2018
Harris
New Jersey
Manufacturers Directory

MERGENT

Exclusive Provider of
Dun & Bradstreet Library Solutions

dun & bradstreet

 HOOVERS™   ☿ First Research    HARRIS INFOSOURCE™

Published December 2018 next update December 2019

Publisher

Mergent Inc.

444 Madison Ave

New York, NY 10022

©Mergent Inc All Rights Reserved

2018 Mergent Business Press

ISSN 1080-2614

ISBN 978-1-62800-799-0

TABLE OF CONTENTS

SUMMARY OF CONTENTS

Number of Companies 12,270
Number of Decision Makers 26,799
Minimum Number of Employees 4

EXPLANATORY NOTES

How to Cross-Reference in This Directory

Sequential Entry Numbers. Each establishment in the Geographic Section is numbered sequentially (G-0000). The number assigned to each establishment is referred to as its "entry number." To make cross-referencing easier, each listing in the Geographic, SIC, Alphabetic and Product Sections includes the establishment's entry number. To facilitate locating an entry in the Geographic Section, the entry numbers for the first listing on the left page and the last listing on the right page are printed at the top of the page next to the city name.

Source Suggestions Welcome

Although all known sources were used to compile this directory, it is possible that companies were inadvertently omitted. Your assistance in calling attention to such omissions would be greatly appreciated. A special form on the facing page will help you in the reporting process.

Analysis

Every effort has been made to contact all firms to verify their information. The one exception to this rule is the annual sales figure, which is considered by many companies to be confidential information. Therefore, estimated sales have been calculated by multiplying the nationwide average sales per employee for the firm's major SIC/NAICS code by the firm's number of employees. Nationwide averages for sales per employee by SIC/NAICS codes are provided by the U.S. Department of Commerce and are updated annually. All sales—sales (est)—have been estimated by this method. The exceptions are parent companies (PA), division headquarters (DH) and headquarter locations (HQ) which may include an actual corporate sales figure—sales (corporate-wide) if available.

Types of Companies

Descriptive and statistical data are included for companies in the entire state. These comprise manufacturers, machine shops, fabricators, assemblers and printers. Also identified are corporate offices in the state.

Employment Data

The employment figure shown in the Geographic Section includes male and female employees and embraces all levels of the company: administrative, clerical, sales and maintenance. This figure is for the facility listed and does not include other plants or offices. It should be recognized that these figures represent an approximate year-round average. These employment figures are broken into codes A through G and used in the Product and SIC Sections to further help you in qualifying a company. Be sure to check the footnotes on the bottom of pages for the code breakdowns.

Standard Industrial Classification (SIC)

The Standard Industrial Classification (SIC) system used in this directory was developed by the federal government for use in classifying establishments by the type of activity they are engaged in. The SIC classifications used in this directory are from the 1987 edition published by the U.S. Government's Office of Management and Budget. The SIC system separates all activities into broad industrial divisions (e.g., manufacturing, mining, retail trade). It further subdivides each division. The range of manufacturing industry classes extends from two-digit codes (major industry group) to four-digit codes (product).

For example:

Industry Breakdown	Code	Industry, Product, etc.
*Major industry group	20	Food and kindred products
Industry group	203	Canned and frozen foods
*Industry	2033	Fruits and vegetables, etc.

*Classifications used in this directory

Only two-digit and four-digit codes are used in this directory.

Arrangement

1. The **Geographic Section** contains complete in-depth corporate data. This section is sorted by cities listed in alphabetical order and companies listed alphabetically within each city. A County/City Index for referencing cities within counties precedes this section.

IMPORTANT NOTICE: It is a violation of both federal and state law to transmit an unsolicited advertisement to a facsimile machine. Any user of this product that violates such laws may be subject to civil and criminal penalties, which may exceed $500 for each transmission of an unsolicited facsimile. Mergent Inc. provides fax numbers for lawful purposes only and expressly forbids the use of these numbers in any unlawful manner.

2. The **Standard Industrial Classification (SIC) Section** lists companies under approximately 500 four-digit SIC codes. An alphabetical and a numerical index precedes this section. A company can be listed under several codes. The codes are in numerical order with companies listed alphabetically under each code.

3. The **Alphabetic Section** lists all companies with their full physical or mailing addresses and telephone number.

4. The **Product Section** lists companies under unique Harris categories. An index preceding this section lists all product categories in alphabetical order. Companies can be listed under several categories.

USER'S GUIDE TO LISTINGS

GEOGRAPHIC SECTION

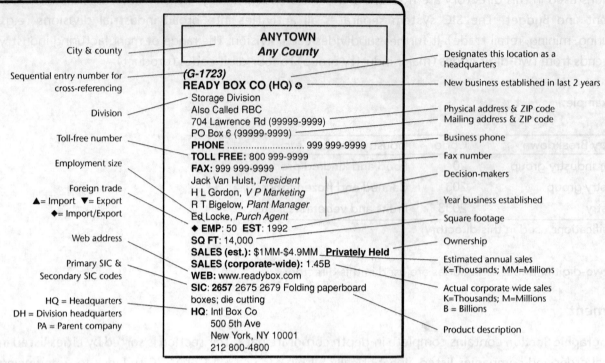

City & county

Sequential entry number for cross-referencing

Division

Toll-free number

Employment size

Foreign trade
▲ = Import ▼ = Export
◆ = Import/Export

Web address

Primary SIC & Secondary SIC codes

HQ = Headquarters
DH = Division headquarters
PA = Parent company

ANYTOWN
Any County

(G-1723)
READY BOX CO (HQ) ✪
Storage Division
Also Called RBC
704 Lawrence Rd (99999-9999)
PO Box 6 (99999-9999)
PHONE 999 999-9999
TOLL FREE: 800 999-9999
FAX: 999 999-9999
Jack Van Hulst, *President*
H L Gordon, *V P Marketing*
R T Bigelow, *Plant Manager*
Ed Locke, *Purch Agent*
◆ **EMP:** 50 **EST:** 1992
SQ FT: 14,000
SALES (est.): $1MM-$4.9MM __Privately Held__
SALES (corporate-wide): 1.45B
WEB: www.readybox.com
SIC: 2657 2675 2679 Folding paperboard
boxes; die cutting
HQ: Intl Box Co
500 5th Ave
New York, NY 10001
212 800-4800

Designates this location as a headquarters

New business established in last 2 years

Physical address & ZIP code
Mailing address & ZIP code

Business phone

Fax number

Decision-makers

Year business established

Square footage

Ownership

Estimated annual sales
K=Thousands; MM=Millions

Actual corporate wide sales
K=Thousands; M=Millions
B = Billions

Product description

SIC SECTION

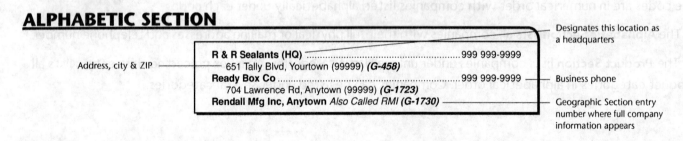

4-digit SIC number & description

Foreign trade
▲ = Import ▼ = Export
◆ = Import/Export

City

2657-Folding Paperboard Boxes
Affordable Inds .... D...999 999-9999
Yourtown *(G-54)*
◆ **Ready Box Co** .... F....999 999-9999
Anytown *(G-1723)*

Indicates approximate employment figure
A = over 500 employees, B = 251–500
C = 101–250, D = 51–100, E = 20–50
F = 10–19, G = 1–9

Business phone

Geographic Section entry number where full company information appears

ALPHABETIC SECTION

Address, city & ZIP

R & R Sealants (HQ) 999 999-9999
651 Tally Blvd, Yourtown (99999) *(G-458)*
Ready Box Co 999 999-9999
704 Lawrence Rd, Anytown (99999) *(G-1723)*
Rendall Mfg Inc, Anytown *Also Called RMI (G-1730)*

Designates this location as a headquarters

Business phone

Geographic Section entry number where full company information appears

PRODUCT SECTION

Product category

City

BOXES: Folding
Edgar & Son Paperboard ....G...999 999-9999
Yourtown *(G-47)*
Ready Box Co .... E...999 999-9999
Anytown *(G-1723)*

Indicates approximate employment figure
A = over 500 employees, B = 251–500
C = 101–250, D = 51–100, E = 20–50
F = 10–19, G = 1–9

Business phone

Geographic Section entry number where full company information appears

GEOGRAPHIC SECTION

Companies sorted by city in alphabetical order

In-depth company data listed

STANDARD INDUSTRIAL CLASSIFICATIONS

Alphabetical index of classifcation descriptions

Numerical index of classifcation descriptions

Companies sorted by SIC product groupings

ALPHABETIC SECTION

Company listings in alphabetical order

PRODUCT INDEX

Product categories listed in alphabetical order

PRODUCT SECTION

Companies sorted by product and manufacturing service classifications

GEOGRAPHIC

SIC

ALPHABETIC

PRDT INDEX

PRODUCT

New Jersey
County Map

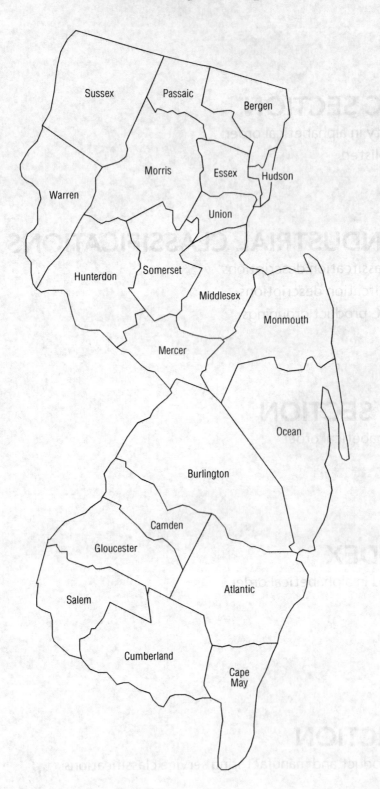

COUNTY/CITY CROSS-REFERENCE INDEX

	ENTRY#		ENTRY#		ENTRY#		ENTRY#		ENTRY#
Atlantic		Old Tappan	(G-7796)	Wrightstown	(G-12242)	Port Elizabeth	(G-8971)	Weehawken	(G-11695)
Absecon	(G-1)	Oradell	(G-7805)	**Camden**		Port Norris	(G-8979)	West New York	(G-11860)
Atlantic City	(G-93)	Palisades Park	(G-7834)	Atco	(G-88)	Rosenhayn	(G-9706)	**Hunterdon**	
Brigantine	(G-917)	Paramus	(G-7852)	Audubon	(G-116)	Vineland	(G-11318)	Annandale	(G-56)
Buena	(G-946)	Park Ridge	(G-7916)	Barrington	(G-170)	**Essex**		Asbury	(G-63)
Cologne	(G-1775)	Ramsey	(G-9229)	Bellmawr	(G-330)	Belleville	(G-293)	Bloomsbury	(G-546)
Dorothy	(G-2073)	Ridgefield	(G-9350)	Berlin	(G-425)	Bloomfield	(G-499)	Califon	(G-1034)
Egg Harbor City	(G-2655)	Ridgefield Park	(G-9395)	Blackwood	(G-469)	Caldwell	(G-1024)	Clinton	(G-1749)
Egg Harbor Township		Ridgewood	(G-9420)	Brooklawn	(G-919)	Cedar Grove	(G-1269)	Flemington	(G-3422)
(G-2675)		River Edge	(G-9463)	Camden	(G-1039)	East Orange	(G-2254)	Frenchtown	(G-3696)
Egg Harbor Twp.	(G-2701)	River Vale	(G-9469)	Cherry Hill	(G-1340)	Essex Fells	(G-3001)	Glen Gardner	(G-3814)
Elwood	(G-2854)	Rochelle Park	(G-9525)	Chesilhurst	(G-1431)	Fairfield	(G-3126)	Hampton	(G-4153)
Galloway	(G-3708)	Rockleigh	(G-9627)	Clementon	(G-1530)	Glen Ridge	(G-3818)	High Bridge	(G-4293)
Hammonton	(G-4126)	Rutherford	(G-9725)	Collingswood	(G-1769)	Irvington	(G-4570)	Lambertville	(G-5209)
Landisville	(G-5229)	Saddle Brook	(G-9747)	Delair	(G-1999)	Livingston	(G-5521)	Lebanon	(G-5274)
Linwood	(G-5465)	Saddle River	(G-9802)	Erial	(G-3000)	Maplewood	(G-5913)	Milford	(G-6244)
Margate City	(G-5933)	South Hackensack	(G-10250)	Gibbsboro	(G-3788)	Millburn	(G-6248)	Oldwick	(G-7803)
Mays Landing	(G-6036)	Teaneck	(G-10740)	Glendora	(G-3832)	Montclair	(G-6404)	Pittstown	(G-8848)
Northfield	(G-7562)	Tenafly	(G-10780)	Gloucester City	(G-3835)	Newark	(G-7062)	Ringoes	(G-9435)
Pleasantville	(G-8902)	Teterboro	(G-10792)	Haddon Heights	(G-4045)	Nutley	(G-7639)	Rosemont	(G-9704)
Pomona	(G-8944)	Twp Washinton	(G-11142)	Haddon Township	(G-4053)	Orange	(G-7816)	Stockton	(G-10611)
Richland	(G-9349)	Upper Saddle River	(G-11273)	Haddonfield	(G-4055)	Roseland	(G-9642)	Three Bridges	(G-10822)
Somers Point	(G-10045)	Waldwick	(G-11441)	Laurel Springs	(G-5232)	Short Hills	(G-9974)	Whitehouse	(G-12045)
Ventnor City	(G-11290)	Wallington	(G-11521)	Lindenwold	(G-5460)	South Orange	(G-10301)	Whitehouse Station	(G-12049)
Bergen		Westwood	(G-11952)	Magnolia	(G-5740)	Verona	(G-11303)	**Mercer**	
Allendale	(G-5)	Wood Ridge	(G-12133)	Mount Ephraim	(G-6762)	West Caldwell	(G-11762)	East Windsor	(G-2339)
Bergenfield	(G-379)	Woodcliff Lake	(G-12179)	Oaklyn	(G-7710)	West Orange	(G-11884)	Ewing	(G-3002)
Bogota	(G-548)	Wyckoff	(G-12244)	Pennsauken	(G-8467)	**Gloucester**		Hamilton	(G-4101)
Carlstadt	(G-1119)	**Burlington**		Pine Hill	(G-8721)	Bridgeport	(G-761)	Hightstown	(G-4310)
Cliffside Park	(G-1536)	Beverly	(G-456)	Runnemede	(G-9717)	Clarksboro	(G-1518)	Hopewell	(G-4541)
Closter	(G-1756)	Birmingham	(G-466)	Sicklerville	(G-10015)	Clayton	(G-1522)	Lawrence Township	(G-5239)
Cresskill	(G-1943)	Bordentown	(G-588)	Somerdale	(G-10038)	Deptford	(G-2063)	Lawrenceville	(G-5249)
Demarest	(G-2026)	Burlington	(G-952)	Stratford	(G-10615)	Franklinville	(G-3629)	Pennington	(G-8444)
Dumont	(G-2115)	Burlington Township	(G-997)	Turnersville	(G-11141)	Gibbstown	(G-3792)	Princeton	(G-8992)
East Rutherford	(G-2274)	Chesterfield	(G-1441)	Voorhees	(G-11419)	Glassboro	(G-3800)	Princeton Junction	(G-9144)
Edgewater	(G-2431)	Cinnaminson	(G-1444)	Waterford Works	(G-11598)	Grenloch	(G-3866)	Robbinsville	(G-9510)
Elmwood Park	(G-2801)	Columbus	(G-1801)	West Berlin	(G-11704)	Logan Township	(G-5610)	Titusville	(G-10855)
Emerson	(G-2855)	Cookstown	(G-1806)	Winslow	(G-12132)	Malaga	(G-5826)	Trenton	(G-11009)
Englewood	(G-2865)	Delanco	(G-2002)	**Cape May**		Mantua	(G-5891)	West Windsor	(G-11909)
Englewood Cliffs	(G-2946)	Delran	(G-2009)	Avalon	(G-120)	Mickleton	(G-6136)	Windsor	(G-12124)
Fair Lawn	(G-3072)	Eastampton	(G-2376)	Cape May	(G-1090)	Mount Royal	(G-6850)	**Middlesex**	
Fairview	(G-3357)	Florence	(G-3476)	Cape May Court House		Mullica Hill	(G-6891)	Avenel	(G-121)
Fort Lee	(G-3541)	Hainesport	(G-4067)	(G-1109)		Newfield	(G-7364)	Carteret	(G-1248)
Franklin Lakes	(G-3607)	Jobstown	(G-4853)	Dennisville	(G-2028)	Paulsboro	(G-8411)	Colonia	(G-1776)
Garfield	(G-3713)	Lumberton	(G-5649)	Marmora	(G-6005)	Pitman	(G-8840)	Cranbury	(G-1809)
Glen Rock	(G-3819)	Maple Shade	(G-5898)	Ocean City	(G-7750)	Sewell	(G-9944)	Dayton	(G-1951)
Hackensack	(G-3872)	Marlton	(G-5963)	Ocean View	(G-7762)	Swedesboro	(G-10681)	Dunellen	(G-2126)
Harrington Park	(G-4169)	Medford	(G-6063)	Rio Grande	(G-9458)	Thorofare	(G-10818)	East Brunswick	(G-2131)
Hasbrouck Heights	(G-4191)	Medford Lakes	(G-6085)	Sea Isle City	(G-9863)	Wenonah	(G-11701)	East Windsor	(G-2371)
Hillsdale	(G-4380)	Moorestown	(G-6555)	Stone Harbor	(G-10613)	West Deptford	(G-11813)	Edison	(G-2444)
Ho Ho Kus	(G-4453)	Mount Holly	(G-6766)	Tuckahoe	(G-11136)	Westville	(G-11936)	Fords	(G-3526)
Leonia	(G-5315)	Mount Laurel	(G-6778)	Villas	(G-11313)	Williamstown	(G-12077)	Green Brook	(G-3854)
Little Ferry	(G-5494)	New Gretna	(G-7020)	West Cape May	(G-11808)	Woodbury	(G-12157)	Helmetta	(G-4286)
Lodi	(G-5573)	Palmyra	(G-7846)	Wildwood	(G-12069)	Woodbury Heights	(G-12173)	Highland Park	(G-4300)
Lyndhurst	(G-5667)	Pemberton	(G-8442)	Wildwood Crest	(G-12076)	Woolwich Township	(G-12241)	Hopelawn	(G-4540)
Mahwah	(G-5743)	Rancocas	(G-9256)	Woodbine	(G-12141)	**Hudson**		Iselin	(G-4608)
Maywood	(G-6045)	Riverside	(G-9492)	**Cumberland**		Bayonne	(G-210)	Jamesburg	(G-4684)
Midland Park	(G-6220)	Riverton	(G-9508)	Bridgeton	(G-776)	Guttenberg	(G-3867)	Keasbey	(G-4924)
Montvale	(G-6440)	Roebling	(G-9638)	Cedarville	(G-1324)	Harrison	(G-4171)	Kendall Park	(G-4933)
Moonachie	(G-6498)	Shamong	(G-9968)	Dividing Creek	(G-2071)	Hoboken	(G-4455)	Laurence Harbor	(G-5235)
New Milford	(G-7021)	Southampton	(G-10469)	Dorchester	(G-2072)	Jersey City	(G-4691)	Metuchen	(G-6093)
North Arlington	(G-7413)	Tabernacle	(G-10737)	Leesburg	(G-5314)	Kearny	(G-4857)	Middlesex	(G-6139)
Northvale	(G-7566)	Vincentown	(G-11317)	Mauricetown	(G-6035)	North Bergen	(G-7425)	Milltown	(G-6267)
Norwood	(G-7615)	Westampton	(G-11910)	Millville	(G-6272)	Secaucus	(G-9865)	Monmouth Junction	(G-6330)
Oakland	(G-7674)	Willingboro	(G-12116)	Newport	(G-7377)	Union City	(G-11239)	Monroe	(G-6373)

City	ENTRY #
Monroe Township	(G-6377)
New Brunswick	(G-6942)
North Brunswick	(G-7499)
Old Bridge	(G-7772)
Parlin	(G-7928)
Perth Amboy	(G-8604)
Piscataway	(G-8723)
Plainsboro	(G-8875)
Port Reading	(G-8984)
Sayreville	(G-9812)
Sewaren	(G-9943)
South Amboy	(G-10233)
South Plainfield	(G-10318)
South River	(G-10456)
Spotswood	(G-10527)
Woodbridge	(G-12144)

Monmouth

City	ENTRY #
Allenhurst	(G-25)
Allentown	(G-27)
Allenwood	(G-36)
Asbury Park	(G-75)
Atlantic Highlands	(G-109)
Belford	(G-286)
Belmar	(G-355)
Bradley Beach	(G-627)
Brielle	(G-911)
Clarksburg	(G-1519)
Cliffwood	(G-1546)
Colts Neck	(G-1779)
Cream Ridge	(G-1931)
Creamridge	(G-1942)
Deal	(G-1997)
Eatontown	(G-2377)
Englishtown	(G-2989)
Fair Haven	(G-3070)
Farmingdale	(G-3376)
Freehold	(G-3634)
Hazlet	(G-4267)
Highlands	(G-4307)
Holmdel	(G-4506)
Howell	(G-4545)
Keansburg	(G-4856)
Keyport	(G-5015)
Lincroft	(G-5336)
Little Silver	(G-5519)
Long Branch	(G-5620)
Manalapan	(G-5836)
Manasquan	(G-5865)
Marlboro	(G-5935)
Matawan	(G-6012)
Middletown	(G-6210)
Millstone Township	(G-6262)
Millstone Twp	(G-6266)
Morganville	(G-6634)
Neptune	(G-6896)
North Middletown	(G-7556)

City	ENTRY #
Oakhurst	(G-7667)
Ocean	(G-7711)
Ocean Grove	(G-7760)
Oceanport	(G-7767)
Perrineville	(G-8602)
Port Monmouth	(G-8973)
Red Bank	(G-9317)
Roosevelt	(G-9639)
Rumson	(G-9713)
Sea Bright	(G-9859)
Sea Girt	(G-9860)
Shrewsbury	(G-9988)
Spring Lake	(G-10532)
Tennent	(G-10790)
Tinton Falls	(G-10823)
Union Beach	(G-11236)
Wall	(G-11458)
Wall Township	(G-11459)
West Long Branch	(G-11843)

Morris

City	ENTRY #
Boonton	(G-551)
Brookside	(G-922)
Budd Lake	(G-923)
Butler	(G-998)
Cedar Knolls	(G-1306)
Chatham	(G-1325)
Chester	(G-1432)
Denville	(G-2029)
Dover	(G-2075)
East Hanover	(G-2198)
Flanders	(G-3399)
Florham Park	(G-3483)
Gillette	(G-3794)
Green Village	(G-3865)
Kenvil	(G-5010)
Kinnelon	(G-5032)
Lake Hiawatha	(G-5054)
Lake Hopatcong	(G-5055)
Landing	(G-5223)
Ledgewood	(G-5304)
Lincoln Park	(G-5325)
Long Valley	(G-5634)
Madison	(G-5716)
Mendham	(G-6086)
Millington	(G-6260)
Mine Hill	(G-6326)
Montville	(G-6482)
Morris Plains	(G-6658)
Morristown	(G-6683)
Mount Arlington	(G-6752)
Mountain Lakes	(G-6853)
Netcong	(G-6941)
Parsippany	(G-7937)
Pequannock	(G-8596)
Pine Brook	(G-8679)
Pompton Plains	(G-8951)

City	ENTRY #
Randolph	(G-9266)
Riverdale	(G-9473)
Rockaway	(G-9540)
Roxbury Township	(G-9711)
Stirling	(G-10599)
Succasunna	(G-10618)
Towaco	(G-10987)
Wharton	(G-11978)
Whippany	(G-12004)

Ocean

City	ENTRY #
Barnegat	(G-159)
Barnegat Light	(G-168)
Bay Head	(G-209)
Bayville	(G-247)
Beach Haven	(G-264)
Brick	(G-733)
Forked River	(G-3532)
Island Heights	(G-4651)
Jackson	(G-4652)
Lakehurst	(G-5059)
Lakewood	(G-5061)
Lavallette	(G-5237)
Long Beach Township (G-5617)	
Ltl Egg Hbr	(G-5640)
Manahawkin	(G-5828)
Manchester	(G-5886)
Mantoloking	(G-5890)
New Egypt	(G-7015)
Pine Beach	(G-8678)
Point Pleasant Beach (G-8920)	
Point Pleasant Boro	(G-8930)
Ship Bottom	(G-9973)
Surf City	(G-10664)
Toms River	(G-10858)
Waretown	(G-11532)
West Creek	(G-11809)
Whiting	(G-12065)

Passaic

City	ENTRY #
Bloomingdale	(G-540)
Clifton	(G-1551)
Haledon	(G-4081)
Haskell	(G-4205)
Hawthorne	(G-4216)
Hewitt	(G-4287)
Little Falls	(G-5468)
Newfoundland	(G-7373)
North Haledon	(G-7547)
Oak Ridge	(G-7659)
Passaic	(G-8121)
Paterson	(G-8191)
Pompton Lakes	(G-8946)
Prospect Park	(G-9168)
Ringwood	(G-9444)

City	ENTRY #
Totowa	(G-10925)
Wanaque	(G-11531)
Wayne	(G-11599)
West Milford	(G-11849)
Woodland Park	(G-12207)

Salem

City	ENTRY #
Carneys Point	(G-1244)
Deepwater	(G-1998)
Elmer	(G-2787)
Hancocks Bridge	(G-4167)
Monroeville	(G-6399)
Norma	(G-7412)
Pedricktown	(G-8433)
Penns Grove	(G-8464)
Pennsville	(G-8592)
Pilesgrove	(G-8676)
Pittsgrove	(G-8847)
Salem	(G-9803)
Woodstown	(G-12237)

Somerset

City	ENTRY #
Basking Ridge	(G-180)
Bedminster	(G-265)
Belle Mead	(G-291)
Bernardsville	(G-447)
Bound Brook	(G-616)
Branchburg	(G-628)
Bridgewater	(G-806)
Far Hills	(G-3374)
Franklin Park	(G-3626)
Gladstone	(G-3798)
Hillsborough	(G-4315)
Kingston	(G-5027)
Liberty Corner	(G-5323)
Manville	(G-5893)
Martinsville	(G-6008)
Neshanic Station	(G-6938)
Peapack	(G-8429)
Pluckemin	(G-8919)
Raritan	(G-9307)
Rocky Hill	(G-9637)
Skillman	(G-10029)
Somerset	(G-10049)
Somerville	(G-10198)
South Bound Brook	(G-10248)
Warren	(G-11533)
Watchung	(G-11591)
Zarephath	(G-12270)

Sussex

City	ENTRY #
Andover	(G-48)
Augusta	(G-119)
Branchville	(G-724)
Byram Township	(G-1021)
Franklin	(G-3593)
Hamburg	(G-4087)
Highland Lakes	(G-4299)

City	ENTRY #
Hopatcong	(G-4533)
Lafayette	(G-5043)
Montague	(G-6402)
Newton	(G-7378)
Ogdensburg	(G-7769)
Sandyston	(G-9811)
Sparta	(G-10485)
Stanhope	(G-10587)
Stockholm	(G-10610)
Sussex	(G-10666)
Tranquility	(G-11008)
Vernon	(G-11295)

Union

City	ENTRY #
Berkeley Heights	(G-398)
Clark	(G-1498)
Cranford	(G-1894)
Elizabeth	(G-2702)
Elizabethport	(G-2783)
Fanwood	(G-3372)
Garwood	(G-3774)
Hillside	(G-4388)
Kenilworth	(G-4936)
Linden	(G-5342)
Mountainside	(G-6865)
Murray Hill	(G-6895)
New Providence	(G-7026)
North Plainfield	(G-7559)
Plainfield	(G-8852)
Rahway	(G-9171)
Roselle	(G-9659)
Roselle Park	(G-9687)
Scotch Plains	(G-9844)
Springfield	(G-10536)
Summit	(G-10630)
Union	(G-11145)
Westfield	(G-11919)
Winfield Park	(G-12131)

Warren

City	ENTRY #
Alpha	(G-38)
Belvidere	(G-366)
Blairstown	(G-494)
Buttzville	(G-1020)
Columbia	(G-1795)
Great Meadows	(G-3848)
Hackettstown	(G-3994)
Hardwick	(G-4168)
Hope	(G-4539)
Johnsonburg	(G-4855)
Oxford	(G-7833)
Phillipsburg	(G-8638)
Port Murray	(G-8974)
Stewartsville	(G-10593)
Washington	(G-11573)

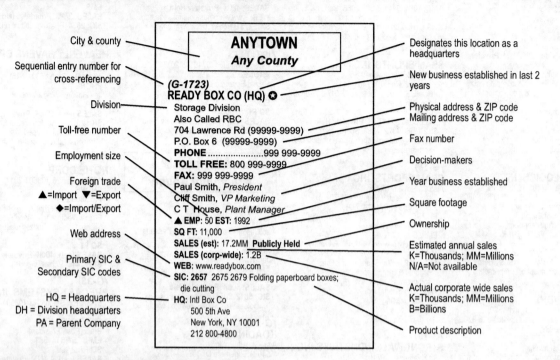

City & county → | **ANYTOWN** *Any County* | ← Designates this location as a headquarters

Sequential entry number for cross-referencing

(G-1723)
READY BOX CO (HQ) ✪ ← New business established in last 2 years

Division → Storage Division
Also Called RBC
704 Lawrence Rd (99999-9999) ← Physical address & ZIP code
P.O. Box 6 (99999-9999) ← Mailing address & ZIP code
Toll-free number → **PHONE** 999 999-9999
TOLL FREE: 800 999-9999 ← Fax number
FAX: 999 999-9999
Employment size → Paul Smith, *President* ← Decision-makers
Cliff Smith, *VP Marketing*
C T House, *Plant Manager*
Foreign trade
▲=Import ▼=Export ▲ **EMP:** 50 **EST:** 1992 ← Year business established
◆=Import/Export **SQ FT:** 11,000 ← Square footage
SALES (est): 17.2MM **Publicly Held** ← Ownership
Web address → **SALES (corp-wide):** 1.2B ← Estimated annual sales K=Thousands; MM=Millions N/A=Not available
WEB: www.readybox.com
Primary SIC & **SIC:** 2657 2675 2679 Folding paperboard boxes; ← Actual corporate wide sales K=Thousands; MM=Millions B=Billions
Secondary SIC codes die cutting
HQ = Headquarters → **HQ:** Intl Box Co ← Product description
DH = Division headquarters 500 5th Ave
PA = Parent Company New York, NY 10001
212 800-4800

See footnotes for symbols and codes identification.
• This section is in alphabetical order by city.
• Companies are sorted alphabetically under their respective cities.
• To locate cities within a county refer to the County/City Cross Reference Index.

IMPORTANT NOTICE: It is a violation of both federal and state law to transmit an unsolicited advertisement to a facsimile machine. Any user of this product that violates such laws may be subject to civil and criminal penalties which may exceed $500 for each transmission of an unsolicited facsimile. Harris InfoSource provides fax numbers for lawful purposes only and expressly forbids the use of these numbers in any unlawful manner.

G E O G R A P H I C

Absecon
Atlantic County

(G-1)
ABSECON ELECTRIC MOTOR WORKS
500 White Horse Pike (08201-2429)
PHONE.............................609 641-1523
Fax: 609 407-9392
Dennis Pruchnicki, *President*
Joseph Pruchincki, *Corp Secy*
EMP: 4
SQ FT: 2,000
SALES (est): 330K **Privately Held**
WEB: www.femyers.com
SIC: 7694 5999 Electric motor repair; motors, electric

(G-2)
DIAMOND SCOOTERS INC
Also Called: Mobility123
645 S Mill Rd Ste 1 (08201-4802)
PHONE.............................609 646-0003
Denise M Penn, *President*
EMP: 7
SALES (est): 1.5MM **Privately Held**
SIC: 1541 1521 3534 3448 Renovation, remodeling & repairs: industrial buildings; general remodeling, single-family houses; elevators & moving stairways; ramps: prefabricated metal

(G-3)
MACO APPLIANCE PARTS & SUP CO
1101 N New Rd (08201-9303)
PHONE.............................609 272-8222

Rich Comunale, *Principal*
EMP: 8
SALES (est): 710K **Privately Held**
SIC: 5063 3585 Electrical supplies; heating & air conditioning combination units

(G-4)
SHOP-RITE SUPERMARKETS INC
Also Called: Shop Rite 633
616 White Horse Pike (08201-2302)
PHONE.............................609 646-2448
Fax: 609 641-6289
Ricky Wilkes, *Branch Mgr*
EMP: 149
SALES (corp-wide): 12.5B **Privately Held**
SIC: 5411 5912 2051 Supermarkets, chain; drug stores & proprietary stores; bread, cake & related products
HQ: Shop Rite Supermarkets, Inc.
5000 Riverside Dr
Keasbey NJ 08832
908 527-3300

Allendale
Bergen County

(G-5)
ACUITIVE TECHNOLOGIES INC
50 Commerce Dr (07401-1623)
PHONE.............................973 617-7175
Alex Khowaylo, *CEO*
Jim Malayter, *Principal*
Mike McCarthy, *Principal*
Dave Washburn, *CFO*
EMP: 11
SQ FT: 8,800

SALES (est): 821.9K **Privately Held**
SIC: 3842 Surgical appliances & supplies

(G-6)
CATALENT CTS LLC
75 Commerce Dr (07401-1600)
PHONE.............................201 785-0275
Vincent Santamaria, *Branch Mgr*
EMP: 110 **Publicly Held**
SIC: 2834 Pharmaceutical preparations
HQ: Catalent Cts, Llc
10245 Hickman Mills Dr
Kansas City MO 64137

(G-7)
COLLAGEN MATRIX INC
110 Commerce Dr (07401-1622)
PHONE.............................201 786-9300
Stuart Heit, *Branch Mgr*
EMP: 11
SALES (corp-wide): 14.3MM **Privately Held**
SIC: 3841 Surgical & medical instruments
PA: Collagen Matrix, Inc.
15 Thornton Rd
Oakland NJ 07436
201 405-1477

(G-8)
DATAPROBE INC (PA)
1 Pearl Ct B (07401-1658)
PHONE.............................201 934-9944
David Weiss, *President*
Sy Weiss, *Chairman*
James Kalymnios, *Vice Pres*
Douglas Osowiecky, *Vice Pres*
Geraldine Weiss, *Treasurer*
▲ EMP: 27
SQ FT: 20,000

SALES (est): 3MM **Privately Held**
WEB: www.dataprobe.com
SIC: 3661 Telephone & telegraph apparatus

(G-9)
EDGEWELL PERSONAL CARE LLC
75 Commerce Dr (07401-1600)
P.O. Box 701 (07401-0701)
PHONE.............................201 785-8000
EMP: 147
SALES (corp-wide): 2.3B **Publicly Held**
WEB: www.playtexproductsinc.com
SIC: 2844 Toilet preparations
HQ: Edgewell Personal Care, Llc
1350 Timberlake Mano
Chesterfield MO 63017
314 594-1900

(G-10)
HEIGHTS JEWELERS LLC
11 Ceely Ct (07401-2101)
PHONE.............................201 825-2381
Deniz Appelbaum, *Director*
Marc Appelbaum,
EMP: 11
SQ FT: 2,000
SALES: 1.2MM **Privately Held**
SIC: 3911 5094 Jewelry, precious metal; jewelry apparel; jewelry

(G-11)
LEISTRITZ ADVANCED TECH CORP (HQ)
Also Called: Leistritz Pump
165 Chestnut St Ste 1 (07401-2230)
PHONE.............................201 934-8262
Fax: 201 934-8266
Jeffrey De Daul, *President*

Dolares Sydoruk, *COO*
Randy Bennett, *Vice Pres*
John Wood, *QC Mgr*
John Babos, *Engineer*
▲ **EMP:** 27
SQ FT: 24,000
SALES (est): 22.5MM
SALES (corp-wide): 289.7MM **Privately Held**
WEB: www.leistritz.com
SIC: 5084 3561 Pumps & pumping equipment; hydraulic systems equipment & supplies; machine tools & accessories; pumps & pumping equipment
PA: Leistritz Ag
    Markgrafenstr. 36-39
    Nurnberg 90459
    911 430-60

(G-12)
LONZA BIOLOGICS INC
90 Boroline Rd (07401-1629)
PHONE..............................603 610-4809
Michael Mietzner, *Engineer*
Jesse Cobb, *Plant Engr*
Jenalyn Coulp-Yu, *Plant Engr*
Mailet Minassian, *VP Human Res*
Bruce Lovett, *Manager*
EMP: 61
SALES (est): 15.3MM **Privately Held**
SIC: 2834 Pharmaceutical preparations

(G-13)
LONZA INC (DH)
90 Boroline Rd Ste 1 (07401-1629)
PHONE..............................201 316-9200
Fax: 201 785-9989
Jeanne Thomas, *CEO*
Paul Lemoi, *District Mgr*
Mike Degennaro, *Vice Pres*
David Doles, *Vice Pres*
Lorenzo Donargo, *Vice Pres*
◆ **EMP:** 100 **EST:** 1958
SQ FT: 50,000
SALES (est): 264.1MM
SALES (corp-wide): 5.1B **Privately Held**
WEB: www.riversidecap.com
SIC: 2899 2869 2819 Chemical preparations; industrial organic chemicals; industrial inorganic chemicals
HQ: Lonza America Inc.
    90 Boroline Rd Ste 1
    Allendale NJ 07401
    201 316-9200

(G-14)
MEDICON INC
17 Beechwood Rd (07401-1801)
PHONE..............................201 669-7456
Robert Marsanico, *President*
EMP: 4
SALES (est): 309K **Privately Held**
SIC: 2834 Pharmaceutical preparations

(G-15)
PRATT INDUSTRIES USA INC
Also Called: Pratt Displays
3 Pearl Ct Unit 3f (07401-1657)
PHONE..............................201 934-1900
EMP: 66
SALES (corp-wide): 2.1B **Privately Held**
SIC: 2653 Display items, corrugated: made from purchased materials
PA: Pratt Industries, Inc.
    1800 Sarasota Busin Ste C
    Conyers GA 30013
    770 918-5678

(G-16)
PROMOTION IN MOTION INC (PA)
Also Called: Promotion In Motion Companies
25 Commerce Dr (07401-1617)
P.O. Box 8 (07401-0008)
PHONE..............................201 962-8530
Michael G Rosenberg, *President*
Kevin Walsh, *President*
Keith Von Zup, *Vice Pres*
Robert Purcell, *CFO*
▲ **EMP:** 55 **EST:** 1986
SQ FT: 45,000

SALES (est): 179.3MM **Privately Held**
WEB: www.promotioninmotion.com
SIC: 2064 5441 5145 2066 Candy & other confectionery products; candy, nut & confectionery stores; confectionery; chocolate & cocoa products

(G-17)
SSAM SPORTS INC (PA)
Also Called: Putterwheel
234 Macintyre Ln (07401-1441)
PHONE..............................917 553-0596
Sang Kim, *President*
▲ **EMP:** 4
SALES (est): 447.4K **Privately Held**
SIC: 7999 7372 7389 Sports instruction, schools & camps; application computer software;

(G-18)
SSAM SPORTS INC
Also Called: 4 D Motion
2 Myrtle Ave Unit 599 (07401-7040)
P.O. Box 599 (07401-0599)
PHONE..............................917 553-0596
Sang Kim, *President*
EMP: 5
SALES (corp-wide): 447.4K **Privately Held**
SIC: 7999 7372 Sports instruction, schools & camps; application computer software
PA: Ssam Sports, Inc.
    234 Macintyre Ln
    Allendale NJ 07401
    917 553-0596

(G-19)
STRONGWALL INDUSTRIES INC
90 Heather Ct (07401-2025)
PHONE..............................201 445-4633
Fax: 201 445-2317
Nicole Kokoletsos, *President*
EMP: 7
SQ FT: 3,000
SALES (est): 910K **Privately Held**
WEB: www.strongwall.com
SIC: 3297 3069 3272 High temperature mortar, nonclay; floor coverings, rubber; concrete products

(G-20)
STRYKER CORPORATION
Stryker Spine
2 Pearl Ct (07401-1611)
PHONE..............................201 760-8000
Spencer Stiles, *Branch Mgr*
EMP: 60
SALES (corp-wide): 12.4B **Publicly Held**
SIC: 3841 Surgical & medical instruments
PA: Stryker Corporation
    2825 Airview Blvd
    Portage MI 49002
    269 385-2600

(G-21)
TELEMETRICS INC
75 Commerce Dr (07401-1600)
PHONE..............................201 848-9818
Fax: 201 848-9819
Tony Cuomo, *General Mgr*
Anthony E Cuomo, *Principal*
▲ **EMP:** 40
SQ FT: 10,000
SALES (est): 9MM **Privately Held**
WEB: www.telemetricsinc.com
SIC: 3663 Television broadcasting & communications equipment

(G-22)
TREASURES LLC
32 Ada Pl (07401-1001)
PHONE..............................201 723-3506
Jeff Bialosky, *Mng Member*
▲ **EMP:** 5
SQ FT: 1,800
SALES: 3MM **Privately Held**
SIC: 3942 Stuffed toys, including animals

(G-23)
WORDMASTERS
213 E Allendale Ave (07401-2016)
PHONE..............................201 327-4201
Fax: 201 327-6219
Nancy McGrath, *Owner*
Julie Whalen, *Marketing Mgr*

Lisa Kennedy, *Exec Dir*
EMP: 6
SALES: 400K **Privately Held**
WEB: www.wordmasterschallenge.com
SIC: 2731 Books: publishing only

(G-24)
ZIRTI LLC
8 Cambridge Dr (07401-2120)
PHONE..............................201 316-4791
Gerald Sugerman, *Director*
Jerald Sugarman,
EMP: 3
SQ FT: 35,000
SALES (est): 10.9MM **Privately Held**
SIC: 3089 Toilets, portable chemical: plastic

Allenhurst
Monmouth County

(G-25)
CRAVINGS
Also Called: Cravings Gourmet Desserts
310 Main St (07711-1038)
PHONE..............................732 531-7122
Jan Walker, *Owner*
EMP: 10
SQ FT: 1,100
SALES: 500K **Privately Held**
SIC: 5812 2051 Eating places; bakery: wholesale or wholesale/retail combined

(G-26)
KOADINGS INC
Also Called: Polymite
540 N Edgemere Dr (07711-1348)
P.O. Box 481 (07711-0481)
PHONE..............................732 517-0784
Mark Midneck, *President*
EMP: 5
SALES: 600K **Privately Held**
SIC: 2952 Roofing materials

Allentown
Monmouth County

(G-27)
AGNO PHARMA
5 Wingate Ct (08501-1936)
PHONE..............................609 223-0638
James Chen, *Owner*
Raymond Dagnino, *Director*
Paul Grover, *Business Dir*
EMP: 4 **EST:** 2007
SALES (est): 293.7K **Privately Held**
SIC: 2834 Pharmaceutical preparations

(G-28)
ALLENTOWN INC (PA)
165 Route 526 (08501-2017)
P.O. Box 698 (08501-0698)
PHONE..............................609 259-7951
Michael A Coiro Sr, *CEO*
John M Coiro, *President*
Steve Benigni, *District Mgr*
Jason Misier, *Production*
David Carmignani, *CFO*
▲ **EMP:** 330
SQ FT: 220,000
SALES (est): 82.3MM **Privately Held**
WEB: www.allentowninc.com
SIC: 3444 3496 5162 Sheet metalwork; cages, wire; plastics products

(G-29)
EDWARD T BRADY
Also Called: Brady Manufacturing Co
12 Waldron Rd (08501-1718)
PHONE..............................732 928-0257
Edward T Brady, *Owner*
EMP: 7
SQ FT: 24,000
SALES (est): 500.4K **Privately Held**
SIC: 3448 Buildings, portable: prefabricated metal

(G-30)
ESJAY PHARMA LLC (PA)
27 Ridgeview Way (08501-1964)
PHONE..............................732 438-1816

Muthusamy Shanmugan, *CEO*
Sivakumar Chinniah, *Vice Pres*
EMP: 10
SALES: 3MM **Privately Held**
SIC: 2834 Pharmaceutical preparations

(G-31)
HEAVENLY HAVENS CREAMERY LLC
33 S Main St (08501-1615)
PHONE..............................609 259-6600
Joy Havens, *Mng Member*
EMP: 4
SALES (est): 59.6K **Privately Held**
SIC: 2024 2656 Ice cream & frozen desserts; dairy based frozen desserts; frozen food & ice cream containers

(G-32)
NOTIE CORP
177 Route 526 (08501-2017)
PHONE..............................609 259-3477
Fax: 609 259-1921
Dave E Weatherholtz, *Ch of Bd*
Elaine Weatherholtz, *Vice Pres*
Michael Weatherholtz, *Treasurer*
EMP: 5
SQ FT: 7,200
SALES (est): 400K **Privately Held**
SIC: 2448 Pallets, wood

(G-33)
PRECAST SYSTEMS INC
57 Sharon Station Rd (08501-1902)
PHONE..............................609 208-0569
Fax: 609 208-1966
Bruce Post, *President*
EMP: 25 **EST:** 1981
SQ FT: 2,000
SALES (est): 4.7MM **Privately Held**
SIC: 3272 Concrete products, precast

(G-34)
RIEPHOFF SAW MILL INC
763 Route 524 (08501-2005)
PHONE..............................609 259-7265
John S Falconio, *President*
Eva Riephoff, *Corp Secy*
EMP: 19
SQ FT: 8,000
SALES: 5MM **Privately Held**
SIC: 2421 2448 Lumber: rough, sawed or planed; wood pallets & skids

(G-35)
SCIMAR TECHNOLOGIES LLC
32 Cliffwood Dr (08501-2041)
PHONE..............................609 208-1796
Michael Conroy,
Donna Conroy,
EMP: 4
SALES (est): 144.5K **Privately Held**
SIC: 7371 7372 7389 Computer software systems analysis & design, custom; prepackaged software; business oriented computer software; home entertainment computer software;

Allenwood
Monmouth County

(G-36)
I F ASSOCIATES INC
Also Called: I F A
3303 Atlantic Ave (08720-7014)
P.O. Box 680 (08720-0680)
PHONE..............................732 223-2900
Pat Iammatteo, *President*
Ester Iammatteo, *Vice Pres*
EMP: 15 **EST:** 1977
SQ FT: 15,000
SALES: 1.4MM **Privately Held**
WEB: www.ifassociatesinc.com
SIC: 7389 3552 Design, commercial & industrial; ; fiber & yarn preparation machinery & equipment

(G-37)
SEALED UNIT PARTS CO INC
Also Called: Supco
2230 Landmark Pl (08720-7038)
P.O. Box 21 (08720-0021)
PHONE..............................732 223-1201

▲ = Import ▼=Export
◆ =Import/Export

Fax: 732 223-1617
Christopher Mancuso, *CEO*
Anthony Mancuso, *Ch of Bd*
Chris Mancuso, *Chairman*
Joe Whelan, *Corp Secy*
Kim Nathaniel, *Purch Agent*
◆ **EMP: 141**
SALES (est): 37.3MM Privately Held
WEB: www.supco.com
SIC: 3585 3625 Parts for heating, cooling & refrigerating equipment; relays, for electronic use

Alpha
Warren County

(G-38)
ALPHA LEHIGH TOOL & MCH CO INC
41 Industrial Rd (08865-4080)
PHONE..................................908 454-6481
Fax: 908 454-9819
William L Green, *President*
Charles Spitale, *Prdtn Mgr*
Teri Green, *Human Res Dir*
David Green, *Manager*
Terry Suiter, *Officer*
EMP: 38 **EST:** 1956
SQ FT: 33,000
SALES (est): 7.2MM Privately Held
WEB: www.alphalehigh.com
SIC: 3599 Machine shop, jobbing & repair

(G-39)
AUTOMATIC TRANSFER INC
2 Industrial Rd (08865-4081)
PHONE..................................908 213-2830
Al Lacosta, *President*
▲ **EMP:** 4
SQ FT: 3,500
SALES (est): 290K Privately Held
SIC: 3861 Toners, prepared photographic (not made in chemical plants)

(G-40)
CORETECH INTERNATIONAL INC
41 Industrial Rd (08865-4080)
PHONE..................................908 454-7999
Lauren Green, *Principal*
EMP: 10 **EST:** 2009
SALES (est): 1.9MM Privately Held
SIC: 3541 Machine tools, metal cutting type

(G-41)
GLEN MAGNETICS INC
1165 3rd Ave (08865-4799)
PHONE..................................908 454-3717
Fax: 908 454-2702
John Di Sarro, *President*
John Disarro, *General Mgr*
Cabot Thomas, *Vice Pres*
Gwendolyn Di Sarro, *Treasurer*
EMP: 35
SQ FT: 53,000
SALES: 2.2MM Privately Held
WEB: www.glenmagnetics.com
SIC: 3612 5065 Power transformers, electric; electronic parts & equipment

(G-42)
HUNTERDON TRANSFORMER CO INC (PA)
75 Industrial Rd (08865-4080)
PHONE..................................908 454-2400
Fax: 908 454-6266
Mark Brock, *President*
Morris Bock, *President*
Donald Gordon, *Chairman*
Peter Droelle, *Treasurer*
Richard McCabe, *VP Sales*
▲ **EMP:** 75 **EST:** 1957
SQ FT: 42,000
SALES (est): 14.2MM Privately Held
WEB: www.hunterdontransformer.com
SIC: 3612 Power transformers, electric

(G-43)
LINDE NORTH AMERICA INC
Also Called: Linde Elec & Specialty Gasses
80 Industrial Rd (08865-4083)
PHONE..................................908 454-7455

William Heintz, *VP Opers*
Fred Hicks, *Safety Mgr*
Ron Robinson, *Safety Mgr*
Monica Caldwell, *Marketing Mgr*
John Ballard, *Manager*
EMP: 100
SALES (corp-wide): 20.1B Privately Held
SIC: 2813 Industrial gases; oxygen, compressed or liquefied
HQ: Linde North America, Inc.
200 Somerset Corporate Bl
Bridgewater NJ 08807
908 464-8100

(G-44)
POWER POOL PLUS INC
7 Edge Rd (08865-9721)
PHONE..................................908 454-1124
Dudley Hulse, *President*
Dona Johnson, *Bookkeeper*
◆ **EMP:** 6
SALES (est): 1.3MM Privately Held
WEB: www.powerpoolplus.com
SIC: 3621 4213 5063 7359 Motors & generators; electric motor & generator parts; coils, for electric motors or generators; power generators; refrigerated products transport; generators; equipment rental & leasing; generator repair

(G-45)
SAFE MAN LLC
801 Vulcanite Ave (08865-4780)
PHONE..................................800 320-2589
Richard N Its, *President*
EMP: 6
SALES (est): 565.8K Privately Held
SIC: 3499 Fabricated metal products

(G-46)
SHERIDAN PRINTING COMPANY INC
Also Called: Sheridan Communications
1425 3rd Ave (08865-4605)
PHONE..................................908 454-0700
Fax: 908 454-2554
James Sheridan, *CEO*
Wayne L Pesaresi, *President*
Elizabeth F Pesaresi, *Treasurer*
Erinn Pesaresi, *VP Sales*
EMP: 40 **EST:** 1956
SQ FT: 40,000
SALES (est): 4.8MM Privately Held
WEB: www.sheridanprinting.com
SIC: 2741 Technical papers: publishing & printing

(G-47)
TORELCO INC
55 Industrial Rd (08865-4080)
PHONE..................................908 387-0814
Matt Peterson, *President*
EMP: 15 **EST:** 2007
SALES (est): 3.5MM Privately Held
SIC: 3677 Electronic coils, transformers & other inductors

Andover
Sussex County

(G-48)
BARRIER ENTERPRISES INC
175 Stanhope Sparta Rd (07821-4905)
PHONE..................................973 770-3983
Thomas Stiffen, *CEO*
EMP: 7
SQ FT: 4,000
SALES (est): 564K Privately Held
SIC: 3713 Truck bodies & parts

(G-49)
BERK GOLD STAMPING CORPORATION (PA)
196 Pequest Rd (07821-2020)
PHONE..................................973 786-6052
Ronald E Stagnari, *President*
EMP: 50
SQ FT: 60,000
SALES (est): 4.4MM Privately Held
WEB: www.berkgoldstamping.com
SIC: 3999 2789 Gold stamping, except books; bookbinding & related work

(G-50)
G R BOWLER INC
511 Maxim Dr (07821-2927)
PHONE..................................973 525-7172
Fax: 973 770-2168
Gary Bowler, *President*
EMP: 4
SALES (est): 282.3K Privately Held
SIC: 3829 Measuring & controlling devices

(G-51)
JA-BAR SILICONE CORP
252 Brighton Rd (07821-5032)
P.O. Box 1249 (07821-1249)
PHONE..................................973 786-5000
Fax: 973 786-6067
Gilbert Jacobs, *President*
Richard Latham, *General Mgr*
Myrtle G Jacobs, *Corp Secy*
Robert J Lisofski, *Exec VP*
Mark Derr, *Vice Pres*
EMP: 83 **EST:** 1965
SQ FT: 24,000
SALES: 13.6MM Privately Held
WEB: www.jabar.com
SIC: 3053 Gaskets, packing & sealing devices

(G-52)
KEURIG DR PEPPER INC
562 Ervey Rd (07821-5625)
PHONE..................................908 684-4400
EMP: 93 **Publicly Held**
SIC: 2086 Soft drinks: packaged in cans, bottles, etc.
PA: Keurig Dr Pepper Inc.
5301 Legacy Dr
Plano TX 75024

(G-53)
NEW JERSEY FENCE & GUARDRAIL
Also Called: Crest Wood Fence
32 Main St (07821-4515)
PHONE..................................973 786-5400
Fax: 973 786-5411
James E Hofmann, *President*
EMP: 15
SQ FT: 1,000
SALES (est): 1.9MM Privately Held
SIC: 2411 Rails, fence: round or split

(G-54)
SUTHERLAND PACKAGING INC
254 Brighton Rd (07821-5032)
P.O. Box 1429 (07821-1429)
PHONE..................................973 786-5141
Fax: 973 786-6030
Tom Sutherland, *President*
Eugene D Sutherland, *Chairman*
Elizabeth Sutherland, *Corp Secy*
Daniel Sutherland, *Vice Pres*
Joe Swistack, *Plant Mgr*
EMP: 60
SQ FT: 100,000
SALES (est): 16.8MM Privately Held
WEB: www.sudsbox.com
SIC: 2653 Boxes, corrugated: made from purchased materials

(G-55)
V E N INC
Also Called: N V E Pharmaceuticals
15 Whitehall Rd (07821-2115)
PHONE..................................973 786-7862
Fax: 973 786-7730
Robert Occhifinto, *President*
Keith Woods, *Facilities Mgr*
Steve Taylor, *Traffic Mgr*
Jenna Gately, *Purchasing*
Edda Kramm, *Research*
▲ **EMP:** 220 **EST:** 1982
SQ FT: 250,000
SALES (est): 51.1MM Privately Held
WEB: www.stacker2.com
SIC: 2023 2086 Dietary supplements, dairy & non-dairy based; carbonated soft drinks, bottled & canned

Annandale
Hunterdon County

(G-56)
BALLANTINE LABORATORIES INC
312 Old Allerton Rd (08801-3214)
PHONE..................................908 713-7742
G Dean McAdoo, *Ch of Bd*
Russell D McAdoo, *President*
Russell Oo, *COO*
Greg McAdoo, *Vice Pres*
Keitha McAdoo, *Admin Sec*
EMP: 7
SQ FT: 6,000
SALES: 2.8MM Privately Held
WEB: www.ballantinelabs.com
SIC: 3825 8734 3829 Test equipment for electronic & electrical circuits; measuring instruments & meters, electric; testing laboratories; measuring & controlling devices

(G-57)
BLUE OCEAN PHARMA LLC
4 Spring Hill Rd (08801-3505)
PHONE..................................908 428-4668
Alden E Masonis, *Principal*
EMP: 4
SALES (est): 236K Privately Held
SIC: 2834 Pharmaceutical preparations

(G-58)
INGERSOLL-RAND COMPANY
1467 Route 31 S (08801-3118)
P.O. Box 970 (08801-0970)
PHONE..................................908 238-7000
Fax: 908 238-7055
Joe Jones, *Branch Mgr*
John Linehan, *Director*
John McCallops, *Director*
EMP: 150 **Privately Held**
WEB: www.ingersoll-rand.com
SIC: 8742 5085 5072 3546 Management consulting services; marketing consulting services; industrial supplies; hardware; power-driven handtools
HQ: Ingersoll-Rand Company
800 Beaty St Ste B
Davidson NC 28036
704 655-4000

(G-59)
INSPIRE WORKS INC
154 River Rd (08801-3512)
PHONE..................................908 730-7447
James Tagliareni, *President*
James Taglarini, *Principal*
EMP: 12
SALES (est): 825.3K Privately Held
WEB: www.inspireworksinc.com
SIC: 7372 Prepackaged software

(G-60)
SONOCO PRODUCTS COMPANY
67 Beaver Ave Ste 11 (08801-3067)
PHONE..................................908 713-6900
Richard Carnali, *Manager*
EMP: 57
SALES (corp-wide): 5B Publicly Held
WEB: www.sonoco.com
SIC: 2631 Paperboard mills
PA: Sonoco Products Company
1 N 2nd St
Hartsville SC 29550
843 383-7000

(G-61)
SUROMA LTD LIABILITY COMPANY
Also Called: Badge Company of New Jersey
223 Hamden Rd (08801-3366)
PHONE..................................908 735-7700
Robert Marlow, *General Mgr*
EMP: 5
SALES (est): 328.3K Privately Held
WEB: www.badgeconj.com
SIC: 3999 5999 Badges, metal: policemen, firemen, etc.; police supply stores

(G-62)
ZETA PRODUCTS INC
18 Westgate Dr (08801-1647)
PHONE..................................908 688-0440

Fax: 908 688-9335
Michael Naso, *President*
Angelo Marzullo, *Sales Mgr*
▲ **EMP:** 38 **EST:** 1977
SQ FT: 20,000
SALES (est): 5.6MM **Privately Held**
WEB: www.zetaproducts.com
SIC: 3861 5044 Microfilm equipment: cameras, projectors, readers, etc.; microfilm equipment

Asbury
Hunterdon County

(G-63)
ALLGRIND PLASTICS INC
6 Vliet Farm Rd (08802-1171)
P.O. Box 363, Bloomsbury (08804-0363)
PHONE..............................908 479-4400
Fax: 908 479-4067
William C Willoughby, *President*
Douglas Slack, *Database Admin*
Regina Willoughby, *Admin Sec*
EMP: 12
SQ FT: 43,550
SALES (est): 2.5MM **Privately Held**
WEB: www.allgrind.com
SIC: 3089 Injection molding of plastics; plastic processing

(G-64)
AMEX TOOL CO
4 Fox Hill Ln (08802-1176)
PHONE..............................908 735-5176
Fax: 908 730-6103
Hubert Stria, *President*
Ronald Stria, *Vice Pres*
EMP: 10
SQ FT: 7,000
SALES: 800K **Privately Held**
SIC: 3599 Machine shop, jobbing & repair

(G-65)
ANTHRACITE INDUSTRIES INC (HQ)
405 Old Main St (08802-1220)
P.O. Box 144 (08802-0144)
PHONE..............................908 537-2155
Marvin Riddle III, *CEO*
Stephen A Riddle, *CEO*
Carol A Kalmar, *President*
Lue Fish, *Vice Pres*
▼ **EMP:** 4
SQ FT: 2,700
SALES (est): 5.5MM
SALES (corp-wide): 131.1MM **Privately Held**
SIC: 3295 Minerals, ground or otherwise treated
PA: Asbury Carbons, Inc.
405 Old Main St
Asbury NJ 08802
908 537-2155

(G-66)
ASBURY CARBONS INC (PA)
405 Old Main St (08802-1077)
PHONE..............................908 537-2155
Stephen A Riddle, *CEO*
H Marvin Riddle III, *Ch of Bd*
Carol A Kalmar, *President*
Sue Rish, *Vice Pres*
William T Meglaughlin Jr, *CFO*
◆ **EMP:** 2
SQ FT: 6,000
SALES (est): 131.1MM **Privately Held**
SIC: 1499 3295 1241 5051 Graphite mining; graphite, natural: ground, pulverized, refined or blended; coal mining services; metals service centers & offices; pencil lead: black, indelible or colored: artists'; erasers: rubber or rubber & abrasive combined

(G-67)
ASBURY GRAPHITE MILLS INC (HQ)
405 Old Main St (08802-1077)
P.O. Box 144 (08802-0144)
PHONE..............................908 537-2155
Fax: 908 537-2908
Steven A Riddle, *CEO*
Lewis Fish, *Vice Pres*

Carol A Kalmar, *Vice Pres*
Susan Rish, *Vice Pres*
H Marvin Riddle III, *Admin Sec*
◆ **EMP:** 35 **EST:** 1895
SQ FT: 100,000
SALES (est): 30.6MM
SALES (corp-wide): 131.1MM **Privately Held**
WEB: www.asbury.com
SIC: 3295 Minerals, ground or treated
PA: Asbury Carbons, Inc.
405 Old Main St
Asbury NJ 08802
908 537-2155

(G-68)
ASBURY GRAPHITE MILLS INC
156 Asbury West Portal Rd (08802-1128)
PHONE..............................908 537-2157
Gary Zeigler, *Branch Mgr*
EMP: 52
SALES (corp-wide): 131.1MM **Privately Held**
WEB: www.asbury.com
SIC: 3295 Minerals, ground or treated
HQ: The Asbury Graphite Mills Inc
405 Old Main St
Asbury NJ 08802
908 537-2155

(G-69)
ASBURY LOUISIANA INC (HQ)
405 Old Main St (08802-1077)
P.O. Box 144 (08802-0144)
PHONE..............................908 537-2155
Stephen A Riddle, *CEO*
H Marvin Riddle III, *Ch of Bd*
Carol Kalmar, *President*
Lewis S Fish, *Vice Pres*
Gary Ziegler, *Vice Pres*
▲ **EMP:** 50
SQ FT: 10,000
SALES (est): 42.8MM
SALES (corp-wide): 131.1MM **Privately Held**
SIC: 3624 Carbon & graphite products
PA: Asbury Carbons, Inc.
405 Old Main St
Asbury NJ 08802
908 537-2155

(G-70)
HART CONSTRUCTION SERVICE
466 Mine Rd (08802-1106)
PHONE..............................908 537-2060
Ronald Hart, *Owner*
EMP: 6
SALES (est): 320K **Privately Held**
SIC: 3531 1521 Plows: construction, excavating & grading; single-family housing construction

(G-71)
JERSEY CIDER WORKS LLC
360 County Road 579 (08802-1231)
PHONE..............................908 940-4115
EMP: 5
SALES (est): 369.4K
SALES (corp-wide): 250K **Privately Held**
SIC: 2084 Wines
PA: Jersey Cider Works, Llc
42 Erwin Park Rd
Montclair NJ 07042
917 604-0067

(G-72)
PACIFIC COAST SYSTEMS LLC
4 Fox Hill Rd (08802-1176)
PHONE..............................908 735-9955
Diana Schaeffer,
Ron Stria,
EMP: 5
SALES (est): 565.4K **Privately Held**
SIC: 3728 Aircraft training equipment

(G-73)
SILVERTHORNE FURNITURE CORP
Also Called: Billiards and Bars
149 Asbury Broadway Rd (08802-1005)
PHONE..............................908 689-6969
Fax: 908 689-0624
John Jones, *President*
Kimberly Jones, *Corp Secy*
EMP: 8
SQ FT: 3,000

SALES: 1.1MM **Privately Held**
SIC: 3949 2517 Billiard & pool equipment & supplies, general; home entertainment unit cabinets, wood

(G-74)
VITAL SIGNS MEDCL LEGL CONSLTN
10 Magnolia Ln (08802-1184)
P.O. Box 157 (08802-0157)
PHONE..............................908 537-7857
William Kaminski, *Principal*
EMP: 11 **EST:** 2001
SALES (est): 1MM **Privately Held**
SIC: 3993 Signs & advertising specialties

Asbury Park
Monmouth County

(G-75)
COASTER INC
Also Called: Coaster, The
1011 Main St Ste B (07712-5963)
PHONE..............................732 775-3010
Fax: 732 775-8345
Ellen Carroll, *President*
Thomas Carroll, *Principal*
Joseph Garrett, *Accounts Exec*
Leah Lamanna, *Marketing Staff*
EMP: 10
SALES: 500K **Privately Held**
WEB: www.thecoaster.net
SIC: 2711 Newspapers

(G-76)
DAYTON GREY CORP
1008 1st Ave (07712-5820)
PHONE..............................732 869-0060
Dan France, *President*
Leven Stein, *Vice Pres*
EMP: 11
SQ FT: 8,000
SALES: 1MM **Privately Held**
WEB: www.daytongrey.com
SIC: 3559 Metal finishing equipment for plating, etc.

(G-77)
F L FELDMAN ASSOCIATES
811 Memorial Dr (07712-5829)
PHONE..............................732 776-8544
Frank L Feldman, *President*
EMP: 10
SQ FT: 8,000
SALES (est): 800K **Privately Held**
WEB: www.customwoodworking.info
SIC: 2431 2434 Woodwork, interior & ornamental; wood kitchen cabinets

(G-78)
GENE MIGNOLA INC
704 Cookman Ave (07712-7008)
PHONE..............................732 775-9291
Gene Mignola, *President*
EMP: 4
SQ FT: 8,000
SALES: 170K **Privately Held**
SIC: 2211 Basket weave fabrics, cotton

(G-79)
KNOCK OUT GRAPHICS INC
522 Cookman Ave Ste 3n (07712-7140)
PHONE..............................732 774-3331
Margaret Brunette, *President*
Kyle Lepree, *Vice Pres*
EMP: 14
SQ FT: 800
SALES (est): 1.8MM **Privately Held**
SIC: 2752 Commercial printing, lithographic

(G-80)
LIGHTHOUSE EXPRESS INC
809 Memorial Dr (07712-5829)
P.O. Box 565, West Long Branch (07764-0565)
PHONE..............................732 776-9555
Isaac Abadi, *President*
EMP: 7 **EST:** 1995
SALES: 800K **Privately Held**
WEB: www.lighthouseexpress.com
SIC: 3499 3961 Giftware, brass goods; costume jewelry

(G-81)
MCLAIN STUDIOS INC
Also Called: Mc Lain Screen Printing
1203 Main St (07712-5940)
P.O. Box 147 (07712-0147)
PHONE..............................732 775-0271
Fax: 732 774-2250
James W Mc Lain, *President*
EMP: 4 **EST:** 1945
SQ FT: 2,000
SALES (est): 406.7K **Privately Held**
WEB: www.mclainstudios.com
SIC: 2396 3993 Screen printing on fabric articles; signs & advertising specialties

(G-82)
PORT A (PA)
911 Kingsley St (07712-6216)
PHONE..............................732 776-6511
EMP: 12
SALES (est): 1.8MM **Privately Held**
SIC: 3421 Table & food cutlery, including butchers'

(G-83)
SPINNINGDESIGNS INC
910 1st Ave (07712-5818)
PHONE..............................732 775-7050
Eileen Herman, *President*
Bob Derosa, *Vice Pres*
Robert Derosa, *Vice Pres*
EMP: 12
SQ FT: 11,000
SALES: 1.4MM **Privately Held**
SIC: 3993 Signs & advertising specialties

(G-84)
STREAMSERVE INC (HQ)
100 Tormee Dr (07712-7502)
PHONE..............................781 863-1510
Dennis Ladd, *President*
Paul Mc Feeters, *CFO*
Ulf Kasshag, *Treasurer*
G Ndor Rentsch, *Director*
Tina Santos, *Admin Sec*
EMP: 28
SALES (est): 25.8MM
SALES (corp-wide): 2.2B **Privately Held**
WEB: www.streamserve.com
SIC: 7372 Prepackaged software
PA: Open Text Corporation
275 Frank Tompa Dr
Waterloo ON N2L 0
519 888-7111

(G-85)
SUPER CHROME INC
1004 1st Ave (07712-5820)
PHONE..............................732 774-2210
Robert Micele, *Principal*
EMP: 5
SALES (est): 261.7K **Privately Held**
SIC: 3471 Anodizing (plating) of metals or formed products

(G-86)
TERRISS CONSOLIDATED INDS
807 Summerfield Ave (07712-6970)
P.O. Box 110 (07712-0110)
PHONE..............................732 988-0909
Fax: 732 502-0526
Judith L Bodnovich, *CEO*
Stephen Bodnovich, *Vice Pres*
Marc J Epstein, *Vice Pres*
Joan Goldberg, *Vice Pres*
Edward Della Zanna, *Sales Mgr*
▼ **EMP:** 12 **EST:** 1895
SQ FT: 30,000
SALES (est): 3.1MM **Privately Held**
WEB: www.terriss.com
SIC: 3556 Beverage machinery

(G-87)
UNIVERSAL FILTERS INC
1207 Main St Ste A (07712-5964)
PHONE..............................732 774-8555
Fax: 732 774-8594
Jerrold D Kolton, *President*
David Tafara, *Vice Pres*
EMP: 20
SALES (est): 3.2MM **Privately Held**
WEB: www.universalfilters.com
SIC: 3569 Filters, general line: industrial

Atco
Camden County

(G-88)
ALAN DUFFY PRINTING
2389 Atco Ave (08004-1824)
PHONE..........................856 768-1046
Fax: 856 768-4742
Alan Duffy, *Owner*
EMP: 4
SALES (est): 224.8K **Privately Held**
SIC: 2752 Commercial printing, lithographic

(G-89)
FORGET ME NOT CHOCOLATES BY NA
121 Lakeside Dr (08004-3036)
PHONE..........................856 753-8916
H Cadet, *Principal*
EMP: 5
SALES (est): 310.2K **Privately Held**
WEB: www.forgetmenotchocolates.com
SIC: 2066 Chocolate

(G-90)
PRE-FAB STRUCTURES INC (PA)
907 Wedgewood Way (08004-1336)
PHONE..........................856 768-4257
Leslie W Johnson, *President*
Terri Johnson, *Vice Pres*
EMP: 5
SALES (est): 592.8K **Privately Held**
WEB: www.pre-fabstructures.com
SIC: 3448 Prefabricated metal buildings

(G-91)
PRECISION SPECIALISTS MCH LLC
1005 Martha Blvd (08004-1452)
PHONE..........................856 768-5990
Fax: 856 768-6394
Richard Bottoni, *President*
Theresa Bottoni, *CFO*
EMP: 10
SQ FT: 10,000
SALES (est): 1.2MM **Privately Held**
WEB: www.precisionspecialists.com
SIC: 3599 Machine shop, jobbing & repair

(G-92)
VI CONCRETE CO
2324 Columbia Ave (08004-1480)
PHONE..........................856 767-0415
Fax: 856 768-7894
EMP: 17
SQ FT: 3,000
SALES (est): 1.1MM **Privately Held**
SIC: 3273 Mfg Ready-Mixed Concrete

Atlantic City
Atlantic County

(G-93)
A C DISPLAY STUDIOS INC
2715 Arctic Ave (08401-3840)
P.O. Box 1174, Brigantine (08203-7174)
PHONE..........................609 345-0814
Fax: 609 345-2715
EMP: 6
SQ FT: 6,000
SALES (est): 611.5K **Privately Held**
SIC: 3993 Mfg Signs/Advertising Specialties

(G-94)
CROCS INC
113 N Arkansas Ave (08401-4105)
PHONE..........................609 344-6300
EMP: 14
SALES (corp-wide): 1B **Publicly Held**
SIC: 3021 Shoes, rubber or rubber soled fabric uppers
PA: Crocs, Inc.
   7477 Dry Creek Pkwy
   Niwot CO 80503
   303 848-7000

(G-95)
DONNA KARAN INTERNATIONAL INC
1931 Atlantic Ave (08401-6705)
PHONE..........................609 345-3402
EMP: 8
SALES (corp-wide): 2.8B **Publicly Held**
SIC: 2335 Women's, juniors' & misses' dresses
HQ: Donna Karan International Inc.
   240 W 40th St
   New York NY 10018
   212 789-1500

(G-96)
FORMICA BROS BAKERY
Also Called: Formica's Bake Shop
2310 Arctic Ave Ste 1 (08401-4044)
PHONE..........................609 348-8934
Fax: 609 344-0304
Frank D Formica, *Owner*
EMP: 11
SQ FT: 3,500
SALES (est): 1.6MM **Privately Held**
SIC: 5149 2051 Baking supplies; bread, cake & related products

(G-97)
FRALINGERS INC (PA)
Also Called: Fralinger's Org Salt Wtr Taffy
1325 Boardwalk Ste 1 (08401-7287)
PHONE..........................609 345-2177
Fax: 609 344-0758
Frank Glaser, *President*
EMP: 37 EST: 1885
SQ FT: 800
SALES (est): 3.9MM **Privately Held**
WEB: www.fralingers.com
SIC: 2066 5145 5441 2064 Chocolate & cocoa products; confectionery; confectionery; candy & other confectionery products

(G-98)
FRALINGERS INC
1519 Boardwalk (08401-7012)
PHONE..........................609 345-2177
Frank Glaser, *Manager*
EMP: 9
SALES (corp-wide): 3.9MM **Privately Held**
WEB: www.fralingers.com
SIC: 2064 Candy & other confectionery products
PA: Fralingers Inc
   1325 Boardwalk Ste 1
   Atlantic City NJ 08401
   609 345-2177

(G-99)
HANDS ON WHEELS
509 Atlantic Ave (08401-7601)
PHONE..........................609 892-4693
Peace Toleito, *Principal*
EMP: 4
SALES (est): 235K **Privately Held**
SIC: 3312 Wheels

(G-100)
HEADQUARTERS PUB LLC
Also Called: Tun Tavern Brewery & Rest
2 Convention Blvd (08401-4137)
PHONE..........................609 347-2579
Fax: 609 347-2536
Montgomery Dahm, *Managing Prtnr*
Diane Tharp, *Manager*
Tom Scannapieco,
EMP: 50 EST: 1998
SQ FT: 7,600
SALES (est): 7.8MM **Privately Held**
WEB: www.tuntavern.com
SIC: 2082 5921 Beer (alcoholic beverage); beer (packaged)

(G-101)
JAMES CANDY COMPANY (PA)
1519 Boardwalk (08401-7012)
PHONE..........................609 344-1519
Frank J Glaser, *President*
Maureen Glaser, *Vice Pres*
▲ EMP: 100
SQ FT: 40,000

SALES: 6MM **Privately Held**
WEB: www.seashoretaffy.com
SIC: 5441 5145 2064 Confectionery; confectionery; candy & other confectionery products

(G-102)
LINDA SPOLITINO
Also Called: Seagull Stain Glass
1917 Kuehnle Ave (08401-1703)
PHONE..........................609 345-3126
Linda Spolitino, *Owner*
Linda Spilitino, *Partner*
EMP: 7
SQ FT: 2,000
SALES: 225K **Privately Held**
SIC: 3231 Stained glass: made from purchased glass

(G-103)
MOTORS AND DRIVES INC
Also Called: Park Electric Motor Co
1413 Marmora Ave (08401-2338)
PHONE..........................609 344-8058
Fax: 609 348-1141
Gene Moir Jr, *Manager*
EMP: 4
SALES (corp-wide): 1.5MM **Privately Held**
WEB: www.motorsanddrives.com
SIC: 5999 7694 Motors, electric; electric motor repair
PA: Motors And Drives, Inc
   5 Asbury Ave
   Freehold NJ 07728
   732 462-7683

(G-104)
MYRIAMS DREAM BOOK BINDERY
1102 Atlantic Ave (08401-4803)
PHONE..........................609 345-5555
Adrienna Epstein, *Principal*
Emma Todd, *Principal*
EMP: 4
SALES: 6K **Privately Held**
SIC: 2789 Bookbinding & related work

(G-105)
OFFSHORE ENTERPRISES INC
433 N Maryland Ave (08401-2533)
P.O. Box 477, Brigantine (08203-0477)
PHONE..........................609 345-9099
Jonathan Weiss, *President*
EMP: 4
SALES (est): 230K **Privately Held**
SIC: 3949 Fishing equipment

(G-106)
PVH CORP
Also Called: Van Heusen
32 N Michigan Ave (08401-4117)
PHONE..........................609 344-6273
EMP: 9
SALES (corp-wide): 8.9B **Publicly Held**
SIC: 2321 Men's & boys' dress shirts
PA: Pvh Corp.
   200 Madison Ave Bsmt 1
   New York NY 10016
   212 381-3500

(G-107)
RAPHEL MARKETING INC
118 S Newton Pl (08401-5615)
PHONE..........................609 348-6646
Fax: 609 347-2455
Neil Raphel, *President*
Neil Raphel, *President*
Ruth Raphel, *President*
Murray Raphel, *Vice Pres*
EMP: 7
SQ FT: 2,000
SALES (est): 630K **Privately Held**
SIC: 8742 2741 Marketing consulting services; miscellaneous publishing

(G-108)
SWAROVSKI NORTH AMERICA LTD
2801 Pacific Ave (08401-6347)
PHONE..........................609 344-1323
Fax: 609 344-1324
Leslie Adam, *Branch Mgr*
EMP: 4
SALES (corp-wide): 3.7B **Privately Held**
SIC: 3961 Costume jewelry

HQ: Swarovski North America Limited
   1 Kenney Dr
   Cranston RI 02920
   401 463-6400

Atlantic Highlands
Monmouth County

(G-109)
BRICK-WALL CORP (PA)
25 1st Ave Ste 200 (07716-1285)
PHONE..........................732 787-0226
Lawrance Hesse, *President*
Larry Mulcahy, *CFO*
EMP: 29
SALES (est): 3.6MM **Privately Held**
SIC: 2951 5032 Asphalt paving mixtures & blocks; gravel; sand, construction

(G-110)
CARTON BREWING COMPANY LLC
6 E Washington Ave (07716-1230)
PHONE..........................732 654-2337
Chris Wecht, *Opers Staff*
Doug Edwards, *Marketing Staff*
La Carton IV,
▲ EMP: 6
SALES (est): 682.3K **Privately Held**
SIC: 2082 5921 Beer (alcoholic beverage); beer (packaged)

(G-111)
FOOD CIRCUS SUPER MARKETS INC
Also Called: Store 266
9 East Ave 36 (07716)
PHONE..........................732 291-4079
Fax: 732 291-5278
Joe Grande, *Controller*
EMP: 100
SALES (corp-wide): 146.4MM **Privately Held**
WEB: www.foodcircus.com
SIC: 5411 5992 5812 2051 Supermarkets; florists; eating places; bread, cake & related products
PA: Food Circus Super Markets, Inc.
   853 State Route 35
   Middletown NJ 07748
   732 671-2220

(G-112)
IWS LICENSE CORP
29 4th Ave (07716-1208)
PHONE..........................732 872-0014
EMP: 15
SALES (est): 1MM **Privately Held**
SIC: 2741 Misc Publishing

(G-113)
JERSEY PRINTING ASSOCIATES INC
153 1st Ave Ste 1 (07716-1292)
P.O. Box 355 (07716-0355)
PHONE..........................732 872-9654
Fax: 732 872-9309
Gregory J Heh, *President*
Charlie McCullagh, *VP Sls/Mktg*
Victor Olefson, *Accounts Exec*
Patricia Pfleger, *Admin Sec*
EMP: 45 EST: 1981
SQ FT: 36,000
SALES (est): 5.6MM **Privately Held**
WEB: www.jerseyprinting.com
SIC: 2752 2789 5112 Commercial printing, offset; bookbinding & related work; social stationery & greeting cards

(G-114)
JULIAN BAIT COMPANY INC
Also Called: Julian Enterprises
990 State Route 36 (07716-2024)
PHONE..........................732 291-0050
Joseph Julian, *President*
Alexandra Julian, *Treasurer*
Josephine Julian, *Admin Sec*
EMP: 6
SQ FT: 1,000
SALES (est): 460.7K **Privately Held**
SIC: 5091 3949 Fishing equipment & supplies; fishing equipment

(G-115)
PREMIER GRAPHICS INC
165 1st Ave C (07716-1265)
PHONE..................................732 872-9933
Fax: 732 872-9335
Sal Madalone, *President*
Toni Madalone, *Vice Pres*
EMP: 20
SQ FT: 10,000
SALES (est): 2.6MM **Privately Held**
WEB: www.premiergraphics.com
SIC: 2752 Commercial printing, offset

Audubon
Camden County

(G-116)
CORBI PRINTING CO INC
Also Called: Municipal Record Service
106 W Atlantic Ave (08106-1439)
PHONE..................................856 547-2444
Fax: 856 547-2999
Thomas G Corbi, *President*
Mary Corbi, *Vice Pres*
EMP: 8
SQ FT: 3,600
SALES (est): 1.2MM **Privately Held**
SIC: 2752 Commercial printing, lithographic

(G-117)
MODERN METRIC MACHINE COMPANY
101 W Nicholson Rd (08106-1411)
PHONE..................................856 547-4044
Paul Volkwine, *President*
Rose Ann Volkwine, *Corp Secy*
EMP: 6 EST: 1977
SQ FT: 4,000
SALES: 750K **Privately Held**
SIC: 3599 Machine shop, jobbing & repair

(G-118)
SIKA CORPORATION
Also Called: Sika Liquid Plasics Division
251 S White Horse Pike (08106-1306)
PHONE..................................856 298-2313
Sam Girgenti, *Director*
EMP: 20
SALES (corp-wide): 213.5MM **Privately Held**
SIC: 2821 Plastics materials & resins
HQ: Sika Corporation
201 Polito Ave
Lyndhurst NJ 07071
201 933-8800

Augusta
Sussex County

(G-119)
CLOGIC LLC
Also Called: Clogic Defense
4 Sunset Ln (07822-2100)
PHONE..................................973 934-5223
Diana-Lynn Herbst, *Branch Mgr*
Michael Voisine, *Director*
EMP: 7
SALES (est): 705.3K
SALES (corp-wide): 2MM **Privately Held**
SIC: 3795 Tanks & tank components
PA: Clogic, Llc
800 Hawks Nest Ct
Ponte Vedra Beach FL 32082
904 686-1641

Avalon
Cape May County

(G-120)
SEVEN MILE PUBG & CREATIVE
355 24th St (08202-1816)
P.O. Box 134 (08202-0134)
PHONE..................................609 967-7707
Monica Coskey, *Mng Member*
David Coskey, *Officer*
EMP: 10

SALES: 800K **Privately Held**
SIC: 2741 Miscellaneous publishing

Avenel
Middlesex County

(G-121)
A&M INDUSTRIAL INC
Also Called: A&M Petro Marine Division
22b Cragwood Rd (07001-2234)
PHONE..................................908 862-1800
John Smickenbecker, *Branch Mgr*
EMP: 10
SALES (corp-wide): 36MM **Privately Held**
WEB: www.am-ind.com
SIC: 3498 Pipe fittings, fabricated from purchased pipe
PA: A&M Industrial, Inc.
37 W Cherry St
Rahway NJ 07065
732 574-1111

(G-122)
ABLE FAB CO
18 Mileed Way (07001-2403)
PHONE..................................732 396-0600
William Demott, *President*
EMP: 36 EST: 1976
SQ FT: 12,000
SALES (est): 4MM **Privately Held**
WEB: www.archerday.com
SIC: 3443 3444 3441 1711 Plate work for the metalworking trade; pipe, sheet metal; fabricated structural metal; plumbing, heating, air-conditioning contractors

(G-123)
ACCELY INC
381 Blair Rd (07001-2201)
PHONE..................................609 598-1882
Nilesh Shah, *CEO*
Alvi Gandhi, *President*
EMP: 10
SALES: 3.3MM **Privately Held**
SIC: 7372 Application computer software

(G-124)
ARCHER DAY INC
18 Mileed Way (07001-2403)
PHONE..................................732 396-0600
William Demott, *President*
EMP: 50
SQ FT: 7,000
SALES (est): 10.8MM **Privately Held**
SIC: 3312 1731 3441 Plate, steel; electrical work; fabricated structural metal

(G-125)
ARTISTIC DOORS AND WINDOWS INC
10 S Inman Ave (07001-1508)
PHONE..................................732 726-9400
Fax: 732 726-9494
Rick Autovino Enrico, *CEO*
John Autovino, *Vice Pres*
Guy Cichy, *Vice Pres*
Jason Adamshick, *Project Mgr*
Samer Gorguis, *Project Mgr*
▲ EMP: 22
SQ FT: 32,000
SALES (est): 5.2MM **Privately Held**
SIC: 2431 Doors & door parts & trim, wood; windows & window parts & trim, wood

(G-126)
AVIONIC INSTRUMENTS LLC
1414 Randolph Ave (07001-2402)
P.O. Box 498 (07001-0498)
PHONE..................................732 388-3500
Fax: 732 382-4996
Carol Soltz, *Vice Pres*
Doris Ulloa, *Prdtn Mgr*
Dan Scardelli, *Materials Mgr*
Eric Padmore, *Traffic Mgr*
Stephen Gross, *Opers Staff*
EMP: 200
SQ FT: 35,000

SALES (est): 50.5MM
SALES (corp-wide): 3.5B **Publicly Held**
WEB: www.avionicinstruments.com
SIC: 3629 Inverters, nonrotating: electrical; power conversion units, a.c. to d.c.: static-electric
HQ: Transdigm, Inc.
4223 Monticello Blvd
Cleveland OH 44121

(G-127)
BARBEITOS INC
6 Pocahont Pl (07001-1516)
PHONE..................................732 726-9543
Martha Amarante, *President*
EMP: 4
SALES (est): 211.5K **Privately Held**
SIC: 2051 Cakes, pies & pastries

(G-128)
CARAVAN INC
160 Essex Ave E (07001-2045)
P.O. Box 427 (07001-0427)
PHONE..................................732 590-0210
Michael Caracapa, *President*
Patricia Caracappa, *Treasurer*
▲ EMP: 16
SQ FT: 5,600
SALES (est): 4MM **Privately Held**
SIC: 3537 Trucks: freight, baggage, etc.: industrial, except mining

(G-129)
D L PRINTING CO INC
283 Prospect Ave (07001-1156)
PHONE..................................732 750-1917
Fax: 732 750-1400
Dave Lospinoso, *President*
Stacie Lospinoso, *Treasurer*
EMP: 5
SQ FT: 2,000
SALES (est): 714K **Privately Held**
WEB: www.dlprinting.net
SIC: 2752 Commercial printing, offset

(G-130)
ESSEX COATINGS LLC
135 Essex Ave E (07001-2019)
PHONE..................................732 855-9400
Josh Feuer, *Manager*
Liz Flott, *Manager*
Sheila Hughes, *Manager*
Ejlat Feuer,
▲ EMP: 10
SQ FT: 2,000
SALES (est): 1.9MM **Privately Held**
SIC: 2435 Hardwood veneer & plywood; hardwood plywood, prefinished

(G-131)
FLAVORS OF ORIGIN INC (PA)
Also Called: Flavor Materials International
10 Engelhard Ave (07001-2205)
PHONE..................................732 499-9700
Fax: 732 499-7090
Paul Ahn, *President*
Deepak Arora, *Vice Pres*
Cinthia Maldonado, *Opers Mgr*
Denise Morris, *Opers Mgr*
Bryan Warren, *Safety Mgr*
◆ EMP: 20
SQ FT: 40,000
SALES (est): 16.9MM **Privately Held**
WEB: www.flavormaterials.com
SIC: 5149 2899 2087 Flavourings & fragrances; essential oils; flavoring extracts & syrups

(G-132)
FUEL ONE INC
869 Us Highway 1 (07001-1357)
PHONE..................................732 726-9500
EMP: 4
SALES (est): 305K **Privately Held**
SIC: 2869 Fuels

(G-133)
G R IMPEX LTD LIABILITY CO (PA)
Also Called: Falcon Papers & Plastics
2 Terminal Way Bldg A (07001)
PHONE..................................732 931-7001
Laura Santiago, *Accountant*
Gautam Bhatia, *Mng Member*
Sam Bhatia,
◆ EMP: 11

SQ FT: 20,000
SALES (est): 7.5MM **Privately Held**
WEB: www.falconpapers.com
SIC: 5111 2621 Printing & writing paper; packaging paper

(G-134)
GENTEK BUILDING PRODUCTS INC
11 Cragwood Rd (07001-2202)
PHONE..................................732 381-0900
Kerry Higgs, *Manager*
EMP: 33 **Privately Held**
WEB: www.gentekinc.com
SIC: 3355 Aluminum rolling & drawing
HQ: Gentek Building Products, Inc.
3773 State Rd
Cuyahoga Falls OH 44223

(G-135)
INTERBAHM INTERNATIONAL INC
10 Engelhard Ave (07001)
PHONE..................................732 499-9700
Paul Ahn, *President*
Mario Natale, *Accountant*
EMP: 45
SALES (est): 4.6MM **Privately Held**
SIC: 2087 2899 5149 Flavoring extracts & syrups; essential oils; flavourings & fragrances

(G-136)
JOY SNACKS LLC
365 Blair Rd Ste A (07001-2231)
PHONE..................................732 272-0707
AVI Weinstein, *Vice Pres*
Mendy Cinner, *Director*
EMP: 15 EST: 2016
SQ FT: 22,000
SALES (est): 2MM **Privately Held**
SIC: 2064 Granola & muesli, bars & clusters; nuts, candy covered

(G-137)
K R ELECTRONICS INC
91 Avenel St (07001-1749)
PHONE..................................732 636-1900
Fax: 732 636-1982
Charles Kiall, *President*
EMP: 13
SQ FT: 10,000
SALES (est): 2.2MM **Privately Held**
WEB: www.krfilters.com
SIC: 3679 Microwave components; electronic circuits

(G-138)
KEURIG DR PEPPER INC
433 Blair Rd (07001-2215)
PHONE..................................732 388-5545
Fax: 732 815-2801
Robert Hofmann, *Branch Mgr*
Martin Bergstein, *Representative*
EMP: 100 **Publicly Held**
SIC: 2086 Soft drinks: packaged in cans, bottles, etc.
PA: Keurig Dr Pepper Inc.
5301 Legacy Dr
Plano TX 75024

(G-139)
MAGIC PRINTING CORP
386 Avenel St (07001-1146)
PHONE..................................732 726-0620
Fax: 732 726-1294
Steven Glassman, *President*
EMP: 14
SQ FT: 3,000
SALES: 1.4MM **Privately Held**
SIC: 2759 5099 Thermography; invitation & stationery printing & engraving; rubber stamps

(G-140)
MICROCAST TECHNOLOGIES CORP
17 Mileed Way (07001-2403)
PHONE..................................732 943-7356
EMP: 6 **Privately Held**
SIC: 3369 White metal castings (lead, tin, antimony), except die
PA: Microcast Technologies Corp.
1611 W Elizabeth Ave
Linden NJ 07036

▲ = Import ▼=Export
◆ =Import/Export

(G-141)
MIZCO INTERNATIONAL INC
Also Called: Cellular Innovations
80 Essex Ave E (07001-2020)
PHONE..............................732 912-2000
Albert Mizrahi, *President*
David Strumeier, *Exec VP*
Sam Mizarahi, *Vice Pres*
Isaac Mizrahi, *Vice Pres*
Richard Healey, *Opers Staff*
▲ EMP: 100
SALES (est): 42.6MM Privately Held
WEB: www.mizco.com
SIC: 5043 3629 3663 3661 Photographic
cameras, projectors, equipment & sup-
plies; battery chargers, rectifying or non-
rotating; mobile communication
equipment; telephone cords, jacks,
adapters, etc.; batteries, rechargeable

(G-142)
MULTI-PLASTICS EXTRUSIONS INC
30 Production Way (07001-1628)
PHONE..............................732 388-2300
Douglas Griswold, *Prdtn Mgr*
Ed McDonald, *Branch Mgr*
Elsy Panitz, *Manager*
Sal Monteleone, *Maintence Staff*
EMP: 17
SALES (corp-wide): 220MM Privately
Held
SIC: 2821 Plastics materials & resins
HQ: Multi-Plastics Extrusions, Inc.
600 Dietrich Ave
Hazleton PA 18201
570 455-2021

(G-143)
NATIONAL FENCE SYSTEMS INC
Also Called: Nfs
1033 Rte One Avenel (07001)
PHONE..............................732 636-5600
Fax: 732 636-5605
Anthony Martinez, *President*
Dennis Grady, *CFO*
Linda Martinez, *Admin Sec*
▲ EMP: 85
SQ FT: 14,500
SALES (est): 17MM Privately Held
WEB: www.nationalfencesystems.com
SIC: 1799 5211 2499 Fence construction;
fencing; fencing, wood

(G-144)
NOURHAN TRADING GROUP INC
27 Engelhard Ave (07001-2204)
PHONE..............................732 381-8110
Mike Ahmed,
▲ EMP: 4
SALES (est): 501.1K Privately Held
SIC: 2011 Canned meats (except baby
food), meat slaughtered on site

(G-145)
PILOT CHEMICAL COMPANY OHIO
267 Homestead Ave (07001-2006)
PHONE..............................732 634-6613
Fax: 732 634-7971
Tom Peterson, *Manager*
EMP: 15
SQ FT: 20,000
SALES (corp-wide): 108.9MM Privately
Held
SIC: 2841 2869 Detergents, synthetic or-
ganic or inorganic alkaline; industrial or-
ganic chemicals
PA: Pilot Chemical Company Of Ohio
2744 E Kemper Rd
Cincinnati OH 45241
513 326-0600

(G-146)
PQ CORPORATION
2 Paddock St (07001)
PHONE..............................732 750-9040
Fax: 732 634-2840
Larry Bodden, *Plant Mgr*
Ted Freeman, *Plant Mgr*
Sue Morris, *Transportation*
Merrill Colmery, *Opers-Prdtn-Mfg*
Christine Salaiz, *Buyer*
EMP: 24

SQ FT: 80,000
SALES (corp-wide): 1.4B Publicly Held
WEB: www.pqcorp.com
SIC: 2819 2842 Industrial inorganic chem-
icals; specialty cleaning, polishes & sani-
tation goods
HQ: Pq Corporation
300 Lindenwood Dr
Malvern PA 19355
610 651-4200

(G-147)
PREMIER DIE CASTING COMPANY
1177 Rahway Ave (07001-2196)
PHONE..............................732 634-3000
Fax: 732 634-0590
Leonard Cordaro, *President*
▲ EMP: 60 EST: 1945
SQ FT: 82,500
SALES (est): 15.7MM Privately Held
WEB: www.diecasting.com
SIC: 3363 Aluminum die-castings

(G-148)
PROCTER & GAMBLE MFG CO
100 Essex Ave E (07001-2020)
PHONE..............................732 602-4500
Fax: 732 634-8946
Kathleen Rasmussen, *Foreman/Supr*
Sandy Moshier, *Branch Mgr*
Phillip Gonzalez, *Technical Staff*
EMP: 100
SALES (corp-wide): 66.8B Publicly Held
SIC: 2841 2079 2099 2844 Detergents,
synthetic organic or inorganic alkaline;
shortening & other solid edible fats;
peanut butter; toilet preparations; cake
mixes, prepared: from purchased flour
HQ: The Procter & Gamble Manufacturing
Company
1 Procter And Gamble Plz
Cincinnati OH 45202
513 983-1100

(G-149)
R L PLASTICS INC
20 Production Way (07001-1628)
PHONE..............................732 340-1100
Melvin Laufer, *Treasurer*
Hindy Laufer, *Controller*
▲ EMP: 5 EST: 1949
SQ FT: 14,000
SALES (est): 767.1K Privately Held
WEB: www.rlplastics.net
SIC: 5023 5131 2392 Home furnishings;
linens, table; yard goods, woven; table-
cloths: made from purchased materials

(G-150)
SAVINO DEL BENE USA INC (HQ)
34 Engelhard Ave (07001-2217)
PHONE..............................347 960-5568
Andrea Fanti, *Ch of Bd*
Silvano Brandani, *President*
Massimiliano Brandani, *Vice Pres*
Fred Sheinblum, *CFO*
Filippo Occaso, *Admin Sec*
▼ EMP: 55
SQ FT: 10,000
SALES (est): 471.6MM
SALES (corp-wide): 453MM Privately
Held
WEB: www.bos.sdbusa.com
SIC: 3799 4731 All terrain vehicles (ATV);
freight forwarding
PA: Trasporti Internazionali Agenzia Marit-
tima Savino Del Bene Spa
Via Delle Nazioni Unite 19
Scandicci FI 50018
055 521-91

(G-151)
SNAPPLE DISTRIBUTORS INC (HQ)
Also Called: Dpsg
433 Blair Rd Ste 1 (07001-2215)
PHONE..............................732 815-2800
Joseph Poli, *President*
Robert Hofmann, *Vice Pres*
Igor Katsman, *Vice Pres*
▲ EMP: 32
SQ FT: 150,000
SALES (est): 31.8MM Publicly Held
SIC: 2086 Bottled & canned soft drinks

(G-152)
STEELSTRAN INDUSTRIES INC (PA)
Also Called: A. L. Don Co.
35 Mileed Way (07001-2403)
P.O. Box 30 (07001-0030)
PHONE..............................732 574-0700
Fax: 732 574-9191
Peter Gronbeck, *CEO*
Susan Gronbeck, *President*
Arthur Jeronimo, *COO*
Thomas Burns, *Vice Pres*
▲ EMP: 21
SQ FT: 33,000
SALES (est): 16.6MM Privately Held
SIC: 5082 2298 3732 5085 Ladders;
ropes & fiber cables; boat building & re-
pairing; industrial supplies; metals service
centers & offices; transportation equip-
ment & supplies

(G-153)
STRETCH-O-RAMA INC
Also Called: Longstreet
5 Paddock St (07001-1856)
PHONE..............................732 855-1400
Fax: 732 283-2798
EMP: 47
SQ FT: 30,000
SALES (est): 5.2MM
SALES (corp-wide): 6.3MM Privately
Held
SIC: 5611 5651 2311 Clothing acces-
sories: men's & boys'; family clothing
stores; men's & boys' uniforms
PA: Stretch-O-Rama Inc.
20 W 33rd St Fl 10-12
New York NY 10001
212 947-4090

(G-154)
SYNERGEM INC
2323 Randolph Ave Ste 2 (07001-2412)
PHONE..............................732 692-6308
Amy P Silverman, *President*
Thomas Demayer, *Chairman*
Jose Rivera, *Opers Mgr*
Jennifer Love, *Opers Staff*
Lisa Cancilla, *Production*
▲ EMP: 20
SQ FT: 17,700
SALES (est): 4.2MM Privately Held
WEB: www.synergem.com
SIC: 3695 Magnetic & optical recording
media

(G-155)
TATARA GROUP INC
Also Called: Nu Steel
381 Blair Rd (07001-2201)
PHONE..............................732 231-6031
Rahul Katyal, *President*
Paresh Mehta, *Vice Pres*
▲ EMP: 6
SALES (est): 592.3K Privately Held
SIC: 5719 5211 4225 2392 Kitchenware;
bathroom fixtures, equipment & supplies;
general warehousing & storage; wash-
cloths & bath mitts: made from purchased
materials

(G-156)
THERMO-GRAPHICS INC
386 Avenel St (07001-1146)
PHONE..............................908 486-0100
Fax: 732 669-0250
Seth Batzar, *President*
Arlene Batzar, *Vice Pres*
▲ EMP: 6
SQ FT: 4,500
SALES (est): 540K Privately Held
WEB: www.thermographics.com
SIC: 2752 Commercial printing, offset

(G-157)
TSI NOMENCLATURE INC
1400 Rahway Ave (07001-2226)
P.O. Box 390 (07001-0390)
PHONE..............................732 340-0646
Shawn Scott, *President*
EMP: 5
SQ FT: 10,000
SALES (est): 818K Privately Held
SIC: 3613 Panelboards & distribution
boards, electric

(G-158)
USA TEALIGHT INC
4 Cragwood Rd (07001-2203)
PHONE..............................732 943-2408
Michael Zohar, *President*
Neal Bochner, *COO*
◆ EMP: 15
SALES (est): 6.3MM Privately Held
SIC: 3999 Candles

Barnegat
Ocean County

(G-159)
AHE MANUFACTURING INC
127 S Main St (08005-2312)
PHONE..............................609 660-8000
John Whitaker, *Principal*
▲ EMP: 15
SALES (est): 451.1K Privately Held
SIC: 3534 Elevators & moving stairways

(G-160)
AIRBRUSH ACTION INC
79 S Main St Ste 1 (08005-2315)
PHONE..............................732 223-7878
Fax: 732 223-2855
Cliff Stieglitz, *President*
▲ EMP: 7
SQ FT: 2,800
SALES (est): 1.1MM Privately Held
WEB: www.airbrushaction.com
SIC: 2721 Magazines: publishing & printing

(G-161)
DL MYERS CORP
446 N Main St (08005-2422)
PHONE..............................609 698-8800
Darren L Myers, *President*
EMP: 10
SALES: 900K Privately Held
SIC: 3443 Fuel tanks (oil, gas, etc.): metal
plate

(G-162)
DOT GRAPHIX INC
79 S Main St Ste 13 (08005-2316)
PHONE..............................609 994-3416
Joe Lopes, *President*
EMP: 10
SALES (est): 520K Privately Held
SIC: 2759 Screen printing

(G-163)
M G S
309 Route 72 (08005-1035)
PHONE..............................609 698-7000
EMP: 4 EST: 2010
SALES (est): 180K Privately Held
SIC: 1321 Natural Gas Liquids Production

(G-164)
S P SHEET METAL CO INC
446 N Main St (08005-2422)
PHONE..............................609 698-8800
Darren Myers, *President*
Clara Dominguez, *Principal*
EMP: 15
SQ FT: 7,000
SALES (est): 2.6MM Privately Held
WEB: www.sptanks.com
SIC: 3444 Sheet metal specialties, not
stamped

(G-165)
SGH INC
Also Called: Southern Ocean Mar Sportswear
79 S Main St Ste 2 (08005-2315)
PHONE..............................609 698-8868
Fax: 609 698-5700
EMP: 7
SQ FT: 2,100
SALES (est): 550K Privately Held
SIC: 2395 Custom Embroidery Silkscreen-
ing & Promitonal Products

(G-166)
STAFFORD PARK SOLAR 1 LLC
500 Barnegat Blvd N (08005-2233)
PHONE..............................609 607-9500
Edward Walters Jr,
EMP: 4

SALES (est): 469.4K **Privately Held**
SIC: 3433 Heating equipment, except electric

(G-167)
THOMAS CLARK FIBERGLASS LLC
145 Old Halfway Rd (08005-1024)
PHONE...................609 492-9257
Thomas Clark,
EMP: 4
SALES (est): 395.9K **Privately Held**
SIC: 2221 3229 Fiberglass fabrics; glass fiber products

Barnegat Light
Ocean County

(G-168)
CAPTAIN JOHN INC
16 E 12th St (08006-1412)
PHONE...................609 494-2094
Marion O Larson, *CEO*
Keith Larson, *Manager*
EMP: 10
SALES (est): 598.6K **Privately Held**
SIC: 3949 Fishing tackle, general

(G-169)
CYCLASE DYNAMICS INC
16 E 27th St (08006-1522)
P.O. Box 339 (08006-0339)
PHONE...................973 420-3259
Stephen F Vatner MD, *Principal*
Patricio Abarzua, *Vice Pres*
EMP: 6
SALES: 200K **Privately Held**
SIC: 2834 Pharmaceutical preparations

Barrington
Camden County

(G-170)
ANCHOR OPTICAL CO
101 E Gloucester Pike (08007-1331)
PHONE...................856 546-1965
Alan Kreutzer, *Manager*
EMP: 200
SQ FT: 1,500
SALES (est): 7.7MM **Privately Held**
WEB: www.anchoroptics.com
SIC: 3827 Magnifying instruments, optical

(G-171)
ANDREW P MC HUGH INC
Also Called: Art Press Printing
124 Clements Bridge Rd # 2 (08007-1834)
PHONE...................856 547-8953
Robert Mc Hugh, *President*
Roberta Mc Hugh, *Corp Secy*
Janet Mc Hugh, *Vice Pres*
EMP: 6
SQ FT: 4,000
SALES: 400K **Privately Held**
SIC: 2752 Commercial printing, offset; lithographing on metal

(G-172)
BERG EAST IMPORTS INC
Also Called: Berg Furniture USA
120 E Gloucester Pike (08007-1330)
PHONE...................908 354-5252
Aharon Lieber, *President*
Almot Liber, *President*
Gideon Adler, *Treasurer*
▲ **EMP:** 76
SQ FT: 144,000
SALES (est): 7.3MM **Privately Held**
SIC: 2511 5021 Juvenile furniture: wood; juvenile furniture

(G-173)
BRIGHT LIGHTS USA INC (PA)
Also Called: Blusa Defense Manufacturing
145 Shreve Ave (08007-1501)
PHONE...................856 546-5656
Fax: 856 546-9191
Daniel ARI Farber, *President*
John Chando, *Plant Mgr*
Ken Bryan, *Project Mgr*
Jennifer Telaar, *Purch Agent*
Christopher Estelow, *Buyer*
▲ **EMP:** 55
SQ FT: 14,000
SALES: 10MM **Privately Held**
WEB: www.brightlightsusa.com
SIC: 3724 5085 3728 Aircraft engines & engine parts; industrial supplies; aircraft parts & equipment

(G-174)
COOPER BURIAL VAULTS CO
621 Atlantic Ave (08007-1108)
PHONE...................856 547-8405
Paul Cooper, *President*
Joanne Cooper, *Treasurer*
EMP: 9 **EST:** 1977
SQ FT: 12,000
SALES (est): 1.5MM **Privately Held**
SIC: 3272 Burial vaults, concrete or precast terrazzo

(G-175)
COOPER-WILBERT VAULT CO INC (PA)
621 Atlantic Ave (08007-1108)
PHONE...................856 547-8405
Fax: 856 547-5454
Paul E Cooper, *President*
Joanne D Cooper, *Corp Secy*
Florence Cooper, *Admin Sec*
EMP: 20
SQ FT: 12,000
SALES (est): 4.5MM **Privately Held**
SIC: 3272 Burial vaults, concrete or precast terrazzo

(G-176)
DERMATOLOGICAL SOC OF NJ INC
208 White Horse Pike (08007-1322)
PHONE...................856 546-5600
Trsr Kerri Hollis, *Principal*
EMP: 4
SALES (est): 83.4K **Privately Held**
SIC: 2834 Dermatologicals

(G-177)
EDMUND OPTICS INC (PA)
Also Called: Edmund Scientific Co
101 E Gloucester Pike (08007-1331)
PHONE...................856 547-3488
Fax: 856 573-6295
Robert Edmund, *CEO*
Paula Bao, *Prdtn Mgr*
Jay Budd, *Safety Mgr*
John Angeles, *Senior Buyer*
Jim Bride, *Buyer*
◆ **EMP:** 220 **EST:** 1942
SQ FT: 96,000
SALES (est): 144.4MM **Privately Held**
WEB: www.edsci.com
SIC: 3211 5961 Flat glass; catalog sales

(G-178)
INTERNATIONAL PAPER COMPANY
100 E Gloucester Pike (08007-1330)
PHONE...................856 546-7000
Fax: 856 546-7924
Robert Conlon, *Buyer*
Andy Fescoe, *Manager*
EMP: 185
SALES (corp-wide): 21.7B **Publicly Held**
WEB: www.internationalpaper.com
SIC: 2621 Paper mills
PA: International Paper Company
6400 Poplar Ave
Memphis TN 38197
901 419-9000

(G-179)
ISCO
1 Commerce Dr Bldg 3 (08007-1515)
PHONE...................856 672-9182
Fax: 856 672-9186
Aaron Snethen, *Manager*
EMP: 4
SALES (est): 449.6K **Privately Held**
SIC: 2448 Wood pallets & skids

Basking Ridge
Somerset County

(G-180)
ARLA FOODS INGREDIENTS N AMER
106 Allen Rd Ste 401 (07920-3851)
PHONE...................908 604-8551
Jasan Jensen, *President*
Michael Currie, *Creative Dir*
EMP: 10
SQ FT: 1,000
SALES (est): 1MM
SALES (corp-wide): 12.2B **Privately Held**
SIC: 2023 5149 Dried & powdered milk & milk products; concentrated whey; milk, canned or dried
HQ: Arla Foods Ingredients Group P/S
Sonderhoj 10-12
Viby 8260
961 377-73

(G-181)
AVAYA INC
211 Mount Airy Rd (07920-2311)
P.O. Box 1934, Morristown (07962-1934)
PHONE...................908 953-6000
Fax: 908 953-7609
Rick Cohen, *President*
Christy Tran, *Partner*
Robert Hake, *Business Mgr*
Robert Lesniak, *Business Mgr*
Jeff Hansen, *Vice Pres*
EMP: 310 **Publicly Held**
SIC: 3661 Telephone & telegraph apparatus
HQ: Avaya Inc.
4655 Great America Pkwy
Santa Clara CA 95054
908 953-6000

(G-182)
CELGENE CORPORATION
106 Allen Rd (07920-3851)
PHONE...................908 673-9000
Sol J Barer, *Branch Mgr*
Eston Mwangi, *Prgrmr*
Bradley Eldon, *Director*
Sreenivas Bhat, *Associate Dir*
Roy Sandry, *Associate Dir*
EMP: 5
SALES (corp-wide): 13B **Publicly Held**
SIC: 2834 Pharmaceutical preparations
PA: Celgene Corporation
86 Morris Ave
Summit NJ 07901
908 673-9000

(G-183)
DAIICHI SANKYO INC
Also Called: Sankyo U S A
211 Mount Airy Rd (07920-2311)
PHONE...................908 992-6400
Glenn Gormley, *President*
Jasmine Harris, *Sales Staff*
Lauren Diorio, *Manager*
Margaret Tierney, *Manager*
EMP: 15
SALES (corp-wide): 9B **Privately Held**
WEB: www.benicar.com
SIC: 2834 Pharmaceutical preparations
HQ: Daiichi Sankyo, Inc.
211 Mount Airy Rd
Basking Ridge NJ 07920
908 992-6400

(G-184)
DEMATIC CORP
150 Allen Rd Ste 102 (07920-3856)
PHONE...................908 991-9900
Fax: 908 991-9901
Poul Lorentzen, *Vice Pres*
EMP: 527
SALES (corp-wide): 9B **Privately Held**
SIC: 3535 Conveyors & conveying equipment
HQ: Dematic Corp.
500 Plymouth Ave Ne
Grand Rapids MI 49505
877 725-7500

(G-185)
DEVCO CORPORATION
131 Morristown Rd Bldg B (07920-1654)
PHONE...................201 337-1600
Fax: 973 781-0234
Bill E Durnan Jr, *Principal*
EMP: 7 **EST:** 1963
SALES (est): 1.6MM **Privately Held**
SIC: 3569 Lubrication equipment, industrial

(G-186)
ELECTROCORE INC
150 Allen Rd Ste 201 (07920-2977)
PHONE...................973 290-0097
Fax: 973 290-9173
Francis R Amato, *CEO*
Carrie S Cox, *Ch of Bd*
Eric J Liebler, *Senior VP*
Michael Romaniw, *Vice Pres*
Mike Romaniw, *Vice Pres*
EMP: 64
SALES: 811.4K **Privately Held**
SIC: 3845 Electromedical equipment

(G-187)
FOUNDATION FOR EMBRYONIC
Also Called: FAEEC
140 Allen Rd (07920-2976)
PHONE...................973 656-2847
Richard Scott, *President*
Heather Garnsey, *Supervisor*
Rebekah Zimmerman, *Director*
EMP: 4 **EST:** 2013
SQ FT: 1,500
SALES: 9.6MM **Privately Held**
SIC: 2835 In vitro diagnostics

(G-188)
FROZEN FALLS LLC
413 King Gorge Rd Ste 202 (07920)
PHONE...................908 350-3939
EMP: 4
SALES (est): 278.2K **Privately Held**
SIC: 2026 Yogurt

(G-189)
GRONIGER USA LLC
180 Mount Airy Rd (07920-2065)
PHONE...................704 588-3873
Horst Groninger, *President*
EMP: 4 **EST:** 2004
SALES (est): 240.6K **Privately Held**
SIC: 3565 Packaging machinery

(G-190)
INVENTIV HEALTH CLINICAL LLC (DH)
131 Morristown Rd (07920-1654)
PHONE...................973 348-1000
EMP: 5 **EST:** 2010
SALES (est): 671.2K **Privately Held**
SIC: 2834 Mfg Pharmaceutical Preparations
HQ: Inventiv Health, Inc.
1 Van De Graaff Dr
Burlington MA 02210
800 416-0555

(G-191)
IPSEN BIOPHARMACEUTICALS INC
106 Allen Rd Ste 301 (07920-3851)
PHONE...................908 275-6300
Fax: 908 275-6301
Richard Paulson, *CEO*
Cynthia Schwalm, *President*
Thorsten V Stein, *Senior VP*
Donald Pearl, *Vice Pres*
Agnes Geniaux, *Purchasing*
EMP: 216
SQ FT: 32,600
SALES (est): 57.9MM **Privately Held**
WEB: www.tercica.com
SIC: 2833 2834 Endocrine products; pharmaceutical preparations
HQ: Ipsen
65 Quai Georges Gorse
Boulogne Billancourt 92100
158 335-000

▲ = Import ▼=Export
◆ =Import/Export

(G-192)
LEXICON PHARMACEUTICALS INC
110 Allen Rd Ste 3 (07920-4500)
P.O. Box 132167, The Woodlands TX (77393-2167)
PHONE......................................609 466-5500
Fax: 609 466-3562
Alan J Main, *Exec VP*
Tim Bingham, *Manager*
EMP: 12 **Publicly Held**
WEB: www.lexgen.com
SIC: 2834 Pharmaceutical preparations
PA: Lexicon Pharmaceuticals, Inc.
  8800 Technology Forest Pl
  The Woodlands TX 77381

(G-193)
M/C COMMUNICATIONS LLC
Also Called: Physician's Weekly
180 Mount Airy Rd Ste 202 (07920-2064)
PHONE......................................908 766-0402
Fax: 908 204-0075
Clay Romweber, *Branch Mgr*
EMP: 15
SALES (corp-wide): 10.6MM **Privately Held**
SIC: 2741 Art copy & poster publishing
PA: M/C Communications, Llc
  180 Mount Airy Rd Ste 102
  Basking Ridge NJ 07920
  908 766-0402

(G-194)
MATHESON TRI-GAS INC
150 Allen Rd Ste 302 (07920-2977)
PHONE......................................908 991-9200
Bobby Downer, *Branch Mgr*
Jeff Medlock, *Manager*
EMP: 16
SALES (corp-wide): 34.9B **Privately Held**
WEB: www.matheson-trigas.com
SIC: 2813 5084 Industrial gases; welding machinery & equipment
HQ: Matheson Tri-Gas, Inc.
  150 Allen Rd Ste 302
  Basking Ridge NJ 07920
  908 991-9200

(G-195)
MATHESON TRI-GAS INC (DH)
150 Allen Rd Ste 302 (07920-2977)
PHONE......................................908 991-9200
Fax: 908 257-9268
Scott Kallman, *Ch of Bd*
Scott Harrison, *President*
Chad Rademacher, *General Mgr*
Keith Spencer, *General Mgr*
Steve Foster, *Exec VP*
◆ **EMP:** 70
SQ FT: 50,000
SALES: 1.7B
SALES (corp-wide): 34.9B **Privately Held**
WEB: www.matheson-trigas.com
SIC: 2813 5084 Industrial gases; nitrogen; oxygen, compressed or liquefied; argon; welding machinery & equipment; safety equipment
HQ: Taiyo Nippon Sanso Corporation
  1-3-26, Koyama
  Shinagawa-Ku TKY 142-0
  357 888-000

(G-196)
MATHESON TRI-GAS INC
Also Called: Matheson Gas Products
150 Allen Rd Ste 301 (07920-2977)
PHONE......................................908 991-9200
Brad Geist, *Site Mgr*
Scott McDaniel, *Site Mgr*
John Pontow, *Site Mgr*
Melissa Diehl, *Accounts Mgr*
Dana McDowell, *Accounts Mgr*
EMP: 30
SQ FT: 14,355
SALES (corp-wide): 34.9B **Privately Held**
WEB: www.matheson-trigas.com
SIC: 2813 5084 Industrial gases; welding machinery & equipment
HQ: Matheson Tri-Gas, Inc.
  150 Allen Rd Ste 302
  Basking Ridge NJ 07920
  908 991-9200

(G-197)
MEDICAL INNOVATION GROUP LLC
416 Mount Airy Rd (07920-2401)
PHONE......................................832 348-6460
Jeremy Pinyard, *Principal*
Harvey Gerhard, *Principal*
Christopher Kinsella, *Principal*
EMP: 6
SALES (est): 275.7K **Privately Held**
SIC: 3841 Diagnostic apparatus, medical

(G-198)
MICROSEMI STOR SOLUTIONS INC
180 Mount Airy Rd (07920-2065)
PHONE......................................908 953-9400
Fax: 908 766-4937
Cheri Russell, *Branch Mgr*
EMP: 5
SALES (corp-wide): 3.9B **Publicly Held**
SIC: 3674 Semiconductors & related devices; modules, solid state; microcircuits, integrated (semiconductor)
HQ: Microsemi Storage Solutions, Inc.
  1380 Bordeaux Dr
  Sunnyvale CA 94089
  408 239-8000

(G-199)
MILLINGTON QUARRY INC
135 Stonehouse Rd (07920-2630)
P.O. Box 367, Millington (07946-0367)
PHONE......................................908 542-0055
Fax: 908 580-3909
Gary A Mahan, *President*
EMP: 100
SQ FT: 3,000
SALES (est): 5.6MM **Privately Held**
SIC: 1429 Trap rock, crushed & broken-quarrying

(G-200)
NOGPO INC
4 Patriot Hill Dr (07920-4214)
PHONE......................................908 642-3545
Ashok Muttin, *CEO*
Rakesh Hate, *Shareholder*
Hot Marlin, *Shareholder*
Dan Stark, *Shareholder*
EMP: 10 **EST:** 2013
SALES (est): 547.4K **Privately Held**
SIC: 7372 Business oriented computer software

(G-201)
ONCODE-MED INC
11 Georgetown Ct (07920-4243)
PHONE......................................908 998-3647
Rongshan LI, *President*
EMP: 6
SALES (est): 227.2K **Privately Held**
SIC: 8071 3841 7389 Pathological laboratory; hypodermic needles & syringes;

(G-202)
PHYSICIANS WEEKLY LLC
180 Mount Airy Rd Ste 202 (07920-2064)
PHONE......................................609 981-7354
EMP: 5
SALES (corp-wide): 10.6MM **Privately Held**
SIC: 2741 Art copy & poster publishing
HQ: Physician's Weekly Llc
  180 Mount Airy Rd Ste 202
  Basking Ridge NJ 07920
  908 766-0421

(G-203)
PHYSICIANS WEEKLY LLC (HQ)
180 Mount Airy Rd Ste 202 (07920-2064)
PHONE......................................908 766-0421
Ezra Ernst, *President*
Rachel Ciufo, *COO*
Mark Elms, *Director*
EMP: 20
SALES: 5MM
SALES (corp-wide): 10.6MM **Privately Held**
SIC: 2741 Art copy & poster publishing
PA: M/C Communications, Llc
  180 Mount Airy Rd Ste 102
  Basking Ridge NJ 07920
  908 766-0402

(G-204)
REGADO BIOSCIENCES INC
106 Allen Rd Ste 401 (07920-3851)
PHONE......................................908 580-2109
EMP: 7
SALES (est): 602.7K **Privately Held**
SIC: 2834 Mfg Pharmaceutical Preparations

(G-205)
SIBI DISTRIBUTORS
1370 Meiners Dr (07920-3540)
PHONE......................................908 658-4448
Joseph Jibis, *Principal*
EMP: 4
SALES (est): 189.4K **Privately Held**
SIC: 2051 Bread, cake & related products

(G-206)
SQUIRE CORRUGATED CONT CORP
110 Allen Rd Ste 3 (07920-4500)
PHONE......................................908 862-9111
Fax: 908 561-2791
James Beneroff, *President*
Elliot Beneroff, *Corp Secy*
Richard Beneroff, *Corp Secy*
EMP: 95 **EST:** 1967
SQ FT: 30,000
SALES (est): 18.4MM **Privately Held**
WEB: www.squirebox.com
SIC: 2653 Corrugated & solid fiber boxes

(G-207)
TORRENT PHARMA INC (DH)
150 Allen Rd Ste 102 (07920-3856)
PHONE......................................269 544-2299
Sanjay Gupta, *CEO*
Kamesh Venugopal, *President*
Dawn Chitty, *Vice Pres*
Tynisha Sims, *Manager*
EMP: 15
SQ FT: 2,000
SALES: 122MM **Privately Held**
WEB: www.torrentpharma.com
SIC: 2834 Pharmaceutical preparations
HQ: Torrent Pharmaceuticals Limited
  Torrent House
  Ahmedabad GJ 38000
  792 659-9000

(G-208)
VERTICAL GROUP INC
106 Allen Rd Ste 207 (07920-3851)
PHONE......................................908 277-3737
Emmitt Richard, *Partner*
EMP: 10
SALES (est): 1.1MM **Privately Held**
SIC: 2591 Blinds vertical

Bay Head
Ocean County

(G-209)
SHORE BET PAINTING AND CNSTR
102 Osborne Ave (08742-4619)
P.O. Box 235 (08742-0235)
PHONE......................................732 996-3455
Jeff Belleth, *Owner*
EMP: 4
SALES (est): 385.9K **Privately Held**
SIC: 3479 Painting, coating & hot dipping

Bayonne
Hudson County

(G-210)
AL RICHRDS HOMEMADE CHOCOLATES
851 Broadway (07002-3018)
PHONE......................................201 436-0915
Fax: 201 436-0485
Alfred Stancampiano, *President*
Richard Stancampiano, *Treasurer*
EMP: 10
SQ FT: 6,000

SALES (est): 847K **Privately Held**
WEB: www.alrichardschocolates.com
SIC: 2064 Chocolate candy, except solid chocolate; licorice candy

(G-211)
AP&G CO INC
Also Called: Catchmaster
75 E 2nd St (07002-4255)
PHONE......................................718 492-3648
Steven Frisch, *Ch of Bd*
Ilona Frisch, *President*
Mordy Shwartz, *Controller*
◆ **EMP:** 80
SALES (est): 31.8MM **Privately Held**
WEB: www.catchmaster.com
SIC: 2879 Pesticides, agricultural or household

(G-212)
AP&G CO INC
Also Called: Atlantic Paste & Glue Co Inc
75 E 2nd St (07002-4255)
PHONE......................................718 492-3648
EMP: 6 **EST:** 2016
SALES (est): 108.9K **Privately Held**
SIC: 2879 Mfg Agricultural Chemicals

(G-213)
BASHA USA LLC
390 Broadway (07002-3624)
PHONE......................................201 339-9770
Fax: 201 339-9771
Akram Dadros, *President*
EMP: 6
SALES (est): 716.1K **Privately Held**
SIC: 3556 Smokers, food processing equipment

(G-214)
BAYONNE COMMUNITY NEWS
447 Broadway (07002-3623)
PHONE......................................201 437-2460
Fax: 201 437-7127
Lusha Malato, *President*
EMP: 22
SQ FT: 1,600
SALES (est): 991.2K **Privately Held**
SIC: 2711 Newspapers: publishing only, not printed on site

(G-215)
BAYONNE DRYDOCK & REPAIR CORP
Also Called: Bdd
100 Military Ocean Trml (07002)
PHONE......................................201 823-9295
Fax: 201 823-9298
Micheal Cranston, *President*
Kevin Sullivan, *General Mgr*
Mike Dimesa, *Superintendent*
Eddie Jordan, *Human Resources*
Elena Nazzaro, *Contract Law*
EMP: 20
SALES (est): 6.7MM **Privately Held**
WEB: www.bayonnedrydock.com
SIC: 3731 4491 Shipbuilding & repairing; marine cargo handling

(G-216)
BOOKAZINE CO INC (PA)
75 Hook Rd (07002-5006)
PHONE......................................201 339-7777
Fax: 201 339-7778
Robert Kallman, *CEO*
Irwin Kallman, *Ch of Bd*
Richard Kallman, *Vice Pres*
David Cisneros, *CFO*
Cindy Raiton, *VP Sales*
◆ **EMP:** 86
SQ FT: 125,000
SALES (est): 458.3MM **Privately Held**
SIC: 5192 2741 Books; catalogs: publishing only, not printed on site

(G-217)
CEJON INC
53 Hook Rd (07002-5061)
PHONE......................................201 437-8780
▲ **EMP:** 23
SQ FT: 11,000
SALES (est): 1.6MM **Publicly Held**
SIC: 3111 5137 Leather Tanning/Finishing Whol Women's/Child's Clothing

PA: Steven Madden, Ltd.
5216 Barnett Ave
Long Island City NY 11104

(G-218)
CLARK STEK-O CORP
148 E 5th St (07002-4252)
P.O. Box 455 (07002-0455)
PHONE..................................201 437-0770
Jim Norton, *President*
Robert Bergfield, *Vice Pres*
Charles Lee Jr, *Treasurer*
EMP: 100 **EST:** 1898
SQ FT: 100,000
SALES (est): 9.2MM **Privately Held**
SIC: 2891 Adhesives & sealants

(G-219)
CLAYTON BLOCK COMPANY LLC (HQ)
440 Hook Rd (07002-5026)
PHONE..................................201 339-8585
Fax: 201 339-0983
William Clayton Jr,
Daniel Clayton,
Douglas Clayton,
EMP: 35 **EST:** 1919
SQ FT: 35,000
SALES (est): 7.2MM
SALES (corp-wide): 44.5MM **Privately Held**
SIC: 3271 3272 Concrete block & brick; concrete products, precast
PA: Clayton Block Company, Inc.
1355 Campus Pkwy Ste 200
Wall Township NJ 07753
732 363-1995

(G-220)
CNS CONFECTIONERY PRODUCTS LLC
33 Hook Rd (07002-5006)
PHONE..................................201 823-1400
Fax: 201 823-2452
Eva Deutsch, *President*
Mirim Gross, *Principal*
Irene Fishman, *CFO*
Carol Ranier, *Finance Mgr*
▲ **EMP:** 12
SQ FT: 45,000
SALES (est): 2.5MM **Privately Held**
SIC: 2064 2068 5149 5145 Fruit & fruit peel confections; salted & roasted nuts & seeds; nuts: dried, dehydrated, salted or roasted; seeds: dried, dehydrated, salted or roasted; milk, canned or dried; nuts, salted or roasted; bakery equipment & supplies

(G-221)
CONTROL INDUSTRIES INC (PA)
Also Called: Control Demolition
197 E 22nd St Ste 4 (07002-5062)
PHONE..................................201 437-3826
Donna Bubnis, *President*
Robert Bubnis, *Vice Pres*
EMP: 10
SALES (est): 1.2MM **Privately Held**
SIC: 1794 1442 1795 Excavation work; construction sand & gravel; concrete breaking for streets & highways; demolition, buildings & other structures; dismantling steel oil tanks

(G-222)
DEE & L LLC
67 Lefante Dr (07002-5024)
P.O. Box 3431 (07002-0288)
PHONE..................................201 858-0138
Morris Helfgott, *COO*
David Herzog, *Mng Member*
▼ **EMP:** 15
SQ FT: 25,000
SALES (est): 2.9MM **Privately Held**
SIC: 2035 Pickles, sauces & salad dressings; mayonnaise

(G-223)
DUNBAR SALES COMPANY INC
Also Called: Steven's Dunbar Companies
39 Avenue C Ste 1 (07002-5403)
P.O. Box 8 (07002-0008)
PHONE..................................201 437-6500
Fax: 201 437-0366
William Rubenstein, *President*
EMP: 7

SALES: 3MM **Privately Held**
SIC: 2851 Paints & allied products

(G-224)
EUROPEAN AMRCN FOODS GROUP INC (PA)
Also Called: Euro American Foods Group
698 Kennedy Blvd (07002-2767)
PHONE..................................201 436-6106
Antonio R Fasolino, *President*
Joseph T Gianasio, *CFO*
▲ **EMP:** 24
SQ FT: 50,000
SALES (est): 33.1MM **Privately Held**
SIC: 2099 2079 2033 Pasta, uncooked: packaged with other ingredients; edible oil products, except corn oil; seasonings, tomato: packaged in cans, jars, etc.; tomato products: packaged in cans, jars, etc.

(G-225)
FLORTEK CORPORATION
39 W 55th St (07002-4112)
PHONE..................................201 436-7700
Fax: 201 436-9132
Warren S Harris, *President*
EMP: 25
SQ FT: 40,000
SALES (est): 7.3MM **Privately Held**
SIC: 2752 2782 Cards, lithographed; looseleaf binders & devices

(G-226)
FLUITEC INTERNATIONAL LLC
179 W 5th St (07002-1102)
PHONE..................................201 946-4584
Frank Magnotti, *CEO*
Andre Annicq, *Chairman*
Simon Bard, *Vice Pres*
April Pannell, *Controller*
Darin Carfaro, *Regl Sales Mgr*
EMP: 4
SALES (est): 1.2MM **Privately Held**
WEB: www.fluitec.com
SIC: 3829 5084 Physical property testing equipment; industrial machinery & equipment

(G-227)
GEL SPICE CO INC (PA)
48 Hook Rd (07002-5007)
P.O. Box 285 (07002-0285)
PHONE..................................201 339-0700
Fax: 201 339-0072
Andre Engel, *President*
John Castrataro, *Senior VP*
Steve Thomas, *Senior VP*
Sherman Engel, *Vice Pres*
Joe Mandel, *Vice Pres*
◆ **EMP:** 300
SQ FT: 184,000
SALES (est): 125MM **Privately Held**
WEB: www.gel-spice.com
SIC: 2099 5149 Spices, including grinding; spices & seasonings

(G-228)
GEL SPICE CO LLC
48 Hook Rd (07002-5007)
P.O. Box 285 (07002-0285)
PHONE..................................201 339-0700
Fax: 201 339-0024
Gershon Engel, *Senior VP*
EMP: 250
SQ FT: 150,000
SALES: 130MM **Privately Held**
SIC: 2099 Seasonings & spices

(G-229)
GORDON TERMINAL SERVICE CO PA
Also Called: Gordon Terminal Service Co. NJ
2 Hook Rd (07002-5007)
P.O. Box 143 (07002-0143)
PHONE..................................201 437-8300
Fax: 201 437-5285
Arthur Nisbeth, *Safety Mgr*
Chuck Fodor, *Production*
Thomas Gordon, *Branch Mgr*
Dave Beears, *Manager*
James Zag, *Info Tech Mgr*
EMP: 100

SALES (corp-wide): 29.8MM **Privately Held**
WEB: www.gtscofnj.com
SIC: 4225 7389 2992 General warehousing; packaging & labeling services; lubricating oils & greases
PA: Gordon Terminal Service Co. Of Pa.
1000 Ella St
Mckees Rocks PA 15136
412 331-9410

(G-230)
GP WINE WORKS LLC
Also Called: Gotham Project
82 E 3rd St (07002-4294)
PHONE..................................201 997-6055
Bruce Schneider,
Charles Bieler,
EMP: 4 **EST:** 2012
SALES (est): 258.7K **Privately Held**
SIC: 2084 Wines

(G-231)
HENRY RAC HOLDING CORP
Also Called: Henry Repeating Arms Company
59 E 1st St (07002-4256)
PHONE..................................201 858-4400
Fax: 201 858-4435
Anthony Imperato, *President*
Lemana Saran, *Controller*
Thomas Kotz, *Supervisor*
Ken Kraft, *Supervisor*
▲ **EMP:** 85
SQ FT: 31,000
SALES (est): 13.6MM **Privately Held**
WEB: www.henryrepeating.com
SIC: 5941 3484 Firearms; rifles or rifle parts, 30 mm. & below

(G-232)
HUDSON AWNING CO INC
Also Called: Hudson Awning & Sign Co
27 Cottage St (07002-4334)
PHONE..................................201 339-7171
Fax: 201 339-9858
Edward Burak, *President*
Lynda Burak, *Vice Pres*
EMP: 30 **EST:** 1881
SQ FT: 6,000
SALES (est): 3.3MM **Privately Held**
WEB: www.hudsonawning.com
SIC: 2394 3444 Canopies, fabric: made from purchased materials; awnings, sheet metal

(G-233)
IN-LINE SHTMTL FABRICATORS
85 E 21st St (07002-4533)
PHONE..................................201 339-8121
Miguel Gutierrez, *President*
Dorthy Gutierrez, *Vice Pres*
Matt Dorans, *Treasurer*
Robert Dorans, *Admin Sec*
EMP: 7
SQ FT: 4,000
SALES (est): 599.4K **Privately Held**
SIC: 1711 1761 3444 Warm air heating & air conditioning contractor; ventilation & duct work contractor; sheet metalwork; sheet metalwork

(G-234)
JERHEL PLASTICS INC
63 Hook Rd (07002-5004)
PHONE..................................201 436-6662
Fax: 201 436-6121
Leonard Mecca, *President*
Peggy Mecca, *Treasurer*
Helen Mecca, *Admin Sec*
◆ **EMP:** 8
SQ FT: 10,000
SALES (est): 2MM **Privately Held**
WEB: www.jerhel.net
SIC: 3089 Plastic containers, except foam

(G-235)
KENRICH PETROCHEMICALS INC
570 Broadway (07002-4280)
P.O. Box 32 (07002-0032)
PHONE..................................201 823-9000
Salvatore J Monte, *President*
Eric Monte, *President*
Charles A Lucania, *Vice Pres*
Erika G Monte, *Vice Pres*
Michelle Monte, *Vice Pres*

▲ **EMP:** 30 **EST:** 1945
SQ FT: 67,700
SALES (est): 6.7MM **Privately Held**
SIC: 2869 Plasticizers, organic: cyclic & acyclic

(G-236)
LAFARGE NORTH AMERICA INC
6 Commerce St (07002-5019)
P.O. Box 273 (07002-0273)
PHONE..................................201 437-2575
Cliff Stripling, *Branch Mgr*
EMP: 5
SALES (corp-wide): 26.4B **Privately Held**
WEB: www.lafargenorthamerica.com
SIC: 3241 Cement, hydraulic
HQ: Lafarge North America Inc.
8700 W Bryn Mawr Ave
Chicago IL 60631
773 372-1000

(G-237)
M & RS MILLER AUTO GEAR & PRT
Also Called: Miller Auto Parts
699 Kennedy Blvd (07002-2713)
PHONE..................................201 339-2270
Fax: 201 339-9054
Mario Protocollo, *President*
Rosalea Protocollo, *Vice Pres*
EMP: 11
SQ FT: 8,500
SALES (est): 1MM **Privately Held**
SIC: 5013 5531 3599 Automotive supplies & parts; automotive supplies; automotive accessories; automotive parts; machine shop, jobbing & repair

(G-238)
MURALO COMPANY INC (PA)
Also Called: Elder & Jenks Co Div
148 E 5th St (07002-4252)
P.O. Box 455 (07002-0455)
PHONE..................................201 437-0770
Fax: 201 437-0664
James S Norton, *President*
Edward Norton III, *Vice Pres*
Shashi Patel, *Vice Pres*
Peter Seaborg, *Vice Pres*
Chuck Lee Jr, *CFO*
◆ **EMP:** 250 **EST:** 1924
SQ FT: 350,000
SALES (est): 43MM **Privately Held**
WEB: www.muralo.com
SIC: 2851 Paints & allied products

(G-239)
NEWSPAPER MEDIA GROUP LLC
Also Called: Hudson Reporter
447 Broadway (07002-3623)
PHONE..................................201 798-7800
EMP: 40
SALES (corp-wide): 6.7MM **Privately Held**
SIC: 2711 Commercial printing & newspaper publishing combined
PA: Newspaper Media Group Llc
2 Executive Campus # 400
Cherry Hill NJ 08002
856 779-3800

(G-240)
P D Q PLASTICS INC
7 Hook Rd (07002-5006)
P.O. Box 1001 (07002-1001)
PHONE..................................201 823-0270
Barry Nathans, *President*
EMP: 20 **EST:** 1969
SQ FT: 50,000
SALES (est): 3.5MM **Privately Held**
WEB: www.pdqplastics.com
SIC: 3089 Pallets, plastic

(G-241)
PRIMETIME TRADING CORP
148 E 5th St (07002-4252)
PHONE..................................646 580-8223
Moses Steinberg, *CEO*
▲ **EMP:** 22
SQ FT: 15,000
SALES: 4.5MM **Privately Held**
SIC: 3944 5023 Games, toys & children's vehicles; kitchenware

(G-242)
PRINCE CHIKOVANI INC
Also Called: Prince-Chikovani
363 Avenue A Fl 1 (07002-1329)
PHONE................................347 622-2789
David Kavleli, *President*
Malkhaz Ramishvili, *Vice Pres*
EMP: 5 EST: 2014
SQ FT: 2,000
SALES (est): 233.6K **Privately Held**
SIC: 2099 Food preparations

(G-243)
ROYAL WINE CORPORATION (PA)
Also Called: Baron Herzog
63 Lefante Dr (07002-5024)
PHONE................................718 384-2400
David Herzog, *Ch of Bd*
ARI Cinner, *General Mgr*
Nathan Herzog, *Exec VP*
Mordechai Herzog, *Senior VP*
Phillip Herzog, *Senior VP*
◆ EMP: 110 EST: 1948
SQ FT: 184,000
SALES (est): 47.4MM **Privately Held**
SIC: 2084 5182 Wines; wine; liquor

(G-244)
ROYAL WINE CORPORATION
Also Called: Hks Marketing
63 Lefante Dr (07002-5024)
PHONE................................201 535-9006
David Herzog, *Branch Mgr*
EMP: 110
SALES (corp-wide): 47.4MM **Privately Held**
SIC: 2084 5182 Wines; wine; liquor
PA: Royal Wine Corporation
63 Lefante Dr
Bayonne NJ 07002
718 384-2400

(G-245)
STEVEN INDUSTRIES INC
39 Avenue C Ste 1 (07002-5403)
P.O. Box 8 (07002-0008)
PHONE................................201 437-6500
Stephen Rubenstein, *President*
William Rubenstein, *Vice Pres*
EMP: 25
SQ FT: 200,000
SALES (est): 3.5MM **Privately Held**
WEB: www.rubensteinprop.com
SIC: 5198 2891 2851 Paints; adhesives; paints & allied products

(G-246)
UNITED MEDICAL PC (PA)
988 Broadway (07002-4036)
PHONE................................201 339-6111
Arnold M Alday, *Principal*
Randa M Hamadeh, *Principal*
Marwa Hazzah, *Principal*
Mark A Hoffman, *Principal*
EMP: 10 EST: 1996
SALES (est): 5.3MM **Privately Held**
SIC: 3841 8011 Diagnostic apparatus, medical; internal medicine practitioners; cardiologist & cardio-vascular specialist

---

Bayville
Ocean County

(G-247)
ACE-CRETE PRODUCTS INC
Also Called: New Jersey Polverizing
250 Hickory Ln (08721-2115)
PHONE................................732 269-1400
Nick Grippaldi, *Manager*
EMP: 12
SALES (corp-wide): 1.3MM **Privately Held**
SIC: 3273 Ready-mixed concrete
PA: Ace-Crete Products Inc
4 Rita St
Syosset NY 11791
516 921-9595

(G-248)
AMERICAN CUSTOM FABRICATORS
Also Called: A C F
215 Hickory Ln Ste A (08721-2114)
PHONE................................732 237-0037
Fax: 732 237-0039
Robert Schinder, *President*
Jacqueline Schinder, *Admin Sec*
EMP: 8
SQ FT: 3,500
SALES (est): 1.2MM **Privately Held**
WEB: www.acfcustom.com
SIC: 3355 Rails, rolled & drawn, aluminum

(G-249)
ANDRITZ SEPARATION INC
555 Hickory Ln (08721-2157)
PHONE................................732 269-5305
Jeff Kravitz, *Manager*
EMP: 7
SALES (corp-wide): 6.9B **Privately Held**
SIC: 2873 Fertilizers: natural (organic), except compost
HQ: Andritz Separation Inc.
1010 Commercial Blvd S
Arlington TX 76001
817 465-5611

(G-250)
ATLANTIC COASTAL WELDING INC
16 Butler Blvd (08721-3002)
PHONE................................732 269-1088
Fax: 732 269-7992
John Gallo, *President*
John J Gallo, *President*
EMP: 10
SQ FT: 6,000
SALES (est): 1.4MM **Privately Held**
SIC: 3599 3444 Machine shop, jobbing & repair; sheet metalwork

(G-251)
B AND G MUSIC LLC
2 Teal Pl (08721-1620)
PHONE................................732 779-4555
Rebecca Barbera,
Gerard McKittrick,
EMP: 5
SALES: 20K **Privately Held**
SIC: 3651 Music distribution apparatus

(G-252)
CC PACKAGING LLC (PA)
93 Storm Jib Ct (08721-1417)
P.O. Box 170 (08721-0170)
PHONE................................732 213-9008
George Cannan Jr, *Exec VP*
Caroline Costante, *Vice Pres*
◆ EMP: 8
SALES (est): 940.6K **Privately Held**
SIC: 2899 Chemical preparations

(G-253)
E-TEC MARINE PRODUCTS INC
245 Hickory Ln (08721-2114)
PHONE................................732 269-0442
Allen Thomas, *Manager*
EMP: 5
SALES (corp-wide): 4.2MM **Privately Held**
WEB: www.etecmarine.com
SIC: 3354 Aluminum extruded products
PA: E-Tec Marine Products, Inc.
7555 Garden Rd Ste B
West Palm Beach FL
561 848-8351

(G-254)
EMPIRE BLENDED PRODUCTS INC
Also Called: Empire Blended Distributors
250 Hickory Ln (08721-2115)
PHONE................................732 269-4949
Fax: 732 269-0497
Jay Gornitzky, *President*
Martin Tanzer, *Vice Pres*
Thomas Bartholomew, *Sales Associate*
Bob Cherry, *Maintence Staff*
▼ EMP: 25
SQ FT: 70,000
SALES (est): 9.6MM **Privately Held**
WEB: www.empireblended.com
SIC: 3272 Concrete products, precast

(G-255)
GREENER CORP (PA)
4 Helmly St (08721-2188)
PHONE................................732 341-3880
Fax: 732 286-7842
Theodore M Wojtech, *President*
Matthew D Wojtech, *Vice Pres*
Susan Tyler, *Opers Staff*
Reggie Bland, *Sales Staff*
Jason Dwulet, *Sales Staff*
EMP: 30
SQ FT: 10,000
SALES (est): 4.5MM **Privately Held**
WEB: www.greenercorp.com
SIC: 3565 Packaging machinery

(G-256)
HENRIQUES YACHTS WORKS
198 Hilton Ave (08721-2136)
PHONE................................732 269-1180
Fax: 732 269-1606
Natalia Henriquescosta, *President*
Natalia Henriques-Costa, *President*
Maria Henriques-Demers, *Vice Pres*
EMP: 6
SQ FT: 28,000
SALES (est): 1.3MM **Privately Held**
WEB: www.integritymarine.com
SIC: 3732 Boats, fiberglass: building & repairing

(G-257)
MACHINERY ELECTRICS
904 Main St (08721-2231)
PHONE................................732 536-0600
Joseph D'Arpa, *Owner*
EMP: 5
SQ FT: 2,000
SALES: 300K **Privately Held**
WEB: www.machineryelectrics.com
SIC: 3613 5084 Control panels, electric; industrial machinery & equipment

(G-258)
MOSSE BEVERAGE INDUSTRIES LLC
15 Osprey Ln (08721-2061)
PHONE................................732 977-5558
Viktoria Peraze, *Mng Member*
EMP: 6
SQ FT: 2,200
SALES: 136K **Privately Held**
SIC: 2086 Fruit drinks (less than 100% juice): packaged in cans, etc.

(G-259)
NEW JERSEY PULVERIZING CO INC
Also Called: Ace Crete Product
250 Hickory Ln (08721-2115)
PHONE................................732 269-1400
Nick Grippaldi, *Manager*
EMP: 14
SALES (corp-wide): 2.8MM **Privately Held**
SIC: 1442 3273 1446 Common sand mining; ready-mixed concrete; industrial sand
PA: New Jersey Pulverizing Co Inc
4 Rita St
Syosset NY 11791
516 921-9595

(G-260)
TOWER SYSTEMS INC
Also Called: Atlantic Towers
235 Hickory Ln (08721-2114)
P.O. Box D (08721-0289)
PHONE................................732 237-8800
Steve Tull, *President*
Shelley Golden, *VP Sales*
▼ EMP: 4
SALES (est): 813.1K **Privately Held**
WEB: www.atlantictowers.com
SIC: 3339 Primary nonferrous metals

(G-261)
TREK INC
43 Cranmer Rd (08721-1713)
P.O. Box 275 (08721-0275)
PHONE................................732 269-6300
John J Dynarski, *President*
Joyce Dynarski, *Admin Sec*
▲ EMP: 5

SALES (est): 724.6K **Privately Held**
WEB: www.treklabel.com
SIC: 2672 8742 Labels (unprinted), gummed: made from purchased materials; management consulting services

(G-262)
WHEELS MOTOR SPORTS INC
13 Penny Ln (08721-1253)
PHONE................................732 606-9208
Thomas Cleary Sr, *President*
EMP: 7
SALES: 4.1MM **Privately Held**
WEB: www.wheelsmotorsports.com
SIC: 3751 Motorcycles, bicycles & parts

(G-263)
ZONE TWO INC
245 Hickory Ln Unit 2 (08721-2114)
PHONE................................732 237-0766
Rick Gettis, *President*
EMP: 12
SQ FT: 10,000
SALES: 700K **Privately Held**
SIC: 2759 2396 Screen printing; automotive & apparel trimmings

---

Beach Haven
Ocean County

(G-264)
CRUST AND CRUMB BAKERY
800 N Bay Ave Ste 9 (08008-2008)
PHONE................................609 492-4966
Lou Richards, *Owner*
Anne Richards, *Owner*
EMP: 4
SALES (est): 140K **Privately Held**
SIC: 2051 Bakery: wholesale or wholesale/retail combined

Bedminster
Somerset County

(G-265)
ALLERGAN INC
1 Crossroads Dr (07921-2688)
PHONE................................908 306-0374
EMP: 51 **Privately Held**
SIC: 2834 Drugs acting on the central nervous system & sense organs
HQ: Allergan, Inc.
5 Giralda Farms
Madison NJ 07940
862 261-7000

(G-266)
AMARIN CORPORATION PLC
1430 Us Highway 206 # 100 (07921-4602)
PHONE................................908 719-1315
Declan Doogan, *Principal*
Joseph T Kennedy, *Exec VP*
Craig B Granowitz, *Chief Mktg Ofcr*
Steven Ketchum, *Principal*
EMP: 29
SALES (est): 3.9MM **Privately Held**
SIC: 2834 Pharmaceutical preparations

(G-267)
AQUARIUS BIOTECHNOLOGIES INC
1545 Rte 206 S Ste 302 (07921)
PHONE................................908 443-1860
Jerome Jabbour JD, *Exec VP*
George Bobotas PHD, *Exec VP*
Addel Fawzy PHD, *Exec VP*
Gary Gaglione, *CFO*
EMP: 5
SALES (est): 74.8K
SALES (corp-wide): 149.6K **Publicly Held**
SIC: 2834 Pharmaceutical preparations
PA: Matinas Biopharma Holdings, Inc.
1545 Route 206 Ste 302
Bedminster NJ 07921
908 443-1860

(G-268)
BRYAN SNOOK
Also Called: Reliable Hermetic Seals
90 Washington Valley Rd (07921-2118)
PHONE..................................888 747-3250
Bryan Snook, *Owner*
EMP: 4
SALES (est): 25K **Privately Held**
SIC: 3643 3679 Bus bars (electrical conductors); hermetic seals for electronic equipment

(G-269)
CEGEDIM INC (DH)
1425 Us Highway 206 (07921-2653)
PHONE..................................908 443-2000
Fax: 908 470-9900
Laurent Schockmel, *President*
Carl L Cohen, *President*
Angela Miccoli, *President*
Christine Kroft, *Vice Pres*
Elaine Van Gunst, *Legal Exec*
EMP: 148
SQ FT: 233,000
SALES (est): 81MM
SALES (corp-wide): 6.8MM **Privately Held**
WEB: www.drte.com
SIC: 7371 7372 Computer software development & applications; prepackaged software

(G-270)
COMPUTER COMPANY NORTH AMERICA
356 Wren Ln (07921-1930)
PHONE..................................909 265-3390
Wendell Wilson, *Owner*
EMP: 12
SALES (est): 805.3K **Privately Held**
SIC: 5045 3575 Computer peripheral equipment; computer terminals, monitors & components

(G-271)
EKR THERAPEUTICS INCORPORATED
1545 Us Highway 206 # 300 (07921-2560)
PHONE..................................877 435-2524
John E Bailye, *CEO*
Bill McKee, *COO*
Susan C Bacso, *VP Opers*
EMP: 102
SQ FT: 9,000
SALES (est): 10.5MM
SALES (corp-wide): 15.4K **Privately Held**
WEB: www.ekrtx.com
SIC: 2834 Druggists' preparations (pharmaceuticals)
HQ: Chiesi Usa, Inc.
    1255 Crescent Green
    Cary NC 27518
    919 678-6611

(G-272)
ETHICON INC
135 Us Highway 202 206 # 4 (07921-2608)
PHONE..................................908 306-0327
Darrell Chilton, *Branch Mgr*
EMP: 225
SALES (corp-wide): 76.4B **Publicly Held**
WEB: www.ethiconinc.com
SIC: 3842 Ligatures, medical
HQ: Ethicon Inc.
    Us Route 22
    Somerville NJ 08876
    732 524-0400

(G-273)
ETHICON INC
Also Called: Ethicon Endo-Surgery
135 Us Highway 202 206 # 4 (07921-2608)
P.O. Box 16509, New Brunswick (08901)
PHONE..................................908 218-0707
Clifford Holland, *Branch Mgr*
EMP: 225
SALES (corp-wide): 76.4B **Publicly Held**
SIC: 3842 Ligatures, medical
HQ: Ethicon Inc.
    Us Route 22
    Somerville NJ 08876
    732 524-0400

(G-274)
INO THERAPEUTICS LLC (DH)
1425 Us Route 206 (07921)
P.O. Box 9001, Hampton (08827-9001)
PHONE..................................908 238-6600
Fax: 908 238-6633
Elizabeth Larkin, *CFO*
Matthew Bennett, *Marketing Mgr*
Ravi Iyer, *Director*
Daniel Tasse,
◆ EMP: 63
SALES (est): 35.9MM **Privately Held**
SIC: 5122 2834 Pharmaceuticals; pharmaceutical preparations
HQ: Therakos, Inc.
    1425 Us Route 206
    Bedminster NJ 07921
    800 828-6316

(G-275)
KYOWA KIRIN INC
135 Rte 202 206 Ste 6 (07921)
PHONE..................................908 234-1096
Tom Stratford, *CEO*
Leonard Paolillo, *President*
Ian Duguid, *Vice Pres*
Len Paolillo, *Vice Pres*
Allan Watson, *CFO*
EMP: 65 EST: 1998
SALES: 30MM
SALES (corp-wide): 16.6B **Privately Held**
SIC: 2834 Pharmaceutical preparations
HQ: Kyowa Kirin International Plc
    Galabank Business Park
    Galashiels TD1 1
    189 666-4000

(G-276)
MALLINCKRODT ARD INC
Also Called: Mallinckrodt Pharmaceuticals
1425 Us Highway 206 (07921-2653)
PHONE..................................510 400-0700
Don M Bailey, *President*
David Dibernardo, *Sales Staff*
EMP: 6 **Privately Held**
SIC: 2834 Pharmaceutical preparations
HQ: Ard Mallinckrodt Inc
    1425 Us Highway 206
    Bedminster NJ 07921
    908 238-6600

(G-277)
MALLINCKRODT ARD INC (HQ)
1425 Us Highway 206 (07921-2653)
PHONE..................................908 238-6600
Don M Bailey, *President*
David J Medeiros, *Exec VP*
Michael H Mulroy, *Exec VP*
Steven C Halladay, *Senior VP*
Eric J Liebler, *Senior VP*
EMP: 9
SALES (est): 92.8MM **Privately Held**
WEB: www.questcor.com
SIC: 2834 Pharmaceutical preparations

(G-278)
MATINAS BIOPHARMA HOLDINGS INC
1545 Route 206 Ste 302 (07921)
PHONE..................................908 443-1860
Addel Fawzy PHD, *Exec VP*
Jerome Jabbour JD, *Exec VP*
Gary Gaglione, *CFO*
Richard Samas, *Accountant*
Douglas Kling, *Executive*
EMP: 10
SQ FT: 5,500
SALES (est): 149.6K **Publicly Held**
SIC: 2833 Fish liver oils: refined or concentrated for medicinal use
PA: Matinas Biopharma Holdings, Inc.
    1545 Route 206 Ste 302
    Bedminster NJ 07921
    908 443-1860

(G-279)
MATINAS BIOPHARMA HOLDINGS INC (PA)
1545 Route 206 Ste 302 (07921)
PHONE..................................908 443-1860
Herbert Conrad, *Ch of Bd*
Jerome D Jabbour, *President*
Abdel A Fawzy, *Exec VP*
Douglas F Kling, *Senior VP*
Raphael J Mannino, *Senior VP*

EMP: 10
SQ FT: 5,900
SALES: 149.6K **Publicly Held**
SIC: 2834 Pharmaceutical preparations

(G-280)
MENTOR GRAPHICS CORPORATION
550 Hills Dr Ste 100 (07921-1537)
PHONE..................................908 604-0800
Bill Dunham, *Engineer*
EMP: 125
SALES (corp-wide): 97.7B **Privately Held**
WEB: www.mentor.com
SIC: 7372 Business oriented computer software
HQ: Mentor Graphics Corporation
    8005 Sw Boeckman Rd
    Wilsonville OR 97070
    503 685-7000

(G-281)
NAUTILUS NEUROSCIENCES INC
135 Rte 202 (07921)
PHONE..................................908 437-1320
Fax: 908 393-7890
William Maichle, *CEO*
James L Fares, *CEO*
Peter A Lankau, *Ch of Bd*
Eric Liebler, *President*
Neil Milano, *CFO*
EMP: 5
SALES (est): 874.4K **Privately Held**
SIC: 2834 Pharmaceutical preparations

(G-282)
PHILIP MORRIS USA INC
2 Crossroads Dr Ste 200b (07921-1565)
PHONE..................................908 781-6400
Fran Telegotis, *Manager*
EMP: 11
SALES (corp-wide): 25.5B **Publicly Held**
WEB: www.philipmorrisusa.com
SIC: 2111 Cigarettes
HQ: Philip Morris Usa Inc.
    6601 W Brd St
    Richmond VA 23230
    804 274-2000

(G-283)
PREMIER HEALTHCARE EXCH CORP (PA)
Also Called: Zelis Healthcare
2 Crossroads Dr Ste 101b (07921-1564)
PHONE..................................908 658-3535
Douglas Klinger, *CEO*
Tina Ellex, *President*
Jay Ver Hulst, *President*
Lori Sempervive, *President*
Terry Harris, *Exec VP*
EMP: 82
SQ FT: 9,000
SALES (est): 76.8MM **Privately Held**
SIC: 7372 Prepackaged software

(G-284)
SILOA INC
2493c Lamington Rd (07921-2619)
PHONE..................................908 234-9040
Mark Bellard, *President*
Joseph Walsh, *Director*
▲ EMP: 4
SALES (est): 220K **Privately Held**
WEB: www.siloa.com
SIC: 2844 Toilet preparations

(G-285)
TAP PHARMACEUTICAL PRODUCTS
500 Hills Dr Ste 125 (07921-1538)
PHONE..................................908 470-9700
EMP: 4
SALES (corp-wide): 16.6B **Privately Held**
SIC: 2834 Mfg Pharmaceutical Preparations
HQ: Tap Pharmaceutical Products Inc.
    675 N Field Dr
    Lake Forest IL 60045
    847 582-2000

(G-286)
BESEECH LTD LIABILITY COMPANY
259 East Rd (07718-1608)
PHONE..................................908 461-7888
William Acevedo,
EMP: 5
SALES (est): 149.4K **Privately Held**
SIC: 7372 7389 Application computer software;

(G-287)
FRANK J ZECHMAN
Also Called: Zeeks Tees
515 Highway 36 (07718-1523)
PHONE..................................732 495-0077
Frank J Zechman, *Owner*
EMP: 9
SQ FT: 1,200
SALES (est): 800K **Privately Held**
SIC: 2759 Commercial printing

(G-288)
KERRY WILKENS INC
Also Called: Jean's Canvas Products
780 State Route 36 (07718-1421)
PHONE..................................732 787-0070
Fax: 732 787-0591
Kerry Wilkens, *President*
▼ EMP: 8
SQ FT: 1,600
SALES (est): 1MM **Privately Held**
WEB: www.jeanscanvas.com
SIC: 2394 Liners & covers, fabric: made from purchased materials

(G-289)
UNIVERSITY PUBLICATIONS INC
562 Morley Ct (07718-1156)
PHONE..................................212 268-4222
EMP: 5
SALES (est): 370K **Privately Held**
SIC: 2759 Commercial Printing

(G-290)
ZEEKS TEES
515 State Route 36 (07718-1523)
PHONE..................................732 291-2700
Fax: 732 291-2745
Frank J Zechman, *Owner*
EMP: 10
SALES (est): 750K **Privately Held**
WEB: www.zeekstees.com
SIC: 2759 Screen printing

(G-291)
FOUNDATION SOFTWARE INC
58 Livingston Dr (08502-4624)
PHONE..................................908 359-0588
Srecko Lazanja, *President*
EMP: 4
SALES (est): 500K **Privately Held**
WEB: www.pengi.com
SIC: 7372 Business oriented computer software

(G-292)
SANHERB BIOTECH INC
Also Called: U-Solution Promo Inc USP
4 Mccullough Close (08502-4323)
PHONE..................................347 946-5896
Albert Tang, *Ch of Bd*
Fan Zhou, *President*
EMP: 9
SALES (est): 1.2MM **Privately Held**
SIC: 2833 Drugs & herbs: grading, grinding & milling

▲ = Import ▼=Export
◆ =Import/Export

Belleville
Essex County

(G-293)
ABBOTT ARTKIVES LLC
Also Called: Abbott Screen Printing
187 Branch Brook Dr (07109-3607)
PHONE.................................201 232-9477
Steven Bornemann,
EMP: 5 **EST:** 1936
SALES: 325K **Privately Held**
WEB: www.abbott-artkives.com
SIC: 2759 Screen printing

(G-294)
AERO PRODUCTS CO INC
21 N 8th St (07109-1117)
PHONE.................................973 759-0959
Fax: 973 759-1818
David Bucci, *President*
Diane Bucci, *Admin Sec*
▲ **EMP:** 12 **EST:** 1932
SQ FT: 10,000
SALES (est): 1.7MM **Privately Held**
SIC: 3599 Machine shop, jobbing & repair

(G-295)
AEROCON INC
Also Called: Subsidiariy of Vac-U-Max
69 William St (07109-3040)
PHONE.................................800 405-2376
Stevens P Pendleton, *President*
EMP: 80
SQ FT: 40,000
SALES (est): 6.5MM **Privately Held**
WEB: www.aerocon.net
SIC: 3535 Conveyors & conveying equipment

(G-296)
BLOOMFIELD IRON CO INC
Also Called: Railing Designs Unlimited
21 Florence Ave (07109-1107)
P.O. Box 246, Mountain Lakes (07046-0246)
PHONE.................................973 748-7040
EMP: 6 **EST:** 1950
SQ FT: 4,800
SALES (est): 450K **Privately Held**
SIC: 3312 3462 Mfg Structural Steel

(G-297)
BRUSSO HARDWARE LLC
67-69 Greylock Ave (07109)
PHONE.................................212 337-8510
Richard Bing, *Mng Member*
EMP: 10
SALES (est): 1.4MM **Privately Held**
SIC: 5072 3599 Hardware; machine & other job shop work

(G-298)
COMMUNIQUE INC
Also Called: Precision Specialties
120 Greylock Ave (07109-3324)
PHONE.................................973 751-7588
Fax: 973 759-8608
Rich Pfuhler, *President*
Eva Pfuhler, *Admin Sec*
EMP: 7
SQ FT: 3,400
SALES (est): 870K **Privately Held**
SIC: 3965 5085 Fasteners; industrial supplies

(G-299)
DANS WOODWORK
37 Branch Brook Dr (07109-3601)
PHONE.................................973 751-4506
Daniel Trujillo, *Principal*
EMP: 7
SALES (est): 1MM **Privately Held**
SIC: 2431 Millwork

(G-300)
DONS DRAPERY MANUFACTURING
145 Heckel St (07109-1095)
PHONE.................................973 751-1544
Joyce Dolan, *President*
Robert Spagnardi, *Corp Secy*
James Dolan, *COO*
EMP: 15

SQ FT: 5,000
SALES: 283.7K **Privately Held**
SIC: 2391 Draperies, plastic & textile: from purchased materials

(G-301)
EASTERN MOLDING CO INC
597 Main St (07109-3494)
PHONE.................................973 759-0220
Fax: 973 759-0294
Peter De Nicholas, *President*
EMP: 8 **EST:** 1947
SQ FT: 15,000
SALES (est): 1.3MM **Privately Held**
SIC: 3069 3061 3053 Molded rubber products; mechanical rubber goods; gaskets, packing & sealing devices

(G-302)
EMPRO PRODUCTS CO INC
47 Montgomery St (07109-1305)
PHONE.................................973 302-4351
Fax: 973 279-5088
Darshan Mehta, *President*
Mehta Kalpi, *Controller*
▲ **EMP:** 8
SQ FT: 10,000
SALES (est): 1MM **Privately Held**
SIC: 3993 Signs, not made in custom sign painting shops

(G-303)
FOAM RUBBER FABRICATORS INC
740 Washington Ave Ste 1 (07109-2897)
PHONE.................................973 751-1445
Irving Lerner, *President*
Arthur Lerner, *Treasurer*
EMP: 22 **EST:** 1950
SQ FT: 30,000
SALES (est): 6.1MM **Privately Held**
SIC: 5199 2821 Foam rubber; plastics materials & resins

(G-304)
J F I PRINTING
357 Cortlandt St (07109-5222)
PHONE.................................973 759-3444
Joe Iannone, *President*
EMP: 5
SALES: 400K **Privately Held**
SIC: 2759 Commercial printing

(G-305)
MAGNETIC TICKET & LABEL CORP
151 Cortlandt St (07109-3130)
PHONE.................................973 759-6500
Michael Hale, *Vice Pres*
Yahya Kashani, *Plant Mgr*
EMP: 30
SALES (corp-wide): 121MM **Privately Held**
SIC: 2679 2771 Labels, paper: made from purchased material; greeting cards
HQ: Magnetic Ticket & Label Corporation
8719 Diplomacy Row
Dallas TX 75247
214 634-8600

(G-306)
MENU SOLUTIONS INC
233 Cortlandt St (07109-3126)
PHONE.................................718 575-5160
Irwin Joel Borracas, *CEO*
Praful Pandya, *Controller*
◆ **EMP:** 75 **EST:** 1996
SALES: 3.2MM **Privately Held**
WEB: www.menucovers.biz
SIC: 2759 Screen printing

(G-307)
MILLER & SON
24 Belleville Ave (07109-3035)
PHONE.................................973 759-6445
Fax: 973 759-1625
Elizabeth Miller, *President*
Ed Milller, *Vice Pres*
George A Miller, *Plant Mgr*
EMP: 8 **EST:** 1913
SQ FT: 20,000
SALES: 1.5MM **Privately Held**
SIC: 3471 Electroplating of metals or formed products

(G-308)
MK WOOD INC
681 Main St (07109-3461)
P.O. Box 9518, Newark (07104-0518)
PHONE.................................973 450-5110
Mourad Khalil, *Principal*
▲ **EMP:** 4 **EST:** 2011
SALES (est): 689.4K **Privately Held**
SIC: 5031 2434 Kitchen cabinets; wood kitchen cabinets

(G-309)
ORTHODOX BAKING CO INC
555 Cortlandt St (07109-3329)
PHONE.................................973 844-9393
Josheph Oberlander, *President*
EMP: 20
SALES (est): 2.2MM **Privately Held**
SIC: 2051 Bakery: wholesale or wholesale/retail combined

(G-310)
PACKAGEMAN
331 Main St (07109-5200)
PHONE.................................201 898-1922
Yashar Novruz, *Administration*
EMP: 4
SALES (est): 146.1K **Privately Held**
SIC: 2631 Container, packaging & boxboard

(G-311)
PETRONIO SHOE PRODUCTS CORP
Also Called: Master Shoe Products
305 Cortlandt St (07109-3292)
PHONE.................................973 751-7579
Fax: 973 759-7324
Donald Rinaldi, *President*
▲ **EMP:** 10 **EST:** 1926
SQ FT: 20,000
SALES (est): 1.5MM **Privately Held**
WEB: www.instantshoeshine.com
SIC: 2891 Adhesives; cement, except linoleum & tile

(G-312)
PRESSURE CONTROLS INC
406 Cortlandt St (07109-3204)
PHONE.................................973 751-5002
Fax: 973 751-9653
Paul Emmarco, *President*
Paul L Emmarco, *Vice Pres*
Tommy Santin, *Vice Pres*
Paul Lind, *Manager*
EMP: 9 **EST:** 1966
SQ FT: 10,000
SALES (est): 890K **Privately Held**
SIC: 3823 3643 3625 Pressure measurement instruments, industrial; current-carrying wiring devices; relays & industrial controls

(G-313)
PULSONICS INC
69 William St (07109-3040)
PHONE.................................800 999-6785
Stevens P Pendleton, *President*
Charlotte Pendleton, *Corp Secy*
Henry Kadel, *Vice Pres*
EMP: 10
SQ FT: 23,000
SALES: 300K **Privately Held**
WEB: www.pulsonics.com
SIC: 3569 3535 3443 Assembly machines, non-metalworking; conveyors & conveying equipment; fabricated plate work (boiler shop)

(G-314)
RED DIAMOND COMPANY
Also Called: National Sports Sales
368 Cortlandt St (07109-3204)
PHONE.................................973 759-2005
Fax: 973 450-0069
Michael Tartaglia, *Owner*
Marc S Tartaglia Jr, *Vice Pres*
EMP: 6 **EST:** 1946
SQ FT: 7,500
SALES (est): 637.3K **Privately Held**
SIC: 2759 7389 2396 2395 Screen printing; embroidering of advertising on shirts, etc.; automotive & apparel trimmings; pleating & stitching

(G-315)
ROBERT FREEMAN
Also Called: N E A Products Co
320 Washington Ave (07109-3249)
PHONE.................................973 751-0082
Fax: 973 751-9151
Robert Freeman, *Principal*
EMP: 6
SQ FT: 7,000
SALES: 600K **Privately Held**
SIC: 3465 7389 Automotive stampings; packaging & labeling services

(G-316)
ROBERT STEWART INC (PA)
120 Little St (07109-3238)
PHONE.................................973 751-5151
Fax: 973 751-2383
▲ **EMP:** 3 **EST:** 1919
SALES (est): 4.6MM **Privately Held**
SIC: 2323 Mfg Men's/Boy's Neckwear

(G-317)
SALEM MANUFACTURING CORP
115 Roosevelt Ave (07109-3403)
PHONE.................................973 751-6331
Fax: 973 751-4711
Jerome Lipiec, *President*
Urairat Lipiec, *Treasurer*
Richard Lipiec, *Shareholder*
EMP: 10
SQ FT: 6,000
SALES: 720K **Privately Held**
SIC: 3451 Screw machine products

(G-318)
SPENCER INDUSTRIES INC (PA)
80 Holmes St (07109-3185)
P.O. Box 128 (07109-0128)
PHONE.................................973 751-2200
Martin J Lawrence, *President*
Martin Lawrence, *General Mgr*
Nicole Lawrence, *Project Mgr*
David Goldstein, *Manager*
▲ **EMP:** 22 **EST:** 1963
SQ FT: 22,000
SALES (est): 4.8MM **Privately Held**
WEB: www.spencerindinc.com
SIC: 3679 Electronic circuits

(G-319)
TERMINAL PRINTING CO
85 Washington Ave (07109-2928)
P.O. Box 30, Hoboken (07030-0030)
PHONE.................................201 659-5924
John Bado III, *Owner*
Virginia Bado, *Corp Secy*
EMP: 4
SALES (est): 300.2K **Privately Held**
SIC: 2759 Commercial printing

(G-320)
TRI-CHEM INC
681 Main St Ste 24 (07109-3471)
PHONE.................................973 751-9200
Andrew D Mc Knight, *Ch of Bd*
Patricia McKnight, *President*
Richard Y Keegan, *Treasurer*
EMP: 10
SQ FT: 12,000
SALES (est): 1.1MM **Privately Held**
SIC: 2397 5092 Schiffli machine embroideries; hobby goods; arts & crafts equipment & supplies

(G-321)
UNIPACK INC
Also Called: UNIPACK,INC.
681 Main St Ste 27 (07109-3471)
PHONE.................................973 450-9880
Jitu Patel, *Branch Mgr*
EMP: 15
SALES (corp-wide): 6.5MM **Privately Held**
WEB: www.unipackinc.com
SIC: 2834 Pharmaceutical preparations
PA: Unipack, Inc.
3253 Old Frankstown Rd
Pittsburgh PA 15239
724 733-7381

(G-322)
VAC-U-MAX (PA)
Also Called: Aerocon
69 William St (07109-3040)
PHONE.................................973 759-4600

Fax: 973 751-5557
Stevens P Pendleton, *President*
Rose Brosius, *Vice Pres*
Mitchell Katz, *Vice Pres*
Doan Pendleton, *Vice Pres*
Mark McGuire, *Purch Mgr*
◆ **EMP:** 50
SQ FT: 27,000
SALES (est): 18.4MM **Privately Held**
WEB: www.vac-u-max.com
SIC: 3494 3563 3535 Valves & pipe fittings; air & gas compressors; pneumatic tube conveyor systems

(G-323)
VAC-U-MAX
69 William St (07109-3040)
PHONE................973 759-4600
Rose Brosius, *Manager*
EMP: 15
SALES (corp-wide): 18.4MM **Privately Held**
WEB: www.vac-u-max.com
SIC: 3589 Vacuum cleaners & sweepers, electric: industrial
PA: Vac-U-Max
        69 William St
        Belleville NJ 07109
        973 759-4600

(G-324)
VERNW PRINTING COMPANY
Also Called: Verna Printing
85 Washington Ave (07109-2928)
PHONE................973 751-6462
Fax: 973 759-4939
John A Vernacchia, *Owner*
EMP: 5 **EST:** 1979
SQ FT: 1,000
SALES: 165K **Privately Held**
SIC: 2759 2752 Letterpress printing; commercial printing, offset

(G-325)
VICTORY TOOL & MFG CO
231 Valley St 233 (07109-3285)
PHONE................973 759-8733
Fax: 973 759-4339
Victor Maccagnan, *President*
Lucille Maccagnan, *Corp Secy*
EMP: 8 **EST:** 1973
SQ FT: 4,000
SALES (est): 857.4K **Privately Held**
SIC: 3544 Special dies & tools

(G-326)
VMC DIE CUTTING CORP
357 Cortlandt St (07109-5222)
PHONE................973 450-4655
Victor Reczynski, *Owner*
EMP: 11
SALES (est): 1.5MM **Privately Held**
SIC: 3544 2675 Special dies & tools; die-cut paper & board

(G-327)
WHEAL-GRACE CORP
300 Ralph St (07109-3381)
P.O. Box 67 (07109-0067)
PHONE................973 450-8100
Fax: 973 450-5394
Nancy Salvini, *President*
Tracy Lockett, *Plant Mgr*
Beth Salvini, *Treasurer*
Emil Salvini, *Marketing Staff*
Tara Wilson, *CTO*
EMP: 35
SALES (est): 8.5MM **Privately Held**
WEB: www.wheal-grace.com
SIC: 2732 2754 Book printing; commercial printing, gravure

(G-328)
WILLIAM R TATZ INDUSTRIES
Also Called: Charcole Products
11 Railroad Pl (07109-3413)
PHONE................973 751-0720
Fax: 973 751-0166
William Tatz, *CEO*
Joseph Tatz, *President*
Richard Tatz, *Treasurer*
EMP: 7 **EST:** 1964
SQ FT: 13,000

SALES (est): 410K **Privately Held**
SIC: 2064 2045 2865 Candy & other confectionery products; cake mixes, prepared: from purchased flour; food dyes or colors, synthetic

(G-329)
WOODPECKERS INC
323 Cortlandt St (07109-3201)
PHONE................973 751-4744
Fax: 973 751-4934
Petros Karantonis, *President*
▲ **EMP:** 12
SQ FT: 60,000
SALES (est): 1.7MM **Privately Held**
WEB: www.woodpeckers-furniture.com
SIC: 2511 Wood household furniture

Bellmawr
Camden County

(G-330)
AIRGAS USA LLC
270 Benigno Blvd Bldg 5 (08031-2514)
PHONE................856 933-0544
Carl Lataze, *Manager*
EMP: 16
SALES (corp-wide): 164.2MM **Privately Held**
SIC: 2813 Industrial gases
HQ: Airgas Usa, Llc
        259 N Radnor Chester Rd # 100
        Radnor PA 19087
        610 687-5253

(G-331)
AMOROSOS BAKING CO
151 Benigno Blvd (08031-2515)
P.O. Box 1145 (08099-5145)
PHONE................215 471-4740
Leonard Amoroso Jr, *President*
Daniel Amoroso Jr, *Vice Pres*
▼ **EMP:** 300 **EST:** 1922
SQ FT: 80,000
SALES (est): 69.5MM **Privately Held**
WEB: www.amorosobaking.com
SIC: 2051 Bakery: wholesale or wholesale/retail combined; bread, all types (white, wheat, rye, etc): fresh or frozen; rolls, bread type: fresh or frozen

(G-332)
BOXWORKS INC
1100 Market St (08031-2810)
P.O. Box 108, Gloucester City (08030-0108)
PHONE................856 456-9030
Ted White, *President*
EMP: 7
SALES (est): 1.1MM **Privately Held**
WEB: www.boxworks.com
SIC: 2653 2441 2449 Corrugated & solid fiber boxes; nailed wood boxes & shook; rectangular boxes & crates, wood

(G-333)
BRENNAN PENROD CONTRACTORS LLC
420 Benigno Blvd Unit B (08031-2519)
PHONE................856 933-1100
Bob Penrod,
Craig Brennan,
EMP: 18
SALES (est): 748.2K **Privately Held**
SIC: 1721 3443 Painting & paper hanging; liners/lining

(G-334)
CAMDEN IRON & METAL LLC (PA)
143 Harding Ave Ste 20 (08031-2434)
PHONE................856 969-7065
Fax: 856 219-3880
Joseph Valzano, *President*
Jelff Omlley, *Treasurer*
◆ **EMP:** 100
SQ FT: 10,000
SALES (est): 47.5MM **Privately Held**
WEB: www.camdeniron.com
SIC: 3312 4953 5093 Blast furnaces & steel mills; refuse systems; metal scrap & waste materials

(G-335)
COUNTRY HOME BAKERS LLC - GA
361 Benigno Blvd Ste C (08031-2557)
PHONE................856 931-7052
Fax: 856 933-4545
Gerald B Shreiber, *CEO*
Dennis Moore, *CFO*
Len Dandrea, *Manager*
EMP: 250
SALES (est): 47.9MM
SALES (corp-wide): 1B **Publicly Held**
WEB: www.jjsnack.com
SIC: 5149 2053 Bakery products; frozen bakery products, except bread
PA: J & J Snack Foods Corp.
        6000 Central Hwy
        Pennsauken NJ 08109
        856 665-9533

(G-336)
DAZZLEDOG LLC
Also Called: You Move ME
143 Harding Ave Ste 7 (08031-2430)
P.O. Box 935 (08099-0935)
PHONE................302 540-6804
Michael Boucher,
EMP: 4
SALES (est): 354.4K **Privately Held**
SIC: 3537 Trucks, tractors, loaders, carriers & similar equipment

(G-337)
DORAZIO FOODS INC
Also Called: D'Orazio Frozen Foods
960 Creek Rd (08031-1672)
P.O. Box 243 (08099-0243)
PHONE................856 931-1900
Fax: 856 931-1907
Anthony Dorazio, *President*
Terri Banks, *Vice Pres*
Terri D'Orazio-Bank, *Vice Pres*
Frank D Orazio, *Vice Pres*
Frank Dorazio, *Plant Mgr*
EMP: 75
SQ FT: 25,000
SALES: 8MM **Privately Held**
WEB: www.dorazio.com
SIC: 2099 Food preparations

(G-338)
EASY ANALYTIC SOFTWARE INC
101 Haag Ave (08031-2506)
P.O. Box 1217 (08099-5217)
PHONE................856 931-5780
Robert Katz, *Branch Mgr*
EMP: 4
SALES (est): 224.3K **Privately Held**
SIC: 7372 Application computer software
PA: Easy Analytic Software Inc
        7359 196th St
        Flushing NY 11366

(G-339)
EMR (USA HOLDINGS) INC (DH)
143 Harding Ave Ste 1 (08031-2430)
PHONE................856 365-7500
David Farnsworth, *CFO*
◆ **EMP:** 13
SALES (est): 642.6MM
SALES (corp-wide): 2.7B **Privately Held**
SIC: 5051 4953 3291 Steel; recycling, waste materials; abrasive metal & steel products

(G-340)
FAMILY SCREEN PRINTING INC
124 Harding Ave Ste 124 (08031-2412)
PHONE................856 933-2780
Fax: 856 933-2782
Robert Armstrong, *President*
EMP: 15
SALES (est): 1.4MM **Privately Held**
WEB: www.familyscreenprinting.com
SIC: 2282 2396 2395 Embroidery yarn: twisting, winding or spooling; automotive & apparel trimmings; pleating & stitching

(G-341)
GREEN HORSE MEDIA LLC
Also Called: Evergreen Printing Company
101 Haag Ave (08031-2506)
P.O. Box 786 (08099-0786)
PHONE................856 933-0222
Fax: 856 933-3924
Steve Danifo, *Vice Pres*

Bob Metzger, *Mfg Dir*
Christine Burt, *Controller*
Jim Lamb, *Sales Staff*
Daniel Wegmann, *Manager*
▲ **EMP:** 130 **EST:** 1955
SQ FT: 90,000
SALES: 22MM **Privately Held**
WEB: www.egpp.com
SIC: 2752 Commercial printing, offset

(G-342)
HIT PROMO LLC
Also Called: Admints & Zagabor
440 Benigno Blvd Unit D (08031-2521)
PHONE................856 739-4474
Fax: 856 931-7384
Arthur W Schmidt III, *CEO*
Christopher John Schmidt, *President*
▲ **EMP:** 110
SALES: 17MM
SALES (corp-wide): 226MM **Privately Held**
SIC: 2759 8743 Promotional printing; promotion service
PA: Hit Promotional Products, Inc.
        7150 Bryan Dairy Rd
        Largo FL 33777
        727 541-5561

(G-343)
INTERNATIONAL PAPER COMPANY
370 Benigno Blvd (08031-2512)
PHONE................856 931-8000
Fax: 856 933-4211
Andy Fescoe, *Manager*
EMP: 137
SALES (corp-wide): 21.7B **Publicly Held**
WEB: www.internationalpaper.com
SIC: 2621 Paper mills
PA: International Paper Company
        6400 Poplar Ave
        Memphis TN 38197
        901 419-9000

(G-344)
J & J SNACK FOODS CORP
361 Benigno Blvd Ste A (08031-2501)
PHONE................856 933-3597
Fax: 856 933-0837
Bob Norbeck, *Purch Agent*
Brenda Usdin, *Controller*
Bill Mullen, *Manager*
EMP: 150
SALES (corp-wide): 1B **Publicly Held**
WEB: www.jjsnack.com
SIC: 2052 2099 2051 2053 Pretzels; cookies; food preparations; bread, cake & related products; frozen bakery products, except bread
PA: J & J Snack Foods Corp.
        6000 Central Hwy
        Pennsauken NJ 08109
        856 665-9533

(G-345)
M PARKER AUTOWORKS INC
Also Called: Factory Fit
150 Heller Pl 17w (08031-2503)
PHONE................856 933-0801
Michael P Manning, *President*
Frank Colonna, *Vice Pres*
EMP: 21
SALES (est): 3.6MM **Privately Held**
WEB: www.factoryfit.com
SIC: 3357 3694 Automotive wire & cable, except ignition sets: nonferrous; engine electrical equipment

(G-346)
MAGGIO PRINTING LLC
Also Called: Maggio Fine
171 Heller Pl (08031-2503)
PHONE................856 931-7805
Jim Kipp, *General Mgr*
Rick Rossano, *Sales Staff*
Ron Fisherkeller, *Manager*
Charles Maggio Jr,
EMP: 48
SALES (est): 598.3K **Privately Held**
SIC: 2759 Business forms: printing

(G-347)
MERCER RUBBER COMPANY
Also Called: Mercer Gasket and Shim
110 Benigno Blvd (08031-2540)
PHONE..............................856 931-5000
Gloria Taraborelli, *Ch of Bd*
Peter Taraborelli Jr, *President*
Dean Taraborelli, *Vice Pres*
▲ **EMP:** 25 **EST:** 1939
SQ FT: 480,000
SALES: 4.5MM **Privately Held**
WEB: www.mercergasket.com
SIC: 3053 5085 Gaskets, packing & sealing devices; gaskets & seals

(G-348)
NATIONAL AUTO DETAILING NETWRK
111 Harding Ave (08031-2413)
PHONE..............................856 931-5529
Peter Moran, *President*
Steven Isreal, *COO*
EMP: 25
SQ FT: 3,500
SALES (est): 1MM **Privately Held**
SIC: 7542 2842 5169 Washing & polishing, automotive; polishing preparations & related products; chemicals & allied products

(G-349)
PIROLLI PRINTING CO INC
860 W Browning Rd (08031-1724)
PHONE..............................856 933-1285
Fax: 856 931-8513
Kathleen Pirolli, *Ch of Bd*
Eugene Pirolli, *President*
Mark Pirolli, *Treasurer*
Matthew J Pirolli, *Admin Sec*
EMP: 18
SQ FT: 5,000
SALES (est): 3.2MM **Privately Held**
WEB: www.pirolliprinting.com
SIC: 2752 Commercial printing, offset

(G-350)
SEALION METAL FABRICATORS INC
776 Creek Rd (08031-2424)
PHONE..............................856 933-3914
Fax: 856 933-3071
Louis D'Orazio, *President*
Michael J Natale, *Corp Secy*
Michael Natale, *CFO*
EMP: 14 **EST:** 1957
SQ FT: 15,000
SALES: 2.5MM **Privately Held**
SIC: 3799 Trailers & trailer equipment; boat trailers

(G-351)
SEVIROLI FOODS INC
960 Creek Rd (08031-1672)
PHONE..............................856 931-1900
Terry Bank, *Manager*
EMP: 5
SALES (est): 393.8K
SALES (corp-wide): 76.9MM **Privately Held**
SIC: 2038 Frozen specialties
PA: Seviroli Foods, Inc.
601 Brook St
Garden City NY 11530
516 222-6220

(G-352)
STAINLESS STEEL FABRICATORS
900 Creek Rd (08031-1676)
PHONE..............................856 464-1999
Daniel Elwell, *President*
Fred Moffitt, *Vice Pres*
Mary Jane Moffitt, *Vice Pres*
EMP: 5
SQ FT: 2,500
SALES (est): 423.4K **Privately Held**
SIC: 3441 Fabricated structural metal

(G-353)
TBT GROUP INC
191 Heller Pl (08031-2503)
PHONE..............................856 753-4500
Daniel Declemnet, *CEO*
Eric M Weiss, *President*
EMP: 8

SQ FT: 1,700
SALES (est): 1.3MM **Privately Held**
SIC: 3675 8711 Electronic capacitors; engineering services

(G-354)
W B MASON CO INC
151 Heller Pl (08031-2503)
PHONE..............................888 926-2766
EMP: 60
SALES (corp-wide): 773MM **Privately Held**
SIC: 5943 5712 2752 Office forms & supplies; office furniture; commercial printing, lithographic
PA: W. B. Mason Co., Inc.
59 Center St
Brockton MA 02301
781 794-8800

Belmar
Monmouth County

(G-355)
A PS INLET MARINA LLC
610 5th Ave (07719-2114)
PHONE..............................732 681-3303
Fax: 732 681-9181
Erika Gerzsenyi,
Robert Gerzsenyi,
Zoltan Gerzsenyi,
EMP: 5
SQ FT: 1,000
SALES (est): 450K **Privately Held**
WEB: www.apsinletmarina.com
SIC: 3732 4493 5551 5541 Boat building & repairing; boat yards, storage & incidental repair; sails & equipment; marine service station

(G-356)
CONSTANTIA BLYTHEWOOD LLC
1111 N Point Blvd (07719)
PHONE..............................732 974-4100
EMP: 57 **Privately Held**
SIC: 3497 Metal foil & leaf
HQ: Constantia Blythewood, Llc
1111 Northpoint Blvd
Blythewood SC 29016
803 404-6581

(G-357)
DEITZ CO INC
1750 Hwy 34 (07719)
P.O. Box 1108, Wall (07719-1108)
PHONE..............................732 295-8212
Fax: 732 681-8468
Steven Deitz, *President*
Stephen J Deitz Jr, *President*
Charles E Deitz, *Vice Pres*
Charles Dietz, *Vice Pres*
EMP: 12 **EST:** 1959
SQ FT: 12,000
SALES (est): 1.9MM **Privately Held**
WEB: www.deitzco.com
SIC: 3565 3559 Packaging machinery; pharmaceutical machinery

(G-358)
GEMCRAFT INC
1921 State Route 71 (07719-3247)
PHONE..............................732 449-8944
John Shenin, *President*
EMP: 4
SALES (est): 300K **Privately Held**
SIC: 2434 Wood kitchen cabinets

(G-359)
HYCHEM CORPORATION
611 Main St Ste B-2 (07719-5103)
PHONE..............................732 280-8803
Henry Yard, *President*
▲ **EMP:** 4
SQ FT: 1,200
SALES (est): 400K **Privately Held**
WEB: www.hychemcorp.com
SIC: 2899 5169 Chemical preparations; chemicals & allied products

(G-360)
NJR CLEAN ENERGY VENTURES CORP
1415 Wyckoff Rd (07719)
PHONE..............................732 938-1000
Warren Downes, *CEO*
Rhonda M Figueroa, *Director*
Valori Mark, *Director*
EMP: 450
SALES (est): 360.7K
SALES (corp-wide): 2.2B **Publicly Held**
SIC: 1311 Natural gas production
PA: New Jersey Resources Corp
1415 Wyckoff Rd
Wall Township NJ 07727
732 938-1000

(G-361)
OCTOPUS YACHTS LTD LBLTY CO
2400 Belmar Blvd Ste C-1 (07719-4098)
PHONE..............................732 698-8550
Aaron Held,
EMP: 10
SALES (est): 1.7MM **Privately Held**
SIC: 3669 Sirens, electric: vehicle, marine, industrial & air raid

(G-362)
RFM PRINTING INC
1715 Hwy 34 (07719)
P.O. Box 1430 (07719-1430)
PHONE..............................732 938-4400
Fax: 732 751-2601
Robert McKenna, *President*
Mike Surowiec, *General Mgr*
EMP: 10
SALES: 2MM **Privately Held**
WEB: www.rfmprinting.com
SIC: 2752 Commercial printing, offset

(G-363)
RKE ATHLETIC LETTERING
1901 State Route 71 1c (07719-3277)
PHONE..............................732 280-1111
Fax: 732 681-4349
Gregory Kapalko, *Owner*
EMP: 7
SALES (est): 977.3K **Privately Held**
SIC: 3949 Sporting & athletic goods

(G-364)
SONETRONICS INC (PA)
1718 State Route 71 (07719-3140)
P.O. Box L (07719-0430)
PHONE..............................732 681-5016
Fax: 732 681-5216
Gary Kuskin, *Ch of Bd*
Debi Kuskin, *Vice Pres*
▲ **EMP:** 80 **EST:** 1961
SQ FT: 19,500
SALES (est): 12.6MM **Privately Held**
WEB: www.sonetronics.com
SIC: 3661 3089 Communication headgear, telephone; injection molding of plastics

(G-365)
WATONKA PRINTING INC
Also Called: Instant Business Cards
1608 State Route 71 (07719-2802)
PHONE..............................732 974-8878
William Reinhard Jr, *President*
EMP: 7
SQ FT: 2,500
SALES (est): 504.5K **Privately Held**
SIC: 2759 2752 2761 2677 Thermography; commercial printing, lithographic; manifold business forms; envelopes

---

Belvidere
Warren County

(G-366)
ARTISAN MODEL MOLD
Also Called: A M M
275 Buckhorn Dr (07823-2708)
PHONE..............................908 453-3524
Ronald Stanwick, *Owner*
EMP: 5
SALES: 160K **Privately Held**
SIC: 3999 Models, general, except toy

(G-367)
CONVEYER INSTALLERS AMERICA
5 Tamarack Rd (07823-2521)
PHONE..............................908 453-4729
Allen Orchard, *Owner*
EMP: 4
SALES: 400K **Privately Held**
SIC: 3535 Belt conveyor systems, general industrial use

(G-368)
COUNTY OF WARREN
Also Called: Road Dept
519 S 185 County Rd (07823)
PHONE..............................908 475-7975
Frederick Miller, *Principal*
EMP: 65 **Privately Held**
WEB: www.co.warren.nj.us
SIC: 3531 Construction machinery
PA: County Of Warren
165 County Road 519 Ste 1
Belvidere NJ 07823
908 475-6500

(G-369)
DSM NUTRITIONAL PRODUCTS LLC
206 Macks Island Dr (07823-1199)
PHONE..............................908 475-7093
Christolph Goppelsrober, *Principal*
EMP: 152
SALES (corp-wide): 10.1B **Privately Held**
SIC: 2834 2836 Pharmaceutical preparations; vitamin, nutrient & hematinic preparations for human use; biological products, except diagnostic; veterinary biological products
HQ: Dsm Nutritional Products, Llc
45 Waterview Blvd
Parsippany NJ 07054
800 526-0189

(G-370)
DSM NUTRITIONAL PRODUCTS LLC
253 260 Macks Island Dr (07823)
PHONE..............................908 475-0150
Michael J Adams, *Opers-Prdtn-Mfg*
EMP: 450
SALES (corp-wide): 10.1B **Privately Held**
WEB: www.nutraaccess.com
SIC: 2834 Pharmaceutical preparations
HQ: Dsm Nutritional Products, Llc
45 Waterview Blvd
Parsippany NJ 07054
800 526-0189

(G-371)
DSM NUTRITIONAL PRODUCTS LLC
200 Roche Dr (07823-2100)
PHONE..............................908 475-5300
Michael Adams, *Branch Mgr*
EMP: 152
SALES (corp-wide): 10.1B **Privately Held**
SIC: 2834 Pharmaceutical preparations
HQ: Dsm Nutritional Products, Llc
45 Waterview Blvd
Parsippany NJ 07054
800 526-0189

(G-372)
DSM NUTRITIONAL PRODUCTS LLC
218 Roche Dr (07823-2100)
PHONE..............................908 475-5300
Dr Christolph Goppelsrober, *Branch Mgr*
EMP: 240
SALES (corp-wide): 10.1B **Privately Held**
WEB: www.nutraaccess.com
SIC: 2834 Pharmaceutical preparations
HQ: Dsm Nutritional Products, Llc
45 Waterview Blvd
Parsippany NJ 07054
800 526-0189

(G-373)
GREAT NORTHERN COMMERCIAL SVCS
401 Greenwich St (07823-1406)
PHONE..............................908 475-8855
Fax: 908 475-3299
Anna Quinn, *President*

GEOGRAPHIC

Dennis Quinn, *Principal*
EMP: 7
SQ FT: 8,000
SALES: 750K **Privately Held**
WEB: www.greatnortherngraphics.com
SIC: 2752 Commercial printing, litho-
graphic

(G-374)
PV DEROCHE LLC
Also Called: Deroche Canvas
283 County Route 519 (07823)
P.O. Box 443 (07823-0443)
PHONE...........................908 475-2266
James Van Stone, *CEO*
Daniel Deroche, *President*
EMP: 34
SQ FT: 20,000
SALES (est): 1.3MM **Privately Held**
SIC: 2394 Convertible tops, canvas or
boat: from purchased materials

(G-375)
RIVERBEND ADVERTISER
401 Greenwich St (07823-1406)
PHONE...........................908 475-3431
Anna Quinn, *Owner*
EMP: 4
SALES (est): 190K **Privately Held**
SIC: 2711 Newspapers

(G-376)
S J SCREW COMPANY INC
Also Called: S Johnson & Son
Front & Hardwick St (07823)
P.O. Box 66 (07823-0066)
PHONE...........................908 475-2155
Sven G Johnson, *President*
Erik H Johnson, *Vice Pres*
EMP: 40 **EST:** 1933
SQ FT: 35,000
SALES (est): 7.3MM **Privately Held**
SIC: 3451 Screw machine products

(G-377)
T M INDUSTRIES INC
2013 Brookfield Glen Dr (07823-2855)
PHONE...........................908 730-7674
Fax: 908 730-6501
Gerda A Tietje, *President*
EMP: 8
SQ FT: 1,500
SALES (est): 1MM **Privately Held**
SIC: 3569 Lubrication equipment, industrial

(G-378)
WESTERN ELECTRONICS DIST
300 5th St (07823-1802)
PHONE...........................908 475-3303
Joe Hyziak, *Vice Pres*
EMP: 5
SALES (est): 447.3K **Privately Held**
SIC: 3679 Electronic circuits

Bergenfield
Bergen County

(G-379)
AIM COMPUTER ASSOCIATES INC
19 Dover Ct (07621-3902)
PHONE...........................201 489-3100
David Hendlish, *President*
EMP: 8
SQ FT: 1,200
SALES (est): 540K **Privately Held**
WEB: www.aimcomputer.com
SIC: 7374 7372 Data entry service; busi-
ness oriented computer software

(G-380)
AMERICAN FORECLOSURES INC
15 W Main St Apt 1 (07621-2131)
P.O. Box 601, Oradell (07649-0601)
PHONE...........................201 501-0200
Craig Laube, *President*
Cynthia Ehrlich, *Vice Pres*
EMP: 12
SALES (est): 950K **Privately Held**
WEB: www.americanforeclosures.com
SIC: 2721 6531 Periodicals: publishing
only; real estate agents & managers

(G-381)
ASTI CORP
Also Called: Asti Magnetics
45 W Broad St (07621-2866)
PHONE...........................201 501-8900
Fax: 201 385-1702
Henry Akiya, *President*
Sal Rutigliano, *Vice Pres*
Paul Rutigliano, *Treasurer*
▲ **EMP:** 14
SQ FT: 10,000
SALES: 9MM **Privately Held**
WEB: www.astimag.com
SIC: 3679 Recording & playback heads,
magnetic

(G-382)
BANICKI SHEET METAL INC
44 Garden St (07621-2744)
PHONE...........................201 385-5938
EMP: 7
SALES (est): 640K **Privately Held**
SIC: 1711 3585 3444 Plumbing/Heat/Ac
Contr Mfg Refrig/Heat Equip Mfg Sheet
Metalwork

(G-383)
BERGEN MARZIPAN & CHOCOLATE
205 S Washington Ave (07621-2918)
PHONE...........................201 385-8343
Fax: 201 385-0042
Serpin Adanan, *President*
Gunter Schott, *Principal*
▲ **EMP:** 4
SALES (est): 250K **Privately Held**
SIC: 2066 2064 Chocolate & cocoa prod-
ucts; marzipan (candy)

(G-384)
CNR PRODUCTS CO
74 Portland Ave (07621-2307)
PHONE...........................201 384-7003
Peter Rebsch, *Owner*
EMP: 5
SQ FT: 3,000
SALES (est): 324.6K **Privately Held**
WEB: www.cnrproducts.com
SIC: 3993 Signs, not made in custom sign
painting shops

(G-385)
GLOBAL EXPRESS FREIGHT INC
136 W Central Ave (07621-1208)
PHONE...........................201 376-6613
Alfonso Rivera, *President*
EMP: 4 **EST:** 2014
SQ FT: 1,000
SALES: 500K **Privately Held**
SIC: 3537 Trucks: freight, baggage, etc.:
industrial, except mining

(G-386)
HARLEY TOOL & MACHINE INC
24 Mcdermott Pl (07621-3706)
PHONE...........................201 244-8899
John Robert Harley, *President*
EMP: 4 **EST:** 1925
SALES: 400K **Privately Held**
SIC: 3599 5051 Machine shop, jobbing &
repair; aluminum bars, rods, ingots,
sheets, pipes, plates, etc.

(G-387)
HITRONS SOLUTIONS INC
88 Portland Ave Ste M (07621-2364)
PHONE...........................201 244-0300
EMP: 10
SQ FT: 2,000
SALES: 2.1MM **Privately Held**
SIC: 3261 Whol Plumbing Equipment/Sup-
plies Mfg Plumbing Fixture Fittings

(G-388)
HITRONS SOLUTIONS INC
88 Portland Ave Ste M (07621-2364)
PHONE...........................201 244-0300
Steve Chung, *President*
Thomas Masters, *Managing Dir*
David Kim, *Vice Pres*
Eun Joung Chung, *CFO*
David Cho, *Accounts Exec*
▲ **EMP:** 10

SALES (est): 4MM **Privately Held**
SIC: 3261 8748 Bidets, vitreous china;
business consulting

MAGIC METAL WORKS INC
40 W Englewood Ave (07621-3714)
PHONE...........................201 384-8457
George Dabaghian, *President*
Vic Dabaghian, *Corp Secy*
Jacques Dabaghian, *Vice Pres*
EMP: 6
SQ FT: 6,400
SALES (est): 510K **Privately Held**
SIC: 3469 Electronic enclosures, stamped
or pressed metal

(G-390)
N B C ENGRAVING CO INC
160 Woodbine St (07621-3521)
P.O. Box 1036, Hackensack (07602-1036)
PHONE...........................201 387-8011
Fax: 201 387-9602
Camillo Scagliotti, *President*
John Scagliotti, *Vice Pres*
EMP: 6
SQ FT: 1,000
SALES: 350K **Privately Held**
WEB: www.nbcengraving.com
SIC: 3555 Plates, metal: engravers'

(G-391)
NEW JERSEY EYE CENTER INC
1 N Washington Ave (07621-2125)
PHONE...........................201 384-7333
Joseph Dello Russo, *Principal*
EMP: 14
SALES (est): 2.3MM **Privately Held**
SIC: 3851 Eyes, glass & plastic

(G-392)
PEACOCK PRODUCTS INC
48 Woodbine St (07621-3520)
P.O. Box 127 (07621-0127)
PHONE...........................201 385-5585
Fax: 201 501-8566
Craig Langslet, *President*
Eric Langslet, *President*
▲ **EMP:** 16
SQ FT: 8,000
SALES (est): 2.4MM **Privately Held**
SIC: 2759 Commercial printing

(G-393)
ROY D SMITH INC
20 Foster St (07621-4302)
P.O. Box 537 (07621-0537)
PHONE...........................201 384-4163
Fax: 201 384-1889
Eric Zymet, *President*
EMP: 5
SQ FT: 1,600
SALES (est): 370K **Privately Held**
SIC: 2752 Commercial printing, litho-
graphic

(G-394)
SAMUEL JEWELS INC
50 Mcdermott Pl (07621-3723)
PHONE...........................201 439-1555
Steve Samuel, *President*
Camille Samuel, *Vice Pres*
EMP: 15
SQ FT: 2,000
SALES (est): 2.1MM **Privately Held**
WEB: www.samueljewels.com
SIC: 3911 Jewelry, precious metal

(G-395)
STARBEAM SOFTWARE SOLUTIONS
373 Wildrose Ave (07621-3409)
PHONE...........................201 384-0017
EMP: 4
SALES (est): 273.4K **Privately Held**
SIC: 7372 Prepackaged Software Services

(G-396)
TECHNOLOGY DYNAMICS INC (PA)
100 School St Ste 1 (07621-2900)
PHONE...........................201 385-0500
Aron Levy, *President*
Daniel J Cavalli, *Vice Pres*
Dwight Dixon, *Vice Pres*

Dan Ellenback, *Vice Pres*
Daniel Ellenback, *Vice Pres*
▲ **EMP:** 49 **EST:** 1976
SQ FT: 30,000
SALES (est): 33.8MM **Privately Held**
WEB: www.theallpower.com
SIC: 5063 3679 3613 Electrical apparatus
& equipment; static power supply convert-
ers for electronic applications; power
switching equipment; regulators, power

(G-397)
TECHNOLOGY DYNAMICS INC
Nova Electric
100 School St (07621-2900)
PHONE...........................201 385-0500
Fax: 201 385-0702
Aron Levy, *President*
Howard Schrier, *Manager*
Dwight Dixon, *Executive*
EMP: 100
SALES (corp-wide): 33.8MM **Privately
Held**
WEB: www.theallpower.com
SIC: 3621 3679 Frequency converters
(electric generators); inverters, rotating:
electrical; power supplies, all types: static
PA: Technology Dynamics, Inc.
100 School St Ste 1
Bergenfield NJ 07621
201 385-0500

Berkeley Heights
Union County

(G-398)
ACE LTHGRAPHERS OF MORRIS CNTY
22 Russo Pl (07922-1606)
PHONE...........................973 428-4911
EMP: 17
SQ FT: 6,700
SALES (est): 3MM **Privately Held**
SIC: 2752 Lithographic Commercial Print-
ing

(G-399)
ALIGN PHARMACEUTICALS LLC
200 Connell Dr Ste 1500 (07922-2811)
PHONE...........................908 834-0960
Greg Preston, *VP Mktg*
Robert Sosnowski,
▲ **EMP:** 5
SALES (est): 106.4K **Publicly Held**
WEB: www.cyclacel.com
SIC: 2834 Pharmaceutical preparations
PA: Cyclacel Pharmaceuticals, Inc.
200 Connell Dr Ste 1500
Berkeley Heights NJ 07922

(G-400)
AT&T TECHNOLOGIES INC
1 Oak Way (07922-2732)
PHONE...........................201 771-2000
Morris Tanenbaum, *Ch of Bd*
Thomas R Thomsen, *President*
William J Warwick, *President*
E Wayne Weeks Jr, *President*
Michael A Brunner, *Exec VP*
▼ **EMP:** 97200 **EST:** 1869
SQ FT: 433,000
SALES: 11.4B
SALES (corp-wide): 160.5B **Publicly
Held**
SIC: 3661 3357 3351 3679 Switching
equipment, telephone; carrier equipment,
telephone or telegraph; fiber optics com-
munications equipment; fiber optic cable
(insulated); wire, copper & copper alloy;
power supplies, all types: static; wiring
boards; nautical instruments; sonar sys-
tems & equipment
HQ: At&T Corp.
1 At&T Way
Bedminster NJ 07921
800 403-3302

(G-401)
BOEING COMPANY
400 Connell Dr Ste 6200 (07922-2810)
PHONE...........................908 464-6959
Matthew M Hoff, *Branch Mgr*

▲ = Import ▼=Export
◆ =Import/Export

EMP: 4518
SALES (corp-wide): 93.3B **Publicly Held**
SIC: 3721 Aircraft
PA: The Boeing Company
100 N Riverside Plz
Chicago IL 60606
312 544-2000

(G-402)
BRIAN LENHART INTERACTIVE LLC
2 Ridge Dr E (07922-2112)
PHONE.............................610 737-5314
Brian Lenhart, *Owner*
EMP: 5
SALES (est): 297.9K **Privately Held**
SIC: 2241 Apparel webbing

(G-403)
CELGENE CORPORATION
300 Connell Dr Ste 6000 (07922-2372)
PHONE.............................908 464-8101
Patricia Tramontana, *Opers Dir*
Monica Cantonetti, *Opers Staff*
Tanesha Duncan, *Opers Staff*
Lisa Serme, *Opers Staff*
Cate Elflein, *Branch Mgr*
EMP: 15
SALES (corp-wide): 13B **Publicly Held**
SIC: 2834 Pharmaceutical preparations
PA: Celgene Corporation
86 Morris Ave
Summit NJ 07901
908 673-9000

(G-404)
CELGENE CORPORATION
400 Connell Dr Ste 4000 (07922-2797)
PHONE.............................908 967-1432
Robert J Hugin, *Principal*
Michael Sturniolo, *Director*
Piyali Chowdhury, *Associate Dir*
EMP: 12
SALES (corp-wide): 13B **Publicly Held**
SIC: 2834 Pharmaceutical preparations
PA: Celgene Corporation
86 Morris Ave
Summit NJ 07901
908 673-9000

(G-405)
CHEMTRADE SOLUTIONS LLC
Also Called: General Chemical
235 Snyder Ave (07922-1140)
PHONE.............................908 464-1500
Jerry Kirwan, *Plant Mgr*
Robert Braddock, *Branch Mgr*
EMP: 15
SALES (corp-wide): 1.1B **Privately Held**
SIC: 2819 Aluminum compounds
HQ: Chemtrade Solutions Llc
90 E Halsey Rd Ste 301
Parsippany NJ 07054

(G-406)
CONNELL MINING PRODUCTS LLC
Also Called: Celco
200 Connell Dr (07922-2805)
PHONE.............................908 673-3700
Howard Jaffe, *Vice Pres*
Paul King, *Vice Pres*
Richard Ringler, *Vice Pres*
Donna Maas, *Opers Mgr*
Michael Gilbert, *Purch Mgr*
◆ **EMP:** 100
SALES (est): 12.1MM
SALES (corp-wide): 464.8MM **Privately Held**
SIC: 1081 Metal mining services
PA: The Connell Company
200 Connell Dr Ste 4100
Berkeley Heights NJ 07922
908 673-3700

(G-407)
CORMEDIX INC (PA)
400 Connell Dr Ste 5000 (07922-2809)
PHONE.............................908 517-9500
Fax: 908 429-4307
Khoso Baluch, *CEO*
Myron Kaplan, *Ch of Bd*
James Alltand, *CFO*
Robert W Cook, *CFO*
Judith R Abrams, *Chief Mktg Ofcr*
EMP: 9

SALES: 329.3K **Publicly Held**
SIC: 2834 Pharmaceutical preparations; drugs acting on the central nervous system & sense organs

(G-408)
CYCLACEL PHARMACEUTICALS INC (PA)
200 Connell Dr Ste 1500 (07922-2811)
PHONE.............................908 517-7330
David U'Prichard, *Ch of Bd*
Christopher S Henney, *Vice Ch Bd*
Spiro Rombotis, *President*
Christopher Henney PHD, *Vice Chairman*
Paul McBarron, *COO*
EMP: 16
SALES (est): 843K **Publicly Held**
WEB: www.cyclacel.com
SIC: 2834 Pharmaceutical preparations

(G-409)
E G L COMPANY INC
Also Called: E G L
100 Industrial Rd (07922-1523)
PHONE.............................908 508-1111
Fax: 908 508-1122
Harold R Cortese Jr, *President*
Douglas Cortese, *Director*
◆ **EMP:** 110 **EST:** 1931
SQ FT: 80,000
SALES (est): 20MM **Privately Held**
WEB: www.egl-neon.com
SIC: 3641 3229 5169 Electrodes, cold cathode fluorescent lamp; tubing, glass; industrial gases

(G-410)
EDGE THERAPEUTICS INC
300 Connell Dr Ste 4000 (07922-2817)
PHONE.............................800 208-3343
Sol Barer, *Ch of Bd*
Isaac Blech, *Vice Ch Bd*
Brian A Leuthner, *President*
W Bradford Middlekauff, *Senior VP*
Alyssa J S Wyant, *Senior VP*
EMP: 31 **EST:** 2009
SQ FT: 20,410
SALES (est): 6.8MM **Privately Held**
SIC: 2834 8731 Pharmaceutical preparations; biological research

(G-411)
GO WADDLE INC
23 Baldwin Dr (07922-1744)
PHONE.............................301 452-5084
Suma Reddy, *Principal*
Vishal Reddy, *Principal*
EMP: 4
SALES (est): 170K **Privately Held**
SIC: 2741

(G-412)
INCOM (AMERICA) INC
330 Snyder Ave (07922-1505)
PHONE.............................908 464-3366
Ahmed G Singer, *President*
Wendell Tomimbang, *Vice Pres*
EMP: 5
SQ FT: 32,000
SALES (est): 433.9K **Privately Held**
WEB: www.incom-america.com
SIC: 3694 Harness wiring sets, internal combustion engines

(G-413)
J K OFFICE MACHINE INC
33 Debbie Pl (07922-1705)
P.O. Box 589, Summit (07902-0589)
PHONE.............................908 273-8811
James Martin, *President*
Neal Pauline, *Vice Pres*
EMP: 5 **EST:** 1969
SQ FT: 2,500
SALES: 625K **Privately Held**
SIC: 3579 7629 Mailing, letter handling & addressing machines; business machine repair, electric

(G-414)
J MICHAELS JEWELERS INC
370 Springfield Ave (07922-1107)
PHONE.............................908 771-9800
Michael Bernardo, *President*
Michael Bernado, *President*
EMP: 4
SQ FT: 1,200

SALES (est): 487.6K **Privately Held**
SIC: 5944 3915 5094 Jewelry, precious stones & precious metals; lapidary work & diamond cutting & polishing; jewelry; diamonds (gems)

(G-415)
KARL NEUWEILER INC
Also Called: Neuweiler, K H
23 Russo Pl (07922-1606)
PHONE.............................908 464-6532
Fax: 908 464-6086
Daniel Neuweiler, *President*
Ann Neuweiler, *Vice Pres*
EMP: 9 **EST:** 1953
SQ FT: 6,000
SALES: 1.5MM **Privately Held**
WEB: www.neuweiler.com
SIC: 3451 Screw machine products

(G-416)
KNOTTS COMPANY INC
350 Snyder Ave (07922-1500)
P.O. Box 611 (07922-0611)
PHONE.............................908 464-4800
Fax: 908 464-7747
Richard L Howe, *President*
Fred Heimall, *Technical Mgr*
George Mehaffey, *Treasurer*
Jerry Ferrante, *Sales Mgr*
Rich Eckhard, *Marketing Staff*
EMP: 36
SQ FT: 14,000
SALES (est): 12.6MM **Privately Held**
WEB: www.knottsco.com
SIC: 3535 5085 Unit handling conveying systems; industrial supplies

(G-417)
LAUDERDALE MILLWORK INC
77 Industrial Rd (07922-1539)
PHONE.............................908 508-9550
John Lauderdale, *President*
EMP: 10
SALES (est): 1.1MM **Privately Held**
SIC: 2431 Millwork

(G-418)
LUMITRON CORP
Also Called: Lumitron Arospc Ltg Components
35 Russo Pl (07922-1622)
P.O. Box 394 (07922-0394)
PHONE.............................908 508-9100
Fax: 908 273-0853
Gil Chassie, *President*
Karen Chassie, *Vice Pres*
Jerry Rosario, *Mfg Staff*
EMP: 10 **EST:** 1970
SQ FT: 1,500
SALES (est): 1.8MM **Privately Held**
WEB: www.lumitroncorp.com
SIC: 3641 Lamps, incandescent filament, electric

(G-419)
MAINSTREAM FLUID & AIR LLC
47 Russo Pl (07922-1606)
P.O. Box 353, Cranford (07016-0353)
PHONE.............................908 931-1010
Derrick Markham, *Mng Member*
James Markham,
EMP: 49
SQ FT: 25,000
SALES (est): 11.5MM **Privately Held**
SIC: 3585 Air conditioning equipment, complete; heating & air conditioning combination units; air conditioning condensers & condensing units

(G-420)
PERCO INC
620 Springfield Ave (07922-1055)
P.O. Box 23 (07922-0023)
PHONE.............................908 464-3000
Jim Dinaio, *President*
Annemarie Dinaio, *Shareholder*
EMP: 10
SQ FT: 6,500
SALES: 1.2MM **Privately Held**
SIC: 2759 Commercial printing

(G-421)
SCIENTIFIC MODELS INC
Also Called: Micro-Mark
340 Snyder Ave (07922-1595)
PHONE.............................908 464-7070
Fax: 908 665-9383
Beth Tobin, *Office Mgr*
Sandra Frisoli, *Director*
▲ **EMP:** 22 **EST:** 1946
SQ FT: 16,000
SALES (est): 5.7MM **Privately Held**
WEB: www.scientificmodels.com
SIC: 5092 3999 Hobby supplies; models, except toy

(G-422)
SHELL PACKAGING CORPORATION (PA)
Also Called: Flexcon Container
200 Connell Dr Ste 1200 (07922-2822)
PHONE.............................908 871-7000
Fax: 908 871-1111
Ken Beckerman, *President*
Stephen M Beckerman, *President*
Edythe Benisrael, *Accounting Mgr*
Jason Grasso, *Sales Staff*
Stephen Beckerman, *Sales Executive*
▲ **EMP:** 49
SQ FT: 6,000
SALES (est): 14MM **Privately Held**
WEB: www.flexcontainer.com
SIC: 2631 3086 3443 Packaging board; packaging & shipping materials, foamed plastic; fabricated plate work (boiler shop)

(G-423)
TWILL INC
22 Russo Pl (07922-1606)
PHONE.............................908 665-1700
Fax: 908 665-9717
George Robert Twill, *President*
Peter Twill, *Vice Pres*
George Wilson, *Prdtn Mgr*
Jeffrey Till, *Producer*
EMP: 15 **EST:** 1947
SQ FT: 17,800
SALES: 2.2MM **Privately Held**
WEB: www.twill.com
SIC: 2752 Commercial printing, offset

(G-424)
WAVE DISPERSION TECH INC (PA)
Also Called: Whisprwave
45 Industrial Rd (07922-1501)
P.O. Box 542407, Greenacres FL (33454-2407)
PHONE.............................908 233-7503
Fax: 908 233-7507
▼ **EMP:** 5 **EST:** 1995
SQ FT: 9,824
SALES: 3.5MM **Privately Held**
SIC: 3531 Mfg Marine Related Equipment

Berlin
Camden County

(G-425)
ARIES FILTERWORKS INC
117 Jackson Rd (08009-9160)
PHONE.............................856 626-1550
Michael C Gottlieb, *President*
Jeffery H Gottlieb, *Vice Pres*
Lawrence Gottlieb, *Vice Pres*
Lynne Gottlieb, *Vice Pres*
Frank Firicano, *Mng Member*
EMP: 43 **EST:** 2010
SALES (est): 1.9MM **Privately Held**
SIC: 3589 Water filters & softeners, household type; water purification equipment, household type

(G-426)
BELTOR MANUFACTURING CORP
50 Union Ave Ste 12 (08009)
PHONE.............................856 768-5570
Derek Torok, *President*
EMP: 5 **EST:** 1945
SQ FT: 2,100

GEOGRAPHIC

SALES: 660K **Privately Held**
SIC: 2391 3841 Curtains, window: made from purchased materials; surgical & medical instruments

(G-427)
BOCCELLA PRECAST LLC
324 New Brooklyn Rd (08009-9506)
P.O. Box 32 (08009-0032)
PHONE..........................856 767-3861
Carol Shahin, *Controller*
Anthony Boccella, *Sales Executive*
Joseph Boccella, *Mng Member*
▲ EMP: 10
SALES (est): 4MM **Privately Held**
SIC: 3272 Concrete products, precast

(G-428)
BRIDGESTATE FOUNDRY CORP
175 Jackson Rd (08009-2608)
PHONE..........................856 767-0400
Ed Ciel, *President*
EMP: 4 EST: 1962
SQ FT: 2,000
SALES (est): 1.3MM
SALES (corp-wide): 11.9MM **Privately Held**
WEB: www.campbellfoundry.com
SIC: 3321 Gray iron castings; manhole covers, metal
PA: Campbell Foundry Company
800 Bergen St
Harrison NJ 07029
973 483-5480

(G-429)
BRINGHURST BROS INC
Also Called: Bringhurst Meats
38 W Taunton Rd (08009-9702)
PHONE..........................856 767-0110
Fax: 856 767-0224
Ralph A Bringhurst Jr, *President*
Jeff Bringhurst, *Corp Secy*
EMP: 22 EST: 1934
SQ FT: 12,000
SALES (est): 1.5MM **Privately Held**
WEB: www.bringhurstmeats.com
SIC: 5421 2011 5812 5147 Meat markets, including freezer provisioners; pork products from pork slaughtered on site; meat by-products from meat slaughtered on site; caterers; meats & meat products; animal & marine fats & oils; sausages & other prepared meats

(G-430)
BUILDERS FIRSTSOURCE INC
210 Williamstown Rd (08009-9730)
PHONE..........................856 767-3153
Manish Kharbanda, *Branch Mgr*
EMP: 20
SALES (corp-wide): 7B **Publicly Held**
WEB: www.hopelumber.com
SIC: 2449 Containers, plywood & veneer wood
PA: Builders Firstsource, Inc.
2001 Bryan St Ste 1600
Dallas TX 75201
214 880-3500

(G-431)
CLASSIC GRAPHIC INC
Also Called: Minuteman Press
35 W White Horse Pike (08009-1273)
PHONE..........................856 753-0055
Kevin J Humphrey, *President*
Karen Humphrey, *Treasurer*
EMP: 5
SQ FT: 1,600
SALES (est): 903.6K **Privately Held**
SIC: 2752 Commercial printing, lithographic

(G-432)
COMPUTA-BASE-MACHINING INC
411 N Grove St (08009-9704)
P.O. Box 340 (08009-0340)
PHONE..........................856 767-9517
Fax: 856 767-8541
EMP: 17 EST: 1981
SQ FT: 22,000
SALES (est): 4.3MM **Privately Held**
SIC: 3599 Mfg Industrial Machinery

(G-433)
DIAL CONNECTION LLC
1040 S Route 73 (08009-2600)
PHONE..........................856 753-6620
Fax: 856 753-6626
Michael Vesper,
EMP: 10
SALES (est): 1.2MM **Privately Held**
WEB: www.dialconnection.com
SIC: 7372 Application computer software

(G-434)
HANSON & ZOLLINGER INC
Also Called: Alliance Contract Mfg
117 Jackson Rd (08009-9160)
PHONE..........................856 626-3440
Robert Zollinger, *President*
Michael Hanson, *Vice Pres*
▲ EMP: 12
SALES: 3MM **Privately Held**
SIC: 3537 3231 Tables, lift: hydraulic; medical & laboratory glassware: made from purchased glass

(G-435)
J B & SONS CONCRETE PRODUCTS (PA)
358 New Brooklyn Rd (08009-9513)
PHONE..........................856 767-4140
Joe Boccella, *President*
◆ EMP: 10
SALES (est): 1.2MM **Privately Held**
SIC: 3272 5211 Concrete products, precast; masonry materials & supplies

(G-436)
JOHNS MANVILLE CORPORATION
437 N Grove St (08009-9704)
P.O. Box 130 (08009-0130)
PHONE..........................856 768-7000
Jason Rogers, *Production*
Mark Uscinowicz, *Engineer*
Glen Wilson, *Plant Engr*
Andrew Reid, *Electrical Engi*
Joseph Catania, *Human Res Mgr*
EMP: 250
SALES (corp-wide): 242.1B **Publicly Held**
WEB: www.jm.com
SIC: 3296 Mineral wool
HQ: Johns Manville Corporation
717 17th St Ste 800
Denver CO 80202
303 978-2000

(G-437)
KESKES PRINTING LLC
5 W Taunton Ave (08009-1441)
PHONE..........................856 767-4733
Joseph C Keskes, *Owner*
Jean Keskes, *Mng Member*
Joseph Keskes, *Mng Member*
EMP: 5 EST: 1972
SQ FT: 2,250
SALES: 300K **Privately Held**
WEB: www.keskes.com
SIC: 2752 2759 Commercial printing, offset; letterpress printing

(G-438)
MOUNTAIN PRINTING COMPANY INC
27 N Atlantic Ave (08009-1694)
P.O. Box 608 (08009-0608)
PHONE..........................856 767-7600
Fax: 856 767-2698
Rose Marie De Pasquale, *President*
Stephen Cammarota, *Marketing Staff*
Millie Clerkin, *Office Mgr*
▲ EMP: 33 EST: 1962
SQ FT: 23,000
SALES (est): 7.8MM **Privately Held**
WEB: www.mountainprinting.com
SIC: 2752 Commercial printing, offset

(G-439)
NATIONAL PAVING CO INC (HQ)
148 Williamstown Rd (08009-9720)
P.O. Box 5 (08009-0005)
PHONE..........................856 767-1950
Fax: 856 767-0806
Bruce Rambo, *President*
Bill Rambo, *Vice Pres*
Rachel Mc Cool, *Admin Sec*

EMP: 10
SQ FT: 2,500
SALES (est): 3MM
SALES (corp-wide): 101.7MM **Privately Held**
SIC: 2951 Asphalt & asphaltic paving mixtures (not from refineries)
PA: Glasgow, Inc.
104 Willow Grove Ave
Glenside PA 19038
215 884-8800

(G-440)
PETERS LABORATORIES
1 Hillside Ln (08009-1703)
PHONE..........................856 767-4144
Peter Serubo, *President*
Susan Zatkins, *Vice Pres*
EMP: 12
SALES (est): 502.8K **Privately Held**
SIC: 3999 Manufacturing industries

(G-441)
SAR INDUSTRIAL FINISHING INC
104 N Route 73 (08009-9636)
PHONE..........................609 567-2772
Fax: 609 567-2494
Ralph Mauro, *President*
EMP: 15
SALES (est): 1.6MM **Privately Held**
SIC: 3471 Finishing, metals or formed products

(G-442)
T J ECKARDT ASSOCIATES INC
Also Called: Honeywell Authorized Dealer
230 Williamstown Rd (08009-9730)
P.O. Box 570, Sicklerville (08081-0570)
PHONE..........................856 767-4111
Fax: 856 768-7499
Thomas J Eckardt, *President*
Bernadette Eckardt, *Corp Secy*
Harry Eckardt, *Marketing Staff*
Sal Marchese, *Supervisor*
Stacy Ammons, *Admin Asst*
EMP: 15
SQ FT: 5,000
SALES (est): 3.2MM **Privately Held**
WEB: www.tjeckardt.com
SIC: 1711 3444 Warm air heating & air conditioning contractor; ducts, sheet metal

(G-443)
UFP BERLIN LLC
Also Called: Universal Forest Products
159 Jackson Rd (08009-2608)
PHONE..........................856 767-0596
Fax: 856 767-1526
Heather Williams, *Executive*
David Goldman,
EMP: 150 EST: 2010
SALES (est): 15.1MM
SALES (corp-wide): 3.9B **Publicly Held**
SIC: 2421 5031 Building & structural materials, wood; building materials, exterior; building materials, interior
PA: Universal Forest Products, Inc.
2801 E Beltline Ave Ne
Grand Rapids MI 49525
616 364-6161

(G-444)
UNITED ASPHALT CO INC
237 N Grove St (08009-9662)
P.O. Box 291, Cedar Brook (08018-0291)
PHONE..........................856 753-9811
Fax: 856 753-9809
Mark Umosella Sr, *President*
Tim McLain, *General Mgr*
James Umosella, *Purch Mgr*
John Laratta, *Controller*
Dave Maimone, *Sales Staff*
▲ EMP: 20 EST: 1963
SQ FT: 20,000
SALES (est): 7.6MM **Privately Held**
SIC: 2952 Roofing materials; roofing felts, cements or coatings

(G-445)
WEILER & SONS LLC
Also Called: W & S Steel Products
170 Jackson Rd (08009-2607)
PHONE..........................856 767-8842
Michael P Weiler, *Mng Member*
EMP: 4

SQ FT: 2,500
SALES (est): 537.5K **Privately Held**
SIC: 3479 Chasing on metals

(G-446)
WINSLOW RENTAL & SUPPLY INC
204 Williamstown Rd (08009-9730)
P.O. Box 517 (08009-0517)
PHONE..........................856 767-5554
Fax: 856 768-7594
Tom Dixon Sr, *President*
Charlotte Dixon, *Vice Pres*
EMP: 7
SQ FT: 4,000
SALES (est): 3.1MM **Privately Held**
WEB: www.winslowrental.com
SIC: 5082 7353 7359 3546 General construction machinery & equipment; concrete processing equipment; heavy construction equipment rental; stores & yards equipment rental; saws & sawing equipment

---

Bernardsville
Somerset County

(G-447)
BABYSMART LLC
174 Hardscrabble Rd (07924-1314)
PHONE..........................908 766-4900
EMP: 5
SALES (est): 778.5K **Privately Held**
WEB: www.abaa.com
SIC: 3944 Games, toys & children's vehicles

(G-448)
BERNARDSVILLE NEWS
17 Morristown Rd (07924-2312)
PHONE..........................908 766-3900
Fax: 908 766-6365
Pete Conover, *Principal*
EMP: 4 EST: 2001
SALES (est): 218.3K **Privately Held**
SIC: 2711 Newspapers

(G-449)
CLASSIC SILKS COM I
131 Roundtop Rd (07924-2106)
PHONE..........................908 204-0940
Ganesh Prasad, *Principal*
EMP: 4
SALES (est): 182.8K **Privately Held**
SIC: 2299 Textile goods

(G-450)
GREENBROOK STAIRS INC
14 Dayton St (07924-2535)
P.O. Box 126, Basking Ridge (07920-0126)
PHONE..........................908 221-9145
Fax: 908 766-2458
Keith Fitting, *President*
Calvin Foots, *Vice Pres*
EMP: 7
SQ FT: 3,500
SALES (est): 1.3MM **Privately Held**
WEB: www.greenbrookstairs.com
SIC: 2431 Staircases & stairs, wood

(G-451)
MEADOWBROOK INVENTIONS INC
260 Mine Brook Rd (07924-2117)
P.O. Box 960 (07924-0960)
PHONE..........................908 696-8470
Harold Sutton, *President*
Joe Colleran, *Principal*
Roberta Ruschmann, *Principal*
Zbigniew Swiderski, *Plant Mgr*
Sarah Snyder, *Executive Asst*
▲ EMP: 30 EST: 1948
SQ FT: 40,000
SALES (est): 6.2MM **Privately Held**
WEB: www.meadowbrookglitter.com
SIC: 3952 Artists' materials, except pencils & leads

(G-452)
OTEX SPECIALTY NARROW FABRICS (PA)
4 Essex Ave Ste 403 (07924-2265)
PHONE..........................908 879-3636

GEOGRAPHIC

Fax: 908 879-3630
Denise A Offray, *President*
Claude V Offray, *Principal*
Barbara Weightman, *Marketing Staff*
Dave Barnes, *Director*
▲ EMP: 9
SALES (est): 36.4MM Privately Held
SIC: 2241 Narrow fabric mills

(G-453)
PARKER PUBLICATIONS INC
Also Called: Caldwell Progress
17 Morristown Rd 19 (07924-2312)
P.O. Box 687 (07924-0687)
PHONE..........................908 766-3900
Steven W Parker, *President*
Cort Parker, *Principal*
Liz Parker, *Principal*
Nancy Parker, *Principal*
EMP: 50
SQ FT: 5,000
SALES (est): 3.7MM Privately Held
WEB: www.parkerexpressions.com
SIC: 2711 Newspapers, publishing & printing

(G-454)
R & B PRINTING INC
Also Called: Bernardsville Print Center
19-21 Mine Brook Rd Fl 1 (07924-2492)
PHONE..........................908 766-4073
Fax: 908 766-7633
Richard Steinberg, *President*
Beth Steinberg, *Vice Pres*
EMP: 9
SQ FT: 2,500
SALES (est): 1.7MM Privately Held
SIC: 2752 7334 2789 2396 Commercial printing, offset; photocopying & duplicating services; bookbinding & related work; automotive & apparel trimmings

(G-455)
SWCE INC (PA)
Also Called: Swce Group, The
360 Mount Harmony Rd (07924-1415)
PHONE..........................908 766-5695
Terrence K Schroeder, *President*
EMP: 20
SALES (est): 2.8MM Privately Held
SIC: 7372 8243 Prepackaged software; data processing schools

Beverly
Burlington County

(G-456)
AE LITHO OFFSET PRINTERS INC (PA)
Also Called: Aelitho Group
450 Broad St (08010-1546)
P.O. Box 9000 (08010-9000)
PHONE..........................800 235-8888
Fax: 609 239-8493
Jeff Bozzi, *CEO*
EMP: 60
SQ FT: 50,000
SALES: 12MM Privately Held
WEB: www.aelitho.com
SIC: 2752 Lithographing on metal; commercial printing, offset

(G-457)
AE LITHO OFFSET PRINTERS INC
450 Broad St (08010-1546)
PHONE..........................609 239-0700
EMP: 9
SALES (corp-wide): 12MM Privately Held
SIC: 2752 Lithographic Commercial Printing
PA: A.E. Litho Offset Printers, Inc.
450 Broad St
Beverly NJ 08010
800 235-8888

(G-458)
ALCOP ADHESIVE LABEL CO
826 Perkins Ln (08010-1619)
P.O. Box 398 (08010-0398)
PHONE..........................609 871-4400
Fax: 609 871-3017

Wilmer Webster III, *President*
Wilmer P Webster III, *President*
Brook Webster, *Vice Pres*
John Webster, *Vice Pres*
EMP: 9
SQ FT: 16,000
SALES (est): 3.7MM Privately Held
SIC: 2759 Labels & seals: printing

(G-459)
ASPEN MANUFACTURING CO INC
Also Called: Aspen Appliance Parts
703 Van Rossum Ave Unit 5 (08010-1739)
PHONE..........................609 871-6400
Fax: 609 871-6430
John De Fulgentis, *President*
▲ EMP: 7 EST: 1998
SQ FT: 4,500
SALES (est): 540K Privately Held
SIC: 3469 Appliance parts, porcelain enameled

(G-460)
CAMPBELL CONVERTING CORP
703 Van Rossum Ave Unit 2 (08010-1739)
PHONE..........................609 835-2720
Claude Campbell, *President*
Gavin Campbell, *Vice Pres*
John Campbell, *Vice Pres*
EMP: 8
SQ FT: 14,000
SALES (est): 847K Privately Held
SIC: 7389 2759 Printers' services: folding, collating; business forms: printing

(G-461)
COLORCRAFT SIGN CO
400 Magnolia St (08010-1526)
PHONE..........................609 386-1115
Fax: 609 386-0429
Stephenson J Molnar, *Principal*
Linda Molnar, *Co-Owner*
EMP: 11
SQ FT: 5,000
SALES: 300K Privately Held
WEB: www.colorcraftsign.com
SIC: 3993 2759 3559 5999 Signs, not made in custom sign painting shops; screen printing; emblems, badges & insignia; trophies & plaques; badges

(G-462)
DISTINCTIVE WDWRK BY ROB HOFFM
703 Van Rossum Ave Unit 1 (08010-1739)
PHONE..........................609 877-8122
Rob Hoffman, *Owner*
EMP: 6
SALES (est): 360K Privately Held
SIC: 2499 Decorative wood & woodwork

(G-463)
FYTH LABS INC
Also Called: Lm PC Products
455 Warren St E (08010-1432)
PHONE..........................856 313-7362
Chad Martin, *President*
EMP: 6
SALES (est): 600.1K Privately Held
WEB: www.fliinvent.com
SIC: 8711 3577 Consulting engineer; electrical or electronic engineering; computer peripheral equipment

(G-464)
PIONEER RAILING INC
401 Railroad Ave (08010)
PHONE..........................609 387-0981
EMP: 6 EST: 1946
SALES (est): 720.8K Privately Held
SIC: 3446 Mfg Custom Ornamental Iron & Metal Work

(G-465)
SMARTPLAY INTERNATIONAL INC
1550 Bridgeboro Rd (08010-2216)
PHONE..........................609 880-1860
David Michaud, *President*
Thomas C Markert, *Exec VP*
Russell Wells, *Project Mgr*
Wayne Ryba, *Foreman/Supr*
Jesse Michaud, *Electrical Engi*
▲ EMP: 30

SQ FT: 15,000
SALES: 5.2MM Privately Held
WEB: www.smartplay.com
SIC: 3999 Coin-operated amusement machines

Birmingham
Burlington County

(G-466)
CABINET TRONICS INC
100 Birmingham Rd (08011)
PHONE..........................609 267-2625
Fax: 609 267-0034
Michael Lockwood, *President*
Lori Lockwood, *Vice Pres*
EMP: 15
SQ FT: 12,000
SALES (est): 2.2MM Privately Held
WEB: www.cabinettronics.com
SIC: 2431 Millwork

(G-467)
CGM US INC (PA)
Also Called: Photon Technology Intl
300 Birmingham Rd (08011)
PHONE..........................609 894-4420
Fax: 609 894-1579
Charles G Marianik, *Ch of Bd*
Ronald Kovach, *Exec VP*
Joseph Marshaleck, *Vice Pres*
EMP: 20
SQ FT: 9,600
SALES (est): 5.6MM Privately Held
WEB: www.pti-nj.com
SIC: 3827 3845 Optical instruments & lenses; laser systems & equipment, medical

(G-468)
LANXESS SYBRON CHEMICALS INC (DH)
200 Birmingham Rd (08011)
PHONE..........................609 893-1100
Markus Linke, *President*
Dwight Tamaki, *Marketing Mgr*
◆ EMP: 199
SQ FT: 200,000
SALES: 117MM
SALES (corp-wide): 11.4B Privately Held
WEB: www.ion-exchange.com
SIC: 2843 2899 3589 Surface active agents; textile processing assistants; water treating compounds; water filters & softeners, household type
HQ: Lanxess Corporation
111 Parkwest Dr
Pittsburgh PA 15275
800 526-9377

Blackwood
Camden County

(G-469)
A & J CARPETS INC
Also Called: A&J Flooring Outlet
4461 Route 42 (08012-1711)
PHONE..........................856 227-1753
James Depaino, *President*
Andrew Depaino, *Vice Pres*
EMP: 5
SQ FT: 15,000
SALES (est): 1MM Privately Held
SIC: 5713 2273 2434 Carpets; carpets & rugs; wood kitchen cabinets

(G-470)
ANSMANN USA CORP
1001 Lower Landing Rd # 101 (08012-3124)
PHONE..........................856 481-3504
Anwar Master, *President*
David Schliep, *Manager*
▲ EMP: 8
SQ FT: 15,028
SALES (est): 1.2MM Privately Held
SIC: 3089 5063 3629 Battery cases, plastic or plastic combination; batteries; battery chargers, rectifying or nonrotating

(G-471)
AROSE INC (PA)
1001 Lower Landing Rd # 412 (08012-3119)
PHONE..........................856 481-4351
Fax: 856 251-0440
Kemp Cook, *President*
Frank Beierschmitt, *Vice Pres*
EMP: 37
SQ FT: 2,500
SALES (est): 3.4MM Privately Held
WEB: www.aroseinc.com
SIC: 1731 5065 5063 3357 Telephone & telephone equipment installation; communication equipment; wire & cable; communication wire; telephone equipment & systems

(G-472)
AVERSAS ITALIAN BAKERY INC
801 Route 168 (08012-1472)
PHONE..........................856 227-8005
Fax: 856 374-0830
Ralph Aversa, *President*
Catherine Aversa, *Treasurer*
EMP: 22
SQ FT: 10,000
SALES (est): 6.4MM Privately Held
WEB: www.aversasbakery.com
SIC: 5149 5461 2051 Bakery products; bakeries; bread, cake & related products

(G-473)
BRADBURY BURIAL VAULT CO INC
Also Called: Delaware Valley Vault
761 Lower Landing Rd (08012-5132)
PHONE..........................856 227-2555
Fax: 856 227-3726
Lawrence A Kenney Sr, *Ch of Bd*
Lawrence A Kenney Jr, *President*
William Kenney, *Vice Pres*
▲ EMP: 20 EST: 1940
SQ FT: 17,000
SALES (est): 3.3MM Privately Held
SIC: 3272 Burial vaults, concrete or precast terrazzo

(G-474)
CAESARS PASTA LLC
1001 Lower Landing Rd (08012-3124)
PHONE..........................856 227-2585
Fax: 856 227-1910
Stephen Leins, *Plant Mgr*
▲ EMP: 40
SQ FT: 24,000
SALES (est): 9.3MM Privately Held
SIC: 2038 Frozen specialties

(G-475)
DELAWARE VALLEY VAULT CO INC
761 Lower Landing Rd (08012-5132)
PHONE..........................856 227-2555
Lawrence A Kenney Jr, *President*
William T Kenney, *Vice Pres*
EMP: 8
SALES (est): 763.8K Privately Held
SIC: 3272 5087 Burial vaults, concrete or precast terrazzo; concrete burial vaults & boxes

(G-476)
DUNE GRASS PUBLISHING LLC
39 Indiana Ave (08012-3819)
PHONE..........................609 774-6562
EMP: 4 EST: 2013
SALES (est): 183.2K Privately Held
SIC: 2741 Miscellaneous publishing

(G-477)
E C D VENTURES INC
Also Called: Qwik Pack & Ship
3501 Route 42 Ste 130 (08012-1780)
PHONE..........................856 875-1100
Fax: 856 875-8555
Eric Dettrey, *President*
EMP: 4

SALES (est): 362.1K **Privately Held**
WEB: www.qwikpackusa.com
SIC: 7389 5113 4822 4731 Mailbox
rental & related service; corrugated &
solid fiber boxes; facsimile transmission
services; agents, shipping; moving services; invitation & stationery printing & engraving

(G-478)
GCE MARKET INC (PA)
1001 Lower Landing Rd # 307
(08012-3120)
PHONE..................856 401-8900
Fax: 856 401-9871
Jaydeep Patel, *President*
Lawrance Kuo, *Sales Staff*
Ajay Kulkarni, *Info Tech Mgr*
▲ **EMP:** 6 **EST:** 2000
SALES (est): 1.2MM **Privately Held**
WEB: www.gcemarket.com
SIC: 3674 Semiconductors & related de-
vices

(G-479)
GLASSBLOWERSCOM LLC (PA)
234 Bells Lake Rd (08012-1640)
P.O. Box 8089 (08012-8089)
PHONE..................856 232-7898
Fax: 856 232-7669
Thomas J Cachaza,
EMP: 4
SALES (est): 643.6K **Privately Held**
WEB: www.glassblowers.com
SIC: 3229 Pressed & blown glass

(G-480)
GRAPHIC IMPRESSIONS PRTG CO
4391 Route 42 (08012-1710)
PHONE..................856 728-2266
Fax: 856 728-1455
Joseph Rocca, *Partner*
Daniel Rocca, *Principal*
EMP: 5
SALES (est): 725.9K **Privately Held**
SIC: 2752 Commercial printing, offset

(G-481)
I SEE OPTICAL LABORATORIES (PA)
44 W Church St (08012-3965)
PHONE..................856 227-9300
Fax: 800 348-4733
Michael Pak, *President*
EMP: 14
SQ FT: 3,000
SALES (est): 1.2MM **Privately Held**
WEB: www.eyeglasslenses.com
SIC: 3851 Lens grinding, except prescrip-
tion: ophthalmic

(G-482)
J L ERECTORS INC
835 Camden Ave (08012-4659)
PHONE..................856 232-9400
Fax: 856 232-0031
Joel Lyons, *President*
James Lyons, *Corp Secy*
EMP: 25
SALES (est): 6.5MM **Privately Held**
WEB: www.jlerectors.com
SIC: 3272 Precast terrazo or concrete
products

(G-483)
JOHNSON & ASSOCIATES INC
Also Called: Johnson Associates Systems
900 Route 168 Ste F4 (08012-3209)
PHONE..................856 228-2175
Fax: 856 232-9364
Hosea Johnson, *President*
EMP: 10
SQ FT: 3,000
SALES: 2MM **Privately Held**
WEB: www.jasystemsinc.com
SIC: 7374 3842 Data processing service;
prosthetic appliances

(G-484)
JOHNSON CONTROLS INC
1001 Lower Landing Rd # 409
(08012-3124)
PHONE..................856 245-9977
Barry Safranek, *Manager*
EMP: 26 **Privately Held**

SIC: 2531 Seats, automobile
HQ: Johnson Controls, Inc.
5757 N Green Bay Ave
Milwaukee WI 53209
414 524-1200

(G-485)
JONTOL UNLIMITED LLC (PA)
1134 S Black Horse Pike (08012-2703)
PHONE..................858 652-1113
Kenneth Robertson, *Exec VP*
Gregory Tolver, *Marketing Staff*
James Jones,
EMP: 7
SALES (est): 1.6MM **Privately Held**
SIC: 1542 3711 5045 5049 Commercial
& office building, new construction; commercial & office buildings, renovation &
repair; military motor vehicle assembly;
computers, peripherals & software; law
enforcement equipment & supplies; industrial supplies; safety equipment & supplies

(G-486)
KARCHER NORTH AMERICA INC
500 University Ct (08012-3230)
PHONE..................856 228-1800
Elliot Younessian, *CEO*
EMP: 12
SALES (corp-wide): 2.3B **Privately Held**
SIC: 3589 Commercial cleaning equip-
ment; dirt sweeping units, industrial; vac-
uum cleaners & sweepers, electric;
industrial
HQ: Karcher North America, Inc.
4555 Airport Way Fl 4
Denver CO 80239
303 762-1800

(G-487)
KITCHEN CABINET
5100 Route 42 (08012-1749)
PHONE..................856 228-8989
WEI Chen, *Principal*
EMP: 4
SALES (est): 389.8K **Privately Held**
SIC: 2434 Wood kitchen cabinets

(G-488)
MJG TECHNOLOGIES INCORPORATED
832 Camden Ave (08012-4660)
P.O. Box 314, Pitman (08071-0314)
PHONE..................856 228-6118
Jeff Genzel, *Vice Pres*
▼ **EMP:** 7
SALES (est): 250K **Privately Held**
WEB: www.electricmatch.com
SIC: 2892 Squibbs, electric

(G-489)
PINTO PRINTING
12 Sycamore Dr (08012-3147)
PHONE..................856 232-2550
Cathy Pinto, *Principal*
EMP: 4
SALES (est): 299.5K **Privately Held**
SIC: 2752 Commercial printing, litho-
graphic

(G-490)
REFAC OPTICAL GROUP (PA)
Also Called: US Vision
1 Harmon Dr (08012-5103)
PHONE..................856 228-1000
Fax: 201 585-2200
Melvin Meskin, *Ch of Bd*
Jerry Bingham, *District Mgr*
Melissa Byrd, *District Mgr*
Kim Demers, *District Mgr*
Tamara Santangelo, *District Mgr*
EMP: 39
SQ FT: 4,800
SALES (est): 492.1MM **Privately Held**
WEB: www.refac.com
SIC: 3827 Optical instruments & lenses

(G-491)
RESIDEX LLC
1001 Lower Landing Rd # 106
(08012-3124)
PHONE..................856 232-0880
Peter Bonsted, *Manager*
EMP: 6

SALES (corp-wide): 3.1B **Privately Held**
WEB: www.residex.com
SIC: 2879 Insecticides & pesticides
HQ: Residex, Llc
29380 Beck Rd
Wixom MI 48393

(G-492)
SCREENDREAMERCOM INC
901 Route 168 Ste 405 (08012-3237)
PHONE..................856 702-6400
Fax: 856 482-2130
Thomas Charrier, *President*
Anthony Severino, *Vice Pres*
Kirk Tegeler, *Vice Pres*
EMP: 4
SALES (est): 395.9K **Privately Held**
WEB: www.crownrealtycorp.com
SIC: 7372 Prepackaged software

(G-493)
STEWART BUSINESS FORMS INC
138 Frankford Ave (08012-3723)
P.O. Box 715, Voorhees (08043-0715)
PHONE..................856 768-2011
Fax: 856 228-7522
Gail Stewart, *President*
James Stewart, *Vice Pres*
EMP: 10
SQ FT: 8,000
SALES (est): 790K **Privately Held**
SIC: 2759 5112 2761 Business forms:
printing; business forms; manifold busi-
ness forms

Blairstown
Warren County

(G-494)
ALEXANDER JAMES CORP
845 State Route 94 (07825-4102)
PHONE..................908 362-9266
Fax: 908 362-5019
Francesca Fazzolari, *President*
Alex Davidson, *Corp Secy*
David Robinson, *Vice Pres*
EMP: 100
SQ FT: 21,000
SALES (est): 15.5MM **Privately Held**
WEB: www.james-alexander.com
SIC: 7389 3842 Packaging & labeling
services; surgical appliances & supplies

(G-495)
CAMBRIDGE SHEET METAL INC
93 Union Brick Rd (07825-2007)
PHONE..................973 386-0788
Patricia Rainey, *President*
Jim Salvatoriello, *General Mgr*
EMP: 24
SQ FT: 12,000
SALES: 4.9MM **Privately Held**
SIC: 3444 Sheet metalwork

(G-496)
HEALTHCARE CART
71 Auble Rd (07825-3011)
PHONE..................201 406-4797
Chris Sunda, *Owner*
EMP: 5 **EST:** 2011
SALES: 1MM **Privately Held**
SIC: 3841 Surgical & medical instruments

(G-497)
INDUSTRIAL METAL INC
169 Cedar Lake Rd (07825-9610)
PHONE..................908 362-0084
Dan Ohern, *President*
▲ **EMP:** 9
SQ FT: 8,640
SALES (est): 1.5MM **Privately Held**
WEB: www.industrialmetal.com
SIC: 3441 Fabricated structural metal

(G-498)
PICTURE WINDOW SOFTWARE LLC
47 Cook Rd (07825-9792)
PHONE..................908 362-4000
Clay Greene, *President*
EMP: 4 **EST:** 1995

SALES (est): 731.5K **Privately Held**
WEB: www.pwin.com
SIC: 7372 Prepackaged software

Bloomfield
Essex County

(G-499)
A PLUS INSTALLS LLC
Also Called: A Plus Installation
29 27 Curtis St Fl 1 Flr 1 (07003)
PHONE..................201 255-4412
Olya Shumilova, *President*
EMP: 5
SALES (est): 438.6K **Privately Held**
SIC: 5719 2591 5963 Venetian blinds;
vertical blinds; window shades; drapes &
curtains, house-to-house

(G-500)
ACKK STUDIOS LLC
411 E Passaic Ave (07003-5312)
PHONE..................973 876-1327
Brian Allanson,
EMP: 7 **EST:** 2012
SALES (est): 202.8K **Privately Held**
SIC: 7372 Prepackaged software

(G-501)
ALLOY SOFTWARE INC
400 Broadacres Dr Ste 100 (07003-3175)
PHONE..................973 661-9700
Vladimir Vinogradskiy, *President*
Edward Medow, *Technical Staff*
EMP: 10
SALES (est): 1MM **Privately Held**
SIC: 7371 7372 Software programming
applications; business oriented computer
software

(G-502)
BANKS BROS CORPORATION (PA)
24 Federal Plz (07003-5636)
PHONE..................973 680-4488
Fax: 973 680-9064
Stanley Banks, *President*
Lawrence Banks, *President*
EMP: 65
SQ FT: 40,000
SALES (est): 21.4MM **Privately Held**
WEB: www.banksbroscorp.com
SIC: 3053 3069 3714 Gasket materials;
sheeting, rubber or rubberized fabric;
motor vehicle parts & accessories

(G-503)
BUDGET PRINT CENTER
332 Broad St (07003-2728)
PHONE..................973 743-0073
Fax: 973 743-2875
Thomas C Destefano, *Owner*
EMP: 8
SQ FT: 1,100
SALES (est): 570K **Privately Held**
SIC: 2752 7389 7334 2791 Commercial
printing, offset; printing broker; photo-
copying & duplicating services; typeset-
ting; bookbinding & related work;
automotive & apparel trimmings

(G-504)
C M FURNACES INC
103 Dewey St (07003-4298)
PHONE..................973 338-6500
Fax: 973 338-1625
David Neill, *President*
Jim Neill, *Vice Pres*
Terry Monaco, *Purch Mgr*
Bryan Sherman, *Research*
John Daiuto, *Engineer*
◆ **EMP:** 30
SQ FT: 25,000
SALES (est): 9.3MM **Privately Held**
WEB: www.cmfurnaces.com
SIC: 3567 Heating units & devices, indus-
trial: electric

(G-505)
CAMBRIDGE BAGELS INC
Also Called: Cambridge Bagel Factory
648 Bloomfield Ave (07003-2511)
PHONE..................973 743-5683

▲ = Import ▼=Export
◆ =Import/Export

Fax: 973 743-4227
Jim Best, *President*
EMP: 15
SQ FT: 2,000
SALES (est): 633.3K **Privately Held**
SIC: 5461 2051 Bagels; bagels, fresh or frozen

(G-506)
CAW LLC
248 Montgomery St (07003-4930)
PHONE..............................973 429-7004
Oscar Costa, *Mng Member*
Maria Costa,
EMP: 16
SQ FT: 11,000
SALES (est): 1.7MM **Privately Held**
SIC: 2431 Millwork

(G-507)
COLES AND BLENMAN NETWORK LLC
117 Orange St (07003-4703)
PHONE..............................973 432-7041
Frank Blenman, *CEO*
EMP: 5
SALES (est): 110.8K **Privately Held**
SIC: 7371 7372 Computer software development & applications; application computer software

(G-508)
COMPLETE OPTICAL LABORATORY
Also Called: Ecca
1255 Broad St Ste 202 (07003-3061)
PHONE..............................973 338-8886
Dwayne Carter, *President*
EMP: 15
SQ FT: 5,000
SALES (est): 2MM **Privately Held**
SIC: 5049 8042 5995 3851 Optical goods; offices & clinics of optometrists; optical goods stores; ophthalmic goods

(G-509)
COSRICH GROUP INC (DH)
51 La France Ave 55 (07003-5681)
PHONE..............................866 771-7473
Laura Hite, *President*
▲ **EMP:** 20
SQ FT: 200,000
SALES (est): 4.7MM
SALES (corp-wide): 2.2B **Privately Held**
WEB: www.cosrich.com
SIC: 2844 Cosmetic preparations
HQ: Pmc, Inc.
12243 Branford St
Sun Valley CA 91352
818 896-1101

(G-510)
COSTA CUSTOM CABINETS INC
Also Called: Costa's Cabinets
248 Montgomery St (07003-4930)
PHONE..............................973 429-7004
Fax: 973 429-8114
Oscar Costa Jr, *President*
Manny Forlenza, *Accountant*
EMP: 13
SQ FT: 12,000
SALES (est): 1.3MM **Privately Held**
SIC: 2541 1751 Cabinets, except refrigerated: show, display, etc.: wood; cabinet building & installation

(G-511)
GENERAL PLASTICS CORPORATION
55 La France Ave (07003-5695)
PHONE..............................973 429-5625
Fax: 973 748-3988
Zetta Bouligaraki, *President*
EMP: 35
SQ FT: 150,000
SALES (est): 5.4MM
SALES (corp-wide): 2.2B **Privately Held**
WEB: www.generalplasticscorp.com
SIC: 3812 Aircraft flight instruments
HQ: Pmc, Inc.
12243 Branford St
Sun Valley CA 91352
818 896-1101

(G-512)
GENERAL PLASTICS GROUP
55 La France Ave (07003-5681)
PHONE..............................973 748-5500
Bob Scher, *President*
EMP: 30
SALES (est): 1.7MM
SALES (corp-wide): 2.2B **Privately Held**
SIC: 3479 2851 Coating of metals & formed products; paints & allied products
HQ: Pmc, Inc.
12243 Branford St
Sun Valley CA 91352
818 896-1101

(G-513)
GLOBAL STRATEGY INSTITUTE A
55 Park Ave Unit 35 (07003-2663)
P.O. Box 1868, Montclair (07042-7868)
PHONE..............................973 615-7447
John Floropoulos, *President*
EMP: 5
SALES (est): 222.7K **Privately Held**
SIC: 2721 7812 8733 Trade journals: publishing only, not printed on site; educational motion picture production, television; noncommercial social research organization; economic research, noncommercial

(G-514)
J T MURDOCH SHOES
Also Called: Murdoch, J T Shoes
623 Bloomfield Ave (07003-2502)
P.O. Box 505 (07003-0505)
PHONE..............................973 748-6484
Fax: 973 748-3466
Mary Murdoch, *President*
EMP: 10 EST: 1949
SQ FT: 1,600
SALES (est): 1MM **Privately Held**
SIC: 5661 2252 Children's shoes; men's shoes; women's shoes; shoes, orthopedic; socks

(G-515)
JANET SHOPS INC
550 Bloomfield Ave (07003-3302)
PHONE..............................973 748-4992
Robert Bluestone, *President*
EMP: 10
SQ FT: 10,000
SALES (est): 780K **Privately Held**
SIC: 5621 2326 Ready-to-wear apparel, women's; medical & hospital uniforms, men's

(G-516)
KANDASAMY LINGESWARAN
Also Called: Noshpeak
38 Patton Dr (07003-5224)
PHONE..............................978 631-7662
Lingeswaran Kandasamy,
Kalaivani Rasalingam,
EMP: 15
SALES (est): 305.2K **Privately Held**
SIC: 7372 7389 Application computer software;

(G-517)
KRYSTAL CLEAR MEDIA GROUP LLC
5 Lawrence St Ste Ph34 (07003-4631)
PHONE..............................302 715-1069
Kokil Chachra, *CEO*
EMP: 4
SALES (est): 130.4K **Privately Held**
SIC: 2721 Periodicals

(G-518)
LOUIS A NELSON INC
224 Glenwood Ave (07003-2416)
PHONE..............................973 743-7404
Fax: 973 743-8480
David Sibilia, *President*
Stephen Cariani, *Exec VP*
EMP: 12 EST: 1947
SQ FT: 6,000
SALES: 1.5MM **Privately Held**
SIC: 2821 Molding compounds, plastics

(G-519)
LS RUBBER INDUSTRIES INC (HQ)
24 Federal Plz (07003-5636)
PHONE..............................973 680-4488
Andrew Banks, *President*
Lawrence Banks, *President*
Anjum Qureshi, *General Mgr*
Stanley F Banks, *Corp Secy*
EMP: 50
SQ FT: 35,000
SALES (est): 15.7MM
SALES (corp-wide): 21.4MM **Privately Held**
SIC: 3069 3714 3053 Foam rubber; motor vehicle parts & accessories; gaskets, packing & sealing devices
PA: Banks Bros Corporation
24 Federal Plz
Bloomfield NJ 07003
973 680-4488

(G-520)
LUMMUS OVERSEAS CORPORATION
Lummus Heat Transf Systems Div
1515 Broad St (07003-3002)
PHONE..............................973 893-3000
Fax: 973 893-2106
Mohammed Tolba, *President*
Michael Blaney, *General Mgr*
Catherine Bensulock, *Principal*
Arthur Carlotti, *Principal*
Kaye Bell-Reiter, *Human Res Dir*
EMP: 40
SALES (corp-wide): 153.1MM **Privately Held**
SIC: 3511 3625 Turbines & turbine generator sets; relays & industrial controls
PA: Lummus Overseas Corporation
1515 Broad St
Bloomfield NJ 07003
973 893-1515

(G-521)
LUMMUS TECHNOLOGY VENTURES LLC
1515 Broad St Ste A110 (07003-3054)
PHONE..............................973 893-1515
Patrick K Mullen, *CEO*
Kirsten B David, *Exec VP*
Michael S Taff, *CFO*
EMP: 7 EST: 1992
SALES (est): 172.6K **Privately Held**
SIC: 8711 4731 3441 1531 Engineering services; freight transportation arrangement; fabricated structural metal; ; general management consultant

(G-522)
MINOR RUBBER CO INC (PA)
Also Called: M R
49 Ackerman St (07003-4299)
PHONE..............................973 338-6800
Fax: 973 893-1399
David C Humphreys, *President*
Sandra Humphreys, *Vice Pres*
Sandy Humphreys, *Vice Pres*
Ray Lagerveld, *Purchasing*
Theresa Trumpore, *Treasurer*
EMP: 50 EST: 1914
SQ FT: 30,000
SALES (est): 6.9MM **Privately Held**
WEB: www.minorrubber.com
SIC: 3061 3052 Appliance rubber goods (mechanical); automotive rubber goods (mechanical); oil & gas field machinery rubber goods (mechanical); rubber & plastics hose & beltings

(G-523)
MUNZING NORTH AMERICA LP (DH)
1455 Broad St Ste 3 (07003-3039)
PHONE..............................973 279-1306
Qun Chu, *Mng Member*
▲ **EMP:** 30
SQ FT: 13,000
SALES (est): 15MM
SALES (corp-wide): 142MM **Privately Held**
SIC: 2819 Industrial inorganic chemicals

HQ: Munzing International Sarl
Rue Aldringen 23
Luxembourg
262 715-

(G-524)
NTE ELECTRONICS INC
44 Farrand St (07003-2516)
PHONE..............................973 748-6224
Fax: 973 748-5089
Andrew Licari, *President*
▲ **EMP:** 72
SALES (est): 7.9MM
SALES (corp-wide): 15.4MM **Privately Held**
WEB: www.nteinc.com
SIC: 3674 3675 3676 Semiconductors & related devices; electronic capacitors; electronic resistors
PA: Solid State, Incorporated
46 Farrand St
Bloomfield NJ 07003
973 429-8700

(G-525)
OBJECTIF LUNE LLC (HQ)
300 Broadacres Dr Ste 410 (07003-3153)
PHONE..............................973 780-0100
Didier Gombert, *CEO*
Ton Van Schaick, *CFO*
Martin Dallaire,
Bertrand Guignat,
Jean Nault,
EMP: 15
SALES (est): 5.1MM
SALES (corp-wide): 6.5MM **Privately Held**
WEB: www.empoweryourprinter.com
SIC: 7372 Prepackaged software
PA: Objectif Lune Inc
2030 Boul Pie-Ix Bureau 500
Montreal QC H1V 2
514 875-5863

(G-526)
OBJECTIF LUNE LLC
300 Broadacres Dr Ste 410 (07003-3153)
PHONE..............................203 878-7206
Bob Ricca, *Branch Mgr*
EMP: 5
SALES (corp-wide): 6.5MM **Privately Held**
WEB: www.empoweryourprinter.com
SIC: 7372 Prepackaged software
HQ: Objectif Lune Llc
300 Broadacres Dr Ste 410
Bloomfield NJ 07003
973 780-0100

(G-527)
PMC INC
General Plastics
55 La France Ave (07003-5681)
PHONE..............................973 748-5500
Robert Scher, *President*
EMP: 13
SQ FT: 91,000
SALES (corp-wide): 2.2B **Privately Held**
SIC: 3812 Aircraft flight instruments
HQ: Pmc, Inc.
12243 Branford St
Sun Valley CA 91352
818 896-1101

(G-528)
RADIX M I S
Also Called: Radix Computer Carrers
50 Hazelwood Rd (07003-5112)
PHONE..............................973 707-2121
Fax: 973 808-9799
Buddy Simpson, *President*
Michael Hart, *Finance Other*
EMP: 3
SQ FT: 1,500
SALES: 2MM **Privately Held**
WEB: www.radixjobs.com
SIC: 7379 7372 Computer related consulting services; prepackaged software

(G-529)
ROMBIOLO LLC
168 Broughton Ave (07003-4006)
PHONE..............................973 680-0405
Natalia Sierpes, *Principal*
EMP: 8

GEOGRAPHIC

SALES (est): 610.2K **Privately Held**
SIC: 2051 Bread, cake & related products

(G-530)
SOLID STATE INTERNATIONAL INC
46 Farrand St (07003-2596)
PHONE..................................201 429-8700
Andrew Dembroski, *President*
Andrew Licari, *Corp Secy*
EMP: 4
SQ FT: 18,000
SALES (est): 461K
SALES (corp-wide): 15.4MM **Privately Held**
SIC: 3674 Integrated circuits, semiconductor networks, etc.
PA: Solid State, Incorporated
46 Farrand St
Bloomfield NJ 07003
973 429-8700

(G-531)
STANEK NETTING CO INC (PA)
111 Orange St (07003-4703)
PHONE..................................973 680-1616
Jeremy Stanek, *President*
Tim Chadwick, *Sales Associate*
Mike Litchman, *Manager*
James Stanek, *Shareholder*
▲ EMP: 8
SQ FT: 15,000
SALES (est): 10.9MM **Privately Held**
WEB: www.staneknetting.com
SIC: 2211 Broadwoven fabric mills, cotton

(G-532)
STANLAR ENTERPRISES INC
24 Federal Plz (07003-5636)
PHONE..................................973 680-4488
Stanley F Banks, *President*
Lawrence Banks, *Vice Pres*
EMP: 24
SQ FT: 35,000
SALES (est): 2.2MM
SALES (corp-wide): 21.4MM **Privately Held**
SIC: 2392 Mattress pads
PA: Banks Bros Corporation
24 Federal Plz
Bloomfield NJ 07003
973 680-4488

(G-533)
STOBBS PRINTING CO INC
18 Washington St (07003-3412)
P.O. Box 91 (07003-0091)
PHONE..................................973 748-4441
Fax: 973 748-2395
Gayle Tungstead, *President*
EMP: 5 EST: 1931
SQ FT: 10,000
SALES (est): 250K **Privately Held**
SIC: 2752 Commercial printing, offset

(G-534)
SURROUND TECHNOLOGIES LLC (PA)
650 Bloomfield Ave # 211 (07003-2512)
PHONE..................................973 743-1277
Douglas Webb, *Software Dev*
Lee Paul,
EMP: 8
SALES (est): 750K **Privately Held**
WEB: www.surroundtech.com
SIC: 7372 Prepackaged software

(G-535)
ULTIMATE HAIR WORLD LTD LBLTY
Also Called: Tnss Enterprises
16 Molter Pl (07003-4706)
PHONE..................................973 622-6900
Natasha James, *Mng Member*
EMP: 10
SALES (est): 277.9K **Privately Held**
SIC: 3999 Doll wigs (hair)

(G-536)
ULTRA ADDITIVES LLC (DH)
Also Called: Munzing
1455 Broad St Ste 3 (07003-3039)
PHONE..................................973 279-1306
Fax: 973 338-0420
Michael Gassney, *Mng Member*

Jean Schaefle,
◆ EMP: 30
SQ FT: 13,000
SALES (est): 16.9MM
SALES (corp-wide): 142MM **Privately Held**
SIC: 2851 Paints & paint additives
HQ: Munzing International Sarl
Rue Aldringen 23
Luxembourg
262 715-

(G-537)
WORRALL COMMUNITY NEWSPAPERS
Also Called: Independent Press, The
266 Liberty St (07003-2673)
P.O. Box 110 (07003-0110)
PHONE..................................973 743-4040
Fax: 973 680-8848
Bill Van Sant, *Editor*
Steve Proctor, *Regional Mgr*
EMP: 5
SALES (corp-wide): 7.1MM **Privately Held**
WEB: www.localsource.com
SIC: 2711 Newspapers
PA: Worrall Community Newspapers Inc
1291 Stuyvesant Ave
Union NJ
908 686-7700

(G-538)
ZALLER STUDIOS INC
265 Watsessing Ave (07003-5726)
PHONE..................................973 743-5175
Gabriel Pereira, *President*
John Szalkowski, *General Mgr*
All Pereira, *Vice Pres*
Jack Pereira, *Vice Pres*
EMP: 5
SQ FT: 30,000
SALES (est): 1.1MM **Privately Held**
SIC: 7336 3577 Silk screen design; graphic displays, except graphic terminals

(G-539)
ZWIER CORP
Also Called: Universal Company
497 Bloomfield Ave (07003-3304)
P.O. Box 4193, Clifton (07012-8193)
PHONE..................................973 748-4009
Fax: 973 748-9884
Michael Zwier, *President*
Joan Bertoli, *Vice Pres*
EMP: 4
SALES (est): 750K **Privately Held**
SIC: 2759 2791 2752 Screen printing; typesetting; commercial printing, lithographic

---
Bloomingdale
Passaic County

(G-540)
AKADEMA INC
Also Called: Academy of Proplayers
46 Star Lake Rd Ste B (07403-1244)
PHONE..................................973 304-1470
Joe Gilligan Jr, *CEO*
Lawrence Gilligan, *President*
Cathy Takter, *Business Mgr*
Kris Totten, *Vice Pres*
Kevin Barrett, *Sales Mgr*
◆ EMP: 23
SQ FT: 25,000
SALES (est): 3.3MM **Privately Held**
WEB: www.akademapro.com
SIC: 3949 5941 5091 Baseball equipment & supplies, general; baseball equipment; athletic goods

(G-541)
CENTRAL SHIPPEE INC
Also Called: Allied Felt Group Div
46 Star Lake Rd (07403-1244)
PHONE..................................973 838-1100
Donald A Hubner, *Ch of Bd*
Eric Hubner, *President*
Cornelius E Hubner Sr, *Vice Pres*
▲ EMP: 29
SQ FT: 17,000

SALES (est): 4.5MM **Privately Held**
WEB: www.centralshippee.com
SIC: 5199 2511 5023 Felt; wood household furniture; linens, table

(G-542)
ELECTRONIC POWER DESIGNS INC
Also Called: Epd
132 Union Ave (07403-1817)
PHONE..................................973 838-7055
Fax: 973 838-7655
Greg Brown, *President*
Sheila Brown, *Corp Secy*
Elaine Barone, *Director*
EMP: 17
SQ FT: 7,500
SALES (est): 2.5MM **Privately Held**
SIC: 3613 3625 Panelboards & distribution boards, electric; control equipment, electric

(G-543)
ENERGY BEAMS INC
185 Hamburg Tpke (07403-1141)
PHONE..................................973 291-6555
Fax: 973 492-1706
John Richard, *CEO*
Tom Richard, *President*
EMP: 15 EST: 1966
SQ FT: 8,000
SALES (est): 3.2MM **Privately Held**
WEB: www.energybeams.com
SIC: 3589 3567 3563 3561 Commercial cleaning equipment; industrial furnaces & ovens; air & gas compressors; pumps & pumping equipment; machine tool accessories; metal heat treating

(G-544)
GERVENS ENTERPRISES INC
122 Hamburg Tpke Ste D (07403-1201)
PHONE..................................973 838-1600
Fax: 973 492-2603
William G Gervens, *President*
Glen M Schumacher, *Vice Pres*
Stacey G Poplawski, *Treasurer*
Deborah G Schumacher, *Treasurer*
EMP: 11
SQ FT: 3,500
SALES (est): 1.5MM **Privately Held**
SIC: 1796 3446 Installing building equipment; machinery installation; railings, bannisters, guards, etc.: made from metal pipe; gates, ornamental metal; fire escapes, metal

(G-545)
VIBRATION MUNTINGS CONTRLS INC (PA)
Also Called: Korfund Dynamics
113 Main St (07403-1673)
P.O. Box 270 (07403-0270)
PHONE..................................800 569-8423
Fax: 973 492-8430
John Wilson Jr, *CEO*
Richard Berger, *Ch of Bd*
John P Giuliano, *President*
James J Nizzo, *Managing Dir*
Tom Steele, *Vice Pres*
▲ EMP: 100 EST: 2005
SQ FT: 70,000
SALES (est): 39.2MM **Privately Held**
WEB: www.vmc-kdc.com
SIC: 3069 3496 Hard rubber & molded rubber products; miscellaneous fabricated wire products

---
Bloomsbury
Hunterdon County

(G-546)
VISUAL ENGINEERING GROUP INC
29 Church St (08804-3132)
P.O. Box 26 (08804-0026)
PHONE..................................908 479-1893
Anthony Casey, *President*
EMP: 4
SALES (est): 1.1MM **Privately Held**
SIC: 2752 Commercial printing, lithographic

(G-547)
WARREN PALLET COMPANY INC
601 County Road 627 (08804-3426)
PHONE..................................908 995-7172
Fax: 908 995-4146
Donald Tigar Sr, *President*
Donald Tigar Jr, *Admin Sec*
EMP: 19
SQ FT: 4,800
SALES: 1.2MM **Privately Held**
SIC: 7699 2448 Pallet repair; pallets, wood

Bogota
Bergen County

(G-548)
JESCO IRON CRAFTS INC
Also Called: Jescraft
201 W Fort Lee Rd (07603-1207)
PHONE..................................201 488-4545
Fax: 201 488-7359
Michael Brown, *President*
Cory Mahady, *Opers Mgr*
Leslie Cappadona, *Office Mgr*
EMP: 15 EST: 1946
SQ FT: 15,000
SALES (est): 2MM **Privately Held**
SIC: 3423 3444 Hand & edge tools; sheet metalwork

(G-549)
ORGANIZE IT ALL INC (PA)
Also Called: Oia
24 River Rd Ste 201 (07603-1522)
PHONE..................................201 488-0808
Fax: 201 931-9408
James Lee, *President*
Michael Chiang, *Vice Pres*
Pauline MA, *Financial Exec*
Peter Hu, *Shareholder*
Spencer Lin, *Shareholder*
▲ EMP: 48
SALES (est): 7.7MM **Privately Held**
SIC: 2599 3639 7699 Factory furniture & fixtures; major kitchen appliances, except refrigerators & stoves; household appliance repair services

(G-550)
OUTWATER PLSTCS/INDUSTRIES INC (PA)
Also Called: Outwater Plastics Industries
24 River Rd Ste 108 (07603-1535)
P.O. Box 500 (07603-0500)
PHONE..................................201 498-8750
Fax: 201 916-1640
Peter Kessler, *President*
David Norburg, *Managing Dir*
Susan Molnar, *Treasurer*
Cheryl McGee, *Admin Sec*
◆ EMP: 86
SQ FT: 160,000
SALES (est): 28.7MM **Privately Held**
WEB: www.outwater.com
SIC: 5072 2599 Hardware; bar furniture

Boonton
Morris County

(G-551)
ADRON INC
94 Fanny Rd (07005-1048)
P.O. Box 270 (07005-0270)
PHONE..................................973 334-1600
Fax: 973 316-8949
Louis J Amaducci, *President*
Robert L Amaducci, *Vice Pres*
Kathleen M Dunne, *Admin Sec*
EMP: 30
SQ FT: 20,000
SALES (est): 5.8MM **Privately Held**
WEB: www.adron.com
SIC: 2869 2844 2087 Industrial organic chemicals; toilet preparations; flavoring extracts & syrups

▲ = Import ▼=Export
◆ =Import/Export

(G-552)
AEROPANEL CORPORATION
661 Myrtle Ave (07005-1916)
PHONE.............................973 335-9636
Fax: 973 263-6304
Jack Miller, *Vice Pres*
Sue Abate, *Sales Mgr*
Jerome Meers, *Technology*
EMP: 59
SALES (corp-wide): 6.5MM **Privately Held**
WEB: www.aeropanel.com
SIC: 3613 3812 3769 5088 Panel & distribution boards & other related apparatus; search & navigation equipment; guided missile & space vehicle parts & auxiliary equipment; aircraft equipment & supplies
PA: Aeropanel Corporation
2200 Post Oak Blvd
Houston TX 77056
713 552-0979

(G-553)
ALPHA TECH SERVICES
121 Hawkins Pl Ste 197 (07005-1127)
PHONE.............................973 283-2011
John Stevens, *President*
EMP: 8
SALES (est): 1MM **Privately Held**
SIC: 3577 Bar code (magnetic ink) printers

(G-554)
AMERICAN INTERNATIONAL CONT
Also Called: Ai Container
3 Mars Ct Ste 4 (07005-9308)
PHONE.............................973 917-3331
Dan Bourneuf, *President*
◆ EMP: 10 EST: 2010
SQ FT: 9,000
SALES: 4MM **Privately Held**
SIC: 3559 2656 Pharmaceutical machinery; frozen food & ice cream containers

(G-555)
AMERICAN MDLAR PWR SLTIONS INC
Also Called: Amps
429 Rockaway Valley Rd (07005-8101)
P.O. Box 604 (07005-0604)
PHONE.............................973 588-4026
Greg Lowndes, *President*
Daryl Killian, *Prdtn Mgr*
Andrea Marrone, *Treasurer*
EMP: 6
SALES (est): 1.6MM **Privately Held**
SIC: 3621 Generating apparatus & parts, electrical

(G-556)
ATIAIR TECHNOLOGY INC
429 Rockaway Valley Rd # 1100 (07005-8101)
P.O. Box 625 (07005-0625)
PHONE.............................973 334-4980
EMP: 4
SALES (est): 182.3K **Privately Held**
SIC: 3312 Stainless steel

(G-557)
BIO-CHEM FLUIDICS INC
Also Called: Bio-Chem Valve
85 Fulton St Unit 12 (07005-1912)
PHONE.............................973 263-3001
Tim O Sullivan, *President*
Bill Heinzmann, *Vice Pres*
Mark Nielsen, *Vice Pres*
Stephen Powell, *Vice Pres*
Joe Turiello, *Vice Pres*
▲ EMP: 60
SQ FT: 8,000
SALES (est): 17MM
SALES (corp-wide): 1.5B **Privately Held**
WEB: www.biochemvalve.com
SIC: 3491 Solenoid valves
HQ: Halma Holdings Inc.
11500 Northlake Dr # 306
Cincinnati OH 45249
513 772-5501

(G-558)
BIOMEDTRIX LLC
50 Intervale Rd Ste 5 (07005-1060)
PHONE.............................973 331-7800

Gregg Huk, *Mfg Mgr*
Matthew Rodriguez, *Opers Staff*
Charles Achonye, *Sales Mgr*
David Helms, *Accounts Mgr*
Betsy Sives, *Marketing Mgr*
EMP: 6
SQ FT: 2,750
SALES (est): 1.1MM **Privately Held**
WEB: www.biomedtrix.com
SIC: 2835 5047 Veterinary diagnostic substances; veterinarians' equipment & supplies

(G-559)
CARBONE AMERICA SCP DIVISION
400 Myrtle Ave 1 (07005-1839)
PHONE.............................973 334-0700
Fax: 973 334-6394
Kenneth Pohing, *Principal*
EMP: 4
SALES (est): 323.2K **Privately Held**
SIC: 3999 Manufacturing industries

(G-560)
COMMUNICATION DEVICES INC (PA)
Also Called: CDI
85 Fulton St Unit 2 (07005-1912)
PHONE.............................973 334-1980
Fax: 973 334-0545
Tadhg Kelly, *President*
Wade Clark, *President*
Loriann Pesci, *Purchasing*
Lillian Kelly, *CFO*
Alexandra Tavarez, *Sales Mgr*
◆ EMP: 17
SALES: 4.1MM **Privately Held**
WEB: www.commdevices.com
SIC: 3663 3825 Multiplex equipment; test equipment for electronic & electric measurement; network analyzers

(G-561)
CREATIVE CABINET DESIGNS INC
301 Main St (07005-1739)
PHONE.............................973 402-5886
Fax: 973 402-1326
Manuel Silva, *President*
Maria Silva, *Vice Pres*
EMP: 10
SQ FT: 3,200
SALES: 190K **Privately Held**
SIC: 5712 2511 5031 1751 Cabinet work, custom; kitchen & dining room furniture; kitchen cabinets; cabinet & finish carpentry

(G-562)
DACO LIMITED PARTNERSHIP (PA)
Also Called: Dauphin North America
100 Fulton St (07005-1910)
PHONE.............................973 263-1100
Fax: 973 263-3551
Nick Bayvel, *CEO*
Gary Chin, *President*
Adam Caldwell, *Manager*
Carol Washor, *Manager*
▲ EMP: 70
SQ FT: 68,000
SALES (est): 28.7MM **Privately Held**
SIC: 5021 5049 2522 Chairs; scientific instruments; chairs, office: padded or plain, except wood

(G-563)
DAVIS SIGN SYSTEMS INC
65 Harrison St (07005-2033)
PHONE.............................973 394-9909
Elaine Davis, *President*
EMP: 4
SQ FT: 7,000
SALES (est): 250K **Privately Held**
WEB: www.davissignsystems.com
SIC: 3993 Signs & advertising specialties

(G-564)
ELECTROMAGNETIC TECH INDS INC
50 Intervale Rd Ste 11 (07005-1060)
PHONE.............................973 394-1719
Fax: 973 394-1710
John Howard, *President*

Chuck Fung, *President*
Thomas Economou, *COO*
▼ EMP: 65
SQ FT: 12,000
SALES: 25MM **Privately Held**
WEB: www.etiworld.com
SIC: 3679 3812 3663 Microwave components; antennas, radar or communications; antennas, transmitting & communications

(G-565)
ENGINEERING DYNAMICS LLC
429 Rockaway Valley Rd # 1300 (07005-8108)
PHONE.............................973 794-4500
Richard G Spitzlei,
Jeffrey J Spitzlei,
EMP: 4
SQ FT: 4,500
SALES (est): 534.7K **Privately Held**
WEB: www.eng-dyn.com
SIC: 3699 Electrical equipment & supplies

(G-566)
ENTERIS BIOPHARMA INC
83 Fulton St (07005-1909)
PHONE.............................973 453-3518
Joel Tune, *CEO*
Brian Zietsman, *President*
Arlyn Peguero, *Principal*
Paul Shields, *COO*
Timothy J Saxon, *Vice Pres*
EMP: 49
SALES (est): 12.7MM **Privately Held**
SIC: 2834 Pharmaceutical preparations

(G-567)
ESCADAUS INC
2 Wood Glen Way (07005-9738)
PHONE.............................973 335-8888
Henry Kuo, *President*
EMP: 5
SQ FT: 3,500
SALES (est): 43.6K **Privately Held**
SIC: 3264 3499 Magnets, permanent: ceramic or ferrite; magnets, permanent: metallic

(G-568)
EVH LLC
Also Called: Audrey Hepburn Collection
6 Mars Ct Unit F5 (07005-9309)
PHONE.............................973 257-0076
Edward Katz, *Mng Member*
EMP: 10
SQ FT: 28,000
SALES (est): 647.9K **Privately Held**
SIC: 2329 Men's & boys' sportswear & athletic clothing

(G-569)
FLOTTEC LLC (PA)
338 W Main St (07005-1148)
PHONE.............................973 588-4717
Frank Cappuccitti,
◆ EMP: 5
SALES (est): 4MM **Privately Held**
WEB: www.flottec.com
SIC: 2879 Trace elements (agricultural chemicals)

(G-570)
FORTUNE BRANDS HOME & SEC INC
603 Cornelia St (07005-1615)
PHONE.............................973 402-6440
EMP: 1898
SALES (corp-wide): 5.2B **Publicly Held**
SIC: 2531 Public building & related furniture
PA: Fortune Brands Home & Security, Inc.
520 Lake Cook Rd
Deerfield IL 60015
847 484-4400

(G-571)
ICON ORTHOPEDIC CONCEPTS LLC
Also Called: Edge Orthopedics
6 Mars Ct Ste 3 (07005-9309)
PHONE.............................973 794-6810
Steven Bridgio, *President*
Anna Kroll, *COO*
EMP: 5 EST: 2012
SQ FT: 3,180

SALES (est): 455.4K **Privately Held**
SIC: 3842 Orthopedic appliances
PA: Plasmology4, Inc.
8502 E Princess Dr # 210
Scottsdale AZ 85255

(G-572)
INSTOCK WIRELESS COMPONENTS
50 Intervale Rd Ste 15 (07005-1060)
PHONE.............................973 335-6550
Fax: 973 335-6770
Michael Davo, *CEO*
▲ EMP: 10
SQ FT: 25,000
SALES (est): 1.8MM **Privately Held**
SIC: 4812 3661 Cellular telephone services; carrier equipment, telephone or telegraph

(G-573)
JANKE & COMPANY INC
Also Called: Electronic Brazing Co Div
283 Myrtle Ave (07005-1753)
PHONE.............................973 334-4477
Fax: 973 334-1706
Edward K Malavarca, *President*
EMP: 5
SALES (est): 707.7K **Privately Held**
SIC: 3825 Electrical power measuring equipment

(G-574)
JOHANSON MANUFACTURING CORP
301 Rockaway Valley Rd (07005-9192)
PHONE.............................973 658-1051
Fax: 973 334-2954
Nancy Johanson, *CEO*
Rocco Melchione, *President*
Walter Hutton, *Exec VP*
Lisa Phillips, *Adv Dir*
Jon Krawczyk, *Branch Mgr*
EMP: 200 EST: 1945
SQ FT: 35,000
SALES (est): 31.8MM **Privately Held**
SIC: 3679 Electronic circuits

(G-575)
MARLO MANUFACTURING CO INC
301 Division St (07005-1826)
PHONE.............................973 423-0226
Salvatore Pirruccio, *CEO*
Sal Pirruccio, *COO*
Corrado Tommasi, *CFO*
EMP: 39
SQ FT: 35,000
SALES (est): 11.1MM **Privately Held**
WEB: www.marlomfg.com
SIC: 2599 3556 1799 Tubing, flexible metallic

(G-576)
MERCHANDISING DISPLAY CORP
Also Called: Mdc
14 Deer Trl (07005-9024)
PHONE.............................973 299-8400
Arthur W Linz, *President*
EMP: 4 EST: 1964
SQ FT: 3,500
SALES (est): 340K **Privately Held**
SIC: 3993 Signs & advertising specialties

(G-577)
MERSEN USA BN CORP (HQ)
400 Myrtle Ave (07005-1839)
PHONE.............................973 334-0700
Bernie Monsalvatge, *President*
Cedrick Fontes, *General Mgr*
Jay Spadaro, *Vice Pres*
Simon Wong, *Buyer*
Gary Pavlosky, *Controller*
▲ EMP: 115
SQ FT: 250,000
SALES (est): 278.6MM
SALES (corp-wide): 1.6MM **Privately Held**
SIC: 3624 Brushes & brush stock contacts, electric

(G-578)
METRO PRTG & PROMOTIONS LLC
311 Mechanic St 2 (07005-1830)
PHONE..............................973 316-1600
Scott Santucci,
EMP: 15
SQ FT: 10,000
SALES (est): 2.1MM **Privately Held**
SIC: 2752 Commercial printing, lithographic

(G-579)
PIPELINE EQP RESOURCES CO LLC
Also Called: Perc
9 Mars Ct Ste 4 (07005-9310)
PHONE..............................888 232-7372
Robert Engdahl, *Mng Member*
EMP: 8
SALES (est): 2.5MM **Privately Held**
SIC: 1321 3449 Natural gas liquids; miscellaneous metalwork

(G-580)
R&D MICROWAVES LLC
301 Rockaway Valley Rd # 3 (07005-9192)
PHONE..............................908 212-1696
Ken Jackson, *Purchasing*
Carl Schraufnagl, *VP Sales*
Marek Antkowiak,
EMP: 20
SALES: 4MM **Privately Held**
WEB: www.rdmicrowaves.com
SIC: 3663 Radio & TV communications equipment

(G-581)
ROYAL PALLET INC
771 Knoll Rd (07005-9633)
PHONE..............................973 299-0445
Dennis G Whipple, *Principal*
EMP: 4
SALES (est): 397.6K **Privately Held**
SIC: 2448 Pallets, wood & wood with metal

(G-582)
S W I INTERNATIONAL INC
Also Called: Super Wash
487 Division St (07005-1828)
PHONE..............................973 334-2525
Edward Smith, *President*
EMP: 4
SALES (est): 190K **Privately Held**
SIC: 2841 Detergents, synthetic organic or inorganic alkaline

(G-583)
SCULPTURED STONE INC
501b Division St (07005)
PHONE..............................973 557-1482
Jerome Matisik, *President*
EMP: 12
SALES: 270K **Privately Held**
SIC: 3281 Cut stone & stone products

(G-584)
SYTHEON LTD
315 Wootton St Ste N (07005-1900)
PHONE..............................973 988-1075
Ratan K Chaudhuri, *President*
Francois Marchio, *COO*
◆ **EMP:** 4
SALES (est): 226K **Privately Held**
SIC: 2833 Organic medicinal chemicals: bulk, uncompounded

(G-585)
TECHNICAL ADVANTAGE INC (PA)
Also Called: Advantage Engineering Group
34 Farber Hill Rd (07005-9223)
PHONE..............................973 402-5500
Stewart Klepesch, *President*
Bruce Hirschorn, *Vice Pres*
Deborah Hirschhorn, *Shareholder*
EMP: 5
SQ FT: 11,000
SALES (est): 754K **Privately Held**
WEB: www.aeg-corp.com
SIC: 3571 7389 Electronic computers; design, commercial & industrial

(G-586)
TELEMARK CNC LLC
429 Rockaway Valley Rd (07005-8101)
PHONE..............................973 794-4857
William Hovey,
EMP: 5
SALES: 990K **Privately Held**
SIC: 3451 Screw machine products

(G-587)
VALLEY PLASTIC MOLDING CO
Also Called: Boonton Plastic Molding Co
30 Plane St Ste 4 (07005-1758)
P.O. Box 30 (07005-0030)
PHONE..............................973 334-2100
Pat Berhman, *Owner*
Mike Berhman, *Co-Owner*
EMP: 10 EST: 1916
SQ FT: 10,000
SALES: 1MM **Privately Held**
SIC: 3089 6512 Molding primary plastic; commercial & industrial building operation

---

Bordentown
Burlington County

(G-588)
A D J GROUP LLC
12 Trainor Cir (08505-4277)
PHONE..............................609 743-2099
Art D Angelo,
EMP: 4
SALES: 350K **Privately Held**
SIC: 3549 Marking machines, metalworking

(G-589)
ADVANCED TECHNICAL SUPPORT INC
Also Called: A T S Rheosystems
231 Crosswicks Rd (08505-2602)
PHONE..............................609 298-2522
Fax: 609 758-3498
Steven M Colo, *President*
Kaj Hedman, *Principal*
Peter Kw Herh, *Principal*
Nick Roye, *Principal*
August J Colo, *CFO*
EMP: 100
SQ FT: 30,000
SALES (est): 13.7MM **Privately Held**
SIC: 3826 Analytical instruments

(G-590)
AONE TOUCH INC
22 Sagamore Ln (08505-4459)
PHONE..............................732 261-6841
George Sara, *CEO*
EMP: 6 EST: 2003
SQ FT: 4,000
SALES: 800K **Privately Held**
SIC: 7374 5044 5045 7372 Computer processing services; calculating machines; calcvlators, electronic; accounting machines using machine readable programs; prepackaged software

(G-591)
ATS MECHANICAL INC
Also Called: Honeywell Authorized Dealer
74 Crosswicks St (08505-1768)
PHONE..............................609 298-2323
Andrew Steward, *President*
EMP: 7
SALES (est): 947.8K **Privately Held**
SIC: 3585 Air conditioning equipment, complete

(G-592)
CARPENTER & PATERSON INC
2 Altran Ct 2 # 2 (08505-9630)
PHONE..............................973 772-1800
Dennis Bourrell, *Opers Mgr*
Tim Gonder, *Sales Staff*
Tom Ferraro, *Branch Mgr*
EMP: 35
SQ FT: 1,500
SALES (corp-wide): 32.3MM **Privately Held**
WEB: www.carpenterandpaterson.com
SIC: 5085 8711 3429 Valves & fittings; engineering services; manufactured hardware (general)

PA: Carpenter & Paterson, Inc.
434 Latigue Rd
Westwego LA 70094
504 431-7722

(G-593)
CARPENTER & PATERSON INC
2 Altran Ct Ste 2 # 2 (08505-9630)
PHONE..............................609 227-2750
Bob Cieslikowski, *Branch Mgr*
Tom Armour, *Manager*
EMP: 30
SALES (corp-wide): 32.3MM **Privately Held**
WEB: www.carpenterpaterson.com
SIC: 8742 3432 Transportation consultant; plumbing fixture fittings & trim
PA: Carpenter & Paterson, Inc.
434 Latigue Rd
Westwego LA 70094
504 431-7722

(G-594)
CCBCC OPERATIONS LLC
948 Farnsworth Ave (08505-2106)
PHONE..............................609 324-7424
Ron Wilson, *President*
EMP: 75
SALES (corp-wide): 4.3B **Publicly Held**
SIC: 2086 Soft drinks: packaged in cans, bottles, etc.
HQ: Ccbcc Operations, Llc
4100 Coca Cola Plz
Charlotte NC 28211
704 364-8728

(G-595)
ELEISON PHARMACEUTICALS INC
311 Farnsworth Ave Ste 1 (08505-1796)
PHONE..............................215 416-7620
Edwin J Thomas, *CEO*
EMP: 5
SALES: 950K **Privately Held**
SIC: 2833 Medicinals & botanicals

(G-596)
FAUBEL PHARMA SERVICES
3 3rd St Ste 102 (08505-1370)
PHONE..............................908 730-7563
▲ **EMP:** 4
SALES (est): 285.8K **Privately Held**
SIC: 2834 Pharmaceutical preparations

(G-597)
GRAHAM PACKAGING COMPANY LP
201 Elizabeth St (08505-1402)
PHONE..............................717 849-8500
Jeff Owens, *Plant Mgr*
Stephen Kearney, *Human Resources*
EMP: 28 **Privately Held**
WEB: www.grahampackaging.com
SIC: 3089 Plastic containers, except foam
HQ: Graham Packaging Company, L.P.
700 Indian Springs Dr # 100
Lancaster PA 17601
717 849-8500

(G-598)
HOMETOWN OFFICE SUPS & PRTG CO
Also Called: Hometown Office Sups & Prtg Co
192 Us Highway 130 (08505-2253)
PHONE..............................609 298-9020
Earl Hall, *President*
EMP: 5
SALES (est): 530K **Privately Held**
SIC: 5943 2752 Office forms & supplies; offset & photolithographic printing

(G-599)
IN-PHASE TECHNOLOGIES INC
401 Bordentown Hedding Rd (08505-4747)
PHONE..............................609 298-9555
Fax: 609 298-0098
Edward J Macmullen, *President*
Howard Salvesen, *Vice Pres*
Robert Twiggs, *Marketing Mgr*
EMP: 27
SQ FT: 20,000

SALES (est): 7.4MM **Privately Held**
WEB: www.in-phasetech.com
SIC: 3663 Microwave communication equipment

(G-600)
M W TRAILER REPAIR INC
400 Rising Sun Rd (08505-4709)
PHONE..............................609 298-1113
Fax: 609 298-7555
Michael Welsh, *President*
EMP: 10
SQ FT: 8,000
SALES: 1.6MM **Privately Held**
WEB: www.mwtrailer.com
SIC: 3715 5012 5013 5511 Truck trailers; trailers for trucks, new & used; trailer parts & accessories; trucks, tractors & trailers: new & used

(G-601)
MEGATRAN INDUSTRIES (PA)
Also Called: Nwl Transformers
312 Rising Sun Rd (08505-9626)
PHONE..............................609 227-4300
Fax: 609 298-1982
James P Seitz, *President*
David Seitz, *Exec VP*
Helmut Herder, *Vice Pres*
Lottie Randow, *Vice Pres*
Philip Atherton, *QC Mgr*
▲ **EMP:** 300
SQ FT: 130,000
SALES (est): 49.1MM **Privately Held**
WEB: www.nwl.com
SIC: 3675 3612 3822 3625 Electronic capacitors; power transformers, electric; reactor transformers; auto controls regulating residntl & coml environmt & applncs; relays & industrial controls

(G-602)
MELTON SALES & SERVICE
Also Called: Melton Industries
1723 Burlington (08505)
PHONE..............................609 699-4800
Fax: 609 699-4819
Kenneth Fairchild, *Opers Staff*
Lori Mlynarski, *Purch Mgr*
Brenda Hedrick, *Finance Mgr*
Skip Melton, *Sales Executive*
Christopher Robles, *Manager*
EMP: 25 **Privately Held**
WEB: www.meltonindustries.com
SIC: 3812 3519 Defense systems & equipment; diesel engine rebuilding
PA: Melton Sales & Service
13 Petticoat Bridge Rd
Columbus NJ 08022

(G-603)
MERSHON CONCRETE LLC
5251 Us Highway 130 (08505-4401)
P.O. Box 254 (08505-0254)
PHONE..............................609 298-2150
Fax: 609 298-7969
Randolph E Mershon Jr, *President*
John Molesworth, *Corp Secy*
Pat Greeber, *Vice Pres*
Beth Petty, *Admin Sec*
EMP: 40
SQ FT: 30,000
SALES (est): 8.7MM **Privately Held**
SIC: 3272 3273 3446 Tanks, concrete; steps, prefabricated concrete; ready-mixed concrete; architectural metalwork

(G-604)
MICRODYSIS INC
1200 Florence Columbus Rd (08505-4200)
PHONE..............................609 642-1184
Joseph Z Huang, *President*
EMP: 5
SQ FT: 300
SALES (est): 276.5K **Privately Held**
WEB: www.microdysis.com
SIC: 3825 3826 3569 Analog-digital converters, electronic instrumentation type; analytical instruments; liquid automation machinery & equipment

▲ = Import ▼=Export
◆ =Import/Export

(G-605)
NATIONAL DIVERSIFIED SALES INC
Also Called: Nds
401 Bordentown Hedding Rd (08505-4747)
PHONE...................................559 562-9888
EMP: 6
SALES (corp-wide): 1.2B Privately Held
SIC: 3089 5083 Plastic containers, except foam; farm equipment parts & supplies
HQ: National Diversified Sales, Inc.
21300 Victory Blvd # 215
Woodland Hills CA 91367
559 562-9888

(G-606)
NWL INC (HQ)
Also Called: Nwl Capacitors
312 Rising Sun Rd (08505-9626)
PHONE...................................609 298-7300
David Seitz, President
Robert Guenther, President
John Scannella, General Mgr
Terry Farmer, Vice Pres
Bob Guenther, Vice Pres
◆ EMP: 280
SQ FT: 130,000
SALES (est): 99.9MM
SALES (corp-wide): 49.1MM Privately Held
SIC: 3612 3679 Power transformers, electric; reactor transformers; power supplies, all types: static
PA: Megatran Industries
312 Rising Sun Rd
Bordentown NJ 08505
609 227-4300

(G-607)
PACOR INC (PA)
333 Rising Sun Rd (08505-9611)
PHONE...................................609 324-1100
Fax: 856 303-8802
Ronald A Latini, President
William Wheatley, Vice Pres
▲ EMP: 50 EST: 1921
SQ FT: 55,000
SALES (est): 35MM Privately Held
WEB: www.pacorinc.com
SIC: 5033 3086 3296 Insulation materials; insulation or cushioning material, foamed plastic; mineral wool

(G-608)
PERDUE FARMS INC
120 Route 130 (08505-2200)
PHONE...................................609 298-4100
Reggie Byrd, Plant Mgr
EMP: 4
SALES (corp-wide): 5.5B Privately Held
SIC: 2015 Poultry slaughtering & processing
PA: Perdue Farms Inc.
31149 Old Ocean City Rd
Salisbury MD 21804
410 543-3000

(G-609)
PRINCE SPORTS INC
Also Called: Ektelon, Viking Athletics
334 Rising Sun Rd (08505)
PHONE...................................609 291-5800
Gordon Boggis, CEO
Alistair Thorburn, Principal
Richard E Margin, Vice Pres
▲ EMP: 80
SQ FT: 35,000
SALES (est): 8.1MM Privately Held
WEB: www.princesports.com
SIC: 3949 Rackets & frames: tennis, badminton, squash, lacrosse, etc; tennis equipment & supplies
PA: Nautic Partners, Llc
100 Westminster St # 1220
Providence RI 02903

(G-610)
RBDEL INC
Also Called: UPS Store 5952
272 Dunns Mill Rd (08505-4748)
PHONE...................................609 324-0040
Fax: 609 324-0070
Richard De Luca, Principal
EMP: 5

SALES (est): 408.2K Privately Held
SIC: 2542 Postal lock boxes, mail racks & related products

(G-611)
STEPAN COMPANY
Also Called: Fieldsboro Plant
4th St Fieldsboro (08505)
PHONE...................................609 298-1222
Fax: 609 298-7950
Gary Traverso, Opers-Prdtn-Mfg
EMP: 75
SALES (corp-wide): 1.9B Publicly Held
WEB: www.stepan.com
SIC: 2869 2843 2842 Industrial organic chemicals; surface active agents; specialty cleaning, polishes & sanitation goods
PA: Stepan Company
22 W Frontage Rd
Northfield IL 60093
847 446-7500

(G-612)
TOMMYS PALLET YARD LLC
2499 Old York Rd (08505-4460)
PHONE...................................609 424-3996
EMP: 4
SALES (est): 501.6K Privately Held
SIC: 2448 Pallets, wood

(G-613)
TOWN FORD INC
860 Us Highway 206 (08505-1510)
PHONE...................................609 298-4990
Randy Johnson, President
EMP: 55
SQ FT: 15,000
SALES (est): 12.2MM Privately Held
SIC: 5511 7538 7532 7515 Automobiles, new & used; general automotive repair shops; top & body repair & paint shops; passenger car leasing; passenger car rental; motor vehicle parts & accessories

(G-614)
VANCO USA LLC
1170 Florence Columbus Rd (08505-4293)
PHONE...................................609 499-4141
Carl Massaro, Mng Member
EMP: 65
SQ FT: 100,000
SALES (est): 4.4MM Privately Held
SIC: 3715 Semitrailers for truck tractors

(G-615)
VANCO USA LLC (DE)
1170 Florence Columbus Rd (08505-4293)
PHONE...................................609 499-4141
Carl Massaro,
EMP: 140
SQ FT: 100,000
SALES (est): 18.2MM Privately Held
SIC: 3715 3537 Truck trailers; industrial trucks & tractors

Bound Brook
Somerset County

(G-616)
ANJU CLINPLUS LLC ✪
1661 Route 22 West (08805-1258)
PHONE...................................732 764-6969
Kurien Jacob, CEO
EMP: 15 EST: 2017
SALES (est): 305.2K
SALES (corp-wide): 2.8MM Privately Held
SIC: 7372 Prepackaged software
PA: Anju Software, Inc.
251 W 19th St
New York NY 10011
480 326-2358

(G-617)
CYALUME SPECIALTY PRODUCTS INC
Also Called: Jfc Technologies
100 W Main St Ste A10 (08805-1972)
PHONE...................................732 469-7760
Fax: 732 469-3666
James G Schleck, President
Zivi Nedivi, Principal

Hemant Desai, Vice Pres
Dina Kisver, Vice Pres
▲ EMP: 50
SQ FT: 40,000
SALES (est): 13MM Publicly Held
WEB: www.jfctechnologies.com
SIC: 2833 2834 8731 Medicinals & botanicals; druggists' preparations (pharmaceuticals); commercial physical research
PA: Cyalume Technologies Holdings, Inc.
910 Se 17th St Ste 300
Fort Lauderdale FL 33316

(G-618)
IMPERIAL METAL PRODUCTS INC
8 W Chimney Rock Rd (08805)
PHONE...................................908 647-8181
EMP: 5
SQ FT: 3,000
SALES (est): 885.7K Privately Held
SIC: 3441 Manufactures Facricated Metal

(G-619)
JOSEPH BURNS INC
Also Called: Versatile Prtg Applications
241 W Union Ave (08805-1334)
PHONE...................................732 356-8355
Mary McClintock, President
EMP: 9
SQ FT: 3,000
SALES: 1.4MM Privately Held
WEB: www.getvpa.com
SIC: 2752 Commercial printing, offset

(G-620)
MARX NJ GROUP LLC
Also Called: Halo Mark
14 Easy St Ste 14e4 (08805-1168)
PHONE...................................732 901-3880
Joseph Marx,
Donald Marx,
Thomas Marx,
EMP: 30 EST: 2016
SALES: 8MM Privately Held
SIC: 3444 Sheet metalwork

(G-621)
POLYMER MOLDED PRODUCTS
10 Easy St (08805-1147)
PHONE...................................732 907-1990
Urena Ayala, Principal
EMP: 6
SALES (est): 643.2K Privately Held
SIC: 3089 Injection molded finished plastic products

(G-622)
ROYAL CABINET COMPANY INC
15 Easy St (08805-1168)
PHONE...................................908 203-8000
Paul Y McDonald, President
EMP: 30
SQ FT: 21,000
SALES (est): 4.2MM Privately Held
WEB: www.royalcabinet.com
SIC: 1799 2434 5712 Kitchen & bathroom remodeling; wood kitchen cabinets; customized furniture & cabinets

(G-623)
SR INTERNATIONAL ROCK INC
7 Easy St Ste E (08805-1147)
PHONE...................................908 864-4700
Raj Raju, President
▲ EMP: 6
SQ FT: 16,000
SALES: 300K Privately Held
SIC: 5032 3281 Granite building stone; marble, building: cut & shaped

(G-624)
STAR PROMOTIONS INC
Also Called: Graphic Concepts
11 Maiden Ln (08805-2023)
PHONE...................................732 356-5959
Fax: 732 469-0889
Gerald Truppelli, President
Jerry Truppelli, Owner
Ryan Devesty, Vice Pres
EMP: 14
SQ FT: 8,000
SALES (est): 2.2MM Privately Held
SIC: 2752 2791 2789 Photo-offset printing; typesetting; bookbinding & related work

(G-625)
STAVOLA CONSTRUCTION MTLS INC
Also Called: Stavola Contracting
810 Thompson Ave (08805-1124)
P.O. Box 482, Red Bank (07701-0482)
PHONE...................................732 356-5700
Fax: 732 356-2175
Juan Berrios, Plant Mgr
Phyllis Delisio, Finance
James M Stavola, Manager
Jim Bean, Info Tech Mgr
EMP: 47
SALES (corp-wide): 9.3MM Privately Held
WEB: www.stavola.com
SIC: 3281 5032 2951 Stone, quarrying & processing of own stone products; stone, crushed or broken; asphalt paving mixtures & blocks
PA: Stavola Construction Materials, Inc.
175 Drift Rd
Tinton Falls NJ 07724
732 542-2328

(G-626)
STEPS TO LITERACY LLC
4 Easy St (08805-1147)
P.O. Box 6737, Bridgewater (08807-0737)
PHONE...................................732 560-8363
Fax: 732 560-8699
Elaine Thompson, COO
Bill Thompson,
EMP: 20
SQ FT: 20,000
SALES (est): 3.7MM Privately Held
SIC: 8748 3999 Business consulting; education aids, devices & supplies

Bradley Beach
Monmouth County

(G-627)
EA PILOT SUPPLY
603 Fletcher Lake Ave (07720-1317)
PHONE...................................201 934-8449
Spencer Ryan, Owner
EMP: 6
SALES (est): 330K Privately Held
SIC: 5999 3669 Electronic parts & equipment; smoke detectors

Branchburg
Somerset County

(G-628)
ADVANCED INDUSTRIAL CONTROLS
Also Called: Aic
10 County Line Rd Ste 30 (08876-6009)
PHONE...................................908 725-7575
Fax: 908 725-2020
Doug Morrison, President
EMP: 6
SQ FT: 4,200
SALES (est): 630K Privately Held
SIC: 3625 8711 Relays & industrial controls; electrical or electronic engineering

(G-629)
AIR LIQUIDE ADVANCED MATERIALS
197 Meister Ave Bldg A (08876-6022)
PHONE...................................908 231-9060
Michael Pikulin, Vice Pres
Paul C Burlingame, Branch Mgr
John D Neufville, Manager
Jay Song, Executive
Michael Mastroianni, Administration
EMP: 10
SALES (corp-wide): 164.2MM Privately Held
SIC: 5169 8733 2813 Industrial gases; noncommercial research organizations; industrial gases
HQ: Air Liquide Advanced Materials Inc.
9811 Katy Fwy Ste 100
Houston TX 77024
713 624-8000

G
E
O
G
R
A
P
H
I
C

(G-630)
ALLOY WELDING CO
6 Culnen Dr Ste A (08876-5463)
Rural Route 6 (08876)
PHONE..................................908 218-1551
Fax: 908 218-1502
Marilyn Scharffenberger, *CEO*
Leonard F Scharffenberger, *President*
EMP: 11 EST: 1946
SQ FT: 27,000
SALES: 4.2MM **Privately Held**
WEB: www.alloyweldingco.com
SIC: 3441 Fabricated structural metal

(G-631)
ALOE SCIENCE INC
Also Called: Aloe Creme Laboratories Div
160 Meister Ave Ste 20 (08876-3474)
PHONE..................................908 231-8888
Fax: 908 231-7388
Douglas Siegel, *President*
EMP: 20
SALES (est): 2.1MM **Privately Held**
SIC: 2844 Suntan lotions & oils; face
creams or lotions

(G-632)
ALTIMA INNOVATIONS INC
211 Evans Way (08876-3766)
PHONE..................................732 474-1500
Fayez Azeez, *Treasurer*
Mohan Devineni, *Director*
EMP: 4 EST: 2014
SALES (est): 208.5K **Privately Held**
SIC: 2834 Pharmaceutical preparations

(G-633)
**AMERICAN LEISTRITZ
EXTRUDER**
169 Meister Ave (08876-3464)
PHONE..................................908 685-2333
Fax: 908 685-0247
Stuart Kapp, *Sales Mgr*
Sarah Scovens, *Marketing Staff*
Janice King, *Manager*
Bill Novak, *Manager*
EMP: 19
SALES (est): 3.5MM
SALES (corp-wide): 289.7MM **Privately
Held**
WEB: www.alec-usa.com
SIC: 3559 Synthetic filament extruding ma-
chines
PA: Leistritz Ag
Markgrafenstr. 36-39
Nurnberg 90459
911 430-60

(G-634)
AMERICAN SPRAYTECH LLC
205 Meister Ave (08876-6032)
PHONE..................................908 725-6060
Allen S Lalwani, *Principal*
Robert Daria, *Business Mgr*
Robert Flaherty, *Opers Mgr*
David Montes, *Facilities Mgr*
Robert Swiatecki, *Opers Staff*
EMP: 35
SQ FT: 24,000
SALES (est): 7.4MM **Privately Held**
WEB: www.americanspraytech.com
SIC: 7389 2844 2813 Packaging & label-
ing services; toilet preparations; aerosols

(G-635)
**AMNEAL PHARMACEUTICALS
LLC**
65 Readington Rd Bldg B (08876-3557)
PHONE..................................908 409-6823
Chirag Patel, *CEO*
EMP: 8
SALES (corp-wide): 74.4K **Publicly Held**
HQ: Amneal Pharmaceuticals Llc
400 Crossing Blvd Fl 3
Bridgewater NJ 08807

(G-636)
**AMNEAL PHARMACEUTICALS
LLC**
131 Chambers Brook Rd (08876-3587)
PHONE..................................908 231-1911
Jiten Parikh, *Branch Mgr*
EMP: 32

SALES (corp-wide): 74.4K **Publicly Held**
SIC: 2834 5122 Pharmaceutical prepara-
tions; pharmaceuticals
HQ: Amneal Pharmaceuticals Llc
400 Crossing Blvd Fl 3
Bridgewater NJ 08807

(G-637)
ARGYLE INDUSTRIES INC
160 Meister Ave Ste 12 (08876-3474)
PHONE..................................908 725-8800
Fax: 908 429-7311
James Kane, *President*
Carrie Troyan, *Accounting Mgr*
▲ EMP: 12
SQ FT: 3,000
SALES (est): 6.3MM **Privately Held**
WEB: www.argyleindustries.com
SIC: 5051 3599 3444 Aluminum bars,
rods, ingots, sheets, pipes, plates, etc.;
machine shop, jobbing & repair; sheet
metalwork

(G-638)
ARNA MARKETING GROUP INC
60 Readington Rd (08876-3540)
PHONE..................................908 625-7395
Mette Brusdal, *President*
EMP: 67
SQ FT: 10,000
SALES (est): 11.6MM **Privately Held**
SIC: 7331 2678 7389 2752 Direct mail
advertising services; writing paper & en-
velopes: made from purchased materials;
presorted mail service; commercial print-
ing, lithographic; promotional printing, lith-
ographic

(G-639)
ARNA MARKETING INC
60 Readington Rd (08876-3540)
P.O. Box 5102, North Branch (08876-1309)
PHONE..................................908 231-1100
Steven Hegna, *President*
Norman Hegna, *Vice Pres*
Anthony Mills, *CFO*
David Hegna, *Sales Executive*
James Archambault, *Manager*
EMP: 40 EST: 1952
SQ FT: 25,000
SALES (est): 14.8MM **Privately Held**
WEB: www.aepcompany.com
SIC: 5112 5961 2754 Envelopes; sta-
tionery; mail order house, order taking of-
fice only; commercial printing, gravure

(G-640)
**ASA HYDRAULIK OF AMERICA
INC**
160 Meister Ave Ste 20a (08876-3499)
PHONE..................................908 541-1500
Thomas Euler-Rolle, *President*
James Matthews, *Vice Pres*
▲ EMP: 7
SQ FT: 5,000
SALES (est): 2.7MM **Privately Held**
WEB: www.asahyd.com
SIC: 5084 3443 Hydraulic systems equip-
ment & supplies; heat exchangers: cool-
ers (after, inter), condensers, etc.

(G-641)
**ATLANTIC CLEAN ENERGY SUP
LLC**
Also Called: Aces Led
18 Culnen Dr (08876-5400)
PHONE..................................888 900-1581
Jinshan Gao, *Mng Member*
▲ EMP: 4
SALES (est): 504K **Privately Held**
SIC: 3674 4911 5074 8711 Light emitting
diodes; ; heating equipment & panels,
solar; energy conservation engineering

(G-642)
AZ-EM USA BRANCHBURG NJ
70 Meister Ave (08876-3440)
PHONE..................................908 429-0020
John Whybrow, *Chairman*
◆ EMP: 7
SALES (est): 905.3K **Privately Held**
SIC: 3679 Electronic circuits

(G-643)
BETTER SLEEP INC
100 Readington Rd (08876-3414)
PHONE..................................908 464-2200
Fax: 908 393-0126
▲ EMP: 17 EST: 1951
SALES (est): 3.7MM **Privately Held**
SIC: 3496 2392 Mfg Misc Fabricated Wire
Products Mfg Household Furnishings

(G-644)
**BIOSEARCH MEDICAL
PRODUCTS INC**
35 Industrial Pkwy (08876-6005)
PHONE..................................908 252-0595
Fax: 908 722-5024
Martin C Dyck, *President*
Robert Lee, *CFO*
Robert J Moravsik, *Admin Sec*
EMP: 70
SQ FT: 35,000
SALES (est): 3.8MM
SALES (corp-wide): 5.8MM **Publicly Held**
WEB: www.biosearch.com
SIC: 3841 Surgical & medical instruments
PA: Hydromer, Inc.
35 Industrial Pkwy
Branchburg NJ 08876
908 526-2828

(G-645)
**BRIDGEWATER WHOLESALERS
INC (PA)**
Also Called: B W I
210 Industrial Pkwy (08876-3450)
PHONE..................................908 526-7555
Fax: 908 526-5013
Jack Cortese, *President*
Bill Asselta, *General Mgr*
Susan Schumer, *Chairman*
Simon Sikora, *COO*
Brock Ryall, *Vice Pres*
▲ EMP: 190
SQ FT: 100,000
SALES (est): 167.4MM **Privately Held**
WEB: www.bwimillwork.com
SIC: 2431 5031 Doors & door parts & trim,
wood; doors & windows; molding, all ma-
terials

(G-646)
**BYRAM LABORATORIES INC
(PA)**
Also Called: Byram Labs
1 Columbia Rd (08876-3518)
PHONE..................................908 252-0852
Fax: 908 252-0822
Monte Prince, *CEO*
Bill Kirk, *Exec VP*
Alex Thompson, *Vice Pres*
Kevin Jezorek, *Mfg Staff*
William Kirk, *VP Sales*
EMP: 30 EST: 1910
SQ FT: 16,000
SALES (est): 8.6MM **Privately Held**
WEB: www.byramlabs.com
SIC: 3825 7629 Measuring instruments &
meters, electric; electrical measuring in-
strument repair & calibration

(G-647)
CLORDISYS SOLUTIONS INC
50 Tannery Rd Ste 1 (08876-6034)
P.O. Box 549, Lebanon (08833-0549)
PHONE..................................908 236-4100
Fax: 908 823-9111
Jennifer Czarneski, *President*
Jenny Winters, *Business Mgr*
Ian Leahy, *Engineer*
Daniel Paznek, *Engineer*
Cheryl Lorcheim, *Treasurer*
▲ EMP: 25
SALES (est): 5MM **Privately Held**
WEB: www.clordisys.com
SIC: 3841 Surgical & medical instru-
ments; pharmaceutical machinery

(G-648)
**COESIA HEALTH & BEAUTY INC
(PA)**
335 Chambers Brook Rd (08876-7213)
PHONE..................................908 707-8008
Goran Adolfsson, *President*
▲ EMP: 16 EST: 2013

SALES (est): 15.1MM **Privately Held**
SIC: 3535 3599 Bucket type conveyor
systems; custom machinery

(G-649)
**COLORON PLASTICS
CORPORATION**
169 Meister Ave (08876-3464)
PHONE..................................908 685-1210
Fax: 908 722-3632
Kenneth Kirchner, *President*
EMP: 24
SQ FT: 16,000
SALES (est): 5.3MM **Privately Held**
SIC: 2865 Dyes & pigments

(G-650)
CONOLOG CORPORATION (PA)
5 Columbia Rd (08876-3518)
PHONE..................................908 722-8081
Fax: 908 722-5461
Michael Horn, *CEO*
EMP: 14 EST: 1968
SQ FT: 7,000
SALES (est): 831.7K **Privately Held**
WEB: www.conolog.com
SIC: 3661 3679 3663 Telephone & tele-
graph apparatus; microwave components;
transmitter-receivers, radio

(G-651)
COVER CO INC
19 Readington Rd (08876-3520)
PHONE..................................908 707-9797
Fax: 908 707-1576
Frank Patel, *President*
▲ EMP: 25
SQ FT: 25,000
SALES (est): 2.3MM **Privately Held**
WEB: www.pegasus-products.com
SIC: 3999 3949 Hot tub & spa covers;
sporting & athletic goods

(G-652)
CROWN GLASS CO INC
990 Evergreen Dr (08876-3898)
PHONE..................................908 642-1764
Fax: 908 526-3238
Erin Adams, *Partner*
Chris Coletti, *Office Mgr*
EMP: 4
SQ FT: 9,000
SALES: 800K **Privately Held**
SIC: 3231 Products of purchased glass

(G-653)
CUSTOM MOLDERS CORP
Also Called: Cmg Plastics
160 Meister Ave Ste 1 (08876-3474)
PHONE..................................908 218-7997
Joseph Caro, *President*
Glenn Loh, *CFO*
EMP: 65
SALES (est): 78.8K **Privately Held**
WEB: www.custommolders.com
SIC: 3089 Injection molding of plastics

(G-654)
**CUSTOM MOLDERS GROUP LLC
(PA)**
Also Called: Cmg
160 Meister Ave Ste 1 (08876-3474)
PHONE..................................908 218-7997
Joseph Caro, *Mng Member*
Glen Loh,
EMP: 5
SALES (est): 2MM **Privately Held**
SIC: 2821 Molding compounds, plastics

(G-655)
CUTTING BOARD COMPANY
2 Dreahook Rd (08876-3729)
PHONE..................................908 725-0187
Theresa Pizzelanti, *Manager*
EMP: 5
SALES (corp-wide): 550K **Privately Held**
SIC: 3613 Distribution cutouts
PA: The Cutting Board Company
291 Route 22 E Bldg 6
Lebanon NJ 08833
908 725-0187

▲ = Import ▼=Export
◆ =Import/Export

(G-656)
ELI LILLY AND COMPANY
1181 Us Highway 202 N (08876-3909)
PHONE..............................908 704-1807
Maria Malabunga, *Research*
Ginny Bogan, *Manager*
Carole Perruzzi, *Manager*
EMP: 26
SALES (corp-wide): 22.8B **Publicly Held**
SIC: 2834 2836 Pharmaceutical prepara-
tions; biological products, except diagnos-
tic
PA: Eli Lilly And Company
Lilly Corporate Ctr
Indianapolis IN 46285
317 276-2000

(G-657)
EMD PERFORMANCE MATERIALS CORP
70 Meister Ave (08876-3440)
PHONE..............................908 429-3500
Xiaoping Ling, *Engineer*
EMP: 450
SALES (corp-wide): 18B **Privately Held**
SIC: 2899 3825 Oils & essential oils; inte-
grated circuit testers
HQ: Emd Performance Materials Corp.
1200 Intrepid Ave Ste 3
Philadelphia PA 19112
888 367-3275

(G-658)
FALCON SAFETY PRODUCTS INC (HQ)
25 Imclone Dr (08876-3998)
P.O. Box 1299, Somerville (08876-1299)
PHONE..............................908 707-4900
Fax: 908 707-8855
Phil Lapin, *CEO*
Dermot McLeers, *Technical Mgr*
Bob Schmalzigan, *Controller*
Wendy Griffin, *Sales Mgr*
Trish Dupuis-Jones, *Cust Mgr*
◆ **EMP:** 70
SQ FT: 55,000
SALES (est): 56.5MM
SALES (corp-wide): 57.8MM **Privately Held**
WEB: www.falconsafety.com
SIC: 3563 Spraying & dusting equipment
PA: The Parker Acquisition Group Inc
25 Imclone Dr
Branchburg NJ 08876
908 707-4900

(G-659)
FEMENELLA & ASSOCIATES INC
10 County Line Rd Ste 24 (08876-6009)
PHONE..............................908 722-6526
Arthur Femenella Jr, *President*
Nancy Femenella, *Corp Secy*
Patrick Baldoni, *Vice Pres*
Karen Gilbert, *Office Mgr*
Allison Unger, *Manager*
EMP: 8
SQ FT: 1,000
SALES: 5.9MM **Privately Held**
SIC: 3231 Stained glass: made from pur-
chased glass

(G-660)
FLEXLINK SYSTEMS INC
Also Called: Hapa
335 Chambers Brook Rd (08876-7213)
PHONE..............................973 983-2700
EMP: 23 **Privately Held**
SIC: 3535 Conveyors & conveying equip-
ment
HQ: Flexlink Systems, Inc.
6580 Snowdrift Rd Ste 200
Allentown PA 18106
610 973-8200

(G-661)
FLEXLINK SYSTEMS INC
Also Called: Gottscho Printing Systems
335 Chambers Brook Rd (08876-7213)
PHONE..............................908 947-2140
EMP: 5 **Privately Held**
SIC: 3535 Conveyors & conveying equip-
ment

HQ: Flexlink Systems, Inc.
6580 Snowdrift Rd Ste 200
Allentown PA 18106
610 973-8200

(G-662)
G M STAINLESS INC (PA)
41 Imclone Dr (08876-3903)
PHONE..............................908 575-1834
Fax: 908 575-1836
Walter W Gauer, *President*
Carol Gauer, *Corp Secy*
EMP: 14
SQ FT: 20,000
SALES (est): 2.2MM **Privately Held**
WEB: www.gmstainless.com
SIC: 3312 5051 Bar, rod & wire products;
bars, metal

(G-663)
GEOLYTICS INC
3322 Us Highway 22 # 806 (08876-3476)
P.O. Box 5336, North Branch (08876-1303)
PHONE..............................908 707-1505
Natasha Vasilev, *President*
EMP: 6
SALES (est): 485.7K **Privately Held**
WEB: www.geolytics.com
SIC: 8732 2741 Market analysis or re-
search; maps: publishing & printing

(G-664)
HAHNS WOODWORKING
181 Meister Ave (08876-3464)
PHONE..............................908 722-2742
Scott Hahn, *President*
EMP: 12
SQ FT: 20,000
SALES (est): 4MM **Privately Held**
WEB: www.hahnswoodworking.com
SIC: 2431 Doors, wood; garage doors,
overhead: wood

(G-665)
HYDROMER INC (PA)
35 Industrial Pkwy (08876-3424)
PHONE..............................908 526-2828
Fax: 908 526-3633
Peter M Von Dyck, *CEO*
Manfred F Dyck, *Ch of Bd*
Martin C Dyck, *Exec VP*
Joseph A Ehrhard Jr, *Exec VP*
John Konar, *Vice Pres*
EMP: 106
SQ FT: 10,400
SALES (est): 5.8MM **Publicly Held**
WEB: www.hydromer.com
SIC: 8731 3841 5047 Biotechnical re-
search, commercial; medical research,
commercial; surgical & medical instru-
ments; medical & hospital equipment;
medical equipment & supplies

(G-666)
IMCLONE LLC
33 Imclone Dr (08876-3903)
PHONE..............................908 218-9588
John H Johnson, *CEO*
Helen Kotanides, *Agent*
Beverly Hiles, *Associate Dir*
EMP: 10
SALES (est): 1.9MM
SALES (corp-wide): 22.8B **Publicly Held**
SIC: 2836 Biological products, except diag-
nostic
HQ: Eli Lilly Sa
Chemin Des Coquelicots 16
Vernier GE
223 060-401

(G-667)
IMCLONE SYSTEMS LLC
33 Imclone Dr (08876-3903)
PHONE..............................908 218-0147
Joe Toronoski, *Principal*
Narine Singh, *Plant Engr*
Robert H Jones, *Manager*
Hershil Patel, *Manager*
Kim Consolino, *Supervisor*
EMP: 75
SALES (corp-wide): 22.8B **Publicly Held**
WEB: www.imclone.com
SIC: 8731 2836 2834 Biotechnical re-
search, commercial; biological products,
except diagnostic; pharmaceutical prepa-
rations

HQ: Imclone Systems Llc
440 Us Highway 22
Bridgewater NJ 08807
908 541-8000

(G-668)
IMCLONE SYSTEMS LLC
50 Imclone Dr (08876-3904)
PHONE..............................908 541-8100
Evelyn Haley, *Branch Mgr*
Timothy Blanc, *Manager*
EMP: 5
SALES (corp-wide): 22.8B **Publicly Held**
WEB: www.imclone.com
SIC: 2834 Pharmaceutical preparations
HQ: Imclone Systems Llc
440 Us Highway 22
Bridgewater NJ 08807
908 541-8000

(G-669)
INIVEN LLC
5 Columbia Rd (08876-3518)
PHONE..............................908 722-3770
Marc Benou, *President*
EMP: 7 EST: 2015
SALES (est): 492.6K **Privately Held**
SIC: 3661 3663 Fiber optics communica-
tions equipment; telemetering equipment,
electronic

(G-670)
JOHNSON & JOHNSON
6 Greenwood Ct (08876-3604)
PHONE..............................732 524-0400
EMP: 80
SALES (corp-wide): 76.4B **Publicly Held**
SIC: 2676 Feminine hygiene paper prod-
ucts
PA: Johnson & Johnson
1 Johnson And Johnson Plz
New Brunswick NJ 08933
732 524-0400

(G-671)
KATADIN INC
53 Dreahook Rd (08876-3728)
PHONE..............................908 526-0166
James Brogan, *President*
Elaine Brogan, *Vice Pres*
EMP: 4 EST: 2001
SALES (est): 260.7K **Privately Held**
SIC: 2431 Interior & ornamental woodwork
& trim

(G-672)
KINEDYNE LLC (HQ)
3040 Us Highway 22 # 150 (08876-3594)
PHONE..............................908 231-1800
James M Klausmann, *President*
Robert L Chamberlin, *Exec VP*
James M Klausmann II, *Exec VP*
Stephen Tucker, *Plant Mgr*
Jason Lueck, *Engineer*
▲ **EMP:** 12
SALES (est): 71.2MM **Privately Held**
WEB: www.kinedyne.com
SIC: 3714 Motor vehicle parts & acces-
sories

(G-673)
LABERN MACHINE PRODUCTS LLC
Also Called: Labern Realty
3388 Us Highway 22 (08876-3500)
PHONE..............................908 722-1970
Lawrence Remaly, *Mng Member*
EMP: 8
SQ FT: 22,000
SALES (est): 726K **Privately Held**
SIC: 3451 Screw machine products

(G-674)
LIFECELL CORPORATION
220 Evans Way Ste 3 (08876-3880)
PHONE..............................908 947-1100
Doris Admin, *Branch Mgr*
EMP: 5 **Privately Held**
SIC: 2836 Biological products, except diag-
nostic
HQ: Lifecell Corporation
1 Millennium Way
Branchburg NJ 08876
908 947-1100

(G-675)
LIFECELL CORPORATION (DH)
1 Millennium Way (08876-3876)
PHONE..............................908 947-1100
Fax: 908 947-1200
Lisa Colleran, *President*
Dianna D Bellavance, *Regional Mgr*
Joe Parella, *Project Mgr*
Richard Maliszewski, *Prdtn Mgr*
Susan Wolf, *Facilities Mgr*
▲ **EMP:** 218
SQ FT: 120,000
SALES: 428MM **Privately Held**
WEB: www.lifecell.com
SIC: 2836 Biological products, except diag-
nostic
HQ: Allergan, Inc.
5 Giralda Farms
Madison NJ 07940
862 261-7000

(G-676)
LUCIANO PACKAGING TECHNOLOGIES
29 County Line Rd (08876-3417)
PHONE..............................908 722-3222
Fax: 908 722-5005
Lawrence Luciano, *President*
Howard Leary, *Vice Pres*
Nancy Smith, *Manager*
EMP: 7
SQ FT: 10,000
SALES (est): 1.4MM **Privately Held**
WEB: www.lucianopackaging.com
SIC: 1796 3565 3742 Machinery installa-
tion; packaging machinery; industry spe-
cialist consultants

(G-677)
LYLE/CARLSTROM ASSOCIATES INC
131 Chambers Brook Rd (08876-3587)
P.O. Box 9, Far Hills (07931-0009)
PHONE..............................908 526-2270
William Carlstrom, *President*
Kimberly Carlstrom, *Exec VP*
Clifford Fisher, *Vice Pres*
Doug Wayner, *Vice Pres*
EMP: 25
SQ FT: 23,000
SALES (est): 2.7MM **Privately Held**
SIC: 2541 2542 Store fixtures, wood; dis-
play fixtures, wood; fixtures, store: except
wood; fixtures: display, office or store: ex-
cept wood

(G-678)
MARCOLIN USA EYEWEAR CORP (DH)
Also Called: Viva International Group
3140 Rte 22 (08876-3548)
P.O. Box 1276, Somerville (08876-1276)
PHONE..............................800 345-8482
Fax: 908 595-6255
Giovanni Zoppas, *CEO*
Sabrizio Gamberini, *CEO*
Vittorio Levi, *Chairman*
Ken Liming, *Senior VP*
John Hecker, *Warehouse Mgr*
◆ **EMP:** 87
SQ FT: 150,000
SALES (est): 98.7MM **Privately Held**
WEB: www.vivagroup.com
SIC: 3851 Eyeglasses, lenses & frames
HQ: Marcolin Spa
Zona Industriale Villanova 4
Longarone BL 32013
043 777-7111

(G-679)
MERCK SHARP & DOHME CORP
203 River Rd (08876-3672)
PHONE..............................908 685-3892
Fax: 908 722-7433
Donald Thompson, *Branch Mgr*
EMP: 9
SALES (corp-wide): 40.1B **Publicly Held**
SIC: 2834 Pharmaceutical preparations
HQ: Merck Sharp & Dohme Corp.
2000 Galloping Hill Rd
Kenilworth NJ 07033
908 740-4000

G E O G R A P H I C

(G-680)
MICHAEL GRAPHICS INC
209 Farmsedge Rd (08853-4113)
PHONE..............................732 846-8680
Fax: 732 846-3490
Michael A Caruso Jr, *President*
EMP: 25
SQ FT: 20,000
SALES (est): 3.2MM **Privately Held**
SIC: 2752 2791 2759 Commercial print-
ing, offset; typesetting; commercial print-
ing

(G-681)
MID OCEAN PARTNERS
Also Called: Agilex Flavors & Fragrances
130 Industrial Pkwy (08876-6004)
PHONE..............................908 707-0100
Fax: 908 963-1584
Kevin Gilbert, *Opers Mgr*
Rick Etter, *Director*
EMP: 90 EST: 2013
SQ FT: 30,000
SALES (est): 8.6MM **Privately Held**
SIC: 2844 Toilet preparations

(G-682)
**NEXT MEDICAL PRODUCTS
LLC**
45 Columbia Rd (08876-3518)
P.O. Box 5148, North Branch (08876-1302)
PHONE..............................908 722-4549
Mary Schlosser, *Engineer*
Dick Smith, *Sales Staff*
John Buday, *Director*
Julia Jacobson,
EMP: 11
SALES (est): 990K **Privately Held**
SIC: 3841 Surgical & medical instruments

(G-683)
NJRLS ENTERPRISES INC
Also Called: R L S Enterprises
3380 Us Highway 22 3a (08876-4000)
PHONE..............................732 846-6010
Fax: 732 846-6012
Richard L Stecklow, *President*
▲ EMP: 12
SQ FT: 10,000
SALES: 3MM **Privately Held**
SIC: 3565 Packaging machinery

(G-684)
**ONGUARD FENCE SYSTEMS
LTD**
18 Culnen Dr (08876-5400)
PHONE..............................908 429-5522
Fax: 908 429-9933
Jinshan Gao, *Ch of Bd*
Thomas Chen, *President*
Karen Gao, *Vice Pres*
Thomas Roche, *Vice Pres*
Sui Ouyang, *Engineer*
▲ EMP: 30
SQ FT: 68,000
SALES (est): 5.8MM **Privately Held**
SIC: 3089 Fences, gates & accessories:
plastic

(G-685)
**ONGUARD FENCE SYSTEMS
LTD**
18 Culnen Dr (08876-5400)
PHONE..............................908 429-5522
EMP: 30
SQ FT: 27,000
SALES (est): 5MM **Privately Held**
SIC: 3089 Mfg Plastic Products
HQ: Crystal Window & Door Systems, Ltd.
3110 Whitestone Expy
Flushing NY 11354
718 961-7300

(G-686)
PARADISE BARXON CORP
Also Called: Symtech Enterprise Intl
185 Industrial Pkwy Ste H (08876-3484)
PHONE..............................908 707-9141
Fax: 908 707-1966
Yeong Lim, *President*
Yatinkumar Patel, *Admin Sec*
EMP: 4
SQ FT: 3,000

SALES (est): 68.1K **Privately Held**
WEB: www.pbcus.com
SIC: 3577 Decoders, computer peripheral
equipment; bar code (magnetic ink) printers; optical scanning devices

(G-687)
**PARKER ACQUISITION GROUP
INC (PA)**
25 Imclone Dr (08876-3903)
P.O. Box 1299, Somerville (08876-1299)
PHONE..............................908 707-4900
Philip M Lapin, *President*
Howard Jacobs, *Director*
David Lowenstein, *Director*
EMP: 1
SQ FT: 55,000
SALES (est): 57.8MM **Privately Held**
SIC: 3861 Photographic equipment & sup-
plies

(G-688)
PEGASUS PRODUCTS INC
19 Readington Rd (08876-3568)
PHONE..............................908 707-1122
Frank Patel, *President*
Roshan Patel, *Cust Mgr*
Sandy Wolwitz, *Manager*
EMP: 40 EST: 1982
SQ FT: 49,900
SALES (est): 6.8MM **Privately Held**
SIC: 3081 Unsupported plastics film &
sheet

(G-689)
PHOENIX CHEMICAL INC
151 Industrial Pkwy (08876-3451)
PHONE..............................908 707-0232
John Imperante, *President*
Carol Horn, *Research*
John Gray, *Regl Sales Mgr*
Sandy Imperante, *Executive*
Phyllis Sica, *Admin Sec*
▲ EMP: 13
SALES (est): 4MM **Privately Held**
WEB: www.phoenix-chem.com
SIC: 2869 Amines, acids, salts, esters; es-
ters of phthalic anhydride

(G-690)
PLASTI FOAM
Also Called: Structural Foam Plastics
68 County Line Rd (08876-3467)
PHONE..............................908 722-5254
Fax: 908 722-7457
Auto Delbro, *Partner*
John Rosania, *Partner*
William S Rosania, *Partner*
EMP: 80
SQ FT: 89,000
SALES (est): 6.5MM **Privately Held**
WEB: www.plastifoam.com
SIC: 3086 Plastics foam products

(G-691)
**POLYCEL STRUCTURAL FOAM
INC**
68 County Line Rd (08876-3467)
PHONE..............................908 722-5254
Kurt Joeger, *Principal*
Otto D Prado, *Principal*
Ayman Sawaged, *Opers Mgr*
Jeremy Geller, *Senior Engr*
Jenny Decker, *Controller*
EMP: 90
SQ FT: 60,000
SALES (est): 17.7K **Privately Held**
SIC: 3089 Injection molding of plastics;
pallets, plastic

(G-692)
**POLYCEL STRUCTURAL FOAM
INC**
68 County Line Rd (08876-3467)
PHONE..............................908 722-5254
Kurt Joerger, *CEO*
Ayman Sawaged, *President*
▲ EMP: 29
SALES: 10.5MM **Privately Held**
WEB: www.polycel.com
SIC: 3089 Injection molding of plastics;
pallets, plastic

(G-693)
PRECISION GRAPHICS INC
21 County Line Rd (08876-3417)
PHONE..............................908 707-8880
Robert T Weissman, *President*
David Weisman, *Vice Pres*
Elaine Arnold, *Sales Staff*
▲ EMP: 58
SQ FT: 25,000
SALES (est): 16.5MM **Privately Held**
SIC: 3672 7389 Circuit boards, television
& radio printed; design, commercial & in-
dustrial

(G-694)
PRO-PACK CORP
160 Meister Ave Ste 18 (08876-3474)
PHONE..............................908 725-5000
Fax: 908 725-6696
Gary Glassman, *President*
EMP: 8
SQ FT: 2,500
SALES (est): 1.1MM **Privately Held**
SIC: 3993 5199 7311 Signs & advertising
specialties; advertising specialties; adver-
tising agencies; advertising consultant

(G-695)
**PURE TECH INTERNATIONAL
INC**
3040 Us Highway 22 # 130 (08876-3594)
PHONE..............................908 722-4968
EMP: 9
SALES (corp-wide): 1B **Privately Held**
SIC: 3052 Garden hose, plastic
HQ: Pure Tech International, Inc.
201 Industrial Pkwy
Branchburg NJ 08876

(G-696)
**PURE TECH INTERNATIONAL
INC (HQ)**
201 Industrial Pkwy (08876-3449)
PHONE..............................908 722-4800
Kenneth Baker, *President*
▲ EMP: 1
SQ FT: 9,900
SALES (est): 35.6MM
SALES (corp-wide): 1B **Privately Held**
SIC: 3052 3082 2821 3089 Garden hose,
plastic; tubes, unsupported plastic; ther-
moplastic materials; vinyl resins; polyvinyl
chloride resins (PVC); injection molding of
plastics; recycling, waste materials
PA: Tekni-Plex, Inc.
460 E Swedesford Rd # 3000
Wayne PA 19087
484 690-1520

(G-697)
**RATHGIBSON NORTH BRANCH
LLC**
100 Aspen Hill Rd (08876-3563)
PHONE..............................908 253-3260
Mike Schwartz, *Mng Member*
Jeff Nelb,
▲ EMP: 180 EST: 2010
SQ FT: 250,000
SALES (est): 173.4MM
SALES (corp-wide): 242.1B **Publicly
Held**
SIC: 3317 Tubing, mechanical or hypoder-
mic sizes: cold drawn stainless
HQ: Rathgibson Holding Co Llc
2505 Foster Ave
Janesville WI 53545

(G-698)
REBTEX INC
40 Industrial Pkwy (08876-6027)
PHONE..............................908 722-3549
Fax: 908 722-8150
Robert P Brandell, *President*
Thomas G Brandell, *Vice Pres*
Michele Senatore, *Admin Sec*
EMP: 110
SQ FT: 108,000
SALES (est): 18.8MM **Privately Held**
WEB: www.rebtex.com
SIC: 2258 2261 Dyeing & finishing lace
goods & warp knit fabric; dyeing cotton
broadwoven fabrics

(G-699)
RED RAY MANUFACTURING
10 County Line Rd Ste 3 (08876-6008)
PHONE..............................908 722-0040
Bannos Thomas, *President*
EMP: 4 EST: 2013
SALES (est): 270K **Privately Held**
SIC: 3999 Manufacturing industries

(G-700)
**ROCHE DIAGNOSTICS
CORPORATION**
1080 Us Highway 202 S (08876-3771)
PHONE..............................908 253-0707
Fax: 908 253-7833
Piyathida Katapituk, *Manager*
Michael Groel, *Manager*
David Hall, *Manager*
EMP: 17
SALES (corp-wide): 53.9B **Publicly Held**
SIC: 3826 Analytical instruments
HQ: Roche Diagnostics Corporation
9115 Hague Rd
Indianapolis IN 46256
800 428-5076

(G-701)
**SANDER MECHANICAL SERVICE
INC**
Also Called: Honeywell Authorized Dealer
55 Columbia Rd (08876-3518)
PHONE..............................732 560-0600
Fax: 908 560-5757
Robert J Bittel, *President*
Robert Vessie, *Director*
EMP: 40 EST: 1965
SALES (est): 11.9MM **Privately Held**
WEB: www.sanmec.com
SIC: 1711 3585 Mechanical contractor;
heating & air conditioning combination
units

(G-702)
SAVOURY SYSTEMS INTL INC
230 Industrial Pkwy Ste C (08876-3580)
P.O. Box 5487, North Branch (08876-1305)
PHONE..............................908 526-2524
David Adams, *President*
Elizabeth Adams, *Vice Pres*
Alex Carillo, *Opers Staff*
Patrick Barrett, *Finance*
Kevin McDermott, *Sales Mgr*
▲ EMP: 19
SQ FT: 28,000
SALES (est): 6.7MM **Privately Held**
WEB: www.savourysystems.com
SIC: 5149 2087 Flavourings & fragrances;
natural & organic foods; concentrates, fla-
voring (except drink)

(G-703)
**SCHUTZ CONTAINER SYSTEMS
INC (DH)**
200 Aspen Hill Rd (08876-3564)
P.O. Box 5950, North Branch (08876-5950)
PHONE..............................908 429-1637
Fax: 908 526-0550
Frederick Wenzel, *President*
David Farenden, *Plant Mgr*
John Cunningham, *Purchasing*
Ian Miller, *Financial Exec*
Nipa Patel, *Financial Analy*
▲ EMP: 75
SQ FT: 76,000
SALES (est): 173.6MM **Privately Held**
SIC: 2655 Fiber cans, drums & containers;
containers, laminated phenolic & vulcan-
ized fiber; drums, fiber: made from pur-
chased material

(G-704)
SCHUTZ CORP (HQ)
200 Aspen Hill Rd (08876-3564)
P.O. Box 5950, North Branch (08876-5950)
PHONE..............................908 526-6161
Udo Schutz, *Ch of Bd*
Peter Schafer, *President*
Gordon Sanderson, *General Mgr*
Joseph Allen, *Purch Mgr*
Harry Kaiser, *Purchasing*
◆ EMP: 90
SQ FT: 76,000
SALES (est): 173.6MM **Privately Held**
SIC: 2655 Fiber cans, drums & similar
products

▲ = Import ▼=Export
◆ =Import/Export

PA: Schutz-Werke Gmbh & Co. Kg
Schutzstr. 12
Selters (Westerwald)
262 677-0

(G-705)
SPECIFIED TECHNOLOGIES INC
Also Called: STI
210 Evans Way (08876-3767)
PHONE....................................908 526-8000
Fax: 908 526-9623
Charbel H Tagher, *President*
Jason Nappi, *Editor*
Joel Campbell, *Regional Mgr*
John Hurley, *Regional Mgr*
Chua Kiang, *Regional Mgr*
◆ **EMP:** 150
SQ FT: 35,000
SALES (est): 48.3MM **Privately Held**
WEB: www.stifirestop.com
SIC: 3569 Firefighting apparatus & related
equipment

(G-706)
SUPERIOR TOOL & MFG CO
42 Columbia Rd Ste 2 (08876-3582)
PHONE....................................908 526-9011
Fax: 908 526-5058
Edward Braunig, *President*
EMP: 8 **EST:** 1959
SQ FT: 11,000
SALES (est): 1.1MM **Privately Held**
WEB: www.superiortoolonline.com
SIC: 3599 Machine shop, jobbing & repair

(G-707)
SYMRISE INC
180 Industrial Pkwy (08876-3452)
PHONE....................................908 429-6824
Fredrick Thor, *Branch Mgr*
EMP: 75
SALES (corp-wide): 3.5B **Privately Held**
SIC: 2869 Perfume materials, synthetic
HQ: Symrise Inc.
300 North St
Teterboro NJ 07608
201 288-3200

(G-708)
**TAYLOR FORGE STAINLESS
INC**
22 Readington Rd (08876-3521)
P.O. Box 610, Somerville (08876-0610)
PHONE....................................908 722-1313
Fax: 908 722-2943
Jim Takacs, *Vice Pres*
George A Guarino, *Vice Pres*
Kim Kanopka, *Vice Pres*
Joseph Del, *Warehouse Mgr*
Tim Kanopka, *Purch Dir*
EMP: 100
SQ FT: 80,000
SALES (est): 22.1MM **Privately Held**
SIC: 3494 5085 Pipe fittings; valves & fit-
tings

(G-709)
TEE-RIFIC GOLF CENTER
3091 Us Highway 22 (08876-3528)
PHONE....................................908 253-9300
EMP: 10
SALES (est): 891.3K **Privately Held**
SIC: 3949 Mfg Sporting/Athletic Goods

(G-710)
TEKNI-PLEX INC
Also Called: Dolco Packaging
201 Industrial Pkwy (08876-3449)
PHONE....................................908 575-7661
Fax: 908 722-4967
John Kratins, *Plant Mgr*
Clark Baubles, *Purch Agent*
Sherry Sternberg, *Purch Agent*
Stephen Schweitzer, *Accountant*
John Brak, *Marketing Mgr*
EMP: 200
SALES (corp-wide): 1B **Privately Held**
SIC: 2679 3089 3081 Egg cartons,
molded pulp: made from purchased mate-
rial; blister or bubble formed packaging,
plastic; packing materials, plastic sheet
PA: Tekni-Plex, Inc.
460 E Swedesford Rd # 3000
Wayne PA 19087
484 690-1520

(G-711)
**TOP SAFETY PRODUCTS
COMPANY**
Also Called: Calgonate
160 Meister Ave Ste 16 (08876-3474)
PHONE....................................908 707-8680
Fax: 908 707-8326
Gerald P Kutsop, *President*
Ken Kallish, *General Mgr*
Marianne Melton, *Info Tech Mgr*
Joe Kutsop, *Sr Consultant*
EMP: 14
SQ FT: 10,000
SALES (est): 2MM **Privately Held**
SIC: 3842 First aid, snake bite & burn kits

(G-712)
TRIAD TOOL & DIE CO
9 Commerce St (08876-6039)
PHONE....................................908 534-1784
Fax: 908 534-1802
Eric P Wichelhaus, *President*
Margaret Hurley, *Corp Secy*
George Romanella, *Mfg Mgr*
Justine Caleca, *Purchasing*
John Van Prooien, *QA Dir*
EMP: 60 **EST:** 1933
SQ FT: 11,000
SALES (est): 4.8MM **Privately Held**
WEB: www.triadtool.com
SIC: 3599 Machine shop, jobbing & repair

(G-713)
**TRIMLINE MEDICAL PRODUCTS
CORP**
34 Columbia Rd (08876-3519)
P.O. Box 220, Skaneateles Falls NY
(13153-0220)
PHONE....................................908 429-0590
Fax: 908 429-0536
Richard Jacobson, *President*
Paul Vonderheyden, *Vice Pres*
▲ **EMP:** 152
SQ FT: 30,000
SALES (est): 8.6MM
SALES (corp-wide): 2.7B **Publicly Held**
WEB: www.trimlinemed.com
SIC: 3841 Blood pressure apparatus
HQ: Welch Allyn Inc
4341 State Street Rd
Skaneateles Falls NY 13153
315 685-4100

(G-714)
**ULTIMATE TRINING MUNITIONS
INC (PA)**
55 Readington Rd (08876-3542)
PHONE....................................908 725-9000
Maxine Nordmeyer, *President*
Tony Lambraia, *Vice Pres*
Steve Cassidy, *Project Engr*
Jessica Michalak, *Cust Mgr*
Joe Overstreet, *Manager*
◆ **EMP:** 32
SALES (est): 5.8MM **Privately Held**
SIC: 5941 3949 Ammunition; shooting
equipment & supplies, general

(G-715)
**VANDERMARK MERRITT GL
STUDIOS**
1 D Angelo Dr (08876-5464)
PHONE....................................908 231-8189
Douglas Merritt, *President*
Steven Smarr, *Vice Pres*
Theodore Merritt, *Treasurer*
▲ **EMP:** 5
SALES (est): 505.7K **Privately Held**
WEB: www.vandermarkmerrittglass.com
SIC: 3229 Glassware, art or decorative

(G-716)
VIS USA LLC
210 Meister Ave (08876-6046)
PHONE....................................908 575-0606
Rene Morph,
▲ **EMP:** 11
SQ FT: 20,000
SALES (est): 920K **Privately Held**
SIC: 3496 Conveyor belts

(G-717)
VIVA INTERNATIONAL INC
Also Called: Viva International Group
3140 Route 22 (08876-3548)
P.O. Box 1275, Somerville (08876-1275)
PHONE....................................908 595-6200
Fabrizio Gamberini, *President*
Donna Harding, *Credit Mgr*
◆ **EMP:** 300
SALES (est): 26.5MM **Privately Held**
SIC: 3851 Eyeglasses, lenses & frames
HQ: Marcolin U.S.A., Inc.
3140 Us Highway 22
Branchburg NJ 08876
800 345-8482

(G-718)
**WOLOCK & LOTT
TRANSMISSION EQP**
25 Chambers Brook Rd (08876-3552)
P.O. Box 5323, North Branch (08876-1303)
PHONE....................................908 218-9292
Fax: 908 218-9868
Richard W Palmer, *President*
J Robert Layman, *Corp Secy*
EMP: 19
SQ FT: 16,000
SALES (est): 6.4MM **Privately Held**
WEB: www.wolocklott.com
SIC: 5063 3612 Transformers & transmis-
sion equipment; transmission & distribu-
tion voltage regulators

(G-719)
WORLD WIDE METRIC INC (PA)
37 Readington Rd (08876-3542)
P.O. Box 5267, North Branch (08876-1303)
PHONE....................................732 247-2300
George Contos, *CEO*
Theo Contos, *President*
Gary Contos, *Admin Sec*
▲ **EMP:** 15
SQ FT: 40,000
SALES (est): 18MM **Privately Held**
WEB: www.worldwidemetric.com
SIC: 5088 3494 Marine supplies; valves &
pipe fittings

(G-720)
ZAHK SALES INC
1405 Boxwood Dr (08876-3674)
PHONE....................................516 633-9179
Husein Kermalli, *President*
EMP: 4
SALES (est): 330K **Privately Held**
SIC: 2821 Plastics materials & resins

(G-721)
**ZEUS INDUSTRIAL PRODUCTS
INC**
134 Chubb Way (08876-3935)
P.O. Box 298, Raritan (08869-0298)
PHONE....................................908 292-6500
Fax: 908 526-5699
Roger Jones, *Director*
EMP: 200
SALES (corp-wide): 258.6MM **Privately
Held**
WEB: www.zeusinc.com
SIC: 3082 Unsupported plastics profile
shapes; tubes, unsupported plastic
PA: Zeus Industrial Products, Inc.
620 Magnolia St
Orangeburg SC 29115
803 531-2174

(G-722)
ZEUS SCIENTIFIC INC
200 Evans Way (08876-3767)
P.O. Box 38, Raritan (08869-0038)
PHONE....................................908 526-3744
Fax: 908 526-2058
Scott Tourville, *CEO*
John Tourville, *COO*
▲ **EMP:** 85 **EST:** 1976
SQ FT: 22,000
SALES (est): 12.5MM **Privately Held**
WEB: www.zeussci.com
SIC: 3841 Diagnostic apparatus, medical

(G-723)
ZZYZX LLC
Also Called: Iniven
5 Columbia Rd (08876-3518)
PHONE....................................908 722-3770

Marc Benou, *President*
EMP: 7 **EST:** 2015
SALES (est): 380.6K **Privately Held**
SIC: 3661 3663 Fiber optics communica-
tions equipment; telemetering equipment,
electronic

Branchville
Sussex County

(G-724)
**ADVANCE PROCESS SYSTEMS
LIM**
130 Gunn Rd (07826-4167)
PHONE....................................201 400-9190
Thomas Todaro, *Manager*
Mark Tarby, *Manager*
EMP: 9
SALES (est): 557.8K **Privately Held**
SIC: 8748 3559 3324 3356 Systems
analysis & engineering consulting serv-
ices; systems engineering consultant, ex.
computer or professional; semiconductor
manufacturing machinery; aerospace in-
vestment castings, ferrous; titanium & tita-
nium alloy: rolling, drawing or extruding

(G-725)
ALECTO SYSTEMS LLC
130 Gunn Rd (07826-4167)
P.O. Box 2976, North Canton OH (44720-
0976)
PHONE....................................973 875-6721
Thomas J Todaro,
EMP: 9
SQ FT: 1,200
SALES (est): 916.4K **Privately Held**
SIC: 3677 8711 Inductors, electronic; engi-
neering services

(G-726)
**BEHRINGER FLUID SYSTEMS
INC**
17 Ridge Rd (07826-4363)
PHONE....................................973 948-0226
Shawn Fantry, *Principal*
EMP: 5
SALES (est): 497.5K **Privately Held**
SIC: 3677 Electronic coils, transformers &
other inductors

(G-727)
BRANCHVILLE BAGELS INC
332 Us Highway 206 N (07826-5086)
P.O. Box 296 (07826-0296)
PHONE....................................973 948-7077
Ricardo Rodregus, *Partner*
Ramon Rogriguez, *Partner*
EMP: 4
SALES (est): 467.2K **Privately Held**
SIC: 5411 5461 2051 Delicatessens;
bagels; bagels, fresh or frozen

(G-728)
**CONCRETE STONE & TILE
CORP (PA)**
Also Called: C S T Pavers
17 Ridge Rd (07826-4366)
P.O. Box 2191 (07826-2191)
PHONE....................................973 948-7193
Fax: 973 948-2771
Ronald Krueger, *President*
Joe Salerno, *General Mgr*
Carey Krueger, *Vice Pres*
Mariusz Rudy, *Plant Mgr*
Vinny Behnke, *Opers Mgr*
▲ **EMP:** 50
SQ FT: 25,000
SALES (est): 9.4MM **Privately Held**
WEB: www.cstpavers.com
SIC: 3272 Paving materials, prefabricated
concrete

(G-729)
**CUSTOM METERING COMPANY
INC**
36 Mattison Ave (07826-4354)
P.O. Box 696, Sparta (07871-0696)
PHONE....................................973 946-4195
Robert Ehling, *CEO*
EMP: 2

GEOGRAPHIC

SALES: 1MM Privately Held
SIC: 3825 Meters: electric, pocket, portable, panelboard, etc.

(G-730)
GEORGES WINE AND SPIRITS GALLE
7 Main St (07826-5526)
PHONE..................973 948-9950
George Delgado, *President*
EMP: 4
SALES (est): 635.6K Privately Held
SIC: 5921 5411 5812 2026 Wine; wine & beer; grocery stores, independent; caterers; farmers' cheese; fresh fruits & vegetables

(G-731)
HB TECHNIK USA LTD LBLTY PRTNR
99 George Hill Rd (07826-4311)
PHONE..................973 875-8688
Sharon Peham, *Principal*
▲ **EMP: 8**
SALES (est): 650K Privately Held
SIC: 2499 Bakers' equipment, wood

(G-732)
R & R DISTRIBUTORS INC
Also Called: Mat
18 Summit Dr (07826-4410)
PHONE..................201 804-0077
Fax: 201 804-8068
Robert Cline, *President*
EMP: 6
SQ FT: 20,000
SALES (est): 1.2MM Privately Held
WEB: www.rjcstudios.com
SIC: 3944 Electronic toys

Brick
Ocean County

(G-733)
AMERICAN RAIL COMPANY INC
1133 Industrial Pkwy B (08724-2582)
P.O. Box 790 (08723-0790)
PHONE..................732 785-1110
Fax: 732 785-0501
Charles Montanye Jr, *President*
EMP: 15 EST: 1998
SALES (est): 1.3MM Privately Held
WEB: www.americanrail.com
SIC: 3743 Railroad locomotives & parts, electric or nonelectric

(G-734)
ANCHOR CONCRETE PRODUCTS INC
975 Burnt Tavern Rd (08724-2003)
PHONE..................732 458-9440
Fax: 732 458-1086
EMP: 70
SALES (corp-wide): 23.5B Privately Held
SIC: 3271 5032 Mfg Of Masonry Blocks And Concrete Slabs
HQ: Anchor Concrete Products, Inc
331 Newman Springs Rd # 236
Red Bank NJ 07701
732 292-2648

(G-735)
AUTOMATED TAPPING SYSTEMS INC
22 Davos Rd (08724-4306)
PHONE..................732 899-2282
Fax: 732 899-0277
William R Pfister, *President*
Craig Wood, *Plant Supt*
EMP: 12
SQ FT: 1,800
SALES: 1.1MM Privately Held
WEB: www.automatedtappingsystems.com
SIC: 3545 3541 Machine tool attachments & accessories; taps, machine tool; machine tools, metal cutting type

(G-736)
CHARLES F KILIAN
Also Called: Essential Machining
682 Rolling Hills Ct (08724-1177)
PHONE..................732 458-3554

Fax: 732 840-5264
Charles Killian, *Owner*
Charles Kilian, *Owner*
EMP: 4 EST: 1966
SQ FT: 5,500
SALES (est): 190K Privately Held
SIC: 3599 3541 Machine shop, jobbing & repair; machine tools, metal cutting type

(G-737)
CNO CORPORATION
Also Called: Floors At Home
611 Yellowbrick Rd (08724-3335)
P.O. Box 936, Point Pleasant Boro (08742-0936)
PHONE..................732 785-5799
Tom Ciano, *Owner*
EMP: 4
SALES (est): 78.9K Privately Held
SIC: 2273 Carpets & rugs

(G-738)
CONSTRUCTION DYNAMICS INC
Also Called: Silvi Concrete of Brick
1381 Sally Ike Rd (08724-1056)
PHONE..................732 840-7766
John Silvi, *President*
EMP: 15
SALES (corp-wide): 24.5MM Privately Held
SIC: 1771 3273 Concrete work; ready-mixed concrete
PA: Construction Dynamics, Inc.
355 Newbold Rd
Fairless Hills PA 19030
215 295-0777

(G-739)
CORIM INTERNATIONAL COFFEE IMP (PA)
Also Called: Corim Industries
1112 Industrial Pkwy (08724-2508)
PHONE..................800 942-4201
Fax: 732 840-1608
Sam Teren, *CEO*
Rame Teren, *President*
Natan Teren, *Treasurer*
▲ **EMP: 78**
SALES (est): 22.8MM Privately Held
WEB: www.corimindustries.com
SIC: 2095 Roasted coffee

(G-740)
CREATIVE DESSERTS
42 Capri Dr (08723-7633)
PHONE..................732 477-0808
Michael Daskalovitz, *President*
EMP: 4
SQ FT: 100
SALES (est): 421.5K Privately Held
WEB: www.creativedesserts.com
SIC: 2051 Bakery: wholesale or wholesale/retail combined

(G-741)
CRH AMERICAS INC
Also Called: Oldcastle Apg Northeast
975 Burnt Tavern Rd (08724-2003)
PHONE..................908 475-1225
Larry Ahlers, *Branch Mgr*
EMP: 5
SALES (corp-wide): 29.7B Privately Held
SIC: 3273 Ready-mixed concrete
HQ: Crh Americas, Inc.
3 Glenlake Pkwy Ste 12
Sandy Springs GA 30328
770 804-3363

(G-742)
EAST COAST STORAGE EQP CO INC (PA)
Also Called: Ecseco
620 Burtis St (08723-5559)
PHONE..................732 451-1316
Audra J Parisis, *President*
John Geddes, *Sales Staff*
Javier Ramirez, *Director*
Paul Parisi, *Business Dir*
Sidney Smith,
EMP: 20
SQ FT: 15,000

SALES (est): 2.9MM Privately Held
WEB: www.eastcoaststorageequipment.com
SIC: 2542 2541 8711 5084 Racks, merchandise display or storage: except wood; garment racks, wood; structural engineering; conveyor systems; steel building construction; structural steel erection

(G-743)
EASTERN REGIONAL WATERWAY
2316 2nd Ave (08723)
PHONE..................732 684-0409
John Okinsky,
EMP: 10 EST: 2014
SALES (est): 642.9K Privately Held
SIC: 3489 Ordnance & accessories

(G-744)
GANGI GRAPHICS INC
1669 Route 88 (08724-3050)
PHONE..................732 840-8680
Fax: 732 840-7665
John Gangi, *President*
Michael Gangi, *Vice Pres*
Paul Gangi, *CFO*
EMP: 7
SALES: 750K Privately Held
WEB: www.gangigraphics.com
SIC: 7336 2752 2791 Graphic arts & related design; commercial printing, offset; typesetting

(G-745)
H & R WELDING LLC
307 Drum Point Rd (08723-6831)
PHONE..................732 920-4881
Fax: 732 920-6466
Robert Hager, *Partner*
Jason Hager, *Partner*
Justin Hager, *Partner*
EMP: 8
SQ FT: 2,000
SALES (est): 1.6MM Privately Held
SIC: 3325 Steel foundries

(G-746)
J A M I ENTERPRISE INC
Also Called: J E I
1129 Industrial Pkwy A (08724-2589)
PHONE..................732 714-6811
Michael Herman, *President*
Jamie Herman, *Vice Pres*
EMP: 4
SALES: 500K Privately Held
SIC: 3679 Electronic circuits

(G-747)
J C ORTHOPEDIC INC
1680 Route 88 (08724-3051)
PHONE..................732 458-7900
Fax: 732 458-7902
Frank Digironomo, *President*
▲ **EMP: 6**
SALES (est): 844.8K Privately Held
SIC: 3842 5999 Orthopedic appliances; orthopedic & prosthesis applications

(G-748)
JERSEY SHORE PUBLICATIONS
Also Called: Jersey Shore Vacation Magazine
749 Bay Ave (08724-4809)
PHONE..................732 892-1276
George Valente, *Owner*
EMP: 8
SALES (est): 46.3K Privately Held
WEB: www.jerseyshorevacation.com
SIC: 2741 Guides: publishing & printing

(G-749)
JOSANTOS CNSTR & DEV LLC
13 Riverview Dr (08723-5752)
PHONE..................732 202-7389
Joe Santos,
EMP: 6 EST: 2008
SALES (est): 611.9K Privately Held
SIC: 3271 1521 Blocks, concrete: landscape or retaining wall; single-family housing construction; patio & deck construction & repair; new construction, single-family houses

(G-750)
LEGGETT & PLATT INCORPORATED
17 Sandy Point Dr (08723-5831)
PHONE..................904 786-0750
Fax: 973 824-0045
EMP: 81
SALES (corp-wide): 3.9B Publicly Held
SIC: 2515 2392 Mfg Mattresses/Bedsprings Mfg Household Furnishings
PA: Leggett & Platt, Incorporated
1 Leggett Rd
Carthage MO 64836
417 358-8131

(G-751)
MARINER SALES AND POWER INC (PA)
Also Called: Marine East
834 Mantoloking Rd (08723-5239)
PHONE..................732 477-7484
Fax: 732 477-4848
David M Thompson, *President*
Barb Thompson, *Vice Pres*
EMP: 8
SQ FT: 7,000
SALES: 2MM Privately Held
WEB: www.marineeast.com
SIC: 3429 Marine hardware

(G-752)
MARKETING ADMINISTRATION ASSOC
Also Called: Milltex Manufacturing
1101 Industrial Pkwy (08724-2507)
PHONE..................732 840-3021
Fax: 732 840-3021
Martin Metzger, *President*
EMP: 5
SQ FT: 3,600
SALES (est): 650K Privately Held
SIC: 5023 2392 Decorative home furnishings & supplies; blankets, comforters & beddings

(G-753)
MASSAGE CHAIR INC
1692 Route 88 Ste 1 (08724-3014)
PHONE..................732 201-7777
Nicholas Fahmie, *President*
EMP: 4
SALES (est): 125.1K Privately Held
SIC: 3999 Manufacturing industries

(G-754)
PARAMOUNT PRODUCTS CO INC
1104 Industrial Pkwy (08724-2508)
PHONE..................732 458-9200
Fax: 732 458-3942
Harold C Vogel Jr, *President*
EMP: 14 EST: 1946
SQ FT: 2,500
SALES (est): 1.4MM Privately Held
SIC: 3469 Stamping metal for the trade

(G-755)
PLASTIC BY ALL LLC
1127 Industrial Pkwy B (08724-2588)
PHONE..................732 785-5900
Wayne Marz, *President*
EMP: 4
SALES (est): 484.9K Privately Held
SIC: 2295 Resin or plastic coated fabrics

(G-756)
RAYGE CANDY CO
11 Beverly Beach Rd (08724-1305)
PHONE..................732 458-2179
Fax: 732 458-1363
George V Erickson, *President*
Lois Erickson, *Corp Secy*
Barbara Angelis, *Vice Pres*
Debbie Kroessig, *Sls & Mktg Exec*
Debbi Smith, *Manager*
EMP: 13
SQ FT: 10,000
SALES: 2MM Privately Held
SIC: 2064 Candy & other confectionery products

▲ = Import ▼=Export
◆ =Import/Export

(G-757)
RUSSO SEAMLESS GUTTER LLC
45 Cherie Dr (08724-8120)
PHONE..............................732 836-0151
Salvator Russo,
EMP: 4
SALES: 87K **Privately Held**
SIC: 3089 Gutters (glass fiber reinforced), fiberglass or plastic

(G-758)
SCORPION CHARTERS SPT FISHING
401 Valley Way (08723-4913)
PHONE..............................732 477-0985
Ray Mumbelardi, *Owner*
EMP: 4
SALES (est): 160K **Privately Held**
SIC: 3732 Fishing boats: lobster, crab, oyster, etc.: small

(G-759)
SEA HABOR MARINE INC
310 Firehouse Rd (08723-6880)
PHONE..............................732 477-8577
Frank Cannella, *President*
EMP: 4
SALES (est): 405.1K **Privately Held**
SIC: 3441 Fabricated structural metal for ships

(G-760)
TERRESTRIAL IMAGING LLC
375 Herbertsville Rd (08724-1636)
PHONE..............................800 359-0530
Christopher Lopresti,
Mike Lopresti,
EMP: 6 **EST:** 2015
SALES (est): 550.2K **Privately Held**
SIC: 3728 Aircraft parts & equipment

Bridgeport
Gloucester County

(G-761)
AMERICAN DAWN INC
520 Pdricktown Rd Ste B (08014)
PHONE..............................856 467-9211
Fax: 856 467-9277
Leslie Sutton, *Principal*
EMP: 9
SALES (corp-wide): 28.5MM **Privately Held**
SIC: 2299 5023 5131 2393 Linen fabrics; linens & towels; textiles, woven; cushions, except spring & carpet: purchased materials; pillows, bed: made from purchased materials
PA: American Dawn, Inc.
    401 W Artesia Blvd
    Compton CA 90220
    310 223-2000

(G-762)
CHELTEN HOUSE PRODUCTS INC
607 Heron Dr (08014)
P.O. Box 434 (08014-0434)
PHONE..............................856 467-1600
Fax: 856 467-4769
Steven Dabrow, *President*
Jason Dabrow, *COO*
Kenneth Pawloski, *CFO*
▼ **EMP:** 110 **EST:** 1965
SQ FT: 138,000
SALES (est): 39.2MM **Privately Held**
WEB: www.cheltenhouse.com
SIC: 2035 Dressings, salad: raw & cooked (except dry mixes); seasonings & sauces, except tomato & dry

(G-763)
EMERSON AUTOMATION SOLUTIONS
4 Killdeer Ct Ste 200 (08014)
PHONE..............................856 542-5252
Steve Oestereicher, *General Mgr*
EMP: 15
SALES (corp-wide): 15.2B **Publicly Held**
SIC: 3491 7699 Industrial valves; valve repair, industrial

HQ: Emerson Automation Solutions Final Control Us Lp
    10707 Clay Rd Ste 200
    Houston TX 77041

(G-764)
FEDERAL PRETZEL BAKING CO (PA)
300 Eagle Ct (08014)
PHONE..............................215 467-0505
Florence Sciambi, *Trustee*
EMP: 20
SQ FT: 3,700
SALES: 1.2MM **Privately Held**
SIC: 2052 Pretzels

(G-765)
FERRO CORPORATION
170 Route 130 S (08014)
P.O. Box 309 (08014-0309)
PHONE..............................856 467-3000
Steve Wood, *Branch Mgr*
EMP: 135
SALES (corp-wide): 1.4B **Publicly Held**
WEB: www.ferro.com
SIC: 2865 2899 Cyclic crudes & intermediates; chemical preparations
PA: Ferro Corporation
    6060 Parkland Blvd # 250
    Mayfield Heights OH 44124
    216 875-5600

(G-766)
FLOWSERVE CORPORATION
401 Heron Dr (08014)
P.O. Box 563 (08014-0563)
PHONE..............................856 241-7800
Dave Siek, *Manager*
EMP: 60
SALES (corp-wide): 3.6B **Publicly Held**
SIC: 3561 Industrial pumps & parts
PA: Flowserve Corporation
    5215 N Oconnor Blvd Connor
    Irving TX 75039
    972 443-6500

(G-767)
J & J SNACK FOODS CORP
Also Called: Uptown Bakeries
300 Eagle Ct (08014)
PHONE..............................856 467-9552
Tom Hunter, *Principal*
Juan Perez, *Facilities Mgr*
Scott Ambruster, *Purch Mgr*
EMP: 100
SALES (corp-wide): 1B **Publicly Held**
WEB: www.jjsnack.com
SIC: 2053 2087 2086 2024 Frozen bakery products, except bread; syrups, drink; mineral water, carbonated: packaged in cans, bottles, etc.; ices, flavored (frozen dessert); cookies; bread, cake & related products
PA: J & J Snack Foods Corp.
    6000 Central Hwy
    Pennsauken NJ 08109
    856 665-9533

(G-768)
MODINE MANUFACTURING COMPANY
244 High Hills Rd (08014)
P.O. Box 370 (08014-0370)
PHONE..............................856 467-9710
EMP: 6
SALES (corp-wide): 1.3B **Publicly Held**
SIC: 3443 5013 Whol Automotive Radiators
PA: Modine Manufacturing Company Inc
    1500 Dekoven Ave
    Racine WI 53403
    262 636-1200

(G-769)
OMEGA ENGINEERING INC
Also Called: Omega Process Controls
1 Omega Cir (08014)
PHONE..............................856 467-4200
Fax: 856 467-1212
William Keating, *Branch Mgr*
EMP: 200
SALES (corp-wide): 2B **Privately Held**
WEB: www.omega.com
SIC: 3625 3823 Relays & industrial controls; pH instruments, industrial process type

HQ: Omega Engineering, Inc.
    800 Connecticut Ave 5n01
    Norwalk CT 06854
    203 359-1660

(G-770)
POLYMER ADDITIVES INC
Also Called: Valtris Specialty Chemicals
170 Us Route 130 S (08014)
P.O. Box 309 (08014-0309)
PHONE..............................856 467-8247
EMP: 13
SALES (corp-wide): 271.6MM **Privately Held**
SIC: 5169 2899 Chemicals & allied products; chemical preparations; fire retardant chemicals
HQ: Polymer Additives, Inc.
    7500 E Pleasant Valley Rd
    Independence OH 44131
    216 875-7200

(G-771)
SEW-EURODRIVE INC
200 High Hill Rd (08014)
P.O. Box 481 (08014-0481)
PHONE..............................856 467-2277
Fax: 856 845-3179
Scott Bansky, *Opers Mgr*
Michael Zlockie, *Opers Staff*
EMP: 40
SALES (corp-wide): 2.7B **Privately Held**
WEB: www.seweurodrive.com
SIC: 3566 5063 Drives, high speed industrial, except hydrostatic; power transmission equipment, electric
HQ: Sew-Eurodrive, Inc.
    1295 Old Spartanburg Hwy
    Lyman SC 29365
    864 439-7537

(G-772)
SEW-EURODRIVE INC
2107 High Hill Rd (08014)
PHONE..............................856 467-2277
Michael Zlockie, *Branch Mgr*
EMP: 57
SALES (corp-wide): 2.7B **Privately Held**
WEB: www.seweurodrive.com
SIC: 3566 Speed changers, drives & gears
HQ: Sew-Eurodrive, Inc.
    1295 Old Spartanburg Hwy
    Lyman SC 29365
    864 439-7537

(G-773)
STATE TECHNOLOGY INC
610 Pedricktown Rd (08014)
P.O. Box 266 (08014-0266)
PHONE..............................856 467-8009
Fax: 856 467-9481
John Dozier, *President*
EMP: 6
SQ FT: 4,000
SALES: 800K **Privately Held**
WEB: www.stiservice.com
SIC: 8734 3841 7699 5047 Calibration & certification; diagnostic apparatus, medical; professional instrument repair services; electro-medical equipment

(G-774)
SULZER PUMP SERVICES (US) INC
Also Called: Sulzer Bingham Pumps
621 Heron Dr (08014)
P.O. Box 487 (08014-0487)
PHONE..............................856 542-5046
Fax: 856 467-0072
Ginny Johnston, *Branch Mgr*
EMP: 16
SQ FT: 15,000
SALES (corp-wide): 3B **Privately Held**
WEB: www.sulzerpumps.com
SIC: 7692 Welding repair
HQ: Sulzer Pump Services (Us) Inc.
    1255 Enclave Pkwy Ste 300
    Houston TX 77077
    346 207-9580

(G-775)
XYLEM DEWATERING SOLUTIONS INC (HQ)
84 Floodgate Rd (08014-1001)
P.O. Box 191 (08014-0191)
PHONE..............................856 467-3636

Fax: 856 467-4841
Colin Sobil, *President*
Grant Salstrom, *President*
Michael Ivory, *District Mgr*
Michael Duffy, *Opers Staff*
Shane Matthews, *Production*
EMP: 225 **EST:** 1976
SQ FT: 51,000
SALES: 330MM **Publicly Held**
WEB: www.godwinpumps.com
SIC: 7353 3561 5084 Heavy construction equipment rental; pumps & pumping equipment; pumps & pumping equipment

Bridgeton
Cumberland County

(G-776)
ADAMS BILL PRINTING & GRAPHICS
Also Called: Adams Printing
300 Ramah Rd (08302-6948)
PHONE..............................856 455-7177
Fax: 856 455-9695
William G Adams II, *Owner*
Mary Adams, *Co-Owner*
EMP: 7
SQ FT: 2,000
SALES: 500K **Privately Held**
SIC: 2752 Commercial printing, offset

(G-777)
AFFORDABLE LEAD SOLUTIONS LLC
26 Blew Valley Ln (08302-6870)
PHONE..............................856 207-1348
Sam Thompson, *Mng Member*
EMP: 6
SALES: 180K **Privately Held**
SIC: 2851 Paint removers

(G-778)
BORTON ENTERPRISES
178 Woodruff Rd (08302-5941)
PHONE..............................856 453-9221
Corrine Borton, *President*
EMP: 10
SALES (est): 402.6K **Privately Held**
SIC: 2711 Newspapers, publishing & printing

(G-779)
BRAMBILA JORGE STUCCO & STONE
148 S Giles St (08302-2432)
PHONE..............................856 451-2039
Jorge Brambila, *Owner*
EMP: 4
SALES (est): 199.1K **Privately Held**
SIC: 3299 Stucco

(G-780)
BUONA VITA INC
1 S Industrial Blvd (08302-3401)
PHONE..............................856 453-7972
Fax: 856 453-7978
Paul Infranco, *President*
EMP: 80
SALES (est): 32.1MM **Privately Held**
WEB: www.buonavitainc.com
SIC: 3556 Food products machinery

(G-781)
BURDOL INC
Also Called: Print Signs and Designs
1791 S Burlington Rd (08302-4303)
PHONE..............................856 453-0336
Susan Lucas, *President*
Aaron Crispin, *Vice Pres*
EMP: 8
SQ FT: 4,200
SALES (est): 1.3MM **Privately Held**
SIC: 2752 2759 Commercial printing, offset; letterpress printing

(G-782)
COVIA HOLDINGS CORPORATION
1660 S Burlington Rd (08302-4338)
P.O. Box 1024 (08302-0713)
PHONE..............................856 451-6400
William P Light, *Manager*

EMP: 22
SALES (corp-wide): 136.2MM **Publicly Held**
WEB: www.unimin.com
SIC: **1446** Industrial sand
HQ: Covia Holdings Corporation
8834 Mayfield Rd
Chesterland OH 44026
800 255-7263

(G-783)
CUMBERLAND DAIRY INC
80 Edward Ave (08302-1230)
P.O. Box 308, Rosenhayn (08302-0308)
PHONE...................................856 451-1300
Carmine Catalana, *President*
Frank Catalana, *Vice Pres*
EMP: 45
SALES (corp-wide): 26MM **Privately Held**
SIC: **2026** 2024 Milk processing (pasteurizing, homogenizing, bottling); yogurt; ice cream & frozen desserts
PA: Cumberland Dairy, Inc.
899 Landis Ave
Rosenhayn NJ 08352
800 257-8484

(G-784)
EURO KRAFT GROUP LLC
71 Bridgeton Ave (08302-1218)
PHONE...................................856 451-7450
Kasper Mitch, *Director*
Henry Michalkiewicz,
▲ EMP: 24
SQ FT: 13,000
SALES: 2.5MM **Privately Held**
WEB: www.eurokraftgroup.com
SIC: **2434** Wood kitchen cabinets

(G-785)
FRANK BURTON & SONS INC
333 W Broad St (08302-1401)
PHONE...................................856 455-1202
Fax: 856 453-1896
Robert J Burton, *President*
William Burton, *Vice Pres*
Thomas R Burton, *Treasurer*
Donald F Burton Jr, *Admin Sec*
EMP: 9 EST: 1933
SALES (est): 1.3MM **Privately Held**
WEB: www.frankburtons.com
SIC: **5074** 2434 1711 Plumbing & hydronic heating supplies; vanities, bathroom: wood; plumbing contractors

(G-786)
INNOVATION FOODS LLC
71 Bridgeton Ave (08302-1218)
PHONE...................................856 455-2209
Rachel Catalana, *President*
John Cowan, *CFO*
▲ EMP: 14
SQ FT: 40,000
SALES (est): 7.2K
SALES (corp-wide): 26MM **Privately Held**
SIC: **3411** Food & beverage containers
PA: Cumberland Dairy, Inc.
899 Landis Ave
Rosenhayn NJ 08352
800 257-8484

(G-787)
JAMES KINKADE
Also Called: Cumberland & Salem Guide
9 Oak Dr (08302-4524)
P.O. Box 735 (08302-0448)
PHONE...................................856 451-1177
Fax: 856 451-5035
James Kinkade, *President*
EMP: 16
SALES (est): 697.1K **Privately Held**
SIC: **2711** Newspapers

(G-788)
LASSONDE PAPPAS AND CO INC
1019 Parsonage Rd (08302-4229)
PHONE...................................856 455-1001
EMP: 30
SALES (corp-wide): 267.2MM **Privately Held**
SIC: **2033** Fruit juices: packaged in cans, jars, etc.; fruits: packaged in cans, jars, etc.

HQ: Lassonde Pappas And Company, Inc.
1 Collins Dr Ste 200
Carneys Point NJ 08069
856 455-1000

(G-789)
LEONE INDUSTRIES INC
443 S East Ave (08302-3498)
P.O. Box 400 (08302-0310)
PHONE...................................856 455-2000
Fax: 856 455-1905
Peter Leone, *President*
David J Leone, *Vice Pres*
◆ EMP: 350
SQ FT: 255,000
SALES (est): 35.8MM **Privately Held**
WEB: www.leoneglass.com
SIC: **3221** Glass containers
PA: Ard Holdings Sa
Rue Charles Martel 56
Luxembourg
262 585-55

(G-790)
MARTIN CORPORATION
171 N Pearl St (08302-1929)
P.O. Box 479 (08302-0373)
PHONE...................................856 451-0900
Fax: 856 451-0975
Will Martin, *President*
Judith S Martin, *Vice Pres*
Peter Martin, *Warehouse Mgr*
Judy Martin, *Executive*
EMP: 19 EST: 1948
SQ FT: 90,000
SALES (est): 3.1MM **Privately Held**
SIC: **2261** 2262 Dyeing cotton broadwoven fabrics; dyeing: manmade fiber & silk broadwoven fabrics

(G-791)
MKS INC
Also Called: Emerging Technologies
7 N Industrial Blvd (08302-3420)
PHONE...................................856 451-5545
Fax: 856 451-9096
Ken Brattlie, *President*
Lauren A Brattlie, *Corp Secy*
Samuel Brattlie, *Shareholder*
James Peery, *Shareholder*
Paula Peery, *Shareholder*
EMP: 30
SQ FT: 9,000
SALES (est): 5.2MM **Privately Held**
WEB: www.quantaflex.com
SIC: **3646** 3641 Commercial indusl & institutional electric lighting fixtures; electric lamps

(G-792)
NATIONAL REFRIGERANTS INC
661 Kenyon Ave (08302-4842)
PHONE...................................856 455-4555
Fax: 856 455-7626
John McDevit, *Plant Mgr*
EMP: 50
SALES (corp-wide): 98.8MM **Privately Held**
WEB: www.refrigerants.com
SIC: **3822** Air conditioning & refrigeration controls
PA: National Refrigerants, Inc.
11401 Roosevelt Blvd
Philadelphia PA 19154
215 698-6620

(G-793)
PALMETTO ADHESIVES COMPANY
1785 S Burlington Rd (08302-4303)
PHONE...................................856 451-0400
Tom Wilson, *Branch Mgr*
EMP: 12
SALES (est): 2.5MM **Privately Held**
SIC: **2891** Adhesives
PA: Palmetto Adhesives Company
112 Guess St
Greenville SC 29605

(G-794)
PERK & PANTRY
97 Trench Rd Ste 4 (08302-5706)
PHONE...................................856 451-4333
EMP: 4

SALES (est): 310K **Privately Held**
SIC: **5411** 2051 2499 5812 Ret Groceries

(G-795)
POOR BOY PALLET LLC
45 Finley Rd (08302-6078)
PHONE...................................856 451-3771
Fax: 856 451-0084
Gary Macklin, *Mng Member*
Dennis Macklin,
EMP: 25
SALES (est): 3.6MM **Privately Held**
SIC: **2448** Pallets, wood

(G-796)
SEABROOK BROTHERS & SONS INC
85 Finley Rd (08302-6078)
P.O. Box 5103 (08302-5103)
PHONE...................................856 455-8080
Fax: 856 455-9282
Charles F Seabrook II, *Vice Ch Bd*
James M Seabrook Jr, *President*
Andrew Carpenter, *COO*
William Seabrook, *Vice Pres*
Joan Turner, *Purch Mgr*
▲ EMP: 200 EST: 1978
SQ FT: 350,000
SALES: 100.8MM **Privately Held**
WEB: www.seabrookfarms.com
SIC: **2037** Vegetables, quick frozen & cold pack, excl. potato products

(G-797)
SEPERS COUNTRYSIDE NURSERY LLC
282 Harmony Rd (08302-5625)
PHONE...................................856 451-0719
Lousi L Sepers,
EMP: 4 EST: 2007
SALES (est): 351.5K **Privately Held**
SIC: **2741** Business service newsletters: publishing & printing

(G-798)
SOUTH JERSEY WATER COND SVC
760 Shiloh Pike (08302-1460)
PHONE...................................856 451-0620
D David Wilson Sr, *President*
EMP: 27 EST: 1967
SQ FT: 9,000
SALES (est): 2.3MM **Privately Held**
SIC: **7389** 5999 0782 3589 Water softener service; product sterilization service; water purification equipment; lawn services; swimming pool filter & water conditioning systems

(G-799)
TERRIGNOS BAKERY
632 N Pearl St (08302-1299)
PHONE...................................856 451-6368
Fax: 856 451-8802
Mario Terrigno Sr, *President*
EMP: 32
SQ FT: 5,000
SALES (est): 1.5MM **Privately Held**
SIC: **5461** 2051 Bakeries: bread, cake & related products

(G-800)
THOMAS COBB & SONS
146 Cobbs Mill Rd (08302-5543)
PHONE...................................856 451-0671
Fax: 856 451-8314
William A Cobb, *Partner*
William Rex Cobb, *Partner*
EMP: 7
SQ FT: 30,000
SALES: 201K **Privately Held**
SIC: **2421** Sawmills & planing mills, general

(G-801)
ULTRA CLEAN TECHNOLOGIES CORP
1274 Highway 77 (08302-5986)
PHONE...................................856 451-2176
Fax: 856 453-4975
Bruce Riley, *CEO*
▲ EMP: 30

SALES: 10MM **Privately Held**
WEB: www.ultracleantechnologies.com
SIC: **3677** Filtration devices, electronic

(G-802)
W W MANUFACTURING CO INC
60 Rosenhayn Ave (08302-1217)
PHONE...................................856 451-5700
Fax: 856 451-4985
Peater Lesche, *President*
Ingrid Hawk, *Treasurer*
EMP: 11 EST: 1964
SQ FT: 8,000
SALES: 1.2MM **Privately Held**
WEB: www.wwmfg.com
SIC: **3524** 3441 7692 Lawn & garden equipment; fabricated structural metal; welding repair

(G-803)
WEBERS CANDY STORE
111 Old Cohansey Rd (08302-5673)
PHONE...................................856 455-8277
William Weber IV, *Owner*
EMP: 7 EST: 1888
SQ FT: 3,000
SALES (est): 210K **Privately Held**
SIC: **2064** 5441 5145 Candy & other confectionery products; candy; confectionery; confectionery

(G-804)
WHIBCO INC (PA)
Also Called: Penn Rillton Div, The
87 E Commerce St (08302-2601)
PHONE...................................856 455-9200
Jane B Sorgren, *Ch of Bd*
Wade R Sjogren, *President*
Walter R Sjogren Jr, *Vice Pres*
EMP: 15
SQ FT: 12,000
SALES (est): 16.5MM **Privately Held**
WEB: www.whibco.com
SIC: **1446** 1442 5051 Industrial sand; foundry sand mining; construction sand mining; foundry products

(G-805)
WWF OPERATING COMPANY
Also Called: Whitewave Foods
70 Rosenhayn Ave (08302-1237)
PHONE...................................856 459-3890
Richard Purdy, *General Mgr*
EMP: 16
SALES (corp-wide): 718.1MM **Privately Held**
SIC: **2026** Fluid milk; milk processing (pasteurizing, homogenizing, bottling); fermented & cultured milk products
HQ: Wwf Operating Company
12002 Airport Way
Broomfield CO 80021
214 303-3400

Bridgewater
Somerset County

(G-806)
3D BIOTEK LLC
1031 Us 206 Ste 202 (08807)
PHONE...................................908 801-6138
Weing Lau, *COO*
Wing Lau, *COO*
James W Fay, *Exec VP*
Qing Liu,
▲ EMP: 5
SQ FT: 1,000
SALES (est): 706.9K **Privately Held**
SIC: **3821** Laboratory apparatus & furniture

(G-807)
ALEMBIC PHARMACEUTICALS INC (DH)
750 Us Highway 202 # 100 (08807-2597)
PHONE...................................908 393-9604
Craig Salmon, *President*
Alexander Villanueva, *Vice Pres*
Cecilia Carfora, *CFO*
Armando Kellum, *VP Sales*
Pranav Amin, *Director*
EMP: 13
SQ FT: 3,300

SALES (est): 1.5MM
SALES (corp-wide): 456.9MM **Privately Held**
SIC: 2834 Tablets, pharmaceutical; powders, pharmaceutical
HQ: Alembic Global Holding Sa
Rue Fritz-Courvoisier 40
La Chaux-De-Fonds NE
329 679-595

(G-808)
ALPHARMA US INC
400 Crossing Blvd Ste 701 (08807-2863)
PHONE..................................201 228-5090
Michael J Locke, President
▲ EMP: 22
SALES (est): 5MM **Privately Held**
SIC: 2834 Pharmaceutical preparations

(G-809)
AMNEAL PHARMACEUTICALS LLC (HQ)
400 Crossing Blvd Fl 3 (08807-2863)
PHONE..................................908 947-3120
Andrew S Boyer, Exec VP
Chirag Patel, Mng Member
Rochelle Fuhrmann,
▲ EMP: 50
SALES (est): 886.8MM
SALES (corp-wide): 74.4K **Publicly Held**
SIC: 2834 3999 Druggists' preparations (pharmaceuticals); atomizers, toiletry
PA: Amneal Pharmaceuticals, Inc.
602 W Office Center Dr
Fort Washington PA 19034
215 558-4388

(G-810)
AMNEAL-AGILA LLC
400 Crossing Blvd Fl 3 (08807-2863)
PHONE..................................908 947-3120
Chirag Patel, President
EMP: 10 EST: 2012
SQ FT: 40,000
SALES: 2MM
SALES (corp-wide): 74.4K **Publicly Held**
SIC: 2834 Pharmaceutical preparations
HQ: Amneal Pharmaceuticals Llc
400 Crossing Blvd Fl 3
Bridgewater NJ 08807

(G-811)
ANN HEMYNG CANDY INC
Also Called: Chocolate Factory
1195 Crim Rd (08807-4602)
PHONE..................................215 536-7004
Louise Spindler, President
EMP: 7
SQ FT: 3,000
SALES (est): 280K **Privately Held**
WEB: www.chocolatefactory.com
SIC: 2064 Candy & other confectionery products

(G-812)
APPLEGATE FARMS LLC
750 Rte 202 Ste 300 (08807-5530)
PHONE..................................908 725-2768
Stephen McDonnell, CEO
Eric Miller, Senior VP
Kerry Collins, Vice Pres
Diane Kull, Vice Pres
Keith Neuman, Vice Pres
▲ EMP: 106
SALES (est): 35.7MM
SALES (corp-wide): 9.1B **Publicly Held**
SIC: 2011 2013 Meat by-products from meat slaughtered on site; sausages & other prepared meats
PA: Hormel Foods Corporation
1 Hormel Pl
Austin MN 55912
507 437-5611

(G-813)
ARGONAUTUS LLC
867 Country Club Rd (08807-1140)
PHONE..................................908 393-4379
Luba Krpenko, General Mgr
EMP: 5
SALES: 500K **Privately Held**
SIC: 3634 Coffee makers, electric: household

(G-814)
ARIBA INC
1160 Us Highway 22 # 110 (08807-2931)
PHONE..................................908 333-3400
Fax: 908 333-2401
Melissa Rado, Manager
William Chung, Sr Consultant
EMP: 43
SALES (corp-wide): 27.6B **Privately Held**
WEB: www.ariba.com
SIC: 7372 Business oriented computer software
HQ: Ariba, Inc.
3420 Hillview Ave Bldg 3
Palo Alto CA 94304

(G-815)
ASHLAND LLC
1005 Route 202/206 (08807-1275)
PHONE..................................908 243-3500
EMP: 5
SALES (corp-wide): 3.2B **Publicly Held**
SIC: 2899 2851 2821 2911 Chemical preparations; water treating compounds; paints & allied products; plastics materials & resins; polyesters; ester gum; heavy distillates; oils, lubricating; trailer maintenance
HQ: Ashland Llc
50 E Rivercenter Blvd # 1600
Covington KY 41011
859 815-3333

(G-816)
ASHLAND SPCALTY INGREDIENTS GP
1005 Route 202/206 (08807-1275)
PHONE..................................908 243-3500
EMP: 146
SALES (corp-wide): 3.2B **Publicly Held**
SIC: 2869 Industrial organic chemicals
HQ: Ashland Specialty Ingredients G.P.
8145 Blazer Dr
Wilmington DE 19808
302 594-5000

(G-817)
AVAIL INC (PA)
Also Called: Service Apex
564a Union Ave (08807-3146)
PHONE..................................732 560-2222
Fax: 732 560-1198
Ken Griggs Sr, President
Ken Griggs Jr, Vice Pres
EMP: 6
SQ FT: 1,200
SALES (est): 929.6K **Privately Held**
WEB: www.serviceapex.com
SIC: 2211 2759 Shirting fabrics, cotton; advertising literature: printing

(G-818)
AVENTIS INC
55 Corporate Dr (08807-1265)
PHONE..................................800 981-2491
Joseph Palladino, President
Gregory Irace, Vice Pres
Richard Thomson, Treasurer
Catherine Crane, Manager
Monica McGill, CTO
▲ EMP: 1358
SALES (est): 185.4MM
SALES (corp-wide): 609.6MM **Privately Held**
SIC: 2834 Vitamin, nutrient & hematinic preparations for human use
PA: Sanofi
54 Rue La Boetie
Paris 75008
153 774-000

(G-819)
AVENTIS PHRMCTICALS FOUNDATION
55 Corporate Dr (08807-1265)
PHONE..................................908 981-5000
Fax: 908 231-4744
G Belle, Principal
Tracy Brennan, Manager
EMP: 20
SALES: 0 **Privately Held**
SIC: 2834 Pharmaceutical preparations

(G-820)
BAUSCH & LOMB INCORPORATED
400 Somerset Corp Blvd (08807-2867)
PHONE..................................908 927-1400
Kimberly Briggs, Vice Pres
Craig Dashefsky, Vice Pres
John Darcy, Project Mgr
Kearsten Hanley, Mfg Staff
David Hodgkinson, Senior Buyer
EMP: 330
SALES (corp-wide): 8.7B **Privately Held**
SIC: 3851 Ophthalmic goods
HQ: Bausch & Lomb Incorporated
1400 N Goodman St
Rochester NY 14609
585 338-6000

(G-821)
BAUSCH HEALTH COMPANIES INC (HQ)
Also Called: Valeant
400 Somerset Corp Blvd (08807-2867)
PHONE..................................908 927-1400
Fax: 949 394-7155
J Michael Pearson, CEO
G Mason Morfit, President
Margaret Mulligan, Exec VP
Robert Chai Onn, Exec VP
Robert Rosiello, Exec VP
▲ EMP: 355 EST: 1960
SQ FT: 110,000
SALES (est): 2.9B
SALES (corp-wide): 8.7B **Privately Held**
WEB: www.icnpharm.com
SIC: 2834 Pharmaceutical preparations
PA: Bausch Health Companies Inc
2150 Boul Saint-Elzear O
Sainte-Rose QC H7L 4
514 744-6792

(G-822)
BIOVAIL DISTRIBUTION COMPANY
700 Us Highway 202/206 (08807-1704)
PHONE..................................908 927-1400
Fax: 908 927-1401
William Wells, Principal
Brenda Perez, Engineer
EMP: 4
SALES (est): 243.4K **Privately Held**
SIC: 2834 Pharmaceutical preparations

(G-823)
BRADDOCK HEAT TREATING COMPANY
123 Chimney Rock Rd (08807-3126)
PHONE..................................732 356-2906
Fax: 732 356-2080
Steven R Braddock, CEO
William K Braddock, President
William Schultz, General Mgr
EMP: 46
SQ FT: 20,000
SALES (est): 11MM
SALES (corp-wide): 18.9MM **Privately Held**
SIC: 3398 Metal heat treating
HQ: Braddock Metallurgical, Inc.
400 Fentress Blvd
Daytona Beach FL 32114
386 267-0955

(G-824)
BRISTOL-MYERS SQUIBB COMPANY
685 Us Highway 202/206 (08807-1750)
PHONE..................................908 218-3700
John Mamone, Branch Mgr
EMP: 500
SALES (corp-wide): 20.7B **Publicly Held**
WEB: www.bms.com
SIC: 2834 Pharmaceutical preparations
PA: Bristol-Myers Squibb Company
430 E 29th St Fl 14
New York NY 10016
212 546-4000

(G-825)
BROTHER INTERNATIONAL CORP (HQ)
200 Crossing Blvd (08807-2861)
PHONE..................................908 704-1700
Fax: 908 704-8235

Tadashi Ishiguro, Ch of Bd
Kazufumi Ikeda, President
Roger T Nakagawa, Senior VP
Dean F Shulman, Senior VP
Brian Vincent, Senior VP
◆ EMP: 340
SQ FT: 93,000
SALES (est): 1.1B
SALES (corp-wide): 6.6B **Privately Held**
WEB: www.brothersupport.com
SIC: 5044 3579 3559 5084 Office equipment; typing & word processing machines; typewriters & parts; word processing equipment; sewing machines & hat & zipper making machinery; sewing machines & attachments, industrial; sewing machines, industrial; sewing machines, household: electric; electronic parts & equipment; facsimile equipment
PA: Brother Industries, Ltd.
15-1, Naeshirocho, Mizuho-Ku
Nagoya AIC 467-0
528 242-511

(G-826)
C TECHNOLOGIES INC
Also Called: Ctechnologiesinc.com
757 Rte 202/206 Ste 102 (08807-1763)
PHONE..................................908 707-1009
Fax: 908 707-1030
Craig Harrison, President
Rob Stoll, Purch Mgr
Joe Ferraiolo, QC Mgr
Anna Santos, Manager
EMP: 40
SALES (est): 7.2MM **Privately Held**
WEB: www.ctechnologiesinc.com
SIC: 3229 Fiber optics strands

(G-827)
CHAPTER ENTERPRISES INC
Also Called: New Jersey Line X
1472 Rte 22 (08807-2910)
PHONE..................................732 560-8500
Michael Terlizzi, President
EMP: 6
SQ FT: 4,000
SALES (est): 1.3MM **Privately Held**
SIC: 5531 3479 Automobile & truck equipment & parts; coating of metals & formed products

(G-828)
CMS TECHNOLOGY INC
10 Finderne Ave Ste A (08807-3365)
PHONE..................................512 913-1898
John Meccia, CEO
EMP: 12
SALES: 917.1K **Privately Held**
SIC: 2819 Industrial inorganic chemicals

(G-829)
CONVATEC INC (DH)
Also Called: Convatec Healthcare A, S.A.R.
1160 Rte 22 Ste 201 (08807-2931)
PHONE..................................908 904-2500
Paul Moraviec, CEO
Dave Johnson, President
Adam Deutsch, Exec VP
Adrienne McNally, Senior VP
David Donnelly, Research
▲ EMP: 253
SALES (est): 3.1B **Privately Held**
WEB: www.convatec.com
SIC: 3841 Surgical & medical instruments
HQ: Nordic Capital Svenska Ab

Stockholm
866 006-80

(G-830)
COUNTY OF SOMERSET
Also Called: Recycling
40 Polhemus Ln (08807-3391)
PHONE..................................732 469-3363
Fax: 908 469-6229
William Saller, Superintendent
EMP: 150 **Privately Held**
WEB: www.rce.rutgers.edu
SIC: 4953 9111 3341 3231 Refuse collection & disposal services; county supervisors' & executives' offices; secondary nonferrous metals; products of purchased glass; pulp mills

PA: County Of Somerset
20 Grove St
Somerville NJ 08876
908 231-7000

(G-831)
CSM WORLDWIDE INC (PA)
36 S Adamsville Rd 7 (08807-3212)
PHONE....................................908 233-2882
Atul Shah, *CEO*
Michael S Torstrup, *President*
▲ **EMP:** 20 **EST:** 1897
SALES (est): 6.1MM **Privately Held**
WEB: www.csmworldwide.com
SIC: 3564 Air purification equipment

(G-832)
D R KENYON & SON INC
400 Us Highway 22 (08807-2463)
PHONE....................................908 722-0001
Fax: 908 722-0002
Loren W Jones, *President*
EMP: 10
SQ FT: 45,000
SALES: 2MM **Privately Held**
SIC: 3552 Finishing machinery, textile

(G-833)
DENBY USA LIMITED
1065 Rte 22 Ste 3b (08807-2949)
PHONE....................................800 374-6479
Susan Beers, *Principal*
Dave Hinrichsen, *Network Mgr*
EMP: 7 **EST:** 2015
SALES (est): 197.8K **Privately Held**
SIC: 2499 Tiles, cork

(G-834)
DEWY MEADOW FARMS INC (PA)
Also Called: Dewy Meadow Foods, Inc.
1018 Rector Rd (08807-1318)
PHONE....................................908 218-5655
Randolph Krogoll, *President*
EMP: 15
SALES (est): 1.3MM **Privately Held**
SIC: 2038 Frozen specialties

(G-835)
ETHICON INC
Also Called: Ethicon Endo - Surgery
520 Us Highway 22 Ste 1 (08807-2410)
P.O. Box 6999 (08807-0999)
PHONE....................................908 253-6464
Eugene T Reilly Jr, *President*
EMP: 24
SALES (corp-wide): 76.4B **Publicly Held**
WEB: www.ethiconinc.com
SIC: 3842 Surgical appliances & supplies
HQ: Ethicon Inc.
Us Route 22
Somerville NJ 08876
732 524-0400

(G-836)
EVAPCO-BLCT DRY COOLING INC
981 Us Highway 22 Ste 103 (08807-2946)
PHONE....................................908 379-2665
William G Bartley, *CEO*
William Wurtz, *President*
Danny Xiao, *Exec VP*
Toby Athron, *Vice Pres*
Raf De Lausnay, *Vice Pres*
▲ **EMP:** 25
SQ FT: 6,000
SALES (est): 8.5MM
SALES (corp-wide): 384.1MM **Privately Held**
SIC: 3629 Condensers, for motors or generators
PA: Evapco, Inc.
5151 Allendale Ln
Taneytown MD 21787
410 756-2600

(G-837)
EXCERPTA MEDICA INC (DH)
Also Called: Instrctnal Cmpt Based Training
685 Us Highway 202/206 (08807-1750)
PHONE....................................908 547-2100
Fax: 908 547-2200
Eric Engstrof, *CEO*
Ronald H Schlosser, *President*
Louis J Andreozzi, *Vice Pres*
Robert Issler, *Treasurer*

Ronald Van Olffen, *Program Mgr*
EMP: 65
SQ FT: 25,000
SALES (est): 18.9MM
SALES (corp-wide): 9.7B **Privately Held**
SIC: 7389 2721 2731 2741 Convention & show services; trade journals: publishing only, not printed on site; pamphlets: publishing only, not printed on site; newsletter publishing
HQ: Relx Inc.
230 Park Ave Ste 700
New York NY 10169
212 309-8100

(G-838)
EYETECH INC
700 Us Highway 202/206 (08807-1704)
PHONE....................................646 454-1779
Steven Bettis, *President*
EMP: 13
SALES (est): 1.3MM
SALES (corp-wide): 8.7B **Privately Held**
SIC: 2834 Pharmaceutical preparations
PA: Bausch Health Companies Inc
2150 Boul Saint-Elzear O
Sainte-Rose QC H7L 4
514 744-6792

(G-839)
EZ-DUMPSTER LLC
829 Madison Ave (08807-1199)
PHONE....................................908 752-2787
Robert Noble, *Principal*
EMP: 4
SALES (est): 119K **Privately Held**
SIC: 2673 Bags: plastic, laminated & coated

(G-840)
GARRETT MOORE
Also Called: Officeclocks.com
1048 Hoffman Rd (08807-2121)
PHONE....................................908 231-9231
Garrett Moore, *Owner*
EMP: 4
SQ FT: 2,200
SALES: 300K **Privately Held**
SIC: 3873 7631 5944 Clocks, assembly of; clock repair; clock & watch stores

(G-841)
HAMAMATSU CORPORATION (DH)
360 Foothill Rd (08807-2932)
P.O. Box 6910 (08807-0910)
PHONE....................................908 231-0960
Fax: 908 231-1218
Craig Walling, *President*
Teresa Moore, *General Mgr*
David Fatlowitz, *Business Mgr*
Shoh Masafumi Asai, *Vice Pres*
Eric Atanda, *Vice Pres*
▲ **EMP:** 90
SQ FT: 74,431
SALES (est): 48.4MM
SALES (corp-wide): 1.1B **Privately Held**
WEB: www.hps-industrial.com
SIC: 3671 5065 3674 3641 Photomultiplier tubes; electronic tubes; receiving & transmitting or industrial; electronic parts; semiconductors & related devices; electric lamps
HQ: Photonics Management Corp.
360 Foothill Rd
Bridgewater NJ 08807
908 231-0960

(G-842)
HAMAMATSU CORPORATION
Hamamatsu Photonic Systems
360 Foothill Rd (08807-2932)
PHONE....................................908 526-0941
Fax: 908 231-0852
Akira Hiruma, *Branch Mgr*
EMP: 20
SALES (corp-wide): 1.1B **Privately Held**
WEB: www.hps-industrial.com
SIC: 3825 3641 Instruments to measure electricity; electric lamps
HQ: Hamamatsu Corporation
360 Foothill Rd
Bridgewater NJ 08807
908 231-0960

(G-843)
HENKEL US OPERATIONS CORP
10 Finderne Ave Ste B (08807-3365)
PHONE....................................908 685-7000
Julio Diaz, *Technical Mgr*
Yuhong Hu, *Technical Mgr*
Cristina Dejesus, *Research*
Darshak Desai, *Research*
Terry Maher, *Research*
EMP: 50
SALES (corp-wide): 23.6B **Privately Held**
SIC: 2891 Adhesives; sealants
HQ: Henkel Us Operations Corporation
1 Henkel Way
Rocky Hill CT 06067
860 571-5100

(G-844)
IMCLONE SYSTEMS LLC (HQ)
Also Called: Lilly
440 Us Highway 22 (08807-2477)
PHONE....................................908 541-8000
John H Johnson, *CEO*
Carl C Icahn, *Ch of Bd*
Richard Crowley, *Senior VP*
Tracy Henrikson, *Vice Pres*
Gregory T Mayes, *Vice Pres*
◆ **EMP:** 180
SQ FT: 45,000
SALES (est): 242.7MM
SALES (corp-wide): 22.8B **Publicly Held**
WEB: www.imclone.com
SIC: 2836 2834 Biological products, except diagnostic; pharmaceutical preparations
PA: Eli Lilly And Company
Lilly Corporate Ctr
Indianapolis IN 46285
317 276-2000

(G-845)
INDUSTRONIC INC
1011 Us Highway 22 # 301 (08807-2950)
PHONE....................................908 393-5960
Wolfgang Stallmeyer, *President*
Axel Breidenbruch, *Vice Pres*
EMP: 4
SQ FT: 2,800
SALES (est): 330.6K
SALES (corp-wide): 30.8MM **Privately Held**
WEB: www.industronic.com
SIC: 3629 3669 5065 5999 Electronic generation equipment; intercommunication systems, electric; communication equipment; communication equipment
PA: Industronic, Industrie-Electronic Gmbh & Co Kg
Carl-Jacob-Kolb-Weg 1
Wertheim 97877
934 287-10

(G-846)
INGREDION INCORPORATED
Also Called: Corn Products International
10 Finderne Ave Ste A (08807-3365)
PHONE....................................908 685-5000
Jan Malecki, *Project Mgr*
Mauricio Osorio, *Project Mgr*
Matthew Seilus, *Project Mgr*
Susan Murphy, *Safety Mgr*
Daryl Kelley, *Production*
EMP: 71
SALES (corp-wide): 5.8B **Publicly Held**
SIC: 2046 Wet corn milling
PA: Ingredion Incorporated
5 Westbrook Corporate Ctr # 500
Westchester IL 60154
708 551-2600

(G-847)
INSMED INCORPORATED (PA)
10 Finderne Ave Bldg 10 # 10 (08807-3365)
PHONE....................................908 977-9900
Donald Hayden Jr, *Ch of Bd*
William H Lewis, *President*
Eugene Sullivan, *Chief*
Wade King, *Senior VP*
S Nicole Schaeffer, *Senior VP*
EMP: 110
SQ FT: 56,617
SALES (est): 41.2MM **Publicly Held**
WEB: www.insmed.com
SIC: 2834 Pharmaceutical preparations; drugs acting on the respiratory system

(G-848)
J C W INC
Also Called: Natural Green
795 E Main St (08807-3338)
PHONE....................................732 560-8061
Clifford Woody, *President*
Jean Woody, *Corp Secy*
EMP: 20
SQ FT: 1,500
SALES (est): 4.8MM **Privately Held**
WEB: www.naturalgreen.com
SIC: 3562 0782 Casters; lawn & garden services

(G-849)
JUNIPER NETWORKS INC
200 Somerset Corp Blvd (08807-2862)
PHONE....................................908 947-4436
Vince Molinaro, *Exec VP*
Chaitanya Kadiyala, *Manager*
EMP: 72 **Privately Held**
WEB: www.juniper.net
SIC: 7373 7372 Computer integrated systems design; prepackaged software
PA: Juniper Networks, Inc.
1133 Innovation Way
Sunnyvale CA 94089

(G-850)
LAVITSKY COMPUTER LABORATORIES
865 Sherwood Rd (08807-1320)
PHONE....................................908 725-6206
Eric Lavitsky, *President*
EMP: 6
SQ FT: 3,000
SALES (est): 1MM **Privately Held**
WEB: www.lavitsky.com
SIC: 3571 7378 7371 Electronic computers; computer maintenance & repair; computer software development

(G-851)
LEGEND MACHINE & GRINDING
36 S Adamsville Rd (08807-3212)
PHONE....................................908 685-1100
Eric Butler, *Manager*
EMP: 12
SALES (est): 980K **Privately Held**
SIC: 3599 Grinding castings for the trade

(G-852)
LIGNO TECH USA INC
Also Called: Lignotech U S A
721 Us Highway 202 (08807-2510)
PHONE....................................908 429-6660
Ray Douglas, *Vice Pres*
EMP: 7 **EST:** 1954
SALES (est): 1MM **Privately Held**
WEB: www.ltus.com
SIC: 2819 2869 Industrial inorganic chemicals; industrial organic chemicals

(G-853)
LINDE GAS NORTH AMERICA LLC (DH)
200 Somerset Corp Blvd # 7000 (08807-2882)
PHONE....................................800 932-0803
Wolfgang Reitzle, *CEO*
Patrick F Murphy, *President*
Mark D Weller, *Chairman*
Philippe D Brunet, *Vice Pres*
Mark Guidroz, *Production*
◆ **EMP:** 750
SQ FT: 215,000
SALES (est): 1.3B
SALES (corp-wide): 20.1B **Privately Held**
SIC: 2813 Oxygen, compressed or liquefied; nitrogen; argon; hydrogen
HQ: Linde North America, Inc.
200 Somerset Corporate Bl
Bridgewater NJ 08807
908 464-8100

(G-854)
LINDE GAS USA LLC (HQ)
200 Somset Cor B Ste 7000 (08807)
P.O. Box 94737, Cleveland OH (44101-4737)
PHONE....................................908 464-8100
Fax: 216 901-5781
Patrick Murphy, *President*
Mark Weller, *Exec VP*
John Brull, *Senior VP*

Jonathan Hoy, *Treasurer*
Elizabeth Nowicki, *Credit Staff*
◆ **EMP:** 131 **EST:** 1917
SQ FT: 20,000
SALES (est) 147.5MM
SALES (corp-wide): 20.1B **Privately Held**
SIC: 2813 5084 Oxygen, compressed or
liquefied; nitrogen; acetylene; hydrogen;
welding machinery & equipment
PA: Linde Ag
Klosterhofstr. 1
Munchen 80331
893 575-701

(G-855)
LINDE LLC (DH)
200 Somerset Corporate Bl (08807-2882)
PHONE.................................908 464-8100
Christian Lafleur, *General Mgr*
Duncan Young, *Business Mgr*
Dean Ferguson, *Engineer*
Matthew Iassogna, *Engineer*
Nick Marco, *Engineer*
◆ **EMP:** 200
SQ FT: 215,000
SALES (est): 1.1B
SALES (corp-wide): 20.1B **Privately Held**
WEB: www.linde.com
SIC: 2813 3569 3561 3823 Oxygen,
compressed or liquefied; nitrogen; argon;
hydrogen; gas separators (machinery);
pumps & pumping equipment; industrial
flow & liquid measuring instruments
HQ: Linde North America, Inc.
200 Somerset Corporate Bl
Bridgewater NJ 08807
908 464-8100

(G-856)
LINDE LLC
Linde Electronics
200 Somerset Corp Blvd # 7000
(08807-2882)
PHONE.................................512 330-0153
Patrick Murphy, *Manager*
EMP: 400
SALES (corp-wide): 20.1B **Privately Held**
SIC: 2813 Oxygen, compressed or lique-
fied
HQ: Linde Llc
200 Somerset Corporate Bl
Bridgewater NJ 08807
908 464-8100

(G-857)
**LINDE NORTH AMERICA INC
(HQ)**
Also Called: Linde Group
200 Somerset Corporate Bl (08807-2882)
PHONE.................................908 464-8100
Pat Murphy, *President*
Sanjiv Lamba, *Managing Dir*
George Kenyon, *Business Mgr*
Michael Yap, *Counsel*
David Johnston, *Vice Pres*
▼ **EMP:** 277
SQ FT: 215,000
SALES (est): 2.6B
SALES (corp-wide): 20.1B **Privately Held**
WEB: www.bocsureflow.com
SIC: 2813 3569 3559 3561 Industrial
gases; oxygen, compressed or liquefied;
nitrogen; argon; gas producers, genera-
tors & other gas related equipment; cryo-
genic machinery, industrial; pumps &
pumping equipment; turbines & turbine
generator sets; flow instruments, indus-
trial process type
PA: Linde Ag
Klosterhofstr. 1
Munchen 80331
893 575-701

(G-858)
LM MATRIX SOLUTIONS LLC
991 Us Highway 22 Ste 200 (08807-2957)
PHONE.................................908 756-7952
Leon M McBride,
EMP: 5

SALES: 250K **Privately Held**
WEB: www.lmmatrixsolutionsllc.com
SIC: 7372 7378 7379 Operating systems
computer software; computer maintenance & repair; computer related maintenance services; computer related
consulting services; computer hardware
requirements analysis

(G-859)
MATRIXX INITIATIVES INC (PA)
Also Called: Zicam
1 Grand Blvd (08807-3161)
P.O. Box 28486, Scottsdale AZ (85255-
0158)
PHONE.................................877 942-2626
Marc L Rovner, *CEO*
Sam Kamdar, *COO*
Raj Shah, *Finance Dir*
Denise Law, *Assistant*
EMP: 25
SQ FT: 23,000
SALES (est): 5.4MM **Privately Held**
SIC: 2834 Pharmaceutical preparations;
drugs acting on the respiratory system

(G-860)
**MEDICIS PHARMACEUTICAL
CORP (HQ)**
700 Us Highway 202/206 (08807-1704)
PHONE.................................866 246-8245
Jonah Shacknai, *CEO*
Jason D Hanson, *COO*
Seth Rodner, *Exec VP*
Mitchell Wortzman PHD, *Exec VP*
Richard D Peterson, *CFO*
◆ **EMP:** 16
SQ FT: 13,000
SALES (est): 81.8MM
SALES (corp-wide): 8.7B **Privately Held**
WEB: www.medicis.com
SIC: 2834 Pharmaceutical preparations;
dermatologicals
PA: Bausch Health Companies Inc
2150 Boul Saint-Elzear O
Sainte-Rose QC H7L 4
514 744-6792

(G-861)
**NATIONAL STRCH CHEM
HOLDG CORP (HQ)**
10 Finderne Ave (08807-3365)
PHONE.................................908 685-5000
Fax: 732 417-5696
Ned W Bandler, *President*
Herbert J Baumgarten, *Vice Pres*
Tony Delio, *Vice Pres*
Clarence L Roberts Jr, *Asst Treas*
David W St Clair, *Admin Sec*
▼ **EMP:** 900
SQ FT: 550,000
SALES (est): 321.8MM
SALES (corp-wide): 5.8B **Publicly Held**
SIC: 2891 2046 2869 Adhesives &
sealants; wet corn milling; industrial or-
ganic chemicals; vinyl acetate
PA: Ingredion Incorporated
5 Westbrook Corporate Ctr # 500
Westchester IL 60154
708 551-2600

(G-862)
NATL ADHESIES DIV OF HENKE
10 Finderne Ave (08807-3365)
PHONE.................................908 685-7000
Brian Henke, *Principal*
▲ **EMP:** 4
SALES (est): 243.1K **Privately Held**
SIC: 2891 Adhesives

(G-863)
**NESTLE HEALTHCARE NTRTN
INC (HQ)**
Also Called: Nestle Health Science
1007 Us Hwy 202206 (08807)
P.O. Box 697, Florham Park (07932-0697)
PHONE.................................952 848-6000
Greg Behar, *CEO*
Barb McCartney, *Manager*
Anna Mohl, *Manager*
◆ **EMP:** 140 **EST:** 1951
SALES: 700MM
SALES (corp-wide): 90.8B **Privately Held**
SIC: 2032 Canned specialties

PA: Nestle S.A.
Avenue Nestle 55
Vevey VD 1800
219 242-111

(G-864)
NEXTGEN IT LLC
991 Us Highway 22 Ste 200 (08807-2957)
PHONE.................................908 837-9443
EMP: 4
SALES (est): 208.7K **Privately Held**
SIC: 8742 7372 Management Consulting
Services Prepackaged Software Services

(G-865)
NISTICA INC
745 Us Highway 202/206 # 201
(08807-1758)
PHONE.................................908 707-9500
Fax: 908 707-9505
Ashish Vengsarkar, *CEO*
Frank W Smith, *COO*
Steven Robinson, *Vice Pres*
Kazuhito Iijima, *CFO*
Nitin Sharma, *Director*
EMP: 30
SQ FT: 15,000
SALES: 10.2MM
SALES (corp-wide): 6.9B **Privately Held**
SIC: 3357 Fiber optic cable (insulated)
HQ: America Fujikura Ltd
170 Ridgeview Cir
Duncan SC 29334
800 235-3423

(G-866)
NITTA CASINGS INC
141 Southside Ave (08807-3256)
PHONE.................................908 218-4400
Rodney Moore, *President*
Francisco Sousa, *COO*
Roseann Salerno, *Vice Pres*
Bruce Zacharias, *Vice Pres*
Gregg Possiel, *Maint Spvr*
▲ **EMP:** 165 **EST:** 1969
SQ FT: 120,000
SALES: 26.1MM
SALES (corp-wide): 354.5MM **Privately
Held**
WEB: www.nittacasings.com
SIC: 2013 5149 Sausage casings, natural;
sausage casings
PA: Nitta Gelatin Inc.
2-22, Futamata
Yao OSK 581-0
729 495-381

(G-867)
NJS ASSOCIATES COMPANY
1170 Route 22 Ste 209 (08807-2928)
PHONE.................................973 960-8688
EMP: 5
SALES (est): 99K **Privately Held**
SIC: 2834 5912 Pharmaceutical prepara-
tions; drug stores

(G-868)
ONPHARMA INC
400 Somerset Corporate Bl (08807-2867)
PHONE.................................408 335-6850
Matt Stepovich, *President*
Michael Parsons, *Vice Pres*
EMP: 6
SALES (est): 765.4K
SALES (corp-wide): 8.7B **Privately Held**
SIC: 2834 Pharmaceutical preparations
HQ: Orapharma, Inc.
700 Route 202/206
Bridgewater NJ 08807
908 927-1400

(G-869)
ORACLE CORPORATION
400 Crossing Blvd Fl 6 (08807-2863)
PHONE.................................908 547-6200
Fax: 908 725-0799
Marty Pattwell, *Sales Staff*
Al Domingo, *Manager*
Jack Coyne, *Technology*
Kevin Kunz, *Director*
Robert Zukowski, *Director*
EMP: 191
SALES (corp-wide): 39.8B **Publicly Held**
WEB: www.oracle.com
SIC: 7372 Business oriented computer
software

PA: Oracle Corporation
500 Oracle Pkwy
Redwood City CA 94065
650 506-7000

(G-870)
**ORION CLOUD CMPT
SOLUTIONS INC**
1200 Rte 22 Ste 2000 (08807-2943)
PHONE.................................732 485-8658
Asim Akram, *CEO*
Venkatesh Iyer, *CEO*
EMP: 6
SALES (est): 164.2K **Privately Held**
SIC: 7372 Application computer software

(G-871)
**ORTHO BIOTECH PRODUCTS
LP**
430 Route 22 (08807-2463)
P.O. Box 6908 (08807-0908)
PHONE.................................908 541-4000
Stephanie Fagan, *Manager*
Carol Webb, *Executive*
EMP: 66
SALES (est): 10.1MM
SALES (corp-wide): 76.4B **Publicly Held**
WEB: www.jnj.com
SIC: 2834 Pharmaceutical preparations
PA: Johnson & Johnson
1 Johnson And Johnson Plz
New Brunswick NJ 08933
732 524-0400

(G-872)
PFIZER INC
400 Crossing Blvd Fl 7 (08807-2863)
PHONE.................................212 733-2323
Fax: 908 566-4137
Mark Bloomfield, *Engineer*
Keith Colmey, *Engineer*
Joe Cully, *Engineer*
Xingong Jiang, *Engineer*
Yingqun Wang, *Engineer*
EMP: 146
SALES (corp-wide): 52.5B **Publicly Held**
WEB: www.pfizer.com
SIC: 2834 2833 Pharmaceutical prepara-
tions; medicinals & botanicals
PA: Pfizer Inc.
235 E 42nd St
New York NY 10017
212 733-2323

(G-873)
PHARMING HEALTHCARE INC
685 Us Highway 202/206 (08807-1775)
PHONE.................................908 376-3058
Robin Wright, *CEO*
Anne-Marie De Groot, *Admin Sec*
EMP: 5
SALES (est): 676.1K
SALES (corp-wide): 11.6MM **Privately
Held**
SIC: 2834 Proprietary drug products
PA: Pharming Group N.V.
Darwinweg 24
Leiden 2333
715 247-400

(G-874)
**PHOTONICS MANAGEMENT
CORP (HQ)**
360 Foothill Rd (08807-2920)
P.O. Box 6910 (08807-0910)
PHONE.................................908 231-0960
Teruo Hiruma, *President*
Akira Hiruma, *Vice Pres*
Kunichika Nakano, *Admin Sec*
EMP: 3
SQ FT: 30,000
SALES (est): 63.8MM
SALES (corp-wide): 1.1B **Privately Held**
SIC: 5065 3825 5047 8732 Electronic
tubes; receiving & transmitting or indus-
trial; measuring instruments & meters,
electric; medical equipment & supplies;
research services, except laboratory
PA: Hamamatsu Photonics K.K.
325-6, Sunayamacho, Naka-Ku
Hamamatsu SZO 430-0
534 522-141

(G-875)
PIPING SOLUTIONS INC
81 Chimney Rock Rd Ste 4 (08807-3179)
PHONE................................732 537-1009
Ernest E Stone III, *President*
Steve Labondra, *Vice Pres*
EMP: 6
SQ FT: 6,000
SALES (est): 1.2MM **Privately Held**
SIC: 3498 Fabricated pipe & fittings

(G-876)
PRESTIGE MILLWORK LLC
27e Kearney St Ste B (08807)
PHONE................................908 526-5100
Daniel Bugasch, *Mng Member*
▲ EMP: 27
SQ FT: 50,000
SALES: 6.7MM **Privately Held**
SIC: 2431 Millwork

(G-877)
PRIME REBAR LLC
36 Adamsville Rd (08807-3110)
PHONE................................908 707-1234
Blima Schwartz,
EMP: 30
SALES (est): 6.4MM **Privately Held**
SIC: 3441 Fabricated structural metal

(G-878)
PRYSMIAN CBLES SYSTEMS USA LLC
111 Chimney Rock Rd (08807-3126)
PHONE................................732 469-5902
EMP: 12
SALES (corp-wide): 1.3B **Privately Held**
SIC: 3357 Building wire & cable, nonferrous
HQ: Prysmian Cables And Systems Usa, Llc
700 Industrial Dr
Lexington SC 29072
803 951-4800

(G-879)
PVH CORP
Also Called: Van Heusen
1001 Frontier Rd Ste 100 (08807-2902)
P.O. Box 6968 (08807-0968)
PHONE................................908 685-0050
Dana Rappe, *President*
Jason Evanchik, *Vice Pres*
Matt M Skinner, *Vice Pres*
Thomas Price, *Store Mgr*
Denise Lentzsch, *Human Res Mgr*
EMP: 8
SALES (corp-wide): 8.9B **Publicly Held**
WEB: www.pvh.com
SIC: 5611 2321 Men's & boys' clothing stores; men's & boys' furnishings
PA: Pvh Corp.
200 Madison Ave Bsmt 1
New York NY 10016
212 381-3500

(G-880)
PVH CORP
Also Called: Van Heusen
1001 Frontier Rd 100 (08807-2902)
PHONE................................908 685-0050
April Delaney, *Manager*
EMP: 4
SALES (corp-wide): 8.9B **Publicly Held**
WEB: www.pvh.com
SIC: 2321 Men's & boys' dress shirts
PA: Pvh Corp.
200 Madison Ave Bsmt 1
New York NY 10016
212 381-3500

(G-881)
PVH CORP
Also Called: Van Heusen
1001 Frontier Rd 100 (08807-2902)
PHONE................................908 685-0148
Christine Grosse, *Manager*
EMP: 6
SALES (corp-wide): 8.9B **Publicly Held**
WEB: www.pvh.com
SIC: 2321 Men's & boys' dress shirts
PA: Pvh Corp.
200 Madison Ave Bsmt 1
New York NY 10016
212 381-3500

(G-882)
QUALCOMM INCORPORATED
500 Smrst Corp Blvd Fl 4 (08807-2856)
PHONE................................908 443-8000
Fax: 908 443-8201
James B Hettesheimer, *Senior Buyer*
Mazhar Alidina, *Engineer*
Madan Kanakamedala, *Engineer*
Mike Meyer, *Engineer*
Madjid Mousavi, *Engineer*
EMP: 79
SALES (corp-wide): 22.2B **Publicly Held**
WEB: www.qualcomm.com
SIC: 3663 Radio & TV communications equipment
PA: Qualcomm Incorporated
5775 Morehouse Dr
San Diego CA 92121
858 587-1121

(G-883)
RENESAS ELECTRONICS AMER INC
Also Called: Intersil Design Center
440 Us Highway 22 Ste 100 (08807-2477)
PHONE................................908 685-6000
Fax: 908 685-6290
Phil Farmer, *Principal*
Donald Preslar, *Principal*
Greg Williams, *Principal*
Glenn Shimomura, *Engineer*
Paul Sferrazza, *Manager*
EMP: 35
SALES (corp-wide): 265.3MM **Privately Held**
WEB: www.intersil.com
SIC: 3674 Semiconductors & related devices
HQ: Renesas Electronics America Inc.
1001 Murphy Ranch Rd
Milpitas CA 95035
408 432-8888

(G-884)
ROUTE 22 FUEL LLC
1240 Us Highway 22 (08807-2978)
PHONE................................908 526-5270
Milkhi Ram, *Manager*
EMP: 7
SALES (est): 797.4K **Privately Held**
SIC: 2869 Fuels

(G-885)
S & W PRECISION TOOL CORP
3 Holly Ct (08807-2559)
PHONE................................908 526-6097
Fax: 201 437-0067
Joseph Wielgus, *President*
Carol Wielgus, *Treasurer*
EMP: 12
SQ FT: 10,000
SALES (est): 930K **Privately Held**
SIC: 3469 Metal stampings

(G-886)
SALIX PHARMACEUTICALS LTD (DH)
400 Somerset Corp Blvd (08807-2867)
PHONE................................866 246-8245
Joseph Papa, *President*
Karen Paff, *Marketing Staff*
Marc Johnson, *Manager*
▲ EMP: 122
SQ FT: 215,000
SALES (est): 197.9MM
SALES (corp-wide): 8.7B **Privately Held**
WEB: www.salix.com
SIC: 2834 Drugs acting on the gastrointestinal or genitourinary system
HQ: Bausch Health Companies Inc.
400 Somerset Corp Blvd
Bridgewater NJ 08807
908 927-1400

(G-887)
SANOFI INC
55 Corporate Dr (08807-1265)
PHONE................................800 981-2491
Serge Weinberg, *Chairman*
Francoise Parisot, *Top Exec*
Susan Esposito, *Vice Pres*
Margaret Fitzgerald, *Project Mgr*
Christopher Mordi, *Project Mgr*
EMP: 426 EST: 2013

SALES (est): 79.7MM **Privately Held**
SIC: 2834 Pharmaceutical preparations

(G-888)
SANOFI US SERVICES INC (HQ)
55 Corporate Dr (08807-1265)
PHONE................................336 407-4994
Fax: 908 981-7838
Christopher A Viehbacher, *CEO*
Timothy Rothwell, *Ch of Bd*
Bhavesh Ashar, *President*
Gerald P Belle, *President*
Kevin Buckle, *President*
▲ EMP: 1500 EST: 1950
SQ FT: 500,000
SALES (est): 5.3B
SALES (corp-wide): 609.6MM **Privately Held**
WEB: www.aventispharma-us.com
SIC: 2834 Pharmaceutical preparations; drugs acting on the cardiovascular system, except diagnostic; drugs acting on the central nervous system & sense organs; drugs acting on the gastrointestinal or genitourinary system
PA: Sanofi
54 Rue La Boetie
Paris 75008
153 774-000

(G-889)
SANOFI US SERVICES INC
200 Cronjing Blvd Fl 2 Flr 2 (08807)
PHONE................................908 231-4000
Barbara Fanelli, *Vice Pres*
Philip Hosbach, *Vice Pres*
Barry Sickels, *Vice Pres*
Ricky Smith, *Vice Pres*
Shefali Goyal, *Project Mgr*
EMP: 23
SALES (corp-wide): 609.6MM **Privately Held**
WEB: www.aventispharma-us.com
SIC: 2834 Pharmaceutical preparations
HQ: Sanofi Us Services Inc.
55 Corporate Dr
Bridgewater NJ 08807
336 407-4994

(G-890)
SANOFI US SERVICES INC
Also Called: Sanofi Avntis Phrmctcals Group
1041 Rte 202/206 (08807-1291)
PHONE................................908 231-4000
Michael Faulkner, *Project Mgr*
Robert Sicola, *Facilities Mgr*
Mark Hem, *Branch Mgr*
Mike Rosano, *Manager*
Alan Harvey, *Consultant*
EMP: 10
SALES (corp-wide): 609.6MM **Privately Held**
WEB: www.aventispharma-us.com
SIC: 8731 2834 Biological research; pharmaceutical preparations
HQ: Sanofi Us Services Inc.
55 Corporate Dr
Bridgewater NJ 08807
336 407-4994

(G-891)
SANOFI-SYNTHELABO INC
55 Corporate Dr (08807-1265)
PHONE................................908 231-2000
Carolina A Isherwood, *Principal*
Dr Jack H Dean, *Enginr/R&D Mgr*
Peter Goethuys, *Human Res Dir*
EMP: 567
SALES (corp-wide): 609.6MM **Privately Held**
WEB: www.sanofi-synthelabous.com
SIC: 8731 2834 Chemical laboratory, except testing; pharmaceutical preparations
HQ: Sanofi-Synthelabo Inc.
55 Corporate Dr
Bridgewater NJ 08807

(G-892)
SAVIENT PHARMACEUTICALS INC (HQ)
400 Crossing Blvd Fl 3 (08807-2863)
PHONE................................732 418-9300
Fax: 732 418-0570
Louis Ferrari, *President*
Richard Crowley, *COO*
Philip K Yachmetz, *Senior VP*

John P Hamill, *CFO*
Kenneth M Bahrt, *Chief Mktg Ofcr*
EMP: 17
SQ FT: 48,469
SALES (est): 1.5MM
SALES (corp-wide): 2.2MM **Privately Held**
WEB: www.savientpharma.com
SIC: 2833 Medicinals & botanicals
PA: Horizon Pharma Rheumatology Llc
500 W Silver Spring Dr
Glendale WI 53217
414 847-6346

(G-893)
SCL
7 Emmons Ct (08807-4700)
PHONE................................908 391-9882
Durga RAO, *CEO*
Chris RAO, *Owner*
EMP: 23 EST: 1988
SALES (est): 1.1MM **Privately Held**
WEB: www.scl.co.uk
SIC: 3672 Printed circuit boards

(G-894)
SEQUEL SOFTWARE INC
1065 Us Highway 22 Ste 3 (08807-2949)
PHONE................................908 575-0252
Kyle Rogh, *President*
William Lee, *Owner*
EMP: 50
SALES (est): 4.6MM **Privately Held**
SIC: 7372 Prepackaged software

(G-895)
SHORT LOAD CONCRETE LLC
81 Chimney Rock Rd Ste 1 (08807-3179)
PHONE................................732 469-4420
Dave Wellema, *President*
EMP: 4 EST: 2016
SALES (est): 110.5K **Privately Held**
SIC: 3273 Ready-mixed concrete

(G-896)
SMS ELECTRIC MOTOR CAR LLC
18 Totten Dr (08807-2367)
PHONE................................215 428-2502
Martin Karo,
Thomas Del Franco,
◆ EMP: 17
SQ FT: 30,000
SALES (est): 980K **Privately Held**
SIC: 7694 Electric motor repair

(G-897)
SOLARIS PHARMA CORPORATION
1031 Rte 202/206 200 (08807-1275)
PHONE................................908 864-0404
Srinivasan Raghavan, *President*
EMP: 5
SALES (est): 689.5K **Privately Held**
SIC: 2834 Pharmaceutical preparations

(G-898)
SPX COOLING TECHNOLOGIES INC
1200 Us Highway 22 Ste 14 (08807-2943)
PHONE................................908 450-8027
Jacqueline Ostrowski, *General Mgr*
Dorothy Sakele, *Branch Mgr*
EMP: 20
SALES (corp-wide): 1.4B **Publicly Held**
WEB: www.cts.spx.com
SIC: 3443 Cooling towers, metal plate
HQ: Spx Cooling Technologies, Inc.
7401 W 129th St
Overland Park KS 66213
913 664-7400

(G-899)
SPX DRY COOLING USA LLC
1200 Rte 22 Ste 1 (08807-2943)
PHONE................................908 450-8027
Andreas Coumnas, *President*
EMP: 20 EST: 2016
SALES: 0
SALES (corp-wide): 129.3MM **Privately Held**
SIC: 3585 Air conditioning units, complete: domestic or industrial

▲ = Import ▼=Export
◆ =Import/Export

PA: Paharpur Cooling Towers Limited
Paharpur House
Kolkata WB 70002
943 316-1240

(G-900)
SS EQUIPMENT HOLDINGS LLC
Also Called: X Hockey Pro Shops
1425 Frontier Rd (08807-2903)
PHONE..............................732 627-0006
Matthew Setola, *President*
EMP: 20 **EST:** 2015
SQ FT: 5,000
SALES: 2MM **Privately Held**
SIC: 5941 3949 Hockey equipment, except skates; hockey equipment & supplies, general

(G-901)
TALON7 LLC
991 Us Highway 22 Ste 200 (08807-2957)
PHONE..............................908 595-2121
Chris Whiteley, *Principal*
EMP: 13 **EST:** 2014
SALES (est): 2.6MM **Privately Held**
SIC: 3699 Security control equipment & systems

(G-902)
TRI-MET INDUSTRIES INC
36 Adamsville Rd (08807-3110)
PHONE..............................908 231-0004
EMP: 6
SALES (est): 150.3K **Privately Held**
SIC: 3999 Atomizers, toiletry

(G-903)
TRI-STATE ALUM & STAINLESS INC
81 Chimney Rock Rd Ste 6 (08807-3179)
PHONE..............................908 693-7337
Charles Fitzsimmons, *Manager*
EMP: 4
SALES (corp-wide): 15MM **Privately Held**
SIC: 2819 Aluminum compounds
PA: Tri-State Aluminum & Stainless, Inc.
6 Ilene Ct Ste 5
Hillsborough NJ 08844
732 667-5600

(G-904)
TRIGEN LABORATORIES LLC
400 Crossing Blvd (08807-2863)
PHONE..............................732 721-0070
Dave Purdy, *President*
JD Schaub, *COO*
Kevin Hudy, *Vice Pres*
Doug Subers, *CFO*
Steve Squashic, *Treasurer*
▲ **EMP:** 3270
SALES (est): 128.7MM
SALES (corp-wide): 862MM **Privately Held**
SIC: 2834 Pharmaceutical preparations
PA: Avista Capital Holdings, L.P.
65 E 55th St Fl 18
New York NY 10022
212 593-6900

(G-905)
UNIONMED TECH INC
1031 Us Highway 202/206 # 101
(08807-1275)
PHONE..............................917 714-3418
Ming Fang, *CEO*
Yong Jing, *COO*
EMP: 5
SALES (est): 245.5K **Privately Held**
SIC: 3841 Surgical lasers

(G-906)
UP UNITED LLC
495 N Bridge St (08807-7500)
PHONE..............................718 383-5700
Kenneth Farina, *Principal*
EMP: 50
SALES (est): 2MM **Privately Held**
SIC: 3081 Plastic film & sheet

(G-907)
V CUSTOM MILLWORK INC
1480 Us Highway 22 (08807-2909)
PHONE..............................732 469-9600
Fax: 732 469-8458
Susan Schumer, *President*

EMP: 15
SQ FT: 30,000
SALES (est): 1.2MM **Privately Held**
SIC: 2431 5031 Millwork; millwork

(G-908)
VALEANT PHRMCTICALS N AMER LLC (DH)
400 Somerset Corp Blvd (08807-2867)
P.O. Box 25169, Lehigh Valley PA (18002-5169)
PHONE..............................908 927-1400
Richard K Masterson, *President*
Rajiv De Silva, *COO*
Brian Stolz, *Exec VP*
Peter Blott, *CFO*
Phillip W Loberg, *CFO*
EMP: 23
SALES (est): 56MM
SALES (corp-wide): 8.7B **Privately Held**
HQ: Bausch Health Companies Inc.
400 Somerset Corp Blvd
Bridgewater NJ 08807
908 927-1400

(G-909)
VALERITAS HOLDINGS INC
750 Route 202 Ste 600 (08807-2597)
PHONE..............................908 927-9920
Peter J Devlin, *Ch of Bd*
John E Timberlake, *President*
Geoffrey Jenkins, *Exec VP*
Erick J Lucera, *CFO*
Mark Conley, *Treasurer*
EMP: 82
SQ FT: 9,700
SALES (est): 20.2MM **Privately Held**
SIC: 2834 Pharmaceutical preparations

(G-910)
ZOETIS PRODUCTS LLC
440 Rte 22 (08807-2477)
P.O. Box 1399 (08807)
PHONE..............................973 660-5000
EMP: 13
SALES (corp-wide): 5.3B **Publicly Held**
WEB: www.alpharma.com
SIC: 2834 Pharmaceutical preparations
HQ: Zoetis Products Llc
100 Campus Dr Ste 3
Florham Park NJ 07932
973 660-5000

Brielle
Monmouth County

(G-911)
COOKMAN CREAMERY LLC
1 Mariners Bnd (08730-1251)
PHONE..............................732 361-5215
Norah Marler, *Principal*
EMP: 5
SALES (est): 199.8K **Privately Held**
SIC: 2021 Creamery butter

(G-912)
L L TEACH INC
Also Called: Lawrence Educational Services
401 Kenli Ln (08730-1615)
PHONE..............................732 223-1605
Paul R Lawrence, *President*
Ann Lawrence, *Vice Pres*
▲ **EMP:** 40
SQ FT: 2,100
SALES (est): 4.4MM **Privately Held**
SIC: 2752 8748 Commercial printing, lithographic; business consulting

(G-913)
MONMOUTH MARINE ENGINES INC
536 Union Ln (08730-1421)
P.O. Box 85 (08730-0085)
PHONE..............................732 528-9290
Paul Mika, *President*
EMP: 13
SQ FT: 3,000

SALES (est): 4.2MM **Privately Held**
WEB: www.monmouthmarineengines.com
SIC: 5084 5551 7699 3731 Engines, gasoline; marine supplies; marine engine repair; barges, building & repairing; fireboats, building & repairing; fishing vessels, large: building & repairing

(G-914)
NEWMAN ORNAMENTAL IRON WORKS
207 Union Ave (08730-1815)
PHONE..............................732 223-9042
Fax: 732 223-6726
Richard Newman, *CEO*
EMP: 12
SQ FT: 4,000
SALES (est): 2.2MM **Privately Held**
WEB: www.newmanironworks.com
SIC: 3446 Architectural metalwork

(G-915)
TOMS RIVER PRINTING CORP
Also Called: Action Instant Printing Center
11 S Tamarack Dr (08730-1245)
PHONE..............................732 240-2033
Fax: 732 244-5697
Birte Hofmann, *President*
Robert Hofmann, *Treasurer*
EMP: 4 **EST:** 1974
SQ FT: 14,000
SALES (est): 433.2K **Privately Held**
SIC: 2752 7334 Commercial printing, offset; photocopying & duplicating services

(G-916)
VALUE ADDED VICE SOLUTIONS LLC
1111 Shore Dr (08730-1127)
PHONE..............................201 400-3247
EMP: 5 **EST:** 2010
SALES (est): 472K **Privately Held**
SIC: 4813 3679 Voice telephone communications; voice controls

---
Brigantine
Atlantic County

(G-917)
BAR LAN INC
Also Called: Kwik Kopy Printing
327 Gull Cv (08203-3637)
PHONE..............................856 596-2330
Fax: 856 596-0308
Paul Barbera, *President*
Joe Nolan, *Corp Secy*
EMP: 4
SQ FT: 1,400
SALES (est): 300K **Privately Held**
SIC: 2752 2791 2789 Commercial printing, lithographic; typesetting; bookbinding & related work

(G-918)
PRIMAL SURF
3106 Revere Blvd (08203-1050)
PHONE..............................609 264-1999
Michael Laielli, *Principal*
EMP: 4
SALES (est): 664.4K **Privately Held**
WEB: www.primalsurf.com
SIC: 5091 3949 Surfing equipment & supplies; surfboards

Brooklawn
Camden County

(G-919)
AMERAL INTERNATIONAL INC
7 Railroad Ln (08030-2619)
PHONE..............................856 456-9000
Fax: 856 456-2522
Louis Grieco, *President*
◆ **EMP:** 16
SQ FT: 11,000
SALES (est): 3.3MM **Privately Held**
WEB: www.ameral.com
SIC: 3679 Harness assemblies for electronic use: wire or cable

(G-920)
C & L MACHINING COMPANY INC
110 S New Broadway (08030-2554)
P.O. Box 167, Gloucester City (08030-0167)
PHONE..............................856 456-1932
Fax: 856 456-4401
George Cohen, *President*
James C Lewis, *Vice Pres*
EMP: 5
SQ FT: 5,000
SALES (est): 650K **Privately Held**
SIC: 3561 3562 Industrial pumps & parts; ball bearings & parts

(G-921)
ROLFERRYS SPECIALTIES INC
601 New Broadway (08030-2625)
PHONE..............................856 456-2999
Fax: 856 456-6141
Francis Ferry, *President*
EMP: 7
SQ FT: 2,400
SALES (est): 881.7K **Privately Held**
SIC: 2261 5947 5999 2759 Screen printing of cotton broadwoven fabrics; gifts & novelties; trophies & plaques; screen printing

---
Brookside
Morris County

(G-922)
ANVIMA TECHNOLOGIES LLC
Also Called: R&D Consulting
68 Woodland Rd (07926)
PHONE..............................973 531-7077
Nelson Pinilla, *Principal*
Victoria Pinilla, *VP Mktg*
EMP: 4
SALES (est): 281.7K **Privately Held**
SIC: 8711 7371 8999 8733 Engineering services; structural engineering; computer software systems analysis & design, custom; search & rescue service; scientific research agency; industrial instrmnts msrmnt display/control process variable

---
Budd Lake
Morris County

(G-923)
AGILENT TECHNOLOGIES INC
Also Called: Keysight Technologies
550 Clark Dr Ste 2 (07828-4317)
PHONE..............................973 448-7129
Tim Buntin, *Manager*
EMP: 22
SALES (corp-wide): 4.4B **Publicly Held**
WEB: www.agilent.com
SIC: 3825 Instruments to measure electricity
PA: Agilent Technologies, Inc.
5301 Stevens Creek Blvd
Santa Clara CA 95051
408 345-8886

(G-924)
AMERICAN SENSOR TECH INC (HQ)
450 Clark Dr Ste 4 (07828-4312)
PHONE..............................973 448-1901
Fax: 973 448-1905
Richard E Tasker, *President*
Michael P Eldredge, *Exec VP*
Karmjit S Sidhu, *VP Bus Dvlpt*
◆ **EMP:** 75
SQ FT: 33,000
SALES: 12.9MM
SALES (corp-wide): 13.1B **Privately Held**
WEB: www.astsensors.com
SIC: 3829 Pressure transducers
PA: Te Connectivity Ltd.
Rheinstrasse 20
Schaffhausen SH
526 336-677

(G-925)
BASF CORPORATION
Also Called: BASF Engineering Plastics
450 Clark Dr Ste 3 (07828-4312)
PHONE..................................973 426-5429
Lynn Griffin, *Administration*
EMP: 33
SALES (corp-wide): 76B **Privately Held**
WEB: www.basf.us
SIC: 2869 Industrial organic chemicals
HQ: Basf Corporation
100 Park Ave
Florham Park NJ 07932
973 245-6000

(G-926)
CHARABOT & CO INC
400 International Dr (07828-4306)
PHONE..................................201 812-2762
Marc Thelott, *President*
Diane Niven, *Vice Pres*
Nathalie Garavagno, *Marketing Staff*
▲ **EMP:** 10 **EST:** 1996
SQ FT: 38,000
SALES (est): 1.9MM
SALES (corp-wide): 127.7MM **Privately
Held**
WEB: www.charabot.com
SIC: 2844 5149 Concentrates, perfume;
flavourings & fragrances
PA: Soc Charabot Sa
10 Avenue Yves Emmanuel Baudoin
Grasse 06130
493 093-333

(G-927)
DSRV INC
330 Waterloo Valley Rd # 200
(07828-1395)
PHONE..................................973 631-1200
Jean-Claude Piel, *CEO*
▲ **EMP:** 12
SQ FT: 10,900
SALES (est): 2MM **Privately Held**
SIC: 2835 In vitro diagnostics

(G-928)
ESG LLC
21 Tall Oaks Ln (07828-2539)
PHONE..................................973 347-2969
Vincent Loconte, *Mng Member*
EMP: 10
SQ FT: 18,000
SALES (est): 1.5MM **Privately Held**
SIC: 3579 Addressing machines, plates &
plate embossers

(G-929)
FRATELLI BERETTA USA INC
750 Clark Dr (07828-4314)
PHONE..................................201 438-0723
Simone Bocchini, *President*
Mike Romano, *Prdtn Mgr*
Giovanni Annoni, *CFO*
▲ **EMP:** 96
SQ FT: 178,000
SALES (est): 20MM **Privately Held**
WEB: www.fratelliberettausa.com
SIC: 2013 Sausages & related products,
from purchased meat

(G-930)
GIVAUDAN FRAGRANCES CORP
300 Waterloo Valley Rd (07828-1384)
PHONE..................................973 448-6500
Fax: 973 448-6517
John Vernieri, *Vice Pres*
Glen Edwards, *Purch Mgr*
John Trombley, *Corp Comm Staff*
Joseph Ciccone, *Manager*
William Drake, *Info Tech Dir*
EMP: 200
SALES (corp-wide): 5.1B **Privately Held**
SIC: 2844 2869 Cosmetic preparations;
perfume materials, synthetic
HQ: Givaudan Fragrances Corporation
1199 Edison Dr Ste 1-2
Cincinnati OH 45216
513 948-3428

(G-931)
**HOWARD A SCHAEVITZ TECH
INC (DH)**
Also Called: Macro Sensors
450 Clark Dr Ste 4 (07828-4312)
PHONE..................................856 662-8000

Howard A Schaevitz, *CEO*
Jeff Childs, *President*
Gene Anderson, *Vice Pres*
James Lang, *Vice Pres*
EMP: 35
SQ FT: 20,000
SALES (est): 6.4MM
SALES (corp-wide): 13.1B **Privately Held**
WEB: www.macrosensors.com
SIC: 3829 Measuring & controlling devices
HQ: American Sensor Technologies, Inc.
450 Clark Dr Ste 4
Budd Lake NJ 07828
973 448-1901

(G-932)
L3 TECHNOLOGIES INC
Also Called: Space and Navigation
450 Clark Dr Ste 1 (07828-4312)
PHONE..................................973 446-4000
Fax: 973 446-4256
Paul Wengen, *Principal*
EMP: 300
SALES (corp-wide): 9.5B **Publicly Held**
SIC: 3812 Defense systems & equipment
PA: L3 Technologies, Inc.
600 3rd Ave Fl 34
New York NY 10016
212 697-1111

(G-933)
LUCAS WORLD INC
100 International Dr (07828-1383)
P.O. Box 840551, Houston TX (77284-
0551)
PHONE..................................832 293-3770
Jose Maria Guerra, *President*
Juan Salinas, *Vice Pres*
EMP: 7
SALES (est): 12.8MM
SALES (corp-wide): 32.1B **Privately Held**
SIC: 2064 Lollipops & other hard candy
HQ: Matre, Inc.
6885 Elm St
Mc Lean VA 22101

(G-934)
M + 4 INC
Also Called: Classic Coves
98 Crease Rd (07828-1002)
PHONE..................................973 527-3262
Robert A Maute, *President*
EMP: 5
SALES (est): 308.3K **Privately Held**
WEB: www.classiccoves.com
SIC: 3645 3646 Residential lighting fix-
tures; commercial indusl & institutional
electric lighting fixtures

(G-935)
MACRO SENSORS
450 Clark Dr Ste 4 (07828-4312)
PHONE..................................856 662-8000
Fax: 856 317-1005
John Magdziak, *Manager*
EMP: 13 **EST:** 2015
SALES (est): 2.3MM **Privately Held**
SIC: 3829 Measuring & controlling devices

(G-936)
MARS INCORPORATED
Also Called: Information Services Intl
100 International Dr (07828-1383)
PHONE..................................973 691-3500
Fax: 973 691-3820
Joe Hennessy, *Manager*
EMP: 10
SALES (corp-wide): 32.1B **Privately Held**
SIC: 2047 2024 2066 Cat food; ice
cream, packaged: molded, on sticks, etc.;
chocolate candy, solid
PA: Mars, Incorporated
6885 Elm St
Mc Lean VA 22101
703 821-4900

(G-937)
MICROELETTRICA-USA LLC
300 International Dr # 2 (07828-4305)
PHONE..................................973 598-0806
Fax: 973 598-0677
Graham Paton, *General Mgr*
Ryan Feeney, *Engineer*
Susan Richards, *Finance*
Vanessa Giordano, *Office Mgr*
▲ **EMP:** 15

SALES (est): 6MM **Privately Held**
SIC: 3999 3564 Railroad models, except
toy; blowers & fans
PA: Stella Vermogensverwaltungs Gmbh
Schlehdornstr. 3
Grunwald
893 547-0

(G-938)
NEW VIEW MEDIA
Also Called: Weekly News, The
1 Old Wolfe Rd Ste 203 (07828-3213)
PHONE..................................973 691-3002
Mary Lalama, *Partner*
Alan Goldsher, *Partner*
Joe Nicastro, *Publisher*
EMP: 25
SALES (est): 1.1MM **Privately Held**
SIC: 2711 Newspapers: publishing only,
not printed on site

(G-939)
ROBERTET INC (HQ)
400 International Dr (07828-4306)
P.O. Box 660, Oakland (07436-0660)
PHONE..................................201 337-7100
Fax: 201 337-0070
Peter N Lombardo, *President*
Kent Swan, *President*
Philippe Maubert, *Chairman*
Bob Weinstein, *Vice Pres*
Gilles Audoli, *CFO*
▲ **EMP:** 35 **EST:** 1979
SQ FT: 25,000
SALES (est): 18.4MM
SALES (corp-wide): 273.9MM **Privately
Held**
WEB: www.robertet.fr
SIC: 5149 2844 2087 Flavourings & fra-
grances; toilet preparations; flavoring ex-
tracts & syrups
PA: Robertet Sa
37 Avenue Sidi Brahim
Grasse 06130
493 403-366

(G-940)
**ROBERTET FRAGRANCES INC
(HQ)**
400 International Dr (07828-4306)
P.O. Box 650, Oakland (07436-0650)
PHONE..................................201 405-1000
Fax: 201 337-6863
Christophe Maubert, *President*
Peter Lombardo, *COO*
Joseph Lattarulo, *Senior VP*
Stephen Dente, *Vice Pres*
Garyy Johnsen, *Vice Pres*
▲ **EMP:** 50
SQ FT: 35,000
SALES (est): 20.7MM
SALES (corp-wide): 273.9MM **Privately
Held**
SIC: 2844 Perfumes & colognes
PA: Robertet Sa
37 Avenue Sidi Brahim
Grasse 06130
493 403-366

(G-941)
RUDOLPH TECHNOLOGIES INC
550 Clark Dr Ste 1 (07828-4317)
P.O. Box 860 (07828-0860)
PHONE..................................973 347-3891
Fax: 973 691-4863
Martin Molan, *General Mgr*
Elvino M Da Silveira, *Vice Pres*
Tim Johnson, *Mfg Spvr*
Todd Curtin, *Buyer*
Prasad Bachiraju, *Engineer*
EMP: 65
SALES (corp-wide): 255.1MM **Publicly
Held**
WEB: www.rudolphtech.com
SIC: 3829 Measuring & controlling devices
PA: Rudolph Technologies, Inc.
16 Jonspin Rd
Wilmington MA 01887
973 691-1300

(G-942)
SAN MAREL DESIGNS INC
Also Called: Mariell
98 Us Highway 46 Ste 10 (07828-1818)
PHONE..................................973 426-9554
Nan Derasmi, *President*

EMP: 8
SQ FT: 3,300
SALES (est): 978.7K **Privately Held**
SIC: 3961 Costume jewelry, ex. precious
metal & semiprecious stones

(G-943)
**SAXTON FALLS SAND &
GRAVEL CO**
Waterloo Valley Rd (07828)
PHONE..................................908 852-0121
Fax: 908 852-1360
Richard P Schindelar, *President*
EMP: 25
SQ FT: 1,000
SALES (est): 3.3MM **Privately Held**
SIC: 1442 5191 Construction sand mining;
gravel mining; soil, potting & planting

(G-944)
SKC POWERTECH INC
850 Clark Dr Ste 2 (07828-4313)
PHONE..................................973 347-7000
Chul Chai, *President*
▲ **EMP:** 13
SALES (est): 5.4MM **Privately Held**
SIC: 3691 Batteries, rechargeable

(G-945)
**TRONEX INTERNATIONAL INC
(PA)**
300 International Dr (07828-4305)
P.O. Box 95000, Philadelphia PA (19195-
0001)
PHONE..................................973 335-2888
Donald L Chu, *President*
Danny Qiu, *Manager*
Steve Rummel, *Manager*
Gustavo Lopez, *Info Tech Mgr*
▲ **EMP:** 65
SALES (est): 17.7MM **Privately Held**
WEB: www.tronexcompany.com
SIC: 3842 5047 Surgical appliances &
supplies; medical & hospital equipment

Buena
Atlantic County

(G-946)
CPB INC
Also Called: Trade Images
701 S Harding Hwy (08310-9732)
PHONE..................................856 697-2700
Fax: 856 697-3737
David Bird, *President*
EMP: 22
SQ FT: 37,000
SALES (est): 1.7MM **Privately Held**
WEB: www.cpb.com
SIC: 7389 2541 2434 Trade show
arrangement; cabinets, except refriger-
ated: show, display, etc.: wood; wood
kitchen cabinets

(G-947)
IMMUNOGENETICS INC
Lincoln Ave & Wheat Rd (08310)
PHONE..................................856 697-1441
Earl Lewis, *Ch of Bd*
Paul Woitach, *President*
John Ambrose, *President*
EMP: 56
SQ FT: 40,000
SALES (est): 3MM
SALES (corp-wide): 67.2MM **Publicly
Held**
WEB: www.askigi.com
SIC: 3999 Pet supplies
PA: Teligent, Inc.
105 Lincoln Ave
Buena NJ 08310
856 697-1441

(G-948)
S P INDUSTRIES INC
Also Called: Hotpack
1002 Harding Hwy (08310-1528)
PHONE..................................215 672-7800
Ronald E Dimaria, *Principal*
EMP: 75
SQ FT: 71,000

SALES (corp-wide): 1.4B **Privately Held**
WEB: www.virtis.com
SIC: **3821** Laboratory apparatus & furniture; incubators, laboratory; ovens, laboratory
HQ: S P Industries, Inc.
935 Mearns Rd
Warminster PA 18974
215 672-7800

(G-949)
TELIGENT INC (PA)
105 Lincoln Ave (08310)
P.O. Box 687 (08310-0687)
PHONE.....................................856 697-1441
Fax: 856 697-2259
James C Gale, *Ch of Bd*
Jason Grenfell-Gardner, *President*
Damian Finio, *CFO*
Martin Wilson, *General Counsel*
Stephen Richardson, *Security Dir*
EMP: 153
SQ FT: 33,000
SALES (est): 67.2MM **Publicly Held**
WEB: www.askigi.com
SIC: **2834** Pharmaceutical preparations; dermatologicals

(G-950)
TELIGENT INC
711 S Harding Hwy (08310)
PHONE.....................................856 697-1441
Carlene Lloyd, *CFO*
EMP: 15
SALES (corp-wide): 67.2MM **Publicly Held**
WEB: www.askigi.com
SIC: **2836 2834** Biological products, except diagnostic; pharmaceutical preparations
PA: Teligent, Inc.
105 Lincoln Ave
Buena NJ 08310
856 697-1441

(G-951)
TRITON ASSOCIATED INDUSTRIES
N Brewster Rd (08310)
P.O. Box 627 (08310-0627)
PHONE.....................................856 697-3050
Fax: 856 697-9597
Leonard G Vanderweel, *President*
Linda M Vanderweel, *Corp Secy*
Wayne T Edwards, *Exec VP*
EMP: 50
SQ FT: 28,000
SALES (est): 3.8MM **Privately Held**
SIC: **3231 3229** Products of purchased glass; scientific & technical glassware: from purchased glass; pressed & blown glass

Burlington
Burlington County

(G-952)
A SMITH & SON INC
300 W Broad St (08016-1412)
PHONE.....................................609 747-0800
John R Smith, *President*
EMP: 8
SQ FT: 4,600
SALES (est): 1.3MM **Privately Held**
SIC: **3479** Etching & engraving

(G-953)
ACTON MOBILE INDUSTRIES INC
2013 Route 130 N (08016-9729)
PHONE.....................................610 485-5100
Carl Bennett, *Principal*
EMP: 8
SALES (est): 1MM **Privately Held**
SIC: **2451** Mobile homes

(G-954)
AMERICAN CASEIN COMPANY (PA)
Also Called: Amoco
109 Elbow Ln (08016-4123)
PHONE.....................................609 387-2988
Fax: 609 387-7204

Adam Cabot, *CEO*
Roger Hare Jr, *Controller*
Sandra Fine, *Hum Res Coord*
Ra Yoo, *Sales Associate*
Nancy Kraus, *Manager*
▲ EMP: 50 EST: 1956
SQ FT: 30,000
SALES (est): 10.9MM **Privately Held**
WEB: www.americancasein.com
SIC: **2023 2891** Dried milk preparations; adhesives & sealants

(G-955)
AMERICAN CUSTOM DRYING CO
Also Called: A C D
109 Elbow Ln (08016-4123)
PHONE.....................................609 387-3933
Adam Cabot, *CEO*
▲ EMP: 42 EST: 1969
SQ FT: 38,000
SALES (est): 8.3MM **Privately Held**
WEB: www.americancustomdrying.com
SIC: **2023 2099** Dry, condensed, evaporated dairy products; food preparations

(G-956)
AMYS OMELETTE HSE BURLINGTON (PA)
637 High St (08016-2736)
PHONE.....................................609 386-4800
Fax: 609 386-4891
Ted Kopsaftis, *Principal*
EMP: 15
SALES (est): 727.9K **Privately Held**
SIC: **5812 2064 2038** Diner; breakfast bars; breakfasts, frozen & packaged

(G-957)
ANIMALS ETC INC
210 Mitchell Ave (08016)
P.O. Box 606 (08016-0606)
PHONE.....................................609 386-8442
Fax: 609 386-8446
Kathleen P Lance, *President*
▲ EMP: 4
SALES (est): 412.8K **Privately Held**
SIC: **5999 3999** Pets; pet supplies

(G-958)
BARTLETT PRINTING & GRAPHIC
4495 Route 130 S (08016-2247)
PHONE.....................................609 386-1525
Fax: 609 386-0661
Clifford Lewis, *CEO*
Cynthia Lewis, *President*
EMP: 6
SQ FT: 6,000
SALES: 200K **Privately Held**
WEB: www.bartlettprinting.com
SIC: **2752 2791** Commercial printing, offset; lithographing on metal; typesetting

(G-959)
BARTON & COONEY LLC (PA)
300 Richards Run (08016-2120)
PHONE.....................................609 747-9300
Fax: 609 747-9700
Kathy Doyle, *Vice Pres*
Steve Angel, *Opers Staff*
Linda Malin, *Financial Exec*
Zlata Seferovic, *Technical Staff*
Mario Fratangeli, *Prgrmr*
EMP: 53
SQ FT: 85,000
SALES (est): 11.7MM **Privately Held**
WEB: www.bartoncooney.com
SIC: **7331 2752** Mailing service; commercial printing, offset

(G-960)
BURLINGTON PRESS CORPORATION
328 High St (08016-4421)
PHONE.....................................609 387-0030
Fax: 609 387-4413
Richard Lewis, *President*
EMP: 10
SQ FT: 3,000
SALES (est): 1.7MM **Privately Held**
WEB: www.burlingtonprint.com
SIC: **2752** Commercial printing, offset

(G-961)
CELLUNET MANUFACTURING COMPNAY
Also Called: Joseph Titone & Sons'
460 Veterans Dr (08016-1259)
PHONE.....................................609 386-3361
John Titone, *CEO*
◆ EMP: 12
SQ FT: 15,000
SALES (est): 1.1MM **Privately Held**
SIC: **3999** Hair & hair-based products

(G-962)
CEMENTEX PRODUCTS INC
Also Called: Cementex Insulated Tools
650 Jacksonville Rd (08016-3333)
P.O. Box 1428 (08016-7028)
PHONE.....................................609 387-1040
Fax: 609 386-8885
Steve Russo, *President*
Tracy Johnson, *Vice Pres*
Jeffrey Russo, *Vice Pres*
Melissa Kyler, *Purchasing*
Phil Stahl, *Sales Staff*
◆ EMP: 34
SQ FT: 20,000
SALES (est): 12.2MM **Privately Held**
WEB: www.cementexusa.com
SIC: **3423** Hand & edge tools

(G-963)
CENTRAL SAFETY EQUIPMENT CO (PA)
Also Called: Centryco
300 W Broad St (08016-1412)
P.O. Box 250 (08016-0250)
PHONE.....................................609 386-6448
Mary T Gordon, *President*
Bill Hartman, *Vice Pres*
Jack Jurechko, *Vice Pres*
William Hartman, *VP Sales*
▲ EMP: 29 EST: 1946
SQ FT: 30,000
SALES (est): 5.9MM **Privately Held**
WEB: www.centryco.com
SIC: **2395** Permanent pleating & pressing, for the trade

(G-964)
CNG PUBLISHING COMPANY
43 Manchester Way (08016-4300)
PHONE.....................................973 768-0978
Catherine Gore, *President*
Mary Gore, *Vice Pres*
EMP: 5
SALES (est): 230.6K **Privately Held**
SIC: **2731** Book publishing

(G-965)
COAST RUBBER AND GASKET INC
1208 Columbus Rd Ste G (08016-3439)
PHONE.....................................609 747-0110
Fax: 609 988-0134
Vito Massa, *President*
Frank J Valenziano, *Vice Pres*
Philip Valenziano, *Treasurer*
EMP: 6
SQ FT: 2,500
SALES (est): 630K **Privately Held**
SIC: **3053 5085** Gaskets, all materials; rubber goods, mechanical

(G-966)
COLGATE-PALMOLIVE COMPANY
400 Elbow Ln (08016-4130)
PHONE.....................................609 239-6001
Fax: 609 386-9134
Owen James, *Branch Mgr*
Jose Borrell, *Manager*
EMP: 25
SALES (corp-wide): 15.4B **Publicly Held**
WEB: www.colgate.com
SIC: **2844** Toothpastes or powders, dentifrices
PA: Colgate-Palmolive Company
300 Park Ave Fl 3
New York NY 10022
212 310-2000

(G-967)
DELAWARE VALLEY SIGN CORP (PA)
Also Called: Dvs Industries
112 Connecticut Dr (08016-4104)
PHONE.....................................609 386-0100
Fax: 609 386-1108
George M Kennedy, *President*
EMP: 95
SALES (est): 7.4MM **Privately Held**
SIC: **1799 3993 3444** Sign installation & maintenance; signs & advertising specialties; sheet metalwork

(G-968)
DELTA PAPER CORPORATION
122 Kissel Rd (08016-4172)
PHONE.....................................856 532-0333
Fax: 609 486-0180
Bill Bregman, *CEO*
Bill Foley, *Sales Associate*
EMP: 50
SQ FT: 48,000
SALES (est): 15.7MM **Privately Held**
WEB: www.deltapaper.com
SIC: **2671 2621** Paper coated or laminated for packaging; newsprint paper

(G-969)
DUBLIN MANAGEMENT ASSOC OF NJ
Also Called: Lynch Industries
7 Campus Dr (08016-2281)
PHONE.....................................609 387-1600
Fax: 609 239-1666
▲ EMP: 120
SQ FT: 200,000
SALES (est): 21.2MM **Privately Held**
WEB: www.lynchexhibits.com
SIC: **3993 7389 7319** Mfg Signs/Ad Specialties Business Services Advertising Services

(G-970)
DYNATEC SYSTEMS INC (PA)
360 Connecticut Dr (08016-4108)
PHONE.....................................609 387-0330
Fax: 609 387-2060
Thomas Doherty, *President*
Judy Doherty, *Treasurer*
William Fisher, *Admin Sec*
▲ EMP: 12
SQ FT: 4,500
SALES (est): 5.9MM **Privately Held**
WEB: www.dynatecsystems.com
SIC: **3826 1629 3589 5074** Environmental testing equipment; waste water & sewage treatment plant construction; water treatment equipment, industrial; water purification equipment

(G-971)
F S BRAINARD & CO
Also Called: West Electronics
5 Terri Ln Ste 15 (08016-4906)
PHONE.....................................609 387-4300
Bradford Brainard Jr, *President*
EMP: 10
SQ FT: 10,000
SALES (est): 2.1MM **Privately Held**
WEB: www.meter-master.com
SIC: **3823** Industrial instrmnts msrmnt display/control process variable

(G-972)
FISHER CANVAS PRODUCTS INC
415 Saint Mary St (08016-1825)
PHONE.....................................609 239-2733
Fax: 609 239-2728
Frederick H Fisher, *President*
EMP: 5
SQ FT: 12,000
SALES: 430K **Privately Held**
WEB: www.boatcanvas.net
SIC: **2394 5551 5091** Canvas & related products; canvas boat seats; marine supplies & equipment; boat accessories & parts

(G-973)
FISHER SERVICE CO
120 Kissel Rd (08016-4172)
PHONE.....................................609 386-5000
Fax: 609 386-5006

Matthew Doyle, *Principal*
EMP: 6
SALES (est): 820.1K **Privately Held**
SIC: 3491 Industrial valves

(G-974)
FRANKLIN ELECTRONIC PUBLS INC (PA)
3 Terri Ln Ste 6 (08016-4903)
P.O. Box 535, Princeton Junction (08550-0535)
PHONE..................................609 386-2500
Fax: 609 387-7420
Barry J Lipsky, *President*
Toshihide Hokari, *COO*
Chealia Fan, *Project Mgr*
Frank A Musto, *CFO*
Debbie Callsen, *Accountant*
▲ **EMP:** 77
SQ FT: 5,000
SALES (est): 12MM **Privately Held**
WEB: www.franklin.com
SIC: 2741 5065 3695 3571 Technical manuals: publishing only, not printed on site; electronic parts & equipment; computer software tape & disks: blank, rigid & floppy; electronic computers; book publishing

(G-975)
GARELICK FARMS LLC
Cumberland Blvd Rr 130 (08016)
PHONE..................................609 499-2600
Ron Loffredo, *Principal*
EMP: 110 **Publicly Held**
WEB: www.overthemoonmilk.com
SIC: 2026 2033 Milk processing (pasteurizing, homogenizing, bottling); canned fruits & specialties
HQ: Garelick Farms, Llc
1199 W Central St Ste 1
Franklin MA 02038
508 528-9000

(G-976)
GARLEY INC
46 Tall Timber Ln (08016-9758)
PHONE..................................215 788-5756
Eugene Whitley, *President*
EMP: 4 EST: 1950
SQ FT: 10,000
SALES (est): 360K **Privately Held**
WEB: www.garleyinc.com
SIC: 2541 Counters or counter display cases, wood; table or counter tops, plastic laminated

(G-977)
GENERATION BRANDS
6 Campus Dr (08016-2280)
PHONE..................................856 764-0500
Kevin M Fagan, *President*
Charlotte Brumbaugh, *Payroll Mgr*
Mark Horning, *Manager*
Sanil Mooken, *Info Tech Dir*
▲ **EMP:** 4
SALES (est): 86.9K **Privately Held**
SIC: 3645 Residential lighting fixtures

(G-978)
INSTRMENT VLVE SVCS BURLINGTON
120 Kissel Rd (08016-4172)
PHONE..................................609 386-5000
Glenn Scott, *Principal*
EMP: 5
SALES (est): 320K **Privately Held**
SIC: 3491 Industrial valves

(G-979)
INTERNATIONAL PRODUCTS CORP (PA)
201 Connecticut Dr (08016-4105)
PHONE..................................609 386-8770
Charles Granito Sr, *President*
Kathy Wyrofsky, *Vice Pres*
Jennifer Sun, *Research*
Laurie Rossman, *Admin Asst*
EMP: 15 EST: 1919
SALES (est): 2MM **Privately Held**
WEB: www.ipcol.com
SIC: 2992 2842 Lubricating oils & greases; specialty cleaning, polishes & sanitation goods

(G-980)
INTERPLAST INC
100 Connecticut Dr (08016-4104)
P.O. Box 1328 (08016-0928)
PHONE..................................609 386-4990
Fax: 609 386-9237
Allen Langman, *President*
Jared Langman, *General Mgr*
A Benjamin Naimoli, *Vice Pres*
◆ **EMP:** 15
SQ FT: 26,000
SALES (est): 4MM **Privately Held**
WEB: www.interplastinc.com
SIC: 2821 Plastics materials & resins

(G-981)
JEMS PHARMA LLC
301 High St (08016-4411)
PHONE..................................609 386-0141
Richard Kozlowski, *President*
EMP: 4 EST: 2013
SALES (est): 279.6K **Privately Held**
SIC: 2834 Pharmaceutical preparations

(G-982)
KLEIN DISTRIBUTORS INC
Also Called: Agway
600 E Route 130 (08016-1846)
PHONE..................................732 446-7632
Fax: 732 446-0192
Michael Klein, *Branch Mgr*
EMP: 6
SALES (corp-wide): 2.3MM **Privately Held**
SIC: 0782 3999 5999 Lawn & garden services; pet supplies; pet food
PA: Klein Distributors Inc
600 N Rte 130
Burlington NJ 08016
609 386-0500

(G-983)
MAG SIGNS
1208 Columbus Rd Ste F (08016-3439)
PHONE..................................609 747-9600
Rob Persichetti, *Owner*
EMP: 12
SQ FT: 10,000
SALES (est): 1.8MM **Privately Held**
WEB: www.effectivesignworks.com
SIC: 3993 Electric signs

(G-984)
MERCHANT & EVANS INC (PA)
Also Called: Zip Rib
308 Connecticut Dr (08016-4108)
PHONE..................................609 387-3033
Fax: 609 387-4383
James Buck, *Ch of Bd*
Steven J Buck, *President*
Ron Jaconelli, *Vice Pres*
Lisa Purden, *Treasurer*
David Handler, *Manager*
◆ **EMP:** 44
SQ FT: 45,000
SALES (est): 7.6MM **Privately Held**
WEB: www.ziprib.com
SIC: 3446 5051 Architectural metalwork; metals service centers & offices

(G-985)
MODERN STORE EQUIPMENT
2045 Route 130 N (08016-9729)
PHONE..................................609 241-7438
David F Dunigan, *President*
John Hamon, *Superintendent*
Shawn Pontoriero, *Purchasing*
Lisa Dunigan, *Admin Sec*
Tyra Woods, *Administration*
EMP: 13
SALES (est): 3.1MM **Privately Held**
SIC: 5021 5078 2542 Shelving; refrigerators, commercial (reach-in & walk-in); pallet racks: except wood

(G-986)
NEW NGC INC
Also Called: National Gypsum Company
1818 River Rd (08016-2132)
PHONE..................................609 499-1323
Fax: 609 499-1589
Joshua Smith, *Opers Staff*
Todd Marker, *Production*
John Hackett, *QC Dir*
Mike Wolverton, *Persnl Mgr*
Steve Cusa, *Sales Staff*

EMP: 70
SALES (corp-wide): 685.8MM **Privately Held**
WEB: www.natgyp.com
SIC: 3275 Wallboard, gypsum
HQ: New Ngc, Inc.
2001 Rexford Rd
Charlotte NC 28211

(G-987)
PENN METAL FINISHING CO INC
700 Jacksonville Rd (08016-3342)
PHONE..................................609 387-3400
Fax: 609 387-3393
Louis F Willa Jr, *President*
Charlotte Willa, *Vice Pres*
EMP: 9 EST: 1966
SQ FT: 26,000
SALES (est): 1.1MM **Privately Held**
WEB: www.pennmetal.net
SIC: 3479 2851 Coating of metals & formed products; paints & allied products

(G-988)
PIXELL CREATIVE GROUP LLC
Also Called: Gary Ell Photography
302 Wood St (08016-4408)
PHONE..................................609 410-3024
Gary Ell, *Owner*
EMP: 5
SALES (est): 170K **Privately Held**
SIC: 7335 3669 Commercial photography; visual communication systems

(G-989)
RIMTEC ENTERPRISES INC
Also Called: Rimtec Corporation
1702 Beverly Rd (08016-1010)
PHONE..................................609 387-0011
Fax: 609 387-0282
Minoru Oba, *President*
Steve Landin, *Business Mgr*
Ray Johnson Jr, *Prdtn Mgr*
Ray Johnston Jr, *Safety Mgr*
Andy Loyer, *Maint Spvr*
▲ **EMP:** 102
SQ FT: 51,000
SALES (est): 42.7MM
SALES (corp-wide): 887.9MM **Privately Held**
WEB: www.rimtec.com
SIC: 2821 Polyvinyl chloride resins (PVC)
HQ: Riken Americas Corporation
342 Riken Ct
Hopkinsville KY 42240
270 874-4131

(G-990)
STULZ-SICKLES STEEL COMPANY (PA)
2 Campus Dr (08016-2280)
PHONE..................................609 531-2172
Fax: 609 387-4762
Rob Ogilvie, *CEO*
Mike Morgan, *Vice Pres*
Michael Harlan, *CFO*
Ron Colla, *Sales Mgr*
Kevin Kolacki, *Manager*
◆ **EMP:** 20 EST: 1916
SQ FT: 32,000
SALES (est): 15MM **Privately Held**
WEB: www.stulzsicklessteel.com
SIC: 5051 3548 Iron & steel (ferrous) products; steel; electrodes, electric welding

(G-991)
THERMO FISHER SCIENTIFIC INC
19 London Rd (08016-2972)
PHONE..................................609 239-3185
Anthony Miles-Sales Rep, *Principal*
EMP: 14
SALES (corp-wide): 20.9B **Publicly Held**
WEB: www.thermo.com
SIC: 3826 Analytical instruments
PA: Thermo Fisher Scientific Inc.
168 3rd Ave
Waltham MA 02451
781 622-1000

(G-992)
TUSCAN/LEHIGH DAIRIES INC (HQ)
Also Called: Lehigh Valley Dairy Farms
117 Cumberland Blvd (08016-9722)
PHONE..................................570 385-1884
Fax: 570 385-1686
Rachel Gonzalez, *President*
Gregg Tanner, *Vice Pres*
Timothy A Smith, *Treasurer*
EMP: 91
SQ FT: 15,000
SALES (est): 43.9MM **Publicly Held**
SIC: 2026 2086 Milk processing (pasteurizing, homogenizing, bottling); milk & cream, except fermented, cultured & flavored; fermented & cultured milk products; cream, sour; fruit drinks (less than 100% juice): packaged in cans, etc.

(G-993)
UNITED HOSPITAL SUPPLY CORP
4422 Route 130 S (08016-2291)
P.O. Box 1238 (08016-0838)
PHONE..................................609 387-7580
Matthew Lyons, *President*
Jonathan Lyons, *Vice Pres*
Adam Lyons, *Treasurer*
Mark Lyons, *Admin Sec*
▼ **EMP:** 110 EST: 1968
SQ FT: 77,000
SALES (est): 25MM **Privately Held**
WEB: www.lab-design.com
SIC: 3499 3821 Safes & vaults, metal; laboratory furniture

(G-994)
UNITED STATES PIPE FNDRY LLC
Also Called: Pressure Pipe Division
1101 E Pearl St Ste 1 (08016-1999)
PHONE..................................609 387-6000
Richard Janicki, *Enginr/R&D Mgr*
EMP: 120
SALES (corp-wide): 1.5B **Publicly Held**
SIC: 3321 Gray & ductile iron foundries
HQ: United States Pipe And Foundry Company Llc
2 Chase Corporate Dr # 200
Hoover AL 35244
205 263-8540

(G-995)
WEBB PRESS
340 E Broad St (08016-1850)
PHONE..................................609 386-0100
Bob Albasi, *Owner*
EMP: 5
SALES (est): 329.9K **Privately Held**
SIC: 2752 Commercial printing, lithographic

(G-996)
WEST ELECTRONICS INC
5 Terri Ln (08016-4906)
P.O. Box 366 (08016-0366)
PHONE..................................609 387-4300
Fax: 609 387-4304
Joseph Bernardo, *Ch of Bd*
Vince Bocchinfuso, *General Mgr*
EMP: 15
SQ FT: 5,000
SALES (est): 1.5MM **Privately Held**
SIC: 3679 Power supplies, all types: static

Burlington Township
Burlington County

(G-997)
ALVA-TECH INC
1208 Columbus Rd Ste G (08016-3439)
PHONE..................................609 747-1133
Fax: 609 747-1136
Philip P Valenziano, *President*
Frank P Valenziano, *Vice Pres*
Kathleen Turner, *Treasurer*
▲ **EMP:** 10
SQ FT: 9,000
SALES (est): 2.5MM **Privately Held**
WEB: www.alva-tech.com
SIC: 3089 2891 Injection molding of plastics; adhesives & sealants

▲ = Import ▼=Export
◆ =Import/Export

Butler
Morris County

(G-998)
BIOS INTERNATIONAL CORP
10 Park Pl Ste 3 (07405-1371)
PHONE..............................973 492-8400
Fax: 973 492-8270
Harvey Padden, *President*
Scott Calvert, *Vice Pres*
EMP: 22
SALES (est): 3.7MM **Privately Held**
SIC: 3826 3564 Environmental testing
  equipment; blowers & fans

(G-999)
BUTLER PRTG & LAMINATING INC
250 Hamburg Tpke (07405-1526)
P.O. Box 836 (07405-0836)
PHONE..............................973 838-8550
Fax: 973 838-1767
Jim Berezny, *President*
◆ EMP: 125
SQ FT: 110,000
SALES (est): 28.3MM **Privately Held**
WEB: www.butlerprinting.com
SIC: 2759 3089 2295 Imprinting; laminat-
  ing of plastic; laminating of fabrics

(G-1000)
CAROLE COSMETICS LLC
Also Called: Posner
10 Park Pl Ste 4 (07405-1371)
P.O. Box 434 (07405-0434)
PHONE..............................973 283-2893
Randy Krupnick,
▲ EMP: 20
SALES (est): 4.4MM **Privately Held**
SIC: 2844 Cosmetic preparations

(G-1001)
COMPUTER CONTROL CORP
10 Park Pl Ste 1 (07405-1371)
PHONE..............................973 492-8265
Harvey Padden, *President*
Scott Calvert, *Vice Pres*
EMP: 14
SQ FT: 13,000
SALES: 2MM **Privately Held**
WEB: www.biosint.com
SIC: 3625 3672 Control equipment, elec-
  tric; printed circuit boards

(G-1002)
DELTA SALES COMPANY INC
Also Called: Airoyal Division
1355 State Rt 23 (07405-1726)
PHONE..............................973 838-0371
Fax: 973 838-2638
Robert Infante, *President*
EMP: 10
SQ FT: 1,500
SALES: 1MM **Privately Held**
WEB: www.airoyal.com
SIC: 3561 Cylinders, pump

(G-1003)
FORCE INDUSTRIES LLC
32 Boonton Ave 1 (07405-1346)
PHONE..............................973 332-1532
Jamie Marie Tacinelli, *Principal*
EMP: 4
SALES (est): 159.3K **Privately Held**
SIC: 3999 Manufacturing industries

(G-1004)
GENERANT COMPANY INC
1865 Route 23 S (07405)
PHONE..............................814 337-0380
Fax: 973 838-4888
Ben Buren, *President*
Christian Grant, *QC Mgr*
Peter Regan, *CFO*
Dennis Prawl, *Regl Sales Mgr*
David Farley, *Mktg Coord*
◆ EMP: 150 EST: 1913
SQ FT: 33,000
SALES (est): 36.9MM **Privately Held**
WEB: www.bilok.com
SIC: 3491 Industrial valves

(G-1005)
GOFFCO INDUSTRIES LLC
10 Park Pl Ste 300 (07405-1310)
PHONE..............................973 492-0150
Leslie Gough Jr, *President*
Leslie R Gough Jr, *Principal*
Gail Gallagher, *Office Mgr*
EMP: 7
SALES (est): 740K **Privately Held**
WEB: www.goffco.co
SIC: 2752 Commercial printing, offset

(G-1006)
HAPPY CHEF INC
22 Park Pl Ste 2 (07405-1380)
PHONE..............................973 492-2525
Fax: 973 492-0303
James R Nadler, *President*
Joseph H Nadler, *Chairman*
Joseph Endres, *Opers Mgr*
Howard Curtin, *VP Sales*
Glenn Donnelly, *Sales Staff*
▼ EMP: 45
SQ FT: 30,000
SALES (est): 14.3MM **Privately Held**
WEB: www.happychefuniforms.com
SIC: 5136 5137 5023 2326 Uniforms,
  men's & boys'; uniforms, women's & chil-
  dren's; linens, table; towels; service ap-
  parel (baker, barber, lab, etc.), washable:
  men's; uniforms, except athletic:
  women's, misses' & juniors'; women's &
  misses' outerwear

(G-1007)
HIGH POINT BREWING CO INC
Also Called: High Point Wheat Beer Company
22 Park Pl (07405-1377)
PHONE..............................973 838-7400
Greg Zaccardi, *President*
Norm Rost, *Vice Pres*
▲ EMP: 4
SQ FT: 3,000
SALES (est): 450.4K **Privately Held**
SIC: 2082 Beer (alcoholic beverage)

(G-1008)
HSH ASSOC FINANCIAL PUBLISHERS
1200 State Rt 23 (07405-2036)
PHONE..............................973 838-3330
EMP: 7
SALES (est): 87.2K **Privately Held**
SIC: 5812 2721 Eating Place Periodicals-
  Publishing/Printing

(G-1009)
INTEGRATED PACKAGING INDS INC (PA)
45 Carey Ave Ste 210 (07405-1475)
PHONE..............................973 839-0500
Keith Traub, *President*
Stephanie Adler, *Project Mgr*
David Golden, *Accounts Exec*
Amy Sova, *Office Mgr*
EMP: 20
SQ FT: 20,000
SALES (est): 6.2MM **Privately Held**
WEB: www.integratedpackaging.net
SIC: 7336 3086 4783 Package design;
  packaging & shipping materials; foamed
  plastic; packing & crating

(G-1010)
JIGSAW PUBLISHING LLC
Also Called: Umbrella Publishing
8 Hemlock Ct (07405-1124)
PHONE..............................973 838-4838
▲ EMP: 1
SALES: 3MM **Privately Held**
SIC: 2741 Misc Publishing

(G-1011)
M S PLASTICS AND PACKG CO
10 Park Pl Ste 100 (07405-1300)
PHONE..............................973 492-2400
Fax: 973 492-7801
Al Saraisky, *President*
Ellen Saraisky, *Vice Pres*
EMP: 19 EST: 1965
SQ FT: 7,500
SALES (est): 3.7MM **Privately Held**
WEB: www.msplastics.com
SIC: 5199 2673 Packaging materials;
  bags: plastic, laminated & coated

(G-1012)
MESA LABORATORIES INC
10 Park Pl (07405-1371)
PHONE..............................973 492-8400
Brian Roberts, *Director*
EMP: 33
SALES (corp-wide): 96.1MM **Publicly Held**
SIC: 3823 Industrial instrmnts msrmnt dis-
  play/control process variable
PA: Mesa Laboratories, Inc.
  12100 W 6th Ave
  Lakewood CO 80228
  303 987-8000

(G-1013)
MESA LABORATORIES- BGI INC
10 Park Pl (07405-1371)
PHONE..............................973 492-8400
John Sullivan, *President*
EMP: 30
SALES (est): 1.7MM **Privately Held**
SIC: 3826 Analytical instruments

(G-1014)
MY WAY PRINTS INC
Also Called: PIP Printing
1376 State Rt 23 Ste E (07405-1742)
PHONE..............................973 492-1212
Myron Friedman, *President*
Gary Friedman, *Vice Pres*
EMP: 5 EST: 1982
SQ FT: 2,900
SALES: 600K **Privately Held**
SIC: 2752 7389 Commercial printing, off-
  set; design services

(G-1015)
PEERLESS CONCRETE PRODUCTS CO
246 Main St (07405-1025)
PHONE..............................973 838-3060
Fax: 973 838-3385
Clara Monaco, *President*
Philip Monaco, *Corp Secy*
Paul Monaco Jr, *Vice Pres*
EMP: 35
SQ FT: 10,000
SALES (est): 5MM **Privately Held**
WEB: www.peerlessconcrete.com
SIC: 3272 Septic tanks, concrete; tanks,
  concrete

(G-1016)
PRECISION FORMS INC
97 Decker Rd (07405-1561)
PHONE..............................973 838-3800
William J Sulski, *President*
Sandra L Sulski, *Corp Secy*
Sandra Sulski, *Vice Pres*
EMP: 26 EST: 1955
SQ FT: 13,000
SALES (est): 4MM **Privately Held**
WEB: www.precisionformsinc.com
SIC: 3599 Amusement park equipment;
  machine shop, jobbing & repair

(G-1017)
ROBERT GAISER INC
292 Main St (07405-1025)
P.O. Box 807 (07405-0807)
PHONE..............................973 838-9254
Fax: 973 838-3706
Mildred Gaiser, *President*
Kurt Gaiser, *Vice Pres*
Stephen Gaiser, *Treasurer*
Lisa Dore, *Admin Sec*
▲ EMP: 12 EST: 1940
SQ FT: 7,200
SALES (est): 1.2MM **Privately Held**
WEB: www.beauveste.com
SIC: 2389 Clergymen's vestments

(G-1018)
RS MICROWAVE CO INC
22 Park Pl (07405-1377)
P.O. Box 273 (07405-0273)
PHONE..............................973 492-1207
Fax: 973 492-2471
Richard V Snyder, *President*
Frank Gangi, *Engineer*
Nemanja Jojic, *Info Tech Mgr*
EMP: 48
SQ FT: 31,000

SALES (est): 7.7MM **Privately Held**
WEB: www.rsmicro.com
SIC: 3679 Microwave components

(G-1019)
STANTON PRECISION PRODUCTS LLC
10 Park Pl Bldg 4 (07405-1371)
PHONE..............................973 838-6951
Charles Stanton,
Sean Stanton,
William Stanton,
EMP: 6
SALES (est): 707.8K **Privately Held**
SIC: 3599 Machine shop, jobbing & repair

Buttzville
Warren County

(G-1020)
CRAMER PLATING INC
4 Hoyt Ln (07829)
PHONE..............................908 453-2887
Fax: 908 453-3739
Jean Cramer, *President*
EMP: 25 EST: 1958
SQ FT: 10,000
SALES (est): 2.5MM **Privately Held**
SIC: 3471 Electroplating of metals or
  formed products

Byram Township
Sussex County

(G-1021)
CARTRIDGE ACTUATED DEVICES
40 Old Indian Spring Rd (07821-3920)
PHONE..............................973 347-2281
Fax: 973 347-3956
Terry Cavalier, *Principal*
Ed Soohoo, *Administration*
EMP: 24
SALES (corp-wide): 374.4MM **Privately Held**
WEB: www.cartactdev.com
SIC: 2892 3489 5169 Detonators, high
  explosives; fuse powder; ordnance & ac-
  cessories; explosives
HQ: Cartridge Actuated Devices, Inc
  51 Dwight Pl
  Fairfield NJ 07004
  973 575-8760

(G-1022)
KANOMAX USA INC
219 Us Highway 206 (07821-3976)
P.O. Box 372, Andover (07821-0372)
PHONE..............................973 786-6386
Minoro Kano, *President*
Toshi Takano, *Business Mgr*
Debra Garrison, *Accountant*
Koji Miyasaka, *Marketing Mgr*
Bob Casale, *Marketing Staff*
▲ EMP: 7
SQ FT: 10,000
SALES: 2.3MM **Privately Held**
SIC: 3829 Geophysical & meteorological
  testing equipment

(G-1023)
TIN SIGH STOP
5 Meteor Trl (07821-3614)
PHONE..............................973 691-2712
James Odonohue, *Principal*
EMP: 4
SALES (est): 236.4K **Privately Held**
SIC: 3356 Tin

Caldwell
Essex County

(G-1024)
AL AND JOHN INC
Also Called: Glen Rock Ham
147 Clinton Rd (07006-6601)
PHONE..............................973 742-4990
Fax: 973 742-5141

GEOGRAPHIC

Alexander Oldja, *President*
Marianne Campana, *Human Res Mgr*
◆ **EMP:** 300
SQ FT: 65,000
SALES (est): 55MM **Privately Held**
SIC: 2013 Ham, boiled: from purchased
　meat; ham, smoked: from purchased
　meat; pork, cured: from purchased
　meat; pork, smoked: from purchased meat

(G-1025)
CROSSFIRE PUBLICATIONS
551 Bloomfield Ave C14 (07006-7502)
PHONE.......................516 352-9087
Gregory Russo, *Owner*
EMP: 4
SALES (est): 188.1K **Privately Held**
WEB: www.crossfirepublications.com
SIC: 2741 Miscellaneous publishing

(G-1026)
DEVON TRADING CORP
5 Fairfield Rd (07006-4732)
PHONE.......................973 812-9190
Fax: 973 812-8384
Fran Orzech, *President*
Susan Orzech, *Treasurer*
Andrew Leichter, *Admin Sec*
▲ **EMP:** 20
SQ FT: 20,000
SALES (est): 4MM **Privately Held**
SIC: 5049 3911 Religious supplies;
　rosaries or other small religious articles,
　precious metal

(G-1027)
**EME ELECTRICAL
CONTRACTORS**
35 Roseland Ave (07006-5901)
PHONE.......................973 228-6608
C Edward Bierals, *President*
EMP: 4
SALES (est): 370K **Privately Held**
SIC: 1731 1711 7692 General electrical
　contractor; plumbing contractors; warm
　air heating & air conditioning contractor;
　welding repair

(G-1028)
**ESSEX PRODUCTS
INTERNATIONAL**
Also Called: Epi
494 Mountain Ave (07006-4571)
PHONE.......................973 226-2424
Kevin Schumacher, *President*
EMP: 26 **EST:** 2000
SQ FT: 1,200
SALES (est): 2.2MM **Privately Held**
WEB: www.epi-inc.net
SIC: 8711 3699 3567 Engineering serv-
　ices; electrical equipment & supplies; in-
　dustrial furnaces & ovens

(G-1029)
GELOTTI CONFECTIONS LLC
194 Bloomfield Ave (07006-5327)
PHONE.......................973 403-9968
Russell Bleeker, *Principal*
EMP: 8
SALES (est): 489.1K **Privately Held**
SIC: 2024 Ice cream & frozen desserts

(G-1030)
LARSON-JUHL US LLC
165 Clinton Rd (07006-6605)
PHONE.......................973 439-1801
Tom McCarthy, *Branch Mgr*
EMP: 31
SALES (corp-wide): 242.1B **Publicly
Held**
SIC: 2499 Picture & mirror frames, wood
HQ: Larson-Juhl Us Llc
　3900 Steve Reynolds Blvd
　Norcross GA 30093
　770 279-5200

(G-1031)
MINUTEMAN PRESS
359 Bloomfield Ave (07006-5118)
PHONE.......................973 403-0146
Fax: 973 403-0145
Anthony Olivri, *Principal*
EMP: 4 **EST:** 2011
SALES (est): 254.1K **Privately Held**
SIC: 2752 Commercial printing, litho-
　graphic

(G-1032)
**PROVOST SQUARE
ASSOCIATES INC**
6 Provost Sq (07006-5130)
PHONE.......................973 403-8755
Barbara Mamchur, *President*
EMP: 10
SALES (est): 1.1MM **Privately Held**
SIC: 3911 Rings, finger: precious metal

(G-1033)
RECORDER NEWSPAPER
6 Brookside Ave (07006-5604)
PHONE.......................973 226-4000
EMP: 4
SALES (est): 212.8K **Privately Held**
SIC: 2711 Newspapers-Publishing/Printing

Califon
Hunterdon County

(G-1034)
**BRITTINGHAM SFTWR DESIGN
INC**
Also Called: Bsdi
440 Hwy 513 (07830)
P.O. Box 357 (07830-0357)
PHONE.......................908 832-2691
Fax: 908 832-2670
Mark Brittingham, *President*
Pamela Brittingham, *Vice Pres*
EMP: 9
SALES (est): 300K **Privately Held**
WEB: www.bsdiweb.com
SIC: 7372 Application computer software;
　business oriented computer software

(G-1035)
POWER BAG AND FILM LLC
189 W Valley Brook Rd (07830-3530)
P.O. Box 534 (07830-0534)
PHONE.......................908 832-6648
Trevor Power, *Mng Member*
EMP: 6
SQ FT: 100,000
SALES (est): 1.6MM **Privately Held**
WEB: www.powerbagandfilm.com
SIC: 2673 Plastic bags: made from pur-
　chased materials

(G-1036)
RAWCO LLC
Also Called: Rawco Precision Manufacturing
452 County Road 513 (07830-4030)
PHONE.......................908 832-7700
Jeffery W Riley,
Lori Riley,
EMP: 8
SALES: 800K **Privately Held**
SIC: 3599 Machine shop, jobbing & repair

(G-1037)
TOLTEC PRODUCTS LLC
68 Beavers Rd (07830-3203)
PHONE.......................908 832-2131
Fax: 908 832-0894
Arnold Shapack,
Becky Shapack,
Michael Shapack,
Nancy Shapack,
Sarah Shapack,
EMP: 5
SALES: 1.4MM **Privately Held**
WEB: www.toltecproducts.com
SIC: 2542 Fixtures, store: except wood

(G-1038)
**TRANSTAR TRUCK BODY &
WLDG CO**
514 County Road 513 (07830-4019)
P.O. Box 226 (07830-0226)
PHONE.......................908 832-2688
Fax: 908 832-5747
Dominick Tranquilli, *President*
EMP: 7
SQ FT: 10,000
SALES (est): 1.2MM **Privately Held**
SIC: 3713 7532 Truck bodies (motor vehi-
　cles); body shop, trucks

Camden
Camden County

(G-1039)
A & A SOFT PRETZEL COMPANY
1100 N 32nd St (08105-4224)
PHONE.......................856 338-0208
Nick Panara, *Partner*
Albert Panara Sr, *Partner*
Albert Panara Jr, *Partner*
Linda S Panara, *Partner*
EMP: 7
SQ FT: 9,100
SALES (est): 430K **Privately Held**
SIC: 2052 5145 Pretzels; pretzels

(G-1040)
**ARCH CUSTOM
MANUFACTURING INC**
1215 S 6th St (08104)
PHONE.......................856 966-3835
Tom Blair, *Owner*
EMP: 4
SALES: 175K **Privately Held**
SIC: 3599 Industrial machinery

(G-1041)
**ARCH MANUFACTURING &
SALES**
1213 S 6th St (08104-1195)
PHONE.......................856 966-3835
Russell Patton Jr, *President*
EMP: 6
SQ FT: 9,000
SALES (est): 623.1K **Privately Held**
SIC: 3599 3577 Machine shop, jobbing &
　repair; computer peripheral equipment

(G-1042)
**ART METALCRAFT PLATING CO
INC**
Also Called: A-1 Fasteners
529 S 2nd St (08103-3307)
PHONE.......................215 923-6625
Fax: 856 365-8539
Cesare Dolente, *President*
EMP: 12 **EST:** 1940
SQ FT: 45,000
SALES (est): 1.4MM **Privately Held**
WEB: www.artmetalcraft.com
SIC: 3471 Plating of metals or formed
　products; polishing, metals or formed
　products

(G-1043)
**BERNARD MILLER
FABRICATORS**
1135 Mount Ephraim Ave (08103-2721)
PHONE.......................856 541-9499
Bernie Miller Sr, *Owner*
EMP: 7
SQ FT: 1,800
SALES (est): 750K **Privately Held**
SIC: 2434 2541 2517 2511 Wood kitchen
　cabinets; counter & sink tops; wood tele-
　vision & radio cabinets; wood household
　furniture

(G-1044)
BESTWALL LLC
Also Called: Georgia-Pacific
1101 S Front St (08103-3200)
PHONE.......................856 966-7600
Mike Kauth, *Manager*
EMP: 100
SALES (corp-wide): 44.4B **Privately Held**
WEB: www.gp.com
SIC: 3275 3299 3531 Gypsum products;
　stucco; construction machinery
HQ: Georgia-Pacific Llc
　133 Peachtree St Nw
　Atlanta GA 30303
　404 652-4000

(G-1045)
**BOMBARDIER
TRANSPORTATION**
700 Beideman Ave (08105-1547)
PHONE.......................856 580-5609
Al Fizio, *Manager*
EMP: 140

SALES (corp-wide): 16.2B **Privately Held**
SIC: 3743 Interurban cars & car equipment
HQ: Bombardier Transportation (Holdings)
　Usa Inc
　1501 Lebanon Church Rd
　Pittsburgh PA 15236
　412 655-5700

(G-1046)
BRIGHT LIGHTS USA INC
9th & Liberty (08104)
PHONE.......................856 546-5656
Daniel Farber, *Manager*
EMP: 40
SALES (corp-wide): 10MM **Privately
Held**
WEB: www.brightlightsusa.com
SIC: 3724 4226 Aircraft engines & engine
　parts; special warehousing & storage
PA: Bright Lights Usa, Inc.
　145 Shreve Ave
　Barrington NJ 08007
　856 546-5656

(G-1047)
**CAMDEN IRON & METAL INC
(DH)**
1500 S 6th St (08104-1402)
PHONE.......................856 365-7500
Fax: 856 365-5294
Joseph Balzano, *CEO*
John Hammerle, *Buyer*
Kristen Campbell, *Controller*
Christina Bunting, *Office Mgr*
Joe Cirillo, *Manager*
EMP: 15
SALES (est): 4.2MM
SALES (corp-wide): 2.7B **Privately Held**
SIC: 3312 Blast furnaces & steel mills

(G-1048)
CAMDEN TOOL INC
129 York St (08102-2799)
P.O. Box 653 (08101-0653)
PHONE.......................856 966-6800
Tony Devlin, *President*
Dennis J Devlin, *Corp Secy*
EMP: 23 **EST:** 1952
SQ FT: 7,600
SALES (est): 5.9MM **Privately Held**
WEB: www.camdentool.com
SIC: 5084 3545 3541 Metalworking tools
　(such as drills, taps, dies, files); reamers;
　tools & accessories for machine tools;
　machine tools, metal cutting type

(G-1049)
**CAMPBELL SOUP COMPANY
(PA)**
1 Campbell Pl (08103-1799)
PHONE.......................856 342-4800
Fax: 856 342-3878
Keith R McLoughlin, *CEO*
Les C Vinney, *Ch of Bd*
Luca Mignini, *COO*
Adam G Ciongoli, *Senior VP*
Emily Waldorf, *Senior VP*
EMP: 1200 **EST:** 1869
SALES: 7.8B **Publicly Held**
WEB: www.campbellsoups.com
SIC: 2032 2038 2033 2052 Canned spe-
　cialties; soups & broths: canned, jarred,
　etc.; spaghetti: packaged in cans, jars,
　etc.; beans & bean sprouts, canned,
　jarred, etc.; frozen specialties; dinners,
　frozen & packaged; breakfasts, frozen &
　packaged; lunches, frozen & packaged;
　canned fruits & specialties; chili sauce,
　tomato: packaged in cans, jars, etc.;
　cookies & crackers; bread, cake & related
　products; potato chips & similar snacks

(G-1050)
**CAMPBELL SOUP SUPPLY CO
LLC (HQ)**
Also Called: Campbell-Soup Company
1 Campbell Pl (08103-1799)
PHONE.......................856 342-4800
Bill Oshea,
◆ **EMP:** 6
SALES (est): 2.2MM
SALES (corp-wide): 7.8B **Publicly Held**
WEB: www.campbellsoups.com
SIC: 2013 2032 Soups & broths: canned,
　jarred, etc.; sausages & other prepared
　meats

▲ = Import ▼=Export
◆ =Import/Export

PA: Campbell Soup Company
1 Campbell Pl
Camden NJ 08103
856 342-4800

(G-1051)
CATHOLIC STAR HERALD
15 N 7th St (08102-1104)
PHONE..................................856 583-6142
Fax: 856 756-7938
Carl Peters, *Director*
EMP: 9
SALES: 1.3MM Privately Held
WEB: www.saintraymonds.cape-mayschools.com
SIC: 2711 2752 Newspapers: publishing only, not printed on site; commercial printing, lithographic

(G-1052)
CENTRAL METALS INC
1054 S 2nd St (08103-3243)
PHONE..................................215 462-7464
Fax: 856 963-1789
Joseph G Giangiullio, *President*
Tabitha Collins, *General Mgr*
Joe Jacovelli, *Vice Pres*
John Kaufman, *Vice Pres*
Bob Russo, *Vice Pres*
EMP: 70
SQ FT: 70,000
SALES (est): 17.4MM Privately Held
WEB: www.centralmetals.com
SIC: 3441 Building components, structural steel

(G-1053)
CHANNEL LOGISTICS LLC
Also Called: Space-Eyes
121 Market St Ste 2 (08102-2409)
PHONE..................................856 614-5441
Brian Breck, *Architect*
Jatin S Bains, *Mng Member*
Brent Baker, *Info Tech Mgr*
Sean Fischer, *Technology*
Stephen Poserina, *Software Dev*
EMP: 15
SQ FT: 2,500
SALES (est): 1.2MM Privately Held
WEB: www.channellogistics.com
SIC: 7372 7371 Prepackaged software; software programming applications

(G-1054)
COMARCO PRODUCTS INC
Also Called: Comarco Quality Pork Products
501 Jackson St (08104-1409)
PHONE..................................856 342-7557
Fax: 856 342-8448
Thomas Hoversen, *President*
Chris Cook, *Vice Pres*
Eric Hoversen, *Vice Pres*
Elizabeth Feliciano, *Cust Mgr*
EMP: 80
SQ FT: 42,000
SALES (est): 5.2MM Privately Held
WEB: www.comarco.com
SIC: 5812 2011 Eating places; meat packing plants

(G-1055)
CONTEMPRARY GRPHICS BNDERY INC
1200 Ferry Ave (08104-1810)
PHONE..................................856 663-7277
Fax: 856 486-1466
Tim Moreton, *President*
Bob Powell, *President*
Pat Quirk, *Production*
Megan Gallagher, *Manager*
Phil Panelli, *Info Tech Dir*
EMP: 200
SQ FT: 115,000
SALES (est): 54.2MM Privately Held
WEB: www.contemporarygraphics.com
SIC: 2657 2752 Folding paperboard boxes; commercial printing, offset

(G-1056)
CRESCENT BOTTLING CO INC
1001 N 25th St (08105-3825)
PHONE..................................856 964-2268
William Holscher, *President*
EMP: 5 EST: 1896
SQ FT: 4,000

SALES (est): 720.2K Privately Held
SIC: 5921 2086 Liquor stores; bottled & canned soft drinks

(G-1057)
CSC BRANDS LP
1 Campbell Pl (08103-1701)
PHONE..................................800 257-8443
Timothy B Hassett, *President*
EMP: 10
SALES (est): 1.2MM
SALES (corp-wide): 7.8B Publicly Held
SIC: 2032 Canned specialties
PA: Campbell Soup Company
1 Campbell Pl
Camden NJ 08103
856 342-4800

(G-1058)
D K TRADING INC
Also Called: State Metal Trading
941 S 2nd St (08103-3208)
PHONE..................................856 225-1130
Yale Dorfman, *President*
▲ EMP: 7
SALES (est): 704.9K
SALES (corp-wide): 27.4MM Privately Held
WEB: www.statemetalindustries.com
SIC: 3499 Aerosol valves, metal
PA: State Metal Industries, Inc.
941 S 2nd St
Camden NJ 08103
856 964-1510

(G-1059)
DIOCESE OF CAMDEN NEW JERSEY (PA)
Also Called: Diocesan Media Center, The
631 Market St (08102-1103)
PHONE..................................856 756-7900
Joseph Pozusa, *Chancellor*
Rev Nicholas A Dimarzio, *Bishop*
Nicholas Dimarzio, *Bishop*
Bartholomew J Eustace, *Bishop*
George H Guilfoyle, *Bishop*
EMP: 1260 EST: 1937
SQ FT: 5,000
SALES (est): 67.4MM Privately Held
WEB: www.saintraymonds.cape-mayschools.com
SIC: 8661 2711 Catholic Church; newspapers: publishing only, not printed on site

(G-1060)
DYNAMIC BLENDING COMPANY INC
1475 S 6th St (08104-1105)
PHONE..................................856 541-6626
Fax: 856 963-8841
Terrence Riley, *CEO*
Julian E West, *President*
Terrance J O Reilly, *Vice Pres*
EMP: 10
SQ FT: 15,000
SALES (est): 1.6MM Privately Held
SIC: 2841 Soap: granulated, liquid, cake, flaked or chip; detergents, synthetic organic or inorganic alkaline

(G-1061)
ELMCO TWO INC
1045 Cambridge Ave (08105-3930)
P.O. Box 561, Pennsauken (08110-0561)
PHONE..................................856 365-2244
Fax: 856 541-2168
Bernard Kofoet, *President*
EMP: 8 EST: 1962
SALES (est): 1MM Privately Held
SIC: 3444 7692 Sheet metal specialties, not stamped; welding repair

(G-1062)
EMDUR METAL PRODUCTS INC
Also Called: Emdur Art Products
1115 Mount Vernon St (08103-2782)
P.O. Box 421, Cherry Hill (08003-0421)
PHONE..................................856 541-1100
Fax: 856 541-1010
Jerome Emdur, *President*
EMP: 10 EST: 1952
SQ FT: 32,000
SALES: 300K Privately Held
SIC: 3999 3873 Plaques, picture, laminated; clocks, assembly of

(G-1063)
ESSROC CORP
2500 S Broadway (08104-2409)
PHONE..................................856 650-9046
Fax: 856 964-2660
Fred Hiatt, *Branch Mgr*
EMP: 7
SALES (corp-wide): 20.3B Privately Held
SIC: 3241 Portland cement
HQ: Essroc Corp.
3251 Bath Pike
Nazareth PA 18064
610 837-6725

(G-1064)
F & R PALLETS INC
Also Called: J & R Pallets
201 Erie St (08102-2619)
PHONE..................................856 964-8516
Fax: 856 635-1129
Ronald Abate, *President*
Frances Abate, *Vice Pres*
EMP: 30
SQ FT: 6,200
SALES (est): 2.4MM Privately Held
SIC: 2448 7699 Pallets, wood & wood with metal; pallet repair

(G-1065)
FAST DOORS LLC
1661 Davis St (08103-3004)
PHONE..................................856 966-3278
Albert David Pooner,
EMP: 5
SALES (est): 489.3K Privately Held
SIC: 3442 Metal doors

(G-1066)
FBM GALAXY INC
Also Called: Specialty Products & Insul Co
2201 Mount Ephraim Ave (08104-3232)
PHONE..................................856 966-1105
Fax: 856 966-1374
Doug Magill, *Branch Mgr*
EMP: 25
SALES (corp-wide): 2B Publicly Held
WEB: www.spi-co.com
SIC: 5033 3296 Insulation materials; glass wool
HQ: Fbm Galaxy, Inc.
1650 Manheim Pike Ste 202
Lancaster PA 17601
717 569-3900

(G-1067)
FW WINTER INC
550 Delaware Ave (08102-2100)
PHONE..................................856 963-7490
Fax: 856 963-7463
Friedrich W Winter, *President*
Ginny Walsh, *Finance Mgr*
Tony Mologne, *Sales Mgr*
Dr Deepak Madan, *Director*
▲ EMP: 25
SQ FT: 60,000
SALES (est): 6.8MM Privately Held
WEB: www.fwwinter.com
SIC: 3399 5051 Powder, metal; metals service centers & offices

(G-1068)
HOARDERS EXPRESS LLC
529 Market St (08102-1216)
PHONE..................................856 963-8471
Ronald Ford Jr, *President*
EMP: 75
SALES (est): 3.7MM Privately Held
SIC: 3579 Sorters, filing (office)

(G-1069)
HOLTEC INTERNATIONAL
1 Holtec Blvd (08104-2413)
PHONE..................................856 797-0900
Robert Galvin, *CFO*
Pankaj Chaudhary, *Manager*
EMP: 400
SALES (corp-wide): 387.9MM Privately Held
SIC: 2819 8711 Nuclear fuel scrap, reprocessing; engineering services
PA: Holtec International
1001 N Us Highway 1
Jupiter FL 33477
561 745-7772

(G-1070)
INDUSTRIAL HYDRAULICS & RUBBER
458 Atlantic Ave (08104-1016)
PHONE..................................856 966-2600
Michael Donaghue,
EMP: 9
SALES (est): 904.2K Privately Held
SIC: 1799 3492 Hydraulic equipment, installation & service; hose & tube couplings, hydraulic/pneumatic

(G-1071)
JAYMAR PRECISION INC
1169 Cooper St (08102-1011)
PHONE..................................856 365-8779
Chuck Vanaltvorst, *President*
EMP: 6
SQ FT: 6,525
SALES (est): 735.8K Privately Held
SIC: 3599 Machine shop, jobbing & repair

(G-1072)
JOSEPH OAT HOLDINGS INC
2500 S Broadway Ste 10 (08104-2433)
PHONE..................................856 541-2900
Martin Kaplan, *CEO*
Michael Holtz, *President*
Ron Kaplan, *President*
Robert Sax, *President*
Jay Murphy, *Vice Pres*
◆ EMP: 68 EST: 1788
SQ FT: 130,000
SALES (est): 17.6MM Privately Held
WEB: www.josephoat.com
SIC: 3443 8711 Heat exchangers, plate type; pressurizers or auxiliary equipment, nuclear: metal plate; engineering services

(G-1073)
KAPLAN & ZUBRIN (PA)
Also Called: K & Z Pickle Co
Second Kaighns Ave (08103)
P.O. Box 1006 (08101-1006)
PHONE..................................856 964-1083
Fax: 856 964-0510
Ronald Kaplan, *President*
Richard Kaplan, *Corp Secy*
EMP: 20 EST: 1940
SQ FT: 25,000
SALES (est): 2.4MM Privately Held
WEB: www.kaplanzubrinpickles.com
SIC: 2035 Pickles, sauces & salad dressings

(G-1074)
L3 TECHNOLOGIES INC
Communication Systems - E Div
1 Federal St (08103-1088)
PHONE..................................856 338-3000
Fax: 856 338-2250
Mark Simon, *President*
Val Snyder, *Division Pres*
Steven Kipp, *Manager*
Julio Martinez, *Manager*
William Hoopes, *Exec Dir*
EMP: 800
SALES (corp-wide): 9.5B Publicly Held
SIC: 3663 Radio & TV communications equipment
PA: L3 Technologies, Inc.
600 3rd Ave Fl 34
New York NY 10016
212 697-1111

(G-1075)
MAFCO WORLDWIDE CORPORATION (DH)
Also Called: Mafco Magnasweet
300 Jefferson St (08104-2113)
PHONE..................................856 964-8840
Steven Taub, *President*
Peter Vora, *Senior VP*
Lisa Armstrong, *Vice Pres*
Lee Collison, *Vice Pres*
Leon Gorgol, *Vice Pres*
◆ EMP: 112
SQ FT: 390,000
SALES (est): 43.1MM Privately Held
WEB: www.mafcolicorice.com
SIC: 2064 Licorice candy
HQ: Flavors Holdings Inc.
35 E 62nd St
New York NY 10065
212 572-8677

(G-1076)
MAGNETIC METALS
CORPORATION (DH)
1900 Hayes Ave (08105-3656)
PHONE..................................856 964-7842
Fax: 856 757-9047
Henry Rowan Jr, *Ch of Bd*
Frank Raneiro, *Owner*
Mark Nguyen, *Buyer*
Eunice Rodriguez, *Buyer*
Rob West, *Marketing Staff*
▲ EMP: 140 EST: 1942
SQ FT: 180,000
SALES (est): 46.8MM
SALES (corp-wide): 930.4MM **Privately Held**
WEB: www.magmet.com
SIC: 3542 Magnetic forming machines
HQ: Indel, Inc.
  10 Indel Ave
  Rancocas NJ 08073
  609 267-9000

(G-1077)
NEW JERSEY RIVET CO LLC
1785 Haddon Ave (08103-3096)
PHONE..................................856 963-2237
Fax: 800 355-1047
Dennis Van Name, *President*
Michael Van Name, *Vice Pres*
Dan Brown, *Plant Mgr*
Ken Landgarten, *Manager*
Dennis Van, *Manager*
▼ EMP: 15 EST: 1938
SQ FT: 27,000
SALES (est): 3.1MM **Privately Held**
WEB: www.njrivet.com
SIC: 3452 Rivets, metal

(G-1078)
NEWMAN GLASS WORKS INC
1515 Haddon Ave (08103-3196)
P.O. Box 18, Lafayette Hill PA (19444-0018)
PHONE..................................215 925-3565
Fax: 856 964-4040
Herb Shore, *President*
Barry Shore, *Vice Pres*
David Shore, *Treasurer*
EMP: 14 EST: 1932
SQ FT: 15,200
SALES (est): 2.1MM **Privately Held**
WEB: www.newmanglass.com
SIC: 1793 5231 3231 Glass & glazing
  work; glass; products of purchased glass

(G-1079)
NOVELTY HAIR GOODS CO
1138 S Broadway 40 (08103-2206)
PHONE..................................856 963-5876
EMP: 6 EST: 1926
SQ FT: 50,000
SALES (est): 45.2K **Privately Held**
SIC: 3999 Mfg Misc Products

(G-1080)
NUTSCO INC
1115 S 2nd St (08103-3232)
PHONE..................................856 966-6400
Fax: 856 966-6544
Francesco Assis, *CEO*
Patricio Assis, *Vice Pres*
▲ EMP: 12
SQ FT: 48,000
SALES (est): 3.1MM **Privately Held**
WEB: www.nutsco.com
SIC: 2068 Nuts: dried, dehydrated, salted
  or roasted

(G-1081)
PATRICK J KELLY DRUMS INC
1810 River Ave (08105-3630)
PHONE..................................856 963-1795
Patrick Kelly, *Shareholder*
EMP: 8
SALES (corp-wide): 12.7MM **Privately Held**
SIC: 3412 Metal barrels, drums & pails
PA: Patrick J. Kelly Drums, Inc.
  6226 Pidcock Creek Rd
  New Hope PA 18938
  215 598-0666

(G-1082)
PLASTICS CONSULTING & MFG CO
Also Called: P C M
1435 Ferry Ave (08104)
PHONE..................................800 222-0317
Fax: 856 964-8977
Steven Schwartz, *President*
Russell G Shallcross, *Vice Pres*
Melissa Schwartz, *Shareholder*
▲ EMP: 25
SQ FT: 49,000
SALES (est): 3.6MM **Privately Held**
WEB: www.pcmc.com
SIC: 3479 Coating of metals with plastic or
  resins

(G-1083)
R F PRODUCTS INC (PA)
1500 Davis St (08103-3013)
PHONE..................................856 365-5500
Fax: 856 342-9757
Robert M Minke, *President*
Carmine Abbondante, *General Mgr*
Rosanne P Minke, *Corp Secy*
Rosanne Minke, *Vice Pres*
William E Smith, *Vice Pres*
EMP: 40
SQ FT: 90,000
SALES (est): 5.4MM **Privately Held**
WEB: www.rfproductsinc.com
SIC: 3663 Radio broadcasting & communi-
  cations equipment

(G-1084)
RECORDED PUBLICATIONS LABS
Also Called: Rpl
1100 E State St (08105-3538)
PHONE..................................856 963-3000
Fax: 856 963-3854
John S Oliano, *Ch of Bd*
Ronald J Oliano, *President*
Lisa Oliano, *Admin Sec*
EMP: 20
SQ FT: 27,000
SALES (est): 1.4MM **Privately Held**
SIC: 7819 7812 3652 Video tape or disk
  reproduction; motion picture & video pro-
  duction; pre-recorded records & tapes

(G-1085)
SCIENCE PUMP CORPORATION
1431 Ferry Ave (08104-1307)
PHONE..................................856 963-7700
Steven Schwartz, *President*
Russell G Fhallcross, *Vice Pres*
Kathy Parker, *Chief Engr*
EMP: 20
SQ FT: 2,000
SALES (est): 2.8MM **Privately Held**
WEB: www.pcmco.com
SIC: 3829 3559 3564 3561 Measuring &
  controlling devices; ozone machines;
  blowers & fans; pumps & pumping equip-
  ment

(G-1086)
SELL ALL PROPERTIES LLC
301 Market St Ste 1 (08102-1528)
PHONE..................................856 963-8800
Eugene Alford,
Norma Sellers,
EMP: 10
SQ FT: 1,400
SALES (est): 905.8K **Privately Held**
SIC: 6531 3088 Selling agent, real estate;
  plastics plumbing fixtures

(G-1087)
STATE METAL INDUSTRIES INC (PA)
941 S 2nd St (08103-3292)
PHONE..................................856 964-1510
Fax: 856 964-0233
Andrew Dorfman, *President*
Yale Dorfman, *Senior VP*
Michael Dorfman, *Vice Pres*
Richard Kuhl, *Vice Pres*
Jim Marmion, *CFO*
▲ EMP: 94 EST: 1948
SQ FT: 15,000
SALES (est): 27.4MM **Privately Held**
WEB: www.statemetalindustries.com
SIC: 3341 Secondary nonferrous metals

(G-1088)
UNITED STATES COLD STORAGE INC (HQ)
2 Aquarium Dr Ste 400 (08103-1000)
PHONE..................................856 354-8181
Fax: 856 772-1876
David M Harlan, *CEO*
Adam Ashley, *General Mgr*
Greg Rohrbaugh, *General Mgr*
Jeff Kunnemann, *Business Mgr*
Larry Alderfer, *Vice Pres*
◆ EMP: 304 EST: 1899
SQ FT: 7,800
SALES (est): 604.7MM
SALES (corp-wide): 9.8B **Privately Held**
WEB: www.uscold.com
SIC: 2097 4222 Block ice; warehousing,
  cold storage or refrigerated
PA: John Swire & Sons Limited
  Swire House
  London
  207 834-7717

(G-1089)
WILLIAM DULING
Also Called: General Metal & Glass Co
613 Kaighn Ave 15 (08103-2308)
PHONE..................................856 365-6323
Fax: 856 541-2553
William Duling, *Owner*
EMP: 6 EST: 1950
SQ FT: 4,000
SALES (est): 401.6K **Privately Held**
SIC: 1793 3231 Glass & glazing work;
  products of purchased glass

Cape May
Cape May County

(G-1090)
ACME MARKETS INC
Lafayette & Ocean Sts (08204)
PHONE..................................609 884-7217
Michael Davis, *Manager*
EMP: 25
SALES (corp-wide): 59.9B **Privately Held**
WEB: www.acmemarkets.com
SIC: 5411 2051 Supermarkets, chain;
  bread, cake & related products
HQ: Acme Markets, Inc.
  75 Valley Stream Pkwy # 100
  Malvern PA 19355
  610 889-4000

(G-1091)
BUMBLE BEE FOODS LLC
Snows
994 Ocean Dr (08204-5400)
PHONE..................................609 884-0440
EMP: 175 **Privately Held**
SIC: 2091 Mfg Canned/Cured
  Fish/Seafood
HQ: Bee Bumble Foods Llc
  280 10th Ave
  San Diego CA 92101
  858 715-4000

(G-1092)
CAPE MAY BREWING LTD LBLTY CO
Also Called: Cape May Brewing Company
1288 Hornet Rd (08204)
PHONE..................................609 849-9933
EMP: 11
SALES (est): 1.6MM
SALES (corp-wide): 4.7MM **Privately Held**
SIC: 2082 Beer (alcoholic beverage)
PA: Cape May Brewing Limited Liability
  Company
  409 Breakwater Rd
  Cape May NJ 08204
  609 849-9933

(G-1093)
CAPE MAY BREWING LTD LBLTY CO (PA)
Also Called: Cape May Brewing Company
409 Breakwater Rd (08204-4537)
PHONE..................................609 849-9933
Edward Belski, *President*
EMP: 26

SALES (est): 4.7MM **Privately Held**
SIC: 2082 Beer (alcoholic beverage)

(G-1094)
CAPE PUBLISHING INC
513 Washington St Fl 2 (08204-1427)
P.O. Box 2383 (08204-7383)
PHONE..................................609 898-4500
Bernar Haas, *Principal*
Kathleen Hayes, *Accounts Exec*
EMP: 5
SALES (est): 345.5K **Privately Held**
SIC: 2741 Miscellaneous publishing

(G-1095)
COHANSEY COVE
705 Jonathan Hoffman Rd (08204-4308)
PHONE..................................609 884-7726
Karen Keirsey, *Principal*
EMP: 4 EST: 2011
SALES (est): 291.7K **Privately Held**
SIC: 2741 Miscellaneous publishing

(G-1096)
COLD SPRING ICE INC
Also Called: Lobster House
906 Schellenger St (08204-1775)
P.O. Box 497 (08204-0497)
PHONE..................................609 884-3405
Keith Laudeman, *President*
Clara Burkhardt, *Manager*
EMP: 5
SALES: 330K **Privately Held**
SIC: 2097 Manufactured ice

(G-1097)
DOUBLE DIAMOND TECHNOLOGIES
705 Route 9 (08204-4611)
P.O. Box 303, Ocean View (08230-0303)
PHONE..................................609 624-1414
David P Catanoso, *President*
EMP: 6
SALES (est): 460K **Privately Held**
WEB: www.doublediamondtech.com
SIC: 3695 Computer software tape &
  disks: blank, rigid & floppy

(G-1098)
EXIT ZERO COOKHOUSE INC
109 Sunset Blvd Ste B (08204-4149)
PHONE..................................609 770-8479
Jack Wright, *Editor*
EMP: 9
SALES (est): 878.3K **Privately Held**
SIC: 2741 Miscellaneous publishing

(G-1099)
FISHERMENS ENERGY NJ LLC
985 Ocean Dr (08204-1855)
PHONE..................................609 286-9650
Chris Wissemann, *CEO*
Daniel Cohen, *Mng Member*
EMP: 13
SALES (est): 2MM **Privately Held**
SIC: 3621 Windmills, electric generating

(G-1100)
GALVANIC LLC
514 Washington St (08204-1428)
PHONE..................................609 600-2604
Ryan Platzer, *Mng Member*
EMP: 5
SALES (est): 568K **Privately Held**
SIC: 2326 Men's & boys' work clothing

(G-1101)
GLOBE ENGINEERING CORP
1213 Delaware Ave (08204-2606)
PHONE..................................609 898-0349
Albert Kuintzle, *President*
EMP: 5 EST: 1962
SQ FT: 6,600
SALES (est): 468.5K **Privately Held**
SIC: 3444 3599 Sheet metal specialties,
  not stamped; machine shop, jobbing & re-
  pair

(G-1102)
LUNDS FISHERIES INC
997 Ocean Dr (08204-1899)
PHONE..................................609 884-7600
Fax: 609 884-0664
Jeffrey Reichle, *President*
Wayne Reichle, *President*

▲ = Import ▼=Export
◆ =Import/Export

Matt Viall, *CFO*
◆ **EMP:** 100 **EST:** 1954
SQ FT: 15,000
SALES (est): 29.4MM **Privately Held**
WEB: www.lundsfish.com
SIC: 2092 Seafoods, frozen: prepared

(G-1103)
MARK I INDUSTRIES INC
910 Shunpike Rd (08204-4333)
PHONE..............................609 884-0051
Robert Bartle, *President*
EMP: 10
SQ FT: 1,000
SALES (est): 670K **Privately Held**
SIC: 3324 Steel investment foundries

(G-1104)
SAMPLE MEDIA INC
Also Called: Cape May Star & Wave
600 Park Blvd Ste 5 (08204-1265)
PHONE..............................609 884-2021
Fax: 609 884-2893
Jennifer Kopp, *Principal*
EMP: 5
SALES (est): 439.2K
SALES (corp-wide): 3.9MM **Privately Held**
SIC: 2711 Newspapers
PA: Sample Media, Inc
112 E 8th St
Ocean City NJ 08226
609 399-5411

(G-1105)
SEA HARVEST INC
985 Ocean Dr (08204-1855)
P.O. Box 555 (08204-0555)
PHONE..............................609 884-3000
Daniel Cohen, *President*
Barry Cohen, *Corp Secy*
Maxi Cohen, *Vice Pres*
EMP: 25
SQ FT: 750
SALES (est): 1.8MM **Privately Held**
SIC: 4499 2091 Boat cleaning; canned & cured fish & seafoods

(G-1106)
TMU INC
Also Called: Tooling & Mfg Unlimited
910 Shunpike Rd Ste A (08204-4334)
PHONE..............................609 884-7656
Fax: 609 884-0778
Robert Bartle, *President*
EMP: 16 **EST:** 1964
SQ FT: 12,000
SALES (est): 2.4MM **Privately Held**
WEB: www.tmuinc.com
SIC: 3469 3556 3549 Machine parts, stamped or pressed metal; food products machinery; metalworking machinery

(G-1107)
W J R B INC
Also Called: Cape May Winery & Vineyard
711 Town Bank Rd (08204-4410)
PHONE..............................609 884-1169
Arthur Craig Jr, *President*
EMP: 7
SALES (est): 942.6K **Privately Held**
WEB: www.wjrb.com
SIC: 2084 5921 Wines; wine

(G-1108)
WILLOW CREEK WINERY INC
160 Stevens St 168 (08204-1092)
PHONE..............................609 770-8782
Barbara Wilde, *President*
EMP: 4
SALES (est): 437.2K **Privately Held**
SIC: 2084 Wines

Cape May Court House
Cape May County

(G-1109)
ANNE ALANNA INC
41 Pierces Point Rd (08210-2518)
PHONE..............................609 465-3787
Ed Obropta, *Owner*
EMP: 5 **EST:** 2001

SALES (est): 654.5K **Privately Held**
WEB: www.alannaanne.com
SIC: 2261 Screen printing of cotton broad-woven fabrics

(G-1110)
BILLY D DUMPSTER SERVICE LLC
1 Kimbles Beach Rd (08210-2077)
PHONE..............................609 465-5990
William Drury, *Principal*
EMP: 8
SALES (est): 833.1K **Privately Held**
SIC: 3443 Dumpsters, garbage

(G-1111)
CANVAS CREATIONS
14 Swainton Goshen Rd (08210-1457)
PHONE..............................609 465-8428
Fax: 609 465-4120
Clinton R Clement Jr, *Partner*
Scott Beck, *Partner*
▲ **EMP:** 4
SQ FT: 1,200
SALES: 300K **Privately Held**
SIC: 2394 Canvas boat seats; convertible tops, canvas or boat: from purchased materials; sails: made from purchased materials

(G-1112)
CHOCOLATE FACE CUPCAKE
1963 Route 9 N (08210-1158)
PHONE..............................609 624-2253
EMP: 4
SALES (est): 255.6K **Privately Held**
SIC: 2051 Bread, cake & related products

(G-1113)
COMMERCIAL WATER SPORTS INC
28 Clermont Dr (08210-1157)
PHONE..............................609 624-3404
Rob Guarini, *CEO*
▼ **EMP:** 5
SALES (est): 735.4K **Privately Held**
SIC: 3732 Boat building & repairing

(G-1114)
INTER REP ASSOCIATES INC (PA)
131 Kimbles Beach Rd (08210-2079)
PHONE..............................609 465-0077
Robert Leafey, *President*
EMP: 1
SALES (est): 1.6MM **Privately Held**
SIC: 5084 3559 7389 Industrial machine parts; glass making machinery: blowing, molding, forming, etc.;

(G-1115)
LICENSEE SERVICES INC
502 S Main St (08210-2350)
P.O. Box 716 (08210-0716)
PHONE..............................609 465-2003
Fred Spiewak, *President*
Ed Paone, *Vice Pres*
Sue Lawrik, *Pub Rel Mgr*
EMP: 15
SQ FT: 400,000
SALES (est): 2MM **Privately Held**
SIC: 2759 Screen printing

(G-1116)
NATALI VINEYARDS LLC
221 Route 47 N (08210-1328)
PHONE..............................609 465-0075
Alfred Natali, *Mng Member*
EMP: 6
SALES (est): 467K **Privately Held**
SIC: 2084 5921 Wines; wine

(G-1117)
THOMAS INSTRUMENTATION INC
118 Kings Hwy (08210-1233)
PHONE..............................609 624-7777
Fax: 609 624-8863
Thomas Gluyas, *President*
Cassandra Gluyas, *President*
EMP: 10

SALES (corp-wide): 1.8MM **Privately Held**
WEB: www.tiweb.net
SIC: 3577 7371 Computer peripheral equipment; custom computer programming services
PA: Thomas Instrumentation Inc.
133 Landing Rd
Cape May Court House NJ 08210
609 624-2630

(G-1118)
THOMAS INSTRUMENTATION INC (PA)
133 Landing Rd (08210-1113)
PHONE..............................609 624-2630
Cassandra Gluyas, *CEO*
Thomas W Gluyas, *President*
Jan Gluyas, *CFO*
Angie Irizzary, *Sales Staff*
Jeff Niccoli, *Marketing Mgr*
EMP: 14
SALES (est): 1.8MM **Privately Held**
WEB: www.tiweb.net
SIC: 8711 7371 3825 3679 Electrical or electronic engineering; custom computer programming services; analog-digital converters, electronic instrumentation type; electronic circuits; harness assemblies for electronic use: wire or cable; printed circuit boards

Carlstadt
Bergen County

(G-1119)
3RD GENERATION ENTERPRISES
283 Veterans Blvd (07072-2708)
P.O. Box 1222, Englewood Cliffs (07632-0222)
PHONE..............................201 528-7274
Mario Lugones, *Exec VP*
Marlen L Bracho, *Vice Pres*
▼ **EMP:** 19
SALES (est): 3.2MM **Privately Held**
WEB: www.toppopsoda.com
SIC: 2086 Soft drinks: packaged in cans, bottles, etc.

(G-1120)
A & S PACKAGING & DISPLAY
120 Kero Rd (07072-2601)
PHONE..............................201 531-1900
Roy Andersen, *President*
Joanne Andersen, *Admin Sec*
EMP: 10
SQ FT: 26,000
SALES (est): 1.6MM **Privately Held**
WEB: www.aspkg.com
SIC: 3086 Packaging & shipping materials, foamed plastic

(G-1121)
AGFA CORPORATION
580 Gotham Pkwy (07072-2405)
PHONE..............................201 440-0111
Bob Caplan, *Principal*
Wolfgang Platter, *Credit Mgr*
Pablo Falter, *Human Res Dir*
Jing Xue, *Accounts Mgr*
Mathias Eichhorn, *Business Anlyst*
EMP: 50
SALES (corp-wide): 526.3MM **Privately Held**
SIC: 2752 3861 Photo-offset printing; photographic equipment & supplies
HQ: Agfa Corporation
611 River Dr Ste 305
Elmwood Park NJ 07407
800 540-2432

(G-1122)
AGFA CORPORATION
580 Gotham Pkwy (07072-2405)
PHONE..............................201 288-4101
Fax: 201 288-3943
EMP: 20
SALES (corp-wide): 633.6MM **Privately Held**
SIC: 2752 Mfg Photo Offset Printing

HQ: Agfa Corporation
10 S Academy St
Greenville SC 07407
800 526-5441

(G-1123)
ALLFASTENERS USA LLC
480 Meadow Ln (07072-3006)
PHONE..............................201 783-8836
EMP: 22
SALES (corp-wide): 2.7MM **Privately Held**
SIC: 3429 Builders' hardware
HQ: Allfasteners Usa, Llc
959 Laker Rd
Medina OH 44256
440 232-6060

(G-1124)
ALLIED ENVELOPE CO INC (PA)
Also Called: Allied Printing Resources
33 Commerce Rd (07072-2504)
PHONE..............................201 440-2000
Fax: 201 507-8812
Robert James Royer, *President*
Jeff Miller, *Vice Pres*
Christopher Royer, *Admin Sec*
▲ **EMP:** 50
SQ FT: 58,000
SALES: 12MM **Privately Held**
SIC: 5112 2752 Envelopes; atlases, lithographed

(G-1125)
AMERICAN CONSOLIDATION INC
500 Washington Ave (07072-2900)
PHONE..............................201 438-4351
Steve Sachs, *CEO*
Dominick Rizzitano, *President*
Jim Casson, *General Mgr*
Bernard Geik, *Chairman*
◆ **EMP:** 90
SQ FT: 200,000
SALES (est): 10.3MM **Privately Held**
WEB: www.americanconsolidation.com
SIC: 3999 Atomizers, toiletry

(G-1126)
ARCY MANUFACTURING CO INC
575 Industrial Rd (07072-1611)
PHONE..............................201 635-1910
Fax: 201 635-1911
Bob Mattesky, *President*
Jackie Nieves, *Manager*
▼ **EMP:** 11
SQ FT: 12,000
SALES (est): 1.9MM **Privately Held**
SIC: 3053 Gaskets, all materials; packing, metallic; packing, rubber; gaskets & sealing devices

(G-1127)
ARDE INC (DH)
Also Called: Arde Barinco or Arde
875 Washington Ave (07072-3001)
PHONE..............................201 784-9880
Warren Boley, *President*
Jim Maser, *Principal*
Joseph Truncale, *Mfg Dir*
Lorrine Kunz, *Opers Mgr*
Estelle Anselmo, *Engineer*
EMP: 57 **EST:** 1951
SQ FT: 40,000
SALES (est): 25.7MM
SALES (corp-wide): 1.8B **Publicly Held**
WEB: www.ardeinc.com
SIC: 3443 Tanks, standard or custom fabricated: metal plate
HQ: Inc Aerojet Rocketdyne Of De
8900 De Soto Ave
Canoga Park CA 91304
818 586-1000

(G-1128)
ARDE INC
875 Washington Ave (07072-3001)
PHONE..............................201 784-9880
EMP: 60
SALES (corp-wide): 1.8B **Publicly Held**
SIC: 3369 Machinery castings, nonferrous: ex. alum., copper, die, etc.
HQ: Arde Inc.
875 Washington Ave
Carlstadt NJ 07072
201 784-9880

(G-1129)
ATLANTIC COOLG TECH & SVCS LLC
Also Called: Atlantank
80 Kero Rd (07072-2604)
PHONE..................................201 939-0900
Kenny Wood, *Opers Mgr*
Jacob Wood, *Purch Mgr*
Mark S Alberti, *Mng Member*
Katherine Cabrera, *Technology*
Raquel Ruiz, *Administration*
▲ EMP: 30
SQ FT: 16,000
SALES: 5.8MM **Privately Held**
WEB: www.atlanticcooling.com
SIC: 2499 Cooling towers, wood or wood & sheet metal combination

(G-1130)
BETA INDUSTRIES CORP
Also Called: Beta Tech
707 Commercial Ave (07072-2602)
PHONE..................................201 939-2400
Arnold Serchuk, *President*
Stuart Serchuk, *VP Sls/Mktg*
Sandra Titsch, *Controller*
Sandy Tish, *Manager*
EMP: 9
SQ FT: 40,000
SALES: 2MM **Privately Held**
SIC: 3861 3826 3442 Photographic equipment & supplies; analytical instruments; metal doors, sash & trim

(G-1131)
BETA PLASTICS
120 Amor Ave (07072-2103)
P.O. Box 808, Lyndhurst (07071-0808)
PHONE..................................201 933-1400
Fax: 201 933-0089
Alfred Teo, *President*
Stanley Band, *Vice Pres*
Annie Teo, *Admin Sec*
Chuck Broo, *Representative*
EMP: 200
SQ FT: 110,000
SALES (est): 31.3MM **Privately Held**
WEB: www.betaplastics.com
SIC: 2673 Plastic bags: made from purchased materials
PA: Alpha Industries Management, Inc.
Page And Schuyler Ave
Lyndhurst NJ 07071

(G-1132)
BM USA INCORPORATED (HQ)
Also Called: Madison Shoe Company
75 Triangle Blvd (07072-2702)
PHONE..................................800 624-5499
Fax: 201 438-5782
James Mullaney, *President*
Mark Koonin, *Admin Sec*
Randy Routh, *Admin Sec*
▲ EMP: 23
SALES: 35MM
SALES (corp-wide): 3MM **Privately Held**
SIC: 3143 Men's footwear, except athletic

(G-1133)
BROOKAIRE COMPANY LLC
329 Veterans Blvd (07072-2708)
PHONE..................................973 473-7527
John Mornan,
EMP: 14
SQ FT: 15,750
SALES: 4MM **Privately Held**
SIC: 3564 Filters, air: furnaces, air conditioning equipment, etc.; air purification equipment

(G-1134)
BURGER MAKER INC
Also Called: Schweid & Sons
666 16th St (07072-1922)
PHONE..................................201 939-4747
Fax: 201 939-1965
David Schweid, *President*
Brad Schweid, *Exec VP*
Jamie Schweid, *Vice Pres*
Felix Sixto, *Plant Mgr*
Tony Crain, *Opers Mgr*
▲ EMP: 30
SALES (est): 13MM **Privately Held**
SIC: 2011 Beef products from beef slaughtered on site

(G-1135)
C AND R PRINTING CORPORATION
400 Gotham Pkwy Ste 4 (07072-2401)
PHONE..................................201 528-8912
EMP: 10
SQ FT: 30,000
SALES (est): 1.3MM **Privately Held**
SIC: 7331 2759 Direct Mail Advertising Services Commercial Printing

(G-1136)
C T A MANUFACTURING CORP
263 Veterans Blvd (07072-2708)
PHONE..................................201 896-1000
Fax: 201 896-0529
Jack Dreyfus, *Ch of Bd*
Michael Borghard, *President*
Fernande Dreyfus, *Corp Secy*
Donna Reiff, *Director*
▲ EMP: 25 EST: 1978
SQ FT: 15,000
SALES: 15MM **Privately Held**
WEB: www.ctatools.com
SIC: 3423 3714 Hand & edge tools; mechanics' hand tools; motor vehicle parts & accessories
PA: Dreyco Inc
263 Veterans Blvd
Carlstadt NJ 07072
201 896-9000

(G-1137)
CARGILLE TAB-PRO CORPORATION
50 Broad St (07072-2006)
PHONE..................................973 267-8883
Fax: 973 267-7998
EMP: 16
SQ FT: 56,000
SALES (est): 1.4MM
SALES (corp-wide): 3.5MM **Privately Held**
SIC: 1799 2899 Trade Contractor Mfg Chemical Preparations/Formulate Chemical
PA: Cargille-Sacher Laboratories Inc.
55 Commerce Rd
Cedar Grove NJ 07009
973 239-6633

(G-1138)
CARNEGIE DELI INC
605 Washington Ave (07072-2901)
PHONE..................................201 507-5557
Fax: 201 507-5854
Jeff Jensen, *Opers Staff*
Gisela Moreno, *Human Res Dir*
Sarri Harper, *Mktg Dir*
Richard O'Donell, *Director*
EMP: 70
SQ FT: 25,000
SALES (est): 9.9MM
SALES (corp-wide): 5.8MM **Privately Held**
WEB: www.carnegiedeli.com
SIC: 2011 2051 Meat packing plants; bread, cake & related products
PA: Carnegie Successors Inc
854 7th Ave Frnt
New York NY 10019
212 757-2245

(G-1139)
CAUDALIE USA INC
30 Commerce Rd (07072-2503)
PHONE..................................201 939-4969
Mathilde Thomas, *Principal*
EMP: 5 EST: 2012
SALES (est): 403.5K **Privately Held**
SIC: 2449 Shipping cases, wood: wirebound

(G-1140)
CIC LETTER SERVICE INC
111 Commerce Rd (07072-2510)
PHONE..................................201 896-1900
Fax: 201 804-8017
Donald Gundry, *President*
Michael Mackey, *Vice Pres*
Kevin Mackey, *CFO*
Raymond Janicki, *Admin Sec*
EMP: 60

SALES (est): 2.9MM **Privately Held**
SIC: 7331 2752 Mailing service; commercial printing, lithographic

(G-1141)
CIRCLE VISUAL INC
Also Called: Circle Fabrics
340 13th St (07072-1918)
PHONE..................................212 719-5153
Oscar Balloveras, *President*
Deborah Nathan, *Project Mgr*
Jasica Mehta, *Opers Mgr*
Sergio Magana, *VP Sales*
◆ EMP: 20 EST: 1958
SQ FT: 15,000
SALES (est): 5.8MM **Privately Held**
SIC: 5131 5023 2396 Piece goods & other fabrics; linens, table; decorative home furnishings & supplies; ribbons & bows, cut & sewed

(G-1142)
CITROIL ENTERPRISES INC
Also Called: Citroil Aromatic
444 Washington Ave (07072-2806)
PHONE..................................201 933-8405
Fax: 201 933-8217
Vivian R Glueck, *President*
Henry Rosenberg, *Exec VP*
Andy Blum, *Vice Pres*
Brian Coady, *Vice Pres*
Elaine Kellman-Grosinger, *Vice Pres*
◆ EMP: 10
SQ FT: 22,000
SALES (est): 1.5MM **Privately Held**
WEB: www.citroil.com
SIC: 2087 Concentrates, drink

(G-1143)
CITROMAX FLAVORS INC
444 Washington Ave (07072-2806)
PHONE..................................201 933-8405
Vivian Glueck, *President*
Murilo Basso, *General Mgr*
Lucas Fornaciari, *General Mgr*
Jacob Glueck, *Principal*
◆ EMP: 9
SALES (est): 1MM **Privately Held**
SIC: 2087 Beverage bases, concentrates, syrups, powders & mixes

(G-1144)
CITROMAX USA INC
444 Washington Ave (07072-2806)
PHONE..................................201 933-8405
Vivian Glueck, *President*
Andy Blum, *Vice Pres*
Michele Distefano, *Purch Mgr*
Glen Camarena, *Sales Staff*
Angela Begley, *Manager*
EMP: 30 EST: 2012
SALES (est): 581.4K **Privately Held**
SIC: 2087 Flavoring extracts & syrups

(G-1145)
CITY THEATRICAL INC
475 Barell Ave (07072-2809)
PHONE..................................201 549-1160
Gary Fails, *CEO*
Carl Camenisch, *Business Mgr*
Gary Vilardi, *Vice Pres*
Andras Joo, *Project Mgr*
Harrison Hohnholt, *Sales Staff*
▲ EMP: 35
SQ FT: 40,000
SALES (est): 10.3MM **Privately Held**
WEB: www.citytheatrical.com
SIC: 5719 3648 Lighting fixtures; lighting equipment

(G-1146)
CMYK PRINTING INC
651 Garden St (07072-1609)
PHONE..................................201 458-1300
Charles Ambrogio, *CEO*
Robert Ryan, *President*
Amy Arrabito, *Production*
EMP: 10
SQ FT: 10,000
SALES: 2.5MM **Privately Held**
SIC: 2752 Commercial printing, offset

(G-1147)
COCA-COLA REFRESHMENTS USA INC
118 Moonachie Ave (07072-2508)
PHONE..................................201 635-6300
Fax: 201 935-5227
Ken Kaprowski, *Branch Mgr*
EMP: 300
SALES (corp-wide): 35.4B **Publicly Held**
WEB: www.cokecce.com
SIC: 2086 Bottled & canned soft drinks
HQ: Coca-Cola Refreshments Usa, Inc.
2500 Windy Ridge Pkwy Se
Atlanta GA 30339
770 989-3000

(G-1148)
COMPONENTS & CONTROLS INC
493 Washington Ave (07072-2803)
P.O. Box 437 (07072-0437)
PHONE..................................201 483-9190
Fax: 201 438-3356
Jerry Orlando, *President*
Anthony Bourne, *General Mgr*
Marc Dinnerman, *Sales Associate*
EMP: 14
SQ FT: 11,000
SALES: 1.5MM **Privately Held**
SIC: 5084 3599 Industrial machinery & equipment; machine & other job shop work

(G-1149)
COORDINATED METALS INC
626 16th St (07072-1929)
PHONE..................................201 460-7280
Fax: 201 460-1821
Frank Grippi, *Ch of Bd*
Paul Santo, *Vice Pres*
Stephen Von Ohlen, *Purchasing*
Scott Eisenberger, *CFO*
▲ EMP: 67
SQ FT: 35,754
SALES: 24.3MM **Privately Held**
WEB: www.cmi-metals.com
SIC: 1799 3441 Ornamental metal work; building components, structural steel

(G-1150)
COSMETIC COATINGS INC
219 Broad St (07072-1903)
P.O. Box 95 (07072-0095)
PHONE..................................201 438-7150
Richard Gottesman, *President*
Robert Fishman, *Admin Sec*
EMP: 20
SALES (est): 3.9MM **Privately Held**
SIC: 2844 Cosmetic preparations

(G-1151)
CRYSTAL WORLD INC
283 Veterans Blvd (07072-2708)
PHONE..................................201 488-0909
Fax: 201 488-7447
Ryuju Nakai, *President*
Kikuko Klawitter, *Corp Secy*
▲ EMP: 25
SQ FT: 14,600
SALES (est): 2.6MM
SALES (corp-wide): 609.9MM **Privately Held**
WEB: www.crystalworld.com
SIC: 3229 Glass furnishings & accessories
HQ: True World Holdings Llc
24 Link Dr Unit D
Rockleigh NJ 07647
201 750-0024

(G-1152)
D AND J INDUSTRIES LLC
435 Meadow Ln (07072-3006)
P.O. Box 32, Wood Ridge (07075-0032)
PHONE..................................201 257-8953
Dan Reiss, *President*
Joseph Deglomini, *Administration*
EMP: 10
SQ FT: 8,800
SALES: 7MM **Privately Held**
SIC: 3646 Commercial indusl & institutional electric lighting fixtures

(G-1153)
DELTA PROCUREMENT INC
Also Called: US Gov Turamco
400 Gotham Pkwy (07072-2400)
PHONE....................................201 623-9353
Mustafa Avci, *President*
Ali Kalkandelen, *Opers Mgr*
▼ EMP: 5
SQ FT: 65,000
SALES: 2.5MM **Privately Held**
SIC: 5932 2899 3429 Building materials, secondhand; chemical preparations; marine hardware

(G-1154)
DESIGN DISPLAY GROUP INC (PA)
105 Amor Ave (07072-2102)
PHONE....................................201 438-6000
Andrew Freedman, *President*
Carmine D'Agosto, *Exec VP*
Jonathon Loew, *Exec VP*
Marsha Chang, *Project Mgr*
Kathy Meneses, *Project Mgr*
▲ EMP: 113
SQ FT: 125,000
SALES (est): 18.9MM **Privately Held**
WEB: www.designdisplaygroup.com
SIC: 3089 3993 2541 Injection molded finished plastic products; injection molding of plastics; displays & cutouts, window & lobby; display fixtures, wood

(G-1155)
DESIGNER SIGN SYSTEMS LLC
Also Called: Barbieri, Anthony J
50 Broad St (07072-2006)
PHONE....................................212 939-5577
Fax: 201 939-7043
Judith Barbieri, *President*
Anthony Barbieri, *Vice Pres*
Monica Rincon, *Project Mgr*
Kathy Rodriguez, *Project Mgr*
Rick Tarrant, *Project Mgr*
EMP: 12
SQ FT: 10,000
SALES (est): 2.2MM **Privately Held**
SIC: 3993 Signs, not made in custom sign painting shops

(G-1156)
DOHRMAN PRINTING CO INC
445 Industrial Rd (07072-1615)
PHONE....................................201 933-0346
Fax: 201 933-0356
Ken Bell, *President*
Lisa Bell, *Vice Pres*
EMP: 7
SALES (est): 621.3K **Privately Held**
WEB: www.dohrmanprinting.com
SIC: 2752 Commercial printing, offset

(G-1157)
DOOR STOP LLC
Also Called: Doorstop
109 Kero Rd (07072-2601)
PHONE....................................718 599-5112
Mike Keller, *Mng Member*
Michael Sklar,
EMP: 10
SALES (est): 1MM **Privately Held**
SIC: 2431 5046 Doors, wood; partitions

(G-1158)
DREYCO INC (PA)
263 Veterans Blvd (07072-2708)
PHONE....................................201 896-9000
Jack Dreyfus, *Ch of Bd*
Michael Borghard, *Exec VP*
Karen Dreyfus Borghard, *Vice Pres*
▼ EMP: 10 EST: 1950
SQ FT: 10,000
SALES (est): 15MM **Privately Held**
WEB: www.dreycoinc.com
SIC: 5013 5072 5085 3423 Automotive supplies & parts; hand tools; industrial supplies; hand & edge tools

(G-1159)
ECCE PANIS INC
447 Gotham Pkwy (07072-2409)
PHONE....................................877 706-0510
EMP: 4
SALES (est): 150K **Privately Held**
SIC: 2051 Mfg Bread/Related Products

(G-1160)
FERRUM INDUSTRIES INC
735 Commercial Ave (07072-2602)
PHONE....................................201 935-1220
Fax: 201 935-1824
Lawrence Wolfin, *President*
Richard Wolfin, *Vice Pres*
EMP: 15
SQ FT: 8,500
SALES (est): 1MM **Privately Held**
SIC: 3451 Screw machine products

(G-1161)
FLAVORS OF ORIGIN INC
Also Called: Flavor Materials International
700 Gotham Pkwy (07072-2402)
PHONE....................................201 460-8306
Ian Gorinsten, *Branch Mgr*
EMP: 4
SALES (est): 215.9K
SALES (corp-wide): 16.9MM **Privately Held**
WEB: www.flavormaterials.com
SIC: 2087 Extracts, flavoring
PA: Flavors Of Origin Inc.
    10 Engelhard Ave
    Avenel NJ 07001
    732 499-9700

(G-1162)
FLEX PRODUCTS LLC
640 Dell Rd Ste 1 (07072-2202)
PHONE....................................201 440-1570
Bradford Philip,
Ed Friedhoff,
EMP: 75
SQ FT: 65,000
SALES (est): 10.6MM
SALES (corp-wide): 118.3MM **Privately Held**
WEB: www.flex-products.com
SIC: 3083 3089 Laminated plastics plate & sheet; plastic containers, except foam; plastic hardware & building products
PA: Sinclair & Rush, Inc.
    123 Manufacturers Dr
    Arnold MO 63010
    636 282-6800

(G-1163)
GLOBE PACKAGING CO INC
Also Called: Globe Casing Co
368 Paterson Plank Rd (07072-2306)
PHONE....................................201 896-1144
Isreal Bank, *President*
David Knoebel, *Vice Pres*
Adam Stein, *Marketing Staff*
Batia Bank, *Admin Sec*
▲ EMP: 9
SQ FT: 4,000
SALES (est): 1.8MM **Privately Held**
WEB: www.globecasing.com
SIC: 3089 Food casings, plastic

(G-1164)
GRAND LIFE INC
40 Broad St (07072-2006)
PHONE....................................201 556-8975
Suk Kan OH, *CEO*
Steve Yi, *Exec VP*
Jason Pak, *CFO*
EMP: 9 EST: 2015
SQ FT: 4,000
SALES: 14MM **Privately Held**
SIC: 2515 Mattresses & bedsprings

(G-1165)
GROBET FILE COMPANY AMER LLC (PA)
Also Called: Grobet USA
750 Washington Ave (07072-3088)
PHONE....................................201 939-6700
Fax: 800 243-2432
Tami McCrickard, *Purch Mgr*
Laurie Fisher, *CFO*
Lori Fisher, *CFO*
Hilal Akhtar, *Controller*
Patricia Vantreuren, *Human Res Mgr*
EMP: 55
SALES (est): 12.5MM **Privately Held**
SIC: 3545 3519 3423 Cutting tools for machine tools; parts & accessories, internal combustion engines; cutting dies, except metal cutting

(G-1166)
H & H GRAPHIC PRINTING INC
400 Gotham Pkwy Ste 1 (07072-2401)
PHONE....................................201 369-9700
Steven Braunstein, *Owner*
EMP: 4
SALES (est): 344.5K **Privately Held**
SIC: 2759 Commercial printing

(G-1167)
HACKENSACK STEEL CORP
645 Industrial Rd (07072-1611)
PHONE....................................201 935-0090
Fax: 201 935-4823
Anthony Fasciano, *President*
EMP: 20 EST: 1963
SQ FT: 8,000
SALES (est): 8.9MM **Privately Held**
SIC: 3441 Fabricated structural metal

(G-1168)
HARTIN PAINT & FILLER CORP
219 Broad St (07072-1903)
P.O. Box 116 (07072-0116)
PHONE....................................201 438-3300
Richard Gotteseman, *President*
Robert Fishman, *Vice Pres*
EMP: 25 EST: 1940
SQ FT: 25,000
SALES (est): 4.3MM **Privately Held**
SIC: 2851 Lacquers, varnishes, enamels & other coatings

(G-1169)
HEINZELMAN HEAT TREATING LLC
790 Washington Ave (07072-3008)
PHONE....................................201 933-4800
Nick Bugliarello-Wondrich, *Principal*
Nick Bugliarello - Wondrich,
EMP: 25 EST: 1915
SQ FT: 30,000
SALES (est): 2.1MM **Privately Held**
SIC: 3398 Metal heat treating

(G-1170)
HOUGHTON CHEMICAL CORPORATION
30 Amor Ave (07072-2103)
PHONE....................................201 460-8071
Walter Engel, *Branch Mgr*
EMP: 16
SQ FT: 60,635
SALES (est): 1.4MM
SALES (corp-wide): 35.1MM **Privately Held**
WEB: www.houghton.com
SIC: 5169 2899 2842 Organic chemicals, synthetic; chemical preparations; antifreeze compounds; specialty cleaning, polishes & sanitation goods
PA: Houghton Chemical Corporation
    52 Cambridge St
    Allston MA 02134
    617 254-1010

(G-1171)
IMPACT DISPLAYS INC
310 13th St (07072-1918)
PHONE....................................201 804-6262
Gill Horowitz, *Co-President*
Brian Mullins, *Co-President*
Michelle Emerson, *Project Mgr*
Rickelle Lewis, *Project Mgr*
Jon Martins, *Prdtn Mgr*
◆ EMP: 32
SQ FT: 11,000
SALES (est): 5.1MM **Privately Held**
SIC: 3993 Signs & advertising specialties

(G-1172)
INNERSPACE TECHNOLOGY INC
728 Garden St (07072-1625)
PHONE....................................201 933-1600
James E Blockburger, *President*
Harold K Fletcher, *President*
EMP: 5
SQ FT: 20,000
SALES: 1MM
SALES (corp-wide): 10MM **Publicly Held**
WEB: www.innerspacetechnology.com
SIC: 3812 7371 3829 Sonar systems & equipment; computer software development; measuring & controlling devices

PA: Tel-Instrument Electronics Corp.
    1 Branca Rd
    East Rutherford NJ 07073
    201 933-1600

(G-1173)
ISOCOLOR INC
631 Central Ave (07072-1538)
PHONE....................................201 935-4494
Henri V Debar, *President*
Christian Voignier, *Vice Pres*
EMP: 6
SQ FT: 150
SALES (est): 520K **Privately Held**
WEB: www.isocolor.com
SIC: 3826 Analytical instruments

(G-1174)
JINPAN INTERNATIONAL USA LTD
Also Called: Patron America
390 Veterans Blvd (07072-2704)
PHONE....................................201 460-8778
Fax: 201 227-0685
LI Zhiyuan, *Ch of Bd*
Ling Xiangsheng, *Vice Ch Bd*
Mark Du, *CFO*
Jing Yuqing, *Admin Sec*
▲ EMP: 4
SQ FT: 130
SALES (est): 40K **Privately Held**
WEB: www.jstusa.net
SIC: 3677 Coil windings, electronic

(G-1175)
JINPAN INTERNATIONAL USA LTD
Also Called: Jing
390 Veterans Blvd (07072-2704)
PHONE....................................201 460-8778
▲ EMP: 5
SALES (est): 1.1MM **Privately Held**
SIC: 3677 Mfg Electronic Coils/Transformers

(G-1176)
KANAR INC
1 Kero Rd (07072-2604)
PHONE....................................201 933-2800
Mehmet Kanar, *Managing Prtnr*
EMP: 10
SALES (est): 430.5K **Privately Held**
SIC: 5122 3999 Cosmetics, perfumes & hair products; barber & beauty shop equipment

(G-1177)
KATZS DELICATESSEN MFG
100 Industrial Rd (07072-1614)
PHONE....................................212 254-2246
Peter Carter,
Jake Dell,
James Jorgeson,
EMP: 20
SQ FT: 30,000
SALES (est): 725.5K **Privately Held**
SIC: 2011 Meat packing plants

(G-1178)
KEURIG DR PEPPER INC
600 Commercial Ave (07072-2607)
PHONE....................................201 933-0070
Jason Williams, *Human Res Dir*
Dan Denisoff, *Manager*
EMP: 100 **Publicly Held**
WEB: www.yoo-hoo.com
SIC: 2086 Soft drinks: packaged in cans, bottles, etc.
PA: Keurig Dr Pepper Inc.
    5301 Legacy Dr
    Plano TX 75024

(G-1179)
KISSLER & CO INC
770 Central Blvd (07072-3009)
PHONE....................................201 896-9600
Fax: 201 896-9190
Jerry Kissler, *President*
Barry Kissler, *Vice Pres*
Doug Tanner, *Purch Mgr*
Glenn Kissler, *VP Sales*
Jeffrey Kissler, *Sales Associate*
◆ EMP: 20

G E O G R A P H I C

SALES (est): 5.1MM **Privately Held**
WEB: www.kissler.com
SIC: 7629 5084 3432 Tool repair, electric;
  industrial machinery & equipment; plumbing fixture fittings & trim

(G-1180)
**KNICKERBOCKER BED
COMPANY**
770 Commercial Ave (07072-2602)
P.O. Box 55, Little Ferry (07643-0055)
PHONE.................................201 933-3100
Fax: 201 933-6963
Milton Polevey, *President*
Joe Hunt, *VP Sales*
Heidi Kleinman, *Sales Staff*
▼ EMP: 20
SALES (est): 3.2MM **Privately Held**
WEB: www.bedbridge.com
SIC: 2514 Frames for box springs or bed-
  springs: metal

(G-1181)
**KOHL & MADDEN PRTG INK
CORP (DH)**
651 Garden St (07072-1609)
PHONE.................................201 935-8666
Brad Bergey, *President*
Eugene Standora, *Treasurer*
EMP: 22 EST: 1905
SQ FT: 7,500
SALES (est): 24.9MM
SALES (corp-wide): 7B **Privately Held**
SIC: 2893 3565 3555 Printing ink; pack-
  aging machinery; printing trades machin-
  ery
HQ: Sun Chemical Corporation
  35 Waterview Blvd Ste 100
  Parsippany NJ 07054
  973 404-6000

(G-1182)
**KROHN TECHNICAL PRODUCTS
INC**
Also Called: Krohn Industries
303 Veterans Blvd (07072-2708)
P.O. Box 98 (07072-0098)
PHONE.................................201 933-9696
John Krohn, *President*
EMP: 18
SALES (est): 1.8MM
SALES (corp-wide): 4MM **Privately Held**
WEB: www.krohnindustries.com
SIC: 2899 3999 Plating compounds; bar-
  ber & beauty shop equipment
PA: Krohn Industries Incorporated
  303 Veterans Blvd
  Carlstadt NJ
  201 933-9696

(G-1183)
LATTA GRAPHICS INC
Also Called: Yes Press
651 Garden St (07072-1609)
P.O. Box 31, Little Ferry (07643-0031)
PHONE.................................201 440-4040
Fax: 201 568-1076
Eileen Latta, *President*
Mark Ehrmann, *Manager*
EMP: 30
SQ FT: 12,000
SALES (est): 6.1MM **Privately Held**
WEB: www.yespress.com
SIC: 2752 2789 2759 Commercial print-
  ing, lithographic; commercial printing, off-
  set; bookbinding & related work;
  commercial printing

(G-1184)
LODOR OFFSET CORPORATION
Also Called: Victoria Offset
111 Amor Ave (07072-2102)
PHONE.................................201 935-7100
Donald Samuels, *President*
Gary Samuels, *Principal*
Lester Samuels, *Vice Pres*
EMP: 10
SALES (est): 1.4MM **Privately Held**
SIC: 2621 2893 2952 2899 Printing
  paper; printing ink; asphalt felts & coat-
  ings; chemical preparations

(G-1185)
LV ADHESIVE INC
341 Michele Pl (07072-2304)
PHONE.................................201 507-0080
Linda Owen, *President*
Steve Owen, *Vice Pres*
Paula Jenkins, *Receptionist*
EMP: 50 EST: 1977
SQ FT: 22,000
SALES (est): 9.9MM **Privately Held**
WEB: www.lvadhesive.com
SIC: 2672 2671 Adhesive papers, labels
  or tapes: from purchased material; plastic
  film, coated or laminated for packaging

(G-1186)
MANHATTAN DOOR CORP
109 Kero Rd (07072-2601)
PHONE.................................718 963-1111
Martin Sklar, *Ch of Bd*
Friment Sklar, *Vice Pres*
EMP: 80 EST: 1962
SQ FT: 33,000
SALES (est): 14.3MM **Privately Held**
SIC: 2431 Doors, wood

(G-1187)
MAR-KAL PRODUCTS CORP
145 Commerce Rd (07072-2501)
PHONE.................................973 783-7155
Hans F Schmid, *President*
Nancy Schmid, *Treasurer*
EMP: 45 EST: 1963
SQ FT: 30,000
SALES (est): 2.2MM **Privately Held**
WEB: www.markalproducts.com
SIC: 3999 2396 Decalcomania work, ex-
  cept on china & glass; automotive & ap-
  parel trimmings

(G-1188)
MASTER PRINTING INC
445 Industrial Rd (07072-1615)
PHONE.................................201 842-9100
Fax: 201 842-9393
John Aresta, *President*
Ralph Castellano, *Prdtn Mgr*
Joseph Aresta Jr, *Admin Sec*
EMP: 20
SQ FT: 25,000
SALES (est): 3.4MM **Privately Held**
WEB: www.masterprintinginc.com
SIC: 2752 Commercial printing, offset

(G-1189)
**METRO SELIGER INDUSTRIES
INC**
330 Washington Ave (07072-2806)
PHONE.................................201 438-4530
Fax: 201 438-7326
Anthony Aveni, *President*
Richard Skolnik, *Sales Staff*
EMP: 160
SQ FT: 125,000
SALES (est): 6.7MM **Privately Held**
SIC: 7331 7374 2752 Direct mail advertis-
  ing services; calculating service (com-
  puter); commercial printing, lithographic;
  promotional printing, lithographic

(G-1190)
MODERN SHOWCASE INC
610 Commercial Ave (07072-2602)
PHONE.................................201 935-2929
John Kang, *President*
▲ EMP: 10
SALES (est): 1.1MM **Privately Held**
WEB: www.modernshowcase.com
SIC: 2542 Office & store showcases & dis-
  play fixtures

(G-1191)
**NATALE MACHINE & TOOL CO
INC**
Also Called: Circle D Light
339 13th St (07072-1917)
PHONE.................................201 933-5500
Fax: 201 933-8146
Dominick Natale, *President*
Karen Natale Conway, *Vice Pres*
Lynn Natale, *Treasurer*
▲ EMP: 11 EST: 1947
SQ FT: 15,000

SALES (est): 1.8MM **Privately Held**
WEB: www.circle-d.com
SIC: 3648 Floodlights

(G-1192)
NES ENTERPRISES INC
513 Washington Ave (07072-2802)
P.O. Box 1377, Springfield (07081-5377)
PHONE.................................201 964-1400
Sheldon Salkovitch, *CEO*
EMP: 9
SQ FT: 6,000
SALES: 960K **Privately Held**
SIC: 2353 2396 Hats, caps & millinery;
  screen printing on fabric articles

(G-1193)
NEW TOP INC
Also Called: Daniel & Elissa
40 Broad St (07072-2006)
PHONE.................................201 438-3990
Fax: 201 438-3994
Bam Le Cho, *President*
◆ EMP: 40
SQ FT: 50,000
SALES (est): 4.4MM **Privately Held**
SIC: 2321 5136 Men's & boys' furnishings;
  men's & boys' clothing

(G-1194)
NMN CLOSET INC
40 Veterans Blvd (07072-2712)
PHONE.................................201 438-2462
Norman Hultz, *President*
EMP: 25
SALES (est): 2.2MM **Privately Held**
SIC: 2434 Wood kitchen cabinets

(G-1195)
**NORTHERN ARCHITECTURAL
SYSTEMS**
599 Gotham Pkwy (07072-2403)
PHONE.................................201 943-6400
Robert Pecorella, *President*
EMP: 27
SALES (corp-wide): 24.7MM **Privately
Held**
SIC: 3442 Metal doors, sash & trim
PA: Northern Architectural Systems, Inc.
  111 Central Ave
  Teterboro NJ 07608
  201 943-6400

(G-1196)
OXBERRY LLC
180 Broad St (07072-1906)
PHONE.................................201 935-3000
Alfred I Thumim,
Anna Ferraro,
EMP: 8
SQ FT: 28,000
SALES (est): 610K **Privately Held**
WEB: www.oxberry.com
SIC: 3861 3641 3577 Photographic
  equipment & supplies; cameras & related
  equipment; electric lamps; computer pe-
  ripheral equipment

(G-1197)
PAN TECHNOLOGY INC
117 Moonachie Ave (07072-2507)
PHONE.................................201 438-7878
Bob Rossomando, *President*
Gary Spero, *Vice Pres*
James Difino, *Plant Mgr*
Debbie Rossomando, *Purch Mgr*
Brian Villardi, *QC Mgr*
▲ EMP: 46 EST: 1949
SQ FT: 60,000
SALES (est): 14.2MM **Privately Held**
WEB: www.pantechnology.com
SIC: 2893 Printing ink

(G-1198)
PARAGON IRON INC
550 Industrial Rd Unit D (07072-1629)
PHONE.................................201 528-7307
John Danubio, *President*
Antoinette Naggio, *Office Mgr*
EMP: 16 EST: 2005
SQ FT: 5,520
SALES (est): 761K **Privately Held**
SIC: 3449 Bars, concrete reinforcing: fabri-
  cated steel

(G-1199)
PENETONE CORPORATION (PA)
Also Called: West Penetone
700 Gotham Pkwy Ste 2 (07072-2402)
PHONE.................................201 567-3000
Fax: 201 510-3973
Elwood W Phares II, *CEO*
Michael Bradford, *Vice Pres*
Bruce Muretta, *Vice Pres*
Michael Nelson, *Vice Pres*
Jean Richard, *Vice Pres*
EMP: 25
SALES (est): 27.5MM **Privately Held**
WEB: www.protectivecream.com
SIC: 2842 2992 Cleaning or polishing
  preparations; degreasing solvent; lubricat-
  ing oils & greases

(G-1200)
PERTECH PRINTING INKS INC
Also Called: Pertech Corp K & E Printing
140 Grand St (07072-2105)
PHONE.................................908 354-1700
Roger Tusche, *President*
Peter Reissig, *Vice Pres*
▲ EMP: 31
SQ FT: 18,000
SALES (est): 5.2MM **Privately Held**
WEB: www.pertechinks.com
SIC: 3952 Ink, drawing: black & colored

(G-1201)
**PETERSON STEEL RULE DIE
CORP**
35 Broad St (07072-2006)
PHONE.................................201 935-6180
Fax: 201 935-9452
Leonard Esposito, *President*
Neal Esposito, *Vice Pres*
Susan Esposito Jacob, *Admin Sec*
EMP: 13 EST: 1963
SQ FT: 13,000
SALES (est): 2.1MM **Privately Held**
SIC: 3544 Special dies & tools

(G-1202)
**PHILIP HOLZER AND ASSOC
LLC**
350 Michele Pl (07072-2304)
PHONE.................................212 691-9500
Stuart Holzer, *Mng Member*
Eric Bernstein,
David Nicholas,
James Nicholas,
Gerry Ritterman,
EMP: 40
SALES (est): 3.6MM **Privately Held**
WEB: www.tanaseybert.com
SIC: 2752 2791 2789 Commercial print-
  ing, lithographic; typesetting; bookbinding
  & related work

(G-1203)
**PLASTIC REEL CORP OF
AMERICA (PA)**
Also Called: PRC of America
40 Triangle Blvd (07072-2701)
PHONE.................................201 933-5100
Ben Zuk, *President*
Pat Baccarella, *Vice Pres*
Robert Basili, *Vice Pres*
John Durkin, *Vice Pres*
▲ EMP: 20
SALES (est): 2.6MM **Privately Held**
WEB: www.prcofamerica.com
SIC: 3089 5043 3572 Plastic containers,
  except foam; cases, plastic; injection
  molding of plastics; motion picture cam-
  eras, equipment & supplies; computer
  storage devices

(G-1204)
POLYAIR INTER PACK INC
Also Called: Polyair Packaging Division
495 Meadow Ln (07072-3006)
PHONE.................................201 804-1725
Fax: 201 804-1711
Joseph Hickey, *Plant Mgr*
Chris Franch, *Branch Mgr*
Lisa Seeley, *Admin Asst*
EMP: 72

2018 Harris New Jersey
Manufacturers Directory
▲ = Import ▼=Export
◆ =Import/Export

SALES (corp-wide): 898.1MM **Privately Held**
WEB: www.polyair.com
SIC: 5199 2671 Packaging materials; packaging paper & plastics film, coated & laminated
HQ: Polyair Inter Pack Inc
330 Humberline Dr
Etobicoke ON M9W 1
416 679-6600

(G-1205)
POLYAIR INTER PACK INC
495 Meadow Ln (07072-3006)
PHONE..............................201 804-1700
Fax: 201 804-1710
Paula Anderson, *President*
Chuck Bergren, *Exec VP*
Tom Irwin, *Plant Mgr*
Joe Hinckley, *Manager*
EMP: 100
SALES (corp-wide): 898.1MM **Privately Held**
SIC: 2394 Liners & covers, fabric: made from purchased materials
HQ: Polyair Inter Pack Inc
330 Humberline Dr
Etobicoke ON M9W 1
416 679-6600

(G-1206)
POTTERS INDUSTRIES LLC
600 Industrial Rd (07072-1619)
PHONE..............................201 507-4169
Andy Gray, *Branch Mgr*
Janet Mizdol, *Office Admin*
Deniece N Dyall, *Technology*
EMP: 28
SALES (corp-wide): 1.4B **Publicly Held**
WEB: www.flexolite.com
SIC: 3231 Reflector glass beads, for highway signs or reflectors
HQ: Potters Industries, Llc
300 Lindenwood Dr
Malvern PA 19355
610 651-4700

(G-1207)
PRECISION METAL MACHINING INC
Also Called: P M M I
800 Central Blvd Ste C (07072-3016)
PHONE..............................201 843-7427
Pat Funicelli, *President*
Ann Funicelli, *Treasurer*
EMP: 28 EST: 1959
SQ FT: 35,000
SALES (est): 5.8MM **Privately Held**
WEB: www.gopmmi.com
SIC: 3599 Machine shop, jobbing & repair

(G-1208)
PREMIUM COLOR GROUP LLC
Also Called: Premium Clor Graphics Handpack
651 Garden St (07072-1609)
PHONE..............................973 472-7007
Andy Griffin, *Managing Prtnr*
Mark Fitzgerald, *Managing Prtnr*
Greg Zoccoli, *Sales Staff*
John Watson,
EMP: 40
SALES (est): 7MM **Privately Held**
SIC: 2759 Commercial printing

(G-1209)
PRINT PEEL
341 Michele Pl (07072-2304)
PHONE..............................201 507-0080
Steve Owen, *Vice Pres*
EMP: 50
SALES (est): 2.3MM **Privately Held**
SIC: 2752 Commercial printing, lithographic

(G-1210)
PROSPECT TRANSPORTATION INC (PA)
630 Industrial Rd (07072-1619)
PHONE..............................201 933-9999
Melissa Eichholz, *President*
Izabela Flot, *Principal*
Charles W Eichholz, *COO*
John Ondrof, *Opers Mgr*
Jackie Cotton, *VP Sales*
EMP: 100 EST: 1986

SQ FT: 26,000
SALES (est): 21.1MM **Privately Held**
WEB: www.prospect-trans.com
SIC: 4212 2869 3443 Petroleum haulage, local; fuels; fuel tanks (oil, gas, etc.); metal plate

(G-1211)
REGGIANI LIGHTING USA INC
372 Starke Rd (07072-2108)
PHONE..............................201 372-1717
John Savoretti, *President*
Matteo Reggiani, *Vice Pres*
Ian Ielfield, *Natl Sales Mgr*
Andrew Scamporino, *Mktg Dir*
▲ EMP: 10
SQ FT: 25,000
SALES (est): 2.4MM
SALES (corp-wide): 488.5K **Privately Held**
SIC: 3646 5063 Commercial indusl & institutional electric lighting fixtures; lighting fixtures, commercial & industrial
HQ: Reggiani Spa Illuminazione
Viale Monza 16
Sovico 20845
039 207-11

(G-1212)
SAFIRE SILK INC
Also Called: Silver Silk
135 Grand St (07072-2106)
PHONE..............................201 636-4061
Paul Kim, *Ch of Bd*
▲ EMP: 7
SQ FT: 4,000
SALES (est): 1.1MM **Privately Held**
SIC: 2329 Men's & boys' sportswear & athletic clothing

(G-1213)
SAPUTO CHEESE USA INC
Advantage International Foods
861 Washington Ave (07072-3001)
PHONE..............................201 508-6400
David Rowan, *Branch Mgr*
EMP: 50
SALES (corp-wide): 1.9B **Privately Held**
SIC: 2022 Cheese spreads, dips, pastes & other cheese products
HQ: Saputo Cheese Usa Inc.
1 Overlook Pt Ste 300
Lincolnshire IL 60069

(G-1214)
SAWITZ STUDIOS INC
Also Called: Sawitz Store Fixture
130 Grand St (07072-2105)
PHONE..............................201 842-9444
Fax: 201 842-8812
Dan Sawitz, *President*
June Sawitz, *Corp Secy*
EMP: 32
SQ FT: 38,000
SALES (est): 5.4MM **Privately Held**
WEB: www.sawitzstorefixture.com
SIC: 2541 2511 Store fixtures, wood; wood household furniture

(G-1215)
SCREEN REPRODUCTIONS CO INC
Also Called: Photo Screen of N J
850 Washington Ave (07072-3014)
PHONE..............................201 935-0830
Fax: 201 935-0471
Larry Weissenberg, *President*
EMP: 30 EST: 1956
SQ FT: 23,000
SALES (est): 4.3MM **Privately Held**
WEB: www.screenreproduction.com
SIC: 2621 Wallpaper (hanging paper)

(G-1216)
SECURITY HOLDINGS LLC (PA)
Also Called: Pioneer Industries
111 Kero Rd (07072-2601)
PHONE..............................201 457-0286
Mitchell Dorf, *Mng Member*
Leinis Santa Maria, *Executive Asst*
Jeffrey Haversat,
Robert Haversat,
EMP: 99
SALES: 17MM **Privately Held**
SIC: 3442 Metal doors

(G-1217)
SHREE JI PRINTING CORPORATION
55 Veterans Blvd (07072-2713)
PHONE..............................201 842-9500
Dilid Patel, *President*
EMP: 30
SQ FT: 22,000
SALES (est): 9MM **Privately Held**
SIC: 2752 Commercial printing, lithographic

(G-1218)
SINCLAIR AND RUSH INC
640 Dell Rd (07072-2202)
PHONE..............................862 262-8189
EMP: 8
SALES (est): 845K **Privately Held**
SIC: 3089 Molding primary plastic; plastic processing

(G-1219)
SNAPPLE BEVERAGE CORP (DEL)
600 Commercial Ave (07072-2607)
PHONE..............................201 933-0070
Bill Pedoto, *Plant Mgr*
EMP: 75 **Publicly Held**
SIC: 2086 Bottled & canned soft drinks
HQ: Snapple Beverage Corp (Del)
900 King St
Rye Brook NY 10573

(G-1220)
SNS ORIENTAL RUGS LLC
455 Barell Ave (07072-2809)
PHONE..............................201 355-8786
Sahigh Kashi, *Mng Member*
▲ EMP: 5
SALES (est): 719.8K **Privately Held**
SIC: 5023 2273 Rugs; carpets & rugs

(G-1221)
SOLAR RIG TECHNOLOGIES LLC
651 Garden St (07072-1609)
PHONE..............................973 600-0500
Richard Hermann, *Principal*
EMP: 4
SALES (est): 284K **Privately Held**
SIC: 7379 7382 5074 3674 ; protective devices, security; heating equipment & panels, solar; semiconductor circuit networks; electronic loads & power supplies

(G-1222)
STANBEE COMPANY INC (PA)
70 Broad St (07072-2006)
P.O. Box 436 (07072-0436)
PHONE..............................201 933-9666
Fax: 201 933-7985
Michael Berkson, *President*
▲ EMP: 30
SQ FT: 52,000
SALES (est): 5.2MM **Privately Held**
WEB: www.stanbee.com
SIC: 2211 Shoe fabrics

(G-1223)
SUN CHEMICAL CORPORATION
631 Central Ave (07072-1599)
PHONE..............................201 933-4500
Fax: 201 933-5658
Joseph Patti, *Vice Pres*
Alexander Chudolij, *Research*
James Luciano, *Engineer*
Jack Powers, *Marketing Mgr*
Dr John Rooney, *Manager*
EMP: 180
SALES (corp-wide): 7B **Privately Held**
WEB: www.sunchemical.com
SIC: 2893 Printing ink
HQ: Sun Chemical Corporation
35 Waterview Blvd Ste 100
Parsippany NJ 07054
973 404-6000

(G-1224)
SUN CHEMICAL CORPORATION
U S Ink
651 Garden St (07072-1609)
PHONE..............................201 935-8666
Fax: 201 933-2441
Frank Costagliola, *Purch Mgr*
Greg Walker, *Design Engr Mgr*

Mimi Chung, *Engineer*
Ron Himawan, *Engineer*
David Benson, *Human Res Dir*
EMP: 13
SALES (corp-wide): 7B **Privately Held**
WEB: www.sunchemical.com
SIC: 2893 Printing ink
HQ: Sun Chemical Corporation
35 Waterview Blvd Ste 100
Parsippany NJ 07054
973 404-6000

(G-1225)
SUN NOODLE NEW JERSEY LLC
40 Kero Rd (07072-2604)
PHONE..............................201 530-1100
Shawn Kim, *Manager*
▲ EMP: 8
SALES (est): 1.3MM **Privately Held**
SIC: 2098 Noodles (e.g. egg, plain & water), dry

(G-1226)
TABCO TECHNOLOGIES LLC (PA)
400 Gotham Pkwy (07072-2400)
PHONE..............................201 438-0422
Turgay Pektas, *Mng Member*
Tony Pak, *Manager*
▲ EMP: 6
SQ FT: 11,000
SALES: 5MM **Privately Held**
WEB: www.tabcotech.com
SIC: 5051 3714 5013 Aluminum bars, rods, ingots, sheets, pipes, plates, etc.; motor vehicle parts & accessories; automotive supplies

(G-1227)
TEC CAST INC (PA)
440 Meadow Ln (07072-3006)
P.O. Box 6596 (07072-0596)
PHONE..............................201 935-3885
Fax: 201 933-7497
Robert Morehardt, *President*
Lynn Biss, *CFO*
EMP: 49
SQ FT: 150,000
SALES: 7.5MM **Privately Held**
SIC: 3365 3544 Aerospace castings, aluminum; industrial molds

(G-1228)
TEXTOL SYSTEMS INC
735 Commercial Ave (07072-2602)
PHONE..............................800 624-8746
Lawrence Wolfin, *President*
Richard Wolfin, *Vice Pres*
▲ EMP: 24
SQ FT: 9,000
SALES (est): 4.6MM **Privately Held**
WEB: www.textol.com
SIC: 2241 3625 Trimmings, textile; actuators, industrial

(G-1229)
THIRD RIVER MANUFACTURING LLC
503 Washington Ave (07072-2802)
PHONE..............................201 935-2795
Jay Shreemal, *General Mgr*
Ameet Shreemal,
EMP: 8
SALES (est): 1.1MM **Privately Held**
SIC: 3599 Machine shop, jobbing & repair

(G-1230)
THUMANN INCORPORATED (PA)
Also Called: THUMANNS
670 Dell Rd Ste 1 (07072-2292)
PHONE..............................201 935-3636
Fax: 201 935-2226
Robert S Burke, *President*
Robert Burke Jr, *Vice Pres*
EMP: 200
SQ FT: 130,000
SALES: 81.1MM **Privately Held**
WEB: www.thumanns.com
SIC: 2013 Sausages from purchased meat; cured meats from purchased meat

GEOGRAPHIC

(G-1231)
TOYO INK AMERICA LLC
350 Starke Rd Ste 400 (07072-2113)
PHONE..............................201 804-0620
Bay Bosco, *Branch Mgr*
EMP: 16
SALES (corp-wide): 2.1B **Privately Held**
SIC: 2893 Printing ink
HQ: Toyo Ink America, Llc
1225 N Michael Dr
Wood Dale IL 60191
630 930-5100

(G-1232)
TRANSGLOBE USA INC
175 Broad St (07072-2002)
PHONE..............................973 465-1998
John L Zhang, *President*
▲ **EMP:** 5
SALES (est): 310K **Privately Held**
SIC: 3161 Luggage

(G-1233)
TRAYCON MANUFACTURING CO INC
555 Barell Ave (07072-2804)
PHONE..............................201 939-5555
Fax: 201 939-4180
August Pisto, *President*
Sandee Goldberg, *VP Admin*
Albert Cialone, *Manager*
EMP: 24 **EST:** 1963
SQ FT: 20,000
SALES (est): 5MM **Privately Held**
WEB: www.traycon.com
SIC: 3535 5084 Conveyors & conveying equipment; food product manufacturing machinery

(G-1234)
TRICO WEB LLC
75 Broad St (07072-2006)
PHONE..............................201 438-3860
Donald Juiliano, *COO*
EMP: 6
SALES (est): 712.9K **Privately Held**
SIC: 2759 Commercial printing

(G-1235)
TUNNEL BARREL & DRUM CO INC
329 Veterans Blvd (07072-2708)
PHONE..............................201 933-1444
Fax: 201 933-3423
Anthony Urcioli, *President*
Joseph Binder, *Corp Secy*
Yolanda Urcioli, *Vice Pres*
▲ **EMP:** 27 **EST:** 1903
SQ FT: 27,500
SALES (est): 9.5MM **Privately Held**
SIC: 5085 2655 Drums, new or reconditioned; drums, fiber: made from purchased material

(G-1236)
UNIMAC GRAPHICS LLC
350 Michele Pl (07072-2304)
PHONE..............................201 372-1000
Gregory C Matonti, *President*
James Sandham, *CFO*
▲ **EMP:** 250
SALES (est): 40.8MM
SALES (corp-wide): 124.2MM **Privately Held**
WEB: www.unimacgraphics.com
SIC: 2759 Commercial printing
PA: Union Graphics Inc
350 Michele Pl
Carlstadt NJ 07072
201 372-1000

(G-1237)
USA INDUSTRIES INC
111 Kero Rd (07072-2601)
PHONE..............................201 438-6606
James Woods, *President*
EMP: 20
SQ FT: 125,000
SALES (est): 2.2MM **Privately Held**
SIC: 3949 3444 Swimming pools, except plastic; radiator shields or enclosures, sheet metal

(G-1238)
VERNON DISPLAY GRAPHICS INC
Also Called: Seri-Arts
145 Commerce Rd (07072-2501)
PHONE..............................201 935-7117
Fax: 201 939-2949
Andrew Gabriel, *General Mgr*
Todd Smith, *Vice Pres*
EMP: 50
SALES (est): 8.3MM
SALES (corp-wide): 69.7MM **Privately Held**
WEB: www.vernoncompany.com
SIC: 2759 Screen printing
PA: The Vernon Company
604 W 4th St N
Newton IA 50208
641 792-9000

(G-1239)
VISION TEN INC
180 Broad St (07072-1906)
PHONE..............................201 935-3000
Dr Alfred I Thumim, *President*
Tiffany Bolen, *Vice Pres*
EMP: 10
SQ FT: 54,232
SALES (est): 840K **Privately Held**
SIC: 3844 3699 X-ray apparatus & tubes; electrical equipment & supplies

(G-1240)
VISUAL GRAPHIC SYSTEMS INC
330 Washington Ave (07072-2806)
PHONE..............................201 528-2700
Paul Theodore, *President*
Kathy Lagerenzi, *General Mgr*
Milton Dipietro, *Chairman*
Patrick Benasillo, *Vice Pres*
Matthew Buksbaum, *Vice Pres*
▲ **EMP:** 130
SQ FT: 106,000
SALES (est): 29.5MM **Privately Held**
WEB: www.vgsonline.com
SIC: 3993 Signs, not made in custom sign painting shops

(G-1241)
WATER-JEL HOLDING COMPANY
50 Brd St (07072)
PHONE..............................201 507-8300
James Hartnett, *CEO*
Herb Baer, *Exec VP*
Joe Dacorta, *Vice Pres*
Jim Geraghty, *Vice Pres*
Paul Slot, *Vice Pres*
▲ **EMP:** 70
SALES (est): 9.5MM **Privately Held**
WEB: www.waterjel.com
SIC: 3842 First aid, snake bite & burn kits

(G-1242)
WATER-JEL TECHNOLOGIES LLC
50 Broad St (07072-2006)
PHONE..............................201 438-1598
Fax: 201 507-8325
James Hartnett, *President*
Mark Lait, *Managing Dir*
Paul Slot, *COO*
Scott Stevenson, *Warehouse Mgr*
Robert Zega, *QC Mgr*
▲ **EMP:** 70
SQ FT: 145,000
SALES (est): 18.2MM **Privately Held**
SIC: 3842 First aid, snake bite & burn kits

(G-1243)
WEIR WELDING COMPANY INC (PA)
316 12th St (07072-1919)
P.O. Box 311 (07072-0311)
PHONE..............................201 939-2284
Fax: 201 929-5525
Charles J Weir, *President*
Chris Little, *VP Admin*
Thomas Weir, *Vice Pres*
Michael Diffley, *Project Mgr*
Paul Emeigh, *Project Mgr*
EMP: 25
SQ FT: 100,000
SALES (est): 16MM **Privately Held**
SIC: 3441 Fabricated structural metal

Carneys Point
Salem County

(G-1244)
BAHADIR USA LLC
431 S Pnnsville Auburn Rd (08069)
PHONE..............................856 517-3080
Ismail Kilic, *President*
EMP: 6
SQ FT: 17,000
SALES (est): 650.4K **Privately Held**
SIC: 3841 Diagnostic apparatus, medical; medical instruments & equipment, blood & bone work

(G-1245)
LASSONDE PAPPAS AND CO INC (DH)
1 Collins Dr Ste 200 (08069-3640)
PHONE..............................856 455-1000
Mark A McNeil, *CEO*
Jean Gattuso, *Chairman*
Craig Ablin, *Vice Pres*
Robert Crawford, *Vice Pres*
Scott Langley, *Vice Pres*
◆ **EMP:** 85
SQ FT: 600,000
SALES (est): 450MM
SALES (corp-wide): 267.2MM **Privately Held**
WEB: www.clementpappas.com
SIC: 2033 Fruit juices: packaged in cans, jars, etc.; fruits: packaged in cans, jars, etc.
HQ: Pappas Lassonde Holdings, Inc.
1 Collins Dr Ste 200
Carneys Point NJ 08069
856 455-1000

(G-1246)
PAPPAS LASSONDE HOLDINGS INC (DH)
1 Collins Dr Ste 200 (08069-3640)
PHONE..............................856 455-1000
Mark A McNeil, *CEO*
Jean Pattuso, *Chairman*
EMP: 5
SALES (est): 450MM
SALES (corp-wide): 267.2MM **Privately Held**
SIC: 2033 6719 Fruit juices: packaged in cans, jars, etc.; fruits: packaged in cans, jars, etc.; investment holding companies, except banks
HQ: Industries Lassonde Inc
755 Rue Principale
Rougemont QC J0L 1
450 469-4926

(G-1247)
TOWNSHIP OF CARNEYS POINT
Also Called: Carneys Point Fire Company Aux
Walker Ave & D St (08069)
PHONE..............................856 299-4973
Dolores Wolfer, *President*
EMP: 14 **Privately Held**
SIC: 9224 3569 ; firefighting apparatus & related equipment
PA: Township Of Carneys Point
303 Harding Hwy
Carneys Point NJ 08069
856 299-0070

Carteret
Middlesex County

(G-1248)
ANGELS BAKERY USA LLC
110 Raskulinecz Rd (07008-1000)
PHONE..............................718 389-1400
Joseph Angel, *President*
Jen McCollum Roberts, *Vice Pres*
EMP: 30
SALES (est): 6MM **Privately Held**
SIC: 2051 Bakery: wholesale or wholesale/retail combined

(G-1249)
ARCHITCTURAL METAL FABRICATORS
66 Grant Ave (07008-2720)
PHONE..............................718 765-0722
Gam Kagan, *Principal*
EMP: 4 **EST:** 2011
SALES (est): 549.8K **Privately Held**
SIC: 3446 Architectural metalwork

(G-1250)
ARCHITECTURAL METALS INC
Also Called: Architctral Metals Fabricaters
66 Grant Ave (07008-2720)
PHONE..............................718 765-0722
Gam Kagan, *President*
EMP: 7
SQ FT: 4,000
SALES (est): 720K **Privately Held**
SIC: 3441 Fabricated structural metal

(G-1251)
ARDAGH GLASS INC
50 Bryla St (07008-1111)
PHONE..............................732 969-0827
Frank Conway, *Manager*
EMP: 500 **Privately Held**
WEB: www.sgcontainers.com
SIC: 3221 Glass containers
HQ: Ardagh Glass Inc.
10194 Crosspoint Blvd
Indianapolis IN 46256

(G-1252)
BASF CATALYSTS LLC
700 Blair Rd (07008-1221)
PHONE..............................732 205-5000
Larry Drummond, *Manager*
EMP: 139
SALES (corp-wide): 76B **Privately Held**
SIC: 2869 Industrial organic chemicals
HQ: Basf Catalysts Llc
25 Middlesex Tpke
Iselin NJ 08830
732 205-5000

(G-1253)
BERJE INCORPORATED (PA)
700 Blair Rd (07008-1221)
PHONE..............................973 748-8980
Fax: 973 680-9618
Kim Bleimann, *CEO*
Dave Herbst, *President*
Carol Dowles, *Business Mgr*
Nehla A Murad, *Senior VP*
Andy O'Shea, *Senior VP*
◆ **EMP:** 125 **EST:** 1950
SQ FT: 235,000
SALES (est): 110.5MM **Privately Held**
WEB: www.berje.com
SIC: 5169 2869 Aromatic chemicals; perfumes, flavorings & food additives

(G-1254)
BRUKER OST LLC
600 Milik St (07008-1115)
P.O. Box 429 (07008-0429)
PHONE..............................732 541-1300
Jeff Parrell, *President*
Joseph Ingato, *Controller*
Karen Taylor, *Human Res Dir*
EMP: 140
SALES (est): 1.3MM
SALES (corp-wide): 1.7B **Publicly Held**
SIC: 3357 Nonferrous wiredrawing & insulating
HQ: Bruker Energy & Supercon Technologies, Inc.
15 Fortune Dr
Billerica MA 01821

(G-1255)
DOW CHEMICAL COMPANY
78 Lafayette St (07008-3521)
PHONE..............................732 969-5723
James Morrison, *Manager*
EMP: 100
SALES (corp-wide): 62.4B **Publicly Held**
WEB: www.dow.com
SIC: 2869 Industrial organic chemicals; alcohols, non-beverage; fuels
HQ: The Dow Chemical Company
2030 Dow Ctr
Midland MI 48674
989 636-1000

(G-1256)
EVERFLOW SUPPLIES INC (PA)
100 Middlesex Ave (07008-3499)
PHONE.................................908 436-1100
Lazar Templer, *President*
David Templer, *Exec VP*
Shragy Apter, *Opers Mgr*
Mark Shaingarten, *Senior Buyer*
Abraham Sharaby, *Finance*
▲ EMP: 25
SALES (est): 11.2MM **Privately Held**
SIC: 5074 3494 Plumbing fittings & sup-
plies; plumbing & heating valves

(G-1257)
FMC CORPORATION
500 Roosevelt Ave (07008-3504)
PHONE.................................732 541-3000
Fax: 732 541-3033
Jerry Sibley, *Branch Mgr*
EMP: 61
SALES (corp-wide): 2.8B **Publicly Held**
SIC: 2812 Soda ash, sodium carbonate
(anhydrous)
PA: Fmc Corporation
2929 Walnut St
Philadelphia PA 19104
215 299-6000

(G-1258)
FOLGORE MOBIL WELDING INC
Also Called: F M W Piping Contractors
526 Roosevelt Ave (07008-3017)
P.O. Box 190 (07008-0190)
PHONE.................................732 541-2974
Fax: 732 541-9202
Joseph Folgore, *President*
EMP: 42
SQ FT: 8,000
SALES: 10MM **Privately Held**
SIC: 7692 Welding repair

(G-1259)
**FUJIPOLY AMERICA
CORPORATION**
900 Milik St (07008-1117)
P.O. Box 119 (07008-0119)
PHONE.................................732 969-0100
Fax: 732 969-3311
Frank Hobler, *President*
Richard Potts, *Controller*
James Hopkins, *Sales Mgr*
Christian Mainegra, *Sales Engr*
▲ EMP: 32
SQ FT: 24,600
SALES: 14MM
SALES (corp-wide): 368.9MM **Privately
Held**
WEB: www.fujipoly.com
SIC: 3678 Electronic connectors
HQ: Fuji Polymer Industries Co.,Ltd.
1-3-18, Nishiki, Naka-Ku
Nagoya AIC 460-0
522 058-911

(G-1260)
INTERTEK USA INC
Also Called: Intertek Caleb Brett
1000 Port Carteret Dr C (07008-3527)
PHONE.................................732 969-5200
Fax: 732 862-0240
Preston Smith, *Branch Mgr*
Roy Pike, *Manager*
Tom Rizzo, *Manager*
Celia Vanpelt, *Technology*
Jyoti Yadav, *Lab Dir*
EMP: 38
SQ FT: 2,500
SALES (corp-wide): 3.6B **Privately Held**
WEB: www.itscb.com
SIC: 2911 Petroleum refining
HQ: Intertek Usa Inc.
200 Westlke Prk Blvd 40
Houston TX 77079
713 543-3600

(G-1261)
KEURIG DR PEPPER INC
1200 Milik St (07008-1119)
PHONE.................................732 969-1600
Laura Tzanavaris, *President*
EMP: 14 **Publicly Held**

SIC: 2086 Soft drinks: packaged in cans,
bottles, etc.; carbonated beverages, nonalcoholic: bottled & canned; iced tea &
fruit drinks, bottled & canned; mineral
water, carbonated: packaged in cans, bottles, etc.
PA: Keurig Dr Pepper Inc.
5301 Legacy Dr
Plano TX 75024

(G-1262)
LM FOODS LLC
100 Raskulinecz Rd (07008-1000)
PHONE.................................732 855-9500
Fax: 732 855-7474
Mark Olivito, *CEO*
Jinha Choi, *General Mgr*
Eok Jeon, *Plant Mgr*
Yong Lee, *Electrical Engi*
Tom Taillon, *Finance*
▲ EMP: 61
SQ FT: 72,000
SALES (est): 11.8MM **Privately Held**
WEB: www.lmfoods.com
SIC: 2092 Fresh or frozen packaged fish;
seafoods, fresh: prepared; seafoods,
frozen: prepared

(G-1263)
NEW YORK POPULAR INC
Also Called: Popularity Products
400 Federal Blvd (07008-1006)
PHONE.................................718 499-2020
Benjamin Tebele, *CEO*
Albert Tebele, *Ch of Bd*
Francine Shokrany, *Buyer*
Edward Tebele, *Admin Sec*
Jennifer Noel, *Assistant*
▲ EMP: 100
SQ FT: 50,000
SALES (est): 18.1MM **Privately Held**
WEB: www.popularityproducts.com
SIC: 2389 5136 5137 Men's miscella-
neous accessories; men's & boys' cloth-
ing; women's & children's clothing

(G-1264)
NU-WORLD CORPORATION (HQ)
Also Called: Nu World
300 Milik St (07008-1113)
PHONE.................................732 541-6300
Fax: 732 541-8911
Jonathan Rosenbaum, *CEO*
Stuart Dolleck, *President*
Peter Greene, *COO*
Joe Moreno, *Vice Pres*
Dianna Ruth, *Vice Pres*
▲ EMP: 211
SQ FT: 131,000
SALES (est): 95.8MM
SALES (corp-wide): 28MM **Privately
Held**
WEB: www.nwcos.com
SIC: 2844 Cosmetic preparations
PA: Cosmax Bti, Inc.
Rm F-801 Pangyo Innovalley
Seongnam 13486
823 178-9330

(G-1265)
**OXFORD INSTRS HOLDINGS INC
(DH)**
600 Milik St (07008-1199)
P.O. Box 429 (07008-0429)
PHONE.................................732 541-1300
Martin Lamaison, *President*
Maarten Kramer, *President*
Peter Williams, *Chairman*
Andrew Mackintosh, *COO*
Peter Dufall, *Prdtn Mgr*
◆ EMP: 44
SQ FT: 100,000
SALES (est): 32.6MM
SALES (corp-wide): 415.9MM **Privately
Held**
SIC: 3264 5047 Magnets, permanent: ce-
ramic or ferrite; medical equipment & sup-
plies

(G-1266)
PERIMETER SOLUTIONS LP
500 Roosevelt Ave (07008-3504)
PHONE.................................732 541-3000
Ron Hannigan, *Opers Staff*
Joseph Keber, *Purchasing*
Renea Medling, *Accounting Mgr*

Chris Philippi, *Accounts Mgr*
Thomas C Falk, *Branch Mgr*
EMP: 108 **Privately Held**
SIC: 2819 Phosphates, except fertilizers:
defluorinated & ammoniated
HQ: Perimeter Solutions Lp
373 Marshall Ave
Saint Louis MO 63119
314 983-7500

(G-1267)
Q-EXIMTRADE INC (PA)
1336 Roosevelt Ave (07008-1302)
P.O. Box 60 (07008-0060)
PHONE.................................732 366-4667
Emilio Quisumbing, *President*
▲ EMP: 5
SQ FT: 4,000
SALES (est): 680.6K **Privately Held**
WEB: www.qeximtrade.com
SIC: 3961 Costume jewelry

(G-1268)
TARMA SALES
641 Roosevelt Ave (07008-2913)
PHONE.................................732 969-3318
Fax: 732 969-2237
Taras Chubencko, *President*
Mary Ann Chubencko, *Vice Pres*
Gregory Chubencko, *Manager*
EMP: 6
SALES: 400K **Privately Held**
SIC: 3089 2396 5699 Plates, plastic;
screen printing on fabric articles; T-shirts,
custom printed

Cedar Grove
Essex County

(G-1269)
AIRDYE SOLUTIONS LLC (PA)
21 Glen Rock Rd (07009-1645)
PHONE.................................540 433-9101
Evan Smith, *CEO*
Jesse Leskanic, *CTO*
EMP: 25
SALES (est): 12.3MM **Privately Held**
SIC: 2899 Ink or writing fluids

(G-1270)
APTIMIZED LLC
579 Pompton Ave (07009-1720)
PHONE.................................203 733-2868
William Mills, *President*
EMP: 4
SQ FT: 500
SALES (est): 253.5K **Privately Held**
SIC: 7372 Application computer software

(G-1271)
AQUA PRODUCTS INC (DH)
25 Rutgers Ave (07009-1443)
PHONE.................................973 857-2700
Fax: 973 857-8981
Giora Erlich, *President*
Kathleen A McClarnon, *Corp Secy*
Mark Raile, *Exec VP*
Joel Flores, *Vice Pres*
Joseph Porat, *Vice Pres*
◆ EMP: 165
SQ FT: 9,700
SALES (est): 36.3MM
SALES (corp-wide): 256K **Privately Held**
SIC: 3589 Swimming pool filter & water
conditioning systems
HQ: Foridra Srl
S.S. Adriatica 16 17/A
Castelfidardo AN 60022
071 721-1048

(G-1272)
**BELLEVILLE WIRE CLOTH CO
INC (PA)**
18 Rutgers Ave (07009-1444)
PHONE.................................973 239-0074
Fax: 973 239-0074
James E Crowley, *President*
Jim Crowely, *Vice Pres*
Kenneth Crowley, *Vice Pres*
Augusto Gujansky, *Research*
Dan Steele, *Sales Staff*
◆ EMP: 43 EST: 1919
SQ FT: 20,000

SALES (est): 6.6MM **Privately Held**
WEB: www.bwire.com
SIC: 3496 Miscellaneous fabricated wire
products

(G-1273)
BLOOMFIELD LIFE INC
632 Pompton Ave (07009-1736)
PHONE.................................973 233-5001
Malcolm A Borg, *CEO*
EMP: 10
SALES (est): 349.5K
SALES (corp-wide): 173.6MM **Privately
Held**
SIC: 2711 Newspapers
HQ: North Jersey Media Group Inc.
1 Garret Mountain Plz # 201
Woodland Park NJ 07424
201 646-4000

(G-1274)
**CARGILLE-SACHER LABS INC
(PA)**
Also Called: Cargille Laboratories
55 Commerce Rd (07009-1289)
PHONE.................................973 239-6633
Fax: 973 239-6096
John J Cargille, *President*
William J Sacher, *Vice Pres*
Cheryl Hosler, *Controller*
Donna Hamersma, *Sales Staff*
Catherine Sacher, *Manager*
▲ EMP: 22 EST: 1924
SQ FT: 16,000
SALES: 3.5MM **Privately Held**
WEB: www.cargille.com
SIC: 3826 Analytical instruments; neph-
elometers, except meteorological; densit-
ometers, analytical; turbidometers

(G-1275)
CONTRACT FILLING INC
10 Cliffside Dr (07009-1227)
PHONE.................................973 433-0053
Fax: 973 239-6692
William Lizzi, *President*
Geoff Handel, *COO*
▲ EMP: 200
SQ FT: 9,500
SALES (est): 31.8MM **Privately Held**
SIC: 2844 Toilet preparations

(G-1276)
**CORRIGAN CENTER FOR
INTEGRATIV**
67 Haller Dr (07009-1704)
PHONE.................................973 239-0700
Dr Lynn Corrigan, *President*
EMP: 5
SALES (est): 114.1K **Privately Held**
SIC: 8093 8322 2834 Weight loss clinic,
with medical staff; general counseling
services; thyroid preparations

(G-1277)
DEGREE DAY SYSTEMS INC
33 Village Park Rd (07009-1286)
P.O. Box 510 (07009-0510)
PHONE.................................973 627-7959
Fax: 973 239-5442
Thomas Saczawa, *President*
Mark Saczawa, *Vice Pres*
▼ EMP: 8
SQ FT: 8,700
SALES (est): 1MM **Privately Held**
WEB: www.degreeday.com
SIC: 2761 Manifold business forms; com-
puter forms, manifold or continuous

(G-1278)
DIGITAL DESIGN INC
67 Sand Park Rd (07009-1281)
PHONE.................................973 857-9500
Edward J Gerri, *President*
Louis Di Cianni, *Vice Pres*
Sam Rankins, *Opers Mgr*
EMP: 30
SQ FT: 25,000
SALES (est): 5.2MM **Privately Held**
WEB: www.genesisinkjet.com
SIC: 8711 3555 3953 Designing: ship,
boat, machine & product; printing trades
machinery; marking devices

(G-1279)
DMS INC
218 Little Falls Rd 7-8 (07009-1277)
PHONE...............................973 928-3040
Gail Stuit, *President*
◆ **EMP:** 9 **EST:** 1993
SALES (est): 1.1MM **Privately Held**
SIC: 2295 Resin or plastic coated fabrics

(G-1280)
DOMINO PRINTING
Control Print Division
67 Sand Park Rd (07009-1243)
PHONE...............................973 857-0900
Richard L Pellegrini, *Principal*
R Coventry, *Opers Mgr*
W Niven, *Technical Mgr*
T Milot, *Internal Med*
EMP: 58
SALES (corp-wide): 6.6B **Privately Held**
WEB: www.domino-printing.com
SIC: 3555 Printing trades machinery
HQ: Domino Uk Limited
Domino House
Cambridge CAMBS CB23
195 478-2551

(G-1281)
ELNIK SYSTEMS LLC
107 Commerce Rd (07009-1207)
PHONE...............................973 239-6066
Clause Joens, *CEO*
Claus Joens, *CEO*
Inge Joens,
Frank Leonard,
▲ **EMP:** 35
SQ FT: 18,000
SALES (est): 6.6MM **Privately Held**
SIC: 3567 Vacuum furnaces & ovens

(G-1282)
FABRICATED SOFTWARE INC
25 Canfield Rd (07009-1201)
PHONE...............................973 857-0524
Fax: 973 695-5400
Gary Hollfelder, *President*
Michael Decaro, *Sr Software Eng*
Maria Graves, *Admin Asst*
EMP: 2
SQ FT: 12,000
SALES: 1.4MM **Privately Held**
SIC: 7372 Business oriented computer software

(G-1283)
FAIRFIELD GOURMET FOOD CORP (PA)
Also Called: Cookie Cupboard
11 Cliffside Dr (07009-1234)
PHONE...............................973 575-4365
Fax: 973 882-6998
ARI Margulies, *CEO*
Harris Beber, *Vice Pres*
Howard Freundlich, *Vice Pres*
Victor Ostreicher, *Vice Pres*
Dawn Fallon, *Regl Sales Mgr*
◆ **EMP:** 95
SALES (est): 31MM **Privately Held**
WEB: www.davidscookies.com
SIC: 2052 5461 Cookies; cookies

(G-1284)
HPC POS SYSTEM CORP (PA)
Also Called: H P C P O S Systems
220 Little Falls Rd # 4 (07009-1255)
PHONE...............................973 239-9666
Fax: 973 239-7757
Mordechai Guttman, *Ch of Bd*
▲ **EMP:** 4
SALES (est): 661.7K **Privately Held**
WEB: www.hpcpossystems.com
SIC: 3578 Point-of-sale devices

(G-1285)
INFOR METAL & TOOLING MFG
16 Commerce Rd (07009-1206)
PHONE...............................973 571-9520
Fax: 973 571-9630
Charles Insel, *President*
George J Insel, *Vice Pres*
Trudy Insel, *Admin Sec*
▼ **EMP:** 10
SQ FT: 20,000
SALES (est): 1.6MM **Privately Held**
SIC: 3544 3469 Special dies & tools; machine parts, stamped or pressed metal

(G-1286)
KLABIN FRAGRANCES INC
71 Village Park Rd (07009-1212)
PHONE...............................973 857-3600
Fax: 973 857-3631
Saul Klabin, *President*
Justin Klabin, *Vice Pres*
EMP: 12
SQ FT: 13,600
SALES (est): 3.3MM **Privately Held**
WEB: www.klabin-usa.com
SIC: 2844 Perfumes & colognes

(G-1287)
KNIGHT FOODS LLC ☉
874 Pompton Ave Ste A2 (07009-1213)
PHONE...............................973 385-1230
Amer Choudhry, *CEO*
EMP: 6 **EST:** 2017
SALES (est): 185.1K **Privately Held**
SIC: 2099 Food preparations

(G-1288)
LARACCAS MANUFACTURING INC
395 Little Falls Rd (07009-1239)
PHONE...............................973 571-1452
Fax: 973 571-1476
Anthony Laracca, *President*
EMP: 20
SQ FT: 10,000
SALES (est): 2.7MM **Privately Held**
SIC: 2452 Prefabricated wood buildings

(G-1289)
M W JENKINS SONS INC
Also Called: Jenkins Brush Co
444 Pompton Ave (07009-1813)
P.O. Box 303 (07009-0303)
PHONE...............................973 239-5150
Fax: 973 239-8087
Craig Sigler, *President*
Eric W Eucker, *Vice Pres*
EMP: 12 **EST:** 1877
SQ FT: 10,000
SALES (est): 1.4MM **Privately Held**
WEB: www.jenkinsbrush.com
SIC: 3991 Brushes, household or industrial

(G-1290)
MAT LOGO CENTRAL LLC
Also Called: Logomatcentral.com
216 Little Falls Rd (07009-1276)
PHONE...............................973 433-0311
Michael Becker,
EMP: 4
SQ FT: 2,500
SALES (est): 788.5K **Privately Held**
SIC: 3069 Rubber floor coverings, mats & wallcoverings; mats or matting, rubber; flooring, rubber: tile or sheet

(G-1291)
METAL CUTTING CORPORATION
Also Called: Mc
89 Commerce Rd (07009-1205)
PHONE...............................973 239-1100
Fax: 973 239-6651
Jordan Jablons, *President*
Joshua Jablons, *Exec VP*
Barbara Osborne, *QC Mgr*
Bob Mekita, *Engineer*
Victor Trzuskot, *Engineer*
▲ **EMP:** 60
SQ FT: 52,000
SALES (est): 21.3MM **Privately Held**
WEB: www.metalcutoff.com
SIC: 5051 3469 3679 Electronic circuits; metals service centers & offices; machine parts, stamped or pressed metal

(G-1292)
MONITEUR DEVICES INC
36 Commerce Rd (07009-1206)
PHONE...............................973 857-1600
John Unoski, *Vice Pres*
Bob Unoski, *Vice Pres*
Robert Unoski, *Vice Pres*
Gene Bohensky, *VP Sales*
▲ **EMP:** 11
SQ FT: 10,000
SALES (est): 2MM **Privately Held**
WEB: www.moniteurdevices.com
SIC: 3669 Intercommunication systems, electric

(G-1293)
O PLAST MATIC VALVES INC
1384 Pompton Ave Ste 1 (07009-1078)
PHONE...............................973 256-3000
James J Kirstein, *President*
Barry Nunno, *Vice Pres*
Anthony Buda, *Mfg Mgr*
Miguel Munoz, *Warehouse Mgr*
Angela Powell, *Purchasing*
▲ **EMP:** 65 **EST:** 1967
SQ FT: 52,000
SALES (est): 14.7MM **Privately Held**
WEB: www.plastomatic.com
SIC: 3491 5085 3083 Industrial valves; industrial supplies; laminated plastics plate & sheet

(G-1294)
OASIS ENTERTAINMENT GROUP
17 Frederick Ct (07009-1340)
P.O. Box 3073, Clifton (07012-0373)
PHONE...............................973 256-7077
Linda Brooks, *Manager*
EMP: 5
SALES (est): 307.1K **Privately Held**
SIC: 2741 Music books: publishing only, not printed on site

(G-1295)
OMNIA INDUSTRIES INC
5 Cliffside Dr (07009-1278)
P.O. Box 330 (07009-0330)
PHONE...............................973 239-7272
Fax: 973 239-5960
Alberto Comini, *President*
Denyse Comini Becker, *Vice Pres*
Alex Comini, *Vice Pres*
Alexander Comini, *Vice Pres*
Fred Marzullo, *Vice Pres*
▲ **EMP:** 40
SQ FT: 24,000
SALES (est): 6.4MM **Privately Held**
WEB: www.omniaindustries.com
SIC: 3446 5039 Architectural metalwork; architectural metalwork

(G-1296)
PRECISION MFG GROUP LLC (DH)
Also Called: Servometer
501 Little Falls Rd (07009-1239)
PHONE...............................973 785-4630
Anatole Penchuk, *CEO*
Glenn Weinrich, *COO*
Gerard O'Donovan, *CFO*
EMP: 75 **EST:** 2014
SQ FT: 26,000
SALES: 17MM
SALES (corp-wide): 169MM **Privately Held**
WEB: www.servometer.com
SIC: 3599 3498 3643 Bellows, industrial: metal; couplings, pipe: fabricated from purchased pipe; contacts, electrical
HQ: Matthew Warren, Inc.
9501 Tech Blvd Ste 401
Rosemont IL 60018
847 349-5760

(G-1297)
PRINTWRAP CORPORATION
95 Sand Park Rd (07009-1270)
PHONE...............................973 239-1144
Fax: 973 239-1233
Richard Neiman, *President*
Roger Neiman, *Vice Pres*
Andrew Neiman, *Admin Sec*
EMP: 17
SQ FT: 20,000
SALES (est): 3.1MM **Privately Held**
WEB: www.printwrap.com
SIC: 2752 2621 5111 Wrappers, lithographed; paper mills; printing paper

(G-1298)
RANDCASTLE EXTRUSION SYSTEMS
220 Little Falls Rd # 6 (07009-1254)
PHONE...............................973 239-1150
Keith Luker, *President*
EMP: 6
SQ FT: 3,000

SALES: 720K **Privately Held**
SIC: 3821 8734 Laboratory apparatus, except heating & measuring; product testing laboratories

(G-1299)
REPROMATIC PRINTING INC
Also Called: Proforma
216 Little Falls Rd # 3 (07009-1276)
PHONE...............................973 239-7610
Fax: 973 239-7613
Paul Molinari, *President*
Alyce Molinari, *Vice Pres*
Joan Molinari, *Admin Sec*
EMP: 4
SQ FT: 2,500
SALES (est): 700K **Privately Held**
WEB: www.repromatic.com
SIC: 2752 Commercial printing, offset

(G-1300)
SAMA PLASTICS CORP
20 Sand Park Rd (07009-1210)
PHONE...............................973 239-7200
Mark Wolsberg, *President*
▼ **EMP:** 35
SQ FT: 3,600
SALES (est): 8.6MM **Privately Held**
SIC: 3089 3993 Plastic processing; displays & cutouts, window & lobby

(G-1301)
TEX GUL INC
874 Pompton Ave Ste A2 (07009-1213)
PHONE...............................973 857-3200
Akram Choudhry, *President*
▲ **EMP:** 9
SQ FT: 2,500
SALES (est): 1.1MM **Privately Held**
SIC: 2211 Broadwoven fabric mills, cotton

(G-1302)
TRANSPORT PRODUCTS INC
20 Village Park Rd (07009-1247)
PHONE...............................973 857-6090
Fax: 973 857-6095
Debbie Petrosino, *President*
Fred Biancone, *Vice Pres*
Lou Saggese, *Purchasing*
EMP: 8
SQ FT: 8,000
SALES (est): 973.5K **Privately Held**
SIC: 3069 5085 Molded rubber products; gaskets; springs

(G-1303)
UMIT INTERNATIONAL TRADING LLC
Also Called: T-Net Technology
14 Village Park Rd A-B (07009-1246)
PHONE...............................973 571-1000
Selim Memis, *Mng Member*
EMP: 14
SQ FT: 3,000
SALES (est): 8.7MM **Privately Held**
SIC: 3577 Computer peripheral equipment

(G-1304)
UNIT PACK COMPANY INC
7 Lewis Rd (07009-1498)
PHONE...............................973 239-4112
Fax: 973 239-0429
Ernest W Loesser Jr, *President*
Benjamin Loesser, *Vice Pres*
EMP: 35 **EST:** 1964
SQ FT: 30,000
SALES (est): 7.1MM **Privately Held**
WEB: www.unitpack.com
SIC: 3089 Plastic containers, except foam

(G-1305)
UNITED SPPORT SLUTIONS-LMT INC
Also Called: U S S
134 Sand Park Rd (07009-1240)
PHONE...............................973 857-9222
Anatoly Lesenskyj, *CEO*
Patrick Lang, *CFO*
EMP: 45 **EST:** 1980
SQ FT: 33,000
SALES: 6MM **Privately Held**
WEB: www.unitedss.com
SIC: 3469 1721 Patterns on metal; industrial painting

PA: Mercer Lmt Group Inc
690 Puritan Ave
Lawrence Township NJ 08648

Cedar Knolls
Morris County

(G-1306)
AMLOID CORPORATION
7 Ridgedale Ave Ste 1a (07927-1120)
PHONE....................................973 328-0654
Michael Albarelli Jr, *President*
Joseph D Albarelli, *Vice Pres*
Michael Albarelli III, *Vice Pres*
Eric Kiel, *Vice Pres*
Daniel McMahon, *Vice Pres*
▲ **EMP:** 10 **EST:** 1916
SQ FT: 9,000
SALES (est): 19.9MM **Privately Held**
SIC: 3944 Games, toys & children's vehicles

(G-1307)
APPLIED NUTRITION CORP
10 Saddle Rd (07927-1901)
PHONE....................................973 734-0023
Richard Finkel, *President*
EMP: 26
SQ FT: 14,000
SALES (est): 2.4MM **Privately Held**
WEB: www.medicalfood.com
SIC: 5499 2099 Health foods; food preparations

(G-1308)
CARGILLE-SACHER LABS INC
4 E Frederick Pl (07927-1801)
PHONE....................................973 267-8888
John J Cargille, *President*
EMP: 16
SALES (corp-wide): 3.5MM **Privately Held**
WEB: www.cargille.com
SIC: 3499 Tablets, bronze or other metal
PA: Cargille-Sacher Laboratories Inc.
55 Commerce Rd
Cedar Grove NJ 07009
973 239-6633

(G-1309)
CELGENE CELLULAR
45 Horsehill Rd (07927-2009)
PHONE....................................908 673-9000
Robert Haviri, *President*
Kelly Nagel, *Manager*
EMP: 800
SALES (est): 74.5MM **Privately Held**
SIC: 2834 Pharmaceutical preparations

(G-1310)
EDGEWELL PERSONAL CARE LLC
240 Cedar Knolls Rd (07927-1621)
PHONE....................................973 753-3000
Mario Soussou, *Branch Mgr*
EMP: 5
SALES (corp-wide): 2.3B **Publicly Held**
SIC: 2844 Shaving preparations; lotions, shaving; suntan lotions & oils; hair preparations, including shampoos
HQ: Edgewell Personal Care, Llc
1350 Timberlake Mano
Chesterfield MO 63017
314 594-1900

(G-1311)
EMPLOYMENT HORIZONS INC
10 Ridgedale Ave (07927-1104)
PHONE....................................973 538-8822
Fax: 973 292-2295
Robert Johnston, *CFO*
Matthew Putts, *Exec Dir*
Jacqueline Burns, *Director*
EMP: 300
SQ FT: 17,500
SALES: 11.1MM **Privately Held**
SIC: 8331 2671 Vocational rehabilitation agency; packaging paper & plastics film, coated & laminated

(G-1312)
FOSTER AND COMPANY INC (PA)
Also Called: Chem Power Mfg Div
15 Wing Dr (07927-1019)
PHONE....................................973 267-4100
Fax: 973 267-9842
Richard Foster, *Ch of Bd*
Robert Foster, *Treasurer*
Ken Foster, *Exec Dir*
EMP: 29
SQ FT: 27,000
SALES (est): 12.2MM **Privately Held**
WEB: www.fostercomfg.com
SIC: 5085 2819 Industrial supplies; chemicals, high purity: refined from technical grade

(G-1313)
HAKAKIAN BEHZAD
52 Horsehill Rd (07927-2004)
PHONE....................................973 267-2506
EMP: 35
SALES (est): 1.3MM **Privately Held**
SIC: 2273 Mfg Carpets/Rugs

(G-1314)
KINLY INC
2 Ridgedale Ave Ste 100 (07927-1108)
PHONE....................................973 585-3000
James De Poortere, *CEO*
Don Sommer, *Vice Pres*
Bill Twomey, *Vice Pres*
Thomas Volk, *Vice Pres*
Michael Mulcahy, *Sales Staff*
EMP: 20
SALES (est): 15.2MM
SALES (corp-wide): 137.2K **Privately Held**
SIC: 3669 5043 Visual communication systems; photographic equipment & supplies
HQ: Kinly Ltd
6 Fleming Road Kirkton Campus
Livingston EH54

(G-1315)
LINDEN GROUP CORPORATION
2b Wing Dr (07927-1020)
PHONE....................................973 983-8809
Fax: 973 983-8803
Ken Chen, *President*
Chris Chen, *Vice Pres*
James Chen, *Vice Pres*
Bob Colaizzo, *QC Mgr*
EMP: 18
SQ FT: 14,000
SALES (est): 2.4MM **Privately Held**
WEB: www.tlgc.com
SIC: 7379 7373 3575 Computer related consulting services; systems software development services; systems integration services; computer system selling services; computer-aided system services; computer terminals, monitors & components

(G-1316)
MARK LITHOGRAPHY INC
Also Called: Mark Lithographers
4 Saddle Rd (07927-1901)
P.O. Box 362 (07927-0362)
PHONE....................................973 538-5557
Charles Tuminello, *President*
Stephen Tumminello, *Admin Sec*
EMP: 40
SQ FT: 17,000
SALES (est): 4.6MM **Privately Held**
WEB: www.marklitho.com
SIC: 2752 Commercial printing, offset

(G-1317)
MORRIS COUNTY DUPLICATING
8 Farview Ave (07927-1527)
PHONE....................................973 993-8484
Fax: 973 605-8828
Ernest D'Angelo, *President*
◆ **EMP:** 80
SQ FT: 25,000
SALES (est): 9.5MM **Privately Held**
WEB: www.mcdonline.com
SIC: 2752 Commercial printing, offset

(G-1318)
MYOS RENS TECHNOLOGY INC
45 Horsehill Rd Ste 106 (07927-2009)
PHONE....................................973 509-0444
Joseph Mannello, *CEO*
Robert J Hariri, *Ch of Bd*
Dominick Commesso, *Exec VP*
Neerav Padliya, *Vice Pres*
Joanne Goodford, *Opers Staff*
EMP: 9
SQ FT: 5,225
SALES: 526K **Privately Held**
SIC: 2834 Pharmaceutical preparations

(G-1319)
NIAGARA CONSERVATION CORP
45 Horsehill Rd Ste 102 (07927-2009)
PHONE....................................973 829-0800
Fax: 973 829-1400
William Cutler, *President*
EMP: 14
SALES (corp-wide): 15.8MM **Privately Held**
WEB: www.niagaraconservation.com
SIC: 3822 Auto controls regulating residntl & coml environmt & applncs
PA: Niagara Conservation Corp.
1200 Lkeside Pkwy Ste 450
Flower Mound TX 75028
682 292-0018

(G-1320)
OLI SYSTEMS INC
240 Cedar Knolls Rd # 301 (07927-1621)
PHONE....................................973 539-4996
Fax: 973 539-5922
Marshall Rafal, *President*
Jane Rafal, *Treasurer*
Denise Llerena, *HR Admin*
Ali Eslamimanesh, *Associate*
EMP: 20
SQ FT: 4,000
SALES (est): 3.7MM **Privately Held**
WEB: www.olisystems.com
SIC: 7372 8731 Business oriented computer software; biotechnical research, commercial

(G-1321)
TRUKMANNS INC
Also Called: Trukmann's Reprographics
4 Wing Dr (07927-1020)
PHONE....................................973 538-7718
Paul Korman, *President*
Ernest Minotti, *Principal*
Will Korman, *Vice Pres*
Erick Mendez, *Prdtn Mgr*
Matt Korman, *Sales Staff*
EMP: 25
SQ FT: 37,000
SALES (est): 4.9MM **Privately Held**
WEB: www.trukmanns-orders.com
SIC: 2759 2752 3993 Screen printing; commercial printing, lithographic; signs & advertising specialties

(G-1322)
UNIQUE SYSTEMS INC
4 Saddle Rd (07927-1901)
PHONE....................................973 455-0440
Fax: 973 455-7214
Olof A Eriksen, *President*
Elaine Eriksen, *Vice Pres*
Kenneth Eriksen, *Vice Pres*
Robert Harris, *Engineer*
Carol McCarthy, *Accounting Mgr*
▲ **EMP:** 12
SQ FT: 15,000
SALES (est): 3MM **Privately Held**
WEB: www.uniquesystems.com
SIC: 3589 Commercial cleaning equipment

(G-1323)
WINERY PAK LLC
3 Wing Dr Ste 101 (07927-1010)
PHONE....................................800 434-4599
Larry Chasin, *Principal*
EMP: 6
SALES (est): 340.9K **Privately Held**
SIC: 2084 Wines

Cedarville
Cumberland County

(G-1324)
OWENS PLASTIC PRODUCTS INC
393 Main St (08311-2542)
P.O. Box 118 (08311-0118)
PHONE....................................856 447-3500
Fax: 856 447-3500
Gloria Owens, *President*
Christopher Owens, *Opers Staff*
Adrienne Debourgion Owens, *Treasurer*
EMP: 7
SQ FT: 15,000
SALES (est): 874.5K **Privately Held**
WEB: www.owensplasticproducts.com
SIC: 3089 3083 Injection molded finished plastic products; laminated plastics plate & sheet

Chatham
Morris County

(G-1325)
AMARYLLIS INC (PA)
418 River Rd (07928-1272)
P.O. Box 208 (07928-0208)
PHONE....................................973 635-0500
Ling Chang, *President*
Jan Chang, *Vice Pres*
▲ **EMP:** 6
SALES: 1.5MM **Privately Held**
SIC: 3999 2771 Novelties, bric-a-brac & hobby kits; greeting cards

(G-1326)
BURLING INSTRUMENTS INC
16 River Rd (07928-1916)
P.O. Box 298 (07928-0298)
PHONE....................................973 665-0601
Fax: 973 635-9530
Harry Bentas, *President*
Roger Nation, *Vice Pres*
Michael Wetterer, *Vice Pres*
EMP: 11
SQ FT: 11,240
SALES (est): 1.1MM **Privately Held**
WEB: www.burlinginstruments.com
SIC: 3822 3823 Auto controls regulating residntl & coml environmt & applncs; temperature instruments: industrial process type

(G-1327)
CHATHAM LAWN MOWLER
Also Called: Chatham Lawnmower Service
14 Commerce St (07928-2703)
PHONE....................................973 635-8855
Fax: 973 701-2340
Scott Sampson, *Owner*
EMP: 4
SQ FT: 3,600
SALES (est): 409.7K **Privately Held**
SIC: 5261 7699 5063 3546 Lawnmowers & tractors; lawn mower repair shop; generators; saws & sawing equipment

(G-1328)
INNOVATION IN MEDTECH LLC
5 Rolling Hill Dr (07928-1609)
P.O. Box 326, Fairfield CT (06824-0326)
PHONE....................................888 202-5939
David Cassak, *Managing Prtnr*
Stephen Levin, *Managing Prtnr*
EMP: 9
SALES (est): 549.5K **Privately Held**
SIC: 2721 Magazines: publishing & printing

(G-1329)
INVESSENCE INC
1 Main St Ste 202 (07928-2426)
PHONE....................................201 977-1955
Jigar Vyas, *CEO*
Michael Frank, *COO*
Christopher Lengle, *Officer*
EMP: 5
SALES (est): 156K **Privately Held**
SIC: 7372 7389 Business oriented computer software; financial services

G
E
O
G
R
A
P
H
I
C

(G-1330)
ISP CHEMICALS LLC
Also Called: Isp Sutton Laboratories
116 Summit Ave (07928-2727)
PHONE.................................973 635-1551
Fax: 973 635-4964
John Cavan, *Branch Mgr*
EMP: 50 Privately Held
WEB: www.ispcorp.com
SIC: 2869 2844 Amines, acids, salts, esters; toilet preparations
HQ: Isp Chemicals Llc
    455 N Main St
    Calvert City KY 42029
    270 395-4165

(G-1331)
JUVENTIO LLC
466 Southern Blvd Ste 2 (07928-1462)
PHONE.................................973 908-8097
Thomas Ford, *CEO*
Michael Graziano, *CFO*
Mike Graziano, *CFO*
Bart Zoni, *Chief Mktg Ofcr*
Lauren Messner, *Marketing Mgr*
EMP: 5
SQ FT: 2,000
SALES (est): 905.8K Privately Held
SIC: 2834 Pharmaceutical preparations

(G-1332)
KILLIAN GRAPHICS
142 Southern Blvd (07928-1324)
P.O. Box 91 (07928-0091)
PHONE.................................973 635-5844
Ron Killian, *Owner*
EMP: 5
SALES: 90K Privately Held
SIC: 7311 2752 Advertising agencies; promotional printing, lithographic

(G-1333)
LIFE LINERS INC (PA)
6 Essex Rd (07928-2056)
PHONE.................................973 635-9234
Stephen Asthalter, *President*
EMP: 2
SQ FT: 5,000
SALES (est): 1.3MM Privately Held
SIC: 2262 3569 Fire resistance finishing: manmade & silk broadwoven; firefighting apparatus & related equipment

(G-1334)
MINDWISE MEDIA LLC
26 Floral St (07928-1660)
PHONE.................................973 701-0685
Mark Scellato, *Director*
Scott Pendergrast,
EMP: 5
SQ FT: 500
SALES (est): 390K Privately Held
WEB: www.mindwise.com
SIC: 4813 2721 ; periodicals

(G-1335)
NATIONAL HOME PLANNING SERVICE
Also Called: Chirgotis, Wm G
79 Thornley Dr (07928-1361)
PHONE.................................973 376-3200
Fax: 973 376-6202
William G Chirgotis, *President*
Lawrence Tranquilli, *Vice Pres*
Wilma Tranquilli, *Admin Sec*
EMP: 4
SQ FT: 3,000
SALES (est): 230K Privately Held
WEB: www.nationalhome.com
SIC: 2741 8712 Miscellaneous publishing; architectural services

(G-1336)
NATIONAL MANUFACTURING CO INC
12 River Rd (07928-1989)
PHONE.................................973 635-8846
Fax: 973 635-0860
Robert Staudinger, *President*
Reggie Zhou, *President*
Peter Colby, *General Mgr*
Kristina Sterni, *General Mgr*
David Carnell, *Business Mgr*
▲ EMP: 150 EST: 1944
SQ FT: 50,000

SALES (est): 35.4MM Privately Held
WEB: www.natlmfg.com
SIC: 3469 Stamping metal for the trade

(G-1337)
QUINNOVA PHARMACEUTICALS INC
1 Main St Ste E (07928-2426)
PHONE.................................877 660-6263
Jeffrey Day, *President*
Jeffrey P McMullen, *Vice Pres*
Christopher Brennan, *Treasurer*
EMP: 30
SALES (est): 3MM Privately Held
SIC: 2834 Dermatologicals
HQ: Exeltis Usa, Inc.
    180 Park Ave Ste 101
    Florham Park NJ 07932
    973 324-0200

(G-1338)
THEWAL INC
Also Called: Chatham Print & Design
12 Center St (07928-2521)
PHONE.................................973 635-1880
Fax: 973 635-1611
Susan Kessel, *President*
Walter Francis III, *Prdtn Mgr*
Ellen Schreiber, *Bookkeeper*
Thelma Francis, *Services*
Debbie Kostibos, *Services*
EMP: 10
SQ FT: 4,500
SALES (est): 1.5MM Privately Held
WEB: www.chatmm.com
SIC: 2752 2791 2789 Commercial printing, offset; typesetting; bookbinding & related work

(G-1339)
UNIKEN INC
466 Southern Blvd Ste 2 (07928-1462)
PHONE.................................917 324-0399
Bimal Gandhi, *CEO*
Robert Levine, *COO*
Ram Gupta, *Director*
EMP: 5 EST: 2013
SALES (est): 141.8K Privately Held
SIC: 7372 Prepackaged software; business oriented computer software

---

Cherry Hill
Camden County

(G-1340)
AGA FOODSERVICE INC (PA)
110 Woodcrest Rd (08003-3648)
PHONE.................................856 428-4200
Iain Whyte, *President*
◆ EMP: 178
SQ FT: 220,000
SALES (est): 16.4MM Privately Held
WEB: www.agafoodservice.com
SIC: 3556 Food products machinery

(G-1341)
AIR DISTRIBUTION SYSTEMS INC
Also Called: ADS
1000 Astoria Blvd (08003-2311)
PHONE.................................856 874-1100
Fax: 856 874-1110
Charles Doyle, *President*
John F Dickson, *Vice Pres*
EMP: 75
SQ FT: 35,000
SALES (est): 17.4MM Privately Held
WEB: www.adsduct.com
SIC: 3444 1711 Ducts, sheet metal; plumbing, heating, air-conditioning contractors

(G-1342)
AIRGAS USA LLC
1910 Old Cuthbert Rd (08034-1416)
PHONE.................................609 685-4241
Joseph Anastasi, *Branch Mgr*
EMP: 19

SALES (corp-wide): 164.2MM Privately Held
SIC: 5169 5084 5085 2813 Industrial gases; gases, compressed & liquefied; carbon dioxide; dry ice; welding machinery & equipment; safety equipment; welding supplies; industrial gases; carbon dioxide; nitrous oxide; dry ice, carbon dioxide (solid); industrial inorganic chemicals; calcium carbide
HQ: Airgas Usa, Llc
    259 N Radnor Chester Rd # 100
    Radnor PA 19087
    610 687-5253

(G-1343)
ALPHAGRAPHICS
5 N Olney Ave Ste 200 (08003-2067)
PHONE.................................856 761-8000
Fax: 856 761-8005
Art Coley, *CEO*
Rudy Baron, *President*
Janet O'Neal, *Project Mgr*
Tommy E Auger, *CFO*
Leah Baron, *Admin Sec*
EMP: 12
SALES (est): 2.6MM Privately Held
SIC: 2752 7336 Commercial printing, offset; graphic arts & related design

(G-1344)
AURORA INFORMATION SYSTEMS
1873 Marlton Pike E # 220 (08003-2034)
PHONE.................................856 596-4180
Fax: 856 596-4181
Jerry Cully, *President*
John Sooy, *Vice Pres*
EMP: 8
SQ FT: 1,100
SALES (est): 869.1K Privately Held
WEB: www.foodpro.com
SIC: 7373 7372 Systems software development services; prepackaged software

(G-1345)
AUTOMATED OFFICE INC
Also Called: DMC Soft
9 Executive Campus (08002-4502)
PHONE.................................888 362-7638
Bruce Bergeron, *President*
Al Giacomucci, *Director*
EMP: 5
SQ FT: 600
SALES (est): 550K Privately Held
SIC: 5734 7372 7379 Software, business & non-game; prepackaged software; computer related consulting services

(G-1346)
BAXTER HEALTHCARE CORPORATION
2 Esterbrook Ln (08003-4002)
PHONE.................................856 489-2104
Shashank Agrawal, *QA Dir*
Clifford Powell Jr, *QC Mgr*
Erick Guevara, *Engineer*
Charles Hosey, *Engineer*
Frank Ricciuti, *Plant Engr*
EMP: 66
SALES (corp-wide): 10.5B Publicly Held
SIC: 3841 Surgical & medical instruments
HQ: Baxter Healthcare Corporation
    1 Baxter Pkwy
    Deerfield IL 60015
    224 948-2000

(G-1347)
BEST DRAPERIES INC
Also Called: Best Drapery & Blind Mfg Co
1 Kresson Rd (08034-3206)
PHONE.................................856 429-5453
Fax: 856 429-2400
James Logan, *President*
EMP: 5
SQ FT: 1,800
SALES (est): 450K Privately Held
SIC: 2591 Shade, curtain & drapery hardware; window blinds

(G-1348)
BEST DRAPERY INC
Also Called: Best Drapery and Design
1 Crescent Way (08002-4201)
PHONE.................................856 429-2242
James Logan, *President*

EMP: 7
SQ FT: 1,800
SALES: 700K Privately Held
WEB: www.ebestdesign.com
SIC: 2591 Shade, curtain & drapery hardware; window blinds

(G-1349)
BESTWORK INDS FOR THE BLIND
1940 Olney Ave 200 (08003-2016)
PHONE.................................856 424-2510
Fax: 856 939-5022
Belinda Moore, *President*
EMP: 70
SALES: 3.1MM Privately Held
SIC: 8331 2326 2339 Sheltered workshop; skill training center; work experience center; men's & boys' work clothing; women's & misses' outerwear

(G-1350)
BIRDS EYE FOODS INC (DH)
121 Woodcrest Rd (08003-3620)
PHONE.................................585 383-1850
Neil Harrison, *President*
David Hogbert, *President*
Robert G Montgomery, *Senior VP*
Carl W Caughran, *Vice Pres*
Chris Puma, *CFO*
◆ EMP: 250
SALES (est): 383.2MM
SALES (corp-wide): 3.1B Publicly Held
WEB: www.agrilinkfoods.com
SIC: 2037 2096 2052 2038 Frozen fruits & vegetables; vegetables, quick frozen & cold pack, excl. potato products; potato chips & other potato-based snacks; corn chips & other corn-based snacks; cheese curls & puffs; cookies & crackers; pretzels; whipped topping, frozen; pickles, sauces & salad dressings; dressings, salad: raw & cooked (except dry mixes); mayonnaise; pickled fruits & vegetables

(G-1351)
BITTNER INDUSTRIES INC
Also Called: Minuteman Press
2060 Springdale Rd # 700 (08003-2099)
PHONE.................................856 817-8400
Fax: 856 817-8404
Frank Bittner, *President*
Cherie L Bittner, *Treasurer*
EMP: 8
SQ FT: 5,000
SALES (est): 1.2MM Privately Held
SIC: 2752 Commercial printing, lithographic

(G-1352)
BPS WORLDWIDE INC
1860 Greentree Rd (08003-2031)
PHONE.................................856 874-0822
Robert Malmud, *Principal*
Cynthia Maiorano, *Vice Pres*
Gary Shull, *Vice Pres*
EMP: 45
SQ FT: 40,000
SALES: 10MM Privately Held
SIC: 3578 Automatic teller machines (ATM)

(G-1353)
BREAD & BAGELS
1600 Church Rd (08002-1203)
PHONE.................................856 667-2333
Fax: 856 667-3568
Heechul Bang, *Owner*
EMP: 10
SQ FT: 2,500
SALES (est): 520K Privately Held
SIC: 2051 Breads, rolls & buns; bagels, fresh or frozen

(G-1354)
BUSINESS DEV SOLUTIONS INC
311 Hadleigh Dr (08003-1979)
PHONE.................................856 433-8005
Fax: 856 787-1510
Robert Bloom, *President*
EMP: 7
SALES (est): 610K Privately Held
WEB: www.bdsdatabase.com
SIC: 8742 7372 Management information systems consultant; prepackaged software

(G-1355)
C JACKSON ASSOCIATES INC
Also Called: AlphaGraphics
2050 Springdale Rd # 700 (08003-4021)
PHONE..................856 761-8000
Charles Jackson, *President*
Frances Jackson, *Vice Pres*
Gary Jackson, *Treasurer*
David Jackson, *Admin Sec*
EMP: 20
SQ FT: 18,000
SALES (est): 236.9K **Privately Held**
SIC: 2752 7331 2789 Commercial printing, offset; mailing service; bookbinding & related work

(G-1356)
CDK INDUSTRIES LLC
Also Called: Whips International
900 Haddonfield Rd Ste 6 (08002-2749)
P.O. Box 444 (08003-0444)
PHONE..................856 488-5456
Fax: 856 488-5524
James Walford, *Mng Member*
EMP: 3
SQ FT: 2,400
SALES: 1.5MM **Privately Held**
SIC: 3949 2395 Sporting & athletic goods; embroidery & art needlework

(G-1357)
CORCENTRIC
457 Haddonfield Rd # 220 (08002-2220)
PHONE..................877 790-7272
Kate Freer, *Principal*
EMP: 12
SALES (est): 1.7MM **Privately Held**
SIC: 7372 Prepackaged software

(G-1358)
CROCES PASTA PODUCTS
Also Called: Croce & Longo Associates
811 Marlton Pike W (08002-3528)
PHONE..................856 795-6000
Fax: 856 795-5755
Joseph Croce, *President*
EMP: 5
SALES: 350K **Privately Held**
SIC: 2099 Pasta, uncooked: packaged with other ingredients

(G-1359)
DAMAN INTERNATIONAL INC
Also Called: Caps Padel
105 Rye Rd (08003-1308)
PHONE..................917 945-9708
Karishma Vohra, *President*
▲ EMP: 2
SQ FT: 400
SALES: 1MM **Privately Held**
SIC: 2329 Riding clothes:, men's, youths' & boys'

(G-1360)
DPI COPIES PRTG & GRAPHICS INC
2070 Marlton Pike E Ste 3 (08003-1281)
PHONE..................856 874-1355
Fax: 856 874-1699
Michael Jones, *President*
EMP: 15
SQ FT: 5,000
SALES (est): 2.4MM **Privately Held**
WEB: www.dpicherryhill.com
SIC: 2752 Commercial printing, offset

(G-1361)
EDWARDS CREATIVE PRODUCTS INC
Also Called: Ecp
910 Beechwood Ave (08002-3497)
PHONE..................856 665-3200
Edward Cohen, *Ch of Bd*
Charles Cohen, *President*
Leona Cohen, *Admin Sec*
EMP: 15 EST: 1953
SQ FT: 9,000
SALES (est): 798.6K **Privately Held**
WEB: www.edwardscreative.com
SIC: 2842 3089 3634 Stain removers; novelties, plastic; electric housewares & fans

(G-1362)
ELITE SURF SNOW SKATEBOARD SP
259 Marlton Pike E (08034-2406)
PHONE..................856 427-7873
EMP: 4 EST: 2007
SALES (est): 160K **Privately Held**
SIC: 3949 Mfg Sporting/Athletic Goods

(G-1363)
EUROPEAN COFFEE CLASSICS INC
Also Called: Melita USA
1401 Berlin Rd Ste A (08034-1402)
PHONE..................856 428-7202
Fax: 856 428-7262
◆ EMP: 20
SQ FT: 104,000
SALES (est): 6MM
SALES (corp-wide): 1.6B **Privately Held**
SIC: 2095 Roasted coffee
HQ: Melitta North America, Inc.
13925 58th St N
Clearwater FL 33760
727 535-2111

(G-1364)
FEDEX OFFICE & PRINT SVCS INC
1160 Route 70 E (08034-2131)
PHONE..................856 427-0099
John Parker, *Manager*
EMP: 20
SALES (corp-wide): 65.4B **Publicly Held**
WEB: www.kinkos.com
SIC: 7334 7312 3993 2791 Photocopying & duplicating services; outdoor advertising services; signs & advertising specialties; typesetting; bookbinding & related work; coated & laminated paper
HQ: Fedex Office And Print Services, Inc.
7900 Legacy Dr
Plano TX 75024
214 550-7000

(G-1365)
FISCHLERS DAWNPOINT
212 Walt Whitman Blvd (08003-3521)
PHONE..................856 428-2092
EMP: 4 EST: 2005
SALES (est): 160K **Privately Held**
SIC: 2759 Commercial Printing

(G-1366)
FRIDAY MORNING QUARTERBACK
1930 Marlton Pike E F36 (08003-4102)
PHONE..................856 424-6873
Fax: 856 424-3881
Kal Rudman, *President*
Lucille Rudman, *Admin Sec*
EMP: 40 EST: 1972
SQ FT: 4,400
SALES (est): 2.7MM **Privately Held**
WEB: www.fmqb.com
SIC: 2741 2721 Miscellaneous publishing; periodicals

(G-1367)
FRONTEND GRAPHICS INC
1951 Old Cuthbert Rd # 414 (08034-1411)
PHONE..................856 547-1600
Fax: 856 547-3837
Elizabeth A Maul, *President*
Karen Ryan, *Production*
EMP: 8
SQ FT: 2,500
SALES (est): 1.2MM **Privately Held**
WEB: www.frontendgraphics.com
SIC: 2759 7336 4212 Screen printing; graphic arts & related design; mail carriers, contract

(G-1368)
G H KRAUSS MANUFACTURING CO
1209 Route 38 (08002-2851)
PHONE..................856 662-0815
Gordon H Krauss, *Owner*
EMP: 4
SQ FT: 2,000
SALES (est): 190K **Privately Held**
SIC: 3643 7389 Current-carrying wiring devices; packaging & labeling services

(G-1369)
GANNETT STLLITE INFO NTWRK LLC
Courier Post
301 Cuthbert Blvd (08002-2905)
P.O. Box 5300 (08034-0430)
PHONE..................856 663-6000
Fax: 856 663-2831
Dan Martin, *President*
EMP: 88
SALES (corp-wide): 3.1B **Publicly Held**
WEB: www.usatoday.com
SIC: 2711 Newspapers
HQ: Gannett Satellite Information Network, Llc
7950 Jones Branch Dr
Mc Lean VA 22102
703 854-6000

(G-1370)
GAW ASSOCIATES INC
Also Called: Gaw Technology
670 Deer Rd Bldg A (08034-1438)
PHONE..................856 608-1428
Kathleen Gaw-Betz, *President*
Chuck Gaw, *Vice Pres*
EMP: 10
SQ FT: 8,000
SALES (est): 5.3MM **Privately Held**
WEB: www.gawtechnology.com
SIC: 3444 2522 5021 3572 Metal housings, enclosures, casings & other containers; office furniture, except wood; office & public building furniture; computer storage devices

(G-1371)
GLAXOSMITHKLINE LLC
24 Cohasset Ln (08003-1964)
PHONE..................609 472-8175
EMP: 27
SALES (corp-wide): 39.8B **Privately Held**
SIC: 2834 Pharmaceutical preparations
HQ: Glaxosmithkline Llc
5 Crescent Dr
Philadelphia PA 19112
215 751-4000

(G-1372)
GRAN ALL MRBLE TILE IMPRTS INC (PA)
932 Marlton Pike W (08002-3509)
PHONE..................856 354-4747
George Siampos, *President*
Foti Tsakiris, *Vice Pres*
▲ EMP: 3 EST: 1995
SQ FT: 5,500
SALES: 2.1MM **Privately Held**
WEB: www.allmarblegranite.com
SIC: 3281 5211 5722 Granite, cut & shaped; tile, ceramic; kitchens, complete (sinks, cabinets, etc.)

(G-1373)
HALDOR USA INC
100 Springdale Rd 83-206 (08003-3300)
PHONE..................856 254-2345
Ilan Kadosh Tamari, *Principal*
Morr Avissara, *COO*
Ram I Alt, *Senior VP*
Pete Koste, *Vice Pres*
EMP: 30
SALES (est): 2.7MM **Privately Held**
SIC: 3841 Surgical instruments & apparatus

(G-1374)
HARSCO CORPORATION
1960 Old Cuthbert Rd # 100 (08034-1456)
PHONE..................856 779-7795
EMP: 20
SALES (corp-wide): 1.6B **Publicly Held**
SIC: 7359 7353 5082 3443 Equipment rental & leasing; heavy construction equipment rental; construction & mining machinery; scaffolding; fuel tanks (oil, gas, etc.): metal plate; cryogenic tanks, for liquids & gases; cylinders, pressure: metal plate; heat exchangers: coolers (after, inter.); condensers, etc.; evaporative condensers, heat transfer equipment; railroad maintenance & repair services

PA: Harsco Corporation
350 Poplar Church Rd
Camp Hill PA 17011
717 763-7064

(G-1375)
HIKMA PHARMACEUTICALS USA INC
Also Called: Injectable Mfg Fcilty
2 Esterbrook Ln (08003-4002)
PHONE..................856 424-3700
Brian Frost, *General Mgr*
Catherine Boettcher, *Opers Staff*
John Reber, *Project Engr*
John Schiller, *Manager*
Joanna Siers, *Technical Staff*
EMP: 200
SQ FT: 372,000
SALES (corp-wide): 1.9B **Privately Held**
SIC: 2834 Pharmaceutical preparations
HQ: Hikma Pharmaceuticals Usa Inc.
246 Industrial Way W
Eatontown NJ 07724
732 542-1191

(G-1376)
ICUP INC
1152 Marlkress Rd Ste 200 (08003-2314)
PHONE..................856 751-2045
Steven Trachtenberg, *CEO*
Erica McKeen, *Buyer*
Preeya Patel, *Accountant*
Ryan Conard, *Sales Associate*
Anthony Lopisi, *Manager*
▲ EMP: 30
SQ FT: 100,000
SALES (est): 6.2MM **Privately Held**
WEB: www.icupinc.com
SIC: 3089 2679 3229 3231 Novelties, plastic; gift wrap & novelties, paper; pressed & blown glass; products of purchased glass; novelties & specialties, metal

(G-1377)
ILKEM MARBLE AND GRANITE INC
Also Called: Ilkem Marble & Granite
2010 Springdale Rd # 300 (08003-2056)
PHONE..................856 433-8714
Fatih Karaca, *Vice Pres*
EMP: 6
SALES (est): 975.8K **Privately Held**
SIC: 3281 5032 Marble, building: cut & shaped; granite building stone

(G-1378)
IMAGINE AUDIO LLC
304 Haddonfield Rd (08002-2204)
PHONE..................856 488-1466
Marc Balzer, *Mng Member*
Mark Balver,
Shira Balver,
EMP: 5
SQ FT: 3,000
SALES (est): 820.4K **Privately Held**
SIC: 2517 Home entertainment unit cabinets, wood

(G-1379)
IMPORTANT PAPERS INC
Also Called: Important Papers & Printing
12 Downing St (08003-1519)
PHONE..................856 751-4544
Fax: 856 751-5433
Ruth Barnett, *President*
EMP: 5
SQ FT: 5,000
SALES (est): 710.8K **Privately Held**
SIC: 2759 5943 5112 5941 Commercial printing; stationery stores; business forms; camping equipment

(G-1380)
INDUSTRIAL STL & FASTENER CORP
167 Old Bilmont Ave Fl 2 Flr 2 (08034)
P.O. Box 2470 (08034-0202)
PHONE..................610 667-2220
Stephen Gelman, *President*
Alan Gelman, *Vice Pres*
Scott Gelman, *Vice Pres*
EMP: 2
SQ FT: 5,000

SALES (est): 5.8MM **Privately Held**
SIC: **5051** 5072 1081 Steel; hardware; metal mining services

(G-1381)
INSIGN INC
1937 Olney Ave (08003-2015)
PHONE...................................856 424-1161
Fax: 856 424-5778
Samuel A Miner, *President*
Chris Custren, *Graphic Designe*
EMP: 35
SQ FT: 30,000
SALES (est): 5.4MM **Privately Held**
WEB: www.insigninc.com
SIC: **3993** 2542 7389 Displays & cutouts, window & lobby; partitions & fixtures, except wood; interior designer; interior decorating

(G-1382)
INTERNATIONAL LASER GROUP INC (DH)
Also Called: Ilg
4 Executive Campus # 104 (08002-4105)
P.O. Box 686, Woodland Hills CA (91365-0686)
PHONE...................................818 888-0400
Fax: 818 888-0331
Timothy Clark, *President*
Fernando Forno, *Vice Pres*
Parcher Kyle, *Vice Pres*
Ling Zito, *Vice Pres*
Al Zortea, *Vice Pres*
EMP: 50
SQ FT: 18,000
SALES (est): 53.1K
SALES (corp-wide): 439.3K **Privately Held**
WEB: www.ilgweb.com
SIC: **3955** 3861 Print cartridges for laser & other computer printers; photographic equipment & supplies
HQ: Turbon Ag
Ruhrdeich 10
Hattingen 45525
232 450-40

(G-1383)
JBAT INC
Also Called: Cherry Hill Precision Co
28 Coles Ave (08002-1224)
PHONE...................................856 667-7307
Fax: 856 667-5966
John Schallenhammer, *President*
Andrew Schallenhammer, *Vice Pres*
Theresa Schallenhammer, *Treasurer*
EMP: 22 EST: 1967
SQ FT: 7,200
SALES (est): 3.8MM **Privately Held**
WEB: www.cherryhillprecision.com
SIC: **3599** Machine shop, jobbing & repair

(G-1384)
JET TEST GLOBAL LLC ✪
800 Kings Hwy N Ste 307 (08034-1511)
PHONE...................................702 785-0011
Taylor Brown, *Project Mgr*
Steven Giordano,
EMP: 5 EST: 2017
SALES: 600K **Privately Held**
SIC: **3429** Aircraft hardware

(G-1385)
K R B PRINTING FOR BUSINESS
1165 Marlkress Rd Ste G (08003-2330)
PHONE...................................856 751-5200
Robert Barbera, *Partner*
Kurt Barbera, *Partner*
Sherre Knable, *Cust Mgr*
EMP: 15
SQ FT: 1,800
SALES: 1.7MM **Privately Held**
SIC: **2752** Commercial printing, offset

(G-1386)
KYOCERA INTERNATIONAL INC
1515 Burnt Mill Rd (08003-3637)
PHONE...................................856 691-7000
Robert Barron, *Branch Mgr*
EMP: 80
SALES (corp-wide): 14.8B **Publicly Held**
SIC: **3674** Semiconductors & related devices; photovoltaic devices, solid state; solar cells

HQ: Kyocera International, Inc.
8611 Balboa Ave
San Diego CA 92123
858 492-1456

(G-1387)
LAP MARKETING MGT SVCS INC
104 Old Carriage Rd (08034-3330)
PHONE...................................609 654-9266
EMP: 10
SALES (est): 694.7K **Privately Held**
SIC: **3661** Mfg Telephone/Telegraph Apparatus

(G-1388)
LIBERTY CNSTR & INV GROUP
Also Called: US Led Installation Group
1878 Marlton Pike E Ste 7 (08003-2090)
PHONE...................................267 784-7931
Shawn Nan, *President*
EMP: 5
SALES (est): 216.8K **Privately Held**
SIC: **3674** Light emitting diodes

(G-1389)
LJ ELEVATOR SERVICE LLC
515 Hanover Ave (08002-2017)
PHONE...................................856 488-5533
Ruzica Pilic,
EMP: 5
SALES (est): 332K **Privately Held**
SIC: **3534** Elevators & moving stairways

(G-1390)
LOCKHEED MARTIN CORPORATION
Also Called: Lockheed Martin Adv
3 Executive Campus # 600 (08002-4160)
P.O. Box 61511, King of Prussia PA (19406-0911)
PHONE...................................856 792-9811
Fax: 856 792-9830
Otto Wilbert, *General Mgr*
Larry Johnson, *Project Mgr*
Greg Barnett, *Engineer*
Kathleen Spivey, *Branch Mgr*
Henry Mendenhall, *Senior Mgr*
EMP: 245 **Publicly Held**
WEB: www.lockheedmartin.com
SIC: **3721** Aircraft
PA: Lockheed Martin Corporation
6801 Rockledge Dr
Bethesda MD 20817

(G-1391)
LRP AND P GRAPHICS
Also Called: Lrp and Profit
1165 Marlkress Rd Ste M (08003-2330)
P.O. Box 1536 (08034-0069)
PHONE...................................856 424-0158
EMP: 20
SALES (est): 1.9MM **Privately Held**
SIC: **2754** Gravure Commercial Printing

(G-1392)
MAARKY THERMAL SYSTEMS INC
1415 Marlton Pike E # 604 (08034-2210)
PHONE...................................856 470-1504
Ranga Nadig, *President*
Michael Phipps, *Vice Pres*
Michael Arico, *Engineer*
Madhura Nadig, *Accounts Mgr*
EMP: 8 EST: 2011
SALES (est): 2.5MM **Privately Held**
WEB: www.maarky.com
SIC: **3443** Condensers, steam; heat exchangers, condensers & components

(G-1393)
MAC COSMETICS INC
2000 Route 38 Ste 200 (08002-2100)
PHONE...................................856 661-9024
Fax: 856 317-1764
Nicole Maze, *Manager*
EMP: 15 **Publicly Held**
WEB: www.danreadcosmetics.com
SIC: **2844** Shampoos, rinses, conditioners: hair
HQ: M.A.C. Cosmetics Inc.
130 Prince St Fl 5
New York NY 10012
212 965-6300

(G-1394)
MANNING PUBLICATION CO
1233 Heartwood Dr (08003-2739)
PHONE...................................856 375-2597
Marjan Bace, *Partner*
Lee Fitzpatrick, *Partner*
▲ EMP: 12
SQ FT: 2,000
SALES (est): 940K **Privately Held**
SIC: **2731** Books: publishing only

(G-1395)
MARLTON PIKE PRECISION LLC
728 Beechwood Ave (08002-2805)
P.O. Box 334, Marlton (08053-0334)
PHONE...................................856 665-1900
Fax: 856 665-8128
Tony Sala, *President*
EMP: 15 EST: 1948
SQ FT: 10,000
SALES: 950K **Privately Held**
SIC: **3599** Machine shop, jobbing & repair

(G-1396)
MASTERPIECE KITCHENS INC
2060 Springdale Rd # 800 (08003-4028)
PHONE...................................609 518-7887
John Nyman, *President*
EMP: 3
SQ FT: 1,400
SALES: 2MM **Privately Held**
WEB: www.masterpiecekitchens.net
SIC: **2434** Wood kitchen cabinets

(G-1397)
MD INTERNATIONAL INC
Also Called: Opalsoft Consulting
383 Kings Hwy N Ste B1 (08034-1014)
PHONE...................................856 779-7633
Dennis Panchal, *President*
EMP: 6
SQ FT: 1,500
SALES (est): 309K **Privately Held**
WEB: www.opalsoftconsult.com
SIC: **7379** 3695 Computer related consulting services; computer software tape & disks: blank, rigid & floppy

(G-1398)
MEDIABRIDGE PRODUCTS LLC
1951 Old Cuthbert Rd (08034-1411)
PHONE...................................856 216-8222
Robert Vezirian, *President*
Jarrod Coburn, *Cust Mgr*
EMP: 37 EST: 2007
SQ FT: 14,000
SALES (est): 25.5MM **Privately Held**
SIC: **3663** Cable television equipment

(G-1399)
MELITTA USA INC
1401 Berlin Rd Ste A (08034-1402)
PHONE...................................856 428-7202
Martin Miller, *Manager*
EMP: 50
SALES (corp-wide): 1.6B **Privately Held**
WEB: www.melitta.com
SIC: **2095** Coffee roasting (except by wholesale grocers)
HQ: Melitta Usa, Inc.
13925 58th St N
Clearwater FL 33760
727 535-2111

(G-1400)
METAL DYNAMIX LLC
670 Deer Rd Ste 201 (08034-1438)
PHONE...................................856 235-4559
Fax: 856 235-4468
Charles Gaw,
EMP: 9
SALES (est): 1.6MM **Privately Held**
WEB: www.metaldynamix.com
SIC: **3444** Sheet metalwork

(G-1401)
MINNITI J HAIR REPLACEMENT INC
Also Called: Joseph Mnniti Hair Replacement
905 Marlton Pike W (08002-3529)
PHONE...................................856 427-9600
Fax: 856 427-0443
Joseph Minniti, *President*
EMP: 6

SALES (est): 602.3K **Privately Held**
SIC: **3999** Hair & hair-based products

(G-1402)
MPLAYER ENTERTAINMENT LLC
329 Greenleigh Ct (08002-2307)
PHONE...................................302 229-3034
Kevin Pineda, *Mng Member*
Kyle Davidson,
EMP: 6
SALES (est): 135.3K **Privately Held**
SIC: **7372** 7389 Application computer software;

(G-1403)
NAVISTAR INC
535 Route 38 Ste 300 (08002-2972)
PHONE...................................856 486-2300
EMP: 70
SALES (corp-wide): 8.5B **Publicly Held**
SIC: **3711** Motor vehicles & car bodies
HQ: Navistar, Inc.
2701 Navistar Dr
Lisle IL 60532
331 332-5000

(G-1404)
NEWSPAPER MEDIA GROUP LLC (PA)
2 Executive Campus # 400 (08002-4102)
PHONE...................................856 779-3800
Angela Smith, *Principal*
EMP: 40
SALES (est): 6.7MM **Privately Held**
SIC: **2711** Newspapers, publishing & printing

(G-1405)
NORTHEAST MEDICAL SYSTEMS CORP
901 Beechwood Ave (08002-3405)
PHONE...................................856 910-8111
Fax: 856 910-8112
Joseph Conte, *President*
David Oberg, *Vice Pres*
EMP: 7
SALES: 1.7MM **Privately Held**
WEB: www.northeastmedicalsystems.com
SIC: **3841** 3845 Diagnostic apparatus, medical; electromedical equipment

(G-1406)
NUCLEAR DIAGNOSTIC PDTS INC
2 Keystone Ave Ste 200 (08003-1629)
PHONE...................................856 489-5733
Rodney Prosser, *President*
EMP: 10
SALES (corp-wide): 2.2MM **Privately Held**
SIC: **2834** Pharmaceutical preparations
PA: Nuclear Diagnostic Products, Inc.
101 Round Hill Dr Ste 4
Rockaway NJ 07866
973 664-9696

(G-1407)
NUMERICAL CONTROL PROGRAM SVC
917 Northwood Ave (08002-3415)
PHONE...................................856 665-8737
EMP: 7 EST: 1966
SQ FT: 9,500
SALES (est): 52.4K **Privately Held**
SIC: **3599** Machine Shop Jobbing

(G-1408)
OPEN SOLUTIONS INC
2091 Springdale Rd Ste 7 (08003-4005)
PHONE...................................856 424-0150
Tim Lenhoff, *Senior VP*
Douglas Jones, *Director*
EMP: 24
SALES (est): 3.3MM **Privately Held**
SIC: **7372** Business oriented computer software

▲ = Import ▼=Export
◆ =Import/Export

(G-1409)
PAD AND PUBL ASSEMBLY CORP
Also Called: Lrp and P Graphics
1165 Markkress Rd Ste M (08003-2330)
P.O. Box 1536 (08034-0069)
PHONE..................................856 424-0158
Fax: 856 424-5730
Joan Buehler, *President*
Carl Buehler, *Vice Pres*
Gwyn Andrews, *Administration*
EMP: 25
SQ FT: 6,600
SALES (est): 4.1MM **Privately Held**
WEB: www.padandpub.com
SIC: 2754 2791 2789 2752 Commercial printing, gravure; typesetting; bookbinding & related work; commercial printing, lithographic

(G-1410)
PANPAC LLC
1971 Old Cuthbert Rd (08034-1417)
PHONE..................................856 376-3576
Rahul Kaushik,
▲ EMP: 15
SQ FT: 25,000
SALES (est): 3.7MM **Privately Held**
SIC: 3555 Printing trades machinery

(G-1411)
PEAK FINANCE HOLDINGS LLC (HQ)
121 Woodcrest Rd (08003-3620)
PHONE..................................856 969-7100
Mark Foley, *Purchasing*
EMP: 1
SALES (est): 2.4B
SALES (corp-wide): 3.1B **Publicly Held**
SIC: 2038 2092 2099 2045 Frozen specialties; breakfasts, frozen & packaged; pizza, frozen; waffles, frozen; prepared fish or other seafood cakes & sticks; pancake syrup, blended & mixed; cake flour: from purchased flour; bread & bread type roll mixes: from purchased flour; pancake mixes, prepared: from purchased flour
PA: Pinnacle Foods Inc.
399 Jefferson Rd
Parsippany NJ 07054
973 541-6620

(G-1412)
PENNANT INGREDIENTS INC
1941 Old Cuthbert Rd (08034-1417)
PHONE..................................856 428-4300
EMP: 7 **Privately Held**
SIC: 2099 Food preparations
HQ: Pennant Ingredients, Inc.
64 Chester St
Rochester NY 14611
585 235-8160

(G-1413)
PHILADELPHIA INQUIRER
53 Haddonfield Rd Ste 300 (08002-4809)
PHONE..................................856 779-3840
Fax: 856 779-3221
Kurt Heine, *Principal*
Jason Di Ridolfo, *Executive*
EMP: 6
SALES (est): 382.8K **Privately Held**
SIC: 2711 Newspapers

(G-1414)
PINNACLE FOOD GROUP INC
6 Executive Campus # 100 (08002-4130)
PHONE..................................856 969-7100
Mark A Clouse, *CEO*
John Butler, *Exec VP*
Mark L Schiller, *Exec VP*
Kelley Maggs Sr, *Senior VP*
Bob Matthews, *Vice Pres*
EMP: 34 EST: 2014
SALES (est): 2.6MM **Privately Held**
SIC: 2038 Breakfasts, frozen & packaged

(G-1415)
POLYSYSTEMS INC
2 Executive Campus # 320 (08002-4102)
PHONE..................................312 332-5670
Graham Bartholomae, *Engineer*
Louis Frano, *Engineer*
Tom Nace, *Accountant*
Cindy Wu, *Manager*
Diane Zapisek, *Manager*
EMP: 8
SALES (corp-wide): 9.4MM **Privately Held**
WEB: www.polysystems.com
SIC: 7372 Application computer software
PA: Polysystems, Inc.
30 N La Salle St Ste 3600
Chicago IL 60602
312 332-2114

(G-1416)
PRESSWORKS
Also Called: Ipp/Pressworks
1879 Old Cuthbert Rd # 28 (08034-1433)
PHONE..................................856 427-9001
Fax: 856 427-9006
Diane Reilly, *Partner*
Dennis Reilly, *Partner*
▲ EMP: 5
SALES: 350K **Privately Held**
SIC: 2759 Promotional printing

(G-1417)
PURATOS CORPORATION (DH)
1941 Old Cuthbert Rd (08034-1417)
PHONE..................................856 428-4300
Fax: 856 428-2939
Karel Zimmermann, *President*
Frdric Duvauchelle, *President*
Ian Rossignol, *Vice Pres*
◆ EMP: 140
SALES: 283.4MM **Privately Held**
WEB: www.puratos.com
SIC: 2099 Food preparations
HQ: Puratos Nv
Industrialaan 25
Dilbeek 1702
248 144-44

(G-1418)
RANDELLS CSTM FNITURE KITCHENS
1864 Marlton Pike E (08003-2029)
PHONE..................................856 216-9400
Fax: 856 216-9494
Randell Wyville, *Owner*
EMP: 12
SALES (est): 970.2K **Privately Held**
SIC: 2499 Decorative wood & woodwork

(G-1419)
SCOTT W SPRINGMAN
Also Called: Architectural Acrylics
5 Rockhill Rd Ste 3 (08003-2384)
PHONE..................................856 751-2411
Fax: 856 751-1428
Scott W Springman, *Owner*
Barbara Springman, *Manager*
EMP: 7
SQ FT: 8,000
SALES: 800K **Privately Held**
SIC: 2519 3089 Lawn & garden furniture, except wood & metal; plastic processing

(G-1420)
SMS BUILDING SYSTEMS LTD LBLTY
5 N Olney Ave Ste 100a (08003-1622)
PHONE..................................856 520-8769
Steven Lulias, *Partner*
William Kanupke, *Partner*
EMP: 10
SALES: 1MM **Privately Held**
SIC: 7382 1731 3646 Confinement surveillance systems maintenance & monitoring; voice, data & video wiring contractor; commercial indusl & institutional electric lighting fixtures

(G-1421)
SPRINGDALE FARM MARKET INC
1638 Springdale Rd (08003-2738)
PHONE..................................856 424-8674
Fax: 856 424-7074
Maryann Jarvis, *President*
John Ebert, *Vice Pres*
Tom Jarvis, *Vice Pres*
Mary Ebert, *Admin Sec*
EMP: 35
SQ FT: 45,000
SALES (est): 1.2MM **Privately Held**
SIC: 0161 5812 5992 5947 Corn farm, sweet; tomato farm; eating places; florists; gift, novelty & souvenir shop; fruit & vegetable markets; bread, cake & related products

(G-1422)
SUN NEON SIGN AND ELECTRIC CO
4 Saddle Ln (08002-1528)
PHONE..................................856 667-6977
Stuart Rosner, *Owner*
EMP: 7 EST: 1947
SALES (est): 570K **Privately Held**
SIC: 1731 1799 3993 General electrical contractor; sign installation & maintenance; neon signs

(G-1423)
SUPERIOR LAMP INC
1060 Kings Hwy N Ste 120 (08034-1910)
PHONE..................................800 257-8353
Frank Zaino, *Branch Mgr*
EMP: 5
SALES (corp-wide): 20.7MM **Privately Held**
SIC: 3641 Electric lamps
HQ: Superior Lamp Inc.
3001 University Dr S
Fargo ND 58103
800 437-4772

(G-1424)
SURGICAL LSER SFETY CUNCIL INC
405 Hialeah Dr (08002-2036)
PHONE..................................216 272-0805
Allen Seftel, *President*
Stephen Nakada, *Vice Pres*
Mandeep Singh, *Treasurer*
Richard Pearl, *Consultant*
Mitchell Humphreys, *Admin Sec*
EMP: 7
SALES (est): 262.6K **Privately Held**
SIC: 3845 3842 Laser systems & equipment, medical; personal safety equipment

(G-1425)
SWAROVSKI NORTH AMERICA LTD
2000 Route 38 (08002-2100)
PHONE..................................856 662-5453
Dana Cooley, *President*
EMP: 7
SALES (corp-wide): 3.7B **Privately Held**
SIC: 3961 Costume jewelry
HQ: Swarovski North America Limited
1 Kenney Dr
Cranston RI 02920
401 463-6400

(G-1426)
TAPESTRY INC
2000 Route 38 Ste 1720 (08002-2178)
PHONE..................................856 488-2220
Marleen Grassia, *Branch Mgr*
EMP: 15
SALES (corp-wide): 5.8B **Publicly Held**
WEB: www.coach.com
SIC: 3171 Handbags, women's
PA: Tapestry, Inc.
10 Hudson Yards
New York NY 10001
212 594-1850

(G-1427)
TASTY CAKE SOUTH JERSEY
1871 Old Cuthbert Rd B (08034-1415)
PHONE..................................856 428-8414
Fax: 856 428-8473
John Zagiel, *Executive*
EMP: 4
SALES (est): 194K **Privately Held**
SIC: 2051 Bakery: wholesale or wholesale/retail combined

(G-1428)
TGZ ACQUISITION COMPANY LLC
Also Called: Jace Systems
5 Rockhill Rd Ste 2 (08003-2384)
PHONE..................................856 669-6600
Fax: 856 669-0017
Tom Zieser, *Mng Member*

EMP: 16
SQ FT: 18,000
SALES (est): 3.4MM **Privately Held**
SIC: 7352 3842 Medical equipment rental; orthopedic appliances

(G-1429)
TOTAL TECHNOLOGY INC
950 Kings Hwy N Ste 105 (08034-1518)
PHONE..................................856 617-0502
Maria C McCabe, *President*
Nicole Hamilton, *Finance*
EMP: 24
SQ FT: 750
SALES (est): 4.8MM **Privately Held**
WEB: www.totaltechnologyinc.net
SIC: 8711 3577 Engineering services; data conversion equipment, media-to-media: computer

(G-1430)
TURBON INTERNATIONAL INC (DH)
Also Called: Turbon USA
4 Executive Campus # 104 (08002-4105)
PHONE..................................800 282-6650
Aldo Deluca, *CEO*
Dean Edwards, *President*
Steven Injaian, *Admin Sec*
◆ EMP: 2
SQ FT: 130,000
SALES (est): 21.9MM
SALES (corp-wide): 439.3K **Privately Held**
SIC: 3955 Print cartridges for laser & other computer printers
HQ: Turbon Ag
Ruhrdeich 10
Hattingen 45525
232 450-40

Chesilhurst
Camden County

(G-1431)
WHIMSY DIDDLES LLC
59 Briarhill Dr (08089-1234)
PHONE..................................609 560-1323
Peter D Connet, *Principal*
EMP: 4 EST: 2007
SALES (est): 387.2K **Privately Held**
SIC: 3499 Novelties & giftware, including trophies

Chester
Morris County

(G-1432)
AB COASTER LLC
Also Called: ABS Company, The
360 State Route 24 Ste 4 (07930-2925)
P.O. Box 9 (07930-0009)
PHONE..................................908 879-2713
Kristin Harrington, *Sales Mgr*
Silvia Milaschewski, *Cust Mgr*
Cindy Ramos, *Mktg Dir*
Dj Hoffman, *Manager*
Kim Healey, *Info Tech Mgr*
EMP: 10
SALES (est): 1.5MM **Privately Held**
SIC: 8742 3949 Marketing consulting services; sporting & athletic goods

(G-1433)
ABACUS ELECTRIC & PLUMBING
95 W Main St Ste 252 (07930-2487)
PHONE..................................908 269-8057
Ken Ryan,
EMP: 4
SALES (est): 250.8K **Privately Held**
SIC: 3699 1711 Electrical equipment & supplies; plumbing, heating, air-conditioning contractors

(G-1434)
BRANDED SCREEN PRINTING
45 Warren St Ste A (07930-3609)
P.O. Box 687 (07930-0687)
PHONE..................................908 879-7411

Chris Smith, *Owner*
EMP: 4
SALES (est): 382.8K **Privately Held**
SIC: 2759 Screen printing

(G-1435)
COMEX SYSTEMS INC
101 Pleasant Hill Rd (07930-2140)
PHONE..............................800 543-6959
Doug Pryblowski, *President*
EMP: 5
SQ FT: 2,400
SALES (est): 390K **Privately Held**
WEB: www.comexsystems.com
SIC: 2731 Books: publishing only

(G-1436)
DOUGLAS MAYBURY ASSOC
385 State Route 24 Ste 3e (07930-2910)
PHONE..............................908 879-5878
Kevin Maybury, *Owner*
EMP: 4
SALES (est): 260K **Privately Held**
SIC: 2752 Business forms, lithographed

(G-1437)
HURRICANE HUTCH
190 Lamerson Rd (07930-2425)
PHONE..............................908 256-5912
Kenneth Hoffman, *Principal*
EMP: 4
SALES: 950K **Privately Held**
SIC: 3499 Fabricated metal products

(G-1438)
PROCESS CONTROLS CO
530 Main St Ste 6a (07930-2669)
P.O. Box 89 (07930-0089)
PHONE..............................908 269-8465
Fax: 908 879-2466
Robert Blanchard Sr, *President*
Susan Blanchard, *Corp Secy*
Stella Myers, *Business Dir*
EMP: 7
SQ FT: 2,400
SALES (est): 1.4MM **Privately Held**
WEB: www.processcontrols.com
SIC: 5084 3823 Power plant machinery;
boiler controls: industrial, power & marine
type

(G-1439)
QUALITY INGREDIENTS CORP
385 State Route 24 Ste 3d (07930-2910)
PHONE..............................908 879-2227
Fax: 908 879-2502
Diane Schmidt, *Ch of Bd*
Thomas A Schmidt, *President*
EMP: 10
SQ FT: 2,000
SALES (est): 1.2MM
SALES (corp-wide): 404MM **Privately Held**
WEB: www.qicusa.com
SIC: 2099 Food preparations
PA: Total Sweeteners, Inc.
1700 E Higgins Rd Ste 300
Des Plaines IL 60018
847 299-1999

(G-1440)
THOMAS PUBLISHING COMPANY LLC
Also Called: Thomas Register
95 W Main St Ste 8 (07930-2487)
PHONE..............................973 543-4994
Robert Probst, *Manager*
EMP: 25
SALES (corp-wide): 166.6MM **Privately Held**
WEB: www.inboundlogistics.com
SIC: 2741 2721 7374 Directories: publishing only, not printed on site; trade journals: publishing only, not printed on site; data processing service
PA: Thomas Publishing Company Llc
5 Penn Plz Fl 9
New York NY 10001
212 695-0500

Chesterfield
Burlington County

(G-1441)
BELLA ACQUA INC
Also Called: Acqua Bella Mfg and Supply
214 Sykesville Rd Ste 1a (08515-2419)
PHONE..............................609 324-9024
Scott Crosbie, *President*
EMP: 10
SALES: 2MM **Privately Held**
WEB: www.acquabella.net
SIC: 3624 Carbon specialties for electrical use

(G-1442)
SOMERSET CPITL MARK TR MGT INC
1 Donlonton Cir (08515-9786)
PHONE..............................848 228-0842
Isaac Inyang, *President*
EMP: 10
SALES (est): 784.5K **Privately Held**
SIC: 3612 Transmission & distribution voltage regulators

(G-1443)
TOWNSEND MACHINE INC
246 Sykesville Rd (08515-2407)
PHONE..............................609 723-2603
Fax: 609 723-3976
Barclay A Townsend, *President*
Barclay Townsend, *President*
Lorraine Townsend, *Corp Secy*
Cindy Von Smith, *Office Mgr*
EMP: 40
SQ FT: 24,000
SALES (est): 5.9MM **Privately Held**
WEB: www.gotownsend.com
SIC: 3599 Machine shop, jobbing & repair

Cinnaminson
Burlington County

(G-1444)
ACTEGA NORTH AMERICA INC
1450 Taylors Ln (08077-2512)
PHONE..............................856 829-6300
Fax: 856 786-2860
Steven Kramer, *Principal*
EMP: 13 **Privately Held**
SIC: 2851 Paints & allied products
HQ: Actega North America, Inc.
950 S Chester Ave Ste B2
Delran NJ 08075
856 829-6300

(G-1445)
AIRGAS USA LLC
600 Union Landing Rd (08077-2002)
PHONE..............................856 829-7878
Joseph Mahan, *Plant Mgr*
Jill Morrison, *Manager*
EMP: 22
SALES (corp-wide): 164.2MM **Privately Held**
SIC: 5169 5084 5085 2813 Industrial gases; gases, compressed & liquefied; carbon dioxide; dry ice; welding machinery & equipment; safety equipment; welding supplies; industrial gases; carbon dioxide; nitrous oxide; dry ice, carbon dioxide (solid); industrial inorganic chemicals; calcium carbide
HQ: Airgas Usa, Llc
259 N Radnor Chester Rd # 100
Radnor PA 19087
610 687-5253

(G-1446)
AQUA PRODUCTS INC
2703 River Rd (08077-1627)
PHONE..............................856 829-8444
Fax: 856 829-8482
Samuel J Jones Sr, *President*
▼ EMP: 25 EST: 1964
SALES (est): 4.4MM **Privately Held**
SIC: 2842 Cleaning or polishing preparations

(G-1447)
ARMADILLO AUTOMATION INC
Also Called: Onyx Valve
835 Industrial Hwy Ste 4 (08077-1929)
PHONE..............................856 829-2888
Fax: 856 829-3080
David Gardellin, *CEO*
▲ EMP: 40
SQ FT: 12,500
SALES (est): 9.9MM **Privately Held**
WEB: www.onyxvalve.com
SIC: 3823 3491 3822 Industrial process control instruments; industrial valves

(G-1448)
BABCOCK & WILCOX COMPANY
1000 Taylors Ln Ste 4 (08077-2026)
PHONE..............................609 261-2424
Fax: 609 702-8550
Paul Kain, *Branch Mgr*
Monica Bowker, *Personnel Assit*
EMP: 7
SALES (corp-wide): 1.5B **Publicly Held**
SIC: 3511 Steam turbines
HQ: The Babcock & Wilcox Company
20 S Van Buren Ave
Barberton OH 44203
330 753-4511

(G-1449)
BOSSEN ARCHITECTURAL MILLWORK
1818 Bannard St (08077-1808)
P.O. Box 133, Riverton (08077-0133)
PHONE..............................856 786-1100
Joseph H Bossen, *President*
Audrey Denyse, *Office Mgr*
Joseph Bossen, *Executive*
EMP: 14
SQ FT: 23,000
SALES (est): 3.1MM **Privately Held**
SIC: 5211 5031 2541 Millwork & lumber; kitchen cabinets; display fixtures, wood

(G-1450)
CAPITAL LABEL AND AFFIXING CO
1100 Taylors Ln Ste 5 (08077-2586)
P.O. Box 2366 (08077-5366)
PHONE..............................856 786-1700
EMP: 2
SQ FT: 15,000
SALES (est): 1.2MM **Privately Held**
SIC: 2672 Mfg Coated/Laminated Paper

(G-1451)
CLOTHES HORSE INTERNATIONAL
2200 Wallace Blvd Ste A (08077-2578)
PHONE..............................856 829-8460
Fax: 856 829-8602
Katrina Coldren, *President*
EMP: 12
SQ FT: 3,000
SALES: 1.1MM **Privately Held**
WEB: www.theclotheshorse.com
SIC: 2399 Horse blankets

(G-1452)
COMPUFAB SALES INC
2303 Garry Rd Ste 1 (08077-2560)
PHONE..............................856 786-0175
Fax: 856 769-9058
Otto Steiner, *President*
EMP: 4
SALES (est): 452.9K **Privately Held**
SIC: 3674 Semiconductors & related devices

(G-1453)
DEB MAINTENANCE INC
1000 Union Landing Rd (08077-2502)
P.O. Box 13, Riverton (08077-0013)
PHONE..............................856 786-0440
Fax: 856 786-1993
Kenneth Williams, *President*
Deborah Hess, *Corp Secy*
EMP: 30
SQ FT: 35,000
SALES (est): 5.2MM **Privately Held**
SIC: 3443 Tanks, lined: metal plate; vessels, process or storage (from boiler shops): metal plate

---

(G-1454)
DEJANA TRCK UTILITY EQP CO LLC
Also Called: Dejana Trck Grter Philadelphia
2502 Route 130 N (08077-3019)
PHONE..............................856 303-1315
Fax: 856 303-1361
Sal Silvestri, *Branch Mgr*
EMP: 24 **Publicly Held**
WEB: www.dejana.com
SIC: 3711 Truck & tractor truck assembly
HQ: Dejana Truck & Utility Equipment Company, Llc
490 Pulaski Rd
Kings Park NY 11754
631 544-9000

(G-1455)
DELVA TOOL & MACHINE CORP (PA)
1603 Industrial Hwy (08077-2503)
P.O. Box 2249 (08077-5249)
PHONE..............................856 786-8700
Fax: 856 786-8708
Stephan J Voellinger, *President*
Steven Griffith, *Vice Pres*
Charles Magro, *Engineer*
Julie Mader, *Human Res Mgr*
Ruth Irizarry, *Manager*
EMP: 76 EST: 1962
SQ FT: 20,000
SALES (est): 31.4MM **Privately Held**
WEB: www.delvatool.com
SIC: 3599 Machine shop, jobbing & repair

(G-1456)
DELVA TOOL & MACHINE CORP
1911 Rowland St (08077-1923)
P.O. Box 2249 (08077-5249)
PHONE..............................856 829-0109
Stephan J Voellinger, *Branch Mgr*
EMP: 53
SALES (corp-wide): 31.4MM **Privately Held**
SIC: 3599 Machine shop, jobbing & repair
PA: Delva Tool & Machine Corp
1603 Industrial Hwy
Cinnaminson NJ 08077
856 786-8700

(G-1457)
DETREX CORPORATION
Also Called: Solvent & Envmtl Svcs Div
835 Industrial Hwy Ste 1 (08077-1929)
PHONE..............................856 786-8686
Fax: 856 786-8288
Una Bauso, *Branch Mgr*
EMP: 6 **Privately Held**
WEB: www.detrex.com
SIC: 3589 Commercial cleaning equipment
HQ: Detrex Corporation
1000 Belt Line Ave
Cleveland OH 44109
216 749-2605

(G-1458)
DU-MOR BLADE CO INC
1002 Union Landing Rd (08077-2502)
PHONE..............................856 829-9384
Fax: 856 829-9303
Harry C Morris, *President*
Margaret Morris, *Corp Secy*
Chris Morris, *Vice Pres*
Elaine Morris, *VP Sales*
▲ EMP: 20
SQ FT: 9,000
SALES (est): 3.2MM **Privately Held**
WEB: www.dumorblade.com
SIC: 3421 Knife blades & blanks

(G-1459)
DYNAMIC MACHINING INC
1920 Bannard St (08077-1901)
PHONE..............................856 273-9830
Fax: 856 273-0393
Harold Budman, *President*
Ginny Zimmer, *Info Tech Mgr*
EMP: 19
SQ FT: 14,600
SALES (est): 5MM **Privately Held**
SIC: 3599 Machine shop, jobbing & repair

▲ = Import ▼=Export
◆ =Import/Export

(G-1460)
EDKER INDUSTRIES INC
1401 Union Landing Rd (08077-2558)
PHONE.................................856 786-1971
Fax: 856 786-8258
Edward C Kerbaugh Jr, *President*
Tom Kerbaugh, *President*
Virginia Kerbaugh, *Admin Sec*
EMP: 45
SQ FT: 12,000
SALES (est): 7.9MM **Privately Held**
SIC: 3444 Sheet metal specialties, not stamped

(G-1461)
ENSER CORPORATION (PA)
1902 Taylors Ln Ste B (08077-2580)
PHONE.................................856 829-5522
Marco Arnone, *President*
Eric Venskytis, *Shareholder*
Michael Wahner, *Shareholder*
EMP: 35
SQ FT: 30,000
SALES (est): 12.8MM **Privately Held**
WEB: www.enser.com
SIC: 8711 7373 3554 7361 Mechanical engineering; computer-aided design (CAD) systems service; computer-aided engineering (CAE) systems service; four-drinier machines, paper manufacturing; labor contractors (employment agency)

(G-1462)
FOUNDATION MONITORING
Also Called: Fmw Drilling
515 Wellfleet Rd (08077-4426)
PHONE.................................856 829-0410
John L Snyder, *President*
Theresa A Snyder, *Vice Pres*
EMP: 4
SALES (est): 411K **Privately Held**
SIC: 1381 8748 Service well drilling; environmental consultant

(G-1463)
G N J INC (PA)
Also Called: Dunkin' Donuts
N Riderton Rd Rr 130 (08077)
PHONE.................................856 786-1127
Fax: 856 461-3908
Shailesh Doshi, *President*
Kal Shah, *Vice Pres*
EMP: 19
SALES (est): 1.7MM **Privately Held**
SIC: 5461 2051 Doughnuts; doughnuts, except frozen

(G-1464)
GAB ELECTRONIC SERVICES LLC
1703 Industrial Hwy Ste 8 (08077-2582)
PHONE.................................856 786-0108
Fax: 856 786-7444
Donald Bogle, *President*
EMP: 25 **EST:** 1976
SQ FT: 6,000
SALES (est): 2MM **Privately Held**
WEB: www.rhrtechnologies.com
SIC: 3672 Printed circuit boards

(G-1465)
GRIFFIN SIGNS INC
484 N Randolph Ave (08077)
PHONE.................................856 786-8517
Michele Angerame, *President*
Robert Perry, *Vice Pres*
EMP: 45
SQ FT: 25,000
SALES (est): 9MM **Privately Held**
WEB: www.griffinsigns.com
SIC: 1799 3993 8748 Sign installation & maintenance; fence construction; signs, not made in custom sign painting shops; traffic consultant

(G-1466)
H-E TOOL & MFG CO INC
800 Industrial Hwy Unit A (08077-1949)
PHONE.................................856 303-8787
Fax: 856 829-8011
Pauline Hamin, *President*
David D'Antonio, *COO*
EMP: 35
SQ FT: 43,000

SALES (est): 4.3MM
SALES (corp-wide): 93.4MM **Privately Held**
WEB: www.h-etool.com
SIC: 3544 Special dies & tools
PA: Sea Box Inc
1 Sea Box Dr
Cinnaminson NJ 08077
856 303-1101

(G-1467)
HENRY OLSEN MACHINE
Also Called: Olsen, H Machine
2504 Route 73 (08077-4113)
PHONE.................................856 662-2121
Henry Olsen, *Owner*
David Olsen, *Co-Owner*
EMP: 5
SQ FT: 1,900
SALES (est): 270K **Privately Held**
SIC: 3599 Machine & other job shop work

(G-1468)
HOEGANAES CORPORATION (DH)
1001 Taylors Ln (08077-2034)
PHONE.................................856 303-0366
Fax: 856 786-2574
Kalathur Narasimhan, *Vice Pres*
Peter Boultbee, *Vice Pres*
Joel Feit, *Vice Pres*
Thomas Lewandowski, *Vice Pres*
Bill Michael, *Vice Pres*
◆ **EMP:** 277
SQ FT: 504,000
SALES (est): 187.9MM
SALES (corp-wide): 12.7B **Privately Held**
WEB: www.hoeganaes.com
SIC: 3312 3399 Blast furnaces & steel mills; metal powders, pastes & flakes

(G-1469)
INTEGRTED LAMINATE SYSTEMS INC
1301 Industrial Hwy (08077-2552)
PHONE.................................856 786-6500
Fax: 856 786-8912
Chris Sparacio, *President*
Alice Schiano, *Project Mgr*
Don Reckeweg, *Purch Mgr*
Kim Staryeu, *Human Res Mgr*
Joanne Butler, *Manager*
EMP: 54
SALES (est): 9.4MM **Privately Held**
SIC: 3843 Cabinets, dental

(G-1470)
INVENTORS SHOP LLC
800 Industrial Hwy Unit A (08077-1949)
PHONE.................................856 303-8787
Gina Tobin, *Sales Associate*
Jim Brennan, *Mng Member*
Maryanne Merritt, *Info Tech Mgr*
EMP: 29
SALES (est): 6.4MM **Privately Held**
SIC: 3544 8999 Special dies, tools, jigs & fixtures; special dies & tools; actuarial consultant

(G-1471)
J A W PRODUCTS INC
835 Industrial Hwy # 125 (08077-1929)
P.O. Box 2593 (08077-4993)
PHONE.................................856 829-3210
Earl Weightman, *President*
Elenore Weightman, *Vice Pres*
EMP: 12
SQ FT: 3,300
SALES (est): 1.8MM **Privately Held**
WEB: www.jawproducts.com
SIC: 3843 5047 3599 Dental equipment & supplies; dental equipment & supplies; machine shop, jobbing & repair

(G-1472)
KOBOLAK & SON INC
1818 Bannard St (08077-1808)
PHONE.................................856 829-6106
Fax: 856 829-4190
Erno Kobolak, *President*
Dana Kobolak, *Software Engr*
EMP: 8
SALES (est): 893.5K **Privately Held**
SIC: 2434 Wood kitchen cabinets

(G-1473)
KT MT CORP (PA)
Also Called: Aall American Fasteners
2303 Garry Rd Unit 12 (08077-2560)
PHONE.................................877 791-4426
Fax: 856 786-8063
Kimberly A Tenenbaum, *President*
Mark D Tenenbaum, *Vice Pres*
EMP: 17 **EST:** 1998
SQ FT: 10,000
SALES (est): 3.5MM **Privately Held**
WEB: www.aallamericanfasteners.com
SIC: 5085 3452 Fasteners, industrial: nuts, bolts, screws, etc.; bolts, nuts, rivets & washers

(G-1474)
LYNN MECHANICAL CONTRACTORS
1810 Rowland St (08077-1852)
PHONE.................................856 829-1717
Fax: 856 829-1331
Raymond W Lynn Sr, *President*
Clare Lynn, *Corp Secy*
Ray Lynn, *Vice Pres*
Raymond W Lynn Jr, *Vice Pres*
EMP: 13 **EST:** 1946
SQ FT: 14,000
SALES (est): 1.4MM **Privately Held**
SIC: 3535 3444 Conveyors & conveying equipment; sheet metal specialties, not stamped

(G-1475)
MARY BRIDGET ENTERPRISES
2305 Garry Rd Ste B (08077-2596)
PHONE.................................609 267-4830
Jim Daly, *Owner*
EMP: 20
SALES (est): 1.8MM **Privately Held**
SIC: 2759 2395 Screen printing; embroidery & art needlework

(G-1476)
MATESON CHEMICAL CORPORATION
510 Whitmore St (08077-1626)
PHONE.................................215 423-3200
Joseph Cammarasana, *President*
James Mateson, *Treasurer*
Christopher Mateson, *Admin Sec*
EMP: 9 **EST:** 1953
SQ FT: 10,000
SALES (est): 2.3MM **Privately Held**
WEB: www.matesonchemical.com
SIC: 2819 Industrial inorganic chemicals

(G-1477)
MICRO-TEK CORPORATION
1600 Taylors Ln (08077-2520)
P.O. Box 2134 (08077-5134)
PHONE.................................856 829-3855
Brian W Gordon, *President*
Ricki Rogers-Gordon, *Sales Staff*
▲ **EMP:** 3
SALES (est): 1.6MM **Privately Held**
SIC: 3357 8711 Nonferrous wiredrawing & insulating; consulting engineer

(G-1478)
MIDLANTIC COLOR GRAPHICS LLC
2303 Garry Rd Ste 9 (08077-2560)
P.O. Box 2388 (08077-5388)
PHONE.................................856 786-3113
Henry Chou, *Technology*
Thomas Gain,
Mike Gain,
EMP: 4
SALES (est): 531.8K **Privately Held**
WEB: www.midlanticonline.com
SIC: 2759 Screen printing

(G-1479)
MONTGOMERY INVESTMENT TECH (PA)
700 Route 130 N Ste 105 (08077-3346)
PHONE.................................610 688-8111
Fax: 610 688-5084
George Montgomery, *President*
Sorin Straja, *Financial Exec*
EMP: 9
SQ FT: 1,000

SALES (est): 1.5MM **Privately Held**
WEB: www.wallstreetnet.com
SIC: 7372 Business oriented computer software

(G-1480)
NATIONAL CASEIN NEW JERSEY INC
401 Marthas Ln (08077-1551)
P.O. Box 226, Riverton (08077-0226)
PHONE.................................856 829-1880
Fax: 856 829-6063
Trever Williams, *Manager*
Vince Lewonski, *Manager*
David Lowery, *Director*
EMP: 30
SALES (corp-wide): 2.6MM **Privately Held**
SIC: 3089 2891 Molding primary plastic; adhesives
PA: National Casein Of New Jersey, Incorporated
601 W 80th St
Chicago IL 60620
773 846-7300

(G-1481)
O & S RESEARCH INC
1912 Bannard St (08077-1901)
P.O. Box 221, Riverton (08077-0221)
PHONE.................................856 829-2800
Fax: 856 829-0482
Anderson Mc Cabe, *President*
Arthur Kania, *Corp Secy*
Warren Thielz, *Mfg Spvr*
Fred Fogleman, *QA Dir*
Ruth A Taylor, *Marketing Staff*
▲ **EMP:** 35
SQ FT: 29,000
SALES (est): 6.8MM
SALES (corp-wide): 7MM **Publicly Held**
WEB: www.osresearch.com
SIC: 3827 Lenses, optical: all types except ophthalmic; prisms, optical
PA: Opt-Sciences Corporation
1912 Bannard St
Cinnaminson NJ 08077
856 829-2800

(G-1482)
OPT-SCIENCES CORPORATION (PA)
1912 Bannard St (08077-1901)
P.O. Box 221, Riverton (08077-0221)
PHONE.................................856 829-2800
Anderson L McCabe, *President*
Anderson McCabe, *CFO*
Lorraine Damask, *Finance*
Arthur J Kania, *Admin Sec*
EMP: 14
SQ FT: 5,000
SALES: 7MM **Publicly Held**
WEB: www.optsciences.com
SIC: 3827 Optical instruments & apparatus

(G-1483)
PECHTERS SOUTHERN NJ LLC
Also Called: Psnj
2 Surrey Ln (08077)
P.O. Box 2069 (08077-5069)
PHONE.................................856 786-8000
Fax: 856 481-2319
James Fisher, *General Mgr*
EMP: 7
SALES (est): 950K **Privately Held**
SIC: 2051 Bread, cake & related products

(G-1484)
PHARMAKON CORP
2200 Wallace Blvd Ste C (08077-2578)
P.O. Box 2174 (08077-5174)
PHONE.................................856 829-3161
Fax: 856 829-3609
William H Shaffer Sr, *President*
Bruce Shaffer, *Vice Pres*
EMP: 15
SQ FT: 5,000
SALES (est): 1.4MM **Privately Held**
SIC: 3999 Advertising display products

(G-1485)
PHOENIX RESINS INC
Also Called: Mas Epoxies
602 Union Landing Rd (08077-2002)
P.O. Box 2310 (08077-5310)
PHONE.................................888 627-3769

Fax: 856 303-2889
James B Currell Jr, *CEO*
Tony Delima, *President*
Maryann Mc Farland, *Corp Secy*
EMP: 10
SQ FT: 2,300
SALES: 500K **Privately Held**
WEB: www.masepoxies.com
SIC: 2821 Epoxy resins

(G-1486)
SAMUEL ELLIOTT INC
Also Called: Apollo Graphics NJ
1818 Bannard St (08077-1808)
P.O. Box 81, Palmyra (08065-0081)
PHONE....................................856 773-6000
Fax: 856 773-6002
Mary Bossen, *President*
John Bossen, *General Mgr*
Sam Bossen, *Treasurer*
EMP: 20
SALES (est): 1.6MM **Privately Held**
WEB: www.samuelelliott.com
SIC: 2759 Commercial printing

(G-1487)
SHELBY MECHANICAL INC
1009 Broad St (08077-1543)
PHONE....................................856 665-4540
Nancy D Bray, *CEO*
Michael P Bray, *President*
Dan McFadden, *Superintendent*
Michael D Mulligan, *Exec VP*
Michael Mulligan, *Exec VP*
EMP: 50
SQ FT: 25,000
SALES (est): 24.7MM **Privately Held**
SIC: 1711 1389 1629 Boiler maintenance
contractor; construction, repair & disman-
tling services; oil refinery construction;
power plant construction

(G-1488)
SOURCE DIRECT INC
Also Called: Source Direct Plastics Div
2200 Garry Rd Ste 3 (08077-2595)
PHONE....................................856 768-7445
Sundeep Thakrar, *President*
Bob Thakrar, *Vice Pres*
▲ **EMP:** 15
SQ FT: 50,000
SALES: 10MM **Privately Held**
WEB: www.sourcedirectinc.com
SIC: 2673 Plastic bags: made from pur-
chased materials

(G-1489)
SPEED RACEWAY
1103 Route 130 S (08077-3003)
PHONE....................................856 314-8264
▲ **EMP:** 5
SALES (est): 406.4K **Privately Held**
SIC: 3644 Raceways

(G-1490)
**T-M VACUUM PRODUCTS INC
(PA)**
630 S Warrington Ave (08077-1898)
P.O. Box 2248 (08077-5248)
PHONE....................................856 829-2000
Fax: 856 829-0990
Fred T Stuffer, *President*
Ken Chew, *Engineer*
David Hartner, *Sales Staff*
Roland Johnson, *Admin Sec*
▼ **EMP:** 35 **EST:** 1965
SQ FT: 25,000
SALES (est): 5MM **Privately Held**
WEB: www.tmvacuum.com
SIC: 3567 Vacuum furnaces & ovens

(G-1491)
T-M VACUUM PRODUCTS INC
630 S Warrington Ave (08077-1898)
P.O. Box 2248 (08077-5248)
PHONE....................................856 829-2000
Rennie Stuffer, *Vice Pres*
EMP: 10
SALES (corp-wide): 5MM **Privately Held**
WEB: www.tmvacuum.com
SIC: 3599 Machine shop, jobbing & repair
PA: T-M Vacuum Products, Inc.
630 S Warrington Ave
Cinnaminson NJ 08077
856 829-2000

(G-1492)
THEPOSITIVE PRESS
2020 Bannard St (08077-1902)
PHONE....................................856 266-8765
EMP: 4
SALES (est): 107.5K **Privately Held**
SIC: 2741 Misc Publishing

(G-1493)
TOMKEN PLATING
625 Pear St (08077-1915)
P.O. Box 2323 (08077-5323)
PHONE....................................856 829-0607
Fax: 856 829-5174
Thomas H Kennedy, *President*
Eric Kennedy, *Vice Pres*
Gertrude M Kennedy, *Treasurer*
EMP: 8
SQ FT: 11,000
SALES (est): 1MM **Privately Held**
SIC: 3471 Chromium plating of metals or
formed products

(G-1494)
TONE KRAFT INC
727 S Randolph Ave (08077-1819)
PHONE....................................856 283-8043
Amalia M Ordonez Paredes, *Principal*
EMP: 4
SALES (est): 164.7K **Privately Held**
SIC: 2022 Processed cheese

(G-1495)
TRANSAXLE LLC (PA)
2501 Route 73 (08077-4114)
P.O. Box 2306 (08077-5306)
PHONE....................................856 665-4445
Fax: 856 661-0092
Bill Clark, *General Mgr*
Doug Everett, *Regional Mgr*
David Gordan, *Controller*
Kathy Pennypacker, *Accounting Mgr*
Liza Koczur, *Human Resources*
▲ **EMP:** 210 **EST:** 1979
SALES (est): 80.9MM **Privately Held**
SIC: 5013 3714 Truck parts & acces-
sories; differentials & parts, motor vehicle

(G-1496)
TRI-DIM FILTER CORPORATION
Also Called: Tri Dim Filter
1306 Sylvania Ave (08077-2715)
PHONE....................................856 786-2447
EMP: 4
SALES (corp-wide): 137.3MM **Privately
Held**
SIC: 3564 Filters, air: furnaces, air condi-
tioning equipment, etc.
PA: Tri-Dim Filter Corporation
93 Industrial Dr
Louisa VA 23093
540 967-2600

(G-1497)
UNITEX INTERNATIONAL INC
2702 Cindel Dr Ste 3 (08077-2035)
PHONE....................................856 786-5000
▲ **EMP:** 4
SALES (est): 621.5K **Privately Held**
SIC: 2869 Mfg Industrial Organic Chemi-
cals

Clark
Union County

(G-1498)
**BOULEVARD LUNCH SERVICE
INC**
251 Willow Way (07066-2835)
PHONE....................................732 381-5772
Fax: 908 241-8427
Henry F Forfa, *President*
Phyllis Forfa, *Corp Secy*
EMP: 15
SQ FT: 4,000
SALES (est): 1.3MM **Privately Held**
SIC: 2099 Ready-to-eat meals, salads &
sandwiches

(G-1499)
**CONTEMPORARY CABLING
COMPANY**
90 Brookside Ter (07066-2862)
PHONE....................................732 382-5064
John Ross, *President*
Gina Ross, *Vice Pres*
EMP: 5
SALES: 500K **Privately Held**
WEB: www.contemporarycable.com
SIC: 1731 2298 Fiber optic cable installa-
tion; cable, fiber

(G-1500)
FALCON GRAPHICS INC
Also Called: Falcon Printing
70 Westfield Ave (07066-3225)
PHONE....................................908 232-1991
Fax: 908 232-8466
Anthony Archambault, *President*
Nicholas Archambault, *Treasurer*
Michael Archambault, *Director*
EMP: 7
SQ FT: 4,500
SALES: 1MM **Privately Held**
SIC: 2752 7336 Commercial printing, off-
set; graphic arts & related design

(G-1501)
J J ORLY INC
67 Walnut Ave Ste 307 (07066-1687)
P.O. Box 945 (07066-0945)
PHONE....................................908 276-9212
William Herbert, *President*
EMP: 15
SALES (est): 2.2MM **Privately Held**
WEB: www.jjorly.com
SIC: 3469 Stamping metal for the trade

(G-1502)
KARNAK CORPORATION (PA)
330 Central Ave (07066-1199)
PHONE....................................732 388-0300
Fax: 732 388-9422
Sarah J Jelin, *President*
Chris Salazar, *COO*
John McDermott, *Vice Pres*
Sean Smith, *Mfg Dir*
Mike Schubick, *Plant Mgr*
▲ **EMP:** 65 **EST:** 1933
SQ FT: 65,000
SALES (est): 18.5MM **Privately Held**
WEB: www.karnakcorp.com
SIC: 2952 Roofing materials; roof cement:
asphalt, fibrous or plastic

(G-1503)
KARNAK MIDWEST LLC (HQ)
330 Central Ave (07066-1199)
PHONE....................................732 388-0300
Robert Andrews, *CFO*
Michael Gada, *Manager*
Sarah Jane Jelin,
James D Hannah,
EMP: 5
SALES (est): 2.3MM
SALES (corp-wide): 18.5MM **Privately
Held**
SIC: 2952 Roofing materials
PA: Karnak Corporation
330 Central Ave
Clark NJ 07066
732 388-0300

(G-1504)
**KERRY FLAVOR SYSTEMS US
LLC**
Also Called: Kerry Ingredients & Flavours
160 Terminal Ave (07066-1319)
PHONE....................................513 771-4682
EMP: 250 **Privately Held**
SIC: 2087 Mfg Flavor Extracts/Syrup
PA: Kerry Flavor Systems Us, Llc
10261 Chester Rd
Cincinnati OH 45215

(G-1505)
LOREAL USA INC
30 Terminal Ave (07066-1322)
PHONE....................................732 499-6617
Jim Murphy, *Branch Mgr*
Jeanne Chang, *Manager*
Gino Devito, *Director*
Donna Kemptner, *Director*
Fred Weisenbacher, *Director*

EMP: 150
SALES (corp-wide): 4.2B **Privately Held**
WEB: www.lorealusa.com
SIC: 2844 Hair preparations, including
shampoos; cosmetic preparations; per-
fumes & colognes
HQ: L'oreal Usa, Inc.
10 Hudson Yards Fl 30
New York NY 10001
212 818-1500

(G-1506)
LOREAL USA INC
100 Terminal Ave (07066-1319)
PHONE....................................212 818-1500
Ken Fischer, *Principal*
Melissa Sabatino, *Marketing Mgr*
EMP: 100
SALES (corp-wide): 4.2B **Privately Held**
WEB: www.lorealparisusa.com
SIC: 2844 5122 Hair preparations, includ-
ing shampoos; drugs, proprietaries & sun-
dries
HQ: L'oreal Usa, Inc.
10 Hudson Yards Fl 30
New York NY 10001
212 818-1500

(G-1507)
LOREAL USA INC
159 Terminal Ave (07066-1320)
PHONE....................................732 499-6690
Anand Mahadeshwar, *Vice Pres*
Gloria Lopez, *Research*
Camilla Wang, *Manager*
EMP: 100
SALES (corp-wide): 4.2B **Privately Held**
WEB: www.lorealparisusa.com
SIC: 2844 8731 Hair preparations, includ-
ing shampoos; cosmetic preparations;
perfumes & colognes; commercial physi-
cal research
HQ: L'oreal Usa, Inc.
10 Hudson Yards Fl 30
New York NY 10001
212 818-1500

(G-1508)
MASTERTASTE INC (DH)
Also Called: Kerry Ingredients and Flavours
160 Terminal Ave (07066-1319)
PHONE....................................732 882-0202
Gerry Behan, *President*
Mike Gransee, *CFO*
William Coole, *Admin Sec*
◆ **EMP:** 101
SALES (est): 61.3MM **Privately Held**
WEB: www.mastertaste.com
SIC: 2087 Flavoring extracts & syrups
HQ: Kerry Inc.
3330 Millington Rd
Beloit WI 53511
608 363-1200

(G-1509)
NB VENTURES INC (PA)
Also Called: Gep
100 Walnut Ave Ste 304 (07066-1247)
PHONE....................................732 382-6565
Fax: 732 382-6363
Subhash Makhija, *CEO*
Roopa Gandhi, *President*
Roopa Makhija, *General Mgr*
Jagadish Turimella, *COO*
Matthew Bardell, *Vice Pres*
EMP: 250
SQ FT: 17,776
SALES (est): 156.2MM **Privately Held**
WEB: www.globaleprocure.com
SIC: 8742 5045 7372 7371 Business
consultant; computer software; applica-
tion computer software; business oriented
computer software; computer software
development & applications

(G-1510)
**NU-PLAN BUSINESS SYSTEMS
INC**
64 Washington St (07066-3223)
PHONE....................................732 231-6944
Howard R Rinn, *President*
EMP: 4 **EST:** 1973
SQ FT: 6,000

SALES (est): 280K **Privately Held**
WEB: www.nu-plan.com
SIC: **2752** 5112 Commercial printing, lithographic; offset & photolithographic printing; stationery & office supplies

(G-1511)
OFFICE NEEDS INC
1120 Raritan Rd Ste 2 (07066-1349)
P.O. Box 5804 (07066-5804)
PHONE......................................732 381-7770
Fax: 732 381-9834
Sharon Katcher, *President*
Gary Katcher, *Vice Pres*
EMP: 9
SQ FT: 2,500
SALES (est): 1.2MM **Privately Held**
SIC: **5112** 2759 5021 Office supplies; letterpress printing; office furniture

(G-1512)
PHILLIP BALDEROSE
Also Called: Budget Instant Printing
70 Westfield Ave (07066-3225)
PHONE......................................732 574-1330
Fax: 732 574-0083
Phillip Balderose, *Owner*
EMP: 4
SQ FT: 1,100
SALES (est): 318.4K **Privately Held**
SIC: **2752** Photo-offset printing

(G-1513)
PLATINUM PLATING SPECIALISTS
11 Blake Dr (07066-1646)
PHONE......................................732 221-2575
EMP: 5 EST: 2011
SALES (est): 260.6K **Privately Held**
SIC: **3471** Plating of metals or formed products

(G-1514)
RAILPACE CO INC
257 Oak Ridge Rd (07066-2761)
PHONE......................................732 388-4984
Dennis Connell, *Partner*
EMP: 4
SALES (est): 180K **Privately Held**
SIC: **2731** Book publishing

(G-1515)
SHANGHAI OPTICS INC
17 Brant Ave Ste 6 (07066-1548)
P.O. Box 846, Old Bridge (08857-0846)
PHONE......................................732 321-6915
Qiao He, *President*
Johnny Lee, *Vice Pres*
EMP: 10
SALES (est): 478.7K **Privately Held**
WEB: www.shanghai-optics.com
SIC: **3827** Optical instruments & apparatus

(G-1516)
TANTER INC
Also Called: Horizon Printing
151 Westfield Ave Ste 3 (07066-2415)
PHONE......................................732 382-3555
Fax: 732 388-4886
Walter Swierc, *President*
Stanley Swierc, *Vice Pres*
EMP: 5
SQ FT: 2,500
SALES (est): 470K **Privately Held**
SIC: **2752** 2791 2789 Commercial printing, offset; typesetting; bookbinding & related work

(G-1517)
THAL PRECISION INDUSTRIES INC
19a Walnut Ave (07066-1605)
P.O. Box 281, Lincroft (07738-0281)
PHONE......................................732 381-6106
Fax: 732 381-5929
James Thal, *President*
Paul Thal, *Vice Pres*
EMP: 9
SQ FT: 5,000
SALES (est): 1.1MM **Privately Held**
WEB: www.thalprecision.com
SIC: **3544** Forms (molds), for foundry & plastics working machinery

Clarksboro
Gloucester County

(G-1518)
DEWALT MANUFACTURING CO INC
88 W Cohawkin Rd (08020-1100)
PHONE......................................856 423-1207
Fax: 856 423-1409
Roger Dewalt, *President*
EMP: 4 EST: 1960
SQ FT: 5,000
SALES (est): 484K **Privately Held**
SIC: **3599** Machine shop, jobbing & repair

Clarksburg
Monmouth County

(G-1519)
FORESIGHT ENVIROPROBE INC
19 Trenton Lakewood Rd (08510-1118)
P.O. Box 6385, Freehold (07728-6385)
PHONE......................................609 259-1244
Tom McChesney, *President*
Ralph Mufgrave, *Vice Pres*
EMP: 6
SALES (est): 900K **Privately Held**
SIC: **1382** Geological exploration, oil & gas field

(G-1520)
HYBRID-TEK LLC
9 Trenton Lakewood Rd # 2 (08510-1114)
PHONE......................................609 259-3355
Fax: 609 259-3539
John Lee, *Mng Member*
Brian Hammond, *Manager*
EMP: 10
SQ FT: 2,000
SALES: 1.5MM **Privately Held**
WEB: www.hybrid-tek.com
SIC: **3674** Hybrid integrated circuits

(G-1521)
MILLSTONE DQ INC
Also Called: Dairy Queen
40 Trenton Lakewood Rd (08510-1110)
PHONE......................................609 259-6733
Sanj Kanwar, *President*
EMP: 9
SALES (est): 510K **Privately Held**
SIC: **5812** 2052 Ice cream stands or dairy bars; cones, ice cream

Clayton
Gloucester County

(G-1522)
ALERIS ROLLED PRODUCTS INC
Also Called: Clayton Rolling Mill
838 N Delsea Dr (08312-1004)
PHONE......................................856 881-3600
EMP: 115 **Privately Held**
SIC: **3341** Aluminum smelting & refining (secondary)
HQ: Aleris Rolled Products, Inc.
25825 Science Park Dr # 400
Beachwood OH 44122
216 910-3400

(G-1523)
AURA BADGE CO
264 W Clayton Ave (08312-1818)
P.O. Box 655 (08312-0655)
PHONE......................................856 881-9026
Fax: 856 881-9359
Philip Barbaro, *President*
Robert Barbaro, *Vice Pres*
▲ EMP: 60 EST: 1952
SQ FT: 40,000
SALES (est): 4.6MM **Privately Held**
WEB: www.aurabadge.com
SIC: **3999** 3993 Identification badges & insignia; advertising novelties

(G-1524)
HUNGERFORD & TERRY INC (PA)
Also Called: H & T
226 N Atlantic Ave (08312-1335)
P.O. Box 650 (08312-0650)
PHONE......................................856 881-3200
Fax: 856 881-6859
Thomas Carrocino, *President*
Harold Aronovitch, *Vice Pres*
Kenneth M Sayell, *Vice Pres*
▼ EMP: 50
SQ FT: 85,000
SALES (est): 25.1MM **Privately Held**
WEB: www.hungerfordterry.com
SIC: **1499** 3589 Greensand mining; water treatment equipment, industrial

(G-1525)
INVERSAND COMPANY INC (HQ)
226 N Atlantic Ave (08312-1335)
PHONE......................................856 881-2345
Alan A Davis, *President*
Kenneth Sayell, *VP Sales*
▲ EMP: 10 EST: 1929
SQ FT: 1,000
SALES (est): 3MM
SALES (corp-wide): 25.1MM **Privately Held**
WEB: www.inversand.com
SIC: **5169** 1446 Industrial chemicals; filtration sand mining
PA: Hungerford & Terry, Inc.
226 N Atlantic Ave
Clayton NJ 08312
856 881-3200

(G-1526)
MARLYN SHEET METAL INC
606 N Delsea Dr (08312-1220)
PHONE......................................856 863-6900
Fax: 856 863-6916
Lynn Brandt, *President*
Julius Brandt, *President*
EMP: 15
SQ FT: 7,000
SALES (est): 3.2MM **Privately Held**
SIC: **3444** Sheet metalwork

(G-1527)
REVERE INDUSTRIES LLC (PA)
Also Called: Revere Packaging
838 N Delsea Dr (08312-1004)
PHONE......................................856 881-3600
David Charles, *President*
David Korus, *Vice Pres*
Ron Lapointe, *Vice Pres*
John Wherry, *Vice Pres*
Gary Stone, *VP Opers*
◆ EMP: 110
SQ FT: 275,000
SALES (est): 65.4MM **Privately Held**
WEB: www.revereindustries.com
SIC: **3497** 3089 Foil containers for bakery goods & frozen foods; food casings, plastic

(G-1528)
SHOREWAY INDUSTRY
260 W Clayton Ave (08312-1818)
PHONE......................................856 307-2020
Kimberly Critchfield, *Partner*
Joann Critchfield, *Partner*
EMP: 4
SQ FT: 5,300
SALES (est): 380K **Privately Held**
SIC: **3561** Industrial pumps & parts

(G-1529)
WILLIAM CROMLEY
Also Called: K & C Fundraising
101 S Delsea Dr (08312-1913)
PHONE......................................856 881-6019
EMP: 4
SQ FT: 2,000
SALES (est): 170K **Privately Held**
SIC: **2395** Pleating/Stitching Services

Clementon
Camden County

(G-1530)
BIMBO BAKERIES USA INC
1340 Blckwood Clemtons Rd (08021-5610)
PHONE......................................856 435-0500
Fax: 856 435-0828
Grace Batten, *Manager*
EMP: 80 **Privately Held**
WEB: www.englishmuffin.com
SIC: **2051** Bread, cake & related products
HQ: Bimbo Bakeries Usa, Inc
255 Business Center Dr # 200
Horsham PA 19044
215 347-5500

(G-1531)
ELECTRONICS BOUTIQUE AMER INC
1468 Blckwood Clemton Rd (08021-5778)
PHONE......................................856 435-3900
Anthony Le Vecchia, *Manager*
EMP: 6
SALES (corp-wide): 9.2B **Publicly Held**
SIC: **3944** Games, toys & children's vehicles
HQ: Electronics Boutique Of America Inc.
625 Westport Pkwy
Grapevine TX 76051
817 424-2000

(G-1532)
GIAMBRIS QUALITY SWEETS INC
Also Called: Giambri's Candy
26 Brand Ave (08021-4211)
PHONE......................................856 783-1099
Fax: 856 783-6377
David Giambri, *President*
EMP: 6
SQ FT: 6,000
SALES (est): 300K **Privately Held**
WEB: www.giambriscandy.com
SIC: **5441** 2064 5961 Candy; candy & other confectionery products; food, mail order

(G-1533)
RACEWAY CARWASH
1471 Blckwood Clmenton Rd (08021-5729)
PHONE......................................215 886-8252
Jack Kim, *Manager*
EMP: 5 EST: 2007
SALES (est): 551.6K **Privately Held**
SIC: **3644** Raceways

(G-1534)
ROBERT WYNN
36 Windmill Dr (08021-5821)
PHONE......................................856 435-6398
Robert Wynn, *Principal*
EMP: 5
SALES (est): 31K **Privately Held**
SIC: **3679** Recording heads, speech & musical equipment

(G-1535)
ROYER GRAPHICS INC
101 Lincoln Dr (08021-2820)
PHONE......................................856 344-7935
Anthony J Cannuli, *President*
Toni Stouhr, *Admin Sec*
EMP: 7
SQ FT: 7,000
SALES: 440K **Privately Held**
SIC: **2752** 7336 Commercial printing, offset; commercial art & illustration

Cliffside Park
Bergen County

(G-1536)
B B SUPPLY CORP
421 Nelson Ave (07010-1819)
PHONE......................................201 313-9021
Slobodan Ristovic, *Branch Mgr*
EMP: 13
SALES (corp-wide): 2MM **Privately Held**
SIC: **3545** Cutting tools for machine tools

PA: B B Supply Corp
40 Arnot St Unit 14
Lodi NJ 07644
201 313-9021

(G-1537)
DAMORE JEWELERS
731 Anderson Ave (07010-2189)
PHONE..............................201 945-0530
Fax: 201 945-3271
Barbara Zaccone, *President*
John D'Amore, *President*
Katherine D'Amore, *Corp Secy*
Eleni Ingenito, *Buyer*
Bea Lhotack, *Sales Mgr*
▲ **EMP:** 10 **EST:** 1946
SQ FT: 5,000
SALES (est): 1.5MM **Privately Held**
WEB: www.damorejewelers.com
SIC: 5944 7631 3911 Jewelry, precious
stones & precious metals; jewelry repair
services; jewelry, precious metal

(G-1538)
EDUCLOUD INC
Also Called: Mathcloud
206 Grant Ave (07010-2502)
PHONE..............................201 944-0445
Penni Ross, *Editor*
Jae Choi, *CFO*
EMP: 20
SQ FT: 20,000
SALES (est): 1.3MM **Privately Held**
SIC: 7372 Educational computer software

(G-1539)
GAURIKA LLC
Also Called: Gaurika Jewels
250 Gorge Rd (07010-1301)
PHONE..............................201 496-1613
Ashish Mookim, *Mng Member*
EMP: 5
SALES (est): 288.7K **Privately Held**
SIC: 3911 Jewelry, precious metal

(G-1540)
GLASSCARE INC
666 Anderson Ave (07010-1921)
PHONE..............................201 943-1122
Mel Neulander, *President*
EMP: 15
SQ FT: 12,000
SALES (est): 2.3MM **Privately Held**
WEB: www.glasscare.com
SIC: 2591 3993 7549 1799 Drapery
hardware & blinds & shades; signs & ad-
vertising specialties; glass tinting, auto-
motive; glass tinting, architectural or
automotive; glass & glazing work

(G-1541)
INTERSTATE ARCHITECTURAL & IR
243 Laird Ave (07010-1206)
PHONE..............................201 941-0393
Fax: 201 941-5938
Richard Papp, *President*
Steve Heaps, *Treasurer*
EMP: 8
SQ FT: 3,300
SALES (est): 490K **Privately Held**
WEB: www.iai.50megs.com
SIC: 3446 Architectural metalwork

(G-1542)
MAIN FUEL LLC
73 Palisade Ave (07010-1014)
PHONE..............................201 941-2707
EMP: 4
SALES (est): 198.9K **Privately Held**
SIC: 2869 Mfg Industrial Organic Chemi-
cals

(G-1543)
NELLSAM GROUP INC
36 Washington Ave Fl 1 (07010-3025)
PHONE..............................201 951-9459
Nelly Reyes, *Principal*
EMP: 4 **EST:** 2015
SALES (est): 338.4K **Privately Held**
SIC: 2844 Toilet preparations

(G-1544)
NORTH BERGEN MARBLE & GRANITE
217 Palisade Ave (07010-1226)
PHONE..............................201 945-9988
Fax: 201 945-6644
Demetrios Markopoulos, *President*
Jim Markopolous, *Manager*
EMP: 4
SALES (est): 420K **Privately Held**
SIC: 2542 5032 Carrier cases & tables,
mail; except wood; marble building stone

(G-1545)
SOUTH AMERICAN IMPORTS CORP
7 Cecelia Ave (07010-2705)
PHONE..............................201 941-2020
Dilia Castanos-Barbosa, *President*
EMP: 7
SALES (est): 538.9K **Privately Held**
SIC: 2022 Cheese, natural & processed

Cliffwood
Monmouth County

(G-1546)
ELKEM INC
443 County Rd (07721-1168)
PHONE..............................732 566-1700
Fax: 732 583-3076
Thomas W Kent, *President*
Peggy C Conrow, *Manager*
EMP: 8
SQ FT: 10,000
SALES (est): 1MM **Privately Held**
WEB: www.elkem-inc.net
SIC: 3471 Electroplating of metals or
formed products

(G-1547)
FLEETSOURCE LLC
Also Called: A G S
423 County Rd (07721-1168)
PHONE..............................732 566-4970
Fax: 732 566-0340
Kenneth Dorward,
Harry Dorward,
▲ **EMP:** 35
SQ FT: 20,000
SALES (est): 4.6MM **Privately Held**
WEB: www.fltsource.com
SIC: 7513 7538 7359 3714 Truck rental
& leasing, no drivers; general truck repair;
equipment rental & leasing; motor vehicle
parts & accessories; engine electrical
equipment

(G-1548)
SPRIALSEAL INC
Also Called: Spiralseal
284 Cliffwood Ave (07721-1128)
PHONE..............................732 738-6113
Fax: 732 738-1343
Gabor Szep, *President*
Dean Georgatos, *Vice Pres*
▲ **EMP:** 7
SQ FT: 5,000
SALES (est): 500K **Privately Held**
SIC: 7699 3053 Precision instrument re-
pair; gaskets, packing & sealing devices

(G-1549)
V P I INDUSTRIES INC
77 Cliffwood Ave Ste 3b (07721-1087)
PHONE..............................732 583-6895
Fax: 732 946-8578
Harry Weisfeld, *President*
Sheila Weisfeld, *Corp Secy*
EMP: 7
SQ FT: 3,700
SALES (est): 1.2MM **Privately Held**
WEB: www.vpiindustries.com
SIC: 3651 5731 Audio electronic systems;
radio, television & electronic stores

(G-1550)
VESTAL PUBLISHING CO INC
Also Called: Vestal Printing
280 Cliffwood Ave Ste A (07721-1196)
PHONE..............................732 583-3232
Fax: 732 583-5207
Robert M Rybnicky, *President*
Sandra Rybnicky, *Co-President*
EMP: 7
SQ FT: 3,750
SALES (est): 650K **Privately Held**
SIC: 2752 Commercial printing, litho-
graphic

Clifton
Passaic County

(G-1551)
21ST CENTURY FINISHING INC
40 Webro Rd (07012-1426)
PHONE..............................201 797-0212
Fax: 201 797-0181
George Olmo, *CEO*
Karen Demaio, *President*
EMP: 23
SQ FT: 40,000
SALES (est): 4.4MM **Privately Held**
WEB: www.21finishing.com
SIC: 3544 Paper cutting dies

(G-1552)
A J P SCIENTIFIC INC
Also Called: ENG SCIENTIFIC
82 Industrial St E (07012-1708)
P.O. Box 1589 (07015-1589)
PHONE..............................973 472-7200
Fax: 973 472-9460
Henry Eng, *President*
Mary Eng, *Admin Sec*
EMP: 7
SQ FT: 10,000
SALES (est): 977.1K **Privately Held**
WEB: www.engscientific.com
SIC: 2385 2899 2836 Waterproof outer-
wear; chemical preparations; biological
products, except diagnostic

(G-1553)
A TO Z PRINTING & PROMOTION
1455 Main Ave Ste 2 (07011-2127)
PHONE..............................973 916-9995
Eyad Asmar, *Principal*
EMP: 7
SALES (est): 764K **Privately Held**
SIC: 2752 Commercial printing, offset

(G-1554)
ACCESSREC LLC
55 Park Slope (07011)
PHONE..............................973 955-0514
Seb Ragon, *Vice Pres*
▲ **EMP:** 4
SALES (est): 210K **Privately Held**
SIC: 3082 Unsupported plastics profile
shapes

(G-1555)
ACCURATE PLASTIC PRINTERS LLC
30 Colfax Ave (07013-2059)
PHONE..............................973 591-0180
Fax: 973 591-0811
Carlos Agudelo, *Mng Member*
Jakie Agudelo,
▲ **EMP:** 20
SQ FT: 10,000
SALES (est): 3.9MM **Privately Held**
WEB: www.accuplastic.com
SIC: 2752 Commercial printing, litho-
graphic

(G-1556)
ACME & DORF DOOR CORP
490 Getty Ave 500 (07011-2152)
PHONE..............................973 772-6774
Leonard Dorf, *President*
Nancy Dorf, *Treasurer*
EMP: 6
SQ FT: 5,000
SALES (est): 570K **Privately Held**
SIC: 3442 Metal doors; window & door
frames

(G-1557)
ACME INTERNATIONAL INC
2a Monhegan St (07013-2008)
PHONE..............................973 594-4866
Fax: 973 594-4888
Aftad Ahmed, *President*
Naila Ahmed, *Vice Pres*
Eli Ahmed, *Admin Sec*
▲ **EMP:** 3
SALES: 2.5MM **Privately Held**
SIC: 3841 Surgical instruments & appara-
tus

(G-1558)
AERO MANUFACTURING CO
310 Allwood Rd (07012-1786)
P.O. Box 1250 (07012-0750)
PHONE..............................973 473-5300
Fax: 973 473-3794
Lloyd Sherman, *General Mgr*
Wayne Phillips, *Principal*
Gloria Phillips, *Treasurer*
Ken Kreiss, *Sales Mgr*
Nancy Ortiz, *Admin Sec*
▲ **EMP:** 73 **EST:** 1946
SQ FT: 150,000
SALES (est): 17.5MM **Privately Held**
WEB: www.aeromfg.com
SIC: 3589 3431 Commercial cooking &
foodwarming equipment; metal sanitary
ware

(G-1559)
AFFIL ENDOSCOPY SERVICES CL
925 Clifton Ave Ste 100 (07013-2724)
PHONE..............................201 842-0020
Fax: 973 405-6435
Donna Benevenga, *Principal*
EMP: 8
SALES (est): 1.2MM **Privately Held**
SIC: 3845 Endoscopic equipment, elec-
tromedical

(G-1560)
AIRFILTRONIX CORP (HQ)
154 Huron Ave (07013-2949)
PHONE..............................973 779-5577
Ronald R Feller, *President*
Christopher Proffitt, *Admin Sec*
EMP: 5
SQ FT: 5,500
SALES: 425K
SALES (corp-wide): 2.8MM **Privately
Held**
WEB: www.airfiltronix.com
SIC: 3821 3444 Laboratory equipment:
fume hoods, distillation racks, etc.; sheet
metalwork
PA: Micro-Tek Laboratories Inc
154 Huron Ave
Clifton NJ 07013
973 779-5577

(G-1561)
ALORIS TOOL TECHNOLOGY CO INC
407 Getty Ave (07011-2121)
P.O. Box 1529 (07015-1529)
PHONE..............................973 772-1201
Fax: 973 772-8606
Rich Roslowski, *President*
Gregory Brajkovic, *Vice Pres*
EMP: 30 **EST:** 1946
SQ FT: 30,000
SALES (est): 4.4MM **Privately Held**
WEB: www.aloris.com
SIC: 3545 Tool holders; tools & acces-
sories for machine tools

(G-1562)
ALPHA PROCESSING CO INC
210 Delawanna Ave (07014-1550)
P.O. Box 936 (07014-0936)
PHONE..............................973 777-1737
Fax: 973 777-1891
Richard Jenny, *President*
Kelly Rodrigues, *Finance Mgr*
Kelly Pereira, *Human Res Mgr*
Kelly Rodriguez, *Manager*
▲ **EMP:** 45 **EST:** 1940
SQ FT: 20,000
SALES: 4.3MM **Privately Held**
SIC: 3479 Coating of metals & formed
products

(G-1563)
AMERICAN MARKING SYSTEMS INC (PA)
Also Called: Paterson Stamp Works
1015 Paulison Ave (07011-3610)
P.O. Box 1677 (07015-1677)
PHONE.................973 478-5600
Fax: 973 478-0039
John A Collins III, *Ch of Bd*
Peter Browlin, *General Mgr*
John Shaughnessy, *Benefits Mgr*
EMP: 81
SQ FT: 10,000
SALES (est): 11.7MM **Privately Held**
WEB: www.ams-stamps.com
SIC: 3953 Embossing seals & hand stamps

(G-1564)
AMERICAN STAMP MFG CO
Also Called: American/Krengel Stamp Mfg Co
1015 Paulison Ave (07011-3610)
PHONE.................212 227-1877
Randy Botc, *President*
EMP: 14
SQ FT: 7,000
SALES: 800K **Privately Held**
SIC: 3953 Embossing seals & hand stamps

(G-1565)
AMERIVATOR SYSTEMS CORPORATION
220 Scoles Ave (07012-1126)
PHONE.................973 471-1200
Daniel Sedrak, *President*
Nabila Sedrak, *Vice Pres*
▲ EMP: 6 EST: 1999
SALES: 2MM **Privately Held**
SIC: 3534 Elevators & equipment

(G-1566)
AROMAC INC
6 Chelsea Rd (07012-1667)
PHONE.................973 365-1090
Fax: 973 472-5686
EMP: 6
SQ FT: 10,000
SALES: 1.5MM **Privately Held**
SIC: 2834 2833 2843 Mfg Pharmaceutical Preparations Mfg Medicinal/Botanical Products Mfg Surface Active Agents

(G-1567)
ATLANTIC CASTING & ENGINEERING
Also Called: ATLANTIC C&E
810 Bloomfield Ave (07012-1199)
P.O. Box 4016 (07012-0416)
PHONE.................973 779-2450
Fax: 973 779-2854
James Binns, *CEO*
Brian Jmcgrady, *President*
Brian McGrady, *President*
Dan Lenino, *Vice Pres*
Gregory Rohrbacker, *Vice Pres*
▲ EMP: 160 EST: 1937
SQ FT: 40,000
SALES: 20MM **Privately Held**
WEB: www.atlantic-ce.com
SIC: 3365 3599 Aluminum foundries; aerospace castings, aluminum; machine & other job shop work; machine shop, jobbing & repair

(G-1568)
ATLAS INDUSTRIAL MFG CO (PA)
81 Somerset Pl (07012-1197)
PHONE.................973 779-3970
Fax: 973 779-7783
Frank De Lorenzo, *President*
Tom Ciampi, *Plant Mgr*
Hasu Darji, *Engineer*
Ramsey Mahadeen, *Treasurer*
Frank J De Lorenzo Jr, *Admin Sec*
▲ EMP: 38 EST: 1922
SQ FT: 41,000
SALES (est): 6.2MM **Privately Held**
SIC: 3443 Heat exchangers, plate type; vessels, process or storage (from boiler shops): metal plate

(G-1569)
AUTOMATED FLEXIBLE CONVEYORS
55 Walman Ave (07011-3416)
PHONE.................973 340-1695
Kevin Devaney, *President*
Grace Faria, *Vice Pres*
EMP: 15
SQ FT: 12,000
SALES: 1.8MM **Privately Held**
WEB: www.afcsolutions.com
SIC: 3535 3564 Conveyors & conveying equipment; blowers & fans

(G-1570)
AVON PRODUCTS INC
1166 Broad St (07013-3343)
PHONE.................973 779-5590
EMP: 4
SALES (corp-wide): 10.7B **Publicly Held**
SIC: 2844 Mfg Cosmetics Fragrances
PA: Avon Products, Inc.
777 3rd Ave Fl 31
New York NY 10017
212 282-5000

(G-1571)
B & B IRON WORKS
1 Broad St (07013-1000)
PHONE.................862 238-7203
Fax: 973 375-9087
Mauro Belgiovine, *President*
Anthony Belgiovine, *Project Engr*
Diane Belgiovine, *Admin Sec*
EMP: 30
SQ FT: 10,000
SALES (est): 7.9MM **Privately Held**
SIC: 3441 Fabricated structural metal

(G-1572)
BARANTEC INC
777 Passaic Ave Ste 345 (07012-1878)
PHONE.................973 779-8774
Fax: 973 779-8768
Diane Bersen, *Vice Pres*
Talia Israel, *Mfg Staff*
Helene Stewart, *Manager*
Ted Bielitz, *Info Tech Mgr*
EMP: 10
SQ FT: 2,100
SALES: 2.5MM **Privately Held**
WEB: www.barantec.com
SIC: 3678 5065 Electronic connectors; electronic parts & equipment
HQ: Baran Advanced Technologies (1986) Ltd
8 Omarim
Omer
732 511-020

(G-1573)
BAY STATE MILLING COMPANY
404 Getty Ave (07011-2122)
PHONE.................973 772-3400
Fax: 973 772-3542
Mike Carlson, *Plant Supt*
Peter Carmony, *Manager*
EMP: 65
SALES (corp-wide): 154.8MM **Privately Held**
WEB: www.bsm.com
SIC: 2041 Wheat mill feed
PA: Bay State Milling Company
100 Congress St Ste 2
Quincy MA 02169
617 328-4423

(G-1574)
BENJAMIN MOORE & CO
203 Kuller Rd (07011-2857)
PHONE.................973 569-5000
Raymond Elustondo, *Manager*
EMP: 70
SALES (corp-wide): 242.1B **Publicly Held**
WEB: www.benjaminmoore.com
SIC: 2851 5231 Paints & allied products; paints: oil or alkyd vehicle or water thinned; enamels; varnishes; paint, glass & wallpaper
HQ: Benjamin Moore & Co.
101 Paragon Dr
Montvale NJ 07645
201 573-9600

(G-1575)
BETTER TEAM USA CORPORATION
95b Industrial St E (07012-1707)
PHONE.................973 365-0947
Horacio Dibattista, *President*
Jensen Dibattista, *Manager*
EMP: 30
SALES (est): 3.9MM **Privately Held**
SIC: 2389 Men's miscellaneous accessories

(G-1576)
BIWAL MANUFACTURING CO INC
48 Industrial St W (07012-1712)
PHONE.................973 778-0105
Fax: 973 778-0322
Joseph Mrocka, *President*
EMP: 30
SQ FT: 12,000
SALES (est): 4.7MM **Privately Held**
SIC: 3599 Machine shop, jobbing & repair

(G-1577)
BLUE DOME INC
Also Called: Blue Dome Press
335 Clifton Ave (07011-2618)
PHONE.................646 415-9331
Ahmet Idil, *Vice Pres*
Katharine Branning, *Vice Pres*
EMP: 5
SALES (est): 331.4K **Privately Held**
SIC: 2731 Books: publishing only

(G-1578)
BREURE SHEET METAL CO INC
Also Called: Bruere Heating & AC
46 Walman Ave (07011-3411)
PHONE.................973 772-6423
Fax: 973 772-7062
Matthew Breure Jr, *President*
Josephine Breure, *Admin Sec*
EMP: 6
SQ FT: 3,000
SALES (est): 630.6K **Privately Held**
SIC: 1711 3444 Heating & air conditioning contractors; sheet metalwork

(G-1579)
BUONAVENTURA BAG AND CASES LLC
Also Called: Burkley Case
95 Main Ave Ste 1 (07014-1749)
PHONE.................212 960-3442
Serkan Demiray,
EMP: 5
SALES (est): 364.5K **Privately Held**
SIC: 3111 Handbag leather

(G-1580)
CARAUSTAR CLIFTON PRIMARY PACK
43 Samworth Rd (07012-1714)
PHONE.................973 472-4900
Carl Oberg, *President*
Ed Goddard, *Vice Pres*
James Walden, *Admin Sec*
EMP: 250
SQ FT: 57,000
SALES (est): 27.8MM
SALES (corp-wide): 1.5B **Privately Held**
WEB: www.caraustar.com
SIC: 2679 Paperboard products, converted
PA: Caraustar Industries, Inc.
5000 Astell Pwdr Sprng Rd
Austell GA 30106
770 948-3101

(G-1581)
CGW NEWS LLC
107 Mount Prospect Ave (07013-1919)
PHONE.................973 473-3972
Christine Witmyer, *Principal*
EMP: 4
SALES (est): 139.2K **Privately Held**
SIC: 2711 Newspapers

(G-1582)
CHALLENGE PRINTING CO INC (PA)
Also Called: Challenge Printing Company The
2 Bridewell Pl (07014-1726)
PHONE.................973 471-4700

Theodore Sasso, *President*
Darrell Sasso, *Exec VP*
Glenn Sola, *Safety Mgr*
Patty Pasterchick, *Purch Agent*
Donna Robertson, *QC Mgr*
▲ EMP: 203 EST: 1911
SQ FT: 55,000
SALES (est): 45.5MM **Privately Held**
WEB: www.challprint.com
SIC: 2752 2754 Commercial printing, off-set; labels: gravure printing; circulars: gravure printing

(G-1583)
CHICAGO PNEUMATIC TOOL (DH)
Also Called: Titan
222 Getty Ave (07011-1827)
PHONE.................973 928-5222
John J Staudinger, *CEO*
Attila Mozsolits, *CFO*
Brad Church, *Sales Staff*
▲ EMP: 16
SQ FT: 10,000
SALES (est): 3MM
SALES (corp-wide): 13.8B **Privately Held**
WEB: www.titanti.com
SIC: 3452 3423 Bolts, nuts, rivets & washers; wrenches, hand tools
HQ: Epiroc Usa Llc
3700 E 68th Ave
Commerce City CO 80022
303 287-8822

(G-1584)
CLIFTON METAL PRODUCTS CO INC
41 Clifton Blvd (07011-3893)
PHONE.................973 777-6100
Fax: 973 473-3587
David Denboer, *President*
Deiter Kemmerich, *Treasurer*
Dorothy Grimes, *Manager*
EMP: 17
SQ FT: 20,000
SALES (est): 3.5MM **Privately Held**
WEB: www.cliftonmetal.com
SIC: 3444 Sheet metal specialties, not stamped

(G-1585)
COINING MFG
35 Monhegan St Ste 4 (07013-2000)
PHONE.................973 253-0500
Edward J Farley, *Principal*
EMP: 8 EST: 2015
SALES (est): 143.1K **Privately Held**
SIC: 3469 Stamping metal for the trade

(G-1586)
COMODO GROUP INC (PA)
1255 Broad St (07013-3398)
PHONE.................888 266-6361
Fax: 201 963-9003
Melih Abdulhayoglu, *CEO*
Steve Subar, *President*
Jon Land, *Exec VP*
Jeffrey Eckhaus, *Vice Pres*
Ugur Gulaydin, *Vice Pres*
EMP: 120
SALES (est): 29.3MM **Privately Held**
WEB: www.comodo.com
SIC: 3663 4813 ;

(G-1587)
COMPONDING ENGRG SOLUTIONS INC
Also Called: C E S
473 Us Highway 46 (07011-1816)
PHONE.................973 340-4000
Arash Kiani, *President*
EMP: 10
SQ FT: 33,000
SALES (est): 2MM **Privately Held**
SIC: 8711 3089 Consulting engineer; pallets, plastic

(G-1588)
COMUS INTERNATIONAL INC (PA)
454 Allwood Rd (07012-1706)
PHONE.................973 777-6900
Robert P Romano, *President*
Joseph Perez, *Vice Pres*
John Rollo, *Vice Pres*

GEOGRAPHIC

Joseph Romano, *Vice Pres*
Jim Simao, *QA Dir*
▲ **EMP:** 125
SQ FT: 40,000
SALES (est): 26.8MM **Privately Held**
WEB: www.comus-intl.com
SIC: 3613 3625 Switches, electric power except snap, push button, etc.; relays, electric power

(G-1589)
CONTINENTAL FOOD & BEV INC
Also Called: Inca Kola
495 River Rd (07014-1520)
PHONE..............................973 815-1600
Elizabeth Berman, *President*
Randall Berman, *COO*
◆ **EMP:** 15
SQ FT: 23,000
SALES (est): 14MM **Privately Held**
SIC: 2086 5149 Soft drinks: packaged in cans, bottles, etc.; soft drinks

(G-1590)
CONVEYORS BY NORTH AMERICAN
156 Huron Ave (07013-2949)
PHONE..............................973 777-6600
Gloria Kolodziej, *President*
Joseph Kolodziej Jr, *Vice Pres*
Josephine Malitsch, *Admin Sec*
EMP: 9
SQ FT: 18,000
SALES: 650K **Privately Held**
SIC: 3535 Conveyors & conveying equipment

(G-1591)
COPACK INTERNATIONAL INC
23 Carol St (07014-1420)
P.O. Box 496, Carlstadt (07072-0496)
PHONE..............................973 405-5151
Peter J Gould, *President*
EMP: 20
SQ FT: 61,000
SALES (est): 1.4MM **Privately Held**
SIC: 7389 3565 Packaging & labeling services; packaging machinery

(G-1592)
CORBO JEWELERS INC
Also Called: Corbo Jewelers of Styertowne
1055 Bloomfield Ave (07012-2198)
PHONE..............................973 777-1635
Fax: 973 777-0927
Michael Corbo, *Manager*
EMP: 10
SALES (corp-wide): 8.7MM **Privately Held**
WEB: www.corbojewelers.com
SIC: 3915 5944 7631 Jewel cutting, drilling, polishing, recutting or setting; jewelry, precious stones & precious metals; watch repair
PA: Corbo Jewelers, Inc.
58 Park Ave
Rutherford NJ 07070
201 438-3855

(G-1593)
CROSS COUNTRY BOX CO INC
474 Getty Ave (07011-2149)
PHONE..............................973 673-8349
Dan Goldman, *President*
Irene Goldman, *Treasurer*
EMP: 11
SQ FT: 3,700
SALES: 700K **Privately Held**
WEB: www.crosscountrybox.com
SIC: 2652 Boxes, newsboard, metal edged: made from purchased materials

(G-1594)
CRYSTEX COMPOSITES LLC
125 Clifton Blvd (07011-3806)
PHONE..............................973 779-8866
George L Flores, *CEO*
Delvis Flores, *VP Opers*
Nart Zakaria, *Maint Spvr*
Donald Van Grouw, *Engineer*
Charles Clement,
EMP: 33
SQ FT: 100,000
SALES (est): 5.4MM **Privately Held**
WEB: www.crystexcomposites.com
SIC: 3299 Ceramic fiber

(G-1595)
CURTAIN CARE PLUS INC
17 Industrial St W (07012-1711)
PHONE..............................800 845-6155
Jimmy Kazanjian, *Principal*
Mason Kirsch, *Principal*
Michael Wargo, *Marketing Mgr*
Alli Glick, *Mktg Coord*
EMP: 5
SALES (est): 397.3K **Privately Held**
SIC: 5714 2259 Curtains; curtains, knit

(G-1596)
CUSTOM BOOK BINDERY INC
9 Sheridan Ave (07011-2731)
PHONE..............................973 815-1400
Fax: 973 804-9746
Lance Belostock, *President*
EMP: 12
SQ FT: 6,000
SALES (est): 900K **Privately Held**
WEB: www.custombookbindery.com
SIC: 2752 2789 Commercial printing, offset; bookbinding & related work

(G-1597)
DATA DELAY DEVICES INC (PA)
3 Mount Prospect Ave (07013-1915)
PHONE..............................973 202-3268
Fax: 973 773-9672
Annibale Lupi, *President*
Lydia Lupi, *Exec VP*
EMP: 23 **EST:** 1964
SQ FT: 24,000
SALES (est): 3.3MM **Privately Held**
WEB: www.datadelay.com
SIC: 3679 3674 3672 Electronic circuits; delay lines; semiconductors & related devices; printed circuit boards

(G-1598)
DELGEN PRESS INC
250 Delawanna Ave (07014-1337)
PHONE..............................973 472-2266
Fax: 973 667-1855
EMP: 5
SQ FT: 3,500
SALES: 700K **Privately Held**
SIC: 2752 2759 Lithographic Commercial Printing Commercial Printing

(G-1599)
DIKEMAN LAMINATING CORPORATION
181 Sargeant Ave (07013-1993)
PHONE..............................973 473-5696
Fax: 973 473-2540
Thomas R Snyder, *President*
Jeffery Snyder, *Vice Pres*
Jean Snyder, *Admin Sec*
▲ **EMP:** 32 **EST:** 1949
SQ FT: 20,000
SALES (est): 5.6MM **Privately Held**
SIC: 2672 3083 Coated & laminated paper; plastic finished products, laminated

(G-1600)
DIOCESE OF PATERSON
Also Called: Beacon, The
597 Valley Rd (07013-2237)
P.O. Box 1887 (07015-1887)
PHONE..............................973 279-8845
Fax: 973 279-2265
Richard Sokerka, *President*
Victor Winkler, *Principal*
EMP: 15
SQ FT: 5,000
SALES (est): 889.9K **Privately Held**
SIC: 2711 Newspapers: publishing only, not printed on site

(G-1601)
DISPOSABLE HYGIENE LLC (PA)
60 Page Rd (07012-1452)
PHONE..............................973 779-1982
Rajesh Prakash, *Mng Member*
◆ **EMP:** 3
SALES (est): 25MM **Privately Held**
SIC: 2844 Toilet preparations; tonics, hair

(G-1602)
DIVERSIFIED FAB PDTS LTD LBLTY
158 River Rd (07014-1571)
PHONE..............................973 773-3189
Michael Fessak, *Mng Member*
EMP: 4
SALES (est): 343.8K **Privately Held**
SIC: 3444 Sheet metal specialties, not stamped

(G-1603)
DOMEL INC
3 Grunwald St (07013-2118)
PHONE..............................973 614-1800
Melvin Cohen, *President*
John Cozza, *President*
John Morse, *Vice Pres*
EMP: 35
SQ FT: 35,000
SALES (est): 6.9MM **Privately Held**
WEB: www.domelinc.com
SIC: 3355 Structural shapes, rolled, aluminum

(G-1604)
DOMINION COLOUR CORP USA
881 Allwood Rd Ste 2 (07012-1900)
PHONE..............................973 279-9591
Fax: 973 279-2133
Ken Tsujiuchi, *Manager*
▲ **EMP:** 10
SALES (est): 1.2MM **Privately Held**
WEB: www.dominioncolour.com
SIC: 2865 Color pigments, organic
HQ: Dominion Colour Corporation
515 Consumers Rd Unit 700
North York ON M2J 4
416 791-4200

(G-1605)
DRITAC FLOORING PRODUCTS LLC
60 Webro Rd (07012-1426)
PHONE..............................973 614-9000
Yale E Block, *Branch Mgr*
EMP: 13
SALES (corp-wide): 24.4MM **Privately Held**
WEB: www.basicadhesives.com
SIC: 2891 Adhesives
PA: Dritac Flooring Products Llc
60 Webro Rd
Clifton NJ 07012
973 614-9000

(G-1606)
DYE INTO PRINT INC
167 Fornelius Ave (07013-1845)
PHONE..............................973 772-8019
Fax: 973 772-6843
Mathew Letterman, *President*
EMP: 62
SQ FT: 60,000
SALES (est): 5.8MM **Privately Held**
WEB: www.dyeintoprint.com
SIC: 2269 2759 2262 Dyeing: raw stock yarn & narrow fabrics; commercial printing; finishing plants, manmade fiber & silk fabrics

(G-1607)
DYNAMETRIC TOOL INC
27 Somerset Pl (07012-1123)
PHONE..............................973 471-8009
Fax: 973 471-8225
Francis Csapo, *President*
EMP: 4 **EST:** 1977
SQ FT: 6,000
SALES: 200K **Privately Held**
SIC: 3599 Machine shop, jobbing & repair

(G-1608)
DYNAMIC PRINTING & GRAPHICS
250 Delawanna Ave (07014-1337)
PHONE..............................973 473-7177
Lou Mascola, *President*
Paul Janacek, *Vice Pres*
EMP: 12
SQ FT: 7,500
SALES (est): 1.7MM **Privately Held**
WEB: www.dynamic-inc.com
SIC: 7336 2752 Graphic arts & related design; commercial printing, offset

(G-1609)
E & M BINDERY INC
11 Peekay Dr (07014-1544)
PHONE..............................973 777-9300
Fax: 973 777-7991
Mark Berkowitz, *CEO*
Gary Markovits, *President*
Steve Schechtman, *Vice Pres*
Lorraine Mann, *Controller*
EMP: 120 **EST:** 1962
SQ FT: 50,000
SALES (est): 18MM **Privately Held**
WEB: www.embindery.com
SIC: 2789 Binding only: books, pamphlets, magazines, etc.

(G-1610)
ECSI INTERNATIONAL INC (HQ)
Also Called: E C S I
790 Bloomfield Ave Ste C1 (07012-1181)
P.O. Box 677 (07012-0677)
PHONE..............................973 574-8555
Fax: 973 574-8562
Arthur Birch, *Ch of Bd*
Stern Rich, *Vice Pres*
Ronald Thomas, *Vice Pres*
Ronald C Thomas, *Vice Pres*
Richard Stern, *VP Mfg*
EMP: 15
SQ FT: 12,500
SALES: 5.9MM
SALES (corp-wide): 981.7K **Publicly Held**
WEB: www.anti-terrorism.com
SIC: 3699 Security control equipment & systems
PA: Electronic Control Security Inc.
790 Bloomfield Ave Ste C1
Clifton NJ 07012
973 574-8555

(G-1611)
EDWARD W HIEMER & CO
141 Wabash Ave (07011-1651)
PHONE..............................973 772-5081
Judith Van Wie, *President*
Gerhard Hiemer, *Admin Sec*
EMP: 12 **EST:** 1929
SQ FT: 6,800
SALES: 970.8K **Privately Held**
SIC: 3231 Stained glass: made from purchased glass

(G-1612)
ELECTRO LIFT INC
204 Sargeant Ave (07013-1932)
P.O. Box 827 (07015-0827)
PHONE..............................973 471-0204
David Erenstoft, *President*
Alice Devereaux, *CFO*
Steve Pilione, *Mktg Dir*
Dolores Erenstoft, *Admin Sec*
EMP: 26 **EST:** 1932
SQ FT: 6,000
SALES (est): 7.4MM **Privately Held**
WEB: www.electrolift.com
SIC: 3536 Hoists

(G-1613)
ELECTRONIC CONTROL SEC INC (PA)
790 Bloomfield Ave Ste C1 (07012-1142)
PHONE..............................973 574-8555
Arthur Barchenko, *President*
Edward Snow, *COO*
Edward V Badolato, *Adv Board Mem*
Juda S Engelmayer, *Adv Board Mem*
Thomas Isdanavich, *Vice Pres*
EMP: 15
SQ FT: 12,200
SALES: 981.7K **Publicly Held**
SIC: 3699 Security control equipment & systems

(G-1614)
ELECTRONIC MFG SVCS INC
48 Industrial St W (07012-1712)
PHONE..............................973 916-1001
Farra Diamond, *CEO*
EMP: 16
SALES (est): 817.7K **Privately Held**
SIC: 3679 Microwave components; loads, electronic; harness assemblies for electronic use; wire or cable

(G-1615)
ELEKTROMEK INC
60 Webro Rd (07012-1426)
PHONE..............................973 614-9000
EMP: 18
SQ FT: 17,000
SALES (est): 2.5MM Privately Held
SIC: 2891 Mfg Adhesives/Sealants

(G-1616)
EXCELLENT PRTG & GRAPHICS LLC
333 Hazel St (07011-2812)
PHONE..............................973 773-6661
Fawzi Abdelgani, General Mgr
Fawzi A Abuyasser, Opers Spvr
Mutasem Abdelghani, Mng Member
EMP: 10
SQ FT: 20,000
SALES (est): 1MM Privately Held
WEB: www.excellent-printing.com
SIC: 2752 Commercial printing, offset

(G-1617)
EXELIS INC/NORTHROP
77 River Rd (07014-2000)
PHONE..............................973 284-4212
Northrop Grumman Systems Corp, Partner
Karen Gelormine, Administration
EMP: 10
SALES (est): 603.4K Privately Held
SIC: 3728 Aircraft parts & equipment

(G-1618)
FASTENATION INC
120 Brighton Rd Ste 2 (07012-1666)
PHONE..............................973 591-1277
David Petak, President
Jayne Petak, Vice Pres
EMP: 20
SQ FT: 18,000
SALES (est): 4.8MM Privately Held
WEB: www.fastenation.com
SIC: 3965 Fasteners

(G-1619)
FIDELITY INDUSTRIES INC
Also Called: Warehouse
750 Bloomfield Ave Ste 1 (07012-1257)
PHONE..............................973 777-2592
Mordecai Rivkin, President
EMP: 45
SALES (est): 3.8MM
SALES (corp-wide): 17.5MM Privately Held
WEB: www.fidelitywall.com
SIC: 3069 Wallcoverings, rubber
PA: Fidelity Industries Inc
559 Rte 23
Wayne NJ 07470
973 696-9120

(G-1620)
FINE ORGANICS CORPORATION (PA)
420 Kuller Rd Ste 2 (07011-2869)
P.O. Box 2277 (07015-2277)
PHONE..............................973 478-7690
William J Reidy, CEO
Gary Straub, President
Joseph Howanitz, Vice Pres
Lew Goldberg, Sales Executive
James Higdon, Info Tech Mgr
EMP: 11
SQ FT: 4,800
SALES (est): 1.5MM Privately Held
WEB: www.fineorganicscorp.com
SIC: 2842 Specialty cleaning preparations

(G-1621)
FIT FABRICATION LLC
310 Colfax Ave (07013-1794)
PHONE..............................973 685-7344
EMP: 8
SALES (est): 934.3K Privately Held
SIC: 3999 Manufacturing industries

(G-1622)
FORREST MFG CO INC
457 River Rd (07014-1520)
PHONE..............................973 473-5236
Fax: 973 471-3333
James S Forrest, President
Jay D Forrest, Vice Pres
EMP: 30 EST: 1946

SQ FT: 17,000
SALES (est): 4.4MM Privately Held
SIC: 3425 Saw blades & handsaws

(G-1623)
FRENCH TEXTILE CO INC
835 Bloomfield Ave Ste 1 (07012-1147)
PHONE..............................973 471-5000
Roy Aibel, CEO
EMP: 10
SALES (est): 982.5K Privately Held
SIC: 2298 2396 Nets, rope; veils & veiling: bridal, funeral, etc.

(G-1624)
FUCHS AUDIO TECH LTD LBLTY CO
407 Getty Ave (07011-2121)
PHONE..............................973 772-4420
Andrew M Fuchs,
Annette J Fuchs,
▲ EMP: 10 EST: 2003
SQ FT: 5,000
SALES: 850K Privately Held
SIC: 3629 Electronic generation equipment

(G-1625)
GENAVITE LLC
235 Clifton Blvd (07011-3646)
PHONE..............................973 779-1532
Bharat Patel, President
EMP: 10
SQ FT: 5,000
SALES (est): 2MM Privately Held
SIC: 2834 Vitamin preparations

(G-1626)
GENUA & MULLIGAN PRINTING
Also Called: Minuteman Press
1 Trenton Ave (07011-1807)
PHONE..............................973 894-1500
Fax: 201 659-6958
Joe Mulligan, President
Joe Genua, Admin Sec
EMP: 21
SQ FT: 4,000
SALES (est): 3.2MM Privately Held
WEB: www.minutemanpress.org
SIC: 2752 Commercial printing, lithographic

(G-1627)
GLOBE INDUSTRIES CORP
48 Industrial St W (07012-1712)
PHONE..............................973 992-8990
Anthony Melillo, President
Mark Melillo, Corp Secy
▲ EMP: 10 EST: 1962
SQ FT: 11,200
SALES (est): 920K Privately Held
SIC: 3544 3599 Special dies, tools, jigs & fixtures; custom machinery

(G-1628)
GLUE FOLD INC
40 Webro Rd (07012-1426)
PHONE..............................973 575-8400
Fax: 973 478-8998
Isabelle Garcia, General Mgr
Paul Delalla, General Mgr
EMP: 80
SALES (est): 7MM Privately Held
SIC: 2621 Envelope paper
PA: Perfect Finishing Inc.
40 Webro Rd
Clifton NJ 07012

(G-1629)
GMPC PRINTING
1 Trenton Ave (07011-1807)
PHONE..............................973 546-6060
Ryan Haessig, President
Mike Finucane, Treasurer
Jim Cox, Accountant
Ruben Velazquez, Accounts Exec
Joseph Genua, Sales Staff
EMP: 8
SALES (est): 823.5K Privately Held
SIC: 2752 Commercial printing, offset

(G-1630)
GRAPHIC EXPRESS MENU CO INC
200 Clifton Blvd Ste 6 (07011-3652)
PHONE..............................973 685-0022

Fax: 973 685-0020
Kathy Heflin, Exec VP
Chris Hesburgh, Exec VP
Evelyn Nugent, Exec VP
Adam Meier, CFO
EMP: 25
SQ FT: 27,000
SALES (est): 4.5MM Privately Held
WEB: www.graphicexpressmenu.com
SIC: 3083 2672 Laminated plastic sheets; coated & laminated paper

(G-1631)
GROSS PRINTING ASSOCIATES INC
180 Brighton Rd (07012-1451)
PHONE..............................718 832-1110
Abraham Lebowitz, President
Samson Gross, Vice Pres
EMP: 16
SQ FT: 13,000
SALES (est): 3.2MM Privately Held
SIC: 2752 Commercial printing, lithographic

(G-1632)
H POWER CORP
1373 Broad St (07013-4200)
PHONE..............................973 249-5444
H Gibbard, Principal
EMP: 4
SALES (est): 292K Privately Held
SIC: 3621 Motors & generators

(G-1633)
HANDI-HUT INC
3 Grunwald St (07013-2118)
PHONE..............................973 614-1800
Melvin Cohen, President
Richard T Cohen, Corp Secy
EMP: 30
SQ FT: 30,000
SALES (est): 5.5MM Privately Held
WEB: www.handi-hut.com
SIC: 3448 3449 3444 3442 Buildings, portable: prefabricated metal; miscellaneous metalwork; sheet metalwork; metal doors, sash & trim

(G-1634)
HARRIS CORPORATION
Also Called: Electronic Systems
77 River Rd (07014-2000)
PHONE..............................973 284-0123
Rich Sorelle, President
Chris Bernhardt, Branch Mgr
EMP: 136
SALES (corp-wide): 5.9B Publicly Held
SIC: 3812 Search & navigation equipment
PA: Harris Corporation
1025 W Nasa Blvd
Melbourne FL 32919
321 727-9100

(G-1635)
HARRIS CORPORATION
77 River Rd (07014-2000)
PHONE..............................973 284-0123
Timothy Ringler, Manager
EMP: 26
SALES (corp-wide): 5.9B Publicly Held
WEB: www.ittind.com
SIC: 3625 Control equipment, electric
PA: Harris Corporation
1025 W Nasa Blvd
Melbourne FL 32919
321 727-9100

(G-1636)
HARRIS CORPORATION
77 River Rd (07014-2000)
PHONE..............................973 284-0123
Mark Chubik, Branch Mgr
EMP: 148
SALES (corp-wide): 5.9B Publicly Held
SIC: 3812 Navigational systems & instruments
PA: Harris Corporation
1025 W Nasa Blvd
Melbourne FL 32919
321 727-9100

(G-1637)
HARRIS CORPORATION
Also Called: Exelis Geospatial Systems
77 River Rd (07014-2000)
PHONE..............................585 269-6600
William Gattle, President
David Melcher, President
Christopher D Young, President
EMP: 163
SALES (corp-wide): 5.9B Publicly Held
SIC: 3812 Search & navigation equipment
PA: Harris Corporation
1025 W Nasa Blvd
Melbourne FL 32919
321 727-9100

(G-1638)
HARVE BENARD LTD (PA)
Also Called: Hb-GM Acquistion
125 Delawanna Ave (07014-1529)
PHONE..............................973 249-1230
Fax: 973 249-1665
Bernard Holtzman, President
Morton Holtzman, Vice Pres
Mariana Perez, Opers Staff
Harvey J Schutzbank, CFO
EMP: 200 EST: 1967
SQ FT: 118,000
SALES (est): 29MM Privately Held
SIC: 2331 2325 2311 2339 Blouses, women's & juniors': made from purchased material; slacks, dress: men's, youths' & boys'; suits, men's & boys': made from purchased materials; women's & misses' jackets & coats, except sportswear; suits: women's, misses' & juniors'

(G-1639)
HEMPEL (USA) INC
127 Kingsland Ave (07014-2034)
PHONE..............................201 939-2801
Joel Benetti, Opers-Prdtn-Mfg
EMP: 5
SALES (corp-wide): 2.1MM Privately Held
WEB: www.us.hempel.com
SIC: 2851 Marine paints
HQ: Hempel (Usa), Inc.
600 Conroe Park North Dr
Conroe TX 77303
936 523-6000

(G-1640)
HICUBE COATING LLC
200 Circle Ave (07011-2870)
P.O. Box 828 (07015-0828)
PHONE..............................973 883-7404
Jonathan Hirsh,
Michael Kahr,
▲ EMP: 4
SALES (est): 480K Privately Held
SIC: 2655 Ammunition cans or tubes, board laminated with metal foil

(G-1641)
HIGH VISION CORPORATION
211 River Rd (07014-1518)
PHONE..............................862 238-7636
Kimi Weing, Owner
▲ EMP: 4
SALES (est): 398.7K
SALES (corp-wide): 41.1MM Privately Held
SIC: 3827 Optical instruments & lenses
PA: Shanghai Dong Da I&E Co., Ltd.
Room 110c, Floor 11, Jia Hua Finance Building, No.133, Tiantong
Shanghai 20008
216 317-3056

(G-1642)
HOUSE OF CUPCAKES
259 Allwood Rd (07012-1703)
PHONE..............................862 225-9536
EMP: 4
SALES (est): 307.7K Privately Held
SIC: 2051 Bread, cake & related products

(G-1643)
HOWARD PACKAGING CORP
86 Cobble St (07013-2224)
P.O. Box 3609, Wayne (07474-3609)
PHONE..............................973 904-0022
Howard Jacobs, President
EMP: 6

SALES (est): 794.3K **Privately Held**
WEB: www.freezaframe.com
SIC: **3861** Photographic equipment & supplies

(G-1644)
HUDSON COSMETIC MFG CORP
Also Called: Paramount Cosmetics
93 Entin Rd Ste 4 (07014-1500)
PHONE..............................973 472-2323
Fax: 973 865-4622
Sanford Salzman, *President*
Dana Graham, *Plant Mgr*
EMP: 65
SQ FT: 40,000
SALES (est): 11.3MM **Privately Held**
WEB: www.paramountcosmetics.net
SIC: **2844** Cosmetic preparations

(G-1645)
ICELANDIRECT INC
127 Kingsland Ave Ste 101 (07014-2034)
PHONE..............................800 763-4690
Mark H Stenberg, *CEO*
Brandon Miller, *President*
Christina Carlini, *Exec VP*
Andrea Patino, *Vice Pres*
Bruce Huff, *Prdtn Mgr*
▲ EMP: 13 EST: 2010
SQ FT: 14,000
SALES (est): 6.3MM **Privately Held**
SIC: **5122** 2023 Vitamins & minerals; dietary supplements, dairy & non-dairy based

(G-1646)
INFRONT MEDICAL LLC
1033 Us Highway 46 A202 (07013-2473)
PHONE..............................888 515-2532
John Kuczynski, *Principal*
EMP: 6 EST: 2013
SQ FT: 1,200
SALES: 50K **Privately Held**
SIC: **3842** Implants, surgical

(G-1647)
INNOVATIVE COSMTC CONCEPTS LLC
Also Called: Llc, Incoco Products
61 Kuller Rd (07011-3475)
PHONE..............................973 225-0264
Fax: 973 773-7007
FA Park, *President*
▲ EMP: 75
SALES (est): 16.9MM **Privately Held**
WEB: www.innovativecosmetics.net
SIC: **2844** Cosmetic preparations

(G-1648)
INTERNATIONAL DELIGHTS LLC
Also Called: Exquisities
230 Brighton Rd (07012-1414)
PHONE..............................973 928-5431
Spiro Sayegh,
Nicolas Sayegh,
▲ EMP: 130
SQ FT: 30,000
SALES (est): 29.7MM **Privately Held**
SIC: **2051** Bread, cake & related products

(G-1649)
INTERNATIONAL PAPER COMPANY
261 River Rd (07014-1551)
PHONE..............................973 405-2400
Jules Derner, *Marketing Mgr*
EMP: 8
SALES (corp-wide): 21.7B **Publicly Held**
SIC: **2621** Paper mills
PA: International Paper Company
6400 Poplar Ave
Memphis TN 38197
901 419-9000

(G-1650)
ITT CORPORATION
Also Called: ITT Defense Electronics & Svcs
100 Kingsland Rd (07014-1919)
PHONE..............................973 284-0123
Fax: 973 284-2210
R Tucci, *Manager*
EMP: 58

SALES (corp-wide): 2.5B **Publicly Held**
WEB: www.ittind.com
SIC: **3625** Control equipment, electric
HQ: Itt Llc
1133 Westchester Ave N-100
White Plains NY 10604
914 641-2000

(G-1651)
JAMES HOWARD INC
1500 Main Ave Ste 3 (07011-2120)
PHONE..............................973 928-1560
Fax: 973 928-1559
Timothy James, *President*
Jackie Nani, *Controller*
Kasia McCarthy, *Art Dir*
Phil Smith, *Graphic Designe*
EMP: 15
SQ FT: 13,000
SALES (est): 2.4MM **Privately Held**
WEB: www.jameshoward.com
SIC: **2759** 7336 Advertising agencies; graphic arts & related design

(G-1652)
JASSMINE CORP
489 Getty Ave (07011-2168)
PHONE..............................848 565-0515
Younes Seddiki, *CEO*
EMP: 6 EST: 1997
SQ FT: 10,000
SALES: 1.2MM **Privately Held**
SIC: **2052** Cookies

(G-1653)
JIMMYS COOKIES LLC
125 Entin Rd (07014-1424)
PHONE..............................973 779-8500
Fax: 201 797-2090
Howard Hirsch, *CEO*
Michael Pisani, *President*
Deborah Kinzley, *CFO*
EMP: 130
SQ FT: 90,000
SALES (est): 20.9MM **Privately Held**
SIC: **2052** 2045 Cookies; doughs, frozen or refrigerated: from purchased flour

(G-1654)
K M MEDIA GROUP LLC
Also Called: Peachtree Kay
220 Entin Rd (07014-1423)
PHONE..............................973 330-3000
Steve Tumminello, *Vice Pres*
Fred Golden, *VP Bus Dvlpt*
Rick Levy, *Director*
Richard Kirschenbaum,
Mike Costello,
EMP: 89
SQ FT: 50,000
SALES: 18.5MM **Privately Held**
SIC: **2759** Commercial printing

(G-1655)
KAY PRINTING & ENVELOPE CO INC
Also Called: Rga Graphics
220 Entin Rd (07014-1423)
PHONE..............................973 330-3000
Fax: 973 330-3301
Richard Kirschenbaum, *President*
Mike Costello, *Vice Pres*
Jackie Thomas, *Vice Pres*
Manny Rosa, *Plant Mgr*
Emil Mirsik, *Production*
EMP: 50 EST: 1974
SQ FT: 50,000
SALES (est): 9.5MM **Privately Held**
WEB: www.kayprinting.com
SIC: **2752** Commercial printing, offset

(G-1656)
LAMART CORP
37 Chestnut St (07011-2805)
PHONE..............................973 772-6262
EMP: 10
SALES (est): 3.1MM **Privately Held**
SIC: **3089** Plastics products

(G-1657)
LAMART CORPORATION (PA)
16 Richmond St (07011-2899)
P.O. Box 1648 (07015-1648)
PHONE..............................973 772-6262
Fax: 973 772-3673
Steven B Hirsh, *President*

Alan Hirsh, *Vice Pres*
◆ EMP: 140
SQ FT: 40,000
SALES (est): 94.2MM **Privately Held**
WEB: www.lamartcorp.com
SIC: **2672** Tape, pressure sensitive: made from purchased materials; adhesive backed films, foams & foils; adhesive papers, labels or tapes: from purchased material; metallic covered paper: made from purchased materials

(G-1658)
LAMART CORPORATION
162 Circle Ave (07011-2810)
PHONE..............................973 772-6262
James Landrum, *Owner*
EMP: 6
SALES (est): 270.2K **Privately Held**
SIC: **3089** Plastic processing

(G-1659)
LEGACY VULCAN LLC
208 Piaget Ave (07011-2255)
PHONE..............................973 253-8828
Voitek Roszkowski, *Principal*
EMP: 26 **Publicly Held**
WEB: www.vulcanmaterials.com
SIC: **1422** Crushed & broken limestone
HQ: Legacy Vulcan, Llc
1200 Urban Center Dr
Vestavia AL 35242
205 298-3000

(G-1660)
LEGEND STONE PRODUCTS
185 River Rd (07014-1518)
PHONE..............................973 473-7088
Emin Aydin, *Owner*
▲ EMP: 6
SALES (est): 619.8K **Privately Held**
SIC: **3423** Stonecutters' hand tools

(G-1661)
LEXINGTON GRAPHICS CORP
161 Elmwood Dr (07013-1129)
PHONE..............................973 345-2493
Henry H Brandhorst, *President*
EMP: 5
SALES (est): 320K **Privately Held**
SIC: **2752** 7336 Commercial printing, lithographic; graphic arts & related design

(G-1662)
LIGHT INC
Also Called: Ant Stores
345 Clifton Ave (07011-2618)
PHONE..............................973 777-2704
Mustafa Ozcan, *President*
Huseyin Senturk, *Vice Pres*
Ahmet Idil, *Treasurer*
▲ EMP: 9
SQ FT: 5,000
SALES (est): 1MM **Privately Held**
SIC: **2741** 5942 8748 Miscellaneous publishing; book stores; business consulting

(G-1663)
LMP PRINTING CORP
Also Called: Minuteman Press
1 Trenton Ave (07011-1807)
PHONE..............................973 428-1987
Mike Finucane, *President*
Patricia Finucane, *Treasurer*
EMP: 4
SALES (est): 433.1K **Privately Held**
SIC: **2752** Commercial printing, lithographic

(G-1664)
LONT & OVERKAMP PUBG CO INC
Also Called: Russco Bindery
200 Entin Rd (07014-1423)
PHONE..............................973 942-2243
Fax: 973 942-4594
Kenneth Lont, *President*
Jeremy Lont, *Vice Pres*
Judy Lont, *Vice Pres*
Dennis Savary, *Marketing Staff*
EMP: 47 EST: 1902
SALES (est): 7.6MM **Privately Held**
SIC: **2752** 7334 2791 2759 Commercial printing, offset; photocopying & duplicating services; typesetting; commercial printing; periodicals

(G-1665)
LUBRIZOL ADVANCED MTLS INC
1 Industrial St W (07012-1711)
PHONE..............................973 471-1300
Stephen K Scher, *CEO*
Roger Williams, *Warehouse Mgr*
Nick Paolazzi, *Technology*
Carlos Garcia, *Maintence Staff*
EMP: 13
SALES (corp-wide): 242.1B **Publicly Held**
WEB: www.pharma.noveoninc.com
SIC: **2869** Industrial organic chemicals; fatty acid esters, aminos, etc.
HQ: Lubrizol Advanced Materials Inc.
9911 Brecksville Rd
Brecksville OH 44141
216 447-5000

(G-1666)
LUKACH INTERIORS INC
208 River Rd (07014-1519)
PHONE..............................973 777-1499
Mike Lukach, *President*
EMP: 10
SQ FT: 10,000
SALES: 1.2MM **Privately Held**
SIC: **2431** 5712 Woodwork, interior & ornamental; customized furniture & cabinets

(G-1667)
MAGNUSON PRODUCTS
6 Chelsea Rd (07012-1667)
PHONE..............................973 472-9292
Albert Reisch Jr, *President*
Pamela Reisch, *Treasurer*
EMP: 12
SQ FT: 23,000
SALES (est): 958.3K
SALES (corp-wide): 9.9MM **Privately Held**
SIC: **2842** 2841 Cleaning or polishing preparations; soap & other detergents
PA: E. M. Sergeant Pulp And Chemical Co., Inc.
6 Chelsea Rd
Clifton NJ 07012
973 472-9111

(G-1668)
MASOULEH CORP (PA)
Also Called: Citgo
301 River Rd (07014-1549)
PHONE..............................973 470-8900
Faramarz Ebrahimi, *President*
Fred Ebrahimi, *Vice Pres*
EMP: 25
SQ FT: 2,000
SALES (est): 4.4MM **Privately Held**
SIC: **5541** 1382 Filling stations, gasoline; oil & gas exploration services

(G-1669)
MASTERS INTERIORS INC
1500 Main Ave Ste 23 (07011-2124)
PHONE..............................973 253-0784
Fax: 973 253-0786
Kevin Costello, *President*
EMP: 35
SALES (est): 1.9MM **Privately Held**
SIC: **7389** 2512 Interior design services; upholstered household furniture

(G-1670)
MAT MANUFACTURING CORPORATION
Also Called: Rush Manufacturing
409 River Rd 3 (07014-1520)
PHONE..............................800 378-7965
Mark Golsdstein, *President*
Jenn Sphere, *Principal*
Sharon Goldstein, *Vice Pres*
EMP: 20
SQ FT: 20,000
SALES: 2MM **Privately Held**
WEB: www.matmfg.com
SIC: **5074** 3431 Plumbing fittings & supplies; plumbing fixtures: enameled iron cast iron or pressed metal

(G-1671)
MAX GURTMAN & SONS INC
622 Lexington Ave (07011-1229)
P.O. Box 1849 (07015-1849)
PHONE..............................973 478-7000
Franklin Gurtman, *President*
EMP: 5 EST: 1934
SQ FT: 10,000
SALES (est): 430K **Privately Held**
SIC: 3444 3441 Sheet metalwork; fabricated structural metal

(G-1672)
MELTOM MANUFACTURING INC
22 Franklin Ave (07011-2214)
PHONE..............................973 546-0058
Joseph Chudzik, *President*
EMP: 5
SQ FT: 3,600
SALES: 158.1K **Privately Held**
SIC: 3451 Screw machine products

(G-1673)
METROPOLITAN FOODS INC (PA)
Also Called: Driscoll Foods
174 Delawanna Ave (07014-1550)
PHONE..............................973 672-9400
Tim Driscoll, *President*
Martin Rapport, *Partner*
Joe Vione, *Area Mgr*
Neil Sheehy, *Business Mgr*
Casey Stangle, *Business Mgr*
▲ EMP: 153
SQ FT: 220,000
SALES (est): 424.6MM **Privately Held**
WEB: www.driscollfoods.com
SIC: 5142 5149 2099 5141 Packaged frozen goods; dried or canned foods; food preparations; food brokers

(G-1674)
MICRO-TEK LABORATORIES INC (PA)
Also Called: Physitemp Instruments
154 Huron Ave (07013-2949)
PHONE..............................973 779-5577
Ronald R Feller, *President*
Chris Proffitt, *Vice Pres*
Christopher Proffitt, *Admin Sec*
EMP: 7
SQ FT: 5,500
SALES (est): 2.8MM **Privately Held**
WEB: www.physitemp.com
SIC: 3823 3821 3829 3822 Temperature instruments: industrial process type; laboratory equipment: fume hoods, distillation racks, etc.; measuring & controlling devices; auto controls regulating residntl & coml environmt & applncs; semiconductors & related devices

(G-1675)
MODERN FUEL INC
158 Colfax Ave (07013-1857)
PHONE..............................973 471-1501
EMP: 5 EST: 2010
SALES (est): 251.5K **Privately Held**
SIC: 2869 Fuels

(G-1676)
MPHASE TECHNOLOGIES INC (PA)
777 Passaic Ave Ste 385 (07012-1874)
PHONE..............................973 256-3737
Ronald A Durando, *President*
Gustave T Dotoli, *COO*
Martin S Smiley, *CFO*
EMP: 12
SALES (est): 1.1MM **Publicly Held**
WEB: www.mphasetech.com
SIC: 3699 3691 3663 Electrical equipment & supplies; storage batteries; radio & TV communications equipment; satellites, communications

(G-1677)
MPOWER TECHNOLOGIES INC
777 Passaic Ave Ste 385 (07012-1874)
PHONE..............................973 256-3737
Ronald Durando, *President*
EMP: 17
SQ FT: 2,144

SALES (est): 652.2K **Privately Held**
SIC: 3621 Storage battery chargers, motor & engine generator type

(G-1678)
NALUCO INC
Also Called: American Flyer
23 Carol St (07014-1420)
PHONE..............................800 601-8198
Fax: 973 523-7912
Joseph Liang, *President*
Grace Liang, *Vice Pres*
EMP: 87
SQ FT: 80,000
SALES (est): 7.6MM **Privately Held**
WEB: www.americanflyer.com
SIC: 5099 3161 Luggage; luggage; clothing & apparel carrying cases; suitcases; attache cases

(G-1679)
NB BOOKBINDING INC
356 Getty Ave Bldg 2 (07011)
PHONE..............................973 247-1200
Nicolas Bassil, *President*
Christine Bassil, *Vice Pres*
Pitiya Bassil, *Manager*
▲ EMP: 8
SQ FT: 20,000
SALES: 550K **Privately Held**
SIC: 2789 Binding only: books, pamphlets, magazines, etc.

(G-1680)
NES JEWELRY INC
43 Samworth Rd (07012-1714)
PHONE..............................646 213-4094
Yosi Arish, *COO*
EMP: 70 **Privately Held**
SIC: 3961 Costume jewelry
PA: Nes Jewelry, Inc.
10 W 33rd St Fl 9
New York NY 10001

(G-1681)
NEW JERSEY WIRE CLOTH CO INC
55 Park Slope (07011)
PHONE..............................973 340-0101
Fax: 973 340-9109
John Rafanello, *President*
EMP: 8
SALES (est): 396.6K **Privately Held**
SIC: 3496 Miscellaneous fabricated wire products

(G-1682)
NEW LINE PRTG & TECH SOLUTIONS
790 Bloomfield Ave Ste 3 (07012-1142)
PHONE..............................973 405-6133
John Luciano, *President*
Maria Russo, *Accounts Exec*
Barry Clark, *Sales Staff*
Art Roselli, *Sales Staff*
Michele Krieger, *Director*
EMP: 7
SQ FT: 750
SALES (est): 881.8K **Privately Held**
SIC: 2759 5045 Business forms: printing; computer software

(G-1683)
NEWARK WIRE CLOTH COMPANY
160 Fornelius Ave (07013-1844)
PHONE..............................973 778-4478
Fax: 973 778-4481
Richard W Campbell, *President*
James L Campbell, *Vice Pres*
Robert D Lucki, *Vice Pres*
▲ EMP: 28 EST: 1911
SQ FT: 30,000
SALES (est): 6.5MM **Privately Held**
WEB: www.newarkwire.com
SIC: 3496 Fabrics, woven wire

(G-1684)
NIJAMA CORPORATION
Also Called: Empanada King
132 Getty Ave (07011-1840)
P.O. Box 213, Little Ferry (07643-0213)
PHONE..............................973 272-3223
Marino Roa, *President*
EMP: 5 EST: 2002

SALES (est): 289.6K **Privately Held**
SIC: 2045 Doughs, frozen or refrigerated: from purchased flour

(G-1685)
NPS PUBLIC FURNITURE CORP
Also Called: National Public Seating
149 Entin Rd (07014-1424)
PHONE..............................973 594-1100
Fax: 973 594-1500
Barry Stauber, *Co-CEO*
Benjamin Grunwald, *Co-CEO*
Devora Mandelbaum, *Admin Sec*
◆ EMP: 93 EST: 1997
SALES (est): 44MM **Privately Held**
WEB: www.nationalpublicseating.com
SIC: 5021 2514 Chairs; chairs, household: metal

(G-1686)
OKLAHOMA SOUND CORP (PA)
Also Called: O S C
149 Entin Rd (07014-1424)
PHONE..............................800 261-4112
Benjamin Grunwald, *CEO*
Barry Stauber, *President*
Jay Leiser, *Software Dev*
Devora Mandelbaum, *Admin Sec*
◆ EMP: 50 EST: 1982
SQ FT: 18,000
SALES (est): 8.7MM **Privately Held**
WEB: www.oklahomasound.com
SIC: 3651 Public address systems

(G-1687)
ORORA VISUAL LLC
1155 Bloomfield Ave (07012-2308)
PHONE..............................973 916-2804
Della Haselman, *Manager*
EMP: 7
SALES (est): 937.9K **Privately Held**
SIC: 2752 Advertising posters, lithographed

(G-1688)
PALLMANN PULVERIZERS CO INC
Also Called: Pallmann Industries
820 Bloomfield Ave (07012-1116)
PHONE..............................973 471-1450
Fax: 973 471-7152
Hartmut Pallmann, *President*
Kevin Moros, *Division Mgr*
Jeff Taylor, *Natl Sales Mgr*
Simon Howard, *Sales Staff*
Ingo Pallmann, *Shareholder*
EMP: 30
SQ FT: 30,000
SALES (est): 6.6MM **Privately Held**
WEB: www.pallmannpulverizers.com
SIC: 3532 5084 Pulverizers (stationary), stone; grinders, stone: stationary; pulverizing machinery & equipment; crushing machinery & equipment

(G-1689)
PAPILLON RIBBON & BOW INC
35 Monhegan St (07013-2000)
PHONE..............................973 928-6128
CHI-Yin Wong, *President*
Igual Pua, *President*
Jimmy Cheung, *Vice Pres*
▲ EMP: 25
SQ FT: 12,000
SALES (est): 5.8MM **Privately Held**
WEB: www.papillonribbon.com
SIC: 5131 2396 Ribbons; ribbons & bows, cut & sewed

(G-1690)
PARAMOUNT COSMETICS INC
93 Entin Rd Ste 4 (07014-1500)
PHONE..............................973 472-2323
Fax: 973 472-5005
Sandy Salzman, *President*
Steven E Schifrien, *Vice Pres*
Dana Graham, *Plant Mgr*
Renata Kowalczyk, *Purch Agent*
Ken Schweizer, *Plant Engr*
▲ EMP: 90
SQ FT: 120,000
SALES (est): 19.9MM **Privately Held**
WEB: www.paramanet.com
SIC: 2844 Cosmetic preparations

(G-1691)
PASSAIC METAL & BLDG SUPS CO (PA)
Also Called: Siding Depot
5 Central Ave Ste 1 (07011-2399)
P.O. Box 1849 (07015-1849)
PHONE..............................973 546-9000
Franklin S Gurtman, *President*
Michael Gurtman, *Vice Pres*
Barry Fishbane, *Sales Staff*
Pete Jimenez, *Sales Staff*
Andrew Wohr, *Sales Staff*
EMP: 80 EST: 1913
SALES (est): 216.8MM **Privately Held**
WEB: www.pampco.com
SIC: 5033 5031 5051 5075 Roofing & siding materials; doors & windows; doors; windows; sheets, metal; air conditioning & ventilation equipment & supplies; sheet metalwork; mineral wool

(G-1692)
PAVEXPRESS
499 River Rd (07014-1520)
PHONE..............................201 330-8300
Fax: 201 330-0096
Kenneth F Pavlik, *Principal*
EMP: 8
SALES (est): 725.4K **Privately Held**
SIC: 2741 Miscellaneous publishing

(G-1693)
PDM LITHO INC
220 Entin Rd (07014-1423)
PHONE..............................718 301-1740
Fax: 718 301-1747
Jeffrey M Alpert, *President*
Aaron Craig, *Chairman*
Joel Sachs, *Chairman*
Bob Sussman, *Vice Pres*
Bart Sussman, *Admin Sec*
EMP: 25
SQ FT: 18,000
SALES (est): 4MM **Privately Held**
WEB: www.pdmlitho.com
SIC: 2752 Commercial printing, lithographic

(G-1694)
PHARM-RX CHEMICAL CORPORATION
Also Called: P R X
4 Brighton Rd Ste 308 (07012-1665)
PHONE..............................973 917-1400
David Lemeshow, *President*
Carlos Doussinague, *President*
▲ EMP: 5
SALES (est): 2.3MM **Privately Held**
WEB: www.pharm-rxchem.com
SIC: 5169 2834 Chemicals & allied products; pharmaceutical preparations

(G-1695)
PHILIPS ELEC N AMER CORP
Gemini Industries
215 Entin Rd (07014-1424)
PHONE..............................973 471-9450
Fax: 973 471-8621
Michael O'Neal, *Manager*
EMP: 100
SALES (corp-wide): 20.9B **Privately Held**
WEB: www.usa.philips.com
SIC: 3663 5064 5065 Antennas, transmitting & communications; electrical entertainment equipment; video cassette recorders & accessories; radio & television equipment & parts; communication equipment; telephone & telegraphic equipment
HQ: Philips North America Llc
3000 Minuteman Rd Ms1203
Andover MA 01810
978 659-3000

(G-1696)
PICTURE KNITS INC
489 Getty Ave (07011-2168)
PHONE..............................973 340-3131
Rory McNamara, *President*
Leon Benitez, *President*
Eduardo Benitez, *Vice Pres*
Mirna Benitez, *Admin Sec*
EMP: 32
SQ FT: 31,500

GEOGRAPHIC

SALES (est): 3MM **Privately Held**
SIC: **2211** 2221 Broadwoven fabric mills, cotton; broadwoven fabric mills, man-made

(G-1697)
PILKINGTON NORTH AMERICA INC
125 Kingsland Ave (07014-2032)
PHONE..................................973 470-5703
EMP: 192
SALES (corp-wide): 5.6B **Privately Held**
SIC: **3211** Flat glass
HQ: Pilkington North America, Inc.
    811 Madison Ave Fl 1
    Toledo OH 43604
    614 802-7027

(G-1698)
PJM SOFTWARE INC
33 Mayer Dr (07012-1651)
P.O. Box 10732, New Brunswick (08906-0732)
PHONE..................................973 330-0405
Peter Moore, *President*
James Krick, *Vice Pres*
EMP: 4
SALES (est): 50K **Privately Held**
WEB: pjmsoftware.com
SIC: **7372** Prepackaged software

(G-1699)
PMJE WELDING LLC
310 Colfax Ave Unit A (07013-1794)
PHONE..................................973 685-7344
EMP: 6
SALES (est): 107.3K **Privately Held**
SIC: **7692** Welding repair

(G-1700)
POLYMER TECHNOLOGIES INC
10 Clifton Blvd Ste 3 (07011-3802)
PHONE..................................973 778-9100
Fax: 973 778-9797
Neal Goldenberg, *President*
J Melvin Goldenberg, *Vice Pres*
▲ EMP: 84
SQ FT: 33,000
SALES (est): 16.7MM **Privately Held**
WEB: www.polymertek.com
SIC: **2821** Plastics materials & resins

(G-1701)
POLYTECH DESIGNS INC
26 W 1st St (07011-2103)
PHONE..................................973 340-1390
Zaki Shasha, *President*
▲ EMP: 11
SQ FT: 6,000
SALES (est): 1.6MM **Privately Held**
WEB: www.polytechdesign.com
SIC: **3052** 3429 Transmission belting, rubber; pulleys metal

(G-1702)
PRECISE CMPNENTS TL DESIGN INC
10 Clifton Blvd Unit A4 (07011-3802)
PHONE..................................973 928-2928
Harry Benedikt, *President*
Lee Kim Benedikt, *Vice Pres*
EMP: 8
SQ FT: 6,400
SALES (est): 800K **Privately Held**
SIC: **3841** 3842 Surgical & medical instruments; surgical appliances & supplies

(G-1703)
PRECISION SAW & TOOL CORP
56 Colfax Ave (07013-1944)
PHONE..................................973 773-7302
James Montesano, *President*
Janet Montesano, *Corp Secy*
EMP: 11
SQ FT: 3,000
SALES (est): 1.1MM **Privately Held**
WEB: www.precisionsaw.com
SIC: **7699** 5251 3546 Knife, saw & tool sharpening & repair; tools; saws & sawing equipment

(G-1704)
PRINCE BLACK DISTILLERY INC
Also Called: Black Prince
691 Clifton Ave (07011-4203)
P.O. Box 1999 (07015-1999)
PHONE..................................212 695-6187
Fax: 973 365-0746
Robert Guttag, *President*
▲ EMP: 29 EST: 1934
SQ FT: 120,000
SALES (est): 5.4MM **Privately Held**
WEB: www.blackprincedistillery.com
SIC: **2085** Distilled & blended liquors

(G-1705)
PRINT FACTORY LTD LIABILITY CO
Also Called: Print Factory Nyc
730 Clifton Ave (07013-1862)
PHONE..................................973 866-5230
Ramsey Contreras,
EMP: 5
SQ FT: 900
SALES (est): 360.4K **Privately Held**
SIC: **2752** 7336 Business form & card printing, lithographic; commercial art & graphic design

(G-1706)
PULSAR MICROWAVE CORP
48 Industrial St W (07012-1712)
PHONE..................................973 779-6262
Fax: 973 779-2727
Charlie Bobroski, *President*
Michael Chilimintris, *President*
Charles Bobroski, *Manager*
EMP: 25
SQ FT: 4,000
SALES (est): 8.6MM **Privately Held**
WEB: www.pulsarmicrowave.com
SIC: **5065** 3825 Radio parts & accessories; radio frequency measuring equipment

(G-1707)
Q10 PRODUCTS LLC
Also Called: Creative Organization
1 Entin Rd Ste 7a (07014-1574)
P.O. Box 475, Tenafly (07670-0475)
PHONE..................................201 567-9299
Alfred Silber,
▲ EMP: 12
SALES (est): 1.5MM **Privately Held**
SIC: **5023** 3999 Home furnishings; pet supplies

(G-1708)
QUALITY INDUSTRIES INC
204 Getty Ave (07011-1804)
PHONE..................................973 478-4425
Fax: 973 478-0172
Jerry K Ponikowski, *President*
EMP: 12
SQ FT: 8,000
SALES (est): 1.1MM **Privately Held**
WEB: www.4qii.com
SIC: **3599** Machine shop, jobbing & repair

(G-1709)
QUALITY STAYS LLC (PA)
10 Underwood Pl Ste 2 (07013-2219)
PHONE..................................800 868-8195
▲ EMP: 5
SALES (est): 511.7K **Privately Held**
SIC: **3965** Fasteners, buttons, needles & pins

(G-1710)
RANCO PRECISION SHEET METAL
40 Colorado St (07014)
PHONE..................................973 472-8808
John Karpi, *President*
EMP: 9 EST: 1959
SQ FT: 5,000
SALES (est): 1.1MM **Privately Held**
SIC: **3444** Sheet metalwork

(G-1711)
RECYCLED PPRBD INC CLIFTON
1 Ackerman Ave (07011-1501)
PHONE..................................201 768-7468
Fax: 973 546-1349
EMP: 23

SQ FT: 200,000
SALES (est): 4.7MM **Privately Held**
SIC: **2675** Mfg Die-Cut Paper/Paperboard

(G-1712)
REGISTER LITHOGRAPHERS LTD
1155 Bloomfield Ave (07012-2308)
PHONE..................................973 916-2804
Fax: 973 916-2810
Joseph Fishman, *President*
Eugene Markowitz, *Vice Pres*
Joseph Goldbrenner, *Treasurer*
EMP: 54
SQ FT: 40,000
SALES (est): 43.7MM **Privately Held**
SIC: **2752** Commercial printing, offset

(G-1713)
SABER ASSOCIATES
1111 Paulison Ave (07011-3600)
PHONE..................................973 777-3800
Dean Emmolo, *Partner*
EMP: 40
SALES (est): 3.6MM **Privately Held**
WEB: www.saberassociates.com
SIC: **3567** Industrial furnaces & ovens

(G-1714)
SAFAS CORPORATION (PA)
2 Ackerman Ave (07011-1502)
PHONE..................................973 772-5252
Fax: 973 772-5858
Akbar Ghahary, *Ch of Bd*
Fateme Ghahary, *President*
Azam Alexander, *Corp Secy*
Steve Mulligan, *VP Opers*
Bill Palowski, *Controller*
▲ EMP: 30
SQ FT: 85,000
SALES (est): 4.7MM **Privately Held**
WEB: www.safascorp.com
SIC: **2821** Plastics materials & resins

(G-1715)
SANDY ALEXANDER INC (PA)
Also Called: Modern Graphic Arts
200 Entin Rd (07014-1494)
PHONE..................................973 470-8100
Fax: 973 470-9269
Michael Graff, *CEO*
Vito Banci, *President*
Louis Scharfstein, *President*
Eric Reinitz, *General Mgr*
Steven Babat, *COO*
◆ EMP: 180
SQ FT: 134,000
SALES (est): 82MM **Privately Held**
WEB: www.sandyinc.com
SIC: **2752** Commercial printing, offset

(G-1716)
SCHER CHEMICALS INC
Industrial West (07012)
PHONE..................................973 471-1300
Fax: 973 471-3783
Stephen K Scher, *President*
Judith Donner, *Vice Pres*
EMP: 2780 EST: 1932
SQ FT: 50,000
SALES (est): 187.7MM
SALES (corp-wide): 242.1B **Publicly Held**
WEB: www.pharma.noveoninc.com
SIC: **2869** Industrial organic chemicals; fatty acid esters, aminos, etc.
HQ: Lubrizol Advanced Materials Inc.
    9911 Brecksville Rd
    Brecksville OH 44141
    216 447-5000

(G-1717)
SCIENTIFIC ALLOYS CORP
5 Troast Ct (07011-2131)
PHONE..................................973 478-8323
Wayne R Connelly, *President*
Phil Jacobs, *Vice Pres*
William Pian, *Vice Pres*
EMP: 14
SQ FT: 27,500
SALES (est): 1.5MM **Privately Held**
WEB: www.bgaspheres.com
SIC: **3443** 3399 Fabricated plate work (boiler shop); metal powders, pastes & flakes

(G-1718)
SEAL TRONICS INC
320 Colfax Ave (07013-1794)
P.O. Box 3068, Wayne (07474-3068)
PHONE..................................864 576-0015
Peter Fleischner, *Principal*
EMP: 15 EST: 1966
SALES (est): 2.2MM **Privately Held**
SIC: **3679** Recording & playback apparatus, including phonograph

(G-1719)
SEMELS EMBROIDERY INC
1078 Route 46 (07013-2420)
PHONE..................................973 473-6868
Charlotte Semel, *President*
Dolly Semel, *Vice Pres*
EMP: 13 EST: 1937
SQ FT: 6,000
SALES (est): 2MM **Privately Held**
SIC: **2395** 7389 2759 2396 Embroidery products, except schiffli machine; printers' services: folding, collating; commercial printing; automotive & apparel trimmings

(G-1720)
SEMI CONDUCTOR MANUFACTURING
Also Called: Semiconductor Manufacturing
5 Troast Ct (07011-2131)
PHONE..................................973 478-2880
Fax: 973 478-6780
Wayne R Connelly, *President*
William Pian, *Corp Secy*
EMP: 43
SQ FT: 12,500
SALES (est): 6.3MM **Privately Held**
WEB:
www.semiconductormanufacturing.com
SIC: **3674** 1793 3341 Microcircuits, integrated (semiconductor); glass & glazing work; secondary nonferrous metals

(G-1721)
SHERMAN PRINTING CO INC
161 Elmwood Dr (07013-1129)
P.O. Box 2304 (07015-2304)
PHONE..................................973 345-2493
Dan Gillan, *President*
Doris Gillan, *Treasurer*
EMP: 4
SALES (est): 320K **Privately Held**
SIC: **2752** 2759 Commercial printing, offset; letterpress printing

(G-1722)
SHINDO INTERNATIONAL INC
200 Entin Rd (07014-1423)
PHONE..................................973 470-8100
Fax: 973 777-1594
Hisako Shindo, *President*
James Lundquist, *Treasurer*
EMP: 35
SQ FT: 5,000
SALES (est): 3.3MM **Privately Held**
SIC: **2752** 7336 Color lithography; commercial art & graphic design
HQ: Flexceed Co., Ltd.
    6701-1, To
    Naka IBR 311-0
    292 970-771

(G-1723)
SHOWTECH INC
40 Entin Rd (07014-1542)
PHONE..................................973 249-6336
Daniel Zazzali, *President*
George P Zazzali, *Vice Pres*
EMP: 8
SALES: 1MM **Privately Held**
SIC: **2541** Cabinets, lockers & shelving; cabinets, except refrigerated: show, display, etc.: wood; lockers, except refrigerated: wood

(G-1724)
SIGN A RAMA
Also Called: Sign-A-Rama
681 Van Houten Ave (07013-2130)
PHONE..................................973 471-5558
Fax: 973 471-2283
Steven Budd, *President*
EMP: 4
SALES (est): 230K **Privately Held**
SIC: **3993** Signs & advertising specialties

(G-1725)
SIGNS OF 2000
421 Broad St (07013-1407)
PHONE..................973 253-1333
Ray Salem, *Owner*
Eva N Cecli, *Manager*
EMP: 10
SALES (est): 889.7K **Privately Held**
SIC: 3993 Electric signs

(G-1726)
SITE DRAINER LLC
18 Sebago St (07013-1924)
PHONE..................862 225-9940
Antonio Perez, *President*
EMP: 6
SQ FT: 4,500
SALES (est): 74.9K **Privately Held**
SIC: 3589 Sewage & water treatment
equipment

(G-1727)
SMARTLITE LLC
Also Called: Smart Candle
25 Madison Ave (07011-2305)
PHONE..................973 470-9400
Marta Lederer,
John Bober,
Gabor Lederer,
William McDaid,
◆ **EMP:** 6
SQ FT: 6,000
SALES: 980K **Privately Held**
SIC: 3999 Candles

(G-1728)
SOMETHING DIFFERENT LINEN INC
167 Fornelius Ave (07013-1845)
PHONE..................973 272-0601
Mitchell Smith, *President*
Melvin Atlas, *Vice Pres*
Araceib Baez, *Vice Pres*
Lina Bonilla, *Vice Pres*
◆ **EMP:** 125
SALES (est): 15.1MM **Privately Held**
WEB: www.tablecloths.net
SIC: 2299 Linen fabrics

(G-1729)
SPARK WIRE PRODUCTS CO INC
158 River Rd (07014-1571)
PHONE..................973 773-6945
Fax: 973 773-0262
Paul Fessak, *President*
EMP: 7 EST: 1956
SQ FT: 7,000
SALES: 700K **Privately Held**
SIC: 2542 Racks, merchandise display or
storage: except wood; stands, merchan-
dise display: except wood

(G-1730)
STAINLESS METAL SOURCE INTL
Also Called: SMS International
207 Piaget Ave (07011-2235)
PHONE..................973 977-2200
Fax: 973 340-5522
Chanoch Shiloh, *President*
Das Meneon, *Vice Pres*
▲ **EMP:** 7
SQ FT: 6,500
SALES: 2MM **Privately Held**
SIC: 5051 3312 Steel; stainless steel

(G-1731)
STANLEY STEEMER INTL INC
Also Called: Stanley Steemer Carpet Clr 79
10 Clifton Blvd Ste B2 (07011-3845)
PHONE..................973 574-1640
Fax: 973 625-0471
Rick Smith, *Manager*
EMP: 22
SALES (corp-wide): 241.9MM **Privately Held**
WEB: www.stanley-steemer.com
SIC: 7217 3635 6794 7513 Carpet & fur-
niture cleaning on location; upholstery
cleaning on customer premises; carpet
shampooer; franchises, selling or licens-
ing; truck rental & leasing, no drivers

PA: Stanley Steemer International, Inc.
5800 Innovation Dr
Dublin OH 43016
614 764-2007

(G-1732)
SUSSEX HUMUS & SUPPLY INC
29 Kenyon St (07013-1717)
PHONE..................973 779-8812
Joseph De Santis, *President*
Laurel Ann De Santis, *Corp Secy*
Glenn De Santis, *Vice Pres*
EMP: 4 EST: 1975
SALES (est): 359.3K **Privately Held**
SIC: 1499 Peat mining & processing

(G-1733)
SWEPCO TUBE LLC
1 Clifton Blvd (07011-3899)
P.O. Box 1899 (07015-1899)
PHONE..................973 778-3000
Fax: 973 778-9289
Ken Schultz,
Victor Battistuz,
Steve Oberhelman,
EMP: 145 EST: 1939
SQ FT: 330,000
SALES (est): 67MM **Privately Held**
WEB: www.swepcotube.com
SIC: 3356 Nonferrous rolling & drawing

(G-1734)
TANZOLA PRINTING INC
Also Called: Sir Speedy
270 Colfax Ave (07013-1700)
PHONE..................973 779-0858
Joe Tanzola, *President*
Ellen Tanzola, *Corp Secy*
EMP: 4 EST: 1980
SQ FT: 1,500
SALES (est): 240K **Privately Held**
SIC: 2752 7334 2789 Commercial print-
ing, offset; photocopying & duplicating
services; bookbinding & related work

(G-1735)
TAPTASK LLC
83 Rolling Hills Rd (07013-4117)
P.O. Box Msc 128449, Atlanta GA (30322-
0001)
PHONE..................201 294-2371
Ekrem Kurucan,
Talha Koc,
Sinan Sahin,
EMP: 4
SALES (est): 98.3K **Privately Held**
SIC: 7372 Business oriented computer
software; application computer software

(G-1736)
TBC COLOR IMAGING INC
Also Called: Tbc Digital
200 Entin Rd (07014-1423)
PHONE..................973 470-8100
Michael Graff, *President*
Steven Borbat, *COO*
Kevin St Germaine, *CFO*
EMP: 26 EST: 1991
SALES (est): 2.5MM **Privately Held**
WEB: www.tbccolor.com
SIC: 2759 Commercial printing

(G-1737)
TIN PANDA INC
875 Bloomfield Ave (07012-1118)
PHONE..................973 916-0707
Edwin Diaz, *Principal*
Brian Cook, *Manager*
EMP: 5
SALES (est): 580.6K **Privately Held**
SIC: 3356 Tin

(G-1738)
VAN NESS PLASTIC MOLDING CO
400 Brighton Rd (07012-1013)
PHONE..................973 778-9500
Fax: 973 778-8588
William Van Ness, *President*
◆ **EMP:** 200
SQ FT: 170,000
SALES (est): 55.3MM **Privately Held**
WEB: www.vannessplastic.com
SIC: 3089 Injection molding of plastics

(G-1739)
VIP INDUSTRIES INC
90 Brighton Rd (07012-1606)
PHONE..................973 472-7500
Fax: 973 472-2404
John Sonatore, *President*
Natalia Sanchez, *Opers Staff*
▲ **EMP:** 50
SQ FT: 24,000
SALES (est): 7.7MM **Privately Held**
WEB: www.vipindustriesinc.com
SIC: 3679 Harness assemblies for elec-
tronic use: wire or cable

(G-1740)
VO-TOYS INC (PA)
Also Called: V I P
179 Entin Rd (07014-1424)
PHONE..................973 482-8915
Fax: 973 484-9569
Arthur Hirschberg, *President*
Gary Hirschberg, *Corp Secy*
▲ **EMP:** 44
SALES (est): 34.8MM **Privately Held**
WEB: www.vo-toys.com
SIC: 5199 3999 Pets & pet supplies; pet
supplies

(G-1741)
WAGNER RACK INC
2 Broad St (07013-1098)
PHONE..................973 278-6966
Fax: 973 278-9514
Ron Wagner, *President*
Wendy Prior, *Corp Secy*
EMP: 25 EST: 1970
SQ FT: 14,500
SALES (est): 4.6MM **Privately Held**
WEB: www.wagnerrack.com
SIC: 2541 Counters or counter display
cases, wood

(G-1742)
WALDEN LANG IN-PAK SERVICE
474 Getty Ave 2 (07011-2149)
PHONE..................973 595-5250
Brian Billes, *President*
Jack Pires, *Corp Secy*
Greg A Regina, *Vice Pres*
EMP: 30 EST: 1992
SQ FT: 20,000
SALES (est): 2.2MM **Privately Held**
SIC: 2782 Blankbooks & looseleaf binders;
sample books

(G-1743)
WESTROCK CP LLC
1401 Broad St Ste 1 (07013-4237)
PHONE..................973 594-6000
Fax: 973 594-6001
Michael Smurfit, *CEO*
EMP: 25
SALES (corp-wide): 14.8B **Publicly Held**
WEB: www.smurfit-stone.com
SIC: 2631 Container board
HQ: Westrock Cp, Llc
504 Thrasher St
Norcross GA 30071

(G-1744)
WRAP-ADE MACHINE CO INC
Also Called: Wrapade
180 Brighton Rd Ste B (07012-1451)
PHONE..................973 773-6150
Robert B Mc Closky, *President*
EMP: 12 EST: 1932
SQ FT: 6,000
SALES (est): 1.2MM **Privately Held**
WEB: www.standuppouch.com
SIC: 3565 5084 Packaging machinery; in-
dustrial machinery & equipment

(G-1745)
X-L PLASTICS INC
Also Called: Champion Plastics Div
220 Clifton Blvd (07011-3695)
PHONE..................973 777-9400
Fax: 800 526-1238
Melvin Fischman, *President*
Arnold Fischman, *Vice Pres*
Erwin Blum, *Purchasing*
John Callahan, *Sales Mgr*
Kelli Terrazzino, *Sales Associate*
▲ **EMP:** 140
SQ FT: 135,000

SALES (est): 44.5MM **Privately Held**
WEB: www.xlplastics.com
SIC: 2673 3082 Plastic bags: made from
purchased materials; tubes, unsupported
plastic

(G-1746)
ZENIA PHARMA LLC
575 Grove St Unit F1 (07013-3178)
PHONE..................973 246-9718
Aurelije Zovko, *Principal*
EMP: 5 EST: 2007
SALES (est): 479.2K **Privately Held**
SIC: 2834 Pharmaceutical preparations

(G-1747)
ZIGGY SNACK FOODS LLC
200 Clifton Blvd Ste 1 (07011-3652)
PHONE..................917 662-6038
Joel Draber, *Mng Member*
Leonid Rofin,
Zigman Sigmond Smitler,
EMP: 30
SQ FT: 20,400
SALES (est): 2.5MM **Privately Held**
SIC: 5963 2096 Snacks, direct sales; pop-
corn, already popped (except candy cov-
ered)

(G-1748)
ZOAG LLC
4305 Harcourt Rd (07013-2691)
PHONE..................862 591-2969
Zoltan Hetzer, *Mng Member*
▲ **EMP:** 6
SALES (est): 620.7K **Privately Held**
SIC: 3965 Fasteners, buttons, needles &
pins

Clinton
Hunterdon County

(G-1749)
APPLIED VOICE SPEECH TECH INC
9 Cypress Ct (08809-2614)
PHONE..................949 699-2300
Susan York, *Branch Mgr*
EMP: 35
SALES (corp-wide): 26.8MM **Privately Held**
SIC: 7372 Prepackaged software
PA: Applied Voice & Speech Technologies,
Inc.
27042 Towne Centre Dr # 200
Foothill Ranch CA 92610
949 699-2300

(G-1750)
GREENROCK RECYCLING LLC
3 Frontage Rd (08809)
PHONE..................908 713-0008
Brian Plushanski, *Owner*
EMP: 6
SALES (est): 147.1K **Privately Held**
SIC: 3271 Concrete block & brick

(G-1751)
GULBRANDSEN TECHNOLOGIES INC (PA)
Also Called: Gulbrandsen Chemicals
2 Main St (08809-1328)
P.O. Box 5523 (08809-5523)
PHONE..................908 735-5458
Donald Gulbrandsen, *CEO*
Peder L Gulbrandsen, *President*
Dave Drolinger, *Vice Pres*
Fredrika Gulbrandsen, *Vice Pres*
Thomas Madsen, *Opers Mgr*
▼ **EMP:** 40
SQ FT: 2,000
SALES (est): 20.4MM **Privately Held**
SIC: 2899 Chemical preparations

(G-1752)
MED-CON TECH LTD LBLTY CO
24 E Main St Unit 5033 (08809-7006)
PHONE..................888 654-0856
Anthony Londino, *CEO*
EMP: 4
SALES (est): 147K **Privately Held**
SIC: 2759 Schedule, ticket & tag printing &
engraving

(G-1753)
PHILLIPS COMPANIES INC (PA)
7 Frontage Rd (08809-1293)
PHONE...............................973 483-4124
Kenneth Phillips, *President*
Michael Sprague, *Vice Pres*
▼ **EMP:** 100
SALES (est): 11MM **Privately Held**
SIC: 3273 3271 Ready-mixed concrete;
concrete block & brick

(G-1754)
SIERRA VIDEO SYSTEMS
6 State Route 173 (08809-1269)
P.O. Box 2462, Grass Valley CA (95945-2462)
PHONE...............................530 478-1000
Fax: 530 478-1105
Adel Ghanem, *President*
David Bright, *Vice Pres*
▲ **EMP:** 44
SQ FT: 28,500
SALES (est): 6.4MM **Privately Held**
WEB: www.sierravideo.com
SIC: 3651 Household audio & video equipment

(G-1755)
SUNFLOWER SEED
38 Old Highway 22 (08809-1305)
PHONE...............................908 735-3822
Edith Stern, *Owner*
EMP: 4
SALES (est): 348.3K **Privately Held**
SIC: 2833 Vitamins, natural or synthetic;
bulk, uncompounded

Closter
Bergen County

(G-1756)
ATLAS WOODWORKING INC
15 Naugle St (07624-1206)
PHONE...............................201 784-1949
Fax: 201 784-7706
Kenneth J Ewald, *President*
Shirl Ewald, *Vice Pres*
EMP: 9
SQ FT: 5,000
SALES (est): 2MM **Privately Held**
SIC: 3553 Cabinet makers' machinery

(G-1757)
EN TECH CORP
91 Ruckman Rd Ste 1 (07624-2118)
PHONE...............................201 784-1034
Eugene Camali, *Branch Mgr*
EMP: 15
SALES (corp-wide): 7.8MM **Privately Held**
SIC: 3321 Sewer pipe, cast iron
PA: En Tech Corp
91 Ruckman Rd
Closter NJ 07624
718 389-2058

(G-1758)
EN TECH CORP (PA)
Also Called: Manhattan Gunite
91 Ruckman Rd (07624-2117)
PHONE...............................718 389-2058
Eugene Camali, *President*
EMP: 17
SQ FT: 8,000
SALES (est): 7.8MM **Privately Held**
SIC: 3321 Sewer pipe, cast iron

(G-1759)
H RITANI LLC
101 Carlson Ct (07624-1336)
PHONE...............................888 974-8264
Harout Aghjayan,
Ani Aghjayan,
▲ **EMP:** 20
SALES (est): 2.5MM **Privately Held**
WEB: www.ritani.com
SIC: 3911 Jewelry, precious metal

(G-1760)
HOME ORGANIZATION LLC
570 Piermont Rd Ste 136 (07624-3100)
PHONE...............................201 351-2121
Aviad Stark, *Mng Member*

EMP: 11
SQ FT: 400
SALES (est): 1.6MM **Privately Held**
SIC: 3089 4813 Organizers for closets,
drawers, etc.: plastic;

(G-1761)
INTECH POWERCORE CORPORATION
250 Herbert Ave (07624-1333)
PHONE...............................201 767-8066
George Bartosch, *President*
EMP: 8 **EST:** 2012
SQ FT: 3,800
SALES (est): 773.2K **Privately Held**
SIC: 3569 3537 Lubricating equipment; tables, lift: hydraulic

(G-1762)
J A MACHINE & TOOL CO INC
84 Herbert Ave (07624-1313)
PHONE...............................201 767-1308
Fax: 201 767-3447
Andrew Petrinic, *President*
Jimmy Petrinic, *Corp Secy*
EMP: 11 **EST:** 1962
SQ FT: 100,000
SALES (est): 1.7MM **Privately Held**
SIC: 3545 3728 Precision tools, machinists'; aircraft parts & equipment

(G-1763)
LUXURY AND TRASH LTD LBLTY CO
Also Called: L & T
1 Closter Cmns 258 (07624-3113)
P.O. Box 939, Alpine (07620-0939)
PHONE...............................201 315-4018
Maureen D Ben Sadigh,
Maureen Ben Sadigh,
EMP: 5
SQ FT: 1,000
SALES: 5MM **Privately Held**
SIC: 2331 2326 Women's & misses'
blouses & shirts; men's & boys' work
clothing

(G-1764)
MORRISON PRESS INC
10 Mckinley St Ste 3 (07624-2727)
PHONE...............................201 488-4848
Fax: 201 488-8415
Irene Morrison, *President*
Jacklyn Morrison, *Treasurer*
Madelyn Morrison, *Admin Sec*
EMP: 10 **EST:** 1920
SQ FT: 3,000
SALES (est): 1.6MM **Privately Held**
WEB: www.morrisonpress.com
SIC: 2752 Commercial printing, offset

(G-1765)
RETROGRAPHICS PUBLISHING INC
3 Reuten Dr (07624-2123)
PHONE...............................201 501-0505
Norman Lavine, *President*
Eric Caren, *Vice Pres*
EMP: 4
SALES (est): 340K **Privately Held**
SIC: 2621 5199 Catalog, magazine &
newsprint papers; gifts & novelties

(G-1766)
SPECTRUM GLASS LLC
360 Homans Ave (07624-2948)
PHONE...............................201 750-1251
Anthony Sorrentino,
Linda Rocco,
EMP: 4
SQ FT: 3,000
SALES (est): 500.2K **Privately Held**
SIC: 3211 3353 Flat glass; aluminum
sheet, plate & foil

(G-1767)
VENTURE STATIONERS INC
570 Piermont Rd (07624-3100)
PHONE...............................212 288-7235
Jamel Ezra, *President*
Effy Barmoshe, *COO*
Joseph Sheena, *Vice Pres*
Benjamin Ezra, *Admin Sec*
EMP: 27
SQ FT: 27,000

SALES (est): 2.8MM **Privately Held**
SIC: 5943 5948 3999 Office forms & supplies; luggage & leather goods stores;
fruits, artificial & preserved

(G-1768)
VINTAGE PRINT GALLERY
3 Reuten Dr (07624-2123)
PHONE...............................201 501-0505
Norman Lavine, *Principal*
▲ **EMP:** 9
SALES (est): 767.9K **Privately Held**
SIC: 2752 Commercial printing, offset

Collingswood
Camden County

(G-1769)
AINSWORTH MEDIA
Also Called: Retrospect The For Local News
732 Haddon Ave (08108-3712)
P.O. Box 296 (08108-0296)
PHONE...............................856 854-1400
Fax: 856 854-8790
Brett Ainsworth, *Owner*
EMP: 6 **EST:** 1970
SQ FT: 4,500
SALES (est): 468.9K **Privately Held**
SIC: 2711 Newspapers, publishing & printing

(G-1770)
GLAXOSMITHKLINE LLC
505 S Vineyard Blvd (08108-1321)
PHONE...............................856 952-6023
Elizabeth Moeller, *Principal*
EMP: 26
SALES (corp-wide): 39.8B **Privately Held**
SIC: 2834 Pharmaceutical preparations
HQ: Glaxosmithkline Llc
5 Crescent Dr
Philadelphia PA 19112
215 751-4000

(G-1771)
JUBILI BEAD & YARN SHOPPE
713 Haddon Ave (08108-3711)
PHONE...............................856 858-7844
Judy Weinstien, *Owner*
EMP: 6
SALES (est): 538.8K **Privately Held**
WEB: www.jubilibeadsandyarns.com
SIC: 2299 5947 5999 Yarns, specialty &
novelty; gift shop; miscellaneous retail
stores

(G-1772)
MCMUNN ASSOCIATES
900 Haddon Ave Ste 302 (08108-2127)
PHONE...............................856 858-3440
Fax: 856 858-5117
Larry McMunn, *President*
Deborah Stephens, *Vice Pres*
EMP: 25
SALES (est): 2.2MM **Privately Held**
SIC: 2721 Statistical reports (periodicals):
publishing & printing

(G-1773)
SEVERINO PASTA MFG CO INC
110 Haddon Ave (08108-1000)
PHONE...............................856 854-3716
Fax: 856 854-6098
Peter Severino, *President*
Louis Severino, *Vice Pres*
Joseph Severino, *Opers Staff*
Cathy Aversa, *Bookkeeper*
Angelica Diodato, *Mktg Dir*
EMP: 22
SQ FT: 7,000
SALES (est): 7.7MM **Privately Held**
SIC: 5149 5499 2098 2038 Pasta & rice;
health & dietetic food stores; macaroni &
spaghetti; frozen specialties

(G-1774)
TECHSETTERS INC
900 Haddon Ave Ste 300 (08108-2112)
PHONE...............................856 240-7905
John Rogosich, *President*
Patricia Anton, *President*
Mildred Jaggard, *Vice Pres*
EMP: 20

SALES (est): 1.9MM **Privately Held**
WEB: www.techsetters.com
SIC: 2731 7336 2791 Books: publishing &
printing; commercial art & graphic design;
typesetting

Cologne
Atlantic County

(G-1775)
ABSECON MILLS INC
901 W Aloe St (08213)
PHONE...............................609 965-5373
Fax: 609 965-7474
Randolph S Taylor, *President*
Douglass A Taylor, *COO*
David Adair, *Exec VP*
▲ **EMP:** 125
SQ FT: 150,000
SALES (est): 20.9MM **Privately Held**
WEB: www.absecon.com
SIC: 2211 2221 Upholstery fabrics, cotton;
broadwoven fabric mills, manmade

Colonia
Middlesex County

(G-1776)
AM CRUZ INTERNATIONAL LLC
13 New York Ave (07067-1741)
PHONE...............................732 340-0066
Lou Cordeiro,
EMP: 5 **EST:** 1970
SQ FT: 800
SALES (est): 560K **Privately Held**
SIC: 3559 Refinery, chemical processing &
similar machinery

(G-1777)
BMA OF COLONIA
1250 State Rt 27 (07067-3416)
PHONE...............................732 382-7333
Sandra Nibbilink, *Manager*
Rosanna Prado, *Manager*
EMP: 24
SALES (est): 1.9MM **Privately Held**
SIC: 3841 8093 Hemodialysis apparatus;
specialty outpatient clinics

(G-1778)
SIGN ENGINEERS INC
13 New York Ave (07067-1741)
PHONE...............................732 382-4224
Jitendra Royal, *President*
Matha Royal, *Admin Sec*
EMP: 5
SALES (est): 360K **Privately Held**
SIC: 3993 Signs & advertising specialties

Colts Neck
Monmouth County

(G-1779)
A KESSLER KREATION INC
31 Continental Ct (07722-1408)
PHONE...............................732 431-2468
Leonard Kessler, *Principal*
EMP: 4 **EST:** 2007
SALES (est): 358.2K **Privately Held**
SIC: 3499 5199 Novelties & giftware, including trophies; gifts & novelties

(G-1780)
CAMTEC INDUSTRIES INC
28 Saddle Ridge Rd (07722-1035)
PHONE...............................732 332-9800
Anthony Mauro, *Owner*
Carol Mauro, *Principal*
EMP: 15
SALES (est): 1.7MM **Privately Held**
WEB: www.camtecindustries.com
SIC: 3449 3089 Miscellaneous metalwork;
plastic hardware & building products

▲ = Import ▼=Export
◆ =Import/Export

(G-1781)
COINING MANUFACTURING LLC
11 Lafayette Ky (07722-1774)
P.O. Box 142 (07722-0142)
PHONE..................................973 253-0500
Courtney Chronley, *General Mgr*
EMP: 40 EST: 2014
SALES (est): 6MM Privately Held
SIC: 3469 Stamping metal for the trade

(G-1782)
COLT MEDIA INC
Also Called: Clover Hill Coffee Co
4 Wedgewood Ave (07722-1137)
PHONE..................................732 946-3276
George Schneider, *President*
EMP: 4
SALES: 500K Privately Held
SIC: 2731 Books: publishing only

(G-1783)
D&S FISHERIES LLC
6 Birch Ln (07722-2018)
PHONE..................................914 438-3197
Michael Sarapochillo, *President*
Michael Lawrence Sarapochillo, *President*
Lawrence Sarapochillo, *Vice Pres*
EMP: 4
SALES (est): 292.4K Privately Held
SIC: 3732 Fishing boats: lobster, crab, oyster, etc.: small

(G-1784)
FERLAND INDUSTRIES INC
14 Evergreen Ln (07722-1276)
PHONE..................................732 246-3200
Jesus Ferro, *President*
Elda Ferro, *Vice Pres*
▲ EMP: 6
SQ FT: 120,000
SALES (est): 841.4K Privately Held
WEB: www.ferlandindustries.com
SIC: 2295 Coated fabrics, not rubberized

(G-1785)
FERRO INDUSTRIES INCORPORATED
14 Evergreen Ln (07722-1276)
PHONE..................................732 246-3200
Fax: 732 246-7417
EMP: 45
SQ FT: 110,000
SALES (est): 6.1MM Privately Held
SIC: 3651 Mfg Home Audio/Video Equipment

(G-1786)
FOLIO ART GLASS INC
73 State Route 34 S (07722-1714)
PHONE..................................732 431-0044
Fax: 732 431-1653
Barbara Folio, *President*
Raymond Folio, *Vice Pres*
EMP: 5
SQ FT: 3,000
SALES: 500K Privately Held
WEB: www.theforgeonline.com
SIC: 3231 3229 5719 Stained glass: made from purchased glass; glass furnishings & accessories; glassware

(G-1787)
GRECO INDUSTRIES LLC
7 Colts Gait Ln (07722-1468)
P.O. Box 547 (07722-0547)
PHONE..................................732 919-6200
Camille M Greco, *Principal*
EMP: 9
SALES (est): 1.4MM Privately Held
SIC: 3089 Garbage containers, plastic

(G-1788)
HERITAGE PUBLISHING
440 State Route 34 Ste 2 (07722-2525)
PHONE..................................732 747-7770
Fax: 732 414-1736
EMP: 4
SALES (est): 320.5K Privately Held
SIC: 2741 Miscellaneous publishing

(G-1789)
LASER DIM GRAPHICS & PRTG INC
Also Called: American Printing
2 Parkwood Ln (07722-2116)
PHONE..................................732 821-9000
Fax: 732 821-0197
Syed Asghar, *President*
Jeff Naqui, *Vice Pres*
EMP: 13
SALES (est): 1.7MM Privately Held
WEB: www.amprc.com
SIC: 2752 7334 2791 2789 Commercial printing, lithographic; photocopying & duplicating services; typesetting; bookbinding & related work

(G-1790)
PMM INC
11 Lafayette Ky (07722-1774)
P.O. Box 142 (07722-0142)
PHONE..................................908 692-1465
Ed Fairful, *CEO*
▲ EMP: 30
SALES: 5MM Privately Held
SIC: 3412 Metal barrels, drums & pails

(G-1791)
R R J CO INC
13 Provincial Pl (07722-1152)
PHONE..................................732 544-1514
Fax: 732 450-8180
Ronald H Holford Jr, *President*
Jeffrey E Holford, *Vice Pres*
Dave Osbourne, *Vice Pres*
▲ EMP: 35
SQ FT: 12,000
SALES (est): 3.7MM Privately Held
WEB: www.rrjco.com
SIC: 3672 Printed circuit boards

(G-1792)
SQUASH BEEF LLC
12 Downing Hill Ln (07722-1415)
PHONE..................................917 577-8723
Anthony Frassetti, *President*
EMP: 5
SALES: 500K Privately Held
SIC: 2741

(G-1793)
TRI G MANUFACTURING LLC
Also Called: Tri-G Manufacturing
8 Iroquois Ct (07722-1821)
PHONE..................................732 460-1881
Justin J Sallusto,
EMP: 10
SALES (est): 603.3K Privately Held
SIC: 2399 Horse & pet accessories, textile

(G-1794)
WESTROCK CP LLC
21 Millpond Ln (07722-1563)
PHONE..................................732 866-1890
EMP: 88
SALES (corp-wide): 14.8B Publicly Held
WEB: www.smurfit-stone.com
SIC: 2631 Paperboard mills
HQ: Westrock Cp, Llc
504 Thrasher St
Norcross GA 30071

Columbia
Warren County

(G-1795)
10-31 INCORPORATED
Also Called: Art Display Essentials
2 W Crisman Rd (07832-2709)
PHONE..................................908 496-4946
Fax: 908 496-4956
William Stender, *President*
Eloise Wierzbicki, *Sales Staff*
▲ EMP: 23
SQ FT: 18,000
SALES: 6.4MM Privately Held
WEB: www.10-31.com
SIC: 2541 2434 2511 5961 Cabinets, except refrigerated: show, display, etc.: wood; wood kitchen cabinets; wood household furniture; catalog & mail-order houses

(G-1796)
BROOK HOLLOW WINERY LLC
594 State Hwy 94 (07832)
PHONE..................................908 496-8200
Paul Ritter,
EMP: 5
SALES (est): 417.7K Privately Held
SIC: 2084 Wines

(G-1797)
GENERAL STAMPING CO INC
Also Called: GSC
309 State Route 94 (07832-2761)
PHONE..................................973 627-9500
Fax: 973 627-6012
EMP: 13
SQ FT: 12,500
SALES (est): 3.2MM Privately Held
SIC: 3469 Mfg Metal Stampings

(G-1798)
IMPERIAL MACHINE & TOOL CO (PA)
8 W Crisman Rd (07832-2709)
PHONE..................................908 496-8100
Fax: 908 496-8102
George H Joest, *CEO*
Christian M Joest, *President*
Mike Clifford, *Opers Staff*
Jeffrey Peterson, *Purchasing*
Tom Golembeski, *CFO*
▼ EMP: 45 EST: 1943
SQ FT: 30,000
SALES (est): 4.2MM Privately Held
SIC: 3825 3599 Instruments to measure electricity; custom machinery

(G-1799)
INTERTEST INC (PA)
303 State Route 94 Ste 1 (07832-2841)
PHONE..................................908 496-8008
Fax: 908 496-8004
Bill Habermann, *President*
Thomas Daly, *Vice Pres*
Deanna Daly, *Cust Mgr*
Brian Hamilton, *Sales Engr*
Stephen Hamilton, *Sales Staff*
EMP: 32
SQ FT: 10,000
SALES (est): 20.2MM Privately Held
SIC: 5084 5046 3861 Industrial machinery & equipment; commercial equipment; cameras & related equipment

(G-1800)
RICKLYN CO INC
43 Centerville Rd (07832-2201)
PHONE..................................908 689-6770
Fax: 908 689-5117
Kevin Nook, *CEO*
Suzanne Nook, *Admin Sec*
EMP: 6 EST: 1963
SALES (est): 851.9K Privately Held
SIC: 7692 3444 Welding repair; sheet metalwork

Columbus
Burlington County

(G-1801)
CORONIS BUILDING SYSTEMS INC
92 Columbus Jobstown Rd (08022-1327)
PHONE..................................609 261-2200
Fax: 609 723-6700
Emanuel A Coronis Jr, *President*
Magdalene Coronis, *Corp Secy*
▼ EMP: 20
SQ FT: 17,000
SALES (est): 4.4MM Privately Held
WEB: www.trussframe.com
SIC: 3441 Building components, structural steel

(G-1802)
CUPCAKE CELEBRATIONS
107 Paddock Dr (08022-9726)
PHONE..................................973 885-0826
EMP: 4
SALES (est): 158.9K Privately Held
SIC: 2051 Bread, cake & related products

(G-1803)
DRAZTIC DESIGNS LLC
Also Called: Tri Tech Telecom
205 Petticoat Bridge Rd (08022-1406)
PHONE..................................609 678-4200
David Camp, *Mng Member*
EMP: 50
SQ FT: 1,200
SALES: 1.7MM Privately Held
SIC: 3663 Radio & TV communications equipment

(G-1804)
K2 MILLWORK LTD LIABILITY CO
Also Called: K 2 Mill Work
2180 Hedding Rd (08022-2069)
PHONE..................................609 379-6411
Michael W Kocubinski, *Principal*
EMP: 4
SALES (est): 199.5K Privately Held
SIC: 2431 Millwork

(G-1805)
MELTON SALES & SERVICE (PA)
Also Called: Melton Industries
13 Petticoat Bridge Rd (08022-1401)
PHONE..................................609 699-4800
John F Melton, *Ch of Bd*
Amber Herbert, *Accounts Mgr*
Jeffrey Pan, *Info Tech Mgr*
EMP: 40
SQ FT: 70,000
SALES: 10MM Privately Held
SIC: 3812 3519 Defense systems & equipment; diesel engine rebuilding

---

Cookstown
Burlington County

(G-1806)
DRYTECH INC
54 Wrghtstown Cookstown Rd (08511-1020)
P.O. Box 128 (08511-0128)
PHONE..................................609 758-1794
Fax: 609 758-1774
Tony Jones, *Principal*
▲ EMP: 25
SQ FT: 6,000
SALES (est): 8MM Privately Held
SIC: 3585 3769 3728 5084 Refrigeration & heating equipment; guided missile & space vehicle parts & auxiliary equipment; aircraft parts & equipment; food industry machinery

(G-1807)
EXPORT MANAGEMENT CONSULTANTS
Also Called: EMC Aviation
54 Wrghtstown Cookstown Rd (08511-1020)
P.O. Box 249 (08511-0249)
PHONE..................................609 758-1166
Fax: 609 758-1879
Anthony Jones, *President*
EMP: 25
SQ FT: 16,500
SALES: 1.8MM Privately Held
WEB: www.drytechinc.com
SIC: 3728 Aircraft assemblies, subassemblies & parts

(G-1808)
RALPH CLAYTON & SONS LLC
Also Called: Clayton Concrete
58 Goldman Dr (08511-1022)
PHONE..................................800 662-3044
Fax: 609 758-3881
William Gangel, *Manager*
EMP: 25
SALES (corp-wide): 96.7MM Privately Held
WEB: www.claytonco.com
SIC: 3273 Ready-mixed concrete
PA: Ralph Clayton & Sons L.L.C.
1355 Campus Pkwy
Wall Township NJ 07753
732 363-1995

G
E
O
G
R
A
P
H
I
C

Cranbury
Middlesex County

(G-1809)
AKORN INC
5 Cedarbrook Dr (08512-3606)
PHONE..................................609 662-9100
Saeed Khan, *Branch Mgr*
EMP: 32
SALES (corp-wide): 841MM **Publicly Held**
SIC: 2834 Pharmaceutical preparations
PA: Akorn, Inc.
1925 W Field Ct Ste 300
Lake Forest IL 60045
847 279-6100

(G-1810)
AMERINDIA TECHNOLOGIES INC
101 Interchange Plz # 201 (08512-3716)
PHONE..................................609 664-2224
Arun Mehta, *President*
Neena Mehta, *Vice Pres*
Rajesh Mittal, *Vice Pres*
Pranshi Gupta, *Finance Dir*
Aabha Sharma, *Manager*
EMP: 35
SQ FT: 3,000
SALES (est): 2.4MM **Privately Held**
WEB: www.amerindia.net
SIC: 1731 7371 7372 7373 Safety & security specialization; computer software systems analysis & design, custom; computer software development & applications; application computer software; systems software development services

(G-1811)
AMICUS THERAPEUTICS INC (PA)
1 Cedarbrook Dr (08512-3618)
PHONE..................................609 662-2000
Fax: 609 662-2001
John F Crowley, *Ch of Bd*
Bradley L Campbell, *President*
Kurt J W Andrews, *Senior VP*
Michael C Diem, *Senior VP*
Daphne Quimi, *Senior VP*
EMP: 134
SQ FT: 90,000
SALES: 36.9MM **Publicly Held**
SIC: 2834 Pharmaceutical preparations

(G-1812)
ANKUR INTERNATIONAL INC
Also Called: Marble and Granite Design Ctr
1206 Cranbury S River Rd (08512)
PHONE..................................609 409-6009
Fax: 609 409-6005
Binod Toshniwal, *President*
Anita Tushinal, *Principal*
Naresh Challa, *Marketing Mgr*
▲ EMP: 12
SQ FT: 45,000
SALES (est): 3.5MM **Privately Held**
WEB: www.ankurinc.com
SIC: 5032 1411 Granite building stone; marble building stone; dimension stone

(G-1813)
ANTRONIX INC (PA)
440 Forsgate Dr (08512-3518)
PHONE..................................609 860-0160
Daniel Tang, *President*
Neil Tang, *Exec VP*
Suphie Tang, *Vice Pres*
Emily Bennett, *Opers Staff*
Christine Chen, *Human Res Mgr*
▲ EMP: 1500 EST: 1980
SQ FT: 36,500
SALES (est): 182.5MM **Privately Held**
WEB: www.antronix.net
SIC: 3663 5063 Cable television equipment; electrical apparatus & equipment

(G-1814)
BERRY GLOBAL INC
4 Aurora Dr Ste 403 (08512-3262)
PHONE..................................609 395-4199
EMP: 127 **Publicly Held**
WEB: www.6sens.com

SIC: 3089 3081 Plastic containers, except foam; cups, plastic, except foam; bottle caps, molded plastic; caps, plastic; unsupported plastics film & sheet
HQ: Berry Global, Inc.
101 Oakley St
Evansville IN 47710
812 424-2904

(G-1815)
BRACCO RESEARCH USA INC
4c Cedarbrook Dr (08512-3612)
PHONE..................................609 514-2517
Fax: 609 514-2446
Michael F Tweedle, *President*
Thomas Nye, *Manager*
EMP: 46
SQ FT: 30,000
SALES (est): 8.6MM **Privately Held**
WEB: www.bru.bracco.com
SIC: 2834 Pharmaceutical preparations
HQ: Bracco U.S.A. Inc.
259 Prospect Plains Rd
Monroe Township NJ 08831
609 514-2200

(G-1816)
BROWN AND PERKINS INC
1193 Cranbury S River Rd (08512)
P.O. Box 412 (08512-0412)
PHONE..................................609 655-1150
Fax: 609 655-1173
Edward T Comly II, *President*
John C Comly, *Vice Pres*
William F Comly, *Treasurer*
Bill Comly, *Sales Staff*
Dave Vactor, *Sales Associate*
▲ EMP: 18
SQ FT: 28,800
SALES (est): 4.6MM **Privately Held**
SIC: 3496 Slings, lifting: made from purchased wire

(G-1817)
BRUNNQUELL IRON WORKS INC
2557 Us Highway 130 Ste 3 (08512-3509)
PHONE..................................609 409-6101
Fax: 609 409-4242
David G Brunnquell, *President*
Gerard J Brunnquell, *Treasurer*
Mary Bellach, *Controller*
EMP: 35 EST: 1925
SALES (est): 5.6MM **Privately Held**
WEB: www.brunnquellironworks.com
SIC: 3441 Fabricated structural metal

(G-1818)
CABLETENNA CORP
Also Called: Antronics
440 Forsgate Dr (08512-3518)
PHONE..................................609 395-9400
Fax: 609 395-1927
Daniel Tang, *President*
Suphie Tang, *Vice Pres*
EMP: 9
SQ FT: 24,000
SALES (est): 880K **Privately Held**
SIC: 3663 5063 Cable television equipment; electrical apparatus & equipment

(G-1819)
CABOKI LLC
3 Corporate Dr (08512-3642)
PHONE..................................609 642-2108
Linda Caboki, *Principal*
▲ EMP: 4 EST: 2012
SALES (est): 240K **Privately Held**
SIC: 2844 Hair preparations, including shampoos

(G-1820)
CARACO PHARMACEUTICAL LABS
270 Prospect Plains Rd (08512-3605)
PHONE..................................609 819-8200
EMP: 7
SALES (est): 506.5K **Privately Held**
SIC: 2834 Pharmaceutical preparations

(G-1821)
CHURCH & DWIGHT CO INC
326 Cranbury Half Acre Rd (08512-5010)
PHONE..................................609 655-6101
Tom Bennis, *Branch Mgr*
EMP: 14

SALES (corp-wide): 3.7B **Publicly Held**
WEB: www.churchdwight.com
SIC: 2812 Sodium bicarbonate
PA: Church & Dwight Co., Inc.
500 Charles Ewing Blvd
Ewing NJ 08628
609 806-1200

(G-1822)
CISPHARMA INC
1212 Cranbury S River Rd (08512)
PHONE..................................609 235-9807
Mukesh Desai, *President*
Ravi Annamaneni, *Chairman*
Peddanna Gumudavelli, *Vice Pres*
Srini Paruchuri, *Vice Pres*
Hasmukh Patel, *Vice Pres*
▲ EMP: 13
SALES (est): 5.2MM **Privately Held**
SIC: 2834 Pharmaceutical preparations

(G-1823)
CLAYTON MANUFACTURING COMPANY
Also Called: Clayton Industries
10 S River Rd Ste 6 (08512-3615)
PHONE..................................609 409-9400
Fax: 609 409-9435
Alan Ulbrecht, *Sales Staff*
Richard Slynn, *Manager*
Gary Wells, *Manager*
EMP: 13
SALES (corp-wide): 114.2MM **Privately Held**
WEB: www.claytonindustries.com
SIC: 3569 Generators: steam, liquid oxygen or nitrogen
PA: Clayton Manufacturing Company
17477 Hurley St
City Of Industry CA 91744
626 443-9381

(G-1824)
CMIC CMO USA CORPORATION
Cedar Brook Corporate Ctr (08512)
PHONE..................................609 395-9700
Kunihide Ichikawa, *President*
Gary Wada, *Vice Pres*
Pramila Agrawal, *QC Mgr*
Timothy Bost, *Engineer*
Dianne Repko, *Manager*
EMP: 41
SALES (est): 17.2MM
SALES (corp-wide): 596.4MM **Privately Held**
SIC: 2834 8731 Pharmaceutical preparations; biotechnical research, commercial
HQ: Cmic Co., Ltd.
1-1-1, Shibaura
Minato-Ku TKY 105-0
367 798-000

(G-1825)
COMM PORT TECHNOLOGIES INC
1 Corporate Dr Ste F (08512-3635)
PHONE..................................732 738-8780
Fax: 732 238-8781
Manny Patel, *President*
Channi Shah, *Vice Pres*
▲ EMP: 2
SQ FT: 10,000
SALES: 4MM **Privately Held**
WEB: www.comm-port.com
SIC: 1731 3663 5731 Fiber optic cable installation; radio & TV communications equipment; video cameras, recorders & accessories

(G-1826)
CONSOLIDATED CONT HOLDINGS LLC
Also Called: Consolidate Cntiner Holdings NJ
4 Pleasant Hill Rd (08512-3637)
PHONE..................................609 655-0855
Sarah Girgis, *Manager*
EMP: 70
SALES (corp-wide): 6.6B **Privately Held**
SIC: 3089 Plastic containers, except foam
HQ: Consolidated Container Holdings Llc
3101 Towercreek Pkwy Se P
Atlanta GA 30339
678 742-4600

(G-1827)
COOPER LIGHTING LLC
1 Broadway Rd (08512-5423)
PHONE..................................609 395-4277
Gary Gredell, *Principal*
EMP: 100 **Privately Held**
WEB: www.corelite.com
SIC: 3645 3646 Residential lighting fixtures; commercial indusl & institutional electric lighting fixtures
HQ: Cooper Lighting, Llc
1121 Highway 74 S
Peachtree City GA 30269
770 486-4800

(G-1828)
DATO COMPANY INC (PA)
Also Called: Sir Speedy
8 Plainsboro Rd (08512-3233)
PHONE..................................732 225-2272
Fax: 732 225-2448
Robert Chido, *President*
▲ EMP: 7
SQ FT: 2,000
SALES (est): 1.4MM **Privately Held**
SIC: 2752 Commercial printing, lithographic

(G-1829)
DOW JONES & COMPANY INC
4300 N Rt 1 & Ridge Rd (08512)
PHONE..................................609 520-4000
Fax: 609 520-4775
Mark Taylor, *Editor*
Bart Ziegler, *Editor*
Peter Fritsch, *Chief*
Henry Osei, *Maint Spvr*
Denise Weir, *Senior Buyer*
EMP: 15
SALES (corp-wide): 9B **Publicly Held**
SIC: 2711 Newspapers, publishing & printing
HQ: Dow Jones & Company, Inc.
1211 Avenue Of The Americ
New York NY 10036
609 627-2999

(G-1830)
E-BEAM SERVICES INC
118 Melrich Rd (08512-3595)
PHONE..................................513 933-0031
Fax: 609 655-3052
Peter Tuzzolo, *Manager*
EMP: 30
SALES (corp-wide): 5MM **Privately Held**
WEB: www.e-beamservices.com
SIC: 7389 3699 2821 Product sterilization service; electrical equipment & supplies; plastics materials & resins
PA: E-Beam Services, Inc.
270 Duffy Ave Ste H
Hicksville NY 11801
516 622-1422

(G-1831)
ENDO PHRMACEUTICALS VALERA INC
8 Clarke Dr (08512-3617)
PHONE..................................609 235-3230
James C Gale, *Ch of Bd*
David Holveck, *President*
Petr F Kuzma, *Vice Pres*
Jeremy D Middleton, *Vice Pres*
Andrew T Drechsler, *CFO*
EMP: 14
SQ FT: 21,274
SALES (est): 3.1MM **Privately Held**
SIC: 2834 Pharmaceutical preparations; drugs affecting neoplasms & endrocine systems; drugs acting on the gastrointestinal or genitourinary system
HQ: Endo Pharmaceuticals, Inc.
1400 Atwater Dr
Malvern PA 19355
484 216-0000

(G-1832)
EXEMPLIFY BIOPHARMA INC
3000 Eastpark Blvd (08512-3532)
PHONE..................................732 500-3208
Yadan Chen, *President*
EMP: 1
SALES (est): 1.3MM **Privately Held**
SIC: 2834 Pharmaceutical preparations

(G-1833)
FBM BAKING MACHINES INC
1 Corporate Dr Ste D (08512-3635)
PHONE..................................609 860-0577
Fax: 609 860-0579
Frank Signorile, *President*
▲ EMP: 7
SQ FT: 15,000
SALES: 3MM **Privately Held**
WEB: www.fbmbakingmachines.com
SIC: 3556 Food products machinery

(G-1834)
GIVAUDAN FLAVORS CORPORATION ✪
6 Santa Fe Way (08512-3288)
PHONE..................................973 463-8192
Joanna Holmes, *Manager*
EMP: 5 EST: 2017
SALES (est): 773.4K **Privately Held**
SIC: 2869 Flavors or flavoring materials, synthetic

(G-1835)
GIVAUDAN FLAVORS CORPORATION
Spicetec Flavors & Seasonings
6 Santa Fe Way (08512-3288)
PHONE..................................609 409-6200
Joanna Holmes, *Branch Mgr*
EMP: 80
SALES (corp-wide): 5.1B **Privately Held**
WEB: www.conagra.com
SIC: 2087 Flavoring extracts & syrups
HQ: Givaudan Flavors Corporation
1199 Edison Dr
Cincinnati OH 45216
513 948-8000

(G-1836)
HALSTED CORPORATION
Also Called: Halsted Bag
51 Commerce Dr Ste 3 (08512-3531)
PHONE..................................201 333-0670
Michael Murphy, *President*
Robert Geraghty, *Vice Pres*
Henry Jaszewski, *Treasurer*
Justin Murphy, *VP Sales*
Patrick Thompson, *Marketing Staff*
◆ EMP: 40 EST: 1876
SQ FT: 40,000
SALES (est): 6.1MM **Privately Held**
WEB: www.halstedbag.com
SIC: 2299 2393 2673 Burlap, jute; canvas bags; plastic bags: made from purchased materials

(G-1837)
ILLINOIS TOOL WORKS INC
Also Called: I T W Covid
32 Commerce Dr Ste 1 (08512-3529)
PHONE..................................609 395-5600
Fax: 609 860-6400
Nick Martino, *Branch Mgr*
EMP: 50
SALES (corp-wide): 14.3B **Publicly Held**
SIC: 2821 2759 Plastics materials & resins; commercial printing
PA: Illinois Tool Works Inc.
155 Harlem Ave
Glenview IL 60025
847 724-7500

(G-1838)
INNOPHOS INC
259 Prospect Plains Rd A (08512-3706)
PHONE..................................973 587-8735
Randolph Gress, *CEO*
Jingwei Mintorovitch, *Research*
EMP: 5
SALES (corp-wide): 722MM **Publicly Held**
SIC: 2819 2874 Industrial inorganic chemicals; phosphates
HQ: Innophos, Inc.
259 Prospect Plains Rd A
Cranbury NJ 08512
609 495-2495

(G-1839)
INNOPHOS HOLDINGS INC (PA)
259 Prospect Plains Rd A (08512-3706)
PHONE..................................609 495-2495
Kim Ann Mink, *President*
Vanessa Herrera, *General Mgr*

Dennis Dean, *Vice Chairman*
Layne Hadley, *COO*
David Lecroy, *Counsel*
EMP: 86
SALES: 722MM **Publicly Held**
SIC: 2874 2819 Phosphatic fertilizers; industrial inorganic chemicals

(G-1840)
INNOPHOS INC (DH)
259 Prospect Plains Rd A (08512-3706)
PHONE..................................609 860-0138
Fax: 609 860-0138
Randolph Gress, *President*
Ricardo Suarez, *COO*
Louis Calvarin PHD, *Vice Pres*
William Farran, *Vice Pres*
Amy Hartzell, *Vice Pres*
◆ EMP: 700
SALES (est): 350.3MM
SALES (corp-wide): 722MM **Publicly Held**
WEB: www.innophos.com
SIC: 2819 Industrial inorganic chemicals
HQ: Innophos Investments Ii, Inc.
259 Prospect Plains Rd
Cranbury NJ 08512
609 495-2495

(G-1841)
INNOPHOS INVESTMENTS II INC (DH)
259 Prospect Plains Rd (08512-3706)
PHONE..................................609 495-2495
Randolph Gress, *Ch of Bd*
Iris Alvarado, *Vice Pres*
Charles Brodheim, *Vice Pres*
William Farran, *Vice Pres*
Mark Feuerbach, *CFO*
EMP: 6 EST: 2012
SALES (est): 350.3MM
SALES (corp-wide): 722MM **Publicly Held**
SIC: 2874 2819 Phosphates; industrial inorganic chemicals
HQ: Innophos Investments Holdings, Inc.
259 Prospect Plains Rd
Cranbury NJ 08512
609 495-2495

(G-1842)
INNOPHOS INVSTMNTS HLDINGS INC (HQ)
259 Prospect Plains Rd (08512-3706)
PHONE..................................609 495-2495
Randy Gress, *President*
William Farran, *Vice Pres*
Wilma Harris, *Vice Pres*
Richard Heyse, *CFO*
Mark Feuerbach, *Treasurer*
EMP: 2
SALES (est): 535.5MM
SALES (corp-wide): 722MM **Publicly Held**
SIC: 2874 2819 Phosphatic fertilizers; industrial inorganic chemicals
PA: Innophos Holdings, Inc.
259 Prospect Plains Rd A
Cranbury NJ 08512
609 495-2495

(G-1843)
IRIS ID SYSTEMS INC
8 Clarke Dr Ste 1 (08512-3617)
PHONE..................................609 819-4747
Fax: 609 819-4736
Charles Koo, *President*
Rami Azzeh, *Regional Mgr*
Tom Dewinter, *Business Mgr*
Monalisa Mazumdar, *Engineer*
Dan Westadt, *Controller*
▲ EMP: 23
SALES (est): 3.9MM **Privately Held**
SIC: 3861 Photographic equipment & supplies

(G-1844)
JAKTOOL LLC
Also Called: Jevek Solutions
259 Prospect Plains Rd (08512-3706)
PHONE..................................609 664-2451
Fax: 732 696-1197
Jeffrey Kinsberg, *President*
Cristy Richards, *Vice Pres*
EMP: 10
SQ FT: 10,100

SALES: 1MM **Privately Held**
SIC: 3841 8711 Surgical & medical instruments; engineering services

(G-1845)
JLI MARKETING & PRINTING CORP
6 Corporate Dr Ste 1 (08512-3616)
PHONE..................................732 828-8877
Fax: 732 828-5368
Charles J Jendrejeski, *President*
Peter Lengyel, *Vice Pres*
EMP: 13
SQ FT: 15,000
SALES (est): 1.8MM **Privately Held**
WEB: www.jlisigns.com
SIC: 2752 Commercial printing, offset

(G-1846)
KEELEY AEROSPACE LTD
2559 Us Highway 130 (08512-3509)
PHONE..................................951 582-2113
Sungtaick Lee, *CEO*
Brian Keeley, *Vice Pres*
EMP: 22
SQ FT: 22,300
SALES (est): 2.6MM
SALES (corp-wide): 4.2B **Privately Held**
WEB: www.kaltd.com
SIC: 3728 7389 Aircraft body & wing assemblies & parts; design services
HQ: Hanwha International Llc
300 Frank W Burr Blvd # 52
Teaneck NJ 07666
201 347-3000

(G-1847)
KLUS PHARMA INC
8 Clarke Dr Ste 4 (08512-3617)
PHONE..................................609 651-4466
EMP: 12
SALES (est): 1.7MM **Privately Held**
SIC: 2834 5122 Druggists' preparations (pharmaceuticals); pharmaceuticals

(G-1848)
KOS PHARMACEUTICALS INC (HQ)
1 Cedarbrook Dr (08512-3618)
PHONE..................................609 495-0500
Fax: 609 495-0920
Adrian Adams, *CEO*
▲ EMP: 19
SALES (est): 47.1MM
SALES (corp-wide): 28.2B **Publicly Held**
WEB: www.kospharm.com
SIC: 2834 Pharmaceutical preparations
PA: Abbvie Inc.
1 N Waukegan Rd
North Chicago IL 60064
847 932-7900

(G-1849)
KRONOS WORLDWIDE INC
5 Cedarbrook Dr Ste 2 (08512-3606)
PHONE..................................609 860-6200
Fax: 609 860-6258
Dr Larry Wigdor, *CEO*
Gregory Swalwell, *Exec VP*
Bob Berthke, *Opers Staff*
Joseph Maas, *Marketing Staff*
EMP: 35
SQ FT: 20,000
SALES (corp-wide): 1.7B **Publicly Held**
SIC: 2816 2899 Titanium dioxide, anatase or rutile (pigments); chemical preparations
PA: Kronos Worldwide, Inc.
5430 Lbj Fwy Ste 1700
Dallas TX 75240
972 233-1700

(G-1850)
KT AMERICA CORP
Also Called: Avanti
2650 Us Highway 130 Ste 1 (08512-3327)
PHONE..................................609 655-5333
Fax: 609 655-8933
Rajiv Toprani, *President*
Ashok Mehta, *Vice Pres*
Ritu Gandhi, *Manager*
▲ EMP: 10
SQ FT: 3,000

SALES (est): 2.4MM **Privately Held**
WEB: www.ktamer.com
SIC: 2221 2393 Polypropylene broadwoven fabrics; textile bags

(G-1851)
LAMITECH INC (DH)
322 Half Acre Rd (08512-3254)
PHONE..................................609 860-8037
Fax: 609 860-8580
Joseph Artiga, *President*
▲ EMP: 34
SQ FT: 120,000
SALES (est): 104.4MM **Privately Held**
SIC: 5113 2631 Paperboard & products; coated paperboard

(G-1852)
LEARNING LINKS-USA INC
26 Haypress Rd (08512-3401)
P.O. Box 326 (08512-0326)
PHONE..................................516 437-9071
Russell Wagner, *President*
Lynda Bradley, *Vice Pres*
EMP: 4
SQ FT: 30,000
SALES (est): 417K **Privately Held**
SIC: 2731 Books: publishing only

(G-1853)
LEGACY CONVERTING INC (PA)
3 Security Dr Ste 301 (08512-3263)
PHONE..................................609 642-7020
Darren Slosberg, *CEO*
Jason Slosberg MD, *President*
Terry Girifalco, *President*
Sirena Carnevale, *Opers Mgr*
▲ EMP: 33
SQ FT: 70,000
SALES (est): 6.6MM **Privately Held**
WEB: www.legacyconverting.com
SIC: 2679 Paper products, converted

(G-1854)
LENG-DOR USA INC (DH)
11 Commerce Dr (08512-3503)
PHONE..................................732 254-4300
Apolo Ruz Martinez, *President*
Sergio Vera, *Manager*
Ricardo Mendoza, *Director*
▲ EMP: 11
SALES (est): 2.9MM
SALES (corp-wide): 978.5K **Privately Held**
WEB: www.lengdor.com
SIC: 2099 Food preparations
HQ: Leng D'or Sa
Calle Industria (Pg Ind Conde Sert) 21
Castellbisbal
937 724-680

(G-1855)
LOREAL USA INC
35 Broadway Rd (08512-5411)
PHONE..................................609 860-7500
Iris Luisi, *General Mgr*
Steve Mund, *Assistant VP*
George Blizzard, *Vice Pres*
Julia Youssef, *Vice Pres*
Jimmy Baecher, *Manager*
EMP: 700
SALES (corp-wide): 4.2B **Privately Held**
WEB: www.lorealparisusa.com
SIC: 2844 5122 Hair preparations, including shampoos; cosmetic preparations; perfumes & colognes; drugs, proprietaries & sundries
HQ: L'oreal Usa, Inc.
10 Hudson Yards Fl 30
New York NY 10001
212 818-1500

(G-1856)
LOVING PETS CORPORATION
110 Melrich Rd Ste 1 (08512-3524)
PHONE..................................609 655-3700
Eric Abbey, *President*
Shane Layton, *Vice Pres*
▲ EMP: 45
SALES: 30MM **Privately Held**
SIC: 5199 3999 Pet supplies; pet supplies

GEOGRAPHIC

(G-1857)
LUMIKO USA INC
Also Called: Heliolite
47 Commerce Dr 3 (08512-3503)
PHONE....................................609 409-6900
Mike Lee, *President*
▲ EMP: 5 EST: 1989
SQ FT: 43,000
SALES (est): 541.6K Privately Held
SIC: 3229 5063 5013 Bulbs for electric
lights; electrical apparatus & equipment;
motor vehicle supplies & new parts

(G-1858)
MAGNIFICA INC
5 Cedarbrook Dr (08512-3606)
PHONE....................................323 202-0386
James Lee, *CEO*
▲ EMP: 3
SALES (est): 6.4MM Privately Held
SIC: 2834 5122 Pharmaceutical prepara-
tions; pharmaceuticals

(G-1859)
MAIN TAPE COMPANY INC (PA)
1 Capital Dr Ste 101 (08512-3264)
PHONE....................................609 395-1704
Joseph Musanti, *President*
Joseph Vanore, *Treasurer*
◆ EMP: 160
SQ FT: 150,000
SALES (est): 44.6MM Privately Held
WEB: www.maintape.com
SIC: 2672 Tape, pressure sensitive: made
from purchased materials

(G-1860)
MARMON INDUSTRIAL LLC
101 Interchange Plz # 106 (08512-3716)
PHONE....................................609 655-4287
Rick Hooper, *Manager*
EMP: 12
SALES (corp-wide): 242.1B Publicly
Held
SIC: 3743 Railway motor cars
HQ: Marmon Industrial Llc
181 W Madison St Fl 26
Chicago IL 60602
312 372-9500

(G-1861)
MASON DISPLAY INNOVATIONS INC
Also Called: M D I
5 Boxal Dr (08512-3521)
P.O. Box 552, Pittstown (08867-0552)
PHONE....................................609 860-0675
Fax: 609 860-1239
John J Mason Jr, *President*
Mark Mason, *Vice Pres*
EMP: 14
SQ FT: 70,000
SALES (est): 1.3MM Privately Held
WEB: www.masondisplay.com
SIC: 7389 3993 Advertising, promotional &
trade show services; convention & show
services; exhibit construction by industrial
contractors; signs & advertising special-
ties; displays & cutouts, window & lobby;
displays, paint process

(G-1862)
MIDSTATE FILIGREE SYSTEMS INC
22 Brick Yard Rd (08512-5002)
P.O. Box 435 (08512-0435)
PHONE....................................609 448-8700
Fax: 609 443-2833
Harry Wise, *President*
Gene McDermott, *Exec VP*
Renee Reilly, *Vice Pres*
Coleen Jones, *Administration*
▲ EMP: 65
SQ FT: 80,000
SALES (est): 10MM Privately Held
SIC: 3272 Slabs, crossing: concrete

(G-1863)
NORLAND PRODUCTS INC
2540 Us Highway 130 # 100 (08512-3519)
PHONE....................................609 395-1966
Fax: 609 395-9006
Tim Norland, *President*
Carroll Foreman, *COO*
Richard Norland, *Vice Pres*

Daniel Beerbohm, *Project Engr*
Neal Wagman, *Sales Mgr*
EMP: 20 EST: 1960
SQ FT: 15,000
SALES (est): 5.7MM Privately Held
WEB: www.norlandprod.com
SIC: 2891 3827 2899 Adhesives; optical
instruments & lenses; gelatin: edible,
technical, photographic or pharmaceutical

(G-1864)
ONCOBIOLOGICS INC
7 Clarke Dr (08512-3627)
PHONE....................................609 619-3990
Fax: 609 619-3980
Randy Thurman, *Ch of Bd*
Lawrence A Kenyon, *President*
Stephen J McAndrew, *Senior VP*
Stephen McAndrew, *Vice Pres*
Elizabeth Yamashita, *Vice Pres*
EMP: 86
SQ FT: 48,000
SALES: 3.8MM Privately Held
SIC: 2834 Pharmaceutical preparations

(G-1865)
ORORA PACKAGING SOLUTIONS
Also Called: Landsberg New Jersey Div 1088
1 Capital Dr Ste 102 (08512-3264)
PHONE....................................609 249-5200
Fax: 609 249-5210
Anthony Panzica, *VP Sales*
Stephen Williams, *Branch Mgr*
EMP: 35
SALES (corp-wide): 3B Privately Held
SIC: 5113 2653 Paper & products, wrap-
ping or coarse; boxes, corrugated: made
from purchased materials
HQ: Orora Packaging Solutions
6600 Valley View St
Buena Park CA 90620
714 562-6000

(G-1866)
PALATIN TECHNOLOGIES INC
4b Cedarbrook Dr (08512-3641)
PHONE....................................609 495-2200
Fax: 609 495-2201
John K A Prendergast, *Ch of Bd*
Carl Spana, *President*
Libby Keating, *Vice Pres*
Jason Winters, *Sr Project Mgr*
Robert Deveer, *Bd of Directors*
EMP: 22
SQ FT: 10,000
SALES (est): 44.7MM Privately Held
WEB: www.palatin.com
SIC: 2834 Pharmaceutical preparations

(G-1867)
PAPA JOHNS NEW JERSEY
Also Called: Pj Food Service
1267 S River Rd Ste 400 (08512-3632)
PHONE....................................609 395-0045
Al Watson, *Manager*
◆ EMP: 75
SALES (est): 11MM
SALES (corp-wide): 1.7B Publicly Held
SIC: 2099 Pizza, refrigerated: except
frozen
HQ: Pj Food Service, Inc.
2002 Papa Johns Blvd
Louisville KY 40299

(G-1868)
PAULAUR CORPORATION
105 Melrich Rd (08512-3589)
PHONE....................................609 395-8844
Fax: 609 395-8850
Vincent Toscano, *President*
Paulette Toscano, *Owner*
Clifford S Rodkey, *Vice Pres*
Michael Toscano, *Vice Pres*
Andrew Toscano, *VP Mfg*
▲ EMP: 100
SQ FT: 144,000
SALES (est): 21.1MM Privately Held
WEB: www.paulaur.com
SIC: 2099 5411 Food preparations; gro-
cery stores

(G-1869)
PEARSON EDUCATION INC
258 Prospect Plains Rd (08512-3605)
PHONE....................................609 395-6000

Fax: 609 395-6038
Glenn Cipriani, *Vice Pres*
Dave Romagnoli, *Branch Mgr*
EMP: 27
SALES (corp-wide): 5.9B Privately Held
WEB: www.phgenit.com
SIC: 2731 Book publishing
HQ: Pearson Education, Inc.
221 River St
Hoboken NJ 07030
201 236-7000

(G-1870)
PLANT FOOD COMPANY INC
38 Hightstwn Crnbry Sta (08512-5099)
P.O. Box 351 (08512-0351)
PHONE....................................609 448-0935
Theodore Platz, *President*
Bill Lubas, *Plant Mgr*
James M Whiteside, *CFO*
William Lubas, *Treasurer*
▼ EMP: 20
SQ FT: 10,000
SALES (est): 6.1MM Privately Held
WEB: www.plantfoodco.com
SIC: 2873 2899 3523 Plant foods, mixed:
from plants making nitrog. fertilizers;
chemical preparations; fertilizing machin-
ery, farm

(G-1871)
PMV PHARMACEUTICALS INC
8 Clarke Dr Ste 3 (08512-3617)
PHONE....................................650 241-2822
David H Mack PHD, *CEO*
Winston Kung, *COO*
Salim Yazji, *Chief Mktg Ofcr*
EMP: 6 EST: 2015
SALES (est): 461.8K Privately Held
SIC: 2834 Solutions, pharmaceutical

(G-1872)
PRINCETON CHROMATOGRAPHY INC
1206 S River Rd Ste 1 (08512-3701)
PHONE....................................609 860-1803
Linda Caldwell, *President*
Walton Caldwell III, *Vice Pres*
EMP: 9
SQ FT: 4,000
SALES: 1.2MM Privately Held
WEB: www.pci-hplc.com
SIC: 3826 Liquid chromatographic instru-
ments

(G-1873)
PRINCETON LIGHTWAVE INC
2555 Route 130 Ste 1 (08512-3527)
PHONE....................................609 495-2600
Fax: 609 395-9114
Mark Itzler, *CEO*
Sabbir Rangwala, *President*
Alfred Mottola, *Marketing Staff*
EMP: 34
SQ FT: 20,000
SALES (est): 8.6MM
SALES (corp-wide): 156.7B Publicly
Held
WEB: www.princetonlightwave.com
SIC: 3699 3674 Laser systems & equip-
ment; semiconductors & related devices
HQ: Argo Ai, Llc
100 W Evelyn Ave Ste 1
Mountain View CA 94041
412 709-6992

(G-1874)
RAFAEL PHARMACEUTICALS INC (PA)
1 Duncan Dr (08512-3643)
PHONE....................................609 409-7050
Fax: 609 409-6035
Steve Carchedi, *CEO*
Robert Rodriguez, *President*
Clifford Straub, *CFO*
Brian Mullaney, *Chief Mktg Ofcr*
Robert Shorr, *Security Dir*
EMP: 15
SQ FT: 10,000
SALES (est): 4.1MM Privately Held
WEB: www.cornerstonepharma.com
SIC: 2834 Solutions, pharmaceutical

(G-1875)
RAHWAY STEEL DRUM CO INC
26 Brick Yard Rd (08512-5002)
PHONE....................................732 382-0113
Fax: 732 382-6713
Anthony Foglia, *President*
Mildred Foglia, *Corp Secy*
Michael Foglia, *Vice Pres*
EMP: 27
SQ FT: 6,000
SALES (est): 8.1MM Privately Held
WEB: www.rahwaysteeldrum.com
SIC: 3412 5085 Metal barrels, drums &
pails; drums, new or reconditioned

(G-1876)
RASI LABORATORIES INC
Also Called: Rasi Labs
320 Half Acre Rd (08512-3254)
PHONE....................................732 873-8500
Fax: 732 873-8571
Ramakrishna Gogineni, *President*
Surendra Vallabhaneni, *Vice Pres*
Suneetha Gogineni, *CFO*
▲ EMP: 70
SQ FT: 180,000
SALES (est): 24MM Privately Held
WEB: www.rasilaboratories.com
SIC: 2834 Vitamin preparations

(G-1877)
ROBOTUNITS INC
8 Corporate Dr Ste 1 (08512-3630)
PHONE....................................732 438-0500
Juergen Roth, *President*
▲ EMP: 6
SQ FT: 7,355
SALES: 750K
SALES (corp-wide): 4.4MM Privately
Held
WEB: www.robotunits.com
SIC: 5084 3535 8742 Conveyor systems;
conveyors & conveying equipment; unit
handling conveying systems; trolley con-
veyors; robotic conveyors; automation &
robotics consultant
HQ: Robotunits Gmbh
Dr. Walter Zumtobel StraBe 2
Dornbirn 6850
557 222-0002

(G-1878)
SCHOLASTIC BOOK FAIRS INC
2540 Us Highway 130 # 105 (08512-3519)
PHONE....................................609 578-4142
Loretta Daddone, *Branch Mgr*
EMP: 6
SALES (corp-wide): 1.6B Publicly Held
WEB: www.scholasticbookfairs.com
SIC: 2741 Miscellaneous publishing
HQ: Scholastic Book Fairs, Inc.
1080 Greenwood Blvd
Lake Mary FL 32746
407 829-7300

(G-1879)
SETARAM INC (DH)
2555 Us Highway 130 Ste 2 (08512-3527)
PHONE....................................908 262-7060
Sylvain Calzaroni, *CEO*
George Levites, *Technical Mgr*
Nelson Garcia, *Sales Mgr*
Noel Liccardi, *Office Mgr*
Yves Cherisien, *Manager*
EMP: 5
SQ FT: 4,700
SALES: 3MM
SALES (corp-wide): 107K Privately Held
WEB: www.setaram.com
SIC: 3826 Instruments measuring thermal
properties; differential thermal analysis in-
struments; thermal analysis instruments,
laboratory type; thermogravimetric ana-
lyzers
HQ: Kep Technologies High Tech Products
Setaram Setaram Instrumentation Ke
Caluire Et Cuire 69300
472 102-525

(G-1880)
SHAW INDUSTRIES INC
1267 S River Rd Ste 100 (08512-3639)
PHONE....................................609 655-8300
Vance Bell, *Manager*
EMP: 350

▲ = Import ▼=Export
◆ =Import/Export

SALES (corp-wide): 242.1B **Publicly Held**
SIC: 2273 Carpets & rugs
HQ: Shaw Industries, Inc.
616 E Walnut Ave
Dalton GA 30721

(G-1881)
SOLVAY USA INC
Cn 1120 (08512)
PHONE..................................609 860-4000
EMP: 79
SALES (corp-wide): 10MM **Privately Held**
WEB: www.food.us.rhodia.com
SIC: 2819 Industrial inorganic chemicals
HQ: Solvay Usa Inc.
504 Carnegie Ctr
Princeton NJ 08540
609 860-4000

(G-1882)
SUN PHARMACEUTICAL INDS INC
1 Commerce Dr (08512-3503)
PHONE..................................609 495-2800
EMP: 50
SALES (corp-wide): 1.2B **Privately Held**
SIC: 2834 Pharmaceutical preparations
HQ: Sun Pharmaceutical Industries, Inc.
270 Prospect Plains Rd
Cranbury NJ 08512
609 495-2800

(G-1883)
SUN PHARMACEUTICAL INDS INC (HQ)
270 Prospect Plains Rd (08512-3605)
PHONE..................................609 495-2800
Fax: 609 495-2715
Subramanian Kalyanasundaram, *CEO*
Arthur Pavlidis, *Business Mgr*
Robert Kurkiewicz, *Senior VP*
Imma Abramowitz, *Vice Pres*
Lorraine Betz, *Vice Pres*
▲ EMP: 400
SQ FT: 82,000
SALES: 565.7MM
SALES (corp-wide): 1.2B **Privately Held**
SIC: 2834 Pharmaceutical preparations
PA: Sun Pharmaceutical Industries Limited
Sun House, Cts No. 201 B/1,
Mumbai MH 40006
224 324-4324

(G-1884)
TARO PHARMACEUTICALS USA INC
1 Commerce Dr (08512-3503)
PHONE..................................609 655-9002
Joel Sokol, *Director*
EMP: 30
SALES (corp-wide): 879.3MM **Privately Held**
WEB: www.taropharma.net
SIC: 5122 2834 Pharmaceuticals; pharmaceutical preparations
HQ: Taro Pharmaceuticals U.S.A., Inc.
3 Skyline Dr Ste 120
Hawthorne NY 10532
914 345-9000

(G-1885)
TRIARCO INDUSTRIES LLC
259 Prospect Plains Rd A (08512-3706)
PHONE..................................973 942-5100
Randy Gress, *CEO*
Jean Marie Mainente, *Senior VP*
Torrie Cantey, *Sales Mgr*
Hermanus Kieftenbeld, *Officer*
EMP: 6
SALES (est): 133.4K
SALES (corp-wide): 722MM **Publicly Held**
SIC: 2834 Vitamin, nutrient & hematinic preparations for human use
PA: Innophos Holdings, Inc.
259 Prospect Plains Rd A
Cranbury NJ 08512
609 495-2495

(G-1886)
TRUMPF INC
2601 Route 130 (08512-5421)
PHONE..................................609 925-8200
Marc Duchesneau, *Engineer*
Stefan Heinemann, *Engineer*
Mark Klawinsky, *Engineer*
Gary Sheridan, *Regl Sales Mgr*
Louis Wegman, *Manager*
EMP: 24
SALES (corp-wide): 3.4B **Privately Held**
WEB: www.us.trumpf.com
SIC: 3542 Sheet metalworking machines
HQ: Trumpf, Inc.
111 Hyde Rd
Farmington CT 06032
860 255-6000

(G-1887)
TRUMPF PHOTONICS INC
2601 Us Highway 130 (08512-5421)
PHONE..................................609 925-8200
Fax: 609 409-7021
Lars Gruenert, *Principal*
S Doughlas Devnew, *Vice Pres*
Mark Mashas, *Engineer*
Ming Shih, *Associate*
▲ EMP: 140
SALES (est): 31.8MM
SALES (corp-wide): 3.4B **Privately Held**
SIC: 3542 Sheet metalworking machines
HQ: Trumpf, Inc.
111 Hyde Rd
Farmington CT 06032
860 255-6000

(G-1888)
TULEX PHARMACEUTICALS INC
5 Cedarbrook Dr (08512-3606)
PHONE..................................609 619-3098
James Lee, *CEO*
▲ EMP: 15
SALES (est): 975.5K **Privately Held**
SIC: 2834 Pharmaceutical preparations

(G-1889)
UTRECHT MANUFACTURING CORP (DH)
Also Called: Utrecht Art Supply
6 Corp Dr Ste 1 (08512)
PHONE..................................609 409-8001
Fax: 609 409-8002
Michael Ippolito, *CEO*
◆ EMP: 85
SQ FT: 54,000
SALES (est): 63.5MM
SALES (corp-wide): 166.4MM **Privately Held**
WEB: www.utrecht.com
SIC: 3952 5999 5961 Artists' materials, except pencils & leads; artists' equipment; drafting materials; artists' supplies & materials; drafting equipment & supplies; arts & crafts equipment & supplies, mail order
HQ: Dick Blick Company
1849 Green Bay Rd Ste 310
Highland Park IL 60035
847 681-6800

(G-1890)
W B MASON CO INC
21 Commerce Dr (08512-3503)
PHONE..................................888 926-2766
Michael Lange, *President*
EMP: 50
SALES (corp-wide): 773MM **Privately Held**
SIC: 5943 5712 2752 Office forms & supplies; office furniture; commercial printing, lithographic
PA: W. B. Mason Co., Inc.
59 Center St
Brockton MA 02301
781 794-8800

(G-1891)
WEST PATTERN WORKS INC
124 S Main St (08512-3145)
PHONE..................................609 443-6241
Fax: 609 443-9466
Doug Trendell, *President*
John Kwiatkowski, *Corp Secy*
William Davis, *Vice Pres*
Lauren Davis, *Manager*
EMP: 13
SQ FT: 11,000

SALES: 1.5MM **Privately Held**
WEB: www.westpatternworks.com
SIC: 3543 3544 Foundry cores; industrial molds

(G-1892)
WORLD AND MAIN LLC (PA)
324a Half Acre Rd (08512-3254)
PHONE..................................609 860-9990
Jack Imszennik, *Treasurer*
Yalile Gonzalez-Deal, *Sales Dir*
Kevin Captan, *Sales Staff*
Steven Quintano, *Sales Staff*
Lauren Vankirk, *Sales Staff*
EMP: 225
SALES (est): 310.3MM **Privately Held**
SIC: 1711 3429 Plumbing contractors; builders' hardware

(G-1893)
YOUR PRINTER V20 LTD
Also Called: AlphaGraphics
6 Corporate Dr Ste 1 (08512-3616)
PHONE..................................609 771-4000
Fax: 609 860-9449
David Kovacs, *President*
Mike Russo, *Principal*
Ellis Galimidi, *Vice Pres*
Charlie Jendrejeski, *Vice Pres*
Ken Seibel, *Vice Pres*
EMP: 32
SALES: 12MM **Privately Held**
SIC: 2752 7331 Commercial printing, offset; mailing service

Cranford
Union County

(G-1894)
AKRIMAX PHARMACEUTICALS LLC
11 Commerce Dr Ste 103 (07016-3513)
PHONE..................................908 372-0506
Fax: 908 272-3084
Gregory Ford, *President*
Donald C Olsen, *President*
Joseph Krivulka, *Chairman*
Leonard Mazur, *Chairman*
Mitchell Arnold, *Vice Pres*
▼ EMP: 75
SQ FT: 12,000
SALES: 85MM **Privately Held**
SIC: 2834 Pharmaceutical preparations

(G-1895)
ALL-STATE INTERNATIONAL INC (PA)
Also Called: All-State Legal
1 Commerce Dr (07016-3508)
PHONE..................................908 272-0800
Fax: 800 634-5184
Robert Busch, *CEO*
Doug Tyler, *Opers Mgr*
Bill Smith, *Facilities Mgr*
Joe Fuzak, *CFO*
Michael Barsa, *Manager*
▲ EMP: 190
SQ FT: 154,000
SALES (est): 28.7MM **Privately Held**
SIC: 2761 2754 2759 3953 Continuous forms, office & business; business forms: gravure printing; stationery: gravure printing; seals: gravure printing; financial note & certificate printing & engraving; embossing seals, corporate & official

(G-1896)
AMICI IMPORTS INC
335 Centennial Ave Unit 7 (07016-6108)
PHONE..................................908 272-8300
Jeffrey Desantis, *CEO*
Charles Cashin, *Senior VP*
▲ EMP: 12
SALES (est): 1.1MM **Privately Held**
SIC: 5713 2273 Rugs; carpets & rugs

(G-1897)
BAB PRINTING JAN SERVICE (PA)
Also Called: Weaver Associates Printing
945 Lincoln Ave E (07016-3155)
PHONE..................................908 272-6224
John Weaver, *President*

Harrison L Weaver, *President*
EMP: 8
SQ FT: 6,000
SALES (est): 1.2MM **Privately Held**
SIC: 2752 Commercial printing, offset

(G-1898)
BADGER BLADES LLC
216 North Ave E Ste 2 (07016-2473)
P.O. Box 269, Green Mountain Falls CO (80819-0269)
PHONE..................................908 325-6587
A Sundiland, *General Mgr*
Ashton Sundiland, *General Mgr*
Jonathan Lin, *Opers Mgr*
EMP: 7
SALES (est): 444.5K **Privately Held**
SIC: 3441 Building components, structural steel

(G-1899)
BERRY BUSINESS PROCEDURE CO
Also Called: Berry Business Forms
6 Park St (07016-3439)
P.O. Box 845 (07016-0845)
PHONE..................................908 272-6464
Fax: 908 272-7607
David Cheek, *President*
Patricia Cheek, *Corp Secy*
EMP: 6 EST: 1956
SQ FT: 5,000
SALES (est): 630K **Privately Held**
WEB: www.berryprinting.com
SIC: 2752 5112 Commercial printing, offset; letters, circular or form: lithographed; business forms

(G-1900)
CITIUS PHARMACEUTICALS INC (PA)
11 Commerce Dr Ste 100 (07016-3513)
PHONE..................................978 938-0338
Leonard Mazur, *Ch of Bd*
Myron Holubiak, *President*
Jaime Bartushak, *CFO*
Howard Safir, *Director*
Suren Dutia, *Bd of Directors*
EMP: 7
SALES (est): 699K **Publicly Held**
SIC: 2834 Pharmaceutical preparations

(G-1901)
COLTWELL INDUSTRIES INC
55 Winans Ave (07016-3144)
PHONE..................................908 276-7600
Fax: 908 276-2679
George J Bengivenga, *Vice Pres*
Anthony J Bengivenga, *Vice Pres*
Alissa Robbins, *Regl Sales Mgr*
▲ EMP: 10
SQ FT: 23,000
SALES (est): 2MM **Privately Held**
WEB: www.coltwell.com
SIC: 3354 Aluminum extruded products

(G-1902)
CONSTRUCTION SPECIALTIES INC
APC Daylighter
49 Meeker Ave (07016-3163)
PHONE..................................908 272-2771
Fax: 908 272-5200
Ronald Dadd, *Branch Mgr*
Arthur La Pointe, *Manager*
EMP: 50
SALES (corp-wide): 367MM **Privately Held**
WEB: www.c-sgroup.com
SIC: 5031 3356 3354 Skylights, all materials; nonferrous rolling & drawing; aluminum extruded products
PA: Construction Specialties Inc.
3 Werner Way Ste 100
Lebanon NJ 08833
908 236-0800

(G-1903)
DURST CORPORATION INC (PA)
Also Called: Jaclo Industries
129 Dermody St (07016-3217)
PHONE..................................800 852-3906
Fax: 908 653-1166
Larry Brody, *Ch of Bd*
Dana Egert, *President*

▲ **EMP:** 25 **EST:** 1911
SQ FT: 50,000
SALES (est): 13.7MM **Privately Held**
WEB: www.durstcorp.com
SIC: 5074 3432 3494 Plumbing fittings &
supplies; lawn hose nozzles & sprinklers;
valves & pipe fittings

(G-1904)
E F BRITTEN & CO INC
22 South Ave W (07016-2695)
PHONE..........................908 276-4800
Fax: 908 276-9153
Richard Stokes, *President*
Margaret M Turner, *Vice Pres*
Emily Petix, *Admin Sec*
▲ **EMP:** 14
SQ FT: 27,500
SALES: 1.2MM **Privately Held**
WEB: www.efbritten.com
SIC: 3443 3398 Cylinders, pressure: metal
plate; brazing (hardening) of metal

(G-1905)
**ENZON PHARMACEUTICALS
INC (PA)**
20 Commerce Dr Ste 135 (07016-3614)
PHONE..........................732 980-4500
Fax: 908 575-9457
Andrew Rackear, *CEO*
Jonathan Christodoro, *Ch of Bd*
Richard L Feinstein, *CFO*
Odysseas Kostas, *Bd of Directors*
Jennifer McNealey, *Bd of Directors*
▲ **EMP:** 3
SQ FT: 500
SALES: 8.3MM **Publicly Held**
WEB: www.enzon.com
SIC: 2834 6794 Pharmaceutical prepara-
tions; franchises, selling or licensing

(G-1906)
FAUST RUDOLPH INC
542 South Ave E (07016-3208)
P.O. Box 335, Lambertville (08530-0335)
PHONE..........................609 298-7334
Peter R Faust Jr, *President*
Bob Paulock, *Vice Pres*
EMP: 10 **EST:** 1922
SQ FT: 6,400
SALES (est): 910K **Privately Held**
WEB: www.faustink.com
SIC: 3952 2893 Lead pencils & art goods;
ink, drawing: black & colored; printing ink

(G-1907)
**FEDERAL PLASTICS
CORPORATION**
570 South Ave E Bldg F1 (07016-3250)
P.O. Box 1789 (07016-5789)
PHONE..........................908 272-5800
Fax: 908 272-9021
Peter T Triano Jr, *President*
Michael Triano, *Vice Pres*
Peter N Triano Sr, *Shareholder*
▲ **EMP:** 32
SQ FT: 86,000
SALES (est): 7.3MM **Privately Held**
WEB: www.federalplastics.com
SIC: 3087 5162 3083 2821 Custom com-
pound purchased resins; plastics resins;
laminated plastics plate & sheet; plastics
materials & resins

(G-1908)
GLITTEREX CORP
7 Commerce Dr (07016-3507)
PHONE..........................908 272-9121
Fax: 908 272-9191
Edward Chumura, *President*
Rene Getler, *Corp Secy*
Frank Eulie, *Vice Pres*
◆ **EMP:** 65 **EST:** 1963
SQ FT: 20,000
SALES (est): 9.9MM **Privately Held**
WEB: www.glitterex.com
SIC: 3081 3497 Plastic film & sheet; metal
foil & leaf

(G-1909)
GORTON HEATING CORP
546 South Ave E (07016-3208)
PHONE..........................908 276-1323
Fax: 908 272-5881
Linda Mast, *President*
Marie Klinefelter, *President*

Linda K Mast, *Admin Sec*
EMP: 6 **EST:** 1887
SQ FT: 3,000
SALES (est): 700K **Privately Held**
WEB: www.gorton-valves.com
SIC: 3494 Valves & pipe fittings

(G-1910)
HHH MACHINE CO
20 Quine St (07016-3130)
PHONE..........................908 276-1220
Fax: 908 276-0317
Howard Hull, *President*
Kenneth Hull, *Vice Pres*
EMP: 9 **EST:** 1965
SQ FT: 5,000
SALES (est): 1.2MM **Privately Held**
WEB: www.hhhmachine.com
SIC: 3599 3561 Machine shop, jobbing &
repair; pumps & pumping equipment

(G-1911)
KITCHEN AND MORE INC
542 South Ave E (07016-3208)
PHONE..........................908 272-3388
Joosub Park, *Owner*
EMP: 14
SALES (est): 2.6MM **Privately Held**
SIC: 3553 Cabinet makers' machinery

(G-1912)
KOPPERS CHOCOLATE LLC
45 Jackson Dr (07016-3503)
PHONE..........................212 243-0220
Lorie Alexander, *Ch of Bd*
Jeffrey Alexander, *Vice Pres*
Leslye Alexander, *Vice Pres*
▲ **EMP:** 100
SALES (est): 15MM **Privately Held**
WEB: www.kopperschocolate.com
SIC: 2064 2066 Candy & other confec-
tionery products; chocolate & cocoa prod-
ucts

(G-1913)
MADAN PLASTICS INC
370 North Ave E (07016-2435)
PHONE..........................908 276-8484
Fax: 908 276-9483
Steven Skoler, *President*
Michael Madan, *General Mgr*
Alexander Friend, *Vice Pres*
Paul Bauer, *MIS Staff*
EMP: 100 **EST:** 1956
SQ FT: 52,000
SALES (est): 1.7MM **Privately Held**
WEB: www.madanplastics.com
SIC: 3089 3471 Thermoformed finished
plastic products; electroplating of metals
or formed products; finishing, metals or
formed products

(G-1914)
MAINSTREAM LLC
230 Cristiani St (07016-3214)
P.O. Box 353 (07016-0353)
PHONE..........................908 931-1010
Derrick Markham,
James Markham,
Rick Markham,
EMP: 4
SALES (est): 320K **Privately Held**
WEB: www.customahu.com
SIC: 3594 Motors: hydraulic, fluid power or
air

(G-1915)
METALICO INC (PA)
135 Dermody St (07016-3217)
PHONE..........................908 497-9610
Fax: 908 497-1097
Carlos E Aguero, *President*
Michael J Drury, *Exec VP*
Arnold S Graber, *Exec VP*
Steven M Alberico, *Vice Pres*
Peter Meyers, *Vice Pres*
◆ **EMP:** 6 **EST:** 1999
SQ FT: 6,190
SALES (est): 476MM **Privately Held**
SIC: 3449 Miscellaneous metalwork

(G-1916)
**METROPOLITAN COMPACTORS
SVC**
21 Quine St (07016-3130)
PHONE..........................908 653-0168

Michael J Walker, *President*
EMP: 8
SQ FT: 10,000
SALES (est): 488.2K **Privately Held**
SIC: 3589 Garbage disposers & com-
pactors, commercial

(G-1917)
**NATIONAL CHRISTMAS PDTS
INC**
Also Called: National Tree Company
2 Commerce Dr (07016-3509)
PHONE..........................908 709-4141
Fax: 908 709-4145
Joseph Puleo, *President*
Richard Puleo, *Vice Pres*
Salvatore Puleo Jr, *Vice Pres*
▲ **EMP:** 30
SQ FT: 50,000
SALES (est): 4.8MM **Privately Held**
SIC: 3999 Christmas trees, artificial;
Christmas tree ornaments, except electri-
cal & glass

(G-1918)
**NORTHROP GRUMMAN
SYSTEMS CORP**
Also Called: Sperry Marine Division
12 Park St (07016-3439)
PHONE..........................908 276-6677
Fax: 908 276-8840
Bonnie Herrington, *Branch Mgr*
EMP: 4 **Publicly Held**
WEB: www.sperry.ngc.com
SIC: 3812 Search & navigation equipment
HQ: Northrop Grumman Systems Corpora-
tion
2980 Fairview Park Dr
Falls Church VA 22042
703 280-2900

(G-1919)
**ORIENT CORPORATION OF
AMERICA (HQ)**
Also Called: Manufacturing Chem Dyestuff
6 Commerce Dr Ste 301 (07016-3515)
PHONE..........................908 298-0990
Fax: 908 298-1833
Akihiro Takahashi, *President*
Masatoshi Matsuura, *Exec VP*
Senta Okada, *Treasurer*
Mike Williston, *Sales Staff*
Maria Silva, *Admin Sec*
▲ **EMP:** 5
SQ FT: 2,000
SALES: 4.2MM
SALES (corp-wide): 57.2MM **Privately
Held**
WEB: www.orient-usa.com
SIC: 2865 Dyes & pigments
PA: Orient Chemical Industries Co., Ltd.
1-7-15, Minamihommachi, Chuo-Ku
Osaka OSK 541-0
662 612-010

(G-1920)
OX GROUP USA LLC
95 Dermody St (07016-3215)
PHONE..........................888 850-6710
John Diplock, *General Mgr*
Jennifer St John, *Finance*
▲ **EMP:** 10
SQ FT: 12,000
SALES (est): 5.5MM
SALES (corp-wide): 138.8K **Privately
Held**
SIC: 5085 5072 3423 Tools; industrial
tools; hand tools; hand & edge tools
HQ: Ox Group International Pty Ltd
2a Hope St
Ermington NSW 2115
288 456-600

(G-1921)
PEM SYSTEMS INC
Also Called: Pem-All Fire Extinguisher Co
39a Myrtle St (07016-3471)
PHONE..........................908 276-0211
Fax: 908 276-8074
Paul Moskaluk, *President*
Joseph Kostecki, *Corp Secy*
Martin Farese, *Vice Pres*
Kathy Kreie, *Controller*
▲ **EMP:** 24
SQ FT: 20,000

SALES (est): 3.8MM **Privately Held**
WEB: www.pemall.com
SIC: 3999 3569 Fire extinguishers,
portable; firefighting apparatus & related
equipment

(G-1922)
PETRO PACKAGING CO INC
16 Quine St (07016-3130)
P.O. Box 546 (07016-0546)
PHONE..........................908 272-4054
Fax: 908 272-2836
Rick Petrozziello, *President*
John Petrozziello, *Vice Pres*
▲ **EMP:** 45 **EST:** 1970
SQ FT: 20,000
SALES (est): 14.2MM **Privately Held**
WEB: www.petropackaging.com
SIC: 2821 3081 Plastics materials &
resins; packing materials, plastic sheet

(G-1923)
**PHARMACEUTIC LITHO LABEL
INC (PA)**
450 North Ave E (07016-2437)
P.O. Box 68 (07016-0068)
PHONE..........................336 785-4000
Fax: 908 276-6566
Keith Dovel, *President*
Howard Auerbach, *Chairman*
Len Dillon, *Admin Sec*
▲ **EMP:** 120 **EST:** 1928
SQ FT: 45,000
SALES (est): 13.6MM **Privately Held**
WEB: www.plymouthprinting.com
SIC: 2752 2759 Commercial printing, litho-
graphic; letterpress printing

(G-1924)
RADNET INC
Also Called: Cranford Diagnostic Imaging
25 S Union Ave (07016-2843)
PHONE..........................908 709-1323
Fax: 908 709-1329
Drew M Netter, *Manager*
EMP: 15 **Publicly Held**
WEB: www.mrii.com
SIC: 8071 3699 Medical laboratories;
electrical equipment & supplies
PA: Radnet, Inc.
1510 Cotner Ave
Los Angeles CA 90025

(G-1925)
RADNET INC
25 S Union Ave (07016-2843)
PHONE..........................908 709-1323
EMP: 21 **Publicly Held**
SIC: 3845 Electromedical equipment
PA: Radnet, Inc.
1510 Cotner Ave
Los Angeles CA 90025

(G-1926)
**ROUSES PT
PHARMACEUTICALS LLC**
11 Commerce Dr Ste 101 (07016-3513)
PHONE..........................239 390-1495
Robert Sanzen, *Mng Member*
EMP: 6
SALES (est): 2.1MM **Privately Held**
SIC: 2834 Dermatologicals

(G-1927)
STAIRWORKS INC
335 Centennial Ave Unit 8 (07016-6108)
PHONE..........................908 276-2829
Mark Freemen, *President*
EMP: 4
SALES: 240K **Privately Held**
SIC: 2431 Staircases & stairs, wood

(G-1928)
TOFUTTI BRANDS INC
50 Jackson Dr (07016-3504)
P.O. Box 786 (07016-0786)
PHONE..........................908 272-2400
Fax: 908 272-9492
David Mintz, *Ch of Bd*
Steven Kass, *CFO*
▼ **EMP:** 9
SQ FT: 6,200
SALES: 14.1MM **Privately Held**
WEB: www.tofutti.com
SIC: 2024 2099 Tofu desserts, frozen;
tofu, except frozen desserts

▲ = Import ▼=Export
◆ =Import/Export

(G-1929)
TOTALCAT GROUP INC (HQ)
186 North Ave E (07016-2439)
PHONE..................................908 497-9610
Carlos E Aguero, *President*
EMP: 3 EST: 2006
SALES (est): 8.6MM
SALES (corp-wide): 476MM **Privately Held**
SIC: 2819 Catalysts, chemical
PA: Metalico, Inc.
    135 Dermody St
    Cranford NJ 07016
    908 497-9610

(G-1930)
US BLADE MFG CO INC
90 Myrtle St (07016-3236)
PHONE..................................908 272-2898
Fax: 908 272-2717
Anthony J Calenda, *President*
Pat Cosgrove, *Principal*
Jessica Ross, *Executive Asst*
▲ EMP: 50
SQ FT: 100,000
SALES (est): 9.4MM **Privately Held**
WEB: www.usblade.com
SIC: 3421 Knife blades & blanks

Cream Ridge
Monmouth County

(G-1931)
CENTRAL ART & ENGINEERING INC
500 Goldman Dr (08514-2529)
PHONE..................................609 758-5922
Fax: 609 758-5923
John Makkay Jr, *President*
EMP: 8
SQ FT: 1,000
SALES (est): 605K **Privately Held**
SIC: 3999 Models, general, except toy

(G-1932)
CENTRAL ART & ENGINEERING INC
Also Called: Impact Visal Systems
500 Goldman Dr (08514-2529)
P.O. Box 289 (08514-0289)
PHONE..................................609 758-5922
John Makkay, *President*
▼ EMP: 9
SQ FT: 17,000
SALES: 895K **Privately Held**
SIC: 3993 Signs, not made in custom sign
    painting shops

(G-1933)
CREAM RIDGE WINERY
145 Route 539 (08514-1520)
P.O. Box 98 (08514-0098)
PHONE..................................609 259-9797
R Thomas Amabile, *President*
Jackie Schlitzer, *Property Mgr*
Aileen Amabile, *Manager*
EMP: 8
SALES (est): 1.3MM **Privately Held**
WEB: www.creamridgewinery.com
SIC: 5921 5947 2084 Wine; gift shop;
    wines

(G-1934)
DENEKA PRINTING SYSTEMS INC (PA)
100c Goldman Dr (08514-2530)
PHONE..................................609 752-0964
Fax: 609 752-0851
P Kenneth Deneka, *President*
EMP: 4
SQ FT: 3,000
SALES (est): 653.9K **Privately Held**
WEB: www.denekaprintingsystems.com
SIC: 3555 Printing trades machinery

(G-1935)
GARDEN STATE FABRICATORS
575 Monmouth Rd (08514-2506)
P.O. Box 156, Adelphia (07710-0156)
PHONE..................................732 928-5006
Fax: 732 928-7473
Michael Jaeger, *Owner*

EMP: 5
SQ FT: 6,000
SALES: 400K **Privately Held**
SIC: 3089 Cases, plastic

(G-1936)
HENRY JACKSON RACING ENGINES
787 Monmouth Rd (08514-2401)
PHONE..................................609 758-7476
Henry A Jackson, *President*
Henry Jackson, *President*
EMP: 5
SQ FT: 5,000
SALES: 300K **Privately Held**
SIC: 3519 Internal combustion engines

(G-1937)
INNOVATIVE PRESSURE CLG LLC
10 Arnytown Hrnerstown Rd (08514-1805)
PHONE..................................609 738-3100
Barbara Vanhandel,
EMP: 8
SALES: 180K **Privately Held**
SIC: 3589 High pressure cleaning equip-
    ment

(G-1938)
NATIONAL ELECTRIC WIRE CO INC
100 Goldman Dr (08514-2530)
PHONE..................................609 758-3600
Fax: 732 240-5433
Steven Herr, *President*
▲ EMP: 36
SQ FT: 18,000
SALES: 7.1MM **Privately Held**
SIC: 3351 Copper rolling & drawing

(G-1939)
OPTEQUIP INC
176 Burlington Path Rd (08514-1603)
P.O. Box 179 (08514-0179)
PHONE..................................609 758-8609
Andrew Jozan, *President*
Daniel Jozan, *Vice Pres*
EMP: 6
SQ FT: 3,000
SALES (est): 520K **Privately Held**
WEB: www.optequip.com
SIC: 3661 Fiber optics communications
    equipment

(G-1940)
RAKO MACHINE PRODUCTS INC
845 Monmouth Rd (08514-2311)
PHONE..................................609 758-1200
John Vandertuyn, *President*
EMP: 7
SQ FT: 2,500
SALES (est): 570K **Privately Held**
SIC: 3599 Machine shop, jobbing & repair

(G-1941)
SIGMA INTERNATIONAL GROUP INC (PA)
700 Goldman Dr (08514-2528)
P.O. Box 300 (08514-0300)
PHONE..................................609 758-0800
Victor Pais, *President*
Ed Eichmann, *General Mgr*
Dave Pietryga, *Regional Mgr*
Raj Upadhyaya, *Exec VP*
Siddharth Bhattacharji, *Vice Pres*
◆ EMP: 13
SQ FT: 15,000
SALES (est): 101.4MM **Privately Held**
SIC: 3494 Valves & pipe fittings

Creamridge
Monmouth County

(G-1942)
BRAYCO INC
951 County Hwy 537 (08514)
PHONE..................................609 758-5235
Randy Bray, *President*
Jody Bray, *Vice Pres*
Lydia Mancini, *Treasurer*
EMP: 15
SQ FT: 4,000

SALES (est): 3.2MM **Privately Held**
WEB: www.brayco.net
SIC: 3441 Fabricated structural metal

Cresskill
Bergen County

(G-1943)
ALTUS PCB LLC
45 Legion Dr (07626-2143)
PHONE..................................973 928-8777
Zohar Shinar, *President*
Rosanne Anderson, *Sales Mgr*
▲ EMP: 10
SALES (est): 1.6MM **Privately Held**
SIC: 3572 Computer storage devices

(G-1944)
CRESTRON ELECTRONICS INC
Also Called: Creston Electronics
101 Broadway (07626-2152)
PHONE..................................201 894-0670
Fax: 201 894-0376
Kor Baydurcan, *Engineer*
Walter Truppe, *Engineer*
Tom Buzzell, *Manager*
EMP: 100
SALES (corp-wide): 500MM **Privately Held**
SIC: 3714 3625 Motor vehicle parts & ac-
    cessories; relays & industrial controls
PA: Crestron Electronics, Inc.
    15 Volvo Dr
    Rockleigh NJ 07647
    201 767-3400

(G-1945)
HELEN MORLEY LLC
35 Buckingham Rd (07626-1630)
PHONE..................................201 348-6459
Helen Morley, *Mng Member*
EMP: 34
SQ FT: 4,000
SALES (est): 2.5MM **Privately Held**
SIC: 2339 Aprons, except rubber or plastic:
    women's, misses', juniors'

(G-1946)
INNOVATIVE DESIGN INC
80 Broadway (07626-2164)
PHONE..................................201 227-2555
Vivian Siegel, *President*
Andrew Siegel, *President*
▲ EMP: 9 EST: 1998
SALES (est): 860.5K **Privately Held**
SIC: 2395 Embroidery & art needlework

(G-1947)
PHOENIX NATIONAL PETROLEUM CO
Also Called: Phoenix Fuels Life
157 Hillside Ave (07626-1611)
PHONE..................................201 568-5568
Robert O Karsian, *President*
Richard Karsian, *Vice Pres*
Joseph Pietrocola, *Admin Sec*
EMP: 7 EST: 1971
SQ FT: 1,100
SALES (est): 401.5K **Privately Held**
SIC: 1311 5541 Crude petroleum & natu-
    ral gas; gasoline service stations

(G-1948)
SILVER PALATE KITCHENS INC
211 Knickerbocker Rd (07626-1830)
P.O. Box 512 (07626-0512)
PHONE..................................201 568-0110
Fax: 201 568-8844
Peter Harris, *President*
◆ EMP: 21 EST: 1977
SALES (est): 6MM **Privately Held**
WEB: www.silverpalate.com
SIC: 2099 2035 2043 2098 Vinegar; sea-
    sonings & sauces, except tomato & dry;
    dressings, salad: raw & cooked (except
    dry mixes); mustard, prepared (wet); pick-
    led fruits & vegetables; oats, rolled: pre-
    pared as cereal breakfast food; macaroni
    products (e.g. alphabets, rings & shells),
    dry; gourmet food stores

(G-1949)
SUN COAST PRECISION INSTRUMENT
80 Broadway Fl 1 (07626-2164)
PHONE..................................646 852-2331
Richard Chitos, *President*
EMP: 4
SALES (est): 291K **Privately Held**
SIC: 3829 Measuring & controlling devices

(G-1950)
VASCULAR THERAPIES LLC
105 Union Ave Ste 2 (07626-2129)
PHONE..................................201 266-8310
Samuel Liang, *Mng Member*
Rosanne Terraciano,
EMP: 5
SALES (est): 1MM **Privately Held**
SIC: 3841 Surgical & medical instruments

Dayton
Middlesex County

(G-1951)
(GT) GLOBAL TECH INC
Also Called: Research Dev & Manufacture
32 Marc Dr (08810-1388)
PHONE..................................732 447-7083
EMP: 10 EST: 1997
SALES (est): 446.2K **Privately Held**
SIC: 3999 Manufacturing industries

(G-1952)
ARCHTECH ELECTRONICS CORP
117 Docks Corner Rd Ste A (08810-2529)
PHONE..................................732 355-1288
Paul Foung, *CEO*
Kirk Lee, *President*
Peggy Foung, *Chairman*
Eva Chen, *Hum Res Coord*
Jerry Wang, *Accounts Exec*
▲ EMP: 39
SQ FT: 20,000
SALES: 7MM **Privately Held**
SIC: 3643 5063 5045 Current-carrying
    wiring devices; electrical apparatus &
    equipment; computer peripheral equip-
    ment

(G-1953)
AUROBINDO PHARMA USA INC
2400 Us Highway 130 (08810-1519)
PHONE..................................732 839-9400
Sanjay Singh, *Vice Pres*
Ashwani Chopra, *Production*
Mahesh K Pinnamaneni, *CIO*
Edwin Rivera, *Administration*
EMP: 5
SALES (corp-wide): 1.6B **Privately Held**
SIC: 2834 Pharmaceutical preparations
HQ: Aurobindo Pharma U.S.A., Inc.
    279 Prnctn Hightstown Rd
    East Windsor NJ 08520
    732 839-9400

(G-1954)
AUROLIFE PHARMA LLC
6 Wheeling Rd (08810-1526)
PHONE..................................732 839-9746
Swaminathan Sambamurty, *Branch Mgr*
EMP: 20
SALES (corp-wide): 1.6B **Privately Held**
SIC: 2834 Pharmaceutical preparations
HQ: Aurolife Pharma Llc
    2400 Us Highway 130
    Dayton NJ 08810

(G-1955)
AUROLIFE PHARMA LLC (DH)
2400 Us Highway 130 (08810-1519)
PHONE..................................732 839-4377
Swaminathan Sambamurty, *CFO*
Beth Fucito, *Human Resources*
Christine Gart, *Human Resources*
▲ EMP: 152
SQ FT: 100,000
SALES: 178MM
SALES (corp-wide): 1.6B **Privately Held**
WEB: www.aurobindousa.com
SIC: 2834 Pharmaceutical preparations

(PA)=Parent Co (HQ)=Headquarters (DH)=Div Headquarters
✪ = New Business established in last 2 years
    2018 Harris New Jersey
    Manufacturers Directory
    87

GEOGRAPHIC

HQ: Aurobindo Pharma U.S.A., Inc.
279 Prnctn Hightstown Rd
East Windsor NJ 08520
732 839-9400

(G-1956)
BROGAN TENNYSON GROUP INC
2245 Us Highway 130 # 102 (08810-2420)
PHONE.................................732 355-0700
William Quinn, *President*
Howard Kenworthy, *Senior VP*
Wendy Schuetz, *Vice Pres*
Shirlene Soos, *CFO*
Sue Thomas, *Manager*
EMP: 11
SQ FT: 1,900
SALES (est): 1.5MM **Privately Held**
WEB: www.brogantennyson.com
SIC: 2741 Catalogs: publishing only, not printed on site

(G-1957)
BWAY CORPORATION
7 Wheeling Rd (08810-1526)
PHONE.................................732 997-4100
Rhode Malivert, *Project Engr*
Arthur Smith, *Branch Mgr*
Anthony Shallo, *Maintence Staff*
Larry Smith, *Maintence Staff*
EMP: 129
SALES (corp-wide): 787.1MM **Privately Held**
SIC: 3411 Metal cans
HQ: Bway Corporation
8607 Roberts Dr Ste 250
Atlanta GA 30350

(G-1958)
CARY COMPOUNDS LLC
5 Nicholas Ct (08810-1558)
PHONE.................................732 274-2626
Fax: 732 274-9003
Abier Baynur, *Purch Mgr*
Cheryl Dorry, *Buyer*
Brad Wright, *QC Mgr*
Kenneth B Cary Jr,
Kevin Bank,
◆ EMP: 20
SQ FT: 67,000
SALES (est): 13.9MM **Privately Held**
WEB: www.carycompounds.com
SIC: 2821 Plastics materials & resins

(G-1959)
CELL DISTRIBUTORS INC (PA)
319 Ridge Rd (08810-1532)
PHONE.................................718 473-0162
Schneur Lang, *President*
Chaim Langsam, *Vice Pres*
Yosef Langsam, *CFO*
EMP: 40 EST: 2008
SQ FT: 28,000
SALES: 35MM **Privately Held**
SIC: 2621 Stationery, envelope & tablet papers

(G-1960)
CENTRAL MILLS INC
Also Called: Imagine Screen Printing
473 Ridge Rd (08810-1323)
PHONE.................................732 329-2009
Mark Fischeain, *Branch Mgr*
EMP: 5
SALES (corp-wide): 73.1MM **Privately Held**
SIC: 2329 2759 Men's & boys' sportswear & athletic clothing; screen printing
PA: Central Mills, Inc.
473 Ridge Rd
Dayton NJ 08810
732 329-2009

(G-1961)
CENTRAL MILLS INC (PA)
Also Called: Freeze
473 Ridge Rd (08810-1323)
PHONE.................................732 329-2009
Fax: 732 355-0233
Charles Tebele, *Ch of Bd*
Solomon Shalam, *President*
Maurice Shalam, *Admin Sec*
◆ EMP: 225
SQ FT: 10,000

SALES (est): 73.1MM **Privately Held**
SIC: 2329 2339 2369 2322 Athletic (warmup, sweat & jogging) suits: men's & boys'; sportswear, women's; girls' & children's outerwear; men's & boys' underwear & nightwear; women's & children's nightwear; men's & boys' furnishings

(G-1962)
FLINT GROUP US LLC
Also Called: Flint Group North America
6 Corn Rd (08810-1527)
PHONE.................................732 329-4627
Fax: 732 329-1428
Donald Witt, *Opers Mgr*
Dennis Noreen, *Branch Mgr*
EMP: 9
SQ FT: 30,000
SALES (corp-wide): 3.5B **Privately Held**
WEB: www.flintink.com
SIC: 2893 Printing ink
PA: Flint Group Us Llc
14909 N Beck Rd
Plymouth MI 48170
734 781-4600

(G-1963)
FOLICA INC (PA)
Also Called: Folica.com
11 Corn Rd Ste B (08810-1527)
PHONE.................................609 860-8430
Carl Gish, *President*
Sylvia Zori, *General Mgr*
Puneet Agrawal, *CFO*
Shuo C Huang, *Shareholder*
▲ EMP: 50
SQ FT: 30,000
SALES (est): 12.4MM **Privately Held**
WEB: www.folica.com
SIC: 3999 Hair, dressing of, for the trade

(G-1964)
FRENCHTOASTCOM LLC
Also Called: French Toast
321 Herrod Blvd (08810-1564)
PHONE.................................732 438-5500
Michael Arking, *President*
EMP: 10
SQ FT: 600,000
SALES (est): 2.6MM **Privately Held**
SIC: 5137 2369 Sportswear, women's & children's; girls' & children's outerwear
PA: Lollytogs, Ltd.
100 W 33rd St Ste 1012
New York NY 10001
212 502-6000

(G-1965)
G-III APPAREL GROUP LTD
Black Rivet Mens
308 Herrod Blvd (08810-1563)
PHONE.................................732 438-0209
EMP: 100
SALES (corp-wide): 2.8B **Publicly Held**
WEB: www.g-iii.com
SIC: 2386 5632 Garments, leather; pants, leather; women's accessory & specialty stores
PA: G-Iii Apparel Group, Ltd.
512 7th Ave Fl 35
New York NY 10018
212 403-0500

(G-1966)
G-III LEATHER FASHIONS INC
308 Herrod Blvd (08810-1563)
PHONE.................................212 403-0500
EMP: 100
SALES (corp-wide): 2.8B **Publicly Held**
SIC: 7323 3172 2386 Credit reporting services; personal leather goods; leather & sheep-lined clothing
HQ: G-Iii Leather Fashions, Inc.
512 Fashion Ave Fl 35
New York NY 10018
212 403-0500

(G-1967)
GRAPHCORR LLC
4 Corn Rd (08810-1527)
PHONE.................................732 355-0088
Louis Federico, *General Mgr*
Nicholas Dottino, *Senior VP*
EMP: 16
SQ FT: 50,630

SALES (est): 3.2MM
SALES (est): 14.8B **Publicly Held**
WEB: www.southerncontainer.com
SIC: 2653 Corrugated boxes, partitions, display items, sheets & pad
HQ: Westrock - Southern Container, Llc
133 River Rd
Cos Cob CT 06807
631 232-5704

(G-1968)
GUARDIAN DRUG COMPANY INC
2 Charles Ct (08810-1508)
PHONE.................................609 860-2600
Fax: 609 860-8008
Arvind B Dhruv, *President*
▲ EMP: 90
SQ FT: 136,000
SALES (est): 31.8MM **Privately Held**
WEB: www.guardiandrug.com
SIC: 2834 Drugs acting on the gastrointestinal or genitourinary system; antacids

(G-1969)
IMAGINE SCREEN PRTG & PROD LLC
473 Ridge Rd (08810-1323)
PHONE.................................732 329-2009
Charles Tebele, *Mng Member*
EMP: 90
SQ FT: 25,000
SALES (est): 7MM **Privately Held**
SIC: 2752 Commercial printing, lithographic

(G-1970)
IMPACT UNLIMITED INC (PA)
Also Called: Impact Xm
250 Ridge Rd (08810-1502)
P.O. Box 558 (08810-0558)
PHONE.................................732 274-2000
Fax: 732 274-2417
Jared Pollacco, *President*
Sandie Stransky, *Exec VP*
Joseph Haggerty, *CFO*
Aaron Miller, *Director*
▲ EMP: 150
SQ FT: 206,000
SALES: 60MM **Privately Held**
WEB: www.impactunlimited.com
SIC: 2541 Store & office display cases & fixtures; drainboards, plastic laminated

(G-1971)
INTER PARFUMS INC
60 Stults Rd (08810-1522)
PHONE.................................609 860-1967
Alex Canavan, *Manager*
EMP: 50
SALES (corp-wide): 591.2MM **Publicly Held**
WEB: www.interparfumsinc.com
SIC: 2844 Toilet preparations
PA: Inter Parfums, Inc.
551 5th Ave
New York NY 10176
212 983-2640

(G-1972)
INTERNTNAL FLVORS FRGRNCES INC
Also Called: I F F
150 Docks Corner Rd (08810-1565)
P.O. Box 439 (08810-0439)
PHONE.................................732 329-4600
Fax: 732 329-5555
Larry Landau, *Vice Pres*
Saumya Dwivedi, *Research*
WEI Qin, *Research*
Allan Coulson, *Branch Mgr*
John Senkovich, *Sr Ntwrk Engine*
EMP: 55
SALES (corp-wide): 3.4B **Publicly Held**
WEB: www.iff.com
SIC: 2087 Extracts, flavoring
PA: International Flavors & Fragrances Inc.
521 W 57th St
New York NY 10019
212 765-5500

(G-1973)
JESE APPAREL LLC (PA)
Also Called: Silverwear
8 Nicholas Ct B (08810-1559)
PHONE.................................732 969-3200
Jay Weitzman, *Mng Member*
Edward Baranoff,
Steven Shalom,
Elias Zakay,
▲ EMP: 17
SQ FT: 5,700
SALES (est): 7.1MM **Privately Held**
SIC: 5137 2389 5139 Women's & children's sportswear & swimsuits; sportswear, women's & children's; apparel for handicapped; footwear

(G-1974)
KATE SPADE & COMPANY
Also Called: Liz Claiborne
120 Herrod Blvd Ste 8 (08810-1528)
P.O. Box 935 (08810-0935)
PHONE.................................609 395-3109
Fax: 609 395-3138
EMP: 20
SALES (corp-wide): 1.2B **Publicly Held**
SIC: 2335 Mfg Women's/Misses' Dresses
PA: Kate Spade & Company
2 Park Ave Rm 8r
New York NY 10016
212 354-4900

(G-1975)
KEYSTONE DYEING AND FINISHING (PA)
10 Pine Hill Ct (08810-1631)
PHONE.................................718 482-7780
Louis Silverman, *President*
Allen Jenkins, *Corp Secy*
▲ EMP: 3
SQ FT: 3,000
SALES: 2.3MM **Privately Held**
SIC: 2258 2262 2261 Dyeing & finishing lace goods & warp knit fabric; dyeing: manmade fiber & silk broadwoven fabrics; dyeing cotton broadwoven fabrics

(G-1976)
L & L WELDING CONTRACTORS
3 Wheeling Rd (08810-1526)
PHONE.................................609 395-1600
Fax: 609 395-1090
Frank Lagattuta, *President*
Thomas Lagattuta, *Shareholder*
EMP: 10
SQ FT: 7,000
SALES (est): 2.2MM **Privately Held**
SIC: 3443 Weldments

(G-1977)
LINDE GAS NORTH AMERICA LLC
Also Called: Lifegas
174 Ridge Rd Ste A (08810-1501)
PHONE.................................732 438-9977
Fax: 732 438-9220
Willie Beale, *Branch Mgr*
EMP: 19
SALES (corp-wide): 20.1B **Privately Held**
SIC: 2813 Nitrogen; oxygen, compressed or liquefied
HQ: Linde Gas North America Llc
200 Somerset Corp Blvd # 7000
Bridgewater NJ 08807

(G-1978)
LOLLYTOGS LTD
Also Called: French Toast
321 Herrod Blvd (08810-1564)
PHONE.................................732 438-5500
Morris Sutton, *Branch Mgr*
EMP: 13
SALES (corp-wide): 2.6MM **Privately Held**
SIC: 5137 2369 2361 1541 Women's & children's clothing; girls' & children's outerwear; girls' & children's dresses, blouses & shirts; industrial buildings & warehouses
PA: Lollytogs, Ltd.
100 W 33rd St Ste 1012
New York NY 10001
212 502-6000

(G-1979)
LOLLYTOGS LTD
Also Called: French Toast
321 Herrod Blvd (08810-1564)
P.O. Box 1001 (08810-1001)
PHONE....................................732 438-5500
EMP: 100
SQ FT: 600,000
SALES (corp-wide): 2.2MM **Privately Held**
SIC: 2369 5137 Mfg Girl/Youth Outerwear Whol Women's/Child's Clothing
PA: Lollytogs, Ltd.
    100 W 33rd St Ste 1012
    New York NY 10001
    212 502-6000

(G-1980)
MINCING TRADING CORPORATION
Also Called: Mincing Overseas Spice Company
10 Tower Rd (08810-1571)
PHONE....................................732 355-9944
Manoj K Ruparelia, *President*
Charlie Armenti, *Plant Mgr*
Harshad K Ruparelia, *Treasurer*
Kaushik Jobanputra, *Controller*
Nagy Beskal, *Manager*
▲ **EMP:** 29 **EST:** 1927
SQ FT: 50,000
SALES (est): 6.7MM
SALES (corp-wide): 3.6MM **Privately Held**
WEB: www.mincing.com
SIC: 2099 5149 Seasonings & spices; spices, including grinding; spices & seasonings
PA: Mincing International Inc.
    10 Tower Rd
    Dayton NJ 08810
    732 355-9944

(G-1981)
NETWORK ACCESS SYSTEMS INCORPR
19 Issac Dr (08810-1314)
PHONE....................................732 355-9770
Bruce Lin, *President*
Roy Jao, *Corp Secy*
Suo Jao, *Vice Pres*
EMP: 9
SQ FT: 6,000
SALES (est): 760K **Privately Held**
WEB: www.naspc.com
SIC: 3695 Computer software tape & disks: blank, rigid & floppy

(G-1982)
PHARMEDIUM SERVICES LLC
36 Stults Rd (08810-1540)
PHONE....................................847 457-2362
William R Spaulding, *CEO*
EMP: 44
SALES (corp-wide): 153.1B **Publicly Held**
SIC: 2834 Pharmaceutical preparations
HQ: Pharmedium Services, Llc
    150 N Field Dr Ste 350
    Lake Forest IL 60045
    800 523-7749

(G-1983)
PIRAMAL GLASS - USA INC (HQ)
329 Herrod Blvd (08810-1564)
PHONE....................................856 293-6400
Niraj Tipre, *CEO*
Daniel Hoover, *Plant Engr*
Jatin Arora, *Accounts Exec*
Gautam Savkar, *Accounts Exec*
Douglas Thompson, *Sales Staff*
▲ **EMP:** 35
SALES (est): 244MM
SALES (corp-wide): 186.3MM **Privately Held**
SIC: 3221 Glass containers
PA: Gujarat Glass Limited
    6th Floor Piramal Tower Annexe
    Mumbai MH 40001
    304 669-69

(G-1984)
RAM PRODUCTS INC
182 Ridge Rd Ste D (08810-1594)
PHONE....................................732 651-5500
Fax: 732 651-6688
Richard L Wiesen, *President*
▲ **EMP:** 9
SQ FT: 4,000
SALES (est): 1.3MM **Privately Held**
WEB: www.1010files.com
SIC: 3545 Drill bits, metalworking

(G-1985)
RHODIUM SOFTWARE INC
10 Scotto Pl (08810-1393)
PHONE....................................848 248-2906
Kandan Kanakaraj, *President*
Rajan Rajarathinam, *Chairman*
EMP: 6
SALES (est): 460K **Privately Held**
WEB: www.rhodiumsoftware.com
SIC: 7372 Prepackaged software

(G-1986)
RICHMOND INDUSTRIES INC
1 Chris Ct (08810-1536)
PHONE....................................732 355-1616
Fax: 732 355-1617
Keith Digrazio, *President*
Jennifer Williams, *Vice Pres*
EMP: 32 **EST:** 1959
SQ FT: 40,000
SALES (est): 7.5MM **Privately Held**
WEB: www.richmond-industries.com
SIC: 3365 Aluminum foundries

(G-1987)
SLT FOODS INC
Also Called: Slt Imports
303 Ridge Rd (08810-1580)
PHONE....................................732 661-1030
Sandip Patel, *President*
Dinesh Jani, *Finance*
Sejal Patel, *Manager*
◆ **EMP:** 16
SQ FT: 75,400
SALES: 38MM **Privately Held**
SIC: 5149 2045 Pasta & rice; prepared flour mixes & doughs

(G-1988)
SONOCO PRODUCTS COMPANY
5 Stults Rd (08810-1541)
PHONE....................................609 655-0300
Fax: 609 655-0745
Jon Greenwalk, *Manager*
EMP: 70
SALES (corp-wide): 5B **Publicly Held**
WEB: www.sonoco.com
SIC: 2655 3411 Cans, composite: foil-fiber & other: from purchased fiber; metal cans
PA: Sonoco Products Company
    1 N 2nd St
    Hartsville SC 29550
    843 383-7000

(G-1989)
SUNSHINE BOUQUET COMPANY (PA)
3 Chris Ct Ste A (08810-1543)
P.O. Box 892 (08810-0892)
PHONE....................................732 274-2900
Fax: 732 274-3378
John Simko, *President*
Andrew Johnston, *CFO*
▲ **EMP:** 150
SQ FT: 65,000
SALES: 208MM **Privately Held**
WEB: www.sunshinebouquet.com
SIC: 5193 3999 Flowers, fresh; flowers, artificial & preserved

(G-1990)
SWISS MADISON LLC
19 Stults Rd (08810-1541)
PHONE....................................434 623-4766
Mendel Gricman, *Mng Member*
Samuel Greisman,
EMP: 19
SQ FT: 2,000
SALES: 500K **Privately Held**
SIC: 2499 Seats, toilet

(G-1991)
TIN MAN SNACKS LLC
351 Herrod Blvd (08810-1564)
PHONE....................................732 329-9100
Joe Glusak, *President*
Charles Fern,
Vincent Mastria,
EMP: 30
SALES (est): 5.4MM **Privately Held**
SIC: 2099 Food preparations

(G-1992)
TOTAL RELIANCE LLC
11b Corn Rd (08810-1527)
PHONE....................................732 640-5079
Brian Kirst, *Co-Owner*
Adam Napoli, *Co-Owner*
EMP: 18
SQ FT: 64,000
SALES (est): 1.5MM **Privately Held**
SIC: 7331 4731 7372 Direct mail advertising services; freight transportation arrangement; prepackaged software

(G-1993)
TRIANGLE HOME FASHIONS LLC
9 Nicholas Ct Ste A (08810-2531)
PHONE....................................732 355-9800
Jenny Zhu, *President*
Jared Cohen, *COO*
Allen Darwin, *Vice Pres*
Jeffrey Swartz, *Vice Pres*
▲ **EMP:** 7
SALES (est): 1MM **Privately Held**
SIC: 2392 5023 Sheets, fabric: made from purchased materials; sheets, textile

(G-1994)
WESTROCK RKT COMPANY
1 Corn Rd (08810-1527)
P.O. Box 440 (08810-0440)
PHONE....................................732 274-2500
Todd Crowell, *Branch Mgr*
EMP: 100
SQ FT: 100,000
SALES (corp-wide): 14.8B **Publicly Held**
WEB: www.rocktenn.com
SIC: 2653 Boxes, corrugated: made from purchased materials
HQ: Westrock Rkt Company
    1000 Abernathy Rd Ste 125
    Atlanta GA 30328
    770 448-2193

(G-1995)
WHOLE YEAR TRADING CO INC
117 Docks Corner Rd Ste B (08810-2529)
PHONE....................................732 238-1196
Jane Han, *President*
Charles Hou, *Vice Pres*
▲ **EMP:** 4
SQ FT: 5,000
SALES: 150K **Privately Held**
SIC: 3089 Planters, plastic

(G-1996)
WOOD TEXTURES
251 Herrod Blvd (08810-1539)
PHONE....................................732 230-5005
Thomas Wu, *Principal*
▲ **EMP:** 10
SALES (est): 1.6MM **Privately Held**
SIC: 2599 Furniture & fixtures

Deal
Monmouth County

(G-1997)
AMBO CONSULTING LLC
Also Called: Smart Gear Toys
82 Norwood Ave Ste 2 (07723-1375)
PHONE....................................732 663-0000
Sam Cohen, *CEO*
Jason Cohen, *President*
▲ **EMP:** 3
SQ FT: 2,500
SALES: 2.4MM **Privately Held**
SIC: 5092 3944 Toys & games; games, toys & children's vehicles

---

Deepwater
Salem County

(G-1998)
CHEMOURS COMPANY
Bldg 603 Rr 130 (08023)
PHONE....................................856 540-3398
John Moriarty, *Manager*
EMP: 7
SALES (corp-wide): 6.1B **Publicly Held**
WEB: www.dupont.com
SIC: 2992 Lubricating oils & greases
PA: The Chemours Company
    1007 Market St
    Wilmington DE 19898
    302 773-1000

Delair
Camden County

(G-1999)
ALUMINUM SHAPES LLC
9000 River Rd (08110-3296)
PHONE....................................888 488-7427
Johnson Shao, *CEO*
EMP: 302
SALES (est): 38MM **Privately Held**
SIC: 3365 3354 Aluminum foundries; aluminum extruded products

(G-2000)
AUDIO AND VIDEO LABS INC
Also Called: Oasis CD Manufacturing
7905 N Crescent Blvd (08110-1402)
PHONE....................................856 661-5772
Micah Solomon, *Principal*
EMP: 20 **Privately Held**
WEB: www.oasiscd.com
SIC: 3652 Compact laser discs, prerecorded
HQ: Audio And Video Labs Inc.
    7905 N Crescent Blvd
    Pennsauken NJ 08110
    856 663-9030

(G-2001)
SHAPES/ARCH HOLDINGS LLC (PA)
Also Called: Arch America
9000 River Rd (08110-3204)
PHONE....................................856 662-5500
Thomas Riddle, *CEO*
Sean Cleary, *Controller*
John May, *Mng Member*
▲ **EMP:** 116
SQ FT: 1,500,000
SALES (est): 113.8MM **Privately Held**
SIC: 3354 3365 Aluminum extruded products; aluminum foundries

---

Delanco
Burlington County

(G-2002)
AMERICAN STRIP STEEL INC
901 Coopertown Rd (08075-5205)
PHONE....................................856 461-8300
Leroy Scheckler, *President*
EMP: 4
SALES (corp-wide): 163.5MM **Privately Held**
SIC: 5051 3441 3316 Steel; fabricated structural metal; cold finishing of steel shapes
HQ: American Strip Steel Inc.
    400 Metuchen Rd
    South Plainfield NJ 07080
    800 526-1216

(G-2003)
ATCO PALLET COMPANY
1000 Creek Rd (08075-5214)
P.O. Box 5115 (08075-0515)
PHONE....................................856 461-8141
Fax: 856 461-8146
David Hajduk, *President*
EMP: 25
SQ FT: 15,000

GEOGRAPHIC

SALES (est): 4.2MM **Privately Held**
SIC: 2448 Pallets, wood

(G-2004)
COLD HEADED FASTENERS INC
401 Creek Rd Ste D (08075-5243)
P.O. Box 5488, Riverside (08075-5488)
PHONE..............................856 461-3244
Fax: 856 461-3299
Charles C Massey, *President*
EMP: 6
SQ FT: 12,000
SALES (est): 1.1MM **Privately Held**
WEB: www.coldheadedfasteners.com
SIC: 3452 3499 5085 Screws, metal; welding tips, heat resistant: metal; fasteners, industrial: nuts, bolts, screws, etc.

(G-2005)
COSTUME GALLERY INC
700 Creek Rd (08075-5212)
PHONE..............................609 386-6601
Fax: 609 386-0677
Ellen Ferreira, *CEO*
Rick Ferreira, *Principal*
Diane Wallace, *Office Mgr*
Kaylee Krogulski, *Manager*
Kim Keller, *Director*
▲ EMP: 42
SALES (est): 6.8MM **Privately Held**
SIC: 2389 Uniforms & vestments; costumes

(G-2006)
HAROLD F FISHER & SONS INC
Also Called: Fisher, Harold & Sons
200 Ash St (08075-4476)
PHONE..............................800 624-2868
Frank Fisher, *President*
Barbara Fisher, *Vice Pres*
EMP: 5
SQ FT: 17,000
SALES (est): 350K **Privately Held**
SIC: 2394 Canvas covers & drop cloths; tarpaulins, fabric: made from purchased materials

(G-2007)
MEDLAUREL INC
Also Called: Laurel Manufacturers
620 Cooper St (08075-4670)
P.O. Box 5306, Riverside (08075-0378)
PHONE..............................856 461-6600
Fax: 856 461-6622
Daniel Iosc, *President*
Ted Gorczynski, *Vice Pres*
Tricia Meyer, *Vice Pres*
Tricia Sell, *Vice Pres*
▲ EMP: 36
SQ FT: 50,000
SALES (est): 7.4MM **Privately Held**
WEB: www.laurelmfg.com
SIC: 2541 3469 3993 3444 Wood partitions & fixtures; machine parts, stamped or pressed metal; signs & advertising specialties; sheet metalwork

(G-2008)
STYLEX INC
740 Coopertown Rd (08075-5252)
P.O. Box 5038 (08075-0438)
PHONE..............................856 461-5600
Fax: 856 461-5574
John Golden, *President*
Bruce Golden, *Corp Secy*
Joe Farrell, *Vice Pres*
Aleksander Calkowski, *Engineer*
Joe Kowalonek, *CFO*
◆ EMP: 185 EST: 1950
SQ FT: 140,000
SALES (est): 35.6MM **Privately Held**
WEB: www.stylexseating.com
SIC: 2522 Chairs, office: padded or plain, except wood

Delran
Burlington County

(G-2009)
ACTEGA NORTH AMERICA INC (DH)
950 S Chester Ave Ste B2 (08075-1271)
PHONE..............................856 829-6300

Mark Westwell, *President*
Brian Long, *CFO*
▼ EMP: 250
SALES (est): 83.7MM **Privately Held**
WEB: www.actega.com/kelstar
SIC: 2851 2952 Paints & allied products; coating compounds, tar
HQ: Actega Gmbh
Abelstr. 43
Wesel 46483
281 670-8

(G-2010)
BILLOWS ELECTRIC SUPPLY CO INC (PA)
1813 Underwood Blvd (08075-1232)
PHONE..............................856 751-2200
Jeffrey Billow, *President*
Bob White, *COO*
Mitch Billows, *Vice Pres*
David Lowenstein, *Vice Pres*
Scott Pressler, *CFO*
EMP: 130
SALES (est): 285MM **Privately Held**
SIC: 5063 3679 3621 3643 Electrical supplies; lighting fixtures; electronic circuits; motors & generators; current-carrying wiring devices; noncurrent-carrying wiring services

(G-2011)
BIOCLIMATIC AIR SYSTEMS LLC
600 Delran Pkwy Ste D (08075-1255)
PHONE..............................856 764-4300
Stephen Zitin,
Michele Bottino,
EMP: 22
SQ FT: 20,000
SALES (est): 4.5MM
SALES (corp-wide): 8.9MM **Privately Held**
WEB: www.bioclimatic.com
SIC: 3564 Air purification equipment
PA: Bioclimatic Inc
600 Delran Pkwy Ste D
Delran NJ 08075
856 764-4300

(G-2012)
BIOCLIMATIC INC (PA)
600 Delran Pkwy Ste D (08075-1255)
PHONE..............................856 764-4300
Fax: 856 764-4301
Stephen Zitin, *President*
Michelle Bottino, *Vice Pres*
EMP: 30
SQ FT: 10,000
SALES (est): 8.9MM **Privately Held**
SIC: 3564 Blowers & fans; air purification equipment

(G-2013)
C R BARD INC
Dabol Division
1822 Underwood Blvd (08075-1233)
PHONE..............................856 461-0946
Alan Grumbling, *Plt & Fclts Mgr*
EMP: 9
SQ FT: 15,640
SALES (corp-wide): 12B **Publicly Held**
WEB: www.crbard.com
SIC: 3841 Surgical & medical instruments
HQ: C. R. Bard, Inc.
730 Central Ave
New Providence NJ 07974
908 277-8000

(G-2014)
CARNEGIE PHARMACEUTICALS LLC
600 Delran Pkwy (08075-1255)
PHONE..............................732 783-7010
Rakesh Grover, *CEO*
EMP: 5 EST: 2015
SALES (est): 731.1K **Privately Held**
SIC: 2834 Pharmaceutical preparations

(G-2015)
CHERUBINI YACHTS LTD LBLTY CO
51 Norman Ave (08075-1009)
PHONE..............................856 764-5319
David Cherubini,
EMP: 9

SALES (est): 138.1K **Privately Held**
WEB: www.cherubiniyachts.com
SIC: 3732 Yachts, building & repairing

(G-2016)
DORALEX INC
403 Saint Mihiel Dr (08075-3030)
P.O. Box 265, Riverside (08075-0285)
PHONE..............................856 764-0694
Fax: 856 764-7402
EMP: 6
SQ FT: 2,000
SALES (est): 510K **Privately Held**
SIC: 8731 3679 Research And Development Of Electronic Components And Mfrs Electronic Components

(G-2017)
LAUDA-BRINKMANN LP
1819 Underwood Blvd Ste 2 (08075-1246)
PHONE..............................856 764-7300
Richard Jezykowski, *CEO*
Susan Colfer, *Opers Mgr*
Jeff Wilson, *Sales Dir*
Mike Andress, *Sales Mgr*
Jillian Kennedy, *Sales Mgr*
▲ EMP: 12
SALES (est): 2.7MM **Privately Held**
SIC: 3585 Parts for heating, cooling & refrigerating equipment

(G-2018)
LAUDA-BRINKMANN MANAGEMENT INC
1819 Underwood Blvd Ste 2 (08075-1246)
PHONE..............................856 764-7300
Richard Jezykowski, *CEO*
EMP: 12
SALES (est): 1.2MM
SALES (corp-wide): 75.3MM **Privately Held**
SIC: 3585 Parts for heating, cooling & refrigerating equipment
PA: Lauda Dr. R. Wobser Gmbh & Co. Kg
Pfarrstr. 41-43
Lauda-Konigshofen 97922
934 350-30

(G-2019)
M & S OPTICS INC
2910 Route 130 (08075-2522)
PHONE..............................856 764-0200
Clifford G Mancine, *President*
Ralph Sollenberger, *Treasurer*
Joseph Mancine, *Admin Sec*
EMP: 10
SALES (est): 1.2MM **Privately Held**
SIC: 3851 Lenses, ophthalmic

(G-2020)
PITNEY BOWES INC
1835 Underwood Blvd Ste 1 (08075-1249)
PHONE..............................856 764-2240
Fax: 856 764-0025
Rcihard Potero, *Manager*
EMP: 200
SALES (corp-wide): 3.5B **Publicly Held**
SIC: 3579 7359 Postage meters; business machine & electronic equipment rental services
PA: Pitney Bowes Inc.
3001 Summer St Ste 3
Stamford CT 06905
203 356-5000

(G-2021)
SEA GULL LIGHTING PRODUCTS LLC (HQ)
Also Called: Woodriver Industries
1829 Underwood Blvd Ste 2 (08075-4135)
P.O. Box 329, Riverside (08075-0329)
PHONE..............................856 764-0500
Bruce Hawkins, *CFO*
Matt Vollmer, *Mng Member*
Alan Hirsch,
Michael Hirsch,
◆ EMP: 400 EST: 1919
SQ FT: 320,000
SALES (est): 160.8MM **Privately Held**
WEB: www.seagulllighting.com
SIC: 3645 Residential lighting fixtures
PA: Quality Home Brands Holdings Llc
125 Rose Feiss Blvd
Bronx NY 10454
718 292-2024

(G-2022)
SIMON & SCHUSTER INC
100 Front St (08075-1181)
P.O. Box 500, Riverside (08075-7500)
PHONE..............................856 461-6500
Fax: 856 461-4205
David Schaesfer, *Vice Pres*
Dave Schaeffer, *Vice Pres*
Pat Kelman, *Plant Mgr*
EMP: 350
SALES (corp-wide): 13.7B **Publicly Held**
SIC: 2741 Miscellaneous publishing
HQ: Simon & Schuster, Inc.
1230 Ave Of The Americas
New York NY 10020
212 698-7000

(G-2023)
SPL HOLDINGS LLC
Also Called: H.N. Lucas & Son
211 Carriage Ln (08075-1237)
PHONE..............................856 764-2400
Fax: 856 764-2678
Pamela S Lloyd,
Stephen H Lloyd,
EMP: 12
SQ FT: 6,700
SALES (est): 1.2MM **Privately Held**
SIC: 3599 Machine shop, jobbing & repair

(G-2024)
WOYSHNER SERVICE COMPANY INC
Also Called: Wsc International
813 Edgewood Ave (08075-1207)
PHONE..............................856 461-9196
EMP: 4
SALES: 1MM **Privately Held**
SIC: 3568 Mfg Power Transmission Equipment

(G-2025)
ZANOTTI TRANSBLOCK USA CORP
1810 Underwood Blvd 1 (08075-1233)
PHONE..............................917 584-9357
John Boschetti, *President*
EMP: 2 EST: 2014
SQ FT: 15,000
SALES: 3MM
SALES (corp-wide): 955.5K **Privately Held**
SIC: 3585 Refrigeration & heating equipment
PA: Mantovani Carlo
Via Ii Giugno 6
Argenta FE 44011

Demarest
Bergen County

(G-2026)
BLU-J2 LLC
Also Called: Strap-Its
91 Alpine Ct (07627-2318)
PHONE..............................201 750-1407
Julie Slavitt, *Mng Member*
Judy Simon,
EMP: 4
SALES (est): 329.7K **Privately Held**
SIC: 2389 Apparel for handicapped

(G-2027)
COINING TECHNOLOGIES INC
35 Monhegan St (07627)
PHONE..............................866 897-2304
Fax: 973 253-9611
Martin G Rosansky, *President*
Jake Allen, *Business Mgr*
Dennis Decker, *Vice Pres*
Donna Parker, *Vice Pres*
Raymond Reboli, *Vice Pres*
▲ EMP: 70
SQ FT: 52,000
SALES (est): 12.9MM **Privately Held**
SIC: 3469 Stamping metal for the trade

Dennisville
Cape May County

(G-2028)
BLUEWATER INDUSTRIES INC
Also Called: Bluewater Wldg & Fabrication
1089 Rt 47 (08214)
PHONE..................609 427-1012
Fax: 609 522-2500
Ed Myland, *President*
EMP: 15
SQ FT: 10,000
SALES: 1.3MM **Privately Held**
WEB: www.bluewaterwelding.com
SIC: 7692 Welding repair

Denville
Morris County

(G-2029)
ACUSTRIP CO INC (PA)
124 E Main St Apt 109b (07834-2169)
PHONE..................973 299-8237
Ron Schornstein, *Principal*
EMP: 18
SALES (est): 2.1MM **Privately Held**
SIC: 3826 Liquid testing apparatus

(G-2030)
ANDIS INC
Also Called: Citizen of Morris County, The
124 E Main St (07834-2100)
P.O. Box 7 (07834-0007)
PHONE..................973 627-0400
Fax: 973 627-0403
EMP: 6
SQ FT: 2,000
SALES (est): 290K **Privately Held**
SIC: 2711 Newspapers-Publishing/Printing

(G-2031)
ANTHONY & SONS BAKERY ITLN BKY
20 Luger Rd (07834-2639)
PHONE..................973 625-2323
Fax: 973 625-7993
Anthony Dattolo, *President*
Joseph Dattolo, *Principal*
Ricky Martinez, *COO*
Baldo Dattolo, *Vice Pres*
Robert Tobia, *Vice Pres*
▲ **EMP:** 98 **EST:** 1984
SQ FT: 30,000
SALES (est): 22MM **Privately Held**
WEB: www.anthonyandsonsbakery.com
SIC: 2051 5812 5149 Bakery: wholesale
or wholesale/retail combined; eating
places; groceries & related products

(G-2032)
CO-PLANAR INC
88 Ford Rd (07834-1378)
P.O. Box 1115 (07834-8115)
PHONE..................973 625-3500
James Cote, *President*
Michael Mullen, *Vice Pres*
▲ **EMP:** 18
SQ FT: 35,000
SALES (est): 4.8MM **Privately Held**
WEB: www.co-planar.com
SIC: 3469 Stamping metal for the trade

(G-2033)
COMPONENTS CORPORATION
6 Kinsey Pl (07834-2692)
PHONE..................866 426-6726
Fax: 973 361-5801
Byron Minter, *President*
Monica Minter, *Corp Secy*
Christopher Minter, *Vice Pres*
William Gordon, *VP Mfg*
Sherry Vanderhoof, *Prdtn Mgr*
EMP: 17 **EST:** 1943
SQ FT: 12,000
SALES (est): 2.6MM **Privately Held**
WEB: www.componentscorp.com
SIC: 3678 Electronic connectors

(G-2034)
CUSTOM DECORATORS SERVICE
415 E Main St Ste 3 (07834-2557)
PHONE..................973 625-0516
Walter Kunzel, *Owner*
EMP: 6
SALES (est): 489K **Privately Held**
SIC: 5023 2512 Draperies; upholstered
household furniture

(G-2035)
DENVILLE DIAGNOSTICS IMAGING
Also Called: Denville Diagnostic Imaging
161 E Main St Ste 101 (07834-2647)
PHONE..................973 586-1212
Michael Dwyre, *CEO*
Peter Barba, *CFO*
Alaina Capozzoli, *Admin Asst*
EMP: 21
SQ FT: 1,000
SALES (est): 4.1MM **Privately Held**
SIC: 3826 Magnetic resonance imaging
apparatus

(G-2036)
DIAGENODE INC
400 Morris Ave Ste 101 (07834-1362)
PHONE..................862 209-4680
Didier Allaer, *CEO*
Ignacio Mazon, *General Mgr*
Rosemarie Koster, *Finance Mgr*
Tracy Faustermann, *Accounts Mgr*
John McShane, *Sales Executive*
▲ **EMP:** 7
SQ FT: 3,000
SALES (est): 1.7MM **Privately Held**
SIC: 3821 Laboratory apparatus & furniture

(G-2037)
DIGITAL XPRESS LLC
3 Luger Rd Ste 3 # 3 (07834-2638)
P.O. Box 545 (07834-0545)
PHONE..................973 627-2609
Rachel Kerr, *Manager*
Jeffrey D Jones,
David Marfiewicz,
EMP: 6
SQ FT: 18,000
SALES (est): 619.7K **Privately Held**
WEB: www.dxp.cc
SIC: 2759 2752 Commercial printing;
commercial printing, lithographic

(G-2038)
EAGLE COMMUNICATIONS INC
2902 Vantage Ct (07834-3452)
PHONE..................973 366-6181
Angelo Salvatore, *President*
EMP: 4
SALES: 400K **Privately Held**
SIC: 3661 Telephone station equipment &
parts, wire

(G-2039)
FGH SYSTEMS INC
10 Prospect Pl (07834-2632)
PHONE..................973 625-8114
Frank G Hohmann, *President*
Eric Hohmann, *Corp Secy*
▲ **EMP:** 17
SQ FT: 12,000
SALES (est): 3MM **Privately Held**
WEB: www.fghsystems.com
SIC: 3599 Machine shop, jobbing & repair

(G-2040)
GENERAL RELIANCE CORPORATION
88 Ford Rd Ste 20 (07834-1357)
PHONE..................973 361-1400
George Michelin, *CEO*
Sheldon Masser, *President*
Steve Stamper, *President*
Doreen Cornelius, *COO*
Chris Schmidt, *Vice Pres*
EMP: 44 **EST:** 1960
SQ FT: 22,000
SALES (est): 9.5MM **Privately Held**
WEB: www.generalreliance.com
SIC: 3679 Harness assemblies for elec-
tronic use: wire or cable; electronic cir-
cuits

(G-2041)
GERARDI PRESS INC
3 Luger Rd Ste 3 # 3 (07834-2638)
P.O. Box 545 (07834-0545)
PHONE..................973 627-2600
Fax: 973 627-2624
Keith Gerardi, *President*
Valerie Bradley, *Accounting Mgr*
Mark Correia, *Manager*
Gus Metz, *Admin Sec*
EMP: 8
SQ FT: 18,800
SALES: 1.6MM **Privately Held**
WEB: www.gerardipress.com
SIC: 2752 Commercial printing, litho-
graphic

(G-2042)
INTEGRATED PACKG SYSTEMS INC
Also Called: Ips
3 Luger Rd Ste 5 (07834-2638)
PHONE..................973 664-0020
Robert W Fields, *President*
Michael T McNeila, *Exec VP*
Janice Mastropaolo, *Manager*
▲ **EMP:** 8
SQ FT: 18,000
SALES (est): 2.1MM **Privately Held**
WEB: www.ipsnj.com
SIC: 3569 5084 Liquid automation ma-
chinery & equipment; packaging machin-
ery & equipment

(G-2043)
J & R CUSTOM WOODWORKING INC
449 E Main St (07834-2515)
PHONE..................973 625-4114
Joel Kriegsfeld, *President*
Rhea Kriegsfeld, *Admin Sec*
EMP: 5 **EST:** 1971
SQ FT: 2,100
SALES (est): 488.6K **Privately Held**
SIC: 2434 Wood kitchen cabinets

(G-2044)
JUSTICE LABORATORY SOFTWARE
Also Called: PC Science Training Center
1 Indian Rd Ste 2 (07834-2000)
P.O. Box 1227 (07834-8227)
PHONE..................973 586-8551
George Schriner, *President*
EMP: 8 **EST:** 1999
SALES (est): 682.7K **Privately Held**
WEB: www.justiceinnovations.com
SIC: 7372 Prepackaged software

(G-2045)
KUDAS INDUSTRIES INC
6 Dorchester Dr (07834-3809)
PHONE..................412 751-0260
Todd G Kudas, *Principal*
EMP: 10
SALES (est): 1MM **Privately Held**
SIC: 3999 Manufacturing industries

(G-2046)
LB ELECTRIC CO LLC
12 Knoll Top Ct (07834-3623)
PHONE..................973 366-2188
Leon Baptiste, *Principal*
Leon K Baptiste, *Principal*
EMP: 8
SALES (est): 805.1K **Privately Held**
SIC: 4911 3699 1731 Electric services;
electrical equipment & supplies; electrical
work

(G-2047)
MECA ELECTRONICS INC
459 E Main St (07834-2515)
PHONE..................973 625-0661
Fax: 973 625-1258
William Davo, *President*
Thomas Hickey, *Vice Pres*
Joseph Scarano, *QC Mgr*
Christopher Connelly, *Chief Engr*
Pierre Kewcharoen, *Engineer*
EMP: 51 **EST:** 1961
SQ FT: 8,000
SALES (est): 4.6MM **Privately Held**
WEB: www.e-meca.com
SIC: 3679 Microwave components

(G-2048)
MEDPEN INC
52 Memory Ln (07834-2455)
PHONE..................973 627-8067
Lauren Cerruto, *CEO*
EMP: 4
SALES (est): 173.9K **Privately Held**
SIC: 8999 3841 Writing for publication;
anesthesia apparatus

(G-2049)
MEMORY INTERNATIONAL CORP
25 Redwood Rd (07834-3502)
PHONE..................973 586-2653
Don Chuan, *President*
EMP: 12
SALES (est): 1MM **Privately Held**
SIC: 3674 Semiconductors & related de-
vices

(G-2050)
MINARDI BAKING CO INC
20 Luger Rd (07834-2639)
PHONE..................973 742-1107
Fax: 973 742-7410
Thomas Minardi, *President*
Joseph Minardi, *Corp Secy*
John C Minardi, *Vice Pres*
EMP: 45 **EST:** 1922
SQ FT: 7,000
SALES (est): 4.5MM **Privately Held**
SIC: 5149 5461 2051 Bakery products;
bakeries; bread, cake & related products

(G-2051)
PLANITROI INC (PA)
Also Called: Plan It Roi
100-10 Ford Rd Ste 10 (07834)
PHONE..................973 664-0700
Paul Baum, *President*
Andrew Bauer, *CFO*
Sharon Berman, *Manager*
Johnny Fischer, *Manager*
▲ **EMP:** 65
SQ FT: 55,000
SALES (est): 22.7MM **Privately Held**
WEB: www.planitroi.com
SIC: 7373 8742 3571 Computer system
selling services; management consulting
services; electronic computers

(G-2052)
QUALSERV IMPORTS INC
Also Called: Pata Pal
3125 State Route 10 (07834-3493)
PHONE..................973 620-9234
David Quincey, *President*
▲ **EMP:** 3
SQ FT: 1,000
SALES: 2.4MM **Privately Held**
SIC: 5199 2631 Gifts & novelties; pets &
pet supplies; container, packaging &
boxboard

(G-2053)
REDMOND BCMS INC
103 Pocono Rd (07834-2948)
PHONE..................973 664-2000
Georgia Redmond, *President*
EMP: 70 **EST:** 1952
SQ FT: 40,000
SALES (est): 9.1MM **Privately Held**
WEB: www.redmondbcms.com
SIC: 2752 2791 2789 2759 Newspapers,
lithographed only; typesetting; bookbind-
ing & related work; commercial printing

(G-2054)
REVELATION GALLERY INC
Also Called: Revelation Art Gallery
22 Broadway (07834-2704)
PHONE..................973 627-6558
Josh Cramer, *President*
EMP: 4
SALES (est): 295.2K **Privately Held**
SIC: 5999 2499 8999 Art dealers; picture
& mirror frames, wood; art restoration

(G-2055)
RICONPHARMA LLC (HQ)
100 Ford Rd Ste 9 (07834-1396)
PHONE..................973 627-4685
Billa Praveen Reddy, *Vice Pres*
Satya Valiveti, *Vice Pres*

GEOGRAPHIC

Akash Arabole, *Project Mgr*
Ravi S Tallapragada, *QA Dir*
Kishore Marimganti, *Research*
EMP: 34
SQ FT: 10,000
SALES (est): 10.2MM **Privately Held**
WEB: www.riconpharma.com
SIC: 2834 Pharmaceutical preparations

(G-2056)
ROLO SYSTEMS
Also Called: Denville Dairy
34a Broadway (07834-2704)
PHONE..........................973 627-4214
Jack Fine, *President*
Lois Fine, *Vice Pres*
EMP: 22
SQ FT: 900
SALES (est): 3.1MM **Privately Held**
WEB: www.denvilleprobarbers.com
SIC: 2024 5812 Ice cream & frozen desserts; ice cream stands or dairy bars

(G-2057)
RUDOLPH INSTRUMENTS INC
Also Called: Digipol Technologies
400 Morris Ave Ste 120 (07834-1362)
PHONE..........................973 227-0139
Fax: 973 983-6290
Kumar Utukuri, *President*
EMP: 5 **EST:** 1948
SQ FT: 6,000
SALES (est): 500K **Privately Held**
WEB: www.rudolphinst.com
SIC: 3826 Analytical instruments

(G-2058)
SENSOR MEDICAL TECHNOLOGY LLC
4 Stewart Ct (07834-1028)
PHONE..........................425 358-7381
Gregory L Heacock, *CEO*
Louise Culham, *Exec VP*
EMP: 5 **EST:** 2012
SALES (est): 629.9K **Privately Held**
SIC: 3851 3841 5048 Lens coating, ophthalmic; lenses, ophthalmic; ophthalmic instruments & apparatus; ophthalmic goods

(G-2059)
SPECIAL OPTICS INC
3 Stewart Ct (07834-1038)
PHONE..........................973 366-7289
Fax: 973 366-7407
Robert Bradford, *Ch of Bd*
David J Manzi, *President*
Bob Stewart, *Plant Mgr*
Christopher Riley, *Engineer*
Steven Morales, *Sales Mgr*
EMP: 18
SQ FT: 25,000
SALES (est): 3.3MM **Privately Held**
WEB: www.specialoptics.com
SIC: 3827 Optical instruments & lenses

(G-2060)
TRI-POWER CONSULTING SVCS LLC
2 Richwood Pl (07834-2615)
PHONE..........................973 227-7100
Fax: 973 227-7959
Steve Woodward, *CFO*
Robert Mastice, *CIO*
Linda M La, *Director*
Anthony La Rosa,
Michael Mastice,
EMP: 30
SALES (est): 13.8MM **Privately Held**
WEB: www.tripower.net
SIC: 5085 3549 Industrial supplies; marking machines, metalworking

(G-2061)
TX TECHNOLOGY CORP
Also Called: Chatlos Systems
100 Ford Rd Ste 18 (07834-1396)
PHONE..........................973 442-7500
Fax: 973 442-7575
Don Black, *Principal*
Nancy Edwards, *Office Mgr*
▲ **EMP:** 120
SQ FT: 12,000

SALES (est): 18.5MM **Privately Held**
WEB: www.txtechnology.com
SIC: 3823 Pressure measurement instruments, industrial

(G-2062)
YANKEE TOOL INC
17 Edgewater Dr (07834-1811)
PHONE..........................973 664-0878
John Pierce, *President*
Linda Pierce, *Vice Pres*
EMP: 10
SQ FT: 6,000
SALES (est): 200K **Privately Held**
SIC: 2844 Manicure preparations

Deptford
Gloucester County

(G-2063)
DEPTFORD PLATING CO INC
Dein Ave Rr 41 (08096)
P.O. Box 5056 (08096-0056)
PHONE..........................856 227-1144
Theodore H Smolenski, *President*
Henrietta Smolenski, *Corp Secy*
EMP: 7 **EST:** 1966
SQ FT: 8,000
SALES (est): 300K **Privately Held**
SIC: 3471 Electroplating of metals or formed products

(G-2064)
G T M SIGNS INC
1960 Harris Dr (08096-3863)
PHONE..........................856 227-2333
Karl Baker, *CEO*
▲ **EMP:** 5
SALES (est): 533.8K **Privately Held**
SIC: 3444 7349 Awnings & canopies; janitorial service, contract basis

(G-2065)
INTERNATIONAL ROLLFORMS INC (PA)
Also Called: Garment Bar
8 International Ave (08096)
P.O. Box 5426 (08096-0426)
PHONE..........................856 228-7100
Fax: 856 228-3126
Jack Vosbikian, *President*
Thomas Vosbikian, *Owner*
Mark Wellner, *Vice Pres*
EMP: 30
SQ FT: 64,500
SALES (est): 21MM **Privately Held**
WEB: www.intl-rollforms.com
SIC: 3356 3469 Nonferrous rolling & drawing; stamping metal for the trade

(G-2066)
PIN POINT CONTAINER CORP
669 Tanyard Rd (08096-6229)
PHONE..........................856 848-2115
Fax: 856 853-6865
Bruce Baelz, *President*
Phyliss Baelz, *Vice Pres*
EMP: 6
SQ FT: 5,000
SALES (est): 1.3MM **Privately Held**
SIC: 2653 3544 Boxes, corrugated: made from purchased materials; dies, steel rule

(G-2067)
SOUTH JERSEY METAL INC
1651 Hurffville Rd (08096)
P.O. Box 5148 (08096-0148)
PHONE..........................856 228-0642
Fax: 856 228-8466
Joseph Wagner III, *President*
Sue Wagner, *Treasurer*
EMP: 25 **EST:** 1945
SQ FT: 17,500
SALES (est): 3.3MM **Privately Held**
WEB: www.southjerseymetal.com
SIC: 2514 3444 Metal kitchen & dining room furniture; sheet metalwork

(G-2068)
SWAROVSKI NORTH AMERICA LTD
1750 Deptford Center Rd (08096-5222)
PHONE..........................856 686-1805

Lorie Summers, *Branch Mgr*
EMP: 4
SALES (corp-wide): 3.7B **Privately Held**
SIC: 3961 Costume jewelry
HQ: Swarovski North America Limited
1 Kenney Dr
Cranston RI 02920
401 463-6400

(G-2069)
WORK ZONE CONTRACTORS LLC
664 Oak Ave (08096-4560)
PHONE..........................856 845-8201
Kathleen M Santanello, *Principal*
EMP: 9
SALES (est): 1.4MM **Privately Held**
SIC: 3669 Signaling apparatus, electric

(G-2070)
ZINNI ELECTRIC LLC
66 Grant Ave (08096-1952)
PHONE..........................856 848-8361
EMP: 4 **EST:** 2015
SALES (est): 273.4K **Privately Held**
SIC: 3699 Electrical equipment & supplies

Dividing Creek
Cumberland County

(G-2071)
COVIA HOLDINGS CORPORATION
1100 Whitehead Rd (08315)
P.O. Box 145, Millville (08332-0145)
PHONE..........................856 785-2700
Fax: 856 785-0538
Waverly Hale, *Branch Mgr*
EMP: 29
SALES (corp-wide): 136.2MM **Publicly Held**
WEB: www.unimin.com
SIC: 1446 Industrial sand
HQ: Covia Holdings Corporation
8834 Mayfield Rd
Chesterland OH 44026
800 255-7263

Dorchester
Cumberland County

(G-2072)
DORCHESTER SHIPYARD INC
13 Front St (08316)
P.O. Box 600 (08316-0600)
PHONE..........................856 785-8040
John Kelleher, *President*
EMP: 16
SALES (est): 3.6MM **Privately Held**
SIC: 3732 Boat building & repairing

Dorothy
Atlantic County

(G-2073)
HAPPLE PRINTING
81 Cape May Ave (08317-9740)
PHONE..........................609 476-0100
Fax: 609 476-2909
Ken Happle, *Owner*
EMP: 5
SALES (est): 122.8K **Privately Held**
SIC: 2752 Commercial printing, offset

(G-2074)
VIKING MOLD & TOOL CORP
64 Tuckahoe Rd (08317-9702)
PHONE..........................609 476-9333
James C Sullivan Jr, *President*
James C Sullivan Sr, *Vice Pres*
EMP: 9
SQ FT: 5,700
SALES (est): 1.3MM **Privately Held**
SIC: 3544 Forms (molds), for foundry & plastics working machinery

Dover
Morris County

(G-2075)
AMSCOT STRUCTURAL PDTS CORP
241 E Blackwell St (07801-4140)
PHONE..........................973 989-8800
Scott Roman, *President*
EMP: 20
SQ FT: 17,000
SALES (est): 4.8MM **Privately Held**
WEB: www.amscotnj.com
SIC: 3568 Bearings, bushings & blocks

(G-2076)
ANGELO BAKERY CORP
330 S Salem St Ste 10 (07801-5628)
PHONE..........................973 537-7220
Angelo Orguilts, *President*
Angelo Orguilsts, *Principal*
EMP: 5
SALES (est): 378.5K **Privately Held**
SIC: 2051 Bakery: wholesale or wholesale/retail combined

(G-2077)
ARIAS MOUNTAIN-COFFEE LLC (PA)
Also Called: La Sierra Coffee Roasters
22 E Blackwell St (07801-3908)
P.O. Box 568, Chester (07930-0568)
PHONE..........................973 927-9595
Fax: 973 989-8995
Jorge H Henao, *Mng Member*
EMP: 4
SALES (est): 1.6MM **Privately Held**
SIC: 2095 Coffee roasting (except by wholesale grocers)

(G-2078)
BLANC INDUSTRIES INC (PA)
88 King St Ste 1 (07801-3655)
PHONE..........................973 537-0090
Fax: 973 537-0906
Didier Blanc, *President*
Edgar Pastrana, *Manager*
▲ **EMP:** 45
SQ FT: 46,500
SALES (est): 12.3MM **Privately Held**
WEB: www.blancind.com
SIC: 3993 Signs & advertising specialties

(G-2079)
BLUEBIRD AUTO RENTL SYSTEMS LP (PA)
200 Mineral Springs Rd (07801-1636)
PHONE..........................973 989-2423
Angela M Margolit, *Partner*
Phil Jones, *Partner*
Andrea Slate, *Bookkeeper*
Nigel Pile, *Manager*
Jeff Swysh, *Manager*
EMP: 34
SQ FT: 5,400
SALES (est): 4.7MM **Privately Held**
WEB: www.bluebird-technologies.com
SIC: 5734 7372 7371 Software, business & non-game; business oriented computer software; computer software systems analysis & design, custom

(G-2080)
BRINKER INDUSTRIES
Also Called: Brinker Displays
88 King St Ste 1 (07801-3655)
PHONE..........................973 678-1200
Didier Blanc, *President*
▲ **EMP:** 35
SQ FT: 120,000
SALES (est): 4.1MM **Privately Held**
WEB: www.brinkerdisplays.com
SIC: 3993 Displays & cutouts, window & lobby

(G-2081)
COCOCARE PRODUCTS INC
85 Franklin Rd Ste 3a (07801-5632)
P.O. Box 311 (07802-0311)
PHONE..........................973 989-8880
Fax: 973 989-1711
Gerald Jay Dubin, *President*

2018 Harris New Jersey
Manufacturers Directory

▲ = Import ▼=Export
◆ =Import/Export

Jane P Dubin, *Admin Sec*
EMP: 30 **EST:** 1969
SALES (est): 5.7MM **Privately Held**
WEB: www.cococare.com
SIC: 2844 Cosmetic preparations; shampoos, rinses, conditioners: hair

(G-2082)
CRYSTAL DELTRONIC INDUSTRIES (PA)
Also Called: Isowave Division
60 Harding Ave (07801-4710)
PHONE..................................973 328-6898
Fax: 973 361-0722
Stuart Samuelson, *President*
Deborah Samuelson, *Corp Secy*
Debbie Cohn, *Mktg Dir*
Glenn Nosti, *Manager*
EMP: 23
SQ FT: 18,000
SALES (est): 2MM **Privately Held**
WEB: www.deltroniccrystal.com
SIC: 3674 3679 Optical isolators; electronic crystals

(G-2083)
CRYSTAL DELTRONIC INDUSTRIES
Also Called: Isowave Division
60 Harding Ave (07801-4710)
PHONE..................................973 328-7000
Fax: 973 328-7036
Stewart Samuelson, *President*
Juanita Washer, *Purch Agent*
EMP: 12
SALES (corp-wide): 2MM **Privately Held**
WEB: www.deltroniccrystal.com
SIC: 3674 7361 Optical isolators; employment agencies
PA: Crystal Deltronic Industries Inc
60 Harding Ave
Dover NJ 07801
973 328-6898

(G-2084)
DABURN WIRE & CABLE CORP
Also Called: Daburn Electronics & Cable
44 Richboynton Rd (07801-2650)
PHONE..................................973 328-3200
Edward A Flaherty, *Principal*
▲ **EMP:** 9
SALES (est): 730K **Privately Held**
SIC: 3357 5063 Nonferrous wiredrawing & insulating; electronic wire & cable

(G-2085)
DANA POLY CORP
85 Harrison St Dover (07801)
PHONE..................................800 474-1020
Mendy Rosner, *President*
Marvin Rosner, *Vice Pres*
Nick Harkavy, *VP Sales*
Ian Turk, *Accounts Exec*
Sol Yudkowsky, *Accounts Exec*
EMP: 40
SQ FT: 65,000
SALES (est): 20MM **Privately Held**
WEB: www.minibagusa.com
SIC: 2673 Plastic bags: made from purchased materials

(G-2086)
ENVIRNMNTAL DSIGN GRPHIC ENTPS
Also Called: Dmr Sign Systems
215 State Route 10 (07869-2413)
PHONE..................................973 361-1829
Andrew K Tunkel, *President*
Grace Tunkel, *Office Mgr*
EMP: 5
SQ FT: 4,400
SALES (est): 250K **Privately Held**
WEB: www.dmrsign.com
SIC: 2759 7336 Screen printing; graphic arts & related design

(G-2087)
FRAMECO INC
158 W Clinton St Ste B (07801-3410)
PHONE..................................973 989-1424
EMP: 25
SQ FT: 35,000
SALES (est): 202.7K **Privately Held**
SIC: 2499 Mfr Wooden Picture Frames

(G-2088)
H & W TOOL CO INC (PA)
22 Lee Ave (07801-4333)
PHONE..................................973 366-0131
Fax: 973 366-9347
Richard Winstead, *President*
Phyllis Winstead, *Corp Secy*
EMP: 17
SQ FT: 5,400
SALES (est): 4.9MM **Privately Held**
WEB: www.hwtool.com
SIC: 3544 3542 3841 3769 Industrial molds; dies, plastics forming; machine tools, metal forming type; surgical & medical instruments; guided missile & space vehicle parts & auxiliary equipment; machine tool accessories

(G-2089)
HIGHLAND PRODUCTS INC
River St (07801)
P.O. Box 794 (07802-0794)
PHONE..................................973 366-0156
Barrett Sangster, *President*
EMP: 4 **EST:** 1957
SQ FT: 3,500
SALES (est): 100K **Privately Held**
SIC: 3089 Plastic processing

(G-2090)
HOWMET CASTINGS & SERVICES INC
Alcoa Howmet, Dover
9 Roy St (07801-4308)
PHONE..................................973 442-2261
Fax: 973 328-7701
Bill Martin, *Production*
Alexander Alford, *Manager*
EMP: 900
SALES (corp-wide): 12.9B **Publicly Held**
SIC: 3324 3369 Commercial investment castings, ferrous; nonferrous foundries
HQ: Howmet Castings & Services, Inc.
1616 Harvard Ave
Newburgh Heights OH 44105
216 641-4400

(G-2091)
HOWMET CASTINGS & SERVICES INC
Also Called: Alcoa Howmet, Dover
9 Roy St (07801-4308)
PHONE..................................973 361-0300
Alexander Alford, *Manager*
EMP: 400
SALES (corp-wide): 12.9B **Publicly Held**
SIC: 3324 Commercial investment castings, ferrous
HQ: Howmet Castings & Services, Inc.
1616 Harvard Ave
Newburgh Heights OH 44105
216 641-4400

(G-2092)
HOWMET CASTINGS & SERVICES INC
Also Called: Alcoa Hwmet Dver Alloy Oprtons
10 Roy St (07801-4325)
PHONE..................................973 361-2310
Alexander Alford, *Manager*
EMP: 331
SALES (corp-wide): 12.9B **Publicly Held**
SIC: 3324 Commercial investment castings, ferrous
HQ: Howmet Castings & Services, Inc.
1616 Harvard Ave
Newburgh Heights OH 44105
216 641-4400

(G-2093)
INSTANT PRINTING OF DOVER INC
241 E Blackwell St (07801-4140)
PHONE..................................973 366-6855
Fax: 973 366-2992
Anna Medore, *President*
Peter Medore, *Vice Pres*
EMP: 7 **EST:** 1968
SQ FT: 5,000
SALES (est): 976.2K **Privately Held**
SIC: 2752 7334 2791 2789 Commercial printing, offset; photocopying & duplicating services; typesetting; bookbinding & related work; commercial printing

(G-2094)
INTERNATIONAL FOODSOURCE LLC
Also Called: Valued Naturals
52 Richboynton Rd (07801-2650)
PHONE..................................973 361-7044
Dan Baron, *CEO*
David Lipson, *President*
◆ **EMP:** 90
SQ FT: 104,000
SALES (est): 23.4MM **Privately Held**
WEB: www.intlfoodsource.com
SIC: 2034 Dehydrated fruits, vegetables, soups

(G-2095)
JAN PACKAGING INC
100 Harrison St (07801-4750)
P.O. Box 448 (07802-0448)
PHONE..................................973 361-7200
Fax: 973 361-3306
Edward Malavarca, *CEO*
Karl R Malavarca, *President*
Katherine Caristia, *COO*
Roger Sorhagen, *Vice Pres*
Colleen Barry, *Opers Mgr*
EMP: 70 **EST:** 1952
SQ FT: 250,000
SALES (est): 21.4MM **Privately Held**
SIC: 4783 4225 2449 Packing goods for shipping; crating goods for shipping; general warehousing & storage; wood containers

(G-2096)
JDV EQUIPMENT CORP
1 Princeton Ave Ste 2 (07801-2557)
PHONE..................................973 366-6556
Robert T Abbott, *President*
Joe Barringer, *Sales Mgr*
Ryan Kelly, *Sales Engr*
▲ **EMP:** 6
SQ FT: 3,000
SALES (est): 1.4MM **Privately Held**
SIC: 3589 5084 Water treatment equipment, industrial; industrial machinery & equipment

(G-2097)
JERSEY SHEET METAL & MACHINE
90 E Dickerson St (07801-4633)
P.O. Box 428 (07802-0428)
PHONE..................................973 366-8628
Fax: 973 989-7591
Richard T Hammond Jr, *President*
Garret Hammond, *Admin Sec*
EMP: 20
SQ FT: 15,000
SALES (est): 3.7MM **Privately Held**
SIC: 3444 Sheet metal specialties, not stamped

(G-2098)
M P T RACING INC
Also Called: Auto Chic
85 Franklin Rd Ste 6b (07801-5632)
PHONE..................................973 989-9220
Fax: 973 989-9234
Michael Trueba Jr, *President*
EMP: 7
SQ FT: 6,500
SALES (est): 1.1MM **Privately Held**
WEB: www.mptindustries.com
SIC: 3714 Motor vehicle parts & accessories

(G-2099)
MANUFACTURERS BRUSH CORP
69 King St Ste 6 (07801-2800)
PHONE..................................973 882-6966
Richard Draudt, *President*
EMP: 5
SQ FT: 3,000
SALES (est): 300K **Privately Held**
SIC: 3991 Brushes, except paint & varnish

(G-2100)
MINITEC CORPORATION
158 W Clinton St Ste V (07801-3410)
PHONE..................................973 989-1426
Scott Mindlin, *President*
Herb Mindlin, *Corp Secy*
Lou Mason, *Vice Pres*

EMP: 7 **EST:** 1963
SQ FT: 5,000
SALES (est): 696K **Privately Held**
SIC: 3469 Metal stampings

(G-2101)
MOTION CONTROL TECH INC
158 W Clinton St Ste Ff (07801-3410)
PHONE..................................973 361-2226
Frank Heidinger, *President*
Bernie Heidinger, *Vice Pres*
▲ **EMP:** 15 **EST:** 1998
SQ FT: 4,000
SALES: 2MM **Privately Held**
WEB: www.mct-inc.net
SIC: 2298 Cable, fiber

(G-2102)
MPT INDUSTRIES
85 Franklin Rd Ste 6b (07801-5632)
PHONE..................................973 989-9220
EMP: 6
SALES (est): 125.8K **Privately Held**
SIC: 3462 Mfg Iron/Steel Forgings

(G-2103)
NEPTUNE PRODUCTS INC
353 E Blackwell St (07801-4302)
P.O. Box 829 (07802-0829)
PHONE..................................973 366-8200
Fax: 973 366-0398
Richard H Schroeder, *President*
Peggy Sinnott, *Admin Sec*
EMP: 10 **EST:** 1948
SQ FT: 4,500
SALES (est): 1.8MM **Privately Held**
SIC: 3594 Fluid power pumps

(G-2104)
NEW STANDARD PRINTING CORP
118 Lincoln Ave (07801-2816)
P.O. Box 276, Blairstown (07825-0276)
PHONE..................................973 366-0006
Fax: 973 366-1534
Michael Wetzel, *President*
EMP: 8
SQ FT: 1,500
SALES (est): 1.1MM **Privately Held**
SIC: 2752 Commercial printing, offset

(G-2105)
NORTHWEST INSTRUMENT INC
69 King St (07801-2800)
PHONE..................................973 347-6830
Bo Xing, *President*
Aili Liu, *Vice Pres*
David Xing, *Manager*
Daniel Ramos, *Technician*
▲ **EMP:** 7
SALES (est): 1.1MM **Privately Held**
SIC: 3829 Surveying & drafting equipment

(G-2106)
PATCHWORKS CO INC
18 N Salem St (07801-4132)
PHONE..................................973 627-2002
Charles Barber, *President*
Greg Barber, *Vice Pres*
Chris Brauchle, *Vice Pres*
EMP: 5
SALES: 510K **Privately Held**
WEB: www.thepatchworks.com
SIC: 2395 2759 2399 Emblems, embroidered; promotional printing; emblems, badges & insignia

(G-2107)
REGION OIL
Also Called: Budd Oil
15 Richboynton Rd (07801-2649)
PHONE..................................973 366-3100
Fax: 973 328-4738
William Olivier, *Managing Prtnr*
EMP: 150
SALES (est): 9.1MM **Privately Held**
SIC: 1389 Building oil & gas well foundations on site

(G-2108)
RIDGE PRECISION PRODUCTS INC
288 Us Highway 46 Ste D (07801-2081)
PHONE..................................973 361-3508
Mark J Leone, *President*

Victoria Ponte, *Admin Sec*
EMP: 9
SQ FT: 12,000
SALES (est): 1.4MM **Privately Held**
SIC: 3599 Machine shop, jobbing & repair

(G-2109)
SCIMEDX CORPORATION
53 Richboynton Rd (07801-2649)
PHONE..............................800 221-5598
Thomas Britten, *Ch of Bd*
Maria Focht, *Supervisor*
EMP: 25
SQ FT: 10,000
SALES (est): 4.7MM **Privately Held**
WEB: www.scimedx.com
SIC: 3841 5049 Diagnostic apparatus,
medical; laboratory equipment, except
medical or dental

(G-2110)
SERVICE METAL FABRICATING INC
Also Called: Precision Shape Solutions
243 E Blackwell St (07801-4140)
PHONE..............................973 989-7199
Fax: 973 989-7196
Corey Akers, *Manager*
EMP: 5
SALES (corp-wide): 20.6MM **Privately Held**
WEB: www.servicemetal.com
SIC: 3444 Sheet metalwork
PA: Service Metal Fabricating Inc
10 Stickle Ave
Rockaway NJ 07866
973 625-8882

(G-2111)
TECHNICAL GLASS PRODUCTS INC
243 E Blackwell St (07801-4140)
PHONE..............................973 989-5500
Fax: 973 989-0121
Joseph Murray, *President*
Al Lorenzo, *Corp Secy*
EMP: 5
SQ FT: 3,000
SALES (est): 427K **Privately Held**
WEB: www.technicalglassinc.com
SIC: 3229 Scientific glassware

(G-2112)
TERRA DESIGNS INC (PA)
241 E Blackwell St Rear (07801-4140)
PHONE..............................973 328-1135
Fax: 973 328-3624
Anna Salibello, *President*
Chris Salibello, *Vice Pres*
Salvatore Salibello, *Treasurer*
▼ **EMP:** 15
SQ FT: 10,000
SALES (est): 1.3MM **Privately Held**
SIC: 3253 1743 Ceramic wall & floor tile;
tile installation, ceramic

(G-2113)
TOTAL TECH MEDICAL LLC
289 Munt Hope Ave Apt J14 (07801)
PHONE..............................973 980-6458
Joseph Scafa,
EMP: 9
SALES (est): 564.4K **Privately Held**
SIC: 3841 5047 3845 Surgical & medical
instruments; diagnostic apparatus, medical; instruments, surgical & medical; diagnostic equipment, medical; ultrasonic
scanning devices, medical; laser systems
& equipment, medical

(G-2114)
WIRE DISPLAYS INC
88 King St Ste 1 (07801-3655)
PHONE..............................973 537-0090
EMP: 12
SQ FT: 5,100
SALES (est): 2.2MM
SALES (corp-wide): 12.3MM **Privately Held**
WEB: www.wiredisplaysinc.com
SIC: 3496 Miscellaneous fabricated wire
products

PA: Blanc Industries Inc.
88 King St Ste 1
Dover NJ 07801
973 537-0090

Dumont
Bergen County

(G-2115)
BAUER SPORT SHOP
48 Dumont Ave (07628-3015)
PHONE..............................201 384-6522
Fax: 201 384-6527
Mike Hegel,
Alan Bergman,
EMP: 4
SQ FT: 1,000
SALES (est): 230.4K **Privately Held**
SIC: 5941 2395 Sporting goods & bicycle
shops; embroidery products, except schif-
fli machine

(G-2116)
BNH ENTERPRISE LLC
Also Called: Samsung Capacitor
76 Romano Dr (07628-2021)
PHONE..............................201 815-0546
Bruce Lee, *CEO*
Hyaeyoung Chung, *Vice Pres*
EMP: 5
SALES: 150K **Privately Held**
SIC: 8748 1521 3555 3648 Business
consulting; single-family housing con-
struction; electrotyping machines; airport
lighting fixtures: runway approach, taxi or
ramp; fuses & fuse equipment

(G-2117)
CRICKET ENTERPRISES
60 Hillcrest Dr (07628-2007)
PHONE..............................201 387-7978
Neil Klein, *Owner*
Judith Klein, *Principal*
EMP: 7
SALES (est): 280K **Privately Held**
SIC: 3669 Emergency alarms

(G-2118)
HOJIBLANCA USA INC
175 Washington Ave Ste 18 (07628-2936)
PHONE..............................201 384-3007
Enrique Escudero, *CEO*
▲ **EMP:** 7
SALES (est): 729.6K **Privately Held**
SIC: 2079 2084 2099 Olive oil; wines;
vinegar

(G-2119)
KEYSTONE PRINTING INC
21c E Madison Ave (07628-2415)
PHONE..............................201 387-7252
Fax: 201 387-2667
Michael C Worner, *Principal*
EMP: 7
SQ FT: 4,400
SALES (est): 1MM **Privately Held**
WEB: www.keystoneprintingnj.com
SIC: 2752 Commercial printing, offset

(G-2120)
KLM MECHANICAL CONTRACTORS
109 W Shore Ave (07628-2332)
PHONE..............................201 385-6965
Fax: 201 385-9497
Kenneth Loehr, *President*
Keith Loehr, *Principal*
Gary Loehr, *Vice Pres*
EMP: 13
SQ FT: 15,000
SALES (est): 1.3MM **Privately Held**
SIC: 1711 1761 3564 3444 Mechanical
contractor; sheet metalwork; blowers &
fans; sheet metalwork

(G-2121)
KODAY PRESS INC
69 Armour Pl (07628-3361)
PHONE..............................201 387-0001
Fax: 201 387-1107
Eugene Koblentz, *President*
EMP: 12 **EST:** 1932
SQ FT: 16,000

SALES (est): 1.1MM **Privately Held**
SIC: 2759 Promotional printing

(G-2122)
PTL SHEET METAL INC
70 Davies Ave (07628-2505)
PHONE..............................201 501-8700
Candice Mac William, *President*
EMP: 4
SQ FT: 6,000
SALES (est): 638.3K **Privately Held**
SIC: 3444 1711 Ducts, sheet metal; venti-
lation & duct work contractor

(G-2123)
RYVAL CMPT SVCS LTD LBLTY CO
111 Washington Ave (07628-3067)
PHONE..............................201 374-1600
Peter De Freitas,
Derrick Henry,
EMP: 8
SALES: 150K **Privately Held**
SIC: 7379 7373 3572 7378 Computer re-
lated maintenance services; computer in-
tegrated systems design; computer
auxiliary storage units; computer periph-
eral equipment repair & maintenance

(G-2124)
SIGN ON INC
149 Washington Ave Apt A (07628-2346)
PHONE..............................201 384-7714
Fax: 201 384-7741
Manohar G Massand, *President*
Kiran Massand, *Vice Pres*
EMP: 4
SQ FT: 3,500
SALES: 250K **Privately Held**
SIC: 3993 2791 Electric signs; typesetting

(G-2125)
WASTE NOT COMPUTERS & SUPPLIES
94 Washington Ave (07628-3026)
PHONE..............................201 384-4444
Fax: 201 384-4024
Peter J Farrell, *President*
EMP: 6
SQ FT: 1,500
SALES (est): 720K **Privately Held**
WEB: www.wastenotcomputers.com
SIC: 5112 3955 Computer & photocopying
supplies; ribbons, inked: typewriter,
adding machine, register, etc.

Dunellen
Middlesex County

(G-2126)
AVENEL PALLET CO INC
1800 S 2nd St (08812)
P.O. Box 276 (08812-0276)
PHONE..............................732 752-0500
Fax: 732 752-0533
Vincent Colonna Jr, *President*
EMP: 10
SQ FT: 9,000
SALES (est): 1.5MM **Privately Held**
SIC: 5031 2448 Pallets, wood; wood pal-
lets & skids

(G-2127)
BEST VALUE RUGS & CARPETS INC
334 Rt 22 W (08812)
PHONE..............................732 752-3528
Daljit Chadha, *President*
EMP: 5 **EST:** 1997
SQ FT: 2,000
SALES: 309.8K **Privately Held**
SIC: 5712 5713 5021 2499 Furniture
stores; carpets; rugs; furniture; tiles, cork;
tile, ceramic

(G-2128)
BLACHER CANVAS PRODUCTS INC
604 Bound Brook Rd (08812-1006)
PHONE..............................732 968-3666
Fax: 732 968-0032
George Rodoussakis, *President*

Irene Rodoussakis, *Vice Pres*
EMP: 7 **EST:** 1947
SQ FT: 6,000
SALES (est): 775K **Privately Held**
SIC: 2394 Awnings, fabric: made from pur-
chased materials

(G-2129)
PEDESTAL PALLET INC
777 N Avenue Ext (08812-1019)
P.O. Box 450 (08812-0450)
PHONE..............................732 968-7488
Fax: 732 968-7499
John Ruotolo, *Principal*
EMP: 8
SALES (est): 1.3MM **Privately Held**
SIC: 2448 Pallets, wood; pallets, wood &
wood with metal

(G-2130)
PFIZER INC
43 Spruce Hollow Rd (08812-1836)
PHONE..............................908 251-5685
Nora Tsivgas, *Branch Mgr*
EMP: 225
SALES (corp-wide): 52.5B **Publicly Held**
SIC: 2834 Pharmaceutical preparations
PA: Pfizer Inc.
235 E 42nd St
New York NY 10017
212 733-2323

East Brunswick
Middlesex County

(G-2131)
ALL SEASONS DOOR & WINDOW INC (PA)
28 Edgeboro Rd (08816-1635)
PHONE..............................732 238-7100
Fax: 732 238-7225
King T Yu, *President*
Steven Yu, *Vice Pres*
Gina Yu, *VP Finance*
Yee Chih, *Manager*
Jeff Chou, *Manager*
▲ **EMP:** 40
SQ FT: 35,000
SALES (est): 5.4MM **Privately Held**
SIC: 2431 Doors & door parts & trim,
wood; windows & window parts & trim,
wood

(G-2132)
ALLU GROUP INC
25 Kimberly Rd Ste A (08816-2038)
PHONE..............................201 288-2236
Mardi Ohanessian, *President*
▲ **EMP:** 14
SQ FT: 10,000
SALES (est): 6MM **Privately Held**
WEB: www.ideachip.com
SIC: 3621 Commutators, electric motor

(G-2133)
AM WOOD INC
18 Kennedy Blvd (08816-1248)
PHONE..............................732 246-1506
Tatiana Elperin, *Manager*
EMP: 10
SALES (corp-wide): 1.3MM **Privately Held**
SIC: 2431 1752 Moldings, wood: unfin-
ished & prefinished; wood floor installa-
tion & refinishing
PA: Am Wood Inc
2901 Nostrand Ave
Brooklyn NY
718 765-1200

(G-2134)
AMERIGEN PHARMACEUTICALS LTD (PA)
197 State Route 18 (08816-1440)
PHONE..............................732 993-9826
John Kratochwil, *Principal*
Al Delia, *Principal*
EMP: 12
SALES (est): 1.5MM **Privately Held**
SIC: 2834 Pharmaceutical preparations

(G-2135)
ART GUILD INC
12 Connerty Ct Unit B (08816-1645)
PHONE..............................732 390-5300
Fax: 732 283-4106
Suzanne Macdougall, *President*
EMP: 14 **EST:** 1954
SQ FT: 20,000
SALES: 1.8MM **Privately Held**
WEB: www.artguildinc.com
SIC: 2759 2396 Screen printing; automotive & apparel trimmings

(G-2136)
BANDEMAR NETWORKS LLC
3 New Dover Rd (08816-2746)
PHONE..............................732 991-5112
Cesar Bandera, *CEO*
Mark Capuano, *Manager*
EMP: 4
SALES: 100K **Privately Held**
SIC: 7371 7372 4813 7812 Computer software systems analysis & design, custom; computer software development & applications; educational computer software; telephone/video communications; motion picture & video production

(G-2137)
BEST TILE OF NEW JERSEY
Also Called: Ceramic Tile Outlet
272 State Route 18 Ste 3 (08816-1916)
PHONE..............................732 390-7700
Jean McBride, *Manager*
Tom Christie, *Contractor*
EMP: 4
SALES (est): 451.4K **Privately Held**
SIC: 3253 Ceramic wall & floor tile
PA: Best Tile Of New Jersey
3 Cass St
Keyport NJ 07735

(G-2138)
BIMBO BAKERIES USA INC
Also Called: Maier's Sunbeam Bakery
5 Alvin Ct (08816-2001)
PHONE..............................732 390-7715
Fax: 732 390-8733
Cris Siddeno, *Manager*
EMP: 60 **Privately Held**
SIC: 2051 Bakery: wholesale or wholesale/retail combined
HQ: Bimbo Bakeries Usa, Inc
255 Business Center Dr # 200
Horsham PA 19044
215 347-5500

(G-2139)
BIOTECH SUPPORT GROUP LLC
29 Hershey Rd (08816-2634)
PHONE..............................732 613-1967
Swapan Roy, *Mng Member*
EMP: 5
SALES: 100K **Privately Held**
SIC: 2869 Laboratory chemicals, organic

(G-2140)
CERAMSOURCE INC
26 Kennedy Blvd Ste B (08816-1260)
P.O. Box 6026 (08816-6026)
PHONE..............................732 257-5002
Yong Gong Wang, *Principal*
Warren Elton, *Regl Sales Mgr*
Howard Yang, *Marketing Staff*
Edwin Wang, *Manager*
▲ **EMP:** 16
SALES (est): 1.9MM **Privately Held**
SIC: 3299 Ceramic fiber

(G-2141)
CHIC LLC
Also Called: Leon Levin
200 State Route 18 Ste 1 (08816-1466)
PHONE..............................732 354-0035
Charles Godfrey, *President*
▲ **EMP:** 8
SQ FT: 2,500

SALES: 6.1MM
SALES (corp-wide): 119.2K **Privately Held**
WEB: www.chic.com
SIC: 5137 2337 2339 2331 Blouses; skirts; skirts, separate: women's, misses' & juniors'; jackets & vests, except fur & leather: women's; slacks: women's, misses' & juniors'; shorts (outerwear): women's, misses' & juniors'; culottes: women's, misses' & juniors'; T-shirts & tops, women's: made from purchased materials
PA: Knitastiks, Inc.
450 Park Ave Ste 2100
New York NY 10022
212 354-7770

(G-2142)
COILHOSE PNEUMATICS INC
Acme Quality Products
19 Kimberly Rd (08816-2010)
PHONE..............................732 432-7177
Gregory Samman, *Principal*
EMP: 20
SALES (corp-wide): 43MM **Privately Held**
WEB: www.coilhose.com
SIC: 3569 3011 Filters; tire & inner tube materials & related products
PA: Coilhose Pneumatics, Inc.
19 Kimberly Rd
East Brunswick NJ 08816
732 390-8480

(G-2143)
COMPUTER PRINTERS & MEDIA SUPS
Also Called: CPM Supplies
6 Alvin Ct (08816-2001)
PHONE..............................732 400-7888
Harsha Desai, *President*
◆ **EMP:** 5
SALES (est): 729.9K **Privately Held**
SIC: 3572 Computer storage devices

(G-2144)
DODSON GLOBAL INC
27 Cotters Ln (08816-2002)
PHONE..............................732 238-7001
Fax: 732 238-7760
Allen Goodrich, *Principal*
▲ **EMP:** 7
SALES (est): 875.7K **Privately Held**
SIC: 3317 Steel pipe & tubes

(G-2145)
DRAKE CORP
110 Tices Ln (08816-2048)
PHONE..............................732 254-1530
Ralph Drake, *President*
Louie Filipe, *General Mgr*
Tom Hohl, *COO*
Diego Discacciati, *Vice Pres*
Alida Maiola, *Vice Pres*
▲ **EMP:** 8
SALES (est): 1.5MM **Privately Held**
WEB: www.plastifin.com
SIC: 2531 2392 Chairs, portable folding; chair covers & pads: made from purchased materials

(G-2146)
DRIFIRE LLC
28 Kennedy Blvd Ste 300 (08816-1255)
PHONE..............................866 266-4035
Darryl Schimeck, *CEO*
Bob Pastene, *Vice Pres*
Scott Willis, *Vice Pres*
Patrick Gainer, *CFO*
Alan Wallis, *Manager*
EMP: 30
SALES (est): 6.7MM **Privately Held**
SIC: 2321 Men's & boys' furnishings

(G-2147)
E R SQUIBB & SONS LLC (HQ)
25 Kennedy Blvd (08816-1259)
PHONE..............................732 246-3195
R Radcliffe, *Principal*
EMP: 7
SALES (est): 53.8MM
SALES (corp-wide): 20.7B **Publicly Held**
WEB: www.bms.com
SIC: 2834 Pharmaceutical preparations

PA: Bristol-Myers Squibb Company
430 E 29th St Fl 14
New York NY 10016
212 546-4000

(G-2148)
EAST BRUNSWICK SEWERAGE AUTH
25 Harts Ln (08816-2034)
PHONE..............................732 257-8313
Fax: 732 257-0605
EMP: 16
SQ FT: 2,000
SALES (est): 2.5MM **Privately Held**
SIC: 3589 Mfg Service Industry Machinery

(G-2149)
ELBEE LITHO INC
292 Dunhams Corner Rd (08816-2624)
PHONE..............................732 698-7738
Barry Zaslavsky, *President*
EMP: 4
SQ FT: 5,000
SALES (est): 280K **Privately Held**
SIC: 2752 7389 Commercial printing, offset; printing broker

(G-2150)
ELITE PACKAGING CORP
40 Cotters Ln Ste E (08816-2043)
PHONE..............................732 651-9955
Mario Magali, *President*
Victor Martinez, *Supervisor*
▲ **EMP:** 18
SQ FT: 50,000
SALES (est): 3.8MM **Privately Held**
SIC: 3565 Packaging machinery

(G-2151)
ELKEM SILICONES USA CORP (DH)
2 Tower Center Blvd # 1601 (08816-1100)
PHONE..............................732 227-2060
Fax: 732 249-7000
J Christopher York, *President*
Luis Guerrero, *Business Mgr*
Bertrand Mollet, *Treasurer*
Rachel Kahan, *HR Admin*
Michael Cook, *Sales Staff*
◆ **EMP:** 25
SALES (est): 33.3MM
SALES (corp-wide): 28.5MM **Privately Held**
WEB: www.bluestarsilicones.com
SIC: 2819 Industrial inorganic chemicals
HQ: Elkem Asa
Drammensveien 169
Oslo 0277
224 501-00

(G-2152)
EMC CORPORATION
Businessedge Solutions
1 Tower Center Blvd Fl 23 (08816-1145)
PHONE..............................732 549-8500
Fax: 732 839-3600
Shail Jain, *Manager*
Nina Hilyard, *Manager*
Alexis Kane, *Director*
EMP: 730
SALES (corp-wide): 78.6B **Publicly Held**
WEB: www.emc.com
SIC: 3572 Computer storage devices
HQ: Emc Corporation
176 South St
Hopkinton MA 01748
508 435-1000

(G-2153)
EMPIRE SPECIALTY FOODS INC
6 Brookdale Rd (08816-4219)
PHONE..............................646 773-2630
Yildiray Hamzacebi, *Principal*
▲ **EMP:** 4 **EST:** 2011
SALES (est): 284.9K **Privately Held**
SIC: 2099 Food preparations

(G-2154)
ESAW INDUSTRIES INC
5 Litchfield Rd (08816-5036)
PHONE..............................732 613-1400
Fax: 732 254-1199
Eddy Chow, *President*
Susan Chow, *Vice Pres*
EMP: 6
SQ FT: 20,000

SALES (est): 570K **Privately Held**
SIC: 3571 Electronic computers

(G-2155)
FOUR BROS VENTURES INC
15 Timothy Ln (08816-4562)
PHONE..............................732 890-9469
Eurya Chauhan, *Co-Owner*
EMP: 4
SALES (est): 137.9K **Privately Held**
SIC: 7372 Prepackaged software

(G-2156)
FU WEI INC
Also Called: Fu WEI International
40 Cotters Ln Bldg B (08816-2043)
PHONE..............................732 937-8388
Jason Nichols, *CEO*
Yugin LI, *President*
▲ **EMP:** 7
SQ FT: 100,000
SALES: 5MM **Privately Held**
SIC: 2759 8743 2521 Commercial printing; promotion service; benches, office: wood

(G-2157)
HERITAGE PHARMA HOLDINGS INC (HQ)
1 Tower Center Blvd # 1700 (08816-1145)
PHONE..............................732 429-1000
William S Marth, *President*
EMP: 1
SALES (est): 43.9MM **Privately Held**
SIC: 2834 Pharmaceutical preparations

(G-2158)
HERITAGE PHARMA LABS INC
8 Elkins Rd (08816-2005)
PHONE..............................732 238-7880
David Aronson, *Manager*
EMP: 10 **Privately Held**
SIC: 2834 Pharmaceutical preparations
HQ: Heritage Pharma Labs Inc.
21 Cotters Ln Ste B
East Brunswick NJ 08816
732 238-7880

(G-2159)
HERITAGE PHARMA LABS INC (DH)
21 Cotters Ln Ste B (08816-2050)
PHONE..............................732 238-7880
Jeffery Glazer, *CEO*
Pankaj Dave, *Vice Pres*
Jayanti Shah, *Plant Engr*
Samir Vij, *Manager*
Bharat Patel, *Director*
▲ **EMP:** 120
SALES (est): 32.4MM **Privately Held**
WEB: www.emcureusa.com
SIC: 2834 8731 Pharmaceutical preparations; commercial physical research
HQ: Heritage Pharma Holdings, Inc.
1 Tower Center Blvd # 1700
East Brunswick NJ 08816
732 429-1000

(G-2160)
HERITAGE PHARMACEUTICALS INC (DH)
1 Tower Center Blvd # 1700 (08816-1145)
PHONE..............................732 429-1000
Fax: 732 429-1001
Fakrul Sayeed MD, *CEO*
Scott Delaney, *President*
John W Denman, *President*
Gary Ruckelshaus, *Vice Pres*
Mike Schmidt, *Vice Pres*
▲ **EMP:** 33
SALES (est): 7.8MM **Privately Held**
WEB: www.heritagepharma.com
SIC: 2834 Pharmaceutical preparations
HQ: Heritage Pharma Holdings, Inc.
1 Tower Center Blvd # 1700
East Brunswick NJ 08816
732 429-1000

(G-2161)
INTERSOURCE USA INC
25 Kimberly Rd Ste A (08816-2038)
P.O. Box 6026 (08816-6026)
PHONE..............................732 257-5002
Edwin Wang, *President*
Hong Jiang, *Vice Pres*

Zane Reed, *Sales Associate*
▲ **EMP:** 10
SQ FT: 5,000
SALES (est): 1.1MM **Privately Held**
WEB: www.intersourceusa.com
SIC: 3299 5085 Ceramic fiber; industrial supplies

(G-2162)
J M FRY PRINTING INKS
124 Tices Ln Ste A (08816-2000)
PHONE..............................732 238-1060
Fax: 732 238-1059
Nick Melillo, *Branch Mgr*
Cris Becilli, *Manager*
EMP: 8
SALES (est): 1.2MM **Privately Held**
SIC: 2893 Lithographic ink

(G-2163)
J S PALUCH CO INC
6 Alvin Ct Ste 1 (08816-2001)
PHONE..............................732 238-2412
Fax: 732 238-1372
David Hoser, *General Mgr*
EMP: 25
SALES (corp-wide): 86.7MM **Privately Held**
WEB: www.jspaluch.com
SIC: 2731 2741 Pamphlets: publishing only, not printed on site; miscellaneous publishing
PA: J. S. Paluch Co., Inc.
   3708 River Rd Ste 400
   Franklin Park IL 60131
   847 678-9300

(G-2164)
LENS DEPOT INC
40c Cotters Ln Ste D (08816-2037)
PHONE..............................732 993-9766
▲ **EMP:** 14
SQ FT: 5,000
SALES (est): 2.4MM **Privately Held**
SIC: 5048 3851 Whol Ophthalmic Goods Mfg Ophthalmic Goods

(G-2165)
MAUSER USA LLC (DH)
2 Tower Center Blvd 20-1 (08816-1100)
PHONE..............................732 353-7100
Hans-Peter Schaefer, *CEO*
Siegfried Weber, *Vice Pres*
John Waddell, *Controller*
Evan Dorries, *Sales Staff*
◆ **EMP:** 25
SALES (est): 569MM **Privately Held**
WEB: www.mausergroup.com
SIC: 3412 2655 Barrels, shipping: metal; fiber cans, drums & containers
HQ: Mauser Holding International Gmbh
   Schildgesstr. 71-163
   Bruhl
   223 278-1000

(G-2166)
MCI SERVICE PARTS
Also Called: Motor Sport Industry
35 Cotters Ln (08816-2032)
PHONE..............................732 967-9081
Todd Brightlow, *Manager*
EMP: 7
SALES (est): 735.3K **Privately Held**
SIC: 2099 Popcorn, packaged: except already popped

(G-2167)
MON-ECO INDUSTRIES INC
Also Called: MEI
5 Joanna Ct Ste G (08816-2285)
PHONE..............................732 257-7942
Fax: 732 257-6525
Sergio Buzzerio, *President*
EMP: 17
SQ FT: 25,000
SALES (est): 3.9MM **Privately Held**
SIC: 2891 Adhesives

(G-2168)
MRC GLOBAL (US) INC
28 Kennedy Blvd Ste 100 (08816-1255)
PHONE..............................732 225-4005
EMP: 11
SALES (corp-wide): 4.5B **Publicly Held**
SIC: 1311 Crude Petroleum/Natural Gas Production

HQ: Mrc Global (Us) Inc.
   1301 Mckinney St Ste 2300
   Houston TX 77010
   877 294-7574

(G-2169)
NEWCO VALVES LLC
Also Called: Newmans
19a Cotters Ln (08816-2002)
PHONE..............................732 257-0300
Fax: 732 238-0132
Charlie Neter, *Branch Mgr*
EMP: 27 **Publicly Held**
WEB: www.newcovalves.com
SIC: 5085 3494 Industrial supplies; valves & pipe fittings
HQ: Newco Valves, Llc
   13127 Trinity Dr
   Stafford TX 77477
   281 325-0041

(G-2170)
NORTHEAST CHEMICALS INC
110 Tices Ln Ste 2-3 (08816-2048)
P.O. Box 188, Milltown (08850-0188)
PHONE..............................732 238-9980
Fred Borelli, *CEO*
Jimmy W Hsu, *President*
Joseph Busch, *Vice Pres*
Frank Russo, *CFO*
▲ **EMP:** 28
SQ FT: 270,000
SALES (est): 32.2MM **Privately Held**
SIC: 2869 2819 5169 Industrial organic chemicals; industrial inorganic chemicals; industrial chemicals

(G-2171)
PEPSI
Also Called: Pepsico
5 Lexington Ave (08816-5033)
PHONE..............................732 238-1598
EMP: 5
SALES (est): 242.2K **Privately Held**
SIC: 2086 Carbonated soft drinks, bottled & canned

(G-2172)
PERL PIGMENTS LLC
400 Cotters Ln (08816)
P.O. Box 1223, Teaneck (07666-1223)
PHONE..............................201 836-1212
Allen Perl,
EMP: 6
SALES (est): 650K **Privately Held**
SIC: 3339 Zinc smelting (primary), including zinc residue

(G-2173)
PINNACLE MATERIALS INC (PA)
39 Edgeboro Rd (08816-1636)
PHONE..............................732 254-7676
Christine Yakman, *President*
Christine Yackman, *Corp Secy*
David Boussmrski, *Project Mgr*
Toni Lynn Bronson, *Finance Mgr*
EMP: 10 **EST:** 1996
SQ FT: 20,000
SALES (est): 3.6MM **Privately Held**
WEB: www.pinnaclematerials.com
SIC: 1442 Construction sand & gravel

(G-2174)
PREM-KHICHI ENTERPRISES INC
Also Called: Metalgraphics
9 Colburn Rd (08816-1102)
PHONE..............................973 242-0300
Fax: 973 242-6750
Peter Permar, *President*
EMP: 14
SQ FT: 20,000
SALES (est): 850K **Privately Held**
SIC: 3471 2851 Finishing, metals or formed products; paints & allied products

(G-2175)
PRIME CODING SERVICES LLC
58 Frost Ave (08816-4509)
PHONE..............................732 254-3036
Flor Bajar, *Owner*
EMP: 8
SALES (est): 659.5K **Privately Held**
SIC: 2833 Codeine & derivatives

(G-2176)
PROHASKA & CO INC
34 Allwood Rd (08816-1349)
PHONE..............................732 238-3420
Bernie Prohaska, *President*
Yvonne Prohaska, *Treasurer*
EMP: 7
SQ FT: 1,000
SALES (est): 1MM **Privately Held**
WEB: www.prohaskaadvertising.com
SIC: 2752 7311 Commercial printing, lithographic; advertising agencies

(G-2177)
R H A AUDIO COMMUNICATIONS
Also Called: R H A Audio Communications
725 State Route 18 (08816-4933)
PHONE..............................732 257-9180
Fax: 732 257-0661
Robert Bielicki, *President*
EMP: 4 **EST:** 1971
SQ FT: 1,000
SALES (est): 600K **Privately Held**
SIC: 3663 Radio & TV communications equipment

(G-2178)
RACEWAY PETROLEUM INC
114 Ryders Ln (08816-1336)
PHONE..............................732 729-7350
EMP: 7 **Privately Held**
SIC: 3644 Raceways
PA: Raceway Petroleum Inc
   1411 Stelton Rd
   Piscataway NJ 08854

(G-2179)
RACEWAY PETROLEUM INC
523 State Route 18 (08816-3044)
PHONE..............................732 613-4404
Pardeep Anand, *Manager*
EMP: 43 **Privately Held**
SIC: 5411 3644 Convenience stores, independent; raceways
PA: Raceway Petroleum Inc
   1411 Stelton Rd
   Piscataway NJ 08854

(G-2180)
RARITAN PHRMCTCALS INCOPORATED
8 Joanna Ct (08816-2108)
PHONE..............................732 238-1685
Fax: 732 432-8255
Vin Nayak, *President*
Sultan Reshamwala, *Vice Pres*
▲ **EMP:** 200
SQ FT: 260,000
SALES (est): 75.5MM **Privately Held**
WEB: www.raritanpharm.com
SIC: 2834 Druggists' preparations (pharmaceuticals)

(G-2181)
RP PRODUCTS LLC
Also Called: Wallscape
646 State Route 18 (08816-3722)
PHONE..............................732 254-4222
Paul Dimaggio,
Ronald Papaleo,
▲ **EMP:** 5
SALES (est): 491.5K **Privately Held**
SIC: 3069 Rubber floor coverings, mats & wallcoverings

(G-2182)
SCREENED IMAGES INC
7 Joanna Ct Ste H (08816-2284)
PHONE..............................732 651-8181
Fax: 732 651-8404
Fred Moskiwitz, *President*
Stuart Weisenfeld, *Vice Pres*
EMP: 30
SQ FT: 35,000
SALES (est): 3MM
SALES (corp-wide): 1.1B **Publicly Held**
SIC: 2261 2262 2396 Screen printing of cotton broadwoven fabrics; screen printing: manmade fiber & silk broadwoven fabrics; automotive & apparel trimmings
HQ: Edge Inc Corporate
   1440 Broadway Fl 22
   New York NY 10018
   212 279-7200

(G-2183)
SHOWTIME EXPRESS
5 Lexington Ave (08816-5033)
PHONE..............................732 238-2701
EMP: 4 **EST:** 2012
SALES (est): 330K **Privately Held**
SIC: 3537 Mfg Industrial Trucks/Tractors

(G-2184)
SIMPLY AMAZING LLC
233 State Route 18 Ste 22 (08816-1903)
PHONE..............................732 249-4151
Jane Jablons, *Branch Mgr*
EMP: 16
SALES (corp-wide): 42.3MM **Privately Held**
SIC: 3643 Outlets, electric: convenience
PA: Simply Amazing Llc
   100 Jaguar Land Rover Way
   Mahwah NJ 07495
   201 529-3700

(G-2185)
SPICE CHAIN CORPORATION
9 Elkins Rd (08816-2006)
PHONE..............................732 518-1100
Dewey Armstrong, *CEO*
Al Gever, *CFO*
Nancy Littleton, *Marketing Staff*
Patrick Mulhern,
▲ **EMP:** 175
SQ FT: 62,000
SALES (est): 42.7MM **Privately Held**
WEB: www.vdvspice.com
SIC: 2099 Seasonings & spices

(G-2186)
SPORTS IMPACT INC
52 Yorktown Rd (08816-3325)
PHONE..............................732 257-1451
Marc Groman, *Manager*
EMP: 5
SALES (corp-wide): 559K **Privately Held**
SIC: 2721 Magazines: publishing only, not printed on site
PA: Sports Impact Inc
   25 Winston Ln
   Garrison NY 10524
   914 232-8890

(G-2187)
STAR PHARMA INC
42 Devon Dr (08816-5331)
PHONE..............................718 466-1790
Krishna Chaluvadi, *CEO*
EMP: 7
SALES (est): 747.1K **Privately Held**
SIC: 2834 Pharmaceutical preparations

(G-2188)
STRIDES PHARMA INC
2 Tower Center Blvd # 1102 (08816-1100)
PHONE..............................609 773-5000
Fayez Azeez, *Finance Dir*
EMP: 5
SALES (corp-wide): 60.3MM **Privately Held**
SIC: 2834 Pharmaceutical preparations
HQ: Strides Pharma, Inc.
   2 Tower Center Blvd # 1102
   East Brunswick NJ 08816
   609 773-5000

(G-2189)
STRIVE PHARMACEUTICALS INC (PA)
19 Lexington Ave (08816-5034)
PHONE..............................609 269-2001
Priyank Pandya, *Director*
EMP: 6
SALES (est): 10MM **Privately Held**
SIC: 2834 5122 Pharmaceutical preparations; pharmaceuticals

(G-2190)
SUPREME MANUFACTURING CO INC
5 Connerty Ct (08816-1633)
PHONE..............................732 254-0087
Fax: 732 254-5736
Clifford Krause, *President*
◆ **EMP:** 46
SQ FT: 19,000

SALES (est): 7.4MM **Privately Held**
WEB: www.supreme-mfg.com
SIC: **2086** Soft drinks: packaged in cans, bottles, etc.

(G-2191)
SUZIE MAC SPECIALTIES INC
3 Joanna Ct Ste C (08816-2283)
PHONE..................................732 238-3500
Fax: 732 238-4106
Suzanne Macdougall, *President*
EMP: 20
SQ FT: 25,000
SALES: 1.6MM **Privately Held**
WEB: www.suziemac.com
SIC: **2752 7311 2396** Decals, lithographed; advertising posters, lithographed; calendars, lithographed; advertising consultant; automotive & apparel trimmings

(G-2192)
SV PHARMA INC
9 Autumn Ln (08816-5500)
PHONE..................................732 651-1336
Purnachandra R Akkineni, *Principal*
EMP: 5
SALES (est): 602.5K **Privately Held**
SIC: **2834** Pharmaceutical preparations

(G-2193)
TECKCHEK (PA)
77 Milltown Rd Ste C4 (08816-2302)
PHONE..................................919 497-0136
William Mundell, *Principal*
Joy Butler, *Opers Mgr*
EMP: 7
SALES (est): 1.9MM **Privately Held**
SIC: **2741** Miscellaneous publishing

(G-2194)
VAHL INC
34 Kennedy Blvd Ste 2 (08816-1261)
PHONE..................................732 249-4042
Henry G Dieken, *President*
EMP: 48 EST: 1938
SQ FT: 42,000
SALES (est): 10.4MM **Privately Held**
SIC: **3728** Aircraft body assemblies & parts; aircraft assemblies, subassemblies & parts

(G-2195)
VANGUARD CONTAINER CORP
35 Cotters Ln Ste 1 (08816-2032)
PHONE..................................732 651-9717
Fax: 732 651-8963
Edward Gunn, *President*
EMP: 40
SQ FT: 85,000
SALES (est): 4.4MM **Privately Held**
SIC: **3089** Plastic containers, except foam
HQ: Mauser-Werke Gmbh
    Schildgesstr. 71-163
    Bruhl 50321
    223 278-1000

(G-2196)
VENDING TRUCKS INC
5 Litchfield Rd (08816-5036)
PHONE..................................732 969-5400
Fax: 732 969-1200
Howard Seasonwein, *President*
Dean Neuman, *Accounts Mgr*
EMP: 25
SQ FT: 5,000
SALES (est): 6.7MM **Privately Held**
WEB: www.vendingtrucks.com
SIC: **3711 8742** Motor vehicles & car bodies; automobile assembly, including specialty automobiles; marketing consulting services

(G-2197)
VITAMIN RETAILER MAGAZINE INC
431 Cranbury Rd Ste C (08816-3698)
PHONE..................................732 432-9600
Fax: 732 432-9288
Daniel McSweeney, *President*
Robert Certo, *Production*
Bryan Zak, *Production*
Russ Fields, *Advt Staff*
Gary Pfaff, *Manager*
EMP: 9

SALES (est): 1MM **Privately Held**
WEB: www.vitaminretailer.com
SIC: **2721** Magazines: publishing only, not printed on site

East Hanover
Morris County

(G-2198)
201 FOOD PACKING INC
Also Called: Tree-Ripe Products
7 Great Meadow Ln (07936-1703)
PHONE..................................973 463-0777
Joel Fishman, *President*
▼ EMP: 15 EST: 1977
SQ FT: 12,000
SALES (est): 1.7MM **Privately Held**
SIC: **2087** Cocktail mixes, nonalcoholic

(G-2199)
ALLIANCE TECHNOLOGIES GROUP
57 Eagle Rock Ave (07936-3169)
PHONE..................................973 664-1151
Phil De Palma, *CEO*
Peter De Palma Jr, *President*
EMP: 6
SQ FT: 6,000
SALES: 1MM **Privately Held**
WEB: www.alliancetechnologies.biz
SIC: **3625** Relays & industrial controls

(G-2200)
ANUCO INC
911 Charles Dr Unit 3 (07936)
PHONE..................................973 887-9465
Bob Nugent, *President*
Marion Nugent, *Corp Secy*
EMP: 10
SQ FT: 4,000
SALES (est): 1.3MM **Privately Held**
SIC: **2752** Commercial printing, offset

(G-2201)
BAVELLE TECH SLTIONS LTD LBLTY
100 Eagle Rock Ave # 301 (07936-3149)
PHONE..................................973 992-8086
Oren David, *Mng Member*
EMP: 10
SALES (est): 209.9K **Privately Held**
SIC: **8748 7371 7372 7373** Systems engineering consultant, ex. computer or professional; custom computer programming services; custom computer programming services; application computer software; systems engineering, computer related

(G-2202)
C & S TOOL CO
304 Ridgedale Ave (07936-2397)
PHONE..................................973 887-6865
Fax: 973 887-9567
Robert Sadowski, *President*
John Sadowski, *Vice Pres*
EMP: 10
SQ FT: 3,300
SALES (est): 1MM **Privately Held**
WEB: www.cstool.com
SIC: **3599 3544** Machine shop, jobbing & repair; special dies, tools, jigs & fixtures

(G-2203)
CADBURY ADAMS USA LLC (HQ)
100 Deforest Ave (07936-2813)
PHONE..................................973 503-2000
Matthew Shattock,
Trevor Bond,
Jim Cali,
Daniel Chung,
Bruce N Futterer,
▲ EMP: 32
SALES (est): 91.7MM **Publicly Held**
WEB: www.cadburyadams.com
SIC: **2064 2844** Candy & other confectionery products; mouthwashes

(G-2204)
CALCULAGRAPH CO (PA)
Also Called: Control Products
280 Ridgedale Ave (07936-2302)
PHONE..................................973 887-9400

Clifford W Moodie, *President*
William C Moodie Jr, *Chairman*
Peter Gagliardi, *Project Mgr*
Nicolas Desalvia, *Prdtn Mgr*
Glenn Heimroth, *QC Mgr*
EMP: 59 EST: 1871
SQ FT: 30,000
SALES (est): 9.9MM **Privately Held**
WEB: www.cpi-nj.com
SIC: **3643 3822** Current-carrying wiring devices; auto controls regulating residntl & coml environmt & applncs

(G-2205)
CALCULAGRAPH CO
T/A Control Products
272 Ridgedale Ave 280 (07936-2393)
PHONE..................................973 887-9400
Fax: 973 887-5083
Cliff Moodie, *Manager*
EMP: 50
SALES (corp-wide): 9.9MM **Privately Held**
WEB: www.cpi-nj.com
SIC: **3643** Electric switches
PA: Calculagraph Co (Inc)
    280 Ridgedale Ave
    East Hanover NJ 07936
    973 887-9400

(G-2206)
CAPCO ENTERPRISES INC
Also Called: Nutibles
34 Deforest Ave Ste 4 (07936-2832)
P.O. Box 335, Florham Park (07932-0335)
PHONE..................................973 884-0044
Fax: 973 884-8711
Carole Lapone, *President*
Brian Henry, *Opers Mgr*
EMP: 12
SQ FT: 12,000
SALES (est): 1MM **Privately Held**
WEB: www.capcoenterprises.com
SIC: **2064** Candy & other confectionery products

(G-2207)
COHERENT INC
Also Called: Coherent Advnced Crystal Group
31 Farinella Dr (07936-2001)
PHONE..................................973 240-6851
Dominic Loiacono, *General Mgr*
Michael Kolesnikov, *Engineer*
Ping Hou, *Director*
Maryellen Wilson, *Director*
EMP: 68
SALES (corp-wide): 1.7B **Publicly Held**
SIC: **3679 3827** Electronic crystals; optical instruments & lenses
PA: Coherent, Inc.
    5100 Patrick Henry Dr
    Santa Clara CA 95054
    408 764-4000

(G-2208)
COMPRELLI EQUIPMENT AND SVC
Also Called: Ces Fence
9 Brace Dr (07936-3023)
PHONE..................................973 428-8687
Jeff Compralli, *President*
EMP: 8
SALES (est): 1.1MM **Privately Held**
SIC: **2499** Fencing, docks & other outdoor wood structural products

(G-2209)
COMVERGE GIANTS INC (DH)
120 Eagle Rock Ave # 190 (07936-3158)
PHONE..................................973 884-5970
Robert Chiste, *CEO*
Rachel Freeman, *Partner*
Tom V Denoer, *Senior VP*
Matthew H Smith, *Senior VP*
Todd St John, *Info Tech Mgr*
EMP: 1
SALES (est): 2.4MM
SALES (corp-wide): 2B **Publicly Held**
SIC: **3822** Hardware for environmental regulators

(G-2210)
CONTROL PRODUCTS INC
272 Ridgedale Ave 280 (07936-2304)
PHONE..................................973 887-5000
Clifford W Moodie, *President*

William C Moodie Jr, *Chairman*
Mary E Moodie, *Admin Sec*
EMP: 60
SQ FT: 30,000
SALES (est): 4.9MM
SALES (corp-wide): 9.9MM **Privately Held**
WEB: www.controlproducts.com
SIC: **3643** Current-carrying wiring devices
PA: Calculagraph Co (Inc)
    280 Ridgedale Ave
    East Hanover NJ 07936
    973 887-9400

(G-2211)
CRAFTSMEN PHOTO LITHOGRAPHERS
38 Beach St (07936-3505)
PHONE..................................973 316-5791
Samuel J Newick, *President*
Ross P Newick, *Corp Secy*
Warren Newick, *Vice Pres*
EMP: 20 EST: 1947
SQ FT: 12,000
SALES (est): 2.4MM **Privately Held**
SIC: **2752 2791 2789** Commercial printing, offset; photolithographic printing; typesetting; bookbinding & related work

(G-2212)
DOS INDUSTRIAL SALES LLC
7d Great Meadow Ln (07936-1721)
PHONE..................................973 887-7800
Justin Kuhn, *Director*
EMP: 4
SALES (est): 317.6K **Privately Held**
SIC: **3613 3444** Power connectors, electric; forming machine work, sheet metal

(G-2213)
DRISCOLL LABEL COMPANY INC
19 West St (07936-2822)
PHONE..................................973 585-7291
Fax: 800 342-1195
John Raguso Jr, *President*
EMP: 18 EST: 1971
SQ FT: 16,000
SALES (est): 1.8MM **Privately Held**
WEB: www.driscolllabel.com
SIC: **2759** Labels & seals: printing

(G-2214)
EDWARD BROWN
Also Called: Ebco Tool
8 Great Meadow Ln B (07936)
PHONE..................................973 887-5255
Edward Brown, *Owner*
EMP: 4 EST: 1957
SQ FT: 3,600
SALES (est): 365.7K **Privately Held**
SIC: **3523** Barn, silo, poultry, dairy & livestock machinery

(G-2215)
ELANA TILE CONTRACTORS INC
8 Merry Ln Ste B (07936-3938)
PHONE..................................973 386-0991
Fax: 973 386-0094
Jeremia Padula, *President*
▲ EMP: 6
SQ FT: 5,600
SALES (est): 420K **Privately Held**
SIC: **1743 3281** Marble installation, interior; tile installation, ceramic; cut stone & stone products

(G-2216)
FASTSIGNS
50 State Route 10 Ste 2 (07936-1015)
PHONE..................................973 887-6700
Fax: 973 887-0020
Linda C Specht,
Scott S Specht,
EMP: 8
SQ FT: 2,000
SALES (est): 970.6K **Privately Held**
SIC: **3993** Signs & advertising specialties

(G-2217)
FOUGERA PHARMACEUTICALS INC
Also Called: Pharmaderm
1 Health Plz (07936-1016)
PHONE..................................973 514-4241
Fax: 973 514-4363
Sandra Anderson, *Sales Staff*
Cristian Pardo, *Sales Staff*
Peter Peach, *Sales Staff*
Brian Markison, *Branch Mgr*
EMP: 40
SALES (corp-wide): 49.1B **Privately Held**
WEB: www.altanapharma-us.com
SIC: 2834 Druggists' preparations (pharmaceuticals)
HQ: Fougera Pharmaceuticals Inc.
60 Baylis Rd
Melville NY 11747
631 454-7677

(G-2218)
GENERAL METAL MANUFACTURING CO
Also Called: G M Fence Co
170 State Route 10 (07936-2107)
PHONE..................................973 386-1818
Fax: 973 503-1706
Lee Rothfeld, *President*
▲ EMP: 20 EST: 1925
SQ FT: 27,000
SALES (est): 2.9MM **Privately Held**
WEB: www.gmfence.com
SIC: 2499 5031 3496 5039 Fencing, wood; fencing, wood; fencing, made from purchased wire; wire fence, gates & accessories

(G-2219)
GIVAUDAN FLAVORS CORPORATION
245 Merry Ln (07936-3900)
P.O. Box 560 (07936-0560)
PHONE..................................973 386-9800
Fax: 973 463-8098
Joseph Fabbri, *Plant Mgr*
Thomas Kirsch, *Research*
Maria Rangos, *Human Res Mgr*
Tracey Mara, *Human Resources*
Ron Gregory, *Info Tech Dir*
EMP: 185
SALES (corp-wide): 5.1B **Privately Held**
SIC: 2869 2087 Perfumes, flavorings & food additives; extracts, flavoring
HQ: Givaudan Flavors Corporation
1199 Edison Dr
Cincinnati OH 45216
513 948-8000

(G-2220)
GIVAUDAN FRAGRANCES CORP
Also Called: Givaudan Flavors
245 Merry Ln (07936-3900)
PHONE..................................973 386-9800
Eileen Moyer, *Director*
EMP: 200
SALES (corp-wide): 5.1B **Privately Held**
SIC: 2087 Flavoring extracts & syrups
HQ: Givaudan Fragrances Corporation
1199 Edison Dr Ste 1-2
Cincinnati OH 45216
513 948-3428

(G-2221)
GIVAUDAN FRAGRANCES CORP
Also Called: Givaudan East
717 Ridgedale Ave (07936-3163)
PHONE..................................973 576-9500
Fax: 973 576-1634
Abenaa Brew, *Research*
Sanjeev Bawa, *Business Anlyst*
John Vernieri, *Branch Mgr*
Josh Denholtz, *Manager*
EMP: 138
SALES (corp-wide): 5.1B **Privately Held**
SIC: 2869 Industrial organic chemicals
HQ: Givaudan Fragrances Corporation
1199 Edison Dr Ste 1-2
Cincinnati OH 45216
513 948-3428

(G-2222)
GIVAUDAN FRAGRANCES CORP
717 Ridgedale Ave (07936-3163)
PHONE..................................973 560-1939

Jun Dizon, *Project Mgr*
Lisa Dahl, *Planning*
EMP: 138
SALES (corp-wide): 5.1B **Privately Held**
SIC: 2869 Perfume materials, synthetic
HQ: Givaudan Fragrances Corporation
1199 Edison Dr Ste 1-2
Cincinnati OH 45216
513 948-3428

(G-2223)
GOLD STAR DISTRIBUTION LLC
Also Called: Goldstar Performance Products
120 Eagle Rock Ave # 326 (07936-3175)
PHONE..................................973 882-5300
Steven Hankin,
EMP: 13 EST: 2014
SQ FT: 1,200
SALES: 2MM **Privately Held**
SIC: 2023 Dietary supplements, dairy & non-dairy based

(G-2224)
IPSCO APOLLO PUNCH & DIE CORP
10 Great Meadow Ln (07936)
PHONE..................................973 884-0900
Fax: 973 884-1682
Claire Tulino, *President*
Robert Gaito, *Vice Pres*
EMP: 7
SQ FT: 20,000
SALES: 300K **Privately Held**
SIC: 3544 Punches, forming & stamping

(G-2225)
ITG BRANDS LLC
50 Williams Pkwy Ste B (07936-2110)
PHONE..................................973 386-9087
Vincent Addona, *Branch Mgr*
EMP: 6
SALES (corp-wide): 38.8B **Privately Held**
SIC: 2121 Cigars
HQ: Itg Brands, Llc
714 Green Valley Rd
Greensboro NC 27408
336 335-7000

(G-2226)
JETTRON PRODUCTS INC
56 State Route 10 (07936-1006)
P.O. Box 337 (07936-0337)
PHONE..................................973 887-0571
Edward C Balzarotti, *President*
Lola R Balzarotti, *Corp Secy*
Jim Lemke, *Engineer*
Edward Balzarotti, *Info Tech Mgr*
EMP: 30 EST: 1959
SQ FT: 12,500
SALES (est): 2.6MM **Privately Held**
SIC: 3498 3679 Tube fabricating (contract bending & shaping); electronic circuits

(G-2227)
LANXESS SOLUTIONS US INC
Anderol Division
215 Merry Ln (07936-3900)
PHONE..................................973 887-7411
Fax: 973 887-6930
Ernest Marcel, *Branch Mgr*
EMP: 150
SALES (corp-wide): 11.4B **Privately Held**
WEB: www.cromptoncorp.com
SIC: 2869 2992 Hydraulic fluids, synthetic base; lubricating oils & greases; oils & greases, blending & compounding
HQ: Lanxess Solutions Us Inc.
199 Benson Rd
Middlebury CT 06762
203 573-2000

(G-2228)
MONDELEZ INTERNATIONAL INC
200 Deforest Ave (07936-2833)
PHONE..................................973 503-2000
EMP: 25 **Publicly Held**
SIC: 2022 Imitation cheese
PA: Mondelez International, Inc.
3 Parkway North Blvd # 300
Deerfield IL 60015

(G-2229)
MOTIF INDUSTRIES INC
299 Ridgedale Ave Ste 5 (07936-2307)
PHONE..................................973 575-1800

Fax: 973 575-1801
Eyal Elkayam, *President*
▲ EMP: 15
SQ FT: 10,000
SALES (est): 3.9MM **Privately Held**
WEB: www.motif-industries.com
SIC: 3851 3543 Eyeglasses, lenses & frames; industrial patterns

(G-2230)
NABISCO ROYAL ARGENTINA INC (HQ)
200 Deforest Ave (07936-2891)
P.O. Box 1944 (07936-1944)
PHONE..................................973 503-2000
Beth Culligan, *President*
EMP: 7
SALES (est): 2.3MM **Publicly Held**
SIC: 2052 Biscuits, dry

(G-2231)
NEW ADVENTURES LLC
6 Deforest Ave Ste 7 (07936-2831)
PHONE..................................973 884-8887
Beth Reiling, *Partner*
Joseph Reiling, *Partner*
▲ EMP: 5
SALES (est): 480K **Privately Held**
SIC: 3942 Dolls & stuffed toys

(G-2232)
NOVARTIS CORPORATION (DH)
1 S Ridgedale Ave (07936-3142)
PHONE..................................212 307-1122
Fax: 973 503-7185
Christi Shaw, *Ch of Bd*
Virginia Lazala, *Vice Pres*
Barbara Warner, *Vice Pres*
Marcia Kayath, *Research*
Harry Kirsch, *CFO*
◆ EMP: 30 EST: 1903
SALES (est): 49.4B
SALES (corp-wide): 49.1B **Privately Held**
WEB: www.novartis.com
SIC: 2834 2879 2032 2865 Pharmaceutical preparations; drugs acting on the cardiovascular system, except diagnostic; drugs acting on the central nervous system & sense organs; veterinary pharmaceutical preparations; agricultural chemicals; canned specialties; cyclic crudes & intermediates
HQ: Novartis International Ag
Lichtstrasse 35
Basel BS 4056
613 241-111

(G-2233)
NOVARTIS CORPORATION
Also Called: Novartis Pharmaceuticals
1 Health Plz (07936-1016)
PHONE..................................862 778-8300
Fax: 973 781-3669
Edgar Arrocha, *Vice Pres*
William Illis, *Vice Pres*
Robert Kowalski, *Vice Pres*
Carol Lynch, *Vice Pres*
Leslie Fields, *Project Mgr*
EMP: 56
SALES (corp-wide): 49.1B **Privately Held**
WEB: www.novartis.com
SIC: 2834 Pharmaceutical preparations
HQ: Novartis Corporation
1 S Ridgedale Ave
East Hanover NJ 07936
212 307-1122

(G-2234)
NOVARTIS CORPORATION
59 State Route 10 (07936-1080)
PHONE..................................973 503-7488
Robert Naidus, *Financial Exec*
Joe Stein, *Manager*
Rajeev Hegde, *Info Tech Mgr*
Gary Cueman, *Director*
Sam Rebello, *Director*
EMP: 500
SALES (corp-wide): 49.1B **Privately Held**
WEB: www.novartis.com
SIC: 2834 Druggists' preparations (pharmaceuticals)
HQ: Novartis Corporation
1 S Ridgedale Ave
East Hanover NJ 07936
212 307-1122

(G-2235)
NOVARTIS PHARMACEUTICALS CORP (DH)
Also Called: NPS
1 Health Plz (07936-1016)
P.O. Box 6656, Saint Louis MO (63125-0656)
PHONE..................................862 778-8300
Fax: 862 778-7185
Paul Hudson, *President*
Anna Frable, *President*
Gary E Rosenthal, *President*
Andre Wyss, *President*
Maria Camacho, *Regional Mgr*
◆ EMP: 4600 EST: 1968
SALES: 49.4B
SALES (corp-wide): 49.1B **Privately Held**
WEB: www.pharma.us.novartis.com
SIC: 2834 Pharmaceutical preparations
HQ: Novartis Corporation
1 S Ridgedale Ave
East Hanover NJ 07936
212 307-1122

(G-2236)
NOVARTIS PHARMACEUTICALS CORP
1 Health Plz (07936-1016)
PHONE..................................862 778-8300
Sean Foster, *Manager*
EMP: 6
SALES (corp-wide): 49.1B **Privately Held**
SIC: 3826 2834 Analytical instruments; pharmaceutical preparations
HQ: Novartis Pharmaceuticals Corporation
1 Health Plz
East Hanover NJ 07936
862 778-8300

(G-2237)
NOVARTIS PHARMACEUTICALS CORP
1 S Ridgedale Ave (07936-3142)
PHONE..................................862 778-8300
Paul Costa, *Principal*
Barbara Frisch, *Personnel*
Antonio Visconti, *Director*
EMP: 9
SALES (corp-wide): 49.1B **Privately Held**
SIC: 2834 Pharmaceutical preparations
HQ: Novartis Pharmaceuticals Corporation
1 Health Plz
East Hanover NJ 07936
862 778-8300

(G-2238)
NOVEL INGREDIENT SERVICES LLC
43 West St (07936-2822)
PHONE..................................973 808-5900
Mindee Green,
EMP: 6
SALES (corp-wide): 722MM **Publicly Held**
SIC: 5149 2087 Health foods; flavoring extracts & syrups
HQ: Novel Ingredient Services, Llc
72 Deforest Ave
East Hanover NJ 07936
973 808-5900

(G-2239)
PEGASUS GROUP PUBLISHING INC
188 State Route 10 Fl 2 (07936-2108)
PHONE..................................973 884-9100
Bruce Warren, *President*
EMP: 12
SQ FT: 2,000
SALES (est): 900K **Privately Held**
SIC: 2731 Books: publishing & printing

(G-2240)
QUEST INTL FLVORS FRGRNCES INC
717 Ridgedale Ave (07936-3163)
PHONE..................................973 576-9500
Fax: 973 691-6871
Damas Thoman, *President*
James Procopio, *Engineer*
Ravi Waran, *Director*
▼ EMP: 450

SALES (est): 50.9MM
SALES (corp-wide): 5.1B **Privately Held**
SIC: 2844 5122 Toilet preparations; perfumes
HQ: Givaudan Fragrances Corporation
1199 Edison Ave Ste 1-2
Cincinnati OH 45216
513 948-3428

(G-2241)
RONED PRINTING & REPRODUCTION
6 Deforest Ave Ste 2 (07936-2831)
PHONE....................973 386-1848
Ron Russo, *President*
EMP: 5
SQ FT: 5,000
SALES (est): 450K **Privately Held**
WEB: www.roned.com
SIC: 2752 Commercial printing, offset

(G-2242)
SANDOZ INC
1 Health Plz (07936-1016)
PHONE....................862 778-8300
Jesus Corchero, *Vice Pres*
Oliver Esman, *Vice Pres*
Patrick Genestin, *Vice Pres*
Scott Higdon, *Vice Pres*
Anthony Maffia, *Vice Pres*
EMP: 528
SALES (corp-wide): 49.1B **Privately Held**
SIC: 2834 5122 Pharmaceutical preparations; drugs, proprietaries & sundries
HQ: Sandoz Inc.
100 College Rd W
Princeton NJ 08540
609 627-8500

(G-2243)
SIGNAL CRAFTERS TECH INC
57 Eagle Rock Ave (07936-3169)
PHONE....................973 781-0880
Fax: 973 781-9044
Al Vnencak, *President*
EMP: 5 **EST:** 1979
SQ FT: 6,000
SALES (est): 1MM **Privately Held**
WEB: www.signalcrafters.com
SIC: 3699 3825 Electronic training devices; test equipment for electronic & electrical circuits

(G-2244)
STATE ELECTRONICS PARTS CORP
36 State Route 10 Ste 6 (07936-1075)
P.O. Box 436 (07936-0436)
PHONE....................973 887-2550
Thomas Sutcliffe, *President*
Tom Sutcliffe, *General Mgr*
Dave Reed, *Vice Pres*
▼ **EMP:** 20 **EST:** 1956
SQ FT: 10,000
SALES (est): 3.7MM **Privately Held**
WEB: www.state-elec.com
SIC: 3676 5065 Electronic resistors; electronic parts

(G-2245)
THERMO X-PRESS PRINTING LLC
12d Great Meadow Ln (07936-1705)
PHONE....................973 585-6505
Stephen Stringas, *President*
EMP: 7 **EST:** 2010
SALES (est): 543.6K **Privately Held**
SIC: 5111 2752 Printing & writing paper; commercial printing, lithographic

(G-2246)
TITANIUM INDUSTRIES INC
64 State Route 10 (07936-1006)
PHONE....................973 428-1900
Fax: 973 428-7250
Bob Reilly, *Principal*
EMP: 7
SALES (est): 640.1K **Privately Held**
SIC: 3356 Titanium

(G-2247)
TRIM BRUSH COMPANY INC
22 Littell Rd Bldg 1 (07936-1002)
PHONE....................973 887-2525
Fax: 973 887-8507

Bruce M Carton, *President*
Diane M Carton, *Corp Secy*
EMP: 6
SQ FT: 15,000
SALES (est): 840K **Privately Held**
SIC: 5087 2842 Cleaning & maintenance equipment & supplies; cleaning or polishing preparations

(G-2248)
VISCOT MEDICAL LLC (PA)
32 West St (07936-2822)
P.O. Box 351 (07936-0351)
PHONE....................973 887-9273
Gary J Pieringer, *President*
Ann Pieringer, *Vice Pres*
◆ **EMP:** 35 **EST:** 1974
SQ FT: 10,000
SALES (est): 7.3MM **Privately Held**
SIC: 3841 3843 Surgical & medical instruments; dental equipment & supplies

(G-2249)
WEISS-AUG CO INC (PA)
220 Merry Ln (07936-3921)
PHONE....................973 887-7600
Fax: 973 887-8109
Dieter Weissenrieder, *President*
Nick Poreman, *Business Mgr*
Robert Zerella, *Business Mgr*
Pierre Y Leonard, *Corp Secy*
Jeffrey Cole, *VP Opers*
▲ **EMP:** 164
SQ FT: 97,000
SALES (est): 36.6MM **Privately Held**
WEB: www.weiss-aug.com
SIC: 3089 3469 Injection molding of plastics; stamping metal for the trade

(G-2250)
WIN-TECH PRECISION PRODUCTS
5a Littell Rd (07936-1001)
PHONE....................973 887-8727
Fax: 973 887-7971
Rashmika Patel, *President*
▲ **EMP:** 4
SQ FT: 2,000
SALES (est): 606.5K **Privately Held**
SIC: 3599 Machine shop, jobbing & repair

(G-2251)
YARDE METALS INC
603 Murray Rd (07936-2201)
PHONE....................973 463-1166
Fax: 973 463-0463
Bryan Doherty, *Manager*
EMP: 27
SALES (corp-wide): 9.7B **Publicly Held**
WEB: www.yarde.com
SIC: 3312 3353 Stainless steel; foil, aluminum
HQ: Yarde Metals, Inc.
45 Newell St
Southington CT 06489
860 406-6061

(G-2252)
ZINAS SALADS INC
11 Great Meadow Ln (07936-1703)
PHONE....................973 428-0660
Fax: 973 503-1666
Zina Shaknovich, *President*
Ruth Sigman, *Treasurer*
William Horstman, *Admin Sec*
EMP: 22
SQ FT: 8,000
SALES (est): 4MM **Privately Held**
SIC: 2099 Food preparations; salads, fresh or refrigerated

(G-2253)
ZYMET INC
7 Great Meadow Ln (07936)
PHONE....................973 428-5245
Karl I Loh, *President*
Sam Ringel, *Vice Pres*
Jay Parton, *Admin Sec*
EMP: 10
SQ FT: 8,000
SALES (est): 1.8MM **Privately Held**
SIC: 2891 Adhesives

East Orange
Essex County

(G-2254)
AFRICAN TELECOM INC
Also Called: African Sun Times
463 N Arlington Ave (07017-3934)
PHONE....................973 675-9919
Chika Onyeani, *President*
EMP: 5
SALES (est): 218.7K **Privately Held**
SIC: 2711 Newspapers: publishing only, not printed on site

(G-2255)
CROSS COUNTER INC (PA)
200 Freeway Dr E (07018-3809)
PHONE....................973 677-0600
Nancy Canavan, *Principal*
EMP: 4
SALES (est): 1.2MM **Privately Held**
SIC: 3131 Counters

(G-2256)
I K CONSTRUCTION INC
174 Evergreen Pl 805 (07018-2001)
P.O. Box 944, South Orange (07079-0944)
PHONE....................908 925-5200
Ian Katwaroo, *President*
EMP: 20
SQ FT: 2,188
SALES (est): 4.4MM **Privately Held**
SIC: 3441 Fabricated structural metal

(G-2257)
JORGENSEN CARR LTD
45 Glenwood Pl (07017-3013)
PHONE....................201 792-2278
Fax: 201 792-1916
Michael Jorgensen, *President*
Kenneth Carr, *Partner*
EMP: 5
SALES (est): 700K **Privately Held**
SIC: 1751 2499 Cabinet building & installation; decorative wood & woodwork

(G-2258)
JUST US BOOKS INC
356 Glenwood Ave Ste 7a (07017-3010)
PHONE....................973 672-7701
Fax: 973 677-7570
Wade Hudson, *President*
Cheryl Willis Hudson, *Vice Pres*
▲ **EMP:** 4
SQ FT: 600
SALES (est): 2MM **Privately Held**
WEB: www.cherylwhudson.com
SIC: 2731 Books: publishing only

(G-2259)
KMBA FASHIONS INC
272 Elmwood Ave Bldg 3 (07018-1802)
PHONE....................973 789-1652
William Cotton Jr, *President*
Andre Wilson, *Vice Pres*
Craig Jones, *Treasurer*
Ronald Parker, *Admin Sec*
EMP: 6
SALES (est): 25K **Privately Held**
WEB: www.kmbafashions.com
SIC: 2329 2339 Men's & boys' sportswear & athletic clothing; athletic clothing: women's, misses' & juniors'

(G-2260)
MACHIAVELLI LLC
64 Eaton Pl (07017-5150)
PHONE....................862 215-5888
John Thompson,
EMP: 6
SALES (est): 398.2K **Privately Held**
SIC: 3714 Motor vehicle parts & accessories

(G-2261)
NEW MANNA INC
426 Prospect St (07017-3329)
P.O. Box 8213, Newark (07108-0213)
PHONE....................973 675-8561
Robert C Morris Jr, *President*
EMP: 4
SALES (est): 150K **Privately Held**
SIC: 2844 Toilet preparations

(G-2262)
NEWARK AUTO TOP CO INC
Also Called: Newark Auto Products
23 Centerway (07017-5354)
P.O. Box 4365 (07019-4365)
PHONE....................973 677-9935
Fax: 973 677-9335
Benjamin Hershkowitz, *Ch of Bd*
EMP: 10 **EST:** 1907
SQ FT: 30,000
SALES (est): 1.5MM **Privately Held**
SIC: 2273 5013 2396 3714 Automobile floor coverings, except rubber or plastic; automotive trim; automotive trimmings; fabric; motor vehicle parts & accessories; synthetic rubber

(G-2263)
PARAMOUNT BAKERIES INC
18-28 Springdale Ave (07019)
PHONE....................973 482-6638
Fernando Frazao, *Manager*
EMP: 4
SALES (corp-wide): 10.8MM **Privately Held**
SIC: 2051 Bread, cake & related products
PA: Paramount Bakeries Inc.
61 Davenport Ave
Newark NJ 07107
973 482-6638

(G-2264)
PARAMOUNT WIRE CO INC
2-8 Central Ave (07018-3912)
PHONE....................973 672-0500
Fax: 973 674-0727
Charles B Coates, *President*
Robert Coates, *Corp Secy*
Marilyn Bergman, *Vice Pres*
▲ **EMP:** 35 **EST:** 1929
SQ FT: 1,000
SALES (est): 2.9MM **Privately Held**
SIC: 3357 Nonferrous wiredrawing & insulating

(G-2265)
PELCO PACKAGING CORPORATION
545 N Arlington Ave Ste 7 (07017-4005)
P.O. Box 196, Stirling (07980-0196)
PHONE....................973 675-4994
Fax: 973 678-4086
Arthur J Brinker, *President*
▲ **EMP:** 15 **EST:** 1949
SQ FT: 20,000
SALES (est): 1.3MM
SALES (corp-wide): 3.2MM **Privately Held**
WEB: www.pelcopackaging.com
SIC: 3089 Pallets, plastic
PA: Engineered Plastic Products, Inc.
269 Mercer St
Stirling NJ 07980
908 647-3500

(G-2266)
PRINTING DELITE INC
279 To 281 Sanford St (07018)
PHONE....................973 676-3033
Fax: 973 676-4845
Phillipe Gomez, *President*
EMP: 6
SQ FT: 2,800
SALES (est): 822K **Privately Held**
SIC: 2752 2791 Commercial printing, offset; typesetting

(G-2267)
QUALLIS BRANDS LLC
211 Glenwood Ave (07017-2009)
PHONE....................862 252-0664
Calvin Quallis, *President*
EMP: 5
SALES (est): 323K **Privately Held**
SIC: 3999 7389 Barber & beauty shop equipment;

(G-2268)
SCI-BORE INC
364 Glenwood Ave Ste 8c (07017-3006)
PHONE....................973 414-9001
Fax: 973 414-9003
EMP: 7
SQ FT: 2,000
SALES: 602.1K **Privately Held**
SIC: 3677 Mfg Machine Parts

(G-2269)
SHEARMAN CABINETS
195 N Munn Ave (07017-4206)
PHONE.....................................973 677-0071
Thomas Shearman, *Owner*
Mark Shearman, *Co-Owner*
EMP: 8
SALES (est): 702.4K Privately Held
SIC: 2434 Wood kitchen cabinets

(G-2270)
TAYLOR WINDOWS INC
Also Called: Taylor Window Factory
61 Central Ave (07018-3908)
PHONE.....................................973 672-3000
Fax: 973 672-3036
Pat Di Gravina, *President*
EMP: 10
SQ FT: 20,000
SALES (est): 880K Privately Held
SIC: 3442 Storm doors or windows, metal

(G-2271)
TECHNICAL AIDS TO INDEPENDENCE
219 S 18th St Unit 2 (07018-3902)
PHONE.....................................973 674-1082
Allan Fenton, *President*
Elfreida Fenton, *Corp Secy*
John Fenton, *Vice Pres*
EMP: 11
SQ FT: 80,000
SALES (est): 1.6MM Privately Held
WEB: www.techaids.com
SIC: 3679 Harness assemblies for electronic use: wire or cable

(G-2272)
TOKEN TORCH LTD LIABILITY CO
3 Hudson Ave (07018-2309)
PHONE.....................................973 629-1805
Bertha Tyson,
Joshua Tyson,
EMP: 11
SALES (est): 650K Privately Held
SIC: 2741 Miscellaneous publishing

(G-2273)
WATER ON TIME BOTTLED
59 N 14th St (07017-5112)
PHONE.....................................862 252-9798
EMP: 5 EST: 2015
SALES (est): 179.2K Privately Held
SIC: 2086 Water, pasteurized: packaged in cans, bottles, etc.

East Rutherford
Bergen County

(G-2274)
A & S FROZEN INC
Also Called: Caravan Products
96 E Union Ave (07073-2125)
PHONE.....................................201 672-0510
John Stone, *President*
EMP: 50
SALES (est): 6.4MM Privately Held
SIC: 2041 2053 Doughs, frozen or refrigerated; frozen bakery products, except bread

(G-2275)
ALPINE GROUP INC (PA)
1 Meadowlands Plz Ste 800 (07073-2152)
PHONE.....................................201 549-4400
Fax: 201 549-4428
Steven S Elbaum, *Ch of Bd*
Joseph Domizio, *COO*
K Mitchell Posner, *Exec VP*
Stewart H Wahrsager, *Senior VP*
Lauren Bazel, *Vice Pres*
EMP: 15
SQ FT: 5,900
SALES (est): 50.9MM Publicly Held
SIC: 2821 3496 Plastics materials & resins; cable, uninsulated wire: made from purchased wire

(G-2276)
AMBER ROAD INC (PA)
1 Meadowlands Plz # 1500 (07073-2151)
PHONE.....................................201 935-8588
James W Preuninger, *CEO*
Barry M V Williams, *Ch of Bd*
Albert C Cooke III, *Senior VP*
Brad Hoffman, *Vice Pres*
Bill Jackowski, *Vice Pres*
EMP: 134
SQ FT: 11,000
SALES (est): 79MM Publicly Held
WEB: www.managementdynamics.com
SIC: 7372 Prepackaged software; business oriented computer software

(G-2277)
APPETIZERS MADE EASY INC
Also Called: Joseph Epstein Food Entps
25 Branca Rd Ste B (07073-2169)
PHONE.....................................201 531-1212
Matt Brown, *President*
Karen Wolf, *Vice Pres*
Lewis Ochs, *CFO*
EMP: 25
SQ FT: 5,500
SALES (est): 7.9MM Privately Held
WEB: www.horsdoeuvresunlimited.com
SIC: 2038 Frozen specialties

(G-2278)
ART MOLD & TOOL CORPORATION
742 Paterson Ave (07073-1028)
PHONE.....................................201 935-3377
Fax: 201 933-2240
Ted Ura, *President*
Mark Ura, *Admin Sec*
EMP: 9
SQ FT: 6,500
SALES (est): 680K Privately Held
WEB: www.artmarkmold.com
SIC: 3544 Industrial molds

(G-2279)
ARTHUR A KAPLAN CO INC
Also Called: Galaxy of Graphics
30 Murray Hill Pkwy # 300 (07073-2181)
PHONE.....................................201 806-2100
Arthur A Kaplan, *CEO*
Reid Alan Fader, *President*
Ellen Fader, *Corp Secy*
EMP: 30 EST: 1956
SQ FT: 30,000
SALES (est): 2.4MM Privately Held
SIC: 2741 2621 Art copy: publishing only, not printed on site; poster & art papers

(G-2280)
ATEKSIS USA CORP (HQ)
1 Meadowlands Plz Ste 200 (07073-2152)
PHONE.....................................646 508-9074
Mehmet Kis, *President*
Emhra Gurpinar, *Vice Pres*
EMP: 4
SALES: 933K
SALES (corp-wide): 2.7MM Privately Held
SIC: 3674 Integrated circuits, semiconductor networks, etc.
PA: Ateksis Profesyonel Ses Ve Goruntu Sistemleri Sanayi Ve Ticaret Limited Sirketi
Bayraktar Bulvari, No:34 Serifali Mahallesi
Istanbul (Anatolia) 34775
216 425-9966

(G-2281)
ATHLON GROUP LLC
1 Meadowlands Plz Ste 200 (07073-2152)
PHONE.....................................201 340-2688
Sean Harley, *Officer*
EMP: 5
SALES: 1.1MM Privately Held
SIC: 8748 3695 Business consulting; computer software tape & disks: blank, rigid & floppy

(G-2282)
AZUMA FOODS INTL INC USA
20 Murray Hill Pkwy # 130 (07073-2295)
PHONE.....................................201 372-1112
Yoshi Sugiura, *Branch Mgr*
EMP: 11

SALES (corp-wide): 25.3MM Privately Held
WEB: www.azumafoods.com
SIC: 2092 Fresh or frozen packaged fish
HQ: Azuma Foods International, Inc. Usa
20201 Mack St
Hayward CA 94545
510 782-1112

(G-2283)
BEACUT ABRASIVES CORP
788 Paterson Ave (07073-1030)
PHONE.....................................973 249-1420
Fax: 973 249-1443
Vladimir Smilovic, *President*
▲ EMP: 11
SQ FT: 6,000
SALES (est): 3.7MM Privately Held
WEB: www.beacutabrasives.com
SIC: 5085 3291 Abrasives; abrasive products

(G-2284)
BELLAQUA INC
Also Called: Water Store, The
251 Paterson Ave (07073-1301)
P.O. Box 344 (07073-0344)
PHONE.....................................201 460-8379
Fax: 201 460-7172
Joel Brizzi, *President*
Jamie Brizzi, *Vice Pres*
EMP: 5
SQ FT: 1,400
SALES: 260K Privately Held
SIC: 5999 5074 5075 3589 Water purification equipment; air purification equipment; water purification equipment

(G-2285)
BERGEN INTERNATIONAL LLC (PA)
196 Paterson Ave Ste 202 (07073-1841)
PHONE.....................................201 299-4499
Fax: 201 909-3769
Dick Leahy, *CEO*
Dennis Keane, *President*
Scott Hunter, *Vice Pres*
Richard Long, *CFO*
Ashley Barfield, *Admin Asst*
EMP: 7 EST: 1998
SALES (est): 4.6MM Privately Held
WEB: www.bergeninternational.com
SIC: 2899 Foam charge mixtures

(G-2286)
BIG APPLE JEWELRY MFG
62 Railroad Ave (07073-2008)
PHONE.....................................201 531-1600
Albert Sirazi, *President*
EMP: 7
SQ FT: 1,500
SALES (est): 530K Privately Held
SIC: 3911 Jewelry, precious metal

(G-2287)
BLOOMFIELD DRAPERY CO INC
948 Paterson Ave Ste A (07073-1062)
PHONE.....................................973 777-3566
Steven Gold, *President*
Madeline Gold, *Vice Pres*
EMP: 11 EST: 1934
SQ FT: 5,000
SALES: 1.4MM Privately Held
SIC: 2391 Curtains, window: made from purchased materials; draperies, plastic & textile: from purchased materials

(G-2288)
BRABANTIA USA INC
20 Murray Hill Pkwy # 260 (07073-2182)
PHONE.....................................201 933-3192
Nicole Gnudi, *Managing Dir*
Anne Slaats, *Comms Mgr*
Thijs Cremers, *Business Anlyst*
Bart Van Elderen, *Manager*
AB Van, *Exec Dir*
▲ EMP: 10
SALES: 1.4MM
SALES (corp-wide): 130.4MM Privately Held
SIC: 3634 Housewares, excluding cooking appliances & utensils
HQ: Bis International Holding B.V.
De Haak 14
Valkenswaard 5555
402 282-222

(G-2289)
C Q CORPORATION
480 Paterson Ave (07073-1281)
PHONE.....................................201 935-8488
EMP: 15 EST: 1975
SQ FT: 65,000
SALES: 2MM Privately Held
SIC: 2396 7336 3953 Mfg Auto/Apparel Trimming Commercial Art/Graphic Design Mfg Marking Devices

(G-2290)
CAMBREX CORPORATION (PA)
1 Meadowlands Plz # 1510 (07073-2214)
PHONE.....................................201 804-3000
Fax: 201 804-9851
Steven M Klosk, *President*
Aldo Magnini, *Managing Dir*
Jonathan Herman, *Area Mgr*
Dieter Plogmann, *Business Mgr*
Shawn P Cavanagh, *COO*
◆ EMP: 97
SALES: 534.4MM Publicly Held
WEB: www.cambrex.com
SIC: 2834 Pharmaceutical preparations; drugs acting on the respiratory system; drugs acting on the gastrointestinal or genitourinary system; drugs acting on the central nervous system & sense organs

(G-2291)
CAPITOL FOAM PRODUCTS INC
75 E Union Ave (07073-2127)
P.O. Box 7564 (07073-7564)
PHONE.....................................201 933-5277
Fax: 201 933-7684
Bart A Krupp, *President*
Isodoro Lerea, *Vice Pres*
Mike Pazar, *Plant Engr*
Paulette Nedrow, *Controller*
Fred Krupp, *Shareholder*
EMP: 45 EST: 1966
SQ FT: 90,000
SALES (est): 7.3MM Privately Held
WEB: www.capitolfoamproducts.com
SIC: 3086 Plastics foam products

(G-2292)
CARAVAN INGREDIENTS INC
96 E Union Ave (07073-2125)
PHONE.....................................201 672-0510
EMP: 32
SALES (corp-wide): 12.9MM Privately Held
SIC: 2099 Food preparations
HQ: Caravan Ingredients Inc.
7905 Quivira Rd
Lenexa KS 66215
913 890-5500

(G-2293)
DAWN BIBLE STUDENTS ASSN
Also Called: Gleeson Agency
199 Railroad Ave (07073-1915)
PHONE.....................................201 438-6421
Fax: 201 531-8225
Kenneth Fernets, *Manager*
EMP: 6 EST: 1932
SQ FT: 15,000
SALES: 357.6K Privately Held
SIC: 2731 7922 Pamphlets: publishing & printing; books: publishing & printing; radio producers; television program, including commercial producers

(G-2294)
ENER-G RUDOX INC
180 E Union Ave (07073-2124)
P.O. Box 467, Carlstadt (07072-0467)
PHONE.....................................201 438-0111
Alan Barlow, *CEO*
Ryan Goodman, *President*
David Suarez, *Vice Pres*
Jonathan Ryba, *Project Engr*
Talal Hindi, *Manager*
▲ EMP: 39
SALES (est): 10MM Privately Held
SIC: 3585 Heating & air conditioning combination units; heating equipment, complete

(G-2295)
FEDEX OFFICE & PRINT SVCS INC
120 Route 17 (07073-2104)
PHONE.....................................201 672-0508

▲ = Import ▼=Export
◆ =Import/Export

Fax: 201 672-0913
EMP: 6
SALES (corp-wide): 65.4B **Publicly Held**
WEB: www.kinkos.com
SIC: **2759** 7334 Commercial printing; photocopying & duplicating services
HQ: Fedex Office And Print Services, Inc.
7900 Legacy Dr
Plano TX 75024
214 550-7000

(G-2296)
FLOORS FOR LESS CORPORATION
94 Carlton Ave (07073-1039)
PHONE..................................201 933-9663
Eric Torres, *President*
▲ EMP: 7
SALES (est): 139.6K **Privately Held**
SIC: **2426** 5713 Flooring, hardwood; floor covering stores

(G-2297)
FLORAL GLASS INDUSTRIES INC
99 Murray Hill Pkwy # 10 (07073-2205)
PHONE..................................201 939-4600
Fax: 201 939-2111
Charles Kaplanek Jr, *President*
Paul Bieber, *Exec VP*
Stanley Lane, *CFO*
EMP: 26
SQ FT: 40,000
SALES (est): 4.1MM **Privately Held**
SIC: **5039** 3211 5023 Glass construction materials; flat glass; home furnishings

(G-2298)
FXI INC
Also Called: Foamex
13 Manor Rd (07073-2119)
PHONE..................................201 933-8540
Fax: 201 933-4148
Jim Darcy, *Manager*
EMP: 65 **Privately Held**
SIC: **3086** Packaging & shipping materials, foamed plastic
HQ: Fxi, Inc.
1400 N Providence Rd # 2000
Media PA 19063

(G-2299)
HELIDEX LLC
Also Called: Helidex Offshore
186 Paterson Ave Ste 303 (07073-1837)
PHONE..................................201 636-2546
Chawki Benteftifa, *President*
Charles Becht,
▼ EMP: 6
SQ FT: 2,500
SALES (est): 1.2MM **Privately Held**
SIC: **3334** 3449 8711 3441 Primary aluminum; landing mats, aircraft: metal; engineering services; fabricated structural metal

(G-2300)
HUDSON GROUP (HG) INC (HQ)
1 Meadowlands Plz (07073-2150)
PHONE..................................201 939-5050
Fax: 201 729-1324
Joseph Didomizio, *President*
Laura Alphran, *President*
Brian Berkner, *President*
Ellen Bramble, *President*
Alan Kessler, *President*
▲ EMP: 277
SQ FT: 20,000
SALES (est): 2.1B
SALES (corp-wide): 8.4B **Privately Held**
SIC: **2731** Book publishing
PA: Dufry Ag
Brunngasslein 12
Basel BS 4052
612 664-444

(G-2301)
KANSAI SPECIAL AMERCN MCH CORP
Also Called: Kansai Special USA
1 Madison St Ste F11 (07073-1605)
PHONE..................................973 470-8321
Chester Hadyka, *Manager*
▲ EMP: 4

SALES (est): 476K
SALES (corp-wide): 19.7MM **Privately Held**
SIC: **3559** Sewing machines & attachments, industrial
PA: Morimoto Mfg.Co.,Ltd.
1-4-17, Suna
Shijonawate OSK 575-0
728 781-177

(G-2302)
KLEIN USA INC
1 Madison St Ste F (07073-1605)
PHONE..................................973 246-8181
Tim Mayhew, *Sales Staff*
Jesse Sevol, *Manager*
▲ EMP: 12
SALES (est): 1.5MM
SALES (corp-wide): 211.4K **Privately Held**
SIC: **3231** Doors, glass: made from purchased glass
HQ: Klein Iberica Sau
Poligono Industrial Can Cuias (Cr N-150 Km 1), Edif. Klein
Montcada I Reixac 08110
935 751-010

(G-2303)
LINK COLOR NA INC
23c Poplar St (07073-1208)
PHONE..................................201 438-8222
Opher Hakem, *Principal*
▲ EMP: 6
SALES (est): 280K **Privately Held**
WEB: www.linkcolorna.com
SIC: **2754** Color printing, gravure

(G-2304)
LINOLEUM SALES COMPANY INC
135 Park Ave (07073-1819)
PHONE..................................201 438-1844
Fax: 201 438-6012
Jeffrey Davidson, *President*
Gregory Davidson, *Vice Pres*
EMP: 4
SQ FT: 2,000
SALES: 500K **Privately Held**
SIC: **3069** Flooring, rubber: tile or sheet; balls, rubber; bath sprays, rubber

(G-2305)
LO GATTO BOOKBINDING
390 Paterson Ave (07073-1339)
P.O. Box 7483 (07073-7483)
PHONE..................................201 438-4344
Fax: 201 438-1775
Medo Lo Gatto, *President*
Michael Lo Gatto, *Treasurer*
Elisa Lo Gatto, *Admin Sec*
EMP: 6 EST: 1967
SQ FT: 4,000
SALES (est): 747.1K **Privately Held**
WEB: www.mtvncontractor.com
SIC: **2789** Binding only: books, pamphlets, magazines, etc.; gold stamping on books

(G-2306)
LUMISCOPE CO INC
33 Whelan Rd (07073-2122)
PHONE..................................678 291-3207
Fax: 732 562-9774
Allen J Beeber, *Ch of Bd*
Marc Bernstein, *President*
▲ EMP: 60
SQ FT: 35,000
SALES (est): 8.7MM **Privately Held**
WEB: www.lumiscope.net
SIC: **3841** 5047 3842 3829 Surgical & medical instruments; surgical equipment & supplies; electro-medical equipment; diagnostic equipment, medical; surgical appliances & supplies; measuring & controlling devices

(G-2307)
MAMAMANCINIS HOLDINGS INC (PA)
25 Branca Rd (07073-2161)
PHONE..................................201 531-1212
Carl Wolf, *Ch of Bd*
Matthew Brown, *President*
Lawrence Morgenstein, *CFO*
EMP: 3
SQ FT: 24,213

SALES: 27.5MM **Publicly Held**
SIC: **2013** 2011 2015 2035 Sausages & other prepared meats; frozen meats from purchased meat; meat packing plants; beef products from beef slaughtered on site; sausages from meat slaughtered on site; turkey, processed: frozen; seasonings & sauces, except tomato & dry

(G-2308)
MARIJON DYEING & FINISHING CO
219 Murray Hill Pkwy (07073-2114)
PHONE..................................201 933-9770
Frank J Mummolo, *President*
John Grimaldi, *CFO*
EMP: 184 EST: 1954
SQ FT: 100,000
SALES (est): 10.2MM **Privately Held**
SIC: **2262** Finishing plants, manmade fiber & silk fabrics

(G-2309)
MCGONEGAL MANUFACTURING CO
Also Called: Themac
405 Railroad Ave (07073-1747)
P.O. Box 444 (07073-0444)
PHONE..................................201 438-2313
Fax: 201 438-8647
Joseph Cremona, *President*
Fran Lundy, *Admin Sec*
EMP: 5
SQ FT: 5,500
SALES: 300K **Privately Held**
SIC: **3541** Grinding machines, metalworking

(G-2310)
METROPOLITAN MANUFACTURING INC
450 Murray Hill Pkwy (07073-2145)
PHONE..................................201 933-8111
Tony Terrigno, *President*
Anthony Terrigno, *President*
Sara Salguero, *Officer*
▲ EMP: 60
SQ FT: 40,000
SALES (est): 4.8MM **Privately Held**
SIC: **2331** 2335 2337 2339 Women's & misses' blouses & shirts; women's, juniors' & misses' dresses; women's & misses' suits & coats; women's & misses' outerwear

(G-2311)
MIL-COMM PRODUCTS COMPANY INC
2 Carlton Ave Ste C (07073-1646)
PHONE..................................201 935-8561
Frances J Furlong, *Ch of Bd*
R Gordon Furlong, *President*
Wendy Servilio, *Business Mgr*
Charley Furlong, *Vice Pres*
John Scheld, *CTO*
EMP: 10
SQ FT: 22,000
SALES (est): 1.6MM **Privately Held**
WEB: www.mil-comm.com
SIC: **2992** Lubricating oils

(G-2312)
MUSHROOM WISDOM INC
1 Madison St Ste F6 (07073-1605)
PHONE..................................973 470-0010
Masaki Shirota, *President*
Donna Noonan, *VP Mktg*
Meagan McLaughlin, *Marketing Staff*
Martin Agurto, *Manager*
▲ EMP: 11
SQ FT: 5,000
SALES (est): 1.8MM **Privately Held**
WEB: www.maitake.com
SIC: **2099** 2032 Food preparations; canned specialties

(G-2313)
NATURAL WIRELESS LLC
23a Poplar St (07073-1208)
PHONE..................................201 438-2865
Dror Shuchman, *Mng Member*
Ralph Hayon,
▲ EMP: 42
SQ FT: 4,000

SALES (est): 11MM **Privately Held**
SIC: **3663** Radio & TV communications equipment

(G-2314)
ORACLE AMERICA INC
1 Meadowlands Plz Ste 700 (07073-2153)
PHONE..................................609 750-0640
Jonathan D Weiner, *Branch Mgr*
Minakshi Dham, *Director*
EMP: 58
SALES (corp-wide): 39.8B **Publicly Held**
SIC: **3571** Electronic computers
HQ: Oracle America, Inc.
500 Oracle Pkwy
Redwood City CA 94065
650 506-7000

(G-2315)
ORACLE CORPORATION
1 Meadowlands Plz # 1400 (07073-2150)
PHONE..................................201 842-7000
Fax: 201 933-0687
Hector Yepez, *Engineer*
Kundan Vyas, *Sales Associate*
Aj Andrews, *Branch Mgr*
Harshivl Shah, *Consultant*
Jerry Abraham, *Technical Staff*
EMP: 302
SALES (corp-wide): 39.8B **Publicly Held**
SIC: **7372** Business oriented computer software
PA: Oracle Corporation
500 Oracle Pkwy
Redwood City CA 94065
650 506-7000

(G-2316)
PANTHERA DENTAL INC
1 Meadowlands Plz Ste 200 (07073-2152)
PHONE..................................201 340-2766
Gabriel Robichaud, *CEO*
Bernard Robichaud, *Vice Pres*
David Solomon, *VP Sales*
EMP: 9
SALES (est): 402.3K **Privately Held**
SIC: **3843** Dental equipment & supplies

(G-2317)
PMC INC
Also Called: General Foam
13 Manor Rd (07073-2119)
PHONE..................................201 933-8540
James Darcy, *Manager*
EMP: 273
SQ FT: 200,000
SALES (corp-wide): 2.2B **Privately Held**
SIC: **3086** Plastics foam products
HQ: Pmc, Inc.
12243 Branford St
Sun Valley CA 91352
818 896-1101

(G-2318)
PRESTIGE LABORATORIES INC
100 Oak St (07073-1220)
PHONE..................................973 772-8922
Gerald Bieber, *President*
▲ EMP: 25
SQ FT: 31,000
SALES (est): 5.9MM **Privately Held**
SIC: **5169** 2842 Industrial chemicals; specialty cleaning, polishes & sanitation goods

(G-2319)
PRIMA-TEC ELECTRONICS CORP
316 Main St (07073-1752)
P.O. Box 436 (07073-0436)
PHONE..................................201 947-4052
Thomas Butler, *President*
Maria Pisano, *Admin Sec*
EMP: 3
SALES: 1MM
SALES (corp-wide): 958.1K **Privately Held**
SIC: **3679** Electronic circuits
HQ: F-T-B International Corp.
26 Broadway Ste 9m1
New York NY 10004
212 514-5400

GEOGRAPHIC

(G-2320)
PURITY LABS
1 Maple St (07073-1221)
PHONE.....................201 372-0236
Joseph Carmello, *General Mgr*
Allison Crispino, *Principal*
Paul Zienkiewicz, *Supervisor*
EMP: 5
SALES (est): 611.7K **Privately Held**
SIC: 3491 Water works valves

(G-2321)
ROBERT COLANERI
Also Called: Colaneri Brothers
236 Park Ave 238 (07073-1919)
PHONE.....................201 939-4405
Fax: 201 939-4406
Robert Colaneri, *Owner*
EMP: 4 EST: 1949
SQ FT: 4,500
SALES (est): 200K **Privately Held**
SIC: 3524 7699 Lawn & garden mowers & accessories; plows (garden tractor equipment); lawn mower repair shop

(G-2322)
ROYCE ASSOCIATES A LTD PARTNR (PA)
35 Carlton Ave (07073-1613)
PHONE.....................201 438-5200
A J Royce IV, *Partner*
Harry Anand, *Partner*
Albert Royce III, *Partner*
Wylie Royce, *Partner*
Victor Villafranca, *Vice Pres*
▲ EMP: 55 EST: 1929
SQ FT: 48,000
SALES (est): 18.3MM **Privately Held**
SIC: 2869 3089 2842 2851 Industrial organic chemicals; plastic processing; polishing preparations & related products; varnishes; chemical preparations

(G-2323)
ROYCE INTERNATIONAL CORP
35 Carlton Ave (07073-1613)
PHONE.....................201 438-5200
A Jay Royce III, *President*
EMP: 5
SALES (est): 395.3K **Privately Held**
SIC: 2869 Industrial organic chemicals

(G-2324)
RUSH INDEX TABS INC
Also Called: Rush Printing and Binding Svcs
60 Willow St (07073-1210)
PHONE.....................201 531-1555
Jay Cohen, *President*
Scott Cohen, *Vice Pres*
EMP: 40
SQ FT: 53,000
SALES (est): 5.4MM **Privately Held**
WEB: www.trustrush.com
SIC: 2732 2752 Book printing; commercial printing, lithographic

(G-2325)
SAMAD BROTHERS INC
419 Murray Hill Pkwy (07073-2107)
PHONE.....................201 372-0909
David Samad, *President*
Malcolm Samad, *Treasurer*
▲ EMP: 12
SQ FT: 20,000
SALES (est): 2.9MM **Privately Held**
SIC: 5023 2273 Rugs; carpets & rugs

(G-2326)
STAR-GLO INDUSTRIES LLC (PA)
2 Carlton Ave (07073-1646)
PHONE.....................201 939-6162
Fax: 201 939-4054
Jeong Cho, *General Mgr*
Dennis Azzolina, *Vice Pres*
Edward Peterhoff, *Vice Pres*
Gene Thomas, *Vice Pres*
Dave Oddo, *Purch Mgr*
▲ EMP: 122
SQ FT: 170,000
SALES (est): 18.1MM **Privately Held**
WEB: www.starglo.com
SIC: 3069 3599 Molded rubber products; machine shop, jobbing & repair

(G-2327)
STEAMIST INC
25 E Union Ave Ste 1 (07073-2254)
PHONE.....................201 933-0700
Fax: 201 933-0746
Jeffrey P Noll, *President*
▲ EMP: 40 EST: 1943
SQ FT: 33,000
SALES (est): 10.6MM
SALES (corp-wide): 353.3MM **Privately Held**
WEB: www.steamist.com
SIC: 3569 Generators: steam, liquid oxygen or nitrogen
PA: R.A.F. Industries, Inc.
165 Township Line Rd # 2100
Jenkintown PA 19046
215 572-0738

(G-2328)
STONE SURFACES INC
890 Paterson Plank Rd (07073-2130)
PHONE.....................201 935-8803
Fax: 201 935-8210
Michael Sakosits, *President*
Felice Cappuccia, *Vice Pres*
▲ EMP: 57
SQ FT: 11,000
SALES (est): 6MM **Privately Held**
SIC: 1411 1429 Granite dimension stone; marble, crushed & broken-quarrying

(G-2329)
SUN CHEMICAL CORPORATION
Also Called: U S Ink Division
390 Central Ave (07073-1216)
PHONE.....................201 438-4831
Fax: 201 896-9137
Bill Griffen, *Plant Mgr*
Julie Dye, *Sales Staff*
EMP: 20
SALES (corp-wide): 7B **Privately Held**
WEB: www.sunchemical.com
SIC: 2893 2899 Printing ink; chemical preparations
HQ: Sun Chemical Corporation
35 Waterview Blvd Ste 100
Parsippany NJ 07054
973 404-6000

(G-2330)
TECHNO CITY INC
1 Meadowlands Plz Ste 200 (07073-2152)
PHONE.....................862 414-3282
Israfil Demir, *Principal*
EMP: 5
SALES (est): 226.9K **Privately Held**
SIC: 3571 Electronic computers

(G-2331)
TECHNTIME BUS SLTONS LTD LBLTY
Also Called: Pro Academy
1 Madison St Ste B4 (07073-1605)
PHONE.....................973 246-8153
Fax: 973 246-8135
Haciee Dinc, *Controller*
Fatih Ormanoglu, *Sr Ntwrk Engine*
Erdem Cosgun,
EMP: 10
SQ FT: 600
SALES: 4MM **Privately Held**
SIC: 3699 7373 5734 5021 Security control equipment & systems; computer integrated systems design; modems, monitors, terminals & disk drives: computers; office furniture; school desks

(G-2332)
TEL-INSTRUMENT ELEC CORP (PA)
Also Called: Tic
1 Branca Rd (07073-2121)
PHONE.....................201 933-1600
Robert H Walker, *Ch of Bd*
Jeffrey C O'Hara, *President*
EMP: 42
SQ FT: 27,000
SALES: 10MM **Publicly Held**
WEB: www.telinst.com
SIC: 3829 3825 Measuring & controlling devices; aircraft & motor vehicle measurement equipment; instruments to measure electricity

(G-2333)
TODD SHELTON LLC
450 Murray Hill Pkwy C2 (07073-2225)
PHONE.....................844 626-6355
Todd Shelton,
▲ EMP: 6
SQ FT: 5,000
SALES (est): 419.2K **Privately Held**
SIC: 2326 5611 Men's & boys' work clothing; men's & boys' clothing stores

(G-2334)
TRANS WORLD MARKETING CORP (PA)
360 Murray Hill Pkwy (07073-2190)
PHONE.....................201 935-5565
William V Carafello, *President*
James Cavaluzzi, *Chairman*
Gerald Molitor, *Exec VP*
▲ EMP: 101 EST: 1966
SQ FT: 140,000
SALES (est): 17.1MM **Privately Held**
WEB: www.transworldmarketing.com
SIC: 3993 Signs & advertising specialties

(G-2335)
UNITED GUTTER SUPPLY INC
Also Called: Eagle Gutter Supply
1 Maple St Ste 1 (07073-1232)
PHONE.....................201 933-6316
Fax: 201 933-7025
Richard Wille, *President*
EMP: 25
SQ FT: 28,000
SALES (est): 3.4MM **Privately Held**
SIC: 3444 Gutters, sheet metal

(G-2336)
VERICO TECHNOLOGY LLC
405 Murray Hill Pkwy (07073-2136)
PHONE.....................201 842-0222
EMP: 152
SALES (corp-wide): 132.7MM **Privately Held**
SIC: 3555 Mfg Printing Trades Machinery
HQ: Verico Technology Llc
230 Shaker Rd
Enfield CT 06082
800 492-7286

(G-2337)
WOODWARD JOGGER AERATORS INC (PA)
45 Carlton Ave (07073-1613)
PHONE.....................201 933-6800
Joseph Giorgio, *President*
▲ EMP: 18
SALES (est): 3MM **Privately Held**
SIC: 3554 Paper industries machinery

(G-2338)
ZENITH PRECISION INC
536 Paterson Ave (07073-1282)
PHONE.....................201 933-8640
Fax: 201 933-0936
Matteo De Gennaro, *President*
John Antico, *Vice Pres*
Andrew D Gennaro, *Vice Pres*
EMP: 10
SQ FT: 5,000
SALES (est): 870K **Privately Held**
SIC: 3545 3769 Precision tools, machinists'; guided missile & space vehicle parts & auxiliary equipment

---

East Windsor
Mercer County

(G-2339)
ABBOTT POINT OF CARE INC
104 Windsor Center Dr (08520-1423)
PHONE.....................609 371-8923
Fax: 609 443-9310
Feth Hunter, *Manager*
EMP: 120
SALES (corp-wide): 27.3B **Publicly Held**
SIC: 3841 Diagnostic apparatus, medical
HQ: Abbott Point Of Care Inc.
400 College Rd E
Princeton NJ 08540
609 454-9000

(G-2340)
ACCELRX LABS LLC
55 Lake Dr (08520-5320)
PHONE.....................609 301-6446
Doug Van Pelt, *Mng Member*
EMP: 4
SQ FT: 30,000
SALES (est): 311.1K **Privately Held**
SIC: 2834 Pharmaceutical preparations

(G-2341)
ADVENTURE INDUSTRIES LLC (PA)
59 Lake Dr (08520-5320)
PHONE.....................609 426-1777
Michael Koretsky,
Frank Koretsky,
EMP: 5
SQ FT: 10,000
SALES: 1MM **Privately Held**
WEB: www.adventureindustries.com
SIC: 3199 5099 Novelties, leather; novelties, durable

(G-2342)
APRECIA PHARMACEUTICALS CO
89 Twin Rivers Dr (08520-5212)
PHONE.....................215 359-3300
Aleece Phillips, *Engineer*
Pat Zafarino, *Branch Mgr*
EMP: 50
SALES (corp-wide): 26.5MM **Privately Held**
SIC: 2834 Pharmaceutical preparations
HQ: Aprecia Pharmaceuticals, Llc
10901 Kenwood Rd
Blue Ash OH 45242
513 864-4107

(G-2343)
AUREX LABS LTD LBLTY CO
10 Lake Dr (08520-5321)
PHONE.....................609 308-2304
Sree Ranga Aravapalli, *Mng Member*
EMP: 12 EST: 2014
SALES (est): 2.3MM **Privately Held**
SIC: 2834 Pharmaceutical preparations

(G-2344)
AUROBINDO PHARMA
279 Prncton Hightstown Rd (08520-1401)
PHONE.....................732 839-9400
Theresa Perniciaro, *Vice Pres*
Vipin Dubey, *Asst Mgr*
Pushpendra Singh, *Asst Mgr*
Paul McMahon, *Director*
Chandra Reddy, *Director*
EMP: 4
SALES (est): 217.8K **Privately Held**
SIC: 2834 Pharmaceutical preparations

(G-2345)
AUROBINDO PHARMA USA INC
Aurohealth
279 Prncton Hightstown Rd (08520-1401)
PHONE.....................732 839-9402
John Segura, *Branch Mgr*
EMP: 5
SALES (corp-wide): 1.6B **Privately Held**
SIC: 2834 Pharmaceutical preparations
HQ: Aurobindo Pharma U.S.A., Inc.
279 Prncton Hightstown Rd
East Windsor NJ 08520
732 839-9400

(G-2346)
AUROBINDO PHARMA USA INC (HQ)
279 Prncton Hightstown Rd (08520-1401)
PHONE.....................732 839-9400
Fax: 732 355-9940
Robert G Cunard, *CEO*
Sandra Martinez, *QC Mgr*
Ujjwala Tammineni, *Manager*
Shrikant Jani, *Technology*
▲ EMP: 40
SQ FT: 45,000
SALES: 854.4MM
SALES (corp-wide): 1.6B **Privately Held**
WEB: www.aurobindousa.com
SIC: 2834 Pharmaceutical preparations

▲ = Import ▼=Export
◆ =Import/Export

PA: Aurobindo Pharma Limited
Survey No. 9, Plot No.11,
Hyderabad TS 50008
406 672-5000

(G-2347)
AUROBINDO PHARMA USA INC
279 Prncton Hightstown Rd (08520-1401)
PHONE..................................609 409-6774
Robert Cunard, *CEO*
G Prasad, *Vice Pres*
EMP: 5
SALES (corp-wide): 1.6B **Privately Held**
SIC: 2834 Pharmaceutical preparations
HQ: Aurobindo Pharma U.S.A., Inc.
279 Prnctn Hightstown Rd
East Windsor NJ 08520
732 839-9400

(G-2348)
AUROBINDO PHARMA USA LLC
279 Prnceton Highstown Rd (08520-1401)
PHONE..................................732 839-9400
Robert Cunard, *CEO*
EMP: 30
SALES (est): 1.6MM
SALES (corp-wide): 1.6B **Privately Held**
SIC: 2834 Pharmaceutical preparations
HQ: Aurobindo Pharma U.S.A., Inc.
279 Prnctn Hightstown Rd
East Windsor NJ 08520
732 839-9400

(G-2349)
AUROLIFE PHARMA LLC
203 Windsor Center Dr (08520-1410)
PHONE..................................732 839-9408
Gangadhar Gorla, *VP Finance*
EMP: 5
SALES (corp-wide): 1.6B **Privately Held**
SIC: 2834 Pharmaceutical preparations
HQ: Aurolife Pharma Llc
2400 Us Highway 130
Dayton NJ 08810

(G-2350)
AUROMEDICS PHARMA LLC
279 Prncton Hightstown Rd (08520-1401)
PHONE..................................732 823-4122
EMP: 10
SALES (est): 676.7K **Privately Held**
SIC: 2834 Mfg Pharmaceutical Preparations

(G-2351)
AUROMEDICS PHARMA LLC
279 Prncton Hightstown Rd (08520-1401)
PHONE..................................732 839-9400
Mark Fedele, *President*
Vincent Andolina, *Vice Pres*
▲ **EMP:** 40
SALES: 855.2MM
SALES (corp-wide): 1.6B **Privately Held**
SIC: 2834 Pharmaceutical preparations
PA: Aurobindo Pharma Limited
Survey No. 9, Plot No.11,
Hyderabad TS 50008
406 672-5000

(G-2352)
AVYAKTA IT SERVICES LLC
37 Sussex Ln (08520-5111)
PHONE..................................609 790-7517
Sirisha Panchagnula, *Principal*
EMP: 10
SALES (est): 439.2K **Privately Held**
SIC: 7371 7372 8331 7389 Computer
software development & applications;
computer software systems analysis &
design, custom; application computer
software; job training & vocational rehabilitation services;

(G-2353)
CONAIR CORPORATION
Also Called: Scunci Division
150 Milford Rd (08520-6124)
PHONE..................................239 673-2125
Fax: 203 965-8348
Alyssa Lucas, *Manager*
Richard Parrish, *Senior Mgr*
EMP: 65
SALES (corp-wide): 2B **Privately Held**
WEB: www.conair.com
SIC: 3634 Electric housewares & fans

PA: Conair Corporation
1 Cummings Point Rd
Stamford CT 06902
203 351-9000

(G-2354)
CONAIR CORPORATION
Also Called: Cuisinarts Division
150 Milford Rd (08520-6124)
PHONE..................................609 426-1300
Fax: 609 426-8766
Alyssa Lucas, *Manager*
EMP: 250
SALES (corp-wide): 2B **Privately Held**
WEB: www.conair.com
SIC: 3634 2844 3999 3661 Dryers, elec-
tric: hand & face; toilet preparations; bar-
ber & beauty shop equipment; telephone
& telegraph apparatus
PA: Conair Corporation
1 Cummings Point Rd
Stamford CT 06902
203 351-9000

(G-2355)
CORE TECH SOLUTIONS INC
50 Lake Dr (08520-5321)
PHONE..................................609 443-1400
Fax: 609 443-1401
Kirti H Valia, *President*
EMP: 12
SQ FT: 10,000
SALES (est): 2.6MM **Privately Held**
SIC: 2834 Pharmaceutical preparations

(G-2356)
DAVLYN INDUSTRIES INC
366 Prncton Hightstown Rd (08520-1411)
PHONE..................................609 655-5974
Tamaki Shimamoto, *President*
▲ **EMP:** 200
SQ FT: 150,000
SALES (est): 39.4MM
SALES (corp-wide): 8.9B **Privately Held**
WEB: www.davlyn-ind.com
SIC: 2844 5122 Cosmetic preparations;
cosmetics, perfumes & hair products; cos-
metics
HQ: Shiseido Americas Corporation
900 3rd Ave Fl 15
New York NY 10022
212 805-2300

(G-2357)
ESJAY PHARMA LLC
70 Lake Dr (08520-5321)
PHONE..................................609 469-5920
Muthusamy Shanmugam, *President*
EMP: 7
SALES (est): 1MM
SALES (corp-wide): 3MM **Privately Held**
SIC: 2834 Pharmaceutical preparations
PA: Esjay Pharma Llc
27 Ridgeview Way
Allentown NJ 08501
732 438-1816

(G-2358)
FORDOZ PHARMA CORP
69 Prnceton Hightstown Rd (08520-1900)
PHONE..................................609 469-5949
Xin He, *CEO*
EMP: 13
SQ FT: 5,000
SALES (est): 715.5K **Privately Held**
SIC: 2834 Solutions, pharmaceutical

(G-2359)
HOVIONE LLC
40 Lake Dr (08520-5321)
PHONE..................................609 918-2600
Fax: 609 918-2615
Lavinia Emery, *General Mgr*
Marco Gil, *General Mgr*
Jorge Pastilha, *General Mgr*
Courtney Smith, *Regional Mgr*
Steven Landelius, *Business Mgr*
▲ **EMP:** 51
SQ FT: 23,000
SALES (est): 17.1MM
SALES (corp-wide): 221.8MM **Privately
Held**
WEB: www.hovione.com
SIC: 2834 Druggists' preparations (phar-
maceuticals)

HQ: Hovione FarmaciEncia, S.A.
Quinta SAo Pedro
Loures 2674-
219 829-000

(G-2360)
INFINLIGHT PRODUCTS INC (PA)
859130 N 126e (08520)
PHONE..................................888 665-7708
Sonora Chiu, *President*
Alex Yeng, *Vice Pres*
EMP: 5
SALES (est): 585.1K **Privately Held**
SIC: 3645 Residential lighting fixtures

(G-2361)
**MCGRAW-HILL GLBL EDCTN
HLDNGS**
104 Windsor Center Dr (08520-1423)
PHONE..................................609 371-8301
James Shanahan, *Publisher*
David Weidinger, *Principal*
EMP: 53
SALES (corp-wide): 164.2MM **Privately
Held**
SIC: 2731 Textbooks: publishing & printing
PA: Mcgraw-Hill Global Education Holdings,
Llc
2 Penn Plz Fl 20
New York NY 10121
800 338-3987

(G-2362)
MUSE MONTHLY LLC
192 Dorchester Dr (08520-1122)
PHONE..................................609 443-3509
Christina Blok, *Principal*
EMP: 4
SALES (est): 124.4K **Privately Held**
SIC: 2711 Newspapers

(G-2363)
NOVITIUM PHARMA LLC
70 Lake Dr (08520-5321)
PHONE..................................609 469-5920
Chad Gassert, *CEO*
EMP: 8
SQ FT: 36,000
SALES (est): 547.5K **Privately Held**
SIC: 2834 Proprietary drug products

(G-2364)
ORGANICA AROMATICS CORP
20 Lake D (08520)
PHONE..................................609 443-3333
Muhammed Majeed, *Chairman*
EMP: 5
SALES: 397.9K **Privately Held**
SIC: 2099 Seasonings & spices

(G-2365)
ROOF DECK INC
Also Called: Rdi
80 Twin Rivers Dr (08520-5213)
P.O. Box 295, Hightstown (08520-0295)
PHONE..................................609 448-6666
Fax: 609 443-0784
Mary Lou Jaroschak, *President*
Frank La, *Comptroller*
EMP: 15
SQ FT: 22,000
SALES: 0 **Privately Held**
WEB: www.roofdeckinc.com
SIC: 3444 Roof deck, sheet metal

(G-2366)
SHISEIDO AMERICA INC (DH)
366 Prncton Hightstown Rd (08520-1411)
PHONE..................................609 371-5800
Fax: 609 371-8170
Tamaki Shimamoto, *President*
▲ **EMP:** 94
SQ FT: 216,000
SALES (est): 159.4MM
SALES (corp-wide): 8.9B **Privately Held**
SIC: 5122 2844 Cosmetics; cosmetic
preparations
HQ: Shiseido Americas Corporation
900 3rd Ave Fl 15
New York NY 10022
212 805-2300

(G-2367)
**SHISEIDO AMERICAS
CORPORATION**
366 Prncton Hightstown Rd (08520-1411)
PHONE..................................609 371-5800
Shyama Dasai, *Branch Mgr*
Shyama Desai, *Director*
EMP: 9
SALES (corp-wide): 8.9B **Privately Held**
WEB: www.davlyn-ind.com
SIC: 2844 Cosmetic preparations
HQ: Shiseido Americas Corporation
900 3rd Ave Fl 15
New York NY 10022
212 805-2300

(G-2368)
THERMO SYSTEMS LLC
84 Twin Rivers Dr (08520-5213)
PHONE..................................609 371-3300
Fax: 609 371-3400
David J Musto,
Gregory Smith,
EMP: 52
SQ FT: 16,000
SALES (est): 18.5MM **Privately Held**
WEB: www.thermosystems.com
SIC: 3822 7373 Auto controls regulating
residntl & coml environmt & applncs; sys-
tems integration services

(G-2369)
TUNNEL NETWORKS INC
53 Winchester Dr (08520-2608)
PHONE..................................609 414-9799
Byron Stokes, *President*
EMP: 8
SQ FT: 2,000
SALES: 195K **Privately Held**
SIC: 7372 Business oriented computer
software

(G-2370)
WINDSOR LABS LLC
55 Lake Dr (08520-5320)
PHONE..................................609 301-6446
Bruce Bassett, *Manager*
Krystal Cole, *Manager*
EMP: 7
SALES (est): 119.8K **Privately Held**
SIC: 2834 Pharmaceutical preparations

East Windsor
Middlesex County

(G-2371)
BRILLIANT LIGHT POWER INC
493 Old Trenton Rd (08512-5601)
PHONE..................................609 490-0427
Lynn Kline, *Executive Asst*
EMP: 30 **EST:** 1991
SALES (est): 1.5MM **Privately Held**
SIC: 5085 8731 3568 Power transmission
equipment & apparatus; energy research;
chain, power transmission

(G-2372)
**ELEMENTIS CHROMIUM INC
(PA)**
469 Old Trenton Rd (08512-5601)
PHONE..................................609 443-2000
Dennis Valentino, *President*
Susan Shaw, *Plant Mgr*
Bill Greer, *Opers Staff*
Jackie Lee, *Buyer*
Jose Gallegos, *Technical Mgr*
EMP: 106
SALES (est): 28.6MM **Privately Held**
SIC: 2819 Industrial inorganic chemicals

(G-2373)
ELEMENTIS GLOBAL LLC (HQ)
Also Called: Elementis Specialities
469 Old Trenton Rd (08512-5601)
PHONE..................................609 443-2000
Dennis Valentino, *President*
Greg McClatchy, *President*
Gary Castellino, *Vice Pres*
Ling Dawes, *Vice Pres*
Jim Gambino, *Vice Pres*
◆ **EMP:** 200
SQ FT: 77,000

GEOGRAPHIC

SALES (est): 161.8MM
SALES (corp-wide): 782.7MM **Privately Held**
SIC: 2899 Vegetable oils, vulcanized or sulfurized
PA: Elementis Plc
Caroline House
London WC1V
207 067-2999

(G-2374)
ELEMENTIS SPECIALTIES INC (HQ)
469 Old Trenton Rd (08512-5601)
PHONE................................609 443-2000
Fax: 609 443-2206
Neil Carr, *President*
Eric Post, *General Mgr*
Marie Yeager, *General Mgr*
William J French, *COO*
Rob Mangold, *Vice Pres*
◆ **EMP:** 145
SQ FT: 70,000
SALES (est): 212.5MM
SALES (corp-wide): 782.7MM **Privately Held**
WEB: www.elementis-specialties.com
SIC: 2851 8731 2899 2865 Paints & paint additives; commercial physical research; chemical preparations; cyclic crudes & intermediates; inorganic pigments
PA: Elementis Plc
Caroline House
London WC1V
207 067-2999

(G-2375)
ELEMENTIS SPECIALTIES INC
469 Old Trenton Rd (08512-5601)
PHONE................................201 432-0800
Howard Bird, *Vice Pres*
Wayne Arndt, *Engineer*
Gene Tesch, *Plant Engr*
Ramon Pineiro, *Technician*
EMP: 21
SALES (corp-wide): 782.7MM **Privately Held**
SIC: 2851 2816 Paints & allied products; inorganic pigments
HQ: Elementis Specialties, Inc.
469 Old Trenton Rd
East Windsor NJ 08512
609 443-2000

Eastampton
Burlington County

(G-2376)
GROWMARK FS LLC
2545 Route 206 (08060-5421)
PHONE................................609 267-7054
EMP: 18
SALES (corp-wide): 7.2B **Privately Held**
SIC: 2875 2873 2874 5191 Fertilizers, mixing only; nitrogenous fertilizers; nitrogen solutions (fertilizer); phosphatic fertilizers; pesticides; seeds: field, garden & flower
HQ: Growmark Fs, Llc
308 Ne Front St
Milford DE 19963
302 422-3002

Eatontown
Monmouth County

(G-2377)
ABOUDI PRINTING LLC
132 Lewis St Ste B (07724-3925)
PHONE................................732 542-2929
EMP: 4
SALES (est): 362.1K **Privately Held**
SIC: 2752 Commercial printing, lithographic

(G-2378)
AEROFLEX CTRL COMPONENTS INC
Also Called: Cobham McRelectronic Solutions
40 Industrial Way E (07724-3317)
PHONE................................732 460-0212
Fax: 973 884-0445
Jill Kale, *CEO*
John Ekis, *General Mgr*
Joseph Lowrey, *VP Finance*
▲ **EMP:** 86
SQ FT: 46,000
SALES: 15MM
SALES (corp-wide): 2.7B **Privately Held**
WEB: www.aeroflex-kdi.com
SIC: 5065 3679 Electronic parts & equipment; microwave components
HQ: Aeroflex Microelectronic Solutions, Inc.
310 Dino Dr
Ann Arbor MI 48103

(G-2379)
ALGEN DESIGN SERVICES INC
40 Industrial Way E (07724-3317)
P.O. Box 188, Colts Neck (07722-0188)
PHONE................................732 389-3630
Fax: 732 389-3811
Edwin Thomas, *President*
Alex Thomas, *Vice Pres*
Genevive Thomas, *Vice Pres*
EMP: 50
SQ FT: 48,000
SALES (est): 7.3MM **Privately Held**
WEB: www.algendesign.com
SIC: 3679 Electronic loads & power supplies

(G-2380)
ALKALINE CORPORATION
Also Called: Allersearch Labs
38 Industrial Way E Ste 2 (07724-3320)
PHONE................................732 531-7830
Isidore Bale, *President*
EMP: 9
SALES (est): 1.4MM **Privately Held**
SIC: 2844 3842 Face creams or lotions; suntan lotions & oils; colognes; sterilizers, hospital & surgical

(G-2381)
AMEDIA NETWORKS INC
Also Called: (A DEVELOPMENT STAGE COMPANY)
541 Industrial Way W B (07724-4242)
PHONE................................732 440-1992
Fax: 732 389-7541
Frank Galuppo, *President*
James D Gardner, *CFO*
John R Colton, *CTO*
Stuart J Waldman, *Internal Med*
William F Lenahan,
EMP: 18 **EST:** 1994
SALES (est): 3.1MM **Privately Held**
WEB: www.ttrtech.com
SIC: 3577 Computer peripheral equipment

(G-2382)
AMERICAN OIL & SUPPLY CO
Also Called: A O S
22 Meridian Rd Ste 6 (07724-2278)
PHONE................................732 389-5514
Stanley J Ziemski, *Ch of Bd*
Victor Papanu, *Vice Pres*
Jenny Jung, *Consultant*
EMP: 11
SQ FT: 25,000
SALES (est): 960K **Privately Held**
WEB: www.americanoilsupply.com
SIC: 2992 Lubricating oils & greases

(G-2383)
AOS THERMAL COMPOUNDS LLC
22 Meridian Rd Ste 6 (07724-2278)
PHONE................................732 389-5514
John Ziemski, *General Mgr*
Vijay Patel, *COO*
Jennifer Decker, *Marketing Mgr*
Steve Ottaviano, *Manager*
EMP: 14
SQ FT: 5,000
SALES (est): 3.6MM **Privately Held**
WEB: www.aosco.com
SIC: 2891 Adhesives, paste

(G-2384)
BAL-EDGE CORPORATION
Also Called: Brim Technologies
151 Industrial Way E (07724-3322)
PHONE................................973 895-8826
Edward Sullivan, *President*
EMP: 4
SALES: 862.8K **Privately Held**
SIC: 2869 Laboratory chemicals, organic

(G-2385)
BIOTECH ATLANTIC INC
6 Industrial Way W Ste E1 (07724-4265)
PHONE................................732 389-4789
Fax: 732 389-3837
▲ **EMP:** 10
SQ FT: 2,400
SALES (est): 740K **Privately Held**
SIC: 2835 Mfg Diagnostic Devices

(G-2386)
BRECOFLEX CO LLC
222 Industrial Way W (07724-2206)
PHONE................................732 460-9500
Fax: 732 542-6725
Bernd Fuellemann, *President*
Bob Beveridge, *Mfg Mgr*
Jonathan Kobialka, *Mfg Spvr*
Michaela Schilling, *Purchasing*
Michael Langston, *Engineer*
▲ **EMP:** 75
SQ FT: 59,800
SALES (est): 15.8MM **Privately Held**
SIC: 3052 Plastic belting

(G-2387)
BURPEE MEDSYSTEMS LLC
15 Christopher Way (07724-3325)
PHONE................................732 544-8900
Fax: 732 544-8910
Victoria Gallardo, *Purch Agent*
Darren Demedici, *Engineer*
Andrew Filachek, *Engineer*
Jie Jiang, *Engineer*
Rob Doty, *Manager*
EMP: 6
SQ FT: 2,500
SALES (est): 2.1MM **Privately Held**
WEB: www.burpeetech.com
SIC: 3841 3842 Surgical & medical instruments; surgical appliances & supplies

(G-2388)
CONCORDE SPECIALTY GASES INC
36 Eaton Rd (07724-2254)
PHONE................................732 544-9899
Gregory Harquail, *President*
Robert Casper, *Chairman*
Bill Horeis, *Sales Staff*
Carla Dinen, *Admin Asst*
◆ **EMP:** 26
SQ FT: 25,000
SALES (est): 6.9MM **Privately Held**
WEB: www.concordegas.com
SIC: 2813 Industrial gases

(G-2389)
DANIEL C HERRING CO INC
Also Called: D C Herring Co
20 Meridian Rd Ste 6 (07724-2270)
PHONE................................732 530-6557
Fax: 732 695-2275
Daniel A Herring, *President*
Joyce Herring, *Vice Pres*
Tom Pedrazzo, *Vice Pres*
EMP: 10
SQ FT: 8,000
SALES: 3MM **Privately Held**
WEB: www.dancingdjs.com
SIC: 3052 Rubber & plastics hose & beltings

(G-2390)
DIAMOND SG INTL LTD LBLTY CO
20 Meridian Rd Ste 9 (07724-2270)
PHONE................................732 861-9850
Hongvan Quan,
EMP: 6
SQ FT: 4,600
SALES: 1MM **Privately Held**
SIC: 3087 Custom compound purchased resins

(G-2391)
EAST COAST DISTRIBUTORS INC
Also Called: Pdec
1 Industrial Way W E (07724-2255)
PHONE................................732 223-5995
Fax: 732 223-8812
Joseph Sodano, *President*
EMP: 15
SQ FT: 16,500
SALES (est): 7MM **Privately Held**
SIC: 5045 2754 Computers, peripherals & software; business forms: gravure printing

(G-2392)
ELECTRONIC CONCEPTS INC (HQ)
526 Industrial Way W (07724-2212)
P.O. Box 1278 (07724-5278)
PHONE................................732 542-7880
Fax: 732 542-0524
Bernard Lavene, *Ch of Bd*
Philip Lepore, *Treasurer*
▲ **EMP:** 132
SQ FT: 64,000
SALES (est): 18.8MM
SALES (corp-wide): 18.8MM **Privately Held**
WEB: www.ecicaps.com
SIC: 3675 Electronic capacitors
PA: Energy Storage Corp.
526 Industrial Way W
Eatontown NJ 07724
732 542-7880

(G-2393)
ELLIS/KUHNKE CONTROLS INC
Also Called: Ellis Controls
132 Lewis St Ste A2 (07724-3925)
PHONE................................732 291-3334
G Corson Ellis Jr, *Ch of Bd*
Howard Boyce, *President*
Ed Leszczack, *Chief Engr*
Frances M Ruane, *Treasurer*
Dale Barney, *Controller*
EMP: 5 **EST:** 1969
SQ FT: 5,000
SALES: 2MM **Privately Held**
WEB: www.ekci.com
SIC: 3824 Controls, revolution & timing instruments; counters, revolution; gauges for computing pressure temperature corrections

(G-2394)
ENERGY STORAGE CORP (PA)
526 Industrial Way W (07724-2212)
P.O. Box 1278 (07724-5278)
PHONE................................732 542-7880
Bernard Lavene, *President*
Philip Lepore, *Treasurer*
Suellen Anton, *Admin Sec*
EMP: 90
SQ FT: 64,000
SALES (est): 18.8MM **Privately Held**
SIC: 3861 3675 Film, sensitized motion picture, X-ray, still camera, etc.; electronic capacitors

(G-2395)
FARGO CONTROLS INC
20 Hampton Rd (07724-2122)
P.O. Box 539 (07724-0539)
PHONE................................732 389-3376
Ernest T Fargo, *President*
EMP: 5
SALES (est): 696.7K **Privately Held**
WEB: www.fargocontrols.com
SIC: 3823 Industrial instrmnts msrmnt display/control process variable

(G-2396)
GLAMOROUS GLO
42 Carolyn Ct (07724-1364)
PHONE................................732 361-3235
Jason Macfarland, *Owner*
EMP: 4 **EST:** 2012
SALES (est): 323.5K **Privately Held**
SIC: 2869 Tanning agents, synthetic organic

(G-2397)
GRAPE BGINNINGS HANDSON WINERY
151 Industrial Way E B (07724-3322)
PHONE..................................732 380-7356
EMP: 4
SALES (est): 343.7K **Privately Held**
SIC: 2084 Wines

(G-2398)
GWF ASSOCIATES LLC
1 Sheila Dr Ste 8 (07724-2658)
PHONE..................................732 933-8780
George Feehan,
EMP: 20
SQ FT: 2,500
SALES (est): 2MM **Privately Held**
SIC: 7372 Educational computer software

(G-2399)
HAMPTON FORGE LTD (PA)
446 Highway 35 Ste 3 (07724-4290)
PHONE..................................877 935-2892
Fax: 732 389-9291
Messod Felix Amar, *President*
Susan Amar, *Treasurer*
Suso Balanza, *Treasurer*
Steve Cohen, *Credit Mgr*
Peter Budzynkiewicz, *Natl Sales Mgr*
◆ EMP: 25
SALES (est): 4MM **Privately Held**
WEB: www.hamptonforge.com
SIC: 3914 Cutlery, stainless steel

(G-2400)
HIGH ENERGY GROUP LTD LBLTY CO
331 Newman Spg Rd (07724)
PHONE..................................732 741-9099
Elaine Coffey,
▲ EMP: 7
SQ FT: 3,500
SALES: 950K **Privately Held**
SIC: 3612 3648 3645 5063 Distribution transformers, electric; lighting equipment; street lighting fixtures; residential lighting fixtures; power wire & cable; miscellaneous fabricated wire products

(G-2401)
HIKMA INJECTABLES USA INC
Also Called: West-Ward Injectables, Inc.
200 Industrial Way W (07724-2206)
PHONE..................................732 542-1191
George J Muench, *Treasurer*
EMP: 5
SALES (est): 99K
SALES (corp-wide): 1.9B **Privately Held**
SIC: 2834 Pharmaceutical preparations
HQ: Eurohealth (U.S.A.), Inc
401 Industrial Way W
Eatontown NJ 07724

(G-2402)
HIKMA PHARMACEUTICALS USA INC (DH)
246 Industrial Way W (07724-4240)
PHONE..................................732 542-1191
Fax: 732 542-6150
Michael Raya, *CEO*
Brian Hoffmann, *President*
Kristy Ronco, *Exec VP*
Robert Berg, *Vice Pres*
Mohammed Obeidat, *CFO*
◆ EMP: 277 EST: 1946
SQ FT: 30,000
SALES (est): 199.4MM
SALES (corp-wide): 1.9B **Privately Held**
WEB: www.west-ward.com
SIC: 2834 Pharmaceutical preparations

(G-2403)
HIKMA PHARMACEUTICALS USA INC
Also Called: Oral Manufacturing
465 Industrial Way W (07724-2209)
PHONE..................................732 542-1191
EMP: 8
SALES (corp-wide): 1.9B **Privately Held**
SIC: 2834 Pharmaceutical preparations
HQ: Hikma Pharmaceuticals Usa Inc.
246 Industrial Way W
Eatontown NJ 07724
732 542-1191

(G-2404)
IACOBUCCI USA INC
151 Industrial Way E A2 (07724-3322)
PHONE..................................732 935-6633
Fax: 732 935-1231
Emilio Iacobucci, *President*
Lucio Iacobucci, *Vice Pres*
EMP: 5 EST: 1996
SALES (est): 49.2K
SALES (corp-wide): 549.8K **Privately Held**
WEB: www.iacobuccigroup.com
SIC: 3161 Luggage
HQ: Iacobucci Hf Aerospace Spa
Strada Sc Asi 1/S 16-18
Ferentino FR 03013
077 539-251

(G-2405)
IMMUNOSTICS INC
38 Industrial Way E Ste 5 (07724-3320)
PHONE..................................732 918-0770
Kenn Kupits, *CEO*
EMP: 5
SALES (est): 133.6K
SALES (corp-wide): 41.7MM **Privately Held**
SIC: 3841 Diagnostic apparatus, medical
PA: Boditech Med Inc.
43 Geodudanji 1-Gil, Dongnae-Myeon
Chuncheon 24398
823 324-3140

(G-2406)
IMMUNOSTICS COMPANY INC
38 Industrial Way E Ste 1 (07724-3334)
PHONE..................................732 918-0770
Fax: 732 918-0618
Kenn Kupits, *President*
Vincent Lastella, *Vice Pres*
▲ EMP: 45
SQ FT: 18,000
SALES (est): 7.9MM **Privately Held**
WEB: www.immunostics.com
SIC: 3841 Diagnostic apparatus, medical

(G-2407)
INNOVATIVE POWER SOLUTIONS LLC
Also Called: Ips
373 South St (07724-1863)
PHONE..................................732 544-1075
Fax: 732 544-1078
Eli Liebermann, *General Mgr*
Santiago Lagunas,
Bill Schatzow,
▲ EMP: 35 EST: 1999
SQ FT: 10,000
SALES (est): 8.7MM
SALES (corp-wide): 650.9MM **Privately Held**
WEB: www.ips-llc.com
SIC: 3621 Motors & generators
HQ: Zodiac Aerospace
Cs20001
Plaisir 78370
161 342-323

(G-2408)
INTERNATIONAL DATA GROUP INC
6 Windsor Dr (07724-2140)
PHONE..................................732 460-9404
Susane Hann, *Branch Mgr*
EMP: 10
SALES (corp-wide): 2.1B **Privately Held**
WEB: www.workscape.net
SIC: 2721 Trade journals: publishing only, not printed on site
PA: International Data Group, Inc.
1 Exeter Plz Fl 15
Boston MA 02116
617 534-1200

(G-2409)
K K S CRITERION CHOCOLATES
125 Lewis St (07724-3454)
PHONE..................................732 542-7847
Fax: 732 542-0045
George Karagias, *President*
EMP: 40 EST: 1929
SQ FT: 4,000
SALES (est): 2.2MM **Privately Held**
WEB: www.criterionchocolates.com
SIC: 5441 2066 Candy; chocolate & cocoa products

(G-2410)
KESSLER-ELLIS PRODUCTS CO (PA)
Also Called: Ket
10 Industrial Way E Ste 6 (07724-3390)
PHONE..................................732 935-1320
Fax: 732 935-9344
G Corson Ellis III, *Ch of Bd*
Peter Sabat, *President*
Anthony Zuccarelli, *Principal*
John Gruskos, *Sales Staff*
▲ EMP: 60
SQ FT: 31,000
SALES (est): 11.3MM **Privately Held**
WEB: www.kep.com
SIC: 3824 3823 Controls, revolution & timing instruments; counter type registers; flow instruments, industrial process type

(G-2411)
LAIRD & COMPANY (PA)
1 Laird Rd (07724-9724)
PHONE..................................732 542-0312
Fax: 732 542-2244
Larrie W Laird, *President*
John E Laird III, *Exec VP*
Ray Murdock, *Plant Mgr*
Susan Herrmann, *Sales Staff*
Vincent Capitolo, *Manager*
◆ EMP: 40
SQ FT: 155,000
SALES: 45MM **Privately Held**
WEB: www.lairdandcompany.com
SIC: 2084 5182 Brandy; brandy & brandy spirits

(G-2412)
MANZI PRINTING
132 Lewis St Ste B2 (07724-3926)
PHONE..................................732 542-1927
Mike Manzi, *Owner*
EMP: 4
SALES (est): 97.5K **Privately Held**
SIC: 2752 Commercial printing, offset

(G-2413)
MICROSOLV TECHNOLOGY CORP
1 Industrial Way W Bldg D (07724-4227)
PHONE..................................732 578-1777
Bill Sciccone, *President*
Suzanne Sciccone, *Vice Pres*
Maria Matyska, *Research*
Bill Ciccone, *Marketing Mgr*
Suzanne Ciccone, *Manager*
▲ EMP: 10
SQ FT: 2,600
SALES (est): 2.4MM **Privately Held**
WEB: www.microsolv.net
SIC: 5049 3826 Laboratory equipment, except medical or dental; automatic chemical analyzers

(G-2414)
MOTION SYSTEMS CORP
600 Industrial Way W (07724-2214)
PHONE..................................732 389-1600
Fax: 732 389-9191
William Wolf, *President*
▼ EMP: 73
SQ FT: 100,000
SALES (est): 17.7MM **Privately Held**
WEB: www.Motionsystems.com
SIC: 3593 Fluid power cylinders & actuators

(G-2415)
NATIONAL PRTECTIVE SYSTEMS INC
1 Meridian Rd (07724-2242)
PHONE..................................732 922-3609
Douglas D'Agata, *CEO*
EMP: 14
SALES (est): 1.9MM **Privately Held**
SIC: 3812 7382 Search & detection systems & instruments; security systems services

(G-2416)
OSTEOTECH INC
51 James Way (07724-2289)
PHONE..................................732 544-5942
EMP: 20 **Privately Held**
SIC: 3841 Surgical & medical instruments
HQ: Osteotech, Inc.
51 James Way
Eatontown NJ 07724
732 542-2800

(G-2417)
OSTEOTECH INC (DH)
51 James Way (07724-2289)
PHONE..................................732 542-2800
Fax: 732 542-9312
Sam Owusu-Akyaw, *President*
Robert M Wynalek, *President*
Robert W Honneffer, *Exec VP*
Mark H Burroughs, *CFO*
EMP: 115
SQ FT: 38,400
SALES (est): 71.3MM **Privately Held**
SIC: 3841 Surgical & medical instruments
HQ: Medtronic, Inc.
710 Medtronic Pkwy
Minneapolis MN 55432
763 514-4000

(G-2418)
OSTEOTECH INC
201 Industrial Way W (07724-2288)
PHONE..................................732 542-2800
Laurie Dunham, *Buyer*
Mike Williams, *Buyer*
Cara Beougher, *Research*
Kim Caballero, *Engineer*
Linda Pedersen, *Engineer*
EMP: 16 **Privately Held**
SIC: 3841 Surgical & medical instruments
HQ: Osteotech, Inc.
51 James Way
Eatontown NJ 07724
732 542-2800

(G-2419)
PROTEC SECURE CARD LTD LBLTY
Also Called: PSC
80 Corbett Way (07724-2263)
PHONE..................................732 542-0700
Mark Goldberg, *COO*
Vincent F Serpico, *CFO*
Juan Mejia, *Mng Member*
Christopher Klostreich, *Supervisor*
▲ EMP: 25
SQ FT: 13,000
SALES (est): 2.3MM **Privately Held**
SIC: 3089 Identification cards, plastic

(G-2420)
QUADRAMED CORPORATION
23 Christopher Way # 303 (07724-3335)
PHONE..................................732 751-0400
Steven McCoy, *Branch Mgr*
EMP: 30
SALES (corp-wide): 2.1B **Privately Held**
WEB: www.quadramed.com
SIC: 7372 7322 8742 Business oriented computer software; collection agency, except real estate; hospital & health services consultant
HQ: Quadramed Corporation
2300 Corp Park Dr Ste 400
Herndon VA 20171
703 709-2300

(G-2421)
QUINTUM TECHNOLOGIES INC (DH)
71 James Way (07724-2272)
PHONE..................................732 460-9000
Fax: 732 544-9119
Cheng T Chen, *CEO*
Kurt Baumann, *President*
Rajiv Bhatia, *Vice Pres*
Chuck Rutledge, *VP Mktg*
Tim Thornton, *CTO*
▲ EMP: 54 EST: 1998
SQ FT: 15,000

G
E
O
G
R
A
P
H
I
C

SALES (est): 4.9MM
SALES (corp-wide): 588.7MM **Publicly Held**
WEB: www.quintumtechnologies.com
SIC: 3661 Telephone & telegraph apparatus
HQ: Network Equipment Technologies, Inc.
4 Technology Park Dr
Westford MA 01886
510 713-7300

(G-2422)
SHORE PRINTED CIRCUITS INC
3 Meridian Rd (07724-2242)
PHONE............................732 380-0590
Fax: 732 380-0591
Charles F Rose, *President*
Steve Pierce, *General Mgr*
David Rose, *Vice Pres*
Glenn Stillwagon, *QC Mgr*
Michele Hulsart, *Human Resources*
▲ **EMP:** 27
SQ FT: 2,500
SALES (est): 6.3MM **Privately Held**
WEB: www.shore-pc.com
SIC: 3672 Circuit boards, television & radio printed

(G-2423)
SPARTON AYDIN LLC
Also Called: Kep Marine
10 Industrial Way E (07724-3332)
PHONE............................732 935-1320
Anthony Zuccarelli, *Principal*
Stan Kurc, *Opers Staff*
Louis Fligor, *Engineer*
Phil Marsh, *Info Tech Dir*
EMP: 10
SALES (corp-wide): 397.5MM **Publicly Held**
WEB: www.kep.com
SIC: 3629 Electronic generation equipment
HQ: Sparton Aydin, Llc
1 Riga Ln
Birdsboro PA 19508
610 404-7400

(G-2424)
T O NAJARIAN ASSOCIATES
1 Industrial Way W Ste D5 (07724-4207)
PHONE............................732 389-0220
Fax: 732 389-8546
Tavit Najarian, *President*
John Freeman, *Research*
Cindy Maynard, *Human Res Dir*
Catherine Lane, *VP Mktg*
Robert Kuhne, *Sr Project Mgr*
EMP: 60
SQ FT: 9,958
SALES (est): 10MM **Privately Held**
WEB: www.najarian.com
SIC: 8711 3535 4499 8713 Consulting engineer; robotic conveyors; marine salvaging & surveying services; surveying services

(G-2425)
TE CONNECTIVITY CORPORATION
250 Industrial Way W (07724-2206)
PHONE............................610 893-9800
EMP: 309
SALES (corp-wide): 13.1B **Privately Held**
SIC: 3678 Electronic connectors
HQ: Te Connectivity Corporation
1050 Westlakes Dr
Berwyn PA 19312
610 893-9800

(G-2426)
THOMAS SMOCK WOODWORKING
Also Called: Smock, Thomas Woodworking
306 Broad St (07724-1602)
PHONE............................732 542-9167
Thomas Smock, *Owner*
EMP: 5
SQ FT: 10,000
SALES (est): 350K **Privately Held**
SIC: 2439 Structural wood members

(G-2427)
TYCO ELEC SBSEA CMMNCTIONS LLC (DH)
Also Called: Te Subcom
250 Industrial Way W (07724-2296)
PHONE............................732 578-7000
Fax: 973 656-8131
Aaron Stucki, *President*
Chris Carobene, *Vice Pres*
Thomas M Lynch, *Vice Pres*
David Van Rossum, *CFO*
Michael Rieger, *VP Sales*
EMP: 270
SALES (est): 241.4MM
SALES (corp-wide): 13.1B **Privately Held**
SIC: 7373 3661 5063 1731 Computer systems analysis & design; communication services; telephone & telegraph apparatus; communications specialization; insulators, electrical
HQ: Te Connectivity Corporation
1050 Westlakes Dr
Berwyn PA 19312
610 893-9800

(G-2428)
UNITED SOUND ARTS INC
Also Called: Kimbo Educational
1 Industrial Way W D-E (07724-4206)
P.O. Box 477, Long Branch (07740-0477)
PHONE............................732 229-4949
Fax: 732 870-3340
James Kimble, *President*
Amy Laufer, *Buyer*
Elaine Murphy, *Marketing Staff*
EMP: 13 **EST:** 1954
SQ FT: 4,000
SALES (est): 3.1MM **Privately Held**
WEB: www.kimboed.com
SIC: 3652 Pre-recorded records & tapes

(G-2429)
VICTORY INTERNATIONAL USA LLC
40 Christopher Way (07724-3327)
PHONE............................732 417-5900
Anil K Monga, *CEO*
Sean Monga, *Vice Pres*
Michael Zemble, *CFO*
Kyle Monga, *Executive*
◆ **EMP:** 15
SQ FT: 60,000
SALES (est): 40MM **Privately Held**
SIC: 5999 2844 Perfumes & colognes; perfumes & colognes

(G-2430)
YORK TELECOM CORPORATION (PA)
Also Called: Yorktel
81 Corbett Way (07724-2264)
PHONE............................732 413-6000
Fax: 732 413-6060
Ron Gaboury, *CEO*
York Wang, *Ch of Bd*
Jim Anderson, *President*
Jim Deblasio, *Exec VP*
Mark Maxey, *Exec VP*
◆ **EMP:** 90
SQ FT: 35,000
SALES (est): 123.6MM **Privately Held**
SIC: 3669 3651 Visual communication systems; recording machines, except dictation & telephone answering

---

Edgewater
Bergen County

(G-2431)
ADORAGE INC
1055 River Rd Apt Th10 (07020-1382)
PHONE............................201 886-7000
EMP: 4
SALES: 360K **Privately Held**
SIC: 2844 Mfg Toilet Preparations

(G-2432)
ANNA J CHUNG LTD
5 Park St (07020-1407)
PHONE............................917 575-8100
Daniel Cho, *President*
Anna Chung, *Vice Pres*
EMP: 12

SALES: 2MM **Privately Held**
SIC: 3911 5944 Jewelry, precious metal; jewelry, precious stones & precious metals

(G-2433)
ANTIQUE BUYING CENTER
725 River Rd Ste 279 (07020-1171)
PHONE............................201 888-0303
D Joleet-Cache, *Principal*
EMP: 5
SALES (est): 231.3K **Privately Held**
SIC: 3171 Women's handbags & purses

(G-2434)
BONDI DIGITAL PUBLISHING LLC
33 Hilliard Ave (07020-1209)
PHONE............................212 405-1655
Murat Aktar, *Mng Member*
David Anthony, *Mng Member*
Carey Taylor, *Mng Member*
EMP: 5
SALES (est): 481.4K **Privately Held**
SIC: 2721 Magazines: publishing & printing

(G-2435)
C S HOT STAMPING
20 Edgewater Pl (07020-1206)
PHONE............................201 840-4004
Carmen Marino, *Owner*
Maria Sabeta, *Managing Dir*
EMP: 6
SALES (est): 320K **Privately Held**
SIC: 2396 Printing & embossing on plastics fabric articles

(G-2436)
COFFEE ASSOCIATES INC (PA)
178 Old River Rd (07020-1699)
P.O. Box 240 (07020-0240)
PHONE............................201 945-1060
Fax: 201 945-4887
Willian D Callas, *Ch of Bd*
▼ **EMP:** 35
SQ FT: 25,000
SALES (est): 17.7MM **Privately Held**
WEB: www.themised.com
SIC: 5149 7389 2095 Coffee, green or roasted; coffee service; roasted coffee

(G-2437)
ECHO THERAPEUTICS INC (PA)
1809 Hudson Park (07020-1575)
PHONE............................732 201-4189
Alan W Schoenbart, *CEO*
EMP: 17
SQ FT: 2,800
SALES (est): 476.8K **Publicly Held**
WEB: www.sontra.com
SIC: 3845 Electromedical equipment; electromedical apparatus; electrotherapeutic apparatus

(G-2438)
EVIGTO INC
327 Undercliff Ave (07020-1216)
PHONE............................201 951-2187
EMP: 5
SQ FT: 2,000
SALES: 300K **Privately Held**
SIC: 2389 2339 Mfg Apparel/Accessories Mfg Women's/Misses' Outerwear

(G-2439)
FRACTAL SOLUTIONS CORP
725 River Rd Unit 32135 (07020-1171)
PHONE............................201 608-6828
EMP: 4
SALES (est): 217.3K **Privately Held**
SIC: 2834 Intravenous solutions

(G-2440)
GUESS INC
39 The Promenade Bldg 300 (07020-2126)
PHONE............................201 941-3683
EMP: 25
SALES (corp-wide): 2.5B **Publicly Held**
SIC: 2325 Mfg Men's/Boy's Trousers
PA: Guess , Inc.
1444 S Alameda St
Los Angeles CA 90021
213 765-3100

(G-2441)
METROLPOLIS MASTERING LP
Also Called: Sterling Sound
33 Hilliard Ave (07020-1209)
PHONE............................212 604-9433
Murat Aktar, *Partner*
EMP: 28
SALES (est): 206K **Privately Held**
WEB: www.sterling-sound.com
SIC: 3652 8999 Master records or tapes, preparation of; music arranging & composing

(G-2442)
TEXTRON INC
143 River Rd (07020-1002)
PHONE............................201 945-1500
EMP: 30
SALES (corp-wide): 12.1B **Publicly Held**
SIC: 2076 Processes Linseed Oils
PA: Textron Inc.
40 Westminster St
Providence RI 02903
401 421-2800

(G-2443)
WILLIAM CARTER COMPANY
17 The Promenade (07020-2126)
PHONE............................201 313-1783
William Carter, *Branch Mgr*
EMP: 6
SALES (corp-wide): 3.4B **Publicly Held**
WEB: www.carters.com
SIC: 2254 Underwear, knit
HQ: The William Carter Company
3438 Peachtree Rd Ne
Atlanta GA 30326
678 791-1000

Edison
Middlesex County

(G-2444)
3I INFOTECH FINANCIAL SOFTWARE
450 Rritan Ctr Pkwy Ste B (08837)
PHONE............................732 710-4444
Kumar Ganesan, *CEO*
EMP: 38
SALES (est): 1.5MM **Privately Held**
SIC: 7372 Business oriented computer software
HQ: 3i Infotech Inc
450 Rritan Ctr Pkwy Ste B
Edison NJ 08837

(G-2445)
3I INFOTECH INC
450 Rritan Ctr Pkwy Ste B (08837)
PHONE............................732 710-4444
Mathew Philip, *CFO*
EMP: 5 **Privately Held**
SIC: 7372 Business oriented computer software
HQ: 3i Infotech Inc
450 Rritan Ctr Pkwy Ste B
Edison NJ 08837

(G-2446)
AAK USA INC (DH)
Also Called: A A K
499 Thornall St Ste 5 (08837-2267)
PHONE............................973 344-1300
Arne Frank, *CEO*
Mark Becker, *President*
Jim Jones, *Vice Pres*
Peter B Maulbeck, *Vice Pres*
Dennis Tagarelli, *Vice Pres*
▲ **EMP:** 95
SALES (est): 94.3MM
SALES (corp-wide): 3.1B **Privately Held**
WEB: www.aak.com
SIC: 2079 Edible oil products, except corn oil
HQ: Aak Sweden Ab
Vastra Kajen
Karlshamn 374 3
454 820-00

(G-2447)
ABBOTT LABORATORIES
18 Mayfield Ave (08837-3821)
PHONE............................732 346-6649

▲ = Import ▼=Export
◆ =Import/Export

EMP: 5
SALES (est): 567.6K **Privately Held**
SIC: 2834 Mfg Pharmaceutical Preparations

(G-2448)
ABSOLUTE PROTECTIVE SYSTEMS
3 Kellogg Ct Ste 13 (08817-2597)
PHONE..............................732 287-4500
Fax: 732 287-4502
Paul Smoley, *President*
EMP: 30
SQ FT: 4,500
SALES (est): 5.9MM **Privately Held**
WEB: www.absps.com
SIC: 1711 5063 3569 3999 Fire sprinkler system installation; alarm systems; sprinkler systems, fire: automatic; fire extinguishers, portable; access control systems specialization; closed circuit television installation; fire detection & burglar alarm systems specialization; closed circuit television services

(G-2449)
ACME DRAPEMASTER AMERICA INC
125 Clearview Rd (08837-3733)
PHONE..............................732 512-0613
Gregory Fromkin, *President*
Daniel McCarren, *Vice Pres*
Marnie McCarren, *Vice Pres*
▲ **EMP:** 8
SQ FT: 7,000
SALES (est): 1.5MM **Privately Held**
WEB: www.acmedrapemaster.com
SIC: 2591 Drapery hardware & blinds & shades

(G-2450)
ACTAVIS LLC
47 Brunswick Ave (08817-2576)
PHONE..............................732 947-5300
Ashesh Dave, *Branch Mgr*
EMP: 85 **Privately Held**
SIC: 5122 2834 Pharmaceuticals; pharmaceutical preparations
HQ: Actavis Llc
400 Interpace Pkwy
Parsippany NJ 07054

(G-2451)
AEROGROUP RETAIL HOLDINGS INC
Also Called: Dmg
207 Meadow Rd Ste A (08817-6033)
PHONE..............................732 819-9843
Jules Schneider, *Manager*
EMP: 55
SALES (corp-wide): 50.8MM **Privately Held**
SIC: 3069 Boot or shoe products, rubber; soles, boot or shoe: rubber, composition or fiber
PA: Aerogroup Retail Holdings Inc
201 Meadow Rd
Edison NJ 08817
732 985-6900

(G-2452)
AFLAG PHARMACEUTICALS LLC
163 Jefferson Blvd (08817-3538)
PHONE..............................732 609-4139
Yujin Bi, *Principal*
EMP: 4
SALES (est): 212.2K **Privately Held**
SIC: 2834 Pharmaceutical preparations

(G-2453)
AFP TRANSFORMERS CORPORATION
206 Talmadge Rd (08817-2824)
PHONE..............................732 248-0305
Fax: 732 287-8546
Gregory S Vongas, *President*
Anthony J Miceli, *CFO*
EMP: 95
SQ FT: 55,000

SALES: 8MM
SALES (corp-wide): 52.2MM **Privately Held**
WEB: www.afp-transformers.com
SIC: 3612 3677 Transformers, except electric; electronic coils, transformers & other inductors
PA: United Capital Corp.
9 Park Pl
Great Neck NY 11021
516 466-6464

(G-2454)
AKZO NOBEL CHEMICALS LLC
Also Called: Akzo Chemicals
340 Meadow Rd (08837-4102)
PHONE..............................732 985-6262
Fax: 732 777-2203
Steve O'Brien, *Branch Mgr*
EMP: 100
SQ FT: 5,000
SALES (corp-wide): 11.3B **Privately Held**
WEB: www.akzo-nobel.com
SIC: 2833 2899 2821 2819 Medicinals & botanicals; chemical preparations; plastics materials & resins; industrial inorganic chemicals
HQ: Akzo Nobel Chemicals Llc
525 W Van Buren St # 1600
Chicago IL 60607
312 544-7000

(G-2455)
ALCAMI NEW JERSEY CORPORATION
Also Called: Analytical Testing
165 Fieldcrest Ave (08837-3633)
PHONE..............................732 346-5100
Stephan Kutzer, *CEO*
Scott Warner, *Vice Pres*
Adam Lauber, *CFO*
Tim Morgan, *Asst Treas*
Burton Ely, *Asst Sec*
EMP: 100
SALES: 12.2MM
SALES (corp-wide): 225MM **Privately Held**
SIC: 8071 2834 Testing laboratories; pharmaceutical preparations
HQ: Alcami Corporation
2320 Scientific Park Dr
Wilmington NC 28405
910 254-7000

(G-2456)
ALLEN FLAVORS INC (PA)
23 Progress St (08820-1102)
PHONE..............................908 561-5995
Fax: 908 561-4164
Joey Allen, *President*
Ira Steinberg, *COO*
Michelle Allen, *Vice Pres*
Dana Allen, *Assoc VP*
Al Handel, *VP Opers*
▲ **EMP:** 115
SQ FT: 150,000
SALES (est): 29.3MM **Privately Held**
WEB: www.allenflavors.com
SIC: 2087 Extracts, flavoring; beverage bases, concentrates, syrups, powders & mixes

(G-2457)
AMERICAN BINDERY DEPOT INC
191 Talmadge Rd (08817-2848)
PHONE..............................732 287-2370
Fax: 732 287-2380
Tony Cuccinello, *Co-President*
Christopher Scarano, *Co-President*
EMP: 150
SQ FT: 65,000
SALES: 8MM **Privately Held**
SIC: 2789 2675 Paper cutting; die-cut paper & board

(G-2458)
AMERICAN PIPE BENDERS & FABRIC
191 Vineyard Rd Ste 5 (08817-4751)
PHONE..............................732 287-1122
Andrew Martingano Jr, *President*
Susan Martingano, *Vice Pres*
EMP: 7 **EST:** 1944
SQ FT: 10,000
SALES (est): 911.8K **Privately Held**
SIC: 3599 Machine shop, jobbing & repair

(G-2459)
AMERICAN TRANSPARENT PLASTIC
180 National Rd (08817-2811)
P.O. Box 556 (08818-0556)
PHONE..............................732 287-3000
Fax: 732 287-1421
Emanuel Parnes, *President*
Herschel Parnes, *Corp Secy*
EMP: 40 **EST:** 1959
SQ FT: 118,000
SALES (est): 6.2MM **Privately Held**
SIC: 3081 2673 Polyethylene film; bags: plastic, laminated & coated

(G-2460)
AMETEK INC
Also Called: Ametek CTS
52 Mayfield Ave (08837-3821)
PHONE..............................732 417-0501
Christopher Walton, *Opers Mgr*
EMP: 5
SALES (corp-wide): 4.3B **Publicly Held**
SIC: 3621 Motors & generators
PA: Ametek, Inc.
1100 Cassatt Rd
Berwyn PA 19312
610 647-2121

(G-2461)
ANTRON TECHNOLOGIES INC
40 Brunswick Ave Ste 104 (08817-2589)
PHONE..............................732 205-0415
Sing-Chang Hung, *President*
Berkuei Hung, *Treasurer*
EMP: 5
SALES (est): 3MM **Privately Held**
WEB: www.antron.com
SIC: 5045 3577 Computer peripheral equipment; computer peripheral equipment

(G-2462)
APCO EXTRUDERS INC
180 National Rd (08817-2811)
P.O. Box 556 (08818-0556)
PHONE..............................732 287-3000
Manny Parnes, *President*
Herb Parnes, *Vice Pres*
David Viera, *Vice Pres*
Shay Parnes, *Manager*
EMP: 42
SALES (est): 9.7MM **Privately Held**
SIC: 2673 Bags: plastic, laminated & coated

(G-2463)
ARCA INDUSTRIAL (NJ) INC
3 Kellogg Ct Ste 2 (08817-2599)
PHONE..............................732 339-0450
Jerry Huang, *President*
◆ **EMP:** 6
SQ FT: 3,000
SALES (est): 2MM **Privately Held**
SIC: 3441 3315 Fabricated structural metal; cable, steel: insulated or armored

(G-2464)
ARCHON VITAMIN LLC (PA)
3775 Park Ave Unit 1 (08820-2566)
PHONE..............................732 537-1220
Thomas F Pugsley, *President*
▲ **EMP:** 62
SQ FT: 45,000
SALES (est): 17.2MM **Privately Held**
WEB: www.archonvitamin.com
SIC: 2834 Vitamin preparations

(G-2465)
ARCHON VITAMIN LLC
3775 Park Ave Unit 1 (08820-2566)
PHONE..............................973 371-1700
Fax: 973 371-1277
Thomas Pugsley, *Manager*
EMP: 6
SALES (est): 963.7K **Privately Held**
SIC: 2834 Vitamin preparations
PA: Archon Vitamin, Llc
3775 Park Ave Unit 1
Edison NJ 08820

(G-2466)
AROMIENS INC
98 Mayfield Ave (08837-3821)
PHONE..............................732 225-8689

Shizhong Wang, *Principal*
▲ **EMP:** 5
SALES (est): 678.9K **Privately Held**
SIC: 2869 Industrial organic chemicals

(G-2467)
ASI COMPUTER TECHNOLOGIES INC
131 Fieldcrest Ave (08837-3622)
PHONE..............................732 343-7100
Rita Chang, *Branch Mgr*
EMP: 11
SALES (corp-wide): 596.6MM **Privately Held**
SIC: 5734 5045 3571 Computer & software stores; computers, peripherals & software; electronic computers
PA: Asi Computer Technologies Inc
48289 Fremont Blvd
Fremont CA 94538
510 226-8000

(G-2468)
ATLAS AUTO TRIM INC
81 Us Highway 1 (08817-5059)
PHONE..............................732 985-6800
Sanford Dubin, *President*
EMP: 5
SQ FT: 3,000
SALES (est): 420K **Privately Held**
WEB: www.atlasautotrim.com
SIC: 7532 2399 Interior repair services; upholstery & trim shop, automotive; seat covers, automobile

(G-2469)
AUSTARPHARMA LLC
18 Mayfield Ave (08837-3821)
PHONE..............................732 225-2930
Rong Liu, *CEO*
Dillon Gao, *Vice Pres*
Hongchun Qiu, *Vice Pres*
David Thang, *Vice Pres*
Jason LI, *Opers Staff*
◆ **EMP:** 80
SQ FT: 40,000
SALES (est): 20.7MM **Privately Held**
SIC: 2834 Adrenal pharmaceutical preparations; tablets, pharmaceutical

(G-2470)
BAXTER HEALTHCARE CORPORATION
100 Raritan Center Pkwy # 120 (08837-3615)
PHONE..............................732 225-4700
Fax: 732 417-4571
Joe Seklecki, *Manager*
EMP: 200
SALES (corp-wide): 10.5B **Publicly Held**
SIC: 2835 Blood derivative diagnostic agents
HQ: Baxter Healthcare Corporation
1 Baxter Pkwy
Deerfield IL 60015
224 948-2000

(G-2471)
BENNETT CABINETS
1251 Us Highway 1 (08837-3197)
PHONE..............................732 548-1616
Michael Bennett, *President*
EMP: 5 **EST:** 1962
SQ FT: 5,000
SALES: 650K **Privately Held**
SIC: 2434 Wood kitchen cabinets

(G-2472)
BENTLEY LABORATORIES LLC (PA)
111 Fieldcrest Ave (08837-3622)
P.O. Box 52209, Newark (07101-0220)
PHONE..............................732 512-0200
Fax: 732 512-0208
Brian Fitzpatrick, *CEO*
Greg Torchiana, *President*
Kathy Fitzpatrick, *Vice Pres*
Ann Marie Hansen, *Vice Pres*
John Kovacevich, *Vice Pres*
▲ **EMP:** 200 **EST:** 1998
SQ FT: 115,000
SALES (est): 66.3MM **Privately Held**
WEB: www.bentleylaboratories.com
SIC: 2844 Cosmetic preparations

(G-2473)
BIG RED PIN LLC
28 May St Apt 1 (08837-3587)
PHONE....................................732 993-9765
Dino Cicala, *CEO*
EMP: 5
SALES (est): 371.7K **Privately Held**
SIC: 2752 Commercial printing, litho-
graphic

(G-2474)
BIO-NATURE LABS LTD LBLTY CO
195 Campus Dr (08837-3937)
PHONE....................................732 738-5550
Michael Kruel, *President*
Lily Kruel, *Vice Pres*
▼ EMP: 50
SQ FT: 35,000
SALES: 1.2MM **Privately Held**
SIC: 2844 5999 Toilet preparations; cos-
metics

(G-2475)
BRILLIANT BRDCSTG CONCEPT INC
1871 Woodbridge Ave Ste 2 (08817-5147)
PHONE....................................732 287-9201
Annur Hamilton, *President*
EMP: 15
SALES (est): 630K **Privately Held**
SIC: 4832 3993 Radio broadcasting sta-
tions; signs & advertising specialties

(G-2476)
BUCKHEAD MEAT COMPANY
Also Called: Buckhead Beef N E
220 Raritan Center Pkwy (08837-3611)
PHONE....................................732 661-4900
Fax: 908 222-1007
Cheyanne Williams, *QC Mgr*
Glenn Ermoian, *Branch Mgr*
EMP: 105
SQ FT: 50,000
SALES (corp-wide): 55.3B **Publicly Held**
WEB: www.buckheadbeef.com
SIC: 2013 2048 2011 Sausages & other
prepared meats; slaughtering of nonfood
animals; lard from carcasses slaughtered
on site
HQ: Buckhead Meat Company
4500 Wickersham Dr
College Park GA 30337
404 355-4400

(G-2477)
C SYSTEMS LLC
510 Thornall St Ste 310 (08837-2207)
PHONE....................................732 338-9347
Roger Abram, *Project Mgr*
Larry Kelly, *Project Mgr*
Annie McIntosh, *Project Mgr*
Heather Austen, *Opers Staff*
Karen Geller, *Manager*
EMP: 12
SALES (est): 1.2MM **Privately Held**
WEB: www.csystemsllc.net
SIC: 7372 Business oriented computer
software

(G-2478)
CAPTIVATE INTERNATIONALLLC
28 May St Apt 1 (08837-3587)
PHONE....................................732 734-0403
Christina Pettola, *Marketing Staff*
Maria Cicala,
EMP: 4
SALES: 20K **Privately Held**
SIC: 2741 Miscellaneous publishing

(G-2479)
CAPUTO INTERNATIONAL INC
112 Northfield Ave (08837-3805)
PHONE....................................732 225-5777
Fax: 732 225-0011
Joseph Caputo, *President*
Paul Caputo, *Vice Pres*
Vincent Caputo, *Vice Pres*
Samantha Caputo, *Accounts Mgr*
▲ EMP: 6 EST: 1941
SQ FT: 9,000
SALES (est): 726.1K **Privately Held**
SIC: 3281 Granite, cut & shaped

(G-2480)
CENTURY CONVEYOR SERVICE INC (PA)
4 Gladys Ct (08817-2275)
P.O. Box 474 (08818-0474)
PHONE....................................732 248-4900
Fax: 732 248-4960
Ron Ferrara, *Principal*
EMP: 28
SALES (est): 8.5MM **Privately Held**
SIC: 3535 Conveyors & conveying equip-
ment

(G-2481)
CHACKO JOHN
Also Called: J S Manufacturing
21 Remington Dr (08820-3626)
PHONE....................................732 494-1088
John Chacko, *Owner*
EMP: 4
SALES (est): 540K **Privately Held**
SIC: 3599 Custom machinery

(G-2482)
CHARLES KERR ENTERPRISES INC
Also Called: Mariners Annual
1090 King Georges Post Rd # 802
(08837-3701)
PHONE....................................732 738-6500
Chris Kerr, *President*
EMP: 6
SQ FT: 1,500
SALES (est): 480K **Privately Held**
SIC: 2741 Miscellaneous publishing

(G-2483)
CINCO STAR LLC
2 Karnell Ct (08820-2947)
PHONE....................................732 744-1617
Vinod Zaveri,
Usha Zaveri,
EMP: 5
SQ FT: 1,000
SALES: 1.5MM **Privately Held**
SIC: 3911 Jewelry, precious metal

(G-2484)
CLAYTON BLOCK COMPANY INC
1025 Route 1 (08837-2904)
PHONE....................................732 549-1234
Fax: 732 494-3305
Mike Ulikowsky, *Manager*
EMP: 25
SALES (corp-wide): 44.5MM **Privately Held**
WEB: www.claytononline.com
SIC: 5211 3271 3273 Concrete & cinder
block; concrete block & brick; ready-
mixed concrete
PA: Clayton Block Company, Inc.
1355 Campus Pkwy Ste 200
Wall Township NJ 07753
732 363-1995

(G-2485)
CLEAN BBQ INC
47 Langstaff Ave (08837-3312)
PHONE....................................732 299-8877
Kyung Rhee, *President*
EMP: 5 EST: 1997
SQ FT: 15,000
SALES: 2MM **Privately Held**
SIC: 3631 Barbecues, grills & braziers
(outdoor cooking)

(G-2486)
COLONIAL WIRE & CABLE CO INC
85 National Rd (08817-2808)
PHONE....................................732 287-1557
Fax: 732 287-1586
Jake Salidino, *Manager*
EMP: 5
SALES (corp-wide): 11.3MM **Privately Held**
WEB: www.colonialwire.com
SIC: 3357 Nonferrous wiredrawing & insu-
lating
PA: Colonial Wire & Cable Co., Inc.
40 Engineers Rd
Hauppauge NY 11788
631 234-8500

(G-2487)
COMMUNICATIONS SUPPLY CORP
104 Sunfield Ave (08837-3845)
PHONE....................................732 346-1864
Fax: 732 346-1750
Andy Fallon, *Financial Exec*
Bill Dalton, *Manager*
Lisa Jacob, *Manager*
EMP: 33 **Publicly Held**
WEB: www.gocsc.com
SIC: 4899 3357 Data communication serv-
ices; building wire & cable, nonferrous
HQ: Communications Supply Corp
200 E Lies Rd
Carol Stream IL 60188
630 221-6400

(G-2488)
COMPREHENSIVE HEALTHCARE SYSTM
2025 Lincoln Hwy (08817-3350)
PHONE....................................732 362-2000
Hassan Mohaideen, *Principal*
Mariam Mohaideen, *Vice Pres*
Satish Kurian, *CFO*
EMP: 100
SQ FT: 2,500
SALES (est): 102.2K **Privately Held**
SIC: 7371 7372 8742 Computer software
development; business oriented computer
software; management information sys-
tems consultant

(G-2489)
CONTI-ROBERT AND CO JV
2045 Lincoln Hwy (08817-3334)
PHONE....................................732 520-5000
William Picken, *Managing Dir*
Lisa Rigatti, *Admin Asst*
EMP: 99
SALES (est): 1MM **Privately Held**
SIC: 1389 Lease tanks, oil field: erecting,
cleaning & repairing

(G-2490)
CONTRAVIR PHARMACEUTICALS INC (PA)
399 Thornall St Ste 1 (08837-2238)
PHONE....................................732 902-4000
Fax: 732 902-4100
Gary S Jacob, *Ch of Bd*
Robert Foster, *Acting CEO*
Theresa Matkovits, *Exec VP*
John Cavan, *CFO*
John Sullivan-Bolyai, *Chief Mktg Ofcr*
EMP: 21 EST: 2013
SQ FT: 4,000
SALES (est): 2.9MM **Publicly Held**
SIC: 2834 Pharmaceutical preparations

(G-2491)
COORS BREWING COMPANY
329 Hana Rd (08817-2061)
PHONE....................................732 767-3300
Fax: 732 548-9368
Vincent Prattico, *Branch Mgr*
EMP: 32
SALES (corp-wide): 11B **Publicly Held**
SIC: 2082 Malt beverages
HQ: Coors Brewing Company
17735 W 32nd Ave
Golden CO 80401
303 279-6565

(G-2492)
COPPER BOSS LTD LIABILITY CO
Also Called: Cross-Dock Solutions
40 Mayfield Ave (08837-3821)
PHONE....................................888 629-2190
Pedro J Cardenas, *Mng Member*
EMP: 27
SQ FT: 55,000
SALES: 850K **Privately Held**
SIC: 4581 3537 Air freight handling at air-
ports; truck trailers, used in plants, docks,
terminals, etc.

(G-2493)
COSPACK AMERICA CORP
3856 Park Ave (08820-2508)
PHONE....................................732 548-5858
Charlie Hou, *President*
Bob Smith, *Principal*
Jack Lo, *Manager*
▲ EMP: 20
SALES (est): 3MM **Privately Held**
WEB: www.cospackamerica.com
SIC: 3443 Metal parts

(G-2494)
CRANIAL TECHNOLOGIES INC
2163 Oak Tree Rd (08820-1083)
PHONE....................................908 754-0572
EMP: 6 **Privately Held**
SIC: 3842 Orthopedic appliances
PA: Cranial Technologies, Inc.
1395 W Auto Dr
Tempe AZ 85284

(G-2495)
CRODA INC (DH)
300 Columbus Cir Ste A (08837-3907)
PHONE....................................732 417-0800
Sandra Breene, *President*
David Shannon, *Senior VP*
Alan Ferguson, *Bd of Directors*
▲ EMP: 75
SQ FT: 36,400
SALES (est): 47.6MM
SALES (corp-wide): 1.8B **Privately Held**
WEB: www.crodausa.com
SIC: 2899 Chemical preparations

(G-2496)
CRODA INVESTMENTS INC (HQ)
300 Columbus Cir Ste A (08837-3907)
PHONE....................................732 417-0800
EMP: 9
SALES (est): 47.6MM
SALES (corp-wide): 1.8B **Privately Held**
SIC: 2899 Chemical preparations
PA: Croda International Public Limited
Company
Cowick Hall
Goole N HUMBS DN14
140 586-0551

(G-2497)
CRYOPAK VERIFICATION TECH INC (PA)
551 Raritan Center Pkwy (08837-3918)
PHONE....................................732 346-9200
Andrew Savarese, *Accounts Mgr*
David Joffe, *Sales Staff*
Darell Pinazo, *Sales Staff*
EMP: 8
SALES (est): 6.1MM **Privately Held**
SIC: 5047 3053 Medical equipment & sup-
plies; packing materials

(G-2498)
CS APPAREL INC
8 Rio Vista Dr (08820-2321)
PHONE....................................732 906-9666
Fax: 732 906-3275
Gopal Karnani, *President*
Phil Mulligan, *Sales Mgr*
▲ EMP: 7
SALES (est): 678.8K **Privately Held**
SIC: 2335 5137 Women's, juniors' &
misses' dresses; women's & children's
clothing

(G-2499)
CURRAN-PFEIFF CORP
Liddle Ave (08837)
PHONE....................................732 225-0555
Fax: 732 225-5012
George C Pfeiff Jr, *President*
Sang Huifang, *Admin Sec*
EMP: 12 EST: 1924
SQ FT: 30,000
SALES: 310K **Privately Held**
WEB: www.curranpfeiffcorp.com
SIC: 3264 3567 3297 Insulators, electri-
cal: porcelain; industrial furnaces &
ovens; nonclay refractories

(G-2500)
CYGATE SFTWR & CONSULTING LLC
Also Called: Sterling System
22 Meridian Rd Unit 9 (08820-2848)
PHONE....................................732 452-1881
Nilesh Dasondi, *President*
Sejal Dasondi, *Vice Pres*
Chhaya Barot, *Human Res Dir*
EMP: 5
SQ FT: 5,000

▲ = Import ▼=Export
◆ =Import/Export

SALES (est): 561.7K **Privately Held**
WEB: www.cygatesoftware.com
SIC: 7372 7379 Prepackaged software; computer related consulting services

(G-2501)
DENTALWORX LAB LTD LBLTY CO
1000 New Durham Rd (08817-2368)
PHONE.....................................732 981-9096
Wayne Wong,
EMP: 6
SALES (est): 586.7K **Privately Held**
SIC: 3843 Dental equipment & supplies

(G-2502)
DOLLFUS MIEG COMPANY INC
Also Called: DMC
86 Northfield Ave (08837-3807)
PHONE.....................................732 662-1005
Fax: 201 589-8931
Jacques Boubal, *CEO*
▲ EMP: 125
SQ FT: 55,000
SALES (est): 18.2MM
SALES (corp-wide): 43.6MM **Privately Held**
SIC: 2231 2259 5199 Apparel & outerwear broadwoven fabrics; convertors, knit goods; yarns
PA: Dmc
    13 Rue De Pfastatt
    Mulhouse 68200
    389 324-444

(G-2503)
DRANETZ TECHNOLOGIES INC (HQ)
1000 New Durham Rd (08817-2368)
P.O. Box 4019 (08818-4019)
PHONE.....................................732 248-4358
Fax: 732 248-1834
Robert Hart, *President*
EMP: 68 EST: 1962
SQ FT: 60,000
SALES (est): 12.7MM **Privately Held**
WEB: www.dranetz-bmi.com
SIC: 3825 3829 3823 3699 Test equipment for electronic & electric measurement; measuring & controlling devices; industrial instrmnts msrmnt display/control process variable; electrical equipment & supplies

(G-2504)
DSE HEALTHCARE SOLUTIONS LLC
164 Northfield Ave (08837-3855)
P.O. Box 6321 (08818-6321)
PHONE.....................................732 417-1870
Moaiz F Daya, *President*
Robert Stites, *Chairman*
Scott R Emerson, *Exec VP*
William Everett, *VP Finance*
Michele Muhammad, *Chief Mktg Ofcr*
▲ EMP: 6
SQ FT: 3,000
SALES (est): 1.5MM **Privately Held**
WEB: www.dsehealth.com
SIC: 2834 Vitamin, nutrient & hematinic preparations for human use

(G-2505)
DSO FLUID HANDLING CO INC
Also Called: Dso Sanitary Supply
300 Mcgaw Dr Ste 2 (08837-3708)
PHONE.....................................732 225-9100
Fax: 973 351-9090
Darrin Oppenheim, *Mng Member*
▲ EMP: 20
SQ FT: 20,000
SALES (est): 3.6MM
SALES (corp-wide): 4.1B **Privately Held**
SIC: 3312 3069 Stainless steel; hard rubber & molded rubber products
HQ: Alfa Laval U.S. Holding Inc.
    5400 Intl Trade Dr
    Richmond VA 23231

(G-2506)
EASY AERIAL CORPORATION ✪
198 Pear Blossom Dr (08837)
PHONE.....................................646 639-4410
Ido Gur, *CEO*
Ivan Stamatovski, *Chief Engr*

Daniel Sirkis,
EMP: 5 EST: 2017
SALES (est): 202.2K **Privately Held**
SIC: 3721 Aircraft

(G-2507)
ECOM 2000 INC (PA)
Also Called: Ecomelectronics
3775 Park Ave Unit 3 (08820-2566)
PHONE.....................................718 504-7355
Alan Cohen, *President*
Abraham Cohen, *Vice Pres*
Ezra Cohen, *Admin Sec*
▲ EMP: 18
SQ FT: 42,000
SALES (est): 25MM **Privately Held**
SIC: 5731 3261 Consumer electronic equipment; vitreous plumbing fixtures

(G-2508)
EDGE ORTHOTICS INC
209 Pierson Ave (08837-3139)
PHONE.....................................732 549-3343
Fax: 732 549-6555
James C Bauman, *President*
Donna Erikson, *Manager*
EMP: 5
SQ FT: 2,500
SALES (est): 617.3K **Privately Held**
SIC: 3842 Limbs, artificial

(G-2509)
EDISON FINISHING
191 Vineyard Rd Ste 3 (08817-4751)
PHONE.....................................732 287-6660
John Autovino, *President*
EMP: 6
SQ FT: 10,000
SALES: 1MM **Privately Held**
WEB: www.edisonfinishing.com
SIC: 2499 Decorative wood & woodwork

(G-2510)
EDISON OPHTHALMOLOGY ASSOC LLC
2177 Oak Tree Rd Ste 203t (08820-1082)
PHONE.....................................908 822-0070
John C Park, *Mng Member*
EMP: 10
SALES (est): 1.2MM **Privately Held**
SIC: 3851 Lenses, ophthalmic

(G-2511)
ENERGY OPTIONS INC
3 Ethel Rd Ste 300 (08817-2855)
PHONE.....................................732 512-9100
Fax: 732 512-1500
Bradley Freeman, *President*
EMP: 30
SQ FT: 10,000
SALES (est): 3.6MM
SALES (corp-wide): 55MM **Privately Held**
SIC: 3822 Air flow controllers, air conditioning & refrigeration; building services monitoring controls, automatic
PA: Albireo Energy, Llc
    3 Ethel Rd Ste 300
    Edison NJ 08817
    732 512-9100

(G-2512)
ENTERIX INC
Also Called: Clincial Genomics
236 Fernwood Ave (08837-3839)
PHONE.....................................732 429-1899
Fax: 732 429-1898
Lawrence Latointe, *President*
Robert Dachille, *Vice Pres*
Richard J Sands, *CFO*
Michele Houldsworth, *Education*
▲ EMP: 25 EST: 1999
SQ FT: 14,000
SALES: 7MM **Privately Held**
WEB: www.enterix.com
SIC: 3845 8733 Ultrasonic scanning devices, medical; medical research
PA: Clinical Genomics Pty Ltd
    U2 Eden Park Dr
    Macquarie Park NSW 2113

(G-2513)
ENVIRO PAK INC
125 National Rd (08817-2810)
PHONE.....................................732 248-1600
Edward Fitzpatrick, *President*

Joseph Otterbine, *Corp Secy*
John S Springer, *Manager*
EMP: 25
SQ FT: 25,000
SALES (est): 5.1MM **Privately Held**
WEB: www.enviropakdrums.com
SIC: 3443 Containers, shipping (bombs, etc.); metal plate

(G-2514)
EOS ENERGY STORAGE LLC
214 Fernwood Ave Bldg B (08837-3839)
PHONE.....................................732 225-8400
Michael Oster, *CEO*
Ebram Megally, *Business Mgr*
Don Humphreys, *Vice Pres*
Joshua Epstein, *Research*
Rob Mohr, *Research*
EMP: 25
SALES (est): 7MM **Privately Held**
SIC: 8731 3699 Energy research; electrical equipment & supplies

(G-2515)
ERCO LIGHTING INC (PA)
160 Rrtan Ctr Pkwy Ste 10 (08837)
PHONE.....................................732 225-8856
Fax: 732 225-8857
Mark Sieber, *President*
▲ EMP: 19
SQ FT: 7,000
SALES (est): 1.9MM **Privately Held**
SIC: 3648 Lighting equipment

(G-2516)
EXCELLENCE IN BAKING INC
Also Called: La Bonbonniere
2062 State Route 27 (08817-3330)
PHONE.....................................732 287-1313
Bryan Pansari, *CEO*
EMP: 4
SALES (est): 294K **Privately Held**
SIC: 2051 Bread, cake & related products

(G-2517)
F & S AWNING AND BLIND CO INC
Also Called: F&S Awning & Sign
13 Coral St (08837-3242)
PHONE.....................................732 738-4110
Fax: 732 738-7255
Robert Trotte, *President*
Carol Trotte, *Vice Pres*
EMP: 7
SQ FT: 850
SALES (est): 720K **Privately Held**
SIC: 1799 3993 5131 Awning installation; electric signs; flags & banners

(G-2518)
FABRICTEX LLC
278 Raritan Center Pkwy (08837-3610)
PHONE.....................................732 225-3990
Ernest Grinacoff,
◆ EMP: 7
SALES (est): 1MM **Privately Held**
SIC: 2297 Nonwoven fabrics

(G-2519)
FERRO CORPORATION
54 Kellogg Ct (08817-2509)
PHONE.....................................732 287-4925
Fax: 732 287-0674
Thomas Loschiazo, *Branch Mgr*
EMP: 50
SALES (corp-wide): 1.4B **Publicly Held**
WEB: www.ferro.com
SIC: 2865 2851 2816 Color lakes or toners; color pigments, organic; lacquers, varnishes, enamels & other coatings; inorganic pigments
PA: Ferro Corporation
    6060 Parkland Blvd # 250
    Mayfield Heights OH 44124
    216 875-5600

(G-2520)
FINE MINERALS INTL INC
11 Progress St (08820-1102)
PHONE.....................................732 318-6760
Daniel Trinchillo, *President*
James Elliott, *Software Dev*
▲ EMP: 5
SALES (est): 573.4K **Privately Held**
SIC: 3295 Minerals, ground or treated

(G-2521)
FOTO FANTASY
2850 Woodbridge Ave (08837-3616)
PHONE.....................................732 548-8446
Lodimer Loyevesky, *CEO*
Gerald Jogan, *Vice Pres*
EMP: 4
SALES (est): 240K **Privately Held**
WEB: www.foto-fantasy.com
SIC: 7929 2759 Entertainers; commercial printing

(G-2522)
FUJI ELECTRIC CORP AMERICA (HQ)
50 Northfield Ave (08837-3807)
PHONE.....................................732 560-9410
Fax: 201 368-8258
Philip Charatz, *CEO*
Darrell Hoffman, *President*
Daisuke Matsuura, *Division Mgr*
Don Woolslayer, *General Mgr*
David Schrader, *Business Mgr*
◆ EMP: 54
SQ FT: 4,916
SALES (est): 52.1MM
SALES (corp-wide): 8.3B **Privately Held**
WEB: www.fujielectric.com
SIC: 5063 3999 3678 Flashlights; bleaching & dyeing of sponges; electronic connectors
PA: Fuji Electric Co., Ltd.
    1-11-2, Osaki
    Shinagawa-Ku TKY 141-0
    354 357-111

(G-2523)
FUJIFILM NORTH AMERICA CORP
1100 King Georges Post Rd (08837-3731)
PHONE.....................................732 857-3000
Jiro Tsukahara, *Division Mgr*
Yuichi Tomaru, *Business Mgr*
Jason Heim, *Vice Pres*
Diku Mandavia, *Vice Pres*
George Otsuka, *Vice Pres*
EMP: 500
SALES (corp-wide): 22.8B **Privately Held**
SIC: 7384 4226 3861 3695 Photofinish laboratories; special warehousing & storage; photographic equipment & supplies; magnetic & optical recording media
HQ: Fujifilm North America Corporation
    200 Summit Lake Dr Fl 2
    Valhalla NY 10595
    914 789-8100

(G-2524)
GALAXY METAL PRODUCTS LLC
2960 Woodbridge Ave (08837-3406)
PHONE.....................................908 668-5200
Joe Makara, *Principal*
Dennis Dickmann, *Engineer*
Mike Ceceri, *Sales Mgr*
Carla Donan,
EMP: 45
SQ FT: 35,000
SALES (est): 7.8MM **Privately Held**
SIC: 3442 Metal doors, sash & trim

(G-2525)
GAMKA SALES CO INC
983 New Durham Rd (08817-2253)
PHONE.....................................732 248-1400
Fax: 732 248-1445
Weiss, *President*
Karl Weiss, *Vice Pres*
Ronald Weiss, *Vice Pres*
EMP: 20
SQ FT: 56,000
SALES (est): 6.9MM **Privately Held**
WEB: www.gamka.com
SIC: 7699 7359 7353 7629 Industrial machinery & equipment repair; construction equipment repair; equipment rental & leasing; tool rental; lawn & garden equipment rental; rental store, general; earth moving equipment, rental or leasing; generator repair; concrete curing & hardening compounds; engine repair

GEOGRAPHIC

(G-2526)
GARDEN STATE RECYCL
EDISON LLC
355 Meadow Rd (08837-4101)
PHONE.....................................732 393-0200
Fax: 732 393-0808
Bill Grove,
Michael Reali,
EMP: 13
SALES (est): 1MM **Privately Held**
WEB: www.gardenstaterecycling.com
SIC: 2611 Pulp manufactured from waste
or recycled paper

(G-2527)
GARRATT-CALLAHAN
COMPANY
306 Talmadge Rd (08817-2300)
PHONE.....................................732 287-2200
Fax: 732 287-1439
Janet Robinson, *Branch Mgr*
EMP: 5
SALES (corp-wide): 69.4MM **Privately Held**
WEB: www.g-c.com
SIC: 2899 Water treating compounds
PA: Garratt-Callahan Company
　　50 Ingold Rd
　　Burlingame CA 94010
　　650 697-5811

(G-2528)
GLOBAL POWER TECHNOLOGY
INC (PA)
Also Called: GMC-I New Wrld Btiligungs
GMBH
1000 New Durham Rd (08817-2368)
P.O. Box 4019 (08818-4019)
PHONE.....................................732 287-3680
Fax: 732 287-9014
Joseph I Gonzalez Rivas, *President*
Robert Hart, *Vice Pres*
Robert Rodgers, *Opers Staff*
Edward May, *Buyer*
Thurman Bridgers, *Engineer*
EMP: 63
SQ FT: 40,000
SALES (est): 19.3MM **Privately Held**
WEB: www.powerqualityseminars.com
SIC: 8711 7371 3825 3823 Engineering
services; custom computer programming
services; test equipment for electronic &
electric measurement; power measuring
equipment, electrical; industrial instrmnts
msrmnt display/control process variable

(G-2529)
GREYCELL LABS INC
190 State Route 27 # 102 (08820-3538)
PHONE.....................................732 444-0123
Jyoti Patel, *President*
Swati Patel, *Manager*
David Vachhani, *Manager*
Amy Patel, *Recruiter*
EMP: 20
SALES (est): 1.6MM **Privately Held**
SIC: 7372 7371 Business oriented com-
puter software; custom computer pro-
gramming services

(G-2530)
H & A GLOBAL ENTERPRISES
INC
Also Called: Evo9x
178 Northfield Ave (08837-3855)
PHONE.....................................732 318-2587
Muhammed Ali, *President*
Steven De, *Sales Staff*
EMP: 14
SQ FT: 9,000
SALES: 1MM **Privately Held**
SIC: 2329 Baseball uniforms: men's,
youths' & boys'; basketball uniforms:
men's, youths' & boys'; football uniforms:
men's, youths' & boys'; hockey uniforms:
men's, youths' & boys'

(G-2531)
HAN HEAN U S A CORP
3856 Park Ave (08820-2508)
PHONE.....................................732 494-3256
Fax: 732 494-9060
Pei Y Hou, *Manager*
▲ EMP: 7

SALES (est): 659.5K **Privately Held**
SIC: 3999 Manufacturing industries
PA: Hanhean Precision Industrial Co., Ltd.
　　2f, 124, Tung Ta Rd., Sec. 4,
　　Hsinchu City 30057
　　353 627-21

(G-2532)
HANES COMPANIES - NJ LLC
104 Sunfield Ave (08837-3845)
PHONE.....................................201 729-9100
Jim Curia, *Manager*
Tom Corrao,
▲ EMP: 16
SALES (est): 2.1MM
SALES (corp-wide): 3.9B **Publicly Held**
WEB: www.leggett.com
SIC: 2261 Dyeing cotton broadwoven fab-
rics
PA: Leggett & Platt, Incorporated
　　1 Leggett Rd
　　Carthage MO 64836
　　417 358-8131

(G-2533)
HANSSEM
50 Idlewild Rd (08817-4170)
PHONE.....................................732 425-7695
Joo Lee, *General Mgr*
EMP: 4
SALES (est): 452.9K **Privately Held**
SIC: 2434 Wood kitchen cabinets

(G-2534)
HANSSEM CORPORATION (HQ)
20 Kilmer Rd (08817-2422)
PHONE.....................................908 754-4949
Fax: 908 754-6969
Sin Hyun Yoon, *President*
Yeon Baik, *Accounting Mgr*
Nam Chul Jeong, *Accounts Mgr*
Ron Hatcher, *Manager*
Eric OH, *Manager*
▲ EMP: 100
SQ FT: 55,000
SALES (est): 20.5MM
SALES (corp-wide): 1.8B **Privately Held**
WEB: www.hanssemmanhattan.com
SIC: 2434 Wood kitchen cabinets
PA: Hanssem
　　144 Beonyeong 2-Ro, Danwon-Gu
　　Ansan 15418
　　822 647-0316

(G-2535)
HB FULLER COMPANY
Also Called: Adhesves Sealants Coatings Div
59 Brunswick Ave (08817-2512)
PHONE.....................................732 287-8330
Fax: 732 287-9495
Nate Ranford, *Opers-Prdtn-Mfg*
EMP: 30
SALES (corp-wide): 2.3B **Publicly Held**
WEB: www.hbfuller.com
SIC: 2891 Adhesives
PA: H.B. Fuller Company
　　1200 Willow Lake Blvd
　　Saint Paul MN 55110
　　651 236-5900

(G-2536)
HEALTHCAREDEPOTONLINECO
M INC
2177 Oak Tree Rd Ste 202 (08820-1082)
PHONE.....................................732 761-9600
Aparna Trivedi, *President*
EMP: 7
SALES (est): 375.6K **Privately Held**
SIC: 3842 Surgical appliances & supplies

(G-2537)
HERCULES LLC
20 Lee St (08817-6404)
PHONE.....................................732 777-4697
Nidia Lujanhercules, *Branch Mgr*
EMP: 9
SALES (corp-wide): 3.2B **Publicly Held**
SIC: 2891 Adhesives
HQ: Hercules Llc
　　500 Hercules Rd
　　Wilmington DE 19808
　　302 594-5000

(G-2538)
HOWMAN ASSOCIATES INC
Also Called: Howman Controls
12 Garden St (08817-4218)
PHONE.....................................732 985-7474
Howard Rood, *President*
EMP: 6
SQ FT: 2,200
SALES (est): 1.3MM **Privately Held**
WEB: www.howman.com
SIC: 3625 Industrial controls: push button,
selector switches, pilot

(G-2539)
HUBER INTERNATIONAL CORP
499 Thornall St Ste 8 (08837-2267)
PHONE.....................................732 549-8600
Mike Marberry, *President*
Brent Flotkoetter, *General Mgr*
Brent McKeen, *Area Mgr*
Sean Smith, *Business Mgr*
Mike Weber, *Vice Pres*
EMP: 5
SALES (est): 277.5K **Privately Held**
SIC: 3443 Industrial vessels, tanks & con-
tainers

(G-2540)
IMPORTERS SERVICE CORP
Also Called: ISC
65 Brunswick Ave (08817-2512)
PHONE.....................................732 248-1946
Eric Berliner, *President*
Patricia Berliner, *Admin Sec*
◆ EMP: 40 EST: 1939
SQ FT: 113,000
SALES (est): 11.3MM **Privately Held**
WEB: www.iscgums.com
SIC: 2861 Gum & wood chemicals

(G-2541)
INNOVATIVE COSMTC
CONCEPTS LLC (PA)
Also Called: Innovative Design
399 Thornall St Ste 26 (08837-2243)
PHONE.....................................212 391-8110
Robert Murello, *Mng Member*
Michael Murello,
▲ EMP: 10
SQ FT: 3,500
SALES (est): 1.4MM **Privately Held**
SIC: 2844 Cosmetic preparations

(G-2542)
ISOMETRIC MICRO FINISH
COATING
477 Plainfield Rd (08820-2630)
PHONE.....................................732 306-6339
Fax: 732 906-8225
Roy Leo, *Owner*
EMP: 4
SQ FT: 5,000
SALES (est): 220K **Privately Held**
SIC: 3479 Painting, coating & hot dipping

(G-2543)
J G MACHINE WORKS INC
2147 State Route 27 Ste D (08817-3365)
PHONE.....................................732 203-2077
John Croddick, *President*
EMP: 9 EST: 1953
SQ FT: 10,200
SALES (est): 1MM **Privately Held**
SIC: 3535 3565 Conveyors & conveying
equipment; packaging machinery

(G-2544)
JFK MEDICAL GROUP PC (PA)
60 James St (08820-3988)
PHONE.....................................732 632-1650
Fax: 732 906-4984
Martin Parker, *President*
Dr David Kingsley, *Treasurer*
Dr Howard Miller, *Director*
Dr Murray Weismann, *Director*
EMP: 20
SQ FT: 12,500
SALES (est): 2.2MM **Privately Held**
SIC: 3826 Magnetic resonance imaging
apparatus

(G-2545)
JFK SUPPLIES INC
85 Lexington Ave (08817-2937)
PHONE.....................................732 985-7800

Fax: 732 339-8391
Fred Schachter, *President*
Russell Epright, *COO*
David Schachter, *COO*
EMP: 10
SALES (est): 1.2MM **Privately Held**
SIC: 5943 5999 5113 3679 Office forms
& supplies; medical apparatus & supplies;
shipping supplies; electronic loads &
power supplies; household appliance
stores; beddings & linens

(G-2546)
JM HUBER CORPORATION (PA)
499 Thornall St Ste 8 (08837-2267)
PHONE.....................................732 603-3630
Fax: 732 549-3805
Mike Marberry, *Ch of Bd*
William B Goodspeed, *President*
Andrew Trott, *President*
David Cotey, *Counsel*
Robert Currie, *Vice Pres*
◆ EMP: 86 EST: 1883
SQ FT: 200,000
SALES (est): 886.9MM **Privately Held**
WEB: www.huber.com
SIC: 0811 1311 1455 2493 Timber tracts;
crude petroleum production; kaolin min-
ing; strandboard, oriented; industrial inor-
ganic chemicals

(G-2547)
JOHN WILEY & SONS INC
41 Saw Mill Pond Rd (08817-6025)
PHONE.....................................732 302-2265
John Wiley, *Manager*
EMP: 80
SALES (corp-wide): 1.8B **Publicly Held**
SIC: 2731 Textbooks: publishing only, not
printed on site
PA: John Wiley & Sons, Inc.
　　111 River St Ste 2000
　　Hoboken NJ 07030
　　201 748-6000

(G-2548)
JOHNS MANVILLE
CORPORATION
Liddle Ave (08837)
PHONE.....................................732 225-9190
Raymond Bruno, *Branch Mgr*
EMP: 45
SALES (corp-wide): 242.1B **Publicly Held**
WEB: www.jm.com
SIC: 2493 3086 Insulation & roofing mate-
rial, reconstituted wood; insulation or
cushioning material, foamed plastic
HQ: Johns Manville Corporation
　　717 17th St Ste 800
　　Denver CO 80202
　　303 978-2000

(G-2549)
JOHNSON CONTROLS INC
264 Fernwood Ave (08837-3839)
PHONE.....................................732 225-6700
Fax: 732 225-6755
Rick Thomas, *Branch Mgr*
EMP: 55 **Privately Held**
SIC: 8711 5084 1731 7629 Electrical or
electronic engineering; controlling instruments & accessories; electronic controls
installation; electronic equipment repair;
auto controls regulating residntl & coml
environmt & applncs
HQ: Johnson Controls, Inc.
　　5757 N Green Bay Ave
　　Milwaukee WI 53209
　　414 524-1200

(G-2550)
JS PALUCH CO INC
510 Thornall St Ste 140 (08837-2230)
PHONE.....................................732 516-1900
Robert J Bober, *Principal*
EMP: 12
SALES (est): 923.1K **Privately Held**
SIC: 2731 2721 7371 2741 Book publish-
ing; periodicals; custom computer pro-
gramming services; miscellaneous
publishing

▲ = Import ▼=Export
◆ =Import/Export

(G-2551)
KABAB & CURRY EXPRESS
4 Brunswick Ave (08817-2500)
PHONE................................732 416-6560
Shabbir Shiliwal, *Owner*
EMP: 4
SALES (est): 286.5K **Privately Held**
SIC: 2741 Miscellaneous publishing

(G-2552)
**KAIZEN TECHNOLOGIES INC
(PA)**
1 State Route 27 Ste 10 (08820-3962)
PHONE................................732 452-9555
Ashok Krisnaswany, *President*
Vijay Patil, *Vice Pres*
Ashok Poddar, *Marketing Staff*
Ramkumar Rajagopal, *Director*
Husena Arvind, *Executive*
EMP: 33
SQ FT: 4,000
SALES (est): 19.2MM **Privately Held**
SIC: 7372 Prepackaged software

(G-2553)
KUMAR & KUMAR INC
57 Denise Dr (08820-4603)
PHONE................................732 322-0435
Ashish Sood, *President*
▲ EMP: 5
SALES: 200K **Privately Held**
SIC: 3462 Iron & steel forgings

(G-2554)
**KWALITY FOODS LTD LIABILITY
CO**
1734 Oak Tree Rd (08820-2855)
PHONE................................732 906-1941
Dr Kanti Parekh,
Anand Parekh,
Jyoti Parekh,
EMP: 5
SALES (est): 290K **Privately Held**
SIC: 2024 Ice cream & frozen desserts

(G-2555)
L A DREYFUS CO
3775 Park Ave (08820-2566)
PHONE................................732 549-1600
Charlean B Gmunder, *President*
William Wrigley, *Chairman*
John Foster, *Vice Pres*
Richard Krema, *Vice Pres*
James Kyle, *Treasurer*
▲ EMP: 170 EST: 1909
SQ FT: 500,000
SALES: 17.7MM
SALES (corp-wide): 32.1B **Privately Held**
WEB: www.wrigley.com
SIC: 2067 Chewing gum base
HQ: Wm. Wrigley Jr. Company
930 W Evergreen Ave
Chicago IL 60642
312 280-4710

(G-2556)
**LEGGETT & PLATT
INCORPORATED**
Also Called: Leggett & Platt 2502
521 Sunfield Ave (08837)
PHONE................................732 225-2440
EMP: 92
SQ FT: 83,000
SALES (corp-wide): 3.7B **Publicly Held**
SIC: 2515 Mfg Mattresses/Bedsprings
PA: Leggett & Platt, Incorporated
1 Leggett Rd
Carthage MO 64836
417 358-8131

(G-2557)
LION SALES CORP
125 Jackson Ave Ste 5 (08837-3147)
PHONE................................732 417-9363
Robert Stella, *President*
EMP: 6
SALES (est): 68.5K **Privately Held**
SIC: 2389 Men's miscellaneous accessories

(G-2558)
LOOK OF LOVE WIGS INC (PA)
1795b State Route 27 (08817-3483)
PHONE................................908 687-9502
Robert A Anzivino, *President*
Ingrid Anzivino, *Vice Pres*
▲ EMP: 17 EST: 1968
SALES: 1.2MM **Privately Held**
WEB: www.lookoflove.com
SIC: 3999 5699 Wigs, including doll wigs,
toupees or wiglets; wigs, toupees &
wiglets

(G-2559)
LOVING CARE PHARMACY
1653 State Route 27 # 102 (08817-3484)
PHONE................................732 832-2862
EMP: 7
SALES (est): 793.4K **Privately Held**
SIC: 2834 Pharmaceutical preparations;
druggists' preparations (pharmaceuticals);
chlorination tablets & kits (water purification)

(G-2560)
LUMINAIRE LIGHTING CORP
5 Sutton Pl (08817-2223)
P.O. Box 2162 (08818-2162)
PHONE................................732 549-0056
Joseph Lipson, *President*
Ralph Peake, *Managing Dir*
Ronald Lipson, *Vice Pres*
Eva Lipson, *Treasurer*
Adam Lipson, *Info Tech Mgr*
▲ EMP: 8
SQ FT: 5,000
SALES (est): 1.2MM **Privately Held**
WEB: www.luminairelighting.com
SIC: 3646 5063 Commercial indusl & institutional electric lighting fixtures; electrical
apparatus & equipment

(G-2561)
**LVMH FRAGRANCE BRANDS US
LLC**
208 Fernwood Ave (08837-3839)
PHONE................................212 931-2668
EMP: 8
SALES (corp-wide): 315.2MM **Privately
Held**
WEB: www.parfumsgivenchy.com
SIC: 5122 2844 Perfumes; toilet preparations
HQ: Lvmh Fragrance Brands Us Llc
80 State St
Albany NY 12207
212 931-2600

(G-2562)
LYONDELLBASELL
340 Meadow Rd (08837-4102)
PHONE................................732 985-6262
Maria Paige, *Purchasing*
John Miano, *QC Mgr*
Catherine Koenig, *Technical Mgr*
Anna Zak, *Accountant*
Len Ostanek, *Sales Executive*
EMP: 19
SALES (est): 2MM **Privately Held**
SIC: 2869 Industrial organic chemicals

(G-2563)
MACHINE TECH
3125 Woodbridge Ave Ste 4 (08837-3259)
PHONE................................732 738-6810
Gordon Scala, *President*
EMP: 12 EST: 2007
SALES (est): 1.7MM **Privately Held**
SIC: 3599 Machine shop, jobbing & repair

(G-2564)
**MAMROUT PAPER GROUP
CORP**
55 Talmadge Rd (08817-3338)
PHONE................................718 510-5484
Simon Mamrout, *Owner*
EMP: 6
SALES (est): 1.7MM **Privately Held**
SIC: 5113 3089 Industrial & personal service paper; air mattresses, plastic

(G-2565)
MAVERICK INDUSTRIES INC
Also Called: Maverick Housewares
94 Mayfield Ave (08837-3821)
PHONE................................732 417-9666
Fax: 732 417-9673
Edward H Mackin, *Ch of Bd*
Peter Chiboucas, *Vice Pres*
▲ EMP: 11 EST: 1980
SQ FT: 9,000
SALES (est): 2.4MM **Privately Held**
WEB: www.maverickhousewares.com
SIC: 3634 5719 Electric household cooking appliances; housewares

(G-2566)
**MAXZONE VEHICLE LIGHTING
CORP**
24 Kilmer Rd (08817-2422)
PHONE................................732 393-9600
Fax: 201 253-8933
Brook Yang, *Branch Mgr*
EMP: 11
SALES (corp-wide): 535.3MM **Privately
Held**
SIC: 3714 Motor vehicle parts & accessories
HQ: Maxzone Vehicle Lighting Corp.
15889 Slover Ave Unit A
Fontana CA 92337
909 822-3288

(G-2567)
MEESHAA INC
Also Called: Diamond Essence
18 Tingley Ln (08820-1463)
PHONE................................908 279-7985
Monali Shah, *President*
EMP: 6
SALES (est): 380K **Privately Held**
SIC: 3961 Jewelry apparel, non-precious
metals

(G-2568)
**MENASHA PACKAGING
COMPANY LLC**
112 Truman Dr (08817-2425)
PHONE................................732 985-0800
Krystian Salwierz, *Sales Staff*
Filip Kucera, *Manager*
Michael Samples, *Manager*
Lee Schiedermayer, *Director*
EMP: 146
SALES (est): 1.8B **Privately Held**
SIC: 2653 Boxes, corrugated: made from
purchased materials
HQ: Menasha Packaging Company, Llc
1645 Bergstrom Rd
Neenah WI 54956
920 751-1000

(G-2569)
**METAL TEXTILES
CORPORATION (HQ)**
970 New Durham Rd (08817-2214)
PHONE................................732 287-0800
Fax: 732 248-8739
Gregory S Vongas, *President*
George Walsh, *Opers Mgr*
Anthony Miceli, *CFO*
Timothy W Miller, *Controller*
Joseph Hodonsky, *VP Sales*
▲ EMP: 72
SQ FT: 53,000
SALES: 30MM
SALES (corp-wide): 52.2MM **Privately
Held**
WEB: www.metexcorp.com
SIC: 3496 Mesh, made from purchased
wire
PA: United Capital Corp.
9 Park Pl
Great Neck NY 11021
516 466-6464

(G-2570)
**METAL TEXTILES
CORPORATION**
Spectrum U V
206 Talmadge Rd (08817-2824)
PHONE................................800 843-1215
Robert Obusek, *Branch Mgr*
Chuck Petersen, *Executive*
EMP: 37
SALES (corp-wide): 52.2MM **Privately
Held**
SIC: 3641 Electric lamps & parts for specialized applications
HQ: Metal Textiles Corporation
970 New Durham Rd
Edison NJ 08817
732 287-0800

(G-2571)
MICRO INNOVATIONS CORP
1090 King Georges Post Rd (08837-3701)
P.O. Box 290399, Brooklyn NY (11229-0399)
PHONE................................732 346-9410
Fax: 732 346-9410
Eddie Mizrahi, *CEO*
Jesse H Grindeland, *President*
Jerry Pasternak, *Vice Pres*
Bruno Ayanian, *CFO*
Daniel Shabat, *Shareholder*
EMP: 84
SQ FT: 70,000
SALES (est): 11.5MM **Privately Held**
WEB: www.microinv.com
SIC: 3577 5065 Computer peripheral
equipment; modems, computer

(G-2572)
MIDDLESEX WATER COMPANY
100 Fairview Ave (08817-2440)
PHONE................................732 579-0290
Jack Lihvarcik, *Plant Engr*
Richard Risoldi, *Manager*
EMP: 147
SALES (corp-wide): 130.7MM **Publicly
Held**
WEB: www.middlesexwater.com
SIC: 3589 4941 Water treatment equipment, industrial; water supply
PA: Middlesex Water Company
1500 Ronson Rd
Iselin NJ 08830
732 634-1500

(G-2573)
MIROAD RUBBER USA LLC
182 Whitman Ave (08817-4724)
PHONE................................480 280-2543
Eric Yu, *Sales Associate*
Anthony Fue,
EMP: 5
SQ FT: 20,000
SALES (est): 500K **Privately Held**
SIC: 3069 Hard rubber products

(G-2574)
MISSRY ASSOCIATES INC
Also Called: Misco Enterprises
250 Carter Dr Ste 3 (08817-2069)
PHONE................................732 752-7500
Morris Missry, *President*
Ezra Missry, *Vice Pres*
◆ EMP: 150
SQ FT: 500,000
SALES (est): 20.2MM **Privately Held**
WEB: www.miscohomeandgarden.com
SIC: 5193 2874 Artificial flowers; phosphatic fertilizers

(G-2575)
**MODEL RECTIFIER
CORPORATION**
80 Newfield Ave Ste 4 (08837-3847)
PHONE................................732 225-2100
Fax: 732 225-0091
Frank Ritota, *President*
Roy C Gelber, *Chairman*
Donald Boyce, *Vice Pres*
Anthony P Iati, *Vice Pres*
Akiko Kimura, *Vice Pres*
▲ EMP: 35
SQ FT: 55,000
SALES (est): 8MM **Privately Held**
WEB: www.modelrec.com
SIC: 3612 5092 Rectifier transformers; toy
transformers; hobby goods

(G-2576)
MOMENTUM USA INC (PA)
Also Called: Autopartsource
120 Fieldcrest Ave (08837-3656)
PHONE................................844 300-1553
John Amalfe, *CEO*
Mark Stewart, *Finance Dir*
Dave Carter, *Director*
EMP: 10
SALES (est): 13.4MM **Privately Held**
SIC: 5075 3714 Air filters; brake drums,
motor vehicle

(G-2577)
MRS MAZZULAS FOOD PRODUCTS
240 Carter Dr (08817-2097)
PHONE.............................732 248-0555
Christopher Lotito, *President*
▲ EMP: 5
SQ FT: 17,000
SALES: 1.5MM **Privately Held**
WEB: www.mazzula.com
SIC: 2032 2034 Italian foods: packaged in cans, jars, etc.; dehydrated fruits, vegetables, soups

(G-2578)
NEILMAX INDUSTRIES INC
15a Progress St (08820-1278)
PHONE.............................908 756-8800
Neil Max, *President*
▲ EMP: 5
SALES (est): 841.5K **Privately Held**
SIC: 3999 Barber & beauty shop equipment

(G-2579)
NETCOM SYSTEMS INC (PA)
200 Metroplex Dr (08817-2601)
PHONE.............................732 393-6100
Niten Ved, *President*
Denise Dennis, *Sls & Mktg Exec*
EMP: 25
SALES (est): 3.4MM **Privately Held**
WEB: www.netcom-sys.com
SIC: 7372 8742 7371 Application computer software; management information systems consultant; computer software development

(G-2580)
NEWARK WIRE WORKS INC
1059 King Georges Rd 10 (08837)
PHONE.............................732 661-2001
Fax: 732 661-2003
Joann Spellman, *President*
John Emmerich, *Opers Staff*
Raju Penematcha, *Marketing Staff*
Joanne Spellman, *Admin Sec*
EMP: 40 EST: 1910
SQ FT: 22,000
SALES (est): 7.2MM **Privately Held**
WEB: www.newarkwireworks.com
SIC: 3496 Miscellaneous fabricated wire products

(G-2581)
NIGHTHAWK INTERACTIVE LLC
1090 King Georges Post Rd # 402 (08837-3732)
PHONE.............................732 243-9922
Joseph Sutton, *Mng Member*
EMP: 4 EST: 2014
SALES (est): 173.6K **Privately Held**
SIC: 2741 Miscellaneous publishing

(G-2582)
NJ ADVANCE MEDIA LLC
2015 State Route 27 # 300 (08817-3392)
PHONE.............................732 902-4300
Matt Kramer, *President*
Joan Mason, *Vice Pres*
EMP: 91
SALES (corp-wide): 13.8MM **Privately Held**
SIC: 2711 Newspapers, publishing & printing
PA: Nj Advance Media Llc
485 Route 1 S Ste 3
Iselin NJ 08830
732 902-4300

(G-2583)
NLYTE SOFTWARE INC
275 Raritan Center Pkwy (08837-3613)
PHONE.............................732 395-6920
Fax: 732 395-6930
Doug Sabella, *CEO*
Owen Nisbett, *CFO*
EMP: 30
SQ FT: 10,000
SALES (est): 4.4MM
SALES (corp-wide): 30.3MM **Privately Held**
SIC: 7372 Prepackaged software
HQ: Nlyte Software Americas Limited
2800 Campus Dr Ste 135
San Mateo CA 94403

(G-2584)
NORTHEAST FOODS INC
Also Called: Automatic Roll
1 Gourmet Ln Ste 1 # 1 (08837-2902)
PHONE.............................732 549-2243
Fax: 732 494-4980
John Lyons, *Branch Mgr*
Rose Grajewski, *Manager*
EMP: 80
SALES (corp-wide): 335.5MM **Privately Held**
SIC: 2051 Bakery: wholesale or wholesale/retail combined
PA: Northeast Foods, Inc.
601 S Caroline St
Baltimore MD 21231
410 276-7254

(G-2585)
NOVEMBAL USA INC
3 Greek Ln (08817-2508)
PHONE.............................732 947-3030
Fax: 732 287-4988
John Fimelliti, *Production*
▲ EMP: 22
SALES (est): 5.7MM
SALES (corp-wide): 7.5B **Privately Held**
SIC: 3089 Injection molding of plastics
HQ: Tetra Pak Closures France Sas
Route De Nantes
Chateaubriant 44110
240 558-200

(G-2586)
NU-WORLD CORPORATION
340 Mill Rd (08817-6026)
PHONE.............................732 541-6300
Susan Pace, *General Mgr*
EMP: 7
SALES (corp-wide): 28MM **Privately Held**
SIC: 2844 Cosmetic preparations
HQ: Nu-World Corporation
300 Milik St
Carteret NJ 07008
732 541-6300

(G-2587)
OFFICEMATE INTERNATIONAL CORP (PA)
90 Newfield Ave Rritan Ctr Raritan Ctr (08837)
P.O. Box 6680 (08818-6680)
PHONE.............................732 225-7422
Fax: 732 225-6466
Shwu-Min Chen, *President*
Peter Chen, *Exec VP*
Martin Yang, *Senior VP*
Lincoln Wu, *Opers Mgr*
Edward Chuang, *Project Engr*
▲ EMP: 88
SQ FT: 140,000
SALES (est): 14MM **Privately Held**
WEB: www.officemate.com
SIC: 2678 5112 Stationery: made from purchased materials; stationery & office supplies

(G-2588)
ONX USA LLC
274 Raritan Center Pkwy (08837-3610)
PHONE.............................440 569-2417
Bruce Vanzo, *Finance Dir*
Sal Ruffino, *Manager*
EMP: 25
SQ FT: 120,000
SALES (corp-wide): 1.2B **Publicly Held**
SIC: 7379 7372 Computer related consulting services; prepackaged software
HQ: Onx Usa Llc
5910 Landerbrook Dr # 250
Cleveland OH 44124

(G-2589)
ORACLE AMERICA INC
399 Thornall St Ste 39 (08837-2265)
PHONE.............................732 623-4821
EMP: 58
SALES (corp-wide): 39.8B **Publicly Held**
SIC: 7372 Prepackaged software
HQ: Oracle America, Inc.
500 Oracle Pkwy
Redwood City CA 94065
650 506-7000

(G-2590)
OSI LASER DIODE INC
4 Olsen Ave (08820-2419)
PHONE.............................732 549-9001
Deepak Chopra, *President*
EMP: 39
SQ FT: 25,000
SALES (est): 5.7MM
SALES (corp-wide): 960.9MM **Publicly Held**
SIC: 3663 Radio & TV communications equipment
PA: Osi Systems, Inc.
12525 Chadron Ave
Hawthorne CA 90250
310 978-0516

(G-2591)
PARIO GROUP LLC
70 Stephenville Pkwy (08820-2609)
PHONE.............................732 906-2302
Sumeer Toteja,
EMP: 4
SQ FT: 500
SALES: 100K **Privately Held**
SIC: 7372 Application computer software

(G-2592)
PARTNERS IN VISION INC
1090 King Georges Post Rd # 103 (08837-3702)
PHONE.............................888 748-1112
Judd Sky, *President*
Angelo Benfante, *Vice Pres*
Ryan Noonan, *VP Opers*
Michael Zuk, *Human Res Mgr*
EMP: 3 EST: 1999
SALES: 23.2MM **Privately Held**
SIC: 5995 3229 Opticians; optical glass

(G-2593)
PATEL METAL PLATING INC
6 Emerson St (08820-1642)
PHONE.............................732 574-1770
EMP: 6
SALES: 1MM **Privately Held**
SIC: 3471 Plating/Polishing Service

(G-2594)
PICTURE IT INC
Also Called: Picture It Awards
1703 State Route 27 Ste 2 (08817-3497)
PHONE.............................732 819-0420
Fax: 732 572-4215
Roy Taetzsch, *President*
EMP: 6
SALES (est): 350K **Privately Held**
WEB: www.picawards.com
SIC: 3914 5999 Trophies, plated (all metals); trophies & plaques

(G-2595)
PLANTFUSION
Also Called: Reliant Vitamins
3775 Park Ave (08820-2566)
PHONE.............................732 537-1220
Phil Dijeant, *Owner*
EMP: 4 EST: 2014
SALES (est): 196.1K **Privately Held**
SIC: 2834 Vitamin preparations

(G-2596)
PRINCETON TECH GROUP INTL CORP
182 Whitman Ave (08817-4724)
PHONE.............................732 328-9308
Tony Fue, *President*
EMP: 4
SQ FT: 1,000
SALES: 500K **Privately Held**
SIC: 3621 Motors & generators

(G-2597)
PROGRESS DISPLAYS INC
39 Progress St (08820-1102)
PHONE.............................908 757-6650
Roger L Robinson, *President*
EMP: 4
SALES (est): 360K **Privately Held**
SIC: 7313 3993 Printed media advertising representatives; signs & advertising specialties

(G-2598)
PROGRESS WOODWORK
225 Pierson Ave (08837-3139)
PHONE.............................732 906-8680
Fax: 732 906-8683
EMP: 4
SALES (est): 406.8K **Privately Held**
SIC: 2431 Millwork

(G-2599)
PROSWEETZ INGREDIENTS INC
Also Called: Panasource Ingredients
98a Mayfield Ave (08837-3821)
PHONE.............................732 512-0886
Fax: 732 512-0188
Hugh Zhang, *President*
Xiaojian Ye, *Vice Pres*
▲ EMP: 26
SALES (est): 7.3MM **Privately Held**
SIC: 2834 Pharmaceutical preparations

(G-2600)
Q-MED SCANDINAVIA INC
2035 State Route 27 # 2150 (08817-3351)
PHONE.............................609 953-8069
Bngt Agerup, *CEO*
Charles Goodwin, *CPA*
Michael Mertel, *Admin Sec*
EMP: 21
SALES (est): 1.3MM
SALES (corp-wide): 90.8B **Privately Held**
SIC: 3842 Implants, surgical
HQ: Q-Med Ab
Seminariegatan 21
Uppsala 752 2
184 749-000

(G-2601)
RAND DIVERSIFIED COMPANIES LLC
112 Truman Dr (08817-2425)
PHONE.............................732 985-0800
Don Garda, *COO*
David Kauffman,
Stuart Sklovsky,
John Wuensch,
EMP: 399
SALES (est): 15.2MM **Privately Held**
SIC: 3993 Signs & advertising specialties

(G-2602)
RCF USA INC
110 Talmadge Rd (08817-2812)
PHONE.............................732 902-6100
Roni Nevo, *President*
Tarik Solangi, *Natl Sales Mgr*
George Goodwin, *Manager*
Ken Voss, *Manager*
▲ EMP: 8 EST: 2002
SQ FT: 2,500
SALES (est): 5.8MM **Privately Held**
SIC: 3651 Speaker monitors
HQ: Rcf Spa
Via Raffaello Sanzio 13
Reggio Emilia RE 42124
052 274-4411

(G-2603)
RELIANCE VITAMIN LLC
3775 Park Ave Unit 1 (08820-2566)
PHONE.............................732 537-1220
Fax: 732 537-1335
Terrell Vigeant, *President*
Phillip Vigeant, *Vice Pres*
James Valenzuela, *VP Opers*
Valerie Leiva, *Buyer*
Linda Naselli, *CFO*
EMP: 212
SALES (est): 20.9MM **Privately Held**
WEB: www.reliancevitamin.com
SIC: 2834 5122 Vitamin preparations; vitamins & minerals

(G-2604)
REUTHER ENGINEERING
154 Silver Lake Ave (08817-5261)
PHONE.............................973 485-5800
Fax: 973 482-5800
Ken Rys, *President*
Bob Cromer, *Manager*
Susan Smith, *Info Tech Mgr*
EMP: 18 EST: 1949
SQ FT: 8,500

SALES (est): 2.8MM **Privately Held**
WEB: www.reutherengineering.com
SIC: 3599 7692 Machine shop, jobbing &
repair; welding repair

(G-2605)
REVLON INC
2147 State Route 27 Fl 3 (08817-3365)
PHONE..................................732 287-1400
Jonathan Brooks, *Senior Mgr*
Steven Doering, *Database Admin*
Ann Pfeffer, *Director*
Raymond Schleckser, *Director*
Donna Ventz, *Director*
EMP: 50 **Publicly Held**
WEB: www.revlon.com
SIC: 2844 3421 5122 5199 Toilet prepa-
rations; hair preparations, including sham-
poos; perfumes & colognes; cosmetic
preparations; clippers, fingernail & toenail;
scissors, hand; cosmetics, perfumes &
hair products; toilet preparations; wigs;
toiletries, cosmetics & perfumes
PA: Revlon, Inc.
1 New York Plz
New York NY 10004

(G-2606)
**REVLON CONSUMER
PRODUCTS CORP**
2121 State Route 27 (08817-3329)
PHONE..................................732 287-1400
Fax: 732 527-4995
Mike Helman, *Vice Pres*
Lynn Lesser, *Branch Mgr*
EMP: 100 **Publicly Held**
SIC: 2844 Cosmetic preparations
HQ: Revlon Consumer Products Corpora-
tion
1 New York Plz
New York NY 10004

(G-2607)
ROMA MOULDING INC
115 Northfield Ave (08837-3856)
PHONE..................................732 346-0999
Fax: 732 346-0223
Barry Zimmerman, *Manager*
EMP: 10
SALES (corp-wide): 11.4MM **Privately
Held**
SIC: 2499 5023 Picture frame molding,
finished; frames & framing, picture & mir-
ror
PA: Roma Moulding Inc
360 Hanlan Rd
Woodbridge ON L4L 3
905 850-1500

(G-2608)
RX TRADE ZONE INC
22 Meridian Rd Unit 15 (08820-2848)
PHONE..................................833 933-6600
Narendar Reddy Yasa, *President*
EMP: 5
SALES: 500K **Privately Held**
SIC: 7371 7372 Computer software devel-
opment & applications; application com-
puter software

(G-2609)
S & S SOCIUS INC
Also Called: S & S Manufacturing
115 Fieldcrest Ave (08837-3622)
PHONE..................................732 698-2400
Fax: 732 698-2424
Steven Silverman, *President*
Mitchell Silverman, *Admin Sec*
EMP: 45
SQ FT: 30,000
SALES (est): 7MM **Privately Held**
WEB: www.handrails.com
SIC: 3446 Architectural metalwork; railings,
prefabricated metal

(G-2610)
SAAD COLLECTION INC
160 Rrtan Ctr Pkwy Unit 5 (08837)
PHONE..................................732 763-4015
Mohammad Younus, *Branch Mgr*
EMP: 8 **Privately Held**
SIC: 2321 2331 Men's & boys' furnishings;
women's & misses' blouses & shirts
PA: Saad Collection Inc.
1165 Broadway Ste 305
New York NY 10001

(G-2611)
SANKET CORPORATION
15 Wood Acres Dr (08820-2303)
PHONE..................................732 287-0201
Daksha Shah, *CEO*
Ketan Shah, *Vice Pres*
▲ EMP: 12
SALES: 300K **Privately Held**
SIC: 2032 Ethnic foods: canned, jarred,
etc.

(G-2612)
**SCONDA CANVAS PRODUCTS
INC**
Also Called: Main Attractions
85 Newfield Ave (08837-3816)
PHONE..................................732 225-3500
Fax: 732 225-2110
Rocky Sconda, *Owner*
Dean Dialfanso, *General Mgr*
Marie Zarra, *Business Mgr*
Thomas Ofarrell, *Engineer*
EMP: 26
SQ FT: 35,000
SALES (est): 1.9MM **Privately Held**
WEB: www.mainattractions.com
SIC: 7359 2394 Party supplies rental serv-
ices; tent & tarpaulin rental; sound & light-
ing equipment rental; awnings, fabric:
made from purchased materials

(G-2613)
SELECT ENTERPRISES INC
71 Executive Ave (08817-6017)
P.O. Box 1353 (08818-1353)
PHONE..................................732 287-8622
Tom Lordi, *President*
Robert Hoffman, *Vice Pres*
EMP: 6
SALES (est): 570K **Privately Held**
WEB: www.selecttp.com
SIC: 2448 4212 Pallets, wood; local truck-
ing, without storage

(G-2614)
SENCO METALS LLC
5056 Woodbridge Ave (08837-3306)
PHONE..................................973 342-1742
Filip Filipovski, *Mng Member*
EMP: 4
SALES (est): 401.5K **Privately Held**
SIC: 3441 7373 Fabricated structural
metal; computer-aided design (CAD) sys-
tems service

(G-2615)
SHAHNAWAZ FOOD LLC
78 Roxy Ave (08820-1947)
PHONE..................................908 413-4206
Feroz Khan, *CEO*
EMP: 10
SQ FT: 10,000
SALES (est): 554.3K **Privately Held**
SIC: 2013 Sausages & other prepared
meats

(G-2616)
SHEKIA GROUP LLC
1130 King Georges Post Rd (08837-3731)
PHONE..................................732 372-7666
Christina Jade, *Mng Member*
▲ EMP: 50
SQ FT: 300,000
SALES (est): 5.7MM **Privately Held**
SIC: 2434 5031 Wood kitchen cabinets;
kitchen cabinets

(G-2617)
**SILGAN CONTAINERS MFG
CORP**
135 National Rd (08817-2810)
PHONE..................................732 287-0300
Bryce Bedford, *Plant Mgr*
Rob Paprota, *QC Mgr*
EMP: 100
SALES (corp-wide): 4B **Publicly Held**
WEB: www.silgancontainers.com
SIC: 3411 Metal cans
HQ: Silgan Containers Manufacturing Cor-
poration
21600 Oxnard St Ste 1600
Woodland Hills CA 91367

(G-2618)
**SIMPLE HOME AUTOMATION
INC**
32 Brunswick Ave (08817-2578)
PHONE..................................877 405-2397
Elie Chemtob, *CEO*
Marco Chemtob, *CFO*
◆ EMP: 200 EST: 2015
SALES (est): 6.4MM **Privately Held**
SIC: 3491 Automatic regulating & control
valves

(G-2619)
**SINO MONTHLY NEW JERSEY
INC**
Also Called: Sino Monthly Jersey
18 Sheppard Pl (08817-3134)
PHONE..................................732 650-0688
Fax: 732 650-7468
Chung Liu, *President*
Ivy Lee, *Chief*
EMP: 10
SQ FT: 1,000
SALES (est): 939.1K **Privately Held**
WEB: www.sino-monthly.com
SIC: 2721 Periodicals

(G-2620)
SJD DIRECT MIDWEST LLC
112 Truman Dr (08817-2425)
PHONE..................................732 985-8405
EMP: 244
SALES (corp-wide): 28.6MM **Privately
Held**
SIC: 3565 Packing & wrapping machinery
PA: Sjd Direct Midwest, Llc
21 Gtewy Cmrc Ctr Dr W
Edwardsville IL 62025
618 931-2151

(G-2621)
SJD DIRECT MIDWEST LLC
3 Ethel Rd Ste 301 (08817-2855)
PHONE..................................732 287-2525
EMP: 102
SALES (corp-wide): 38.5MM **Privately
Held**
SIC: 3565 Mfg Packaging Machinery
PA: Sjd Direct Midwest, Llc
21 Gtewy Cmrc Ctr Dr W
Edwardsville IL 62025
618 931-2151

(G-2622)
SMALL QUANTITIES NJ INC
66 Ethel Rd (08817-2249)
P.O. Box 4167, Metuchen (08840-4167)
PHONE..................................732 248-9009
Fax: 732 248-9559
Harry Mathis, *President*
Michael Mathis, *Vice Pres*
Wayne Bruck, *VP Opers*
Yenibel Morales, *Human Res Mgr*
Tom Schindel, *Sales Staff*
EMP: 57 EST: 1958
SQ FT: 22,000
SALES (est): 11.1MM **Privately Held**
SIC: 3469 Stamping metal for the trade

(G-2623)
**SMARTLINX SOLUTIONS LLC
(PA)**
333 Thornall St Ste 401 (08837-2237)
PHONE..................................732 385-5507
Marina Aslanyan, *CEO*
Alex Gardner, *CFO*
EMP: 65
SQ FT: 4,000
SALES: 13.9MM **Privately Held**
SIC: 7371 7372 7373 Computer software
development; business oriented computer
software; systems software development
services

(G-2624)
**SOLGEN PHARMACEUTICALS
INC**
1514 Edison Glen Ter (08837-2940)
PHONE..................................732 983-6025
Arpit Patel, *President*
EMP: 20
SALES (est): 1.2MM **Privately Held**
SIC: 2834 Pharmaceutical preparations

(G-2625)
**SPOTLESS VENETIAN BLIND
SERVIC**
Also Called: Spotless Shade
1217 Us Highway 1 (08837-3114)
PHONE..................................732 548-1711
Fax: 732 548-9782
Scott Fitzgerald, *President*
EMP: 4 EST: 1961
SQ FT: 2,500
SALES (est): 370K **Privately Held**
SIC: 2591 7699 Venetian blinds; window
shades; venetian blind repair shop

(G-2626)
ST MARTIN CABINETRY INC
100 Newfield Ave Ste B (08837-3849)
PHONE..................................732 902-6020
EMP: 4 EST: 2016
SALES (est): 173.9K **Privately Held**
SIC: 2434 Wood kitchen cabinets

(G-2627)
STELFAST INC
104 Sunfield Ave (08837-3845)
PHONE..................................440 879-0077
Oj Simpson, *Natl Sales Mgr*
EMP: 30
SALES (corp-wide): 24.7MM **Privately
Held**
SIC: 3449 Miscellaneous metalwork
PA: Stelfast Inc.
22979 Stelfast Pkwy
Strongsville OH 44149
440 879-0077

(G-2628)
**STRIKEFORCE TECHNOLOGIES
INC**
1090 King Georges Post Rd (08837-3701)
PHONE..................................732 661-9641
Fax: 732 661-9647
Mark L Kay, *Ch of Bd*
George Waller, *Exec VP*
Philip E Blocker, *CFO*
George Stout Jr, *Controller*
Mike Brenner, *Technical Staff*
EMP: 8
SALES: 274.1K **Privately Held**
SIC: 7372 Prepackaged software

(G-2629)
**SUITE K VALUE ADDED SVCS
LLC**
31 Executive Ave (08817-6035)
PHONE..................................732 590-0647
Kathleen C Molyneaux, *Branch Mgr*
EMP: 10 **Privately Held**
SIC: 2844 Cosmetic preparations
PA: Suite K Value Added Services Llc
31 Executive Ave
Edison NJ 08817

(G-2630)
**SUITE K VALUE ADDED SVCS
LLC**
Also Called: Suite-K
31 Executive Ave (08817-6035)
PHONE..................................609 655-6890
Alexandra De Markoff, *Principal*
Joseph Pereira, *Administration*
EMP: 18 **Privately Held**
SIC: 2844 Cosmetic preparations
PA: Suite K Value Added Services Llc
31 Executive Ave
Edison NJ 08817

(G-2631)
**SUITE K VALUE ADDED SVCS
LLC (PA)**
Also Called: Suite-K
31 Executive Ave (08817-6035)
PHONE..................................609 655-6890
Kathleen Molyneaux, *President*
Kathleen C Molyneaux,
Waiming Chan,
▲ EMP: 72
SQ FT: 156,211
SALES (est): 20.7MM **Privately Held**
SIC: 2844 Cosmetic preparations

(G-2632)
SUNLIGHT PHOTONICS INC
2045 State Route 27 1w (08817-3334)
PHONE..........................732 362-7501
Michael Cyrus, *President*
Sergey Frolov, *President*
Jodi Ciongoli, *Executive*
EMP: 4
SALES (est): 340K **Privately Held**
SIC: 3674 Semiconductors & related devices

(G-2633)
SUPER STUD BUILDING PDTS INC
2960 Woodbridge Ave (08837-3406)
PHONE..........................732 662-6200
Raymond Frobosilo, *President*
Ed Frobosilo, *General Mgr*
Annette Frobosilo, *Corp Secy*
Jainarine Maniram, *Opers Mgr*
John Sullivan, *Materials Mgr*
▲ **EMP:** 100
SQ FT: 100,000
SALES (est): 27.1MM **Privately Held**
WEB: www.buysuperstud.com
SIC: 3444 Studs & joists, sheet metal

(G-2634)
SWAROVSKI NORTH AMERICA LTD
55 Parsonage Rd Unit 333 (08837-2497)
PHONE..........................732 632-1856
Fax: 732 632-1857
EMP: 7
SALES (corp-wide): 3.7B **Privately Held**
SIC: 3961 Costume jewelry
HQ: Swarovski North America Limited
1 Kenney Dr
Cranston RI 02920
401 463-6400

(G-2635)
SWEET SOLUTIONS INC
117 Fieldcrest Ave (08837-3622)
PHONE..........................732 512-0777
Nick Chao, *President*
▲ **EMP:** 8 **EST:** 2006
SQ FT: 15,000
SALES (est): 1MM **Privately Held**
SIC: 2869 Sweeteners, synthetic

(G-2636)
SWISSRAY INTERNATIONAL INC (HQ)
1090 King Georges Rd 1203 (08837)
PHONE..........................800 903-5543
Gilbert Wai, *CEO*
John Monahan, *Vice Pres*
Jack Lee, *Officer*
EMP: 15
SQ FT: 2,500
SALES: 1.6MM **Privately Held**
WEB: www.swissray.com
SIC: 3844 X-ray generators
PA: Swissray Medical Ag
Turbistrasse 25-27
Hochdorf LU
419 141-212

(G-2637)
TAYLOR PRODUCTS INC
255 Raritan Center Pkwy (08837-3613)
P.O. Box 6748 (08818-6748)
PHONE..........................732 225-4620
Fax: 732 225-4630
Wayne Schwacke, *Principal*
Jason Rossi, *District Mgr*
Richard P Guerra, *Vice Pres*
Matt Fab, *Sales Staff*
Mike Ryder, *Manager*
▲ **EMP:** 41
SQ FT: 16,000
SALES (est): 19.9MM **Privately Held**
SIC: 5046 7699 2024 Restaurant equipment & supplies; restaurant equipment repair; ices, flavored (frozen dessert)

(G-2638)
TCP RELIABLE INC (PA)
551 Raritan Center Pkwy (08817-3918)
PHONE..........................848 229-2466
Fax: 732 346-0295
Maurice Barakat, *CEO*
Anthony Spina, *CFO*

Carlene Spencer, *Controller*
▲ **EMP:** 5
SQ FT: 62,000
SALES (est): 33.8MM **Privately Held**
WEB: www.tcpreliable.com
SIC: 3086 3825 Packaging & shipping materials, foamed plastic; instruments to measure electricity

(G-2639)
TONYS AUTO ENTP LTD LBLTY CO
98 Loring Ave (08817-4322)
PHONE..........................203 223-5776
Anthony F Filippone, *Mng Member*
EMP: 4
SALES (est): 309.7K **Privately Held**
SIC: 4212 3465 Local trucking, without storage; body parts, automobile: stamped metal

(G-2640)
UNITED NATURAL TRADING CO
Also Called: Woodstock Farms
96 Executive Ave (08817-6016)
PHONE..........................732 650-9905
Fax: 732 650-9909
Daniel V Atwood, *President*
◆ **EMP:** 100 **EST:** 1971
SQ FT: 100,000
SALES (est): 13.6MM **Publicly Held**
WEB: www.unfi.com
SIC: 2099 5149 Food preparations; dried or canned foods
PA: United Natural Foods, Inc.
313 Iron Horse Way
Providence RI 02908

(G-2641)
VASWANI INC (PA)
75 Carter Dr Ste 1 (08817-2067)
PHONE..........................877 376-4425
Vinay Vaswani, *CEO*
Ishwar Vaswani, *President*
◆ **EMP:** 52
SALES (est): 27MM **Privately Held**
WEB: www.vaswani.com
SIC: 2499 Picture & mirror frames, wood

(G-2642)
VASWANI INC
75 Carter Dr Ste 1 (08817-2067)
PHONE..........................877 376-4425
EMP: 10
SALES (corp-wide): 33.4MM **Privately Held**
SIC: 2521 4226 4783 Mfg Wood Office Furniture Special Warehouse/Storage Packing/Crating Service
PA: Vaswani Inc.
75 Carter Dr Ste 1
Edison NJ 08817
877 376-4425

(G-2643)
VERMONT CABLEWORKS INC
31 National Rd (08817-2808)
P.O. Box 71, Windsor VT (05089-0071)
PHONE..........................802 674-6555
Fax: 802 674-6699
Richard Sincerbeaux, *President*
Winthrop Townsend, *Admin Sec*
EMP: 7
SQ FT: 6,000
SALES (est): 1.1MM **Privately Held**
SIC: 3643 Current-carrying wiring devices

(G-2644)
VERTIV SERVICES INC
3a Fernwood Ave (08837-3800)
PHONE..........................732 225-3741
Fax: 732 225-0667
Bob Jones, *Branch Mgr*
EMP: 32
SALES (corp-wide): 242.6MM **Privately Held**
SIC: 3823 7378 Industrial instrmnts msrmnt display/control process variable; computer maintenance & repair
HQ: Vertiv Services, Inc.
610 Executive Campus Dr
Westerville OH 43082
614 841-6400

(G-2645)
VICMARR AUDIO INC
9 Kilmer Ct (08817-2428)
PHONE..........................732 289-9111
Richard Cohen, *Ch of Bd*
Victor Cohen, *President*
Mal Cohen, *Vice Pres*
Ron Cohen, *Admin Sec*
◆ **EMP:** 20
SQ FT: 50,000
SALES: 6.7MM **Privately Held**
SIC: 3699 Electrical equipment & supplies

(G-2646)
VIGO INDUSTRIES LLC (PA)
220 Mill Rd (08817-6009)
PHONE..........................866 591-7792
Jacob Belenitsky, *Partner*
Nabila Dellil, *Partner*
Todd Alexander, *Vice Pres*
Denise Sias, *Human Res Mgr*
Nikki Williams, *Accounts Exec*
◆ **EMP:** 32
SALES (est): 14.1MM **Privately Held**
SIC: 3431 3469 Bathroom fixtures, including sinks; kitchen fixtures & equipment: metal, except cast aluminum

(G-2647)
VIKING MARINE PRODUCTS INC
Also Called: Viking Fender Company
977 New Durham Rd (08817-2253)
PHONE..........................732 826-4552
Kurt Grimsgaard, *President*
Guy Grimsgaard, *Vice Pres*
▼ **EMP:** 9
SALES (est): 1.2MM **Privately Held**
SIC: 3429 Marine hardware

(G-2648)
W C OMNI INCORPORATED
Also Called: Omni Wall Coverings
166 National Rd (08817-2811)
PHONE..........................732 248-0999
Fax: 732 248-0930
Gary Tumminello, *President*
Nino Pasqua, *Vice Pres*
▲ **EMP:** 20
SQ FT: 33,000
SALES (est): 6.4MM **Privately Held**
WEB: www.omniwcinc.com
SIC: 2295 Laminating of fabrics

(G-2649)
WAKEFERN FOOD CORP
Also Called: Wakefern Personnel
Old Post Rd Rr 1 (08837)
P.O. Box 7812 (08818-7812)
PHONE..........................732 819-0140
Fax: 732 906-5215
Alan Aront, *President*
Dawn Hudacko, *Buyer*
Steve Penk, *Engineer*
Robert Matyas, *Accountant*
Daniel Tarnopol, *Corp Counsel*
EMP: 300
SALES (corp-wide): 12.5B **Privately Held**
SIC: 5411 5149 4213 2026 Grocery stores; supermarkets, chain; groceries & related products; contract haulers; milk processing (pasteurizing, homogenizing, bottling)
PA: Wakefern Food Corp.
5000 Riverside Dr
Keasbey NJ 08832
908 527-3300

(G-2650)
WEATHERBEETA USA INC
201 Mill Rd (08837-3801)
PHONE..........................732 287-1182
Darren Nann, *President*
Paul Pels, *Treasurer*
Chris Corn, *Sales Staff*
Donna Young, *Manager*
▲ **EMP:** 24
SQ FT: 99,000
SALES (est): 8.7MM **Privately Held**
WEB: www.weatherbeetausa.com
SIC: 5023 2399 Blankets; horse & pet accessories, textile; horse blankets
HQ: Weatherbeeta Pty Ltd
8 Moncrief Rd
Nunawading VIC 3131
398 450-600

(G-2651)
WORLDWIDE WHL FLR CVG INC (PA)
1055 Us Highway 1 (08837-2904)
PHONE..........................732 906-1400
Fax: 732 906-1412
Alan Braunstein, *President*
Barbara Braunstein, *Corp Secy*
Darren Braunstein, *COO*
Melissa Dixon, *Accounting Mgr*
James Fitzsimmons, *Marketing Staff*
▲ **EMP:** 80
SQ FT: 40,000
SALES (est): 34.5MM **Privately Held**
WEB: www.worldwidefloors.com
SIC: 5713 5023 2273 2591 Carpets; floor tile; wood flooring; carpets & rugs; window blinds

(G-2652)
YIPIN FOOD PRODUCTS INC
Also Called: Yi Pin Food Prods
29 Mack Dr (08817-2807)
PHONE..........................718 788-3059
Chiwan Cheung, *CEO*
Siu Hang Lai, *Vice Pres*
Kevin Zhang, *Manager*
Ping Chan, *Admin Sec*
▲ **EMP:** 12
SQ FT: 15,000
SALES (est): 1.2MM **Privately Held**
SIC: 2035 5149 Seasonings & sauces, except tomato & dry; soy sauce; seasonings, sauces & extracts

(G-2653)
YORK INTERNATIONAL CORPORATION
160 Rritan Ctr Pkwy Ste 6 (08837)
PHONE..........................732 346-0606
Tony Natale, *Branch Mgr*
EMP: 13 **Privately Held**
SIC: 3585 Refrigeration & heating equipment
HQ: York International Corporation
631 S Richland Ave
York PA 17403
717 771-7890

(G-2654)
ZINK HOLDINGS LLC
114 Tived Ln E (08837-3076)
PHONE..........................781 761-5400
Akiva Klein, *CFO*
Chaim Piekarski
EMP: 184 **EST:** 2015
SALES: 10MM **Privately Held**
SIC: 3861 Photographic film, plate & paper holders

Egg Harbor City
Atlantic County

(G-2655)
ACCENT FENCE INC
1450 Bremen Ave (08215-2820)
P.O. Box 656 (08215-0656)
PHONE..........................609 965-6400
Fax: 609 965-6403
Greg Carnesale, *President*
EMP: 35
SQ FT: 400
SALES (est): 7.5MM **Privately Held**
SIC: 3496 1799 Miscellaneous fabricated wire products; fence construction

(G-2656)
ATLANTIC INDUS WD PDTS LLC
411 S London Ave (08215-3014)
P.O. Box 1234, Hammonton (08037-5234)
PHONE..........................609 965-4555
Michael Perrone,
Peter Scaffidi,
EMP: 5
SALES: 500K **Privately Held**
SIC: 2448 Pallets, wood

(G-2657)
BARRETTE OUTDOOR LIVING INC
545 Tilton Rd Ste 100 (08215-5136)
PHONE..........................609 965-5450

EMP: 15
SALES (corp-wide): 67.8K **Privately Held**
SIC: 3315 Fence gates posts & fittings: steel
HQ: Barrette Outdoor Living, Inc.
7830 Freeway Cir
Middleburg Heights OH 44130
440 891-0790

(G-2658)
BUSINESS CARDS TOMORROW INC
Also Called: BCT
129 Cincinnati Ave (08215-1998)
PHONE..............................609 965-0808
Fax: 609 965-5930
Brian D'Agostino, *President*
Madeline D'Agostino, *Corp Secy*
EMP: 10 **EST:** 1980
SQ FT: 2,700
SALES (est): 1.3MM **Privately Held**
WEB: www.bctsouthjersey.com
SIC: 2752 Commercial printing, lithographic

(G-2659)
C HARRY MAREAN PRINTING
1717 Philadelphia Ave (08215-1627)
P.O. Box 294 (08215-0294)
PHONE..............................609 965-4708
C Harry Marean, *Partner*
Lee M Marean, *Partner*
EMP: 5
SQ FT: 2,800
SALES: 75K **Privately Held**
SIC: 2752 2759 Lithographing on metal; letterpress printing

(G-2660)
COSTA MAR CNVAS ENCLOSURES LLC
1324 Moss Mill Rd (08215-3130)
PHONE..............................609 965-1538
Joseph Costa, *Owner*
Christopher Costa, *General Mgr*
Chris Costa, *Project Mgr*
Jennifer Smith, *Project Mgr*
Donna Costa, *Sales Mgr*
EMP: 10
SQ FT: 2,000
SALES (est): 949.3K **Privately Held**
WEB: www.costamarinecanvas.com
SIC: 7641 3732 2394 Reupholstery; boat building & repairing; canvas & related products

(G-2661)
DEMAIO INC
543 Columbia Rd (08215-4131)
PHONE..............................609 965-4094
George V Demaio, *President*
Michele L Demaio, *Vice Pres*
EMP: 20
SQ FT: 3,000
SALES: 2.9MM **Privately Held**
WEB: www.demaios.com
SIC: 4959 1081 8748 Environmental cleanup services; draining or pumping of metal mines; systems analysis & engineering consulting services

(G-2662)
DOUGLASS INDUSTRIES INC
Also Called: Douglass Weave Appeal
412 Boston Ave (08215-2603)
P.O. Box 701 (08215-0701)
PHONE..............................609 804-6040
Fax: 609 965-7271
F Naomi Taylor, *CEO*
Howard Taylor, *Principal*
Douglass A Taylor, *COO*
Randolph S Taylor, *Treasurer*
Gail McKinney, *Mktg Dir*
▼ **EMP:** 33
SQ FT: 50,000
SALES: 22MM **Privately Held**
WEB: www.dougind.com
SIC: 5131 2299 Upholstery fabrics, woven; batting, wadding, padding & fillings

(G-2663)
EGG HARBOR ROPE PRODUCTS INC
5105 White Horse Pike (08215-4016)
P.O. Box 294 (08215-0294)
PHONE..............................609 965-2435
C Harry Marean, *President*
Fred Good, *Treasurer*
EMP: 4 **EST:** 1963
SQ FT: 5,600
SALES (est): 240K **Privately Held**
SIC: 2298 Rope, except asbestos & wire

(G-2664)
EH YACHTS LLC
Also Called: Egg Harbor Boats
801 Philadelphia Ave (08215-1609)
P.O. Box 702 (08215-0702)
PHONE..............................609 965-2300
Ira Trocki, *Mng Member*
EMP: 84
SALES (est): 14.8MM **Privately Held**
WEB: www.ehyachts.com
SIC: 3732 Yachts, building & repairing

(G-2665)
JERSEY CAPE YACHTS INC
2143 River Rd (08215-4745)
PHONE..............................609 965-8650
Wayne Puglise, *President*
EMP: 52
SQ FT: 90,000
SALES (est): 8.7MM **Privately Held**
SIC: 3732 Boat building & repairing

(G-2666)
LAUREATE PRESS
1336 W Central Ave (08215-1798)
P.O. Box 343 (08215-0343)
PHONE..............................609 646-1545
Fax: 609 965-4032
Janet Rotellini, *President*
Henry Sartorio, *Admin Sec*
EMP: 6 **EST:** 1928
SQ FT: 3,872
SALES (est): 962.8K **Privately Held**
SIC: 2752 Commercial printing, lithographic; photo-offset printing

(G-2667)
MARINE ACQUISITION INC
Also Called: Egg Harbor Yacht-Div
801 Philadelphia Ave (08215-1609)
P.O. Box 702 (08215-0702)
PHONE..............................609 965-2300
Rick Trapp, *Ch of Bd*
William C Robinson, *President*
Doug Finney, *Vice Pres*
Joan Sgorbati, *Treasurer*
EMP: 100
SQ FT: 65,480
SALES (est): 12.6MM **Privately Held**
SIC: 3732 5551 Boat building & repairing; boat dealers

(G-2668)
NEW JRSEY SFOOD MKTG GROUP LLC
143 Leektown Rd (08215-4809)
PHONE..............................609 296-7026
George W Mathis,
EMP: 5
SALES (est): 304.4K **Privately Held**
SIC: 2092 Fresh or frozen packaged fish

(G-2669)
RENAULT WINERY INC
Also Called: Renault Winery Restaurant
72 N Bremen Ave (08215-3195)
PHONE..............................609 965-2111
Fax: 609 965-1847
Joseph P Milza Sr, *President*
Joseph Milza, *Owner*
Damon Scalasro, *Vice Pres*
Dave Demarsico, *Opers Mgr*
Brian Crompton, *Buyer*
▲ **EMP:** 50 **EST:** 1864
SQ FT: 52,000
SALES (est): 4MM **Privately Held**
WEB: www.renaultwinery.com
SIC: 5812 7299 2084 Restaurant, family: independent; banquet hall facilities; wine cellars, bonded: engaged in blending wines

(G-2670)
SCHAIRER BROTHERS
254 S Bremen Ave (08215-3101)
PHONE..............................609 965-0996
Fax: 609 965-4040
Paul Schairer, *Partner*
Anthony Schairer, *Partner*
EMP: 6 **EST:** 1936
SALES (est): 666.2K **Privately Held**
SIC: 2421 Sawmills & planing mills, general

(G-2671)
TASTE ITALY MANUFACTURING LLC
1301 Bremen Ave (08215-2860)
P.O. Box 1146, Mullica Hill (08062-1146)
PHONE..............................856 223-0707
Eric Brennan, *VP Opers*
Luigi Illiano, *Mng Member*
EMP: 5
SALES (est): 875.8K **Privately Held**
SIC: 2099 Pizza, refrigerated: except frozen

(G-2672)
TF YACHTS LLC
801 Philadelphia Ave (08215-1609)
PHONE..............................609 965-2300
Robert Weidhaas, *President*
EMP: 23
SALES (est): 1MM **Privately Held**
SIC: 3732 Yachts, building & repairing

(G-2673)
TIME LOG INDUSTRIES INC
312 N Leipzig Ave (08215-3308)
PHONE..............................609 965-5017
Frank Tomasello, *President*
Melissa Tomasello, *Vice Pres*
EMP: 5
SQ FT: 1,500
SALES: 200K **Privately Held**
SIC: 3953 Time stamps, hand: rubber or metal

(G-2674)
WELDING & RADIATOR SUPPLY CO
1144 W White Horse Pike (08215-3136)
P.O. Box 609, Allenwood (08720-0609)
PHONE..............................609 965-0433
EMP: 5 **EST:** 1947
SQ FT: 2,500
SALES: 200K **Privately Held**
SIC: 5172 5984 5084 7692 Whol Petroleum Products Ret Liquefied Petroleum Gas Whol Industrial Equipment Welding Services

Egg Harbor Township
Atlantic County

(G-2675)
A E STONE INC (PA)
1435 Doughty Rd (08234-2229)
PHONE..............................609 641-2781
Thomas Ritter, *President*
Tom Collard, *Vice Pres*
Steven C Kurtz, *Vice Pres*
Ross Williamson, *Vice Pres*
Walt Noll, *Project Mgr*
EMP: 40 **EST:** 1955
SQ FT: 6,600
SALES (est): 11.7MM **Privately Held**
WEB: www.aestone.com
SIC: 2951 1611 1429 Asphalt & asphaltic paving mixtures (not from refineries); highway & street paving contractor; igneous rock, crushed & broken-quarrying

(G-2676)
ABSECON ISLAND BEVERAGE CO
6754 Washington Ave B (08234-3807)
PHONE..............................609 653-8123
Matt Helm, *President*
EMP: 4
SQ FT: 7,000
SALES: 1.5MM **Privately Held**
SIC: 3556 Beverage machinery

(G-2677)
ADVANTAGE FIBERGLASS INC
4 Prospect Ave (08234-8519)
PHONE..............................609 926-4606
Thomas Kampert, *President*
EMP: 4
SALES (est): 265.7K **Privately Held**
SIC: 3296 Mineral wool

(G-2678)
ANTHONY EXCAVATING & DEM
22 English Ln (08234-7034)
PHONE..............................609 926-8804
Fax: 609 926-7760
Steven R Anthony, *President*
Laurie Anthony, *Admin Sec*
EMP: 1
SALES: 1MM **Privately Held**
SIC: 1629 1795 2499 Dredging contractor; land clearing contractor; wrecking & demolition work; mulch, wood & bark

(G-2679)
AST CONSTRUCTION INC
5 Canale Dr (08234-5131)
PHONE..............................609 277-7101
Ted Gendron, *President*
Brian Gerner, *Vice Pres*
EMP: 50
SQ FT: 2,000
SALES (est): 12.3MM **Privately Held**
WEB: www.astconstruction.com
SIC: 3795 Tanks & tank components

(G-2680)
ATLANTIC MASONRY SUPPLY INC
6422 Black Horse Pike (08234-5542)
PHONE..............................609 909-9292
Fax: 609 641-6744
Deborah Tower, *President*
Darlene Tower, *Vice Pres*
EMP: 10
SALES (est): 1.3MM **Privately Held**
WEB: www.atlanticmasonrynj.com
SIC: 3273 Ready-mixed concrete

(G-2681)
BALLY TECHNOLOGIES INC
Also Called: Bally Gaming
3133 Fire Rd (08234-9601)
PHONE..............................609 641-7711
Fax: 609 641-7711
Stan Kozlowski, *Branch Mgr*
Victoria Simon, *Manager*
Jon Rickert, *Data Proc Exec*
EMP: 12
SALES (corp-wide): 3B **Publicly Held**
WEB: www.ballygaming.com
SIC: 3944 Games, toys & children's vehicles
HQ: Bally Technologies, Inc.
6650 El Camino Rd
Las Vegas NV 89118
702 897-2284

(G-2682)
BATTISTINI FOODS
20 Brandywine Ct (08234-4882)
PHONE..............................609 476-2184
Timothy Datig, *Owner*
EMP: 4
SQ FT: 5,000
SALES: 900K **Privately Held**
SIC: 2038 Ethnic foods, frozen

(G-2683)
CAPE ATLANTIC SOFTWARE LLC
6523 Mill Rd (08234-9655)
PHONE..............................609 442-1331
Gaey Schaefer,
EMP: 6
SALES (est): 340K **Privately Held**
SIC: 7372 Prepackaged software

(G-2684)
ENROUTE COMPUTER SOLUTIONS INC
Also Called: E C S
2511 Fire Rd Ste A4 (08234-5618)
PHONE..............................609 569-9255
Fax: 609 569-9256
Anthony Curatolo, *President*
John Rodolico, *Business Mgr*

Charles Wiemer, *COO*
Theresa Boyle, *Vice Pres*
Dallas Hepler, *VP Opers*
EMP: 303
SQ FT: 11,000
SALES: 47.5MM **Privately Held**
WEB: www.enroute-computer.com
SIC: 7371 3721 8734 Computer software development & applications; research & development on aircraft by the manufacturer; testing laboratories

(G-2685)
INNOVATIVE CUTNG CONCEPTS LLC
203 Cates Rd (08234-5286)
PHONE..................................609 484-9960
Fax: 609 484-4739
Mike Isley,
Ronald Simmoni,
Martin Sokolski,
EMP: 8
SALES (est): 825.9K **Privately Held**
SIC: 3281 1499 Cut stone & stone products; gem stones (natural) mining

(G-2686)
INTERACTIVE ADVISORY SOFTWARE
3393 Bargaintown Rd # 200 (08234-5955)
PHONE..................................770 951-2929
Stephen Hartney, *Project Mgr*
Nathan Berk, *Mng Member*
EMP: 38
SQ FT: 10,000
SALES (est): 5MM
SALES (corp-wide): 11.7MM **Privately Held**
SIC: 7372 Application computer software
PA: Optima Technologies Inc
1110 Northchase Pkwy Se # 250
Marietta GA 30067
800 821-7355

(G-2687)
JOMAR CORP
115 E Parkway Dr (08234-5112)
P.O. Box 1020, Pleasantville (08232-6020)
PHONE..................................609 646-8000
Fax: 609 645-9166
Carlos R Castro, *President*
Kevin Adams, *Plant Mgr*
Jesse Boyington, *Purch Agent*
James Chukinas, *Controller*
Ron Gabriele, *Sales Staff*
▲ **EMP:** 34 **EST:** 1968
SQ FT: 40,000
SALES: 5MM
SALES (corp-wide): 930.4MM **Privately Held**
WEB: www.jomarcorp.com
SIC: 3559 Plastics working machinery
HQ: Indel, Inc.
10 Indel Ave
Rancocas NJ 08073
609 267-9000

(G-2688)
LNS INC
Also Called: L N S Industries
24 Buckingham Dr (08234-7253)
PHONE..................................609 927-6656
Lisa Fasola, *President*
Nicholas Fasola, *Vice Pres*
EMP: 12 **EST:** 2000
SALES: 20K **Privately Held**
SIC: 3089 Injection molded finished plastic products

(G-2689)
M & W FRANKLIN LLC
Also Called: Eastern Sign Company
3011 Ocean Heights Ave B (08234-7748)
PHONE..................................609 927-0885
Fax: 609 927-8955
Mike Franklin, *Principal*
Wendy Franklin,
EMP: 5
SQ FT: 1,500
SALES (est): 602.9K **Privately Held**
WEB: www.easternsignco.com
SIC: 3993 Signs & advertising specialties

(G-2690)
MID ATLANTIC GRAPHIXINC
Also Called: Signal Graphics
2558 Tilton Rd (08234-1833)
PHONE..................................609 569-9990
Fax: 609 569-9993
Kathryn Gunnles, *President*
John R Gunnels, *Vice Pres*
John Gunnels, *Vice Pres*
EMP: 8
SQ FT: 5,000
SALES (est): 1.3MM **Privately Held**
SIC: 2752 Commercial printing, offset

(G-2691)
PENN-JERSEY BLDG MTLS CO INC (PA)
6761 Washington Ave (08234-1917)
P.O. Box 981, Pleasantville (08232-0981)
PHONE..................................609 641-6994
Fax: 609 485-0350
Eileen L Johnston, *President*
Pat Phillips, *Plant Mgr*
Timothy Karaso, *Opers Mgr*
Joe Rich, *Sales Executive*
EMP: 55
SQ FT: 7,000
SALES (est): 11.3MM **Privately Held**
WEB: www.penn-jersey.net
SIC: 3273 Ready-mixed concrete

(G-2692)
POST TO POST LLC
2545 Fire Rd Ste 1 (08234-5667)
PHONE..................................609 646-9300
Richard Sonsini, *Principal*
EMP: 7 **EST:** 2003
SALES (est): 931.2K **Privately Held**
SIC: 3446 Railings, bannisters, guards, etc.: made from metal pipe

(G-2693)
RALPH CLAYTON & SONS LLC
103 Chestnut Ave (08234-5147)
PHONE..................................609 383-1818
Fax: 609 383-1638
Damian Haaf, *Manager*
EMP: 20
SALES (corp-wide): 96.7MM **Privately Held**
WEB: www.claytonco.com
SIC: 3273 Ready-mixed concrete
PA: Ralph Clayton & Sons L.L.C.
1355 Campus Pkwy
Wall Township NJ 07753
732 363-1995

(G-2694)
RSL WOODWORKING PRODUCTS CO (PA)
Also Called: Rsl
3092 English Creek Ave (08234-5245)
PHONE..................................609 484-1600
Bernd Lewkowitz, *Ch of Bd*
Ron Lewkowitz, *President*
Kevin Kavanagh, *Vice Pres*
Conor Fleming, *Marketing Staff*
Sharon Oran, *Shareholder*
▲ **EMP:** 75 **EST:** 1964
SQ FT: 300,000
SALES: 30MM **Privately Held**
SIC: 2431 3442 Door frames, wood; sash, door or window: metal

(G-2695)
RSL WOODWORKING PRODUCTS CO
3049 Fernwood Ave (08234-5235)
PHONE..................................609 645-9777
Fax: 609 645-8349
Charles Nixon, *Manager*
EMP: 31
SALES (corp-wide): 30MM **Privately Held**
SIC: 2431 3429 Door frames, wood; manufactured hardware (general)
PA: R.S.L. Woodworking Products, Co.
3092 English Creek Ave
Egg Harbor Township NJ 08234
609 484-1600

(G-2696)
SF LUTZ LLC
Also Called: Bon-Ton Instant Blnds Intriors
3143 Fire Rd Ste F (08234-9640)
P.O. Box 534, Longport (08403-0534)
PHONE..................................609 646-9490
Fax: 609 645-3413
Frederic M Lutz,
EMP: 4
SALES: 400K **Privately Held**
SIC: 2591 Drapery hardware & blinds & shades

(G-2697)
TASTY BAKING COMPANY
Also Called: Tasty Bake Distributing Center
203 Cates Rd (08234-5286)
PHONE..................................609 641-8588
Sean Flynn, *Manager*
EMP: 6
SALES (corp-wide): 3.9B **Publicly Held**
WEB: www.tastykake.com
SIC: 2051 Bakery: wholesale or wholesale/retail combined
HQ: Tasty Baking Company
4300 S 26th St
Philadelphia PA 19112
215 221-8500

(G-2698)
VERIZON COMMUNICATIONS INC
2546 Fire Rd (08234-5651)
PHONE..................................609 646-9939
Bill Beloff, *Manager*
EMP: 100
SALES (corp-wide): 126B **Publicly Held**
WEB: www.verizon.com
SIC: 4813 4812 2741 7373 Local telephone communications; voice telephone communications; data telephone communications; cellular telephone services; directories, telephone: publishing only, not printed on site; computer integrated systems design; direct mail advertising services; electrical work
PA: Verizon Communications Inc.
1095 Ave Of The Americas
New York NY 10036
212 395-1000

(G-2699)
W B MASON CO INC
350 Commerce Dr (08234-9589)
PHONE..................................888 926-2766
EMP: 40
SALES (corp-wide): 773MM **Privately Held**
SIC: 5943 5712 2752 Office forms & supplies; office furniture; commercial printing, lithographic
PA: W. B. Mason Co., Inc.
59 Center St
Brockton MA 02301
781 794-8800

(G-2700)
WINSOME DIGITAL INC
Also Called: Gotham Group, The
202 W Parkway Dr (08234-5107)
PHONE..................................609 645-2211
Qiang Wang, *President*
Keith Ogorek, *Editor*
Sarah Bodtmann, *Sales Staff*
Julie Meschko, *Admin Asst*
▲ **EMP:** 16
SALES (est): 3MM **Privately Held**
WEB: www.gothamgroup.com
SIC: 2759 Commercial printing

Egg Harbor Twp
Atlantic County

(G-2701)
TUCKAHOE BREWING COMPANY LLC
3092 English Creek Ave (08234-5245)
PHONE..................................609 645-2739
Stuart Stromfeld, *Mng Member*
Tim Hanna,
Chris Konicki,
James McAfee,
Matt McDevitt,

EMP: 15
SQ FT: 1,000
SALES (est): 589.4K **Privately Held**
SIC: 2082 Beer (alcoholic beverage)

Elizabeth
Union County

(G-2702)
A 1 FENCING INC
166 7th St (07201-2831)
PHONE..................................908 527-1066
Fax: 908 289-6307
Ray Camajo, *Owner*
EMP: 12 **EST:** 1960
SQ FT: 3,000
SALES (est): 1.1MM **Privately Held**
WEB: www.a1fencing.com
SIC: 1799 7692 Fence construction; welding repair

(G-2703)
A&B HEATING & COOLING
107 Trumbull St (07206-2165)
PHONE..................................908 289-2231
Allmon Banks, *Owner*
EMP: 4
SALES (est): 178.1K **Privately Held**
SIC: 3444 Sheet metalwork

(G-2704)
ACTAVIS ELIZABETH LLC (DH)
Also Called: Actavis US
200 Elmora Ave (07202-1106)
PHONE..................................908 527-9100
Fax: 973 993-4303
Sigurbar Olafsson, *President*
Paul M Bisaro, *Principal*
Aleksandr Yarmola, *Regional Mgr*
George Long, *Vice Pres*
Renzo Rodriguez, *Project Mgr*
▲ **EMP:** 300
SQ FT: 245,000
SALES (est): 287MM **Privately Held**
SIC: 2834 Pharmaceutical preparations; druggists' preparations (pharmaceuticals)

(G-2705)
ADCO SIGNS OF NJ INC
57 Westfield Ave (07208-3662)
PHONE..................................908 965-2112
Fax: 908 965-1379
Clara Molski, *President*
EMP: 30
SQ FT: 20,000
SALES (est): 3.9MM **Privately Held**
SIC: 3993 3953 Signs, not made in custom sign painting shops; marking devices

(G-2706)
AIR CLEAN CO INC
1135 Chestnut St (07201-1049)
PHONE..................................908 355-1515
Alex Drucker, *President*
EMP: 5
SQ FT: 6,000
SALES (est): 500K **Privately Held**
SIC: 3564 Air purification equipment; air cleaning systems

(G-2707)
ALEX AND ANI LLC
651 Kapkowski Rd Ste 1274 (07201-4913)
PHONE..................................908 965-1510
EMP: 9 **Privately Held**
SIC: 3911 Jewelry, precious metal
PA: Alex And Ani, Llc
2000 Chapel View Blvd # 360
Cranston RI 02920

(G-2708)
ALPHA WIRE CORPORATION (PA)
Also Called: Alphawire
711 Lidgerwood Ave (07202-3115)
PHONE..................................908 925-8000
Fax: 908 925-3346
Philip R Cowen, *Ch of Bd*
Willis E Bye, *President*
Mike Dugar, *President*
Marc Tousignant, *Regional Mgr*
Tim Yontek, *District Mgr*
EMP: 175

SQ FT: 320,000
SALES (est): 225.8MM **Privately Held**
SIC: 5063 3082 3357 Wire & cable; tubes, unsupported plastic; shipboard cable, nonferrous

(G-2709)
AMERICAN BABY HEADWEAR CO INC (PA)
1000 Jefferson Ave (07201-1394)
PHONE..................908 558-0017
Joseph Templer, *President*
Julius Templer, *Vice Pres*
Laser Templer, *Vice Pres*
EMP: 80
SQ FT: 35,000
SALES (est): 4.6MM **Privately Held**
SIC: 2369 2381 2353 Headwear: girls', children's & infants'; fabric dress & work gloves; hats, caps & millinery

(G-2710)
AMERICAN CHEMICAL & COATING CO
410 Division St (07201-1962)
PHONE..................908 353-2260
Fax: 908 353-3641
Qamar V Zaman, *President*
EMP: 4
SQ FT: 7,000
SALES (est): 410K **Privately Held**
SIC: 2865 2851 2891 Dyes, synthetic organic; lacquer: bases, dopes, thinner; adhesives

(G-2711)
ATTITUDES IN DRESSING INC (PA)
Also Called: Body Wrappers
107 Trumbull St Bldg B8 (07206-2165)
PHONE..................908 354-7218
Marie West, *President*
Michael Rubin, *Corp Secy*
Nicholas Karant, *Vice Pres*
▲ **EMP:** 320
SQ FT: 185,000
SALES (est): 55.8MM **Privately Held**
SIC: 2339 2369 5137 Athletic clothing: women's, misses' & juniors'; leotards: women's, misses' & juniors'; girls' & children's outerwear; women's & children's clothing

(G-2712)
BELDEN INC
Also Called: Alpha Wire
711 Lidgerwood Ave (07202-3115)
P.O. Box 711 (07207-0711)
PHONE..................908 925-8000
Christine Birkner, *Principal*
EMP: 13
SALES (corp-wide): 2.3B **Publicly Held**
WEB: www.belden.com
SIC: 3351 5063 3498 3496 Copper rolling & drawing; electrical apparatus & equipment; fabricated pipe & fittings; miscellaneous fabricated wire products; sheet metalwork
PA: Belden Inc.
  1 N Brentwood Blvd Fl 15
  Saint Louis MO 63105
  314 854-8000

(G-2713)
BELL ARTE INC
Also Called: Bell'arte
10 W Mravlag Pl (07201-2515)
P.O. Box 8912 (07201-0812)
PHONE..................908 355-1199
Fax: 908 355-6979
Giuseppe Chillemi, *President*
Frank Arena, *Vice Pres*
EMP: 17
SQ FT: 15,000
SALES: 1.7MM **Privately Held**
WEB: www.artebellagallery.com
SIC: 2431 Interior & ornamental woodwork & trim; exterior & ornamental woodwork & trim

(G-2714)
BERRY GLOBAL INC
100 Dowd Ave (07206-2130)
PHONE..................908 353-3850
Scott Christ, *Plant Mgr*

Tahir Khan, *Controller*
Raymond Panek, *Manager*
Frances Villaman, *Manager*
EMP: 120 **Publicly Held**
WEB: www.6sens.com
SIC: 3089 3081 Bottle caps, molded plastic; unsupported plastics film & sheet
HQ: Berry Global, Inc.
  101 Oakley St
  Evansville IN 47710
  812 424-2904

(G-2715)
BERRY GLOBAL INC
322 3rd St (07206-2007)
PHONE..................718 205-3115
EMP: 127 **Publicly Held**
SIC: 3089 Bottle caps, molded plastic
HQ: Berry Global, Inc.
  101 Oakley St
  Evansville IN 47710
  812 424-2904

(G-2716)
BURLINGTON COAT FACTORY
651 Kapkowski Rd Ste 30 (07201-4928)
PHONE..................908 994-9562
Roberto Manresa, *Manager*
EMP: 68
SALES (corp-wide): 6.1B **Publicly Held**
SIC: 5137 5136 2311 Women's & children's clothing; men's & boys' clothing; coats, overcoats & vests
HQ: Burlington Coat Factory Warehouse Corporation
  1830 N Route 130
  Burlington NJ 08016
  609 387-7800

(G-2717)
CARGILL INCORPORATED
132 Corbin St (07201-2910)
PHONE..................908 820-9800
Fax: 908 820-9808
Alfred Rieger, *Branch Mgr*
EMP: 4
SALES (corp-wide): 88.8B **Privately Held**
SIC: 2087 Flavoring extracts & syrups
PA: Cargill, Incorporated
  15407 Mcginty Rd W
  Wayzata MN 55391
  952 742-7575

(G-2718)
CHECK-IT ELECTRONICS CORP
560 Trumbull St (07206-1409)
PHONE..................973 520-8435
Fax: 908 354-9564
Richard E Bettle, *President*
George T Van Brunt, *Corp Secy*
EMP: 20
SALES (est): 1.7MM **Privately Held**
WEB: www.check-it-electronics.com
SIC: 3823 3822 3812 Industrial instrmnts msrmnt display/control process variable; auto controls regulating residntl & coml environmt & applncs; search & navigation equipment

(G-2719)
COCKPIT USA INC
725 New Point Rd (07201-2861)
PHONE..................212 575-1616
Tammy Butler, *Production*
Nicole Grab, *Sales Staff*
Jeffrey Clyman, *Branch Mgr*
Steve Lehmann, *Manager*
EMP: 10
SALES (corp-wide): 10.5MM **Privately Held**
SIC: 2386 5136 5611 5961 Coats & jackets, leather & sheep-lined; sportswear, men's & boys'; clothing, sportswear, men's & boys'; clothing, mail order (except women's)
PA: Cockpit Usa, Inc.
  15 W 39th St Fl 12
  New York NY 10018
  212 575-1616

(G-2720)
CONSOLIDATED CONTAINER CO LP
Also Called: Contech
28-36 Slater Dr (07206)
PHONE..................908 289-5862

Fax: 908 351-7980
Dan Citus, *Manager*
EMP: 70
SALES (corp-wide): 6.6B **Privately Held**
SIC: 3085 Plastics bottles
HQ: Consolidated Container Company Lp
  3101 Towercreek Pkwy Se
  Atlanta GA 30339
  678 742-4600

(G-2721)
CRINCOLI WOODWORK CO INC
160 Spring St (07201-2660)
PHONE..................908 352-9332
Fax: 908 289-7449
Peter Crincoli, *President*
EMP: 11
SQ FT: 17,000
SALES (est): 1.5MM **Privately Held**
WEB: www.crincoliwoodwork.com
SIC: 1521 1542 2431 5712 General remodeling, single-family houses; commercial & office buildings, renovation & repair; woodwork, interior & ornamental; custom made furniture, except cabinets; cabinet work, custom

(G-2722)
DAVES SALAD HOUSE INC
577 Pennsylvania Ave (07201-1101)
PHONE..................908 965-0773
David Miles, *President*
Michelle Miles, *Vice Pres*
EMP: 6
SQ FT: 1,500
SALES (est): 400K **Privately Held**
SIC: 2099 Salads, fresh or refrigerated

(G-2723)
DEARBORN A BELDEN CDT COMPANY (HQ)
Also Called: Kerrigan Lewis Wire/Cdt
711 Lidgerwood Ave (07202-3115)
PHONE..................908 925-8000
Scott Blackwood, *CEO*
Robert Canny, *President*
Ray Grabowski, *Vice Pres*
▲ **EMP:** 100
SQ FT: 110,000
SALES (est): 10.1MM
SALES (corp-wide): 2.3B **Publicly Held**
WEB: www.dearborn-cdt.com
SIC: 3643 3699 3694 3496 Current-carrying wiring devices; electrical equipment & supplies; engine electrical equipment; miscellaneous fabricated wire products; nonferrous wiredrawing & insulating; steel wire & related products
PA: Belden Inc.
  1 N Brentwood Blvd Fl 15
  Saint Louis MO 63105
  314 854-8000

(G-2724)
DEXMED INC
433 N Broad St Fl 1 (07208-3398)
PHONE..................732 831-0507
Joseph Stern, *CEO*
Rochel Leah Stern, *Principal*
Toby Schleisinger, *Principal*
EMP: 5
SALES (est): 423.8K **Privately Held**
WEB: www.dexmed.com
SIC: 5047 3842 3841 Medical equipment & supplies; cotton, including cotton balls: sterile & non-sterile; surgical & medical instruments

(G-2725)
DEXMED LLC
433 N Broad St Fl 1 (07208-3398)
PHONE..................732 831-0507
Joseph Stern,
Toby Schleslinger,
Rochel Leah Stern,
EMP: 5
SQ FT: 1,500
SALES (est): 264K **Privately Held**
SIC: 3841 5047 Surgical & medical instruments; instruments, surgical & medical

(G-2726)
DUBON CORP
1356 Stanley Ter (07208-2613)
PHONE..................212 812-2171
Egmaldo Bonilla, *President*

Lucas Bonilla, *Vice Pres*
EMP: 8
SALES (est): 386.7K **Privately Held**
SIC: 2013 Sausages & other prepared meats

(G-2727)
DURO BAG MANUFACTURING COMPANY
750 Dowd Ave (07201-2108)
PHONE..................908 351-2400
Karl Kalkbrenner, *Manager*
EMP: 200
SALES (corp-wide): 2.9B **Privately Held**
SIC: 2674 Paper bags: made from purchased materials
HQ: Duro Bag Manufacturing Company
  7600 Empire Dr
  Florence KY 41042
  859 371-2150

(G-2728)
ELEGANT HEADWEAR CO INC (PA)
Also Called: ABG Accessories
1000 Jefferson Ave (07201-1394)
PHONE..................908 558-1200
Fax: 908 558-0082
Joseph Templer, *President*
Abraham Ausch, *Vice Pres*
Emma Fonseca, *Design Engr*
John Guevara, *Design Engr*
Frank Martinez, *Sales Executive*
▲ **EMP:** 180
SQ FT: 250,000
SALES (est): 28.3MM **Privately Held**
WEB: www.elegantheadwear.com
SIC: 2253 Hats & headwear, knit

(G-2729)
EVOQUA WATER TECHNOLOGIES LLC
624 Evans St (07201-2009)
PHONE..................908 353-7400
Andrew Lees, *Manager*
EMP: 12
SALES (corp-wide): 1.1B **Publicly Held**
SIC: 2819 Charcoal (carbon), activated
HQ: Evoqua Water Technologies Llc
  210 6th Ave Ste 3300
  Pittsburgh PA 15222
  724 772-0044

(G-2730)
FAULDING HOLDINGS INC
200 Elmora Ave (07202-1106)
PHONE..................908 527-9100
Mark Stier, *Vice Pres*
EMP: 250
SQ FT: 300,000
SALES (est): 24.4MM **Publicly Held**
SIC: 2834 Druggists' preparations (pharmaceuticals)
HQ: Mayne Pharma International Pty Ltd
  1538 Main North Rd
  Salisbury South SA 5106

(G-2731)
FEDERAL LORCO PETROLEUM LLC
Also Called: Federal Petroleum
450 S Front St (07202-3009)
PHONE..................908 352-0542
John Lionetti,
Frank Lo Bello Jr,
EMP: 70
SALES (est): 6.7MM **Privately Held**
WEB: www.federalpetroleum.com
SIC: 4491 4953 2992 Marine terminals; refuse systems; lubricating oils & greases

(G-2732)
FEROLITO VULTAGGIO & SONS
535 Dowd Ave (07201-2103)
PHONE..................908 282-4480
Don Ferolito, *President*
EMP: 30
SALES (est): 1.5MM **Privately Held**
SIC: 2086 Carbonated beverages, nonalcoholic: bottled & canned

(G-2733)
FINE LINEN INC
107 Trumbull St (07206-2165)
PHONE..................908 469-3634

Isaac Braun, *President*
EMP: 10
SALES: 383.3K **Privately Held**
SIC: 2392 Household furnishings

(G-2734)
FREEPORT MINERALS CORPORATION
Also Called: Phelps Dodge
48 94 Bayway Ave (07202)
PHONE..............................908 351-3200
Fax: 908 351-9475
William Spellman, *Branch Mgr*
EMP: 86
SQ FT: 200,000
SALES (corp-wide): 16.4B **Publicly Held**
WEB: www.phelpsdodge.com
SIC: 3351 Copper rolling & drawing
HQ: Freeport Minerals Corporation
333 N Central Ave
Phoenix AZ 85004
602 366-8100

(G-2735)
FREEPORT-MCMORAN INC
48-94 Bayway Ave (07202)
PHONE..............................908 558-4361
EMP: 5
SALES (corp-wide): 16.4B **Publicly Held**
SIC: 1041 1044 1021 Gold ores; silver ores; copper ores
PA: Freeport-Mcmoran Inc.
333 N Central Ave
Phoenix AZ 85004
602 366-8100

(G-2736)
FULL CIRCLE MFG GROUP
534 S Front St (07202-3009)
PHONE..............................908 353-8933
Joseph Ioia, *President*
EMP: 10
SALES (est): 1.7MM **Privately Held**
SIC: 2899 Antifreeze compounds

(G-2737)
GARYLIN TOGS
Also Called: Body Wrappers
107 Trumbull St (07206-2165)
PHONE..............................908 354-7218
Fax: 908 354-4023
Michael Rubin, *President*
Robert Rubin, *Principal*
Eleanor Rubin, *Admin Sec*
EMP: 90 **EST:** 1955
SQ FT: 50,000
SALES (est): 9.2MM **Privately Held**
WEB: www.bodywrappers.com
SIC: 2339 2369 Women's & misses' athletic clothing & sportswear; girls' & children's outerwear

(G-2738)
GENERAL FILM PRODUCTS INC
107 Trumbull St Ste 302 (07206-2172)
PHONE..............................908 351-0454
Fax: 908 351-0482
Richard Eisner, *President*
Louis Antonacci, *President*
EMP: 50
SQ FT: 40,000
SALES (est): 9.3MM
SALES (corp-wide): 81.9MM **Privately Held**
SIC: 2673 Plastic & pliofilm bags
PA: Poly-Pak Industries, Inc
125 Spagnoli Rd
Melville NY 11747
631 293-6767

(G-2739)
GIBBONS COMPANY LTD
614 Progress St (07201-2057)
PHONE..............................441 294-5047
▲ **EMP:** 30
SALES (est): 1.9MM **Privately Held**
SIC: 5311 3161 Department stores; clothing & apparel carrying cases

(G-2740)
GRAY OVERHEAD DOOR CO
439 3rd Ave (07206-1034)
PHONE..............................908 355-3889
Grayton Acosta, *President*
Benazir Acosta, *Corp Secy*
EMP: 10

SQ FT: 10,000
SALES (est): 1.2MM **Privately Held**
SIC: 3442 1751 Garage doors, overhead: metal; garage door, installation or erection

(G-2741)
HAYWARD INDUSTRIAL PRODUCTS (HQ)
Also Called: Hayward Plastic Products Div
620 Division St (07201-2004)
PHONE..............................908 351-5400
Fax: 908 351-8721
Robert Davis, *CEO*
Oscar Davis, *CEO*
Dave Rudiger, *Manager*
◆ **EMP:** 250 **EST:** 1980
SALES (est): 87.5MM
SALES (corp-wide): 542.8MM **Privately Held**
SIC: 3089 3492 3491 3494 Plastic hardware & building products; control valves, fluid power: hydraulic & pneumatic; pressure valves & regulators, industrial; line strainers, for use in piping systems; sporting & athletic goods; blowers & fans
PA: Hayward Industries, Inc.
620 Division St
Elizabeth NJ 07201
908 351-5400

(G-2742)
HAYWARD INDUSTRIES INC (PA)
Also Called: Haywood Pool Products
620 Division St (07201-2004)
PHONE..............................908 351-5400
Fax: 908 351-4492
Oscar Davis, *Ch of Bd*
Robert Davis, *President*
Clark Hale, *President*
Sharon Bahr, *Vice Pres*
David Macnair, *Vice Pres*
◆ **EMP:** 350 **EST:** 1925
SQ FT: 30,000
SALES (est): 542.8MM **Privately Held**
WEB: www.haywardnet.com
SIC: 3589 3561 3423 3494 Swimming pool filter & water conditioning systems; pumps & pumping equipment; pumps, domestic: water or sump; leaf skimmers or swimming pool rakes; valves & pipe fittings; filters & strainers, pipeline; plastic hardware & building products; fittings for pipe, plastic

(G-2743)
HAYWARD INDUSTRIES INC
628 Henry St Bldg 6 (07201-2016)
PHONE..............................908 351-0899
Reuven Har-Even, *Vice Pres*
EMP: 5
SALES (corp-wide): 542.8MM **Privately Held**
SIC: 3589 Swimming pool filter & water conditioning systems
PA: Hayward Industries, Inc.
620 Division St
Elizabeth NJ 07201
908 351-5400

(G-2744)
HAYWARD POOL PRODUCTS INC
Also Called: Hayward Flow Control
620 Division St (07201-2004)
PHONE..............................908 351-5400
Fax: 908 351-1532
Oscar Davis, *Ch of Bd*
Margaret B Costello, *Vice Pres*
George Metkovich, *Vice Pres*
Erick Anderson, *Project Mgr*
Jim Kinney, *Facilities Mgr*
◆ **EMP:** 900 **EST:** 1980
SQ FT: 20,000
SALES (est): 5.2MM
SALES (corp-wide): 542.8MM **Privately Held**
SIC: 5091 3569 Swimming pools, equipment & supplies; heaters, swimming pool: electric
PA: Hayward Industries, Inc.
620 Division St
Elizabeth NJ 07201
908 351-5400

(G-2745)
HEDAYA HOME FASHIONS INC (PA)
1111 Jefferson Ave (07201-1371)
PHONE..............................908 352-0808
Joseph Hedaya, *Ch of Bd*
Nathan Hedaya, *President*
▲ **EMP:** 110
SQ FT: 50,000
SALES (est): 10.8MM **Privately Held**
SIC: 2392 2339 5131 Placemats, plastic or textile; towels, fabric & nonwoven: made from purchased materials; aprons, except rubber or plastic: women's, misses', juniors'; piece goods & notions

(G-2746)
IMPERIAL WELD RING CORP INC
80 Front St 88 (07206-1755)
P.O. Box 6646 (07206-6646)
PHONE..............................908 354-0011
Calvin Sierra, *President*
Alicia Borrero, *Office Mgr*
EMP: 20 **EST:** 1959
SQ FT: 12,000
SALES: 1.9MM **Privately Held**
SIC: 3429 3498 3494 Metal fasteners; fabricated pipe & fittings; valves & pipe fittings

(G-2747)
INNOVATIVE CONCEPTS DESIGN LLC
Also Called: Gemini Sound
107 Trumbull St Ste 203 (07206-2170)
PHONE..............................732 346-0061
Artie Cabasso, *CEO*
EMP: 10 **EST:** 2014
SQ FT: 100,000
SALES (est): 2.3MM **Privately Held**
SIC: 3651 Audio electronic systems

(G-2748)
INTERNATIONAL COCONUT CORP
225 W Grand St (07202-1205)
P.O. Box 3326 (07207-3326)
PHONE..............................908 289-1555
Fax: 908 289-1556
Arthur Kesselhaut, *President*
Richard Kesselhaut, *Vice Pres*
▲ **EMP:** 15 **EST:** 1978
SQ FT: 15,000
SALES (est): 2.4MM **Privately Held**
WEB: www.internationalcoconut.com
SIC: 2099 Coconut, desiccated & shredded

(G-2749)
JASPER FASHION LTD LBLTY CO
336 Murray St (07202-1723)
PHONE..............................917 561-4533
Moheuddin Ahmed, *President*
▲ **EMP:** 10 **EST:** 2008
SALES (est): 825.7K **Privately Held**
SIC: 5137 2361 Women's & children's clothing; dresses: girls', children's & infants'

(G-2750)
JF BRAUN & SONS INC
2 Slater Dr (07206-2128)
P.O. Box 1188 (07207-1188)
PHONE..............................908 393-7400
Stephen O Mara, *Chairman*
Ed Howard, *Exec VP*
Pierre La Plante, *Vice Pres*
Joann McRoberts, *CFO*
Pierre Laplante, *Sales Executive*
▲ **EMP:** 20
SQ FT: 7,116
SALES (est): 4.3MM **Privately Held**
WEB: www.jfbny.com
SIC: 2034 Dehydrated fruits, vegetables, soups

(G-2751)
LEGGS HNS BLI PLYTX FCTRY OUTL
651 Kapkowski Rd Ste 1008 (07201-4931)
PHONE..............................908 289-7262
Lasaunja Pretlow, *Manager*

EMP: 5
SALES (est): 366.4K **Privately Held**
SIC: 2211 Underwear fabrics, cotton

(G-2752)
LITHUANIAN BAKERY T J INC
131 Inslee Pl (07206-2010)
PHONE..............................908 354-0970
John Backiel, *President*
Janina Backiel, *Vice Pres*
EMP: 14 **EST:** 1968
SQ FT: 5,000
SALES (est): 1.7MM **Privately Held**
SIC: 2051 Breads, rolls & buns

(G-2753)
M HAND PALLETS
864 North Ave E (07201-2104)
PHONE..............................908 887-2100
EMP: 7
SALES (est): 545.8K **Privately Held**
SIC: 2448 Pallets, wood & wood with metal

(G-2754)
MARINE OIL SERVICE INC
450 S Front St (07202-3009)
PHONE..............................908 282-6440
Fax: 908 282-6444
Joseph Olivieri, *Manager*
Herminio Perez, *Manager*
EMP: 9
SALES (corp-wide): 29.3MM **Privately Held**
WEB: www.marineoilservice.com
SIC: 2992 Lubricating oils
PA: Marine Oil Service, Inc.
201 E City Hall Ave
Norfolk VA 23510
757 543-1446

(G-2755)
MASTERCRAFT ELECTROPLATING
801 Magnolia Ave Ste 4 (07201-1900)
PHONE..............................908 354-4404
Pat Obrien, *Principal*
EMP: 5
SQ FT: 5,500
SALES (est): 420K **Privately Held**
SIC: 3559 Automotive related machinery

(G-2756)
MASTERCRAFT METAL FINISHING
801 Magnolia Ave (07201-1900)
PHONE..............................908 354-4404
EMP: 5 **EST:** 2016
SALES (est): 291.2K **Privately Held**
SIC: 3471 Plating/Polishing Service

(G-2757)
METROFUSER LLC (PA)
475 Division St Bldg 1 (07201-2000)
PHONE..............................908 245-2100
Eric Katz, *CFO*
Marissa Rodriuez, *Administration*
EMP: 65
SQ FT: 10,000
SALES (est): 14MM **Privately Held**
WEB: www.metrofuser.com
SIC: 3575 Computer terminals

(G-2758)
NINE WEST HOLDINGS INC
Also Called: Kasper
651 Kapkowski Rd Ste 2032 (07201-4919)
PHONE..............................908 354-8895
EMP: 8
SALES (corp-wide): 2.2B **Privately Held**
WEB: www.kasper.net
SIC: 2337 Women's & misses' suits & coats
HQ: Nine West Holdings, Inc.
180 Rittenhouse Cir
Bristol PA 19007
215 785-4000

(G-2759)
NORTH EASTERN PALLET EXCHANGE
725 Spring St Ste 2 (07201-2045)
PHONE..............................908 289-0018
Toll Free:..............................888 -
EMP: 50 **EST:** 1996
SQ FT: 15,000

▲ = Import ▼=Export
◆ =Import/Export

SALES (est): 4.7MM **Privately Held**
SIC: 2448 Mfg Pallets

(G-2760)
NORTHEAST BINDERY INC
419 Trumbull St (07206-2114)
PHONE...............................908 436-3737
Fax: 908 436-3738
Bel Ramlochan, *President*
EMP: 16
SALES: 1.7MM **Privately Held**
SIC: 2789 Binding only: books, pamphlets, magazines, etc.

(G-2761)
NYP CORP (FRMR NY-PTERS CORP) (PA)
805 E Grand St (07201-2721)
PHONE...............................908 351-6550
Fax: 908 351-0108
Gerald La Belle, *President*
Jerry Labelle, *Vice Pres*
Don Yale, *Opers Mgr*
Don Ament, *Facilities Mgr*
Katie Coffey, *Purch Mgr*
▲ EMP: 100 EST: 1945
SQ FT: 60,000
SALES (est): 16.8MM **Privately Held**
WEB: www.nyp-corp.com
SIC: 2393 5199 2221 Textile bags; burlap; broadwoven fabric mills, manmade

(G-2762)
OBARE SERVICES LTD LBLTY CO
593 Meadow St (07201-1513)
P.O. Box 2437 (07207-2437)
PHONE...............................908 456-1887
Dan Obare, *CEO*
EMP: 4
SQ FT: 1,000
SALES (est): 242.1K **Privately Held**
SIC: 2541 Store & office display cases & fixtures

(G-2763)
ON DEMAND MACHINERY
Also Called: American Graphix
150 Broadway (07206-1856)
P.O. Box 240, Elizabethport (07206-0240)
PHONE...............................908 351-7137
John Jacobson, *Owner*
Mark Williamson, *Prdtn Mgr*
EMP: 12
SALES (est): 1.9MM **Privately Held**
WEB: www.odmachinery.com
SIC: 3555 Bookbinding machinery

(G-2764)
PABST ENTERPRISES EQUIPMENT CO
676 Pennsylvania Ave (07201-1214)
PHONE...............................908 353-2880
Fax: 908 353-1916
Robert D Verkouille, *CEO*
David E Bechtold, *President*
Jody Sackett, *Corp Secy*
Lidia Almeida, *Office Mgr*
EMP: 20 EST: 1934
SQ FT: 35,000
SALES: 2.1MM **Privately Held**
SIC: 3441 3599 3444 7692 Fabricated structural metal; machine shop, jobbing & repair; sheet metalwork; welding repair

(G-2765)
PAO BA AVO LLC
545 Edgar Rd (07202-3301)
PHONE...............................908 962-9090
Fernando Santos, *Manager*
EMP: 4
SALES (est): 172.5K **Privately Held**
SIC: 2051 Cakes, bakery: except frozen

(G-2766)
PEGASUS HOME FASHIONS INC
107 Trumbull St (07206-2165)
PHONE...............................908 965-1919
Carmine Spinella, *President*
◆ EMP: 80
SALES (est): 21.1MM **Privately Held**
WEB: www.pegasushomefashions.com
SIC: 2392 Cushions & pillows

(G-2767)
PPG ARCHITECTURAL FINISHES INC
Also Called: Glidden Professional Paint Ctr
1001 Newark Ave (07208-3576)
PHONE...............................908 353-2477
Cliff Brocker, *Owner*
EMP: 5
SALES (corp-wide): 14.2B **Publicly Held**
WEB: www.gliddenpaint.com
SIC: 2891 Adhesives
HQ: Ppg Architectural Finishes, Inc.
1 Ppg Pl
Pittsburgh PA 15272
412 434-3131

(G-2768)
PRIDE PRODUCTS MFG LLC
5 Slater Dr (07206-2151)
PHONE...............................908 353-1900
Joseph Yuan, *Principal*
EMP: 12
SALES (est): 387.8K **Privately Held**
SIC: 3944 Games, toys & children's vehicles

(G-2769)
PVH CORP
Also Called: Van Heusen
651 Kapkowski Rd Ste 1416 (07201-4934)
PHONE...............................908 685-0050
Philip Gallina, *Manager*
EMP: 7
SALES (corp-wide): 8.9B **Publicly Held**
WEB: www.pvh.com
SIC: 2321 Men's & boys' furnishings
PA: Pvh Corp.
200 Madison Ave Bsmt 1
New York NY 10016
212 381-3500

(G-2770)
QUALITY SWISS SCREW MACHINE CO
849 4th Ave (07202-3853)
PHONE...............................908 289-4334
Fax: 908 289-8451
Juan Monserrate, *Branch Mgr*
EMP: 4
SALES (corp-wide): 2.1MM **Privately Held**
WEB: www.qualityswiss.com
SIC: 3469 Machine parts, stamped or pressed metal
PA: Quality Swiss Screw Machine Co Inc
960 Mountain Ave
Mountainside NJ
908 654-1881

(G-2771)
RAPSOCO INC
648 Newark Ave (07208-3539)
PHONE...............................908 977-7321
Richard Atuahene, *CEO*
EMP: 4
SALES: 500K **Privately Held**
SIC: 3999 Manufacturing industries

(G-2772)
RENAE TELECOM LLC
745 Thomas St (07202-2743)
PHONE...............................908 362-8112
Raymond C Meyers,
EMP: 99
SALES (est): 9MM **Privately Held**
SIC: 3663 Radio & TV communications equipment

(G-2773)
ROYAL PRIME INC
1027 Newark Ave Ste 1 (07208-3592)
PHONE...............................908 354-7600
Fax: 908 354-6341
Andrew Inelli, *President*
◆ EMP: 60 EST: 1978
SQ FT: 85,000
SALES (est): 7.3MM **Privately Held**
SIC: 3442 Window & door frames

(G-2774)
SMITHFIELD PACKAGED MEATS CORP
Also Called: 814 Americas
814 2nd Ave (07202-3804)
PHONE...............................908 354-2674

Michael Patraceolla, *General Mgr*
Alex Tanquino, *Supervisor*
EMP: 30 **Privately Held**
SIC: 2013 Sausages from purchased meat
HQ: Smithfield Packaged Meats Corp.
805 E Kemper Rd
Cincinnati OH 45246
513 782-3800

(G-2775)
STARPHIL INC
107 Trumbull St R12 (07206-2165)
PHONE...............................908 353-8943
EMP: 5
SQ FT: 12,000
SALES: 500K **Privately Held**
SIC: 2511 Mfg Wood Household Furniture

(G-2776)
SUPERIOR LIGHTING INC
1245 Virginia St (07208-3068)
PHONE...............................908 759-0199
Abraham Knopfler, *CEO*
Chaya Knoppler, *President*
▲ EMP: 10
SQ FT: 8,000
SALES: 3.4MM **Privately Held**
SIC: 3646 3645 Commercial indusl & institutional electric lighting fixtures; residential lighting fixtures

(G-2777)
SUPERIOR POWDER COATING INC (PA)
Also Called: Spct
600 Progress St (07201-2018)
PHONE...............................908 351-8707
Fax: 908 351-0870
Peter G Markey, *President*
Charles D Briggs, *Vice Pres*
Susan Santiago, *Corp Comm Staff*
Glenn Ashton, *Director*
▲ EMP: 111
SQ FT: 112,000
SALES (est): 17.5MM **Privately Held**
WEB: www.superiorpowder.com
SIC: 3479 Varnishing of metal products; coating of metals & formed products

(G-2778)
SWISSRAY AMERICA INC
Also Called: Swissray Medical Systems
1180 Mclester St Ste 2 (07201-2931)
PHONE...............................908 353-0971
Fax: 908 644-6498
Ueli Laupper, *CEO*
Michael J Baker, *CEO*
Rudy Laupper, *Chairman*
▲ EMP: 34 EST: 1997
SALES (est): 1.2MM **Privately Held**
SIC: 3844 X-ray apparatus & tubes
HQ: Swissray International, Inc.
1090 King Georges Rd 1203
Edison NJ 08837

(G-2779)
TOTAL INSTALLATIONS
Also Called: Total Remodeling
941 Olive St (07201-1922)
PHONE...............................908 943-3211
Javier Barrera, *Owner*
EMP: 4
SALES: 80K **Privately Held**
SIC: 3442 Metal doors, sash & trim

(G-2780)
UNIVERSAL VALVE COMPANY INC
478 Schiller St (07206-2183)
PHONE...............................908 351-0606
Fax: 908 351-0369
Martin Pettesch, *Principal*
Mike Farinha, *Prdtn Mgr*
Peter Mascis, *Natl Sales Mgr*
Joe Zulewski, *Mktg Coord*
▲ EMP: 15
SALES (est): 3.7MM **Privately Held**
WEB: www.universalvalve.com
SIC: 3492 3321 Fluid power valves & hose fittings; manhole covers, metal

(G-2781)
VF OUTDOOR LLC
Also Called: Tbl Licencing
651 Kapkowski Rd Ste 2034 (07201-4935)
PHONE...............................908 352-5390

EMP: 4
SALES (corp-wide): 11.8B **Publicly Held**
SIC: 3143 Men's footwear, except athletic
HQ: Vf Outdoor, Llc
2701 Harbor Bay Pkwy
Alameda CA 94502
510 618-3500

(G-2782)
WILD FLAVORS INC
Also Called: Wild Juice US
132 Corbin St Bldg 1200 (07201-2910)
PHONE...............................908 820-9800
EMP: 11
SALES (corp-wide): 60.8B **Publicly Held**
SIC: 2087 Flavoring extracts & syrups
HQ: Wild Flavors, Inc.
1261 Pacific Ave
Erlanger KY 41018

Elizabethport
Union County

(G-2783)
EDDIE DOMANI
20 Butler St (07206-1527)
PHONE...............................908 469-8863
Eddie Domani, *Owner*
▲ EMP: 4
SALES (est): 444.4K **Privately Held**
SIC: 2325 Slacks, dress: men's, youths' & boys'

(G-2784)
GENESIS LIGHTING MFG INC
107 Trumbull St Ste 104 (07206-2171)
PHONE...............................908 352-6720
Jay Gindoff, *President*
▲ EMP: 5
SQ FT: 85,000
SALES (est): 5MM **Privately Held**
SIC: 3646 Commercial indusl & institutional electric lighting fixtures

(G-2785)
IMPACT DESIGN INC
248 3rd St (07206-2052)
PHONE...............................908 289-2900
Martin Templer, *President*
▲ EMP: 25
SQ FT: 15,000
SALES (est): 1.5MM **Privately Held**
SIC: 5137 2353 Women's & children's clothing; hats, caps & millinery

(G-2786)
PAPETTIS HYGRADE EGG PDTS INC (DH)
Also Called: Michael Foods
1 Papetti Plz (07206-1421)
PHONE...............................908 282-7900
Fax: 908 354-8660
Arthur Papetti, *President*
Stephen Papetti, *Exec VP*
Alfred Papetti, *Vice Pres*
Anthony Papetti, *Vice Pres*
Jack Novak, *Human Res Dir*
▼ EMP: 550
SQ FT: 75,000
SALES (est): 136.1MM **Publicly Held**
SIC: 2015 Egg processing; eggs, processed: desiccated (dried); eggs, processed: frozen; eggs, processed: dehydrated
HQ: M.G. Waldbaum Company
301 Carlson Pkwy Ste 400
Minnetonka MN 55305
952 258-4000

Elmer
Salem County

(G-2787)
A CHEERFUL GIVER INC
300 Front St (08318-2143)
PHONE...............................856 358-4438
Fax: 856 358-7763
Tony Gross, *President*
▲ EMP: 10
SQ FT: 15,000

SALES (est): 1.7MM **Privately Held**
WEB: www.acheerfulgiver.com
SIC: **2099** 5945 5999 5947 Sauces:
gravy, dressing & dip mixes; arts & crafts
supplies; candle shops; gift shop; candles

(G-2788)
AKS PHARMA INC
201 Front St (08318-2141)
PHONE.................................856 521-0710
EMP: 4
SALES (est): 251.5K **Privately Held**
SIC: **2834** Pharmaceutical preparations

(G-2789)
ARCHER PLASTICS INC
Also Called: Archer Seating Clearing House
1510 Jesse Bridge Rd (08318-4563)
PHONE.................................856 692-0242
Ruth Archer, *President*
Steve Archer, *Vice Pres*
EMP: 5
SALES: 700K **Privately Held**
WEB: www.msequip.com
SIC: **2531** Stadium seating

(G-2790)
COLE BROTHERS MARBLE & GRANITE
892 Parvin Mill Rd (08318-4005)
PHONE.................................856 455-7989
Ruth Cole, *President*
Benjamin Cole, *Vice Pres*
EMP: 6
SQ FT: 8,000
SALES (est): 767K **Privately Held**
WEB: www.colebrothersgranite.com
SIC: **3281** 1752 Marble, building: cut &
shaped; granite, cut & shaped; carpet lay-
ing; ceramic floor tile installation; linoleum
installation; vinyl floor tile & sheet installa-
tion

(G-2791)
ELMER TIMES CO INC
21 State St (08318-2145)
PHONE.................................856 358-6171
Fax: 856 358-7951
Mark Foster, *President*
Preston Foster III, *President*
Pamela S Brunner, *Corp Secy*
EMP: 5
SQ FT: 3,000
SALES (est): 310K **Privately Held**
SIC: **2711** Newspapers: publishing only,
not printed on site

(G-2792)
FAVS CORP
Also Called: Enviro Safe Wtr Trtmnt Systems
331 Husted Station Rd (08318-3804)
PHONE.................................856 358-1515
Fax: 856 358-4341
Anthony Favorito, *President*
EMP: 6
SALES (est): 820K **Privately Held**
SIC: **5074** 5999 3589 1711 Water purifi-
cation equipment; water purification
equipment; sewage & water treatment
equipment; plumbing, heating, air-condi-
tioning contractors

(G-2793)
J SPINELLI & SONS INC
Also Called: J Spinelli & Sons Excavating
615 Gershal Ave (08318-4216)
PHONE.................................856 691-3133
Joseph Spinelli III, *President*
Dino Spinelli, *President*
EMP: 50
SALES (est): 7.3MM **Privately Held**
SIC: **4212** 2041 7549 Dump truck
haulage; doughs, frozen or refrigerated;
towing services

(G-2794)
MANUTECH INC
29 State St (08318-2145)
P.O. Box 758 (08318-0758)
PHONE.................................856 358-6136
Fax: 856 358-6279
Ed Deinarowicz, *CEO*
Hendrick Severe, *Warehouse Mgr*
EMP: 4
SQ FT: 6,000

SALES (est): 275K **Privately Held**
SIC: **3469** Metal stampings

(G-2795)
PERFECT SHAPES INC
Also Called: Things 2 B
110 Salem St (08318-2271)
PHONE.................................856 783-3844
Fax: 856 627-5665
Colin Broecker, *President*
EMP: 4
SQ FT: 44,000
SALES: 1MM **Privately Held**
SIC: **5032** 3299 Stucco; stucco

(G-2796)
RICHARD SHAFER
Also Called: Shafer Brothers Trailers
38 Martin Ave (08318-4400)
PHONE.................................856 358-3483
Richard Shafer, *Owner*
EMP: 4 EST: 1967
SQ FT: 2,400
SALES: 500K **Privately Held**
SIC: **3715** 7539 Trailer bodies; trailer re-
pair

(G-2797)
S J QUARRY MATERIALS INC
615 Gershal Ave (08318-4216)
PHONE.................................856 691-3133
Joseph Spinelli III, *President*
Dino Spinelli, *Assistant VP*
EMP: 55
SALES (est): 5.5MM **Privately Held**
SIC: **1411** Dimension stone

(G-2798)
SIGN SPEC INC
602 Centerton Rd (08318-3918)
PHONE.................................856 663-2292
Charles Jacques, *Vice Pres*
Michael A Pagliuso, *Vice Pres*
EMP: 55
SQ FT: 43,000
SALES (est): 4.5MM **Privately Held**
WEB: www.signspec.com
SIC: **3993** Electric signs

(G-2799)
UNITED RESIN INC
321 Willow Grove Rd (08318-2046)
PHONE.................................856 358-2574
Fax: 856 358-6464
Albert O'Brien, *President*
EMP: 12
SQ FT: 22,000
SALES (est): 885.7K **Privately Held**
WEB: www.unitedresincorp.com
SIC: **2821** Acrylic resins

(G-2800)
VANGUARD PRINTING
531 Garden Rd (08318-3933)
PHONE.................................856 358-2665
Fax: 856 358-7234
Charles Panek, *Owner*
Lynn Hickey, *Purch Mgr*
William Wilcox, *Marketing Staff*
EMP: 4
SALES (est): 240K **Privately Held**
SIC: **2752** Commercial printing, offset

Elmwood Park
Bergen County

(G-2801)
ADAGIO TEAS INC (PA)
170 Kipp Ave (07407-1123)
PHONE.................................973 253-7400
Michael Cramer, *CEO*
Nicholas Lin, *Engineer*
Ashley Williams, *Admin Asst*
◆ EMP: 5
SALES (est): 2MM **Privately Held**
WEB: www.adagio.com
SIC: **5149** 5499 5719 2095 Tea; tea;
kitchenware; coffee extracts

(G-2802)
AGFA CORPORATION (HQ)
Also Called: AGFA Graphics
611 River Dr Ste 305 (07407-1338)
P.O. Box 471500, Tulsa OK (74147-1500)
PHONE.................................800 540-2432
Gunther Mertenes, *President*
Michael Patrick, *President*
Steve White, *President*
Annelies Daenen, *Vice Pres*
Nancy Murray, *Facilities Mgr*
▲ EMP: 400
SALES (est): 6.6MM
SALES (corp-wide): 526.3MM **Privately Held**
WEB: www.agfa.com
SIC: **3861** Photographic equipment & sup-
plies; film, sensitized motion picture, X-
ray, still camera, etc.; photographic
processing chemicals
PA: Agfa-Gevaert Nv
Septestraat 27
Mortsel 2640
344 421-11

(G-2803)
AGFA CORPORATION
611 River Dr Ste 305 (07407-1338)
PHONE.................................201 440-0111
Fax: 201 342-4742
Brian Paradis, *Business Mgr*
Hubert Uytdewilligen, *Plant Mgr*
Luc Colijn, *Project Mgr*
Jim Supple, *Project Mgr*
Thomas Zaher, *Warehouse Mgr*
EMP: 50
SALES (corp-wide): 526.3MM **Privately Held**
SIC: **3861** Photographic equipment & sup-
plies
HQ: Agfa Corporation
611 River Dr Ste 305
Elmwood Park NJ 07407
800 540-2432

(G-2804)
AGFA FINANCE CORP
Also Called: AGFA Corporation, Elmwood
Park
611 River Dr (07407-1325)
PHONE.................................201 796-0058
▲ EMP: 112
SALES (est): 5.4MM
SALES (corp-wide): 526.3MM **Privately Held**
SIC: **3861** Photographic equipment & sup-
plies
HQ: Agfa Corporation
611 River Dr Ste 305
Elmwood Park NJ 07407
800 540-2432

(G-2805)
B&F AND SON MASONRY COMPANY
Also Called: B & F Mason Contractors
10 North St (07407-2246)
P.O. Box 187 (07407-0187)
PHONE.................................201 791-7630
Fax: 201 791-0513
Gino Fasolo, *President*
EMP: 45
SALES (est): 5.4MM **Privately Held**
SIC: **3271** 1741 1771 Blocks, concrete:
acoustical; masonry & other stonework;
concrete work

(G-2806)
BLACK & DECKER (US) INC
Also Called: Dewalt Industrial Tools
213 Us Highway 46 (07407-1902)
PHONE.................................201 475-3524
Fax: 201 475-3526
Dan Calabresse, *Principal*
EMP: 6
SALES (corp-wide): 12.7B **Publicly Held**
WEB: www.dewalt.com
SIC: **3546** Power-driven handtools
HQ: Black & Decker (U.S.) Inc.
1000 Stanley Dr
New Britain CT 06053
860 225-5111

(G-2807)
C & S FENCING INC
75 Midland Ave 77 (07407-2414)
PHONE.................................201 797-5440
Ciro Spinella, *President*
Antonino Spinella, *Vice Pres*
Graciela Locancore, *Treasurer*
EMP: 30
SQ FT: 8,400
SALES: 3.4MM **Privately Held**
SIC: **1799** 3446 Fence construction;
fences, gates, posts & flagpoles

(G-2808)
CARIB CHEMICAL CO INC
Also Called: Carib International
103 Main Ave (07407-3203)
PHONE.................................201 791-6700
Michael Granatell, *President*
EMP: 13
SALES (corp-wide): 1.6MM **Privately Held**
SIC: **2865** Dyes & pigments
PA: Carib Chemical Co Inc
125 Main Ave
Elmwood Park NJ 07407
201 791-6700

(G-2809)
CARIB CHEMICAL CO INC (PA)
Also Called: Grant Industries
125 Main Ave (07407-3203)
PHONE.................................201 791-6700
Michael Granatell, *President*
▲ EMP: 13
SQ FT: 1,000
SALES (est): 1.6MM **Privately Held**
SIC: **2865** 5169 Dyes & pigments;
dyestuffs

(G-2810)
COLEX IMAGING INC
55-57 Bushes Ln (07407)
PHONE.................................201 414-5575
Werner Waden, *President*
EMP: 4
SALES (est): 458.2K **Privately Held**
SIC: **3861** Printing equipment, photo-
graphic

(G-2811)
COMPUTER SOURCES
37 Leliarts Ln (07407-3201)
PHONE.................................201 791-9443
Igor Kholostoy, *President*
EMP: 2
SQ FT: 800
SALES: 3MM **Privately Held**
SIC: **7373** 7372 Value-added resellers,
computer systems; application computer
software; educational computer software;
operating systems computer software;
publishers' computer software

(G-2812)
CORBAN ENERGY GROUP CORP
418 Falmouth Ave (07407-3305)
PHONE.................................201 509-8555
Daniel Chung, *President*
Howard Adams, *General Mgr*
▲ EMP: 20 EST: 2012
SQ FT: 20,000
SALES: 150MM **Privately Held**
SIC: **1623** 3443 5085 Natural gas com-
pressor station construction; cryogenic
tanks, for liquids & gases; tanks, pressur-
ized

(G-2813)
CUMMINS - ALLISON CORP
Also Called: Cummins-Allison
495 Boulevard Ste 6 (07407-2041)
PHONE.................................201 791-2394
Ralph Nabors, *Manager*
EMP: 6
SALES (corp-wide): 377.9MM **Privately Held**
WEB: www.gsb.com
SIC: **5044** 7629 3519 Office equipment;
business machine repair, electric; internal
combustion engines
PA: Cummins - Allison Corp.
852 Feehanville Dr
Mount Prospect IL 60056
847 759-6403

(G-2814)
CUSTOM CHEMICALS CORP
30 Paul Kohner Pl (07407-2621)
PHONE..............................201 791-5100
Robert C Vielee, *President*
EMP: 600
SQ FT: 105,000
SALES (est): 47.1MM **Privately Held**
SIC: 2893 2851 2816 Printing ink; lacquers, varnishes, enamels & other coatings; inorganic pigments

(G-2815)
DOR-WIN MANUFACTURING CO
109 Midland Ave (07407-2441)
PHONE..............................201 796-4300
Marco Cangialosi, *President*
Rosalba Scaravilli, *Corp Secy*
Sarah Calderone, *Vice Pres*
EMP: 50 EST: 1962
SQ FT: 75,000
SALES (est): 5MM **Privately Held**
WEB: www.dor-winmfg.com
SIC: 3089 3442 2431 Doors, folding: plastic or plastic coated fabric; window frames & sash, plastic; storm doors or windows, metal; millwork

(G-2816)
DORWIN MANUFACTURING CO
109 Midland Ave (07407-2441)
PHONE..............................201 796-4300
Fax: 201 791-1962
Marco Cangialosi, *President*
Sara Caldiron, *General Mgr*
Roslba Scaravilli, *General Mgr*
EMP: 48
SALES (est): 3.5MM **Privately Held**
SIC: 3442 Metal doors

(G-2817)
DR PREGERS SENSIBLE FOODS INC
9 Boumar Pl (07407-2615)
PHONE..............................201 703-1300
Larry Praeger, *CEO*
Eric Somberg, *Ch of Bd*
Adam Somberg, *President*
Jeff Cohen, *COO*
David Horvath, *Exec VP*
▲ **EMP:** 100
SQ FT: 60,000
SALES (est): 30.9MM **Privately Held**
SIC: 2038 Frozen specialties

(G-2818)
ELMWOOD PRESS INC
85 Main Ave (07407-3203)
PHONE..............................201 794-6273
Fax: 201 794-9085
Gene Murphy, *President*
Al Cowie, *Treasurer*
EMP: 13
SQ FT: 5,000
SALES (est): 1.6MM **Privately Held**
SIC: 2752 Commercial printing, offset

(G-2819)
EMDEON CORPORATION
Also Called: Medical Manager
669 River Dr Ste 240 (07407-1361)
PHONE..............................201 703-3400
EMP: 2258
SQ FT: 14,000
SALES (est): 92.1MM **Privately Held**
SIC: 7373 3089 Computer Systems Design Mfg Plastic Products

(G-2820)
G & H SOHO INC
413 Market St (07407-2605)
PHONE..............................201 216-9400
Fax: 201 216-1778
James Harris, *President*
Robert Tinkham, *General Mgr*
Gerald F Burstein, *Vice Pres*
Gerry Burstein, *Vice Pres*
▲ **EMP:** 15
SQ FT: 9,500
SALES (est): 2.3MM **Privately Held**
WEB: www.ghsoho.com
SIC: 2732 Book printing

(G-2821)
GF SUPPLIES LLC (PA)
Also Called: Sigo Signs
319 E 54th St (07407-2712)
PHONE..............................336 539-1666
Jacob Gluck, *CEO*
Joel Freund,
EMP: 2
SQ FT: 10,000
SALES: 2MM **Privately Held**
SIC: 5099 3993 Signs, except electric; signs & advertising specialties

(G-2822)
GRANT INDUSTRIES INC
103 Main Ave (07407-3203)
PHONE..............................201 791-8700
Fax: 201 791-0038
Steven Grant, *Principal*
EMP: 100
SALES (corp-wide): 29.4MM **Privately Held**
SIC: 2834 Pharmaceutical preparations
PA: Grant Industries, Inc.
125 Main Ave
Elmwood Park NJ 07407
201 791-6700

(G-2823)
GRANT INDUSTRIES INC (PA)
125 Main Ave (07407-3203)
PHONE..............................201 791-6700
Steven Grant, *CEO*
Michael Granatell, *President*
David Granatell, *Vice Pres*
Joseph Granatell, *Vice Pres*
Paul Granatell, *Vice Pres*
▲ **EMP:** 56
SQ FT: 40,000
SALES (est): 29.4MM **Privately Held**
SIC: 2834 Pharmaceutical preparations

(G-2824)
GRANT INDUSTRIES INC
125 Main Ave (07407-3203)
PHONE..............................201 791-6700
Tom Granatell, *Manager*
EMP: 10
SALES (corp-wide): 29.4MM **Privately Held**
SIC: 2834 Pharmaceutical preparations
PA: Grant Industries, Inc.
125 Main Ave
Elmwood Park NJ 07407
201 791-6700

(G-2825)
INDUSTRIE BITOSSI INC (DH)
Also Called: Italian Tile Decor
410 Market St (07407-2607)
PHONE..............................201 796-0722
Fax: 201 796-2313
Rittoriano Bittosi, *President*
Giacomo Bandino, *CFO*
▲ **EMP:** 38
SQ FT: 10,000
SALES (est): 2MM **Privately Held**
SIC: 3253 Mosaic tile, glazed & unglazed: ceramic
HQ: Industrie Bitossi Spa
Via Pietramarina 53
Vinci FI 50059
057 170-9535

(G-2826)
INTERNTNAL GLOBL SOLUTIONS INC
Also Called: Green Life America
130 Kipp Ave (07407-1011)
PHONE..............................201 791-1500
Kozo Okada, *Owner*
▲ **EMP:** 4
SALES (est): 280K **Privately Held**
SIC: 3949 Sporting & athletic goods

(G-2827)
JOHN WM MACY CHEESESTICKS INC
Also Called: JOHN WM. MACY'S CHEESESTICKS
80 Kipp Ave (07407-1011)
PHONE..............................201 791-8036
Fax: 201 797-5068
John W Macy, *President*
Tim Macy, *Vice Pres*
Elizabeth Schwartz, *Sales Dir*
Joy Macy, *Admin Sec*
▲ **EMP:** 60
SQ FT: 45,000
SALES: 11.2MM **Privately Held**
WEB: www.cheesesticks.com
SIC: 2052 Cookies & crackers

(G-2828)
KEYENCE CORPORATION AMERICA (HQ)
669 River Dr Ste 403 (07407-1361)
PHONE..............................201 930-0100
Fax: 201 930-1883
Tiffany Stallworth, *General Mgr*
Katsuhiro Yoshii, *Principal*
Greg Glover, *Project Mgr*
Ron Maul, *Project Mgr*
Wesley McBride, *Technical Mgr*
▲ **EMP:** 50
SQ FT: 15,000
SALES (est): 162.4MM
SALES (corp-wide): 4.9B **Privately Held**
SIC: 3825 5084 3674 Instruments to measure electricity; measuring & testing equipment, electrical; semiconductors & related devices
PA: Keyence Corporation
1-3-14, Higashinakajima, Higashiyo-dogawa-Ku
Osaka OSK 533-0
663 791-111

(G-2829)
KREISLER INDUSTRIAL CORP (HQ)
180 Van Riper Ave (07407-2622)
PHONE..............................201 773-6829
Fax: 201 791-8015
Edward A Stern, *Ch of Bd*
Michael D Stern, *President*
Kalman Morocz, *Manager*
EMP: 83 EST: 1956
SQ FT: 1,000
SALES (est): 19.9MM
SALES (corp-wide): 51.1MM **Publicly Held**
SIC: 3724 Aircraft engines & engine parts
PA: Kreisler Manufacturing Corp
180 Van Riper Ave
Elmwood Park NJ 07407
201 791-0700

(G-2830)
KREISLER MANUFACTURING CORP (PA)
Also Called: Kreisler Industrial
180 Van Riper Ave (07407-2610)
PHONE..............................201 791-0700
Michael D Stern, *President*
Edward A Stern, *President*
EMP: 9 EST: 1968
SQ FT: 52,000
SALES (est): 51.1MM **Publicly Held**
WEB: www.kreisler-ind.com
SIC: 3728 3724 Aircraft body assemblies & parts; turbines, aircraft type

(G-2831)
LACOA INC
21 Wallace St (07407-2612)
P.O. Box 839 (07407-0839)
PHONE..............................973 754-1000
Hector Baralt, *President*
Marilyn Van Vink, *Manager*
▲ **EMP:** 9
SALES (est): 1.7MM **Privately Held**
SIC: 2672 2261 2796 Coated & laminated paper; embossing cotton broadwoven fabrics; platemaking services; commercial printing

(G-2832)
LOCAL CONCRETE SUP & EQP CORP
Also Called: Nyc Concrete Materials
475 Market St Ste 3fl (07407-3100)
PHONE..............................201 797-7979
Tino Lemanna, *President*
EMP: 7
SQ FT: 1,435
SALES (est): 501K **Privately Held**
SIC: 3241 Masonry cement

(G-2833)
MARCAL MANUFACTURING LLC (DH)
Also Called: Soundview Paper Company
1 Market St (07407-1401)
PHONE..............................201 703-6225
Ray Heuchling, *Vice Pres*
John McLean, *Vice Pres*
William Schlenger, *Vice Pres*
David Freeswick, *VP Mfg*
Donna McGauley, *Safety Mgr*
◆ **EMP:** 9
SQ FT: 10,000
SALES (est): 281.1MM
SALES (corp-wide): 473.3MM **Privately Held**
SIC: 2676 Sanitary paper products; towels, paper: made from purchased paper; napkins, paper: made from purchased paper; toilet paper: made from purchased paper
HQ: Soundview Paper Mills Llc
1 Sound Shore Dr Ste 203
Greenwich CT 06830
201 796-4000

(G-2834)
MARCAL PAPER MILLS LLC
1 Market St (07407-1493)
PHONE..............................800 631-8451
Fax: 201 796-0470
Debi Mims, *Vice Pres*
Paul Lowry, *Opers Staff*
Nancy Damone, *Manager*
Fred Smagorinsky,
EMP: 800
SALES (est): 200.6MM
SALES (corp-wide): 473.3MM **Privately Held**
SIC: 2676 Sanitary paper products
HQ: Soundview Paper Mills Llc
1 Sound Shore Dr Ste 203
Greenwich CT 06830
201 796-4000

(G-2835)
MEDICRAFT INC
50 Bushes Ln (07407-3204)
PHONE..............................201 797-8820
Francis Phillips, *President*
Michael Phillips, *President*
Ian Tnocman, *Engineer*
Jeanne Phillips, *Admin Sec*
EMP: 35
SQ FT: 4,000
SALES (est): 5.9MM **Privately Held**
WEB: www.medicraftinc.com
SIC: 3841 3354 Surgical & medical instruments; aluminum extruded products

(G-2836)
MINIATURE FOLDING INC
14 Wenzel St (07407-2601)
PHONE..............................201 773-6477
Christopher Taliercio, *President*
EMP: 10
SALES (est): 1.4MM **Privately Held**
WEB: www.miniaturefolding.com
SIC: 2789 Trade binding services

(G-2837)
ML WOODWORK INC
255 Falmouth Ave (07407-2809)
PHONE..............................201 953-2175
Michal Lenczewski, *Principal*
EMP: 4
SALES (est): 370.8K **Privately Held**
SIC: 2431 Millwork

(G-2838)
NAN BREAD DISTRIBUTION
41 Leliarts Ln (07407-3201)
PHONE..............................201 475-9311
Alaa Moustafa, *Owner*
EMP: 4
SALES (est): 212.7K **Privately Held**
SIC: 2051 Bread, cake & related products

(G-2839)
O E M MANUFACTURERS LTD INC
65 Leliarts Ln (07407-3201)
PHONE..............................201 475-8585
Westley Zion, *President*
Stephanie McFarlane, *Vice Pres*
EMP: 8

SQ FT: 5,000
SALES (est): 674.8K **Privately Held**
SIC: 3451 Screw machine products

(G-2840)
PAIGE COMPANY CONTAINERS INC (PA)
1 Paul Kohner Pl (07407-2614)
PHONE..............................201 461-7800
Fax: 201 461-2677
Allan Levine, *President*
Michael Levine, *Vice Pres*
Thomas Quinn, *Production*
Jonathan Chazin, *Treasurer*
▼ **EMP:** 25
SQ FT: 10,000
SALES (est): 5.5MM **Privately Held**
WEB: www.paigecompany.com
SIC: 2653 Boxes, corrugated: made from purchased materials

(G-2841)
PATH SILICONES INC (PA)
21 Wallace St (07407-2612)
P.O. Box 430 (07407-0430)
PHONE..............................201 796-0833
Robert Baldanzi, *CEO*
Ted A Baldanzi, *Admin Sec*
▲ **EMP:** 10
SQ FT: 30,000
SALES (est): 1.1MM **Privately Held**
SIC: 3339 5169 Silicon refining (primary, over 99% pure); silicon lubricants

(G-2842)
PENN COLOR INC
30 Kohner Dr (07407-2614)
PHONE..............................201 791-5100
Bob Vielee, *General Mgr*
John Palumbo, *Marketing Staff*
EMP: 175
SALES (corp-wide): 183.9MM **Privately Held**
SIC: 2865 Color pigments, organic
PA: Penn Color, Inc.
    400 Old Dublin Pike
    Doylestown PA 18901
    215 345-6550

(G-2843)
PHILLIPS PRECISION INC
Also Called: Phillips Precision Medicraft
7 Paul Kohner Pl (07407-2614)
PHONE..............................201 797-8820
Fax: 201 797-3039
Michael Phillips, *President*
John Phillips, *President*
Francis Phillips, *Principal*
Vadim Shpak, *Engineer*
Jose Valentin, *Engineer*
EMP: 120
SQ FT: 40,000
SALES (est): 28.2MM **Privately Held**
WEB: www.phillipsprecision.com
SIC: 3841 Medical instruments & equipment, blood & bone work

(G-2844)
PHYTOCEUTICALS INC
37 Midland Ave Ste 1 (07407-2506)
PHONE..............................201 791-2255
Mostafa Omar, *President*
Amira Omar, *Vice Pres*
Iris Wong, *Marketing Staff*
▲ **EMP:** 6
SQ FT: 2,000
SALES: 700K **Privately Held**
WEB: www.phytoc-usa.com
SIC: 5122 2834 Pharmaceuticals; dermatologicals

(G-2845)
POTTI-BAGS INC
120 Ackerman Ave (07407-1605)
PHONE..............................201 796-5555
H Scott Price, *President*
EMP: 5
SALES (est): 714.2K **Privately Held**
SIC: 5113 2673 Bags, paper & disposable plastic; plastic bags: made from purchased materials

(G-2846)
RAMSEY GRAPHICS AND PRINTING
262 Market St Ste 1 (07407-2048)
PHONE..............................201 300-2912
David Ramsey, *President*
EMP: 6
SALES (est): 495.6K **Privately Held**
SIC: 7336 2759 Graphic arts & related design; commercial printing

(G-2847)
RECYCLE-TECH CORP
418 Falmouth Ave (07407-3305)
PHONE..............................201 475-5000
Fax: 201 475-5001
Daniel Chung, *President*
Howard Adams, *General Mgr*
John Kim, *General Mgr*
Joon Park, *Marketing Mgr*
▲ **EMP:** 10
SALES (est): 4MM **Privately Held**
WEB: www.recycletech.net
SIC: 5093 3559 Plastics scrap; recycling machinery

(G-2848)
RELIABLE ENVELOPE AND GRAPHICS
85 Main Ave (07407-3203)
PHONE..............................201 794-7756
Fax: 201 794-1319
Eugene Murphy, *President*
EMP: 35
SQ FT: 26,000
SALES (est): 5.2MM **Privately Held**
WEB: www.reliableenvelope.com
SIC: 2759 2752 Envelopes: printing; commercial printing, lithographic

(G-2849)
SEALED AIR HOLDINGS
200 Riverfront Blvd # 301 (07407-1038)
PHONE..............................201 791-7600
Warren Kudman, *Principal*
EMP: 5
SALES (est): 482.5K
SALES (corp-wide): 4.4B **Publicly Held**
SIC: 3089 2621 5162 Cases, plastic; paper mills; plastics products
PA: Sealed Air Corporation
    2415 Cascade Pointe Blvd
    Charlotte NC 28208
    980 221-3235

(G-2850)
SOUNDVIEW PAPER HOLDINGS LLC (PA)
1 Market St (07407-1401)
PHONE..............................201 796-4000
Karl Meyers, *CEO*
Rob Baron, *President*
John Glaze, *Exec VP*
Carrie Williamson, *Senior VP*
Jim Andrews, *CFO*
▲ **EMP:** 925
SALES (est): 473.3MM **Privately Held**
SIC: 2676 2656 Sanitary paper products; towels, paper: made from purchased paper; napkins, paper: made from purchased paper; toilet paper: made from purchased paper; sanitary food containers; straws, drinking: made from purchased material

(G-2851)
STRAVAL MACHINE CO INC
20 Bushes Ln (07407-3204)
PHONE..............................973 340-9955
Fax: 973 340-9933
Ed Simin, *President*
Maria Nienajadlo, *General Mgr*
Wilson Diaz, *Project Engr*
Zaneta Spoljarik, *Administration*
EMP: 25
SALES (est): 1.2MM **Privately Held**
SIC: 3592 3599 Valves; machine shop, jobbing & repair

(G-2852)
TUFF MFG CO INC
4 Midland Ave (07407-3115)
PHONE..............................201 796-5319
Howard Klein, *President*
EMP: 4

SQ FT: 600
SALES (est): 330K **Privately Held**
SIC: 3531 Construction machinery

(G-2853)
UNIQUE EMBROIDERY INC
64 Bushes Ln (07407-3204)
PHONE..............................201 943-9191
Robby Moutran, *President*
Sonia Besenia, *Corp Secy*
EMP: 11
SQ FT: 2,500
SALES (est): 822.5K **Privately Held**
WEB: www.uniqueembroidery.com
SIC: 2395 Embroidery & art needlework

Elwood
Atlantic County

(G-2854)
SPECIALTY RUBBER INC
4500 White Horse Pike (08217)
P.O. Box 483 (08217-0483)
PHONE..............................609 704-2555
Richard Orosz, *President*
Kevin Orosz, *Vice Pres*
EMP: 5
SQ FT: 2,000
SALES (est): 1.3MM **Privately Held**
WEB: www.specialtyrubber.com
SIC: 5085 3053 Rubber goods, mechanical; gaskets, all materials

---

Emerson
Bergen County

(G-2855)
ACCURATE DIAMOND TOOL CORP
1 Palisade Ave (07630-1880)
PHONE..............................201 265-8868
Fax: 201 265-8865
Daniel Michael, *President*
Muriam Michael, *CFO*
EMP: 29
SQ FT: 25,000
SALES (est): 5.2MM **Privately Held**
WEB: www.accuratediamondtool.com
SIC: 3545 Diamond cutting tools for turning, boring, burnishing, etc.

(G-2856)
AESYS INC
27 Bland St (07630-1153)
PHONE..............................201 871-3223
Guiseppe Biava, *President*
Colin McGregor, *Principal*
Mae Bogdansky, *Administration*
▲ **EMP:** 7
SALES (est): 1MM **Privately Held**
SIC: 3993 Electric signs

(G-2857)
ARTEMIS OPTICS AND COATINGS
Also Called: Arrow Thin Films
9 Ackerman Ave (07630-1801)
PHONE..............................201 847-0887
Jon Herringer, *President*
EMP: 5
SALES (est): 420K **Privately Held**
SIC: 3827 Optical instruments & lenses

(G-2858)
INTERNATIONAL TECH LASERS (PA)
Also Called: Itl
70 Kinderkamack Rd Ste 7 (07630-1812)
PHONE..............................201 262-4580
Fax: 201 634-1311
Isaac Goldlust, *President*
EMP: 2
SQ FT: 1,500
SALES: 3.7MM **Privately Held**
SIC: 3949 Hunting equipment

(G-2859)
JAMOL LABORATORIES INC
13 Ackerman Ave (07630-1801)
P.O. Box 313 (07630-0313)
PHONE..............................201 262-6363
Emil Scott Lucia, *President*
EMP: 6
SQ FT: 2,500
SALES (est): 880.1K **Privately Held**
SIC: 2834 Vitamin preparations; iodine, tincture of

(G-2860)
KITTYHAWK DIGITAL LLC
35 Linwood Ave (07630-1851)
PHONE..............................269 767-8399
Richard Narvadez,
EMP: 5
SALES (est): 278.1K **Privately Held**
SIC: 7371 7372 7373 Computer software development; computer software systems analysis & design, custom; computer software writing services; educational computer software; systems software development services

(G-2861)
ONT SUTTER
17c Palisade Ave (07630-1821)
PHONE..............................201 265-0262
Fax: 201 265-0588
Ralph Ocker, *President*
Milleis Sutter, *Owner*
EMP: 4 **EST:** 1964
SQ FT: 6,800
SALES (est): 401.4K **Privately Held**
SIC: 2789 Binding only: books, pamphlets, magazines, etc.

(G-2862)
RAYS REPRODUCTION INC
39 Bland St (07630-1153)
PHONE..............................201 666-5650
Fax: 201 666-7784
Raymond Stuart, *President*
Irene Stuart, *Vice Pres*
EMP: 9
SQ FT: 3,300
SALES (est): 1.6MM **Privately Held**
WEB: www.raysreproductions.com
SIC: 2752 7336 Commercial printing, offset; commercial art & graphic design

(G-2863)
TOLIN DESIGN INC
16 Bland St (07630-1154)
PHONE..............................201 261-4455
Fax: 201 261-0018
Tony Suarez, *President*
EMP: 5
SALES: 500K **Privately Held**
WEB: www.tolindesign.com
SIC: 3728 Aircraft parts & equipment

(G-2864)
WEATHERCRAFT MANUFACTURING CO
13 Emerson Plz E (07630-1823)
PHONE..............................201 262-0055
Fax: 201 262-8860
Salvatore Gebbia, *President*
EMP: 15
SALES (est): 1.9MM **Privately Held**
SIC: 3444 3442 Awnings, sheet metal; metal doors

Englewood
Bergen County

(G-2865)
A P M HEXSEAL CORPORATION
44 Honeck St (07631-4134)
PHONE..............................201 569-5700
Fax: 201 569-4106
David Morse, *President*
EMP: 30
SQ FT: 22,000
SALES (est): 6.7MM **Privately Held**
SIC: 3679 3648 Hermetic seals for electronic equipment; lighting equipment

(G-2866)
ACME GEAR CO INC
130 W Forest Ave (07631-4526)
PHONE....................................201 568-2245
Fax: 201 568-0282
Joseph Gelles, *President*
Joey Gelles, *Purch Mgr*
Rob Faro, *Controller*
Michelle Gelles, *Sales Mgr*
▲ EMP: 60 EST: 1929
SQ FT: 45,000
SALES (est): 16.7MM **Privately Held**
WEB: www.acmegear.com
SIC: 3566 Speed changers, drives & gears

(G-2867)
ALPINE TRADING COMPANY INC
Also Called: Image First Uniforms
400 Overpeck Pl (07631-4629)
PHONE....................................201 871-6111
Fax: 201 871-6112
Jacob Ardon, *President*
Marjorie Lors, *Treasurer*
Luis Jerez, *Sales Staff*
David Zylbershlag, *Director*
▲ EMP: 34 EST: 1999
SQ FT: 45,000
SALES (est): 6.4MM **Privately Held**
WEB: www.atcuniforms.com
SIC: 2311 Policemen's uniforms: made from purchased materials

(G-2868)
AMD FINE LINENS LLC
Also Called: Bellino
471 S Dean St (07631-4920)
PHONE....................................201 568-5255
Arnaldo Miccoli,
▲ EMP: 7
SALES (est): 4MM **Privately Held**
SIC: 2299 Linen fabrics

(G-2869)
AMERSHOE CORP
456 Nordhoff Pl (07631-4808)
PHONE....................................201 569-7300
Josh Nathel, *General Mgr*
Neal Liber, *Principal*
Rod Sunga, *Purch Dir*
Dan Nathel, *Info Tech Mgr*
EMP: 5 EST: 2014
SALES (est): 135K **Privately Held**
SIC: 3965 Fasteners

(G-2870)
ANU INDUSTRIES LLC
209 Wilbur St (07631-3326)
PHONE....................................201 735-7475
Yusef Assaan, *Principal*
EMP: 5
SALES (est): 194.1K **Privately Held**
SIC: 3999 Manufacturing industries

(G-2871)
ARRO-MARK COMPANY LLC
158 W Forest Ave (07631-4526)
PHONE....................................201 567-4112
George Pappageorge,
Stephanie Pappageorge,
◆ EMP: 18
SALES (est): 3.5MM **Privately Held**
SIC: 2899 Ink or writing fluids

(G-2872)
ARTISTIC TYPOGRAPHY CORP
161 Coolidge Ave (07631-4523)
PHONE....................................845 783-1990
Paul Weinstein, *Branch Mgr*
EMP: 9
SALES (corp-wide): 2.2MM **Privately Held**
WEB: www.tagimage.com
SIC: 2759 Commercial printing
PA: Artistic Typography Corp.
151 W 30th St Fl 8
New York NY 10001
212 463-8880

(G-2873)
ARTUS CORP
201 S Dean St (07631-4179)
P.O. Box 511 (07631-0511)
PHONE....................................201 568-1000
Fax: 201 568-8865

Edwin Katzenstein, *President*
Margaret Levi, *Vice Pres*
Samuel Levi, *Plant Mgr*
Raphael Levi, *Treasurer*
EMP: 41 EST: 1941
SQ FT: 22,000
SALES (est): 7.3MM **Privately Held**
WEB: www.artuscorp.com
SIC: 3089 3444 Plastic hardware & building products; washers, plastic; sheet metalwork

(G-2874)
AUDIO DYNAMIX INC
170 Coolidge Ave (07631-4522)
PHONE....................................201 567-5488
Fax: 201 567-5411
Esmat Gayed, *President*
EMP: 10
SQ FT: 9,000
SALES (est): 1.5MM **Privately Held**
SIC: 3577 7336 Disk & diskette equipment, except drives; package design

(G-2875)
BEN AHARON & SON INC
Also Called: Nyc Rugs
15 Smith St (07631-4607)
PHONE....................................201 541-2388
Fax: 201 541-2389
Ofer B Aharon, *President*
Elya B Aharon, *Vice Pres*
▲ EMP: 8
SQ FT: 5,000
SALES (est): 823.1K **Privately Held**
SIC: 2273 Carpets & rugs; carpets, hand & machine made

(G-2876)
BIODYNAMICS LLC (HQ)
84 Honeck St (07631-4133)
PHONE....................................201 227-9255
Jane A Grinch, *President*
James D Ralph, *Vice Pres*
Paul S Starr, *Vice Pres*
Patrick J Darcy, *CFO*
EMP: 7
SALES (est): 1.1MM **Privately Held**
SIC: 3841 8011 Inhalation therapy equipment; orthopedic physician

(G-2877)
BLITZ SAFE OF AMERICA INC
33 Honeck St (07631-4125)
PHONE....................................201 569-5000
Fax: 201 569-5042
Ira Marlowe, *President*
Melanie Kerr, *Manager*
◆ EMP: 17
SQ FT: 4,500
SALES (est): 3.1MM **Privately Held**
WEB: www.blitzsafe.com
SIC: 3663 3669 Radio broadcasting & communications equipment; emergency alarms

(G-2878)
BRITE CONCEPTS INC
90 W Palisade Ave (07631-2642)
PHONE....................................201 270-8544
David Siegel, *President*
EMP: 5
SALES (est): 500K **Privately Held**
SIC: 8732 2759 Market analysis or research; advertising literature: printing

(G-2879)
BURGESS STEEL HOLDING LLC
200 W Forest Ave (07631-4526)
P.O. Box 5629 (07631-5629)
PHONE....................................201 871-3500
EMP: 3
SALES: 38.1MM **Privately Held**
SIC: 3441 1791 Building components, structural steel; structural steel erection

(G-2880)
C & C METAL PRODUCTS CORP (PA)
Also Called: Knobware
456 Nordhoff Pl (07631-4877)
PHONE....................................201 569-7300
Fax: 201 569-4112
Gerald Nathel, *President*
Mitchell Chalfin, *Vice Pres*
Michael Nathel, *Vice Pres*

Armondo Haro, *Foreman/Supr*
Willy Clark, *Buyer*
▲ EMP: 100 EST: 1914
SQ FT: 149,000
SALES (est): 7.1MM **Privately Held**
WEB: www.ccmetal.com
SIC: 3965 3544 3961 Fasteners; buttons & parts; eyelets, metal: clothing, fabrics, boots or shoes; fasteners, snap; die sets for metal stamping (presses); industrial molds; jewelry apparel, non-precious metals

(G-2881)
CANAC KITCHENS OF NJ INC
99 N Dean St (07631-2806)
PHONE....................................201 567-9585
Fax: 201 567-9541
Linda Reiter, *President*
Jeff Chinman, *Vice Pres*
EMP: 12
SALES (est): 2.4MM **Privately Held**
WEB: www.canackitchensnj.com
SIC: 2499 Kitchen, bathroom & household ware: wood

(G-2882)
CANTONE PRESS INC
161 Coolidge Ave (07631-4523)
PHONE....................................201 569-3435
Frank W Cantone Jr, *President*
Daryl Schambach, *Accounts Exec*
Lynda McErlean, *Technology*
EMP: 40
SQ FT: 11,000
SALES (est): 7.1MM **Privately Held**
SIC: 2752 Commercial printing, offset

(G-2883)
CENTRAL ADMXTURE PHRM SVCS INC
Also Called: C A P S
160 W Forest Ave (07631-4526)
PHONE....................................201 541-0080
Fax: 201 541-0088
Daniel Buchner, *Branch Mgr*
Charles Mason, *Pharmacist*
Bill Jones, *Director*
Richard Maude, *Director*
EMP: 50 **Privately Held**
WEB: www.capspharmacy.com
SIC: 2834 5122 Pharmaceutical preparations; pharmaceuticals
HQ: Central Admixture Pharmacy Services, Inc.
2525 Mcgaw Ave
Irvine CA 92614

(G-2884)
CLYDE OTIS MUSIC GROUP
Also Called: Iza and Vanessa Music
494 N Woodland St (07631-2028)
P.O. Box 325 (07631-0325)
PHONE....................................845 425-8198
Clyde Otis, *Owner*
EMP: 5
SALES (est): 220K **Privately Held**
WEB: www.tcomg.com
SIC: 2741 Music, sheet: publishing only, not printed on site

(G-2885)
D & I PRINTING CO INC
23 Chestnut St (07631-2412)
PHONE....................................201 871-3620
Fax: 201 569-3134
Gus Dovi, *President*
Diane Alessi, *Treasurer*
EMP: 14
SQ FT: 10,000
SALES (est): 1.1MM **Privately Held**
SIC: 2752 2789 Commercial printing, offset; bookbinding & related work

(G-2886)
DELL AQUILA BAKING COMPANY
308 W Hudson Ave (07631-1406)
PHONE....................................201 886-0613
Laura Aguilar, *Principal*
EMP: 8
SALES (est): 640.8K **Privately Held**
SIC: 2051 Bread, cake & related products

(G-2887)
DELTA LAMBSKIN PRODUCTS INC
595 Ridge Rd (07631-5119)
PHONE....................................201 871-9233
Millie Dimitriou, *President*
◆ EMP: 20
SQ FT: 50,000
SALES (est): 1.9MM **Privately Held**
SIC: 3991 Paint rollers

(G-2888)
DISYS COMMERCE INC
100 W Forest Ave Ste H (07631-4033)
PHONE....................................201 567-0457
Sangwoo Han, *Administration*
EMP: 6
SALES (est): 87K
SALES (corp-wide): 33.3MM **Privately Held**
SIC: 3111 Accessory products, leather
PA: Ise Commerce Co., Ltd.
Saman Bldg.
Seoul 06078
822 321-8301

(G-2889)
EDUCHAT INC
17 Lane Dr (07631-3734)
PHONE....................................201 871-8649
Ross Kopelman, *CEO*
EMP: 5
SALES (est): 117.2K **Privately Held**
SIC: 7372 Business oriented computer software

(G-2890)
EMPIRE TELECOMMUNICATIONS INC
15 S Van Brunt St (07631-3427)
PHONE....................................201 569-3339
Sidney Kaplan, *President*
EMP: 11 EST: 1978
SQ FT: 5,000
SALES (est): 880K **Privately Held**
SIC: 3679 Electronic circuits

(G-2891)
ENGLEWOOD LAB LLC (PA)
88 W Sheffield Ave (07631-4809)
PHONE....................................201 567-2267
David Chung, *CEO*
John H Kim, *COO*
Ken Saavedra, *Project Mgr*
Jay Jim, *Warehouse Mgr*
Frank Dittrick, *Purch Mgr*
▲ EMP: 140
SQ FT: 30,000
SALES (est): 47.1MM **Privately Held**
WEB: www.englewoodlab.com
SIC: 2844 Toilet preparations

(G-2892)
ENOR CORPORATION
Also Called: Progard
246 S Dean St (07631-4139)
PHONE....................................201 750-1680
Fax: 201 750-1418
Steven Udwin, *CEO*
David Tarica, *President*
Merle T Udwin, *Corp Secy*
Justin Tarica, *Natl Sales Mgr*
▲ EMP: 225 EST: 1958
SQ FT: 40,000
SALES (est): 37.1MM **Privately Held**
SIC: 3089 Plastic processing; injection molding of plastics

(G-2893)
ENTERPRISE PRESS INC
1 W Forest Ave Ste 2d (07631-4085)
PHONE....................................212 741-2111
Daniel Hort, *Ch of Bd*
Benjamin Hort, *President*
Robert Hort, *Shareholder*
▲ EMP: 38
SQ FT: 40,000
SALES: 8MM **Privately Held**
WEB: www.enterprise-press.com
SIC: 2759 Commercial printing

(G-2894)
EUROPROJECTS INTL INC (PA)
Also Called: Adotta America
500 Nordhoff Pl Ste 5 (07631-4800)
PHONE.................................917 262-0795
Luigi Zannier, *President*
Mila Piazzo, *Asst Controller*
▲ EMP: 8
SALES: 13MM **Privately Held**
SIC: 3211 1751 Structural glass; window
& door (prefabricated) installation

(G-2895)
EZCOM SOFTWARE INC
25 Rockwood Pl Ste 420 (07631-4971)
PHONE.................................201 731-1800
Fax: 201 883-1909
Carol Weidner, *CEO*
Adele Rosenblum, *Sales Staff*
Bernie Byrne, *CTO*
Felice Levine, *Prgrmr*
Ted Cancila, *Director*
EMP: 28
SALES: 4.4MM **Privately Held**
WEB: www.ezcomsoftware.com
SIC: 7372 Business oriented computer
software

(G-2896)
**FIRMA FOODS USA
CORPORATION**
25 Rockwood Pl Ste 220 (07631-4959)
PHONE.................................201 794-1181
Claudia Vitelli, *Vice Pres*
▲ EMP: 5
SQ FT: 3,000
SALES (est): 266.3K **Privately Held**
SIC: 2099 Pasta, uncooked: packaged with
other ingredients

(G-2897)
FORBO SIEGLING LLC
130 Coolidge Ave (07631-4522)
PHONE.................................201 567-6100
Fax: 201 567-2981
Ron Supino, *Branch Mgr*
EMP: 13
SALES (corp-wide): 1.2B **Privately Held**
SIC: 3052 Rubber & plastics hose & belt-
ings
HQ: Forbo Siegling, Llc
12201 Vanstory Dr
Huntersville NC 28078
704 948-0800

(G-2898)
**FRENCH COLOR FRAGRANCE
CO INC (PA)**
488 Grand Ave (07631-4950)
PHONE.................................201 567-6883
Fax: 201 567-5749
Peter A French, *President*
Angie Dorrity, *Admin Asst*
▲ EMP: 25
SQ FT: 8,500
SALES (est): 3.6MM **Privately Held**
WEB: www.frenchcolor.com
SIC: 2865 2844 2816 Dye (cyclic) inter-
mediates; perfumes & colognes; inorganic
pigments

(G-2899)
G & A PAVERS LLC
2123 Sterling Blvd (07631-4827)
PHONE.................................201 562-5947
EMP: 4 EST: 2010
SALES (est): 267.7K **Privately Held**
SIC: 3531 Pavers

(G-2900)
**GEMINI CUT GLASS COMPANY
INC**
4 E Forest Ave (07631-4137)
PHONE.................................201 568-7722
Eric Zelwiam, *President*
▲ EMP: 7 EST: 1942
SQ FT: 6,000
SALES (est): 996.5K **Privately Held**
SIC: 5719 5063 3645 Lighting, lamps &
accessories; lighting fixtures; lighting fix-
tures; chandeliers, residential

(G-2901)
GLENWOOD LLC
Also Called: Glenwood-Palisades
111 Cedar Ln (07631-4803)
P.O. Box 5419 (07631-5419)
PHONE.................................201 569-0050
Judith Gacita, *Controller*
Cynthia Shachar, *Manager*
Suzanne Israel, *Consultant*
Eric Goodwine, *Supervisor*
Christopher Fuhrmann,
▲ EMP: 194
SQ FT: 54,000
SALES (est): 25.4MM **Privately Held**
WEB: www.glenwood-llc.com
SIC: 2834 Pharmaceutical preparations

(G-2902)
**HEINRICH BAUER PUBLISHING
LP**
270 Sylvan Ave Ste 100 (07632-2521)
PHONE.................................201 569-6699
Hubert Boehle, *President*
EMP: 19
SALES (est): 696.9K
SALES (corp-wide): 2.3B **Privately Held**
SIC: 2721 Magazines: publishing only, not
printed on site
HQ: Heinrich Bauer Verlag Beteiligungs
Gmbh
270 Sylvan Ave Ste 100
Englewood Cliffs NJ 07632
201 569-0006

(G-2903)
HOWMEDICA OSTEONICS CORP
Also Called: Stryker Orthopaedics
53 Bancker St (07631-4105)
PHONE.................................201 541-6569
Fax: 201 567-9151
Mike Zurnili, *Manager*
EMP: 20
SALES (corp-wide): 12.4B **Publicly Held**
SIC: 3841 Surgical & medical instruments
HQ: Howmedica Osteonics Corp.
325 Corporate Dr
Mahwah NJ 07430
201 831-5000

(G-2904)
HOYT CORPORATION
520 S Dean St (07631-4952)
PHONE.................................201 894-0707
William H Nixon, *CEO*
Michael Bradford, *President*
Donald McGuire, *President*
Ted Hoyt, *COO*
Dennis Maas, *CFO*
EMP: 60 EST: 1961
SQ FT: 30,000
SALES (est): 11MM **Privately Held**
WEB: www.hoyt-corp.com
SIC: 3624 3999 5063 Brushes & brush
stock contacts, electric; atomizers, toi-
letry; switchgear

(G-2905)
INFOSEAL LLC
Also Called: A Division NJ Bus Forms
55 W Sheffield Ave (07631-4804)
PHONE.................................201 569-4500
David Harnett,
Ian Ashton,
Andrew Harnett,
◆ EMP: 79
SALES (est): 10.3MM **Privately Held**
WEB: www.infoseal.com
SIC: 2761 Manifold business forms

(G-2906)
JAD BAGELS LLC
52 E Palisade Ave (07631-2902)
PHONE.................................201 567-4500
Mark Urich, *Owner*
EMP: 4
SALES (est): 315.9K **Privately Held**
SIC: 2051 Bagels, fresh or frozen

(G-2907)
KINZEE INDUSTRIES INC
80 Brayton St (07631-3116)
PHONE.................................201 408-4301
Jeffrey Solomon, *President*
EMP: 18
SQ FT: 117,000

SALES (est): 1.4MM **Privately Held**
SIC: 2434 5031 Wood kitchen cabinets;
vanities, bathroom: wood; kitchen cabinets; building materials, interior

(G-2908)
LBD CORP
Also Called: Cassies Restaurant
18 S Dean St (07631-3515)
PHONE.................................201 541-6760
Larry Drucker, *President*
EMP: 30
SALES (est): 2.3MM **Privately Held**
SIC: 2599 Food wagons, restaurant

(G-2909)
LEO PRAGER INC
2322 Sterling Blvd (07631-4829)
PHONE.................................201 266-8888
Peter Schoenfeld, *Ch of Bd*
EMP: 5
SALES (est): 506.5K **Privately Held**
SIC: 2542 Racks, merchandise display or
storage: except wood

(G-2910)
LIZ FIELDS LLC
41 Smith St (07631-4607)
PHONE.................................201 408-5640
Lizette Brodsky,
▲ EMP: 6 EST: 2009
SALES (est): 538.2K **Privately Held**
SIC: 2335 Wedding gowns & dresses

(G-2911)
LUNZER INC
1 W Forest Ave Ste 1i (07631-4038)
PHONE.................................201 794-2800
Jay K R Lunzer, *CEO*
EMP: 7
SQ FT: 10,000
SALES (est): 749K **Privately Held**
SIC: 3291 Abrasive products

(G-2912)
**MARATHON ENTERPRISES INC
(PA)**
Also Called: Sabett Hot Dog
9 Smith St (07631-4607)
PHONE.................................201 935-3330
Boyd G Adelman, *President*
Mark Rosen, *Vice Pres*
Philip Venturini, *Vice Pres*
Patricia Bowie, *Accounts Exec*
▲ EMP: 15
SQ FT: 4,500
SALES (est): 25.5MM **Privately Held**
WEB: www.sabrett.com
SIC: 2013 Sausages & other prepared
meats; frankfurters from purchased meat;
ham, boneless: from purchased meat;
bologna from purchased meat

(G-2913)
MARLOW CANDY & NUT CO INC
65 Honeck St (07631-4125)
PHONE.................................201 569-7606
Fax: 201 569-9533
Eric Lowenthal, *President*
EMP: 25
SQ FT: 18,000
SALES (est): 8.7MM **Privately Held**
WEB: www.marlowcandy.net
SIC: 5145 2064 Candy; nuts, salted or
roasted; candy & other confectionery
products

(G-2914)
**MATISSE CHOCOLATIER INC
(PA)**
260 Grand Ave Ste 6 (07631-4360)
PHONE.................................201 568-2288
Lucille Skroce, *President*
Valdo Skroce, *Vice Pres*
EMP: 4
SQ FT: 700
SALES (est): 445.2K **Privately Held**
SIC: 2066 5441 5947 Chocolate; candy;
gifts & novelties

(G-2915)
**MERCURY FLOOR MACHINES
INC**
110 S Van Brunt St (07631-3438)
PHONE.................................201 568-4606

Fax: 201 568-7962
Bill Allen, *President*
Marcos De La O', *CFO*
▲ EMP: 20 EST: 1958
SQ FT: 8,000
SALES (est): 2.6MM **Privately Held**
WEB: www.mercuryfloormachines.com
SIC: 3291 3589 Abrasive products; floor
washing & polishing machines, commer-
cial

(G-2916)
MICROSURFACES INC
1 W Forest Ave Ste 2b (07631-4038)
PHONE.................................201 408-5596
Athena Guo, *President*
EMP: 6
SQ FT: 1,518
SALES: 500K **Privately Held**
WEB: www.memsurface.com
SIC: 3479 Coating of metals with silicon

(G-2917)
**MIDDLE EAST MARKETING
GROUP (PA)**
Also Called: Mem Group
266 S Dean St (07631-4139)
PHONE.................................201 503-0150
Henri Dimidjian, *President*
Sabrina Kalfayan, *Vice Pres*
Alex Kalfayan, *Admin Sec*
▼ EMP: 7 EST: 1974
SQ FT: 50,000
SALES (est): 1.7MM **Privately Held**
SIC: 3999 Bric-a-brac

(G-2918)
MUSIC TRADES CORP
Also Called: Music Trades Magazine
80 West St Ste 200 (07631-2743)
PHONE.................................201 871-1965
Fax: 201 871-0455
Brian Majeski, *President*
Richard Watson, *Editor*
Paul Majeski, *Vice Pres*
EMP: 6
SQ FT: 1,000
SALES (est): 613.7K **Privately Held**
WEB: www.musictrades.com
SIC: 2721 5736 Magazines: publishing
only, not printed on site; musical instru-
ment stores

(G-2919)
NINE WEST HOLDINGS INC
Also Called: Kasper
33 E Palisade Ave (07631-2901)
PHONE.................................201 541-7004
EMP: 8
SALES (corp-wide): 2.2B **Privately Held**
SIC: 2337 Mfg Women's/Misses'
Suits/Coats
PA: Nine West Holdings, Inc.
1411 Broadway Fl 15
New York NY 10007
212 642-3860

(G-2920)
PALISADES DENTAL LLC
Also Called: Impact Air 45
111 Cedar Ln (07631-4803)
P.O. Box 5419 (07631-5419)
PHONE.................................201 569-0050
John Gruen,
EMP: 12
SALES (est): 1.7MM **Privately Held**
WEB: www.palisadesdental-llc.com
SIC: 3843 Drills, dental

(G-2921)
PDQ PRINT & COPY INC
Also Called: P D Q Digital
161 Coolidge Ave (07631-4523)
PHONE.................................201 569-2288
Kelly Rozansky, *President*
Tim Rozansky, *Principal*
EMP: 12
SQ FT: 4,500
SALES (est): 1.4MM **Privately Held**
WEB: www.pdqdigital.com
SIC: 2752 Commercial printing, offset

(G-2922)
PLATON INTERIORS
180 S Van Brunt St (07631-3438)
PHONE.................................201 567-5533

▲ = Import ▼=Export
◆ =Import/Export

Fax: 201 567-3335
▲ EMP: 8
SALES (est): 620K **Privately Held**
SIC: 2434 Architectural And Furniture Mfg

(G-2923)
PREMIER CONSUMER PRODUCTS INC
106 Grand Ave Ste 120 (07631-3570)
PHONE..................................201 568-9700
Michael Zeher, *President*
William Delayo, *Treasurer*
EMP: 6
SQ FT: 12,500
SALES (est): 538.8K
SALES (corp-wide): 3MM **Privately Held**
SIC: 2844 Toilet preparations
PA: Scott Chemical Co, Inc
106 Grand Ave
Englewood NJ
201 568-9700

(G-2924)
PRINT SOLUTIONS LLC
320 S Dean St (07631-4138)
PHONE..................................201 567-9622
John Vartanian, *Mng Member*
Paul Vartanian,
EMP: 14
SQ FT: 7,000
SALES (est): 1.1MM **Privately Held**
SIC: 2759 Commercial printing

(G-2925)
PROGRESSIVE OFFSET INC
161 Coolidge Ave (07631-4523)
PHONE..................................201 569-3900
Fax: 201 569-1747
Frank W Cantone Jr, *President*
Miesha Dimeglio, *Creative Dir*
EMP: 30
SQ FT: 20,000
SALES (est): 7.3MM **Privately Held**
WEB: www.prooffset.com
SIC: 2752 Commercial printing, offset

(G-2926)
PROVENCE LLC
Also Called: Balthazar Bakery
214 S Dean St (07631-4139)
PHONE..................................201 503-9717
Paula Oland, *Mng Member*
EMP: 120
SQ FT: 14,000
SALES (est): 20.2MM **Privately Held**
SIC: 2051 Bakery: wholesale or wholesale/retail combined

(G-2927)
R YATES CONSUMER PRD LLC
204 Green St (07631-3818)
PHONE..................................201 569-1030
Russell Yates, *Owner*
EMP: 4 EST: 1996
SALES (est): 220K **Privately Held**
SIC: 3843 Dental equipment & supplies

(G-2928)
RENAISSANCE HOUSE
465 Westview Ave (07631-5106)
PHONE..................................201 408-4048
Sam Laredo, *President*
Raquel Laredo, *Vice Pres*
▲ EMP: 3
SALES (est): 1.2MM **Privately Held**
SIC: 2731 Book publishing

(G-2929)
SELWAY PARTNERS LLC (PA)
74 Grand Ave B (07631-3506)
PHONE..................................201 712-7974
Yaron Eitan, *Mng Member*
Winston Churchill,
EMP: 10
SQ FT: 5,000
SALES (est): 11.6MM **Privately Held**
SIC: 3663 Television closed circuit equipment

(G-2930)
SHERMAN NAT INC (HQ)
10 Sterling Blvd Ste 302 (07631-4835)
PHONE..................................201 735-9000
Shannon Leistra, *General Mgr*
William M Sherman, *Vice Pres*
Brendon B Scott, *CFO*

◆ EMP: 40
SQ FT: 7,000
SALES (est): 28.4MM
SALES (corp-wide): 25.5B **Publicly Held**
WEB: www.natsherman.com
SIC: 5194 5993 5947 2111 Cigarettes; cigarette store; novelties; cigarettes; cigars
PA: Altria Group, Inc.
6601 W Broad St
Richmond VA 23230
804 274-2200

(G-2931)
SHERMANS 1400 BRDWAY N Y C LTD
10 Sterling Blvd (07631-4834)
PHONE..................................201 735-9000
Shannon Leistra, *General Mgr*
Brendon Scott, *CFO*
EMP: 60
SALES (est): 1.9MM
SALES (corp-wide): 25.5B **Publicly Held**
SIC: 2111 Cigarettes
PA: Altria Group, Inc.
6601 W Broad St
Richmond VA 23230
804 274-2200

(G-2932)
SNIDERMAN JOHN
Also Called: Allied Embroidery
133 E Palisade Ave Apt H (07631-2249)
PHONE..................................201 569-5482
John Sniderman, *Owner*
EMP: 16
SALES (est): 590K **Privately Held**
SIC: 2395 2396 Embroidery products, except schiffli machine; automotive & apparel trimmings

(G-2933)
SOUTH EAST INSTRUMENTS LLC
111 Cedar Ln (07631-4803)
P.O. Box 5657 (07631-5657)
PHONE..................................201 569-0050
Judith Gacita,
Maureen McGovern,
EMP: 8
SQ FT: 5,000
SALES (est): 429.8K **Privately Held**
SIC: 3843 Ultrasonic dental equipment

(G-2934)
STARFUELS INC
285 Grand Ave (07631-4369)
PHONE..................................201 685-0400
EMP: 6
SALES (corp-wide): 1MM **Privately Held**
SIC: 1241 2911 3339 Coal mining services; oils, fuel; precious metals
HQ: Starfuels, Inc.
50 Main St
White Plains NY 10606
914 289-4800

(G-2935)
STRUCTURED HEALTHCARE MGT INC
Also Called: Shm
456 Nordhoff Pl (07631-4808)
PHONE..................................201 569-3290
Maurice Reifman, *President*
EMP: 28
SQ FT: 4,200
SALES (est): 2.1MM **Privately Held**
WEB: www.shminc.com
SIC: 7372 7371 Prepackaged software; custom computer programming services

(G-2936)
TANGENT GRAPHICS INC
23 Chestnut St (07631-2412)
PHONE..................................201 488-2840
Fax: 201 489-1254
Daniel Canner, *President*
John Wehle, *Treasurer*
EMP: 8
SQ FT: 9,200
SALES (est): 1.3MM **Privately Held**
SIC: 2752 2796 2791 Commercial printing, offset; platemaking services; typesetting

(G-2937)
TIME SYSTEMS INTERNATIONAL CO
142 S Van Brunt St (07631-3438)
PHONE..................................201 871-1200
Fax: 201 871-1202
Samuel Gleich, *President*
Augie Caruso, *VP Sales*
EMP: 30 EST: 1961
SQ FT: 9,600
SALES (est): 4.8MM **Privately Held**
WEB: www.timesystemsint.com
SIC: 5044 3579 Office equipment; time clocks & time recording devices

(G-2938)
TRUSS ENGINEERING
120 Charlotte Pl Ste 206 (07632-2607)
PHONE..................................201 871-4800
William F Loftus, *Principal*
EMP: 4
SALES (est): 33.2K **Privately Held**
SIC: 2439 Trusses, wooden roof

(G-2939)
UMBRELLA & CHAIRS LLC
Also Called: Schmutzerland
8 Old Quarry Rd (07631-5123)
PHONE..................................973 284-1240
Donald Berkowitz,
Bonnie Berish,
David Rubin,
EMP: 4
SALES (est): 204.6K **Privately Held**
SIC: 3961 7389 Costume jewelry;

(G-2940)
UNITY GRAPHICS & ENGRAVING CO
Also Called: Unity Engraving Company
210 S Van Brunt St (07631-4012)
P.O. Box 88 (07631-0088)
PHONE..................................201 541-5462
Fax: 201 569-2956
Jerry Mandel, *President*
EMP: 50 EST: 1930
SQ FT: 20,000
SALES (est): 7.1MM **Privately Held**
SIC: 2752 2796 Commercial printing, lithographic; platemaking services

(G-2941)
UNITY STEEL RULE DIE CO
210 S Van Brunt St (07631-4012)
PHONE..................................201 569-6400
Jerry Mandel, *Owner*
Jim Lyons, *Accounts Mgr*
Dennis Mayer, *Technology*
EMP: 40
SALES (est): 4.3MM **Privately Held**
SIC: 3312 3544 Tool & die steel; special dies, tools, jigs & fixtures

(G-2942)
VICTOR SECURITIES INC
285 Grand Ave Bldg No3 (07631-4369)
PHONE..................................646 481-4835
Kevin Bakhler, *Principal*
Michael Elia, *Manager*
EMP: 7
SALES (est): 751.9K **Privately Held**
SIC: 2621 Parchment, securites & bank note papers

(G-2943)
WESTBURY PRESS INC
1 W Forest Ave (07631-4038)
PHONE..................................201 894-0444
Sanford Zenker, *President*
Al Zenker, *Corp Secy*
EMP: 60
SQ FT: 40,000
SALES (est): 5.8MM **Privately Held**
WEB: www.westburypress.com
SIC: 2752 2789 Commercial printing, offset; bookbinding & related work

(G-2944)
WOHNERS (PA)
29 Bergen St (07631-2907)
PHONE..................................201 568-7307
Robert Vadas Wohner, *General Mgr*
John Wohner, *Vice Pres*
Robert Wohner Jr, *Vice Pres*
EMP: 6

SQ FT: 4,000
SALES (est): 760.5K **Privately Held**
WEB: www.wohners.com
SIC: 5211 2431 Millwork & lumber; millwork

(G-2945)
YORK STREET CATERERS INC
196 Coolidge Ave (07631-4522)
PHONE..................................201 868-9088
John Lorenzo, *President*
Joseph Lorenzo, *Vice Pres*
EMP: 250
SALES (est): 45MM **Privately Held**
WEB: www.lorenzofoodgroup.com
SIC: 5812 2011 Caterers; cured meats from meat slaughtered on site

Englewood Cliffs
Bergen County

(G-2946)
ACE BOX LANDAU CO INC
Also Called: Ace Box Co
600 E Palisade Ave Ste 23 (07632-1898)
PHONE..................................201 871-4776
Fax: 201 871-1327
Leonard Landau, *President*
EMP: 8
SQ FT: 1,500
SALES (est): 1.7MM **Privately Held**
SIC: 5113 2673 2653 3842 Corrugated & solid fiber boxes; bags, paper & disposable plastic; plastic & pliofilm bags; boxes, corrugated: made from purchased materials; adhesive tape & plasters, medicated or non-medicated

(G-2947)
AMATI INTERNATIONAL LLC
560 Sylvan Ave Ste 2053 (07632-3165)
PHONE..................................201 569-1000
David Yarin,
Robert Leopold,
Naoko T Yarin,
Peter Yarin,
▲ EMP: 26
SALES (est): 3MM **Privately Held**
WEB: www.amatiintl.com
SIC: 3645 3646 3641 Residential lighting fixtures; commercial indusl & institutional electric lighting fixtures; electric lamps

(G-2948)
AMERICA TECHMA INC
385 Sylvan Ave Ste 28 (07632-2722)
PHONE..................................201 894-5887
Chris S Yu, *CEO*
▲ EMP: 7
SQ FT: 1,200
SALES (est): 4.5MM **Privately Held**
SIC: 5047 5063 3841 Medical & hospital equipment; electrical apparatus & equipment; surgical & medical instruments

(G-2949)
BARNET PRODUCTS CORPORATION
920 Sylvan Ave 210 (07632-3301)
PHONE..................................201 346-4620
Steve Kosann, *President*
Carol Kosann, *General Mgr*
Herve Offredo, *VP Sales*
▲ EMP: 15
SQ FT: 5,000
SALES (est): 4.9MM **Privately Held**
WEB: www.barnetproducts.com
SIC: 2869 Fatty acid esters, aminos, etc.

(G-2950)
BAUER PUBLISHING COMPANY LP (DH)
Also Called: First For Women Magazine
270 Sylvan Ave Ste 210 (07632-2523)
PHONE..................................201 569-6699
Fax: 201 510-3297
Hubert Boehle, *Partner*
Heinz Bauer, *Partner*
Richard Buchert, *Partner*
Henning Lauer, *Partner*
Richard Teehan, *Partner*
▲ EMP: 8
SQ FT: 27,000

SALES (est): 85.3MM
SALES (corp-wide): 2.3B **Privately Held**
WEB: www.bauerpublishing.com
SIC: 2721 Magazines: publishing only, not printed on site
HQ: Heinrich Bauer Verlag Beteiligungs Gmbh
     Burchardstr. 11
     Hamburg
     403 019-0

(G-2951)
CAPORALE ENGRAVING CO INC
30 Roberts Rd (07632-2212)
PHONE...................................201 569-8711
Louis Caporale, *President*
Tom Caporale, *Treasurer*
Gary Caporale, *Admin Sec*
EMP: 22
SQ FT: 26,000
SALES (est): 2.1MM **Privately Held**
SIC: 2796 Engraving platemaking services; engraving on copper, steel, wood or rubber: printing plates

(G-2952)
CASTLE INDUSTRIES INC
120 Sylvan Ave Ste 3 (07632-2501)
PHONE...................................201 585-8400
Fax: 201 592-8419
Arthur Schloss, *President*
▲ EMP: 20
SQ FT: 2,500
SALES (est): 2.3MM **Privately Held**
SIC: 3699 Electronic training devices

(G-2953)
COMPETECH SMRTCARD SLTIONS INC
Also Called: CSS
440 Sylvan Ave Ste 250 (07632-2700)
PHONE...................................201 256-4184
Gregory Thornton, *CEO*
Laura Pace, *Treasurer*
EMP: 9
SQ FT: 2,500
SALES (est): 465.8K **Privately Held**
SIC: 3089 3999 Identification cards, plastic; identification badges & insignia; buttons: Red Cross, union, identification

(G-2954)
CONOPCO INC
940 Sylvan Ave (07632-3301)
PHONE...................................201 894-7760
EMP: 5
SALES (corp-wide): 63B **Privately Held**
SIC: 2035 Pickles, sauces & salad dressings
HQ: Conopco, Inc.
     700 Sylvan Ave
     Englewood Cliffs NJ 07632
     201 894-2727

(G-2955)
CONOPCO INC
Also Called: Good Humor/Breyers
800 Sylvan Ave (07632-3201)
PHONE...................................920 499-2509
Eric Walsh, *President*
Harold Vastag, *President*
EMP: 240
SALES (corp-wide): 63B **Privately Held**
SIC: 2024 Ice cream, packaged: molded, on sticks, etc.; ices, flavored (frozen dessert)
HQ: Conopco, Inc.
     700 Sylvan Ave
     Englewood Cliffs NJ 07632
     201 894-2727

(G-2956)
CUSTOM GASKET MFG LLC
640 E Palisade Ave (07632-1827)
PHONE...................................201 331-6363
Eric Helf, *CEO*
EMP: 12
SALES (est): 556.3K **Privately Held**
SIC: 3053 5085 Gaskets & sealing devices; gaskets & seals

(G-2957)
DOOSAN HEAVY INDS AMER LLC
140 Sylvan Ave (07632-2514)
PHONE...................................201 944-4554

EMP: 4
SALES (est): 590.5K **Privately Held**
SIC: 3999 Barber & beauty shop equipment

(G-2958)
ENERGY CHEM AMERICA INC
920 Sylvan Ave (07632-3301)
PHONE...................................201 816-2307
Steven Park, *President*
▲ EMP: 60
SALES (est): 4.4MM **Privately Held**
SIC: 2869 Industrial organic chemicals

(G-2959)
ET BROWNE DRUG CO INC (PA)
Also Called: Palmer's Cocoa Butter Formula
440 Sylvan Ave (07632-2727)
PHONE...................................201 894-9020
Arnold Hayward Neis, *Ch of Bd*
Robert Neis, *President*
Susan Crook, *Accounts Mgr*
◆ EMP: 60
SQ FT: 15,000
SALES (est): 84.7MM **Privately Held**
WEB: www.etbrowne.com
SIC: 2844 Cosmetic preparations; face creams or lotions; toilet preparations

(G-2960)
FYI MARKETING INC
Also Called: Ciao Milano
22 Laurie Dr (07632-2222)
PHONE...................................646 546-5226
Timothy Delton, *CEO*
EMP: 5
SALES (est): 98.1K **Privately Held**
SIC: 2339 2337 Down-filled coats, jackets & vests: women's & misses'; women's & misses' capes & jackets

(G-2961)
GALAXY LED INC
600 Sylvan Ave Ste 106 (07632-3151)
PHONE...................................201 541-5461
Jae Hong Choi, *President*
Robert Uhl, *Vice Pres*
▲ EMP: 4
SALES: 500K **Privately Held**
SIC: 3648 Lighting equipment

(G-2962)
GUYLIAN USA INC
560 Sylvan Ave Ste 2105 (07632-3174)
PHONE...................................201 871-4144
Fax: 201 871-3632
Michael Cobb, *President*
Conchetta Sturm, *Office Mgr*
◆ EMP: 4
SQ FT: 1,500
SALES (est): 541.8K
SALES (corp-wide): 97.2MM **Privately Held**
WEB: www.guylian.us
SIC: 2064 Candy & other confectionery products
PA: Chocolaterie Guylian Nv
     Europark-Oost 1
     Sint-Niklaas 9100
     376 097-00

(G-2963)
HEINRICH BAUER VERLAG (HQ)
Also Called: Woman's World Magazine
270 Sylvan Ave Ste 100 (07632-2521)
PHONE...................................201 569-0006
Fax: 201 569-3584
Hubert Boehle, *President*
Richard Teehan, *Corp Secy*
Sebastian Raatz, *Exec VP*
Richard Buchert, *Senior VP*
Dennis Cohen, *Senior VP*
EMP: 22
SQ FT: 7,000
SALES (est): 40.4MM
SALES (corp-wide): 2.3B **Privately Held**
SIC: 2721 Magazines: publishing only, not printed on site
PA: Heinrich Bauer Verlag Kg
     Burchardstr. 11
     Hamburg 20077
     403 019-0

(G-2964)
HITECHONE INC
440 Sylvan Ave Ste 2508 (07632-2727)
PHONE...................................201 500-8864
Richard Kimsen, *President*
Park Kyu Tae, *Principal*
▲ EMP: 7
SALES (est): 702K **Privately Held**
SIC: 3621 7373 3571 Generators for storage battery chargers; systems engineering, computer related; electronic computers

(G-2965)
IMMUNE PHARMACEUTICALS INC (PA)
550 Sylvan Ave Ste 101 (07632-3115)
PHONE...................................201 464-2677
Elliot Maza, *President*
Tony Fiorino, *Chief Mktg Ofcr*
EMP: 12
SQ FT: 1,674
SALES (est): 2.3MM **Publicly Held**
WEB: www.epicept.com
SIC: 2834 Pharmaceutical preparations; analgesics

(G-2966)
INSTITUTATIONAL EDGE LLC
120 Van Nostrand Ave # 201 (07632-1555)
PHONE...................................201 944-5447
EMP: 6
SQ FT: 900
SALES (est): 490K **Privately Held**
SIC: 2621 Security Broker

(G-2967)
INTEGRATED DENTAL SYSTEMS LLC
Also Called: IDS
300 Sylvan Ave Ste 104 (07632-2536)
PHONE...................................201 676-2457
Carey Lyons, *CEO*
David Singh, *COO*
EMP: 21
SQ FT: 40,000
SALES (est): 3.4MM **Privately Held**
SIC: 3843 Dental equipment & supplies

(G-2968)
INTELLECT NEUROSCIENCES INC
550 Sylvan Ave Ste 101 (07632-3115)
PHONE...................................201 608-5101
Elliot M Maza, *Ch of Bd*
EMP: 1
SQ FT: 900
SALES (est): 1.2MM **Privately Held**
SIC: 2834 Druggists' preparations (pharmaceuticals)

(G-2969)
KAIROS ENTERPRISES LLC
210 Sylvan Ave Ste 22 (07632-2503)
PHONE...................................201 731-3181
Jae Y Kim, *Mng Member*
EMP: 10
SALES: 4.5MM **Privately Held**
SIC: 2282 2821 8742 Manmade & synthetic fiber yarns: twisting, winding, etc.; plastics materials & resins; marketing consulting services

(G-2970)
KIKUICHI NEW YORK INC
560 Sylvan Ave Ste 3110 (07632-3131)
PHONE...................................201 567-8388
Ikuyo Yanagisawa, *President*
EMP: 8
SALES (est): 860K **Privately Held**
SIC: 3421 Knives: butchers', hunting, pocket, etc.

(G-2971)
KOREAN BERGEN NEWS INC
210 Sylvan Ave Ste 23 (07632-2503)
PHONE...................................201 894-9061
Hyuk Bae, *President*
EMP: 10
SALES (est): 470K **Privately Held**
SIC: 2711 Newspapers

(G-2972)
LG ELCTRNICS MBILECOMM USA INC (DH)
Also Called: Lg Infocomm U.S.A.
1000 Sylvan Ave (07632-3302)
PHONE...................................201 816-2000
Wayne Park, *CEO*
Kyung Joo Hwang, *President*
John Hollen, *Vice Pres*
M Ehtisham Rabbani, *Vice Pres*
Jae Dong Han, *Treasurer*
▲ EMP: 100
SQ FT: 67,500
SALES (est): 136.9MM
SALES (corp-wide): 29.2B **Privately Held**
SIC: 5065 3663 Mobile telephone equipment; radio & TV communications equipment
HQ: Lg Electronics U.S.A., Inc.
     1000 Sylvan Ave
     Englewood Cliffs NJ 07632
     201 816-2000

(G-2973)
LG ELECTRONICS USA INC (HQ)
Also Called: Lg Group Aic
1000 Sylvan Ave (07632-3318)
PHONE...................................201 816-2000
William Cho, *President*
Jae C Lee, *General Mgr*
Eugene Yoo, *General Mgr*
Jong Choi, *Vice Pres*
Richard Wingate, *Vice Pres*
◆ EMP: 500
SQ FT: 57,000
SALES: 12.1B
SALES (corp-wide): 29.2B **Privately Held**
WEB: www.lge.com
SIC: 5064 3651 Electrical appliances, television & radio; electrical appliances, major; electrical entertainment equipment; air conditioning appliances; household audio & video equipment
PA: Lg Electronics, Inc.
     128 Yeoui-Daero, Yeongdeungpo-Gu
     Seoul 07336
     822 377-7111

(G-2974)
LIMOSYS LLC
550 Sylvan Ave Ste 100 (07632-3115)
PHONE...................................212 222-4433
Issac Yehuda,
Kornel Cyrzyk,
EMP: 15
SQ FT: 2,500
SALES (est): 1.3MM **Privately Held**
SIC: 7371 7372 Computer software development & applications; business oriented computer software

(G-2975)
LITTLE FOX INC
720 E Palisade Ave # 104 (07632-3054)
PHONE...................................609 919-9691
Kyung Sook Sung, *Administration*
EMP: 4
SALES (est): 207.8K **Privately Held**
SIC: 2741 Guides: publishing & printing

(G-2976)
OSEM USA INC
333 Sylvan Ave Ste 302 (07632-2733)
PHONE...................................201 871-4433
Fax: 201 871-3007
Gad Propper, *Ch of Bd*
Izzet Ozdogan, *President*
Ron Wise, *Vice Pres*
Philip Gisondi, *Natl Sales Mgr*
Kobi Afek, *Marketing Staff*
▲ EMP: 8
SALES (est): 1.5MM
SALES (corp-wide): 1B **Privately Held**
WEB: www.osemusa.com
SIC: 2034 Soup mixes
PA: Osem Investments Ltd.
     2 Rimon
     Shoham 60829
     372 050-50

(G-2977)
PAUL WINSTON FINE JEWELRY GROU (PA)
Also Called: True Romance
619 E Palisade Ave Ste 1 (07632-1834)
PHONE...................................800 232-2728
Isaac Gad, *CEO*
Benjamin Yekutiel, *President*
Xavier Bretillion, *Vice Pres*
Ahuva Nazarian, *Vice Pres*
James Van Nostrand, *Assoc Prof*
▼ EMP: 15
SALES (est): 2.5MM **Privately Held**
SIC: 3911 Jewelry, precious metal

(G-2978)
PCS REVENUE CTRL SYSTEMS INC
560 Sylvan Ave Ste 2050 (07632-3174)
PHONE...................................201 568-8300
Abe Halpern, *President*
David Yaniv, *General Mgr*
Judi Dugan, *Project Mgr*
Rich Purcell, *Sales Staff*
David Smith, *Program Mgr*
▲ EMP: 48
SQ FT: 11,000
SALES (est): 16.2MM **Privately Held**
WEB: www.pcsrcs.com
SIC: 5045 3577 3571 Computers, peripherals & software; computer software; computer peripheral equipment; electronic computers

(G-2979)
PRIMACY ENGINEERING INC (PA)
560 Sylvan Ave Ste 1212 (07632-3163)
PHONE...................................201 731-3272
Jaewan Lee, *President*
Albert OH, *Vice Pres*
John Devlin, *Director*
John Salak,
Sun Young Han, *Executive Asst*
EMP: 15
SQ FT: 1,500
SALES (est): 4.1MM **Privately Held**
SIC: 3613 8711 3621 3812 Switchgear & switchboard apparatus; engineering services; motors & generators; search & navigation equipment

(G-2980)
TALENTI GELATO LLC (HQ)
800 Sylvan Ave (07632-3201)
PHONE...................................800 298-4020
Steve Gill, *Mng Member*
EMP: 31
SALES (est): 21.6MM
SALES (corp-wide): 63B **Privately Held**
SIC: 2024 Ice cream, bulk
PA: Unilever Plc
Unilever House
London EC4Y
207 822-5252

(G-2981)
TELLAS LTD
600 Sylvan Ave Ste 4 (07632-3120)
PHONE...................................201 399-8888
Richard Helfenbein, *President*
EMP: 21 **Privately Held**
SIC: 2326 2339 Men's & boys' work clothing; women's & misses' athletic clothing & sportswear
HQ: Tellas Ltd.
95 Madison Ave
New York NY 10016
212 213-1709

(G-2982)
TOPIFRAM LABORATORIES INC
440 Sylvan Ave Ste 100 (07632-2711)
P.O. Box 1613 (07632-0613)
PHONE...................................201 894-9020
Robert Neis, *President*
Arnold Neis, *Chairman*
Charmane Halas, *Controller*
EMP: 50

SALES (est): 3.3MM
SALES (corp-wide): 84.7MM **Privately Held**
WEB: www.etbrowne.com
SIC: 2834 8731 2844 Dermatologicals; commercial physical research; toilet preparations
PA: E.T. Browne Drug Co., Inc.
440 Sylvan Ave
Englewood Cliffs NJ 07632
201 894-9020

(G-2983)
TRILOGY PUBLICATIONS LLC
560 Sylvan Ave Ste 1240 (07632-3171)
PHONE...................................201 816-1211
Lenore Clark, *Office Mgr*
Rose Reichman,
EMP: 6
SALES (est): 351.4K **Privately Held**
SIC: 2731 Book publishing

(G-2984)
TRIMTEX COMPANY INC
Also Called: St Louis Trimming Div
325 Sylvan Ave Ste 102 (07632-2753)
PHONE...................................201 945-2151
William C Henderson, *President*
Howard Mann, *Chairman*
EMP: 100
SQ FT: 300,000
SALES (est): 3.8MM **Privately Held**
WEB: www.trimtex.com
SIC: 2241 2257 2211 Trimmings, textile; braids, textile; weft knit fabric mills; broadwoven fabric mills, cotton

(G-2985)
UNILEVER BESTFOODS NORTH AMER (DH)
800 Sylvan Ave (07632-3201)
PHONE...................................201 894-4000
Fax: 201 894-2244
Charles R Shoemate, *President*
Julio Del Cioppo, *Manager*
◆ EMP: 12
SALES (est): 659.7MM
SALES (corp-wide): 63B **Privately Held**
WEB: www.bestfoods.com
SIC: 2046 2034 2035 2098 Wet corn milling; dextrose; high fructose corn syrup (HFCS); glucose; soup mixes; mayonnaise; macaroni products (e.g. alphabets, rings & shells); dry; noodles (e.g. egg, plain & water); dry; peanut butter; cakes, bakery: except frozen; pastries, e.g. danish: except frozen; bagels, fresh or frozen; bread, all types (white, wheat, rye, etc): fresh or frozen
HQ: Unilever United States, Inc.
700 Sylvan Ave
Englewood Cliffs NJ 07632
201 894-4000

(G-2986)
UNILEVER UNITED STATES INC (HQ)
Also Called: Unilever Hpc-USA
700 Sylvan Ave (07632-3113)
P.O. Box 210253, Dallas TX (75211-0253)
PHONE...................................201 894-4000
Fax: 201 871-8257
Michael B Polk, *President*
Siobhan Moore, *President*
John Bird, *Senior VP*
Julio Del Cioppo, *Mktg Dir*
Laura Klauberg, *Marketing Staff*
▲ EMP: 1180 EST: 1977
SALES (est): 5.6B
SALES (corp-wide): 63B **Privately Held**
WEB: www.unilever.com
SIC: 2035 2086 2024 2038 Pickles, sauces & salad dressings; dressings, salad: raw & cooked (except dry mixes); mayonnaise; spreads, sandwich: salad dressing base; bottled & canned soft drinks; ice cream & frozen desserts; frozen specialties; toilet preparations; toothpastes or powders, dentifrices; hair preparations, including shampoos; cosmetic preparations; detergents, synthetic organic or inorganic alkaline; dishwashing compounds; soap: granulated, liquid, cake, flaked or chip

PA: Unilever Plc
Unilever House
London EC4Y
207 822-5252

(G-2987)
UNILEVER UNITED STATES INC
800 Sylvan Ave (07632-3201)
PHONE...................................800 298-5018
Michell Largmann, *Branch Mgr*
EMP: 6
SALES (corp-wide): 63B **Privately Held**
SIC: 2035 Pickles, sauces & salad dressings
HQ: Unilever United States, Inc.
700 Sylvan Ave
Englewood Cliffs NJ 07632
201 894-4000

(G-2988)
ZENITH ELECTRONICS CORPORATION
1000 Sylvan Ave Fl 1 (07632-3302)
PHONE...................................201 816-2071
Tj Lee, *CEO*
EMP: 40
SALES (corp-wide): 29.2B **Privately Held**
WEB: www.zenith.com
SIC: 3651 Household audio & video equipment
HQ: Zenith Electronics Corporation
2000 Millbrook Dr
Lincolnshire IL 60069
847 941-8000

Englishtown
Monmouth County

(G-2989)
ACORN INDUSTRY INC
Also Called: Raason Cabinetry
6 Hoffer Ct (07726-8414)
PHONE...................................732 536-6256
David Langner, *President*
EMP: 11
SALES: 1.5MM **Privately Held**
SIC: 2599 Cabinets, factory

(G-2990)
CHEVEUX COSMETICS CORPORATION
30 Park Ave (07726-1607)
P.O. Box 449 (07726-0449)
PHONE...................................732 446-7516
Mabel Richardson, *President*
Sharon Griffith, *Corp Secy*
Bill Covey Jr, *Vice Pres*
EMP: 60
SQ FT: 35,000
SALES (est): 6.6MM **Privately Held**
SIC: 2844 Hair preparations, including shampoos

(G-2991)
DAVID BRADLEY CHOCOLATIER INC
520 Us Highway 9 (07726-8264)
PHONE...................................732 536-7719
Bradley David, *Branch Mgr*
EMP: 22
SALES (corp-wide): 2.2MM **Privately Held**
SIC: 2066 2064 Chocolate & cocoa products; candy & other confectionery products
PA: David Bradley Chocolatier Inc.
92 N Main St Bldg 19
Windsor NJ 08561
609 443-4747

(G-2992)
GOLDEN TREASURE IMPORTS INC
Also Called: Alisa
522 Us Highway 9 (07726-8241)
PHONE...................................732 723-1830
Lisa Morgan, *President*
Fred Morgan, *Sales Staff*
Alfred Morgan, *Marketing Staff*
EMP: 4
SQ FT: 600

SALES: 641K **Privately Held**
SIC: 5094 3961 Diamonds (gems); costume jewelry

(G-2993)
GREATER MEDIA NEWSPAPERS (DH)
198 Us Highway 9 Ste 100 (07726-3073)
PHONE...................................732 358-5200
Fax: 732 780-4257
Peter Smyth, *President*
John Zielinski, *Principal*
Donna Kenyon, *Editor*
Toni Smith, *Production*
Linda Hecht, *Accounts Exec*
EMP: 22 EST: 1888
SQ FT: 6,500
SALES (est): 45.5MM
SALES (corp-wide): 232.1MM **Publicly Held**
WEB: www.gmnews.com
SIC: 2711 Newspapers: publishing only, not printed on site; newspapers, publishing & printing
HQ: Greater Media, Inc.
3033 Riviera Dr Ste 200
Naples FL 34103
239 263-5000

(G-2994)
HAIR SYSTEMS INC
30 Park Ave (07726-1607)
P.O. Box 449 (07726-0449)
PHONE...................................732 446-2202
William Covey Jr, *President*
Marjorie M Covey, *Chairman*
Sunny Shah, *Plant Mgr*
Uzma Shah, *Purch Agent*
Nancy Lastra, *Purchasing*
▲ EMP: 70
SQ FT: 55,000
SALES: 18MM **Privately Held**
WEB: www.hairsystemsinc.com
SIC: 2844 3565 Bleaches, hair; hair coloring preparations; packing & wrapping machinery

(G-2995)
KUMAR BROS USA LLC (PA)
74 Oxford Ct (07726-1571)
PHONE...................................732 266-3091
Siddharth Khattar,
▲ EMP: 6
SQ FT: 500
SALES (est): 787.5K **Privately Held**
SIC: 3714 Motor vehicle parts & accessories

(G-2996)
PACKET MEDIA LLC (PA)
198 Us Highway 9 Ste 100 (07726-3073)
P.O. Box 350, Princeton (08542-0350)
PHONE...................................856 779-3800
James B Kilgore, *President*
EMP: 3
SALES (est): 41.7MM **Privately Held**
SIC: 2711 3993 Newspapers; signs & advertising specialties

(G-2997)
QUADRANGLE PRODUCTS INC
28 Harrison Ave Unit D (07726-1579)
PHONE...................................732 792-1234
Fax: 732 792-8305
Michael Levine, *President*
▲ EMP: 10
SQ FT: 5,000
SALES: 1.2MM **Privately Held**
WEB: www.quadrangleproducts.com
SIC: 3679 5045 Harness assemblies for electronic use: wire or cable; computer peripheral equipment

(G-2998)
STAVOLA CONTRACTING CO INC
120 Old Bergen Mill Rd (07726)
PHONE...................................732 935-0156
Joe Stavola, *Manager*
EMP: 4
SALES (est): 447.4K
SALES (corp-wide): 29.9MM **Privately Held**
SIC: 2951 Concrete, bituminous

G E O G R A P H I C

PA: Stavola Contracting Co Inc
175 Drift Rd
Tinton Falls NJ 07724
732 542-2328

(G-2999)
UNION HILL CORP
29 Park Ave (07726-1622)
PHONE..................................732 786-9422
Fax: 732 786-9423
Mike Conforth, *CEO*
▲ EMP: 5
SALES (est): 624.3K **Privately Held**
SIC: 2399 Horse & pet accessories, textile

Erial
Camden County

(G-3000)
ERIAL CONCRETE INC
965 Hickstown Rd (08081-1090)
P.O. Box 309, Blackwood (08012-0309)
PHONE..................................856 784-8884
Fax: 856 627-1979
Steve Rowanowski, *President*
Emma Rowanowski, *Admin Sec*
EMP: 15
SQ FT: 3,000
SALES (est): 2.8MM **Privately Held**
SIC: 3273 Ready-mixed concrete

Essex Fells
Essex County

(G-3001)
WINSTAR WINDOWS LLC
217 Roseland Ave (07021-1111)
PHONE..................................973 403-0574
Gene Kelly, *Mng Member*
EMP: 7
SALES (est): 625.9K **Privately Held**
SIC: 3442 Window & door frames

Ewing
Mercer County

(G-3002)
AFRICA WORLD PRESS
541 W Ingham Ave Ste B (08638-5001)
P.O. Box 1892, Trenton (08607-1892)
PHONE..................................609 695-3200
Fax: 609 844-0198
Kassahun Checole, *President*
EMP: 6
SQ FT: 15,000
SALES: 743.7K **Privately Held**
SIC: 2731 Books: publishing only

(G-3003)
ANTARES PHARMA INC (PA)
100 Princeton S Ste 300 (08628)
PHONE..................................609 359-3020
Fax: 484 359-3015
Leonard S Jacob, *Ch of Bd*
Robert F Apple, *President*
Leonard Jacob, *COO*
Peter Graham, *Exec VP*
Steven Knapp, *Vice Pres*
EMP: 110
SQ FT: 16,400
SALES: 54.5MM **Publicly Held**
WEB: www.antarespharma.com
SIC: 2834 3841 Pharmaceutical prepara-
tions; surgical & medical instruments

(G-3004)
ARCTIC PRODUCTS CO INC
Also Called: Arctic Ice Cream Co
22 Arctic Pkwy (08638-3041)
PHONE..................................609 393-4264
Fax: 609 392-3663
Thomas G Green, *President*
EMP: 12 EST: 1931
SQ FT: 6,000
SALES: 1MM **Privately Held**
WEB: www.arcticicecreamco.com
SIC: 2024 Ice cream, bulk

(G-3005)
CAPITAL STEEL SERVICE LLC
82 Stokes Ave (08638-3726)
PHONE..................................609 882-6983
Fax: 609 882-7458
Robert Hickman, *President*
Kim Fox, *Purch Agent*
▲ EMP: 22
SALES: 6MM **Privately Held**
WEB: www.capitalsteel.org
SIC: 5051 3441 Steel; fabricated structural
metal

(G-3006)
CAPITOL BINDERY INC
312 Stokes Ave (08638-3732)
PHONE..................................609 883-5971
Fax: 609 883-9104
Robert Gugger, *President*
Marilyn Gugger, *Vice Pres*
EMP: 4
SQ FT: 5,000
SALES (est): 385.7K **Privately Held**
WEB: www.capitolbindery.com
SIC: 2789 Binding only: books, pamphlets,
magazines, etc.

(G-3007)
**CELATOR PHARMACEUTICALS
INC (HQ)**
200 Princeton S (08628)
PHONE..................................609 243-0123
Fax: 609 243-0202
Bruce C Cozadd, *President*
Karen Smith, *Vice Pres*
Matthew P Young, *Treasurer*
Donna C Alvarez, *Manager*
Michael Chiarella, *Director*
EMP: 25
SQ FT: 4,785
SALES (est): 3MM **Privately Held**
SIC: 2834 Pharmaceutical preparations

(G-3008)
CHESSCO INDUSTRIES INC
Process Research Products
1013 Whitehead Road Ext (08638-2418)
PHONE..................................609 882-0400
Fax: 609 882-9608
Anthony Broomer, *Vice Pres*
John Broomer, *Sales Engr*
EMP: 20
SALES (corp-wide): 8.5MM **Privately
Held**
WEB: www.processresearch.com
SIC: 2819 3291 Industrial inorganic chem-
icals; abrasive products
PA: Chessco Industries, Inc.
1330 Post Rd E Ste 2
Westport CT 06880
203 255-2804

(G-3009)
**CHURCH & DWIGHT CO INC
(PA)**
500 Charles Ewing Blvd (08628-3448)
PHONE..................................609 806-1200
Fax: 609 497-7177
James R Craigie, *Ch of Bd*
Matthew T Farrell, *President*
Patrick D De Maynadier, *Exec VP*
Steven J Katz, *Vice Pres*
Richard A Dierker, *CFO*
◆ EMP: 350
SQ FT: 250,000
SALES: 3.7B **Publicly Held**
WEB: www.churchdwight.com
SIC: 2841 2812 2842 2844 Detergents;
synthetic organic or inorganic alkaline;
sodium bicarbonate; bleaches, house-
hold: dry or liquid; fabric softeners; de-
odorants, nonpersonal; toothpastes or
powders, dentifrices; ammonium com-
pounds, except fertilizers

(G-3010)
CMF LTD INC
599 W Ingham Ave (08638-5001)
PHONE..................................609 695-3600
Fax: 609 695-3763
Gerald P Donahue, *President*
Michael Donahue, *Vice Pres*
Keith Schultz, *Vice Pres*
EMP: 45
SQ FT: 56,000

SALES (est): 6.3MM **Privately Held**
WEB: www.cmflimited.com
SIC: 3429 Metal fasteners

(G-3011)
**CREST ULTRASONICS CORP
(HQ)**
18 Graphics Dr (08628-1546)
P.O. Box 7266, Trenton (08628-0266)
PHONE..................................609 883-4000
Fax: 609 530-0872
J Michael Goodson, *CEO*
Sami Awad, *President*
Mitchelle Vitarelli, *CFO*
Tom Lipski, *Manager*
Lo Kang, *Software Engr*
▲ EMP: 7
SQ FT: 55,000
SALES: 27.4MM
SALES (corp-wide): 41.3MM **Privately
Held**
WEB: www.crest-ultrasonics.com
SIC: 3841 Ultrasonic medical cleaning
equipment
PA: Crestek, Inc.
18 Graphics Dr
Ewing NJ 08628
609 883-4000

(G-3012)
CRESTEK INC (PA)
18 Graphics Dr (08628-1546)
PHONE..................................609 883-4000
J Michael Goodson, *CEO*
▲ EMP: 22
SQ FT: 50,000
SALES: 41.3MM **Privately Held**
WEB: www.crestek.com
SIC: 3699 3841 3679 Cleaning equip-
ment, ultrasonic, except medical & dental;
ultrasonic medical cleaning equipment;
power supplies, all types: static

(G-3013)
DAVIS HYUNDAI
Also Called: Davis Hyundai & Mitsubishi
1655 N Olden Avenue Ext (08638-3205)
PHONE..................................609 883-3500
Ron Derouin, *Principal*
EMP: 18
SALES (est): 5.3MM **Privately Held**
SIC: 5511 3519 Automobiles, new & used;
parts & accessories, internal combustion
engines

(G-3014)
**DISCOVERY SEMICONDUCTORS
INC**
119 Silvia St (08628-3200)
PHONE..................................609 434-1311
Fax: 609 434-1317
Abhay Joshi, *President*
Sharon V Joshi, *Vice Pres*
Aaron Berry, *Sales Engr*
EMP: 25
SQ FT: 10,000
SALES: 3.8MM **Privately Held**
WEB: www.discoverysemi.com
SIC: 3674 Semiconductors & related de-
vices

(G-3015)
EASTERN PODIATRY LABS INC
1702 5th St (08638-3039)
PHONE..................................609 882-4444
Thomas Mc Guigan, *President*
EMP: 4
SQ FT: 3,000
SALES (est): 477.1K **Privately Held**
SIC: 3842 Orthopedic appliances

(G-3016)
ESQUIRE BUSINESS FORMS
Also Called: Esquire Graphics & Bus Forms
1668 N Olden Avenue Ext (08638-3209)
PHONE..................................609 883-1155
Fax: 609 883-2406
Roger Melick, *Owner*
EMP: 4
SQ FT: 3,100
SALES (est): 700K **Privately Held**
SIC: 2752 Commercial printing, offset

(G-3017)
EWING RECOVERY CORP
Also Called: Century Metals
1565 6th St (08638-3001)
PHONE..................................609 883-0318
Betty Wallace, *Vice Pres*
Ronald Mc Closkey, *Vice Pres*
Brian Mc Closkey, *Treasurer*
James Wallace, *Admin Sec*
EMP: 6
SALES (est): 564.5K **Privately Held**
WEB: www.centurymetalsco.com
SIC: 3339 Precious metals

(G-3018)
FMC CORPORATION
Also Called: F M C Research and Dev Div
801-701 Princeton S (08628)
PHONE..................................609 963-6200
Shaaban Elnaggar, *President*
Richard Police, *Branch Mgr*
Upender Garlapati, *Programmer Anys*
Luanne McGovern, *Director*
Deepesh Singh, *Associate Dir*
EMP: 120
SQ FT: 10,000
SALES (corp-wide): 2.8B **Publicly Held**
WEB: www.fmc.com
SIC: 2869 Industrial organic chemicals
PA: Fmc Corporation
2929 Walnut St
Philadelphia PA 19104
215 299-6000

(G-3019)
HALBERD MATCH CORP
1230 Parkway Ave Ste 306 (08628-3018)
PHONE..................................609 882-7000
Fax: 609 882-7000
Michael Shutt, *CEO*
Julia Freedman, *Vice Pres*
Julia Price, *Marketing Staff*
EMP: 6
SALES (est): 362.8K **Privately Held**
WEB: www.halberdmatch.com
SIC: 3812 Search & navigation equipment

(G-3020)
**HARRISON MACHINE AND TOOL
INC**
21 Lexington Ave (08618-2301)
PHONE..................................609 883-0800
Steven Harrison, *President*
Marie Harrison, *Admin Sec*
EMP: 4
SQ FT: 4,000
SALES (est): 440K **Privately Held**
WEB: www.harrisonmachine.com
SIC: 3599 Machine shop, jobbing & repair

(G-3021)
HEIGHTS USA INC
1445 Lower Ferry Rd (08618-1424)
PHONE..................................609 530-1300
Fax: 609 530-9430
Leigh Jezorek, *President*
Tim Philburn, *COO*
Sheri Petrone, *Human Res Dir*
Julie Mc Clain, *Mktg Dir*
▲ EMP: 24
SQ FT: 38,000
SALES (est): 4MM
SALES (corp-wide): 4.6MM **Privately
Held**
WEB: www.heights-usa.com
SIC: 3861 Photographic equipment & sup-
plies
HQ: Heights (U.K.) Limited
The Old Mill
Halifax HX2 7
142 224-0914

(G-3022)
**HERMITAGE PRESS OF NEW
JERSEY (PA)**
1595 5th St (08638-3099)
PHONE..................................609 882-3600
Fax: 609 882-1137
Mary L Stoeckle, *Ch of Bd*
Michael Stoeckle, *President*
Michael W Stoeckle, *President*
Joseph Fallon, *Vice Pres*
Thomas Stoeckle, *CFO*
EMP: 57
SQ FT: 10,000

2018 Harris New Jersey
Manufacturers Directory

▲ = Import ▼=Export
◆ =Import/Export

SALES (est): 8.9MM **Privately Held**
SIC: 2752 7331 Commercial printing, offset; mailing service

(G-3023)
HESS CORPORATION
601 Jack Stephan Way (08628-3019)
PHONE..............................609 882-8477
EMP: 4
SALES (corp-wide): 5.4B **Publicly Held**
SIC: 1382 Oil & gas exploration services
PA: Hess Corporation
1185 Ave Of The Amer
New York NY 10036
212 997-8500

(G-3024)
HOMASOTE COMPANY
932 Lower Ferry Rd (08628-3298)
P.O. Box 7240, Trenton (08628-0240)
PHONE..............................609 883-3300
Fax: 609 530-1584
Warren L Flicker, *President*
Pete Tindall, *VP Opers*
Ronald Fasano, *CFO*
Jennifer Birtkovich, *Admin Sec*
EMP: 107 EST: 1909
SQ FT: 537,000
SALES: 20MM **Privately Held**
WEB: www.homasote.com
SIC: 2493 2671 Insulation board, cellular fiber; paper coated or laminated for packaging

(G-3025)
HPH PRODUCTS INC
182 Carlton Ave (08618-1402)
PHONE..............................609 883-0052
Jim Deiner, *President*
EMP: 5
SALES: 950K **Privately Held**
SIC: 3643 Current-carrying wiring devices

(G-3026)
ITECH INSTRUMENTS LLC
816 Silvia St (08628-3240)
PHONE..............................609 924-7310
Scott Gater, *Manager*
Marius Casile,
Thomas Cautzsch,
◆ EMP: 5
SQ FT: 5,000
SALES: 400K **Privately Held**
SIC: 3674 Radiation sensors

(G-3027)
JOHN PATRICK PUBLISHING LLC
Also Called: Jppc
1707 4th St (08638-3032)
P.O. Box 5469, Trenton (08638-0469)
PHONE..............................609 883-2700
Fax: 609 883-8821
Carol Schmerbeck, *Opers Mgr*
Celeste Gama, *Sales Mgr*
Patricia Graham, *Sales Staff*
Glenn Wassmer, *Sales Staff*
Tom Zukofski, *Sales Staff*
EMP: 52
SQ FT: 13,000
SALES (est): 6.4MM **Privately Held**
WEB: www.jppc.net
SIC: 2741 2759 Miscellaneous publishing; newsletter publishing; yearbooks: publishing & printing; envelopes: printing

(G-3028)
JOSEPH NATICCHIA
Also Called: Naticchia's Custom Woodworking
1597 5th St (08638-3034)
PHONE..............................609 882-7709
Fax: 609 882-2442
Joseph Naticchia, *Owner*
EMP: 12
SQ FT: 1,500
SALES: 600K **Privately Held**
SIC: 2431 Millwork

(G-3029)
KELLEIGH USA INC
1445 Lower Ferry Rd Ste 2 (08618-1424)
PHONE..............................732 248-1161
EMP: 6

SALES (est): 607.1K **Privately Held**
SIC: 2822 Ethylene-propylene rubbers, EPDM polymers

(G-3030)
KINETICS INDUSTRIES INC
Also Called: Kinetics Control Systems
140 Stokes Ave (08638-3796)
PHONE..............................609 883-9700
Ronald H Secrest, *President*
Kenneth Morris, *Vice Pres*
Keith Secrest, *Vice Pres*
EMP: 29 EST: 1939
SQ FT: 20,000
SALES (est): 8.4MM **Privately Held**
WEB: www.kinetics-industries.com
SIC: 3679 5063 Rectifiers, electronic; electrical apparatus & equipment

(G-3031)
KNITE INC
18 W Piper Ave Ste 201 (08628-1307)
PHONE..............................609 258-9550
Art Suckewer, *President*
Lynda Sacharov, *Office Mgr*
David Boyer, *Director*
EMP: 4
SALES (est): 250K **Privately Held**
WEB: www.knite.com
SIC: 3694 Ignition apparatus, internal combustion engines

(G-3032)
KNUDSEN PRECISION MFG
113 Walters Ave (08638-1829)
PHONE..............................609 538-1100
Don Hoven, *President*
Janet Hoven, *Exec VP*
EMP: 12
SQ FT: 7,500
SALES (est): 1.2MM **Privately Held**
SIC: 3599 Machine shop, jobbing & repair

(G-3033)
KRAFTWORK CUSTOM DESIGN
182 Homecrest Ave (08638-3634)
PHONE..............................609 883-8444
Fax: 609 882-3424
EMP: 15
SALES (est): 740K **Privately Held**
SIC: 2759 Commercial Printing

(G-3034)
LAWRENCE CUSTOM DRAPERY SHOP
Also Called: Shuren Upholstery
323 4th St (08638-2703)
PHONE..............................609 882-4007
Fax: 609 278-9059
Charles C Cullen, *President*
Cathy Stone, *Vice Pres*
EMP: 18
SQ FT: 7,000
SALES (est): 3.2MM **Privately Held**
SIC: 5023 7641 5714 2391 Draperies; reupholstery; draperies; upholstery materials; curtains & draperies

(G-3035)
LAWRENCE KATONA
Also Called: Precision Cut Kits
63 Carlton Ave (08618-1418)
PHONE..............................609 538-1388
Lawrence Katona, *Owner*
EMP: 5
SALES (est): 346.9K **Privately Held**
WEB: www.precisioncutkits.com
SIC: 3944 Airplane models, toy & hobby

(G-3036)
M K WOODWORKING INC
Also Called: Majer Design
1476 Prospect St (08638-4802)
PHONE..............................609 771-1350
Fax: 609 771-1306
George Majer, *President*
Roland Majer, *Vice Pres*
EMP: 5
SQ FT: 4,000
SALES: 700K **Privately Held**
SIC: 2431 2434 Millwork; wood kitchen cabinets

(G-3037)
MICRODOSE THERAPEUTX INC
Also Called: Microdose Defense Products
7 Graphics Dr (08628-1547)
PHONE..............................732 355-2100
Fax: 732 355-2101
Anand Gumaste, *CEO*
Scott Fleming, *President*
F Scott Fleming, *Senior VP*
Dave Byron, *Vice Pres*
Michael Martin, *Vice Pres*
EMP: 49
SQ FT: 16,000
SALES (est): 6.6MM **Privately Held**
WEB: www.mdtx.com
SIC: 3841 Inhalation therapy equipment

(G-3038)
NANOPV CORPORATION (PA)
Also Called: Nanopv Technology
122 Mountainview Rd (08560-1202)
PHONE..............................609 851-3666
Anna Selvan John, *President*
▲ EMP: 12
SQ FT: 40,000
SALES (est): 9.4MM **Privately Held**
WEB: www.nano-pv.com
SIC: 3674 Solar cells

(G-3039)
NAVINTA LLC
1499 Lower Ferry Rd (08618-1414)
PHONE..............................609 883-1135
Fax: 609 883-1137
Mahendra Patel, *Mng Member*
Pankaj Dave,
Jay Patel,
▲ EMP: 10
SALES (est): 2.7MM **Privately Held**
WEB: www.navinta.com
SIC: 2833 Drugs & herbs: grading, grinding & milling

(G-3040)
NEUROTRON MEDICAL INC
800 Silvia St (08628-3239)
P.O. Box 6480, Trenton (08648-0480)
PHONE..............................609 896-3444
Jack Guldalian, *President*
EMP: 4
SALES (est): 290K **Privately Held**
WEB: www.neumedinc.com
SIC: 3845 Electromedical apparatus

(G-3041)
PFIZER INC
1001 Jack Stephan Way (08628-3015)
PHONE..............................609 434-4920
Brian Clark, *Manager*
EMP: 50
SALES (corp-wide): 52.5B **Publicly Held**
WEB: www.pfizer.com
SIC: 2834 Pharmaceutical preparations
PA: Pfizer Inc.
235 E 42nd St
New York NY 10017
212 733-2323

(G-3042)
PFLAUMER BROTHERS INC (PA)
1008 Whitehead Road Ext (08638-2406)
P.O. Box 309, Norristown PA (19404-0309)
PHONE..............................609 883-0360
Fax: 609 883-4610
Harley McNair, *President*
Craig McNair, *Vice Pres*
Lorraine McNair, *Vice Pres*
Diann Rupprecht, *Treasurer*
Danielle Hamilton, *Manager*
▲ EMP: 6 EST: 1934
SQ FT: 6,000
SALES (est): 5.1MM **Privately Held**
WEB: www.pflaumer.com
SIC: 2843 2992 8742 Surface active agents; lubricating oils & greases; industry specialist consultants

(G-3043)
PIERCE-ROBERTS RUBBER COMPANY
1450 Heath Ave (08638-3832)
P.O. Box 5007, Trenton (08638-0007)
PHONE..............................609 394-5245
Fax: 609 394-0709

Christopher Weber, *Vice Pres*
Matthew Hoffman, *Manager*
Dan Pogo, *Manager*
Marilynn Williams, *Manager*
EMP: 18 EST: 1911
SQ FT: 65,000
SALES (est): 4.2MM **Privately Held**
WEB: www.pierceroberts.com
SIC: 2822 3069 3061 Synthetic rubber; molded rubber products; mechanical rubber goods

(G-3044)
POWTEK POWDER COATING INC
233 Dickinson St (08638-3450)
PHONE..............................609 394-1144
Fred Martucci, *President*
EMP: 6
SALES (est): 520.2K **Privately Held**
SIC: 3479 Painting, coating & hot dipping

(G-3045)
PRECISION DEVICES INC
20 Lexington Ave Ste 3 (08618-2323)
PHONE..............................609 882-2230
Fax: 609 882-2278
Mark Hoover, *Principal*
EMP: 4
SALES (est): 313.8K **Privately Held**
SIC: 5063 7694 Electrical supplies; electric motor repair

(G-3046)
PURDUE PHARMA LP
100 Prnctn S Corpt Ctr # 250 (08628-3459)
PHONE..............................203 588-8000
Fax: 609 409-5799
Franz Azuolas, *Branch Mgr*
EMP: 153 **Privately Held**
SIC: 2834 Pharmaceutical preparations
PA: Purdue Pharma L.P.
201 Tresser Blvd Fl 1
Stamford CT 06901

(G-3047)
QUANTEM CORP
1457 Lower Ferry Rd Ste 1 (08618-1493)
PHONE..............................609 883-9191
Fax: 609 883-9879
Christopher Bromberg, *Ch of Bd*
John Brienza, *Senior VP*
EMP: 25
SQ FT: 15,000
SALES (est): 4.3MM **Privately Held**
SIC: 3825 Measuring instruments & meters, electric

(G-3048)
RBC BEARINGS INCORPORATED
400 Sullivan Way (08628-3438)
PHONE..............................609 882-5050
Sandi Mease, *Purch Mgr*
Kevin Hoekzema, *Engineer*
Robert Pallini, *Engineer*
Michele Jordan, *Sales Staff*
George Sabochick, *Branch Mgr*
EMP: 105
SQ FT: 110,000
SALES (corp-wide): 674.9MM **Publicly Held**
SIC: 3562 Roller bearings & parts
PA: Rbc Bearings Incorporated
102 Willenbrock Rd
Oxford CT 06478
203 267-7001

(G-3049)
RED SEA PRESS INC
Also Called: Africa World Red Sea Press
541 W Ingham Ave Ste B (08638-5001)
PHONE..............................609 695-3200
Kassahun Checole, *President*
EMP: 5
SQ FT: 15,000
SALES (est): 625.8K **Privately Held**
SIC: 2731 Books: publishing only

(G-3050)
REES SCIENTIFIC CORPORATION
1007 Whitehead Road Ext # 1 (08638-2428)
PHONE..............................609 530-1055

Fax: 609 530-1854
Dr Rees Thomas, *President*
Eric Hammond, *Regional Mgr*
William Harrington, *Regional Mgr*
Alex Rivera, *Project Mgr*
Mae Fraley-Hall, *Prdtn Mgr*
▲ **EMP:** 104
SQ FT: 26,000
SALES (est): 24MM **Privately Held**
WEB: www.reesscientific.com
SIC: 3822 3823 Auto controls regulating residntl & coml environmt & applncs; industrial instrmnts msrmnt display/control process variable

(G-3051)
RIEGEL CMMUNICATIONS GROUP INC
1 Graphics Dr (08628-1547)
P.O. Box 7430, Trenton (08628-0430)
PHONE..............................609 771-0555
Lou Vassallo, *President*
Jim Esca, *CFO*
▼ **EMP:** 26
SALES (est): 4.9MM **Privately Held**
SIC: 2759 Letterpress printing

(G-3052)
RIEGEL HOLDING COMPANY INC
Also Called: Riegel Printing Company
1 Graphics Dr (08628-1547)
P.O. Box 7430, Trenton (08628-0430)
PHONE..............................609 771-0361
Fax: 609 771-0947
Kathleen Adkins, *President*
Susan Heath, *Exec VP*
Kevin Brown, *Vice Pres*
Brian Haley, *Vice Pres*
Zuzana Heath, *Vice Pres*
EMP: 53
SQ FT: 42,000
SALES (est): 16MM **Privately Held**
WEB: www.riegelprintinginc.com
SIC: 2752 Commercial printing, offset

(G-3053)
RIVER HORSE BREWERY CO INC
2 Graphics Dr (08628-1546)
PHONE..............................609 883-0890
Chris Walsh, *CEO*
Jack Bryan, *President*
Andrea Whaley, *Office Mgr*
EMP: 10
SQ FT: 10,000
SALES (est): 1.5MM **Privately Held**
SIC: 2082 Beer (alcoholic beverage)

(G-3054)
S L ENTERPRISES INC (PA)
Also Called: Fixturecraft
1603 N Olden Ave (08638-3205)
PHONE..............................908 272-8145
Fax: 908 272-8149
William P Mooney, *President*
Michael Rossetti, *Vice Pres*
EMP: 4
SQ FT: 2,000
SALES: 3.5MM **Privately Held**
WEB: www.fixturecraft.com
SIC: 4225 7389 2541 2542 General warehousing; coupon redemption service; store & office display cases & fixtures; partitions & fixtures, except wood

(G-3055)
SPECIALTY MEASURES
15 Dawes Ave (08638-4609)
PHONE..............................609 882-6071
EMP: 4
SALES (est): 408.9K **Privately Held**
SIC: 3449 7692 Custom roll formed products; automotive welding

(G-3056)
SPECIALTY VHCL SOLUTIONS LLC
804 Silvia St (08628-3239)
PHONE..............................609 882-1900
J Michael Burke, *CEO*
Karen Burke, *General Mgr*
Brian Tomchik, *Principal*
Frank Schwalenberg, *VP Finance*
◆ **EMP:** 25

SQ FT: 22,000
SALES (est): 5.4MM **Privately Held**
WEB: www.vehiclesolutionsnow.com
SIC: 3711 Bus & other large specialty vehicle assembly

(G-3057)
SUPERIOR INTL SRGICAL SUPS LLC
46 Oak Ln (08618-4002)
PHONE..............................609 695-6591
James Smith,
Joshua Baker,
▲ **EMP:** 10
SALES (est): 1.4MM **Privately Held**
SIC: 3842 Surgical appliances & supplies

(G-3058)
SURFACE TECHNOLOGY INC
Also Called: STI
1405 Lower Ferry Rd (08618-1414)
P.O. Box 8585, Trenton (08650-0585)
PHONE..............................609 259-0099
Michael D Feldstein, *President*
Mary A Stephenson, *Human Res Dir*
Barry McCoy, *Sales Staff*
Jijeesh Thottathil, *Technician*
EMP: 15 **EST:** 1973
SQ FT: 20,000
SALES (est): 2.5MM **Privately Held**
WEB: www.diamondcoating.com
SIC: 8734 2869 Testing laboratories; industrial organic chemicals

(G-3059)
T A C TECHNICAL INSTR CORP
Also Called: Tactic
152 Mercer Cty Airport (08628-1390)
PHONE..............................609 882-2894
Fax: 609 882-3147
Kenneth H Beck, *Ch of Bd*
Frederick Beck, *President*
Howard Hunter, *Treasurer*
Ruth Kontura, *Admin Sec*
▼ **EMP:** 14 **EST:** 1962
SQ FT: 10,000
SALES (est): 3MM **Privately Held**
WEB: www.tactictest.com
SIC: 3823 7389 3541 Industrial instrmnts msrmnt display/control process variable; inspection & testing services; machine tools, metal cutting type

(G-3060)
TEDCO INC
Also Called: Minuteman Press
35 Scotch Rd (08628-2512)
PHONE..............................609 883-0799
Fax: 609 538-0701
Ted Blumenthal, *President*
EMP: 7
SQ FT: 5,000
SALES: 850K **Privately Held**
SIC: 2752 2791 2789 Commercial printing, offset; typesetting; bookbinding & related work

(G-3061)
TRENTON CORRUGATED PRODUCTS
17 Shelton Ave (08618)
PHONE..............................609 695-0808
Fax: 609 695-7530
Anthony Pecoraro, *President*
Brad Pecoraro, *Vice Pres*
Gail Pecoraro, *Treasurer*
Cathy Dillon, *Sales Mgr*
M Helen Pecoraro, *Admin Sec*
EMP: 50
SQ FT: 150,000
SALES (est): 9.8MM **Privately Held**
WEB: www.trentoncorrugated.com
SIC: 2653 Boxes, corrugated: made from purchased materials; boxes, solid fiber: made from purchased materials

(G-3062)
TRENTYPO INC
304 Stokes Ave (08638-3732)
PHONE..............................609 883-5971
Fax: 609 883-2428
EMP: 15 **EST:** 1960
SQ FT: 6,000

SALES (est): 1MM **Privately Held**
SIC: 2791 2752 2759 Typesetting Services Lithographic Commercial Printing Commercial Printing

(G-3063)
TUSA PRODUCTS INC
1515 Parkway Ave (08628-2730)
PHONE..............................609 448-8333
Matthew Chow, *Principal*
Chad Lippincott, *Graphic Designe*
EMP: 8
SQ FT: 40,000
SALES (est): 601.8K **Privately Held**
SIC: 3651 3369 3625 Home entertainment equipment, electronic; machinery castings, nonferrous: ex. alum., copper, die, etc.; switches, electronic applications

(G-3064)
UNIVERSAL DISPLAY CORPORATION (PA)
375 Phillips Blvd Ste 1 (08618-1455)
PHONE..............................609 671-0980
Fax: 609 671-0995
Sherwin I Seligsohn, *Ch of Bd*
Steven V Abramson, *President*
Sidney Rosenblatt, *Exec VP*
Julia J Brown, *Senior VP*
Julie Brown, *Vice Pres*
EMP: 138
SALES: 335.6MM **Publicly Held**
WEB: www.universaldisplay.com
SIC: 3674 Semiconductors & related devices; light emitting diodes

(G-3065)
UNIVERSAL MEDICAL INC
275 Phillips Blvd (08618-1452)
PHONE..............................800 606-5511
EMP: 19
SQ FT: 1,200
SALES: 300.5K **Privately Held**
SIC: 3845 Mfg Electromedical Equipment

(G-3066)
UNLIMITED SILK SCREEN PRODUCTS
41 Lexington Ave (08618-2320)
PHONE..............................609 882-0653
Fax: 609 882-5221
Alan Heayn, *President*
Karen Yerkes, *Corp Secy*
EMP: 8 **EST:** 1981
SQ FT: 3,600
SALES (est): 1.2MM **Privately Held**
SIC: 2759 Screen printing

(G-3067)
VEHICLE TECHNOLOGIES INC
Also Called: Vetex
17 Decou Ave (08628-2908)
PHONE..............................609 406-9626
Nicholas Fenelli, *President*
Mary Fenelli, *Vice Pres*
EMP: 4
SALES (est): 380K **Privately Held**
SIC: 3537 Lift trucks, industrial: fork, platform, straddle, etc.

(G-3068)
W GERRIETS INTERNATIONAL INC
130 Winterwood Ave (08638-1836)
PHONE..............................609 771-8111
Walter Gerriets, *President*
Bernd Baumeisteer, *Vice Pres*
Hannes Gerriets, *Vice Pres*
Claudia Baldenhofer, *Technology*
▲ **EMP:** 8
SALES (est): 2MM **Privately Held**
WEB: www.gi-info.com
SIC: 5049 5045 2391 Theatrical equipment & supplies; computers, peripherals & software; curtains & draperies

(G-3069)
WASTE MANAGEMENT NJ INC (HQ)
107 Silvia St (08628-3200)
PHONE..............................609 434-5200
Fax: 609 882-8715
James E Trevathan, *President*
Jim Dancy, *Senior VP*
William Trubeck, *CFO*

Larry Faschan, *Human Res Mgr*
Brenda Byles, *Network Analyst*
▼ **EMP:** 200
SALES (est): 1.4B
SALES (corp-wide): 14.4B **Publicly Held**
SIC: 3087 Custom compound purchased resins
PA: Waste Management, Inc.
1001 Fannin St Ste 4000
Houston TX 77002
713 512-6200

Fair Haven
Monmouth County

(G-3070)
ART FLAG CO INC
Also Called: Artflag
890 River Rd (07704-3348)
PHONE..............................212 334-1890
Fax: 212 941-9631
George Weiner, *President*
Carmen Weiner, *Vice Pres*
EMP: 18 **EST:** 1929
SQ FT: 5,000
SALES: 1MM **Privately Held**
SIC: 2399 2396 Flags, fabric; banners, made from fabric; screen printing on fabric articles

(G-3071)
DADDY DONKEY LABS LLC
115 Park Rd (07704-3136)
PHONE..............................646 461-4677
EMP: 6
SALES (est): 211K **Privately Held**
SIC: 7372 Prepackaged Software Services

Fair Lawn
Bergen County

(G-3072)
A ZEREGAS SONS INC (PA)
Also Called: Zerega Pasta
20-01 Broadway (07410-2059)
P.O. Box 241 (07410-0241)
PHONE..............................201 797-1400
Fax: 201 797-0148
John B Vermylen, *President*
Paul A Vermylen, *Chairman*
Mark E Vermylen, *Vice Pres*
Robert A Vermylen, *Vice Pres*
Nicholas Pugliese, *Treasurer*
◆ **EMP:** 170 **EST:** 1848
SQ FT: 125,000
SALES (est): 78.6MM **Privately Held**
WEB: www.zerega.com
SIC: 2098 Macaroni products (e.g. alphabets, rings & shells), dry; noodles (e.g. egg, plain & water), dry

(G-3073)
ABG LAB LLC
20-21 Wagaraw Rd Bldg 31b (07410-1322)
PHONE..............................973 559-5663
Dr Elina Tester, *President*
Louis Rinaldi, *COO*
EMP: 5
SALES (est): 337.4K **Privately Held**
SIC: 2834 2844 Pharmaceutical preparations; toilet preparations

(G-3074)
ADVANCED PROTECTIVE PRODUCTS
17-10 River Rd Ste 4c (07410-1250)
PHONE..............................201 794-2000
Thomas Heiss, *President*
Charlotte Heiss, *Treasurer*
▼ **EMP:** 11
SQ FT: 4,500
SALES (est): 2.5MM **Privately Held**
WEB: www.rust007.com
SIC: 2851 Paints & allied products

(G-3075)
AMERICAN FITTINGS CORP (PA)
Also Called: Amfico
17-10 Willow St (07410-2057)
PHONE..............................201 664-0027
Fax: 201 664-1175

▲ = Import ▼=Export
◆ =Import/Export

Henry Fischbein, *President*
Allen Fischbein, *Vice Pres*
Dan Fischbein, *Vice Pres*
Robert Fischbein, *Vice Pres*
Rachell Fischbein, *VP Opers*
EMP: 5
SQ FT: 5,000
SALES (est): 2.3MM **Privately Held**
WEB: www.americanfittingscorp.com
SIC: 5063 3644 Conduits & raceways;
noncurrent-carrying wiring services

(G-3076)
**AMERICAN GRAPHIC SYSTEMS
INC**
39-26 Broadway (07410-5401)
PHONE....................................201 796-0666
Fax: 201 796-7997
Stanley Schechter, *President*
Steven C Schechter, *Vice Pres*
Diane Schechter, *Treasurer*
Sandra Schechter, *Admin Sec*
EMP: 4
SQ FT: 9,600
SALES (est): 607.5K **Privately Held**
SIC: 2752 7389 3993 2791 Commercial
printing, offset; sign painting & lettering
shop; signs & advertising specialties;
typesetting; bookbinding & related work;
commercial printing

(G-3077)
ARTICULIGHT INC
15-06 Morlot Ave (07410-2115)
PHONE....................................201 796-2690
Israel Simchi, *President*
Pamela Simchi, *Vice Pres*
EMP: 6
SALES (est): 1.4MM **Privately Held**
WEB: www.articulight.com
SIC: 3646 5063 Commercial indusl & insti-
tutional electric lighting fixtures; ornamen-
tal lighting fixtures, commercial; lighting
fixtures

(G-3078)
**ASSOCIATED FABRICS
CORPORATION**
Also Called: A F C
15-01 Pollitt Dr Ste 7 (07410-2769)
PHONE....................................201 300-6053
Martin Marckowrtz, *President*
Bruce Nocera, *Vice Pres*
Samuel Samson, *Vice Pres*
▲ **EMP:** 5 **EST:** 1928
SQ FT: 6,000
SALES: 1.5MM **Privately Held**
WEB: www.afcnewyork.com
SIC: 5131 2396 Piece goods & other fab-
rics; textiles, woven; knit fabrics; furniture
trimmings, fabric

(G-3079)
AUTO REMIND INC
Also Called: Mbox Usa, Inc
14-25 Plaza Rd Ste N35 (07410-3547)
P.O. Box 105 (07410-0105)
PHONE....................................800 277-1299
Bo Nielsen, *CEO*
Yoav Amiri, *Vice Pres*
EMP: 5
SALES (est): 450K **Privately Held**
SIC: 3679 Electronic switches

(G-3080)
**AVERY DENNISON
CORPORATION**
16-00 Pollitt Dr Ste 3 (07410-2765)
PHONE....................................201 956-6100
Susan Guerin, *Branch Mgr*
EMP: 4
SALES (corp-wide): 6.6B **Publicly Held**
SIC: 2672 Coated & laminated paper
PA: Avery Dennison Corporation
207 N Goode Ave Ste 500
Glendale CA 91203
626 304-2000

(G-3081)
B-TEA BEVERAGE LLC
12-17 River Rd (07410-1812)
PHONE....................................201 512-8400
Michael Tseytin,
Felix Belferman,
Leon Bitelman,

EMP: 20
SQ FT: 1,600
SALES: 1MM **Privately Held**
SIC: 5149 2086 Tea; tea, iced: packaged
in cans, bottles, etc.

(G-3082)
BEILIS DEVELOPMENT LLC
20-21 Wagaraw Rd Bldg 31b (07410-1322)
PHONE....................................862 203-3650
Maddy Rubenstein, *CEO*
Natty Rubenstien, *Mng Member*
Eugene Beilis,
▲ **EMP:** 10
SQ FT: 3,500
SALES: 6MM **Privately Held**
SIC: 2844 Cosmetic preparations

(G-3083)
BEST OF FARMS LLC
12-17 River Rd (07410-1812)
PHONE....................................201 512-8400
Felix Belferman, *Managing Prtnr*
EMP: 5
SALES: 1MM **Privately Held**
SIC: 2024 Dairy based frozen desserts

(G-3084)
BIOMET FAIR LAWN LP
20-01 Pollitt Dr (07410-2823)
PHONE....................................201 797-7300
Jeffrey Anto, *Principal*
▲ **EMP:** 15
SALES (est): 2.5MM
SALES (corp-wide): 7.8B **Publicly Held**
WEB: www.biomet.com
SIC: 3842 Surgical appliances & supplies
HQ: Biomet, Inc.
345 E Main St
Warsaw IN 46580
574 267-6639

(G-3085)
**CALMAC MANUFACTURING
CORP**
3-00 Banta Pl (07410-3011)
PHONE....................................201 797-1511
Fax: 201 797-1522
Mark M Maccracken, *Chairman*
Brian Silvetti, *Vice Pres*
Dorothy Sullivan, *Treasurer*
Theresa Zambrano, *Admin Sec*
EMP: 50
SQ FT: 79,100
SALES (est): 11.3MM **Privately Held**
WEB: www.calmac.com
SIC: 3585 Refrigeration equipment, com-
plete; air conditioning equipment, com-
plete

(G-3086)
CATALOGUE PUBLISHERS INC
20-10 Maple Ave 35f-2 (07410-1591)
PHONE....................................973 423-3600
Fax: 973 423-4886
Gary Hegger, *President*
EMP: 11
SALES (est): 1.4MM **Privately Held**
WEB: www.cataloguepublishers.com
SIC: 2741 Catalogs: publishing only, not
printed on site

(G-3087)
CIBO VITA INC
16-00 Pollitt Dr Ste 3 (07410-2765)
PHONE....................................201 773-4873
Emre Imamoglu, *CEO*
Ahmet Celik, *President*
▲ **EMP:** 219 **EST:** 2009
SQ FT: 75,000
SALES (est): 71MM **Privately Held**
SIC: 2068 5145 2041 2034 Salted &
roasted nuts & seeds; nuts: dried, dehy-
drated, salted or roasted; nuts, salted or
roasted; grain cereals, cracked; dried &
dehydrated fruits

(G-3088)
CREATIVE INNOVATIONS INC
Also Called: Metropolitan Cabinet Works
20-21 Wagaraw Rd Bldg 31b (07410-1322)
PHONE....................................973 636-9060
Fax: 973 636-9061
Joseph Batavia, *President*
Anita L Batavia, *Managing Dir*
EMP: 10

SQ FT: 13,500
SALES: 1MM **Privately Held**
SIC: 1751 2522 1799 Cabinet building &
installation; office furniture, except wood;
counter top installation

(G-3089)
DE ZAIO PRODUCTIONS INC
Also Called: Center Stage Productions
20-10 Maple Ave Bldg 31c (07410-1591)
PHONE....................................973 423-5000
Fax: 973 423-6000
Michael Dezaio, *President*
Jim McGrath, *Exec VP*
Michael Guzik, *Director*
Christina Riojas, *Director*
Sangeeta Datta, *Assistant*
EMP: 65
SQ FT: 56,095
SALES (est): 8.1MM **Privately Held**
SIC: 7389 3949 3942 Decoration service
for special events; playground equipment;
dolls & stuffed toys

(G-3090)
**EDGEWATER MANUFACTURING
CO INC (PA)**
17-10 Willow St (07410-2057)
PHONE....................................201 664-0022
Allen Fischbein, *President*
Dan Fischbein, *Vice Pres*
Rachell Fischbein, *Vice Pres*
Edith Fischbein, *Admin Sec*
▲ **EMP:** 37
SQ FT: 4,500
SALES (est): 8.2MM **Privately Held**
SIC: 3599 Machine shop, jobbing & repair

(G-3091)
**EXCALIBUR BAGEL BKY EQUIP
INC**
4-1 Banta Pl (07410)
PHONE....................................201 797-2788
Fax: 201 797-2711
Richard Zinn, *President*
Erich Zinn, *Corp Secy*
Shelly Kuo, *Vice Pres*
▲ **EMP:** 20 **EST:** 1995
SQ FT: 10,000
SALES (est): 3.4MM **Privately Held**
WEB: www.excalibur-equipment.com
SIC: 3556 Food products machinery

(G-3092)
**FISHER SCIENTIFIC CHEMICAL
DIV**
1 Reagent Ln (07410-2885)
PHONE....................................609 633-1422
Ebony Taileur-David, *Vice Pres*
Corina Fisher, *Director*
EMP: 25
SALES (est): 6.1MM **Privately Held**
SIC: 3826 Analytical instruments

(G-3093)
**FISHER SCIENTIFIC COMPANY
LLC**
Fisher Fair Lawn
1 Reagent Ln (07410-2885)
PHONE....................................201 796-7100
Fax: 201 796-1329
Melinda N Hazelman, *Principal*
Gerald Smith, *Opers Mgr*
Kevin Ford, *Buyer*
David Muntz, *QC Mgr*
Kathy Pangle, *Accounts Mgr*
EMP: 260
SALES (corp-wide): 20.9B **Publicly Held**
WEB: www.fishersci.com
SIC: 2833 8748 2899 Medicinals & botan-
icals; business consulting; chemical
preparations
HQ: Fisher Scientific Company Llc
300 Industry Dr
Pittsburgh PA 15275
724 517-1500

(G-3094)
**HENRY BROS ELECTRONICS
INC (HQ)**
17-01 Pollitt Dr Ste 5 (07410-2808)
PHONE....................................201 794-6500
James Henry, *CEO*
Ben Goodwin, *President*
Jim Henry, *President*

Fred Thomas, *Exec VP*
Jim Cotter, *Senior VP*
EMP: 58
SQ FT: 31,801
SALES (est): 48.2MM **Publicly Held**
SIC: 7373 3699 Computer integrated sys-
tems design; electrical equipment & sup-
plies; security control equipment &
systems

(G-3095)
**HISPANIC OUTLOOK-12 MAG
INC**
42-32 Debruin Dr (07410-5914)
P.O. Box 68, Paramus (07653-0068)
PHONE....................................201 587-8800
Jose Lopez ISA, *President*
Nicole Lopez ISA, *Vice Pres*
Meredith Cooper, *Advt Staff*
EMP: 7 **EST:** 2015
SALES (est): 489.6K **Privately Held**
SIC: 2731 Book publishing

(G-3096)
**INDUSTRIAL CONSULTING
MKTG INC**
Also Called: ICM
20-21 Wagaraw Rd Bldg 39 (07410-1322)
PHONE....................................973 427-2474
▲ **EMP:** 23 **EST:** 1996
SQ FT: 40,000
SALES (est): 3.8MM **Privately Held**
SIC: 3281 Stone Fabrication Services

(G-3097)
J M M R INC
Also Called: Arthroglide
25-9 Broadway (07410)
PHONE....................................201 612-5104
Joseph Molino, *President*
Michael Rebarber, *Exec VP*
EMP: 4
SALES (est): 264.1K **Privately Held**
WEB: www.jmmr.org
SIC: 8731 3842 Commercial physical re-
search; prosthetic appliances

(G-3098)
JDV PRODUCTS INC
22-01 Raphael St (07410-3043)
PHONE....................................201 794-6467
Fax: 201 796-9399
Eva Dvorak, *President*
▲ **EMP:** 17
SQ FT: 16,000
SALES (est): 5.3MM **Privately Held**
WEB: www.jdvproducts.com
SIC: 5072 3423 3545 3546 Hand tools;
hand & edge tools; machine tool acces-
sories; power-driven handtools; engineer-
ing services

(G-3099)
**KA-LOR CUBICLE AND SUP CO
INC**
14-24 Abbott Rd (07410-9698)
P.O. Box 804 (07410-0804)
PHONE....................................201 891-8077
Dennis Brett, *President*
Adelle Brett, *Vice Pres*
EMP: 7
SQ FT: 2,500
SALES (est): 837.6K **Privately Held**
SIC: 3429 Manufactured hardware (gen-
eral)

(G-3100)
**KUIKEN BROTHERS COMPANY
(PA)**
6-02 Fair Lawn Ave (07410-1219)
P.O. Box 1040 (07410-8040)
PHONE....................................201 796-2082
Douglas Kuiken, *President*
Henry Kuiken, *Vice Pres*
Kenneth H Kuiken, *Vice Pres*
Matthew D Kuiken, *Vice Pres*
Nicholas M Kuiken, *Vice Pres*
EMP: 38
SQ FT: 60,000
SALES: 156MM **Privately Held**
SIC: 5211 5031 3272 Millwork & lumber;
building materials, exterior; concrete stuc-
tural support & building material

(G-3101)
MADE SOLUTIONS LLC
18-01 River Rd (07410-1257)
PHONE..........................201 254-3693
Jenna Saccurato,
EMP: 4
SQ FT: 6,000
SALES (est): 167.4K Privately Held
SIC: 2842 2841 Specialty cleaning, polishes & sanitation goods; soap & other detergents

(G-3102)
MAURICE S DESSAU CO INC
Also Called: Dessau Company
15-01 Pollitt Dr Ste 10 (07410-2769)
PHONE..........................201 791-2005
Fax: 201 791-2115
Richard Dessau, President
◆ EMP: 20
SQ FT: 15,000
SALES: 4.5MM Privately Held
WEB: www.dessaudiamond.com
SIC: 3545 Cutting tools for machine tools

(G-3103)
MONDELEZ GLOBAL LLC
Also Called: Nabisco
22-11 State Rt 208 (07410-2608)
PHONE..........................201 794-4000
Calvin Reed, Manager
EMP: 850 Publicly Held
WEB: www.kraftfoods.com
SIC: 2052 2051 8731 Biscuits, dry; bakery: wholesale or wholesale/retail combined; commercial physical research
HQ: Mondelez Global Llc
3 N Pkwy Ste 300
Deerfield IL 60015
847 943-4000

(G-3104)
MONDELEZ GLOBAL LLC
Also Called: Nabisco
21-05 Route 208 (07410-2601)
PHONE..........................201 794-4080
John Ferri, Manager
EMP: 1000 Publicly Held
WEB: www.kraftfoods.com
SIC: 4212 4225 2052 Local trucking, without storage; general warehousing; cookies & crackers
HQ: Mondelez Global Llc
3 N Pkwy Ste 300
Deerfield IL 60015
847 943-4000

(G-3105)
MY MAGIC
0 Plaza Rd (07410)
PHONE..........................201 703-1171
Meir Yeid, Owner
EMP: 5 EST: 1979
SALES (est): 226.1K Privately Held
SIC: 3999 Magic equipment, supplies & props

(G-3106)
NITKA GRAPHICS INC
13-63 Henrietta Ct (07410-5801)
PHONE..........................201 797-3000
Hy Nitka, President
EMP: 10
SQ FT: 6,000
SALES (est): 1.6MM Privately Held
WEB: www.nitkainc.com
SIC: 2752 Commercial printing, offset

(G-3107)
PRIVATE LABEL PRODUCTS INC
20-21 Wagaraw Rd Bldg 34 (07410-1322)
PHONE..........................201 773-4230
David Naor, President
▲ EMP: 20
SALES (est): 2.4MM Privately Held
WEB: www.foodoodler.com
SIC: 3953 Marking devices

(G-3108)
RANGECRAFT MANUFACTURING INC
4-40 Banta Pl (07410-3059)
PHONE..........................201 791-0440
Ramona Panus, President
EMP: 10

SQ FT: 5,500
SALES (est): 2MM Privately Held
SIC: 3444 Hoods, range: sheet metal

(G-3109)
RINKO ORTHOPEDIC APPLIANCES
25-09 Broadway Ste 1 (07410-3898)
PHONE..........................201 796-3121
Fax: 201 796-1551
Stephen Rinko, President
Terri Wassel, Office Mgr
EMP: 9 EST: 1955
SQ FT: 3,250
SALES (est): 1.4MM Privately Held
WEB: www.rinko.com
SIC: 3842 Orthopedic appliances; prosthetic appliances

(G-3110)
ROBERT MAIN SONS INC
20-21 Wagaraw Rd (07410-1324)
P.O. Box 159, Wyckoff (07481-0159)
PHONE..........................201 447-3700
Robert Main Jr, President
Zachary Main, Principal
Susan Main, Corp Secy
Timothy Den Bleyker, Vice Pres
William Main, Vice Pres
EMP: 40 EST: 1955
SQ FT: 29,000
SALES (est): 7.4MM
SALES (corp-wide): 28.7MM Privately Held
WEB: www.ramsco-inc.com
SIC: 3496 Miscellaneous fabricated wire products
PA: Main, Robert A & Sons Holding Company Inc
555 Goffle Rd
Wyckoff NJ 07481
201 447-3700

(G-3111)
ROBERT WEIDENER
Also Called: Weidener Construction
9 12th St (07410)
PHONE..........................201 703-5700
Robert Weidener, President
EMP: 7
SALES (est): 1.8MM Privately Held
SIC: 1389 Construction, repair & dismantling services

(G-3112)
SANDVIK INC (DH)
Also Called: Sandvik & Coromant
17-02 Nevins Rd (07410-2886)
P.O. Box 428 (07410-0428)
PHONE..........................201 794-5000
Fax: 201 794-5042
Rick Askin, President
Claes Akarblom, President
Sunil Joshi, President
Michel Obolensky, General Mgr
Hosea Molife, Business Mgr
◆ EMP: 250 EST: 1919
SQ FT: 168,000
SALES (est): 917.2MM
SALES (corp-wide): 10.7B Privately Held
SIC: 3316 3317 3356 3315 Strip steel, cold-rolled: from purchased hot-rolled; wire, flat, cold-rolled strip: not made in hot-rolled mills; tubes, seamless steel; zirconium & zirconium alloy: rolling, drawing or extruding; titanium & titanium alloy: rolling, drawing or extruding; wire products, ferrous/iron: made in wiredrawing plants; machine tool accessories; bits, oil & gas field tools: rock; drilling tools for gas, oil or water wells
HQ: Sandvik Finance B.V.
's-Gravelandseweg 401
Schiedam
102 080-208

(G-3113)
SANDVIK INC
Also Called: Sandvik Coromant
17-2 Nevins Rd (07410)
PHONE..........................281 275-4800
Fax: 281 275-4940
Ray Benson, Plant Mgr
Bert Schmidt, Facilities Mgr
Perry Birkner, Sales Mgr
John Pusatera, Sales Mgr

Tim Tobin, Sales Mgr
EMP: 129
SQ FT: 50,790
SALES (corp-wide): 10.7B Privately Held
SIC: 5084 5251 3545 Industrial machinery & equipment; tools; machine tool accessories
HQ: Sandvik, Inc.
17-02 Nevins Rd
Fair Lawn NJ 07410
201 794-5000

(G-3114)
SK LIFE SCIENCE INC
Also Called: Sklsi
22-10 State Rt 208 (07410-2605)
PHONE..........................201 421-3800
Jaeyon Yoon, Vice Pres
Joanne Song, Accounting Mgr
Joon Hyun, Info Tech Mgr
Hunwoo Harry Shin, Director
Augustin Pegan, Director
▲ EMP: 30 EST: 1989
SALES (est): 7.5MM
SALES (corp-wide): 2.2B Privately Held
SIC: 2833 Medicinals & botanicals
HQ: Sk Biopharmaceuticals Co., Ltd.
221 Pangyoyeok-Ro Bundang-Gu
Seongnam 13494
822 212-1533

(G-3115)
STEPPIN OUT MAGAZINE
21-07 Maple Ave (07410-1524)
P.O. Box 626, Allendale (07401-0626)
PHONE..........................201 703-0911
Fax: 201 703-0211
Larry Collins, Owner
EMP: 5
SALES (est): 291.9K Privately Held
SIC: 2721 Magazines: publishing only, not printed on site

(G-3116)
STINGRAY SPORT PDTS LTD LBLTY
20-10 Maple Ave Bldg 35e (07410-1591)
PHONE..........................201 300-6482
Brad Lieberman,
EMP: 4
SQ FT: 2,000
SALES (est): 245.9K Privately Held
SIC: 3949 Winter sports equipment; water sports equipment; protective sporting equipment

(G-3117)
SYLVAN CHEMICAL CORPORATION
7 Prescott Pl (07410-4916)
PHONE..........................201 934-4224
Fax: 201 934-4274
Eugene Darvin, President
M W Edelstein, Vice Pres
Garrett Darvin, Admin Sec
EMP: 22
SQ FT: 3,500
SALES (est): 3MM Privately Held
WEB: www.sylvanchemical.com
SIC: 2899 5169 Chemical preparations; chemicals & allied products

(G-3118)
T G TYPE-O-GRAPHICS INC
19-03 Maple Ave Ste 3 (07410-1553)
PHONE..........................973 253-3333
Ruth Valdez, President
John F Valdez, Vice Pres
EMP: 5
SQ FT: 2,600
SALES: 1.2MM Privately Held
SIC: 2759 Commercial printing

(G-3119)
TANIS CONCRETE
17-68 River Rd (07410-1206)
PHONE..........................201 796-1556
Charles Tanis, President
Mark Tanis, President
Evelyn Tanis, Treasurer
Rosemary Gerson, Financial Exec
Lou Terletsky, Sales Mgr
EMP: 35
SQ FT: 15,000

SALES (est): 6.4MM Privately Held
SIC: 3241 3273 8711 1771 Cement, hydraulic; ready-mixed concrete; construction & civil engineering; concrete work

(G-3120)
TARGET COATINGS INC
17-12 River Rd (07410-1206)
P.O. Box 1582, Rutherford (07070-0582)
PHONE..........................800 752-9922
Jeff Weiss, President
▼ EMP: 5
SQ FT: 10,000
SALES: 618K Privately Held
WEB: www.targetcoatings.com
SIC: 5198 2851 Paints; paints & allied products

(G-3121)
TEX PRINT USA LLC
20-21 Wagaraw Rd 31a-1 (07410-1346)
PHONE..........................201 773-6531
Eduardo Margarucci Jr, CEO
▲ EMP: 20
SALES: 2.3MM Privately Held
SIC: 2752 Commercial printing, lithographic

(G-3122)
UNIVERCLEAN LTD
8-46 Susan Pl (07410-1616)
PHONE..........................201 674-1563
EMP: 5
SQ FT: 10,000
SALES: 250K Privately Held
SIC: 2841 3589 Mfg Soap/Other Detergents Mfg Service Industry Machinery

(G-3123)
WAREHOUSE SOLUTIONS INC
3-29 27th St Fl 4 (07410-3817)
PHONE..........................201 880-1110
Hannah Lebovich, Manager
EMP: 14
SALES (corp-wide): 4.2MM Privately Held
SIC: 2541 5046 7373 6794 Cabinets, lockers & shelving; shelving, commercial & industrial; computer-aided design (CAD) systems service; patent buying, licensing, leasing
PA: Warehouse Solutions Inc.
365 W Passaic St Ste 235
Rochelle Park NJ 07662
201 880-1110

(G-3124)
WAYSIDE FENCE COMPANY INC
38-06 Broadway (07410-5400)
PHONE..........................201 791-7979
John Weglarz, President
EMP: 22
SQ FT: 5,000
SALES: 2.2MM Privately Held
WEB: www.waysidefenceco.com
SIC: 5211 5039 3446 Fencing; wire fence, gates & accessories; partitions & supports/studs, including accoustical systems

(G-3125)
ZOLUU LLC
0-74 Saddle River Rd (07410-5509)
PHONE..........................862 686-1774
Mark Trujillo, Mng Member
EMP: 5
SALES: 1.5MM Privately Held
SIC: 7372 7389 Business oriented computer software;

```
┌─────────────────────────┐
│       Fairfield         │
│      Essex County       │
└─────────────────────────┘
```

(G-3126)
ACCURATE SCREW MACHINE CORP
Also Called: A S M
10 Audrey Pl (07004-3402)
PHONE..........................973 276-0379
Fax: 973 244-9177
Paul Stupinski, Vice Pres
James Callaghan, Vice Pres
Greg Corsi, Safety Mgr

▲ = Import ▼=Export
◆ =Import/Export

Pete Fuentes, *Mfg Staff*
Peter Kaczor, *QC Mgr*
EMP: 60
SQ FT: 16,000
SALES (est): 14.1MM
SALES (corp-wide): 169MM **Privately Held**
WEB: www.accuratescrew.com
SIC: 3451 3999 Screw machine products; atomizers, toiletry
HQ: Matthew Warren, Inc.
9501 Tech Blvd Ste 401
Rosemont IL 60018
847 349-5760

(G-3127)
ADHERENCE SOLUTIONS LLC
75 Lane Rd Ste 404 (07004-1000)
PHONE...................................800 521-2269
Dann Ferara, *CEO*
EMP: 4
SALES (est): 214.7K **Privately Held**
SIC: 8748 7372 Business consulting; business oriented computer software

(G-3128)
AIR POWER INC
25 Commerce Rd Ste N (07004-1620)
P.O. Box 1449, West Caldwell (07007-1449)
PHONE...................................973 882-5418
Hugh Rooney Jr, *President*
Victor Giambattista, *Vice Pres*
EMP: 35
SQ FT: 13,000
SALES: 5.3MM **Privately Held**
SIC: 1711 3444 Plumbing, heating, air-conditioning contractors; refrigeration contractor; ducts, sheet metal

(G-3129)
ALFA MACHINE & TOOL CO INC
19 Just Rd (07004-3407)
P.O. Box 11181 (07004-7181)
PHONE...................................973 227-1962
Fax: 973 808-8541
EMP: 17 **EST:** 1961
SQ FT: 12,000
SALES (est): 2.4MM **Privately Held**
SIC: 3599 3544 3541 Mfg Industrial Machinery Mfg Dies/Tools/Jigs/Fixtures Mfg Machine Tools-Cutting

(G-3130)
ALISON CONTROL INC
35 Daniel Rd W (07004-2558)
PHONE...................................973 575-7100
Fax: 973 575-3647
Gene Benzenberg, *President*
EMP: 20
SQ FT: 13,500
SALES (est): 4.1MM **Privately Held**
WEB: www.alisoncontrol.com
SIC: 3829 Fire detector systems, non-electric

(G-3131)
ALL MTALS FRGE GROUP LTD LBLTY (PA)
75 Lane Rd Ste 303 (07004-1061)
PHONE...................................973 276-5000
Lewis A Weiss, *Mng Member*
Lewis Weiss, *Mng Member*
Christine Casati, *Director*
▲ **EMP:** 15
SALES (est): 6.7MM **Privately Held**
SIC: 3462 Iron & steel forgings

(G-3132)
ALLIED PRINTING-GRAPHICS INC
4 Madison Rd (07004-2309)
PHONE...................................973 227-0520
Fax: 973 227-7664
Dominick Pascarella, *President*
Ralph Magliocchetti, *Shareholder*
EMP: 5
SALES (est): 1.3MM **Privately Held**
WEB: www.printallied.com
SIC: 2752 Commercial printing, offset

(G-3133)
AM-MAC INCORPORATED
311 Route 46 W Ste C (07004-2419)
PHONE...................................973 575-7567
Judith Spritzer, *President*

John M Spritzer, *Vice Pres*
▲ **EMP:** 10
SQ FT: 12,000
SALES (est): 5.1MM **Privately Held**
WEB: www.am-mac.com
SIC: 3556 5046 5084 Food products machinery; commercial cooking & food service equipment; food industry machinery

(G-3134)
AMARK WIRE LLC
18 Passaic Ave Unit 6 (07004-3834)
PHONE...................................973 882-7818
Joseph Whittaker,
Trac Dam,
Mario Salerno,
George Whittaker,
EMP: 5 **EST:** 2011
SQ FT: 5,000
SALES (est): 472.8K **Privately Held**
SIC: 3315 Steel wire & related products

(G-3135)
AMERICAN NATIONAL RED CROSS
209 Fairfield Rd (07004-2420)
PHONE...................................973 797-3300
Jocelyn Gilman, *Exec Dir*
EMP: 39
SALES (corp-wide): 2.5B **Privately Held**
WEB: www.redcross.org
SIC: 3999 Buttons: Red Cross, union, identification
PA: The American National Red Cross
430 17th St Nw
Washington DC 20006
202 737-8300

(G-3136)
ANDERSON & VREELAND INC (PA)
8 Evans St (07004-2200)
P.O. Box 1246, Caldwell (07007-1246)
PHONE...................................973 227-2270
Fax: 973 882-6621
Howard Vreeland Jr, *Ch of Bd*
Thomas O Gavin, *President*
Darin Lyon, *President*
Lonnie Grieser, *Principal*
Sean Sawa, *Regional Mgr*
▲ **EMP:** 25 **EST:** 1978
SALES (est): 47.5MM **Privately Held**
WEB: www.andersonvreeland.com
SIC: 3555 5084 Printing trades machinery; printing plates; printing trades machinery, equipment & supplies

(G-3137)
API INC
10 Industrial Rd (07004-3018)
PHONE...................................973 227-9335
Irwan Rusli, *Principal*
Ruo Xu, *Principal*
EMP: 15 **EST:** 2001
SALES (est): 2.8MM **Privately Held**
SIC: 2834 Pharmaceutical preparations

(G-3138)
ARLINGTON PRCSION CMPNENTS LLC
Also Called: Arlington Machine & Tool Co
90 New Dutch Ln (07004-2515)
PHONE...................................973 276-1377
Fax: 973 276-1378
John J Staudinger, *President*
▲ **EMP:** 50
SQ FT: 56,000
SALES (est): 354.4K
SALES (corp-wide): 23.9MM **Privately Held**
SIC: 3728 Aircraft body assemblies & parts; bodies, aircraft
HQ: Whi Global, Llc
13914 E Admiral Pl
Tulsa OK 74116
918 933-6500

(G-3139)
ARTHUR SCHUMAN INC (PA)
Also Called: Schuman Cheese
40 New Dutch Ln (07004-2514)
PHONE...................................973 227-0030
Fax: 973 227-1525
Neal Schuman, *CEO*
Ellen Schum, *President*

Tom Deangelo, *COO*
Patrick O'Callaghan, *Vice Pres*
Glenn Carrara, *Opers Staff*
◆ **EMP:** 85
SQ FT: 90,000
SALES (est): 177.2MM **Privately Held**
WEB: www.arthurschuman.com
SIC: 2022 Cheese, natural & processed

(G-3140)
ASHA44 LLC
175 Us Highway 46 Unit A (07004-2327)
PHONE...................................201 306-3600
Lester Samuels, *Managing Dir*
Andrea C Samuels, *Managing Dir*
◆ **EMP:** 25
SQ FT: 60,000
SALES (est): 10MM **Privately Held**
SIC: 2752 2269 Commercial printing, lithographic; printing of narrow fabrics

(G-3141)
ASPE INC
2 Daniel Rd Ste 101 (07004-2516)
PHONE...................................973 808-1155
Fax: 973 808-5666
Rudolph Sachs, *CEO*
Khanh Dim, *Office Mgr*
EMP: 20
SQ FT: 30,000
SALES (est): 2.1MM **Privately Held**
WEB: www.aspeusa.com
SIC: 3679 3469 3053 Hermetic seals for electronic equipment; metal stampings; gaskets, packing & sealing devices

(G-3142)
AW MACHINERY LLC
7 Just Rd (07004-3407)
PHONE...................................973 882-3223
Rudy Fernandez, *Sales Staff*
Nestor E Gener,
Arthur K Watson,
▼ **EMP:** 11
SQ FT: 9,000
SALES (est): 1.9MM **Privately Held**
WEB: www.awmachinery.com
SIC: 3357 3496 Fiber optic cable (insulated); miscellaneous fabricated wire products; cable, uninsulated wire: made from purchased wire

(G-3143)
BABCOCK & WILCOX POWR GENERATN
277 Fairfield Rd Ste 331a (07004-1942)
PHONE...................................973 227-7008
Mike Grady, *Vice Pres*
Steve Dutkiewicz, *Branch Mgr*
Ann Shuster, *Clerk*
EMP: 14
SALES (corp-wide): 1.5B **Publicly Held**
SIC: 3511 Steam turbines
HQ: The Babcock & Wilcox Company
20 S Van Buren Ave
Barberton OH 44203
330 753-4511

(G-3144)
BAR-LO CARBON PRODUCTS INC
31 Daniel Rd (07004-2520)
P.O. Box 10031 (07004-6031)
PHONE...................................973 227-2717
Fax: 973 575-7164
Barry M Flowers, *President*
Lois S Flowers, *Admin Sec*
▲ **EMP:** 26
SQ FT: 25,000
SALES (est): 5.3MM **Privately Held**
WEB: www.barlocarbon.com
SIC: 3545 Precision tools, machinists'

(G-3145)
BELLWOOD AEROMATICS INC
4 Spielman Rd (07004-3404)
PHONE...................................201 670-4617
Eric Beldner, *President*
Adam Beldner, *Vice Pres*
EMP: 4
SALES: 1MM **Privately Held**
WEB: www.belwoodaromatics.com
SIC: 2844 Toilet preparations

(G-3146)
BENCO INC
Also Called: Benco Products New York
10 Madison Rd Ste E (07004-2325)
P.O. Box 866, Pine Brook (07058-0866)
PHONE...................................973 575-4440
Fax: 973 575-4558
Karen Pyonin, *CEO*
Paul Pyonin, *President*
Chris Carey, *Partner*
Mike Benco, *Vice Pres*
Bill Beirne, *Sales Staff*
EMP: 17
SQ FT: 9,200
SALES: 2MM **Privately Held**
SIC: 1796 3444 5039 5211 Installing building equipment; sheet metalwork; prefabricated buildings; prefabricated buildings; partitions & fixtures, except wood; vitreous plumbing fixtures

(G-3147)
BERGEN CABLE TECHNOLOGY LLC (PA)
343 Kaplan Dr (07004-2510)
PHONE...................................973 276-9596
Fax: 973 276-9566
Terry Boboige, *President*
Peter Bartholomew, *General Mgr*
Ken Vandervelde, *Plant Mgr*
Debbie Hillman, *Purch Agent*
Surendra Patel, *QC Dir*
▲ **EMP:** 25 **EST:** 1942
SQ FT: 15,000
SALES (est): 4.3MM **Privately Held**
WEB: www.bergencable.com
SIC: 3542 3315 Crimping machinery, metal; cable, steel: insulated or armored

(G-3148)
BERGIO INTERNATIONAL INC (PA)
12 Daniel Rd (07004-2536)
PHONE...................................973 227-3230
Berge Abajian, *Ch of Bd*
EMP: 6
SQ FT: 1,730
SALES: 557.3K **Publicly Held**
SIC: 3911 Jewelry, precious metal; jewelry mountings & trimmings; necklaces, precious metal; rings, finger: precious metal

(G-3149)
BEVERAGE WORKS NJ INC
10 Dwight Pl (07004-3414)
PHONE...................................973 439-5700
Erich Becker, *Manager*
EMP: 19
SALES (est): 2MM **Privately Held**
SIC: 2086 Bottled & canned soft drinks
PA: The Beverage Works Nj Inc
1800 State Route 34 # 203
Wall Township NJ 07719

(G-3150)
BILT RITE TOOL & DIE CO INC
29 Montesano Rd (07004-3387)
PHONE...................................973 227-2882
Fax: 973 808-1962
Dennis George, *President*
Frank Mannuzza, *CPA*
EMP: 8 **EST:** 1956
SQ FT: 4,000
SALES: 2MM **Privately Held**
SIC: 3312 3469 Tool & die steel & alloys; metal stampings

(G-3151)
BONO USA INC
19 Gardner Rd Ste E (07004-2204)
PHONE...................................973 978-7361
Salvatore Russotiesi, *President*
Salvatore Bono, *General Mgr*
▲ **EMP:** 3
SALES: 5MM **Privately Held**
SIC: 2032 Italian foods: packaged in cans, jars, etc.

(G-3152)
C & M SHADE CORP
53 Dwight Pl (07004-3311)
P.O. Box 2388, South Hackensack (07606-0988)
PHONE...................................201 807-1200
Fax: 201 807-1930

Allen Francus, *President*
Blaise Domino, *Sales Mgr*
EMP: 32
SQ FT: 21,000
SALES (est): 4.7MM **Privately Held**
SIC: 2591 Window shades

(G-3153)
C & S MACHINE INC
22 Commerce Rd Ste Q (07004-1604)
PHONE.....................973 882-1097
Fax: 973 882-3242
Ronald J Woods, *President*
EMP: 15
SQ FT: 12,500
SALES (est): 1.5MM **Privately Held**
SIC: 7699 3552 Industrial equipment services; textile machinery

(G-3154)
CALIZ - MALKO LLC
66 Clinton Rd (07004-2910)
PHONE.....................973 207-5200
Cris Caliz, *CEO*
Alla Malko,
EMP: 4
SQ FT: 5,000
SALES: 200K **Privately Held**
SIC: 2052 Cookies

(G-3155)
CANFIELD PROPERTY GROUP INC
Also Called: Canfield Clinic Systems
253 Passaic Ave Ste 1 (07004-2524)
PHONE.....................973 276-0300
Douglas Canfield, *President*
Lisa Cramer, *Project Mgr*
Bill Halas, *CFO*
Dennis P Dasilva, *CTO*
Dan Cherill, *Network Mgr*
▲ **EMP:** 15
SALES (est): 2.2MM **Privately Held**
SIC: 3841 Surgical & medical instruments

(G-3156)
CARECAM INTERNATIONAL INC
10 Plog Rd (07004-3302)
PHONE.....................973 227-0720
Fax: 973 227-7395
Haren Gupta MD, *CEO*
Ravinder Jain PHD, *President*
EMP: 20
SQ FT: 8,500
SALES (est): 1.8MM **Privately Held**
SIC: 3089 Blister or bubble formed packaging, plastic

(G-3157)
CARTRIDGE ACTUATED DEVICES (HQ)
Also Called: C A D
51 Dwight Pl (07004-3311)
PHONE.....................973 575-8760
James Yake, *Ch of Bd*
Jim Yeats, *President*
John Grant, *Exec Dir*
EMP: 30 **EST:** 1962
SALES (est): 8.3MM
SALES (corp-wide): 374.4MM **Privately Held**
WEB: www.cartactdev.com
SIC: 2892 Explosives
PA: The Fike Corporation
704 Sw 10th St
Blue Springs MO 64015
816 229-3405

(G-3158)
CHICAGO PNEUMATIC TOOL
90 New Dutch Ln (07004-2515)
PHONE.....................973 276-1377
John J Staudinger, *Manager*
EMP: 7
SALES (corp-wide): 13.8B **Privately Held**
SIC: 3451 Screw machine products
HQ: Chicago Pneumatic Tool
222 Getty Ave
Clifton NJ 07011
973 928-5222

(G-3159)
CK MANUFACTURING INC
8 Gardner Rd (07004-2206)
PHONE.....................973 808-3500
Brian W Kaltner, *President*

Daniel Dall'ava, *Chairman*
Richard Cafaro, *Vice Pres*
Ruth Stern, *Admin Sec*
▲ **EMP:** 20 **EST:** 1953
SQ FT: 5,000
SALES (est): 2.5MM **Privately Held**
SIC: 3544 Industrial molds

(G-3160)
CLAREMONT DISTILLED SPIRITS
25 Commerce Rd (07004-1619)
PHONE.....................973 227-7027
EMP: 10
SALES (est): 1.2MM **Privately Held**
SIC: 2085 Distilled & blended liquors

(G-3161)
CLARK PRINTING INC
6 Audrey Pl (07004-3402)
PHONE.....................201 845-4888
Fax: 201 845-5888
Richard Lisa, *President*
Cecelia Ventrice, *Manager*
John Gambino, *Director*
Jim Lomicky, *Executive*
Joanne Scielzo, *Graphic Designe*
EMP: 30
SQ FT: 17,500
SALES (est): 4.7MM **Privately Held**
SIC: 2752 Commercial printing, lithographic

(G-3162)
CNI CERAMIC NOZZLES INC
23 Commerce Rd Ste L (07004-1609)
PHONE.....................973 276-1535
Fax: 973 276-1537
Stephen Ziegler, *President*
Thomas Calandrillo, *Vice Pres*
EMP: 8 **EST:** 1964
SQ FT: 5,000
SALES (est): 710K **Privately Held**
SIC: 3548 Welding & cutting apparatus & accessories

(G-3163)
COLUMBIA PRESS INC
12 Industrial Rd (07004-3018)
P.O. Box 10723 (07004-6723)
PHONE.....................973 575-6535
Fax: 973 575-6344
Charles Puleo, *President*
Alan Puleo, *Vice Pres*
EMP: 32 **EST:** 1977
SALES (est): 4MM **Privately Held**
SIC: 2752 Commercial printing, offset

(G-3164)
COMMAND NUTRITIONALS LLC
10 Washington Ave Ste 1 (07004-3840)
PHONE.....................973 227-8210
Rosa Figueiredo, *Office Mgr*
Akshi Patel, *Manager*
Scott Biedron,
Shyvonne Grimes, *Admin Asst*
▲ **EMP:** 40 **EST:** 1972
SQ FT: 55,000
SALES (est): 10.2MM **Privately Held**
WEB: www.commandnutritionals.com
SIC: 2834 Vitamin, nutrient & hematinic preparations for human use

(G-3165)
CONSTANT SERVICES INC
Also Called: Csi
17 Commerce Rd Ste 2 (07004-1662)
PHONE.....................973 227-2990
Fax: 973 227-2705
Vincent Pepe, *President*
Anthony Pepe, *Vice Pres*
Dominick Pepe, *Admin Sec*
EMP: 35
SQ FT: 39,000
SALES (est): 4.5MM **Privately Held**
SIC: 2754 Commercial printing, gravure

(G-3166)
CONTINUITY LOGIC LLC
55 Lane Rd Ste 303 (07004-1015)
PHONE.....................866 321-5079
Tejas Katwala,
Peter Christensen,
EMP: 59
SALES (est): 6.9MM **Privately Held**
SIC: 7372 Application computer software

(G-3167)
CONTROL & POWER SYSTEMS INC
Also Called: Dmz Industries
17 Spielman Rd (07004-3409)
PHONE.....................973 439-0500
Fax: 973 575-5300
Dov Shevich, *President*
David Lyon, *Vice Pres*
Tim Hecht, *Project Mgr*
Gregory Balcerek, *Engineer*
Rafal Skrzypczak, *Engineer*
▲ **EMP:** 34
SQ FT: 14,584
SALES (est): 9.5MM **Privately Held**
WEB: www.c-p-s.com
SIC: 3625 Electric controls & control accessories, industrial

(G-3168)
CONTROL INSTRUMENTS CORP
25 Law Dr (07004-3206)
PHONE.....................973 575-9114
Fax: 973 575-0013
Christopher Schaeffer, *President*
Matthew Schaeffer, *Chairman*
James M Schaeffer, *Vice Pres*
John Schaeffer, *Vice Pres*
Pravin Patel, *Engineer*
EMP: 31
SQ FT: 24,000
SALES (est): 7.7MM **Privately Held**
WEB: www.controlinstruments.com
SIC: 3823 On-stream gas/liquid analysis instruments, industrial

(G-3169)
CRISPY GREEN INC
10 Madison Rd Ste D (07004-2325)
PHONE.....................973 679-4515
Angela Liu, *President*
▲ **EMP:** 10
SQ FT: 15,000
SALES (est): 1.6MM **Privately Held**
SIC: 2099 Food preparations

(G-3170)
CUSTOM LABELS INC
345 Kaplan Dr (07004-2510)
PHONE.....................973 473-1934
Fax: 973 473-1509
Abraham Rubin, *President*
EMP: 4
SQ FT: 7,100
SALES (est): 380K **Privately Held**
WEB: www.cpp-flexo.com
SIC: 2759 Labels & seals: printing

(G-3171)
DATASCOPE CORP (HQ)
Also Called: Maquet
15 Law Dr (07004-3206)
PHONE.....................973 244-6100
Fax: 973 244-6243
Donald R Lemma, *Vice Pres*
Mark Rappaport, *Vice Pres*
S Arieh Zak, *Vice Pres*
Shrenik Daftary, *Engineer*
Bob Hoff, *Engineer*
◆ **EMP:** 200 **EST:** 1964
SQ FT: 75,000
SALES (est): 126.2MM
SALES (corp-wide): 2.6B **Privately Held**
WEB: www.datascope.com
SIC: 3845 Electrotherapeutic apparatus; electromedical apparatus
PA: Getinge Ab
Lindholmspiren 7a
Goteborg 417 5
103 350-000

(G-3172)
DAUM INC (DH)
368 Passaic Ave Ste 300 (07004-2008)
PHONE.....................862 210-8522
Henri Dequatrebarbes, *CEO*
Thierry Collot, *Exec VP*
▲ **EMP:** 4
SALES (est): 86.1K **Privately Held**
WEB: www.daumusa.com
SIC: 3229 Pressed & blown glass
HQ: Daum
22 Rue De La Tremoille
Paris 75008
383 322-165

(G-3173)
DAVEN INDUSTRIES INC
55 Dwight Pl (07004-3311)
PHONE.....................973 808-8848
Fax: 973 808-8777
Lou Lever, *President*
Phillip Stahl, *Vice Pres*
EMP: 20
SQ FT: 26,000
SALES (est): 3MM **Privately Held**
WEB: www.davenindustries.com
SIC: 3599 3568 3545 Custom machinery; power transmission equipment; machine tool accessories

(G-3174)
DEE JAY PRINTING INC
16 Passaic Ave Unit 3 (07004-3835)
PHONE.....................973 227-7787
Fax: 973 227-3773
Jeff Jaffe, *President*
EMP: 8
SQ FT: 5,000
SALES (est): 900K **Privately Held**
SIC: 2752 Commercial printing, offset

(G-3175)
DELTA CIRCUITS INC
26 Spielman Rd (07004-3412)
PHONE.....................973 575-3000
Fax: 973 575-8682
Pravin Bhuva, *President*
Dimple Bhuva, *Vice Pres*
▲ **EMP:** 26
SQ FT: 30,000
SALES (est): 4.6MM **Privately Held**
WEB: www.deltacircuits-nj.com
SIC: 3672 Printed circuit boards

(G-3176)
DENTISTRY TODAY INC
100 Passaic Ave Ste 220 (07004-3508)
PHONE.....................973 882-4700
Fax: 973 882-3622
Paul Radcliffe, *President*
John Lannon, *President*
Damon C Adams, *Principal*
Richard Gawel, *Editor*
Andrew Goodman, *Editor*
EMP: 20
SQ FT: 3,700
SALES (est): 3.2MM **Privately Held**
WEB: www.dentistrytoday.net
SIC: 2721 Trade journals: publishing only, not printed on site

(G-3177)
DESIGN OF TOMORROW INC
Also Called: Educational & Lab Systems
24 Sherwood Ln (07004-3602)
PHONE.....................973 227-1000
David Roitburg, *President*
Alex Gizersky, *Vice Pres*
Leon Roitburg, *Treasurer*
▲ **EMP:** 15
SQ FT: 12,000
SALES (est): 4MM **Privately Held**
SIC: 2431 8734 3553 Millwork; testing laboratories; scarfing machines, woodworking

(G-3178)
DM GRAPHIC CENTER LLC
26 Commerce Rd Ste L (07004-1606)
PHONE.....................973 882-8990
Fax: 973 882-0899
Jeannette Matin,
Kaweh K Matin,
EMP: 10
SQ FT: 5,000
SALES (est): 1.5MM **Privately Held**
WEB: www.dmgraphiccenter.com
SIC: 7389 7336 2789 Printers' services: folding, collating; graphic arts & related design; binding only: books, pamphlets, magazines, etc.

(G-3179)
DREW & ROGERS INC (PA)
30 Plymouth St Ste 2 (07004-1622)
P.O. Box 2040, West Caldwell (07007-2040)
PHONE.....................973 575-6210
Fax: 973 575-7180
Thomas M Rogers, *President*
Eugene Aleshevich, *Vice Pres*

Greg McDermott, *Vice Pres*
Michael Monteleone, *Vice Pres*
Brad Paxson, *Vice Pres*
▲ EMP: 31 EST: 1944
SQ FT: 30,000
SALES (est): 20.6MM **Privately Held**
WEB: www.drew-rogers.com
SIC: 5112 5199 7336 2761 Business forms; advertising specialties; commercial art & graphic design; manifold business forms

(G-3180)
DRIVE-MASTER CO INC
37 Daniel Rd (07004-2521)
PHONE.....................973 808-9709
Peter B Ruprecht Sr, *President*
Christina Knapik, *Vice Pres*
Peter B Ruprecht Jr, *Vice Pres*
Adrienne Ruprecht, *CFO*
Shelby Wells, *Sales Staff*
EMP: 14
SQ FT: 20,185
SALES (est): 3.3MM **Privately Held**
WEB: www.drive-master.com
SIC: 7532 5511 3711 Top & body repair & paint shops; automobiles, new & used; motor vehicles & car bodies

(G-3181)
ECB USA INC
Also Called: Ets Claude Blandin
333 Fairfield Rd (07004-1961)
PHONE.....................973 575-3226
Fax: 973 461-2348
Alain Voss, *Ch of Bd*
Claude Blandin, *Vice Chairman*
Arnaud Leoni, *Treasurer*
Bruno Blandin, *Admin Sec*
EMP: 6 EST: 2014
SALES (est): 410.2K **Privately Held**
SIC: 2022 Processed cheese
PA: Establissements Claude Blandin Et Fils
17 Rue Achille Rene Boisneuf
Pointe A Pitre

(G-3182)
EDSTON MANUFACTURING COMPANY
125 Clinton Rd Unit 2 (07004-2929)
PHONE.....................908 647-0116
Fax: 908 647-0901
Paul Zuzock, *President*
Emily B Weston, *President*
Jonathan P Weston, *Vice Pres*
Charles F Weston, *Admin Sec*
EMP: 6 EST: 1947
SQ FT: 4,900
SALES: 646.2K **Privately Held**
SIC: 3451 3542 Screw machine products; thread rolling machines

(G-3183)
ELMI MACHINE TOOL CORP
15 Spielman Rd 2 (07004-3403)
P.O. Box 1112, Caldwell (07007-1112)
PHONE.....................973 882-1277
Victor Vitencz, *President*
David Hyde, *Vice Pres*
Roy Olson, *Sales Dir*
EMP: 5 EST: 1966
SQ FT: 1,700
SALES: 900K **Privately Held**
WEB: www.elmimachine.com
SIC: 3599 Machine shop, jobbing & repair

(G-3184)
EMSE CORP
Also Called: Emseco
10 Plog Rd (07004-3302)
PHONE.....................973 227-9221
Fax: 973 227-9223
K Alex Rothenberg, *President*
Larry Savastano, *Vice Pres*
Gary Kroeger, *Treasurer*
▼ EMP: 13
SQ FT: 8,500
SALES (est): 1.4MM **Privately Held**
WEB:
SIC: 3821 3841 3563 Vacuum pumps, laboratory; surgical & medical instruments; air & gas compressors

(G-3185)
ESSEX WEST GRAPHICS INC (PA)
305 Fairfield Ave (07004-3831)
PHONE.....................973 227-2400
Fax: 973 227-2588
Donald Alldian, *President*
Thomas Guth, *Exec VP*
EMP: 45
SQ FT: 16,700
SALES (est): 8.1MM **Privately Held**
WEB: www.westessexgraphics.com
SIC: 2796 Platemaking services

(G-3186)
EVS BROADCAST EQUIPMENT INC (HQ)
9 Law Dr Ste 4 (07004-3233)
PHONE.....................973 575-7811
Gregory Macchia, *Senior VP*
Anne-Sophie Dupont, *Human Res Mgr*
EMP: 25 EST: 2007
SALES (est): 2.9MM
SALES (corp-wide): 115.7MM **Privately Held**
SIC: 3663 Studio equipment, radio & television broadcasting
PA: Evs Broadcast Equipment Sa
Rue Du Bois Saint-Jean 13
Seraing 4102
436 170-00

(G-3187)
EVS BROADCAST EQUIPMENT INC
Also Called: Evs
700 Route 46 E Ste 300 (07004-1532)
PHONE.....................973 575-7811
Frederic Garroy, *General Mgr*
Marc Caeymaex, *Senior VP*
James Stellpflug, *Vice Pres*
Pierre Matelart, *QC Mgr*
Armando Orellano, *Engineer*
EMP: 15
SALES (corp-wide): 115.7MM **Privately Held**
WEB: www.evs-global.com
SIC: 3577 Disk & diskette equipment, except drives
HQ: E.V.S. Broadcast Equipment, Inc.
9 Law Dr Ste 4
Fairfield NJ 07004
973 575-7811

(G-3188)
EXCALIBUR MIRETTI GROUP LLC
285 Eldridge Rd (07004-2508)
PHONE.....................973 808-8399
Roberto Santilli, *Engineer*
Michael Topf, *CFO*
Carl Palumbo, *Sales Staff*
Angelo Miretti,
▲ EMP: 15
SALES (est): 4.9MM **Privately Held**
WEB: www.exequipment.com
SIC: 3537 5084 Industrial trucks & tractors; forklift trucks; trucks, industrial

(G-3189)
EXCELLENT BAKERY EQUIPMENT CO
19 Spielman Rd (07004-3409)
PHONE.....................973 244-1664
Fax: 973 244-1696
Karin M Seruga, *President*
▲ EMP: 20
SQ FT: 30,000
SALES (est): 3.5MM **Privately Held**
WEB: www.excellent-bagels.com
SIC: 3556 Food products machinery

(G-3190)
EXCELLENTIA FLAVOURS LLC (PA)
Also Called: Excellentia International
30 Stewart Pl (07004-1631)
PHONE.....................732 749-9840
Tommas Buco, *Owner*
Steve Manning,
◆ EMP: 12
SQ FT: 20,000
SALES (est): 3.4MM **Privately Held**
SIC: 2099 Seasonings & spices

(G-3191)
EXPRESS PRINTING SERVICES INC
26 Commerce Rd Ste L (07004-1606)
PHONE.....................973 585-7355
Val Digiacinto, *Owner*
EMP: 4
SALES (est): 122.8K **Privately Held**
SIC: 2752 Commercial printing, lithographic

(G-3192)
EXTREME DIGITAL GRAPHICS INC
7 Kingsbridge Rd Ste 1 (07004-2141)
PHONE.....................973 227-5599
Fax: 973 227-5699
Pat Basile, *President*
Lynn Basile, *Vice Pres*
John Destefano, *Production*
Steve Nebesni, *Manager*
EMP: 10
SALES (est): 1.2MM **Privately Held**
SIC: 2732 Book printing

(G-3193)
FAIRFIELD LAUNDRY MCHY CORP
5 Montesano Rd Ste 1 (07004-3309)
PHONE.....................973 575-4330
Fax: 973 575-8507
Raymond Hall, *President*
Patrick Niland Sr, *Vice Pres*
EMP: 25
SQ FT: 12,000
SALES (est): 4.2MM **Privately Held**
WEB: www.flmcorp.com
SIC: 3582 Commercial laundry equipment

(G-3194)
FAIRFIELD METAL LTD LBLTY CO
9 Audrey Pl (07004-3401)
PHONE.....................973 276-8440
Arkadiuxz Baginksi, *Mng Member*
Luigi Colella Jr,
EMP: 12
SALES (est): 2.1MM **Privately Held**
SIC: 3444 Siding, sheet metal

(G-3195)
FINN & EMMA LLC
Also Called: Finn Emma
1275 Bloomfield Ave Ste 5 (07004-2736)
PHONE.....................973 227-7770
Maya Heenan, *Accounts Mgr*
Anna Schwengle, *Mng Member*
Marybeth Pasquariello, *Director*
▲ EMP: 5
SALES (est): 406.4K **Privately Held**
SIC: 2329 2261 5651 Athletic (warmup, sweat & jogging) suits: men's & boys'; calendering of cotton fabrics; unisex clothing stores

(G-3196)
FLM GRAPHICS CORPORATION (PA)
123 Lehigh Dr (07004-3010)
PHONE.....................973 575-9450
Fax: 973 575-6421
Frank Misischia, *Ch of Bd*
Karl Dewyngaert, *Business Mgr*
Tony Gagliardi, *Exec VP*
Vincent Gagliardi, *Exec VP*
Mike Monk, *Vice Pres*
EMP: 60 EST: 1972
SQ FT: 44,000
SALES: 18.8MM **Privately Held**
SIC: 2752 7374 Commercial printing, offset; computer graphics service

(G-3197)
FLOR LIFT OF N J INC
Also Called: Florlift of NJ
19 Gardner Rd Ste M (07004-2204)
PHONE.....................973 429-2200
Casper Vivona, *President*
Louisa Vivona, *Vice Pres*
EMP: 20
SQ FT: 12,000
SALES (est): 328.4K **Privately Held**
SIC: 3534 3535 Elevators & equipment; conveyors & conveying equipment

(G-3198)
FLOWSERVE CORPORATION
142 Clinton Rd (07004-2914)
PHONE.....................973 227-4565
Amy Hartman, *Controller*
EMP: 55
SALES (corp-wide): 3.6B **Publicly Held**
SIC: 3561 Industrial pumps & parts
PA: Flowserve Corporation
5215 N Oconnor Blvd Connor
Irving TX 75039
972 443-6500

(G-3199)
FORDHAM INC
20 Gloria Ln (07004-3306)
PHONE.....................973 575-7840
Thomas R Buckley, *CEO*
James Lombard, *President*
Karen Morgan, *Vice Pres*
EMP: 40
SQ FT: 15,000
SALES (est): 2.6MM **Privately Held**
WEB: www.fordhamjackets.com
SIC: 5999 2759 2339 2337 Banners, flags, decals & posters; commercial printing; women's & misses' outerwear; women's & misses' suits & coats; men's & boys' suits & coats
PA: Redi-Direct Marketing, Inc.
107 Little Falls Rd
Fairfield NJ 07004

(G-3200)
FOREMOST MACHINE BUILDERS INC
23 Spielman Rd (07004-3488)
P.O. Box 10155 (07004-6155)
PHONE.....................973 227-0700
Marlene C Heydenreich, *President*
Clifford J Weinpel, *Exec VP*
Clifford Weinpel, *Vice Pres*
Tim Downing, *Engineer*
Dave Revette, *Electrical Engi*
▲ EMP: 51 EST: 1947
SQ FT: 48,000
SALES (est): 12.8MM **Privately Held**
WEB: www.foremostmachine.com
SIC: 3559 3535 3532 Plastics working machinery; conveyors & conveying equipment; crushing, pulverizing & screening equipment

(G-3201)
FRAMEWARE INC
Also Called: Profiles of Frameware
8 Audrey Pl (07004-3402)
PHONE.....................800 582-5608
Fax: 973 808-0262
Dean De Luccia, *President*
Carmen Luccia, *VP Opers*
Francklin Ermeus, *Purchasing*
Wanda Chandler, *CFO*
Jim Stemper, *Marketing Staff*
◆ EMP: 18
SALES (est): 4.3MM **Privately Held**
WEB: www.framewareinc.com
SIC: 3469 2499 3354 7389 Metal stampings; picture frame molding, finished; shapes, extruded aluminum;

(G-3202)
FRIMPEKS INC
30 Sherwood Ln Ste 6 (07004-3603)
PHONE.....................201 266-0116
Sonay Karamanci, *President*
◆ EMP: 11
SALES: 3MM **Privately Held**
SIC: 2891 Adhesives

(G-3203)
FUJITSU GENERAL AMERICA INC
353 Route 46 W (07004)
PHONE.....................973 575-0380
Tedd Rozylowicz, *President*
Roy Kuczera, *Senior VP*
Cameron S Brown, *Engineer*
Susumu Ohkawara, *CFO*
Cathy Miller, *Accountant*
◆ EMP: 51 EST: 1995
SQ FT: 25,000

SALES (est): 180.5MM
SALES (corp-wide): 2.4B **Privately Held**
WEB: www.fujitsugeneral.com
SIC: 3585 Heating & air conditioning combination units
PA: Fujitsu General Limited
3-3-17, Suenaga, Takatsu-Ku
Kawasaki KNG 213-0
448 661-111

(G-3204)
G P R COMPANY INC
8 Spielman Rd (07004-3404)
PHONE.............................973 227-6160
Fax: 973 808-8350
George H Verhoest, *President*
Richard Verhoest, *Corp Secy*
Paul R Verhoest, *Vice Pres*
Vicky Huynh, *Office Mgr*
Devin Verhoest, *Program Mgr*
EMP: 47
SQ FT: 25,000
SALES: 8.5MM **Privately Held**
WEB: www.gprco.com
SIC: 3599 Machine shop, jobbing & repair

(G-3205)
GALLERIA ENTERPRISES INC
26 Commerce Rd Ste I (07004-1606)
PHONE.............................646 416-6683
Joe Simeone, *President*
Davis Lin, *Vice Pres*
Anthony Margulis, *Vice Pres*
▲ **EMP:** 5
SQ FT: 3,400
SALES (est): 2.5MM **Privately Held**
SIC: 3999 Umbrellas, canes & parts

(G-3206)
GARFIELD INDUSTRIES INC
62 Clinton Rd Ste 1 (07004-6216)
P.O. Box 839, Caldwell (07007-0839)
PHONE.............................973 575-3322
Fax: 973 575-6840
Deborah Gladstone, *President*
Steven Gelvan, *Vice Pres*
▲ **EMP:** 32 **EST:** 1949
SQ FT: 33,000
SALES: 4.3MM **Privately Held**
WEB: www.garfieldindustries.com
SIC: 3291 Buffing or polishing wheels, abrasive or nonabrasive

(G-3207)
GASFLO PRODUCTS INC
19 Industrial Rd (07004-3017)
PHONE.............................973 276-9011
Fax: 973 276-9014
David Panetta, *CEO*
Bill Wagner, *Vice Pres*
Chris Vernieri, *Engineer*
Timothy Galvin, *Treasurer*
John Galasso, *Office Mgr*
EMP: 37
SQ FT: 16,000
SALES (est): 10.3MM **Privately Held**
WEB: www.gasflo.com
SIC: 3494 3491 Valves & pipe fittings; industrial valves

(G-3208)
GATOR COMMUNICATIONS GROUP LLC
Also Called: Harvard Printing Group
175 Us Highway 46 (07004-2327)
P.O. Box 4148, Clifton (07012-8148)
PHONE.............................973 233-6700
Fax: 973 233-6701
Charles Stuto, *Mng Member*
Richard Bitetti,
Michael D'Allesandro,
Gene Palecco,
EMP: 47
SQ FT: 35,000
SALES: 11MM **Privately Held**
SIC: 2759 Commercial printing

(G-3209)
GIBRALTAR LABORATORIES INC (PA)
122 Fairfield Rd (07004-2405)
PHONE.............................973 227-6882
Fax: 973 227-0812
Daniel L Prince, *President*
Jozef Mastej, *VP Opers*
Remy Varughese, *Facilities Mgr*

Shiri Hechter, *QA Dir*
Kristah Kohan, *Sales Staff*
EMP: 50
SQ FT: 40,000
SALES (est): 10.1MM **Privately Held**
WEB: www.gibraltarlabsinc.com
SIC: 3841 8734 Diagnostic apparatus, medical; testing laboratories

(G-3210)
GLOBAL PRTNERS IN SHELDING INC
Also Called: Gps Specialty Doors
5 Just Rd (07004-3407)
PHONE.............................973 574-9077
Fax: 973 574-9078
Mark Holder, *President*
Bryan Bordeman, *Project Mgr*
Taylor Brady, *Project Mgr*
Nef Canelo, *Purch Mgr*
Robert Roman, *QC Mgr*
◆ **EMP:** 33
SQ FT: 17,000
SALES: 7MM **Privately Held**
WEB: www.gps-door.com
SIC: 3353 Aluminum sheet, plate & foil

(G-3211)
GMS LITHO CORP
16 Passaic Ave Unit 3 (07004-3835)
PHONE.............................973 575-9400
Gregory Enright, *President*
EMP: 5
SALES (est): 787.3K **Privately Held**
SIC: 2752 Commercial printing, lithographic

(G-3212)
GRANULATION TECHNOLOGY INC
12 Industrial Rd (07004-3018)
PHONE.............................973 276-0740
Fax: 973 276-0741
Ashok Niganaye, *President*
EMP: 15
SQ FT: 11,000
SALES (est): 1.9MM **Privately Held**
SIC: 2834 Pharmaceutical preparations

(G-3213)
GRAPH TECH SALES & SERVICE
6 Farmstead Ln (07004-1229)
PHONE.............................201 218-1749
Walter Petronczak, *Principal*
EMP: 13 **EST:** 2009
SALES (est): 1.9MM **Privately Held**
SIC: 2752 Commercial printing, lithographic

(G-3214)
H & T TOOL CO INC
19 Gardner Rd Ste C (07004-2204)
PHONE.............................973 227-4858
Fax: 973 227-4479
Thomas Schall, *President*
Raymond Mundrick, *Vice Pres*
EMP: 10
SQ FT: 10,000
SALES (est): 1.3MM **Privately Held**
SIC: 3469 Stamping metal for the trade

(G-3215)
HANOVIA SPECIALTY LIGHTING LLC
Also Called: Hanovia Colight
6 Evans St (07004-2210)
PHONE.............................973 651-5510
Liming Du, *Mng Member*
Jeffrey Andrews,
▲ **EMP:** 10
SQ FT: 53,000
SALES (est): 1.6MM **Privately Held**
WEB: www.hanovia-uv.com
SIC: 3641 Ultraviolet lamps

(G-3216)
HARVARD PRINTING GROUP
175 Us Highway 46 (07004-2327)
PHONE.............................973 672-0800
Fax: 973 672-3780
Richard Bitetti, *President*
EMP: 60 **EST:** 1946
SQ FT: 133,000

SALES (est): 6.2MM **Privately Held**
WEB: www.harvardpress.com
SIC: 2752 Commercial printing, lithographic; commercial printing, offset

(G-3217)
HBS ELECTRONICS INC
1275 Bloomfield Ave # 17 (07004-2735)
PHONE.............................973 439-1147
Hans Bisesar, *President*
Rocky Bisesar, *Vice Pres*
EMP: 4
SALES: 400K **Privately Held**
WEB: www.hbselectronics.com
SIC: 3612 Specialty transformers

(G-3218)
HEAT-TIMER CORPORATION (PA)
20 New Dutch Ln (07004-2513)
PHONE.............................973 575-4004
Fax: 973 575-4052
Michael Pitonyak, *CEO*
Vincent Clerico, *VP Sls/Mktg*
▲ **EMP:** 30
SQ FT: 39,000
SALES (est): 7.7MM **Privately Held**
WEB: www.heat-timer.com
SIC: 3822 3669 3491 3625 Electric heat controls; smoke detectors; valves, automatic control; relays & industrial controls; heating equipment, except electric

(G-3219)
HEAT-TIMER CORPORATION
Also Called: Heat-Timer Service
20 New Dutch Ln (07004-2513)
PHONE.............................212 481-2020
Fax: 212 684-5444
John Winston, *Manager*
EMP: 30
SALES (est): 4.2MM
SALES (corp-wide): 7.7MM **Privately Held**
WEB: www.heat-timer.com
SIC: 3824 1711 7623 Controls, revolution & timing instruments; heating & air conditioning contractors; refrigeration service & repair
PA: Heat-Timer Corporation
20 New Dutch Ln
Fairfield NJ 07004
973 575-4004

(G-3220)
HEISLER MACHINE & TOOL CO
Also Called: Heisler Industries
224 Passaic Ave (07004-3581)
PHONE.............................973 227-6300
Fax: 973 227-7627
Richard A Heisler, *President*
Ron Heisler, *Vice Pres*
Ronald A Heisler, *Vice Pres*
James Lamb, *Vice Pres*
Rich Heerema, *Parts Mgr*
◆ **EMP:** 40 **EST:** 1920
SQ FT: 24,000
SALES (est): 12.1MM **Privately Held**
WEB: www.heislerind.com
SIC: 3565 Packaging machinery; carton packing machines

(G-3221)
HERMA US INC
39 Plymouth St Unit 300 (07004-1643)
PHONE.............................973 521-7254
Peter Goff, *President*
EMP: 6 **EST:** 2016
SALES (est): 291.4K **Privately Held**
SIC: 3565 Labeling machines, industrial

(G-3222)
HILL PHARMA INC
6 Madison Rd (07004-2309)
PHONE.............................973 521-7400
Charles Dong, *President*
Thomas Kelly, *Marketing Staff*
WEI Zheng, *Executive Asst*
▲ **EMP:** 12
SALES (est): 1.5MM **Privately Held**
SIC: 2834 Druggists' preparations (pharmaceuticals)

(G-3223)
HOBART SALES AND SERVICE INC
Also Called: Hobart Feg Service Center
4 Gloria Ln (07004-3306)
PHONE.............................973 227-9265
Fax: 973 227-1654
Gordon De Block, *Branch Mgr*
EMP: 50
SALES (corp-wide): 46.3MM **Privately Held**
WEB: www.hobartcorp.com
SIC: 3589 Dishwashing machines, commercial; cooking equipment, commercial; commercial cooking & foodwarming equipment
PA: Hobart Sales And Service, Inc.
701 S Ridge Ave
Troy OH 45373
937 332-3000

(G-3224)
HT STAMPING CO LLC
19 Gardner Rd Ste C (07004-2204)
PHONE.............................973 227-4858
Thomas Schall, *Mng Member*
EMP: 9
SQ FT: 14,000
SALES (est): 567K **Privately Held**
SIC: 3469 Metal stampings

(G-3225)
HUDSON INDUSTRIES CORPORATION (HQ)
Also Called: Milligan & Higgins Div
271 Us Highway 46 F207 (07004-2448)
PHONE.............................973 402-0100
Fax: 973 402-9520
Arnold Palmer, *Ch of Bd*
Lee Kornbluh, *Corp Secy*
Barry Karpf, *Vice Pres*
▲ **EMP:** 4 **EST:** 1935
SQ FT: 1,500
SALES (est): 4.5MM **Privately Held**
WEB: www.milligan1868.com
SIC: 2891 2899 Glue; gelatin: edible, technical, photographic or pharmaceutical

(G-3226)
IMPERIAL DAX CO INC
Also Called: Dax Haircare
120 New Dutch Ln (07004-2598)
P.O. Box 10002 (07004-6002)
PHONE.............................973 227-6105
Fax: 973 808-8533
David Joy, *President*
Donald Joy, *General Mgr*
▼ **EMP:** 25
SQ FT: 41,000
SALES (est): 4.8MM **Privately Held**
WEB: www.imperialdax.com
SIC: 2844 Cosmetic preparations; hair preparations, including shampoos

(G-3227)
INDEPENDENT MACHINE COMPANY
Also Called: Smartwinders
2 Stewart Pl (07004-2202)
PHONE.............................973 882-0060
Fax: 973 808-9505
Jack S Lucia, *President*
Bruce Butler, *Vice Pres*
Andrew Lenkiewicz, *Mfg Mgr*
Melanie Pimont, *Manager*
EMP: 20 **EST:** 1968
SQ FT: 34,000
SALES (est): 6.2MM **Privately Held**
SIC: 3569 Assembly machines, non-metalworking

(G-3228)
INDUSTRIAL BRUSH CO INC
Also Called: Indusco
105 Clinton Rd Ste 1 (07004-2988)
PHONE.............................800 241-9860
Fax: 973 575-6169
Tim Enchelmaier, *President*
David Enchelmaier, *Vice Pres*
▲ **EMP:** 22
SQ FT: 44,000
SALES (est): 4.1MM **Privately Held**
WEB: www.indbrush.com
SIC: 3991 3545 Brooms & brushes; precision tools, machinists'

▲ = Import ▼=Export
◆ =Import/Export

(G-3229)
INDUSTRIAL FILTERS COMPANY
9 Industrial Rd (07004-3043)
PHONE...................973 575-0533
Fax: 973 575-9238
Steven Donker, *President*
Steve Donker, *President*
Marilyn Donker, *Treasurer*
EMP: 7
SQ FT: 12,600
SALES: 1.5MM **Privately Held**
WEB: www.indfilco.com
SIC: 3569 Filters, general line: industrial;
filters

(G-3230)
INDUSTRIAL LBELING SYSTEMS INC
Also Called: Ilsi
50 Kulick Rd (07004-3308)
PHONE...................973 808-8188
Yimin Shiuey, *President*
Brad Mack, *CFO*
Wai K Tsang, *Director*
EMP: 23
SQ FT: 25,000
SALES (est): 5.7MM **Privately Held**
SIC: 2759 Labels & seals: printing

(G-3231)
INFINITE CLASSIC INC
30 Sherwood Ln Ste 8 (07004-3603)
PHONE...................973 227-2790
Baek H Kim, *Ch of Bd*
▲ EMP: 6
SALES (est): 392.3K **Privately Held**
SIC: 3961 Costume jewelry

(G-3232)
INTERNATIONAL CORD SETS INC
Also Called: I C S
6 Spielman Rd (07004-3404)
PHONE...................973 227-2118
Fax: 973 882-8918
Dieter Baars, *President*
Ralph Mezza, *Vice Pres*
▲ EMP: 16 EST: 1981
SQ FT: 12,500
SALES (est): 2MM **Privately Held**
SIC: 3699 Electrical equipment & supplies

(G-3233)
INTERNATIONAL TOOL AND MFG INC
30 Sherwood Ln Ste 10 (07004-3603)
PHONE...................973 227-6767
Fax: 973 227-6711
Susan Brock, *President*
Thomas Brock, *Vice Pres*
Ryan Brock, *Treasurer*
EMP: 9
SQ FT: 4,500
SALES (est): 1.2MM **Privately Held**
SIC: 3599 3545 Machine shop, jobbing &
repair; precision tools, machinists'

(G-3234)
IVY-DRY INC
299b Fairfield Ave (07004-3863)
P.O. Box 596, Caldwell (07007-0596)
PHONE...................973 575-1992
Stephen Heydt, *President*
Harry Reicherz, *Vice Pres*
EMP: 8
SQ FT: 10,100
SALES (est): 1.8MM **Privately Held**
SIC: 5122 2833 Medicinals & botanicals;
medicinals & botanicals

(G-3235)
JERSEY BORING & DRLG CO INC
36 Pier Ln W (07004-2505)
PHONE...................973 242-3800
Shelley Lach, *President*
EMP: 35
SQ FT: 2,500
SALES (est): 5MM **Privately Held**
WEB: www.jerseyboring.com
SIC: 1481 Test boring for nonmetallic min-
erals

(G-3236)
JMC DESIGN & GRAPHICS INC
144 Fairfield Rd (07004-2407)
PHONE...................973 276-9033
Fax: 973 322-2222
Joseph M Caniano, *President*
EMP: 5
SQ FT: 10,000
SALES (est): 1.3MM **Privately Held**
SIC: 2752 Commercial printing, offset

(G-3237)
JOHN N FEHLINGER CO INC
16 Passaic Ave Unit 8 (07004-3835)
PHONE...................973 633-0699
John Fehlinger, *Owner*
EMP: 6
SALES (est): 930K **Privately Held**
SIC: 3559 Sewing machines & attach-
ments, industrial

(G-3238)
JRC WEB ACCESSORIES
46 Passaic Ave (07004-3522)
PHONE...................973 625-3888
Ralph Ryan, *President*
Todd Ryan, *Manager*
▲ EMP: 11 EST: 1976
SQ FT: 20,000
SALES (est): 2MM **Privately Held**
SIC: 2655 Cores, fiber: made from pur-
chased material

(G-3239)
KATHY JEANNE INC
7 Industrial Rd (07004-3017)
PHONE...................973 575-9898
Fax: 973 575-7988
Jeanne Gerish, *President*
Jay M Gerish, *Vice Pres*
▲ EMP: 15
SQ FT: 11,500
SALES: 2MM **Privately Held**
WEB: www.kathyjeanneinc.com
SIC: 2353 5137 Hats & caps; hats,
trimmed: women's, misses' & children's;
hats: women's, children's & infants'

(G-3240)
KEYPOINT INTELLIGENCE LLC (HQ)
Also Called: Buyers Laboratory, LLC
80 Little Falls Rd (07004-2135)
PHONE...................973 797-2100
Michael Danziger, *CEO*
Mark Lerch, *COO*
EMP: 37
SQ FT: 26,000
SALES (est): 7.6MM **Privately Held**
WEB: www.buyerslab.com
SIC: 2721 Statistical reports (periodicals):
publishing only

(G-3241)
KIDS OF AMERICA CORP
103 Route 46 W (07004-3235)
P.O. Box 411, Pine Brook (07058-0411)
PHONE...................973 808-8242
Stephen Chan, *President*
Peter Joseph, *Senior VP*
▲ EMP: 26
SQ FT: 3,000
SALES (est): 3MM **Privately Held**
WEB: www.kidsofamericacorp.com
SIC: 5092 3942 Toys & hobby goods &
supplies; dolls & stuffed toys

(G-3242)
KINECT AUTO PARTS CORPORATION
75 Lane Rd Ste 201 (07004-1000)
PHONE...................862 702-8252
Adam Wang, *President*
EMP: 3 EST: 2015
SALES (est): 6MM **Privately Held**
SIC: 3089 Automotive parts, plastic

(G-3243)
KITCHEN TABLE BAKERS INC
100 Passaic Ave Ste 155 (07004-3563)
PHONE...................516 941-5113
Barry Novick, *President*
Seth Novick, *Vice Pres*
EMP: 25

SALES: 2MM **Privately Held**
WEB: www.kitchentablebakers.com
SIC: 2052 Cookies & crackers

(G-3244)
KTB ACQUISITION SUB INC (HQ)
100 Passaic Ave (07004-3520)
PHONE...................973 240-0200
Aldo Zuppichini, *CEO*
EMP: 4
SALES (est): 726.1K
SALES (corp-wide): 958.9K **Privately Held**
SIC: 2096 Potato chips & similar snacks
PA: That's How We Roll Llc
100 Passaic Ave Ste 155
Fairfield NJ 07004
973 240-0200

(G-3245)
L&M ARCHITECTURAL GRAPHICS INC
Also Called: L&M Signs
20 Montesano Rd (07004-3310)
PHONE...................973 575-7665
Fax: 973 575-6709
Justin Lorenzo, *President*
Paul Lorenzo, *Vice Pres*
Peter Lorenzo, *Vice Pres*
Thomas Vitale, *Accounts Exec*
◆ EMP: 16
SQ FT: 10,000
SALES (est): 2.5MM **Privately Held**
WEB: www.lmsigns.com
SIC: 2221 3993 7336 Wall covering fab-
rics, manmade fiber & silk; signs & adver-
tising specialties; commercial art &
graphic design

(G-3246)
LA COUR INC (PA)
36 Kulick Rd (07004-3308)
PHONE...................973 227-3300
Paul M Lacour, *President*
Tom Ruggieri, *General Mgr*
Athea Novello, *Production*
EMP: 30
SQ FT: 35,000
SALES (est): 3.4MM **Privately Held**
WEB: www.lacourinc.com
SIC: 2521 2522 5021 5712 Wood office
furniture; office furniture, except wood; of-
fice furniture; office furniture

(G-3247)
LAB EXPRESS INC
Also Called: Lab Express International
10 Madison Rd Ste A (07004-2325)
PHONE...................973 227-1700
David Mazzarell, *President*
▲ EMP: 10
SQ FT: 10,000
SALES (est): 2.7MM **Privately Held**
WEB: www.labexpress.com
SIC: 2834 5169 Pharmaceutical prepara-
tions; chemicals & allied products

(G-3248)
LABEL GRAPHICS MFG INC
Also Called: Label Graphics II
315 Fairfield Rd (07004-1930)
PHONE...................973 276-1555
Ali Kahn, *General Mgr*
Edgar Cruz, *Mfg Mgr*
EMP: 9
SALES (corp-wide): 8.4MM **Privately Held**
WEB: www.labelgraphicsmfg.com
SIC: 2672 Labels (unprinted), gummed:
made from purchased materials
PA: Label Graphics Manufacturing, Inc.
175 Paterson Ave
Little Falls NJ 07424
973 890-5665

(G-3249)
LB BOOK BINDERY LLC
19 Gardner Rd Ste I (07004-2204)
PHONE...................973 244-0442
Fax: 973 244-0732
Ralph Lozito, *Mng Member*
Frank Lozito,
Michael Lozito,
Sandy Lozito,
▲ EMP: 15

SALES: 1MM **Privately Held**
SIC: 2789 Binding only: books, pamphlets,
magazines, etc.

(G-3250)
LEADING PHARMA LLC (PA)
3 Oak Rd (07004-2903)
PHONE...................201 746-9160
Ronald F Gold, *CEO*
Rasik M Gondalia, *President*
Richard Monica, *Treasurer*
EMP: 50
SQ FT: 30,000
SALES: 10.6MM **Privately Held**
SIC: 1541 2834 Pharmaceutical manufac-
turing plant construction; pharmaceutical
preparations

(G-3251)
LEVINE PACKAGING SUPPLY CORP
400 Us Highway 46 (07004-1906)
PHONE...................973 575-3456
Fax: 973 575-1411
Sanford I Levine, *President*
Neal Levine, *Vice Pres*
Larry Levine, *Treasurer*
Edith Levine, *Admin Sec*
EMP: 30
SQ FT: 40,000
SALES (est): 6.2MM **Privately Held**
SIC: 2653 Boxes, corrugated: made from
purchased materials; pallets, solid fiber:
made from purchased materials

(G-3252)
LIBERTY SPORT INC
107 Fairfield Rd (07004-2546)
PHONE...................973 882-0986
Fax: 973 575-1274
Anthony M Di Chiara, *Ch of Bd*
Carmine Di Chiara, *Vice Pres*
Franco Tommasino, *CFO*
Ken Slattery, *Sales Associate*
Jon Phillips, *Director*
▲ EMP: 35 EST: 1938
SQ FT: 60,000
SALES (est): 7.2MM **Privately Held**
WEB: www.libertyoptical.com
SIC: 3851 5048 Frames & parts, eyeglass
& spectacle; frames, ophthalmic

(G-3253)
LINK COMPUTER GRAPHICS INC
Also Called: Link Instruments
17a Daniel Rd (07004-2527)
PHONE...................973 808-8990
Hung-WEI Yeh, *President*
Ken Wong, *Vice Pres*
Todd Schreibman, *Treasurer*
EMP: 9
SQ FT: 4,000
SALES (est): 1.6MM **Privately Held**
WEB: www.linkins.com
SIC: 3577 5045 5065 3825 Computer
peripheral equipment; computers, periph-
erals & software; electronic parts & equip-
ment; instruments to measure electricity

(G-3254)
LIZARD LABEL CO (PA)
Also Called: Intergrated Scales Systems
20 Kulick Rd Ste A (07004-3308)
PHONE...................973 808-3322
Fax: 973 882-8829
Joseph Winter, *President*
John Winter, *Vice Pres*
▲ EMP: 10
SQ FT: 8,800
SALES (est): 946.2K **Privately Held**
WEB: www.lizardlabel.com
SIC: 2759 Labels & seals: printing

(G-3255)
MAR COR PURIFICATION INC
341 Kaplan Dr (07004-2510)
PHONE...................973 521-7032
Pam Fritzler, *President*
EMP: 4
SALES (corp-wide): 770.1MM **Publicly
Held**
SIC: 3569 Filters

GEOGRAPHIC

HQ: Mar Cor Purification, Inc.
4450 Township Line Rd
Skippack PA 19474
800 633-3080

(G-3256)
MEDIMTRIKS PHARMACEUTICALS INC
383 Us Highway 46 (07004-2473)
PHONE.....................................973 882-7512
Bradley Glassman, *CEO*
Eric Licwinko, *District Mgr*
Alan Goldstein, *Exec VP*
David Addis, *Vice Pres*
Brent Lenczycki, *CFO*
EMP: 38
SQ FT: 11,000
SALES (est): 13.5MM **Privately Held**
SIC: 5122 2834 Pharmaceuticals; dermatologicals; ointments

(G-3257)
MEGADYNE AMERICA LLC (HQ)
Also Called: Jason Industrial Inc.
340 Kaplan Dr (07004-2511)
P.O. Box 10004 (07004-6004)
PHONE.....................................973 227-4904
Fax: 973 227-1651
Philip Cohenca, *CEO*
Emilia Cohenca, *Ch of Bd*
Glen Taylor, *Warehouse Mgr*
Diane Fobert, *Controller*
Rosemary Greene, *Human Resources*
◆ **EMP: 45 EST:** 1965
SQ FT: 30,000
SALES (est): 114MM **Privately Held**
WEB: www.jasonindustrial.com
SIC: 5084 3052 Textile machinery & equipment; rubber & plastics hose & beltings

(G-3258)
MENNEKES ELECTRONICS INC
277 Fairfield Rd Ste 111 (07004-1931)
PHONE.....................................973 882-8333
Fax: 973 882-5585
Walter Mennekes, *President*
Paul Di Antonio, *Corp Secy*
Thomas Bodnar, *Vice Pres*
Robert Nimeth, *Engineer*
Paul Diantonio, *VP Sls/Mktg*
▲ **EMP:** 25
SQ FT: 24,000
SALES (est): 12.6MM **Privately Held**
SIC: 5063 3679 Wiring devices; safety switches; electronic switches

(G-3259)
MERCURY LIGHTING PDTS CO INC
20 Audrey Pl (07004-3416)
PHONE.....................................973 244-9444
Fax: 973 244-9522
John Fedinec, *President*
Scott Fleischer, *Exec VP*
Jorge Correa, *Prdtn Mgr*
Manny Garrido, *Purch Agent*
Lou Dina, *Sales Mgr*
▲ **EMP: 110 EST:** 1946
SQ FT: 100,000
SALES (est): 27.8MM **Privately Held**
WEB: www.mercltg.com
SIC: 3646 Commercial indusl & institutional electric lighting fixtures

(G-3260)
MICHELE MADDALENA
Also Called: GM Construction
1275 Bloomfield Ave (07004-2708)
PHONE.....................................973 244-0033
Eugene M Maddalena, *Principal*
Michael Maddalena, *Vice Pres*
EMP: 7
SALES (est): 570.3K **Privately Held**
SIC: 3993 3648 1799 Signs & advertising specialties; lighting equipment; sign installation & maintenance

(G-3261)
MIDDLE ATLANTIC PRODUCTS INC (DH)
Also Called: Datatel
300 Fairfield Rd (07004-1932)
PHONE.....................................973 839-1011
Michael L Baker, *President*

Patrick Cuddy, *Business Mgr*
Gordon Wason, *Business Mgr*
Robert Julian, *Vice Pres*
Bill Poling, *Vice Pres*
◆ **EMP:** 320
SQ FT: 250,000
SALES (est): 104.9MM
SALES (corp-wide): 20.7MM **Privately Held**
WEB: www.middleatlantic.com
SIC: 3444 Casings, sheet metal
HQ: Legrand Holding, Inc.
60 Woodlawn St
West Hartford CT 06110
860 233-6251

(G-3262)
MOD MEDIA LTD LIABILITY CO
15 Oak Rd Ste 2 (07004-2939)
PHONE.....................................973 249-6157
Shannon Steitz, *President*
EMP: 7
SALES (est): 641.5K **Privately Held**
SIC: 2721 Magazines: publishing & printing

(G-3263)
MODERN DRUMMER PUBLICATIONS
271 Us Highway 46 H212 (07004-2458)
PHONE.....................................973 239-4140
Fax: 973 239-7139
Isabel Spagnardi, *President*
EMP: 15 EST: 1976
SQ FT: 3,000
SALES (est): 1.9MM **Privately Held**
WEB: www.moderndrummer.com
SIC: 2721 2731 Magazines: publishing only, not printed on site; books: publishing only

(G-3264)
MORGAN ADVANCED CERAMICS INC
26 Madison Rd (07004-2309)
PHONE.....................................973 808-1621
John Stang, *Branch Mgr*
EMP: 50
SALES (corp-wide): 1.3B **Privately Held**
WEB: www.morganelectroceramics.com
SIC: 2899 3251 3644 3297 Fluxes: brazing, soldering, galvanizing & welding; brick & structural clay tile; noncurrent-carrying wiring services; nonclay refractories; porcelain electrical supplies
HQ: Morgan Advanced Ceramics, Inc
2425 Whipple Rd
Hayward CA 94544

(G-3265)
MW INDUSTRIES INC
Also Called: Accurate Screw Machine
10 Audrey Pl (07004-3402)
PHONE.....................................973 244-9200
EMP: 100
SALES (corp-wide): 169MM **Privately Held**
SIC: 3451 Screw machine products
HQ: Mw Industries, Inc.
9501 Tech Blvd Ste 401
Rosemont IL 60018
847 349-5760

(G-3266)
NATIONAL PRECISION TOOL CO
24 Sherwood Ln (07004-3602)
PHONE.....................................973 227-5005
Fax: 973 227-5077
Leon Roitburg, *President*
Henry Solorzano, *Mfg Staff*
EMP: 21
SQ FT: 12,000
SALES (est): 3.5MM **Privately Held**
SIC: 3599 Machine shop, jobbing & repair

(G-3267)
NEMA FOOD DISTRIBUTION INC
18 Commerce Rd Ste D (07004-1603)
PHONE.....................................973 256-4415
Beyhan Nakiboglu, *President*
Galip Kiyakli, *Vice Pres*
▲ **EMP:** 6
SQ FT: 10,000

SALES (est): 1.3MM **Privately Held**
SIC: 2053 2032 2015 5142 Frozen bakery products, except bread; ethnic foods: canned, jarred, etc.; luncheon meat, poultry; meat, frozen: packaged; bakery products, frozen

(G-3268)
NEW AGE METAL FABG CO INC
Also Called: Namf
26 Daniel Rd W (07004-2522)
PHONE.....................................973 227-9107
Fax: 973 227-6039
Mario Costa, *President*
Frank Melchiorre, *Materials Mgr*
Margaret Goble, *Office Mgr*
Helen Pritchard, *Office Mgr*
EMP: 70
SQ FT: 40,000
SALES (est): 19.6MM **Privately Held**
SIC: 3444 Sheet metal specialties, not stamped

(G-3269)
NEW JERSEY BUSINESS MAGAZINE
310 Passaic Ave Ste 201 (07004-2523)
PHONE.....................................973 882-5004
Fax: 973 882-4648
Philip Kirschner, *President*
EMP: 8
SALES (est): 643K
SALES (corp-wide): 9.2MM **Privately Held**
SIC: 2721 Magazines: publishing & printing
PA: New Jersey Business & Industry Association
10 W Lafayette St
Trenton NJ 08608
609 393-7707

(G-3270)
NEXTRON MEDICAL TECH INC
Also Called: Nextron Infusion Services
45 Kulick Rd (07004-3307)
PHONE.....................................973 575-0614
Eric Nemeth, *CEO*
Silvio Eruzzi, *Ch of Bd*
Loriann Rubino-Chang, *Principal*
Simone Cimino, *CFO*
▲ **EMP:** 72
SALES (est): 7.1MM
SALES (corp-wide): 129MM **Privately Held**
SIC: 2834 3845 Intravenous solutions; pacemaker, cardiac
HQ: Amerita, Inc.
7307 S Revere Pkwy # 200
Centennial CO 80112

(G-3271)
NIKO TRADE LTD-USA INC
271 Us Highway 46 D107 (07004-2440)
PHONE.....................................973 575-4353
Jacob Katz, *President*
EMP: 3
SQ FT: 3,000
SALES (est): 2MM **Privately Held**
WEB: www.niko-nikcole.com
SIC: 3545 Cutting tools for machine tools

(G-3272)
NJ COPY CENTER LLC
10 Madison Rd Ste C (07004-2325)
PHONE.....................................973 788-1600
Bradley Gimbel,
EMP: 4
SALES (est): 414.9K **Privately Held**
SIC: 2732 Book printing

(G-3273)
NOMADIC NORTH AMERICA LLC
46 Just Rd (07004-3413)
PHONE.....................................703 866-9200
Jim Laganke, *Branch Mgr*
EMP: 4
SALES (corp-wide): 24.8MM **Privately Held**
SIC: 3993 Signs & advertising specialties
HQ: Nomadic North America Llc
10505 Furnace Rd Ste 108
Lorton VA 22079
703 866-9200

(G-3274)
NOUVEAUTES INC
70 Clinton Rd Ste 1 (07004-2928)
P.O. Box 1198, Caldwell (07007-1198)
PHONE.....................................973 882-8850
David W Little, *President*
EMP: 15
SQ FT: 6,000
SALES (est): 2.3MM **Privately Held**
WEB: www.nouveautesusa.com
SIC: 2066 5199 Chocolate & cocoa products; gifts & novelties

(G-3275)
NOVA POLYMERS INC
8 Evans St (07004-2210)
PHONE.....................................973 227-6695
Patrick Avallone, *Client Mgr*
Diane Milliman, *Manager*
EMP: 12
SALES (est): 2.4MM **Privately Held**
SIC: 2822 Ethylene-propylene rubbers, EPDM polymers

(G-3276)
OMP TECHNOLOGIES INC
24 Commerce Rd Ste H (07004-1665)
PHONE.....................................973 808-8500
Fax: 973 808-5618
Yufeng Hsiao, *President*
Kanhan Hsiao, *Officer*
EMP: 15
SQ FT: 4,500
SALES (est): 1.8MM **Privately Held**
WEB: www.omptech.com
SIC: 3599 Machine shop, jobbing & repair

(G-3277)
OTIS ELEVATOR INTL INC
105 Fairfield Rd (07004-2546)
PHONE.....................................973 575-7030
Fax: 973 575-8673
Chris Dlugolecki, *Branch Mgr*
EMP: 125
SALES (corp-wide): 59.8B **Publicly Held**
WEB: www.otis.com
SIC: 3534 1796 7699 5084 Elevators & equipment; elevator installation & conversion; elevators: inspection, service & repair; elevators
HQ: Otis Elevator Company
1 Carrier Pl
Farmington CT 06032
860 674-3000

(G-3278)
OUTFRONT MEDIA LLC
185 Us Highway 46 (07004-2321)
PHONE.....................................973 575-6900
Tameria Killeen, *Accounts Exec*
George Gross, *Manager*
EMP: 100
SALES (corp-wide): 1.5B **Publicly Held**
SIC: 7312 3993 2759 Outdoor advertising services; signs & advertising specialties; commercial printing
HQ: Outfront Media Llc
405 Lexington Ave Fl 14
New York NY 10174
212 297-6400

(G-3279)
PACE PACKAGING LLC
3 Sperry Rd (07004-2004)
PHONE.....................................973 227-1040
Mark W Anderson, *President*
Dave Rosequist, *Sales Staff*
Sam Jarkas, *Network Mgr*
▼ **EMP:** 55
SQ FT: 30,000
SALES (est): 13.3MM
SALES (corp-wide): 641.6MM **Privately Held**
WEB: www.pacepkg.com
SIC: 3565 Packaging machinery
PA: Pro Mach, Inc.
50 E Rivercntr Blvd 180
Covington KY 41011
513 831-8778

(G-3280)
PAR TROY SHEET METAL & AC LLC
122 Clinton Rd (07004-2921)
PHONE.....................................973 227-1150
Fax: 973 227-2757

Lino Rocha, *Owner*
EMP: 6
SQ FT: 4,800
SALES (est): 732.7K **Privately Held**
SIC: 3444 3446 Ducts, sheet metal; architectural metalwork

(G-3281)
PARAVISTA INC
Also Called: Paravista Imaging and Printing
123 Lehigh Dr (07004-3010)
PHONE....................732 752-1222
Michael Spallucci, *President*
James Connell, *Vice Pres*
Mark Spallucci, *Vice Pres*
▲ **EMP:** 27
SQ FT: 30,000
SALES (est): 4.9MM **Privately Held**
WEB: www.paravistainc.com
SIC: 2752 Commercial printing, offset; advertising posters, lithographed

(G-3282)
PARKER LABS
286 Eldridge Rd (07004-2509)
PHONE....................973 276-9500
Kevin Mc Dermott, *Engineer*
Martin King, *Director*
EMP: 4
SALES (est): 202.2K **Privately Held**
SIC: 2834 5122 Pharmaceutical preparations; pharmaceuticals

(G-3283)
PHARMATECH INTERNATIONAL INC
Also Called: Mironova Labs
21 Just Rd (07004-3407)
PHONE....................973 244-0393
Miroslav Trampota, *President*
EMP: 15
SQ FT: 26,000
SALES (est): 4.1MM **Privately Held**
WEB: www.pharmatech.org
SIC: 5122 2834 Pharmaceuticals; pharmaceutical preparations

(G-3284)
POOF-ALEX HOLDINGS LLC
40 Lane Rd (07004-1012)
PHONE....................734 454-9552
John Belniak,
EMP: 4
SALES (corp-wide): 11.7MM **Privately Held**
SIC: 3944 Blocks, toy
PA: Poof-Alex Holdings, Llc
10 Glenville St Ste 1
Greenwich CT 06831
203 930-7711

(G-3285)
PPI/TIME ZERO INC (PA)
11 Madison Rd (07004-2308)
PHONE....................973 278-6500
Dana Pittman, *President*
Joe Litavis, *Exec VP*
Michael J Shelor, *Exec VP*
Trudy Ganguzza, *Senior Buyer*
Michael Hatfield, *Engineer*
EMP: 145
SQ FT: 45,000
SALES (est): 42.9MM **Privately Held**
WEB: www.ppi-timezero.com
SIC: 3672 Printed circuit boards

(G-3286)
PRINCE STERILIZATION SVCS LLC
122 Fairfield Rd (07004-2405)
PHONE....................973 227-6882
Daniel Prince, *Principal*
EMP: 25
SQ FT: 3,000
SALES (est): 10MM **Privately Held**
SIC: 2834 Pharmaceutical preparations

(G-3287)
PRINT COMMUNICATIONS GROUP INC
Also Called: P C G
175 Us Highway 46 Unit A (07004-2327)
PHONE....................973 882-9444
Fax: 973 882-9434
James Purcaro, *CEO*

Michael D Alessandro, *COO*
Gene Palecco, *Chief Mktg Ofcr*
EMP: 60
SQ FT: 35,000
SALES (est): 7.7MM **Privately Held**
WEB: www.pcgnj.com
SIC: 2759 Thermography

(G-3288)
PROTECH POWDER COATINGS INC (PA)
Also Called: Protech Oxyplast
21 Audrey Pl (07004-3415)
PHONE....................973 276-1292
David Ades, *President*
Robinya Roberts, *Human Res Mgr*
▲ **EMP:** 54
SQ FT: 42,000
SALES (est): 15MM **Privately Held**
WEB: www.protechpowder.com
SIC: 2851 Lacquers, varnishes, enamels & other coatings

(G-3289)
RAINBOW CLOSETS INC (PA)
Also Called: California Closet Co
4 Gardner Rd Ste 5 (07004-2211)
PHONE....................973 882-3800
Fax: 973 882-9171
Ruth Ginsberg, *President*
Martin Ginsberg, *Vice Pres*
Rochelle Topper, *Asst Sec*
EMP: 52
SQ FT: 6,400
SALES (est): 6.8MM **Privately Held**
SIC: 1799 2511 Closet organizers, installation & design; wardrobes, household: wood

(G-3290)
RECTICO INC
12 Gloria Ln Ste 1 (07004-3315)
PHONE....................973 575-7117
Fax: 973 575-7117
Scott Sandler, *President*
Fulton W Sandler, *President*
EMP: 16
SQ FT: 14,000
SALES: 1MM **Privately Held**
WEB: www.rectico.com
SIC: 7389 2653 Packaging & labeling services; corrugated boxes, partitions, display items, sheets & pad

(G-3291)
REDI-DATA INC (PA)
5 Audrey Pl (07004-3401)
PHONE....................973 227-4380
Dori Bruno, *General Mgr*
EMP: 15 **EST:** 1991
SALES (est): 33.3MM **Privately Held**
SIC: 7375 7372 Data base information retrieval; prepackaged software

(G-3292)
REDI-DIRECT MARKETING INC (PA)
107 Little Falls Rd (07004-2105)
PHONE....................973 808-4500
James Weaver, *President*
Thomas R Buckley, *CFO*
EMP: 350
SQ FT: 15,000
SALES (est): 52.5MM **Privately Held**
WEB: www.redidata.com
SIC: 7319 7331 7389 7375 Sample distribution; direct mail advertising services; telemarketing services; data base information retrieval; prepackaged software

(G-3293)
RESEARCH AND PVD MATERIALS
373 Us Highway 46 Bldg E (07004-2442)
PHONE....................973 575-4245
Fax: 973 575-6460
Irene Wasnick, *President*
Melvin Hollander, *Vice Pres*
EMP: 6
SQ FT: 6,000
SALES (est): 806.8K **Privately Held**
SIC: 3499 Tablets, bronze or other metal

(G-3294)
RIGZTOOLS LLC
1275 Bloomfield Ave (07004-2708)
PHONE....................908 361-5433
Rodrigo Jesus Ponce, *Mng Member*
EMP: 6
SQ FT: 1,800
SALES (est): 251.5K **Privately Held**
SIC: 3663 Radio & TV communications equipment

(G-3295)
ROBERTET FRAGRANCES INC
30 Stewart Pl (07004-1631)
PHONE....................973 575-4550
Joseph Rainone, *Branch Mgr*
EMP: 30
SALES (corp-wide): 273.9MM **Privately Held**
SIC: 2844 Perfumes & colognes
HQ: Robertet Fragrances Inc.
400 International Dr
Budd Lake NJ 07828
201 405-1000

(G-3296)
ROBINSON TECH INTL CORP
Also Called: Rti
310 Fairfield Rd (07004-1932)
PHONE....................973 287-6458
Mark Lin, *President*
Gary Xu, *Vice Pres*
▲ **EMP:** 9
SQ FT: 26,000
SALES (est): 1.5MM **Privately Held**
SIC: 3291 3312 Abrasive products; fence posts, iron & steel

(G-3297)
RSI COMPANY
Also Called: Rsi-Fairfield Division
333 Us Highway 46 (07004-2427)
PHONE....................973 227-7800
Mike Thailer, *Manager*
EMP: 4
SALES (corp-wide): 3.2MM **Privately Held**
WEB: www.rsicomp.com
SIC: 7629 7694 Generator repair; electric motor repair
PA: Rsi Company
24050 Commerce Park # 200
Beachwood OH 44122
216 360-9800

(G-3298)
RUBBER & SILICONE PRODUCTS CO
17 Montesano Rd (07004-3309)
P.O. Box 1215, Caldwell (07007-1215)
PHONE....................973 227-2300
Fax: 973 227-8747
Jeffery Dylla, *President*
John Cox, *Vice Pres*
Gustave G Dylla, *Vice Pres*
Deborah Dylla, *Admin Sec*
▲ **EMP:** 20
SQ FT: 12,500
SALES (est): 3.3MM **Privately Held**
SIC: 3061 Mechanical rubber goods

(G-3299)
SAFEGUARD COINBOX INC
101 Clinton Rd (07004-2912)
P.O. Box 1266, Caldwell (07007-1266)
PHONE....................973 575-0040
Susan Macina, *President*
EMP: 15
SALES (est): 966.3K
SALES (corp-wide): 2MM **Privately Held**
WEB: www.safeguardcoinbox.com
SIC: 3469 Boxes: tool, lunch, mail, etc.: stamped metal
PA: Bloomfield Manufacturing Co Inc
29 Crosby Ln
Oakland NJ 07436
973 575-8900

(G-3300)
SAPPHIRE FLVORS FRAGRANCES LLC
6 Commerce Rd (07004-1602)
PHONE....................973 200-8849
Paul Braccia,
EMP: 10

SQ FT: 35,000
SALES: 1.2MM **Privately Held**
SIC: 2087 Concentrates, flavoring (except drink)

(G-3301)
SAS STRESSTEEL INC
100 New Dutch Ln (07004-2515)
PHONE....................973 244-5995
Felix E Ferrer, *President*
Jaime Silva, *General Mgr*
Kevin Dowling, *Vice Pres*
Nicholas J Mauro, *Sr Project Mgr*
▲ **EMP:** 16 **EST:** 2002
SQ FT: 30,000
SALES (est): 9.2MM **Privately Held**
WEB: www.stressteel.com
SIC: 5051 3325 Forms, concrete construction (steel); steel foundries

(G-3302)
SCANDIA PACKAGING MACHINERY CO
15 Industrial Rd (07004-3017)
PHONE....................973 473-6100
W B Bronander III, *President*
Cecelia Bronander, *Vice Pres*
Lewis Dallegro, *Purch Mgr*
Paul De Ghetto, *Engineer*
Charles Vanriper, *Manager*
▲ **EMP:** 26 **EST:** 1918
SQ FT: 32,000
SALES (est): 8MM **Privately Held**
WEB: www.scandiapack.com
SIC: 3565 Packaging machinery

(G-3303)
SCHULKE INC
30 Two Bridges Rd Ste 225 (07004-1515)
PHONE....................973 521-7163
Linda Sedlewicz, *Branch Mgr*
EMP: 4
SALES (corp-wide): 164.2MM **Privately Held**
SIC: 2842 Disinfectants, household or industrial plant
HQ: Schulke & Mayr Gmbh
Robert-Koch-Str. 2
Norderstedt 22851
405 210-00

(G-3304)
SCREEN PLAY INC
1275 Bloomfield Ave Ste 5 (07004-2736)
PHONE....................973 227-9014
Stephen Wacker, *President*
James Hill, *Vice Pres*
EMP: 6
SALES: 400K **Privately Held**
WEB: www.screenplay.com
SIC: 2759 Screen printing

(G-3305)
SENSOR SCIENTIFIC INC (PA)
6 Kingsbridge Rd Ste 4 (07004-2100)
PHONE....................973 227-7790
Fax: 973 227-8063
G Robert Brinley, *President*
Russ Bolton PHD, *Vice Pres*
▼ **EMP:** 20
SQ FT: 8,000
SALES (est): 2.1MM **Privately Held**
WEB: www.sensorsci.com
SIC: 3829 Thermometers & temperature sensors

(G-3306)
SGS USTESTING COMPANY (DH)
291 Fairfield Ave (07004-3833)
PHONE....................973 575-5252
Fax: 973 575-7175
Christian Jilch, *Ch of Bd*
Nancy Rivera, *Managing Dir*
Mark Connors, *Treasurer*
Ken Bridwell, *Admin Sec*
EMP: 10 **EST:** 1880
SALES (est): 9.7MM
SALES (corp-wide): 6.4B **Privately Held**
SIC: 8732 8734 8071 8731 Commercial nonphysical research; hazardous waste testing; forensic laboratory; soil analysis; product testing laboratory, safety or performance; testing laboratories; biotechnical research, commercial; environmental research; physical property testing equipment

HQ: Sgs North America Inc.
201 Route 17
Rutherford NJ 07070
201 508-3000

(G-3307)
SOFRADIR EC INC
Also Called: Electrophysics
373 Us Highway 46 (07004-2442)
PHONE.....................................973 882-0211
Bob Demarco, *President*
Frank J Vallese, *President*
Philippe Bensussan, *Chairman*
Richard Ryan, *Vice Pres*
Arthur Stout, *Vice Pres*
EMP: 35
SQ FT: 10,000
SALES (est): 7.2MM **Privately Held**
WEB: www.electrophysics.com
SIC: 3823 Industrial instrmnts msrmnt display/control process variable

(G-3308)
SOLBERN LLC
8 Kulick Rd (07004-3308)
PHONE.....................................973 227-3030
Fax: 973 227-3069
Gil Foulon, *Mng Member*
EMP: 37
SQ FT: 23,000
SALES (est): 11.2MM
SALES (corp-wide): 6B **Publicly Held**
WEB: www.solbern.com
SIC: 5084 3556 Food product manufacturing machinery; food products machinery
HQ: Markel Ventures, Inc.
4521 Highwoods Pkwy
Glen Allen VA 23060

(G-3309)
SPARKS BELTING COMPANY INC
5 Spielman Rd (07004-3480)
PHONE.....................................973 227-4100
Fax: 973 227-7369
David Engelhard, *Regional Mgr*
EMP: 8
SALES (corp-wide): 596.1MM **Privately Held**
SIC: 3535 Conveyors & conveying equipment
HQ: Sparks Belting Company, Inc.
3800 Stahl Dr Se
Grand Rapids MI 49546

(G-3310)
SPRINGWORKS GROUP LTD
123 Lehigh Dr (07004-3010)
PHONE.....................................973 276-7940
Neil Rice, *President*
George Colotti, *Vice Pres*
Diana L Rice, *Vice Pres*
Bob Groves, *VP Sales*
EMP: 4
SALES (est): 1.3MM **Privately Held**
SIC: 7336 3999 7389 Commercial art & graphic design; preparation of slides & exhibits; design services

(G-3311)
STANDARD PRTG & MAIL SVCS INC
30 Plymouth St Ste A (07004-1622)
P.O. Box 11021 (07004-7021)
PHONE.....................................973 790-3333
Kevin Walsh, *President*
EMP: 14
SALES (est): 2.5MM **Privately Held**
WEB: www.standprint.com
SIC: 2752 7331 2791 2789 Photo-offset printing; mailing service; typesetting; bookbinding & related work

(G-3312)
STAR LITHO INC
175 Us Highway 46 Unit C (07004-2327)
PHONE.....................................973 641-1603
Anthony Aquila Jr, *President*
Anthony Aquila III, *Vice Pres*
Anne Aquila, *Admin Sec*
EMP: 8 EST: 1961
SQ FT: 10,000
SALES: 1MM **Privately Held**
SIC: 2752 Commercial printing, offset

(G-3313)
STONE SYSTEMS NEW JERSEY LLC
5 Washington Ave (07004-3812)
PHONE.....................................973 778-5525
Thomas Landers, *Manager*
EMP: 13
SALES (est): 1.6MM **Privately Held**
SIC: 3281 Granite, cut & shaped

(G-3314)
STONE TRUSS SYSTEMS INC (PA)
23 Commerce Rd Ste O (07004-1609)
PHONE.....................................973 882-7377
Francisco Tauriello, *President*
Anthony Tauriello, *Chairman*
Joanne Di Benedetto, *Controller*
Dina M Tauriello, *Admin Sec*
▲ EMP: 25
SQ FT: 4,200
SALES (est): 4.8MM **Privately Held**
WEB: www.stonetrusssystems.com
SIC: 1741 3281 Stone masonry; granite, cut & shaped

(G-3315)
STONEWORK DSIGN CONSULTING INC (PA)
25 Pier Ln W (07004-2504)
PHONE.....................................973 575-0835
Anthony Abdy, *President*
EMP: 40 EST: 1998
SALES: 15MM **Privately Held**
SIC: 3253 1743 Ceramic wall & floor tile; terrazzo, tile, marble, mosaic work; tile installation, ceramic

(G-3316)
SUN DIAL & PANEL CORPORATION
Also Called: Sun Display Systems
2 Daniel Rd Ste 102 (07004-2516)
PHONE.....................................973 226-4334
Fax: 973 808-6759
EMP: 23
SQ FT: 10,000
SALES: 2.9MM **Privately Held**
SIC: 3812 Mfg Search/Navigation Equipment

(G-3317)
SUN DISPLAY SYSTEMS LLC
2 Daniel Rd (07004-2516)
PHONE.....................................973 226-4334
James Lloyd, *Vice Pres*
Liam Rafferty, *Engineer*
Roger Lokker,
EMP: 35
SALES (est): 5.9MM **Privately Held**
SIC: 3647 Vehicular lighting equipment

(G-3318)
SYNCOM PHARMACEUTICALS INC (PA)
125 Clinton Rd Unit 5 (07004-2929)
P.O. Box 11320 (07004-7320)
PHONE.....................................973 787-2405
Fax: 973 787-2406
James W De Coursin, *President*
Fred Mc Ilreath, *Vice Pres*
Gerald Aust, *Sales Staff*
Jon Black, *Info Tech Mgr*
▼ EMP: 25
SALES (est): 14.2MM **Privately Held**
WEB: www.syncom.net
SIC: 2023 Dietary supplements, dairy & non-dairy based

(G-3319)
TADBIK NJ INC
17 Madison Rd (07004-2308)
PHONE.....................................973 882-9595
Fax: 973 882-0902
Leslie Gurland, *President*
Aryeh Silbert, *Chairman*
▲ EMP: 34
SQ FT: 14,400
SALES: 5.6MM
SALES (corp-wide): 200.8MM **Privately Held**
WEB: www.logotech-inc.com
SIC: 2754 Labels: gravure printing

PA: Tadbik Ltd.
4 Boltimor
Petah Tikva 49510
392 780-00

(G-3320)
TALLY DISPLAY CORP
19 Gardner Rd Ste A (07004-2204)
PHONE.....................................973 777-7760
Steve Rose, *President*
Sheldon Hoffman, *Vice Pres*
EMP: 9
SALES (est): 894.1K **Privately Held**
WEB: www.tallydisplay.com
SIC: 3993 Signs & advertising specialties

(G-3321)
TBMC INC
340 Kaplan Dr (07004-2511)
PHONE.....................................864 288-9916
Fax: 864 458-8729
Philip Cohenca, *President*
Nevine Michaan, *Corp Secy*
▲ EMP: 50
SQ FT: 35,000
SALES (est): 6.4MM **Privately Held**
WEB: www.tbmcinc.com
SIC: 3061 Mechanical rubber goods
HQ: Megadyne America, Llc
340 Kaplan Dr
Fairfield NJ 07004
973 227-4904

(G-3322)
TECHNOGYM USA CORP (DH)
700 Us Highway 46 (07004-1591)
PHONE.....................................800 804-0952
Claudio Bellini, *President*
Andrea Severi, *Treasurer*
◆ EMP: 12
SQ FT: 6,000
SALES (est): 4.7MM **Privately Held**
WEB: www.technogym.com
SIC: 3949 Exercise equipment
HQ: Technogym Spa
Via Calcinaro 2861
Cesena FC 47521
054 765-0650

(G-3323)
TEVA PHARMACEUTICALS USA INC
8 Gloria Ln Ste 10 (07004-3306)
PHONE.....................................973 575-2775
Robert Tarra, *Manager*
Kanta Solanki, *Manager*
Jj Devine, *Director*
Brahma Singh, *Director*
EMP: 102
SALES (corp-wide): 22.3B **Privately Held**
WEB: www.lemmon.com
SIC: 2834 Pharmaceutical preparations
HQ: Teva Pharmaceuticals Usa, Inc.
1090 Horsham Rd
North Wales PA 19454
215 591-3000

(G-3324)
TEXAS CANVAS CO INC (PA)
Also Called: Awnings By Texas Canvas
1275 Bloomfield Ave 54b (07004-2708)
PHONE.....................................973 278-3802
EMP: 4
SALES (est): 913.3K **Privately Held**
SIC: 2394 Mfg Canvas/Related Products

(G-3325)
THIN STONE SYSTEMS LLC
23 Commerce Rd Ste O (07004-1609)
PHONE.....................................973 882-7377
Frank Tauriello,
▲ EMP: 8
SALES (est): 368.3K
SALES (corp-wide): 4.8MM **Privately Held**
WEB: www.stonetrusssystems.com
SIC: 1741 3281 Masonry & other stonework; cut stone & stone products
PA: Stone Truss Systems, Llc.
23 Commerce Rd Ste O
Fairfield NJ 07004
973 882-7377

(G-3326)
TILTON RACK & BASKET CO
66 Passaic Ave (07004-3522)
PHONE.....................................973 226-6010
Fax: 973 227-4155
Joseph Tilton, *President*
EMP: 25 EST: 1963
SQ FT: 15,000
SALES (est): 6MM **Privately Held**
WEB: www.tiltonrackandbasket.com
SIC: 3559 Electroplating machinery & equipment

(G-3327)
TITANIUM FABRICATION CORP (PA)
Also Called: Tifab
110 Lehigh Dr (07004-3013)
PHONE.....................................973 227-5300
Fax: 973 227-2141
Brent Willey, *President*
Troy Bartley, *COO*
Dan Williams, *Vice Pres*
Paul Holdstock, *Sales Dir*
Carl Clendennen, *Manager*
▲ EMP: 60
SQ FT: 50,000
SALES (est): 44.1MM **Privately Held**
WEB: www.tifab.com
SIC: 3443 Fabricated plate work (boiler shop); heat exchangers: coolers (after, inter), condensers, etc.

(G-3328)
TORPAC INC
Also Called: Torpac Capsules
333 Us Highway 46 (07004-2427)
PHONE.....................................973 244-1125
Fax: 973 244-1365
Raj Tahil, *President*
▲ EMP: 25
SQ FT: 6,000
SALES (est): 5.9MM **Privately Held**
WEB: www.torpac.com
SIC: 2899 Gelatin capsules

(G-3329)
TQ3 NORTH AMERICA INC (PA)
23 Commerce Rd Ste I (07004-1609)
PHONE.....................................973 882-7900
Aidan Bradley, *President*
▲ EMP: 6
SQ FT: 3,500
SALES (est): 4MM **Privately Held**
SIC: 2851 Paints, waterproof

(G-3330)
TREMONT PRINTING CO
72 Deer Park Rd (07004-1431)
PHONE.....................................973 227-0742
Daniel Cerami, *Owner*
EMP: 4
SALES: 170K **Privately Held**
SIC: 2759 2752 Commercial printing; commercial printing, lithographic

(G-3331)
TRIM AND TASSELS LLC
Also Called: Graduation Outlet
204 Passaic Ave Unit 3 (07004-3503)
PHONE.....................................973 808-1566
Pradeep Jalan,
Rashmi Jalan,
Ritu Jalan,
▲ EMP: 4
SALES (est): 416.3K **Privately Held**
SIC: 2431 5023 7389 Window trim, wood; decorative home furnishings & supplies;

(G-3332)
ULTIMATE TRADING CORP
Also Called: U T C
4 Just Rd (07004-3408)
PHONE.....................................973 228-7700
Fax: 973 228-7100
James Geswelli, *President*
Todd Knichel, *Vice Pres*
Raul Blancas, *Production*
Douglas Roberts, *Controller*
Stacie Androsky, *Director*
EMP: 100
SQ FT: 21,000
SALES (est): 12.8MM **Privately Held**
SIC: 3911 5094 3961 3369 Jewelry, precious metal; jewelry & precious stones; costume jewelry; nonferrous foundries

(G-3333)
UNICORN GROUP INC
23 Daniel Rd (07004-2527)
PHONE..................................973 360-5904
James S Devine, *Branch Mgr*
EMP: 76
SALES (corp-wide): 20.9MM **Privately Held**
WEB: www.open4.com
SIC: 7372 7379 Business oriented computer software; computer related consulting services
PA: The Unicorn Group Inc
25b Hanover Rd
Florham Park NJ 07932
973 360-0688

(G-3334)
UNIFOIL CORPORATION
12 Daniel Rd (07004-2536)
PHONE..................................973 244-9900
Fax: 973 244-5555
Joseph Funicelli, *President*
Milica Bubalo, *Sales Staff*
Megan Bronkowski, *Marketing Staff*
Patricia Shane, *Admin Asst*
▲ EMP: 62 EST: 1971
SQ FT: 135,000
SALES (est): 28.1MM **Privately Held**
WEB: www.unifoil.com
SIC: 2672 Metallic covered paper: made from purchased materials

(G-3335)
UNITED STATES BOX CORP
Also Called: U S Box
14 Madison Rd Ste E (07004-2326)
PHONE..................................973 481-2000
Fax: 973 481-2002
Alan S Kossoff, *President*
Chris Belli, *General Mgr*
Evan Don Kossoff, *Vice Pres*
Tom Kossoff, *Vice Pres*
Grace Conway, *Traffic Mgr*
▼ EMP: 35
SQ FT: 50,000
SALES (est): 3.5MM **Privately Held**
WEB: www.usbox.com
SIC: 2631 2652 3089 5113 Folding boxboard; setup paperboard boxes; boxes, plastic; industrial & personal service paper

(G-3336)
V & L MACHINE AND TOOL CO INC
Also Called: Www.vandlmachinetool.com
30 Sherwood Ln Ste 11 (07004-3603)
PHONE..................................973 808-5858
EMP: 6
SQ FT: 7,400
SALES (est): 900.2K **Privately Held**
SIC: 3599 Mfg Industrial Machinery

(G-3337)
VCOM INTL MULTI-MEDIA CORP (PA)
Also Called: Comprehensive Connectivity Com
80 Little Falls Rd (07004-2135)
P.O. Box 10005 (07004-6005)
PHONE..................................201 814-0405
Fax: 201 814-0615
Sheldon Goldstein, *President*
Randall Cole, *Vice Pres*
Madelyn Picone, *Vice Pres*
Isreal Gautier, *Warehouse Mgr*
Charlie Mena, *Purchasing*
▲ EMP: 93
SQ FT: 45,000
SALES (est): 27.1MM **Privately Held**
WEB: www.vcomimc.com
SIC: 3651 5999 5065 Electronic kits for home assembly: radio, TV, phonograph; communication equipment; communication equipment

(G-3338)
VCOM INTL MULTI-MEDIA CORP
Also Called: Alltec Stores
80 Little Falls Rd (07004-2135)
P.O. Box 10005 (07004-6005)
PHONE..................................201 296-0600
Sheldon Goldstein, *President*
William Kurtzer, *General Mgr*

EMP: 85
SALES (corp-wide): 27.1MM **Privately Held**
SIC: 5999 3651 5065 Alarm & safety equipment stores; household audio & video equipment; electronic parts & equipment
PA: Vcom International Multi-Media Corp.
80 Little Falls Rd
Fairfield NJ 07004
201 814-0405

(G-3339)
VECTOR FOILTEC LLC
55 Lane Rd Ste 110 (07004-1018)
PHONE..................................862 702-8909
Christina Borecki, *General Mgr*
Stefan Lehnert, *Mng Member*
▲ EMP: 4
SALES (est): 938.4K **Privately Held**
WEB: www.foiltecna.com
SIC: 2952 1761 Roofing materials; roofing contractor

(G-3340)
VELA DIAGNOSTICS USA INC
353c Rte 46 W Ste 250 (07004)
PHONE..................................973 852-3740
Gerard Lee, *President*
Tine Normann, *President*
Charlie Lee, *Top Exec*
Wen Huang, *Vice Pres*
Gary Raff, *Controller*
EMP: 9
SALES (est): 1.1MM **Privately Held**
SIC: 3841 Diagnostic apparatus, medical
PA: Vela Diagnostics Holding Pte. Ltd.
50 Science Park Road
Singapore
667 260-60

(G-3341)
VERTICAN TECHNOLOGIES INC
55 Lane Rd Ste 210 (07004-1015)
PHONE..................................800 435-7257
Stevan H Goldman, *CEO*
Isaac Goldman, *COO*
Kurt Sund, *CTO*
EMP: 6 EST: 1981
SALES (est): 168.2K **Privately Held**
SIC: 7372 Prepackaged software

(G-3342)
VICINITY MEDIA GROUP INC
165 Passaic Ave (07004-3521)
PHONE..................................973 276-1688
David Black, *Principal*
Michael Reidy, *Art Dir*
EMP: 12 EST: 2012
SALES (est): 729.3K **Privately Held**
SIC: 2711 Newspapers, publishing & printing

(G-3343)
VICINITY PUBLICATIONS INC
Also Called: Suburban Essex Magazine
165 Passaic Ave Ste 107 (07004-3592)
PHONE..................................973 276-1688
Fax: 973 276-1466
David Black, *President*
Cathy Black, *Publisher*
EMP: 9 EST: 1992
SQ FT: 2,000
SALES (est): 960K **Privately Held**
WEB: www.vpmagazines.com
SIC: 2721 Magazines: publishing only, not printed on site

(G-3344)
VITAQUEST INTERNATIONAL LLC
Also Called: Windmill Health Products
21 Dwight Pl (07004-3303)
PHONE..................................973 575-9200
Howard Munk, *Branch Mgr*
EMP: 10 **Privately Held**
WEB: www.gardenstatenutritionals.com
SIC: 2834 5122 5149 8742 Vitamin preparations; vitamins & minerals; health foods; marketing consulting services
PA: Vitaquest International, Llc
8 Henderson Dr
West Caldwell NJ 07006

(G-3345)
VIVREAU ADVANCED WATER SYSTEMS
14 Madison Rd Ste 30 (07004-2326)
PHONE..................................212 502-3749
Andrew Hamilton, *Principal*
EMP: 14
SALES (est): 1.4MM **Privately Held**
SIC: 3221 3589 5963 Bottles for packing, bottling & canning: glass; water purification equipment, household type; bottled water delivery

(G-3346)
VOLTIS LLC
55 Dwight Pl Unit A (07004-3311)
PHONE..................................607 349-9411
Byron James, *Mng Member*
Patrick Cupo
EMP: 6
SALES: 950K **Privately Held**
SIC: 3612 Power & distribution transformers

(G-3347)
W & H SYSTEMS INC
Also Called: DMW&h
253 Passaic Ave Ste 1 (07004-2524)
PHONE..................................201 933-7840
Fax: 201 933-2144
Joe Colleti, *President*
Ken Knapp, *COO*
Joe Esquilin, *Engineer*
Peter Lukowicz, *Controller*
Christopher Castaldi, *VP Sales*
▲ EMP: 132
SQ FT: 31,000
SALES: 68MM
SALES (corp-wide): 176.4MM **Privately Held**
WEB: www.whsystems.com
SIC: 3535 Conveyors & conveying equipment
PA: Dearborn Mid-West Company, Llc
20334 Superior Rd
Taylor MI 48180
734 288-4400

(G-3348)
W R CHESNUT ENGINEERING INC
2 Industrial Rd 101 (07004-3018)
PHONE..................................973 227-6995
Fax: 973 227-7873
Richard Chesnut, *President*
Norma Chesnut, *Corp Secy*
Bob Pozner, *Production*
Albert Mirra, *Purch Agent*
Anthony Zisa, *Controller*
EMP: 19
SQ FT: 16,000
SALES (est): 4.5MM **Privately Held**
WEB: www.chesnuteng.com
SIC: 3555 Printing trades machinery

(G-3349)
W T WINTER ASSOCIATES INC
Also Called: Winter Scale & Equipment
20a Kulick Rd (07004-3308)
PHONE..................................888 808-3611
Fax: 973 808-3344
William T Winter Jr, *President*
Jonathon S Winter, *Vice Pres*
Joseph W Winter, *Treasurer*
Laura C Winter, *Admin Sec*
EMP: 25
SQ FT: 8,600
SALES (est): 4.5MM **Privately Held**
WEB: www.wtwinter.com
SIC: 7629 5064 5084 5046 Electrical repair shops; electrical appliances, television & radio; industrial machinery & equipment; commercial equipment; scales & balances, except laboratory

(G-3350)
WAVELINE INCORPORATED
160 Passaic Ave (07004-3596)
P.O. Box 718, Caldwell (07007-0718)
PHONE..................................973 226-9100
Fax: 973 226-1565
James A Mc Gregor, *President*
Fred Henningsen, *Managing Dir*
Chris Del Plato, *Manager*
Don Morsillo, *Manager*

Timothy Alexander, *Asst Mgr*
▼ EMP: 35 EST: 1946
SQ FT: 32,000
SALES (est): 7MM **Privately Held**
WEB: www.wavelineinc.com
SIC: 3825 3679 Microwave test equipment; microwave components

(G-3351)
WEST ESSEX GRAPHICS INC
305 Fairfield Ave (07004-3831)
PHONE..................................973 227-2400
Thomas Guth, *Owner*
EMP: 30
SALES (corp-wide): 8.1MM **Privately Held**
WEB: www.westessexgraphics.com
SIC: 3861 Plates, photographic (sensitized)
PA: Essex West Graphics Inc
305 Fairfield Ave
Fairfield NJ 07004
973 227-2400

(G-3352)
WHITEHOUSE PRTG & LABELING LLC
50 Kulick Rd (07004-3308)
PHONE..................................973 521-7648
Fax: 908 526-6626
Yimin Shiuey, *Principal*
David P Matto, *Principal*
Allison Lavallato,
Alyssa Newton,
Patrick Newton,
EMP: 8
SALES: 1MM **Privately Held**
SIC: 2759 Commercial printing

(G-3353)
WM HBREWSTER JR INCORPORATED
Also Called: Wm.h. Brewster Jr
16 Kulick Rd (07004-3308)
PHONE..................................973 227-1050
Fax: 973 227-2363
Salvatore T Freda Jr, *CEO*
Mary Freda, *Officer*
EMP: 9 EST: 1919
SQ FT: 7,500
SALES (est): 1.8MM **Privately Held**
WEB: www.brewster-washers.com
SIC: 3499 3452 Shims, metal; bolts, nuts, rivets & washers; washers, metal

(G-3354)
WOODWORKING INC CORPORATE
368 Passaic Ave Ste 300 (07004-2008)
P.O. Box 10362 (07004-6362)
PHONE..................................973 227-2211
Daniel Andersen, *President*
Michael Andersen, *Vice Pres*
Bob Brennan, *Project Mgr*
Dennis Drew, *Project Mgr*
Scott Solvang, *CFO*
EMP: 25
SQ FT: 24,000
SALES (est): 6.6MM **Privately Held**
SIC: 2431 Millwork

(G-3355)
WRAPADE PACKAGING SYSTEMS LLC
15 Gardner Rd Ste 200 (07004-2207)
PHONE..................................973 787-1788
Fax: 973 773-6010
William Beattie, *President*
Laurene Beattie,
▲ EMP: 18
SQ FT: 15,000
SALES (est): 5.3MM **Privately Held**
WEB: www.wrapade.com
SIC: 3565 Packaging machinery

(G-3356)
ZKTECO USA LLC
6 Kingsbridge Rd Ste 8 (07004-2133)
PHONE..................................862 505-2101
Manish Dalal, *President*
Larry Reed, *Vice Pres*
Sherry Zemanek, *Finance*
EMP: 20
SQ FT: 1,500

G
E
O
G
R
A
P
H
I
C

SALES (est): 819.9K **Privately Held**
SIC: 3575 Computer terminals

Fairview
Bergen County

(G-3357)
ARAMANI INC
369 Henry St (07022-1910)
PHONE....................................201 945-1160
ARA Milkonean, *President*
EMP: 4
SQ FT: 1,112
SALES (est): 360K **Privately Held**
SIC: 2732 Books: printing & binding

(G-3358)
BERTOLOTTI LLC
54 Industrial Ave (07022-1605)
PHONE....................................201 941-3116
Fax: 201 941-3361
John Camisa, *President*
Ronald Camisa, *Vice Pres*
Albert Camisa, *Treasurer*
EMP: 10
SALES (est): 1.2MM **Privately Held**
WEB: www.bertolottidesserts.com
SIC: 2024 5812 Ice cream, bulk; spumoni; ice cream stands or dairy bars

(G-3359)
CLIFFSIDE BODY CORPORATION
130 Broad Ave (07022-1502)
P.O. Box 206 (07022-0206)
PHONE....................................201 945-3970
Fax: 201 945-7534
Edward Greenwald, *President*
Robert Greenwald, *Vice Pres*
Warren Greenwald, *Treasurer*
Bill Kerwick, *Sales Staff*
Guy Bradford, *Marketing Staff*
EMP: 32 EST: 1919
SQ FT: 28,000
SALES (est): 9.9MM **Privately Held**
WEB: www.cliffsidebody.com
SIC: 7532 3711 5012 5013 Body shop, trucks; truck & tractor truck assembly; truck bodies; truck parts & accessories; truck & bus bodies

(G-3360)
CUTLER BROS BOX & LUMBER CO (PA)
711 W Prospect Ave (07022-1523)
P.O. Box 217 (07022-0217)
PHONE....................................201 943-2535
Fax: 201 943-8532
Gregory Cutler, *President*
Adam Cutler, *Vice Pres*
Jed Cutler, *Vice Pres*
Carolyn Sands, *Treasurer*
EMP: 30
SQ FT: 20,000
SALES (est): 5.9MM **Privately Held**
WEB: www.cutlerpallets.com
SIC: 2448 2441 3412 2449 Pallets, wood; skids, wood; boxes, wood; metal barrels, drums & pails; wood containers

(G-3361)
EURO MECHANICAL INC
16 Industrial Ave (07022-1605)
PHONE....................................201 313-8050
Ante Pestic, *President*
Robin Taylor, *Division Mgr*
Francis Franklin, *Opers Mgr*
Jenifer Kalaw, *Accountant*
Sancho Varghese, *Accountant*
EMP: 12
SALES (est): 2.4MM **Privately Held**
WEB: www.euromechanical.com
SIC: 3498 Pipe fittings, fabricated from purchased pipe

(G-3362)
IWEISS INC
815 Fairview Ave Ste 10 (07022-1571)
PHONE....................................201 402-6500
David Rosenberg, *CEO*
Jennifer Tankleaf, *Vice Pres*
▲ EMP: 36
SQ FT: 18,000

SALES (est): 5.7MM **Privately Held**
WEB: www.iweiss.com
SIC: 2391 Curtains, window: made from purchased materials; draperies, plastic & textile: from purchased materials

(G-3363)
JOHN M SNIDERMAN INC (PA)
405 Henry St (07022-1911)
P.O. Box 278 (07022-0278)
PHONE....................................201 450-4291
Anita Sniderman, *President*
EMP: 9
SQ FT: 10,800
SALES (est): 2MM **Privately Held**
WEB: www.johnmsniderman.com
SIC: 2397 5131 Schiffli machine embroideries; piece goods & notions

(G-3364)
KRAUSES HOMEMADE CANDY INC
461 Fairview Ave 465 (07022-1836)
PHONE....................................201 943-4790
Fax: 201 943-8329
Nicole Cinquegrana, *President*
EMP: 10
SQ FT: 3,000
SALES (est): 1.2MM **Privately Held**
SIC: 2064 5441 Candy & other confectionery products; candy

(G-3365)
MARKO ENGRAVING & ART CORP
439 Fairview Ave (07022-1857)
PHONE....................................201 945-6555
EMP: 13
SALES (corp-wide): 1.2MM **Privately Held**
SIC: 3555 2796 Mfg Printing Trades Machinery Platemaking Services
PA: Marko Engraving & Art Corp
19 Baldwin Ave
Weehawken NJ 07086
201 864-6500

(G-3366)
NIKKO CERAMICS INC (HQ)
815 Fairview Ave Ste 9 (07022-1571)
PHONE....................................201 840-5200
Kenji Anzai, *President*
Akiko Mitani, *Chairman*
Kaz Suzuki, *Vice Pres*
▲ EMP: 11
SQ FT: 32,000
SALES: 2MM
SALES (corp-wide): 131MM **Privately Held**
SIC: 5023 5199 3262 China; glassware; gifts & novelties; vitreous china table & kitchenware
PA: Nikko Company
383, Ainokimachi
Hakusan ISH 924-0
762 762-121

(G-3367)
O BERK COMPANY LLC
Aql Decorating
215 Bergen Blvd (07022-1358)
PHONE....................................201 941-1610
Fax: 201 941-5079
EMP: 26
SALES (corp-wide): 53.3MM **Privately Held**
SIC: 2759 Commercial Printing
PA: The O Berk Company L L C
3 Milltown Ct
Union NJ 07083
908 810-2267

(G-3368)
PCS CRANE SERVICES INC
83 Broad Ave (07022-1501)
PHONE....................................201 366-4250
Robert Williams, *President*
EMP: 10
SQ FT: 60,000
SALES: 2MM **Privately Held**
SIC: 3536 Cranes, industrial plant
PA: Pro Crane Services (Pty) Ltd
53-55 Rigger Road Rtan
Johannesburg GP
945 550-

(G-3369)
PRIME FUR & LEATHER INC
Also Called: New York Fur
29 Industrial Ave 31 (07022-1605)
PHONE....................................201 941-9600
Fax: 201 941-7888
Brian S Han, *President*
▲ EMP: 15 EST: 1997
SQ FT: 8,000
SALES (est): 1.8MM **Privately Held**
SIC: 2386 Garments, leather; leather & sheep-lined garments

(G-3370)
PRINTING CRAFTSMAN INC
Also Called: Printing Craftsmen
130 Bergen Blvd (07022-1998)
PHONE....................................201 943-0276
Fax: 201 943-0278
EMP: 11 EST: 1935
SQ FT: 8,000
SALES (est): 1.2MM **Privately Held**
SIC: 2752 2791 2789 2759 Lithographic Coml Print Typesetting Services Bookbinding/Related Work Commercial Printing

(G-3371)
TONE EMBROIDERY CORP
Also Called: Touch of Lace
333 Bergen Blvd (07022-1213)
PHONE....................................201 943-1082
Haim Sasson, *President*
Gabriel Sasson, *Vice Pres*
Henriette Sasson, *Admin Sec*
▲ EMP: 36
SQ FT: 50,000
SALES (est): 7.2MM **Privately Held**
WEB: www.touchoflace.com
SIC: 5131 5949 2397 2395 Lace fabrics; sewing, needlework & piece goods; schiffli machine embroideries; pleating & stitching

Fanwood
Union County

(G-3372)
EAGLEVISION USA LLC
150 North Ave (07023-1209)
PHONE....................................908 322-1892
Nicholaos S Galakis, *Mng Member*
▼ EMP: 6
SALES (est): 231.1K **Privately Held**
SIC: 1459 Clays, except kaolin & ball

(G-3373)
REBUTH METAL SERVICES (PA)
130 Farley Ave (07023-1005)
PHONE....................................908 889-6400
Fax: 908 889-6400
Michael J Rebuth, *President*
Ralph W Rebuth, *Corp Secy*
EMP: 10 EST: 1958
SQ FT: 23,000
SALES (est): 1.9MM **Privately Held**
SIC: 5051 3544 3469 Steel; special dies & tools; stamping metal for the trade

Far Hills
Somerset County

(G-3374)
EDGEMONT PHARMACEUTICALS LLC
92 Roxiticus Rd (07931-2222)
PHONE....................................908 375-8039
Fax: 908 375-8039
Douglas Saltel, *Executive*
EMP: 4
SALES (est): 314.6K **Privately Held**
SIC: 2834 Vitamin, nutrient & hematinic preparations for human use

(G-3375)
ENGRAVED IMAGES LTD
Demunn Pl Rr 202 (07931)
P.O. Box 966 (07931-0966)
PHONE....................................908 234-0323
Fax: 908 234-0024

Heidi P Gammon, *President*
Heide Gammon, *President*
Heide Pfluger, *President*
EMP: 6
SALES (est): 317.9K **Privately Held**
SIC: 5947 2759 Gift shop; invitation & stationery printing & engraving

Farmingdale
Monmouth County

(G-3376)
ALLTEST INSTRUMENTS INC
500 Central Ave (07727-3790)
PHONE....................................732 919-3339
Fax: 732 919-1916
Nathan Nelson, *Principal*
Jeremy Nelson, *Principal*
Duane Sankar, *Opers Staff*
Jeremiah Nelson, *Info Tech Mgr*
Carl Mayer, *Technology*
◆ EMP: 17
SQ FT: 18,000
SALES (est): 6.9MM **Privately Held**
SIC: 3825 Instruments to measure electricity

(G-3377)
ANS NUTRITION INC
700 Central Ave (07727-3787)
PHONE....................................212 235-5205
Solomon Brander, *Principal*
EMP: 23
SALES (est): 5.6MM **Privately Held**
SIC: 2834 Vitamin preparations

(G-3378)
BELFER
10 Ruckle Ave (07727-3691)
PHONE....................................732 493-2666
Judi Handel, *Principal*
Debra Grimm, *Accounts Mgr*
EMP: 5
SALES (est): 739.7K **Privately Held**
SIC: 3646 Commercial indusl & institutional electric lighting fixtures

(G-3379)
CENTRAL METAL FABRICATORS INC
300 Central Ave (07727-3789)
PHONE....................................732 938-6900
Fax: 732 938-6902
Frank Crisafulli, *President*
Margaret Crisafulli, *Admin Sec*
EMP: 19
SQ FT: 10,000
SALES: 2.1MM **Privately Held**
WEB: www.central-metal.com
SIC: 3443 3444 Tanks, standard or custom fabricated: metal plate; sheet metalwork

(G-3380)
COLWOOD ELECTRONICS INC
44 Main St (07727-1325)
PHONE....................................732 938-5556
Richard Colaguori, *President*
Steven Colaguori, *Corp Secy*
Donna Colaguori, *Vice Pres*
▲ EMP: 9
SQ FT: 3,500
SALES (est): 1.2MM **Privately Held**
WEB: www.woodburning.com
SIC: 3544 3546 Special dies, tools, jigs & fixtures; power-driven handtools

(G-3381)
COMPOUNDERS INC
15 Marl Rd (07727-1413)
P.O. Box 413 (07727-0413)
PHONE....................................732 938-5007
Fax: 732 938-5008
Harold K Saunders, *President*
EMP: 4
SQ FT: 10,000
SALES (est): 810K **Privately Held**
SIC: 2891 Sealants

▲ = Import ▼=Export
◆ =Import/Export

(G-3382)
CROWN ENGINEERING CORP
550 Sqnkum Yellowbrook Rd (07727-3744)
P.O. Box 846 (07727-0846)
PHONE..........................800 631-2153
Fax: 732 938-3969
Michael J Palmer, *President*
Jackie Palmer, *Treasurer*
Steven Pereira, *Marketing Mgr*
Ken Mercure, *Manager*
▲ EMP: 25
SQ FT: 22,500
SALES (est): 5.1MM **Privately Held**
WEB: www.crownengineering.com
SIC: 3443 Fabricated plate work (boiler shop)

(G-3383)
D&E NUTRACEUTICALS INC
700 Central Ave (07727-3787)
PHONE..........................212 235-5200
Sam Zeldes, *President*
Dariusz Michalski, *Prdtn Mgr*
David Cohen, *Controller*
Michelle Rodriguez, *Executive Asst*
EMP: 20
SALES (est): 8.7MM **Privately Held**
SIC: 5122 2834 Drugs, proprietaries & sundries; pharmaceuticals; pharmaceutical preparations

(G-3384)
DOERRE FENCE CO LLC
392 Adelphia Rd (07727-3529)
PHONE..........................732 751-9700
Chris Doerre, *Mng Member*
Christine Bosse, *Mng Member*
EMP: 10
SQ FT: 3,000
SALES (est): 901.5K **Privately Held**
SIC: 2499 5211 1799 Fencing, wood; fencing; fence construction

(G-3385)
ENVIRONMENTAL TECHNICAL DRLG
Also Called: Environmental Technical Drlg
408 Cranberry Rd (07727-3511)
PHONE..........................732 938-3222
Fax: 732 919-0524
Michael Ryan Jr, *President*
Ann C Ryan, *Vice Pres*
EMP: 7
SALES: 425K **Privately Held**
SIC: 1799 1389 Core drilling & cutting; bailing, cleaning, swabbing & treating of wells

(G-3386)
HANRAHAN TOOL CO INC
Also Called: Howell Precision Tool Co
415 Cranberry Rd (07727-3512)
PHONE..........................732 919-7300
Fax: 732 919-7750
David W Hanrahan Jr, *President*
Elizabeth Hanrahan, *Vice Pres*
EMP: 7
SQ FT: 4,300
SALES (est): 936K **Privately Held**
WEB: www.howellprecision.com
SIC: 3599 3544 Machine shop, jobbing & repair; industrial molds

(G-3387)
IDEAL TILE FABRICATIONS LLC
304a Squankum Rd (07727-3754)
PHONE..........................732 751-0074
David Cupko,
EMP: 12
SALES (est): 1.7MM **Privately Held**
SIC: 3441 Fabricated structural metal

(G-3388)
LIGHTING WORLD INC
Also Called: Belfer Lighting Manufacturing
10 Ruckle Ave (07727-3691)
P.O. Box 2079, Asbury Park (07712-2079)
PHONE..........................732 919-1224
Bruce Belfer, *President*
Norman Armbrust, *President*
Evelyn Maldonado, *Vice Pres*
Elaine Belfer, *Treasurer*
◆ EMP: 48
SQ FT: 22,000

SALES (est): 7.2MM **Privately Held**
WEB: www.belfer.com
SIC: 3646 3645 Commercial indusl & institutional electric lighting fixtures; residential lighting fixtures

(G-3389)
MARINE CONT EQP CRTFCTION CORP
160 Sqnkum Yellowbrook Rd (07727-3736)
PHONE..........................732 938-6622
Fax: 732 938-6622
Kenneth Allen, *President*
Jennifer Allen, *Vice Pres*
Joyce M Allen, *Treasurer*
EMP: 6
SQ FT: 5,000
SALES (est): 540K **Privately Held**
SIC: 3829 Physical property testing equipment

(G-3390)
MASTER TOOL CORP
342 Sqnkum Yellowbrook Rd (07727-3740)
P.O. Box 711 (07727-0711)
PHONE..........................732 919-1010
Fax: 732 919-1010
Tom Didonato, *President*
EMP: 4
SALES (est): 110K **Privately Held**
SIC: 3599 Machine shop, jobbing & repair

(G-3391)
PATTY-O-MATIC INC
Lakewood Farmingdale Rd (07727)
P.O. Box 404 (07727-0404)
PHONE..........................732 938-2757
Fax: 732 938-5809
Bernard Miles, *President*
June Miles, *Treasurer*
EMP: 12
SQ FT: 10,000
SALES (est): 2.6MM **Privately Held**
WEB: www.pattyomatic.com
SIC: 3556 7389 Meat processing machinery; personal service agents, brokers & bureaus

(G-3392)
PEKAY INDUSTRIES INC
452 Sqnkum Yellowbrook Rd (07727-3775)
P.O. Box 559 (07727-0559)
PHONE..........................732 938-2722
Fax: 732 919-0224
Peter Kowalenko Jr, *President*
EMP: 10
SQ FT: 5,000
SALES: 1MM **Privately Held**
SIC: 3674 3643 3429 3296 Solid state electronic devices; current-carrying wiring devices; manufactured hardware (general); mineral wool; porcelain electrical supplies

(G-3393)
ROSANO ASPHALT LLC
Asbury Rd Ste 360 (07727)
PHONE..........................732 620-8400
Fax: 732 542-5014
Frank Rosano, *Manager*
EMP: 8
SALES (est): 850K **Privately Held**
SIC: 2951 Road materials, bituminous (not from refineries)

(G-3394)
STEVE GREEN ENTERPRISES
Also Called: Stephan L Green Trailers
74 Sqankum Yellowbrook Rd (07727-3734)
PHONE..........................732 938-5572
Stephan L Green, *President*
Stephan Green, *Owner*
EMP: 14
SQ FT: 50,000
SALES (est): 3.1MM **Privately Held**
SIC: 3523 3799 7549 Trailers & wagons, farm; trailers & trailer equipment; trailer maintenance

(G-3395)
TEA ELLE WOODWORKS
53 Main St (07727-1326)
PHONE..........................732 938-9660
Todd Gleason, *Owner*
EMP: 4

SALES (est): 404.8K **Privately Held**
SIC: 2431 Millwork

(G-3396)
WELD TECH FAB
282 Lemon Rd (07727-3538)
PHONE..........................732 919-2185
Dave Hanick, *Owner*
EMP: 4
SALES (est): 20K **Privately Held**
SIC: 7692 Welding repair

(G-3397)
WM LEIBER INC
190 Georgia Tavern Rd (07727-3549)
PHONE..........................732 938-2080
William Leiber, *Principal*
EMP: 4
SALES (est): 288.4K **Privately Held**
SIC: 2448 Wood pallets & skids

(G-3398)
YATES SIGN CO INC
Also Called: Allied Enviornmental Signage
69 Megill Rd (07727-3678)
PHONE..........................732 578-1818
Fax: 732 578-1808
Kevin R White, *President*
Michael McClellan, *President*
Kevin White, *Export Mgr*
Clara Wasshem, *Sales Staff*
Kim Rasmussen, *Office Mgr*
EMP: 25 EST: 1923
SQ FT: 17,500
SALES (est): 3.9MM **Privately Held**
WEB: www.yatessignco.com
SIC: 3993 Electric signs

Flanders
Morris County

(G-3399)
AFFINITY CHEMICAL WOODBINE LLC
82 Crenshaw Dr (07836-4725)
PHONE..........................973 873-4070
EMP: 11
SALES (est): 3.5MM **Privately Held**
SIC: 2819 Industrial inorganic chemicals

(G-3400)
ALT SHIFT CREATIVE LLC
15 Mountain Ave (07836-9130)
PHONE..........................609 619-0009
Paul Reidinger,
EMP: 7
SALES: 900K **Privately Held**
SIC: 7372 Application computer software

(G-3401)
ANALYTICAL SALES AND SVCS INC
179 Rte 206 (07836-9262)
PHONE..........................973 616-0700
Fax: 973 616-0133
David A Isom, *President*
Rosanne Isom, *Vice Pres*
◆ EMP: 10
SQ FT: 14,500
SALES (est): 4.7MM **Privately Held**
WEB: www.analytical-sales.com
SIC: 3826 8732 Chromatographic equipment, laboratory type; research services, except laboratory

(G-3402)
BON VENTURE SERVICES LLC
34 Ironia Rd (07836-9111)
P.O. Box 850 (07836-0850)
PHONE..........................973 584-5699
Fax: 973 252-7403
Mike Garde, *Ch of Bd*
Tom Garde, *President*
Stuart Frazier, *Vice Pres*
Mary Beth Piazza, *Human Res Mgr*
John Slootmaker, *Sales Mgr*
EMP: 60
SQ FT: 10,000
SALES (est): 9.3MM **Privately Held**
WEB: www.bonventure.net
SIC: 2731 Pamphlets: publishing & printing

(G-3403)
DANI LEATHER USA INC
37 Ironia Rd Ste 2 (07836-4422)
PHONE..........................973 598-0890
Silvano Fumei, *Principal*
▲ EMP: 6
SQ FT: 15,000
SALES (est): 1.1MM **Privately Held**
SIC: 3111 Leather tanning & finishing
HQ: Dani Spa
Via Della Concia 186
Arzignano VI 36071
044 445-4111

(G-3404)
DELTA COOLING TOWERS INC (PA)
185 Us Highway 206 (07836-9238)
PHONE..........................973 586-2201
Fax: 973 586-2243
John C Flaherty, *President*
▼ EMP: 9
SALES (est): 7.4MM **Privately Held**
WEB: www.deltacooling.com
SIC: 3443 3589 Cooling towers, metal plate; water treatment equipment, industrial

(G-3405)
DPC CIRRUS
62 Flanders Bartley Rd (07836-4715)
PHONE..........................973 927-2828
Douglas Olson, *Principal*
EMP: 14
SALES (est): 2.2MM **Privately Held**
SIC: 2835 In vitro & in vivo diagnostic substances

(G-3406)
ELECTRONIC MEASURING DEVICES
Also Called: E M D
15 Mill Rd (07836-9611)
PHONE..........................973 691-4755
Frank Allia, *CEO*
Klaus Ulbrich, *COO*
▲ EMP: 10
SQ FT: 2,600
SALES (est): 1.2MM **Privately Held**
WEB: www.emdsceptre.com
SIC: 3823 8748 Industrial process measurement equipment; business consulting

(G-3407)
ENERGY TRACKING LLC
16 Southwind Dr (07836-9734)
PHONE..........................973 448-8660
Keith Mistry, *Mng Member*
Raji Mistry,
EMP: 8
SALES: 300K **Privately Held**
SIC: 3825 7371 7389 Electrical energy measuring equipment; computer software development;

(G-3408)
FIRST PRIORITY GLOBAL LTD (PA)
160 Gold Mine Rd (07836-9284)
PHONE..........................973 347-4321
Alex N Cherepakhov,
EMP: 15
SALES (est): 7.3MM **Privately Held**
SIC: 3711 Ambulances (motor vehicles), assembly of

(G-3409)
G E INSPECTION TECHNOLOGIES LP
199 Us Highway 206 (07836-4501)
PHONE..........................973 448-0077
Fax: 973 448-9147
John Farrow, *Opers Mgr*
Bruce Pellegrino, *Branch Mgr*
EMP: 89 **Privately Held**
SIC: 3829 3844 Ultrasonic testing equipment; radiographic X-ray apparatus & tubes
HQ: G E Inspection Technologies, Lp
721 Visions Dr
Skaneateles NY 13152
315 554-2000

(G-3410)
HAAS LASER TECHNOLOGIES INC (PA)
37 Ironia Rd (07836-4422)
PHONE...................................973 598-1150
Gilbert Haas, *President*
Ann Haas, *Vice Pres*
Stephen Roe, *Design Engr*
◆ EMP: 16
SQ FT: 34,600
SALES (est): 2.2MM **Privately Held**
WEB: www.haaslti.com
SIC: 3699 Laser systems & equipment

(G-3411)
INSTANT IMPRINTS
286 Us Highway 206 119b (07836-9582)
PHONE...................................973 252-9500
EMP: 4
SALES (est): 190K **Privately Held**
SIC: 2752 Lithographic Commercial Printing

(G-3412)
JOHNSTON LETTER CO INC
209 Pleasant Hill Rd (07836-9179)
PHONE...................................973 482-7535
Fax: 973 482-4535
James Johnston, *President*
EMP: 4 EST: 1921
SQ FT: 10,000
SALES (est): 194.8K **Privately Held**
SIC: 7338 7331 2791 2789 Letter writing service; direct mail advertising services; typesetting; bookbinding & related work; commercial printing, lithographic

(G-3413)
NORTH JERSEY SPECIALISTS INC
Also Called: N J S
5 Laurel Dr Unit 6 (07836-4701)
PHONE...................................973 927-1616
Fax: 973 927-6228
Richard A Lettorale, *President*
EMP: 5 EST: 1976
SQ FT: 2,500
SALES (est): 838.5K **Privately Held**
WEB: www.northjerseyspecialists.net
SIC: 2851 Epoxy coatings

(G-3414)
ROBERT H HOOVER & SONS INC
Also Called: Transfer Truck & Equipment
149 Gold Mine Rd (07836-9138)
P.O. Box 719 (07836-0719)
PHONE...................................973 347-4210
Robert C Hoover, *Manager*
EMP: 7
SALES (corp-wide): 8MM **Privately Held**
WEB: www.hoovertruckcenters.com
SIC: 5511 7538 5531 3492 Trucks, tractors & trailers: new & used; truck engine repair, except industrial; truck equipment & parts; hose & tube fittings & assemblies, hydraulic/pneumatic
PA: Robert H Hoover & Sons Inc
   1784 Route 9
   Toms River NJ 08755
   732 341-2128

(G-3415)
SHIVA SOFTWARE GROUP INC
2 Fennimore Ct (07836-9660)
PHONE...................................973 691-5475
Chandrareddy Vallapureddy, *CEO*
EMP: 35
SALES (est): 4MM **Privately Held**
SIC: 7372 Prepackaged software

(G-3416)
SIEMENS MED SLTONS DIAGNOSTICS
Also Called: Dpc Instrument Systems
62 Flanders Bartley Rd (07836-4715)
PHONE...................................973 927-2828
Douglas R Olson, *President*
Jim Guille, *Vice Pres*
David Herzog, *Vice Pres*
Brenda Lynch, *Buyer*
Jim Meredith, *Purchasing*
▲ EMP: 2100
SQ FT: 89,000

SALES (est): 228.8MM
SALES (corp-wide): 97.7B **Privately Held**
WEB: www.dpconline.com
SIC: 3826 Analytical instruments
HQ: Siemens Healthcare Diagnostics Inc.
   511 Benedict Ave
   Tarrytown NY 10591
   914 631-8000

(G-3417)
SPECIAL TECHNICAL SERVICES
11 Carlton Rd (07836-4409)
PHONE...................................609 259-2626
Fax: 609 259-0044
Ronald Dunster, *President*
Alan Dunster, *Vice Pres*
Allan Dunster, *Research*
Myrtle Dunster, *Treasurer*
EMP: 6 EST: 1966
SQ FT: 6,300
SALES (est): 490K **Privately Held**
SIC: 3625 Relays & industrial controls

(G-3418)
TARGA INDUSTRIES INC
Also Called: Cherokee Rubber Company
5 Laurel Dr Unit 13 (07836-4701)
P.O. Box 339, Chester (07930-0339)
PHONE...................................973 584-3733
Gilbert Stroming II, *President*
Jacquelyn M Stroming, *Vice Pres*
EMP: 10
SQ FT: 4,000
SALES (est): 2MM **Privately Held**
SIC: 3052 Rubber & plastics hose & beltings

(G-3419)
TECHNICAL COATINGS CO (DH)
Also Called: Benjamin Moore
360 Us Highway 206 (07836-9577)
P.O. Box 4000 (07836-4000)
PHONE...................................973 927-8600
Fax: 973 252-2727
Robert J Hodgson, *President*
Thomas O Cassidy, *Treasurer*
EMP: 20
SQ FT: 3,200
SALES (est): 35.2MM
SALES (corp-wide): 242.1B **Publicly Held**
SIC: 2851 Lacquers, varnishes, enamels & other coatings; paints & paint additives; varnishes
HQ: Benjamin Moore & Co.
   101 Paragon Dr
   Montvale NJ 07645
   201 573-9600

(G-3420)
TRI-STATE QUIKRETE
150 Gold Mine Rd (07836-9171)
PHONE...................................973 347-4569
Jeffrey R Nanfeldt, *Partner*
Anthony Casavecchia, *Cust Mgr*
EMP: 50
SALES (est): 7.4MM **Privately Held**
SIC: 3272 Dry mixture concrete

(G-3421)
TRIUMPH PLASTICS LLC
99 Bartley Flanders Rd (07836-9642)
PHONE...................................973 584-5500
EMP: 5
SALES (est): 620.1K **Privately Held**
SIC: 3089 Kits, plastic

Flemington
Hunterdon County

(G-3422)
3M COMPANY
500 Rte 202 (08822-6031)
PHONE...................................908 788-4000
David Marston, *Branch Mgr*
EMP: 200
SALES (corp-wide): 31.6B **Publicly Held**
WEB: www.mmm.com
SIC: 5047 3841 Medical equipment & supplies; surgical & medical instruments
PA: 3m Company
   3m Center
   Saint Paul MN 55144
   651 733-1110

(G-3423)
ABILITY2WORK A NJ NNPRFIT CORP
42 State Route 12 (08822-1540)
P.O. Box 368, Whitehouse (08888-0368)
PHONE...................................908 782-3458
Karen Monroy, *CEO*
EMP: 10
SALES (est): 672.7K **Privately Held**
SIC: 2051 Cakes, bakery: except frozen

(G-3424)
ACTIVE LEARNING ASSOCIATES
Also Called: Children's Tecnology Review
126 Main St (08822-1652)
PHONE...................................908 284-0404
Warren Buckleiter, *President*
Lisa Fave, *Editor*
Ellen Wolock, *Vice Pres*
Chris Grabowich, *Manager*
EMP: 5
SQ FT: 1,000
SALES (est): 266.2K **Privately Held**
WEB: www.littleclickers.com
SIC: 2759 Publication printing

(G-3425)
AMBRO MANUFACTURING INC
Also Called: Special T S Screen Prtg & EMB
6 Kings Ct (08822-6004)
PHONE...................................908 806-8337
Robert Amato, *President*
Linda Amato, *Principal*
Ryan Amato, *Vice Pres*
Darren Amato, *VP Sales*
EMP: 12
SQ FT: 5,000
SALES (est): 880K **Privately Held**
SIC: 2396 2395 Screen printing on fabric articles; embroidery & art needlework

(G-3426)
AMPAL INC
408 Us Highway 202 (08822-6020)
P.O. Box 2270 (08822-2270)
PHONE...................................908 782-5454
Fax: 908 782-3489
K Ramsey, *Branch Mgr*
EMP: 4
SALES (corp-wide): 10.5MM **Privately Held**
SIC: 3471 Coloring & finishing of aluminum or formed products
HQ: Ampal Inc.
   2115 Little Gap Rd
   Palmerton PA 18071
   610 826-7020

(G-3427)
ANTI HYDRO INTERNATIONAL INC
45 River Rd Ste 200 (08822-6026)
P.O. Box 2467 (08822-2467)
PHONE...................................908 284-9000
Fax: 908 284-9464
Pankaj Desai, *CEO*
Piyush Patel, *President*
Suresh Patel, *Vice Pres*
Anil Chokshi, *Opers Staff*
▼ EMP: 10
SQ FT: 30,000
SALES (est): 1.9MM **Privately Held**
WEB: www.anti-hydro.com
SIC: 2821 3241 1799 Epoxy resins; cement, hydraulic; waterproofing

(G-3428)
ARNO THERAPEUTICS INC
200 Route 31 Ste 104 (08822-5812)
P.O. Box 571, Kingston (08528-0571)
PHONE...................................862 703-7170
Fax: 973 267-0101
Arie S Belldegrun, *Ch of Bd*
Alexander Zukiwski, *Chief Mktg Ofcr*
David M Tanen, *Admin Sec*
EMP: 4
SQ FT: 4,168
SALES (est): 780.5K **Privately Held**
SIC: 2834 Druggists' preparations (pharmaceuticals)

(G-3429)
BAGEL CLUB
20 Commerce St Ste 5 (08822-7700)
PHONE...................................908 806-6022

Fax: 908 806-7022
Jeff Stern, *President*
EMP: 16
SALES: 575K **Privately Held**
SIC: 5812 2051 5411 Delicatessen (eating places); bagels, fresh or frozen; delicatessens

(G-3430)
CELLULAR SCIENCES INC
84 Park Ave (08822-1172)
PHONE...................................908 237-1561
Allan Martin, *President*
EMP: 5
SALES (est): 446.5K **Privately Held**
WEB: www.cellularsciences.com
SIC: 2834 Pharmaceutical preparations

(G-3431)
CORNERSTONE PRINTS IMAGING LLC
Also Called: Cornerstone Imaging
179 State Route 31 Ste 8 (08822-5743)
PHONE...................................908 782-7966
Arthur Clark, *Owner*
Carol Clark, *Manager*
EMP: 5
SQ FT: 2,300
SALES (est): 350K **Privately Held**
WEB: www.cornerstone-print.com
SIC: 2752 2791 2789 Commercial printing, lithographic; typesetting; bookbinding & related work

(G-3432)
CRETER VAULT CORP (PA)
417 Us Highway 202 (08822-6021)
PHONE...................................908 782-7771
Fax: 908 782-4381
Richard E Creter, *President*
Camille Creter, *Corp Secy*
EMP: 48 EST: 1918
SQ FT: 35,000
SALES (est): 12.1MM **Privately Held**
WEB: www.beachsaver.com
SIC: 3272 Burial vaults, concrete or precast terrazzo

(G-3433)
DAKA MANUFACTURING LLC
19 Floral Rd (08822-3321)
PHONE...................................908 782-0360
Fax: 908 782-0360
Shelly Sobel,
Martin Sobel,
EMP: 5
SALES: 100K **Privately Held**
SIC: 3423 Hand & edge tools

(G-3434)
DEX MEDIA INC
27 Minneakoning Rd # 204 (08822-5761)
PHONE...................................908 237-0956
Ellen Green, *Branch Mgr*
EMP: 15
SALES (corp-wide): 1.8B **Privately Held**
WEB: www.rhdonnelley.com
SIC: 2741 Directories: publishing only, not printed on site
PA: Dex Media Holdings, Inc.
   2200 W Airfield Dr
   Dfw Airport TX 75261
   972 453-7000

(G-3435)
DIGITAL ARTS IMAGING LLC
105 State Route 31 Ste 10 (08822-5745)
PHONE...................................908 237-4646
Fax: 908 237-4644
Robert Vernon, *President*
EMP: 12
SQ FT: 7,500
SALES (est): 1.6MM **Privately Held**
SIC: 7336 3993 Graphic arts & related design; signs & advertising specialties

(G-3436)
DMS LABORATORIES INC
2 Darts Mill Rd (08822-7090)
PHONE...................................908 782-3353
Nicholas A Gallo III, *President*
Denise G Darmanian, *Admin Sec*
EMP: 6
SQ FT: 2,000

▲ = Import ▼=Export
◆ =Import/Export

SALES: 1MM
SALES (corp-wide): 3.4MM **Privately Held**
WEB: www.rapidvet.com
SIC: 5047 2835 Veterinarians' equipment & supplies; veterinary diagnostic substances
PA: Fed Corporate Services Ag
C/O Bmo Treuhand Ag
Neuhausen Am Rheinfall SH 8212
526 755-922

(G-3437)
DONALD MASON BAKER CONTRACTOR (PA)
Also Called: Baker General Contracting
188 Thatchers Hill Rd (08822-4650)
PHONE..................908 782-2115
Donald Baker, *President*
Gregory Baker, *Principal*
Jordan Baker, *Corp Secy*
Mary Baker, *Corp Secy*
EMP: 3
SALES: 4MM **Privately Held**
SIC: 3272 1741 Concrete stuctural support & building material

(G-3438)
ENERGY BATTERY
1200 County Road 523 (08822-7097)
PHONE..................908 751-5918
▲ **EMP:** 5
SALES (est): 657.5K **Privately Held**
SIC: 3691 Storage batteries

(G-3439)
ENERGY BATTERY GROUP INC
1200 County Road 523 (08822-7097)
PHONE..................404 255-7529
Rick Hallock, *President*
EMP: 5
SALES (corp-wide): 210MM **Privately Held**
SIC: 3621 5063 Storage battery chargers, motor & engine generator type; storage batteries, industrial
PA: Energy Battery Group, Inc.
1800 Roswell Rd Ste 2200
Marietta GA 30062
404 255-7529

(G-3440)
FLEMINGTON ALUMININUM & BRASS
24 Junction Rd (08822-5721)
PHONE..................908 782-6333
Fax: 908 782-8078
James Kozicki, *President*
Lynne Kozicki, *Vice Pres*
Jim Kozicki, *Sales Executive*
EMP: 6 **EST:** 1940
SQ FT: 12,000
SALES: 954.7K **Privately Held**
WEB: www.fabonline.net
SIC: 3364 Brass & bronze die-castings

(G-3441)
FLEMINGTON BITUMINOUS CORP
356 State Route 31 (08822-5741)
PHONE..................908 782-2722
Fax: 908 782-6292
Richard D Mannon, *President*
Hilda Mannon, *Treasurer*
EMP: 10 **EST:** 1960
SQ FT: 1,200
SALES (est): 1.5MM **Privately Held**
SIC: 2951 Road materials, bituminous (not from refineries)

(G-3442)
FLEMINGTON PRECAST & SUP LLC
18 Allen St (08822-1120)
PHONE..................908 782-3246
Garrett Hoffman, *Prdtn Mgr*
Jeffrey W Hoffman,
EMP: 12 **EST:** 1951
SQ FT: 4,000
SALES: 1.2MM **Privately Held**
SIC: 5084 3272 Pumps & pumping equipment; septic tanks, concrete; burial vaults, concrete or precast terrazzo; concrete products, precast

(G-3443)
FLUID DYNAMICS INC
18 Commerce St Ste 1819 (08822-7708)
P.O. Box 7, Rosemont (08556-0007)
PHONE..................908 200-5823
Fax: 908 237-0884
Rita Rounds, *President*
EMP: 4
SQ FT: 3,000
SALES (est): 451K **Privately Held**
WEB: www.fluiddynamics.com
SIC: 3821 Laboratory apparatus & furniture

(G-3444)
GEM VAULT INC
23 Turntable Jct (08822-1541)
P.O. Box 997 (08822-0997)
PHONE..................908 788-1770
William Brewer, *President*
Bill Brewer, *President*
EMP: 5
SQ FT: 1,500
SALES: 480K **Privately Held**
SIC: 5944 3911 Jewelry, precious stones & precious metals; jewelry, precious metal

(G-3445)
GENERAL PALLET LLC
97 River Rd (08822-5732)
P.O. Box 1000, Readington (08870-1000)
PHONE..................732 549-1000
Toll Free:..................888 -
Fax: 908 806-5555
Chet Czaplicki, *Opers Mgr*
Paula Baldwin, *Marketing Staff*
Donald W Baldwin,
Pam Vail, *Administration*
EMP: 7 **EST:** 1966
SALES (est): 730K **Privately Held**
WEB: www.generalpallet.com
SIC: 2448 Pallets, wood

(G-3446)
HEALIOS INC
56 Main St Ste 1d (08822-1474)
PHONE..................908 731-5061
Dupont Guilhem, *Principal*
EMP: 6
SALES (est): 305.9K
SALES (corp-wide): 2MM **Privately Held**
SIC: 2879 Agricultural chemicals
PA: Healios Llc
Sevogelstrasse 32
Basel BS 4052
613 112-009

(G-3447)
HITRAN CORPORATION
362 Highway 31 (08822-5741)
PHONE..................908 782-5525
Fax: 908 782-9733
John Hindle Jr, *Ch of Bd*
John C Hindle III, *President*
James S Hindle, *Vice Pres*
William Hindle, *Treasurer*
▲ **EMP:** 150 **EST:** 1944
SALES (est): 60.2MM **Privately Held**
WEB: www.hitrancorp.com
SIC: 3612 Power transformers, electric; line voltage regulators

(G-3448)
HUNTERDON COUNTY DEMOCRAT INC (PA)
Also Called: Hunterdon Observer
200 State Route 31 # 202 (08822-5727)
PHONE..................908 782-4747
Fax: 908 782-6572
Catherine T Langley, *President*
Robert Bell, *Info Tech Mgr*
Anne M Thomas, *Admin Sec*
EMP: 90 **EST:** 1825
SQ FT: 25,000
SALES (est): 4.9MM **Privately Held**
WEB: www.hcdems.com
SIC: 2711 Commercial printing & newspaper publishing combined

(G-3449)
INN-CLIENT SERVER SYSTEMS LLC
45 River Rd Ste 301 (08822-6026)
PHONE..................908 782-9500
Fax: 973 782-9607
Piyush Patel, *President*

Sharad Yagnik, *Sales Mgr*
EMP: 12 **EST:** 1993
SALES (est): 833.4K **Privately Held**
WEB: www.inn-client.com
SIC: 7372 Prepackaged software

(G-3450)
JEM PRINTING INC
Also Called: Printech
35 Main St (08822-1486)
PHONE..................908 782-9986
Fax: 908 806-7820
Joseph E Mastrull, *President*
Robert Celentano, *Accounts Exec*
EMP: 5
SQ FT: 1,200
SALES (est): 122.9K **Privately Held**
WEB: www.prin-tech.com
SIC: 2752 2741 2791 Commercial printing, lithographic; commercial printing, offset; miscellaneous publishing; typesetting

(G-3451)
JERSEY SHORE COSMETICS LLC
23 Pleasant View Way (08822-4617)
PHONE..................908 500-9954
Jacquelyn Quattro,
EMP: 10
SQ FT: 2,500
SALES (est): 917.3K **Privately Held**
SIC: 2844 Toilet preparations; face creams or lotions

(G-3452)
JOHANNA FOODS INC (PA)
20 Johanna Farms Rd (08822)
P.O. Box 272 (08822-0272)
PHONE..................908 788-2200
Fax: 908 788-2331
Robert A Facchina, *President*
Richard Cook, *CFO*
▲ **EMP:** 277 **EST:** 1944
SQ FT: 500,000
SALES (est): 178.1MM **Privately Held**
WEB: www.johannafoods.com
SIC: 2033 2026 Fruit juices: packaged in cans, jars, etc.; fruit juices: fresh; yogurt

(G-3453)
KERRY INC
Also Called: Kerry Ingredients
26 Minneakoning Rd (08822-5725)
PHONE..................908 237-1595
Simon G Statter, *Branch Mgr*
EMP: 60 **Privately Held**
SIC: 2087 Flavoring extracts & syrups
HQ: Kerry Inc.
3330 Millington Rd
Beloit WI 53511
608 363-1200

(G-3454)
KUHL CORP
39 Kuhl Rd (08822-6801)
P.O. Box 26 (08822-0026)
PHONE..................908 782-5696
Fax: 908 782-2751
Henry Y Kuhl, *President*
Jeffrey Kuhl, *Vice Pres*
Kevin Kuhl, *Vice Pres*
Paul R Kuhl Jr, *CFO*
Naomi Nierenberg, *Teacher*
◆ **EMP:** 62
SQ FT: 60,000
SALES (est): 19.5MM **Privately Held**
SIC: 3556 Poultry processing machinery

(G-3455)
MAGNA-POWER ELECTRONICS
39 Royal Rd (08822-6001)
PHONE..................908 237-2200
Fax: 908 237-2201
Ira J Pitel, *President*
Bob Collins, *Managing Dir*
Adam Pitel, *Vice Pres*
Grant Pitel, *Vice Pres*
Jim Williams, *Prdtn Mgr*
EMP: 85
SQ FT: 73,500
SALES (est): 19.3MM **Privately Held**
WEB: www.magna-power.com
SIC: 3629 Electronic generation equipment

(G-3456)
MEL CHEMICALS INC (DH)
Also Called: M E I
500 Brbrtown Pt Breeze Rd (08822-4702)
PHONE..................908 782-5800
Fax: 908 782-7768
Alan Foster, *Ch of Bd*
Pat Jones, *Business Mgr*
Jack Fisher, *Purch Dir*
Oliver Butler, *Purch Agent*
Janet Raphagen, *Treasurer*
▲ **EMP:** 103 **EST:** 1951
SQ FT: 135,000
SALES (est): 54.4MM
SALES (corp-wide): 441.3MM **Privately Held**
WEB: www.meichem.com
SIC: 5169 3295 2819 3339 Chemicals & allied products; minerals, ground or otherwise treated; industrial inorganic chemicals; primary nonferrous metals; chemical preparations
HQ: Luxfer Group Limited
Anchorage Gateway
Salford LANCS M50 3
161 300-0600

(G-3457)
METRO OPTICS LLC
38 Winding Way (08822-7039)
P.O. Box 275, Whitehouse Station (08889-0275)
PHONE..................908 413-0004
Nick T Cloutier, *Manager*
Nick Clothier,
EMP: 15
SQ FT: 20,000
SALES: 1.9MM **Privately Held**
SIC: 3229 Fiber optics strands

(G-3458)
ON SITE MANUFACTURING INC
1042 County Road 523 (08822-7034)
P.O. Box 250, Austin IN (47102-0250)
PHONE..................812 794-6040
Irvin L French, *President*
EMP: 9
SALES (est): 1.6MM **Privately Held**
SIC: 3585 Refrigeration & heating equipment

(G-3459)
POWERCOMM SOLUTIONS LLC
15 Minneakoning Rd # 311 (08822-5749)
PHONE..................908 806-7025
Fax: 908 806-4433
Leila Gabel, *Office Mgr*
Raymond Fella,
EMP: 5
SALES (est): 570K **Privately Held**
SIC: 3825 Instruments to measure electricity

(G-3460)
PRECISION DEALER SERVICES INC
4 Ryerson Rd (08822-7004)
P.O. Box 74, Whitehouse Station (08889-0074)
PHONE..................908 237-1100
Mark Berry, *President*
EMP: 25
SALES (est): 2.3MM **Privately Held**
SIC: 8742 2541 4731 2431 Materials mgmt. (purchasing, handling, inventory) consultant; cabinets, lockers & shelving; freight transportation arrangement; millwork; fluid meters & counting devices

(G-3461)
PRETTY JEWELRY CO
80 Main St 82 (08822-1482)
PHONE..................908 806-3377
Mario Marcel, *Owner*
EMP: 4
SALES (est): 103K **Privately Held**
SIC: 7631 3911 Jewelry repair services; jewelry, precious metal

(G-3462)
PRINT SHOPPE INC
15 Minneakoning Rd # 305 (08822-5749)
PHONE..................908 782-9213
Fax: 908 782-2959
Denise Hayes, *President*
Nicole Smith, *Sales Staff*

Sandra Bakos, *Administration*
EMP: 9
SQ FT: 5,000
SALES (est): 1.4MM **Privately Held**
WEB: www.printshoppe.com
SIC: 2752 Commercial printing, offset

(G-3463)
PRINTCO
Also Called: Prentco
12 Minneakoning Rd 103b (08822-5810)
PHONE..............................908 687-9518
Ron Steinberg, *Owner*
EMP: 4
SALES (est): 408.1K **Privately Held**
SIC: 3544 Special dies & tools

(G-3464)
PVH CORP
Also Called: Van Heusen
41 Liberty Vlg (08822-1561)
PHONE..............................908 788-5880
Fax: 908 780-5880
Catherine Perkins, *Manager*
EMP: 10
SALES (corp-wide): 8.9B **Publicly Held**
WEB: www.pvh.com
SIC: 2321 5621 Men's & boys' dress
shirts; sport shirts, men's & boys': from
purchased materials; ready-to-wear ap-
parel, women's
PA: Pvh Corp.
200 Madison Ave Bsmt 1
New York NY 10016
212 381-3500

(G-3465)
SERVICE TECH
109 Rake Factory Rd (08822-5626)
PHONE..............................908 788-0072
Todd De Vito, *Owner*
EMP: 4
SALES (est): 490.5K **Privately Held**
SIC: 3357 Appliance fixture wire, nonfer-
rous

(G-3466)
SIMPLEX AMERICAS LLC
20 Bartles Corner Rd (08822-5716)
PHONE..............................908 237-9099
Flip Harris, *Opers Staff*
Jeremy Cantilina, *Controller*
Chuck Autrey, *Manager*
Paul Cooper, *Manager*
Donald Vogler,
▲ **EMP:** 4
SALES (est): 907.5K **Privately Held**
SIC: 3731 Shipbuilding & repairing

(G-3467)
**SOMERVILLE ACQUISITIONS CO
INC (PA)**
45 River Rd Ste 300 (08822-6026)
PHONE..............................908 782-9500
Piyush J Patel, *President*
Milton Rosen, *Vice Pres*
Richard Rosen, *Vice Pres*
◆ **EMP:** 15 EST: 1959
SALES (est): 27.3MM **Privately Held**
SIC: 2819 Aluminum compounds

(G-3468)
STEVENS PUBLISHING CO
5 Hageman Dr (08822-7186)
PHONE..............................908 284-9326
John Wolfangle, *Principal*
Patricia Wolfangel, *Principal*
EMP: 20
SALES (est): 1.1MM **Privately Held**
SIC: 2731 Books: publishing only

(G-3469)
**SUMMIT RESEARCH
LABORATORY**
45 River Rd Ste 300 (08822-6026)
PHONE..............................908 782-9500
Tiyush Patel, *President*
Sherry Milisivana, *Office Mgr*
▼ **EMP:** 20
SALES (est): 3.8MM **Privately Held**
SIC: 2819 Industrial inorganic chemicals

(G-3470)
TECHNIMOLD INC
112 Pine Bank Rd (08822-7165)
PHONE..............................908 232-8331
William Mc Namara, *President*
Carole Mc Namara, *Corp Secy*
EMP: 18
SQ FT: 8,200
SALES (est): 2.2MM **Privately Held**
WEB: www.technimold.com
SIC: 3089 Injection molding of plastics

(G-3471)
TEKNI-PLEX INC
112 Church St (08822-1645)
PHONE..............................908 782-4000
Jeff Wright, *Plant Mgr*
Frank Strachan, *Manager*
EMP: 64
SQ FT: 130,000
SALES (corp-wide): 1B **Privately Held**
WEB: www.dolco.net
SIC: 3089 2631 2671 7336 Blister or
bubble formed packaging, plastic; coated
paperboard; packaging paper & plastics
film, coated & laminated; package design
PA: Tekni-Plex, Inc.
460 E Swedesford Rd # 3000
Wayne PA 19087
484 690-1520

(G-3472)
**TITANIUM TECHNICAL
SERVICES**
21 New York Ave (08822-1437)
PHONE..............................908 323-9899
Justin Moss, *Principal*
EMP: 5 EST: 2016
SALES (est): 133K **Privately Held**
SIC: 3356 Titanium

(G-3473)
U S ALUMINUM INC
408 Us Highway 202 (08822-6020)
PHONE..............................908 782-5454
K Clive Ramsey, *President*
William Cwieka, *Vice Pres*
Vincent J Vaccaro, *Vice Pres*
Arun K Chattopadhyay, *Research*
◆ **EMP:** 4
SQ FT: 1,200
SALES (est): 598.8K **Privately Held**
SIC: 3365 Aluminum foundries

(G-3474)
**UNITED STTES METAL
POWDERS INC (PA)**
Also Called: Royal Powdered Metals
408 Us Highway 202 (08822-6020)
PHONE..............................908 782-5454
K Clive Ramsey, *President*
Vincent J Vaccaro, *Vice Pres*
Shirley Davis, *Plant Mgr*
Joao Baptiste Dos Santos, *Purch Mgr*
Barry Schmutter, *Credit Mgr*
▲ **EMP:** 18
SQ FT: 100,000
SALES (est): 10.5MM **Privately Held**
SIC: 3399 Powder, metal; brads: alu-
minum, brass or other nonferrous metal
or wire; nails: aluminum, brass or other
nonferrous metal or wire

(G-3475)
WELSCH METAL PRODUCTS INC
8 Bartles Corner Rd # 13 (08822-5712)
PHONE..............................908 782-5996
Forest Earl, *President*
John Smith, *Vice Pres*
EMP: 4
SQ FT: 5,600
SALES (est): 480.5K **Privately Held**
SIC: 2816 Metallic & mineral pigments

Florence
Burlington County

(G-3476)
BOYDS PHARMACY INC
Also Called: Good Neighbor Pharmacy
306 Broad St (08518-1912)
P.O. Box 1 (08518-0001)
PHONE..............................609 499-0100

Fax: 609 499-9628
Lardner C Boyd III, *President*
EMP: 12
SALES (est): 1.9MM **Privately Held**
WEB: www.boydspharmacy.com
SIC: 2834 5912 Medicines, capsuled or
ampuled; drug stores

(G-3477)
DC FABRICATORS INC
801 W Front St (08518-1121)
PHONE..............................609 499-3000
John Frieling, *Ch of Bd*
Michael Salerno, *Shareholder*
EMP: 135
SQ FT: 1,000
SALES (est): 62MM **Privately Held**
WEB: www.dcfab.com
SIC: 3443 Condensers, steam

(G-3478)
ENDURANCE NET INC
763 B Railroad Ave (08518)
P.O. Box 127, Roebling (08554-0127)
PHONE..............................609 499-3450
Joseph R Scarperia, *President*
▲ **EMP:** 12
SQ FT: 40,000
SALES (est): 1.6MM **Privately Held**
WEB: www.endurancenetinc.com
SIC: 2258 3949 Net & netting products;
netting, knit; sporting & athletic goods

(G-3479)
**MIDWAY MACHINE PRODUCT
CORP**
763a Railroad Ave (08518)
P.O. Box 129 (08518-0129)
PHONE..............................609 499-4377
Fax: 609 499-0084
William Green, *President*
EMP: 9
SQ FT: 6,500
SALES (est): 992.8K **Privately Held**
SIC: 3599 Machine shop, jobbing & repair

(G-3480)
READY PAC PRODUCE INC
Also Called: Ready-Pac Club Chef
700 Railroad Ave (08518)
P.O. Box 6 (08518-0006)
PHONE..............................609 499-1900
Fax: 609 499-0042
Tom Hunter, *Manager*
EMP: 100
SALES (corp-wide): 30.4MM **Privately
Held**
WEB: www.readypacproduce.com
SIC: 2099 5148 Food preparations; sal-
ads, fresh or refrigerated; cole slaw, in
bulk; vegetables, peeled for the trade;
fresh fruits & vegetables
PA: Ready Pac Produce, Inc.
4401 Foxdale St
Irwindale CA 91706
800 800-4088

(G-3481)
TEX-NET INC
763 Railroad Ave B (08518)
P.O. Box 92 (08518-0092)
PHONE..............................609 499-9111
John Scarperia, *President*
Joseph Scarperia, *Vice Pres*
EMP: 20
SQ FT: 18,000
SALES (est): 2.4MM **Privately Held**
WEB: www.powercage.com
SIC: 2221 5941 Textile mills, broadwoven:
silk & manmade, also glass; golf goods &
equipment

(G-3482)
**TOTAL CONTROL OTHOTICS
LAB**
14 W Front St (08518-1319)
PHONE..............................609 499-2200
Dominick Ciccone, *President*
EMP: 7
SALES (est): 919.2K **Privately Held**
SIC: 3842 Orthopedic appliances

Florham Park
Morris County

(G-3483)
ASCO LP (HQ)
160 Park Ave (07932-1049)
PHONE..............................800 972-2726
◆ **EMP:** 313
SALES (est): 234.2MM
SALES (corp-wide): 15.2B **Publicly Held**
SIC: 3491 Industrial valves
PA: Emerson Electric Co.
8000 West Florissant Ave
Saint Louis MO 63136
314 553-2000

(G-3484)
ASCO INVESTMENT CORP
50-60 Hanover Rd (07932-1503)
PHONE..............................973 966-2000
Fax: 973 966-2054
Jean-Pierre Yaouanc, *President*
Albert Giarrusso, *Senior Buyer*
Eamon Rowan, *VP Finance*
Shawn Burke, *Natl Sales Mgr*
Kent Fowler, *Sales Dir*
▲ **EMP:** 107
SQ FT: 13,000
SALES (est): 20.1MM **Privately Held**
SIC: 3625 Switches, electronic applications

(G-3485)
**ASCO POWER SERVICES INC
(DH)**
160 Park Ave (07932-1049)
PHONE..............................973 966-2000
Fax: 973 966-6586
Armand J Visioli, *President*
Jack Petro, *Vice Pres*
EMP: 10
SALES (est): 13.9MM
SALES (corp-wide): 200.4K **Privately
Held**
WEB: www.redhat3.com
SIC: 3643 Electric switches
HQ: Schneider Electric Usa, Inc.
800 Federal St
Andover MA 01810
978 975-9600

(G-3486)
**ASCO POWER TECHNOLOGIES
LP**
50 Hanover Rd (07932-1419)
PHONE..............................209 547-8874
Cal Alford, *Principal*
EMP: 11
SALES (corp-wide): 200.4K **Privately
Held**
SIC: 3699 7629 Electrical equipment &
supplies; electrical repair shops
HQ: Asco Power Technologies, L.P.
160 Park Ave
Florham Park NJ 07932

(G-3487)
**ASCO POWER TECHNOLOGIES
LP (DH)**
160 Park Ave (07932-1049)
PHONE..............................973 966-2000
Fax: 973 966-5709
Michael Quinn, *President*
◆ **EMP:** 300
SQ FT: 126,000
SALES (est): 806.8MM
SALES (corp-wide): 200.4K **Privately
Held**
SIC: 3699 Electrical equipment & supplies
HQ: Schneider Electric Usa, Inc.
800 Federal St
Andover MA 01810
978 975-9600

(G-3488)
ASCO VALVE LLC (PA)
Also Called: Asco Valve Mfg
50-60 Hanover Rd (07932-1503)
PHONE..............................973 966-2437
Fax: 973 966-7320
▲ **EMP:** 90
SQ FT: 200,000

▲ = Import ▼=Export
◆ =Import/Export

SALES (est): 407.8MM **Privately Held**
WEB: www.rapcoassoc.com
SIC: **3443** 3491 3492 3625 Mfg Fabricated Plate Wrk Mfg Industrial Valves Mfg Fluid Power Valves Mfg Relay/Indstl Control Whol Electrical Equip

(G-3489)
AUTOMATIC SWITCH COMPANY (DH)
50-60 Hanover Rd (07932-1591)
PHONE....................................973 966-2000
Fax: 973 966-2628
Jean-Pierre Yaouanc, *President*
Gregory C Schreiber, *President*
Ed Amaducci, *Plant Mgr*
John Kovach, *Engineer*
Chris Myers, *Manager*
▲ EMP: 1200 EST: 1906
SQ FT: 220,000
SALES (est): 345.1MM
SALES (corp-wide): 15.2B **Publicly Held**
WEB: www.ascoval.com
SIC: **3491** 3625 3677 3674 Solenoid valves; control equipment, electric; electronic coils, transformers & other inductors; semiconductors & related devices; switchgear & switchboard apparatus; fluid power valves & hose fittings
HQ: Emerson Electric (U.S.) Holding Corporation
850 Library Ave Ste 204c
Saint Louis MO 63136
314 553-2000

(G-3490)
AUTOMATIC SWITCH COMPANY
Also Called: Asco Power Technology
50 Hanover Rd (07932-1419)
PHONE....................................209 941-4111
Phil Tibbits, *Branch Mgr*
EMP: 601
SALES (corp-wide): 15.2B **Publicly Held**
SIC: **3491** Solenoid valves
HQ: Automatic Switch Company
50-60 Hanover Rd
Florham Park NJ 07932
973 966-2000

(G-3491)
BANDING CENTERS OF AMERICA
83 Hanover Rd Ste 160 (07932-1518)
PHONE....................................973 805-9977
EMP: 4
SALES (est): 470K **Privately Held**
SIC: **3842** Mfg Surgical Appliances/Supplies

(G-3492)
BASF CORPORATION (HQ)
100 Park Ave (07932-1089)
P.O. Box 685 (07932-0685)
PHONE....................................973 245-6000
Fax: 973 895-8002
Wayne T Smith, *CEO*
Peter Eckes, *President*
Kenneth Lane, *President*
Teressa Szelest, *President*
Mike Grindle, *Business Mgr*
◆ EMP: 277 EST: 1873
SQ FT: 325,000
SALES: 16.2B
SALES (corp-wide): 76B **Privately Held**
WEB: www.basf.com
SIC: **2869** 2819 2899 2843 Industrial organic chemicals; industrial inorganic chemicals; antifreeze compounds; surface active agents; pharmaceutical preparations; vitamin preparations; agricultural chemicals
PA: Basf Se
Carl-Bosch-Str. 38
Ludwigshafen Am Rhein 67056
621 600-

(G-3493)
BASFIN CORPORATION (HQ)
100 Park Ave (07932-1049)
PHONE....................................973 245-6000
Peter Oakley, *President*
Frank A Bozich, *President*
Martin Brudermller, *Principal*
Hans-Ulrich Engel, *Principal*
Joseph Falsone, *Principal*
▲ EMP: 1000

SALES (est): 3.1B
SALES (corp-wide): 76B **Privately Held**
SIC: **2869** 2819 2899 2843 Industrial organic chemicals; industrial inorganic chemicals; antifreeze compounds; surface active agents; agricultural chemicals; pharmaceutical preparations
PA: Basf Se
Carl-Bosch-Str. 38
Ludwigshafen Am Rhein 67056
621 600-

(G-3494)
BOOMERANG SYSTEMS INC (PA)
30a Vreeland Rd (07932-1904)
PHONE....................................973 538-1194
James V Gelly, *CEO*
James Gelly, *CEO*
Mark R Patterson, *Ch of Bd*
Christopher Mulvihill, *President*
George Gelly, *COO*
EMP: 39 EST: 1979
SQ FT: 7,350
SALES: 5.4MM **Privately Held**
SIC: **3549** 3535 7521 Assembly machines, including robotic; robotic conveyors; automobile storage garage

(G-3495)
CAPINTEC INC (DH)
7 Vreeland Rd Ste 101 (07932-1511)
PHONE....................................201 825-9500
Fax: 201 825-1336
Jeff Miller, *Prdtn Mgr*
Roman Zaikin, *Electrical Engi*
Ralph J Monaco, *CFO*
Michael Flynn, *Controller*
Earle Mulrane, *Manager*
▲ EMP: 23
SQ FT: 41,000
SALES (est): 12.7MM **Privately Held**
SIC: **3829** 3823 3845 5045 Nuclear radiation & testing apparatus; temperature instruments: industrial process type; patient monitoring apparatus; computer peripheral equipment; surgical appliances & supplies; surgical & medical instruments
HQ: Eczacibasi Monrol Nukleer Urunler Sanayi Ve Ticaret Anonim Sirketi
Tubitak Mahallesi
Kocaeli 41400
262 648-0200

(G-3496)
COMVERGE GIANTS INC
25a Vreeland Rd Ste 300 (07932-1933)
PHONE....................................973 884-5970
John Bunyan, *Branch Mgr*
EMP: 6
SALES (corp-wide): 2B **Publicly Held**
SIC: **3822** Hardware for environmental regulators
HQ: Comverge Giants, Inc.
120 Eagle Rock Ave # 190
East Hanover NJ 07936

(G-3497)
CREATIONS BY SHERRY LYNN LLC
90 Park Ave Ste 414 (07932-1068)
PHONE....................................800 742-3448
Andrew Greenberger,
Sherry Greenberger,
EMP: 4
SALES: 50K **Privately Held**
SIC: **3911** Jewelry apparel

(G-3498)
DATAMOTION INC (PA)
200 Park Ave Ste 302 (07932-1040)
PHONE....................................973 455-1245
Bob Bales, *CEO*
Mahesh Muchhala, *Ch of Bd*
Bob Janacek, *Exec VP*
Derek Czernikowski, *Technology*
EMP: 28 EST: 1999
SALES (est): 7.8MM **Privately Held**
WEB: www.datamotion.com
SIC: **7373** 7374 7372 7372 Systems integration services; data verification service; ; business oriented computer software

(G-3499)
EAGLE WORK CLOTHES INC (PA)
20 Quail Run (07932-1755)
PHONE....................................908 964-8888
Fax: 908 964-7759
Charles J Fruchter, *President*
Dennis Fruchter, *Vice Pres*
◆ EMP: 37 EST: 1946
SQ FT: 35,000
SALES (est): 3.5MM **Privately Held**
WEB: www.eaglewc.com
SIC: **2326** 5136 2337 Work garments, except raincoats: waterproof; work uniforms; uniforms, men's & boys'; uniforms, except athletic: women's, misses' & juniors'

(G-3500)
EXELTIS USA INC (DH)
180 Park Ave Ste 101 (07932-1054)
PHONE....................................973 324-0200
Fax: 973 324-0795
Maria Carell, *President*
Everett Felper, *President*
John Giordano, *Exec VP*
Tova Friede, *Vice Pres*
Jane Chen, *Senior Mgr*
▲ EMP: 63 EST: 1971
SALES (est): 11.7MM **Privately Held**
WEB: www.everettlabs.com
SIC: **2834** 5122 Pharmaceutical preparations; drugs & drug proprietaries
HQ: Chemo Iberica Sa
Calle Gran Via Carles Iii, 98 - 7 Planta
Barcelona 08028
913 021-560

(G-3501)
EXELTIS USA DERMATOLOGY LLC
180 Park Ave Ste 101 (07932-1054)
PHONE....................................973 805-4060
Maria Carell, *President*
Manuel Barro, *Director*
Ignacio Ponce, *Director*
Sandra Martin Moran, *Admin Sec*
Eduardo Fernandez, *Asst Sec*
EMP: 50 EST: 2012
SALES (est): 5.8MM **Privately Held**
SIC: **2834** Pharmaceutical preparations
HQ: Exeltis Usa, Inc.
180 Park Ave Ste 101
Florham Park NJ 07932
973 324-0200

(G-3502)
EZOSE SCIENCES INC
300 Campus Dr Ste 300 (07932-1039)
PHONE....................................862 926-1950
Kiyoshi Nagata, *CEO*
Scott A Siegel, *COO*
Hidehisa Asada, *Vice Pres*
▲ EMP: 17
SQ FT: 12,000
SALES (est): 2.7MM **Privately Held**
SIC: **3826** Amino acid analyzers

(G-3503)
FTI INC
Also Called: Tetra Lubricants
8 Vreeland Rd (07932-1501)
PHONE....................................973 443-0004
W B Smith, *CEO*
◆ EMP: 4
SQ FT: 20,000
SALES (est): 923.2K **Privately Held**
SIC: **2992** 2851 2952 Lubricating oils & greases; paints & paint additives; coating compounds, tar
PA: Troy Corporation
8 Vreeland Rd
Florham Park NJ 07932

(G-3504)
GERBER PRODUCTS COMPANY (DH)
Also Called: Nestle Infant Nutrition
12 Vreeland Rd Fl 2 (07932-1521)
PHONE....................................973 593-7500
Fax: 973 593-7600
Kurt T Schmidt, *President*
Kevin L Goldberg, *Vice Pres*
Craig Thompson, *Vice Pres*
Saumya Mishra, *Engineer*
Mia Insabella, *Design Engr*

▲ EMP: 212 EST: 1867
SALES (est): 602MM
SALES (corp-wide): 90.8B **Privately Held**
WEB: www.gerber.com
SIC: **2023** 2043 2037 2052 Baby formulas; cereal breakfast foods; fruit juices; cookies & crackers; pasteurized & mineral waters, bottled & canned; canned & cured fish & seafoods
HQ: Nestle Holdings, Inc.
800 N Brand Blvd
Glendale CA 91203
818 549-6000

(G-3505)
HELLER INDUSTRIES INC (PA)
4 Vreeland Rd Ste 1 (07932-1593)
PHONE....................................973 377-6800
Fax: 973 377-3862
David Heller, *President*
Marc Peo, *President*
David Gross, *Vice Pres*
Hemang Patel, *Facilities Mgr*
Simon Etin, *Engineer*
▲ EMP: 60
SQ FT: 50,000
SALES (est): 21.5MM **Privately Held**
WEB: www.hellerindustries.com
SIC: **3569** Assembly machines, non-metalworking

(G-3506)
HISAMITSU PHRM CO INC
100 Campus Dr Ste 117 (07932-1006)
PHONE....................................973 765-0122
Keniehi Suruta, *President*
EMP: 13
SALES (est): 1.3MM **Privately Held**
SIC: **2834** 8731 Pharmaceutical preparations; medical research, commercial

(G-3507)
HR ACUITY LLC
25a Vreeland Rd Ste 101 (07932-1903)
PHONE....................................888 598-0161
Deborah Muller, *CEO*
EMP: 12
SALES (est): 1MM **Privately Held**
SIC: **8742** 7372 Human resource consulting services; business oriented computer software

(G-3508)
LAPP CABLE WORKS INC
29 Hanover Rd (07932-1408)
PHONE....................................973 660-9632
Roland Keller, *President*
Andreas Lapp, *Chairman*
Marc Mackin, *Corp Secy*
Keith Myrick, *COO*
▲ EMP: 24
SQ FT: 25,000
SALES (est): 6.6MM **Privately Held**
SIC: **3357** Nonferrous wiredrawing & insulating
HQ: Lapp Holding Na Inc.
29 Hanover Rd
Florham Park NJ 07932

(G-3509)
LAPP HOLDING NA INC (HQ)
29 Hanover Rd (07932-1408)
PHONE....................................973 660-9700
Marc Mackin, *President*
Christian Abambari, *Engineer*
Maureen Hedden, *Human Resources*
Rick Fiorey, *Supervisor*
▲ EMP: 26
SALES (est): 123.3MM **Privately Held**
SIC: **3355** Aluminum wire & cable
PA: Lapp Beteiligungs-Kg
Oskar-Lapp-Str. 2
Stuttgart
711 783-801

(G-3510)
LAPP USA INC
29 Hanover Rd (07932-1408)
PHONE....................................973 660-9700
Andreas Lapp, *President*
Michael Christiansen, *Vice Pres*
Patti Piotrowski, *Warehouse Mgr*
Anayanci Hinojosa, *Purch Mgr*
Brian Bookamer, *Engineer*
EMP: 4

SALES (est): 249.3K **Privately Held**
SIC: 3643 Power line cable

(G-3511)
LAPP USA LLC
29 Hanover Rd (07932-1408)
PHONE....................................973 660-9700
Fax: 973 660-9330
Andreas Lapp, *President*
Tracey Timmons, *Business Mgr*
Marc K Mackin, *COO*
Rob Conway, *Exec VP*
George Dann, *Vice Pres*
◆ EMP: 132
SALES (est): 99.4MM **Privately Held**
SIC: 5063 3678 Control & signal wire & cable, including coaxial; electronic connectors
HQ: Lapp Holding Na Inc.
     29 Hanover Rd
     Florham Park NJ 07932

(G-3512)
NOVARTIS CORPORATION
25 Vreeland Rd B (07932-1902)
PHONE....................................973 377-4794
EMP: 120
SALES (corp-wide): 49.1B **Privately Held**
WEB: www.novartis.com
SIC: 2834 Pharmaceutical preparations
HQ: Novartis Corporation
     1 S Ridgedale Ave
     East Hanover NJ 07936
     212 307-1122

(G-3513)
OLON USA INC
100 Campus Dr Ste 105 (07932-1006)
PHONE....................................973 577-6038
Aldo Donati, *President*
Francesco Saletta, *Vice Pres*
EMP: 15 EST: 2012
SALES (est): 808.1K **Privately Held**
SIC: 2899 Gelatin: edible, technical, photographic or pharmaceutical
HQ: Olon Spa
     Strada Provinciale Rivoltana 6/7
     Rodano MI 20090
     029 523-1

(G-3514)
PIEMONTE & LIEBHAUSER LLC
325 Columbia Tpke Ste 108 (07932-1220)
PHONE....................................973 937-6200
Robin Kerrs, *Principal*
EMP: 13
SALES (est): 1.8MM **Privately Held**
SIC: 2024 Ice cream & frozen desserts

(G-3515)
PRECISION ROLL PRODUCTS INC
306 Columbia Tpke (07932-1217)
PHONE....................................973 822-9100
Fax: 973 822-9400
▲ EMP: 10 EST: 2009
SALES (est): 1MM **Privately Held**
SIC: 3356 Nonferrous Rolling/Drawing

(G-3516)
PROFOTO US INC
220 Park Ave Ste 120 (07932-1047)
PHONE....................................973 822-1300
Mark Rezzonico, *President*
Ron Eglentowicz, *Principal*
▲ EMP: 14
SQ FT: 6,500
SALES (est): 2.3MM **Privately Held**
SIC: 3861 Photographic equipment & supplies
HQ: Profoto Ab
     Landsvagen 57
     Sundbyberg 172 6
     844 753-00

(G-3517)
QUATRX PHARMACEUTICALS COMPANY (PA)
300 Campus Dr Ste 300 (07932-1039)
PHONE....................................734 913-9900
Fax: 734 913-0743
Robert Zerbe MD, *President*
Christopher Nicholas, *COO*
Gary Onn, *CFO*
EMP: 57
SQ FT: 9,742

SALES (est): 8.5MM **Privately Held**
WEB: www.quatrx.com
SIC: 2834 Pharmaceutical preparations

(G-3518)
TRISYS INC
215 Ridgedale Ave Ste 2 (07932-1355)
PHONE....................................973 360-2300
Fax: 973 360-2222
Mark Karpilovsky, *President*
Michelle Karpilovsky, *Marketing Mgr*
Christina Laraia, *Info Tech Mgr*
George Tsintsadze, *Software Dev*
EMP: 16
SQ FT: 4,600
SALES: 2.1MM **Privately Held**
WEB: www.born2e.com
SIC: 7372 Publishers' computer software

(G-3519)
TROPAR MANUFACTURING CO INC (PA)
5 Vreeland Rd (07932-1505)
PHONE....................................973 765-0380
Fax: 973 822-2891
Peter V Ilaria, *President*
Bob Oshea, *President*
Jason Larkey, *Plant Mgr*
Phyllis Chiappa, *Manager*
Della Gregorybabia, *Info Tech Mgr*
◆ EMP: 30
SALES (est): 5.5MM **Privately Held**
SIC: 3499 Trophies, metal, except silver

(G-3520)
TROPAR TROPHY MANUFACTURING CO (PA)
5 Vreeland Rd (07932-1596)
PHONE....................................973 822-2400
Peter V Ilaria, *President*
Peter E Ilaria, *Treasurer*
Gregory D Badia, *Admin Sec*
▲ EMP: 65 EST: 1958
SQ FT: 58,000
SALES (est): 8.9MM **Privately Held**
WEB: www.airflyte.com
SIC: 3499 Trophies, metal, except silver

(G-3521)
TROY CORPORATION (PA)
8 Vreeland Rd (07932-1501)
P.O. Box 434 (07932-0434)
PHONE....................................973 443-4200
Fax: 973 443-4402
Daryl D Smith, *President*
Sonia Silva, *General Mgr*
Brian Dirk, *Vice Chairman*
David Koehl, *Business Mgr*
Richard Rotherham, *COO*
◆ EMP: 98
SQ FT: 75,000
SALES (est): 201.8MM **Privately Held**
SIC: 2869 Industrial organic chemicals

(G-3522)
UNICORN GROUP INC (PA)
25b Hanover Rd (07932-1442)
PHONE....................................973 360-0688
Frank Diassi, *Chairman*
EMP: 30
SQ FT: 12,000
SALES (est): 20.9MM **Privately Held**
WEB: www.open4.com
SIC: 7379 7372 Computer related consulting services; business oriented computer software

(G-3523)
WASHINGTON STAMP EXCHANGE INC
Also Called: Art Craft
2 Vreeland Rd (07932-1501)
PHONE....................................973 966-0001
Fax: 973 966-0888
Michael August, *President*
Tim Devany, *Corp Secy*
Robin Devany, *Admin Sec*
EMP: 13
SQ FT: 35,000
SALES (est): 2.7MM **Privately Held**
WEB: www.washpress.com
SIC: 2677 2789 3083 2752 Envelopes; binding & repair of books, magazines & pamphlets; laminated plastic sheets; commercial printing, lithographic

(G-3524)
WORLD WIDE PACKAGING LLC (PA)
15 Vreeland Rd Ste 4 (07932-1506)
PHONE....................................973 805-6500
Fax: 973 805-6500
Barry A Freda, *CEO*
Michael Milano, *VP Finance*
David Ditchfield, *VP Sales*
▲ EMP: 60
SQ FT: 20,000
SALES (est): 15MM **Privately Held**
SIC: 2844 Cosmetic preparations

(G-3525)
ZOETIS PRODUCTS LLC (HQ)
100 Campus Dr Ste 3 (07932-1006)
PHONE....................................973 660-5000
David R Jackson, *Vice Pres*
Adrian Del Valle, *Technical Mgr*
Matthew Farrell,
Juan Ramon Alaix,
Joseph Del Buono,
◆ EMP: 200
SALES (est): 366.9MM
SALES (corp-wide): 5.3B **Publicly Held**
WEB: www.alpharma.com
SIC: 2834 2833 Pharmaceutical preparations; medicinals & botanicals
PA: Zoetis Inc.
     10 Sylvan Way Ste 105
     Parsippany NJ 07054
     973 822-7000

Fords
Middlesex County

(G-3526)
ALLIED PHARMA INC
20 Corrielle St (08863-1909)
PHONE....................................732 738-3295
Mayur Doshi, *President*
EMP: 7
SALES: 5.2MM **Privately Held**
SIC: 2834 Pharmaceutical preparations

(G-3527)
BAI LAR INTERIOR SERVICES INC
554 New Brunswick Ave (08863-2195)
PHONE....................................732 738-0350
Fax: 732 738-0074
James E Quinn, *President*
Patrick M Quinn, *Vice Pres*
Denise Sims, *Admin Sec*
EMP: 5
SQ FT: 3,000
SALES: 1MM **Privately Held**
SIC: 2211 5131 7389 Draperies & drapery fabrics, cotton; millinery supplies; interior designer

(G-3528)
CLAUSEN COMPANY INC
1055 King George Rd (08863)
PHONE....................................732 738-1165
Fax: 732 738-1618
Donald J Peck, *Ch of Bd*
EMP: 15 EST: 1957
SQ FT: 12,800
SALES (est): 3.1MM **Privately Held**
WEB: www.clausencompany.com
SIC: 2851 2821 Paints & allied products; plastics materials & resins

(G-3529)
JOHNNYS SERVICE CENTER
53 Lawrence St (08863-2019)
PHONE....................................732 738-0569
Fax: 732 738-5978
Gary English, *Owner*
Karen Klemm, *Admin Sec*
EMP: 5
SQ FT: 3,000
SALES (est): 429.6K **Privately Held**
SIC: 7694 7539 Motor repair services; automotive repair shops

(G-3530)
LANXESS SOLUTIONS US INC
Hatco Division
1020 King George Post Rd (08863-2329)
PHONE....................................732 738-1000

Micheal Raab, *Branch Mgr*
EMP: 165
SALES (corp-wide): 11.4B **Privately Held**
WEB: www.cromptoncorp.com
SIC: 2869 2992 Plasticizers, organic: cyclic & acyclic; lubricating oils & greases
HQ: Lanxess Solutions Us Inc.
     199 Benson Rd
     Middlebury CT 06762
     203 573-2000

(G-3531)
ZACK PAINTING CO INC
900 King George Rd (08863-2140)
P.O. Box 120 (08863-0120)
PHONE....................................732 738-7900
Fax: 732 738-4225
David Zack, *President*
Robert Zack, *Vice Pres*
EMP: 50 EST: 1923
SQ FT: 15,000
SALES (est): 6.9MM **Privately Held**
WEB: www.zackpainting.com
SIC: 1721 1799 3081 Commercial painting; spraying contractor, non-agricultural; floor or wall covering, unsupported plastic

Forked River
Ocean County

(G-3532)
A B C MACHINERY CORP
712 Old Shore Rd Ste 1 (08731-5906)
P.O. Box 1212 (08731-6212)
PHONE....................................609 971-0990
Edwin S Palecek, *President*
Berry Cerino, *Vice Pres*
Linda Cerino, *Admin Sec*
Anne Luckhurst, *Admin Sec*
EMP: 5
SQ FT: 2,000
SALES (est): 360K **Privately Held**
SIC: 3552 Textile machinery

(G-3533)
ADE INC
719 Old Shore Rd (08731-5905)
P.O. Box 538, Lanoka Harbor (08734-0538)
PHONE....................................609 693-6050
Earnie Cretola, *Vice Pres*
Ernie Tretola, *President*
EMP: 10
SALES (est): 2.6MM **Privately Held**
SIC: 3585 Heating & air conditioning combination units

(G-3534)
BRICK-WALL CORP
Also Called: CJS Hesse
2215 Lacey Rd (08731-5810)
PHONE....................................609 693-6223
Fax: 609 971-7212
Charles Stout, *Manager*
EMP: 20
SALES (est): 2.4MM
SALES (corp-wide): 3.6MM **Privately Held**
SIC: 1611 2951 Highway & street paving contractor; asphalt paving mixtures & blocks
PA: Brick-Wall Corp.
     25 1st Ave Ste 200
     Atlantic Highlands NJ 07716
     732 787-0226

(G-3535)
CLAYTON BLOCK COMPANY INC
2011 Lacey Rd (08731-5806)
PHONE....................................609 693-9600
Ron Mc Millan, *Manager*
EMP: 13
SALES (corp-wide): 44.5MM **Privately Held**
WEB: www.claytononline.com
SIC: 3271 Blocks, concrete or cinder: standard
PA: Clayton Block Company, Inc.
     1355 Campus Pkwy Ste 200
     Wall Township NJ 07753
     732 363-1995

(G-3536)
CORBCO INC
40 Canterbury Dr (08731-5644)
PHONE..........................609 549-6299
Paul Corbacho, *President*
Rose Corbacho, *Corp Secy*
EMP: 5
SQ FT: 4,700
SALES: 300K **Privately Held**
SIC: 3081 Unsupported plastics film & sheet

(G-3537)
CUSTOM AUTO RADIATOR INC
Also Called: C A R
441 S Main St (08731-4638)
PHONE..........................609 242-9700
Charles Monjoy, *President*
Sylvia Monjoy, *Admin Sec*
EMP: 11
SQ FT: 5,000
SALES (est): 1.5MM **Privately Held**
SIC: 3714 5531 Radiators & radiator shells & cores, motor vehicle; automotive parts

(G-3538)
IACOVELLI STAIRS INCORPORATED
707 Challenger Way (08731-5915)
PHONE..........................609 693-3476
Fax: 609 971-6766
Joseph Iacovelli, *President*
EMP: 13
SQ FT: 2,000
SALES: 2MM **Privately Held**
SIC: 2431 Staircases & stairs, wood; stair railings, wood

(G-3539)
PIONEER CONCRETE CORP
Also Called: Central Concrete Aggregates
2011 Lacey Rd (08731-5806)
PHONE..........................609 693-6151
Fax: 609 693-5642
Nelson K Walling, *President*
Gary O Walling, *Vice Pres*
EMP: 20 **EST:** 1986
SALES: 1.9MM **Privately Held**
SIC: 1442 Construction sand mining

(G-3540)
PLASTICS FOR CHEMICALS INC (PA)
710 Old Shore Rd (08731-5900)
PHONE..........................609 242-9100
Fax: 609 242-9137
John T Donovan, *President*
John Donavan, *Partner*
Edward T Norman, *Vice Pres*
EMP: 7
SQ FT: 2,500
SALES (est): 832.3K **Privately Held**
WEB: www.plastkemiforetagen.se
SIC: 3089 Bearings, plastic

Fort Lee
Bergen County

(G-3541)
ACTAVIS ELIZABETH LLC
Actavis US
1 Executive Dr (07024-3309)
PHONE..........................908 527-9100
Lee Dress, *Branch Mgr*
EMP: 140 **Privately Held**
SIC: 2834 Pharmaceutical preparations; druggists' preparations (pharmaceuticals)
HQ: Actavis Elizabeth Llc
200 Elmora Ave
Elizabeth NJ 07202
908 527-9100

(G-3542)
AEON ENGINEERING LLC
442 Main St Ste 5 (07024-2830)
PHONE..........................518 253-7681
Kim James Kyung-Hwan, *Administration*
EMP: 5
SALES (est): 131.8K **Privately Held**
SIC: 3679 8711 Electronic circuits; engineering services

(G-3543)
AMERICAN BANKNOTE CORPORATION (PA)
2200 Fletcher Ave Ste 501 (07024-5016)
PHONE..........................203 941-4090
Fax: 201 224-2762
Steven G Singer, *CEO*
David Kober, *Vice Pres*
Steve Andrews, *CFO*
Ken Gruber, *VP Finance*
◆ **EMP:** 6
SQ FT: 8,020
SALES (est): 389.5MM **Privately Held**
WEB: www.americanbanknote.com
SIC: 2759 2752 2621 Commercial printing; cards, lithographed; card paper

(G-3544)
ANATOLIAN NATURALS INC
1 Bridge Plz N Ste 275 (07024-7586)
PHONE..........................201 893-0142
Volkan Sonmez, *Vice Pres*
EMP: 4
SALES (est): 367.1K **Privately Held**
SIC: 2844 Cosmetic preparations

(G-3545)
BAETA CORP
Also Called: (A DEVELOPMENTAL STAGE COMPANY)
1 Bridge Plz N Ste 2 (07024-7586)
PHONE..........................201 471-0988
Leonid Pushkantser, *CEO*
Alexander Gak MD, *Ch of Bd*
Jeff Burkland, *CFO*
Lee Smith, *Chief Mktg Ofcr*
Eugene Gribov, *CTO*
EMP: 6
SALES (est): 410K **Privately Held**
SIC: 3841 Surgical & medical instruments

(G-3546)
BETERRIFIC CORP (PA)
900 Palisade Ave Apt 1d (07024-4136)
PHONE..........................201 735-7711
Michael Artsis, *CEO*
David M Milch, *Ch of Bd*
EMP: 4
SALES (est): 444.1K **Privately Held**
SIC: 7819 2741 Visual effects production;

(G-3547)
BINEX LINE CORP
2 Executive Dr Ste 755 (07024-3302)
PHONE..........................201 662-7600
Fax: 201 662-9088
Mimi Ji, *Manager*
EMP: 13 **Privately Held**
SIC: 3999 Barber & beauty shop equipment
PA: Binex Line Corp.
19515 S Vermont Ave
Torrance CA 90502

(G-3548)
BLACK SEA FISHERIES
306 Whiteman St Apt 6 (07024-5627)
PHONE..........................973 553-1580
EMP: 4
SALES (est): 304.1K **Privately Held**
SIC: 2092 Fresh or frozen packaged fish

(G-3549)
CHOCMOD USA INC
2200 Fletcher Ave Ste 3 (07024-5005)
PHONE..........................201 585-8730
Stephen Picard, *President*
▲ **EMP:** 20
SQ FT: 3,500
SALES (est): 2.4MM
SALES (corp-wide): 99.7K **Privately Held**
SIC: 2066 Chocolate & cocoa products
HQ: Chocmod
1 Avenue De Flandre
Roncq
320 289-282

(G-3550)
DAINIPPON SUMITOMO PHARMA AMER (DH)
1 Bridge Plz N Ste 510 (07024-7102)
PHONE..........................201 592-2050
▲ **EMP:** 20

SALES (est): 690.7MM
SALES (corp-wide): 20.5B **Privately Held**
SIC: 2834 Mfg Pharmaceutical Preparations
HQ: Sumitomo Dainippon Pharma Co., Ltd.
2-6-8, Doshomachi, Chuo-Ku
Osaka OSK 541-0
662 035-321

(G-3551)
DIAMOND UNIVERSE LLC
2460 Lemoine Ave Ste 302 (07024-6210)
PHONE..........................201 592-9500
Sneha Kheskwani, *Mng Member*
Tony Kheskwani,
▲ **EMP:** 10
SQ FT: 1,700
SALES (est): 1.1MM **Privately Held**
SIC: 3915 5094 Jewelers' castings; jewelry

(G-3552)
E W WILLIAMS PUBLICATIONS (HQ)
2125 Center Ave Ste 305 (07024-5874)
PHONE..........................201 592-7007
Andrew Williams, *President*
Ew Williams, *Founder*
EMP: 16
SALES (est): 1.8MM
SALES (corp-wide): 42.3MM **Privately Held**
WEB: www.williamspublications.com
SIC: 2721 Magazines: publishing only, not printed on site
PA: Pioneer Associates, Inc.
2125 Center Ave Ste 305
Fort Lee NJ 07024
201 592-7007

(G-3553)
EVEREAST TRADING INC
2125 Center Ave Ste 215 (07024-5810)
PHONE..........................201 944-6484
Bum Suk Shim, *President*
EMP: 1
SQ FT: 600
SALES: 2MM **Privately Held**
SIC: 2024 2086 Ice cream & frozen desserts; bottled & canned soft drinks

(G-3554)
FINE WEAR U S A
22 E Columbia Ave (07024)
PHONE..........................201 313-3777
Ben Huh, *CEO*
EMP: 4
SALES (est): 400K **Privately Held**
SIC: 2389 7219 Uniforms & vestments; laundry, except power & coin-operated

(G-3555)
FRANKLIN MINT LLC
Also Called: Franklin Mint Trading
400 Kelby St Ste 15 (07024-2938)
PHONE..........................800 843-6468
Robert H Book, *CEO*
Scott Book, *President*
◆ **EMP:** 42 **EST:** 1964
SALES (est): 4.4MM **Privately Held**
WEB: www.franklinmint.com
SIC: 3942 3911 3999 2731 Dolls, except stuffed toy animals; bracelets, precious metal; necklaces, precious metal; pins (jewelry), precious metal; models, general, except toy; books: publishing & printing; figures: pottery, china, earthenware & stoneware

(G-3556)
HERBORIUM GROUP INC (PA)
1 Bridge Plz N Ste 275 (07024-7586)
PHONE..........................201 849-4431
Dr Agnes P Olszewski, *CEO*
EMP: 1
SALES (est): 2.9MM **Publicly Held**
SIC: 2833 5122 Medicinals & botanicals; medicinals & botanicals

(G-3557)
HRP CAPITAL INC (PA)
173 Bridge Plz N (07024-7575)
PHONE..........................201 242-4938
A Alberto Lugo, *Principal*
EMP: 2 **EST:** 2008

SALES (est): 12.4MM **Privately Held**
SIC: 2834 Pharmaceutical preparations

(G-3558)
HUB PRINT & COPY CENTER LLC
Also Called: Hub, The
2037 Lemoine Ave (07024-5704)
PHONE..........................201 585-7887
Fax: 201 585-1560
Gerard Tonner, *President*
Donna Tonner, *Vice Pres*
EMP: 4
SQ FT: 1,600
SALES (est): 359.3K **Privately Held**
WEB: www.hubprint.com
SIC: 2752 7334 2791 2789 Commercial printing, offset; photocopying & duplicating services; typesetting; bookbinding & related work; agents, shipping; packing goods for shipping

(G-3559)
INTERNATIONAL TELEMATICS CORP
1 Bridge Plz N Ste 100 (07024-7535)
PHONE..........................888 887-0935
EMP: 15
SQ FT: 2,000
SALES (est): 3.5MM **Privately Held**
SIC: 7373 3663 Computer Systems Design Mfg Radio/Tv Communication Equipment
HQ: International Telematics Holdings Limited
Level 2 135 Broadway
Auckland
937 972-11

(G-3560)
INTERNTNAL DIGITAL SYSTEMS INC
Also Called: IDS
400 Kelby St Ste 6 (07024-2938)
PHONE..........................201 983-7700
Fax: 201 482-6446
Anthony Han, *CEO*
Jung Ye Han, *President*
Han Park, *Consultant*
EMP: 18
SALES (est): 1.5MM **Privately Held**
SIC: 7379 7371 7372 7373 Computer related consulting services; custom computer programming services; custom computer programming services; business oriented computer software; office computer automation systems integration; systems engineering consultant, ex. computer or professional

(G-3561)
J-TECH CREATIONS INC
1 Bridge Plz N Ste 275 (07024-7586)
PHONE..........................201 944-2968
Masaki Yamaguchi, *President*
EMP: 5 **EST:** 2013
SALES: 440K **Privately Held**
SIC: 7372 Application computer software; business oriented computer software; home entertainment computer software

(G-3562)
K & S DRUG & SURGICAL INC
Also Called: Junction Drugs
266 Columbia Ave (07024-4125)
PHONE..........................201 886-9191
Fax: 201 886-2101
Khoren Nalbandian, *President*
Seta Nalbandian, *Treasurer*
EMP: 4
SQ FT: 1,000
SALES (est): 850K **Privately Held**
SIC: 5912 3842 5921 Drug stores; surgical appliances & supplies; liquor stores

(G-3563)
KEDRION BIOPHARMA INC (DH)
400 Kelby St Ste 11 (07024-2938)
PHONE..........................201 242-8900
Paolo Marcucci, *President*
Kenneth Moran, *Purch Agent*
Jeffrey Wyman, *Buyer*
Michele Barcia, *QC Mgr*
Richard Califano, *Engineer*
EMP: 100

GEOGRAPHIC

SQ FT: 10,078
SALES (est): 214MM **Privately Held**
SIC: 2836 Plasmas
HQ: Kedrion Spa
     Localita' Ai Conti
     Barga LU 55051
     058 376-7100

(G-3564)
LINK2CONSULT INC
1 Bridge Plz N Ste 275 (07024-7586)
PHONE.................................888 522-0902
Fax: 201 608-7129
Peter McCree, *President*
EMP: 10
SQ FT: 500
SALES (est): 1.2MM **Privately Held**
WEB: www.link2consult.com
SIC: 7372 Prepackaged software

(G-3565)
LLC DUNN MEADOW
Also Called: Dunn Meadow Pharmacy
1555 Center Ave Ste 1 (07024-4612)
PHONE.................................201 297-4603
Craig Cohen, *Owner*
EMP: 9 **EST:** 2014
SALES (est): 864.5K **Privately Held**
SIC: 2834 Pharmaceutical preparations

(G-3566)
MAXENTRIC TECHNOLOGIES LLC (PA)
2071 Lemoine Ave Ste 302 (07024-6007)
PHONE.................................201 242-9800
Per Johansson, *Vice Pres*
Pouria Khaliliadl, *Design Engr*
Paul Theilmann, *Design Engr*
Brian Woods, *Design Engr*
Grisel Perez, *Office Admin*
EMP: 25
SALES (est): 6.1MM **Privately Held**
WEB: www.maxentric.com
SIC: 1623 3663 7379 Transmitting tower (telecommunication) construction; satellites, communications;

(G-3567)
METALLIA USA LLC
2200 Fletcher Ave Ste 7 (07024-5005)
PHONE.................................201 585-5000
Avy Buchen,
Morris Weinstein,
▲ **EMP:** 9
SALES (est): 2.1MM **Privately Held**
SIC: 3315 Steel wire & related products

(G-3568)
MICROFEED LLC
1053 Anderson Ave (07024-4248)
P.O. Box 916 (07024-0916)
PHONE.................................201 886-9200
Fax: 201 886-9233
Elizabeth Guiza, *Mng Member*
Myriam Serrano, *Relations*
EMP: 1
SQ FT: 2,200
SALES (est): 2MM **Privately Held**
SIC: 2048 Feed supplements

(G-3569)
MICROTELECOM LTD LIABILITY CO (PA)
1 Bridge Plz N Ste 275 (07024-7586)
PHONE.................................866 676-5679
Yonathan Shechter,
EMP: 3
SQ FT: 2,000
SALES (est): 2MM **Privately Held**
SIC: 7371 7372 7373 Custom computer programming services; prepackaged software; computer systems analysis & design

(G-3570)
MTEIXEIRA SOAPSTONE VA LLC
1100 Palisade Ave (07024-6328)
PHONE.................................201 757-8608
EMP: 4
SALES (est): 223.7K **Privately Held**
SIC: 1499 Soapstone mining

(G-3571)
N J W MAGAZINE
Also Called: Advantage Publications
177 Main St Ste 232 (07024-6936)
PHONE.................................201 886-2185
Louise Hafesh, *President*
Joseph Hafesh, *Vice Pres*
▼ **EMP:** 11
SALES (est): 750K **Privately Held**
SIC: 2721 Periodicals

(G-3572)
NADRI INC
2 Executive Dr Ste 500 (07024-3307)
PHONE.................................201 585-0088
Young Tae Choi, *President*
Mickey Walters, *Vice Pres*
Yool Lee, *Accountant*
▲ **EMP:** 5
SALES (est): 704.3K **Privately Held**
SIC: 3911 Jewelry, precious metal

(G-3573)
NANA CREATIONS INC
329 Lincoln Ave (07024-6106)
PHONE.................................201 263-1112
EMP: 14
SQ FT: 10,000
SALES (est): 787K **Privately Held**
SIC: 2337 Mfgs Ladies Coats

(G-3574)
NATAL LAMP & SHADE CORP
Also Called: Natalie Lamp & Shade
5 Horizon Rd Apt 2601 (07024-6646)
PHONE.................................201 224-7844
George Reisman, *President*
EMP: 50 **EST:** 1935
SQ FT: 90,000
SALES (est): 3.2MM **Privately Held**
SIC: 3641 5023 3999 Lamps, incandescent filament, electric; lamps: floor, boudoir, desk; shades, lamp or candle

(G-3575)
OBJECUTIVE INC
2125 Center Ave Ste 411 (07024-5812)
PHONE.................................201 242-0990
Fax: 201 242-0990
Constantinos Kelleas, *CEO*
Christoper Leeming, *President*
Robert Arvanitis, *Vice Pres*
Ariana Franciscovic, *Marketing Staff*
Gordana Dimoska, *Project Leader*
EMP: 13 **EST:** 1998
SQ FT: 1,000
SALES (est): 1.8MM **Privately Held**
WEB: www.objecutive.com
SIC: 7372 Business oriented computer software

(G-3576)
OLIVOS USA INC (DH)
1 Bridge Plz N Ste 275 (07024-7586)
PHONE.................................201 893-0142
Selcuk Atalay, *CEO*
▲ **EMP:** 5
SQ FT: 10,000
SALES (est): 801.6K
SALES (corp-wide): 25.9MM **Privately Held**
WEB: www.olivosusa.com
SIC: 2079 Olive oil
HQ: Olivos Gida Yag Tarim Sanayi Ithalat Ihracat Ve Ticaret Anonim Sirketi
     1. Organize Sanayi Bolgesi, No:9
     Ticaret Ve Sanayi Odasi Bulvar
     Manisa 45400
     236 332-5032

(G-3577)
PIONEER ASSOCIATES INC (PA)
2125 Center Ave Ste 305 (07024-5874)
PHONE.................................201 592-7007
Andrew Williams, *President*
Timothy Denman, *Assoc Editor*
Joanne Gambert, *Director*
EMP: 40
SQ FT: 3,000
SALES (est): 42.3MM **Privately Held**
WEB: www.idhonline.com
SIC: 1623 2721 Electric power line construction; trade journals: publishing only, not printed on site

(G-3578)
PIONEER POWER SOLUTIONS INC (PA)
400 Kelby St Ste 12 (07024-2938)
PHONE.................................212 867-0700
Fax: 212 867-1325
Nathan J Mazurek, *Ch of Bd*
Thomas Klink, *CFO*
Mark Malinosky, *Controller*
David Landes PHD, *Bd of Directors*
David Tesler, *Bd of Directors*
EMP: 47
SQ FT: 2,700
SALES: 101.3MM **Publicly Held**
SIC: 3612 Transformers, except electric; control transformers

(G-3579)
QUICK FROZEN FOODS INTL
2125 Center Ave Ste 305 (07024-5874)
PHONE.................................201 592-7007
Fax: 201 592-7171
Andrew Williams, *President*
▲ **EMP:** 30
SALES (est): 1.2MM **Privately Held**
SIC: 2721 Periodicals: publishing only

(G-3580)
SA RICHARDS INC
1600 Parker Ave Apt 23a (07024-7007)
PHONE.................................201 947-3850
Fax: 201 947-3910
Richard Aquino, *President*
EMP: 4
SALES: 800K **Privately Held**
SIC: 2653 Boxes, solid fiber: made from purchased materials

(G-3581)
SADELCO INC
96 Linwood Plz (07024-3701)
PHONE.................................201 569-3323
Fax: 201 569-6285
Les Kaplan, *President*
Gail Kaplan, *Admin Sec*
▲ **EMP:** 70 **EST:** 1960
SQ FT: 13,500
SALES (est): 10.1MM **Privately Held**
WEB: www.sadelco.com
SIC: 3825 Test equipment for electronic & electrical circuits

(G-3582)
SHERMAN GROUP HOLDINGS
2200 Fletcher Ave Office (07024-5005)
PHONE.................................201 735-9000
Brendon Scott, *CFO*
EMP: 5
SALES (est): 468.6K **Privately Held**
SIC: 2111 Cigarettes

(G-3583)
STAMM INTERNATIONAL CORP (PA)
1530 Palisade Ave Ste Phd (07024-5471)
P.O. Box 1929 (07024-8429)
PHONE.................................201 947-1700
Fax: 201 947-9662
Marilyn Skony Stamm, *President*
Maria Vilardi, *Controller*
EMP: 3
SQ FT: 1,000
SALES (est): 64.4MM **Privately Held**
WEB: www.stamminternational.com
SIC: 6719 3585 3564 3433 Investment holding companies, except banks; refrigeration & heating equipment; blowers & fans; heating equipment, except electric

(G-3584)
SUNOVION PHARMACEUTICALS INC
1 Bridge Plz N Ste 510 (07024-7102)
PHONE.................................201 592-2050
Bonnie Neuhardt, *Managing Dir*
Lisa Haase, *Facilities Mgr*
Doreen Simonelli, *Opers Staff*
Godson Lomax, *Research*
Rica Minatoya, *Financial Analy*
EMP: 85
SALES (corp-wide): 20.5B **Privately Held**
SIC: 2834 Pharmaceutical preparations

HQ: Sunovion Pharmaceuticals Inc.
     84 Waterford Dr
     Marlborough MA 01752
     508 481-6700

(G-3585)
TOPAZ SKIN CARE INC
1530 Palisade Ave Ste 1 (07024-5470)
PHONE.................................201 489-0686
Fax: 201 489-0167
Stephanie I Kiriak, *President*
Moe Marshall, *Vice Pres*
EMP: 2
SQ FT: 1,000
SALES (est): 3MM **Privately Held**
SIC: 2844 Toilet preparations

(G-3586)
TYPECOM LLC (PA)
1275 15th St Apt 19a (07024-1936)
P.O. Box 1163 (07024-1163)
PHONE.................................201 969-1901
Richard Barnett, *Mng Member*
Cathy Coda,
EMP: 5
SQ FT: 1,200
SALES (est): 702.6K **Privately Held**
SIC: 2759 7311 Commercial printing; advertising agencies

(G-3587)
US CHINA ALLIED PRODUCTS INC
Also Called: Uscap
555 North Ave Apt 12h (07024-2414)
PHONE.................................201 461-9886
▲ **EMP:** 6 **EST:** 1995
SQ FT: 1,000
SALES (est): 480K **Privately Held**
SIC: 3841 Mfg Surgical/Medical Instruments

(G-3588)
VATECH AMERICA INC
2200 Fletcher Ave Ste 605 (07024-5016)
PHONE.................................201 210-5028
Jai Hoon Kim, *President*
Brian Hwang, *Business Dir*
▲ **EMP:** 30
SALES (est): 5.2MM
SALES (corp-wide): 140.2MM **Privately Held**
SIC: 8021 3844 Dental clinics & offices; radiographic X-ray apparatus & tubes
PA: Value Added Technology Co., Ltd.
     13 Samsung 1-Ro 2-Gil
     Hwaseong 18449
     823 167-9200

(G-3589)
VIVA CHEMICAL CORPORATION (PA)
1512 Palisade Ave Apt 5m (07024-5310)
PHONE.................................201 461-5281
Veniamin Nilva, *President*
Constantine Lutsenko, *Vice Pres*
EMP: 6
SQ FT: 2,000
SALES (est): 559K **Privately Held**
SIC: 2869 Industrial organic chemicals

(G-3590)
WHALE COMMUNICATIONS INC
400 Kelby St Ste 8 (07024-2938)
PHONE.................................201 947-0054
Roger J Pilc, *CEO*
Daniel Steiner, *President*
Joseph Gleberman, *Principal*
Neal Moszkowski, *Principal*
Eli Barkat, *Chairman*
EMP: 35
SQ FT: 7,300
SALES (est): 4.2MM **Privately Held**
SIC: 3577 Computer peripheral equipment
PA: Whale Communications Ltd.
     13 Shenkar Arie
     Herzliya 48091
     390 311-01

(G-3591)
WORLD CLASS MARKETING CORP (DH)
Also Called: A A World Class Corp
2147 Hudson Ter (07024-7729)
PHONE.................................201 313-0022

▲ = Import ▼=Export
◆ =Import/Export

Fax: 201 313-0044
Coleman Schneider, *CEO*
Benjamin Amoruso, *President*
EMP: 40
SQ FT: 24,000
SALES (est): 9.5MM
SALES (corp-wide): 54MM **Privately Held**
WEB: www.aaworld.com
SIC: 2395 3911 2258 2281 Emblems, embroidered; jewelry, precious metal; lace & lace products; yarn spinning mills
HQ: Carolace Industries, Inc.
325 Sylvan Ave Ste 102
Englewood Cliffs NJ 07632
201 945-2151

(G-3592)
WYSSMONT COMPANY INC
1470 Bergen Blvd (07024-2197)
PHONE..............................201 947-4600
Fax: 201 947-0324
Joseph Bevacqua, *CEO*
Robert Schuit, *Regional Mgr*
Jim Ulrich, *VP Engrg*
James McGuire, *Sales Engr*
Jayne Kraljic, *Technology*
▲ **EMP:** 24
SQ FT: 6,000
SALES (est): 2.5MM **Privately Held**
WEB: www.wyssmont.com
SIC: 3567 3559 3556 Driers & redriers, industrial process; chemical machinery & equipment; cutting, chopping, grinding, mixing & similar machinery

Franklin
Sussex County

(G-3593)
ADVANCED IMAGING ASSOC LLC (PA)
190 Munsonhurst Rd Ste 1 (07416-1810)
PHONE..............................973 823-8999
Clifford Barker MD, *Principal*
EMP: 6
SALES (est): 730.2K **Privately Held**
WEB: www.advancedimagingassoc.com
SIC: 3826 Magnetic resonance imaging apparatus

(G-3594)
AMERICAN PRVATE LABEL PDTS LLC
24b Munsonhurst Rd (07416-1819)
P.O. Box 1025, Goshen NY (10924-8025)
PHONE..............................845 733-8151
Robert Kozic, *COO*
EMP: 4
SALES (est): 208.5K **Privately Held**
SIC: 2844 Depilatories (cosmetic)

(G-3595)
AURORA RESEARCH COMPANY INC
200 Munsonhurst Rd # 201 (07416-1813)
PHONE..............................973 827-8055
Fax: 973 827-0591
Donna Barbetta, *President*
Richard Barbetta, *Vice Pres*
EMP: 5
SQ FT: 3,000
SALES (est): 608K **Privately Held**
WEB: www.auroraresearchgroup.com
SIC: 3572 7373 Tape storage units, computer; systems software development services

(G-3596)
B & C MACHINE CO INC
22 Lasinski Rd Ste I (07416-9715)
PHONE..............................973 823-1120
Robert Van Dyke, *President*
EMP: 5
SQ FT: 4,000
SALES (est): 800K **Privately Held**
SIC: 3599 Machine shop, jobbing & repair

(G-3597)
CLINICAL IMAGE RETRIEVAL SYSTE
Also Called: Cir Systems
12 Cork Hill Rd Ste 2 (07416-1302)
P.O. Box 6081, Parsippany (07054-7081)
PHONE..............................888 482-2362
Douglas D Haas Jr, *Owner*
Karen Toepper, *Treasurer*
EMP: 6
SQ FT: 1,000
SALES (est): 906.4K **Privately Held**
SIC: 3841 Diagnostic apparatus, medical

(G-3598)
DOUBLE TWENTIES INC
Also Called: Franklin Precast Tanks
20 Park Dr (07416-9758)
PHONE..............................973 827-7563
Fax: 973 827-4746
Alex Kovach, *President*
Wendy Kovach, *Vice Pres*
EMP: 10
SQ FT: 2,500
SALES (est): 1.7MM **Privately Held**
SIC: 3272 Septic tanks, concrete

(G-3599)
FUTURREX INC
24 Munsonhurst Rd Ste F (07416-1803)
P.O. Box 823, Denville (07834-0823)
PHONE..............................973 209-1563
Zbigniew Sobczak, *President*
Dusty Weaver, *Project Mgr*
Krzysztof Konopka, *Manager*
Kerri Leto, *Director*
▲ **EMP:** 19
SALES (est): 5.1MM **Privately Held**
SIC: 2819 Industrial inorganic chemicals

(G-3600)
GORDON BRUSH MFG CO INC
15 Park Dr (07416-9758)
PHONE..............................973 827-4600
EMP: 8
SALES (corp-wide): 15MM **Privately Held**
SIC: 3991 Brooms & brushes
PA: Gordon Brush Mfg. Co., Inc.
3737 Capitol Ave
City Of Industry CA 90601
323 724-7777

(G-3601)
MJS PRECISION INC
12 Cork Hill Rd Ste 3 (07416-1302)
PHONE..............................973 209-1300
Michael Sanclementi, *President*
EMP: 4
SQ FT: 3,000
SALES (est): 514.7K **Privately Held**
SIC: 3599 Machine & other job shop work

(G-3602)
NEWTON SCREEN PRINTING CO
Also Called: Newton Screenprinting
75 Main St (07416-1422)
PHONE..............................973 827-0486
Paula Lavorgna, *President*
Frank Newton Jr, *Corp Secy*
Mark Cunnington, *Mktg Dir*
EMP: 8
SQ FT: 7,000
SALES (est): 780K **Privately Held**
WEB: www.newtonscreen.com
SIC: 2759 5199 Screen printing; advertising specialties

(G-3603)
NUMERITOOL MANUFACTURING CORP
58 Woodland Rd (07416-1315)
PHONE..............................973 827-7714
Curtis Allen, *President*
EMP: 5
SQ FT: 2,500
SALES (est): 2.5MM **Privately Held**
SIC: 3566 Drives, high speed industrial, except hydrostatic

(G-3604)
NUTRI SPORT PHARMACAL INC
200 N Church Rd (07416-1211)
PHONE..............................973 827-9287
Vince Paternoster, *President*

William D Bernared, *Vice Pres*
Mario Ebanietti, *Shareholder*
▲ **EMP:** 15 **EST:** 1997
SALES (est): 1.7MM **Privately Held**
WEB: www.e-nutrisport.com
SIC: 2023 2834 Dietary supplements, dairy & non-dairy based; vitamin, nutrient & hematinic preparations for human use

(G-3605)
TECHNOLOGY GENERAL CORPORATION (PA)
Also Called: Clawson Machine Division
12 Cork Hill Rd (07416-1304)
PHONE..............................973 827-8209
Fax: 973 827-4613
Charles J Fletcher, *President*
Helen S Fletcher, *Treasurer*
EMP: 10
SQ FT: 34,100
SALES (est): 1.3MM **Publicly Held**
WEB: www.eclipsesystem.com
SIC: 3634 3999 Ice crushers, electric; dock equipment & supplies, industrial

(G-3606)
UNITED SILICA PRODUCTS INC
3 Park Dr (07416-9758)
PHONE..............................973 209-8854
Lynn Marie Kane, *President*
John Boccuzzo, *General Mgr*
James Campbell, *Vice Pres*
Jim Campbell, *Vice Pres*
Lisa Burke, *Purchasing*
▲ **EMP:** 18
SQ FT: 7,500
SALES (est): 2.1MM **Privately Held**
WEB: www.unitedsilica.com
SIC: 3229 Industrial-use glassware

Franklin Lakes
Bergen County

(G-3607)
BAXTER CORPORATION (PA)
511 Commerce St (07417-1309)
P.O. Box 645 (07417-0645)
PHONE..............................201 337-1212
Fax: 201 337-9469
George Bowen, *President*
Michael Bolton, *Counsel*
Michael Kelley, *Treasurer*
Ty Shockley, *Marketing Mgr*
Lisa Keltner, *Corp Comm Staff*
EMP: 13
SQ FT: 10,000
SALES (est): 5.8MM **Privately Held**
SIC: 3552 5085 5084 7373 Jacquard loom parts & attachments; twine; textile machinery & equipment; computer systems analysis & design

(G-3608)
BD BISCNCES SYSTEMS RGENTS INC (PA)
1 Becton Dr (07417-1815)
PHONE..............................201 847-6800
Fax: 201 847-4442
EMP: 9
SALES (est): 1.2MM **Privately Held**
SIC: 2819 Mfg Industrial Inorganic Chemicals

(G-3609)
BD VENTURES LLC
1 Becton Dr (07417-1815)
PHONE..............................201 847-6800
Fax: 201 847-4874
Steve Barbato, *CEO*
Paul Marini, *Opers Mgr*
Irma Arochi, *Buyer*
Charles Houston, *Buyer*
Corey Christensen, *Engineer*
EMP: 20
SALES (est): 5.7MM
SALES (corp-wide): 12B **Publicly Held**
SIC: 3841 Surgical & medical instruments
PA: Becton, Dickinson And Company
1 Becton Dr
Franklin Lakes NJ 07417
201 847-6800

(G-3610)
BECTON DICKINSON AND COMPANY (PA)
Also Called: B D
1 Becton Dr (07417-1880)
PHONE..............................201 847-6800
Fax: 201 847-4845
Vincent A Forlenza, *Ch of Bd*
Thomas E Polen, *President*
Bill Tozzi, *Interim Pres*
James W Borzi, *Exec VP*
John A Deford, *Exec VP*
EMP: 1500 **EST:** 1897
SALES: 12B **Publicly Held**
SIC: 3841 3842 3829 3826 Hypodermic needles & syringes; IV transfusion apparatus; catheters; surgical knife blades & handles; gloves, safety; surgical appliances & supplies; elastic hosiery, orthopedic (support); thermometers & temperature sensors; analytical instruments; blood testing apparatus; hemoglobinometers; laboratory apparatus & furniture; pipettes, hemocytometer

(G-3611)
BECTON DICKINSON RE INC
1 Becton Dr (07417-1880)
PHONE..............................201 847-6800
EMP: 11
SALES (est): 1.4MM
SALES (corp-wide): 12B **Publicly Held**
SIC: 2834 Mfg Pharmaceutical Preparations
PA: Becton, Dickinson And Company
1 Becton Dr
Franklin Lakes NJ 07417
201 847-6800

(G-3612)
COLUMBIA INDUSTRIES INC (PA)
567 Commerce St (07417-1309)
PHONE..............................201 337-7332
Richard Pearson, *Ch of Bd*
Mary Ann Pearson, *Corp Secy*
▲ **EMP:** 8
SQ FT: 30,000
SALES (est): 18.9MM **Privately Held**
SIC: 3713 Truck bodies (motor vehicles)

(G-3613)
DIFCO LABORATORIES INC (HQ)
1 Becton Dr (07417-1815)
PHONE..............................410 316-4113
Michael Meehan, *Vice Pres*
EMP: 5
SQ FT: 46,680
SALES (est): 4.3MM
SALES (corp-wide): 12B **Publicly Held**
SIC: 2836 5122 3841 2834 Biological products, except diagnostic; culture media; biologicals & allied products; surgical & medical instruments; pharmaceutical preparations; industrial instrmnts msrmnt display/control process variable; laboratory apparatus & furniture
PA: Becton, Dickinson And Company
1 Becton Dr
Franklin Lakes NJ 07417
201 847-6800

(G-3614)
DIRECT COMPUTER RESOURCES INC (PA)
Also Called: D C R
120 Birch Rd (07417-2718)
PHONE..............................201 848-0018
George Lang, *Ch of Bd*
Joseph J Buonomo, *President*
William Vitiello, *Vice Pres*
Don Hughes, *QC Mgr*
Valerie Burke, *Accounts Exec*
EMP: 25
SQ FT: 2,500
SALES (est): 3.4MM **Privately Held**
WEB: www.datavantage.com
SIC: 7372 Prepackaged software

(G-3615)
DOUGHERTY FOUNDATION PRODUCTS
851 Meadow Ln (07417-1112)
P.O. Box 688 (07417-0688)
PHONE..............................201 337-5748

John Dougherty, *President*
Barbara Dougherty, *Vice Pres*
EMP: 5
SALES (est): 568.6K **Privately Held**
SIC: 3531 Construction machinery

(G-3616)
DOVER TOOL CONNECTICUT LLC (PA)
620 Franklin Lake Rd (07417-2205)
PHONE..................203 367-6376
Michael F James, *Mng Member*
EMP: 18
SQ FT: 12,000
SALES (est): 2.6MM **Privately Held**
WEB: www.dovertool.com
SIC: 3724 Aircraft engines & engine parts

(G-3617)
FLEET EQUIPMENT CORPORATION (PA)
Also Called: FEC
567 Commerce St (07417-1309)
PHONE..................201 337-3294
Fax: 201 337-3294
Richard Pearson, *Ch of Bd*
Scott Pearson, *Vice Pres*
Mary Ann Pearson, *Treasurer*
Rick Pearson, *CTO*
EMP: 15
SQ FT: 30,000
SALES (est): 6MM **Privately Held**
SIC: 5012 3713 3563 Truck bodies; truck & bus bodies; air & gas compressors

(G-3618)
GLEN ROCK STAIR CORP
551 Commerce St (07417-1309)
PHONE..................201 337-9595
Fax: 201 337-3470
James Veenstra, *President*
Nick Veenstra, *President*
Alan Jeltema, *Vice Pres*
Lyn Veenstra, *Treasurer*
Kathy Jeltema, *Admin Sec*
EMP: 35
SQ FT: 15,000
SALES (est): 3.3MM **Privately Held**
SIC: 1751 2431 Finish & trim carpentry; millwork

(G-3619)
GOLDEN RULE CREATIONS INC
250 Terrace Rd (07417-1621)
P.O. Box 123 (07417-0123)
PHONE..................201 337-4050
Eric Shicker, *President*
EMP: 4
SALES (est): 173.9K **Privately Held**
WEB: www.goldenrulepatriot.com
SIC: 2395 Emblems, embroidered

(G-3620)
M R C MILLWORK & TRIM INC
319 Hobar Ct (07417-2018)
PHONE..................201 954-2176
Marc McKeon, *President*
EMP: 4
SQ FT: 4,400
SALES (est): 494.2K **Privately Held**
SIC: 2431 Millwork

(G-3621)
MECHTRONICS CORPORATION (PA)
939 Huron Rd (07417-2210)
PHONE..................845 231-1400
Fax: 914 989-2726
Richard J Fellinger, *Ch of Bd*
Anthony Squitieri, *President*
Alejandro Reyes, *Engineer*
Jose Morales, *Manager*
Kevin Fellinger, *Director*
▲ **EMP:** 40 EST: 1944
SQ FT: 20,000
SALES (est): 22.8MM **Privately Held**
WEB: www.mech-tronics.com
SIC: 3993 Displays, paint process

(G-3622)
NUTECH CORP
Also Called: Nu Tech
322 Freemans Ln (07417-1012)
PHONE..................908 707-2097
Nagi Awad, *President*

Jacob Hauser, *Vice Pres*
EMP: 8
SQ FT: 1,800
SALES (est): 829.6K **Privately Held**
SIC: 2843 2899 Textile processing assistants; chemical preparations

(G-3623)
RIPE LIFE WINES LLC
253 Indian Trail Dr (07417-1014)
PHONE..................201 560-3233
Mary McAuley,
EMP: 6 EST: 2012
SALES (est): 246.3K **Privately Held**
SIC: 2084 Wines

(G-3624)
ROMAR MACHINE & TOOL COMPANY
521 Commerce St (07417-1309)
PHONE..................201 337-7111
Fax: 201 337-5385
Robert Thum, *President*
URS Haller, *Electrical Engi*
Maria Thum, *Treasurer*
EMP: 20
SQ FT: 5,600
SALES (est): 3MM **Privately Held**
WEB: www.romarmachine.com
SIC: 3599 3544 Machine shop, jobbing & repair; special dies, tools, jigs & fixtures

(G-3625)
VOZEH EQUIPMENT CORP
Also Called: S C T
509 Commerce St Ste 1 (07417-1314)
PHONE..................201 337-3729
Fax: 201 337-3278
Gregory Vozeh, *CEO*
Christopher Vozeh, *VP Sales*
Karen Vozeh, *Admin Sec*
EMP: 50
SQ FT: 9,000
SALES (est): 10.2MM **Privately Held**
SIC: 3841 5072 Surgical & medical instruments; hand tools

Franklin Park
Somerset County

(G-3626)
CONFECTIONATELY YOURS LLC
3391 State Route 27 # 121 (08823-1360)
PHONE..................732 821-6863
Fax: 732 821-1536
Mary Gondek, *Owner*
EMP: 20
SQ FT: 2,800
SALES (est): 645.4K **Privately Held**
SIC: 5812 2024 Ice cream stands or dairy bars; ice cream, bulk

(G-3627)
CRESCENT UNIFORMS LLC
33 Hasbrouck Dr (08823-1825)
PHONE..................732 398-1866
Asma Usmani, *Mng Member*
Uzma Khan, *Director*
EMP: 10
SALES: 225K **Privately Held**
SIC: 2299 Batting, wadding, padding & fillings

(G-3628)
M D LABORATORY SUPPLIES INC
4 Minebrook Ln (08823-1784)
PHONE..................732 322-0773
Harsha J Shah, *President*
Jadinkumar C Shah, *Vice Pres*
EMP: 2
SALES: 1.3MM **Privately Held**
SIC: 3229 3826 7389 Glassware, industrial; analytical instruments;

Franklinville
Gloucester County

(G-3629)
CORE 3 BREWERY LTD LBLTY CO
3171 Coles Mill Rd (08322-3012)
PHONE..................856 562-0386
Alexsandros Skriapas, *Principal*
EMP: 4
SALES (est): 106K **Privately Held**
SIC: 2082 Malt beverages

(G-3630)
EASTERN MACHINING CORPORATION
1197 Fries Mill Rd (08322-2619)
PHONE..................856 694-3303
Fax: 856 964-2128
Joe Davis, *President*
EMP: 5
SQ FT: 10,000
SALES: 440K **Privately Held**
WEB: www.em-corp.com
SIC: 3599 3451 3541 Machine shop, jobbing & repair; screw machine products; machine tools, metal cutting type

(G-3631)
SPECTRUM DESIGN LLC
1106 Grant Ave (08322-3107)
P.O. Box 438 (08322-0438)
PHONE..................856 694-1870
Fax: 856 694-1966
Steve Monteleone, *Mng Member*
Brenda Monteleone,
EMP: 4
SQ FT: 700
SALES (est): 490K **Privately Held**
WEB: www.designedbyspectrum.com
SIC: 7389 3599 Design, commercial & industrial; custom machinery

(G-3632)
STAR BINDERY INC
963 Lincoln Ave (08322-2704)
PHONE..................609 519-5732
David Moskowitz, *President*
Annette Moskowitz, *Corp Secy*
EMP: 35
SQ FT: 18,000
SALES: 3MM **Privately Held**
SIC: 2782 Receipt, invoice & memorandum books

(G-3633)
UNI-TECH DRILLING COMPANY INC
61 Grays Ferry Rd (08322-3692)
P.O. Box 407 (08322-0407)
PHONE..................856 694-4200
Gerald Freck, *President*
David Conover, *Treasurer*
Rita Lawrence, *Controller*
Marlene Mueller, *Admin Sec*
EMP: 25
SQ FT: 10,000
SALES (est): 5.1MM **Privately Held**
WEB: www.unitechdrilling.com
SIC: 1781 1799 5084 1381 Water well servicing; boring for building construction; pumps & pumping equipment; drilling water intake wells

Freehold
Monmouth County

(G-3634)
ACCESS NORTHERN SECURITY INC (PA)
Also Called: Access Controls International
303 W Main St Ste 4 (07728-2522)
PHONE..................732 462-2500
Paul Grossman, *CEO*
Bill Borowik, *Senior VP*
Paul Kelly, *Vice Pres*
David Steinmetz, *Vice Pres*
EMP: 12
SQ FT: 4,500

SALES (est): 2.8MM **Privately Held**
WEB: www.acisecurity.com
SIC: 3822 1731 Auto controls regulating residntl & coml environmt & applncs; access control systems specialization

(G-3635)
AGINOVA INC (PA)
3 Chambry Ct (07728-9064)
PHONE..................732 804-3272
Ashok Sabata, *CEO*
Chris Plummer, *CFO*
Bikash Sabata, *Admin Sec*
EMP: 8
SQ FT: 1,100
SALES (est): 1MM **Privately Held**
WEB: www.aginova.com
SIC: 3822 7371 Thermostats & other environmental sensors; computer software development & applications

(G-3636)
ALERE INC
500 Halls Mill Rd (07728-8811)
PHONE..................732 620-4244
Greg Menke, *General Mgr*
Pooja S Pathak, *Vice Pres*
Melissa Pearson, *Vice Pres*
Steve Sevy, *Vice Pres*
Daniel Sullivan, *Vice Pres*
EMP: 375
SALES (corp-wide): 27.3B **Publicly Held**
SIC: 2835 2834 In vivo diagnostics; vitamin, nutrient & hematinic preparations for human use
HQ: Alere Inc.
51 Sawyer Rd Ste 200
Waltham MA 02453
781 647-3900

(G-3637)
ALERE INC
Also Called: Alere Distribution
569 Halls Mill Rd (07728-8812)
PHONE..................732 358-5921
EMP: 375
SALES (corp-wide): 27.3B **Publicly Held**
SIC: 2835 In vitro & in vivo diagnostic substances
HQ: Alere Inc.
51 Sawyer Rd Ste 200
Waltham MA 02453
781 647-3900

(G-3638)
APPLIED IMAGE INC
800 Business Park Dr (07728-9393)
PHONE..................732 410-2444
Fax: 732 919-7791
EMP: 34
SQ FT: 25,000
SALES (est): 6.8MM **Privately Held**
SIC: 7336 2759 Commercial Art/Graphic Design Commercial Printing

(G-3639)
ART OF SHAVING - FL LLC
3710 Us Highway 9 (07728-4801)
PHONE..................732 410-2520
EMP: 6
SALES (corp-wide): 66.8B **Publicly Held**
SIC: 5999 2844 3421 5122 Hair care products; toilet preparations; razor blades & razors; razor blades
HQ: The Art Of Shaving - Fl Llc
6100 Blue Lagoon Dr # 150
Miami FL 33126

(G-3640)
AVALON GLOBOCARE CORP (PA)
4400 Route 9 N (07728-1383)
PHONE..................646 762-4517
David Jin, *CEO*
Meng LI, *COO*
Luisa Ingargiola, *CFO*
EMP: 5
SALES: 1MM **Publicly Held**
SIC: 7372 Prepackaged software

(G-3641)
BARTELL MORRISON (USA) LLC
200 Commerce Ave (07728-9379)
PHONE..................732 566-5400
Jeff Durgin, *President*
▲ **EMP:** 19

SALES (est): 3.8MM **Privately Held**
SIC: 3443 Mixers, for hot metal

(G-3642)
BENTON BINDERY INC
43 Sycamore Ave (07728-2916)
PHONE..................................732 431-9064
Phil Engel, *President*
EMP: 10
SALES (est): 1.1MM **Privately Held**
SIC: 2789 Binding only: books, pamphlets, magazines, etc.

(G-3643)
CAMPUS COORDINATES LLC
1711 Ginesi Dr Ste 1 (07728-8592)
PHONE..................................732 866-6060
Fax: 732 866-6044
Kevin Drake, *Owner*
Roy Piper, *Sales Associate*
EMP: 7
SQ FT: 3,400
SALES: 1MM **Privately Held**
SIC: 2759 Screen printing

(G-3644)
CENNTRO AUTOMOTIVE CORPORATION (PA)
Also Called: Cenntro Motors
125 Halls Mill Rd Unit 4 (07728-9395)
PHONE..................................732 863-0777
Peter Wang, *CEO*
Susan Yuqing Xu, *President*
Tony Tsai, *Vice Pres*
David Ming He, *CFO*
▲ EMP: 7
SQ FT: 78,000
SALES (est): 1MM **Privately Held**
SIC: 3711 Automobile assembly, including specialty automobiles

(G-3645)
CENTRAL TECHNOLOGY INC
Also Called: Laser Save
843 State Route 33 Ste 11 (07728-8493)
P.O. Box 294, Marlboro (07746-0294)
PHONE..................................732 431-3339
Fax: 732 431-3706
Alan D Yoss, *President*
Howard D Topal, *President*
Judith L Topal, *Vice Pres*
Kay Yoss, *Vice Pres*
Jerrold Landau, *Sales Executive*
EMP: 16
SQ FT: 8,500
SALES (est): 1.8MM **Privately Held**
WEB: www.lasersave.com
SIC: 7378 5045 5112 3861 Computer peripheral equipment repair & maintenance; computers; computer & photocopying supplies; photographic equipment & supplies

(G-3646)
CHARTWELL PROMOTIONS LTD INC
1 Chartwell Ct (07728-8115)
PHONE..................................732 780-6900
Vincent Rinaldi, *President*
EMP: 4
SALES: 1MM **Privately Held**
SIC: 2261 2262 5136 Screen printing of cotton broadwoven fabrics; screen printing: manmade fiber & silk broadwoven fabrics; sportswear, men's & boys'

(G-3647)
CLAYTON BLOCK COMPANY INC
225 Throckmorton St (07728-8298)
PHONE..................................732 462-1860
Fax: 732 462-7285
Justin Errickson, *Sales Staff*
Ron Smith, *Manager*
EMP: 7
SALES (corp-wide): 44.5MM **Privately Held**
WEB: www.claytononline.com
SIC: 3271 Blocks, concrete or cinder: standard
PA: Clayton Block Company, Inc.
1355 Campus Pkwy Ste 200
Wall Township NJ 07753
732 363-1995

(G-3648)
CRITERION SOFTWARE LLC
205 Us Highway 9 30 (07728-8561)
PHONE..................................908 754-1166
Alag Arasan, *CEO*
Shashi Alagarasan, *Opers Staff*
Anusha Alagarasan, *Director*
Natasha Alagarasan, *Director*
Kiran Bambulkar,
EMP: 17
SQ FT: 500
SALES (est): 887K **Privately Held**
WEB: www.criterion-software.com
SIC: 7376 7372 Computer facilities management; prepackaged software

(G-3649)
CUSTOM BUSINESS SOFTWARE LLC
Also Called: Twisted Networking
87 Broad St (07728-1943)
P.O. Box 6930 (07728-6930)
PHONE..................................732 534-9557
David Mound,
EMP: 9
SALES: 250K **Privately Held**
WEB: www.custombs.com
SIC: 7372 Application computer software

(G-3650)
DEPENDABLE MACHINING CO
53 Weaverville Rd (07728-8192)
PHONE..................................732 462-0262
Fax: 732 462-0262
Frank Minervini, *Owner*
EMP: 4
SQ FT: 1,700
SALES (est): 220K **Privately Held**
WEB: www.francominervini.com
SIC: 3599 Machine shop, jobbing & repair

(G-3651)
DR TECHNOLOGY INC
73 South St (07728-2317)
PHONE..................................732 780-4664
Fax: 732 780-1545
Doris Schwartz, *Ch of Bd*
Richard Schwartz, *President*
Lucas Young, *Engng Exec*
Debra Krueger, *Manager*
EMP: 5
SQ FT: 2,500
SALES (est): 670K **Privately Held**
WEB: www.drtechnologyinc.com
SIC: 3564 3443 Air purification equipment; heat exchangers, condensers & components

(G-3652)
ELCO GLASS INDUSTRIES CO INC
16 Tree Line Dr (07728-9287)
PHONE..................................732 363-6550
Fax: 732 905-2086
Eli Bavarsky, *President*
Zippi Bavarsky, *CFO*
EMP: 50
SQ FT: 40,000
SALES: 3.8MM **Privately Held**
SIC: 3211 Window glass, clear & colored

(G-3653)
ELITE LANDSCAPING & PAVERS
3102 Kapalua Ct (07728-5915)
P.O. Box 6752 (07728-6752)
PHONE..................................732 252-6152
Richard A Castaldi Jr, *President*
EMP: 1
SALES (est): 2.8MM **Privately Held**
SIC: 3531 Pavers

(G-3654)
ENSYNC INTRCTIVE SOLUTIONS INC
83 South St Ste 202 (07728-2491)
PHONE..................................732 542-4001
Claude Jones, *President*
Simonetta Brown, *Network Enginr*
EMP: 5
SQ FT: 2,600

SALES: 300.4K **Privately Held**
SIC: 8711 3663 7379 7376 Consulting engineer; radio & TV communications equipment; computer related maintenance services; computer facilities management; custom computer programming services; computer integrated systems design

(G-3655)
FALCON PRINTING & GRAPHICS
339 W Main St (07728-2517)
PHONE..................................732 462-6862
Fax: 732 462-2184
William E Britland, *President*
Greg Pfremmer, *Vice Pres*
EMP: 5
SQ FT: 1,500
SALES (est): 697.3K **Privately Held**
WEB: www.falconprint.com
SIC: 2752 Commercial printing, offset

(G-3656)
FREEHOLD PNTIAC BICK GMC TRCKS
Also Called: Freehold Buick
4404 Us Highway 9 (07728-8311)
PHONE..................................732 462-7093
Fax: 732 303-5473
Robert Thugut, *President*
Nick Guarino, *General Mgr*
EMP: 58
SQ FT: 18,000
SALES (est): 12.7MM **Privately Held**
SIC: 5511 7532 7515 7538 Automobiles, new & used; body shop, automotive; passenger car leasing; general automotive repair shops; motor vehicle parts & accessories

(G-3657)
GENEXOSOME TECHNOLOGIES INC
4400 Route 9 N (07728-1383)
PHONE..................................646 762-4517
David Jin, *CEO*
Meng Li, *COO*
Luisa Ingargiola, *CFO*
EMP: 10
SALES (est): 165.6K
SALES (corp-wide): 1MM **Publicly Held**
SIC: 7372 Prepackaged software
PA: Avalon Globocare Corp.
4400 Route 9 N
Freehold NJ 07728
646 762-4517

(G-3658)
GORDON INTERNATIONAL INC
6 Paragon Way Ste 110 (07728-5925)
PHONE..................................732 431-3361
Peter Spaldaning, *President*
EMP: 11
SALES (est): 962.3K **Privately Held**
SIC: 2521 Chairs, office: padded, upholstered or plain: wood

(G-3659)
HOBBY PUBLICATIONS INC
Also Called: Picture Framing Magazine
83 South St Ste 307 (07728-2492)
PHONE..................................732 536-5160
Fax: 732 536-5761
David Gherman, *President*
Tammy Keck, *Publisher*
Patrick Sarver, *Editor*
Debbie Fintz, *Accountant*
Marlene Jaeger, *Accounts Mgr*
▲ EMP: 35
SQ FT: 4,800
SALES (est): 4.5MM **Privately Held**
WEB: www.hobbypub.com
SIC: 2721 Magazines: publishing only, not printed on site

(G-3660)
ICEBERG COFFEE LLC
865 Rte 33 Ste 4 (07728-8475)
PHONE..................................908 675-6972
Jeff Burkard,
Joe Burkard,
EMP: 4 EST: 2015
SALES (est): 127.4K **Privately Held**
SIC: 2086 Bottled & canned soft drinks

(G-3661)
IT SURPLUS LIQUIDATORS
179 South St Ste 1 (07728-2647)
PHONE..................................732 308-1935
Igor Gleyzer, *Principal*
EMP: 4
SALES (est): 501.5K **Privately Held**
SIC: 3679 Antennas, receiving

(G-3662)
JANICO INC
88 Industrial Ct (07728-8898)
PHONE..................................732 370-2223
Saul Siegman, *President*
▲ EMP: 10
SALES (est): 1.5MM **Privately Held**
SIC: 2392 3589 3089 Mops, floor & dust; janitors' carts; garbage containers, plastic

(G-3663)
JDM ENGINEERING INC
60 Jerseyville Ave (07728-2369)
PHONE..................................732 780-0770
Fax: 732 780-1715
James P D'Amore, *President*
Jim D'Amore, *Sales Staff*
EMP: 5
SALES (est): 742.1K **Privately Held**
WEB: www.teamjdm.com
SIC: 3462 Automotive & internal combustion engine forgings

(G-3664)
KOLE DESIGN LLC
35 Cedar Ct (07728-1589)
P.O. Box 6095 (07728-6095)
PHONE..................................732 409-0211
Fax: 732 409-7145
Lawrence Kolodny, *Owner*
Terry Kolodny,
EMP: 9
SALES (est): 800K **Privately Held**
SIC: 3911 Jewelry, precious metal

(G-3665)
LASER XPRESSIONS INC
3710 Us Highway 9 Fl 2 (07728-4801)
PHONE..................................732 303-9530
Fax: 732 303-9531
Aco Sokolovski, *President*
Constantine Spannos, *Vice Pres*
▲ EMP: 14
SQ FT: 2,000
SALES (est): 1.4MM **Privately Held**
WEB: www.laserxpressions.com
SIC: 2759 Laser printing

(G-3666)
LECTRO PRODUCTS INC
22 Francis Mills Rd (07728-7944)
PHONE..................................732 462-2463
Fax: 732 446-5851
Wolfgang Storch, *President*
Alfred Pound, *Treasurer*
Ann Pound, *Admin Sec*
EMP: 6 EST: 1958
SQ FT: 12,000
SALES (est): 500K **Privately Held**
SIC: 3444 Sheet metalwork

(G-3667)
LIGHTFIELD AMMUNITION CORP
912 State Route 33 (07728-8439)
P.O. Box 162, Adelphia (07710-0162)
PHONE..................................732 462-9200
Peter J Saker Jr, *Owner*
Lou Saker, *Co-Owner*
▲ EMP: 8
SALES (est): 2.5MM **Privately Held**
SIC: 3482 3483 Small arms ammunition; ammunition, except for small arms

(G-3668)
LIGHTFIELD LLR CORPORATION
912 State Route 33 (07728-8439)
P.O. Box 162, Adelphia (07710-0162)
PHONE..................................732 462-9200
Peter J Saker Jr, *President*
Louis J Saker, *Corp Secy*
EMP: 4
SALES (est): 270K **Privately Held**
SIC: 3842 Surgical appliances & supplies

GEOGRAPHIC

(G-3669)
LYMPHA PRESS USA
265 Willow Brook Rd # 4
PHONE.................................732 792-9677
Charlie Berhang, *Principal*
▲ EMP: 9
SALES (est): 647.9K **Privately Held**
SIC: 2741 Miscellaneous publishing

(G-3670)
MIKE DOLLY SCREEN PRINTING
17 Elm St (07728-2203)
PHONE.................................732 294-8979
Fax: 732 294-5599
Mike Dolly, *President*
EMP: 12 EST: 1993
SQ FT: 14,000
SALES: 2.5MM **Privately Held**
SIC: 2759 Commercial printing

(G-3671)
MONMOUTH BIOPRODUCTS LLC
918 State Route 33 Ste 3 (07728-8439)
PHONE.................................732 863-0300
Sean Duddy,
EMP: 5
SQ FT: 4,500
SALES (est): 842K **Privately Held**
SIC: 2836 Bacteriological media

(G-3672)
MOTORS AND DRIVES INC (PA)
Also Called: Best Electric Motor Co
5 Asbury Ave (07728-8111)
PHONE.................................732 462-7683
Gene Moir Jr, *Vice Pres*
EMP: 5
SQ FT: 3,000
SALES (est): 1.5MM **Privately Held**
WEB: www.motorsanddrives.com
SIC: 7694 Electric motor repair

(G-3673)
NESTLE USA INC
Also Called: Nestle Beverage Division
61 Jerseyville Ave (07728-2328)
PHONE.................................732 462-1300
Jean-Marc Garnier, *Branch Mgr*
EMP: 200
SALES (corp-wide): 90.8B **Privately Held**
WEB: www.nestleusa.com
SIC: 2095 2099 Roasted coffee; food preparations
HQ: Nestle Usa, Inc.
    1812 N Moore St
    Rosslyn VA 22209
    818 549-6000

(G-3674)
OLD MONMOUTH PEANUT BRITTLE CO
Also Called: Old Monmouth Candy Co
627 Park Ave (07728-2351)
PHONE.................................732 462-1311
Fax: 732 462-6820
Harold Gunther, *President*
Susan Gunther, *Vice Pres*
David Gunther, *Manager*
EMP: 5 EST: 1939
SQ FT: 22,000
SALES (est): 517.6K **Privately Held**
WEB: www.oldmonmouthcandies.com
SIC: 2064 5441 Candy & other confectionery products; confectionery

(G-3675)
ONE SOURCE SOLUTIONS LLC
3 Industrial Ct Ste 3 # 3 (07728-9553)
PHONE.................................732 536-0578
Fax: 732 536-1347
Tim O Hanley,
John Ford,
EMP: 10
SQ FT: 1,700
SALES (est): 1.3MM **Privately Held**
WEB: www.onesourcesolution.com
SIC: 7372 Business oriented computer software

(G-3676)
OXFORD LAMP INC
Also Called: Oxford Lighting Co
17 Bannard St Ste 30 (07728-1686)
PHONE.................................732 462-3755

Sy Janowsky, *President*
Carol Janowsky, *Vice Pres*
EMP: 12
SALES (est): 1.6MM **Privately Held**
SIC: 3641 Electric lamp (bulb) parts

(G-3677)
PLANET POPCORN LLC
Freehold Mall (07728)
PHONE.................................732 294-8680
EMP: 8
SQ FT: 200
SALES: 150K **Privately Held**
SIC: 2096 Mfg Potato Chips/Snacks

(G-3678)
POLY SOURCE ENTERPRISES LLC
17 Duchess Ct (07728-7758)
PHONE.................................732 580-5409
Robert Macdougall,
EMP: 4
SALES (est): 187.2K **Privately Held**
SIC: 3089 Extruded finished plastic products

(G-3679)
POSTAGE BIN
31 E Main St Ste 4 (07728-2286)
PHONE.................................732 333-0915
Marc G Cooper, *Principal*
EMP: 8
SALES (est): 864.6K **Privately Held**
SIC: 3444 Mail (post office) collection or storage boxes, sheet metal

(G-3680)
PRECISION FILAMENTS INC
17 Bannard St Ste 30 (07728-1686)
PHONE.................................732 462-3755
Fax: 732 462-3758
Robert McLean, *President*
EMP: 7 EST: 1955
SQ FT: 12,500
SALES (est): 590K **Privately Held**
SIC: 3641 Electric lamps & parts for generalized applications; filaments, for electric lamps

(G-3681)
PREMIER MARBLE AND GRAN 2 INC
Also Called: Pg Marble
200 Commerce Ave Ste 200 # 200 (07728-9379)
PHONE.................................732 294-7891
Umit Kellegoz, *President*
Ayhan Sahin, *Vice Pres*
EMP: 4
SQ FT: 12,000
SALES (est): 492.3K **Privately Held**
SIC: 3281 Marble, building: cut & shaped; granite, cut & shaped

(G-3682)
PRESTONE PRODUCTS CORPORATION
Also Called: Kik Custom Products
250 Halls Mill Rd (07728-8832)
PHONE.................................732 577-7800
Thomas Hines, *Manager*
Tom Hines, *Manager*
EMP: 40
SQ FT: 5,000
SALES (corp-wide): 990.7K **Privately Held**
WEB: www.honeywell.com
SIC: 2899 Antifreeze compounds
HQ: Prestone Products Corporation
    1900 W Field Ct
    Lake Forest IL 60045

(G-3683)
PRINCETON SEPARATIONS INC
100 Commerce Ave (07728-9380)
P.O. Box 296, Adelphia (07710-0296)
PHONE.................................732 431-3338
Fax: 732 431-3768
Paul Nix, *President*
Stuart Levinson, *President*
Kiran Desai, *Mfg Dir*
Regina Hatton, *Finance Mgr*
Wilma Crescente, *Manager*
EMP: 20
SQ FT: 12,000

SALES (est): 4.1MM **Privately Held**
WEB: www.prinsep.com
SIC: 3826 Blood testing apparatus

(G-3684)
QUIET TONE INC
12 Vine St (07728-1620)
PHONE.................................732 431-2826
David Loendorf, *President*
Karen Friberg, *Education*
EMP: 5
SALES (est): 330K **Privately Held**
SIC: 3161 Luggage

(G-3685)
RAPTOR RESOURCES HOLDINGS INC (PA)
41 Howe Ln (07728-3336)
PHONE.................................732 252-5146
Stan Baron, *President*
Craig Gimbel, *Vice Pres*
EMP: 6
SALES (est): 787.5K **Publicly Held**
SIC: 3843 Dental equipment & supplies

(G-3686)
ROTTA PHARMACEUTICALS INC
86 W Main St (07728-2134)
PHONE.................................732 751-9020
Fax: 732 544-4085
John Barone, *President*
EMP: 5
SALES (est): 376.2K **Privately Held**
WEB: www.rottapharmaceuticals.com
SIC: 2834 Pharmaceutical preparations

(G-3687)
SCHER FABRICS INC
18 Duncan Way (07728-4350)
PHONE.................................212 382-2266
▲ EMP: 17 EST: 1923
SQ FT: 12,000
SALES: 2MM **Privately Held**
SIC: 5131 2396 Whol Piece Goods/Notions Mfg Auto/Apparel Trimming

(G-3688)
SHORE POINT DISTRG CO INC
100 Shore Point Dr (07728-8568)
PHONE.................................732 308-3334
James Annarella, *President*
Chip Thompson, *Regional Mgr*
Joanne Augustine, *Inv Control Mgr*
John Macrae, *CFO*
William Gutierrez, *Controller*
▲ EMP: 120
SQ FT: 100,000
SALES (est): 21.8MM **Privately Held**
WEB: www.njcoors.com
SIC: 2082 Beer (alcoholic beverage)

(G-3689)
TAG MINERALS INC
41 Howe Ln (07728-3336)
PHONE.................................732 252-5146
Al Pietrangelo, *President*
EMP: 4
SALES (est): 175.7K **Publicly Held**
SIC: 1481 Mine exploration, nonmetallic minerals
PA: Raptor Resources Holdings Inc.
    41 Howe Ln
    Freehold NJ 07728

(G-3690)
US PROPACK INC
341 Fairfield Rd (07728-7829)
P.O. Box 298, Adelphia (07710-0298)
PHONE.................................732 294-4500
Fax: 732 294-4501
Stephen Miller, *President*
Mary Jane Esposito, *Manager*
▲ EMP: 6
SQ FT: 12,500
SALES (est): 1.2MM **Privately Held**
WEB: www.uspropack.com
SIC: 3086 3993 5199 Packaging & shipping materials, foamed plastic; signs & advertising specialties; packaging materials

(G-3691)
VIDEONET COMM GROUP LLC
7 Seaman Rd (07728-8583)
PHONE.................................732 863-5310
Dave Sellick, *Owner*

EMP: 12
SALES (est): 1MM **Privately Held**
WEB: www.bigbandnet.com
SIC: 3663 Digital encoders

(G-3692)
W & E BAUM BRONZE TABLET CORP
Also Called: Baum, W & E
89 Bannard St (07728-1607)
PHONE.................................732 866-1881
Richard Baum, *President*
Heidi King, *Vice Pres*
Maurice Zagha, *Vice Pres*
Lane King, *Prdtn Mgr*
Anna Paczedlik, *Bookkeeper*
EMP: 23 EST: 1920
SQ FT: 15,000
SALES (est): 4.9MM **Privately Held**
WEB: www.webaum.com
SIC: 3364 3479 Brass & bronze die-castings; etching & engraving

(G-3693)
WINGOLD EMBROIDERY LLC
5 Monarch Ln (07728-8577)
PHONE.................................732 845-9802
EMP: 3
SQ FT: 5,500
SALES: 1.5MM **Privately Held**
SIC: 2241 Mfg Lace & Embroidery

(G-3694)
WOODHUT LLC
210 Jerseyville Ave (07728-2329)
PHONE.................................732 414-6440
Merrill Hassell,
EMP: 10
SQ FT: 700
SALES: 1.6MM **Privately Held**
SIC: 2435 Hardwood veneer & plywood

(G-3695)
WYNNPHARM INC
86 W Main St (07728-2134)
PHONE.................................732 409-1005
John Barone, *President*
Mariella Scardino, *Vice Pres*
Giuseppe Barone, *Marketing Staff*
EMP: 7
SALES (est): 4.5MM **Privately Held**
SIC: 2834 Pharmaceutical preparations

Frenchtown
Hunterdon County

(G-3696)
ARCHITECTURAL WDWKG ASSOC
4 7th St (08825-1146)
PHONE.................................908 996-7866
Fax: 908 996-7933
John Gehman, *Partner*
Matthias Ritzmann, *Partner*
Patrick Hagerty, *Opers Mgr*
EMP: 7
SQ FT: 12,000
SALES (est): 550K **Privately Held**
SIC: 2431 2499 Woodwork, interior & ornamental; decorative wood & woodwork

(G-3697)
BLUE FISH CLOTHING INC
62 Trenton Ave Frnt Frnt (08825-1256)
PHONE.................................908 996-3720
Fax: 908 996-7095
Jennifer Barclay, *Co-COB*
EMP: 155
SQ FT: 18,000
SALES (est): 17.8MM **Privately Held**
SIC: 2339 2369 5621 Women's & misses' outerwear; girls' & children's outerwear; women's clothing stores

(G-3698)
CARAUSTAR INDUSTRIES INC
Also Called: Frenchtown Partition Plant
869 State Route 12 (08825-4223)
PHONE.................................908 782-0505
Alan Sochats, *Manager*
EMP: 50

▲ = Import ▼=Export
◆ =Import/Export

SALES (corp-wide): 1.5B **Privately Held**
WEB: www.caraustar.com
SIC: 2631 Paperboard mills
PA: Caraustar Industries, Inc.
5000 Astell Pwdr Sprng Rd
Austell GA 30106
770 948-3101

(G-3699)
CERBACO LTD
809 Harrison St (08825-1122)
PHONE..................908 996-1333
Fax: 908 996-0023
Alan Flash, *President*
Keith McClean, *Vice Pres*
Michelle Flash, *Treasurer*
EMP: 35
SQ FT: 10,000
SALES: 1.9MM **Privately Held**
WEB: www.cerbaco.com
SIC: 3599 3548 3496 Machine shop, job-bing & repair; welding apparatus; miscellaneous fabricated wire products

(G-3700)
F & R GRINDING INC
138 County Road 513 (08825-3732)
PHONE..................908 996-0440
Ronald Nicolato, *President*
Peter Nicolato, *Vice Pres*
EMP: 15
SQ FT: 5,000
SALES (est): 2.4MM **Privately Held**
SIC: 3545 3452 Machine tool accessories; bolts, nuts, rivets & washers

(G-3701)
HUNTERDON COUNTY DEMOCRAT INC
Also Called: Delaware Valley News
207 Harrison St (08825-1110)
PHONE..................908 996-4047
Fax: 908 996-2238
Betty Crouse, *Branch Mgr*
EMP: 4
SALES (corp-wide): 4.9MM **Privately Held**
WEB: www.hcdems.com
SIC: 2711 Newspapers, publishing & print-ing
PA: Hunterdon County Democrat Inc
200 State Route 31 # 202
Flemington NJ 08822
908 782-4747

(G-3702)
INSTRUMENT SCIENCES & TECH
1131 State Route 12 (08825-4160)
PHONE..................908 996-9920
Thomas Mitchell, *President*
James Sheridan, *Corp Secy*
EMP: 70
SQ FT: 10,000
SALES: 7.4MM **Privately Held**
WEB: www.instrumentsciencesandtech-nologies.com
SIC: 3829 Geophysical & meteorological testing equipment

(G-3703)
LONGVIEW COFFEE CO NJ INC
Also Called: Longview Coffee Company
843 State Route 12 B10 (08825-4233)
P.O. Box 538, Stockton (08559-0538)
PHONE..................908 788-4186
Andrew Esserman, *President*
Margaret Esserman, *Vice Pres*
EMP: 25
SQ FT: 10,000
SALES: 5.5MM **Privately Held**
SIC: 2099 2095 Tea blending; roasted cof-fee

(G-3704)
MV LABORATORIES INC (PA)
843 State Route 12 B17 (08825-4234)
PHONE..................908 788-6906
Fax: 908 996-6697
Warren Miller, *President*
Phillip Blacher, *Vice Pres*
EMP: 5
SQ FT: 6,000
SALES (est): 688.3K **Privately Held**
WEB: www.mvlaboratories.com
SIC: 3399 Metal powders, pastes & flakes

(G-3705)
ROSTEK INNOVATIONS LLC
2 7th St (08825-1146)
PHONE..................908 996-6007
Edward Jozowski, *Principal*
EMP: 4
SALES: 800K **Privately Held**
SIC: 4731 3469 Agents, shipping; furniture components, porcelain enameled

(G-3706)
RTS PACKAGING LLC
869 State Hwy 12 (08825)
PHONE..................908 782-0505
Greg Lawrence, *Manager*
EMP: 70
SALES (corp-wide): 14.8B **Publicly Held**
WEB: www.rtspackaging.com
SIC: 2653 Corrugated & solid fiber boxes
HQ: Rts Packaging, Llc
504 Thrasher St
Norcross GA 30071
800 558-6984

(G-3707)
ZERO SURGE INC
889 State Route 12 Ste 2 (08825-4223)
PHONE..................908 996-7700
Fax: 908 996-7773
James Minadeo, *President*
Brian Warner, *Engineer*
Deborah Peru, *Admin Sec*
◆ **EMP:** 11
SQ FT: 4,000
SALES: 1.9MM **Privately Held**
WEB: www.zerosurge.com
SIC: 3612 Voltage regulators, transmission & distribution

Galloway
Atlantic County

(G-3708)
ALLEGRO PRINTING CORPORATION
Also Called: Express Press
408 S 4th Ave (08205-9501)
PHONE..................609 641-7060
Fax: 609 383-0340
Richard H Lamkin, *President*
Ruth Lamkin, *Corp Secy*
David Lore, *Vice Pres*
EMP: 5 **EST:** 1977
SQ FT: 1,500
SALES (est): 560.8K **Privately Held**
WEB: www.expresspressnj.com
SIC: 2759 2791 2789 2752 Letterpress printing; typesetting; bookbinding & re-lated work; commercial printing, litho-graphic

(G-3709)
B T PARTNERS INC
3 N New York Rd Ste 23 (08205-3037)
PHONE..................609 652-6511
Robert Koch, *President*
EMP: 4
SALES (est): 317.3K **Privately Held**
SIC: 2392 Placemats, plastic or textile

(G-3710)
CASINO PLAYER PUBLISHING LLC
333 E Jimmie Leeds Rd # 7 (08205-4123)
PHONE..................609 404-0600
Derek James, *CFO*
Glenn Fine, *Mng Member*
Adam Fine
EMP: 32
SQ FT: 6,100
SALES (est): 3.9MM **Privately Held**
WEB: www.casinocenter.com
SIC: 2721 Magazines: publishing only, not printed on site

(G-3711)
GREATER ATL CY GOLF ASSN LLC
Also Called: Seaview Golf Resort
401 S New York Rd (08205-9753)
PHONE..................609 652-1800
Brian Rashley, *Principal*

EMP: 13
SALES (est): 1.2MM **Privately Held**
SIC: 3949 Golf equipment

(G-3712)
INFRASTRUCTURE LLC
124 Old Port Republic Rd (08205-9607)
PHONE..................609 748-1229
Christine Jordan, *Mng Member*
EMP: 5
SALES: 1.4MM **Privately Held**
SIC: 3531 1629 Graders, road (construc-tion machinery); drainage system con-struction

Garfield
Bergen County

(G-3713)
ABCO TOOL & MACHINE CORP
2 Elm St (07026-3804)
PHONE..................973 772-8160
Fax: 973 772-1455
Dominick Riccelli, *President*
EMP: 9 **EST:** 1944
SQ FT: 3,500
SALES (est): 946.7K **Privately Held**
SIC: 3599 Machine shop, jobbing & repair

(G-3714)
ACE FINE ART INC
141 Lanza Ave Bldg 3d (07026-3533)
PHONE..................201 960-4447
Dong H Jo, *Owner*
▲ **EMP:** 2
SALES: 1MM **Privately Held**
SIC: 3231 Stained glass: made from pur-chased glass

(G-3715)
ACON WATCH CROWN COMPANY
260 Division Ave (07026-2521)
P.O. Box 800 (07026-0800)
PHONE..................973 546-8585
Fax: 973 478-4067
Arnold Cohen, *Owner*
▲ **EMP:** 11 **EST:** 1935
SQ FT: 4,000
SALES: 550K **Privately Held**
SIC: 3873 3423 Watches & parts, except crystals & jewels; jewelers' hand tools

(G-3716)
ALGENE MARKING EQUIPMENT CO
232 Palisade Ave (07026-2998)
PHONE..................973 478-9041
Fax: 973 478-7644
Gary Mann, *President*
Milton Mann, *Vice Pres*
EMP: 5 **EST:** 1946
SQ FT: 5,000
SALES: 1MM **Privately Held**
SIC: 3555 3952 3544 Printing trades ma-chinery; ink, drawing: black & colored; special dies & tools

(G-3717)
ANATECH MICROWAVE COMPANY INC
70 Outwater Ln Ste 3 (07026-3854)
PHONE..................973 772-7369
Sam Benzacar, *President*
EMP: 5
SALES: 950K **Privately Held**
SIC: 3663 Radio & TV communications equipment

(G-3718)
ARTIC ICE MANUFACTURING CO
158 Semel Ave (07026-3743)
PHONE..................973 772-7000
Fax: 973 772-7675
John Minechetti, *President*
Steven Lengel, *Co-Owner*
Gerri Minichetti, *Manager*
Rose Marie Minichetti, *Admin Sec*
EMP: 5 **EST:** 1950
SQ FT: 5,000

SALES (est): 637.5K **Privately Held**
WEB: www.articiceco.com
SIC: 2097 5169 Block ice; ice cubes; dry ice

(G-3719)
ARTISTIC RAILINGS INC (PA)
500 River Dr (07026-3220)
P.O. Box 110, Pottersville (07979-0110)
PHONE..................973 772-8540
Fax: 973 772-4395
Thomas Zuzik, *President*
Elaine Zuzik, *Vice Pres*
Paul Zuzik, *Vice Pres*
Thomas Zuzik Jr, *Vice Pres*
EMP: 7
SQ FT: 7,600
SALES (est): 959.2K **Privately Held**
WEB: www.artisticrail.com
SIC: 3446 Railings, bannisters, guards, etc.: made from metal pipe

(G-3720)
ATEKSIS USA CORP
141 Lanza Ave (07026-3538)
PHONE..................201 340-2655
Mehmet Kis, *CEO*
EMP: 6
SALES (est): 1.2MM
SALES (corp-wide): 2.7MM **Privately Held**
SIC: 3674 Integrated circuits, semiconduc-tor networks, etc.
HQ: Ateksis Usa Corp
1 Meadowlands Plz Ste 200
East Rutherford NJ 07073
646 508-9074

(G-3721)
BANKERS PEN INC
Also Called: Bankers Line, The
141 Lanza Ave Bldg 12 (07026-3530)
PHONE..................800 499-7367
Richard Danzinger, *President*
EMP: 30
SQ FT: 18,000
SALES (est): 3.4MM **Privately Held**
WEB: www.bankerspens.com
SIC: 2759 3993 Advertising specialties; coin rollers, plastics

(G-3722)
BAR-MAID CORPORATION
362 Midland Ave Ste 2 (07026-1736)
PHONE..................973 478-7070
Fax: 973 478-2106
George Steele, *President*
▲ **EMP:** 150
SQ FT: 2,000
SALES (est): 5.8MM **Privately Held**
WEB: www.bar-maid.com
SIC: 5078 5044 3632 Refrigeration equip-ment & supplies; vaults & safes; house-hold refrigerators & freezers

(G-3723)
BELMONT WHL FENCE MFG INC
112 Monroe St (07026-2913)
PHONE..................973 472-5121
Fax: 973 472-9260
Aldo Sibeni, *President*
Lucille Marino Harvey, *Vice Pres*
Maria Elena Ponterio, *Treasurer*
EMP: 25
SQ FT: 18,000
SALES (est): 5.4MM **Privately Held**
SIC: 3315 3496 Chain link fencing; miscel-laneous fabricated wire products

(G-3724)
BRIMAR INDUSTRIES INC
Also Called: Safetysign.com
64 Outwater Ln Ste 2 (07026-3845)
PHONE..................973 340-7889
Fax: 973 340-7809
Brian D Costello, *President*
Gianni Gallorini, *General Mgr*
Kevin McColl, *Accounts Exec*
Joseph Saia, *Sales Staff*
Jason Hodulik, *Chief Mktg Ofcr*
EMP: 50
SQ FT: 90,000
SALES (est): 9.7MM **Privately Held**
WEB: www.brimar-online.com
SIC: 2759 Labels & seals: printing

(G-3725)
CALORIC COLOR CO INC
176 Saddle River Rd A (07026)
PHONE.................................973 471-4748
Fax: 973 471-4748
June Anton, *President*
Connie Sink, *Vice Pres*
Linda Craner, *Admin Sec*
EMP: 10 EST: 1963
SQ FT: 7,800
SALES (est): 1.8MM **Privately Held**
SIC: 2899 3081 Ink or writing fluids; plastic film & sheet

(G-3726)
CLEAR PLUS WINDSHIELD WIPERS
Also Called: Advantage Asia
100 Outwater Ln (07026-2647)
PHONE.................................973 546-8800
Rej Chawla, *Owner*
▲ EMP: 10
SQ FT: 10,000
SALES (est): 720K **Privately Held**
WEB: www.clearplus.com
SIC: 3714 Windshield frames, motor vehicle

(G-3727)
COSMETIC CONCEPTS INC
20 Chestnut St (07026-2820)
PHONE.................................973 546-1234
Fax: 973 546-0387
Atul Desai, *President*
▲ EMP: 150
SQ FT: 25,000
SALES (est): 20.7MM **Privately Held**
SIC: 2844 Cosmetic preparations

(G-3728)
DAS INSTALLATIONS INC
176 Saddle River Rd D (07026)
PHONE.................................973 473-6858
Fax: 973 473-2626
Louis Skvarca, *President*
EMP: 11
SALES: 800K **Privately Held**
SIC: 3535 5084 Conveyors & conveying equipment; conveyor systems

(G-3729)
DENTAL MODELS & DESIGNS INC
Also Called: Dental Designs
20 Passaic St Ste 3 (07026-3151)
PHONE.................................973 472-8009
Fax: 973 472-8011
David Lauchheimer, *President*
Sheryl Lauchheimer, *Treasurer*
EMP: 4
SQ FT: 1,500
SALES (est): 478.1K **Privately Held**
WEB: www.dentalmodelsanddesigns.com
SIC: 3843 Teeth, artificial (not made in dental laboratories)

(G-3730)
DIRECT SALES AND SERVICES INC
Also Called: Aunt Gussies Cookies Crackers
141 Lanza Ave Bldg 8 (07026-3533)
PHONE.................................973 340-4480
Marilyn Caine, *CEO*
David Caine, *Ch of Bd*
EMP: 25
SQ FT: 15,000
SALES (est): 5.3MM **Privately Held**
WEB: www.auntgussies.com
SIC: 2052 Cookies & crackers

(G-3731)
E C ELECTROPLATING INC
125 Clark St (07026-1799)
PHONE.................................973 340-0227
Fax: 973 340-0672
Mary Pettit, *Ch of Bd*
James E Calderio, *President*
Anthony Calderio, *Vice Pres*
Theresa Cusmano, *Admin Sec*
EMP: 25
SQ FT: 28,000
SALES (est): 2.9MM **Privately Held**
SIC: 3471 3312 Electroplating of metals or formed products; blast furnaces & steel mills

(G-3732)
ECLIPSE MANUFACTURING LLC
438 Lanza Ave (07026-2004)
PHONE.................................973 340-9939
Ziggy Nieradka, *President*
EMP: 4
SQ FT: 4,000
SALES (est): 600K **Privately Held**
SIC: 3469 Machine parts, stamped or pressed metal

(G-3733)
FLUID COATING SYSTEMS INC
13 Barthold St (07026-2708)
PHONE.................................973 767-1028
Janusz Styga, *President*
EMP: 5
SQ FT: 3,600
SALES: 760K **Privately Held**
SIC: 3999 5033 Sprays, artificial & preserved; insulation materials

(G-3734)
FLUID FILTRATION CORP
102 Van Winkle Ave (07026-2940)
PHONE.................................973 253-7070
Fax: 973 253-0070
Farzad Alborzi, *President*
EMP: 10
SQ FT: 5,000
SALES (est): 1.7MM **Privately Held**
WEB: www.fluidfiltr.com
SIC: 3599 Gasoline filters, internal combustion engine, except auto; oil filters, internal combustion engine, except automotive

(G-3735)
FRAGALES BAKERY INC
6874 Gaston Ave (07026)
PHONE.................................973 546-0327
Andrew Fragale, *President*
EMP: 15
SQ FT: 7,500
SALES (est): 1.7MM **Privately Held**
SIC: 2051 Bread, all types (white, wheat, rye, etc): fresh or frozen

(G-3736)
GEMINI PLASTIC FILMS CORP
535 Midland Ave (07026-1658)
P.O. Box 360 (07026-0360)
PHONE.................................973 340-0700
Fax: 973 340-1045
Andrew Del Presto, *President*
Richard Hulbert, *Vice Pres*
EMP: 40 EST: 1971
SQ FT: 31,000
SALES (est): 7.9MM **Privately Held**
SIC: 2673 3081 Bags: plastic, laminated & coated; polyethylene film

(G-3737)
GENEVIEVES INC
Also Called: Genevieves Home Made Candy Sp
174 Ray St (07026-3670)
PHONE.................................973 772-8816
David Dzwilewski, *President*
Anne Dzwilewski, *Admin Sec*
EMP: 12 EST: 1944
SQ FT: 3,000
SALES (est): 1.6MM **Privately Held**
WEB: www.genevieves.com
SIC: 2066 2064 5961 5441 Chocolate candy, solid; chocolate candy, except solid chocolate; food, mail order; candy; confectionery; gift shop; greeting cards

(G-3738)
GREEN APPLE HOME IMPRV LLC
96 Belmont Ave Apt 2 (07026-2837)
PHONE.................................201 300-5554
Amro Alaeddin, *Principal*
EMP: 5
SALES (est): 577.5K **Privately Held**
SIC: 3571 Personal computers (microcomputers)

(G-3739)
INTERNATIONAL CRYSTAL LABS (PA)
Also Called: Lens Savers Division
11 Erie St Ste 2 (07026-2302)
PHONE.................................973 478-8944
Fax: 973 478-4201
Robert D Herpst, *Ch of Bd*
Theresa Herpst, *President*
Irene Ascuitto, *Vice Pres*
Vladimir Yakimovich, *Vice Pres*
Steven Hanst, *Executive*
◆ EMP: 25 EST: 1962
SQ FT: 9,500
SALES: 3.8MM **Privately Held**
WEB: www.lenssavers.com
SIC: 3827 Optical elements & assemblies, except ophthalmic

(G-3740)
J GENNARO TRUCKING
13 Garfield Pl (07026-1901)
P.O. Box 215, Lodi (07644-0215)
PHONE.................................973 773-0805
Angelo Annuzzi, *President*
Dominick Annuzzi, *Treasurer*
Delores Annuzzi, *Admin Sec*
EMP: 15
SQ FT: 3,500
SALES: 1.6MM **Privately Held**
SIC: 4959 1794 1442 Snowplowing; excavation & grading, building construction; construction sand & gravel

(G-3741)
KOHOUTS BAKERY
75 Jewell St Fl 1 (07026-3749)
PHONE.................................973 772-7270
Charles Kohout Jr, *Owner*
EMP: 4
SQ FT: 1,000
SALES: 750K **Privately Held**
SIC: 2051 5461 5411 Bakery: wholesale or wholesale/retail combined; bread; grocery stores, independent; delicatessens

(G-3742)
LATIN PERCUSSION INC (DH)
Also Called: L P Music Group
160 Belmont Ave Ste 1 (07026-2394)
PHONE.................................973 478-6903
Fax: 973 772-3568
Martin Cohen, *Ch of Bd*
David McAllister, *President*
Barry Granet, *COO*
Marilyn Cohen, *Exec VP*
Wayne Cohen, *Exec VP*
▲ EMP: 50 EST: 1970
SQ FT: 23,000
SALES (est): 14.6MM
SALES (corp-wide): 816.3MM **Privately Held**
WEB: www.lpmusic.com
SIC: 5099 3931 Musical instruments; percussion instruments & parts
HQ: Rokr Distribution Us, Inc.
　310 W Newberry Rd
　Bloomfield CT 06002
　860 509-8888

(G-3743)
NORTH AMERICAN ILLUMINATION
Also Called: American Lighting
79 Commerce Ave Ste 2 (07026-1853)
PHONE.................................973 478-4700
Alfred Binder, *President*
Geoffrey Binder, *Vice Pres*
Paul Binder, *Treasurer*
▲ EMP: 18 EST: 1961
SQ FT: 14,000
SALES (est): 3.3MM **Privately Held**
SIC: 3646 Commercial indusl & institutional electric lighting fixtures

(G-3744)
PALMER ELECTRONICS INC
Also Called: Palmer Industries Div
156 Belmont Ave (07026-2395)
PHONE.................................973 772-5900
Fax: 973 772-6054
Victor R Palmeri, *President*
Olga Palmeri, *Admin Sec*
▲ EMP: 16 EST: 1962
SQ FT: 8,000
SALES: 700K **Privately Held**
WEB: www.palmer-electronics.com
SIC: 3829 3569 3823 Temperature sensors, except industrial process & aircraft; assembly machines, non-metalworking; industrial instrmnts msrmnt display/control process variable

(G-3745)
PAN GRAPHICS INC
45 Hartmann Ave (07026-2299)
PHONE.................................973 478-2100
Fax: 973 478-1481
Bruce Leskanic, *Vice Pres*
EMP: 65 EST: 1962
SALES (est): 4.3MM **Privately Held**
SIC: 2796 Engraving platemaking services

(G-3746)
PAVAN & KIEVIT ENTERPRISES
Also Called: Uehling Instrument Company
113 Dewitt St Ste 210 (07026-2755)
PHONE.................................973 546-4615
Richard Pavan Jr, *President*
John Kievit, *Vice Pres*
EMP: 25
SQ FT: 6,200
SALES (est): 3.9MM **Privately Held**
WEB: www.uehling.com
SIC: 3823 5084 Industrial instrmnts msrmnt display/control process variable; industrial machinery & equipment

(G-3747)
PENTA GLASS INDUSTRIES INC
71 Hepworth Pl (07026-1817)
PHONE.................................973 478-2110
Jim Huddleston, *President*
EMP: 8
SQ FT: 3,200
SALES (est): 940K **Privately Held**
SIC: 1793 3231 Glass & glazing work; products of purchased glass; mirrored glass; glass sheet, bent: made from purchased glass

(G-3748)
PERSONLZED EXPRSSONS BY AUDREY
63 Harrison Ave (07026-1501)
PHONE.................................973 478-5115
Audrey Singer, *President*
Craig Singer, *Vice Pres*
Irwin Singer, *Vice Pres*
▲ EMP: 11
SQ FT: 4,000
SALES: 900K **Privately Held**
WEB: www.personalizedexpressionsbyaudrey.com
SIC: 3231 Art glass: made from purchased glass

(G-3749)
POLO MACHINE INC
223 Banta Ave (07026-3632)
P.O. Box 403 (07026-0403)
PHONE.................................973 340-9984
John Pszpnizzny, *President*
EMP: 4
SALES (est): 370K **Privately Held**
SIC: 3599 Machine shop, jobbing & repair

(G-3750)
PRIMEX COLOR COMPOUNDING (DH)
Also Called: O'Neil Color Compounding Corp
61 River Dr (07026-3145)
PHONE.................................800 282-7933
Fax: 973 777-9886
Mark Bruner, *President*
Paul Dechard, *COO*
Bob R Anthony, *Plant Mgr*
Robert Hillyer, *Opers Mgr*
Guy Millard, *Maint Spvr*
EMP: 50 EST: 1955
SALES (est): 31MM
SALES (corp-wide): 1.1B **Privately Held**
WEB: www.oneilcolor.com
SIC: 2865 Dyes & pigments
HQ: Primex Plastics Corporation
　1235 N F St
　Richmond IN 47374
　765 966-7774

(G-3751)
PRIMEX PLASTICS CORPORATION
65 River Dr (07026-3196)
PHONE...................973 470-8000
Fax: 973 470-8728
Juan Choy, *Project Mgr*
Cecibel Quinones, *Human Res Mgr*
Aaron Putnam, *Branch Mgr*
Fernando Barboto, *Manager*
EMP: 110
SALES (corp-wide): 1.1B **Privately Held**
WEB: www.primexplastics.com
SIC: 3081 Plastic film & sheet
HQ: Primex Plastics Corporation
1235 N F St
Richmond IN 47374
765 966-7774

(G-3752)
PRODO-PAK CORP
130 Monroe St (07026-1826)
PHONE...................973 772-4500
EMP: 4
SALES (est): 435.1K **Privately Held**
SIC: 3565 Packaging machinery

(G-3753)
PRODO-PAK CORPORATION
77 Commerce St (07026-1811)
P.O. Box 363 (07026-0363)
PHONE...................973 777-7770
Fax: 973 772-0471
John Mueller, *President*
Ralph Isler, *Plant Mgr*
▲ EMP: 20
SQ FT: 20,000
SALES (est): 5.7MM **Privately Held**
WEB: www.prodo-pak.com
SIC: 3565 Packaging machinery

(G-3754)
PRODUCT IDENTIFICATION CO INC
141 Lanza Ave Bldg 19 (07026-3530)
PHONE...................973 227-7770
Les Weinstock, *President*
Jeff Weinstock, *General Mgr*
Arlene Weinstock, *Corp Secy*
Rich Carlisle, *Plant Mgr*
Dante Cuoco, *Manager*
EMP: 17 EST: 1964
SQ FT: 2,700
SALES: 72.1K **Privately Held**
SIC: 2752 2759 Decals, lithographed; labels & seals: printing

(G-3755)
QUALITY SOLID SURFACE INC
333 Vreeland Ave (07026)
PHONE...................973 772-8600
Fax: 973 357-9773
Offer Bok, *President*
EMP: 7
SQ FT: 3,500
SALES (est): 720.5K **Privately Held**
SIC: 2541 Counter & sink tops

(G-3756)
RICKS CLEANOUTS INC
654 River Dr (07026-3822)
PHONE...................973 340-7454
Rifat Ferhatovic, *President*
EMP: 30
SALES (est): 5.7MM **Privately Held**
WEB: www.rickscleanouts.com
SIC: 2851 Removers & cleaners

(G-3757)
ROYAL SLIDE SALES CO INC (PA)
42 Hepworth Pl (07026-3039)
PHONE...................973 777-1177
Fax: 973 777-1443
Abraham Levine, *Vice Pres*
▲ EMP: 8 EST: 1947
SQ FT: 40,000
SALES (est): 1.8MM **Privately Held**
SIC: 3965 5131 5199 Zipper; zippers; bags, baskets & cases

(G-3758)
ROYAL ZIPPER MANUFG COMPANY
Also Called: Royal Slide Sales
42 Hepworth Pl (07026-3039)
PHONE...................973 777-1177
Abraham Levine, *Vice Pres*
Lewis Neuman, *Vice Pres*
EMP: 13
SQ FT: 30,000
SALES (est): 895.7K
SALES (corp-wide): 1.8MM **Privately Held**
SIC: 3965 Zipper
PA: Royal Slide Sales Co Inc
42 Hepworth Pl
Garfield NJ 07026
973 777-1177

(G-3759)
RPL SUPPLIES INC
Also Called: R P L
141 Lanza Ave Bldg 3a (07026-3533)
PHONE...................973 767-0880
Larry Milazzo, *President*
Henry Fishman, *Vice Pres*
Ken Baitala, *Technology*
◆ EMP: 18
SQ FT: 17,000
SALES (est): 3.3MM **Privately Held**
WEB: www.rplsupplies.com
SIC: 3861 5699 5947 Photographic equipment & supplies; customized clothing & apparel; novelties

(G-3760)
S & M PRESS INC
169 Semel Ave Ste 2 (07026-2582)
P.O. Box 296 (07026-0296)
PHONE...................973 546-6111
Fax: 973 778-3609
Marc Elving, *President*
Eileen Vaughan, *Vice Pres*
Kelly Brown, *Manager*
EMP: 10
SQ FT: 6,000
SALES (est): 1MM **Privately Held**
SIC: 2759 2791 2789 2752 Commercial printing; typesetting; bookbinding & related work; commercial printing, lithographic

(G-3761)
SHARP IMPRESSIONS INC
163 Belmont Ave Ste 1 (07026-2336)
PHONE...................201 573-4943
Fax: 201 488-5750
Thomas G Difiore, *President*
Arlene J Difiore, *Treasurer*
EMP: 4
SQ FT: 3,000
SALES (est): 200K **Privately Held**
SIC: 2759 Invitation & stationery printing & engraving

(G-3762)
SIGNS OF SECURITY INC
64 Outwater Ln Ste 2 (07026-3845)
P.O. Box 468 (07026-0468)
PHONE...................973 340-8404
Stephanie Gunning, *President*
Gianni Gallorini, *Manager*
EMP: 30
SALES (est): 1.9MM **Privately Held**
WEB: www.signsofsecurity.com
SIC: 3993 2752 Signs & advertising specialties; commercial printing, lithographic

(G-3763)
SOPHIES FASHIONS
352 Lanza Ave Apt 1 (07026-2453)
PHONE...................973 272-8321
Fax: 973 772-4314
Zosia Rostkowski, *Owner*
EMP: 4 EST: 1996
SALES (est): 180K **Privately Held**
SIC: 2335 2253 Women's, juniors' & misses' dresses; dresses & skirts

(G-3764)
STAR DYNAMIC CORP
100 Outwater Ln (07026-2647)
PHONE...................732 257-7488
Fax: 973 340-1530
Michelle Schwartzman, *CEO*
David Alster, *Vice Pres*

Hung Anqui, *Controller*
EMP: 60 EST: 1975
SQ FT: 25,000
SALES (est): 8.9MM **Privately Held**
WEB: www.stardynamic.com
SIC: 3661 Telephone & telegraph apparatus

(G-3765)
STEFAN ENTERPRISES INC
141 Lanza Ave Bldg 16e (07026-3533)
PHONE...................973 253-6005
Fax: 973 253-6005
Stefan Missbrenner, *President*
Walter Beck, *Vice Pres*
▲ EMP: 20
SALES (est): 3.2MM **Privately Held**
WEB: www.stefanenterprises.com
SIC: 2262 2396 Printing: manmade fiber & silk broadwoven fabrics; automotive & apparel trimmings

(G-3766)
SUMATIC CO INC
102 Dewitt St (07026-2712)
P.O. Box 435 (07026-0435)
PHONE...................973 772-1288
Fax: 973 772-1927
Michael Sunier, *President*
EMP: 5
SQ FT: 3,000
SALES (est): 611.4K **Privately Held**
SIC: 3451 Screw machine products

(G-3767)
TECHNO DESIGN INC
11 Erie St Ste 1 (07026-2302)
PHONE...................973 478-0930
Reuben Diaz, *President*
Kris Krol, *Manager*
EMP: 5 EST: 1976
SQ FT: 8,000
SALES (est): 733.5K **Privately Held**
WEB: www.techno-design.com
SIC: 3556 Food products machinery

(G-3768)
TOBY-YANNI INCORPORATED
62 Plauderville Ave (07026-2242)
PHONE...................973 253-9800
Elizabeth Tobias, *Principal*
EMP: 17
SALES (est): 1.9MM **Privately Held**
SIC: 3672 Printed circuit boards

(G-3769)
TOYDRIVER LLC
100 Outwater Ln (07026-2647)
PHONE...................678 637-8500
Lauren Levy,
EMP: 1
SQ FT: 10,000
SALES: 2MM **Privately Held**
SIC: 3546 Drill attachments, portable

(G-3770)
US MAGIC BOX INC
Also Called: Designer
221 Macarthur Ave (07026-1215)
PHONE...................973 772-2070
Sam Khattap, *President*
▼ EMP: 4
SALES (est): 481.8K **Privately Held**
WEB: www.usmagicbox.com
SIC: 2671 Packaging paper & plastics film, coated & laminated

(G-3771)
VENETIAN CORP
Also Called: Venetian Caterers, The
546 River Dr (07026-3818)
PHONE...................973 546-2250
James Kourgelis, *President*
Christos Gourmos, *Principal*
EMP: 16
SALES (est): 3.4MM **Privately Held**
SIC: 2099 Food preparations

(G-3772)
WEARBEST SIL-TEX MILLS LTD (PA)
325 Midland Ave (07026-1718)
P.O. Box 589 (07026-0589)
PHONE...................973 340-8844
Fax: 973 340-2066
Irwin Gasner, *President*

▲ EMP: 100 EST: 1940
SQ FT: 60,000
SALES (est): 21.3MM **Privately Held**
SIC: 2221 Broadwoven fabric mills, manmade

(G-3773)
WJJ AND COMPANY LLC
Also Called: Papertec
141 Lanza Ave Bldg 29 (07026-3530)
PHONE...................973 246-7480
Kevin Bielen, *Vice Pres*
Theodore Bielen,
Todd Bielen,
EMP: 10
SALES (est): 3.1MM **Privately Held**
SIC: 2631 Paperboard mills

Garwood
Union County

(G-3774)
ACCURATE BUSHING COMPANY INC
Also Called: Smith Bearing
443 North Ave Ste 1 (07027-1090)
P.O. Box 52 (07027-0052)
PHONE...................908 789-1121
Peter Dubinsky, *President*
Richard Picut, *Vice Pres*
Robert Picut, *Vice Pres*
Russel Picut, *Vice Pres*
Paul Robuck, *QC Mgr*
▲ EMP: 50
SQ FT: 45,000
SALES (est): 12MM **Privately Held**
WEB: www.accuratebushing.com
SIC: 3325 3562 3728 3568 Steel foundries; ball & roller bearings; aircraft parts & equipment; power transmission equipment; copper foundries

(G-3775)
ALMARK TOOL & MANUFACTURING CO
27 South Ave (07027-1337)
P.O. Box 189 (07027-0189)
PHONE...................908 789-2440
Fax: 908 789-2465
Mark Bowman, *President*
Norma Bowman, *Treasurer*
EMP: 10
SQ FT: 6,000
SALES (est): 1.6MM **Privately Held**
WEB: www.almarktool.com
SIC: 3545 3544 Precision tools, machinists'; special dies, tools, jigs & fixtures

(G-3776)
BEN VENUTI
512 North Ave (07027-1017)
PHONE...................908 389-9999
Jason White, *General Mgr*
Ben Venuti, *Principal*
EMP: 4 EST: 2008
SALES (est): 431.2K **Privately Held**
SIC: 3421 Table & food cutlery, including butchers'

(G-3777)
CREATIVE COLOR LITHOGRAPHERS
611 South Ave (07027-1238)
PHONE...................908 789-2295
Fax: 908 789-2270
Frank Adams, *President*
Helen Christodoulou, *Vice Pres*
Tara Szopinski, *VP Human Res*
Kevin Sadler, *Art Dir*
EMP: 15
SALES (est): 2MM **Privately Held**
WEB: www.creativecolor.net
SIC: 2752 2791 2789 2759 Commercial printing, offset; color lithography; typesetting; bookbinding & related work; commercial printing

(G-3778)
GRILL CREATIONS
100 North Ave Ste 8 (07027-1137)
PHONE...................908 264-8426
Ivin Alvarez, *Manager*
EMP: 4

SALES (est): 301.9K **Privately Held**
SIC: 3949 Bowling alleys & accessories

(G-3779)
MOLD POLISHING COMPANY INC
45 North Ave Ste 3 (07027-1158)
P.O. Box 96 (07027-0096)
PHONE..................................908 518-9191
Fax: 908 518-9192
Joseph Guerrero, *President*
Susan Guerrero, *Vice Pres*
Paulo Desousa, *Manager*
Alice Giler, *Manager*
EMP: 8
SQ FT: 8,000
SALES (est): 939.5K **Privately Held**
SIC: 3544 3471 Industrial molds; plating & polishing

(G-3780)
NEW JERSEY REPROGRAPHICS INC
Also Called: Precision Press
110 Center St (07027-1241)
P.O. Box 161 (07027-0161)
PHONE..................................908 789-1616
Fax: 908 789-2474
Joseph M Bizzarro, *President*
EMP: 4
SQ FT: 3,500
SALES: 510K **Privately Held**
SIC: 2752 Commercial printing, offset

(G-3781)
NORCO INC
237 South Ave (07027-1341)
P.O. Box 186 (07027-0186)
PHONE..................................908 789-1550
Fax: 908 654-0812
Michael Rosenberg, *President*
Marc R Krattenstein, *Treasurer*
Adriana Curbelo, *Technology*
Elizabeth Ojeda, *Technology*
▲ EMP: 45
SQ FT: 18,000
SALES (est): 5.6MM **Privately Held**
WEB: www.norcopins.com
SIC: 3911 3499 2672 3961 Medals, precious or semiprecious metal; pins (jewelry), precious metal; novelties & giftware, including trophies; labels (unprinted), gummed: made from purchased materials; costume jewelry

(G-3782)
OCSIDOT INC
Also Called: Advance Printing Co
116 South Ave (07027-1340)
PHONE..................................908 789-3300
Fax: 908 789-0509
John Todisco, *President*
Ed Cristilles, *Vice Pres*
Marina Todisco, *Manager*
Ed Christilles, *Prgrmr*
EMP: 17 EST: 1953
SQ FT: 17,000
SALES (est): 3.1MM **Privately Held**
SIC: 2752 2759 Commercial printing, offset; commercial printing

(G-3783)
P K WELDING LLC
520 South Ave (07027-1237)
PHONE..................................908 928-1002
Fax: 908 928-1004
Paul Gucker, *Mng Member*
Jean Johnson, *Administration*
Robert Parmentier,
EMP: 10
SQ FT: 2,000
SALES: 2.6MM **Privately Held**
SIC: 7692 Welding repair

(G-3784)
PEN COMPANY OF AMERICA LLC
502 South Ave (07027-1237)
PHONE..................................908 374-7949
EMP: 41
SALES (est): 7.2MM
SALES (corp-wide): 166.2MM **Privately Held**
SIC: 3951 Pens & mechanical pencils

HQ: Pen Company Of America Llc
1401 S Park Ave
Linden NJ 07036

(G-3785)
PMC LIQUIFLO EQUIPMENT CO INC
443 North Ave (07027-1014)
PHONE..................................908 518-0666
Fax: 908 518-1847
Richard Picut, *CEO*
Marla Sattler, *Manager*
Cezary Elmanowski, *Technology*
▲ EMP: 25 EST: 1972
SALES (est): 5.3MM **Privately Held**
WEB: www.endurapumps.com
SIC: 3594 Fluid power pumps & motors
PA: Picut Industries Inc
140 Mount Bethel Rd
Warren NJ 07059

(G-3786)
ROSCO INC
55 South Ave (07027-1337)
P.O. Box 427, Lanoka Harbor (08734-0427)
PHONE..................................908 789-1020
John K Burton, *President*
EMP: 5 EST: 1946
SQ FT: 3,700
SALES (est): 728.7K **Privately Held**
WEB: www.roscoincnj.com
SIC: 3365 Aluminum & aluminum-based alloy castings

(G-3787)
STANDARD PIPE PRODUCTS INC
15 North Ave (07027-1116)
PHONE..................................908 264-8284
Henry Rudorfer, *President*
▲ EMP: 8
SALES: 2MM **Privately Held**
SIC: 3317 Steel pipe & tubes

Gibbsboro
Camden County

(G-3788)
NICKS WORKSHOP INC
171 Clementon Rd W (08026-1107)
PHONE..................................856 784-6097
Nick Rulli, *President*
Mathew Rulli, *Vice Pres*
Rosemary Rulli, *Admin Sec*
EMP: 8
SALES (est): 1MM **Privately Held**
SIC: 2542 Fixtures: display, office or store: except wood

(G-3789)
PENN JERSEY PRESS INC
10 United States Ave E (08026-1125)
PHONE..................................856 627-2200
Fax: 856 627-3821
Richard Fichter, *President*
EMP: 5 EST: 1931
SQ FT: 5,400
SALES (est): 409.9K **Privately Held**
WEB: www.pennjerseypress.com
SIC: 2752 7334 2759 Commercial printing, offset; photocopying & duplicating services; commercial printing

(G-3790)
WILLIER ELC MTR REPR CO INC (PA)
1 Linden Ave (08026-1315)
P.O. Box 98 (08026-0098)
PHONE..................................856 627-3535
Fax: 856 627-5271
Donald P Willier Sr, *President*
Kathleen Willier, *Corp Secy*
James Willier, *Vice Pres*
Kurt Schneider, *Sales Staff*
Don Willier, *Executive*
EMP: 32 EST: 1954
SQ FT: 12,000
SALES: 9.7MM **Privately Held**
WEB: www.willierelectric.com
SIC: 5063 7694 Motors, electric; electric motor repair

(G-3791)
WILLIER ELC MTR REPR CO INC
Also Called: Willier Technical Services
3 Democrat Rd Ste Td (08026-1303)
P.O. Box 98 (08026-0098)
PHONE..................................856 627-2262
Don Willard, *Manager*
EMP: 40
SALES (corp-wide): 9.7MM **Privately Held**
WEB: www.willierelectric.com
SIC: 7694 Electric motor repair
PA: Willier Electric Motor Repair Co., Inc.
1 Linden Ave
Gibbsboro NJ 08026
856 627-3535

Gibbstown
Gloucester County

(G-3792)
MYCONE DENTAL SUPPLY CO INC (PA)
Also Called: Keystone Industries
480 S Democrat Rd (08027-1239)
PHONE..................................856 663-4700
Fax: 856 317-9769
Fred Robinson, *Ch of Bd*
Cary Robinson, *President*
▲ EMP: 150
SQ FT: 45,000
SALES (est): 106MM **Privately Held**
SIC: 5047 3843 2844 Dental equipment & supplies; dental equipment & supplies; toilet preparations

(G-3793)
WAGNER PROVISION CO INC
54 E Broad St (08027-1475)
P.O. Box 95 (08027-0095)
PHONE..................................856 423-1630
Fax: 856 423-8690
Herbold Wagner Jr, *President*
Caroline Wagner, *Treasurer*
EMP: 10
SQ FT: 3,000
SALES (est): 3MM **Privately Held**
SIC: 2013 Sausages & other prepared meats

Gillette
Morris County

(G-3794)
ELEMENTS GLOBAL GROUP LLC
527 Meyersville Rd (07933-1331)
PHONE..................................908 468-8407
▲ EMP: 5 EST: 2015
SALES (est): 336.3K **Privately Held**
SIC: 2819 Industrial inorganic chemicals

(G-3795)
MITRONICS PRODUCTS INC
239 Morristown Rd (07933-1818)
P.O. Box 196 (07933-0196)
PHONE..................................908 647-5006
Fax: 908 647-7070
Eric Bergman, *President*
EMP: 8 EST: 1971
SQ FT: 2,750
SALES: 250K **Privately Held**
SIC: 3264 Insulators, electrical: porcelain

(G-3796)
NINE WEST HOLDINGS INC
Also Called: Jones New York
977 Valley Rd (07933-1813)
PHONE..................................908 647-6168
Rebecca White, *Manager*
EMP: 22
SALES (corp-wide): 2.2B **Privately Held**
SIC: 2339 Sportswear, women's
HQ: Nine West Holdings, Inc.
180 Rittenhouse Cir
Bristol PA 19007
215 785-4000

(G-3797)
SOUND CHICE ASSSTIVE LISTENING
498 Long Hill Rd (07933-1345)
PHONE..................................908 647-2651
Phyllis R Wald, *President*
Lawrence Fast, *Vice Pres*
EMP: 4
SALES (est): 320K **Privately Held**
WEB: www.assistivelistening.net
SIC: 3651 Amplifiers: radio, public address or musical instrument

Gladstone
Somerset County

(G-3798)
HOBART GROUP HOLDINGS LLC
240 Main St (07934-2016)
PHONE..................................908 470-1780
Fax: 908 470-1784
Dan Renick, *President*
Nicole Sweeney, *Manager*
Jillian Flynn, *Supervisor*
David Melvin, *Director*
Ronald Rosich, *Director*
EMP: 140 EST: 2003
SALES (est): 12.1MM
SALES (corp-wide): 65.8MM **Privately Held**
SIC: 2834 Pharmaceutical preparations
PA: Precision Medicine Group, Llc
2 Bethesda Metro Ctr # 850
Bethesda MD 20814
240 654-0730

(G-3799)
WEXFORD INTERNATIONAL INC
190 Main St Ste 102 (07934-2064)
P.O. Box 715 (07934-0715)
PHONE..................................908 781-7200
Fax: 973 543-6820
Donald L Brown, *President*
Daniel T Kelly, *Partner*
▲ EMP: 5
SQ FT: 3,200
SALES (est): 2MM **Privately Held**
SIC: 2821 Molding compounds, plastics

Glassboro
Gloucester County

(G-3800)
ADVANTAGE DS LLC
8 Deptford Rd (08028-2449)
PHONE..................................856 307-9600
James Madosky, *President*
EMP: 10
SALES: 700K **Privately Held**
SIC: 2395 2759 Embroidery products, except schiffli machine; screen printing

(G-3801)
ASTRO OUTDOOR ADVERTISING INC (PA)
Also Called: Astro Sign Co
230 E High St (08028-2310)
PHONE..................................856 881-4300
Fax: 856 881-2399
Gerald H Painter, *CEO*
Joann Painter, *Corp Secy*
Jason Painter, *Accounts Mgr*
Michael Fratini, *Sales Staff*
Linda Danner, *Office Mgr*
EMP: 10
SQ FT: 3,500
SALES (est): 1.1MM **Privately Held**
SIC: 3993 Signs & advertising specialties

(G-3802)
CWI ARCHITECTURAL MILLWORK LLC
8 Deptford Rd Dept D (08028-2449)
PHONE..................................856 307-7900
Fax: 856 307-7500
David Ganor, *Mng Member*
Kimberly Ganor,
EMP: 8
SQ FT: 6,200

SALES: 650K **Privately Held**
WEB: www.certainlywoodinc.com
SIC: **2431** 5211 1751 Woodwork, interior
& ornamental; millwork & lumber; cabinet
& finish carpentry

(G-3803)
DEMOUNTABLE CONCEPTS INC
200 Acorn Rd (08028-3299)
PHONE....................................856 863-3081
Fax: 856 863-6704
Frank Fisher, *CEO*
Rustin Cassway, *President*
David Fisher, *Vice Pres*
▼ EMP: 30
SQ FT: 50,000
SALES (est): 7.9MM **Privately Held**
WEB: www.demount.com
SIC: **3713** Truck bodies & parts

(G-3804)
**ELRAY MANUFACTURING
COMPANY**
17 Liberty St (08028-2305)
PHONE....................................856 881-1935
Fax: 856 881-4928
Edward Stopper, *President*
Betty Stopper, *Vice Pres*
EMP: 30 EST: 1952
SQ FT: 33,000
SALES (est): 6.1MM **Privately Held**
WEB: www.elrayman.com
SIC: **3469** 3544 Machine parts, stamped
or pressed metal; die sets for metal
stamping (presses)

(G-3805)
FAZZIO MACHINE & STEEL INC
3278 Glassboro Crs Kys Rd (08028-2716)
P.O. Box 232 (08028-0232)
PHONE....................................609 653-1098
Fax: 856 881-4129
Felix P Fazzio, *President*
James Fazzio, *Vice Pres*
Mike Fazzio, *Vice Pres*
EMP: 6 EST: 1943
SQ FT: 2,500
SALES (est): 2.2MM **Privately Held**
SIC: **5051** 3599 Steel; machine shop, job-
bing & repair

(G-3806)
**GLASSBORO NEWS & FOOD
STORE**
255 E High St (08028-2309)
PHONE....................................856 881-1181
Preg Shah, *Principal*
EMP: 4
SALES (est): 154.5K **Privately Held**
SIC: **2711** 5411 Newspapers, publishing &
printing; convenience stores

(G-3807)
KERK CABINETRY LLC
45 Dogwood Ave (08028-2819)
PHONE....................................856 881-4213
Kristian Van Dexter, *Principal*
EMP: 4
SALES (est): 373K **Privately Held**
SIC: **2434** Wood kitchen cabinets

(G-3808)
MADHOUZ LLC
8 Deptford Rd Dept A (08028-2449)
PHONE....................................609 206-8009
▲ EMP: 4
SALES (est): 453.5K **Privately Held**
SIC: **5199** 3993 7319 7389 Gifts & novelties; signs & advertising specialties; display advertising service; embroidering of
advertising on shirts, etc.; direct mail advertising services

(G-3809)
MCALISTER WELDING & FABG
112 Maple Leaf Ct (08028-2644)
PHONE....................................856 740-3890
Dave McAlister, *Owner*
David McAlister, *Owner*
Lynn McAlister, *Co-Owner*
EMP: 15
SALES (est): 1.7MM **Privately Held**
SIC: **7692** 3312 Welding repair; structural
shapes & pilings, steel

(G-3810)
NER DATA PRODUCTS INC (HQ)
307 Delsea Dr S (08028-2647)
PHONE....................................888 637-3282
Fax: 856 881-2393
Francis C Oatway, *Ch of Bd*
Stephen F Oatway, *President*
Scott Steele, *Exec VP*
Robert Belvin, *Production*
Christopher Oatway, *CFO*
▲ EMP: 40
SQ FT: 60,000
SALES (est): 56MM
SALES (corp-wide): 24.4MM **Privately
Held**
WEB: www.nerdata.com
SIC: **3577** 3955 3861 3572 Computer
peripheral equipment; carbon paper &
inked ribbons; photographic equipment &
supplies; computer storage devices; parti-
tions & fixtures, except wood
PA: Ner Data Corporation
307 Delsea Dr S
Glassboro NJ 08028
856 881-5524

(G-3811)
S&W FABRICATORS INC
100 Delsea Dr S (08028-2662)
P.O. Box 664 (08028-0664)
PHONE....................................856 881-7418
Andrea Sebastiani, *President*
EMP: 7
SALES (est): 1.1MM **Privately Held**
SIC: **3498** Fabricated pipe & fittings

(G-3812)
SPORTS STOP INC
Also Called: Two Vic's Sports Stop
31 Delsea Dr N (08028-1930)
PHONE....................................856 881-2763
Fax: 856 863-0537
Fitz Duer, *President*
Maureen Duer, *Vice Pres*
EMP: 10
SQ FT: 3,800
SALES: 1MM **Privately Held**
WEB: www.twovics.com
SIC: **5941** 5091 2759 Sporting goods &
bicycle shops; sporting & recreation
goods; screen printing

(G-3813)
WECOM INC
20 Warrick Ave (08028-2500)
PHONE....................................856 863-8400
Fax: 856 863-8408
Eric Sprengle Sr, *President*
E Carl Sprengle Jr, *Vice Pres*
EMP: 29
SQ FT: 50,000
SALES: 3MM **Privately Held**
WEB: www.wecom.com
SIC: **3444** Sheet metal specialties, not
stamped

Glen Gardner
Hunterdon County

(G-3814)
**EASTERN CONCRETE
MATERIALS INC**
1 Railroad Ave (08826-3537)
PHONE....................................908 537-2135
EMP: 4
SALES (corp-wide): 1.3B **Publicly Held**
SIC: **3273** 1411 Ready-mixed concrete;
granite dimension stone
HQ: Eastern Concrete Materials, Inc.
250 Pehle Ave Ste 503
Saddle Brook NJ 07663
201 797-7979

(G-3815)
HUP & SONS
10 White Tail Ln (08826-3048)
PHONE....................................908 832-7878
Martin Hup Jr, *Owner*
EMP: 4
SALES (est): 480.1K **Privately Held**
SIC: **3292** 1794 Floor tile, asphalt; exca-
vation work

(G-3816)
OFF-ROAD WELDING INC
417 Little Brook Rd (08826-3319)
PHONE....................................908 832-2967
Frances Edwards, *President*
EMP: 4
SALES (est): 220K **Privately Held**
SIC: **7692** Welding repair

(G-3817)
VISION RAILINGS LTD LBLTY CO
Also Called: Ultimate Outdoors
213 Dee Dee Dr (08826-3220)
PHONE....................................908 310-8926
Andrea Nicolai,
EMP: 10
SALES (est): 790K **Privately Held**
SIC: **3441** Fabricated structural metal

Glen Ridge
Essex County

(G-3818)
G J HAERER CO INC (PA)
372 Ridgewood Ave (07028-1513)
PHONE....................................973 614-8090
Timothy J Kelleher, *President*
Richard B Colledge, *Vice Pres*
Sabina Prendergast, *Vice Pres*
EMP: 69 EST: 1938
SQ FT: 15,000
SALES (est): 3.6MM **Privately Held**
WEB: www.gjhaerer.com
SIC: **2752** Commercial printing, offset

Glen Rock
Bergen County

(G-3819)
AMERICAN STENCYL INC
Also Called: American Sten-Cyl
479 S Broad St (07452-1309)
PHONE....................................201 251-6460
Thomas Nardini, *President*
Mary Nardini, *Corp Secy*
EMP: 5 EST: 1982
SQ FT: 4,000
SALES (est): 484.5K **Privately Held**
WEB: www.americansten-cyl.com
SIC: **3993** 3953 Signs & advertising spe-
cialties; stencils, painting & marking

(G-3820)
ARTIQUE GLASS STUDIO INC
483 S Broad St (07452-1309)
PHONE....................................201 444-3500
J De Mauro, *President*
EMP: 5
SALES (est): 400K **Privately Held**
SIC: **3211** 5231 Antique glass; glass,
leaded or stained

(G-3821)
ASH INGREDIENTS INC
65 Harristown Rd Ste 307 (07452-3317)
PHONE....................................201 689-1322
Shawna Kriplani, *CEO*
Anil Kripalani, *President*
▲ EMP: 8
SQ FT: 1,500
SALES (est): 26MM **Privately Held**
SIC: **2834** Extracts of botanicals: pow-
dered, pilular, solid or fluid; powders,
pharmaceutical

(G-3822)
B E C MFG CORP
Also Called: Specialized Metal Stamping
649 Lincoln Ave (07452-2518)
PHONE....................................201 414-0000
Bart Sciaino, *President*
Jim Clavan, *Vice Pres*
Elizabeth Sciaino, *Admin Sec*
EMP: 25 EST: 1964
SQ FT: 60,000
SALES (est): 2.9MM **Privately Held**
WEB: www.becmfg.com
SIC: **3544** 3469 Special dies & tools;
metal stampings

(G-3823)
**CLASSIC DESIGNER
WOODWORK INC**
60 Hazelhurst Ave (07452-2840)
PHONE....................................201 280-3711
Keith Richter, *Principal*
EMP: 4
SALES (est): 260.2K **Privately Held**
SIC: **2431** Millwork

(G-3824)
**COLIBRI SCENTIQUE LTD LBLTY
CO**
68 Chadwick Pl (07452-3105)
PHONE....................................201 445-5715
Cheryl Sarno, *Mng Member*
EMP: 9
SALES (est): 1.2MM **Privately Held**
SIC: **2869** Industrial organic chemicals

(G-3825)
**CUNNINGHAM CLASSICS LTD
LBLTY**
Also Called: Leather Head Sports
536 S Broad St Ste 2 (07452-1301)
PHONE....................................201 857-4647
Debbie Wiele, *Production*
Paul Cunningham, *Mng Member*
Catherine Leonard, *Director*
EMP: 8
SQ FT: 1,100
SALES (est): 540K **Privately Held**
SIC: **3199** Novelties, leather

(G-3826)
MELISSA SPICE TRADING CORP
Also Called: Marian
123 Glen Ave (07452-2111)
PHONE....................................862 262-7773
Melissa Mifsud, *Mng Member*
▲ EMP: 12
SQ FT: 10,000
SALES: 3MM **Privately Held**
SIC: **5149** 2099 Spices & seasonings;
spices, including grinding

(G-3827)
OPICI IMPORT CO INC
25 De Boer Dr (07452-3301)
PHONE....................................201 689-3256
Tom Hopper, *Principal*
Dottie Dipatria, *Vice Pres*
Lorie Woolums, *Purch Agent*
Michael Palese, *Sales Staff*
George Palmieri, *Sales Staff*
▲ EMP: 39
SALES (est): 6.4MM **Privately Held**
SIC: **2084** Wines

(G-3828)
**RESPIRERX
PHARMACEUTICALS INC (PA)**
126 Valley Rd Ste C (07452-1796)
PHONE....................................201 444-4947
Arnold S Lippa, *Ch of Bd*
James S J Manuso, *President*
Robert N Weingarten, *CFO*
Jeff E Margolis, *Treasurer*
EMP: 5
SALES: 86.9K **Publicly Held**
WEB: www.cortexpharm.com
SIC: **2834** Pharmaceutical preparations

(G-3829)
RICHARD DANZ & SONS INC
390 Prospect St (07452-1533)
PHONE....................................212 697-5722
William Danz, *President*
Richard Danz, *President*
EMP: 50 EST: 1851
SALES (est): 4.7MM **Privately Held**
SIC: **3851** 8011 Eyes, glass & plastic;
oculist

(G-3830)
WORLD ELECTRONICS INC
Also Called: Lowell Electronics
37 Hanover Pl (07452-2705)
PHONE....................................201 670-1177
Fax: 201 447-1633
Murray Rinzler, *President*
Joan Rinzler, *Corp Secy*
Robert Baylor Rinzle, *Vice Pres*
EMP: 10
SQ FT: 5,200

GEOGRAPHIC

SALES: 2MM **Privately Held**
WEB: www.worldtubes.com
SIC: 3671 5065 Electron tubes; electronic parts & equipment

(G-3831)
WORLD SOFTWARE CORPORATION
Also Called: Worldox
266 Harristown Rd Ste 201 (07452-3321)
PHONE.....................................201 444-3228
Thomas W Burke, *Ch of Bd*
Ray Zwiefelhofer, *President*
Kristina Burke, *Vice Pres*
EMP: 25
SALES (est): 4.2MM **Privately Held**
WEB: www.worldox.com
SIC: 7372 7371 Prepackaged software; computer software development

Glendora
Camden County

(G-3832)
NICKOLAOS KAPPATOS ENTPS INC
Also Called: Signpros
1215 Black Horse Pike (08029-1305)
PHONE.....................................856 939-1099
Nickolaos Kappatos, *President*
EMP: 19
SQ FT: 9,000
SALES (est): 2MM **Privately Held**
SIC: 3993 Advertising artwork

(G-3833)
US VISION INC (HQ)
Also Called: J C Penney Optical
1 Harmon Dr (08029)
PHONE.....................................856 227-8339
Fax: 856 228-7256
Mark Robinski, *Regional Mgr*
Thomas Spaulding, *District Mgr*
Caroline Flagler, *Senior VP*
Sean Keegan, *Prdtn Mgr*
Brian Seay, *Inv Control Mgr*
▲ **EMP:** 412
SQ FT: 20,000
SALES (est): 384.1MM
SALES (corp-wide): 492.1MM **Privately Held**
WEB: www.usvision.com
SIC: 5995 3827 Optical goods stores; eyeglasses, prescription; contact lenses, prescription; optical instruments & lenses
PA: Refac Optical Group
    1 Harmon Dr
    Blackwood NJ 08012
    856 228-1000

(G-3834)
USV OPTICAL INC (DH)
Also Called: J C Penney Optical
1 Harmon Dr Glen Oaks Par (08029)
P.O. Box 124 (08029-0124)
PHONE.....................................856 228-1000
William A Schwartz Jr, *CEO*
Carmen J Nepa III, *Exec VP*
Dorit Bannett, *Controller*
Tobe Finseth, *Human Resources*
Uzma Ali, *Manager*
EMP: 412
SQ FT: 20,000
SALES (est): 241.3MM
SALES (corp-wide): 492.1MM **Privately Held**
WEB: www.ntouchcomm.net
SIC: 5995 3851 Eyeglasses, prescription; ophthalmic goods
HQ: U.S. Vision, Inc.
    1 Harmon Dr
    Glendora NJ 08029
    856 227-8339

Gloucester City
Camden County

(G-3835)
D&N MACHINE MANUFACTURING INC
Also Called: D & N Machine Co
334 Nicholson Rd (08030-1229)
P.O. Box 67 (08030-0067)
PHONE.....................................856 456-1366
Fax: 856 456-5334
Robert B Doble Jr, *President*
Sandy Doble, *Corp Secy*
EMP: 20 **EST:** 1949
SQ FT: 15,000
SALES (est): 3.2MM **Privately Held**
SIC: 3444 3556 3679 Sheet metal specialties, not stamped; food products machinery; electronic circuits

(G-3836)
G & M PRINTWEAR
549 S Broadway Ste 2 (08030-2455)
PHONE.....................................856 742-5551
Fax: 856 742-5549
Rob Dill, *Owner*
EMP: 12
SQ FT: 4,800
SALES (est): 940K **Privately Held**
WEB: www.gmprintwear.com
SIC: 2759 Screen printing

(G-3837)
GLOUCESTER CITY BOX WORKS LLC
775 Charles St (08030-2456)
P.O. Box 2 (08030-0002)
PHONE.....................................856 456-9032
Kathleen White, *Mng Member*
EMP: 10
SALES (est): 1MM **Privately Held**
SIC: 3565 Packaging machinery

(G-3838)
H BARRON IRON WORKS INC
316 Water St (08030-2426)
PHONE.....................................856 456-9092
Fax: 856 456-7836
Dennis Barron, *President*
Michael Barron, *Vice Pres*
EMP: 15 **EST:** 1955
SALES (est): 3.8MM **Privately Held**
SIC: 3441 1799 Building components, structural steel; fence construction

(G-3839)
IMPERIAL DESIGN
729 Charles St (08030-2456)
PHONE.....................................856 742-8480
Derek Cohen, *Owner*
EMP: 7
SALES (est): 400K **Privately Held**
SIC: 2542 Partitions & fixtures, except wood

(G-3840)
MID-LANTIC PRECISION INC
940 Market St (08030-1861)
P.O. Box 105 (08030-0105)
PHONE.....................................856 456-3810
Fax: 856 456-3704
Lauri Wilke, *President*
William Wilke, *Vice Pres*
EMP: 14
SQ FT: 5,000
SALES: 900K **Privately Held**
SIC: 3599 Machine shop, jobbing & repair

(G-3841)
NEWS INC GLOUCESTER CITY
34 S Broadway (08030-1710)
P.O. Box 151 (08030-0151)
PHONE.....................................856 456-1199
Albert Countryman, *President*
EMP: 4
SALES (est): 250K **Privately Held**
SIC: 2711 Newspapers, publishing & printing

(G-3842)
PIERANGELI GROUP INC
Also Called: Window Repairs & Restoration
221 Jersey Ave (08030-2027)
PHONE.....................................856 582-4060
Raymond Depiano, *Div Sub Head*
EMP: 4
SALES (corp-wide): 17.1MM **Privately Held**
WEB: www.strybuc.com
SIC: 7699 3211 Door & window repair; flat glass
PA: Pierangeli Group, Inc.
    2006 Elmwood Ave
    Sharon Hill PA 19079
    610 534-3200

(G-3843)
QUIK FLEX CIRCUIT INC
Also Called: Flextron Systems
85 Nicholson Rd (08030-1308)
PHONE.....................................856 742-0550
Ishwar Chauhan, *President*
B Thakroe, *Vice Pres*
Piyush Patel, *Director*
H L Patel, *Admin Sec*
EMP: 15
SQ FT: 10,000
SALES: 620.9K **Privately Held**
WEB: www.flextronsystems.com
SIC: 3672 Printed circuit boards

(G-3844)
QUIK-FLEX CIRCUIT INC
85 Nicholson Rd (08030-1308)
PHONE.....................................856 742-0550
Ishwar Chauhan, *President*
EMP: 20
SALES (est): 2.9MM **Privately Held**
SIC: 3625 Control circuit devices, magnet & solid state

(G-3845)
REDKEYS DIES INC
1307 Market St (08030-1605)
P.O. Box 360 (08030-0360)
PHONE.....................................856 456-7890
Fax: 856 456-6393
Morgan Reichner, *President*
EMP: 6
SQ FT: 1,200
SALES (est): 807.6K **Privately Held**
WEB: www.redkeysdies.com
SIC: 3544 Dies, steel rule; special dies & tools

(G-3846)
TELEFLEX INCORPORATED
860 Charles St (08030-2450)
PHONE.....................................856 349-7234
Debra Gorges, *Manager*
EMP: 100
SALES (corp-wide): 2.1B **Publicly Held**
WEB: www.teleflex.com
SIC: 3841 3842 Surgical & medical instruments; surgical appliances & supplies
PA: Teleflex Incorporated
    550 E Swedesford Rd # 400
    Wayne PA 19087
    610 225-6800

(G-3847)
THERMOSEAL INDUSTRIES LLC
600 Jersey Ave (08030-2361)
PHONE.....................................856 456-3109
Fax: 856 456-0989
Richard Chubb, *President*
Patrick McMullen, *CFO*
Jeffrey Stark, *Admin Sec*
◆ **EMP:** 60 **EST:** 1996
SQ FT: 45,000
SALES: 14MM
SALES (corp-wide): 5.7B **Privately Held**
WEB: www.thermoseal.com
SIC: 3231 Insulating glass: made from purchased glass
HQ: Chase Industries, Inc.
    10021 Commerce Park Dr
    West Chester OH 45246
    513 860-5565

Great Meadows
Warren County

(G-3848)
CLASSIC IMPRESSIONS
2 Witte Ln (07838-2055)
PHONE.....................................908 689-3137
Christine Witte, *President*
EMP: 4 **EST:** 2013
SALES (est): 351.3K **Privately Held**
SIC: 2752 Commercial printing, lithographic

(G-3849)
D N D CORP
13 Cemetery Rd (07838-2012)
PHONE.....................................908 637-4343
Robert Drechsel, *President*
William De Marco Jr, *General Mgr*
EMP: 8
SQ FT: 5,000
SALES (est): 510K **Privately Held**
SIC: 3599 7692 Machine shop, jobbing & repair; welding repair

(G-3850)
PARTAC PEAT CORP
95 Shades Of Death Rd (07838)
PHONE.....................................908 637-4191
Fax: 908 637-8421
James Kelsey, *President*
EMP: 18
SQ FT: 45,000
SALES (est): 1.1MM **Privately Held**
WEB: www.partac.com
SIC: 0181 0782 1499 1459 Sod farms; turf installation services, except artificial; peat mining; clays (common) quarrying; sand mining; gravel mining

(G-3851)
PARTAC PEAT CORPORATION
Also Called: Kelsey Humus
95 Kelsey Park (07838)
PHONE.....................................908 637-4631
Maria B Kelsey, *President*
Janes Kelsey, *President*
EMP: 15 **EST:** 1945
SALES (est): 1.1MM **Privately Held**
SIC: 1499 Peat mining

(G-3852)
PAUL ENGLEHARDT
Island Rd (07838)
P.O. Box 13 (07838-0013)
PHONE.....................................908 637-4556
Paul Englehardt, *Owner*
EMP: 8
SQ FT: 2,000
SALES: 430K **Privately Held**
SIC: 2822 Silicone rubbers

(G-3853)
WORKS ENDURO RIDER INC
1 Jenny Jump Ave (07838-2415)
PHONE.....................................908 637-6385
Andrew F Smith, *President*
EMP: 6
SALES (est): 520K **Privately Held**
SIC: 3751 Motorcycles & related parts

Green Brook
Middlesex County

(G-3854)
ANDYS CUSTOM CABINETS
143 Jefferson Ave (08812-2607)
PHONE.....................................732 752-6443
A Hopeck, *Principal*
EMP: 4
SALES (est): 363.1K **Privately Held**
SIC: 3553 Cabinet makers' machinery

(G-3855)
CORPORATE ENVELOPE & PRTG CO
299r Us Highway 22 (08812-1701)
PHONE.....................................732 752-4333
James Bidne, *President*
Paul Psak, *President*

▲ = Import ▼=Export
◆ =Import/Export

EMP: 7
SQ FT: 8,000
SALES: 2MM **Privately Held**
WEB: www.corpenvelope.com
SIC: 2677 Envelopes

(G-3856)
GREATER NEW JERSEY DIAMND EXCH
Also Called: Ski Setting Company
299 Us Highway 22 Ste 22 (08812-1716)
PHONE..........................732 752-6446
Fax: 732 752-6637
Joseph M Sulovski, *President*
Jim Ford, *Vice Pres*
Maryann Bazicka, *Admin Sec*
EMP: 8
SALES (est): 1.4MM **Privately Held**
SIC: 3911 Jewel settings & mountings, precious metal

(G-3857)
HOZRIC LLC
11 Ridge Rd (08812-1831)
PHONE..........................908 420-8821
Faizan Ahmed, *Vice Pres*
EMP: 4
SALES (est): 55.6K **Privately Held**
SIC: 7213 7371 7372 Linen supply, nonclothing; linen supply, clothing; computer software systems analysis & design, custom; computer software development & applications; prepackaged software

(G-3858)
IWC
12 Red Bud Ln (08812-1820)
PHONE..........................732 968-8122
Mark Kang, *General Mgr*
▲ EMP: 15
SALES (est): 1.3MM **Privately Held**
SIC: 3315 Wire & fabricated wire products

(G-3859)
J G SCHMIDT CO INC
Also Called: Jgs
354 U S Rt 22 (08812)
PHONE..........................732 563-9500
Fax: 732 563-4946
George R Schmidt, *CEO*
Thomas Schmidt, *President*
Theresa Schmidt, *Corp Secy*
▲ EMP: 80 EST: 1920
SQ FT: 70,000
SALES (est): 14.4MM **Privately Held**
WEB: www.jgschmidt.com
SIC: 3469 Stamping metal for the trade

(G-3860)
K JABAT INC
342 Us Highway 22 (08812-1703)
P.O. Box 68, Middlesex (08846-0068)
PHONE..........................732 469-8177
Theresa Kulkaski, *President*
Stanley Kulkaski, *Admin Sec*
▲ EMP: 15
SQ FT: 5,500
SALES (est): 3MM **Privately Held**
SIC: 3083 3082 Laminated plastics plate & sheet; tubes, unsupported plastic

(G-3861)
PAINTON STUDIOS INC
299 Us Highway 22 Ste 21 (08812-1716)
PHONE..........................732 752-8842
EMP: 4
SQ FT: 2,000
SALES (est): 390K **Privately Held**
SIC: 2791 Typesetting Computer Graphics

(G-3862)
POOL TABLES PLUS INC (PA)
Also Called: Loree Jon Pool Tables Plus
299 Us Highway 22 Ste 24 (08812-1716)
PHONE..........................732 968-8228
Fax: 732 968-8161
Nancy Skalaski, *President*
Mark Ogonowski, *President*
Tom Wharton, *Sales Staff*
▲ EMP: 6
SQ FT: 10,000
SALES (est): 2.4MM **Privately Held**
SIC: 5941 5091 5021 2542 Pool & billiard tables; specialty sport supplies; billiard equipment & supplies; bar furniture; bar fixtures, except wood

(G-3863)
PRETTY UGLY LLC
290 Us Highway 22 (08812-1808)
PHONE..........................908 620-0931
Drew Matilsky,
▲ EMP: 15 EST: 2011
SALES (est): 2MM **Privately Held**
SIC: 3942 5092 Dolls & stuffed toys; dolls

(G-3864)
STAINLESS SURPLUS LLC
6 Pheasant Run (08812-2042)
PHONE..........................914 661-3800
Sam Desi,
◆ EMP: 5
SALES (est): 3.6MM **Privately Held**
SIC: 3341 Secondary nonferrous metals

Green Village
Morris County

(G-3865)
KLEEMEYER & MERKEL INC
Also Called: Green Village Packing Co
68 Britten Rd (07935-3000)
P.O. Box 204 (07935-0204)
PHONE..........................973 377-0875
Fax: 973 377-5774
William Kleemeyer Jr, *President*
Carl Kleemeyer, *Corp Secy*
EMP: 15
SQ FT: 5,000
SALES (est): 4MM **Privately Held**
SIC: 5147 5421 2011 Meats, fresh; meat markets, including freezer provisioners; meat packing plants

Grenloch
Gloucester County

(G-3866)
ENSINGER GRENLOCH INC (DH)
Also Called: Ensinger Hyde
1 Main St (08032)
PHONE..........................856 227-0500
Fax: 856 232-1754
Robert Racchini, *Vice Pres*
Chris Ranallo, *Vice Pres*
Larry Resavage, *Vice Pres*
▲ EMP: 75
SQ FT: 90,000
SALES (est): 36.7MM
SALES (corp-wide): 434.6MM **Privately Held**
WEB: www.insulbar.com
SIC: 3083 Thermoplastic laminates: rods, tubes, plates & sheet; thermosetting laminates: rods, tubes, plates & sheet
HQ: Ensinger Industries, Inc.
365 Meadowlands Blvd
Washington PA 15301
724 746-6050

Guttenberg
Hudson County

(G-3867)
CARIBE EXPRESS ASSOCIATES INC (PA)
6710 Bergenline Ave (07093-1700)
PHONE..........................201 869-2822
Alberto Diequez, *Vice Pres*
EMP: 5
SALES (est): 1MM **Privately Held**
SIC: 2819 Carbides

(G-3868)
CRAIG FABRICS INC (PA)
7014 Jackson St (07093-2283)
PHONE..........................201 869-9126
Craig Goldman, *President*
Saul Goldman, *Treasurer*
EMP: 12 EST: 1977
SQ FT: 5,000

SALES (est): 3MM **Privately Held**
SIC: 5131 2395 Silk piece goods, woven; pleating & stitching

(G-3869)
DEERBROOK FABRICS
427 69th St (07093-2413)
PHONE..........................201 945-4141
Fax: 201 945-8446
Edward Parseghian, *President*
EMP: 14 EST: 1969
SQ FT: 4,000
SALES (est): 2.4MM **Privately Held**
SIC: 5131 8741 2395 Lace fabrics; management services; pleating & stitching

(G-3870)
O STITCH MATIC INC
Also Called: Deerbrook Fabrics
427 69th St (07093-2413)
PHONE..........................201 861-3045
Edward Parseghian, *President*
EMP: 6
SALES (corp-wide): 915.3K **Privately Held**
SIC: 2397 2395 Schiffli machine embroideries; pleating & stitching
PA: O Stitch Matic Inc
430 Walker St
Fairview NJ
201 945-4141

(G-3871)
SOFA DOCTOR INC
Also Called: Dr Sofa
148 71st St (07093-3410)
PHONE..........................718 292-6300
Shlomie Eini, *President*
EMP: 8 EST: 2004
SALES (est): 873.5K **Privately Held**
SIC: 2512 7641 Upholstered household furniture; furniture upholstery repair

Hackensack
Bergen County

(G-3872)
AAS TECHNOLOGIES INC
290 Lodi St (07601-3118)
PHONE..........................201 342-7300
Ralph Varano, *Ch of Bd*
EMP: 6
SALES (est): 663.9K **Privately Held**
SIC: 3699 5946 Security control equipment & systems; cameras

(G-3873)
ALLURE BOX & DISPLAY CO
216 Charles St (07601-3111)
PHONE..........................212 807-7070
Dov Baum, *Principal*
EMP: 10
SQ FT: 30,000
SALES (est): 1.1MM **Privately Held**
SIC: 2671 2631 2621 2541 Paper coated or laminated for packaging; container, packaging & boxboard; wrapping & packaging papers; store & office display cases & fixtures

(G-3874)
ARCADIA EQUIPMENT INC
140 Lawrence St (07601-4195)
PHONE..........................201 342-3308
Fax: 201 342-3334
Doug White, *President*
Sally White, *Admin Sec*
EMP: 12
SQ FT: 8,000
SALES (est): 8.8MM **Privately Held**
WEB: www.arcadiaequipment.com
SIC: 5084 3823 Pumps & pumping equipment; industrial instrmnts msrmnt display/control process variable

(G-3875)
ARTISAN OVEN INC
Also Called: Central Bakery
105 S State St (07601-3919)
PHONE..........................201 488-6261
Carlos A Garcia, *President*
EMP: 6 EST: 2010

SALES (est): 141.7K **Privately Held**
SIC: 5461 2051 Bread; bakery: wholesale or wholesale/retail combined

(G-3876)
AURORA APPAREL INC
Also Called: Aurora Apparels
1 Riverside Sq Mall # 146 (07601-6358)
PHONE..........................201 646-4590
EMP: 4
SQ FT: 3,000
SALES (est): 330K **Privately Held**
SIC: 2211 Cotton Broadwoven Fabric Mill

(G-3877)
B & S TOOL AND CUTTER SERVICE
99 John St (07601-4129)
PHONE..........................201 488-3545
Fax: 201 488-3861
Frederick Lindenau, *President*
Thomas Lindenau, *Vice Pres*
EMP: 9 EST: 1959
SQ FT: 5,000
SALES: 800K **Privately Held**
WEB: www.cncsharptools.com
SIC: 7699 3545 Knife, saw & tool sharpening & repair; cutting tools for machine tools

(G-3878)
BASSIL BOOKBINDING COMPANY INC
535 S River St (07601-6621)
PHONE..........................201 440-4925
Fax: 201 440-4975
Elias Bassil, *President*
EMP: 27
SQ FT: 20,000
SALES (est): 4.9MM **Privately Held**
SIC: 2789 Bookbinding & related work; binding only: books, pamphlets, magazines, etc.

(G-3879)
BCG MARBLE GRAN FABRICATORS CO
167 Sussex St (07601-3317)
PHONE..........................201 343-8487
Fax: 201 343-8273
Giuseppe Guerini, *President*
◆ EMP: 10
SQ FT: 5,000
SALES (est): 1.3MM **Privately Held**
SIC: 3281 2511 2434 5032 Granite, cut & shaped; marble, building: cut & shaped; wood household furniture; wood kitchen cabinets; marble building stone

(G-3880)
BEACON OFFSET PRINTING LLC
204 Russell Pl (07601-3315)
PHONE..........................201 488-4241
Fax: 201 488-6776
Vivian Hollenbeck, *Corp Secy*
Daniel Communali,
EMP: 5
SQ FT: 6,000
SALES (est): 600K **Privately Held**
SIC: 2752 Commercial printing, offset

(G-3881)
BIB AND TUCKER INC (PA)
51 Main St (07601-7001)
PHONE..........................201 489-9600
Fax: 201 489-1660
Ross Arrabito, *President*
Robin Arrabito, *Vice Pres*
EMP: 6
SQ FT: 5,000
SALES (est): 699.3K **Privately Held**
SIC: 2369 5641 Girls' & children's outerwear; infants' wear; children's wear

(G-3882)
BIOGENESIS INC
Also Called: Biogenesis-Labs
296 Washington Ave (07601-6727)
PHONE..........................201 678-1992
Ann Rabbani, *President*
Kevin Rabbani, *COO*
Carl Barthole, *Director*
▲ EMP: 10 EST: 1998
SQ FT: 10,000

SALES (est): 2.4MM **Privately Held**
WEB: www.biogenesis-labs.com
SIC: 2844 Cosmetic preparations

(G-3883)
BITRO GROUP INC
300 Lodi St (07601-3143)
PHONE..............................201 641-1004
Wha Lee, *President*
Ki S Lee, *President*
Sy Chang, *CFO*
Fritz Meyne, *VP Sales*
Rob Riley, *Sales Staff*
▲ EMP: 25
SQ FT: 22,000
SALES (est): 7MM **Privately Held**
SIC: 3641 Electric lamps & parts for spe-
cialized applications

(G-3884)
BOSTON TEA COMPANY LLC
560 Hudson St Ste 1-5 (07601-6638)
P.O. Box 1844, South Hackensack (07606-
0444)
PHONE..............................201 440-3004
Andrew Jacob, *President*
▲ EMP: 8
SALES (est): 1.1MM **Privately Held**
SIC: 2086 5149 Iced tea & fruit drinks,
bottled & canned; tea

(G-3885)
**BRAINSTORM CELL
THRPEUTICS INC**
3 University Plaza Dr (07601)
PHONE..............................201 488-0460
Fax: 201 430-7555
Irit Arbel, *Ch of Bd*
Chaim Lebovits, *President*
Uri Yablonka, *COO*
Joseph Petroziello, *Vice Pres*
Mary Kay Turner, *Vice Pres*
EMP: 20
SALES (est): 2.7MM **Privately Held**
SIC: 2836 Biological products, except diag-
nostic

(G-3886)
**C & K PUNCH & SCREW MCH
PDTS**
160 Hobart St (07601-3922)
PHONE..............................201 343-6750
Fax: 201 343-1814
Donald Kuder, *President*
Alan Conrad, *Vice Pres*
Carole Kuder, *Treasurer*
EMP: 6
SQ FT: 4,000
SALES (est): 858.6K **Privately Held**
WEB: www.candkpunches.com
SIC: 3544 3451 Special dies & tools; die
sets for metal stamping (presses); jigs &
fixtures; screw machine products

(G-3887)
CAD SIGNS LLC
169 Lodi St (07601-3942)
PHONE..............................201 267-0457
Oscar F Galeano,
EMP: 5 EST: 2005
SALES (est): 641.1K **Privately Held**
SIC: 3993 Electric signs

(G-3888)
CAD SIGNS NYC CORP
169 Lodi St (07601-3942)
PHONE..............................201 525-5415
Alex Galeano, *President*
EMP: 30 EST: 2013
SALES (est): 1.3MM **Privately Held**
SIC: 3993 Signs & advertising specialties

(G-3889)
CADENCE DISTRIBUTORS LLC
200 S Newman St Unit 8 (07601-3124)
PHONE..............................646 808-3031
Ankur Ahuja, *Mng Member*
▲ EMP: 3 EST: 2010
SALES: 1.7MM **Privately Held**
SIC: 2844 Perfumes & colognes

(G-3890)
**CALIFORNIA STUCCO
PRODUCTS**
85 Zabriskie St Ste 1 (07601-4934)
PHONE..............................201 457-1900
Fax: 201 342-2114
Edwin Gorter, *President*
EMP: 6 EST: 1927
SQ FT: 4,000
SALES (est): 615K **Privately Held**
WEB: www.californiastucco.net
SIC: 3299 Stucco

(G-3891)
**CALLAGHAN PUMP CONTROLS
INC**
106 Hobart St (07601-3911)
PHONE..............................201 621-0505
John Callaghan, *CEO*
Eileen Latona, *Vice Pres*
EMP: 4
SALES (est): 627.1K **Privately Held**
WEB: www.callaghanpump.com
SIC: 3561 Pumps & pumping equipment

(G-3892)
**CAMBRIDGE THERAPEUTIC
TECH LLC**
90 Main St Ste 107 (07601-7130)
PHONE..............................914 420-5555
John Klein, *CEO*
Mark Adams Jr, *Exec VP*
Barry Posner, *Exec VP*
EMP: 6
SALES (est): 315.6K **Privately Held**
SIC: 2834 Pharmaceutical preparations

(G-3893)
**CANADA DRY BOTTLING CO NY
LP**
Also Called: Seven Up Bottling Company
88 Polifly Rd (07601-3292)
PHONE..............................201 489-6600
Fax: 201 489-5852
Dave Barba, *Manager*
EMP: 35
SALES (corp-wide): 210.2MM **Privately
Held**
SIC: 2086 Soft drinks: packaged in cans,
bottles, etc.
PA: Canada Dry Bottling Company Of New
York, L.P.
11202 15th Ave
College Point NY 11356
718 358-2000

(G-3894)
CAVALLA INC
111 Union St (07601-4083)
PHONE..............................201 343-3338
Fax: 201 487-1096
Arthur Pisani, *President*
Alfred Neri, *Treasurer*
Mirella Bortone, *Finance Mgr*
Bryan Kafka, *Sales Engr*
Robert Pisani, *Admin Sec*
▲ EMP: 20 EST: 1925
SQ FT: 12,000
SALES (est): 3.5MM **Privately Held**
WEB: www.cavalla.net
SIC: 3544 5084 Special dies & tools;
packaging machinery & equipment

(G-3895)
CERAMIC PRODUCTS INC
221 Park St (07601-4215)
PHONE..............................201 342-8200
Ante Vidacic, *President*
Susan Giacobone, *President*
Richard Giacobone, *Vice Pres*
Mark Vidacic, *Manager*
▲ EMP: 4
SQ FT: 800
SALES: 950K **Privately Held**
SIC: 3299 Ceramic fiber

(G-3896)
**CHAMPIONS ONCOLOGY INC
(PA)**
1 University Plz Ste 307 (07601-6205)
PHONE..............................201 808-8400
Ronnie Morris, *CEO*
Joel Ackerman, *Ch of Bd*
David Miller, *CFO*

David Sidransky, *Director*
Abba Poliakoff, *Bd of Directors*
EMP: 92
SQ FT: 3,800
SALES: 20.2MM **Publicly Held**
WEB: www.championsbiotechnology.com
SIC: 2834 Pharmaceutical preparations

(G-3897)
CLIP STRIP CORP
343 S River St (07601-6838)
PHONE..............................201 342-9155
Fax: 201 342-1438
Edward Spitaletta, *President*
Buddy Mickolajczyk, *Exec VP*
Stuart Morrison, *Sales Staff*
Kamala Goldman, *Manager*
Robert Spitaletta, *Manager*
▲ EMP: 6
SQ FT: 12,000
SALES (est): 1.4MM **Privately Held**
WEB: www.clipstrip.com
SIC: 2542 Office & store showcases & dis-
play fixtures

(G-3898)
**CONCRETE CUTTING
PARTNERS INC**
508 Hudson St (07601-6608)
PHONE..............................201 440-2233
Fax: 201 440-2277
Barry Maillet, *President*
EMP: 8
SQ FT: 6,000
SALES (est): 995.7K **Privately Held**
SIC: 3559 1771 Concrete products ma-
chinery; concrete work

(G-3899)
CONTINENTAL COOKIES INC
185 S Newman St (07601-3125)
PHONE..............................201 498-1966
Fax: 201 498-1969
Steve Gavosto, *President*
EMP: 14
SQ FT: 15,000
SALES (est): 2.4MM **Privately Held**
WEB: www.continentalcookies.com
SIC: 2052 Cookies

(G-3900)
CONTRACT COATINGS INC
161 Beech St (07601-3424)
PHONE..............................201 343-3131
Fax: 201 343-3512
Jayant Amin, *President*
Bharat Patel, *Vice Pres*
EMP: 10
SQ FT: 6,700
SALES (est): 2.2MM **Privately Held**
WEB: www.contractcoatings.com
SIC: 2834 Pharmaceutical preparations

(G-3901)
CUTTING RECORDS INC
190 Main St Ste 403 (07601-7319)
PHONE..............................201 488-8444
Amado Marin, *President*
Louie Garcia, *General Mgr*
EMP: 7
SALES (est): 765.9K **Privately Held**
WEB: www.cuttingnyc.com
SIC: 2782 Record albums

(G-3902)
D & G LLC
Also Called: Hai Tai Boutique
29 1st St Apt 605 (07601-2067)
PHONE..............................201 289-5750
Ty Dobson, *CEO*
Madison Dey, *Exec Sec*
EMP: 5 EST: 2008
SQ FT: 2,200
SALES (est): 387.7K **Privately Held**
SIC: 2253 2341 2322 Knit outerwear
mills; women's & children's underwear;
underwear, men's & boys': made from
purchased materials

(G-3903)
DANSON SHEET METAL INC
Also Called: Hutcheon and Simon
140 Atlantic St (07601-4114)
PHONE..............................201 343-4876
Fax: 201 487-6332
Dan Cubicciotti Jr, *President*

EMP: 25
SQ FT: 8,000
SALES: 4MM **Privately Held**
SIC: 3444 1761 Sheet metalwork; sheet
metalwork

(G-3904)
DESIGN N STITCH INC
107 Pink St (07601-5207)
PHONE..............................201 488-1314
Fax: 201 488-1335
John Fitzpatrick, *President*
Robert Fitzpatrick, *Corp Secy*
EMP: 8
SQ FT: 2,000
SALES: 1MM **Privately Held**
WEB: www.design-n-stitch.com
SIC: 2262 2395 Screen printing: man-
made fiber & silk broadwoven fabrics; em-
broidery products, except schiffli machine

(G-3905)
DIE TECH LLC
58 Mckinley St (07601-4007)
PHONE..............................201 343-8324
Fax: 201 489-0803
Jim Galbreath,
EMP: 8
SALES (est): 939.1K **Privately Held**
SIC: 3544 Special dies & tools

(G-3906)
DISPLAY EQUATION LLC
135 Spring Valley Ave (07601-2947)
PHONE..............................201 343-4135
Frank J Cristiano,
Rosa Cristiano,
EMP: 6
SALES: 350K **Privately Held**
SIC: 2542 Office & store showcases & dis-
play fixtures

(G-3907)
DUCT MATE INC
190 Lexington Ave (07601-4021)
PHONE..............................201 488-8002
Joseph Tasca, *President*
Patricia Tasca, *Corp Secy*
EMP: 8
SALES (est): 900K **Privately Held**
WEB: www.ductmatehvac.com
SIC: 1711 3444 3585 Heating & air condi-
tioning contractors; sheet metalwork;
heating & air conditioning combination
units

(G-3908)
EBSCO PUBLISHING INC
Also Called: Salem Press
2 University Plz Ste 310 (07601-6202)
PHONE..............................201 968-9899
Veronica Kelly, *Sales Mgr*
Kristen Marino, *Regl Sales Mgr*
Deborah Lapierre, *Accounts Exec*
Ryan Mooney, *Accounts Exec*
Ian Collins, *Sales Staff*
EMP: 8
SALES (corp-wide): 2.8B **Privately Held**
SIC: 2741 Miscellaneous publishing
HQ: Ebsco Publishing, Inc.
10 Estes St
Ipswich MA 01938
978 356-6500

(G-3909)
**ELECTRO-CERAMIC
INDUSTRIES**
Also Called: Eci
75 Kennedy St (07601-5262)
PHONE..............................201 342-2630
Fax: 201 342-1823
Herbert Schlomann, *President*
Frank Floystad, *Vice Pres*
Leslie Vanderlaan, *Production*
EMP: 25
SQ FT: 6,500
SALES (est): 3.4MM **Privately Held**
WEB: www.electroceramic.com
SIC: 3264 3675 3053 Porcelain parts for
electrical devices, molded; electronic ca-
pacitors; gaskets, packing & sealing de-
vices

(G-3910)
FENCE AMERICA NEW JERSEY INC
210 S Newman St Ste 1 (07601-3145)
PHONE..............................973 472-5121
EMP: 5 EST: 2014
SALES (est): 575K **Privately Held**
SIC: 4789 4212 3315 Pipeline terminal facilities, independently operated; local trucking, without storage; fencing made in wiredrawing plants

(G-3911)
FIFTY/FIFTY GROUP INC
Also Called: Lola Products
343 S River St (07601-6838)
PHONE..............................201 343-1243
Fax: 201 489-6477
Richard Spitaletta, *President*
Edward Spitaletta, *Chairman*
Charles Spitaletta, *Vice Pres*
Jonathan Rento, *Purch Agent*
Nicole Kulhawy, *Sales Staff*
▲ EMP: 35
SQ FT: 27,000
SALES (est): 7.1MM **Privately Held**
WEB: www.lolaproducts.com
SIC: 3991 Brooms & brushes

(G-3912)
FIT GRAPHIX (PA)
390 Maple Hill Dr (07601-1411)
PHONE..............................201 488-4670
Lawrence Eisen, *President*
Marsha Eisen, *Treasurer*
EMP: 8
SQ FT: 5,000
SALES: 810K **Privately Held**
SIC: 2759 Commercial printing

(G-3913)
FITNESS TECHNOLOGIES INC
10 Banta Pl Ste 202 (07601-5605)
PHONE..............................201 457-0030
Opher Pail, *President*
Teresa Williams, *Officer*
EMP: 20
SQ FT: 3,500
SALES (est): 2.3MM **Privately Held**
SIC: 3625 Switches, electronic applications

(G-3914)
FLEX MOULDING INC
22 E Lafayette St (07601-6831)
PHONE..............................201 487-8080
Fax: 201 487-6637
Milton Glicksman, *Principal*
EMP: 8
SQ FT: 16,000
SALES: 1MM **Privately Held**
WEB: www.flexiblemoulding.com
SIC: 3089 2821 Injection molded finished plastic products; plastics materials & resins

(G-3915)
FORD FASTENERS INC
110 S Newman St (07601-3294)
PHONE..............................201 487-3151
Fax: 201 487-1919
Steve Cellary, *President*
Rossana Palatucci, *Office Mgr*
▲ EMP: 6 EST: 1963
SQ FT: 25,000
SALES (est): 2.5MM **Privately Held**
WEB: www.fordfasteners.com
SIC: 5072 3312 Screws; bolts; stainless steel

(G-3916)
FORDION PACKAGING LTD
185 Linden St Ste 3 (07601-4672)
PHONE..............................201 692-1344
Francis Harvey, *President*
John B Landers, *Vice Pres*
Brian Mc Manus, *Vice Pres*
Daniel J Ryan, *Vice Pres*
James Flanagan, *Treasurer*
EMP: 17
SQ FT: 2,000
SALES (est): 5MM **Privately Held**
SIC: 3081 Unsupported plastics film & sheet; polypropylene film & sheet

(G-3917)
FORM LECTRO INC
1 University Plaza Dr (07601-6229)
PHONE..............................973 777-0621
Fax: 973 777-7791
Thomas Schaffran, *President*
Nick Sans, *Vice Pres*
Thomas Kim, *Admin Sec*
▲ EMP: 30
SQ FT: 5,000
SALES (est): 4.6MM **Privately Held**
WEB: www.lectroform.com
SIC: 3535 2741 Conveyors & conveying equipment; miscellaneous publishing

(G-3918)
FOSTER ENGRAVING CORPORATION
174 S Main St Ste B (07601-5209)
PHONE..............................201 489-5979
Fax: 201 489-0112
Giovanni Osorio, *President*
EMP: 4 EST: 1959
SQ FT: 5,000
SALES: 300K **Privately Held**
SIC: 3089 3479 Engraving of plastic; etching & engraving

(G-3919)
FULL SERVICE MAILERS INC
123 S Newman St (07601-3211)
PHONE..............................973 478-8813
Evelio Velez Jr, *President*
EMP: 22
SQ FT: 154,000
SALES: 1.5MM **Privately Held**
SIC: 7331 2752 Mailing service; commercial printing, lithographic

(G-3920)
GENERAL AVIATION & ELEC MFG CO
Also Called: General A & E
30 Jersey Pl (07601-3103)
P.O. Box 2245, South Hackensack (07606-0845)
PHONE..............................201 487-1700
Fax: 201 487-8606
John Baker, *CEO*
Bella Baker, *Vice Pres*
Nancy Detoma, *Accountant*
Stella Baker, *Software Dev*
EMP: 25 EST: 1954
SQ FT: 25,000
SALES (est): 2.9MM **Privately Held**
WEB: www.generalae.com
SIC: 3444 Sheet metal specialties, not stamped

(G-3921)
GRAPHIC IMPRESSIONS INC
316 Prospect Ave Apt 10f (07601-2575)
PHONE..............................201 487-8788
Allan Bauer, *President*
Sharyn Bauer, *Treasurer*
▲ EMP: 9
SQ FT: 2,500
SALES (est): 858.9K **Privately Held**
WEB: www.graphic-impressions.com
SIC: 2752 Commercial printing, offset

(G-3922)
GRAPHIC SOLUTIONS & SIGNS LLC
82 Burlews Ct (07601-4829)
PHONE..............................201 343-7446
Felipe Alarcon,
EMP: 11
SQ FT: 10,000
SALES (est): 1.3MM **Privately Held**
WEB: www.graphicsolutionsandsigns.com
SIC: 3993 Signs & advertising specialties

(G-3923)
GREAT NOTCH INDUSTRIES INC
140 Liberty St (07601-3181)
PHONE..............................201 343-8110
Fax: 201 343-8327
Paul Galinski, *President*
James Galinski, *Vice Pres*
EMP: 5 EST: 1971
SQ FT: 3,200
SALES (est): 340K **Privately Held**
WEB: www.greatnotch.com
SIC: 3599 Machine shop, jobbing & repair

(G-3924)
GREY HOUSE PUBLISHING INC
Also Called: Salem Publishing
2 University Plz (07601-6202)
PHONE..............................201 968-0500
EMP: 8 **Privately Held**
SIC: 2741 Misc Publishing

(G-3925)
HARTMANN TOOL CO INC
147 Lodi St (07601-3928)
P.O. Box 405, Blairstown (07825-0405)
PHONE..............................201 343-8700
Fax: 201 343-8701
Thomas Hartmann, *President*
Dianne Hartmann, *Vice Pres*
EMP: 5
SQ FT: 1,300
SALES: 475K **Privately Held**
SIC: 3089 3544 Molding primary plastic; dies, plastics forming

(G-3926)
HIGH-TECHNOLOGY CORPORATION (PA)
144 South St (07601-3109)
PHONE..............................201 488-0010
Fax: 201 488-4318
Veronica Alroy, *President*
Aline Alroy, *Vice Pres*
Robert Crue, *Project Engr*
Violeta Enciu, *Project Engr*
Kim McCoy, *Technology*
EMP: 18
SQ FT: 13,500
SALES (est): 4.4MM **Privately Held**
SIC: 8731 3542 Commercial physical research; machine tools, metal forming type

(G-3927)
HIROX - USA INC (HQ)
100 Commerce Way Ste 4 (07601-6307)
PHONE..............................201 342-2600
Yusuke Kajiro, *President*
Steve Buck, *General Mgr*
Yasuo Monno, *Sales Engr*
Hideyuki Masui, *Manager*
EMP: 6
SALES (est): 1MM
SALES (corp-wide): 13.1MM **Privately Held**
WEB: www.hirox-usa.com
SIC: 3944 Science kits: microscopes, chemistry sets, etc.
PA: Hirox Co., Ltd.
2-15-17, Koenjiminami
Suginami-Ku TKY 166-0
333 119-911

(G-3928)
HOFFMAN/NEW YORKER INC (PA)
46 Clinton Pl (07601-4523)
PHONE..............................201 488-1800
Fax: 973 748-1341
Terrance Rothlisberger, *General Mgr*
Terence V Rothlisberger, *Vice Pres*
Richard J Greco, *Treasurer*
Jeffrey A Rabinowitz, *Admin Sec*
▲ EMP: 7
SALES (est): 7.9MM **Privately Held**
WEB: www.hoffmanpressing.com
SIC: 3582 Pressing machines, commercial laundry & drycleaning; drycleaning equipment & machinery, commercial

(G-3929)
INTENZE PRODUCTS INC (PA)
15 Van Orden Pl (07601-6012)
PHONE..............................201 342-4446
Mario Barth, *CEO*
EMP: 6
SALES (est): 1.8MM **Privately Held**
SIC: 2899 Ink or writing fluids

(G-3930)
INTERIOR ART & DESIGN INC
59 Oak St (07601-4927)
PHONE..............................201 488-8855
Fax: 201 487-4488
Ori Katzin, *President*
Ronit Katzin, *Treasurer*
EMP: 23
SQ FT: 9,615
SALES: 1.2MM **Privately Held**
WEB: www.interiorart.com
SIC: 2392 2391 Household furnishings; curtains & draperies

(G-3931)
INTERNATIONAL CONTAINER CO
Also Called: Paper Board Products
409 S River St (07601-6616)
PHONE..............................201 440-1600
Fax: 201 440-6740
Jonathan A Marks, *President*
Peter L Kirsch, *Vice Pres*
Sean Searles, *Sales Staff*
Victoria Marks, *Admin Sec*
EMP: 46
SQ FT: 5,000
SALES (est): 9MM **Privately Held**
SIC: 2653 2657 Boxes, corrugated: made from purchased materials; folding paperboard boxes

(G-3932)
JACQUELINE EMBROIDERY CO
445 Thompson St Apt G (07601-1261)
PHONE..............................732 278-8121
Frank Cervantes, *Owner*
EMP: 4
SQ FT: 5,000
SALES (est): 228.4K **Privately Held**
SIC: 2397 Schiffli machine embroideries

(G-3933)
JOHN COOPER COMPANY INC
Also Called: Beers Steel Erecting
250 Maywood Ave Ste C (07601)
PHONE..............................201 487-4018
Darby L Diedrich, *President*
EMP: 12
SQ FT: 20,000
SALES (est): 1.1MM **Privately Held**
SIC: 1761 1791 3441 Siding contractor; structural steel erection; fabricated structural metal

(G-3934)
JOHNSON & MAYER INC
Also Called: Skinwear Temporary Tattoos
58 Hobart St (07601-3909)
PHONE..............................201 646-1717
Fax: 201 646-1115
Mitchell Perdue, *President*
EMP: 12
SQ FT: 15,000
SALES: 1.8MM **Privately Held**
WEB: www.jmtattoos.com
SIC: 2679 Novelties, paper: made from purchased material

(G-3935)
KAYDEN MANUFACTURING INC
Also Called: Pool Ladder
83a Burlews Ct Ste A (07601-4839)
PHONE..............................201 880-9898
Jeff Kayden, *President*
Jess Kayden, *President*
Erika Kayden, *Vice Pres*
◆ EMP: 12
SQ FT: 3,500
SALES: 1MM **Privately Held**
WEB: www.kaydenmfg.com
SIC: 3949 Swimming pools, except plastic

(G-3936)
KEYPOINT INTELLIGENCE LLC
108 John St (07601-4130)
PHONE..............................201 489-6439
Dan Narbone, *Director*
EMP: 5 **Privately Held**
WEB: www.buyerslab.com
SIC: 2721 Statistical reports (periodicals): publishing only
HQ: Keypoint Intelligence Llc
80 Little Falls Rd
Fairfield NJ 07004
973 797-2100

(G-3937)
KRAISSL COMPANY INC
299 Williams Ave (07601-5225)
P.O. Box 2363, South Hackensack (07606-0963)
PHONE..............................201 342-0008
Fax: 201 342-0025
Richard C Michel, *Ch of Bd*

GEOGRAPHIC

Angela Di Palma, *Controller*
EMP: 25
SQ FT: 13,000
SALES: 1.9MM **Privately Held**
WEB: www.kraissl.com
SIC: 3494 3561 3563 Valves & pipe fittings; pumps & pumping equipment; air & gas compressors including vacuum pumps

(G-3938)
LECO PLASTICS INC
130 Gameville St (07601)
PHONE.................................201 343-3330
Fax: 201 343-0558
Barry Schwartz, *President*
Seth Haubenstock, *Sales Dir*
Burt Schwartz, *Sales Staff*
◆ **EMP:** 10 **EST:** 1946
SQ FT: 20,000
SALES (est): 2.2MM **Privately Held**
WEB: www.lecoplastics.com
SIC: 3089 Extruded finished plastic products; injection molding of plastics

(G-3939)
LIVEU INC
2 University Plz Ste 505 (07601-6210)
PHONE.................................201 742-5229
Avichai Cohen, *President*
EMP: 60 **EST:** 2008
SALES (est): 16.2MM **Privately Held**
SIC: 3861 Cameras & related equipment

(G-3940)
LOSURDO FOODS INC (PA)
Also Called: Bel-Capri
20 Owens Rd (07601-3297)
PHONE.................................201 343-6680
Fax: 201 343-8078
Marc Jx Losurdo, *President*
Marc Losurdo, *Vice Pres*
Maria Losurdo, *Treasurer*
Michael Losurdo Sr, *Officer*
Mary Losurdo, *Admin Sec*
▲ **EMP:** 50
SQ FT: 20,000
SALES (est): 81.7MM **Privately Held**
WEB: www.losurdofoods.com
SIC: 5141 2022 2033 2045 Food brokers; natural cheese; tomato sauce: packaged in cans, jars, etc.; pizza doughs, prepared: from purchased flour

(G-3941)
M B C FOOD MACHINERY CORP
78 Mckinley St (07601-4009)
PHONE.................................201 489-7000
Fax: 201 489-0614
Mario Battaglia, *CEO*
John Battaglia, *President*
Chris Guilianti, *Foreman/Supr*
Rosa Battaglia, *Admin Sec*
EMP: 6
SQ FT: 4,410
SALES (est): 1.1MM **Privately Held**
WEB: www.mbcfoodmachinery.com
SIC: 3556 Food products machinery

(G-3942)
MACROMEDIA INCORPORATED (PA)
150 River St (07601-7110)
P.O. Box 75 (07602-0075)
PHONE.................................201 646-4000
Fax: 201 646-4135
Malcolm A Borg, *Ch of Bd*
Stephen A Borg, *Vice Pres*
Charles W Gibney, *Treasurer*
EMP: 21
SQ FT: 360,000
SALES (est): 173.6MM **Privately Held**
WEB: www.mmsconnect.com
SIC: 2711 2721 Newspapers, publishing & printing; periodicals

(G-3943)
MASTER BOND INC
154 Hobart St (07601-3922)
PHONE.................................201 343-8983
James Brenner, *President*
Susan Edwards, *Corp Secy*
Robert Brenner, *Vice Pres*
Michaels Robert, *Vice Pres*
Hillary Evans, *Research*
▲ **EMP:** 30

SQ FT: 16,000
SALES (est): 7.7MM **Privately Held**
SIC: 2891 2851 Adhesives; epoxy coatings

(G-3944)
MAVERICK CATERERS LLC
20 Railroad Ave (07601-3309)
PHONE.................................718 433-3776
AVI Moche,
Erik Gross,
EMP: 30
SQ FT: 4,000
SALES (est): 3.1MM **Privately Held**
SIC: 5149 2099 Natural & organic foods; food preparations

(G-3945)
MDJ INC
25 Dicarolis Ct 21 (07601-4115)
PHONE.................................201 457-9260
Fax: 201 457-9265
Donald Hahn, *President*
Peter Sowinski, *Vice Pres*
EMP: 40
SQ FT: 8,000
SALES (est): 4.3MM **Privately Held**
WEB: www.mdjco.com
SIC: 3672 Printed circuit boards

(G-3946)
MEDCO WEST ELECTRONICS INC
25 Dicarolis Ct 21 (07601-4115)
PHONE.................................201 457-9260
Guy Intoci, *President*
Peter Sowinski, *Vice Pres*
EMP: 6
SALES (est): 629.3K **Privately Held**
SIC: 3672 Printed circuit boards

(G-3947)
MERC USA INC
Also Called: Inserch By Merc U.S.a
41 Newman St (07601-3324)
PHONE.................................201 489-3527
Fax: 201 489-7636
Jahangir Astaneha, *President*
Mostafa Astaneha, *Vice Pres*
▲ **EMP:** 11
SALES (est): 2.8MM **Privately Held**
SIC: 5136 2329 Men's & boys' clothing; men's & boys' sportswear & athletic clothing

(G-3948)
MUL-T-LOCK USA INC
100 Commerce Way Ste 2 (07601-6307)
PHONE.................................973 778-3320
Fax: 973 778-4007
Nava Efrati, *President*
▲ **EMP:** 20
SQ FT: 10,000
SALES (est): 9.6MM
SALES (corp-wide): 9B **Privately Held**
WEB: www.mul-t-lockusa.com
SIC: 5072 3429 Security devices, locks; keys, locks & related hardware; padlocks; door locks, bolts & checks
HQ: Assa Abloy Inc.
　　110 Sargent Dr
　　New Haven CT 06511
　　203 624-5225

(G-3949)
MULTI-PAK CORPORATION
180 Atlantic St (07601-3301)
PHONE.................................201 342-7474
Fax: 201 342-6525
Phil Cahill, *President*
Niel Cavanaugh, *Chairman*
EMP: 24 **EST:** 1956
SQ FT: 8,500
SALES (est): 5.4MM **Privately Held**
WEB: www.compactors1.com
SIC: 3589 3531 Garbage disposers & compactors, commercial; construction machinery

(G-3950)
MURRAY PAVING & CONCRETE LLC
210 S Newman St Ste 1 (07601-3145)
PHONE.................................201 670-0030
William Murray,
EMP: 35 **EST:** 2004

SALES: 12.3MM **Privately Held**
SIC: 1611 1771 1741 3281 Highway & street paving contractor; blacktop (asphalt) work; masonry & other stonework; concrete block masonry laying; curbing, paving & walkway stone

(G-3951)
NEI GOLD PRODUCTS OF NJ
Also Called: Nei House of Chains
44 Burlews Ct (07601-4829)
PHONE.................................201 488-5858
John Nanasi, *President*
Ernie Tacktill, *Exec VP*
Andy Kardos, *Vice Pres*
Ernie Reinetz, *Treasurer*
EMP: 30
SQ FT: 15,000
SALES (est): 369.8K **Privately Held**
SIC: 3911 Jewelry, precious metal

(G-3952)
NEI JEWELMASTERS OF NEW JERSEY (PA)
Also Called: Nanasi Enterprises
44 Burlews Ct (07601-4829)
PHONE.................................201 488-5858
Fax: 201 488-1926
John Nanasi, *President*
Norman Diamond, *Vice Pres*
Andy Kardos, *Vice Pres*
Marc Nanasi, *Sales Staff*
Sarah Nanasi, *Mktg Dir*
EMP: 60 **EST:** 1972
SQ FT: 15,000
SALES (est): 6.1MM **Privately Held**
SIC: 3911 Jewelry, precious metal

(G-3953)
NETWORK COMMUNICATIONS CONS
Also Called: Netcom
20 E Kennedy St (07601-6807)
PHONE.................................201 968-0684
Fax: 201 968-0688
Virginia Connors, *President*
James Tronolone, *Treasurer*
EMP: 10
SQ FT: 5,000
SALES: 1.3MM **Privately Held**
WEB: www.netcom-stl.com
SIC: 3663 8711 Radio & TV communications equipment; consulting engineer

(G-3954)
NJIW LIMITED LIABILITY COMPANY
Also Called: J A Visual Group
87 Burlews Ct (07601-4839)
PHONE.................................201 355-2955
Jeffrey Weissman, *Mng Member*
Terumi Uto,
EMP: 14
SALES (est): 187.7K **Privately Held**
SIC: 2759 8742 7389 Promotional printing; merchandising consultant;

(G-3955)
NU-EZ CUSTOM BINDERY LLC
111 Essex St Ste 1 (07601-4043)
PHONE.................................201 488-4140
Julia Paulucci,
EMP: 25
SALES (est): 7.2MM **Privately Held**
SIC: 2631 Binders' board

(G-3956)
OCEANIC GRAPHIC INTL INC
Also Called: Oceanic Graphic Printing
105 Main St Ste 1 (07601-8103)
PHONE.................................201 883-1816
David LI, *President*
Michael Lok, *Vice Pres*
EMP: 10
SALES (est): 933.8K **Privately Held**
WEB: www.ogprinting.com
SIC: 8742 2732 Marketing consulting services; book printing

(G-3957)
OSHEA SERVICES INC
Also Called: O'Shea's Printing Services
483 Main St (07601-5932)
PHONE.................................201 343-8668
Fax: 201 343-2105

Kathleen Bracken, *President*
Mildred O'Shea, *Director*
EMP: 9
SQ FT: 5,000
SALES: 800K **Privately Held**
SIC: 2752 2791 2789 2759 Commercial printing, offset; typesetting; bookbinding & related work; commercial printing

(G-3958)
OVEN ART LLC
Also Called: Oven Arts
200 S Newman St Unit 7 (07601-3124)
PHONE.................................973 910-2266
Manish Wadia,
EMP: 40
SQ FT: 20,000
SALES: 4.5MM **Privately Held**
SIC: 2052 5149 Cookies & crackers; crackers, cookies & bakery products

(G-3959)
P & A AUTO PARTS INC (PA)
530 River St (07601-5907)
PHONE.................................201 655-7117
Anne De Pasque, *President*
Bill Freedman, *VP Opers*
Robert Samarati, *Opers Mgr*
Steve Blitzstein, *Store Mgr*
Jackie De Pasque-Cupoli, *Treasurer*
EMP: 30
SQ FT: 13,000
SALES (est): 65.8MM **Privately Held**
WEB: www.paautoparts.com
SIC: 5531 5013 5015 3714 Automotive parts; automotive supplies & parts; motor vehicle parts, used; motor vehicle parts & accessories

(G-3960)
P L M MANUFACTURING COMPANY
Also Called: Progressive Machine Company
293 Hudson St (07601-6732)
P.O. Box 1663, South Hackensack (07606-0263)
PHONE.................................201 342-3636
Fax: 201 342-3568
Peter Wysocki, *President*
Kazmier Wysocki, *Vice Pres*
EMP: 27
SQ FT: 7,500
SALES (est): 3.6MM **Privately Held**
SIC: 3599 3444 Machine shop, jobbing & repair; sheet metalwork

(G-3961)
PATCHAMP INC
20 E Kennedy St (07601-6807)
PHONE.................................201 457-1504
Fax: 201 457-1507
Virginia Connors, *President*
James Tronolone, *Vice Pres*
EMP: 7
SQ FT: 5,000
SALES: 1MM **Privately Held**
WEB: www.patchamp.com
SIC: 3663 Television broadcasting & communications equipment

(G-3962)
PETNET SOLUTIONS INC
86-110 Orchard St Ste 2 (07601-4833)
PHONE.................................865 218-2000
Frank Chapman, *Branch Mgr*
EMP: 4
SALES (corp-wide): 97.7B **Privately Held**
SIC: 2835 Radioactive diagnostic substances
HQ: Petnet Solutions, Inc.
　　810 Innovation Dr
　　Knoxville TN 37932
　　865 218-2000

(G-3963)
PMC INDUSTRIES INC
275 Hudson St (07601-6753)
P.O. Box 1663, South Hackensack (07606-0263)
PHONE.................................201 342-3684
Kazmier Wysocki, *President*
Peter Wysocki, *Vice Pres*
Mary Wysocki, *Treasurer*
Jim Harris, *Sales Executive*
Dominic Delia, *Manager*
EMP: 25

SQ FT: 10,000
SALES (est): 5.7MM **Privately Held**
WEB: www.pmc-industries.com
SIC: 3565 Packaging machinery

(G-3964)
PREFORM LABORATORIES INC
Also Called: Performance Laboratories Inc
34 George St (07601-3907)
P.O. Box 2208, South Hackensack (07606-0808)
PHONE....................................973 523-8610
Fax: 973 523-3865
Michael Bozzaotra, *CEO*
▲ EMP: 44
SQ FT: 5,400
SALES: 2.6MM **Privately Held**
WEB: www.performlab.com
SIC: 3842 Supports: abdominal, ankle, arch, kneecap, etc.

(G-3965)
PRISMATIX DECAL INC
324 Railroad Ave (07601-3401)
PHONE....................................201 525-2800
Fax: 201 525-2828
Ira Salomon, *President*
▲ EMP: 8
SQ FT: 5,000
SALES: 1.5MM **Privately Held**
WEB: www.prismatixdecal.com
SIC: 5199 2396 Gifts & novelties; automotive & apparel trimmings

(G-3966)
RENNSTEIG TOOLS INC (DH)
411 Hackensack Ave # 200 (07601-6328)
PHONE....................................330 315-3044
Sascha Zmiskol, *President*
Mirko Reffke, *Vice Pres*
Feven Mekkonen, *Train & Dev Mgr*
Ralf Putsch, *Director*
Hans Michael Kraus, *Admin Sec*
▲ EMP: 3
SALES: 1.5MM
SALES (corp-wide): 49.4MM **Privately Held**
SIC: 5084 5251 3546 Machine tools & accessories; tools, power; cartridge-activated hand power tools
HQ: Rennsteig Werkzeuge Gmbh
An Der Koppel 1
Viernau 98547
368 474-410

(G-3967)
ROY ANANIA
Also Called: South State Speed Shop
149 S State St (07601-3902)
PHONE....................................201 498-1555
Roy Anania, *Owner*
EMP: 6
SALES (est): 410K **Privately Held**
WEB: www.southstatespeed.com
SIC: 3519 Gasoline engines

(G-3968)
RUFFINO PAPER BOX MFG CO
Also Called: Ruffino Packaging Co
63 Green St (07601-4082)
PHONE....................................201 487-1260
Fax: 201 487-3926
Raymond Ruffino, *President*
Rosario Ruffino, *President*
EMP: 12
SQ FT: 12,000
SALES (est): 4.9MM **Privately Held**
SIC: 2652 Setup paperboard boxes

(G-3969)
S GOLDBERG & CO INC (PA)
Also Called: Sgfootwear Company
3 University Plz Ste 400 (07601-6222)
PHONE....................................201 342-1200
Fax: 201 935-4837
Matthew Feiner, *CEO*
Bernard Leifer, *President*
Helen B King, *Chairman*
Paul Kingslow, *COO*
Stanley Altscher, *CFO*
◆ EMP: 105 EST: 1896
SQ FT: 23,000

SALES (est): 27.5MM **Privately Held**
WEB: www.sgfootwear.com
SIC: 3149 3142 5139 Sandals, except rubber or plastic: children's; house slippers; slipper socks, made from purchased socks; footwear

(G-3970)
SAGE CHEMICAL INC
2 University Plz Ste 204 (07601-6211)
PHONE....................................201 489-5172
Daniel Newman, *President*
Colleen Dominguez, *President*
Nathan Barishan, *Vice Pres*
EMP: 4
SQ FT: 1,400
SALES (est): 469.2K **Privately Held**
SIC: 2899 5169 Chemical supplies for foundries; chemicals & allied products

(G-3971)
SAMUEL H FIELDS DENTAL LABS
Also Called: Fields Samuel H Dental Labs
197 Union St (07601-4236)
PHONE....................................201 343-4626
Fax: 201 343-1480
Samuel Fields, *President*
Robert Fields, *Corp Secy*
Richard Fields, *Vice Pres*
EMP: 25
SQ FT: 5,000
SALES (est): 1.8MM **Privately Held**
WEB: www.samfieldslab.com
SIC: 8072 8021 3843 Crown & bridge production; offices & clinics of dentists; dental equipment & supplies

(G-3972)
SENSIBLE COLLECTION INC
Also Called: Toweltails
2 University Plz Ste 100 (07601-6210)
PHONE....................................201 831-1063
Ziv Kopolovitz,
EMP: 1
SQ FT: 1,000
SALES: 1MM **Privately Held**
SIC: 5719 5023 2211 Towels; towels; towels & toweling, cotton

(G-3973)
SGB PACKAGING GROUP INC
401 Hackensack Ave Fl 7 (07601-6411)
PHONE....................................201 488-3030
Shoshana Gibli, *President*
Benjamin Gibli, *Vice Pres*
Christin Meizinger-Kiene, *Opers Staff*
EMP: 4
SALES (est): 598.2K **Privately Held**
WEB: www.sgbpackaging.com
SIC: 8748 2844 7389 Agricultural consultant; cosmetic preparations; cosmetic kits, assembling & packaging

(G-3974)
SGI APPAREL LTD
3 University Plz Ste 400 (07601-6222)
PHONE....................................201 342-1200
Bernard Leifer, *CEO*
Michael Diablo, *President*
Paul Kingslow, *Vice Pres*
Stanley Altscher, *CFO*
◆ EMP: 7
SQ FT: 23,000
SALES (est): 720.9K
SALES (corp-wide): 27.5MM **Privately Held**
WEB: www.sgfootwear.com
SIC: 2341 2322 Women's & children's nightwear; men's & boys' underwear & nightwear
PA: S. Goldberg & Co., Inc.
3 University Plz Ste 400
Hackensack NJ 07601
201 342-1200

(G-3975)
SIGN A RAMA
Also Called: Sign-A-Rama
379 Main St (07601-5806)
PHONE....................................201 489-6969
Fax: 201 489-1429
Jonathan Sklar, *President*
Michael Fried, *Vice Pres*
EMP: 4

SALES (est): 403.4K **Privately Held**
SIC: 3993 Signs & advertising specialties

(G-3976)
SOLUTION AND SYSTEM INC
Also Called: Internl Traders Asso Silicon
411 Hackensack Ave (07601-6328)
PHONE....................................201 488-7770
Byeong Keon Son, *President*
EMP: 5
SALES (est): 773.6K **Privately Held**
SIC: 3674 Solar cells

(G-3977)
SOMES UNIFORMS INC (PA)
314 Main St (07601-5707)
P.O. Box 68 (07602-0068)
PHONE....................................201 843-1199
Jerome S Some, *President*
Diane Some, *Treasurer*
Jason Some, *Sales Staff*
▲ EMP: 18
SQ FT: 40,000
SALES (est): 2.9MM **Privately Held**
SIC: 5699 2326 5961 Uniforms; men's & boys' work clothing; clothing, mail order (except women's); women's apparel, mail order

(G-3978)
SOUTH RIVER MACHINERY CORP
Also Called: South River Food Machinery
115 S River St (07601-6909)
PHONE....................................201 487-1736
Frank Chessari, *President*
Lisa Asala, *President*
EMP: 4
SALES (est): 310K **Privately Held**
SIC: 3599 Machine shop, jobbing & repair

(G-3979)
SPARTECH LLC
Also Called: Polycast
215 S Newman St (07601)
PHONE....................................201 489-4000
Fax: 201 489-0923
John Alfano, *General Mgr*
EMP: 35
SALES (corp-wide): 1.4B **Privately Held**
WEB: www.spartech.com
SIC: 2821 Plastics materials & resins
PA: Spartech Llc
11650 Lkeside Crossing Ct
Saint Louis MO 63105
314 569-7400

(G-3980)
SPECTRUM INSTRUMENTATION CORP
15 Warren St Ste 25 (07601-5436)
PHONE....................................201 562-1999
Gisela Hassler, *CEO*
EMP: 20
SALES (est): 157K **Privately Held**
SIC: 3825 Oscillographs & oscilloscopes

(G-3981)
STOREMAXX INC
343 S River St (07601-6838)
PHONE....................................201 440-8800
Edward Spitaletta, *President*
◆ EMP: 11 EST: 2010
SALES (est): 1.5MM **Privately Held**
SIC: 3089 Plastic containers, except foam

(G-3982)
STUDIO L CONTRACTING LLC
18 Dicarolis Ct (07601-4115)
PHONE....................................201 837-1650
David Lehmann,
EMP: 6
SQ FT: 2,400
SALES: 1MM **Privately Held**
SIC: 2434 2499 Wood kitchen cabinets; decorative wood & woodwork

(G-3983)
TECH ART INC
Also Called: Techart
25 Green St (07601-4003)
P.O. Box 1556, South Hackensack (07606-0156)
PHONE....................................201 525-0044
Gerald Pfund, *President*

Paul McDonald, *Vice Pres*
EMP: 10
SQ FT: 16,000
SALES (est): 790K **Privately Held**
SIC: 3999 Education aids, devices & supplies

(G-3984)
TESTRITE INSTRUMENT CO INC
Also Called: Testrite Visual Products
216 S Newman St (07601-3124)
PHONE....................................201 543-0240
Fax: 201 589-4196
Laurence S Rubin, *CEO*
Mitchell Lewis, *President*
Jeffrey Rubin, *President*
Jenae Rubin, *Business Mgr*
Ken Allen, *Vice Pres*
▲ EMP: 130 EST: 1919
SQ FT: 88,000
SALES (est): 31.5MM **Privately Held**
WEB: www.TESTRITE.com
SIC: 2542 5046 3599 3993 Fixtures: display, office or store: except wood; store fixtures & display equipment; tubing, flexible metallic; signs & advertising specialties

(G-3985)
TOTAL INK SOLUTIONS LLC
200 S Newman St Unit 4 (07601-3124)
PHONE....................................201 487-9600
Luis Uribe, *President*
Marc Jelinsky, *Vice Pres*
Andrew Maniotis, *VP Sales*
Michael D Savino, *Marketing Staff*
EMP: 10
SQ FT: 20,000
SALES (est): 2MM **Privately Held**
SIC: 2893 2396 Printing ink; screen printing on fabric articles

(G-3986)
TRIUMPH KNITTING MACHINE SVC (PA)
Also Called: Truimph Knitting Mills
238 Main St Ste 102 (07601-7318)
PHONE....................................201 646-0022
Fax: 201 646-1198
Trudy Gerber, *President*
Steve Gerber, *Treasurer*
▲ EMP: 4
SQ FT: 20,000
SALES (est): 2.9MM **Privately Held**
WEB: www.triumphknittinginc.com
SIC: 2253 Knit outerwear mills

(G-3987)
TYPESTYLE INC
Also Called: Blue Dog Graphics
222 River St (07601-7516)
PHONE....................................201 343-3343
Donald Perlman, *President*
EMP: 5
SQ FT: 3,000
SALES (est): 791.7K **Privately Held**
SIC: 2752 Commercial printing, offset

(G-3988)
TYZ-ALL PLASTICS LLC
130 Gamewell St (07601-4230)
PHONE....................................201 343-1200
Burt Schwartz,
EMP: 7
SALES (est): 872.6K **Privately Held**
SIC: 3089 Food casings, plastic

(G-3989)
UNIVERSAL ELECTRIC CO
131 S Newman St (07601-3211)
PHONE....................................201 968-1000
Fax: 201 678-9511
Bill Stagg, *President*
EMP: 44
SQ FT: 17,900
SALES (est): 3.7MM **Privately Held**
SIC: 7694 5063 3621 Electric motor repair; motors, electric; motors, electric; generators & sets, electric

(G-3990)
UNIVERSAL ELECTRIC MTR SVC INC
131 S Newman St (07601-3211)
PHONE....................................201 968-1000
Stephen Adzima Jr, *President*

Steve Stagg, *Sales Staff*
EMP: 17 **EST:** 1947
SQ FT: 10,000
SALES (est): 5.8MM **Privately Held**
SIC: 5063 7694 Motors, electric; electric motor repair

(G-3991)
WHAT A TEE 2 INC
82 Sussex St (07601-4104)
PHONE..............................201 457-0060
Fax: 201 457-0064
Craig Laskow, *President*
Harry Poulos, *President*
EMP: 16
SQ FT: 6,500
SALES (est): 1.4MM **Privately Held**
SIC: 2339 2329 Women's & misses' athletic clothing & sportswear; men's & boys' sportswear & athletic clothing

(G-3992)
WORLD SCIENTIFIC PUBLISHING CO
27 Warren St Ph 401 (07601-8918)
PHONE..............................201 487-9655
Doreen Phua, *President*
Nancy Merino, *General Mgr*
K K Phua, *Vice Pres*
Allan Barnett, *Sales Executive*
Ruth Zhou, *Marketing Mgr*
▲ **EMP:** 10
SQ FT: 1,500
SALES (est): 974.7K
SALES (corp-wide): 13.1MM **Privately Held**
WEB: www.wspc.com
SIC: 2731 Textbooks: publishing only, not printed on site
PA: World Scientific Publishing Co Pte Ltd
5 Toh Tuck Link
Singapore 59622
646 230-83

(G-3993)
ZAIYA INC
185 Kenneth St (07601)
PHONE..............................201 343-3988
Hirokazu Sano, *President*
EMP: 24
SALES (est): 1.7MM **Privately Held**
SIC: 2051 Bakery: wholesale or wholesale/retail combined

Hackettstown
Warren County

(G-3994)
A AND P PHARMACY
Also Called: A&P
7 Naughright Rd Ste V (07840-5660)
PHONE..............................908 850-7640
EMP: 6
SALES (est): 380K **Privately Held**
SIC: 2834 Mfg Pharmaceutical Preparations

(G-3995)
AJJ POWERNUTRITION LLC
Also Called: Nutrition Zone
1930 State Route 57 (07840-3484)
PHONE..............................908 452-5164
Jon Aid Anwar, *Owner*
Jawad Anwar,
Jonaid Anwar,
EMP: 7
SALES (est): 978.1K **Privately Held**
SIC: 2834 Vitamin, nutrient & hematinic preparations for human use

(G-3996)
ALMETEK INDUSTRIES INC
2 Joy Dr (07840-5331)
PHONE..............................908 850-9700
Fax: 908 850-9618
Lori Mc Mahon, *CEO*
Lori McMahon, *President*
Albert Burlando, *Principal*
Joyce Burlando, *Vice Pres*
Mike Quagliana, *Vice Pres*
EMP: 50
SQ FT: 42,000

SALES (est): 8.7MM **Privately Held**
WEB: www.almetek.com
SIC: 3999 3699 Identification badges & insignia; security devices

(G-3997)
ANDREX INC
101 Bilby Rd Ste E (07840-1753)
PHONE..............................908 852-2400
William T Pote, *President*
Thomas W Pote, *Vice Pres*
Marion Pote, *Admin Sec*
EMP: 15
SQ FT: 18,200
SALES (est): 2.3MM **Privately Held**
WEB: www.andrex.com
SIC: 3599 3679 3429 Hose, flexible metallic; harness assemblies for electronic use: wire or cable; manufactured hardware (general)

(G-3998)
ASTRODYNE CORPORATION (PA)
36 Newburgh Rd (07840-3904)
PHONE..............................908 850-5088
Peter Murphy, *President*
Peter Resca, *VP Sls/Mktg*
Lisa Gorman, *CFO*
Mary Ellen Gilson, *Contract Mgr*
▲ **EMP:** 62
SQ FT: 20,000
SALES (est): 172.3MM **Privately Held**
WEB: www.astrodyne.com
SIC: 3625 3621 3613 Switches, electric power; motors & generators; switchgear & switchboard apparatus

(G-3999)
B & H PRINTERS INC
Also Called: Jbq Printing & Marketing
470 Schooleys Mountain Rd # 1 (07840-4012)
PHONE..............................908 688-6990
Holly Harvey, *President*
Robert Harvey, *Vice Pres*
EMP: 7
SQ FT: 4,000
SALES (est): 1.2MM **Privately Held**
SIC: 2759 Commercial printing

(G-4000)
CEODEUX INCORPORATED
101 Bilby Rd Ste B (07840-1753)
PHONE..............................724 696-4340
Isabelle Schmitz, *President*
▲ **EMP:** 25
SQ FT: 65,041
SALES (est): 4.8MM **Privately Held**
WEB: www.rotarex.com
SIC: 3494 5085 Valves & pipe fittings; valves & fittings
HQ: Ceodeux Sa
Rue De Diekirch 24
Lintgen 7440
327 832-

(G-4001)
CLASSIC CHESS AND GAMES INC
52 Main St (07840-1331)
PHONE..............................908 850-6553
Ken Tomchek, *President*
EMP: 4
SALES (est): 216.3K **Privately Held**
WEB: www.classicchessandgames.com
SIC: 3944 Board games, children's & adults'

(G-4002)
DALE BEHRE
Also Called: Dales's Custom Auto & Sign
108 East Ave Ste 6 (07840-2661)
PHONE..............................908 850-4225
Fax: 908 850-1545
Dale Behre, *Owner*
EMP: 5
SQ FT: 2,500
SALES (est): 484.2K **Privately Held**
WEB: www.dalescustomauto.com
SIC: 7532 3993 Body shop, automotive; signs & advertising specialties

(G-4003)
EDHARD CORP
279 Blau Rd (07840-5221)
PHONE..............................908 850-8444
Edgar Bars, *President*
Ilze Bars, *Vice Pres*
Gints Gulbis, *Prdtn Mgr*
Daina Lazdins, *Purch Agent*
Andy Millers, *Purchasing*
EMP: 35
SQ FT: 33,000
SALES (est): 6.6MM **Privately Held**
WEB: www.edhard.com
SIC: 3599 Machine shop, jobbing & repair

(G-4004)
EMIL DIPALMA INC
182 Stephens State Pk Rd (07840-5007)
PHONE..............................973 477-2766
Emil Dipalma, *President*
EMP: 5 **EST:** 1978
SALES (est): 439.9K **Privately Held**
SIC: 1429 Trap rock, crushed & broken-quarrying

(G-4005)
EP SYSTEMS INC
470 Schooleys Mountain Rd (07840-4012)
PHONE..............................570 424-0581
EMP: 7
SALES (est): 655.6K **Privately Held**
SIC: 2842 Mfg Polish/Sanitation Goods

(G-4006)
EXPERT PROCESS SYSTEMS LLC
470 Schooleys Mountain Rd A (07840-4012)
PHONE..............................570 424-0581
EMP: 7
SQ FT: 6,500
SALES (est): 1.2MM **Privately Held**
SIC: 8711 3559 3556 1796 Engineering Services Mfg Misc Industry Mach Mfg Food Prdts Mach Bldg Equip Installation

(G-4007)
FILTRATION SOLUTIONS INC
432 Sand Shore Rd Ste 8 (07840-5528)
PHONE..............................908 684-4000
Fax: 908 684-4100
Chang Jen, *President*
Guanghua Yu, *Vice Pres*
Vin Ardcizzone, *Info Tech Mgr*
Bill Marscher, *Shareholder*
EMP: 8 **EST:** 2000
SALES (est): 1.3MM **Privately Held**
WEB: www.filtsol.com
SIC: 3569 Filters

(G-4008)
FRED S BURROUGHS NORTH JERSEY
6 Rushmore Ln (07840-2831)
PHONE..............................908 850-8773
Glen Zeeck, *Principal*
Tom Mount, *Principal*
John Nordstedt, *Principal*
Susan Reed, *Principal*
EMP: 99 **EST:** 2015
SALES (est): 2.8MM **Privately Held**
SIC: 3949 7389 Rods & rod parts, fishing;

(G-4009)
GREENE BROS SPCLTY COF RASTERS (PA)
Also Called: Greene's Beans Cafe
313 High St (07840-1955)
PHONE..............................908 979-0022
Fax: 908 979-0526
David Greene, *President*
Brian Greene, *Vice Pres*
EMP: 13
SQ FT: 1,200
SALES (est): 1.9MM **Privately Held**
SIC: 2095 5499 Roasted coffee; beverage stores

(G-4010)
HACKETTSTOWN PUBLIC WORKS
Also Called: Town of Hackettstown, The
309 E Plane St (07840-2015)
PHONE..............................908 852-2320
Thomas Kitchen, *Superintendent*

EMP: 8
SALES (est): 1.2MM **Privately Held**
SIC: 3531 1611 Road construction & maintenance machinery; highway & street construction

(G-4011)
HOMESTYLE KITCHENS & BATHS LLC
453 Route 46 E (07840-2693)
PHONE..............................908 979-9000
Fax: 908 979-9901
George Journey,
EMP: 5
SALES (est): 407.5K **Privately Held**
SIC: 2493 Reconstituted wood products

(G-4012)
INTEGRATED MICROWAVE TECH LLC (HQ)
Also Called: Vislink
101 Bilby Rd Ste 15 (07840-1753)
PHONE..............................908 852-3700
John Payne, *President*
Paul Norridge, *Finance*
EMP: 75
SQ FT: 40,000
SALES (est): 7.2MM **Publicly Held**
WEB: www.imt-solutions.com
SIC: 3663 Radio & TV communications equipment

(G-4013)
JEROME INDUSTRIES CORP (HQ)
36 Newburgh Rd (07840-3904)
PHONE..............................908 353-5700
Pete Kaczmarek, *CEO*
Theresa Di Girolamo, *Admin Sec*
▲ **EMP:** 38
SQ FT: 15,000
SALES (est): 4.9MM **Privately Held**
WEB: www.jeromeindustries.com
SIC: 3677 5065 3612 3674 Electronic coils, transformers & other inductors; electronic parts & equipment; transformers, except electric; semiconductors & related devices; power supplies, all types: static

(G-4014)
JERSEY GIRL BREWING COMPANY
426 Sand Shore Rd (07840-5535)
PHONE..............................908 269-5523
Mike Bigger, *Partner*
EMP: 7
SALES (est): 100.4K **Privately Held**
SIC: 2082 Malt beverages

(G-4015)
KINGWOOD INDUSTRIAL PDTS INC
261 Main St Unit 12 (07840-2062)
PHONE..............................908 852-8655
Kevin Smith, *President*
EMP: 5
SALES (est): 37.8K **Privately Held**
WEB: www.kingwoodindustrial.com
SIC: 3842 Hearing aids

(G-4016)
LAMB PRINTING INC
700 Grand Ave (07840-1145)
PHONE..............................908 852-0837
Fax: 908 813-0906
Michael Lamb, *President*
Teresa Lamb, *Vice Pres*
EMP: 5
SQ FT: 2,500
SALES (est): 776.5K **Privately Held**
SIC: 5943 2759 2752 Office forms & supplies; directories (except telephone): printing; offset & photolithographic printing

(G-4017)
LODI WELDING CO INC
133 Willow Grove St (07840-2017)
PHONE..............................908 852-8367
Donald W Buschgans, *President*
EMP: 4
SQ FT: 8,700
SALES (est): 576K **Privately Held**
SIC: 7692 Welding repair

▲ = Import ▼=Export
◆ =Import/Export

(G-4018)
LORDON INC
453 Us Highway 46 E Ste 1 (07840-2694)
PHONE..................908 813-1143
Fax: 908 813-1610
Donna Quagliana, *President*
Lori McMahon, *Vice Pres*
EMP: 6
SQ FT: 1,000
SALES (est): 650.2K **Privately Held**
WEB: www.britesidepanels.com
SIC: 3479 Coating of metals & formed
products

(G-4019)
MANGO CUSTOM CABINETS INC
216 W Stiger St (07840-1269)
PHONE..................908 813-3077
Richard W Mango, *President*
EMP: 14
SQ FT: 14,000
SALES (est): 2.1MM **Privately Held**
SIC: 2511 5031 1751 Kitchen & dining
room furniture; kitchen cabinets; cabinet
& finish carpentry

(G-4020)
MARS INCORPORATED
Also Called: M & M Mars
700 High St (07840-1502)
PHONE..................908 852-1000
Fax: 908 850-2624
Joanne Walker, *Manager*
EMP: 700
SALES (corp-wide): 32.1B **Privately Held**
SIC: 2064 2066 Candy & other confec-
tionery products; chocolate & cocoa prod-
ucts
PA: Mars, Incorporated
6885 Elm St
Mc Lean VA 22101
703 821-4900

(G-4021)
MARS INCORPORATED
800 High St (07840-1552)
P.O. Box 731 (07840-0731)
PHONE..................908 850-2420
Rick Hampton, *President*
EMP: 55
SALES (corp-wide): 32.1B **Privately Held**
SIC: 2066 2064 Chocolate & cocoa prod-
ucts; candy & other confectionery prod-
ucts
PA: Mars, Incorporated
6885 Elm St
Mc Lean VA 22101
703 821-4900

(G-4022)
**MARS CHOCOLATE NORTH
AMER LLC (HQ)**
800 High St (07840-1552)
PHONE..................908 852-1000
Todd R Lachman, *President*
Jim Murphy, *Vice Pres*
Mike Wittman, *Vice Pres*
Yassine El Quarzazi, *Project Mgr*
◆ EMP: 850
SALES (est): 1.1B
SALES (corp-wide): 32.1B **Privately Held**
WEB: www.kilic-kalkan.com
SIC: 2064 2066 Candy & other confec-
tionery products; chocolate & cocoa prod-
ucts
PA: Mars, Incorporated
6885 Elm St
Mc Lean VA 22101
703 821-4900

(G-4023)
**MARS CHOCOLATE NORTH
AMER LLC**
Masterfoods USA
700 High St (07840-1502)
PHONE..................908 979-5070
David Prybylowski, *Branch Mgr*
EMP: 589
SALES (corp-wide): 32.1B **Privately Held**
WEB: www.kilic-kalkan.com
SIC: 2064 Candy & other confectionery
products

HQ: Mars Chocolate North America, Llc
800 High St
Hackettstown NJ 07840
908 852-1000

(G-4024)
MARS FOOD US LLC
800 High St (07840-1552)
PHONE..................908 852-1000
Charlie Smith, *Branch Mgr*
EMP: 13
SALES (corp-wide): 32.1B **Privately Held**
SIC: 2047 Dog & cat food
HQ: Mars Food Us, Llc
2001 E Cashdan St Ste 201
Rancho Dominguez CA 90220
310 933-0670

(G-4025)
MARS WRIGLEY CONF US LLC
800 High St (07840-1552)
PHONE..................908 852-1000
EMP: 4
SALES (est): 691.3K
SALES (corp-wide): 32.1B **Privately Held**
SIC: 2064 Candy bars, including chocolate
covered bars
PA: Mars, Incorporated
6885 Elm St
Mc Lean VA 22101
703 821-4900

(G-4026)
MOBILE POWER INC
392 Watters Rd (07840-5704)
PHONE..................908 852-3117
Fax: 908 852-2941
Paul F Mitchell, *President*
EMP: 8
SALES: 550K **Privately Held**
WEB: www.mobilepowerinc.com
SIC: 3694 Alternators, automotive

(G-4027)
MS HEALTH SOFTWARE CORP
128 Willow Grove St (07840-2018)
PHONE..................908 850-5564
Michael Sedita, *President*
Dorothy Higgins, *Vice Pres*
EMP: 7
SQ FT: 4,500
SALES: 735K **Privately Held**
WEB: www.mshealth.com
SIC: 7372 7371 Business oriented com-
puter software; computer software sys-
tems analysis & design, custom

(G-4028)
**NATIONAL ENVIRONMENTAL
SVCS CO**
700 Grand Ave (07840-1145)
PHONE..................908 813-1195
Fax: 908 813-1124
Peter Foley, *General Mgr*
EMP: 4
SALES (est): 543.3K **Privately Held**
WEB: www.drdust.com
SIC: 3564 8748 Air purification equipment;
environmental consultant
PA: National Environmental Services Com-
pany, Inc
7 Hampshire Dr
Mendham NJ 07945

(G-4029)
NORMS AUTO PARTS INC
Also Called: NAPA Auto Parts
135 Willow Grove St (07840-2017)
PHONE..................908 852-5080
Fax: 908 852-6219
Norman Lemasters, *President*
EMP: 4
SALES (est): 364.8K **Privately Held**
SIC: 5531 3599 Automobile & truck equip-
ment & parts; machine shop, jobbing &
repair

(G-4030)
**NORTHLAND TOOLING
TECHNOLOGIES**
999 Willow Grove St Ste 2 (07840-5001)
PHONE..................908 850-0023
Brian Zuber, *President*
EMP: 5
SQ FT: 3,250

SALES: 600K **Privately Held**
SIC: 3089 3599 Injection molding of plastics; blow molded finished plastic products; machine shop, jobbing & repair

(G-4031)
**PACKAGING CORPORATION
AMERICA**
Also Called: PCA
101 Bilby Rd Bldg 1 (07840-1753)
PHONE..................908 452-9271
EMP: 5
SQ FT: 9,000
SALES (corp-wide): 6.4B **Publicly Held**
SIC: 2653 Boxes, corrugated: made from
purchased materials
PA: Packaging Corporation Of America
1955 W Field Ct
Lake Forest IL 60045
847 482-3000

(G-4032)
ROLLON CORPORATION
101 Bilby Rd Ste B (07840-1753)
PHONE..................973 300-5492
Erlado Bianchessi, *President*
Andrew Cook, *General Mgr*
Marta Kalawur, *Purch Mgr*
Jose Barreto, *Engineer*
Diana Santos, *Financial Analy*
▲ EMP: 26
SQ FT: 20,000
SALES (est): 7.8MM
SALES (corp-wide): 111.6MM **Privately
Held**
WEB: www.rolloncorp.com
SIC: 3562 Ball & roller bearings
HQ: Rollon Spa
Via Trieste 26
Vimercate 20871
039 625-91

(G-4033)
ROTAREX INC NORTH AMERICA
Also Called: Rotarex Trade
101 Bilby Rd Ste B (07840-1753)
PHONE..................724 696-3345
Jean Claude Schmitz, *President*
Bert Pistor, *Vice Pres*
▲ EMP: 100
SALES (est): 14.7MM **Privately Held**
SIC: 3592 5085 Valves; valves & fittings

(G-4034)
**RUDOLPH RES ANALYTICAL
CORP**
55 Newburgh Rd (07840-3903)
PHONE..................973 584-1558
Richard C Spainer, *President*
Robert Taggart, *Vice Pres*
Bruce Gilliland, *Purch Mgr*
Elizabeth Nithz, *VP Finance*
Debra Beyer, *Accountant*
EMP: 68
SQ FT: 30,000
SALES (est): 14.2MM **Privately Held**
WEB: www.rudolphresearch.com
SIC: 3827 Optical instruments & apparatus

(G-4035)
**SALTOPIA ARTISAN INFUSED
SEA S**
9 Reservoir Rd (07840-5646)
PHONE..................917 628-8433
Kimarie Santiago, *Mng Member*
EMP: 6 EST: 2012
SQ FT: 2,000
SALES: 275K **Privately Held**
SIC: 2899 Salt; salt, edible; alcoholic bev-
erage making equipment & supplies

(G-4036)
SHARMATEK INC
999 Willow Grove St (07840-5001)
PHONE..................908 852-5087
Vinay Sharma, *Ch of Bd*
Sonia Sharma, *President*
EMP: 7
SQ FT: 3,500
SALES (est): 490K **Privately Held**
SIC: 2834 Pharmaceutical preparations

(G-4037)
SMR RESEARCH CORPORATION
300 Valentine St Ste A (07840-2160)
PHONE..................908 852-7677
Fax: 908 852-6884
Stuart Feldstein, *President*
EMP: 6
SQ FT: 10,450
SALES: 1.1MM **Privately Held**
WEB: www.smrresearch.com
SIC: 2721 8742 8732 7389 Statistical re-
ports (periodicals): publishing only; busi-
ness consultant; business research
service; financial services

(G-4038)
ST JUDE MEDICAL
999 Willow Grove St (07840-5001)
PHONE..................908 979-3200
Hillary Paulison, *Mng Member*
Tracy Albright, *IT/INT Sup*
EMP: 14
SALES (est): 1.3MM **Privately Held**
SIC: 3845 Electromedical equipment

(G-4039)
T C S TECHNOLOGIES INC
430 Sand Shore Rd Ste 1 (07840-5519)
PHONE..................908 852-7555
Fax: 908 852-7216
Gerard W Fitzgerald, *President*
Pat Ward, *Vice Pres*
EMP: 12
SQ FT: 6,000
SALES (est): 1.4MM **Privately Held**
SIC: 3645 Residential lighting fixtures

(G-4040)
**THOMAS & BETTS
CORPORATION**
ABB
1 Esna Park (07840-3906)
PHONE..................908 852-1122
Allan Bordstrom, *General Mgr*
Joseph Luzasky, *Buyer*
EMP: 250
SALES (corp-wide): 34.3B **Privately Held**
WEB: www.tnb.com
SIC: 3643 3678 3644 3679 Connectors &
terminals for electrical devices; solderless
connectors (electric wiring devices); elec-
tronic connectors; electric conduits & fit-
tings; raceways; insulators & insulation
materials, electrical; electronic circuits
HQ: Thomas & Betts Corporation
8155 T&B Blvd
Memphis TN 38125
901 252-5000

(G-4041)
TRANSISTOR DEVICES INC (PA)
Also Called: Astrodyne Tdi
36 Newburgh Rd (07840-3904)
PHONE..................908 850-5088
Fax: 908 850-1614
Chris Viola, *CEO*
James M Feely, *President*
Hector Fuentes, *General Mgr*
Robert Smolinski, *COO*
Ruth Otte, *Exec VP*
▲ EMP: 250 EST: 1951
SQ FT: 150,000
SALES (est): 221.3MM **Privately Held**
WEB: www.transdev.com
SIC: 3612 3625 3672 3812 Power trans-
formers, electric; switches, electric power;
printed circuit boards; search & navigation
equipment; measuring & controlling de-
vices

(G-4042)
TRANSISTOR DEVICES INC
Also Called: Astrodyne Tdi
36 Newburgh Rd (07840-3904)
PHONE..................908 850-5088
James Feely, *Branch Mgr*
EMP: 250
SALES (corp-wide): 221.3MM **Privately
Held**
WEB: www.transdev.com
SIC: 3612 3679 Power transformers, elec-
tric; power supplies, all types: static
PA: Transistor Devices, Inc.
36 Newburgh Rd
Hackettstown NJ 07840
908 850-5088

(G-4043)
WOODTEC INC
300 W Stiger St (07840-1276)
PHONE..............................908 979-0180
John Marra, *President*
EMP: 7
SQ FT: 4,000
SALES (est): 990K **Privately Held**
SIC: 5712 2431 5211 Customized furniture & cabinets; millwork; millwork & lumber

(G-4044)
ZONE DEFENSE INC
428 Sand Shore Rd 7 (07840-5510)
PHONE..............................973 328-0436
Fax: 973 927-0608
George Mandas, *President*
EMP: 10
SQ FT: 7,500
SALES (est): 1.6MM **Privately Held**
SIC: 2431 3446 Interior & ornamental woodwork & trim; bank fixtures, ornamental metal

Haddon Heights
Camden County

(G-4045)
ARTSIGN STUDIO
916 Kings Hwy Ste C (08035-1251)
PHONE..............................856 546-4889
Mark Zito, *Owner*
EMP: 5
SALES: 225K **Privately Held**
SIC: 3993 Signs, not made in custom sign painting shops

(G-4046)
CHILDRENS RESEARCH & DEV CO
216 9th Ave (08035-1633)
PHONE..............................856 546-8814
Robert Petrillo, *President*
EMP: 4
SALES (est): 158.6K **Privately Held**
SIC: 2731 Textbooks: publishing only, not printed on site

(G-4047)
DEL BUONO BAKERY INC
319 Black Horse Pike (08035-1097)
PHONE..............................856 546-9585
Constantino Del Buono Jr, *Owner*
EMP: 30 EST: 1932
SQ FT: 7,500
SALES (est): 3.2MM **Privately Held**
SIC: 2051 5461 5149 Bread, all types (white, wheat, rye, etc): fresh or frozen; rolls, bread type: fresh or frozen; bakeries; groceries & related products

(G-4048)
MAXWELL MCKENNEY INC
116 White Horse Pike # 6 (08035-1936)
PHONE..............................856 310-0700
Larry Schultz, *President*
Kathleen Lawler, *Assistant*
EMP: 6 EST: 1982
SALES (est): 770.6K **Privately Held**
SIC: 3731 Shipbuilding & repairing

(G-4049)
PEDIBRUSH LLC
211 7th Ave (08035-1623)
PHONE..............................856 796-2963
Christian Klemash, *CEO*
EMP: 6
SALES (est): 430K **Privately Held**
WEB: www.pedibrush.com
SIC: 3089 Handles, brush or tool: plastic

(G-4050)
RELAY SPECIALTIES INC
1810 Prospect Ridge Blvd (08035-1139)
PHONE..............................856 547-5000
Walter Woodward, *Manager*
EMP: 4
SALES (corp-wide): 9.9MM **Privately Held**
WEB: www.relayspec.com
SIC: 3625 Relays & industrial controls

PA: Relay Specialties, Inc.
17 Raritan Rd
Oakland NJ 07436
201 337-1000

(G-4051)
SENSONICS INC
Also Called: Sensonics International
125 White Horse Pike (08035-1909)
P.O. Box 112 (08035-0112)
PHONE..............................856 547-7702
Fax: 856 547-5665
Richard L Doty, *CEO*
EMP: 11
SQ FT: 6,000
SALES (est): 887.2K **Privately Held**
WEB: www.smelltest.com
SIC: 2835 5999 8999 In vitro diagnostics; medical apparatus & supplies; scientific consulting

(G-4052)
W C DAVIS INC
126 W Atlantic Ave (08035-1902)
PHONE..............................856 547-4750
Richard Davis, *President*
EMP: 10
SALES (corp-wide): 1.5MM **Privately Held**
WEB: www.wcdavis.com
SIC: 3432 Plastic plumbing fixture fittings, assembly
PA: W C Davis Inc
605 Station Ave
Haddon Heights NJ 08035
856 547-4750

Haddon Township
Camden County

(G-4053)
NEW JERSEY STEEL CORPORATION
2840 Mount Ephraim Ave (08104-3214)
P.O. Box 2506, Cherry Hill (08034-0205)
PHONE..............................856 337-0054
EMP: 18
SQ FT: 2,000
SALES (est): 2.1MM **Privately Held**
SIC: 3449 1541 Mfg Misc Structural Metalwork Industrial Building Construction

(G-4054)
NORWOOD INDUSTRIES INC
107 Norwood Ave (08108-3518)
P.O. Box 2056, Haddonfield (08033-0816)
PHONE..............................856 858-6195
Fax: 856 858-6241
Francis Kernan, *President*
Catherine Kernan, *Vice Pres*
EMP: 15
SALES: 500K **Privately Held**
WEB: www.norwoodind.com
SIC: 4783 5031 3952 Packing goods for shipping; lumber: rough, dressed & finished; palettes, artists'

Haddonfield
Camden County

(G-4055)
ANDREW TECHNOLOGIES LLC
3 S Haddon Ave Ste 3 # 3 (08033-1882)
PHONE..............................215 990-0754
Tom Albright, *CEO*
Mark Andrew, *General Mgr*
Tina Kang, *Cust Mgr*
Bruce Osborn, *Executive*
EMP: 5
SALES (est): 430.1K **Privately Held**
SIC: 3845 Electromedical equipment

(G-4056)
BERNARD D ASCENZO
61 Centre St (08033-1801)
PHONE..............................856 795-0511
Bernard Ascenzo, *Principal*
EMP: 4
SALES (est): 369.5K **Privately Held**
SIC: 3911 Jewelry, precious metal

(G-4057)
CELESTECH INC
221 Kngs Hwy W Hddonfield (08033)
PHONE..............................856 986-2221
Celeste Todaro, *President*
EMP: 7
SQ FT: 2,500
SALES: 4MM **Privately Held**
SIC: 3569 Centrifuges, industrial

(G-4058)
COMMUNITY NEWS NETWORK INC
Also Called: What's On In Haddonfield
6 S Haddon Ave Ste 1 (08033-1880)
PHONE..............................856 428-3399
Fax: 856 428-7695
David Hunter, *President*
Susan W Hunter, *Vice Pres*
EMP: 7
SALES (est): 285.4K **Privately Held**
SIC: 2711 Newspapers: publishing only, not printed on site

(G-4059)
DORADO SYSTEMS LLC
8 Kings Hwy E (08033-2002)
PHONE..............................856 354-0048
Michael Matt, *COO*
Joseph Malcarney, *Client Mgr*
Corey Katzen, *Accounts Exec*
Steffi Silva, *Director*
Paul Yauger, *Officer*
EMP: 15
SALES (est): 1.6MM **Privately Held**
SIC: 2741 Business service newsletters: publishing & printing

(G-4060)
GLOBAL DIRECT MARKETING GROUP
Also Called: Paramount Packaging
229 Kings Hwy E (08033-1909)
PHONE..............................856 427-6116
Curt J Byerley, *President*
EMP: 3
SQ FT: 3,300
SALES: 2MM **Privately Held**
WEB: www.gdm-group.com
SIC: 2448 2653 2652 2657 Wood pallets & skids; corrugated & solid fiber boxes; setup paperboard boxes; folding paperboard boxes; bags: plastic, laminated & coated

(G-4061)
PFK COACH PHYLLIS FLOOD KNERR
119 Walnut St (08033-1854)
PHONE..............................856 429-5425
Phyllis Knerr, *Principal*
EMP: 4
SALES (est): 292.3K **Privately Held**
SIC: 3089 Organizers for closets, drawers, etc.: plastic

(G-4062)
PRINCETON HOSTED SOLUTIONS LLC
30 Washington Ave Ste D2 (08033-3400)
P.O. Box 2078 (08033-0836)
PHONE..............................856 470-2350
Brad Bono, *CEO*
Sara Trivedi, *Accounts Mgr*
EMP: 10 EST: 2011
SALES (est): 1.3MM **Privately Held**
SIC: 8748 4812 3229 1731 Telecommunications consultant; cellular telephone services; fiber optics strands; telephone & telephone equipment installation

(G-4063)
PROFESSIONAL PRINTING SERVICES
116 N Haddon Ave Ste G (08033-2388)
PHONE..............................856 428-6300
Fax: 856 429-8522
Joseph Mc Elroy, *President*
EMP: 5
SALES (est): 490K **Privately Held**
SIC: 2752 Commercial printing, offset

(G-4064)
REVIVA LABS INC
705 Hopkins Rd (08033-3096)
PHONE..............................856 428-3885
Fax: 856 429-0767
Stephen Strassler, *President*
Terry French, *COO*
Melissa Baylis, *Vice Pres*
Mellisa Baylis, *Vice Pres*
Charles Ricefield, *Vice Pres*
EMP: 40
SQ FT: 7,000
SALES (est): 7.3MM **Privately Held**
WEB: www.revivalabs.com
SIC: 5122 2844 Cosmetics; toilet preparations

(G-4065)
UM EQUITY CORP (HQ)
56 N Haddon Ave Ste 300 (08033-2438)
PHONE..............................856 354-2200
Joan Carter, *President*
John Aglialoro, *Chairman*
Arthur Hicks Jr, *Treasurer*
EMP: 3
SQ FT: 5,000
SALES (est): 13.1MM
SALES (corp-wide): 234MM **Privately Held**
SIC: 7371 3949 8099 8093 Custom computer programming services; treadmills; exercise equipment; physical examination service, insurance; specialty outpatient clinics
PA: Um Holding Company
56 N Haddon Ave Ste 300
Haddonfield NJ 08033
856 354-2200

(G-4066)
W E WAMSLEY RESTORATIONS INC
26 Tanner St (08033-2404)
PHONE..............................856 795-4001
Wilbur E Wamsley, *President*
EMP: 6
SALES: 750K **Privately Held**
SIC: 5932 3931 7699 Musical instruments, secondhand; violins & parts; musical instrument repair services

Hainesport
Burlington County

(G-4067)
3 IS TECHNOLOGIES INC
4 Colfax Ln (08036-4818)
PHONE..............................609 238-8213
John Pettit, *President*
EMP: 5
SALES (est): 466.5K **Privately Held**
SIC: 3523 Farm machinery & equipment

(G-4068)
ACCURATE THERMAL SYSTEMS LLC
4104 Sylon Blvd (08036-3730)
PHONE..............................609 326-3190
Darren Sager, *President*
EMP: 7
SALES: 300K **Privately Held**
SIC: 3823 Temperature instruments: industrial process type

(G-4069)
ATLANTIC SWITCH GENERATOR LLC
4108 Sylon Blvd (08036-3730)
PHONE..............................609 518-1900
Steve Louden, *Partner*
Hank Bevillard, *Mng Member*
Steven Louden,
William Shields,
EMP: 10
SALES (est): 2.6MM **Privately Held**
SIC: 7694 7699 Electric motor repair; industrial machinery & equipment repair

(G-4070)
ATLANTIC WOOD INDUSTRIES INC
1517 Hwy 38 (08036)
PHONE..............................609 267-4700
Phil Taylor, *Manager*
EMP: 15
SALES (corp-wide): 87.8MM **Privately Held**
SIC: 2491 Preserving (creosoting) of wood
PA: Atlantic Wood Industries, Inc.
    405 E Perry St
    Savannah GA 31401
    912 966-7008

(G-4071)
CRYOVATION LLC (PA)
9b Mary Way (08036)
PHONE..............................609 914-4792
Fax: 609 914-4795
Troy Saylor, *Business Dir*
Ric Boyd,
◆ EMP: 7
SQ FT: 5,000
SALES (est): 1.4MM **Privately Held**
WEB: www.cryovation.com
SIC: 3559 Cryogenic machinery, industrial

(G-4072)
HAINESPORT INDUSTRIAL RAILROAD
5900 Delaware Ave (08036-3667)
PHONE..............................609 261-8036
Ronald W Bridges, *President*
EMP: 10
SALES (est): 5.4MM **Privately Held**
SIC: 3743 Railroad equipment

(G-4073)
HOPPECKE BATTERIES INC
2 Berry Dr (08036-4858)
PHONE..............................856 616-0032
Marc Zoellner, *CEO*
Stefan Keuthen, *Vice Pres*
Hans-Peter Czernietzki, *Sales Staff*
Christian Stampfer, *Sales Staff*
Susan Grout, *Office Mgr*
▲ EMP: 25
SALES (est): 6.8MM
SALES (corp-wide): 429.3MM **Privately Held**
WEB: www.hoppecke-us.com
SIC: 5999 3691 Batteries
PA: Accumulatorenwerke Hoppecke Carl
    Zoellner & Sohn Gmbh
    Bontkirchener Str. 1
    Brilon 59929
    296 361-0

(G-4074)
INDEPENDENT METAL SALES INC
1900 Park Ave W (08036-3734)
P.O. Box 17 (08036-0017)
PHONE..............................609 261-8090
Edward Kligerman, *President*
Jason Sheffield, *Sales Mgr*
Collen Spector, *Manager*
EMP: 16
SQ FT: 48,000
SALES (est): 4.7MM **Privately Held**
WEB: www.independentmetalsales.com
SIC: 3444 5051 Sheet metalwork; metals
    service centers & offices

(G-4075)
JORDAN TOOLING & MANUFACTURING
1307 Maine Ave (08036-2957)
PHONE..............................609 261-2636
Fax: 609 267-2210
EMP: 7
SQ FT: 3,000
SALES (est): 390K **Privately Held**
SIC: 3599 Machine Shop

(G-4076)
PERRY PRODUCTS CORPORATION
25 Mount Laurel Rd (08036-2711)
P.O. Box 327 (08036-0327)
PHONE..............................609 267-1600
Fax: 609 267-4986
Jerome Epstein, *CEO*

Gregg Epstein, *President*
Philip Wallace, *General Mgr*
Kenneth Miller, *Exec VP*
Annie Harris, *Project Mgr*
▲ EMP: 25
SQ FT: 190,000
SALES (est): 6.3MM **Privately Held**
SIC: 3443 Heat exchangers: coolers (after,
    inter), condensers, etc.

(G-4077)
SIGN A RAMA
Also Called: Sign-A-Rama
1413 Rte 38 (08036)
PHONE..............................609 702-1444
Gary Kuffer, *Owner*
EMP: 4 EST: 2001
SALES (est): 327.2K **Privately Held**
SIC: 3993 Signs & advertising specialties

(G-4078)
SOUND PROFESSIONALS INC
3444 Sylon Blvd (08036-3664)
PHONE..............................609 267-4400
Fax: 609 267-0054
Chris Carfagno, *CEO*
Joseph Carfagno, *Technician*
EMP: 6
SALES (est): 1.5MM **Privately Held**
SIC: 5099 3651 Video & audio equipment;
    microphones

(G-4079)
T WIKER ENTERPRISES INC
Also Called: Total Logistics
5900 Delaware Ave (08036-3667)
P.O. Box 44 (08036-0044)
PHONE..............................609 261-9494
Fax: 609 265-1599
Thomas Wiker, *President*
EMP: 5
SQ FT: 46,500
SALES (est): 520K **Privately Held**
SIC: 8742 3325 4225 Materials mgmt.
    (purchasing, handling, inventory) consult-
    ant; steel foundries; warehousing, self-
    storage

(G-4080)
TWO JAYS BINGO SUPPLY INC (PA)
Also Called: Two Jays Specialties
709 Park Ave E (08036-3656)
PHONE..............................609 267-4542
Fax: 609 267-9687
Donald Plucinski, *President*
Cynthia Plucinski, *Corp Secy*
EMP: 10
SQ FT: 3,500
SALES: 900K **Privately Held**
WEB: www.twojays.com
SIC: 5092 5021 3993 Amusement goods;
    office furniture; advertising novelties

Haledon

Passaic County

(G-4081)
DOORSILLS LLC
302 Legion Pl (07508-1420)
PHONE..............................973 904-0270
Donald Kuehn,
EMP: 5
SALES: 450K **Privately Held**
SIC: 3728 Aircraft assemblies, subassem-
    blies & parts

(G-4082)
E & W PIECE DYE WORKS
293 Morrissee Ave (07508-1436)
PHONE..............................973 942-8718
Joseph Pizzoli Jr, *President*
Joseph Pizzoli Sr, *Admin Sec*
EMP: 20 EST: 1959
SQ FT: 42,000
SALES: 3MM **Privately Held**
SIC: 2261 Finishing plants, cotton; dyeing
    cotton broadwoven fabrics

(G-4083)
J P ROTELLA CO INC
20 E Barbour St (07508-1524)
P.O. Box 8438 (07538-0438)
PHONE..............................973 942-2559
Fax: 973 942-5135
John P Rotella, *President*
EMP: 12
SQ FT: 3,000
SALES: 500K **Privately Held**
SIC: 3679 3599 7692 3544 Electronic cir-
    cuits; machine shop, jobbing & repair;
    welding repair; special dies, tools, jigs &
    fixtures; gaskets, packing & sealing de-
    vices

(G-4084)
MRL MANUFACTURING CORP
59 Lee Ave (07508-1201)
P.O. Box 8440 (07538-0440)
PHONE..............................973 790-1744
Fax: 973 790-1414
John De Napoli, *President*
Lorraine Paone, *Vice Pres*
EMP: 16
SQ FT: 12,000
SALES (est): 2.6MM **Privately Held**
SIC: 3452 Bolts, nuts, rivets & washers

(G-4085)
STONE INDUSTRIES INC (PA)
Also Called: Braen Stone Company
400 Central Ave 402 (07508-1116)
P.O. Box 8310 (07538-8310)
PHONE..............................973 595-6250
Janet R Braen, *CEO*
Scott A Braen, *President*
Sam Braen III, *Vice Pres*
Charles Veldran, *Vice Pres*
Victor Coleson, *Mng Member*
EMP: 85
SQ FT: 6,000
SALES (est): 41.1MM **Privately Held**
WEB: www.braenstone.com
SIC: 1423 5032 2951 Crushed & broken
    granite; asphalt mixture; asphalt paving
    mixtures & blocks

(G-4086)
TEEFX SCREEN PRINTING LLC
250 Belmont Ave (07508-1404)
PHONE..............................973 942-6800
Mario Guarriello,
EMP: 3
SQ FT: 125,000
SALES: 1.2MM **Privately Held**
SIC: 2211 Print cloths, cotton

Hamburg

Sussex County

(G-4087)
ACCURATE FORMING LLC
24 Ames Blvd (07419-1518)
PHONE..............................973 827-7155
Fax: 973 827-3678
Rich Regole, *CEO*
R Mark Baker, *CFO*
◆ EMP: 47
SQ FT: 100,000
SALES (est): 10.8MM **Privately Held**
WEB: www.accurateforming.com
SIC: 3469 Stamping metal for the trade

(G-4088)
AMES RUBBER CORPORATION (PA)
19 Ames Blvd (07419-1514)
P.O. Box 15240, Newark (07192-5240)
PHONE..............................973 827-9101
Fax: 973 827-8893
Charles A Roberts, *President*
Timothy Marvil, *Principal*
William J Kovach, *CFO*
▲ EMP: 100 EST: 1949
SQ FT: 112,700
SALES (est): 32.9MM **Privately Held**
WEB: www.amesrubber.com
SIC: 3069 Rubber rolls & roll coverings;
    rubber automotive products

(G-4089)
CAVA WINERY AND VINEYARD INC
3619 State Rt 94 (07419-9651)
PHONE..............................973 823-9463
Anthony Riccio, *Principal*
▲ EMP: 12
SALES (est): 1.6MM **Privately Held**
SIC: 2084 Wines

(G-4090)
DAUSON CORRUGATED CONTAINER
Also Called: Poly Bag Division
3627 State Rt 23 (07419-1821)
P.O. Box 331, Franklin (07416-0331)
PHONE..............................973 827-1494
Mark Taylor, *President*
EMP: 11
SALES: 5MM **Privately Held**
SIC: 2653 5113 Boxes, corrugated: made
    from purchased materials; boxes, solid
    fiber: made from purchased materials;
    boxes & containers

(G-4091)
EASTERN CONCRETE MATERIALS INC
3620 State Rt 23 N (07419-1426)
PHONE..............................973 827-7625
Michael Benza, *Manager*
EMP: 30
SALES (corp-wide): 1.3B **Publicly Held**
SIC: 1411 2951 1442 Dimension stone;
    asphalt & asphaltic paving mixtures (not
    from refineries); construction sand &
    gravel
HQ: Eastern Concrete Materials, Inc.
    250 Pehle Ave Ste 500
    Saddle Brook NJ 07663
    201 797-7979

(G-4092)
EASY STOP FOOD & FUEL CORP
19 Exeter Ln (07419-9662)
PHONE..............................973 517-0478
Kirit M Patel, *Owner*
EMP: 5
SALES (est): 369.2K **Privately Held**
SIC: 2869 Fuels

(G-4093)
EBELLE DEBELLE PHRM INC
Also Called: Ede Pharmaceutical
5 Witherwood Dr (07419-1273)
PHONE..............................973 823-0665
Renay Ebelle, *CEO*
Steve Alexander, *Vice Pres*
Jacqueline Williams-Phillips, *Vice Pres*
EMP: 10
SALES (est): 518.2K **Privately Held**
SIC: 2834 Drugs acting on the cardiovas-
    cular system, except diagnostic; drugs af-
    fecting parasitic & infective diseases;
    tablets, pharmaceutical

(G-4094)
ELASTOGRAF INC
19 Ames Blvd (07419-1514)
PHONE..............................973 209-3161
Charles Roberts, *Admin Sec*
EMP: 88
SALES (est): 2.4MM **Privately Held**
SIC: 3069 Molded rubber products

(G-4095)
LEVEL TEN PRODUCTS INC
3670 State Rt 94 (07419-9613)
PHONE..............................973 827-0900
Patrick Barrett, *President*
EMP: 18
SALES (est): 2.6MM **Privately Held**
SIC: 3714 Transmissions, motor vehicle

(G-4096)
ROBERTAS JEWELERS INC
Also Called: Roberta's Hut
175 State Rt 23 S Ste D (07419-1627)
PHONE..............................973 875-5318
Roberta Bootsma, *President*
Deborah Falanga, *Vice Pres*
Harry Bootsma, *Treasurer*
EMP: 4 EST: 1977

GEOGRAPHIC

SALES (est): 594K **Privately Held**
WEB: www.robertasjewelers.com
SIC: 5944 3911 Jewelry, precious stones
& precious metals; jewelry, precious metal

(G-4097)
TRILLIUM US
3627 State Rt 23 (07419-1821)
PHONE..........................973 827-1661
Albert Citarella, *Manager*
▲ EMP: 6
SALES (est): 777.7K **Privately Held**
SIC: 3563 Air & gas compressors

(G-4098)
UNITED VACUUM LLC
Also Called: UNI-Vac
3627 State Rt 23 Bldg 3 (07419-1821)
PHONE..........................973 827-1661
Fax: 973 788-8883
Al Citarella, *Mng Member*
▲ EMP: 17
SQ FT: 3,000
SALES (est): 3MM
SALES (corp-wide): 46.3MM **Privately Held**
WEB: www.unitedvacuum.com
SIC: 3563 Vacuum pumps, except laboratory
PA: Trillium Us Inc.
13011 Se Jennifer St # 204
Clackamas OR 97015
503 607-0393

(G-4099)
WEB-COTE LTD
Also Called: Web-Cote Industries
141 Wheatsworth Rd (07419-2607)
P.O. Box 120 (07419-0120)
PHONE..........................973 827-2299
James Cowen, *President*
Andrew Kozdron, *Plant Mgr*
▲ EMP: 18
SQ FT: 16,000
SALES (est): 4.3MM **Privately Held**
SIC: 2672 Tape, pressure sensitive: made from purchased materials
PA: L2f, Llc
1 Barker Ave
White Plains NY

(G-4100)
WILCOX PRESS
6 Main St (07419-1508)
PHONE..........................973 827-7474
Fax: 973 827-5373
Jodie Palmasano, *Partner*
Judy Ehrich, *Partner*
EMP: 5 EST: 1919
SQ FT: 2,400
SALES: 550K **Privately Held**
SIC: 2759 2752 5112 Letterpress printing; commercial printing, offset; office supplies

---

Hamilton
Mercer County

(G-4101)
ACINO PRODUCTS LTD LBLTY CO
9b S Gold Dr (08691-1642)
P.O. Box 3093, Trenton (08619-0093)
PHONE..........................609 695-4300
Ravi Deshpande,
Sandy Desphande,
EMP: 10
SALES (est): 1.4MM **Privately Held**
SIC: 2834 Medicines, capsuled or ampuled

(G-4102)
AFTEK INC
2960 E State Street Ext (08619-4504)
PHONE..........................609 588-0900
Dennis Cumbest, *General Mgr*
Neville Richards, *Manager*
EMP: 4
SALES (est): 719.3K **Privately Held**
SIC: 3634 Sauna heaters, electric

(G-4103)
ANDLOGIC COMPUTERS
866 Nj 33 6 (08619)
PHONE..........................609 610-5752

Swapan Nandy, *Principal*
EMP: 4
SALES (est): 230K **Privately Held**
SIC: 5734 3571 Computer & software stores; personal computers (microcomputers)

(G-4104)
ASSA ABLOY ENTRANCE SYSTEMS US
Also Called: Besam Entrance Solutions
300 Horizon Center Blvd # 309 (08691-1919)
PHONE..........................609 528-2580
Cameron Cary, *Branch Mgr*
Thomas Epke, *Director*
EMP: 22
SALES (corp-wide): 9B **Privately Held**
SIC: 3699 1796 3442 Door opening & closing devices, electrical; installing building equipment; metal doors
HQ: Assa Abloy Entrance Systems Us Inc.
1900 Airport Rd
Monroe NC 28110
704 290-5520

(G-4105)
CONISTICS INC
1800 E State St Ste 148 (08609-2013)
PHONE..........................609 584-2600
Christian Leeser, *President*
▲ EMP: 4 EST: 2010
SALES (est): 429.4K **Privately Held**
SIC: 3829 Thermometers & temperature sensors

(G-4106)
DENMATT INDUSTRIES LLC
Also Called: Closets By Dsign - Cntl Jersey
2080 E State Street Ext (08619-3308)
PHONE..........................609 689-0099
Dennis Mattessich, *Co-Owner*
EMP: 17
SALES (est): 701.8K **Privately Held**
SIC: 2522 Wallcases, office: except wood

(G-4107)
GRAM EQUIPMENT (PA)
1 S Gold Dr (08691-1606)
PHONE..........................201 750-6500
Neil Whyte, *President*
John Irwin, *Parts Mgr*
Christopher Heckler, *Senior Mgr*
▲ EMP: 40
SALES (est): 11.2MM **Privately Held**
WEB: www.wcbicecream.com
SIC: 3565 3556 Packing & wrapping machinery; ice cream manufacturing machinery

(G-4108)
HOUZER INC (HQ)
2605 Kuser Rd (08691-1805)
PHONE..........................609 584-1900
Tyler Byun, *President*
▲ EMP: 16
SQ FT: 43,000
SALES (est): 3.8MM
SALES (corp-wide): 78.7MM **Privately Held**
WEB: www.enexsink.com
SIC: 3431 5084 Sinks: enameled iron, cast iron or pressed metal; industrial machinery & equipment
PA: Hamat Group Ltd
41 Hayozma
Ashdod 77524
885 138-17

(G-4109)
LINEAR PHOTONICS LLC
3 Nami Ln Ste 7c (08619-1285)
PHONE..........................609 584-5747
Elen Catz, *President*
Debbie Kamens, *General Mgr*
John McDonald, *Senior VP*
Eugene Hoffman, *Vice Pres*
Lou Pedrini, *Production*
EMP: 5
SQ FT: 2,500
SALES (est): 1.2MM **Privately Held**
WEB: www.linphotonic.com
SIC: 3671 Electronic tube parts, except glass blanks

(G-4110)
LINEARIZER TECHNOLOGY INC (PA)
3 Nami Ln Unit C9 (08619-1285)
PHONE..........................609 584-5747
Fax: 609 631-0177
Allen Katz, *President*
Roger Dorval, *Vice Pres*
Eugene Hoffman, *Vice Pres*
John Macdonald, *Opers Staff*
Daniel P Chokola, *Engineer*
EMP: 56
SQ FT: 20,000
SALES (est): 10.4MM **Privately Held**
WEB: www.lintech.com
SIC: 3671 Electronic tube parts, except glass blanks

(G-4111)
LINEARIZER TECHNOLOGY INC
3 Nami Ln Unit C9 (08619-1285)
PHONE..........................609 584-8424
John Macdonald, *President*
Roger Dorval, *VP Opers*
Allen Katz, *Branch Mgr*
EMP: 5 **Privately Held**
SIC: 3663 Radio & TV communications equipment
PA: Linearizer Technology Inc.
3 Nami Ln Unit C9
Hamilton NJ 08619

(G-4112)
M/C COMMUNICATIONS LLC
5 Commerce Way Ste 202 (08691-3384)
PHONE..........................609 838-7952
EMP: 20
SALES (corp-wide): 10.6MM **Privately Held**
SIC: 2741 Art copy & poster publishing
PA: M/C Communications, Llc
180 Mount Airy Rd Ste 102
Basking Ridge NJ 07920
908 766-0402

(G-4113)
MEDAVANTE INC (HQ)
100 American Metro Blvd # 106 (08619-2319)
PHONE..........................609 528-9400
Paul M Gilbert, *CEO*
Ian C Neilson, *Senior VP*
Peter Sorantin, *Senior VP*
Thomas Weir, *Senior VP*
Christopher Randolph, *Vice Pres*
EMP: 9
SALES (est): 8.2MM
SALES (corp-wide): 75.5MM **Privately Held**
WEB: www.medavante.net
SIC: 2834 Solutions, pharmaceutical
PA: Wirb-Copernicus Group Inc.
212 Carnegie Ctr Ste 301
Princeton NJ 08540
609 945-0101

(G-4114)
MEDICAL INDICATORS INC
16 Thmas J Rhdes Indus Dr (08619-1263)
PHONE..........................609 737-1600
Larry Gentile, *Principal*
Bedwuine Senatus, *QA Dir*
Michael Minakowski, *VP Sales*
Cara Lapolla, *Sales Staff*
▼ EMP: 14
SQ FT: 10,500
SALES (est): 5.2MM **Privately Held**
WEB: www.medicalindicators.com
SIC: 5047 3829 Medical equipment & supplies; thermometers, including digital: clinical

(G-4115)
MEJ SIGNS INC
Also Called: Sign-A-Rama
3100 Quakerbridge Rd # 5 (08619-1658)
P.O. Box 9993, Trenton (08650-2993)
PHONE..........................609 584-6881
Mark Jarvis, *President*
EMP: 4
SALES: 360K **Privately Held**
SIC: 3993 Signs & advertising specialties

(G-4116)
MERCER C ALPHAGRAPHICS
100 Youngs Rd (08619-1025)
PHONE..........................609 921-0959
Mark Wilhelm, *President*
EMP: 6
SQ FT: 5,200
SALES (est): 1MM **Privately Held**
SIC: 2752 2759 Offset & photolithographic printing; commercial printing

(G-4117)
MERLIN INDUSTRIES INC (PA)
2904 E State Street Ext (08619-4504)
PHONE..........................609 807-1000
Fax: 609 807-1001
Andrew Maggion, *President*
▲ EMP: 81
SQ FT: 30,000
SALES (est): 23.4MM **Privately Held**
SIC: 3999 5999 7389 Hot tub & spa covers; swimming pool chemicals, equipment & supplies; swimming pool & hot tub service & maintenance

(G-4118)
MILLNER KITCHENS INC
200b Whitehead Rd Ste 108 (08619-3283)
PHONE..........................609 890-7300
EMP: 4
SALES (est): 312.7K **Privately Held**
SIC: 2434 Wood kitchen cabinets

(G-4119)
NEU INC
1 N Johnston Ave Ste 2 (08609-1855)
PHONE..........................281 648-9751
Jack Morin, *President*
▲ EMP: 4
SALES (est): 2.6MM
SALES (corp-wide): 453K **Privately Held**
WEB: www.neu-inc.com
SIC: 3531 Railroad related equipment
HQ: Neu Railways
Neu Solids Handling & Processing
Marcq En Baroeul 59700
320 456-464

(G-4120)
OAVCO LTD LIABILITY COMPANY
Also Called: Oav Air Bearings
1800 E State St Ste 130 (08609-2013)
P.O. Box 7421, Princeton (08543-7421)
PHONE..........................609 454-5340
Murat Erturk, *CEO*
EMP: 12
SALES (corp-wide): 2MM **Privately Held**
SIC: 3366 Bushings & bearings
PA: Oavco Limited Liability Company
103 Carnegie Ctr
Princeton NJ 08540
855 535-4227

(G-4121)
POWER BROOKS CO LLC
Also Called: Brooks Power Systems
2 Marlen Dr (08691-1601)
PHONE..........................609 890-0100
Avinash Diwan,
Ambika Diwan,
Anuraj Diwan,
Veena Diwan,
EMP: 13
SQ FT: 6,000
SALES (est): 1.3MM **Privately Held**
SIC: 3699 Electrical equipment & supplies

(G-4122)
PRINCETEL INC (PA)
2560 E State Street Ext (08619-3318)
PHONE..........................609 588-8801
Fax: 609 895-9552
Barry Zhang, *President*
Louis Violante, *QC Mgr*
Mark Knudsen, *Manager*
Michael O'Boyle, *Info Tech Mgr*
EMP: 30
SQ FT: 44,000
SALES: 8.5MM **Privately Held**
WEB: www.princetel.com
SIC: 3678 Electronic connectors

▲ = Import ▼=Export
◆ =Import/Export

(G-4123)
PRINCETON IDENTITY INC
300 Horizon Center Blvd # 306
(08691-1919)
PHONE.....................609 256-6994
Mark Clifton, *CEO*
EMP: 20
SALES (est): 986.1K **Privately Held**
SIC: 3571 Personal computers (microcomputers)

(G-4124)
ROMACO NORTH AMERICA INC
8 Commerce Way Ste 115 (08691-3373)
PHONE.....................609 584-2500
EMP: 7 **EST:** 2014
SALES (est): 749.2K **Privately Held**
SIC: 3053 3412 Packing materials; metal barrels, drums & pails

(G-4125)
ROYAL AQUARIUS EMPIRE
Also Called: Royal Aquarius Engrg Inds
2462 Yardville (08690)
PHONE.....................646 847-3322
Muhammad A Ali, *President*
EMP: 55
SALES (est): 877.8K **Privately Held**
SIC: 7699 3599 3535 3559 Industrial machinery & equipment repair; custom machinery; gasoline filters, internal combustion engine, except auto; robotic conveyors; automotive maintenance equipment

Hammonton
Atlantic County

(G-4126)
AG&E HOLDINGS INC (PA)
223 Pratt St (08037-1719)
PHONE.....................609 704-3000
Robert M Pickus, *Ch of Bd*
Anthony Tomasello, *President*
Francis X McCarthy, *CFO*
▲ **EMP:** 28 **EST:** 1925
SQ FT: 15,000
SALES: 13.2MM **Publicly Held**
WEB: www.wellsgardner.com
SIC: 3944 7993 Video game machines, except coin-operated; coin-operated amusement devices; game machines

(G-4127)
AMERICAN FLUX & METAL LLC
352 Fleming Pike (08037-2522)
PHONE.....................609 561-7500
Joachim Rudoler, *Mng Member*
▲ **EMP:** 20
SQ FT: 35,000
SALES (est): 12.3MM **Privately Held**
SIC: 2899 Chemical preparations; fluxes; brazing, soldering, galvanizing & welding

(G-4128)
AMERICAN GALVANIZING CO INC
1919 S 12th St (08037)
P.O. Box 408 (08037-0408)
PHONE.....................609 567-2090
Fax: 609 567-2822
John Gregor, *President*
George Cheesman, *Plant Mgr*
John Greenough, *Maint Spvr*
Allen Ivins, *Manager*
Jeff Scagnelli, *Manager*
EMP: 55 **EST:** 1965
SQ FT: 65,000
SALES: 9MM
SALES (corp-wide): 2.7B **Publicly Held**
SIC: 3479 Galvanizing of iron, steel or end-formed products
PA: Valmont Industries, Inc.
    1 Valmont Plz Ste 500
    Omaha NE 68154
    402 963-1000

(G-4129)
AMERICAN GAMING & ELEC INC (HQ)
Also Called: Wells-Gardner
233 Pratt St (08037)
PHONE.....................609 704-3000

Fax: 708 290-2200
Anthony Tomasello, *President*
Joe Karlowicz, *Sales Staff*
▲ **EMP:** 65
SALES: 6MM
SALES (corp-wide): 13.2MM **Publicly Held**
SIC: 3575 Computer terminals, monitors & components
PA: Ag&E Holdings Inc.
    223 Pratt St
    Hammonton NJ 08037
    609 704-3000

(G-4130)
ARAWAK PAVING CO INC (PA)
Also Called: Aztek Sand Grav Cmpny-Division
7503 Weymouth Rd (08037-3410)
PHONE.....................609 561-4100
Fax: 609 567-4750
Jack Barrett Sr, *President*
EMP: 23 **EST:** 1973
SQ FT: 5,000
SALES: 24MM **Privately Held**
WEB: www.arawakpci.com
SIC: 1611 2951 Highway & street paving contractor; asphalt & asphaltic paving mixtures (not from refineries)

(G-4131)
ASPHALT PAVING SYSTEMS INC (PA)
500 N Egg Harbor Rd (08037-3201)
P.O. Box 530 (08037-0530)
PHONE.....................609 561-4161
Fax: 609 561-0920
Robert Capoferri, *President*
Joseph Capoferri, *Admin Sec*
EMP: 164
SALES (est): 62.3MM **Privately Held**
SIC: 2951 Asphalt paving mixtures & blocks

(G-4132)
BARRETT ASPHALT INC
7503 Weymouth Rd (08037-3410)
PHONE.....................609 561-4100
John Barrett, *President*
Susan Barrett, *Admin Sec*
EMP: 25
SQ FT: 5,000
SALES (est): 6.7MM
SALES (corp-wide): 24MM **Privately Held**
WEB: www.arawakpci.com
SIC: 2951 Paving mixtures
PA: Arawak Paving Co., Inc.
    7503 Weymouth Rd
    Hammonton NJ 08037
    609 561-4100

(G-4133)
BASIC COMMERCE & INDUSTRIES
Also Called: BCI
856 S Route 30 Ste 5a (08037-2032)
PHONE.....................609 482-3740
Tom McParland, *Vice Pres*
EMP: 21
SALES (corp-wide): 31.6MM **Privately Held**
SIC: 7372 Prepackaged software
PA: Basic Commerce And Industries, Inc.
    303 Harper Dr
    Moorestown NJ 08057
    856 778-1660

(G-4134)
BUCCI MANAGEMENT CO INC
Also Called: Marbleworld Manufacturing
603 N 1st Rd (08037-3124)
PHONE.....................609 567-8808
Guy Bucci Sr, *President*
Guy Bucci Jr, *Vice Pres*
Henrietta Bucci, *Treasurer*
EMP: 7
SQ FT: 1,000
SALES (est): 797.3K **Privately Held**
SIC: 3479 Marbles (toys)

(G-4135)
C & E CANNERS INC
1249 Mays Landing Rd (08037-2816)
P.O. Box 229 (08037-0229)
PHONE.....................609 561-1078

Fax: 609 567-2776
Robert Cappuccio, *President*
▼ **EMP:** 15 **EST:** 1933
SQ FT: 40,000
SALES (est): 2.7MM **Privately Held**
SIC: 2033 Fruits & fruit products in cans, jars, etc.; vegetables & vegetable products in cans, jars, etc.

(G-4136)
CUSTOM SALES & SERVICE INC
Also Called: Custom Mobile Food Equipment
275 S 2nd Rd (08037-8445)
P.O. Box 635 (08037-0635)
PHONE.....................800 257-7855
Fax: 609 567-9318
Lynda Sikora, *President*
Bill Sikora, *Plant Mgr*
David Kyle, *Director*
▼ **EMP:** 48 **EST:** 1961
SQ FT: 22,000
SALES (est): 11MM **Privately Held**
WEB: www.foodcart.com
SIC: 3713 2599 Truck bodies (motor vehicles); carts, restaurant equipment

(G-4137)
GARVEY CORPORATION (PA)
208 S Route 73 (08037-9565)
PHONE.....................609 561-2450
Fax: 609 561-2328
William Garvey, *President*
Steve Ferrante, *Vice Pres*
Frank Scancella, *Foreman/Supr*
Robert Schaeffer, *Production*
Mark Jackson, *Purchasing*
◆ **EMP:** 70 **EST:** 1926
SQ FT: 55,000
SALES (est): 30.9MM **Privately Held**
WEB: www.garvey.com
SIC: 3535 3444 Conveyors & conveying equipment; sheet metalwork

(G-4138)
HAMMONTON GAZETTE INC
14 Tilton St (08037-1951)
P.O. Box 1228 (08037-5228)
PHONE.....................609 704-1939
Gabriel Donio, *President*
EMP: 5
SALES (est): 530.3K **Privately Held**
WEB: www.hammontongazette.com
SIC: 2721 Periodicals

(G-4139)
INTEGRITY MEDICAL DEVICES DEL
360 Fairview Ave (08037-1902)
PHONE.....................609 567-8175
Fax: 609 567-8086
Carleton Kimber, *President*
George Hughes Sr, *Vice Pres*
Hector Rodriguez, *Plant Mgr*
Roe Capaccio, *Executive*
EMP: 87
SQ FT: 15,000
SALES (est): 12.8MM **Privately Held**
WEB: www.integritymedical.com
SIC: 2211 Bandages, gauzes & surgical fabrics, cotton

(G-4140)
JOHN H ABBOTT INC
2101 Woodland Ave (08037-3732)
PHONE.....................609 561-0303
Fax: 609 561-1336
Sophie Abbott, *President*
Howard Abbott, *Corp Secy*
EMP: 6
SALES (est): 450K **Privately Held**
WEB: www.johnhabbott.com
SIC: 2421 Siding (dressed lumber)

(G-4141)
KELLOGG COMPANY
Also Called: Kellogg's Eggo
322 S Egg Harbor Rd (08037-9439)
PHONE.....................609 567-1688
Fax: 609 567-4849
Jeff Kirberg, *Branch Mgr*
EMP: 100
SALES (corp-wide): 12.9B **Publicly Held**
SIC: 2043 Cereal breakfast foods
HQ: Kellogg Usa Inc.
    1 Kellogg Sq
    Battle Creek MI 49017

(G-4142)
LUCCAS BAKERY INC
631 Egg Harbor Rd (08037-8507)
P.O. Box 97, Winslow (08095-0097)
PHONE.....................609 561-5558
Fax: 609 561-0310
Anthony Lucca, *President*
Mary Ann Lucca, *Corp Secy*
EMP: 20 **EST:** 1959
SQ FT: 10,000
SALES: 900K **Privately Held**
SIC: 5149 2051 Bakery products; bread, cake & related products

(G-4143)
MASSARELLIS LAWN ORNAMENTS INC
500 S Egg Harbor Rd (08037-3341)
PHONE.....................609 567-9700
Fax: 609 567-8844
Mario Massarelli, *President*
Christine L Massarelli, *Vice Pres*
Christine Massarelli, *Purchasing*
Eleanor Gaskill, *Technology*
▲ **EMP:** 36 **EST:** 1972
SALES (est): 6.7MM **Privately Held**
WEB: www.massarelli.com
SIC: 3272 Precast terrazo or concrete products

(G-4144)
MASTER WIRE MANUFACTURING CO
Also Called: Master Wire Fence
1019 Black Horse Pike (08037-2824)
P.O. Box 328 (08037-0328)
PHONE.....................609 561-2900
Brian Hefferon, *President*
Geraldin Hefferon, *Vice Pres*
EMP: 25
SALES (est): 5.3MM **Privately Held**
WEB: www.masterwiremfg.com
SIC: 3496 Fencing, made from purchased wire

(G-4145)
NINSA LLC
125 Lincoln St (08037-1219)
PHONE.....................609 561-7103
Greg Fondacaro, *President*
Olga Applegate, *CFO*
EMP: 8
SALES (est): 1.3MM **Privately Held**
SIC: 3315 Wire & fabricated wire products

(G-4146)
PLAGIDOS WINERY LLC
570 N 1st Rd (08037-9103)
PHONE.....................609 567-4633
Ollie Tomasello,
EMP: 5
SALES (est): 413.4K **Privately Held**
SIC: 2084 Wines

(G-4147)
POLYVEL INC
100 9th St (08037-3362)
PHONE.....................609 567-0080
Fax: 609 567-9522
Brian Tidwell, *President*
Gary Losasso, *Vice Pres*
Albert Losasso, *Admin Sec*
▼ **EMP:** 26
SQ FT: 46,000
SALES: 12MM **Privately Held**
WEB: www.polyvel.com
SIC: 2821 Plastics materials & resins

(G-4148)
SHARROTT WINE
370 S Egg Harbor Rd (08037-2460)
PHONE.....................609 567-9463
Larry Sharrott, *Owner*
Evelyn Tisch, *Marketing Staff*
EMP: 4 **EST:** 2007
SALES (est): 390K **Privately Held**
SIC: 2084 Wines

(G-4149)
SOUTH JERSEY INDUSTRIES INC
1 S Jersey Plz (08037-9109)
PHONE.....................609 561-9000
EMP: 99

SALES (corp-wide): 1.2B Publicly Held
SIC: 3999 Barber & beauty shop equipment
PA: South Jersey Industries, Inc.
1 S Jersey Plz
Hammonton NJ 08037
609 561-9000

(G-4150)
T G MANUFACTURING INC
Also Called: Tgm
206 Old Forks Rd (08037-9017)
PHONE..................................609 561-0022
Fax: 609 561-2972
Thomas G Garvey III, *President*
▲ EMP: 15
SQ FT: 9,000
SALES (est): 2.5MM Privately Held
WEB: www.tgmfg.com
SIC: 3441 Fabricated structural metal

(G-4151)
TOMASELLO WINERY INC (PA)
225 N White Horse Pike (08037-1868)
P.O. Box 440 (08037-0440)
PHONE..................................609 561-0567
Fax: 609 561-8617
Charles J Tomasello Sr, *Ch of Bd*
Charles J Tomasello Jr, *President*
John K Tomasello, *Vice Pres*
Margaret Tomasello, *Treasurer*
Stephen Smith, *Manager*
▲ EMP: 12 EST: 1933
SQ FT: 18,000
SALES (est): 3.8MM Privately Held
WEB: www.tomasellowinery.com
SIC: 2084 5812 Wine cellars, bonded: engaged in blending wines; eating places

(G-4152)
TRI DIAMOND ENTERPRISES LLC
Also Called: Tri Diamond Electric
735 Wiltseys Mill Rd (08037-9013)
PHONE..................................609 927-6018
Harry Bernstein,
Joseph Carusso,
EMP: 6 EST: 2006
SALES (est): 1.2MM Privately Held
SIC: 3699 Electrical equipment & supplies

Hampton
Hunterdon County

(G-4153)
AMEC FSTER WHEELER N AMER CORP (HQ)
53 Frontage Rd (08827-4031)
P.O. Box 9000 (08827-9000)
PHONE..................................936 448-6323
Fax: 908 730-5300
Gary Nedelka, *CEO*
Byron Roth, *President*
Peter Coppola, *Exec VP*
David Parham, *Exec VP*
Anthony Scerbo, *Exec VP*
◆ EMP: 59 EST: 1992
SQ FT: 72,000
SALES (est): 295.4MM
SALES (corp-wide): 5.3B Privately Held
WEB: www.fwcparts.com
SIC: 3433 3443 3532 3569 Steam heating apparatus; burners, furnaces, boilers & stokers; oil burners, domestic or industrial; gas burners, industrial; condensers, steam; boilers: industrial, power, or marine; process vessels, industrial: metal plate; coal breakers, cutters & pulverizers; generators: steam, liquid oxygen or nitrogen
PA: John Wood Group P.L.C.
15 Justice Mill Lane
Aberdeen AB12
122 485-1000

(G-4154)
BEHR TECHNOLOGY INC
223 State Route 31 (08827-5417)
PHONE..................................908 537-9960
Fax: 908 537-9980
Thomas Behr, *President*
EMP: 4
SQ FT: 4,000

SALES: 2MM Privately Held
SIC: 5045 3577 Computers, peripherals & software; computer peripheral equipment

(G-4155)
CELLDEX THERAPEUTICS INC (PA)
53 Frontage Rd Ste 220 (08827-4034)
PHONE..................................908 200-7500
Fax: 908 238-6773
Larry Ellberger, *Ch of Bd*
Anthony S Marucci, *President*
Tibor Keler, *Exec VP*
Ronald Pepin, *Senior VP*
Sam Martin, *CFO*
EMP: 135
SQ FT: 49,600
SALES: 12.7MM Publicly Held
WEB: www.avantimmune.com
SIC: 2834 8731 Pharmaceutical preparations; biotechnical research, commercial

(G-4156)
FOSTER WHEELER ARABIA LTD
53 Frontage Rd (08827-4031)
PHONE..................................908 730-4000
Umberto Della Sala, *CEO*
EMP: 6
SALES (est): 184K
SALES (corp-wide): 6.7B Privately Held
SIC: 8711 1629 3443 Engineering services; chemical plant & refinery construction; boiler shop products: boilers, smokestacks, steel tanks
PA: Amec Foster Wheeler Limited
4th Floor Old Change House
London EC4V
207 429-7500

(G-4157)
FOSTER WHEELER INTL CORP (DH)
Also Called: Foster Wheeler
Perryville Corporate Pk 5 (08827)
PHONE..................................908 730-4000
Fax: 908 730-4404
Umberto Della Sala, *President*
Filippo Abba, *Exec VP*
Chris Covert, *Exec VP*
James Gibson, *Exec VP*
Marco Moresco, *Exec VP*
EMP: 11
SQ FT: 294,000
SALES (est): 3.4MM
SALES (corp-wide): 5.3B Privately Held
SIC: 8711 1629 3443 Engineering services; chemical plant & refinery construction; boiler shop products: boilers, smokestacks, steel tanks
HQ: Wheeler Foster International Holdings Inc
Perryville Corporate Pk 5
Hampton NJ 08827
908 730-4000

(G-4158)
FOSTER WHEELER ZACK INC (HQ)
53 Frontage Rd (08827-4031)
P.O. Box 9000 (08827-9000)
PHONE..................................908 730-4000
Chris Covert, *President*
John Paul Archambault, *Vice Pres*
Jimmy Collins, *Vice Pres*
Michelle Davies, *Vice Pres*
Rakesh Jindal, *Vice Pres*
◆ EMP: 87
SQ FT: 600,000
SALES (est): 61.8MM
SALES (corp-wide): 6.7B Privately Held
WEB: www.fwc.com
SIC: 8711 1629 3569 4931 Industrial engineers; industrial plant construction; oil refinery construction; chemical plant & refinery construction; generators: steam, liquid oxygen or nitrogen; electric & other services combined
PA: Amec Foster Wheeler Limited
4th Floor Old Change House
London EC4V
207 429-7500

(G-4159)
FOSTER WHLER INTL HOLDINGS INC (DH)
Also Called: Foster Wheeler
Perryville Corporate Pk 5 (08827)
PHONE..................................908 730-4000
Kent Masters, *President*
Michelle Davies, *Exec VP*
Rakesh Jindal, *Vice Pres*
Peter Kuchler, *Vice Pres*
Lisa Wood, *Vice Pres*
EMP: 4 EST: 2001
SALES (est): 41MM
SALES (corp-wide): 5.3B Privately Held
SIC: 8711 3443 1629 Consulting engineer; boilers: industrial, power, or marine; chemical plant & refinery construction; oil refinery construction
HQ: Amec Foster Wheeler North America Corp.
53 Frontage Rd
Hampton NJ 08827
936 448-6323

(G-4160)
IKARIA THERAPEUTICS LLC
Perryvle 3 Corp Park Fl 3 (08827)
P.O. Box 9001 (08827-9001)
PHONE..................................908 238-6600
Douglas Greene, *Exec VP*
Bryan Ball, *Vice Pres*
Darrell Breaux, *Manager*
Thomas Rosenberg, *Manager*
Dianne Burns, *Supervisor*
EMP: 6
SALES (est): 660K Privately Held
SIC: 2834 Pharmaceutical preparations

(G-4161)
INFINITI COMPONENTS INC (PA)
223 State Route 31 (08827-5417)
PHONE..................................908 537-9950
Thomas Behr, *President*
Andy Lifshin, *Vice Pres*
EMP: 4
SQ FT: 3,700
SALES: 2.3MM Privately Held
WEB: www.infiniticomponents.com
SIC: 5065 3679 Electronic parts; static power supply converters for electronic applications

(G-4162)
INTEL CORPORATION
53 Frontage Rd Ste 210 (08827-4032)
PHONE..................................908 894-6035
EMP: 4
SALES (corp-wide): 62.7B Publicly Held
SIC: 3674 Semiconductors & related devices; microprocessors; microcircuits, integrated (semiconductor); memories, solid state
PA: Intel Corporation
2200 Mission College Blvd
Santa Clara CA 95054
408 765-8080

(G-4163)
KAPPUS PLASTIC COMPANY INC
61 State Route 31 65 (08827-2751)
P.O. Box 151 (08827-0151)
PHONE..................................908 537-2288
Fax: 908 537-7192
Kathleen Plenkers, *CEO*
John Kappus, *Ch of Bd*
Annette Gormly, *President*
Noel Kappus, *Vice Pres*
Rob Slater, *Purch Agent*
EMP: 60
SQ FT: 35,000
SALES (est): 13.5MM Privately Held
WEB: www.kappusplastic.com
SIC: 3081 3069 Polyvinyl film & sheet; rubber rolls & roll coverings

(G-4164)
MALLINCKRODT LLC
Also Called: Mallinckrodt Parmaceuticals
53 Frontage Rd (08827-4031)
PHONE..................................908 238-6600
Paul Coiante, *Vice Pres*
Dianne Burns, *Project Mgr*
Heather Arnold, *Natl Sales Mgr*
Lauren Riley, *Sales Staff*

Roy Bjellquist, *Manager*
EMP: 17 Privately Held
SIC: 3841 3829 2834 2833 Surgical & medical instruments; catheters; anesthesia apparatus; medical diagnostic systems, nuclear; pharmaceutical preparations; analgesics; codeine & derivatives; opium derivatives
HQ: Mallinckrodt Llc
675 Jmes S Mcdonnell Blvd
Hazelwood MO 63042
314 654-2000

(G-4165)
MONITORING SOLUTIONS INC (PA)
78 State Route 173 Ste 7 (08827-4020)
PHONE..................................908 713-0172
Fax: 908 713-0221
Mike Sroka, *President*
EMP: 7
SQ FT: 15,000
SALES (est): 2.3MM Privately Held
WEB: www.monsol.com
SIC: 3589 Sewage & water treatment equipment

(G-4166)
R & M CHEMICAL TECHNOLOGIES
7 Imlaydale Rd (08827-4500)
PHONE..................................908 537-9516
William Supplee, *President*
▲ EMP: 10
SQ FT: 12,800
SALES (est): 1.1MM Privately Held
SIC: 2819 4731 Nonmetallic compounds; freight forwarding

Hancocks Bridge
Salem County

(G-4167)
PSEG NUCLEAR LLC
80 Park Plz (08038)
P.O. Box 232 (08038-0232)
PHONE..................................856 339-1002
Fax: 856 339-1136
Ralph Izzo, *CEO*
William Levis, *President*
Glenn Figueroa, *Opers Staff*
Andrew Bauer, *Engineer*
Jennifer Holland, *Engineer*
▲ EMP: 2408
SALES (est): 228.8MM
SALES (corp-wide): 9B Publicly Held
SIC: 3462 Nuclear power plant forgings, ferrous
HQ: Pseg Power Llc
80 Park Plz T-9
Newark NJ 07102

Hardwick
Warren County

(G-4168)
M T D INC
24 Slabtown Creek Rd (07825-3211)
PHONE..................................908 362-6807
Fax: 908 362-5068
Thomas Nichols, *President*
Mary Nichols, *Corp Secy*
Dave Nichols, *Vice Pres*
EMP: 3
SALES: 1.8MM Privately Held
SIC: 3844 X-ray apparatus & tubes

Harrington Park
Bergen County

(G-4169)
A M GRAPHICS INC
68 Schraalenburg Rd Ste 6 (07640-1932)
P.O. Box 2185, River Vale (07675-9005)
PHONE..................................201 767-5320
John Motta, *President*
Vera Motta, *Vice Pres*
EMP: 4

▲ = Import ▼=Export
◆ =Import/Export

SQ FT: 2,000
SALES (est): 1MM Privately Held
SIC: 2752 2791 7336 Commercial printing, offset; hand composition typesetting; graphic arts & related design

(G-4170)
APPETITO PROVISIONS COMPANY
406 Lafayette Rd (07640-1324)
P.O. Box 715, Osprey FL (34229-0715)
PHONE..............................201 864-3410
Fax: 201 864-8017
Michael Tota, *President*
EMP: 35
SQ FT: 30,000
SALES (est): 6.8MM Privately Held
WEB: www.appetitosausage.com
SIC: 2013 Sausages from purchased meat

Harrison
Hudson County

(G-4171)
B & A GRAFX INC
1 Cape May St (07029-2402)
PHONE..............................646 302-8849
Jose Morales, *Principal*
EMP: 10 **EST:** 2015
SQ FT: 800
SALES (est): 427.2K Privately Held
SIC: 3993 Signs & advertising specialties

(G-4172)
BARNETT MACHINE TOOLS INC
401 Supor Blvd Bldg 3n (07029-2059)
PHONE..............................973 482-6222
Fax: 973 482-6012
Antonio Ferreira, *President*
Angelo Tamburri, *Vice Pres*
Steven Ferreira, *Manager*
▲ **EMP:** 17
SALES (est): 3MM Privately Held
WEB: www.barnettmachinetools.com
SIC: 3599 Machine shop, jobbing & repair

(G-4173)
BNG INDUSTRIES LLC
1 Cape May St Ste 2 (07029-2413)
PHONE..............................862 229-2414
Ian Grunes, *Mng Member*
EMP: 15
SALES: 250K Privately Held
SIC: 2511 4225 7922 Wood household furniture; miniwarehouse, warehousing; entertainment promotion

(G-4174)
BRADLEY CORRUGATED BOX CO INC
900 S 2nd St (07029-2323)
PHONE..............................973 483-0505
James Robinson, *President*
EMP: 4
SALES (est): 181.7K Privately Held
SIC: 2653 Boxes, corrugated: made from purchased materials

(G-4175)
CAMPBELL FOUNDRY COMPANY (PA)
Also Called: Campbell Group
800 Bergen St (07029-2034)
PHONE..............................973 483-5480
Fax: 973 483-1843
Chris Campbell, *President*
Greg Campbell, *Vice Pres*
John R Campbell III, *Vice Pres*
Beth A Skrenta, *Human Res Dir*
Ken Farrelly, *Sales Staff*
▲ **EMP:** 30
SQ FT: 5,000
SALES (est): 11.9MM Privately Held
WEB: www.campbellfoundry.com
SIC: 3321 Manhole covers, metal

(G-4176)
CEM INDUSTRIES INC
300 Somerset St Apt 217 (07029-2343)
PHONE..............................908 244-8080
Calvin Moore, *Principal*
EMP: 5

SALES (est): 175.5K Privately Held
SIC: 3999 Manufacturing industries

(G-4177)
CS OSBORNE & CO (PA)
Also Called: Parmelee Wrench
125 Jersey St (07029-1700)
PHONE..............................973 483-3232
Fax: 973 484-3621
I Jackson Angell III, *President*
D M Amador, *Vice Pres*
Jake Angell, *Opers Staff*
▲ **EMP:** 100 **EST:** 1826
SALES (est): 16.7MM Privately Held
WEB: www.csosborne.com
SIC: 3423 Hand & edge tools

(G-4178)
DOLCE VITA INTIMATES LLC (PA)
Also Called: Bebe Girdle
1000 1st St (07029-2332)
PHONE..............................973 482-8400
Jack Thekkekara, *President*
Diana Baradarian, *Vice Pres*
Allen Solomon, *CFO*
Michael Goldberg, *Accounts Mgr*
Anita Moran, *Accounts Exec*
◆ **EMP:** 60
SALES (est): 11.3MM Privately Held
SIC: 2342 2341 Girdles & panty girdles; slips: women's, misses', children's & infants'

(G-4179)
E-LO SPORTSWEAR LLC
Also Called: Sharagano
1 Cape May St (07029-2402)
PHONE..............................862 902-5220
David Lomita, *Principal*
Christine Ruffie, *Manager*
EMP: 15
SALES (corp-wide): 138MM Privately Held
SIC: 2337 Women's & misses' suits & skirts
PA: E-Lo Sportswear Llc
469 7th Ave Fl 15
New York NY 10018
862 902-5225

(G-4180)
EASTERN GLASS RESOURCES INC (PA)
770 Supor Blvd (07029-2035)
PHONE..............................973 483-8411
Fax: 973 482-2717
Phil Fisher, *President*
Cathy Hewitt, *Bookkeeper*
Richard Zmijewski, *Info Tech Mgr*
Joe Shary, *Technology*
▲ **EMP:** 35
SALES (est): 10.4MM Privately Held
SIC: 5023 3231 Glassware; products of purchased glass

(G-4181)
EMPORIA FOUNDRY INC
800 Bergen St (07029-2034)
PHONE..............................973 483-5480
Christopher Campbell, *President*
J Greg Campbell, *Vice Pres*
John R Campbell III, *Vice Pres*
EMP: 40
SQ FT: 30,000
SALES (est): 5.8MM
SALES (corp-wide): 11.9MM Privately Held
WEB: www.campbellfoundry.com
SIC: 3321 Manhole covers, metal
PA: Campbell Foundry Company
800 Bergen St
Harrison NJ 07029
973 483-5480

(G-4182)
FEDERAL CASTERS CORP (PA)
785 Harrison Ave (07029)
PHONE..............................973 483-6700
Fax: 973 483-5030
Salvatore Cumella, *Ch of Bd*
Charles Cumella, *President*
EMP: 58
SQ FT: 53,000
SALES (est): 26.3MM Privately Held
SIC: 5051 3562 Sheets, metal; casters

(G-4183)
FLEXO-CRAFT PRINTS INC
1000 1st St (07029-2332)
PHONE..............................973 482-7200
Fax: 973 482-9574
Mendel Klein, *Ch of Bd*
Abraham Klein, *President*
Dov Klein, *Senior VP*
Herschel Klein, *Vice Pres*
Joel Perlman, *Accounts Mgr*
▲ **EMP:** 45 **EST:** 1978
SQ FT: 150,000
SALES (est): 12MM Privately Held
WEB: www.flexocraft.com
SIC: 2679 2759 2621 2674 Gift wrap, paper: made from purchased material; flexographic printing; wrapping & packaging papers; shipping bags or sacks, including multiwall & heavy duty

(G-4184)
FMB SYSTEMS INC
Also Called: F M B Systems
70 Supor Blvd (07029-1921)
PHONE..............................973 485-5544
Fax: 973 485-3005
Bradley A Yount, *President*
Boris Kromis, *Vice Pres*
Gary Paolella, *Vice Pres*
Timothy Smith, *CFO*
▲ **EMP:** 70
SQ FT: 60,000
SALES (est): 15.7MM Privately Held
SIC: 3446 3441 Architectural metalwork; stairs, staircases, stair treads: prefabricated metal; railings, prefabricated metal; fabricated structural metal

(G-4185)
HOCKMEYER EQUIPMENT CORP (PA)
610 Supor Blvd (07029-1911)
PHONE..............................973 482-0225
Fax: 973 484-6114
Herman Hockmeyer Jr, *President*
Randall Seaman, *Vice Pres*
Mike Villardi, *VP Mfg*
Walter Audersch, *Purch Agent*
Rick Rimmer, *Technical Mgr*
▼ **EMP:** 67
SQ FT: 18,500
SALES (est): 17.2MM Privately Held
WEB: www.hockmeyer.com
SIC: 3559 7699 Refinery, chemical processing & similar machinery; industrial machinery & equipment repair

(G-4186)
INTERNATIONAL DIODE CORP
229 Cleveland Ave (07029-1395)
PHONE..............................973 482-6518
Lee Toong, *President*
Lee-Min Toong, *President*
EMP: 5 **EST:** 1959
SQ FT: 15,000
SALES (est): 460K Privately Held
SIC: 3674 Semiconductors & related devices; semiconductor diodes & rectifiers

(G-4187)
PRECISE CORPORATE PRINTING INC
Also Called: Precise Continental
1 Cape May St Ste 250 (07029-2409)
PHONE..............................973 350-0330
James P Donnelly, *CEO*
Frank Polizzi, *Vice Pres*
EMP: 38
SQ FT: 35,000
SALES (est): 5.4MM Privately Held
WEB: www.precisecorp.com
SIC: 2759 Engraving; thermography

(G-4188)
PRETTY LIL CUPCAKES
317 Essex St (07029-2119)
PHONE..............................201 256-1205
Gabriela Sandwith, *President*
EMP: 4
SALES (est): 178.7K Privately Held
SIC: 2051 Bread, cake & related products

(G-4189)
R P BAKING LLC
Also Called: Pechter's
840 Jersey St (07029-2056)
PHONE..............................973 483-3374
Sal Battaglia, *President*
Anthony Battaglia, *Vice Pres*
Ignazio Battaglia,
Joseph Battaglia,
Mario Battaglia,
EMP: 22
SALES (est): 3.5MM Privately Held
SIC: 2051 Bread, cake & related products

(G-4190)
TRI-STATE BUNS LLC
Also Called: Tsb
808 Warren St 810 (07029-2022)
PHONE..............................973 418-8323
Anthony Bataglia,
Ignazio Battaglia,
EMP: 45
SQ FT: 1,000
SALES (est): 8.8MM Privately Held
SIC: 2051 Bread, cake & related products

Hasbrouck Heights
Bergen County

(G-4191)
AMFINE CHEMICAL CORPORATION (HQ)
777 Perrace Ave Ste 602b (07604)
PHONE..............................201 818-0159
Fax: 201 818-0259
Koji Tajima, *President*
Takeyuki Mototani, *Exec VP*
Jay Kolaya, *Vice Pres*
Pete Goman, *Research*
Eduardo Rios, *Sales Mgr*
◆ **EMP:** 11
SQ FT: 5,000
SALES: 31.1MM
SALES (corp-wide): 2.2B Privately Held
WEB: www.amfine.com
SIC: 5169 2899 Industrial chemicals; chemical preparations
PA: Adeka Corporation
7-2-35, Higashiogu
Arakawa-Ku TKY 116-0
344 552-811

(G-4192)
FUJIKIN OF AMERICA INC
777 Terrace Ave Ste 110 (07604-3111)
PHONE..............................201 641-1119
John Crawford, *Manager*
EMP: 7
SALES (corp-wide): 829MM Privately Held
SIC: 3592 Valves
HQ: Fujikin Of America, Inc.
454 Kato Ter
Fremont CA 94539

(G-4193)
GULF CABLE LLC (PA)
777 Terrace Ave Ste 101 (07604-3112)
PHONE..............................201 242-9906
Bonita Singh, *CFO*
Orin Brian Singh, *Mng Member*
Sherie Singh-Cho,
▲ **EMP:** 150
SQ FT: 70,000
SALES: 4.3MM Privately Held
SIC: 3351 Copper rolling & drawing

(G-4194)
H & L PRINTING CO
309 Boulevard (07604-1302)
PHONE..............................201 288-0877
Tossi Henry, *Owner*
EMP: 6
SALES (est): 473.9K Privately Held
SIC: 2759 Commercial printing

(G-4195)
JCDECAUX MALLSCAPE LLC
440 State Rt 17 Ste 9 (07604-3000)
PHONE..............................201 288-2024
Abraham Lee, *Branch Mgr*
EMP: 6

SALES (corp-wide): 10.2MM **Privately Held**
SIC: **2531** Benches for public buildings
HQ: Jcdecaux Mallscape, Llc
　350 5th Ave Fl 73
　New York NY 10118
　646 834-1200

(G-4196)
M & M PRINTING CORP
Also Called: Minuteman Press
216 Boulevard (07604-1920)
PHONE.............................201 288-7787
Fax: 201 288-3476
Steven Cifaldi, *President*
Joyce Cifaldi, *Principal*
EMP: 4
SALES (est): 571.8K **Privately Held**
SIC: **2752** 2759 Commercial printing, off-set; commercial printing

(G-4197)
PABIN ASSOCIATES INC (PA)
Also Called: Gregory Associates
281 Springfield Ave (07604-1625)
PHONE.............................201 288-7216
John Pabin, *President*
EMP: 5
SALES (est): 584.5K **Privately Held**
SIC: **8742** 3565 Materials mgmt. (purchasing, handling, inventory) consultant; packaging machinery

(G-4198)
SPINDLERS BAKE SHOP
247 Boulevard (07604-1902)
PHONE.............................201 288-1345
Vinnie Pertuzzella, *Partner*
Ippolita Pertuzzella, *Partner*
EMP: 6 EST: 1956
SQ FT: 1,500
SALES (est): 288.6K **Privately Held**
SIC: **5461** 2051 Cakes; bakery: wholesale or wholesale/retail combined

(G-4199)
TAPE GRAPHICS
208 Boulevard Ste A (07604-1839)
PHONE.............................201 393-9500
Joe Bassani, *President*
EMP: 4
SALES: 2.3MM **Privately Held**
SIC: **2752** Wrapper & seal printing, lithographic

(G-4200)
TOP RATED SHOPPING BARGAINS
92 Railroad Ave (07604-2800)
P.O. Box 272, Edgewater (07020-0272)
PHONE.............................201 630-0770
Zoe Skyy, *CEO*
EMP: 10
SQ FT: 20,000
SALES (est): 274.2K **Privately Held**
SIC: **5092** 5014 3714 3911 Toys & hobby goods & supplies; hobby goods; automobile tires & tubes; wheel rims, motor vehicle; rosaries or other small religious articles, precious metal; men's & boys' work clothing; rubber coated fabrics & clothing

(G-4201)
TRACK SYSTEMS INC
Also Called: Mmp Ergonomics Co
174 Boulevard Ste 6 (07604-1844)
PHONE.............................201 462-0095
Robert Bogaczyk, *President*
Stuart Hirsh, *Vice Pres*
EMP: 12
SQ FT: 2,000
SALES (est): 2.7MM **Privately Held**
WEB: www.mmpergo.com
SIC: **3535** 5046 Conveyors & conveying equipment; commercial equipment

(G-4202)
UNIPLAST INDUSTRIES INC
1-5 Plant Rd (07604-2804)
P.O. Box 2367, South Hackensack (07606-0967)
PHONE.............................201 288-4672
A Joel Goldman, *President*
Lawrence H Goldman, *Vice Pres*
Bertram Goldman, *Treasurer*

▲ EMP: 40
SQ FT: 50,000
SALES (est): 9MM **Privately Held**
WEB: www.uniplastindustries.com
SIC: **3089** Clothes hangers, plastic

(G-4203)
UNITED WIRE HANGER CORP
1-5 Plant Rd (07604-2804)
P.O. Box 2367, South Hackensack (07606-0967)
PHONE.............................201 288-3212
Fax: 201 288-7212
Lawrence H Goldman, *President*
A Joel Goldman, *Exec VP*
Bertram Goldman, *Treasurer*
▲ EMP: 210 EST: 1962
SQ FT: 151,000
SALES (est): 33.9MM **Privately Held**
SIC: **3315** Hangers (garment), wire

(G-4204)
ZYMES LLC
777 Terrace Ave Ste 203 (07604-3112)
PHONE.............................201 727-1520
Benjamin D Mamola,
Randy Frank,
Vincent Morano,
EMP: 16
SALES (est): 2.9MM **Privately Held**
SIC: **2836** Biological products, except diagnostic

Haskell
Passaic County

(G-4205)
AMERICAN BERYLLIA INC
16 1st Ave (07420-1502)
PHONE.............................973 248-8080
Dino Nicoletta, *President*
Nussy Brauner, *General Mgr*
Larry Feinsinger, *Shareholder*
Mark Feinsinger, *Shareholder*
Hirsch Wolf, *Shareholder*
▲ EMP: 20 EST: 2001
SQ FT: 70,000
SALES (est): 5.7MM **Privately Held**
WEB: www.americanberyllia.com
SIC: **2869** Oxalic acid & metallic salts

(G-4206)
ARROW SHED LLC
1 3rd Ave (07420-1101)
PHONE.............................973 835-3200
Ed Paisker, *Vice Pres*
Joann Trezza, *Vice Pres*
EMP: 35
SALES (corp-wide): 38.1MM **Privately Held**
WEB: www.spacemakersheds.com
SIC: **3448** 3443 Buildings, portable: prefabricated metal; fabricated plate work (boiler shop)
HQ: Arrow Shed, Llc
　1101 N 4th St
　Breese IL 62230
　618 526-4546

(G-4207)
GILBERT STORMS JR
Also Called: Gilbys
1456 Ringwood Ave Apt 1 (07420-1577)
PHONE.............................973 835-5729
Fax: 973 835-2941
EMP: 5
SQ FT: 2,500
SALES: 450K **Privately Held**
SIC: **2395** 2262 5611 Mfg Embroidery & Art Needlework Screen Printing Fabrics & Ret Clothing Accessories

(G-4208)
INTERNTNAL DMNSIONAL STONE LLC
14 Doty Rd Unit B (07420-1411)
PHONE.............................973 729-0359
Michael Nestico,
EMP: 4
SALES (est): 83.3K **Privately Held**
SIC: **3281** 3272 Building stone products; furniture, cut stone; building stone, artificial: concrete

(G-4209)
LAKELAND TRANSFORMER CORP
6 Paul Pl (07420-1048)
PHONE.............................973 835-0818
Michael Golas, *Principal*
EMP: 5
SALES (est): 504.5K **Privately Held**
SIC: **3679** Cores, magnetic

(G-4210)
MACHINE PLUS INC
97 4th Ave (07420-1141)
PHONE.............................973 839-8884
Fax: 973 835-5361
Ford Robbins, *President*
Joyce Robbins, *Corp Secy*
Alan Pittelkow, *Vice Pres*
EMP: 8
SQ FT: 6,000
SALES (est): 660K **Privately Held**
SIC: **3599** 7699 7692 Machine shop, jobbing & repair; industrial machinery & equipment repair; welding repair

(G-4211)
NEW AMERICAN THERAPEUTICS INC
1069 Ringwood Ave 311b (07420-1452)
PHONE.............................908 282-7444
Bryan Sendrowski, *Principal*
EMP: 4
SALES (est): 285.9K **Privately Held**
SIC: **3841** Medical instruments & equipment, blood & bone work

(G-4212)
PHOENIX POWDER COATING LLC
400 Union Ave Ste 2 (07420-1554)
PHONE.............................973 907-7500
Steve Maus,
EMP: 4
SALES (est): 334.2K **Privately Held**
SIC: **3479** Coating of metals & formed products

(G-4213)
POLY MOLDING LLC
96 4th Ave (07420-1140)
PHONE.............................973 835-7161
Fax: 973 835-2138
Adam Corn, *Owner*
Sebastian Williams, *Sales Mgr*
Damien Choma, *Sales Associate*
Joann Doty, *Office Mgr*
◆ EMP: 19
SQ FT: 30,000
SALES (est): 3.9MM **Privately Held**
WEB: www.polytek.com
SIC: **3086** Insulation or cushioning material, foamed plastic

(G-4214)
STAMPEX CORP
75 4th Ave (07420-1141)
PHONE.............................973 839-4040
Fax: 973 616-1707
Detmar Nieshalla, *President*
Tom Nieshalla, *Vice Pres*
EMP: 10
SQ FT: 4,000
SALES (est): 700K **Privately Held**
SIC: **3544** 3469 Die sets for metal stamping (presses); metal stampings

(G-4215)
TECHLINE EXTRUSION SYSTEMS
89 4th Ave (07420-1141)
PHONE.............................973 831-0317
Fax: 973 831-7923
Victor Norman, *President*
Wilma Norman, *Treasurer*
EMP: 9
SQ FT: 3,200
SALES: 900K **Privately Held**
SIC: **3565** Packaging machinery

Hawthorne
Passaic County

(G-4216)
ACCURACY DEVICES
321 Central Ave (07506-1223)
PHONE.............................973 427-8829
Dave Van Derzee, *Owner*
EMP: 6
SALES: 450K **Privately Held**
SIC: **3821** Laboratory equipment: fume hoods, distillation racks, etc.

(G-4217)
ALEX SILK CO INC
53 Braen Ave (07506-2201)
PHONE.............................973 427-0499
Fax: 973 427-6858
John A Hryncewich Jr, *President*
Gloria Hryncewich, *Corp Secy*
EMP: 4 EST: 1932
SQ FT: 9,000
SALES: 1MM **Privately Held**
WEB: www.thegunglove.com
SIC: **2221** Broadwoven fabric mills, manmade; silk broadwoven fabrics; rayon broadwoven fabrics; apparel & outerwear fabric, manmade fiber or silk

(G-4218)
B & S SHEET METAL CO INC
60 5th Ave (07506-2140)
PHONE.............................973 427-3739
Fax: 973 427-5981
Robert Buchmann, *President*
Gary Buchmann, *Vice Pres*
EMP: 10 EST: 1960
SQ FT: 19,000
SALES (est): 1.9MM **Privately Held**
SIC: **3444** Sheet metalwork

(G-4219)
B WITCHING BATH COMPANY LLC (PA)
174 Lincoln Ave (07506-1302)
PHONE.............................973 423-1820
Barbara Ross,
EMP: 6 EST: 2010
SALES (est): 559K **Privately Held**
SIC: **2844** Deodorants, personal; toilet preparations

(G-4220)
BASSANO PRTRS & LITHOGRAPHERS
Also Called: Bassano Graphics
67 Royal Ave (07506-1916)
PHONE.............................973 423-1400
Fax: 973 427-0810
Ronald C Bassano, *President*
Donna Bassano, *Corp Secy*
EMP: 30
SQ FT: 2,800
SALES (est): 5.1MM **Privately Held**
WEB: www.bassanoprinting.com
SIC: **2752** 2759 Commercial printing, offset; letterpress printing

(G-4221)
BEAVER RUN FARMS (PA)
10 Wagaraw Rd (07506-2704)
P.O. Box 204 (07507-0204)
PHONE.............................973 427-1000
Charles Shotmeyer, *President*
Henry Shotmeyer Jr, *Corp Secy*
EMP: 5
SQ FT: 20,000
SALES (est): 1.4MM **Privately Held**
SIC: **2951** Asphalt & asphaltic paving mixtures (not from refineries)

(G-4222)
BRAWER BROS INC (PA)
375 Diamond Bridge Ave (07506-1323)
P.O. Box 640 (07507-0640)
PHONE.............................973 238-0163
Fax: 973 238-1545
Shartel Smith, *President*
Larry Haney, *Opers Mgr*
Adolfo Castillo, *Controller*
Scott Hartzell, *Sales Mgr*
Chris Schultz, *Sales Staff*
◆ EMP: 140 EST: 1899

SQ FT: 8,700
SALES (est): 21.5MM **Privately Held**
WEB: www.brawerbros.com
SIC: 2282 Textured yarn

(G-4223)
BROADHURST SHEET METAL WORKS
230 Warburton Ave (07506-1834)
PHONE......................973 304-4001
Fax: 973 427-1323
Kris Lill, *President*
EMP: 8
SALES (est): 1.5MM **Privately Held**
SIC: 3444 Sheet metal specialties, not stamped

(G-4224)
CAKE SPECIALTY INC
255 Goffle Rd (07506-3606)
PHONE......................973 238-0500
Fax: 973 238-1829
Joseph De Spirito, *President*
Nick Dispirito, *Vice Pres*
Nicholas De Spirito Fr, *Vice Pres*
Mike De Spirito, *Admin Sec*
EMP: 12 **EST:** 1965
SALES (est): 1.3MM **Privately Held**
WEB: www.cakespecialty.com
SIC: 2051 5461 Bakery: wholesale or wholesale/retail combined; bakeries

(G-4225)
CAST LIGHTING LLC (PA)
1120 Goffle Rd (07506-2024)
PHONE......................973 423-2303
Fax: 973 423-2304
Jim Hespe, *General Mgr*
Jeff Hesser, *Regl Sales Mgr*
Dave Beasoleil, *Mng Member*
Robert Beasoleil,
◆ **EMP:** 11
SALES (est): 2.9MM **Privately Held**
WEB: www.cast-lighting.com
SIC: 3645 Garden, patio, walkway & yard lighting fixtures: electric

(G-4226)
COLLINS AND COMPANY LLC
121 Wagaraw Rd (07506-2711)
PHONE......................973 427-4068
John Collins,
EMP: 9
SALES (est): 1.5MM **Privately Held**
SIC: 2679 Wallpaper

(G-4227)
COMMERCIAL PRODUCTS CO INC
117 Ethel Ave Ste 143 (07506-1526)
P.O. Box 504 (07507-0504)
PHONE......................973 427-6887
Fax: 973 427-0549
Charles Arnoldi, *President*
Elaine Arnoldi, *Admin Sec*
EMP: 12 **EST:** 1944
SALES (est): 1.7MM **Privately Held**
SIC: 2843 2295 Softeners (textile assistants); resin or plastic coated fabrics

(G-4228)
COMPUTER CRAFTS INC
57 Thomas Rd N (07506-2717)
P.O. Box 645 (07507-0645)
PHONE......................973 423-3500
Fax: 973 423-1648
John J Harkins, *Ch of Bd*
Donald Harkins, *President*
Robert Harkins, *Vice Pres*
▲ **EMP:** 250
SQ FT: 100,000
SALES (est): 35.9MM **Privately Held**
WEB: www.computer-crafts.com
SIC: 3679 3357 Harness assemblies for electronic use: wire or cable; fiber optic cable (insulated)

(G-4229)
CONTINENTAL AROMATICS
1 Thomas Rd S (07506-2701)
P.O. Box 567 (07507-0567)
PHONE......................973 238-9300
Fax: 973 345-0028
Ira Schneider, *President*
Beatrice Spitzer, *Accountant*
EMP: 20

SQ FT: 22,000
SALES (est): 3.6MM **Privately Held**
WEB: www.continentalaromatics.com
SIC: 2844 Perfumes & colognes

(G-4230)
E NEVIN MILLER INC
Also Called: Sir Speedy
21 Debra Ct (07506-2234)
PHONE......................201 444-5784
Fax: 201 444-6170
E Nevin Miller, *President*
Mary Miller, *Vice Pres*
EMP: 16 **EST:** 1974
SQ FT: 4,000
SALES (est): 1.5MM **Privately Held**
SIC: 2752 7334 2791 2789 Commercial printing, offset; photocopying & duplicating services; typesetting; bookbinding & related work

(G-4231)
ENCORE INTERNATIONAL LLC
270 Lafayette Ave (07506-1920)
PHONE......................973 423-3880
Fax: 973 423-3885
Rose Smith, *Accountant*
Nicole Chinnici, *Marketing Staff*
Dorys Spiegler, *Officer*
Peggi Geissler,
▲ **EMP:** 11
SQ FT: 2,500
SALES (est): 2.8MM **Privately Held**
WEB: www.encoreintl.com
SIC: 2844 Cosmetic preparations

(G-4232)
EPPLEY BUILDING & DESIGN INC
220 Goffle Rd Ste B (07506-3605)
PHONE......................973 636-9499
Fax: 973 636-9808
Paul Eppley, *President*
Brian Langford, *Project Mgr*
David Rowell, *Project Mgr*
Eric Schenk, *Supervisor*
EMP: 25
SQ FT: 5,000
SALES (est): 4MM **Privately Held**
WEB: www.ebandd.com
SIC: 2426 Furniture stock & parts, hardwood

(G-4233)
FISK ALLOY CONDUCTORS INC (HQ)
10 Thomas Rd N (07506-2716)
P.O. Box 26 (07507-0026)
PHONE......................973 825-8500
Eric Fisk, *President*
Brian Fisk, *Vice Pres*
Arelis Valenzuela, *Controller*
▲ **EMP:** 173
SQ FT: 65,000
SALES (est): 23MM **Privately Held**
WEB: www.fiskalloy.com
SIC: 3496 Miscellaneous fabricated wire products

(G-4234)
FISK ALLOY INC (PA)
10 Thomas Rd N (07506-2716)
P.O. Box 26 (07507-0026)
PHONE......................973 427-7550
Eric Fisk, *President*
Janet M Green, *CFO*
William Ward, *Sales Executive*
Bill Griglak, *Manager*
Maximin Basanaga, *Director*
EMP: 22
SQ FT: 140,000
SALES (est): 48MM **Privately Held**
SIC: 3496 3356 3351 3339 Miscellaneous fabricated wire products; nonferrous rolling & drawing; copper rolling & drawing; primary nonferrous metals; steel wire & related products

(G-4235)
FISK ALLOY WIRE INCORPORATED
Also Called: Electro Plated Wire
10 Thomas Rd N (07506-2716)
P.O. Box 26 (07507-0026)
PHONE......................973 949-4491

Fax: 973 427-4585
Eric Fisk, *President*
Brian Fisk, *Vice Pres*
Randy Martin, *Vice Pres*
Jim Mednteklidis, *Safety Mgr*
Brian Gerard, *Technical Mgr*
◆ **EMP:** 130
SQ FT: 140,000
SALES (est): 39.6MM **Privately Held**
SIC: 3496 3356 3351 3339 Miscellaneous fabricated wire products; nonferrous rolling & drawing; copper rolling & drawing; primary nonferrous metals; steel wire & related products

(G-4236)
FLAVOR ASSOCIATES INC
1 Thomas Rd N (07506-2717)
PHONE......................973 238-9300
Ira Schneider, *President*
EMP: 15
SQ FT: 22,000
SALES (est): 1.5MM **Privately Held**
SIC: 2087 Extracts, flavoring

(G-4237)
GRAPHIC ARTS PRINTING
170 Parmelee Ave (07506-2925)
PHONE......................201 343-6554
EMP: 5
SALES (est): 430K **Privately Held**
SIC: 2759 Commercial Printing

(G-4238)
HAWTHORNE KITCHENS INC
120 5th Ave (07506-2134)
PHONE......................973 427-9010
Kia Olsen, *President*
Annelise Olsen, *Corp Secy*
EMP: 10
SQ FT: 40,000
SALES (est): 1.5MM **Privately Held**
SIC: 5712 2541 5719 1751 Cabinet work, custom; sink tops, plastic laminated; bath accessories; cabinet building & installation

(G-4239)
HAWTHORNE PRESS
463 Lafayette Ave (07506-2521)
P.O. Box 1 (07507-0001)
PHONE......................973 427-3330
Fax: 973 427-8781
Linda Cmissonelli, *President*
Linda C Missonelli, *President*
Stephen Boswell, *Engineer*
EMP: 12
SALES (est): 500K **Privately Held**
SIC: 2711 Newspapers: publishing only, not printed on site

(G-4240)
HAWTHORNE RUBBER MFG CORP
35 4th Ave (07506-2150)
P.O. Box 171 (07507-0171)
PHONE......................973 427-3337
Fax: 973 427-8233
Michael J Morton, *President*
Dennis Dec, *Managing Dir*
Donald Morton, *Chairman*
John Morton, *Vice Pres*
Charlotte Morton, *Admin Sec*
EMP: 50 **EST:** 1943
SQ FT: 14,000
SALES (est): 9MM **Privately Held**
WEB: www.hawthornerubber.com
SIC: 3069 3061 Molded rubber products; mechanical rubber goods

(G-4241)
INTEK PLASTICS INC
150 5th Ave (07506-2159)
PHONE......................973 427-7331
Rich Theurer, *General Mgr*
EMP: 28
SALES (corp-wide): 43.8MM **Privately Held**
SIC: 3089 Plastic processing
PA: Intek Plastics, Inc.
1000 Spiral Blvd
Hastings MN 55033
651 437-3805

(G-4242)
IW TREMONT CO INC
Also Called: I W Tremont Co
18 Utter Ave (07506-2127)
PHONE......................973 427-3800
Fax: 973 427-3778
Sal Averso, *President*
Andrew S Averso, *Vice Pres*
James Averso, *Vice Pres*
▲ **EMP:** 25
SQ FT: 17,000
SALES (est): 5.8MM **Privately Held**
WEB: www.iwtremont.com
SIC: 2621 Specialty or chemically treated papers

(G-4243)
J BLANCO ASSOCIATES INC
280 9th Ave 1 (07506-1549)
PHONE......................973 427-0619
Victor Ramos, *President*
EMP: 11
SALES (est): 3.5MM **Privately Held**
WEB: www.jblanco.com
SIC: 3429 8711 Manufactured hardware (general); mechanical engineering

(G-4244)
JET PRECISION METAL INC
7 Schoon Ave (07506-1435)
PHONE......................973 423-4350
Fax: 973 423-1570
Nick Di Maggio, *President*
Luciano Iannucci, *Vice Pres*
Lou Iannucci, *Director*
Jill Vanhouten, *Admin Asst*
▲ **EMP:** 35
SQ FT: 30,000
SALES (est): 7MM **Privately Held**
WEB: www.jetprecision.com
SIC: 3444 Sheet metalwork

(G-4245)
LA FORCHETTA
27 Utter Ave (07506-2163)
PHONE......................973 304-4797
Peter Michienzi, *Owner*
EMP: 6
SALES (est): 594.3K **Privately Held**
SIC: 2273 Carpets & rugs

(G-4246)
MAGNATROL VALVE CORPORATION
21 Horton Ave (07506-1718)
PHONE......................973 427-4341
Bill Hagan, *Branch Mgr*
EMP: 6
SALES (est): 645K
SALES (corp-wide): 14.2MM **Privately Held**
SIC: 3491 Industrial valves
PA: Magnatrol Valve Corporation
67 5th Ave
Hawthorne NJ 07506
973 427-4341

(G-4247)
MID-STATE ENTERPRISES INC
Also Called: Latex Products Division
155 Van Winkle Ave (07506-2143)
P.O. Box 25 (07507-0025)
PHONE......................973 427-6040
Fax: 973 427-9750
David C Humphreys, *President*
Sandra Humphreys, *Admin Sec*
EMP: 10
SQ FT: 6,000
SALES (est): 1.1MM **Privately Held**
SIC: 3061 Oil & gas field machinery rubber goods (mechanical)

(G-4248)
MIDDLEBURG YARN PROCESSING CO (PA)
375 Diamond Bridge Ave (07506-1323)
P.O. Box 639 (07507-0639)
PHONE......................973 238-1800
Shartel Smith, *CEO*
Howard Reece, *President*
▲ **EMP:** 33 **EST:** 1946
SQ FT: 2,000
SALES (est): 9.9MM **Privately Held**
SIC: 2282 Throwing yarn; winding yarn; spooling yarn

(G-4249)
NEXUS PLASTICS INCORPORATED
1 Loretto Ave (07506-1300)
P.O. Box 667 (07507-0667)
PHONE...................................973 427-3311
Fax: 973 427-4847
Marwan Sholakh, *President*
▼ EMP: 90
SQ FT: 82,000
SALES (est): 26.8MM **Privately Held**
WEB: www.nexusplastics.com
SIC: 3081 2673 Plastic film & sheet; plastic bags: made from purchased materials

(G-4250)
NYLOK CORPORATION
Also Called: Aerospace Nylok
S11 Thomas Rd S (07506)
P.O. Box 651 (07507-0651)
PHONE...................................201 427-8555
Fax: 201 337-0040
John E Johnson, *Ch of Bd*
Richard Nolan, *President*
Leon Drake, *Vice Pres*
EMP: 16 EST: 1960
SQ FT: 10,000
SALES (est): 2.4MM **Privately Held**
SIC: 3452 Nuts, metal

(G-4251)
PASCACK DATA SERVICES INC
200 Central Ave Ste 100 (07506-1821)
PHONE...................................973 304-4858
Howard Adler, *President*
EMP: 12
SQ FT: 2,600
SALES (est): 3.1MM **Privately Held**
WEB: www.pascackdata.com
SIC: 7373 5045 7379 3571 Computer systems analysis & design; computer peripheral equipment; computer related consulting services; personal computers (microcomputers); computer installation; computer tape drives & components

(G-4252)
PEERLESS COATINGS LLC
Also Called: Peerless Coating Services
220a Goffle Rd (07506-3605)
PHONE...................................973 427-8771
Richard Bottoni,
Joe Hyer,
EMP: 45
SALES (est): 5.2MM **Privately Held**
SIC: 3479 Coating of metals & formed products; painting, coating & hot dipping

(G-4253)
PETER YAGED
Also Called: Hawthorne Machine Products
58 Braen Ave (07506-2202)
P.O. Box 259 (07507-0259)
PHONE...................................973 427-4219
Fax: 973 427-4160
Peter Yaged, *Owner*
EMP: 4 EST: 1948
SALES (est): 264.4K **Privately Held**
SIC: 3451 Screw machine products

(G-4254)
PHARMA SYSTEMS INC
662 Goffle Rd Ste 3 (07506-3420)
PHONE...................................973 636-9007
Fax: 973 636-9630
Bernard Giletta, *President*
EMP: 5
SALES (est): 519.2K **Privately Held**
WEB: www.pharmasystemsusa.com
SIC: 3559 Pharmaceutical machinery

(G-4255)
PREMIO FOODS INC (PA)
50 Utter Ave (07506-2117)
PHONE...................................800 864-7622
Marc Cinque, *President*
Steven Cinque, *Vice Pres*
Dan Gerrity, *CFO*
Sue Huang, *Controller*
▲ EMP: 150 EST: 1978
SQ FT: 60,000
SALES (est): 34.4MM **Privately Held**
WEB: www.premiofoods.com
SIC: 2013 2011 Sausages from purchased meat; meat packing plants

(G-4256)
RADIANT ENERGY SYSTEMS INC
175 N Ethel Ave (07506-1515)
PHONE...................................973 423-5220
Fax: 973 423-5220
Sarvejit Narang, *President*
Bob Narang, *President*
Cornel Polnyj, *Project Engr*
James Margiotta, *Sales Mgr*
Nicole Burchell, *Technology*
▲ EMP: 30
SQ FT: 16,000
SALES (est): 8.4MM **Privately Held**
WEB: www.radiantenergy.com
SIC: 3567 Infrared ovens, industrial

(G-4257)
RUSH GRAPHICS INC
1122 Goffle Rd 32 (07506-2024)
PHONE...................................973 427-9393
Fax: 973 427-1901
Zora Agheli, *President*
Sam Kassaii, *Vice Pres*
Manee Kassaii, *Marketing Mgr*
EMP: 20
SQ FT: 10,000
SALES (est): 3.4MM **Privately Held**
WEB: www.rushgraphics.com
SIC: 2752 Commercial printing, offset

(G-4258)
SERVO-TEK PRODUCTS COMPANY INC
1096 Goffle Rd (07506-2009)
PHONE...................................973 427-4249
Fax: 973 427-4249
EMP: 40
SQ FT: 25,000
SALES (est): 4.3MM **Privately Held**
SIC: 3625 3621 Mfg Relays/Industrial Controls Mfg Motors/Generators

(G-4259)
SIGNATURE MARKETING & MFG
Also Called: Signature Crafts
301 Wagaraw Rd (07506-1411)
PHONE...................................973 427-3700
Fax: 973 427-2906
Michael Assile, *President*
Hala Assile, *Treasurer*
EMP: 8
SQ FT: 8,000
SALES (est): 1.3MM **Privately Held**
WEB: www.signaturecrafts.com
SIC: 2891 Glue

(G-4260)
TEKNO INC
Also Called: Conexion Printing
86 5th Ave (07506-2138)
PHONE...................................973 423-2004
Elliot Montalvo, *President*
Claudia Montalvo, *Manager*
EMP: 6
SQ FT: 10,000
SALES (est): 569.5K **Privately Held**
SIC: 2759 Commercial printing

(G-4261)
ULMA FORM-WORKS INC (HQ)
58 5th Ave (07506-2160)
PHONE...................................201 882-1122
Fax: 973 636-2045
Alberto Arocena, *President*
Frank Deluccia, *General Mgr*
Frank Cola, *Vice Pres*
Eugenio Pedrao, *CFO*
Charles Polesovsky, *Regl Sales Mgr*
▲ EMP: 52
SQ FT: 9,500
SALES (est): 9.6MM
SALES (corp-wide): 102.7MM **Privately Held**
WEB: www.ulmaforms.com
SIC: 3443 3272 3444 Fabricated plate work (boiler shop); concrete stuctural support & building material; concrete forms, sheet metal
PA: Ulma C Y E S Coop
    Calle Obispo Otadui, 3 - Apdo 13
    Onati 20560
    943 034-900

(G-4262)
USSECURENET LLC
1086 Goffle Rd Ste 101 (07506-2012)
PHONE...................................201 447-0130
Kathryn Zegarra, *Manager*
Debra Deffaa,
EMP: 4
SQ FT: 10,000
SALES (est): 569.2K **Privately Held**
SIC: 3663 4899 Satellites, communications; satellite earth stations

(G-4263)
VANDEREEMS MANUFACTURING CO
40 Schoon Ave (07506-1408)
PHONE...................................973 427-2355
Fax: 973 427-2356
John Van Der Eems, *President*
EMP: 10 EST: 1933
SQ FT: 12,000
SALES (est): 1.4MM **Privately Held**
SIC: 2449 Shipping cases & drums, wood: wirebound & plywood; berry crates, wood: wirebound

(G-4264)
VIVITONE INC (PA)
111 Ethel Ave (07506-1528)
PHONE...................................973 427-8114
Gerald Sandler, *President*
EMP: 18
SQ FT: 35,000
SALES (est): 1MM **Privately Held**
SIC: 2816 2893 Inorganic pigments; printing ink

(G-4265)
VYRAL SYSTEMS INC
Also Called: Vyral Entertainment
300 Mountain Ave (07506-3314)
PHONE...................................201 321-2488
David Kaplan, *CEO*
EMP: 5 EST: 2011
SQ FT: 650
SALES (est): 186.4K **Privately Held**
SIC: 7372 Prepackaged software; application computer software; home entertainment computer software

(G-4266)
WARP PROCESSING INC (PA)
375 Diamond Bridge Ave (07506-1323)
P.O. Box 640 (07507-0640)
PHONE...................................973 238-1800
Shartel Smith, *President*
▲ EMP: 2
SQ FT: 7,000
SALES (est): 11.4MM **Privately Held**
SIC: 2282 Throwing & winding mills; winding yarn

Hazlet
Monmouth County

(G-4267)
A SIGN OF EXCELLENCE INC
6 Surrey Dr (07730-1829)
PHONE...................................732 264-0404
Sue Cosnoski, *President*
EMP: 4
SALES: 250K **Privately Held**
SIC: 3993 Signs & advertising specialties

(G-4268)
ADMARTEC INC
12 Crown Plz Ste 204 (07730-2441)
PHONE...................................732 888-8248
Anatoly Nemiroski, *President*
EMP: 4
SQ FT: 2,500
SALES (est): 494.4K **Privately Held**
SIC: 3625 Control circuit devices, magnet & solid state

(G-4269)
ARGLEN INDUSTRIES INC
1 Bethany Rd Ste 44 (07730-1681)
PHONE...................................732 888-8100
Fax: 732 888-7876
Andrew Strahl, *President*
EMP: 10
SALES (est): 1.5MM **Privately Held**
WEB: www.arglen-us.com
SIC: 2752 Commercial printing, lithographic

(G-4270)
ASTRA CLEANERS OF HAZLET
35 Hazlet Ave (07730-1844)
PHONE...................................732 264-4144
David Lee, *Owner*
Paula Saeber, *Owner*
Ron Silver, *Owner*
EMP: 5
SALES (est): 103.4K **Privately Held**
SIC: 7216 2842 Curtain cleaning & repair; specialty cleaning, polishes & sanitation goods

(G-4271)
BURLINGTON ATLANTIC CORP
Burlington Battery
1 Crown Plz (07730-2441)
PHONE...................................732 888-7776
Fax: 732 888-0157
Randolph Resch, *Manager*
EMP: 5
SALES (corp-wide): 1.4MM **Privately Held**
WEB: www.sierratechnologies.net
SIC: 3692 Primary batteries, dry & wet
PA: Burlington Atlantic Corporation
    277 Frank Applegate Rd
    Jackson NJ 08527
    732 888-7799

(G-4272)
CARWIN PHRM ASSOC LLC
1301 Hwy 36 Ste 12 (07730-1755)
PHONE...................................732 344-6987
Kevin Hudy, *President*
Jason Melfi,
EMP: 5
SALES (est): 370K **Privately Held**
SIC: 2834 Pharmaceutical preparations

(G-4273)
CIRCA PROMOTIONS INC
58 Village Ct (07730-1537)
P.O. Box 360, Atlantic Highlands (07716-0360)
PHONE...................................732 264-1200
Fax: 732 264-9414
Karen Kantor, *President*
EMP: 8
SQ FT: 3,000
SALES (est): 1.3MM **Privately Held**
WEB: www.circapromotions.com
SIC: 5199 2759 Advertising specialties; commercial printing

(G-4274)
FRAGRANCE RESOURCES INC (HQ)
600 State Route 36 (07730-1704)
PHONE...................................973 777-2979
Fax: 973 458-5224
◆ EMP: 18
SQ FT: 13,000
SALES (est): 8.6MM
SALES (corp-wide): 3.4B **Publicly Held**
WEB: www.fragranceresources.com
SIC: 2844 Mfg Toilet Preparations
PA: International Flavors & Fragrances Inc.
    521 W 57th St
    New York NY 10019
    212 765-5500

(G-4275)
INDUSTRIAL WATER TECH INC
6 Village Ct (07730-1530)
PHONE...................................732 888-1233
Fax: 732 888-9441
Richard Demartino, *President*
Joy Lacy, *Opers Mgr*
Marie Cantelmo, *Controller*
EMP: 7
SQ FT: 2,000
SALES (est): 2MM **Privately Held**
WEB: www.iwtnj.com
SIC: 2899 8748 Water treating compounds; business consulting

(G-4276)
INTERNTNAL FLVORS FRGRNCES INC
Also Called: Interntonal Flavors Fragrances
600 Highway 36 (07730-1704)
PHONE..............................732 264-4500
Fax: 732 335-2551
David Smith, *Branch Mgr*
EMP: 200
SALES (corp-wide): 3.4B **Publicly Held**
SIC: 2869 5999 2844 Flavors or flavoring materials, synthetic; perfumes & colognes; toilet preparations
PA: International Flavors & Fragrances Inc.
521 W 57th St
New York NY 10019
212 765-5500

(G-4277)
LAZAR TECHNOLOGIES INC
Also Called: LAZAR CAPPER
39 Evergreen St (07730-4033)
PHONE..............................732 739-9622
Fax: 732 739-9610
Carlos Gaviria, *President*
Isabel Gaviria, *Vice Pres*
Sabrina Gaviria, *Sales Staff*
▼ EMP: 10
SQ FT: 10,000
SALES (est): 1.8MM **Privately Held**
WEB: www.lazartec.com
SIC: 3599 Custom machinery

(G-4278)
LUMBER SUPER MART
State Hwy No 36 (07730)
P.O. Box 333 (07730-0333)
PHONE..............................732 739-1428
EMP: 4
SALES (est): 280K **Privately Held**
SIC: 5261 3089 Ret Nursery/Garden Supplies Mfg Plastic Products

(G-4279)
MID-STATE CONTROLS INC
8 Crown Plz Ste 102 (07730-2472)
PHONE..............................732 335-0500
Robert Rosko, *Principal*
EMP: 14
SALES (est): 2.2MM **Privately Held**
SIC: 3625 Control equipment, electric

(G-4280)
NOUVEAU PROSTHETICS LTD
984 State Route 36 (07730-1700)
PHONE..............................732 739-0888
Fax: 732 739-5351
Stuart Weiner, *President*
Camille Levin, *Administration*
EMP: 10
SQ FT: 3,200
SALES (est): 1MM **Privately Held**
SIC: 3842 5999 Limbs, artificial; braces, orthopedic; medical apparatus & supplies

(G-4281)
NOUVEAU PROSTHETICS ORTHOTICS
984 State Route 36 (07730-1700)
PHONE..............................732 739-0888
Stuart Weiner, *President*
Evett Weiner, *Corp Secy*
Camille Levin, *Asst Director*
EMP: 10
SQ FT: 1,400
SALES (est): 1.3MM **Privately Held**
SIC: 3842 Limbs, artificial; prosthetic appliances

(G-4282)
PETER MORLEY LLC
Also Called: Safeguard Business Systems
21 Village Ct (07730-1532)
PHONE..............................732 264-0010
Peter Morley,
EMP: 4
SQ FT: 1,000
SALES (est): 602K **Privately Held**
SIC: 5112 2621 Business forms; stationery, envelope & tablet papers

(G-4283)
SILAB INC
1301 State Route 36 Ste 8 (07730-1751)
PHONE..............................732 335-1030

Jean Paufique, *CEO*
▲ EMP: 10
SALES (est): 1.3MM **Privately Held**
SIC: 2834 Extracts of botanicals: powdered, pilular, solid or fluid
HQ: Societe Industrielle Limousine D'application Biologique
Lieu Dit Madrias
Objat 19130
555 845-840

(G-4284)
TALENT INVESTMENT LLC
Also Called: Talent Technology Center
12 Crown Plz (07730-2441)
PHONE..............................732 931-0088
Grace Wang, *Manager*
Yuhinin Hwang,
EMP: 7
SALES (est): 873.4K **Privately Held**
SIC: 2869 Silicones

(G-4285)
TRETINA PRINTING INC
1301 Cncrd Hwy 36 101 (07730)
PHONE..............................732 264-2324
Fax: 732 264-0180
Jan Tretina, *President*
Olga Tretina, *Corp Secy*
EMP: 15
SQ FT: 22,000
SALES (est): 1.9MM **Privately Held**
WEB: www.tretinaprinting.com
SIC: 2752 Photo-offset printing; commercial printing, offset

Helmetta
Middlesex County

(G-4286)
MILLER SIGNS LLC
14 Main St (08828-1210)
PHONE..............................732 521-0904
Tabitha Miller, *Principal*
EMP: 6
SALES (est): 89.8K **Privately Held**
SIC: 3993 Signs & advertising specialties

Hewitt
Passaic County

(G-4287)
A & A IRONWORK CO INC
955 Burnt Meadow Rd (07421-3503)
P.O. Box 1090 (07421-2090)
PHONE..............................973 728-4300
Fax: 973 208-8663
Adam G Muzer, *President*
Adam E Muzer, *Vice Pres*
Mark Muzer, *Vice Pres*
EMP: 14
SQ FT: 4,500
SALES: 3MM **Privately Held**
SIC: 3312 3446 Structural & rail mill products; architectural metalwork

(G-4288)
COM-FAB INC
921 Burnt Meadow Rd B (07421-3503)
Rural Route 7 Cane Rd, Greenwood Lake NY (10925)
PHONE..............................973 296-0433
Michael Fattal, *President*
EMP: 4
SQ FT: 1,875
SALES (est): 324K **Privately Held**
SIC: 3441 Building components, structural steel

(G-4289)
ECO-PLUG-SYSTEM LLC
1946 Union Valley Rd (07421-4100)
P.O. Box 12 (07421-0012)
PHONE..............................855 326-7584
Peter Esposito, *President*
▼ EMP: 6
SQ FT: 5,600
SALES: 156K **Privately Held**
SIC: 3559 Automotive related machinery

(G-4290)
MACK TRADING LLC
486 Lake Shore Dr (07421-1324)
PHONE..............................973 794-4904
EMP: 4 EST: 1999
SALES: 40K **Privately Held**
SIC: 2066 Mfg Chocolate/Cocoa Products

(G-4291)
NORTHEAST CON PDTS & SUP INC
937 Burnt Meadow Rd (07421-3503)
P.O. Box 963 (07421-0963)
PHONE..............................973 728-1667
Nancy Vitale, *President*
John Vitale, *Vice Pres*
EMP: 5
SALES (est): 785.7K **Privately Held**
SIC: 3272 Septic tanks, concrete

(G-4292)
ROBERT YOUNG AND SON INC
830 Burnt Meadow Rd (07421-3506)
PHONE..............................973 728-8133
William Young, *President*
Karen Young, *Admin Sec*
EMP: 8
SQ FT: 100
SALES (est): 343.9K **Privately Held**
SIC: 3531 Asphalt plant, including gravel-mix type

High Bridge
Hunterdon County

(G-4293)
ADVANCED PRECISION SYSTEMS LLC
6 Sunset Dr (08829-1307)
PHONE..............................908 730-8892
Michael Manzella,
EMP: 5
SQ FT: 1,300
SALES (est): 230K **Privately Held**
WEB: www.advancedprecisionsystems.com
SIC: 3499 Metal household articles

(G-4294)
CUSTOM ALLOY CORPORATION (PA)
3 Washington Ave Ste 5 (08829-2108)
PHONE..............................908 638-0257
Fax: 908 638-5623
Adam F Ambielli, *President*
Blair Woodring, *Business Mgr*
John M Ambielli, *Exec VP*
Patricia Schriver, *Assistant VP*
Roger Carroll, *Prdtn Mgr*
▲ EMP: 170
SQ FT: 150,000
SALES (est): 44.2MM **Privately Held**
WEB: www.customalloy.us
SIC: 3498 Fabricated pipe & fittings

(G-4295)
ENVIRO-CLEAR COMPANY INC
152 Cregar Rd (08829-1003)
PHONE..............................908 638-5507
J J Muldowney, *President*
Cindy Meyer, *President*
Kevin Muldowney, *Project Mgr*
Michael Leicht, *Project Engr*
▲ EMP: 15
SQ FT: 15,000
SALES (est): 3.7MM **Privately Held**
WEB: www.enviro-clear.com
SIC: 3569 3532 Filters; clarifying machinery, mineral

(G-4296)
GLASSMAN HIGH VOLTAGE INC (PA)
124 W Main St (08829-1707)
P.O. Box 317 (08829-0317)
PHONE..............................908 638-3800
Fax: 908 638-3700
Sanford Glassman, *CEO*
Bill Smith, *Facilities Mgr*
Scott N Jarmicki, *Sales Staff*
Jeanne Fleck, *Admin Sec*
EMP: 100 EST: 1977

SQ FT: 60,000
SALES (est): 17.1MM **Privately Held**
SIC: 3679 Power supplies, all types: static

(G-4297)
J & M MANUFACTURING INC
54 Main St (08829-1915)
P.O. Box 43 (08829-0043)
PHONE..............................908 638-4298
Fax: 908 638-5077
John Gargas, *President*
EMP: 8
SQ FT: 6,000
SALES (est): 912K **Privately Held**
SIC: 3599 Machine shop, jobbing & repair

(G-4298)
NORSAL DISTRIBUTION ASSOCIATES
150 Cregar Rd (08829-1003)
P.O. Box 264 (08829-0264)
PHONE..............................908 638-6430
Fax: 908 638-4320
Sal Moscato Sr, *Ch of Bd*
Sal Moscato Jr, *President*
Norma Moscato, *Vice Pres*
Russell Lown, *Opers Mgr*
EMP: 10
SQ FT: 11,700
SALES (est): 1MM **Privately Held**
WEB: www.norsalnda.com
SIC: 1731 3679 Electric power systems contractors; electronic circuits

---

Highland Lakes
Sussex County

(G-4299)
NORTH STAR SIGNS INC
3 Callan Ct (07422-1002)
PHONE..............................973 244-1144
Jesse Guzman, *Principal*
EMP: 9 EST: 2008
SALES (est): 133.6K **Privately Held**
SIC: 3993 Signs & advertising specialties

Highland Park
Middlesex County

(G-4300)
ALL COLORS SCREEN PRINTING LLC
176 Woodbridge Ave (08904-3767)
PHONE..............................732 777-6033
Gayle Brill Mittler, *Mng Member*
EMP: 6
SQ FT: 5,700
SALES (est): 821.3K **Privately Held**
SIC: 2759 3993 7389 5199 Screen printing; signs & advertising specialties; embroidering of advertising on shirts, etc.; advertising specialties

(G-4301)
BIRNN CHOCOLATES INC
314 Cleveland Ave (08904-1845)
PHONE..............................732 214-8680
John Cunnell, *President*
EMP: 4
SQ FT: 5,000
SALES (est): 424K **Privately Held**
WEB: www.birnnchocolates.com
SIC: 5441 5145 2066 Candy; candy; chocolate & cocoa products

(G-4302)
COLGATE-PALMOLIVE COMPANY
251 S 8th Ave (08904-3107)
PHONE..............................732 878-6062
EMP: 279
SALES (corp-wide): 15.4B **Publicly Held**
SIC: 2844 Toothpastes or powders, dentifrices
PA: Colgate-Palmolive Company
300 Park Ave Fl 3
New York NY 10022
212 310-2000

GEOGRAPHIC

(G-4303)
ENERGY RECYCLING CO LLC
233 Cleveland Ave (08904-1841)
P.O. Box 4762 (08904-4762)
PHONE..............................732 545-6619
Larry Schrager, *President*
Rosella Sabatini, *Vice Pres*
EMP: 5
SALES: 700K **Privately Held**
WEB: www.energyrecyclingco.com
SIC: 3559 5084 Recycling machinery; recycling machinery & equipment

(G-4304)
RESPONSIBLE MACHINES LLC
70 Lawrence Ave (08904-1834)
PHONE..............................917 740-2269
Manoj Khanna, *Owner*
EMP: 5
SALES (est): 167.6K **Privately Held**
SIC: 3599 Industrial machinery

(G-4305)
WATER MASTER CO
13 S 3rd Ave (08904-2509)
PHONE..............................732 247-1900
Marvin Cheiten, *Owner*
▼ **EMP:** 6 **EST:** 1947
SQ FT: 3,000
SALES (est): 380K **Privately Held**
SIC: 3069 3471 Molded rubber products; polishing, metals or formed products

(G-4306)
YAMATE CHOCOLATIER INC
320 Cleveland Ave (08904-1845)
PHONE..............................732 249-4847
EMP: 7
SALES (est): 716.6K **Privately Held**
SIC: 2026 Mfg Chocolate

Highlands
Monmouth County

(G-4307)
CERTIFIED CLAM CORP
190 Bay Ave Ste 1 (07732-1665)
P.O. Box 383 (07732-0383)
PHONE..............................732 872-6650
Fax: 732 872-6653
Cathy Armstrong, *President*
Janis Hartsgrove, *Sales Staff*
EMP: 14
SALES: 4.2MM **Privately Held**
SIC: 5146 2092 Seafoods; fresh or frozen packaged fish

(G-4308)
DRONE GO HOME LLC
25 Grand Tour (07732-2001)
PHONE..............................732 991-3605
Linda Ziemba, *General Mgr*
EMP: 9
SALES (est): 187K **Privately Held**
SIC: 3721 3728 Autogiros; target drones

(G-4309)
GARDNER RESOURCES INC
188 Bay Ave (07732-1624)
P.O. Box 363 (07732-0363)
PHONE..............................732 872-0755
Blair Lazar, *President*
Gary Tucker, *Sales Mgr*
Karin Swan, *Manager*
▲ **EMP:** 4
SALES (est): 476.9K **Privately Held**
SIC: 5499 5149 2033 Gourmet food stores; sauces; chili sauce, tomato: packaged in cans, jars, etc.

Hightstown
Mercer County

(G-4310)
B-HIVE LTD LIABILITY COMPANY
10 Olivia Rd (08520-4762)
PHONE..............................302 438-2769
Tara Prabhakar,
EMP: 8
SALES: 100K **Privately Held**
SIC: 3572 Computer storage devices

(G-4311)
CCL LABEL INC
120 Stockton St (08520-3706)
PHONE..............................609 443-3700
Jason Rudolph, *Opers Mgr*
Larry Joseph, *Facilities Mgr*
Dave Lore, *Purch Agent*
Jack Lang, *Branch Mgr*
Melinda Eger, *Director*
EMP: 100
SALES (corp-wide): 3.7B **Privately Held**
SIC: 2679 2673 2672 Paper products, converted; paperboard products, converted; bags: plastic, laminated & coated; coated & laminated paper
HQ: Ccl Label, Inc.
　161 Worcester Rd Ste 504
　Framingham MA 01701
　508 872-4511

(G-4312)
HIGHTS ELECTRIC MOTOR SERVICE
156 Stockton St (08520-3706)
PHONE..............................609 448-2298
Fax: 609 448-4778
Bernard E Stella Jr, *President*
Therese A Stella, *Corp Secy*
EMP: 4
SQ FT: 7,000
SALES (est): 1.4MM **Privately Held**
SIC: 5063 5084 7694 7699 Motors, electric; generators; pumps & pumping equipment; motor repair services; pumps & pumping equipment repair; generator repair

(G-4313)
NATIONAL CERTIFIED PRINTING
Also Called: Michael's Quick Printing
387 Mercer St A (08520-4409)
PHONE..............................609 443-6323
Fax: 609 490-0266
Joseph Sharoff, *Owner*
EMP: 4
SALES (est): 448.2K **Privately Held**
SIC: 2752 Commercial printing, offset

(G-4314)
ROMULUS EMPRISES INC
60 Woodside Ave (08520-4900)
PHONE..............................609 683-4549
Harold D Romulus, *Ch of Bd*
Antoine Francis, *President*
Hymler Geffrard, *CFO*
EMP: 6
SALES: 70K **Privately Held**
SIC: 2076 Vegetable oil mills

Hillsborough
Somerset County

(G-4315)
4 WAY LOCK LLC
5 Ilene Ct Ste 12 (08844-1915)
PHONE..............................908 359-2002
Ann Magiash, *Mng Member*
EMP: 4
SQ FT: 25,000
SALES (est): 482.9K **Privately Held**
SIC: 3442 3429 Metal doors; keys, locks & related hardware

(G-4316)
ADAM GATES & COMPANY LLC
249 Homestead Rd Ste 5 (08844-1912)
P.O. Box 2248, East Millstone (08875-2248)
PHONE..............................908 829-3386
Chester Swasey,
EMP: 10
SQ FT: 5,000
SALES (est): 1.6MM **Privately Held**
WEB: www.adamgatescompany.com
SIC: 2899 8711 Chemical supplies for foundries; engineering services

(G-4317)
AURA SIGNS INC
Also Called: Triaddisplay
6 Ilene Ct Ste 9 (08844-1921)
PHONE..............................866 963-7446
Deval Soni, *President*
EMP: 4
SALES (est): 465.2K **Privately Held**
SIC: 3993 Signs & advertising specialties

(G-4318)
BELLEMEAD HOT GLASS
884 Route 206 (08844-1509)
PHONE..............................908 281-5516
Robert Kuster, *Mng Member*
EMP: 6
SALES (est): 408.1K **Privately Held**
SIC: 3646 Chandeliers, commercial

(G-4319)
BELLEVUE PARFUMS USA LLC
2 Jill Ct Bldg 21 (08844-1935)
PHONE..............................908 262-7774
Narinder Manghani, *CEO*
EMP: 10 **EST:** 2016
SQ FT: 13,500
SALES (est): 906.7K **Privately Held**
SIC: 2844 Perfumes & colognes

(G-4320)
BEZWADA BIOMEDICAL LLC
15 Ilene Ct Ste 1 (08844-1920)
P.O. Box 6357 (08844-6357)
PHONE..............................908 281-7529
Fax: 908 534-5789
RAO S Bezwada, *President*
Sujata Moton, *CFO*
Neeti Srivastava, *Manager*
EMP: 4
SQ FT: 6,000
SALES (est): 559.3K **Privately Held**
WEB: www.bezwadabiomedical.com
SIC: 2822 8731 Ethylene-propylene rubbers, EPDM polymers; biotechnical research, commercial

(G-4321)
BNS ENTERPRISES INC
186 Wildflower Ln (08844-4868)
PHONE..............................908 285-6556
Bruce E Hemstock, *President*
EMP: 4
SALES: 100K **Privately Held**
SIC: 5063 3663 Batteries; radio & TV communications equipment

(G-4322)
BRENT RIVER CORP (HQ)
Also Called: Tri-Delta Plastics
208 Cougar Ct (08844-4105)
PHONE..............................908 722-6021
Thomas J Dolan, *President*
Paul Rolando, *Opers Staff*
Brian J Dolan, *VP Sls/Mktg*
▲ **EMP:** 40
SQ FT: 88,000
SALES (est): 18.1MM
SALES (corp-wide): 746.6MM **Privately Held**
SIC: 3089 Injection molding of plastics
PA: Pretium Packaging, L.L.C.
　15450 S Outer Forty Dr St
　Chesterfield MO 63017
　314 727-8200

(G-4323)
BRENT RIVER CORP
Tri Delta Technology
208 Cougar Ct (08844-4105)
PHONE..............................908 722-6021
Thomas J Dolan, *Branch Mgr*
EMP: 8
SALES (corp-wide): 746.6MM **Privately Held**
SIC: 3085 Plastics bottles
HQ: Brent River Corp.
　208 Cougar Ct
　Hillsborough NJ 08844
　908 722-6021

(G-4324)
C AND C TOOL CO LLC
198 Us Highway 206 Ste 1 (08844-4138)
PHONE..............................908 431-0330
Steven A Calello,
EMP: 4
SQ FT: 1,600
SALES (est): 300K **Privately Held**
SIC: 3544 Industrial molds

(G-4325)
CLANTECH INC
198 Us Highway 206 Ste 10 (08844-4138)
PHONE..............................908 281-7667
Fax: 908 281-7671
John Gracie, *President*
David Gracie, *Admin Sec*
▲ **EMP:** 4 **EST:** 1975
SQ FT: 3,500
SALES: 1MM **Privately Held**
WEB: www.clantech.com
SIC: 3679 Power supplies, all types: static; commutators, electronic

(G-4326)
COUNTER EFX INC
301 Roycefield Rd Bldg 5 (08844-4097)
PHONE..............................908 203-0155
EMP: 9
SALES: 975K **Privately Held**
SIC: 2541 Contractor Specializing In Counter-Top

(G-4327)
DISTRIBUTOR LABEL PRODUCTS
Also Called: Certified Labeling Solutions
51 Old Camplain Rd (08844-4227)
PHONE..............................908 704-9997
Fax: 908 704-8188
Joseph Braun, *President*
Petra Braun, *Treasurer*
EMP: 25
SQ FT: 10,000
SALES (est): 5MM **Privately Held**
SIC: 2759 Labels & seals: printing

(G-4328)
EAST COAST ELECTRONICS INC
216 Us Highway 206 20a (08844-4384)
PHONE..............................908 431-7555
Fax: 908 431-7556
Sidney A Lentz, *President*
EMP: 3
SQ FT: 2,500
SALES: 1.5MM **Privately Held**
WEB: www.eastcoastelectronics.com
SIC: 5065 3643 Electronic parts; power line cable

(G-4329)
EAST COAST MEDIA LLC
14 Park Ave (08844-4125)
PHONE..............................908 575-9700
Theresa Distasio, *President*
Andy Fresco III, *Mng Member*
Mark B Arnold,
▲ **EMP:** 22 **EST:** 1999
SQ FT: 20,000
SALES (est): 4.4MM **Privately Held**
WEB: www.companyflair.com
SIC: 2752 Commercial printing, lithographic

(G-4330)
EDSALL GROUP USA INC
115 Stryker Ln (08844-1910)
PHONE..............................908 874-6953
Michael S Sultan, *President*
▼ **EMP:** 86
SQ FT: 5,800
SALES: 35MM **Privately Held**
SIC: 2035 5046 5149 2099 Seasonings & sauces, except tomato & dry; commercial equipment; seasonings, sauces & extracts; food preparations

(G-4331)
ESCO PRECISION INC
71 Old Camplain Rd (08844-4297)
PHONE..............................908 722-0800
Samy Elkholy, *President*
Ryan Elkholy, *Project Mgr*
Emir Elkholy, *Engineer*
▲ **EMP:** 20
SQ FT: 8,000
SALES: 2MM **Privately Held**
WEB: www.escoprecision.com
SIC: 3451 Screw machine products

(G-4332)
FISCHL MACHINE & TOOL
Also Called: F M T
5 Ilene Ct Ste 7 (08844-1915)
PHONE......................908 829-5621
Fax: 973 227-1867
EMP: 4
SQ FT: 2,500
SALES (est): 476.6K **Privately Held**
SIC: 3599 Mfg Industrial Machinery

(G-4333)
FREWITT USA INC
249 Homestead Rd (08844-1912)
PHONE......................908 829-5245
EMP: 20
SALES (est): 2.4MM **Privately Held**
SIC: 2041 Flour & other grain mill products

(G-4334)
G & J STEEL & TUBING INC
406 Roycefield Rd (08844-4099)
PHONE......................908 526-4445
Fax: 908 526-9487
John Tursky, President
Jitender Yadav, QC Mgr
Gary Borowicz, Controller
Peter Narcizykiewicz, Manager
▲ EMP: 67
SQ FT: 25,000
SALES (est): 15.5MM **Privately Held**
WEB: www.gjsteel.com
SIC: 3498 Tube fabricating (contract bending & shaping)

(G-4335)
GENERAL TOOL SPECIALTIES INC
284 Sunnymeade Rd (08844-4630)
PHONE......................908 874-3040
Fax: 908 874-5777
John K Domici Jr, President
EMP: 12
SQ FT: 7,000
SALES (est): 2.6MM **Privately Held**
SIC: 3544 Special dies, tools, jigs & fixtures

(G-4336)
GLEN-GERY CORPORATION
Also Called: Glen-Gery Brick
75 Hamilton Rd (08844-4671)
PHONE......................908 359-5111
Fax: 908 359-5576
Brendan Meagan, Sales/Mktg Mgr
EMP: 40
SALES (corp-wide): 571K **Privately Held**
WEB: www.glengerybrick.com
SIC: 5032 3251 Brick, except refractory; brick & structural clay tile
HQ: Glen-Gery Corporation
1166 Spring St
Reading PA 19610
610 374-4011

(G-4337)
GRAB EM SNACKS LTD LBLTY CO
216 Us Highway 206 (08844-4140)
PHONE......................908 333-3229
Geetha Jayaraman, Principal
EMP: 7
SALES (est): 818.5K **Privately Held**
SIC: 2052 2096 Cookies & crackers; potato chips & similar snacks

(G-4338)
HANKIN ACQUISITIONS INC
1 Harvard Way Ste 6 (08844-4294)
P.O. Box 5759 (08844-5759)
PHONE......................908 722-9595
David W Chou, President
Harshad Modi, Vice Pres
EMP: 13
SQ FT: 6,000
SALES (est): 1.6MM **Privately Held**
SIC: 3567 Incinerators, metal: domestic or commercial

(G-4339)
HANKIN ENVMTL SYSTEMS INC
1 Harvard Way Ste 6 (08844-4294)
P.O. Box 5759 (08844-5759)
PHONE......................908 722-9595
Fax: 908 722-9514

David W Chou, CEO
David C Chen, President
Harshad S Modi, Exec VP
Luis A Velazquez, Vice Pres
Richard Sun, Controller
EMP: 13
SQ FT: 6,000
SALES: 10MM
SALES (corp-wide): 290.2MM **Privately Held**
SIC: 3567 Incinerators, metal: domestic or commercial
PA: Cse Global Limited
202 Bedok South Avenue 1
Singapore 46933
651 203-33

(G-4340)
HERCULES ENTERPRISES LLC
321 Valley Rd (08844-4056)
PHONE......................908 369-0000
Fax: 908 369-0620
Carl Massaro,
▲ EMP: 100
SQ FT: 189,000
SALES (est): 26.6MM **Privately Held**
SIC: 3715 Truck trailers

(G-4341)
HILLSBOROUGH VACUUM LLC
54 Buckland Dr (08844-1127)
PHONE......................908 904-6600
Fax: 908 904-6600
Frank R Scrofani,
Patty G Scrofani,
EMP: 6
SQ FT: 2,000
SALES (est): 670K **Privately Held**
WEB: www.hillsboroughvacuum.com
SIC: 3635 5722 Household vacuum cleaners; vacuum cleaners

(G-4342)
HOT RUNNER TECHNOLOGY
216 Us Highway 206 (08844-4140)
PHONE......................908 431-5711
EMP: 9
SALES (est): 939.3K **Privately Held**
SIC: 3089 Injection molding of plastics

(G-4343)
ICOTE USA INC (PA)
465 Amwell Rd (08844-1207)
PHONE......................908 359-7575
Renata Jesionka, President
EMP: 4
SQ FT: 2,300
SALES: 89K **Privately Held**
SIC: 2952 Roofing materials

(G-4344)
IDEON LLC
249 Homestead Rd Ste 1 (08844-1912)
PHONE......................908 431-3126
Mikhail Laksin,
Brijesh Nigam,
Bhalendra Patel,
EMP: 4
SQ FT: 2,500
SALES (est): 1MM **Privately Held**
SIC: 2893 Printing ink

(G-4345)
INDUSTRIAL TUBE CORPORATION
297 Valley Rd (08844-4057)
P.O. Box 957, Somerville (08876-0957)
PHONE......................908 369-3737
Fax: 908 369-8805
Gustav Imhauser, President
Lydia Imhauser, Vice Pres
Kenneth Imhauser, Controller
Marion Imhauser, Admin Sec
▲ EMP: 40
SALES (est): 10.2MM **Privately Held**
WEB: www.industrialtubecorp.com
SIC: 3366 3351 3356 Brass foundry; tubing, copper & copper alloy; nickel; precious metals

(G-4346)
INNOVATIVE MANUFACTURING INC
198 Us Highway 206 Ste 4 (08844-4138)
PHONE......................908 904-1884
Fax: 908 904-6433

Kevin J Lovell, President
Heather Lovell, Vice Pres
EMP: 18 EST: 1996
SALES (est): 3.4MM **Privately Held**
SIC: 3541 Machine tools, metal cutting type

(G-4347)
INSTRIDE SHOES LLC
29 Polhemus Dr (08844-1808)
PHONE......................908 874-6670
Erica Werremeyer,
▲ EMP: 20
SQ FT: 8,000
SALES: 13.5MM **Privately Held**
SIC: 3841 Surgical & medical instruments

(G-4348)
INTEGRATED PHOTONICS INC (HQ)
132 Stryker Ln Ste 1 (08844-1937)
PHONE......................908 281-8000
Robert T David, CEO
Ron Glass, President
Steven J Licht, Vice Pres
Shanthi Subramanian, Vice Pres
▼ EMP: 80 EST: 1999
SQ FT: 22,000
SALES (est): 5.4MM
SALES (corp-wide): 972MM **Publicly Held**
WEB: www.integratedphotonics.com
SIC: 3827 Optical elements & assemblies, except ophthalmic
PA: Ii-Vi Incorporated
375 Saxonburg Blvd
Saxonburg PA 16056
724 352-4455

(G-4349)
INTEGRATED PHOTONICS INC
132 Stryker Ln Ste 1 (08844-1937)
PHONE......................908 281-8000
Robert Abbott, Branch Mgr
EMP: 4
SALES (corp-wide): 972MM **Publicly Held**
WEB: www.integratedphotonics.com
SIC: 3827 Optical elements & assemblies, except ophthalmic
HQ: Integrated Photonics, Inc.
132 Stryker Ln Ste 1
Hillsborough NJ 08844
908 281-8000

(G-4350)
INTERGANIC FZCO LLC
Also Called: MII Organics
125 Stryker Ln Ste 3 (08844-1938)
PHONE......................224 436-0372
Craig Sirota, CEO
▲ EMP: 4 EST: 2014
SQ FT: 3,000
SALES: 1MM **Privately Held**
SIC: 2676 Infant & baby paper products

(G-4351)
J K DESIGN INC
Also Called: J K Print Management
465 Amwell Rd (08844-1207)
PHONE......................908 428-4700
Jerry Kaulius, President
Sean Schools, Editor
John Geoghegan, Vice Pres
Andrea Wolkofsky, Vice Pres
Joanna Karausz, Project Mgr
EMP: 48
SQ FT: 900
SALES (est): 3.6MM **Privately Held**
SIC: 7336 2791 Graphic arts & related design; typesetting

(G-4352)
JOYCE LESLIE INC (PA)
401 Towne Centre Dr (08844-4698)
PHONE......................201 804-7800
Celia Clancy, CEO
Peter Left, CFO
Hermine Gewirtz, Treasurer
◆ EMP: 70 EST: 1947
SQ FT: 45,000
SALES (est): 315.6MM **Privately Held**
WEB: www.xion.com
SIC: 3087 Custom compound purchased resins

(G-4353)
K B ENTERPRISES OF NEW JERSEY
15 Ilene Ct Ste 1211 (08844-1920)
PHONE......................908 451-5282
Thomas Griffin, President
EMP: 4
SQ FT: 1,500
SALES: 900K **Privately Held**
SIC: 3911 Jewelry, precious metal

(G-4354)
KWG INDUSTRIES LLC
330 Roycefield Rd Unit B (08844-4148)
PHONE......................908 218-8900
Oguz Aydogan, Engineer
Kurt W Grimm,
EMP: 30
SQ FT: 25,000
SALES (est): 4.6MM **Privately Held**
SIC: 7389 5051 3354 3599 Metal cutting services; aluminum bars, rods, ingots, sheets, pipes, plates, etc.; steel; tubing, metal; aluminum extruded products; machine shop, jobbing & repair

(G-4355)
LIEDL
462 Long Hill Rd (08844-1012)
PHONE......................908 359-8335
EMP: 5
SALES (est): 469.8K **Privately Held**
SIC: 3272 Mfg Concrete Products

(G-4356)
MALLIKA ASHWIN MAYA CORP
Also Called: Mam
10 Old Camplain Rd (08844-4228)
PHONE......................908 393-2571
Kanaka Tatikola, President
Seshu Tatikola, Manager
▲ EMP: 3
SQ FT: 6,000
SALES: 2.6MM **Privately Held**
SIC: 3677 Electronic coils, transformers & other inductors

(G-4357)
NATURAL DENTAL STUDIOS INC
216 Us Highway 206 Ste 23 (08844-4384)
PHONE......................908 281-0089
Fax: 908 281-9562
Charles Palmieri, President
Lori Palmieri, Corp Secy
EMP: 6
SQ FT: 1,800
SALES (est): 730K **Privately Held**
SIC: 3843 Teeth, artificial (not made in dental laboratories)

(G-4358)
NEWTON BIOPHARMA SOLUTIONS LLC
8 Fine Rd (08844-5268)
PHONE......................908 874-7145
Niya D Bowers, Principal
EMP: 5
SALES (est): 394.9K **Privately Held**
SIC: 2834 Pharmaceutical preparations

(G-4359)
NJ PAVER RESTORATIONS LLC
857 Amwell Rd (08844-3902)
PHONE......................732 558-6011
Pamela Mazuch, Owner
EMP: 4
SALES (est): 548.6K **Privately Held**
SIC: 3531 Pavers

(G-4360)
NU-STENT TECHNOLOGIES INC
1 Ilene Ct (08844-1916)
PHONE......................732 729-6270
EMP: 4
SALES (est): 260K **Privately Held**
SIC: 3841 Mfg Surgical/Medical Instruments

(G-4361)
ONYX GRAPHICS LLC
115 Stryker Ln Ste 4 (08844-1910)
PHONE......................908 281-0038
Robert Ceceri, President
David Perry, Principal

EMP: 5
SALES (est): 412.2K **Privately Held**
SIC: 7336 3089 Commercial art & graphic design; corrugated panels, plastic

(G-4362)
PERMADUR INDUSTRIES INC
Also Called: SISSCO DIVISION
186 Route 206 (08844-4123)
P.O. Box 1032, Somerville (08876-1032)
PHONE..................................908 359-9767
Fax: 908 359-9773
William A Schneider, *President*
Bill Schneider Jr, *VP Opers*
▲ **EMP:** 73 **EST:** 1972
SQ FT: 32,000
SALES: 24.4MM **Privately Held**
WEB: www.permadur.com
SIC: 5084 5072 5085 7699 Materials handling machinery; hardware; industrial supplies; construction equipment repair; magnets, permanent: metallic; industrial trucks & tractors

(G-4363)
PREMIUM SERVICE PRINTING
Also Called: B & L Printing Co
46 Old Complain Rd (08844-4228)
PHONE..................................908 707-1311
Gerry Harris, *President*
EMP: 6
SQ FT: 6,000
SALES (est): 1MM **Privately Held**
SIC: 2752 Commercial printing, offset

(G-4364)
PROSCAPE TECHNOLOGIES INC
14 Dogwood Dr (08844-2516)
PHONE..................................215 441-0300
Fax: 215 441-0600
Timothy Healy, *President*
EMP: 49
SQ FT: 10,000
SALES (est): 5.7MM **Privately Held**
WEB: www.proscape.com
SIC: 7372 Business oriented computer software

(G-4365)
R & R PRINTING & COPY CENTER
46 Old Complain Rd (08844-4228)
PHONE..................................732 249-9450
Fax: 732 249-5662
Robert Sepe, *President*
Maria Sepe, *Vice Pres*
EMP: 4
SQ FT: 500
SALES (est): 475.1K **Privately Held**
WEB: www.randrprinting.com
SIC: 2759 Screen printing

(G-4366)
R C FINE FOODS INC
139 Stryker Ln (08844-1930)
P.O. Box 236, Belle Mead (08502-0236)
PHONE..................................908 359-5500
Susan Goldman, *President*
Gary Cohen, *Vice Pres*
Jim Boganski, *Opers Staff*
Cathy Shaw, *Purchasing*
Cari Young, *Research*
EMP: 70
SQ FT: 40,000
SALES (est): 13.3MM **Privately Held**
WEB: www.rcfinefoods.com
SIC: 2099 5149 2087 2045 Food preparations; groceries & related products; flavoring extracts & syrups; prepared flour mixes & doughs; pickles, sauces & salad dressings

(G-4367)
RB MANUFACTURING LLC
799 Us Highway 206 (08844-1530)
PHONE..................................908 533-2000
Fax: 908 533-2050
Saurabh Joshi, *Project Mgr*
Adarsh Mathur, *Project Mgr*
Ian Corkhill, *Engineer*
Lillian In, *Engineer*
Lou Borzone, *Project Engr*
EMP: 250

SALES (corp-wide): 15.2B **Privately Held**
WEB: www.reckittprofessional.com
SIC: 2035 2842 Mustard, prepared (wet); deodorants, nonpersonal; disinfectants, household or industrial plant; laundry cleaning preparations; specialty cleaning preparations
HQ: Rb Manufacturing Llc
    399 Interpace Pkwy
    Parsippany NJ 07054
    973 404-2600

(G-4368)
REDKOH INDUSTRIES INC (PA)
Also Called: Redkoh Datatest Industries
300 Valley Rd (08844-4059)
P.O. Box 801, Belle Mead (08502-0801)
PHONE..................................908 369-1590
Fax: 908 369-1594
Paul Ford, *President*
Phil Blockus, *Business Mgr*
John Jannone, *Exec VP*
Robert Prendeville, *Vice Pres*
April Coughlin, *Accounting Mgr*
EMP: 4
SQ FT: 10,000
SALES (est): 4.4MM **Privately Held**
WEB: www.redkoh.com
SIC: 3672 3625 7373 Printed circuit boards; industrial controls: push button, selector switches, pilot; computer systems analysis & design

(G-4369)
RICH DESIGNS
867 Amwell Rd (08844-3902)
PHONE..................................908 369-5035
April Dombey, *Principal*
EMP: 4
SALES (est): 354.2K **Privately Held**
SIC: 7532 5099 3993 Truck painting & lettering; signs, except electric; signs & advertising specialties

(G-4370)
S G A BUSINESS SYSTEMS INC
83 Haverford Ct (08844-5211)
PHONE..................................908 359-4626
Fax: 908 359-4861
Wayne Scarano, *President*
Nancy Spadavecchia, *Business Anlyst*
EMP: 5
SALES (est): 350K **Privately Held**
WEB: www.isga.com
SIC: 7374 3571 Data processing service; personal computers (microcomputers)

(G-4371)
SEBASTIAN & KING LTD LBLTY CO
816 Robin Rd (08844-4408)
PHONE..................................908 874-6953
Michael Sultan, *President*
Joanna Witas, *Vice Pres*
▲ **EMP:** 16
SALES (est): 39.5MM **Privately Held**
SIC: 2099 Sauces: gravy, dressing & dip mixes

(G-4372)
SPECIALTY TUBE FILLING LLC
1 Ilene Ct Bldg 8u6 (08844-1916)
PHONE..................................908 262-2219
Kevin Hagerman, *Mng Member*
EMP: 6
SALES (est): 617.1K **Privately Held**
SIC: 3565 Bottling machinery: filling, capping, labeling

(G-4373)
STERIS INSTRUMENT MGT SVCS INC
10 Ilene Ct (08844-1922)
PHONE..................................908 904-1317
Christian Mills, *President*
EMP: 5
SALES (corp-wide): 2.6B **Privately Held**
SIC: 3841 Surgical & medical instruments
HQ: Steris Instrument Management Services, Inc.
    3316 2nd Ave N
    Birmingham AL 35222

(G-4374)
SULTAN FOODS INC
115 Stryker Ln Ste 13 (08844-1910)
P.O. Box 6293 (08844-6293)
PHONE..................................908 874-6953
Michael S Sultan, *President*
John Cummings, *Vice Pres*
EMP: 16
SQ FT: 5,800
SALES: 30MM **Privately Held**
SIC: 2099 Seasonings & spices

(G-4375)
SWISS ORTHOPEDIC INC
188 Us Highway 206 (08844-4123)
PHONE..................................908 874-5522
Fax: 908 874-8821
Peter Seitz, *President*
EMP: 8
SQ FT: 2,500
SALES (est): 978.6K **Privately Held**
SIC: 3842 5999 Prosthetic appliances; orthopedic & prosthesis applications

(G-4376)
THINFILMS INC
15 Ilene Ct Ste 6 (08844-1920)
PHONE..................................908 359-7014
Fax: 908 359-7015
Arshad Mumtaz, *President*
Zareen Arshad, *Vice Pres*
Marc Diamond, *Engineer*
EMP: 14
SQ FT: 10,000
SALES (est): 2MM **Privately Held**
WEB: www.thinfilmsinc.com
SIC: 3674 Semiconductors & related devices; thin film circuits

(G-4377)
TIFA INTERNATIONAL LLC
Also Called: Tifa Worldwide
109 Stryker Ln Ste 4 (08844-1911)
PHONE..................................908 647-4570
Fax: 908 647-7338
Gamal Osman, *Mng Member*
EMP: 11
SQ FT: 20,000
SALES (est): 1.2MM **Privately Held**
WEB: www.tifausa.com
SIC: 3523 Sprayers & spraying machines, agricultural

(G-4378)
UAC PACKAGING LLC
330 Roycefield Rd Unit C (08844-4148)
PHONE..................................908 595-6890
Charles Bernius, *Mng Member*
EMP: 5
SALES (est): 430K **Privately Held**
SIC: 3499 Machine bases, metal

(G-4379)
ZALA MACHINE CO INC
Also Called: Zala Machine Shop
109 Stryker Ln Ste 11 (08844-1911)
PHONE..................................908 431-9106
Fax: 908 431-9430
Stanislaw Zala, *President*
Elzeieta Zala, *Vice Pres*
EMP: 15
SQ FT: 16,000
SALES (est): 3.5MM **Privately Held**
SIC: 3599 Machine shop, jobbing & repair

Hillsdale
Bergen County

(G-4380)
BUILDING PERFORMANCE EQP INC
80 Broadway Ste 101 (07642-2745)
PHONE..................................201 722-1414
Klas Haglid, *CEO*
EMP: 10
SQ FT: 1,000
SALES (est): 1MM **Privately Held**
WEB: www.bpequip.com
SIC: 3564 3822 Ventilating fans: industrial or commercial; energy cutoff controls; residential or commercial types

(G-4381)
CAROL S MILLER CORPORATION
98 Saddlewood Dr (07642-1364)
PHONE..................................201 406-4578
Carol Schepker, *President*
▲ **EMP:** 4
SQ FT: 2,000
SALES (est): 190K **Privately Held**
SIC: 3171 Women's handbags & purses

(G-4382)
FORNAZOR INTERNATIONAL INC (PA)
455 Hillsdale Ave (07642-2710)
PHONE..................................201 664-4000
John Fornazor, *CEO*
Kevin Sinnott, *President*
◆ **EMP:** 25
SQ FT: 4,500
SALES (est): 21.1MM **Privately Held**
SIC: 0119 2034 2044 2045 Feeder grains; vegetable flour, meal & powder; rice milling; flours & flour mixes, from purchased flour; soybean oil, cake or meal; intracoastal (freight) transportation

(G-4383)
GENERAL GRAPHICS CORPORATION (PA)
63 Briarcliff Rd (07642-1358)
PHONE..................................201 664-4083
Evelyn F Meyer, *President*
EMP: 4
SALES (est): 833.3K **Privately Held**
SIC: 3841 Blood pressure apparatus

(G-4384)
I C SYSTEM SOLUTIONS INC
270 Broadway (07642-1415)
PHONE..................................201 666-1122
Nancy Nolan, *President*
EMP: 12
SQ FT: 3,800
SALES (est): 1.6MM **Privately Held**
WEB: www.icssolutions.com
SIC: 3577 Computer peripheral equipment

(G-4385)
KEN BAUER INC
Also Called: Ken Bauer & Sons
277 Broadway Ste A (07642-1436)
PHONE..................................201 664-6881
Fax: 201 664-0538
Ken Bauer, *President*
Sandy Martucci, *Treasurer*
Scott Bauer, *Admin Sec*
EMP: 21
SQ FT: 12,000
SALES (est): 2MM **Privately Held**
WEB: www.kenbauer.com
SIC: 1521 1799 2434 2541 General remodeling, single-family houses; new construction, single-family houses; kitchen & bathroom remodeling; wood kitchen cabinets; wood partitions & fixtures

(G-4386)
OROSZLANY LASZLO
Also Called: Apollo Machine Shop
121 Patterson St (07642-2010)
PHONE..................................201 666-2101
EMP: 5
SQ FT: 5,000
SALES (est): 247.2K **Privately Held**
SIC: 5049 3541 3452 3451 Whol Professional Equip Mfg Machine Tool-Cutting Mfg Bolts/Screws/Rivets Mfg Screw Machine Prdts

(G-4387)
TEXX TEAM LLC
589 Hillsdale Ave (07642-2650)
P.O. Box 65, Carlstadt (07072-0065)
PHONE..................................201 289-1039
Teodor Stanchev, *COO*
▼ **EMP:** 23 **EST:** 2016
SQ FT: 3,000
SALES: 1MM
SALES (corp-wide): 2.4MM **Privately Held**
SIC: 2299 Textile mill waste & remnant processing

PA: Green Team Worldwide Recycling
Group Limited Liability Company
589 Hillsdale Ave
Hillsdale NJ 07642
201 289-1039

Hillside
Union County

(G-4388)
AMERICAN STONE INC
215 Us Highway 22 (07205-1832)
PHONE.................................973 318-7707
Steven Young, *Manager*
EMP: 26 Privately Held
SIC: 3281 Marble, building: cut & shaped
PA: American Stone Inc.
215 Us Highway 22
Hillside NJ 07205

(G-4389)
AMERICAN STONE INC (PA)
215 Us Highway 22 (07205-1832)
PHONE.................................973 318-7707
Fax: 973 318-7667
Steven Young, *President*
EMP: 14
SALES (est): 3.9MM **Privately Held**
SIC: 3281 Marble, building: cut & shaped;
granite, cut & shaped

(G-4390)
ARCH CROWN INC
460 Hillside Ave Ste 1 (07205-1100)
PHONE.................................973 731-6300
Fax: 973 731-2228
Craig Meadow, *President*
Norman Liebman, *Chairman*
Miriam Corcino, *Marketing Staff*
Rose Liebman, *Shareholder*
Kristina Herberg, *Receptionist*
◆ **EMP:** 36 **EST:** 1907
SALES (est): 6.6MM **Privately Held**
WEB: www.archcrown.com
SIC: 3081 2679 2791 2671 Unsupported
plastics film & sheet; tags, paper (un-
printed): made from purchased paper; la-
bels, paper: made from purchased
material; typesetting; packaging paper &
plastics film, coated & laminated

(G-4391)
ARROW ENGINEERING CO INC
260 Pennsylvania Ave (07205-2636)
PHONE.................................908 353-5229
Fax: 908 353-8362
Louis Spitzer, *President*
Ray Fluet, *Vice Pres*
Jenny Fluet, *Admin Sec*
EMP: 4 **EST:** 1920
SQ FT: 9,000
SALES (est): 430K **Privately Held**
WEB: www.arroweng.com
SIC: 3821 3826 Shakers & stirrers; analyt-
ical instruments

(G-4392)
ATLAS MODEL RAILROAD CO INC
378 Florence Ave (07205-1134)
PHONE.................................908 687-0880
Fax: 908 851-2550
Thomas A Haedrich, *CEO*
Diane S Haedrich, *Ch of Bd*
Jarrett Haedrich, *Vice Pres*
Joe Kolnoski, *VP Opers*
Robert Allard, *Engineer*
▲ **EMP:** 80 **EST:** 1925
SQ FT: 100,000
SALES (est): 14.2MM **Privately Held**
WEB: www.atlasrr.com
SIC: 3944 Trains & equipment, toy: electric
& mechanical

(G-4393)
ATLAS O LLC
378 Florence Ave (07205-1134)
PHONE.................................908 687-9590
Tom Haedrich, *Mng Member*
EMP: 50

SALES (est): 1.8MM **Privately Held**
WEB: www.atlaso.com
SIC: 7389 5945 3944 Convention & show
services; hobby, toy & game shops;
games, toys & children's vehicles

(G-4394)
AWARDS TROPHY COMPANY
611 Us Highway 22 (07205-1916)
PHONE.................................908 687-5775
Fax: 908 687-3451
Mary Anne Kilgarriss, *President*
Steve Zall, *General Mgr*
▲ **EMP:** 7 **EST:** 1959
SALES (est): 700K **Privately Held**
SIC: 3499 3479 Trophies, metal, except
silver; engraving jewelry silverware, or
metal

(G-4395)
BANNER DESIGN INC
600 N Union Ave Ste 11 (07205-1031)
PHONE.................................908 687-5335
Peter Schapira, *President*
EMP: 35
SQ FT: 35,000
SALES (est): 3.2MM **Privately Held**
WEB: www.bannerdesignco.com
SIC: 1799 3993 2541 7336 Sign installa-
tion & maintenance; signs & advertising
specialties; display fixtures, wood; graphic
arts & related design

(G-4396)
BEAU LABEL
385 Hillside Ave (07205-1123)
PHONE.................................973 318-7800
Vincent Mela, *Owner*
Tom Savona, *Plant Mgr*
Vincent Melapioni, *Executive*
EMP: 60 **EST:** 2008
SALES (est): 5.9MM **Privately Held**
SIC: 2241 Labels, woven

(G-4397)
BEAUTY-FILL LLC
1319 N Broad St (07205-2460)
PHONE.................................908 353-1600
Gregory Harmon,
Robert Harmon,
Kurt Lueken,
▲ **EMP:** 30
SQ FT: 120,000
SALES (est): 5.3MM **Privately Held**
SIC: 3565 5999 5149 Bottling machinery:
filling, capping, labeling; toiletries, cos-
metics & perfumes; flavourings & fra-
grances

(G-4398)
BEST AMERICAN HANDS
475 Bloy St (07205-1707)
PHONE.................................203 247-2028
Nitzy Cohen, *Mng Member*
EMP: 27
SALES (est): 853K **Privately Held**
SIC: 2599 Furniture & fixtures

(G-4399)
BRISTOL-MYERS SQUIBB COMPANY
171 Long Ave (07205-2350)
PHONE.................................212 546-4000
Shuyan Du, *Branch Mgr*
EMP: 40
SALES (corp-wide): 20.7B **Publicly Held**
WEB: www.bms.com
SIC: 2834 8731 2844 Pharmaceutical
preparations; drugs acting on the cardiovascular system, except diagnostic; antibiotics, packaged; drugs acting on the
central nervous system & sense organs;
commercial physical research; toilet
preparations
PA: Bristol-Myers Squibb Company
430 E 29th St Fl 14
New York NY 10016
212 546-4000

(G-4400)
CAMEO NOVELTY & PEN CORP
400 Hillside Ave (07205-1117)
PHONE.................................973 923-1600
Sol Oberlander, *President*
▲ **EMP:** 20
SQ FT: 12,000

SALES (est): 2.5MM **Privately Held**
SIC: 3951 Pens & mechanical pencils

(G-4401)
CARTOLITH GROUP
28 Sager Pl (07205-1014)
PHONE.................................908 624-9833
Fax: 908 624-9834
Roy Sayroo, *Manager*
▼ **EMP:** 5
SALES (est): 484.4K **Privately Held**
SIC: 2679 Paper products, converted

(G-4402)
CERTIFIED PROCESSING CORP
184 Us Highway 22 (07205-1895)
PHONE.................................973 923-5200
Paul P Iacono, *President*
Kenneth P Iacono, *Treasurer*
EMP: 3 **EST:** 1960
SQ FT: 36,000
SALES (est): 1MM **Privately Held**
SIC: 2833 Caffeine & derivatives

(G-4403)
COOPER ALLOY CORPORATION
201 Sweetland Ave Ste 1 (07205-1756)
PHONE.................................908 688-4120
Fax: 908 686-9314
Gerald Lewis, *President*
Stuart F Cooper, *Vice Pres*
John Brodeur, *Admin Sec*
EMP: 11 **EST:** 1931
SQ FT: 40,000
SALES (est): 3MM **Privately Held**
SIC: 3561 5084 Pumps & pumping equip-
ment; industrial pumps & parts; pumps &
pumping equipment

(G-4404)
DESIGN FACTORY NJ INC
1210 Liberty Ave (07205-2023)
PHONE.................................908 964-8833
Fax: 908 964-8840
Johnathon Simons, *Owner*
EMP: 4
SQ FT: 2,000
SALES (est): 529.6K **Privately Held**
SIC: 2752 7336 Commercial printing, off-
set; graphic arts & related design

(G-4405)
DIVERSIFIED DISPLAY PDTS LLC
Also Called: D D P
777 Ramsey Ave (07205-1011)
P.O. Box 913 (07205-0913)
PHONE.................................908 686-2200
David Rosen,
EMP: 25
SQ FT: 5,600
SALES (est): 13.8MM **Privately Held**
WEB: www.ddpmsc.com
SIC: 5199 3577 Foams & rubber; printers
& plotters

(G-4406)
DORAN SLING AND ASSEMBLY CORP
1285 Central Ave Ste 2 (07205-2645)
PHONE.................................908 355-1101
Barry Lemberg, *President*
Michael Cuccinello, *Vice Pres*
Charlie Voigt, *Marketing Mgr*
EMP: 9
SQ FT: 60,000
SALES (est): 4.6MM **Privately Held**
SIC: 5051 3496 Rope, wire (not insu-
lated); cable, wire; slings, lifting: made
from purchased wire

(G-4407)
FLUETS CORP
260 Pennsylvania Ave (07205-2696)
PHONE.................................908 353-5229
Ray Fluet, *President*
Raymond Fluet, *President*
Angie Fluet, *Vice Pres*
EMP: 30 **EST:** 1965
SQ FT: 9,000
SALES (est): 5.2MM **Privately Held**
WEB: www.fluetscorp.com
SIC: 3599 Machine shop, jobbing & repair

(G-4408)
G & H SHEET METAL WORKS INC
1423 Chestnut Ave (07205-1179)
PHONE.................................973 923-1100
Carl W Heide, *CEO*
Nancy Heide, *Principal*
Don Shaffer, *Principal*
EMP: 11 **EST:** 1938
SQ FT: 15,000
SALES: 1.2MM **Privately Held**
WEB: www.ghsmw.com
SIC: 3821 2599 Laboratory apparatus &
furniture; factory furniture & fixtures

(G-4409)
GOLDEN METAL PRODUCTS CORP
100 Hoffman Pl Ste 1 (07205-1000)
PHONE.................................973 399-1157
Thomas Abella, *President*
EMP: 41 **EST:** 1949
SQ FT: 16,000
SALES (est): 5.4MM **Privately Held**
WEB: www.goldenmetal.com
SIC: 3444 3469 Sheet metalwork; metal
stampings

(G-4410)
H & H SWISS SCREW MACHINE PR
Also Called: H&H Swiss
1478 Chestnut Ave (07205-1174)
PHONE.................................908 688-6390
Darryl Stacy, *President*
Diane Lucas, *Corp Secy*
John Auburger, *Opers Mgr*
Michael Jaffe, *QC Mgr*
Brett Hardman, *Sales Dir*
EMP: 48 **EST:** 1943
SQ FT: 28,500
SALES (est): 11.5MM **Privately Held**
WEB: www.hhswiss.com
SIC: 3451 Screw machine products

(G-4411)
HERSHEY INDUSTRIES INC
1209 Central Ave (07205-2613)
PHONE.................................908 353-3344
Henry Herbst, *President*
Miriam Herbst, *Corp Secy*
David Rubin, *Vice Pres*
EMP: 12 **EST:** 1975
SQ FT: 115,000
SALES (est): 1.1MM **Privately Held**
SIC: 2673 Plastic bags: made from pur-
chased materials

(G-4412)
HILLSIDE BOTTLING CORP
1 Evans Terminal (07205-2406)
PHONE.................................908 353-6773
Carlos Prior, *President*
EMP: 8
SALES (est): 1MM **Privately Held**
SIC: 2086 Soft drinks: packaged in cans,
bottles, etc.

(G-4413)
HILLSIDE CANDY LLC (PA)
35 Hillside Ave (07205-1833)
PHONE.................................973 926-2300
Ted Cohen, *President*
Henry Adamkowski, *Plant Mgr*
Socorro Nuguid, *QC Mgr*
Ray Laconte, *CFO*
Ray La Conte, *Human Res Dir*
▼ **EMP:** 10
SQ FT: 15,000
SALES (est): 6MM **Privately Held**
WEB: www.hillsidecandy.com
SIC: 2064 Candy & other confectionery
products

(G-4414)
HILLSIDE PLASTICS CORPORATION
125 Long Ave (07205-2350)
P.O. Box 609 (07205-0609)
PHONE.................................973 923-2700
Fax: 973 923-2056
Harold Kaufman, *President*
Jim Kern, *Vice Pres*
Debbie Haas, *Hum Res Coord*
Karen Triebenbacher, *Sales Staff*

(PA)=Parent Co (HQ)=Headquarters (DH)=Div Headquarters
✿ = New Business established in last 2 years

2018 Harris New Jersey
Manufacturers Directory

181

GEOGRAPHIC

EMP: 60
SQ FT: 65,500
SALES (est): 22.5MM **Privately Held**
WEB: www.hillsideplasticscorp.com
SIC: 3081 Plastic film & sheet

(G-4415)
**INB MANHATTAN DRUG
COMPANY INC (HQ)**
225 Long Ave Ste 15 (07205-2356)
P.O. Box 278 (07205-0278)
PHONE...............................973 926-0816
E Gerald Kay, *Chairman*
Christina Kay, *Vice Pres*
Riva Sheppard, *Vice Pres*
Dina Masi, *CFO*
Eleanor D Martino, *Admin Sec*
▼ **EMP:** 59
SQ FT: 40,000
SALES (est): 19.6MM
SALES (corp-wide): 46.9MM **Publicly
Held**
WEB: www.chemintl.com
SIC: 2834 Vitamin preparations
PA: Integrated Biopharma, Inc.
225 Long Ave Ste 13
Hillside NJ 07205
888 319-6962

(G-4416)
**INB MANHATTAN DRUG
COMPANY INC**
210 Route 22 (07205)
PHONE...............................973 926-0816
Fax: 973 926-1735
E Gerald Kay, *Chairman*
EMP: 60
SALES (corp-wide): 46.9MM **Publicly
Held**
SIC: 2834 Pharmaceutical preparations
HQ: Inb Manhattan Drug Company, Inc.
225 Long Ave Ste 15
Hillside NJ 07205
973 926-0816

(G-4417)
**INB MANHATTAN DRUG
COMPANY INC**
225 Long Ave Ste 6 (07205-2356)
PHONE...............................973 926-0816
Gerald Kay, *Branch Mgr*
EMP: 21
SALES (corp-wide): 46.9MM **Publicly
Held**
SIC: 2834 Vitamin preparations
HQ: Inb Manhattan Drug Company, Inc.
225 Long Ave Ste 15
Hillside NJ 07205
973 926-0816

(G-4418)
**INTEGRATED BIOPHARMA INC
(PA)**
225 Long Ave Ste 13 (07205-2368)
PHONE...............................888 319-6962
E Gerald Kay, *Ch of Bd*
Christina Kay, *Exec VP*
Riva Sheppard, *Exec VP*
Dina L Masi, *CFO*
EMP: 32
SQ FT: 76,161
SALES (est): 46.9MM **Publicly Held**
WEB: www.ibiopharma.com
SIC: 2834 Vitamin, nutrient & hematinic
preparations for human use

(G-4419)
**INTERNATIONAL TOOL & MCH
LLC**
Also Called: ITM
446 Hillside Ave (07205-1118)
PHONE...............................908 687-5580
Fax: 908 687-5368
Chris Hoeker, *President*
▲ **EMP:** 5 **EST:** 1967
SQ FT: 12,000
SALES (est): 370K **Privately Held**
SIC: 3451 Screw machine products

(G-4420)
J R ENGINEERING & MACHINE
663 Ramsey Ave (07205-1009)
PHONE...............................908 810-6300
Joseph E Kloss, *President*
Andrew Wakeman, *Vice Pres*

F Joseph Kilroy, *Director*
EMP: 10
SQ FT: 15,000
SALES: 1.6MM **Privately Held**
SIC: 3599 Machine shop, jobbing & repair

(G-4421)
JOMEL INDUSTRIES INC
140 Central Ave Ste 1 (07205-2377)
PHONE...............................973 282-0300
Phillip Iuliano, *President*
Jeff Spitz, *Vice Pres*
◆ **EMP:** 10
SQ FT: 20,000
SALES (est): 1.3MM **Privately Held**
WEB: www.jomel.net
SIC: 2515 5712 2296 Mattresses & bed-
springs; mattresses; tire cord & fabrics

(G-4422)
**JOMEL SEAMS REASONABLE
LLC (PA)**
Also Called: J S R
140 Cent Ave (07205)
PHONE...............................973 282-0300
Phil Iuliano, *President*
Jeffrey Spitz, *Vice Pres*
EMP: 7
SQ FT: 30,000
SALES (est): 5MM **Privately Held**
SIC: 2515 5712 2296 Mattresses & bed-
springs; mattresses; tire cord & fabrics

(G-4423)
**K & A ARCHITECTURAL MET GL
LLC**
766b Ramsey Ave (07205-1039)
P.O. Box 544, Oceanport (07757-0544)
PHONE...............................908 687-0247
Allen Jackson,
Kimberly Demott,
EMP: 15
SQ FT: 3,000
SALES (est): 4.2MM **Privately Held**
SIC: 3446 Architectural metalwork

(G-4424)
LALLY-PAK INC
1209 Central Ave (07205-2613)
PHONE...............................908 351-4141
Fax: 908 351-4411
Henry Herbst, *President*
▲ **EMP:** 75
SQ FT: 120,000
SALES (est): 20.9MM **Privately Held**
WEB: www.lallypak.com
SIC: 3081 2759 2671 Packing materials,
plastic sheet; bags, plastic: printing; plas-
tic film, coated or laminated for packaging

(G-4425)
LEOPARD INC
1 Montgomery St (07205-1106)
PHONE...............................908 964-3600
Fax: 908 964-6066
Wendy Chen, *President*
Mark Merezio, *Vice Pres*
◆ **EMP:** 11 **EST:** 2000
SQ FT: 11,000
SALES (est): 2.3MM **Privately Held**
SIC: 3011 Truck or bus tires, pneumatic

(G-4426)
LOVE PALLET LLC
460 Mundet Pl (07205-1115)
P.O. Box 774 (07205-0774)
PHONE...............................908 964-3385
Fax: 908 688-1525
Brenda Bardoza, *Managing Prtnr*
Susanne Lanzafama, *Managing Prtnr*
EMP: 7 **EST:** 1977
SQ FT: 700
SALES (est): 1.1MM **Privately Held**
WEB: www.lovepallet.com
SIC: 2448 Pallets, wood

(G-4427)
M DEITZ & SONS INC
Also Called: Deitz, Michael & Sons
490 Hillside Ave (07205-1119)
PHONE...............................908 686-8800
Fax: 908 686-6602
Ken Deitz, *President*
Steve Deitz, *Vice Pres*
▲ **EMP:** 15
SQ FT: 45,000

SALES (est): 2.3MM **Privately Held**
WEB: www.mdeitz.com
SIC: 2599 Bar, restaurant & cafeteria furni-
ture

(G-4428)
M S C PAPER PRODUCTS CORP
777 Ramsey Ave (07205-1011)
P.O. Box 913 (07205-0913)
PHONE...............................908 686-2200
Edward Brody, *Vice Pres*
EMP: 20 **EST:** 1938
SQ FT: 34,000
SALES (est): 2MM **Privately Held**
SIC: 2679 2631 Gift wrap & novelties,
paper; paperboard mills

(G-4429)
**MARK RONALD ASSOCIATES
INC (PA)**
Also Called: R M A
1227 Central Ave (07205-2613)
P.O. Box 776 (07205-0776)
PHONE...............................908 558-0011
Fax: 908 558-9366
Leslie J Satz, *President*
Jeffrey Riotto, *General Mgr*
Nate Sofer, *General Mgr*
Charles Riotto, *Vice Pres*
Ronald M Satz, *Vice Pres*
▲ **EMP:** 70
SQ FT: 40,000
SALES (est): 50MM **Privately Held**
WEB: www.ronaldmark.com
SIC: 3081 5162 Polyvinyl film & sheet;
plastics materials

(G-4430)
MCINTOSH INDUSTRIES INC
Also Called: Electro Mechanical Tech
676 Ramsey Ave (07205-1023)
PHONE...............................908 688-7475
Peter McIntosh, *President*
▲ **EMP:** 21
SALES (est): 2.1MM **Privately Held**
WEB: www.mcintoshindustries.com
SIC: 7694 Electric motor repair

(G-4431)
NATURES RULE LLC
1319 N Broad St (07205-2460)
PHONE...............................888 819-4220
Mohamad Hammod, *Mng Member*
EMP: 10
SALES (est): 1.3MM **Privately Held**
SIC: 2834 Vitamin, nutrient & hematinic
preparations for human use; vitamin
preparations

(G-4432)
**NEW YORK BLACKBOARD OF
NJ INC**
83 Us Highway 22 (07205-1884)
PHONE...............................973 926-1600
Fax: 973 926-3440
Henry Ruggiero, *President*
Regina Ruggiero, *Admin Sec*
EMP: 6 **EST:** 1958
SQ FT: 12,000
SALES (est): 1MM **Privately Held**
WEB: www.nyblackboard.com
SIC: 2493 Bulletin boards, cork; bulletin
boards, wood

(G-4433)
OASIS TRADING CO INC
Also Called: Oasis Foods Co
635 Ramsey Ave (07205-1032)
PHONE...............................908 964-0477
Fax: 908 688-4375
Anthony Alves, *President*
Ron Cronk, *Project Mgr*
Liliana Ferreira, *Buyer*
Vicky Veloso, *Buyer*
Steve Brandenburg, *Sales Staff*
◆ **EMP:** 150
SQ FT: 200,000
SALES (est): 54.4MM
SALES (corp-wide): 3.1B **Privately Held**
WEB: www.oasisfoodsco.com
SIC: 2079 2035 4783 2084 Cooking oils,
except corn: vegetable refined; dressings,
salad: raw & cooked (except dry mixes);
mayonnaise; packing goods for shipping;
wines, brandy & brandy spirits; wines

HQ: Aak Sweden Ab
Vastra Kajen
Karlshamn 374 3
454 820-00

(G-4434)
PTY LIGHTING LLC (PA)
Also Called: Pwg Lighting
100 Hoffman Pl (07205-1033)
PHONE...............................855 303-4500
Joe Espinosa, *President*
▲ **EMP:** 8
SALES (est): 2.1MM **Privately Held**
SIC: 1731 3645 Lighting contractor; chan-
deliers, residential

(G-4435)
QUALITY FILMS CORP
500 Hillside Ave (07205-1119)
PHONE...............................718 246-7150
Soloman Phillips, *President*
Moses Friedman, *Vice Pres*
▲ **EMP:** 5
SALES (est): 895.1K **Privately Held**
WEB: www.qualityshrinkfilm.com
SIC: 3861 Cameras & related equipment

(G-4436)
RAMCO EQUIPMENT CORP
Also Called: Randall Manufacturing Co
32 Montgomery St (07205-1107)
PHONE...............................908 687-6700
Fax: 908 687-0653
Fred Randall, *President*
Jenny Ranall, *Vice Pres*
Oretta Tigges, *Materials Mgr*
Genny Randall, *Human Resources*
▲ **EMP:** 22
SQ FT: 10,000
SALES: 671.7K **Privately Held**
SIC: 3559 Metal finishing equipment for
plating, etc.

(G-4437)
**RANDALL MANUFACTURING CO
INC**
Also Called: Ramco
32 Montgomery St (07205-1192)
PHONE...............................973 746-2111
EMP: 20 **EST:** 1920
SQ FT: 20,000
SALES (est): 6MM **Privately Held**
SIC: 5072 3589 Whol Hardware Mfg Serv-
ice Industry Machinery

(G-4438)
**RELIABLE PALLET SERVICES
LLC**
460 Hillside Ave Ste 1 (07205-1100)
PHONE...............................973 900-2260
EMP: 5
SALES (est): 254.5K **Privately Held**
SIC: 2448 Pallets, wood & wood with metal

(G-4439)
SAM HAK FOOD CORP
10 Montgomery St Ste 20 (07205-1107)
PHONE...............................908 688-4993
Elizabeth Kwon, *President*
▲ **EMP:** 20
SALES (est): 3.4MM **Privately Held**
SIC: 2099 Rice, uncooked: packaged with
other ingredients

(G-4440)
SINGE CORPORATION
Also Called: Addressing Machine & Sup Div
1290 Central Ave (07205-2615)
PHONE...............................908 289-7900
Fax: 908 289-7911
Herbert J Singe, *President*
Margaret Singe, *Treasurer*
▲ **EMP:** 9
SQ FT: 28,000
SALES (est): 1.1MM **Privately Held**
SIC: 5044 7629 3546 Mailing machines;
electronic equipment repair; power-driven
handtools

(G-4441)
**SNAPCO MANUFACTURING
CORP**
140 Central Ave Ste 1 (07205-2377)
PHONE...............................973 282-0300
Fax: 973 282-7627

Arnold A Spitz, *Ch of Bd*
Jeffrey Spitz, *President*
Phillip Iuliano, *Vice Pres*
▲ EMP: 25 EST: 1941
SQ FT: 34,000
SALES (est): 3.9MM Privately Held
SIC: 2241 3965 3552 Fabric tapes; trimmings, textile; zipper; fasteners, snap; finishing machinery, textile

(G-4442)
SURVIVOR II INC
Also Called: Survirvor Windows II
1239 Central Ave (07205-2613)
PHONE...............................908 353-1155
Antonio Casas, *President*
EMP: 20
SQ FT: 14,000
SALES: 3MM Privately Held
SIC: 3089 Windows, plastic

(G-4443)
SUSAN MILLS INC (PA)
1285 Central Ave (07205-2645)
PHONE...............................908 355-1400
Luis Lee, *President*
▲ EMP: 10
SQ FT: 55,000 Privately Held
WEB: www.susanmills.com
SIC: 2257 Pile fabrics, circular knit

(G-4444)
THOMAS ERECTORS INC
630 Ramsey Ave (07205-1042)
PHONE...............................908 810-0030
Jeffrey Lukowiak, *Principal*
EMP: 8
SALES (est): 950.4K Privately Held
SIC: 3442 Window & door frames

(G-4445)
THOMAS MANUFACTURING INC
630 Ramsey Ave Ste 1 (07205-1042)
PHONE...............................908 810-0030
Fax: 908 810-1551
Thomas Lukowiak, *President*
Jeff Lukowiak, *COO*
Mitch Kapsaskis, *Vice Pres*
George Lukowiak, *Director*
EMP: 20
SALES (est): 6.4MM Privately Held
WEB: www.thomasmfg.com
SIC: 3442 Window & door frames

(G-4446)
UNION BEVERAGE PACKERS LLC
600 N Union Ave Ste 7 (07205-1030)
PHONE...............................908 206-9111
Yaron Gohar, *CEO*
Dwight Deming, *Vice Pres*
Marcin Mierzejewski, *Project Mgr*
Carol Viviano, *Production*
AVI Saunders, *Office Admin*
◆ EMP: 170
SALES (est): 33.9MM Privately Held
SIC: 2086 Soft drinks: packaged in cans, bottles, etc.

(G-4447)
UNIQUE WIRE WEAVING CO INC
762 Ramsey Ave (07205-1094)
PHONE...............................908 688-4600
Fax: 908 688-4601
Ken Beyer, *President*
Alex Cedeno, *Engineer*
Howard Gabriel, *Sales Mgr*
Bill Bard, *Sales Executive*
▲ EMP: 20 EST: 1946
SQ FT: 10,000
SALES (est): 6MM Privately Held
WEB: www.uniquewire.com
SIC: 3496 3643 Woven wire products; current-carrying wiring devices

(G-4448)
UNITED FORMS FINISHING CORP
Also Called: Uff
1413 Chestnut Ave Ste 2 (07205-1132)
PHONE...............................908 687-0494
Fax: 908 687-9211
Elizabeth Demkin, *President*
Liz Demkin, *Vice Pres*
Paul A Dick Jr, *Vice Pres*
Paul Dick, *Vice Pres*

James Damico, *VP Opers*
EMP: 13
SQ FT: 30,000
SALES (est): 2.3MM Privately Held
WEB: www.uffcorp.net
SIC: 7331 2759 Mailing service; laser printing

(G-4449)
URBAN STATE
209 Hollywood Ave (07205-2446)
PHONE...............................646 836-4311
Jonathan Hunter,
Albertha Hunter,
EMP: 5
SALES (est): 216.1K Privately Held
SIC: 2111 7389 Cigarettes;

(G-4450)
VANTON PUMP & EQUIPMENT CORP
201 Sweetland Ave Ste 1 (07205-1756)
PHONE...............................908 688-4120
Larry Lewis, *President*
Johannes Tang, *Regional Mgr*
John Brodeur, *Corp Secy*
Kenneth Comerford, *Vice Pres*
Stuart Cooper, *Vice Pres*
▲ EMP: 39 EST: 1948
SQ FT: 30,000
SALES (est): 10MM Privately Held
WEB: www.vanton.com
SIC: 3561 Pump jacks & other pumping equipment

(G-4451)
WIREWORKS CORPORATION
380 Hillside Ave (07205-1339)
PHONE...............................908 686-7400
Gerald Krulewicz, *President*
Larry J Williams, *CFO*
Larry Williams, *CFO*
Richard N Chilvers, *Sales Mgr*
EMP: 22
SQ FT: 4,500
SALES (est): 4.4MM Privately Held
WEB: www.wireworks.com
SIC: 3679 3672 3663 3651 Electronic circuits; printed circuit boards; radio & TV communications equipment; household audio & video equipment; nonferrous wiredrawing & insulating

(G-4452)
YALE HOOK & EYE CO INC
33 Race St (07205-2316)
PHONE...............................973 824-1440
Ann Roseman, *President*
Morton A Roseman, *Vice Pres*
▲ EMP: 10 EST: 1914
SQ FT: 54,000
SALES (est): 4.2MM Privately Held
WEB: www.snaptape.com
SIC: 3965 Fasteners, buttons, needles & pins

Ho Ho Kus
Bergen County

(G-4453)
ATOMIZING SYSTEMS INC
1 Hollywood Ave Ste 1 # 1 (07423-1438)
PHONE...............................201 447-1222
Fax: 201 447-6932
Michael Elkas, *President*
Thomas Pagliaroni, *Purchasing*
▼ EMP: 14
SQ FT: 9,200
SALES (est): 2.6MM Privately Held
WEB: www.coldfog.com
SIC: 3822 3585 Air conditioning & refrigeration controls; refrigeration & heating equipment

(G-4454)
JMP PRESS INC
Also Called: Minuteman Press
19 Sheridan Ave (07423-3507)
PHONE...............................201 444-0236
Prebin Karlsmark, *President*
Maja Karlsmark, *Vice Pres*
EMP: 6

SALES (est): 898.2K Privately Held
SIC: 2752 2791 2789 Commercial printing, offset; typesetting; bookbinding & related work

Hoboken
Hudson County

(G-4455)
A A SAYIA & COMPANY INC
1 Newark St Ste 29 (07030-5698)
P.O. Box M9 (07030-0009)
PHONE...............................201 659-1179
Fax: 201 659-3167
Garret Sayia, *President*
Peter Sayia, *Vice Pres*
Edward A Deep, *Treasurer*
◆ EMP: 8 EST: 1917
SQ FT: 2,000
SALES (est): 2.6MM Privately Held
WEB: www.aasayia.com
SIC: 5149 2087 Spices & seasonings; extracts, flavoring

(G-4456)
AF PHARMA LLC
1500 Garden St Apt 2I (07030-4493)
PHONE...............................908 769-7040
Fax: 908 769-7041
Susan Navarro, *QC Mgr*
Lars Peitersen,
▲ EMP: 5
SALES (est): 780.7K Privately Held
SIC: 2834 Pharmaceutical preparations

(G-4457)
ANTIQUE BAKERY & PIZZERIA
122 Willow Ave Ste A (07030-3602)
PHONE...............................201 714-9323
Ivan Rodriquez, *President*
EMP: 4
SQ FT: 2,500
SALES (est): 371.8K Privately Held
WEB: www.antiquebakery.com
SIC: 2051 Bakery: wholesale or wholesale/retail combined

(G-4458)
AUGMENTUS LLC
306 Wshngton Blvd Ste 303 (07030)
PHONE...............................855 240-1100
▲ EMP: 7 EST: 2005
SALES (est): 1.1MM Privately Held
SIC: 2819 Phosphorus, elemental

(G-4459)
BEN & JERRYS OF HOBOKEN
405 Washington St (07030-4980)
PHONE...............................201 792-1966
Fax: 201 792-2192
Sibel Berberogru, *Partner*
Pierre Berberogru, *Partner*
EMP: 12
SALES (est): 740.7K Privately Held
SIC: 2023 5812 Ice cream mix, unfrozen: liquid or dry; caterers

(G-4460)
BRAYNIAC LLC
80 River St Ste 5d (07030-5619)
PHONE...............................212 993-7222
Christopher Bray, *President*
EMP: 10
SALES (est): 215.9K
SALES (corp-wide): 774.5K Privately Held
SIC: 7379 7372 ; application computer software
PA: Bray Media Limited Liability Company
80 River St Ste 5d
Hoboken NJ 07030
212 993-7222

(G-4461)
BURGISS GROUP LLC
111 River St Fl 10th (07030-5773)
PHONE...............................201 427-9600
Leslie Halladay, *Managing Dir*
Brian Schmid, *Managing Dir*
James Rearden, *Project Mgr*
Najmul Suvo, *QA Dir*
Fuhchun Tsay, *Controller*
EMP: 55

SQ FT: 30,000
SALES (est): 9.1MM Privately Held
WEB: www.burgiss.com
SIC: 7379 7372 7371 Computer related consulting services; prepackaged software; computer software development

(G-4462)
C M H HELE-SHAW INC
Also Called: Cunningham Marine Hydraulics
1714 Willow Ave (07030-3414)
PHONE...............................201 974-0570
Fax: 201 974-0574
Robert F Cunningham, *President*
John Miner Vini, *Vice Pres*
Edwin Tracy, *Treasurer*
Craig Haese, *Admin Sec*
EMP: 12
SQ FT: 10,000
SALES (est): 93.6K
SALES (corp-wide): 670.5K Privately Held
SIC: 3069 Pump sleeves, rubber
PA: Cunningham Marine Hydraulics Co, Inc
1714 Willow Ave
Hoboken NJ
201 792-0500

(G-4463)
CARPATHIAN INDUSTRIES LLC
51 Newark St Ste 508 (07030-4543)
PHONE...............................201 386-5356
Paul Lichstein, *General Mgr*
▲ EMP: 14
SQ FT: 1,500
SALES: 14.5MM Privately Held
WEB: www.carpathianinc.com
SIC: 3491 Industrial valves

(G-4464)
CHAMBORD PRINTS INC
38 Jackson St (07030-6072)
PHONE...............................201 795-2007
Fax: 201 792-1713
Dennis Shah, *President*
Rose Robertsson, *Purch Mgr*
Rose Robertson, *Office Mgr*
Mike Desai, *Admin Sec*
▲ EMP: 25 EST: 1945
SQ FT: 70,000
SALES (est): 2.5MM Privately Held
SIC: 2759 Screen printing

(G-4465)
COLLEGE SPUN MEDIA INC
95 River St Ste 408 (07030-5612)
PHONE...............................973 945-5040
Matthew Lombardi, *President*
EMP: 6
SALES: 900K Privately Held
SIC: 2741

(G-4466)
COSMOPOLITAN FOOD GROUP INC
50 Harrison St Ste 208 (07030-6087)
PHONE...............................908 998-1818
Baris Kantarci, *President*
◆ EMP: 5
SQ FT: 20,000
SALES: 15MM Privately Held
SIC: 5149 2079 2099 2035 Cooking oils; olive oil; vinegar; pickles, sauces & salad dressings

(G-4467)
D KWITMAN & SON INC (PA)
1015 Adams St (07030-2147)
PHONE...............................201 798-5511
Fax: 201 798-9147
Harold Kwitman, *President*
▲ EMP: 10 EST: 1934
SQ FT: 2,500
SALES (est): 4.4MM Privately Held
WEB: www.dkwitman.com
SIC: 5023 2391 2392 Curtains; curtains, window: made from purchased materials; bedspreads & bed sets: made from purchased materials

(G-4468)
D KWITMAN & SON INC
1015 Adams St (07030-2147)
PHONE...............................201 798-5511
Robert Quackenbush, *Manager*
EMP: 18

SALES (corp-wide): 4.4MM **Privately Held**
WEB: www.dkwitman.com
SIC: 2259 2391 Curtains & bedding, knit; curtains & draperies
PA: D. Kwitman & Son Inc.
1015 Adams St
Hoboken NJ 07030
201 798-5511

(G-4469)
DOMS BAKERY GRAND INC
506 Grand St (07030-2708)
PHONE...............................201 653-1948
Dominick Castellitto, *President*
Florence Castellitto, *Vice Pres*
Francisco Castellitto, *Manager*
EMP: 9
SALES (est): 759.7K **Privately Held**
SIC: 2051 Bakery: wholesale or wholesale/retail combined

(G-4470)
FULL HOUSE PRINTING INC
303 1st St (07030-2433)
PHONE...............................201 798-7073
Rose Capaptorto, *President*
Larry Weiss, *President*
EMP: 5
SQ FT: 1,000
SALES: 250K **Privately Held**
WEB: www.fullhouseprinting.com
SIC: 2752 Commercial printing, offset

(G-4471)
GENDELL ASSOCIATES PA
Also Called: Folditure
1031 Bloomfield St (07030-5203)
PHONE...............................201 656-4498
Alexander Gendell, *Principal*
EMP: 5 **EST:** 2005
SQ FT: 2,000
SALES (est): 100K **Privately Held**
SIC: 2519 Furniture, household: glass, fiberglass & plastic

(G-4472)
HARRISON SCOTT PBLICATIONS INC
Also Called: Asset Backed Alert
5 Marine View Plz Ste 400 (07030-5722)
PHONE...............................201 659-1700
Andrew Albert, *Ch of Bd*
Daniel Cowles, *President*
Thomas J Ferris, *Editor*
Tj Foderaro, *Editor*
Ben Lebowitz, *Editor*
EMP: 34
SQ FT: 7,200
SALES: 19MM **Privately Held**
WEB: www.abalert.com
SIC: 2741 Newsletter publishing

(G-4473)
HOBOKEN EXECUTIVE ART INC
Also Called: Right Angle
320 Washington St Ste A (07030-4831)
PHONE...............................201 420-8262
Toni Sullivan, *President*
EMP: 6
SQ FT: 1,000
SALES (est): 685.7K **Privately Held**
SIC: 2499 8748 Picture & mirror frames, wood; business consulting

(G-4474)
HOBOKEN MARY LTD LIABILITY CO
1109 Washington St Apt 2 (07030-5327)
PHONE...............................201 234-9910
Ryan Grace, *Mng Member*
EMP: 4
SALES (est): 155.5K **Privately Held**
SIC: 2085 5182 Cocktails, alcoholic; cocktails, alcoholic: premixed

(G-4475)
HORPHAG RESEARCH (USA) INC
5 Marine View Plz Ste 403 (07030-5722)
PHONE...............................201 459-0300
Bruce Nadler, *President*
Peter Rohdewald, *Research*
EMP: 4 **EST:** 2010
SQ FT: 2,100

SALES (est): 16.2MM **Privately Held**
SIC: 2023 Dietary supplements, dairy & non-dairy based

(G-4476)
INTANGIBLE LABS INC
2 Hudson Pl Fl 7 (07030-5594)
PHONE...............................917 375-1301
Nader Al-Naji, *CEO*
EMP: 13
SALES (est): 272.7K
SALES (corp-wide): 562.8K **Privately Held**
SIC: 7372 Business oriented computer software
PA: Intangible Labs Llc
2 Hudson Pl Fl 7
Hoboken NJ 07030
917 375-1301

(G-4477)
JARDEN CORPORATION (HQ)
Also Called: Newell Brands
221 River St (07030-5989)
PHONE...............................201 610-6600
Michael B Polk, *CEO*
Cheryl Johnson, *Executive*
◆ **EMP:** 20
SALES: 8.6B
SALES (corp-wide): 14.7B **Publicly Held**
WEB: www.jarden.com
SIC: 3089 3634 3631 Plastic containers, except foam; plastic kitchenware, tableware & houseware; electric housewares & fans; electric household cooking appliances; electric household cooking utensils; personal electrical appliances; barbecues, grills & braziers (outdoor cooking)
PA: Newell Brands Inc.
221 River St Ste 13
Hoboken NJ 07030
201 610-6600

(G-4478)
JOHN B STETSON COMPANY
86 Hudson St (07030-5617)
PHONE...............................212 563-1848
Paul Guilden, *Ch of Bd*
Steve Kantor, *President*
Richard Adler, *COO*
Jean Ebert, *Controller*
Kinao LI Tan, *Director*
EMP: 5
SQ FT: 900
SALES (est): 510K **Privately Held**
SIC: 5611 2353 Clothing, men's & boys': everyday, except suits & sportswear; hats, caps & millinery

(G-4479)
JOHN WILEY & SONS INC (PA)
111 River St Ste 2000 (07030-5790)
P.O. Box 1569 (07030-1569)
PHONE...............................201 748-6000
Fax: 201 748-6088
Matthew S Kissner, *Ch of Bd*
Brian A Napack, *President*
James Weeks, *Publisher*
Anne Badal, *Editor*
Tracy Boggier, *Editor*
◆ **EMP:** 100
SQ FT: 303,000
SALES: 1.8B **Publicly Held**
WEB: www.wiley.com
SIC: 2731 2721 Textbooks: publishing only, not printed on site; books: publishing only; statistical reports (periodicals): publishing only; trade journals: publishing only, not printed on site

(G-4480)
JOHN WILEY & SONS INC
111 River St Ste 4 (07030-5773)
PHONE...............................201 748-6000
Pamela Reh, *Manager*
EMP: 6
SALES (corp-wide): 1.8B **Publicly Held**
WEB: www.wiley.com
SIC: 2731 Textbooks: publishing only, not printed on site
PA: John Wiley & Sons, Inc.
111 River St Ste 2000
Hoboken NJ 07030
201 748-6000

(G-4481)
JOSEMI INC
1201 Hudson St Apt 216s (07030-7408)
PHONE...............................917 710-2110
Jonaf Tamir, *President*
EMP: 5
SALES (est): 338.8K **Privately Held**
SIC: 2387 Apparel belts

(G-4482)
KHANNA PAPER INC
50 Harrison St Ste 118 (07030-8843)
P.O. Box 1170, Little Falls (07424-8170)
PHONE...............................201 706-8050
Mike Diplacido, *General Mgr*
Saurabh Khanna, *Exec VP*
Navdeep Singh, *Sales Staff*
Sandeep Pundir, *Asst Mgr*
Pawan Sharma, *Asst Mgr*
▼ **EMP:** 7
SALES (est): 60MM **Privately Held**
SIC: 5093 3554 Scrap & waste materials; paper industries machinery
PA: Khanna Paper Mills Limited
B-26, Infocity-1,
Gurgaon HR 12200

(G-4483)
L&W AUDIO/VIDEO INC
Also Called: Lowell / Edwards
1034 Clinton St Apt 101 (07030-3166)
PHONE...............................212 980-2862
Lowell Kaps, *President*
EMP: 7
SQ FT: 1,600
SALES: 1.2MM **Privately Held**
WEB: www.lowelledwards.com
SIC: 2511 2517 5031 5064 Wood household furniture; wood television & radio cabinets; lumber, plywood & millwork; kitchen cabinets; electrical appliances, television & radio; electrical work; sound equipment specialization; wood kitchen cabinets

(G-4484)
LIQUID HOLDINGS GROUP INC
111 River St Ste 1204 (07030-5777)
PHONE...............................212 293-1836
Peter R Kent, *CEO*
Victor Simone Jr, *Ch of Bd*
Robert O'Boyle, *Exec VP*
James Lee, *Officer*
Jose Ibietatorremendia, *Admin Sec*
EMP: 53
SALES (est): 4.8MM **Privately Held**
SIC: 7372 Prepackaged software; business oriented computer software

(G-4485)
MOSAIC GOLF LLC
900 Monroe St Apt 312 (07030-6245)
PHONE...............................201 906-6136
John Murphy, *Mng Member*
EMP: 6
SALES (est): 135.3K **Privately Held**
SIC: 7372 Application computer software

(G-4486)
NEWELL BRANDS INC (PA)
221 River St Ste 13 (07030-5990)
PHONE...............................201 610-6600
Michael B Polk, *CEO*
Mark S Tarchetti, *President*
William A Burke III, *COO*
Fiona Laird, *Exec VP*
Nate Young, *Senior VP*
▲ **EMP:** 300
SALES: 14.7B **Publicly Held**
WEB: www.newell-rubbermaid.com
SIC: 3089 3469 2591 3951 Plastic kitchenware, tableware & houseware; household cooking & kitchen utensils; porcelain enameled; household cooking & kitchen utensils, metal; drapery hardware & blinds & shades; pens & mechanical pencils; markers, soft tip (felt, fabric, plastic, etc.); hair & hair-based products; power-driven handtools

(G-4487)
NRG BLUEWATER WIND LLC
22 Hudson Pl Ste 3 (07030-5512)
PHONE...............................201 748-5000
David Blazer, *Principal*
EMP: 5

SALES (est): 380K **Privately Held**
SIC: 3822 Temperature sensors for motor windings

(G-4488)
OBSERVER PARK
51 Garden St (07030-3558)
PHONE...............................201 798-7007
Jennifer Mortellaro, *Principal*
EMP: 10 **EST:** 2009
SALES (est): 676.6K **Privately Held**
SIC: 2711 Newspapers, publishing & printing

(G-4489)
PAN AMERICAN COFFEE COMPANY (PA)
500 16th St (07030-2336)
PHONE...............................201 963-2329
Roy Montes, *CEO*
EMP: 40 **EST:** 1964
SQ FT: 40,000
SALES (est): 46MM **Privately Held**
WEB: www.panamericancoffee.com
SIC: 5149 2095 Coffee, green or roasted; roasted coffee

(G-4490)
PEARSON EDUCATION INC (DH)
221 River St (07030-5989)
PHONE...............................201 236-7000
Fax: 201 236-7696
Will Ethridge, *CEO*
John Fallon, *President*
Leeanne Fisher, *President*
Ravi Joag, *Business Mgr*
Kelly Doyle, *Sales Staff*
◆ **EMP:** 1583
SQ FT: 1,000
SALES (est): 2.4B
SALES (corp-wide): 5.9B **Privately Held**
WEB: www.phgenit.com
SIC: 2731 Book publishing
HQ: Pearson Education Holdings Inc.
330 Hudson St Fl 9
New York NY 10013
201 236-6716

(G-4491)
PEARSON EDUCATION INC
Also Called: Pearson Longman
221 River St (07030-5989)
PHONE...............................914 287-8000
Owen Mitchell, *President*
Joanne Dresner, *Manager*
EMP: 99
SALES (corp-wide): 5.9B **Privately Held**
WEB: www.phgenit.com
SIC: 7372 Educational computer software
HQ: Pearson Education, Inc.
221 River St
Hoboken NJ 07030
201 236-7000

(G-4492)
PEARSON EDUCATION INC
Prentice Hall
221 River St Ste 200 (07030-5990)
PHONE...............................201 785-2721
Fax: 201 767-5225
Barbara Puegner, *Sales Staff*
Boris Kerdman, *Business Anlyst*
Vanessa Stclair, *Business Anlyst*
Maria Gleason, *Manager*
Josh Richards, *Manager*
EMP: 19
SALES (corp-wide): 5.9B **Privately Held**
WEB: www.phgenit.com
SIC: 2731 Books: publishing only
HQ: Pearson Education, Inc.
221 River St
Hoboken NJ 07030
201 236-7000

(G-4493)
R NEUMANN & CO
300 Observer Hwy (07030-8410)
PHONE...............................201 659-3400
William Bernheim, *Vice Pres*
Richard Bernheim, *Manager*
▲ **EMP:** 14 **EST:** 1863
SQ FT: 30,000
SALES (est): 1.5MM **Privately Held**
WEB: www.rneumann.com
SIC: 3172 3199 Personal leather goods; novelties, leather

(G-4494)
RCDC CORPORATION
Also Called: Radiant Cut Diamond
59 Madison St 2 (07030-1805)
PHONE.................................212 382-0386
Fax: 212 869-1038
Stanley M Grossbard, *President*
Rebecca Grossbard, *Vice Pres*
EMP: 5
SQ FT: 1,600
SALES (est): 946.8K **Privately Held**
WEB: www.radiantcut.com
SIC: 5094 3915 Diamonds (gems); diamond cutting & polishing

(G-4495)
REUGE MANAGEMENT GROUP INC
Also Called: Retawa
89 River St Unit 1002 (07030-9643)
PHONE.................................888 306-3253
EMP: 4
SALES (est): 290K **Privately Held**
SIC: 3674 8331 Mfg Semiconductors/Related Devices Job Training/Related Services

(G-4496)
SIMS PUMP VALVE COMPANY INC
1314 Park Ave (07030-4404)
PHONE.................................201 792-0600
Fax: 201 792-4803
John A Kozel, *President*
Dr Charles Post, *Vice Pres*
Edwin Van Keuren, *Sales Staff*
Laura Kozel, *Marketing Staff*
John Franklin, *Manager*
EMP: 20 EST: 1919
SQ FT: 10,000
SALES (est): 5.7MM **Privately Held**
WEB: www.simsite.com
SIC: 3494 5085 Valves & pipe fittings; valves & fittings

(G-4497)
SLENDERTONE DISTRIBUTION INC
221 River St Ste 9 (07030-5990)
P.O. Box 5179 (07030-1502)
PHONE.................................732 660-1177
Andy Leyland, *CEO*
Joseph Petracca, *President*
▲ EMP: 6
SALES (est): 981K **Privately Held**
SIC: 3949 7311 Exercise equipment; advertising agencies

(G-4498)
SMALL MOLECULES INC
38 Jackson St (07030-6072)
PHONE.................................201 918-4664
Julia Zhu, *Principal*
▲ EMP: 4
SALES (est): 440K **Privately Held**
SIC: 2869 Industrial organic chemicals

(G-4499)
SUMMIT PROFESSIONAL NETWORKS
33 41 Newark St Fl 2 (07030)
P.O. Box 770 (07030-0770)
PHONE.................................201 526-1230
Fax: 201 526-1260
John Whelan, *Manager*
EMP: 20
SALES (corp-wide): 186.9MM **Privately Held**
WEB: www.nationalunderwriter.com
SIC: 2711 Newspapers
HQ: Summit Professional Networks
4157 Olympic Blvd Ste 225
Erlanger KY 41018
859 692-2100

(G-4500)
TAXSTREAM LLC
95 River St Ste 5c (07030-5612)
PHONE.................................201 610-0390
Fax: 201 356-6521
EMP: 75
SQ FT: 10,000
SALES (est): 4.7MM
SALES (corp-wide): 3.2B **Publicly Held**
SIC: 7372 Prepackaged Software Services

HQ: Thomson Reuters Corporation
3 Times Sq
New York NY 10036
646 223-4000

(G-4501)
UNION DRY DOCK & REPAIR CO (PA)
51 Newark St Ste 504 (07030-4543)
P.O. Box 1539 (07030-1539)
PHONE.................................201 792-9090
Robert J Burke, *President*
Robert Ferrie, *Vice Pres*
Bruce Southern, *Vice Pres*
Carlotta Crissy, *Treasurer*
Carol A Barnes, *Admin Sec*
EMP: 4 EST: 1908
SQ FT: 1,500
SALES (est): 5.1MM **Privately Held**
SIC: 3731 Barges, building & repairing; scows, building & repairing; tugboats, building & repairing

(G-4502)
UNION DRY DOCK & REPAIR CO
Also Called: Yard
901 Sinatra Dr (07030-5797)
PHONE.................................201 963-5833
Fax: 201 792-4977
Bruce Southern, *General Mgr*
EMP: 45
SALES (corp-wide): 5.1MM **Privately Held**
SIC: 3731 3732 Shipbuilding & repairing; boat building & repairing
PA: Union Dry Dock & Repair Co Inc
51 Newark St Ste 504
Hoboken NJ 07030
201 792-9090

(G-4503)
W KODAK JEWELERS INC (PA)
Also Called: Kodak W Jewelers of Bayonne
60 Newark St (07030-4581)
PHONE.................................201 710-5491
Carol Kodak Walden, *President*
Bradley Kodak, *Vice Pres*
Creighton Kodak, *Vice Pres*
EMP: 5
SQ FT: 2,500
SALES (est): 2.2MM **Privately Held**
WEB: www.wkodakjewelers.com
SIC: 5944 3911 Jewelry, precious stones & precious metals; jewelry, precious metal

(G-4504)
WILEY PUBLISHING LLC (HQ)
Also Called: John Wiley and Sons
111 River St (07030-5773)
PHONE.................................201 748-6000
Stephen M Smith, *CEO*
William J Arlington, *Senior VP*
David Checkley, *Vice Pres*
Ellis E Cousens, *Vice Pres*
Edward J Melando, *Vice Pres*
▲ EMP: 500
SALES (est): 393.5MM
SALES (corp-wide): 1.8B **Publicly Held**
WEB: www.mcp.com
SIC: 2731 Books: publishing & printing
PA: John Wiley & Sons, Inc.
111 River St Ste 2000
Hoboken NJ 07030
201 748-6000

(G-4505)
WILEY SUBSCRIPTION SERVICES
Also Called: Wiley-Interscience
111 River St (07030-5773)
PHONE.................................201 748-6000
Bradford Wiley II, *President*
EMP: 13
SQ FT: 230,000
SALES (est): 1.3MM
SALES (corp-wide): 1.8B **Publicly Held**
WEB: www.wiley.com
SIC: 2731 Textbooks: publishing only, not printed on site
PA: John Wiley & Sons, Inc.
111 River St Ste 2000
Hoboken NJ 07030
201 748-6000

(G-4506)
A&E PROMOTIONS LLC
118 Woodlake Ct A (07733-2544)
P.O. Box 355, Atlantic Highlands (07716-0355)
PHONE.................................732 382-2300
Mae Veltri,
Anthony Veltri,
Eugene Veltri,
EMP: 7
SQ FT: 20,000
SALES (est): 1.1MM **Privately Held**
SIC: 5199 2752 Advertising specialties; commercial printing, lithographic

(G-4507)
ACTION PRESS PARK SLOPE
5 Rustic Ln (07733-2318)
PHONE.................................718 624-3457
EMP: 4
SALES (est): 189.2K **Privately Held**
SIC: 2741 Miscellaneous publishing

(G-4508)
AER X DUST CORPORATION
12 Windingbrook Way (07733-2330)
P.O. Box 93, Tennent (07763-0093)
PHONE.................................732 946-9462
Guy D Cusumano, *President*
EMP: 6
SALES (est): 500K **Privately Held**
SIC: 5087 3564 3563 Vacuum cleaning systems; blowers & fans; air & gas compressors

(G-4509)
BKT EXIM US INC (HQ)
960 Holmdel Rd Ste 2-02 (07733-2138)
PHONE.................................732 817-1400
Shawn Rasey, *President*
EMP: 6
SALES (est): 5.3MM
SALES (corp-wide): 675.2MM **Privately Held**
SIC: 3011 Pneumatic tires, all types
PA: Balkrishna Industries Limited
Bkt House, C/15
Mumbai MH 40001
226 666-3800

(G-4510)
BKT TIRES INC
960 Holmdel Rd Ste 2 (07733-2100)
PHONE.................................844 258-8473
Minoo Mehta, *President*
EMP: 9
SQ FT: 2,000
SALES: 5.3MM
SALES (corp-wide): 675.2MM **Privately Held**
SIC: 3011 Pneumatic tires, all types
HQ: Bkt Exim Us, Inc.
960 Holmdel Rd Ste 2-02
Holmdel NJ 07733
732 817-1400

(G-4511)
CEI HOLDINGS INC (PA)
2182 State Route 35 (07733-1125)
PHONE.................................732 888-7788
John F Croddick, *President*
▲ EMP: 36
SALES (est): 265.8MM **Privately Held**
SIC: 2844 7389 4225 5122 Toilet preparations; cosmetic kits, assembling & packaging; general warehousing & storage; cosmetics, perfumes & hair products

(G-4512)
COSMETIC ESSENCE LLC (HQ)
2182 Hwy 35 (07733-1125)
PHONE.................................732 888-7788
Fax: 732 888-6194
Peter G Martin, *CEO*
Kurt Polinger, *General Mgr*
Tina Caputo, *Principal*
Christian Algarin, *Prdtn Mgr*
Abdul Tahboub, *Purch Mgr*
▲ EMP: 237

SALES (est): 265.8MM **Privately Held**
WEB: www.ceidistribution.com
SIC: 2844 7389 4225 Cosmetic preparations; cosmetic kits, assembling & packaging; general warehousing & storage
PA: Cei Holdings Inc.
2182 State Route 35
Holmdel NJ 07733
732 888-7788

(G-4513)
COSMETIC ESSENCE INC
2182 State Route 35 (07733-1125)
PHONE.................................732 888-7788
EMP: 21 EST: 1982
SALES (est): 3.8MM **Privately Held**
SIC: 2844 7389 Mfg Toilet Preparations Business Services

(G-4514)
CRS INK INTL LTD LBLTY CO
11 Main St (07733-2105)
PHONE.................................732 817-0401
Luis Uribe, *Principal*
Eve McDonald, *Vice Pres*
Jeff Bossen, *VP Opers*
EMP: 5 EST: 2011
SQ FT: 5,400
SALES (est): 543.8K **Privately Held**
SIC: 2893 3479 Screen process ink; painting, coating & hot dipping

(G-4515)
EIGENT TECHNOLOGIES INC
10 Cindy Ln (07733-2027)
PHONE.................................732 673-0402
Robert Warner, *President*
EMP: 8
SALES (est): 681.4K **Privately Held**
WEB: www.eigent.com
SIC: 3663 Radio & TV communications equipment

(G-4516)
FULLVIEW INC
3 Fieldpoint Dr (07733-1227)
PHONE.................................732 275-6500
Vic Nalwa, *President*
Joe Lazaroff, *Admin Sec*
▼ EMP: 5 EST: 2000
SALES: 1MM **Privately Held**
SIC: 3861 Cameras & related equipment

(G-4517)
HOLMDEL ACPNCTR & NTRL MED CTR
721 N Beers St Ste Suite (07733-1518)
PHONE.................................732 888-4910
Liping Wang, *Owner*
EMP: 8 EST: 2007
SALES (est): 700.2K **Privately Held**
SIC: 2834 8049 Medicines, capsuled or ampuled; acupuncturist

(G-4518)
J F C MACHINE WORKS LLC
2182 State Route 35 (07733-1125)
P.O. Box 133, Marlboro (07746-0133)
PHONE.................................732 203-2077
John F Croddick,
EMP: 12
SALES (est): 2MM **Privately Held**
SIC: 3565 Bag opening, filling & closing machines

(G-4519)
M P M BUILDING SERVICE
6 Brook Ln (07733-2002)
P.O. Box 97 (07733-0097)
PHONE.................................732 946-2600
Raymond Morgan, *Owner*
EMP: 9
SALES: 200K **Privately Held**
SIC: 3714 Cleaners, air, motor vehicle

(G-4520)
MAGNETIC PRODUCTS AND SVCS INC
Also Called: M P S
2135 State Route 35 Ste 1 (07733-1077)
PHONE.................................732 264-6651
Fax: 732 264-6876
Paul I Nippes, *President*
Marilyn B Nippes, *Corp Secy*
Philip Giglio, *Engineer*

Marilyn Nippes, *CFO*
EMP: 9
SQ FT: 15,000
SALES (est): 1.3MM **Privately Held**
SIC: 8711 5049 3829 Engineering services; scientific & engineering equipment & supplies; measuring & controlling devices

(G-4521)
MAGRUDER COLOR COMPANY INC
14 Takolusa Dr (07733-1232)
PHONE.....................817 837-3293
Allan Weissglass, *Ch of Bd*
Abdul Saleh, *President*
Jay R Weissglass, *Vice Pres*
Joel Weissglass, *Admin Sec*
EMP: 200
SQ FT: 250,000
SALES (est): 24.1MM **Privately Held**
WEB: www.magruder.com
SIC: 2865 Dyes & pigments; color pigments, organic

(G-4522)
METUCHEN CAPACITORS INC
2139 Highway 35 Ste 2 (07733-1095)
PHONE.....................800 899-6969
Fax: 732 888-7811
Gary Ficsor, *Ch of Bd*
Stephen P Ficsor, *President*
Nancy Masterson, *Buyer*
Robert Boyd, *QC Dir*
Cathy Hoehl, *Accounting Dir*
EMP: 35
SQ FT: 20,000
SALES (est): 6.6MM **Privately Held**
WEB: www.metcaps.net
SIC: 3675 Electronic capacitors

(G-4523)
MOBILE INTELLIGENT ALERTS INC
72 Middletown Rd (07733-2206)
PHONE.....................201 410-5324
Tom Santora, *CEO*
EMP: 4 **EST:** 2013
SALES: 162K **Privately Held**
SIC: 3699 7371 7389 Security control equipment & systems; software programming applications;

(G-4524)
MODELWARE INC
28 Red Coach Ln (07733-1137)
PHONE.....................732 264-3020
Anthony Dalleggio, *President*
EMP: 10 **EST:** 1995
SQ FT: 1,800
SALES (est): 1MM
SALES (corp-wide): 2.5B **Publicly Held**
WEB: www.modelware.com
SIC: 3674 7372 3672 Microcircuits, integrated (semiconductor); application computer software; printed circuit boards
PA: Xilinx, Inc.
2100 All Programable
San Jose CA 95124
408 559-7778

(G-4525)
MTN GOVERNMENT SERVICES INC (DH)
200 Telegraph Rd (07733)
PHONE.....................703 443-6738
Peg Grayson, *President*
Margaret Grayson, *President*
Quais Hassan, *President*
Ty Narkmon, *President*
Catherine Melquist, *Vice Pres*
EMP: 15
SALES: 30MM **Publicly Held**
SIC: 3448 Prefabricated metal buildings
HQ: Emerging Markets Communications, Llc
3044 N Commerce Pkwy
Miramar FL 33025
954 538-4000

(G-4526)
MVN USA INC
960 Holmdel Rd (07733-2138)
PHONE.....................732 817-1400
Atul Nalhotra, *President*
EMP: 5

SALES (est): 308.4K **Privately Held**
SIC: 7372 Educational computer software

(G-4527)
NOVEGA VENTURE PARTNERS INC
Also Called: Vonage
23 Main St (07733-2136)
PHONE.....................732 528-2600
David Pearson, *President*
Gerald Maloney, *Treasurer*
Kurt Rogers, *Admin Sec*
EMP: 5
SALES (est): 436K
SALES (corp-wide): 1B **Publicly Held**
SIC: 7372 4813 Application computer software; local & long distance telephone communications
PA: Vonage Holdings Corp.
23 Main St
Holmdel NJ 07733
732 528-2600

(G-4528)
OPTHERIUM LABS OU
21 Riverside Ln (07733-2084)
PHONE.....................516 253-1777
Sergey Beck, *Principal*
EMP: 6
SALES (est): 135.3K **Privately Held**
SIC: 7372 7389 Application computer software; financial services

(G-4529)
SAXA PHARMACEUTICALS LLC
22 Candlelight Dr (07733-2362)
PHONE.....................862 571-7630
Joseph Todisco, *Administration*
EMP: 4
SALES (est): 216K **Privately Held**
SIC: 2834 Pharmaceutical preparations

(G-4530)
SPIRENT COMMUNICATIONS INC
101 Crawfords Corner Rd (07733-1976)
PHONE.....................732 946-4018
EMP: 5
SALES (corp-wide): 454.8MM **Privately Held**
SIC: 5065 4899 4813 3679 Telephone & telegraphic equipment; data communication services; local & long distance telephone communications; electronic circuits
HQ: Spirent Communications Inc.
27349 Agoura Rd
Calabasas CA 91301
818 676-2300

(G-4531)
WILLOW TECHNOLOGY INC
12 Valley Point Dr (07733-1325)
PHONE.....................732 671-1554
William O Wurtz, *President*
EMP: 5
SALES (est): 400K **Privately Held**
WEB: www.willowtechnology.com
SIC: 3556 Mixers, commercial, food

(G-4532)
WORKWAVE LLC (DH)
101 Crawfords Corner Rd (07733-1976)
PHONE.....................866 794-1658
Chris Sullens, *President*
Shawn Cantor, *COO*
Perry Pappas, *Senior VP*
Bill Hazard, *Vice Pres*
Bill Fahrbach, *CFO*
EMP: 12
SALES (est): 4.2MM
SALES (corp-wide): 393.9MM **Privately Held**
SIC: 7372 Application computer software

Hopatcong
Sussex County

(G-4533)
ALLSTAR DISPOSAL
118 Hudson Ave (07843-1708)
PHONE.....................973 398-8808
Michael A Lombardi, *Principal*
EMP: 4

SALES (est): 314.1K **Privately Held**
SIC: 3089 Garbage containers, plastic

(G-4534)
ARCHLIT INC
42 Ithanell Rd (07843-1846)
PHONE.....................973 577-4400
Gaspar M Glusberg, *Principal*
EMP: 4
SALES (est): 513.7K **Privately Held**
SIC: 3648 Outdoor lighting equipment

(G-4535)
CORRVIEW INTERNATIONAL LLC
9 Pahaquarry Rd (07843-1419)
P.O. Box 8513, Landing (07850-8513)
PHONE.....................973 770-0571
William Duncan, *CEO*
EMP: 4
SQ FT: 2,000
SALES: 300K **Privately Held**
WEB: www.corrview.com
SIC: 7389 3531 Pipeline & power line inspection service; concrete grouting equipment

(G-4536)
GREEN POWER CHEMICAL LLC
Also Called: Green Power Chemical Sciences
151 Sparta Stanhope Rd (07843)
PHONE.....................973 770-5600
Fax: 973 770-1158
Tom Hawkins, *Controller*
August Peter Dangelo, *Mng Member*
Peter D'Angelo, *Manager*
Jake Wilson, *Manager*
EMP: 10
SQ FT: 3,000
SALES: 1.5MM **Privately Held**
SIC: 2842 3559 Degreasing solvent; degreasing machines, automotive & industrial

(G-4537)
HOPATCONG FUEL ON YOU LLC
107 Tulsa Trl (07843-1236)
PHONE.....................973 770-0854
John Corrente, *Principal*
EMP: 4
SALES (est): 280.1K **Privately Held**
SIC: 2869 Fuels

(G-4538)
SONRISE METAL INC
32 Shore Rd (07843-1328)
PHONE.....................973 423-4717
Fax: 973 423-0338
EMP: 18
SQ FT: 8,000
SALES (est): 3.1MM **Privately Held**
SIC: 3444 Mfg Sheet Metalwork

Hope
Warren County

(G-4539)
CHRISTOPHER F MAIER
Also Called: Jenny Jump Farm
352 Great Meadows Rd (07844)
PHONE.....................908 459-5100
Fax: 908 459-4770
Christopher F Maier, *Owner*
EMP: 10
SQ FT: 10,000
SALES (est): 1MM **Privately Held**
WEB: www.thelandofmakebelieve.org
SIC: 7999 3089 Tourist attraction, commercial; novelties, plastic

---
Hopelawn
Middlesex County

(G-4540)
F & A SIGNS INC
Also Called: Stand Out Signs
49 W Pond Rd (08861-1540)
PHONE.....................732 442-9399
Fax: 732 442-9292
Joe Musuruca, *President*

EMP: 5
SQ FT: 6,000
SALES: 800K **Privately Held**
SIC: 3993 Signs & advertising specialties

Hopewell
Mercer County

(G-4541)
DOOR CENTER ENTERPRISES INC
Also Called: The Door Center Publishing
105 Crusher Rd (08525-2203)
PHONE.....................609 333-1233
Fax: 609 466-3377
Charles M Huebner, *President*
Louise Huebner, *Corp Secy*
Lucia Huebner, *Vice Pres*
EMP: 7
SQ FT: 2,000
SALES: 1MM **Privately Held**
WEB: www.doorposter.com
SIC: 5211 5031 5251 2741 Garage doors, sale & installation; doors & windows; door locks & lock sets; posters: publishing only, not printed on site

(G-4542)
L & S CONTRACTING INC
259 Route 31 N (08525-2702)
PHONE.....................609 397-1281
Leon A Walters IV, *Partner*
Steven Walters, *Principal*
EMP: 6
SALES (est): 580K **Privately Held**
SIC: 4212 2875 5261 Local trucking, without storage; compost; top soil

(G-4543)
ORAL FIXATION LLC
53 Railroad Pl A (08525-1826)
PHONE.....................609 937-9972
Jeremy H Kahn, *Mng Member*
Henry M Rich,
▲ **EMP:** 5
SQ FT: 1,000
SALES (est): 449.3K **Privately Held**
WEB: www.oralfix.com
SIC: 2064 Candy & other confectionery products

(G-4544)
WELL MANAGER LLC
371 Route 31 N (08525-2802)
PHONE.....................609 466-4347
Daniel Serlenga, *Mng Member*
EMP: 4
SQ FT: 5,000
SALES: 500K **Privately Held**
SIC: 3714 Water pump, motor vehicle

Howell
Monmouth County

(G-4545)
AMERICAN BRAIDING & MFG CORP
247 Old Tavern Rd (07731-8814)
PHONE.....................732 938-6333
Fax: 732 938-6377
Jerry Bailey, *CEO*
Jason Bailey, *President*
▲ **EMP:** 11
SQ FT: 24,000
SALES (est): 1.1MM **Privately Held**
SIC: 3053 3069 Packing materials; gaskets, all materials; rubberized fabrics

(G-4546)
ARNOLD STEEL CO INC
79 Randolph Rd (07731-8611)
PHONE.....................732 363-1079
Felix Pflaster, *President*
Leon Pflaster, *Vice Pres*
Dave Brunnquell, *Project Mgr*
Vincent Digioia, *Project Mgr*
Jason Watkins, *Project Mgr*
EMP: 70
SQ FT: 60,000

SALES (est): 23.3MM Privately Held
WEB: www.arnoldsteel.com
SIC: 3441 2439 1791 Building components, structural steel; structural wood members; structural steel erection

(G-4547)
BR WELDING INC
3 Brook Rd (07731-8675)
PHONE..................................732 363-8253
Fax: 732 363-0155
Brandon REO, *President*
EMP: 19
SQ FT: 1,000
SALES (est): 3.6MM Privately Held
WEB: www.brwelding.com
SIC: 1799 7692 3444 Welding on site; welding repair; sheet metalwork

(G-4548)
CHIPS ICE CREAM LLC
149 Newtons Corner Rd (07731-2890)
PHONE..................................732 840-6332
Robin Almeida,
EMP: 5
SALES (est): 272.3K Privately Held
SIC: 2052 Cones, ice cream

(G-4549)
CORNER STONE SOFTWARE INC
1246 Hwy 33 (07731)
P.O. Box 180 (07731-0180)
PHONE..................................732 938-5229
Paul Crooks, *CEO*
EMP: 4
SALES (est): 261.1K Privately Held
WEB: www.cornerstonesoft.com
SIC: 7372 Prepackaged software

(G-4550)
CUTTER DRILL & MACHINE INC
175 Ramtown Greenville Rd # 7 (07731-3829)
P.O. Box 140, Lakewood (08701-0140)
PHONE..................................732 206-1112
Michael C Tellier, *President*
William Young, *Corp Secy*
EMP: 7
SQ FT: 6,000
SALES (est): 2.1MM Privately Held
WEB: www.cutterdrill.com
SIC: 3541 3545 Machine tools, metal cutting type; drills (machine tool accessories)

(G-4551)
CUTTING EDGE GROWER SUPPLY LLC
97 Glen Arden Dr (07731-1639)
PHONE..................................732 905-9220
Jackie Barendregt, *Sales Executive*
Anthonie D Barendregt,
▲ EMP: 4
SALES (est): 1MM Privately Held
SIC: 5191 4971 3999 Greenhouse equipment & supplies; irrigation systems; atomizers, toiletry

(G-4552)
DON SHRTS PCTURE FRMES MOLDING
Also Called: Don Shurts Frames & Molding
294 Lanes Mill Rd (07731-2524)
PHONE..................................732 363-1323
Donald Shurts, *Owner*
Kasimiera Shurts, *Owner*
EMP: 4
SQ FT: 8,000
SALES: 300K Privately Held
SIC: 2499 3089 Picture frame molding, finished; molding primary plastic

(G-4553)
EMIL A SCHROTH INC
Copper Av Yellow Brook Rd (07731)
PHONE..................................732 938-5015
Fax: 732 938-2363
Emil A Schroth Jr, *President*
Benjamin U Jackson, *Vice Pres*
EMP: 40
SQ FT: 55,000
SALES (est): 8.1MM Privately Held
SIC: 5093 3341 Nonferrous metals scrap; secondary nonferrous metals

(G-4554)
ERVIN ADVERTISING CO INC (PA)
Also Called: Garden State Sign
4880 Us Hwy Rte 9 S (07731)
PHONE..................................732 363-7645
Fax: 732 363-7655
Joseph Ervin, *President*
Robert Ervin, *Vice Pres*
Mary Burns, *Office Mgr*
EMP: 6 EST: 1951
SQ FT: 4,000
SALES: 748.3K Privately Held
SIC: 3993 Electric signs; neon signs

(G-4555)
GOGREEN POWER INC
Also Called: Power By Gogreen
4675 Us Highway 9 (07731-3384)
PHONE..................................732 994-5901
James Murry, *CEO*
Elliot Buzil, *Exec VP*
◆ EMP: 10
SALES: 4.5MM Privately Held
SIC: 3691 3699 3648 Alkaline cell storage batteries; extension cords; flashlights

(G-4556)
HOWELL TOWNSHIP POLICE
Also Called: HOWELL TOWNSHIP PAL
115 Kent Rd (07731-2420)
P.O. Box 713 (07731-0713)
PHONE..................................732 919-2805
Christopher Hill, *President*
Howard Dunbar, *CFO*
John Stevens, *Exec Dir*
Chris Hill, *Exec Dir*
Rochelle Hill, *Administration*
EMP: 55
SALES: 126K Privately Held
SIC: 2499 Policemen's clubs, wood

(G-4557)
JCH PARTNERS & CO LLC
8 Man O War Ln (07731-1161)
PHONE..................................732 664-6440
Timothy Harshaw,
EMP: 12
SALES (est): 553.1K Privately Held
SIC: 2899 Peppermint oil

(G-4558)
KARLA LANDSCAPING PAVERS
11 Woodland Dr (07731-1437)
PHONE..................................732 333-5852
Jorge Ortizdeorue, *Principal*
EMP: 4 EST: 2010
SALES (est): 561.5K Privately Held
SIC: 3531 Pavers

(G-4559)
KOEHLER INDUSTRIES INC
25 Arnold Blvd (07731-2792)
PHONE..................................732 364-2700
Raymond F Koehler, *President*
Patricia Koehler, *Corp Secy*
EMP: 4
SQ FT: 4,000
SALES: 300K Privately Held
WEB: www.flashlight.com
SIC: 3479 7336 Engraving jewelry silverware, or metal; etching on metals; silk screen design

(G-4560)
LAKEWOOD ELC MTR SLS & SVC
6850 Us Highway 9 (07731-3364)
PHONE..................................732 363-2865
Fax: 732 363-2990
Marc Lipman, *President*
EMP: 4
SALES (est): 310K Privately Held
SIC: 7694 5999 5063 Electric motor repair; motors, electric; motors, electric

(G-4561)
MARK-O-LITE SIGN CO INC
1420 Us Highway 9 (07731-3331)
PHONE..................................732 462-8530
Howard Mark, *President*
EMP: 10
SQ FT: 3,000
SALES: 300K Privately Held
SIC: 3993 Electric signs; neon signs

(G-4562)
PALUDE ENTERPRISES INC
1933 Hwy 35 Ste 105-144 (07731)
PHONE..................................732 241-5478
David Marsh, *President*
EMP: 5
SALES: 99K Privately Held
SIC: 3564 Air cleaning systems

(G-4563)
PASTEL COMPANIES INC (PA)
Also Called: China Assured
4 Hummingbird Ct (07731-8835)
PHONE..................................732 508-0635
Moses Grossman, *CEO*
EMP: 4 EST: 2015
SALES (est): 689.5K Privately Held
SIC: 3999 7389 Barber & beauty shop equipment; design services

(G-4564)
PHOENIX PACKING & GASKET CO
Also Called: Phoenix Pkg & Gasket Mfg Co
247 Old Tavern Rd (07731-8814)
PHONE..................................732 938-7377
Gerald D Bailey, *President*
EMP: 13
SQ FT: 24,000
SALES: 548.9K Privately Held
SIC: 3053 Gaskets, all materials; packing, metallic; packing, rubber

(G-4565)
SAWDUST DEPOT LLC
704 Hulses Corner Rd (07731-8551)
PHONE..................................973 344-5255
James Ippolito, *Mng Member*
EMP: 12
SALES (est): 1.2MM Privately Held
SIC: 2421 Sawdust & shavings

(G-4566)
SKRIPAK METAL FABRICATORS INC
15 Berkshire Dr (07731-2355)
PHONE..................................732 364-9662
Fax: 732 364-8345
John Skripak, *President*
Victoria Skripak, *Corp Secy*
EMP: 8
SQ FT: 6,000
SALES: 645K Privately Held
WEB: www.skripakmetal.com
SIC: 3441 Fabricated structural metal

(G-4567)
SOUTHWEST STAINLESS LP
Multalloy 9070
507 Oak Glen Rd (07731-8933)
PHONE..................................732 961-1520
Tim Robert, *Manager*
EMP: 8
SALES (corp-wide): 618.5MM Privately Held
SIC: 2819 Elements
HQ: Southwest Stainless, L.P.
    3730 S Main St
    Pearland TX 77581

(G-4568)
SURBURBAN BUILDING PDTS INC (PA)
Also Called: Suburban Aluminum Mfg
1178 Lkwood Frmingdale Rd (07731-8659)
PHONE..................................732 901-8900
Fax: 732 901-2155
Vincent P Bochiaro, *President*
Art Perlman, *Sales Executive*
EMP: 30
SQ FT: 25,000
SALES (est): 5MM Privately Held
WEB: www.suburbanbuildingproducts.com
SIC: 3442 5031 Storm doors or windows, metal; window frames, all materials

(G-4569)
UNITED ENERGY CORP (PA)
3598 Us Highway 9 Ste 303 (07731-3345)
PHONE..................................732 994-5225
Jack Silver, *President*
Adam Hershey, *Corp Secy*
▼ EMP: 8
SQ FT: 4,800

SALES (est): 1.2MM Publicly Held
SIC: 2899 2911 Chemical preparations; solvents

Irvington
Essex County

(G-4570)
AGAPE INC
Also Called: Dairyland
487 Chancellor Ave (07111-4002)
PHONE..................................973 923-7625
Fax: 973 923-2557
Arthur Anastasio, *President*
EMP: 11
SQ FT: 6,000
SALES (est): 490K Privately Held
SIC: 2024 5812 Ice cream & ice milk; ice cream stands or dairy bars

(G-4571)
ALBERT PAPER PRODUCTS COMPANY
464 Coit St (07111-4607)
P.O. Box 989, Hillside (07205-0989)
PHONE..................................973 373-0330
Richard Kenah, *President*
Mark Kenah, *Vice Pres*
EMP: 25 EST: 1944
SQ FT: 38,500
SALES (est): 6.5MM Privately Held
SIC: 2657 2653 5199 Folding paperboard boxes; boxes, corrugated: made from purchased materials; packaging materials

(G-4572)
ALBOUM W HAT COMPANY INC
1439 Springfield Ave (07111-1357)
PHONE..................................201 399-4110
Fax: 973 399-4110
Stuart Alboum, *President*
Sophia Saketos, *Manager*
▲ EMP: 22
SQ FT: 30,000
SALES (est): 1.4MM Privately Held
SIC: 2353 Uniform hats & caps; hats: cloth, straw & felt; caps: cloth, straw & felt

(G-4573)
AMERICAN ALUMINUM CASTING CO (PA)
324 Coit St (07111-4087)
PHONE..................................973 372-3200
Fax: 973 375-4958
Robert W Hartl, *President*
Clifford Hartl, *Vice Pres*
James Murray, *Sales Executive*
EMP: 28 EST: 1921
SQ FT: 50,000
SALES (est): 5.2MM Privately Held
WEB: www.americanalum.com
SIC: 3365 Aluminum foundries; aluminum & aluminum-based alloy castings

(G-4574)
ARNOLD DESKS INC
Also Called: Arnolds Desk
120 Coit St (07111-4117)
PHONE..................................908 686-5656
Fax: 908 686-9401
Joseph Weuste, *President*
Julius Arnold, *Vice Pres*
Toni Heidrich, *Sls & Mktg Exec*
Matt Stoffers, *Sales Mgr*
EMP: 35
SQ FT: 31,500
SALES (est): 4.5MM Privately Held
SIC: 2521 Cabinets, office: wood

(G-4575)
ARNOLD FURNITURE MFRS INC (PA)
400 Coit St (07111-4607)
PHONE..................................973 399-0505
Fax: 973 399-7638
Julius Arnold, *President*
Barbara Arnold, *Manager*
EMP: 10 EST: 1962
SQ FT: 70,000 Privately Held
WEB: www.arnoldfurniture.com
SIC: 2521 3993 Wood office furniture; signs & advertising specialties

(G-4576)
ARNOLD KOLAX FURNITURE INC
Also Called: Arnold Gisler Furn Fabricators
146 Coit St (07111-4117)
PHONE...................................973 375-3344
Fax: 973 375-6024
Eric Arnold, *President*
Benjamin Kolax, *Vice Pres*
EMP: 25
SQ FT: 18,000
SALES (est): 4.8MM **Privately Held**
WEB: www.arnoldkolax.com
SIC: 2521 Wood office furniture

(G-4577)
ARNOLD RECEPTION DESKS INC
120 Coit St (07111-4117)
PHONE...................................973 375-8101
Fax: 973 375-8090
William Kolax, *President*
Ben Kolax, *General Mgr*
Julius Arnold, *Vice Pres*
Jose Gonzalez, *Project Mgr*
Melissa Nieves, *Project Mgr*
▲ EMP: 26
SQ FT: 18,000
SALES (est): 3.9MM **Privately Held**
WEB: www.arnoldreceptiondesks.com
SIC: 2521 5712 Wood office desks & tables; custom made furniture, except cabinets

(G-4578)
BESTMARK NATIONAL LLC
171 Coit St (07111-4104)
PHONE...................................862 772-4863
Mark Weglicka, *President*
EMP: 30 EST: 2016
SALES (est): 72K **Privately Held**
SIC: 2431 Millwork

(G-4579)
BISTIS PRESS PRINTING CO
1310 Clinton Ave (07111-1403)
PHONE...................................973 373-8033
Fax: 973 373-1066
Matthew Bistis, *Partner*
Nicholas Bistis, *Partner*
EMP: 4 EST: 1939
SALES: 250K **Privately Held**
SIC: 2759 Commercial printing; financial note & certificate printing & engraving

(G-4580)
BLEEMA MANUFACTURING CORP
517 Lyons Ave (07111-4717)
PHONE...................................973 371-1771
Bruce Bier, *President*
Robert Bier, *Vice Pres*
Steve Weinerman, *CFO*
EMP: 32
SQ FT: 36,000
SALES: 5MM **Privately Held**
SIC: 3643 Electric connectors

(G-4581)
DIVERSIFIED IMPRESSIONS INC
Also Called: Diversfield Impressions
119 Coit St (07111-4104)
PHONE...................................973 399-9041
Richard Feldman, *President*
EMP: 4
SQ FT: 3,600
SALES: 500K **Privately Held**
SIC: 2752 Commercial printing, offset

(G-4582)
E J M STORE FIXTURES INC
460 Coit St (07111-4630)
PHONE...................................973 372-7907
Marcos Zos Santos, *Partner*
EMP: 6
SALES (est): 480K **Privately Held**
SIC: 2542 Fixtures, store: except wood

(G-4583)
ELECTRONIC TECHNOLOGY INC
Also Called: Eti
511 Lyons Ave (07111-4717)
PHONE...................................973 371-5160
Victor Mohl, *President*
Bruce Bier, *Corp Secy*

Joseph Bier, *Vice Pres*
Mike De Oliveira, *Purchasing*
Arthur Diem, *Engineer*
▲ EMP: 130
SQ FT: 23,000
SALES (est): 31.8MM **Privately Held**
WEB: www.eti-nj.com
SIC: 3625 Electric controls & control accessories, industrial

(G-4584)
ENGINE COMBO LLC
Also Called: TEC
300 Nye Ave (07111-4713)
PHONE...................................201 290-4399
Kumal Pasawala, *Managing Prtnr*
▼ EMP: 16 EST: 2013
SQ FT: 25,000
SALES: 4.5MM **Privately Held**
SIC: 3465 Body parts, automobile: stamped metal

(G-4585)
FEHLBERG MFG INC
10 Renee Pl 16 (07111-4609)
PHONE...................................973 399-1905
Harold Fehlberg, *President*
EMP: 6
SQ FT: 15,000
SALES: 500K **Privately Held**
SIC: 2522 Office furniture, except wood

(G-4586)
FLAME CUT STEEL INC
300 Coit St (07111-4006)
P.O. Box 524, Matawan (07747-0524)
PHONE...................................973 373-9300
Ramesh Nuthi, *President*
EMP: 10
SALES (est): 1MM **Privately Held**
SIC: 3441 Fabricated structural metal for bridges

(G-4587)
FRONTLINE INDUSTRIES INC
990 Chancellor Ave (07111-1262)
PHONE...................................973 373-7211
Alfredo A Ciotola, *President*
Alfred Ciotola, *Project Mgr*
Dan Gural, *Production*
Justin Mackey, *Manager*
Yolanda Ramirez, *Admin Asst*
EMP: 17
SQ FT: 15,000
SALES (est): 5MM **Privately Held**
SIC: 7699 5084 3053 Pumps & pumping equipment repair; pumps & pumping equipment; gaskets & sealing devices

(G-4588)
HARVESTER INC
Also Called: Harvester Chemical
31 Cordier St (07111-4035)
PHONE...................................201 445-1122
Fax: 973 705-3255
EMP: 15
SALES (corp-wide): 5.9MM **Privately Held**
SIC: 2842 Mfg Polish/Sanitation Goods
PA: Harvester, Inc.
    85 Carver Ave
    Westwood NJ 07675
    201 664-4884

(G-4589)
HIGH TECH MANUFACTURING INC
460 Coit St Bldg D (07111-4630)
PHONE...................................973 372-7907
Azad Mehta, *CEO*
Victor Salgado, *President*
Jorge Salazar, *Vice Pres*
▲ EMP: 5
SQ FT: 8,000
SALES: 1MM **Privately Held**
SIC: 2542 Fixtures, office: except wood

(G-4590)
ICYKIDZ
539 Union Ave (07111-2855)
PHONE...................................973 342-9665
Sharon Hand, *Owner*
EMP: 5
SALES: 12K **Privately Held**
SIC: 2024 Fruit pops, frozen; ices, flavored (frozen dessert); juice pops, frozen

(G-4591)
IMPERIAL SEWING MACHINE CO
584 S 21st St (07111-4202)
PHONE...................................973 374-3405
Fax: 973 374-1185
Philip Pantusco, *President*
EMP: 5 EST: 1957
SQ FT: 14,000
SALES: 700K **Privately Held**
SIC: 3559 Sewing machines & attachments, industrial

(G-4592)
INTERNATIONAL VITAMIN CORP
209 40th St (07111-1154)
PHONE...................................973 371-4400
Ray Mulbey, *Manager*
EMP: 203 **Privately Held**
WEB: www.invernessmedical.com
SIC: 2834 Vitamin preparations
PA: International Vitamin Corp
    1 Park Plz Ste 800
    Irvine CA 92614

(G-4593)
INTERNATIONAL VITAMIN CORP
191 40th St (07111-1184)
PHONE...................................973 416-2000
Arthur Edell, *President*
Steve Citron, *Facilities Mgr*
EMP: 5
SQ FT: 30,000 **Privately Held**
WEB: www.invernessmedical.com
SIC: 2834 2899 Vitamin, nutrient & hematinic preparations for human use; gelatin capsules
PA: International Vitamin Corp
    1 Park Plz Ste 800
    Irvine CA 92614

(G-4594)
INTERNTNAL ARCHTCTRAL IRNWORKS
181 Coit St (07111-4104)
PHONE...................................973 741-0749
Fax: 973 399-6398
Pedro Varela, *Owner*
▲ EMP: 40
SALES (est): 5.3MM **Privately Held**
SIC: 3446 Architectural metalwork

(G-4595)
JERSEY PLASTIC MOLDERS INC
Also Called: Primo Division
149 Shaw Ave (07111-4779)
PHONE...................................973 926-1800
Fax: 973 926-1745
Joseph Zazzara, *President*
▲ EMP: 125
SQ FT: 120,000
SALES (est): 18.9MM **Privately Held**
SIC: 3089 Molding primary plastic

(G-4596)
M CHASEN & SON INC
123 S 20th St (07111-4704)
PHONE...................................973 374-8956
Tedro Silveira, *Manager*
EMP: 19
SALES (corp-wide): 14.6MM **Privately Held**
SIC: 2299 Batting, wadding, padding & fillings
PA: M Chasen & Son Inc
    117 S 20th St 123
    Irvington NJ 07111
    973 374-8956

(G-4597)
M P M DISPLAY INC
74 Woolsey St (07111-4012)
PHONE...................................973 374-3477
Fax: 973 374-0078
Michael Bertko, *President*
Margaret Baker, *Admin Sec*
EMP: 10
SQ FT: 10,762
SALES: 750K **Privately Held**
SIC: 2542 3496 Stands, merchandise display: except wood; miscellaneous fabricated wire products

(G-4598)
MANCO INDUSTRIES
673 S 21st St (07111-4101)
PHONE...................................973 971-3131
Donald Mangione, *President*
EMP: 7
SQ FT: 5,200
SALES (est): 500K **Privately Held**
SIC: 3599 Machine shop, jobbing & repair

(G-4599)
P A K MANUFACTURING INC
704 S 21st St (07111-4109)
PHONE...................................973 372-1090
Fax: 973 372-1091
Alex Even-Esh, *President*
Peter Wester, *Opers Mgr*
Peter Scranton, *VP Sls/Mktg*
▲ EMP: 19
SQ FT: 28,000
SALES (est): 5.5MM **Privately Held**
WEB: www.pakmanufacturing.com
SIC: 3841 Surgical instruments & apparatus

(G-4600)
PLASTICO PRODUCTS LLC
34 Loretto St (07111-4710)
PHONE...................................973 923-1944
Edd Griffith,
EMP: 5
SQ FT: 45,000
SALES (est): 916.5K **Privately Held**
SIC: 3086 Cups & plates, foamed plastic

(G-4601)
PRINTMAKER INTERNATIONAL LTD (DH)
503 Chancellor Ave (07111-4002)
PHONE...................................212 629-9260
Angus R Petrie, *Ch of Bd*
Edward Berkise, *President*
Paul Shen, *President*
▲ EMP: 8 EST: 1981
SQ FT: 10,000
SALES (est): 4.5MM **Privately Held**
WEB: www.printmakerintl.com
SIC: 5131 2335 2339 Textile converters; women's, juniors' & misses' dresses; sportswear, women's
HQ: First National Trading Co Inc
    9114 90th St
    Woodhaven NY 11421
    917 359-3469

(G-4602)
RICHARDS MANUFACTURING CO INC
517 Lyons Ave (07111-4717)
P.O. Box 18109, Newark (07191-8109)
PHONE...................................973 371-1771
Spencer Fox, *Senior VP*
EMP: 6
SALES (est): 450K **Privately Held**
SIC: 3674 Semiconductors & related devices

(G-4603)
RICHARDS MFG A NJ LTD PARTNR
517 Lyons Ave (07111-4717)
PHONE...................................973 371-1771
Bruce Bier, *President*
Richards M Sales, *General Ptnr*
◆ EMP: 175
SQ FT: 80,000
SALES (est): 25.3MM **Privately Held**
SIC: 3643 Electric connectors

(G-4604)
RICHARDS MFG CO SALES INC
517 Lyons Ave (07111-4717)
PHONE...................................973 371-1771
Fax: 973 371-9538
Bruce Bier, *CEO*
Joseph Bier, *President*
Steve Weinerman, *CFO*
Steven Weinerman, *CFO*
Robert Bier, *Treasurer*
▲ EMP: 25 EST: 1955
SQ FT: 36,000

SALES (est): 17.7MM Privately Held
WEB: www.richards-mfg.com
SIC: 5063 3678 3643 Lugs & connectors, electrical; electronic connectors; current-carrying wiring devices

(G-4605)
STUYVESANT PRESS INC
119 Coit St (07111-4104)
PHONE................................973 399-3880
Fax: 973 399-0480
Michael A Roesch, *President*
Theodore Roesch, *Vice Pres*
Lillian Roesch, *Admin Sec*
Mary Sandre, *Assistant*
EMP: 19
SQ FT: 10,000
SALES (est): 3.6MM **Privately Held**
WEB: www.stuyvesantpress.com
SIC: 2752 2761 2759 Commercial printing, offset; continuous forms, office & business; letterpress printing

(G-4606)
TIGER SUPPLIES INC
27 Selvage St (07111-4722)
P.O. Box 5395, Hillside (07205-5395)
PHONE................................973 854-8635
Fax: 973 854-8652
Herman Goldberger, *President*
Jack Wise, *General Mgr*
Chaya Hoffer, *Associate Dir*
Christopher Dahlman, *Executive*
◆ **EMP:** 6
SALES (est): 2.2MM **Privately Held**
SIC: 3699 Laser systems & equipment

(G-4607)
WAYNE COUNTY FOODS INC
360 Coit St (07111-4627)
PHONE................................973 399-0101
Fax: 973 399-2070
Vincent P Nemeth, *President*
Louise Nemeth, *Purch Mgr*
Josephine Nemeth, *Admin Sec*
EMP: 32
SQ FT: 7,500
SALES (est): 11.3MM **Privately Held**
WEB: www.waynecountyfoods.com
SIC: 5149 2033 Seasonings, sauces & extracts; juices; canned fruits & specialties

---

Iselin
Middlesex County

(G-4608)
ADVANSTAR COMMUNICATIONS INC
Also Called: Biopharm International
485 Us Highway 1 S # 200 (08830)
PHONE................................732 596-0276
Tom Brown, *Opers Mgr*
Lori Dennis, *Credit Staff*
Mick Tessalone, *Branch Mgr*
Deb Stokes, *Director*
Francine Rich, *Executive*
EMP: 50
SALES (corp-wide): 1B **Privately Held**
WEB: www.advanstar.com
SIC: 2721 Magazines: publishing only, not printed on site
HQ: Advanstar Communications Inc.
2501 Colorado Ave Ste 280
Santa Monica CA 90404
310 857-7500

(G-4609)
AMERICAN BUS & COACH LLC
1020 Green St (08830-2146)
PHONE................................732 283-1982
George Dapper,
EMP: 34
SALES (est): 3.3MM **Privately Held**
SIC: 3713 Bus bodies (motor vehicles)

(G-4610)
ANSELL HAWKEYE INC (HQ)
111 Wood Ave S Ste 210 (08830-2700)
PHONE................................662 258-3200
Tablo Bebetti, *General Mgr*
Donald Rodenborn Jr, *Director*
James P Rodenborn, *Director*
EMP: 50

SQ FT: 28,000
SALES (est): 26.2MM
SALES (corp-wide): 1.3B **Privately Held**
WEB: www.hawkeyeglove.com
SIC: 3151 Leather gloves & mittens; gloves, leather: work
PA: Ansell Limited
L3 678 Victoria St
Richmond VIC 3121
392 707-270

(G-4611)
ANSELL HEALTHCARE PRODUCTS LLC (DH)
111 Wood Ave S Ste 210 (08830-2700)
PHONE................................732 345-5400
Fax: 732 219-5114
Douglas Tough, *CEO*
Glenn L L Barnes, *Chairman*
John Rossi, *Business Mgr*
William Reilly Jr, *Senior VP*
Darryl Nazareth, *Vice Pres*
◆ **EMP:** 200
SALES (est): 123.2MM
SALES (corp-wide): 1.3B **Privately Held**
SIC: 3069 3842 2822 2326 Balloons, advertising & toy: rubber; birth control devices, rubber; finger cots, rubber; surgical appliances & supplies; synthetic rubber; men's & boys' work clothing

(G-4612)
ANSELL LIMITED
111 Wood Ave S Ste 210 (08830-2700)
PHONE................................732 345-5400
Magnus R Nicolin, *Branch Mgr*
Lucy Reday, *Manager*
Scott Johnson, *Technology*
EMP: 26
SALES (corp-wide): 1.3B **Privately Held**
SIC: 3842 Personal safety equipment
PA: Ansell Limited
L3 678 Victoria St
Richmond VIC 3121
392 707-270

(G-4613)
ANSELL PROTECTIVE PRODUCTS LLC
111 Wood Ave S Ste 210 (08830-2700)
PHONE................................732 345-5400
Douglas Tough, *President*
William Reed, *Senior VP*
William Reilly Jr, *Senior VP*
Rustom Jilla, *CFO*
Jim McBride, *Sales Mgr*
▲ **EMP:** 1900
SALES (est): 2.5MM
SALES (corp-wide): 1.3B **Privately Held**
WEB: www.ansellpro.com
SIC: 3842 3069 Gloves, safety; rubber coated fabrics & clothing; aprons, vulcanized rubbed or rubberized fabric
HQ: Pacific Dunlop Holdings (Usa) Llc
200 Schulz Dr
Red Bank NJ 07701

(G-4614)
AUTO INJURY SOLUTIONS INC
485 Us Highway 1 S (08830)
PHONE................................240 245-3117
Matthew Elges, *Manager*
EMP: 10
SALES (corp-wide): 3.7B **Privately Held**
SIC: 7372 Prepackaged software
HQ: Auto Injury Solutions, Inc.
222 Merchandise Mart Plz # 900
Chicago IL 60654
312 229-2704

(G-4615)
AXIOM INGREDIENTS LLC
33 Wood Ave S Ste 600 (08830-2717)
PHONE................................732 669-2458
Michael Desantis, *Mng Member*
EMP: 10
SALES (est): 2MM **Privately Held**
SIC: 1479 Mineral pigment mining

(G-4616)
BASF CATALYSTS LLC (DH)
Also Called: Engelhard
25 Middlesex Tpke (08830-2721)
P.O. Box 770 (08830-0770)
PHONE................................732 205-5000
Fax: 732 205-5687

Fried-Walter M Nstermann, *CFO*
Jer Nimo Cruz, *Director*
Wayne Smith,
◆ **EMP:** 100
SQ FT: 168,000
SALES (est): 361.4MM
SALES (corp-wide): 76B **Privately Held**
WEB: www.catalysts.basf.com
SIC: 2819 2816 5094 3339 Catalysts, chemical; inorganic pigments; white pigments; color pigments; bullion, precious metals; precious metals; platinum group metal refining (primary); silver refining (primary); gold refining (primary)
HQ: Basf Corporation
100 Park Ave
Florham Park NJ 07932
973 245-6000

(G-4617)
BASF CORPORATION
Catalysts Division
25 Middlesex Tpke (08830-2721)
P.O. Box 770 (08830-0770)
PHONE................................732 205-5086
Maurica Fedors, *Manager*
EMP: 163
SALES (corp-wide): 76B **Privately Held**
SIC: 2869 Industrial organic chemicals
HQ: Basf Corporation
100 Park Ave
Florham Park NJ 07932
973 245-6000

(G-4618)
BULKHAUL (USA) LIMITED (DH)
485 Us Highway 1 S E230b (08830)
PHONE................................908 272-3100
Dennis McCullough, *Vice Pres*
EMP: 11
SQ FT: 5,000
SALES (est): 3.2MM **Privately Held**
SIC: 4412 4424 3443 Deep sea foreign transportation of freight; deep sea domestic transportation of freight; industrial vessels, tanks & containers
HQ: Bulkhaul Limited
Brignell Road
Middlesbrough TS2 1
164 223-0423

(G-4619)
BUSINESS CONTROL SYSTEMS CORP
1173 Green St (08830-2011)
PHONE................................732 283-1301
Alexander Want, *President*
Marc R Want, *Treasurer*
EMP: 12
SQ FT: 6,000
SALES (est): 2.3MM **Privately Held**
SIC: 3578 7373 Point-of-sale devices; computer integrated systems design

(G-4620)
CISCO SYSTEMS INC
111 Wood Ave S Ste 2 (08830-2700)
PHONE................................732 635-4200
Fax: 732 635-3058
Andy Brajkovic, *Vice Pres*
Luis Geronimo, *Engineer*
Romulus Pestano, *Engineer*
Blue Somogyi, *Engineer*
Jack Dejovin, *Accounts Mgr*
EMP: 200
SALES (corp-wide): 48B **Publicly Held**
WEB: www.cisco.com
SIC: 3577 Data conversion equipment, media-to-media: computer
PA: Cisco Systems, Inc.
170 W Tasman Dr
San Jose CA 95134
408 526-4000

(G-4621)
CLIENTSRVER TECH SOLUTIONS LLC
2 Austin Ave Fl 2 # 2 (08830-3058)
PHONE................................732 710-4495
Srinivas Arra, *President*
EMP: 7
SQ FT: 1,000

SALES: 250K **Privately Held**
SIC: 7371 7372 8748 Computer software development & applications; business oriented computer software; systems engineering consultant, ex. computer or professional

(G-4622)
COUNTRY OVEN
1585 Oak Tree Rd Ste 207 (08830-1555)
PHONE................................732 494-4838
Sudhakar RAO Polsani, *Principal*
EMP: 5
SALES (est): 240.9K **Privately Held**
SIC: 2053 Cakes, bakery: frozen

(G-4623)
DOMINO FOODS INC (DH)
Also Called: Domino Sugar
99 Wood Ave S Ste 901 (08830-2733)
PHONE................................732 590-1173
Brian O' Malley, *CEO*
Veronica Escalante, *Business Anlyst*
John Damiano, *Manager*
Jack Giovinco, *Director*
Robert Studer, *Planning*
▼ **EMP:** 47
SQ FT: 2,222
SALES (est): 89.3MM
SALES (corp-wide): 1.8B **Privately Held**
WEB: www.dominofoods.com
SIC: 2062 5149 Cane sugar refining; refined cane sugar from purchased raw sugar or syrup; granulated cane sugar from purchased raw sugar or syrup; powdered cane sugar from purchased raw sugar or syrup; sugar, honey, molasses & syrups
HQ: American Sugar Refining, Inc.
1 N Clematis St Ste 200
West Palm Beach FL 33401
561 366-5100

(G-4624)
E PRO INC (PA)
555 Us Highway 1 S # 330 (08830-3179)
PHONE................................732 283-0499
Fax: 732 283-0489
Sadeesh Venugopal, *President*
Vivek Chaturvedi, *Vice Pres*
Christa Benedetto, *Financial Exec*
Christa Di Benedetto, *Manager*
Girish Chandran, *Info Tech Mgr*
EMP: 12
SQ FT: 2,000
SALES (est): 8.8MM **Privately Held**
SIC: 7372 7379 Business oriented computer software; computer related consulting services

(G-4625)
ENGELHARD CORPORATION
101 Wood Ave S (08830-2749)
PHONE................................732 205-5000
Fax: 732 205-6711
EMP: 19
SALES (est): 2.3MM **Privately Held**
SIC: 2819 Industrial inorganic chemicals

(G-4626)
EPCOS INC (DH)
Also Called: Epcos Inc A Tdk Group Company
485b Us Highway 1 S # 200 (08830-3013)
PHONE................................732 906-4300
Fax: 732 906-4395
Jon Nelson, *President*
Marlene Cortez, *Controller*
Richard Michelson, *Sales Mgr*
Tracey Dewitt, *Manager*
▲ **EMP:** 100
SQ FT: 22,477
SALES (est): 119.5MM
SALES (corp-wide): 11.9B **Privately Held**
SIC: 3679 3546 5065 3671 Electronic crystals; power-driven handtools; electronic parts & equipment; electron tubes
HQ: Epcos Ag
Rosenheimer Str. 141e
Munchen 81671
895 402-00

GEOGRAPHIC *(vertical tab, right margin)*

(G-4627)
FEDEX OFFICE & PRINT SVCS INC
1 Quality Way (08830-2924)
PHONE.....................................732 636-3580
Fax: 732 636-3581
Deon Young, *Manager*
EMP: 20
SALES (corp-wide): 65.4B **Publicly Held**
WEB: www.kinkos.com
SIC: 7334 2759 4731 Photocopying & duplicating services; commercial printing; freight transportation arrangement
HQ: Fedex Office And Print Services, Inc.
    7900 Legacy Dr
    Plano TX 75024
    214 550-7000

(G-4628)
HELSINN THERAPEUTICS US INC
170 Wood Ave S Fl 1 (08830-2742)
PHONE.....................................908 231-1435
Riccardo Braglia, *CEO*
Franco De Vecchi, *Ch of Bd*
Paolo Guainazzi, *General Mgr*
Padraig Somers, *General Mgr*
John Friend, *Vice Pres*
EMP: 21
SALES (est): 6.5MM **Privately Held**
SIC: 2834 Pharmaceutical preparations
PA: Helsinn Holding Sa
    Via Pian Scairolo 9
    Pazzallo TI 6912
    919 852-121

(G-4629)
INFINEON TECH AMERICAS CORP
186 Wood Ave S (08830-2763)
PHONE.....................................732 603-5914
Cheris Rickalla, *President*
EMP: 15
SALES (corp-wide): 8.3B **Privately Held**
WEB: www.infineon-ncs.com
SIC: 3674 Semiconductors & related devices
HQ: Infineon Technologies Americas Corp.
    101 N Pacific Coast Hwy
    El Segundo CA 90245
    310 726-8000

(G-4630)
LABNET INTERNATIONAL INC
33 Wood Ave S Ste 600 (08830-2717)
PHONE.....................................732 417-0700
Gerald Cooney, *CEO*
Sandra Burke, *Manager*
▲ EMP: 30
SALES (est): 4.9MM
SALES (corp-wide): 10.1B **Publicly Held**
WEB: Www.labnetlink.com
SIC: 3821 Laboratory equipment: fume hoods, distillation racks, etc.
PA: Corning Incorporated
    1 Riverfront Plz
    Corning NY 14831
    607 974-9000

(G-4631)
MAGLIONES ITALIAN ICES LLC
Also Called: Little Jimmy's
    111 Madison St (08830-1918)
PHONE.....................................732 283-0705
Fax: 732 283-3290
Mike Maglione, *Mng Member*
George Maglione,
EMP: 10
SQ FT: 2,500
SALES: 900K **Privately Held**
SIC: 2024 5143 5451 Ice cream & frozen desserts; ice cream & ices; ice cream (packaged)

(G-4632)
MAIDENFORM
485 Us Highway 1 S (08830)
PHONE.....................................732 621-2216
Anthony Esposito, *Manager*
▲ EMP: 1200
SQ FT: 12,000
SALES (est): 47.6MM **Privately Held**
SIC: 2341 Women's & children's underwear

(G-4633)
MAIDENFORM BRANDS INC (HQ)
485 Us Highway 1 S (08830)
PHONE.....................................888 573-0299
Maurice S Reznik, *CEO*
Malcolm Robinson, *President*
Christopher W Vieth, *COO*
Patrick J Burns, *Exec VP*
Nanci Prado, *Exec VP*
▲ EMP: 27
SQ FT: 81,300
SALES (est): 97.1MM
SALES (corp-wide): 6.4B **Publicly Held**
SIC: 2341 2342 5621 Women's & children's underwear; women's & children's undergarments; bras, girdles & allied garments; brassieres; foundation garments, women's; girdles & panty girdles; women's specialty clothing stores; ready-to-wear apparel, women's
PA: Hanesbrands Inc.
    1000 E Hanes Mill Rd
    Winston Salem NC 27105
    336 519-8080

(G-4634)
MICROSOFT CORPORATION
101 Wood Ave S Ste 900 (08830-2750)
PHONE.....................................732 476-5600
Harsha Bennur, *Partner*
Richard Shi, *Principal*
Nilesh Parikh, *Engineer*
Himani Sharma, *Engineer*
Paula Warfield, *Accounts Mgr*
EMP: 80
SALES (corp-wide): 110.3B **Publicly Held**
WEB: www.microsoft.com
SIC: 7372 Application computer software
PA: Microsoft Corporation
    1 Microsoft Way
    Redmond WA 98052
    425 882-8080

(G-4635)
NANKING EXPRESS
1538 Oak Tree Rd (08830-1502)
PHONE.....................................732 549-7788
Fax: 732 549-7797
J Sohan, *Manager*
EMP: 4
SALES (est): 219.7K **Privately Held**
SIC: 2741 Miscellaneous publishing

(G-4636)
NATIONAL LABNET CO
33 Wood Ave S Ste 600 (08830-2717)
PHONE.....................................732 417-0700
Fax: 732 549-2120
Walter Demsia, *Owner*
▲ EMP: 22
SALES (est): 1.8MM **Privately Held**
WEB: www.labnetlink.com
SIC: 5049 3821 3826 Laboratory equipment, except medical or dental; scientific instruments; laboratory equipment: fume hoods, distillation racks, etc.; analytical instruments

(G-4637)
NOVAERA SOLUTIONS INC
33 Wood Ave S Ste 600 (08830-2717)
PHONE.....................................732 452-3605
Dan Vaper, *President*
EMP: 81
SALES (est): 2.1MM **Privately Held**
SIC: 8748 7379 2836 Business consulting; computer related consulting services; ; biological products, except diagnostic

(G-4638)
OS33 SERVICES CORP (PA)
120 Wood Ave S Ste 505 (08830-2709)
PHONE.....................................866 796-0310
David Matalon, *Principal*
EMP: 5
SALES (est): 4.3MM **Privately Held**
SIC: 7372 7371 Prepackaged software; computer software development

(G-4639)
OTI AMERICA INC
517 Us Highway 1 S # 2150 (08830-3069)
PHONE.....................................732 429-1900
Shlomi Cohen, *CEO*

Udi Abramovic, *Vice Pres*
Amir Eilam, *Vice Pres*
Yishay Curelaru, *CFO*
Yenis Torres, *Controller*
EMP: 9 EST: 1998
SALES (est): 2MM
SALES (corp-wide): 20.5MM **Privately Held**
SIC: 3571 Electronic computers
PA: On Track Innovations Ltd
    Industrial Zone
    Rosh Pina 12000
    468 680-00

(G-4640)
PARTH ENTERPRISES INC
665 State Route 27 (08830-1820)
PHONE.....................................732 404-0665
EMP: 4
SALES: 500K **Privately Held**
SIC: 2752 Lithographic Commercial Printing

(G-4641)
QUALITY SWEETS
1396 Oak Tree Rd (08830-1661)
PHONE.....................................732 283-3799
Krishan Ram, *Owner*
EMP: 4
SALES (est): 302.4K **Privately Held**
SIC: 2869 Sweeteners, synthetic

(G-4642)
RF360 TECHNOLOGIES INC
485b Us Highway 1 S # 210 (08830-3013)
PHONE.....................................848 999-3582
James Wilson, *President*
Akash Palkhiwala, *Treasurer*
John Delmastro, *Admin Sec*
EMP: 42 EST: 2016
SALES (est): 85.3K
SALES (corp-wide): 165.4MM **Privately Held**
SIC: 3559 Electronic component making machinery
PA: Rf360 Europe Gmbh
    Anzinger Str. 13
    Munchen 81671
    892 080-50

(G-4643)
S S P ENTERPRISES INC
Also Called: Signs By Tomorrow
    825 Us Highway 1 S (08830-2660)
PHONE.....................................732 602-7878
Fax: 732 602-0889
Rajeez Krishna, *President*
EMP: 5
SQ FT: 1,700
SALES (est): 470K **Privately Held**
SIC: 3993 Signs & advertising specialties

(G-4644)
SHOWCASE PRINTING OF ISELIN
181 E James Pl (08830-1226)
PHONE.....................................732 283-0438
Fax: 732 283-4988
Vivian Hoppock, *President*
Glenn Hoppock, *Vice Pres*
EMP: 5
SALES: 250K **Privately Held**
SIC: 2752 Commercial printing, offset

(G-4645)
SIEMENS CORPORATION
170 Wood Ave S Fl 1 (08830-2726)
PHONE.....................................732 590-6895
Stephanie Marinello, *Vice Pres*
Thomas McCausland, *Manager*
EMP: 80
SALES (corp-wide): 97.7B **Privately Held**
WEB: www.usa.siemens.com
SIC: 3612 Distribution transformers, electric; voltage regulators, transmission & distribution
HQ: Siemens Corporation
    300 New Jersey Ave Nw # 10
    Washington DC 20001
    202 434-4800

(G-4646)
SUNRISE GLAMOUR LLC
33 Wood Ave S Ste 600 (08830-2717)
PHONE.....................................800 960-2426
Sunita Attarde,

EMP: 5
SALES: 400K **Privately Held**
SIC: 2844 Toilet preparations

(G-4647)
SXWELL USA LLC
111 Wood Ave S Ste 210 (08830-2700)
PHONE.....................................732 345-5400
EMP: 450
SALES (est): 851.8K **Privately Held**
SIC: 3069 Medical & laboratory rubber sundries & related products

(G-4648)
TECHENZYME INC
75 State Route 27 Ste 300 (08830-1536)
PHONE.....................................732 632-8600
Manu Rajvanshi, *Branch Mgr*
EMP: 4
SALES (est): 272.6K
SALES (corp-wide): 2.2MM **Privately Held**
SIC: 2869 Enzymes
PA: Techenzyme Inc
    1091 Amboy Ave Ste A
    Edison NJ 08837
    732 662-3429

(G-4649)
THROMBOGENICS INC
101 Wood Ave S Ste 610 (08830-2750)
PHONE.....................................732 590-2900
Patrick De Haes, *CEO*
Claudia Alexandrou, *CFO*
Jose Lemos, *Manager*
EMP: 50
SALES (est): 10.2MM **Privately Held**
WEB: www.thrombogenics.com
SIC: 2834 Pharmaceutical preparations

(G-4650)
VST CONSULTING INC
200 Middlesex Tpke # 102 (08830-2033)
PHONE.....................................732 404-0025
Suresh Chatakondu, *President*
Priya Gupta, *Manager*
Subba RAO, *Manager*
Sandeeep Kumar, *IT/INT Sup*
EMP: 80
SQ FT: 2,500
SALES (est): 7.4MM **Privately Held**
SIC: 7372 7373 Application computer software; systems integration services

---

Island Heights
Ocean County

(G-4651)
BEACHWOOD CANVAS WORKS LLC
39 Lake Ave (08732-7790)
P.O. Box 137 (08732-0137)
PHONE.....................................732 929-1783
Dan Janquitto,
EMP: 10
SQ FT: 12,000
SALES (est): 858.8K **Privately Held**
SIC: 2394 Canvas & related products

Jackson
Ocean County

(G-4652)
AK ASSOCIATES LLC
33 Sherwood Ct (08527-4554)
P.O. Box 407, Montville (07045-0407)
PHONE.....................................732 786-0002
Sidharth Sharma, *CEO*
Archana Sharma,
EMP: 4
SALES (est): 1.6MM **Privately Held**
SIC: 2295 Coated fabrics, not rubberized

(G-4653)
AMERIMOLD TECH INC
150 Park Ave (08527-3752)
PHONE.....................................732 462-7577
Michael Schon, *President*
John Schon, *Chairman*
James Schon, *Vice Pres*

▲ = Import ▼=Export
◆ =Import/Export

Russell Schon, *Vice Pres*
EMP: 35
SQ FT: 17,500
SALES (est): 4.7MM **Privately Held**
WEB: www.amerimoldtech.com
SIC: 5085 3544 Rubber goods, mechanical; special dies, tools, jigs & fixtures

(G-4654)
APPAREL STRGC ALLIANCES LLC
41 Greenwich Dr (08527-4878)
PHONE....................732 833-7771
James Saar,
EMP: 15 **EST:** 2015
SALES: 10MM **Privately Held**
SIC: 2389 Apparel for handicapped

(G-4655)
BCG MARBLE & GRANITE SOUTH LLC
150 Faraday Ave (08527-5034)
PHONE....................732 367-3788
Fax: 732 367-2849
Tony Cianvhetta, *President*
Pasquale Petrocelli, *Vice Pres*
▲ **EMP:** 8
SQ FT: 7,000
SALES (est): 968.2K **Privately Held**
SIC: 3281 5999 5032 Marble, building: cut & shaped; granite, cut & shaped; monuments & tombstones; marble building stone

(G-4656)
CENTRAL JERSEY HOT MIX ASP LLC
577 S Hope Chapel Rd (08527-5056)
PHONE....................732 323-0226
Fax: 732 323-3244
James Johnson Jr,
Pamela Flockhart,
Carolyn Hordichuk,
David Johnson,
EMP: 4
SALES (est): 640K **Privately Held**
SIC: 5032 2951 Asphalt mixture; asphalt paving mixtures & blocks

(G-4657)
CLAYTON BLOCK COMPANY INC
Also Called: Clayton Concrete
1215 E Veterans Hwy (08527-5004)
PHONE....................732 364-2404
EMP: 18
SALES (corp-wide): 46.8MM **Privately Held**
SIC: 3273 Mfg Ready-Mixed Concrete
PA: Clayton Block Company, Inc.
1355 Campus Pkwy Ste 200
Wall Township NJ 07753
732 363-1995

(G-4658)
CLEANZONES LLC
640 Herman Rd Ste 2 (08527-3068)
PHONE....................732 534-5590
David McClelland, *Mng Member*
Toni McClelland,
EMP: 10 **EST:** 2000
SQ FT: 5,000
SALES: 1MM **Privately Held**
WEB: www.cleanzones.com
SIC: 3564 3821 Blowers & fans; purification & dust collection equipment; air cleaning systems; dust or fume collecting equipment, industrial; laboratory equipment: fume hoods, distillation racks, etc.; laboratory furniture

(G-4659)
CREATIVE CONCEPTS OF NJ LLC
580 N County Line Rd (08527-4431)
PHONE....................732 833-1776
Thomas Jonin, *Senior Partner*
Tyler Jonin, *Prdtn Mgr*
Michael Jonin, *Mktg Dir*
EMP: 4
SALES (est): 79.2K **Privately Held**
SIC: 2431 Interior & ornamental woodwork & trim

(G-4660)
CREATIVE WOOD PRODUCTS INC
370 Whitesville Rd Ste 8 (08527-5063)
PHONE....................732 370-0051
Fax: 732 370-2442
George Tomaszewioz, *President*
Marion Romanowski, *Vice Pres*
EMP: 11
SQ FT: 8,000
SALES: 1.3MM **Privately Held**
SIC: 2431 Moldings, wood: unfinished & prefinished

(G-4661)
D DEPASQUALE PAVING LLC
1 Reagan Dr (08527-5155)
PHONE....................301 674-9775
Stephany Green,
EMP: 4 **EST:** 2012
SALES (est): 253.6K **Privately Held**
SIC: 2951 4212 Asphalt paving blocks (not from refineries); local trucking, without storage

(G-4662)
D J B WELDING INC
1461 Toms River Rd (08527-5211)
PHONE....................732 657-7478
Daniel J Black, *President*
Vickie Black, *Manager*
EMP: 4
SALES (est): 250K **Privately Held**
SIC: 7692 Welding repair

(G-4663)
DESIGNER KITCHENS
250 Faraday Ave (08527-5035)
PHONE....................732 370-5500
Fax: 732 363-2929
Edwin Rivera, *Partner*
Hector Rivera,
EMP: 10
SQ FT: 6,400
SALES (est): 640K **Privately Held**
SIC: 2511 2434 Kitchen & dining room furniture; wood kitchen cabinets

(G-4664)
DMD STAIRS & RAILS LLC
370 Whitesville Rd Ste 8 (08527-5063)
PHONE....................732 901-0102
Fax: 732 730-3886
Douglas Diani, *Owner*
EMP: 7
SALES (est): 1MM **Privately Held**
SIC: 2431 Staircases, stairs & railings

(G-4665)
EARLE THE WALTER R CORP
655 S Hope Chapel Rd (08527-5202)
P.O. Box 757, Farmingdale (07727-0757)
PHONE....................732 657-8551
Fax: 732 657-9230
Walter R Earle, *President*
Tj Earle, *Vice Pres*
EMP: 5
SALES (corp-wide): 3.8MM **Privately Held**
WEB: www.theearlecompanies.com
SIC: 2951 Concrete, bituminous
PA: Earle, The Walter R Corp
1800 State Route 34 # 205
Wall Township NJ 07719
732 308-1113

(G-4666)
EARLE ASPHALT COMPANY
655 S Hope Chapel Rd (08527-5202)
P.O. Box 757, Farmingdale (07727-0757)
PHONE....................732 657-8551
Mike Corsi, *Project Mgr*
Darlene Rasmussen, *Human Res Mgr*
Debbi Nichols, *Human Resources*
Walter Earle, *Branch Mgr*
EMP: 87
SALES (corp-wide): 40.5MM **Privately Held**
SIC: 2951 Asphalt & asphaltic paving mixtures (not from refineries)
PA: Earle Asphalt Company
1800 State Route 34 # 205
Wall Township NJ 07719
732 308-1113

(G-4667)
ECS ENERGY LTD
16 Meadow Run Ct (08527-4070)
PHONE....................201 341-5044
James Carbone, *President*
Peter Ramsey, *Exec VP*
EMP: 4 **EST:** 2007
SQ FT: 3,000
SALES: 1MM **Privately Held**
SIC: 3674 8742 Solar cells; management consulting services

(G-4668)
GALE NEWSON INC (PA)
460 Faraday Ave Ste 7 (08527-5072)
PHONE....................732 961-7610
Fax: 732 791-2182
Graham Tyers, *President*
EMP: 24
SALES (est): 2.6MM **Privately Held**
SIC: 3599 Electrical discharge machining (EDM)

(G-4669)
INTELLIGENTPROJECT LLC
15 Walter Dr Ste 4 (08527-3419)
PHONE....................732 928-3421
Jeffrey Raker,
EMP: 5
SALES (est): 320K **Privately Held**
WEB: www.intelligentproject.net
SIC: 1442 Construction sand & gravel

(G-4670)
JERSEY SHORE STEEL INC
636 Herman Rd (08527-3008)
PHONE....................732 833-8855
Theresa Loveland, *Principal*
EMP: 5
SALES (est): 1MM **Privately Held**
SIC: 1751 3449 Lightweight steel framing (metal stud) installation; bars, concrete reinforcing: fabricated steel

(G-4671)
MACHINE CONTROL SYSTEMS INC
47 Portchester Dr (08527-4395)
PHONE....................732 529-6888
Frank Chipchase, *President*
EMP: 4 **EST:** 1998
SALES (est): 449.4K **Privately Held**
WEB: www.machinecontrolsys.com
SIC: 3556 Bakery machinery

(G-4672)
MBS INSTALLATIONS INC
29 Summerhill Ave (08527-4366)
PHONE....................888 446-9135
Scott Shack, *CEO*
EMP: 10
SALES (est): 81.5K **Privately Held**
SIC: 7641 2521 Office furniture repair & maintenance; panel systems & partitions (free-standing), office: wood

(G-4673)
MSG FIRE & SAFETY INC
8 Short Hills Blvd (08527-4883)
PHONE....................732 833-8500
Michael Granit, *President*
EMP: 6
SALES (est): 899.7K **Privately Held**
SIC: 3432 5082 Lawn hose nozzles & sprinklers; construction & mining machinery

(G-4674)
OLD HIGHTS PRINT SHOP INC
16 Nancy Ct (08527-4669)
PHONE....................609 443-4700
Fax: 609 443-8053
Cathy M Simmons, *President*
Richard J Simmons, *Vice Pres*
EMP: 7
SQ FT: 5,500
SALES (est): 800.1K **Privately Held**
SIC: 2752 2791 7384 Commercial printing, lithographic; typesetting; photograph developing & retouching

(G-4675)
PRESENTATION SOLUTIONS INC
432 Clearstream Rd (08527-2040)
PHONE....................732 961-1960
Margo Sweeney, *President*
EMP: 4
SALES (est): 350K **Privately Held**
WEB: www.presentationsolution.com
SIC: 3993 Signs & advertising specialties

(G-4676)
PVH CORP
Also Called: Van Heusen
537 Monmouth Rd Ste 332 (08527-5368)
PHONE....................732 833-9602
Rochelle Kuhn, *Branch Mgr*
EMP: 9
SALES (corp-wide): 8.9B **Publicly Held**
SIC: 2321 Men's & boys' dress shirts
PA: Pvh Corp.
200 Madison Ave Bsmt 1
New York NY 10016
212 381-3500

(G-4677)
SCHON J TOOL & MACHINE CO
Also Called: Schon Tool
150 Park Ave (08527-3752)
PHONE....................732 928-6665
James B Schon, *President*
John O Schon, *Shareholder*
EMP: 5 **EST:** 1944
SALES (est): 416.5K **Privately Held**
SIC: 3069 Hard rubber & molded rubber products

(G-4678)
SIMI GRANOLA LLC
10 S New Prospect Rd (08527-1645)
PHONE....................848 459-5619
Frank D'Angelo, *Principal*
EMP: 13
SALES (est): 1.3MM **Privately Held**
SIC: 2043 Granola & muesli, except bars & clusters

(G-4679)
T & B SPECIALTIES INC
479 Wright Debow Rd (08527-5420)
PHONE....................732 928-4500
Fax: 732 928-1819
Thomas E Barchie, *President*
EMP: 5
SQ FT: 6,000
SALES (est): 2.3MM **Privately Held**
SIC: 5085 5087 5169 3052 Rubber goods, mechanical; hose, belting & packing; janitors' supplies; chemicals & allied products; rubber belting; rubber hose; mechanical rubber goods; extruded finished plastic products

(G-4680)
TRADEMARKSIGN
631 Herman Rd (08527-3009)
PHONE....................848 223-4548
Thomas Menshouse, *Principal*
Sue Campbell, *Project Mgr*
EMP: 17
SALES (est): 2.3MM **Privately Held**
SIC: 3993 Signs & advertising specialties

(G-4681)
VEP MANUFACTURING
575 S Hope Chapel Rd (08527-5056)
PHONE....................732 657-0666
Robert Pfluger, *President*
Frances Pfluger, *Corp Secy*
Tom Pfluger, *Vice Pres*
Ryan Pfluger, *Plant Mgr*
Tim Pfluger, *Marketing Staff*
EMP: 10
SQ FT: 8,000
SALES (est): 1MM **Privately Held**
WEB: www.vepmfg.com
SIC: 3599 7692 Machine shop, jobbing & repair; welding repair

(G-4682)
VET CONSTRUCTION INC
29 N County Line Rd # 218 (08527)
PHONE....................732 987-4922
Travis Glover,
EMP: 10

SALES: 500K **Privately Held**
SIC: **8741** 1799 1389 Construction management; construction site cleanup; construction, repair & dismantling services

(G-4683)
YOGURT PARADISE LLC
10 S New Prospect Rd (08527-1645)
PHONE.................................732 534-6395
EMP: 4
SALES (est): 266.6K **Privately Held**
SIC: **2026** Mfg Fluid Milk

Jamesburg
Middlesex County

(G-4684)
CHEROKEE PHARMA LLC
1085 Cranbury S Riv 1 (08831-3410)
PHONE.................................732 422-7800
Suresh Balaswamy,
Suresh Palaniswamy,
EMP: 8
SALES (est): 660K **Privately Held**
SIC: **2834** Pharmaceutical preparations

(G-4685)
FORM TOPS LMINATORS OF TRENTON
37 Merlot Ct (08831-5307)
PHONE.................................609 409-4357
Fax: 609 426-1551
Joseph Hadad, *President*
Sylvia Hadad, *Corp Secy*
John Dawes, *Vice Pres*
EMP: 6
SQ FT: 1,875
SALES: 250K **Privately Held**
SIC: **2541** 5031 Cabinets, lockers & shelving; table or counter tops, plastic laminated; building materials, exterior; building materials, interior

(G-4686)
LESLI KATCHEN STEEL CNSTR INC
300 Buckelew Ave Ste 109 (08831-1400)
PHONE.................................732 521-2600
Leslie Katchen, *President*
EMP: 3
SALES (est): 1.1MM **Privately Held**
SIC: **3441** Fabricated structural metal

(G-4687)
MOLDERS FISHING PRESERVE
318 John Wall Rd (08831-3208)
PHONE.................................732 446-2850
John Genoese, *Manager*
EMP: 4
SALES (est): 331K **Privately Held**
SIC: **3089** Molding primary plastic

(G-4688)
MONROE MACHINE & DESIGN INC
566 Buckelew Ave (08831-2971)
PHONE.................................732 521-3434
Fax: 732 521-3050
Mozes Kovacs, *President*
Robert Kovacs, *Vice Pres*
Susan Kovacs, *Treasurer*
Ericka Kovacs, *Admin Sec*
EMP: 12
SQ FT: 3,500
SALES: 1MM **Privately Held**
WEB: www.monroemachine.com
SIC: **3599** Machine shop, jobbing & repair

(G-4689)
RANX PHARMACEUTICALS INC
1085 Cranbury S River Rd (08831-3410)
PHONE.................................571 214-8989
Sivakumar Rangasamy, *Principal*
EMP: 4
SALES (est): 249.5K **Privately Held**
SIC: **2834** Pharmaceutical preparations

(G-4690)
SWEET SIGN SYSTEMS INC
9 Davison Ave Ste 5 (08831-1373)
PHONE.................................732 521-9300
Richard Dawson, *President*

EMP: 5 EST: 1920
SQ FT: 400
SALES (est): 697.1K **Privately Held**
SIC: **3993** Electric signs

Jersey City
Hudson County

(G-4691)
3DIMENSION DGNSTC SLUTION CORP
394 Union St Fl 1 (07304-1212)
PHONE.................................201 780-4653
Farrukh Babar, *President*
EMP: 8 EST: 2009
SALES: 1MM **Privately Held**
SIC: **3845** Ultrasonic scanning devices, medical

(G-4692)
67 POLLOCK AVE CORP
Also Called: Willow Iron Works
67 Pollock Ave (07305-1109)
PHONE.................................201 432-1156
Fax: 201 432-0042
Michael Zaccaria, *President*
Delores Zaccaria, *Treasurer*
EMP: 7
SQ FT: 2,500
SALES (est): 560K **Privately Held**
SIC: **1799** 3446 3444 Ornamental metal work; architectural metalwork; sheet metalwork

(G-4693)
9001 CORPORATION
Also Called: Dunkin' Donuts
507 Summit Ave Ste 7 (07306-2933)
PHONE.................................201 963-2233
Fax: 201 963-2233
Peter Matarazzo, *President*
EMP: 25
SALES (est): 837.4K **Privately Held**
SIC: **5461** 2051 Doughnuts; doughnuts, except frozen

(G-4694)
9002 CORPORATION
Also Called: Dunkin' Donuts
318 Central Ave (07307-2911)
PHONE.................................201 792-9595
Peter Matarazzo, *President*
EMP: 30
SALES (est): 815.9K **Privately Held**
SIC: **5461** 2051 Doughnuts; doughnuts, except frozen

(G-4695)
A & R SEWING COMPANY INC
451 Communipaw Ave (07304-3601)
PHONE.................................201 332-0622
Fax: 201 332-8538
Jerry Ragoobir, *President*
EMP: 12
SQ FT: 2,300
SALES: 100K **Privately Held**
SIC: **2392** 5949 7389 Tablecloths & table settings; sewing, needlework & piece goods; sewing contractor

(G-4696)
A B TEES LLC
7 Sherman Ave Fl 3 (07307-2338)
PHONE.................................201 239-0022
Anthony J Blunda, *Partner*
▲ EMP: 4 EST: 1998
SALES (est): 450.4K **Privately Held**
WEB: www.abtees1.com
SIC: **2759** Screen printing

(G-4697)
ACADIA SCENIC INC
130 Bay St (07302-2923)
P.O. Box 197 (07303-0197)
PHONE.................................201 653-8889
Fax: 201 653-4717
David Lawson, *President*
EMP: 30
SQ FT: 20,000
SALES (est): 4MM **Privately Held**
SIC: **3999** 7922 7812 Theatrical scenery; equipment rental, theatrical; motion picture production & distribution, television

(G-4698)
ACRILEX INC (PA)
230 Culver Ave (07305-1122)
PHONE.................................201 333-1500
Fax: 201 333-1237
Steve Sullivan, *President*
David Grunberg, *CFO*
Shaun Madary, *Accounts Mgr*
Trevor Butler, *Sales Staff*
Edward Wolkowicz, *Branch Mgr*
▲ EMP: 45 EST: 1972
SQ FT: 50,000
SALES (est): 21MM **Privately Held**
WEB: www.acrilex.com
SIC: **5162** 3081 Plastics materials; plastic film & sheet

(G-4699)
ADVANCE DIGITAL INC
185 Hudson St Ste 3100 (07311-1217)
PHONE.................................201 459-2808
Peter Weinberger, *President*
Stuart Schauman, *Vice Pres*
Mike Schiller, *Technical Staff*
EMP: 250
SALES (est): 29.2MM **Privately Held**
WEB: www.advancecars.com
SIC: **7372** Publishers' computer software

(G-4700)
AFL TELECOMMUNICATIONS LLC
123 Town Square Pl (07310-1756)
PHONE.................................864 486-7303
Kenny Nara, *Branch Mgr*
EMP: 63
SALES (corp-wide): 6.9B **Privately Held**
SIC: **3357** Nonferrous wiredrawing & insulating
HQ: Afl Telecommunications Llc
170 Ridgeview Center Dr
Duncan SC 29334
864 433-0333

(G-4701)
ALL AMRCAN RECYCL CORP CLIFTON
Also Called: Aarc
2 Hope St (07307-1306)
PHONE.................................201 656-3363
Fax: 201 656-8188
Vincent M Ponte, *President*
Vincent F Ponte, *Vice Pres*
Charlie Jacobsen, *CFO*
EMP: 130
SQ FT: 90,000
SALES (est): 37.1MM **Privately Held**
SIC: **4953** 2611 Recycling, waste materials; pulp manufactured from waste or recycled paper

(G-4702)
ALLIED BIAS PRODUCTS CORP
430 Communipaw Ave Ste 3 (07304-3699)
PHONE.................................201 432-6050
Fax: 201 432-8881
Leonard Staloff, *President*
Steve Moskovitz, *Principal*
▲ EMP: 13 EST: 1964
SQ FT: 15,000
SALES (est): 1.4MM **Privately Held**
SIC: **2241** Bindings, textile; trimmings, textile

(G-4703)
ALPINE CUSTOM FLOORS
173 Sherman Ave (07307-2040)
P.O. Box 441, Elmwood Park (07407-0441)
PHONE.................................201 533-0100
Fax: 201 533-0200
Paul Benson, *Owner*
EMP: 15
SALES (est): 1.4MM **Privately Held**
WEB: www.alpinegroupusa.com
SIC: **2426** Flooring, hardwood

(G-4704)
ALSTER IMPORT CO INC
16 Burma Rd (07305-4634)
PHONE.................................201 332-7245
Al Barletta, *President*
Paul Ling, *Vice Pres*
▲ EMP: 10
SQ FT: 10,000

SALES: 1.6MM **Privately Held**
SIC: **5094** 3961 Jewelry; costume jewelry, ex. precious metal & semiprecious stones

(G-4705)
ANCRAFT PRESS CORP
234 16th St Fl 8 (07310-1196)
PHONE.................................201 792-9200
Marlon Curtis, *Principal*
Toni Andors, *Admin Sec*
▲ EMP: 15
SQ FT: 10,000
SALES (est): 1.1MM **Privately Held**
SIC: **2752** 3555 2789 Commercial printing, lithographic; printing trades machinery; bookbinding & related work

(G-4706)
ANGELOS PANETTERIA INC
14 Wales Ave (07306-6412)
P.O. Box 1792, Englewood Cliffs (07632-1192)
PHONE.................................201 435-4659
EMP: 6
SALES (est): 469K **Privately Held**
SIC: **2051** Manufactures Bread

(G-4707)
ANHEUSER-BUSCH LLC
30 Montgomery St Ste 700 (07302-3841)
PHONE.................................973 645-7700
Fax: 973 645-7950
Carla Powell, *Buyer*
James Correll, *Manager*
Eugene Bocis, *Manager*
Carolina Guerra, *Director*
EMP: 162
SALES (corp-wide): 1.9B **Privately Held**
WEB: www.hispanicbud.com
SIC: **2082** Beer (alcoholic beverage)
HQ: Anheuser-Busch, Llc
1 Busch Pl
Saint Louis MO 63118
314 632-6777

(G-4708)
ANTENNA SOFTWARE INC (HQ)
111 Town Square Pl # 520 (07310-1725)
PHONE.................................201 217-3824
Fax: 201 239-2315
James J Hemmer, *President*
Adele Freedman, *Exec VP*
Ken Nicolson, *Exec VP*
Gregg Plekan, *Exec VP*
Pmp Arthur Punla, *Project Mgr*
EMP: 35
SQ FT: 13,000
SALES (est): 28.6MM
SALES (corp-wide): 840.5MM **Publicly Held**
WEB: www.antennasoftware.com
SIC: **7372** 7371 Prepackaged software; computer systems writing services
PA: Pegasystems Inc.
1 Rogers St
Cambridge MA 02142
617 374-9600

(G-4709)
APPRENTICE FS INC
155 Palisade Ave (07306-1113)
PHONE.................................201 819-1575
Angelo Stracquatanio, *CEO*
Gary Pignata, *Security Dir*
EMP: 30
SALES (est): 971.3K **Privately Held**
SIC: **7372** Prepackaged software

(G-4710)
ARRAY SOLDERS LTD LIABILITY CO
329 Mercer Loop (07302-3232)
PHONE.................................201 432-0095
Fax: 201 997-7920
Rolando Pavon, *Sales Staff*
Rosario Murillo,
Joseph Portelo,
EMP: 5
SQ FT: 14,000
SALES: 350K **Privately Held**
WEB: www.arraysolders.com
SIC: **3541** Machine tools, metal cutting type

(G-4711)
AUBREY DAVID INC
186 Griffith St (07307-2927)
PHONE....................201 653-2200
Fax: 201 653-6344
Jennifer Arago, *President*
Vj Curtis, *Admin Dir*
▲ EMP: 20
SALES (est): 2.5MM **Privately Held**
WEB: www.aubreydavid.com
SIC: 3911 5944 Jewelry, precious metal; jewelry stores

(G-4712)
B2X CORPORATION
10 Exchange Pl Fl 25 (07302-4914)
PHONE....................201 714-2373
Joseph A Sorisi, *CEO*
Alessandra Coderoni, *President*
Mark Bonilla, *CFO*
▲ EMP: 6
SALES (est): 530K **Privately Held**
SIC: 2326 3571 Men's & boys' work clothing; electronic computers

(G-4713)
BANAREZ ENTERPRISES INC
175 Baldwin Ave (07306-1901)
PHONE....................201 222-7515
Miguel Banarez, *President*
EMP: 4
SALES: 185K **Privately Held**
SIC: 3565 Packaging machinery

(G-4714)
BANNON GROUP LTD
234 16th St Fl 8 (07310-1196)
PHONE....................201 451-6500
Fax: 201 451-5697
Michael Falcone, *President*
EMP: 6 EST: 1996
SQ FT: 60,000
SALES (est): 971.5K **Privately Held**
WEB: www.bannongroup.com
SIC: 2752 Commercial printing, lithographic

(G-4715)
BEL FUSE INC (PA)
206 Van Vorst St (07302-4421)
PHONE....................201 432-0463
Fax: 201 432-9542
Daniel Bernstein, *President*
Dennis Ackerman, *Vice Pres*
Raymond Cheung, *Vice Pres*
Craig Brosious, *CFO*
EMP: 128 EST: 1949
SQ FT: 19,000
SALES: 491.6MM **Publicly Held**
SIC: 3679 3674 3613 3677 Cores, magnetic; semiconductors & related devices; modules, solid state; fuses, electric; inductors, electronic

(G-4716)
BEL HYBRIDS & MAGNETICS INC (HQ)
206 Van Vorst St (07302-4421)
PHONE....................201 432-0463
Daniel Bernstein, *President*
Peter Christopher, *Vice Pres*
Joyce Fitzpatrick, *Purch Agent*
Brian Gaultney, *Purchasing*
EMP: 10 EST: 1948
SQ FT: 12,600
SALES (est): 2.5MM
SALES (corp-wide): 491.6MM **Publicly Held**
SIC: 8731 8711 3677 Electronic research; engineering services; electronic coils, transformers & other inductors
PA: Bel Fuse Inc.
206 Van Vorst St
Jersey City NJ 07302
201 432-0463

(G-4717)
BETHEL INDUSTRIES INC
3423 John F Kennedy Blvd (07307-4107)
PHONE....................201 656-8222
Fax: 201 656-9964
Sun Kim, *President*
▲ EMP: 250
SQ FT: 45,000

SALES (est): 49.5MM **Privately Held**
SIC: 2326 7389 Jackets, overall & work; sewing contractor

(G-4718)
BILLYKIRK
150 Bay St Fl 3 (07302-2900)
PHONE....................201 222-9092
Chris Bray, *Principal*
▲ EMP: 16
SALES (est): 2.5MM **Privately Held**
SIC: 3199 3172 Leather garments; leather cases

(G-4719)
BINDING PRODUCTS INC
430 Communipaw Ste 1 (07304-3699)
PHONE....................212 947-1192
Freddie Brooks, *President*
EMP: 26
SQ FT: 16,000
SALES (est): 4.4MM **Privately Held**
SIC: 7334 2711 2732 5044 Photocopying & duplicating services; newspapers; book printing; office equipment; bookbinding & related work; electrical repair shops

(G-4720)
BORAK GROUP INC
255 Us Highway 1 And 9 (07306-6727)
PHONE....................718 665-8500
Marc Borak, *President*
▲ EMP: 88
SALES (est): 49.3MM
SALES (corp-wide): 998.6MM **Privately Held**
WEB: www.boraxpaper.com
SIC: 5113 2621 5085 Industrial & personal service paper; packaging paper; clean room supplies
PA: Imperial Bag & Paper Co. Llc
255 Us Highway 1 And 9
Jersey City NJ 07306
201 437-7440

(G-4721)
BRUCE TELEKY INC
430 Communipaw Ave Ste 2 (07304-3699)
PHONE....................718 965-9694
Bruce Teleky, *President*
EMP: 8
SQ FT: 14,000
SALES (est): 580K **Privately Held**
WEB: www.bruceteleky.com
SIC: 2741 Art copy & poster publishing

(G-4722)
C2 IMAGING LLC (HQ)
201 Plaza Two (07311-1100)
PHONE....................646 557-6300
Tim Wieland, *President*
EMP: 20
SALES (est): 26.2MM
SALES (corp-wide): 155MM **Privately Held**
WEB: www.C2imagingllc.com
SIC: 7334 2759 7336 Photocopying & duplicating services; commercial printing; commercial art & graphic design
PA: Vomela Specialty Company
274 Fillmore Ave E
Saint Paul MN 55107
651 228-2200

(G-4723)
CARLASCIO CUSTOM & ORTHOPEDIC (PA)
283 Grove St Apt 1 (07302-3660)
PHONE....................201 333-8716
Fax: 201 200-9391
Louis Carlascio, *Owner*
EMP: 7 EST: 1923
SQ FT: 1,200
SALES (est): 587.5K **Privately Held**
WEB: www.carlorth.com
SIC: 5661 3143 3149 Shoes, orthopedic; orthopedic shoes, men's; orthopedic shoes, women's; orthopedic shoes, children's

(G-4724)
CAROLE HCHMAN DESIGN GROUP INC (HQ)
Also Called: Sara Beth Division
90 Hudson St Fl 9 (07302-3900)
P.O. Box 101166, Atlanta GA (30392-1166)
PHONE....................866 267-3945
Charlie Komar, *CEO*
Peter J Gabbe, *Ch of Bd*
Seth Morris, *President*
Carole Hochman, *Principal*
Paul Shreck, *Principal*
▲ EMP: 150
SQ FT: 26,000
SALES (est): 56.2MM
SALES (corp-wide): 310.7MM **Privately Held**
SIC: 2342 2341 2384 7389 Bras, girdles & allied garments; women's & children's underwear; nightgowns & negligees: women's & children's; women's & children's undergarments; bathrobes, men's & women's: made from purchased materials; interior designer; interior decorating
PA: Charles Komar & Sons, Inc.
90 Hudson St Fl 9
Jersey City NJ 07302
212 725-1500

(G-4725)
CENVEO INC
Also Called: Mail-Well Envelope
25 Linden Ave E (07305-4726)
PHONE....................201 434-2100
Fax: 201 434-4048
Calvin Boles, *Controller*
Allan Rose, *Maintence Staff*
EMP: 65 **Publicly Held**
WEB: www.mail-well.com
SIC: 2677 2679 5112 Envelopes; tags, paper (unprinted): made from purchased paper; envelopes
PA: Cenveo, Inc.
200 1st Stamford Pl # 200
Stamford CT 06902

(G-4726)
CHARLES KOMAR & SONS INC (PA)
Also Called: Komar Company, The
90 Hudson St Fl 9 (07302-3900)
PHONE....................212 725-1500
Charles E Komar Jr, *CEO*
Harold Komar, *Co-COB*
Herman H Komar, *Co-COB*
Jay Harris, *COO*
Donna Nadeau, *Vice Pres*
◆ EMP: 428 EST: 1908
SALES (est): 310.7MM **Privately Held**
WEB: www.komar-ny.com
SIC: 2341 2384 5137 Women's & children's nightwear; nightgowns & negligees: women's & children's; robes & dressing gowns; nightwear: women's, children's & infants'

(G-4727)
CITY ENVELOPE INC
235 Orient Ave 1 (07305-1608)
PHONE....................201 792-9292
Randy Leif, *President*
EMP: 4
SALES (est): 695.3K **Privately Held**
SIC: 3555 2621 Presses, envelope, printing; stationery, envelope & tablet papers

(G-4728)
CITY OF JERSEY CITY
Also Called: Street Lights Dept
575 State Rt 440 (07305-4823)
PHONE....................201 547-4470
Fax: 201 547-4703
Joe D'Souza, *Principal*
EMP: 15 **Privately Held**
WEB: www.cityofjerseycity.com
SIC: 3648 Street lighting fixtures
PA: City Of Jersey City
280 Grove St
Jersey City NJ 07302
201 547-5000

(G-4729)
COCOA PROCESSING CORP
580 Luis Munoz Marin Blvd (07310-1416)
PHONE....................908 688-0415

Helen Mecca, *President*
Peggy Mecca, *Vice Pres*
EMP: 5
SQ FT: 20,000
SALES (est): 400K **Privately Held**
WEB: www.cocoaprocessingcorp.com
SIC: 2066 Cacao bean processing

(G-4730)
COLOR CODED LLC
249 Thomas Mcgovern Dr # 3 (07305-4633)
PHONE....................718 482-1063
Anthony Telesford,
EMP: 4
SALES: 370K **Privately Held**
SIC: 2752 Commercial printing, offset

(G-4731)
COLUMBIA PAINT LAB INC
452 Communipaw Ave (07304-3659)
PHONE....................201 435-4884
George Pahiakos, *President*
John Liapakis, *Admin Sec*
EMP: 20
SQ FT: 30,000
SALES (est): 4.6MM **Privately Held**
SIC: 2851 Paints & paint additives; varnishes

(G-4732)
CONNEAUT CREEK SHIP REPR INC
333 Washington St Ste 201 (07302-3095)
PHONE....................212 863-9406
Joseph Craine, *President*
EMP: 4
SALES (est): 264.4K
SALES (corp-wide): 2.3B **Privately Held**
SIC: 3731 Shipbuilding & repairing
HQ: Rand Logistics, Inc.
333 Washington St Ste 201
Jersey City NJ 07302
212 863-9427

(G-4733)
CONNECTOR MFG CO ✪
123 Town Square Pl (07310-1756)
PHONE....................513 860-4455
EMP: 8 EST: 2017
SALES (est): 1.3MM **Privately Held**
SIC: 3999 Manufacturing industries

(G-4734)
CORGI SPIRITS LLC
150 Pacific Ave Bldg P (07304-3201)
PHONE....................862 219-3114
Robert Hagemann, *Mng Member*
EMP: 6
SALES (est): 70.1K **Privately Held**
SIC: 2085 Distilled & blended liquors

(G-4735)
CRAFT SIGNS
136 Franklin St (07307-2330)
PHONE....................201 656-1991
Fax: 201 656-4764
Michael Tepper, *President*
Robert Iezzi, *Owner*
EMP: 4
SQ FT: 2,000
SALES: 300K **Privately Held**
WEB: www.craftsigns.com
SIC: 3993 5999 Electric signs; decals

(G-4736)
DAILY NEWS LP
Also Called: New York Daily News
125 Theodore Conrad Dr (07305-4615)
PHONE....................212 210-2100
Fax: 201 946-7046
Michael Aiello, *Branch Mgr*
EMP: 11
SALES (corp-wide): 1.5B **Publicly Held**
WEB: www.nydailynews.com
SIC: 2621 2759 2711 Catalog, magazine & newspaper papers; commercial printing; newspapers
HQ: Daily News, L.P.
4 New York Plz Fl 6
New York NY 10004

(G-4737)
DATAYOG INC
155 Morgan St (07302-2932)
PHONE....................714 253-6558

Bharat Bhate,
EMP: 10
SQ FT: 4,500
SALES (est): 350.3K **Privately Held**
SIC: 7372 Prepackaged software

(G-4738)
DELIGHT FOODS USA LLC
Also Called: Impex
438 Saint Pauls Ave (07306-6126)
P.O. Box 1555, Livingston (07039-7155)
PHONE.................................201 369-1199
Joseph Parayil, *President*
Philip Parayil, *Vice Pres*
Mathew Parayil, *Director*
Alapatt Thomas, *Director*
◆ **EMP:** 11
SQ FT: 5,500
SALES (est): 7MM **Privately Held**
SIC: 5142 2092 Meat, frozen: packaged;
fish, frozen: packaged; fish, frozen: pre-
pared

(G-4739)
DG3 GROUP AMERICA INC (DH)
Also Called: Cgi North America
100 Burma Rd (07305-4623)
PHONE.................................201 793-5000
Fax: 201 333-8428
Tom Saggiomo, *CEO*
Michael Cunningham, *President*
Constantino Riviello, *Project Mgr*
Ricky Franchino, *Production*
Thomas Kelly, *Production*
EMP: 9
SALES (est): 49.5MM
SALES (corp-wide): 352MM **Privately
Held**
WEB: www.cgii.net
SIC: 2752 Commercial printing, offset
HQ: Dg3 Holdings, Llc
100 Burma Rd
Jersey City NJ 07305
201 793-5000

(G-4740)
DG3 HOLDINGS LLC (HQ)
Also Called: Diversfied Globl Grphics Group
100 Burma Rd (07305-4623)
PHONE.................................201 793-5000
Tom Saggiomo, *CEO*
George Iczkovitz, *Production*
Gerald Baillargeon, *CFO*
Brian C Paoli, *VP Sales*
Tom Hunter, *Sales Staff*
EMP: 8 **EST:** 2008
SALES (est): 147.7MM
SALES (corp-wide): 352MM **Privately
Held**
SIC: 2752 Commercial printing, offset
PA: Arsenal Capital Partners Lp
100 Park Ave Fl 31
New York NY 10017
212 771-1717

(G-4741)
DG3 NORTH AMERICA INC
Also Called: Diversfied Globl Grphics Group
100 Burma Rd (07305-4623)
PHONE.................................201 793-5000
Steven Babat, *CEO*
Joe Lindfeldt, *Exec VP*
Robert Needle, *Exec VP*
Seth Diamond, *Senior VP*
Fred Gorra, *Senior VP*
EMP: 405
SQ FT: 167,000
SALES: 160MM
SALES (corp-wide): 205.8MM **Privately
Held**
WEB: www.dg3.com
SIC: 2752 Commercial printing, offset
PA: Resilience Capital Partners Llc
25101 Chagrin Blvd # 350
Cleveland OH 44122
216 292-0200

(G-4742)
DIACRITECH LLC
201 Marin Blvd Apt 1112 (07302-6499)
PHONE.................................732 238-1157
Madhu Rajamani,
Kavitha Rajamani,
EMP: 525
SQ FT: 18,000

SALES: 4MM **Privately Held**
WEB: www.diacritech.com
SIC: 7372 7313 Prepackaged software;
radio, television, publisher representatives

(G-4743)
**DIAMOND HUT JEWELRY
EXCHANGE**
Hudson Mall Rr 440 (07304)
PHONE.................................201 332-5372
Fax: 201 332-2222
Sachin Gupta, *Partner*
Neera Gupta, *General Mgr*
EMP: 7
SALES (est): 862.5K **Privately Held**
SIC: 3911 7631 5094 3479 Jewelry, pre-
cious metal; jewelry repair services; jew-
elry & precious stones; engraving jewelry
silverware, or metal; jewelry stores

(G-4744)
DISCOUNT DIGITAL PRINT LLC
629 Grove St Fl 3 (07310-1249)
PHONE.................................201 659-9600
James Dilworth, *Principal*
EMP: 12 **EST:** 2010
SALES (est): 704.7K **Privately Held**
SIC: 2752 Commercial printing, offset

(G-4745)
**DURABRITE LTG SOLUTIONS
LLC**
4 Beacon Way Apt 514 (07304-6123)
PHONE.................................201 915-0555
Mark Larson, *VP Sales*
Steven Cronley, *Director*
EMP: 6
SALES (est): 602K **Privately Held**
SIC: 3646 7389 Commercial indusl & insti-
tutional electric lighting fixtures;

(G-4746)
EBAOTECH INC USA
2500 Plaza Five Fl 25 (07311-4026)
PHONE.................................917 977-1145
Brenda Anaya, *Administration*
EMP: 4
SALES (est): 79.2K **Privately Held**
SIC: 7372 Prepackaged software
HQ: Ebaotech Corporation
No. 3 Building, Kic Plaza, No. 270,
Songhu Road
Shanghai 20043
216 140-7777

(G-4747)
ELECTROHEAT INDUCTION INC
81 Oakland Ave 3 (07306-2203)
PHONE.................................908 494-0726
Shame Prsna, *Principal*
▲ **EMP:** 4 **EST:** 2011
SALES (est): 266K **Privately Held**
SIC: 3567 Industrial furnaces & ovens

(G-4748)
ELEMENTS TRUFFLES LLC
2 2nd St Apt 1002 (07302-7030)
PHONE.................................908 731-2088
Alak Vasa, *Principal*
EMP: 5 **EST:** 2016
SALES (est): 108.9K **Privately Held**
SIC: 2819 Elements

(G-4749)
**ENTERPRISECC LTD LIABILITY
CO**
521 Palisade Ave (07307-1409)
PHONE.................................201 266-0020
Marco L Chaffiotte, *CEO*
EMP: 7 **EST:** 2013
SALES (est): 807.6K **Privately Held**
SIC: 8711 3699 4813 5065 Construction
& civil engineering; security devices; se-
curity control equipment & systems; tele-
phone/video communications;
communication equipment; telecommuni-
cations consultant

(G-4750)
**FABRIC CHEMICAL
CORPORATION**
61 Cornelison Ave (07304-3403)
PHONE.................................201 432-0440
Fax: 201 432-7997

Andrew Jacobson, *President*
EMP: 9 **EST:** 1936
SQ FT: 15,000
SALES (est): 1.8MM **Privately Held**
SIC: 2842 Cleaning or polishing prepara-
tions

(G-4751)
FABUWOOD CABINETRY CORP
99 Caven Point Rd (07305-4605)
PHONE.................................201 432-6555
Moshe Panzer, *CEO*
Solomon Eidlisz, *General Mgr*
Joel Epstein, *COO*
Joel Weinstein, *VP Opers*
Jay Nussenzweig, *Purch Agent*
◆ **EMP:** 500
SQ FT: 500,000
SALES (est): 115MM **Privately Held**
SIC: 2434 Wood kitchen cabinets

(G-4752)
FLEXICIOUS LLC
57 Sip Ave Apt 4b (07306-3173)
P.O. Box 6350 (07306-0350)
PHONE.................................646 340-5066
Suha Ozal, *Partner*
EMP: 5
SALES (est): 207.4K **Privately Held**
SIC: 7372 Prepackaged software

(G-4753)
FLORENTINE PRESS INC
234 16th St (07310-1196)
PHONE.................................201 386-9200
Timothy Meredith, *Principal*
EMP: 4
SALES (est): 165.2K **Privately Held**
SIC: 2741 Miscellaneous publishing

(G-4754)
FORBES MEDIA LLC
Also Called: Forbes Magazine
499 Washington Blvd (07310-1995)
PHONE.................................212 620-2200
Mike Perlis, *President*
Ann Marinovich, *Vice Pres*
Jorge Consuegra, *Chief Mktg Ofcr*
Mark Howard, *Risk Mgmt Dir*
Sean P Hegarty,
EMP: 80
SALES (est): 20.7MM **Privately Held**
SIC: 2732 2752 Book printing; advertising
posters, lithographed

(G-4755)
FOREST LABORATORIES LLC
185 Hudson St (07311-1209)
PHONE.................................631 436-4534
Taglietti Marco, *Branch Mgr*
EMP: 15 **Privately Held**
SIC: 2834 Pharmaceutical preparations
HQ: Forest Laboratories, Llc
909 3rd Ave Fl 23
New York NY 10022
212 421-7850

(G-4756)
FOREST LABORATORIES LLC
1900 Plaza Five (07311-4032)
PHONE.................................631 501-5399
EMP: 35 **Privately Held**
SIC: 2834 Mfg Pharmaceutical Prepara-
tions
HQ: Forest Laboratories, Llc
909 3rd Ave Fl 23
New York NY 10022
212 421-7850

(G-4757)
**FORSTERS CLEANING &
TAILORING**
Also Called: Hudson Drapery Service
248 Central Ave (07307-3084)
PHONE.................................201 659-4411
Robert Iezzi, *President*
EMP: 5
SQ FT: 5,400
SALES (est): 202.2K **Privately Held**
SIC: 7216 7219 2391 Drycleaning collect-
ing & distributing agency; curtain cleaning
& repair; tailor shop, except custom or
merchant tailor; draperies, plastic & tex-
tile: from purchased materials

(G-4758)
FROYO SKYVIEW LLC
42 Dales Ave (07306-6802)
PHONE.................................718 607-5656
Xuyan Chen, *CEO*
Xiang Wu, *Finance*
Jialin Zhang,
EMP: 8
SALES (est): 550.7K **Privately Held**
SIC: 3944 7389 Games, toys & children's
vehicles;

(G-4759)
**GENERAL PENCIL COMPANY
INC (PA)**
Also Called: Semi-Hex
67 Fleet St (07306-2213)
PHONE.................................201 653-5351
Fax: 650 369-7169
James S Weissenborn, *President*
Katie Vanonconi, *President*
Helmut Bode, *Vice Pres*
David Seeber, *Vice Pres*
Rose Pica, *Purch Dir*
▲ **EMP:** 3 **EST:** 1888
SQ FT: 70,000
SALES (est): 4.9MM **Privately Held**
WEB: www.generalpencil.com
SIC: 3952 Pencil lead: black, indelible or
colored: artists'; crayons: chalk, gypsum,
charcoal, fusains, pastel, wax, etc.

(G-4760)
GL CONSULTING INC (PA)
Also Called: GL Associates
210 Hudson St Ste 1000 (07311-1208)
PHONE.................................201 938-0200
Fax: 201 451-0849
George Lambrianakos, *President*
Roger Elwell, *Vice Pres*
Amelia Ortiz, *Treasurer*
Dino Panayiotarakos, *Admin Sec*
EMP: 20
SALES (est): 3.6MM **Privately Held**
WEB: www.cetova.com
SIC: 7372 Business oriented computer
software

(G-4761)
GLOCAL EXPERTISE LLC
185 Zabriskie St (07307-4316)
P.O. Box 17341 (07307-7341)
PHONE.................................718 928-3839
Yasmin Obriwala,
EMP: 5
SQ FT: 100
SALES: 5MM **Privately Held**
SIC: 3229 8748 5023 Glass furnishings &
accessories; business consulting; decora-
tive home furnishings & supplies

(G-4762)
GRAYDEN INDUSTRIES INC
84 Constitution Way (07305-5487)
PHONE.................................201 761-0788
Claude S Bruell, *President*
EMP: 31
SQ FT: 3,000
SALES (est): 2.6MM **Privately Held**
SIC: 3533 2899 Oil & gas drilling rigs &
equipment; essential oils

(G-4763)
GUM RUNNERS LLC
Also Called: Jolt Energy Gum
333 Washington St 2 (07302-3066)
P.O. Box 201, Lebanon (08833-0201)
PHONE.................................201 333-0756
Laurence Molloy,
Kevin M Gass,
▲ **EMP:** 12
SQ FT: 2,500
SALES (est): 1.5MM **Privately Held**
WEB: www.joltgum.com
SIC: 2067 Chewing gum

(G-4764)
HEALQU LLC
210 Fairmount Ave (07306-3304)
PHONE.................................844 443-2578
Yoel Katz, *Mng Member*
Stanley Salot,
EMP: 5 **Privately Held**
SIC: 3842 Ligatures, medical

(G-4765)
HMS MONACO ET CIE LTD
629 Grove St Fl 5 (07310-1249)
PHONE..............................201 533-0007
Ira Erstling, *President*
Steven Schulman, *Vice Pres*
▲ EMP: 25
SQ FT: 15,000
SALES: 4MM Privately Held
WEB: www.hmsmonaco.com
SIC: 3961 5199 Costume jewelry; gifts & novelties

(G-4766)
HOPE CENTER
43 Charles St (07307-2830)
PHONE..............................201 798-1234
Liz Vidal-Cintron, *President*
EMP: 10
SALES: 1.1MM Privately Held
SIC: 3669 8661 8299 Visual communication systems; Assembly of God Church; musical instrument lessons

(G-4767)
IMAAN TRADING INC ✪
286 Bergen Ave (07305-1620)
PHONE..............................201 779-2062
Liza Azim, *President*
EMP: 5 EST: 2017
SALES (est): 245.4K Privately Held
SIC: 2844 Toilet preparations; perfumes & colognes; cosmetic preparations; toilet preparations

(G-4768)
IPC SYSTEMS INC (PA)
Also Called: IPC Information Systems
3 2nd St Fl Plz10 (07311-4045)
PHONE..............................201 253-2000
Neil Barua, *CEO*
David Brown, *Senior VP*
Lionel Grosclaude, *Senior VP*
Don Henderson, *Senior VP*
Tracy Terrebush, *Research*
▲ EMP: 120
SQ FT: 35,000
SALES (est): 792.4MM Privately Held
SIC: 3661 Telephone & telegraph apparatus

(G-4769)
JON-DA PRINTING CO INC
234 16th St (07310-1196)
PHONE..............................201 653-6200
John Malluzzo, *President*
EMP: 15
SQ FT: 4,000
SALES (est): 2.1MM Privately Held
SIC: 2752 Commercial printing, offset

(G-4770)
JOSEPH C HANSEN COMPANY INC
Also Called: J C Hansen
629 Grove St Ste 26 (07310-1263)
PHONE..............................201 222-1677
Harold Simon, *President*
Joseph Hansen, *Administration*
EMP: 6 EST: 1980
SALES (est): 44.9K Privately Held
WEB: www.josephchansen.com
SIC: 3999 Theatrical scenery

(G-4771)
KENNAMETAL INC
123 Town Square Pl (07310-1756)
PHONE..............................412 248-8200
EMP: 126
SALES (corp-wide): 2.3B Publicly Held
SIC: 3545 Cutting tools for machine tools
PA: Kennametal Inc.
600 Grant St Ste 5100
Pittsburgh PA 15219
412 248-8000

(G-4772)
KOMAR INC
Also Called: Komar Sleepwear
90 Hudson St Fl 9 (07302-3900)
PHONE..............................212 725-1500
Charles Komar, *CEO*
David L Komar, *President*
Herman H Komar, *Director*
EMP: 450 EST: 1994

SALES (est): 74.7K
SALES (corp-wide): 310.7MM Privately Held
SIC: 5651 5641 5139 3149 Unisex clothing stores; children's & infants' wear stores; shoes; athletic shoes, except rubber or plastic
PA: Charles Komar & Sons, Inc.
90 Hudson St Fl 9
Jersey City NJ 07302
212 725-1500

(G-4773)
KOMAR INTIMATES LLC (HQ)
90 Hudson St (07302-3900)
P.O. Box 5227, New York NY (10087-5227)
PHONE..............................212 725-1500
Charles Komar, *CEO*
EMP: 14
SQ FT: 2,400
SALES: 57.7MM
SALES (corp-wide): 310.7MM Privately Held
SIC: 2341 2254 5621 Panties: women's, misses', children's & infants'; nightwear (nightgowns, negligees, pajamas), knit; women's clothing stores; women's sportswear
PA: Charles Komar & Sons, Inc.
90 Hudson St Fl 9
Jersey City NJ 07302
212 725-1500

(G-4774)
KOMAR KIDS LLC (HQ)
90 Hudson St (07302-3900)
PHONE..............................212 725-1500
Charlie Komar, *CEO*
Jay Harris, *COO*
Harry Gaffney, *CFO*
David Komar, *Admin Sec*
▲ EMP: 10
SQ FT: 15,000
SALES (est): 6MM
SALES (corp-wide): 310.7MM Privately Held
SIC: 2254 Nightwear (nightgowns, negligees, pajamas), knit; underwear, knit
PA: Charles Komar & Sons, Inc.
90 Hudson St Fl 9
Jersey City NJ 07302
212 725-1500

(G-4775)
L A S PRINTING CO
3035 John F Kennedy Blvd (07306-3669)
PHONE..............................201 991-5362
Fax: 201 991-7367
Joseph R Conti, *President*
Peter Miliotis, *Vice Pres*
EMP: 4
SQ FT: 6,000
SALES (est): 379.1K Privately Held
WEB: www.lasprinting.com
SIC: 2752 2791 Commercial printing, lithographic; photocomposition, for the printing trade

(G-4776)
LIBERTY PARK RACEWAY LLC
99 Caven Point Rd (07305-4605)
PHONE..............................201 333-7223
Eyal Farage, *Mng Member*
EMP: 9
SALES (est): 1.3MM Privately Held
SIC: 3644 Raceways

(G-4777)
LINDER & COMPANY INC
Also Called: Linder Graphics
1183 W Side Ave (07306-6112)
PHONE..............................201 386-8788
Fax: 201 386-1222
George Linder, *President*
Camille Linder, *Treasurer*
EMP: 17 EST: 1852
SQ FT: 32,000
SALES (est): 3.3MM Privately Held
WEB: www.linderco.com
SIC: 2752 Photolithographic printing

(G-4778)
LOGOMANIA INC
Also Called: Composition Printing
110 1/2 Erie St (07302-2076)
P.O. Box 55 (07303-0055)
PHONE..............................201 798-0531
Allen Gradin, *President*
Lynn Gradin, *Admin Sec*
EMP: 4
SQ FT: 1,000
SALES: 400K Privately Held
SIC: 5943 2759 Stationery stores; commercial printing

(G-4779)
LOREAL USA PRODUCTS INC
Also Called: It Cosmetics
111 Town Square Pl # 317 (07310-1755)
PHONE..............................732 873-3520
EMP: 4
SALES (corp-wide): 4.2B Privately Held
SIC: 2844 Hair coloring preparations
HQ: L'oreal Usa Products, Inc.
10 Hudson Yards
New York NY 10001

(G-4780)
M LONDON INC (PA)
629 Grove St Fl 8 (07310-1264)
PHONE..............................201 459-6460
Michael Bannout, *President*
▲ EMP: 30
SQ FT: 30,000
SALES: 2.9MM Privately Held
SIC: 3171 3172 Women's handbags & purses; wallets; billfolds

(G-4781)
M2 COMMUNICATIONS INC
30 Montgomery St Ste 700 (07302-3841)
PHONE..............................201 433-1746
Fax: 201 433-9393
Roy Wilschut, *President*
Didier Merle, *Exec VP*
EMP: 25 EST: 1997
SQ FT: 10,000
SALES: 1.5MM Privately Held
WEB: www.informedonline.com
SIC: 8748 2721 Business consulting; trade journals: publishing & printing

(G-4782)
MAYA TRADING CORPORATION
Also Called: Maya Liquidation
746-748 Tonnelle Ave (07307)
PHONE..............................201 533-1400
Antounyous Gurguis, *President*
EMP: 5
SQ FT: 15,000
SALES (est): 507K Privately Held
SIC: 3253 Floor tile, ceramic

(G-4783)
METAL MGT PITTSBURGH INC
Also Called: Sims Metal Management
1 Linden Ave E (07305-4726)
PHONE..............................201 333-2902
Galdino Claro, *CEO*
Bob Kelman, *President*
Dennis O'Loughlin, *President*
Robert C Larry, *CFO*
Kyle Mills, *Treasurer*
▼ EMP: 43 EST: 1958
SQ FT: 12,000
SALES (est): 43.3MM Privately Held
WEB: www.mtlm.com
SIC: 5093 3341 Nonferrous metals scrap; secondary nonferrous metals
HQ: Metal Management, Inc.
200 W Madison St Ste 3600
Chicago IL 60606
312 645-0700

(G-4784)
MITSUBISHI TANABE PHARMA (DH)
525 Wshngton Blvd Fl 1400 Flr 1400 (07310)
PHONE..............................908 607-1950
Eiji Tanaka, *President*
Armand Famiglietti, *VP Opers*
Partha Banerjee, *Research*
Julie Reinhart, *Human Res Mgr*
EMP: 21

SALES (est): 17.2MM
SALES (corp-wide): 34.9B Privately Held
SIC: 2834 Pharmaceutical preparations
HQ: Mitsubishi Tanabe Pharma Corporation
3-2-10, Doshomachi, Chuo-Ku
Osaka OSK 541-0
662 055-085

(G-4785)
MOJO ORGANICS INC
101 Hudson St Fl 21 (07302-3929)
PHONE..............................201 633-6519
Glenn Simpson, *Ch of Bd*
Peter Spinner, *COO*
EMP: 3
SALES: 1.3MM Privately Held
SIC: 2037 Fruit juices

(G-4786)
MOSCOVA ENTERPRISES INC
101 Hudson St (07302-3915)
PHONE..............................848 628-4873
Vickens Moscova, *Principal*
EMP: 10
SQ FT: 1,000
SALES (est): 468.5K Privately Held
SIC: 7311 2741 8742 Advertising agencies; advertising consultant; ; management consulting services; new business start-up consultant

(G-4787)
NAUTICA RETAIL USA
545 Washington Blvd Fl 8 (07310-1619)
PHONE..............................212 541-5757
EMP: 5 EST: 2015
SALES (est): 130.6K Privately Held
SIC: 2329 Men's & boys' sportswear & athletic clothing

(G-4788)
NES COMPANY INC
2500 Plz 5 Haborsde Finan (07395-0001)
PHONE..............................973 795-1519
Jared Sandman, *President*
▲ EMP: 5
SALES (est): 1MM Privately Held
SIC: 3821 3561 Vacuum pumps, laboratory; pumps & pumping equipment; industrial pumps & parts

(G-4789)
NICHOLAS GALVANIZING CO INC
120 Duffield Ave (07306-6123)
PHONE..............................201 795-1010
Robert Gregory, *President*
Angel Torres, *General Mgr*
EMP: 30 EST: 1949
SQ FT: 18,000
SALES (est): 3.5MM Privately Held
SIC: 3479 Galvanizing of iron, steel or end-formed products

(G-4790)
NILSSON ELECTRICAL LABORATORY
333 W Side Ave (07305-1127)
PHONE..............................201 521-4860
John Brown, *President*
EMP: 6 EST: 1919
SQ FT: 4,500
SALES (est): 500K Privately Held
WEB: www.nilssoneleclab.com
SIC: 3612 5065 7629 Electronic meter transformers; electronic parts & equipment; electrical repair shops

(G-4791)
NIRWANA FOODS LLC
778 Newark Ave (07306-3807)
PHONE..............................201 659-2200
Jagdar Singh, *President*
▲ EMP: 11
SALES (est): 1.6MM Privately Held
SIC: 2086 Iced tea & fruit drinks, bottled & canned

(G-4792)
NORTH AMERICAN FRONTIER CORP
195 New York Ave (07307-1654)
PHONE..............................201 222-1931
Vincent Manz, *Principal*
EMP: 25

G E O G R A P H I C

SQ FT: 27,000
SALES (est): 1.8MM **Privately Held**
SIC: 3199 Leather garments

(G-4793)
NSGV INC
Also Called: Forbes Magazine
499 Washington Blvd Fl 9 (07310-2055)
PHONE....................212 620-2200
Jill Harris, *Manager*
EMP: 4
SALES (corp-wide): 181.1MM **Privately Held**
WEB: www.forbes.com
SIC: 2721 Magazines: publishing only, not printed on site
HQ: Nsgv Inc.
　499 Washington Blvd Fl 9
　Jersey City NJ 07310
　212 620-2200

(G-4794)
NU GRAFIX INC
430 Communipaw Ave (07304-3663)
PHONE....................201 413-1776
Charles Chaffey, *CEO*
EMP: 50
SALES (est): 4.9MM **Privately Held**
SIC: 2891 Laminating compounds

(G-4795)
ORENS DAILY ROAST INC
430 Communipaw Ave Ste 13
(07304-3667)
PHONE....................201 432-2008
Judd Meyerson, *Branch Mgr*
EMP: 15
SALES (corp-wide): 14.1MM **Privately Held**
SIC: 2095 5149 Roasted coffee; coffee & tea
PA: Oren's Daily Roast Inc
　12 E 46th St Fl 6
　New York NY 10017
　212 348-5400

(G-4796)
ORIENT ORIGINALS INC
Also Called: Home Warehouse Outlet
55 Edward Hart Dr (07305-4607)
PHONE....................201 332-5005
Rituraaj Baijal, *President*
Rahul Bhargava, *Merchandise Mgr*
▲ EMP: 30
SQ FT: 25,000
SALES (est): 5.9MM **Privately Held**
WEB: www.textileshop.com
SIC: 1541 2392 Industrial buildings & warehouses; cushions & pillows

(G-4797)
PALISADE LUMBER & SUPPLY INC (PA)
432 Palisade Ave (07307-1608)
P.O. Box 7075 (07307-0075)
PHONE....................201 656-4400
Fax: 201 653-6890
Daniel Goff, *President*
EMP: 6
SQ FT: 16,000
SALES (est): 3.4MM **Privately Held**
WEB: www.palisadelumber.com
SIC: 5211 2431 Lumber products; millwork

(G-4798)
PENNETTA & SONS
428 Hoboken Ave (07306-2696)
PHONE....................201 420-1693
Fax: 201 420-9424
May Pennetta, *President*
Mike Ventresca, *General Mgr*
Victor Pennetta Jr, *Vice Pres*
David Taylor, *VP Sales*
EMP: 30
SQ FT: 18,000
SALES (est): 4.8MM **Privately Held**
WEB: www.pennetta.com
SIC: 1711 8748 7692 Mechanical contractor; warm air heating & air conditioning contractor; energy conservation consultant; welding repair

(G-4799)
PENTA DIGITAL INCORPORATED
234 16th St Fl 8 (07310-1196)
PHONE....................201 839-5392

Jonathan Chung, *President*
EMP: 8
SALES (est): 509.8K **Privately Held**
WEB: www.pentadigitalinc.com
SIC: 2759 Commercial printing

(G-4800)
PENTAGRAPHIX OFFSET PRTG INC
629 Grove St Ste 701 (07310-1264)
PHONE....................201 526-9300
Fax: 201 526-9298
EMP: 13
SQ FT: 27,000
SALES: 4.5MM **Privately Held**
SIC: 2752 Lithographic Commercial Printing

(G-4801)
PIC GRAPHICS
926 Newark Ave Ste 400 (07306-6337)
PHONE....................201 420-5040
Nat Zucker, *President*
Howard Zucker, *Vice Pres*
Julia Zucker, *Vice Pres*
Phillip Zucker, *Vice Pres*
▲ EMP: 32
SQ FT: 30,000
SALES: 9MM **Privately Held**
WEB: www.picgraphics.com
SIC: 3953 Marking devices

(G-4802)
POLAR TRUCK SALES
350 Sip Ave (07306-6525)
PHONE....................201 246-1010
Raymond Higgins, *President*
EMP: 30
SALES (est): 5.2MM **Privately Held**
SIC: 5521 3711 Pickups & vans, used; truck & tractor truck assembly

(G-4803)
POLARIS CONSULTING & SVCS LTD
111 Town Square Pl # 340 (07310-1755)
PHONE....................732 590-8151
Naveen Tiwari, *Manager*
EMP: 10
SALES (corp-wide): 91.5MM **Privately Held**
SIC: 7372 Prepackaged software
HQ: Polaris Consulting & Services Ltd.
　20 Corporate Pl S
　Piscataway NJ 08854

(G-4804)
POLY-VERSION INC
49 Fisk St (07305-1100)
PHONE....................201 451-7600
Phillip Goldschmiedt, *President*
Teresa Mert, *Vice Pres*
▲ EMP: 35
SQ FT: 120,000
SALES (est): 6MM **Privately Held**
SIC: 3089 Work gloves, plastic

(G-4805)
POWERTRUNK INC
66 York St Ste 4 (07302-3839)
PHONE....................201 630-4520
Jose Martin, *CEO*
David Domingo, *President*
Morne Stramrood, *Vice Pres*
Javier Murad, *Technical Mgr*
Christopher Ramsden, *VP Sales*
EMP: 4
SALES (est): 709.6K
SALES (corp-wide): 66.5MM **Privately Held**
SIC: 3663 Radio & TV communications equipment
HQ: Teltronic Sa
　Calle F (Poligono Industrial Malpica)
　(Oeste), Parc. 12
　Zaragoza 50016
　976 465-656

(G-4806)
PROGRESS PRINTING CO
338 Montgomery St (07302-4009)
P.O. Box 442 (07303-0442)
PHONE....................201 433-3133
Fax: 201 433-0005
Manny Portnoy, *President*
Lois Porco, *Vice Pres*

EMP: 11
SQ FT: 6,000
SALES (est): 1.2MM **Privately Held**
WEB: www.progressprinting.com
SIC: 2752 Commercial printing, offset

(G-4807)
PROJECT FEED USA INC
127a Dwight St (07305-3227)
PHONE....................201 443-7143
Kevin Wolfe, *Director*
EMP: 10
SALES (est): 283.4K **Privately Held**
SIC: 2032 Canned specialties

(G-4808)
PROTECTION INDUSTRIES CORP
107 York St (07302-3701)
P.O. Box 348 (07303-0348)
PHONE....................201 333-8050
William J Hill, *Ch of Bd*
EMP: 17
SALES (corp-wide): 2.6MM **Privately Held**
SIC: 5063 3669 Control & signal wire & cable, including coaxial; fire detection systems, electric
PA: Protection Industries Corp
　2897 Main St
　Stratford CT 06614
　203 375-9393

(G-4809)
PROXIMO DISTILLERS LLC
333 Washington St Fl 4 (07302-3066)
PHONE....................201 204-1718
Mark Teasdale, *President*
EMP: 82
SALES (est): 12.2MM **Privately Held**
SIC: 2082 Malt beverages
PA: Proximo Spirits, Inc.
　333 Washington St Ste 401
　Jersey City NJ 07302

(G-4810)
PURELY ORGANIC SA LLC
142 Liberty Ave (07306-4920)
PHONE....................201 942-0400
Raul Munoz, *CEO*
Raul Muoz, *CEO*
John Justiniano, *Principal*
Marcelo Muoz, *COO*
EMP: 4
SALES (est): 109.8K **Privately Held**
SIC: 2911 5191 Residues; fertilizers & agricultural chemicals; pesticides

(G-4811)
R WORLD ENTERPRISES
197 Congress St (07307-3415)
PHONE....................201 795-2428
Marian Pacailler, *Partner*
Gene Pacailler, *Partner*
EMP: 5
SALES (est): 497.6K **Privately Held**
SIC: 2048 5199 Bird food, prepared; pet supplies

(G-4812)
RAJBHOG FOODS INC
60 Amity St (07304-3510)
PHONE....................551 222-4700
Ajit Mody, *Branch Mgr*
EMP: 5 **Privately Held**
SIC: 3556 Food products machinery
PA: Rajbhog Foods Inc.
　812 Newark Ave
　Jersey City NJ 07306

(G-4813)
RAJBHOG FOODS INC (PA)
812 Newark Ave (07306-3809)
PHONE....................201 395-9400
Sanjiv Mod, *President*
Sachin Mody, *Vice Pres*
Satish Patel, *Sales Staff*
▲ EMP: 7
SQ FT: 37,000
SALES (est): 1.9MM **Privately Held**
SIC: 3556 Food products machinery

(G-4814)
RAJBHOG FOODS(NJ) INC
60 Amity St (07304-3510)
PHONE....................551 222-4700

Sanjiv Mody, *President*
Sachin Mody, *Vice Pres*
Ajit Mody, *Admin Sec*
EMP: 125
SQ FT: 35,000
SALES: 8MM **Privately Held**
SIC: 2096 2013 5143 2038 Potato chips & similar snacks; frozen meats from purchased meat; frozen dairy desserts; breakfasts, frozen & packaged; dinners, frozen & packaged; ice cream & frozen desserts

(G-4815)
RAMBUSCH DECORATING COMPANY
Also Called: Rambusch Lighting
160 Cornelison Ave (07304-3513)
PHONE....................201 333-2525
Fax: 201 433-3355
Martin V Rambusch, *Ch of Bd*
Edwin P Rambusch, *President*
▲ EMP: 41 **EST:** 1891
SQ FT: 5,000
SALES: 7.5MM **Privately Held**
WEB: www.rambusch.com
SIC: 3646 3231 3446 8742 Commercial indusl & institutional electric lighting fixtures; stained glass: made from purchased glass; architectural metalwork; industry specialist consultants

(G-4816)
RECRUIT CO LTD
Also Called: Recruit USA
111 Pavonia Ave (07310-1755)
PHONE....................201 216-0600
Fax: 201 216-3116
Janet Chalmers, *Branch Mgr*
EMP: 35
SALES (corp-wide): 20.4B **Privately Held**
SIC: 2721 6512 Magazines: publishing only, not printed on site; commercial & industrial building operation
PA: Recruit Holdings Co.,Ltd.
　1-9-2, Marunouchi
　Chiyoda-Ku TKY 100-0
　368 351-111

(G-4817)
REDSTAGE NETWORKS LLC
111 Town Square Pl (07310-1755)
PHONE....................888 335-2747
Adam Morris, *CEO*
Anthony Latona, *Chief Mktg Ofcr*
Kristopher Silva, *Sr Project Mgr*
EMP: 18
SALES (est): 785K
SALES (corp-wide): 1.1MM **Privately Held**
SIC: 7372 7371 Application computer software; custom computer programming services
PA: Fulcrum Worldwide, Inc.
　111 Town Square Pl # 1215
　Jersey City NJ 07310
　201 523-7555

(G-4818)
RELAYWARE INC
30 Montgomery St Ste 1210 (07302-3821)
PHONE....................201 433-3331
Debra Padula, *Business Anlyst*
Jonathan Pack, *Marketing Staff*
EMP: 12
SALES (est): 1.2MM
SALES (corp-wide): 7.1MM **Privately Held**
SIC: 7372 Business oriented computer software
HQ: Relayware, Inc.
　303 Twin Dolphin Dr Fl 6
　Redwood City CA 94065
　650 632-4520

(G-4819)
RELIABLE PAPER RECYCLING INC
1 Caven Point Ave (07305-4603)
PHONE....................201 333-5244
Leonard Pirrello, *President*
Kiki Emmons, *Credit Mgr*
Gina Marquez, *Office Mgr*
Joseph Pirrello, *CTO*
▼ EMP: 105
SQ FT: 45,000

SALES (est): 21.2MM **Privately Held**
SIC: **4953** 2611 5093 Recycling, waste
materials; pulp mills; waste paper

(G-4820)
RONALD PERRY
Also Called: Uniquiwa's
14 Westervelt Pl 1 (07304-3428)
PHONE.............................201 702-2407
Ronald Perry, *Owner*
EMP: 10 EST: 2015
SALES (est): 319.7K **Privately Held**
SIC: **2326** Service apparel (baker, barber,
lab, etc.), washable: men's

(G-4821)
SAKSOFT INC (HQ)
30 Montgomery St Ste 1240 (07302-3834)
PHONE.............................201 451-4609
Aditya Krishna, *CEO*
Suman Kumar Mukherji, *Regl Sales Mgr*
EMP: 110
SQ FT: 950
SALES (est): 27.1MM **Privately Held**
WEB: www.saksoft.com
SIC: **7371** 7372 Computer software devel-
opment & applications; prepackaged soft-
ware

(G-4822)
SANDKAMP WOODWORKS LLC
430 Communipaw Ave Ste 1 (07304-3699)
PHONE.............................201 200-0101
Anthony Sandkamp,
EMP: 4
SALES (est): 420K **Privately Held**
WEB: www.sandkampwoodworks.com
SIC: **2431** Interior & ornamental woodwork
& trim

(G-4823)
SARA EMPORIUM INC
833 Newark Ave (07306-3808)
PHONE.............................201 792-7222
Ahmed Akbary, *President*
EMP: 4 EST: 1997
SQ FT: 1,100
SALES: 3.5MM **Privately Held**
SIC: **3911** Jewelry, precious metal

(G-4824)
SCIVANTAGE INC (PA)
499 Washington Blvd Fl 11 (07310-2017)
PHONE.............................646 452-0001
Fax: 646 452-0049
Adnane Charchour, *CEO*
Bill Wagner, *President*
Christian J Farber, *Exec VP*
Susan Massaro, *Exec VP*
Cameron Routh, *Exec VP*
EMP: 80
SQ FT: 30,000
SALES (est): 46.7MM **Privately Held**
WEB: www.scivantage.com
SIC: **7372** Business oriented computer
software

(G-4825)
SCYNEXIS INC
1 Evertrust Plz Fl 13 (07302-3051)
PHONE.............................201 884-5485
Guy Macdonald, *Ch of Bd*
Marco Taglietti, *President*
Eric Francois, *CFO*
David Angulo, *Chief Mktg Ofcr*
Scott Sukenick, *General Counsel*
EMP: 19 EST: 1999
SQ FT: 10,141
SALES: 257K **Privately Held**
WEB: www.scynexis.com
SIC: **2834** 8731 Pharmaceutical prepara-
tions; commercial physical research; bio-
logical research

(G-4826)
SELFMADE LLC
Also Called: Selfmade Boutique
290 Hoboken Ave (07306-1692)
PHONE.............................201 792-8968
EMP: 5
SALES (est): 359.7K **Privately Held**
SIC: **2329** 3161 5136 5621 Men's &
boys' sportswear & athletic clothing; cloth-
ing & apparel carrying cases; men's &
boys' clothing; boutiques

(G-4827)
SIGNS & CUSTOM METAL INC
62 Monitor St (07304-4019)
PHONE.............................201 200-0110
Fax: 201 200-1717
Shan Kumar, *President*
EMP: 12
SQ FT: 8,000
SALES (est): 1.8MM **Privately Held**
WEB: www.signscm.com
SIC: **5099** 3993 Signs, except electric;
signs & advertising specialties

(G-4828)
SIMS LEE INC (PA)
Also Called: Lee Sims Chocolates
743 Bergen Ave (07306-4795)
PHONE.............................201 433-1308
Fax: 201 433-0288
Nicholas Vlahakis, *CEO*
Allison McKernan, *President*
Valerie Vlahakis, *Corp Secy*
Susan Coviello, *Manager*
EMP: 7
SQ FT: 2,000
SALES (est): 772.8K **Privately Held**
WEB: www.leesims.com
SIC: **2064** 5441 Candy & other confec-
tionery products; chocolate candy, except
solid chocolate; jellybeans; candy

(G-4829)
SIRMA GROUP INC
1 Evertrust Plz Ste 1103 (07302-3086)
PHONE.............................646 357-3067
EMP: 400
SQ FT: 700
SALES (est): 3.9MM **Privately Held**
SIC: **7371** 7372 Computer Programming
Svc Prepackaged Software Svc

(G-4830)
SOH LLC
150 Bay St Apt 715 (07302-5917)
PHONE.............................646 943-4066
Song OH, *President*
Glen Conn, *Vice Pres*
EMP: 46 EST: 2009
SQ FT: 1,500
SALES (est): 665.5K **Privately Held**
SIC: **2231** Apparel & outerwear broadwo-
ven fabrics

(G-4831)
STANLEY BLACK & DECKER INC
Also Called: Stanley Tools
123 Town Square Pl (07310-1756)
PHONE.............................860 225-5111
EMP: 11
SALES (corp-wide): 12.7B **Publicly Held**
WEB: www.stanleyworks.com
SIC: **3423** Hand & edge tools
PA: Stanley Black & Decker, Inc.
1000 Stanley Dr
New Britain CT 06053
860 225-5111

(G-4832)
STAR SNACKS CO LLC
111 Port Jersey Blvd (07305-4513)
PHONE.............................201 200-9820
Fax: 201 200-9827
Jacob Fleischer, *Site Mgr*
David Giuliani, *QC Mgr*
Don Markey, *QC Mgr*
Rafie Miller, *CFO*
Sruly Weinberger, *Sales Staff*
◆ EMP: 500
SQ FT: 160,000
SALES: 242MM **Privately Held**
SIC: **2068** Seeds: dried, dehydrated, salted
or roasted

(G-4833)
STATEWIDE GRANITE AND MARBLE
Also Called: Statewide Granite & Marble
109 Carlton Ave (07306-3403)
PHONE.............................201 653-1700
Linda Coviello, *President*
Donato Capozza, *Vice Pres*
EMP: 11
SQ FT: 20,000

SALES (est): 1.2MM **Privately Held**
SIC: **5032** 3281 Granite building stone;
marble building stone; marble, building:
cut & shaped; granite, cut & shaped;
switchboard panels, slate

(G-4834)
STEPS CLOTHING INC
30 Mall Dr W Unit B59a (07310-1615)
PHONE.............................201 420-1496
Susan Yu, *Branch Mgr*
EMP: 21
SALES (corp-wide): 15.5MM **Privately Held**
SIC: **5137** 2389 Women's & children's
clothing; apparel for handicapped
PA: Steps Clothing, Inc.
662 Dell Rd
Carlstadt NJ 07072
201 438-9311

(G-4835)
STUDIO DELLARTE
234 16th St Fl 1 (07310-1196)
PHONE.............................718 599-3715
Fax: 718 599-4738
Jeremy Lebensohn, *Owner*
EMP: 5
SALES (est): 513.4K **Privately Held**
WEB: www.studiodellarte.com
SIC: **3446** Architectural metalwork

(G-4836)
SURUCHI FOODS LLC
114 Baldwin Ave Ste A (07306-2050)
PHONE.............................201 432-2201
▲ EMP: 5
SALES (est): 340K **Privately Held**
SIC: **2099** Mfg Food Preparations

(G-4837)
THOMAS RUSSO & SONS INC
854 Communipaw Ave (07304-1305)
PHONE.............................201 332-4159
Fax: 201 332-1940
Thomas Russo, *President*
Concetta Russo, *Admin Sec*
EMP: 5 EST: 1919
SQ FT: 5,500
SALES (est): 467.5K **Privately Held**
SIC: **3441** Fabricated structural metal

(G-4838)
TOTAL AMERICAN SERVICES INC (PA)
100 Town Square Pl # 401 (07310-2778)
PHONE.............................206 626-3500
Ronald W Haddock, *President*
◆ EMP: 12 EST: 1999
SALES (est): 169.4MM **Privately Held**
SIC: **2911** 4612 5541 2895 Petroleum re-
fining; crude petroleum pipelines; gaso-
line service stations; carbon black

(G-4839)
U I S INDUSTRIES INC (PA)
15 Exchange Pl Ste 1120 (07302-4937)
PHONE.............................201 946-2600
Andrew Pietrini, *President*
Joseph F Arrigo, *Vice Pres*
▲ EMP: 800
SQ FT: 6,000
SALES (est): 26.8MM **Privately Held**
SIC: **2064** Candy & other confectionery
products

(G-4840)
U S TECH SOLUTIONS INC (PA)
10 Exchange Pl Ste 1710 (07302-4934)
PHONE.............................201 524-9600
Manoj Agarwal, *CEO*
Debabrata Ghosh, *Technical Staff*
Shaik Mohsin, *Technical Staff*
Sunny Nalkari, *Technical Staff*
Sorav Rana, *Technical Staff*
EMP: 78
SQ FT: 20,000
SALES: 120MM **Privately Held**
SIC: **7379** 7372 Computer related consult-
ing services; prepackaged software

(G-4841)
US NEWS & WORLD REPORT INC
125 Theodore Conrad Dr (07305-4615)
PHONE.............................212 716-6800
Mort Zuckerman, *Principal*
EMP: 11
SALES (corp-wide): 108.3MM **Privately Held**
SIC: **2721** Periodicals
PA: U.S. News & World Report, Inc.
120 5th Ave Fl 7
New York NY 10011
212 716-6800

(G-4842)
UTAX USA INC
30 Montgomery St Ste 1320 (07302-3858)
PHONE.............................201 433-1200
Yasuhiro Sasho, *President*
▲ EMP: 8
SQ FT: 1,700
SALES (est): 929.2K **Privately Held**
SIC: **3582** Commercial laundry equipment

(G-4843)
VIGILANT DESIGN
535 Communipaw Ave (07304-2940)
PHONE.............................201 432-3900
Fax: 973 694-5805
Darren Vigilant, *Owner*
EMP: 5
SALES (est): 661.5K **Privately Held**
WEB: www.vigilantdesign.com
SIC: **3471** Finishing, metals or formed
products

(G-4844)
VIVIS LIFE LLC
Also Called: Partake Foods
25 Park Ln S Apt 709 (07310-3121)
P.O. Box 1108, Hoboken (07030-1108)
PHONE.............................201 798-1938
Denise Woodard, *Mng Member*
Jeremy Woodard,
EMP: 2 EST: 2016
SALES: 1MM **Privately Held**
SIC: **2043** 7389 Cereal breakfast foods;
oatmeal: prepared as cereal breakfast
food;

(G-4845)
W W JEWELERS INC
Also Called: W W Manufacturing Jewelers
35 Journal Sq Ste 231 (07306-4024)
PHONE.............................718 392-4500
William Jacoby, *CEO*
David Bellman, *Vice Pres*
Stuart Kuropatkin, *Vice Pres*
Shirley Jacoby, *Treasurer*
Lynn Jacoby, *Admin Sec*
EMP: 75 EST: 1946
SQ FT: 20,000
SALES (est): 9.1MM **Privately Held**
WEB: www.wwjewelers.com
SIC: **3911** Jewelry, precious metal; rings,
finger: precious metal

(G-4846)
WALTER MACHINE CO INC
84 Cambridge Ave 98 (07307-2101)
P.O. Box 7700 (07307-0700)
PHONE.............................201 656-5654
Fax: 201 656-0318
Donald R Chatrnuck, *President*
Donald W Chatrnuck, *Vice Pres*
Karen Chatrnuck, *Treasurer*
Elinor Chatrnuck, *Admin Sec*
▲ EMP: 30
SQ FT: 35,000
SALES (est): 6.4MM **Privately Held**
WEB: www.waltergear.com
SIC: **3566** 3585 Gears, power transmis-
sion, except automotive; coolers, milk &
water: electric

(G-4847)
WEINMAN BROS INC
111 Town Square Pl # 434 (07310-2766)
PHONE.............................212 695-8116
Robert Weinman, *President*
EMP: 25
SALES (est): 2.7MM **Privately Held**
SIC: **3911** Jewelry, precious metal

GEOGRAPHIC

(G-4848)
WILLIAM ROBERT GRAPHICS INC
234 16th St Fl 7 (07310-1196)
PHONE....................................201 239-7400
Robert William Horneck, *President*
EMP: 6
SQ FT: 7,000
SALES (est): 750K **Privately Held**
SIC: 2752 Commercial printing, offset

(G-4849)
WILLOW RUN CONSTRUCTION INC
67 Pollock Ave (07305-1109)
PHONE....................................201 659-7266
Michael Zaccaria, *President*
Marilyn Zaccaria, *Admin Sec*
EMP: 10
SALES (est): 538.5K **Privately Held**
SIC: 7692 Welding repair

(G-4850)
WISELY PRODUCTS LLC
77 Hudson St Apt 2406 (07302-8525)
PHONE....................................929 329-9188
Douglass Lee,
EMP: 6
SQ FT: 1,000
SALES: 9.9MM **Privately Held**
SIC: 5021 3648 Outdoor lighting equipment; outdoor & lawn furniture

(G-4851)
WRENCH BROTHERS LLC
327 Newark Ave (07302-2209)
PHONE....................................201 222-0301
EMP: 5
SALES (est): 570.6K **Privately Held**
SIC: 2911 Petroleum Refiner

(G-4852)
XCEEDIUM INC
30 Montgomery St Ste 1020 (07302-3836)
PHONE....................................201 536-1000
Fax: 201 536-1200
Glenn C Hazard, *CEO*
Richard Rose, *CFO*
Aimee Rhodes, *VP Mktg*
Larry Lennhoff, *Software Dev*
EMP: 53
SQ FT: 5,000
SALES (est): 7.1MM **Privately Held**
WEB: www.xceedium.com
SIC: 3571 Electronic computers

Jobstown
Burlington County

(G-4853)
ALMA PARK ALPACAS
2800 Monmouth Rd (08041-2214)
PHONE....................................732 620-1052
Alma Park, *Principal*
EMP: 5
SALES (est): 492.7K **Privately Held**
SIC: 2231 Alpacas, mohair: woven

(G-4854)
ATLANTIC LINING CO INC
2206 Saylors Pond Rd 2 (08041-9990)
PHONE....................................609 723-2400
Fax: 609 620-1101
Nancy L Taylor, *President*
Joshua Pell, *General Mgr*
John Brancato, *Superintendent*
Barry Garland, *Superintendent*
Nick Lascala, *Superintendent*
EMP: 45
SQ FT: 1,200
SALES (est): 13.5MM **Privately Held**
WEB: www.atlanticlining.com
SIC: 1799 2821 Protective lining installation, underground (sewage, etc.); polypropylene resins

Johnsonburg
Warren County

(G-4855)
RUBBER FAB & MOLDING INC
1100 Rte 519 (07846)
PHONE....................................908 852-7725
William Washer, *President*
Sharon Washer, *Vice Pres*
EMP: 6
SQ FT: 4,000
SALES (est): 1.2MM **Privately Held**
WEB: www.rubber-fab.com
SIC: 3052 Rubber hose

Keansburg
Monmouth County

(G-4856)
J AND S SPORTING APPAREL LLC
Also Called: Smitteez Sportswear
224 Main St (07734-1752)
P.O. Box 274 (07734-0274)
PHONE....................................732 787-5500
James W Smith, *Mng Member*
EMP: 4
SQ FT: 2,400
SALES: 250K **Privately Held**
SIC: 3949 2759 2395 Sporting & athletic goods; screen printing; embroidery & art needlework

Kearny
Hudson County

(G-4857)
A L WILSON CHEMICAL CO
Also Called: Novel Technology Labs
1050 Harrison Ave (07032-5941)
P.O. Box 207 (07032-0207)
PHONE....................................201 997-3300
Fax: 201 997-5122
Fred G Schwarzmann Sr, *CEO*
Bob Edwards, *President*
Jeff Schwarz, *President*
Fred G Schwarzmann Jr, *President*
Rich Lindemann, *Facilities Mgr*
▼ EMP: 17
SQ FT: 22,000
SALES (est): 4MM **Privately Held**
WEB: www.alwilson.com
SIC: 2842 Drycleaning preparations

(G-4858)
ALDEN - LEEDS INC
100 Hackensack Ave (07032-4657)
PHONE....................................973 344-7986
Jeffery Houtz, *Branch Mgr*
EMP: 4
SALES (est): 264.4K
SALES (corp-wide): 38MM **Privately Held**
SIC: 5091 3949 Swimming pools, equipment & supplies; water sports equipment
PA: Alden - Leeds, Inc.
55 Jacobus Ave Ste 1
Kearny NJ 07032
973 589-3544

(G-4859)
ALDEN - LEEDS INC (PA)
Also Called: Alden Leeds
55 Jacobus Ave Ste 1 (07032-4584)
PHONE....................................973 589-3544
Fax: 973 589-5093
Mark Epstein, *President*
Andy Epstein, *Vice Pres*
Larry Epstein, *Vice Pres*
Lawrence Epstein, *Vice Pres*
Steven Epstein, *Vice Pres*
◆ EMP: 75
SQ FT: 180,000
SALES (est): 38MM **Privately Held**
WEB: www.aldenleeds.com
SIC: 2899 Water treating compounds

(G-4860)
AMERICAN INGREDIENTS INC
265 Harrison Tpke (07032-4315)
PHONE....................................714 630-6000
David A Holmes, *President*
Colin Mac Intyre, *Vice Pres*
Andrea Bauer, *Treasurer*
Roberto Garcia, *Sales Mgr*
Catherine Holmes, *Admin Sec*
EMP: 15
SQ FT: 26,000
SALES (est): 1.1MM
SALES (corp-wide): 3.2B **Publicly Held**
SIC: 2833 Medicinals & botanicals
HQ: Pharmachem Laboratories, Llc
265 Harrison Tpke
Kearny NJ 07032
201 246-1000

(G-4861)
APELIO INNOVATIVE INDS LLC
46 Sellers St (07032-4216)
PHONE....................................973 777-8899
Michael Zelenkoz, *Mng Member*
Boris Bregman,
Michael Bregman,
Alison Hine,
Michael Zelenko,
EMP: 18 EST: 2014
SALES: 2.2MM **Privately Held**
SIC: 3646 3645 3613 1731 Commercial indusl & institutional electric lighting fixtures; residential lighting fixtures; switchgear & switchboard apparatus; electrical work

(G-4862)
ART PLAQUE CREATIONS INC
70 Arlington Ave (07032-4007)
PHONE....................................973 482-2536
Ed Marcus, *President*
Minerva Marquez, *Treasurer*
EMP: 10 EST: 1987
SQ FT: 11,100
SALES (est): 860K **Privately Held**
SIC: 3299 3263 3275 Statuary: gypsum, clay, papier mache, metal, etc.; semivitreous table & kitchenware; gypsum products

(G-4863)
BELLEVILLE CORP
Also Called: Gild-N-Son Manufacturing
328 Belleville Tpke (07032-3801)
PHONE....................................201 991-6222
Fax: 201 991-6203
Alan Gildenberg, *President*
EMP: 10 EST: 1947
SQ FT: 10,000
SALES (est): 1.4MM **Privately Held**
SIC: 3442 Screens, window, metal; screen doors, metal; storm doors or windows, metal

(G-4864)
BERNARDAUD NA INC
1 Jacobus Ave (07032-4532)
PHONE....................................973 274-3555
Isabelle Darocha, *Manager*
EMP: 4
SALES (corp-wide): 32.3MM **Privately Held**
SIC: 3469 Table tops, porcelain enameled
HQ: Bernardaud Na, Inc.
499 Park Ave
New York NY 10022
212 371-4300

(G-4865)
BINDI NORTH AMERICA INC (PA)
Also Called: Bindi Dessert
630 Belleville Tpke (07032-4407)
PHONE....................................973 812-8118
Fax: 973 751-5443
Attilio Bindi, *President*
Christopher Klemensowicz, *Opers Mgr*
Gianfranco Orlando, *Controller*
Alberto Carrotta, *Manager*
Stefano Del Verme, *Manager*
◆ EMP: 50
SALES (est): 13.3MM **Privately Held**
SIC: 2024 Dairy based frozen desserts

(G-4866)
BOMBARDIER TRANSPORTATION
Also Called: Adtranz
1148 Newark Tpke (07032-4311)
PHONE....................................201 955-5874
Mark Ives, *Manager*
EMP: 4
SALES (corp-wide): 16.2B **Privately Held**
SIC: 3743 Train cars & equipment, freight or passenger
HQ: Bombardier Transportation (Holdings) Usa Inc
1501 Lebanon Church Rd
Pittsburgh PA 15236
412 655-5700

(G-4867)
CAMPBELL FOUNDRY COMPANY
Campbell Materials
1235 Harrison Tpke (07032-4310)
PHONE....................................201 998-3765
George Campbell, *Sales Staff*
John Pisciotto, *Branch Mgr*
EMP: 40
SALES (corp-wide): 11.9MM **Privately Held**
WEB: www.campbellfoundry.com
SIC: 3321 Manhole covers, metal
PA: Campbell Foundry Company
800 Bergen St
Harrison NJ 07029
973 483-5480

(G-4868)
CP TEST & VALVE PRODUCTS INC
234 Sanford Ave (07032-5920)
P.O. Box 311 (07032-0311)
PHONE....................................201 998-1500
Pamela Krieg, *President*
Jim Krieg, *Vice Pres*
William Conklin, *Admin Sec*
▲ EMP: 8
SALES (est): 704K **Privately Held**
SIC: 3494 Valves & pipe fittings; pipe fittings

(G-4869)
CRYSTAL BEVERAGE CORPORATION (PA)
174 Sanford Ave (07032-5920)
PHONE....................................201 991-2342
John Apolinario, *President*
Victor Apolinario, *Treasurer*
▲ EMP: 2
SQ FT: 14,000
SALES: 5MM **Privately Held**
SIC: 2086 Carbonated beverages, nonalcoholic: bottled & canned

(G-4870)
CUMMINS INC
435 Bergen Ave (07032-3938)
PHONE....................................973 491-0100
Fax: 973 578-8873
Whityeld Whylie, *General Mgr*
Richard Boyer, *Manager*
Richard Perry, *Manager*
EMP: 100
SALES (corp-wide): 20.4B **Publicly Held**
SIC: 5084 3519 Engines & parts, diesel; internal combustion engines
PA: Cummins Inc.
500 Jackson St
Columbus IN 47201
812 377-5000

(G-4871)
DERV2000
420 Belgrove Dr (07032-1628)
PHONE....................................503 470-9158
Rosa Vernazza, *Vice Pres*
EMP: 4
SALES (est): 154.7K **Privately Held**
SIC: 3069 Reclaimed rubber (reworked by manufacturing processes)

(G-4872)
DYNASTY METALS INC
183 Garfield Ave (07032-4017)
P.O. Box 695, Rockaway (07866-0695)
PHONE....................................800 225-3962
Fax: 201 997-7488

Richard A Kolodin, *President*
John M Tolpa Jr, *Treasurer*
Sam Adorno, *Sales Staff*
Brian Gill, *Sales Staff*
EMP: 45
SQ FT: 15,000
SALES (est): 5.6MM **Privately Held**
SIC: 3471 5051 Polishing, metals or formed products; nonferrous metal sheets, bars, rods, etc.

(G-4873)
FEED YOUR SOUL LTD LBLTY CO
78 John Miller Way # 100 (07032-6500)
PHONE..........................201 204-0720
Mya Zoracki, *Mng Member*
EMP: 4
SALES (est): 443.7K **Privately Held**
SIC: 2051 Bakery: wholesale or wholesale/retail combined

(G-4874)
FUSAR TECHNOLOGIES INC
78 John Miller Way # 310 (07032-6531)
PHONE..........................201 563-0189
Ryan Shearman, *CEO*
Frank Bober, *Chairman*
Clayton Patton, *CFO*
Todd Rushing, *Exec Dir*
EMP: 9
SALES (est): 1.5MM **Privately Held**
SIC: 5045 7371 7372 Computer peripheral equipment; custom computer programming services; application computer software

(G-4875)
G & S MOTOR EQUIPMENT CO INC
Also Called: G & S Technologies
1800 Harrison Ave (07032)
P.O. Box 493 (07032-0493)
PHONE..........................201 998-9244
Fax: 201 998-3349
Gabor Newmark, *President*
Zoltan Lefkovits, *Corp Secy*
Jeffery Lefkovits, *Vice Pres*
George Newmark, *Vice Pres*
◆ **EMP:** 100
SQ FT: 60,000
SALES (est): 21.3MM **Privately Held**
WEB: www.gstechnologies.com
SIC: 3612 Distribution transformers, electric

(G-4876)
GALAXY SWITCHGEAR INDS LLC
46 Sellers St (07032-4216)
PHONE..........................914 668-8200
Isak Lamberg, *President*
Boris Bregman,
Charles Casquarelli,
Brett Sagona,
EMP: 30
SQ FT: 17,000
SALES (est): 5.4MM **Privately Held**
SIC: 3613 3645 Switchgear & switchboard apparatus; residential lighting fixtures

(G-4877)
GARDEN STATE BTLG LTD LBLTY CO
174 Sanford Ave (07032-5920)
PHONE..........................201 991-2342
John Apolinario, *Ch of Bd*
Alan Silverstein, *Vice Pres*
EMP: 14
SQ FT: 14,000
SALES: 4.4MM
SALES (corp-wide): 5MM **Privately Held**
SIC: 2086 Carbonated beverages, nonalcoholic: bottled & canned
PA: Crystal Beverage Corporation
174 Sanford Ave
Kearny NJ 07032
201 991-2342

(G-4878)
GIFFORD GROUP INC
Also Called: Just Plastics
35 Obrien St (07032-4212)
PHONE..........................212 569-8500
Fax: 212 569-6970

Robert C Vermann, *President*
Tammy Espaillat, *Vice Pres*
Lois Vermann, *Vice Pres*
EMP: 15
SQ FT: 25,000
SALES: 1.5MM **Privately Held**
WEB: www.justplastics.com
SIC: 3089 Injection molding of plastics

(G-4879)
GRAPHIC MANAGEMENT
21 Lafayette Pl (07032-2228)
PHONE..........................908 654-8400
Fax: 908 654-0312
Scott Wright, *President*
EMP: 40
SQ FT: 50,000
SALES (est): 4.3MM **Privately Held**
WEB: www.graphicmgt.com
SIC: 2752 Commercial printing, lithographic

(G-4880)
HONEYWARE INC (PA)
244 Dukes St (07032-3929)
PHONE..........................201 997-5900
Fax: 201 997-4420
Tony Sheng, *President*
Lambert Sheng, *Vice Pres*
Raymond Sheng, *Vice Pres*
James Sheng, *Shareholder*
◆ **EMP:** 65
SQ FT: 86,000
SALES (est): 11.5MM **Privately Held**
SIC: 3089 2899 2865 Injection molding of plastics; ink or writing fluids; dyes, synthetic organic

(G-4881)
HUDSON & BERGEN COMPANY
350 Belleville Tpke (07032-3841)
P.O. Box 264 (07032-0264)
PHONE..........................201 991-4900
Fax: 201 998-4949
Steven Boyd, *President*
June Kresga, *Corp Secy*
EMP: 7 **EST:** 1948
SALES (est): 780K **Privately Held**
WEB: www.century21turi.com
SIC: 2591 5719 5211 Venetian blinds; window shade rollers & fittings; window shades; windows, storm: wood or metal; doors, storm: wood or metal

(G-4882)
HUDSON WEST PUBLISHING CO
Also Called: Observer, The
39 Seeley Ave (07032-1806)
PHONE..........................201 991-1600
Fax: 201 991-8941
Mary Tortoreti, *President*
Lisa Pezzolla, *Publisher*
EMP: 15
SQ FT: 3,000
SALES (est): 1.1MM **Privately Held**
SIC: 2711 2741 Newspapers: publishing only, not printed on site; shopping news: publishing only, not printed on site

(G-4883)
HUGO NEU RECYCLING LLC
78 John Miller Way Ste 1 (07032-6528)
PHONE..........................914 530-2350
Robert Houghton, *CEO*
Jill Vaske, *President*
EMP: 25
SALES: 11MM
SALES (corp-wide): 15.5MM **Privately Held**
SIC: 3399 5093 Staples, nonferrous metal or wire; laminating steel; metal scrap & waste materials
HQ: Sage Sustainable Electronics Llc
2801 Charter St
Columbus OH 43228
844 472-4373

(G-4884)
INFINITE MFG GROUP INC
35 Obrien St (07032-4212)
PHONE..........................973 649-9950
Bernard Alloysius, *Branch Mgr*
EMP: 10

SALES (est): 901.9K
SALES (corp-wide): 5.1MM **Privately Held**
SIC: 2542 Fixtures: display, office or store: except wood
PA: Infinite Manufacturing Group, Inc.
35 Obrien St
Kearny NJ 07032
973 649-9950

(G-4885)
INFINITE MFG GROUP INC (PA)
Also Called: Infinite Sign
35 Obrien St (07032-4212)
PHONE..........................973 649-9950
Bernard Alloysius, *CEO*
▼ **EMP:** 20
SQ FT: 45,000
SALES (est): 5.1MM **Privately Held**
SIC: 3993 2431 7389 2599 Signs & advertising specialties; displays & cutouts, window & lobby; letters for signs, metal; woodwork, interior & ornamental; styling of fashions, apparel, furniture, textiles, etc.; factory furniture & fixtures; fabricated structural metal; construction project management consultant

(G-4886)
INFINITE SIGN INDUSTRIES INC
35 Obrien St (07032-4212)
PHONE..........................973 649-9950
Fax: 973 649-9951
Bernard Alloysius, *President*
EMP: 50
SQ FT: 30,000
SALES (est): 6.8MM **Privately Held**
WEB: www.infinitesign.com
SIC: 3993 Signs, not made in custom sign painting shops

(G-4887)
INTELLICON INC
46 Sellers St (07032-4216)
PHONE..........................201 791-9499
Lenny Novikov, *President*
EMP: 4
SQ FT: 2,000
SALES: 820K **Privately Held**
WEB: www.intelliconinc.com
SIC: 3625 Industrial controls: push button, selector switches, pilot

(G-4888)
JAI GANESH FUEL LLC
815 Kearny Ave (07032-3147)
PHONE..........................201 246-8995
Jai Ganesh, *Mng Member*
EMP: 4
SALES (est): 238.5K **Privately Held**
SIC: 2869 Fuels

(G-4889)
JIMENEZ PALLETS LLC
244 Dukes St (07032-3929)
PHONE..........................862 267-3900
Russell Jimenez, *Principal*
Alexander Jimenez, *Buyer*
EMP: 6 **EST:** 2013
SALES (est): 510K **Privately Held**
SIC: 2448 Pallets, wood

(G-4890)
JOSE MOREIRA
Also Called: Moreira, Jose B, Attorney
712 Kearny Ave (07032-3004)
PHONE..........................201 991-9001
Jose Moreira, *Owner*
EMP: 4
SALES (est): 348.8K **Privately Held**
WEB: www.josemoreira.com
SIC: 8111 2711 General practice attorney, lawyer; newspapers

(G-4891)
KEARNY SMELTING & REF CORP
936 Harrison Ave Ste 5 (07032-5999)
PHONE..........................201 991-7276
Francine Rothschild, *President*
EMP: 21 **EST:** 1945
SQ FT: 12,000

SALES (est): 3.6MM **Privately Held**
SIC: 3356 3351 3341 Nonferrous rolling & drawing; brass rolling & drawing; bronze rolling & drawing; brass smelting & refining (secondary); bronze smelting & refining (secondary)

(G-4892)
KENNEY STEEL TREATING CORP
100 Quincy Pl (07032-4012)
P.O. Box 6 (07032-0006)
PHONE..........................201 998-4420
Fax: 201 998-4429
John Patrick Dunphy Jr, *President*
James Dunphy, *Vice Pres*
EMP: 20
SQ FT: 16,000
SALES: 752K **Privately Held**
SIC: 3398 Metal heat treating

(G-4893)
KUEHNE CHEMICAL COMPANY INC (PA)
86 N Hackensack Ave (07032-4673)
PHONE..........................973 589-0700
Fax: 973 589-4866
Donald Nicolai, *President*
Kelly Ward, *General Mgr*
Ken Corolla, *Vice Pres*
Manuel Cunha, *Vice Pres*
Martina Hanna, *Engineer*
◆ **EMP:** 50
SQ FT: 10,000
SALES (est): 120.1MM **Privately Held**
SIC: 2819 4226 2812 Sodium & potassium compounds, exc. bleaches, alkalies, alum.; special warehousing & storage; alkalies & chlorine

(G-4894)
L & R MANUFACTURING CO INC (PA)
577 Elm St (07032-3699)
P.O. Box 607 (07032-0607)
PHONE..........................201 991-5330
Fax: 201 991-5870
James J Lazarus, *CEO*
Robert Lazarus, *President*
David Romanok, *Exec VP*
Ralph Devito, *Finance Mgr*
Carmen Distano, *Manager*
◆ **EMP:** 95 **EST:** 1928
SQ FT: 21,000
SALES (est): 19.5MM **Privately Held**
WEB: www.lrultrasonics.com
SIC: 2842 3841 3843 3699 Cleaning or polishing preparations; ultrasonic medical cleaning equipment; ultrasonic dental equipment; cleaning equipment, ultrasonic, except medical & dental

(G-4895)
L & R MANUFACTURING CO INC
John Hay Ave (07032)
P.O. Box 607 (07032-0607)
PHONE..........................201 991-5330
Robert J Lazarus, *President*
EMP: 110
SALES (corp-wide): 19.5MM **Privately Held**
WEB: www.lrultrasonics.com
SIC: 3699 Cleaning equipment, ultrasonic, except medical & dental
PA: L & R Manufacturing Co Inc
577 Elm St
Kearny NJ 07032
201 991-5330

(G-4896)
MAC PRODUCTS INC
Also Called: Mac Power
60 Pennsylvania Ave (07032-4595)
P.O. Box 469 (07032-0469)
PHONE..........................973 344-5149
Fax: 973 344-5891
Edward Gollob, *President*
Ed Russnow, *Vice Pres*
Christopher Oneill, *Purch Agent*
Peter Haenchen, *Buyer*
Michelle Soares, *Buyer*
◆ **EMP:** 60 **EST:** 1960
SQ FT: 195,000

SALES (est): 16.6MM **Privately Held**
WEB: www.macproducts.net
SIC: 3643 5063 3549 Connectors & terminals for electrical devices; electrical apparatus & equipment; metalworking machinery

(G-4897)
MARBLE ONLINE CORPORATION
260 Schuyler Ave Fl 1 (07032-4002)
PHONE..........................201 998-9100
Allan Lan, *President*
▲ EMP: 5 EST: 2014
SALES (est): 632.8K **Privately Held**
SIC: 3281 Marble, building: cut & shaped

(G-4898)
MARCOTEX INTERNATIONAL INC
Also Called: Ultimate Home Products Div
69 Sellers St (07032-4227)
PHONE..........................201 991-8200
Fax: 973 471-3380
Marc Moyal, *President*
▼ EMP: 35
SQ FT: 200,000
SALES (est): 4.8MM **Privately Held**
SIC: 5131 2211 Piece goods & other fabrics; sheets, bedding & table cloths: cotton

(G-4899)
MILLAR SHEET METAL
39 Rizzolo Rd Ste 2 (07032-4288)
PHONE..........................201 997-1990
Fax: 201 997-2240
Peter Millar, *President*
Margaret Millar, *Vice Pres*
EMP: 5
SQ FT: 3,000
SALES (est): 530K **Privately Held**
SIC: 1711 3444 Ventilation & duct work contractor; warm air heating & air conditioning contractor; sheet metalwork

(G-4900)
MIRACLE VERDE GROUP LLC
47 Sellers St (07032-4215)
PHONE..........................201 399-2222
Milton Dsouza, *Mng Member*
▼ EMP: 7
SQ FT: 35,000
SALES (est): 450.6K **Privately Held**
SIC: 2873 Fertilizers: natural (organic), except compost

(G-4901)
MOHAWK INDUSTRIES
150 Western Rd (07032-6508)
PHONE..........................973 982-6200
EMP: 4
SALES (est): 97.7K **Privately Held**
SIC: 2273 Finishers of tufted carpets & rugs

(G-4902)
MULTI-TEX PRODUCTS CORP
54 2nd Ave (07032-4014)
PHONE..........................201 991-7262
Michaelene Dwulet, *President*
▲ EMP: 35 EST: 1971
SQ FT: 22,000
SALES (est): 4.1MM **Privately Held**
SIC: 2269 2299 2281 Finishing plants; yarns, specialty & novelty; yarn spinning mills

(G-4903)
NEW ENGLAND BEDDING TRNSPT INC
102 3rd Ave (07032-4028)
PHONE..........................631 484-0147
Douglas Daly, *President*
EMP: 8
SQ FT: 1,000
SALES (est): 1MM **Privately Held**
SIC: 2515 Mattresses & bedsprings

(G-4904)
OWENS CORNING SALES LLC
1249 Newark Tpke (07032-4398)
PHONE..........................201 998-5666
Fax: 201 998-5938
Tom Messlli, *Manager*

EMP: 125 **Publicly Held**
WEB: www.owenscorning.com
SIC: 3296 Mineral wool
HQ: Owens Corning Sales, Llc
1 Owens Corning Pkwy
Toledo OH 43659
419 248-8000

(G-4905)
PEPSI-COLA METRO BTLG CO INC
680 Belleville Tpke (07032-4407)
PHONE..........................201 955-2691
Tony Pessolano, *Branch Mgr*
EMP: 9
SALES (corp-wide): 63.5B **Publicly Held**
SIC: 2086 Soft drinks: packaged in cans, bottles, etc.
HQ: Pepsi-Cola Metropolitan Bottling Company, Inc.
1111 Westchester Ave
White Plains NY 10604
914 767-6000

(G-4906)
PERCEPTIONS INC
280 Central Ave (07032-4609)
PHONE..........................973 344-5333
Barry Pessar, *President*
Sy Blechman, *Vice Pres*
▲ EMP: 45
SQ FT: 5,600
SALES (est): 3.5MM **Privately Held**
WEB: www.perceptionsdress.com
SIC: 2335 Ensemble dresses: women's, misses' & juniors'; gowns, formal

(G-4907)
PERFECTO FOODS LLC
79 Stuyvesant Ave (07032-3139)
PHONE..........................201 889-5328
David P Perez, *Principal*
EMP: 5
SALES (est): 250.4K **Privately Held**
SIC: 2099 Food preparations

(G-4908)
PHARMACHEM LABORATORIES LLC (DH)
Also Called: Pharmachem Laboratories, Inc.
265 Harrison Tpke (07032-4315)
PHONE..........................201 246-1000
Fax: 201 991-5674
David Holmes, *President*
Lynn Dahle, *Vice Pres*
George Joseph, *Vice Pres*
Mike Stefanelli, *Transptn Dir*
Jodie Adams, *Project Mgr*
◆ EMP: 70
SQ FT: 54,000
SALES (est): 132.3MM
SALES (corp-wide): 3.2B **Publicly Held**
WEB: www.pharmachem.com
SIC: 2099 2834 Food preparations; pharmaceutical preparations
HQ: Ashland Llc
50 E Rivercenter Blvd # 1600
Covington KY 41011
859 815-3333

(G-4909)
PICASSO LIGHTING INDS LLC
Also Called: Lightingindustries Picasso
46 Sellers St (07032-4216)
PHONE..........................201 246-8188
Alex Chernoknyzhnyy, *Prdtn Mgr*
Lenny Novikov, *Prdtn Mgr*
Andrew Bregman, *Engineer*
Alister Mallet, *Engineer*
Yuri Khaskin, *Design Engr*
EMP: 20
SQ FT: 2,000
SALES (est): 3.3MM **Privately Held**
SIC: 3646 Commercial indusl & institutional electric lighting fixtures

(G-4910)
PRO SCREEN PRINTING INC
590 Belleville Tpke # 24 (07032-4241)
PHONE..........................201 246-7600
Fax: 201 246-9046
EMP: 6
SQ FT: 12,000
SALES (est): 580K **Privately Held**
SIC: 2752 Commercial Printer On Plastic Containers

(G-4911)
PROFESSIONAL ENVMTL SYSTEMS
1806 Harrison Ave (07032)
PHONE..........................201 991-3000
Perry Mentore, *President*
Robert Mentore, *Vice Pres*
Dola Ilyas, *Treasurer*
EMP: 24 EST: 1977
SQ FT: 54,000
SALES (est): 3.1MM **Privately Held**
WEB: www.pesworldwide.com
SIC: 3444 1711 Metal ventilating equipment; ventilation & duct work contractor

(G-4912)
REFRIG-IT WAREHOUSE
77 Hackensack Ave (07032-4656)
PHONE..........................973 344-4545
Brian Doliner, *Branch Mgr*
EMP: 50
SALES (corp-wide): 11.2MM **Privately Held**
SIC: 2673 Food storage & frozen food bags, plastic
PA: Refrig-It Warehouse
80 Campus Dr
Kearny NJ 07032
973 344-4545

(G-4913)
SCHUYLER PRINTING INC
71 Kearny Ave (07032-2334)
PHONE..........................201 997-8083
EMP: 4
SQ FT: 1,200
SALES (est): 310K **Privately Held**
SIC: 2752 Offset Printers

(G-4914)
SMITH LIME FLOUR CO INC
60 Central Ave (07032-4603)
PHONE..........................973 344-1700
Mark Veca, *President*
Thomas Veca, *Corp Secy*
Robert Veca, *Vice Pres*
EMP: 18 EST: 1895
SQ FT: 14,000
SALES (est): 1.7MM **Privately Held**
SIC: 3274 Lime

(G-4915)
SOLID COLOR INC
78 John Miller Way # 420 (07032-6532)
PHONE..........................212 239-3930
Frank Ferreiras, *President*
Robert Ellis, *Treasurer*
EMP: 6
SQ FT: 5,000
SALES (est): 1.3MM **Privately Held**
SIC: 2752 Advertising posters, lithographed

(G-4916)
STANSON CORPORATION (PA)
2 N Hackensack Ave (07032-4611)
PHONE..........................973 344-8666
Fax: 973 344-8505
Robert Holuba, *President*
Angela Holuba, *Corp Secy*
Stanley Holuba Jr, *COO*
EMP: 75
SQ FT: 500,000
SALES (est): 6.5MM **Privately Held**
WEB: www.stanson.com
SIC: 2841 2842 Detergents, synthetic organic or inorganic alkaline; specialty cleaning, polishes & sanitation goods

(G-4917)
TILCON NEW YORK INC
Also Called: Kearny Recycle
411 Bergen Ave (07032-3920)
PHONE..........................800 789-7625
EMP: 63
SALES (corp-wide): 29.7B **Privately Held**
SIC: 1429 Dolomitic marble, crushed & broken-quarrying
HQ: Tilcon New York Inc.
9 Entin Rd
Parsippany NJ 07054
800 789-7625

(G-4918)
UNITED DIE COMPANY INC
Also Called: Udico
199 Devon Ter (07032-3916)
P.O. Box 490 (07032-0490)
PHONE..........................201 997-0250
Fax: 201 997-3297
John Kontra, *President*
Mary Kontra, *Vice Pres*
Marion Martin, *CFO*
EMP: 50 EST: 1940
SQ FT: 12,000
SALES (est): 8.7MM **Privately Held**
WEB: www.uniteddie.com
SIC: 3544 Wire drawing & straightening dies; special dies & tools

(G-4919)
WELDON MATERIALS INC
1100 Harrison Ave (07032-5922)
PHONE..........................201 991-3200
Todd Philips, *Manager*
EMP: 7 **Privately Held**
WEB: www.weldonmaterials.com
SIC: 2951 Road materials, bituminous (not from refineries)
PA: Weldon Materials, Inc.
141 Central Ave
Westfield NJ 07090

(G-4920)
WEST HUDSON LUMBER & MLLWK CO
60 Arlington Ave (07032-4007)
PHONE..........................201 991-7191
Fax: 201 991-4987
Johnathon Giordano, *President*
Patricia Giordano, *Vice Pres*
EMP: 5 EST: 1945
SQ FT: 7,500
SALES: 500K **Privately Held**
SIC: 2599 2431 Cabinets, factory; millwork

(G-4921)
WESTERN PACIFIC FOODS INC
650 Belleville Tpke Ste 2 (07032-4409)
PHONE..........................908 838-0186
Zheng Cheo, *Managing Dir*
EMP: 14 EST: 2016
SQ FT: 23,000
SALES (est): 548.9K **Privately Held**
SIC: 2079 Edible fats & oils; margarine & margarine oils; cooking oils, except corn: vegetable refined

(G-4922)
WILLIAMS SCOTSMAN INC
Also Called: Williams Scotsman - NY Cy
150 Western Rd (07032-6508)
PHONE..........................856 429-0315
Arnold Sobral, *Branch Mgr*
EMP: 8
SALES (corp-wide): 54.7MM **Publicly Held**
WEB: www.willscot.com
SIC: 3412 3499 3542 Barrels, shipping: metal; fire- or burglary-resistive products; metal container making machines: cans, etc.
HQ: Williams Scotsman, Inc.
901 S Bond St Ste 600
Baltimore MD 21231
410 931-6000

(G-4923)
WILPAK INDUSTRIES INC
244 Dukes St (07032-3929)
PHONE..........................201 997-7600
Tony Sheng, *President*
Lambert Sheng, *Vice Pres*
Raymond Sheng, *Treasurer*
James Sheng, *Shareholder*
▲ EMP: 6
SQ FT: 3,000
SALES: 500K
SALES (corp-wide): 11.5MM **Privately Held**
WEB: www.honeyware.com
SIC: 2899 3089 Ink or writing fluids; injection molded finished plastic products
PA: Honeyware Inc.
244 Dukes St
Kearny NJ 07032
201 997-5900

▲ = Import ▼=Export
◆ =Import/Export

Keasbey
Middlesex County

(G-4924)
BAYSHORE RECYCLING CORP
75 Crows Mill Rd (08832-1004)
P.O. Box 290 (08832-0290)
PHONE..................................732 738-6000
Fax: 732 738-9150
Valerie Montecalvo, *President*
Stephen Thomas, *General Mgr*
Frank Montecalvo, *COO*
Al Ludwig, *Senior VP*
John Davies, *Vice Pres*
EMP: 25
SALES (est): 10.6MM **Privately Held**
WEB: www.bayshorerecycling.com
SIC: 4953 3087 Recycling, waste materials; custom compound purchased resins

(G-4925)
BRUCE SUPPLY CORP
300 Smith St (08832-1017)
PHONE..................................732 661-0500
EMP: 10
SALES (corp-wide): 168.3MM **Privately Held**
SIC: 3432 Plumbing fixture fittings & trim
PA: Bruce Supply Corp.
8805 18th Ave
Brooklyn NY 11214
718 259-4900

(G-4926)
CHARLES M JESSUP INC
177 Smith St (08832-1158)
PHONE..................................732 324-0430
Fax: 732 324-1616
Caren Jessup, *President*
Jay Jessup, *Vice Pres*
EMP: 6 EST: 1948
SQ FT: 7,000
SALES (est): 1.1MM **Privately Held**
SIC: 5084 3555 Screening machinery & equipment; printing trades machinery

(G-4927)
COASTAL METAL RECYCLING CORP
75 Crows Mill Rd (08832-1004)
PHONE..................................732 738-6000
Daniel A Scwartz Esq, *President*
EMP: 4
SALES (est): 400K **Privately Held**
SIC: 1081 Metal mining services

(G-4928)
MAINETTI USA INC (HQ)
300 Mac Ln (08832-1200)
PHONE..................................201 215-2900
Roberto Peruzzo, *President*
Steve Regino, *Co-President*
Bala Balakrishnan, *Vice Pres*
Jim Logan, *Opers Mgr*
David Provine, *Opers Mgr*
◆ EMP: 17
SALES (est): 12.5MM **Privately Held**
SIC: 3089 Clothes hangers, plastic
PA: Mainetti Americas, Inc.
115 Enterprise Ave S
Secaucus NJ 07094
201 215-2900

(G-4929)
NESTLE USA INC
326 Smith St (08832-1029)
PHONE..................................973 390-9555
EMP: 132
SALES (corp-wide): 90.8B **Privately Held**
SIC: 2023 Evaporated milk
HQ: Nestle Usa, Inc.
1812 N Moore St
Rosslyn VA 22209
818 549-6000

(G-4930)
PRAXAIR INC
60 Crows Mill Rd (08832-1028)
P.O. Box 127 (08832-0127)
PHONE..................................732 738-4150
Gary Wilson, *Branch Mgr*
Mike Wilday, *Info Tech Dir*
Mike Beaudrow, *Executive Asst*

EMP: 13
SQ FT: 100,000
SALES (corp-wide): 11.4B **Publicly Held**
SIC: 2813 Industrial gases
PA: Praxair, Inc.
10 Riverview Dr
Danbury CT 06810
203 837-2000

(G-4931)
PRAXAIR CRYOMAG SERVICES INC
Industrial Ave (08832)
PHONE..................................732 738-4000
Fax: 732 738-9586
Jack Quinn, *General Mgr*
▲ EMP: 10
SALES (est): 1.6MM
SALES (corp-wide): 11.4B **Publicly Held**
SIC: 2813 Industrial gases
PA: Praxair, Inc.
10 Riverview Dr
Danbury CT 06810
203 837-2000

(G-4932)
WAKEFERN FOOD CORP (PA)
Also Called: Wakefern General Merchandise
5000 Riverside Dr (08832-1209)
PHONE..................................908 527-3300
Joseph Colalillo, *CEO*
Joseph Sheridan, *President*
Joe Amorim, *District Mgr*
Allison Berger, *Vice Pres*
Chris Lane, *Senior VP*
◆ EMP: 400 EST: 1946
SALES (est): 12.5B **Privately Held**
WEB: www.shoprite.com
SIC: 5141 5149 5411 4213 Groceries, general line; groceries & related products; supermarkets, chain; contract haulers; milk processing (pasteurizing, homogenizing, bottling)

Kendall Park
Middlesex County

(G-4933)
ABRAZIL LLC
1 Jacques Ave (08824-1601)
PHONE..................................732 658-5191
Fax: 732 783-0397
Hugh Liang, *Purchasing*
Steven Shen, *Marketing Staff*
Tony Chuang, *Business Dir*
◆ EMP: 9
SALES (est): 1.2MM **Privately Held**
WEB: www.abrazil.com
SIC: 2833 Medicinals & botanicals

(G-4934)
COOLENHEAT INC
11 Clinton Ct (08824-1837)
P.O. Box 1368, Linden (07036-0004)
PHONE..................................908 925-4473
Fax: 908 862-1506
Jeffrey Bossert, *President*
Randall Bossert, *Vice Pres*
Jonathan Bossert, *Treasurer*
EMP: 30
SQ FT: 18,000
SALES (est): 5.4MM **Privately Held**
SIC: 3498 3585 Fabricated pipe & fittings; evaporative condensers, heat transfer equipment

(G-4935)
NEWTECH GROUP CORP
Also Called: N G C
54 Inverness Dr (08824-7012)
PHONE..................................732 355-0392
Peggy Foung, *President*
Austin Yang,
EMP: 5
SALES: 50K **Privately Held**
WEB: www.newtechgc.com
SIC: 3357 2298 3678 3643 Nonferrous wiredrawing & insulating; cable, fiber; electronic connectors; current-carrying wiring devices

Kenilworth
Union County

(G-4936)
ALLOY CAST PRODUCTS INC
700 Swenson Dr (07033-1326)
PHONE..................................908 245-2255
Fax: 908 245-3267
Frank Panico Jr, *President*
EMP: 12
SQ FT: 14,850
SALES (est): 1.3MM **Privately Held**
WEB: www.alloycastproducts.com
SIC: 3369 3544 3545 Castings, except die-castings, precision; extrusion dies; cutting tools for machine tools

(G-4937)
ARBEE COMPANY INC
Also Called: Abbey Commemoratives
16 N 26th St (07033-1714)
PHONE..................................908 241-7717
Fax: 908 241-6466
Margaret A Beute, *Principal*
William M Beute, *Vice Pres*
Robert Boak, *Vice Pres*
EMP: 10
SQ FT: 3,500
SALES (est): 800K **Privately Held**
SIC: 3089 Laminating of plastic

(G-4938)
AUTO ACTION GROUP INC
Also Called: Installations Unlimited
121 N Michigan Ave Ste A (07033-1261)
PHONE..................................908 964-6290
Jared Cohen, *CEO*
Joe Cardinale, *Manager*
Brenda Cohen, *Shareholder*
EMP: 50
SQ FT: 12,000
SALES (est): 9.8MM **Privately Held**
SIC: 3694 Automotive electrical equipment

(G-4939)
B & B MILLWORK & DOORS INC
327 Monroe Ave (07033-1129)
PHONE..................................973 249-0300
EMP: 5
SALES (est): 1.7MM **Privately Held**
SIC: 5031 2431 Millwork; millwork

(G-4940)
B & M FINISHERS INC
201 S 31st St (07033-1305)
PHONE..................................908 241-5640
Fax: 908 241-5061
Robert Bramson, *President*
Donald Marcus, *Plant Mgr*
▲ EMP: 35 EST: 1956
SALES (est): 4.5MM **Privately Held**
WEB: www.bmfinishers.com
SIC: 3471 Anodizing (plating) of metals or formed products

(G-4941)
B AND W PRINTING COMPANY INC
730 Fairfield Ave (07033-2012)
P.O. Box 65 (07033-0065)
PHONE..................................908 241-3060
Fax: 908 298-9248
Claire Butler, *CEO*
Gary L Butler, *President*
EMP: 8
SQ FT: 2,560
SALES (est): 450K **Privately Held**
WEB: www.bwprinting.com
SIC: 2752 2759 Commercial printing, offset; letterpress printing

(G-4942)
BEACON C M P CORP
295 N Michigan Ave Ste G (07033-1270)
P.O. Box 103 (07033-0103)
PHONE..................................908 851-9393
Fax: 908 851-9894
Richard M Loncar, *President*
Lenore Rodino, *Vice Pres*
EMP: 5
SQ FT: 1,400
SALES (est): 580K **Privately Held**
SIC: 2899 Chemical preparations

(G-4943)
BELLA PALERMO PASTRY SHOP
541 Boulevard (07033-1656)
PHONE..................................908 931-0298
Joe Oliveira, *Principal*
EMP: 23 **Privately Held**
SIC: 5461 2051 Pastries; cakes, pies & pastries
PA: Bella Palermo Pastry Shop
619 Elizabeth Ave
Elizabeth NJ 07206

(G-4944)
BENEDICT-MILLER LLC (PA)
123 N 8th St (07033-1108)
PHONE..................................908 497-1477
Richard Hayes, *Purch Mgr*
Nancy Nadolny, *Accounting Mgr*
Ed Halpin, *Sales Mgr*
Walter Las, *Marketing Staff*
Jeremiah H Shaw, *Mng Member*
EMP: 10
SQ FT: 50,000
SALES (est): 1.5MM **Privately Held**
WEB: www.benedict-miller.com
SIC: 3312 5051 Plate, sheet & strip, except coated products; metals service centers & offices

(G-4945)
BLUE BLADE CORP
Also Called: Blue Blade Steel
123 N 8th St (07033-1108)
P.O. Box 40 (07033-0040)
PHONE..................................908 272-2620
Fax: 908 272-8252
Jeremiah H Shaw Jr, *President*
Gail Snyder, *Accounting Mgr*
Don Lindewirth, *Manager*
Robert Van Laere, *Supervisor*
▲ EMP: 46 EST: 1933
SQ FT: 130,000
SALES (est): 23.4MM **Privately Held**
WEB: www.blubladesteel.com
SIC: 3398 Metal heat treating

(G-4946)
BRENT MATERIAL COMPANY
308 N 14th St (07033-1168)
PHONE..................................908 686-3832
Bill Fiorenzo, *Manager*
Shane Dobke, *Manager*
EMP: 8
SALES (corp-wide): 11.4MM **Privately Held**
SIC: 3272 5031 Sewer pipe, concrete; lumber, plywood & millwork
PA: Brent Material Company
325 Columbia Tpke Ste 308
Florham Park NJ 07932
973 325-3030

(G-4947)
CAMPTOWN TOOL & DIE CO INC
25 Sidney Cir (07033-1051)
P.O. Box 274 (07033-0274)
PHONE..................................908 688-8406
Fax: 908 964-0747
Albert W Bossert Jr, *President*
Mary Ann Bossert, *Corp Secy*
Lee R Rosander, *Vice Pres*
EMP: 8
SQ FT: 18,000
SALES: 1MM **Privately Held**
WEB: www.camptownauto.com
SIC: 3544 3469 Dies & die holders for metal cutting, forming, die casting; stamping metal for the trade

(G-4948)
CONSOLDATED STL ALUM FENCE INC
Also Called: Consolidated Stl Alum Fence I
316 N 12th St (07033-1162)
P.O. Box 643 (07033-0643)
PHONE..................................908 272-0494
Fax: 908 272-0494
Paul A Cacicedo Sr, *Ch of Bd*
Paul Cacicedo Jr, *President*
Armando Orsini, *Corp Secy*
John De Rosa, *Exec VP*
Rose Ann De Rosa, *Vice Pres*
EMP: 35 EST: 1958
SQ FT: 1,000

GEOGRAPHIC

SALES (est): 6MM **Privately Held**
WEB: www.csafinc.com
SIC: 1799 3496 3446 Fence construction;
miscellaneous fabricated wire products;
architectural metalwork

(G-4949)
CUBIST PHARMACEUTICALS
LLC (HQ)
2000 Galloping Hill Rd (07033-1310)
PHONE.................................908 740-4000
Michael W Bonney, *CEO*
Robert Perez, *President*
Kerry A Flynn, *Owner*
Thomas Desrosier, *Exec VP*
Steven Gilman, *Exec VP*
◆ EMP: 195
SALES (est): 202MM
SALES (corp-wide): 40.1B **Publicly Held**
WEB: www.cubist.com
SIC: 2834 Pharmaceutical preparations
PA: Merck & Co., Inc.
2000 Galloping Hill Rd
Kenilworth NJ 07033
908 740-4000

(G-4950)
DAYSOL INC
Also Called: Display Pro Manufacturing
40 Boright Ave (07033-1015)
PHONE.................................908 272-5900
Fax: 908 272-8320
Dennis Polvere, *President*
Dean Polvere, *Vice Pres*
William Silver, *Vice Pres*
Shirley Cook, *Accounting Dir*
EMP: 100
SQ FT: 60,000
SALES (est): 8.6MM **Privately Held**
SIC: 3993 Signs & advertising specialties

(G-4951)
DEWITT BROS TOOL CO INC
140 Market St (07033-2018)
PHONE.................................908 298-3700
Michael De Witt, *President*
Wenny Dewitt, *Treasurer*
▲ EMP: 8 EST: 1923
SQ FT: 3,500
SALES (est): 1.9MM **Privately Held**
SIC: 5084 3545 Metalworking tools (such
as drills, taps, dies, files); diamond cutting
tools for turning, boring, burnishing, etc.

(G-4952)
DIGITRON ELECTRONIC CORP
144 Market St (07033-2018)
PHONE.................................908 245-2012
Fax: 908 245-0555
Joel Schwartz, *President*
Douglas Berry, *Engineer*
EMP: 30
SQ FT: 25,000
SALES (est): 6.2MM **Privately Held**
WEB: www.digitroncorp.com
SIC: 3674 5065 Integrated circuits, semi-
conductor networks, etc.; semiconductor
devices; transistors

(G-4953)
EXOTHERMIC MOLDING INC
50 Lafayette Pl (07033-1105)
PHONE.................................908 272-2299
Fax: 908 272-3355
Paul K Steck, *President*
EMP: 25
SQ FT: 10,000
SALES (est): 6MM **Privately Held**
WEB: www.exothermic.com
SIC: 3089 Injection molding of plastics

(G-4954)
F & G TOOL & DIE INC
195 Sumner Ave (07033-1318)
PHONE.................................908 241-5880
Fax: 908 241-6831
Norman Friedrich, *President*
John Friedrich, *Vice Pres*
EMP: 5
SQ FT: 14,000
SALES (est): 490K **Privately Held**
SIC: 3544 3469 Special dies & tools;
stamping metal for the trade

(G-4955)
F & M MACHINE CO INC
751 Lexington Ave (07033-2015)
PHONE.................................908 245-8830
Richard Rutledge, *President*
Norman Radick, *Vice Pres*
EMP: 10
SQ FT: 11,000
SALES (est): 1.7MM **Privately Held**
WEB: www.fmmachineco.com
SIC: 3469 3599 Stamping metal for the
trade; machine shop, jobbing & repair

(G-4956)
FLEXLINE INC
Also Called: Service Seal Div
11 Columbus Ave (07033-1054)
PHONE.................................908 486-3322
Fax: 908 486-6176
Jeffrey C Scheininger, *President*
▲ EMP: 18
SQ FT: 20,000
SALES (est): 4MM **Privately Held**
WEB: www.flexlineus.com
SIC: 3599 5085 Flexible metal hose, tub-
ing & bellows; hose, belting & packing;
seals, industrial

(G-4957)
FOLEY-WAITE ASSOCIATES INC
746 Colfax Ave (07033-2051)
P.O. Box 164, Bloomfield (07003-0164)
PHONE.................................908 298-0700
Fax: 973 680-0453
Kathryn W Schackner, *Partner*
James Kelley Conklin, *Partner*
EMP: 10
SQ FT: 8,000
SALES (est): 1.1MM **Privately Held**
SIC: 2434 2511 Wood kitchen cabinets;
wood household furniture

(G-4958)
GAUER METAL PRODUCTS CO
INC
175 N Michigan Ave (07033-1259)
P.O. Box 158 (07033-0158)
PHONE.................................908 241-4080
Walter W Gauer, *CEO*
Dennis J Schultz, *President*
John Gotsch, *Senior VP*
Arturo Bermudez, *Engineer*
Sharon Schultz, *Admin Sec*
EMP: 50 EST: 1946
SQ FT: 70,000
SALES (est): 10MM **Privately Held**
WEB: www.gauermetal.com
SIC: 3541 3535 3444 5051 Machine
tools, metal cutting: exotic (explosive,
etc.); conveyors & conveying equipment;
sheet metalwork; bars, metal; racks, mer-
chandise display or storage: except wood

(G-4959)
GR STONE LLC
91 Market St (07033-1723)
PHONE.................................908 925-7290
Melvin Peralta, *Mng Member*
EMP: 8
SALES (est): 251.1K **Privately Held**
SIC: 3281 Marble, building: cut & shaped

(G-4960)
GREGORY PRESS INC
7 Mark Rd Ste A (07033-1000)
PHONE.................................908 686-6473
EMP: 12
SALES (est): 2.1MM **Privately Held**
SIC: 2752 Lithographic Commercial Print-
ing

(G-4961)
HI-GRADE PRODUCTS MFG CO
752 Jefferson Ave (07033-1718)
P.O. Box 273 (07033-0273)
PHONE.................................908 245-4133
Fax: 908 241-1260
Jeffrey Pfingst, *President*
Donna Pfingst, *Admin Sec*
EMP: 10 EST: 1960
SQ FT: 5,000
SALES: 1.1MM **Privately Held**
SIC: 3451 Screw machine products

(G-4962)
IDL TECHNI-EDGE LLC
30 Boright Ave (07033-1086)
PHONE.................................908 497-9818
Fax: 201 641-0835
Karl Gunkel, *Engineer*
Mike Donath, *CFO*
Janice Ecochard, *Accountant*
Elena Camaraza, *Cust Mgr*
Krista Maslowski, *Marketing Staff*
▲ EMP: 140
SALES (est): 29.7MM
SALES (corp-wide): 29.2MM **Privately
Held**
SIC: 3421 3425 3423 3841 Razor blades
& razors; saw blades & handsaws; hand
& edge tools; surgical & medical instru-
ments
PA: I.D.L. Tools International Llc
30 Boright Ave
Kenilworth NJ 07033
908 276-2330

(G-4963)
INK WELL PRINTERS LLC
38 S 21st St (07033-1626)
PHONE.................................908 272-8090
Fax: 908 272-7934
Edward Ensslin III,
Elizabeth Ensslin,
EMP: 5
SQ FT: 1,500
SALES: 700K **Privately Held**
SIC: 2752 Commercial printing, offset

(G-4964)
J M C TOOL & MFG CO
845 Fairfield Ave (07033-2013)
PHONE.................................908 241-8950
Fax: 908 241-8965
Mario J Giaimo, *President*
Charles V Giaimo, *Corp Secy*
EMP: 9
SQ FT: 6,400
SALES (est): 1.2MM **Privately Held**
SIC: 3599 Machine shop, jobbing & repair

(G-4965)
J-MAC PLASTICS INC (PA)
40 Lafayette Pl (07033-1105)
PHONE.................................908 709-1111
John Mc Namara, *President*
Jill Farawell, *Vice Pres*
Dan Mc Namara, *Manager*
Elizabeth Mc Namara, *Admin Sec*
EMP: 20
SQ FT: 12,500
SALES (est): 3.5MM **Privately Held**
SIC: 3089 3544 Injection molding of plas-
tics; industrial molds

(G-4966)
KELLES INCORPORATED
Also Called: Kelles Machining Center
20 Hoiles Dr Ste D (07033-1314)
PHONE.................................908 241-9300
Fax: 908 241-9654
Michael J Patrick, *President*
Tony Pace, *Vice Pres*
▲ EMP: 19
SALES (est): 1.6MM **Privately Held**
WEB: www.kelles.com
SIC: 3599 Machine shop, jobbing & repair

(G-4967)
KENECO INC
123 N 8th St (07033-1108)
P.O. Box 121 (07033-0121)
PHONE.................................908 241-3700
Fax: 908 272-0344
William Van Loan III, *President*
Thomas Hoefenkrieg, *Vice Pres*
EMP: 3
SQ FT: 800
SALES: 350MM **Privately Held**
WEB: www.kenecoinc.com
SIC: 3535 Conveyors & conveying equip-
ment

(G-4968)
KENILWORTH ANODIZING CO
201 S 31st St Ste A (07033-1305)
PHONE.................................908 241-5640
Robert Bramson, *President*
EMP: 30 EST: 1957
SQ FT: 20,000

SALES (est): 2.7MM **Privately Held**
SIC: 3471 Anodizing (plating) of metals or
formed products

(G-4969)
KNA GRAPHICS INC
Also Called: Sign-A-Rama
303 N 14th St (07033-1167)
PHONE.................................908 272-4232
Fax: 908 272-2233
Kamal Assad, *President*
Nada Assad, *Vice Pres*
EMP: 8
SQ FT: 4,000
SALES: 460K **Privately Held**
SIC: 3993 Signs, not made in custom sign
painting shops

(G-4970)
KONECRANES INC
834 Fairfield Ave (07033-2014)
PHONE.................................908 259-9696
Suzanne Barich, *Manager*
EMP: 14
SALES (corp-wide): 3.7B **Privately Held**
SIC: 3536 Hoists, cranes & monorails
HQ: Konecranes, Inc.
4401 Gateway Blvd
Springfield OH 45502

(G-4971)
M & S HOLES CORP
20 Hoiles Dr Ste A1 (07033-1314)
PHONE.................................908 298-6900
EMP: 5
SQ FT: 3,000
SALES (est): 596.9K **Privately Held**
SIC: 3599 Mfg Industrial Machinery

(G-4972)
MAINGEAR INC
206 Market St (07033-2032)
PHONE.................................888 624-6432
Wallace Santos, *CEO*
Jake Vance, *Business Mgr*
Ron Reed, *Senior Mgr*
EMP: 22
SQ FT: 5,000
SALES: 7.6MM **Privately Held**
SIC: 7373 3571 3575 3577 Turnkey ven-
dors, computer systems; personal com-
puters (microcomputers); computer
terminals; computer peripheral equip-
ment; computers & accessories, personal
& home entertainment; computer & soft-
ware stores

(G-4973)
MASTER DRAPERY
WORKROOM INC
220 N 14th St (07033-1166)
PHONE.................................908 272-4404
Fax: 908 709-3740
Philip Ricca, *President*
Anne Ricca, *Corp Secy*
Philip A Ricca, *Vice Pres*
EMP: 10
SQ FT: 3,000
SALES (est): 520K **Privately Held**
SIC: 2391 Curtains & draperies

(G-4974)
MERCK & CO INC (PA)
2000 Galloping Hill Rd (07033-1310)
P.O. Box 100, Whitehouse Station (08889-
0100)
PHONE.................................908 740-4000
Fax: 908 735-1220
Kenneth C Frazier, *Ch of Bd*
James Hall, *President*
David Rubin, *Managing Dir*
Minesh Sangani, *District Mgr*
David King, *Counsel*
EMP: 277 EST: 1928
SALES: 40.1B **Publicly Held**
SIC: 2834 2836 2844 5122 Pharmaceuti-
cal preparations; druggists' preparations
(pharmaceuticals); drugs acting on the
respiratory system; drugs affecting para-
sitic & infective diseases; vaccines; veteri-
nary biological products; suntan lotions &
oils; animal medicines

▲ = Import ▼=Export
◆ =Import/Export

(G-4975)
MERCK & CO INC
251 S 31st St (07033-1305)
PHONE..................908 740-4000
EMP: 41
SALES (corp-wide): 40.1B Publicly Held
SIC: 2834 Pharmaceutical preparations
PA: Merck & Co., Inc.
    2000 Galloping Hill Rd
    Kenilworth NJ 07033
    908 740-4000

(G-4976)
MERCK & CO INC
2000 Galloping Hill Rd (07033-1310)
PHONE..................908 298-4000
Fax: 908 822-7048
EMP: 56
SALES (corp-wide): 40.1B Publicly Held
SIC: 2834 Mfg Pharmaceutical Preparations
PA: Merck & Co., Inc.
    2000 Galloping Hill Rd
    Kenilworth NJ 07033
    908 740-4000

(G-4977)
MERCK SHARP & DOHME CORP (HQ)
2000 Galloping Hill Rd (07033-1310)
P.O. Box 982122, El Paso TX (79998-2122)
PHONE..................908 740-4000
Fax: 908 298-4690
Kenneth C Frazier, Ch of Bd
Sanat Chattopadhyay, Exec VP
Richard R Deluca Jr, Exec VP
Julie L Gerberding, Exec VP
Mirian M Graddick-Weir, Exec VP
◆ EMP: 1600 EST: 1935
SALES (est): 6B
SALES (corp-wide): 40.1B Publicly Held
WEB: www.schering.com
SIC: 2834 8741 Pharmaceutical preparations; druggists' preparations (pharmaceuticals); drugs acting on the respiratory system; drugs affecting parasitic & infective diseases; management services
PA: Merck & Co., Inc.
    2000 Galloping Hill Rd
    Kenilworth NJ 07033
    908 740-4000

(G-4978)
MERCK SHARP & DOHME CORP
2000 Galloping Hill Rd (07033-1310)
PHONE..................908 423-1000
Fax: 908 236-1702
Michael Pohleven, Opers Dir
April Cobb, Project Mgr
Leif Matzon, Project Mgr
Scott Baker, Opers Mgr
Stan Avery, Research
EMP: 275
SALES (corp-wide): 40.1B Publicly Held
SIC: 2834 Pharmaceutical preparations
HQ: Merck Sharp & Dohme Corp.
    2000 Galloping Hill Rd
    Kenilworth NJ 07033
    908 740-4000

(G-4979)
NATUREE NUTS INC
Also Called: Sungood
636 N Michigan Ave (07033-1042)
PHONE..................732 786-4663
Abraham Rosman, Vice Pres
EMP: 10
SQ FT: 9,150
SALES (est): 409.3K Privately Held
SIC: 2064 2068 Nuts, glace; nuts: dried, dehydrated, salted or roasted

(G-4980)
NEW JERSEY AIR PRODUCTS INC
4 Mark Rd Ste D (07033-1025)
PHONE..................908 964-9001
Fax: 908 964-9003
Pete Petracco, President
EMP: 10
SALES (est): 1.5MM Privately Held
SIC: 3999 Atomizers, toiletry

(G-4981)
NICKS INC
Also Called: Nick's Railings
39 N 23rd St (07033-1619)
PHONE..................908 272-3739
Fax: 908 931-6692
Nicholas Patella, President
Catheren Patella, Admin Sec
EMP: 4
SALES (est): 220K Privately Held
SIC: 3446 3441 3354 Railings, prefabricated metal; fabricated structural metal; aluminum extruded products

(G-4982)
NORDIC METAL LLC
500 S 31st St (07033-1398)
PHONE..................908 245-8900
Fax: 908 245-5345
Bo Johansson,
Lars Johansson,
EMP: 4
SQ FT: 7,000
SALES (est): 800K Privately Held
SIC: 3444 Sheet metalwork

(G-4983)
OCEAN DRIVE INC
Also Called: Ocean Drive Clothing Co.
530 N Michigan Ave (07033-1023)
PHONE..................908 964-2591
Abraham Shiloach, President
Joseph Shiloach, Vice Pres
◆ EMP: 7 EST: 1992
SQ FT: 10,000
SALES (est): 1.1MM Privately Held
WEB: www.oceandriveclothing.com
SIC: 2339 Sportswear, women's

(G-4984)
OPTIMER PHARMACEUTICALS LLC
2000 Galloping Hill Rd (07033-1310)
PHONE..................858 909-0736
Henry A McKinnell, CEO
John Womelsdorf, President
Eric Sirota, COO
Linda E Amper, Senior VP
Sherwood L Gorbach, Senior VP
EMP: 281
SQ FT: 24,000
SALES (est): 27.7MM
SALES (corp-wide): 40.1B Publicly Held
WEB: www.optimerpharma.com
SIC: 2834 Pharmaceutical preparations
HQ: Cubist Pharmaceuticals Llc
    2000 Galloping Hill Rd
    Kenilworth NJ 07033

(G-4985)
OPTIMUM PRECISION INC
Also Called: Optimum Precision Machine & Tl
147 N Michigan Ave (07033-1275)
PHONE..................908 259-9017
Fax: 908 259-9013
Gregory Maroukian, President
EMP: 4
SALES (est): 242K Privately Held
SIC: 3599 Machine shop, jobbing & repair

(G-4986)
PETERSON STAMPING & MFG CO
75 N Michigan Ave (07033-1750)
P.O. Box 190 (07033-0190)
PHONE..................908 241-0900
Fax: 908 241-0706
Robert Olsen, President
Lynette Peterson Olander, Vice Pres
Laura M Peterson, CFO
Laura Peterson, CFO
Donna Olsen, Treasurer
EMP: 15 EST: 1945
SQ FT: 10,000
SALES (est): 1.5MM Privately Held
WEB: www.petersonstamping.com
SIC: 3469 Stamping metal for the trade

(G-4987)
PETRO PLASTICS COMPANY INC
500 Hoiles Dr (07033-1330)
PHONE..................908 789-1200
Fax: 908 789-1381
Lewis Petrozzielo, President

EMP: 30
SQ FT: 24,000
SALES (est): 4.4MM Privately Held
SIC: 3089 Extruded finished plastic products; plastic processing

(G-4988)
PINNACLE COSMETIC PACKG LLC
Also Called: Pinnacle Cosmetics Packaging
80 Market St (07033-1722)
P.O. Box 733 (07033-0733)
PHONE..................908 241-7777
Fax: 908 241-9449
Ed Halsch,
▲ EMP: 12
SQ FT: 25,000
SALES (est): 2.3MM Privately Held
WEB: www.pcp-llc.com
SIC: 2631 Container, packaging & boxboard

(G-4989)
PLASTPAC INC (PA)
30 Boright Ave (07033-1086)
PHONE..................908 272-7200
Mark Porges, President
EMP: 15
SALES (est): 9.3MM Privately Held
SIC: 3086 Packaging & shipping materials, foamed plastic

(G-4990)
PROGRESSIVE TOOL & MFG CORP
708 Fairfield Ave (07033-2012)
PHONE..................908 245-7010
Fax: 908 245-7011
Gunther Heim, President
Willy Heim, Corp Secy
EMP: 4
SQ FT: 2,100
SALES (est): 270K Privately Held
SIC: 3544 Special dies & tools; jigs & fixtures

(G-4991)
RAMCO MANUFACTURING CO INC (PA)
365 Carnegie Ave (07033-2004)
PHONE..................908 245-4500
Kevin Nee, President
Gerald Nee, Principal
Virginia Nee, Vice Pres
Bryan Argenbright, Natl Sales Mgr
Kathleen Russell, Sales Staff
EMP: 25 EST: 1938
SALES (est): 5MM Privately Held
WEB: www.ramco-safetyshields.com
SIC: 3494 3545 3463 Pipe fittings; files, machine tool; nonferrous forgings

(G-4992)
RESOURCES INC IN DISPLAY (PA)
Also Called: Unified Resources
40 Boright Ave (07033-1015)
PHONE..................908 272-5900
Dennis Polvere, President
Dean Polvere, Vice Pres
William Silver, Vice Pres
John Pillarella, Controller
Gregory Gannon, Shareholder
▲ EMP: 30
SQ FT: 38,000
SALES (est): 3.8MM Privately Held
SIC: 3993 Displays & cutouts, window & lobby

(G-4993)
ROTECH TOOL & MOLD CO INC
824 Fairfield Ave (07033-2014)
PHONE..................908 241-9669
Robert F Leschinski, President
Theresa J Leschinski, Corp Secy
EMP: 9
SQ FT: 5,018
SALES (est): 790K Privately Held
SIC: 3544 3542 Forms (molds), for foundry & plastics working machinery; industrial molds; machine tools, metal forming type

(G-4994)
SEAGRAVE COATINGS CORP
Also Called: Plextone
209 N Michigan Ave (07033-1264)
PHONE..................201 933-1000
H Peter Tepperman, CEO
David Walden, Accounts Exec
▲ EMP: 50 EST: 1846
SQ FT: 30,000
SALES (est): 10MM Privately Held
WEB: www.seagravecoatings.com
SIC: 2851 Paints & allied products

(G-4995)
SEATING EXPERT INC
721 Boulevard (07033-1703)
PHONE..................201 299-9109
▼ EMP: 50
SALES (est): 6.5MM Privately Held
SIC: 2521 Mfg Wood Office Furniture

(G-4996)
SECURITY FABRICATORS INC
321 Lafayette Ave (07033-1078)
P.O. Box 643 (07033-0643)
PHONE..................908 272-9171
Paul Cacicedo Sr, Ch of Bd
Paul Cacicedo Jr, President
Armando Orsini, Corp Secy
John De Rosa, Exec VP
Roseann De Rosa, Vice Pres
EMP: 18
SQ FT: 2,500
SALES (est): 7.6MM Privately Held
SIC: 3315 3496 3446 3354 Chain link fencing; miscellaneous fabricated wire products; architectural metalwork; aluminum extruded products

(G-4997)
STOLLEN MACHINE & TOOL COMPANY
761 Lexington Ave (07033-2015)
PHONE..................908 241-0622
Doug Stollen, President
EMP: 6 EST: 1954
SQ FT: 10,000
SALES: 500K Privately Held
SIC: 3599 Machine shop, jobbing & repair

(G-4998)
SYNRAY CORPORATION
209 N Michigan Ave (07033-1264)
PHONE..................908 245-2600
Fax: 908 245-2460
H Peter Tepperman, CEO
Stanley Lesnewski, President
Colleen Merendino, Office Mgr
Peter H Tepperman, CTO
▲ EMP: 25
SQ FT: 30,000
SALES (est): 7.7MM Privately Held
WEB: www.synray.com
SIC: 2821 Plastics materials & resins

(G-4999)
TASTE IT PRESENTS INC
200 Sumner Ave (07033-1319)
PHONE..................908 241-9191
John Alair, President
Carol Devine, Vice Pres
Paula Perlis, Vice Pres
Vincent Caminiti, CFO
Nellie Mnich, Accountant
▲ EMP: 75
SQ FT: 85,000
SALES (est): 15.6MM Privately Held
WEB: www.tasteitpresents.com
SIC: 2099 Food preparations

(G-5000)
TOO COOL OF OCEAN CITY
530 N Michigan Ave (07033-1023)
PHONE..................908 810-6363
Eli Shiloach, Manager
EMP: 4
SALES (est): 355.1K Privately Held
SIC: 2389 Apparel & accessories

(G-5001)
TOP LINE SEATING INC
540 S 31st St (07033-1306)
PHONE..................908 241-9051
Carl Friedrich, CEO
Norman Friedrich, President

John Friedrich, *Vice Pres*
EMP: 15
SQ FT: 14,000
SALES: 1.5MM **Privately Held**
SIC: 2522 Office chairs, benches & stools, except wood; chairs, office: padded or plain, except wood; benches, office: except wood; stools, office: except wood

(G-5002)
UNION COUNTY SEATING & SUP CO
135 N Michigan Ave (07033-1269)
PHONE..................................908 241-4949
Fax: 908 241-2979
Bruce Bussell, *President*
EMP: 26
SQ FT: 4,500
SALES: 1.2MM **Privately Held**
WEB: www.unioncountyseating.com
SIC: 2531 Seats, automobile

(G-5003)
VS SYSTEMATICS CORP
300 S Michigan Ave (07033-2036)
PHONE..................................908 241-5110
Fax: 908 241-0052
Tony Esteves, *Principal*
Sarah Esteves, *Vice Pres*
EMP: 5
SQ FT: 5,000
SALES (est): 1.5MM **Privately Held**
WEB: www.vssystematics.com
SIC: 5999 3714 Motors, electric; motor vehicle parts & accessories

(G-5004)
WAAGE ELECTRIC INC
720 Colfax Ave (07033-2050)
P.O. Box 337 (07033-0337)
PHONE..................................908 245-9363
Fax: 908 245-8477
Curtis Marc Waage, *President*
Marc Waage, *President*
Marcia McBurney, *Principal*
Bruce Waage, *Vice Pres*
EMP: 9 EST: 1908
SQ FT: 11,800
SALES: 1MM **Privately Held**
WEB: www.waage.com
SIC: 3567 7629 3821 3548 Heating units & devices, industrial: electric; electrical equipment repair services; laboratory apparatus & furniture; welding apparatus; fabricated plate work (boiler shop); heating equipment, except electric

(G-5005)
WAGNER FOTO SCREEN PROCESS
4 Mark Rd (07033-1025)
PHONE..................................908 624-0800
Fax: 908 624-0801
Jim Lucadema, *Partner*
Robert Mosucci, *Partner*
EMP: 4
SALES (est): 352.1K **Privately Held**
SIC: 2759 Screen printing

(G-5006)
WELTON V JOHNSON ENGINEERING
22 N 26th St (07033-1724)
PHONE..................................908 241-3100
Fax: 908 241-3101
Paul Damjanovic, *President*
EMP: 10 EST: 1946
SALES (est): 1.3MM **Privately Held**
SIC: 3451 Screw machine products

(G-5007)
WESTFIELD SHTMTL WORKS INC
261 Monroe Ave (07033-1131)
P.O. Box 128 (07033-0128)
PHONE..................................908 276-5500
Fax: 908 276-6808
Campbell Johnstone, *CEO*
Thomas Johnstone, *Vice Pres*
Tom Johnstone, *Vice Pres*
Gregg Wheatley, *CFO*
Greg Wheatley, *Human Res Dir*
EMP: 45 EST: 1928
SQ FT: 50,000

SALES (est): 9.9MM **Privately Held**
WEB: www.westfieldsheetmetal.com
SIC: 3444 3441 Sheet metal specialties, not stamped; fabricated structural metal

(G-5008)
WHITE HOME PRODUCTS INC
30 Boright Ave 4 (07033-1086)
PHONE..................................908 226-2501
Donald Weiss, *CEO*
Tamara Owens, *President*
▲ **EMP:** 6
SALES (est): 570.7K **Privately Held**
SIC: 3634 Electric housewares & fans

(G-5009)
YUHL PRODUCTS INC
15 N 7th St (07033-1406)
PHONE..................................908 276-5180
Ron Yuhl, *President*
EMP: 4
SQ FT: 1,000
SALES: 500K **Privately Held**
SIC: 5084 3089 Plastic products machinery; injection molded finished plastic products

---

Kenvil
Morris County

(G-5010)
COUNTY CONCRETE CORPORATION (PA)
Also Called: CCC
50 Railroad Ave (07847-2606)
P.O. Box F (07847-1005)
PHONE..................................973 744-2188
Fax: 908 584-4370
John C Crimi, *President*
Peter Crimi, *Exec VP*
EMP: 80
SQ FT: 1,500
SALES (est): 30.2MM **Privately Held**
WEB: www.countyconcretenj.com
SIC: 3273 5032 Ready-mixed concrete; sand, construction

(G-5011)
MAJOR AUTO INSTALLATIONS INC
Also Called: Spectrum Communications
47 N Dell Ave Ste 10 (07847-2640)
PHONE..................................973 252-4262
Fax: 973 584-5022
Edward A Windt, *CEO*
J Bradley Badal, *President*
Kent Meinhold, *COO*
EMP: 20
SQ FT: 4,500
SALES (est): 3.8MM **Privately Held**
SIC: 3663 5065 Radio broadcasting & communications equipment; electronic parts & equipment

(G-5012)
PINTO OF MONTVILLE INC
25 Pine St (07847-2603)
PHONE..................................973 584-2002
John Pinto, *President*
EMP: 8
SQ FT: 5,000
SALES: 1.2MM **Privately Held**
SIC: 3589 Commercial cooking & food-warming equipment

(G-5013)
PRO IMAGE PROMOTIONS INC
Also Called: Brian's Embroidery
480 Us Highway 46 (07847-2675)
PHONE..................................973 252-8000
Fax: 973 252-8340
Brian Hewitt, *President*
EMP: 5
SALES (est): 454.4K **Privately Held**
SIC: 2395 Embroidery & art needlework

(G-5014)
TROY-ONIC INC
90 N Dell Ave (07847-2559)
P.O. Box 494 (07847-0494)
PHONE..................................973 584-6830
Fax: 973 584-7205
Michael Murphy, *President*

Edna Murphy, *Corp Secy*
EMP: 40
SQ FT: 5,000
SALES (est): 3MM **Privately Held**
SIC: 3671 3545 Electron tubes; machine tool accessories

Keyport
Monmouth County

(G-5015)
AMP CUSTOM RUBBER INC
3 Cass St Ste 8 (07735-1425)
P.O. Box 377, Hazlet (07730-0377)
PHONE..................................732 888-2714
John Petrizzo, *President*
EMP: 12
SQ FT: 15,000
SALES (est): 1.6MM **Privately Held**
WEB: www.ampcustomrubber.com
SIC: 3061 2499 2493 Mechanical rubber goods; cork & cork products; reconstituted wood products

(G-5016)
ENCUR INC
200 Division St (07735-1604)
P.O. Box 92 (07735-0092)
PHONE..................................732 264-2098
Fax: 732 264-0126
Mark Curcio, *President*
Maureen Del Popolo, *Manager*
EMP: 7
SQ FT: 5,000
SALES (est): 1.8MM **Privately Held**
WEB: www.encur.com
SIC: 3564 5074 Air purification equipment; heating equipment (hydronic)

(G-5017)
FAST COPY PRINTING CENTER
Also Called: Fast T'S
81 Broad St (07735-1242)
PHONE..................................732 739-4646
Fax: 732 739-8862
William Sacks, *Owner*
EMP: 10
SQ FT: 4,500
SALES (est): 500K **Privately Held**
WEB: www.fastcopynj.com
SIC: 2752 Commercial printing, offset

(G-5018)
FRAGRANCE RESOURCES INC
275 Clark St (07735-1107)
P.O. Box 110 (07735-0110)
PHONE..................................973 458-5231
Fax: 732 264-2933
EMP: 55
SALES (corp-wide): 3.4B **Publicly Held**
SIC: 2899 2844 Mfg Chemical Preparations Mfg Toilet Preparations
HQ: Fragrance Resources, Inc.
600 State Route 36
Hazlet NJ 07730
973 777-2979

(G-5019)
G & M CUSTOM FORMICA WORK
120 Francis St Ste 5 (07735-1363)
PHONE..................................732 888-0360
Fax: 732 888-4450
George Macchia, *Partner*
James Macchia, *Partner*
Michael Macchia, *Partner*
EMP: 5
SALES: 150K **Privately Held**
WEB: www.sgprinting.net
SIC: 2434 Wood kitchen cabinets

(G-5020)
METHOD ASSOC INC
120 Francis St Ste 2 (07735-1363)
PHONE..................................732 888-0444
Fax: 732 264-8769
Malcolm Will, *President*
Stephen Will, *General Mgr*
Debbie Grant, *Manager*
▲ **EMP:** 12
SQ FT: 20,000
SALES: 1.2MM **Privately Held**
WEB: www.methodassociates.com
SIC: 3543 7389 Industrial patterns; design, commercial & industrial

(G-5021)
MR GREEN TEA ICE CREAM CORP
25 Church St Unit 104 (07735-1508)
P.O. Box 70255, Staten Island NY (10307-0255)
PHONE..................................732 446-9800
EMP: 21
SQ FT: 3,500
SALES: 2.5MM **Privately Held**
SIC: 2024 Mfg Ice Cream/Frozen Desert

(G-5022)
MR GREEN TEA ICE CREAM CORP
42 E Front St (07735-1544)
PHONE..................................732 446-9800
Richard Emanuele, *CEO*
Marcus Lemonis, *CEO*
Lori Emanuele, *Purch Dir*
EMP: 15
SQ FT: 10,000
SALES (est): 581.4K **Privately Held**
SIC: 2024 Ice cream & frozen desserts

(G-5023)
REEDY INTERNATIONAL CORP
25 E Front St Ste 200 (07735-1564)
P.O. Box 38486, Charlotte NC (28278-1008)
PHONE..................................732 264-1777
Fax: 732 264-1189
Michael Reedy, *Owner*
Anne Reedy, *Vice Pres*
Patricia Roberts, *Purchasing*
Bryan Burgess, *Sales Staff*
Kristen Reedy, *Director*
EMP: 13
SALES (est): 1.1MM **Privately Held**
SIC: 3089 Plastic processing

(G-5024)
TASK INTERNATIONAL (USA) INC
3 Cass St (07735-1425)
PHONE..................................732 739-0377
Fax: 914 337-5404
Richard Hopwood, *President*
Loretta Hopwood, *Corp Secy*
Thomas Saporita, *Vice Pres*
▲ **EMP:** 13
SQ FT: 5,000
SALES (est): 1.1MM **Privately Held**
SIC: 3585 Air conditioning equipment, complete

(G-5025)
TIRE PLACE LLC (PA)
408 State Route 35 (07735-5032)
PHONE..................................732 970-6667
Michael Travers, *CEO*
EMP: 5
SALES (est): 741.2K **Privately Held**
SIC: 3061 Automotive rubber goods (mechanical)

(G-5026)
WCD ENTERPRISES INC
1 Main St (07735-1213)
PHONE..................................732 888-4422
Fax: 732 332-0303
Hank Freeman, *CFO*
EMP: 9
SALES (est): 934.4K **Privately Held**
WEB: www.adultsights.com
SIC: 4813 2741 ;

Kingston
Somerset County

(G-5027)
CIVIC RESEARCH INSTITUTE INC (PA)
4478 Route 27 Ste 202 (08528-9613)
P.O. Box 585 (08528-0585)
PHONE..................................609 683-4450
Fax: 609 683-7291
Mark E Peel, *President*
Arthur H Rosenfeld, *Chairman*
Deborah J Launer, *Vice Pres*
Felicia A Rosenfeld, *Vice Pres*
EMP: 3

▲ = Import ▼=Export
◆ =Import/Export

SQ FT: 1,000
SALES: 1.5MM **Privately Held**
WEB: www.civicresearchinstitute.com
SIC: 2721 Periodicals

(G-5028)
JOSEPH AND WILLIAM STAVOLA (PA)
460 River Rd (08528)
P.O. Box 419 (08528-0419)
PHONE..................................609 924-0300
Joseph W Stavola, *President*
William Stavola, *Corp Secy*
EMP: 50
SQ FT: 5,000
SALES (est): 15.7MM **Privately Held**
SIC: 3273 2951 1429 1611 Ready-mixed concrete; concrete, bituminous; trap rock, crushed & broken-quarrying; highway & street paving contractor

(G-5029)
KINGSTON NURSERIES LLC
Also Called: Mapleton Nurseries
140 Mapleton Rd (08528)
P.O. Box 396 (08528-0396)
PHONE..................................609 430-0366
Fax: 609 430-0367
EMP: 12
SALES (est): 880K **Privately Held**
SIC: 3299 Mfg Nonmetallic Mineral Products

(G-5030)
TRAP ROCK INDUSTRIES INC (PA)
460 River Rd (08528)
P.O. Box 419 (08528-0419)
PHONE..................................609 924-0300
Fax: 609 924-5734
Joseph M Stavola, *President*
Wayne Byard, *Vice Pres*
Michael Crowley, *Vice Pres*
Ronald Lapinski, *Buyer*
EMP: 300 EST: 1860
SQ FT: 90,000
SALES (est): 131.7MM **Privately Held**
WEB: www.traprock.com
SIC: 3273 3272 1429 1611 Ready-mixed concrete; concrete products; trap rock, crushed & broken-quarrying; highway & street paving contractor

(G-5031)
TRAP ROCK INDUSTRIES LLC
460 River Rd (08528)
PHONE..................................609 924-0300
Michael Crowley, *Principal*
EMP: 99
SQ FT: 8,000
SALES (est): 3.4MM **Privately Held**
SIC: 1429 Trap rock, crushed & broken-quarrying

Kinnelon
Morris County

(G-5032)
ACME WIRE FORMING LLC
18 Pepperidge Tree Ter (07405-2228)
PHONE..................................201 218-2912
Kevin Skvorecz,
EMP: 12
SALES (est): 851.7K **Privately Held**
SIC: 3496 Miscellaneous fabricated wire products

(G-5033)
ARCHI-TREAD INC
191 Brook Valley Rd (07405-3326)
PHONE..................................973 725-5738
Scott Akin, *President*
EMP: 9
SALES (est): 920K **Privately Held**
SIC: 3534 Stair elevators, motor powered

(G-5034)
DIAMEX INTERNATIONAL CORP (PA)
23 Birch Rd (07405-2504)
PHONE..................................973 838-8844
Andreas Ladjias, *President*
EMP: 7

SALES (est): 957.8K **Privately Held**
SIC: 2653 Corrugated & solid fiber boxes

(G-5035)
GP JAGER INC
143 Miller Rd (07405-3005)
P.O. Box 50, Boonton (07005-0050)
PHONE..................................973 750-1180
Gregory Jager, *President*
Zuzanna Stolc, *Administration*
EMP: 4 EST: 2015
SALES (est): 598K **Privately Held**
SIC: 3589 Water treatment equipment, industrial; sewage treatment equipment

(G-5036)
HILLCREST OPTICIANS
11 Kiel Ave Ste D-1 (07405-2557)
PHONE..................................973 838-6666
Fax: 973 838-3579
Eric Shnayder, *Owner*
EMP: 4
SALES (est): 190K **Privately Held**
SIC: 3851 5995 Ophthalmic goods; opticians

(G-5037)
JTWO INC
Also Called: Storybook Knits
4 Birch Rd (07405-2505)
PHONE..................................201 410-1616
Jamie Gries, *President*
EMP: 4
SQ FT: 2,000
SALES (est): 1.9MM **Privately Held**
SIC: 2253 Sweaters & sweater coats, knit

(G-5038)
LIFE RECOVERY SYSTEMS HD LLC (PA)
170 Kinnelon Rd Rm 5 (07405-2323)
PHONE..................................973 283-2800
John Diliddo, *President*
Robert Schock, *Vice Pres*
Rick Hettenbach, *Mng Member*
EMP: 4
SALES (est): 753.7K **Privately Held**
SIC: 3829 Personnel dosimetry devices

(G-5039)
OLYMPIC EDM SERVICES INC
Also Called: Olympic Custom Tools
20 Kiel Ave (07405-2552)
PHONE..................................973 492-0664
Donald Ferrante, *President*
Jody Laufer, *Manager*
EMP: 8 EST: 1977
SQ FT: 4,000
SALES (est): 1.2MM **Privately Held**
SIC: 3544 3599 Special dies & tools; electrical discharge machining (EDM)

(G-5040)
PUREVOLUTION
62 Fayson Lake Rd (07405-3124)
PHONE..................................973 919-4047
Jeffrey Schirripa, *CEO*
EMP: 10
SALES (est): 552.9K **Privately Held**
SIC: 2833 Medicinals & botanicals

(G-5041)
TUFF MUTTERS LLC
2 Kiel Ave Unit 155 (07405-2572)
PHONE..................................973 291-6679
Michelle Bonus, *Mng Member*
EMP: 4
SALES (est): 185.8K **Privately Held**
SIC: 2399 5199 5999 Horse & pet accessories, textile; pet supplies; pet supplies

(G-5042)
TYPEN GRAPHICS INC
170 Kinnelon Rd Rm 12 (07405-2324)
PHONE..................................973 838-6544
Fax: 973 838-8161
Mary Weber, *President*
John Weber, *Vice Pres*
EMP: 8
SQ FT: 1,500
SALES (est): 797.4K **Privately Held**
WEB: www.typengraphics.com
SIC: 2791 Typesetting

Lafayette
Sussex County

(G-5043)
ACRYLICS UNLIMITED
11 Millpond Dr Unit 2 (07848-3826)
PHONE..................................973 862-6014
EMP: 7 EST: 2013
SALES (est): 1MM **Privately Held**
SIC: 3089 Plastic processing

(G-5044)
BEAVER RUN FARMS
Also Called: Shotmeyer Bros
300 Beaver Run Rd (07848-3131)
PHONE..................................973 875-5555
Kevin Joan, *Manager*
EMP: 15
SALES (corp-wide): 1.4MM **Privately Held**
SIC: 2951 Asphalt & asphaltic paving mixtures (not from refineries)
PA: Beaver Run Farms
10 Wagaraw Rd
Hawthorne NJ 07506
973 427-1000

(G-5045)
BON CHEF INC (PA)
205 State Route 94 (07848-4617)
PHONE..................................973 383-8848
Salvatore Torre, *President*
Tina Crowley, *General Mgr*
Paul McGreevy, *Opers Mgr*
Adel Salem, *VP Sales*
Maryanne Torre, *Sales Staff*
◆ EMP: 65
SQ FT: 63,000
SALES (est): 33.2MM **Privately Held**
WEB: www.bonchef.com
SIC: 5046 3365 Commercial cooking & food service equipment; aluminum foundries

(G-5046)
F W BENNETT & SON INC
403 Sparta Rd (07848-3643)
PHONE..................................973 383-4050
Frank W Bennet, *President*
EMP: 4 EST: 1929
SALES (est): 262.2K **Privately Held**
SIC: 1442 Common sand mining; gravel mining

(G-5047)
JAMES ZYLSTRA ENTERPRISES INC
Also Called: Fredon Welding & Iron Works
52 State Route 15 (07848-2424)
P.O. Box 260 (07848-0260)
PHONE..................................973 383-6768
Fax: 973 383-8018
James S Zylstra, *President*
Laura Silvero, *Admin Asst*
EMP: 30
SQ FT: 9,200
SALES (est): 4.7MM **Privately Held**
WEB: www.fredonwelding.com
SIC: 3446 Architectural metalwork

(G-5048)
JORDAN MANUFACTURING LLC
28 Randazzo Rd (07848-2221)
P.O. Box 226 (07848-0226)
PHONE..................................973 383-8363
Gary Wilson, *Mayor*
Zdenek Fremund, *Manager*
EMP: 5
SQ FT: 6,000
SALES: 1MM
SALES (corp-wide): 273.6MM **Privately Held**
WEB: www.jordanmanufacturing.com
SIC: 3469 3544 Stamping metal for the trade; special dies & tools
HQ: Carl Stahl Sava Industries, Inc.
4 N Corporate Dr
Riverdale NJ 07457
973 835-0882

(G-5049)
LAMSON AIRTUBES LLC
10 Millpond Dr Unit 4 (07848-3825)
PHONE..................................973 300-4267
Fax: 973 300-1932
Scott Begraft, *CEO*
Bryan Neuman, *Vice Pres*
Arlene Matos, *Project Mgr*
Pamela Struble, *Office Mgr*
Pam Spruble, *Admin Sec*
EMP: 11
SALES: 2.8MM **Privately Held**
WEB: www.airlinkans.com
SIC: 3535 Pneumatic tube conveyor systems

(G-5050)
LIMECREST QUARRY DEVELOPER LLC
217 Limecrest Rd (07848-3646)
PHONE..................................973 383-7100
Pam Kelley, *General Mgr*
Howard Goddard, *Superintendent*
EMP: 15
SALES (est): 1.5MM **Privately Held**
WEB: www.limecrest.com
SIC: 1422 Crushed & broken limestone

(G-5051)
METAPORT MANUFACTURING LLC
28 Randazzo Rd (07848-2221)
P.O. Box 226 (07848-0226)
PHONE..................................973 383-8363
Zdenek Fremund, *Mng Member*
EMP: 7
SALES (est): 750K **Privately Held**
SIC: 5084 3541 Machine tools & metalworking machinery; machine tools, metal cutting type

(G-5052)
RT COM USA INC
10 Millpond Dr Unit 2 (07848-3825)
P.O. Box 135, Ogdensburg (07439-0135)
PHONE..................................973 862-4210
Chanyi Ryu, *President*
Joon Ryu, *President*
EMP: 6
SALES (est): 577.8K **Privately Held**
WEB: www.rtcomusa.com
SIC: 3571 Electronic computers

(G-5053)
TECH-NI FOLD USA INC
4 Wisteria Rd (07848-3648)
PHONE..................................973 383-6691
Andre Palko, *President*
Gina Palko, *Vice Pres*
EMP: 4
SALES (est): 365.4K **Privately Held**
SIC: 2796 Platemaking services

Lake Hiawatha
Morris County

(G-5054)
EMPIRICAL LABS INC
41 N Beverwyck Rd (07034-2605)
PHONE..................................973 541-9446
David Derr, *President*
Judith Saiya-Berr, *Vice Pres*
Judith Saiya-Derr, *Vice Pres*
EMP: 7
SALES (est): 800K **Privately Held**
WEB: www.empiricallabs.com
SIC: 3651 Audio electronic systems; video & audio equipment

Lake Hopatcong
Morris County

(G-5055)
CRETT CONSTRUCTION INC
18 Cella St (07849-2233)
PHONE..................................973 663-1184
Fax: 973 663-4360
John Starger, *President*
Ed Poskit, *Vice Pres*
EMP: 13

SALES (est): 1.1MM **Privately Held**
SIC: **1761** 3444 Sheet metalwork; sheet metalwork

(G-5056)
DIGITIZE INC
158 Edison Rd (07849-2217)
PHONE.................................973 663-1011
Fax: 973 663-4333
Abraham Brecher, *President*
Linda Brecher, *Treasurer*
EMP: 17
SQ FT: 6,800
SALES (est): 3.2MM **Privately Held**
WEB: www.digitize-inc.com
SIC: **3669** 3699 Fire alarm apparatus, electric; security devices

(G-5057)
STACKS ENVMTL LTD LBLTY CO
5 Crescent Dr (07849-1339)
P.O. Box 278 (07849-0278)
PHONE.................................973 885-2036
Raymond F Evans, *President*
EMP: 7
SQ FT: 30,000
SALES (est): 1.2MM **Privately Held**
SIC: **3443** Boiler shop products: boilers, smokestacks, steel tanks; breechings, metal plate

(G-5058)
WATER MARK TECHNOLOGIES INC
762 State Route 15 S 2d (07849-2410)
PHONE.................................973 663-3438
Phil Reilly, *President*
Kim Logsdon, *Vice Pres*
▲ EMP: 8
SALES (est): 1.5MM **Privately Held**
SIC: **2819** Brine; calcium chloride & hypochlorite

Lakehurst
Ocean County

(G-5059)
MICRO MEDIA PUBLICATIONS INC
Also Called: Berkeley Times
15 Union Ave (08733-3023)
P.O. Box 521 (08733-0521)
PHONE.................................732 657-7344
Fax: 732 657-7388
Stewart Swann, *President*
Jason Allentoff, *General Mgr*
Chris Lundy, *Editor*
Robin Weather, *Vice Pres*
Allison Gradzki, *Prdtn Mgr*
EMP: 7
SALES (est): 410K **Privately Held**
WEB: www.micromediapubs2.com
SIC: **2711** Newspapers: publishing only, not printed on site

(G-5060)
YERG INC
Also Called: Yerg Accounting Supplies
7 Fawnhollow Ln (08759-7312)
PHONE.................................973 759-4041
Fax: 973 759-5446
Kathleen Yerg-Marmo, *President*
Kathleen Yerg Marmo, *President*
Frank Marmo Jr, *Admin Sec*
EMP: 5 EST: 1909
SQ FT: 10,000
SALES (est): 567.6K **Privately Held**
WEB: www.yergpads.com
SIC: **2678** Stationery products

Lakewood
Ocean County

(G-5061)
10X DAILY LLC
10 Blue Jay Way (08701-4746)
PHONE.................................732 276-6407
Yitzchok Liebes, *Owner*
EMP: 4

SALES (est): 136.4K **Privately Held**
SIC: **2711** Newspapers, publishing & printing

(G-5062)
A&R PRINTING CORPORATION
Also Called: Printers Plus
421 W County Line Rd (08701-1204)
PHONE.................................732 886-0505
Jacob Stendig, *President*
EMP: 6
SQ FT: 5,700
SALES (est): 851K **Privately Held**
SIC: **2752** Commercial printing, offset

(G-5063)
ABSOLUME LLC
1153 Tiffany Ln (08701-5863)
PHONE.................................732 523-1231
Yisroel Berkowitz, *CEO*
Michael Greenberg, *COO*
EMP: 4
SQ FT: 300
SALES (est): 500K **Privately Held**
SIC: **3646** Commercial indusl & institutional electric lighting fixtures

(G-5064)
ACCUPAC INC
1700 Oak St (08701-5926)
PHONE.................................215 256-7094
Paul H Alvater, *Branch Mgr*
EMP: 144
SALES (corp-wide): 141.2MM **Privately Held**
SIC: **3823** Liquid analysis instruments, industrial process type
PA: Accupac, Inc.
1501 Industrial Blvd
Mainland PA 19451
215 256-7000

(G-5065)
ACKERSON DRAPERY DECORATOR SVC
500 James St Ste 14 (08701-4043)
PHONE.................................732 797-1967
Fax: 732 905-9606
Ronni L Leddy, *President*
Christina Ackerson, *Principal*
Michael K Leddy, *Vice Pres*
▲ EMP: 9
SQ FT: 6,500
SALES (est): 1.3MM **Privately Held**
WEB: www.ackersondrapery.com
SIC: **2391** 2392 2591 Curtains & draperies; bedspreads & bed sets: made from purchased materials; slipcovers: made of fabric, plastic etc.; curtain & drapery rods, poles & fixtures; blinds vertical

(G-5066)
ADVANCED PRODUCTS LLC
1915 Swarthmore Ave (08701-4567)
PHONE.................................800 724-5464
Klink Stanley, *Mng Member*
Larry S Stanley, *Mng Member*
Andrew Davidson,
EMP: 20
SQ FT: 15,000
SALES (est): 5MM **Privately Held**
SIC: **3446** Architectural metalwork

(G-5067)
ALPHA ASSOCIATES INC
145 Lehigh Ave (08701-4527)
PHONE.................................732 730-1800
Steve Prinn, *Managing Prtnr*
Susan Ferreira, *Purch Mgr*
Venecia Mercedes, *Purch Agent*
Josie Marcinczyk, *Buyer*
Kathryn Cosentino, *Research*
EMP: 25
SALES (corp-wide): 31MM **Privately Held**
WEB: www.alphainc.com
SIC: **5131** 3535 2295 Textile converters; conveyors & conveying equipment; coated fabrics, not rubberized
PA: Alpha Engineered Composites, Llc
145 Lehigh Ave
Lakewood NJ 08701
732 634-5700

(G-5068)
ALPHA ENGNEERED COMPOSITES LLC (PA)
145 Lehigh Ave (08701-4527)
PHONE.................................732 634-5700
Fax: 732 634-1430
Christopher J Avallone, *CEO*
John Baxter, *Vice Pres*
Kevin Burton, *Plant Mgr*
Scott Flaherty, *Opers Mgr*
Spyros Tsielepas, *Opers Mgr*
◆ EMP: 108
SQ FT: 112,000
SALES (est): 31MM **Privately Held**
WEB: www.alphainc.com
SIC: **2295** Resin or plastic coated fabrics

(G-5069)
AMERICAN BUSINESS PAPER INC
Also Called: American Graphic Solutions
222 River Ave (08701-4807)
PHONE.................................732 363-5788
Jeffrey Berger, *President*
EMP: 12
SALES (est): 1.6MM **Privately Held**
SIC: **2754** 5113 Commercial printing, gravure; industrial & personal service paper

(G-5070)
AMERICAN STAIRS INC
Also Called: Stair Store, The
687 Prospect St Ste 420 (08701-4648)
PHONE.................................732 363-3734
Fax: 732 363-1120
Richard Kaplan, *President*
Susan Kaplan, *Treasurer*
EMP: 12 EST: 1979
SQ FT: 20,000
SALES (est): 1.7MM **Privately Held**
WEB: www.americanstairs.com
SIC: **2431** Staircases & stairs, wood; doors & door parts & trim, wood; stair railings, wood

(G-5071)
AMERICAN VAN EQUIPMENT INC (PA)
149 Lehigh Ave (08701-4527)
PHONE.................................732 905-5900
Charles B Richter, *President*
Martin Richter, *Vice Pres*
Joseph Fallon, *VP Sales*
Richard Gebbia, *VP Mktg*
◆ EMP: 140
SQ FT: 130,000
SALES (est): 74.7MM **Privately Held**
WEB: www.americanvan.com
SIC: **5531** 3429 Automotive accessories; motor vehicle hardware

(G-5072)
AMERICHEM ENTERPRISES INC
6 Round Valley Ln (08701-5755)
PHONE.................................732 363-4840
Fax: 732 363-4244
Deanna Robinson, *President*
EMP: 7
SALES (est): 845.1K **Privately Held**
WEB: www.americanenterprisesllc.com
SIC: **5087** 2842 Janitors' supplies; cleaning or polishing preparations; waxes for wood, leather & other materials

(G-5073)
AMETEK INC
485 Oberlin Ave S (08701-6904)
PHONE.................................732 370-9100
Scot Rapoza, *Purch Mgr*
Kim Murphy, *Branch Mgr*
EMP: 6
SALES (corp-wide): 4.3B **Publicly Held**
SIC: **3643** Current-carrying wiring devices
PA: Ametek, Inc.
1100 Cassatt Rd
Berwyn PA 19312
610 647-2121

(G-5074)
AMICO TECHNOLOGIES INC
Also Called: Keco Engineered Controls
1200 River Ave Ste 3a (08701-5657)
PHONE.................................732 901-5900
Fax: 732 901-5904

Joseph W Mitchell, *President*
EMP: 6
SQ FT: 1,000
SALES (est): 2.7MM **Privately Held**
WEB: www.kecocontrols.com
SIC: **5085** 3823 Valves & fittings; industrial instrmnts msrmnt display/control process variable

(G-5075)
ARCHITECTURAL METAL AND GLASS
644 Cross St Ste 14 (08701-4654)
P.O. Box 177, Forked River (08731-0177)
PHONE.................................732 994-7575
Anjennette Panebianco,
EMP: 4
SALES (est): 607.5K **Privately Held**
SIC: **5231** 1542 3449 Glass; store front construction; curtain wall, metal

(G-5076)
ASBURY TOWEL COMPANY INC
1295 Towbin Ave (08701-5934)
PHONE.................................732 370-3908
Tomas Cughan, *General Mgr*
▲ EMP: 10
SQ FT: 20,000
SALES (est): 587.5K **Privately Held**
SIC: **2392** Towels, fabric & nonwoven: made from purchased materials

(G-5077)
ASTOR CHOCOLATE CORP (PA)
651 New Hampshire Ave (08701-5452)
PHONE.................................732 901-1000
Fax: 732 901-1003
Erwin Grunhut, *CEO*
David Grunhut, *President*
Toni Grunhut, *Admin Sec*
◆ EMP: 120 EST: 1950
SALES (est): 56.5MM **Privately Held**
WEB: www.astorchocolate.com
SIC: **2064** Candy & other confectionery products

(G-5078)
AUGENBRAUNS BRIDAL PASSAIC INC
200 Central Ave (08701-3134)
PHONE.................................845 425-3439
Joseph Augenbraun, *CEO*
Malky Augenbraun, *COO*
Chanie Coplowitz, *CFO*
Adina Fride, *CFO*
EMP: 7
SQ FT: 1,450
SALES (est): 516.4K **Privately Held**
SIC: **2335** Bridal & formal gowns

(G-5079)
AVANTEGARDE IMAGE LLC
535 E County Line Rd (08701-1486)
PHONE.................................732 363-8701
Sidney Welz,
EMP: 15
SALES (est): 794K **Privately Held**
WEB: www.avantgardeimage.com
SIC: **2514** Metal household furniture

(G-5080)
B P GRAPHICS INC
315 4th St (08701-3231)
PHONE.................................732 942-2315
Fax: 732 905-1320
Benjamin Heineman, *President*
EMP: 20
SQ FT: 6,000
SALES: 1.2MM **Privately Held**
SIC: **2759** Commercial printing

(G-5081)
BASIC LTD
575 Prospect St Ste 241 (08701-5040)
PHONE.................................718 871-6106
Harris Mermelstein, *President*
▲ EMP: 25
SALES (est): 5MM **Privately Held**
WEB: www.basic.net
SIC: **2673** Garment & wardrobe bags, (plastic film)

▲ = Import ▼ =Export
◆ =Import/Export

(G-5082)
BBG SURGICAL LTD LIABILITY CO
1995 Rutgers Blvd (08701-4538)
PHONE..................................551 404-7920
Steven Gluck,
Mark Bakst,
Alan Berman,
EMP: 8
SQ FT: 6,000
SALES: 6MM **Privately Held**
SIC: 5047 3841 Instruments, surgical & medical; surgical instruments & apparatus

(G-5083)
BELAIR TIME CORPORATION
1995 Swarthmore Ave Ste 3 (08701-4572)
PHONE..................................732 905-0100
Fax: 732 367-3215
Alan Grunwald, *President*
Adrienne Grunwald, *Principal*
Joan Grunwald, *Principal*
Bill Peak, *Natl Sales Mgr*
Johny Gupton, *VP Sales*
▲ **EMP:** 60 **EST:** 1945
SQ FT: 30,000
SALES (est): 9.8MM **Privately Held**
WEB: www.beltime.com
SIC: 3873 Watches & parts, except crystals & jewels

(G-5084)
BGS INC
Also Called: Buildgreen Solutions
910 E County Line Rd # 101 (08701-2092)
PHONE..................................732 442-5000
Elkana Tombak, *CEO*
EMP: 15
SQ FT: 3,500
SALES: 2.8MM **Privately Held**
SIC: 3585 Parts for heating, cooling & refrigerating equipment

(G-5085)
BIMBO BAKERIES USA INC
160 Airport Rd Ste 4 (08701-6927)
PHONE..................................732 886-1881
EMP: 56 **Privately Held**
SIC: 2051 Bakery: wholesale or wholesale/retail combined
HQ: Bimbo Bakeries Usa, Inc
   255 Business Center Dr # 200
   Horsham PA 19044
   215 347-5500

(G-5086)
BORUCH TRADING LTD LBLTY CO
69 Gudz Rd (08701-2913)
PHONE..................................718 614-9575
Boruch Kirschenbaum, *Mng Member*
EMP: 8
SALES (est): 284.4K **Privately Held**
SIC: 3999 5064 Barber & beauty shop equipment; electric household appliances

(G-5087)
BP PRINT GROUP INC
315 4th St (08701-3231)
PHONE..................................732 905-9830
Ben Heinemann, *President*
EMP: 70 **EST:** 2015
SQ FT: 9,000
SALES (est): 8.3MM **Privately Held**
SIC: 2752 Commercial printing, offset; letters, circular or form: lithographed; business form & card printing, lithographic; periodicals, lithographed

(G-5088)
BRAND AROMATICS INTL INC
1600 Oak St (08701-5924)
P.O. Box 3033 (08701-9033)
PHONE..................................732 363-1204
Fax: 732 363-8041
Karl E Brand, *President*
Dennis Shea Jr, *Vice Pres*
Patty Joyce, *Opers Staff*
Nancy Moore, *Purchasing*
Dianna Derosa, *Receptionist*
▲ **EMP:** 7
SQ FT: 100,000

SALES (est): 1.8MM
SALES (corp-wide): 4.8B **Publicly Held**
WEB: www.brandaromatics.com
SIC: 2087 Manufactures Flavor Extracts/Syrup
PA: Mccormick & Company Incorporated
   18 Loveton Cir
   Sparks MD 21152
   410 771-7301

(G-5089)
BRIGHT IDEAS USA LLC
890 Morris Ave (08701-5520)
PHONE..................................732 886-8865
Deena Leiman,
▲ **EMP:** 4
SALES (est): 377.2K **Privately Held**
SIC: 2399 Fabricated textile products

(G-5090)
BRISCO APPAREL CO INC
575 Prospect St Ste 230 (08701-5075)
PHONE..................................718 715-7110
Scott Gartner, *CEO*
EMP: 20
SALES (corp-wide): 14.9MM **Privately Held**
SIC: 2329 Shirt & slack suits: men's, youths' & boys'
PA: Brisco Apparel Co., Inc.
   4315 13th Ave Fl 3
   Brooklyn NY 11219
   718 832-2080

(G-5091)
BSD INDUSTRIES LTD LIABILITY
110 Columbus Ave S (08701-2951)
PHONE..................................732 534-4341
EMP: 5 **EST:** 2011
SALES (est): 174.5K **Privately Held**
SIC: 3999 Manufacturing industries

(G-5092)
CHERRI STONE INTERACTIVE LLC
Also Called: Zaffre
182 N Crest Pl (08701-3282)
PHONE..................................844 843-7765
AMI Bielinki, *Mng Member*
EMP: 5
SALES: 350K **Privately Held**
SIC: 2844 7389 7311 8742 Deodorants, personal; face creams or lotions; ; advertising consultant; marketing consulting services

(G-5093)
CHURCH & DWIGHT CO INC
800 Airport Rd (08701-5909)
PHONE..................................732 730-3100
Fax: 732 730-3191
Tom Volz, *Manager*
EMP: 14
SALES (corp-wide): 3.7B **Publicly Held**
WEB: www.churchdwight.com
SIC: 2812 Sodium bicarbonate
PA: Church & Dwight Co., Inc.
   500 Charles Ewing Blvd
   Ewing NJ 08628
   609 806-1200

(G-5094)
CLAYTON ASSOCIATES INC
1650 Oak St (08701-5924)
PHONE..................................732 363-2100
Fax: 732 364-6084
James Clayton, *President*
Brad Clayton, *Vice Pres*
Janice Clayton, *Vice Pres*
Margaret Candiano, *Office Mgr*
▲ **EMP:** 11
SQ FT: 18,500
SALES (est): 3.2MM **Privately Held**
WEB: www.jclayton.com
SIC: 3589 3569 Vacuum cleaners & sweepers, electric: industrial; brake burnishing or washing machines

(G-5095)
COMPONENT HARDWARE GROUP INC (PA)
1890 Swarthmore Ave (08701-4530)
P.O. Box 2020 (08701-8020)
PHONE..................................800 526-3694
Fax: 732 364-8110
Harry Franze, *President*

Chris Guarnieri, *Business Mgr*
Dan Hazard, *Business Mgr*
Aj Kraft, *Business Mgr*
Lenny Munyer, *Business Mgr*
▲ **EMP:** 90
SQ FT: 85,000
SALES (est): 26.5MM **Privately Held**
WEB: www.componenthardware.com
SIC: 5251 3429 Hardware; manufactured hardware (general)

(G-5096)
COUNTYLINE ELEC CONTRS CORP
2037 Lanes Mill Rd (08701-4506)
PHONE..................................732 961-6738
Zvi H Kohn, *Principal*
EMP: 4
SALES (est): 268.1K **Privately Held**
SIC: 3699 Electrical equipment & supplies

(G-5097)
CREATIVE FILM CORP
Also Called: Griff Decorative Film
700 Vassar Ave Ste 2 (08701-6957)
PHONE..................................732 367-2166
Fax: 732 367-6203
Joseph Coburn, *CEO*
Gene Silvestro, *General Mgr*
Chip Adams, *Vice Pres*
EMP: 15
SALES (est): 2.4MM **Privately Held**
WEB: www.creativefilmcorp.net
SIC: 3081 Plastic film & sheet

(G-5098)
CREOH TRADING CORP
Also Called: Creoh Packaging
910 E County Line Rd (08701-2091)
PHONE..................................718 821-0570
Daryl Hagler, *President*
Yuri Fromowitz, *COO*
Chany Mendlowitz, *Admin Sec*
▲ **EMP:** 13
SQ FT: 4,000
SALES: 6.5MM **Privately Held**
WEB: www.creoh.com
SIC: 3993 Signs & advertising specialties

(G-5099)
CREOH USA LLC
1771 Madison Ave Ste 7 (08701-1251)
PHONE..................................718 821-0570
EMP: 5 **EST:** 2014
SALES (est): 226.8K **Privately Held**
SIC: 2653 Solid fiber boxes, partitions, display items & sheets

(G-5100)
CRIJUODAMA BAKING CORP T
1900 Highway 70 Ste 209 (08701-7324)
PHONE..................................732 451-1250
EMP: 4
SALES (est): 179.1K **Privately Held**
SIC: 2051 Bread, cake & related products

(G-5101)
CUISINE INNVTONS UNLIMITED LLC
180 Lehigh Ave (08701-4526)
PHONE..................................732 730-9310
Ron Rexroth,
EMP: 150
SALES (est): 21.1MM **Privately Held**
SIC: 2038 Frozen specialties

(G-5102)
CUSTOM EXTRUSION TECH INC
Also Called: CET Films
1650 Corporate Rd W (08701-5920)
PHONE..................................732 367-5511
Paul Charapata, *CEO*
Guy Leigh, *Vice Pres*
Tom Kennedy, *CFO*
Tim Reimer, *Controller*
EMP: 15
SALES (est): 10.2MM **Privately Held**
SIC: 3544 Extrusion dies
HQ: R Tape Corporation
   6 Ingersoll Rd
   South Plainfield NJ 07080
   908 753-5570

(G-5103)
CW INTERNATIONAL SALES LLC
Also Called: Crystal Ware
600 James St (08701-4023)
PHONE..................................732 367-4444
Sam Greenwald, *Opers Staff*
Fred Katz, *Sales Dir*
Nicole Aquino, *Office Mgr*
Nisson Kugler, *Mng Member*
Tzaley Zombo, *Manager*
◆ **EMP:** 27
SQ FT: 150,000
SALES (est): 7MM **Privately Held**
SIC: 2621 2656 Towels, tissues & napkins: paper & stock; paper cups, plates, dishes & utensils

(G-5104)
D & A GRANULATION LLC
1970 Rutgers Univ Blvd (08701-4573)
PHONE..................................732 994-7480
Tyson Pritchard, *President*
EMP: 4 **EST:** 2016
SALES (est): 124.1K **Privately Held**
SIC: 2833 Medicinals & botanicals

(G-5105)
DALEMARK INDUSTRIES INC
575 Prospect St Ste 211 (08701-5040)
PHONE..................................732 367-3100
Fax: 732 367-7031
Michael Delli Gatti, *President*
EMP: 10 **EST:** 1955
SQ FT: 12,000
SALES: 1MM **Privately Held**
WEB: www.dalemark.com
SIC: 3953 3565 Marking devices; labeling machines, industrial

(G-5106)
DCM CLEAN AIR PRODUCTS INC
1650 Oak St (08701-5924)
PHONE..................................732 363-2100
James Clayton, *President*
Brad Clayton, *Vice Pres*
EMP: 7 **EST:** 2012
SALES (est): 851.2K **Privately Held**
SIC: 3546 3589 Cartridge-activated hand power tools; vacuum cleaners & sweepers, electric: industrial

(G-5107)
DEB MANUFACTURING INC
850 Towbin Ave (08701-5928)
PHONE..................................732 364-7007
Fax: 732 364-7299
Hollis Mueller, *President*
Ronald Lyons, *Corp Secy*
David Armstrong, *Vice Pres*
EMP: 8
SQ FT: 6,500
SALES (est): 1.3MM **Privately Held**
WEB: www.debmfg.com
SIC: 3544 3728 Industrial molds; aircraft parts & equipment

(G-5108)
DESTINY FOUNDATION
564 Marc Dr (08701-5115)
PHONE..................................732 987-9008
Elaine Gilbert, *Owner*
EMP: 5
SALES: 617.3K **Privately Held**
SIC: 3999 5999 Education aids, devices & supplies; education aids, devices & supplies

(G-5109)
DISPERSION TECHNOLOGY INC
1885 Swarthmore Ave (08701-4574)
P.O. Box 300 (08701-0300)
PHONE..................................732 364-4488
Fax: 732 364-1018
Yogesh Parikh, *President*
Rosanne Heitner, *Admin Sec*
EMP: 10
SQ FT: 15,000
SALES (est): 1.2MM **Privately Held**
WEB: www.dispersion.com
SIC: 2816 Inorganic pigments

GEOGRAPHIC

(G-5110)
DRAGON ASPHALT EQUIPMENT LLC
845 Towbin Ave (08701-5929)
PHONE..................................732 922-9290
Tathiana Carrasco, *CEO*
Todd Bullivant,
EMP: 10
SQ FT: 25,000
SALES (est): 2MM **Privately Held**
SIC: 3531 Asphalt plant, including gravel-mix type; mixers, bituminous; road construction & maintenance machinery

(G-5111)
E P HOMIEK SHTMTL SUPS INC
1352 River Ave Ste 4 (08701-5646)
PHONE..................................732 364-7644
Fax: 732 364-5806
Edward P Homiek, *President*
EMP: 20
SQ FT: 2,300
SALES (est): 9.3MM **Privately Held**
SIC: 3444 Sheet metalwork; metal ventilating equipment

(G-5112)
EAGLE RACING INC
810 Cross St Ste 4 (08701-4045)
PHONE..................................732 367-8487
Dale Barlet, *President*
EMP: 4
SQ FT: 8,960
SALES (est): 489.3K **Privately Held**
SIC: 3559 Automotive related machinery

(G-5113)
ELAUT USA INC (PA)
1000 Towbin Ave (08701-7022)
PHONE..................................732 364-9900
Glenn Kramer, *CEO*
Steve Paris, *COO*
Drew Maniscalco, *Vice Pres*
Fred Madsen, *Opers Staff*
John Dondzila, *Engineer*
◆ EMP: 15
SQ FT: 25,000
SALES (est): 4.1MM **Privately Held**
SIC: 7993 3599 Game machines; carnival machines & equipment, amusement park

(G-5114)
ELECTRONIC CONNECTIONS INC (PA)
Also Called: Eci
195 Lehigh Ave Ste 3 (08701-4555)
PHONE..................................732 367-5588
Fax: 732 367-4580
Steven Jordan, *President*
Tom Vella, *General Mgr*
Jim Greene, *Sales Staff*
Laura Martin, *Sales Staff*
Matt Smith, *Sales Staff*
EMP: 15
SQ FT: 8,100
SALES (est): 7.7MM **Privately Held**
WEB: www.ecinj.com
SIC: 5065 3679 Electronic parts; harness assemblies for electronic use: wire or cable

(G-5115)
ELITE EMRGNCY LIGHTS LTD LBLTY
1000 Bennett Blvd Ste 6 (08701-5944)
PHONE..................................732 534-2377
Nate Herskovits, *Principal*
EMP: 12
SALES (est): 253.9K **Privately Held**
SIC: 1731 3647 3711 3714 Standby or emergency power specialization; flasher lights, automotive; automobile assembly, including specialty automobiles; motor vehicle parts & accessories

(G-5116)
EOM WORLDWIDE SALES CORP
39 Harmony Dr (08701-5841)
PHONE..................................732 994-7352
David Teller, *President*
EMP: 1 EST: 2016
SQ FT: 1,100
SALES: 19.5MM **Privately Held**
SIC: 5946 3571 Cameras; personal computers (microcomputers)

(G-5117)
EPI GROUP LTD LIABILITY CO
410 Monmouth Ave (08701-3711)
PHONE..................................917 710-6607
Benjamin Klein, *President*
EMP: 5
SQ FT: 800
SALES: 4MM **Privately Held**
SIC: 3469 Kitchen fixtures & equipment: metal, except cast aluminum

(G-5118)
EROOMSYSTEM TECHNOLOGIES INC (PA)
150 Airport Rd Ste 1200 (08701-6924)
PHONE..................................732 730-0116
Fax: 732 810-0380
David A Gestetner, *Ch of Bd*
Herbert Hardt, *Director*
James Savas, *Bd of Directors*
EMP: 15
SQ FT: 1,600
SALES: 903.6K **Publicly Held**
WEB: www.eroomsystem.com
SIC: 7372 Business oriented computer software

(G-5119)
EXCLUSIVE MATERIALS LLC
Also Called: Exma Industries
1385 Pasadena St (08701-3922)
PHONE..................................732 886-9956
Yehudah Kirshenbaum,
▲ EMP: 8 EST: 2002
SALES (est): 543.7K **Privately Held**
SIC: 3494 Pipe fittings

(G-5120)
EZRIRX LLC (PA)
1525 Prospect St Ste 203 (08701-4662)
PHONE..................................718 502-6610
Ezriel Green, *CEO*
EMP: 2
SALES: 5MM **Privately Held**
SIC: 5122 7372 Pharmaceuticals; application computer software

(G-5121)
FASHION CENTRAL LLC
556 Warren Ave (08701-4813)
PHONE..................................732 887-7683
Yizhaq Chkory, *Manager*
▲ EMP: 8
SALES (est): 618.5K **Privately Held**
SIC: 2341 Women's & children's underwear; women's & children's undergarments; chemises, camisoles & teddies: women's & children's; panties: women's, misses', children's & infants'

(G-5122)
FEDPLAST INC
1174 Buckwald Ct (08701-1263)
PHONE..................................732 901-1153
Fax: 732 363-1246
Andre Grunberger, *President*
Ben Schechter, *Sales Mgr*
EMP: 14
SQ FT: 25,000
SALES (est): 1.1MM **Privately Held**
WEB: www.fedplast.com
SIC: 3083 Laminated plastics plate & sheet

(G-5123)
FLEXABAR CORPORATION (PA)
1969 Rutgers Blvd (08701-4538)
PHONE..................................732 901-6500
Fax: 732 901-6504
Andy Guglielmo, *CEO*
Richard J Guglielmo Sr, *President*
Anita Guglielmo, *Corp Secy*
Daniel Guglielmo, *Plant Mgr*
Greg Devine, *Mktg Dir*
▼ EMP: 22 EST: 1955
SQ FT: 40,000
SALES (est): 4.3MM **Privately Held**
WEB: www.flexabar.com
SIC: 2851 Vinyl coatings, strippable

(G-5124)
FLEXDELL CORP
1969 Rutgers Blvd (08701-4538)
PHONE..................................732 901-7771
Richard Guglielmo Sr, *President*
EMP: 4 EST: 1952

SQ FT: 50,000
SALES (est): 395.2K
SALES (corp-wide): 4.3MM **Privately Held**
WEB: www.flexabar.com
SIC: 2851 Marine paints
PA: Flexabar Corporation
1969 Rutgers Blvd
Lakewood NJ 08701
732 901-6500

(G-5125)
FRANCIS METALS COMPANY INC
Also Called: Francis Cable Systems
687 Prospect St Ste 430 (08701-4747)
PHONE..................................732 761-0500
Matt Deiner, *President*
James Deiner, *Vice Pres*
John McLaughlin, *Sales Mgr*
EMP: 10
SQ FT: 24,000
SALES (est): 3.3MM **Privately Held**
SIC: 3441 3357 3699 Fabricated structural metal; nonferrous wiredrawing & insulating; electrical equipment & supplies

(G-5126)
G & S PRECISION PROTOTYPE
115 Somerset Ave (08701-3629)
P.O. Box 18, Allenwood (08720-0018)
PHONE..................................732 370-3010
Fax: 732 370-3122
Guenter K Schindler, *Owner*
EMP: 5
SALES (est): 320K **Privately Held**
SIC: 3429 Manufactured hardware (general)

(G-5127)
GARDEN STATE MEDICAL SUP LLC
1995 Rutgers Univ Blvd (08701-4538)
PHONE..................................732 348-0312
Steven Gluck, *COO*
EMP: 5
SALES (corp-wide): 325K **Privately Held**
SIC: 5047 3841 Beds, hospital; hospital furniture; patient monitoring equipment; surgical & medical instruments
PA: Garden State Medical Supply Llc
203 Arlington Ave
Lakewood NJ 08701
888 200-2797

(G-5128)
GATEWAY PROPERTY SOLUTIONS LTD
730 Airport Rd Unit 1 (08701-5994)
PHONE..................................732 901-9700
Eli Kessler, *CEO*
EMP: 20
SALES (est): 882.7K **Privately Held**
SIC: 1522 1389 1542 Hotel/motel & multi-family home construction; construction; repair & dismantling services; hospital construction; institutional building construction

(G-5129)
GLASSEAL PRODUCTS INC
485 Oberlin Ave S (08701-6996)
PHONE..................................732 370-9100
Fax: 732 370-7107
Ian McGavisk, *President*
William Hubbard, *Vice Pres*
Renato Madarang, *Opers Mgr*
Ceasar Morte, *Engineer*
EMP: 130
SQ FT: 50,000
SALES (est): 19.3MM
SALES (corp-wide): 4.3B **Publicly Held**
WEB: www.glasseal.com
SIC: 3643 3679 3471 3812 Connectors & terminals for electrical devices; hermetic seals for electronic equipment; plating of metals or formed products; search & navigation equipment; electronic connectors
HQ: Hcc Industries Inc.
4232 Temple City Blvd
Rosemead CA 91770
626 443-8933

(G-5130)
GOLDEN FLUFF INC
118 Monmouth Ave (08701-3347)
PHONE..................................732 367-5448
Ephraim Schwinder, *President*
Sara Schwinder, *Vice Pres*
▲ EMP: 13
SQ FT: 21,000
SALES (est): 1.5MM **Privately Held**
WEB: www.goldenfluff.com
SIC: 2096 5149 Potato chips & similar snacks; specialty food items

(G-5131)
GWENSTONE INC
Also Called: Big Dog Natural
1790 Swarthmore Ave (08701-4593)
P.O. Box 531 (08701-0531)
PHONE..................................732 785-2600
Christiane De Rijk, *Principal*
Carlo Van Bael, *Principal*
EMP: 5
SALES (est): 409.2K **Privately Held**
SIC: 2047 3999 Dog food; pet supplies

(G-5132)
HAROLD R HENRICH INC
300 Syracuse Ct (08701-6919)
PHONE..................................732 370-4455
Fax: 732 370-5566
Harold Henrich Jr, *CEO*
Tom Henrich, *President*
Mike Henrich, *Vice Pres*
Tom Sofia, *Plant Mgr*
Ryan Henrich, *Foreman/Supr*
▲ EMP: 55
SALES (est): 14.4MM **Privately Held**
WEB: www.haroldhenrich.com
SIC: 3441 3444 Fabricated structural metal; sheet metalwork

(G-5133)
HAT BOX
605 E County Line Rd # 1 (08701-1491)
PHONE..................................732 961-2262
Chester Golombeck, *Branch Mgr*
EMP: 23
SALES (corp-wide): 3.1MM **Privately Held**
SIC: 2389 5611 Men's miscellaneous accessories; men's & boys' clothing stores
PA: Hat Box
1837 Coney Island Ave
Brooklyn NY 11230
718 951-9533

(G-5134)
HERR FOODS INCORPORATED
100 Kenyon Dr (08701-4500)
PHONE..................................732 905-1600
Fax: 732 905-7749
Ike Neff, *Manager*
EMP: 38
SQ FT: 7,500
SALES (corp-wide): 448.6MM **Privately Held**
WEB: www.herrs.com
SIC: 2096 Potato chips & similar snacks
PA: Herr Foods Incorporated
20 Herr Dr
Nottingham PA 19362
610 932-9330

(G-5135)
HPI INTERNATIONAL INC
301 1st St (08701-3322)
PHONE..................................732 942-9900
Amy Berger, *Manager*
EMP: 10
SALES (est): 607.3K
SALES (corp-wide): 19.9MM **Privately Held**
WEB: www.hpi.com
SIC: 3861 Photographic equipment & supplies
PA: Hpi International Inc.
1040 E 17th St
Brooklyn NY 11230
718 768-8800

(G-5136)
IBOCO CORP
1205 Paco Way Ste B (08701-6126)
PHONE..................................732 417-0066
Fax: 732 417-1166
▲ EMP: 9

▲ = Import ▼=Export
◆ =Import/Export

SQ FT: 10,000
SALES (est): 1.6MM **Privately Held**
WEB: www.iboco.com
SIC: 3357 Nonferrous wiredrawing & insulating

(G-5137)
JA CISSEL MANUFACTURING CO
1995 Rutgers Blvd (08701-4538)
P.O. Box 2035 (08701-8035)
PHONE.................................732 901-0300
Fax: 732 901-1166
George Spisak, *President*
David Morgen, *President*
EMP: 20
SALES (est): 2.1MM
SALES (corp-wide): 5.1MM **Privately Held**
WEB: www.jacissel.net
SIC: 3949 Golf equipment
PA: Century Sports, Inc.
1715 Oak St Ste 1
Lakewood NJ
732 905-4422

(G-5138)
JACQUARD FABRICS INC
Also Called: Jacquard Fabrics Co
1965 Swarthmore Ave (08701-4534)
PHONE.................................732 905-4545
Fax: 732 905-5334
Leonard Gliner, *President*
Shelton Cagle, *Plant Mgr*
▲ **EMP:** 38 **EST:** 1985
SQ FT: 34,000
SALES (est): 6.3MM **Privately Held**
SIC: 2211 Jacquard woven fabrics, cotton

(G-5139)
JERSEY JACK PINBALL INC
1645 Oak St (08701-5925)
PHONE.................................732 364-9900
Jack Guarnieri, *President*
▲ **EMP:** 47
SALES (est): 7.6MM **Privately Held**
SIC: 3999 Coin-operated amusement machines

(G-5140)
JESEL INC
1985 Cedarbridge Ave # 2 (08701-7031)
PHONE.................................732 901-1800
Fax: 732 901-2043
Daniel Jesel, *President*
EMP: 65
SQ FT: 40,000
SALES (est): 14.6MM **Privately Held**
WEB: www.jeselonline.com
SIC: 3714 Motor vehicle parts & accessories

(G-5141)
KOMO MACHINE INC
Also Called: Komo Innovative Cnc Solutions
1 Komo Dr (08701-5923)
P.O. Box 918801, Denver CO (80291-8801)
PHONE.................................732 719-6222
Mike Kolibas, *President*
Jennifer Dempsey, *General Mgr*
Jeff Erickson, *Exec VP*
Doreen Romanowski, *Purch Agent*
Bryan Minue, *Engineer*
▲ **EMP:** 55
SALES (est): 18.3MM
SALES (corp-wide): 2.2B **Privately Held**
WEB: www.komo.com
SIC: 3541 Machine tools, metal cutting type
PA: Pmc Global, Inc.
12243 Branford St
Sun Valley CA 91352
818 896-1101

(G-5142)
KRAEMER PROPERTIES INC (PA)
Also Called: Luminer Converting Group
1925 Swarthmore Ave Ste 3 (08701-4552)
PHONE.................................732 886-6557
Fax: 732 886-6692
Thomas N Spina, *CEO*
John Lubisco, *QC Mgr*
Daniel Goldstein, *Marketing Staff*
John Borelli, *Shareholder*

Paul Kraemer, *Shareholder*
▲ **EMP:** 35
SQ FT: 5,000
SALES (est): 8.1MM **Privately Held**
WEB: www.luminer.com
SIC: 2672 Labels (unprinted), gummed: made from purchased materials; tape, pressure sensitive: made from purchased materials

(G-5143)
KRFC CUSTOM WOODWORKING INC
Also Called: Krfc Design Center
1328 River Ave Ste 25 (08701-5645)
PHONE.................................732 363-0522
Chris Cooper, *President*
Barbara Salerno, *Office Mgr*
EMP: 7
SQ FT: 4,000
SALES (est): 730K **Privately Held**
SIC: 2499 Decorative wood & woodwork

(G-5144)
LAMINETICS INC
1151 River Ave (08701-5658)
PHONE.................................732 367-1116
Yechiel Malichy, *President*
EMP: 8
SQ FT: 3,700
SALES (est): 814K **Privately Held**
SIC: 2541 Table or counter tops, plastic laminated

(G-5145)
LARDIERI CUSTOM WOODWORKING
1830 Swarthmore Ave Ste 6 (08701-4556)
PHONE.................................732 905-6334
Fax: 732 370-2186
Robert Lardieri, *President*
EMP: 11
SALES (est): 1.4MM **Privately Held**
SIC: 2499 Decorative wood & woodwork

(G-5146)
LIFE SCIENCE LABORATORIES LLC
170 Oberlin Ave N Ste 26 (08701-4548)
PHONE.................................732 367-1900
Fax: 732 367-4146
Elke Isbee, *Purchasing*
Sam Brownstein, *VP Sales*
Yochanan Bulka,
Adeena Zabrowsky,
EMP: 9
SQ FT: 9,500
SALES (est): 2.3MM **Privately Held**
SIC: 2834 Vitamin preparations

(G-5147)
LIFE SCIENCE LABS MFG LLC
170 Oberlin Ave N Ste 26 (08701-4548)
PHONE.................................732 367-9937
Yochanan Bulka, *President*
EMP: 14
SQ FT: 9,000
SALES (est): 629K **Privately Held**
SIC: 2833 Vitamins, natural or synthetic: bulk, uncompounded

(G-5148)
LIFE SCNCE LABS SPPLEMENTS LLC
Also Called: Lsl Supplements
216 River Ave (08701-4807)
PHONE.................................732 367-1749
Yochanan Bulka, *CEO*
EMP: 14
SQ FT: 18,000
SALES: 3.1MM **Privately Held**
SIC: 2834 Vitamin preparations

(G-5149)
LITTLE MISS CUPCAKE LLC
200 Tudor Ct (08701-1473)
PHONE.................................732 370-3083
Jonathan Platschek, *Principal*
EMP: 4
SALES (est): 205.7K **Privately Held**
SIC: 2051 Bread, cake & related products

(G-5150)
M AND R MANUFACTURING
Also Called: Mister Boardwalk
575 Prospect St Ste 202 (08701-5040)
PHONE.................................732 905-1061
Warren McLeod, *Principal*
EMP: 5
SALES (est): 212K **Privately Held**
SIC: 2499 Decorative wood & woodwork

(G-5151)
MAGNA INDUSTRIES INC
1825 Swarthmore Ave Ste 1 (08701-4570)
PHONE.................................732 905-0957
Walter Ostrowicki, *CEO*
Jerry Krzemiresk, *President*
▲ **EMP:** 28
SQ FT: 32,000
SALES (est): 6.1MM **Privately Held**
WEB: www.magnaindustries.com
SIC: 3556 Bakery machinery

(G-5152)
MANLEY PERFORMANCE PDTS INC (PA)
1960 Swarthmore Ave (08701-4547)
PHONE.................................732 905-3366
Fax: 732 905-3010
Henry Manley, *President*
Gil Morejon, *CFO*
Tom Razzano, *Manager*
Trip Manley, *Shareholder*
▲ **EMP:** 63
SQ FT: 40,000
SALES (est): 15MM **Privately Held**
WEB: www.manleyvalves.com
SIC: 3714 Motor vehicle engines & parts

(G-5153)
MASCO CABINETRY LLC
450 Oberlin Ave S (08701-6903)
PHONE.................................732 363-3797
EMP: 127
SALES (corp-wide): 7.1B **Publicly Held**
SIC: 2541 Mfg Wood Partitions/Fixtures
HQ: Masco Cabinetry Llc
4600 Arrowhead Dr
Ann Arbor MI 48105
313 274-7400

(G-5154)
MASCO CABINETRY LLC
Also Called: Tfi OEM Commercial Group
440-450 Oberlin Ave S (08701)
PHONE.................................732 942-5138
EMP: 143
SALES (corp-wide): 7.1B **Publicly Held**
SIC: 2541 Mfg Wood Partitions/Fixtures
HQ: Masco Cabinetry Llc
4600 Arrowhead Dr
Ann Arbor MI 48105
313 274-7400

(G-5155)
MASTER PRESENTATIONS INC
182 Hadassah Ln (08701-5561)
PHONE.................................732 239-7093
Maurice Pachtinger, *President*
◆ **EMP:** 10
SALES (est): 1MM **Privately Held**
SIC: 3915 Jewel preparing: instruments, tools, watches & jewelry

(G-5156)
MAY NATIONAL ASSOCIATES NJ INC
Also Called: Sika
995 Towbin Ave (08701-5930)
PHONE.................................973 473-3330
Mark Yamout, *President*
▲ **EMP:** 55
SQ FT: 5,000
SALES (est): 12.8MM
SALES (corp-wide): 213.5MM **Privately Held**
SIC: 2891 Caulking compounds
HQ: Sika Corporation
201 Polito Ave
Lyndhurst NJ 07071
201 933-8800

(G-5157)
MDI MANUFACTURING INC
100 Syracuse Ct (08701-6909)
PHONE.................................732 994-5599

Fax: 732 458-7030
Mark Daugherty, *President*
Eileen Savage, *Executive Asst*
EMP: 19
SQ FT: 8,000
SALES (est): 3.9MM **Privately Held**
SIC: 3599 Machine shop, jobbing & repair

(G-5158)
MEDICAL SCRUBS COLLECTN NJ LLC (HQ)
1655 Corporate Rd W (08701-5921)
PHONE.................................732 719-8600
Mark Bakst, *CEO*
EMP: 6
SALES: 2.8MM
SALES (corp-wide): 5MM **Privately Held**
SIC: 2211 Scrub cloths
PA: Avaline Medical Nj Limited Liability Company
1665 Corporate Rd W
Lakewood NJ 08701
732 746-5030

(G-5159)
MILSPRAY LLC (HQ)
Also Called: Milspray Military Technologies
845 Towbin Ave (08701-5929)
PHONE.................................732 886-2223
Fax: 732 886-2250
Liz Shivers, *President*
Joseph Gerschutz, *Engineer*
Liz Deserio, *Controller*
Janet Armitt, *Finance*
Chad Vroman, *Sales Staff*
▲ **EMP:** 40
SQ FT: 18,000
SALES (est): 24.8MM
SALES (corp-wide): 353.3MM **Privately Held**
SIC: 5169 2851 3812 Aerosols; paints & paint additives; defense systems & equipment
PA: R.A.F. Industries, Inc.
165 Township Line Rd # 2100
Jenkintown PA 19046
215 572-0738

(G-5160)
MIRACLE MILE AUTOMOTIVE INC
Also Called: Kraemer Koating
1925 Swarthmore Ave Ste 1 (08701-4552)
PHONE.................................732 886-6315
Fax: 732 886-6317
Paul Kraemer, *President*
Barbara Kraemer, *Vice Pres*
EMP: 5
SQ FT: 30,000
SALES (est): 5.1MM **Privately Held**
WEB: www.kraemerkoating.com
SIC: 3559 Chemical machinery & equipment

(G-5161)
MISTER COOKIE FACE INC
Also Called: Mrs Fieldbrook Food
1989 Rutgers Blvd (08701-4538)
P.O. Box 1318, Dunkirk NY (14048-6318)
PHONE.................................732 370-5533
Frank R Koenemund, *President*
Mahesh Khemraj, *Plant Mgr*
David Edelstein, *Director*
Ed Grosso, *Maintence Staff*
Kevin Shaw, *Maintence Staff*
◆ **EMP:** 125
SQ FT: 40,000
SALES (est): 30.9MM **Privately Held**
WEB: www.cookieface.com
SIC: 2024 Ice cream, bulk
HQ: Fieldbrook Foods Corporation
1 Ice Cream Dr
Dunkirk NY 14048
716 366-5400

(G-5162)
MJ GROSS COMPANY - NJ
Also Called: David Gross Group
2 Commonwealth Dr (08701-4163)
Rural Route 40 Canary Dr (08701)
PHONE.................................212 542-3199
David Gross, *Owner*
EMP: 7
SQ FT: 1,500

SALES (est): 680K **Privately Held**
SIC: 5094 3911 Jewelry; jewelry, precious
metal

(G-5163)
NICKELS N DIMES LLC
80 Gudz Rd (08701-2912)
PHONE...................................732 886-5528
Mattil Kahn, *Owner*
EMP: 5
SALES (est): 337.5K **Privately Held**
SIC: 3356 Nickel

(G-5164)
NITTO INC (HQ)
Also Called: Nitto Denko Automotive
1990 Rutgers Blvd (08701-4537)
PHONE...................................732 901-7905
Hideo Takasaki, *President*
Yoichiro Sakuma, *President*
Maggie Charles, *General Mgr*
Takei Nishioka, *General Mgr*
Toshihiko Omote, *Exec VP*
▲ EMP: 240
SALES: 144MM
SALES (corp-wide): 8B **Privately Held**
SIC: 3714 Motor vehicle parts & acces-
sories
PA: Nitto Denko Corporation
4-20, Ofukacho, Kita-Ku
Osaka OSK 530-0
676 322-101

(G-5165)
NITTO AMERICAS INC
1990 Rutgers Blvd (08701-4537)
PHONE...................................732 901-7905
Christopher Quinn, *Branch Mgr*
EMP: 12
SALES (corp-wide): 8B **Privately Held**
SIC: 2672 3589 5162 5065 Tape, pres-
sure sensitive: made from purchased ma-
terials; water treatment equipment,
industrial; plastics products; electronic
parts
HQ: Nitto Americas, Inc.
48500 Fremont Blvd
Fremont CA 94538
510 445-5400

(G-5166)
NITTO INC
1975 Swarthmore Ave (08701-4534)
PHONE...................................732 901-0035
Chad Joldersma, *Manager*
EMP: 7 EST: 2014
SALES (est): 1.1MM **Privately Held**
SIC: 2672 Tape, pressure sensitive: made
from purchased materials

(G-5167)
NOVASOM INDUSTRIES INC
15 Enclave Blvd (08701-5788)
PHONE...................................732 994-5652
Christian Carrieri, *CEO*
Terry Manton, *Vice Pres*
▼ EMP: 1
SALES: 1MM **Privately Held**
SIC: 3571 Electronic computers

(G-5168)
**OLD FASHION KITCHEN INC
(PA)**
Also Called: Old Fashioned Kitchen
1045 Towbin Ave (08701-5931)
PHONE...................................732 364-4100
Fax: 732 905-7352
Jay Conzen, *President*
Jeff Brown, *CFO*
▲ EMP: 90
SQ FT: 30,000
SALES (est): 15.6MM **Privately Held**
WEB: www.oldfashionedkitchen.com
SIC: 2038 Ethnic foods, frozen

(G-5169)
ORNATE MILLWORK LLC
15 Hazelwood Ln (08701-5131)
PHONE...................................866 464-5596
Tovia Halpern, *Mng Member*
EMP: 5
SALES (est): 250K **Privately Held**
SIC: 2431 Millwork

(G-5170)
PERMA PURE LLC (DH)
1001 New Hampshire Ave (08701-6037)
PHONE...................................732 244-0010
Fax: 732 244-8140
Craig Sunada, *President*
Doug Hasbrouck, *General Mgr*
Tim Blanke, *Vice Pres*
Ken Geiser, *Materials Mgr*
Tom Kmec, *Facilities Mgr*
EMP: 5 EST: 1972
SQ FT: 25,000
SALES (est): 1.5MM
SALES (corp-wide): 1.5B **Privately Held**
WEB: www.permapure.com
SIC: 3826 Gas analyzing equipment
HQ: Halma Holdings Inc.
11500 Northlake Dr # 306
Cincinnati OH 45249
513 772-5501

(G-5171)
PINE PARK KITCHENS INC
225 2nd St (08701-3326)
PHONE...................................732 987-6520
Lisa Kaszirer, *President*
EMP: 4
SALES (est): 401.6K **Privately Held**
SIC: 2434 Wood kitchen cabinets

(G-5172)
PLASTICS GALORE LLC
1970 Swarthmore Ave Ste 8 (08701-4553)
PHONE...................................732 363-8447
Chris Wollerman,
EMP: 8
SALES (est): 1MM **Privately Held**
SIC: 3089 Air mattresses, plastic

(G-5173)
PMC INC
1 Gusmer Dr (08701)
PHONE...................................732 370-1163
Mike Kolibas, *Branch Mgr*
EMP: 159
SALES (corp-wide): 2.2B **Privately Held**
SIC: 3086 Plastics foam products
HQ: Pmc, Inc.
12243 Branford St
Sun Valley CA 91352
818 896-1101

(G-5174)
**POLARIS AMERICA LTD LBLTY
CO**
1985 Rutgers Blvd (08701-4569)
P.O. Box 486, Allenwood (08720-0486)
PHONE...................................614 540-1710
Chris Filos,
EMP: 35
SQ FT: 40,000
SALES (est): 6MM **Privately Held**
SIC: 3511 Turbines & turbine generator
sets

(G-5175)
QUICK FAB ALUMINUM MFG CO
Also Called: Quik-Fab Aluminum Mfg
1830 Swarthmore Ave Ste 1 (08701-4556)
PHONE...................................732 367-7200
Fax: 732 370-4659
Joseph Leary, *President*
EMP: 25 EST: 1974
SQ FT: 52,000
SALES (est): 2.9MM **Privately Held**
WEB: www.quikfab.com
SIC: 3334 3442 Primary aluminum; metal
doors, sash & trim

(G-5176)
**RED THE UNIFORM TAILOR INC
(PA)**
Also Called: Red The Tailor
475 Oberlin Ave S Ste 2 (08701-7024)
PHONE...................................848 299-0100
Patricia Klein, *CEO*
Harvey Klein, *President*
Tracy Gluck, *Vice Pres*
Barry Klein, *Treasurer*
Bob Entrekin, *Manager*
◆ EMP: 30
SQ FT: 17,000

SALES (est): 10.8MM **Privately Held**
SIC: 5699 2339 2326 Military goods & regalia; uniforms; women's & misses' outerwear; men's & boys' work clothing

(G-5177)
**REGAL LITHO PRTRS LTD
LBLTY CO**
1725 Oak St (08701-5927)
PHONE...................................732 901-1500
Simon Zeldes, *Mng Member*
Ben Zeldes,
EMP: 8 EST: 2013
SQ FT: 3,500
SALES: 700K **Privately Held**
SIC: 2752 Commercial printing, litho-
graphic

(G-5178)
REGENCY CABINETRY LLC
525 Oberlin Ave S (08701-7037)
PHONE...................................732 363-5630
Reuvan Sternstein, *Principal*
EMP: 4 **Privately Held**
WEB: www.regentcabinetry.com
SIC: 2434 Wood kitchen cabinets
PA: Regency Cabinetry Llc
525 Oberlin Ave S
Lakewood NJ 08701

(G-5179)
REGENCY CABINETRY LLC (PA)
Also Called: Regent
525 Oberlin Ave S (08701-7037)
PHONE...................................732 363-5630
Norman Shapiro, *Principal*
Leon Welcher, *Principal*
Reuvan Sternstein,
▲ EMP: 16
SALES (est): 2.3MM **Privately Held**
WEB: www.regentcabinetry.com
SIC: 2434 Wood kitchen cabinets

(G-5180)
**REMOTE LANDLORD SYSTEMS
LLC**
525 E County Line Rd (08701-1405)
PHONE...................................732 534-4445
David Lieberman,
EMP: 6
SALES (est): 148.8K **Privately Held**
SIC: 7372 Business oriented computer
software

(G-5181)
**RENAISSANCE LAKEWOOD
LLC (DH)**
Also Called: Renaissance Pharmaceuticals
1200 Paco Way (08701-5938)
PHONE...................................732 901-2052
Serge Maltais, *President*
John W Feik, *COO*
Mark Fite, *Senior VP*
Rick Bentzinger, *Vice Pres*
Kuljit Bhatia, *Vice Pres*
▲ EMP: 11
SALES: 73.1MM
SALES (corp-wide): 656.4MM **Privately
Held**
SIC: 2834 Druggists' preparations (phar-
maceuticals); cold remedies; lip balms;
ointments
HQ: Renaissance Ssp Holdings, Inc.
272 E Deerpath Ste 350
Lake Forest IL 60045
210 476-8194

(G-5182)
**RENAISSANCE LAKEWOOD
LLC**
Also Called: Renaissance Pharmaceuticals
1720 Oak St (08701-5926)
PHONE...................................732 367-9000
Antonio Di Nicola, *Plant Mgr*
EMP: 440
SQ FT: 750,000
SALES (corp-wide): 656.4MM **Privately
Held**
SIC: 2834 Druggists' preparations (phar-
maceuticals)
HQ: Renaissance Lakewood, Llc
1200 Paco Way
Lakewood NJ 08701
732 901-2052

(G-5183)
REVIEW AND JUDGE LLC
910 E County Line Rd 202c (08701-2093)
PHONE...................................732 987-3905
Malky Paskes, *Mng Member*
EMP: 5
SALES: 92K **Privately Held**
SIC: 2741 Miscellaneous publishing

(G-5184)
**ROBEN MANUFACTURING CO
INC**
760 Vassar Ave (08701-6907)
PHONE...................................732 364-6000
Fax: 732 905-9703
Gary R Huhn, *CEO*
Jennifer Adams-Hoffman, *Purchasing*
Allen Hoffman, *Sales Staff*
Nev Heimall, *Manager*
EMP: 31 EST: 1955
SQ FT: 30,000
SALES: 6.2MM **Privately Held**
WEB: www.robenmfg.com
SIC: 3443 Industrial vessels, tanks & con-
tainers

(G-5185)
ROELYNN LITHO INC
687 Prospect St Ste 410 (08701-4649)
PHONE...................................732 942-9650
Fax: 732 942-9655
Vincent J Praino, *President*
Rosemarie Praino, *Vice Pres*
▲ EMP: 15
SQ FT: 10,000
SALES (est): 2.4MM **Privately Held**
WEB: www.roelynn.com
SIC: 2752 Commercial printing, offset

(G-5186)
**ROYAL SEAMLESS
CORPORATION**
1000 Airport Rd Ste 203 (08701-5960)
PHONE...................................732 901-9595
Hedwig Obara, *President*
Hedy Obara, *Vice Pres*
EMP: 14
SQ FT: 20,000
SALES (est): 1.7MM **Privately Held**
SIC: 3498 Fabricated pipe & fittings

(G-5187)
SEABOARD INDUSTRIES
1957 Rutgers University B (08701-4568)
PHONE...................................732 901-5700
Samtha Fullerton, *Manager*
EMP: 10
SALES (corp-wide): 16.4MM **Privately
Held**
WEB: www.seaboard-usa.com
SIC: 5091 2899 Swimming pools, equip-
ment & supplies; water treating com-
pounds
PA: Seaboard Industries
185 Van Winkle Ave
Hawthorne NJ 07506
973 427-8500

(G-5188)
SHACHIHATA INC (USA)
525 Oberlin Ave S (08701-7037)
PHONE...................................732 905-7159
Fax: 732 370-3339
Youngsint Park, *Branch Mgr*
Maureen McGurk, *Manager*
Young Park, *Manager*
EMP: 12
SALES (corp-wide): 151.9MM **Privately
Held**
WEB: www.xstamper.com
SIC: 3953 Embossing seals & hand
stamps
HQ: Shachihata Inc. (U.S.A.)
20775 S Wstn Ave Ste 105
Torrance CA
310 530-4445

(G-5189)
SMARTPOOL LLC
687 Prospect St (08701-4648)
PHONE...................................732 730-9880
Fax: 732 730-9881
Richard Holstein, *President*
Bill Baker, *CFO*
Lewis Dubrofsky, *Mng Member*

◆ **EMP:** 24
SALES (est): 5.3MM **Privately Held**
WEB: www.smartpool.com
SIC: 3648 3569 Swimming pool lighting fixtures; heaters, swimming pool: electric

(G-5190)
SS WHITE BURS INC
1145 Towbin Ave (08701-5932)
PHONE................................732 905-1100
William Bobcock, *CEO*
EMP: 180
SALES (corp-wide): 29.9MM **Privately Held**
WEB: www.sswhiteburs.com
SIC: 3843 7699 5047 Burs, dental; dental instrument repair; dental equipment & supplies
PA: Ss White Burs, Inc.
1145 Towbin Ave
Lakewood NJ 08701
732 905-1100

(G-5191)
STEICO USA INC
Also Called: Juvenile Planet
250 Carey St (08701-1836)
PHONE................................732 364-6200
Fax: 732 364-2617
James Stein, *President*
EMP: 10
SQ FT: 2,000
SALES (est): 1.8MM **Privately Held**
SIC: 3944 5999 Games, toys & children's vehicles; infant furnishings & equipment

(G-5192)
STERN KNIT INC
3 Fillmore Ave (08701-5665)
PHONE................................732 364-8055
Mark Stern, *President*
▲ **EMP:** 9 **EST:** 1950
SALES (est): 481.7K **Privately Held**
SIC: 2258 Warp & flat knit products

(G-5193)
TARYAG LEGACY FOUNDATION INC
1136 Somerset Ave (08701-2138)
PHONE................................732 569-2467
Judy Wax, *President*
EMP: 15
SALES (est): 837.7K **Privately Held**
SIC: 2731 Book publishing

(G-5194)
TEX SPAR CO INC
155 Oberlin Ave N (08701-4525)
PHONE................................732 367-9439
Fax: 732 367-4172
Charles Sparasino, *President*
Joe Sparasino, *Corp Secy*
EMP: 200
SQ FT: 25,000
SALES (est): 6.5MM **Privately Held**
SIC: 7389 2392 Sewing contractor; household furnishings

(G-5195)
TIPICO PRODUCTS CO INC
490 Oberlin Ave S (08701-6903)
PHONE................................732 942-8820
Fax: 732 942-8837
William Gellert, *President*
Peggy Zimmerman, *Purchasing*
David Schreiner, *Manager*
Deniss Sossa, *Technology*
▲ **EMP:** 81
SALES (est): 18MM **Privately Held**
WEB: www.tipicoproducts.com
SIC: 2022 5143 Cheese, natural & processed; cheese

(G-5196)
TLW BATH LTD LIABILITY COMPANY
Also Called: Quality Bath
1144 E Cnty Ln Rd (08701)
PHONE................................732 942-7117
Steven Loeb, *Mktg Dir*
Mordi Lercher, *Mng Member*
Bayla Nussbaum, *Software Dev*
▼ **EMP:** 30

SALES: 30MM **Privately Held**
SIC: 2499 5999 Kitchen, bathroom & household ware: wood; plumbing & heating supplies

(G-5197)
TRI-STATE PHARMACEUTICAL LLC
1985 Swarthmore Ave Ste 3 (08701-4554)
PHONE................................732 905-7592
EMP: 7
SALES (est): 1MM **Privately Held**
SIC: 2834 Pharmaceutical preparations

(G-5198)
TWO 12 FASHION LLC
1525 Prospect St Ste 205 (08701-4662)
PHONE................................848 222-1562
Aron S Weiner, *Administration*
EMP: 4 **EST:** 2015
SQ FT: 16,000
SALES: 550K **Privately Held**
SIC: 7389 2387 Apparel designers, commercial; apparel belts

(G-5199)
UNEX MANUFACTURING INC (PA)
691 New Hampshire Ave (08701-5452)
PHONE................................732 928-2800
Fax: 732 928-2828
Brian Neuwirth, *President*
Mark Neuwirth, *Vice Pres*
◆ **EMP:** 65 **EST:** 1965
SQ FT: 60,000
SALES (est): 18.3MM **Privately Held**
WEB: www.unex.com
SIC: 3535 Conveyors & conveying equipment

(G-5200)
VINYLAST INC
Also Called: Quik-Sab
1830 Swarthmore Ave Ste 1 (08701-4556)
PHONE................................732 367-7200
Joseph L Leary, *President*
▲ **EMP:** 20
SALES (est): 3.7MM **Privately Held**
WEB: www.vinylast.com
SIC: 3089 1521 Windows, plastic; single-family housing construction

(G-5201)
VITILLO & SONS INC
Also Called: Diversified Fixtures
1930 Swarthmore Ave (08701-4547)
PHONE................................732 886-1393
Fax: 732 886-0911
Jerry Vitillo, *President*
Jerry Castoral, *Manager*
EMP: 18
SQ FT: 20,000
SALES (est): 3.6MM **Privately Held**
WEB: www.diversifiedfixture.com
SIC: 2542 3993 3841 2434 Office & store showcases & display fixtures; signs & advertising specialties; surgical & medical instruments; wood kitchen cabinets

(G-5202)
VOGEL PRECAST INC
1509 Prospect St (08701-4659)
PHONE................................732 552-8837
Kathy Vogel, *President*
Timothy Vogel, *Vice Pres*
EMP: 6 **EST:** 1948
SALES (est): 440K **Privately Held**
SIC: 3271 1711 Sewer & manhole block, concrete; septic system construction

(G-5203)
W G I CORP
Also Called: Webco Graphics
1875 Swarthmore Ave (08701-4533)
P.O. Box 1478 (08701-1016)
PHONE................................732 370-2900
Fax: 732 367-4621
Glenn A Davis, *President*
Maureen Davis, *Admin Sec*
EMP: 15
SQ FT: 23,000
SALES (est): 1.8MM **Privately Held**
SIC: 2731 2752 Books: publishing & printing; commercial printing, lithographic

(G-5204)
WARDALE CORP
Also Called: Mister Boardwalk
575 Prospect St Ste 202 (08701-5040)
P.O. Box 736, Arkansas City KS (67005-0736)
PHONE................................800 813-4050
Fax: 732 905-1724
Warren Mc Leod, *President*
Warren McLeod, *President*
Dale Mc Leod, *Corp Secy*
EMP: 20
SQ FT: 15,000
SALES (est): 1.6MM **Privately Held**
WEB: www.misterboardwalk.com
SIC: 2499 Fencing, docks & other outdoor wood structural products

(G-5205)
WEST PHRM SVCS LAKEWOOD INC
1200 Paco Way (08701-5938)
PHONE................................732 730-3295
EMP: 4
SALES (est): 189K
SALES (corp-wide): 1.6B **Publicly Held**
SIC: 3069 Medical & laboratory rubber sundries & related products
PA: West Pharmaceutical Services, Inc.
530 Herman O West Dr
Exton PA 19341
610 594-2900

(G-5206)
WOODHAVEN LUMBER & MILLWORK (PA)
200 James St (08701-4103)
PHONE................................732 901-0030
Fax: 732 886-5088
James T Robinson, *CEO*
Robert Rhodes, *Vice Pres*
David Robinson, *Vice Pres*
Glenn Simons, *Vice Pres*
Russell Gilbert, *Opers Staff*
▲ **EMP:** 180
SALES (est): 48.5MM **Privately Held**
WEB: www.woodhavenlumber.com
SIC: 5211 2431 Millwork & lumber; cabinets, kitchen; paneling; interior & ornamental woodwork & trim

(G-5207)
WORTHINGTON BIOCHEMICAL CORP (PA)
730 Vassar Ave (08701-6907)
PHONE................................732 942-1660
Fax: 732 942-9270
Von Worthington, *President*
Joseph M Berardo Sr, *Vice Pres*
Rick Schmitz, *Vice Pres*
James Zacka, *Vice Pres*
Theodore Worthington, *CFO*
EMP: 50
SQ FT: 30,000
SALES (est): 7.6MM **Privately Held**
WEB: www.worthington-biochem.com
SIC: 2835 2836 Enzyme & isoenzyme diagnostic agents; biological products, except diagnostic

(G-5208)
Y & J BAKERS INC
Also Called: Gelbsteins Bakery
415 Clifton Ave (08701-3235)
PHONE................................732 363-3636
Fax: 732 363-1124
Joseph Gruenepaum, *President*
Joel Tesser, *Vice Pres*
EMP: 25
SQ FT: 4,000
SALES (est): 1MM **Privately Held**
SIC: 5461 5149 2051 Bakeries; bakery products; bread, cake & related products

---

Lambertville
Hunterdon County

(G-5209)
ADVANCED CERAMETRICS INC (PA)
245 N Main St (08530-1416)
P.O. Box 128 (08530-0128)
PHONE................................609 397-2900
Fax: 609 397-2708
Richard B Cass, *President*
Michael R Hendricks, *Exec VP*
Robert D Frawley, *Admin Sec*
EMP: 8
SQ FT: 20,000
SALES (est): 3.1MM **Privately Held**
WEB: www.advancedcerametrics.com
SIC: 3299 Ceramic fiber

(G-5210)
BREEN COLOR CONCENTRATES LLC
11 Kari Dr (08530-3411)
PHONE................................609 397-8200
Howard Demonte, *President*
Paul Wheeler, *Plant Mgr*
Scott Senour, *CFO*
Paul Legnetti, *CTO*
Andrew Diamatteo, *IT/INT Sup*
◆ **EMP:** 10
SALES (est): 1MM **Privately Held**
SIC: 2821 2851 2816 Polyvinyl chloride resins (PVC); paints & allied products; inorganic pigments

(G-5211)
BUCKS COUNTY BREWING CO INC
80 Lambert Ln Ste 120 (08530-1920)
PHONE................................609 929-0148
Fax: 609 397-4715
Jack Bryan, *President*
EMP: 5
SALES (est): 270K **Privately Held**
WEB: www.riverhorse.com
SIC: 2082 Beer (alcoholic beverage)

(G-5212)
G-FORCE RIVER SIGNS LLC
9 S Main St (08530-2135)
PHONE................................609 397-4467
David Gerrity, *President*
EMP: 6
SALES (est): 253.7K **Privately Held**
SIC: 3993 Signs, not made in custom sign painting shops

(G-5213)
GRENADE SUPPLY CO
278 N Union St Ste 135 (08530-1506)
PHONE................................267 968-3115
Bradley Newcomer, *President*
EMP: 4
SQ FT: 5,000
SALES (est): 229.4K **Privately Held**
SIC: 2844 Deodorants, personal

(G-5214)
JOHNSON & JOHNSON
10 Stymiest Rd (08530-3107)
PHONE................................732 524-0400
EMP: 80
SALES (corp-wide): 76.4B **Publicly Held**
SIC: 2676 Feminine hygiene paper products
PA: Johnson & Johnson
1 Johnson And Johnson Plz
New Brunswick NJ 08933
732 524-0400

(G-5215)
JULIUS E HOLLAND-MORITZ CO INC
Also Called: J.E. Holland-Moritz Co., Inc.
599 Brunswick Pike (08530-2720)
PHONE................................609 397-1231
Jeanne Maier, *Corp Secy*
John Maier, *Vice Pres*
▲ **EMP:** 5
SQ FT: 3,200

SALES: 1MM **Privately Held**
WEB: www.jehmco.com
SIC: 3499 Aquarium accessories, metal

(G-5216)
KANSAS CITY DESIGN INC
201 S Main St (08530-1800)
PHONE..............................609 460-4629
William Arnold, *President*
EMP: 4
SALES (est): 567.9K **Privately Held**
SIC: 2671 Plastic film, coated or laminated for packaging

(G-5217)
L S P INDUSTRIAL CERAMICS INC
34 Mount Airy Village Rd (08530-3511)
PHONE..............................609 397-8330
Fax: 609 397-4660
Frank D Smith, *President*
▲ **EMP:** 5
SQ FT: 900
SALES: 900K **Privately Held**
WEB: www.lspceramics.com
SIC: 3253 Floor tile, ceramic

(G-5218)
LOCAL WISDOM INC
287 S Main St Ste 2 (08530-1830)
PHONE..............................609 269-2320
Nicole Dimeglio, *Partner*
Derrick Larane, *Principal*
Michael Alfaro, *Principal*
Pinaki Kathiari, *Principal*
Ryan Czepiel, *Graphic Designe*
EMP: 35
SQ FT: 5,000
SALES (est): 2.4MM **Privately Held**
SIC: 7371 7372 7379 Computer software development & applications; computer software development; prepackaged software;

(G-5219)
NXLEVEL INC
Also Called: Nxlevel Solutions
201 S Main St Ste 5 (08530-1800)
PHONE..............................609 483-6900
Fax: 609 466-4322
Robert Christensen, *President*
Peter Sandford, *Exec VP*
Daniel O'Connor, *Vice Pres*
Pam Dorini, *Project Mgr*
Sean Murphy, *Manager*
EMP: 20
SQ FT: 5,100
SALES (est): 3.3MM **Privately Held**
WEB: www.nxlevelsolutions.com
SIC: 7372 Educational computer software

(G-5220)
PULSETOR LLC
243 N Union St Ste 207 (08530-1521)
PHONE..............................609 303-0578
Fax: 609 303-0581
Nicholas C Barbi,
Richard B Mott,
James A Nicolino,
EMP: 5
SALES (est): 858.4K **Privately Held**
SIC: 3826 Analytical instruments

(G-5221)
SOUTH COUNTY SOCCER LEAGUE INC
3 Ferry St (08530-1802)
PHONE..............................908 310-9052
Regina Skrebel, *President*
Howard Young, *Vice Pres*
Richard Eyre, *Treasurer*
Robin Wedeking, *Admin Sec*
EMP: 4
SALES (est): 132.7K **Privately Held**
SIC: 3949 Guards: football, basketball, soccer, lacrosse, etc.

(G-5222)
TRIUMPH BREWING OF PRINCETON
287 S Main St Ste 16 (08530-1869)
PHONE..............................609 773-0111
Torri Thompson, *Branch Mgr*
EMP: 5 **Privately Held**
WEB: www.triumphbrew.com

SIC: 2082 Malt beverages
PA: Triumph Brewing Company Of Princeton Inc
138 Nassau St Ste A
Princeton NJ 08542

Landing
Morris County

(G-5223)
EDMUND KISS
Also Called: Ej Machine & Tool Co
12 Orben Dr Unit 1 (07850-1800)
PHONE..............................973 810-2312
Edmund Kiss, *Owner*
EMP: 5
SQ FT: 2,600
SALES (est): 605K **Privately Held**
SIC: 8711 3599 Machine tool design; machine shop, jobbing & repair

(G-5224)
GAMMA MACHINE & TOOL CO INC
32 Oneida Ave (07850-1318)
PHONE..............................973 398-8821
EMP: 4
SQ FT: 2,500
SALES (est): 280K **Privately Held**
SIC: 3599 Machine Shop

(G-5225)
ORCAS INTERNATIONAL INC
Also Called: Orcas Naturals
9 Lenel Rd (07850-1844)
PHONE..............................973 448-2801
K Gnaneshwar RAO, *President*
Kuldip RAO, *Vice Pres*
Marlene Bencel, *Purch Mgr*
▲ **EMP:** 16
SQ FT: 10,000
SALES (est): 2.6MM **Privately Held**
SIC: 2023 5122 Dietary supplements, dairy & non-dairy based; drugs, proprietaries & sundries

(G-5226)
PRC LASER CORPORATION (DH)
Also Called: ROFIN-SINAR TECHNOLOGIES INC.
350 N Frontage Rd (07850-1526)
PHONE..............................973 347-0100
Fax: 973 347-8932
Walter Wilson, *President*
Nancy Mc Namara, *Vice Pres*
William Ondish, *Opers Mgr*
Doug Myers, *Senior Buyer*
Kenneth Tuluo, *Engineer*
▲ **EMP:** 43
SQ FT: 65,000
SALES: 8.7MM
SALES (corp-wide): 1.7B **Publicly Held**
WEB: www.prclaser.com
SIC: 3699 Laser systems & equipment

(G-5227)
PRUDENT PUBLISHING CO INC
400 N Frontage Rd (07850-1516)
PHONE..............................973 347-4554
Fax: 973 347-5855
Sharon Ruthman, *Branch Mgr*
Yuhen Abreu, *CTO*
EMP: 22
SALES (corp-wide): 27.4MM **Privately Held**
WEB: www.bizgreetingcards.com
SIC: 2771 Greeting cards
PA: Prudent Publishing Co., Inc.
65 Challenger Rd Ste 501
Ridgefield Park NJ 07660
201 641-7900

(G-5228)
UNIQUE ENCAPSULATION TECH LLC
Also Called: Unique Encapsulation Tech Orca
9 Lenel Rd (07850-1844)
PHONE..............................973 448-2801
Gnaneshwar K RAO, *Mng Member*
EMP: 27 **EST:** 2012
SQ FT: 12,000

SALES (est): 1.1MM **Privately Held**
SIC: 2023 Dietary supplements, dairy & non-dairy based

Landisville
Atlantic County

(G-5229)
APPLAUSE MUSICAL PRODUCTS
Also Called: Musikraft
108 Buena Vista Ave (08326-1440)
P.O. Box 331 (08326-0331)
PHONE..............................856 697-8333
Gulab Gidwani, *Owner*
▲ **EMP:** 5
SALES (est): 423.1K **Privately Held**
SIC: 3931 Guitars & parts, electric & non-electric

(G-5230)
BELLVIEW FARMS INC
Also Called: Bellview Winery
150 Atlantic St (08326-1204)
PHONE..............................856 697-7172
Fax: 856 697-7183
James Quarella, *President*
Sofia Zych, *Manager*
EMP: 7
SALES (est): 746.2K **Privately Held**
WEB: www.bellviewwinery.com
SIC: 2084 Wines

(G-5231)
FIBERTECH GROUP INC (DH)
Also Called: Pgi Nonwovens
450 N East Blvd (08326-1212)
PHONE..............................856 697-1600
Jerry Zucker, *Ch of Bd*
Jim Schaeffer, *COO*
Jay Tiedemann, *Vice Pres*
Gregg Wilkinson, *Vice Pres*
James Boyd, *Treasurer*
▲ **EMP:** 205
SQ FT: 240,000
SALES (est): 39.1MM **Publicly Held**
SIC: 2297 Spunbonded fabrics

Laurel Springs
Camden County

(G-5232)
BODY BOOST LABS LTD LBLTY CO
36 W Brookline Dr (08021-4854)
PHONE..............................609 519-1070
Christopher Gaudio,
EMP: 10
SALES: 120K **Privately Held**
SIC: 2023 Dietary supplements, dairy & non-dairy based

(G-5233)
J & R REBUILDERS INC
330 Washington Ave (08021-2050)
PHONE..............................856 627-1414
Robert Visconti, *President*
EMP: 8
SALES (est): 600K **Privately Held**
SIC: 7539 3714 3694 Automotive repair shops; motor vehicle parts & accessories; engine electrical equipment

(G-5234)
VACUUM SALES INC
51 Stone Rd (08021-2137)
PHONE..............................856 627-7790
Fax: 856 627-3044
James Redstreake, *President*
Bill Bax, *Parts Mgr*
Mike Downey, *Sales Staff*
Mike Vittese, *Sales Staff*
▼ **EMP:** 21
SQ FT: 10,000
SALES: 8MM **Privately Held**
WEB: www.vacuumsalesinc.com
SIC: 3713 Tank truck bodies

Laurence Harbor
Middlesex County

(G-5235)
TELCONTEL CORP
11 Industrial Dr (08879)
PHONE..............................732 441-0800
Eugene Norden, *President*
EMP: 10
SALES (est): 1MM **Privately Held**
SIC: 3661 3663 Telephone & telegraph apparatus; radio & TV communications equipment

(G-5236)
VOLTA CORPORATION (PA)
11 Industrial Dr (08879)
P.O. Box 1027 (08879-4027)
PHONE..............................732 583-3300
Fax: 732 583-4900
Alexander R Norden, *President*
Arden Penton, *Mktg Dir*
EMP: 22
SQ FT: 6,000
SALES (est): 2.9MM **Privately Held**
SIC: 3643 Connectors, electric cord

Lavallette
Ocean County

(G-5237)
SIGNAL SYSTEMS INTERNATIONAL (PA)
Also Called: Coastal Creations
1700 Grand Central Ave (08735-2432)
PHONE..............................732 793-4668
Fax: 732 793-4679
Tom M Kinney, *President*
William D Kinney, *Chairman*
Doris Kinney, *Vice Pres*
EMP: 4 **EST:** 1975
SQ FT: 3,750
SALES (est): 975.5K **Privately Held**
WEB: www.signalsystem.com
SIC: 3823 5699 3643 Liquid level instruments, industrial process type; bathing suits; current-carrying wiring devices

(G-5238)
Z LINE BEACHWEAR
Also Called: Z-Line
3263 Route 35 N (08735-1535)
PHONE..............................732 793-1234
Fax: 732 793-2939
Bruce Zabelski, *Owner*
Terry Zabelski, *Co-Owner*
EMP: 4
SQ FT: 3,000
SALES (est): 350.9K **Privately Held**
SIC: 7336 2396 Silk screen design; automotive & apparel trimmings

Lawrence Township
Mercer County

(G-5239)
ADVISORY DUMAS GROUP LLC
Also Called: Bert's Cake Studio
7 Van Buren Pl (08648-4346)
PHONE..............................850 778-1624
Bertrand Dumas, *Principal*
EMP: 15
SALES (est): 390K **Privately Held**
SIC: 5461 8742 2051 Bakeries; restaurant & food services consultants; cakes, bakery: except frozen

(G-5240)
AURO HEALTH LLC (DH)
2572 Brunswick Pike (08648-4128)
PHONE..............................732 839-9400
Nivaran Kapur, *President*
Gangadhar RAO Gorla, *Vice Pres*
Swami Iyer, *CFO*
Kiran Kumar Nagabandhi, *Controller*
EMP: 2 **EST:** 2012
SQ FT: 175,000

▲ = Import ▼=Export
◆ =Import/Export

SALES (est): 5.3MM
SALES (corp-wide): 1.6B **Privately Held**
SIC: 2834 Pharmaceutical preparations
HQ: Aurobindo Pharma U.S.A., Inc.
279 Prnctn Hightstown Rd
East Windsor NJ 08520
732 839-9400

(G-5241)
BROOK METAL PRODUCTS INC
Also Called: Venture Shuffelbuard
16 Sunset Rd (08648-2712)
PHONE..............................908 355-1601
Fax: 908 527-0305
Russ McKay, *President*
Christopher McKay, *Exec VP*
▲ EMP: 14
SQ FT: 17,000
SALES (est): 1.8MM **Privately Held**
SIC: 3444 Sheet metalwork

(G-5242)
DKSH LUXURY & LIFESTYLE N AMER
9 Princess Rd Ste D (08648-2318)
PHONE..............................609 750-8800
Philipp Von Bueren, *President*
EMP: 6
SQ FT: 4,000
SALES (est): 740.5K **Privately Held**
SIC: 3873 5944 Watches, clocks, watchcases & parts; clock & watch stores

(G-5243)
LMT MERCER GROUP INC (PA)
690 Puritan Ave (08648-4600)
PHONE..............................888 570-5252
Anthony Lesenskyj, *President*
Jim Fattori, *President*
Bernie Henry, *President*
Pete Fischel, *COO*
George Lesenskyj, *Vice Pres*
◆ EMP: 45
SQ FT: 40,000
SALES (est): 13.3MM **Privately Held**
WEB: www.lmtproducts.com
SIC: 3446 Fences, gates, posts & flagpoles

(G-5244)
MUALEMA LLC
Also Called: Sohha Savory Yogurt
2214 Town Ct N (08648-4736)
PHONE..............................609 820-6098
Angela Fout, *Mng Member*
John Fout,
EMP: 6
SALES: 600K **Privately Held**
SIC: 2026 Yogurt

(G-5245)
NASSAU COMMUNICATIONS INC
Also Called: Nassau Printers
650 Whitehead Rd (08648-4404)
PHONE..............................609 208-9099
Fax: 609 208-9855
Kenneth M Fisher, *President*
EMP: 10
SQ FT: 8,000
SALES (est): 1.2MM **Privately Held**
SIC: 2752 2791 2796 Lithographing on metal; typesetting, computer controlled; platemaking services

(G-5246)
RAMCO SYSTEMS CORPORATION (HQ)
3150 Us Highway 1 Ste 206 (08648-2420)
PHONE..............................609 620-4800
Fax: 609 620-2860
Venkatesh Viswanathan, *CEO*
James Fitzgerald, *President*
Rajesh Kumar Ranganathan, *Finance*
EMP: 30
SQ FT: 6,700
SALES (est): 11.3MM
SALES (corp-wide): 44.2MM **Privately Held**
WEB: www.rsc.ramco.com
SIC: 7372 Prepackaged software
PA: Ramco Systems Limited
No-64 Ramco Building
Chennai TN 60011
442 235-2880

(G-5247)
RICHARD REIN
Also Called: U S 1 Publishing Co
15 Princess Rd K (08648-2301)
PHONE..............................609 452-7000
Richard Rein, *Owner*
Diana Riley, *Advt Staff*
EMP: 10
SALES (est): 390K **Privately Held**
WEB: www.princetoninfo.com
SIC: 2711 Newspapers: publishing only, not printed on site

(G-5248)
SOFTWARE SERVICES & SOLUTIONS
15 Laurel Wood Dr (08648-1043)
PHONE..............................203 630-2000
Elisabeth Masterson, *President*
Robert Masterson, *Vice Pres*
EMP: 10
SALES (est): 507.2K **Privately Held**
WEB: www.sss.com
SIC: 7379 7372 Computer related consulting services; prepackaged software

Lawrenceville
Mercer County

(G-5249)
ABI INC
227 Bakers Basin Rd (08648-3307)
PHONE..............................609 588-8225
James A Britton, *President*
EMP: 20 EST: 1998
SQ FT: 2,100
SALES (est): 1.5MM **Privately Held**
SIC: 3273 Ready-mixed concrete

(G-5250)
ATGI ADVANCED TECH GROUP INTL
1217 Colts Cir (08648-3267)
PHONE..............................609 271-8666
EMP: 50 EST: 2012
SALES (est): 4.7MM **Privately Held**
SIC: 3812 Mfg Search/Navigation Equipment

(G-5251)
BOT LLC
Also Called: Bot Beverages
12 Clementon Way (08648-3742)
PHONE..............................609 439-1537
Fax: 609 530-1675
Cricket Allen, *Mng Member*
Brian Allen,
Craig Carlson,
Tom Connor,
EMP: 8
SQ FT: 225
SALES: 350K **Privately Held**
SIC: 2086 Bottled & canned soft drinks

(G-5252)
BRISTOL-MYERS SQUIBB COMPANY
3401 Princeton Pike (08648-1205)
PHONE..............................609 302-3000
Fax: 609 897-6791
Peter Dolan, *Branch Mgr*
EMP: 2500
SQ FT: 650,000
SALES (corp-wide): 20.7B **Publicly Held**
WEB: www.bms.com
SIC: 2834 Pharmaceutical preparations
PA: Bristol-Myers Squibb Company
430 E 29th St Fl 14
New York NY 10016
212 546-4000

(G-5253)
CELSION CORPORATION (PA)
997 Lenox Dr Ste 100 (08648-2317)
PHONE..............................609 896-9100
Fax: 609 896-2200
Michael H Tardugno, *Ch of Bd*
Khursheed Anwer, *Exec VP*
Marianne Lambertson, *Vice Pres*
Jeffrey W Church, *CFO*
Nicholas Borys, *Chief Mktg Ofcr*
EMP: 19

SQ FT: 10,870
SALES: 500K **Publicly Held**
WEB: www.celsion.com
SIC: 2834 Pharmaceutical preparations

(G-5254)
COMMUNITY NEWS SERVICE LLC
15 Princess Rd K (08648-2301)
PHONE..............................609 396-1511
Joseph Emanski, *Manager*
EMP: 10
SALES (est): 648.1K **Privately Held**
SIC: 2711 Commercial printing & newspaper publishing combined

(G-5255)
CORE LABORATORIES LP
Core Lab Refinery Systems
11 Princess Rd Ste H (08648-2319)
PHONE..............................609 896-2673
Fax: 609 520-1224
Craig Tournay, *General Mgr*
Craig A Tournay, *Branch Mgr*
Harvey Feller, *Manager*
EMP: 10
SALES (corp-wide): 659.8MM **Privately Held**
SIC: 1382 Oil & gas exploration services
HQ: Core Laboratories Lp
6316 Windfern Rd
Houston TX 77040

(G-5256)
DATACOLOR INC (HQ)
Also Called: Applied Color Systems
5 Princess Rd (08648-2301)
P.O. Box 200834, Pittsburgh PA (15251-0834)
PHONE..............................609 924-2189
Fax: 609 895-7449
Albert Busch, *CEO*
Jim Jenkins, *Project Mgr*
Clifford Chuba, *Manager*
▲ EMP: 65
SQ FT: 72,000
SALES (est): 22.9MM
SALES (corp-wide): 72.8MM **Privately Held**
WEB: www.datacolor.com
SIC: 3827 3695 Optical test & inspection equipment; computer software tape & disks: blank, rigid & floppy
PA: Datacolor Ag
Waldstatterstrasse 12
Luzern LU 6003
448 353-711

(G-5257)
HALO FARM INC
Also Called: Milk Farm
970 Spruce St (08648-4548)
PHONE..............................609 695-3311
Fax: 609 695-3372
Jerry Reilly, *President*
Ann T Reilly, *Vice Pres*
EMP: 8
SQ FT: 2,500
SALES (est): 1MM **Privately Held**
WEB: www.milkfarm.com
SIC: 2033 5451 2026 5499 Fruit juices: packaged in cans, jars, etc.; dairy products stores; milk processing (pasteurizing, homogenizing, bottling); juices, fruit or vegetable

(G-5258)
HEL INC
4 Princess Rd Ste 208 (08648-2322)
PHONE..............................440 208-7360
Fax: 609 912-1552
Jasbir Singh, *President*
EMP: 6
SQ FT: 1,200
SALES: 4.2MM
SALES (corp-wide): 1.6MM **Privately Held**
WEB: www.helgroup.com
SIC: 3821 Laboratory apparatus & furniture
PA: Hel Limited
9-10 Capital Business Park
Borehamwood HERTS WD6 1
208 736-0640

(G-5259)
KIDCUTETURE LLC
5 Rosalind Dr (08648-3212)
PHONE..............................609 532-0149
Olga Pantelyat, *President*
Yury Pantelyat, *General Mgr*
Nataliya Pantelyat, *Vice Pres*
▲ EMP: 6
SALES (est): 576.6K **Privately Held**
SIC: 2335 Women's, juniors' & misses' dresses; gowns, formal

(G-5260)
LAWRENCE MOLD AND TOOL CORP (PA)
1412 Ohio Ave (08648-4638)
PHONE..............................609 392-5422
Fax: 609 392-5861
George Lesenskyj Jr, *President*
◆ EMP: 45
SQ FT: 10,000
SALES (est): 6.9MM **Privately Held**
WEB: www.lawrencemold.net
SIC: 3544 Industrial molds

(G-5261)
LE BON MAGOT LTD LIABILITY CO
69 Lawrncvlle Pnnngton Rd (08648-1483)
PHONE..............................609 895-0211
Rohit Bansal,
EMP: 6
SALES (est): 203.6K **Privately Held**
SIC: 2099 Food preparations

(G-5262)
MEADOWGATE FARM ALPACAS
Also Called: Meadowfarmalpacas Aol.com
3071 Lawrenceville Rd (08648-1108)
PHONE..............................609 219-0529
Diane Rosenberg, *Owner*
▲ EMP: 7
SALES: 500K **Privately Held**
WEB: www.meadowgatefarmalpacas.com
SIC: 2211 Alpacas, cotton

(G-5263)
MERCER DIGITAL PRINTING LLC
650 Whitehead Rd 2 (08648-4404)
PHONE..............................609 919-9190
EMP: 6
SALES (est): 679.1K **Privately Held**
SIC: 2752 Commercial printing, offset

(G-5264)
MOA INSTRUMENTATION INC
20 Carla Way (08648-1500)
PHONE..............................215 547-8308
Marshall Borlaug, *Manager*
EMP: 7
SALES (est): 1.3MM
SALES (corp-wide): 2.6MM **Privately Held**
SIC: 3826 Spectrometers
PA: Moa Instrumentation, Inc.
1606 Manning Blvd Ste 1
Levittown PA 19057
609 352-9329

(G-5265)
NATIONAL REPROGRAPHICS INC
Bluedge
3175 Princeton Pike (08648-2331)
PHONE..............................609 896-4100
Frank Plum, *Vice Pres*
EMP: 42
SALES (corp-wide): 70.3MM **Privately Held**
SIC: 2759 Commercial printing
PA: National Reprographics Inc.
44 W 18th St Fl 2
New York NY 10011
212 366-7250

(G-5266)
NOAH LLC
610 Lawrenceville Rd (08648-4208)
PHONE..............................609 637-0039
Emery Cappola,
EMP: 5
SALES (est): 354.6K **Privately Held**
SIC: 3679 Electronic circuits

G
E
O
G
R
A
P
H
I
C

(G-5267)
PRINCETON POWER SYSTEMS INC
3175 Princeton Pike (08648-2331)
PHONE..............................609 955-5390
Fax: 609 751-9225
Ken McCauley, *President*
Darren Hammell, *President*
Ed Howell, *COO*
Kevin Wells, *Buyer*
Martin Becker, *Engineer*
▲ EMP: 55
SQ FT: 38,000
SALES (est): 14.8MM Privately Held
WEB: www.princetonpower.com
SIC: 3629 Power conversion units, a.c. to d.c.; static-electric

(G-5268)
SCIENTIFIC SALES INC
3 Glenbrook Ct (08648-5556)
P.O. Box 6725 (08648-0725)
PHONE..............................609 844-0055
Fax: 609 844-0466
Thomas Tesauro, *President*
◆ EMP: 12
SALES (est): 2.9MM Privately Held
WEB: www.scientificsales.com
SIC: 3829 Measuring & controlling devices

(G-5269)
SHERWOOD INDUSTRIES INC
1333 Brunswick Ave # 200 (08648-4502)
PHONE..............................609 396-7600
EMP: 56
SALES (corp-wide): 42.7MM Privately Held
SIC: 3999 Barber & beauty shop equipment
PA: Sherwood Industries, Inc.
   1333 Brunswick Ave Ste 2
   Lawrenceville NJ 08648
   609 396-7600

(G-5270)
TLG SIGNS INC
Also Called: Fastsigns
2901 Us Highway 1 Ste 3 (08648-2419)
PHONE..............................609 912-0500
Fax: 609 912-0554
William Belmont, *President*
Joan Belmont, *Vice Pres*
EMP: 8 EST: 1998
SALES: 1.2MM Privately Held
SIC: 3993 Signs & advertising specialties

(G-5271)
VARSITY SOFTWARE INC
124 Lwrncvlle Pnnngton Rd (08648)
PHONE..............................609 309-9955
John Weaver, *President*
EMP: 5
SALES (est): 210.4K Privately Held
SIC: 7372 Prepackaged software

(G-5272)
WRIGHTWORKS ENGINEERING LLC
12 Rosetree Ln (08648-3233)
PHONE..............................609 882-8840
Craig Wright,
Lois Wright,
EMP: 8
SALES (est): 690K Privately Held
SIC: 3545 Precision tools, machinists'

(G-5273)
XYBION CORPORATION (PA)
2000 Lenox Dr Ste 101 (08648-2314)
PHONE..............................973 538-2067
Fax: 973 540-9712
Pradip K Banerjee, *President*
Kamal Biswas, *President*
Nagraj Lanka, *General Mgr*
Bob Friedman, *CTO*
Santhosh Saravanan, *Software Engr*
EMP: 138
SQ FT: 11,000
SALES (est): 15.6MM Privately Held
SIC: 8731 3625 7371 3861 Electronic research; relays & industrial controls; computer software development; cameras, still & motion picture (all types); integrated circuits, semiconductor devices, etc.

Lebanon
Hunterdon County

(G-5274)
AIRSCAN INC
291 Rt 22 Ste 12 (08833)
PHONE..............................908 823-9425
Fax: 908 823-9428
Stephen Shoemaker, *President*
Sharon Dechant, *Manager*
EMP: 7
SQ FT: 3,000
SALES: 1MM Privately Held
WEB: www.airscan1.com
SIC: 3826 Gas testing apparatus

(G-5275)
ALAQUEST INTERNATIONAL INC
28 Molasses Hill Rd (08833-3206)
PHONE..............................908 713-9399
Fax: 908 713-9288
Marcia Magazzu, *President*
Ronald Magazzu, *Director*
EMP: 10
SALES (est): 750K Privately Held
WEB: www.alaquest.com
SIC: 7372 7373 7374 Prepackaged software; computer integrated systems design; service bureau, computer

(G-5276)
AUTODRILL LLC
1221 Us Highway 22 Ste 6 (08833-2228)
PHONE..............................908 542-0244
Fax: 908 542-0242
Joseph Agro,
▲ EMP: 6
SQ FT: 1,500
SALES (est): 1.1MM Privately Held
WEB: www.autodrill.com
SIC: 5084 3541 Machine tools & accessories; drilling machine tools (metal cutting)

(G-5277)
AVSTAR PUBLISHING CORP
3 Burlinghoff Ln (08833-4383)
PHONE..............................908 236-6210
Alvin Silverstein, *President*
Virginia Silverstein, *Vice Pres*
Laura Nunn, *Admin Sec*
EMP: 5
SALES (est): 400K Privately Held
SIC: 2731 Books: publishing & printing

(G-5278)
B & B PRESS INC
24 Cokesbury Rd Ste 11 (08833-2218)
PHONE..............................908 840-4093
Fax: 908 840-4358
Mark Bistis, *President*
Christopher Koch, *Prdtn Mgr*
John Bistis, *Treasurer*
EMP: 9 EST: 1922
SQ FT: 3,200
SALES (est): 1.5MM Privately Held
WEB: www.bbpress.com
SIC: 2752 2791 Commercial printing, offset; typesetting, computer controlled

(G-5279)
CANDY TREASURE LLC
66 Welsh Rd (08833-4316)
P.O. Box 201 (08833-0201)
PHONE..............................201 830-3600
Agnes Kaszycki, *Treasurer*
Oleg Yarmolenko,
▲ EMP: 8
SALES (est): 2.4MM Privately Held
SIC: 5947 2064 2066 Gift shop; candy & other confectionery products; chocolate & cocoa products

(G-5280)
CELIMMUNE
110 Old Driftway Ln (08833-4628)
PHONE..............................908 399-2954
EMP: 4 EST: 2016
SALES (est): 265.8K Privately Held
SIC: 2834 Pharmaceutical preparations

(G-5281)
CHATHAM CONTROLS CORPORATION
6 Corral Cir (08833-4021)
PHONE..............................908 236-6019
Fax: 908 236-6345
Richard H Perst, *President*
Marcia Bernstein, *Office Mgr*
EMP: 6 EST: 1954
SALES (est): 1MM Privately Held
SIC: 3822 Thermostats, except built-in

(G-5282)
CONSTRUCTION SPECIALTIES INC (PA)
Also Called: C/S Corporate
3 Werner Way Ste 100 (08833-2230)
PHONE..............................908 236-0800
Fax: 908 236-0801
Tom Hakes, *President*
Charles Van Koten, *Vice Pres*
Timothy Cobbs, *Engineer*
Robert Olsen, *Engineer*
Gregory Casey, *Asst Treas*
▲ EMP: 50 EST: 1948
SQ FT: 20,000
SALES (est): 367MM Privately Held
WEB: www.c-sgroup.com
SIC: 3446 3354 3443 3272 Railings, prefabricated metal; railings, bannisters, guards, etc.: made from metal pipe; guards, made from pipe; aluminum extruded products; columns (fractioning, etc.): metal plate; floor slabs & tiles, precast concrete; air conditioning units, complete: domestic or industrial

(G-5283)
CUTTING BOARD COMPANY (PA)
291 Route 22 E Bldg 6 (08833)
PHONE..............................908 725-0187
Theresa Pizzelanti, *Owner*
Tony Pizzelanti, *Co-Owner*
▲ EMP: 4
SQ FT: 5,000
SALES (est): 550K Privately Held
SIC: 3613 Distribution cutouts

(G-5284)
ENGINE FACTORY INC
24 Cokesbury Rd Ste 15 (08833-2218)
PHONE..............................908 236-9915
Bruce T Nelson, *Executive*
EMP: 4
SALES (est): 408.8K Privately Held
WEB: www.enginefactory.com
SIC: 3694 Engine electrical equipment

(G-5285)
ENPRO INC
1401 Us Highway 22 (08833-4215)
P.O. Box 418 (08833-0418)
PHONE..............................908 236-2137
Fax: 908 236-7394
Vincent Cioffi, *President*
Pearl Cioffi, *Treasurer*
EMP: 30 EST: 1961
SQ FT: 7,500
SALES (est): 2.8MM Privately Held
SIC: 3589 Water treatment equipment, industrial

(G-5286)
FLEXBIOSYS INC
291 Us Highway 22 Ste 32 (08833-5071)
PHONE..............................908 300-3244
Gayle Tarry, *CEO*
Stanley Tarry, *President*
EMP: 12
SALES (est): 920.2K Privately Held
SIC: 2673 3085 Plastic bags: made from purchased materials; plastics bottles

(G-5287)
GLEN G COATS
Also Called: Lebanon Door Company
119 Main St (08833-2162)
P.O. Box 168 (08833-0168)
PHONE..............................908 236-2620
Glen G Coats, *Owner*
EMP: 4
SQ FT: 2,000

SALES: 600K Privately Held
SIC: 5211 3442 Garage doors, sale & installation; doors, storm: wood or metal; garage doors, overhead: metal

(G-5288)
HOWMAN ELECTRONICS INC
Also Called: Howman Engineering
291 Us Highway 22 Ste 40 (08833-5072)
PHONE..............................908 534-2247
Fax: 908 534-9357
Salvatore Treppiccione, *President*
David Ward, *Vice Pres*
EMP: 15
SQ FT: 6,000
SALES: 2.5MM Privately Held
SIC: 3625 3643 Industrial controls: push button, selector switches, pilot; current-carrying wiring devices

(G-5289)
IAM INTERNATIONAL INC
4 Saddle Ridge Dr (08833-3249)
PHONE..............................908 713-9651
Neera Tulshian, *President*
Deen Tulshian, *CFO*
EMP: 2
SALES (est): 1.5MM Privately Held
SIC: 8748 2099 Business consulting; food preparations

(G-5290)
INTER CITY PRESS INC
143 Petticoat Ln (08833-4122)
PHONE..............................908 236-9911
Jack Aquila, *President*
EMP: 26 EST: 1905
SALES (est): 1.5MM Privately Held
SIC: 2759 Commercial printing

(G-5291)
INTREPID INDUSTRIES INC
291 Us Highway 22 Ste 3 (08833-5066)
PHONE..............................908 534-5300
A John Haley, *President*
Martha Lynn Haley, *Corp Secy*
EMP: 7
SQ FT: 5,000
SALES (est): 1MM Privately Held
WEB: www.intrepidindustries.com
SIC: 3471 Plating & polishing

(G-5292)
JAEGER THOMAS & MELISSA DDS
1128 State Rd 31 (08833)
PHONE..............................908 735-2722
Fax: 908 735-0640
Thomas Jaeger, *Partner*
Melissa Jaeger, *Partner*
EMP: 14
SALES (est): 861.9K Privately Held
SIC: 8021 1799 3443 Orthodontist; sandblasting of building exteriors; liners/lining

(G-5293)
JOHNTHAN LEASING CORP
Also Called: Don Schreiber Co
17 Water St (08833-4528)
PHONE..............................908 226-3434
Eugene R Kistler, *President*
Nathan Connell, *Manager*
Alene Reed, *Shareholder*
Barry Reed, *Shareholder*
EMP: 30
SQ FT: 40,000
SALES (est): 3.6MM Privately Held
WEB: www.donschreiber.com
SIC: 2782 Looseleaf binders & devices

(G-5294)
JRH SERVICE & SALES LLC
30 Boulder Hill Rd (08833-4526)
PHONE..............................908 832-9266
EMP: 4 EST: 2008
SALES (est): 330K Privately Held
SIC: 3841 Mfg Surgical/Medical Instruments

(G-5295)
LEBANON CHEESE COMPANY INC
3 Railroad Ave (08833-2156)
P.O. Box 63 (08833-0063)
PHONE..............................908 236-2611

Joe Lotito, *President*
EMP: 8
SQ FT: 5,000
SALES: 3MM **Privately Held**
SIC: 2022 Natural cheese

(G-5296)
MDB CONSTRUCTION
236 Cokesbury Rd (08833-4538)
PHONE..................................908 628-8010
Michael Barnard, *Owner*
EMP: 5
SALES (est): 272.5K **Privately Held**
SIC: 5719 1522 1521 2452 Fireplaces &
wood burning stoves; residential construction; single-family home remodeling,
additions & repairs; farm & agricultural
buildings, prefabricated wood; renovation,
remodeling & repairs: industrial buildings;
demolition, buildings & other structures

(G-5297)
MEDALCO METALS INC
5 Chrystal Dr (08833-3243)
PHONE..................................908 238-0513
Richard Feldman, *Marketing Staff*
Ken Booth, *Manager*
EMP: 4
SALES (est): 406.1K
SALES (corp-wide): 4.6MM **Privately
Held**
SIC: 3364 Nonferrous die-castings except
aluminum
PA: Medalco Metals, Inc.
1 Corticelli St
Florence MA 01062
413 586-6010

(G-5298)
MOUNTAIN TOP LOGGING LLC
99 Main St (08833-2132)
P.O. Box 324 (08833-0324)
PHONE..................................908 413-2982
Matthew Good, *Principal*
EMP: 5 **EST:** 2010
SALES (est): 415.6K **Privately Held**
SIC: 2411 Logging

(G-5299)
PLATE CONCEPTS INC
Also Called: PCI
1221 Us Highway 22 Ste 3 (08833-2228)
PHONE..................................908 236-9570
James C Gooch, *President*
John Loiacona, *Principal*
Hank Shamsi, *Vice Pres*
Karl Duerwald, *Sales Staff*
EMP: 5
SQ FT: 5,000
SALES: 3MM **Privately Held**
WEB: www.plateconcepts.com
SIC: 3443 Heat exchangers, condensers &
components

(G-5300)
RACEWELD CO INC
1120 Us Highway 22 (08833-4209)
P.O. Box 378 (08833-0378)
PHONE..................................908 236-6533
EMP: 4
SQ FT: 10,000
SALES: 175K **Privately Held**
SIC: 3499 3599 Mfgs Fabricated Metal
Products & Job Machine Shop

(G-5301)
**REED PRESENTATIONS INC
(PA)**
Also Called: R P I
17 Water St (08833-4528)
PHONE..................................908 832-0007
Barry A Reed, *CEO*
Alene Reed, *Treasurer*
Beth Connell, *VP Sales*
Sandra D'Emilio, *Director*
EMP: 5
SQ FT: 40,000
SALES (est): 3.5MM **Privately Held**
SIC: 2782 Library binders, looseleaf

(G-5302)
**SPECIALTY MEASUREMENTS
INC**
Also Called: SMI Incorprated
1309 Us Highway 22 (08833-2216)
P.O. Box 356 (08833-0356)
PHONE..................................908 534-1500
Fax: 908 534-1546
Mary Ann Kulawiec, *President*
Gary Bubb, *Vice Pres*
Gary E Bubb, *Vice Pres*
Jennifer McGonigle, *Purch Mgr*
Brian Dilley, *Manager*
EMP: 10 **EST:** 1982
SQ FT: 3,000
SALES: 3MM **Privately Held**
SIC: 3559 2833 5084 Pharmaceutical
machinery; medicinals & botanicals; in-
dustrial machinery & equipment

(G-5303)
**WEBER AND SCHER MFG CO
INC**
Also Called: George Scher Engineering
1231 Us Highway 22 (08833-2213)
P.O. Box 366 (08833-0366)
PHONE..................................908 236-8484
Fax: 908 236-7001
J William Scher, *CEO*
Gregory K Scher, *President*
J Douglas Scher, *Vice Pres*
Jim Kling, *Mfg Mgr*
Joan Scher, *Admin Sec*
▲ **EMP:** 24 **EST:** 1915
SALES (est): 5.3MM **Privately Held**
WEB: www.webscher.com
SIC: 3549 Metalworking machinery

(G-5304)
CATHETER PRECISION INC
1705 Us Highway 46 Ste 6 (07852-9720)
PHONE..................................973 691-2000
Steve Adler, *CEO*
David A Jenkins, *Ch of Bd*
Dan Whitehead, *Opers Mgr*
Robert Pacheco, *Engineer*
James Caruso, *CFO*
EMP: 11
SALES (est): 774.2K **Privately Held**
SIC: 3841 Catheters

(G-5305)
IDENTITY DEPOT INC
Also Called: Sign-A-Rama
244 Main St (07852-9615)
PHONE..................................973 584-9301
Fax: 973 584-9332
Micheal Grivalsky, *CEO*
Steven Grivalsky, *Vice Pres*
Carole Grivalsky, *Admin Sec*
EMP: 8
SQ FT: 5,800
SALES (est): 534.5K **Privately Held**
SIC: 3993 Signs & advertising specialties

(G-5306)
JT FUELS LLC
1470 Us Highway 46 (07852-9606)
PHONE..................................973 527-4470
John Farnsworth, *Manager*
EMP: 6
SALES (est): 504K **Privately Held**
SIC: 2869 Fuels

(G-5307)
PHILIPS ELEC N AMER CORP
1 Samsung Pl (07852-9760)
PHONE..................................973 804-2100
Glen McMail, *Exec VP*
EMP: 100
SALES (corp-wide): 20.9B **Privately Held**
WEB: www.usa.philips.com
SIC: 3651 Household audio & video equip-
ment
HQ: Philips North America Llc
3000 Minuteman Rd Ms1203
Andover MA 01810
978 659-3000

(G-5308)
R B B CORP
Also Called: Adam Metal Products Company
7 Orben Dr (07852-9719)
P.O. Box 450 (07852-0450)
PHONE..................................973 770-1100
Fax: 973 770-1105
Raymond Bentley, *President*
▲ **EMP:** 35
SQ FT: 72,000
SALES (est): 7.5MM **Privately Held**
SIC: 3646 3645 Fluorescent lighting fix-
tures, commercial; ceiling systems, lumi-
nous; residential lighting fixtures

(G-5309)
RUDOLPH TECHNOLOGIES INC
1705 Us Highway 46 Ste 3 (07852-9720)
PHONE..................................973 448-4307
Jule Von Sternberg, *Branch Mgr*
EMP: 6
SALES (corp-wide): 255.1MM **Publicly
Held**
WEB: www.rudolphtech.com
SIC: 3674 Semiconductors & related de-
vices; transistors
PA: Rudolph Technologies, Inc.
16 Jonspin Rd
Wilmington MA 01887
973 691-1300

(G-5310)
STEB INC (PA)
Also Called: Castle Printing Center
1501 Us Highway 46 (07852-9718)
PHONE..................................973 584-0990
Kevin Ebner, *President*
James Storms, *Vice Pres*
Wilkin Vargas, *Prdtn Mgr*
EMP: 7
SQ FT: 1,400
SALES (est): 912.3K **Privately Held**
WEB: www.steb.com
SIC: 2752 2791 2789 Commercial print-
ing, offset; typesetting; bookbinding & re-
lated work

(G-5311)
STEB INC
Also Called: Castle Printing
1501 Us Highway 46 (07852-9718)
PHONE..................................973 584-0990
Jim Storms, *Owner*
Carmella Mustachio, *Production*
EMP: 11
SALES (est): 1.4MM
SALES (corp-wide): 912.3K **Privately
Held**
WEB: www.steb.com
SIC: 2752 Commercial printing, offset
PA: Steb Inc.
1501 Us Highway 46
Ledgewood NJ 07852
973 584-0990

(G-5312)
TONYMACX86 LLC
23 Lookout Dr (07852-9730)
PHONE..................................973 584-5273
Michael Wallace, *Co-Owner*
Gabriel Rohmann, *Co-Owner*
EMP: 4
SALES (est): 27.3K **Privately Held**
SIC: 2741 7389 ;

(G-5313)
VANDERMOLEN CORP
106 Hillcrest Ave (07852-9731)
PHONE..................................973 992-8506
Fax: 973 992-4219
Aldo H Vandermolen, *President*
EMP: 4 **EST:** 1954
SQ FT: 9,000
SALES (est): 522.2K **Privately Held**
WEB: www.vandermolencorp.com
SIC: 3699 5083 Fly traps, electrical; lawn
& garden machinery & equipment; agri-
cultural machinery

(G-5314)
ALLEN STEEL CO
202 High St (08327-2020)
P.O. Box 211 (08327-0211)
PHONE..................................856 785-1171
James P Allen III, *President*
Dorothy Allen, *Admin Sec*
EMP: 5 **EST:** 1952
SALES: 400K **Privately Held**
SIC: 3731 3556 Fishing vessels, large:
building & repairing; food products ma-
chinery

(G-5315)
CARRY EASY INC
Also Called: Quality Medical Supplies
131 Fort Lee Rd Fl 2 (07605-2216)
PHONE..................................201 944-0042
EMP: 25
SALES: 950K **Privately Held**
SIC: 4119 5047 3842 Local Passenger
Trans Whol Med/Hospital Equip Mfg Sur-
gical Appliances

(G-5316)
**EBIC PRPAREDNESS
SOLUTIONS LLC**
236 Overlook Ave (07605-1519)
PHONE..................................719 244-6209
EMP: 4
SALES: 500K **Privately Held**
SIC: 7371 7372 Custom Computer Pro-
graming Prepackaged Software Services

(G-5317)
LABRADA INC
41 Palmer Pl (07605-1314)
PHONE..................................201 461-2641
David Labrada, *President*
Orquidea La Brada, *Corp Secy*
Nidia La Brada, *Vice Pres*
EMP: 5 **EST:** 1967
SQ FT: 1,500
SALES (est): 430K **Privately Held**
WEB: www.labrada.com
SIC: 3911 Jewelry, precious metal

(G-5318)
MINMETALS INC (PA)
120 Schor Ave (07605-2208)
PHONE..................................201 809-1898
Shili Jing, *President*
Donald Kimball, *President*
Chu Wenguo, *General Mgr*
David Cheng, *Managing Dir*
Zhou Addressing, *Vice Pres*
◆ **EMP:** 12
SQ FT: 25,000
SALES (est): 10.6MM **Privately Held**
WEB: www.minmetals.com
SIC: 5052 5051 3341 3295 Coal; steel;
secondary nonferrous metals; minerals,
ground or treated

(G-5319)
SOLGAR INC (DH)
Also Called: Solgar Vitamin & Her
500 Willow Tree Rd (07605-2232)
P.O. Box 9010, Ronkonkoma NY (11779-
9010)
PHONE..................................201 944-2311
Fax: 201 861-3651
Floriam Bernodat, *CEO*
William Arthur, *Vice Pres*
Jay Cook, *Vice Pres*
Edgar Deutsch, *Vice Pres*
Steve Cook, *Materials Mgr*
◆ **EMP:** 15
SQ FT: 50,000
SALES (est): 337.8K **Publicly Held**
WEB: www.solgar.com
SIC: 2833 Vitamins, natural or synthetic:
bulk, uncompounded

HQ: The Nature's Bounty Co
2100 Smithtown Ave
Ronkonkoma NY 11779
631 200-2000

(G-5320)
SUEZ TREATMENT SOLUTIONS INC
600 Willow Tree Rd (07605-2211)
PHONE.........................201 676-2525
EMP: 60
SALES (corp-wide): 86.1MM **Privately Held**
SIC: 3559 Ozone machines
HQ: Suez Treatment Solutions Inc.
461 From Rd Ste 400
Paramus NJ 07652
201 767-9300

(G-5321)
TEKKOTE CORPORATION
580 Willow Tree Rd (07605-2211)
PHONE.........................201 585-1708
Lawrence Goldman, *President*
Matthew Cain, *Vice Pres*
Thomas Chanqanqui, *Vice Pres*
Irwin Kowal, *Vice Pres*
Ted Waterhouse, *Buyer*
◆ EMP: 100
SQ FT: 65,000
SALES (est): 38.5MM **Privately Held**
SIC: 2679 Filter paper: made from pur-
chased material
PA: Mondi Plc
Building 1 1st Floor Aviator Park
Addlestone KT15

(G-5322)
TURNING STAR INC
600 Willow Tree Rd (07605-2211)
PHONE.........................201 944-3462
Thomas Andrews, *President*
▼ EMP: 9 EST: 1998
SQ FT: 5,000
SALES (est): 1.8MM **Privately Held**
WEB: www.turningstar.com
SIC: 2899 Fire retardant chemicals

Liberty Corner
Somerset County

(G-5323)
NEW HORIZON PRESS PUBLISHERS
34 Church St (07938)
P.O. Box 669, Far Hills (07931-0669)
PHONE.........................908 604-6311
Fax: 908 604-6330
Joan Dunphy, *President*
T J Dermot Dunphy, *Vice Pres*
EMP: 5
SALES (est): 568.7K **Privately Held**
WEB: www.newhorizonpressbooks.com
SIC: 2731 5942 Books: publishing only;
book stores

(G-5324)
SEAL-SPOUT CORP
50 Allen Rd (07938)
P.O. Box 74 (07938-0074)
PHONE.........................908 647-0648
Fax: 908 647-0648
EMP: 12 EST: 1944
SQ FT: 16,000
SALES (est): 1.1MM **Privately Held**
SIC: 3549 3444 3089 Mfg Metalworking
Machinery Mfg Sheet Metalwork Mfg
Plastic Products

Lincoln Park
Morris County

(G-5325)
ACTION GRAPHICS INC (PA)
600 Ryerson Rd Ste G (07035-2054)
PHONE.........................973 633-6500
Fax: 973 633-0660
Leonard Wynbeek, *President*
David J Corby, *Vice Pres*
Dale Park, *Treasurer*

EMP: 20
SQ FT: 20,000
SALES (est): 4.2MM **Privately Held**
WEB: www.actiongraphicsnj.com
SIC: 2752 Catalogs, lithographed

(G-5326)
D S JH LLC
Also Called: Structural Steel Fabricators
107 Beaverbrook Rd Ste 3 (07035-1448)
PHONE.........................973 782-4086
Santosh Salvi, *Mng Member*
Jorge Hermida,
EMP: 20
SQ FT: 1,000
SALES: 1.2MM **Privately Held**
SIC: 3325 3441 Steel foundries; fabricated
structural metal

(G-5327)
INDOOR ENVIRONMENTAL TECH
Also Called: Tri-Dim Filter
600 Ryerson Rd Ste F (07035-2054)
PHONE.........................973 709-1122
Fax: 973 709-9508
John C Stanley Sr, *President*
EMP: 50
SALES (est): 3.4MM
SALES (corp-wide): 137.3MM **Privately Held**
WEB: www.tridim.com
SIC: 8731 3564 Environmental research;
blowers & fans
PA: Tri-Dim Filter Corporation
93 Industrial Dr
Louisa VA 23093
540 967-2600

(G-5328)
J & S ENTERPRISES LLC
Also Called: Sports Factory
175 Beaverbrook Rd (07035-1411)
PHONE.........................973 696-9199
Jay Yang, *Mng Member*
Mark White, *Manager*
Steve Beneventine,
EMP: 18
SQ FT: 38,000
SALES (est): 1.2MM **Privately Held**
WEB: www.sportsfactory.net
SIC: 3949 Guards: football, basketball,
soccer, lacrosse, etc.

(G-5329)
MEDITERRANEAN CHEF INC
3 Borinski Dr (07035-2060)
PHONE.........................855 628-0903
Rafael Montekio, *Principal*
▲ EMP: 10
SQ FT: 10,000
SALES (est): 618.5K **Privately Held**
SIC: 2099 Food preparations

(G-5330)
NASA MACHINE TOOLS INC
1 Frassetto Way Ste B (07035-2056)
P.O. Box 157, Pompton Plains (07444-0157)
PHONE.........................973 633-5200
Robert De George Sr, *President*
▲ EMP: 25
SQ FT: 16,200
SALES (est): 4.8MM **Privately Held**
WEB: www.nassamachine.com
SIC: 3541 Machine tools, metal cutting
type

(G-5331)
NOVAPAC LABORATORIES INC
510 Ryerson Rd Ste 1 (07035-2016)
PHONE.........................973 414-8800
Fax: 973 414-8888
Jean Marcperez, *President*
Jessie Desrouleaux, *Research*
▲ EMP: 11
SALES (est): 2.2MM **Privately Held**
SIC: 2844 Face creams or lotions

(G-5332)
ROMACO INC
6 Frassetto Way Ste D (07035-2055)
PHONE.........................973 709-0691
▲ EMP: 23

SALES (est): 5.5MM
SALES (corp-wide): 21.4B **Publicly Held**
SIC: 3565 Mfg Packaging Machinery
HQ: Robbins & Myers, Inc.
10586 N Highway 75
Willis TX 77378
936 890-1064

(G-5333)
TEKNICS INDUSTRIES INC
Also Called: Teknics Sales
170 Beaverbrook Rd Ste 1 (07035-1441)
PHONE.........................973 633-7575
Bruce T Robertson, *President*
Dave Robertson, *Vice Pres*
David Robertson, *Vice Pres*
▲ EMP: 56
SQ FT: 20,000
SALES (est): 5.2MM **Privately Held**
SIC: 3545 Machine tool attachments & ac-
cessories

(G-5334)
TRANSMISSION TECHNOLOGY CO
1 High Mountain Trl (07035-1937)
PHONE.........................973 305-3600
Fax: 973 305-1313
Dezi Folenta, *President*
Margaret Folenta, *Vice Pres*
EMP: 6
SQ FT: 1,000
SALES (est): 370K **Privately Held**
SIC: 3714 7389 Motor vehicle transmis-
sions, drive assemblies & parts; design,
commercial & industrial

(G-5335)
TRI-DIM FILTER CORPORATION
600 Ryerson Rd Ste F (07035-2054)
PHONE.........................973 709-1122
John Stanley, *Branch Mgr*
EMP: 10
SALES (corp-wide): 137.3MM **Privately Held**
SIC: 3564 Blowers & fans
PA: Tri-Dim Filter Corporation
93 Industrial Dr
Louisa VA 23093
540 967-2600

Lincroft
Monmouth County

(G-5336)
AVAYA INC
307 Mddletown Lincroft Rd (07738-1526)
PHONE.........................732 852-2030
Tara Molnar, *Manager*
EMP: 250 **Publicly Held**
WEB: www.avaya.com
SIC: 3661 7372 Telephone & telegraph
apparatus; business oriented computer
software
HQ: Avaya Inc.
4655 Great America Pkwy
Santa Clara CA 95054
908 953-6000

(G-5337)
HOUSE OF PRILL INC
716 Newman Springs Rd # 303
(07738-1523)
PHONE.........................732 442-2400
Steven Lazar, *President*
Rachel Lazar, *Treasurer*
EMP: 20 EST: 1905
SQ FT: 11,500
SALES (est): 1.8MM **Privately Held**
WEB: www.houseofprill.com
SIC: 5023 5199 3264 Home furnishings;
gifts & novelties; porcelain electrical sup-
plies

(G-5338)
J & L CONTROLS INC
15 Leland Ter (07738)
P.O. Box 504 (07738-0504)
PHONE.........................732 460-0380
John Stocker, *President*
EMP: 4
SQ FT: 1,200

SALES: 200K **Privately Held**
SIC: 3822 Building services monitoring
controls, automatic

(G-5339)
MEDICAL STRATEGIC PLANNING INC
5 Shelbern Dr (07738-1324)
PHONE.........................732 219-5090
Fax: 732 219-5066
Arthur Gasch, *CEO*
Ken Happel, *CTO*
Richard Dick, *Officer*
Betty Gasch, *Admin Sec*
EMP: 5
SQ FT: 1,000
SALES (est): 670.8K **Privately Held**
WEB: www.medsp.com
SIC: 2721 7371 7373 7376 Periodicals;
custom computer programming services;
computer integrated systems design;
computer facilities management; manage-
ment consulting services

(G-5340)
NJ SERVICE TESTING & INSPTN
26 Oak St (07738-1821)
PHONE.........................732 221-6357
John Gillen, *Principal*
EMP: 4
SALES (est): 768.9K **Privately Held**
SIC: 3569 General industrial machinery

(G-5341)
SAINT LA SALLE AUXILIARY INC
850 Newman Springs Rd (07738-1608)
PHONE.........................732 842-4359
William Martin, *President*
EMP: 4 EST: 1956
SALES (est): 318.1K **Privately Held**
WEB: www.dlsaux.org
SIC: 2771 Greeting cards

Linden
Union County

(G-5342)
A&C CATALYSTS INC
Also Called: AC Catalysts
1600 W Blancke St (07036-6228)
PHONE.........................908 474-9393
Fax: 908 474-9388
David Rawlins, *Opers Staff*
John Wolfe, *Sales Executive*
Abe Goldstein, *Director*
◆ EMP: 23 EST: 1995
SQ FT: 26,000
SALES: 10MM **Privately Held**
WEB: www.ac-catalyst.com
SIC: 2821 Thermosetting materials

(G-5343)
ADVANCE MACHINE INC
531 Pennsylvania Ave (07036-2898)
PHONE.........................908 486-7244
Fax: 908 925-3267
Richard J Walano Sr, *President*
Carl M Walano, *Vice Pres*
Robert Boccadutre, *Treasurer*
Richard J Walano Jr, *Admin Sec*
EMP: 11 EST: 1971
SQ FT: 4,800
SALES (est): 1.5MM **Privately Held**
SIC: 3599 Machine shop, jobbing & repair

(G-5344)
AIR PROTECTION PACKAGING CORP
Also Called: AP Packaging
1200 Fuller Rd Ste 2 (07036-5774)
PHONE.........................973 577-4343
Eli Green, *CEO*
Joel Green, *CEO*
EMP: 17
SALES: 8MM **Privately Held**
SIC: 3081 Packing materials, plastic sheet

(G-5345)
AJAY METAL FABRICATORS INC
355 Dalziel Rd (07036-6229)
PHONE.........................908 523-0557
Fax: 908 523-0560

▲ = Import ▼=Export
◆ =Import/Export

Tony Zambell Jr, *President*
Carolyn Zambell, *Admin Sec*
EMP: 8
SALES (est): 1MM **Privately Held**
SIC: 3441 3444 Fabricated structural metal; sheet metalwork

(G-5346)
ALL RACKS INDUSTRIES INC
101 Roselle St (07036-2636)
PHONE..................212 244-1069
Joseph Desimone, *President*
Charles Desimone, *Vice Pres*
EMP: 5
SQ FT: 7,000
SALES: 500K **Privately Held**
SIC: 2542 Garment racks: except wood

(G-5347)
ALUMA SYSTEMS CON CNSTR LLC
1800 Lower Rd (07036-6512)
PHONE..................908 418-5073
Martin Berger, *General Mgr*
EMP: 9
SALES (corp-wide): 3.6B **Privately Held**
SIC: 3444 1799 Forming machine work, sheet metal; shoring & underpinning work
HQ: Aluma Systems Concrete Construction, Llc
5045 N 12th St Ste 119
Phoenix AZ 85014
602 212-0350

(G-5348)
AMERICAN ENVELOPE
Also Called: American Micro Technologies
612 E Elizabeth Ave (07036-2662)
PHONE..................908 241-9900
Edward Nodelman, *Owner*
▲ **EMP:** 4 **EST:** 1957
SQ FT: 4,200
SALES: 600K **Privately Held**
WEB: www.americanenvelope.com
SIC: 2759 Envelopes: printing

(G-5349)
ANDERSON TOOL & DIE CORP
1430 W Blancke St (07036-6299)
PHONE..................908 862-5550
▲ **EMP:** 30 **EST:** 1947
SQ FT: 28,000
SALES (est): 410.8K **Privately Held**
SIC: 3841 Mfg Surgical/Medical Instruments

(G-5350)
ARTALE GRAPHICS
2614 Summit Ter (07036-4934)
PHONE..................212 868-0015
Michael Artale, *Owner*
Gerard Artale, *Co-Owner*
EMP: 13 **EST:** 1960
SQ FT: 2,000
SALES (est): 1.4MM **Privately Held**
WEB: www.artalegraphics.com
SIC: 2752 Photolithographic printing

(G-5351)
BAR FIELDS INC
Also Called: AB Aerospace
1400 W Elizabeth Ave (07036-6321)
PHONE..................347 587-7795
Rose Ranna, *Ch of Bd*
EMP: 10 **EST:** 2011
SALES (est): 478.2K **Privately Held**
SIC: 3728 Aircraft parts & equipment

(G-5352)
BATHWARE HOUSE LTD LBLTY CO
524 W Edgar Rd (07036-6502)
PHONE..................732 546-3220
Mario Talavera,
EMP: 4
SALES: 800K **Privately Held**
SIC: 2499 Kitchen, bathroom & household ware: wood

(G-5353)
BP CORPORATION NORTH AMER INC
Also Called: Air BP
Park And Brunswick Ave (07036)
PHONE..................908 474-5000

Dan Murphy, *Manager*
EMP: 20
SALES (corp-wide): 240.2B **Privately Held**
WEB: www.bpamoco.com
SIC: 2911 2899 Petroleum refining; chemical preparations
HQ: Bp Corporation North America Inc.
501 Westlake Park Blvd
Houston TX 77079
281 366-2000

(G-5354)
BRODIE SYSTEM INC
1539 W Elizabeth Ave (07036-6322)
PHONE..................908 862-8620
Thomas W Nielsen, *President*
Nicholas Lloyd, *Manager*
Jane Nielsen, *Administration*
▲ **EMP:** 16 **EST:** 1929
SQ FT: 22,000
SALES (est): 2.8MM **Privately Held**
WEB: www.brodiesystem.com
SIC: 3599 3479 Machine shop, jobbing & repair; painting, coating & hot dipping

(G-5355)
CAPITAL FOODS INC
1701 E Elizabeth Ave (07036-1726)
PHONE..................908 587-9050
Fax: 908 587-9052
Joseph Falcone, *President*
EMP: 24 **EST:** 1992
SQ FT: 11,000
SALES (est): 3.9MM **Privately Held**
WEB: www.capitalfoods.com
SIC: 2022 Cheese, natural & processed

(G-5356)
CDI GROUP INC
1135 W Elizabeth Ave (07036-6314)
PHONE..................908 862-1493
Jordan Ruddy, *CEO*
Norman L Constant, *Ch of Bd*
Bart Shulman, *President*
Richard Constant, *Vice Pres*
EMP: 18
SQ FT: 40,000
SALES (est): 4.3MM **Privately Held**
WEB: www.cdigroupinc.com
SIC: 5046 3993 Display equipment, except refrigerated; displays & cutouts, window & lobby

(G-5357)
CELLULAR EMPIRE INC
Also Called: Pom Gear
1400 W Elizabeth Ave (07036-6321)
PHONE..................800 778-3513
Doris Mosseri, *President*
Steve Jacobs, *President*
EMP: 56
SQ FT: 8,500
SALES: 2MM **Privately Held**
SIC: 3629 Electronic generation equipment

(G-5358)
CENTRAL POLY-BAG CORP
2400 Bedle Pl (07036-1313)
PHONE..................908 862-7570
Fax: 908 862-9019
Andrew Hoffer, *President*
Agnes Serhofer, *Treasurer*
EMP: 14
SQ FT: 35,000
SALES: 9.9MM **Privately Held**
WEB: www.centralpoly.com
SIC: 2673 5113 Plastic bags: made from purchased materials; bags, paper & disposable plastic

(G-5359)
CHEMIQUIP PRODUCTS CO INC
109 Bradford Ave (07036-6339)
PHONE..................201 868-4445
Jack Diamond, *President*
Kim C KY, *Admin Sec*
EMP: 9
SQ FT: 6,000
SALES (est): 1.7MM **Privately Held**
SIC: 3824 3491 Gauges for computing pressure temperature corrections; pressure valves & regulators, industrial

(G-5360)
COLORFLO INC
Also Called: Color Company
1261 W Elizabeth Ave (07036-6316)
P.O. Box 1398 (07036-0004)
PHONE..................908 862-3010
Phillip Kasper, *President*
Jose M Garcia, *Vice Pres*
Diane Galgoci, *Office Mgr*
Kenneth Frenchu, *Shareholder*
Robert Frenchu, *Shareholder*
EMP: 5
SQ FT: 7,000
SALES (est): 901.1K **Privately Held**
WEB: www.colorco-flo.com
SIC: 2851 Paints & allied products

(G-5361)
CORP AMERICAN MICA
1015 Pennsylvania Ave (07036-2240)
PHONE..................908 587-5237
Fax: 908 382-0013
Ray Bailey, *Owner*
EMP: 6
SALES (est): 591.5K **Privately Held**
SIC: 3295 Mica, ground or otherwise treated

(G-5362)
COUNTY GRAPHICS FORMS MGT LLC
2 Stercho Rd (07036-6222)
PHONE..................908 474-9797
Fax: 908 474-5232
Vincent Martino, *Production*
Gina Scarola, *Finance Mgr*
Robert Scarola, *VP Sales*
Fabienne Francois, *Sales Dir*
Robert Gaudiosi,
EMP: 30 **EST:** 1976
SALES (est): 5.5MM **Privately Held**
WEB: www.countygraphics.com
SIC: 2752 Commercial printing, offset

(G-5363)
COX STATIONERS AND PRINTERS
1634 E Elizabeth Ave (07036-1725)
PHONE..................908 928-1010
Michael Kaufman, *CEO*
EMP: 30
SALES (est): 2.5MM **Privately Held**
SIC: 7389 2396 Printers' services: folding, collating; automotive & apparel trimmings

(G-5364)
CUBALAS EMERGENCY LIGHTING LLC
811 Roselle St (07036-2520)
PHONE..................908 943-1615
Robert Cubala, *Principal*
EMP: 5 **EST:** 2007
SALES (est): 719.9K **Privately Held**
SIC: 3648 Lighting equipment

(G-5365)
CUSTOM FABRICATORS INC
400 Commerce Rd (07036-2429)
PHONE..................908 862-4244
Fax: 908 862-4245
Joseph Bonanno, *President*
Chiffon Bonanno, *Corp Secy*
EMP: 7 **EST:** 1966
SQ FT: 12,000
SALES (est): 570K **Privately Held**
WEB: www.metalfab.net
SIC: 3444 Sheet metal specialties, not stamped

(G-5366)
CUTTING EDGE CASTING INC
Also Called: Cutting Edge Industries
1233 W Saint Georges Ave (07036-6117)
PHONE..................908 925-7500
Fax: 908 925-9240
Steve Filler, *President*
Tom Hazel, *Vice Pres*
Jessica Ramirez, *Project Mgr*
▲ **EMP:** 40
SQ FT: 40,000
SALES (est): 4MM **Privately Held**
WEB: www.cuttingedgecatalog.com
SIC: 3599 3645 Machine shop, jobbing & repair; residential lighting fixtures

(G-5367)
DANGELO METAL PRODUCTS INC
360 Dalziel Rd (07036-6291)
PHONE..................908 862-8220
Fax: 908 862-0826
John D'Angelo Jr, *President*
Rosemary Scamardella, *Treasurer*
Pauline Gajek, *Admin Sec*
EMP: 12
SQ FT: 14,000
SALES (est): 870K **Privately Held**
SIC: 3471 3432 3494 3312 Plating of metals or formed products; polishing, metals or formed products; plumbing fixture fittings & trim; valves & pipe fittings; blast furnaces & steel mills

(G-5368)
DAVID LEIZ CUSTOM WOODWORK
Also Called: Leiz Custom Woodworking
2301 E Edgar Rd Bldg 5a (07036-1200)
PHONE..................908 486-1533
David Leiz, *President*
EMP: 4 **EST:** 1975
SQ FT: 6,000
SALES: 500K **Privately Held**
SIC: 2434 Wood kitchen cabinets

(G-5369)
DIM INC
Also Called: Le BEC Fin Fine Foods
10 Grant St (07036-1735)
PHONE..................908 925-2043
Daniel Monneaux, *President*
Irene Khlevner, *Vice Pres*
EMP: 10 **EST:** 1999
SALES (est): 1.2MM **Privately Held**
SIC: 2043 Cereal breakfast foods

(G-5370)
EASTSIDE EXPRESS CORPORATION
2025 E Linden Ave (07036-1147)
PHONE..................908 486-3300
Michael Mac Farlane, *Owner*
EMP: 9
SALES (est): 785.6K **Privately Held**
SIC: 2741 Miscellaneous publishing

(G-5371)
EXCEL DIE SHARPENING CORP
19 Grant St (07036-1734)
PHONE..................908 587-2606
Hanna Krysa, *President*
Jerry Krysa, *Manager*
EMP: 6
SQ FT: 3,400
SALES: 360K **Privately Held**
SIC: 7699 3444 Knife, saw & tool sharpening & repair; sheet metalwork

(G-5372)
EXPRESS PRINTING INC
Also Called: Noble Metals
209 W Saint Georges Ave (07036-3948)
PHONE..................908 925-6300
Fax: 908 925-6302
Arvind Patel, *President*
EMP: 4
SQ FT: 1,500
SALES (est): 526.8K **Privately Held**
SIC: 2752 Commercial printing, offset

(G-5373)
EXXON MOBIL CORPORATION
Also Called: Chemical Products Division
1900 E Linden Ave Ste A (07036-1133)
PHONE..................732 321-6100
Fax: 732 321-3303
Tim Spenner, *Branch Mgr*
John R Boyea, *Director*
EMP: 70
SQ FT: 32,000
SALES (corp-wide): 244.3B **Publicly Held**
SIC: 2821 Plastics materials & resins
PA: Exxon Mobil Corporation
5959 Las Colinas Blvd
Irving TX 75039
972 444-1000

(G-5374)
FAUST THERMOGRAPHIC
SUPPLY
325 Cantor Ave (07036-6230)
PHONE......................................908 474-0555
Fax: 908 474-8042
Craig Schwartzer, *President*
Helen Corrigan, *Manager*
Mark Serafinas, *Manager*
▲ EMP: 14
SALES (est): 3.4MM **Privately Held**
WEB: www.faustusa.com
SIC: 2899 Ink or writing fluids

(G-5375)
FILIPE CUSTOM WOODWORK
Also Called: Kitchen & Bath Design Center
1600 E Edgar Rd (07036-1512)
PHONE......................................908 486-0033
Filipe Augustino, *President*
Filipe Agostinha, *President*
EMP: 30
SQ FT: 15,000
SALES (est): 3.1MM **Privately Held**
WEB: www.filipecw.com
SIC: 2431 Millwork

(G-5376)
FIVE STAR SUPPLIES NJ CORP
1301 W Elizabeth Ave A (07036-6389)
PHONE......................................908 862-8801
Maohua Dong, *President*
▲ EMP: 20
SALES (est): 3.5MM **Privately Held**
SIC: 2834 Pharmaceutical preparations

(G-5377)
G & S DESIGN &
MANUFACTURING
Also Called: Galvanotech
330 Dalziel Rd (07036-6232)
PHONE......................................908 862-2444
Gennady Volkov, *President*
Sofya Volkov, *Vice Pres*
EMP: 15
SQ FT: 12,000
SALES (est): 2.7MM **Privately Held**
WEB: www.galvanotech.com
SIC: 3559 Electroplating machinery &
equipment

(G-5378)
G-TECH ELEVATOR
ASSOCIATES LLC
12 Sherman St (07036-1954)
PHONE......................................866 658-9296
Kendra Glenn, *Project Mgr*
Brock Glenn, *Opers Mgr*
EMP: 13
SQ FT: 5,000
SALES: 16.1MM **Privately Held**
SIC: 1796 3534 3446 Elevator installation
& conversion; elevators & moving stair-
ways; elevators & equipment; elevator
guide rails

(G-5379)
GENERAL MAGNAPLATE
CALIFORNIA
1331 W Edgar Rd (07036-6496)
PHONE......................................805 642-6262
Candida C Aversenti, *CEO*
Charles P Covino, *Chairman*
Billy Bowne, *Manager*
EMP: 14
SQ FT: 35,000
SALES (est): 1.7MM
SALES (corp-wide): 25.1MM **Privately**
Held
WEB: www.magnaplate.com
SIC: 3479 3471 Coating of metals &
formed products; plating of metals or
formed products; electroplating of metals
or formed products
PA: General Magnaplate Corporation
1331 W Edgar Rd
Linden NJ 07036
908 862-6200

(G-5380)
GENERAL MAGNAPLATE
CORPORATION (PA)
1331 W Edgar Rd (07036-6496)
PHONE......................................908 862-6200

Fax: 908 862-0497
Candida C Aversenti, *Ch of Bd*
Edmund V Aversenti Jr, *President*
Larry Campbell, *Vice Pres*
EMP: 58
SQ FT: 90,000
SALES (est): 25.1MM **Privately Held**
SIC: 3479 3471 Coating of metals &
formed products; electroplating of metals
or formed products

(G-5381)
GENERAL MAGNAPLATE
WISCONSIN
1331 W Edgar Rd (07036-6496)
PHONE......................................800 441-6173
Candida C Aversenti, *CEO*
Edmund V Aversenti, *COO*
EMP: 15 EST: 1973
SQ FT: 30,000
SALES (est): 1.3MM
SALES (corp-wide): 25.1MM **Privately**
Held
WEB: www.magnaplate.com
SIC: 3479 Coating of metals & formed
products; coating, rust preventive
PA: General Magnaplate Corporation
1331 W Edgar Rd
Linden NJ 07036
908 862-6200

(G-5382)
HANSOME ENERGY SYSTEMS
INC (PA)
365 Dalziel Rd (07036-6292)
PHONE......................................908 862-9044
Fax: 908 862-8195
Albert Reposi, *Ch of Bd*
Selma Rossen, *President*
Neil Bonner, *Vice Pres*
Thomas Costello, *Vice Pres*
George Shuhan, *Engineer*
▲ EMP: 40 EST: 1969
SQ FT: 30,000
SALES (est): 6.8MM **Privately Held**
SIC: 7629 8711 3625 3621 Electrical re-
pair shops; consulting engineer; noise
control equipment; motors & generators

(G-5383)
HEINZ GLAS USA INC
360 Hurst St (07036-6221)
PHONE......................................908 474-0300
Emanuele Mazzei, *CEO*
Carl August Heinz, *Ch of Bd*
▲ EMP: 13 EST: 1978
SQ FT: 55,000
SALES (est): 2.1MM
SALES (corp-wide): 317MM **Privately**
Held
SIC: 3221 3544 Cosmetic jars, glass; bot-
tles for packing, bottling & canning: glass;
industrial molds
PA: Heinz-Glas Gmbh & Co. Kgaa
Glashuttenplatz 1-7
Tettau 96355
926 977-0

(G-5384)
IFC PRODUCTS INC
568 E Elizabeth Ave (07036-2816)
P.O. Box 2175 (07036-0011)
PHONE......................................908 587-1221
Joseph Christiano, *President*
Maria Christiano, *Vice Pres*
EMP: 10
SQ FT: 6,000
SALES (est): 1.2MM **Privately Held**
SIC: 2087 Extracts, flavoring

(G-5385)
IFC SOLUTIONS INC
1601 E Linden Ave (07036-1508)
PHONE......................................908 862-8810
Fax: 908 862-8825
David J Dukes, *President*
Judith Grossman, *Business Dir*
▼ EMP: 25
SQ FT: 28,000
SALES (est): 6.7MM **Privately Held**
SIC: 2087 Food colorings

(G-5386)
INDUSTRIAL MACHINE &
ENGRG CO
Also Called: Industrial Machine & Engrg Co
1807 W Elizabeth Ave (07036-6391)
PHONE......................................908 862-8874
Valeria Peti, *President*
Steven R Peti, *Treasurer*
Sheree Peti, *Shareholder*
EMP: 10
SQ FT: 25,000
SALES (est): 2.5MM **Privately Held**
SIC: 3451 Screw machine products

(G-5387)
INFINEUM USA LP (DH)
1900 E Linden Ave (07036-1133)
PHONE......................................908 474-0100
Fax: 908 474-3241
Mark Struglinski, *President*
Fernando Martin, *Business Mgr*
Carl Howard, *Counsel*
Jacob Levine, *Counsel*
Bryan Boyle, *Opers Mgr*
◆ EMP: 600
SQ FT: 300,000
SALES (est): 228.8MM
SALES (corp-wide): 1.3B **Privately Held**
WEB: www.infineum.com
SIC: 2899 Chemical preparations
HQ: Infineum International Limited
Milton Hill Business And Technology
Centre
Abingdon OXON OX13
123 554-9500

(G-5388)
INSULATION MATERIALS
DISTRS
Also Called: Insulation Material Distrs
501 S Park Ave (07036-1192)
P.O. Box 2134 (07036-0010)
PHONE......................................908 925-2323
Harold Faske, *President*
EMP: 8
SALES (est): 750K **Privately Held**
SIC: 3296 Fiberglass insulation

(G-5389)
INTERLINK PRODUCTS INTL INC
1315 E Elizabeth Ave (07036-1951)
PHONE......................................908 862-8090
Eli Zhadanov, *President*
▲ EMP: 21
SQ FT: 5,000
SALES: 10MM **Privately Held**
SIC: 3431 Shower stalls, metal

(G-5390)
INTERMARK INC
601 E Linden Ave (07036-2413)
PHONE......................................908 474-1311
Fax: 908 474-1367
EMP: 6
SQ FT: 6,000
SALES: 1MM **Privately Held**
SIC: 3499 Metal Working Machinery Cnc

(G-5391)
INTERNATIONAL DESIGN & MFG
LLC
1217 Pennsylvania Ave (07036-2050)
PHONE......................................908 587-2884
Heidi Bravo, *Mng Member*
EMP: 5
SALES (est): 785K **Privately Held**
SIC: 3446 Architectural metalwork

(G-5392)
JOBE INDUSTRIES INC
1600 W Elizabeth Ave (07036-6325)
P.O. Box 1367 (07036-0004)
PHONE......................................908 862-0400
Sheila W Reicher, *President*
EMP: 8
SALES (est): 1.3MM **Privately Held**
WEB: www.jobe-industries.com
SIC: 2842 Specialty cleaning preparations

(G-5393)
JUST IN TIME CHEMICAL SALES
&
Also Called: Chemicals Services
1711 W Elizabeth Ave (07036-6326)
PHONE......................................908 862-7726

Fax: 908 523-1999
Stan Jakubowycz, *President*
Halyna Jakubowycz, *Vice Pres*
▲ EMP: 9
SALES (est): 6MM **Privately Held**
SIC: 5169 2869 Chemicals, industrial &
heavy; plasticizers, organic: cyclic &
acyclic

(G-5394)
JVM SALES CORP
3401a Tremley Point Rd (07036-3533)
PHONE......................................908 862-4866
Fax: 908 862-4867
Mary Beth Tomasino, *President*
Robert Boyle, *President*
Anthony Caliendo, *Vice Pres*
Linda Braunsberg, *Manager*
EMP: 100 EST: 1983
SQ FT: 30,000
SALES (est): 29.1MM **Privately Held**
WEB: www.jvmsales.com
SIC: 2022 Natural cheese

(G-5395)
K & S INDUSTRIES INC
333 Dalziel Rd (07036-6229)
PHONE......................................908 862-3030
Peter Sklenar, *President*
Peter Korcasko, *Vice Pres*
▲ EMP: 14
SQ FT: 6,500
SALES: 2.1MM **Privately Held**
SIC: 3549 3565 Coil winding machines for
springs; packaging machinery

(G-5396)
KASHMIR CROWN BAKING LLC
(PA)
710 W Linden Ave (07036-6527)
PHONE......................................908 474-1470
Fax: 908 474-1159
Sajjad Ahmed, *Owner*
▲ EMP: 21
SALES (est): 9.1MM **Privately Held**
SIC: 2051 Bread, cake & related products

(G-5397)
KERNEY SERVICE GROUP INC
(PA)
Also Called: Kerney Ship Repair
1700 E Elizabeth Ave (07036-1727)
P.O. Box 1830, Tampa FL (33601-1830)
PHONE......................................908 486-2644
Fax: 908 486-6354
Frank Kerney Sr, *President*
Frank Karney Jr, *Vice Pres*
EMP: 25
SQ FT: 12,000
SALES (est): 6.5MM **Privately Held**
WEB: www.kerneyservice.com
SIC: 3731 Shipbuilding & repairing

(G-5398)
KT WELDING
328 Spruce St (07036-5066)
PHONE......................................908 862-7370
EMP: 4 EST: 1986
SALES (est): 170K **Privately Held**
SIC: 7692 Welding Repair

(G-5399)
LAEGER METAL SPINNING CO
INC
1514 E Elizabeth Ave (07036-1919)
PHONE......................................908 925-5530
Frederick W Laeger, *President*
Chris Sparrer, *General Mgr*
Mary Ann Laeger, *Vice Pres*
EMP: 7 EST: 1942
SQ FT: 6,000
SALES (est): 1MM **Privately Held**
SIC: 3469 Spinning metal for the trade

(G-5400)
LAMINATED INDUSTRIES INC
2000 Brunswick Ave (07036-2400)
PHONE......................................908 862-5995
Chaim Schvimmer, *President*
Sam Schwimmer, *Vice Pres*
▲ EMP: 28
SQ FT: 100,000
SALES (est): 6.3MM **Privately Held**
SIC: 2679 2611 Paper products, con-
verted; pulp mills

▲ = Import ▼=Export
◆ =Import/Export

(G-5401)
LAMINATED PAPERBOARD CORP
2000 Brunswick Ave (07036-2400)
PHONE..................908 862-5995
Fax: 908 862-5891
Mendel Schwimmer, *President*
Sam Schwimmer, *Vice Pres*
EMP: 7
SALES (est): 790K **Privately Held**
WEB: www.laminated-industries.com
SIC: 2679 Cardboard products, except die-cut

(G-5402)
LENTINE SHEET METAL INC
Also Called: A Andersen Shtmtl Fabrication
1210 E Elizabeth Ave (07036-2049)
PHONE..................908 486-8974
Fax: 908 486-8751
John Lentine, *President*
EMP: 12 EST: 1927
SQ FT: 16,000
SALES (est): 2.1MM **Privately Held**
WEB: www.aandersensheetmetal.com
SIC: 3444 5051 Sheet metal specialties, not stamped; metals service centers & offices

(G-5403)
LINDEN WELL DRILLING
2020 Clinton St (07036-3452)
P.O. Box 1247 (07036-0003)
PHONE..................908 862-6633
Richard Lutz, *Principal*
Henry Lutz, *Vice Pres*
EMP: 25
SALES (est): 1.6MM **Privately Held**
SIC: 3443 8748 Liners/lining; environmental consultant

(G-5404)
LONGO ELCTRICAL-MECHANICAL INC
1625 Pennsylvania Ave (07036-1761)
P.O. Box 1397 (07036-0004)
PHONE..................973 537-0400
Fax: 908 925-9427
Bill Valente, *Manager*
EMP: 30
SALES (corp-wide): 21MM **Privately Held**
WEB: www.longo-ind.com
SIC: 7629 7699 5999 7694 Electrical equipment repair, high voltage; pumps & pumping equipment repair; motors, electric; electric motor repair
PA: Longo Electrical-Mechanical, Inc.
1 Harry Shupe Blvd
Wharton NJ 07885
973 537-0400

(G-5405)
MAGNALUBE INC
1331 W Edgar Rd (07036-6402)
P.O. Box 1250 (07036-0003)
PHONE..................718 729-1000
Kerby Saunders, *President*
Luke Saunders, *COO*
EMP: 8
SALES (est): 1.3MM **Privately Held**
WEB: www.magnalube.com
SIC: 2911 Greases, lubricating

(G-5406)
MATCHLESS UNITED COMPANIES (HQ)
801 E Linden Ave Ste 1 (07036-2487)
PHONE..................908 862-7300
Fax: 908 862-7305
Frank Ungari, *CEO*
Gary Slonski, *CFO*
EMP: 8
SQ FT: 30,000
SALES (est): 1.2MM
SALES (corp-wide): 14.5MM **Privately Held**
SIC: 2842 5085 Specialty cleaning, polishes & sanitation goods; industrial supplies
PA: The Matchless Metal Polish Company
840 W 49th Pl
Chicago IL 60609
773 924-1515

(G-5407)
METAL HOSE FABRICATORS INC
1122 Fedirko Ct (07036-6137)
PHONE..................908 925-7345
Fax: 973 473-6056
Charles Hartmann, *President*
Emanuele Dirubba, *Vice Pres*
EMP: 6
SQ FT: 6,000
SALES: 1.1MM **Privately Held**
SIC: 3599 Hose, flexible metallic

(G-5408)
METALS PLUS
200 Marion Ave (07036-6337)
PHONE..................908 862-7677
Farid Mensi, *Owner*
Daniel Mensi, *Project Mgr*
EMP: 24
SALES (est): 2.2MM **Privately Held**
SIC: 3441 Fabricated structural metal

(G-5409)
MICROCAST TECHNOLOGIES CORP (PA)
1611 W Elizabeth Ave (07036-6342)
PHONE..................908 523-9503
Fax: 908 523-0910
Dean Fushcetti, *President*
Leonard Cordaro, *President*
Richard Fuschetti Jr, *Vice Pres*
Dean Fuschetti, *VP Opers*
Kasia Kozlowski, *VP Opers*
▲ EMP: 60
SQ FT: 20,000
SALES (est): 29.4MM **Privately Held**
WEB: www.mtcnj.com
SIC: 3364 8711 3089 5051 Zinc & zinc-base alloy die-castings; engineering services; injection molding of plastics; stampings, metal; silk screen design; zinc & zinc-base alloy castings, except die-castings

(G-5410)
MIRE ENTERPRISES LLC
Also Called: Reggie's Roast Coffees
1501 W Blancke St Ste 3 (07036-6238)
PHONE..................732 882-1010
Fax: 908 862-3711
▲ EMP: 4
SALES: 350K **Privately Held**
SIC: 2095 Mfg Roasted Coffee

(G-5411)
MM PACKAGING GROUP LLC
2401 E Linden Ave (07036-1121)
PHONE..................908 759-0101
Moshe Sofer, *Principal*
▲ EMP: 6
SQ FT: 17,000
SALES: 500K **Privately Held**
SIC: 5199 2043 Packaging materials; cereal breakfast foods

(G-5412)
MODERNLINEFURNITURE INC
531 N Stiles St (07036-5771)
PHONE..................908 486-0200
Vladimir Spivak, *President*
Robert Deli, *Vice Pres*
Bertila Rodriguez, *Sales Staff*
EMP: 25
SQ FT: 70,000
SALES: 9MM **Privately Held**
SIC: 5712 2599 Office furniture; cabinets, factory

(G-5413)
MOLDWORKS WORLDWIDE LLC
985 E Linden Ave (07036-2416)
PHONE..................908 474-8082
Fax: 908 474-1113
Howard Hyams, *President*
Terry Hyams, *Chairman*
▲ EMP: 7
SQ FT: 6,500
SALES (est): 877.8K **Privately Held**
SIC: 2329 Men's & boys' sportswear & athletic clothing

(G-5414)
NAPCO SEPARATION EQUIPMENT INC
200 Marion Ave (07036-6337)
PHONE..................908 862-7677
Farid E Mensi, *President*
EMP: 4
SQ FT: 10,000
SALES: 1.2MM **Privately Held**
SIC: 3441 Fabricated structural metal

(G-5415)
NATIONAL STEEL RULE COMPANY (PA)
750 Commerce Rd (07036-2496)
PHONE..................908 862-3366
Fax: 908 862-5339
Edmund Mucci Jr, *President*
Eddie Mucci, *General Mgr*
Gregory Zimmer, *Senior VP*
Joseph E Bialoglow, *Vice Pres*
Bethann Bialoglow-Masiello, *Vice Pres*
▲ EMP: 90
SALES (est): 38.3MM **Privately Held**
SIC: 3423 3546 3425 Rules or rulers, metal; power-driven handtools; saw blades & handsaws

(G-5416)
NATIONAL STEEL RULE COMPANY
620 Commerce Rd (07036-2425)
PHONE..................800 922-0885
Jim Lheureux, *Principal*
EMP: 10
SALES (corp-wide): 38.3MM **Privately Held**
SIC: 3423 Rules or rulers, metal
PA: National Steel Rule Company
750 Commerce Rd
Linden NJ 07036
908 862-3366

(G-5417)
NATIONAL STEEL RULE COMPANY
712 Commerce Rd (07036-2423)
PHONE..................908 862-3366
Ed Mucci, *President*
EMP: 100
SALES (corp-wide): 38.3MM **Privately Held**
SIC: 3423 Hand & edge tools
PA: National Steel Rule Company
750 Commerce Rd
Linden NJ 07036
908 862-3366

(G-5418)
NEMA ASSOCIATES INC
408 E Elizabeth Ave (07036-3041)
PHONE..................973 274-0052
Juan Lopez, *President*
Claudia Lopez, *Treasurer*
EMP: 14
SALES (est): 2.3MM **Privately Held**
WEB: www.nemadesign.com
SIC: 7311 7336 2752 Advertising agencies; advertising consultant; commercial art & graphic design; creative services to advertisers, except writers; graphic arts & related design; package design; commercial printing, lithographic

(G-5419)
NEW YORK POULTRY CO
3351 Tremley Point Rd # 2 (07036-3575)
PHONE..................908 523-1600
Abdul Nasaoy, *President*
EMP: 15
SALES (est): 948.8K **Privately Held**
SIC: 2048 Poultry feeds

(G-5420)
NOBLE METALS CORP
Also Called: Ex-Press Printing
209 W Saint Georges Ave (07036-3948)
PHONE..................908 925-6300
Arvind Patel, *President*
EMP: 4
SQ FT: 1,000
SALES (est): 279.3K **Privately Held**
SIC: 2752 Commercial printing, offset

(G-5421)
NVS INTERNATIONAL INC
1600 Lower Rd (07036-6516)
PHONE..................908 523-0266
Natalie Soltys, *President*
◆ EMP: 25
SALES (est): 3.9MM **Privately Held**
SIC: 3731 Shipbuilding & repairing

(G-5422)
OIL TECHNOLOGIES SERVICES INC
Also Called: Seahawk Services
1177 W Elizabeth Ave (07036)
PHONE..................856 845-4142
Wajdi Abdmessih, *President*
EMP: 6
SALES (corp-wide): 1MM **Privately Held**
SIC: 1389 5551 Testing, measuring, surveying & analysis services; oil consultants; marine supplies & equipment
PA: Oil Technologies Services Inc.
1501 Grandview Ave Ste 1
Paulsboro NJ 08066
856 845-4142

(G-5423)
PANOS BRANDS LLC
Also Called: Walden Farms
1209 W Saint Georges Ave (07036-6117)
PHONE..................800 229-1706
Santo Gonzalez, *Plant Mgr*
EMP: 22
SALES (corp-wide): 669.8K **Privately Held**
SIC: 2035 2023 Dressings, salad: raw & cooked (except dry mixes); powdered cream
HQ: Panos Brands, Llc
395 W Passaic St Ste 240
Rochelle Park NJ 07662

(G-5424)
PARAMOUNT METAL FINISHING CO
Also Called: Paramount Plating
1515 W Elizabeth Ave (07036-6322)
PHONE..................908 862-0772
Fax: 908 862-9477
Vincent Fuschetti, *President*
Michael Fuschetti, *President*
Richard Fuschetti, *Corp Secy*
Richard Fuschetti Jr, *Vice Pres*
Mark Andres, *Prdtn Mgr*
EMP: 120 EST: 1949
SQ FT: 54,000
SALES (est): 18.8MM **Privately Held**
WEB: www.pmf1.com
SIC: 3479 3471 1796 Coating of metals & formed products; finishing, metals or formed products; machinery installation

(G-5425)
PARAMOUNT PLATING CO INC
1515 W Elizabeth Ave (07036-6322)
PHONE..................908 862-0772
Vincent Fuschetti, *President*
Richard A Fuschetti, *Corp Secy*
▲ EMP: 45
SQ FT: 54,000
SALES: 8.8MM **Privately Held**
SIC: 3471 Electroplating of metals or formed products; anodizing (plating) of metals or formed products

(G-5426)
PATWIN PLASTICS INC
2300 E Linden Ave (07036-1194)
PHONE..................908 486-6600
Fax: 908 486-6605
Thomas Hannon Sr, *President*
Eva Hannon, *Corp Secy*
Thomas Hannon Jr, *Vice Pres*
Timothy Hannon, *Vice Pres*
Mike Staryak, *Sales Mgr*
▲ EMP: 45
SQ FT: 42,000
SALES (est): 11.5MM **Privately Held**
WEB: www.patwin.com
SIC: 3089 Extruded finished plastic products; plastic processing

GEOGRAPHIC

(G-5427)
PEN COMPANY OF AMERICA LLC (HQ)
1401 S Park Ave (07036-1609)
PHONE................................908 374-7949
Adam Bell, *President*
Mark Littwin, *Vice Pres*
Jim Blumenfeld, *VP Opers*
Greg Shea, *Opers Mgr*
EMP: 45
SQ FT: 20,000
SALES: 13.3MM
SALES (corp-wide): 166.2MM **Privately Held**
SIC: 3951 Pens & mechanical pencils
PA: Plaskolite, Llc
400 W Nationwide Blvd # 400
Columbus OH 43215
614 294-3281

(G-5428)
PI METAL PRODUCTS INC
1717 Pennsylvania Ave (07036-1762)
PHONE................................201 955-0800
Jincheng Wu, *President*
EMP: 6
SALES (est): 275.2K **Privately Held**
SIC: 3444 Sheet metalwork

(G-5429)
PIC CORPORATION
1101 W Elizabeth Ave (07036-6314)
P.O. Box 1458 (07036-0005)
PHONE................................908 862-7977
Fax: 908 862-5386
Allen Rubel, *President*
David Lowe, *Vice Pres*
David Hennessey, *Project Mgr*
James Mitchell, *Director*
Phyllis Rubel, *Director*
▲ **EMP:** 30
SQ FT: 45,000
SALES (est): 9.6MM **Privately Held**
WEB: www.pic-corp.com
SIC: 2879 5191 Insecticides, agricultural or household; insecticides

(G-5430)
PRAXAIR DISTRIBUTION INC
515 E Edgar Rd (07036-2403)
PHONE................................908 862-7200
Michael Solomon, *Principal*
EMP: 18
SALES (corp-wide): 11.4B **Publicly Held**
SIC: 2813 5169 5084 Industrial gases; industrial gases; welding machinery & equipment
HQ: Praxair Distribution, Inc.
10 Riverview Dr
Danbury CT 06810
203 837-2000

(G-5431)
PRO PLASTICS INC
1190 Sylvan St (07036-6417)
P.O. Box 1489 (07036-0005)
PHONE................................908 925-5555
George C Sievewright, *President*
Dennis Krokosc, *Vice Pres*
Lynn Fullem, *Sales Staff*
John Scanlon, *Asst Sec*
EMP: 20 **EST:** 1968
SQ FT: 10,000
SALES (est): 3.2MM **Privately Held**
WEB: www.proplasticsinc.com
SIC: 3089 5162 Injection molded finished plastic products; plastics materials

(G-5432)
PULASKI MEAT PRODUCTS CO
Also Called: Pulasky Meat Products Co
123 N Wood Ave (07036-4227)
PHONE................................908 925-5380
Fax: 908 925-6547
Ronald Preiss, *President*
Else Preiss, *Corp Secy*
Paul Preiss, *Vice Pres*
Alfred Preiss, *Shareholder*
EMP: 30
SQ FT: 18,000
SALES (est): 5MM **Privately Held**
SIC: 2013 2011 Sausages from purchased meat; ham, smoked: from purchased meat; meat packing plants

(G-5433)
RESEARCH & MFG CORP AMER (PA)
Also Called: Research Manufacturing
1130 W Elizabeth Ave (07036-6315)
PHONE................................908 862-6744
Fax: 908 659-5729
Charles Semah, *President*
Shlomo Kanarek, *President*
Joseph Berta, *Vice Pres*
Murray Walters, *Treasurer*
▲ **EMP:** 12
SQ FT: 22,000
SALES (est): 3MM **Privately Held**
SIC: 3061 3714 3083 Mechanical rubber goods; motor vehicle parts & accessories; laminated plastics plate & sheet

(G-5434)
REX TOOL & MANUFACTURING INC
544 E Elizabeth Ave (07036-2816)
P.O. Box 1423 (07036-0005)
PHONE................................908 925-2727
Fax: 908 925-0797
John Haydu, *President*
Patricia Haydu, *Corp Secy*
Jennifer Haydu, *Vice Pres*
EMP: 4 **EST:** 1953
SQ FT: 3,800
SALES (est): 496.7K **Privately Held**
SIC: 3544 Special dies & tools

(G-5435)
ROUND CUPS LLC
1301 W Elizabeth Ave D (07036-6389)
PHONE................................732 734-0244
Ewa Skoneczny-Glab, *Mng Member*
Joanna Pasek,
Robert Pasek,
▲ **EMP:** 8
SALES (est): 1.1MM **Privately Held**
SIC: 2656 Cups, paper: made from purchased material

(G-5436)
S & H R INC
Also Called: Furs By Severyn
401 N Wood Ave Ste 1 (07036-4156)
PHONE................................908 925-3797
Fax: 908 925-7011
Chester Lebrow Severyn, *President*
Jadwiga Lobrow, *Vice Pres*
EMP: 5
SQ FT: 1,750
SALES (est): 472.1K **Privately Held**
WEB: www.lobrow.com
SIC: 5632 4226 2371 Furriers; fur storage; coats, fur

(G-5437)
SAKER SHOPRITES INC
Also Called: World Class Intl Kit 712
1911 Pennsylvania Ave (07036-1422)
PHONE................................908 925-1550
Fax: 908 925-5294
Brant Walsh, *Manager*
EMP: 10 **Privately Held**
SIC: 5411 2099 Supermarkets, chain; food preparations
HQ: Saker Shoprites, Inc.
10 Centerville Rd
Holmdel NJ 07733
732 462-4700

(G-5438)
SAYBOLT LP
1026 W Elizabeth Ave # 5 (07036-6341)
PHONE................................908 523-2000
Howard Scholl, *Manager*
EMP: 6
SALES (corp-wide): 659.8MM **Privately Held**
WEB: www.corelab.com
SIC: 1389 Testing, measuring, surveying & analysis services
HQ: Saybolt Lp
6316 Windfern Rd
Houston TX 77040
713 328-2673

(G-5439)
SCREEN TECH INC OF NEW JERSEY
1800 W Blancke St (07036-6224)
PHONE................................908 862-8000
Fax: 908 862-2629
Dennis Berthiaume, *President*
Jose Caria, *Treasurer*
Terri Krawec, *Executive*
▲ **EMP:** 60
SQ FT: 10,000
SALES (est): 7.7MM **Privately Held**
SIC: 2759 Screen printing

(G-5440)
SENTREX INGREDIENTS LLC
350 Cantor Ave (07036-6230)
PHONE................................908 862-4440
Naushad Lalani,
Arthur Gurerrera,
▲ **EMP:** 5
SALES (est): 783.7K
SALES (corp-wide): 7.6MM **Privately Held**
SIC: 2087 Extracts, flavoring
PA: Flavor Producers, Llc
8521 Fllbrook Ave Ste 380
West Hills CA 91304
818 307-4062

(G-5441)
SHALLCROSS BOLT & SPECIALTIES
1 Mccandless St (07036-2318)
PHONE................................908 925-4700
Fax: 908 925-8451
Jeffrey Kaden, *President*
Todd Kaden, *General Mgr*
Loretta Kaden, *Corp Secy*
Charles Meder, *Marketing Staff*
Shirley Lake, *Info Tech Mgr*
EMP: 30
SQ FT: 18,000
SALES (est): 9.8MM **Privately Held**
WEB: www.shallcrossbolt.com
SIC: 5072 3452 Hardware; bolts; miscellaneous fasteners; bolts, nuts, rivets & washers

(G-5442)
SHORT RUN STAMPING COMPANY INC (PA)
925 E Linden Ave (07036-2416)
PHONE................................908 862-1070
Fax: 908 862-6260
Robert Speir, *CEO*
Randall Speir, *President*
Carol Speir, *Corp Secy*
Nigel F Hewett, *Vice Pres*
EMP: 25
SQ FT: 20,000
SALES (est): 30.2MM **Privately Held**
WEB: www.shortrun.com
SIC: 3469 Patterns on metal; stamping metal for the trade

(G-5443)
SLYS EXPRESS LLC
518 Lindegar St (07036-5750)
PHONE................................908 787-7516
Slawomir M Polchlopek, *Principal*
EMP: 4 **EST:** 2010
SALES (est): 330.4K **Privately Held**
SIC: 2655 Fiber shipping & mailing containers

(G-5444)
SOLAR COMPOUNDS CORPORATION
1201 W Blancke St (07036-6213)
P.O. Box 1097 (07036-1097)
PHONE................................908 862-2813
Fax: 908 862-8061
Harry Bockus, *CEO*
Alice Thomsen, *Manager*
▼ **EMP:** 24 **EST:** 1920
SQ FT: 60,000
SALES (est): 6.4MM **Privately Held**
WEB: www.solarcompounds.com
SIC: 2891 Adhesives

(G-5445)
SOLUTIA INC
2000 Brunswick Ave (07036-2400)
PHONE................................908 862-0278

EMP: 4
SALES (est): 158K **Publicly Held**
SIC: 2824 Organic fibers, noncellulosic
PA: Eastman Chemical Company
200 S Wilcox Dr
Kingsport TN 37660

(G-5446)
SOUTH BRUNSWICK FURNITURE INC
1015 Edward St (07036-6408)
PHONE................................732 658-8850
William Schafer, *President*
EMP: 198
SQ FT: 60,000
SALES: 30MM **Privately Held**
SIC: 5712 2519 Furniture stores; office furniture; household furniture, except wood or metal: upholstered

(G-5447)
SS TOOL & MANUFACTURING CO
1 Garfield St (07036-1415)
PHONE................................908 486-5497
Fax: 908 486-8864
Stephen Kanyo Sr, *President*
Stephen Kanyo Jr, *Corp Secy*
EMP: 4 **EST:** 1976
SQ FT: 4,000
SALES (est): 600K **Privately Held**
SIC: 3545 Machine tool attachments & accessories

(G-5448)
STAR METAL PRODUCTS
1125 W Elizabeth Ave (07036-6314)
PHONE................................908 474-9860
Fax: 908 474-9868
Donald Eckloff, *President*
Robert Sarnecki, *Treasurer*
EMP: 38
SALES (est): 6MM **Privately Held**
WEB: www.starmetalproducts.com
SIC: 3444 Sheet metalwork

(G-5449)
STEEL MOUNTAIN FABRICATORS LLC (PA)
Also Called: Smf
1312 W Elizabeth Ave (07036-6319)
PHONE................................908 862-2800
Michael Dell'aquila,
Joseph Dell'aquila,
Justin Heald,
EMP: 12
SALES (est): 2.5MM **Privately Held**
SIC: 3599 Machine & other job shop work

(G-5450)
STYLUS CUSTOM APPAREL INC
729 E Elizabeth Ave (07036-2621)
PHONE................................908 587-0800
Domenico Muscillo, *President*
EMP: 5
SALES (est): 82.8K **Privately Held**
SIC: 2389 Men's miscellaneous accessories

(G-5451)
SUBURBAN SIGN CO INC
210 Marion Ave (07036-6337)
PHONE................................908 862-7222
EMP: 20 **EST:** 1946
SQ FT: 12,000
SALES (est): 3.2MM **Privately Held**
SIC: 3993 Mfg Signs/Advertising Specialties

(G-5452)
TED-STEEL INDUSTRIES LTD
Also Called: Ted-Steel Indstries
101 Roselle St (07036-2636)
PHONE................................212 279-3878
Fax: 212 279-3878
Charles Desimone, *President*
Joseph Desimone, *Vice Pres*
Saml T Grayburn,
EMP: 6 **EST:** 1959
SQ FT: 10,000
SALES (est): 711.5K **Privately Held**
SIC: 2542 Garment racks: except wood

▲ = Import ▼ =Export
◆ =Import/Export

(G-5453)
THOMAS H COX & SON INC
Also Called: Spectraform
1634 E Elizabeth Ave (07036-1725)
PHONE.....................................908 928-1010
Fax: 973 928-1212
Michael Kaufman, *President*
Sally Kaufman, *CFO*
Todd Pifher, *Marketing Staff*
Jill Kaufman, *Admin Sec*
EMP: 28
SQ FT: 21,000
SALES: 4.2MM **Privately Held**
WEB: www.coxprinters.com
SIC: 5112 2752 Office supplies; commercial printing, offset

(G-5454)
TOTAL SPECIALTIES USA INC
Also Called: Total Lubricants USA
5 N Stiles St (07036-4208)
PHONE.....................................908 862-9300
Fax: 908 862-1647
Barry Martin, *Plant Mgr*
Joe Squilleante, *Plant Mgr*
Bernie Kordelski, *Safety Mgr*
Steve Daubert, *Human Res Mgr*
Karen Lin, *Manager*
EMP: 51
SALES (corp-wide): 8.3B **Publicly Held**
SIC: 2992 Oils & greases, blending & compounding
HQ: Total Specialties Usa, Inc.
1201 La St Ste 1800
Houston TX 77002

(G-5455)
TRIPLE S INDUSTRIES
1108 E Linden Ave (07036-2419)
P.O. Box 1293 (07036-0003)
PHONE.....................................908 862-0110
Robert Schulte, *President*
John H Schulte, *Vice Pres*
Walter Bradshaw, *Treasurer*
Patricia Bradshaw, *Shareholder*
Ruth Schulte, *Admin Sec*
EMP: 7 **EST:** 1961
SALES (est): 760K **Privately Held**
SIC: 3599 Machine shop, jobbing & repair

(G-5456)
UNIQUE SCREEN PRINTING CORP
10 Mckinley St 16 (07036-1747)
PHONE.....................................908 925-3773
Fax: 908 925-3087
Jose Grajeda, *President*
EMP: 50
SQ FT: 15,000
SALES (est): 5.5MM **Privately Held**
WEB: www.uniquescreenprinting.com
SIC: 2262 2261 2396 Screen printing: manmade fiber & silk broadwoven fabrics; screen printing of cotton broadwoven fabrics; automotive & apparel trimmings

(G-5457)
VELOSO INDUSTRIES INC
1020 E Elizabeth Ave (07036-2230)
PHONE.....................................908 925-0999
Carlos Veloso, *President*
▲ **EMP:** 5
SQ FT: 3,600
SALES (est): 697K **Privately Held**
SIC: 3089 Thermoformed finished plastic products

(G-5458)
WELL BILT INDUSTRIES INC
2 Maple Ave (07036-2820)
PHONE.....................................908 486-6002
Les Zalewski, *President*
EMP: 15
SQ FT: 8,000
SALES (est): 3MM **Privately Held**
WEB: www.wellbiltind.com
SIC: 3469 3544 Stamping metal for the trade; special dies, tools, jigs & fixtures

(G-5459)
WGJF MANUFACTURING CORP
Also Called: Hammer Manufacturing
417 Commerce Rd (07036-2428)
P.O. Box 1340 (07036-0004)
PHONE.....................................908 862-1730
William J Fig, *President*

EMP: 26
SQ FT: 15,000
SALES (est): 5MM **Privately Held**
SIC: 3469 Stamping metal for the trade

Lindenwold
Camden County

(G-5460)
ACTION GRAPHICS INC
424 E Gibbsboro Rd (08021-1907)
PHONE.....................................856 783-1825
Fax: 856 783-3467
Barry Balliet, *Owner*
EMP: 6
SALES (est): 500.6K **Privately Held**
WEB: www.actiongraphicsusa.com
SIC: 2759 Commercial printing

(G-5461)
ADVANCE SCALE COMPANY INC (PA)
2400 Egg Harbor Rd (08021-1431)
PHONE.....................................856 784-4916
Fax: 856 627-7800
Jim Santarpio, *President*
Sheila Santarpio, *Vice Pres*
EMP: 30
SQ FT: 16,000
SALES (est): 11.1MM **Privately Held**
WEB: www.advancescale.com
SIC: 5046 3596 Scales, except laboratory; weighing machines & apparatus; industrial scales

(G-5462)
PAUL BURKHARDT & SONS INC
Also Called: Pe Burkhardt & Sons
648 7th Ave (08021-3549)
PHONE.....................................856 435-2020
Fax: 856 435-1089
Paul Burkhardt Sr, *President*
Paul Burkhardt Jr, *President*
Winona Burkhardt, *Treasurer*
EMP: 6 **EST:** 1982
SQ FT: 600
SALES (est): 200K **Privately Held**
SIC: 5712 2434 Cabinet work, custom; wood kitchen cabinets

(G-5463)
PAVERART LLC
2512 Egg Harbor Rd Ste C (08021-1405)
PHONE.....................................856 783-7000
Michael K Bull, *Vice Pres*
Kenneth R Bull,
John M Seroka,
EMP: 7
SQ FT: 10,000
SALES (est): 680K **Privately Held**
WEB: www.paverartllc.com
SIC: 3271 Concrete block & brick

(G-5464)
WILLIAM R HALL CO
901 E Gibbsboro Rd (08021-1209)
PHONE.....................................856 784-6700
George Aho, *President*
EMP: 40
SQ FT: 22,000
SALES (est): 5.5MM
SALES (corp-wide): 9.3MM **Privately Held**
WEB: www.ecmoore.com
SIC: 3843 3291 Dental equipment & supplies; abrasive products
PA: E C Moore Company
13325 Leonard St
Dearborn MI 48126
313 581-7878

Linwood
Atlantic County

(G-5465)
ATLANTIC PRSTHTIC ORTHOTIC SVC
199 New Rd Ste 56 (08221-2025)
PHONE.....................................609 927-6330
Rich Kathrins, *President*

Leonard Hollander, *President*
Joan Gatti, *Manager*
Paul Rutledge, *Exec Dir*
Jill Ojserkis, *Admin Sec*
EMP: 5
SALES: 1.4MM **Privately Held**
SIC: 3842 5999 Prosthetic appliances; limbs, artificial; orthopedic appliances; orthopedic & prosthesis applications; convalescent equipment & supplies

(G-5466)
HANGER PRSTHETCS & ORTHO INC
210 New Rd Ste 7 (08221-1371)
PHONE.....................................609 653-8323
Thomas Delsey, *Manager*
EMP: 7
SALES (corp-wide): 1B **Publicly Held**
SIC: 3842 Limbs, artificial
HQ: Hanger Prosthetics & Orthotics, Inc.
10910 Domain Dr Ste 300
Austin TX 78758
512 777-3800

(G-5467)
PROCRETE LLC
4 Evergreen Rd (08221-1346)
P.O. Box 492 (08221-0592)
PHONE.....................................609 365-2922
David McBride,
EMP: 4
SALES: 90K **Privately Held**
SIC: 1741 3271 7389 Masonry & other stonework; concrete block & brick;

Little Falls
Passaic County

(G-5468)
AMERICAN SOC OF MECH ENGINEERS
Also Called: Asme
150 Clove Rd Ste 6 (07424-2139)
PHONE.....................................973 244-2282
Fax: 973 882-8113
Jim Barrett, *General Mgr*
Nicholas Jankowski, *Electrical Engi*
Michael T Young, *HR Admin*
Paul Scott, *Exec Dir*
Kimberly Verderber, *Admin Sec*
EMP: 82
SALES (corp-wide): 61.2MM **Privately Held**
WEB: www.asmestaff.org
SIC: 2741 8711 Technical manual & paper publishing; engineering services
PA: The American Society Of Mechanical Engineers
2 Park Ave
New York NY 10016
212 591-7000

(G-5469)
ANDON BRUSH CO INC
1 Merrit Ave (07424-1145)
PHONE.....................................973 256-6611
Fax: 973 256-7965
Robert Newell, *President*
Charles Newell, *Production*
Kenneth Kuter, *VP Sales*
▲ **EMP:** 25
SALES (est): 5.4MM **Privately Held**
WEB: www.andonbrush.com
SIC: 5085 5113 3991 Brushes, industrial; closures, paper & disposable plastic; brooms & brushes

(G-5470)
ARTS WEEKLY INC
Also Called: The Aquarian Weekly
52 Sindle Ave (07424-1619)
P.O. Box 1140 (07424-8140)
PHONE.....................................973 812-6766
Fax: 973 812-5420
Diane Casazza, *President*
Chris Farinas, *Vice Pres*
Mark Sterman, *Treasurer*
Delores Atkinson, *Mktg Dir*
EMP: 50
SQ FT: 2,400

SALES: 1MM **Privately Held**
WEB: www.theaquarian.com
SIC: 2721 2711 Magazines: publishing & printing; newspapers

(G-5471)
CANTEL MEDICAL CORP (PA)
150 Clove Rd Ste 36 (07424-2100)
PHONE.....................................973 890-7220
Charles M Diker, *Ch of Bd*
George L Fotiades, *Vice Ch Bd*
Jorgen B Hansen, *President*
Eric W Nodiff, *Exec VP*
Seth M Yellin, *Exec VP*
◆ **EMP:** 8 **EST:** 1963
SALES: 770.1MM **Publicly Held**
WEB: www.cantelmedical.com
SIC: 3841 3589 Surgical & medical instruments; water purification equipment, household type

(G-5472)
CARET CORPORATION (PA)
101 E Main St Ste 1202 (07424-2263)
PHONE.....................................973 423-5999
Ivonne Ruggles, *President*
EMP: 7
SALES (est): 1.3MM **Privately Held**
SIC: 2844 Toilet preparations

(G-5473)
CASE DAVENPORT INC
280 Main St Apt 211 (07424-1374)
PHONE.....................................973 812-7180
Keith Caggiano, *Principal*
EMP: 7
SALES (est): 138.4K **Privately Held**
SIC: 3523 Farm machinery & equipment

(G-5474)
CHEM FLOWTRONIC INC
195 Paterson Ave Ste 4 (07424-4656)
P.O. Box 4635, Wayne (07474-4635)
PHONE.....................................973 785-0001
Kevin Mooney, *President*
▲ **EMP:** 8
SQ FT: 1,500
SALES (est): 1.7MM **Privately Held**
WEB: www.chem-flowtronics.com
SIC: 3824 Mechanical & electromechanical counters & devices

(G-5475)
EVERGREEN INFORMATION SVCS INC
275 Paterson Ave Ste 101 (07424-1658)
PHONE.....................................973 339-9672
John Gilrain, *President*
Lisa Gilrain, *Vice Pres*
Karen Stuart, *Department Mgr*
EMP: 10 **EST:** 2008
SALES: 1.6MM **Privately Held**
SIC: 2731 2711 2721 Book publishing; newspapers: publishing only, not printed on site; magazines: publishing only, not printed on site

(G-5476)
HOFFMANN-LA ROCHE INC (DH)
150 Clove Rd Ste 88th (07424-2138)
PHONE.....................................973 890-2268
Fax: 973 235-3775
Kurt Seiler, *President*
David McDede, *Principal*
Gregg Scheideler, *Principal*
Jim Porter, *Business Mgr*
Sean Johnston, *Vice Pres*
◆ **EMP:** 3000 **EST:** 1905
SALES (est): 1B
SALES (corp-wide): 53.9B **Publicly Held**
WEB: www.rocheusa.com
SIC: 2834 8733 Pharmaceutical preparations; medical research

(G-5477)
HYCRETE INC
409 Main St (07424-1207)
PHONE.....................................201 386-8110
Fax: 201 386-8155
Jason Guerack, *CEO*
Richard Guinn, *CEO*
Christopher Worthington, *Opers Mgr*
Andrea Reynolds, *Finance*
Andrew Rhodes, *Sales Mgr*
▼ **EMP:** 32

SALES (est): 6.8MM **Privately Held**
SIC: 3271 Concrete block & brick

(G-5478)
JOHN W KENNEDY COMPANY
60 Sindle Ave (07424-1649)
PHONE..................................973 256-5525
Dalton Pemberton, *Manager*
EMP: 5
SALES (corp-wide): 24.3MM **Privately Held**
SIC: 3559 Petroleum refinery equipment
PA: John W. Kennedy Co.
990 Waterman Ave
East Providence RI 02914
401 434-1246

(G-5479)
JW PARR LEADBURING CO (PA)
Also Called: Parr, J W Leadburing Co
87 Parkway (07424-1227)
PHONE..................................973 256-8093
Gary Parr, *Owner*
EMP: 4
SALES: 1MM **Privately Held**
WEB: www.garyparr.com
SIC: 7699 3443 8742 Tank repair; tanks,
lined: metal plate; management consult-
ing services

(G-5480)
LABEL GRAPHICS MFG INC (PA)
175 Paterson Ave (07424-1607)
PHONE..................................973 890-5665
Fax: 973 890-1164
Thomas Silvano, *President*
Victor Paravati, *QC Mgr*
Denise Silvano, *Treasurer*
▲ EMP: 43
SQ FT: 26,000
SALES (est): 8.4MM **Privately Held**
WEB: www.labelgraphicsmfg.com
SIC: 2672 Labels (unprinted); gummed:
made from purchased materials

(G-5481)
LITTLE FALLS SHOP RITE SUPER
171 Browertown Rd Ste 2 (07424-1718)
PHONE..................................973 256-0909
Charles M Infusino, *President*
Carol Tokar, *Treasurer*
EMP: 282
SALES (est): 24.5MM **Privately Held**
SIC: 5912 5411 7384 5992 Drug stores;
supermarkets, chain; photofinish labora-
ries; florists; cookies & crackers; bread,
cake & related products

(G-5482)
METALIX INC
9 Villa Rd (07424-2315)
PHONE..................................973 546-2500
Gary Nardino, *President*
Charles Nardino, *Vice Pres*
EMP: 8 EST: 1951
SQ FT: 14,000
SALES (est): 42.9K **Privately Held**
SIC: 3444 Sheet metal specialties, not
stamped

(G-5483)
OVADIA CORPORATION
101 E Main St Ste 501 (07424-2265)
PHONE..................................973 256-9200
Susan Ovadia, *President*
Steven Ovadia, *Vice Pres*
Michael Bender, *Mktg Dir*
Ed Ovadia, *Marketing Mgr*
▲ EMP: 50
SQ FT: 20,000
SALES (est): 7.2MM **Privately Held**
SIC: 3089 3993 Plastic containers, except
foam; signs & advertising specialties

(G-5484)
PACKOM LLC (PA)
385 Main St (07424-1207)
PHONE..................................201 378-8382
Peter Dobirc, *Director*
EMP: 15
SQ FT: 12,000
SALES: 2.5MM **Privately Held**
SIC: 2064 Candy & other confectionery
products

(G-5485)
PAPER CLIP COMMUNICATION INC
125 Paterson Ave Ste 4 (07424-4626)
PHONE..................................973 256-1333
Fax: 973 256-8088
Andy Mc Laughlin, *President*
Doris McLaughlin, *Editor*
Dorris Laughlin, *Vice Pres*
Samantha Neil, *Cust Mgr*
Marisa Portuesi, *Cust Mgr*
EMP: 10 EST: 1993
SQ FT: 1,600
SALES (est): 1.3MM **Privately Held**
WEB: www.paper-clip.com
SIC: 2759 Publication printing

(G-5486)
PRIORE CONSTRUCTION SVCS LLC
5 Peckman Rd (07424-1631)
PHONE..................................973 785-2262
Fax: 973 785-2261
Dominick Priore, *President*
Michael Priore, *Vice Pres*
EMP: 19
SQ FT: 13,000
SALES: 3MM **Privately Held**
SIC: 3441 Fabricated structural metal;
tower sections, radio & television trans-
mission

(G-5487)
RUBIGO COSMETICS
101 E Main St Bldg 12 (07424-5608)
PHONE..................................973 636-6573
Fax: 973 636-6585
Jules Schlesinger, *President*
Carol Cozin, *Vice Pres*
Steve Schisrien, *Vice Pres*
Michael J Assante, *Treasurer*
EMP: 6
SQ FT: 10,000
SALES (est): 460K **Privately Held**
WEB: www.rubigo.com
SIC: 2844 5122 3991 Cosmetic prepara-
tions; cosmetics; brooms & brushes

(G-5488)
SIMTEK USA INC
13 Fairfield Ave (07424-1264)
PHONE..................................862 757-8130
EMP: 5
SALES (est): 484.3K **Privately Held**
SIC: 3728 Aircraft power transmission
equipment

(G-5489)
SRE VENTURES LLC
Also Called: UPS Store, The
163 E Main St (07424-1711)
PHONE..................................973 785-0099
Steve Eldrige, *President*
EMP: 6
SQ FT: 2,000
SALES: 250K **Privately Held**
SIC: 7389 4215 4513 2621 Mailbox
rental & related service; package delivery,
vehicular; parcel delivery, vehicular; letter
delivery, private air; package delivery, pri-
vate air; parcel delivery, private air; print-
ing paper

(G-5490)
STORY ELECTRIC MTR REPR CO INC
20 Francisco Ave (07424-2317)
P.O. Box 379 (07424-0379)
PHONE..................................973 256-1636
Fax: 973 256-1384
David R Wilberton, *President*
EMP: 6
SQ FT: 28,000
SALES: 3.5MM **Privately Held**
SIC: 1731 7694 General electrical con-
tractor; electric motor repair

(G-5491)
TAURUS PRECISION INC
129 Paterson Ave (07424-1643)
PHONE..................................973 785-9254
Michael E Jakubas, *President*
EMP: 14
SQ FT: 5,000

SALES (est): 2.2MM **Privately Held**
SIC: 3599 3429 Machine shop, jobbing &
repair; metal fasteners

(G-5492)
TSG INC
Also Called: Technical Systems Group
28 Muller Pl (07424-1133)
PHONE..................................973 785-1118
Fax: 973 785-4585
Peter Chin, *President*
EMP: 15
SALES (est): 1.4MM **Privately Held**
WEB: www.tompat.com
SIC: 3625 8711 Industrial controls: push
button, selector switches, pilot; consulting
engineer

(G-5493)
UTZ TECHNOLOGIES INC (PA)
4 Peckman Rd (07424-1631)
PHONE..................................973 339-1100
Fax: 973 778-4239
Dennis Curtis, *President*
Arthur Wein, *President*
Kristian Guidi, *General Mgr*
Donald Utz, *Chairman*
EMP: 30
SQ FT: 8,000
SALES: 5MM **Privately Held**
WEB: www.utz.com
SIC: 3679 Electronic circuits

Little Ferry
Bergen County

(G-5494)
ALTONA BLOWER & SHTMTL WORK
Also Called: Altona Blower & Shtmtl Works
23 N Washington Ave (07643-1602)
PHONE..................................201 641-3520
Walter Martin, *President*
Robert Class, *Vice Pres*
Chip Martin, *Vice Pres*
Abe Ingersoll, *Project Mgr*
Kelly B Battaglia, *Purch Mgr*
EMP: 9
SQ FT: 5,000
SALES (est): 1.5MM **Privately Held**
WEB: www.altonametal.com
SIC: 1711 3444 Ventilation & duct work
contractor; pipe, sheet metal

(G-5495)
BRIX CITY BREWING
4 Alsan Way (07643-1001)
PHONE..................................201 440-0865
EMP: 5
SALES (est): 174.1K **Privately Held**
SIC: 2082 Beer (alcoholic beverage)

(G-5496)
CHIZZYS SERVICE CENTER
Also Called: Chizzy's Truck & Auto Repair
44 Bergen Tpke (07643-1609)
PHONE..................................201 641-7222
Mike Dizmadia, *President*
Matt Dizmadia, *Vice Pres*
EMP: 6
SALES (est): 624.8K **Privately Held**
SIC: 7538 7692 General truck repair;
welding repair

(G-5497)
CITY DESIGN GROUP INC
201 Gates Rd Ste C (07643-1919)
PHONE..................................201 329-7711
Lee John, *President*
▲ EMP: 6
SALES (est): 631.9K **Privately Held**
SIC: 2339 Women's & misses' accessories

(G-5498)
CLINTON INDUSTRIES INC
207 Redneck Ave (07643-1320)
PHONE..................................201 440-0400
Harry Klein, *President*
Larry Paricio, *Vice Pres*
Dara Silver, *Vice Pres*
Bob Pulliam, *Marketing Staff*
▲ EMP: 45
SQ FT: 25,000

SALES (est): 7MM **Privately Held**
WEB: www.clintonind.com
SIC: 3559 Sewing machines & attach-
ments, industrial

(G-5499)
COMPCO ANALYTICAL INC
215 Gates Rd Ste U (07643-1928)
PHONE..................................201 641-3936
Mark Barenburg, *President*
Helene Barenburg, *Vice Pres*
EMP: 7
SQ FT: 2,500
SALES (est): 730K **Privately Held**
SIC: 7699 7372 5963 Hospital equipment
repair services; prepackaged software; di-
rect selling establishments

(G-5500)
DASSAULT AIRCRAFT SVCS CORP (DH)
200 Riser Rd (07643-1226)
PHONE..................................201 440-6700
Peter S Rothwell, *Principal*
Remy St-Martin, *COO*
EMP: 8
SALES (est): 986.7K **Privately Held**
SIC: 3721 Aircraft
HQ: Dassault Falcon Jet Corp.
200 Riser Rd
Little Ferry NJ 07643
201 440-6700

(G-5501)
DASSAULT PROCUREMENT SVCS INC (DH)
200 Riser Rd (07643-1226)
PHONE..................................201 261-4130
Patrick Duterpre, *President*
Robin Willson, *Vice Pres*
EMP: 15
SQ FT: 4,500
SALES (est): 41.9MM **Privately Held**
SIC: 5088 3812 Aircraft equipment & sup-
plies; aircraft flight instruments
HQ: Dassault Aviation
Marcel Dassault
Paris 75008
153 754-895

(G-5502)
DREW-WAL MACHINE & TOOL CORP
76 Monroe St (07643-2131)
PHONE..................................201 641-3887
Fax: 201 641-3888
Andrew J Kovach, *President*
Gloria Kovach, *Treasurer*
EMP: 4 EST: 1961
SALES (est): 468.3K **Privately Held**
SIC: 3599 Machine shop, jobbing & repair

(G-5503)
EASYFLEX EAST INC
101 Industrial Ave (07643-1936)
PHONE..................................201 853-9005
Sunmin Kim OH, *CEO*
Yoonsuk OH, *Principal*
▲ EMP: 4
SALES (est): 622K **Privately Held**
SIC: 3312 Stainless steel

(G-5504)
FERRY MACHINE CORP
75 Industrial Ave (07643-1996)
PHONE..................................201 641-9191
Fax: 201 641-7320
Louis Ferretti Jr, *President*
Tom Brock, *Vice Pres*
Susan Brock, *Treasurer*
EMP: 25 EST: 1952
SQ FT: 12,000
SALES (est): 5.2MM **Privately Held**
WEB: www.ferrymachine.com
SIC: 3599 7692 3841 3812 Machine
shop, jobbing & repair; welding repair;
surgical & medical instruments; search &
navigation equipment

(G-5505)
FLAVOUR TEE INTERNATIONAL LLC
66 Industrial Ave (07643-1913)
PHONE..................................201 440-3281
Greg Carrandza, *General Mgr*

Cosmo Verni, *Principal*
EMP: 7
SQ FT: 5,000
SALES (est): 410K **Privately Held**
SIC: 2099 Food preparations

(G-5506)
GLOBE PHOTO ENGRAVING CO LLC
19 N Washington Ave Ste 1 (07643-1693)
PHONE..................................201 489-2300
Charles Mesropian, *Administration*
EMP: 25
SALES (est): 481.3K **Privately Held**
SIC: 2796 Platemaking services

(G-5507)
GLOBE PHOTO ENGRAVING CORP
19 N Washington Ave (07643-1693)
PHONE..................................201 489-2300
Fax: 201 641-7682
Charles Mesropian, *Principal*
Alan Soojian, *Principal*
EMP: 16
SQ FT: 30,000
SALES (est): 2.2MM **Privately Held**
SIC: 2796 7384 Photoengraving plates, linecuts or halftones; photographic services

(G-5508)
IMPACT PRINTING
15 Vogt Ln 1 (07643-1801)
PHONE..................................862 225-9167
Frank Corbiserie, *President*
EMP: 8
SALES (est): 385.4K **Privately Held**
SIC: 2752 Commercial printing, offset

(G-5509)
IMPERIUM ENTERPRISES LLC
Also Called: Avalon Pearls
100 Industrial Ave Ste 1 (07643-1934)
PHONE..................................908 206-4970
Dennis Canlas, *Mng Member*
Hike Larson,
Anna Raynes,
▲ **EMP:** 5 EST: 2006
SQ FT: 1,700
SALES (est): 100K **Privately Held**
SIC: 3911 5094 Jewelry, precious metal; jewelry & precious stones

(G-5510)
JJS OWN LTD LIABILITY COMPANY
71 Pickens St (07643-1911)
PHONE..................................551 486-8510
Joy Ortiz,
EMP: 8
SALES (est): 162.2K **Privately Held**
SIC: 2035 Pickles, sauces & salad dressings

(G-5511)
JNT TECHNICAL SERVICES INC
85 Industrial Ave (07643-1901)
PHONE..................................201 641-2130
Fax: 201 641-2309
Glenn F Jorgensen, *President*
EMP: 20
SQ FT: 10,000
SALES (est): 2.9MM **Privately Held**
WEB: www.jnt-tech-serv.com
SIC: 3545 5085 Machine tool accessories; industrial tools

(G-5512)
MAJOR PRODUCTS CO INC (HQ)
66 Industrial Ave (07643-1923)
P.O. Box 675 (07643-0675)
PHONE..................................201 641-5555
Fax: 201 641-6331
Daniel Derose Jr, *President*
Rich Eberhardt, *Business Mgr*
Valerie Leimer, *COO*
Ralph D Rose, *Vice Pres*
George Dipaola, *Plant Mgr*
▲ **EMP:** 20 EST: 1951
SQ FT: 54,000

SALES (est): 4.8MM
SALES (corp-wide): 3.7MM **Privately Held**
SIC: 2034 7389 Soup mixes; packaging & labeling services
PA: Major International Limited
Major House, Higham Business Park
Rushden NORTHANTS NN10
193 335-6012

(G-5513)
PAPER DOVE PRESS LLC
16 Monnett St (07643-1212)
PHONE..................................201 641-7938
Laurel Nakai, *Principal*
EMP: 4
SALES (est): 83.8K **Privately Held**
SIC: 2711 Newspapers

(G-5514)
REVERE PLASTICS INC
16 Industrial Ave (07643-1913)
P.O. Box 191480, Boston MA (02119-0028)
PHONE..................................201 641-0777
Fax: 201 641-1086
EMP: 6 EST: 1953
SQ FT: 10,000
SALES (est): 592.3K **Privately Held**
SIC: 3089 2394 Mfg Plastic Products Mfg Canvas/Related Products

(G-5515)
RIEDEL SIGN COMPANY INC
15 Warren St (07643-2006)
PHONE..................................201 641-9121
Fax: 201 641-8338
William F Riedel, *President*
Regina Riedel, *Office Mgr*
EMP: 5
SALES (est): 591.8K **Privately Held**
WEB: www.riedelsignco.com
SIC: 3993 7389 Signs, not made in custom sign painting shops; sign painting & lettering shop

(G-5516)
SCIENTIFIC DESIGN COMPANY (PA)
49 Industrial Ave (07643-1922)
PHONE..................................201 641-0500
Fax: 201 807-0149
Paul R Lamb, *Principal*
Ashok S Padia, *Principal*
Paul Ellis, *Vice Pres*
Allan S West, *Vice Pres*
Randy Murillo, *Opers Staff*
EMP: 124
SALES (est): 48.1MM **Privately Held**
WEB: www.scidesign.com
SIC: 8711 2819 Chemical engineering; catalysts, chemical

(G-5517)
SPIDENT USA INCORPORATED
205 Redneck Ave (07643-1320)
PHONE..................................201 944-0511
Kwang Soon Choi, *President*
▲ **EMP:** 4
SALES (est): 483.3K **Privately Held**
SIC: 3843 Dental equipment & supplies

(G-5518)
SPIRIT TEX LLC
201 Gates Rd Ste E (07643-1919)
PHONE..................................201 440-1113
Ammar Artani,
EMP: 6 EST: 2006
SQ FT: 18,000
SALES (est): 800K **Privately Held**
SIC: 2325 2339 2369 2331 Jeans: men's, youths' & boys'; jeans: women's, misses' & juniors'; jeans: girls', children's & infants'; women's & misses' blouses & shirts; shirts, men's & boys'

Little Silver
Monmouth County

(G-5519)
ALL STRUCTURES LLC
Also Called: Yardworks
21 Rumson Rd (07739-1331)
PHONE..................................732 233-7071

James Mc Allister,
Jamie Mc Allister,
EMP: 5
SALES (est): 272.9K **Privately Held**
SIC: 2452 Panels & sections, prefabricated, wood

(G-5520)
SIMTRONICS CORPORATION
50 Birch Ave Ste 100 (07739-1107)
P.O. Box 38 (07739-0038)
PHONE..................................732 747-0322
Thomas B Judge, *President*
EMP: 10
SALES (est): 898.5K **Privately Held**
WEB: www.simtronics.com
SIC: 7372 7371 3652 Prepackaged software; application computer software; computer software writing services; compact laser discs, prerecorded

Livingston
Essex County

(G-5521)
A C L EQUIPMENT CORP (PA)
Northfield Rd (07039)
PHONE..................................973 740-9800
Martin Reinfeld, *President*
Nancy Reinfeld, *Vice Pres*
Richard Greenburg, *Treasurer*
EMP: 7
SQ FT: 3,000
SALES (est): 549.3K **Privately Held**
WEB: www.aclequipment.com
SIC: 3993 3669 Electric signs; traffic signals, electric

(G-5522)
ACCESSION DATA SYSTEMS
25 Hickory Pl (07039-3614)
PHONE..................................973 992-7392
Ken Bernstein, *CEO*
EMP: 4
SALES (est): 200K **Privately Held**
WEB: www.accessiondata.com
SIC: 7372 Prepackaged software

(G-5523)
ALLISON CORP (PA)
15-33 Okner Pkwy (07039-1626)
PHONE..................................973 992-3800
Fax: 973 992-3095
David Dennison, *President*
Stanley Saltz, *Controller*
Cheryl Dennison, *Admin Sec*
Ben Adams, *Real Est Agnt*
▲ **EMP:** 7 EST: 1960
SQ FT: 100,000
SALES (est): 4.7MM **Privately Held**
WEB: www.allisoncorp.com
SIC: 2211 2221 3714 2842 Automotive fabrics, cotton; automotive fabrics, man-made fiber; motor vehicle parts & accessories; deodorants, nonpersonal; motor vehicle supplies & new parts

(G-5524)
AMARK INDUSTRIES INC (PA)
Also Called: Kenlen Wire Products Division
293 Eisenhower Pkwy # 100 (07039-1719)
PHONE..................................973 992-8900
Fax: 973 992-9203
Mark Venturi, *CEO*
J P Venturi, *Vice Pres*
EMP: 2
SQ FT: 14,000
SALES (est): 1.5MM **Privately Held**
SIC: 3315 3451 Wire & fabricated wire products; screw machine products

(G-5525)
ATM AFICIONADO LLC
184 S Livingston Ave (07039-3014)
PHONE..................................973 251-2115
Mark Teitelbaum,
EMP: 7 EST: 2010
SALES (est): 707.7K **Privately Held**
SIC: 3629 Electrical industrial apparatus

(G-5526)
CAMPAK INC
Also Called: Tecnicam
119 Naylon Ave (07039-1005)
PHONE..................................973 994-4888
Fax: 973 992-4497
Thomas Miller, *CEO*
Brian Pomponio, *Engineer*
Brian Oliver, *Sales Engr*
Thomas Turner, *Sales Executive*
▲ **EMP:** 9
SQ FT: 25,000
SALES (est): 3.3MM **Privately Held**
WEB: www.campak.com
SIC: 5084 3565 Packaging machinery & equipment; packaging machinery

(G-5527)
CUSTOM CONVERTERS INC
115 Naylon Ave (07039-1005)
PHONE..................................201 994-9000
Fax: 973 994-6679
Mark Krause, *President*
▲ **EMP:** 23 EST: 1982
SQ FT: 15,000
SALES (est): 2.8MM **Privately Held**
WEB: www.customconverters.com
SIC: 7694 3531 2675 Rewinding services

(G-5528)
DMF ASSOCIATED ENGINES LLC
W Hobart Gap Rd (07039)
PHONE..................................973 535-9773
Dennis Bodor,
EMP: 100
SALES (est): 5.9MM **Privately Held**
SIC: 3694 Engine electrical equipment

(G-5529)
FERRATEX SERVICES INC
354 Eisenhower Pkwy (07039-1022)
PHONE..................................973 609-5449
Ej Solimine, *CEO*
EMP: 25
SALES (est): 987.6K **Privately Held**
SIC: 3523 Water troughs

(G-5530)
FORMOSA PLASTICS CORP USA (PA)
Also Called: Fpc USA
9 Peach Tree Hill Rd (07039-5702)
PHONE..................................973 992-2090
Fax: 973 992-9627
David Lin, *President*
Jason Lin, *President*
Jim Liu, *General Mgr*
Paula Ellentuch, *Editor*
C T Lee, *Chairman*
◆ **EMP:** 340
SQ FT: 225,000
SALES (est): 1.3B **Privately Held**
WEB: www.fpcusa.com
SIC: 2821 2812 Polyvinyl chloride resins (PVC); vinyl resins; caustic soda, sodium hydroxide

(G-5531)
FRANKLIN MILLER INC
60 Okner Pkwy (07039-1604)
PHONE..................................973 535-9200
Fax: 973 533-6456
William Galanty, *President*
Beth Rothenberg, *Corp Secy*
Galanty Trust, *Shareholder*
◆ **EMP:** 50 EST: 1918
SQ FT: 12,000
SALES (est): 15.2MM **Privately Held**
WEB: www.franklinmiller.com
SIC: 3559 3589 Refinery, chemical processing & similar machinery; sewage treatment equipment

(G-5532)
G L TOOL & MANUFACTURING CO
26 Okner Pkwy (07039-1604)
PHONE..................................973 740-0001
Fax: 973 740-9243
Gerhard Liepold, *President*
EMP: 20
SQ FT: 15,000

SALES (est): 3.2MM **Privately Held**
SIC: 3599 3549 3544 8748 Machine shop, jobbing & repair; metalworking machinery; special dies, tools, jigs & fixtures; systems analysis & engineering consulting services

(G-5533)
GEORGE PRESS INC
74 S Livingston Ave (07039-3009)
PHONE..................................973 992-7797
Fax: 973 992-2618
George Press, *President*
▲ EMP: 13
SALES (est): 1.5MM **Privately Held**
SIC: 5944 3911 Jewelry, precious stones & precious metals; jewelry, precious metal

(G-5534)
HYMAN W FISHER INC
121 E Northfield Rd (07039-4506)
PHONE..................................973 992-9155
Hyman Fisher, *President*
EMP: 7
SALES (est): 348.7K **Privately Held**
SIC: 8742 2741 7389 Incentive or award program consultant; technical papers: publishing only, not printed on site; convention & show services

(G-5535)
INTEPLAST GROUP CORPORATION (PA)
Also Called: Bopp Films
9 Peach Tree Hill Rd (07039-5702)
PHONE..................................973 994-8000
Fax: 973 994-8028
John Young, *Ch of Bd*
Homer Shieh, *President*
Marie Zagada, *President*
Andy Chen, *General Mgr*
Dan Taylor, *Regional Mgr*
◆ EMP: 300
SQ FT: 20,000
SALES (est): 1B **Privately Held**
WEB: www.inteplast.com
SIC: 2673 Bags: plastic, laminated & coated

(G-5536)
INTRINSIQ SPCLTY SOLUTIONS INC
354 Eisenhower Pkwy # 2025 (07039-1022)
PHONE..................................973 251-2039
Michael Custode, *President*
Nestor Olivier, *CFO*
Larry Drappi, *Director*
EMP: 42
SQ FT: 6,300
SALES (est): 2.4MM **Privately Held**
WEB: www.meridianemr.net
SIC: 7372 Business oriented computer software

(G-5537)
IP MOULDING INC
9 Peach Tree Hill Rd (07039-5702)
PHONE..................................574 825-6554
EMP: 5
SALES (est): 786.2K **Privately Held**
SIC: 2821 Plastics materials & resins

(G-5538)
J-M MANUFACTURING COMPANY INC
Also Called: J-M Eagle
9 Peach Tree Hill Rd (07039-5702)
PHONE..................................800 621-4404
Fax: 800 451-4170
Walter Wang, *Manager*
EMP: 83
SALES (corp-wide): 1B **Privately Held**
SIC: 2821 Polyvinyl chloride resins (PVC)
PA: J-M Manufacturing Company, Inc.
 5200 W Century Blvd
 Los Angeles CA 90045
 800 621-4404

(G-5539)
LITHOS ESTIATORIO LTD LBLTY CO
405 Eisenhower Pkwy (07039-1000)
PHONE..................................973 758-1111
Lithos Estiatorio, *Principal*

EMP: 5
SALES (est): 337.6K **Privately Held**
SIC: 2752 Commercial printing, lithographic

(G-5540)
LIVINGSTON BAGEL WARREN INC
37 E Northfield Rd (07039-4501)
P.O. Box 1638 (07039-7238)
PHONE..................................973 994-1915
Fax: 973 994-1701
Sol Snyder, *President*
Rita Snyder, *Corp Secy*
EMP: 28
SQ FT: 2,500
SALES (est): 1.6MM **Privately Held**
SIC: 5461 5149 5812 2051 Bagels; bakery products; delicatessen (eating places); bread, cake & related products

(G-5541)
M4 MACHINE LLC
7 Industrial Pkwy 18 (07039-1613)
PHONE..................................718 928-9695
Matthew Allen, *President*
EMP: 5
SALES (est): 167.6K **Privately Held**
SIC: 3599 Machine & other job shop work

(G-5542)
MAX PRO SERVICES LLC
Also Called: Total Relief Services
184 S Livingston Ave (07039-3014)
PHONE..................................973 396-2373
Donald Dauphin, *Mng Member*
EMP: 6
SALES (est): 244.5K **Privately Held**
WEB: www.maxproservices.com
SIC: 6531 6163 7389 3953 Selling agent, real estate; buying agent, real estate; agents, farm or business loan; legal & tax services; seal presses, notary & hand

(G-5543)
MEP ALASKA LLC
Also Called: Magnum Energy Partners
29 Vanderbilt Dr (07039-6120)
PHONE..................................646 535-9005
Mark Steinmetz, *Owner*
Terrence Manning, *COO*
EMP: 5
SALES (est): 228.4K **Privately Held**
SIC: 1389 3569 1382 Construction, repair & dismantling services; gas producers, generators & other gas related equipment; oil & gas exploration services

(G-5544)
MILESTONE EDUCATION LLC
220 S Orange Ave (07039-5804)
PHONE..................................973 535-2717
EMP: 4 EST: 2013
SALES (est): 182.2K
SALES (corp-wide): 2.7MM **Privately Held**
SIC: 3843 Dental equipment & supplies
PA: Shenzhen Superline Technology Co.,Ltd
 Room B-314, Century Holidays Plaza,9030 Shennan Ave, Nanshan
 Shenzhen 51805
 755 267-5628

(G-5545)
MILESTONE SCIENTIFIC INC (PA)
220 S Orange Ave Ste 102 (07039-5800)
PHONE..................................973 535-2717
Fax: 973 535-2829
Leonard A Osser, *CEO*
Leslie Bernhard, *Ch of Bd*
Joseph D'Agostino, *COO*
Eugene Casagrande, *Director*
Mark Hochman, *Director*
▲ EMP: 17 EST: 1989
SQ FT: 7,625
SALES: 11.2MM **Publicly Held**
WEB: www.milesci.com
SIC: 3843 Dental equipment & supplies; dental equipment; dental hand instruments; dental laboratory equipment

(G-5546)
MIND-ALLIANCE SYSTEMS LLC
21 Herbert Ter (07039-4803)
PHONE..................................212 920-1911
David Kamien, *Mng Member*
Jf Cloutier, *CTO*
EMP: 7
SALES (est): 433.1K **Privately Held**
SIC: 7372 8741 7379 Prepackaged software; business management; computer related consulting services

(G-5547)
MOBLTY INC
651 W Mount Pleasant Ave # 270 (07039-1642)
PHONE..................................973 535-3600
Rajesh Saggi, *CEO*
EMP: 20
SQ FT: 8,000
SALES: 1MM **Privately Held**
SIC: 7372 Business oriented computer software

(G-5548)
MORRIS PLAINS PIP INC
Also Called: PIP Printing
465 W Mount Pleasant Ave (07039-1720)
PHONE..................................973 533-9330
Steven Solotoss, *President*
Sandra Colyer, *Corp Secy*
EMP: 8
SQ FT: 1,800
SALES (est): 866.5K **Privately Held**
SIC: 2752 2791 2789 Commercial printing, offset; typesetting; bookbinding & related work

(G-5549)
NAN YA PLASTICS CORP AMERICA (PA)
9 Peach Tree Hill Rd (07039-5702)
P.O. Box 478 (07039-0478)
PHONE..................................973 992-1775
Fax: 973 716-7470
Chia-Chau Wu, *President*
William Wong, *Chairman*
David Lin, *Treasurer*
George Chang, *Controller*
Max Ll, *Accounts Mgr*
◆ EMP: 20
SQ FT: 5,000
SALES: 973.8MM **Privately Held**
WEB: www.npcam.com
SIC: 2824 2869 3083 Polyester fibers; ethylene glycols; laminated plastics plate & sheet

(G-5550)
NAN YA PLASTICS CORP USA (HQ)
9 Peach Tree Hill Rd (07039-5702)
P.O. Box 478 (07039-0478)
PHONE..................................973 992-1775
William Wong, *Ch of Bd*
Chia-Chau Wu, *President*
David Lin, *Treasurer*
Kevin Tsay, *Controller*
Norman Lee, *Accounting Mgr*
▲ EMP: 20
SQ FT: 5,000
SALES: 116.7MM
SALES (corp-wide): 10.1B **Privately Held**
WEB: www.npcusa.com
SIC: 3081 Vinyl film & sheet
PA: Nan Ya Plastics Corporation
 201, Dunhua N. Rd.,
 Taipei City TAP 10508
 227 122-211

(G-5551)
NANION TECHNOLOGIES INC
1 Naylon Pl Ste 3 (07039-1041)
PHONE..................................973 369-7960
Niels Fertig, *CEO*
Professor Jan Behrends, *Ch of Bd*
Rodolfo Haedo, *Senior VP*
Sonja Stlzle-Feix, *Director*
EMP: 8
SALES (est): 474.3K **Privately Held**
SIC: 3825 Instruments to measure electricity

(G-5552)
NIAFLEX CORPORATION
9 Peach Tree Hill Rd (07039-5702)
PHONE..................................407 851-6620
Jo Chen, *President*
James Smell, *Vice Pres*
EMP: 10 EST: 2010
SALES (est): 1.4MM **Privately Held**
SIC: 3081 Unsupported plastics film & sheet

(G-5553)
P D SALCO INC
61 Shrewsbury Dr (07039-3401)
PHONE..................................973 716-0517
Jeffrey Namer, *President*
Brandi Namer, *Vice Pres*
EMP: 11
SALES (est): 579.3K **Privately Held**
SIC: 2721 5192 Periodicals; books, periodicals & newspapers

(G-5554)
PENTA INTERNATIONAL CORP
Also Called: Penta Manufacturing Company
50 Okner Pkwy (07039-1604)
P.O. Box 1448, Caldwell (07007-1448)
PHONE..................................973 740-2300
Fax: 973 740-1839
Grace M Volpe, *President*
George Volpe Sr, *Senior VP*
Christine Tavares, *Vice Pres*
◆ EMP: 75
SQ FT: 100,000
SALES (est): 15.9MM **Privately Held**
WEB: www.pentamfg.com
SIC: 2087 Extracts, flavoring

(G-5555)
PET DEVICES LLC
184 S Livingston Ave (07039-3014)
PHONE..................................929 244-0012
Dimitri Vorona, *Mng Member*
EMP: 4
SQ FT: 1,000
SALES: 1MM **Privately Held**
SIC: 2048 Feed supplements

(G-5556)
PLASTPRO 2000 INC
Also Called: Plastpro Doors
9 Peach Tree Hill Rd (07039-5702)
PHONE..................................973 992-2090
Walter Wang, *Branch Mgr*
EMP: 6 **Privately Held**
WEB: www.plastproinc.com
SIC: 3089 Plastic hardware & building products
PA: Plastpro 2000, Inc.
 5200 W Century Blvd Fl 9
 Los Angeles CA 90045

(G-5557)
RECOMBINE LLC
3 Regent St Ste 301 (07039-1638)
PHONE..................................646 470-7422
Alicia Pagano, *Sales Mgr*
Alexander Bisignano,
Kelly Ketterson,
Santiago Munne,
Stephany Foster, *Associate*
▲ EMP: 6 EST: 2011
SQ FT: 4,000
SALES (est): 300K **Privately Held**
SIC: 2835 In vitro diagnostics

(G-5558)
ROSEVILLE TOOL & MANUFACTURING
22 Okner Pkwy (07039-1604)
PHONE..................................973 992-5405
Gideon Schuftan, *President*
Louise Schuftan, *Corp Secy*
EMP: 25 EST: 1945
SQ FT: 13,000
SALES (est): 4.1MM **Privately Held**
SIC: 3469 3544 Stamping metal for the trade; special dies, tools, jigs & fixtures

(G-5559)
SELDOM SEEN DESIGNS LLC
6215 Town Center Way (07039-2986)
PHONE..................................973 535-8805
Len Braunstein, *Mng Member*
▲ EMP: 5

SALES (est): 727.2K **Privately Held**
SIC: 2273 5023 Carpets & rugs; rugs

(G-5560)
SERVICES EQUIPMENT COM LLC
4 Tamarack Dr (07039-1115)
P.O. Box 2032 (07039-7632)
PHONE..................973 992-4404
Harvey Kahn, *Partner*
EMP: 4
SALES (est): 220.7K **Privately Held**
SIC: 3999 5131 Military insignia; flags & banners

(G-5561)
SHARKK LLC
70 S Orange Ave Ste 105 (07039-4916)
PHONE..................302 377-3974
Dov Brafman, *CEO*
Isaac Rubinstein, *CTO*
Dovi Vogel, *Director*
EMP: 11 EST: 2011
SALES (est): 90.3K **Privately Held**
SIC: 3651 Speaker systems

(G-5562)
SIGNAL SIGN COMPANY LLC
105 Dorsa Ave (07039-1002)
PHONE..................973 535-9277
Fax: 973 535-9276
Peggy Johnson, *Plant Mgr*
Bruce J Fish,
EMP: 12 EST: 1956
SQ FT: 15,000
SALES: 2.2MM **Privately Held**
WEB: www.signalsign.com
SIC: 3993 Electric signs; neon signs; letters for signs, metal

(G-5563)
SPARE PAIR VISION CENTER LLC
184 S Lvingston Ave Ste 8 (07039-3013)
PHONE..................973 758-1151
Micheal Isenburge, *Partner*
EMP: 4
SALES (est): 280K **Privately Held**
SIC: 3841 Eye examining instruments & apparatus

(G-5564)
STEVEN MADDEN LTD
112 Eisenhower Pkwy (07039-4995)
PHONE..................973 533-0121
EMP: 75 **Publicly Held**
SIC: 3143 Men's footwear, except athletic
PA: Steven Madden, Ltd.
5216 Barnett Ave
Long Island City NY 11104

(G-5565)
STRIVR INC
20 Downing Pl (07039-3613)
PHONE..................973 216-7379
Zachary Gray, *President*
Michael Manuccia, *COO*
Brian Murphy, *Vice Pres*
Jeannette Francia, *Marketing Mgr*
Mike Colucci, *Manager*
EMP: 4
SALES (est): 214.1K **Privately Held**
SIC: 7372 7389 Application computer software;

(G-5566)
TRINITY PLASTICS INC (DH)
9 Peach Tree Hill Rd (07039-5702)
PHONE..................973 994-8018
Joe Chen, *President*
▲ EMP: 135 EST: 2013
SALES (est): 98.5MM **Privately Held**
SIC: 2673 3081 Bags: plastic, laminated & coated; unsupported plastics film & sheet

(G-5567)
UTILITY DEVELOPMENT CORP
112 Naylon Ave (07039-1006)
PHONE..................973 994-4334
Harry S Katz, *President*
Dr Radha Agarwal, *Vice Pres*
Toby Katz, *Shareholder*
EMP: 6
SQ FT: 5,000

SALES (est): 1MM **Privately Held**
SIC: 3086 8742 Packaging & shipping materials, foamed plastic; business consultant

(G-5568)
VANCO MILLWORK INC
18 Microlab Rd (07039-1639)
PHONE..................973 992-3061
Fax: 973 992-3253
Lyn F Vanadia, *President*
Steven Vanadia, *Vice Pres*
EMP: 12
SALES (est): 1.9MM **Privately Held**
WEB: www.vancoconstruction.com
SIC: 5211 2431 Millwork & lumber; millwork

(G-5569)
VANGUARD PACKAGING CORP
15 Stratford Dr (07039-5115)
PHONE..................973 391-9200
Michael Wische, *President*
EMP: 5 EST: 1996
SALES (est): 741.3K **Privately Held**
WEB: www.vanguardpkg.net
SIC: 2631 Packaging board

(G-5570)
VERSATILE DISTRIBUTORS INC
Also Called: American Jewel Window Systems
293 Eisenhower Pkwy # 100 (07039-1711)
PHONE..................973 773-0550
Fax: 973 473-1788
Joel Cuccio, *CEO*
Todd Cuccio, *Plant Mgr*
EMP: 55 EST: 1946
SQ FT: 42,000
SALES (est): 9.4MM **Privately Held**
WEB: www.grovehomeproducts.com
SIC: 3089 Window frames & sash, plastic

(G-5571)
WEST ESSEX TRIBUNE INC
495 S Livingston Ave (07039-4327)
P.O. Box 65 (07039-0065)
PHONE..................973 992-1771
Fax: 973 992-7015
Jennifer Cheiuk, *President*
Ellen Haerte, *Corp Secy*
EMP: 10 EST: 1929
SQ FT: 2,000
SALES (est): 580K **Privately Held**
SIC: 2711 Newspapers: publishing only, not printed on site

(G-5572)
WIRE FABRICATORS & INSULATORS
20 Harding Pl (07039-1804)
PHONE..................973 768-2839
Frank Basile, *President*
Tom Palmisano, *Manager*
EMP: 25 EST: 1963
SQ FT: 34,000
SALES: 952K **Privately Held**
SIC: 3357 3315 3496 Coaxial cable, non-ferrous; cable, steel: insulated or armored; miscellaneous fabricated wire products

---
Lodi
Bergen County

(G-5573)
AERONAUTICAL INSTR & RDO CO (PA)
234 Garibaldi Ave (07644-2506)
P.O. Box 340 (07644-0340)
PHONE..................973 473-0034
Fax: 973 473-8748
Wilfred Burke, *President*
Mario Lousada, *Controller*
Cyril Burke, *Manager*
Anne Burke, *Admin Sec*
EMP: 32
SQ FT: 10,000
SALES (est): 6.3MM **Privately Held**
SIC: 3812 3825 Radio magnetic instrumentation; test equipment for electronic & electrical circuits

(G-5574)
ALBA TRANSLATIONS CPA
436 Main St (07644-1856)
PHONE..................973 340-1130
Alba Translations, *Principal*
EMP: 8
SALES (est): 88.7K **Privately Held**
SIC: 7692 Welding repair

(G-5575)
ALL STATE MEDAL CO INC
Also Called: Hock & Mandel
16 Adams Pl (07644-2928)
PHONE..................973 458-1458
Fax: 973 458-1678
Richard J Micucci Sr, *President*
Richard J Micucci Jr, *Vice Pres*
EMP: 6
SALES (est): 490K **Privately Held**
SIC: 3499 5999 3911 Trophies, metal, except silver; trophies & plaques; jewelry, precious metal

(G-5576)
AMERIFAB CORP
196 Garibaldi Ave Ste 1 (07644-2506)
PHONE..................973 777-2120
Fax: 973 777-9242
Tom Castell, *President*
EMP: 6
SQ FT: 4,000
SALES (est): 1MM **Privately Held**
SIC: 3444 Sheet metalwork

(G-5577)
BLUTEK POWER INC
300 1 State Rte 17 Ste B2 (07644)
PHONE..................973 594-1800
Fax: 973 594-1804
Angelo Lopresti, *President*
▲ EMP: 10
SALES (est): 1.5MM **Privately Held**
WEB: www.blutekpower.com
SIC: 3621 Motors & generators

(G-5578)
BRIM ELECTRONICS INC
120 Home Pl (07644-1514)
PHONE..................201 796-2886
Fax: 973 778-2792
Barry Danziger, *President*
EMP: 15
SQ FT: 5,000
SALES: 1MM **Privately Held**
WEB: www.brimelectronics.com
SIC: 3357 3678 3643 3429 Nonferrous wiredrawing & insulating; electronic connectors; current-carrying wiring devices; manufactured hardware (general)

(G-5579)
CHARLES DELUCA
Also Called: Associated Marble Co
239 Garibaldi Ave (07644-2505)
PHONE..................973 778-5621
Fax: 973 778-7853
Charles Deluca, *Owner*
Charles De Luca Jr, *Manager*
EMP: 6
SQ FT: 4,600
SALES (est): 480K **Privately Held**
SIC: 3281 Cut stone & stone products; marble, building: cut & shaped

(G-5580)
CRONOS-PRIM COLORADO LLC
Also Called: Cronos Design
300-2 State Rt 17 S (07644-3822)
P.O. Box 221762, Denver CO (80222-1020)
PHONE..................303 369-7477
Gary Yurkovetskiy,
EMP: 5
SQ FT: 1,500
SALES (est): 262.6K **Privately Held**
SIC: 7389 2541 Interior design services; cabinets, lockers & shelving

(G-5581)
DINA HERNANDEZ
Also Called: Orlando's Italian Bakery
236 Harrison Ave Ste A (07644-1051)
PHONE..................973 772-8883
Dina Hernandez, *Partner*
EMP: 7
SQ FT: 6,000

SALES (est): 410K **Privately Held**
SIC: 2051 5461 Breads, rolls & buns; bakeries

(G-5582)
DO PRODUCTIONS LLC
11 Gregg St (07644-2704)
PHONE..................856 866-3566
Christian Von Twinkle,
EMP: 80
SALES (est): 12.1MM
SALES (corp-wide): 12.4B **Privately Held**
SIC: 2038 Frozen specialties
HQ: Dr. Oetker Gmbh
Lutterstr. 14
Bielefeld 33617
521 155-0

(G-5583)
DUX PAINT LLC
18 Mill St (07644-2604)
PHONE..................973 473-2376
Howard Goldstein, *President*
EMP: 10
SALES (est): 1.4MM **Privately Held**
SIC: 2851 1721 7532 Paints & paint additives; exterior residential painting contractor; truck painting & lettering

(G-5584)
FEDERAL EQUIPMENT & MFG CO INC
Also Called: Femco
194 Westervelt Pl (07644-1100)
PHONE..................973 340-7600
Fax: 973 340-9575
Joan Giani, *President*
Douglas Howard, *Vice Pres*
EMP: 7
SQ FT: 3,400
SALES (est): 4.4MM **Privately Held**
SIC: 5085 2676 Industrial supplies; towels, napkins & tissue paper products

(G-5585)
H K METAL CRAFT MFG CORP
35 Industrial Rd (07644-2607)
PHONE..................973 471-7770
Fax: 201 471-9666
Raymond Hopp, *President*
Nancy Hopp, *Corp Secy*
Robert Osborn, *COO*
▲ EMP: 38 EST: 1927
SQ FT: 58,000
SALES (est): 8.9MM **Privately Held**
WEB: www.hkmetalcraft.com
SIC: 3469 3452 3053 Stamping metal for the trade; washers, metal; gaskets & sealing devices

(G-5586)
HAWTHORNE PAINT COMPANY INC
18 Mill St (07644-2604)
P.O. Box 157, Hawthorne (07507-0157)
PHONE..................973 423-2335
Fax: 973 423-9363
Murray Greene, *CEO*
EMP: 9
SQ FT: 15,000
SALES (est): 1.9MM **Privately Held**
WEB: www.hawthornepaints.com
SIC: 2851 5231 Paints & paint additives; paint & painting supplies

(G-5587)
HOOD PRODUCTS LLC
18 Mill St (07644-2604)
PHONE..................201 426-0700
Howard Goldstein,
Donna Kruegel, *Admin Asst*
EMP: 9
SQ FT: 12,126
SALES (est): 405.6K **Privately Held**
SIC: 2851 Lacquers, varnishes, enamels & other coatings; paint removers; putty, wood fillers & sealers; varnish removers

(G-5588)
HOUSE PEARL FASHIONS (US) LTD (HQ)
300-2 D&E Rr 17 (07644)
PHONE..................973 778-7551
Mehesh Seth, *President*
Paritosh Nath, *COO*

Sanjay Kapoor, *CFO*
▼ **EMP:** 15
SQ FT: 22,000
SALES: 15.5MM
SALES (corp-wide): 116.8MM **Privately Held**
SIC: 2329 2339 Coats (oiled fabric, leatherette, etc.): men's & boys'; women's & misses' outerwear; women's & misses' accessories
PA: Pearl Global Industries Limited
Pearl Tower, Plot No. 51, Sector 32
Gurgaon HR 12200
124 465-1000

(G-5589)
INTERPLAST UNIVERSAL INDS
199 Garibaldi Ave (07644-2505)
P.O. Box 40 (07644-0040)
PHONE...................................973 471-4100
H R Gulati, *President*
EMP: 50 **EST:** 1936
SQ FT: 75,000
SALES (est): 3.2MM **Privately Held**
SIC: 2295 Resin or plastic coated fabrics

(G-5590)
J D M ASSOCIATES INC
127 Kipp Ave (07644-3037)
PHONE...................................973 773-8699
Fax: 973 773-6488
Joseph Mastropaolo, *President*
Dorothy Mastropaolo, *Vice Pres*
EMP: 8
SALES (est): 811.6K **Privately Held**
SIC: 7336 2752 7313 2741 Art design services; promotional printing, lithographic; printed media advertising representatives; miscellaneous publishing

(G-5591)
LABEL MASTER INC
89 Dell Glen Ave (07644-1707)
PHONE...................................973 546-3110
Robert Mazzella, *President*
EMP: 9 **EST:** 1978
SQ FT: 6,500
SALES (est): 1MM **Privately Held**
WEB: www.labelmaster.net
SIC: 2754 2672 Labels: gravure printing; tape, pressure sensitive: made from purchased materials

(G-5592)
LOBSTER LIFE SYSTEMS INC
10 Dell Glen Ave Ste 5a (07644-1759)
P.O. Box 839, Saddle Brook (07663-0839)
PHONE...................................201 398-0303
Thomas Olsen, *President*
EMP: 11 **EST:** 1987
SALES (est): 1.7MM **Privately Held**
WEB: www.lobsterlife.com
SIC: 3443 Water tanks, metal plate

(G-5593)
LODI CML COOPERATIVE LLC
170 Gregg St Ste 5 (07644-2620)
PHONE...................................201 820-2380
Wael Kioumji, *Principal*
EMP: 8
SALES (est): 987K **Privately Held**
SIC: 2051 Doughnuts, except frozen

(G-5594)
MARCO BOOK CO INC
Also Called: Everbind Marco
60 Industrial Rd (07644-2608)
P.O. Box 695 (07644-0695)
PHONE...................................973 458-0485
Stewart Penn, *CEO*
EMP: 50 **EST:** 1954
SQ FT: 52,000
SALES (est): 24.5MM **Privately Held**
SIC: 5192 2789 Books; bookbinding & related work

(G-5595)
MCCAIN ELLIOS FOODS INC
11 Gregg St (07644-2704)
PHONE...................................201 368-0600
Fax: 201 368-8771
Tim Driscoll, *President*
Van S Chaayk, *President*
Mark Bohen, *Vice Pres*
H McCain, *Vice Pres*
Peter Reijula, *Vice Pres*

EMP: 160
SQ FT: 150,000
SALES (est): 17.7MM
SALES (corp-wide): 3.7B **Privately Held**
SIC: 2038 Pizza, frozen
HQ: Mccain Usa, Inc.
1 Tower Ln Ste Uppr
Oakbrook Terrace IL 60181

(G-5596)
MINT PRINTING LLC
475 Westminster Pl (07644-1234)
PHONE...................................973 546-2060
Thomas Davis,
Nick Tarthelia,
EMP: 4 **EST:** 1993
SALES (est): 978.3K **Privately Held**
SIC: 2752 Commercial printing, lithographic

(G-5597)
PRECIOUS COSMETICS PACKAGING
40 Meta Ln (07644-3807)
PHONE...................................973 478-4633
Fax: 201 478-4670
Sam Mikhail, *President*
Sanaa Mikhail, *Vice Pres*
Michael Mikhail, *Prdtn Mgr*
James Mikhail, *Research*
Kathy Digirolamo, *Office Mgr*
▲ **EMP:** 14
SALES (est): 1.3MM **Privately Held**
SIC: 2844 5122 Cosmetic preparations; cosmetics

(G-5598)
RHINGO PRO LLC
32 Us Highway 46 E (07644-1309)
PHONE...................................201 728-9099
Kevin Jung,
EMP: 4
SALES (est): 200.7K **Privately Held**
SIC: 3641 Electric lamps & parts for generalized applications; electric light bulbs, complete; tubes, electric light

(G-5599)
SANTANGELO PRINTING CO INC
Also Called: H & S Graphics
196 Garibaldi Ave (07644-2506)
PHONE...................................973 779-5880
Fax: 973 779-5859
Thomas Santangelo, *President*
John A Santangelo, *Exec VP*
Michael Santangelo, *Plant Mgr*
Stephan Sylvester, *Graphic Designe*
EMP: 10
SQ FT: 13,000
SALES (est): 2.8MM **Privately Held**
WEB: www.h-sgraphics.com
SIC: 2752 2759 Commercial printing, offset; letterpress printing

(G-5600)
SILVERSTONE WIRELESS LLC (PA)
6 9 Park Pl (07644)
PHONE...................................845 458-5197
Jay Friedman, *CEO*
Joel Friedman,
▲ **EMP:** 8
SQ FT: 3,000
SALES (est): 8MM **Privately Held**
SIC: 3679 5271 Electronic circuits; mobile homes

(G-5601)
STAR BINDING & TRIMMING LLC
80 Industrial Rd (07644-2608)
PHONE...................................201 864-2220
Fax: 201 864-1051
Michael Friedman, *Owner*
Rebecca Holloway, *Technology*
◆ **EMP:** 35 **EST:** 1914
SQ FT: 35,500
SALES (est): 3.7MM **Privately Held**
WEB: www.starnj.com
SIC: 2241 2396 2221 Bindings, textile; labels, woven; trimming, fabric; broadwoven fabric mills, manmade

(G-5602)
STAR NARROW FABRICS INC
Also Called: Star Group, The
80a Industrial Rd (07644-2619)
PHONE...................................973 778-8600
Michael Freidman, *President*
Marc Abeles, *Vice Pres*
Marc Rosenstrauch, *Vice Pres*
Carolina Risso, *Accounts Exec*
▲ **EMP:** 6
SQ FT: 26,600
SALES (est): 722.5K **Privately Held**
SIC: 2759 2269 7336 2282 Labels & seals: printing; labels, cotton: printed; commercial art & graphic design; throwing & winding mills

(G-5603)
SUBURBAN AUTO SEAT CO INC (PA)
35 Industrial Rd (07644-2607)
PHONE...................................973 778-9227
Robert G Winfield, *President*
Jane Lee Winfield, *Admin Sec*
▼ **EMP:** 13
SQ FT: 3,000
SALES (est): 1.7MM **Privately Held**
WEB: www.suburbanseats.com
SIC: 2531 5013 7532 Vehicle furniture; seats, automobile; truck parts & accessories; automotive supplies & parts; interior repair services; upholstery & trim shop, automotive

(G-5604)
SUFFERN PLATING CORP
210 Garibaldi Ave (07644-2506)
P.O. Box 755 (07644-0755)
PHONE...................................973 473-4404
Fax: 973 473-6802
Philip Landau, *President*
David French, *CFO*
EMP: 42 **EST:** 1949
SQ FT: 25,000
SALES (est): 6.1MM **Privately Held**
SIC: 3471 Electroplating of metals or formed products

(G-5605)
SYNTHETIC GRASS SURFACES INC
Also Called: Synthetic Grass Surfaces NJ
6 Robert Ct (07644-3504)
PHONE...................................973 778-9594
Robert McLaren, *President*
EMP: 4
SALES: 15K **Privately Held**
SIC: 3999 Grasses, artificial & preserved

(G-5606)
TONY JONES APPAREL INC
Also Called: Clench
300-1 State Rt 17 S 1c (07644-3821)
PHONE...................................973 773-6200
John Yi, *President*
▲ **EMP:** 6
SALES: 5.4MM **Privately Held**
SIC: 2329 5136 Men's & boys' sportswear & athletic clothing; men's & boys' outerwear

(G-5607)
UVITEC PRINTING INK CO INC
14 Mill St (07644-2604)
PHONE...................................973 778-0737
Fax: 973 778-5981
George Dakos, *Ch of Bd*
Andrew Dakos, *President*
EMP: 20
SQ FT: 12,000
SALES (est): 4.1MM **Privately Held**
WEB: www.uvitec.com
SIC: 2893 2851 2821 Printing ink; coating, air curing; plastics materials & resins

(G-5608)
VITAMIA PASTA BOY INC
Also Called: Vitamia & Sons
206 Harrison Ave Ste 214 (07644-1013)
PHONE...................................973 546-1140
Fax: 973 546-3882
Anthony Vitamia, *President*
Maria Vitamia, *Vice Pres*
Joseph Vitamia, *Treasurer*
Paul Vitamia, *Admin Sec*

▲ **EMP:** 10
SQ FT: 2,500
SALES (est): 1MM **Privately Held**
SIC: 2026 2098 2099 5451 Pot cheese; macaroni & spaghetti; pasta, uncooked: packaged with other ingredients; cheese; bakery: wholesale or wholesale/retail combined; pickles, sauces & salad dressings

(G-5609)
WOOD & LAMINATES INC
102 Us Highway 46 E (07644-3608)
PHONE...................................973 773-7475
Fax: 973 773-8344
Gabriel Salazar, *President*
Julio Botero, *Manager*
Olga Botero, *Bd of Directors*
▲ **EMP:** 7
SQ FT: 5,000
SALES (est): 1MM **Privately Held**
WEB: www.wlbars.com
SIC: 1751 3083 Cabinet building & installation; laminated plastics plate & sheet

---

Logan Township
Gloucester County

(G-5610)
ADVANCED DRAINAGE SYSTEMS INC
Also Called: ADS
300 Progress Ct (08085-4539)
PHONE...................................856 467-4779
Bruce Schlichter, *Manager*
EMP: 60
SALES (corp-wide): 1.3B **Publicly Held**
WEB: www.ads-pipe.com
SIC: 3084 Plastics pipe
PA: Advanced Drainage Systems, Inc.
4640 Trueman Blvd
Hilliard OH 43026
614 658-0050

(G-5611)
ARYSTA LLC
Also Called: Arysta/ Labrea Bakery
11 Technology Dr (08085-1761)
PHONE...................................856 417-8100
Tom Bent, *General Mgr*
EMP: 7 **EST:** 2012
SALES (est): 928.8K **Privately Held**
SIC: 2052 Bakery products, dry

(G-5612)
CUSTOM BUILDING PRODUCTS INC
2115 High Hill Rd (08085-4529)
PHONE...................................856 467-9226
Sharon Dahllof, *Purch Agent*
Dianna Lavender, *Human Res Mgr*
David Debear, *Sales Executive*
Steven Sabatino, *Manager*
EMP: 60 **Privately Held**
WEB: www.custombuildingproducts.com
SIC: 2891 Adhesives & sealants
HQ: Custom Building Products, Inc.
7711 Center Ave Ste 500
Huntington Beach CA 92647
800 272-8786

(G-5613)
ENGINRED ARRSTING SYSTEMS CORP
Also Called: Engineered Mtl Arresting Sys
2239 High Hill Rd (08085-4531)
PHONE...................................856 241-8620
Fax: 856 241-8621
John Matish, *Maint Spvr*
Kevin Keller, *Buyer*
Kevin Quan, *Engineer*
Trip Thomas, *Engineer*
Hong Zou, *Engineer*
EMP: 26
SALES (corp-wide): 650.9MM **Privately Held**
SIC: 3728 Aircraft landing assemblies & brakes
HQ: Engineered Arresting Systems Corporation
2550 Market St
Upper Chichester PA 19014
610 494-8000

(G-5614)
INFINITY COMPOUNDING LLC
Also Called: Infinity Ltl Engnred Compounds
2079 Center Square Rd (08085-1790)
PHONE..................................856 467-3030
Fax: 856 467-3033
Carlos Carreno, *President*
Alicia McCready, *Cert Phar Tech*
Dave Vautour, *Manager*
▲ EMP: 40
SQ FT: 57,000
SALES: 15MM
SALES (corp-wide): 228.8MM **Privately Held**
WEB: www.infinitycompounding.com
SIC: 2821 Molding compounds, plastics
PA: Americhem, Inc.
2000 Americhem Way
Cuyahoga Falls OH 44221
330 929-4213

(G-5615)
UPTOWN BAKERIES
Also Called: Uptown Bagels
300 Eagle Ct (08085-1847)
PHONE..................................856 467-9552
Alfred Neuhauser, *Owner*
EMP: 150
SALES (est): 13MM **Privately Held**
SIC: 2051 5149 Bagels, fresh or frozen;
bakery products

(G-5616)
VERONI USA INC
1110 Commerce Blvd # 200 (08085-1765)
PHONE..................................609 970-0320
Antonio Corsano, *CEO*
Marco Veroni, *President*
EMP: 28
SQ FT: 50,000
SALES (est): 130.7MM **Privately Held**
SIC: 2011 Cured meats from meat slaughtered on site

Long Beach Township
Ocean County

(G-5617)
MELTDOWN
13302 Long Beach Blvd (08008-2742)
PHONE..................................609 207-0527
Drew Merlo, *Manager*
EMP: 4
SALES (est): 287.8K **Privately Held**
SIC: 2052 Cones, ice cream

(G-5618)
NETX INFORMATION SYSTEMS INC (PA)
76 Auburn Rd (08008-7009)
PHONE..................................609 298-9118
Keith Saltstein, *President*
EMP: 20
SALES (est): 3.8MM **Privately Held**
WEB: www.netxinc.com
SIC: 7371 7372 Computer software development; educational computer software

(G-5619)
ROBEL RECEPTACLES INC
180 Marina Blvd (08008-6146)
PHONE..................................609 882-8065
Robert Bard, *Owner*
EMP: 4
SALES (est): 131.4K **Privately Held**
SIC: 3999 Manufacturing industries

Long Branch
Monmouth County

(G-5620)
ACCUCOLOR LLC (PA)
Also Called: Jamm Litho
185 Broadway (07740-7005)
PHONE..................................732 870-1999
Fax: 732 870-1414
Robert Labella, *President*
EMP: 4
SQ FT: 5,000

SALES (est): 613.9K **Privately Held**
SIC: 2752 Commercial printing, offset

(G-5621)
BRAD GARMAN DESIGNS
30 New Ct (07740-5103)
PHONE..................................732 229-6670
Brad Garman, *Owner*
EMP: 5
SALES (est): 220K **Privately Held**
SIC: 3911 Jewelry mountings & trimmings

(G-5622)
CREATIVE PRODUCTS INC
92 Shrewsbury Dr (07740-7619)
PHONE..................................732 614-9035
Mary Amgers, *President*
Barry Papp, *Vice Pres*
EMP: 52
SALES: 65K **Privately Held**
SIC: 5083 3524 7389 Lawn & garden machinery & equipment; lawn & garden equipment;

(G-5623)
DERMATOLOGY & LASER CENTER PA
279 3rd Ave Ste 603 (07740-6205)
PHONE..................................732 222-8323
Andrea Jude, *Office Mgr*
EMP: 6
SALES (est): 1.7MM **Privately Held**
SIC: 2834 Dermatologicals

(G-5624)
GAMIT FORCE ATHC LTD LBLTY CO
459 Atlantic Ave (07740-6807)
P.O. Box 303, West Long Branch (07764-0303)
PHONE..................................908 675-0733
Barbara Hill, *CEO*
Arlene Smith, *Vice Pres*
EMP: 10
SALES (est): 950K **Privately Held**
SIC: 5091 3949 Athletic goods; sporting & athletic goods

(G-5625)
J & R FOODS INC
309 Morris Ave Ste 5 (07740-6580)
PHONE..................................732 229-4020
Rocco F Raimondi III, *President*
EMP: 10
SQ FT: 2,000
SALES: 1MM **Privately Held**
SIC: 2092 Seafoods, fresh: prepared

(G-5626)
JAMES SMITH (PA)
Also Called: Smitteez Sportswear
375 Broadway (07740-6825)
P.O. Box 274, Keansburg (07734-0274)
PHONE..................................732 229-8273
James Smith, *Owner*
EMP: 4
SALES: 162K **Privately Held**
WEB: www.smitteez.com
SIC: 2396 5699 Screen printing on fabric articles; T-shirts, custom printed

(G-5627)
JERSEY JOB GUIDE INC
422 Morris Ave Ste 5 (07740-6574)
PHONE..................................732 263-9675
Fax: 732 263-0494
Mike Beson, *President*
EMP: 5
SALES (est): 380K **Privately Held**
WEB: www.jerseyjobguide.com
SIC: 2741 Guides: publishing only, not printed on site

(G-5628)
LATINO U S A
Also Called: Latino USA Newspaper
647 Broadway (07740-5442)
PHONE..................................732 870-1475
Gio Simoes, *President*
EMP: 4 EST: 2003
SALES (est): 142.1K **Privately Held**
SIC: 2711 Newspapers

(G-5629)
LINK NEWS
176 Broadway (07740-7006)
P.O. Box 120 (07740-0120)
PHONE..................................732 222-4300
Patty Oneill, *Principal*
EMP: 5
SALES (est): 188.7K **Privately Held**
SIC: 2711 Newspapers

(G-5630)
MONMOUTH RUBBER CORP
Also Called: Monmouth Rubber & Plastics
75 Long Branch Ave (07740-7155)
PHONE..................................732 229-3444
Fax: 732 229-0711
John M Bonforte, *President*
▲ EMP: 48 EST: 1964
SQ FT: 30,000
SALES (est): 9.1MM **Privately Held**
WEB: www.monmouthrubber.com
SIC: 3061 3083 3053 Mechanical rubber goods; laminated plastic sheets; gasket materials

(G-5631)
RPM PRFRMNCE CATINGS GROUP INC (HQ)
280 West Ave (07740-6139)
PHONE..................................888 788-4323
David Reif, *CEO*
Peggy Fynan, *President*
Margaret Fynan, *Exec VP*
Frederick Pfaff, *Vice Pres*
EMP: 15
SALES (est): 7.6MM
SALES (corp-wide): 5.3B **Publicly Held**
SIC: 2851 Coating, air curing
PA: Rpm International Inc.
2628 Pearl Rd
Medina OH 44256
330 273-5090

(G-5632)
SECURED MBL HLTH APPLCTONS INC
29 Long Branch Ave (07740-7121)
PHONE..................................732 997-9609
Joseph P Nardone IV, *President*
EMP: 5
SALES (est): 120.3K **Privately Held**
SIC: 7371 7373 7379 7372 Computer software development & applications; computer systems analysis & design; computer related consulting services; application computer software

(G-5633)
SHORE MICROSYSTEMS INC (PA)
45 Memorial Pkwy (07740-6720)
PHONE..................................732 870-0800
Fax: 732 229-2324
Gordon Elam, *President*
Jiri Hlataey, *Vice Pres*
EMP: 6
SALES (est): 1MM **Privately Held**
SIC: 3661 Telephones & telephone apparatus

Long Valley
Morris County

(G-5634)
ALL SEASONS CONSTRUCTION INC
43 Flocktown Rd (07853-3534)
PHONE..................................908 852-0955
Nina Dorlon, *President*
Kevin B Dorlon, *Vice Pres*
EMP: 4
SALES (est): 464.1K **Privately Held**
SIC: 1521 1799 1542 1389 New construction, single-family houses; building site preparation; commercial & office building, new construction; construction, repair & dismantling services; building construction consultant; snowplowing

(G-5635)
BLUE MARLIN SYSTEMS INC
2 Ranney Rd (07853-3169)
P.O. Box 241, Succasunna (07876-0241)
PHONE..................................973 722-0816
Dan Gupta, *President*
EMP: 55
SALES (est): 2.7MM **Privately Held**
WEB: www.bmsmail.com
SIC: 7372 Prepackaged software

(G-5636)
DIGITAL BINSCOM LLC
59 E Mill Rd Ste 1-103 (07853-6215)
PHONE..................................908 867-7055
Bruce Bender, *President*
EMP: 5 EST: 2008
SALES (est): 540K **Privately Held**
SIC: 3823 3829 Industrial process measurement equipment; measuring & controlling devices

(G-5637)
FRAZIER INDUSTRIAL COMPANY (PA)
91 Fairview Ave (07853-3381)
PHONE..................................908 876-3001
Fax: 908 876-3615
William L Mascharka, *CEO*
Carlos Oliver, *President*
Donald Frazier, *Chairman*
Domenick Iellimo, *Vice Pres*
Peter Acerra, *CFO*
▼ EMP: 110 EST: 1949
SQ FT: 33,000
SALES: 288MM **Privately Held**
WEB: www.ecologic.com
SIC: 3441 2542 Fabricated structural metal; pallet racks: except wood

(G-5638)
GARDEN STATE WOMAN MAG LLC
210 Parker Rd (07853-3055)
PHONE..................................908 879-7143
Judy Chapman, *Mng Member*
EMP: 5
SALES (est): 310K **Privately Held**
WEB: www.gswoman.com
SIC: 2721 Magazines: publishing only, not printed on site

(G-5639)
MILLENNIUM RESEARCH LLC
Also Called: Advanced Formulations
99 W Mill Rd (07853-3465)
PHONE..................................908 867-7646
Fax: 908 769-3234
Sean Campbell,
▲ EMP: 7
SALES (est): 1.3MM **Privately Held**
WEB: www.advancedformulations.com
SIC: 2844 Face creams or lotions

Ltl Egg Hbr
Ocean County

(G-5640)
ATLANTIC COAST WOODWORK INC
160 Country Club Blvd (08087-1832)
PHONE..................................609 294-2478
EMP: 7
SALES: 200K **Privately Held**
SIC: 2521 2599 2542 Mfg Custom Commercial Cabinets

(G-5641)
ATLANTIC FLOORING LLC
121 Middle Holly Ln (08087-2046)
PHONE..................................609 296-7700
Christohper King, *Principal*
EMP: 11
SALES (est): 1.8MM **Privately Held**
SIC: 3069 1771 2426 Flooring, rubber: tile or sheet; flooring contractor; flooring, hardwood

(G-5642)
BETHEL BINDERY
1500 Route 539 (08087-9754)
PHONE..................................609 296-5043

Fax: 609 296-9483
Thomas Giger, *President*
Velma Giger, *Corp Secy*
EMP: 10
SQ FT: 5,000
SALES: 500K **Privately Held**
WEB: www.bethelbindery.com
SIC: 2789 Binding only: books, pamphlets, magazines, etc.

(G-5643)
CUSTOM ALLEY
36 Ship Dr (08087-1520)
PHONE..................................609 294-1875
Allison Brown, *Principal*
EMP: 4 **EST:** 2010
SALES (est): 168.9K **Privately Held**
SIC: 2392 Slip covers & pads

(G-5644)
EAGLE FABRICATION INC
63 Ohio Dr (08087-1025)
PHONE..................................732 739-5300
Fax: 732 739-6978
Philip J De Caro Jr, *President*
Debra Decaro, *Vice Pres*
EMP: 30
SQ FT: 16,000
SALES (est): 4.5MM **Privately Held**
WEB: www.eaglefabrication.com
SIC: 2493 2821 2541 Marbleboard (stone face hard board); plastics materials & resins; wood partitions & fixtures

(G-5645)
MIEMIE DESIGN SERVICES INC
1341 Radio Rd (08087-1036)
PHONE..................................609 857-3688
Winston Chit, *CEO*
EMP: 25
SALES (est): 1.5MM **Privately Held**
SIC: 3599 Industrial machinery

(G-5646)
PINELANDS BREWING LTD LBLTY CO
140 7th Ave Unit 15 (08087-4259)
PHONE..................................609 296-6169
Lucas McCooley, *Mng Member*
Micheal Broderson,
Jason Chapman,
Sean Collin,
EMP: 10
SALES: 337K **Privately Held**
SIC: 2082 Beer (alcoholic beverage)

(G-5647)
REPRO TRONICS INC
348 Golf View Dr (08087-4230)
PHONE..................................201 722-1880
David Skrivanek, *President*
Janice Skrivanek, *Treasurer*
EMP: 5 **EST:** 1981
SQ FT: 1,800
SALES (est): 585K **Privately Held**
WEB: www.repro-tronics.com
SIC: 2752 Commercial printing, offset

(G-5648)
STEPHEN L FEILINGER
Also Called: Marlin Candle Co
655 Route 9 N (08087-3519)
P.O. Box 1068, Tuckerton (08087-5068)
PHONE..................................609 294-1884
Fax: 609 294-2019
Stephen L Feilinger, *Owner*
EMP: 2
SALES: 1MM **Privately Held**
WEB: www.marlincandle.com
SIC: 3999 Candles

Lumberton
Burlington County

(G-5649)
AAA PHARMACEUTICAL (PA)
681 Main St (08048-5013)
PHONE..................................609 288-6060
Fax: 856 423-2808
Shashikant Sheth, *President*
Surbhi Sheth, *Vice Pres*
Tejash Sheth, *Vice Pres*
EMP: 75

SQ FT: 31,000
SALES: 20MM **Privately Held**
WEB: www.aaapharm.com
SIC: 2834 Pharmaceutical preparations

(G-5650)
ABATETECH INC
30 Maple Ave (08048-2918)
P.O. Box 25 (08048-0025)
PHONE..................................609 265-2107
Fax: 609 265-2109
William J White, *President*
Robert Gunst, *Vice Pres*
John Mullarkey, *Vice Pres*
Elizabeth M Odonnell, *Treasurer*
EMP: 20
SQ FT: 6,500
SALES: 6.6MM **Privately Held**
WEB: www.abatetechinc.com
SIC: 1799 2431 8744 Asbestos removal & encapsulation; insulation of pipes & boilers; moldings & baseboards, ornamental & trim;

(G-5651)
BLUE RING STENCILS LLC (PA) ✪
140 Mount Holly By Pass (08048-1114)
PHONE..................................866 763-3873
Fred Cox, *President*
EMP: 25 **EST:** 2017
SALES: 10MM **Privately Held**
SIC: 3953 Marking devices

(G-5652)
BURLINGTON CNTY ENDOSCOPY CTR
140 Mount Holly By Pass # 5 (08048-1114)
PHONE..................................609 267-1555
Elaine Lang, *Administration*
EMP: 40
SALES (est): 4MM **Privately Held**
WEB: www.bcendoscopycenter.com
SIC: 3845 Endoscopic equipment, electromedical

(G-5653)
CCL LABEL INC
Also Called: CCL Label Tubedec
92 Ark Rd (08048-4103)
PHONE..................................856 273-0700
Lisa Robinson, *Purch Mgr*
Karen Houssell, *Buyer*
Ronald Hoffman, *Engineer*
EMP: 28
SALES (corp-wide): 3.7B **Privately Held**
SIC: 2759 Labels & seals: printing
HQ: Ccl Label, Inc.
    161 Worcester Rd Ste 504
    Framingham MA 01701
    508 872-4511

(G-5654)
CELEBRATION (US) INC
681 Main St (08048-5013)
P.O. Box 188, Sunman IN (47041-0188)
PHONE..................................609 261-5200
Fax: 609 265-1493
Tom Kleen, *President*
EMP: 180
SALES (est): 17.5MM
SALES (corp-wide): 3.5B **Privately Held**
SIC: 2796 Platemaking services
HQ: The Occasions Group Inc
    1750 Tower Blvd
    North Mankato MN 56003
    800 296-9029

(G-5655)
CHAMPION FASTENERS INC (PA)
707 Smithville Rd (08048-5302)
PHONE..................................609 267-5222
Fax: 609 267-2745
Robert Santare, *President*
Ronald E Doane, *Chairman*
EMP: 25
SQ FT: 28,000
SALES (est): 4.5MM **Privately Held**
SIC: 3451 5085 Screw machine products; fasteners, industrial: nuts, bolts, screws, etc.

(G-5656)
DISTINCTIVE WOODWORK INC
70 Stacy Haines Rd Ste D (08048-4107)
PHONE..................................609 714-8505
Fax: 609 714-8544
Jim Cherubino, *President*
EMP: 7
SALES: 600K **Privately Held**
SIC: 2499 1751 Decorative wood & woodwork; cabinet & finish carpentry

(G-5657)
EPCOS INC
120 Munt Holly Byp Unit 2 (08048)
PHONE..................................732 603-5941
Joann Melusky, *General Mgr*
EMP: 10
SALES (corp-wide): 11.9B **Privately Held**
SIC: 3679 5065 3546 Electronic crystals; diskettes, computer; power-driven hand-tools; grinders, portable: electric or pneumatic
HQ: Epcos, Inc.
    485a Us Highway 1 S # 200
    Iselin NJ 08830
    732 906-4300

(G-5658)
HEILIND ELECTRONICS INC
Also Called: Heilind Electronics Inc
120 Mount Holly Byp (08048)
PHONE..................................888 881-5420
Fax: 856 722-9425
Scott Jacobs, *President*
Miriam Jacobs, *Treasurer*
Craig Alan Jacobs, *Admin Sec*
▲ **EMP:** 93
SQ FT: 33,000
SALES (est): 45.4MM
SALES (corp-wide): 729.8MM **Privately Held**
WEB: www.5015.com
SIC: 5065 3678 Connectors, electronic; electronic connectors
PA: Heilind Electronics, Inc
    58 Jonspin Rd
    Wilmington MA 01887
    978 657-4870

(G-5659)
HEILIND MIL-AERO LLC (HQ)
Also Called: Interstate Cnncting Components
100c Mount Holly Byp (08048)
P.O. Box 419186, Boston MA (02241-9186)
PHONE..................................856 722-5535
Robert Clapp, *President*
▲ **EMP:** 110 **EST:** 2012
SALES (est): 24.6MM
SALES (corp-wide): 729.8MM **Privately Held**
SIC: 3678 Electronic connectors
PA: Heilind Electronics, Inc
    58 Jonspin Rd
    Wilmington MA 01887
    978 657-4870

(G-5660)
IMPRINTZ CSTM PRINTED GRAPHICS
691 Main St (08048-5013)
PHONE..................................609 386-5673
Leah Arter, *President*
Don Arter, *Vice Pres*
EMP: 8
SQ FT: 5,000
SALES (est): 1MM **Privately Held**
WEB: www.imprintz.net
SIC: 5199 2759 Advertising specialties; screen printing

(G-5661)
NEW JERSEY TECH GROUP LLC
Also Called: 1800iprint
1632 Route 38 (08048-2923)
PHONE..................................609 301-6405
Henry Vasquez,
EMP: 4
SALES (est): 273.9K **Privately Held**
SIC: 2759 Commercial printing

(G-5662)
PROCO INC
Also Called: Glass House, The
15 Queen St (08048-1111)
PHONE..................................609 265-8777
Fax: 609 265-8773

David Prouse, *President*
Ron Glembocki, *Vice Pres*
EMP: 4
SQ FT: 1,200
SALES (est): 380.1K **Privately Held**
SIC: 3231 Novelties, glass: fruit, foliage, flowers, animals, etc.

(G-5663)
RANSOME EQUIPMENT SALES LLC
106 Ark Rd (08048-4104)
PHONE..................................856 797-8100
Percy Ransome, *Principal*
◆ **EMP:** 6
SALES (est): 600.2K **Privately Held**
SIC: 3531 5082 Subgraders (construction equipment); road construction equipment

(G-5664)
TREK CONNECT INC
120 Munt Holly Byp Unit 7 (08048)
PHONE..................................856 608-0901
Fax: 856 608-0902
Craig Jacobs, *President*
Scott Jacobs, *Vice Pres*
EMP: 35
SQ FT: 60,000
SALES (est): 6.4MM **Privately Held**
WEB: www.trekconnect.com
SIC: 3679 Harness assemblies for electronic use: wire or cable

(G-5665)
UNITED STEEL PRODUCTS CO INC
130 Mount Holly By Pass # 5 (08048-1115)
PHONE..................................609 518-9230
Fax: 609 518-9231
Don Sitzer, *Branch Mgr*
EMP: 7
SALES (corp-wide): 242.1B **Publicly Held**
WEB: www.uspconnectors.com
SIC: 3441 Fabricated structural metal
HQ: United Steel Products Company, Inc.
    703 Rogers Dr
    Montgomery MN 56069
    507 364-7333

(G-5666)
VU SOUND INCORPORATED
Also Called: Vu World
1 Cameron Ln (08048-5231)
PHONE..................................215 990-2864
Victor Stott Jr, *President*
▲ **EMP:** 10
SALES: 1.5MM **Privately Held**
SIC: 7812 7372 3822 7389 Audio-visual program production; home entertainment computer software; appliance controls except air-conditioning & refrigeration;

Lyndhurst
Bergen County

(G-5667)
ALPHA INDUSTRIES MGT INC (PA)
Also Called: Sigma Plastics Group, The
Page And Schuyler Ave (07071)
P.O. Box 808 (07071-0808)
PHONE..................................201 933-6000
Alfred Teo, *Ch of Bd*
Daniel Murphy, *General Mgr*
Chuck Magee, *Regional Mgr*
William Lenchinsky, *Vice Pres*
Cheryl Odonnell, *Controller*
▲ **EMP:** 180
SQ FT: 205,000
SALES (est): 1.3B **Privately Held**
WEB: www.sigma-plastics.com
SIC: 2673 Plastic & pliofilm bags

(G-5668)
APEX SAW & TOOL CO INC
595 New York Ave (07071-1506)
P.O. Box 497 (07071-0497)
PHONE..................................201 438-8777
Fax: 201 438-8792
John Ferrie Jr, *President*
EMP: 8
SQ FT: 5,000

SALES (est): 590K **Privately Held**
SIC: 7699 3423 Knife, saw & tool sharpening & repair; hand & edge tools

(G-5669)
ATLANTIC BUSINESS PRODUCTS
230 Clay Ave (07071-3507)
PHONE..............................201 672-0773
Larry Weiss, *President*
Juan Vilchez, *Accounts Exec*
EMP: 4
SALES (est): 336.1K **Privately Held**
SIC: 3579 Office machines

(G-5670)
AXIM CONCRETE TECHNOLOGIES
201 Polito Ave (07071-3601)
PHONE..............................330 966-0444
David Nethercutt, *Vice Pres*
Don Lane, *Vice Pres*
▼ EMP: 62
SQ FT: 20,000
SALES (est): 5.9MM
SALES (corp-wide): 20.3B **Privately Held**
WEB: www.aximconcrete.com
SIC: 2899 Concrete curing & hardening compounds
HQ: Essroc Corp.
3251 Bath Pike
Nazareth PA 18064
610 837-6725

(G-5671)
BARNES & NOBLE BOOKSELLERS INC
Also Called: Barnes & Noble.com
125 Chubb Ave Fl 3 (07071-3504)
PHONE..............................201 272-3635
Diedra Hughes, *Director*
EMP: 30
SALES (corp-wide): 3.6B **Publicly Held**
WEB: www.bnn.com
SIC: 5942 5961 2731 Book stores; catalog & mail-order houses; book publishing
HQ: Barnes & Noble Booksellers, Inc.
1166 Ave Americas
New York NY 10036
212 403-2580

(G-5672)
BUZZBOARD INC
1050 Wall St W Ste 630 (07071-3600)
PHONE..............................201 820-0697
Umesh Tibrewal, *CEO*
Anil Bansal, *Chairman*
Marilyn Sartori, *Opers Staff*
EMP: 15 EST: 2013
SALES (est): 838K **Privately Held**
SIC: 7372 Application computer software

(G-5673)
CAMBRIDGE PAVERS INC
Also Called: Cambridge Pavingstones
1 Jerome Ave (07071-2915)
P.O. Box 157 (07071-0157)
PHONE..............................201 933-5000
Charles H Gamarekian, *President*
Chris Gamarekian, *Vice Pres*
Jack Callahan, *Opers Mgr*
Jim Latona, *Purch Mgr*
Chuck Domencetti, *Sales Mgr*
◆ EMP: 155
SQ FT: 65,000
SALES (est): 22MM **Privately Held**
WEB: www.cambridgepavers.com
SIC: 3281 Paving blocks, cut stone

(G-5674)
CAPITAL COOLING SYSTEMS LLC
1050 Wall St W Ste 202 (07071-3615)
PHONE..............................973 773-8700
Michael Chen,
EMP: 2
SALES: 2MM **Privately Held**
SIC: 3724 Cooling systems, aircraft engine

(G-5675)
CASE IT INC
1050 Valley Brook Ave B (07071-3634)
PHONE..............................800 441-4710
Adam Merzon, *Ch of Bd*
John Bogut, *Principal*

Jeffrey Fine, *VP Prdtn*
Lina Valencia, *Accounts Exec*
Richard Haase, *Creative Dir*
▲ EMP: 40
SQ FT: 35,000
SALES (est): 6.6MM **Privately Held**
WEB: www.caseit.com
SIC: 3965 2621 3952 3089 Zipper; bag paper; pencil holders; cases, plastic

(G-5676)
CCA INDUSTRIES INC
1099 Wall St W Ste 275 (07071-3617)
PHONE..............................201 935-3232
Fax: 201 935-0675
Lance Funston, *Ch of Bd*
Douglas Haas, *President*
Stephen Weiss, *Vice Pres*
Blanca Melendez, *Opers Staff*
Stephen A Heit, *CFO*
EMP: 20
SQ FT: 81,000
SALES: 19.8MM **Privately Held**
WEB: www.ccaindustries.com
SIC: 2844 Cosmetic preparations; shampoos, rinses, conditioners: hair; toothpastes or powders, dentifrices; face creams or lotions

(G-5677)
CHASE MACHINE CO
127 Park Ave (07071-1419)
P.O. Box 148 (07071-0148)
PHONE..............................201 438-2214
Fax: 201 438-8590
Donald La Scola Jr, *President*
EMP: 15
SQ FT: 5,000
SALES (est): 2.2MM **Privately Held**
SIC: 3541 3491 Machine tools, metal cutting type; industrial valves

(G-5678)
COM TEK WRKPLACE SOLUTIONS LLC
Also Called: Drawbase Software
1099 Wall St W Ste 269 (07071-3617)
PHONE..............................973 927-6814
Cynthia Kontos, *Technology*
Evangelos Kontos,
EMP: 16
SQ FT: 2,000
SALES (est): 913.2K **Privately Held**
SIC: 7372 7373 7371 Prepackaged software; computer integrated systems design; custom computer programming services

(G-5679)
ELEGANT DESSERTS INC
275 Warren St (07071-2017)
PHONE..............................201 933-7309
Fax: 201 933-7309
John Mazur, *President*
EMP: 16
SQ FT: 10,000
SALES (est): 2.8MM **Privately Held**
SIC: 2024 Dairy based frozen desserts

(G-5680)
EPSILON PLASTICS INC (HQ)
Also Called: Alpha Industries
Page & Schuyler Ave 8 (07071)
P.O. Box 808 (07071-0808)
PHONE..............................201 933-6000
Mark Teo, *CEO*
Alfred S Teo, *CEO*
John Reier, *CFO*
Donna McGowan, *Human Res Mgr*
Bill Lenchinsky, *Sales Staff*
EMP: 100
SALES (est): 22.4MM **Privately Held**
SIC: 2821 Polyethylene resins

(G-5681)
FABIAN COUTURE GROUP INTL INC
205 Chubb Ave Bldg C (07071-3520)
PHONE..............................800 367-6251
Allan Weiss, *Principal*
Kelly Sherman, *CFO*
Maurice Doran, *Controller*
Mark Harabedian, *Controller*
▲ EMP: 15

SALES (est): 2MM **Privately Held**
SIC: 2311 5136 Tailored suits & formal jackets; shirts, men's & boys'

(G-5682)
FABIAN FORMALS INC
Also Called: First Nighter Formals
205 Chubb Ave Ste 2 (07071-3520)
PHONE..............................201 460-7776
Fax: 201 460-0343
Allan Weiss, *President*
Mark Harabedian, *CFO*
Neil Weiss, *Treasurer*
▲ EMP: 50
SQ FT: 30,000
SALES (est): 6MM **Privately Held**
WEB: www.fabiancouture.com
SIC: 2311 Formal jackets, men's & youths': from purchased materials; tuxedos: made from purchased materials

(G-5683)
FER PLATING INC
Also Called: Imperial Electro-Plating
52 Park Ave (07071-1012)
PHONE..............................201 438-1010
Fax: 201 438-2341
Fred L Engelhardt, *President*
Richard Engelhardt, *Corp Secy*
Edward F Engelhardt, *Vice Pres*
EMP: 27 EST: 1950
SQ FT: 35,000
SALES (est): 3.1MM **Privately Held**
SIC: 3471 Electroplating of metals or formed products

(G-5684)
GRAYTOR PRINTING COMPANY INC
149 Park Ave (07071-1419)
PHONE..............................201 933-0100
Fax: 201 933-2587
Stephen Toron, *President*
Nissim Shenova, *COO*
Anthony De Benedetto, *CFO*
Lisa Gebhardt, *Admin Sec*
Armand S Toron, *Asst Sec*
EMP: 50 EST: 1948
SQ FT: 43,000
SALES: 3.8MM
SALES (corp-wide): 11.9MM **Privately Held**
WEB: www.graytor.com
SIC: 2752 Commercial printing, lithographic
PA: Dolce Brothers Printing, Inc
29 Brook Ave
Maywood NJ 07607
201 843-0400

(G-5685)
LEADER NEWSGROUP LLC
Also Called: Pulse Magazine, The
251 Ridge Rd (07071-1903)
PHONE..............................201 438-6801
Fax: 201 438-9022
Joann Merklinghaus, *Mng Member*
EMP: 21 EST: 1894
SQ FT: 3,000
SALES (est): 1.2MM **Privately Held**
SIC: 2711 Newspapers: publishing only, not printed on site

(G-5686)
LEDONNE LEATHER CO INC
730 5th St (07071-3214)
PHONE..............................201 531-2100
Robert Le Donne, *President*
EMP: 10
SQ FT: 5,000
SALES (est): 1.6MM **Privately Held**
SIC: 5199 3171 3161 Leather, leather goods & furs; women's handbags & purses; luggage

(G-5687)
LONG ISLAND PIPE OF NJ
Also Called: Neill Supply Co
700 Schuyler Ave (07071-2913)
PHONE..............................201 939-1100
Fax: 201 939-6095
Robert Moss, *Principal*
EMP: 32
SALES (est): 8.8MM **Privately Held**
SIC: 3317 Steel pipe & tubes

(G-5688)
M & E PACKAGING CORP
900 Page Ave Fl 2 (07071-2534)
P.O. Box 808 (07071-0808)
PHONE..............................201 635-1381
Arezer Rosborough II, *General Mgr*
◆ EMP: 7
SALES (est): 892.1K **Privately Held**
SIC: 5199 2673 Packaging materials; plastic bags: made from purchased materials

(G-5689)
MAIL DIRECT PAPER COMPANY LLC
515 Vly Brook Ave Ste A (07071-1951)
PHONE..............................201 933-2782
Fax: 201 933-7533
Paul Cimicata,
Michele Cimicata,
EMP: 12
SALES (est): 1.8MM **Privately Held**
SIC: 2396 Fabric printing & stamping

(G-5690)
MARCHIONE INDUSTRIES INC
Also Called: Trylon
136 Park Ave (07071-1420)
PHONE..............................718 317-4900
Ralph Marchione, *President*
Barbara Marchione, *Vice Pres*
EMP: 15
SQ FT: 20,000
SALES (est): 2.2MM **Privately Held**
WEB: www.trylon.com
SIC: 3995 3446 Grave vaults, metal; architectural metalwork

(G-5691)
MEDIEVAL TIMES USA INC
Also Called: Meadowlands Castle
149 Polito Ave (07071-3601)
PHONE..............................201 933-2220
Fax: 201 438-2062
Jose Tejdor, *Manager*
EMP: 250
SALES (corp-wide): 31.5MM **Privately Held**
SIC: 2711 5813 5812 Newspapers; drinking places; eating places
PA: Medieval Times U.S.A., Inc.
6363 N State Highway 161 # 400
Irving TX 75038
214 596-7600

(G-5692)
MEGAS YEEROS LLC
165 Chubb Ave (07071-3503)
PHONE..............................212 777-6342
Nikos Stergiou, *General Mgr*
George Vanis, *Director*
◆ EMP: 20
SALES (est): 9.7MM **Privately Held**
SIC: 5147 2099 3556 Meats & meat products; food preparations; food products machinery

(G-5693)
MENASHA PACKAGING COMPANY LLC
160 Chubb Ave Ste 101 (07071-3526)
PHONE..............................973 893-1300
Fax: 201 287-2511
Gioacchino Uccello, *Facilities Mgr*
Byron Herald, *Accounts Mgr*
EMP: 146
SALES (corp-wide): 1.8B **Privately Held**
SIC: 2653 Display items, corrugated: made from purchased materials
HQ: Menasha Packaging Company, Llc
1645 Bergstrom Rd
Neenah WI 54956
920 751-1000

(G-5694)
MSC MARKETING & TECHNOLOGY
808 Page Ave 8 (07071)
PHONE..............................201 507-9100
Fax: 201 507-0447
Per Nylen, *President*
Bob Nocek, *President*
William Lenchinsky, *Executive*
Thomas Fowles, *Administration*
EMP: 30

SALES (est): 5.8MM **Privately Held**
SIC: 2671 Plastic film, coated or laminated for packaging

(G-5695)
NCS PEARSON INC
1099 Wall St W (07071-3678)
PHONE..............................201 896-1011
Isabella Elliott, *Manager*
EMP: 99
SALES (corp-wide): 5.9B **Privately Held**
SIC: 3577 Optical scanning devices
HQ: Ncs Pearson Inc
5601 Green Valley Dr # 220
Bloomington MN 55437
952 681-3000

(G-5696)
NORTHCOTT SILK USA INC
1099 Wall St W Ste 250 (07071-3605)
PHONE..............................201 672-9600
Fax: 201 672-9675
Brian O'Rourke, *President*
▲ **EMP:** 8
SALES: 10.2MM **Privately Held**
SIC: 2399 Fabricated textile products

(G-5697)
OMEGA PLASTICS CORP (HQ)
Also Called: Sigma Plastics Group
Page & Schuyler Ave Ste 5 (07071)
PHONE..............................201 507-9100
Fax: 201 933-8921
Alfred Teo, *President*
Stanley Band, *Exec VP*
John Reier, *CFO*
Laurie Lightfoot, *Controller*
Robert Levine, *Sales Staff*
▲ **EMP:** 100
SQ FT: 205,000
SALES (est): 73.9MM **Privately Held**
SIC: 2673 Plastic bags: made from purchased materials

(G-5698)
ON DEMAND PRINT GROUP
442 Valley Brook Ave (07071-1925)
PHONE..............................201 636-2270
Allen Jack Fakhouri, *President*
EMP: 6
SQ FT: 6,000
SALES: 1MM **Privately Held**
SIC: 2752 Commercial printing, lithographic

(G-5699)
OPTICS PLASTICS
537 New York Ave (07071-1506)
P.O. Box 375 (07071-0375)
PHONE..............................201 939-3344
Mike Mazzolla, *President*
EMP: 5 EST: 1999
SALES (est): 209.8K **Privately Held**
SIC: 3089 Plastics products

(G-5700)
OTIS GRAPHICS INC
290 Grant Ave (07071-1911)
P.O. Box 116 (07071-0116)
PHONE..............................201 438-7120
Fax: 201 438-5546
Patricia McKnight, *President*
Don Lyst, *Manager*
EMP: 11
SQ FT: 8,200
SALES (est): 1.3MM **Privately Held**
WEB: www.otisgraphics.com
SIC: 2791 2752 Typesetting; commercial printing, offset

(G-5701)
PM SWAPCO INC
Also Called: Select Records
1099 Wall St W Ste 390 (07071-3617)
PHONE..............................201 438-7700
Fredrick Munao, *President*
▲ **EMP:** 10 EST: 1980
SALES (est): 1.1MM **Privately Held**
WEB: www.selectrecords.com
SIC: 3652 Pre-recorded records & tapes

(G-5702)
POPNFOLD PAPERS INC
Also Called: Digital Dimension Three
205 Chubb Ave Fl 2 (07071-3520)
PHONE..............................201 933-2015

Harvey Hirsch, *President*
EMP: 5
SQ FT: 1,500
SALES (est): 490K **Privately Held**
WEB: www.mediaconsultants.net
SIC: 2621 Copy paper

(G-5703)
PRESTIGE INDUSTRIES LLC
1099 Wall St W Ste 353 (07071-3617)
PHONE..............................866 492-2244
EMP: 28
SALES (est): 22.4K **Privately Held**
SIC: 3999 Advertising curtains
PA: Prestige Hospitality Services Llc
2 Wood St
Paterson NJ 07524

(G-5704)
RALPH LAUREN CORPORATION
9 Polito Ave Fl 5 (07071-3406)
PHONE..............................201 531-6000
Stephen Mannello, *President*
Elizabeth Dipietro, *Vice Pres*
Lauren Flusser, *Vice Pres*
Marie Fogel, *Vice Pres*
Dan Holdefehr, *Vice Pres*
EMP: 88
SALES (corp-wide): 6.1B **Publicly Held**
SIC: 2325 2321 2253 5621 Men's & boys' trousers & slacks; men's & boys' furnishings; men's & boys' sports & polo shirts; men's & boys' dress shirts; knit outerwear mills; shirts (outerwear), knit; sweaters & sweater coats, knit; women's clothing stores
PA: Ralph Lauren Corporation
650 Madison Ave Fl C1
New York NY 10022
212 318-7000

(G-5705)
ROLLS OFFSET GROUP INC (PA)
264 Castle Ter (07071-2002)
PHONE..............................201 727-1110
Fax: 201 727-9229
Richard Schlanger, *CEO*
Carl Schlanger, *Vice Pres*
Stewart Avrick, *Shareholder*
Robert Fishbine, *Shareholder*
EMP: 20 EST: 1953
SQ FT: 250,000
SALES (est): 2MM **Privately Held**
WEB: www.rollsoffsetgroup.com
SIC: 2752 Commercial printing, offset

(G-5706)
SCAFA-TORNABENE ART PUBG CO
Also Called: Scafa Modern Art Group, The
165 Chubb Ave Ste 4 (07071-3503)
PHONE..............................201 842-8500
Fax: 201 842-8546
John Bridgewater, *President*
Cyrus Bhote, *CFO*
▲ **EMP:** 25 EST: 1970
SQ FT: 25,000
SALES (est): 4.3MM
SALES (corp-wide): 152.5MM **Privately Held**
WEB: www.theartpublishinggroup.com
SIC: 5199 2741 Art goods; art copy: publishing & printing
PA: Quarto Group Inc(The)
The Old Brewery
London N7 9B
207 700-6700

(G-5707)
SIGMA EXTRUDING CORP (HQ)
Also Called: Sigma Stretch Film
Page & Schuyler Ave (07071)
P.O. Box 808 (07071-0808)
PHONE..............................201 933-5353
Fax: 201 933-6429
Alfred S Teo, *CEO*
Stanley Band, *Vice Pres*
Covarrubias Tamayo, *Plant Mgr*
Kevin Plesa, *Sales Staff*
◆ **EMP:** 80
SQ FT: 38,000
SALES (est): 39.6MM **Privately Held**
WEB: www.sigmaplastics.com
SIC: 2673 Garment bags (plastic film): made from purchased materials

(G-5708)
SIKA CORPORATION (DH)
201 Polito Ave (07071-3601)
P.O. Box 710 (07071-0710)
PHONE..............................201 933-8800
Fax: 201 804-6166
Christoph Ganz, *President*
Patrick O'Byrne, *General Mgr*
John Rivers, *Regional Mgr*
Kurt Anderson, *District Mgr*
Greg Illig, *District Mgr*
◆ **EMP:** 258
SALES: 1B
SALES (corp-wide): 213.5MM **Privately Held**
WEB: www.sikacorp.com
SIC: 2891 2899 2851 2821 Epoxy adhesives; chemical preparations; epoxy coatings; epoxy resins; concrete products
HQ: Sika Ag
Zugerstrasse 50
Baar ZG
584 366-800

(G-5709)
SIKA CORPORATION
875 Valley Brook Ave (07071-1331)
PHONE..............................201 933-8800
Fax: 201 804-1040
Steve Gill, *Principal*
EMP: 157
SALES (corp-wide): 213.5MM **Privately Held**
WEB: www.sikacorp.com
SIC: 2899 2821 2851 2891 Concrete curing & hardening compounds; epoxy resins; epoxy coatings; sealants; epoxy adhesives
HQ: Sika Corporation
201 Polito Ave
Lyndhurst NJ 07071
201 933-8800

(G-5710)
TECHNOVISION INC
10 Stuyvesant Ave Bsmt 7 (07071-1028)
PHONE..............................732 381-0200
Anju Aggarwal, *President*
Dinesh Goel, *Vice Pres*
EMP: 24
SALES: 3MM **Privately Held**
WEB: www.etechnovision.com
SIC: 7372 Application computer software

(G-5711)
TENEYCK INC
700 Schuyler Ave (07071-2913)
PHONE..............................201 939-1100
Brad Moss, *CEO*
Neil Shyman, *Vice Pres*
Tim Nowell, *Sales Staff*
EMP: 70
SQ FT: 56,000
SALES (est): 10.6MM
SALES (corp-wide): 59.6MM **Privately Held**
WEB: www.neillsupply.com
SIC: 3569 5085 Sprinkler systems, fire: automatic; valves & fittings
PA: Long Island Pipe Supply Inc
586 Commercial Ave
Garden City NY 11530
516 222-8008

(G-5712)
VERINT SYSTEMS INC
9 Polito Ave Fl 9 # 9 (07071-3406)
PHONE..............................201 438-1429
William Durr, *Principal*
Aron Dovrat, *VP Sales*
Trang Dam, *Sales Associate*
Israel Targeting, *Branch Mgr*
Alistair Mearns, *Consultant*
EMP: 60 **Publicly Held**
WEB: www.verintsystems.com
SIC: 7373 5045 7372 3577 Systems software development services; computers, peripherals & software; prepackaged software; computer peripheral equipment
PA: Verint Systems Inc.
175 Broadhollow Rd # 100
Melville NY 11747

(G-5713)
WACOAL AMERICA INC (DH)
1 Wacoal Plz (07071-3400)
PHONE..............................201 933-8400
Robert Vitale, *President*
◆ **EMP:** 200 EST: 1952
SQ FT: 131,000
SALES (est): 190.7MM
SALES (corp-wide): 1.8B **Privately Held**
WEB: www.wacoal-america.com
SIC: 2342 2341 Brassieres; panties: women's, misses', children's & infants'; women's & children's nightwear
HQ: Wacoal International Corp
1 Wacoal Plz
Lyndhurst NJ 07071
201 933-8400

(G-5714)
WACOAL INTERNATIONAL CORP (DH)
1 Wacoal Plz (07071-3400)
PHONE..............................201 933-8400
Ken Yamamoto, *President*
Lisa Reid, *Credit Mgr*
Anthony Banasiak, *Finance*
Laura Shifflett, *Sales Staff*
Trish Shapland, *Consultant*
◆ **EMP:** 3
SQ FT: 50,000
SALES (est): 173.9MM
SALES (corp-wide): 1.8B **Privately Held**
SIC: 2341 Women's & children's undergarments
HQ: Wacoal Corp.
29, Nakajimacho, Kisshoin, Minami-Ku
Kyoto KYO 601-8
756 825-111

(G-5715)
YKK (USA) INC
1099 Wall St W Ste 244 (07071-3623)
PHONE..............................201 935-4200
William Langley, *Manager*
Mike Blunt, *Manager*
EMP: 7
SALES (corp-wide): 7B **Privately Held**
SIC: 3965 5131 Fasteners, slide zippers; zippers
HQ: Ykk (U.S.A.), Inc.
1300 Cobb Industrial Dr
Marietta GA 30066
770 427-5521

Madison
Morris County

(G-5716)
ACTAVIS ELIZABETH LLC
5 Giralda Farms (07940-1027)
PHONE..............................973 442-3200
Elizabeth Cooper, *Manager*
Richard Lang, *Manager*
Enzo Smeriglio, *Network Mgr*
Marty Shindler, *Director*
James Bloem, *Bd of Directors*
EMP: 193 **Privately Held**
SIC: 2834 Druggists' preparations (pharmaceuticals)
HQ: Actavis Elizabeth Llc
200 Elmora Ave
Elizabeth NJ 07202
908 527-9100

(G-5717)
ALFRED SPORTS INC
Also Called: Sunset Lettering
30 Main St (07940)
PHONE..............................973 822-8987
Fax: 973 966-1889
David Chiarolanzio, *President*
EMP: 15
SQ FT: 1,000
SALES: 890K **Privately Held**
SIC: 2759 Screen printing

(G-5718)
ALLERGAN INC (HQ)
5 Giralda Farms (07940-1027)
P.O. Box 19534, Irvine CA (92623-9534)
PHONE..............................862 261-7000
A Robert D Bailey, *Ch of Bd*
Charles Hugh-Jones, *Chief Mktg Ofcr*

▲ **EMP:** 1300
SALES (est): 4.6B **Privately Held**
WEB: www.allergan.com
SIC: 2834 3841 Solutions, pharmaceutical; dermatologicals; drugs acting on the central nervous system & sense organs; proprietary drug products; surgical & medical instruments

(G-5719)
AMERICAN MICROSEMICONDUCTOR
133 Kings Rd (07940-2122)
P.O. Box 104 (07940-0104)
PHONE...............................973 377-9566
Fax: 973 377-3078
William F Foley, *President*
Rosemarie Foley, *Corp Secy*
EMP: 45
SALES (est): 10.1MM **Privately Held**
WEB: www.americanmicrosemi.com
SIC: 5065 3674 Semiconductor devices; semiconductors & related devices

(G-5720)
CHATHAM BOOKSELLER INC
8 Green Village Rd (07940-1817)
PHONE...............................973 822-1361
Frank Deodene, *President*
Carolyn Deodene, *Corp Secy*
EMP: 4
SQ FT: 2,000
SALES (est): 300K **Privately Held**
SIC: 5961 5932 2731 Book club, mail order; book stores, secondhand; books: publishing only

(G-5721)
E P HELLER COMPANY
21 Samson Ave 25 (07940-2261)
P.O. Box 26 (07940-0026)
PHONE...............................973 377-2878
Fax: 973 514-1022
Eugene P Heller, *Ch of Bd*
August Daub, *President*
Douglas Heller, *Vice Pres*
Peter Heller, *Vice Pres*
Jeananne Heller, *Treasurer*
EMP: 25
SQ FT: 10,000
SALES (est): 6.3MM **Privately Held**
WEB: www.ephco.com
SIC: 3545 5072 Cutting tools for machine tools; power tools & accessories

(G-5722)
ELLIS INSTRUMENTS INC
21 Cook Ave (07940-1935)
PHONE...............................973 593-9222
Chuck Ellis, *President*
Andy Ellis, *Vice Pres*
EMP: 4
SQ FT: 2,000
SALES (est): 2MM **Privately Held**
WEB: www.ellisinstruments.com
SIC: 5047 3841 Medical equipment & supplies; surgical instruments & apparatus

(G-5723)
GENERAL COMMIS ARCHIVES & HSTR
Also Called: Gcah
36 Madison Ave (07940-1434)
P.O. Box 127 (07940-0127)
PHONE...............................973 408-3189
Mark Shenise, *VP Mktg*
Jay Rollins, *Comms Dir*
Robert Williams, *Admin Sec*
Charles Yrigoyen Jr, *Admin Sec*
EMP: 5
SALES (est): 456.4K **Privately Held**
WEB: www.gcah.org
SIC: 2721 8412 Periodicals; museum

(G-5724)
IMPACT PROTECTIVE EQP LLC
8 Westerly Ave (07940-1606)
PHONE...............................973 377-0903
Fax: 973 263-6125
Mark Monica,
Theodore Monica,
EMP: 8
SALES (est): 680K **Privately Held**
WEB: www.impactpads.com
SIC: 3949 Pads: football, basketball, soccer, lacrosse, etc.

(G-5725)
INTERVET INC
Also Called: Merck Animal Health
2 Giralda Farms (07940-1026)
PHONE...............................908 423-6273
Rick Deluca, *President*
Darren Kong, *Business Mgr*
Richard Spotts, *Opers Mgr*
Stuart Waters, *Production*
Sandy Rogers, *QC Mgr*
EMP: 4 **EST:** 2015
SALES (est): 368.2K
SALES (corp-wide): 40.1B **Publicly Held**
SIC: 2836 Biological products, except diagnostic
PA: Merck & Co., Inc.
2000 Galloping Hill Rd
Kenilworth NJ 07033
908 740-4000

(G-5726)
J HARRIS COMPANY
57 Barnsdale Rd (07940-2807)
PHONE...............................917 731-5080
Scott Goldstone, *President*
EMP: 4
SALES: 1MM **Privately Held**
SIC: 2329 Athletic (warmup, sweat & jogging) suits: men's & boys'

(G-5727)
KRIECK ENTERPRISES LLC
Also Called: Home Care America
125 Park Ave (07940-1122)
PHONE...............................908 789-8600
Richard Kantor, *General Mgr*
Tom Krieck,
Rich Kantor,
▲ **EMP:** 9
SQ FT: 2,500
SALES (est): 1MM **Privately Held**
SIC: 5999 3534 5047 Medical apparatus & supplies; wheelchair lifts; elevators & moving stairways; medical & hospital equipment

(G-5728)
LEO PHARMA INC
7 Giralda Farms Ste 2 (07940-1051)
PHONE...............................973 637-1690
Fax: 973 637-1682
John Koconis, *President*
Christian Antoni, *Senior VP*
Mitch Johnson, *Vice Pres*
Judit H Nyirady, *Vice Pres*
George Padden, *Vice Pres*
▲ **EMP:** 261
SALES (est): 117.8MM
SALES (corp-wide): 1.6B **Privately Held**
SIC: 5122 8731 2834 Pharmaceuticals; biotechnical research, commercial; drugs affecting parasitic & infective diseases
HQ: Leo Pharma A/S
Industriparken 55
Ballerup 2750
449 458-88

(G-5729)
MERCK & CO INC
2 Giralda Farms (07940-1026)
PHONE...............................800 224-5318
Kim Novick, *Associate*
EMP: 38
SALES (corp-wide): 40.1B **Publicly Held**
SIC: 2834 Pharmaceutical preparations
PA: Merck & Co., Inc.
2000 Galloping Hill Rd
Kenilworth NJ 07033
908 740-4000

(G-5730)
PARKER PUBLICATIONS
Also Called: Madison Eagle
155 Main St (07940-2156)
PHONE...............................908 766-3900
Fax: 973 377-7721
Steven Parker, *Owner*
Elizabeth K Parker, *Co-Owner*
EMP: 14
SQ FT: 1,800
SALES (est): 512.3K **Privately Held**
SIC: 2711 4215 Newspapers: publishing only, not printed on site; courier services, except by air

(G-5731)
PFIZER INC
1 Giralda Farms (07940-1021)
PHONE...............................973 660-5000
Julia Cumberbatch, *President*
Christian Velmer, *Senior VP*
Rich Rezek, *Assistant VP*
Ann Czar, *Technical Mgr*
Ghouse Shaik, *Applctn Conslt*
EMP: 13
SALES (corp-wide): 52.5B **Publicly Held**
SIC: 2834 2833 Pharmaceutical preparations; drugs acting on the cardiovascular system, except diagnostic; drugs affecting parasitic & infective diseases; veterinary pharmaceutical preparations; antibiotics
PA: Pfizer Inc.
235 E 42nd St
New York NY 10017
212 733-2323

(G-5732)
RED FEATHER MKTG GROUP LLC
332 Main St (07940-2336)
PHONE...............................973 377-1988
Steve Becker, *Principal*
Jeff Roberts, *Principal*
Susan Becker, *Project Mgr*
Vivian Roberts, *Technology*
EMP: 11
SALES (est): 1MM **Privately Held**
WEB: www.red-feather.com
SIC: 7336 3993 Creative services to advertisers, except writers; signs & advertising specialties

(G-5733)
ROBERT A EICK QLTY BOOKBINDING
Also Called: Eick-Rbert A Qulty Bookbinding
34 Central Ave (07940-1811)
PHONE...............................973 822-2100
Robert A Eick, *Owner*
EMP: 15
SALES (est): 550K **Privately Held**
SIC: 2789 Binding only: books, pamphlets, magazines, etc.

(G-5734)
SENSOR PRODUCTS INC
300 Madison Ave Ste 200 (07940-1868)
PHONE...............................973 884-1755
Dimitri Raitzin, *CEO*
Carlos Pais, *Prdtn Mgr*
Ying Liu, *Electrical Engi*
Rui LI, *Electrical Engi*
Rick Sklar, *Electrical Engi*
EMP: 23
SQ FT: 1,400
SALES (est): 3.9MM **Privately Held**
WEB: www.sensorprod.com
SIC: 3599 5084 Custom machinery; instruments & control equipment

(G-5735)
SHOR INTERNATIONAL
77 Fairwood Rd (07940-1460)
PHONE...............................973 520-8777
John Scott, *General Mgr*
EMP: 30
SALES (est): 2.3MM **Privately Held**
SIC: 3541 5084 5251 Machine tools, metal cutting type; machine tools & accessories; tools

(G-5736)
STEWART-MORRIS INC
71 Kings Rd Ste 1 (07940-2697)
PHONE...............................973 822-2777
Fax: 973 822-0451
John R Morris, *President*
John Morris, *President*
EMP: 5
SQ FT: 3,000
SALES (est): 558.6K **Privately Held**
SIC: 5999 2399 Trophies & plaques; flags; flags, fabric

(G-5737)
WYETH HOLDINGS LLC (DH)
Also Called: Wyeth Holdings Corporation
5 Giralda Farms (07940-1027)
PHONE...............................973 660-5000
Greg Norden, *Ch of Bd*

Andre Petrunoff, *Director*
Lawrence V Stein, *Director*
▲ **EMP:** 35
SALES (est): 38.3MM
SALES (corp-wide): 52.5B **Publicly Held**
SIC: 2834 2836 Pharmaceutical preparations; analgesics; cough medicines; veterinary pharmaceutical preparations; biological products, except diagnostic; allergens, allergenic extracts; vaccines; veterinary biological products
HQ: Wyeth Llc
235 E 42nd St
New York NY 10017
973 660-5000

(G-5738)
WYETH LLC
5 Giralda Farms (07940-1027)
PHONE...............................973 660-5000
Anne Radestad, *Manager*
Edgar Rodriguez, *Manager*
Stephanie King, *Consultant*
Michael West, *Info Tech Mgr*
Guy Lamothe, *Director*
EMP: 500
SALES (corp-wide): 52.5B **Publicly Held**
SIC: 2834 Pharmaceutical preparations
HQ: Wyeth Llc
235 E 42nd St
New York NY 10017
973 660-5000

(G-5739)
WYETH-AYERST (ASIA) LTD (DH)
5 Giralda Farms (07940-1027)
PHONE...............................973 660-5500
Joan Chen, *Principal*
EMP: 4
SALES (est): 1.5MM
SALES (corp-wide): 52.5B **Publicly Held**
SIC: 2834 Pharmaceutical preparations
HQ: Wyeth Llc
235 E 42nd St
New York NY 10017
973 660-5000

Magnolia
Camden County

(G-5740)
GREASE N GO
334 S White Horse Pike (08049-1059)
PHONE...............................856 784-6555
Joe Panchella, *General Mgr*
EMP: 4 **EST:** 2012
SALES (est): 167.6K **Privately Held**
SIC: 7549 3559 Lubrication service, automotive; degreasing machines, automotive & industrial

(G-5741)
J J L & W INC
Also Called: Komfort & Kare
424 N White Horse Pike (08049-1405)
PHONE...............................856 854-3100
Fax: 856 854-5204
Seth Auerbach, *President*
EMP: 25
SQ FT: 3,600
SALES (est): 1.8MM **Privately Held**
WEB: www.komfortkare.com
SIC: 5999 3842 Hospital equipment & supplies; prosthetic appliances

(G-5742)
SAPPHIRE ENVELOPE & GRAPHICS
214 Davis Rd (08049-1215)
PHONE...............................856 782-2227
Fax: 856 782-8479
Anthony Mellace, *President*
Stephen Bressi, *Vice Pres*
EMP: 20
SQ FT: 7,000
SALES (est): 3.5MM **Privately Held**
SIC: 2759 2752 Envelopes: printing; commercial printing, lithographic

GEOGRAPHIC

Mahwah
Bergen County

(G-5743)
ACUPAC PACKAGING INC
55 Ramapo Valley Rd (07430-1118)
PHONE.................................201 529-3434
Fax: 201 529-1319
Rob Edmonds, *President*
Stephanie Hayano, *Vice Pres*
EMP: 200
SQ FT: 66,000
SALES (est): 69MM
SALES (corp-wide): 91.8MM **Privately Held**
WEB: www.acupac.com
SIC: 2844 Cosmetic preparations
PA: Corporation Developpement Knowlton
Inc
255 Boul Roland-Therrien
Longueuil QC J4H 4
450 243-2000

(G-5744)
ADVA OPTICAL NETWORKING INC
1 International Blvd # 705 (07495-0027)
PHONE.................................201 258-8300
Fax: 201 684-9200
EMP: 40 EST: 1998
SQ FT: 1,000
SALES (est): 4.7MM **Privately Held**
SIC: 3661 Mfg Telephone/Telegraph Apparatus

(G-5745)
AIR WORLD INC
126 Christie Ave (07430-1351)
PHONE.................................201 831-0700
Sam OH, *President*
Micheal OH, *Vice Pres*
▲ EMP: 20
SQ FT: 4,000
SALES: 3.8MM **Privately Held**
SIC: 3582 Commercial laundry equipment

(G-5746)
ALPHAGRAPHICS
1 Lethbridge Plz Ste 22 (07430-2113)
PHONE.................................201 327-2200
John Chrisostomou, *President*
EMP: 5
SALES: 950K **Privately Held**
SIC: 2752 8743 Commercial printing, offset; promotion service

(G-5747)
ALTIBASE INCORPORATED
1 International Blvd (07495-0027)
PHONE.................................888 837-7333
Chris Chung, *CEO*
Jung Nahm, *Finance Mgr*
EMP: 6
SQ FT: 411
SALES (est): 449.9K **Privately Held**
SIC: 7372 Prepackaged software

(G-5748)
AMMOSA ENTERPRISES INC (PA)
Also Called: Ammosa Jewelry
1 Lethbridge Plz Ste 12 (07430-2113)
PHONE.................................212 779-2890
Russell Yang, *President*
Fung Chin Yang, *Vice Pres*
▲ EMP: 5
SQ FT: 1,000
SALES (est): 673.9K **Privately Held**
SIC: 3961 Costume jewelry, ex. precious
metal & semiprecious stones

(G-5749)
ARIES PRECISION TOOL INC
300 State Rt 17 Ste H (07430-2141)
PHONE.................................201 252-8550
Fax: 201 666-0335
Stephen Bachman, *Mng Member*
Lynn Bachman,
EMP: 8
SQ FT: 2,400
SALES (est): 1.1MM **Privately Held**
SIC: 3599 Machine shop, jobbing & repair

(G-5750)
AT INFORMATION PRODUCTS INC (PA)
575 Corporate Dr Ste 401 (07430-3703)
PHONE.................................201 529-0202
Fax: 201 529-5603
Joseph Traut, *Ch of Bd*
Roger Angrick, *President*
Joseph Rau, *Senior VP*
Alexander Redel, *Prdtn Mgr*
CJ Sgro, *Sales Mgr*
EMP: 8
SQ FT: 10,000
SALES: 3MM **Privately Held**
WEB: www.atip-usa.com
SIC: 3555 3565 5045 5084 Printing
trades machinery; labeling machines, industrial; computers; printing trades machinery, equipment & supplies

(G-5751)
AVADA SOFTWARE LLC
1 International Blvd # 400 (07495-0027)
P.O. Box 2271, Oak Ridge (07438-2271)
PHONE.................................973 697-1043
Peter D'Agosta, *COO*
Peter Ohrenberger, *Sales Mgr*
Allison Fierro, *Sales Staff*
Sarah Brush, *Marketing Staff*
Janine Loweth, *Manager*
EMP: 15
SALES: 2.2MM **Privately Held**
WEB: www.avadasoftware.com
SIC: 7372 Business oriented computer
software

(G-5752)
BIMINI BAY OUTFITTERS LTD
43 Mckee Dr Ste 1 (07430-2122)
PHONE.................................201 529-3550
Fax: 201 529-0258
Robert Feldsott, *President*
Edward Feldsott, *Vice Pres*
▼ EMP: 19
SQ FT: 15,000
SALES (est): 2.5MM **Privately Held**
WEB: www.biminibayoutfitters.com
SIC: 2311 2321 2329 5136 Tailored
dress & sport coats: men's & boys'; men's
& boys' sports & polo shirts; men's &
boys' sportswear & athletic clothing;
sportswear, men's & boys'

(G-5753)
BIONOMIC INDUSTRIES INC
777 Corporate Dr (07430-2008)
PHONE.................................201 529-1094
Fax: 201 529-0252
John Enhoffer, *President*
EMP: 12
SQ FT: 7,500
SALES (est): 3.6MM **Privately Held**
WEB: www.bionomicind.com
SIC: 3564 Air purification equipment

(G-5754)
BOGEN COMMUNICATIONS INC
1200 Macarthur Blvd # 303 (07430-2331)
PHONE.................................201 934-8500
Fax: 201 934-9832
Jonathan Guss, *CEO*
Michael P Fleischer, *President*
David Delbrocco, *Principal*
Jeffrey E Schwarz, *Chairman*
Yoav Stern, *Chairman*
▲ EMP: 100
SQ FT: 6,000
SALES (est): 20.3MM
SALES (corp-wide): 23.4MM **Privately Held**
WEB: www.bogen-es.com
SIC: 3651 3661 3663 3669 Amplifiers:
radio, public address or musical instrument; audio electronic systems; telephone & telegraph apparatus; telephones
& telephone apparatus; radio broadcasting & communications equipment; intercommunication systems, electric;
communication equipment
PA: Bogen Corporation
50 Spring St Ste 1
Ramsey NJ 07446
201 934-8500

(G-5755)
BUHLER INC
40 Whitney Rd (07430-3130)
PHONE.................................201 847-0600
Rene Steiner, *President*
Larry Wedll, *Project Engr*
Allan Cooney, *Senior Engr*
EMP: 21
SALES (corp-wide): 2.7B **Privately Held**
SIC: 3556 3542 3535 3564 Food products machinery; die casting machines;
conveyors & conveying equipment; dust
or fume collecting equipment, industrial
HQ: Buhler Inc.
13105 12th Ave N
Plymouth MN 55441
763 847-9900

(G-5756)
CASES BY SOURCE INC
Also Called: Source Packaging
215 Island Rd (07430-2130)
PHONE.................................201 831-0005
Alan Adler, *President*
Matthew Adler, *Vice Pres*
Adam Rinaldi, *Accounts Mgr*
Jim Wahler, *Sales Staff*
Jeff Chookazian, *Marketing Mgr*
▲ EMP: 24
SQ FT: 7,500
SALES (est): 7.1MM **Privately Held**
WEB: www.casesbysource.com
SIC: 2653 Display items, solid fiber: made
from purchased materials

(G-5757)
CELCO
Also Called: Constantine Engrg Labs Co
14 Industrial Ave Ste 2 (07430-4201)
P.O. Box 555 (07430-0555)
PHONE.................................201 327-1123
Fax: 201 327-7047
EMP: 16 EST: 1947
SQ FT: 25,500
SALES (est): 3.4MM **Privately Held**
SIC: 3651 3677 3825 3823 Mfg Home
Audio/Video Eqp Mfg Elec Coil/Transfrmrs Mfg Elec Measuring Instr Mfg
Process Cntrl Instr

(G-5758)
CHEFMAN DIRECT INC
10 Sharp Plz (07495)
PHONE.................................888 315-8407
Ralph Newhouse, *CEO*
Eli Weiss, *Exec Sec*
EMP: 30
SQ FT: 10,000
SALES (est): 1MM **Privately Held**
SIC: 3631 Indoor cooking equipment

(G-5759)
CLEAR CUT WINDOW DISTRS OF NJ
127 Tam O Shanter Dr (07430-3270)
PHONE.................................201 512-1804
Stanley Freimark, *President*
EMP: 4
SALES: 175K **Privately Held**
SIC: 2431 Windows & window parts & trim,
wood

(G-5760)
CODA INC (PA)
30 Industrial Ave Ste 1 (07430-2207)
PHONE.................................201 825-7400
Fax: 201 825-8133
Lee Coda, *President*
Alfred Coda, *Vice Pres*
EMP: 24 EST: 1946
SQ FT: 45,000
SALES (est): 4MM **Privately Held**
WEB: www.codamount.com
SIC: 3861 Photographic equipment & supplies

(G-5761)
CUPCAKE KITSCHEN
1042 Ash Dr (07430-2350)
PHONE.................................862 221-8872
EMP: 4
SALES (est): 178.9K **Privately Held**
SIC: 2051 Bread, cake & related products

(G-5762)
DATASCOPE CORP
Also Called: Datascope Patient Monitoring
800 Macarthur Blvd (07430-2001)
PHONE.................................201 995-8000
Fax: 201 995-8605
Don Southard, *Manager*
EMP: 36
SALES (corp-wide): 2.6B **Privately Held**
WEB: www.datascope.com
SIC: 3841 3845 Medical instruments &
equipment, blood & bone work; catheters;
electromedical equipment
HQ: Datascope Corp.
15 Law Dr
Fairfield NJ 07004
973 244-6100

(G-5763)
DATASCOPE CORP
Also Called: Maquet
1300 Macarthur Blvd (07430-2052)
PHONE.................................800 777-4222
Fax: 201 995-8929
EMP: 15
SALES (est): 1.4MM **Privately Held**
SIC: 3841 Mfg Surgical/Medical Instruments

(G-5764)
DATASCOPE CORP
Also Called: Maquet Cardiac Assist
1300 Macarthur Blvd (07430-2052)
PHONE.................................201 995-8000
Dan Pitkowski, *Principal*
Fox Wade, *Marketing Staff*
EMP: 8
SALES (corp-wide): 2.6B **Privately Held**
WEB: www.datascope.com
SIC: 3845 Electromedical equipment
HQ: Datascope Corp.
15 Law Dr
Fairfield NJ 07004
973 244-6100

(G-5765)
DILIGAF ENTERPRISES INC (DH)
Also Called: Gsds
500 Corporate Dr (07430-2005)
PHONE.................................201 684-0900
Christopher Petro, *President*
Winne Nienhuijs, *General Mgr*
Arthur Manzo, *COO*
Rick Lidestri, *Opers Mgr*
John Poalillo, *Opers Staff*
▲ EMP: 40
SQ FT: 29,850
SALES (est): 10.7MM
SALES (corp-wide): 3.6B **Publicly Held**
WEB: www.globalsoftdigital.com
SIC: 2752 2759 Commercial printing, offset; commercial printing
HQ: Creel Printing, Llc
6330 W Sunset Rd
Las Vegas NV 89118
702 735-8161

(G-5766)
DIMENSIONAL COMMUNICATIONS INC
1595 Macarthur Blvd (07430-3601)
PHONE.................................201 767-1500
Fax: 201 767-9696
Douglas Fixell, *President*
Steve Witzke, *Vice Pres*
Ray Schutz, *Plant Mgr*
Jerry Cardillo, *Prdtn Mgr*
Tim Higgins, *Prdtn Mgr*
▲ EMP: 80 EST: 1963
SQ FT: 75,000
SALES (est): 16.6MM **Privately Held**
WEB: www.dimcom.com
SIC: 3993 Signs & advertising specialties

(G-5767)
DUN-RITE COMMUNICATIONS INC
31 Industrial Ave (07430-2223)
PHONE.................................201 444-0080
Steve Rogalinski, *President*
EMP: 6

▲ = Import ▼=Export
◆ =Import/Export

SALES (est): 647.8K **Privately Held**
SIC: **1623** 1799 2298 Communication line & transmission tower construction; antenna installation; cable, fiber

(G-5768)
DXL ENTERPRISES INC
575 Corporate Dr Ste 420 (07430-2330)
PHONE.............................201 891-8718
Fax: 201 891-9629
Ulrich Gernhardt, *President*
Patricia Clark Jones, *Assistant*
EMP: 11
SQ FT: 20,000
SALES (est): 2.8MM **Privately Held**
WEB: www.dxl.com
SIC: **7363** 3571 5094 Help supply services; industrial help service; electronic computers; precious metals

(G-5769)
EDAX INC (HQ)
91 Mckee Dr (07430-2105)
PHONE.............................201 529-4880
Fax: 201 529-3156
Alan Devenish, *President*
James Abramson, *Corp Secy*
Brian Adams, *Senior Buyer*
Josh Feldman, *Manager*
Tara Nylese, *Manager*
EMP: 99
SALES (est): 26.1MM
SALES (corp-wide): 4.3B **Publicly Held**
WEB: www.edax.com
SIC: **3826** 3829 Analytical instruments; measuring & controlling devices
PA: Ametek, Inc.
     1100 Cassatt Rd
     Berwyn PA 19312
     610 647-2121

(G-5770)
ENVIRNMNTAL MGT CHEM WSTE SVCS (PA)
Also Called: Turnkey Solutions
45 Whitney Rd Bldg B (07430-3170)
PHONE.............................201 848-7676
Fax: 201 848-1643
David Lyman, *President*
EMP: 8
SQ FT: 10,000
SALES (est): 3MM **Privately Held**
WEB: www.turnkey-solutions-inc.com
SIC: **3589** 5084 Water treatment equipment, industrial; industrial machinery & equipment

(G-5771)
FECKEN-KIRFEL AMERICA INC
6 Leighton Pl Ste 1 (07430-3195)
PHONE.............................201 891-5530
Fax: 201 891-0129
Rudolf Schiffler, *President*
Michael Anders, *Vice Pres*
Marc Eskind, *Representative*
▲ EMP: 11
SQ FT: 22,000
SALES (est): 2.2MM
SALES (corp-wide): 41.2MM **Privately Held**
WEB: www.fk-am.com
SIC: **3541** Machine tools, metal cutting type
PA: Fecken - Kirfel Gmbh & Co. Kg
     Prager Ring 1-15
     Aachen 52070
     241 182-020

(G-5772)
FLANAGAN HOLDINGS INC (PA)
Also Called: F & M Expressions Unlimited
211 Island Rd (07430-2130)
PHONE.............................201 512-3338
Fax: 201 512-3240
Frank E Flanagan, *President*
Buck Anderson, *Prdtn Mgr*
Sidney Diaz, *Art Dir*
▲ EMP: 90 EST: 1983
SQ FT: 40,000
SALES (est): 12.8MM **Privately Held**
WEB: www.fmexpressions.com
SIC: **2759** Fashion plates: printing

(G-5773)
FLAVOR & FRAGRANCE SPC INC (PA)
3 Industrial Ave (07430-2204)
PHONE.............................201 828-9400
Fax: 201 825-4785
Michael C Bloom, *President*
William H Palmer, *Vice Pres*
Jeffery Wichman, *Plant Mgr*
Garrick Campbell, *Facilities Mgr*
Melanie Deritter, *Purch Mgr*
▲ EMP: 100
SQ FT: 45,000
SALES (est): 23.9MM **Privately Held**
SIC: **2087** 2869 2844 Extracts, flavoring; perfumes, flavorings & food additives; toilet preparations

(G-5774)
FLOXITE COMPANY INC
31 Industrial Ave Ste 2 (07430-3591)
PHONE.............................201 529-2019
Bruce Pitot, *President*
Pat Ely, *Vice Pres*
▲ EMP: 15
SQ FT: 6,000
SALES (est): 5.6MM **Privately Held**
SIC: **3843** Dental equipment

(G-5775)
FMDK TECHNOLOGIES INC
Also Called: Merlin Controls
63 Ramapo Valley Rd 63w (07430-1133)
PHONE.............................201 828-9822
Frank Gallo, *President*
Bill Miller, *Consultant*
EMP: 8 EST: 1978
SQ FT: 5,000
SALES (est): 1.1MM **Privately Held**
WEB: www.fmdkinc.com
SIC: **3564** Blowers & fans

(G-5776)
GLASCO UV LLC
126 Christie Ave (07430-1351)
PHONE.............................201 934-3348
Steven Martin, *Director*
Julie Donnellan,
EMP: 10
SALES: 2.5MM **Privately Held**
SIC: **3589** Water purification equipment, household type

(G-5777)
GLENMARK PHRMCEUTICALS INC USA (HQ)
750 Corporate Dr (07430-2009)
PHONE.............................201 684-8000
Robert Mapsuk, *President*
Vijay Soni, *Exec VP*
Prakash Chainani, *CFO*
Andrew Chromey, *Manager*
Atul Garg, *Manager*
◆ EMP: 91
SQ FT: 68,627
SALES (est): 26.3MM
SALES (corp-wide): 258.7MM **Privately Held**
WEB: www.glenmark-generics.com
SIC: **2834** Pharmaceutical preparations
PA: Glenmark Pharmaceuticals Limited
     Glenmark House Hdo-Corporate Building, Wing-A
     Mumbai MH 40009
     224 018-9999

(G-5778)
GLENMARK THERAPEUTICS INC USA
750 Corporate Dr (07430-2009)
PHONE.............................201 684-8000
EMP: 341
SALES (est): 55.2MM
SALES (corp-wide): 258.7MM **Privately Held**
SIC: **2834** Pharmaceutical preparations
PA: Glenmark Pharmaceuticals Limited
     Glenmark House Hdo-Corporate Building, Wing-A
     Mumbai MH 40009
     224 018-9999

(G-5779)
GOLD BUYERS AT MALL LLC (PA)
1 International Blvd # 200 (07495-0027)
PHONE.............................201 512-5780
Danny Baruch,
EMP: 4
SALES (est): 1.5MM **Privately Held**
SIC: **3911** Jewelry, precious metal

(G-5780)
HEALTHSTAR COMMUNICATIONS INC (PA)
1000 Wyckoff Ave Ste 202 (07430-3164)
PHONE.............................201 560-5370
Fax: 201 891-2380
Jerry Brager, *CEO*
John Corcoran, *President*
Myron Holubiak, *President*
Peter Cossman, *Exec VP*
Ken Dutcher, *Exec VP*
EMP: 620
SQ FT: 10,000
SALES (est): 68.4MM **Privately Held**
SIC: **7372** 7311 6719 Prepackaged software; advertising agencies; personal holding companies, except banks

(G-5781)
HNST MOLD INSPECTIONS LLC
143 Church St (07430-1256)
PHONE.............................201 733-0091
EMP: 19
SALES (corp-wide): 1.6MM **Privately Held**
SIC: **3544** Industrial molds
PA: H.N.S.T. Mold Inspections Llc
     87 S Nauraushaun Rd
     Pearl River NY 10965
     845 215-9258

(G-5782)
HOLLYWOOD TANNING SYSTEMS INC
Also Called: Hollywood Tans
380 Franklin Tpke (07430-2212)
PHONE.............................856 302-1368
Joe Venuto, *Manager*
EMP: 20
SALES (est): 178K **Privately Held**
WEB: www.hollywoodtan.com
SIC: **7299** 3949 Tanning salon; sporting & athletic goods
PA: Hollywood Tanning Systems, Inc.
     380 Franklin Tpke
     Mahwah NJ 07430

(G-5783)
HOWMEDICA OSTEONICS CORP (HQ)
Also Called: Stryker Orthopaedics
325 Corporate Dr (07430-2006)
PHONE.............................201 831-5000
Fax: 201 831-4000
Kevin A Lobo, *President*
David Floyd, *President*
Yin C Becker, *Vice Pres*
Steven P Benscoter, *Vice Pres*
Dean H Bergy, *Vice Pres*
▲ EMP: 153
SALES (est): 1B
SALES (corp-wide): 12.4B **Publicly Held**
SIC: **5047** 3842 Orthopedic equipment & supplies; surgical appliances & supplies
PA: Stryker Corporation
     2825 Airview Blvd
     Portage MI 49002
     269 385-2600

(G-5784)
I FCB HOLDINGS INC (HQ)
933 Macarthur Blvd (07430-2045)
PHONE.............................201 934-2000
Camille Shayka, *President*
EMP: 4
SALES (est): 1.4MM
SALES (corp-wide): 9.8MM **Privately Held**
SIC: **2834** Pharmaceutical preparations; drugs acting on the cardiovascular system, except diagnostic; drugs affecting parasitic & infective diseases

PA: Footstar, Inc.
     45 Rockefeller Plz # 2260
     New York NY 10111
     201 934-2000

(G-5785)
I TRADE TECHNOLOGY LTD (PA)
115 Franklin Tpke Ste 144 (07430-1325)
PHONE.............................615 348-7233
Shia Lebreche, *President*
▲ EMP: 1
SALES: 1.5MM **Privately Held**
SIC: **3678** 5999 5065 Electronic connectors; electronic parts & equipment; connectors, electronic

(G-5786)
JETYD CORPORATION
218 Island Rd (07430-2101)
PHONE.............................201 512-9500
Jason Junkers, *Branch Mgr*
EMP: 10
SALES (corp-wide): 2.6MM **Privately Held**
WEB: www.jetyd.com
SIC: **3423** 3566 Wrenches, hand tools; torque converters, except automotive
PA: Jetyd Corporation
     120 Wesley St
     South Hackensack NJ 07606
     201 343-4570

(G-5787)
JSN HOLDINGS LLC
1 International Blvd (07495-0027)
PHONE.............................201 857-5900
Brian Tedesco, *President*
▲ EMP: 10
SQ FT: 1,200
SALES: 5.2MM **Privately Held**
SIC: **3629** Battery chargers, rectifying or nonrotating

(G-5788)
LEMNISCATE INC
Also Called: Enchantmints
1 International Blvd # 400 (07495-0027)
PHONE.............................707 824-2272
Marke Levene, *President*
▲ EMP: 9
SQ FT: 1,400
SALES (est): 1.3MM **Privately Held**
WEB: www.lemniscateinc.com
SIC: **3944** Board games, puzzles & models, except electronic

(G-5789)
LEVER MANUFACTURING CORP
420 State Rt 17 (07430-2135)
PHONE.............................201 684-4400
Irving V Gerstein, *President*
Mel B Gerstein, *Corp Secy*
William M Corbett, *Vice Pres*
David B Gerstein, *Vice Pres*
▲ EMP: 25 EST: 1905
SQ FT: 100,000
SALES (est): 4.6MM **Privately Held**
WEB: www.levercorp.com
SIC: **3552** 3549 3541 Winders, textile machinery; metalworking machinery; machine tools, metal cutting type

(G-5790)
MICRO LOGIC INC (PA)
31 Industrial Ave Ste 7 (07430-2210)
PHONE.............................201 962-7510
James Lewis, *President*
EMP: 15
SQ FT: 2,000
SALES (est): 1.8MM **Privately Held**
WEB: www.miclog.com
SIC: **7371** 2741 Computer software development; technical manual & paper publishing

(G-5791)
MINDRAY DS USA INC
Also Called: Mindray North America
800 Macarthur Blvd (07430-2001)
PHONE.............................201 995-8000
Fax: 201 992-8906
George Solomon, *President*
Maria Capuano-Weachoc, *Business Mgr*
Rich Cipolli, *Vice Pres*
John Du, *Vice Pres*

Jack Mori, *Vice Pres*
◆ **EMP:** 4050
SALES (est): 228.8MM
SALES (corp-wide): 1.6B **Privately Held**
WEB: www.mindray.com.cn
SIC: 3845 2835 3841 Electromedical
equipment; patient monitoring apparatus;
in vitro diagnostics; surgical & medical in-
struments
PA: Shenzhen Mindray Bio-Medical Elec-
tronics Co., Ltd.
Mindray Building, Keji South No.12
Road, High-Tech Inductrial Zo
Shenzhen 51805
755 818-8881

(G-5792)
MISSIONARY SOCIETY OF ST PAUL
Also Called: Polish Press
997 Macarthur Blvd (07430-2045)
PHONE...................................201 825-7300
EMP: 50
SALES (corp-wide): 5.9MM **Privately Held**
WEB: www.paulistpress.com
SIC: 2721 2731 Periodicals; book publish-
ing
PA: Missionary Society Of St Paul The
Apostle Of Ny
8611 Midland Pkwy
Jamaica NY

(G-5793)
MONTAGE MEDIA CORPORATION
1000 Wyckoff Ave (07430-3164)
PHONE...................................201 891-3200
Fax: 201 891-2626
Stephen Sweeney, *Chairman*
EMP: 35
SALES (est): 3.2MM **Privately Held**
WEB: www.mmcpub.com
SIC: 2721 Trade journals: publishing only,
not printed on site

(G-5794)
MYAT INC (PA)
360 Franklin Tpke (07430-2258)
PHONE...................................201 529-0145
Philip Cindrich, *President*
Tom Teel, *Traffic Mgr*
Art White, *Project Engr*
Bea Porta, *Human Res Mgr*
Virginia Cindrich, *Director*
▲ **EMP:** 35 **EST:** 1951
SALES (est): 5.1MM **Privately Held**
WEB: www.myat.com
SIC: 3663 Transmitting apparatus, radio or
television

(G-5795)
NEW YORK-NJ TRAIL CONFERENCE (PA)
600 Ramapo Valley Rd (07430-1633)
PHONE...................................201 512-9348
Fax: 201 512-9012
Jane Daniels, *Ch of Bd*
Edward Goodell, *Exec Dir*
Maureen Walsh, *Administration*
EMP: 11
SQ FT: 5,200
SALES: 2.5MM **Privately Held**
WEB: www.nynjtc.org
SIC: 8699 2741 2731 Athletic organiza-
tions; atlas, map & guide publishing; book
publishing

(G-5796)
NMP WATER SYSTEMS LLC
63 Ramapo Valley Rd # 103 (07430-1133)
PHONE...................................201 252-8333
Timothy Van Overloop, *Mng Member*
EMP: 7
SALES (est): 138.7K **Privately Held**
SIC: 7389 3589 3677 Water softener
service; swimming pool filter & water con-
ditioning systems; filtration devices, elec-
tronic

(G-5797)
NOBEL BIOCARE PROCERA LLC
800 Corporate Dr (07430-2011)
PHONE...................................201 529-7100
Richard Laube, *CEO*

▲ **EMP:** 40
SALES (est): 10.1MM
SALES (corp-wide): 18.3B **Publicly Held**
SIC: 3087 8021 Custom compound pur-
chased resins; specialized dental practi-
tioners
PA: Danaher Corporation
2200 Penn Ave Nw Ste 800w
Washington DC 20037
202 828-0850

(G-5798)
NORTH JERSEY MEDIA GROUP INC
6 Leighton Pl (07430-3198)
PHONE...................................201 485-7800
M O'Neill, *Owner*
EMP: 194
SQ FT: 10,000
SALES (corp-wide): 173.6MM **Privately Held**
WEB: www.njmg.com
SIC: 2711 Newspapers, publishing & print-
ing
HQ: North Jersey Media Group Inc.
1 Garret Mountain Plz # 201
Woodland Park NJ 07424
201 646-4000

(G-5799)
NUANCE COMMUNICATIONS INC
1111 Macarthur Blvd (07430-2038)
PHONE...................................201 252-9100
Irene Papp, *Branch Mgr*
EMP: 150 **Publicly Held**
SIC: 7372 Prepackaged software
PA: Nuance Communications, Inc.
1 Wayside Rd
Burlington MA 01803

(G-5800)
PAULIST PRESS INC
997 Macarthur Blvd (07430-2096)
PHONE...................................201 825-7300
Fax: 201 825-6921
Lawrence Boadt, *President*
▲ **EMP:** 3
SQ FT: 76,665
SALES (est): 1.8MM **Privately Held**
SIC: 2731 Books: publishing only

(G-5801)
POLYTYPE AMERICA CORP
10 Industrial Ave Ste 4 (07430-3530)
PHONE...................................201 995-1000
Fax: 201 995-1080
Pieter S Van Der Griendt, *President*
▲ **EMP:** 50 **EST:** 1946
SALES (est): 11.5MM **Privately Held**
SIC: 3555 Printing trades machinery; print-
ing trade parts & attachments
HQ: Polytype S.A.
Route De La Glane 26
Fribourg FR
264 261-111

(G-5802)
PRESCRIPTION DYNAMICS INC
310 Ridge Rd (07430-3613)
PHONE...................................201 746-6262
Michael De Giglio, *CEO*
EMP: 10
SALES (est): 1MM **Privately Held**
SIC: 2834 Medicines, capsuled or ampuled

(G-5803)
PRINTING & SIGNS EXPRESS INC
634 Wyckoff Ave (07430-3057)
PHONE...................................201 368-1255
Fax: 201 368-1464
Joseph Busto, *President*
EMP: 4
SALES (est): 454.6K **Privately Held**
SIC: 3993 2759 Signs & advertising spe-
cialties; commercial printing

(G-5804)
PTC ELECTRONICS INC
45 Whitney Rd Ste B9 (07430-3160)
P.O. Box 72, Wyckoff (07481-0072)
PHONE...................................201 847-0500
Fax: 201 847-1394
Alan Kicks, *President*

Alan F Kicks, *President*
Janet Kicks, *Vice Pres*
John Kicks, *Vice Pres*
EMP: 7
SQ FT: 2,000
SALES (est): 750K **Privately Held**
WEB: www.ptcelectronics.com
SIC: 5046 3052 3829 Scales, except lab-
oratory; hose, pneumatic: rubber or rub-
berized fabric; pressure & vacuum
indicators, aircraft engine; pressure trans-
ducers

(G-5805)
QUALITY CARTON INC (PA)
1 International Blvd # 610 (07495-0020)
PHONE...................................201 529-6900
Jack Bartta, *President*
Dan Baratta, *Vice Pres*
EMP: 11
SALES (est): 1.3MM **Privately Held**
WEB: www.qualitycarton.com
SIC: 3565 Carton packing machines

(G-5806)
RADWIN INC
900 Corporate Dr (07430-3611)
PHONE...................................201 252-4224
Ilan Moshe, *President*
Aaron Barnes, *Manager*
EMP: 5
SALES (est): 980.2K **Privately Held**
SIC: 3663 Radio & TV communications
equipment
PA: Radwin Ltd
27 Habarzel
Tel Aviv-Jaffa
376 629-00

(G-5807)
RAPID TRANSFER CO INC
1 Lethbridge Plz Ste 16 (07430-2113)
PHONE...................................201 529-0002
Harvey Wortzel, *CEO*
Barry Finn, *President*
Andrew O'Connell, *Vice Pres*
EMP: 14
SQ FT: 3,000
SALES (est): 1.2MM **Privately Held**
WEB: www.rapidtransfer.com
SIC: 2399 Emblems, badges & insignia

(G-5808)
REICH USA CORPORATION
300 Rte 17 Ste H (07430-2141)
P.O. Box 916 (07430-0916)
PHONE...................................201 684-9400
Joel G Poganski, *President*
Sarah McChesney, *Engineer*
Mauricio Alvarez, *Regl Sales Mgr*
Corey Schwab, *Regl Sales Mgr*
Loucas Nestoros, *Technology*
▲ **EMP:** 11
SALES (est): 1.9MM **Privately Held**
SIC: 3429 3568 Clamps, couplings, noz-
zles & other metal hose fittings; power
transmission equipment

(G-5809)
RJ BRANDS LLC (PA)
Also Called: Chefman
200 Performance Dr # 207 (07495-1101)
PHONE...................................888 315-8407
Ralph Newhouse, *CEO*
Joseph Ritterman, *CFO*
Eli Weiss, *Officer*
▲ **EMP:** 140
SQ FT: 270,000
SALES (est): 150MM **Privately Held**
SIC: 3634 Electric household cooking ap-
pliances

(G-5810)
RUSSELL W ANDERSON INC
1 Fyke Rd (07430-2411)
PHONE...................................201 825-2092
Russell Anderson, *Principal*
EMP: 5 **EST:** 2013
SALES (est): 372.7K **Privately Held**
SIC: 3443 Tanks, lined: metal plate

(G-5811)
SHARP ELECTRONICS CORPORATION (HQ)
Also Called: Sharp Manufacturing Co Amer
100 Jaguar Land Rover Way (07495-1100)
PHONE...................................201 529-8200
Fax: 201 529-8820
Toshiyiki Osawa, *Ch of Bd*
John Herrington, *President*
James Sanduski, *President*
Tim O'Brien, *Partner*
Michael Guenther, *Business Mgr*
◆ **EMP:** 850
SQ FT: 500,000
SALES (est): 954.1MM
SALES (corp-wide): 22.7B **Privately Held**
WEB: www.sharp-usa.com
SIC: 5044 5064 3651 3631 Office equip-
ment; calcvlators, electronic; photocopy
machines; cash registers; electrical appli-
ances, television & radio; television sets;
tape players & recorders; high fidelity
equipment; television receiving sets; microwave ovens, including portable:
household; projectors, still or motion picture, silent or sound; semiconductors &
related devices
PA: Sharp Corporation
1, Takumicho, Sakai-Ku
Sakai OSK 590-0
722 821-221

(G-5812)
SHOCK TECH INC (PA)
211 Island Rd (07430-2130)
PHONE...................................845 368-8600
Fax: 845 368-8799
Serge Seguin, *Ch of Bd*
Kevork Kayayan, *President*
Bernadette King, *Facilities Dir*
Peter Valy, *Mfg Mgr*
Michael Alvarez, *Engineer*
EMP: 40 **EST:** 1998
SQ FT: 50,000
SALES (est): 11.1MM **Privately Held**
WEB: www.shocktech.com
SIC: 8711 3061 3829 3714 Engineering
services; mechanical rubber goods;
measuring & controlling devices; motor
vehicle parts & accessories; springs,
shock absorbers & struts; automobiles

(G-5813)
SOUND UNITED LLC
100 Corporate Dr (07430-2041)
PHONE...................................201 762-6500
Kevin Zarow, *Branch Mgr*
EMP: 242 **Privately Held**
SIC: 3651 5065 Electronic kits for home
assembly: radio, TV, phonograph; elec-
tronic parts & equipment
HQ: Sound United, Llc
1 Viper Way
Vista CA 92081

(G-5814)
STARNET BUSINESS SOLUTIONS
46 Industrial Ave Ste 2 (07430-2206)
PHONE...................................201 252-2863
Doug Arbolino, *CEO*
EMP: 50
SQ FT: 34,000
SALES (est): 9.3MM **Privately Held**
SIC: 2759 Bank notes: engraved

(G-5815)
STARNET PRINTING INC
46 Industrial Ave Ste 2 (07430-2206)
PHONE...................................201 760-2600
Lorraine Brink, *President*
EMP: 5
SALES (est): 171.1K **Privately Held**
SIC: 2732 2741 Book printing; catalogs:
publishing & printing

(G-5816)
STRATEGIC MKTG PROMOTIONS INC (PA)
Also Called: S M P
1200 Macarthur Blvd # 251 (07430-2325)
PHONE...................................845 623-7777
Jennifer Pagels-Caglione, *Ch of Bd*
Robert Russo, *President*
Greg Caglione, *Vice Pres*

▲ = Import ▼=Export
◆ =Import/Export

▼ **EMP:** 15
SQ FT: 3,000
SALES (est): 2.3MM **Privately Held**
SIC: 3999 Advertising display products

(G-5817)
STS TECHNOLOGIES LLC
282 Franklin Tpke (07430-1923)
PHONE.....................973 277-5416
Steven Sciaino, *General Mgr*
Patricia Sciaino, *Principal*
EMP: 10 **EST:** 2012
SQ FT: 10,000
SALES (est): 555.8K **Privately Held**
SIC: 8711 3544 3599 Mechanical engineering; die sets for metal stamping (presses); crankshafts & camshafts, machining

(G-5818)
TAM METAL PRODUCTS INC
55 Whitney Rd (07430-3129)
PHONE.....................201 848-7800
Fax: 201 848-8479
Mark Cariddi, *President*
Frank Cariddi, *Vice Pres*
Jason Cariddi, *Vice Pres*
Rohit Bhalla, *Opers Staff*
Mike Pallotta, *Purch Agent*
EMP: 48
SQ FT: 50,000
SALES (est): 9.9MM **Privately Held**
WEB: www.tam-ind.com
SIC: 3599 3444 Machine shop, jobbing & repair; sheet metalwork

(G-5819)
THEORY DEVELOPMENT CORP
Also Called: Phillips Scientific Co
31 Industrial Ave Ste 1 (07430-2210)
PHONE.....................201 783-8770
Fax: 201 934-8269
Thomas M Phillips, *President*
Rob Ehrhart, *Purch Mgr*
EMP: 15
SQ FT: 13,000
SALES (est): 1.3MM **Privately Held**
WEB: www.phillipsscientific.com
SIC: 3829 3823 Nuclear radiation & testing apparatus; industrial instrmnts msrmnt display/control process variable

(G-5820)
THERMWELL PRODUCTS CO INC (PA)
Also Called: Frost King
420 State Rt 17 (07430-2135)
PHONE.....................201 684-4400
Fax: 201 529-0289
David B Gerstein, *President*
Vincent Giarratana, *Exec VP*
Mel B Gerstein, *Vice Pres*
Chris Riccio, *VP Mfg*
Mark Heitlinger, *CFO*
◆ **EMP:** 400 **EST:** 1910
SQ FT: 100,000
SALES (est): 191.8MM **Privately Held**
WEB: www.frostking.com
SIC: 3442 Moldings & trim, except automobile: metal; weather strip, metal

(G-5821)
THERMWELL PRODUCTS CO INC
Filmco Industries
420 State Rt 17 (07430-2135)
PHONE.....................201 684-4400
Joe Scarpa, *Manager*
EMP: 5
SALES (corp-wide): 191.8MM **Privately Held**
WEB: www.frostking.com
SIC: 2672 Adhesive papers, labels or tapes: from purchased material
PA: Thermwell Products Co., Inc.
  420 State Rt 17
  Mahwah NJ 07430
  201 684-4400

(G-5822)
TRAFFIC SAFETY & EQUIPMENT CO
457 State Rt 17 (07430-2143)
PHONE.....................201 327-6050
Fax: 201 327-4807

Mark Simpson, *CEO*
Peter J Simpson, *President*
Robert Simpson, *Treasurer*
EMP: 10
SQ FT: 16,000
SALES (est): 1.4MM **Privately Held**
WEB: www.trafficsafetydirect.com
SIC: 3993 5084 Signs, not made in custom sign painting shops; industrial machinery & equipment

(G-5823)
UNION INSTITUTE INC
Also Called: National Tax Training School
67 Ramapo Valley Rd # 102 (07430-1170)
P.O. Box 767 (07430-0767)
PHONE.....................800 914-8138
Fax: 201 684-0829
Akiva J Eisenberg, *President*
Sarah Eisenberg, *Treasurer*
EMP: 28
SQ FT: 2,000
SALES (est): 1.1MM **Privately Held**
WEB: www.nattax.com
SIC: 8249 2721 Vocational schools; periodicals: publishing only

(G-5824)
WIND TUNNEL INC
60 Whitney Rd Ste 13 (07430-3180)
PHONE.....................201 485-7793
Jason Friedman, *CEO*
EMP: 5 **EST:** 2010
SALES (est): 571.1K **Privately Held**
SIC: 3443 Wind tunnels

(G-5825)
YOLO CANDY LLC
1 International Blvd # 208 (07495-0027)
PHONE.....................201 252-8765
Brent Greer, *Sales Staff*
John Budd, *Chief Mktg Ofcr*
Scott Silverstein, *Mng Member*
▲ **EMP:** 4 **EST:** 2012
SQ FT: 3,000
SALES (est): 1.5MM **Privately Held**
SIC: 2064 Candy & other confectionery products; chewing candy, not chewing gum; lollipops & other hard candy

Malaga
Gloucester County

(G-5826)
HYPER BICYCLES INC
177 Malaga Park Dr (08328-4241)
PHONE.....................856 694-0352
Clay Goldsmid, *CEO*
Joe Dechamp, *Vice Pres*
Eric Carter, *Manager*
◆ **EMP:** 7
SQ FT: 4,000
SALES (est): 30MM **Privately Held**
SIC: 3751 Bicycles & related parts

(G-5827)
R H VASSALLO INC
Us Rte 40 & State 47 (08328)
P.O. Box 375 (08328-0905)
PHONE.....................856 358-8841
Ron Vassallo, *President*
Diane Vassallo, *Treasurer*
EMP: 6
SQ FT: 5,000
SALES (est): 691.5K **Privately Held**
SIC: 2511 2452 5039 Lawn furniture: wood; prefabricated buildings, wood; prefabricated structures

Manahawkin
Ocean County

(G-5828)
ASAP POSTAL PRINTING
775 N Main St (08050-3025)
PHONE.....................609 597-7421
EMP: 6 **EST:** 2009
SALES (est): 390K **Privately Held**
SIC: 2759 Commercial Printing

(G-5829)
CLEARWATER WELL DRILLING CO
1073 Prospect Ave (08050-3049)
PHONE.....................609 698-1800
Fax: 609 698-1504
Leslie A Pascale, *President*
Yvonne Pascale, *Vice Pres*
EMP: 4
SQ FT: 3,500
SALES (est): 450K **Privately Held**
SIC: 3589 1781 Water filters & softeners, household type; water well drilling

(G-5830)
COPY-RITE PRINTING
378 N Main St Ste A (08050-3092)
PHONE.....................609 597-9182
Fax: 609 597-1311
Gail Moro, *Owner*
EMP: 4
SALES (est): 504.3K **Privately Held**
SIC: 2752 2791 Commercial printing, offset; typesetting

(G-5831)
JETTY LIFE LLC
509 N Main St 3 (08050-3021)
PHONE.....................800 900-6435
Edmund Townsend, *Manager*
Anthony Hediger, *Manager*
EMP: 5
SALES (est): 830.5K **Privately Held**
SIC: 3577 Printers & plotters

(G-5832)
NJ LOGO WEAR LLC
100 Mckinley Ave Ste 6 (08050-6056)
PHONE.....................609 597-9400
Keith Anderson,
EMP: 5
SQ FT: 2,500
SALES (est): 75K **Privately Held**
SIC: 7389 2759 2395 3499 Engraving service; advertising, promotional & trade show services; screen printing; embroidery & art needlework; trophies, metal, except silver

(G-5833)
PACE BUSINESS SOLUTIONS INC
297 Route 72 W (08050-2890)
PHONE.....................908 451-0355
Joseph Tornabene, *President*
EMP: 33 **EST:** 2009
SALES (est): 3.8MM **Privately Held**
SIC: 7371 7372 7379 Computer software systems analysis & design, custom; prepackaged software; computer related consulting services

(G-5834)
TAYLOR MADE CABINETS INC
516 E Bay Ave (08050-3325)
PHONE.....................609 978-6900
Fax: 609 978-6764
David Taylor, *President*
Chris Taylor, *Vice Pres*
Pete Holzwarth, *Technology*
EMP: 24
SQ FT: 10,000
SALES (est): 4.6MM **Privately Held**
WEB: www.taylormadecabinets.com
SIC: 2514 5031 5211 Metal kitchen & dining room furniture; lumber, plywood & millwork; cabinets, kitchen

(G-5835)
WEAVERS FIBERGLASS
19 Parker St (08050-3163)
PHONE.....................609 597-4324
Patrick Weaver, *President*
EMP: 5
SALES (est): 563K **Privately Held**
SIC: 2821 Plastics materials & resins

Manalapan
Monmouth County

(G-5836)
ABRIS DISTRIBUTION INC (PA)
522 Us Highway 9 Ste 377 (07726-8241)
PHONE.....................732 252-9819
Leonid Khegay, *President*
Albert Martirosyan, *Principal*
Vladimir Sim, *Vice Pres*
EMP: 5
SALES (est): 5.5MM **Privately Held**
SIC: 5045 3669 7629 Computer peripheral equipment; intercommunication systems, electric; telecommunication equipment repair (except telephones)

(G-5837)
AIR PRODUCTS AND CHEMICALS INC
405 Route 33 (07726-8308)
PHONE.....................732 446-5676
Fax: 732 446-2698
Dan Nettina, *Branch Mgr*
EMP: 23
SALES (corp-wide): 8.1B **Publicly Held**
WEB: www.airproducts.com
SIC: 2813 Industrial gases
PA: Air Products And Chemicals, Inc.
  7201 Hamilton Blvd
  Allentown PA 18195
  610 481-4911

(G-5838)
ALWAYS BE SECURE LLC
195 Route 9 Ste 109 (07726-8294)
PHONE.....................917 887-2286
Michael Kaplun, *CEO*
Michael Zeidner, *COO*
EMP: 8
SQ FT: 2,500
SALES (est): 300.6K **Privately Held**
SIC: 3172 Wallets

(G-5839)
BASIC SOLUTIONS LTD
330 Adams Ct (07726-8701)
PHONE.....................201 978-7691
Lawrence Meltzer, *President*
Ken Kloff, *COO*
Bobby Choueke, *Vice Pres*
EMP: 4
SALES (est): 248.5K **Privately Held**
SIC: 2322 Men's & boys' underwear & nightwear

(G-5840)
CCARD
Also Called: Manufacturing / Consultants
17 Belle Terre Dr (07726-4521)
PHONE.....................732 303-8264
Chris Cardinale, *President*
EMP: 6
SALES: 440K **Privately Held**
SIC: 3679 Electronic circuits

(G-5841)
COBYCO INC
65 Wilson Ave (07726-3813)
PHONE.....................732 446-4448
Coby Keinan, *President*
Elana Keinan, *Vice Pres*
◆ **EMP:** 4
SQ FT: 6,000
SALES: 310.5K **Privately Held**
SIC: 2284 Embroidery thread

(G-5842)
EAST COAST PALLETS LLC
17 Sweetmans Ln (07726-8349)
PHONE.....................732 308-3616
Enrique Martinez,
EMP: 4
SALES (est): 320K **Privately Held**
SIC: 2448 Wood pallets & skids

(G-5843)
EDESIA OIL LLC
225 County Road 522 B (07726-8824)
PHONE.....................732 851-7979
Joseph Calcagno, *Mng Member*
EMP: 10
SQ FT: 2,300

GEOGRAPHIC

SALES (est): 1.2MM **Privately Held**
SIC: 2079 Olive oil

(G-5844)
ELKOM NORTH AMERICA INC
680 Madison Ave (07726-9594)
PHONE................................732 786-0490
Angelika Uphoff, *Principal*
▲ EMP: 5
SALES (est): 457.3K **Privately Held**
SIC: 3353 Foil, aluminum

(G-5845)
EVERTLAST INTERIORS
52 Main St Ste 6 (07726-1529)
PHONE................................732 252-9965
EMP: 5
SALES (est): 287.4K **Privately Held**
SIC: 2431 Millwork

(G-5846)
EWC CONTROLS INC
385 State Route 33 (07726-8306)
PHONE................................732 446-3110
Fax: 800 635-8646
Mike Reilly, *President*
Stan Plepis, *President*
David Imig, *Regional Mgr*
Dave Dreskin, *Purch Mgr*
Paul Zimmerman, *Engineer*
▲ EMP: 50
SQ FT: 26,000
SALES (est): 8.6MM **Privately Held**
WEB: www.ewccontrols.com
SIC: 3679 1711 3621 3585 Electronic circuits; plumbing, heating, air-conditioning contractors; motors & generators; refrigeration & heating equipment; sheet metalwork; heating equipment, except electric

(G-5847)
FERNANDES CUSTOM CABINETS
233 Pease Rd (07726-2643)
PHONE................................732 446-2829
Jonathan Fernandes, *Principal*
EMP: 5
SALES (est): 227.1K **Privately Held**
SIC: 2434 Wood kitchen cabinets

(G-5848)
FLOORING CONCEPTS NJ LLC
211 Park Ave (07726-8372)
PHONE................................732 409-7600
John Pilot,
EMP: 11
SALES (est): 171.2K **Privately Held**
SIC: 1752 3069 1771 2426 Floor laying & floor work; flooring, rubber: tile or sheet; flooring contractor; flooring, hardwood

(G-5849)
GPT INC
227 State Route 33 (07726-8362)
PHONE................................732 446-2400
Michael Witt, *President*
Niels E Scholer, *Corp Secy*
Michael Monica, *Sales Staff*
EMP: 10
SQ FT: 2,200
SALES: 1MM **Privately Held**
WEB: www.gpt.net
SIC: 5169 3564 Industrial chemicals; purification & dust collection equipment

(G-5850)
HUB SIGN CRANE CORP
67 Wood Ave (07726-8062)
PHONE................................732 252-9090
Chris Barber, *Principal*
EMP: 5
SALES (est): 540.9K **Privately Held**
SIC: 3993 Signs & advertising specialties

(G-5851)
JACQUAR FUEL
107 Hawkins Rd (07726-8420)
PHONE................................732 441-0700
Steve Pielli, *Principal*
EMP: 4 EST: 2009
SALES (est): 467.5K **Privately Held**
SIC: 2869 Fuels

(G-5852)
JEMCO INC
85 Tracy Station Rd (07726-8048)
PHONE................................732 446-1112
EMP: 8
SQ FT: 9,000
SALES (est): 890K **Privately Held**
SIC: 3441 Structural Metal Fabrication

(G-5853)
LEAD CONVERSION PLUS
Also Called: Intergrated Media Solutions
500 Craig Rd Ste 101 (07726-8748)
PHONE................................802 497-1557
John Bean,
EMP: 15 EST: 2010
SALES (est): 903.7K **Privately Held**
SIC: 2721 Magazines: publishing only, not printed on site

(G-5854)
MINUTEMAN PRESS
349 Us Highway 9 Ste 5 (07726-5105)
PHONE................................732 536-8788
Fax: 732 536-0579
Joe Lorenz, *Partner*
Elaine Lorenz, *Partner*
EMP: 6
SALES (est): 1MM **Privately Held**
WEB: www.mmpmanalapan.com
SIC: 2752 Commercial printing, lithographic

(G-5855)
NICE INSTRUMENTATION
205 Park Ave (07726-8372)
PHONE................................732 851-4300
EMP: 14 EST: 2005
SQ FT: 5,000
SALES (est): 2MM **Privately Held**
SIC: 4941 3825 Water Supply Service Mfg Electrical Measuring Instruments

(G-5856)
NJ GRASS CHOPPERS
254 Monmouth Rd (07726-8808)
PHONE................................732 414-2850
Christopher Colosi, *Principal*
EMP: 7 EST: 2011
SALES (est): 975.7K **Privately Held**
SIC: 3751 Motorcycles & related parts

(G-5857)
NUTRI-PET RESEARCH INC
227 State Route 33 Ste 10 (07726-8363)
PHONE................................732 786-8822
Janis Gianforte, *President*
Bruce Horner, *Vice Pres*
EMP: 7
SQ FT: 1,200
SALES (est): 1.1MM **Privately Held**
WEB: www.nuprosupplements.com
SIC: 2834 Veterinary pharmaceutical preparations

(G-5858)
ONE CLICK CLEANERS
43 Kipling Way (07726-3743)
PHONE................................732 804-9802
EMP: 4
SALES (est): 41.8K **Privately Held**
SIC: 7219 3582 Hand laundries; commercial laundry equipment

(G-5859)
ONWARDS INC
Also Called: Bestar
10 Connor Dr (07726-1662)
PHONE................................732 309-7348
Yang Sup Cha, *President*
▲ EMP: 3
SALES: 1MM **Privately Held**
SIC: 2329 Men's & boys' sportswear & athletic clothing

(G-5860)
PANATECH CORPORATION
5 Elkridge Way (07726-3179)
PHONE................................732 331-5692
Jay Panchal, *President*
▲ EMP: 5
SALES (est): 608K **Privately Held**
SIC: 3433 1711 Solar heaters & collectors; solar energy contractor

(G-5861)
REX LUMBER COMPANY
1 Station St (07726-1608)
PHONE................................732 446-4200
Fax: 732 446-5036
Benjamin Forester, *Manager*
EMP: 70
SALES (corp-wide): 58.7MM **Privately Held**
WEB: www.rexlumber.com
SIC: 2421 2431 Custom sawmill; kiln drying of lumber; lumber: rough, sawed or planed; millwork
PA: Rex Lumber Company
840 Main St
Acton MA 01720
800 343-0567

(G-5862)
S&A MOLDERS INC
75 Mount Vernon Rd (07726-8071)
PHONE................................732 851-7770
EMP: 7 EST: 2015
SALES (est): 258.3K **Privately Held**
SIC: 3089 Injection molded finished plastic products

(G-5863)
STEINER PAPER CORP
72 Lone Star Ln (07726-3878)
PHONE................................732 651-6009
Jeffrey Nichols, *President*
Mark Nichols, *Vice Pres*
▲ EMP: 8
SALES (est): 2MM **Privately Held**
WEB: www.steinerpaper.com
SIC: 2679 5113 2823 2621 Paper products, converted; industrial & personal service paper; cellulosic manmade fibers; paper mills

(G-5864)
SUN PACIFIC POWER CORP
215 Gordons Corner Rd 1a (07726-3352)
PHONE................................888 845-0242
Nicholas Campanella, *President*
▲ EMP: 10
SQ FT: 2,000
SALES (est): 3.7MM **Privately Held**
SIC: 5074 3433 5719 5211 Heating equipment & panels, solar; solar heaters & collectors; lighting fixtures; solar heating equipment

---
Manasquan
Monmouth County

(G-5865)
AHERN BLUEPRINTING INC
Also Called: A1 Copying Center
231 Parker Ave (08736-2806)
PHONE................................732 223-1476
Matthew J Ahern, *President*
Patricia Ahern, *Vice Pres*
Patrick Ahern, *Vice Pres*
Edward Ahern, *Treasurer*
EMP: 11
SQ FT: 5,000
SALES (est): 1.9MM **Privately Held**
WEB: www.aherncopy.com
SIC: 7334 2759 Blueprinting service; commercial printing

(G-5866)
APLNOW LLC (PA)
Also Called: Apl2000
2640 Highway 70 Ste 4 (08736-2610)
P.O. Box 361, Brielle (08730-0361)
PHONE................................732 223-5575
Douglas Masto, *Partner*
EMP: 9
SALES (est): 1.6MM **Privately Held**
SIC: 7371 7379 7372 Computer software development & applications; computer related consulting services; business oriented computer software

(G-5867)
ARMSTRONG AND SONS INC
2335 Highway 34 (08736-1423)
PHONE................................732 223-1555
Linda Pietsch, *President*
Michael Pickell, *Vice Pres*

EMP: 5 EST: 1930
SQ FT: 2,200
SALES (est): 564.2K **Privately Held**
WEB: www.armstrongandsons.com
SIC: 7359 3541 Equipment rental & leasing; cutoff machines (metalworking machinery)

(G-5868)
ARTHUR A TOPILOW WILLIAM LRNER
Also Called: Atlantic Hemotology & Oncology
1707 Atlantic Ave (08736-1147)
PHONE................................732 528-0760
Fax: 732 528-0764
Arthur Topilow MD, *Partner*
Carol Henningson, *Partner*
William Lerner MD, *Partner*
EMP: 23
SQ FT: 22,000
SALES (est): 3.2MM **Privately Held**
SIC: 8011 2835 Oncologist; hemotology diagnostic agents

(G-5869)
COAST STAR
13 Broad St (08736-2906)
PHONE................................732 223-0076
Fax: 732 223-8212
James Manser, *President*
EMP: 35 EST: 1877
SQ FT: 2,000
SALES (est): 2.1MM **Privately Held**
WEB: www.thecoaststar.com
SIC: 2711 2752 Newspapers: publishing only, not printed on site; commercial printing, lithographic

(G-5870)
GAMMON TECHNICAL PRODUCTS INC (PA)
2300 Highway 34 (08736-1499)
P.O. Box 400 (08736-0400)
PHONE................................732 223-4600
Fax: 732 223-5778
James H Gammon, *President*
Howard M Gammon, *Vice Pres*
Howard Gammon, *Vice Pres*
Stan Zelek, *Project Engr*
Wanda Gammon, *Treasurer*
▲ EMP: 60 EST: 1960
SQ FT: 34,440
SALES: 12.1MM **Privately Held**
WEB: www.gammontech.com
SIC: 3823 Liquid analysis instruments, industrial process type; liquid level instruments, industrial process type

(G-5871)
INTERNATIONAL OLIVE OIL INC
2271 Landmark Pl Ste C (08736-1026)
PHONE................................732 612-3338
Chris Wall, *Officer*
EMP: 7 EST: 2011
SALES (est): 210.5K **Privately Held**
SIC: 2079 5169 2099 Olive oil; essential oils; vinegar

(G-5872)
J & G GRAPHICS INC
Also Called: Doctor Tee Shirt
221 Parker Ave (08736-2806)
PHONE................................732 223-6660
Fax: 732 223-3565
Robert Giaquinto, *President*
Mary O'Brien, *Treasurer*
EMP: 4
SQ FT: 1,000
SALES: 550K **Privately Held**
WEB: www.jerseyrunner.com
SIC: 2759 Screen printing

(G-5873)
MC RENEWABLE ENERGY LLC
Also Called: Azimuth Renewable Energy
50 Fletcher Ave (08736-3132)
PHONE................................732 369-9933
Jim Alberts, *Vice Pres*
EMP: 14
SALES (est): 771.1K **Privately Held**
SIC: 1711 5211 5074 3674 Solar energy contractor; solar heating equipment; heating equipment & panels, solar; solar cells

(G-5874)
MICHAEL LUBRICH
Also Called: Custom Kitchen By Lubrich
5 Mount Ln (08736-3600)
PHONE..................................732 223-4235
Michael Lubrich, *Owner*
EMP: 5
SQ FT: 3,000
SALES (est): 395.7K **Privately Held**
SIC: 2434 Wood kitchen cabinets

(G-5875)
MR PAULS CUSTOM CABINETS
2416 Highway 35 Ste E (08736-1154)
PHONE..................................732 528-9427
Fax: 732 528-6131
Paul Waltsak Jr, *President*
Claire Waltsak, *Treasurer*
▲ **EMP:** 6 **EST:** 1966
SQ FT: 8,000
SALES (est): 834.6K **Privately Held**
SIC: 2434 Wood kitchen cabinets

(G-5876)
NORTH SALES
Also Called: Bossett Sailmakers
2422 Highway 34 (08736-1808)
PHONE..................................732 528-8899
Henry P Bossett, *Owner*
Ron Laneve, *Sales Associate*
EMP: 5 **EST:** 1979
SQ FT: 7,500
SALES (est): 332.2K **Privately Held**
SIC: 2394 Sails: made from purchased
materials

(G-5877)
P L CUSTOM BODY & EQP CO INC
Also Called: Pl Custom Emergency Vehicles
2201 Atlantic Ave (08736-1097)
PHONE..................................732 223-1411
Fax: 732 223-8456
Jean S Smock, *CEO*
Deborah Thomson, *President*
Nancy Buhagiar, *Vice Pres*
Daniel Feliciano, *Warehouse Mgr*
Lisa Croasmun, *QC Mgr*
EMP: 175 **EST:** 1946
SQ FT: 110,000
SALES (est): 44.5MM **Privately Held**
WEB: www.plcustom.com
SIC: 3711 5012 Ambulances (motor vehicles), assembly of; automobiles & other motor vehicles

(G-5878)
REDA FURNITURE LLC
25 Ocean Ave (08736-3219)
PHONE..................................732 948-1703
Colin Wynd,
EMP: 12
SALES (est): 979.5K **Privately Held**
SIC: 2521 Wood office furniture

(G-5879)
ROYAL PHARMACEUTICALS LLC
2317 Highway 34 Ste 1d (08736-1443)
PHONE..................................732 292-2661
Matthew Regan,
Matt Regan,
EMP: 4
SQ FT: 2,500
SALES (est): 560.6K **Privately Held**
SIC: 2834 Druggists' preparations (pharmaceuticals)

(G-5880)
SANFORD & BIRDSALL INC
Also Called: George Pnterman Kitchens Baths
1704 Atlantic Ave (08736-1116)
PHONE..................................732 223-6966
Virginia Sanford-Birdsall, *President*
John Birdsall, *Vice Pres*
EMP: 6 **EST:** 1950
SQ FT: 3,000
SALES (est): 620K **Privately Held**
WEB: www.penterman.com
SIC: 1799 3281 Kitchen & bathroom remodeling; bathroom fixtures, cut stone

(G-5881)
SUSTANBLE BLDG INNOVATIONS INC
2435 Highway 34 Ste 204 (08736-1819)
PHONE..................................800 560-4143
Tristram Collins, *President*
EMP: 7
SALES (est): 630K **Privately Held**
SIC: 2452 Prefabricated wood buildings

(G-5882)
TRIAD SCIENTIFIC INC
6 Stockton Lake Blvd (08736-3024)
PHONE..................................732 292-1994
Tom Leskow, *President*
Bill Aronoff, *Vice Pres*
EMP: 5
SQ FT: 8,500
SALES (est): 1.2MM **Privately Held**
WEB: www.triadsci.com
SIC: 5049 3821 Laboratory equipment, except medical or dental; laboratory apparatus & furniture

(G-5883)
W F SHERMAN & SON INC
84 Broad St (08736-2907)
PHONE..................................732 223-1505
Donald Lee Sherman Jr, *President*
Alan Lee Sherman, *Corp Secy*
EMP: 15 **EST:** 1878
SQ FT: 7,500
SALES (est): 1.9MM **Privately Held**
SIC: 2431 Doors, wood

(G-5884)
WINEMILLER PRESS INC
Also Called: Toadhall Promotions
2411 Atlantic Ave Ste 6 (08736-1030)
PHONE..................................732 223-0100
Fax: 732 223-9740
Carol Hutchinson, *President*
EMP: 8
SQ FT: 10,000
SALES (est): 540K **Privately Held**
WEB: www.winemiller-press.com
SIC: 2754 3993 2759 Posters: gravure printing; signs & advertising specialties; engraving

(G-5885)
WITTICH BROS MARINE INC
25a Abe Voorhees Dr (08736-3560)
PHONE..................................732 722-8656
George Wittich, *President*
William Wittich, *COO*
Luke Wittich, *Accounting Mgr*
EMP: 30
SALES (est): 2.2MM **Privately Held**
SIC: 4492 7389 3731 Towing & tugboat service; ; dredges, building & repairing

Manchester
Ocean County

(G-5886)
FIRST PRIORITY EMERGENCY VHICL (HQ)
Also Called: First Priority Specialty Pdts
2444 Ridgeway Blvd # 500 (08759-5703)
PHONE..................................732 657-1104
Fax: 732 657-7955
Robert Freeman, *President*
Ken Rudnicky, *Prdtn Mgr*
Trevor Foster, *Manager*
Henry Oneil, *Manager*
Henry Piller, *Manager*
▼ **EMP:** 21
SQ FT: 12,000
SALES (est): 7.3MM **Privately Held**
SIC: 3711 Ambulances (motor vehicles), assembly of
PA: First Priority Global Ltd.
160 Gold Mine Rd
Flanders NJ 07836
973 347-4321

(G-5887)
ORGO-THERMIT INC (PA)
3500 Colonial Dr (08759-5799)
PHONE..................................732 657-5781
Fax: 732 657-1047
Michael Madden, *President*

Pete Capiak, *Business Mgr*
Stephanie Amiano, *Human Resources*
Brian Dry, *Marketing Staff*
Teresa Hefer, *Manager*
▲ **EMP:** 35
SQ FT: 60,000
SALES (est): 7.1MM **Privately Held**
WEB: www.orgothermit.com
SIC: 1799 3548 7692 Welding on site; welding & cutting apparatus & accessories; welding repair

(G-5888)
READE MANUFACTURING COMPANY (HQ)
Also Called: Magnesium Elektron Powders NJ
2590 Ridgeway Blvd (08759-5798)
PHONE..................................732 657-6451
James Gardella, *President*
Nuala Kelly, *Human Res Mgr*
Amith Furtardo, *Sales Mgr*
◆ **EMP:** 50
SALES (est): 13MM
SALES (corp-wide): 441.3MM **Privately Held**
WEB: www.luxfer.com
SIC: 2819 5169 Industrial inorganic chemicals; chemicals & allied products
PA: Luxfer Holdings Plc
Ancorage Gateway
Salford LANCS M50 3
161 300-0611

(G-5889)
RED WALLET CONNECTION INC
Also Called: Barkin Expanding Envelope Co
106 Cardigan Ct (08759-4632)
PHONE..................................201 223-2644
Fax: 201 223-1055
Linda Lafferty, *President*
Edward Lafferty, *Vice Pres*
EMP: 55
SALES (est): 9.6MM **Privately Held**
WEB: www.redwalletconnection.com
SIC: 2677 2675 Envelopes; folders, filing, die-cut: made from purchased materials

Mantoloking
Ocean County

(G-5890)
JOHN J CHANDO JR INC
209 Downer Ave (08738)
P.O. Box 731, Normandy Beach (08739-0731)
PHONE..................................732 793-2122
Fax: 732 793-8649
John J Chando Jr, *President*
EMP: 15 **EST:** 1978
SQ FT: 1,200
SALES: 4MM **Privately Held**
SIC: 1521 8711 1542 2655 New construction, single-family houses; single-family home remodeling, additions & repairs; consulting engineer; nonresidential construction; fiber cans, drums & containers; radioactive waste materials, disposal

Mantua
Gloucester County

(G-5891)
C BENNETT SCOPES INC
550 Bridgeton Pike (08051-1318)
PHONE..................................856 464-6889
Carolyn Bennett, *President*
EMP: 4
SALES (est): 270K **Privately Held**
SIC: 3999 5199 5947 Fire extinguishers, portable; gifts & novelties; gift, novelty & souvenir shop

(G-5892)
KINNARNEY RUBBER CO INC
450 Main St (08051-1064)
P.O. Box 37 (08051-0037)
PHONE..................................856 468-1320
Fax: 856 468-7438
Luke Kinnarney, *President*

Brian Kiannarney, *Vice Pres*
EMP: 14 **EST:** 1959
SQ FT: 6,000
SALES: 1MM **Privately Held**
WEB: www.kinnarney.com
SIC: 3069 3061 Hard rubber & molded rubber products; boot or shoe products, rubber; mechanical rubber goods

Manville
Somerset County

(G-5893)
CREATIONSREWARDS NET LLC
116 S 19th Ave (08835-1634)
PHONE..................................908 526-3127
Christopher Basista, *President*
EMP: 7 **EST:** 2008
SALES (est): 474.4K **Privately Held**
SIC: 2741

(G-5894)
DARBY LITHO INC
301 N Main St (08835-1346)
PHONE..................................908 231-8883
EMP: 10
SALES (est): 880K **Privately Held**
SIC: 2752 Lithographic Commercial Printing

(G-5895)
ESTRIN CALABRESE SALES AGENCY
17 S Main St Ste 3 (08835-1966)
PHONE..................................908 722-9980
Michael Estrin, *President*
Frank Calabrese, *Vice Pres*
EMP: 7
SQ FT: 1,800
SALES (est): 1.1MM **Privately Held**
WEB: www.estrincalabrese.com
SIC: 3645 Residential lighting fixtures

(G-5896)
MANVILLE RUBBER PRODUCTS INC
1009 Kennedy Blvd (08835-2031)
PHONE..................................908 526-9111
Fax: 908 526-7123
Sophia Gajewski, *President*
▲ **EMP:** 35 **EST:** 1964
SQ FT: 7,500
SALES (est): 3.8MM **Privately Held**
WEB: www.manvillerubber.com
SIC: 3069 3061 Molded rubber products; mechanical rubber goods

(G-5897)
MOLECU-WIRE CORPORATION
1215 Kennedy Blvd (08835-2035)
P.O. Box 5426, Somerset (08875-5426)
PHONE..................................908 429-0300
Vinod K Barot, *President*
Hung K Chan, *Vice Pres*
EMP: 12 **EST:** 1958
SQ FT: 45,000
SALES (est): 1.7MM **Privately Held**
WEB: www.molecu.com
SIC: 3357 Nonferrous wiredrawing & insulating

Maple Shade
Burlington County

(G-5898)
A QUICK CUT STAMPING EMBOSSING
803 N Forklanding Rd (08052-1007)
PHONE..................................856 321-0050
Fax: 856 755-9669
Holly Zahradnick, *President*
John Zahradnick, *Principal*
EMP: 10
SALES: 175K **Privately Held**
SIC: 3953 Embossing seals & hand stamps

(G-5899)
ANSWERS IN MOTION LLC
204 S Lippincott Ave (08052-3251)
PHONE..............................732 267-7792
Gregg Pembleton, *Mng Member*
EMP: 5
SALES: 400K **Privately Held**
SIC: 3944 Games, toys & children's vehicles

(G-5900)
CITI-CHEM INC
122 E Kings Hwy Ste 503 (08052-3424)
PHONE..............................609 231-6655
Calvin King, *President*
Lafayette Turner, *Vice Pres*
EMP: 38
SQ FT: 7,000
SALES (est): 3.1MM **Privately Held**
SIC: 2819 Industrial inorganic chemicals

(G-5901)
CPS METALS INC
450 S Fellowship Rd (08052-1880)
PHONE..............................856 779-0846
Fax: 856 779-0905
Edwin Pelczarski, *President*
Paul Pelczarski, *Shareholder*
Thomas Pelczarski, *Shareholder*
EMP: 12
SQ FT: 12,000
SALES (est): 1.1MM **Privately Held**
WEB: www.cpsmetals.com
SIC: 3444 Sheet metalwork

(G-5902)
FRANKS UPHOLSTERY &
DRAPERIES
621 S Forklanding Rd (08052-2916)
PHONE..............................856 779-8585
Fax: 856 779-8007
Frank A Troso, *Owner*
Frank Troso, *Owner*
EMP: 4
SQ FT: 2,700
SALES: 350K **Privately Held**
SIC: 2391 7641 1752 Curtains, window: made from purchased materials; reupholstery; carpet laying

(G-5903)
INNOVATIVE SFTWR
SOLUTIONS INC
3000 S Lenola Rd (08052-1613)
PHONE..............................856 910-9190
Fax: 856 910-9192
James Barling, *President*
Mary Beth Imondi, *Manager*
EMP: 78
SQ FT: 13,000
SALES (est): 14.1MM **Privately Held**
WEB: www.issisystems.com
SIC: 7372 7379 7378 Operating systems computer software; computer related consulting services; computer & data processing equipment repair/maintenance
PA: Advanced Solutions International, Inc.
　901 N Pitt St Ste 200
　Alexandria VA 22314

(G-5904)
LIQUID ELEMENTS
1000 E Park Ave (08052-1200)
PHONE..............................856 321-7646
Edward Moore, *Principal*
EMP: 4 EST: 2011
SALES (est): 211.1K **Privately Held**
SIC: 2819 Industrial inorganic chemicals

(G-5905)
MAIN STREET GRAPHICS INC
30 W Main St (08052-2432)
PHONE..............................856 755-3523
Eileen Cusumano, *President*
EMP: 4
SALES (est): 555.7K **Privately Held**
WEB: www.mainstreetgraphics.net
SIC: 2759 Commercial printing

(G-5906)
MARKS MANAGEMENT
SYSTEMS INC
Also Called: Sir Speedy
590 E Kings Hwy (08052)
PHONE..............................856 866-0588

Dennis Marks, *President*
Darlene Marks, *Vice Pres*
EMP: 8
SQ FT: 2,000
SALES (est): 798.8K **Privately Held**
SIC: 7334 2791 2789 2752 Photocopying & duplicating services; typesetting; bookbinding & related work; commercial printing, lithographic

(G-5907)
PIONEER MACHINE & TOOL CO
INC
425 E Broadway (08052-1242)
PHONE..............................856 779-8800
Fax: 856 779-9233
Michael Czuzak, *President*
John Cuthbert, *Manager*
EMP: 26 EST: 1953
SQ FT: 20,000
SALES: 2.5MM **Privately Held**
WEB: www.pioneermachine.net
SIC: 3444 Sheet metal specialties, not stamped

(G-5908)
SJ MAGAZINE
1000 S Lenola Rd Ste 102 (08052-1630)
PHONE..............................856 722-9300
Fax: 856 234-0115
Marianne Aleardi, *Owner*
Heather Morse, *Editor*
EMP: 10
SALES (est): 966.7K **Privately Held**
SIC: 2721 Magazines: publishing & printing

(G-5909)
STONCOR GROUP INC (DH)
Also Called: Stonhard
1000 E Park Ave (08052-1200)
P.O. Box 308 (08052-0308)
PHONE..............................800 257-7953
Fax: 856 321-7525
David Reif, *CEO*
Michael Jewell, *President*
Michael Barton, *General Mgr*
Ryan Engel, *Superintendent*
Jeff Angstadt, *Regional Mgr*
◆ EMP: 120
SQ FT: 75,000
SALES (est): 476.2MM
SALES (corp-wide): 5.3B **Publicly Held**
WEB: www.stoncor.com
SIC: 2851 Coating, air curing
HQ: Republic Powdered Metals, Inc.
　2628 Pearl Rd
　Medina OH 44256
　330 225-3192

(G-5910)
STONHARD MANUFACTURING
CO INC (DH)
1000 E Park Ave (08052-1200)
P.O. Box 308 (08052-0308)
PHONE..............................856 779-7500
Fax: 856 321-7510
Stork H Donald, *CEO*
Dave Reis, *CFO*
Beth Powers, *Human Res Mgr*
Pam Russell, *Human Resources*
◆ EMP: 44
SALES (est): 13.5MM
SALES (corp-wide): 5.3B **Publicly Held**
WEB: www.stoncor.com
SIC: 2899 Chemical preparations
HQ: Stoncor Group, Inc.
　1000 E Park Ave
　Maple Shade NJ 08052
　800 257-7953

(G-5911)
SUPERIOR PRINTING INK CO
INC
540 E Linwood Ave (08052-1213)
PHONE..............................856 482-9066
Fax: 856 482-1078
Jim La Rocca, *Vice Pres*
EMP: 30
SALES (corp-wide): 117.1MM **Privately Held**
SIC: 2893 5085 Printing ink; ink, printers'
PA: Superior Printing Ink Co Inc
　100 North St
　Teterboro NJ 07608
　201 478-5600

(G-5912)
THOMSON LAMINATION CO INC
504 E Linwood Ave (08052-1213)
PHONE..............................856 779-8521
Fax: 856 779-8819
Sterling A Martin, *President*
Sterling Martin III, *Vice Pres*
Nicholas Gombos, *QA Dir*
Keith Boswick, *Controller*
Debra Martin, *Human Res Mgr*
▲ EMP: 88 EST: 1964
SQ FT: 75,000
SALES (est): 24.1MM **Privately Held**
WEB: www.tlclam.net
SIC: 3544 3679 Special dies & tools; cores, magnetic

━━━━━━━━━━━━━━━━━━━━━━━━
Maplewood
Essex County
━━━━━━━━━━━━━━━━━━━━━━━━

(G-5913)
2A HOLDINGS INC
Also Called: Constitution Arms
12 Hoffman St (07040-1114)
PHONE..............................973 378-8011
EMP: 10
SALES (est): 961.9K **Privately Held**
SIC: 8748 8742 3484 Business Consulting Svcs Mgmt Consulting Svcs Mfg Small Arms

(G-5914)
BARRASSO & BLASI
INDUSTRIES
Also Called: Acme Ring Div
1581 Springfield Ave (07040-2474)
PHONE..............................973 761-0595
EMP: 10 EST: 1916
SALES (est): 700K **Privately Held**
SIC: 3911 Mfg Precious Metal Jewelry

(G-5915)
BLUE APPLE BOOKS LLC
515 Valley St Ste 170 (07040-1389)
PHONE..............................973 763-8191
Kip Jacobson, *Opers Staff*
Harriet Ziefert, *Mng Member*
▲ EMP: 4
SALES (est): 1.9MM **Privately Held**
SIC: 2731 Books: publishing only

(G-5916)
COLUMBIA MARKETING CORP
221 Rutgers St (07040-3229)
PHONE..............................973 275-1700
Fax: 973 275-3998
Alan H Beck, *President*
EMP: 6
SQ FT: 1,500
SALES (est): 420K **Privately Held**
SIC: 2741 Maps: publishing only, not printed on site; directories: publishing only, not printed on site

(G-5917)
CUSTOM BEDDING CO
Also Called: Orange Mattress
1677 Springfield Ave (07040-2967)
PHONE..............................973 761-1100
Fax: 973 378-3464
Marcel Segal, *President*
EMP: 6
SQ FT: 12,500
SALES (est): 675.3K **Privately Held**
WEB: www.mycustombedding.com
SIC: 2515 5712 Mattresses, innerspring or box spring; mattresses

(G-5918)
DIPIETRO FOODS INC
269 Wyoming Ave (07040-2001)
PHONE..............................973 762-4077
EMP: 5
SQ FT: 4,000
SALES: 100K **Privately Held**
SIC: 2099 5411 Mfg Food Preparations Ret Groceries

(G-5919)
ELEMENTS ACCESSORIES INC
Also Called: Lava Lunch
16 Essex Rd (07040-2308)
PHONE..............................646 801-5187

Melissa Zimberg, *Principal*
▲ EMP: 4
SALES (est): 318.1K **Privately Held**
SIC: 2393 Bags & containers, except sleeping bags: textile

(G-5920)
GORDON FRGSON INTR DSIGNS
SVCS
Also Called: Gordon Fergusson Intr Dctg Ser
205 Rutgers St (07040-3229)
PHONE..............................973 378-2330
Gary N Reusch, *President*
EMP: 6
SQ FT: 1,700
SALES: 500K **Privately Held**
SIC: 2391 7389 Curtains & draperies; interior designer

(G-5921)
HAIR DEPOT LIMITED
53 Peachtree Rd (07040-1641)
PHONE..............................973 251-9924
Marlon Mendoza, *President*
EMP: 10
SALES (est): 480.2K **Privately Held**
SIC: 3999 Wigs, including doll wigs, toupees or wiglets; hair & hair-based products; hair curlers, designed for beauty parlors; hair driers, designed for beauty parlors

(G-5922)
IDEAL JACOBS CORPORATION
515 Valley St Bsmt 1 (07040-4301)
PHONE..............................973 275-5100
Fax: 973 275-5161
Andrew C Jacobs, *President*
Wendy Jacobs, *Corp Secy*
Alice Prager, *Vice Pres*
Mike Valentine, *Technology*
▲ EMP: 30
SQ FT: 16,000
SALES (est): 6.7MM **Privately Held**
WEB: www.idealjacobs.com
SIC: 2759 2431 Tags: printing; labels & seals: printing; schedule, ticket & tag printing & engraving; millwork

(G-5923)
MAPLEWOOD BEVERAGE
PACKERS LLC
Also Called: Arizona Iced Tea
45 Camptown Rd (07040-3034)
PHONE..............................973 416-4582
Fax: 973 416-4583
Nick Dimaria, *Plant Mgr*
Nick Dimirio, *Plant Mgr*
Vincent Paturzo, *Manager*
Nick De Maria,
▼ EMP: 165
SQ FT: 10,000
SALES (est): 48.8MM **Privately Held**
SIC: 2086 Carbonated beverages, nonalcoholic: bottled & canned

(G-5924)
PEACOCK COMMUNICATIONS
INC (PA)
215 Rutgers St (07040-3229)
P.O. Box 339, Montville (07045-0339)
PHONE..............................973 763-3311
Bernard Cicirelli, *Chairman*
Loretta Cicirelli, *Treasurer*
EMP: 5
SQ FT: 13,000
SALES (est): 401.6K **Privately Held**
WEB: www.peacockcommunications.com
SIC: 2752 Commercial printing, lithographic; commercial printing, offset

(G-5925)
R G DUNN ACQUISITIONS CO
INC
Also Called: Electronic Manufacturing Co
71 Newark Way (07040-3309)
PHONE..............................973 762-1300
Martin Peterson, *President*
EMP: 27 EST: 1935
SQ FT: 10,000
SALES (est): 5.1MM **Privately Held**
WEB: www.elecmfgco.com
SIC: 3599 Machine shop, jobbing & repair

(G-5926)
RAILS COMPANY INC (PA)
101 Newark Way (07040-3309)
PHONE..................................973 763-4320
Fax: 973 763-2585
Garwood N Burwell, *President*
Joan Maldonado, *Vice Pres*
Satish Shankar, *Purch Mgr*
Mik Kinda, *Treasurer*
Miklos Kinda, *Treasurer*
▼ EMP: 30 EST: 1932
SQ FT: 31,000
SALES (est): 4.5MM Privately Held
WEB: www.railsco.com
SIC: 3743 3469 3444 Railroad equipment; stamping metal for the trade; sheet metalwork

(G-5927)
SUPERMEDIA LLC
Also Called: Verizon
50 Burnett Ave (07040-2968)
PHONE..................................973 649-9900
Joseph Gibbs, *Branch Mgr*
EMP: 254
SALES (corp-wide): 1.8B Privately Held
WEB: www.verizon.superpages.com
SIC: 2741 Directories, telephone: publishing only, not printed on site
HQ: Supermedia Llc
2200 W Airfield Dr
Dfw Airport TX 75261
972 453-7000

(G-5928)
TOVATECH LLC
Also Called: Iultrasonic
205 Rutgers St (07040-3229)
PHONE..................................973 913-9734
Robert Sandor,
Rachel Kohn,
EMP: 5
SALES (est): 1.5MM Privately Held
SIC: 5047 3821 5049 Medical laboratory equipment; laboratory equipment: fume hoods, distillation racks, etc.; laboratory equipment, except medical or dental

(G-5929)
TRIMARCO INC
Also Called: New Art Ring Co
1847 Springfield Ave # 1849 (07040-2904)
PHONE..................................973 762-7380
Fax: 973 762-5772
Nick Trimarco, *President*
EMP: 4
SQ FT: 4,000
SALES (est): 520K Privately Held
SIC: 5094 3911 Jewelry; diamonds (gems); rings, finger: precious metal

(G-5930)
TURBOT HQ INC
105 Oakview Ave (07040-2303)
PHONE..................................973 922-0297
Nathan Wallace, *Principal*
EMP: 20
SALES (est): 880.6K Privately Held
SIC: 7372 Prepackaged software

(G-5931)
UNION TOOL & MOLD CO INC
220 Rutgers St (07040-3228)
PHONE..................................973 763-6611
Fax: 973 763-7643
Bob Arrighi, *CEO*
Joyce Arrighi, *Corp Secy*
▲ EMP: 25 EST: 1956
SQ FT: 20,000
SALES (est): 6.1MM Privately Held
WEB: www.uniontool-mold.com
SIC: 3544 Industrial molds

(G-5932)
VISUAL IMPACT ADVERTISING INC
Also Called: Matter Magazine
9 Highland Pl Apt 3 (07040-2568)
PHONE..................................973 763-4900
Karen Duncan, *President*
EMP: 10
SALES (est): 844.2K Privately Held
SIC: 2721 Magazines: publishing only, not printed on site

Margate City
Atlantic County

(G-5933)
PET SALON INC
8510 Ventnor Ave (08402-2522)
PHONE..................................609 350-6480
Beth Simons, *President*
EMP: 11
SALES (corp-wide): 1.3MM Privately Held
SIC: 3999 0752 Pet supplies; grooming services, pet & animal specialties
PA: The Pet Salon Inc
3 S Franklin Ave
Margate City NJ 08402
609 350-6480

(G-5934)
PET SALON INC (PA)
Also Called: Groomershelper.com
3 S Franklin Ave (08402-2747)
PHONE..................................609 350-6480
Fax: 609 822-2920
Beth Simons, *President*
Charles Simons, *Vice Pres*
▲ EMP: 4
SALES: 1.3MM Privately Held
WEB: www.petshots.com
SIC: 3999 0752 Pet supplies; grooming services, pet & animal specialties

---

Marlboro
Monmouth County

(G-5935)
A PLUS PRODUCTS INCORPORATED
8 Timber Ln (07746-1444)
PHONE..................................732 866-9111
Mike Schriber, *Principal*
Jerry Carbonaro, *Purchasing*
◆ EMP: 28
SALES (est): 5.3MM Privately Held
SIC: 3469 Metal stampings

(G-5936)
CERTIFIED CABINET CORP
9 S Main St (07746-1539)
PHONE..................................732 741-0755
Mark Forman, *President*
EMP: 4 EST: 2011
SALES (est): 465.8K Privately Held
SIC: 2434 Wood kitchen cabinets

(G-5937)
DB DESIGNS INC
10 Damascus Dr (07746-1953)
PHONE..................................732 616-5018
David Belasco, *President*
EMP: 5
SALES (est): 210K Privately Held
SIC: 2326 Service apparel (baker, barber, lab, etc.), washable: men's

(G-5938)
EFCO CORP
Also Called: Econ Forms
77 Vanderburg Rd (07746-1450)
PHONE..................................732 308-1010
Joe Capazi, *Manager*
EMP: 13
SALES (corp-wide): 259.3MM Privately Held
SIC: 5051 5211 3444 Steel; masonry materials & supplies; concrete forms, sheet metal
HQ: Efco Corp
1800 Ne Broadway Ave
Des Moines IA 50313
515 266-1141

(G-5939)
EXPERT APPLIANCE CENTER LLC
460 County Road 520 (07746-1041)
PHONE..................................732 946-0999
Oleg Gampel, *Principal*
EMP: 4

(G-5940)
FLEXCO BLDG PDTS LTD LBLTY CO
15 Timber Ln (07746-1443)
PHONE..................................732 780-1700
Michael W O'Gorman, *Mng Member*
Robert Lombardi,
EMP: 15
SQ FT: 18,000
SALES: 3.6MM Privately Held
SIC: 3272 Building materials, except block or brick: concrete

(G-5941)
FUTUREX PROPERTIES INC (PA)
4 Timber Ln (07746-1480)
PHONE..................................732 414-6211
Fax: 609 860-8770
Kathleen Fitzsimmons, *President*
Susan McCaffrey, *Office Mgr*
EMP: 28
SQ FT: 36,000
SALES (est): 5.7MM Privately Held
WEB: www.fitzpak.com
SIC: 3086 Packaging & shipping materials, foamed plastic

(G-5942)
GP ACOUSTICS (US) INC
Also Called: Kef America
10 Timber Ln (07746-1444)
PHONE..................................732 683-2356
▲ EMP: 19 EST: 1973
SALES (est): 3.2MM
SALES (corp-wide): 750.2MM Privately Held
SIC: 3651 Loudspeakers, electrodynamic or magnetic
PA: Gold Peak Industries (Holdings) Limited
9/F Bldg 12w Hong Kong Science Park Ph 3
Sha Tin NT
242 711-33

(G-5943)
HILMAN INCORPORATED (PA)
Also Called: Hillman Rollers
12 Timber Ln (07746-1444)
P.O. Box 45 (07746-0045)
PHONE..................................732 462-6277
Fax: 732 462-6355
Norman A Hill, *Ch of Bd*
David A Hill, *Principal*
Susan Montgomery, *Vice Pres*
◆ EMP: 65 EST: 1953
SQ FT: 76,000
SALES (est): 20.5MM Privately Held
WEB: www.hilmaninc.com
SIC: 3537 Forklift trucks; dollies (hand or power trucks), industrial except mining; lift trucks, industrial: fork, platform, straddle, etc.

(G-5944)
INSUL-STOP INC
240 Boundary Rd (07746-1478)
PHONE..................................732 706-1978
Harry Bussey III, *President*
EMP: 5
SQ FT: 150,000
SALES (est): 506.9K Privately Held
SIC: 2899 Insulating compounds

(G-5945)
INTERNTONAL RIDING HELMETS INC
15 Timber Ln (07746-1443)
PHONE..................................732 772-0165
Frank Plastino, *President*
▲ EMP: 20
SQ FT: 23,000
SALES (est): 135.6K Privately Held
SIC: 3949 5699 Helmets, athletic; riding apparel

(G-5946)
KEF AMERICA INC
10 Timber Ln (07746-1444)
PHONE..................................732 414-2074
Fax: 732 683-9790
SALES (est): 334K Privately Held
SIC: 5064 3634 Electrical appliances, television & radio; housewares, excluding cooking appliances & utensils

Alec Chanin, *President*
▲ EMP: 24
SALES (est): 8.3MM Privately Held
WEB: www.kefamerica.com
SIC: 5065 3677 3663 3651 Electronic parts & equipment; electronic coils, transformers & other inductors; radio & TV communications equipment; household audio & video equipment

(G-5947)
MASTER STRAP LLC
20 Hastings Rd Ste B (07746-1365)
PHONE..................................888 503-7779
Abraham Ovadia, *President*
EMP: 4
SALES: 69K Privately Held
SIC: 3931 7389 Drums, parts & accessories (musical instruments);

(G-5948)
MULTI-TECH INDUSTRIES INC
64 S Main St (07746-1893)
P.O. Box 159 (07746-0159)
PHONE..................................732 431-0550
Fax: 732 409-6695
James L Bernard, *President*
Cindy Stanziola, *Admin Sec*
▲ EMP: 10 EST: 1969
SQ FT: 8,000
SALES: 930K Privately Held
WEB: www.multi-tech-industries.com
SIC: 3644 3643 3812 3825 Noncurrent-carrying wiring services; current-carrying wiring devices; electric switches; detection apparatus: electronic/magnetic field, light/heat; antennas, radar or communications; instruments to measure electricity; semiconductors & related devices; motors & generators

(G-5949)
NEW JERSEY GOLD BUYERS CORP (PA)
460 County Road 520 (07746-1041)
PHONE..................................732 765-4653
Raymond Benz, *Owner*
EMP: 4
SALES (est): 309.7K Privately Held
SIC: 3356 Gold & gold alloy: rolling, drawing or extruding

(G-5950)
NYC WOODWORKING INC
39 Kingfisher Ct (07746-2504)
PHONE..................................718 222-1221
Mark Spelczak, *Owner*
EMP: 4
SALES (est): 381K Privately Held
SIC: 2431 Millwork

(G-5951)
PARKWAY PRINTING INC
52 N Main St Ste 11 (07746-1428)
PHONE..................................732 308-0300
Steven Meringolo, *President*
Robin Meringolo, *Admin Sec*
EMP: 5
SALES (est): 666.1K Privately Held
SIC: 2752 Commercial printing, offset

(G-5952)
PLASMA POWDERS & SYSTEMS INC
228 Boundary Rd Ste 2 (07746-1446)
P.O. Box 132 (07746-0132)
PHONE..................................732 431-0992
Fax: 732 308-1075
Peter Foy, *President*
Iris Copeland, *Office Mgr*
◆ EMP: 7
SQ FT: 6,000
SALES (est): 2.7MM Privately Held
WEB: www.plasmapowders.com
SIC: 5169 5051 3315 Metal polishes; metal wires, ties, cables & screening; steel wire & related products

(G-5953)
PRO SPORTS INC
Also Called: Champion Sports Products Co
1 Champion Way (07746-1457)
P.O. Box 368 (07746-0368)
PHONE..................................732 294-5561
Howard Meller, *President*
Steven Meller, *Vice Pres*

◆ EMP: 34 EST: 1961
SQ FT: 60,000
SALES (est): 3.8MM **Privately Held**
SIC: 5941 3949 Specialty sport supplies;
sporting & athletic goods

(G-5954)
**PROFESSIONAL
REPRODUCTIONS INC**
75 Vanderburg Rd (07746-1450)
PHONE..............................212 268-1222
Dominic Manzi, *President*
Chris Manzi, *Vice Pres*
EMP: 14
SQ FT: 5,000
SALES (est): 2.3MM **Privately Held**
WEB: www.professionalrepro.com
SIC: 7334 2752 Blueprinting service; com-
mercial printing, offset

(G-5955)
QCOM INC
475 County Road 520 # 200 (07746-1059)
PHONE..............................732 772-0990
Daniel Wang, *Ch of Bd*
John Sun, *President*
EMP: 30
SQ FT: 8,100
SALES: 2MM **Privately Held**
SIC: 7372 Business oriented computer
software

(G-5956)
SAM GRAPHICS INC
Also Called: Millenium Graphics
35 Vanderburg Rd (07746-1418)
PHONE..............................732 431-0440
Robert Klepner, *Principal*
EMP: 26
SQ FT: 8,000
SALES (est): 379.4K **Privately Held**
SIC: 2752 Commercial printing, litho-
graphic

(G-5957)
SCORPIO POSTERS INC
4 Timber Ln Ste B (07746-1481)
PHONE..............................718 499-2001
Frank Wolsky, *President*
▲ EMP: 38
SQ FT: 20,000
SALES (est): 4.3MM **Privately Held**
SIC: 2759 5199 6794 5112 Poster &
decal printing & engraving; posters;
patent owners & lessors; stationery & of-
fice supplies

(G-5958)
SHOPINDIA INC
3 Topaz Ct (07746-2161)
PHONE..............................732 409-0656
Tarun Chandra, *CEO*
EMP: 5
SALES (est): 442K **Privately Held**
WEB: www.shopindia.com
SIC: 5023 3911 Decorative home furnish-
ings & supplies; jewelry apparel

(G-5959)
SINE TRU TOOL COMPANY INC
238 Boundary Rd Ste 2 (07746-1485)
P.O. Box 280, Morganville (07751-0280)
PHONE..............................732 591-1100
Fax: 732 591-0386
Kenny Klawunn, *President*
Bruce Klawunn, *Production*
EMP: 6 EST: 1956
SQ FT: 12,000
SALES (est): 925.8K **Privately Held**
SIC: 3545 7692 3423 Cutting tools for
machine tools; machine knives, metal-
working; welding repair; hand & edge
tools

(G-5960)
**SYNERGETICA INTERNATIONAL
INC**
9 Inverness Dr (07746-2129)
PHONE..............................732 780-5865
Heng Michael Su, *President*
Nancy Yeh, *Accountant*
▲ EMP: 5
SALES: 8.5MM **Privately Held**
WEB: www.synergeticainc.com
SIC: 2834 Pharmaceutical preparations

(G-5961)
**TOWN & COUNTRY PLASTICS
INC**
Also Called: T & C
10b Timber Ln (07746-1444)
P.O. Box 269, Morganville (07751-0269)
PHONE..............................732 780-5300
Fax: 732 294-0001
Harold Mermel, *President*
Leslie Mermel, *Vice Pres*
▲ EMP: 15
SQ FT: 5,000
SALES (est): 2MM **Privately Held**
SIC: 3089 3088 3822 Plastic processing;
plastics plumbing fixtures; auto controls
regulating residntl & coml environmt & ap-
plncs

(G-5962)
**TUSCANY ESPECIALLY ITLN
FOODS**
13a S Main St Store 5 (07746)
PHONE..............................732 308-1118
Vincent Lafranca, *President*
Sal Faenza, *Vice Pres*
EMP: 10
SALES (est): 866.8K **Privately Held**
SIC: 2032 Italian foods: packaged in cans,
jars, etc.

Marlton
Burlington County

(G-5963)
ABBOTT LABORATORIES
10000 Lincoln Dr E # 201 (08053-3108)
PHONE..............................856 988-5572
Stephen Fortino, *Branch Mgr*
EMP: 11
SALES (corp-wide): 27.3B **Publicly Held**
WEB: www.abbott.com
SIC: 2834 Pharmaceutical preparations
PA: Abbott Laboratories
    100 Abbott Park Rd
    Abbott Park IL 60064
    224 667-6100

(G-5964)
ACS QUALITY SERVICES INC
20 Elmgate Rd (08053-2402)
P.O. Box 266 (08053-0266)
PHONE..............................856 988-6550
Norm Skversky, *President*
EMP: 4
SALES (est): 619.7K **Privately Held**
SIC: 3823 Water quality monitoring & con-
trol systems

(G-5965)
BOBIT BUSINESS MEDIA INC
49 S Maple Ave (08053-2031)
PHONE..............................856 596-0999
Fax: 856 596-0168
Frank Digiacomo, *Publisher*
Marykay Duff, *Branch Mgr*
EMP: 5
SQ FT: 1,900
SALES (corp-wide): 29.7MM **Privately
Held**
WEB: www.bobit.com
SIC: 2721 Magazines: publishing only, not
printed on site
PA: Bobit Business Media Inc.
    3520 Challenger St
    Torrance CA 90503
    310 533-2400

(G-5966)
**CAPE PROSTHETICS-
ORTHOTICS**
Also Called: Prosthetic Orthotic Solutions
100 Brick Rd Ste 315 (08053-2146)
PHONE..............................856 810-7900
Kevin Powers, *Principal*
EMP: 7 **Privately Held**
SIC: 3842 Limbs, artificial
HQ: Cape Prosthetics-Orthotics Inc
    855 Springdale Dr Ste 200
    Exton PA 19341
    610 644-7824

(G-5967)
**CENTURUM INFORMATION
TECH INC (HQ)**
651 Route 73 N Ste 107 (08053-3445)
PHONE..............................856 751-1111
Robert M Matteucci, *CEO*
Samuel R Seymour, *Exec VP*
Thomas J Botulinski, *Vice Pres*
Steve Golle, *Vice Pres*
Jeffrey S Hughes Sr, *CFO*
EMP: 8
SQ FT: 2,000
SALES (est): 45MM
SALES (corp-wide): 57.1MM **Privately
Held**
SIC: 8742 8711 3661 3663 Management
consulting services; engineering services;
telephone & telegraph apparatus; radio &
TV communications equipment; commer-
cial physical research; radio telephone
communication
PA: Centurum Inc.
    651 Route 73 N Ste 107
    Marlton NJ 08053
    856 751-1111

(G-5968)
**COVENTRY OF NEW JERSEY
INC**
10000 Lincoln Dr E # 201 (08053-3108)
PHONE..............................856 988-5521
Mark Recchiniti, *President*
Harry Orth, *Vice Pres*
EMP: 20
SALES (est): 1.1MM **Privately Held**
SIC: 2759 2752 Commercial printing;
commercial printing, lithographic

(G-5969)
CUSTOM QUICK LABEL INC
300 Greentree Rd # 207 (08053-9418)
PHONE..............................856 596-7555
Judy Tagen, *President*
Martin Tagen, *Treasurer*
EMP: 7
SALES (est): 1.2MM **Privately Held**
SIC: 5131 2679 Labels; bridal supplies; la-
bels, paper: made from purchased mate-
rial

(G-5970)
**DEFENSE SPPORT SVCS INTL 2
LLC**
901 Lincoln Dr W Ste 200 (08053-3131)
PHONE..............................856 866-2200
Kathleen Bates, *Manager*
Donald Smith, *Manager*
Tara Rush, *Info Tech Mgr*
John Keating,
Clinton Bickett,
EMP: 11
SALES (est): 957.7K **Privately Held**
SIC: 3721 4581 8711 8742 Airplanes,
fixed or rotary wing; aircraft servicing &
repairing; engineering services; manage-
ment consulting services; systems analy-
sis & engineering consulting services

(G-5971)
**DEFENSE SUPPORT SVCS INTL
LLC (DH)**
901 Lincoln Dr W Ste 200 (08053-3131)
PHONE..............................850 390-4737
Fax: 856 988-0100
John F Keating, *Mng Member*
Donald W Smith,
EMP: 12
SALES (est): 8.9MM **Privately Held**
SIC: 4581 3728 8742 Airports, flying
fields & services; aircraft parts & equip-
ment; materials mgmt. (purchasing, han-
dling, inventory) consultant
HQ: Pae Aviation And Technical Services
    Llc
    1320 N Courthouse Rd # 800
    Arlington VA 22201
    856 866-2200

(G-5972)
DEX MEDIA INC
401 Route 73 N Bldg 20 (08053-3427)
PHONE..............................856 988-2700
Andrea Drioli, *Manager*
EMP: 42

SALES (corp-wide): 1.8B **Privately Held**
SIC: 2741 Telephone & other directory
publishing
PA: Dex Media Holdings, Inc.
    2200 W Airfield Dr
    Dfw Airport TX 75261
    972 453-7000

(G-5973)
**DOOLAN INDUSTRIES
INCORPORATED (PA)**
Also Called: Emc3
5 Blue Anchor St (08053-3011)
PHONE..............................856 985-1880
Timothy W Stein, *President*
EMP: 4
SQ FT: 5,000
SALES (est): 5.6MM **Privately Held**
SIC: 4959 3694 5051 7363 Environmen-
tal cleanup services; motor generator
sets, automotive; metals service centers
& offices; labor resource services

(G-5974)
**DYNAMIC DEFENSE MATERIALS
LLC**
100 Sharp Rd (08053-5547)
P.O. Box 1339 (08053-6339)
PHONE..............................856 552-4150
Robert A Lipinski, *CEO*
John Yarsinsky, *CFO*
Elizabeth Pineiro-Doyle, *Sales Staff*
▲ EMP: 8
SQ FT: 5,000
SALES (est): 820K **Privately Held**
WEB: www.ddmat.com
SIC: 3312 Armor plate

(G-5975)
FIVE MACS INC
Also Called: Business Card Express
8 E Stow Rd Ste 140 (08053-3161)
PHONE..............................856 596-3150
John McTigue Jr, *President*
Madeline McTigue, *Vice Pres*
EMP: 31
SALES (est): 4.4MM **Privately Held**
WEB: www.bcex.com
SIC: 2754 5112 2759 Cards, except
greeting: gravure printing; envelopes:
gravure printing; stationery: gravure print-
ing; invitations: gravure printing; en-
velopes; stationery; commercial printing

(G-5976)
GALLANT LABORATORIES INC
2407 Delancey Way (08053-8513)
PHONE..............................609 654-4146
Gary Gallant, *President*
Barbara Gallant, *Admin Sec*
EMP: 8
SQ FT: 6,000
SALES (est): 1MM **Privately Held**
SIC: 2844 Cosmetic preparations

(G-5977)
GLOBAL INDUSTRIES INC (PA)
Also Called: Evolve Furniture Group
17 W Stow Rd (08053-3116)
P.O. Box 562 (08053-0562)
PHONE..............................856 596-3390
Fax: 856 596-5684
Joel Appel, *Ch of Bd*
Jon Abraham, *Exec VP*
Jon Soll, *Exec VP*
Mark Walker, *Sales Mgr*
Michael Fishman, *Chief Mktg Ofcr*
◆ EMP: 180 EST: 1990
SALES (est): 138.7MM **Privately Held**
WEB: www.evolvefurnituregroup.com
SIC: 2522 5021 Office furniture, except
wood; furniture

(G-5978)
**HOLTEC GOVERNMENT
SERVICES LLC**
525 Route 73 N Ste 304 (08053-3422)
PHONE..............................856 291-0600
Kalyan Niyogi, *President*
Joy Russell, *Vice Pres*
Martha Singh, *Treasurer*
EMP: 4

SALES (est): 271.5K **Privately Held**
SIC: 3273 3536 4013 Ready-mixed concrete; cranes, industrial plant; belt line railroads

(G-5979)
INTERNTNAL BSCITS CNFCTONS INC
10000 Lincoln Dr E # 102 (08053-3108)
PHONE.............................856 813-1008
Don Demato, *Principal*
Monica Mattar, *Business Mgr*
EMP: 4
SALES (est): 188.8K **Privately Held**
SIC: 2052 Biscuits, dry

(G-5980)
ISLAND BREEZE INTL INC
Also Called: (A DEVELOPMENT STAGE COMPANY)
24 S Maple Ave (08053-2002)
PHONE.............................856 931-1505
Bradley T Prader, *Ch of Bd*
Sean F McManimon, *COO*
Thomas L Schneider, *Exec VP*
Steven G Weismann, *CFO*
Michael C Hovdestad, *Admin Sec*
EMP: 14
SALES (est): 1.5MM **Privately Held**
SIC: 3731 Commercial passenger ships, building & repairing

(G-5981)
LAWLESS JERKY LLC
37 N Maple Ave Apt 30 (08053-1758)
PHONE.............................310 869-5733
Matt Tolnick, *CEO*
EMP: 6
SALES (est): 283.4K **Privately Held**
SIC: 2013 Snack sticks, including jerky: from purchased meat

(G-5982)
LIBERTY COCA-COLA BEVS LLC
5 E Stow Rd Ste G (08053-3145)
PHONE.............................856 988-3844
Fax: 856 988-6948
Margaret Bailey, *Manager*
EMP: 20
SALES (corp-wide): 210K **Privately Held**
SIC: 2086 Bottled & canned soft drinks
PA: Liberty Coca-Cola Beverages Llc
725 E Erie Ave
Philadelphia PA 19134
215 427-4500

(G-5983)
LOCKHEED MARTIN
3000 Lincoln Dr E Ste E (08053-1500)
PHONE.............................856 762-2222
Ron Street, *Manager*
EMP: 104 **Publicly Held**
SIC: 3812 Search & navigation equipment
HQ: Lockheed Martin Integrated Systems, Llc
6801 Rockledge Dr
Bethesda MD 20817

(G-5984)
LOCKHEED MARTIN
Also Called: Mission Systems & Training
3000 Lincoln Dr E Ste E (08053-1500)
PHONE.............................856 722-7782
Peggy Koenitzer, *Manager*
EMP: 100 **Publicly Held**
SIC: 3812 Search & navigation equipment
HQ: Lockheed Martin Integrated Systems, Llc
6801 Rockledge Dr
Bethesda MD 20817

(G-5985)
LOCKHEED MARTIN
3000 Lincoln Dr E Ste E (08053-1500)
PHONE.............................856 722-2418
John R Busca, *Manager*
EMP: 250 **Publicly Held**
SIC: 3812 Search & navigation equipment
HQ: Lockheed Martin Integrated Systems, Llc
6801 Rockledge Dr
Bethesda MD 20817

(G-5986)
MC DOES INC
Also Called: Fastsigns
906 Route 73 N (08053-1230)
PHONE.............................856 985-8730
Fax: 856 985-8531
Mark Esposito, *President*
John Downing, *Principal*
EMP: 9
SALES (est): 1.3MM **Privately Held**
SIC: 3993 Signs & advertising specialties

(G-5987)
MEDFORD SOFT PRETZELS INC
102 Williamsburg Ct (08053-3748)
PHONE.............................856 662-8792
Patrick Scott, *President*
Michael Loose, *Principal*
Karen Scott, *Principal*
Mindy Loose, *Vice Pres*
EMP: 8
SALES (est): 341.5K **Privately Held**
SIC: 2052 Pretzels

(G-5988)
MUNIPOL SYSTEMS
1 Eves Dr Ste 111 (08053-3125)
PHONE.............................856 985-2929
Jack Brownstein, *President*
Richmond Cooper, *Vice Pres*
James Mc Farland, *Vice Pres*
William Olsen, *Vice Pres*
EMP: 15
SALES: 700K **Privately Held**
WEB: www.munipol.com
SIC: 7372 Application computer software

(G-5989)
NEIGHBORHOOD SHOPPERS (PA)
Also Called: Shopper Discount Guide
10000 Grntree Ctr Ste 201 (08053)
PHONE.............................856 988-7722
EMP: 7 EST: 2008
SALES: 875K **Privately Held**
SIC: 8742 2721 7311 Management Consulting Services Periodicals-Publishing/Printing Advertising Agency

(G-5990)
NETSCOUT SYSTEMS INC
2000 Lincoln Dr E (08053-1557)
PHONE.............................609 518-4100
Felix Houvig, *Engineer*
EMP: 9
SALES (corp-wide): 986.7MM **Publicly Held**
SIC: 7373 3577 Computer integrated systems design; computer peripheral equipment
PA: Netscout Systems, Inc.
310 Littleton Rd
Westford MA 01886
978 614-4000

(G-5991)
OMNITESTER CORP (PA)
101 Flintlock Ln (08053-1111)
PHONE.............................856 985-8960
James M Lamy, *CEO*
James Wehman, *President*
Ben Broomhead, *Mfg Staff*
Joseph M Donovan, *Controller*
EMP: 15
SQ FT: 5,000
SALES (est): 1.1MM **Privately Held**
SIC: 3825 Test equipment for electronic & electrical circuits

(G-5992)
PACKAGING CORPORATION AMERICA
Also Called: Marlton Creative Design Center
8 E Stow Rd Ste 100 (08053-3161)
PHONE.............................856 596-5020
EMP: 4
SALES (corp-wide): 6.4B **Publicly Held**
SIC: 2653 Boxes, corrugated: made from purchased materials
PA: Packaging Corporation Of America
1955 W Field Ct
Lake Forest IL 60045
847 482-3000

(G-5993)
PAPERY OF MARLTON LLC
300 Route 73 S Ste B (08053-3029)
PHONE.............................856 985-1776
Fax: 856 985-3199
Edmund Brandhorst,
Marylou Brandhorst,
EMP: 6
SALES: 600K **Privately Held**
SIC: 5943 5947 2759 Stationery stores; greeting cards; gift shop; invitation & stationery printing & engraving

(G-5994)
PLESCIA & COMPANY INC
Also Called: Compliance Educational Systems
205 Shady Ln (08053-2718)
PHONE.............................856 793-0137
Gary Plescia, *President*
Joanne Plescia, *Vice Pres*
Christine Castile, *Treasurer*
EMP: 10
SALES (est): 844K **Privately Held**
SIC: 7372 Prepackaged software

(G-5995)
PREMIER PRODUCTS INC
1002 Lincoln Dr W Ste B (08053-1533)
PHONE.............................856 231-1800
Eric Alpert, *President*
Rich Holderman, *Vice Pres*
▲ EMP: 65
SQ FT: 3,000
SALES (est): 9.8MM **Privately Held**
SIC: 3714 Air conditioner parts, motor vehicle

(G-5996)
REDI-DATA INC
Km Lists
600 Route 73 N Ste 10a (08053-1611)
PHONE.............................856 988-0551
Fax: 856 988-6662
Pam Holden, *Vice Pres*
EMP: 835
SALES (corp-wide): 33.3MM **Privately Held**
SIC: 7375 7372 Data base information retrieval; prepackaged software
PA: Redi-Data Inc.
5 Audrey Pl
Fairfield NJ 07004
973 227-4380

(G-5997)
RVS PUBLISHING INC
Also Called: S J Magazine
875 Route 73 N Ste H (08053-1273)
PHONE.............................856 810-7743
Fax: 856 810-7796
Richard V Smith, *President*
Todd Moreland, *VP Sales*
EMP: 11
SALES: 1.8MM **Privately Held**
SIC: 2721 Magazines: publishing & printing

(G-5998)
SCHURMAN FINE PAPERS
Also Called: Papyrus
300 State Hwy Rte 73 (08053)
PHONE.............................856 985-1776
EMP: 21
SALES (corp-wide): 751.7MM **Privately Held**
SIC: 5113 2679 2771 5947 Industrial & personal service paper; paper & products, wrapping or coarse; gift wrap & novelties, paper; greeting cards; gift, novelty & souvenir shop; greeting cards
PA: Schurman Fine Papers
300 Oak Bluff Ln
Goodlettsville TN 37072
707 425-8006

(G-5999)
SHEEX INC
Also Called: Sheex Performance Sleep
10000 Lincoln Dr E # 303 (08053-3108)
PHONE.............................856 334-3021
Michelle Brooke-Marciniak, *CEO*
Susan K Walvius, *President*
Joel Ginsparg, *CFO*
▲ EMP: 20
SQ FT: 5,000
SALES (est): 5MM **Privately Held**
WEB: www.sheex.com
SIC: 2515 2392 Sleep furniture; household furnishings

(G-6000)
STONE MAR NATURAL STONE CO LLC (PA)
8 E Stow Rd Ste 200 (08053-3161)
PHONE.............................856 988-1802
Simon Katan, *President*
▲ EMP: 6
SALES (est): 1MM **Privately Held**
SIC: 3281 Cut stone & stone products

(G-6001)
TEST TECHNOLOGY INC (HQ)
5 E Stow Rd (08053-3145)
PHONE.............................856 596-1215
Fax: 856 552-0262
Linda A Austin, *President*
▲ EMP: 94
SQ FT: 71,000
SALES (est): 8.6MM
SALES (corp-wide): 15.4MM **Privately Held**
WEB: www.testtech.com
SIC: 7629 3672 Electronic equipment repair; printed circuit boards
PA: Revertech Solutions, Llc
4 E Stow Rd Ste 2
Marlton NJ 08053
877 207-2836

(G-6002)
VAN BRILL POOL & SPA CENTER
Also Called: All Seasons Pool & Spa
850 Route 70 W (08053-1646)
P.O. Box 844 (08053-0844)
PHONE.............................856 424-4333
Fax: 856 424-4093
Armand J Savaiano, *President*
Armand Savaiano, *President*
EMP: 8
SQ FT: 4,500
SALES (est): 1.7MM **Privately Held**
SIC: 5999 3272 Spas & hot tubs; fireplace & chimney material: concrete

(G-6003)
WESTROCK CONVERTING COMPANY
5000 Lincoln Dr E (08053-1562)
PHONE.............................856 438-2200
Rhonda Hall, *General Mgr*
EMP: 8
SALES (corp-wide): 14.8B **Publicly Held**
SIC: 3999 Advertising display products
HQ: Westrock Converting Company
1000 Abernathy Rd Ste 125
Atlanta GA 30328
770 246-9982

(G-6004)
WESTROCK RKT COMPANY
Also Called: Rock Team Alliance
5000 Lincoln Dr E (08053-1562)
PHONE.............................856 596-8604
Bill Atcheson, *Branch Mgr*
EMP: 161
SALES (corp-wide): 14.8B **Publicly Held**
SIC: 2653 Partitions, solid fiber: made from purchased materials
HQ: Westrock Rkt Company
1000 Abernathy Rd Ste 125
Atlanta GA 30328
770 448-2193

Marmora
Cape May County

(G-6005)
BUSTED KNUCKLE
100 Route Us 9 S Unit A (08223-1285)
PHONE.............................609 432-7383
Fax: 609 390-5940
Ronald Liberati, *Principal*
EMP: 6 EST: 2012
SALES (est): 350K **Privately Held**
SIC: 3531 Automobile wrecker hoists

(G-6006)
SJSHORE MARKETING LTD LBLTY CO
Also Called: Allegra Marketing Print & Mail
533 S Shore Rd Ste 1 (08223-1258)
PHONE................................609 390-1400
Nicholas Wieand,
Denise Wieand,
EMP: 14
SQ FT: 5,400
SALES (est): 825K Privately Held
SIC: 2759 3993 7331 8742 Commercial printing; advertising literature: printing; signs & advertising specialties; mailing service; marketing consulting services

(G-6007)
TEC ELEVATOR INC
510 Route Us 9 S (08223-1329)
PHONE................................609 938-0647
Robert Shaw Jr, CEO
David Hollingsworth, General Mgr
Jim Koch, Sales Staff
Margaret Dromgoole, Admin Sec
Dan Sabia, Representative
EMP: 10
SALES (est): 2.3MM Privately Held
SIC: 3534 Elevators & equipment

Martinsville
Somerset County

(G-6008)
CHEMTRACT LLC
2144 Gilbride Rd (08836-2231)
PHONE................................732 820-0427
James Balkovec, Owner
EMP: 4 EST: 2012
SALES (est): 231.5K Privately Held
SIC: 2834 Pharmaceutical preparations

(G-6009)
COMPUTER DOC ASSOCIATES INC
2007 Washington Valley Rd (08836-2010)
P.O. Box 184, Gillette (07933-0184)
PHONE................................908 647-4445
Parveen Khattar, President
EMP: 68 EST: 1994
SALES (est): 6.8MM Privately Held
WEB: www.cdaus.com
SIC: 5734 7372 8243 8748 Computer & software stores; business oriented computer software; operating systems computer software; software training, computer; systems engineering consultant, ex. computer or professional

(G-6010)
MRS SULLIVANS INC (PA)
Also Called: Mrs. Sullivan's Pies
1990 Washington Valley Rd (08836-7000)
P.O. Box 446, Jackson TN (38302-0446)
PHONE................................908 246-8937
James Lawrence, President
Rodney Myrick, President
Ed Novy, CFO
EMP: 21
SQ FT: 12,000
SALES (est): 1.9MM Privately Held
WEB: www.mrssullivans.com
SIC: 2051 Cakes, pies & pastries

(G-6011)
WINTERS STAMP MFG CO INC
Also Called: Winters Bank Signs
1024 Mayflower Ct (08836-2324)
PHONE................................908 352-3725
Fax: 908 352-3324
J Carl Apsley Jr, CEO
Jane Apsley - Williams, President
▲ EMP: 10
SQ FT: 48,000
SALES (est): 835K Privately Held
SIC: 3953 3479 Marking devices; name plates: engraved, etched, etc.

Matawan
Monmouth County

(G-6012)
AGAU INC
Also Called: Print Shop, The
1077 State Route 34 Ste M (07747-2151)
PHONE................................732 583-4343
Paul Silvergold, President
EMP: 8 EST: 1979
SALES (est): 720K Privately Held
WEB: www.printshoppenj.com
SIC: 2752 Commercial printing, offset

(G-6013)
B SPINELLI FARM CONTAINERS
3992 Highway 516 (07747-7017)
PHONE................................732 566-5619
Fax: 732 566-0387
Benjamin Spinelli Jr, President
Benjamin Spinelli Sr, Vice Pres
Margaret Spinelli, Vice Pres
Helen Spinelli, Admin Sec
EMP: 6
SALES (est): 807.3K Privately Held
SIC: 2449 2653 Boxes, wood: wirebound; boxes, corrugated: made from purchased materials

(G-6014)
CARIB-DISPLAY CO (PA)
18 Northland Ln (07747-1321)
P.O. Box 306 (07747-0306)
PHONE................................732 583-1648
Fax: 718 851-7965
Cary Binder, Owner
EMP: 5
SALES (est): 497.2K Privately Held
WEB: www.caribdisplay.com
SIC: 2542 Partitions & fixtures, except wood

(G-6015)
CERONICS INC
5 Dock St (07747-2506)
P.O. Box 75 (07747-0075)
PHONE................................732 566-5600
Fax: 732 566-9317
Richard Patton, President
George Curchin, Vice Pres
EMP: 7
SQ FT: 3,000
SALES (est): 756.1K Privately Held
WEB: www.ceronicsinc.com
SIC: 3479 Coating of metals & formed products; painting, coating & hot dipping

(G-6016)
D R TIELMANN INC
Also Called: Fibercontrol
1208 State Route 34 Ste 1 (07747-1966)
P.O. Box 198, Holmdel (07733-0198)
PHONE................................732 332-1860
D R Tielmann, President
EMP: 5
SQ FT: 3,000
SALES (est): 410K Privately Held
WEB: www.fibercontrol.com
SIC: 3661 Telegraph & related apparatus

(G-6017)
DIGIVAC COMPANY
105 B Church St Ste 4 (07747)
PHONE................................732 765-0900
Timothy Collins, President
Heather Maitree, Treasurer
Kerry Obrien, Marketing Staff
Christine Diab, Manager
Marilyn Simone, Manager
EMP: 12
SQ FT: 3,300
SALES (est): 1.3MM Privately Held
WEB: www.digivac.com
SIC: 3545 3823 3829 Gauges (machine tool accessories); industrial instrmnts msrmnt display/control process variable; measuring & controlling devices

(G-6018)
DULCE A DESSERT BAR LLC
609 S Atlantic Ave (07747-2225)
PHONE................................908 461-2418
Erica Townes,
EMP: 7
SALES (est): 210.5K Privately Held
SIC: 2099 Desserts, ready-to-mix

(G-6019)
DYNAMIC COATINGS LLC
253 Main St Ste 120 (07747-3222)
PHONE................................732 998-6625
Gregory Guga, President
EMP: 4 EST: 2015
SALES (est): 518.8K Privately Held
SIC: 3479 Metal coating & allied service

(G-6020)
ELIS HOT BAGELS INC
1055c Hwy 34 (07747)
PHONE................................732 566-4523
Fax: 732 566-1715
Stuart Rauchman, President
EMP: 45
SQ FT: 4,000
SALES (est): 3.8MM Privately Held
SIC: 2051 5812 5149 5461 Bagels, fresh or frozen; eating places; groceries & related products; bakeries

(G-6021)
GEMTOR INC
1 Johnson Ave (07747-2595)
PHONE................................732 583-6200
Fax: 732 290-9391
Craig Neustater, President
Ruth Ullrich, Admin Sec
▲ EMP: 40
SQ FT: 18,000
SALES (est): 6MM Privately Held
WEB: www.gemtor.com
SIC: 3842 Personal safety equipment

(G-6022)
ITEC CONSULTANTS LLC
38 Hyer Ct (07747-1252)
PHONE................................732 784-8322
Robert Smith, Mng Member
Mario Rodrigues, Mng Member
EMP: 6
SALES (est): 570K Privately Held
SIC: 3651 Household audio & video equipment

(G-6023)
KITCHEN CRAFTERS PLUS
Also Called: B & B Custom Cabinets
1 Suydam Pl (07747-1024)
PHONE................................732 566-7995
Al Brisebois, President
Roger Buchko, Vice Pres
EMP: 4
SQ FT: 4,500
SALES (est): 330K Privately Held
WEB: www.kitchencraftersplus.com
SIC: 2434 1751 Wood kitchen cabinets; cabinet building & installation

(G-6024)
MAJOR BS GENERAL QUARTERS LLC
46 Oak Knoll Dr (07747-2650)
PHONE................................732 710-6088
EMP: 4
SALES (est): 333.3K Privately Held
SIC: 3131 Quarters

(G-6025)
NEW JERSEY STAIR AND RAIL INC
746 Lloyd Rd (07747-1401)
PHONE................................732 583-8400
Fax: 732 583-6303
Robert Barrett, President
Cathrine Barrett, Corp Secy
EMP: 5
SQ FT: 8,000
SALES (est): 467.1K Privately Held
SIC: 3446 Stairs, staircases, stair treads: prefabricated metal

(G-6026)
OPEN TERRA INC
20 Reddington Dr (07747-6647)
PHONE................................732 765-9600
David Sasson, CEO
Tim Kehrer, Marketing Staff
Ted Bielenda, CTO
EMP: 7
SALES: 500K Privately Held
WEB: www.openterra.com
SIC: 3663 Mobile communication equipment

(G-6027)
PARWAN ELECTRONICS CORPORATION (PA)
Also Called: PEC
1230 Hwy 34 (07747-1952)
PHONE................................732 290-1900
Fax: 732 566-8771
Suraj Tschand, President
Vinay Tschand, COO
Chand Tschand, CFO
Ajay Tschand, CTO
EMP: 23
SQ FT: 7,000
SALES (est): 5.6MM Privately Held
WEB: www.voicesaver.com
SIC: 3661 Carrier equipment, telephone or telegraph

(G-6028)
PENN POWER GROUP LLC
Also Called: Carrier Transicold of NJ
4118 Hiway 34 (07747)
PHONE................................732 441-1489
Gary Meyers, Branch Mgr
EMP: 10
SALES (corp-wide): 92MM Privately Held
SIC: 3519 Engines, diesel & semi-diesel or dual-fuel
PA: Penn Power Group, Llc
8330 State Rd
Philadelphia PA 19136
215 335-0500

(G-6029)
POMI USA INC
253 Main St Ste 380 (07747-3222)
PHONE................................732 541-4115
Constantino Vaia, President
Angela Crane, Manager
▲ EMP: 7
SQ FT: 60
SALES: 470.9K
SALES (corp-wide): 274.3MM Privately Held
SIC: 2033 Canned fruits & specialties
PA: Consorzio Casalasco Del Pomodoro Societa' Agricola Cooperativa
Strada Provinciale 32
Rivarolo Del Re Ed Uniti CR 26036
037 553-6211

(G-6030)
RAZER SCANDINAVIA INC
432 State Route 34 Ste 1a (07747-2193)
PHONE................................732 441-1250
Charles Goodwin, CFO
▲ EMP: 4 EST: 2013
SALES: 158K Privately Held
SIC: 3462 Horseshoes

(G-6031)
ROSSOW COSMETIQUES - USA INC
Also Called: Rossow USA
100 Matawan Rd Ste 350 (07747-3902)
PHONE................................732 872-1464
Tara Tobin, Opers Mgr
Paul Kretzer, Sales Dir
Carrie Kutzkowski, Office Mgr
▲ EMP: 5
SQ FT: 1,200
SALES (est): 490K Privately Held
SIC: 2844 Cosmetic preparations

(G-6032)
SOUTH SHORE SIGN CO INC
Also Called: South Shore Signs
550 Morristown Rd (07747-3580)
PHONE................................718 984-5624
Anthony Nuzzolo, Chairman
EMP: 12
SQ FT: 1,400
SALES (est): 1.2MM Privately Held
WEB: www.signbrothers.com
SIC: 3993 Advertising artwork

▲ = Import ▼=Export
◆ =Import/Export

(G-6033)
STEELSTRAN INDUSTRIES INC
Also Called: A L Don Co
Foot Of Dock St (07747)
PHONE..................................732 566-5040
Fax: 732 566-5365
Bob Bauer, *Opers-Prdtn-Mfg*
EMP: 6
SQ FT: 9,000
SALES (corp-wide): 16.6MM **Privately Held**
SIC: 2499 3429 Poles, wood; ladders, wood; oars & paddles, wood; manufactured hardware (general)
PA: Steelstran Industries, Inc.
35 Mileed Way
Avenel NJ 07001
732 574-0700

(G-6034)
UNITED DIAM INC
12 Grenoble Ct (07747-9651)
PHONE..................................732 619-0950
Vivek Diora, *Exec Dir*
EMP: 5
SALES (est): 349.3K **Privately Held**
SIC: 5094 3911 Jewelry & precious stones; jewelry; jewelry, precious metal

---

Mauricetown
Cumberland County

(G-6035)
U S SILICA COMPANY
9035 Noble St (08329)
P.O. Box 254 (08329-0254)
PHONE..................................856 785-0720
Scott Eves, *Branch Mgr*
Bill Davis, *Maintence Staff*
EMP: 50
SALES (corp-wide): 1.2B **Publicly Held**
WEB: www.u-s-silica.com
SIC: 1446 Foundry sand mining
HQ: U. S. Silica Company
8490 Progress Dr Ste 300
Frederick MD 21701
301 682-0600

Mays Landing
Atlantic County

(G-6036)
AMERICAN YOUTH ENTERPRISES INC
120 Marlin Ln (08330-1635)
P.O. Box 653 (08330-0653)
PHONE..................................609 909-1900
Fax: 609 909-8860
David Hagan Jr, *President*
EMP: 8
SQ FT: 5,000
SALES (est): 1MM **Privately Held**
WEB: www.americanyouth.org
SIC: 2759 Promotional printing

(G-6037)
BAU-LO WOODEN FURNITURE INC
63 Chancellor Park Dr (08330-2047)
PHONE..................................212 664-9188
Baolian Yang, *President*
EMP: 8
SALES (est): 852.2K
SALES (corp-wide): 75.8MM **Privately Held**
WEB: www.sanmu.com
SIC: 5712 2511 Furniture stores; wood household furniture
PA: Rizhao Sanmu Group Co., Ltd.
Andongwei Sub-District, Lanshan Dist.
Rizhao 27680
633 261-1299

(G-6038)
CASTELLANE MANUFACTURING CO
1405 Cantillon Blvd (08330-2023)
P.O. Box 921 (08330-0921)
PHONE..................................609 625-3427
Fax: 609 625-3428

Nicholas R Castellane, *President*
Elizabeth M Castellane, *Corp Secy*
EMP: 12 EST: 1958
SQ FT: 10,000
SALES (est): 1.2MM **Privately Held**
SIC: 2353 Uniform hats & caps

(G-6039)
INTEX MILLWORK SOLUTIONS LLC
45 Mill St (08330-1511)
PHONE..................................856 293-4100
Fax: 856 293-4102
Joe Umosella, *President*
Ned Lawrence, *Regl Sales Mgr*
EMP: 36
SALES (est): 11MM **Privately Held**
SIC: 2431 Millwork

(G-6040)
NICKELS CARPET CLEANING
957 Morningside Dr (08330-1913)
PHONE..................................609 892-5783
Daniel Nickels, *Principal*
EMP: 6 EST: 2011
SALES (est): 480.1K **Privately Held**
SIC: 3356 Nickel

(G-6041)
NORTH AMERICAN COMPOSITES CO
5450 Atlantic Ave (08330-2006)
PHONE..................................609 625-8101
Simon Bula, *Manager*
EMP: 14
SALES (corp-wide): 302.9MM **Privately Held**
SIC: 2821 Plastics materials & resins
HQ: North American Composites Company
300 Apollo Dr
Circle Pines MN 55014
651 766-6892

(G-6042)
PRECISION WELDING MACHINE
13th St (08330)
P.O. Box 216 (08330-0216)
PHONE..................................609 625-1465
Dave Birch, *Owner*
EMP: 6
SALES (est): 601.7K **Privately Held**
SIC: 7692 Welding repair

(G-6043)
VAN DUYNE BROS INC
5112 Oakwood Blvd (08330-2016)
PHONE..................................609 625-0299
Eileen Van Duyne, *President*
John L Van Duyne Jr, *Vice Pres*
Thomas Van Duyne, *Treasurer*
John L Van Duyne Sr, *Shareholder*
EMP: 5 EST: 1948
SALES (est): 530K **Privately Held**
SIC: 3732 1521 Lifeboats, building & repairing; new construction, single-family houses

(G-6044)
VANTAGE BUSINESS SYSTEMS INC
6019 Main St (08330-1845)
PHONE..................................609 625-7020
EMP: 6
SALES (est): 550K **Privately Held**
SIC: 7372 Prepackaged Software Services

Maywood
Bergen County

(G-6045)
ADLER INTERNATIONAL LTD (PA)
205 Maywood Ave (07607-1027)
PHONE..................................201 843-4525
Donald James Adler, *President*
▲ EMP: 7
SALES (est): 654K **Privately Held**
WEB: www.adlerinternational.com
SIC: 2678 5112 Stationery products; stationery & office supplies; writing instruments & supplies

(G-6046)
CIRCUIT REPRODUCTION CO
219 Hergesell Ave (07607-1140)
PHONE..................................201 712-9292
Fax: 201 712-9155
Paul Kabaria, *President*
Ashok Kabaria, *Vice Pres*
EMP: 12
SQ FT: 20,000
SALES (est): 1.6MM **Privately Held**
SIC: 3672 Printed circuit boards

(G-6047)
DE SAUSSURE EQUIPMENT CO INC
Also Called: Maywood Furniture
23 W Howcroft Rd (07607-1089)
PHONE..................................201 845-6517
Fax: 201 845-4586
Thomas McMullen, *CEO*
William P De Saussure IV, *President*
Jack Desaussure, *COO*
Kenneth Persson, *Vice Pres*
Barbara Jenkins, *CFO*
▲ EMP: 34
SQ FT: 44,700
SALES (est): 4.5MM **Privately Held**
WEB: www.maywood.com
SIC: 2514 Tables, household: metal

(G-6048)
DOLCE BROTHERS PRINTING INC (PA)
29 Brook Ave (07607-1130)
PHONE..................................201 843-0400
James Dolce, *President*
Glenn Dolce, *Vice Pres*
EMP: 33
SQ FT: 35,000
SALES (est): 11.9MM **Privately Held**
WEB: www.dolceprint.com
SIC: 2752 Commercial printing, offset

(G-6049)
DOLCE PRINTING
29 Brook Ave (07607-1130)
PHONE..................................201 843-0400
Matthew Yeranian, *President*
Bill Camarco, *General Mgr*
Aimee Cuevas, *Principal*
Jay Maidenberg, *Vice Pres*
Joann Smolen, *Production*
EMP: 16 EST: 2012
SALES (est): 2.3MM **Privately Held**
SIC: 2752 Commercial printing, offset

(G-6050)
ENCORE POLY
240 W Passaic St Ste 7 (07607-1264)
PHONE..................................201 845-4510
Kay Kyff, *Owner*
EMP: 5
SALES (est): 826.4K **Privately Held**
SIC: 2673 Bags: plastic, laminated & coated

(G-6051)
INTERNATIONAL MOLASSES CORP
121 E Hunter Ave (07607-1831)
PHONE..................................201 368-8036
Ronald Targan, *President*
EMP: 30
SQ FT: 18,000
SALES (est): 2.8MM **Privately Held**
SIC: 2062 Blackstrap molasses from purchased raw sugar or syrup

(G-6052)
JACLYN INC
Bonnie International
197 W Spring Valley Ave # 101 (07607-1729)
PHONE..................................201 909-6000
Fax: 201 226-7801
Allan Ginsburg, *Branch Mgr*
EMP: 120
SALES (corp-wide): 32.8MM **Publicly Held**
SIC: 2389 Costumes
HQ: Jaclyn Llc
197 W Spring Valley Ave # 101
Maywood NJ 07607
201 909-6000

(G-6053)
JACLYN HOLDINGS PARENT LLC (PA)
197 W Spring Valley Ave (07607-1730)
PHONE..................................201 909-6000
Robert Chestnov, *President*
EMP: 2
SALES (est): 32.8MM **Publicly Held**
SIC: 3199 3111 2824 3172 Equestrian related leather articles; bag leather; vinyl fibers; cosmetic bags; investment holding companies, except banks

(G-6054)
JACLYN LLC (HQ)
197 W Spring Valley Ave # 101 (07607-1729)
PHONE..................................201 909-6000
Robert Chestnov, *President*
Anthony Christon, *CFO*
▲ EMP: 62
SQ FT: 16,000
SALES (est): 32.8MM **Publicly Held**
WEB: www.jaclyninc.com
SIC: 3199 3111 2824 3172 Equestrian related leather articles; bag leather; handbag leather; vinyl fibers; cosmetic bags
PA: Jaclyn Holdings Parent Llc
197 W Spring Valley Ave
Maywood NJ 07607
201 909-6000

(G-6055)
JIMCAM PUBLISHING INC
Also Called: Our Town
19 W Pleasant Ave Fl 1 (07607-1320)
PHONE..................................201 843-5700
Jim Hornes, *President*
Camille Hornes, *CFO*
EMP: 5
SQ FT: 250
SALES (est): 440.5K **Privately Held**
SIC: 2759 Commercial printing

(G-6056)
JOSEPH CASTINGS INC
25 Brook Ave (07607-1130)
PHONE..................................201 712-0717
Fax: 201 712-0818
Albert Hess, *President*
Marion Hess, *Corp Secy*
Robert Hess, *Vice Pres*
EMP: 16 EST: 1957
SQ FT: 5,000
SALES (est): 1.7MM **Privately Held**
WEB: www.josephcastings.com
SIC: 3915 Jewelers' castings

(G-6057)
JP GROUP INTERNATIONAL LLC
Also Called: Lisabelle
525 Palmer Ave (07607-1325)
P.O. Box 748 (07607-0748)
PHONE..................................201 820-1444
Lisa Begega Mignano,
EMP: 4
SALES (est): 308.6K **Privately Held**
SIC: 2369 Girls' & children's outerwear

(G-6058)
MIDAS DESIGNS LTD
124 Lafayette Ave (07607-2035)
PHONE..................................201 567-2700
Adam Haber, *President*
Yvonne Wasilewski, *Corp Secy*
EMP: 6
SQ FT: 2,000
SALES (est): 1MM **Privately Held**
SIC: 3911 Jewelry, precious metal

(G-6059)
PARSELLS PRINTING INC
938 Spring Valley Rd # 1 (07607-1446)
PHONE..................................973 473-2700
Fax: 973 473-6383
James Parsells, *President*
Ron Parsells, *Vice Pres*
EMP: 4
SQ FT: 2,800
SALES (est): 270K **Privately Held**
WEB: www.parsellsprinting.com
SIC: 2752 Commercial printing, offset

(PA)=Parent Co (HQ)=Headquarters (DH)=Div Headquarters
✪ = New Business established in last 2 years

(G-6060)
PRECISION PRODUCTS CO INC
219 Hergesell Ave (07607-1140)
PHONE..............................201 712-5757
Fax: 201 712-5757
Amit Kabaria, *President*
EMP: 25 EST: 1955
SQ FT: 13,000
SALES: 779.1K Privately Held
WEB: www.precisionproductsco.com
SIC: 3672 Printed circuit boards

(G-6061)
STEPAN COMPANY
Maywood Division
100 W Hunter Ave (07607-1021)
PHONE..............................201 845-3030
Fax: 201 845-6754
Scott Behrens, *Vice Pres*
Deb Stefaniak, *Vice Pres*
Joe Gartelmann, *Opers Mgr*
Warren Kaplan, *Research*
Steven Clauss, *Engineer*
EMP: 91
SALES (corp-wide): 1.9B Publicly Held
WEB: www.stepan.com
SIC: 2842 2899 Polishing preparations &
  related products; sanitation preparations,
  disinfectants & deodorants; chemical
  preparations
PA: Stepan Company
  22 W Frontage Rd
  Northfield IL 60093
  847 446-7500

(G-6062)
VICTORS THREE-D INC
Also Called: Victors Settings
25 Brook Ave (07607-1130)
PHONE..............................201 845-4433
Albert Hess, *President*
Marion Hess, *Corp Secy*
Robert Hess, *Vice Pres*
Joseph De Poto, *Sales Staff*
Paul M Low, *Technology*
EMP: 100 EST: 1958
SQ FT: 27,000
SALES (est): 17.4MM Privately Held
WEB: www.victorsettings.com
SIC: 3339 3915 Primary nonferrous met-
  als; jewelers' findings & materials

Medford
Burlington County

(G-6063)
ADAPTIVE TECHNOLOGY ENTPS LLC
Also Called: Adaptech
141 Taunton Blvd (08055-3412)
PHONE..............................877 847-6272
Adam Berr,
Donyce Flanagan,
Darren Pedersen,
EMP: 5
SALES (est): 210.3K Privately Held
SIC: 8243 7373 5734 3999 Software
  training, computer; value-added resellers;
  computer systems; personal computers;
  wheelchair lifts; wheelchair lifts;

(G-6064)
AMEGA SCIENTIFIC CORPORATION
617 Stokes Rd (08055-3097)
PHONE..............................609 953-7295
Anthony Amato, *President*
Hope McCorristin, *Mktg Coord*
EMP: 12
SQ FT: 2,500
SALES (est): 1.6MM
SALES (corp-wide): 96.1MM Publicly
Held
WEB: www.amegascientific.com
SIC: 3822 5084 Auto controls regulating
  residntl & coml environmt & applncs; in-
  struments & control equipment
PA: Mesa Laboratories, Inc.
  12100 W 6th Ave
  Lakewood CO 80228
  303 987-8000

(G-6065)
BERAT CORPORATION
Also Called: Shop Rite of Medford
208 Route 70 (08055-9522)
PHONE..............................609 953-7700
Anthony Massony, *Manager*
EMP: 200
SALES (corp-wide): 194.8MM Privately
Held
SIC: 5411 5992 5912 5812 Grocery
  stores, independent; florists; drug stores
  & proprietary stores; eating places; bread,
  cake & related products
PA: Berat Corporation
  1230 Blckwood Clmenton Rd
  Clementon NJ 08021
  856 627-6501

(G-6066)
CHEMTREAT INC
520 Stokes Rd Ste B11 (08055-2904)
PHONE..............................609 654-9522
EMP: 8
SALES (corp-wide): 19.1B Publicly Held
SIC: 2899 Ret Misc Merchandise
HQ: Chemtreat, Inc.
  5640 Cox Rd Ste 300
  Glen Allen VA 23060
  804 965-0154

(G-6067)
CONTINENTAL WOODWORKING CO
617 Stokes Rd Ste 4305 (08055-3097)
PHONE..............................609 654-0820
Michael Dovell, *President*
EMP: 4
SQ FT: 70,000
SALES: 1MM Privately Held
SIC: 2426 Flooring, hardwood

(G-6068)
DUBELL LUMBER CO (PA)
148 Route 70 (08055-2373)
P.O. Box 1449 (08055-6449)
PHONE..............................609 654-4143
Gene S Dimedio, *President*
Dennis Dimedio, *Corp Secy*
David Dimedio, *Vice Pres*
Ronald Dimedio, *Vice Pres*
EMP: 45
SQ FT: 50,000
SALES (est): 49MM Privately Held
WEB: www.dubell.com
SIC: 5211 5031 1521 1542 Lumber &
  other building materials; lumber: rough,
  dressed & finished; single-family housing
  construction; nonresidential construction;
  cabinets, lockers & shelving

(G-6069)
FAULKNER INFORMATION SVCS LLC
143 Old Marlton Pike (08055-8750)
PHONE..............................856 662-2070
Fax: 856 662-0905
Tom Hogan, *President*
Michael Flaherty, *President*
Barbara Forkel, *Vice Pres*
Jeanne Andricola, *Accounts Mgr*
Paula Sherman, *Accounts Mgr*
EMP: 100
SQ FT: 14,000
SALES (est): 6.4MM Privately Held
WEB: www.faulkner.com
SIC: 2741 Technical manuals: publishing &
  printing

(G-6070)
HOMAN COMMUNICATIONS INC
194 Route 70 Ste 9 (08055-2377)
PHONE..............................609 654-9594
Jack Acconey, *Owner*
EMP: 5
SALES (est): 413.7K Privately Held
WEB: www.homancom.com
SIC: 5731 7622 3663 Radios, two-way,
  citizens' band, weather, short-wave, etc.;
  home entertainment repair services; radio
  broadcasting & communications equip-
  ment

(G-6071)
INFORMATION TODAY INC (PA)
143 Old Marlton Pike (08055-8750)
PHONE..............................609 654-6266
Roger R Bilboul, *Ch of Bd*
Thomas H Hogan, *President*
Michael Baumann, *Editor*
Donovan Griffin, *Editor*
Stephen Nathans, *Editor*
EMP: 50
SQ FT: 5,000
SALES (est): 19.2MM Privately Held
WEB: www.infotoday.com
SIC: 2721 7389 Trade journals: publishing
  only, not printed on site; convention &
  show services

(G-6072)
J & S PRECISION PRODUCTS CO
16 Medford Evesboro Rd (08055-9592)
PHONE..............................609 654-0900
Fax: 609 654-7098
Steven Janssen, *President*
Barbara Janssen, *Corp Secy*
David Janssen, *Vice Pres*
◆ EMP: 40 EST: 1964
SQ FT: 25,000
SALES (est): 7.5MM Privately Held
SIC: 3451 Screw machine products

(G-6073)
JOE MIKE PRECISION FABRICATION
6 Tidswell Ave (08055-2708)
PHONE..............................609 953-1144
Fax: 609 953-9603
Joseph Evans, *President*
EMP: 10
SALES: 750K Privately Held
SIC: 3541 3556 Gear cutting & finishing
  machines; food products machinery

(G-6074)
L E ROSELLIS FOOD SPECIALTIES
Also Called: Roselli, L E
155 Church Rd (08055-9595)
P.O. Box 610 (08055-0610)
PHONE..............................609 654-4816
Fax: 609 953-5673
Dolores Roselli, *President*
Leo Roselli, *Vice Pres*
Leo P Roselli, *Vice Pres*
EMP: 10
SQ FT: 5,000
SALES (est): 1.5MM Privately Held
WEB: www.rosellisfood.com
SIC: 5411 2038 0161 2099 Frozen food
  & freezer plans, except meat; ethnic
  foods, frozen; vegetables & melons; food
  preparations; macaroni & spaghetti

(G-6075)
LASER CONTRACTORS LLC
433 Mckendimen Rd (08055-9773)
PHONE..............................609 517-2407
Cheryl Ann Pereira, *Mng Member*
EMP: 4
SALES (est): 311.3K Privately Held
SIC: 3699 Laser systems & equipment

(G-6076)
LEOS ICE CREAM COMPANY
Also Called: Leo's Famous Yum Yum
7 Tomlinson Mill Rd Ste 5 (08055-3480)
PHONE..............................856 797-8771
Rick Cirelli, *CEO*
EMP: 7
SALES (est): 434.7K Privately Held
WEB: www.leosicecream.com
SIC: 2024 Ice cream & frozen desserts

(G-6077)
MFB SOFT PRETZELS INC
617 Stokes Rd (08055-3097)
PHONE..............................609 953-6773
Mark Butterfoss, *Principal*
EMP: 4
SALES (est): 302.7K Privately Held
SIC: 2051 Bakery: wholesale or whole-
  sale/retail combined

(G-6078)
PLEXUS PUBLISHING INC
143 Old Marlton Pike (08055-8750)
PHONE..............................609 654-6500
Fax: 609 654-4309
Thomas H Hogan, *President*
Amy Reeve, *Vice Pres*
Rob Colding, *Marketing Staff*
▲ EMP: 30
SQ FT: 2,000
SALES (est): 3MM Privately Held
WEB: www.plexuspublishing.com
SIC: 2721 2731 Trade journals: publishing
  only, not printed on site; book clubs: pub-
  lishing only, not printed on site

(G-6079)
REILYS CANDY INC
719 Stokes Rd 721 (08055-3002)
PHONE..............................609 953-0040
Fax: 609 953-5478
Susan Pulkon, *President*
Michael Collins, *Plant Mgr*
EMP: 10
SQ FT: 3,600
SALES: 250K Privately Held
SIC: 2064 5441 Candy & other confec-
  tionery products; candy

(G-6080)
RPI INDUSTRIES INC
220 Route 70 (08055-9522)
PHONE..............................609 714-2330
Peter C Palko, *President*
P J Gavin, *Vice Pres*
▲ EMP: 100
SQ FT: 59,475
SALES (est): 22.1MM Privately Held
SIC: 2431 Doors, wood

(G-6081)
SIRCHIE ACQUISITION CO LLC
Also Called: Sirchie Finger Print Labs
612 Gravelly Hollow Rd (08055-8464)
P.O. Box 789 (08055-0789)
PHONE..............................609 654-0777
Tony Saggiomo, *Vice Pres*
Anthony Saggiomo, *Info Tech Mgr*
EMP: 35
SALES (corp-wide): 6.5B Publicly Held
WEB: www.sirchie.com
SIC: 2899 Chemical preparations; oils &
  essential oils
HQ: Sirchie Acquisition Company, Llc
  100 Hunter Pl
  Youngsville NC 27596
  800 356-7311

(G-6082)
SOLV-TEC INCORPORATED
75 N Main St (08055-2718)
PHONE..............................609 261-4242
Patrick O'Brien, *President*
Michael Schult, *Vice Pres*
EMP: 8
SQ FT: 2,400
SALES: 3.5MM Privately Held
SIC: 2843 Surface active agents

(G-6083)
STAUTS PRINTING & GRAPHICS
12 Maine Trl (08055-8916)
PHONE..............................609 654-5382
Paul Stauts, *President*
EMP: 5
SQ FT: 700
SALES (est): 500K Privately Held
SIC: 2752 Commercial printing, offset

(G-6084)
WECOOL TOYS INC
19 N Lakeside Dr W (08055-9205)
PHONE..............................856 296-9766
Jeff Osnato, *President*
Ross Alber, *COO*
◆ EMP: 20
SQ FT: 3,500
SALES: 15MM Privately Held
SIC: 3944 Games, toys & children's vehi-
  cles

▲ = Import ▼=Export
◆ =Import/Export

Medford Lakes
Burlington County

(G-6085)
FULFILLMENT PRINTING AND MAIL
77 Oswego Trl (08055-1110)
P.O. Box 1415, Medford (08055-6415)
PHONE....................................609 953-9500
Kathleen Schindler,
Irvin Chip Schindler,
EMP: 4
SALES (est): 733.8K **Privately Held**
SIC: 2752 Commercial printing, lithographic

Mendham
Morris County

(G-6086)
ALLIED GROUP INC
5 Cold Hill Rd S Ste 19 (07945-3208)
P.O. Box 209 (07945-0209)
PHONE....................................973 543-4994
Fax: 973 543-9737
Vernon Pansmith, *President*
Edward Thomas, *Opers Staff*
▲ **EMP:** 20
SQ FT: 1,400
SALES (est): 5MM **Privately Held**
WEB: www.alliedfilters.com
SIC: 2679 Filter paper: made from purchased material

(G-6087)
JUDITH ROTH STUDIO COLLECTION
3 Stone House Rd (07945-3125)
P.O. Box 351 (07945-0351)
PHONE....................................973 543-4455
Judith Roth, *President*
▲ **EMP:** 6
SALES (est): 900K **Privately Held**
SIC: 2759 5199 Calendars: printing; calendars

(G-6088)
MACIE PUBLISHING COMPANY
13 E Main St Ste 3 (07945-1537)
PHONE....................................973 983-8700
Fax: 973 983-1415
Edward Sueta Jr, *President*
Julie S Kaufmann, *Vice Pres*
▲ **EMP:** 12
SALES (est): 1.2MM **Privately Held**
SIC: 2741 Miscellaneous publishing

(G-6089)
MENDHAM GARDEN CENTER
11 W Main St (07945-1220)
PHONE....................................973 543-4178
Fax: 973 543-4132
Jack Broadhead, *Branch Mgr*
EMP: 5
SALES (corp-wide): 5.8MM **Privately Held**
WEB: www.mendhamgardencenter.com
SIC: 5999 5261 3546 1799 Feed & farm supply; lawn & garden supplies; lawn & garden equipment; saws & sawing equipment; fence construction
PA: Mendham Garden Center
1306 State Route 31 N
Annandale NJ
908 730-9664

(G-6090)
NATIONAL ENVIRONMENTAL SVCS CO (PA)
Also Called: Nesco
7 Hampshire Dr (07945-2003)
PHONE....................................973 543-4586
Mark Kestner, *President*
Peter Foley, *Vice Pres*
Paul Kestner, *CFO*
EMP: 1
SALES: 1MM **Privately Held**
WEB: www.drdust.com
SIC: 3822 Electric air cleaner controls, automatic

(G-6091)
SUETA MUSIC ED PUBLICATIONS
13 E Main St Ste 3 (07945-1537)
PHONE....................................888 725-2333
Edward Sueta Sr, *President*
▲ **EMP:** 10
SALES (est): 813K **Privately Held**
SIC: 2741 7389 Music, sheet: publishing only, not printed on site; financial services

(G-6092)
SURVIVING LIFE CORP
Also Called: Sunshine Lane Mixed Media
3 Muirfield Ln (07945-1234)
PHONE....................................973 543-3370
Ronald C Striano PHD, *President*
EMP: 6
SALES: 360K **Privately Held**
SIC: 2732 Book printing

Metuchen
Middlesex County

(G-6093)
ACE ELECTRONICS INC
235 Liberty St (08840-1217)
P.O. Box 4215 (08840-4215)
PHONE....................................732 603-9800
Edward Di Villa, *President*
Susan Di Villa, *Business Mgr*
Tammy Kielian, *Business Mgr*
Ashley Morris, *Business Mgr*
Vinn Patel, *Corp Secy*
EMP: 60
SQ FT: 15,000
SALES (est): 20.2MM **Privately Held**
WEB: www.aceelectronics.com
SIC: 3496 5051 Miscellaneous fabricated wire products; cable, wire

(G-6094)
ACND PARTNERS INC
1 Honey Ct (08840-2600)
PHONE....................................848 200-7460
EMP: 4
SALES (est): 330.3K **Privately Held**
SIC: 2819 Elements

(G-6095)
AVANTIER INC (PA)
148 Main St (08840-2745)
PHONE....................................732 491-8150
Keng Stencer, *Principal*
EMP: 4
SALES (est): 852.2K **Privately Held**
SIC: 3827 Optical instruments & lenses

(G-6096)
BERKELEY VARITRONICS SYSTEMS
Also Called: B V S
255 Liberty St (08840-1217)
PHONE....................................732 548-3737
Fax: 732 548-3404
Scott Schober, *CEO*
Gary W Schober, *President*
Eva Villanueva, *Controller*
Corinne Jaracz, *Sales Mgr*
Eileen Schober, *Office Mgr*
EMP: 30
SQ FT: 20,000
SALES (est): 6MM **Privately Held**
WEB: www.bvsystems.com
SIC: 3577 8731 Computer peripheral equipment; computer (hardware) development

(G-6097)
BLUE PARACHUTE LLC
263 Amboy Ave Ste 1 (08840-2477)
PHONE....................................732 767-1320
David Frietberg, *Mng Member*
Angela Pineiro,
EMP: 4
SQ FT: 1,800
SALES (est): 428.3K **Privately Held**
SIC: 3861 7336 Commercial printing, lithographic; commercial art & illustration

(G-6098)
C & K PLASTICS INC
Also Called: CK
159 Liberty St (08840-1215)
PHONE....................................732 549-0011
Fax: 732 549-1889
Robert Carrier, *President*
Hetal Amin, *Project Mgr*
Bridgette Carrier, *Project Mgr*
Nikita Patel, *Project Mgr*
Bill Butler, *Warehouse Mgr*
EMP: 80
SALES (est): 19.8MM **Privately Held**
WEB: www.candkplastics.com
SIC: 3089 3083 Plastic containers, except foam; laminated plastics plate & sheet

(G-6099)
CHARTER MACHINE COMPANY
55 Wester Ave (08840-2537)
PHONE....................................732 494-5350
Michael Greenlaw, *Principal*
Mike Greenlaw, *VP Mfg*
Heinz Goetz, *Engineer*
Anthony Tesoriero, *Design Engr*
Bill Wright, *Natl Sales Mgr*
EMP: 14 **EST:** 2014
SALES (est): 1.9MM **Privately Held**
SIC: 3599 Machine shop, jobbing & repair

(G-6100)
CHEM-IS-TRY INC
160 Liberty St Ste 4 (08840-1255)
PHONE....................................732 372-7311
Prafulla Kumar Porwal, *President*
▲ **EMP:** 5
SQ FT: 2,000
SALES: 1MM **Privately Held**
SIC: 2819 2833 2865 2869 Industrial inorganic chemicals; medicinals & botanicals; cyclic crudes & intermediates; industrial organic chemicals; agricultural chemicals; chemical preparations

(G-6101)
CRITERION PUBLISHING CO
87 Forrest St (08840-1213)
P.O. Box 4278 (08840-4278)
PHONE....................................732 548-8300
Fax: 732 548-8338
William Crane Sr, *Owner*
EMP: 8 **EST:** 1952
SALES (est): 330K **Privately Held**
SIC: 2741 Miscellaneous publishing

(G-6102)
DIVINE PRINTING
131 Liberty St (08840-1215)
PHONE....................................732 632-8800
Devina Rodriguez, *Owner*
Jim Mann, *Manager*
EMP: 4
SALES (est): 426.8K **Privately Held**
SIC: 2752 Commercial printing, offset

(G-6103)
ENAMEL ART STUDIO
120 Liberty St (08840-1216)
PHONE....................................732 321-0774
Helen Radchenko, *Principal*
EMP: 4
SALES (est): 379.2K **Privately Held**
SIC: 3911 5094 Jewelry, precious metal; jewelry & precious stones

(G-6104)
FRANCO MANUFACTURING CO INC (PA)
555 Prospect St (08840-2271)
PHONE....................................732 494-0500
Fax: 732 494-8270
Louis D Franco, *President*
Raymond Franco, *General Mgr*
Jack D Franco, *Exec VP*
Morris Franco, *Exec VP*
Edmund Rossi, *Senior VP*
◆ **EMP:** 175
SQ FT: 71,000

SALES (est): 150.9MM **Privately Held**
WEB: www.francomfg.com
SIC: 2269 2392 2211 5023 Finishing plants; printing of narrow fabrics; towels, fabric & nonwoven: made from purchased materials; washcloths & bath mitts: made from purchased materials; towels, dishcloths & washcloths: cotton; dishcloths; washcloths; towels & toweling, cotton; towels; textiles, woven; cotton goods

(G-6105)
GLOBE DIE-CUTTING PRODUCTS INC
76 Liberty St (08840-1237)
P.O. Box 4339 (08840-4339)
PHONE....................................732 494-7744
Fax: 732 548-9755
Irwin Brody, *President*
Bruce Brody, *Corp Secy*
▲ **EMP:** 200 **EST:** 1961
SQ FT: 30,000
SALES (est): 33.6MM **Privately Held**
SIC: 3544 2675 Special dies & tools; cardboard cut-outs, panels & foundations: diecut

(G-6106)
GRAPHIC EQUIPMENT CORPORATION (PA)
Also Called: G E C
55 Wester Ave (08840-2590)
PHONE....................................732 494-5350
Fax: 732 494-4596
Karl Kuehnrich, *President*
Barbara Kuehnrich, *Corp Secy*
Michael Greenlaw, *Vice Pres*
Frank Markle, *Purch Mgr*
Walter Kuehnrich, *Purchasing*
EMP: 45
SQ FT: 47,000
SALES (est): 9MM **Privately Held**
WEB: www.gecorp.com
SIC: 3599 3555 Machine shop, jobbing & repair; printing trades machinery

(G-6107)
GRAPHIC EQUIPMENT CORPORATION
Also Called: Charter Machine
19 Wester Ave (08840-2537)
PHONE....................................732 548-4400
Fax: 732 548-4407
James A Vertes, *General Mgr*
Heinz Goetz, *Engineer*
Christopher Boyd, *Sales Staff*
James Vertes, *Manager*
EMP: 48
SALES (corp-wide): 9MM **Privately Held**
WEB: www.gecorp.com
SIC: 3599 Machine shop, jobbing & repair
PA: Graphic Equipment Corporation
55 Wester Ave
Metuchen NJ 08840
732 494-5350

(G-6108)
HARD CROME SOLUTIONS
195 Central Ave (08840-1848)
PHONE....................................732 500-2568
Frank Nicholas, *Owner*
▲ **EMP:** 5
SQ FT: 5,000
SALES (est): 170.5K **Privately Held**
SIC: 3471 Plating & polishing

(G-6109)
HOLLER METAL FABRICATORS INC
215 Liberty St (08840-1217)
PHONE....................................732 635-9050
Dan Holler, *President*
EMP: 8
SQ FT: 20,000
SALES: 1.5MM **Privately Held**
SIC: 3443 Tanks, standard or custom fabricated: metal plate

(G-6110)
HYDRACORE INC
60 Liberty St (08840-1237)
PHONE....................................732 548-5500
Sam Lotfy, *President*
Ken Greiff, *General Mgr*
EMP: 5

SALES: 400K **Privately Held**
SIC: 3599 Machine shop, jobbing & repair

(G-6111)
IT WORQS LLC
16 Pearl St Ste 102 (08840-1962)
PHONE................................732 494-0009
Noorali Sonawalla, *Mng Member*
EMP: 50
SALES (est): 2.7MM **Privately Held**
WEB: www.itworqs.com
SIC: 7372 Prepackaged software

(G-6112)
J & E METAL FABRICATORS INC
1 Coan Pl (08840-2589)
PHONE................................732 548-9650
Fax: 732 548-9589
Mark E Brazina, *President*
EMP: 28
SQ FT: 40,000
SALES: 2.5MM **Privately Held**
WEB: www.metalfab.com
SIC: 3444 Sheet metal specialties, not stamped

(G-6113)
JEFFERY S ZLOTNICK OD
39 Bridge St Ste A (08840-2277)
PHONE................................732 549-3555
Fax: 732 549-3595
Jeffery Zlotnick, *Owner*
EMP: 5
SQ FT: 1,500
SALES (est): 370K **Privately Held**
SIC: 8042 3851 Offices & clinics of optometrists; eyes, glass & plastic

(G-6114)
MAXISIT INC
203 Main St (08840-2727)
PHONE................................732 494-2005
Maulik Shah, *President*
Priti Sanjeev, *General Mgr*
Divya Reddy, *COO*
Arati Kaps, *Manager*
Banupriya Priya, *Manager*
EMP: 110
SQ FT: 5,000
SALES (est): 13.9MM **Privately Held**
WEB: www.maxisit.com
SIC: 7371 7373 7374 7372 Computer software development; computer integrated systems design; data processing & preparation; prepackaged software; information retrieval services

(G-6115)
MSI HOLDINGS LLC
203 Norcross Ave (08840-1253)
PHONE................................732 549-7144
EMP: 4
SALES (est): 303.4K **Privately Held**
SIC: 3821 Mfg Laboratory Apparatus

(G-6116)
O S I INC
101 Hillside Ave (08840-1936)
PHONE................................732 754-6271
Bogie Bosha, *President*
Martha Kelly, *Vice Pres*
EMP: 15
SQ FT: 10,000
SALES (est): 1.4MM **Privately Held**
WEB: www.osi-inc.com
SIC: 3699 Laser systems & equipment

(G-6117)
PETROLEUM TRENDS INTERNATIONAL
312 Amboy Ave Ste 2 (08840-2455)
PHONE................................732 494-0405
Fax: 732 494-0588
Thomas F Glenn, *President*
EMP: 5
SALES (est): 750K **Privately Held**
WEB: www.petrotrends.com
SIC: 1389 Oil consultants

(G-6118)
RELIABLE PALLET SERVICES LLC
74 Liberty St (08840-1237)
PHONE................................732 243-9642
Lisa Quaglieri, *Principal*

EMP: 8 **EST:** 2016
SALES (est): 729.5K **Privately Held**
SIC: 2448 Pallets, wood & wood with metal

(G-6119)
S G MANUFACTURING CO INC
15 Oliver St (08840-1728)
PHONE................................732 494-6520
Murray Melnick, *President*
EMP: 60
SQ FT: 24,000
SALES: 5MM **Privately Held**
SIC: 3462 3568 Iron & steel forgings; power transmission equipment

(G-6120)
SAVIANCE TECHNOLOGIES
16 Bridge St (08840-2274)
PHONE................................609 448-7095
Guruda Sarkar, *CEO*
Jatin Mahajan, *Vice Pres*
Harish Naidu, *Vice Pres*
Arjun Mahajan, *VP Sales*
Anuj Sakhuja, *Manager*
EMP: 15
SQ FT: 1,000
SALES: 20MM **Privately Held**
SIC: 7371 7379 7372 Computer software development & applications; computer related consulting services; prepackaged software

(G-6121)
SPEX CERTIPREP INC (PA)
203 Norcross Ave (08840-1253)
PHONE................................732 549-7144
Michel Baudron, *Chairman*
Neil A Stein, *Chairman*
Gilbert Hayat, *Treasurer*
▲ **EMP:** 53
SQ FT: 16,587
SALES (est): 13.1MM **Privately Held**
WEB: www.spexcsp.com
SIC: 3821 8734 2899 Chemical laboratory apparatus; testing laboratories; chemical preparations

(G-6122)
SPEX CERTIPREP GROUP LLC
203 Norcross Ave (08840-1253)
PHONE................................208 204-6656
Michel Baudron, *Chairman*
EMP: 11 **EST:** 2013
SALES (est): 1.7MM **Privately Held**
SIC: 3821 Chemical laboratory apparatus

(G-6123)
SPEX CERTPREP GROUP LLC
203 Norcross Ave (08840-1253)
PHONE................................732 549-7144
William Hahn, *General Mgr*
Neil A Stein,
Ralph H Obenauf,
EMP: 9
SQ FT: 10,000
SALES (est): 1.1MM **Privately Held**
WEB: www.prostds.com
SIC: 2819 Industrial inorganic chemicals

(G-6124)
SPEX SAMPLE PREP LLC
65 Liberty St (08840-1221)
PHONE................................732 549-7144
Ralph Obenauf, *Branch Mgr*
EMP: 14
SALES (est): 2.6MM
SALES (corp-wide): 7.8MM **Privately Held**
SIC: 3821 Chemical laboratory apparatus
PA: Spex Sample Prep, Llc
　　203 Norcross Ave
　　Metuchen NJ 08840
　　732 549-7144

(G-6125)
SPEX SAMPLE PREP LLC (PA)
203 Norcross Ave (08840-1253)
PHONE................................732 549-7144
Fax: 732 603-9647
Ralph Obenauf,
EMP: 25
SQ FT: 15,000
SALES (est): 7.8MM **Privately Held**
WEB: www.spexsampleprep.net
SIC: 3821 Chemical laboratory apparatus

(G-6126)
SYNASIA INC
240 Amboy Ave (08840-2441)
PHONE................................732 205-9880
Howard Z Qiu, *President*
Kevin Qiu, *Principal*
Linda LI, *Business Mgr*
Kevin Greene, *Mktg Dir*
▲ **EMP:** 4
SQ FT: 3,000
SALES (est): 520K **Privately Held**
WEB: www.synasia.com
SIC: 2819 5169 Industrial inorganic chemicals; chemicals & allied products

(G-6127)
T & E SALES OF MARLBORO INC
913 Middlesex Ave (08840-2201)
P.O. Box 791, Edison (08818-0791)
PHONE................................732 549-7551
Fax: 732 549-5810
Martin Wachtel, *President*
EMP: 6
SALES (est): 1.1MM **Privately Held**
SIC: 3589 7542 Car washing machinery; washing & polishing, automotive

(G-6128)
TMC CORPORATION
335 High St Bldg B1 (08840-2285)
PHONE................................609 860-1830
▲ **EMP:** 6
SQ FT: 5,000
SALES (est): 520K **Privately Held**
SIC: 3661 7389 Mfg Telephone Systems

(G-6129)
TRINITY MANUFACTURING LLC
Also Called: Trinity LLC
60 Leonard St (08840-1220)
PHONE................................732 549-5521
Fax: 732 549-2866
Randy Riley, *President*
Bella Gutman, *President*
Jay Myers, *President*
George Mitchell, *General Mgr*
George Cox Jr, *Exec VP*
▲ **EMP:** 120
SQ FT: 120,000
SALES (est): 31.2MM **Privately Held**
WEB: www.trinityinstore.com
SIC: 3648 2541 3646 Store & office display cases & fixtures; commercial indusl & institutional electric lighting fixtures; decorative area lighting fixtures

(G-6130)
WEST MACHINE WORKS INC
101 Liberty St (08840-1215)
PHONE................................732 549-2183
Fax: 732 549-2930
Jan H Van Hoesen, *President*
Peter Van Hoesen, *Vice Pres*
EMP: 7 **EST:** 1945
SALES (est): 300K **Privately Held**
SIC: 3599 3544 Machine shop, jobbing & repair; special dies, tools, jigs & fixtures

(G-6131)
WINDOW SHAPES INC
225 Liberty St (08840-1217)
PHONE................................732 549-0708
Tom Change, *President*
▲ **EMP:** 90 **EST:** 1997
SQ FT: 45,000
SALES (est): 12.9MM **Privately Held**
SIC: 3442 Storm doors or windows, metal

(G-6132)
WIRELESS COMMUNICATIONS INC
55 Liberty St (08840-1221)
PHONE................................732 926-1000
EMP: 12
SALES (est): 1.9MM **Privately Held**
SIC: 3663 Radio broadcasting & communications equipment
PA: Wireless Communications, Inc.
　　1803 Old Slphur Spring Rd
　　Baltimore MD 21227

(G-6133)
WLXT LLC
Also Called: WI Ring
16 Wernik Pl (08840-2422)
PHONE................................732 906-7979
Mary Durocher, *Vice Pres*
Howard Kaye,
Joe Clapper,
EMP: 73
SALES (est): 6.2MM **Privately Held**
SIC: 3911 Jewelry, precious metal

(G-6134)
WORLD JOURNAL LLC
41a Bridge St (08840-2277)
PHONE................................732 632-8890
Fax: 732 632-9595
Harver Lee, *Manager*
EMP: 12
SALES (corp-wide): 53.3MM **Privately Held**
WEB: www.wjnews.net
SIC: 2711 Newspapers, publishing & printing
HQ: World Journal Llc
　　14107 20th Ave Fl 2
　　Whitestone NY 11357
　　718 746-8889

(G-6135)
ZENITH ENERGY US LP (PA)
1 Highland Ave (08840-1956)
PHONE................................732 515-7410
Jeffrey R Armstrong, *CEO*
EMP: 2
SALES (est): 105.3MM **Privately Held**
SIC: 1311 Crude petroleum & natural gas

Mickleton
Gloucester County

(G-6136)
ATLAS FLASHER & SUPPLY CO INC
430 Swedesboro Ave (08056-1208)
P.O. Box 488 (08056-0488)
PHONE................................856 423-3333
Fax: 856 423-3313
Karenanne Brown, *CEO*
Jason Morse, *Vice Pres*
Gary P Ottey, *Vice Pres*
Mike Scheufele, *Opers Mgr*
Brian Stevens, *Materials Mgr*
EMP: 30
SQ FT: 5,000
SALES (est): 7.1MM **Privately Held**
WEB: www.atlasflasher.com
SIC: 5999 7359 3993 Safety supplies & equipment; equipment rental & leasing; signs & advertising specialties

(G-6137)
MARTINS SPECIALTY SAUSAGE CO (PA)
150 Harmony Rd (08056-1210)
PHONE................................856 423-4000
Fax: 856 423-5130
Martin Guinta, *President*
Tom Maschino, *Plant Engr*
Ed Hall, *Sales Mgr*
EMP: 14
SQ FT: 8,800
SALES (est): 2.8MM **Privately Held**
SIC: 2013 Spiced meats from purchased meat

(G-6138)
SAINT-GOBAIN PRFMCE PLAS CORP
Also Called: Division Name Process Systems
210 Harmony Rd (08056-1209)
P.O. Box 248 (08056-0248)
PHONE................................856 423-6630
Vincent Hurst, *Branch Mgr*
EMP: 75
SALES (corp-wide): 213.5MM **Privately Held**
SIC: 3083 3082 Thermoplastic laminates: rods, tubes, plates & sheet; unsupported plastics profile shapes

HQ: Saint-Gobain Performance Plastics
Corporation
31500 Solon Rd
Solon OH 44139
440 836-6900

Middlesex
Middlesex County

(G-6139)
150 DEVELOPMENT GROUP LLC
400 South Ave Ste 10 (08846-2567)
PHONE..................................732 546-3812
Massimo Pinelli, *Mng Member*
EMP: 5 EST: 2012
SALES (est): 612.3K **Privately Held**
SIC: 3572 Computer storage devices

(G-6140)
250 LACKLAND HOLDING INC
Also Called: Micro-Tube Fabricators
250 Lackland Dr (08846-2562)
PHONE..................................732 469-7420
Fax: 732 469-4314
Dave Brewer, *Production*
EMP: 65
SQ FT: 24,000
SALES (est): 21.8MM
SALES (corp-wide): 24.9MM **Privately Held**
SIC: 3351 Tubing, copper & copper alloy
PA: Wytech Industries Inc
960 E Hazelwood Ave
Rahway NJ 07065
732 396-3900

(G-6141)
A T C COMPANIES INC (PA)
207 Blackford Ave (08846-2503)
P.O. Box 310 (08846-0310)
PHONE..................................732 560-0900
Fax: 732 560-9699
Stephen J Gajarsky, *President*
James Winship, *Opers Staff*
John Tullo, *Info Tech Dir*
Elaine Gajarsky, *Admin Sec*
EMP: 30
SQ FT: 6,300
SALES (est): 2.9MM **Privately Held**
SIC: 3822 7629 Hydronic pressure or temperature controls; electrical equipment repair, high voltage

(G-6142)
ACC COATINGS LLC
201 Pond Ave (08846-2220)
PHONE..................................732 469-8600
David Steele, *President*
EMP: 10
SQ FT: 8,000
SALES (est): 4MM **Privately Held**
SIC: 2851 Coating, air curing

(G-6143)
ADM CORPORATION
100 Lincoln Blvd (08846-1090)
PHONE..................................732 469-0900
Fax: 732 469-0785
Mary Mota, *Ch of Bd*
Susan Mota, *COO*
Gene Potts, *Plant Mgr*
Joe Tattegrain, *QC Mgr*
Michael Turner, *CFO*
▲ EMP: 100 EST: 1964
SQ FT: 100,000
SALES: 30MM **Privately Held**
WEB: www.packing-list.com
SIC: 2393 3081 2678 Bags & containers, except sleeping bags: textile; plastic film & sheet; writing paper & envelopes: made from purchased materials

(G-6144)
ADVANCE MACHINE PLANNING INC
200 Egel Ave (08846-2506)
PHONE..................................732 356-4438
Henry A Phillips Sr, *President*
Susan Delaney, *Manager*
EMP: 10
SQ FT: 17,000

SALES (est): 640K **Privately Held**
SIC: 3559 8711 Rubber working machinery, including tires; engineering services

(G-6145)
AGATE LACQUER TRI-NAT LLC
824 South Ave (08846-2259)
PHONE..................................732 968-1080
Fax: 732 968-1269
Jane Natalini, *President*
▲ EMP: 5
SQ FT: 25,000
SALES (est): 940.9K **Privately Held**
SIC: 2851 2842 Lacquer: bases, dopes, thinner; lacquers, varnishes, enamels & other coatings; metal polish

(G-6146)
ANALYTIC STRESS RELIEVING INC
190 Egel Ave (08846-2504)
PHONE..................................732 629-7232
David Herzog, *President*
EMP: 57
SALES (corp-wide): 250MM **Privately Held**
SIC: 3398 Metal heat treating
PA: Analytic Stress Relieving, Inc.
3118 W Pinhook Rd Ste 202
Lafayette LA 70508
337 237-8790

(G-6147)
ANGUS SYSTEMS GROUP INC
Also Called: Angus Anywhere
1273 Bound Brook Rd # 11 (08846-1490)
PHONE..................................770 521-5553
Garry Gale, *President*
Rick Randolph, *Vice Pres*
EMP: 50
SALES (est): 3.8MM **Privately Held**
SIC: 8743 7372 Sales promotion; prepackaged software

(G-6148)
ANSUN PROTECTIVE METALS INC
130 Lincoln Blvd (08846-1022)
P.O. Box 4260, Dunellen (08812-4260)
PHONE..................................732 302-0616
George Whalen, *President*
Anthony Mendel, *Vice Pres*
◆ EMP: 8
SQ FT: 10,000
SALES: 1MM **Privately Held**
WEB: www.ansunmetals.com
SIC: 3599 5051 Machine shop, jobbing & repair; metals service centers & offices

(G-6149)
ATC SYSTEMS INC
207 Blackford Ave (08846-2503)
P.O. Box 310 (08846-0310)
PHONE..................................732 560-0900
Stephen Gajarsky, *Principal*
Kevin O'Rourke, *Vice Pres*
John Tullo, *Info Tech Dir*
EMP: 4 EST: 2009
SALES (est): 720.8K **Privately Held**
SIC: 3625 Control equipment, electric

(G-6150)
BAMCO INC
30 Baekeland Ave (08846-2601)
PHONE..................................732 302-0889
Michael Biviano, *President*
Scott Parneg, *Superintendent*
Chris Riolo, *Superintendent*
Allan Pasternak, *Corp Secy*
Bob Balaam, *Vice Pres*
▲ EMP: 80
SQ FT: 14,000
SALES (est): 23.5MM **Privately Held**
WEB: www.bamcoinc.org
SIC: 3446 Architectural metalwork

(G-6151)
BERRY GLOBAL INC
87 Lincoln Blvd (08846-1020)
PHONE..................................732 356-2870
Fax: 732 356-4745
Christian Chuquibala, *Opers Spvr*
Jim Deming, *Branch Mgr*
Carolyn Caldwell, *Admin Sec*
EMP: 127 **Publicly Held**
SIC: 3089 Bottle caps, molded plastic

HQ: Berry Global, Inc.
101 Oakley St
Evansville IN 47710
812 424-2904

(G-6152)
BOMAR EXO LTD LIABILITY CO
Also Called: Bomar Crystal Company
200b Wood Ave (08846-2553)
P.O. Box 10 (08846-0010)
PHONE..................................732 356-7787
Fax: 732 356-7362
Ermina Lirio, *CEO*
Dave Miskov, *Plant Mgr*
EMP: 11 EST: 1960
SQ FT: 20,000
SALES: 356.7K **Privately Held**
WEB: www.bomarcrystal.com
SIC: 3679 Quartz crystals, for electronic application

(G-6153)
CAPITAL PRINTING CORPORATION
420 South Ave (08846-2532)
PHONE..................................732 560-1515
Fax: 732 560-8895
Brett Russo, *President*
Nolan Russo Sr, *Principal*
Nolan Russo Jr, *CFO*
EMP: 80
SQ FT: 60,000
SALES (est): 25MM **Privately Held**
WEB: www.capitalprintingcorp.com
SIC: 2752 Commercial printing, offset

(G-6154)
CENTRAL COMPONENTS MFG LLC
440 Lincoln Blvd (08846-2439)
PHONE..................................732 469-5720
Greg Lane, *Opers Staff*
Tom Stiff, *Accounting Mgr*
Tom Winfough,
Howard Chiou,
Gregg Lane,
▲ EMP: 6 EST: 1993
SALES (est): 650K **Privately Held**
WEB: www.centralcm.com
SIC: 3678 8742 Electronic connectors; management consulting services

(G-6155)
CONTAINER MFG INC
Also Called: Container Manufacturing
50 Baekeland Ave (08846-2601)
P.O. Box 428 (08846-0428)
PHONE..................................732 563-0100
Fax: 732 563-0704
J Thomas Jennings, *President*
Robert Jennings, *Vice Pres*
EMP: 40
SQ FT: 32,000
SALES (est): 9.7MM **Privately Held**
WEB: www.containermanufacturing.com
SIC: 3089 Plastic containers, except foam

(G-6156)
CORE ACQUISITION LLC (PA)
215 Wood Ave Ste 215 # 215 (08846-2554)
PHONE..................................732 983-6025
Arpit Patel, *CEO*
Vithal Dhaduk, *President*
Payal Dhaduk, *CFO*
Ameeshi Chovatia,
EMP: 3
SQ FT: 32,000
SALES: 5MM **Privately Held**
SIC: 2834 Pills, pharmaceutical

(G-6157)
COREPHARMA LLC
215 Wood Ave Ste 215 # 215 (08846-2554)
PHONE..................................732 983-6025
Fax: 732 868-1091
Arpit Patel, *CEO*
Vithal Dhaduk, *President*
Payal Dhaduk, *CFO*
▲ EMP: 3
SQ FT: 32,000
SALES: 5MM **Privately Held**
WEB: www.corepharma.com
SIC: 2834 Pills, pharmaceutical

PA: Core Acquisition, Llc
215 Wood Ave Ste 215 # 215
Middlesex NJ 08846
732 983-6025

(G-6158)
COVALNCE SPCALTY ADHESIVES LLC
87 Lincoln Blvd (08846-1020)
PHONE..................................732 356-2870
Seth Salano, *Branch Mgr*
EMP: 600 **Publicly Held**
SIC: 2891 Adhesives & sealants
HQ: Covalence Specialty Adhesives Llc
101 Oakley St
Evansville IN 47710

(G-6159)
COVALNCE SPCIALTY COATINGS LLC
Also Called: Tapes and Coatings
87 Lincoln Blvd (08846-1020)
PHONE..................................732 356-2870
Seth Salano, *Manager*
Elizabeth Curran,
EMP: 85
SALES (est): 4.8MM **Privately Held**
SIC: 2399 2821 2851 Fabricated textile products; plastics materials & resins; paints & allied products

(G-6160)
CRT INTERNATIONAL INC
260 Wagner St (08846-2501)
PHONE..................................973 887-7737
Carmine Tarantino, *President*
Rosa Tarantino, *Senior VP*
Mario Schiavone, *Finance*
Leonardo Orozco, *Webmaster*
EMP: 12
SALES (est): 1.8MM **Privately Held**
SIC: 2752 Business forms, lithographed

(G-6161)
DELISA PALLET CORP
116 South Ave (08846-2526)
PHONE..................................732 667-7070
Fax: 973 344-0689
John P Delisa, *President*
James A Chichelo, *Corp Secy*
David Colavita, *Manager*
▼ EMP: 11 EST: 1958
SQ FT: 5,000
SALES (est): 5.5MM **Privately Held**
WEB: www.delisapallet.com
SIC: 5031 2448 Pallets, wood; wood pallets & skids

(G-6162)
DISHMAN USA INC
476 Union Ave Ste 2 (08846-1968)
PHONE..................................732 560-4300
Fax: 732 560-4343
Jay R Vyas, *Chairman*
Bhavesh Oza, *Administration*
▲ EMP: 10
SQ FT: 2,200
SALES (est): 2.2MM
SALES (corp-wide): 73.6MM **Privately Held**
WEB: www.dishman-usa.com
SIC: 2834 Pharmaceutical preparations
PA: Dishman Carbogen Amcis Limited
Bhadr-Raj Chambers, Swastik
Ahmedabad GJ 38000
792 644-3053

(G-6163)
DOUBLE O MANUFACTURING INC
2b Smalley Ave (08846-2231)
PHONE..................................732 752-9423
Al Oslislo, *President*
Jim Oslislo, *Vice Pres*
EMP: 7
SQ FT: 7,500
SALES: 1MM **Privately Held**
WEB: www.doubleomfg.com
SIC: 3325 Steel foundries

(G-6164)
DYNAFLOW ENGINEERING INC
106 Egel Ave (08846-2504)
PHONE..................................732 356-9790
Fax: 732 356-9794

GEOGRAPHIC

Ross Block, *President*
EMP: 5
SQ FT: 1,100
SALES (est): 1.1MM **Privately Held**
WEB: www.dynafloweng.com
SIC: 5084 3561 Pumps & pumping equipment; pumps & pumping equipment

(G-6165)
F S T PRINTING INC
1324 Bound Brook Rd (08846-1401)
PHONE..................................732 560-3749
Salvatore Buonocore, *President*
Frank Buonocore, *Vice Pres*
Timothy Hurley, *Vice Pres*
Patty Hurley, *Treasurer*
EMP: 5
SQ FT: 2,500
SALES: 600K **Privately Held**
SIC: 2759 Commercial printing, offset; business forms: printing; alcoholic beverage making equipment & supplies

(G-6166)
FLAVOR AND FD INGREDIENTS INC
256 Lackland Dr (08846-2511)
PHONE..................................201 298-6964
Sandy Feld, *Principal*
EMP: 21
SALES (corp-wide): 7.6MM **Privately Held**
WEB: www.summithillflavors.com
SIC: 2087 Flavoring extracts & syrups
PA: Flavor And Food Ingredients Inc.
21 Worlds Fair Dr
Somerset NJ 08873
732 805-0335

(G-6167)
FRAM TRAK INDUSTRIES INC
Also Called: Alpha Plastics
205 Hallock Ave (08846-2280)
PHONE..................................732 424-8400
Fax: 732 424-8811
Albert Santelli, *President*
Paul Houston, *Admin Sec*
▲ **EMP:** 40
SQ FT: 66,000
SALES (est): 8.1MM **Privately Held**
WEB: www.framtrak.com
SIC: 3089 Injection molding of plastics

(G-6168)
GEMCO VALVE CO LLC
301 Smalley Ave (08846-2232)
PHONE..................................732 752-7900
John Muench, *Ch of Bd*
Jim Lenihan, *President*
Victoria Stratoudakis, *Opers Staff*
Douglas Krok, *Engineer*
Amy Repole, *Admin Asst*
EMP: 20
SQ FT: 20,000
SALES (est): 2.4MM **Privately Held**
SIC: 3491 Industrial valves

(G-6169)
HANDYTUBE CORPORATION
250 Lackland Dr Ste 1 (08846-2562)
PHONE..................................732 469-7420
Bill Glas, *Manager*
EMP: 50
SQ FT: 7,000
SALES (corp-wide): 1.3B **Publicly Held**
SIC: 3351 3498 Tubing, copper & copper alloy; fabricated pipe & fittings
HQ: Handytube Corporation
12244 Willow Grove Rd
Camden DE 19934

(G-6170)
IMAGE SCREEN PRINTING INC
532 Lincoln Blvd (08846-2441)
PHONE..................................732 560-1817
Fax: 732 560-0795
Nancy Mangee, *President*
Charles Mangee, *Corp Secy*
EMP: 8
SQ FT: 5,400
SALES: 640K **Privately Held**
SIC: 2759 Screen printing

(G-6171)
J G CARPENTER CONTRACTOR
Also Called: JG Tire
300 Lincoln Blvd (08846-2370)
PHONE..................................732 271-8991
Fax: 732 271-1814
John Giaretta, *President*
John Giarretta, *Owner*
EMP: 8
SALES (est): 897.8K **Privately Held**
SIC: 4212 3011 Dump truck haulage; tires & inner tubes

(G-6172)
JEMA-AMERICAN INC
824 South Ave (08846-2259)
P.O. Box 206, Dunellen (08812-0206)
PHONE..................................732 968-5333
Fax: 732 968-1269
James Natalini, *President*
EMP: 7 **EST:** 1957
SQ FT: 10,000
SALES (est): 1.9MM **Privately Held**
WEB: www.jema-american.com
SIC: 3479 Coating of metals & formed products

(G-6173)
KOBA CORP
60 Baekeland Ave (08846-2601)
PHONE..................................732 469-0110
Fax: 732 469-0835
Joseph Koelmel Jr, *President*
Franz Bach, *Corp Secy*
EMP: 60
SQ FT: 35,000
SALES (est): 10MM **Privately Held**
WEB: www.kobacorp.com
SIC: 3089 3544 Injection molding of plastics; special dies, tools, jigs & fixtures

(G-6174)
KRS AUTOMOTIVE DEV GROUP INC
Also Called: Phoenix Friction Products
278 Lincoln Blvd Ste 2 (08846-2281)
PHONE..................................732 667-7937
Louis Riveccio, *President*
William Sanders, *Vice Pres*
EMP: 10
SQ FT: 26,000
SALES (est): 1.3MM **Privately Held**
SIC: 3714 Clutches, motor vehicle

(G-6175)
L AND DS SAPORE RAVIOLI CHEESE
Also Called: Sapore Ravioli & Cheese
429b Lincoln Blvd (08846-2440)
PHONE..................................732 563-9190
Fax: 732 563-9195
Dominic Discenza, *President*
Anthony Florano, *Managing Prtnr*
Michael Discenza, *Vice Pres*
EMP: 15
SQ FT: 1,500
SALES: 750K **Privately Held**
WEB: www.saporeravioli.com
SIC: 2099 Pasta, uncooked: packaged with other ingredients

(G-6176)
LOUIS N ROTHBERG & SON INC
550 Cedar Ave (08846-2433)
P.O. Box 550 (08846-0550)
PHONE..................................732 356-9505
Fax: 732 356-0974
Louis N Rothberg, *President*
John Rothberg, *Vice Pres*
Snyder Russell, *Foreman/Supr*
Dick Kimsey, *Controller*
Chris Pudimott, *Manager*
EMP: 30
SQ FT: 12,200
SALES (est): 9MM **Privately Held**
WEB: www.lnrothberg.com
SIC: 1794 2951 Excavation & grading, building construction; asphalt paving mixtures & blocks

(G-6177)
LOWDER ELECTRIC AND CNSTR
250 Hallock Ave Ste B (08846-2281)
PHONE..................................732 764-6000
Jeremy Lowder, *President*

EMP: 5
SALES (est): 200.5K **Privately Held**
SIC: 7694 1731 Electric motor repair; general electrical contractor; electric power systems contractors; standby or emergency power specialization; voice, data & video wiring contractor

(G-6178)
MARITIME SOLUTIONS INC
Also Called: MSI
200 Pond Ave (08846-2219)
PHONE..................................732 752-3831
Richard Fredricks, *President*
Christopher Constantine, *Senior VP*
Gerard J Lynch, *VP Engrg*
EMP: 7 **EST:** 2007
SALES (est): 532.6K **Privately Held**
SIC: 3531 Marine related equipment

(G-6179)
MEDPLAST MEDICAL INC
Also Called: Medtech Precision Molds
278 Lincoln Blvd (08846-2373)
PHONE..................................732 356-0689
Bob McKaba, *Branch Mgr*
EMP: 15
SALES (corp-wide): 189.2MM **Privately Held**
WEB: www.medtech-grp.com
SIC: 3841 Surgical & medical instruments
HQ: Medplast Medical, Inc.
6 Century Ln
South Plainfield NJ 07080
908 561-0717

(G-6180)
MID STATE BINDERY
262 Lackland Dr (08846-2511)
PHONE..................................908 755-9388
Steve Stout, *Owner*
Sidney Stoddard, *Vice Pres*
EMP: 4
SALES (est): 140K **Privately Held**
SIC: 2789 Bookbinding & related work

(G-6181)
MORELLI CONTRACTING LLC
201 Egel Ave Ste B (08846-2574)
PHONE..................................732 356-8800
Anthony Morelli, *Mng Member*
Colleen Morelli
EMP: 5 **EST:** 2004
SQ FT: 6,500
SALES: 600K **Privately Held**
SIC: 1411 Dimension stone

(G-6182)
MULBRO MANUFACTURING & SVC CO
488 Lincoln Blvd (08846-2439)
P.O. Box 386 (08846-0386)
PHONE..................................732 805-0290
Ray Mullen, *President*
EMP: 4 **EST:** 1954
SQ FT: 5,000
SALES (est): 310K **Privately Held**
WEB: www.mulbro.com
SIC: 7699 3949 5941 Bowling pins, refinishing or repair; sporting & athletic goods; bowling equipment & supplies

(G-6183)
NATIONAL MTAL FNSHNGS CORP INC (PA)
Also Called: National Metals
897 South Ave (08846-2569)
P.O. Box 486 (08846-0486)
PHONE..................................732 752-7770
Fax: 732 752-6579
Lou Fahsbender, *President*
▲ **EMP:** 12
SQ FT: 12,000
SALES (est): 2.5MM **Privately Held**
SIC: 3599 3471 Custom machinery; electroplating of metals or formed products

(G-6184)
NEW BRUNSWICK SAW SERVICE INC
400 Lincoln Blvd (08846-2439)
PHONE..................................732 287-4466
Michael Schaefer, *Principal*
EMP: 14

SALES (est): 2.3MM **Privately Held**
SIC: 3541 Saws & sawing machines

(G-6185)
NEWBOLD INC
Also Called: Newbold Target
200 Egel Ave (08846-2506)
PHONE..................................732 469-5654
Henry A Phillips Jr, *President*
EMP: 5
SALES (est): 180K **Privately Held**
WEB: www.newboldtargets.com
SIC: 3949 Target shooting equipment

(G-6186)
PETERSON BROTHERS MFG CO
10 Baekeland Ave (08846-2601)
PHONE..................................732 271-8240
Fax: 732 271-8230
Gary Lewis, *President*
Marlys Lewis, *Corp Secy*
EMP: 25 **EST:** 1951
SQ FT: 14,000
SALES (est): 3.9MM **Privately Held**
WEB: www.petersonbrothersmanufacturing.com
SIC: 3469 Stamping metal for the trade

(G-6187)
PETRO EXTRUSION TECH INC
Also Called: Petro Extrusion Technology
205 Hallock Ave Ste B (08846-2280)
P.O. Box 99, Garwood (07027-0099)
PHONE..................................908 789-3338
Fax: 908 789-0434
Robert Petrozziello, *President*
Joseph Petrozziello, *Vice Pres*
Alan Pinsky, *Chief Engr*
Frances Petrozziello, *Treasurer*
Bill Gathercole, *Sales Staff*
EMP: 42
SQ FT: 20,000
SALES (est): 9MM **Privately Held**
WEB: www.petroextrusion.com
SIC: 3089 Extruded finished plastic products

(G-6188)
PHILLIPS SAFETY PRODUCTS INC
123 Lincoln Blvd Ste 2 (08846-1071)
PHONE..................................732 356-1493
Robert Phillips, *President*
Ryan Phillips, *Vice Pres*
Geri Baitz, *Accounts Mgr*
Mike Richard, *Cust Mgr*
Brian Struble, *Technology*
▲ **EMP:** 20
SALES (est): 4MM **Privately Held**
WEB: www.phillips-safety.com
SIC: 3851 Ophthalmic goods

(G-6189)
POLISH NAIL
570 Union Ave (08846-1960)
PHONE..................................732 627-9799
Tuan Nguyen, *Owner*
EMP: 7
SALES: 420K **Privately Held**
SIC: 3999 Fingernails, artificial

(G-6190)
PREMIER SPECIALTIES INC
201 Egel Ave Ste 3a (08846-2574)
PHONE..................................732 469-6615
Fax: 732 469-6772
Roger Rich, *President*
Marnie McBreen, *Vice Pres*
Megan Daly, *Marketing Staff*
Talysha Marcellus, *Manager*
Zeke Salazar, *Manager*
▲ **EMP:** 19
SQ FT: 15,000
SALES (est): 5.7MM **Privately Held**
WEB: www.premierfragrances.com
SIC: 2087 2844 Flavoring extracts & syrups; cosmetic preparations

(G-6191)
PROMO GRAPHIC INC
Also Called: Graphic Impressions
112 Wood Ave (08846-2551)
PHONE..................................732 629-7300
Fax: 908 688-6999
Debra Rossello, *President*
EMP: 7

▲ = Import ▼ =Export
◆ =Import/Export

SQ FT: 3,500
SALES: 450K **Privately Held**
WEB: www.promographics.com
SIC: 2759 7336 Screen printing; commercial art & graphic design

(G-6192)
R & R IRRIGATION CO INC
283 Lincoln Blvd (08846-1734)
PHONE..................................732 271-7070
Fax: 732 271-0721
Stephen C Dobossy, *President*
Paul W Maiwaldt, *Vice Pres*
EMP: 18
SQ FT: 4,500
SALES (est): 2.6MM **Privately Held**
WEB: www.rirrigation.com
SIC: 1731 3259 Electrical work; clay sewer & drainage pipe & tile

(G-6193)
SCARLET PRINTING
Also Called: Minuteman Press
253 Beechwood Ave (08846-1107)
PHONE..................................732 560-1415
Fax: 908 687-8065
Robert Oconner,
Erich Peter,
EMP: 6
SQ FT: 1,000
SALES: 300K **Privately Held**
WEB: www.mmpunion.net
SIC: 2752 2791 2789 Commercial printing, offset; typesetting; bookbinding & related work

(G-6194)
SCHIFANO CONSTRUCTION CORP
1 Smalley Ave (08846-2272)
P.O. Box 288 (08846-0288)
PHONE..................................732 752-3450
Fax: 732 752-3473
Dale Schifano, *President*
John Schifano, *Vice Pres*
Paul Schifano, *Treasurer*
Philip Schifano, *Admin Sec*
EMP: 12
SQ FT: 12,800
SALES (est): 3.7MM **Privately Held**
SIC: 1611 2951 Highway & street paving contractor; asphalt paving mixtures & blocks

(G-6195)
SCIENTIFIC MACHINE AND SUP CO
700 Cedar Ave (08846-2448)
P.O. Box 67 (08846-0067)
PHONE..................................732 356-1553
Fax: 732 356-7127
Elizabeth Landau, *President*
EMP: 20 EST: 1956
SQ FT: 10,000
SALES: 980K **Privately Held**
WEB: www.scientificmachine.com
SIC: 3821 3829 3494 Laboratory equipment: fume hoods, distillation racks, etc.; shakers & stirrers; evaporation apparatus, laboratory type; measuring & controlling devices; valves & pipe fittings

(G-6196)
SERMACH INC
Also Called: Service Machine Co
311 Lincoln Blvd Ste C (08846-2364)
PHONE..................................732 356-9021
Fax: 732 563-9753
Peter D'Elia, *President*
Lori D'Elia, *Treasurer*
EMP: 5
SQ FT: 3,500
SALES: 600K **Privately Held**
SIC: 3599 Machine shop, jobbing & repair

(G-6197)
SIGMA ENGINEERING & CONSULTING
220 Lincoln Blvd Ste A (08846-1738)
PHONE..................................732 356-3046
Fax: 732 356-7360
Robert Bruno, *President*
EMP: 18
SQ FT: 36,600

SALES (est): 2.6MM **Privately Held**
WEB: www.sigmaeca.com
SIC: 3599 1796 8711 3462 Machine shop, jobbing & repair; machinery installation; mechanical engineering; iron & steel forgings

(G-6198)
SILVER LINE BUILDING PDTS LLC
207 Pond Ave (08846-2220)
PHONE..................................732 752-8704
Fax: 732 752-7924
Kris Edwards, *Sales Mgr*
Brian Traynor, *Manager*
EMP: 220
SALES (corp-wide): 3B **Privately Held**
WEB: www.silverlinewindow.com
SIC: 3089 3442 Windows, plastic; window frames & sash, plastic; awnings, fiberglass & plastic combination; injection molded finished plastic products; metal doors, sash & trim
HQ: Silver Line Building Products Llc
     1 Silverline Dr
     North Brunswick NJ 08902
     732 435-1000

(G-6199)
SOMA LABS INC
248 Wagner St 252 (08846-2501)
PHONE..................................732 271-3444
Fax: 732 271-3446
John Botzolakis, *President*
EMP: 17 EST: 1998
SQ FT: 11,000
SALES (est): 4MM **Privately Held**
WEB: www.somalabs.com
SIC: 2834 Vitamin preparations

(G-6200)
SPADIX TECHNOLOGIES INC
110 Egel Ave (08846-2504)
PHONE..................................732 356-6906
Fax: 732 356-6907
Albert Simone, *President*
Ann Marie Wolliver, *Manager*
▲ EMP: 4 EST: 1995
SQ FT: 13,000
SALES (est): 200.4K **Privately Held**
WEB: www.spadixtechnologies.com
SIC: 3559 Glass cutting machinery

(G-6201)
SPRAY-TEK INC (PA)
344 Cedar Ave (08846-2433)
PHONE..................................732 469-0050
Fax: 732 302-0866
Mark Epstein, *Ch of Bd*
David Brand, *Vice Pres*
Melvin Denholtz, *Vice Pres*
EMP: 50
SQ FT: 22,000
SALES (est): 16.3MM **Privately Held**
SIC: 2834 Pharmaceutical preparations

(G-6202)
STAINLESS STOCK
Also Called: Diamond Bright Metal Proc
333 Cedar Ave Ste 1 (08846-2400)
PHONE..................................732 564-1164
Fax: 732 564-1169
George Karpus, *President*
EMP: 8
SALES (est): 936.3K **Privately Held**
SIC: 3471 Plating & polishing

(G-6203)
STANDEX INTERNATIONAL CORP
Also Called: Mason Candlelight Company
820 Lincoln Blvd (08846-2148)
P.O. Box 367 (08846-0367)
PHONE..................................732 469-8452
Fax: 732 469-4978
Robert Gasbarro, *Vice Pres*
EMP: 7
SALES (corp-wide): 755.2MM **Publicly Held**
SIC: 3999 3641 Candles; electric lamps
PA: Standex International Corporation
     11 Keewaydin Dr Ste 300
     Salem NH 03079
     603 893-9701

(G-6204)
STIRLING AUDIO SERVICES LLC
201 Wood Ave (08846-2554)
PHONE..................................732 560-0707
Fax: 732 417-1010
Jim Ferrate Jr,
Mary Ann Mason,
EMP: 5
SALES (est): 612.5K **Privately Held**
WEB: www.stirlingaudioservices.com
SIC: 3651 Household audio & video equipment

(G-6205)
TESS-COM INC (PA)
400 South Ave Ste 11 (08846-2567)
PHONE..................................412 233-5782
Lou Colonna, *President*
David Colonna, *Vice Pres*
EMP: 20
SQ FT: 10,000
SALES (est): 5.2MM **Privately Held**
WEB: www.tesscom.com
SIC: 3826 5084 Environmental testing equipment; pollution control equipment, air (environmental)

(G-6206)
TOOLING ETC LLC
Also Called: Wagner Carbide Saw Division
250 Hallock Ave (08846-2281)
PHONE..................................732 752-8080
Fax: 732 752-8209
Ernest Jesacher, *Mng Member*
Erika Jesacher,
Markus Jesacher,
▲ EMP: 8 EST: 1980
SQ FT: 16,000
SALES (est): 1.1MM **Privately Held**
WEB: www.toolingetc.com
SIC: 3425 3541 7699 Saw blades for hand or power saws; machine tools, metal cutting type; knife, saw & tool sharpening & repair

(G-6207)
UNIQUE ALUMINUM EXTRUSION LLC
333 Cedar Ave Ste 6 (08846-2400)
PHONE..................................732 271-0006
Selim Uzel, *Principal*
Edith Bellotti, *COO*
EMP: 13
SALES (est): 2.3MM **Privately Held**
SIC: 3354 Aluminum extruded products

(G-6208)
VEOLIA ES
125 Factory Ln (08846-1043)
PHONE..................................732 469-5100
James Nerger, *President*
EMP: 40
SALES (corp-wide): 572.2MM **Privately Held**
WEB: www.marisolinc.com
SIC: 7389 5169 2869 Solvents recovery service; chemicals & allied products; industrial organic chemicals
HQ: Veolia Environmental Services
     125 Factory Ln
     Middlesex NJ
     732 469-5100

(G-6209)
VINOS CUSTOM MLLWK & FINSHG
Also Called: Vino's Kitchen Renovation
562 Lincoln Blvd (08846-2441)
PHONE..................................732 356-1147
Fax: 732 356-0080
EMP: 10
SQ FT: 5,000
SALES (est): 1.3MM **Privately Held**
SIC: 5031 2521 Whol Lumber/Plywood/Millwork Mfg Wood Office Furniture

(G-6210)
AT&T SERVICES INC
200 S Laurel Ave (07748-1998)
PHONE..................................732 420-3131
Randall Stephensen, *CEO*
EMP: 1000
SALES (est): 73.9MM
SALES (corp-wide): 160.5B **Publicly Held**
SIC: 3669 Intercommunication systems, electric
HQ: At&T Communications Americas, Inc
     900 Us Highway 202 206
     Bedminster NJ 07921
     404 861-9188

(G-6211)
BAY SHORE PRESS INC
Also Called: Courier Newspaper, The
320 Kings Hwy E (07748-3511)
PHONE..................................732 957-0070
Fax: 732 957-0143
EMP: 25
SALES (est): 1.3MM **Privately Held**
SIC: 2711 Newspapers-Publishing/Printing

(G-6212)
BIRDS BEWARE CORPORATION
50 Townsend Dr (07748-3130)
PHONE..................................732 671-6377
EMP: 4 EST: 2011
SALES (est): 274K **Privately Held**
SIC: 3089 Garbage containers, plastic

(G-6213)
DREAMSTAR CONSTRUCTION LLC
248 Clubhouse Dr (07748-1325)
PHONE..................................732 393-2572
Ronald D Denig, *Mng Member*
EMP: 15 EST: 2006
SALES (est): 1.3MM **Privately Held**
WEB: www.dreamstarconstruction.com
SIC: 1541 1522 8741 2431 Industrial buildings & warehouses; residential construction; construction management; millwork; doors & windows

(G-6214)
ENGINEERED PRECISION CAST CO
Also Called: Epco
952 Palmer Ave (07748-1255)
PHONE..................................732 671-2424
Fax: 732 671-8615
Walter Dubovick, *President*
William Dubovick, *General Mgr*
EMP: 90 EST: 1946
SQ FT: 55,000
SALES (est): 19.3MM **Privately Held**
WEB: www.epcast.com
SIC: 3324 3369 Commercial investment castings, ferrous; nonferrous foundries

(G-6215)
GRAVITY VAULT
37 Kanes Ln (07748-3501)
PHONE..................................732 856-9599
Nick Hohn, *Principal*
EMP: 5
SALES (est): 361.2K **Privately Held**
SIC: 3272 Burial vaults, concrete or pre-cast terrazzo

(G-6216)
HEALTH CARE ALERT LLC
1715 State Route 35 # 208 (07748-1870)
PHONE..................................732 676-2630
Jerry Cariello, *CEO*
EMP: 10
SALES (est): 1.3MM **Privately Held**
SIC: 3841 Diagnostic apparatus, medical

(G-6217)
HEKIKAT LLC
24 Doherty Dr (07748-3303)
PHONE..................................908 232-1145
EMP: 5 EST: 2008

GEOGRAPHIC

SALES (est): 414.2K **Privately Held**
SIC: 3565 Packaging machinery

(G-6218)
POWERWASH PLUS
25 Oriole Rd (07748-3236)
PHONE..................................732 671-6767
Christopher Nickel, *Principal*
EMP: 4
SALES (est): 346.9K **Privately Held**
SIC: 3589 High pressure cleaning equipment

(G-6219)
UNIVERSAL PARTS NEW JERSEY LLC
3 Chanowich Ct (07748-2200)
PHONE..................................732 615-0626
Mark T Merezio, *Principal*
EMP: 4
SALES (est): 245.2K **Privately Held**
SIC: 3715 Truck trailer chassis

Midland Park
Bergen County

(G-6220)
ALTECH MACHINE & TOOL INC
230 Bank St (07432-1708)
PHONE..................................201 652-4409
Ishmael Ciera, *President*
EMP: 6
SQ FT: 2,500
SALES: 416.7K **Privately Held**
WEB: www.altechmachine.com
SIC: 3599 Machine shop, jobbing & repair

(G-6221)
ATHLETIC ORGANIZATIONAL AIDS
54 Fairhaven Dr (07432-1017)
PHONE..................................201 652-1485
Adolph Santorine, *Partner*
Helen Santorine, *Partner*
EMP: 26
SALES: 1.6MM **Privately Held**
WEB: www.starscheduler.com
SIC: 2732 7372 Book printing; prepackaged software

(G-6222)
BERGEN CNTY CRTRDGE XCHNGE LLC
268 Greenwood Ave (07432-1445)
PHONE..................................201 493-8182
Mark Giannella, *Sales Mgr*
EMP: 8
SALES (est): 788.3K **Privately Held**
SIC: 3955 Print cartridges for laser & other computer printers
PA: American Internet Holdings L.L.C.
268 Greenwood Ave
Midland Park NJ 07432

(G-6223)
COMMERCE REGISTER INC
190 Godwin Ave (07432-1841)
P.O. Box 190 (07432-0190)
PHONE..................................201 445-3000
Fax: 201 670-7066
Charles Greer, *President*
Frank Castellvi, *Vice Pres*
Joel Rosano, *Vice Pres*
Ken Spittler, *Accounts Mgr*
Deb Rader, *Office Mgr*
EMP: 40
SQ FT: 7,500
SALES: 4.1MM **Privately Held**
WEB: www.comreg.com
SIC: 2741 7374 Directories: publishing & printing; service bureau, computer

(G-6224)
CONVENTION NEWS COMPANY INC (PA)
Also Called: Aviation International News
214 Franklin Ave (07432-1842)
PHONE..................................201 444-5075
Fax: 201 612-8125
Wilson Leach, *President*
Jeff Burger, *Editor*
Nigel Moll, *Editor*

Matt Thurber, *Editor*
Randall Padfield, *Chief*
EMP: 10
SQ FT: 4,800
SALES (est): 5.8MM **Privately Held**
WEB: www.ainonline.com
SIC: 2711 2721 8742 Newspapers, publishing & printing; periodicals; new products & services consultants

(G-6225)
DELUXE INNOVATIONS INC
140 Greenwood Ave Ste 2a (07432-1462)
P.O. Box 141 (07432-0141)
PHONE..................................201 857-5880
David Ferrari, *President*
Linda Ferrari, *Vice Pres*
EMP: 5
SQ FT: 2,550
SALES: 800K **Privately Held**
WEB: www.deluxeinnovations.com
SIC: 3944 Railroad models: toy & hobby

(G-6226)
GEORGE GLOVE COMPANY INC
301 Greenwood Ave Ste 1 (07432-1484)
PHONE..................................201 251-1200
Fax: 201 251-8431
Andy Wilson, *CEO*
Steve Orr, *Sales Staff*
Roy Miller, *Marketing Staff*
▲ EMP: 8
SQ FT: 15,000
SALES: 1.7MM **Privately Held**
WEB: www.georgeglove.com
SIC: 2381 Fabric dress & work gloves

(G-6227)
GRAFWED INTERNET MEDIA STUDIOS
37 Millington Dr (07432-1110)
P.O. Box 121, Ridgewood (07451-0121)
PHONE..................................201 632-1771
Timothy Graf, *President*
EMP: 5
SALES: 410K **Privately Held**
WEB: www.grafweb.com
SIC: 4899 2741 7319 7389 Data communication services; miscellaneous publishing; transit advertising services; design services

(G-6228)
HAFCO FOUNDRY & MACHINE CO
301 Greenwood Ave Ste 2 (07432-1484)
PHONE..................................201 447-0433
Fax: 201 447-1065
Michael J Fornaci, *President*
Bill Fornaci, *Manager*
▲ EMP: 12 EST: 1969
SQ FT: 300
SALES (est): 2.7MM **Privately Held**
SIC: 3322 3462 3469 Malleable iron foundries; iron & steel forgings; machine parts, stamped or pressed metal

(G-6229)
HERITAGE INC
225 Franklin Ave Ste 4 (07432-1865)
PHONE..................................201 447-2600
Fax: 201 447-1414
Paul Mortola, *President*
EMP: 5
SQ FT: 1,300
SALES (est): 637.4K **Privately Held**
SIC: 2759 Screen printing

(G-6230)
IRON MOUNTAIN PLASTICS INC
112 Greenwood Ave (07432-1456)
PHONE..................................201 445-0063
Richard Ver Hage, *President*
Doris Ver Hage, *Corp Secy*
Glenn Ver Hage, *Vice Pres*
Henry Ver Hage, *Vice Pres*
EMP: 10
SQ FT: 10,000
SALES: 1.7MM **Privately Held**
SIC: 3089 Injection molded finished plastic products; extruded finished plastic products

(G-6231)
MASTER REPRO INC
95 Greenwood Ave (07432-1423)
PHONE..................................201 447-4800
Mark Shishmanian, *President*
George Shismanian, *Vice Pres*
EMP: 7
SQ FT: 4,000
SALES: 700K **Privately Held**
WEB: www.masterrepro.com
SIC: 2752 Commercial printing, offset

(G-6232)
MC GINLEY PACKAGING METHODS
80 Greenwood Ave (07432-1413)
P.O. Box 150 (07432-0150)
PHONE..................................201 493-9330
John T Mc Ginley, *President*
EMP: 4
SQ FT: 7,500
SALES (est): 537K **Privately Held**
SIC: 2891 Adhesives & sealants

(G-6233)
MR QUICK SIGN
30 Dairy St (07432-1317)
PHONE..................................201 670-1690
Fax: 201 444-8162
Trena Greenfield, *Owner*
Bernard Greenfield, *Principal*
EMP: 4
SALES: 150K **Privately Held**
SIC: 3993 Signs & advertising specialties

(G-6234)
PINNACLE PRESS INC
41 Prospect St (07432-1645)
PHONE..................................201 652-0500
Fax: 201 652-0503
Howard Siegel, *President*
Ray Huber, *Vice Pres*
EMP: 5
SQ FT: 900
SALES: 750K **Privately Held**
WEB: www.printatpinnacle.com
SIC: 2752 Commercial printing, offset

(G-6235)
PIPER SERVICES LLC
Also Called: Piper Heating and Cooling
268 Greenwood Ave (07432-1445)
P.O. Box 734, Belleville (07109-0734)
PHONE..................................844 567-3900
Joe Rogers, *Mng Member*
John Celentano,
Kevin Frerich,
EMP: 17
SQ FT: 10,000
SALES: 2.5MM **Privately Held**
SIC: 3585 Parts for heating, cooling & refrigerating equipment

(G-6236)
PRECISION MULTIPLE CONTRLS INC (PA)
Also Called: Ramsey Building Supply
33 Greenwood Ave (07432-1717)
PHONE..................................201 444-0600
Fax: 201 445-8575
Peter H Zecher, *President*
Darren Lilley, *Vice Pres*
Todd Zecher, *Vice Pres*
Jane Zecher, *Admin Sec*
▲ EMP: 50 EST: 1957
SQ FT: 70,000
SALES (est): 5.6MM **Privately Held**
WEB: www.precisionmulticontrols.com
SIC: 3625 3613 5211 5031 Electric controls & control accessories, industrial; time switches, electrical switchgear apparatus; lumber & other building materials; masonry materials & supplies; tile, ceramic; lumber, plywood & millwork; building materials, exterior; building materials, interior; masons' materials; tile, clay or other ceramic, excluding refractory

(G-6237)
PRECISION MULTIPLE CONTRLS INC
Also Called: PMC
33 Greenwood Ave (07432-1717)
PHONE..................................201 444-0600
Arnot Charles, *Branch Mgr*

EMP: 100
SALES (corp-wide): 5.6MM **Privately Held**
WEB: www.precisionmulticontrols.com
SIC: 3625 3613 5211 5031 Electric controls & control accessories, industrial; time switches, electrical switchgear apparatus; lumber & other building materials; masonry materials & supplies; tile, ceramic; lumber, plywood & millwork; building materials, exterior; building materials, interior; masons' materials; tile, clay or other ceramic, excluding refractory
PA: Precision Multiple Controls Inc.
33 Greenwood Ave
Midland Park NJ 07432
201 444-0600

(G-6238)
PRINTOLOGY
229 Godwin Ave (07432-1807)
PHONE..................................201 345-4632
Jon Bognar, *Owner*
Jonathan Boguar, *Principal*
EMP: 4
SALES (est): 567K **Privately Held**
SIC: 2759 Laser printing

(G-6239)
TECH PRODUCTS CO INC
300 Greenwood Ave (07432-1426)
PHONE..................................201 444-7777
Fax: 201 444-1909
Robert White, *President*
EMP: 10
SQ FT: 5,000
SALES (est): 1MM **Privately Held**
SIC: 8711 3599 3089 Engineering services; machine shop, jobbing & repair; injection molding of plastics

(G-6240)
TIMES THE VILLADOM INC
Also Called: Vierheilig Publishing
333 Godwin Ave (07432-1533)
P.O. Box 96 (07432-0096)
PHONE..................................201 652-0744
Fax: 201 670-4745
Albert Vierheilig, *President*
Ester Vierheilig, *Vice Pres*
Nicky Warner, *Accounts Exec*
Joan Wilkinson, *Accounts Exec*
Janine Mistretta, *Graphic Designe*
EMP: 10
SALES (est): 524.8K **Privately Held**
SIC: 2711 Newspapers: publishing only, not printed on site; newspapers, publishing & printing

(G-6241)
VAIRTEC CORPORATION
265 Greenwood Ave (07432-1446)
PHONE..................................201 445-6965
Robert Marlow, *President*
Johanna Poletti, *Treasurer*
Joan Miller, *Admin Sec*
EMP: 4
SALES: 1.7MM **Privately Held**
WEB: www.nortechcorp.com
SIC: 3563 Vacuum (air extraction) systems, industrial

(G-6242)
WILKER GRAPHICS LLC
Also Called: AlphaGraphics
95 Greenwood Ave (07432-1423)
PHONE..................................201 447-4800
Nyree Shishmanian, *Consultant*
Bernie Wilker,
EMP: 6
SQ FT: 1,800
SALES (est): 760.4K **Privately Held**
SIC: 2752 2791 2789 Commercial printing, offset; typesetting; bookbinding & related work

(G-6243)
WOSTBROCK EMBROIDERY INC
11 Paterson Ave Ste 1 (07432-1873)
PHONE..................................201 445-3074
Henry Wostbrock, *President*
Barbara Wostbrock, *Corp Secy*
EMP: 4
SQ FT: 3,000

SALES (est): 200K Privately Held
WEB: www.chiefneckerchief.com
SIC: **2395** Embroidery products, except schiffli machine

Milford
Hunterdon County

(G-6244)
FLEMINGTON KNITTING MILLS
123 Dawn Rd (08848-1133)
P.O. Box 5186, North Branch (08876-1302)
PHONE..................................908 995-9590
Sven Klinge, *President*
EMP: 12 EST: 1993
SQ FT: 16,000
SALES: 1MM **Privately Held**
SIC: **2253** Knit outerwear mills

(G-6245)
GEORGIA-PACIFIC LLC
623 Riegelsville Rd (08848-1732)
PHONE..................................908 995-2228
Fax: 908 995-9143
Fred Majewski, *General Mgr*
Michael Diehl, *Project Engr*
Fred Huff, *Manager*
Brian Trapp, *Manager*
Arul Govindasami, *Director*
EMP: 112
SALES (corp-wide): 44.4B **Privately Held**
WEB: www.gp.com
SIC: **2653** 2679 Boxes, corrugated: made from purchased materials; paper products, converted
HQ: Georgia-Pacific Llc
133 Peachtree St Nw
Atlanta GA 30303
404 652-4000

(G-6246)
HOME AND GARDEN KRAFT LLC
93 Crab Apple Hill Rd (08848-1804)
P.O. Box 547 (08848-0547)
PHONE..................................908 995-9355
Chris E Wettstein, *Principal*
EMP: 4
SALES (est): 272.8K Privately Held
SIC: **2022** Processed cheese

(G-6247)
PERMANORE ARCHTCTURAL FINISHES
3 Parkland Dr (08848-1976)
PHONE..................................908 797-4177
Monica Y Johnson, *President*
Robert Johnson, *Manager*
Robert J Johnson, *Officer*
EMP: 5
SQ FT: 3,000
SALES: 210K **Privately Held**
WEB: www.permanore.com
SIC: **3446** Architectural metalwork

Millburn
Essex County

(G-6248)
BEHRMAN HOUSE INC
241 Millburn Ave B (07041-1739)
PHONE..................................973 379-7200
Fax: 973 379-7280
David Behrman, *President*
Matthew Israel, *Controller*
Benjamin Lewis, *Director*
Robert Tinkham,
▲ **EMP: 15 EST:** 1922
SQ FT: 23,400
SALES (est): 2.3MM **Privately Held**
WEB: www.behrmanhouse.com
SIC: **2731** 5192 Books: publishing only; books

(G-6249)
ELIE TAHARI LTD (PA)
16 Bleeker St (07041-1415)
PHONE..................................973 671-6300
Elie Tahari, *Ch of Bd*
▲ **EMP:** 180

SALES (est): 182.1MM Privately Held
WEB: www.elietahari.com
SIC: **2331** 2339 2335 2337 Blouses, women's & juniors': made from purchased material; slacks: women's, misses' & juniors'; women's, juniors' & misses' dresses; suits: women's, misses' & juniors'; jackets & vests, except fur & leather: women's; women's clothing stores; men's & boys' clothing stores

(G-6250)
ENFORSYS INC (PA)
Also Called: Enforsys Systems
27 Bleeker St 222 (07041-1414)
PHONE..................................973 515-8126
Lois Primovic, *CEO*
Vincent Tortoriello PHD, *President*
Lisa Klein, *CFO*
Colette Van Dyke, *Admin Asst*
EMP: 40 EST: 2000
SALES (est): 4.1MM **Privately Held**
WEB: www.enforsys.com
SIC: **7372** Application computer software

(G-6251)
GRASSMAN-BLAKE INC
58 E Willow St (07041-1417)
P.O. Box 737 (07041-0737)
PHONE..................................973 379-6170
Richard Blake Jr, *President*
Susan Mathias, *Manager*
EMP: 25 EST: 1946
SALES (est): 3.9MM **Privately Held**
WEB: www.gbclasp.com
SIC: **3911** 3915 Pearl jewelry, natural or cultured; jewelers' materials & lapidary work

(G-6252)
HUDSON MANUFACTURING CORP
12 E Willow St (07041-1417)
P.O. Box 683, New Providence (07974-0683)
PHONE..................................973 376-7070
Jeffrey Stapfer, *President*
Craig Stapfer, *Vice Pres*
EMP: 10 EST: 1940
SQ FT: 7,200
SALES (est): 814.3K **Privately Held**
SIC: **3544** Punches, forming & stamping

(G-6253)
INNOVI MOBILE LLC
45 Essex St Ste 201 (07041-1668)
PHONE..................................646 588-0165
Alex Zaltsman, *General Mgr*
EMP: 10
SALES (est): 524.2K **Privately Held**
SIC: **7371** 7372 7379 Computer software development & applications; software programming applications; application computer software; computer related consulting services

(G-6254)
KASON CORPORATION (PA)
6771 E Willow St (07041)
PHONE..................................973 467-8140
Fax: 973 258-9533
Hossein Alamzad, *President*
◆ **EMP:** 60
SQ FT: 37,000
SALES (est): 18.7MM **Privately Held**
WEB: www.kason.com
SIC: **3569** Sifting & screening machines

(G-6255)
LENS MODE INC
Also Called: Contact Len Lab
150 Main St Ste 1 (07041-1179)
PHONE..................................973 467-2000
Fax: 973 912-3323
Daniel Strulowitz, *President*
EMP: 4
SQ FT: 5,000
SALES (est): 350K **Privately Held**
WEB: www.lensmode.com
SIC: **3851** Contact lenses

(G-6256)
MCT DAIRIES INC (HQ)
Also Called: Trugman-Nash
15 Bleeker St Ste 103 (07041-1458)
P.O. Box 738 (07041-0738)
PHONE..................................973 258-9600
Fax: 973 258-9222
Ken Meyers, *President*
David Raff, *Exec VP*
Peter Levitan, *Opers Staff*
Vincent McCann, *CFO*
Stephanie Angelis, *Human Resources*
◆ **EMP:** 10
SQ FT: 2,000
SALES (est): 22.7MM
SALES (corp-wide): 23.8MM **Privately Held**
WEB: www.mctdairies.com
SIC: **5084** 5963 8999 3999 Food industry machinery; beverage services, direct sales; artists & artists' studios; barber & beauty shop equipment
PA: Allied Dairy Products, Inc.
15 Bleeker St
Millburn NJ 07041
973 258-9600

(G-6257)
MCT MANUFACTURING INC
15 Bleeker St Ste 101 (07041-1463)
PHONE..................................877 258-9600
Ken Meyers, *President*
EMP: 4
SALES (est): 526.8K **Privately Held**
SIC: **3999** Manufacturing industries

(G-6258)
MILLBURN BAGEL INC
Also Called: Bagel Chateau
321 Millburn Ave Ste 14 (07041-1616)
PHONE..................................973 258-1334
Martin Wayne, *President*
EMP: 30
SQ FT: 3,000
SALES (est): 3.6MM **Privately Held**
SIC: **2051** 5812 5461 Bagels, fresh or frozen; coffee shop; bakeries

(G-6259)
TAHARI ASL LLC (PA)
Also Called: Tahari Arthur S Levine
16 Bleeker St (07041-1415)
PHONE..................................888 734-7459
Mark Smith, *President*
Elie Tahari,
Arthur S Levine,
Lester E Schreiber,
▲ **EMP:** 41
SALES (est): 85.1MM **Privately Held**
SIC: **2331** 2335 2339 Blouses, women's & juniors': made from purchased material; women's, juniors' & misses' dresses; slacks: women's, misses' & juniors'

Millington
Morris County

(G-6260)
BLUEWATER INC
Also Called: Wild Bills Olde Fashioned Soda
50 Division Ave Ste 42 (07946-1377)
PHONE..................................973 532-1225
Christine Kropp, *CEO*
Derek Kropp, *Partner*
EMP: 13
SALES (est): 1.7MM **Privately Held**
SIC: **2087** Beverage bases

(G-6261)
RW DELIGHTS INC
Also Called: Heavenly Souffle
50 Division Ave Ste 44 (07946-1377)
P.O. Box 31, Short Hills (07078-0031)
PHONE..................................718 683-1038
Wendy Freidmann, *President*
Roxanne Kam, *Treasurer*
EMP: 5
SQ FT: 5,000
SALES (est): 250K **Privately Held**
SIC: **2024** Dairy based frozen desserts

Millstone Township
Monmouth County

(G-6262)
ARQUEST INC (PA)
14 Scotto Farm Ln (08535-9426)
PHONE..................................609 395-9500
Fax: 609 395-9778
John R Rinaldi, *CEO*
Matthew J Rinaldi, *President*
Paul Destefano, *Vice Pres*
Eddie Everett, *Vice Pres*
Reed Macfarland, *Vice Pres*
▲ **EMP:** 500
SQ FT: 7,000
SALES (est): 65.2MM **Privately Held**
WEB: www.arquest.com
SIC: **2676** Diapers, paper (disposable): made from purchased paper; feminine hygiene paper products

(G-6263)
COBRA POWER SYSTEMS INC (PA)
304 Monmouth Rd (08510-7936)
PHONE..................................908 486-1800
Doug Cohen, *President*
EMP: 7
SQ FT: 3,800
SALES: 2MM **Privately Held**
SIC: **3621** Motors & generators

(G-6264)
GREIF INC
200 Rike Dr (08535-8548)
PHONE..................................609 448-5300
Geoff Eaton, *Branch Mgr*
EMP: 40
SALES (corp-wide): 3.6B **Publicly Held**
WEB: www.greif.com
SIC: **2655** Fiber cans, drums & containers
PA: Greif, Inc.
425 Winter Rd
Delaware OH 43015
740 549-6000

(G-6265)
SAFEGAURD DOCUMENT DESTRUCTION
800 Rike Dr (08535-8526)
PHONE..................................609 448-6695
Frank Vitarelli, *Principal*
EMP: 4
SALES (est): 558.6K **Privately Held**
SIC: **3559** Tire shredding machinery

Millstone Twp
Monmouth County

(G-6266)
CHRISTOPHER SZUCO
Also Called: Westwood Construction
1061 Windsor Rd (08535-6017)
PHONE..................................732 684-7643
Christopher Szuco, *Owner*
EMP: 4
SALES (est): 365.6K **Privately Held**
SIC: **2514** 1742 Frames for box springs or bedsprings: metal; household furniture: upholstered on metal frames; drywall

Milltown
Middlesex County

(G-6267)
BANNISTER COMPANY INC
216 Brook Dr (08850-1596)
PHONE..................................732 828-1353
Fax: 732 545-0846
Lionel Bannister, *President*
EMP: 12 EST: 1956
SQ FT: 12,000
SALES (est): 1.5MM **Privately Held**
WEB: www.bannistercompany.com
SIC: **3479** 7389 Etching & engraving; engraving service

GEOGRAPHIC

(G-6268)
INTERNATIONAL PAPER COMPANY
101 Ford Ave (08850-1565)
P.O. Box 36 (08850-0036)
PHONE..................................732 828-1700
Richard Hostinsky, *Owner*
Rob Marquis, *Plant Mgr*
Vinny Marricco, *Safety Mgr*
Bill Waldron, *Branch Mgr*
EMP: 60
SALES (corp-wide): 21.7B **Publicly Held**
WEB: www.tin.com
SIC: 2653 Corrugated & solid fiber boxes
PA: International Paper Company
    6400 Poplar Ave
    Memphis TN 38197
    901 419-9000

(G-6269)
JASON MILLS LLC
440 S Main St Ste 7 (08850-1727)
PHONE..................................732 651-7200
Michael L Lavroff, *President*
Brenda Stamboulian, *Sales Dir*
◆ EMP: 6
SQ FT: 2,000
SALES (est): 930.3K **Privately Held**
SIC: 2258 Lace & warp knit fabric mills

(G-6270)
OSSB AND L PHARMA LLC
6 Bel Air Ct (08850-2183)
PHONE..................................732 940-8701
Prabhavathi V K Maddula, *Principal*
EMP: 4
SALES (est): 227.4K **Privately Held**
SIC: 2834 Pharmaceutical preparations

(G-6271)
SALLY MILLER LLC
30 N Main St (08850-1549)
PHONE..................................732 729-4840
Sally Miller,
▲ EMP: 7
SALES (est): 1MM **Privately Held**
SIC: 2361 Girls' & children's dresses,
blouses & shirts

Millville
Cumberland County

(G-6272)
AAVOLYN CORP
207 Bogden Blvd Ste M (08332-4844)
P.O. Box 1097 (08332-8097)
PHONE..................................856 327-8040
Fax: 856 327-9595
Lynn Farrell, *President*
Carolyn Shourds, *Purch Mgr*
Venkat Koganti, *Engineer*
EMP: 25
SALES (est): 5MM **Privately Held**
WEB: www.aavolyn.com
SIC: 3563 Air & gas compressors

(G-6273)
ABSOLUTE BUSINESS SERVICES INC
325 Maurice St (08332-4113)
PHONE..................................856 265-9447
Jaysen Rose, *President*
EMP: 4
SALES (est): 269K **Privately Held**
SIC: 2752 Business forms, lithographed

(G-6274)
ADVANCED METAL PROCESSING
326 S Wade Blvd (08332-3544)
PHONE..................................856 327-0048
Shane Callahan, *General Mgr*
▲ EMP: 5
SALES (est): 572.8K **Privately Held**
SIC: 3471 Finishing, metals or formed
products

(G-6275)
AMCOR FLEXIBLES LLC
Also Called: Amcor Flexibles Mil
1633 Wheaton Ave (08332-2013)
PHONE..................................856 825-1400

Hutton Ward, *Director*
EMP: 135
SALES (corp-wide): 9.1B **Privately Held**
SIC: 2671 2621 2821 3081 Plastic film,
coated or laminated for packaging; packaging paper; plastics materials & resins;
packing materials, plastic sheet; closures,
stamped metal
HQ: Amcor Flexibles Llc
    2150 E Lake Cook Rd
    Buffalo Grove IL 60089
    224 313-7000

(G-6276)
AMCOR PHRM PACKG USA INC
Nipro Glass
1600 Malone St (08332-4831)
PHONE..................................856 825-3050
Jack Chebra, *Sales/Mktg Mgr*
EMP: 108
SALES (corp-wide): 9.1B **Privately Held**
WEB: www.alcanpackaging.com
SIC: 3221 Glass containers
HQ: Amcor Pharmaceutical Packaging Usa,
    Llc
    625 Sharp St N
    Millville NJ 08332
    856 327-1540

(G-6277)
AMCOR PHRM PACKG USA LLC (HQ)
625 Sharp St N (08332-2862)
PHONE..................................856 327-1540
Peter Brues, *President*
Peter Bruess, *President*
David White, *President*
▲ EMP: 170 EST: 1888
SQ FT: 1,000,000
SALES (est): 572MM
SALES (corp-wide): 9.1B **Privately Held**
WEB: www.alcanpackaging.com
SIC: 3221 3085 Cosmetic jars, glass;
medicine bottles, glass; plastics bottles
PA: Amcor Ltd
    L11 60 City Rd
    Southbank VIC 3006
    392 269-000

(G-6278)
AMCOR PHRM PACKG USA LLC
1200 N 10th St (08332-2032)
PHONE..................................856 825-1400
Richard Calabro, *Manager*
EMP: 108
SALES (corp-wide): 9.1B **Privately Held**
WEB: www.alcanpackaging.com
SIC: 3221 Cosmetic jars, glass
HQ: Amcor Pharmaceutical Packaging Usa,
    Llc
    625 Sharp St N
    Millville NJ 08332
    856 327-1540

(G-6279)
AMCOR PHRM PACKG USA LLC
Tube Drawing Division
1633 Wheaton Ave (08332-2013)
PHONE..................................856 825-1400
Bob Griffin, *Manager*
EMP: 150
SALES (corp-wide): 9.1B **Privately Held**
WEB: www.alcanpackaging.com
SIC: 3221 Cosmetic jars, glass; medicine
bottles, glass
HQ: Amcor Pharmaceutical Packaging Usa,
    Llc
    625 Sharp St N
    Millville NJ 08332
    856 327-1540

(G-6280)
AMCOR PHRM PACKG USA LLC
Also Called: Wheaton Science Products
1501 N 10th St (08332-2038)
PHONE..................................856 825-1100
Steve Drozdow, *Manager*
EMP: 200
SQ FT: 1,000
SALES (corp-wide): 9.1B **Privately Held**
WEB: www.alcanpackaging.com
SIC: 3221 3829 3231 3229 Glass con-
tainers; measuring & controlling devices;
products of purchased glass; pressed &
blown glass

HQ: Amcor Pharmaceutical Packaging Usa,
    Llc
    625 Sharp St N
    Millville NJ 08332
    856 327-1540

(G-6281)
AMCOR PHRM PACKG USA LLC
Nipro Glass
1101 Wheaton Ave (08332-2003)
PHONE..................................856 825-1400
Walter Dolson, *Manager*
EMP: 22
SALES (corp-wide): 9.1B **Privately Held**
WEB: www.alcanpackaging.com
SIC: 3559 Pharmaceutical machinery
HQ: Amcor Pharmaceutical Packaging Usa,
    Llc
    625 Sharp St N
    Millville NJ 08332
    856 327-1540

(G-6282)
AMCOR RIGID PLASTICS USA LLC
625 Sharp St N (08332-2862)
PHONE..................................856 327-1540
Bruce Clungeon, *Branch Mgr*
EMP: 58
SALES (corp-wide): 9.1B **Privately Held**
SIC: 3085 Plastics bottles
HQ: Amcor Rigid Plastics Usa, Llc
    935 Technology Dr Ste 100
    Ann Arbor MI 48108

(G-6283)
AMERICAN SIGN INSTLLATIONS LLC ✪
209 S 15th St (08332-3446)
PHONE..................................856 506-0610
Stephen Armstrong, *CEO*
EMP: 4 EST: 2017
SALES (est): 138.4K **Privately Held**
SIC: 3993 Signs & advertising specialties

(G-6284)
ARC INTERNATIONAL N AMER LLC (HQ)
Also Called: Cardinal Millville DC ARC Intl
601 S Wade Blvd (08332-3550)
PHONE..................................856 825-5620
Hubert Ibled, *President*
Dominick Miletta, *Production*
Ken Turner, *Purch Mgr*
Bertrand Lenglart, *CFO*
Bill Calvert, *Controller*
▲ EMP: 140
SQ FT: 750,000
SALES (est): 981.5MM
SALES (corp-wide): 4.9MM **Privately
Held**
SIC: 5023 2821 Glassware; plastics mate-
rials & resins
PA: Arc Holdings
    104 Avenue Du General De Gaulle
    Arques 62510
    321 954-647

(G-6285)
ARCHITCTURAL METAL DESIGNS INC
Also Called: A M D
1505 Pineland Ave (08332-3505)
PHONE..................................856 765-3000
Martin J Schelmbach, *President*
Jennifer Schelmbach, *Vice Pres*
Joe Paradise, *Project Mgr*
Michael Smith, *Manager*
Donna Louden, *Software Dev*
EMP: 35
SALES (est): 4MM **Privately Held**
SIC: 3444 Sheet metalwork

(G-6286)
BETCO GLASS INC
824 Columbia Ave (08332-3733)
P.O. Box 1099 (08332-8099)
PHONE..................................856 327-4301
Fax: 856 825-9142
Neil Betchner, *President*
EMP: 5
SALES (est): 386.6K **Privately Held**
SIC: 3229 Glass tubes & tubing

(G-6287)
BIG 3 PRECISION PRODUCTS INC
30 Gorton Rd (08332-6202)
PHONE..................................856 293-1400
Alan Scheidt, *Branch Mgr*
EMP: 8 **Privately Held**
SIC: 3089 Blow molded finished plastic
products
HQ: Big 3 Precision Products, Inc.
    2923 S Wabash Ave
    Centralia IL 62801
    618 533-3251

(G-6288)
BIG DADDYS SPORTS HAVEN
595 Sherman Ave (08332-7424)
PHONE..................................856 453-9009
EMP: 5 EST: 1999
SALES (est): 440K **Privately Held**
SIC: 3949 Fishing Hunting Guns & Atvs

(G-6289)
BODYBIO INC (PA)
45 Reese Rd (08332-6227)
PHONE..................................856 825-8338
Fax: 856 825-2143
Edward Kane, *CEO*
Patricia Kane MD, *Vice Pres*
EMP: 26
SALES (est): 3.2MM **Privately Held**
WEB: www.bodybio.com
SIC: 2833 Medicinal chemicals

(G-6290)
BREWSTER VAULTS & MONUMENTS
1017 Steep Run Rd (08332-7544)
PHONE..................................856 785-1412
Fax: 856 785-0939
Steven W Brewster, *President*
Joseph E Brewster, *Vice Pres*
Asa Brewster, *Treasurer*
EMP: 11
SALES (est): 1.7MM **Privately Held**
SIC: 3272 5999 Burial vaults, concrete or
precast terrazzo; monuments, finished to
custom order

(G-6291)
CAIN MACHINE INC
1501 Oakland Ave Ste R (08332-0015)
PHONE..................................856 825-7225
Fax: 856 825-3126
Doug Cain, *President*
Jesse Cain, *Vice Pres*
Eleanor Cain, *Treasurer*
EMP: 10
SQ FT: 6,000
SALES (est): 1MM **Privately Held**
SIC: 3559 2821 3643 3444 Glass making
machinery: blowing, molding, forming,
etc.; polytetrafluoroethylene resins
(teflon); current-carrying wiring devices;
sheet metalwork

(G-6292)
CAPE MAY FOODS LLC
48 Gorton Rd (08332-6202)
PHONE..................................856 825-8111
Peter L Lamonica, *Principal*
Tom Considine, *CFO*
Ronald Labuda, *Director*
EMP: 22 EST: 2003
SALES (est): 3.8MM **Privately Held**
SIC: 2091 Canned & cured fish & seafoods

(G-6293)
CARLISLE MACHINE WORKS INC
412 S Wade Blvd Ste 5 (08332-3534)
P.O. Box 746 (08332-0746)
PHONE..................................856 825-0627
Mary Dougherty, *President*
Mary Hedges, *Financial Exec*
EMP: 24
SQ FT: 10,000
SALES (est): 4.6MM **Privately Held**
WEB: www.carlislemachine.com
SIC: 3433 3535 3823 Gas burners, do-
mestic; conveyors & conveying equip-
ment; combustion control instruments

(G-6294)
CREAMER GLASS LLC
2201 Quince Ln (08332-3661)
R Wayne Miskelly, *Owner*
PHONE..................................856 327-2023
R Wayne Miskelly, *Owner*
Todd Miskelly, *General Mgr*
EMP: 5
SQ FT: 800
SALES (est): 430K **Privately Held**
WEB: www.creamerglass.com
SIC: 3229 Tubing, glass

(G-6295)
CREAMER GLASS LLC
411 N 10th St (08332-3145)
PHONE..................................856 327-2023
Fax: 856 327-2077
Todd Miskelly, *Mng Member*
EMP: 4
SALES: 500K **Privately Held**
SIC: 3229 1389 Tubing, glass; running, cutting & pulling casings, tubes & rods

(G-6296)
CUMBERLAND RCYCL CORP S JERSEY
Also Called: Luciano Brothers
N Delsea Dr (08332)
P.O. Box 2304, Vineland (08362-2304)
PHONE..................................856 825-4153
Fax: 856 825-3633
George Luciano Sr, *President*
EMP: 35
SALES (corp-wide): 11.6MM **Privately Held**
SIC: 4953 3341 3231 Recycling, waste materials; secondary nonferrous metals; products of purchased glass
PA: Cumberland Recycling Corporation Of South Jersey
702 S West Blvd
Vineland NJ 08360
856 692-7650

(G-6297)
DELTRONICS CORPORATION
224 Bogden Blvd (08332-4801)
P.O. Box 446 (08332-0446)
PHONE..................................856 825-8200
Robert Hignutt, *President*
Kenneth Hignutt, *Vice Pres*
EMP: 15
SQ FT: 8,000
SALES: 1.6MM **Privately Held**
SIC: 7699 3625 5085 Mechanical instrument repair; industrial controls: push button, selector switches, pilot; industrial supplies

(G-6298)
DEMATTE OIL SERVICE INC
1780 Hance Bridge Rd (08332-1216)
PHONE..................................856 692-9125
John J Braiti, *President*
EMP: 5
SALES (est): 256.2K **Privately Held**
SIC: 1389 Oil field services

(G-6299)
DEMCO SCIENTIFIC GLASSWARE INC
25 N 6th St (08332-3341)
PHONE..................................856 327-7898
Clyde Demary, *President*
EMP: 8
SALES (est): 363K **Privately Held**
SIC: 3231 Medical & laboratory glassware: made from purchased glass; scientific & technical glassware: from purchased glass

(G-6300)
DURAND GLASS MFG CO INC
901 S Wade Blvd (08332-3531)
PHONE..................................856 327-1850
Fax: 856 691-1245
Susan Saidman, *CEO*
Ken Bell, *Vice Pres*
Emmanuel Gauffeny, *Vice Pres*
Shannon Merson, *Vice Pres*
Steve Obrian, *Vice Pres*
▲ **EMP:** 1100
SQ FT: 800,000

SALES (est): 228.8MM
SALES (corp-wide): 4.9MM **Privately Held**
SIC: 3229 3269 5023 Tableware, glass or glass ceramic; kitchen articles, coarse earthenware; glassware
HQ: Arc International North America, Llc
601 S Wade Blvd
Millville NJ 08332
856 825-5620

(G-6301)
DWK LIFE SCIENCES INC (DH)
Also Called: Wheaton Science Products
1501 N 10th St (08332-2038)
PHONE..................................856 825-1100
Fax: 856 825-1368
Wayne L Brinster, *President*
David Koi, *President*
Kirsti Dare, *Regional Mgr*
Karla Melendez, *Regional Mgr*
Gregory W Bianco, *Vice Pres*
◆ **EMP:** 202
SALES: 50.9MM
SALES (corp-wide): 306.4MM **Privately Held**
WEB: www.wheatonsci.com
SIC: 3231 3089 Products of purchased glass; laboratory glassware; plastic containers, except foam
HQ: Dwk Life Sciences Gmbh
Otto-Schott-Str. 21
Wertheim 97877
934 280-20

(G-6302)
FRIEDRICH AND DIMMOCK INC
Also Called: F & D
2127 Wheaton Ave (08332-1421)
PHONE..................................856 825-0305
Fax: 856 327-4299
Joseph Plumbo, *CEO*
John T Plumbo, *CEO*
Bob Goffredi, *President*
Victor G Plumbo, *Chairman*
Steve Cimer, *CFO*
▲ **EMP:** 48 EST: 1919
SQ FT: 25,000
SALES (est): 7.6MM **Privately Held**
WEB: www.fdglass.com
SIC: 3229 5047 3231 3221 Scientific glassware; medical laboratory equipment; products of purchased glass; glass containers

(G-6303)
GARDEN STATE HIGHWAY PDTS INC (PA)
301 Riverside Dr D (08332-6717)
PHONE..................................856 692-7572
Fax: 856 692-6797
Sharon Green, *President*
Robert Green, *Vice Pres*
Robert A Green, *Vice Pres*
EMP: 46
SQ FT: 28,000
SALES (est): 11.9MM **Privately Held**
WEB: www.gardenstatehwy.com
SIC: 3993 5099 3499 Signs & advertising specialties; safety equipment & supplies; barricades, metal

(G-6304)
GENERAL POLYGON SYSTEMS INC
203 Peterson St (08332-4803)
PHONE..................................800 825-1655
Joseph Pitassi Jr, *President*
William Anderson, *Principal*
Rich Shea, *Principal*
Michael Sormanto, *Vice Pres*
EMP: 10
SQ FT: 6,000
SALES (est): 1.6MM **Privately Held**
WEB: www.generalpolygon.com
SIC: 3599 Machine shop, jobbing & repair

(G-6305)
GLASS WAREHOUSE
Also Called: Wheaton Sands Products
1101 Wheaton Ave (08332-2003)
PHONE..................................856 825-1400
Fax: 856 825-9014
Steve Drozdow, *President*
James Smith, *Vice Pres*
▼ **EMP:** 8

SALES (est): 947.7K **Privately Held**
WEB: www.glass-warehouse.com
SIC: 3229 Scientific glassware

(G-6306)
GROUPE SEB USA
2121 Eden Rd (08332-4060)
PHONE..................................856 825-6300
Cyril Buxtorf, *Senior VP*
Luc Gaudemard, *Senior VP*
Virginia Flower, *Accounting Mgr*
Sheri Zakher, *Human Resources*
Judy Phillips, *Natl Sales Mgr*
EMP: 10 **Privately Held**
SIC: 3639 Floor waxers & polishers, electric: household
HQ: Groupe Seb Usa
5 Woodhollow Rd Fl 2
Parsippany NJ 07054

(G-6307)
HENDERSON AQUATIC INC (PA)
1 Whitall Ave (08332-3988)
PHONE..................................856 825-4771
Allan G Edmund, *President*
◆ **EMP:** 25 EST: 1954
SQ FT: 15,000
SALES (est): 4.1MM **Privately Held**
WEB: www.hendersonusa.com
SIC: 3069 Wet suits, rubber

(G-6308)
HOLLY PACKAGING INC
1101 N 10th St (08332-2029)
P.O. Box 356 (08332-0356)
PHONE..................................856 327-8281
Preston Hickman, *President*
Gregory Fink, *Exec VP*
EMP: 50
SQ FT: 36,000
SALES (est): 11.9MM **Privately Held**
SIC: 2653 7389 Partitions, corrugated: made from purchased materials; packaging & labeling services

(G-6309)
J AND J CONTRACTORS
604 5th St N (08332-2614)
PHONE..................................856 765-7521
Fax: 609 765-0007
Julian Mendez, *Owner*
Janet Mendez, *Co-Owner*
EMP: 10
SALES: 351K **Privately Held**
SIC: 3545 Drill bushings (drilling jig)

(G-6310)
JACQUET JONPAUL
25 E Main St Ste D (08332-4289)
PHONE..................................856 825-4259
Jon Paul Jacquet, *Principal*
EMP: 4
SALES (est): 368.6K **Privately Held**
SIC: 3843 Enamels, dentists'

(G-6311)
LAMONICA FINE FOODS LLC
Also Called: Cape May Foods
48 Gorton Rd (08332-6202)
P.O. Box 309 (08332-0309)
PHONE..................................856 776-2126
Danny Lavecchia, *President*
Steve Schwartz, *Regional Mgr*
Chris Douthett, *Vice Pres*
Michael Lavecchia, *Vice Pres*
Sandy Ritchie, *Buyer*
▲ **EMP:** 200 EST: 1949
SQ FT: 95,000
SALES (est): 38MM **Privately Held**
WEB: www.capemayfoods.com
SIC: 2091 2092 Clams: packaged in cans, jars, etc.; juice, clam: packaged in cans, jars, etc.; seafoods, fresh: prepared

(G-6312)
LLOYDS OF MILLVILLE INC
Also Called: Lloyd's Awnings
208 S Wade Blvd (08332-3542)
PHONE..................................856 825-0345
Fax: 856 825-0345
Benjamin H Lloyd Jr, *President*
Linda Lloyd, *Vice Pres*
EMP: 6
SALES: 250K **Privately Held**
SIC: 2394 Canvas & related products

(G-6313)
MCQUADE ENTERPRISES LLC ✪
511 N 6th St (08332-2707)
PHONE..................................609 501-2437
Robert McQuade,
EMP: 5 EST: 2017
SALES (est): 138.7K **Privately Held**
SIC: 6798 3524 6531 Real estate investment trusts; lawn & garden equipment; real estate managers

(G-6314)
NIPRO GLASS AMERICAS CORP
1633 Wheaton Ave (08332-2013)
PHONE..................................856 825-1400
EMP: 11
SALES (corp-wide): 3.7B **Privately Held**
SIC: 3221 Vials, glass
HQ: Nipro Pharmapackaging Americas Corp.
1200 N 10th St
Millville NJ 08332

(G-6315)
NIPRO PHRMPCKGING AMRICAS CORP (HQ)
Also Called: Millville Vials
1200 N 10th St (08332-2032)
PHONE..................................856 825-1400
Kurt Van Dal, *President*
Bob Luderitz, *Engineer*
Anthony Lieske, *Finance*
◆ **EMP:** 192
SQ FT: 4,000,000
SALES (est): 98.7MM
SALES (corp-wide): 3.7B **Privately Held**
SIC: 3221 Vials, glass
PA: Nipro Corporation
3-9-3, Honjonishi, Kita-Ku
Osaka OSK 531-0
663 722-331

(G-6316)
NM KNIGHT CO INC
Also Called: Knight Gas Burner Co
1001 S 2nd St (08332-4234)
P.O. Box 1099 (08332-8099)
PHONE..................................856 327-4855
Jack Narbut, *President*
Reinhold Nutz, *General Mgr*
Connie Sparks, *Finance Mgr*
Scott Nagao, *Sales Executive*
▲ **EMP:** 25
SQ FT: 12,000
SALES (est): 4.6MM **Privately Held**
WEB: www.nmknight.com
SIC: 3823 3433 5084 Combustion control instruments; heating equipment, except electric; industrial machinery & equipment

(G-6317)
NORTHEAST PRECAST LTD LBLTY CO
92 Reese Rd (08332-6228)
PHONE..................................856 765-9088
John Ruga, *Principal*
Ken Baur, *Chief Engr*
Peter Gorgas, *Project Engr*
Heidi Ahlquist, *Sales Staff*
Don Heiken, *Sales Staff*
EMP: 80
SQ FT: 65,000
SALES (est): 19.3MM **Privately Held**
SIC: 1799 3599 Fence construction; custom machinery

(G-6318)
OHM EQUIPENT LLC
2525 S 2nd St (08332-9606)
PHONE..................................856 765-3011
Douglas OHM, *Principal*
EMP: 4
SALES (est): 308.3K **Privately Held**
WEB: www.ohmequipment.com
SIC: 3699 Electrical equipment & supplies

(G-6319)
PARKER-HANNIFIN CORPORATION
525 Orange St (08332-4030)
PHONE..................................856 825-8900
Ronald McBride, *Supervisor*
EMP: 12

SALES (corp-wide): 12B **Publicly Held**
SIC: 3577 Computer peripheral equipment
PA: Parker-Hannifin Corporation
    6035 Parkland Blvd
    Cleveland OH 44124
    216 896-3000

(G-6320)
PENTAGON PERFORMANCE INC
Also Called: Ppi
112 Leddon St (08332-4811)
PHONE..973 975-0400
Anthony Lasure, *President*
Alfred Rosu, *COO*
Nolan Ryon, *Marketing Staff*
Candace Rosu, *Admin Sec*
EMP: 8 EST: 2012
SQ FT: 1,000
SALES: 4.1MM **Privately Held**
SIC: 7335 3861 4899 Aerial photography,
except mapmaking; photographic equip-
ment & supplies; data communication
services

(G-6321)
RAILING DYNAMICS INC
1201 N 10th St (08332-2031)
PHONE..609 593-5400
Fax: 856 327-2343
EMP: 13
SALES (corp-wide): 94.2K **Privately Held**
SIC: 2411 Mfg And Distributes Vinyl Railing
And Fencing
HQ: Railing Dynamics Inc
    135 Steelmanville Rd
    Egg Harbor Township NJ 08226
    609 601-1300

(G-6322)
REMINDER NEWSPAPER
2 W Vine St (08332-3823)
P.O. Box 1600 (08332-8600)
PHONE..856 825-8811
Fax: 856 825-0011
Darrell Kopp, *President*
EMP: 15
SALES (est): 845.8K **Privately Held**
WEB: www.nreminder.com
SIC: 2711 Newspapers

(G-6323)
RICHARD ANDRUS
Also Called: Andrus Bait Company
708 E Main St (08332-3441)
PHONE..856 825-1782
Richard Andrus, *Owner*
EMP: 5
SALES (est): 406.6K **Privately Held**
SIC: 2298 3949 Fishing lines, nets,
seines: made in cordage or twine mills;
lures, fishing: artificial

(G-6324)
SHURE-PAK CORPORATION
1500 N Ten St (08332)
PHONE..856 825-0808
Fax: 856 825-1562
Aaron B Sheppard, *President*
Cynthia Sheppard, *Corp Secy*
George B Sheppard, *Vice Pres*
EMP: 8 EST: 1944
SQ FT: 22,000
SALES: 1.6MM **Privately Held**
WEB: www.shure-pak.com
SIC: 2631 2652 Folding boxboard; setup
paperboard boxes

(G-6325)
SOUTHWIND EQUESTRIAN
385 Lebanon Rd (08332-7446)
PHONE..856 364-9690
Jeannie Dickison Allan, *Owner*
Lorrie D Allen, *Manager*
EMP: 6
SALES: 150K **Privately Held**
SIC: 2084 Wines

Mine Hill
Morris County

(G-6326)
FIABILA USA INC
114 Iron Mountain Rd (07803-2300)
PHONE..973 659-9510
Fax: 973 659-9504
Pierre Miasnik, *President*
Mitchell Schlossman, *Vice Pres*
▲ EMP: 28
SQ FT: 11,000
SALES (est): 11.5MM **Privately Held**
WEB: www.fiabilausa.com
SIC: 5999 2841 Cosmetics; soap & other
detergents

(G-6327)
M2 ELECTRIC LLC
Also Called: M2 Enterprises
3 Iron Mountain Rd (07803-2312)
Rural Route 311 Maxim, Hopatcong
(07843)
PHONE..973 770-4596
Aimee Oliva, *Mng Member*
Michael Oliva,
EMP: 14
SALES (est): 1.4MM **Privately Held**
WEB: www.m2enterprisesusa.com
SIC: 1731 2521 7389 General electrical
contractor; panel systems & partitions
(free-standing), office: wood;

(G-6328)
MINE HILL SPARTAN
274 Us Highway 46 (07803-3030)
PHONE..973 442-2280
Cengiz Unal, *Owner*
EMP: 5 EST: 2007
SALES (est): 417.8K **Privately Held**
SIC: 1389 Oil field services

(G-6329)
**WIRE CLOTH MANUFACTURERS
INC (PA)**
110 Iron Mountain Rd (07803-2300)
PHONE..973 328-1000
Kathleen Hegarty, *President*
Brian Blaber, *General Mgr*
Jim Beyer, *Managing Dir*
Kathleen H Blaber, *Vice Pres*
James P Hegarty Sr, *Vice Pres*
▲ EMP: 25 EST: 1965
SQ FT: 65,000
SALES: 4.9MM **Privately Held**
SIC: 3496 3564 3494 Wire cloth & woven
wire products; blowers & fans; valves &
pipe fittings

Monmouth Junction
Middlesex County

(G-6330)
ACCELEDEV CHEMICAL LLC
11 Deerpark Dr Ste 119 (08852-1923)
PHONE..732 274-1451
Charles Lewis, *President*
EMP: 5
SALES (corp-wide): 613K **Privately Held**
SIC: 2869 Laboratory chemicals, organic
PA: Acceledev Chemical, L.L.C.
    18 Apple Ln
    Wayne NJ 07470
    862 239-1524

(G-6331)
AMPERICON INC
1 Tamaron Ct (08852-2967)
PHONE..609 945-2591
Vivek Bhatnagar, *President*
EMP: 11
SALES (est): 211.7K **Privately Held**
SIC: 3433 Heating equipment, except elec-
tric

(G-6332)
BRIARS USA
891 Georges Rd (08852-3057)
P.O. Box 7092, North Brunswick (08902-
7092)
PHONE..732 821-7600
Joseph De Marco, *Ch of Bd*
Herbert Schloss, *President*
Guy Battaglia, *Vice Pres*
Maurie Motto, *Admin Sec*
EMP: 6 EST: 1921
SQ FT: 85,000
SALES (est): 919.1K **Privately Held**
WEB: www.briars.com
SIC: 2086 2087 Soft drinks: packaged in
cans, bottles, etc.; syrups, drink

(G-6333)
**BRIGHT HRZONS FMLY SLTIONS
LLC**
890 Ridge Rd (08852-2726)
PHONE..609 520-7501
Fax: 609 520-7504
Sandy Alu, *Principal*
Surya Mylavarapu, *Info Tech Mgr*
Greg Russell, *Director*
EMP: 20
SALES (corp-wide): 1.7B **Publicly Held**
SIC: 2711 Newspapers
HQ: Bright Horizons Family Solutions Llc
    200 Talcott Ave
    Watertown MA 02472
    617 673-8000

(G-6334)
BWI CHEMICALS
Also Called: Aroma Chemicals
6 Libby Dr (08852-2921)
PHONE..732 689-0913
Yunus Bandukwala, *Owner*
▼ EMP: 2 EST: 2007
SALES: 1MM **Privately Held**
SIC: 2911 Aromatic chemical products

(G-6335)
CARDOLITE CORPORATION (PA)
11 Deerpark Dr Ste 124 (08852-1923)
PHONE..609 436-0902
Fax: 973 344-1197
Anthony Stonis, *President*
Timothy Stonis, *President*
Tom Claessen, *Business Mgr*
Angel Soto, *Vice Pres*
Shannon Donohue, *Purchasing*
◆ EMP: 50
SQ FT: 88,000
SALES (est): 14.5MM **Privately Held**
WEB: www.cardolite.com
SIC: 3479 3499 2891 Coating of metals &
formed products; friction material, made
from powdered metal; adhesives

(G-6336)
CHEM-AQUA INC
34 Stouts Ln (08852-1911)
PHONE..972 438-0211
Bill Bolton, *President*
Jim Lorditch, *Regional Mgr*
Kevin Battaglini, *District Mgr*
Jeffrey Kazio, *Consultant*
EMP: 11
SALES (corp-wide): 996.6MM **Privately
Held**
SIC: 3589 1629 Water treatment equip-
ment, industrial; waste water & sewage
treatment plant construction
HQ: Chem-Aqua, Inc.
    2727 Chemsearch Blvd
    Irving TX 75062
    972 438-0232

(G-6337)
**COCA COLA BOTTLING CO MID
AMER**
Coca-Cola
60 Deans Rhode Hall Rd (08852-3031)
PHONE..732 398-4800
Fax: 732 897-8585
Ed Rowan, *Branch Mgr*
EMP: 10
SALES (corp-wide): 35.4B **Publicly Held**
WEB: www.phillycoke.com
SIC: 2086 Soft drinks: packaged in cans,
bottles, etc.

HQ: Coca Cola Bottling Company Of Mid
    America
    435 Se 70th St
    Topeka KS 66619
    785 243-1071

(G-6338)
**COCA-COLA REFRESHMENTS
USA INC**
60 Deans Rhode Hall Rd (08852-3031)
PHONE..732 398-4800
Gina Kurdewan, *Manager*
EMP: 11
SALES (corp-wide): 35.4B **Publicly Held**
SIC: 2086 Bottled & canned soft drinks
HQ: Coca-Cola Refreshments Usa, Inc.
    2500 Windy Ridge Pkwy Se
    Atlanta GA 30339
    770 989-3000

(G-6339)
**CYTOSORBENTS
CORPORATION (PA)**
7 Deerpark Dr Ste K (08852-1977)
PHONE..732 329-8885
Al W Kraus, *Ch of Bd*
Phillip P Chan, *President*
Vincent J Capponi, *COO*
Kathleen P Bloch, *CFO*
Eric R Mortensen, *Chief Mktg Ofcr*
EMP: 24
SQ FT: 15,745
SALES: 15.1MM **Publicly Held**
SIC: 3841 Surgical & medical instruments

(G-6340)
**CYTOSORBENTS MEDICAL INC
(HQ)**
7 Deerpark Dr Ste K (08852-1977)
PHONE..732 329-8885
Al W Kraus, *Ch of Bd*
Phillip P Chan, *President*
Vincent J Capponi, *COO*
Christopher Cramer, *Vice Pres*
Matthew Sheahan, *Opers Mgr*
EMP: 41
SQ FT: 12,400
SALES (est): 7.6MM
SALES (corp-wide): 15.1MM **Publicly
Held**
SIC: 3841 Surgical & medical instruments
PA: Cytosorbents Corporation
    7 Deerpark Dr Ste K
    Monmouth Junction NJ 08852
    732 329-8885

(G-6341)
DOW JONES & COMPANY INC
4300 Us Highway 1 (08852-1963)
P.O. Box 300, Princeton (08543-0300)
PHONE..609 520-5238
EMP: 100
SQ FT: 3,000
SALES (corp-wide): 9B **Publicly Held**
SIC: 2711 Newspapers, publishing & print-
ing
HQ: Dow Jones & Company, Inc.
    1211 Avenue Of The Americ
    New York NY 10036
    609 627-2999

(G-6342)
DRIVE TECHNOLOGY INC
2031 Us Highway 130 1l (08852-3014)
PHONE..732 422-6500
Thomas R Doscher, *President*
Marjorie Doscher, *Vice Pres*
EMP: 4
SQ FT: 5,400
SALES: 800K **Privately Held**
SIC: 8711 5063 3566 Consulting engi-
neer; motor controls, starters & relays:
electric; motors, electric; speed changers,
drives & gears

(G-6343)
ELITE GRAPHIX LLC
45 Stouts Ln Ste 2 (08852-1914)
P.O. Box 1430, Belmar (07719-1430)
PHONE..732 274-2356
Joseph Angelone, *CEO*
EMP: 10
SALES (est): 1.1MM **Privately Held**
SIC: 2752 Business form & card printing,
lithographic

(G-6344)
FILTER TECHNOLOGIES INC
Also Called: Filter Process & Supply
45 Stouts Ln Ste 3 (08852-1914)
PHONE....................................732 329-2500
Fax: 732 251-9503
Peter Wojnarowicz, *President*
EMP: 5
SQ FT: 10,000
SALES: 400K **Privately Held**
WEB: www.filterselect.com
SIC: 5075 3589 5085 Air filters; water filters & softeners, household type; water treatment equipment, industrial; filters, industrial

(G-6345)
FIRMENICH
21 Distribution Way (08852-3001)
PHONE....................................609 580-4498
Jim Henson, *Manager*
▲ EMP: 5
SALES (est): 479.8K **Privately Held**
SIC: 2869 Flavors or flavoring materials, synthetic

(G-6346)
I PHYSICIAN HUB
Also Called: Iphysicianhub
462 New Rd (08852-2653)
PHONE....................................732 274-0155
Ramdev Regulapati, *President*
EMP: 99
SALES (est): 2.8MM **Privately Held**
SIC: 7372 7379 8011 8099 Business oriented computer software; ; group health association; medical services organization

(G-6347)
INFINOVA CORPORATION
Also Called: Infinova Networks
51 Stouts Ln Ste 1 (08852-1916)
PHONE....................................732 355-9100
Jeffrey Z Liu, *President*
Steve Cannellos, *Senior VP*
Nathan Needel, *Vice Pres*
Adolph Salas, *Vice Pres*
Ciprian Suciu, *Vice Pres*
▲ EMP: 50
SQ FT: 20,000
SALES (est): 10MM **Privately Held**
WEB: www.infinova.com
SIC: 3663 3661 3699 3625 Television closed circuit equipment; fiber optics communications equipment; security devices; electric controls & control accessories, industrial

(G-6348)
INNOVTIVE PHTNICS SLUTION CORP
Also Called: Innovative Photonic Solutions
4250 Us Highway 1 Ste 1 (08852-1966)
PHONE....................................732 355-9300
Dieter Strohm, *President*
Nancy Morris, *Vice Pres*
Scott Rudder, *Vice Pres*
Tina Gong, *Sales Staff*
EMP: 8
SQ FT: 5,000
SALES (est): 2MM **Privately Held**
WEB: www.innovativephotonics.com
SIC: 3648 Lighting equipment

(G-6349)
KAREBAY BIOCHEM INC
11 Deerpark Dr Ste 102a (08852-1923)
PHONE....................................732 823-1545
Lijun Dai, *Ch of Bd*
Drew Dai, *Vice Pres*
EMP: 4
SALES (est): 319.6K **Privately Held**
SIC: 2869 Laboratory chemicals, organic; high purity grade chemicals, organic

(G-6350)
M G X INC
Also Called: Mastergraphx
45 Stouts Ln (08852-1914)
P.O. Box 567 (08852-0567)
PHONE....................................732 329-0088
Fax: 732 329-0024
Robert Townsend, *President*
Harry A Copeland, *Officer*
James G Copeland, *Officer*

Robert E Copeland, *Officer*
EMP: 11 EST: 1980
SQ FT: 5,000
SALES (est): 2.1MM **Privately Held**
WEB: www.mgxprint.com
SIC: 2752 Commercial printing, offset

(G-6351)
MEDCHEM EXPRESS LLC
11 Deerpark Dr (08852-1923)
PHONE....................................732 783-7915
James Dal, *Mng Member*
EMP: 5
SALES (est): 340.7K **Privately Held**
SIC: 2836 Biological products, except diagnostic

(G-6352)
NANONEX CORP
1 Deerpark Dr Ste O (08852-1962)
PHONE....................................732 355-1600
Fax: 732 355-1608
Lin W Chou, *President*
Hua Tan, *President*
Larry Koecher, *COO*
Lin Hu, *Engineer*
Yanjun Wang, *Engineer*
EMP: 12
SALES (est): 1.2MM **Privately Held**
WEB: www.nanonex.com
SIC: 3674 Semiconductors & related devices

(G-6353)
PARABOLE LLC
1100 Cornwall Rd (08852-2410)
PHONE....................................609 917-8479
Rajib Kumar Saha, *CEO*
Manesh Murali, *President*
EMP: 9 EST: 2014
SALES (est): 450K **Privately Held**
SIC: 7372 Business oriented computer software

(G-6354)
PETRO PALLET LLC
575 Ridge Rd (08852-2638)
PHONE....................................732 230-3287
Anthony Lanza Jr, *Mng Member*
EMP: 20
SQ FT: 1,000
SALES: 2MM **Privately Held**
SIC: 2448 Pallets, wood; pallets, wood & wood with metal

(G-6355)
PHARMASEQ INC
11 Deerpark Dr Ste 104 (08852-1923)
PHONE....................................732 355-0100
Fax: 732 355-0102
Richard Morris, *CEO*
Wlodek Mandecki, *President*
▲ EMP: 5
SQ FT: 1,500
SALES (est): 1MM **Privately Held**
WEB: www.pharmaseq.com
SIC: 2835 8731 In vitro & in vivo diagnostic substances; commercial physical research

(G-6356)
PRINCETON BIOMEDITECH CORP (PA)
Also Called: P B M
4242 Us Highway 1 (08852-1905)
P.O. Box 7139, Princeton (08543-7139)
PHONE....................................732 274-1000
Fax: 732 274-1010
Jemo Kang, *President*
Young Kim, *Facilities Mgr*
Gabriel Chan, *Plant Engr*
Brian Lee, *Sales Executive*
Roger Kang, *Marketing Staff*
▲ EMP: 100
SQ FT: 25,000
SALES (est): 18.3MM **Privately Held**
SIC: 2835 3826 In vitro diagnostics; pregnancy test kits; environmental testing equipment

(G-6357)
PRINCETON ENDURING BIOTECH INC
190 Major Rd (08852-2303)
PHONE....................................732 406-3041
Shu-Min Liu, *CEO*

Howard Chen, *Principal*
Dechun Wu, *COO*
EMP: 4
SALES (est): 288.5K **Privately Held**
SIC: 2834 2836 Pharmaceutical preparations; biological products, except diagnostic

(G-6358)
PRINCETON ENDURING BIOTECH INC
190 Major Rd (08852-2303)
PHONE....................................732 406-3041
EMP: 4
SALES (est): 180K **Privately Held**
SIC: 2836 2834 Mfg Biological Products Mfg Pharmaceutical Preparations

(G-6359)
PRINCETONIAN GRAPHICS INC
45 Stouts Ln Ste 4 (08852-1914)
PHONE....................................732 329-8282
Fax: 732 329-6441
Jack E Norsworthy, *President*
Tony Catania, *Art Dir*
EMP: 15
SQ FT: 10,000
SALES (est): 2.4MM **Privately Held**
WEB: www.pringraph.com
SIC: 2752 Commercial printing, offset

(G-6360)
REAL SOFT INC
Also Called: Diversity Direct
68 Culver Rd Ste 100 (08852-2820)
PHONE....................................609 409-3636
Fax: 609 409-3637
Rajan Desai, *President*
Joel Jerva, *Vice Pres*
Eabu Mathson, *Accounting Mgr*
Barkha Patni, *Accounts Mgr*
Anirban Singh, *Accounts Mgr*
EMP: 550
SQ FT: 58,000
SALES (est): 58.1MM **Privately Held**
WEB: www.realsoftinc.com
SIC: 7379 7373 7371 7372 Computer related consulting services; computer integrated systems design; custom computer programming services; computer software systems analysis & design, custom; computer software development; application computer software; human resource consulting services

(G-6361)
RIVE TECHNOLOGY INC
1 Deerpark Dr Ste A (08852-1970)
PHONE....................................732 329-4441
David C Aldous, *CEO*
Andrew Dougherty, *Vice Pres*
Janak Patel, *Research*
Scott Babitz, *Project Leader*
Adrian Humphries, *Technical Staff*
EMP: 20
SALES (est): 9.2MM **Privately Held**
SIC: 2819 Catalysts, chemical

(G-6362)
SALUS PHARMA LLC
11 Deerpark Dr Ste 118 (08852-1923)
PHONE....................................732 329-8089
Fax: 732 329-8083
Nuo Wang, *CEO*
Fan Zhou, *CFO*
▲ EMP: 10
SQ FT: 7,000
SALES (est): 1.6MM **Privately Held**
SIC: 2834 Druggists' preparations (pharmaceuticals)

(G-6363)
SCIECURE PHARMA INC
11 Deerpark Dr Ste 120 (08852-1923)
PHONE....................................732 329-8089
Nuo Wang, *CEO*
▲ EMP: 34
SALES: 6.5MM
SALES (corp-wide): 5.1MM **Privately Held**
SIC: 2834 Pharmaceutical preparations

PA: Beijing Sciecure Pharmaceutical Co., Ltd.
Zhongbei Industrial Park, Beishicao Town, Shunyi Dist.
Beijing 10130
106 042-5456

(G-6364)
SUVEN LIFE SCIENCES LTD
1100 Cornwall Rd Ste 5 (08852-2410)
PHONE....................................732 274-0037
Venkat Jasti, *CEO*
Padmakumar Kumar, *Research*
Pardha Uppalapati, *CIO*
Venkateswar Jasti, *Director*
Padmakumar Kaimal, *Director*
EMP: 10
SQ FT: 4,000
SALES (est): 1.7MM **Privately Held**
WEB: www.synthoncorp.com
SIC: 2899 Chemical preparations

(G-6365)
TRIS PHARMA INC
Also Called: Customer Complaint Dept
2031 Us Highway 130 Ste H (08852-3014)
PHONE....................................732 940-0358
Ketan Mehta, *CEO*
Amanda Wohlleber, *Vice Pres*
Jonathan Parker, *Sales Staff*
Peter Currie, *Director*
Joe Gilhooly, *Director*
EMP: 76
SQ FT: 130,350 **Privately Held**
SIC: 2834 Syrups, pharmaceutical
PA: Tris Pharma, Inc.
2033 Rte 130 Ste D
Monmouth Junction NJ 08852

(G-6366)
TRIS PHARMA INC (PA)
2033 Rte 130 Ste D (08852)
PHONE....................................732 940-2800
Fax: 732 940-2855
Ketan Mehta, *President*
Peter Ciano, *Senior VP*
Norma Cappetti, *Vice Pres*
Dominick Dipaolo, *Vice Pres*
Jeffery Palmer, *Vice Pres*
EMP: 249
SQ FT: 28,000
SALES (est): 87MM **Privately Held**
WEB: www.trispharma.com
SIC: 2834 Druggists' preparations (pharmaceuticals); drugs acting on the central nervous system & sense organs

(G-6367)
TYRX INC
1 Deerpark Dr Ste G (08852-1920)
PHONE....................................732 246-8676
Fax: 732 246-8677
Robert White, *CEO*
Bill Young, *Ch of Bd*
George D Landau, *Vice Pres*
Ray Imp, *CFO*
Gail O'Brien Turner, *VP Sales*
EMP: 50
SALES (est): 9.4MM **Privately Held**
WEB: www.tyrx.com
SIC: 3842 Surgical appliances & supplies
HQ: Medtronic, Inc.
710 Medtronic Pkwy
Minneapolis MN 55432
763 514-4000

(G-6368)
UNITED SILICON CARBIDE INC
7 Deerpark Dr Ste E (08852-1921)
PHONE....................................732 355-0550
John Christopher Dries, *CEO*
Bhalla Anup, *President*
Betsy Cotton, *CFO*
EMP: 18 EST: 1997
SALES: 5.2MM **Privately Held**
SIC: 8731 3674 Commercial research laboratory; transistors

(G-6369)
VALEUR CORPORATION
Also Called: Oilco Liquid Handling Systems
596 Ridge Rd (08852-2638)
P.O. Box 226 (08852-0226)
PHONE....................................732 329-4666
Richard C Slawinski Sr, *Ch of Bd*
Richard C Slawinski Jr, *President*

Patricia A Skochial, *Vice Pres*
Margaret Slawinski, *Treasurer*
EMP: 22
SQ FT: 25,000
SALES (est): 4.6MM **Privately Held**
SIC: 3569 Liquid automation machinery & equipment

(G-6370)
WALL STREET JOURNAL
4300 Us Highway 1 (08852-1906)
PHONE..................................609 520-4000
Fax: 609 520-4274
EMP: 7
SALES (est): 429.8K **Privately Held**
SIC: 2711 Newspapers-Publishing/Printing

(G-6371)
WALLY ENTERPRISES INC
Also Called: Active Imprints
4266 Us Route 1 (08852)
PHONE..................................732 329-2613
Fax: 732 329-2454
Duane Watlington, *President*
Nancy Watlington, *Vice Pres*
Diane Reznik, *Manager*
Jody Grzyb, *Consultant*
EMP: 12
SQ FT: 2,880
SALES (est): 1.7MM **Privately Held**
WEB: www.activeimprints.com
SIC: 7336 5199 5699 2395 Silk screen design; advertising specialties; T-shirts, custom printed; emblems, embroidered; embroidering of advertising on shirts, etc.; screen printing on fabric articles

(G-6372)
WYETH-AYERST PHARMACEUTICAL
865 Ridge Rd (08852-2718)
PHONE..................................732 274-4221
EMP: 16
SALES (est): 2MM
SALES (corp-wide): 52.5B **Publicly Held**
SIC: 2834 Mfg Pharmaceutical Preparations
HQ: Wyeth Llc
235 E 42nd St
New York NY 10017
973 660-5000

Monroe
Middlesex County

(G-6373)
EDISON DESIGN GROUP INC (PA)
95 Cobblestone Blvd (08831-7944)
PHONE..................................732 993-3341
John Spicer, *President*
William Miller, *Design Engr*
Mike Herrick, *Software Dev*
EMP: 1
SALES: 1.6MM **Privately Held**
WEB: www.edg.com
SIC: 7372 Prepackaged software

(G-6374)
HRA INTERNATIONAL INC (PA)
489 Hillrose Way (08831-3778)
PHONE..................................609 395-0939
Howard Rosenthal, *President*
EMP: 2
SQ FT: 2,000
SALES: 1MM **Privately Held**
WEB: www.hra-nca.org
SIC: 2323 5136 Neckties, men's & boys': made from purchased materials; scarves, men's & boys'

(G-6375)
UNIVERSAL SYSTEMS INSTALLERS
10 Red Oak Ct (08831-4067)
PHONE..................................732 656-9002
Salvatore Filiano, *President*
Teresa Filiano, *Vice Pres*
EMP: 20

SALES (est): 2.6MM **Privately Held**
SIC: 2541 5031 1751 Store fixtures, wood; cabinets, lockers & shelving; lumber, plywood & millwork; millwork; cabinet & finish carpentry; store fixture installation

(G-6376)
WEBANNUITIESCOM INC (PA)
Also Called: United State Annuities
8 Talmadge Dr (08831-2910)
PHONE..................................732 521-5110
Hersh Stern, *President*
EMP: 7
SQ FT: 1,600
SALES: 1.8MM **Privately Held**
WEB: www.webannuities.com
SIC: 6411 2721 Insurance brokers; trade journals: publishing only, not printed on site

Monroe Township
Middlesex County

(G-6377)
AKELA LASER CORPORATION
1095 Cranbury S Riv 14 (08831-3411)
PHONE..................................732 305-7105
Bob Sellers, *President*
Mikhail Maiorov, *COO*
Vladimir Zeidel, *Mfg Dir*
Maria Kudryashova, *Controller*
EMP: 10
SQ FT: 6,200
SALES: 1MM **Privately Held**
WEB: www.akelalaser.com
SIC: 3674 Semiconductors & related devices

(G-6378)
BRACCO DIAGNOSTICS INC (DH)
259 Prospect Plains Rd (08831-3820)
PHONE..................................609 514-2200
Fax: 609 514-2440
Vittorio Puppo, *President*
▲ **EMP:** 135
SQ FT: 59,500
SALES (est): 167.3MM **Privately Held**
WEB: www.diag.bracco.com
SIC: 2835 In vitro & in vivo diagnostic substances
HQ: Bracco U.S.A. Inc.
259 Prospect Plains Rd
Monroe Township NJ 08831
609 514-2200

(G-6379)
BRACCO USA INC (HQ)
259 Prospect Plains Rd (08831-3820)
PHONE..................................609 514-2200
Diana Bracco, *President*
Alberto Sana Maria, *Treasurer*
Dennis J Block, *Admin Sec*
Curtis Landherr,
Antonio Cantaluppi, *Asst Sec*
▲ **EMP:** 4
SQ FT: 66,187
SALES (est): 176MM **Privately Held**
SIC: 2835 In vitro & in vivo diagnostic substances
PA: Bracco Spa
Via Caduti Di Marcinelle 13
Milano MI
022 177-1

(G-6380)
BROADWAY KLEER-GUARD CORP
Also Called: Shipmaster
1 S Middlesex Ave (08831-3726)
PHONE..................................609 662-3970
Steve Kohn, *President*
▲ **EMP:** 30 **EST:** 1946
SQ FT: 30,000
SALES (est): 8.2MM **Privately Held**
WEB: www.shipmasterbags.com
SIC: 3081 5113 Packing materials, plastic sheet; bags, paper & disposable plastic

(G-6381)
DAILY DOLLAR LLC
48 E Sedgwick St (08831-1211)
PHONE..................................732 236-9709

Krystina Mendez, *Principal*
EMP: 4
SALES (est): 157K **Privately Held**
SIC: 2711 Newspapers, publishing & printing

(G-6382)
FRAGRANCE EXCHANGE INC
1075 Cranbury Rd Ste 7 (08831-3409)
PHONE..................................732 641-2210
▲ **EMP:** 5 **EST:** 2006
SALES (est): 995.2K **Privately Held**
SIC: 2844 Perfumes & colognes

(G-6383)
LG ELECTRONICS USA INC
380 Deans Rhode Hall Rd (08831-3004)
PHONE..................................732 605-0385
John Cummings, *Branch Mgr*
EMP: 6
SALES (corp-wide): 29.2B **Privately Held**
SIC: 3679 Antennas, receiving
HQ: Lg Electronics U.S.A., Inc.
1000 Sylvan Ave
Englewood Cliffs NJ 07632
201 816-2000

(G-6384)
METROPLEX PRODUCTS COMPANY INC
377 Deans Rhode Hall Rd (08831-3006)
PHONE..................................732 249-0653
EMP: 8
SQ FT: 2,000
SALES (est): 4.7MM **Privately Held**
SIC: 5031 1751 2499 Whol Lumber/Plywood/Millwork Carpentry Contractor Mfg Wood Products

(G-6385)
NOODLE FAN
557 Englishtown Rd (08831-3042)
PHONE..................................732 446-2820
EMP: 4
SALES (est): 149K **Privately Held**
SIC: 2098 Noodles (e.g. egg, plain & water), dry

(G-6386)
NOVOTEC PHARMA LLC
Also Called: Accelis Pharma
20 Spruce Meadows Dr (08831-3103)
PHONE..................................609 632-2239
Patrick Patel, *Managing Prtnr*
Snehal Patel, *Managing Prtnr*
EMP: 4
SQ FT: 5,000
SALES: 1MM **Privately Held**
SIC: 2834 8731 Pharmaceutical preparations; proprietary drug products; commercial research laboratory

(G-6387)
OCEAN POWER TECHNOLOGIES INC (PA)
Also Called: Opt
28 Engelhard Dr Ste B (08831-3720)
PHONE..................................609 730-0400
Fax: 609 730-0404
George H Kirby III, *CEO*
Terence J Cryan, *Ch of Bd*
Dean J Glover, *Vice Ch Bd*
Christopher Phebus, *VP Engrg*
Matthew T Shafer, *CFO*
◆ **EMP:** 28
SQ FT: 22,000
SALES: 511K **Publicly Held**
WEB: www.oceanpowertechnologies.com
SIC: 4911 3621 3629 Generation, electric power; distribution, electric power; generating apparatus & parts, electrical; electronic generation equipment

(G-6388)
ONEAL FLAT ROLLED METALS LLC
1 Fitzgerald Ave (08831-3729)
PHONE..................................609 395-7007
Fax: 609 395-9555
Mickey Claudio, *Plant Mgr*
Luke Babb, *Sales Associate*
Jeff Katz, *Branch Mgr*
Mary McBride, *Manager*
EMP: 33

SALES (corp-wide): 2B **Privately Held**
SIC: 5051 3441 Steel; fabricated structural metal
HQ: O'neal Flat Rolled Metals, Llc
1229 Fulton St
Brighton CO 80601
303 654-0300

(G-6389)
PAGE STAMP LLC
110 Kings Mill Rd (08831-8903)
PHONE..................................732 390-1700
Aaron Weinberger,
Michelle Horowitz,
Joseph Weinberger,
Naomi Weinberger,
EMP: 7
SALES: 700K **Privately Held**
WEB: www.pagestamp.com
SIC: 2759 Commercial printing

(G-6390)
R & M MANUFACTURING INC
20 Abeel Rd (08831-2036)
PHONE..................................609 495-8032
Thomas Marvel, *President*
David Rudolph, *Vice Pres*
Gary Taylor, *Plant Mgr*
Tom Marvel, *Technology*
▲ **EMP:** 20
SQ FT: 30,000
SALES (est): 4MM **Privately Held**
SIC: 2434 2431 Wood kitchen cabinets; millwork

(G-6391)
SETCO LLC
34 Engelhard Dr (08831-3796)
PHONE..................................610 321-9760
EMP: 7 **Publicly Held**
SIC: 3085 Plastics bottles
HQ: Setco, Llc
101 Oakley St
Evansville IN 47710
812 424-2904

(G-6392)
SHELAN CHEMICAL COMPANY INC
174 Tournament Dr (08831-2543)
PHONE..................................732 796-1003
Shelly Weiss, *President*
EMP: 9
SQ FT: 4,500
SALES (est): 8.9MM **Privately Held**
SIC: 5162 2493 2865 Resins; reconstituted wood products; dyes & pigments; color pigments, organic

(G-6393)
SILVERTON PACKAGING CORP
75 Fairway Blvd (08831-2711)
PHONE..................................732 341-0986
Fax: 732 505-1877
Manolita Gadaleta, *President*
EMP: 1
SALES: 1MM **Privately Held**
WEB: www.silvertonpackagingcorp.com
SIC: 3081 Polyethylene film

(G-6394)
ST THOMAS CREATIONS (HQ)
3a S Middlesex Ave (08831-6809)
P.O. Box 100410, Pasadena CA (91189-0003)
PHONE..................................800 536-2284
▲ **EMP:** 42
SQ FT: 78,000
SALES (est): 6.9MM
SALES (corp-wide): 867.1MM **Privately Held**
SIC: 5023 3231 Whol Homefurnishings Mfg Products-Purchased Glass
PA: Villeroy & Boch Ag
Saaruferstr. 1-3
Mettlach 66693
686 481-0

(G-6395)
STERLING PUBLISHING CO INC
Also Called: Sterling Publishing Warehouse
1 Barnes And Noble Way (08831-3417)
PHONE..................................732 248-6563
Robert A Ciofalo, *Manager*
EMP: 21

SALES (corp-wide): 3.6B **Publicly Held**
WEB: www.sterlingpub.com
SIC: 2731 5192 Books: publishing only;
books
HQ: Sterling Publishing Co., Inc.
1166 Avenue Of The Flr 17
New York NY 10036
212 532-7160

(G-6396)
STEVEN ORROS
Also Called: Winetree Publishing
106 Timber Hill Dr (08831-7961)
PHONE..................................732 972-1104
Steven Orros, *Owner*
EMP: 6
SALES (est): 258.7K **Privately Held**
SIC: 2741 Miscellaneous publishing

(G-6397)
TAYLOR COMMUNICATIONS INC
7 Costco Dr (08831-1129)
PHONE..................................732 561-8210
Mack Jim, *General Mgr*
EMP: 31
SALES (corp-wide): 3.5B **Privately Held**
SIC: 2754 Commercial printing, gravure
HQ: Taylor Communications, Inc.
4205 S 96th St
Omaha NE 68127
402 898-6422

(G-6398)
VSAR RESOURCES LLC
30 Engelhard Dr (08831-3720)
PHONE..................................973 233-6000
Ashvin Vaghani, *Mng Member*
Vijay Vaghani,
▲ **EMP:** 15
SQ FT: 5,000
SALES (est): 3MM **Privately Held**
SIC: 2844 Face creams or lotions

Monroeville
Salem County

(G-6399)
GARDEN STATE FUEL
600 Buck Rd (08343-2534)
PHONE..................................856 442-0061
Baokar Saini, *President*
EMP: 6
SALES (est): 208.7K **Privately Held**
SIC: 1389 Oil & gas field services

(G-6400)
KRAMME CONSOLIDATED INC (PA)
Main St (08343)
PHONE..................................856 358-8151
Paul E Kramme Jr, *President*
Richard Kramme, *Treasurer*
Gerald A Kramme, *Admin Sec*
EMP: 3
SQ FT: 20,000
SALES (est): 19.4MM **Privately Held**
SIC: 4213 3229 Trucking, except local;
scientific glassware

(G-6401)
MONROEVILLE VINEYARD & WINERY
314 Richwood Rd (08343-1847)
PHONE..................................856 521-0523
Debra Basile, *CEO*
John Basile, *Owner*
EMP: 13
SALES (est): 91.3K **Privately Held**
SIC: 2084 Brandy & brandy spirits

Montague
Sussex County

(G-6402)
CRAIG ROBERTSON
Also Called: Robertson Industries
19 State Route 23 (07827-3303)
P.O. Box 720, New Hampton NY (10958-0720)
PHONE..................................973 293-8666

Fax: 973 293-8601
Craig Robertson, *Owner*
EMP: 9
SQ FT: 43,000
SALES (est): 1.1MM **Privately Held**
SIC: 3086 Packaging & shipping materials,
foamed plastic

(G-6403)
THOMPSON STONE
3 Myrtle Dr (07827-3024)
PHONE..................................973 293-7237
Fax: 973 293-3107
William Thompson, *Owner*
EMP: 5
SALES: 1MM **Privately Held**
WEB: www.thompsonstone.com
SIC: 3559 Stone working machinery

Montclair
Essex County

(G-6404)
ACTION COPY CENTERS INC
Also Called: Sir Speedy
590 Valley Rd Ste 2 (07043-1851)
PHONE..................................973 744-5520
Fax: 973 744-3853
Dave Pradip, *President*
Dave Moxa, *Vice Pres*
EMP: 6
SQ FT: 2,000
SALES (est): 841.5K **Privately Held**
SIC: 2752 2791 2789 Commercial print-
ing, lithographic; typesetting; bookbinding
& related work

(G-6405)
ALCARO & ALCARO PLATING CO
112 Pine St (07042-4812)
P.O. Box 1215 (07042-1215)
PHONE..................................973 746-1200
Anthony Alcaro, *President*
EMP: 22
SQ FT: 2,500
SALES (est): 1.9MM **Privately Held**
WEB: www.platingservicesonline.com
SIC: 3471 Electroplating of metals or
formed products

(G-6406)
APPLEGATE FARM HOMEMADE ICE CR (PA)
616 Grove St (07043-2017)
PHONE..................................973 744-5900
Fax: 973 744-0334
Jason Street, *Owner*
Harold Thompson, *Opers Mgr*
Melinda Street, *Shareholder*
EMP: 10
SQ FT: 130,000
SALES (est): 973.8K **Privately Held**
SIC: 2024 Ice cream & frozen desserts

(G-6407)
ARCTIC GLACIER USA INC
363 Bloomfield Ave Ste 3b (07042-3655)
PHONE..................................973 771-3391
EMP: 11
SALES (corp-wide): 132MM **Privately Held**
SIC: 2097 Manufactured ice
HQ: Arctic Glacier U.S.A., Inc.
1654 Marthaler Ln
Saint Paul MN 55118
204 784-5873

(G-6408)
BEDLAM CORP
Also Called: Carpet Hardware Systems
33 Church St (07042-2701)
PHONE..................................973 774-8770
Richard Grabowsky, *President*
Jane Kaine, *General Mgr*
EMP: 13
SQ FT: 7,500

SALES: 767.7K **Privately Held**
WEB: www.bedlam.com
SIC: 3446 5051 Brasswork, ornamental:
structural; stairs, staircases, stair treads:
prefabricated metal; railings, prefabricated metal; metals service centers & offices

(G-6409)
CRAVE FOODS LLC
19 Club Rd (07043-2503)
PHONE..................................973 233-1220
Shahida Sayed,
Riaz Surti,
EMP: 12
SQ FT: 2,000
SALES (est): 970K **Privately Held**
WEB: www.cravefoods.com
SIC: 2032 Ethnic foods: canned, jarred,
etc.

(G-6410)
D L V LOUNGE INC
300 Bloomfield Ave (07042-3602)
PHONE..................................973 783-6988
George Marable Jr, *Treasurer*
EMP: 4
SQ FT: 1,200
SALES (est): 340K **Privately Held**
SIC: 2253 Lounge, bed & leisurewear; T-
shirts & tops, knit

(G-6411)
DOCBOX SOLUTIONS LTD LBLTY CO
140 Upper Mountain Ave (07042-1918)
PHONE..................................201 650-0970
Brian Cole, *CEO*
Stephanie Aranowitz, *COO*
Alain Espinosa, *CIO*
EMP: 6 **EST:** 2013
SALES: 100K **Privately Held**
SIC: 7372 7389 Business oriented com-
puter software;

(G-6412)
ELEMENTAL INTERIORS
204 Bellevue Ave (07043-1893)
PHONE..................................646 861-3596
Megan Downing, *Owner*
EMP: 4 **EST:** 2016
SALES (est): 119.7K **Privately Held**
SIC: 2819 Elements

(G-6413)
ENVIRONMENTAL COATINGS & CNSTR
36 Eagle Rock Way (07042-2017)
PHONE..................................973 509-9456
Joseph Cusenza, *President*
Mary Beth Cusenza, *Vice Pres*
EMP: 17
SQ FT: 2,000
SALES: 3.5MM **Privately Held**
WEB: www.eciproducts.com
SIC: 2851 Paints & allied products

(G-6414)
FLUOROPHARMA MEDICAL INC
8 Hillside Ave Ste 108 (07042-2129)
P.O. Box 1297, Clifton (07012-0797)
PHONE..................................973 744-1565
Walter Witoshkin, *Ch of Bd*
Thomas H Tulip, *President*
Edward L Lyons, *Vice Pres*
Tamara Rhein, *CFO*
Johan Spoor, *Director*
EMP: 4
SALES (est): 435K **Privately Held**
SIC: 2835 In vitro & in vivo diagnostic sub-
stances; in vitro diagnostics; in vivo diag-
nostics

(G-6415)
HAL LEONARD LLC
Hal Leonard Publishing
33 Plymouth St Ste 302 (07042-2677)
PHONE..................................973 337-5034
Michael Mecina, *Branch Mgr*
EMP: 230
SALES (corp-wide): 142.3MM **Privately Held**
SIC: 2741 Music, sheet: publishing only,
not printed on site

PA: Hal Leonard Llc
7777 W Bluemound Rd
Milwaukee WI 53213
414 774-3630

(G-6416)
HYP HAIR INC
Also Called: Magna Publishing
372 Orange Rd (07042-4312)
PHONE..................................201 843-4004
EMP: 30
SALES (est): 2.8MM **Privately Held**
SIC: 2721 Publish Magazines

(G-6417)
IMMTECH PHARMACEUTICALS INC
93 Prospect Ave (07042-1920)
PHONE..................................212 791-2911
Eric L Sorkin, *CEO*
Cecilia Chan, *Vice Ch Bd*
Norman A Abood, *Vice Pres*
Dolores Kapral, *Opers Staff*
Gary C Parks, *Admin Sec*
EMP: 24
SQ FT: 2,500
SALES (est): 3.9MM **Privately Held**
WEB: www.immtechpharma.com
SIC: 2834 8731 Drugs affecting parasitic &
infective diseases; medical research,
commercial

(G-6418)
INTERCHANGE GROUP INC
Also Called: Soyka-Smith Design Research
52 Watchung Ave (07043-1338)
PHONE..................................973 783-7032
Bridget Soyka-Smith, *President*
EMP: 10
SALES: 3.2MM **Privately Held**
SIC: 7389 2511 Design services; wood
household furniture

(G-6419)
INTERCURE INC
Also Called: Intercure Limited and Resperat
356 Bloomfield Ave Ste 5 (07042-3625)
PHONE..................................973 893-5653
Erez Gavish, *President*
Judy Chodirker, *Principal*
Arik Kleinstein, *CFO*
EMP: 20
SQ FT: 3,000
SALES (est): 2.3MM **Privately Held**
SIC: 3841 Blood pressure apparatus

(G-6420)
JERSEY CIDER WORKS LLC (PA)
42 Erwin Park Rd (07042-3020)
PHONE..................................917 604-0067
Charles Rosen, *CEO*
EMP: 5
SQ FT: 10,000
SALES: 250K **Privately Held**
SIC: 2084 Wines

(G-6421)
LURE LASH
416 Bloomfield Ave (07042-3537)
PHONE..................................973 783-5274
Anna Abraham, *Owner*
Carlean Martinez, *Co-Owner*
EMP: 10
SQ FT: 2,000
SALES (est): 871.9K **Privately Held**
SIC: 5087 3949 Beauty salon & barber
shop equipment & supplies; lures, fishing:
artificial

(G-6422)
MONTCLAIR FUEL LLC
651 Bloomfield Ave (07042-2213)
PHONE..................................973 744-4300
Barry's Flooring, *Administration*
EMP: 8
SALES (est): 731.6K **Privately Held**
SIC: 2869 Fuels

(G-6423)
MONTCLAIR LOCAL NEWS LLC ✪
132 High St (07042-2418)
PHONE..................................973 744-6243
Heeten Choxi, *Principal*

EMP: 4 **EST:** 2017
SALES (est): 159.9K **Privately Held**
SIC: 2711 Newspapers, publishing & printing

(G-6424)
NATIONAL HOUSING INSTITUTE
Also Called: SHELTERFORCE MAGAZINE
60 S Fullerton Ave # 206 (07042-2663)
PHONE..............................973 509-1600
Fax: 973 509-1602
John Atlas, *President*
Bob Zdenek, *Vice Pres*
Harold Simon, *Exec Dir*
Patrick Morrissy, *Admin Sec*
Keli Tianga, *Associate*
EMP: 4
SQ FT: 1,200
SALES: 668.3K **Privately Held**
WEB: www.nhi.org
SIC: 2721 8733 Magazines: publishing only, not printed on site; noncommercial research organizations

(G-6425)
NORLO OF NEW JERSEY LLC
105 Alexander Ave (07043-2620)
PHONE..............................646 492-3293
EMP: 5 **EST:** 2010
SALES (est): 326K **Privately Held**
SIC: 3089 Molding primary plastic

(G-6426)
NORTH JERSEY MEDIA GROUP INC
Also Called: Montclair Times Editorial
130 Valley Rd Ste D (07042-2355)
PHONE..............................973 233-5000
Kathy Hivish, *Manager*
EMP: 30
SALES (corp-wide): 173.6MM **Privately Held**
WEB: www.njmg.com
SIC: 2711 Newspapers, publishing & printing
HQ: North Jersey Media Group Inc.
1 Garret Mountain Plz # 201
Woodland Park NJ 07424
201 646-4000

(G-6427)
OXFORD BIOCHRONOMETRICS LLC
29 S Willow St (07042-3309)
PHONE..............................201 755-5932
William Scheckel, *General Mgr*
EMP: 1 **EST:** 2016
SALES: 2.5MM **Privately Held**
SIC: 7372 7389 Prepackaged software; application computer software; business oriented computer software;

(G-6428)
P O V INCORPORATED (PA)
Also Called: Pov Reports
29 Park St (07042-3407)
PHONE..............................914 258-4361
David Ogden, *President*
Robert Hannan, *President*
Henry McCarter, *Vice Pres*
EMP: 15
SQ FT: 3,000
SALES (est): 1.1MM **Privately Held**
SIC: 2741 Newsletter publishing

(G-6429)
PAM OPTICAL CO
107 Park St (07042-3465)
PHONE..............................973 744-8882
Kenneth Testa, *President*
Margaret Testa, *Vice Pres*
EMP: 4 **EST:** 1963
SQ FT: 100
SALES (est): 395.1K **Privately Held**
SIC: 3851 5995 Lenses, ophthalmic; optical goods stores

(G-6430)
PARSONS CABINETS INC
79 Beverly Rd (07043-1729)
PHONE..............................973 279-4954
Winfield Parsons, *President*
Stephen Parsons, *Treasurer*
EMP: 8

SALES (est): 408.1K **Privately Held**
SIC: 2711 Wood kitchen cabinets; wood partitions & fixtures; wood television & radio cabinets; cabinet & finish carpentry

(G-6431)
PATTERSON SMITH PUBLISHING
23 Prospect Ter (07042-3204)
PHONE..............................973 744-3291
Patterson Smith, *President*
Thomas Kelly, *Corp Secy*
EMP: 5
SQ FT: 5,000
SALES (est): 470.8K **Privately Held**
WEB: www.patterson-smith.com
SIC: 2731 Books: publishing only

(G-6432)
PRINTERS PLACE INC (PA)
8 S Fullerton Ave (07042-3359)
PHONE..............................973 744-8889
Fax: 973 744-7201
Bill Coutts Sr, *President*
EMP: 5
SQ FT: 1,200
SALES (est): 1.3MM **Privately Held**
WEB: www.theprintersplace.com
SIC: 2752 5943 Commercial printing, offset; office forms & supplies

(G-6433)
PUENT-ROMER COMMUNICATIONS INC
Also Called: Studio042
423 Bloomfield Ave (07042-3505)
PHONE..............................973 509-7591
Scott Kennedy, *CEO*
Pilar P Kennedy, *President*
Carol Castelluccio, *Graphic Designe*
EMP: 4
SQ FT: 3,200
SALES (est): 689.4K **Privately Held**
WEB: www.weprintfast.com
SIC: 2752 2789 2791 Commercial printing, offset; bookbinding & related work; typesetting

(G-6434)
RETAIL MANAGEMENT PUBG INC
Also Called: Instore Magazine
28 Valley Rd (07042-2709)
PHONE..............................212 981-0217
Fred Mouawad, *Ch of Bd*
EMP: 13
SALES (est): 1.8MM **Privately Held**
SIC: 2721 7313 8741 Magazines: publishing only, not printed on site; electronic media advertising representatives; management services

(G-6435)
SITETRACKER INC (PA)
491 Bloomfield Ave # 301 (07042-3406)
PHONE..............................551 486-2087
Giuseppe Incitti, *CEO*
Tim May, *CTO*
Bob Amelung, *Director*
EMP: 16
SALES (est): 7MM **Privately Held**
SIC: 7372 Prepackaged software

(G-6436)
STERLING NET & TWINE CO INC (PA)
Also Called: Sterling Marine Products
18 Label St (07042-3823)
P.O. Box 411, Basking Ridge (07920-0411)
PHONE..............................973 783-9800
Fax: 973 783-9808
James C Van Loon Jr, *President*
EMP: 10 **EST:** 1950
SQ FT: 12,000
SALES (est): 871.9K **Privately Held**
WEB: www.sterlingnets.com
SIC: 2399 3949 2298 Fishing nets; nets, launderers & dyers; sporting & athletic goods; nets, rope

(G-6437)
TEN ONE DESIGN LTD LBLTY CO
149 Chestnut St (07042-2945)
PHONE..............................201 474-8232

Peter Skinner,
EMP: 4
SALES: 950K **Privately Held**
SIC: 3999 Manufacturing industries

(G-6438)
TOSCA
15 Church St (07042-2701)
PHONE..............................973 337-5724
EMP: 4
SALES (est): 295.7K **Privately Held**
SIC: 3559 Foundry machinery & equipment

(G-6439)
WELLSPRING INFO INC
251 Park St (07043-1798)
PHONE..............................800 268-3682
Scott Cohen, *President*
◆ **EMP:** 7 **EST:** 2010
SALES (est): 570.6K **Privately Held**
SIC: 2732 Book printing

Montvale
Bergen County

(G-6440)
ACCURATE TOOL & DIE CO INC
Also Called: Accurate Transmissions
6 Westminster Ct (07645-1353)
PHONE..............................201 476-9348
Fax: 201 955-0099
Dominick Costantino, *President*
Joseph Manderano, *Vice Pres*
▲ **EMP:** 4
SQ FT: 30,000
SALES (est): 744.1K **Privately Held**
SIC: 3714 3469 3544 Motor vehicle parts & accessories; metal stampings; special dies & tools

(G-6441)
ADVANSTAR COMMUNICATIONS INC
5 Paragon Dr (07645-1791)
PHONE..............................973 944-7777
Fax: 973 944-7778
Claren Copany, *Manager*
EMP: 40
SALES (corp-wide): 1B **Privately Held**
WEB: www.advanstar.com
SIC: 2721 8742 Magazines: publishing only, not printed on site; sales (including sales management) consultant
HQ: Advanstar Communications Inc.
2501 Colorado Ave Ste 280
Santa Monica CA 90404
310 857-7500

(G-6442)
AMERICAN MEDICAL & DENTAL SUPS
240 W Grand Ave (07645-1716)
PHONE..............................877 545-6837
Dinesh Sakhrani, *CEO*
EMP: 13 **EST:** 2008
SALES (est): 1.3MM **Privately Held**
SIC: 3843 Dental equipment & supplies

(G-6443)
AUTOMATED RESOURCE GROUP INC
135 Chestnut Ridge Rd # 2 (07645-1152)
PHONE..............................201 391-8357
Fax: 201 391-8357
Ray Butkus, *CEO*
Thomas Amoriello Sr, *Ch of Bd*
Alexander Amoriello, *COO*
James N Slack, *CFO*
EMP: 60
SQ FT: 17,000
SALES (est): 3.7MM **Privately Held**
WEB: www.callargi.com
SIC: 7374 7372 Data processing service; publishers' computer software

(G-6444)
BENJAMIN MOORE & CO (HQ)
101 Paragon Dr (07645-1727)
PHONE..............................201 573-9600
Fax: 201 573-0046
Michael Searles, *President*
Tom Jozefowicz, *Executive*

◆ **EMP:** 147 **EST:** 1891
SQ FT: 57,000
SALES (est): 1.3B
SALES (corp-wide): 242.1B **Publicly Held**
WEB: www.benjaminmoore.com
SIC: 2851 5231 Paints & allied products; paints: oil or alkyd vehicle or water thinned; enamels; varnishes; paint, glass & wallpaper
PA: Berkshire Hathaway Inc.
3555 Farnam St Ste 1140
Omaha NE 68131
402 346-1400

(G-6445)
BENJAMIN MOORE & CO
1 Paragon Dr Ste 255 (07645-1728)
PHONE..............................201 573-9600
Jim Henderson, *Branch Mgr*
EMP: 56
SALES (corp-wide): 242.1B **Publicly Held**
WEB: www.benjaminmoore.com
SIC: 2851 Paints & allied products
HQ: Benjamin Moore & Co.
101 Paragon Dr
Montvale NJ 07645
201 573-9600

(G-6446)
BERRY GLOBAL FILMS LLC (DH)
95 Chestnut Ridge Rd (07645-1801)
P.O. Box 959, Evansville IN (47706-0959)
PHONE..............................201 641-6600
Fax: 201 807-2239
Tom Salmon, *CEO*
Jason K Greene, *Exec VP*
Mark W Miles, *CFO*
Stacy Lemaster, *Manager*
Jerzy Kowalczyk, *Technician*
▼ **EMP:** 110 **EST:** 1970
SQ FT: 48,000
SALES (est): 1.1B **Publicly Held**
WEB: www.aepinc.com
SIC: 3081 2821 Unsupported plastics film & sheet; plastic film & sheet; polyethylene film; polypropylene film & sheet; polyvinyl chloride resins (PVC); polyethylene resins
HQ: Berry Global, Inc.
101 Oakley St
Evansville IN 47710
812 424-2904

(G-6447)
BFHJ HOLDINGS INC (PA)
26 Chestnut Ridge Rd (07645-1825)
PHONE..............................908 730-6280
EMP: 3 **EST:** 2015
SALES (est): 2MM **Privately Held**
SIC: 1731 3585 Energy management controls; heat pumps, electric

(G-6448)
CISCO SYSTEMS INC
1 Paragon Dr Ste 275 (07645-1751)
PHONE..............................201 782-0842
Fax: 201 782-5099
Zakariya Abbassi, *Engineer*
Rick Frothingham, *Engineer*
Ashish Modi, *Engineer*
Andrew Wozniak, *Branch Mgr*
Jennifer McCarron, *Technology*
EMP: 40
SALES (corp-wide): 48B **Publicly Held**
WEB: www.cisco.com
SIC: 3825 5063 3577 Network analyzers; electrical apparatus & equipment; computer peripheral equipment
PA: Cisco Systems, Inc.
170 W Tasman Dr
San Jose CA 95134
408 526-4000

(G-6449)
COINING INC
15 Mercedes Dr (07645-1815)
PHONE..............................201 791-4020
Gary Holcomb, *CEO*
Kenneth Whited, *President*
Peter Pachella, *General Mgr*
Julie Scelzo, *Vice Pres*
Vito Tanzi, *Vice Pres*
▲ **EMP:** 114 **EST:** 1963
SQ FT: 30,000

▲ = Import ▼ =Export
◆ =Import/Export

SALES (est): 16.9MM
SALES (corp-wide): 4.3B **Publicly Held**
WEB: www.coiningcorp.com
SIC: **3469** Stamping metal for the trade
HQ: Coining Holding Company
    15 Mercedes Dr
    Montvale NJ 07645

(G-6450)
COINING HOLDING COMPANY (HQ)
Also Called: Coining Manufactures
15 Mercedes Dr (07645-1815)
PHONE...................................201 791-4020
Fax: 201 791-1637
Ken Whited, *Vice Pres*
Paul Nikac, *Vice Pres*
Julie Scelzo, *Vice Pres*
Vito Tanzi, *Vice Pres*
Martin Oud, *Research*
▲ EMP: 15
SALES (est): 28.1MM
SALES (corp-wide): 4.3B **Publicly Held**
SIC: **3469** Stamping metal for the trade
PA: Ametek, Inc.
    1100 Cassatt Rd
    Berwyn PA 19312
    610 647-2121

(G-6451)
CREATIVE PAVERS
45 Akers Ave (07645-2004)
PHONE...................................201 782-1661
Brett Unger, *Owner*
EMP: 8
SALES (est): 882.7K **Privately Held**
SIC: **3271** Paving blocks, concrete

(G-6452)
DATA CNTRUM COMMUNICATIONS INC
Also Called: Health Monitor Network
135 Chestnut Ridge Rd # 2 (07645-1152)
PHONE...................................201 391-1911
Eric Jensen, *President*
Maria Lissandrello, *Editor*
Dave Dolton, *Vice Pres*
Alex Dong, *Vice Pres*
Lixin Du, *Vice Pres*
EMP: 18
SQ FT: 4,300
SALES (est): 3.4MM **Privately Held**
WEB: www.healthmonitor.com
SIC: **2721** Magazines: publishing only, not printed on site

(G-6453)
DOWDEN HEALTH MEDIA INC (HQ)
110 Summit Ave Ste 1 (07645-1776)
PHONE...................................201 740-6100
Fax: 201 740-6136
J Roger Friedman, *President*
Dobbs Obrien Sarah, *Editor*
Daniel J Mills, *CFO*
EMP: 60
SQ FT: 30,000
SALES (est): 7.9MM
SALES (corp-wide): 109.5MM **Privately Held**
WEB: www.dowdenhealthmedia.com
SIC: **2721** Magazines: publishing only, not printed on site
PA: Lebhar-Friedman, Inc.
    150 W 30th St Fl 19
    New York NY 10001
    212 756-5000

(G-6454)
ECOCOM INC
221 W Grand Ave Ste 168 (07645-1729)
PHONE...................................201 393-0786
Stephen Shen, *President*
Lin LI, *Vice Pres*
▲ EMP: 6 EST: 1998
SALES: 10MM **Privately Held**
WEB: www.ecocom.com
SIC: **3496** Garment hangers, made from purchased wire

(G-6455)
EIGHT OCLOCK COFFEE COMPANY (DH)
155 Chestnut Ridge Rd # 2 (07645-1156)
PHONE...................................201 571-9214

Barbara Roth, *President*
EMP: 99
SQ FT: 13,000
SALES (est): 131.9MM
SALES (corp-wide): 485.8MM **Privately Held**
WEB: www.eightoclock.com
SIC: **5149** 2095 Coffee & tea; roasted coffee

(G-6456)
EMPIRICAL GROUP LLC
155 Chestnut Ridge Rd (07645-1156)
PHONE...................................201 571-0300
John Petrizzo, *Principal*
▲ EMP: 25
SALES (est): 3.5MM
SALES (corp-wide): 485.8MM **Privately Held**
WEB: www.empiricalgroup.com
SIC: **2099** Tea blending
PA: Tata Global Beverages Limited
    3rd Floor, Block C
    Bengaluru KA 56002
    806 717-1200

(G-6457)
GOOD EARTH TEAS INC
155 Chestnut Ridge Rd (07645-1156)
PHONE...................................831 423-7913
Ben Zaricor, *President*
Louise V Zaricor, *Corp Secy*
Lynn Rodriguez, *Accounts Mgr*
◆ EMP: 70
SQ FT: 41,000
SALES (est): 10.6MM
SALES (corp-wide): 485.8MM **Privately Held**
WEB: www.flagcollection.com
SIC: **2099** Tea blending; spices, including grinding
PA: Tata Global Beverages Limited
    3rd Floor, Block C
    Bengaluru KA 56002
    806 717-1200

(G-6458)
GRASS VALLEY USA LLC
135 Chestnut Ridge Rd # 3 (07645-1153)
PHONE...................................201 818-4050
EMP: 35
SALES (corp-wide): 2.3B **Publicly Held**
SIC: **3663** Radio & TV communications equipment
HQ: Grass Valley Usa, Llc
    125 Crown Point Ct
    Grass Valley CA 95945

(G-6459)
HIGHLANDS ACQUISITION CORP
1 Paragon Dr Ste 125 (07645-1744)
PHONE...................................201 573-8400
Robert Pangia, *CEO*
EMP: 4
SALES (est): 271.2K **Privately Held**
SIC: **3845** Electromedical equipment

(G-6460)
INVESTMENT CASTING INSTITUTE
Also Called: Incast
1 Paragon Dr Ste 110 (07645-1744)
PHONE...................................201 573-9770
Michael C Perry, *Exec Dir*
EMP: 5
SQ FT: 2,200
SALES: 1.3MM **Privately Held**
WEB: www.investmentcasting.org
SIC: **8621** Education & teacher association; magazines: publishing only, not printed on site

(G-6461)
IVY CAPITAL PARTNERS LLC
102 Chestnut Ridge Rd # 1 (07645-1856)
PHONE...................................201 573-8400
Dennis O' Dowd, *Partner*
EMP: 5
SALES (est): 471.6K **Privately Held**
SIC: **3842** Orthopedic appliances

(G-6462)
IVY SPORTS MEDICINE LLC
102 Chestnut Ridge Rd # 1 (07645-1856)
PHONE...................................201 573-5423

Robert Pangia, *CEO*
EMP: 4
SALES (est): 919K
SALES (corp-wide): 12.4B **Publicly Held**
SIC: **3841** Surgical & medical instruments
PA: Stryker Corporation
    2825 Airview Blvd
    Portage MI 49002
    269 385-2600

(G-6463)
KFT FIRE TRAINER LLC
Also Called: Kidde Fire Trainers
17 Philips Pkwy (07645-1810)
PHONE...................................201 300-8100
Fax: 201 300-8101
William R Lane, *President*
Lucille Mathews, *Admin Sec*
Arlene Rosenberg, *Asst Sec*
▲ EMP: 35
SQ FT: 25,755
SALES (est): 10.2MM
SALES (corp-wide): 2.2MM **Privately Held**
WEB: www.kiddeft.com
SIC: **3699** Electronic training devices
PA: Kidde Fire Trainer Holdings, Llc
    155 N Wacker Dr Ste 4150
    Chicago IL

(G-6464)
KURT VERSEN INC
1 Paragon Dr Ste 157 (07645-1728)
PHONE...................................201 664-5283
Steve Siversten, *President*
▼ EMP: 15
SALES (est): 3.1MM
SALES (corp-wide): 3.6B **Publicly Held**
WEB: www.hubbell-ltg.com
SIC: **3645** Residential lighting fixtures
HQ: Hubbell Lighting, Inc.
    701 Millennium Blvd
    Greenville SC 29607

(G-6465)
LEADING PHARMA LLC
155 Chestnut Ridge Rd # 3 (07645-1156)
PHONE...................................201 746-9160
Ronald F Gold, *CEO*
EMP: 40
SALES (corp-wide): 10.6MM **Privately Held**
SIC: **5122** 2834 Pharmaceuticals; pharmaceutical preparations
PA: Leading Pharma, Llc
    3 Oak Rd
    Fairfield NJ 07004
    201 746-9160

(G-6466)
LEXMARK INTERNATIONAL INC
135 Chestnut Ridge Rd # 2 (07645-1152)
PHONE...................................201 307-4601
Michael Chisholm, *Engineer*
John O'Sullivan, *Sales Mgr*
Joshua Vance, *Accounts Exec*
Matt Ellis, *Sales Associate*
Jason Williams, *Business Anlyst*
EMP: 10
SALES (corp-wide): 3.5B **Privately Held**
WEB: www.lexmark.com
SIC: **3577** Printers, computer
PA: Lexmark International Inc.
    740 W New Circle Rd
    Lexington KY 40511
    859 232-2000

(G-6467)
MICRONET ENERTEC TECH INC
28 W Grand Ave Ste 3 (07645-2100)
PHONE...................................201 225-0190
David Lucatz, *Ch of Bd*
EMP: 89
SALES: 18.3MM **Privately Held**
SIC: **3572** Computer storage devices

(G-6468)
PENTAX OF AMERICA INC
Pentax Medical Company
3 Paragon Dr (07645-1782)
PHONE...................................973 628-6200
John M Crump, *Vice Pres*
EMP: 45

SALES (corp-wide): 5B **Privately Held**
WEB: www.pentaximaging.com
SIC: **3841** Surgical instruments & apparatus; diagnostic apparatus, medical; computer software development & applications
HQ: Pentax Of America, Inc.
    3 Paragon Dr
    Montvale NJ 07645
    201 571-2300

(G-6469)
PEOPLES EDUCATION INC
25 Philips Pkwy 105 (07645-1810)
P.O. Box 513, Saddle Brook (07663-0513)
PHONE...................................201 712-0090
Brian Beckwith, *CEO*
James Peoples, *Ch of Bd*
Diane Miller, *Vice Pres*
Matti Prima, *Vice Pres*
Michael Demarco, *CFO*
▲ EMP: 110
SQ FT: 18,000
SALES (est): 11.3MM
SALES (corp-wide): 25.6MM **Publicly Held**
WEB: www.standardshelpdata.com
SIC: **2731** Textbooks: publishing only, not printed on site
PA: Peoples Educational Holdings, Inc.
    299 Market St Ste 240
    Saddle Brook NJ 07663
    201 712-0090

(G-6470)
PIN PEOPLE LLC
1 Paragon Dr Ste 150 (07645-1751)
PHONE...................................888 309-7467
Andrew Dale,
EMP: 10
SQ FT: 12,000
SALES: 9.5MM **Privately Held**
WEB: www.thepinpeople.com
SIC: **3911** Pins (jewelry), precious metal

(G-6471)
RECKITT BENCKISER LLC
1 Philips Pkwy (07645-1810)
PHONE...................................973 404-2600
Fax: 201 573-6046
Sharon James, *Vice Pres*
Laura Mateo, *Vice Pres*
Brenda Beckman, *Research*
Marcia Bole, *Research*
Aleksandra Kruszewska, *Research*
EMP: 125
SALES (corp-wide): 15.2B **Privately Held**
WEB: www.reckittprofessional.com
SIC: **2842** 2035 Specialty cleaning, polishes & sanitation goods; pickles, sauces & salad dressings
HQ: Reckitt Benckiser Llc
    399 Interpace Pkwy # 101
    Parsippany NJ 07054
    973 404-2600

(G-6472)
RIDGEWOOD ENERGY O FUND LLC
14 Philips Pkwy (07645-1811)
PHONE...................................201 447-9000
Robert E Swanson, *CEO*
EMP: 1
SALES: 15.7MM **Privately Held**
SIC: **1389** Gas field services; oil field services; servicing oil & gas wells

(G-6473)
RIDGEWOOD ENERGY S FUND LLC
14 Philips Pkwy (07645-1811)
PHONE...................................201 307-0470
Robert E Swanson, *CEO*
EMP: 3
SALES: 5.3MM
SALES (corp-wide): 4.3MM **Privately Held**
SIC: **1382** Oil & gas exploration services
PA: Ridgewood Energy Corporation
    14 Philips Pkwy
    Montvale NJ 07645
    201 307-0470

(G-6474)
RIDGEWOOD ENERGY T FUND LLC
14 Philips Pkwy (07645-1811)
PHONE................................800 942-5550
Robert E Swanson, *Principal*
EMP: 2
SALES: 4.9MM **Privately Held**
SIC: 1382 Oil & gas exploration services

(G-6475)
RIDGEWOOD ENERGY U FUND LLC
14 Philips Pkwy (07645-1811)
PHONE................................201 447-9000
Robert E Swanson, *CEO*
EMP: 1
SALES: 5.7MM **Privately Held**
SIC: 1382 Oil & gas exploration services

(G-6476)
RIDGEWOOD ENERGY V FUND LLC
14 Philips Pkwy (07645-1811)
PHONE................................800 942-5550
Jonathan Keehner, *Principal*
EMP: 2
SALES: 6.5MM **Privately Held**
SIC: 1382 Oil & gas exploration services

(G-6477)
RIDGEWOOD ENERGY Y FUND LLC
14 Philips Pkwy (07645-1811)
PHONE................................201 447-9000
Robert E Swanson, *CEO*
EMP: 1
SALES: 9.9MM **Privately Held**
SIC: 1382 Oil & gas exploration services

(G-6478)
RODMAN MEDIA CORP
Also Called: Household and Per Pdts Indust
25 Philips Pkwy Fl 2 (07645-1810)
PHONE................................201 825-2552
Rodman Zilenziger Jr, *President*
Matt Carey, *Publisher*
Jay Gorga, *Publisher*
Damaris Kope, *Publisher*
Art Largar, *Publisher*
EMP: 45
SQ FT: 12,000
SALES (est): 8.8MM **Privately Held**
WEB: www.rodmanpublishing.com
SIC: 2721 Magazines: publishing only, not printed on site

(G-6479)
SILBO INDUSTRIES INC
50 Chestnut Ridge Rd # 204 (07645-1845)
PHONE................................201 307-0900
Fax: 201 307-0932
James Mullally, *President*
Alan Shalom, *Partner*
Howard Jakob, *Partner*
Jeff Shalom, *Partner*
Mitchell Shalom, *Partner*
▲ EMP: 14 EST: 1965
SQ FT: 5,700
SALES (est): 6.4MM **Privately Held**
SIC: 5085 3317 Valves & fittings; steel pipe & tubes

(G-6480)
SRS SOFTWARE LLC
155 Chestnut Ridge Rd (07645-1156)
PHONE................................201 802-1300
Fax: 201 802-1301
Scott Ciccarelli, *CEO*
Robert Harmonay, *COO*
EMP: 14
SALES (est): 2MM **Privately Held**
SIC: 7372 Prepackaged software

(G-6481)
THOMSOM HEALTH CARE INC
5 Paragon Dr (07645-1791)
PHONE................................201 358-7300
Barry Gray, *Vice Pres*
Mary Rodrigues, *Executive Asst*
EMP: 150
SALES (est): 5.8MM **Privately Held**
SIC: 8733 2741 Medical research; miscellaneous publishing

Montville
Morris County

(G-6482)
AIRZONE SYSTEMS
28 Valhalla Rd (07045-9760)
PHONE................................201 207-6593
Tym Koda, *Owner*
EMP: 4 EST: 2010
SALES: 1.2MM **Privately Held**
SIC: 3443 Air coolers, metal plate

(G-6483)
BLAVOR INC
1 Mountain Ave (07045-9408)
PHONE................................973 265-4165
Ratko Nedich, *President*
EMP: 5
SALES (est): 307.8K **Privately Held**
SIC: 3292 Asbestos products

(G-6484)
BOZZONE CUSTOM WOODWORK INC
4 Taylortown Rd (07045-9744)
PHONE................................973 334-5598
EMP: 4
SQ FT: 3,000
SALES: 300K **Privately Held**
SIC: 2511 2541 5712 Mfg & Ret Custom Furniture

(G-6485)
CATBRIDGE MACHINERY LLC
115 Main Rd (07045-9225)
PHONE................................973 808-0029
Michael Pappas, *President*
William Christman, *Vice Pres*
John Michel, *Sales Executive*
Glenn Bartholomew, *Manager*
Matt Unger, *Supervisor*
▲ EMP: 40
SQ FT: 4,500
SALES (est): 11.7MM **Privately Held**
WEB: www.catbridgemachine.com
SIC: 3552 Textile machinery

(G-6486)
COMPUTERADIO
7 Brittany Rd (07045-9549)
P.O. Box 282, Pine Brook (07058-0282)
PHONE................................973 220-0087
Yurri Blanarovich, *Owner*
EMP: 5
SALES: 120K **Privately Held**
SIC: 3663 Radio & TV communications equipment

(G-6487)
DRUG DELIVERY TECHNOLOGY LLC
219 Changebridge Rd (07045-9514)
PHONE................................973 299-1200
James N Czaban, *Partner*
John Kiesewetter, *Sales Staff*
Ralph Eaccaro, *Partner*
EMP: 25
SALES (est): 2.5MM **Privately Held**
WEB: www.drugdeliverytech.com
SIC: 2721 Magazines: publishing & printing

(G-6488)
FILLIMERICA INC
170 Chngbrdge Rd Bldg A42 (07045)
PHONE................................800 435-7257
Fax: 973 808-1384
Thomas Filliman, *President*
Lucille Filliman, *Vice Pres*
EMP: 5
SQ FT: 1,600
SALES: 433.5K **Privately Held**
SIC: 7379 3571 5734 Computer related consulting services; electronic computers; computer peripheral equipment

(G-6489)
HICKOK MATTHEWS CO INC
Also Called: Schroth's Gold & Silversmiths
337 Main Rd (07045-9729)
PHONE................................973 335-3400
Fax: 973 335-7964
Win Schroth, *President*
Susan Schroth, *Corp Secy*
EMP: 6 EST: 1919
SQ FT: 4,200
SALES (est): 1.1MM **Privately Held**
WEB: www.hickokmatthews.com
SIC: 5944 5094 3914 Jewelry, precious stones & precious metals; precious metals; precious stones (gems); holloware, silver; holloware, pewter

(G-6490)
MAROTTA CONTROLS INC (PA)
78 Boonton Ave (07045)
P.O. Box 427 (07045-0427)
PHONE................................973 334-7800
Fax: 973 334-1219
Lance W Lord, *CEO*
Thomas S Marotta, *Ch of Bd*
Patrick A Marotta, *President*
Mark Hallock, *COO*
Steven A Fox, *Vice Pres*
▲ EMP: 150 EST: 1943
SQ FT: 100,000
SALES (est): 29.8MM **Privately Held**
WEB: www.marotta.com
SIC: 3494 3823 Valves & pipe fittings; industrial instrmnts msrmnt display/control process variable

(G-6491)
P J MURPHY FOREST PDTS CORP (PA)
150 River Rd Ste L1 (07045-8924)
P.O. Box 300 (07045-0300)
PHONE................................973 316-0800
Fax: 973 316-9455
Fred A Faehner, *President*
Roger Faehner, *Corp Secy*
Josh Faehnaer, *Vice Pres*
Kyle Faehner, *Vice Pres*
EMP: 6
SQ FT: 900
SALES: 25MM **Privately Held**
WEB: www.pjmurphy.net
SIC: 2421 Sawmills & planing mills, general

(G-6492)
PKC FINEWOODWORKING LLC
31 Springbrook Rd E (07045-9163)
PHONE................................201 951-8880
Ciambruschini Paul, *Principal*
EMP: 4 EST: 2011
SALES (est): 325.3K **Privately Held**
SIC: 2431 Millwork

(G-6493)
ROCKLINE INDUSTRIES INC
1 Kramer Way (07045-9593)
P.O. Box 189 (07045-0189)
PHONE................................973 257-2884
Fax: 973 257-9672
Lourdes Phr, *Human Res Mgr*
Chris Bruno, *Branch Mgr*
Lourdes Jesus, *Manager*
EMP: 135
SALES (corp-wide): 476.7MM **Privately Held**
WEB: www.rocklineind.com
SIC: 2679 5046 Filter paper; made from purchased material; coffee brewing equipment & supplies
PA: Rockline Industries, Inc.
4343 S Taylor Dr
Sheboygan WI 53081
800 558-7790

(G-6494)
SPERRO METAL PRODUCTS LLC
2 Skyline Dr (07045-9455)
P.O. Box 393, Kearny (07032-0393)
PHONE................................973 335-2000
Fax: 973 335-2656
James Fernandez, *Mng Member*
Joseph Roman,
EMP: 25 EST: 1970
SQ FT: 17,000
SALES (est): 4.9MM **Privately Held**
WEB: www.sperro.com
SIC: 3444 Sheet metalwork

(G-6495)
SR SHIRTS & STUFF LLC
4 Hickory Dr (07045-9348)
PHONE................................973 335-3086
Steven Riback,
EMP: 5
SQ FT: 1,000
SALES: 1MM **Privately Held**
SIC: 2329 Athletic (warmup, sweat & jogging) suits: men's & boys'

(G-6496)
UNIVERSAL BUSINESS AUTOMATION
170 Changebridge Rd D3 (07045-9112)
PHONE................................973 575-3568
Fax: 973 575-7259
Scott Liu, *President*
Ai-Ju Liu, *Vice Pres*
John Liu, *Vice Pres*
EMP: 7
SQ FT: 3,000
SALES: 634.8K **Privately Held**
SIC: 7372 Application computer software

(G-6497)
WEB INDUSTRIES INC
5 Mars Ct (07045)
P.O. Box 237 (07045-0237)
PHONE................................973 335-1200
Fax: 973 335-7054
William J Burgoyne, *President*
EMP: 14 EST: 1969
SQ FT: 24,000
SALES (est): 1MM **Privately Held**
SIC: 3541 Grinding, polishing, buffing, lapping & honing machines; grinding machines, metalworking

---

Moonachie
Bergen County

(G-6498)
4 OVER INC
4 Empire Blvd (07074-1303)
PHONE................................201 440-1656
Luis Mateo, *Manager*
EMP: 12
SALES (corp-wide): 190.6MM **Privately Held**
SIC: 2759 7336 Commercial printing; commercial art & graphic design
HQ: 4 Over, Llc
5900 San Fernando Rd D
Glendale CA 91202
818 246-1170

(G-6499)
ACRISON INC (PA)
Also Called: Acrison International
20 Empire Blvd (07074-1382)
PHONE................................201 440-8300
Fax: 201 440-4939
Ronald J Ricciardi, *President*
Ronald Ricciardi, *General Mgr*
Ralph N Ricciardi, *Vice Pres*
Carmen Pagano, *VP Mfg*
Phil Pergola, *Project Mgr*
◆ EMP: 135 EST: 1963
SQ FT: 65,000
SALES (est): 24.3MM **Privately Held**
WEB: www.acrison.com
SIC: 3823 3443 3545 Industrial process control instruments; hoppers, metal plate; hopper feed devices

(G-6500)
ALFRED HEITZMAN MACHINE WORKS
303 E Park St (07074-1137)
PHONE................................201 489-8888
Fax: 201 641-5554
Alfred C Heitzman, *President*
EMP: 4 EST: 1933
SQ FT: 6,500
SALES (est): 280K **Privately Held**
SIC: 3552 3571 Textile machinery; electronic computers

(G-6501)
ALGAR/DISPLAY CONNECTION CORP
131 W Commercial Ave (07074-1704)
PHONE................................201 438-1000
Fax: 201 438-2224
Richard Urso, *President*
Deian Urso, *Vice Pres*

Barbara Urso, *Treasurer*
▲ **EMP:** 70
SQ FT: 83,000
SALES (est): 17.7MM **Privately Held**
WEB: www.displayconnection.com
SIC: 2653 Display items, solid fiber: made from purchased materials

(G-6502)
ALLMIKE METAL TECHNOLOGY INC
Also Called: Almike Metal Products
65 Anderson Ave (07074-1621)
PHONE..............................201 935-2306
Tom Fischetti, *President*
EMP: 19 **EST:** 1956
SQ FT: 20,000
SALES (est): 2.5MM **Privately Held**
SIC: 3444 Sheet metal specialties, not stamped

(G-6503)
ALU INC
240 Anderson Ave (07074-1632)
PHONE..............................201 935-2213
Dan Kestleman, *Branch Mgr*
EMP: 25 **Privately Held**
WEB: www.alu.com
SIC: 4225 3993 General warehousing & storage; signs & advertising specialties
HQ: Alu Inc.
240 Anderson Ave
Moonachie NJ 07074

(G-6504)
AMF GRAPHICS INC
12 Empire Blvd (07074-1303)
PHONE..............................201 994-1500
Fax: 201 994-1180
David Goldberg, *President*
Linda Goldberg, *CFO*
EMP: 10
SQ FT: 25,000
SALES (est): 1MM **Privately Held**
WEB: www.amfgraphics.com
SIC: 2752 Commercial printing, offset

(G-6505)
AMKO DISPLAYS CORPORATION
Also Called: Alliance Store Fixture
7 Purcell Ct (07074-1606)
PHONE..............................201 460-7199
Hansang Lim, *CEO*
Heedeuk Lim, *President*
Eric Um, *Representative*
▲ **EMP:** 15
SQ FT: 25,000
SALES (est): 3MM **Privately Held**
WEB: www.ahjunam.com
SIC: 2541 Store & office display cases & fixtures

(G-6506)
AVANTI LINENS INC (PA)
234 Moonachie Rd Ste 1 (07074-1391)
PHONE..............................201 641-7766
Fax: 201 641-1712
Arthur Tauber, *President*
Jeff Kaufman, *COO*
◆ **EMP:** 159
SQ FT: 125,000
SALES (est): 41.9MM **Privately Held**
WEB: www.avantilinens.com
SIC: 2395 Decorative & novelty stitching, for the trade; embroidery & art needlework

(G-6507)
BERGEN HOMESTATE CORP
Also Called: All Smith Spinning and Turning
9 Willow St (07074-1502)
PHONE..............................201 372-9740
Fax: 201 372-9742
Michael Noback, *President*
Diane Van Blarcon, *Administration*
EMP: 7 **EST:** 1948
SQ FT: 4,500
SALES (est): 475.7K **Privately Held**
SIC: 3444 Forming machine work, sheet metal

(G-6508)
BIO COMPRESSION SYSTEMS INC
120 W Commercial Ave (07074-1703)
PHONE..............................201 939-0716
Robert Freidenrich, *CEO*
Donald Warren, *President*
◆ **EMP:** 24
SALES (est): 4.4MM **Privately Held**
WEB: www.biocompression.com
SIC: 3841 8011 3561 Surgical & medical instruments; offices & clinics of medical doctors; pumps & pumping equipment

(G-6509)
BULBRITE INDUSTRIES INC
145 W Commercial Ave (07074-1704)
P.O. Box 4108, South Hackensack (07606-4108)
PHONE..............................201 531-5900
Cathy Choi, *President*
Myrna Agustin, *Business Mgr*
Barbara Eun Choi, *Corp Secy*
Addie Cinquino, *Vice Pres*
Bill Drysdale, *Vice Pres*
◆ **EMP:** 40
SALES (est): 8.1MM **Privately Held**
WEB: www.bulbrite.com
SIC: 3229 5063 Bulbs for electric lights; light bulbs & related supplies

(G-6510)
BYLADA FOODS LLC (PA)
140 W Commercial Ave (07074-1703)
PHONE..............................201 933-7474
Bob Silverman,
Donald Pompliano,
Eric Silverman,
Michael Silverman,
Robert Silverman,
▼ **EMP:** 4
SQ FT: 30,000
SALES (est): 8.5MM **Privately Held**
SIC: 2099 Food preparations

(G-6511)
CARLYLE CUSTOM CONVERTIBLES (PA)
6 Empire Blvd (07074-1303)
PHONE..............................973 546-4502
Albert De Matteo, *CEO*
Donna De Matteo, *President*
EMP: 60
SQ FT: 28,000
SALES (est): 15.4MM **Privately Held**
SIC: 5712 2515 2512 2392 Furniture stores; sofa beds (convertible sofas); wood upholstered chairs & couches; household furnishings; comforters & quilts: made from purchased materials; sofas & couches; beds & bedding

(G-6512)
CARTER MANUFACTURING CO INC
55 Anderson Ave (07074-1677)
PHONE..............................201 935-0770
Fax: 201 935-2812
John Scholz, *Ch of Bd*
Mark Casatelli, *Vice Pres*
▲ **EMP:** 23
SQ FT: 15,000
SALES (est): 4.4MM **Privately Held**
SIC: 3469 Stamping metal for the trade

(G-6513)
COGNATI CHEESE COMPANY INC
205 Moonachie Rd (07074-1309)
PHONE..............................201 807-9100
Alain Voss, *Principal*
▲ **EMP:** 27
SALES (est): 5.3MM **Privately Held**
SIC: 2022 Cheese spreads, dips, pastes & other cheese products

(G-6514)
DIAMOND WHOLESALE CO
30 Congress Dr (07074-1406)
PHONE..............................201 727-9595
Fax: 201 672-4018
David Rothenberg, *President*
▲ **EMP:** 35
SQ FT: 65,000
SALES (est): 6.6MM **Privately Held**
SIC: 1499 5094 Gemstone & industrial diamond mining; diamonds (gems)

(G-6515)
DU TECHNOLOGIES INC
300 W Commercial Ave (07074-1607)
PHONE..............................201 729-0070
Phil L Morar, *President*
▲ **EMP:** 15
SALES (est): 2.5MM **Privately Held**
SIC: 3089 Ducting, plastic

(G-6516)
ELECTRO-MINIATURES CORP (PA)
68 W Commercial Ave (07074-1703)
PHONE..............................201 460-0510
Fax: 201 935-8153
Mark Pollack, *President*
Jamie Pollack, *Vice Pres*
▼ **EMP:** 58 **EST:** 1952
SQ FT: 20,000
SALES: 9MM **Privately Held**
WEB: www.emcsales.com
SIC: 3621 Sliprings, for motors or generators

(G-6517)
FLEXI PRINTING PLATE CO INC
50 Commercial Ave (07074-1705)
PHONE..............................201 939-3600
John Moss, *Vice Pres*
Joel Berlin, *Marketing Staff*
EMP: 18
SQ FT: 25,000
SALES (est): 3.9MM **Privately Held**
SIC: 2759 Commercial printing

(G-6518)
GALVANIC PRTG & PLATE CO INC
50 Commercial Ave (07074-1705)
PHONE..............................201 939-3600
John Moss, *President*
Lou Santiago, *Mfg Mgr*
Keith Pires, *Foreman/Supr*
Glendon Sabiel, *Sales Staff*
Larry Snyder, *Manager*
EMP: 25
SQ FT: 25,000
SALES (est): 5.5MM **Privately Held**
WEB: www.galvanicprinting.com
SIC: 2752 3555 Commercial printing, offset; printing plates

(G-6519)
H CROSS COMPANY
Also Called: Cross H Co
150 W Commercial Ave (07074-1706)
PHONE..............................201 964-9380
Fax: 201 964-9385
Edward McClary, *President*
Robert Vitali, *Plant Mgr*
Diane McClary, *Manager*
EMP: 32 **EST:** 1939
SQ FT: 31,500
SALES (est): 7.2MM **Privately Held**
WEB: www.hcrosscompany.com
SIC: 3356 3351 3355 3353 Nickel & nickel alloy: rolling, drawing or extruding; zirconium & zirconium alloy bars, sheets, strip, etc.; strip, copper & copper alloy; coils, wire aluminum: made in rolling mills; coils, sheet aluminum

(G-6520)
HAIN CELESTIAL GROUP INC
Also Called: Terra Chips
50 Knickerbocker Rd (07074-1613)
PHONE..............................201 935-4500
Fax: 201 935-8264
Urmikant Sheth, *QC Mgr*
Helene Miller, *Branch Mgr*
EMP: 29 **Publicly Held**
WEB: www.hain-celestial.com
SIC: 2096 Potato chips & similar snacks
PA: The Hain Celestial Group Inc
1111 Marcus Ave Ste 100
New Hyde Park NY 11042

(G-6521)
HIGHROAD PRESS LLC
220 Anderson Ave (07074-1632)
PHONE..............................201 708-6900
Eric Denburg, *VP Sales*
Hallie Denburg Satz,
EMP: 48
SQ FT: 38,000
SALES (est): 15.3MM **Privately Held**
WEB: www.highroadpress.com
SIC: 2752 Commercial printing, lithographic

(G-6522)
INOAC USA INC
Also Called: Crest Foam Industries
100 Carol Pl (07074-1300)
PHONE..............................201 807-0809
Amberley Babbage, *Plant Mgr*
Charles Hernandez, *Senior Buyer*
Akiko Eto, *Sales Staff*
Tom Myers, *Marketing Mgr*
EMP: 66
SALES (corp-wide): 7.2MM **Privately Held**
SIC: 3069 Foam rubber
HQ: Inoac Usa, Inc.
1515 Equity Dr Ste 200
Troy MI 48084
248 619-7031

(G-6523)
INTERNATIONAL AROMATICS INC (PA)
200 Anderson Ave (07074-1632)
PHONE..............................201 964-0900
Fax: 201 964-0807
Gary Gerardi, *President*
Jen Boyer, *Executive*
EMP: 15
SALES (est): 3.8MM **Privately Held**
WEB: www.iaromatics.com
SIC: 2844 Perfumes & colognes

(G-6524)
JADE EASTERN TRADING INC (PA)
Also Called: Marquis
13 Division St Ste A (07074)
PHONE..............................201 440-8500
Fax: 201 440-1012
Jae R Lee, *President*
Stella Lee, *Co-Owner*
Edward Lee, *Vice Pres*
◆ **EMP:** 15
SQ FT: 41,000
SALES: 8MM **Privately Held**
SIC: 5136 2321 Trousers, men's & boys'; men's & boys' outerwear; shirts, men's & boys'; men's & boys' furnishings

(G-6525)
JOHN F PEARCE
76 Frederick St (07074-1007)
PHONE..............................201 440-8765
John F Pearce, *Owner*
EMP: 5
SALES (corp-wide): 850K **Privately Held**
SIC: 3441 Fabricated structural metal
PA: John F Pearce
155 S River St
Hackensack NJ 07601
201 488-0434

(G-6526)
JUNE JACOBS LABS LLC (PA)
46 Graphic Pl (07074-1106)
PHONE..............................201 329-9100
Fax: 201 329-9166
June Jacobs, *President*
Matthew E Silpe, *COO*
Matthew Silpe, *COO*
Jennifer Hardell, *Opers Staff*
Danny Ng, *Accounts Mgr*
▲ **EMP:** 2
SALES (est): 16.4MM **Privately Held**
SIC: 2844 Cosmetic preparations

(G-6527)
KARIS GRAPHIC CORP
43 Romeo St (07074-1612)
PHONE..............................201 935-8774
Hawewon Min Norton, *President*
Fred Shin, *Vice Pres*
EMP: 5
SALES (est): 64.8K **Privately Held**
SIC: 3555 Printing presses

(G-6528)
KEY HANDLING SYSTEMS INC
137 W Commercial Ave (07074-1704)
P.O. Box 1489, Summit (07902-1489)
PHONE...................................201 933-9333
Fax: 201 933-5732
William E Stefan, *President*
Ron Baptista, *Senior VP*
Rudy Jaochico, *Vice Pres*
Steven V Melis, *Info Tech Dir*
Paul Hendrikse, *Director*
EMP: 40 EST: 1964
SQ FT: 53,350
SALES (est): 9.6MM **Privately Held**
WEB: www.keyhandling.com
SIC: 3535 Conveyors & conveying equipment

(G-6529)
LPS INDUSTRIES INC (PA)
Also Called: Lawrence Packaging
10 Caesar Pl (07074-1701)
P.O. Box 18858, Newark (07191-8858)
PHONE...................................201 438-3515
Fax: 201 438-1326
Madeleine D Robinson, *CEO*
Larry Costa, *Manager*
◆ EMP: 150 EST: 1959
SQ FT: 164,000
SALES (est): 53.4MM **Privately Held**
WEB: www.lpsind.com
SIC: 2671 5046 3081 2673 Packaging paper & plastics film, coated & laminated; scales, except laboratory; packing materials, plastic sheet; plastic bags: made from purchased materials; labels: gravure printing; packaging paper; bag paper

(G-6530)
MASSIMO ZANETTI BEVERAGE USA
10 Empire Blvd (07074-1303)
PHONE...................................201 440-1700
Jack Rush, *Principal*
▲ EMP: 19 EST: 2011
SALES (est): 3.3MM **Privately Held**
SIC: 2095 Roasted coffee

(G-6531)
MATERIAL IMPORTS
10 Oxford Dr (07074-1010)
PHONE...................................201 229-1180
Shaheryar Irshad, *Owner*
▲ EMP: 6
SALES: 5MM **Privately Held**
SIC: 2211 2299 Towels & toweling, cotton; batting, wadding, padding & fillings

(G-6532)
MEADOWLANDS BINDERY INC
146 W Commercial Ave (07074-1706)
PHONE...................................201 935-6161
Fax: 201 935-9014
Carmine Idone, *President*
Maria Molfetas, *Admin Sec*
EMP: 42
SQ FT: 12,000
SALES (est): 5.9MM **Privately Held**
WEB: www.meadowlandsbindery.com
SIC: 2789 Binding only: books, pamphlets, magazines, etc.

(G-6533)
MODERN SPORTSWEAR CORPORATION
102 W Commercial Ave (07074-1704)
PHONE...................................201 804-2700
Chris Park, *President*
Holmshiek Park, *Corp Secy*
Scott Park, *Vice Pres*
Beth Luiszer, *Sales Executive*
▲ EMP: 10
SQ FT: 25,000
SALES (est): 1.9MM **Privately Held**
SIC: 3429 Aircraft & marine hardware, inc. pulleys & similar items

(G-6534)
PACE PRESS INCORPORATED
1 Caesar Pl (07074-1702)
PHONE...................................201 935-7711
Fax: 201 507-7138
Jack Mangi, *President*
Seth Diamond, *Vice Pres*
Jonathan Vitale, *Vice Pres*

EMP: 75 EST: 1914
SQ FT: 78,000
SALES (est): 20.5MM **Privately Held**
SIC: 2752 Commercial printing, lithographic

(G-6535)
PERMAGRAPHICS INC
25 Graphic Pl (07074-1106)
PHONE...................................201 814-1200
Fax: 201 814-1600
Rita Caloni, *President*
Michael Caloni, *Vice Pres*
EMP: 13
SQ FT: 25,000
SALES (est): 2.1MM **Privately Held**
SIC: 2752 2789 2791 Commercial printing, offset; bookbinding & related work; typesetting

(G-6536)
PRESIDENT CONT GROUP II LLC (PA)
200 W Commercial Ave (07074-1610)
PHONE...................................201 933-7500
Marvin Grossbard,
Lawrence Grossbard,
Richard Grossbard,
▲ EMP: 450
SALES (est): 203.8MM **Privately Held**
SIC: 2653 Boxes, corrugated: made from purchased materials; sheets, corrugated: made from purchased materials; display items, corrugated: made from purchased materials

(G-6537)
R SQUARED SLS & LOGISTICS LLC
30 Congress Dr (07074-1406)
PHONE...................................201 329-9745
Dave Rothenberg, *President*
Gary Darwin, *Vice Pres*
Lee Rothman, *Vice Pres*
▲ EMP: 8 EST: 2012
SQ FT: 63,000
SALES (est): 1.1MM **Privately Held**
SIC: 3089 Plastic kitchenware, tableware & houseware

(G-6538)
RAFFETTOS CORP
62 W Commercial Ave (07074-1703)
PHONE...................................201 372-1222
Richard Raffetto, *President*
EMP: 13
SALES (est): 1.5MM **Privately Held**
SIC: 2098 Macaroni & spaghetti

(G-6539)
REACHMAN INTERNATIONAL CORP
Also Called: Global Plastics
75 Knickerbocker Rd (07074-1613)
PHONE...................................718 388-6565
Robert Chen, *President*
▲ EMP: 10
SQ FT: 10,000
SALES (est): 1.1MM **Privately Held**
SIC: 3089 5162 Plastic processing; plastics materials & basic shapes

(G-6540)
ROYAL BAKING CO INC
Also Called: Leonard's Novelty Bakery
8 Empire Blvd (07074-1303)
PHONE...................................201 296-0888
Fax: 201 296-0950
Jack Di Piazza, *President*
Marann Carro, *Principal*
Darman Di Piazza, *Principal*
Leonard Di Piazza, *Vice Pres*
▲ EMP: 80 EST: 1945
SQ FT: 50,000
SALES (est): 15.8MM **Privately Held**
SIC: 2051 2052 2053 Pastries (danish): frozen; cakes, bakery: frozen; cookies

(G-6541)
SCHRATTER FOODS INCORPORATED
Also Called: Anco Fine Cheese
205 Moonachie Rd (07074-1309)
PHONE...................................973 575-3226
Fax: 973 575-5010

Arnald Fusco, *Branch Mgr*
EMP: 6
SALES (corp-wide): 6.3B **Privately Held**
SIC: 2022 5143 Cheese, natural & processed; dairy products, except dried or canned
HQ: Schratter Foods Incorporated
3001 Sw 3rd Ave
Miami FL 33129
305 651-8884

(G-6542)
SCREEN-TRANS DEVELOPMENT CORP
Also Called: Foil-On
100 Grand St (07074-1623)
PHONE...................................201 933-7800
Fax: 201 804-6371
Robert Devries, *President*
Diana Lopez, *Opers Mgr*
David Devries, *Marketing Staff*
Joe Kierych, *Art Dir*
Roy Devries, *Shareholder*
EMP: 22
SQ FT: 18,800
SALES (est): 4.5MM **Privately Held**
WEB: www.screentrans.com
SIC: 2759 Commercial printing

(G-6543)
STAR RAVIOLI MANUFACTURING CO
2 Anderson Ave Ste 2 # 2 (07074-1678)
PHONE...................................201 933-6427
Fax: 201 933-0484
Lawrence J Piretra, *President*
Eileen Pisani, *Admin Sec*
EMP: 12 EST: 1946
SQ FT: 9,000
SALES (est): 2MM **Privately Held**
WEB: www.starravioli.com
SIC: 2098 Noodles (e.g. egg, plain & water), dry

(G-6544)
SUGAR & PLUMM UPPER WEST LLC
146 Redneck Ave (07074-1002)
PHONE...................................201 334-1600
Lamia Jacobs, *Mng Member*
EMP: 60
SALES (est): 4.7MM **Privately Held**
SIC: 2053 Cakes, bakery: frozen

(G-6545)
SUGAR AND PLUMM LLC
146 Redneck Ave (07074-1002)
PHONE...................................201 334-1600
Thierry Atlan, *Principal*
EMP: 7
SALES (est): 100.4K **Privately Held**
SIC: 2053 Frozen bakery products, except bread

(G-6546)
SUN TAIYANG CO LTD
Also Called: Sun Trading
85 Oxford Dr 2 (07074-1020)
PHONE...................................201 549-7100
Kyungja Park, *Chairman*
Kyung Ja Choi, *Treasurer*
◆ EMP: 90
SALES (est): 1.6MM **Privately Held**
SIC: 3999 Barber & beauty shop equipment

(G-6547)
SUPPLY TECHNOLOGIES LLC
50 Graphic Pl (07074-1106)
PHONE...................................201 641-7600
EMP: 35
SALES (corp-wide): 1.4B **Publicly Held**
SIC: 3462 3732 Mfg Iron/Steel Forgings Boatbuilding/Repairing
HQ: Supply Technologies Llc
6065 Parkland Blvd Ste 1
Cleveland OH 44124
440 947-2100

(G-6548)
SWINTEC CORP (PA)
320 W Coml Ave Ste 1 (07074)
P.O. Box 356, Wood Ridge (07075-0356)
PHONE...................................201 935-0115
Fax: 201 935-6021

Dominic Vespia, *President*
Matt Arki, *Vice Pres*
Noelle Aversano, *Cust Mgr*
◆ EMP: 15 EST: 1978
SQ FT: 38,000
SALES (est): 2.9MM **Privately Held**
WEB: www.swintec.com
SIC: 3579 3578 3661 Typewriters & parts; calculators & adding machines; facsimile equipment

(G-6549)
TEC CAST INC
2 W Commercial Ave (07074-1703)
P.O. Box 6596, Carlstadt (07072-0596)
PHONE...................................201 935-3885
Edgard Gotthold, *President*
EMP: 70
SALES (est): 9.5MM
SALES (corp-wide): 7.5MM **Privately Held**
SIC: 3365 7389 Aluminum foundries; inspection & testing services
PA: Tec Cast Inc
440 Meadow Ln
Carlstadt NJ 07072
201 935-3885

(G-6550)
ULTIMATE SPINNING TURNING CORP
9 Willow St (07074-1502)
PHONE...................................201 372-9740
Michael Novack, *President*
EMP: 7
SALES (est): 1.1MM **Privately Held**
SIC: 3542 3451 7389 Spinning machines, metal; screw machine products;

(G-6551)
VICTORY PRESS
1 Caesar Pl (07074-1702)
P.O. Box 218, Rochelle Park (07662-0218)
PHONE...................................201 729-1007
Joe Damico,
EMP: 4
SALES (est): 230K **Privately Held**
WEB: www.victoryprint.com
SIC: 2741 Miscellaneous publishing

(G-6552)
WISE FOODS INC
150 Carol Pl (07074-1300)
PHONE...................................201 440-2876
Chris Raftery, *President*
EMP: 8 **Privately Held**
SIC: 2096 Potato chips & similar snacks
HQ: Wise Foods, Inc.
228 Rasely St
Berwick PA 18603

(G-6553)
WOODBRIDGE INOAC TECHNICAL
Also Called: Crest Foam Industries Inc
100 Carol Pl (07074-1300)
PHONE...................................201 807-0809
Fax: 201 584-0274
Kyle Schultz, *General Mgr*
Amberley Babbage, *Plant Mgr*
Florence Depippa, *Purch Mgr*
Kedar Muzumdar, *Engineer*
William Hughes, *Sales Mgr*
◆ EMP: 66 EST: 1955
SALES (est): 18.9MM
SALES (corp-wide): 7.2MM **Privately Held**
WEB: www.crestfoam.com
SIC: 3069 Foam rubber
HQ: Inoac Usa, Inc.
1515 Equity Dr Ste 200
Troy MI 48084
248 619-7031

(G-6554)
WOODBRIDGE INOAC TECHNICAL PRO
100 Carol Pl (07074-1300)
PHONE...................................201 807-0809
Yosuke Nakano, *Exec VP*
John Zianis, *Manager*
EMP: 64
SQ FT: 65,000
SALES (est): 2MM **Privately Held**
SIC: 3069 Foam rubber

Moorestown
Burlington County

(G-6555)
ACKLEY MACHINE CORPORATION
1273 N Church St Ste 106 (08057-1194)
PHONE..................................856 234-3626
Fax: 856 234-8657
E Michael Ackley, *President*
Walter Kohler, *Sales Engr*
Philip Gulotta, *Mktg Dir*
Steve Hickey, *Software Engr*
Richard J Braemer, *Admin Sec*
▼ EMP: 34
SQ FT: 8,000
SALES (est): 7.9MM **Privately Held**
WEB: www.ackleymachine.com
SIC: 3555 Printing trades machinery

(G-6556)
ALADDIN COLOR INC
19 E Main St Ste D (08057-3338)
P.O. Box 500, Lumberton (08048-0500)
PHONE..................................609 518-9858
Fax: 856 727-0097
David Bard, *Ch of Bd*
Eric Bard, *President*
EMP: 6
SQ FT: 5,000
SALES (est): 750K **Privately Held**
WEB: www.aladdincolor.com
SIC: 2752 Commercial printing, offset

(G-6557)
AMERICAN BILTRITE INC
Tape Products Division
105 Whittendale Dr (08057-1313)
PHONE..................................856 778-0700
Fax: 856 231-9477
Michel Merkx, *Vice Pres*
Bonita Posnak, *Vice Pres*
John Mauro, *Plant Mgr*
Bill Evans, *Safety Mgr*
Sam Veitz, *Production*
EMP: 150
SQ FT: 119,000
SALES (corp-wide): 2MM **Publicly Held**
WEB: www.ambilt.com
SIC: 2672 Adhesive backed films, foams & foils
PA: American Biltrite Inc.
57 River St Ste 302
Wellesley MA 02481
781 237-6655

(G-6558)
AMERICAN HARLEQUIN CORPORATION
Also Called: Harlequin Floors
1531 Glen Ave (08057-1103)
PHONE..................................856 234-5505
Bob Dagger, *President*
Chantal Lagniau, *General Mgr*
Guenther Goetz, *Managing Dir*
Patricia A Basileo, *Exec VP*
Ray Lloyds, *VP Admin*
◆ EMP: 22
SQ FT: 24,000
SALES (est): 6.7MM
SALES (corp-wide): 425.6K **Privately Held**
WEB: www.harlequinfloors.com
SIC: 3069 5049 Mats or matting, rubber; theatrical equipment & supplies
PA: Harlequin Holdings International Limited
150 High Street
Sevenoaks

(G-6559)
AMERICAN PLASTIC WORKS INC
1270 Glen Ave (08057-1133)
PHONE..................................800 494-7326
Judith Zimmermann, *President*
EMP: 40
SALES (est): 3.4MM **Privately Held**
WEB: www.lwipromo.com
SIC: 2821 Plastics materials & resins

(G-6560)
ANDEK CORPORATION
850 Glen Ave (08057-1122)
P.O. Box 392 (08057-0392)
PHONE..................................856 866-7600
Harvey Liss, *President*
Andrew Liss, *Vice Pres*
◆ EMP: 13
SALES (est): 1.6MM **Privately Held**
WEB: www.andek.com
SIC: 3479 2851 2891 Coating of metals & formed products; lacquers, varnishes, enamels & other coatings; adhesives & sealants

(G-6561)
AUNTIE ANNES SOFT PRETZELS
400 W Route 38 (08057-3219)
PHONE..................................856 722-0433
Fax: 856 722-1692
Mel Sickler, *Owner*
EMP: 20
SALES (est): 429.9K **Privately Held**
SIC: 5461 2096 2051 Pretzels; potato chips & similar snacks; bread, cake & related products

(G-6562)
AUTOMATION & CONTROL INC
Also Called: Aci
1491 Lancer Dr (08057-4207)
P.O. Box 386 (08057-0386)
PHONE..................................856 234-2300
Fax: 856 234-5223
Ron Iannacone, *President*
Joe McKenna, *Opers Staff*
Brian Garwood, *Engineer*
Tom George, *Engineer*
George Cramer, *Sales Staff*
EMP: 32
SQ FT: 4,500
SALES: 8MM **Privately Held**
WEB: www.automation-control.com
SIC: 8711 3613 1731 Electrical or electronic engineering; panel & distribution boards & other related apparatus; electrical work

(G-6563)
BIOMEDICON
30 E Central Ave (08057-2519)
PHONE..................................856 778-1880
Mark Singer, *Owner*
EMP: 19
SQ FT: 5,200
SALES: 1.7MM **Privately Held**
WEB: www.biomedicon.com
SIC: 3841 3826 5047 Surgical & medical instruments; analytical instruments; hospital equipment & furniture

(G-6564)
BODINE TOOL AND MACHINE CO INC
1273 N Church St Ste 104 (08057-1115)
PHONE..................................856 234-7800
Fax: 856 234-4281
William Lauth, *President*
Paul Donegan, *Vice Pres*
Eleanor Kerr, *Admin Sec*
EMP: 30 EST: 1937
SQ FT: 25,000
SALES (est): 6.4MM **Privately Held**
WEB: www.bodinetool.com
SIC: 3544 Special dies & tools; jigs & fixtures; industrial molds

(G-6565)
BRAINSTORM SOFTWARE CORP
16 Apple Orchard Rd (08057-3844)
PHONE..................................856 234-4945
Bruce Kratz, *President*
EMP: 4
SALES (est): 182.9K **Privately Held**
WEB: www.brainstorm-software.com
SIC: 7372 Prepackaged software

(G-6566)
CIRCUIT TECH ASSEMBLY LLC
341 New Albany Rd Ste 130 (08057-1151)
PHONE..................................856 231-0777
Fax: 856 231-7878
Bill Sherlock Jr, *President*

William Sherlock,
EMP: 15
SQ FT: 16,000
SALES (est): 2.5MM **Privately Held**
WEB: www.circuittechassembly.com
SIC: 3679 Electronic circuits

(G-6567)
CISCO SYSTEMS INC
308 Harper Dr Ste 100 (08057-3244)
PHONE..................................856 642-7000
Fred Zalupski, *Partner*
Chuck Adams, *Regional Mgr*
Jim Clothier, *Opers Staff*
Ronald Solometo, *Engineer*
Fran Terlingo, *Engineer*
EMP: 8
SALES (corp-wide): 48B **Publicly Held**
SIC: 3577 Computer peripheral equipment
PA: Cisco Systems, Inc.
170 W Tasman Dr
San Jose CA 95134
408 526-4000

(G-6568)
COCOA SERVICES INC
905 N Lenola Rd (08057-1042)
PHONE..................................856 234-1700
John Lyons, *President*
EMP: 10
SALES (est): 1.1MM **Privately Held**
SIC: 2066 Cocoa butter

(G-6569)
COMTREX SYSTEMS CORPORATION (PA)
101 Foster Rd B (08057-1118)
PHONE..................................856 778-0090
Fax: 856 778-9322
Nathan I Lipson, *Ch of Bd*
Jeffrey C Rice, *President*
Charles A Hardin, *Vice Pres*
Matthew R Carter, *VP Sales*
EMP: 31
SQ FT: 19,000
SALES (est): 6.7MM **Publicly Held**
WEB: www.comtrex.com
SIC: 7373 3578 Computer integrated systems design; point-of-sale devices

(G-6570)
CR LAURENCE CO INC
Also Called: Thiladel Phia
1511 Lancer Dr (08057-4232)
PHONE..................................856 727-1022
Fax: 856 727-3299
Jason Key, *Manager*
EMP: 10
SALES (corp-wide): 29.7B **Privately Held**
WEB: www.crlaurence.com
SIC: 2891 Sealants
HQ: C.R. Laurence Co., Inc.
2503 E Vernon Ave
Vernon CA 90058
323 588-1281

(G-6571)
CVC SPECIALTY CHEMICALS INC (HQ)
Also Called: Cvc Thermoset Specialties
844 N Lenola Rd V (08057-1052)
PHONE..................................856 533-3000
Fax: 856 533-3003
John Cech, *President*
▼ EMP: 19 EST: 1982
SQ FT: 20,400
SALES (est): 10.6MM
SALES (corp-wide): 228.8MM **Privately Held**
WEB: www.cvcchem.com
SIC: 2869 2821 5169 Industrial organic chemicals; epoxy resins; chemicals & allied products
PA: Emerald Performance Materials Llc
1499 Se Tech Center Pl
Vancouver WA 98683
360 954-7100

(G-6572)
DENTON VACUUM LLC
1259 N Church St (08057-1169)
PHONE..................................856 439-9100
EMP: 0
SQ FT: 80,000
SALES (est): 22.9MM **Privately Held**
SIC: 3821 Mfg Lab Apparatus/Furniture

PA: Denton Vacuum L.L.C.
1259 N Church St Bldg 3
Moorestown NJ 08057
856 439-9100

(G-6573)
EASTERN INSTRUMENTATION OF
710 E Main St Ste 1a (08057-3066)
PHONE..................................856 231-0668
Fax: 856 231-9022
Jerry Lomurno, *President*
Kevin Mays, *Sales Engr*
Dominic Giarratano, *Administration*
EMP: 8
SALES (est): 890K **Privately Held**
WEB: www.eiphila.com
SIC: 3825 5065 3661 Instruments to measure electricity; electronic parts & equipment; fiber optics communications equipment

(G-6574)
ECOLAB INC
110 Marter Ave Ste 411 (08057-3124)
PHONE..................................856 596-4845
Ursula Carvale, *Branch Mgr*
EMP: 205
SALES (corp-wide): 13.8B **Publicly Held**
WEB: www.ecolab.com
SIC: 2841 Soap & other detergents
PA: Ecolab Inc.
1 Ecolab Pl
Saint Paul MN 55102
800 232-6522

(G-6575)
ELECTRO MAGNETIC PRODUCTS INC
355 Crider Ave (08057-1241)
PHONE..................................856 235-3011
Fax: 856 722-0566
Gordon Mason, *President*
Andrew Lipenta, *Vice Pres*
Eric M Mason, *Sales Mgr*
EMP: 40 EST: 1966
SQ FT: 30,000
SALES (est): 6.3MM **Privately Held**
WEB: www.empmags.com
SIC: 3544 Die sets for metal stamping (presses)

(G-6576)
EMS AVIATION INC
121 Whittendale Dr Ste A (08057-1373)
P.O. Box 7700, Norcross GA (30091-7700)
PHONE..................................856 234-5020
Fax: 856 234-5242
John Jarrell, *President*
John Byard Mowell, *Chairman*
Paul R Kuphal, *Senior VP*
EMP: 140
SQ FT: 34,000
SALES (est): 33MM
SALES (corp-wide): 40.5B **Publicly Held**
SIC: 3577 Computer peripheral equipment
PA: Honeywell International Inc.
115 Tabor Rd
Morris Plains NJ 07950
973 455-2000

(G-6577)
ESSENTRA PACKAGING US INC
1224 N Church St (08057-1102)
PHONE..................................856 439-1700
EMP: 6
SALES (corp-wide): 1.3B **Privately Held**
SIC: 2673 Plastic bags: made from purchased materials
HQ: Essentra Packaging U.S. Inc.
2 Westbrook Corp Ctr
Westchester IL 60154
704 418-8692

(G-6578)
FRINTON LABORATORIES INC
204 Winding Way (08057-2632)
PHONE..................................856 722-7037
George Inglessis, *President*
EMP: 4
SALES (est): 356.6K **Privately Held**
SIC: 2899 Chemical preparations

GEOGRAPHIC

(G-6579)
GRANITE PACKAGING SUPPLY CO (HQ)
Also Called: Supply One Plastics
111 Whittendale Dr (08057-1364)
PHONE..................................856 727-1010
Fax: 856 727-1020
Brian Cassano, *Corp Secy*
EMP: 75
SQ FT: 93,000
SALES (est): 30.7MM
SALES (corp-wide): 488.7MM **Privately Held**
WEB: www.granitepackaging.com
SIC: 5199 3086 5113 5085 Packaging materials; packaging & shipping materials, foamed plastic; industrial & personal service paper; industrial supplies; setup paperboard boxes
PA: Supplyone Holdings Company, Inc.
11 Campus Blvd Ste 150
Newtown Square PA 19073
484 582-5005

(G-6580)
GRAYDON PRODUCTS INC
800 Glen Ave (08057-1122)
PHONE..................................856 234-9513
George Semanko, *President*
EMP: 35
SQ FT: 30,000
SALES (est): 5.4MM **Privately Held**
WEB: www.omnimedbeam.com
SIC: 3841 Surgical & medical instruments
PA: Omni Acquisition Corp
101 N Pine Ave
Maple Shade NJ

(G-6581)
GWYNN-E CO
222 Cedar St (08057-1709)
PHONE..................................215 423-6400
Michael L Gwynne, *Principal*
EMP: 6
SALES (est): 671.7K **Privately Held**
SIC: 2426 Hardwood dimension & flooring mills

(G-6582)
H G SCHAEVITZ LLC
Also Called: Alliance Sensors Group
102 Commerce Dr Ste 8 (08057-4205)
PHONE..................................856 727-0250
Harold Schaevitz, *President*
John Matmack, *Mng Member*
Howard Schaevitz, *Mng Member*
Ed Herceg, *CTO*
John Matlack, *Executive*
EMP: 6
SALES: 1,000K **Privately Held**
SIC: 3699 Electrical equipment & supplies

(G-6583)
HARRIS FREEMAN & CO INC
Also Called: Harris Tea Company
344 New Albany Rd (08057-1167)
PHONE..................................856 787-9026
Kishore Shah, *Partner*
EMP: 71
SALES (corp-wide): 400.8MM **Privately Held**
SIC: 5149 2099 2673 Tea; coffee, green or roasted; spices & seasonings; tea blending; food storage & trash bags (plastic)
PA: Harris Freeman & Co., Inc.
3110 E Miraloma Ave
Anaheim CA 92806
714 765-1190

(G-6584)
HILL-ROM HOLDINGS INC
202 Commerce Dr Ste 2 (08057-4226)
PHONE..................................856 486-2117
Peter Soderberg, *CEO*
EMP: 8
SALES (corp-wide): 2.7B **Publicly Held**
SIC: 2599 Hospital furniture, except beds; hospital beds
PA: Hill-Rom Holdings, Inc.
130 E Randolph St # 1000
Chicago IL 60601
312 819-7200

(G-6585)
HONEYWELL INTERNATIONAL INC
121 Whittendale Dr (08057-1373)
PHONE..................................856 234-5020
EMP: 708
SALES (corp-wide): 40.5B **Publicly Held**
SIC: 3724 Aircraft engines & engine parts
PA: Honeywell International Inc.
115 Tabor Rd
Morris Plains NJ 07950
973 455-2000

(G-6586)
INNOVASYSTEMS INC
1245 N Church St Ste 6 (08057-1142)
PHONE..................................856 722-0410
Fax: 856 722-0042
John J Waters, *President*
Nick Schreier, *Vice Pres*
EMP: 12
SQ FT: 5,000
SALES (est): 2.6MM **Privately Held**
WEB: www.innovasystems.com
SIC: 3821 8711 Laboratory equipment: fume hoods, distillation racks, etc.; chemical engineering

(G-6587)
ION360 USA LLC
513 S Lenola Rd Ste 208 (08057-1550)
PHONE..................................866 901-0073
Ron Garriqes, *CEO*
EMP: 2
SALES: 1.9MM **Privately Held**
SIC: 3861 Cameras & related equipment

(G-6588)
JET PULVERIZER CO INC
1255 N Church St (08057-1136)
P.O. Box 212, Palmyra (08065-0212)
PHONE..................................856 235-5554
Fax: 856 778-7712
Ed Fay, *President*
William S Henry, *Vice Pres*
Jeff Conn, *Engineer*
Christine E Henry, *Treasurer*
▲ EMP: 27
SQ FT: 20,000
SALES (est): 6.6MM **Privately Held**
WEB: www.jetpul.com
SIC: 3541 3559 Grinding machines, metalworking; chemical machinery & equipment

(G-6589)
KATIS KUPCAKES
233 Hedgeman Rd (08057-1308)
PHONE..................................609 332-2172
Kati Angelini, *Owner*
EMP: 4 EST: 2010
SALES (est): 172K **Privately Held**
SIC: 2051 Biscuits, baked: baking powder & raised

(G-6590)
KERN & SZALAI CO
Also Called: Kern & Szalai Machine Company
351 Crider Ave (08057-1238)
PHONE..................................856 802-1500
Robert Santare, *President*
EMP: 14
SQ FT: 4,000
SALES: 1.6MM
SALES (corp-wide): 4.5MM **Privately Held**
WEB: www.champfast.com
SIC: 3599 Machine shop, jobbing & repair
PA: Champion Fasteners, Inc.
707 Smithville Rd
Lumberton NJ 08048
609 267-5222

(G-6591)
KETEC
1256 N Church St Ste A (08057-1146)
PHONE..................................856 778-4343
Fax: 856 778-8337
Ronald Kenney, *President*
Michael Vergilio, *Managing Dir*
George Kaltner, *Vice Pres*
Bob Plizak, *Purchasing*
EMP: 18
SQ FT: 2,000
SALES (est): 1.8MM **Privately Held**
WEB: www.ketec.com
SIC: 7382 3699 Protective devices, security; security control equipment & systems

(G-6592)
LANTIER CONSTRUCTION COMPANY
12 Greenvale Rd (08057-2235)
PHONE..................................856 780-6366
Douglas Lantier, *Owner*
EMP: 35
SALES (est): 4.8MM **Privately Held**
SIC: 3479 4932 Name plates: engraved, etched, etc.; gas & other services combined

(G-6593)
LIBERTY COCA-COLA BEVS LLC
1250 Glen Ave (08057-1112)
PHONE..................................215 427-4500
Fax: 856 866-1372
Leon Ivey, *Manager*
EMP: 54
SALES (corp-wide): 210K **Privately Held**
SIC: 2086 Bottled & canned soft drinks
PA: Liberty Coca-Cola Beverages Llc
725 E Erie Ave
Philadelphia PA 19134
215 427-4500

(G-6594)
LOCKHEED MARTIN CORPORATION
199 Bortons Landing Rd (08057-3048)
PHONE..................................856 722-7782
EMP: 99 **Publicly Held**
SIC: 3812 8711 3721 Search & navigation equipment; engineering services; aircraft
PA: Lockheed Martin Corporation
6801 Rockledge Dr
Bethesda MD 20817

(G-6595)
LOCKHEED MARTIN CORPORATION
Lockheed Martin Naval Electron
199 Bortons Landing Rd (08057-3048)
P.O. Box 1027 (08057-0927)
PHONE..................................856 722-3336
Robert Coutts, *Principal*
Don Fleenor, *Research*
Justin Gallagher, *Engineer*
Ilya Gershkovich, *Engineer*
Matthew Hibshman, *Engineer*
EMP: 230 **Publicly Held**
WEB: www.lockheedmartin.com
SIC: 8733 8734 3812 Research institute; product testing laboratory, safety or performance; search & navigation equipment
PA: Lockheed Martin Corporation
6801 Rockledge Dr
Bethesda MD 20817

(G-6596)
LOCKHEED MARTIN CORPORATION
199 Bortons Landing Rd (08057-3048)
PHONE..................................856 722-4100
Fax: 856 722-4619
Fred Moosally, *Division Pres*
Sarah Rivera, *Project Mgr*
Kelly Michael, *Purch Agent*
Tom Yeaple, *Purch Agent*
Kelly Forrester, *Engineer*
EMP: 4500 **Publicly Held**
WEB: www.lockheedmartin.com
SIC: 3812 Defense systems & equipment
PA: Lockheed Martin Corporation
6801 Rockledge Dr
Bethesda MD 20817

(G-6597)
LOCKHEED MARTIN OVERSEAS LLC
199 Bortons Landing Rd (08057-3048)
PHONE..................................856 787-3105
Richard D'Alesandro, *Manager*
EMP: 6
SALES (est): 156.8K **Publicly Held**
SIC: 3761 Space vehicles, complete
PA: Lockheed Martin Corporation
6801 Rockledge Dr
Bethesda MD 20817

(G-6598)
LONGPORT SHIELDS INC
Also Called: Shields Business Solutions
5 Twosome Dr (08057-1367)
PHONE..................................856 727-0227
Richard Grossman, *CEO*
Bonnie Hill, *Controller*
EMP: 8
SALES (est): 827.8K
SALES (corp-wide): 196.3K **Privately Held**
SIC: 3578 7699 Automatic teller machines (ATM); automated teller machine (ATM) repair
PA: Longport Shields Re Holdings, Llc
5 Twosome Dr
Moorestown NJ 08057
856 727-0227

(G-6599)
LUKOIL N ARLINGTON LTD LBLTY
302 Harper Dr Ste 303 (08057-4701)
PHONE..................................856 722-6425
Julia Gureyea, *Office Mgr*
EMP: 20
SALES (est): 1MM **Privately Held**
SIC: 2396 Automotive & apparel trimmings

(G-6600)
MCLEAN PACKAGING CORPORATION (PA)
1504 Glen Ave (08057-1104)
PHONE..................................856 359-2600
Fax: 856 359-2910
Joseph Fenkel, *CEO*
Stuart Fenkel, *President*
Jeffrey Besnick, *Vice Pres*
David Seidenberg, *Vice Pres*
Rj Howarth, *Plant Mgr*
▲ EMP: 325 EST: 1961
SQ FT: 110,000
SALES (est): 82MM **Privately Held**
SIC: 2652 2653 3089 2657 Setup paperboard boxes; boxes, corrugated: made from purchased materials; boxes, plastic; folding paperboard boxes

(G-6601)
MESA VETERANS POWER LLC
365 New Albany Rd Ste C (08057-1105)
PHONE..................................856 222-1000
Howard B Gartland,
EMP: 4
SALES (est): 364.3K **Privately Held**
SIC: 3612 Transformers, except electric

(G-6602)
MORGAN TOWERS INC
212 W Route 38 Ste 300 (08057-3271)
PHONE..................................856 786-7200
Diane Lauro, *Manager*
EMP: 5
SALES (est): 376.4K **Privately Held**
SIC: 3441 Tower sections, radio & television transmission

(G-6603)
NW SIGN INDUSTRIES INC
Also Called: N W Sign Industries
360 Crider Ave (08057-1239)
PHONE..................................856 802-1677
Fax: 704 782-2887
Chris Reedel, *Branch Mgr*
EMP: 30 **Privately Held**
SIC: 3993 Electric signs
PA: Nw Sign Industries, Inc.
360 Crider Ave
Moorestown NJ 08057

(G-6604)
NW SIGN INDUSTRIES INC (PA)
360 Crider Ave (08057-1239)
PHONE..................................856 802-1677
Fax: 856 802-0412
Ronald Brodie, *President*
Joe Piemonte, *Controller*
Pat Scala, *Accountant*
Christopher Depaolo, *Manager*
EMP: 100
SQ FT: 65,000
SALES (est): 37.4MM **Privately Held**
SIC: 3993 Signs & advertising specialties

(G-6605)
OLDCASTLE BUILDINGENVELOPE INC
1500 Glen Ave (08057-1104)
PHONE..................................856 234-9222
Dave Mailhiot, *General Mgr*
Brian Mello, *Vice Pres*
Dave Myer, *Branch Mgr*
Dan Kerr, *Director*
EMP: 100
SQ FT: 66,470
SALES (corp-wide): 29.7B **Privately Held**
WEB: www.oldcastleglass.com
SIC: 3231 5039 3211 Products of purchased glass; exterior flat glass: plate or window; flat glass
HQ: Oldcastle Buildingenvelope, Inc.
5005 Lndn B Jnsn Fwy 10
Dallas TX 75244
214 273-3400

(G-6606)
OPEX CORPORATION
835 Lancer Dr (08057-4225)
PHONE..................................856 727-1100
Albert Stevens, *Owner*
Thomas Goraj, *Project Mgr*
EMP: 15
SALES (corp-wide): 221.8MM **Privately Held**
SIC: 3579 Mailing, letter handling & addressing machines
PA: Opex Corporation
305 Commerce Dr
Moorestown NJ 08057
856 727-1100

(G-6607)
OTIS ELEVATOR COMPANY
30 Twosome Dr Ste 4 (08057-1370)
PHONE..................................856 235-5200
Fax: 856 642-4910
Joe Frask, *President*
EMP: 35
SALES (corp-wide): 59.8B **Publicly Held**
WEB: www.otis.com
SIC: 5084 3534 1796 Elevators; elevators & moving stairways; installing building equipment
HQ: Otis Elevator Company
1 Carrier Pl
Farmington CT 06032
860 674-3000

(G-6608)
PARKEON INC
40 Twosome Dr Ste 7 (08057-1369)
PHONE..................................856 234-8000
Naples A S, *CEO*
Yves Chambeau, *President*
Sheila Laut, *Business Mgr*
Ronald Kroes, *CFO*
Robert Barnes, *Treasurer*
◆ EMP: 50
SQ FT: 15,000
SALES (est): 15.2MM
SALES (corp-wide): 37.1MM **Privately Held**
WEB: www.moorestown.parkeon.com
SIC: 3824 Parking meters
HQ: Parkeon
100 A 102
Paris 75015
158 098-110

(G-6609)
PARTS LIFE INC
30 Twosome Dr Ste 1 (08057-1370)
PHONE..................................856 786-8675
Samuel Thevanayagam, *President*
Renee Lynn Schoppe, *Bookkeeper*
▲ EMP: 32
SALES: 3MM **Privately Held**
WEB: www.partslifeinc.com
SIC: 3799 3724 Electrocars for transporting golfers; aircraft engines & engine parts

(G-6610)
PATIENTSTAR LLC
308 Harper Dr Ste 105 (08057-3245)
PHONE..................................856 722-0808
Lucine A King, *President*
Laureen Gonnella, *Opers Staff*
Lauren Brejcak, *Manager*
Chris Newbern, *Senior Mgr*

Sarah Vellner, *Analyst*
EMP: 11
SQ FT: 3,000
SALES (est): 1MM **Privately Held**
SIC: 7372 Business oriented computer software

(G-6611)
PERFECT PRINTING INC
1533 Glen Ave (08057-1103)
PHONE..................................856 787-1877
Fax: 856 787-0054
Joseph Olivo, *CEO*
Ann Olivo, *President*
Chris Buoni, *Vice Pres*
Charlie Olivo, *Vice Pres*
Brian Riggs, *Vice Pres*
EMP: 25
SALES (est): 4.1MM **Privately Held**
SIC: 2752 Commercial printing, lithographic

(G-6612)
PETIT POIS CORP
Also Called: Sussex Wine Merchants
50 Twosome Dr Ste 3 (08057-1379)
PHONE..................................856 608-9644
James Weinrott, *President*
David Akry, *Treasurer*
▲ EMP: 7
SQ FT: 600
SALES (est): 1.8MM **Privately Held**
WEB: www.petitpois.net
SIC: 5182 2084 Wine; wines

(G-6613)
PIONEER & CO INC
97 Foster Rd Ste 5 (08057-1154)
PHONE..................................856 866-9191
Fax: 856 866-8615
Wolfgang Harms, *President*
Sven Harms, *Exec VP*
Bjorn Harms, *Vice Pres*
Patrick Morio, *CFO*
Karl Schuster, *Sales Associate*
◆ EMP: 20
SQ FT: 7,200
SALES: 57.4K **Privately Held**
WEB: www.pioneer-research.com
SIC: 5699 3648 Sports apparel; underwater lighting fixtures

(G-6614)
POPLAR BINDERY INC
300 Mill St (08057-2522)
PHONE..................................856 727-8030
Fax: 856 727-1677
Steve Heisler, *President*
John Heisler, *Principal*
▲ EMP: 12
SALES (est): 1.4MM **Privately Held**
SIC: 2789 Binding only: books, pamphlets, magazines, etc.

(G-6615)
PRISM COLOR CORPORATION
31 Twosome Dr Ste 1 (08057-1390)
PHONE..................................856 234-7515
Fax: 856 234-7516
Edward Brown, *President*
Dennis O'Sullivan, *General Mgr*
Tom Krisak, *Vice Pres*
Bill Drexel Sr, *Plant Mgr*
Chris Elser, *Prdtn Mgr*
EMP: 84
SQ FT: 38,000
SALES (est): 14.3MM **Privately Held**
WEB: www.prismcolorcorp.com
SIC: 2752 7335 Commercial printing, offset; color separation, photographic & movie film

(G-6616)
PROTEUS DESIGNS LLC
900 N Lenola Rd Bldg 9 (08057-1043)
PHONE..................................215 519-0135
Joseph Herron, *Mng Member*
Patrick Barry,
Therese Barry,
Richard Skettini,
EMP: 4
SQ FT: 1,100
SALES: 360K **Privately Held**
SIC: 3944 Games, toys & children's vehicles

(G-6617)
QUANTUM COATING INC
1259 N Church St Bldg 1 (08057-1169)
PHONE..................................856 234-5444
Daniel Patriarca Jr, *CEO*
EMP: 30
SQ FT: 15,000
SALES (est): 7.1MM **Privately Held**
WEB: www.quantumcoating.com
SIC: 3827 Optical instruments & lenses

(G-6618)
RAMSAY DAVID CABINETMAKERS
Also Called: David Ramsay
310 Mill St (08057-2536)
PHONE..................................856 234-7776
Fax: 856 234-2618
David Ramsay, *President*
EMP: 12
SQ FT: 8,000
SALES (est): 1.9MM **Privately Held**
WEB: www.ramsaycabinetmakers.com
SIC: 5712 3429 7389 Cabinet work, custom; furniture builders' & other household hardware; interior design services

(G-6619)
ROTARY DIE SYSTEMS INC
876 N Lenola Rd Ste 9a (08057-1046)
PHONE..................................856 234-3994
Robert Donahue, *President*
Maureen Donahue, *Shareholder*
EMP: 5
SQ FT: 9,000
SALES: 600K **Privately Held**
SIC: 3554 3599 Die cutting & stamping machinery, paper converting; machine shop, jobbing & repair

(G-6620)
S W ELECTRONICS & MFG (PA)
Also Called: Swemco
1215 N Church St (08057-1101)
PHONE..................................856 222-9900
Fax: 856 222-0700
Carl Szczepkowski, *CEO*
Albert Szczepkowski, *Ch of Bd*
Richard Szczepkowski, *President*
Richard Sepkowski, *Vice Pres*
Richard Lafalce, *Engineer*
▲ EMP: 115 EST: 1965
SQ FT: 54,000
SALES (est): 49.5MM **Privately Held**
WEB: www.swemco.com
SIC: 3577 Computer peripheral equipment

(G-6621)
SCHINDLER ELEVATOR CORPORATION
840 N Lenola Rd Ste 4 (08057-1055)
PHONE..................................856 234-2220
Fax: 856 437-2322
Steve Ryan, *Branch Mgr*
EMP: 20
SALES (corp-wide): 10.3B **Privately Held**
WEB: www.us.schindler.com
SIC: 3534 7699 1796 Elevators & equipment; elevators: inspection, service & repair; miscellaneous building item repair services; elevator installation & conversion
HQ: Schindler Elevator Corporation
20 Whippany Rd
Morristown NJ 07960
973 397-6500

(G-6622)
SENTRY MFG LLC
351 Crider Ave (08057-1238)
PHONE..................................856 642-0480
Mike Vermes, *Principal*
EMP: 4 EST: 2001
SALES (est): 526.7K **Privately Held**
SIC: 3399 Primary metal products

(G-6623)
STAR LINEN INC (PA)
Also Called: Linen Enterprises
1501 Lancer Dr (08057-4233)
PHONE..................................800 782-7999
Fax: 856 778-1771
Joseph W Ranieri, *President*
Cathy Bryant, *General Mgr*
Louis A Gutman, *Vice Pres*

David Middleberg, *Mfg Dir*
Sandra Moreno, *Prdtn Mgr*
◆ EMP: 45
SQ FT: 64,500
SALES (est): 9.8MM **Privately Held**
WEB: www.starlinen.com
SIC: 2299 2392 Linen fabrics; blankets, comforters & beddings

(G-6624)
STUD WELDING CO THE INC
750 Glen Ave (08057-1124)
PHONE..................................856 866-9300
Fax: 856 866-1818
Ralph Kohart Jr, *President*
Douglas Oyama, *Sls & Mktg Exec*
EMP: 5
SQ FT: 8,000
SALES (est): 600K **Privately Held**
WEB: www.studweldingco.com
SIC: 5072 5085 5084 3699 Bolts; nuts (hardware); rivets; fasteners, industrial: nuts, bolts, screws, etc.; welding machinery & equipment; electrical welding equipment

(G-6625)
SWEMCO LLC (HQ)
121 Whittendale Dr Ste A (08057-1373)
PHONE..................................856 222-9900
Carl Szczepkowski,
Richard Szczepkowski,
EMP: 115
SQ FT: 30,000
SALES (est): 20.8MM
SALES (corp-wide): 49.5MM **Privately Held**
SIC: 3672 Printed circuit boards
PA: S W Electronics & Manufacturing Corp
1215 N Church St
Moorestown NJ 08057
856 222-9900

(G-6626)
SYMPHONY INC
Also Called: Symphony Pastries
1263 Glen Ave Ste 220 (08057-1178)
PHONE..................................856 727-9596
Fax: 856 727-9665
Yann Machard, *President*
Susan Cohen, *Opers Staff*
▲ EMP: 17
SQ FT: 2,500
SALES (est): 2.5MM **Privately Held**
WEB: www.symphonypastries.com
SIC: 2051 5461 Cakes, pies & pastries; pastries

(G-6627)
SYSCOM TECHNOLOGIES CORP
1537 Glen Ave (08057-1103)
PHONE..................................856 642-7661
Fax: 856 642-1111
Peter Anninos, *President*
Anthony Maladra, *Vice Pres*
EMP: 100
SQ FT: 36,000
SALES (est): 30.7MM **Privately Held**
SIC: 3672 Printed circuit boards

(G-6628)
THOMA INC (PA)
1640 Nixon Dr 323 (08057-2675)
PHONE..................................856 608-6887
Fax: 856 608-7982
Brian Thoma, *President*
▲ EMP: 14
SQ FT: 2,100
SALES (est): 2.3MM **Privately Held**
WEB: www.thomainc.com
SIC: 3821 Laboratory furniture

(G-6629)
V H EXACTA CORP
107 Whittendale Dr (08057-1364)
PHONE..................................856 235-7379
Francis A Hubler, *President*
Wayne Hubler, *Vice Pres*
Susan Hileman, *Treasurer*
Barbara Hubler, *Admin Sec*
EMP: 9
SQ FT: 10,000
SALES (est): 1.5MM **Privately Held**
SIC: 3469 Machine parts, stamped or pressed metal

(G-6630)
VERMES MACHINE CO INC
351 Crider Ave (08057-1238)
PHONE..................................856 642-9300
Fax: 856 642-9302
Erwin Vermes, *President*
Michael Vermes Jr, *Vice Pres*
Mike Vermes, *Vice Pres*
▲ EMP: 25
SQ FT: 5,000
SALES (est): 5.1MM **Privately Held**
WEB: www.vermesmachine.com
SIC: 3599 7692 Machine shop, jobbing & repair; welding repair

(G-6631)
WAY IT WAS SPORTING SVC INC
620 Chestnut St (08057-2004)
PHONE..................................856 231-0111
Henry Peters, *President*
John R Peters, *Corp Secy*
EMP: 4
SQ FT: 1,000
SALES (est): 338.2K **Privately Held**
SIC: 5941 3484 Sporting goods & bicycle shops; rifles or rifle parts, 30 mm. & below; shotguns or shotgun parts, 30 mm. & below

(G-6632)
WEILER LABELING SYSTEMS LLC
1256 N Church St (08057-1129)
PHONE..................................856 273-3377
Ted Geiselman, *President*
Mary Lawrence, *Parts Mgr*
Dana Breese, *Engineer*
Jim Esposito, *Project Engr*
Lisa Propati, *Controller*
◆ EMP: 60
SQ FT: 33,000
SALES (est): 14.2MM
SALES (corp-wide): 641.6MM **Privately Held**
WEB: www.weilerls.com
SIC: 3565 Labeling machines, industrial
PA: Pro Mach, Inc.
50 E Rivercntr Blvd 180
Covington KY 41011
513 831-8778

(G-6633)
WILSONART LLC
11 Twosome Dr (08057-1367)
PHONE..................................800 822-7613
Fax: 856 866-1812
James Kane, *Manager*
EMP: 17
SALES (corp-wide): 14.3B **Publicly Held**
WEB: www.wilsonart.com
SIC: 2821 2541 Plastics materials & resins; table or counter tops, plastic laminated
HQ: Wilsonart Llc
2501 Wilsonart Dr
Temple TX 76504
254 207-7000

Morganville
Monmouth County

(G-6634)
ABLE GROUP TECHNOLOGIES INC
281 State Route 79 N (07751-1157)
PHONE..................................732 591-9299
Alan Rogolsky, *Sales Staff*
EMP: 5
SALES (est): 565.3K **Privately Held**
SIC: 7378 7372 8731 Computer maintenance & repair; application computer software; computer (hardware) development

(G-6635)
ADS SALES CO INC
Also Called: Room Service Amenities
1010 Campus Dr (07751-1260)
PHONE..................................732 591-0500
Fax: 732 591-2765
Ann Summer, *President*
Dennis Summer, *Vice Pres*
Marshall Summer, *Vice Pres*
Robert Sutton, *Purchasing*

Victoria McMillin, *Design Engr*
◆ EMP: 20
SQ FT: 7,000
SALES (est): 5.2MM **Privately Held**
WEB: www.roomserviceamenities.com
SIC: 5046 2844 5199 Hotel equipment & supplies; toilet preparations; advertising specialties

(G-6636)
AMERICAN SOFT SOLUTIONS CORP
704 Ginesi Dr Ste 26 (07751-1280)
PHONE..................................732 272-0052
Tariq Chaudhry, *President*
Yasmin Chaudhry, *Vice Pres*
EMP: 5
SALES (est): 240.2K **Privately Held**
SIC: 7372 Business oriented computer software

(G-6637)
AURORA MULTIMEDIA CORPORATION
205 Commercial Ct (07751-1070)
PHONE..................................732 591-5800
Paul E Harris, *CEO*
Michael Twerdak, *COO*
Nicholas Reiser, *Prdtn Mgr*
Len Edwards, *Purch Mgr*
Lawrence S Waldron, *CFO*
▲ EMP: 25
SQ FT: 11,000
SALES (est): 7.2MM **Privately Held**
WEB: www.auroramultimedia.com
SIC: 3669 Visual communication systems

(G-6638)
CENOGENICS CORPORATION (PA)
100 County Road 520 (07751-1270)
P.O. Box 308 (07751-0308)
PHONE..................................732 536-6457
Fax: 732 972-8527
Michael Katz, *President*
Nitza Hernandez, *Vice Pres*
EMP: 25
SQ FT: 3,000
SALES (est): 3.7MM **Privately Held**
SIC: 3841 2835 Surgical & medical instruments; in vitro & in vivo diagnostic substances

(G-6639)
CHROMA TRADING USA INC
Also Called: Chroma Inks USA
18 Guest Dr (07751-1431)
PHONE..................................732 956-4431
Shakher Puntambekar, *Manager*
EMP: 5
SALES (est): 634.2K **Privately Held**
SIC: 2893 Duplicating ink

(G-6640)
CITY MASTER BARBERS INC
12 Us Highway 9 Ste 4 (07751-1575)
PHONE..................................732 536-6400
Renat Nekhamiyev, *Principal*
EMP: 4 EST: 2008
SALES (est): 338.3K **Privately Held**
SIC: 2741 Directories: publishing & printing

(G-6641)
EMBROIDERY IN STITCHES INC
1020 Campus Dr (07751-1260)
PHONE..................................732 460-2660
Fax: 732 460-2662
Harry Harkavy, *President*
Debra Harkavy, *Principal*
EMP: 16
SQ FT: 4,000
SALES (est): 910K **Privately Held**
SIC: 2395 Embroidery & art needlework

(G-6642)
HY-TEK MATERIAL HANDLING INC
704 Ginesi Dr Ste 25 (07751-1280)
PHONE..................................732 490-6282
Thomas Mann, *President*
Sam Grooms, *Branch Mgr*
Scott Blum, *Officer*
EMP: 33

SALES (corp-wide): 81.4MM **Privately Held**
SIC: 5084 3535 Materials handling machinery; belt conveyor systems, general industrial use; bulk handling conveyor systems; overhead conveyor systems; robotic conveyors
PA: Hy-Tek Material Handling, Inc.
2222 Rickenbacker Pkwy W
Columbus OH 43217
614 497-2500

(G-6643)
IDA AUTOMOTIVE INC
600 Texas Rd (07751-4128)
PHONE..................................732 591-1245
Robert Ida, *President*
EMP: 4
SQ FT: 3,000
SALES (est): 550.1K **Privately Held**
SIC: 3714 5531 Motor vehicle parts & accessories; automotive & home supply stores

(G-6644)
INDAMPHARM INC
281 Route 79 N Ste 219 (07751-1157)
PHONE..................................732 970-0002
Radha Sayyaparaju, *CEO*
EMP: 10
SALES (est): 999.1K **Privately Held**
SIC: 2834 Pharmaceutical preparations

(G-6645)
INVITATION STUDIO
12 Hemingway Ct (07751-2017)
PHONE..................................732 740-5558
Kira Kogan, *Principal*
EMP: 4
SALES (est): 223K **Privately Held**
SIC: 2221 Paper broadwoven fabrics

(G-6646)
LABORATORY DIAGNOSTICS CO INC (HQ)
100 County Road 520 (07751-1270)
P.O. Box 160 (07751-0160)
PHONE..................................732 536-6300
Michael Katz, *President*
Nitza Hernandez, *Vice Pres*
EMP: 15
SALES (est): 2.3MM
SALES (corp-wide): 3.7MM **Privately Held**
WEB: www.cenogenics.com
SIC: 3841 2835 2295 Surgical & medical instruments; in vitro & in vivo diagnostic substances; coated fabrics, not rubberized
PA: Cenogenics Corporation
100 County Road 520
Morganville NJ 07751
732 536-6457

(G-6647)
LABORATORY DIAGNOSTICS CO INC
712 Ginesi Dr (07751-1206)
PHONE..................................732 972-2145
Michael Katz, *Manager*
EMP: 7
SALES (corp-wide): 3.7MM **Privately Held**
WEB: www.cenogenics.com
SIC: 3841 Surgical & medical instruments
HQ: Laboratory Diagnostics Co Inc
100 County Road 520
Morganville NJ 07751
732 536-6300

(G-6648)
MEDALCO METALS INC
281 Highway 79 N (07751-1157)
PHONE..................................732 591-0913
Laryy Dansky, *Branch Mgr*
EMP: 4
SALES (est): 782.2K
SALES (corp-wide): 4.6MM **Privately Held**
SIC: 3364 Nonferrous die-castings except aluminum
PA: Medalco Metals, Inc.
1 Corticelli St
Florence MA 01062
413 586-6010

(G-6649)
NEXAGEN NETWORKS INC (PA)
704 Ginesi Dr Ste 21 (07751-1249)
PHONE..................................732 598-1277
Rupal Parikh, *President*
Rajesh Parikh, *COO*
Carl Swenson, *Vice Pres*
EMP: 100
SALES (est): 15.6MM **Privately Held**
WEB: www.nexagen.com
SIC: 7372 Prepackaged software

(G-6650)
PAT BRY ADVERTISING SPC
Tennant Rd Rr 79 (07751)
P.O. Box 369 (07751-0369)
PHONE..................................732 591-0999
Gary Bernie, *President*
Joseph Burn, *Treasurer*
EMP: 4
SQ FT: 1,250
SALES: 300K **Privately Held**
SIC: 3993 Signs & advertising specialties

(G-6651)
PLATYPUS PRINT PRODUCTIONS LLC
253 State Route 79 N (07751-2000)
PHONE..................................732 772-1212
Jason Gerbsman,
Richard Trager,
EMP: 5
SQ FT: 2,000
SALES (est): 350K **Privately Held**
SIC: 2759 Catalogs: printing; circulars: printing

(G-6652)
POLARITY LLC
330 Mockingbird Ln (07751-4603)
PHONE..................................732 970-3855
Al Belfer, *Principal*
EMP: 4
SALES (est): 223.6K **Privately Held**
SIC: 3827 Polarizers

(G-6653)
TRESKY CORP
704 Ginesi Dr Ste 11 (07751-1278)
PHONE..................................732 536-8600
Thorlief Brandsberg, *CEO*
Alex Tresky, *President*
EMP: 4
SALES (est): 270K **Privately Held**
SIC: 3479 Bonderizing of metal or metal products

(G-6654)
TRILENIUM SALVAGE CO
147 Tennent Rd (07751-1131)
PHONE..................................732 462-2909
Fred Smith, *Owner*
EMP: 4
SALES (est): 519.4K **Privately Held**
SIC: 3531 Automobile wrecker hoists

(G-6655)
VYTRAN CORPORATION
1400 Campus Dr (07751-1283)
PHONE..................................732 972-2880
Fax: 732 972-4410
Eric Mies, *President*
Jeorge Jiarette, *Vice Pres*
Bernd Kaliske, *Prdtn Mgr*
Scott Bartolett, *Design Engr*
Kevin Lin, *Technician*
EMP: 45
SALES (est): 4.8MM **Privately Held**
SIC: 3661 Telephone & telegraph apparatus

(G-6656)
VYTRAN LLC
1400 Campus Dr (07751-1283)
PHONE..................................732 972-2880
Jean Michel Pelaprat, *CEO*
John Hanogofsky, *Vice Pres*
Jeorge Jiarette, *Vice Pres*
Larry Winderg, *Vice Pres*
EMP: 27

▲ = Import ▼=Export
◆ =Import/Export

SALES (est): 3.8MM
SALES (corp-wide): 211.7MM **Privately
Held**
WEB: www.vytran.com
SIC: 3357 3661 Fiber optic cable (insulated); switching equipment, telephone
PA: Thorlabs, Inc.
56 Sparta Ave
Newton NJ 07860
973 579-7227

(G-6657)
ZIXEL LTD
4 Pegasus Ct (07751-1188)
PHONE...................................732 972-3287
Zosim Ioffe, *President*
▲ EMP: 5
SQ FT: 750
SALES (est): 490K **Privately Held**
SIC: 3825 Test equipment for electronic &
electric measurement

Morris Plains
Morris County

(G-6658)
COTY US LLC
Also Called: Coty Research and Development
410 American Rd (07950-2461)
PHONE...................................973 490-8700
Francesca P Pitsker, *COO*
Ralph Macchio, *Vice Pres*
Alan Farer, *Vice Pres*
Michael A Knopf, *Research*
Brian Kolman, *Research*
EMP: 100 **Publicly Held**
SIC: 2844 Perfumes & colognes; cosmetic
preparations
HQ: Coty Us Llc
350 5th Ave
New York NY 10118

(G-6659)
DOUBLE CHECK
101 Gibraltar Dr Ste 1e (07950-1287)
PHONE...................................973 984-2229
Joe Cincotta, *CEO*
Sandy Brown, *Managing Dir*
Tim Ihde, *Principal*
Daniel Carlucci, *Director*
EMP: 6
SALES (est): 453.1K **Privately Held**
WEB: www.omnie.com
SIC: 7372 Application computer software

(G-6660)
DUCTS INC
8 Moraine Rd (07950-2711)
PHONE...................................973 267-8482
Nicholas Roccaforte, *President*
Arlene Roccaforte, *Treasurer*
EMP: 8
SQ FT: 8,000
SALES (est): 600K **Privately Held**
WEB: www.ducts.com
SIC: 3444 Ducts, sheet metal

(G-6661)
**ENCORE PHARMACEUTICAL
INC**
Also Called: Enspharma
49 Moraine Rd (07950-2721)
PHONE...................................973 267-9331
Bhanu Godhani, *President*
Rakash Methpara, *General Mgr*
EMP: 7
SALES (est): 721.1K **Privately Held**
SIC: 2834 Pharmaceutical preparations

(G-6662)
**HONEYWELL ASIA PACIFIC INC
(HQ)**
115 Tabor Rd (07950-2546)
PHONE...................................973 455-2000
John Tus, *President*
EMP: 19
SALES (est): 53.7MM
SALES (corp-wide): 40.5B **Publicly Held**
SIC: 3822 Auto controls regulating residntl
& coml environmt & applncs

PA: Honeywell International Inc.
115 Tabor Rd
Morris Plains NJ 07950
973 455-2000

(G-6663)
**HONEYWELL INTERNATIONAL
INC**
115 Tabor Rd (07950-2546)
PHONE...................................800 601-3099
Shariful Haque, *Purchasing*
John Sharkey, *Financial Analy*
Louis Vuoncino, *Branch Mgr*
Michael Dobson, *Programmer Anys*
David Rogers, *Analyst*
EMP: 130
SALES (corp-wide): 40.5B **Publicly Held**
WEB: www.honeywell.com
SIC: 3724 Aircraft engines & engine parts
PA: Honeywell International Inc.
115 Tabor Rd
Morris Plains NJ 07950
973 455-2000

(G-6664)
**HONEYWELL INTERNATIONAL
INC**
8 Waterloo Dr (07950-1438)
PHONE...................................973 285-5321
Michael Bonsignore, *Branch Mgr*
EMP: 48
SALES (corp-wide): 40.5B **Publicly Held**
WEB: www.honeywell.com
SIC: 3724 Aircraft engines & engine parts
PA: Honeywell International Inc.
115 Tabor Rd
Morris Plains NJ 07950
973 455-2000

(G-6665)
**HONEYWELL INTERNATIONAL
INC**
115 Tabor Rd (07950-2546)
PHONE...................................973 455-2000
Frank Medrano, *Technical Mgr*
Brett Daire, *Engineer*
Rick Ross, *Engineer*
Jonathan Farmer, *Software Engr*
Roger Reinholdt, *Network Enginr*
EMP: 97
SALES (corp-wide): 40.5B **Publicly Held**
SIC: 3724 Aircraft engines & engine parts
PA: Honeywell International Inc.
115 Tabor Rd
Morris Plains NJ 07950
973 455-2000

(G-6666)
**HONEYWELL INTERNATIONAL
INC (PA)**
115 Tabor Rd (07950-2546)
PHONE...................................973 455-2000
Fax: 973 455-6761
Darius Adamczyk, *Ch of Bd*
Vimal Kapur, *President*
Mark R James, *Senior VP*
Anne T Madden, *Senior VP*
Krishna Mikkilineni, *Senior VP*
◆ EMP: 1400
SALES: 40.5B **Publicly Held**
WEB: www.honeywell.com
SIC: 3724 3812 3585 2824 Aircraft engines & engine parts; turbines, aircraft
type; research & development on aircraft
engines & parts; aircraft control systems,
electronic; cabin environment indicators;
radar systems & equipment; aircraft flight
instruments; air conditioning equipment,
complete; heating equipment, complete;
humidifiers & dehumidifiers; nylon fibers;
polyester fibers; polyethylene resins;
motor vehicle parts & accessories; filters:
oil, fuel & air, motor vehicle; motor vehicle
brake systems & parts; PVC valves

(G-6667)
**HONEYWELL INTERNATIONAL
INC**
115 Tabor Rd (07950-2546)
PHONE...................................800 601-3099
Louis Vuoncino, *Branch Mgr*
EMP: 4
SALES (corp-wide): 40.5B **Publicly Held**
WEB: www.honeywell.com
SIC: 3724 Aircraft engines & engine parts

PA: Honeywell International Inc.
115 Tabor Rd
Morris Plains NJ 07950
973 455-2000

(G-6668)
**HONEYWELL INTERNATIONAL
INC**
115 Tabor Rd (07950-2546)
PHONE...................................973 455-2000
EMP: 135
SALES (corp-wide): 40.5B **Publicly Held**
WEB: www.honeywell.com
SIC: 2999 5169 2819 Waxes, petroleum:
not produced in petroleum refineries;
waxes, except petroleum; industrial inorganic chemicals
PA: Honeywell International Inc.
115 Tabor Rd
Morris Plains NJ 07950
973 455-2000

(G-6669)
HOUSES MAGAZINE INC
173 Morris St (07950)
PHONE...................................973 605-1877
Fax: 973 605-1883
Gene Petraglia, *President*
Peter Best, *Vice Pres*
EMP: 18
SALES (est): 1.4MM **Privately Held**
SIC: 2721 Periodicals: publishing only

(G-6670)
IBC PHARMACEUTICALS INC
300 The American Rd (07950-2460)
PHONE...................................973 540-9595
Cynthia Sullivan, *President*
Ken Chang, *Vice Pres*
EMP: 10
SALES (est): 895.3K
SALES (corp-wide): 3MM **Publicly Held**
WEB: www.immunomedics.com
SIC: 2834 Pharmaceutical preparations
PA: Immunomedics, Inc.
300 The American Rd
Morris Plains NJ 07950
973 605-8200

(G-6671)
IMMUNOMEDICS INC (PA)
300 The American Rd (07950-2460)
PHONE...................................973 605-8200
Behzad Aghazadeh, *Ch of Bd*
Michael Garone, *VP Finance*
Brendan Delaney, *Ch Credit Ofcr*
Brian Markison, *Director*
Scott Canute, *Bd of Directors*
▲ EMP: 138
SQ FT: 85,000
SALES: 3MM **Publicly Held**
WEB: www.immunomedics.com
SIC: 2835 2834 In vitro & in vivo diagnostic substances; in vitro diagnostics; in vivo
diagnostics; pharmaceutical preparations

(G-6672)
J&E BUSINESS SERVICES LLC
Also Called: Pinnacle Grphic Communications
39 E Hanover Ave Ste C7 (07950-2456)
PHONE...................................973 984-8444
Jeffrey P Green,
EMP: 6
SALES (est): 507.2K **Privately Held**
SIC: 7389 3993 2759 7334 Packaging &
labeling services; signs & advertising specialties; commercial printing; photocopying & duplicating services; advertising
specialties

(G-6673)
JOHNSON & JOHNSON
201 Tabor Rd (07950-2614)
PHONE...................................908 874-1000
Cheryl Miller, *Branch Mgr*
EMP: 147

SALES (corp-wide): 76.4B **Publicly Held**
WEB: www.jnj.com
SIC: 3842 3841 2834 2844 Surgical appliances & supplies; dressings, surgical;
ligatures, medical; sutures, absorbable &
non-absorbable; surgical & medical instruments; ophthalmic instruments & apparatus; diagnostic apparatus, medical;
surgical instruments & apparatus; pharmaceutical preparations; drugs acting on
the central nervous system & sense organs; dermatologicals; drugs affecting
parasitic & infective diseases; toilet
preparations; oral preparations; toilet
preparations; powder: baby, face, talcum
or toilet; feminine hygiene paper products;
napkins, sanitary: made from purchased
paper; panty liners: made from purchased
paper; infant & baby paper products
PA: Johnson & Johnson
1 Johnson And Johnson Plz
New Brunswick NJ 08933
732 524-0400

(G-6674)
**NOVARTIS PHARMACEUTICALS
CORP**
220 E Hanover Ave (07950-2445)
PHONE...................................973 538-1296
Andrew S Sandler, *Vice Pres*
Jeff Boyd, *Vice Pres*
EMP: 15
SALES (corp-wide): 49.1B **Privately Held**
SIC: 2834 Pharmaceutical preparations
HQ: Novartis Pharmaceuticals Corporation
1 Health Plz
East Hanover NJ 07936
862 778-8300

(G-6675)
NPT PUBLISHING GROUP INC
Also Called: Non Profit Times
201 Littleton Rd Ste 2 (07950-2939)
PHONE...................................973 401-0202
Fax: 973 401-0404
John McIlquham, *President*
Kevin M Landers, *Publisher*
Ted Olczak, *Publisher*
Ivan Goodinho, *Accounts Mgr*
Lisa Pinto, *Webmaster*
EMP: 15
SQ FT: 5,700
SALES (est): 2.5MM **Privately Held**
WEB: www.nptimes.com
SIC: 2721 8742 Magazines: publishing
only, not printed on site; management
consulting services

(G-6676)
PACIFIC MICROTRONICS INC
8 Laurel Ln (07950-3216)
PHONE...................................973 993-8665
Bob Grossman, *Principal*
EMP: 8
SALES (est): 340K **Privately Held**
SIC: 3721 Aircraft

(G-6677)
PALSGAARD INCORPORATED
101 Gibraltar Dr Ste 2b (07950-1287)
PHONE...................................973 998-7951
Rosa Regalado, *General Mgr*
▲ EMP: 19
SALES (est): 2.5MM
SALES (corp-wide): 200.2MM **Privately
Held**
SIC: 2099 5145 Food preparations; snack
foods
HQ: Palsgaard A/S
Palsgaardvej 10
Juelsminde 7130
768 276-82

(G-6678)
PFIZER INC
182 Tabor Rd (07950)
PHONE...................................973 993-0977
Michael Krupar, *Research*
Joe Perez, *Sales Staff*
Dave Davis, *Manager*
Lorraine Brong, *Manager*
Veronica Casier, *Manager*
EMP: 146

SALES (corp-wide): 52.5B **Publicly Held**
WEB: www.pfizer.com
SIC: 2834 Pharmaceutical preparations; veterinary pharmaceutical preparations
PA: Pfizer Inc.
235 E 42nd St
New York NY 10017
212 733-2323

(G-6679)
Q&Q PHARMA RESEARCH COMPANY
19 Meadow Bluff Rd (07950-1952)
PHONE................973 267-0160
Rui Yu, *Principal*
EMP: 7
SALES (est): 790.7K **Privately Held**
SIC: 2834 Pharmaceutical preparations

(G-6680)
TEMPTIME CORPORATION (HQ)
116 The American Rd (07950-2443)
PHONE................973 984-6000
Fax: 973 984-2186
Renaat Van Den Hooffm, *CEO*
Emily Moore, *President*
Nicholos Puro, *President*
Curt Selquist, *Chairman*
Jeff Gutkind, *Business Mgr*
▲ EMP: 74
SQ FT: 55,000
SALES (est): 14.7MM
SALES (corp-wide): 478.8MM **Privately Held**
WEB: www.heatmarker.com
SIC: 3826 Instruments measuring thermal properties
PA: Water Street Healthcare Partners Llc
444 W Lake St Ste 1800
Chicago IL 60606
312 506-2900

(G-6681)
WALPOLE WOODWORKERS INC
540 Tabor Rd (07950-2726)
PHONE................973 539-3555
Fax: 973 539-2796
Ben Lowell, *Branch Mgr*
EMP: 25
SALES (corp-wide): 85.8MM **Privately Held**
WEB: www.walpolewoodworkers.com
SIC: 2499 5211 5712 2452 Fencing, wood; fencing; outdoor & garden furniture; prefabricated wood buildings; prefabricated metal buildings; wood household furniture
PA: Walpole Woodworkers, Inc.
767 East St
Walpole MA 02081
508 668-2800

(G-6682)
ZION INDUSTRIES INC
39 E Hanover Ave Ste G (07950-2456)
P.O. Box 362 (07950-0362)
PHONE................973 998-0162
Gilbert Carpete, *President*
EMP: 20
SALES (est): 720.7K **Privately Held**
SIC: 1389 8742 Construction, repair & dismantling services; maintenance management consultant

Morristown
Morris County

(G-6683)
ACTAVIS LLC
360 Mount Kemble Ave # 3 (07960-6662)
PHONE................800 272-5525
Fax: 973 355-8301
Diane Miranda, *VP Opers*
Rich Devivo, *Research*
Ralph Manning, *Manager*
EMP: 150 **Privately Held**
WEB: www.watsonpharm.com
SIC: 2834 Pharmaceutical preparations
HQ: Actavis Llc
400 Interpace Pkwy
Parsippany NJ 07054

(G-6684)
ALLERGAN INC
16 Airport Rd (07960-4624)
PHONE................862 261-7000
George Hrichak II, *Principal*
EMP: 5 **Privately Held**
SIC: 2834 Drugs acting on the central nervous system & sense organs
HQ: Allergan, Inc.
5 Giralda Farms
Madison NJ 07940
862 261-7000

(G-6685)
ALLIED-SIGNAL CHINA LTD
101 Columbia Rd (07960-4640)
PHONE................973 455-2000
Fax: 973 455-3881
Lawrence Bossidy, *Principal*
EMP: 32
SALES (est): 3.9MM
SALES (corp-wide): 40.5B **Publicly Held**
WEB: www.honeywell.com
SIC: 3724 3714 3812 2824 Aircraft engines & engine parts; motor vehicle parts & accessories; search & navigation equipment; organic fibers, noncellulosic; plastics materials & resins
PA: Honeywell International Inc.
115 Tabor Rd
Morris Plains NJ 07950
973 455-2000

(G-6686)
ALPHAGRAPHICS PRINTSHOPS OF TH
60 Speedwell Ave (07960-6830)
PHONE................973 984-0066
Fax: 973 984-9755
Aaron Grohs, *President*
Brian Harrigan, *Chairman*
Tommy E Auger, *CFO*
EMP: 6
SQ FT: 8,000
SALES: 700K **Privately Held**
SIC: 2752 2759 Commercial printing, offset; commercial printing

(G-6687)
APPLETON GRP LLC
55 Madison Ave (07960-7337)
PHONE................973 285-3261
David Appleton, *Branch Mgr*
EMP: 108
SALES (corp-wide): 15.2B **Publicly Held**
SIC: 3644 Electric conduits & fittings
HQ: Appleton Grp Llc
9377 W Higgins Rd
Rosemont IL 60018
847 268-6000

(G-6688)
ASTRAZENECA PHARMACEUTICALS LP
Fl 2 Flr (07960)
PHONE................973 975-0324
Brian Handlon, *Research*
Kevin Moy, *Research*
Ray Phan, *Engineer*
Konstantine Lachaouri, *Auditor*
Chadwick Orevillo, *Branch Mgr*
EMP: 10
SALES (corp-wide): 22.4B **Privately Held**
SIC: 2834 Druggists' preparations (pharmaceuticals)
HQ: Astrazeneca Pharmaceuticals Lp
1 Medimmune Way
Gaithersburg MD 20878

(G-6689)
AVAYA CALA INC
350 Mount Kemble Ave (07960-6646)
PHONE................866 462-8292
EMP: 8 EST: 2000
SALES (est): 252.1K **Publicly Held**
SIC: 3661 Telephone & telegraph apparatus
HQ: Sierra Communication International Llc
350 Mount Kemble Ave
Morristown NJ 07960
866 462-8292

(G-6690)
AVAYA WORLD SERVICES INC
350 Mount Kemble Ave (07960-6646)
PHONE................908 953-6000
Adele C Freeman, *Officer*
Nidal Abou-Itaif,
◆ EMP: 20
SALES (est): 1.7MM **Publicly Held**
SIC: 3661 7372 Telephone & telegraph apparatus; prepackaged software
HQ: Avaya Inc.
4655 Great America Pkwy
Santa Clara CA 95054
908 953-6000

(G-6691)
AVIGDOR LTD LIABILITY COMPANY
Also Called: Avigdor Jewelry
25 Tikvah Way (07960-3607)
PHONE................973 898-4770
Ezra Solomon, *CEO*
EMP: 23 EST: 2012
SQ FT: 2,000
SALES (est): 1.7MM **Privately Held**
SIC: 3911 Jewelry, precious metal

(G-6692)
BARRETT INDUSTRIES CORPORATION (DH)
73 Headquarters Plz (07960-3964)
PHONE................973 533-1001
Georges Ausseil, *President*
Zach Green, *Vice Pres*
Fred Shelton, *CFO*
Michael Macrina, *Controller*
Xiong Zeng, *Accountant*
EMP: 20
SALES (est): 369.1MM
SALES (corp-wide): 95.5MM **Privately Held**
SIC: 1611 2951 4213 1799 Highway & street paving contractor; road materials, bituminous (not from refineries); trucking, except local; building site preparation; excavation work
HQ: Colas Inc.
73 Headquarters Plz 10t
Morristown NJ 07960
973 290-9082

(G-6693)
BAYER CONSUMER CARE INC
36 Columbia Rd (07960-4526)
PHONE................973 267-6198
Fax: 973 254-4854
Adrienne M Pavan, *Principal*
Grant Macdougall, *Business Mgr*
Sarah Heineman, *Counsel*
Jeremy R Jessen, *Counsel*
Kimberly Harris, *Project Mgr*
EMP: 535
SALES (est): 47MM **Privately Held**
SIC: 2834 Pharmaceutical preparations

(G-6694)
BAYER HEALTHCARE LLC
Qa Release Group
36 Columbia Rd (07960-4526)
PHONE................973 254-5000
Fax: 973 254-4859
Thomas Lupo, *Principal*
Ying Ng, *QC Mgr*
Todd M Stich, *Human Resources*
Alois Bachmaier, *Sales Staff*
Kent Taylor, *Sales Staff*
EMP: 10
SALES (corp-wide): 41.2B **Privately Held**
SIC: 2834 Pharmaceutical preparations
HQ: Bayer Healthcare Llc
100 Bayer Blvd
Whippany NJ 07981
862 404-3000

(G-6695)
BERTOT INDUSTRIES INC
23 Malcolm St Ste 1 (07960-4298)
PHONE................973 267-0006
Fax: 973 267-1922
Harold Jelonnek, *President*
Curtis Jelonnek, *Vice Pres*
Frank Gaden, *Admin Sec*
EMP: 9 EST: 1973
SQ FT: 10,000

SALES: 750K **Privately Held**
SIC: 3599 Machine shop, jobbing & repair

(G-6696)
CAPSUGEL INC (DH)
Also Called: Capsugel US
412 Mount Kemble Ave 200c (07960-6674)
PHONE................862 242-1700
Guido Driesen, *CEO*
Fabrice Quaghebeur, *COO*
Keith Hutchison, *Vice Pres*
George Manteghi, *Senior Buyer*
Christen Davis, *QC Mgr*
▲ EMP: 70
SALES (est): 668MM **Privately Held**
WEB: www.capsugel.com
SIC: 2834 Antibiotics, packaged

(G-6697)
CAPSUGEL HOLDINGS US INC (DH)
412 Mount Kemble Ave 200c (07960-6666)
PHONE................862 242-1700
Guido Driesen, *CEO*
EMP: 8
SALES (est): 695MM **Privately Held**
SIC: 6799 2834 Investors; pharmaceutical preparations

(G-6698)
CAPSUGEL US LLC
412 Mount Kemble Ave (07960-6666)
PHONE................862 242-1700
Guido Driesen,
EMP: 350
SALES (est): 67.6K **Privately Held**
SIC: 2834 Antibiotics, packaged
HQ: Capsugel Holdings Us, Inc.
412 Mount Kemble Ave 200c
Morristown NJ 07960

(G-6699)
CITY DIECUTTING INC
1 Cory Rd Ste C (07960-3112)
PHONE................973 270-0370
Eric Devos, *President*
EMP: 13
SALES (est): 2.1MM **Privately Held**
SIC: 3544 Special dies & tools

(G-6700)
COLAS INC (DH)
73 Headquarters Plz 10t (07960-3964)
PHONE................973 290-9082
Fax: 973 290-9088
Louis R Gabanna, *Ch of Bd*
Jean Vidal, *COO*
James E Weeks, *Senior VP*
Gordon R Crawley, *Vice Pres*
Anthony L Martino II, *Vice Pres*
▲ EMP: 1
SQ FT: 12,500
SALES (est): 1.5B
SALES (corp-wide): 95.5MM **Privately Held**
SIC: 1611 1622 2951 Highway & street paving contractor; bridge construction; road materials, bituminous (not from refineries)
HQ: Colas Canada Inc
181 University Ave Suite 2011
Toronto ON M5H 3
416 717-7912

(G-6701)
CORENTEC AMERICA INC
60 Washington St Ste 202 (07960-6844)
PHONE................949 379-6227
Sung Taek Hong, *CEO*
EMP: 9
SALES (est): 991.3K **Privately Held**
SIC: 3845 Ultrasonic scanning devices, medical

(G-6702)
COUNTY CONCRETE CORPORATION
Ridgedale Ave (07960)
P.O. Box F, Kenvil (07847-1005)
PHONE................973 538-3113
Fax: 973 538-3281
Bill Space, *Manager*
EMP: 15

SALES (corp-wide): 30.2MM **Privately Held**
WEB: www.countyconcretenj.com
SIC: **3273** 1442 5039 5032 Ready-mixed concrete; construction sand & gravel; septic tanks; stone, crushed or broken
PA: County Concrete Corporation
50 Railroad Ave
Kenvil NJ 07847
973 744-2188

(G-6703)
CYPRESS PHARMACEUTICALS INC
10 N Park Pl Ste 201 (07960-7101)
P.O. Box 399, Madison MS (39130-0399)
PHONE..........................601 856-4393
Max Draughn, *President*
Jason Sanderson, *CFO*
EMP: 150
SQ FT: 60,000
SALES (est): 16.9MM
SALES (corp-wide): 146MM **Publicly Held**
WEB: www.cypressrx.com
SIC: **2834** Pharmaceutical preparations
PA: Pernix Therapeutics Holdings, Inc.
10 N Park Pl Ste 201
Morristown NJ 07960
800 793-2145

(G-6704)
DATASCAN GRAPHICS INC
55 Madison Ave Ste 400 (07960-7397)
PHONE..........................973 543-4803
Roy House, *President*
▲ EMP: 25
SQ FT: 8,500
SALES (est): 4.1MM **Privately Held**
SIC: **2752** Promotional printing, lithographic

(G-6705)
DAYBROOK HOLDINGS INC (PA)
161 Madison Ave Ste 200 (07960-7329)
P.O. Box 1931 (07962-1931)
PHONE..........................973 538-6766
Gregory Holt, *President*
Steven Morganstern, *CFO*
Thomas Kenny, *Treasurer*
Joe Malin, *Admin Sec*
Leonard Guber, *Asst Sec*
EMP: 5
SQ FT: 2,700
SALES (est): 52.9MM **Privately Held**
SIC: **2077** Menhaden oil; fish meal, except as animal feed

(G-6706)
DUSENBERY ENGINEERING CO INC
309 E Hanover Ave (07960-4077)
P.O. Box 1001 (07962-1001)
PHONE..........................973 539-2200
Fax: 973 538-5186
Phillip N Williams, *President*
William Janus, *Vice Pres*
EMP: 9
SQ FT: 10,000
SALES: 2MM **Privately Held**
SIC: **3443** Process vessels, industrial: metal plate

(G-6707)
ENJOU CHOCOLAT MORRISTOWN INC
8 Dehart St Ste 1 (07960-8205)
PHONE..........................973 993-9090
Fax: 973 993-8299
Wendy Jacobs Tafett, *President*
EMP: 6
SQ FT: 3,000
SALES (est): 706.1K **Privately Held**
SIC: **2064** 5441 5812 Chocolate candy, except solid chocolate; candy; ice cream stands or dairy bars

(G-6708)
EPIC HOLDING INC
Also Called: Epic Industries
15 Footes Ln (07960-6304)
PHONE..........................732 249-6867
Ted Bustany, *President*
Sam Levine, *Vice Pres*
EMP: 40

SQ FT: 60,000
SALES (est): 9.8MM **Privately Held**
WEB: www.epicindustries.com
SIC: **2841** 2869 2842 Detergents, synthetic organic or inorganic alkaline; industrial organic chemicals; floor waxes

(G-6709)
GARDEN STATE ORTHOPEDIC CENTER
Also Called: Garden State Alnce Orthopaedic
95 Mount Kemble Ave (07960-5155)
PHONE..........................973 538-4948
Fax: 973 605-8481
Louis J Haberman, *Owner*
EMP: 5
SALES (est): 561.6K
SALES (corp-wide): 989.9K **Privately Held**
SIC: **3842** 5999 Limbs, artificial; orthopedic appliances; orthopedic & prosthesis applications
PA: Garden State Orthopedic Center Inc
9 Post Rd Ste Op1
Oakland NJ 07436
201 337-5566

(G-6710)
GLASSWORKS STUDIO INC
151 South St Ste B103 (07960-9576)
PHONE..........................973 656-0800
Fax: 973 656-0881
Stacey Schlosser, *President*
EMP: 9
SQ FT: 3,500
SALES (est): 125K **Privately Held**
SIC: **3229** Glassware, art or decorative

(G-6711)
GRIFFEN LLC
44 Prospect St Apt 531 (07960-7816)
PHONE..........................973 723-5344
EMP: 5 EST: 2011
SQ FT: 1,500
SALES: 1.8MM **Privately Held**
SIC: **3089** Mfg Plastic Products

(G-6712)
HARRIS DRIVER CO (PA)
200 Madison Ave Ste 2 (07960-6167)
PHONE..........................973 267-8100
Frank L Driver IV, *Ch of Bd*
Lavinia Z Emery, *Corp Secy*
EMP: 4 EST: 1899
SALES (est): 5.3MM **Privately Held**
SIC: **3357** Nonferrous wiredrawing & insulating

(G-6713)
HEALTH SCIENCE FUNDING LLC
55 Madison Ave (07960-7337)
PHONE..........................973 984-6159
EMP: 11 EST: 2004
SQ FT: 1,051
SALES (est): 890K **Privately Held**
SIC: **2834** Mfg Pharmaceutical Preparations

(G-6714)
HONEYWELL INTERNATIONAL INC
20 Airport Rd (07960-4624)
PHONE..........................973 455-6633
Jerry Norton, *Director*
EMP: 30
SALES (corp-wide): 40.5B **Publicly Held**
WEB: www.honeywell.com
SIC: **3724** Aircraft engines & engine parts
PA: Honeywell International Inc.
115 Tabor Rd
Morris Plains NJ 07950
973 455-2000

(G-6715)
HONEYWELL INTERNATIONAL INC
Columbia Tpke (07962)
PHONE..........................973 455-2000
EMP: 214
SALES (corp-wide): 40.5B **Publicly Held**
WEB: www.honeywell.com
SIC: **3714** 3812 Motor vehicle parts & accessories; aircraft/aerospace flight instruments & guidance systems

PA: Honeywell International Inc.
115 Tabor Rd
Morris Plains NJ 07950
973 455-2000

(G-6716)
HONEYWELL SPAIN HOLDINGS LLC (HQ)
101 Columbia Rd (07960-4640)
PHONE..........................973 455-2000
David M Cote,
EMP: 5
SALES (est): 771.8K
SALES (corp-wide): 40.5B **Publicly Held**
SIC: **3724** Aircraft engines & engine parts
PA: Honeywell International Inc.
115 Tabor Rd
Morris Plains NJ 07950
973 455-2000

(G-6717)
HONEYWELL SPECLTY WAX & ADDITV (HQ)
101 Columbia Rd (07960-4640)
PHONE..........................973 455-2000
David Cote, *CEO*
John Gottshall, *President*
Brad Grantham, *Software Dev*
George Paz, *Director*
▼ EMP: 14
SALES (est): 123.7MM
SALES (corp-wide): 40.5B **Publicly Held**
WEB: www.honeywellspecialtymaterials.com
SIC: **2999** 5169 Waxes, petroleum: not produced in petroleum refineries; waxes, except petroleum
PA: Honeywell International Inc.
115 Tabor Rd
Morris Plains NJ 07950
973 455-2000

(G-6718)
ISDIN CORP
36 Cattano Ave (07960-9602)
PHONE..........................862 242-8129
Juan Emilio Naya Ariste, *CEO*
Robert Durso, *Principal*
EMP: 45
SALES (est): 6.2MM **Privately Held**
SIC: **2834** Chlorination tablets & kits (water purification)

(G-6719)
KAHLE AUTOMATION
89 Headquarters Plz S (07960-6834)
PHONE..........................973 993-1850
EMP: 4
SALES (est): 128.3K
SALES (corp-wide): 21.3MM **Privately Held**
SIC: **3559** Pharmaceutical machinery
PA: Kahle Automation Srl
Viale Europa Unita 57
Caravaggio BG 24043
036 335-5511

(G-6720)
LA PACE IMPORTS INC
3 Ascot Ln (07960-3202)
P.O. Box 337, Mendham (07945-0337)
PHONE..........................973 895-5420
Fax: 973 895-8824
Peter Carolan, *President*
Elena Carolan, *Vice Pres*
▲ EMP: 10 EST: 1974
SQ FT: 5,000
SALES: 8MM **Privately Held**
WEB: www.pasta.com
SIC: **5149** 2099 Pasta & rice; crackers, cookies & bakery products; bakery products; cookies; pasta, uncooked: packaged with other ingredients

(G-6721)
LAUTUS PHRMCEUTICALS LTD LBLTY
Also Called: Glyderm
7 Kitchell Rd (07960-6547)
PHONE..........................908 273-2777
Steven Bosacki,
EMP: 5
SALES: 900K **Privately Held**
SIC: **2834** Pharmaceutical preparations

(G-6722)
LEVY INNOVATION
3 Brigade Hill Rd (07960-4920)
PHONE..........................908 303-4492
Mark Levy, *Principal*
EMP: 4
SALES (est): 172K **Privately Held**
SIC: **2711** Newspapers, publishing & printing

(G-6723)
LIGHTFOX INC
67 E Park Pl Ste 750 (07960-7103)
PHONE..........................973 209-9112
Tony Carrella, *CEO*
EMP: 20
SALES (est): 1MM **Privately Held**
SIC: **3648** Lighting equipment

(G-6724)
M J POWERS & CO PUBLISHERS
65 Madison Ave Ste 220 (07960-7307)
PHONE..........................973 898-1200
Fax: 973 898-1201
Michael J Powers, *President*
EMP: 4
SALES (est): 321.3K **Privately Held**
WEB: www.alertpubs.com
SIC: **2741** Business service newsletters: publishing & printing

(G-6725)
MAJESCO (HQ)
412 Mount Kemble Ave 110c (07960-6675)
PHONE..........................973 461-5200
Arun K Maheshwari, *Ch of Bd*
Ketan Mehta, *President*
Edward Ossie, *COO*
Prateek Kumar, *Exec VP*
Ganesh Pai, *Exec VP*
EMP: 7
SQ FT: 31,030
SALES: 122.9MM **Publicly Held**
WEB: www.majesco.com
SIC: **7372** 7371 Prepackaged software; computer software development

(G-6726)
MENNEN COMPANY (HQ)
191 E Hanover Ave (07960-3100)
PHONE..........................973 630-1500
William S Shanahan, *President*
Andrew Hendry, *Vice Pres*
Stephanie Bereday, *Project Engr*
Brian J Heidtke, *Treasurer*
▲ EMP: 403 EST: 1878
SQ FT: 570,000
SALES (est): 27.5MM
SALES (corp-wide): 15.4B **Publicly Held**
SIC: **2844** 2842 Toilet preparations; shampoos, rinses, conditioners: hair; lotions, shaving; deodorants, personal; deodorants, nonpersonal
PA: Colgate-Palmolive Company
300 Park Ave Fl 3
New York NY 10022
212 310-2000

(G-6727)
MFV INTERNATIONAL CORPORATION
89 Headquarters Plz (07960-6834)
PHONE..........................973 993-1687
Yoshiyuki Takahashi, *CEO*
Yoshifumi Tokuhara, *Chairman*
Keika Takahashi, *Corp Secy*
▲ EMP: 3
SQ FT: 280
SALES (est): 1.2MM
SALES (corp-wide): 28.6MM **Privately Held**
SIC: **3089** 3069 3999 Plastic containers, except foam; bags, rubber or rubberized fabric; atomizers; toiletry
PA: Mfv Co.,Ltd.
15-8, Kashitahonmachi
Higashi-Osaka OSK 577-0
667 286-080

(G-6728)
MORRIS COUNTY IMAGING
310 Madison Ave Ste 110 (07960-6967)
PHONE..........................973 532-7900
Mary Ann Gomez, *Principal*

EMP: 5
SALES (est): 414.2K **Privately Held**
SIC: 3845 CAT scanner (Computerized Axial Tomography) apparatus

(G-6729)
MORRISTOWN CYCLE
103 Washington St (07960-8623)
PHONE................................973 540-1244
David Shaw, *Owner*
EMP: 4 **EST:** 1971
SQ FT: 3,000
SALES (est): 440K **Privately Held**
SIC: 5571 7699 3751 Motorcycle parts & accessories; motorcycle repair service; motorcycles & related parts

(G-6730)
NEW JERSEY MONTHLY LLC
55 S Park Pl (07960-3924)
PHONE................................973 539-8230
Fax: 973 538-2953
Kate Tomlinson, *Publisher*
Susan Brierly, *Editor*
Carla Gouraige, *Natl Sales Mgr*
Danielle Cortina, *Accounts Exec*
Ann M Kramer, *Marketing Staff*
EMP: 40
SALES (est): 2.9MM **Privately Held**
SIC: 2721 Magazines: publishing & printing

(G-6731)
OMNIACTIVE HLTH TCHNLOGIES INC (HQ)
67 E Park Pl Ste 500 (07960-7138)
PHONE................................866 588-3629
Hiren Doshi, *President*
Abhijit Bhattacharya, *President*
Chaitanya Desai, *COO*
Janice Rodriguez, *Opers Mgr*
Ashoke Roy, *CFO*
▲ **EMP:** 20
SALES (est): 2.4MM **Privately Held**
SIC: 2834 Vitamin, nutrient & hematinic preparations for human use

(G-6732)
PARADISE
1098 Mount Kemble Ave # 2 (07960-8004)
PHONE................................973 425-0505
Paul Haley, *Principal*
EMP: 4
SALES (est): 140K **Privately Held**
SIC: 2389 5137 5621 Men's miscellaneous accessories; women's & children's outerwear; women's specialty clothing stores

(G-6733)
PERNIX THERAPEUTICS LLC
10 N Park Pl Ste 201 (07960-7101)
P.O. Box 40, Gonzales LA (70707-0040)
PHONE................................800 793-2145
Cooper Collins, *President*
EMP: 45
SQ FT: 4,000
SALES (est): 7.8MM
SALES (corp-wide): 146MM **Publicly Held**
WEB: www.zyberrx.com
SIC: 2834 5122 Pharmaceutical preparations; pharmaceuticals
PA: Pernix Therapeutics Holdings, Inc.
10 N Park Pl Ste 201
Morristown NJ 07960
800 793-2145

(G-6734)
PERNIX THRPEUTICS HOLDINGS INC (PA)
10 N Park Pl Ste 201 (07960-7101)
PHONE................................800 793-2145
John A Sedor, *Ch of Bd*
Angus W Smith, *CFO*
Kenneth Pina,
Glenn Whaley,
EMP: 77 **EST:** 1996
SQ FT: 15,990
SALES: 146MM **Publicly Held**
WEB: www.golftrust.com
SIC: 2834 Pharmaceutical preparations

(G-6735)
PICA PRINTINGS INC
Also Called: Digital Printed Communications
103 Ridgedale Ave Ste 4 (07960-4290)
PHONE................................973 540-0420
Thomas Malphrus, *President*
EMP: 4
SQ FT: 1,400
SALES: 475K **Privately Held**
SIC: 2752 Commercial printing, lithographic

(G-6736)
PLUS PACKAGING INC
10 Mount Pleasant Rd (07960-3317)
P.O. Box 12, Madison (07940-0012)
PHONE................................973 538-2216
Lee Dornfeld, *President*
◆ **EMP:** 6
SQ FT: 5,000
SALES (est): 1.1MM **Privately Held**
WEB: www.pluspackaging.com
SIC: 5199 2673 2672 Packaging materials; plastic bags: made from purchased materials; adhesive papers, labels or tapes: from purchased material

(G-6737)
PORTASEAL LLC
1 John St (07960-4237)
P.O. Box B, Convent Station (07961-0160)
PHONE................................973 539-0100
Fax: 973 539-4101
Stanley Garbowy, *Principal*
Stanley Grabowy, *Mng Member*
EMP: 9 **EST:** 1959
SQ FT: 8,500
SALES (est): 1.1MM **Privately Held**
WEB: www.portaseal.com
SIC: 1799 5211 3442 Weather stripping; lumber & other building materials; garage doors, overhead: metal

(G-6738)
PTC INC
89 Headquarters Plz (07960-6834)
PHONE................................973 631-6195
EMP: 19
SALES (corp-wide): 1.1B **Publicly Held**
WEB: www.ptc.com
SIC: 7372 Prepackaged software
PA: Ptc Inc.
140 Kendrick St
Needham MA 02494
781 370-5000

(G-6739)
RESTORTIONS BY PETER SCHICHTEL
10 New St (07960-4049)
PHONE................................973 605-8818
Peter Schichtel, *Partner*
EMP: 9
SALES (est): 366.4K **Privately Held**
SIC: 7641 2499 1751 Antique furniture repair & restoration; decorative wood & woodwork; cabinet & finish carpentry

(G-6740)
SCHINDLER ELEVATOR CORPORATION (DH)
20 Whippany Rd (07960-4539)
P.O. Box 1935 (07962-1935)
PHONE................................973 397-6500
Fax: 973 397-6485
Greg Ergenbright, *President*
John Kenner, *President*
John Albrecht, *General Mgr*
Mark Bernhard, *General Mgr*
John Dull, *General Mgr*
◆ **EMP:** 325
SQ FT: 162,500
SALES (est): 1.2B
SALES (corp-wide): 10.3B **Privately Held**
WEB: www.us.schindler.com
SIC: 3534 7699 1796 Elevators & equipment; elevators: inspection, service & repair; miscellaneous building item repair services; elevator installation & conversion
HQ: Schindler Enterprises Inc.
20 Whippany Rd
Morristown NJ 07960
973 397-6500

(G-6741)
SCHINDLER ENTERPRISES INC (HQ)
20 Whippany Rd (07960-4539)
PHONE................................973 397-6500
David J Bauhs, *President*
John R Impellizeeri, *Vice Pres*
Jujudhan Jena, *Treasurer*
Jeff Degier, *Technology*
Jacques G Lovenbach, *Admin Sec*
◆ **EMP:** 10
SQ FT: 2,000
SALES (est): 1.2B
SALES (corp-wide): 10.3B **Privately Held**
SIC: 3534 7699 1796 Elevators & moving stairways; elevators: inspection, service & repair; elevator installation & conversion
PA: Schindler Holding Ag
Seestrasse 55
Hergiswil NW 6052
848 821-821

(G-6742)
SIERRA COMMUNICATION INTL LLC (DH)
350 Mount Kemble Ave (07960-6646)
PHONE................................866 462-8292
Eric S Koza,
EMP: 5
SALES (est): 777.1K **Publicly Held**
SIC: 3661 7372 Telephone & telegraph apparatus; telephones & telephone apparatus; telephone dialing devices, automatic; prepackaged software
HQ: Avaya Inc.
4655 Great America Pkwy
Santa Clara CA 95054
908 953-6000

(G-6743)
SPEEDY SIGN-A-RAMA
166 Ridgedale Ave Ste 4 (07960-4085)
PHONE................................973 605-8313
Fax: 973 605-8306
David Fan, *President*
EMP: 4
SQ FT: 2,500
SALES: 950K **Privately Held**
SIC: 3993 1799 Signs & advertising specialties; sign installation & maintenance

(G-6744)
TECHNOLOGY CORP AMERICA INC
350 Mount Kemble Ave (07960-6646)
PHONE................................866 462-8292
EMP: 4 **EST:** 1995
SALES (est): 190.8K **Publicly Held**
SIC: 3661 Telephones & telephone apparatus
HQ: Sierra Communication International Llc
350 Mount Kemble Ave
Morristown NJ 07960
866 462-8292

(G-6745)
TRANSMAR GROUP LLC
200 South St Ste 4 (07960-5370)
PHONE................................973 359-4040
Peter B Johnson, *President*
Peter Johnson, *Managing Dir*
Anne Berges, *Manager*
Caitlin Frevert, *Manager*
EMP: 6 **EST:** 2015
SALES (est): 70.1K **Privately Held**
SIC: 2066 Cocoa & cocoa products

(G-6746)
TYCOM LIMITED (DH)
10 Park Ave (07960-4700)
PHONE................................973 753-3040
Fax: 973 753-3805
Neil R Garvey, *President*
David Van Rossam, *CFO*
EMP: 250
SALES (est): 104.9MM **Privately Held**
SIC: 3643 1623 Current-carrying wiring devices; cable laying construction
HQ: Tyco International Management Company, Llc
9 Roszel Rd Ste 2
Princeton NJ 08540
609 720-4200

(G-6747)
U V INTERNATIONAL LLC (PA)
Also Called: U V International
360 Mount Kemble Ave # 2 (07960-6662)
PHONE................................973 993-9454
Vinod Jhunjhunwala, *CEO*
▲ **EMP:** 14
SQ FT: 800
SALES (est): 4.2MM **Privately Held**
WEB: www.uvintl.com
SIC: 5074 3589 3498 Plumbing fittings & supplies; sewage & water treatment equipment; fabricated pipe & fittings

(G-6748)
VERMEER PHARMA LLC
36 Canfield Rd (07960-6933)
PHONE................................973 270-0073
Mark Vanarendonk, *Principal*
EMP: 4 **EST:** 2014
SALES (est): 218.8K **Privately Held**
SIC: 2834 Pharmaceutical preparations

(G-6749)
VICTOR INTERNATIONAL MARKETING
35 Airport Rd Ste LI25 (07960-4642)
PHONE................................973 267-8900
Fax: 973 267-0098
Christopher Anderson, *President*
EMP: 4
SALES (est): 320K **Privately Held**
WEB: www.victorinternational.com
SIC: 8742 3559 Marketing consulting services; pharmaceutical machinery

(G-6750)
WARNER CHILCOTT (US) LLC
17 Airport Rd Ste 2 (07960-4665)
PHONE................................973 442-3200
EMP: 4 **Privately Held**
SIC: 2834 Pharmaceutical preparations
HQ: Warner Chilcott (Us), Llc
400 Interpace Pkwy
Parsippany NJ 07054

(G-6751)
WASAK INC
45 S Park Pl Ste 224 (07960-3924)
PHONE................................973 605-8122
Daryl Reigel, *President*
◆ **EMP:** 2
SALES: 1.2MM **Privately Held**
SIC: 2899 Water treating compounds

Mount Arlington
Morris County

(G-6752)
CABLETIME LTD
Also Called: Cabletime USA
100 Valley Rd Ste 203 (07856-1324)
PHONE................................973 770-8070
Edward Carabetta, *General Mgr*
Ed Carabetta, *Vice Pres*
Chad Potenzone, *Manager*
EMP: 4
SALES (est): 623.5K **Privately Held**
WEB: www.cabletime.com
SIC: 3695 Video recording tape, blank

(G-6753)
DOVE CHOCOLATE DISCOVERIES LLC
400 Valley Rd Ste 200 (07856-2316)
PHONE................................866 922-3683
John Wyckoff, *President*
EMP: 20
SALES (est): 7.8MM
SALES (corp-wide): 32.1B **Privately Held**
SIC: 5141 2066 Groceries, general line; chocolate & cocoa products
PA: Mars, Incorporated
6885 Elm St
Mc Lean VA 22101
703 821-4900

(G-6754)
EXODON LLC
111 Howard Blvd Ste 204 (07856-1315)
PHONE................................973 398-2900
Gerald Tramontano,

EMP: 10
SALES (est): 1.4MM **Privately Held**
SIC: 3821 Clinical laboratory instruments,
except medical & dental

(G-6755)
GRAY STAR INC
200 Valley Rd Ste 103 (07856-1320)
PHONE..................................973 398-3331
Fax: 973 398-8310
Martin H Stein, *President*
Russell Stein, *Vice Pres*
EMP: 4
SALES: 1MM **Privately Held**
WEB: www.graystarinc.com
SIC: 3844 Irradiation equipment

(G-6756)
KONGSBERG PROTECH
200 Valley Rd Ste 204 (07856-1320)
PHONE..................................973 770-0574
EMP: 5
SALES (corp-wide): 38.1MM **Privately
Held**
SIC: 3489 Mfg Ordnance/Accessories
HQ: Kongsberg Protech Systems Usa Cor-
poration
210 Industrial Park Rd # 105
Johnstown PA 15904
814 269-5700

(G-6757)
MARS RETAIL GROUP INC
Also Called: Ethel M Chocolates
400 Valley Rd Ste 204 (07856-2316)
PHONE..................................973 398-2078
Lowell Barry, *Branch Mgr*
EMP: 34
SALES (corp-wide): 32.1B **Privately Held**
SIC: 2066 Chocolate & cocoa products
HQ: Mars Retail Group, Inc.
2 Cactus Garden Dr
Henderson NV 89014
702 458-8864

(G-6758)
**MICHELLE STE WINE ESTATES
LTD**
Also Called: Stimson Lane Wine & Spirit
200 Valley Rd Ste 200 (07856-1320)
PHONE..................................973 770-8100
Frank Genovese, *Vice Pres*
EMP: 5
SALES (corp-wide): 42.8MM **Privately
Held**
WEB: www.columbia-crest.com
SIC: 2084 Wines
PA: Michelle Ste Wine Estates Ltd
14111 Ne 145th St
Woodinville WA 98072
425 488-1133

(G-6759)
**PDS PRCLNICAL DATA
SYSTEMS INC**
100 Valley Rd Ste 204 (07856-1324)
PHONE..................................973 398-2800
Sayed Badrawi, *CEO*
Maro Schuster, *Exec VP*
Craig Sonntag, *Manager*
Michael Wasko, *Manager*
EMP: 50
SQ FT: 4,000
SALES (est): 3.2MM
SALES (corp-wide): 5MM **Privately Held**
SIC: 7372 7371 8243 7374 Business ori-
ented computer software; computer soft-
ware development & applications;
software training, computer; data pro-
cessing & preparation; computer process-
ing services; computer related
maintenance services
PA: Pds Pathology Data Systems Ag
Durrenhubelstrasse 9
Pratteln BL 4133
613 778-777

(G-6760)
STORIS INC (PA)
Also Called: Storis Management Systems
400 Valley Rd Ste 302 (07856-2316)
PHONE..................................888 478-6747
Fax: 973 601-0078
Donald J Surdoval, *President*
Brian Robinson, *Business Mgr*
Lindsey Scapicchio, *Business Mgr*

Greg Strosnider, *Business Mgr*
Kevin R Hond, *Senior VP*
EMP: 83
SQ FT: 24,000
SALES (est): 16MM **Privately Held**
WEB: www.storis.com
SIC: 3629 7372 5719 Battery chargers,
rectifying or nonrotating; application com-
puter software; bedding (sheets, blankets,
spreads & pillows)

(G-6761)
**UNIVERSAL TECHNCL RESRCE
SVCS**
Also Called: Utrs
200 Valley Rd Ste 102 (07856-1320)
PHONE..................................973 663-7930
Steve George, *Owner*
EMP: 130
SALES (corp-wide): 69.4MM **Privately
Held**
SIC: 7372 Prepackaged software
PA: Universal Technical Resource Services,
Inc.
950 Kings Hwy N Ste 208
Cherry Hill NJ 08034
856 667-6770

Mount Ephraim
Camden County

(G-6762)
BARBS HARLEY-DAVIDSON
Also Called: Harley Davidson Camden
County
926 Black Horse Pike (08059-1815)
PHONE..................................856 456-4141
Fax: 856 456-2013
Barbara Boroweic, *President*
Mary Duffy, *General Mgr*
Jay Jaconetti, *Business Mgr*
Tom Beatty, *Manager*
Barbara Borowiec, *Manager*
EMP: 24
SQ FT: 12,500
SALES (est): 7.2MM **Privately Held**
WEB: www.harleydavidsoncc.com
SIC: 5571 7699 3751 3519 Motorcycles;
motorcycle parts & accessories; motorcy-
cle repair service; motorcycle acces-
sories; diesel, semi-diesel or duel-fuel
engines, including marine

(G-6763)
GADREN MACHINE CO INC (PA)
Also Called: Gade Float Valves
108 Main St (08059-1846)
P.O. Box 117 (08059-0117)
PHONE..................................856 456-4329
Fax: 856 456-2238
George Gadren, *President*
George S Gadren Sr, *President*
Gary S Gadren, *Vice Pres*
George S Gadren Jr, *Vice Pres*
Francis J Gadren, *VP Sales*
▲ EMP: 19 EST: 1937
SQ FT: 15,000
SALES (est): 2.4MM **Privately Held**
WEB: www.gadrenmachine.com
SIC: 3492 3451 3494 3491 Fluid power
valves & hose fittings; screw machine
products; valves & pipe fittings; industrial
valves

(G-6764)
SELECT MACHINE TOOL INC
19 Thompson Ave (08059-2108)
PHONE..................................856 933-2100
Jay Brad, *President*
Margaret Brad, *Treasurer*
EMP: 9
SQ FT: 1,500
SALES: 600K **Privately Held**
SIC: 3599 Machine shop, jobbing & repair

(G-6765)
WINDOW FACTORY INC
603 N Black Horse Pike (08059-1319)
PHONE..................................856 546-5050
Fax: 856 546-8600
John D Merryfield, *President*
Joyce Merryfield, *Corp Secy*
EMP: 25

SQ FT: 20,000
SALES (est): 3.3MM **Privately Held**
WEB: www.windowfactory.com
SIC: 2431 5211 1761 3442 Windows &
window parts & trim, wood; door & window products; siding contractor; metal
doors, sash & trim

Mount Holly
Burlington County

(G-6766)
AMCOR FLEXIBLES INC
Also Called: Amcor Flexibles Mount Holly
220 Shreve St (08060-2220)
PHONE..................................609 267-5900
Jim Lacanna, *Branch Mgr*
EMP: 32
SALES (corp-wide): 9.1B **Privately Held**
SIC: 3081 5199 3497 3353 Packing ma-
terials, plastic sheet; packaging materials;
metal foil & leaf; aluminum sheet, plate &
foil; packaging paper & plastics film,
coated & laminated
HQ: Amcor Flexibles Llc
2150 E Lake Cook Rd
Buffalo Grove IL 60089
224 313-7000

(G-6767)
DEANS GRAPHICS
16 Mill St Ste D (08060-2154)
P.O. Box 809 (08060-0809)
PHONE..................................609 261-8817
Fax: 609 261-9372
Mark Deans, *Owner*
EMP: 5
SQ FT: 3,500
SALES (est): 526.5K **Privately Held**
WEB: www.deansgraphics.com
SIC: 2759 Screen printing

(G-6768)
EATON CORPORATION
96 Stemmers Ln (08060-5652)
PHONE..................................609 835-4230
Fax: 609 835-4777
Alexander Cutler, *CEO*
EMP: 40
SALES (est): 3MM **Privately Held**
WEB: www.eatoncutlerhammer.com
SIC: 3999 Barber & beauty shop equip-
ment

(G-6769)
**ELECTRONIC PARTS
SPECIALTY CO**
10 Eagle Ave Ste 1100 (08060-1602)
PHONE..................................609 267-0055
EMP: 9 EST: 1945
SQ FT: 30,000
SALES (est): 730K **Privately Held**
SIC: 3469 Mfg Metal Stampings

(G-6770)
EPICORE NETWORKS USA INC
4 Lina Ln (08060-5414)
PHONE..................................609 267-9118
William P Long, *President*
EMP: 20
SQ FT: 11,990
SALES: 11MM
SALES (corp-wide): 228.6K **Privately
Held**
WEB: www.epicorebionet.com
SIC: 2077 2836 8731 Animal & marine
fats & oils; biological products, except di-
agnostic; biotechnical research, commer-
cial
PA: Epicore Bionetworks Inc
150 6 Ave Sw
Calgary AB T2P 3

(G-6771)
**GLOBAL SPCLTY PRODUCTS-
USA INC**
10 Eagle Ave Ste 500 (08060-1601)
PHONE..................................609 518-7577
Davood Faghani, *President*
Cameron Faghani, *Natl Sales Mgr*
◆ EMP: 10
SQ FT: 15,000

SALES: 500K **Privately Held**
WEB: www.gsp-usa-inc.com
SIC: 5169 2842 Chemical additives; specialty cleaning, polishes & sanitation
goods

(G-6772)
**HAINESPORT TOOL & MACHINE
CO**
Also Called: Haineport Tools & Maintenance
1924 Ark Rd (08060)
PHONE..................................609 261-0016
Gerhard Zwick, *President*
EMP: 18 EST: 1950
SQ FT: 8,000
SALES (est): 2.7MM **Privately Held**
SIC: 3545 Machine tool attachments & ac-
cessories

(G-6773)
HIGH GATE CORP
Also Called: Mech-Tronics
100 Campus Dr (08060-9664)
PHONE..................................609 267-0680
Fax: 609 267-7621
Peter Reed, *President*
EMP: 10
SQ FT: 1,500
SALES (est): 1.6MM **Privately Held**
SIC: 3612 Specialty transformers

(G-6774)
**INNOVATIVE METAL SOLUTIONS
LLC**
10 Eagle Ave Ste 400b (08060-1649)
PHONE..................................609 784-8406
Kevin Hocking,
EMP: 4
SQ FT: 1,800
SALES (est): 649.8K **Privately Held**
SIC: 3441 Fabricated structural metal

(G-6775)
**METAL SPECIALTIES NEW
JERSEY**
1 Compass Ln (08060-5417)
PHONE..................................609 261-9277
Michael Ems, *Principal*
EMP: 8
SALES (est): 1.2MM **Privately Held**
SIC: 3444 7539 Sheet metal specialties,
not stamped; machine shop, automotive

(G-6776)
R B BADAT LANDSCAPING INC
507 Woodlane Rd (08060-3808)
PHONE..................................609 877-7138
Fax: 609 880-9677
Robert B Badat, *President*
EMP: 5
SALES (est): 287K **Privately Held**
SIC: 1429 5032 Igneous rock, crushed &
broken-quarrying; stone, crushed or bro-
ken

(G-6777)
VERTIS INC
80 Stemmers Ln (08060-5652)
PHONE..................................215 781-1668
Steve King, *Manager*
EMP: 100
SALES (est): 10.6MM **Privately Held**
SIC: 2759 Commercial printing

Mount Laurel
Burlington County

(G-6778)
**AMERICAN HARVEST BAKING
CO INC (PA)**
Also Called: Ahb Foods
823 E Gate Dr Ste 3 (08054-1202)
PHONE..................................856 642-9955
Fax: 856 642-9799
Jay Roseman, *President*
Barry Kratchman, *Vice Pres*
Betty Ann Peard, *Controller*
Betty Peard, *Controller*
EMP: 30
SALES (est): 13.7MM **Privately Held**
SIC: 2051 Bakery: wholesale or whole-
sale/retail combined

GEOGRAPHIC

(G-6779)
AUS INC (PA)
Also Called: Valuation Services Group
155 Gaither Dr Ste A (08054-1753)
PHONE..................................856 234-9200
John L Ringwood, *President*
Jack Ringwood, *Principal*
Stuart G McDaniel, *Senior VP*
Pauline Ahern, *Vice Pres*
Barbara Marshall, *Vice Pres*
EMP: 5
SALES (est): 60.8MM Privately Held
WEB: www.ingnews.com
SIC: 8742 2711 2752 8249 Business
consultant; newspapers, publishing &
printing; lithographing on metal; aviation
school; janitorial service, contract basis;
market analysis or research

(G-6780)
BAE SYSTEMS TECH SOL SRVC INC
Also Called: Technology Solutions Sector
8000 Midlantic Dr 700n (08054-1549)
PHONE..................................856 638-1003
Beryl Moore, *Manager*
EMP: 50
SALES (corp-wide): 24.2B Privately Held
SIC: 3728 Countermeasure dispensers,
aircraft
HQ: Bae Systems Technology Solutions &
Services Inc.
520 Gaither Rd
Rockville MD 20850
703 847-5820

(G-6781)
BASYS INC
1200 S Church St Ste 7 (08054-2936)
PHONE..................................732 616-5276
Jeffrey Marino, *President*
Jeff Marino, *Engineer*
EMP: 3 EST: 2009
SALES: 1MM Privately Held
SIC: 7372 Prepackaged software

(G-6782)
BELLE PRINTING GROUP LLC (PA)
3838 Church Rd (08054-1106)
PHONE..................................856 235-5151
William C Shanley IV, *Mng Member*
Thomas R Shanley,
William C Shanley III,
EMP: 7
SALES (est): 5.7MM Privately Held
SIC: 3082 2759 8741 Unsupported plas-
tics profile shapes; commercial printing;
management services

(G-6783)
BLADES LANDSCAPING INC
Also Called: Blades Ldscpg Lawn Maint & Ir
2028 Briggs Rd (08054-4607)
P.O. Box 729, Marlton (08053-0729)
PHONE..................................856 779-7665
Keith Haitz, *President*
Joseph Butkus, *Admin Sec*
EMP: 13
SALES: 470K Privately Held
SIC: 0781 4959 0782 3271 Landscape
services; snowplowing; lawn services;
blocks, concrete: landscape or retaining
wall

(G-6784)
BSRM INC
691 Cornwallis Dr (08054-3216)
PHONE..................................888 509-0668
Bruce Rotkowitz, *President*
Matt Rotkowitz, *Vice Pres*
Russell Rotkowitz, *Vice Pres*
Scott Rotkowitz, *Vice Pres*
EMP: 4
SALES (est): 540.5K Privately Held
SIC: 3069 Reclaimed rubber (reworked by
manufacturing processes)

(G-6785)
BURLINGTON DESIGN CENTER INC
3019 Marne Hwy (08054-2038)
PHONE..................................856 778-7772
Fax: 856 778-7732
Stephen F Tremain, *President*

Michael Keane, *Vice Pres*
John Keane, *Admin Sec*
EMP: 12
SQ FT: 3,300
SALES: 1.2MM Privately Held
SIC: 2679 Wallpaper

(G-6786)
CARILETHA COMPANY INC
2206 Sedgefield Dr (08054-1862)
PHONE..................................609 222-3055
Joseph M Doyle, *President*
EMP: 10
SALES (est): 261K Privately Held
SIC: 2741 Miscellaneous publishing

(G-6787)
CHERISH DESIGNS LLC
3111 Route 38 Unit 316 (08054-9754)
PHONE..................................856 751-8034
Catherine Radley, *President*
Douglas Radley Jr,
EMP: 7
SALES: 500K Privately Held
WEB: www.cherishdesigns.com
SIC: 3911 Jewelry, precious metal

(G-6788)
CINCHSEAL ASSOCIATES INC
23b Roland Ave (08054-1011)
PHONE..................................856 662-5162
David M Pitchko, *President*
Jessica Amato, *Mktg Coord*
▲ EMP: 22
SQ FT: 10,000
SALES: 4MM Privately Held
WEB: www.cinchseal.com
SIC: 3053 Gaskets & sealing devices

(G-6789)
CLOVER GARDEN CTR LTD LBLTY CO
1017 S Church St (08054-2507)
PHONE..................................856 235-4625
Fax: 856 235-5426
Paula Brandimarte, *President*
Thal Le, *Partner*
EMP: 8
SALES (est): 440.8K Privately Held
SIC: 5992 3999 0781 Flowers, fresh;
plants, artificial & preserved; landscape
planning services

(G-6790)
CONOPCO INC
305 Fellowship Rd Ste 114 (08054-1232)
PHONE..................................856 722-1664
Brentt Vandebovenkamp, *Manager*
EMP: 25
SALES (corp-wide): 63B Privately Held
SIC: 2844 Toilet preparations
HQ: Conopco, Inc.
700 Sylvan Ave
Englewood Cliffs NJ 07632
201 894-2727

(G-6791)
CUTMARK INC
102 Gaither Dr Ste 2 (08054-1714)
PHONE..................................856 234-3428
Fax: 856 273-2837
George Gibson, *President*
EMP: 4
SQ FT: 2,000
SALES (est): 560.4K Privately Held
WEB: www.cutmark.com
SIC: 3444 3599 Sheet metalwork; ma-
chine shop, jobbing & repair

(G-6792)
DELAWARE TECHNOLOGIES INC
641 Mount Laurel Rd (08054-9555)
PHONE..................................856 234-7692
Fax: 856 231-7943
Donald Dawson, *President*
Almeta Dawson, *Corp Secy*
EMP: 10
SALES: 500K Privately Held
WEB: www.delawaretechnologies.com
SIC: 3821 3823 7629 Sample preparation
apparatus; water quality monitoring &
control systems; electronic equipment re-
pair

(G-6793)
E & T SALES CO INC
824 E Gate Dr Ste E (08054-1254)
PHONE..................................856 787-0900
Ed Godshok, *Manager*
Ed Godshaldt, *Manager*
EMP: 9
SALES (corp-wide): 31.4MM Privately
Held
SIC: 3089 5162 Plastic containers, except
foam; plastics sheets & rods
PA: E. & T. Sales Co., Inc.
4545 37th St
Long Island City NY 11101
718 729-6226

(G-6794)
E BERKOWITZ & CO INC
Also Called: Security Systems Unlimited
520 Fellowship Rd B202 (08054-3407)
PHONE..................................856 608-1118
Fax: 856 608-1112
Eric Berkowitz, *President*
EMP: 7
SQ FT: 3,200
SALES (est): 680K Privately Held
SIC: 1731 2541 Sound equipment special-
ization; telephone & telephone equipment
installation; fire detection & burglar alarm
systems specialization; closed circuit tele-
vision installation; store fixtures, wood

(G-6795)
E GROUP INC
129 Gaither Dr Ste M (08054-1708)
PHONE..................................856 320-9688
Wade Xu, *President*
EMP: 8
SQ FT: 18,000
SALES: 10MM Privately Held
SIC: 4812 3691 Radio telephone commu-
nication; storage batteries

(G-6796)
E LOC TOTAL LOGISTICS LLC
144 Canterbury Rd (08054-1416)
P.O. Box 1521 (08054-7521)
PHONE..................................609 685-6117
Robert Gittens, *Mng Member*
EMP: 6
SALES (est): 390.3K Privately Held
SIC: 3715 Truck trailers

(G-6797)
FEDEX OFFICE & PRINT SVCS INC
1211 Route 73 Ste E (08054-2236)
PHONE..................................856 273-5959
Bryan Hill, *Branch Mgr*
EMP: 15
SALES (corp-wide): 65.4B Publicly Held
WEB: www.kinkos.com
SIC: 7334 2791 2789 Photocopying & du-
plicating services; typesetting; bookbind-
ing & related work
HQ: Fedex Office And Print Services, Inc.
7900 Legacy Dr
Plano TX 75024
214 550-7000

(G-6798)
FOOD SCIENCES CORP (PA)
Also Called: Robard
821 E Gate Dr (08054-1239)
PHONE..................................856 778-4192
Fax: 856 778-4192
Robert Schwartz, *President*
Mj Matrazzo, *Business Mgr*
Mary Mitchell, *Business Mgr*
Jay Satinsky, *Business Mgr*
Mario Testa, *Vice Pres*
EMP: 149
SQ FT: 58,000
SALES (est): 24MM Privately Held
WEB: www.foodsciences.com
SIC: 2023 Dietary supplements, dairy &
non-dairy based

(G-6799)
FOX STEEL PRODUCTS LLC
8 Fox Run Dr (08054-3255)
PHONE..................................856 778-4661
Rose M Burns, *President*
EMP: 4

SALES (est): 280K Privately Held
SIC: 3312 3317 3316 3498 Blast furnaces & steel mills; steel pipe & tubes;
cold finishing of steel shapes; fabricated
pipe & fittings

(G-6800)
GLENBURNIE FEED & GRAIN
87 Chapel Hill Rd (08054-8510)
PHONE..................................856 986-8128
Charles E Connell Jr, *President*
David Estey, *Principal*
Marion J Connell, *Corp Secy*
EMP: 2
SALES: 1MM Privately Held
WEB: www.glenburniefeedandgrain.com
SIC: 5191 2048 Feed; prepared feeds

(G-6801)
GRAY HAIR SOFTWARE INC
124 Gaither Dr Ste 160 (08054-1719)
PHONE..................................856 924-2253
Fax: 856 727-1315
Cameron Bellamy, *President*
Scott Kushner, *CFO*
Susan Gallucci, *Manager*
Lisa Miller, *Manager*
Thad Wellington, *Manager*
EMP: 42
SQ FT: 3,000
SALES (est): 9.6MM Privately Held
WEB: www.grayhairsoftware.com
SIC: 7372 Business oriented computer
software

(G-6802)
HOLMAN ENTERPRISES INC
Also Called: Holman Jaguar and Infinite
1311 Route 73 (08054-2215)
PHONE..................................609 383-6100
Ann Williams, *Manager*
EMP: 35
SALES (corp-wide): 1.7B Privately Held
WEB: www.holmanenterprises.com
SIC: 5511 7538 7532 7516 Automobiles,
new & used; general automotive repair
shops; top & body repair & paint shops;
passenger car leasing; motor vehicle
parts & accessories
PA: Holman Enterprises Inc.
244 E Kings Hwy
Maple Shade NJ 08052
856 663-5200

(G-6803)
INGERSOLL-RAND COMPANY
3001 Irwin Rd (08054-4636)
PHONE..................................856 793-7000
Tim Lowery, *Branch Mgr*
EMP: 50 Privately Held
WEB: www.ingersoll-rand.com
SIC: 3562 3561 3429 3546 Ball & roller
bearings; roller bearings & parts; ball
bearings & parts; pumps & pumping
equipment; furniture builders' & other
household hardware; keys, locks & related hardware; power-driven handtools;
air & gas compressors including vacuum
pumps; winches
HQ: Ingersoll-Rand Company
800 Beaty St Ste B
Davidson NC 28036
704 655-4000

(G-6804)
INJECTION WORKS INC
104 Gaither Dr (08054-1702)
PHONE..................................856 802-6444
Christopher A Rapacki, *President*
Irene Connolly, *General Mgr*
Robert Weiss, *General Mgr*
Dan Ferrante, *Opers Mgr*
Steven Beck, *QC Mgr*
▲ EMP: 35
SQ FT: 46,000
SALES: 7.1MM Privately Held
WEB: www.injectionworks.com
SIC: 3089 Injection molding of plastics

(G-6805)
INSTITUTE FOR RESPNSBLE ONLINE
82 Hillside Ln (08054-4517)
PHONE..................................856 722-1048
Richard Guerry, *Exec Dir*
EMP: 5

SALES (est): 484.9K **Privately Held**
SIC: 3669 Communications equipment

(G-6806)
INTERNTNAL INGRDENT SLTONS INC
3001 Irwin Rd Ste A (08054-4636)
PHONE........................856 778-6623
George Shapirl, *President*
EMP: 25
SALES: 3MM **Privately Held**
SIC: 2099 5149 Seasonings & spices; spices, including grinding; spices & seasonings

(G-6807)
INTEST CORPORATION (PA)
804 E Gate Dr Ste 200 (08054-1209)
PHONE........................856 505-8800
Fax: 856 505-8801
Robert E Matthiessen, *Ch of Bd*
James Pelrin, *President*
Hugh T Regan Jr, *CFO*
▲ EMP: 3
SQ FT: 54,897
SALES: 66.8MM **Publicly Held**
WEB: www.intest.com
SIC: 3825 3823 Digital test equipment, electronic & electrical circuits; semiconductor test equipment; temperature measurement instruments, industrial

(G-6808)
INVENTEK COLLOIDAL CLRS LLC
106 Gaither Dr (08054-1702)
PHONE........................856 206-0058
Yasmin Andrecola, *President*
Paul Andrecola,
EMP: 45
SQ FT: 25,000
SALES (est): 7.9MM **Privately Held**
SIC: 2841 Soap & other detergents

(G-6809)
J K P DONUTS INC
Also Called: Dunkin' Donuts
807 Route 73 (08054-1165)
PHONE........................856 234-9844
Peter Amin, *President*
Vipul Patel, *Vice Pres*
Mukesh Patel, *Admin Sec*
EMP: 6
SALES (est): 270K **Privately Held**
SIC: 5461 2051 Doughnuts; doughnuts, except frozen

(G-6810)
JERSEY TEMPERED GLASS INC
2035 Briggs Rd (08054-4608)
P.O. Box 205 (08054-0205)
PHONE........................856 273-8700
Fax: 856 273-1999
Nicholas Concio, *President*
EMP: 45
SQ FT: 48,000
SALES (est): 10.7MM **Privately Held**
WEB: www.jerseytemperedglass.com
SIC: 3211 3231 Tempered glass; products of purchased glass

(G-6811)
KUBIK MALTBIE INC
7000 Commerce Pkwy Ste C (08054-2288)
PHONE........................856 234-0052
Fax: 856 234-0760
Sam Kohn, *CEO*
Chuck Maltbie, *President*
George Mayer, *President*
Gary Brooks, *Vice Pres*
A J Higgs, *Vice Pres*
◆ EMP: 40 EST: 1962
SQ FT: 36,000
SALES: 7.6MM
SALES (corp-wide): 17.8MM **Privately Held**
WEB: www.maltbie.com
SIC: 3993 2541 3231 Displays, paint process; displays & cutouts, window & lobby; wood partitions & fixtures; products of purchased glass
PA: Kubik Inc
1680 Mattawa Ave
Mississauga ON L4X 3
905 272-2818

(G-6812)
LINGO INC
Also Called: Acme Flagpole Division
10 Opal Ct (08054-3062)
PHONE........................856 273-6594
John E Lingo Jr, *President*
Gail P Lingo, *Admin Sec*
EMP: 11 EST: 1897
SQ FT: 12,000
SALES: 890K **Privately Held**
SIC: 3441 3446 Tower sections, radio & television transmission; flagpoles, metal

(G-6813)
LOCKHEED MARTIN CORPORATION
750 Centerton Rd (08054-1625)
PHONE........................856 234-1261
John Skiba, *Engineer*
Andrew Takacs, *Engineer*
EMP: 1265 **Publicly Held**
SIC: 3812 Aircraft/aerospace flight instruments & guidance systems
PA: Lockheed Martin Corporation
6801 Rockledge Dr
Bethesda MD 20817

(G-6814)
LOCKHEED MARTIN CORPORATION
532 Fellowship Rd (08054-3405)
P.O. Box 1027, Moorestown (08057-0927)
PHONE........................856 787-3104
Fax: 856 273-5249
Thomas Rogers, *Vice Pres*
Jacek J Brach, *Engineer*
Nicholas Coretti, *Engineer*
Tim Martino, *Engineer*
Shelly Carr, *Branch Mgr*
EMP: 435 **Publicly Held**
WEB: www.lockheedmartin.com
SIC: 3721 3761 3663 3764 Research & development on aircraft by the manufacturer; guided missiles & space vehicles, research & development; airborne radio communications equipment; guided missile & space vehicle engines, research & devel.; space vehicle guidance systems & equipment
PA: Lockheed Martin Corporation
6801 Rockledge Dr
Bethesda MD 20817

(G-6815)
LTS NJ INC
109 W Park Dr Unit C (08054-1260)
PHONE........................856 780-9888
Wing Pang, *Principal*
Serena Zhang, *Sales Mgr*
Kelly Breitton, *Accounts Mgr*
Ling Tang, *Consultant*
EMP: 7
SALES (est): 1.4MM **Privately Held**
SIC: 3699 Security control equipment & systems

(G-6816)
MANNA GROUP LLC
137 Gaither Dr Ste F (08054-1711)
PHONE........................856 881-7650
Dennis McCullough,
EMP: 10
SALES (est): 215.9K **Privately Held**
SIC: 7379 2741 ;

(G-6817)
MDR DIAGNOSTICS LLC
199 6th Ave Ste C (08054-9749)
PHONE........................609 396-0021
David Katz,
EMP: 20
SALES (est): 2.5MM **Privately Held**
SIC: 3829 Medical diagnostic systems, nuclear

(G-6818)
METROLOGIC INSTRUMENTS INC (HQ)
Also Called: Honeywell
534 Fellowship Rd (08054-3405)
PHONE........................856 228-8100
Fax: 856 232-2932
Benny A Noens, *CEO*
Dipanjan Deb, *President*
Joseph Sawitsky, *Exec VP*

Mark Schmidt, *Exec VP*
Gregory Dinoia, *Vice Pres*
▲ EMP: 150
SQ FT: 116,000
SALES (est): 128.5MM
SALES (corp-wide): 40.5B **Publicly Held**
WEB: www.metrologic.com
SIC: 3577 3699 Magnetic ink & optical scanning devices; optical scanning devices; laser systems & equipment
PA: Honeywell International Inc.
115 Tabor Rd
Morris Plains NJ 07950
973 455-2000

(G-6819)
MJ CORPORATE SALES INC
109 W Park Dr Unit A (08054-1260)
PHONE........................856 778-0055
Robert Madosky, *Principal*
Richard Schwerdtmann, *Sales Staff*
Toni Mascantonio, *Marketing Staff*
Penny Petty, *Manager*
Tim Trotman, *Manager*
▲ EMP: 25
SQ FT: 28,000
SALES (est): 4.3MM **Privately Held**
WEB: www.mjsales.com
SIC: 2759 5947 Screen printing; gifts & novelties

(G-6820)
MNEMONICS INC
102 Gaither Dr Ste 4 (08054-1714)
P.O. Box 877 (08054-0877)
PHONE........................856 234-0970
Fax: 856 234-6793
Michael Negin, *President*
Carolyn Rosner, *Marketing Staff*
▼ EMP: 4
SQ FT: 1,600
SALES (est): 651.9K **Privately Held**
SIC: 3826 Laser scientific & engineering instruments

(G-6821)
MONARCH ART PLASTICS CO LLC
Also Called: Monarch Plastics
3838 Church Rd (08054-1106)
PHONE........................856 235-5151
Fax: 856 778-9032
William C Shanley, *CEO*
Kimberton E Messner, *CFO*
EMP: 25
SQ FT: 26,500
SALES (est): 4.5MM
SALES (corp-wide): 5.7MM **Privately Held**
WEB: www.monarchplastics.com
SIC: 2759 Screen printing
PA: Belle Printing Group Llc
3838 Church Rd
Mount Laurel NJ 08054
856 235-5151

(G-6822)
NETQUEST CORPORATION
523 Fellowship Rd Ste 205 (08054-3434)
PHONE........................856 866-0505
Fax: 856 866-2852
Slobodan Pocek, *President*
Jesse Price, *Principal*
Chuck Hellings, *Purchasing*
Edward Kravets, *Design Engr*
John Pye, *Design Engr*
EMP: 20
SQ FT: 10,000
SALES (est): 3MM **Privately Held**
WEB: www.netquestcorp.com
SIC: 3669 7371 3829 3823 Intercommunication systems, electric; custom computer programming services; measuring & controlling devices; industrial instrmnts msrmnt display/control process variable

(G-6823)
PAI SERVICES LLC
Also Called: Sage Payroll Services
305 Fellowship Rd Ste 300 (08054-1232)
PHONE........................856 231-4667
William Scott,
EMP: 130

SALES (corp-wide): 2.2B **Privately Held**
SIC: 7372 7371 Prepackaged software; business oriented computer software; computer software development & applications
HQ: Pai Services, Llc
305 Fellowship Rd Ste 300
Mount Laurel NJ

(G-6824)
PENNY PLATE LLC (DH)
1400 Horizon Way Ste 300 (08054)
PHONE........................856 429-7583
Paul Cobb, *President*
George Buff III, *Exec VP*
John Charles Buff, *Vice Pres*
▲ EMP: 75 EST: 1949
SQ FT: 40,000
SALES (est): 102.4MM
SALES (corp-wide): 901.9MM **Privately Held**
WEB: www.pennyplate.com
SIC: 3411 Food containers, metal
HQ: Replanet, Llc
800 N Haven Ave Ste 120
Ontario CA 91764
951 520-1700

(G-6825)
PGW AUTO GLASS LLC
Also Called: P P G Auto Glass
823 E Gate Dr (08054-1202)
PHONE........................856 234-1600
Sally Neher, *Manager*
EMP: 21
SALES (corp-wide): 9.7B **Publicly Held**
SIC: 5013 7536 3365 Automobile glass; automotive glass replacement shops; aerospace castings, aluminum
HQ: Pgw Auto Glass, Llc
30 Isabella St Ste 500
Pittsburgh PA 15212
888 774-2886

(G-6826)
PHILLY MOTORS AND DRIVES INC
103 Central Ave Ste 400b (08054-1200)
PHONE........................856 840-8011
Jeffrey Peterson, *President*
EMP: 21
SALES: 2.5MM **Privately Held**
SIC: 3632 Household refrigerators & freezers

(G-6827)
PLCS INC
102 Gaither Dr Ste 1 (08054-1754)
PHONE........................856 722-1333
Fax: 856 273-9723
Howard Hardwick, *President*
David R Payne, *Exec VP*
Joe Tete, *Vice Pres*
John Klimek, *Warehouse Mgr*
Kathleen Hatch, *Treasurer*
◆ EMP: 22
SQ FT: 14,000
SALES: 9.8MM **Privately Held**
WEB: www.plcsusa.com
SIC: 2891 5084 Sealing compounds for pipe threads or joints; industrial machinery & equipment

(G-6828)
PMC GROUP INC (PA)
1288 Route 73 Ste 401 (08054-2237)
PHONE........................856 533-1866
Fax: 856 533-1867
Paritosh M Chakrabarti, *CEO*
John Woods, *VP Mfg*
Terry Stapleton, *Opers Mgr*
Jim Foerster, *Manager*
James Mountain, *CTO*
◆ EMP: 15
SQ FT: 10,000
SALES (est): 302.8MM **Privately Held**
SIC: 3089 2812 Injection molding of plastics; plastic hardware & building products; alkalies & chlorine

(G-6829)
POLYTECHNIC INDUSTRIES INC
14 Roland Ave (08054-1012)
PHONE........................856 235-6550
Fax: 856 235-6522
Alvin C Lanson, *President*

Steven Lanson, *Vice Pres*
Sheri Levinson, *Manager*
Lori Miller, *Shareholder*
Eric Miller, *Admin Sec*
EMP: 10
SQ FT: 24,000
SALES (est): 2MM **Privately Held**
WEB: www.polytechnicind.com
SIC: 3728 Military aircraft equipment & armament

(G-6830)
PPG INDUSTRIES INC
823 E Gate Dr Ste 4 (08054-1202)
PHONE..........................856 273-7870
Amy Lee, *Branch Mgr*
EMP: 23
SALES (corp-wide): 14.2B **Publicly Held**
SIC: 2851 Shellac (protective coating)
PA: Ppg Industries, Inc.
1 Ppg Pl
Pittsburgh PA 15272
412 434-3131

(G-6831)
PRECISION PRINTING GROUP INC
606 Stamford Dr # 606 (08054-3515)
PHONE..........................856 753-0900
Joseph Cartafalsn, *President*
EMP: 45
SQ FT: 52,000
SALES (est): 10.3MM **Privately Held**
WEB: www.hamiltonpress.com
SIC: 2752 Commercial printing, lithographic

(G-6832)
PRODUCTIVE PLASTICS INC (PA)
103 W Park Dr (08054-1278)
PHONE..........................856 778-4300
Fax: 856 234-3310
Harold Gilham, *President*
Kevin Davis, *Business Mgr*
John Zerillo, *Vice Pres*
Jose Lamboy, *Prdtn Mgr*
Todd Mitchell, *VP Finance*
EMP: 78
SQ FT: 24,000
SALES (est): 17MM **Privately Held**
SIC: 3089 3083 3081 Thermoformed finished plastic products; laminated plastics plate & sheet; unsupported plastics film & sheet

(G-6833)
QAD INC
10000 Midlantic Dr 100w (08054-1542)
PHONE..........................856 273-1717
Fax: 856 273-1030
Robin Lubin, *Human Resources*
Jane Barrett, *Sales Staff*
Roland Desilets, *Branch Mgr*
Michael Montesanti, *Manager*
Bruce Edwards, *Senior Mgr*
EMP: 150
SALES (corp-wide): 305MM **Publicly Held**
WEB: www.qad.com
SIC: 7372 5045 Application computer software; computers, peripherals & software
PA: Qad Inc.
100 Innovation Pl
Santa Barbara CA 93108
805 566-6000

(G-6834)
RAMBLEWOOD CLEANERS INC (PA)
Also Called: Rumblewood Cleaners
1155 Route 73 Ste B (08054-2352)
PHONE..........................856 235-6051
Sung Kim, *President*
Fung Oak Kim, *President*
EMP: 4
SQ FT: 2,000
SALES: 200K **Privately Held**
SIC: 2842 Drycleaning preparations

(G-6835)
RHYTHMEDIX LLC
Also Called: Rmx
5000 Atrium Way Ste 1 (08054-3915)
PHONE..........................856 282-1080

Brian Pike, *Managing Prtnr*
Keith Gartland, *Vice Pres*
Dmitri Mezhevich, *CIO*
Patricia Oliver, *Director*
Kaye Bryson, *Administration*
EMP: 6 **EST:** 2013
SQ FT: 13,000
SALES (est): 1MM **Privately Held**
SIC: 3845 Electromedical equipment

(G-6836)
S FRANKFORD & SONS INC
Also Called: Frankford Umbrellas
110 Gaither Dr Ste A (08054-1703)
PHONE..........................856 222-4134
Marc Kaufer, *Principal*
Angela Rampson, *Sales Mgr*
Kristina Mendenhall, *Sales Staff*
Shawn McDonald, *Manager*
◆ **EMP:** 10 **EST:** 1898
SALES (est): 1.5MM **Privately Held**
WEB: www.umbrellausa.com
SIC: 3999 5136 Garden umbrellas; umbrellas, men's & boys'

(G-6837)
SAGE SOFTWARE INC
305 Fellowship Rd Ste 300 (08054-1232)
PHONE..........................856 231-4667
Bryan Regan, *General Mgr*
EMP: 80
SALES (corp-wide): 2.2B **Privately Held**
SIC: 7372 8721 Prepackaged software; payroll accounting service
HQ: Sage Software International, Inc.
271 17th St Nw Ste 1100
Atlanta GA 30363
866 996-7243

(G-6838)
SCIENTIFIX LLC
Also Called: Sfx Installations
520 Fellowship Rd E508 (08054-3417)
PHONE..........................856 780-5871
Fax: 908 753-5604
George Lynch, *Marketing Mgr*
George F Lynch, *Mng Member*
Brian Foresta,
▲ **EMP:** 8
SQ FT: 1,600
SALES (est): 2.1MM **Privately Held**
WEB: www.scientifix.net
SIC: 3821 Chemical laboratory apparatus

(G-6839)
SENSIGRAPHICS INC
105 W Park Dr (08054-1278)
PHONE..........................856 853-9100
Fax: 856 853-6966
Tony Ciccatelli, *Principal*
EMP: 6
SALES (est): 1.1MM **Privately Held**
WEB: www.sensigraphics.com
SIC: 3613 3679 Control panels, electric; electronic switches

(G-6840)
SFP SOFTWARE INC
162 Knotty Oak Dr (08054-2115)
PHONE..........................856 235-7778
Steven Pipe, *President*
Janeane Pipe, *Vice Pres*
EMP: 4
SALES (est): 100K **Privately Held**
SIC: 7372 Prepackaged software

(G-6841)
SIEMENS INDUSTRY INC
Also Called: Siemens Fire Safety
2000 Crawford Pl Ste 300 (08054-3920)
PHONE..........................856 234-7666
Fax: 856 234-5690
Albert Meloni, *Branch Mgr*
Albert Melloni, *Manager*
EMP: 50
SALES (corp-wide): 97.7B **Privately Held**
WEB: www.sibt.com
SIC: 3822 5085 Air conditioning & refrigeration controls; industrial supplies
HQ: Siemens Industry, Inc.
100 Technology Dr
Alpharetta GA 30005
770 740-3000

(G-6842)
SMITH ENTERPRISES
100 Hillside Ln (08054-4522)
PHONE..........................215 416-9881
Damian Smith, *Owner*
EMP: 4
SALES (est): 210K **Privately Held**
SIC: 2759 3993 Promotional printing; signs & advertising specialties

(G-6843)
SODASTREAM USA INC
136 Gaither Dr Ste 200 (08054-1725)
PHONE..........................856 755-3400
Daniel Birnbaum, *CEO*
Scott Guthrie, *President*
Yossi Azarzar, *COO*
Jack Thompson, *Senior VP*
Dorit Bannett, *Vice Pres*
▲ **EMP:** 72
SALES (est): 218.1MM
SALES (corp-wide): 543.3MM **Privately Held**
WEB: www.sodaclubusa.com
SIC: 2087 3585 Syrups, drink; soda fountain & beverage dispensing equipment & parts
PA: Sodastream International Ltd
2 Gilboa
Lod 71256
397 623-23

(G-6844)
TELVUE CORPORATION (PA)
16000 Horizon Way Ste 100 (08054-4317)
PHONE..........................800 885-8886
Fax: 856 866-7411
Jesse Lerman, *President*
Paul Andrews, *Senior VP*
Stanley Greene, *Vice Pres*
Mark Steele, *CIO*
Randy Gilson, *Info Tech Dir*
EMP: 26
SQ FT: 8,732
SALES (est): 6.8MM **Privately Held**
WEB: www.telvue.com
SIC: 3663 4813 Television broadcasting & communications equipment; studio equipment, radio & television broadcasting;

(G-6845)
UTAH INTERMEDIATE HOLDING CORP
1020 Briggs Rd (08054-4101)
PHONE..........................856 787-2700
Tom Gores, *CEO*
EMP: 203
SALES (est): 6.3MM **Privately Held**
SIC: 7372 7371 Business oriented computer software; software programming applications

(G-6846)
WHITTLE & MUTCH INC
712 Fellowship Rd (08054-1004)
PHONE..........................856 235-1165
Fax: 856 235-0902
John Mutch Jr, *President*
Samuel Mutch, *Vice Pres*
Richard Mutch, *Treasurer*
Peter Sauer, *Supervisor*
John Mutch III, *Admin Sec*
EMP: 14 **EST:** 1892
SQ FT: 20,000
SALES (est): 2.6MM **Privately Held**
WEB: www.wamiflavor.com
SIC: 2087 Extracts, flavoring

(G-6847)
WILLIAM SPENCER (PA)
Also Called: Spencer's
20 Lake Dr (08054-2077)
PHONE..........................856 235-1830
Fax: 856 235-8552
Valerie Houser, *President*
Orin G Houser, *Corp Secy*
Isabel Michalski, *Bookkeeper*
▼ **EMP:** 9
SQ FT: 15,800
SALES (est): 1.5MM **Privately Held**
SIC: 5712 3645 Furniture stores; residential lighting fixtures

(G-6848)
ZIMMER INC
Also Called: Tri-State Orthopedic
1001 Briggs Rd Ste 275 (08054-4105)
PHONE..........................856 778-8300
Stan Smoyer, *Branch Mgr*
EMP: 6
SALES (corp-wide): 7.8B **Publicly Held**
WEB: www.zimmer.com
SIC: 3842 Surgical appliances & supplies
HQ: Zimmer, Inc.
1800 W Center St
Warsaw IN 46580
330 343-8801

(G-6849)
ZOUNDS INC
Also Called: Zounds Hearing
3131 Route 38 Ste 19 (08054-9764)
PHONE..........................856 234-8844
EMP: 10 **Privately Held**
WEB: www.zoundshearing.com
SIC: 3842 3845 Surgical appliances & supplies; electromedical equipment
PA: Zounds, Inc.
6825 W Galveston St Ste 9
Chandler AZ 85226

Mount Royal
Gloucester County

(G-6850)
CW BROWN FOODS INC (PA)
Also Called: Bottos Gnine Itln Style Susage
161 Kings Hwy (08061-1011)
P.O. Box 243 (08061-0243)
PHONE..........................856 423-3700
Vince Botto, *President*
Dominic Botto, *Vice Pres*
Enrico Botto, *Treasurer*
Robert Botto Jr, *Admin Sec*
EMP: 29
SQ FT: 25,000
SALES: 10MM **Privately Held**
SIC: 2013 Sausages from purchased meat

(G-6851)
CW BROWN FOODS INC
Also Called: C W Brown & Company
161 Kings Hwy (08061-1011)
PHONE..........................856 423-3700
Fax: 856 423-8894
Vincent Botto, *Manager*
EMP: 21
SALES (corp-wide): 10MM **Privately Held**
SIC: 5411 2013 Grocery stores, independent; sausages & other prepared meats
PA: C.W. Brown Foods Inc.
161 Kings Hwy
Mount Royal NJ 08061
856 423-3700

(G-6852)
S GENO CARPET AND FLOORING
153 Sunset Dr (08061-1047)
PHONE..........................215 669-1400
Eugene Reilly, *Owner*
EMP: 4
SALES (est): 140K **Privately Held**
SIC: 3996 Hard surface floor coverings

Mountain Lakes
Morris County

(G-6853)
ACUSTRIP CO INC
10 Craven Rd (07046-1424)
P.O. Box 413 (07046-0413)
PHONE..........................973 299-8237
Francine Schornstein, *CFO*
Ronald Schornstein, *Branch Mgr*
EMP: 4
SALES (corp-wide): 2.1MM **Privately Held**
WEB: www.acustrip.com
SIC: 3826 Liquid testing apparatus

PA: Acustrip Co Inc
124 E Main St Apt 109b
Denville NJ 07834
973 299-8237

(G-6854)
ALEXANDER COMMUNICATIONS GROUP
Also Called: Alexander Marketing Services
36 Midvale Rd Ste 2e (07046-1330)
PHONE....................973 265-2300
Fax: 973 402-6056
Lawrence Alexander, *President*
Margaret Dewitt, *Publisher*
EMP: 11
SQ FT: 5,000
SALES: 2MM **Privately Held**
WEB: www.alexcommgrp.com
SIC: 2721 2731 Periodicals: publishing & printing; book publishing

(G-6855)
CIRE TECHNOLOGIES INC
251 Boulevard (07046-1209)
PHONE....................973 402-8301
Fax: 973 402-8302
Eric Becht, *President*
EMP: 5
SALES (est): 953.6K **Privately Held**
WEB: www.ciretechnologies.com
SIC: 3567 3552 8711 Incinerators, metal: domestic or commercial; drying machines, textile: for stock, yarn & cloth; consulting engineer

(G-6856)
DATA BASE ACCESS SYSTEMS INC
Also Called: Codenoll
60 Midvale Rd Ste 206 (07046-1309)
PHONE....................973 335-0800
Fax: 973 335-1956
Michael Palazzi, *President*
John Bazin, *Vice Pres*
Frank Eppes, *Treasurer*
EMP: 14
SALES (est): 1.9MM **Privately Held**
WEB: www.dbasinc.com
SIC: 3577 Computer peripheral equipment

(G-6857)
DELUXE CORPORATION
Also Called: Deluxe Check Printers
105 Route 46 W (07046-1645)
PHONE....................973 334-8000
Fax: 973 334-4292
Steve Tenna, *Manager*
EMP: 167
SALES (corp-wide): 1.9B **Publicly Held**
WEB: www.dlx.com
SIC: 2782 Checkbooks
PA: Deluxe Corporation
3680 Victoria St N
Shoreview MN 55126
651 483-7111

(G-6858)
EUROIMMUN US INC
1 Bloomfield Ave 1 # 1 (07046-1429)
PHONE....................973 656-1000
Hamid Ersanian, *CEO*
Theresa Gilosa, *Accounting Mgr*
Susan Goodhand, *Accountant*
Greg Stock, *Sales Mgr*
Lauren Basile, *Technology*
▲ EMP: 20
SQ FT: 5,500
SALES (est): 4.4MM **Privately Held**
WEB: www.euroimmunus.com
SIC: 3829 Medical diagnostic systems, nuclear
HQ: Euroimmun Medizinische Labordiagnostika Ag
Seekamp 31
Lubeck 23560
451 585-50

(G-6859)
FBN NEW JERSEY MFG INC
8 Morris Ave (07046-1011)
P.O. Box 125 (07046-0125)
PHONE....................973 402-1443
Phillip Motyka, *President*
Richard Beuke, *Vice Pres*
Gary Petersen, *Vice Pres*
Cynthia Pensinger, *Project Mgr*

Raymond Grasso, *Mfg Staff*
▲ EMP: 32
SQ FT: 20,000
SALES (est): 3.7MM **Privately Held**
WEB: www.ocom.com
SIC: 3231 Products of purchased glass
HQ: Fabrinet Company Limited
5/6 Moo 6
Khlong Luang 12120
252 496-00

(G-6860)
RED OAK SOFTWARE INC (PA)
115 Us Highway 46 F1000 (07046-1668)
PHONE....................973 316-6064
George Cummings, *President*
EMP: 16
SQ FT: 4,300
SALES (est): 1.3MM **Privately Held**
WEB: www.redoaksw.com
SIC: 7372 Prepackaged software

(G-6861)
RICOH PRTG SYSTEMS AMER INC
Also Called: Ricoh Systems
115 Route 46 Bldg F (07046-1673)
PHONE....................973 316-6051
Cheryl Taylor, *Branch Mgr*
EMP: 5
SALES (corp-wide): 19.3B **Privately Held**
WEB: www.hitachi-printingsolutions.us
SIC: 3577 3861 3955 Printers, computer; toners, prepared photographic (not made in chemical plants); ribbons, inked: typewriter, adding machine, register, etc.
HQ: Ricoh Printing Systems America, Inc.
2390 Ward Ave Ste A
Simi Valley CA 93065
805 578-4000

(G-6862)
TIMES TIN CUP
35 Rainbow Trl (07046-1725)
PHONE....................973 983-1095
Laurel Durenberger, *Principal*
EMP: 4
SALES (est): 410.2K **Privately Held**
SIC: 3356 Tin

(G-6863)
TURNER ENGINEERING INC
14 Morris Ave (07046-1011)
PHONE....................973 263-1000
John J Turner Jr, *President*
Nancy Mattson, *Corp Secy*
EMP: 15
SQ FT: 2,200
SALES (est): 3.6MM **Privately Held**
WEB: www.turnereng.com
SIC: 3663 8711 Television closed circuit equipment; television monitors; engineering services; consulting engineer

(G-6864)
WESTERN SCIENTIFIC COMPUTERS
28 W Shore Rd (07046-1523)
PHONE....................973 263-9311
Fax: 973 263-1976
Joseph Lutz, *President*
Jody Klinghoffer, *Vice Pres*
EMP: 13
SQ FT: 4,500
SALES: 1.8MM **Privately Held**
SIC: 3577 Computer peripheral equipment

Mountainside
Union County

(G-6865)
A K STAMPING CO INC
Also Called: Globe Manufacturing Sales Co
1159 Us Highway 22 (07092-2808)
P.O. Box 1213 (07092-0213)
PHONE....................908 232-7300
Fax: 908 232-4729
Arthur A Kurz, *President*
Linda Bonnel, *Purchasing*
Marlene M Kurz, *Treasurer*
Carlo Montesa, *Info Tech Mgr*
Kathleen Holmes, *Technology*
▲ EMP: 75 EST: 1954

SQ FT: 100,000
SALES (est): 17.5MM **Privately Held**
WEB: www.akstamping.com
SIC: 3469 3544 Stamping metal for the trade; special dies & tools; jigs & fixtures

(G-6866)
AIR & SPECIALTIES SHEET METAL
276 Sheffield St (07092-2303)
PHONE....................908 233-8306
Fax: 908 233-8323
Kim Deitrich, *President*
Bruce Deitrich, *Vice Pres*
EMP: 15
SQ FT: 14,500
SALES (est): 3.7MM **Privately Held**
WEB: www.airconsonline.com
SIC: 3549 3444 3441 Metalworking machinery; sheet metalwork; fabricated structural metal

(G-6867)
ALL PRINT RESOURCES GROUP INC
256 Sheffield St (07092-2303)
P.O. Box 1455 (07092-0455)
PHONE....................201 994-0600
Joseph Dec, *President*
EMP: 4
SALES (est): 549.7K **Privately Held**
SIC: 2752 Commercial printing, offset

(G-6868)
AMERICAN ALUMINUM COMPANY
Also Called: Amalco
230 Sheffield St (07092-2303)
PHONE....................908 233-3500
Fax: 908 233-3241
Robert Brucker, *President*
Daniel Osworth, *General Mgr*
Henry Brucker II, *Vice Pres*
Eldar Sukurlu, *Prdtn Mgr*
Karen Alifante, *Purch Mgr*
EMP: 70
SQ FT: 70,000
SALES (est): 18.7MM **Privately Held**
WEB: www.amalco.com
SIC: 3356 3489 3728 Battery metal; ordnance & accessories; aircraft parts & equipment

(G-6869)
AMERICAN TELETIMER CORP
1167 Globe Ave (07092-2903)
PHONE....................908 654-4200
Fax: 908 653-1155
Joel Rosenzweig, *CEO*
Ron Couturier, *COO*
Matt Rosenzweig, *Manager*
Ford Cook, *Director*
EMP: 40
SQ FT: 6,400
SALES (est): 3.7MM **Privately Held**
WEB: www.teletimer.com
SIC: 3625 7384 Timing devices, electronic; photofinish laboratories

(G-6870)
CREATONE INC
1011 Us Highway 22 Ste 1 (07092-2803)
PHONE....................908 789-8700
Arun Patel, *President*
Asha Patel, *Treasurer*
EMP: 11
SQ FT: 6,000
SALES (est): 980K **Privately Held**
WEB: www.assetor.net
SIC: 8711 3679 Electrical or electronic engineering; electronic circuits

(G-6871)
CSM ENVIRONMENTAL SYSTEMS LLC
269 Sheffield St Ste 1 (07092-2318)
PHONE....................908 789-5431
Michael Torstrup, *Owner*
Jim Castillo, *Principal*
EMP: 12
SALES (est): 1.2MM **Privately Held**
SIC: 3564 Blowers & fans

(G-6872)
D PAGLIA & SONS INC
280 Sheffield St (07092-2303)
PHONE....................908 654-5999
Daniel Paglia Sr, *President*
EMP: 14
SQ FT: 2,500
SALES: 1.5MM **Privately Held**
WEB: www.dpaglia.com
SIC: 3911 Jewelry, precious metal

(G-6873)
DANFOSS HAGO INC
1120 Globe Ave (07092-2904)
PHONE....................908 232-8687
Phil Emond, *President*
Eleanor Smith, *Chairman*
Christine Oschmann, *Exec VP*
Susan Fleming, *Shareholder*
▲ EMP: 110 EST: 1937
SQ FT: 33,500
SALES (est): 14.1MM
SALES (corp-wide): 6.8B **Privately Held**
WEB: www.hagonozzles.com
SIC: 3432 Plumbing fixture fittings & trim
HQ: Danfoss A/S
Nordborgvej 81
Nordborg 6430
748 822-22

(G-6874)
DAVID E CONNOLLY INC
1091 Bristol Rd (07092-2301)
P.O. Box 2331, New Preston CT (06777-0331)
PHONE....................908 654-4600
David E Connolly, *President*
Nora Connolly, *Vice Pres*
EMP: 18 EST: 1982
SQ FT: 3,000
SALES (est): 251.9K **Privately Held**
SIC: 3911 Jewelry, precious metal

(G-6875)
DE DITRICH PROCESS SYSTEMS INC (PA)
244 Sheffield St (07092-2303)
P.O. Box 345, Union (07083-0345)
PHONE....................908 317-2585
Donald Doell, *CEO*
Helen Wilson, *CFO*
Jim Friedrich, *Regl Sales Mgr*
Sara Gerity, *Mktg Coord*
Mark Banfield, *Manager*
EMP: 35 EST: 1976
SQ FT: 100,000
SALES (est): 44.9MM **Privately Held**
WEB: www.ddpsinc.com
SIC: 8711 3443 Consulting engineer; industrial vessels, tanks & containers

(G-6876)
DESMAR CORPORATION
Also Called: Desisti Lighting
1011 Us Highway 22 Ste 3 (07092-2803)
PHONE....................908 317-0020
Fabio Desisti, *Ch of Bd*
Mario Desisti, *Ch of Bd*
Greg Semper, *Treasurer*
▲ EMP: 9
SQ FT: 10,000
SALES: 6MM **Privately Held**
SIC: 5063 3648 Lighting fixtures; lighting equipment

(G-6877)
DIGITAL COLOR CONCEPTS INC
256 Sheffield St (07092-2303)
PHONE....................908 264-0504
Fax: 908 264-0514
Don Cerwilliter, *Exec VP*
John Rock, *Sales Staff*
David Morin, *Department Mgr*
James Rehfuss, *Info Tech Mgr*
Ramona Pauley, *Executive*
EMP: 79 **Privately Held**
SIC: 2759 Publication printing
PA: Digital Color Concepts, Inc.
30 W 21st St Fl 5
New York NY 10010

(G-6878)
DORF FEATURE SERVICE INC
187 Mill Ln Ste 3 (07092-2919)
PHONE..................................908 518-1802
Fax: 908 518-2761
Sid Dorfman, *President*
EMP: 35
SALES (est): 1.8MM **Privately Held**
WEB: www.starledger.com
SIC: 7383 2711 News reporting services for newspapers & periodicals; newspapers

(G-6879)
E Z HI-TECH SERVICES INC (PA)
Also Called: E Z HI Tech International
1140 Route 22 (07092-2810)
PHONE..................................908 317-8203
Fax: 908 317-8269
Zeev Sela, *President*
Karrie Dipiazzo, *Credit Mgr*
▲ EMP: 9
SQ FT: 1,000
SALES (est): 1.5MM **Privately Held**
WEB: www.ezhitech.com
SIC: 3861 Printing equipment, photographic

(G-6880)
EATON CORPORATION
1115 Globe Ave A (07092-2903)
PHONE..................................732 767-9600
Fax: 732 205-2642
Russ Brodsky, *Senior Engr*
Doug Carolan, *Manager*
EMP: 20 **Privately Held**
WEB: www.eaton.com
SIC: 3699 5065 Electrical equipment & supplies; electronic parts & equipment
HQ: Eaton Corporation
1000 Eaton Blvd
Cleveland OH 44122
440 523-5000

(G-6881)
ELENA CONSULTANTS & ELEC
1175 Globe Ave (07092-2903)
P.O. Box 1339 (07092-0339)
PHONE..................................908 654-8309
Rick Miller, *President*
Karen Miller, *Vice Pres*
EMP: 20
SQ FT: 15,000
SALES (est): 2.3MM **Privately Held**
SIC: 3674 8742 Solid state electronic devices; industrial consultant

(G-6882)
G & A COML SEATING PDTS CORP
152 Glen Rd (07092-2915)
PHONE..................................908 233-8000
Yuri Libson, *President*
◆ EMP: 9
SALES (est): 1.8MM **Privately Held**
SIC: 2521 Wood office furniture

(G-6883)
M P TUBE WORKS INC
237 Sheffield St (07092-2313)
P.O. Box 1430 (07092-0430)
PHONE..................................908 317-2500
Fax: 908 317-2969
Michael J McGinley, *President*
Paul W Kelman, *Vice Pres*
EMP: 8 EST: 1981
SQ FT: 15,000
SALES (est): 1.5MM **Privately Held**
SIC: 3498 5051 Tube fabricating (contract bending & shaping); cast iron pipe; tubing, metal

(G-6884)
NEWLINE PRTG & TECH SOLUTIONS
1011 Us Highway 22 Ste 1 (07092-2803)
PHONE..................................973 405-6133
John Luciano, *President*
Michelle Krieger, *Accountant*
Elena Manzi, *Office Mgr*
▲ EMP: 10 EST: 1998
SALES: 3MM **Privately Held**
SIC: 2752 Commercial printing, offset

(G-6885)
NJ PRECISION TECH INC
1081 Bristol Rd (07092-2301)
PHONE..................................800 409-3000
Fax: 908 232-8867
Robert Tarantino, *President*
Michal Obloj, *Engineer*
Mohammad Oudeh, *Engineer*
EMP: 50
SQ FT: 10,500
SALES (est): 10.1MM **Privately Held**
WEB: www.njpt.com
SIC: 3599 Machine shop, jobbing & repair

(G-6886)
PRISM DGTAL COMMUNICATIONS LLC
1011 Us Highway 22 Ste A (07092-2803)
PHONE..................................973 232-5038
Jack Ayan, *Mng Member*
EMP: 10
SQ FT: 23,000
SALES (est): 2MM **Privately Held**
SIC: 2752 8742 Commercial printing, offset; marketing consulting services

(G-6887)
REMINGTON INDUSTRIES INC
Also Called: Cordes Machine Div
269 Sheffield St Ste 2 (07092-2318)
PHONE..................................908 233-0153
Fax: 908 223-2606
Harold Feigel, *President*
Nancy Feigel, *Corp Secy*
Diana Devito, *Administration*
EMP: 12
SQ FT: 6,000
SALES (est): 2.1MM **Privately Held**
SIC: 3569 3565 Assembly machines, non-metalworking; packaging machinery

(G-6888)
SPRINGFIELD HEATING & AC CO
Also Called: Spring Aire
217 Sheffield St (07092-2302)
PHONE..................................908 233-8400
Joseph Gallini Jr, *President*
Louis Gallini, *President*
George Gallini, *Vice Pres*
EMP: 11
SQ FT: 5,000
SALES (est): 1.1MM **Privately Held**
SIC: 1711 3444 Heating & air conditioning contractors; sheet metalwork

(G-6889)
TRANO BRUCE PLUMBING & HEATING
872 Woodland Ave (07092-2524)
PHONE..................................908 654-3685
Bruce Trano, *Owner*
Craig Trano, *Partner*
EMP: 4
SALES (est): 290K **Privately Held**
SIC: 3431 1711 Plumbing fixtures: enameled iron cast iron or pressed metal; plumbing, heating, air-conditioning contractors

(G-6890)
WRITERS & POETS
Also Called: Best Pmbooks.com
1625 Nottingham Way (07092-1348)
P.O. Box 1307 (07092-0307)
PHONE..................................908 233-2399
Earl Cox, *President*
EMP: 5
SALES: 225K **Privately Held**
SIC: 2731 Books: publishing only

<hr>
Mullica Hill
Gloucester County
<hr>

(G-6891)
ALBERT FORTE NECKWEAR CO INC
127 Fellowship Ln (08062-2207)
PHONE..................................856 423-2342
Albert Forte Jr, *President*
Brian Forte, *Admin Sec*
EMP: 6

SQ FT: 5,000
SALES (est): 683.3K **Privately Held**
SIC: 2323 Men's & boys' neckwear

(G-6892)
ANNA K PARK
50 N Main St (08062-9409)
PHONE..................................856 478-9500
Anna Park, *Principal*
EMP: 4
SALES (est): 327.3K **Privately Held**
SIC: 3843 Enamels, dentists'

(G-6893)
WJM TRUCKING INC
515 Macintosh Dr (08062-9475)
P.O. Box 54 (08062-0054)
PHONE..................................856 381-3635
William J Macmillan, *President*
EMP: 9
SALES (est): 750K **Privately Held**
SIC: 3715 Truck trailers

(G-6894)
ZIPPITYPRINT LLC
Also Called: Zippityprint.com
182 Harrisonville Rd (08062-2832)
PHONE..................................216 438-0001
Joseph P Dell Aquila, *CEO*
EMP: 12
SQ FT: 17,000
SALES: 1.7MM **Privately Held**
SIC: 2752 7331 7336 Commercial printing, offset; direct mail advertising services; graphic arts & related design

<hr>
Murray Hill
Union County
<hr>

(G-6895)
NOKIA INC
600-700 Mountain Ave (07974)
PHONE..................................908 582-3149
John Wu, *Opers Mgr*
Laurie Abyazi, *Engineer*
Shon Winters, *Engineer*
Julie Liptak, *VP Human Res*
Patrick Moran, *Security Mgr*
EMP: 15 EST: 1987
SALES (est): 2.7MM **Privately Held**
SIC: 3661 Telephone dialing devices, automatic

<hr>
Neptune
Monmouth County
<hr>

(G-6896)
5 KIDS GROUP LTD LIABILITY CO
37 State Route 35 N (07753-4745)
PHONE..................................732 774-5331
▲ EMP: 12
SALES (est): 809.7K **Privately Held**
SIC: 2284 Thread Mill

(G-6897)
A H HOFFMANN LLC
209 W Sylvania Ave (07753-6233)
PHONE..................................732 988-6000
Arthur Hoffmann, *CEO*
EMP: 5
SQ FT: 9,600
SALES (est): 308.3K **Privately Held**
SIC: 1389 Oil consultants

(G-6898)
A PLUS POWERWASHING
503 Moore Rd (07753-5510)
PHONE..................................732 245-3816
Brian Hegarty, *Owner*
EMP: 4
SALES (est): 180K **Privately Held**
SIC: 3589 High pressure cleaning equipment

(G-6899)
ALLEGRO NUTRITION INC
Also Called: Gaspari Nutrition
1023 Waverly Ave (07753-3195)
PHONE..................................732 364-3777

Richard Gaspari, *President*
Oscar Iturralde, *Treasurer*
Lynn Brabant, *Executive Asst*
▼ EMP: 25
SQ FT: 65,000
SALES (est): 4.8MM **Privately Held**
SIC: 2023 Dietary supplements, dairy & non-dairy based
HQ: Allegro Limited
Jamestown House
Dublin 11
185 806-00

(G-6900)
ASBURY PARK PRESS INC
Also Called: Home News & Tribune
3600 Route 66 (07753-2605)
P.O. Box 1550 (07754-1550)
PHONE..................................732 922-6000
Fax: 732 643-4014
Thomas M Donovan, *President*
Robert T Collins, *Principal*
W Raymond Ollwerther, *Vice Pres*
Kristen Janet Materese, *Prdtn Mgr*
Brian Johnston, *Production*
▲ EMP: 1200 EST: 1879
SQ FT: 172,000
SALES (est): 193.8MM
SALES (corp-wide): 3.1B **Publicly Held**
WEB: www.app.com
SIC: 2711 2752 Commercial printing & newspaper publishing combined; commercial printing, lithographic
PA: Gannett Co., Inc.
7950 Jones Branch Dr
Mc Lean VA 22102
703 854-6000

(G-6901)
AUTOMATED CONTROL CONCEPTS INC (PA)
Also Called: A C C
3535 State Route 66 # 14 (07753-2625)
PHONE..................................732 922-6611
Fax: 732 922-9611
Robert J Tomasetta, *Ch of Bd*
Michael Blechman, *President*
Victor Ronchetti, *Vice Pres*
Alfredo Prieto, *Project Mgr*
Satgurusharan Thakkar, *Project Mgr*
EMP: 32
SQ FT: 15,000
SALES: 10.2MM **Privately Held**
WEB: www.automated-control.com
SIC: 7373 3577 Systems integration services; computer peripheral equipment

(G-6902)
BROWNS WELDING SERVICE
105 Oxonia Ave (07753-4523)
PHONE..................................732 988-9530
Al Brown, *Owner*
EMP: 4
SALES (est): 200K **Privately Held**
SIC: 7692 Welding repair

(G-6903)
CARL STREIT & SON CO
703 Atkins Ave (07753-5169)
P.O. Box 157 (07754-0157)
PHONE..................................732 775-0803
Fax: 732 775-2274
James E Robinson Jr, *President*
Judith E Robinson, *Vice Pres*
EMP: 9
SQ FT: 1,344
SALES (est): 3.4MM **Privately Held**
SIC: 5147 2011 2015 Meats, fresh; meat packing plants; poultry slaughtering & processing

(G-6904)
CONTAINER GRAPHICS CORP
3535 Highway 66 Ste 2 (07753-2624)
PHONE..................................732 922-1180
Fax: 732 922-1696
Jeff McCready, *Branch Mgr*
EMP: 50
SQ FT: 5,000
SALES (corp-wide): 3MM **Privately Held**
WEB: www.containergraphics.com
SIC: 3953 3544 2796 Marking devices; special dies, tools, jigs & fixtures; platemaking services

PA: Container Graphics Corp.
114 Ednbrgh S Dr Ste 104
Cary NC 27511
919 481-4200

(G-6905)
COTTAGE LACE AND RIBBON CO INC (PA)
Also Called: Ribbon Bazaar
210 3rd Ave Ste 21 (07753)
PHONE....................732 776-9353
Fax: 732 776-9375
Shahid Waseem, *President*
▲ EMP: 4
SALES (est): 950K **Privately Held**
SIC: 5131 2241 Ribbons; ribbons

(G-6906)
CRAFTMASTER PRINTING INC (PA)
2024 State Route 33 (07753-6115)
PHONE....................732 775-0011
Fax: 732 775-1771
Jeanne A Baumgartner, *President*
Robert Baumgartner, *Corp Secy*
Curtis Baumgartner, *Vice Pres*
EMP: 4
SQ FT: 1,200
SALES (est): 584.6K **Privately Held**
WEB: www.craftmasterprinting.com
SIC: 2752 Commercial printing, offset

(G-6907)
CREATIVE DISPLAY INC
349 Essex Rd (07753-2637)
PHONE....................732 918-8010
Fax: 732 918-8999
Danette Bussey, *President*
David Longo, *Vice Pres*
▲ EMP: 7
SALES (est): 1.1MM **Privately Held**
SIC: 3999 Plants, artificial & preserved

(G-6908)
DYMAX SYSTEMS INC
3455 State Route 66 Ste 6 (07753-2759)
PHONE....................732 918-2424
Ralph Barnhart, *President*
Russell Nielson, *Engineer*
EMP: 15
SQ FT: 1,000
SALES (est): 922K **Privately Held**
WEB: www.dymaxsystems.com
SIC: 7379 7372 5045 Computer related consulting services; prepackaged software; computers

(G-6909)
EDMONDMARKS TECHNOLOGIES INC
3535 State Route 66 Ste 3 (07753-2624)
PHONE....................732 643-0290
Fax: 732 612-1119
James Williams, *CEO*
Michael Marks, *President*
Susan Williams, *Vice Pres*
Kristy Capak, *Buyer*
Shawn Sena, *Engineer*
EMP: 35
SQ FT: 11,600
SALES (est): 6.7MM **Privately Held**
SIC: 3699 8711 Electrical equipment & supplies; electrical or electronic engineering

(G-6910)
ELECTRO IMPULSE LABORATORY INC
1805 State Route 33 (07753-4847)
P.O. Box 278 (07754-0278)
PHONE....................732 776-5800
Fax: 732 776-6793
Mark Rubin, *Ch of Bd*
Lucille P Gardner, *Vice Pres*
Carol Rubin, *Vice Pres*
Theresa Carmicheal, *Senior Buyer*
Tyler Kanter, *Engineer*
EMP: 45 EST: 1947
SQ FT: 53,000

SALES: 6.9MM **Privately Held**
WEB: www.electroimpulse.com
SIC: 3585 3825 Refrigeration equipment, complete; power measuring equipment, electrical; radio frequency measuring equipment; test equipment for electronic & electrical circuits

(G-6911)
EXCELSIOR MEDICAL LLC (HQ)
1933 Heck Ave (07753-4428)
PHONE....................732 776-7525
James Abrams, *COO*
Sandra Rigopoulos, *CFO*
Robert Raia, *Manager*
◆ EMP: 144
SALES (est): 75.8MM
SALES (corp-wide): 5.6B **Privately Held**
WEB: www.excelsiormedical.com
SIC: 3841 Surgical & medical instruments
PA: Medline Industries, Inc.
3 Lakes Dr
Northfield IL 60093
847 949-5500

(G-6912)
FIVE KIDS GROUP INC
37 Highway 35 N Fl 2 (07753-4745)
PHONE....................732 774-5331
Glen Suchecki, *President*
EMP: 1
SQ FT: 8,500
SALES: 1.4MM **Privately Held**
SIC: 5699 3999 Uniforms & work clothing; embroidery kits

(G-6913)
G G TAUBER COMPANY INC
3535 State Route 66 Ste 1 (07753-2623)
PHONE....................800 638-6667
Dana Belser Jr, *CEO*
Judith Bryant, *President*
EMP: 25 EST: 1947
SQ FT: 12,000
SALES (est): 1.8MM **Privately Held**
WEB: www.ggtauber.com
SIC: 3999 5699 5199 Identification badges & insignia; belts, apparel: custom; customized clothing & apparel; sports apparel; T-shirts, custom printed; advertising specialties

(G-6914)
GERIN CORPORATION INC
1109 7th Ave (07753-5189)
P.O. Box 307, Avon By The Sea (07717-0307)
PHONE....................732 774-3256
Fax: 732 774-0274
Robert Gerin, *President*
EMP: 6
SQ FT: 4,550
SALES: 300K **Privately Held**
SIC: 3823 Viscosimeters, industrial process type

(G-6915)
GLUEFAST COMPANY INC
3535 State Route 66 Ste 1 (07753-2623)
PHONE....................732 918-4600
Fax: 732 918-4646
Lester Mallet, *President*
Amy Altman, *Corp Secy*
▲ EMP: 12 EST: 1939
SQ FT: 17,500
SALES (est): 3.5MM **Privately Held**
WEB: www.gluefast.com
SIC: 2891 3559 Glue; chemical machinery & equipment

(G-6916)
GOURMET KITCHEN LLC
1238 Corlies Ave (07753-5069)
PHONE....................732 775-5222
Fax: 732 775-5225
Micheal Lacey, *President*
Ray Walsh, *Principal*
Pat Duffey, *Vice Pres*
Ryan Walsh, *Admin Sec*
▲ EMP: 140
SQ FT: 7,000
SALES (est): 26MM **Privately Held**
SIC: 2099 Food preparations

(G-6917)
GROEZINGER PROVISIONS INC
1200 7th Ave (07753-5190)
PHONE....................732 775-3220
Fax: 732 775-3223
Laurie Cummins, *President*
EMP: 17
SQ FT: 18,000
SALES (est): 2.9MM **Privately Held**
WEB: www.alexianpate.com
SIC: 2013 Sausages & other prepared meats; sausages from purchased meat; bologna from purchased meat

(G-6918)
HINCK TURKEY FARM INC
3930 Belmar Blvd (07753-7111)
PHONE....................732 681-0508
Fax: 732 681-8791
Robert Longo, *President*
EMP: 9
SQ FT: 12,000
SALES (est): 611.9K **Privately Held**
SIC: 2015 0253 Turkey processing & slaughtering; turkey farm

(G-6919)
HOLOCRAFT CORPORATION (PA)
Also Called: Flexcraft Company
50 Flexcraft Dr (07753-6276)
PHONE....................732 502-9500
Fax: 732 502-9503
Ben Smith, *CEO*
Adrian Mendez, *Plant Mgr*
Ben Bamberger, *Engineer*
Russ Smith Jr, *CFO*
David Schutzer, *Manager*
▼ EMP: 81
SQ FT: 34,000
SALES (est): 20MM **Privately Held**
WEB: www.flexcraftcompany.com
SIC: 3089 Blow molded finished plastic products; air mattresses, plastic

(G-6920)
KIRMS PRINTING CO INC
1520 Washington Ave (07753-4912)
P.O. Box 1067 (07754-1067)
PHONE....................732 774-8000
Albert G Kirms, *President*
Norris D Kirms, *Corp Secy*
EMP: 20 EST: 1924
SQ FT: 9,600
SALES (est): 3MM **Privately Held**
SIC: 2752 2791 Commercial printing, offset; typesetting

(G-6921)
KRELL TECHNOLOGIES INC
11 Evergreen Ave (07753-6501)
PHONE....................732 617-7091
EMP: 8
SQ FT: 1,300
SALES (est): 1.2MM **Privately Held**
SIC: 8711 3827 Engineering Services Mfg Optical Instruments/Lenses

(G-6922)
MALLETECH LLC
1107 11th Ave (07753-5165)
PHONE....................732 774-0011
Leigh Stevens,
▲ EMP: 17
SALES (est): 2.4MM **Privately Held**
SIC: 3931 Musical instruments

(G-6923)
MARLO PLASTIC PRODUCTS INC
3535 State Route 66 Ste 1 (07753-2623)
PHONE....................732 792-1988
Fax: 732 792-1996
Arthur Livingston, *President*
▲ EMP: 40 EST: 1945
SQ FT: 25,000
SALES (est): 6.7MM **Privately Held**
WEB: www.marloplastics.com
SIC: 3089 2759 Novelties, plastic; promotional printing

(G-6924)
MASTERCRAFT IRON INC
1111 10th Ave (07753-5130)
P.O. Box 748 (07754-0748)
PHONE....................732 988-3113
Fax: 732 988-3321
P Peter Stagaard III, *President*
Bryan Newhook, *Project Mgr*
Pete Stagaard, *Executive*
Robert Van Norman, *Admin Sec*
EMP: 15
SQ FT: 3,500
SALES (est): 3MM **Privately Held**
SIC: 1761 3542 Sheet metalwork; punching, shearing & bending machines

(G-6925)
NEW DAWN INC
Also Called: Rex Sign
60 Steiner Ave (07753-6639)
PHONE....................732 774-1377
Jacqueline Janocha, *President*
EMP: 8
SALES (est): 937.3K **Privately Held**
SIC: 3993 Signs, not made in custom sign painting shops

(G-6926)
NJ PRESS MEDIA
3601 State Route 66 (07753-2604)
P.O. Box 1550 (07754-1550)
PHONE....................732 643-3604
Bill Ditty, *Sales Staff*
Paul C Grzella, *Manager*
EMP: 8 EST: 2012
SALES (est): 415.2K **Privately Held**
SIC: 2711 Newspapers, publishing & printing

(G-6927)
PARK STEEL & IRON CO (PA)
9 Evergreen Ave (07753-6501)
P.O. Box 365, Bradley Beach (07720-0365)
PHONE....................732 775-7500
Fax: 732 776-8494
Garet J Pilling, *CEO*
Scot Pilling, *Vice Pres*
EMP: 10
SQ FT: 19,000
SALES (est): 1.4MM **Privately Held**
SIC: 3441 3444 3341 Fabricated structural metal; sheet metalwork; secondary nonferrous metals

(G-6928)
SCAASIS ORIGINALS INC
Also Called: Oceanic Trading
1006 11th Ave (07753-5174)
PHONE....................732 775-7474
Fax: 732 775-7535
Brenda Saada, *President*
Esther Saada, *Treasurer*
▲ EMP: 30
SQ FT: 18,000
SALES (est): 4.3MM **Privately Held**
WEB: www.scaasis.com
SIC: 3961 5094 5199 Jewelry apparel, non-precious metals; costume jewelry, ex. precious metal & semiprecious stones; jewelry; gifts & novelties

(G-6929)
SCHOOL PUBLICATIONS CO INC
Also Called: Spc Publication
1520 Washington Ave (07753-4912)
P.O. Box 1067 (07754-1067)
PHONE....................732 988-1100
Albert G Kirms, *President*
Bill Kirms, *Human Res Mgr*
Norris D Kirms, *Admin Sec*
EMP: 20
SALES (est): 1.3MM **Privately Held**
WEB: www.schoolpub.com
SIC: 2741 2752 2732 2731 Miscellaneous publishing; commercial printing, lithographic; book printing; book publishing; periodicals; newspapers

(G-6930)
SCHULTZ COMPANY
2530 Asbury Ave (07753-2501)
PHONE....................732 922-4334
Robert Schultz, *President*
Mike Carpenter, *Manager*
▲ EMP: 4
SQ FT: 5,000

SALES (est): 400K **Privately Held**
WEB: www.schultzproducts.com
SIC: 3728 Aircraft parts & equipment

(G-6931)
SEAJAY MANUFACTURING CORP
9 Memorial Dr Ste 1 (07753-5083)
PHONE.............................732 774-0900
Jeffrey Finn, *President*
Carl Flury, *President*
Robert Musanti, *Controller*
EMP: 11
SQ FT: 20,000
SALES: 800K **Privately Held**
SIC: 3089 3069 3559 3544 Blow molded finished plastic products; molded rubber products; plastics working machinery; special dies, tools, jigs & fixtures

(G-6932)
SHOP RITE SUPERMARKETS INC
Also Called: Shop Rite 299
2200 Highway 66 (07753-4062)
PHONE.............................732 775-4250
Don Brennan, *Manager*
EMP: 180
SALES (corp-wide): 12.5B **Privately Held**
SIC: 5411 5912 5992 2051 Supermarkets; drug stores & proprietary stores; florists; bread, cake & related products
HQ: Shop Rite Supermarkets, Inc.
5000 Riverside Dr
Keasbey NJ 08832
908 527-3300

(G-6933)
STAR PROCESS HEAT SYSTEMS LLC
208 Iris Dr (07753-3654)
PHONE.............................732 282-1002
Steven A Robinson,
Mary E Bass,
Steven A Robertson,
EMP: 5
SQ FT: 2,100
SALES: 500K **Privately Held**
WEB: www.starphs.com
SIC: 3599 Air intake filters, internal combustion engine, except auto

(G-6934)
TFH PUBLICATIONS INC
85 W Sylvania Ave (07753-6775)
PHONE.............................732 897-6860
Marcy Cortez, *Controller*
EMP: 100
SALES (corp-wide): 2B **Publicly Held**
WEB: www.tfh.com
SIC: 2731 Books: publishing & printing
HQ: T.F.H. Publications, Inc.
85 W Sylvania Ave
Neptune NJ 07753
732 988-8400

(G-6935)
TFH PUBLICATIONS INC
211 W Sylvania Ave (07753-6296)
PHONE.............................732 988-8400
Marcy Cortez, *Branch Mgr*
Albert Connelly, *Manager*
EMP: 40
SALES (corp-wide): 2B **Publicly Held**
WEB: www.tfh.com
SIC: 2731 Books: publishing & printing
HQ: T.F.H. Publications, Inc.
85 W Sylvania Ave
Neptune NJ 07753
732 988-8400

(G-6936)
TOLL COMPACTION SERVICE INC (PA)
Also Called: Toll Compaction Group
14 Memorial Dr (07753-5051)
PHONE.............................732 776-8225
Fax: 732 776-8306
Paul B Pritchard, *CEO*
Tyson Pritchard, *President*
Kevin Thor, *Plant Mgr*
Jim Margl, *Maint Spvr*
Stacy Ritchie, *Admin Asst*
▲ EMP: 40
SQ FT: 23,000

SALES (est): 6.6MM **Privately Held**
WEB: www.tollcompaction.com
SIC: 2833 Medicinals & botanicals

(G-6937)
ZIMPLI KIDS INC
3301 Route 66 Ste 130 (07753-2705)
PHONE.............................732 945-5995
Thomas Whale, *Principal*
EMP: 7
SALES (est): 231.3K **Privately Held**
SIC: 3944 Games, toys & children's vehicles

Neshanic Station
Somerset County

(G-6938)
AROME AMERICA LLC
2 Van Fleet Rd (08853-4300)
PHONE.............................908 806-7003
John F Nobile, *Managing Prtnr*
▲ EMP: 7
SALES (est): 548.4K **Privately Held**
WEB: www.aromeamerica.com
SIC: 2099 Food preparations

(G-6939)
SOURLAND MOUNTAIN WDWKG LLC T
17 Higginsville Rd (08853-3612)
PHONE.............................908 806-7661
EMP: 4 EST: 2009
SALES (est): 373.1K **Privately Held**
SIC: 2431 Millwork

(G-6940)
WESTCON ORTHOPEDICS INC
4 Craig Rd (08853-3504)
P.O. Box 342, Adelphia (07710-0342)
PHONE.............................908 806-8981
Fax: 908 806-6664
Don Gordon, *President*
Robert Schultz, *Corp Secy*
Marcella Schultz, *Vice Pres*
EMP: 4
SALES: 250K **Privately Held**
SIC: 3841 Ophthalmic instruments & apparatus

Netcong
Morris County

(G-6941)
HOOKWAY ENTERPRISES INC
Also Called: Megasafe
130 Allen St (07857-1236)
PHONE.............................973 691-0382
Michael J Hookway, *President*
EMP: 10
SQ FT: 5,000
SALES: 2MM **Privately Held**
SIC: 7382 3499 Protective devices, security; locks, safe & vault: metal

---

New Brunswick
Middlesex County

(G-6942)
ACCU SEAL RUBBER INC
18f Home News Row (08901-3644)
PHONE.............................732 246-4333
Fax: 732 246-4609
Pravin Tejani, *President*
Surekse Tejani, *Accountant*
Shawn Tejani, *Manager*
Manjula Tejani, *Admin Sec*
EMP: 4
SQ FT: 4,200
SALES: 500K **Privately Held**
WEB: www.accusealrubber.com
SIC: 3069 Molded rubber products

(G-6943)
AKCROS CHEMICALS INC
500 Jersey Ave (08901-3502)
PHONE.............................800 500-7890
Paul Angus, *CEO*

Mike Bogdan, *Production*
Erin Maietta, *Human Res Mgr*
Vini Shah, *Manager*
George W Turk, *Manager*
◆ EMP: 72
SQ FT: 124,000
SALES (est): 24MM
SALES (corp-wide): 271.6MM **Privately Held**
WEB: www.akcros.com
SIC: 2869 Industrial organic chemicals
HQ: Polymer Additives, Inc.
7500 E Pleasant Valley Rd
Independence OH 44131
216 875-7200

(G-6944)
ANS PLASTICS CORPORATION
625 Jersey Ave Ste 11a (08901-3679)
PHONE.............................732 247-2776
Fax: 732 247-1594
Adel Samuel, *President*
Ramy Samuel, *Vice Pres*
▲ EMP: 14
SQ FT: 14,000
SALES (est): 3.9MM **Privately Held**
WEB: www.ansplastics.com
SIC: 2673 2671 5162 5113 Plastic bags: made from purchased materials; plastic film, coated or laminated for packaging; plastics film; bags, paper & disposable plastic

(G-6945)
AP DEAUVILLE LLC
594 Jersey Ave Ste 1 (08901-3569)
PHONE.............................732 545-0200
Fred Horowitz, *CEO*
Bruce Lazare, *Senior VP*
Robert J Myszka, *Vice Pres*
Alfred Efremoff, *VP Opers*
Frank Bollaci, *Opers Staff*
▲ EMP: 49
SQ FT: 97,000
SALES: 40MM **Privately Held**
WEB: www.apdeauville.com
SIC: 2844 Cosmetic preparations

(G-6946)
AQUASPORTS POOLS LLC
999 Jersey Ave (08901-3609)
PHONE.............................732 247-6298
EMP: 15
SALES (est): 1.3MM **Privately Held**
SIC: 3949 Swimming pools, plastic

(G-6947)
ART MATERIALS SERVICE INC
Also Called: AMS
625 Joyce Kilmer Ave (08901-3307)
PHONE.............................732 545-8888
Fax: 732 545-9166
Joseph Eichert, *President*
Wilson Cubides, *President*
Manuel Lopez, *Manager*
Gary Roark, *Admin Sec*
▲ EMP: 70 EST: 1977
SQ FT: 21,000
SALES (est): 12.5MM **Privately Held**
WEB: www.artmaterialsservice.com
SIC: 3429 Manufactured hardware (general)

(G-6948)
BRISTOL-MYERS SQUIBB COMPANY
104 Georges Rd (08901-3901)
PHONE.............................800 332-2056
Brant Bulgarelli, *Principal*
▲ EMP: 8
SALES (est): 2.9MM **Privately Held**
SIC: 2834 Pharmaceutical preparations

(G-6949)
BUCKETS PLUS INC
Also Called: Mr Ice Buckets
345 Sandford St (08901-2320)
PHONE.............................732 545-0420
Fred Haleluk, *President*
Sudesh Rajpal, *Opers Mgr*
Giorgi Bitsadze, *Manager*
◆ EMP: 6
SALES (est): 590K **Privately Held**
SIC: 3089 3229 Plastic kitchenware, tableware & housewares; barware

(G-6950)
CHALMERS & KUBECK INC
8 Jules Ln (08901-3636)
PHONE.............................732 993-1251
Fax: 732 993-1252
Wayne Salvi, *Manager*
EMP: 7
SALES (corp-wide): 52.2MM **Privately Held**
WEB: www.candk.com
SIC: 3599 5085 Machine shop, jobbing & repair; valves & fittings
PA: Chalmers & Kubeck, Inc.
150 Commerce Dr
Aston PA 19014
610 494-4300

(G-6951)
CHANDLER PHARMACY LLC
Also Called: Chandler Pharmacy & Surgicals
272 George St (08901-1314)
PHONE.............................732 543-1568
Janak Patel,
EMP: 5
SALES (est): 507.5K **Privately Held**
SIC: 2834 Pharmaceutical preparations

(G-6952)
CIELITO LINDO
224 French St (08901-2334)
PHONE.............................580 286-1127
Dari R Almonte Peralta, *Principal*
EMP: 4 EST: 2010
SALES (est): 232.9K **Privately Held**
SIC: 2024 Ice cream, bulk

(G-6953)
CORDIS INTERNATIONAL CORP
1 Johnson And Johnson Plz (08933-0001)
P.O. Box 25700, Miami FL (33102-5700)
PHONE.............................732 524-0400
Fax: 305 824-2080
Donald O'Dwer, *President*
Jesse Pin, *President*
Wayne C Casebolt, *Treasurer*
Daniel G Hall, *Admin Sec*
EMP: 531
SQ FT: 400,000
SALES (est): 120.8MM
SALES (corp-wide): 76.4B **Publicly Held**
WEB: www.jnj.com
SIC: 3841 Surgical & medical instruments
PA: Johnson & Johnson
1 Johnson And Johnson Plz
New Brunswick NJ 08933
732 524-0400

(G-6954)
DETERGENT 20 LLC
594 Jersey Ave (08901-3569)
PHONE.............................732 545-0200
Eddie Greenstein, *Director*
Fred Horowitz,
EMP: 10
SALES: 1MM **Privately Held**
SIC: 5169 2841 Detergents; soap & other detergents

(G-6955)
DOWNTOWN PRINTING CENTER INC
46 Paterson St Ste 1 (08901-2092)
PHONE.............................732 246-7990
Fax: 732 246-3425
Juan E Ruiz, *President*
EMP: 14
SQ FT: 4,000
SALES (est): 1MM **Privately Held**
WEB: www.downtownprinting.com
SIC: 2752 2796 2791 2759 Photo-offset printing; letterpress plates, preparation of; typesetting; letterpress printing; thermography

(G-6956)
DREAM WELL COLLECTION INC
Also Called: Dreamwell
633 Nassau St (08902-2940)
PHONE.............................732 545-5900
Amanda Edna Srour, *Ch of Bd*
Isaac Srour, *Vice Pres*
▲ EMP: 12
SQ FT: 20,000
SALES (est): 3.5MM **Privately Held**
SIC: 2515 Mattresses & bedsprings

▲ = Import ▼=Export
◆ =Import/Export

(G-6957)
ECLIPSE SLEEP PRODUCTS LLC
1375 Jersey Ave Ste 1 (08902-1600)
PHONE..................................732 628-0002
Stuart Carlitz,
EMP: 80
SQ FT: 90,000
SALES (est): 5.6MM **Privately Held**
WEB: www.eclipsebedding.com
SIC: 2515 Mattresses & bedsprings

(G-6958)
ELAINE K JOSEPHSON INC
Also Called: Lawn Doctor of Mercer County
7f Jules Ln (08901-3675)
PHONE..................................609 259-2256
Elaine Josephson, *President*
Michael Josephson, *Vice Pres*
EMP: 5 EST: 1971
SQ FT: 1,500
SALES (est): 590K **Privately Held**
SIC: 2034 Vegetables, dried or dehydrated (except freeze-dried)

(G-6959)
EXCEL DISPLAY CORP
100 Jersey Ave Ste A6 (08901-3268)
P.O. Box 10045 (08906-0045)
PHONE..................................732 246-3724
Fax: 908 246-3753
Tony Chuang, *President*
EMP: 4 EST: 2003
SALES (est): 882.4K **Privately Held**
SIC: 3679 Liquid crystal displays (LCD)

(G-6960)
FEDEX OFFICE & PRINT SVCS INC
212 Rte 18 (08901)
PHONE..................................732 249-9222
Steven Cohn, *Branch Mgr*
EMP: 15
SALES (corp-wide): 65.4B **Publicly Held**
WEB: www.kinkos.com
SIC: 7334 2791 2789 Photocopying & duplicating services; typesetting; bookbinding & related work
HQ: Fedex Office And Print Services, Inc.
7900 Legacy Dr
Plano TX 75024
214 550-7000

(G-6961)
GATEHUSE MEDIA PA HOLDINGS INC
Snowden Pulications
104 Church St (08901-2002)
PHONE..................................732 246-7677
George Taber, *Branch Mgr*
EMP: 28
SALES (corp-wide): 1.3B **Publicly Held**
WEB: www.journalpub.com
SIC: 2711 Newspapers: publishing only, not printed on site
HQ: Gatehouse Media Pennsylvania Holdings, Inc.
175 Sullys Trl Fl 3
Pittsford NY 14534
585 598-0030

(G-6962)
GDB INTERNATIONAL INC (PA)
1 Home News Row (08901-3601)
PHONE..................................732 246-3001
Sanjeev Bagaria, *CEO*
Sunil Bagaria, *President*
Rajesh Dhir, *Senior VP*
Vanessa Downey, *Vice Pres*
Francisco Suarez, *Vice Pres*
◆ EMP: 100
SQ FT: 102,000
SALES (est): 66.2MM **Privately Held**
WEB: www.gdbinternational.com
SIC: 2851 5162 5111 5093 Paints & allied products; paints & paint additives; plastics materials & basic shapes; printing & writing paper; plastics scrap

(G-6963)
GLOBE PHARMA INC
2b Janine Pl (08901-3646)
PHONE..................................732 296-9700
Fax: 732 296-9898
Sanni Raju, *Owner*

▲ EMP: 8
SALES (est): 1.1MM **Privately Held**
SIC: 2834 Pharmaceutical preparations

(G-6964)
GLOBEPHARMA INC
2b Janine Pl (08901-3646)
P.O. Box 7307, North Brunswick (08902-7307)
PHONE..................................732 296-9700
Sanni Raju, *President*
◆ EMP: 10
SQ FT: 5,000
SALES (est): 2.2MM **Privately Held**
WEB: www.globepharma.com
SIC: 3559 Pharmaceutical machinery

(G-6965)
GREENWAY PRODUCTS & SVCS LLC (PA)
14 Home News Row (08901-3602)
PHONE..................................732 442-0200
Anthony Fabrizio, *CFO*
Dominick Davi, *Mng Member*
EMP: 200
SQ FT: 3,000
SALES (est): 15MM **Privately Held**
SIC: 2448 2499 3089 Pallets, wood & wood with metal; mulch or sawdust products, wood; plastic processing

(G-6966)
I I GALAXY INC
235 Jersey Ave Ste 3 (08901-3281)
PHONE..................................732 828-2686
Earl Creighton II, *President*
Earl Creighton Sr, *Vice Pres*
EMP: 5
SALES: 200K **Privately Held**
SIC: 3599 Custom machinery

(G-6967)
ILLUMINATING EXPERIENCES LLC
625 Jersey Ave Ste 7 (08901-3679)
PHONE..................................800 734-5858
Stephen Blackman, *Mng Member*
▲ EMP: 7
SALES (est): 548.8K **Privately Held**
SIC: 3229 3646 Glass lighting equipment parts; ceiling systems, luminous

(G-6968)
INTERNATIONAL SWIMMING POOLS
14c Van Dyke Ave (08901-3578)
P.O. Box 7367, Watchung (07069-0796)
PHONE..................................732 565-9229
Fax: 732 565-1203
Bradley Korbel, *President*
Nicholas J Pietrone, *Corp Secy*
Douglas F Colson, *Vice Pres*
Mary Turner, *Sales Executive*
Danielle Wehrle, *Marketing Mgr*
▲ EMP: 25
SQ FT: 53,000
SALES (est): 4.3MM **Privately Held**
WEB: www.internationalswimmingpools.com
SIC: 3444 Sheet metalwork

(G-6969)
INTERNTIONAL CNSLD CHEMEX CORP
235 Jersey Ave (08901-3281)
PHONE..................................732 828-7676
Fax: 732 828-8677
Walter M Geslak, *President*
Walter Geslak, *Principal*
EMP: 35
SQ FT: 48,974
SALES (est): 5.2MM **Privately Held**
SIC: 3589 2842 3561 5087 Car washing machinery; commercial cleaning equipment; cleaning or polishing preparations; pumps & pumping equipment; carwash equipment & supplies; soap & other detergents

(G-6970)
J & G DIVERSIFIED
235 Jersey Ave Ste 5 (08901-3281)
PHONE..................................732 543-2537
Eli Komm, *President*
EMP: 5

SALES (est): 320K **Privately Held**
SIC: 3993 Signs & advertising specialties

(G-6971)
JANSSEN ORTHO LLC (HQ)
1 Johnson And Johnson Plz (08901-1241)
PHONE..................................609 730-2000
Alex Gorsky, *CEO*
Charles OH, *Research*
Mark Tsai, *Engineer*
Stan Cooley, *Sales Staff*
Fiona Diram, *Manager*
▲ EMP: 2
SALES (est): 1.4MM
SALES (corp-wide): 76.4B **Publicly Held**
WEB: www.ncsca.jnj.com
SIC: 3842 Surgical appliances & supplies
PA: Johnson & Johnson
1 Johnson And Johnson Plz
New Brunswick NJ 08933
732 524-0400

(G-6972)
JETSTREAM OF HOUSTON LLP
Also Called: Fs Solutions
17 Jules Ln (08901-3643)
PHONE..................................732 448-7830
EMP: 5
SALES (corp-wide): 898.5MM **Publicly Held**
SIC: 5087 3563 Vacuum cleaning systems; spraying & dusting equipment
HQ: Jetstream Of Houston, Llp
5905 Thomas Rd
Houston TX 77041
832 590-1300

(G-6973)
JNJ INTERNATIONAL INV LLC
One Johnson/Johnson Plaza (08933-0001)
PHONE..................................732 524-0400
EMP: 6
SALES (est): 513.1K
SALES (corp-wide): 76.4B **Publicly Held**
SIC: 2676 2844 3841 3842 Feminine hygiene paper products; napkins, sanitary: made from purchased paper; panty liners: made from purchased paper; infant & baby paper products; toilet preparations; oral preparations; toilet preparations; powder: baby, face, talcum or toilet; surgical & medical instruments; surgical instruments & apparatus; diagnostic apparatus, medical; ophthalmic instruments & apparatus; surgical appliances & supplies; ligatures, medical; sutures, absorbable & non-absorbable; dressings, surgical; pharmaceutical preparations; drugs acting on the central nervous system & sense organs; dermatologicals; drugs affecting parasitic & infective diseases
PA: Johnson & Johnson
1 Johnson And Johnson Plz
New Brunswick NJ 08933
732 524-0400

(G-6974)
JOHNSON & JOHNSON (PA)
1 Johnson And Johnson Plz (08933-0002)
P.O. Box 767, Neenah WI (54957-0767)
PHONE..................................732 524-0400
Fax: 732 524-0332
Alex Gorsky, *Ch of Bd*
Paulus Stoffels, *Exec VP*
Michael H Ullmann, *Exec VP*
Joseph Wolk, *CFO*
Peter M Fasolo, *Officer*
◆ EMP: 1000 EST: 1886
SALES: 76.4B **Publicly Held**
WEB: www.jnj.com
SIC: 2834 3842 3841 2844 Pharmaceutical preparations; drugs acting on the central nervous system & sense organs; dermatologicals; drugs affecting parasitic & infective diseases; surgical appliances & supplies; ligatures, medical; sutures, absorbable & non-absorbable; dressings, surgical; surgical & medical instruments; surgical instruments & apparatus; diagnostic apparatus, medical; ophthalmic instruments & apparatus; toilet preparations; oral preparations; toilet preparations; powder: baby, face, talcum or toilet; feminine hygiene paper products; napkins, sanitary: made from purchased paper; panty liners: made from purchased paper; infant & baby paper products

(G-6975)
JOHNSON & JOHNSON
100 Albany St Ste 100 # 100 (08901-1296)
PHONE..................................732 524-0400
Martes P Stepper, *Project Mgr*
Gabry Kuijten, *Manager*
Laura Zimmermann, *Admin Asst*
EMP: 147
SALES (corp-wide): 76.4B **Publicly Held**
WEB: www.jnj.com
SIC: 3842 3841 2834 2844 Surgical appliances & supplies; surgical & medical instruments; pharmaceutical preparations; toilet preparations; feminine hygiene paper products
PA: Johnson & Johnson
1 Johnson And Johnson Plz
New Brunswick NJ 08933
732 524-0400

(G-6976)
KVK USA INC
19 Home News Row Bldg A (08901-3601)
PHONE..................................732 846-2355
Fax: 732 846-2355
Robert Sliner, *General Mgr*
◆ EMP: 10
SALES (est): 980K **Privately Held**
SIC: 2816 Inorganic pigments

(G-6977)
LASERWAVE GRAPHICS INC
24a Joyce Kilmer Ave N (08901-1950)
PHONE..................................732 745-7764
Fax: 732 745-7765
Albert Hakim, *President*
Vince Lam, *Manager*
Jamie Hakim, *Teacher*
Millie Hakim, *Clerk*
▲ EMP: 11
SQ FT: 2,000
SALES (est): 1.5MM **Privately Held**
WEB: www.laserwave.com
SIC: 2759 7336 2791 Commercial printing; graphic arts & related design; typesetting

(G-6978)
MANTTRA INC
1130 Somerset St (08901-3623)
PHONE..................................877 962-6887
TT Jagannathan, *CEO*
S Ravichandran, *President*
T Jagannathan, *Principal*
K Shankaran, *Treasurer*
EMP: 4 EST: 1995
SALES: 2.6MM **Privately Held**
WEB: www.manttra.com
SIC: 3469 Pressure cookers, stamped or drawn metal

(G-6979)
MCNICHOLS COMPANY
2 Home News Row (08901-3602)
PHONE..................................877 884-4653
Fax: 732 846-5555
Arlene Schneier, *Sales Staff*
Glenn Stewart, *Branch Mgr*
EMP: 17
SALES (corp-wide): 177.1MM **Privately Held**
SIC: 5051 3446 Steel; architectural metalwork
PA: Mcnichols Company
2502 N Rocky Point Dr # 750
Tampa FL 33607
877 884-4653

(G-6980)
MEDICAL DEVICE BUS SVCS INC
1 Johnson And Johnson Plz (08933-0001)
PHONE..................................732 524-0400
Laurie Snyder, *Production*
Jeff Parker, *Buyer*
Phil Bly, *Branch Mgr*
Katy Cain, *Director*
EMP: 5
SALES (corp-wide): 76.4B **Publicly Held**
SIC: 3842 Surgical appliances & supplies
HQ: Medical Device Business Services, Inc.
700 Orthopaedic Dr
Warsaw IN 46582

(G-6981)
METALLO GASKET COMPANY INC
16 Bethany St (08901-2324)
P.O. Box 550 (08903-0550)
PHONE................................732 545-7223
Fax: 732 545-9848
Frederick W Haleluk, *President*
N Lawrence Catanese, *Vice Pres*
EMP: 14
SQ FT: 16,000
SALES (est): 2.7MM **Privately Held**
WEB: www.metallogasket.com
SIC: 3053 5085 Gaskets, all materials; industrial supplies

(G-6982)
MISS SPORTSWEAR INC
745 Joyce Kilmer Ave (08901-3308)
PHONE................................212 391-2535
EMP: 9 **Privately Held**
SIC: 2329 Men's & boys' sportswear & athletic clothing
PA: M.I.S.S. Sportswear, Inc.
117 9th St
Brooklyn NY 11215

(G-6983)
NBS GROUP SUP MED PDTS DIV LLC
Also Called: Nbs Medical
257 Livingston Ave Fl 3 (08901-3054)
P.O. Box 157, Milltown (08850-0157)
PHONE................................732 745-9292
Fax: 732 745-1192
Osman Boraie, *Mng Member*
EMP: 6
SQ FT: 2,000
SALES (est): 797.1K **Privately Held**
SIC: 3061 5047 Medical & surgical rubber tubing (extruded & lathe-cut); medical & hospital equipment

(G-6984)
NCONNEX INC
1 Richmond St Apt 3079 (08901-4508)
PHONE................................413 658-5582
Dan Xie, *Principal*
Yun Lin, *Principal*
EMP: 4
SALES (est): 270K **Privately Held**
SIC: 7372 Prepackaged software

(G-6985)
NETFRUITS INC
Also Called: Iweddingband.com
100 Jersey Ave (08901-3200)
PHONE................................732 249-2588
Hyun Yi, *President*
EMP: 4
SALES: 450K **Privately Held**
WEB: www.iweddingband.com
SIC: 3911 Jewelry, precious metal

(G-6986)
NEW BRUNSWICK LAMP SHADE CO
7 Terminal Rd (08901-3615)
PHONE................................732 545-0377
Fax: 732 545-6993
Nathan Zankel, *President*
Paul Zankel, *Vice Pres*
Richard Zankel, *Treasurer*
▲ EMP: 26 EST: 1943
SALES (est): 2.8MM **Privately Held**
WEB: www.nbls.com
SIC: 3999 Shades, lamp or candle

(G-6987)
NEW BRUNSWICK PLATING INC (PA)
596 Jersey Ave (08901-3502)
P.O. Box 7280, North Brunswick (08902-7280)
PHONE................................732 545-6522
Fax: 732 846-9779
Robert Sica, *CEO*
Red Melchione, *President*
Brain Patterson, *COO*
Anthony Melchione, *Plant Mgr*
Bobbi Gumbinger, *CFO*
EMP: 52
SQ FT: 28,000

SALES (est): 6.9MM **Privately Held**
WEB: www.nbplating.com
SIC: 3471 Electroplating of metals or formed products

(G-6988)
NIPPON BENKAN KAGYO
Also Called: Tube Line
475 Jersey Ave (08901-3297)
PHONE................................732 435-0777
Fax: 732 435-0013
Bob Sheldon, *Vice Pres*
EMP: 20
SALES (corp-wide): 19.8MM **Privately Held**
SIC: 3317 3494 Steel pipe & tubes; valves & pipe fittings
PA: Nihon Bankin Kogyo K.K.
798-8, Shimokobashi, Sakaimachi
Sashima-Gun IBR 306-0
280 874-531

(G-6989)
OHM LABORATORIES INC
14 Terminal Rd (08901-3616)
PHONE................................732 514-1072
Fax: 732 514-4405
Narendra Bhojraj, *Engineer*
Phanindra Potineni, *Engineer*
Charles Woods, *Engineer*
Sanjay Shaw, *Branch Mgr*
EMP: 100
SALES (corp-wide): 1.2B **Privately Held**
WEB: www.ranbaxy.com
SIC: 2834 Pharmaceutical preparations
HQ: Ohm Laboratories Inc.
1385 Livingston Ave
North Brunswick NJ 08902
732 418-2235

(G-6990)
OMEGA CIRCUIT AND ENGINEERING
8 Terminal Rd (08901-3616)
PHONE................................732 246-1661
Fax: 732 246-1643
James C Genes, *President*
Tyler Genes, *Info Tech Mgr*
EMP: 30 EST: 1980
SQ FT: 16,000
SALES (est): 5.3MM **Privately Held**
WEB: www.omegacircuits.com
SIC: 3672 Circuit boards, television & radio printed

(G-6991)
PLUMBING SUPPLY NOW LLC
167 Black Horse Ln (08902-4321)
PHONE................................732 228-8852
Evan Gartenberg,
EMP: 10
SQ FT: 250
SALES (est): 400.4K **Privately Held**
SIC: 3432 Plastic plumbing fixture fittings, assembly

(G-6992)
POLVAC INC
235 Jersey Ave Ste 1 (08901-3281)
PHONE................................732 828-1662
Fax: 732 828-4148
Marek Ringwelski, *Owner*
EMP: 4
SQ FT: 2,600
SALES (est): 280K **Privately Held**
WEB: www.polvac.net
SIC: 3563 Vacuum pumps, except laboratory

(G-6993)
PRESTIGE FORKLIFT MAINT SVC
31 Timber Ridge Rd (08902-5514)
PHONE................................732 297-1001
Phil Hill, *President*
EMP: 4 EST: 2001
SALES (est): 337.2K **Privately Held**
SIC: 3537 Forklift trucks

(G-6994)
PRIMESOURCE BUILDING PDTS INC
20 Van Dyke Ave (08901-3253)
P.O. Box 6330, Edison (08818-6330)
PHONE................................732 296-0600

Fax: 732 296-8797
Dan Javitt, *Branch Mgr*
EMP: 25
SALES (corp-wide): 828.2MM **Privately Held**
WEB: www.primesourcebp.com
SIC: 3965 Fasteners, buttons, needles & pins
PA: Primesource Building Products, Inc.
1321 Greenway Dr
Irving TX 75038
972 999-8500

(G-6995)
PRINCETON CORP GRAPHICS INC
Also Called: Universal Nutrition
3 Terminal Rd (08901-3615)
PHONE................................732 545-6163
Fax: 732 214-1210
Clyde Rockoff, *President*
Micheal Rockoff, *Vice Pres*
◆ EMP: 100
SQ FT: 15,000
SALES (est): 25.2MM **Privately Held**
SIC: 2671 2759 Packaging paper & plastics film, coated & laminated; commercial printing

(G-6996)
PROCEDYNE CORP (PA)
11 Industrial Dr (08901-3657)
PHONE................................732 249-8347
Fax: 732 249-7220
Thomas R Parr, *President*
Bob Schulz, *Vice Pres*
Robert Schulz, *Safety Dir*
EMP: 40
SQ FT: 60,000
SALES (est): 11.9MM **Privately Held**
WEB: www.procedyne.com
SIC: 3567 5065 8711 5051 Industrial furnaces & ovens; electronic parts & equipment; engineering services; metals service centers & offices; chemical preparations

(G-6997)
PUBLISHING TECHNOLOGY INC
317 George St Ste 320 (08901-2091)
PHONE................................732 563-9292
EMP: 7
SALES (corp-wide): 19.4MM **Privately Held**
WEB: www.publishingtechnology.com
SIC: 2711 Newspapers, publishing & printing
PA: Ingenta Plc
8100 Alec Issigonis Way
Oxford OXON OX4 2
186 539-7800

(G-6998)
R J BLEN GRPHIC ARTS CNVERTING
Also Called: Rj Bielan Graphic Arts
6 Jules Ln (08901-3636)
PHONE................................732 545-3501
Fax: 732 545-9842
Robert J Bielen, *President*
EMP: 22 EST: 1956
SQ FT: 18,000
SALES (est): 3.6MM **Privately Held**
SIC: 2675 2657 Paper die-cutting; paperboard die-cutting; folding paperboard boxes

(G-6999)
RARITAN PACKAGING INDUSTRIES
Also Called: Raritan Container
570 Jersey Ave (08901-3502)
P.O. Box 7237, North Brunswick (08902-7237)
PHONE................................732 246-7200
Fax: 732 246-4942
Bernard L Newman, *President*
Sandra Newman, *Vice Pres*
EMP: 26
SQ FT: 40,000
SALES: 3MM **Privately Held**
WEB: www.raritancontainer.com
SIC: 2653 5085 Boxes, corrugated: made from purchased materials; packing, industrial

(G-7000)
RELIABOTICS LLC
24 Van Dyke Ave (08901-3253)
PHONE................................732 791-5500
Mina Nassar, *Electrical Engi*
Marci Tapper, *Office Mgr*
Richard Delewsky, *Manager*
Juan Vega, *CTO*
EMP: 5
SALES (est): 715.9K **Privately Held**
SIC: 3535 Robotic conveyors

(G-7001)
RETRIEVEX
5 Home News Row (08901-3601)
PHONE................................732 247-3200
Leon Kroll, *CEO*
EMP: 5
SALES (est): 548.4K **Privately Held**
SIC: 3554 Cutting machines, paper

(G-7002)
ROYAL COSMETICS CORPORATION
Also Called: Royale Cosmetics
4 Jules Ln A (08901-3636)
PHONE................................732 246-7275
Fax: 732 246-0578
Doodnauth Tulshi, *President*
Deancalli Tulshi, *Vice Pres*
▲ EMP: 14
SQ FT: 4,000
SALES (est): 2.2MM **Privately Held**
SIC: 2844 Cosmetic preparations

(G-7003)
SHERWOOD BRANDS CORPORATION
120 Jersey Ave (08901-3289)
PHONE................................973 249-8200
Steven Deutsch, *CEO*
EMP: 10
SALES (est): 456.4K **Privately Held**
SIC: 2064 Candy bars, including chocolate covered bars

(G-7004)
SPECTRUM LABORATORY PDTS INC (PA)
Also Called: Spectrum Chemicals & Lab Pdts
769 Jersey Ave (08901-3605)
PHONE................................732 214-1300
Fax: 732 220-6553
Randy Burg, *President*
Nathalie Burg, *Principal*
Paul Burg, *Principal*
Rodica Cohen Burg, *Principal*
Erik Hawkinson, *Vice Pres*
◆ EMP: 110 EST: 1971
SQ FT: 140,000
SALES: 60.4MM **Privately Held**
SIC: 2869 2899 5047 Laboratory chemicals, organic; chemical preparations; diagnostic equipment, medical; electro-medical equipment

(G-7005)
SPECTRUM LABORATORY PDTS INC
Also Called: Spectrum Quality Products
755 769 & 777 Jersey Ave (08901)
PHONE................................732 214-1300
George Wachter, *Sales Staff*
Grant Gibson, *VP Mktg*
Paul Burg, *Branch Mgr*
Adan Hernandez, *Manager*
Zelene Valencia, *Admin Asst*
EMP: 35
SALES (corp-wide): 60.4MM **Privately Held**
SIC: 5169 2819 2869 2899 Organic chemicals, synthetic; industrial inorganic chemicals; laboratory chemicals, organic; chemical preparations
PA: Spectrum Laboratory Products, Inc.
769 Jersey Ave
New Brunswick NJ 08901
732 214-1300

▲ = Import ▼=Export
◆ =Import/Export

(G-7006)
TARGUM PUBLISHING COMPANY
Also Called: Daily Targum
126 College Ave Ste 431 (08901-1166)
PHONE................................732 247-1286
Fax: 732 932-1681
M Stefanelli, *Business Mgr*
Michelle Stefanelli, *Business Mgr*
Christopher Mahon, *Bd of Directors*
Selene Maugeri, *Bd of Directors*
Edwin Gano, *Associate*
EMP: 50
SQ FT: 1,000
SALES: 1.3MM **Privately Held**
WEB: www.dailytargum.com
SIC: 2711 Newspapers, publishing & printing

(G-7007)
TREK II PRODUCTS INC
400 Jersey Ave Ste 1 (08901-3589)
PHONE................................732 214-9200
Michael Smokowicz, *Principal*
EMP: 7
SALES (est): 725.3K **Privately Held**
WEB: www.trekii.com
SIC: 8748 3931 Business consulting; musical instruments

(G-7008)
UNITED MIJOVI AMER LTD LBLTY
21 Roseland Pl (08902-2909)
PHONE................................732 718-1001
Marcos Carrington,
EMP: 10
SALES (est): 660K **Privately Held**
SIC: 2095 5149 Instant coffee; coffee & tea

(G-7009)
UNITED SILICON CARBIDE INC
100 Jersey Ave Bldg A (08901-3200)
PHONE................................732 565-9500
Jhi Yong, *Principal*
EMP: 4 EST: 2010
SALES (est): 559.1K **Privately Held**
SIC: 2819 Carbides

(G-7010)
UNIVERSAL PRTEIN SPPLMNTS CORP (PA)
Also Called: Universal Labs
3 Terminal Rd (08901-3615)
PHONE................................732 545-3130
Michael Rockoff, *CEO*
Clyde Rockoff, *President*
▼ EMP: 100
SQ FT: 100,000
SALES (est): 41.9MM **Privately Held**
SIC: 2834 2032 Vitamin, nutrient & hematinic preparations for human use; vitamin preparations; canned specialties

(G-7011)
WATCHITUDE LLC
24a Joyce Kilmer Ave N (08901-1950)
PHONE................................732 745-2626
Dan Hakim,
EMP: 5
SALES (est): 178.2K **Privately Held**
SIC: 3873 Watches & parts, except crystals & jewels

(G-7012)
WENNER BREAD PRODUCTS INC
571 Jersey Ave (08901-3501)
PHONE................................631 563-6262
EMP: 96
SALES (corp-wide): 127.7MM **Privately Held**
SIC: 2051 2053 5461 Bread, all types (white, wheat, rye, etc); fresh or frozen; frozen bakery products, except bread; bakeries
PA: Wenner Bread Products, Inc.
33 Rajon Rd
Bayport NY 11705
800 869-6262

(G-7013)
WHITE LOTUS HOME LTD LBLTY CO
745 Joyce Kilmer Ave (08901-3308)
PHONE................................732 828-2111
Marlon Pando, *President*
Elizabeth Pando-Nieves, *Vice Pres*
EMP: 16
SQ FT: 6,000
SALES (est): 2.4MM **Privately Held**
WEB: www.whitelotus.net
SIC: 2515 2392 5712 Mattresses & bedsprings; mattresses & foundations; blankets, comforters & beddings; cushions & pillows; furniture stores; unfinished furniture

(G-7014)
WOODLINE WORKS CORPORATION
625 Jersey Ave Ste 9 (08901-3679)
PHONE................................732 828-9100
Fax: 732 828-9102
Song Wu, *President*
▲ EMP: 30
SQ FT: 10,000
SALES (est): 2.4MM **Privately Held**
SIC: 2511 Wood household furniture

New Egypt
Ocean County

(G-7015)
GO R DESIGN LLC
74 Hemlock Dr (08533-2738)
PHONE................................609 286-2146
Tim Klein, *Mng Member*
EMP: 30
SQ FT: 3,000
SALES (est): 2.1MM **Privately Held**
SIC: 3499 3645 7336 Novelties & giftware, including trophies; residential lighting fixtures; commercial art & graphic design

(G-7016)
KINI PRODUCTS INC
7 Forest Hill Dr (08533-2731)
PHONE................................732 299-5555
Nancy Gingrich, *President*
Neil B Gingrich Jr, *Vice Pres*
EMP: 5
SALES (est): 450K **Privately Held**
SIC: 2822 5099 Silicone rubbers; cases, carrying

(G-7017)
LITTLE HOUSE CANDLES INC
20 Province Line Rd (08533-1008)
PHONE................................609 758-2996
Jennifer Ingalls, *President*
EMP: 5
SALES: 1MM **Privately Held**
WEB: www.littlehousecandles.com
SIC: 3999 5947 Candles; gift, novelty & souvenir shop

(G-7018)
VAHLCO RACING WHEELS LLC
849 Route 539 (08533-2004)
PHONE................................609 758-7013
Fred Vahlsing, *President*
EMP: 4 EST: 2014
SALES (est): 442.4K **Privately Held**
SIC: 3714 Motor vehicle wheels & parts

(G-7019)
W2F INC (PA)
167 Archertown Rd (08533-1904)
P.O. Box 1291, Browns Mills (08015-8291)
PHONE................................609 735-0135
Bob Jenkins, *President*
EMP: 6
SQ FT: 1,200
SALES: 980K **Privately Held**
SIC: 3449 3711 Miscellaneous metalwork; automobile assembly, including specialty automobiles

New Gretna
Burlington County

(G-7020)
VIKING YACHT COMPANY (PA)
On The Bass Riv Rr 9 (08224)
P.O. Box 308 (08224-0308)
PHONE................................609 296-6000
Fax: 609 296-3956
Robert T Healey, *CEO*
William J Healey, *President*
Patrick Healey, *Exec VP*
Dana Cusack, *Buyer*
Bob Keller, *Research*
▲ EMP: 271
SQ FT: 400,000
SALES: 280MM **Privately Held**
WEB: www.vikingyachts.com
SIC: 3732 Yachts, building & repairing

New Milford
Bergen County

(G-7021)
DMJ TECHNOLOGIES LLC
775 Maple St (07646-3005)
PHONE................................201 261-5560
Steven Robert Lehr,
Julie Walder,
EMP: 6
SALES (est): 722.5K **Privately Held**
SIC: 3651 Audio electronic systems

(G-7022)
K & R PRECISION MACHINING LLC
336 Birchwood Rd (07646-2506)
PHONE................................201 385-8855
Fax: 201 385-2640
Richard Penser, *Partner*
Kevin Smith, *Partner*
EMP: 11
SQ FT: 1,900
SALES (est): 1.5MM **Privately Held**
SIC: 3545 Precision tools, machinists'

(G-7023)
METRO PUBLISHING GROUP INC
Also Called: Metro Features
626 Mccarthy Dr (07646-1029)
PHONE................................201 385-2000
Robert Nesoff, *President*
EMP: 10
SALES (est): 480K **Privately Held**
SIC: 2791 Typesetting

(G-7024)
PETER-LISAND MACHINE CORP
262 Voorhis Ave (07646-1924)
PHONE................................201 943-5600
Fax: 201 943-6913
Peter Guasti, *President*
EMP: 4
SQ FT: 7,600
SALES: 200K **Privately Held**
WEB: www.peterlisand.com
SIC: 3651 3663 Household video equipment; radio & TV communications equipment

(G-7025)
SCOTT GRAPHICS PRINTING CO INC
690 River Rd Ste D (07646-2903)
PHONE................................201 262-0473
Fax: 201 262-0210
Scott McNiff, *President*
Charles McNiff, *Vice Pres*
Joanne McNiff, *Treasurer*
Margaret McNiff, *Admin Sec*
EMP: 9
SQ FT: 6,000
SALES (est): 1.3MM **Privately Held**
WEB: www.scottgraphicsprinting.com
SIC: 2752 2791 2789 Commercial printing, offset; typesetting; bookbinding & related work

New Providence
Union County

(G-7026)
ALCATEL-LUCENT USA INC
600 Mountain Ave 700 (07974-2008)
PHONE................................908 582-3275
Mex White, *Regional Mgr*
Jacek Slowinski, *Vice Pres*
Steven Kingscott, *Vice Pres*
Andrew Ambrose, *Technical Mgr*
Tze-Wah Chan, *Engineer*
EMP: 61
SALES (corp-wide): 27.3B **Privately Held**
SIC: 3661 7372 3663 3674 Telephone & telegraph apparatus; prepackaged software; radio broadcasting & communications equipment; integrated circuits, semiconductor networks, etc.
HQ: Nokia Of America Corporation
600 Mountain Ave Ste 700
New Providence NJ 07974

(G-7027)
BARD DEVICES INC (DH)
730 Central Ave (07974-1139)
PHONE................................908 277-8000
Timothy Ring, *CEO*
William Longfield, *Chairman*
Todd Schermerhorn, *Vice Pres*
Greg Bentley, *Info Tech Dir*
Wendy Lemke, *Info Tech Dir*
▲ EMP: 32
SQ FT: 48,000
SALES (est): 14MM
SALES (corp-wide): 12B **Publicly Held**
SIC: 3842 Surgical appliances & supplies
HQ: C. R. Bard, Inc.
730 Central Ave
New Providence NJ 07974
908 277-8000

(G-7028)
BARD HEALTHCARE INC
730 Central Ave (07974-1139)
PHONE................................908 277-8000
John H Weiland, *President*
John Moran, *Vice Pres*
Todd C Schermerhorn, *Vice Pres*
Scott T Lowry, *Treasurer*
Jean F Miller, *Asst Sec*
▲ EMP: 12
SALES (est): 2.8MM
SALES (corp-wide): 12B **Publicly Held**
WEB: www.crbard.com
SIC: 3841 3845 3842 Surgical & medical instruments; blood transfusion equipment; surgical instruments & apparatus; electromedical equipment; electrocardiographs; surgical support systems: heart-lung machine, exc. iron lung; patient monitoring apparatus; surgical appliances & supplies; surgical appliances & supplies; implants, surgical
HQ: C. R. Bard, Inc.
730 Central Ave
New Providence NJ 07974
908 277-8000

(G-7029)
BARD INTERNATIONAL INC (DH)
Also Called: Bard Asia Pacific Division
111 Spring St (07974-1146)
PHONE................................908 277-8000
William Longfield, *President*
Mike Flores, *General Mgr*
Tim Waitkus, *Manager*
Andy Medina, *Director*
EMP: 64
SQ FT: 48,000
SALES (est): 11.3MM
SALES (corp-wide): 12B **Publicly Held**
WEB: www.bardinternational.com
SIC: 5047 3842 Medical equipment & supplies; surgical appliances & supplies
HQ: C. R. Bard, Inc.
730 Central Ave
New Providence NJ 07974
908 277-8000

(G-7030)
BOC GROUP INC
575 Mountain Ave (07974-2078)
PHONE..................908 665-2400
Fax: 908 771-1460
Trevor J Burt, *President*
Gabriel McNabola, *General Mgr*
Suzanne Jurkovic, *General Ptnr*
Michael Tasca, *Opers Spvr*
David L Brooks, *Treasurer*
▲ **EMP:** 856
SQ FT: 215,000
SALES (est): 406MM
SALES (corp-wide): 1.7B **Privately Held**
SIC: 2813 3569 3559 3561 Industrial
　gases; oxygen, compressed or liquefied;
　nitrogen; argon; gas producers, genera-
　tors & other gas related equipment; cryo-
　genic machinery, industrial; pumps &
　pumping equipment; turbines & turbine
　generator sets; flow instruments, indus-
　trial process type
HQ: B O C Holdings
　Chertsey Rd
　Windlesham

(G-7031)
BOWMAR ENTERPRISES INC
Also Called: Accent Printing Solutions
558 Cent Ave (07974)
PHONE..................908 277-3000
Michael Tan, *President*
EMP: 9
SQ FT: 3,500
SALES (est): 1.5MM **Privately Held**
SIC: 2752 2791 Commercial printing, off-
　set; photo-offset printing; typesetting

(G-7032)
C R BARD INC (HQ)
730 Central Ave (07974-1199)
PHONE..................908 277-8000
Fax: 908 277-8412
Timothy M Ring, *Ch of Bd*
Jim C Beasley, *President*
Douglas Church, *President*
Timothy P Collins, *President*
John P Groetelaars, *President*
▲ **EMP:** 210 **EST:** 1907
SALES: 3.7B
SALES (corp-wide): 12B **Publicly Held**
WEB: www.crbard.com
SIC: 3841 3845 3842 Surgical & medical
　instruments; blood transfusion equipment;
　surgical instruments & apparatus; surgical
　electromedical equipment; electrocardio-
　graphs; surgical support systems:
　heart-lung machine, exc. iron lung; patient
　monitoring apparatus; surgical appliances
　& supplies; surgical appliances & sup-
　plies; bandages & dressings; implants,
　surgical
PA: Becton, Dickinson And Company
　1 Becton Dr
　Franklin Lakes NJ 07417
　201 847-6800

(G-7033)
CHEMETALL US INC (HQ)
Also Called: Chemetall Americas
675 Central Ave (07974-1560)
PHONE..................908 464-6900
Ronald Felber, *President*
Mark Bruner, *President*
Gregory V Poff, *Vice Pres*
Kevin Filipski, *CFO*
Melissa Glick, *Manager*
◆ **EMP:** 80
SQ FT: 37,000
SALES (est): 127.2MM
SALES (corp-wide): 76B **Privately Held**
WEB: www.chemetall.com
SIC: 2842 2899 2851 Specialty cleaning,
　polishes & sanitation goods; sanitation
　preparations, disinfectants & deodorants;
　metal treating compounds; rust resisting
　compounds; water treating compounds;
　paints & allied products; paint removers
PA: Basf Se
　Carl-Bosch-Str. 38
　Ludwigshafen Am Rhein 67056
　621 600-

(G-7034)
FABLOK MILLS INC
140 Spring St (07974-1152)
P.O. Box 900 (07974-0900)
PHONE..................908 464-1950
Fax: 908 464-6520
Alex Fisher, *President*
Jim Malure, *Manager*
▲ **EMP:** 40 **EST:** 1952
SQ FT: 32,000
SALES (est): 5.3MM **Privately Held**
WEB: www.fablokmills.com
SIC: 2221 2258 Broadwoven fabric mills,
　manmade; lace & warp knit fabric mills

(G-7035)
FLODYNE CONTROLS INC
48 Commerce Dr (07974-1142)
PHONE..................908 464-6200
Fax: 908 464-1553
Carol Perrin, *President*
Michael Perrin, *Vice Pres*
Robert Hartje, *Purchasing*
Craig Kalugin, *Info Tech Mgr*
EMP: 25 **EST:** 1960
SQ FT: 30,000
SALES (est): 5.1MM **Privately Held**
WEB: www.flodynecontrols.com
SIC: 3491 Industrial valves

(G-7036)
FRC ELECTRICAL INDUSTRIES INC
705 Central Ave Ste 3 (07974-1151)
PHONE..................908 464-3200
Ahmed El-Mahdawy, *Manager*
EMP: 44 **Privately Held**
SIC: 3679 3444 3643 3053 Hermetic
　seals for electronic equipment; sheet met-
　alwork; current-carrying wiring devices;
　gaskets, packing & sealing devices; elec-
　trical equipment & supplies
PA: Frc Electrical Industries Inc
　1260 Clearmont St Ne
　Palm Bay FL 32905

(G-7037)
FREEMAN TECHNICAL SALES INC
148 Maple St (07974-2405)
PHONE..................908 464-4784
David Freeman, *President*
EMP: 1 **EST:** 2008
SQ FT: 400
SALES (est): 3.2MM **Privately Held**
SIC: 3999 Barber & beauty shop equip-
　ment

(G-7038)
GRAPHIC IMAGERY INC
556 Central Ave Ste 1 (07974-1563)
PHONE..................908 755-2882
Fax: 908 752-9588
Linda Maher, *President*
EMP: 10
SQ FT: 1,600
SALES (est): 1.1MM **Privately Held**
WEB: www.graphicimagery.com
SIC: 7336 2759 Graphic arts & related de-
　sign; promotional printing

(G-7039)
GRAVER WATER SYSTEMS LLC (DH)
Also Called: Graver Water Division
675 Central Ave Ste 3 (07974-1560)
PHONE..................908 516-1400
Robert Gluth,
Gregory Allemano,
Patrick Allen,
Michael O'Brien,
▼ **EMP:** 2
SQ FT: 40,000
SALES (est): 8.8MM
SALES (corp-wide): 242.1B **Publicly
Held**
WEB: www.graver.com
SIC: 3589 Water treatment equipment, in-
　dustrial
HQ: Marmon Industrial Llc
　181 W Madison St Fl 26
　Chicago IL 60602
　312 372-9500

(G-7040)
INFORMATION TODAY INC
630 Central Ave Fl 2 (07974-1506)
PHONE..................908 219-0279
Thomas Hogan Sr, *President*
Theresa Cramer, *Editor*
EMP: 17
SALES (corp-wide): 19.2MM **Privately
Held**
SIC: 2741 Directories: publishing only, not
　printed on site
PA: Information Today, Inc.
　143 Old Marlton Pike
　Medford NJ 08055
　609 654-6266

(G-7041)
LAWYERS DIARY AND MANUAL LLC
890 Mountain Ave Ste 300 (07974-1218)
PHONE..................973 642-1440
Andrew Strauss, *Chairman*
David Stein, *CFO*
EMP: 35
SALES (est): 2.7MM **Privately Held**
SIC: 2721 Periodicals: publishing only

(G-7042)
LINDE GLOBAL HELIUM INC
575 Mountain Ave (07974-2097)
PHONE..................908 464-8100
Stephen Penn, *Principal*
▲ **EMP:** 24
SALES (est): 2.2MM
SALES (corp-wide): 20.1B **Privately Held**
SIC: 2813 Helium
HQ: Linde Gas North America Llc
　200 Somerset Corp Blvd # 7000
　Bridgewater NJ 08807

(G-7043)
LINDE LLC
100 Mountain Ave (07974-2069)
PHONE..................908 464-8100
William Gerristead, *Manager*
Josef Petermeier, *Manager*
EMP: 50
SALES (corp-wide): 20.1B **Privately Held**
SIC: 2813 Oxygen, compressed or lique-
　fied
HQ: Linde Llc
　200 Somerset Corporate Bl
　Bridgewater NJ 08807
　908 464-8100

(G-7044)
LINDE MERCHANT PRODUCTION INC (DH)
575 Mountain Ave (07974-2097)
PHONE..................908 464-8100
Patrick F Murphy, *President*
EMP: 11
SALES (est): 1.7MM
SALES (corp-wide): 20.1B **Privately Held**
SIC: 2813 Oxygen, compressed or lique-
　fied

(G-7045)
LINDE NORTH AMERICA INC
575 Mountain Ave (07974-2097)
PHONE..................908 464-8100
Danielle Deller, *Counsel*
Amy Ficon, *Marketing Staff*
Kent Masters, *Manager*
Robert Parkanyi, *Manager*
Norbert Ingenerf, *Director*
EMP: 98
SALES (corp-wide): 20.1B **Privately Held**
SIC: 2813 3569 3559 3561 Industrial
　gases; argon; nitrogen; oxygen, com-
　pressed or liquefied; gas producers, gen-
　erators & other gas related equipment;
　cryogenic machinery, industrial; pumps &
　pumping equipment; turbines & turbine
　generator sets; flow instruments, indus-
　trial process type
HQ: Linde North America, Inc.
　200 Somerset Corporate Bl
　Bridgewater NJ 08807
　908 464-8100

(G-7046)
LUCENT TECHNOLOGIES WORLD SVCS
600 Mountain Ave (07974-2008)
PHONE..................908 582-3000
Fax: 908 582-6245
Holly Anderson, *Partner*
Alain Viallix, *Partner*
Derek Wright, *Business Mgr*
Dave Bolka, *Vice Pres*
Javier Falcon, *Vice Pres*
EMP: 200
SALES (est): 50.6MM
SALES (corp-wide): 27.3B **Privately Held**
WEB: www.bell-labs.com
SIC: 5065 7622 3674 3663 Electronic
　parts & equipment; communication equip-
　ment repair; semiconductors & related de-
　vices; radio & TV communications
　equipment; telephone & telegraph appa-
　ratus; computer peripheral equipment
HQ: Alcatel-Lucent Technologies Holdings
　Inc.
　600 Mountain Ave 700
　New Providence NJ 07974
　908 582-8500

(G-7047)
MARQUIS - WHOS WHO INC
Also Called: National Register Publishing
430 Mountain Ave Ste 403 (07974-2732)
PHONE..................908 673-1006
Fax: 908 673-1179
Fred Marks, *Managing Dir*
Gene McGovern, *Principal*
James Finkelstein, *Principal*
Charles Lillis, *Vice Pres*
John Macdonald, *Vice Pres*
EMP: 80
SQ FT: 22,000
SALES (est): 9.9MM **Privately Held**
WEB: www.marquiswhoswho.com
SIC: 2741 Miscellaneous publishing

(G-7048)
MGL PRINTING SOLUTION LLC
Also Called: Mgl Forms
154 South St Ste 1 (07974-2933)
PHONE..................908 665-1999
Fred Smith, *CEO*
Darren Lowe, *General Ptnr*
Christopher Lowe,
Gregory Lowe,
Matthew Lowe,
EMP: 5
SQ FT: 2,300
SALES (est): 931.7K **Privately Held**
WEB: www.mglforms.com
SIC: 3555 Printing presses

(G-7049)
NEW VENTURE PARTNERS LLC
430 Mountain Ave Ste 404 (07974-2732)
P.O. Box 881 (07974-0881)
PHONE..................908 464-8131
Anthony Abrahams, *CFO*
Chris Winter,
Harry Berry,
Dror Futter,
Franklin Rimalovski,
EMP: 600
SALES (est): 26.6MM **Privately Held**
WEB: www.nvpllc.com
SIC: 7372 Prepackaged software; busi-
　ness oriented computer software

(G-7050)
NOKIA OF AMERICA CORPORATION (DH)
Also Called: Alcatel-Lucent USA Inc.
600 Mountain Ave Ste 700 (07974-2008)
P.O. Box 696526, San Antonio TX (78269-
6526)
PHONE..................908 582-3275
Michel Combes, *CEO*
Jeff Cortley, *President*
Satoshi Fujita, *President*
Frank Noviello, *President*
Shashank Deulkar, *General Mgr*
◆ **EMP:** 1300
SALES (est): 8.9B
SALES (corp-wide): 27.3B **Privately Held**
WEB: www.lucent.com
SIC: 3674 7372 Integrated circuits, semi-
　conductor networks, etc.; hybrid inte-
　grated circuits; prepackaged software

▲ = Import ▼ =Export
◆ =Import/Export

GEOGRAPHIC

(G-7051)
ONTIMEWORKS LLC
Also Called: Everythingbenefits
1253 Springfield Ave (07974-2931)
PHONE..........................800 689-3568
Rachel Lyubovitzky,
EMP: 19
SALES (est): 489.3K Privately Held
SIC: 7372 Business oriented computer
software

(G-7052)
REEVES ENTERPRISES INC
Also Called: Templar Food Products
562 Central Ave (07974-1555)
PHONE..........................800 883-6752
Fax: 908 665-9122
Edward Reeves Jr, *President*
Ann Reeves, *Corp Secy*
Michael Murray, *Vice Pres*
Michael Eagan, *Opers Mgr*
Trudy Jenna, *Finance Mgr*
▼ EMP: 7 EST: 1971
SQ FT: 1,700
SALES (est): 908.3K Privately Held
WEB: www.icedtea.com
SIC: 2087 Beverage bases

(G-7053)
RR BOWKER LLC (HQ)
630 Central Ave (07974-1506)
PHONE..........................908 286-1090
Fax: 908 219-0090
Annie Callanan, *CEO*
Rhonda McKendrick, *Editor*
Peter Ashekian, *Manager*
Gary Aiello,
Michael Cairns,
EMP: 155
SALES (est): 22.4MM
SALES (corp-wide): 370.8MM Privately
Held
WEB: www.bowker.com
SIC: 2731 Books: publishing only
PA: Cambridge Information Group, Inc.
888 7th Ave Ste 1701
New York NY 10106
301 961-6700

(G-7054)
SKINDER-STRAUSS LLC (PA)
Also Called: Lawyers Diary & Manual
890 Mountain Ave Ste 300 (07974-1218)
P.O. Box 1027, Summit (07902-1027)
PHONE..........................973 642-1440
Fax: 973 642-3731
Andrew Strauss, *CEO*
Robert W Pladek, *President*
Karen Harris, *Partner*
Jerrold Krivitzky, *Partner*
Trudi Krivitzky, *Partner*
EMP: 40
SQ FT: 24,000
SALES (est): 19.8MM Privately Held
WEB: www.lawdiary.com
SIC: 2721 7389 Periodicals: publishing &
printing; courier or messenger service

(G-7055)
SUNHAM HOME FASHIONS LLC
700 Central Park Ave (07974)
PHONE..........................908 363-1100
Edward Silver, *Opers Staff*
Richard Landis, *Manager*
Sandra Rodrigues, *Manager*
Simon Lee, *Info Tech Mgr*
Tim Dong, *Technology*
EMP: 75 Privately Held
SIC: 2392 Blankets, comforters & beddings
PA: Sunham Home Fashions, Llc
136 Madison Ave Fl 16
New York NY 10016

(G-7056)
TAP INTO LLC
66 W 4th St (07974-1923)
P.O. Box 794 (07974-0794)
PHONE..........................908 370-1158
Michael Shapiro, *CEO*
Nathan Rudy, *Publisher*
Fred Smith, *Publisher*
Jennifer Popper, *Editor*
Natalie Hackett, *Manager*
EMP: 4 EST: 2013

SALES (est): 377.9K Privately Held
SIC: 7311 2741 7389 Advertising consultant; miscellaneous publishing;

(G-7057)
TAPINTONET
598 Central Ave Ste 7 (07974-1500)
PHONE..........................908 279-0303
Michael Shapiro, *Publisher*
Jessica Marrone, *Administration*
EMP: 9
SALES (est): 232.7K Privately Held
SIC: 2711 Newspapers

(G-7058)
TETLEY USA INC (HQ)
890 Mountain Ave Ste 105 (07974-1218)
PHONE..........................800 728-0084
Micheal Camp, *Principal*
Michael Fischle, *Principal*
▲ EMP: 28
SQ FT: 20,000
SALES (est): 35.6MM
SALES (corp-wide): 485.8MM Privately
Held
WEB: www.tetleyusa.com
SIC: 2099 Tea blending
PA: Tata Global Beverages Limited
3rd Floor, Block C
Bengaluru KA 56002
806 717-1200

(G-7059)
UNISPHERE MEDIA LLC
630 Central Ave (07974-1506)
PHONE..........................908 795-3701
Fax: 973 665-1124
Thomas J Wilson,
Calvin Carr,
Daniel Fishman,
Elliot King,
EMP: 10
SQ FT: 800
SALES (est): 942.9K Privately Held
SIC: 2721 Magazines: publishing & printing

(G-7060)
VERTICE PHARMA LLC (PA)
630 Central Ave (07974-1506)
PHONE..........................877 530-1633
Don Degolyer, *President*
Scott Meyers, *COO*
Ozgur Kilic, *CFO*
EMP: 200
SALES (est): 45MM Privately Held
SIC: 2834 5122 Pharmaceutical prepara-
tions; pharmaceuticals

(G-7061)
VISTAPHARM INC (HQ)
630 Central Ave (07974-1506)
PHONE..........................908 376-1622
Don Degolyer, *CEO*
Ozgur Kilic, *CFO*
EMP: 200 EST: 1998
SALES (est): 49.6MM
SALES (corp-wide): 45MM Privately
Held
WEB: www.vistapharm.com
SIC: 2834 Proprietary drug products
PA: Vertice Pharma, Llc
630 Central Ave
New Providence NJ 07974
877 530-1633

Newark
Essex County

(G-7062)
24 HORAS INC
68 Madison St Ste A (07105-7109)
PHONE..........................973 817-7400
Fax: 973 817-8383
Victor Alves, *President*
Manuel Ricardo, *Editor*
EMP: 10
SALES (est): 487K Privately Held
WEB: www.24horasinc.com
SIC: 2711 1751 Newspapers: publishing
only, not printed on site; carpentry work

(G-7063)
26 FLAVORS LLC
Also Called: Crazy Cups
29 Riverside Ave (07104-4238)
PHONE..........................855 662-7299
Brian Sanders,
EMP: 8
SALES (est): 387.7K Privately Held
SIC: 2095 Roasted coffee

(G-7064)
A & L INDUSTRIES INC
Also Called: Ace Powder Coating
23 George St (07105-3526)
PHONE..........................973 589-8070
Elton Lima, *President*
EMP: 22
SQ FT: 35,000
SALES (est): 3MM Privately Held
SIC: 3471 Finishing, metals or formed
products

(G-7065)
A C TRANSFORMER CORP
89 Madison St (07105-2191)
PHONE..........................973 589-8574
Fax: 973 589-3155
Robert Giangrande, *President*
Irene Giangrande, *Corp Secy*
EMP: 6 EST: 1949
SQ FT: 11,000
SALES (est): 780K Privately Held
WEB: www.actransformer.com
SIC: 3612 3677 Autotransformers, electric
(power transformers); electronic coils,
transformers & other inductors

(G-7066)
A V HYDRAULICS LTD LBLTY CO
2 Avenue C (07114-2602)
PHONE..........................973 621-6800
EMP: 5
SALES (est): 544.8K Privately Held
SIC: 3492 Control valves, aircraft: hy-
draulic & pneumatic

(G-7067)
A-1 PLASTIC BAGS INC
136 Tichenor St (07105-1018)
PHONE..........................973 344-4441
Fax: 973 344-4411
Benjamin A Schwartz, *President*
▲ EMP: 75
SQ FT: 57,000
SALES (est): 13.5MM Privately Held
WEB: www.complast.com
SIC: 2673 Plastic bags: made from pur-
chased materials

(G-7068)
AARHUSKARLSHAMN USA INC (PA)
131 Marsh St (07114-3238)
PHONE..........................973 344-1300
Fax: 973 344-9049
Arne Frank, *CEO*
Terrence Thomas, *President*
David Smith, *Opers Dir*
Kevin Doyle, *Purch Mgr*
Ann C Andersson, *Research*
▲ EMP: 42 EST: 1998
SALES (est): 37.8MM Privately Held
SIC: 2079 Edible fats & oils

(G-7069)
ABBY BINDERY CO INC
Also Called: Bmo Bindery
121 Christie St (07105-3915)
PHONE..........................973 690-5509
Fax: 973 690-5876
Mark Burkowitz, *President*
Lawrence Monahan, *Vice Pres*
Johnny Almeida, *Buyer*
EMP: 20
SQ FT: 20,000
SALES (est): 2.6MM Privately Held
SIC: 2789 Bookbinding & repairing: trade,
edition, library, etc.

(G-7070)
ABCO DIE CASTERS INC
39 Tompkins Point Rd (07114-2814)
PHONE..........................973 624-7030
Fax: 973 624-7425
Joseph Vitollo, *President*

Steve Vitollo, *Vice Pres*
Orlando Torres, *Opers Mgr*
Fred Vitollo, *Treasurer*
▲ EMP: 80 EST: 1971
SQ FT: 60,000
SALES (est): 11.1MM Privately Held
SIC: 3479 3364 Coating of metals &
formed products; coating, rust preventive;
zinc & zinc-base alloy die-castings

(G-7071)
ACE BAG & BURLAP COMPANY INC
Also Called: Aceco Industrial Packaging Co
166 Frelinghuysen Ave (07114-1694)
PHONE..........................973 242-2200
Fax: 973 242-1044
Richard J Sherman, *President*
Linda Sherman, *Treasurer*
EMP: 12
SQ FT: 36,400
SALES (est): 2.3MM Privately Held
SIC: 5199 2393 Packaging materials; tex-
tile bags

(G-7072)
ADCO CHEMICAL COMPANY INC
49 Rutherford St (07105-4820)
PHONE..........................973 589-0880
George Parker, *President*
Eleanor Parker, *Corp Secy*
Richard Carr, *Asst Sec*
EMP: 35 EST: 1936
SQ FT: 10,000
SALES (est): 6.1MM Privately Held
SIC: 2821 Plastics materials & resins

(G-7073)
ADVOCATE PUBLISHING CORP
Also Called: Directory & Almanac
171 Clifton Ave (07104-1019)
PHONE..........................973 497-4200
Fax: 973 497-4192
Isabel Kirchner, *Ch of Bd*
Archbishop John J Myers, *President*
Archbishop J Myers, *Principal*
EMP: 20
SQ FT: 8,000
SALES (est): 1MM
SALES (corp-wide): 61.5MM Privately
Held
WEB: www.ourladyofsorrowsschool.org
SIC: 2711 Newspapers: publishing only,
not printed on site
PA: Roman Catholic Archdiocese Of
Newark
171 Clifton Ave
Newark NJ 07104
973 497-4000

(G-7074)
AIRMET INC
Also Called: Airmet Metal Works
794 N 6th St (07107-2717)
PHONE..........................973 481-5550
Fax: 973 481-5551
Stephen Yavorski, *President*
Cynthia Yavorski, *Office Mgr*
EMP: 7
SQ FT: 10,000
SALES (est): 731.9K Privately Held
WEB: www.airmet.com
SIC: 1711 3444 3446 3443 Mechanical
contractor; sheet metalwork; architectural
metalwork; fabricated plate work (boiler
shop); fabricated structural metal

(G-7075)
AIVA NATURALS LLC
50 Park Pl Ste 1100 (07102-4301)
P.O. Box 96, Hightstown (08520-0096)
PHONE..........................201 825-0749
Alexander P Roubian, *President*
EMP: 4
SALES (est): 268.6K Privately Held
SIC: 2053 Cakes, bakery: frozen

(G-7076)
ALL METAL POLISHING CO INC
23 George St (07105-3526)
PHONE..........................973 589-8070
Fax: 973 589-0035
Elton Lima, *President*
EMP: 25
SQ FT: 15,000

SALES (est): 1.7MM **Privately Held**
SIC: 3471 Polishing, metals or formed products; plating of metals or formed products

(G-7077)
ALLIED METAL INDUSTRIES INC
Also Called: Allied Steel Dist & Svc Ctr
118 Harper St 144 (07114-2804)
PHONE..................................973 824-7347
Toll Free:..................................888 -
Fax: 973 624-8404
Donald De Faria Jr, *CEO*
Donald De Faria Sr, *Ch of Bd*
Lou Calderon, *Manager*
Lynn Turiello, *Information Mgr*
EMP: 43
SQ FT: 18,000
SALES (est): 37.3MM **Privately Held**
WEB: www.alliedsteel.com
SIC: 5051 3441 3444 Steel; structural shapes, iron or steel; fabricated structural metal for ships; sheet metalwork

(G-7078)
ALLIED PLASTICS HOLDINGS LLC (PA)
560 Ferry St (07105-4402)
PHONE..................................718 729-5500
Menash Oratz, *Mng Member*
▼ **EMP:** 51
SQ FT: 70,000
SALES: 70K **Privately Held**
SIC: 3081 Plastic film & sheet

(G-7079)
ALLSTATE PAPER BOX CO INC (PA)
223 Raymond Blvd (07105)
PHONE..................................973 589-2600
Fax: 973 817-9326
Matthew Elias, *President*
Robert Levine, *Vice Pres*
◆ **EMP:** 65
SQ FT: 138,000
SALES (est): 14.5MM **Privately Held**
WEB: www.allstatepaperbox.com
SIC: 2653 Boxes, corrugated: made from purchased materials

(G-7080)
ALM MEDIA LLC
New Jersey Law Journal
238 Mulberry St Fl 2 (07102-3528)
P.O. Box 20081 (07101-6081)
PHONE..................................973 642-0075
Fax: 973 642-0075
Robert Steinbaum, *Publisher*
Jennifer Thompson, *Editor*
Jonathan Erway, *Assoc Editor*
Peter Arthur, *Systems Staff*
EMP: 45
SALES (corp-wide): 186.9MM **Privately Held**
WEB: www.alm.com
SIC: 2711 Newspapers
HQ: Alm Media, Llc
120 Broadway Fl 5
New York NY 10271
212 457-9400

(G-7081)
ALVARO P ESCANDON INC
528 Ferry St (07105-4489)
PHONE..................................973 274-1040
Fax: 973 274-1092
Gary Escandon, *President*
EMP: 8
SALES: 3.5MM **Privately Held**
WEB: www.apescandon.com
SIC: 5199 2655 Bags, textile; reels (fiber), textile: made from purchased material

(G-7082)
AMERICAN FUR FELT LLC
53 Rome St (07105-3317)
PHONE..................................973 344-3026
Maria Dasilva, *Mng Member*
Lou Pereira,
▲ **EMP:** 19
SALES: 3.6MM **Privately Held**
SIC: 2371 Fur goods

(G-7083)
AMERICAN SHALE OIL LLC (HQ)
520 Broad St Ste 1 (07102-3111)
PHONE..................................973 438-3500
Joseph Giancaspro, *Controller*
Claude Popkin, *Mng Member*
Liore Alroy, *Manager*
Yoni Jonas, *Director*
EMP: 9
SALES (est): 2MM **Publicly Held**
SIC: 1382 Oil & gas exploration services

(G-7084)
AMROD CORP (PA)
305a Craneway St (07114-3114)
P.O. Box 445, Kearny (07032-0445)
PHONE..................................973 344-2978
Fax: 973 344-0365
Edward Gollob, *Ch of Bd*
Mark Woehnker, *President*
▲ **EMP:** 5
SQ FT: 175,000
SALES (est): 17.5MM **Privately Held**
WEB: www.amrod.com
SIC: 3351 Extruded shapes, copper & copper alloy

(G-7085)
AMROD CORP
305a Craneway St (07114-3114)
PHONE..................................973 344-3806
Mark Winkler, *President*
EMP: 60
SALES (corp-wide): 17.5MM **Privately Held**
WEB: www.amrod.com
SIC: 3351 3331 3366 3312 Extruded shapes, copper & copper alloy; primary copper; copper foundries; blast furnaces & steel mills
PA: Amrod Corp.
305a Craneway St
Newark NJ 07114
973 344-2978

(G-7086)
ANHYDRIDES & CHEMICALS INC
2 Margaretta St (07105)
PHONE..................................973 465-0077
Fax: 973 465-7713
Philip Rhodes, *President*
Micheal Rhodes, *President*
EMP: 8
SQ FT: 16,000
SALES (est): 690K **Privately Held**
SIC: 2821 Thermosetting materials

(G-7087)
ANTONIO MOZZARELLA FACTORY INC (PA)
631 Frelinghuysen Ave (07114-1330)
PHONE..................................973 353-9411
Thomas Pugliese, *President*
◆ **EMP:** 10
SQ FT: 51,000
SALES (est): 2.3MM **Privately Held**
WEB: www.antoniomozzarella.com
SIC: 5812 2032 Italian restaurant; Italian foods: packaged in cans, jars, etc.

(G-7088)
ANTONIO MOZZARELLA FACTORY INC
631 Frelinghuysen Ave # 2 (07114-1330)
PHONE..................................973 353-9411
Thomas Pugliese, *President*
EMP: 25
SALES (corp-wide): 2.3MM **Privately Held**
SIC: 5812 2032 Italian restaurant; Italian foods: packaged in cans, jars, etc.
PA: Antonio Mozzarella Factory Inc.
631 Frelinghuysen Ave
Newark NJ 07114
973 353-9411

(G-7089)
APPLECHEM INC
105 Lock St Ste 205 (07103-3565)
PHONE..................................862 210-8344
Samuel Lin, *President*
EMP: 5
SQ FT: 1,000

SALES: 350K **Privately Held**
WEB: www.applechem.com
SIC: 2834 Proprietary drug products

(G-7090)
ARCHIVE DESIGNS INC
238 Emmet St (07114-2731)
PHONE..................................973 242-6400
John Dubicki, *President*
Bernard Morchelles, *Vice Pres*
EMP: 6
SQ FT: 14,000
SALES: 2MM **Privately Held**
WEB: www.archivedesigns.com
SIC: 3579 Sorters, filing (office)

(G-7091)
ARDMORE INC
29 Riverside Ave Bldg 14 (07104-4237)
PHONE..................................973 481-2406
Fax: 973 481-2637
Albert Sharphouse, *President*
EMP: 8
SQ FT: 18,000
SALES: 1.2MM **Privately Held**
WEB: www.ardmore.com
SIC: 2841 Soap & other detergents

(G-7092)
ARISAPH PHARMACEUTICALS INC
Also Called: Triad Pharmaceutical
1037 Raymond Blvd # 1520 (07102-5429)
PHONE..................................617 986-4500
Christopher Kiritsy, *President*
William Bachovchin, *Vice Pres*
Joseph J Suarez, *VP Finance*
EMP: 5
SQ FT: 3,773
SALES (est): 1.8MM **Privately Held**
WEB: www.arisaph.com
SIC: 2834 Pharmaceutical preparations

(G-7093)
ARMETEC CORP
166 Abington Ave (07107-2633)
PHONE..................................973 485-2525
E Ginzburg, *Director*
EMP: 9
SALES (est): 993.6K **Privately Held**
SIC: 3446 Architectural metalwork

(G-7094)
AROL CHEMICAL PRODUCTS CO
649 Ferry St (07105-4601)
PHONE..................................973 344-1510
Sal Coppola, *President*
EMP: 8
SQ FT: 20,000
SALES (est): 1.6MM **Privately Held**
SIC: 2841 2842 2843 2899 Detergents; synthetic organic or inorganic alkaline; textile soap; degreasing solvent; textile finishing agents; textile processing assistants; oil treating compounds; oils & greases, blending & compounding; chemicals & allied products

(G-7095)
ARROW MACHINE COMPANY INC
117 Norfolk St (07103-3226)
PHONE..................................973 642-2430
Fax: 973 642-2431
George Ambandos, *President*
Sophie Ambandos, *Treasurer*
EMP: 6
SQ FT: 7,500
SALES: 350K **Privately Held**
SIC: 3519 Gas engine rebuilding; diesel engine rebuilding

(G-7096)
ATLAS REFINERY INC
142 Lockwood St (07105-4776)
PHONE..................................973 589-2002
Fax: 973 589-7377
Steven Schroeder Sr, *CEO*
Steven Schroeder Jr, *President*
◆ **EMP:** 22 **EST:** 1887
SQ FT: 90,000

SALES (est): 15MM **Privately Held**
WEB: www.atlasrefinery.com
SIC: 2843 2899 Softeners (textile assistants); leather processing assistants; chemical preparations

(G-7097)
ATLAS WOODWORK INC
212 Wright St (07114-2629)
PHONE..................................973 621-9595
Antonio Martins, *President*
George Costa, *Vice Pres*
EMP: 12
SALES (est): 1.8MM **Privately Held**
WEB: www.atlaswoodwork.com
SIC: 2499 Decorative wood & woodwork

(G-7098)
AUDIO TECHNOLOGIES AND CODECS (PA)
Also Called: Atc Labs
105 Lock St Ste 411 (07103-3575)
PHONE..................................973 624-1116
Deepen Sinha, *President*
John Glover, *Financial Exec*
EMP: 17
SQ FT: 1,000
SALES (est): 1.7MM **Privately Held**
SIC: 7371 3651 Computer software development & applications; audio electronic systems

(G-7099)
AURA DETERGENT LLC
649 Ferry St (07105-4601)
PHONE..................................718 824-2162
EMP: 36
SALES (corp-wide): 5MM **Privately Held**
SIC: 2841 Soap & other detergents
PA: Aura Detergent, Llc
1811 Mayflower Ave
Bronx NY 10461
718 824-2162

(G-7100)
AVANT INDUSTRIES LTD INC (PA)
780 Frelinghuysen Ave (07114-2294)
PHONE..................................973 242-1700
Rino Baranes, *President*
Bob De Prospo, *Vice Pres*
Antonio Matos, *Treasurer*
Edwardo Fernandez, *Admin Sec*
EMP: 4
SQ FT: 78,000
SALES (est): 1.2MM **Privately Held**
SIC: 6512 3231 3221 Nonresidential building operators; products of purchased glass; glass containers

(G-7101)
AVITEX CO INC (PA)
461 Frelinghuysen Ave (07114-1404)
PHONE..................................973 242-2410
Fax: 973 242-7258
AVI N Lazarovitz, *President*
Angela Olivo, *Vice Pres*
▲ **EMP:** 30
SQ FT: 50,000
SALES (est): 4MM **Privately Held**
WEB: www.selectofficesuites.com
SIC: 2241 Narrow fabric mills; trimmings, textile

(G-7102)
AVITEX CO INC
32 Noble St (07114-1363)
PHONE..................................973 242-2410
Ray Lindenberg, *Branch Mgr*
EMP: 4
SALES (corp-wide): 4MM **Privately Held**
SIC: 2241 Narrow fabric mills
PA: Avitex Co Inc
461 Frelinghuysen Ave
Newark NJ 07114
973 242-2410

(G-7103)
BABY TIME INTERNATIONAL INC
250 Passaic St (07104-3700)
PHONE..................................973 481-7400
Mandy Battap, *President*
▲ **EMP:** 5

▲ = Import ▼=Export
◆ =Import/Export

SALES (est): 424.7K **Privately Held**
SIC: 3069 5137 Baby pacifiers, rubber; baby goods

(G-7104)
BELL CONTAINER CORP
615 Ferry St (07105-4404)
P.O. Box 5728 (07105-7728)
PHONE................................973 344-4400
Fax: 973 344-0817
Arnold Kaplan, *Principal*
Keith Jones, *Vice Pres*
Steve Jones, *Vice Pres*
Steven Jones, *Vice Pres*
Michael Schwarzmann, *CFO*
▲ EMP: 200
SQ FT: 220,000
SALES (est): 100.8MM **Privately Held**
WEB: www.bellcontainer.com
SIC: 2653 Boxes, corrugated: made from purchased materials; solid fiber boxes, partitions, display items & sheets

(G-7105)
BENJAMIN MOORE & CO
134 Lister Ave (07105-4566)
PHONE................................973 344-1200
Glenn Cooper, *Principal*
EMP: 200
SALES (corp-wide): 242.1B **Publicly Held**
WEB: www.benjaminmoore.com
SIC: 2851 Paints & allied products; varnishes
HQ: Benjamin Moore & Co.
101 Paragon Dr
Montvale NJ 07645
201 573-9600

(G-7106)
BENNETT HEAT TRTING BRZING INC (PA)
690 Ferry St (07105-4619)
PHONE................................973 589-0590
David J Quaglia, *President*
Mark Fiore, *Vice Pres*
Lidia Galvez, *Vice Pres*
Tom De Fillipo, *Prdtn Mgr*
John Quaglia, *QC Mgr*
EMP: 32 EST: 1954
SQ FT: 70,000
SALES (est): 6.4MM **Privately Held**
WEB: www.bennetheat.com
SIC: 3398 Brazing (hardening) of metal

(G-7107)
BEST PROVISION CO INC (PA)
144 Avon Ave (07108-1995)
PHONE................................973 242-5000
Leonard Karp, *Ch of Bd*
Floyd Jayson, *President*
Richard Dolinko, *Co-Owner*
Kevin Karp, *Co-Owner*
Bernard Karp, *Exec VP*
EMP: 94 EST: 1938
SQ FT: 65,000
SALES (est): 18.8MM **Privately Held**
WEB: www.bestprovision.com
SIC: 2013 Sausages & other prepared meats; frankfurters from purchased meat; bologna from purchased meat; pastrami from purchased meat

(G-7108)
BLANKETS INC
26 Blanchard St (07105-4702)
PHONE................................973 589-7800
Bruce Liroff, *President*
Harriet Liroff, *Treasurer*
▲ EMP: 20
SQ FT: 4,000
SALES (est): 3.5MM **Privately Held**
WEB: www.blankets.com
SIC: 3555 Printing trades machinery

(G-7109)
BOMBARDIER TRANSPORTATION
60 Earhart Dr (07114-3703)
PHONE................................973 624-9300
Raymond T Betler, *Branch Mgr*
EMP: 400

SALES (corp-wide): 16.2B **Privately Held**
SIC: 4111 3536 7538 4581 Monorails, regular route: except amusement & scenic; monorail systems; general automotive repair shops; airports, flying fields & services
HQ: Bombardier Transportation (Holdings) Usa Inc
1501 Lebanon Church Rd
Pittsburgh PA 15236
412 655-5700

(G-7110)
BOYKO METAL FINISHING CO INC (PA)
100 Poinier St (07114-1711)
PHONE................................973 623-4254
Fax: 973 623-3529
John Boyko Jr, *President*
John Boyko III, *Vice Pres*
EMP: 65
SQ FT: 2,500
SALES (est): 6.9MM **Privately Held**
SIC: 3479 3471 Coating of metals & formed products; plating & polishing

(G-7111)
BOYKO METAL FINISHING CO INC
100 Poinier St (07114-1711)
PHONE................................973 623-4254
John Boyko Jr, *Branch Mgr*
EMP: 5
SALES (corp-wide): 6.9MM **Privately Held**
SIC: 3471 Plating & polishing
PA: Boyko Metal Finishing Co Inc
100 Poinier St
Newark NJ 07114
973 623-4254

(G-7112)
BRAZILIAN PRESS & ADVERTISING
78 Fillmore St Ste 1 (07105-3682)
PHONE................................973 344-4555
Fax: 973 344-7683
Silvio Desouza, *President*
EMP: 10
SALES (est): 650K **Privately Held**
WEB: www.brazilianpress.com
SIC: 2711 Newspapers: publishing only, not printed on site

(G-7113)
BRAZILIAN VOICE
412 Chestnut St (07105-2433)
P.O. Box 5686 (07105-0686)
PHONE................................973 491-6200
Fax: 973 491-6287
Roberto Leman, *CEO*
Fabianne Lima, *Adv Mgr*
EMP: 5
SALES (est): 230K **Privately Held**
SIC: 2711 Newspapers, publishing & printing

(G-7114)
BRICK CITY WHEELCHAIR RPS LLC
92 Hansbury Ave (07112-2205)
PHONE................................862 371-4311
Bradford James Sr,
EMP: 5
SALES (est): 223.9K **Privately Held**
SIC: 3842 Wheelchairs

(G-7115)
BRISTOL-DONALD COMPANY INC
50 Roanoke Ave (07105-4398)
PHONE................................973 589-2640
Fax: 973 589-2610
Robert P Greeley Jr, *President*
Daniel Greeley, *Vice Pres*
Dan Greeley, *Finance*
Jerry Duffy, *Sales Mgr*
EMP: 25 EST: 1945
SQ FT: 30,000
SALES (est): 5.7MM **Privately Held**
SIC: 3713 5012 5084 5088 Truck & bus bodies; truck bodies; hydraulic systems equipment & supplies; transportation equipment & supplies

(G-7116)
BROADVIEW TECHNOLOGIES INC
7 Amsterdam St 33 (07105-3801)
PHONE................................973 465-0077
Philip S Rhodes, *President*
Phillip Rhodes, *Vice Pres*
Jason Tuerack, *Vice Pres*
▲ EMP: 20
SQ FT: 2,500
SALES (est): 4.6MM **Privately Held**
WEB: www.broadview-tech.com
SIC: 2851 Epoxy coatings

(G-7117)
BROADWAY EMPRESS ENTRMT INC
15-21 Oraton St (07104-4172)
PHONE................................973 991-0009
Jean Rey, *CEO*
EMP: 8
SALES (est): 850K **Privately Held**
SIC: 3651 Household audio & video equipment

(G-7118)
CALANDRA ITALIAN & FRENCH BKY
Also Called: Calandra's Bakery
204 1st Ave W (07107-2436)
PHONE................................973 484-5598
Luciano Calandra, *President*
Anthony Calandra, *Vice Pres*
Ortenza Calandra, *Vice Pres*
EMP: 60 EST: 1962
SQ FT: 30,000
SALES (est): 2.4MM **Privately Held**
SIC: 5461 2051 Bread; cakes; cookies; pastries; bread, cake & related products

(G-7119)
CAMBRIDGE INDUSTRIES CO INC
7 Amsterdam St 33 (07105-3801)
PHONE................................973 465-4565
Philip Rhodes, *Vice Pres*
Joseph Stone, *Vice Pres*
EMP: 7
SQ FT: 10,000
SALES (est): 480K **Privately Held**
SIC: 2869 Plasticizers, organic: cyclic & acyclic

(G-7120)
CHARLES E GREEN & SON INC
625 3rd St (07107-2620)
P.O. Box 8277, Glen Ridge (07028-8277)
PHONE................................973 485-3630
John V Green III, *President*
John V Green III, *President*
▲ EMP: 41 EST: 1870
SQ FT: 100,000
SALES (est): 7.9MM **Privately Held**
WEB: www.charlesegreen.com
SIC: 3429 3991 3544 3469 Manufactured hardware (general); paint rollers; special dies & tools; metal stampings

(G-7121)
CHEM-FLEUR INC
Also Called: Firmenich
150 Firmench Way (07114-3124)
P.O. Box 5880, Princeton (08543-5880)
PHONE................................973 589-4266
Fax: 973 344-2999
David Shipman, *President*
Jean-Philippe Lebudel, *Vice Pres*
Johan Firmenich, *Project Mgr*
Nehal Gandhi, *Research*
Eric Jorgensen, *Treasurer*
▼ EMP: 80
SQ FT: 1,600
SALES (est): 6.1MM
SALES (corp-wide): 3.1B **Privately Held**
SIC: 2869 Industrial organic chemicals
HQ: Firmenich Incorporated
250 Plainsboro Rd
Plainsboro NJ 08536
609 452-1000

(G-7122)
CLEARWAY LLC
414 Wilson Ave (07105-4203)
PHONE................................973 578-4578
Stephen Winer, *Principal*

▼ EMP: 2
SALES: 4MM **Privately Held**
SIC: 3728 Deicing equipment, aircraft

(G-7123)
COBON PLASTICS CORP
90 South St (07114-2719)
PHONE................................973 344-6330
Michael Nelson, *President*
EMP: 10
SQ FT: 18,000
SALES (est): 860K **Privately Held**
WEB: www.cobonplastics.com
SIC: 3082 Tubes, unsupported plastic

(G-7124)
COLONIAL CONCRETE COMPANY (HQ)
1196 Mccarter Hwy (07104-3710)
PHONE................................973 482-1920
Fax: 973 482-7524
Martin Lucibello, *President*
Frank Rizzo, *Vice Pres*
EMP: 50
SQ FT: 1,000
SALES (est): 12.5MM
SALES (corp-wide): 1.3B **Publicly Held**
WEB: www.colonialconcrete.com
SIC: 3273 Ready-mixed concrete
PA: U.S. Concrete, Inc.
331 N Main St
Euless TX 76039
817 835-4105

(G-7125)
COLOR SCREEN PROS INC
100 Verona Ave (07104-3608)
PHONE................................973 268-5080
Oscar Cano, *CEO*
▲ EMP: 14
SQ FT: 5,000
SALES (est): 660K **Privately Held**
SIC: 2759 Screen printing

(G-7126)
CONDUENT STATE HEALTHCARE LLC
60 Park Pl Ste 605 (07102-5516)
PHONE................................973 824-3250
Fax: 609 689-6853
Jacqueline Fischer, *Branch Mgr*
EMP: 5
SALES (corp-wide): 6B **Publicly Held**
SIC: 3577 8099 Computer peripheral equipment; blood related health services
HQ: Conduent State Healthcare, Llc
12410 Milestone Dr Ste 500
Germantown MD 20876
301 820-4200

(G-7127)
CORPORATE COMPUTER SYSTEMS
Also Called: C C S
33 Washington St Ste 1002 (07102-3129)
PHONE................................732 739-5600
Fax: 732 739-1818
Mike D'Agostino, *Manager*
EMP: 19
SQ FT: 11,000
SALES (est): 2.2MM **Privately Held**
WEB: www.musicamusa.com
SIC: 7371 3577 3823 7361 Custom computer programming services; computer software development & applications; computer software development; computer peripheral equipment; computer interface equipment for industrial process control; placement agencies

(G-7128)
COUNTING SHEEP COFFEE INC
41 Malvern St (07105-1510)
PHONE................................973 589-4104
Deland Jessop, *CEO*
EMP: 4
SALES (est): 246.1K **Privately Held**
SIC: 2095 Roasted coffee

(G-7129)
COUSE & BOLTEN CO
90 S St Dock 5 (07114)
PHONE................................973 344-6330
Michael Nelson, *President*
Charles Mans, *Vice Pres*

EMP: 9 **EST:** 1899
SQ FT: 18,000
SALES: 1MM **Privately Held**
SIC: 3052 Plastic hose; rubber hose; plastic belting; rubber belting

(G-7130)
CREATIVE EMBROIDERY CORP
305 3rd Ave W Ste 3 (07107-2387)
PHONE..................................973 497-5700
Fax: 973 497-5520
Steven Diamond, *President*
Marlene Diamond, *Corp Secy*
EMP: 20
SQ FT: 65,000
SALES: 6MM **Privately Held**
SIC: 2395 2396 Embroidery products, except schiffli machine; automotive & apparel trimmings

(G-7131)
D & H PALLETS LLC
45 Verona Ave (07104-4409)
P.O. Box 8563, Elizabeth (07208-0563)
PHONE..................................973 481-2981
Hugo Munoz, *Mng Member*
Ramon Munoz,
EMP: 6 **EST:** 1999
SALES (est): 734.4K **Privately Held**
SIC: 2448 Pallets, wood & wood with metal

(G-7132)
DAMASCUS BAKERY NJ LLC
60 Mcclellan St (07114-2112)
PHONE..................................718 855-1456
James P Sweeney, *Principal*
▼ **EMP:** 55
SALES (est): 10.3MM **Privately Held**
SIC: 2051 Bakery: wholesale or wholesale/retail combined

(G-7133)
DARLING INGREDIENTS INC
Also Called: Quaker Soap Div
825 Wilson Ave (07105-4813)
PHONE..................................973 465-1900
Fax: 973 465-9247
Ed Schlagenhaft, *General Mgr*
William Frish, *Vice Pres*
John Latino, *Manager*
EMP: 104
SALES (corp-wide): 3.6B **Publicly Held**
WEB: www.darlingii.com
SIC: 2077 2048 Animal & marine fats & oils; prepared feeds
PA: Darling Ingredients Inc.
251 Oconnor Ridge Blvd
Irving TX 75038
972 717-0300

(G-7134)
DCI SIGNS & AWNINGS INC
110 Riverside Ave (07104-4202)
PHONE..................................973 350-0400
Danny Castillo, *President*
EMP: 25
SQ FT: 12,000
SALES (est): 4.2MM **Privately Held**
WEB: www.dcisigns.com
SIC: 3993 1799 Electric signs; sign installation & maintenance

(G-7135)
DCM GROUP INC
Also Called: I3 Software
563 Broad St (07102-4503)
PHONE..................................732 516-1173
Kumar Chaluvadi, *President*
Sachin Patil, *Manager*
EMP: 6
SALES (est): 816.9K **Privately Held**
WEB: www.dcmgroup.com
SIC: 7372 Prepackaged software

(G-7136)
DEB EL FOOD PRODUCTS LLC (PA)
Also Called: Deb El Foods
520 Broad St Fl 6 (07102-3121)
P.O. Box 876, Elizabeth (07207-0876)
PHONE..................................908 282-0120
Elliott Gibber, *President*
Oscar Reyes, *General Mgr*
Richard Mensh, *Buyer*
Michael Gibber, *Purchasing*
Alex Karmondi, *Engineer*

◆ **EMP:** 5
SQ FT: 30,000
SALES (est): 38.1MM **Privately Held**
SIC: 2015 Egg processing

(G-7137)
DEB-EL FOODS CORPORATION
520 Broad St (07102-3121)
P.O. Box 876, Elizabeth (07207-0876)
PHONE..................................908 351-0330
Elliot Gibber, *President*
◆ **EMP:** 135
SQ FT: 30,000
SALES (est): 19MM **Privately Held**
SIC: 2015 Eggs, processed: dehydrated

(G-7138)
DEBORAH SALES & MFG CO
109 Meeker Ave (07114-1300)
PHONE..................................973 344-8466
Fax: 973 344-3981
Carlos Rei, *President*
EMP: 4 **EST:** 1957
SQ FT: 5,000
SALES (est): 428.2K **Privately Held**
SIC: 3469 3496 Stamping metal for the trade; miscellaneous fabricated wire products

(G-7139)
DELEET MERCHANDISING CORP (PA)
Also Called: Prisco Printers Service
26 Blanchard St (07105-4784)
PHONE..................................212 962-6565
Fax: 973 589-0343
Bruce Liroff, *President*
Richard Liroff, *Chairman*
Mauro Marcatili, *Business Mgr*
Jay Friedman, *Vice Pres*
Mike White, *Vice Pres*
◆ **EMP:** 40
SQ FT: 30,000
SALES (est): 22MM **Privately Held**
SIC: 2869 5084 Industrial organic chemicals; printing trades machinery, equipment & supplies

(G-7140)
DELTECH RESINS CO (PA)
49 Rutherford St (07105-4820)
PHONE..................................973 589-0880
Bob Elfante, *President*
▲ **EMP:** 20
SALES (est): 12.2MM **Privately Held**
WEB: www.deltechresins.com
SIC: 2821 Plastics materials & resins

(G-7141)
DORZAR CORPORATION
Also Called: New Great American Veal
50 Avenue L Ste 5 (07105-3841)
PHONE..................................973 589-6363
Fax: 973 589-1188
Zarko Grgas, *President*
Dorothy Burke, *Corp Secy*
EMP: 35
SQ FT: 9,500
SALES (est): 7.2MM **Privately Held**
SIC: 2011 Veal from meat slaughtered on site

(G-7142)
DOSIS FRAGRANCE LLC
250 Passaic St (07104-3700)
PHONE..................................718 874-0074
Abraham Hartman, *Manager*
▲ **EMP:** 4
SQ FT: 700
SALES (est): 671.8K **Privately Held**
SIC: 2844 5122 Perfumes & colognes; perfumes

(G-7143)
DRS LEONARDO INC
95 William St (07102-1318)
PHONE..................................973 775-4440
EMP: 28
SALES (corp-wide): 9.2B **Privately Held**
SIC: 3812 Navigational systems & instruments
HQ: Leonardo Drs, Inc.
2345 Crystal Dr Ste 1000
Arlington VA 22202
703 416-8000

(G-7144)
DURAAMEN ENGINEERED PDTS INC (PA)
457 Frelinghuysen Ave (07114-1426)
PHONE..................................973 230-1301
Fax: 973 241-7830
Victor Pachade, *President*
EMP: 3
SQ FT: 1,750
SALES: 1.2MM **Privately Held**
SIC: 3272 2851 Dry mixture concrete; epoxy coatings; polyurethane coatings

(G-7145)
DURON CO INC
238 Emmet St (07114-2731)
PHONE..................................973 242-5704
John A Dubicki, *President*
EMP: 11
SQ FT: 14,000
SALES (est): 1.3MM **Privately Held**
WEB: www.flatfile.com
SIC: 3469 Stamping metal for the trade

(G-7146)
DYNA VEYOR INC
10 Hudson St (07103-2804)
PHONE..................................908 276-5384
Fax: 973 484-7790
Beverly Ayre, *CEO*
Stephen Ayre II, *President*
Stephen Ayre, *CFO*
Anthony M Ayre, *Treasurer*
EMP: 8
SQ FT: 26,000
SALES (est): 1.7MM **Privately Held**
WEB: www.dyna-veyor.com
SIC: 3535 3052 5085 Conveyors & conveying equipment; plastic belting; hose, belting & packing

(G-7147)
DYNAMIC DIE CUTTING & FINSHG
104-110 South St (07114-2719)
PHONE..................................973 589-8338
Fax: 973 589-4123
Emilio Esteva, *President*
George Esteva, *Vice Pres*
EMP: 10 **EST:** 1958
SQ FT: 13,000
SALES: 500K **Privately Held**
SIC: 2675 3544 Die-cut paper & board; special dies & tools

(G-7148)
E & J GALLO WINERY
1037 Raymond Blvd Ste 220 (07102-5425)
PHONE..................................973 877-0118
Fax: 973 884-1575
John Tripp, *Manager*
Marjorie Stern, *Admin Asst*
EMP: 40
SALES (corp-wide): 2.5B **Privately Held**
WEB: www.gallo.com
SIC: 2084 Wines
PA: E. & J. Gallo Winery
600 Yosemite Blvd
Modesto CA 95354
209 341-3111

(G-7149)
ELAN FOOD LABORATORIES INC
Also Called: Elan Vanilla
268 Doremus Ave (07105-4879)
PHONE..................................973 344-8014
Jerome Scharf, *President*
Ira Kapp, *Chairman*
Dr Jerry Guerrera, *Vice Pres*
David Weissman, *Vice Pres*
Thomas Jones, *Plant Mgr*
EMP: 15
SQ FT: 45,000
SALES (est): 3.4MM **Privately Held**
SIC: 2869 Vanillin, synthetic

(G-7150)
ELAN INC (PA)
268 Doremus Ave (07105-4879)
PHONE..................................973 344-8014
Fax: 973 344-1948
David R Weisman, *CEO*
Ira Kapp, *Ch of Bd*
Jocelyn Manship, *President*

Art Guerrera, *Vice Pres*
David Pimentel, *Vice Pres*
▲ **EMP:** 67
SQ FT: 45,000
SALES (est): 14.8MM **Privately Held**
WEB: www.elan-chemical.com
SIC: 2087 2899 2869 Extracts, flavoring; chemical preparations; industrial organic chemicals; flavors or flavoring materials, synthetic; perfume materials, synthetic

(G-7151)
ELDON GLASS & MIRROR CO INC
Also Called: Luso Glass
58 Stockton St 76 (07105-3013)
PHONE..................................973 589-2099
Fax: 973 589-7529
Carlos Firmino, *President*
Anna Firmino, *Admin Sec*
John Jroe, *Admin Sec*
EMP: 12
SALES (est): 1.4MM **Privately Held**
SIC: 1793 3229 Glass & glazing work; glassware, art or decorative

(G-7152)
ELITE CABINETRY CORP
97 Main St (07105-3520)
PHONE..................................973 583-0194
Marcio Rodrigues, *Principal*
EMP: 4 **EST:** 2009
SALES (est): 200.6K **Privately Held**
SIC: 2434 Wood kitchen cabinets

(G-7153)
EMPIRE LUMBER & MILLWORK CO
Also Called: Empire Architectural Millwork
377 Frelinghuysen Ave (07114-1422)
P.O. Box 2070 (07114-0070)
PHONE..................................973 242-2700
Fax: 973 242-3970
Ira Kent, *Ch of Bd*
Wayne Kent, *President*
Charlie Shields, *Vice Pres*
Ross Weinick, *Vice Pres*
Karl Kaiser, *Manager*
EMP: 40 **EST:** 1949
SQ FT: 1,000
SALES (est): 7.4MM **Privately Held**
WEB: www.elmdoor.com
SIC: 2421 2431 3446 Lumber: rough, sawed or planed; millwork; architectural metalwork

(G-7154)
ENDOMEDIX
Also Called: Medical Device
211 Warren St Ste 1 (07103-3569)
PHONE..................................848 248-1883
Richard Russo, *CEO*
John M Abrahams MD, *Principal*
Piyush Modak, *Research*
EMP: 5
SALES (est): 450K **Privately Held**
SIC: 3841 Surgical & medical instruments

(G-7155)
ENSEMBLEIQ INC
Also Called: Edgell Communications
1 Gateway Ctr Fl 1 # 1 (07102-5322)
PHONE..................................973 252-0100
Albert Guffanti, *Managing Dir*
Peter Breen, *Chief*
Noell Dimmig, *Accounts Exec*
Luis Santos, *Marketing Mgr*
Michele Rowe, *Marketing Staff*
EMP: 63
SALES (corp-wide): 26.8MM **Privately Held**
SIC: 2721 Magazines: publishing & printing
PA: Ensembleiq, Inc.
8550 W Bryn Mawr Ave # 200
Chicago IL 60631
773 992-4450

(G-7156)
EPIQ SYSTEMS INC
50 Park Pl Ste 701 (07102-4308)
PHONE..................................973 622-6111
Fax: 973 622-6333
Maria Celi, *Manager*
EMP: 7

▲ = Import ▼=Export
◆ =Import/Export

SALES (corp-wide): 588.4MM Privately Held
SIC: 3577 Computer peripheral equipment
HQ: Epiq Systems, Inc.
2 Ravinia Dr Ste 850
Atlanta GA 30346
913 621-9500

(G-7157)
EPOLIN CHEMICAL LLC (HQ)
Also Called: Epolin Inc
358-364 Adams St (07105)
PHONE....................973 465-9495
Greg Amato, CEO
James Ivchenko, President
Morton Lefar, Vice Pres
▲ EMP: 8
SQ FT: 19,500
SALES (est): 1.5MM Privately Held
WEB: www.epolin.com
SIC: 2865 6512 Dyes & pigments; nonresidential building operators
PA: Polymathes Holdings I Llc
20 Nassau St Ste M
Princeton NJ 08542
609 945-1690

(G-7158)
EVERTILE FLOORING CO INC
127 Frelinghuysen Ave (07114-1631)
PHONE....................973 242-7474
Nigel Mandel, Branch Mgr
EMP: 8
SALES (corp-wide): 1.4MM Privately Held
WEB: www.locktile-usa.com
SIC: 3996 Hard surface floor coverings
PA: Evertile Flooring Co. Inc
127 Frelinghuysen Ave
Newark NJ 07114
973 242-7474

(G-7159)
EXTREME PALLET INC
315 Astor St (07114-2822)
PHONE....................973 286-1717
Eddie Sanchez, President
EMP: 9
SALES (est): 1.6MM Privately Held
SIC: 2448 Pallets, wood

(G-7160)
FAPS INC (PA)
371 Craneway St (07114-3114)
PHONE....................973 589-5656
Fax: 973 589-5147
Gary L Lobue, President
William Mazur, General Mgr
August Lobue, Vice Pres
Gary Love, Vice Pres
Mike Mazzeo, Opers Mgr
▲ EMP: 200 EST: 1991
SQ FT: 6,000
SALES (est): 87.9MM Privately Held
WEB: www.fapsinc.com
SIC: 3499 3711 7538 Metal household articles; motor vehicles & car bodies; general automotive repair shops

(G-7161)
FEDERAL BRONZE CAST INDS INC (PA)
9 Backus St (07105-3087)
PHONE....................973 589-7575
Fax: 973 589-7078
Douglas J Reichard, CEO
Raj Mittal, Vice Pres
Frank J Reilly, Vice Pres
▲ EMP: 45
SQ FT: 40,000
SALES (est): 5.9MM Privately Held
SIC: 3366 Castings (except die); bronze

(G-7162)
FIRST FRIDAY GLOBAL INC
130 Mount Pleasant Ave (07104)
PHONE....................201 776-6709
Antonio M Francisco, President
EMP: 4
SALES (est): 219.4K Privately Held
SIC: 2711 Newspapers, publishing & printing

(G-7163)
FLEXCRAFT INDUSTRIES INC
390 Adams St (07114-2802)
P.O. Box 2098 (07114-0098)
PHONE....................973 589-3403
Fax: 973 589-0015
Bruce Machleder, President
EMP: 6
SALES: 500K Privately Held
WEB: www.flexcraftindustries.com
SIC: 3479 2891 Coating of metals with plastic or resins; adhesives & sealants

(G-7164)
FOREM PACKAGING INC
2 Joseph St (07105-4710)
P.O. Box 50090 (07105-8090)
PHONE....................973 589-0402
Aron Forem, President
Mitchell Lewites, CFO
▲ EMP: 12
SQ FT: 70,000
SALES: 4.9MM Privately Held
SIC: 2671 Plastic film, coated or laminated for packaging

(G-7165)
FORM CUT INDUSTRIES INC
195 Mount Pleasant Ave (07104-3814)
PHONE....................973 483-5154
Charles M Alberto, President
Joan Alberto, Corp Secy
Steve Alberto, Vice Pres
Ken Degraaf, Sales Mgr
EMP: 49 EST: 1961
SQ FT: 24,000
SALES (est): 8.8MM Privately Held
WEB: www.formcut.com
SIC: 3496 3451 Miscellaneous fabricated wire products; screw machine products

(G-7166)
G & R FUEL CORP
822 Clinton Ave (07108-1031)
PHONE....................973 732-0530
Sonny Singh, Manager
EMP: 5
SALES (est): 456.2K Privately Held
SIC: 2869 Fuels

(G-7167)
G BIG CORP
189 Frelinghuysen Ave (07114-1531)
PHONE....................973 242-6521
Trevor Blackwell, Principal
EMP: 5 EST: 2010
SALES (est): 374.3K Privately Held
SIC: 3469 Metal stampings

(G-7168)
GAMBERT SHIRT CORP
Also Called: Gambert Custom Shirts
436 Ferry St Ste 2 (07105-3929)
PHONE....................973 424-9105
Theodore Gambert, CEO
EMP: 50 EST: 1933
SQ FT: 7,200
SALES (est): 5.3MM Privately Held
SIC: 2321 2331 Men's & boys' furnishings; women's & misses' blouses & shirts

(G-7169)
GANN LAW BOOKS INC
1 Washington Park # 1300 (07102-3194)
PHONE....................973 268-1200
Fax: 973 268-1330
Michael Protzel, President
Howard Dubner, Vice Pres
EMP: 19
SQ FT: 2,500
SALES (est): 1.7MM Privately Held
WEB: www.gannlaw.com
SIC: 2731 8111 Textbooks: publishing only, not printed on site; legal services

(G-7170)
GLASSROOTS INC
10 Bleeker St (07102-1903)
PHONE....................973 353-9555
Fax: 973 353-9551
Katie Witzig, COO
Barbara Heisler, Exec Dir
Jenny Pollack, Program Dir
Yazmine Graham, Assistant
EMP: 20

SALES: 787.9K Privately Held
SIC: 3229 Pressed & blown glass

(G-7171)
GLOBAL COMMODITIES EXPORTACAO
126 Jackson St (07105-2157)
PHONE....................201 613-1532
Benjamin Allen, CEO
EMP: 8 EST: 2013
SALES: 602.6K Privately Held
SIC: 7389 0116 2061 4412 Weighing, food & commodity; soybeans; granulated cane sugar; deep sea foreign transportation of freight

(G-7172)
GLOBAL MANUFACTURING LLC
Also Called: Global Force and Artic Bloc
35 William St Fl 2 (07102-2714)
PHONE....................973 494-5413
Fax: 973 656-1500
David Slossberg, Mng Member
EMP: 4
SQ FT: 1,000
SALES (est): 458.1K Privately Held
WEB: www.globalmfgllc.com
SIC: 2389 Uniforms & vestments

(G-7173)
GLOBAL WEAVERS CORP
Also Called: J & S Housewares Corp
9-13 Dey St (07103)
PHONE....................973 824-5500
Simon Belfer, President
EMP: 8
SALES (est): 187K Privately Held
SIC: 2392 Comforters & quilts: made from purchased materials; home furnishings; beds & accessories

(G-7174)
GLOBE METALS INC
7 Avenue L (07105-3805)
P.O. Box 5029 (07105-0029)
PHONE....................973 589-2563
Alfred H Rueff, President
EMP: 20 EST: 1977
SQ FT: 16,000
SALES (est): 3MM Privately Held
SIC: 5093 4953 3341 Nonferrous metals scrap; refuse systems; secondary nonferrous metals

(G-7175)
GOLDEN PLATTER FOODS INC
37 Tompkins Point Rd (07114-2814)
PHONE....................973 344-8770
Fax: 973 242-5892
Scott Bennett, CEO
William Louttit, Exec VP
▲ EMP: 50
SQ FT: 20,000
SALES: 30MM Privately Held
SIC: 2015 Poultry, processed: frozen

(G-7176)
GOLDEN TROPICS LTD
1489-1495 Mccarter Hwy (07104-3966)
PHONE....................973 484-0202
Carlos Favaro, President
Alicia Favaro, Vice Pres
▲ EMP: 25
SALES (est): 4.6MM Privately Held
SIC: 2099 2092 Food preparations; fresh or frozen packaged fish

(G-7177)
GRAVER WATER SYSTEMS LLC
Also Called: Graver Chemical Products
72 Lockwood St (07105-4719)
PHONE....................973 465-2380
Walter Bass, VP Mfg
Al Tavares, Director
EMP: 16
SALES (corp-wide): 242.1B Publicly Held
WEB: www.graver.com
SIC: 3589 Water filters & softeners, household type
HQ: Graver Water Systems Llc
675 Central Ave Ste 3
New Providence NJ 07974
908 516-1400

(G-7178)
GREEN LABS LLC
211 Warren St Ste 206 (07103-3568)
PHONE....................220-4845
Oscar Melancia De La Cruz Roma, Vice Pres
Erick Salgado, Mng Member
EMP: 6 EST: 2009
SALES (est): 615.8K Privately Held
SIC: 2099 5149 Food preparations; seasonings: dry mixes; spices & seasonings

(G-7179)
GREWE PLASTICS INC
123 S 15th St (07107-1097)
PHONE....................973 485-7602
Fax: 973 485-7650
Allen D Blum, President
EMP: 8
SQ FT: 46,500
SALES (est): 620K Privately Held
WEB: www.greweco.com
SIC: 3089 5162 Plastic processing; plastics sheets & rods

(G-7180)
GROUP MARTIN LLC JJ
90 South St (07114-2719)
PHONE....................862 240-1813
John Ra, Principal
▲ EMP: 10
SALES (est): 1MM Privately Held
SIC: 2082 2038 Ale (alcoholic beverage); snacks, including onion rings, cheese sticks, etc.

(G-7181)
GUARDRITE STEEL DOOR CORP
81-87 Springdale Ave (07107-1232)
PHONE....................973 481-4424
Fax: 973 482-5347
Todd Santana, President
▲ EMP: 6
SQ FT: 30,000
SALES (est): 965.5K Privately Held
SIC: 3442 1751 Rolling doors for industrial buildings or warehouses, metal; window & door installation & erection

(G-7182)
HAENSSLER SHTMTL WORKS INC
592 Hawthorne Ave (07112-1122)
PHONE....................973 373-6360
Wendy Haenssler, President
Richard Haenssler, Vice Pres
EMP: 14
SQ FT: 7,900
SALES (est): 1.2MM Privately Held
SIC: 3444 Sheet metalwork

(G-7183)
HAL-O MANUFACTURING CO INC
137 Meeker Ave Ste 143 (07114-1333)
PHONE....................973 824-6122
Fax: 973 824-4047
Hal Roth, President
Lois Roth, Principal
Harold S Roth, Corp Secy
▲ EMP: 9
SQ FT: 23,000
SALES (est): 870K Privately Held
SIC: 3646 Commercial indusl & institutional electric lighting fixtures

(G-7184)
HALSEY NEWS
2 Prudential Dr (07102-3075)
PHONE....................973 645-0017
EMP: 4
SALES (est): 76.2K Privately Held
SIC: 2711 Newspapers

(G-7185)
HANDCRAFT MANUFACTURING CORP
640 Frelinghuysen Ave # 1 (07114-1360)
PHONE....................973 565-0077
Fax: 973 733-2152
Erwin Mizrahy, President
EMP: 39

GEOGRAPHIC

SALES (est): 3.9MM
SALES (corp-wide): 17.1MM **Privately Held**
WEB: www.handcraftmfg.com
SIC: 2389 5137 5136 Men's miscellaneous accessories; women's & children's clothing; men's & boys' clothing
PA: Handcraft Manufacturing Corp.
　　34 W 33rd St Rm 401
　　New York NY 10001
　　212 251-0022

(G-7186)
HANDY STORE FIXTURES INC
337 Sherman Ave (07114-1507)
PHONE....................973 242-1600
Fax: 973 733-2185
Paul Kurland, *President*
Richard Kurland, *Vice Pres*
Joe O'Brien, *VP Sales*
Jim Lackey, *Regl Sales Mgr*
▼ **EMP:** 55 **EST:** 1952
SQ FT: 200,000
SALES (est): 10.3MM **Privately Held**
WEB: www.handysf.com
SIC: 2542 2541 Fixtures, store: except wood; store fixtures, wood

(G-7187)
HAWK DAIRY INC
30 Jabez St (07105-3021)
PHONE....................973 466-9030
Fax: 973 466-1139
Jack Taranto, *President*
EMP: 6
SQ FT: 16,000
SALES (est): 510K **Privately Held**
SIC: 2022 Natural cheese

(G-7188)
HEADWEAR CREATIONS INC
Also Called: Bold Hat Makers
200 Wright St (07114-2663)
PHONE....................973 622-1144
Fax: 973 622-4309
Ruben Spitz, *President*
EMP: 48
SQ FT: 15,000
SALES (est): 4.8MM **Privately Held**
SIC: 2353 Hats & caps

(G-7189)
HILIN LIFE PRODUCTS INC
211 Warren St Ste 211 # 211 (07103-3568)
PHONE....................973 648-0265
Helen Denise, *CEO*
EMP: 8
SALES (est): 708.6K **Privately Held**
SIC: 3845 Electromedical equipment

(G-7190)
HOLBY VALVE CO INC
24 Ferdon St (07105-3011)
PHONE....................973 465-7400
Arthur Brown, *President*
Michael Fleischer, *Treasurer*
Timothy Devine, *Sales Associate*
EMP: 10 **EST:** 1945
SQ FT: 8,000
SALES (est): 1.1MM **Privately Held**
SIC: 3494 Valves & pipe fittings

(G-7191)
HOLISTIC SOLAR USA INC
105 Lock St Ste 407 (07103-3567)
PHONE....................732 757-5500
Scott Blow, *Corp Secy*
EMP: 5
SALES (est): 175K **Privately Held**
SIC: 3433 1711 3356 3674 Solar cells; battery metal; ; solar heaters & collectors; solar energy contractor

(G-7192)
HONIG CHEMICAL & PROC CORP
414 Wilson Ave (07105-4203)
PHONE....................973 344-0881
Fax: 973 344-5743
Robert Honig, *President*
Jim Cahill, *Manager*
Eloise Honig, *Admin Sec*
EMP: 32 **EST:** 1970
SQ FT: 70,000
SALES (est): 4.6MM **Privately Held**
SIC: 2869 Industrial organic chemicals

(G-7193)
HUDSON DISPLAYS CO
687 Frelinghuysen Ave # 1 (07114-1349)
PHONE....................973 623-8255
Maggie Marin, *President*
Tito Marin, *Vice Pres*
Nelson Marin, *Treasurer*
EMP: 25
SQ FT: 20,000
SALES (est): 2.4MM **Privately Held**
WEB: www.hudsondisplays.com
SIC: 3999 Advertising display products

(G-7194)
IDT ENERGY INC (HQ)
520 Broad St Fl 9 (07102-3111)
PHONE....................877 887-6866
Geoffrey Rochwarger, *CEO*
Alan Schwab, *COO*
Brad Martin, *Vice Pres*
Stuart Naftel, *Vice Pres*
Sara Miller, *Opers Staff*
EMP: 30
SALES (est): 4.4MM **Publicly Held**
SIC: 3679 Power supplies, all types: static

(G-7195)
IDT GLOBAL PROCESSING SVCS INC
520 Broad St (07102-3121)
PHONE....................973 438-3556
Bill Pereira, *CEO*
EMP: 5 **EST:** 2013
SALES (est): 33.8K **Privately Held**
SIC: 7372 Application computer software
PA: Idt International Telecom, Inc.
　　550 Broad St Bsmt B05
　　Newark NJ 07102

(G-7196)
INDUSTRIAL HARD CHROMIUM CO
7 Rome St (07105-3317)
P.O. Box 605, Allendale (07401-0605)
PHONE....................973 344-2265
Fax: 973 344-2261
Marilyn Foote, *President*
Craig Foote, *Vice Pres*
Rj Anderson, *Prdtn Mgr*
Nancy Lanzalott, *Controller*
EMP: 12
SQ FT: 13,000
SALES (est): 1.4MM **Privately Held**
WEB: www.ihcco.com
SIC: 3471 Chromium plating of metals or formed products; electroplating of metals or formed products

(G-7197)
INNOVATIVE RESIN SYSTEMS INC
257 Wilson Ave (07105-3826)
PHONE....................973 465-6887
John Khosdeghian, *Manager*
EMP: 7
SALES (est): 956.8K
SALES (corp-wide): 6.1MM **Privately Held**
SIC: 2821 Epoxy resins
PA: Innovative Resin Systems, Inc.
　　70 Verkade Dr
　　Wayne NJ 07470
　　973 465-6887

(G-7198)
IRONBOUND EXPRESS INC
65 Jabez St (07105-3047)
PHONE....................973 491-5151
Carmen Pizzuto, *Principal*
EMP: 4 **EST:** 1996
SALES (est): 518.6K **Privately Held**
SIC: 2655 Fiber cans, drums & similar products

(G-7199)
IRONBOUND INTERMODAL INDS INC
65 Jabez St (07105-3047)
PHONE....................973 491-5151
Frank Borland, *President*
Danny Lastra, *Manager*
Wendy Cruz, *Technology*
EMP: 15
SALES (est): 4.4MM **Privately Held**
SIC: 2655 Fiber cans, drums & containers

(G-7200)
IRONBOUND METAL
Also Called: Metal Fabrication
238 Emmet St (07114-2731)
PHONE....................973 242-5704
John Dubicki, *Owner*
EMP: 4
SALES: 250K **Privately Held**
SIC: 3499 3699 Fabricated metal products; laser welding, drilling & cutting equipment

(G-7201)
IRONBOUND WELDING INC
156 Walnut St (07105-1216)
PHONE....................973 589-3128
Fax: 973 589-1183
Louis J Tamasco Jr, *President*
Antoinette Tamasco, *Corp Secy*
EMP: 6
SQ FT: 4,000
SALES (est): 450K **Privately Held**
SIC: 7692 5211 5051 Welding repair; lumber & other building materials; steel

(G-7202)
IVEY KATRINA OWNER
Also Called: Fritnationalsupply
95 Montrose St (07106-2315)
PHONE....................973 951-8328
Ivey Katrina, *Owner*
EMP: 4
SALES (est): 175.4K **Privately Held**
SIC: 3334 3366 3613 3612 Primary aluminum; bushings & bearings; control panels, electric; machine tool transformers

(G-7203)
J P EGAN INDUSTRIES INC
676 S 14th St (07103-1411)
PHONE....................973 642-1500
Jan P Egan Jr, *President*
EMP: 8
SALES (est): 670K **Privately Held**
SIC: 2515 Mattresses & foundations

(G-7204)
J&S HOUSEWARE CORP
9 Dey St Ste 13 (07103-3609)
PHONE....................973 824-5500
Semen Belfer, *President*
◆ **EMP:** 8
SQ FT: 30,000
SALES (est): 1MM **Privately Held**
SIC: 2392 Comforters & quilts: made from purchased materials

(G-7205)
JARCHEM INDUSTRIES INC
Malec Don Specialty Chem Div
414 Wilson Ave (07105-4287)
PHONE....................973 344-0600
Arnold Stern, *Branch Mgr*
EMP: 12
SALES (est): 1MM
SALES (corp-wide): 11.3MM **Privately Held**
WEB: www.jarchem.com
SIC: 2869 Acetates: amyl, butyl & ethyl
PA: Jarchem Industries, Inc.
　　414 Wilson Ave
　　Newark NJ 07105
　　973 344-0600

(G-7206)
JEFFERSON PRINTING SERIVCE
184 Jefferson St (07105-1204)
PHONE....................973 491-0019
Julio Depaula, *President*
EMP: 10
SALES (est): 4MM **Privately Held**
SIC: 2759 Commercial printing

(G-7207)
JERSEY STEEL DOOR INC
95 N 11th St (07107-1117)
PHONE....................973 482-4020
Rolin Gonzalez, *President*
EMP: 5
SALES (est): 671.6K **Privately Held**
SIC: 3442 1799 5211 Metal doors, sash & trim; antenna installation; door & window products

(G-7208)
JONAS MEDIA GROUP INC
520 Broad St Ste 400 (07102-3121)
PHONE....................973 438-1900
Howard Jonas, *President*
EMP: 11
SALES (est): 550.8K **Publicly Held**
WEB: www.idt.net
SIC: 2721 2741 Magazines: publishing only, not printed on site; directories: publishing only, not printed on site
PA: Idt Corporation
　　520 Broad St Fl 9
　　Newark NJ 07102

(G-7209)
JOYCE FOOD LLC (PA)
80 Avenue K (07105-3803)
PHONE....................973 491-9696
Fax: 973 491-9236
Howard Freundlich,
Victor Ostreicher,
▲ **EMP:** 180 **EST:** 1945
SQ FT: 35,000
SALES (est): 15.9MM **Privately Held**
WEB: www.rokeach.com
SIC: 2034 2052 2099 2045 Soup mixes; cookies; crackers, dry; gelatin dessert preparations; seasonings & spices; pancake mixes, prepared: from purchased flour

(G-7210)
KAMPACK INC (HQ)
100 Frontage Rd (07114-3718)
PHONE....................973 589-7400
Fax: 973 817-8223
Karen Mehiel, *CEO*
Karen Aguerosmehiel, *President*
Randy Baer, *Vice Pres*
Irving Levine, *Vice Pres*
Chris Scallan, *Plant Supt*
EMP: 200 **EST:** 1959
SQ FT: 180,000
SALES (est): 68.6MM
SALES (corp-wide): 113.2MM **Privately Held**
WEB: www.mannkraft.com
SIC: 2653 Sheets, corrugated: made from purchased materials; boxes, corrugated: made from purchased materials; display items, corrugated: made from purchased materials
PA: U.S. Corrugated, Inc.
　　95 W Beau St Ste 430
　　Washington PA 15301
　　724 345-2050

(G-7211)
KAMPACK INC
100 Frontage Rd (07114-3718)
PHONE....................973 589-7400
Dennis Mehiel, *Manager*
EMP: 145
SALES (corp-wide): 113.2MM **Privately Held**
WEB: www.mannkraft.com
SIC: 2653 Boxes, corrugated: made from purchased materials
HQ: Kampack Inc.
　　100 Frontage Rd
　　Newark NJ 07114
　　973 589-7400

(G-7212)
KEYSTONE FOLDING BOX COMPANY
367 Verona Ave (07104-1713)
PHONE....................973 483-1054
Fax: 973 483-5853
Wade E Hartman, *President*
William Hartman, *Vice Pres*
Richard Rossbach, *QC Mgr*
Scott Pajewski, *Comptroller*
Kim Vigilante, *Accounts Exec*
EMP: 75 **EST:** 1890
SQ FT: 85,000
SALES (est): 30MM **Privately Held**
WEB: www.keyboxco.com
SIC: 2657 Folding paperboard boxes

(G-7213)
KP FUEL CORPORATION
864 Mount Prospect Ave (07104-3620)
PHONE....................973 350-1202
EMP: 4

▲ = Import ▼=Export
◆ =Import/Export

SALES (est): 228.5K **Privately Held**
SIC: 2869 Fuels

(G-7214)
KRAFTAPE PRINTERS INC
124 Orchard St (07102-3304)
PHONE..................................973 824-3005
Fax: 973 824-3364
Frank Hirtler, *President*
Robert Hirtler, *Vice Pres*
EMP: 6 **EST:** 1931
SQ FT: 5,000
SALES: 600K **Privately Held**
SIC: 2759 Commercial printing

(G-7215)
L GAMBERT LLC
Also Called: L Gambert Shirts
61 Freeman St Ste 4 (07105-4000)
PHONE..................................973 344-3440
Lorraine Gambert, *Owner*
Bill Epps, *Controller*
EMP: 85
SQ FT: 9,000
SALES (est): 612.2K **Privately Held**
WEB: www.gambertshirts.com
SIC: 2321 Men's & boys' dress shirts;
men's & boys' sports & polo shirts

(G-7216)
LANDEW SAWDUST CO INC
21 Poinier St (07114-1725)
PHONE..................................973 344-5255
Seymour Landew, *President*
EMP: 12 **EST:** 1914
SQ FT: 8,000
SALES: 400K **Privately Held**
SIC: 2421 Sawdust & shavings

(G-7217)
LEFT-HANDED LIBRA LLC
Also Called: Jane Carter Solution
50 Park Pl Ste 1001 (07102-4300)
PHONE..................................973 623-1112
Valli W APM, *Opers Mgr*
Jane Carter,
Michael Hellerman,
▼ **EMP:** 10
SALES: 4MM **Privately Held**
SIC: 3999 Hair & hair-based products

(G-7218)
LEXORA INC
Also Called: Lexora Home
80 Wheeler Point Rd (07105-3033)
PHONE..................................855 453-9672
Andrey Bogan, *President*
EMP: 3
SQ FT: 5,000
SALES: 1MM **Privately Held**
SIC: 2434 2499 Vanities, bathroom: wood;
kitchen, bathroom & household ware:
wood

(G-7219)
LIME ENERGY CO
100 Mulberry St 4 (07102-4056)
PHONE..................................732 791-5380
Scott Fertig, *Branch Mgr*
EMP: 7
SALES (corp-wide): 112.6MM **Privately
Held**
SIC: 3274 Lime
PA: Lime Energy Co.
4 Gateway Ctr Fl 4 # 4
Newark NJ 07102
201 416-2575

(G-7220)
LION EXTRUDING CORP
106 Rutherford St (07105-4823)
PHONE..................................973 344-4648
Fax: 973 465-1055
Gary Demarco, *President*
Carl Demarco, *Vice Pres*
▼ **EMP:** 16
SQ FT: 15,000
SALES: 2.5MM **Privately Held**
SIC: 5093 3087 Plastics scrap; custom
compound purchased resins

(G-7221)
LIPOID LLC
744 Broad St Ste 1801 (07102-3805)
PHONE..................................973 735-2692
C Matthias Rebmann, *Mng Member*

Michael Kahn, *Senior Mgr*
Joy Romulus, *Senior Mgr*
Eisaku Takai, *Senior Mgr*
▼ **EMP:** 4
SALES (est): 380K **Privately Held**
WEB: www.lipoidllc.com
SIC: 2834 Pharmaceutical preparations

(G-7222)
LMC PRECISION INC
91 Rome St (07105-3405)
PHONE..................................973 522-0005
Fax: 973 522-0007
Manuel Lobo, *Owner*
Napoleon Cruz, *Vice Pres*
EMP: 10
SALES (est): 1.1MM **Privately Held**
SIC: 3469 Machine parts, stamped or
pressed metal

(G-7223)
LOCAL BAKING PRODUCTS INC
Also Called: Joey's Fine Foods
135 Manchester Pl (07104-1722)
PHONE..................................973 482-1400
Fax: 973 482-1597
Aaron Aihini, *CEO*
Joseph Aihini, *President*
Barbara Aihini, *Financial Exec*
Joe Aihini, *Sales Executive*
Selma Aihini, *Admin Sec*
EMP: 40
SQ FT: 15,000
SALES (est): 6.6MM **Privately Held**
SIC: 2052 2051 Cookies & crackers;
bread, cake & related products; cakes,
pies & pastries

(G-7224)
LOCKTILE INDUSTRIES LLC
127 Frelinghuysen Ave (07114-1631)
PHONE..................................888 562-5845
Nigel Mandel, *Mng Member*
Aaron Silberberg,
EMP: 10
SALES (est): 466K **Privately Held**
SIC: 3996 1752 Tile, floor: supported plas-
tic; ceramic floor tile installation

(G-7225)
LOPES SAUSAGE CO
304 Walnut St (07105-1717)
PHONE..................................973 344-3063
Hermino R Lopes, *Owner*
EMP: 5
SQ FT: 8,800
SALES: 400K **Privately Held**
SIC: 2013 Sausages from purchased meat

(G-7226)
LOUIS IRON WORKS INC
218 Lackawanna Ave (07103-3236)
PHONE..................................973 624-2700
Louis Velasco, *President*
EMP: 9
SALES (est): 640K **Privately Held**
WEB: www.louisironworks.com
SIC: 7692 Welding repair

(G-7227)
LUSO AMERICANO
66 Union St (07105-1417)
PHONE..................................973 344-3200
Natalie Matinho, *Principal*
Paul Matinho, *Opers Staff*
EMP: 20
SALES (est): 1MM **Privately Held**
SIC: 2711 Newspapers: publishing only,
not printed on site

(G-7228)
LUSO MACHINE INC
29 Avenue C (07114-2601)
PHONE..................................973 242-1717
Fax: 973 242-1728
Sergio Remelgado, *President*
Harold Schultz, *Sales Mgr*
EMP: 10
SALES (est): 726.2K **Privately Held**
SIC: 3449 3469 3599 Miscellaneous met-
alwork; metal stampings; custom machin-
ery; machine shop, jobbing & repair

(G-7229)
LUSO-AMERICANO CO INC
88 Ferry St Ste 1 (07105-1817)
PHONE..................................973 344-3200
Fax: 973 589-3848
Antonio Matinho, *President*
Luis Pires, *Editor*
Natalie Matinho, *Corp Secy*
Paul Matinho, *Vice Pres*
Gloria Afonso, *Office Mgr*
EMP: 23
SQ FT: 6,000
SALES (est): 1.1MM **Privately Held**
WEB: www.lusoamericano.com
SIC: 2711 Newspapers: publishing only,
not printed on site

(G-7230)
LUSOTECH LLC
82-84 Vanderpool St (07114-1765)
P.O. Box 237, Elizabeth (07207-0237)
PHONE..................................973 332-3861
Fax: 973 465-9517
Filipe M Daluz, *Mng Member*
EMP: 4
SALES: 500K **Privately Held**
SIC: 1711 7692 3449 Mechanical con-
tractor; welding repair; bars, concrete re-
inforcing: fabricated steel

(G-7231)
LYCA TEL LLC (PA)
Also Called: Lycatel
24 Commerce St Ste 100 (07102-4024)
PHONE..................................973 286-0771
Jarmi Lopez, *Regional Mgr*
Ilanko Ponnampalam, *Business Mgr*
Hiral Patel, *Engineer*
Thaya Soma, *Accounting Mgr*
Carmela Monti, *Human Res Dir*
EMP: 24
SQ FT: 4,000
SALES (est): 5.8MM **Privately Held**
WEB: www.lycatel.com
SIC: 3661 Telegraph & related apparatus

(G-7232)
**LYONDELL CHEMICAL
COMPANY**
Also Called: Equistar Chemicals
300 Doremus Ave (07105-4882)
PHONE..................................973 578-2200
Josh Squillante, *Manager*
EMP: 8
SALES (corp-wide): 34.5B **Privately Held**
WEB: www.lyondell.com
SIC: 2869 2822 Olefins; ethylene; polyeth-
ylene, chlorosulfonated (hypalon)
HQ: Lyondell Chemical Company
1221 Mckinney St Ste 300
Houston TX 77010
713 309-7200

(G-7233)
MACHINE PARTS INC
Also Called: M P I
17 Ferdon St (07105-3010)
PHONE..................................973 491-5444
Douglas Reicard, *President*
EMP: 10 **EST:** 1995
SALES (est): 1.3MM **Privately Held**
WEB: www.machineparts.com
SIC: 3599 Machine shop, jobbing & repair

(G-7234)
**MANCO PLATING
INCORPORATED**
390 Park Ave (07107-1112)
P.O. Box 7025 (07107-0025)
PHONE..................................973 485-6800
Fax: 973 485-8444
Luis Garcia, *President*
EMP: 9 **EST:** 1966
SQ FT: 9,800
SALES: 700K **Privately Held**
SIC: 3471 Electroplating of metals or
formed products; finishing, metals or
formed products

(G-7235)
MANISCHEWITZ COMPANY (HQ)
Also Called: Horowitz
80 Avenue K (07105-3803)
PHONE..................................201 553-1100
Paul Bensabat, *CEO*

Alain Bankier, *President*
Mark Weinsten, *President*
Michael Schrob, *Materials Mgr*
Jose Ruiz, *Warehouse Mgr*
◆ **EMP:** 60 **EST:** 1888
SQ FT: 139,100
SALES (est): 54MM
SALES (corp-wide): 330.1MM **Privately
Held**
SIC: 2052 2045 2032 2091 Matzos; cake
mixes, prepared: from purchased flour;
soups, except seafood: packaged in
cans, jars, etc.; fish: packaged in cans,
jars, etc.
PA: Tmci Holdings, Inc
80 Avenue K
Newark NJ 07105
201 553-1100

(G-7236)
**MARA POLISHING & PLATING
CORP**
105 W Peddie St (07112-2753)
PHONE..................................973 242-0800
Fax: 973 242-5205
Louis Galarza, *President*
Eugene Maykish, *Vice Pres*
EMP: 7
SQ FT: 5,000
SALES (est): 777.9K **Privately Held**
SIC: 3471 Plating of metals or formed
products; polishing, metals or formed
products

(G-7237)
**MATTHEW BENDER & COMPANY
INC (DH)**
Also Called: Lexisnexis Matthew Bender
744 Broad St Fl 8 (07102-3803)
PHONE..................................518 487-3000
Fax: 973 820-2007
Andrew Prozes, *CEO*
EMP: 43 **EST:** 1915
SALES (est): 75.6MM
SALES (corp-wide): 9.7B **Privately Held**
SIC: 2731 Books: publishing only
HQ: Relx Inc.
230 Park Ave Ste 700
New York NY 10169
212 309-8100

(G-7238)
MEADOWS KNITTING CORP
Also Called: Safer Textiles
1875 Mccarter Hwy (07104-4211)
PHONE..................................973 482-6400
Albert Safer, *President*
Ricardo Guerrero, *Plant Mgr*
EMP: 45 **EST:** 1977
SQ FT: 130,000
SALES (est): 7.2MM **Privately Held**
SIC: 2257 Weft knit fabric mills

(G-7239)
**MEDITERRANEAN STUCCO
CORP**
111 Main St (07105-3520)
P.O. Box 5562 (07105-0562)
PHONE..................................973 491-0160
Fax: 973 491-0162
Ernesto Andrade, *Owner*
EMP: 12
SQ FT: 10,000
SALES (est): 1.1MM **Privately Held**
SIC: 3299 5032 Stucco; stucco

(G-7240)
MERRILL CORPORATION
60 Park Pl Ste 400 (07102-5513)
PHONE..................................973 643-4403
Mike James, *Manager*
EMP: 87
SALES (corp-wide): 566.6MM **Privately
Held**
SIC: 2759 Commercial printing
PA: Merrill Corporation
1 Merrill Cir
Saint Paul MN 55108
651 646-4501

(G-7241)
**METAL USA PLATES AND
SHAPES**
178-204 Frelinghuyen Ave (07114)
PHONE..................................973 242-1000

EMP: 50
SALES (corp-wide): 9.7B **Publicly Held**
SIC: 3441 Fabricated structural metal
HQ: Metals Usa Plates And Shapes, Inc.
50 Cabot Blvd E
Langhorne PA 19047
267 580-2100

(G-7242)
MIMEOCOM INC
158 Mount Olivet Ave (07114-2114)
PHONE.................................973 286-2901
Jesse Squire, *Engineer*
Richard Barone, *Natl Sales Mgr*
Joseph Hanley, *Accounts Exec*
Steve Scott, *Manager*
Carol Maher, *Manager*
EMP: 15
SALES (corp-wide): 215MM **Privately Held**
SIC: 2759 Commercial printing
PA: Mimeo.Com, Inc.
3 Park Ave Fl 22
New York NY 10016
212 847-3000

(G-7243)
MITZI INTL HANDBAG & ACC LTD
Tucker Distribution
250 Passaic St (07104-3700)
PHONE.................................973 483-5015
Richard Freeman, *Opers-Prdtn-Mfg*
EMP: 125
SALES (corp-wide): 65.6MM **Privately Held**
WEB: www.beteshgroup.com
SIC: 4225 3171 General warehousing & storage; women's handbags & purses
PA: Mitzi International Handbag & Accessories, Ltd.
250 Passaic St
Newark NJ 07104
212 686-4666

(G-7244)
MONTANA ELECTRICAL DECORATING
Perdeco Displays
62 Mcwhorter St (07105-1413)
PHONE.................................973 344-1815
Fax: 212 368-4681
John Montano, *Manager*
EMP: 5
SQ FT: 10,000
SALES (corp-wide): 1.9MM **Privately Held**
SIC: 3993 Displays & cutouts, window & lobby
PA: Montana Electrical Decorating Corp
126 E 131st St 2
New York NY 10037
212 368-4600

(G-7245)
MOTION SYSTEMS LLC (HQ)
250 Passaic St (07104-3700)
PHONE.................................212 686-4666
Mike Betesh,
Elliot Betesh,
Steven Betesh,
Chris Cassidy,
EMP: 17
SALES (est): 4MM **Privately Held**
SIC: 3161 Cases, carrying
PA: The Betesh Group Holding Corp
250 Passaic St
Newark NJ 07104
212 686-4666

(G-7246)
N & J MACHINE PRODUCTS CORP
52 Bruen St (07105-1423)
PHONE.................................973 589-0031
Nino Pereira, *President*
Philippe Moinot, *Electrical Engi*
EMP: 5
SQ FT: 5,000
SALES (est): 580.3K **Privately Held**
SIC: 3599 Machine shop, jobbing & repair

(G-7247)
N C CARPET BINDING & EQUIPMENT
Also Called: NC Carpet
858 Summer Ave (07104-3618)
PHONE.................................973 481-3500
Fax: 973 481-0839
Mark J Caplan, *President*
Mel Maher Jr, *Vice Pres*
◆ **EMP:** 15
SQ FT: 25,000
SALES (est): 3.5MM **Privately Held**
WEB: www.n-ccarpet.com
SIC: 3559 Sewing machines & hat & zipper making machinery

(G-7248)
NATURAL FLAVORS INC
268 Doremus Ave (07105-4879)
PHONE.................................973 589-1230
Fax: 973 589-0016
Herb Stein, *President*
Robert Maxwell, *Opers Staff*
Jason Stein, *Research*
Joanne Hoffman, *Admin Sec*
▲ **EMP:** 25
SQ FT: 4,500
SALES (est): 5.1MM
SALES (corp-wide): 3.1B **Privately Held**
SIC: 2087 5149 Extracts, flavoring; flavourings & fragrances
HQ: Firmenich Sa
Route Des Jeunes 1
Les Acacias GE
227 802-211

(G-7249)
NEW COMMUNITY CORP
Also Called: Fashion Institute of Ncc
200 S Orange Ave (07103-2724)
PHONE.................................973 643-5300
Linda Arrell, *Manager*
EMP: 30
SALES (corp-wide): 19MM **Privately Held**
SIC: 2326 2339 2337 2321 Work uniforms; women's & misses' outerwear; women's & misses' suits & coats; men's & boys' furnishings; men's & boys' suits & coats; broadwoven fabric mills, manmade
PA: New Community Corp
233 W Market St
Newark NJ 07103
973 623-2800

(G-7250)
NEW JERSEY HEADWEAR CORP
Also Called: Unionwear
305 3rd Ave W Ste 5 (07107-2387)
P.O. Box 7009 (07107-0009)
PHONE.................................973 497-0102
Fax: 973 731-1600
Mitchell Cahn, *President*
Mitch Cahn, *President*
Maria Guido, *Purch Mgr*
Gloria Montoya, *Accounting Mgr*
Harris Cahn, *Director*
▲ **EMP:** 105
SQ FT: 50,000
SALES (est): 12.7MM **Privately Held**
WEB: www.unionwear.com
SIC: 2353 2331 2321 Baseball caps; women's & misses' blouses & shirts; men's & boys' furnishings

(G-7251)
NEW JRSY GLVNZNG & TNNNG WKS
139 Haynes Ave (07114-2207)
PHONE.................................973 242-3200
Fax: 973 242-6461
Robert Gregory, *President*
EMP: 53 **EST:** 1902
SQ FT: 2,500
SALES (est): 7MM **Privately Held**
SIC: 3479 Galvanizing of iron, steel or end-formed products

(G-7252)
NEWAGE PAINTING CORPORATION
78 Fillmore St Ste 7 (07105-3682)
PHONE.................................908 547-4734
Rossiny Dacosta, *President*

EMP: 6
SALES (est): 1.4K **Privately Held**
SIC: 2851 1799 1721 Paints, waterproof; epoxy application; bridge painting

(G-7253)
NEWARK ASPHALT CORP
1500 Mccarter Hwy (07104-3997)
PHONE.................................973 482-3503
Joseph Napp, *President*
Micheal Manno, *Vice Pres*
Raymond Lesoine, *Plant Supt*
Daniel Corvelli, *Admin Sec*
EMP: 9 **EST:** 1964
SQ FT: 5,000
SALES (est): 2.3MM
SALES (corp-wide): 17.6MM **Privately Held**
WEB: www.napp-grecco.com
SIC: 2951 2952 Asphalt & asphaltic paving mixtures (not from refineries); asphalt felts & coatings
PA: Napp-Grecco Company
1500 Mccarter Hwy
Newark NJ 07104
973 482-3500

(G-7254)
NEWARK INDUSTRIAL SPRAYING
12 Amsterdam St (07105-3802)
PHONE.................................973 344-6855
Fax: 973 344-1773
Richard D Wantz, *President*
Susan Farmen, *Corp Secy*
EMP: 15
SQ FT: 12,000
SALES: 1.7MM **Privately Held**
WEB: www.rwdi.com
SIC: 3479 Painting of metal products

(G-7255)
NEWARK IRONWORKS INC
Also Called: Newark Steel & Orna Sup Co
41 Frelinghuysen Ave # 43 (07114)
PHONE.................................973 424-9790
Jose Martinez, *President*
EMP: 10
SQ FT: 5,000
SALES (est): 1.8MM **Privately Held**
SIC: 3441 5211 Fabricated structural metal; lumber & other building materials

(G-7256)
NEWARK LINER & WASHER INC
819 Broadway (07104-4300)
PHONE.................................973 482-5400
Fax: 973 482-1127
George Figueroa, *President*
Avelina Figueroa, *President*
Antonio Figueroa, *Vice Pres*
EMP: 12
SQ FT: 1,500
SALES (est): 1.8MM **Privately Held**
SIC: 3089 Bottle caps, molded plastic

(G-7257)
NEWARK MORNING LEDGER CO (PA)
Also Called: Sunday Star Ledger
1 Gateway Ctr Ste 1100 (07102-5323)
PHONE.................................973 392-4141
Fax: 973 392-5845
Donald E Newhouse, *President*
Laura J Evans, *Editor*
Kevin Shea, *Governor*
Brad Young, *Vice Pres*
Joe Laratta, *Foreman/Supr*
EMP: 500
SQ FT: 20,000
SALES (est): 217.5MM **Privately Held**
SIC: 2711 Commercial printing & newspaper publishing combined

(G-7258)
NEWARK STAMP & DIE WORKS INC
35 Verona Ave (07104-4409)
PHONE.................................973 485-7111
Fax: 973 485-6905
Denis Bruce McNab, *President*
Barbara McNab, *Corp Secy*
EMP: 6 **EST:** 1917
SQ FT: 10,000

SALES: 850K **Privately Held**
WEB: www.newarkstampdie.com
SIC: 3953 Embossing seals & hand stamps

(G-7259)
NICHEM CO
750 Frelinghuysen Ave (07114-2221)
PHONE.................................973 399-9810
Peigeng Lu, *President*
Geoff Misek, *Sr Software Eng*
Ryan Bell, *Analyst*
Laura Linn, *Analyst*
▲ **EMP:** 7
SALES (est): 2.6MM **Privately Held**
WEB: www.nichemcompany.com
SIC: 5199 3569 Smokers' supplies; filters

(G-7260)
NORPAK CORPORATION (PA)
70 Blanchard St (07105-4702)
PHONE.................................973 589-4200
Fax: 973 578-8845
Anthony Coraci, *President*
James Coraci, *Vice Pres*
Pedro Oliveira, *Plant Mgr*
Louis Rebol, *Purchasing*
Andrew Crumrine, *Engineer*
▲ **EMP:** 50
SQ FT: 140,000
SALES (est): 17.5MM **Privately Held**
WEB: www.norpak.net
SIC: 2671 Wrapping paper, waterproof or coated; bread wrappers, waxed or laminated: purchased material

(G-7261)
PANASONIC CORP NORTH AMERICA
Panasonic Ind Dev Sales Co Div
2 Riverfront Plz Ste 200 (07102-5490)
PHONE.................................201 348-7000
Samip Patel, *Sales Staff*
Erwin Wu, *Marketing Mgr*
EMP: 80
SALES (corp-wide): 74.9B **Privately Held**
SIC: 5065 3625 Electronic parts & equipment; relays, for electronic use
HQ: Panasonic Corporation Of North America
2 Riverfront Plz Ste 200
Newark NJ 07102
201 348-7000

(G-7262)
PANASONIC CORP NORTH AMERICA
Panasonic Entp Solutions Co
2 Riverfront Plz Ste 200 (07102-5490)
PHONE.................................201 348-7000
Jim Doyle, *President*
EMP: 4
SALES (corp-wide): 74.9B **Privately Held**
SIC: 3663 Television broadcasting & communications equipment
HQ: Panasonic Corporation Of North America
2 Riverfront Plz Ste 200
Newark NJ 07102
201 348-7000

(G-7263)
PARAMOUNT BAKERIES INC (PA)
61 Davenport Ave (07107-2533)
PHONE.................................973 482-6638
Shraga Zabludovsky, *President*
Linda Zabludovsky, *Admin Sec*
▲ **EMP:** 7 **EST:** 1920
SQ FT: 5,000
SALES (est): 10.8MM **Privately Held**
WEB: www.paramountbakeries.com
SIC: 2051 Bakery: wholesale or wholesale/retail combined

(G-7264)
PARAMOUNT BAKERIES INC
412 428 N 5th St (07107)
PHONE.................................973 481-4763
Fax: 973 482-3285
Jose Montalvo, *Manager*
EMP: 30
SQ FT: 25,000

SALES (est): 2.1MM
SALES (corp-wide): 10.8MM **Privately Held**
WEB: www.paramountbakeries.com
SIC: 2051 Bakery: wholesale or wholesale/retail combined
PA: Paramount Bakeries Inc.
61 Davenport Ave
Newark NJ 07107
973 482-6638

(G-7265)
PARAMOUNT FIXTURE CORPORATION
Also Called: Paramount Fixture Sales
175 Mount Pleasant Ave (07104-3814)
PHONE..................973 485-1585
Fax: 973 485-3366
Danniel Moore, *President*
Steve Porcelli, *Corp Secy*
Jorge Lopes, *Vice Pres*
EMP: 38
SQ FT: 45,000
SALES (est): 6.2MM **Privately Held**
WEB: www.paramountfixturecorp.com
SIC: 2541 Store fixtures, wood

(G-7266)
PAUL DYEING COMPANY
626 Orange St (07107-1030)
P.O. Box C, Whippany (07981-0402)
PHONE..................973 484-1121
Fax: 973 242-3427
Laurie Braun, *President*
EMP: 15 **EST:** 1934
SQ FT: 7,000
SALES (est): 2MM **Privately Held**
WEB: www.pauldyeing.com
SIC: 2261 Dyeing cotton broadwoven fabrics

(G-7267)
PEERLESS UMBRELLA CO INC (PA)
427 Ferry St (07105-3903)
PHONE..................973 578-4900
Fax: 973 578-2626
Gene Moscowitz, *President*
Bryan McKatten, *Regl Sales Mgr*
Andy Reichert, *Regl Sales Mgr*
Rosalind Leonessa, *Sales Staff*
Megan Schulze, *Manager*
◆ **EMP:** 110 **EST:** 1929
SQ FT: 100,000
SALES (est): 12.1MM **Privately Held**
WEB: www.peerlessumbrella.com
SIC: 3999 5136 Umbrellas, canes & parts; candles; umbrellas, men's & boys'

(G-7268)
PENICK CORPORATION
33 Industrial Park Rd (07114)
PHONE..................856 678-3601
Dr Stuart A Rose, *President*
John Mc Roberts Jr, *Vice Pres*
Robert J Nilsen, *Treasurer*
EMP: 5
SQ FT: 100,000
SALES (est): 550.4K
SALES (corp-wide): 759MM **Privately Held**
WEB: www.penickcorp.com
SIC: 2834 Pharmaceutical preparations
HQ: Siegfried Usa Llc
33 Industrial Park Rd
Pennsville NJ 08070
856 678-3601

(G-7269)
PERSONALITY HANDKERCHIEFS INC
Also Called: Hand Craft Mfg
640 Frelinghuysen Ave (07114-1360)
PHONE..................973 565-0077
Morris Mizrahi, *President*
Joseph I Mizrahi, *Corp Secy*
Irwin Mizrahi, *Exec VP*
Isaac Mizrahi, *Exec VP*
EMP: 30 **EST:** 1969
SQ FT: 65,000
SALES (est): 3.3MM **Privately Held**
SIC: 2389 5137 5136 Handkerchiefs, except paper; men's miscellaneous accessories; women's & children's clothing; men's & boys' clothing

(G-7270)
PHARMACEUTICAL INNOVATIONS
897 Frelinghuysen Ave (07114-2122)
PHONE..................973 242-2900
Fax: 973 242-0578
Gilbert Buchalter, *President*
▲ **EMP:** 25
SQ FT: 45,000
SALES (est): 6.8MM **Privately Held**
WEB: www.pharminnovations.com
SIC: 2834 Pharmaceutical preparations

(G-7271)
PITNEY BOWES INC
158 Mount Olivet Ave (07114-2114)
PHONE..................800 521-0080
Robert Divincenzo, *Principal*
EMP: 150
SALES (corp-wide): 3.5B **Publicly Held**
SIC: 3579 7359 Postage meters; business machine & electronic equipment rental services
PA: Pitney Bowes Inc.
3001 Summer St Ste 3
Stamford CT 06905
203 356-5000

(G-7272)
PRAXAIR DISTRIBUTION INC
425 Avenue P (07105-4800)
PHONE..................973 589-7895
Mike Anuszewski, *Branch Mgr*
EMP: 25
SALES (corp-wide): 11.4B **Publicly Held**
SIC: 5085 5169 2813 Welding supplies; compressed gas; industrial gases
HQ: Praxair Distribution, Inc.
10 Riverview Dr
Danbury CT 06810
203 837-2000

(G-7273)
PREMIER RIBBON COMPANY
223 Raymond Blvd (07105-4733)
PHONE..................973 589-2600
Matthew Elias, *President*
Robert Levine, *Vice Pres*
EMP: 9
SQ FT: 108,000
SALES (est): 621.3K
SALES (corp-wide): 14.5MM **Privately Held**
WEB: www.allstatepaperbox.com
SIC: 2396 Ribbons & bows, cut & sewed
PA: Allstate Paper Box Co Inc
223 Raymond Blvd
Newark NJ 07105
973 589-2600

(G-7274)
PRINCETON KEYNES GROUP INC
470 Mulberry St (07114-2738)
PHONE..................609 208-1777
Douglas Stewart, *Branch Mgr*
EMP: 10
SALES (corp-wide): 1.6MM **Privately Held**
WEB: www.princetonkeynes.com
SIC: 2891 Adhesives & sealants
PA: The Princeton Keynes Group Inc
116 Village Blvd Ste 200
Princeton NJ 08540
609 951-2239

(G-7275)
PRINT POST
274 Chestnut St (07105)
PHONE..................973 732-0950
William Lion, *Principal*
EMP: 4
SALES (est): 542.1K **Privately Held**
SIC: 2752 Commercial printing, offset

(G-7276)
PRINTERS SERVICE FLORIDA INC (PA)
26 Blanchard St (07105-4784)
PHONE..................973 589-7800
Richard Liroff, *Ch of Bd*
David Schwartz, *President*
Brian Blackburn, *Prdtn Mgr*
Carla Zandick, *Purchasing*
Daryll Engle, *Sales Staff*

▼ **EMP:** 2
SQ FT: 10,000
SALES (est): 3.4MM **Privately Held**
SIC: 5199 3555 Art goods; printing trades machinery

(G-7277)
PRISCO DIGITAL LTD LBLTY CO (PA)
26 Blanchard St (07105-4702)
PHONE..................973 589-7800
Eric Gutwillig, *Vice Pres*
EMP: 13
SALES (est): 6MM **Privately Held**
SIC: 2752 Commercial printing, lithographic; commercial printing, offset

(G-7278)
PROFESSIONAL LAUNDRY SOLUTIONS
443 Orange St (07107-2901)
PHONE..................973 392-0837
Francisco Mercado-Ebanks, *CEO*
EMP: 4
SALES (est): 187.3K **Privately Held**
SIC: 5719 5023 7349 3582 Beddings & linens; linens & towels; building & office cleaning services; washing machines, laundry: commercial, incl. coin-operated

(G-7279)
PURE H2O TECHNOLOGIES INC
211 Warren St Ste 19 (07103-3571)
PHONE..................973 622-0440
Fax: 973 859-7889
Matthew Rela, *President*
EMP: 10
SQ FT: 30,000
SALES (est): 2MM **Privately Held**
SIC: 3589 Water treatment equipment, industrial

(G-7280)
PYRAMID FOOD SERVICES CORP
93-105 Albert Ave (07105)
PHONE..................973 900-6513
Luis Ferreira, *President*
EMP: 17
SQ FT: 24,000
SALES (est): 586.7K **Privately Held**
SIC: 2099 Food preparations

(G-7281)
Q-PAK CORPORATION
2145 Mccarter Hwy (07104-4407)
PHONE..................973 483-4404
Fax: 973 484-7896
Michael Formica, *President*
Anthony Formica, *Vice Pres*
EMP: 30 **EST:** 1964
SALES (est): 5MM **Privately Held**
WEB: www.qpakcorp.com
SIC: 3085 2842 Plastics bottles; ammonia, household; bleaches, household: dry or liquid

(G-7282)
R G SMITH TOOL & MFG CO
245 South St (07114-2990)
PHONE..................973 344-1395
Fax: 973 344-1387
Edgar Blaus Jr, *President*
Christopher A Blaus, *Admin Sec*
EMP: 10 **EST:** 1921
SQ FT: 13,500
SALES (est): 1.3MM **Privately Held**
SIC: 3599 3544 Custom machinery; special dies, tools, jigs & fixtures

(G-7283)
R J HOPPE STORE CONSTRUCTION
Also Called: Ge-Ro Desk Company
340 N 5th St (07107-2306)
PHONE..................973 485-5665
Fax: 973 485-9003
Rolf J Hoppe, *President*
Rolf B Hoppe Jr, *Vice Pres*
EMP: 8
SQ FT: 12,500
SALES (est): 968K **Privately Held**
SIC: 2541 2521 2431 Display fixtures, wood; desks, office: wood; millwork

(G-7284)
RANDALL MFG CO INC
200 Sylvan Ave (07104-3691)
PHONE..................973 482-8603
Cary S Tinfow, *President*
Deborah Tinfow, *Vice Pres*
Laurie A Holey, *Treasurer*
Charlotte S Tinfow, *Admin Sec*
▲ **EMP:** 36 **EST:** 1955
SQ FT: 33,000
SALES (est): 7.4MM **Privately Held**
SIC: 3442 2431 Moldings & trim, except automobile: metal; moldings, wood: unfinished & prefinished

(G-7285)
RAZAC PRODUCTS INC
Also Called: So Many Waves
25 Brenner St (07108-1610)
PHONE..................973 622-3700
Darren Dowdy, *President*
Devon Dowdy, *Principal*
Jalil Dowdy, *Principal*
Madeline Dowdy, *Principal*
Menbere Tesfaye, *Administration*
EMP: 5
SALES (est): 751.5K **Privately Held**
SIC: 3999 Hair, dressing of, for the trade; hair nets

(G-7286)
REAL KOSHER LLC
146 Christie St (07105-3916)
PHONE..................973 690-5394
Irving Braun, *President*
EMP: 6
SALES (est): 886.6K **Privately Held**
SIC: 2013 Sausages & other prepared meats

(G-7287)
REDDAWAY MANUFACTURING CO INC
32 Euclid Ave (07105-4599)
PHONE..................973 589-1410
Fax: 973 589-8223
Pamela Barton, *Ch of Bd*
Todd Walker, *President*
Daisey Gonzalez, *Vice Pres*
▲ **EMP:** 15 **EST:** 1890
SQ FT: 60,000
SALES (est): 2.2MM **Privately Held**
SIC: 2241 Manmade fiber narrow woven fabrics
PA: Rossendale Reddaway Company Inc
32 Euclid Ave
Newark NJ 07105
973 690-6097

(G-7288)
REGINA WINE CO
Also Called: Rex Vinegar Co
828 Raymond Blvd (07105-2905)
PHONE..................973 589-6911
B Vincent Carlesimo, *President*
▲ **EMP:** 5 **EST:** 1968
SQ FT: 10,000
SALES (est): 344.8K **Privately Held**
SIC: 2099 Vinegar

(G-7289)
REX WINE VINEGAR COMPANY
Also Called: Roma Vinegar
828 Raymond Blvd Ste 830 (07105-2905)
PHONE..................973 589-6911
B Vincent Carlesimo, *President*
EMP: 8 **EST:** 1948
SQ FT: 10,000
SALES (est): 886.7K **Privately Held**
SIC: 2099 Vinegar

(G-7290)
ROBDEN ENTERPRISES INC
Also Called: Fastsigns
210 Market St (07102-3708)
PHONE..................973 273-1200
Robert S Acquaye, *CEO*
Denise Acquaye, *President*
EMP: 7
SALES (est): 716.7K **Privately Held**
SIC: 3993 Signs & advertising specialties

(G-7291)
ROBERT YOUNG & SONS INC
25 Grafton Ave (07104-4239)
PHONE.....................................973 483-0451
Fax: 973 483-0185
David Young, *President*
Nancy Young, *Admin Sec*
◆ EMP: 4 EST: 1885
SQ FT: 2,500
SALES: 650K **Privately Held**
SIC: 3281 Cut stone & stone products;
granite, cut & shaped; limestone, cut &
shaped; marble, building: cut & shaped

(G-7292)
**ROSSENDALE REDDAWAY
COMPANY (PA)**
32 Euclid Ave (07105-4527)
PHONE.....................................973 690-6097
William T Walker, *CEO*
Pamela Barton, *Chairman*
EMP: 6
SQ FT: 60,000
SALES (est): 2.2MM **Privately Held**
SIC: 6512 3069 Nonresidential building
operators; brake linings, rubber

(G-7293)
ROYAL ALUMINUM CO INC
620 Market St Ste 1 (07105-3693)
PHONE.....................................973 589-8880
Fax: 973 589-3954
John D Inelli, *President*
Pamela Inelli, *Corp Secy*
▲ EMP: 60
SQ FT: 45,000
SALES (est): 7.8MM **Privately Held**
SIC: 3089 1751 3442 Window frames &
sash, plastic; carpentry work; storm doors
or windows, metal

(G-7294)
RUGGIERO SEA FOOD INC (PA)
Also Called: Fisherman's Pride
474 Wilson Ave (07105-4833)
P.O. Box 5369 (07105-0369)
PHONE.....................................973 589-0524
Fax: 973 589-5690
Rocco Ruggiero, *President*
Teresa Gomes, *Sales Staff*
Mario Pereira, *Admin Sec*
◆ EMP: 52
SALES (est): 51.5MM **Privately Held**
WEB: www.ruggieroseafood.com
SIC: 5146 5812 2092 Seafoods; eating
places; fresh or frozen packaged fish

(G-7295)
RUGGIERO SEA FOOD INC
117 Avenue L (07105-3809)
PHONE.....................................973 589-0524
Rocco Ruggiero, *Branch Mgr*
EMP: 8
SALES (est): 945.4K
SALES (corp-wide): 51.5MM **Privately
Held**
SIC: 5146 5812 2092 Seafoods; eating
places; fresh or frozen packaged fish
PA: Ruggiero Sea Food, Inc.
474 Wilson Ave
Newark NJ 07105
973 589-0524

(G-7296)
RUST-OLEUM CORPORATION
480 Frelinghuysen Ave (07114-1428)
PHONE.....................................732 652-2378
EMP: 10
SALES (corp-wide): 5.3B **Publicly Held**
SIC: 2891 Adhesives & sealants
HQ: Rust-Oleum Corporation
11 E Hawthorn Pkwy
Vernon Hills IL 60061
847 367-7700

(G-7297)
S & G TOOL AID CORPORATION
43 E Alpine St (07114-1629)
PHONE.....................................973 824-7730
George Gering, *President*
Steven Gering, *Vice Pres*
Brad Gering, *Plant Mgr*
▲ EMP: 61 EST: 1971
SQ FT: 15,000

SALES (est): 8.5MM
SALES (corp-wide): 37.6MM **Privately
Held**
SIC: 3546 3829 3423 3714 Power-driven
handtools; testing equipment: abrasion,
shearing strength, etc.; hand & edge
tools; motor vehicle parts & accessories
PA: M. Eagles Tool Warehouse, Inc.
178-192 Sherman Ave
Newark NJ 07114
973 824-6951

(G-7298)
S H P C INC
Also Called: Star National
187 Christie St (07105-3915)
PHONE.....................................973 589-5242
Fax: 973 589-2163
Paul Sacks, *President*
Louis D Sacks, *President*
▲ EMP: 24 EST: 1950
SQ FT: 20,000
SALES (est): 3.7MM **Privately Held**
WEB: www.starheelplate.com
SIC: 3469 5072 Metal stampings; hard-
ware

(G-7299)
SAFER HOLDING CORP
Also Called: Safer Textile
1875 Mccarter Hwy (07104-4211)
PHONE.....................................973 485-1458
Fax: 973 481-7773
Albert Safer, *President*
Bill Garrity, *VP Admin*
Ray Dawson, *VP Sales*
▲ EMP: 700
SQ FT: 100,000
SALES (est): 73.6MM **Privately Held**
SIC: 2282 Knitting yarn: twisting, winding
or spooling

(G-7300)
**SAFER TEXTILE PROCESSING
CORP**
1875 Mccarter Hwy (07104-4211)
PHONE.....................................973 482-6400
Fax: 973 482-5694
Albert Safer, *President*
AMI Inbal, *General Mgr*
Niso Barokas, *Vice Pres*
Stephen Hermann, *Vice Pres*
Richard Menken, *Vice Pres*
EMP: 400
SQ FT: 100,000
SALES (est): 171.5K **Privately Held**
SIC: 7389 2396 2295 2261 Textile & ap-
parel services; automotive & apparel trim-
mings; coated fabrics, not rubberized;
finishing plants, cotton

(G-7301)
SAMAX ENTERPRISE INC
29-75 Riverside Ave Ste 2 (07104)
PHONE.....................................973 350-9400
Fax: 973 350-9538
Pessy Fleischman, *President*
Aniko Lebowitz, *Vice Pres*
◆ EMP: 10
SALES (est): 2.1MM **Privately Held**
SIC: 2851 Lacquer: bases, dopes, thinner;
varnishes; paint removers; varnish re-
movers

(G-7302)
SANCON SERVICES INC
Also Called: Sancon Dumpster Rental Svcs
50 E Peddie St (07114-1411)
P.O. Box 466, Kenilworth (07033-0466)
PHONE.....................................973 344-2500
Jose Conde, *President*
EMP: 4
SALES (est): 686.6K **Privately Held**
SIC: 3089 Garbage containers, plastic

(G-7303)
**SCHIFFENHAUS INDUSTRIES
INC (DH)**
2013 Mccarter Hwy (07104-4301)
PHONE.....................................973 484-5000
Steven C Voorhees, *President*
James A Rubright, *Chairman*
Robert B McIntosh, *Exec VP*
Paul W Stecher, *Senior VP*
EMP: 130
SQ FT: 170,000

SALES (est): 26.3MM
SALES (corp-wide): 14.8B **Publicly Held**
SIC: 2653 2679 Boxes, corrugated: made
from purchased materials; display items,
corrugated: made from purchased materials; corrugated paper: made from purchased material
HQ: Westrock - Southern Container, Llc
133 River Rd
Cos Cob CT 06807
631 232-5704

(G-7304)
SCORIES INC
28 Vassar Ave (07112-2310)
PHONE.....................................973 923-1372
Fax: 973 705-9624
William Hall, *President*
Yvonne Hall, *Vice Pres*
EMP: 10
SQ FT: 1,800
SALES (est): 780K **Privately Held**
WEB: www.scories.com
SIC: 2844 7231 Hair preparations, includ-
ing shampoos; face creams or lotions;
beauty shops

(G-7305)
SEABRITE CORP
Also Called: Corte Provisions
574 Ferry St (07105-4402)
PHONE.....................................973 491-0399
Fax: 973 589-7320
Antonio Seabra, *President*
Albano Seabra, *Vice Pres*
EMP: 32
SALES (est): 4.2MM **Privately Held**
SIC: 2011 Meat packing plants

(G-7306)
SEKO WORLDWIDE
Also Called: Seko Logistics
74 Avenue L (07105-3805)
PHONE.....................................973 465-6868
Fax: 973 465-7364
Joe Trigueros, *Supervisor*
Chet Spencer,
◆ EMP: 9
SALES (est): 62.3K **Privately Held**
SIC: 3537 Containers (metal), air cargo

(G-7307)
**SERRATELLI HAT COMPANY
INC**
418 Central Ave (07107-3023)
P.O. Box 7069 (07107-0069)
PHONE.....................................973 623-4133
Dean Serratelli, *President*
Peter Serratelli, *Vice Pres*
EMP: 5
SQ FT: 18,000
SALES: 3MM **Privately Held**
SIC: 2353 Hats & caps

(G-7308)
**SHABAZZ FRUIT COLA
COMPANY LLC**
24 Wyndmoor Ave (07112-1217)
PHONE.....................................973 230-4641
Frankie Shabazz, *Principal*
EMP: 8
SALES (est): 360.7K **Privately Held**
SIC: 2086 Soft drinks: packaged in cans,
bottles, etc.

(G-7309)
**SHAMROCK TECHNOLOGIES
INC (PA)**
Foot Of Pacific St (07114)
PHONE.....................................973 242-2999
Fax: 973 242-8074
William B Neuberg, *Ch of Bd*
Al Pape, *President*
Joon S Choo, *Vice Pres*
Manshi Sui, *Vice Pres*
Cameron Brown, *Purchasing*
▲ EMP: 190
SQ FT: 150,000
SALES: 70MM **Privately Held**
WEB: www.shamrocktechnologies.com
SIC: 2899 Chemical preparations

(G-7310)
SHEET METAL PRODUCTS INC
794 N 6th St (07107-2798)
PHONE.....................................973 482-0450
Fax: 973 482-0180
William F Kovacs, *President*
James A Kovacs, *Corp Secy*
▲ EMP: 51
SQ FT: 27,000
SALES (est): 12.9MM **Privately Held**
SIC: 3443 3444 Plate work for the metal-
working trade; sheet metalwork

(G-7311)
SHERIS COOKERY INC
33 Delancey St (07105-1508)
PHONE.....................................973 589-2060
Fax: 973 589-3260
Murray Forman, *President*
EMP: 15
SQ FT: 10,000
SALES (est): 2MM **Privately Held**
SIC: 2099 Salads, fresh or refrigerated;
cole slaw, in bulk

(G-7312)
SHEROY PRINTING INC
Also Called: Sir Speedy
40 Commerce St (07102-4003)
PHONE.....................................973 242-4040
Fax: 973 242-8344
Roy Winters, *President*
Sherry Winters, *Admin Sec*
EMP: 15
SALES (est): 2.2MM **Privately Held**
SIC: 2752 2791 2789 Commercial print-
ing, lithographic; typesetting; bookbinding
& related work

(G-7313)
SILVER EDMAR
Also Called: G R P Signs
186 Van Buren St (07105-2638)
PHONE.....................................973 817-7483
Edmar Silver, *Owner*
EMP: 5
SALES (est): 152.3K **Privately Held**
SIC: 7319 2759 Bus card advertising; pro-
motional printing

(G-7314)
SINAI MANUFACTURING CORP
Also Called: Jade Apparel Group
133 Kossuth St (07105-3485)
PHONE.....................................973 522-1003
Florence Lee, *President*
Ajay Watts, *Controller*
EMP: 99
SALES (est): 3.2MM **Privately Held**
SIC: 2329 Field jackets, military

(G-7315)
SK & P INDUSTRIES INC (PA)
Also Called: Metrolab Division
73 Norfolk St (07103-3229)
PHONE.....................................973 482-1864
Lynda Davidson, *President*
Edmund Davidson, *Vice Pres*
EMP: 8 EST: 1881
SALES (est): 1.2MM **Privately Held**
SIC: 3822 8734 3823 Auto controls regu-
lating residntl & coml environmt & ap-
plncs; testing laboratories; industrial
instrmnts msrmnt display/control process
variable

(G-7316)
SK & P INDUSTRIES INC
Also Called: Metrolab Div
73 Norfolk St (07103-3229)
PHONE.....................................973 482-1864
Edmond Davidson, *Manager*
EMP: 8
SALES (corp-wide): 1.2MM **Privately
Held**
SIC: 3545 8734 7699 Machine tool ac-
cessories; testing laboratories; profes-
sional instrument repair services
PA: Sk & P Industries Inc
73 Norfolk St
Newark NJ 07103
973 482-1864

(G-7317)
SKIP GAMBERT & ASSOCIATES INC
Also Called: S G A Custom Shirtmakers
436 Ferry St Ste 2 (07105-3929)
PHONE..................................973 344-3373
Fax: 973 344-3581
David G Gambert Jr, *President*
Claire Corcoran, *Human Res Dir*
Carla Pinheiro, *Director*
Patrice C Gambert, *Admin Sec*
EMP: 150
SQ FT: 28,000
SALES (est): 49.1MM **Privately Held**
SIC: 5136 2321 Shirts, men's & boys'; men's & boys' dress shirts

(G-7318)
SOCAFE LLC
41-43 Malvern St (07105)
PHONE..................................973 589-4104
Fax: 973 589-4429
Joseph Fernandes III, *CEO*
EMP: 10 EST: 2011
SALES (est): 1MM **Privately Held**
SIC: 2095 0179 Roasted coffee; coffee farm

(G-7319)
SOLBRIGHT GROUP INC (PA)
1 Gateway Ctr Ste 26 (07102-5308)
PHONE..................................973 339-3855
Fax: 732 465-9600
Terrence Defranco, *Ch of Bd*
Cem Alptekin, *CIO*
Michael Davies, *Officer*
EMP: 15
SALES: 2.3MM **Publicly Held**
WEB: www.arkados.com
SIC: 7372 4813 Prepackaged software;

(G-7320)
SOLMOR MANUFACTURING CO INC
164 Emmet St Ste 2 (07114-4710)
PHONE..................................973 824-7203
Robert Ulmer, *President*
EMP: 4 EST: 1946
SQ FT: 4,500
SALES: 500K **Privately Held**
SIC: 3915 Jewelers' findings & materials

(G-7321)
SOWA CORP
223 Murray St (07114-2646)
PHONE..................................973 297-0008
Fax: 973 297-1210
Chris Garstka, *President*
EMP: 4
SALES (est): 540.2K **Privately Held**
SIC: 3469 Household cooking & kitchen utensils, metal

(G-7322)
SPARTECH LLC
297 Ferry St (07105-3443)
PHONE..................................973 344-2700
Julie A McAlindon, *Manager*
EMP: 8
SALES (corp-wide): 1.4B **Privately Held**
SIC: 2821 Plastics materials & resins
PA: Spartech Llc
11650 Lkeside Crossing Ct
Saint Louis MO 63105
314 569-7400

(G-7323)
SPECIALNEEDSWARE INC
Also Called: Oneder
60 Park Pl Ste 504 (07102-5513)
PHONE..................................646 278-9959
Jonathan Izak, *CEO*
EMP: 14 EST: 2014
SQ FT: 2,200
SALES (est): 1.1MM **Privately Held**
SIC: 7372 Educational computer software

(G-7324)
SPECTRUM FOILS INC
29 Riverside Ave Bldg 1 (07104-4237)
PHONE..................................973 481-0808
Carl Sowa, *President*
William Paczkowski, *Corp Secy*
William Huddleston, *Vice Pres*
Paul McCready, *Vice Pres*

EMP: 6
SQ FT: 11,000
SALES: 1.5MM **Privately Held**
SIC: 3497 Metal foil & leaf

(G-7325)
SPECTRUM PAINT APPLICATOR
425 Ferry St Fl 2 (07105-3903)
PHONE..................................973 732-9180
Arthur Edelson, *President*
Vicki Edelson, *Corp Secy*
▲ EMP: 40 EST: 1948
SQ FT: 25,000
SALES (est): 5.2MM **Privately Held**
WEB: www.spectrumbrush.com
SIC: 3991 Paint brushes; paint rollers

(G-7326)
SPRING EUREKA CO INC
9 Manufacturers Pl (07105-4405)
P.O. Box 5067 (07105-0067)
PHONE..................................973 589-4960
Jeffrey Suckow, *President*
Dorothy Cherry, *Shareholder*
Douglas Suckow, *Shareholder*
EMP: 20 EST: 1908
SQ FT: 13,000
SALES (est): 2.8MM **Privately Held**
SIC: 3493 3495 Coiled flat springs; flat springs, sheet or strip stock; wire springs

(G-7327)
STANDARD EMBOSSING PLATE MFG
129 Pulaski St (07105-2410)
PHONE..................................973 344-6670
Fax: 973 344-6730
Christian Fleissner IV, *President*
Richard Fleissner, *Vice Pres*
Susan Fleissner, *Admin Sec*
EMP: 5 EST: 1888
SQ FT: 15,000
SALES (est): 390K **Privately Held**
WEB: www.immigration-usa.com
SIC: 2796 Embossing plates for printing

(G-7328)
STAR EMBROIDERY CORP
305 3rd Ave W Ste 7 (07107-1242)
PHONE..................................973 481-4300
Uluwehi Lovell-Gannet, *President*
▲ EMP: 22
SALES (est): 1.5MM **Privately Held**
WEB: www.starembroidery.com
SIC: 2395 Embroidery & art needlework; embroidery products, except schiffli machine

(G-7329)
STATE TOOL GEAR CO INC
211 Camden St (07103-2404)
PHONE..................................973 642-6181
Fax: 973 642-0649
Michael Insabella, *President*
Ross Insabella, *Vice Pres*
Camille Tedesco, *Treasurer*
EMP: 15 EST: 1962
SQ FT: 7,500
SALES (est): 2.4MM **Privately Held**
SIC: 3462 5085 3566 Gears, forged steel; gears; speed changers, drives & gears; reduction gears & gear units for turbines, except automotive

(G-7330)
STIRRUP METAL PRODUCTS CORP
215 Emmet St (07114-2732)
PHONE..................................973 824-7086
Fax: 973 824-7088
Todd Stirrup, *President*
George Stirrup, *Vice Pres*
▲ EMP: 18 EST: 1871
SQ FT: 20,000
SALES (est): 4.6MM **Privately Held**
WEB: www.stirrupmetal.com
SIC: 3469 3444 3471 3443 Stamping metal for the trade; sheet metalwork; plating & polishing; fabricated plate work (boiler shop); fabricated structural metal

(G-7331)
STR8LINE PUBLISHING COMPANY
511 Frelinghuysen Ave (07114-1425)
P.O. Box 4240 (07112-0240)
PHONE..................................919 717-6740
Sonja Wilkerson, *CEO*
EMP: 4
SALES (est): 99.5K **Privately Held**
SIC: 2711 Newspapers

(G-7332)
SUBURBAN MONUMENT & VAULT
203 Sherman Ave (07114-1611)
PHONE..................................973 242-7007
Clyde Brooks, *President*
EMP: 7 EST: 1968
SQ FT: 2,500
SALES: 500K **Privately Held**
SIC: 3272 Monuments, concrete

(G-7333)
SUCCESS SEWING INC
50 Columbia St Ste 2 (07102-4831)
PHONE..................................973 622-0328
Fax: 973 504-8575
Yalcin Mizrak, *President*
EMP: 5
SQ FT: 7,000
SALES: 300K **Privately Held**
WEB: www.mizrak.com
SIC: 2337 2335 Skirts, separate: women's, misses' & juniors'; ensemble dresses: women's, misses' & juniors'

(G-7334)
SUPERIOR PRINTING INK CO INC
252 Wright St (07114-2631)
PHONE..................................973 242-5868
Jeff Simmons, *President*
EMP: 8
SALES (corp-wide): 117.1MM **Privately Held**
SIC: 2893 2899 Printing ink; chemical preparations
PA: Superior Printing Ink Co Inc
100 North St
Teterboro NJ 07608
201 478-5600

(G-7335)
SUPREME INK CORP
65 Mcwhorter St (07105-1412)
PHONE..................................973 344-2922
Fax: 973 344-3888
John T Ahmed, *President*
EMP: 10
SQ FT: 8,000
SALES (est): 1.6MM **Privately Held**
WEB: www.supremeink.com
SIC: 2893 2752 Lithographic ink; commercial printing, lithographic

(G-7336)
SYMBIOMIX THERAPEUTICS LLC (DH)
105 Lock St Ste 409 (07103-3576)
PHONE..................................609 722-7250
David L Stern, *CEO*
Robert Jacks, *President*
David Palling, *VP Mfg*
Joseph Amprey, *Officer*
Tom Beck, *Officer*
EMP: 13
SQ FT: 1,083
SALES (est): 1.8MM
SALES (corp-wide): 1.5B **Privately Held**
SIC: 2834 Druggists' preparations (pharmaceuticals)
HQ: Lupin Inc.
111 S Calvert St Fl 21
Baltimore MD 21202
410 576-2000

(G-7337)
TBB INC (PA)
Also Called: Teixeira's Bakery
115-129 Kossuth St (07105)
PHONE..................................973 589-8875
Manuel Teixeira, *President*
Maria Teixeira, *Vice Pres*
▲ EMP: 5

SALES (est): 1.8MM **Privately Held**
SIC: 2051 Breads, rolls & buns

(G-7338)
TEG NEW JERSEY INC
Also Called: Journal of Commerce Inc
2 Penn Plz E 12 (07105-2257)
PHONE..................................973 776-8660
Fax: 973 848-7165
Bill Ralph, *President*
William Ralph, *President*
Willy Morgan, *Publisher*
Rhiannon James, *COO*
Doug Weber, *Senior VP*
EMP: 681
SQ FT: 28,000
SALES (est): 39.7MM
SALES (corp-wide): 440.4MM **Privately Held**
SIC: 7375 2711 2721 Data base information retrieval; newspapers: publishing only, not printed on site; magazines: publishing only, not printed on site
PA: Economist Newspaper Limited(The)
The Adelphi
London WC2N
207 830-7000

(G-7339)
TENAX FINISHING PRODUCTS CO
390 Adams St (07114-2899)
PHONE..................................973 589-9000
Fax: 973 589-7067
James A O'Neill, *President*
John F O'Neill, *Vice Pres*
Muriel Miller, *Manager*
EMP: 18 EST: 1948
SQ FT: 25,000
SALES (est): 2.9MM **Privately Held**
WEB: www.tenaxfp.com
SIC: 2851 Paints & allied products

(G-7340)
THIBAUT & WALKER CO INC
49 Rutherford St (07105-4820)
PHONE..................................973 589-3331
George Parker, *President*
Steven Holland, *Vice Pres*
EMP: 4 EST: 1880
SQ FT: 5,000
SALES (est): 970K **Privately Held**
SIC: 5162 2821 Resins; plastics materials & resins

(G-7341)
THIRTY-THREE QUEEN REALTY INC (PA)
Also Called: Flexon Industries
1 Flexon Plz (07114-1421)
PHONE..................................973 824-5527
Joseph Folkman, *Ch of Bd*
David Rauch, *President*
Rickie Folkman, *Corp Secy*
Henry Rosenbaum, *Controller*
Chris Cardone, *Marketing Staff*
▲ EMP: 11
SQ FT: 2,000,000
SALES (est): 28.6MM **Privately Held**
WEB: www.flexonhose.com
SIC: 5085 3423 3052 Hose, belting & packing; hand & edge tools; rubber & plastics hose & beltings

(G-7342)
THOMSON REUTERS (MARKETS) LLC
Also Called: Thomson Financial
2 Gateway Ctr Fl 11 (07102-5006)
PHONE..................................973 286-7200
EMP: 5
SALES (corp-wide): 4.5B **Publicly Held**
SIC: 2731 Books-Publishing/Printing
HQ: Thomson Reuters (Markets) Llc
195 Broadway Fl 4
New York NY 10036
646 822-2000

(G-7343)
THOMSON REUTERS CORPORATION
Also Called: Research Institute of America
2 Gateway Ctr Fl 11 (07102-5006)
PHONE..................................212 337-4281
Robyn Staatorman, *Manager*

EMP: 500
SALES (corp-wide): 3.2B **Publicly Held**
SIC: 2731 Books: publishing only
HQ: Thomson Reuters Corporation
3 Times Sq
New York NY 10036
646 223-4000

(G-7344)
TITAN AMERICA LLC
178 Marsh St (07114-3237)
PHONE...................................973 690-5896
Ted Marousas, *Branch Mgr*
EMP: 5
SALES (corp-wide): 275.7MM **Privately Held**
SIC: 1499 Gypsum & calcite mining
HQ: Titan America Llc
1151 Azalea Garden Rd
Norfolk VA 23502
757 858-6500

(G-7345)
TKO VISUAL COMMUNICATIONS
108-136 Martin Luther (07104)
PHONE...................................610 770-7700
Fax: 610 770-7709
Thomas K Ortalano, *President*
Michael Briere, *Vice Pres*
EMP: 11
SQ FT: 8,000
SALES (est): 1.3MM **Privately Held**
WEB: www.tkovisual.com
SIC: 7384 2759 Photofinishing laboratory;
commercial printing; screen printing

(G-7346)
TOVLI INC
49 Hunter St (07114-1609)
P.O. Box 50320, Brooklyn NY (11205-0320)
PHONE...................................718 417-6677
Abraham Leser, *President*
Chana J Ostreicher, *Vice Pres*
▲ **EMP:** 50
SQ FT: 32,000
SALES (est): 4.8MM **Privately Held**
SIC: 2038 Frozen specialties

(G-7347)
TRADEMARK PLASTICS CORPORATION
494 Broad St Rm 202 (07102-3217)
PHONE...................................908 925-5900
Melvyn Schaffer, *CEO*
Robert Schaffer, *President*
Ann Schaffer, *Corp Secy*
EMP: 30
SALES (est): 24.2MM **Privately Held**
WEB: www.trademarkplasticscorp.com
SIC: 2821 Plastics materials & resins

(G-7348)
TRUCKTECH PARTS & SERVICES
13 Avenue C (07114-2601)
PHONE...................................973 799-0500
Fax: 973 799-0020
Anderson Vieira, *Principal*
EMP: 4 **EST:** 2008
SALES (est): 822.1K **Privately Held**
SIC: 3537 7538 7539 7532 Industrial
trucks & tractors; truck engine repair, except industrial; general truck repair; wheel
alignment, automotive; trailer repair; body
shop, trucks

(G-7349)
U J RAMELSON CO INC
165 Thomas St (07114-2709)
PHONE...................................973 589-5422
Fax: 973 589-5429
John Ramella, *President*
Daniel Ramella, *Vice Pres*
EMP: 8 **EST:** 1937
SQ FT: 2,400
SALES (est): 500K **Privately Held**
WEB: www.ramelson.com
SIC: 3952 Artists' materials, except pencils
& leads

(G-7350)
U S SCREENING CORP
780 Frelinghuysen Ave (07114-2221)
PHONE...................................973 242-1110
Fax: 973 242-5755

Rino Baranes, *Ch of Bd*
Robert Deprospo, *Exec VP*
Carlos Matos, *Controller*
Carmen Peak, *Manager*
Jean Simpson, *Supervisor*
◆ **EMP:** 250
SQ FT: 140,000
SALES (est): 28.9MM **Privately Held**
SIC: 2759 2396 Screen printing; automotive & apparel trimmings

(G-7351)
UNION CONTAINER CORP
439 Frelinghuysen Ave (07114-1426)
PHONE...................................973 242-3600
A George Onufer, *President*
Robert Blakley, *Corp Secy*
EMP: 33 **EST:** 1940
SQ FT: 40,000
SALES (est): 3.4MM **Privately Held**
SIC: 2655 2631 Spools, fiber: made from
purchased material; tubes, fiber or paper:
made from purchased material; paper-
board mills

(G-7352)
UNIPHY HEALTH HOLDINGS LLC
211 Warren St (07103-3568)
PHONE...................................866 874-8616
Adam Turinas, *Principal*
Chad Stoerp, *CFO*
Edward Guy, *Officer*
Stewart Hochron, *Officer*
EMP: 20
SALES: 2.5MM **Privately Held**
SIC: 7372 Application computer software

(G-7353)
UNITED EQP FABRICATORS LLC
175 Orange St (07103-4009)
PHONE...................................973 242-2737
Fax: 973 242-2738
Robert Ayars, *President*
Charles Corbett, *Purchasing*
EMP: 6
SQ FT: 120,000
SALES (est): 570K **Privately Held**
SIC: 3089 3449 1799 5084 Plastic processing; miscellaneous metalwork; fiberglass work; pumps & pumping equipment;
fiberglass fabrics

(G-7354)
UNITED LABEL CORP
65 Chambers St (07105-2893)
P.O. Box 5311 (07105-0311)
PHONE...................................973 589-6500
Fax: 973 589-4465
John O'Conner, *President*
EMP: 10 **EST:** 1965
SQ FT: 20,000
SALES: 1.5MM **Privately Held**
WEB: www.unitedlabelcorp.com
SIC: 2679 3479 2759 2672 Labels,
paper: made from purchased material;
name plates: engraved, etched, etc.;
commercial printing; coated & laminated
paper

(G-7355)
US WIRE & CABLE CORPORATION (PA)
Also Called: Flexon Inds Div US Wire Cable
366 Frelinghuysen Ave (07114-1424)
PHONE...................................973 824-5530
Fax: 973 824-1208
David Rauch, *President*
Joseph Folkman, *Vice Pres*
Alex Folkman, *Admin Sec*
◆ **EMP:** 482
SALES (est): 141.9MM **Privately Held**
WEB: www.uswireandcable.com
SIC: 3052 3315 Garden hose, plastic;
cable, steel: insulated or armored

(G-7356)
VEHICLE SAFETY MFG LLC (HQ)
Also Called: V S M
408 Central Ave (07107-3021)
PHONE...................................973 643-3000
Fax: 973 643-2167
James Pineau, *CEO*
Fernando Columbro, *Senior VP*
Fernando Zambrano, *Safety Mgr*
Edward Errico, *Mfg Staff*

Daviel Rivera, *CFO*
▲ **EMP:** 43
SQ FT: 50,000
SALES: 12MM
SALES (corp-wide): 24MM **Privately Held**
WEB: www.vehiclesafetymfg.com
SIC: 3647 Vehicular lighting equipment
PA: Aftermarket Controls Corp.
2519 Dana Dr
Laurinburg NC 28352
910 291-2500

(G-7357)
VIEIRAS BAKERY INC
Also Called: Vieiras Bakery
34-48 Ave K (07105)
PHONE...................................973 589-7719
Carlos Vieira, *President*
◆ **EMP:** 60
SALES (est): 8MM **Privately Held**
WEB: www.vieirasbakery.com
SIC: 2051 Bread, all types (white, wheat,
rye, etc): fresh or frozen

(G-7358)
WELDED PRODUCTS CO INC
330 Raymond Blvd Ste 336 (07105-4698)
PHONE...................................973 589-0180
Francis Zurica, *President*
EMP: 25 **EST:** 1930
SALES (est): 4MM **Privately Held**
SIC: 3312 7692 3443 3444 Sheet or
strip, steel, hot-rolled; welding repair;
tanks, standard or custom fabricated:
metal plate; sheet metalwork

(G-7359)
WESTROCK RKT COMPANY
2013 Mccarter Hwy (07104-4301)
PHONE...................................973 484-5000
Steven Donohoe, *Branch Mgr*
EMP: 110
SALES (corp-wide): 14.8B **Publicly Held**
SIC: 5113 2653 Boxes & containers; corrugated & solid fiber boxes
HQ: Westrock Rkt Company
1000 Abernathy Rd Ste 125
Atlanta GA 30328
770 448-2193

(G-7360)
WICKR INC
211 Warren St Ste 34 (07103-3574)
PHONE...................................516 637-2882
EMP: 4
SALES (est): 241.6K **Privately Held**
SIC: 3699 Mfg Electrical Equipment/Supplies

(G-7361)
XANTHUS INC
105 Lock St Ste 215 (07103-3565)
PHONE...................................973 643-0920
EMP: 5 **EST:** 1984
SALES: 500K **Privately Held**
SIC: 7372 Prepackaged Software Services

(G-7362)
ZAGO MANUFACTURING COMPANY
21 E Runyon St (07114-1510)
PHONE...................................973 643-6700
Fax: 973 643-4433
Jackie Luciano-Brito, *General Mgr*
Gail Friedberg, *Vice Pres*
Thomas Nicolicchia, *Project Mgr*
Jessica Reyes, *Purchasing*
Alejandra Sanchez, *Sales Staff*
EMP: 25
SQ FT: 8,000
SALES (est): 5.1MM **Privately Held**
WEB: www.flexibletrim.com
SIC: 3451 3679 3648 3452 Screw machine products; hermetic seals for electronic equipment; lighting equipment;
bolts, nuts, rivets & washers

(G-7363)
ZVONKO STULIC & SON INC
21 Main St (07105-3509)
PHONE...................................973 589-3773
Fax: 973 589-3860
Zvonko Stulic, *President*
EMP: 5
SQ FT: 5,000

SALES: 350K **Privately Held**
WEB: www.zssfabrication.com
SIC: 3556 Cutting, chopping, grinding, mixing & similar machinery

---
Newfield
Gloucester County

(G-7364)
CS INDUSTRIAL SERVICES LLC
303 Catawba Ave (08344-9515)
PHONE...................................609 381-4380
Carman Simonetti, *Mng Member*
EMP: 6
SALES (est): 899.9K **Privately Held**
SIC: 3441 Fabricated structural metal

(G-7365)
ERNEST R MILES CONSTRUCTION CO
Also Called: Miles Concrete Co
1445 Catawba Ave (08344-5332)
P.O. Box 39 (08344-0039)
PHONE...................................856 697-2311
Fax: 856 697-3611
Ernest Miles Jr, *President*
Ernest R Miles, *President*
Eleanor Miles, *Corp Secy*
EMP: 12
SQ FT: 8,000
SALES (est): 909.7K **Privately Held**
SIC: 1741 5032 3273 Foundation & retaining wall construction; stone masonry;
concrete mixtures; ready-mixed concrete

(G-7366)
FENCEMAX
1624 Harding Hwy (08344-5221)
PHONE...................................609 646-2265
Mark Amechi, *Branch Mgr*
EMP: 5 **Privately Held**
SIC: 3089 Fences, gates & accessories:
plastic
PA: Fencemax
664 Mantua Pike
Woodbury NJ 08096

(G-7367)
MILES CONCRETE COMPANY INC
1445 Catawba Ave (08344-5332)
P.O. Box 39 (08344-0039)
PHONE...................................856 697-2311
Ernest Miles Jr, *President*
Lisa Santoro, *Administration*
EMP: 17
SALES (est): 1.5MM **Privately Held**
SIC: 1771 3273 Concrete work; ready-
mixed concrete

(G-7368)
NEW ERA ENTERPRISES INC
208 N West Blvd (08344-9556)
P.O. Box 747, Vineland (08362-0747)
PHONE...................................856 794-2005
Fax: 856 697-8727
Frank L Bosco, *President*
Lynda Bosco, *Treasurer*
EMP: 6
SQ FT: 1,700
SALES (est): 866.2K **Privately Held**
WEB: www.newera-spectro.com
SIC: 3826 Analytical instruments

(G-7369)
NOOPYS RESEARCH INC
108 Harding Hwy (08344-8409)
PHONE...................................856 358-6001
Fax: 856 358-0206
Lester Morgan, *President*
Pearl E Morgan, *Corp Secy*
EMP: 4
SQ FT: 9,500
SALES (est): 530.3K **Privately Held**
SIC: 2851 Paint removers; varnish removers

(G-7370)
PAUL BROS INC
113 Church St (08344-9595)
P.O. Box 10 (08344-0010)
PHONE...................................856 697-5895
Fax: 856 697-5897

Thomas D Paul, *President*
Nancy M Paul, *Treasurer*
William R Paul, *Admin Sec*
EMP: 25
SQ FT: 7,500
SALES: 2MM **Privately Held**
SIC: 3272 Concrete products

(G-7371)
RF VII INC
104 Church St (08344-9583)
PHONE..............................856 875-2121
Fax: 856 875-2119
Steve Barber, *CEO*
Kelly Barber, *President*
▲ **EMP:** 14
SALES (est): 1.8MM **Privately Held**
WEB: www.rfvii.com
SIC: 7699 3825 Professional instrument
repair services; precision instrument re-
pair; mechanical instrument repair; radio
frequency measuring equipment

(G-7372)
SOLID CAST STONE
470 Grubb Rd (08344-4813)
P.O. Box 343 (08344-0343)
PHONE..............................856 694-5245
Tiffany Brown, *President*
EMP: 4
SALES (est): 400K **Privately Held**
SIC: 3272 Concrete products

Newfoundland
Passaic County

(G-7373)
**ATLANTIC RUBBER
ENTERPRISES**
Also Called: Hercules World Industries
35 Union Valley Rd (07435-1649)
PHONE..............................973 697-5900
Fax: 973 208-0709
Phillip Corbae, *President*
Josephine M Corbae, *Corp Secy*
▲ **EMP:** 8
SQ FT: 8,000
SALES (est): 1.5MM **Privately Held**
SIC: 5085 3053 3052 Hose, belting &
packing; gaskets, packing & sealing de-
vices; rubber & plastics hose & beltings

(G-7374)
ESP ASSOCIATES INC
Also Called: Electronic Specialty Products
2713 State Rt 23 Ste 8a (07435-1415)
P.O. Box 349 (07435-0349)
PHONE..............................973 208-9045
Fax: 973 208-1533
James R Johnson, *President*
EMP: 16
SALES (est): 2.5MM **Privately Held**
WEB: www.espnj.com
SIC: 3672 Printed circuit boards

(G-7375)
PHOENIX PRECISION CO
2963 State Rt 23 (07435-1419)
PHONE..............................973 208-8877
Fax: 973 208-8883
Edward Wolos III, *President*
Edward Wolos Jr, *Vice Pres*
EMP: 12
SQ FT: 10,000
SALES (est): 1.6MM **Privately Held**
SIC: 3599 Machine shop, jobbing & repair

(G-7376)
RGI INC
27 Union Valley Rd (07435-1649)
PHONE..............................973 697-2624
Fax: 973 697-0550
Barry Maloney, *President*
Raymond Christian, *Vice Pres*
EMP: 15 EST: 1977
SQ FT: 11,000
SALES (est): 2.8MM **Privately Held**
WEB: www.rgi.net
SIC: 3494 Valves & pipe fittings

Newport
Cumberland County

(G-7377)
**MAYS LANDING SAND &
GRAVEL CO (DH)**
1101 Railroad Ave (08345-2199)
PHONE..............................856 447-4294
Dan Harrington, *President*
EMP: 1 EST: 1948
SQ FT: 2,000
SALES (est): 3.9MM
SALES (corp-wide): 20.3B **Privately Held**
SIC: 1442 Construction sand & gravel

Newton
Sussex County

(G-7378)
A B SCANTLEBURY CO INC
108 Phil Hardin Rd (07860-5223)
PHONE..............................973 770-3000
Arthur B Scantlebury, *President*
Lora Grant, *Vice Pres*
John Spinelli, *Finance Mgr*
EMP: 12
SQ FT: 5,000
SALES: 1MM **Privately Held**
WEB: www.absco.com
SIC: 3599 3444 Machine shop, jobbing &
repair; sheet metal specialties, not
stamped

(G-7379)
**ALESSANDRA MISCELLANEOUS
METAL**
75 Mill St Ste B (07860-1453)
PHONE..............................973 786-6805
Scott Alessandra, *President*
EMP: 17
SQ FT: 3,000
SALES: 2.5MM **Privately Held**
SIC: 3446 Stairs, staircases, stair treads:
prefabricated metal

(G-7380)
**AUTOMATIC MACHINE
PRODUCT**
56 Paterson Ave (07860-2349)
PHONE..............................973 383-9929
Don Schanstra, *Owner*
EMP: 4
SQ FT: 2,000
SALES (est): 170K **Privately Held**
SIC: 3451 Screw machine products

(G-7381)
BACKROADS INC
160 County Road 521 (07860-6453)
PHONE..............................973 948-4176
Fax: 973 948-0823
Brian Rathjen, *President*
Shila Kamil, *Vice Pres*
EMP: 7
SALES (est): 300K **Privately Held**
WEB: www.backroadsusa.com
SIC: 2721 Magazines: publishing only, not
printed on site

(G-7382)
BROOK MEADOW INVENTIONS
1 Brooks Plz (07860-2626)
PHONE..............................973 300-0419
Zbigniew Swiderski, *Manager*
EMP: 30
SALES (est): 1.7MM **Privately Held**
SIC: 5162 3089 Plastics materials & basic
shapes; plastics products

(G-7383)
BROTHERS SHEET METAL (PA)
15 Grandview Dr (07860-6409)
PHONE..............................973 579-1788
Tracey Dube, *President*
Chris Dube, *Vice Pres*
Kevin Dube, *Vice Pres*
EMP: 19 EST: 1998
SALES (est): 3.4MM **Privately Held**
SIC: 3444 Sheet metalwork

(G-7384)
CARSTENS PUBLICATIONS INC
Also Called: Flying Models
108 Phil Hardin Rd (07860-5223)
P.O. Box 700 (07860-0070)
PHONE..............................973 383-3355
Fax: 973 383-4064
Harold H Carstens, *President*
Frank Fanelli, *Editor*
Henry Carstens, *Treasurer*
Phyllis Carstens, *Admin Sec*
EMP: 24
SQ FT: 11,000
SALES (est): 2.5MM **Privately Held**
WEB: www.carstens-publications.com
SIC: 2721 2731 Magazines: publishing
only, not printed on site; books: publishing
only

(G-7385)
**CUSTOM WOOD FURNITURE
INC**
37 E Clinton St Ste 1 (07860-1870)
P.O. Box 3034 (07860-3034)
PHONE..............................973 579-4880
Fax: 973 579-0070
John K Kweselait, *President*
EMP: 19
SQ FT: 10,000
SALES (est): 2.4MM **Privately Held**
WEB: www.customwoodfurnitureinc.com
SIC: 2431 Millwork

(G-7386)
EM SIGNS
80 Merriam Ave (07860-2420)
PHONE..............................973 300-9703
Eric M Martino, *Principal*
EMP: 5
SALES (est): 409.5K **Privately Held**
SIC: 3993 Signs, not made in custom sign
painting shops

(G-7387)
**ENGINEERED SILICONE PDTS
LLC**
Also Called: ESP
75 Mill St Ste 2 (07860-1453)
PHONE..............................973 300-5120
Louis Haberman, *Mng Member*
Lynn Snyder,
EMP: 5
SALES: 1.7MM **Privately Held**
WEB: www.wearesp.com
SIC: 2869 Silicones

(G-7388)
**FOUR STAR REPRODUCTIONS
INC**
Also Called: Four Star Color
52 Paterson Ave Ste 2 (07860-2363)
PHONE..............................862 268-8200
Fax: 973 227-1578
Charles Cioppa, *President*
EMP: 27 EST: 1963
SQ FT: 28,000
SALES (est): 6.3MM **Privately Held**
WEB: www.fourstarcolor.com
SIC: 2752 2631 Commercial printing, off-
set; milk carton board

(G-7389)
**FREDON DEVELOPMENT INDS
LLC**
393 State Route 94 S (07860-5154)
PHONE..............................973 383-7576
Tom Krisanda, *Opers Staff*
Gerald Wildrick, *Mng Member*
EMP: 17
SQ FT: 11,000
SALES (est): 3MM **Privately Held**
SIC: 3089 Injection molding of plastics

(G-7390)
G A D INC
Also Called: Pro Gad Sales
914 Cedar Ridge Rd (07860-4400)
PHONE..............................973 383-3499
Patricia Barone, *President*
Vincent D Barone, *Corp Secy*
EMP: 4
SALES (est): 402.2K **Privately Held**
WEB: www.progadsales.com
SIC: 3949 Sporting & athletic goods

(G-7391)
GOETZ & RUSCHMANN INC
1 Brooks Plz (07860-2626)
P.O. Box 960, Bernardsville (07924-0960)
PHONE..............................973 383-9270
Fax: 973 761-1039
Harold A Sutton, *President*
Bertha Ruschmann, *Corp Secy*
EMP: 35 EST: 1933
SQ FT: 9,000
SALES (est): 1.5MM **Privately Held**
SIC: 2675 2673 2679 3354 Paper die-
cutting; bags: plastic, laminated & coated;
foil board: made from purchased material;
aluminum extruded products

(G-7392)
IMAGE POINT
69 Water St (07860-1414)
PHONE..............................908 684-1768
Fax: 908 684-8955
John Fernicola, *President*
EMP: 5
SALES (est): 401K **Privately Held**
SIC: 2396 Fabric printing & stamping

(G-7393)
J & S TOOL
56 Paterson Ave Ste 4 (07860-2350)
PHONE..............................973 383-5059
Roman Sleszar, *Owner*
EMP: 5 EST: 1941
SQ FT: 15,000
SALES (est): 900K **Privately Held**
WEB: www.jstool.com
SIC: 3541 5084 Machine tools, metal cut-
ting type; industrial machinery & equip-
ment

(G-7394)
KATIES CLOSETS
3 Lower Hill Rd (07860-5310)
PHONE..............................973 300-4007
Mike Higgins, *Owner*
EMP: 6
SALES (est): 583.6K **Privately Held**
SIC: 2673 Wardrobe bags (closet acces-
sories): from purchased materials

(G-7395)
MAGAZINEXPERTS LLC
103 Spring St (07860-2145)
PHONE..............................973 383-0888
Donald Berry, *Mng Member*
EMP: 8
SALES: 792K **Privately Held**
SIC: 2741 Miscellaneous publishing

(G-7396)
MAXWELL & MOLLYS CLOSET
218 Spring St (07860-2012)
PHONE..............................973 300-0101
Bonnie Bitondo, *Principal*
EMP: 8
SALES (est): 793.1K **Privately Held**
SIC: 3999 Pet supplies

(G-7397)
MRI INTERNATIONAL
Also Called: Photographic Tech Intl
44 Clinton St (07860-1404)
P.O. Box 406 (07860-0406)
PHONE..............................973 383-3645
Fax: 973 383-6672
William Foltyn, *President*
Cynthia Dizeso, *Vice Pres*
▲ **EMP:** 7
SQ FT: 25,000
SALES (est): 973K **Privately Held**
SIC: 5043 2899 Photographic processing
equipment; chemical preparations

(G-7398)
NATIONAL LECITHIM INC (PA)
93 Spring St Ste 303 (07860-2079)
PHONE..............................973 940-8920
Patricia Bruno, *President*
Glenn Geisler, *Vice Pres*
Jean Geisler, *Treasurer*
▲ **EMP:** 2 EST: 1977
SALES: 1.3MM **Privately Held**
SIC: 2099 Emulsifiers, food

GEOGRAPHIC

(G-7399)
NEW JERSEY HERALD (HQ)
2 Spring St (07860-2077)
PHONE..................................973 383-1500
Fax: 973 383-8477
Thomas Oakley, *President*
Oakley Ralph M, *Director*
EMP: 130
SQ FT: 22,000
SALES (est): 54.1MM
SALES (corp-wide): 224.3MM **Privately Held**
WEB: www.njherald.com
SIC: 2711 Commercial printing & newspaper publishing combined
PA: Quincy Media, Inc..
   130 S 5th St
   Quincy IL 62301
   217 223-5100

(G-7400)
PIN CANCER CAMPAIGN
34 County Road 519 (07860-6231)
PHONE..................................973 600-4170
EMP: 4 EST: 2011
SALES: 168.1K **Privately Held**
SIC: 3452 Pins

(G-7401)
RIOTSOUND INC
Also Called: Millenium Worldwide
17 Hampton House Rd # 15 (07860-3404)
P.O. Box 3112 (07860-3112)
PHONE..................................917 273-5814
Alexander Shtaerman, *President*
Jennifer Shtaerman, *Vice Pres*
EMP: 4
SQ FT: 3,000
SALES: 1MM **Privately Held**
SIC: 5735 3651 5064 Records; audio electronic systems; high fidelity equipment

(G-7402)
SCHNEIDER & MARQUARD INC
Also Called: S & M Retaining Rings
112 Phil Hardin Rd (07860-5223)
P.O. Box 39 (07860-0039)
PHONE..................................973 383-2200
Fax: 973 383-6529
Michael O'Shea, *President*
Cheryl Foster, *Admin Sec*
EMP: 20
SQ FT: 23,000
SALES (est): 4.2MM **Privately Held**
WEB: www.schneidermarquard.com
SIC: 3544 Dies & die holders for metal cutting, forming, die casting; special dies & tools

(G-7403)
SCHRADER & COMPANY INC
188 Halsey Rd (07860-7058)
PHONE..................................973 579-1160
Fax: 973 579-1806
David Lake, *President*
Margaret Lake, *Treasurer*
EMP: 12
SALES (est): 1.6MM **Privately Held**
SIC: 3444 Sheet metalwork

(G-7404)
SKYLANDS PRESS
Also Called: Jmd Printing
57 Trinity St (07860-1824)
P.O. Box 809 (07860-0809)
PHONE..................................973 383-5006
John Daly, *Owner*
EMP: 4
SALES (est): 269.7K **Privately Held**
SIC: 2759 Commercial printing

(G-7405)
STUART MILLS INC (PA)
25 Stillwater Rd (07860-5037)
PHONE..................................973 579-5717
Fax: 973 579-2507
Stuart Mills, *President*
EMP: 6 EST: 1993
SQ FT: 3,500
SALES: 500K **Privately Held**
SIC: 3599 Machine shop, jobbing & repair

(G-7406)
STUART MILLS INC
25 Stillwater Rd (07860-5037)
PHONE..................................973 579-5717
Stuart Mills, *Owner*
EMP: 4
SALES (corp-wide): 500K **Privately Held**
SIC: 3599 Machine shop, jobbing & repair
PA: Stuart Mills Inc
   25 Stillwater Rd
   Newton NJ 07860
   973 579-5717

(G-7407)
T & M NEWTON CORPORATION
Also Called: Newton Tool
119 Fredon Springdale Rd (07860-5218)
PHONE..................................973 383-1232
Fax: 973 383-3819
Ralph Meola Jr, *President*
EMP: 7
SQ FT: 11,000
SALES (est): 1.1MM **Privately Held**
SIC: 3089 Injection molding of plastics

(G-7408)
TECHNICAL OIL PRODUCTS CO INC (PA)
93 Spring St Ste 303 (07860-2079)
PHONE..................................973 940-8920
Alan S Geisler, *President*
Alan Geisler, *Owner*
Patricia Bruno, *Vice Pres*
Jean Geisler, *Admin Sec*
EMP: 9 EST: 1961
SALES (est): 828.5K **Privately Held**
SIC: 2079 2035 2869 Edible fats & oils; pickles, sauces & salad dressings; sorbitol

(G-7409)
TERCO CONSTRUCTION LLC
Also Called: Excavating
71 Newton Sparta Rd (07860-2745)
PHONE..................................973 551-7759
Brian P Hendricks, *Principal*
EMP: 11
SALES (est): 3.3MM **Privately Held**
WEB: www.tercoconstructionllc.com
SIC: 3531 1794 1541 1542 Construction machinery; excavation & grading, building construction; industrial buildings, new construction; commercial & office building, new construction; highway & street construction; irrigation system construction

(G-7410)
THORLABS INC (PA)
56 Sparta Ave (07860-2402)
PHONE..................................973 579-7227
Fax: 973 300-3600
Alex Cable, *President*
David Beatson, *General Mgr*
Peter Heim, *General Mgr*
Pauline Non, *Project Mgr*
Jack Meharg, *Facilities Mgr*
▲ EMP: 128
SQ FT: 121,277
SALES (est): 211.7MM **Privately Held**
WEB: www.thorlabs.com
SIC: 3826 Analytical optical instruments

(G-7411)
VINE HILL FARM
100 Parsons Rd (07860-6340)
PHONE..................................973 383-0100
Andrew Napolitano, *Owner*
EMP: 4
SALES (est): 234.7K **Privately Held**
SIC: 5099 0115 2099 2511 Firewood; corn; maple syrup; cedar chests

Norma
Salem County

(G-7412)
B & B POULTRY CO INC
Almond Rd (08347)
P.O. Box 307 (08347-0307)
PHONE..................................856 692-8893
Benjamin Fisher, *President*
Dorothy Fisher, *Corp Secy*
Mark Fisher, *Vice Pres*
EMP: 175 EST: 1945
SQ FT: 75,000
SALES (est): 28.8MM **Privately Held**
WEB: www.bandbpoultry.com
SIC: 2015 2011 Poultry, slaughtered & dressed; meat packing plants

North Arlington
Bergen County

(G-7413)
A-ONE MERCHANDISING CORP
170 Schuyler Ave (07031-5424)
PHONE..................................718 773-7500
Yakov Spritzer, *Ch of Bd*
▲ EMP: 13
SQ FT: 60,000
SALES (est): 12MM **Privately Held**
SIC: 5113 3089 Industrial & personal service paper; disposable plates, cups, napkins & eating utensils; holders: paper towel, grocery bag, etc.: plastic

(G-7414)
ALBERT H HOPPER INC
329 Ridge Rd (07031-5304)
PHONE..................................201 991-2266
Fax: 201 991-8887
Kenneth A Roberts, *President*
Doreen Schafer, *Manager*
Bernadeth Logan, *Admin Sec*
EMP: 6
SQ FT: 1,000
SALES: 150K **Privately Held**
WEB: www.ahhopper.com
SIC: 3281 5999 Monuments, cut stone (not finishing or lettering only); tombstones, cut stone (not finishing or lettering only); burial vaults, stone; monuments & tombstones

(G-7415)
ANGO ELECTRONICS CORPORATION
Also Called: Par Metal Products
29 Ewing Ave (07031-5001)
PHONE..................................201 955-0800
John Ango, *President*
▲ EMP: 10
SQ FT: 8,500
SALES (est): 1.9MM **Privately Held**
WEB: www.par-metal.com
SIC: 3679 3444 3354 Electronic circuits; sheet metalwork; aluminum extruded products

(G-7416)
ATLANTIC KENMARK ELECTRIC INC
11 Ewing Ave (07031-5001)
PHONE..................................201 991-2117
Salvatore Gaccione, *President*
Frank Gaccione, *Vice Pres*
Vincent Gaccione, *Treasurer*
▲ EMP: 17 EST: 1945
SQ FT: 5,000
SALES (est): 3.1MM **Privately Held**
SIC: 7694 Electric motor repair

(G-7417)
C & F BURNER CO
39 River Rd (07031-6101)
P.O. Box 7189 (07031-7189)
PHONE..................................201 998-8080
Robert A Dunn, *President*
Elizabeth Dunn, *Owner*
EMP: 34 EST: 1960
SQ FT: 1,000
SALES (est): 1.9MM **Privately Held**
SIC: 3433 Heating equipment, except electric

(G-7418)
CLAYTON BLOCK CO
2 Porete Ave (07031-6722)
PHONE..................................201 955-6292
John Cherchio, *President*
Richard Cherchio, *Treasurer*
EMP: 75
SQ FT: 15,000
SALES (est): 7.2MM
SALES (corp-wide): 44.5MM **Privately Held**
SIC: 3272 3271 Concrete products, precast; concrete block & brick
HQ: Clayton Block Company Llc
   440 Hook Rd
   Bayonne NJ 07002
   201 339-8585

(G-7419)
FIRST INTERNET SYSTEMS
16 Geraldine Rd (07031-5407)
PHONE..................................201 991-1889
Balaji Modhagala, *Owner*
EMP: 13
SALES (est): 505.9K **Privately Held**
SIC: 7372 Prepackaged software

(G-7420)
IDEAL DATA INC
420 River Rd (07031-5163)
PHONE..................................201 998-9440
Fax: 201 998-5590
Linda A Rueda, *President*
EMP: 15
SALES: 2MM **Privately Held**
WEB: www.idealdata.com
SIC: 7374 7331 3571 Data entry service; direct mail advertising services; electronic computers

(G-7421)
MINHURA INC
24 William St (07031-6153)
PHONE..................................862 763-4078
Jose Monteiro, *Owner*
EMP: 5
SALES (est): 285.4K **Privately Held**
SIC: 2064 Candy bars, including chocolate covered bars

(G-7422)
PAR METAL PRODUCTS INC
21 Ewing Ave (07031-5001)
PHONE..................................201 955-0800
John Ngo, *Principal*
EMP: 10
SALES (est): 1.3MM **Privately Held**
SIC: 3469 Electronic enclosures, stamped or pressed metal

(G-7423)
PROACTIVE LTG SOLUTIONS LLC
21 Ewing Ave (07031-5001)
PHONE..................................800 747-1209
Alfred Heyer, *CEO*
▼ EMP: 10
SQ FT: 25,000
SALES (est): 1.1MM **Privately Held**
SIC: 3648 Lighting equipment

(G-7424)
SCOTTS COMPANY LLC
125 Baler Blvd (07031-4415)
PHONE..................................201 246-0180
David Irwin, *Principal*
Kip Edwardson, *Marketing Staff*
EMP: 15
SALES (corp-wide): 2.6B **Publicly Held**
WEB: www.scottscompany.com
SIC: 2873 Fertilizers: natural (organic), except compost
HQ: The Scotts Company Llc
   14111 Scottslawn Rd
   Marysville OH 43040
   937 644-3729

North Bergen
Hudson County

(G-7425)
A R C PLASMET CORP
4131 Bergen Tpke (07047-2509)
PHONE..................................201 867-8533
Fax: 201 867-7023
Ricardo Perez, *President*
Tony Palama, *President*
Genoveva Perez, *Corp Secy*
EMP: 11 EST: 1972
SQ FT: 8,000

SALES: 675K **Privately Held**
WEB: www.arcplasmet.com
SIC: **3089** Injection molding of plastics; plastic processing

(G-7426)
ALCO TRIMMING
8608 Grand Ave Rear (07047-4337)
PHONE..............................201 854-8608
Fax: 201 854-6387
Michael Colon, *Partner*
Momeena Colon, *Partner*
EMP: 5
SQ FT: 7,000
SALES (est): 240K **Privately Held**
SIC: **2396** 5131 Trimming, fabric; trimmings, apparel

(G-7427)
ALL-LACE PROCESSING CORP
1109 Grand Ave Ste 4 (07047-1628)
PHONE..............................201 867-1974
Fax: 201 867-4232
Achille Gaetano, *President*
Frank Gaetano, *Vice Pres*
EMP: 18
SQ FT: 15,000
SALES (est): 2.1MM **Privately Held**
WEB: www.alllace.com
SIC: **2258** Lace & warp knit fabric mills

(G-7428)
ALLIED SPECIALTY GROUP INC (PA)
Also Called: Allied Metal
3223 Dell Ave (07047-2369)
PHONE..............................201 223-4600
Fax: 201 223-1884
Henry H Bilge, *President*
Keyur Patel, *Controller*
EMP: 19
SQ FT: 16,000
SALES (est): 2.2MM **Privately Held**
WEB: www.alliedmetal.com
SIC: **2819** Aluminum compounds

(G-7429)
ALVARO STAIRS LLC
4201 Tonnelle Ave Ste 12 (07047-2431)
PHONE..............................201 864-6754
Fax: 201 864-1521
Enrique Bernar,
EMP: 5
SALES (est): 470.8K **Privately Held**
SIC: **2431** Staircases & stairs, wood

(G-7430)
AMPERITE CO INC
4201 Tonnelle Ave Ste 6 (07047-2431)
PHONE..............................201 864-9503
Frank M Kretkowski, *Vice Pres*
EMP: 35 EST: 1922
SQ FT: 12,000
SALES (est): 4.9MM **Privately Held**
WEB: www.amperite.com
SIC: **3679** 3625 3647 3612 Delay lines; industrial electrical relays & switches; flasher lights, automotive; lamp ballasts; voltage regulating transformers, electric power; lighting equipment; current-carrying wiring devices

(G-7431)
ARAFAT LAFI
7329 Broadway (07047-5738)
PHONE..............................201 854-7300
Lafi Arafat, *Owner*
EMP: 7
SALES: 400K **Privately Held**
SIC: **3999** Artificial flower arrangements

(G-7432)
ARMCO COMPRESSOR PRODUCTS
Also Called: Armco Machine
2042 46th St (07047-2633)
P.O. Box 105 (07047-0105)
PHONE..............................201 866-6766
Fax: 201 866-0360
ARA Zadourian, *President*
Silva Zadourian, *Admin Sec*
▲ EMP: 4
SQ FT: 3,000
SALES (est): 784.8K **Privately Held**
WEB: www.armcocompressor.com
SIC: **3563** Air & gas compressors

(G-7433)
ARMEL ELECTRONICS INC
1601 75th St (07047-4094)
PHONE..............................201 869-4300
Ed Johnsen, *CEO*
EMP: 36
SQ FT: 27,000
SALES (est): 5.9MM **Privately Held**
WEB: www.armelelectronics.com
SIC: **3644** 3643 3678 Terminal boards; connectors & terminals for electrical devices; electronic connectors

(G-7434)
BERGEN MANUFACTURING & SUPPLY
2025 85th St (07047-4714)
PHONE..............................201 854-3461
Ida Petrone, *President*
Michael Dimick, *Vice Pres*
EMP: 25
SQ FT: 15,000
SALES (est): 3.1MM **Privately Held**
SIC: **5047** 3949 2821 Medical equipment & supplies; surgical equipment & supplies; incontinent care products & supplies; sporting & athletic goods; plastics materials & resins

(G-7435)
BERGENLINE GELATO LLC
7903 Bergenline Ave (07047-4943)
PHONE..............................201 861-1100
EMP: 4
SALES (est): 202.9K **Privately Held**
SIC: **2024** Ice cream, bulk

(G-7436)
BT INDUSTRIES INC
Also Called: Bal-Togs
6605-09 Smith Ave (07047)
PHONE..............................201 866-0201
Bruce Kopelman, *President*
▲ EMP: 60
SQ FT: 40,000
SALES (est): 8.6MM **Privately Held**
SIC: **2339** Women's & misses' outerwear; women's & misses' athletic clothing & sportswear; leotards: women's, misses' & juniors'

(G-7437)
C3 CONCEPTS INC
Also Called: Christopher Fischer
1435 51st St Ste 2d (07047-3100)
PHONE..............................212 840-1116
Christopher Fischer, *President*
Charlene Kuo, *Vice Pres*
▲ EMP: 31 EST: 1996
SALES (est): 9.3MM **Privately Held**
WEB: www.c3concepts.com
SIC: **5137** 2231 Women's & children's clothing; broadwoven fabric mills, wool

(G-7438)
CAPITOL BOX CORP (PA)
1300 6th St (07047-1714)
PHONE..............................201 867-6018
Fax: 201 867-4159
Edward B Maleh, *President*
Shirley Maleh, *Vice Pres*
EMP: 23 EST: 1936
SQ FT: 12,700
SALES (est): 2.3MM **Privately Held**
WEB: www.capitolbox.com
SIC: **2652** 5113 Setup paperboard boxes; set-up paperboard boxes

(G-7439)
CHAMPION INK CO INC
2045 88th St (07047-4794)
PHONE..............................201 868-4100
Fax: 201 868-3449
Raymond Czorniewy, *President*
EMP: 5
SQ FT: 9,700
SALES (est): 951.8K **Privately Held**
SIC: **2893** Screen process ink

(G-7440)
CHIHA INC
Also Called: Chiha Sales
5711 Kennedy Blvd (07047-3202)
PHONE..............................201 861-2000
Edward Chiha, *President*

George A Chiha, *Vice Pres*
EMP: 12
SQ FT: 13,263
SALES (est): 1MM **Privately Held**
WEB: www.chiha.com
SIC: **2384** 2253 Dressing gowns, men's & women's: from purchased materials; lounge, bed & leisurewear

(G-7441)
COLLECTION XIIX LTD
7001 Anpesil Dr Ste 2 (07047-4517)
PHONE..............................201 854-7740
Andrew Pizzo, *Branch Mgr*
EMP: 10
SALES (corp-wide): 29.9MM **Privately Held**
WEB: www.collection18.com
SIC: **2339** Women's & misses' accessories
PA: Collection Xiix Ltd.
1370 Broadway Fl 17
New York NY 10018
212 686-8990

(G-7442)
COLONIAL CONCRETE COMPANY
9301 Railroad Ave Ste 1 (07047-1419)
PHONE..............................201 869-0055
Fax: 201 869-2504
Frank Rizzo, *Owner*
EMP: 15
SALES (corp-wide): 1.3B **Publicly Held**
WEB: www.colonialconcrete.com
SIC: **3273** Ready-mixed concrete
HQ: Colonial Concrete Company
1196 Mccarter Hwy
Newark NJ 07104
973 482-1920

(G-7443)
COLONNA BROTHERS INC (PA)
4102 Bergen Tpke (07047-2510)
P.O. Box 808 (07047-0808)
PHONE..............................800 626-8384
Fax: 201 864-0144
Peter Colonna, *President*
Diane Maniscalco, *Corp Secy*
Mark Colonna, *Executive*
▲ EMP: 100 EST: 1918
SQ FT: 50,000
SALES (est): 35.5MM **Privately Held**
SIC: **2022** 2099 5143 5149 Natural cheese; seasonings & spices; bread crumbs, not made in bakeries; cheese; groceries & related products; salt, edible

(G-7444)
D3 LED LLC
1609 54th St (07047-3016)
PHONE..............................201 583-9486
EMP: 5
SALES (corp-wide): 14.5MM **Privately Held**
SIC: **3993** Mfg Signs/Advertising Specialties
PA: D3 Led, Llc
11370 Sunrise Park Dr
Rancho Cordova CA 95742
916 669-7408

(G-7445)
DATA MEDICAL INC
2075 91st St (07047-4795)
P.O. Box 10124, Fairfield (07004-6124)
PHONE..............................800 790-9978
Chuck Ward, *CEO*
Harry Marmora, *President*
EMP: 12
SALES (est): 900K **Privately Held**
SIC: **3841** Surgical & medical instruments

(G-7446)
DERMARITE INDUSTRIES LLC
7777 W Side Ave (07047-6436)
PHONE..............................973 247-3491
Fax: 973 569-9001
Norman Braunstein, *President*
Mark Friedman, *Vice Pres*
Rick Vesely, *Vice Pres*
Hetal Sopariwala, *Materials Dir*
Maximiliano Sanchez, *QA Dir*
◆ EMP: 115
SQ FT: 14,000

SALES (est): 36.2MM **Privately Held**
WEB: www.dermarite.com
SIC: **2834** 2841 Dermatologicals; ointments; soap: granulated, liquid, cake, flaked or chip

(G-7447)
DRAPERY & MORE INC
2321 Kennedy Blvd Ste 1 (07047-2039)
PHONE..............................201 271-9661
Ally Espana, *Owner*
EMP: 5
SALES (est): 420.3K **Privately Held**
SIC: **2391** Curtains, window: made from purchased materials

(G-7448)
DRU WHITACRE MEDIA SVCS LTD (PA)
Also Called: Drapekings
3200 Liberty Ave Ste 2c (07047-2394)
PHONE..............................201 770-9950
Drape Kings, *CEO*
Kevin Goodrich, *President*
Linda Brisco, *Project Mgr*
Margie Gilbert, *Admin Sec*
◆ EMP: 85
SQ FT: 20,000
SALES (est): 19.2MM **Privately Held**
SIC: **2391** Draperies, plastic & textile: from purchased materials

(G-7449)
EDISON LITHOG & PRTG CORP (PA)
3725 Tonnelle Ave (07047-2421)
PHONE..............................201 902-9191
Fax: 201 902-0475
George Gross, *President*
Anthony Lagattuta, *General Mgr*
Mel Schwartz, *General Mgr*
Kevin Neureuter, *COO*
Joseph Ostreicher, *Vice Pres*
▲ EMP: 90 EST: 1958
SQ FT: 80,000
SALES: 36.2MM **Privately Held**
WEB: www.edisonlitho.com
SIC: **2752** Commercial printing, offset

(G-7450)
ENSIGN OVERSEAS (USA) LTD
Also Called: Ensign Vidal USA
8800 Boulevard East 4a (07047-6054)
PHONE..............................201 662-7150
Antoine Akar, *President*
Catherine Akar, *Vice Pres*
▲ EMP: 4
SQ FT: 2,000
SALES (est): 355.7K **Privately Held**
SIC: **2064** Candy & other confectionery products

(G-7451)
EUROPEAN PRETZEL ONE LLC
Also Called: Heidi's European Pretzel
1619 54th St (07047-3016)
PHONE..............................201 867-6117
Fax: 201 867-8085
Robert Johnson, *President*
EMP: 13
SALES (est): 760K **Privately Held**
WEB: www.heidispretzel.com
SIC: **2052** Pretzels

(G-7452)
FIVE STAR ALUMINUM PRODUCTS
Also Called: Five Star Building Products
2012 86th St (07047-4719)
PHONE..............................201 869-4181
Fax: 201 869-4187
Daniel Polito, *President*
EMP: 12
SQ FT: 18,300
SALES (est): 3.6MM **Privately Held**
SIC: **5031** 3442 Metal doors, sash & trim; window frames, all materials; metal doors, sash & trim

(G-7453)
GENERAL ELECTRIC COMPANY
6001 Tonnelle Ave (07047-3307)
PHONE..............................201 866-2161
Fax: 201 553-5229
Raymond Shellhimer, *Manager*

EMP: 200
SALES (corp-wide): 122B **Publicly Held**
SIC: 7694 4911 Electric motor repair; electric services
PA: General Electric Company
41 Farnsworth St
Boston MA 02210
617 443-3000

(G-7454)
GP CHEMICALS INC
7225 Bergenline Ave 3b (07047-5497)
PHONE...................................201 869-2200
Michael Politopoulos, *President*
Alexandra Stringli, *Controller*
▲ EMP: 4
SQ FT: 1,000
SALES: 2.9MM **Privately Held**
WEB: www.gpchemicals.com
SIC: 2869 Industrial organic chemicals

(G-7455)
GRAND DISPLAYS INC
3725 Tonnelle Ave (07047-2421)
PHONE...................................201 994-1500
EMP: 12 **Privately Held**
SIC: 2675 Die-cut paper & board
PA: Grand Displays, Inc.
1700 Suckle Hwy
Pennsauken NJ 08110

(G-7456)
HICKORY INDUSTRIES INC
4900 W Side Ave (07047-6411)
PHONE...................................201 223-4382
Fax: 201 223-0950
Steven Maroti, *President*
Aniko Heller, *Corp Secy*
Jeffrey Petrik, *CFO*
EMP: 25 EST: 1953
SQ FT: 43,000
SALES (est): 6.1MM **Privately Held**
WEB: www.hickorybbq.com
SIC: 3589 Cooking equipment, commercial

(G-7457)
HOBOKEN REPORTER
4400 Dell Ave (07047-2637)
PHONE...................................201 553-0130
Roberto Lopez, *Manager*
EMP: 4
SALES (est): 193.2K **Privately Held**
SIC: 2711 Newspapers, publishing & printing

(G-7458)
I PRINT NB
9252 Kennedy Blvd (07047-9300)
PHONE...................................201 662-1133
Guillermo Melendrez, *Administration*
EMP: 4
SALES (est): 122.8K **Privately Held**
SIC: 2752 Commercial printing, lithographic

(G-7459)
K H MACHINE WORKS
4322 Grand Ave (07047-2622)
PHONE...................................201 867-2338
Fax: 201 867-8783
Bob Koehler, *Partner*
Grace Koehler, *Partner*
Shereelynn Koehler, *Partner*
EMP: 6 EST: 1918
SQ FT: 3,700
SALES: 450K **Privately Held**
WEB: www.pccom.net
SIC: 3469 7692 Machine parts, stamped or pressed metal; welding repair

(G-7460)
KATE SPADE & COMPANY
Also Called: Liz Claiborne
5901 W Side Ave (07047-6451)
PHONE...................................201 295-7569
EMP: 13
SALES (corp-wide): 1.2B **Publicly Held**
SIC: 2335 Mfg Women's/Misses' Dresses
PA: Kate Spade & Company
2 Park Ave Rm 8r
New York NY 10016
212 354-4900

(G-7461)
KATHY GIBSON DESIGNS INC (PA)
Also Called: Ansonia Bridal Veils
1435 51st St Ste 2 (07047-3100)
PHONE...................................201 420-0088
Fax: 201 656-4732
Ruth Wiener, *President*
Marie Sanchez, *Marketing Staff*
▲ EMP: 17 EST: 1946
SQ FT: 4,000
SALES (est): 1.9MM **Privately Held**
WEB: www.ansoniabridal.com
SIC: 2353 Millinery

(G-7462)
LAWRENCE M GICHAN INCORPORATED
900 Dell Ave (07047-1555)
PHONE...................................201 330-3222
Larry Gichan, *President*
EMP: 12
SALES (est): 1MM **Privately Held**
SIC: 2448 Pallets, wood

(G-7463)
MARKS ICE CREAM
Also Called: Mark's Hmmade Ice Cream Dlghts
8205 Bergenline Ave (07047-5051)
PHONE...................................201 861-5099
Mark Russo, *Owner*
EMP: 4
SALES (est): 260.8K **Privately Held**
SIC: 2024 Ice cream & frozen desserts

(G-7464)
MARLENE TRIMMINGS LLC
Also Called: Marlene Lace
407 77th St (07047-5505)
PHONE...................................201 926-3108
Stephen Hepperle, *President*
EMP: 6
SALES: 68K **Privately Held**
SIC: 2241 8712 Trimmings, textile; house designer

(G-7465)
MARTY ANDERSON & ASSOC INC
4200 Grand Ave (07047-2518)
P.O. Box 1595, Hoboken (07030-1595)
PHONE...................................201 798-0507
Marty Anderson, *President*
EMP: 7
SQ FT: 1,100
SALES: 330K **Privately Held**
SIC: 1751 2431 Finish & trim carpentry; staircases, stairs & railings

(G-7466)
MAYABEQUE PRODUCTS INC
7424 Bergenline Ave Ste 1 (07047-5496)
PHONE...................................201 869-0531
Antonio Idavoy, *President*
Andre Idavoy, *President*
Rita Idavoy, *Admin Sec*
EMP: 7
SQ FT: 1,700
SALES (est): 720K **Privately Held**
SIC: 2013 5421 Sausages from purchased meat; meat markets, including freezer provisioners

(G-7467)
METRO WEB CORP
5901 Tonnelle Ave (07047-3221)
PHONE...................................201 553-0700
Fax: 201 553-7840
Tristan Vogel, *President*
William E Vogel, *Chairman*
Bob Irving, *Vice Pres*
Richard Moore, *CFO*
Chris Hanson, *Treasurer*
EMP: 50
SQ FT: 70,000
SALES (est): 9.1MM **Privately Held**
WEB: www.metrowebnj.com
SIC: 2752 Commercial printing, offset

(G-7468)
MIRIC INDUSTRIES INC
Also Called: Miric Revolving Swinging Doors
1516 Union Tpke (07047-2597)
PHONE...................................201 864-0233

Michael Petricko, *President*
EMP: 15
SQ FT: 7,000
SALES (est): 3.4MM **Privately Held**
WEB: www.miricdoors.com
SIC: 7699 3442 3231 Door & window repair; metal doors, sash & trim; products of purchased glass

(G-7469)
ML METTLER CORP
Also Called: Mettler Mechanical
8905 Bergenwood Ave (07047-5309)
P.O. Box 161 (07047-0161)
PHONE...................................201 869-0170
Fax: 201 758-9395
Lawrence Mettler, *President*
EMP: 4
SALES (est): 395.4K **Privately Held**
SIC: 3585 5075 Refrigeration & heating equipment; air conditioning & ventilation equipment & supplies

(G-7470)
NAPA CONCEPTS LTD LIABILITY CO
36-3 Bergen Ridge Rd (07047-7235)
PHONE...................................201 673-2381
Fersun Senolsun, *Mng Member*
▲ EMP: 4
SALES (est): 206.5K **Privately Held**
SIC: 3714 Differentials & parts, motor vehicle

(G-7471)
NORCO MANUFACTURING INC
2025 85th St (07047-4714)
PHONE...................................201 854-3461
Steven Petrone, *President*
EMP: 10 EST: 1980
SQ FT: 2,500
SALES (est): 760K **Privately Held**
SIC: 3069 Hard rubber & molded rubber products

(G-7472)
NUCHAS TSQ LLC
5905 Kennedy Blvd (07047-3210)
PHONE...................................212 913-9682
Ariel Barbouth, *President*
Michael Quinones, *Opers Mgr*
Hannah Choy, *Social Dir*
EMP: 18
SQ FT: 160
SALES (est): 3.1MM **Privately Held**
SIC: 2051 5812 Pastries, e.g. danish: except frozen; eating places; fast food restaurants & stands

(G-7473)
PARTY CITY OF NORTH BERGEN
3111 Kennedy Blvd (07047-2378)
PHONE...................................201 865-0040
Fax: 201 865-4813
Phillip David, *President*
Michael Brent, *Vice Pres*
Lloyd Breslin, *Vice Pres*
EMP: 17
SQ FT: 7,300
SALES (est): 1MM **Privately Held**
SIC: 5947 7299 2759 Party favors; costume rental; invitation & stationery printing & engraving

(G-7474)
PDM PACKAGING INC
4102 Bergen Tpke (07047-2510)
P.O. Box 808 (07047-0808)
PHONE...................................201 864-1115
Peter Colonna, *President*
Mark Colonna, *Vice Pres*
Diane Maniscalco, *Treasurer*
▲ EMP: 10
SQ FT: 50,000
SALES (est): 1.7MM **Privately Held**
WEB: www.pdmfoam.com
SIC: 2099 5149 5499 Spices, including grinding; spices & seasonings; spices & herbs

(G-7475)
PFIZER INC
8810 Durham Ave (07047-4434)
PHONE...................................201 294-8060
Corwin Nunez, *Principal*

EMP: 146
SALES (corp-wide): 52.5B **Publicly Held**
SIC: 2834 Pharmaceutical preparations
PA: Pfizer Inc.
235 E 42nd St
New York NY 10017
212 733-2323

(G-7476)
PRESTIGE BREAD JERSEY CY INC
Also Called: Hudson Bread
5601-5711 Tonnelle Ave (07047-3399)
PHONE...................................201 422-7900
Mariusz Kolodziej, *President*
◆ EMP: 60
SQ FT: 26,000
SALES (est): 12MM **Privately Held**
WEB: www.hudsonbread.com
SIC: 2051 Bread, all types (white, wheat, rye, etc): fresh or frozen

(G-7477)
QUES APRV A R KNITWEAR INC
2201 74th St (07047-6407)
PHONE...................................201 869-1333
Fax: 201 869-5855
Dionisio Garcia, *Principal*
EMP: 7
SALES (est): 698.6K **Privately Held**
SIC: 2258 Fabric finishing, warp knit

(G-7478)
RELIABLE WELDING & MCH WORK
Also Called: Reliable Rbr Plastic McHy Div
2008 Union Tpke (07047-2499)
PHONE...................................201 865-1073
Helga Liccardo, *President*
Joseph Liccardo III, *Vice Pres*
Thomas S Liccardo, *Vice Pres*
Zsolt Racz, *Engineer*
▲ EMP: 20 EST: 1935
SQ FT: 125,000
SALES (est): 5.3MM **Privately Held**
SIC: 3559 3599 Rubber working machinery, including tires; machine shop, jobbing & repair

(G-7479)
REMCO PRESS INC
4201 Tonnelle Ave Ste 4 (07047-2431)
PHONE...................................201 751-5703
Fax: 201 751-5705
Anthony Skalicky Jr, *President*
EMP: 4
SQ FT: 5,000
SALES: 900K **Privately Held**
WEB: www.remcopress.com
SIC: 2752 7336 2759 Business form & card printing, lithographic; commercial art & graphic design; invitation & stationery printing & engraving

(G-7480)
REUTHER CONTRACTING CO INC
Also Called: Reuther Material
5303 Tonnelle Ave 5311 (07047-3036)
P.O. Box 106 (07047-0106)
PHONE...................................201 863-3550
Andrew Reuther, *President*
Margaret Diehl, *Vice Pres*
Robert Diehl, *Vice Pres*
Lois Marrone, *Vice Pres*
EMP: 20
SQ FT: 4,500
SALES (est): 3.1MM **Privately Held**
SIC: 3271 Blocks, concrete or cinder: standard

(G-7481)
REUTHER MATERIAL CO INC
5303 Tonnelle Ave (07047-3090)
P.O. Box 106 (07047-0106)
PHONE...................................201 863-3550
Fax: 201 863-0950
Andrew Reuther, *President*
Nick Marrone, *Vice Pres*
Douglas Reuther, *VP Opers*
Bill Bringas, *Sales Mgr*
Carmine Covello, *Manager*
EMP: 20 EST: 1927
SQ FT: 4,500

▲ = Import ▼=Export
◆ =Import/Export

SALES (est): 4.9MM **Privately Held**
SIC: 3273 5032 Ready-mixed concrete; masons' materials

(G-7482)
SAHAR USA INC
2029 83rd St (07047-4710)
PHONE....................201 868-4900
Farhat Khan, *President*
▼ **EMP:** 4
SQ FT: 600
SALES (est): 1.3MM **Privately Held**
SIC: 2844 Perfumes & colognes

(G-7483)
SANT-TEC ELECTRIC INC (PA)
2017 41st St (07047-2412)
PHONE....................201 865-4100
Olga Pena, *Principal*
Juan Gonzalez, *Manager*
EMP: 20
SALES (est): 5.6MM **Privately Held**
SIC: 3699 Electrical equipment & supplies

(G-7484)
SATEX FABRICS LTD
704 76th St (07047-4962)
PHONE....................212 221-5555
Albert Abergel, *President*
▼ **EMP:** 6 **EST:** 1992
SALES (est): 940.9K **Privately Held**
WEB: www.satexfabrics.com
SIC: 5084 2221 Textile & leather machinery; textile mills, broadwoven: silk & man-made, also glass

(G-7485)
SCHRIPPS EUROPEAN BREAD INC
5410 Tonnelle Ave (07047-3038)
PHONE....................201 867-0909
Dan Marcus, *President*
Sharone Marcus, *Opers Staff*
Dragana Milic, *Sales Mgr*
Tali Marcus, *Admin Sec*
EMP: 35
SQ FT: 17,000
SALES (est): 3MM **Privately Held**
SIC: 2051 Bread, all types (white, wheat, rye, etc): fresh or frozen

(G-7486)
SEQUINS OF DISTINCTION INC
Also Called: Sequin City
1302 13th St (07047-1859)
PHONE....................201 348-8111
Fax: 201 330-9050
EMP: 6 **EST:** 1971
SALES (est): 420K **Privately Held**
SIC: 2395 Mfg Embroidery Sequins On Fabric

(G-7487)
STEEL MOUNTAIN FABRICATORS LLC
2712 Secaucus Rd (07047-1549)
PHONE....................201 741-3019
Michael Dell'aquila, *Branch Mgr*
EMP: 4
SALES (corp-wide): 2.5MM **Privately Held**
SIC: 3599 Machine & other job shop work
PA: Steel Mountain Fabricators Llc
1312 W Elizabeth Ave
Linden NJ 07036
908 862-2800

(G-7488)
SUUCHI INC
2321 Kennedy Blvd Ste S4 (07047-2039)
PHONE....................201 284-0789
Suchitra Ramesh, *CEO*
Miguel Astacio, *Production*
Al Gaviria, *Sales Staff*
Toolsie Raghoo, *Manager*
Ben Yehooda, *CTO*
✪ **EMP:** 109
SQ FT: 12,000
SALES: 1.2MM **Privately Held**
SIC: 7389 2331 Apparel designers, commercial; women's & misses' blouses & shirts

(G-7489)
TILCON NEW YORK INC
Also Called: North Bergen Asphalt
2414 95th St (07047-1414)
PHONE....................800 789-7625
Fax: 201 854-2816
EMP: 63
SALES (corp-wide): 29.7B **Privately Held**
SIC: 2951 Asphalt paving mixtures & blocks
HQ: Tilcon New York Inc.
9 Entin Rd
Parsippany NJ 07054
800 789-7625

(G-7490)
TRIPP NYC INC
5200 W Side Ave (07047-6440)
PHONE....................201 520-0420
Fax: 201 520-0418
Natharorn Daang Goodman, *President*
Ray Michael Goodman, *Vice Pres*
▲ **EMP:** 20
SQ FT: 9,000
SALES (est): 2.6MM **Privately Held**
WEB: www.trippnyc.com
SIC: 2339 Sportswear, women's

(G-7491)
VITAMIN SHOPPE INDUSTRIES INC (HQ)
Also Called: Vitamin Shoppe, The
2101 91st St (07047-4731)
PHONE....................201 868-5959
Fax: 201 624-3010
Colin Watts, *CEO*
Jerome Williams, *General Mgr*
Tammi Aqueche, *District Mgr*
Michelle Mevissen, *District Mgr*
Joseph Patalano, *District Mgr*
EMP: 540
SQ FT: 230,000
SALES (est): 915.6MM **Publicly Held**
WEB: www.ourmothernature.com
SIC: 5499 5961 2833 Vitamin food stores; pharmaceuticals, mail order; vitamins, natural or synthetic: bulk, uncompounded

(G-7492)
VS HERCULES LLC (DH)
Also Called: Nutri-Force Nutrition
2101 91st St (07047-4731)
PHONE....................201 868-5959
Colin Watts, *CEO*
Brenda Galgano, *CFO*
EMP: 5
SALES (est): 93.1MM **Publicly Held**
SIC: 2834 Vitamin, nutrient & hematinic preparations for human use
HQ: Vitamin Shoppe Industries Inc
2101 91st St
North Bergen NJ 07047
201 868-5959

(G-7493)
W R GRACE & CO - CONN
Also Called: W R Grace Construction Pdts
2133 85th St (07047-4788)
PHONE....................201 869-5220
Gary Hutchison, *Branch Mgr*
Brian O'Connell, *Technology*
EMP: 15
SQ FT: 25,000
SALES (corp-wide): 1.7B **Publicly Held**
WEB: www.grace.com
SIC: 2899 Concrete curing & hardening compounds
HQ: W. R. Grace & Co.-Conn.
7500 Grace Dr
Columbia MD 21044
410 531-4000

(G-7494)
WALKER EIGHT CORP
Also Called: Universal Thd & Scallop Cutng
510 73rd St (07047-5407)
PHONE....................201 861-4208
Fax: 201 861-4218
Joseph Simeone, *President*
Vinh Tran, *Corp Secy*
EMP: 5
SALES (est): 270K **Privately Held**
SIC: 2395 Scalloping, for the trade

(G-7495)
WESTCHESTER LACE & TEXTILES
3901 Liberty Ave (07047-2595)
PHONE....................201 864-2150
Leonard Edelson, *President*
▲ **EMP:** 120
SQ FT: 150,000
SALES (est): 11MM **Privately Held**
WEB: www.westchesterlace.com
SIC: 2258 Lace & lace products

(G-7496)
WY INDUSTRIES INC
Also Called: W Y Industries
2500 Secaucus Rd (07047-1553)
PHONE....................201 617-8000
Fax: 201 617-7688
Bill Cheng, *President*
Brian Buchalski, *Plant Mgr*
Chen Zhang, *Sales Dir*
Kent Cheng, *Manager*
◆ **EMP:** 75
SALES (est): 27MM **Privately Held**
WEB: www.wyindustries.com
SIC: 3089 Plastic containers, except foam

(G-7497)
XCESSORY LLC
5901 W Side Ave Fl 7n (07047-6451)
PHONE....................917 647-7523
Darren Cohen, *President*
EMP: 5 **EST:** 2014
SALES (est): 186.2K **Privately Held**
SIC: 2389 Masquerade costumes

(G-7498)
ZEON US INC
5903 W Side Ave (07047-6451)
PHONE....................516 532-7167
Charles Kreite, *President*
EMP: 2
SALES: 1MM **Privately Held**
SIC: 3873 Watches, clocks, watchcases & parts

North Brunswick
Middlesex County

(G-7499)
3R BIOPHARMA LLC
324 Perry Dr (08902-5594)
PHONE....................914 486-1898
Suman Garlaphei,
EMP: 5
SALES (est): 81.8K **Privately Held**
SIC: 2834 Pharmaceutical preparations

(G-7500)
ABP INDUCTION LLC
1460 Livingston Ave 200-1 (08902-1873)
PHONE....................732 932-6400
Fax: 732 932-6294
Boris Kon, *Engineer*
German M Gallegos, *Branch Mgr*
Andrew Perzanowski, *Manager*
EMP: 15
SALES (corp-wide): 8.1MM **Privately Held**
WEB: www.abpinduction.com
SIC: 3567 Industrial furnaces & ovens
PA: Abp Induction, Llc
1440 13th Ave
Union Grove WI 53182
262 317-5300

(G-7501)
ACHIEVEMENT JOURNAL LLC
5 Larson Ct (08902-9636)
PHONE....................732 297-1570
Joseph Mancuso, *Principal*
EMP: 5
SALES (est): 255.5K **Privately Held**
SIC: 2711 Newspapers, publishing & printing

(G-7502)
ACTAVIS LLC
661 Us Highway 1 (08902-3390)
PHONE....................732 843-4904
EMP: 130 **Privately Held**
SIC: 2834 Pharmaceutical preparations

HQ: Actavis Llc
400 Interpace Pkwy
Parsippany NJ 07054

(G-7503)
AGRIUM ADVANCED TECH US INC
1470 Jersey Ave (08902-1659)
PHONE....................732 296-8448
Gary Sosnowski, *Branch Mgr*
EMP: 12
SALES (corp-wide): 14.1B **Privately Held**
SIC: 2873 Nitrogenous fertilizers
HQ: Agrium Advanced Technologies (U.S.) Inc.
2915 Rocky Mountain Ave # 400
Loveland CO 80538

(G-7504)
ARTEGRAFT INC
206 N Center Dr (08902-4246)
P.O. Box 7305 (08902-7305)
PHONE....................732 422-8333
Fax: 732 422-8647
Rick Gibson, *President*
Warren Kirschbaum, *VP Sales*
Teddy Williams, *Sales Staff*
Cathleen Vanderveer, *Manager*
EMP: 14 **EST:** 1993
SQ FT: 5,000
SALES: 3MM **Privately Held**
WEB: www.artegraft.com
SIC: 3841 Surgical & medical instruments

(G-7505)
ASCENDIA PHARMACEUTICALS LLC
661 Us Highway 1 2 (08902-3390)
PHONE....................732 638-4028
Jingjun Huang, *CEO*
EMP: 6 **EST:** 2012
SALES (est): 932.8K **Privately Held**
SIC: 2834 Druggists' preparations (pharmaceuticals)

(G-7506)
ATLANTIC PRECISION TECH LLC
432 Quarry Ln (08902-4727)
PHONE....................732 658-3060
Carol Patrick,
EMP: 5 **EST:** 2007
SALES: 700K **Privately Held**
SIC: 3441 Fabricated structural metal

(G-7507)
BASU GROUP
227 Us Hwy One (08902)
PHONE....................908 517-9138
Bhaskar Basu, *President*
▼ **EMP:** 5
SALES (est): 658.4K **Privately Held**
SIC: 3171 Handbags, women's

(G-7508)
BRUNSWICK SIGNS & EXHIBIT
1510 Jersey Ave (08902-1606)
PHONE....................732 246-2500
Walter S Talan, *CEO*
EMP: 8
SQ FT: 15,000
SALES (est): 560K **Privately Held**
SIC: 3993 Signs & advertising specialties; displays & cutouts, window & lobby; signs, not made in custom sign painting shops; letters for signs, metal

(G-7509)
C D E INC
Also Called: Eastern Cold Drawn
950 Schweitzer Pl (08902-3235)
PHONE....................732 297-2540
Fax: 973 926-1632
Anthony Russo, *President*
William Hughes, *Exec VP*
Cheryl Coelho, *Vice Pres*
Paul Finne, *Vice Pres*
▲ **EMP:** 55 **EST:** 1971
SQ FT: 100,000
SALES (est): 8.7MM **Privately Held**
SIC: 3315 Wire products, ferrous/iron: made in wiredrawing plants; wire, steel: insulated or armored

(G-7510)
CARL A VENABLE INC
Also Called: AlphaGraphics 321
65 Hidden Lake Dr (08902-1213)
PHONE......................732 985-6677
Carl A Venable, *President*
EMP: 6
SQ FT: 1,610
SALES (est): 863.4K **Privately Held**
SIC: 2752 Commercial printing, offset

(G-7511)
CHEMSPEED TECHNOLOGIES INC
113 N Center Dr (08902-4909)
PHONE......................732 329-1225
Fax: 732 329-1226
Rolf Gueller, *CEO*
Ed Halpin, *General Mgr*
Mark Meyers, *Vice Pres*
EMP: 5
SALES (est): 1MM **Privately Held**
WEB: www.chemspeed.com
SIC: 3821 Laboratory equipment: fume hoods, distillation racks, etc.
PA: Chemspeed Technologies Ag
    Wolferstrasse 8
    FUllinsdorf BL 4302
    618 169-500

(G-7512)
CHROMOCELL CORPORATION (PA)
685 Us Highway 1 (08902-3390)
PHONE......................732 565-1113
Fax: 732 565-1183
Christian Kopfli, *CEO*
Kenneth Kashkin, *COO*
Olga Dedova, *Research*
Stuart Hayden, *Research*
Deshou Jiang, *Research*
EMP: 70
SALES (est): 32.5MM **Privately Held**
WEB: www.chromocell.com
SIC: 2834 Pharmaceutical preparations

(G-7513)
CLOUDAGEIT LTD LIABILITY CO
1308 Plymouth Rd (08902-4592)
PHONE......................888 205-4128
Safia Djennane,
Donna Eastman,
EMP: 6 EST: 2012
SALES (est): 413.4K **Privately Held**
SIC: 7372 8748 7371 7389 Business oriented computer software; utility computer software; systems engineering consultant, ex. computer or professional; custom computer programming services;

(G-7514)
DAVION INC (PA)
2 Progress Rd (08902-4324)
PHONE......................973 485-0793
Fax: 973 485-0025
James Placa Jr, *President*
◆ EMP: 20
SQ FT: 150,000
SALES (est): 18.1MM **Privately Held**
WEB: www.haba-davion.com
SIC: 2844 Cosmetic preparations

(G-7515)
DIAMOND FOODS USA INC
832 Ridgewood Ave (08902-2200)
PHONE......................732 543-2186
Sardar M Sultani, *President*
▲ EMP: 3
SQ FT: 5,500
SALES (est): 1.5MM **Privately Held**
SIC: 2044 5149 Rice milling; groceries & related products

(G-7516)
DISTEK INC
121 N Center Dr (08902-4910)
PHONE......................732 422-7585
Fax: 732 422-7310
Gerald Brinker, *Founder*
Pierre Parks, *Opers Mgr*
Michael Baldino, *Prdtn Mgr*
Ray Rodriguez, *Buyer*
Tracy Yu, *Buyer*
EMP: 63

SALES (est): 16.3MM **Privately Held**
WEB: www.distekinc.com
SIC: 3826 5047 3999 Analytical instruments; medical equipment & supplies; atomizers, toiletry

(G-7517)
GENERAL FOUNDRIES INC (PA)
1 Progress Rd (08902-4325)
PHONE......................732 951-9001
Fax: 732 951-9002
Rita J Todani, *President*
Alok Todani, *Principal*
Alex Todani, *Vice Pres*
▲ EMP: 30
SQ FT: 5,000
SALES: 22.5MM **Privately Held**
SIC: 3321 Gray iron castings

(G-7518)
IMAGE REMIT INC
205 N Center Dr (08902-4246)
PHONE......................732 940-7900
Fax: 732 940-7237
Herman Velasquez, *Vice Pres*
EMP: 25
SALES (est): 3.8MM **Privately Held**
WEB: www.imageremit.com
SIC: 3861 7374 Trays, photographic printing & processing; data processing & preparation

(G-7519)
IN MOCEAN GROUP LLC
2400 Rte 1 (08902-4303)
PHONE......................732 960-2415
EMP: 9
SALES (est): 1.1MM
SALES (corp-wide): 14.6MM **Privately Held**
SIC: 2369 Bathing suits & swimwear: girls', children's & infants'
PA: In Mocean Group, Llc
    463 Fashion Ave Fl 21
    New York NY 10018
    212 944-0317

(G-7520)
INTENSE INC
1200 Airport Rd Ste A (08902-1892)
PHONE......................732 249-2228
Kevin Laughlin, *CEO*
John Marsh, *CTO*
Martin Burdash, *Administration*
EMP: 29
SALES (est): 6.4MM **Privately Held**
WEB: www.hpdinc.com
SIC: 3674 5995 Semiconductor diodes & rectifiers; contact lenses, prescription

(G-7521)
JOHN MALTESE IRON WORKS INC
1453 Jersey Ave (08902-1622)
P.O. Box 7161 (08902-7161)
PHONE......................732 249-4350
Fax: 732 249-9182
Laurence Danza, *President*
Mary G Danza, *Treasurer*
Lauren Kokinos, *Manager*
EMP: 21 EST: 1954
SQ FT: 50,000
SALES: 3.2MM **Privately Held**
WEB: www.jmiw.com
SIC: 3441 1791 Building components, structural steel; structural steel erection

(G-7522)
JOHNSON & JOHNSON
691 Rte 1 (08902-3390)
PHONE......................732 422-5000
Steve Bowlan, *Manager*
EMP: 79
SALES (corp-wide): 76.4B **Publicly Held**
WEB: www.jnj.com
SIC: 2834 2844 2676 Pharmaceutical preparations; toilet preparations; sanitary paper products
PA: Johnson & Johnson
    1 Johnson And Johnson Plz
    New Brunswick NJ 08933
    732 524-0400

(G-7523)
KAMAT PHARMATECH LLC
675 Us Highway 1 (08902-3378)
PHONE......................732 406-6421
Madhav Kamat,
EMP: 9 EST: 2013
SALES (est): 1.3MM **Privately Held**
SIC: 2834 Pharmaceutical preparations

(G-7524)
LIFE OF PARTY LLC
832 Ridgewood Ave Ste 4 (08902-2200)
PHONE......................732 828-0886
Fax: 732 828-0980
Deb Rodriguez, *Executive*
Carol Krinsky,
▲ EMP: 40
SQ FT: 30,000
SALES (est): 7.8MM **Privately Held**
WEB: www.soapplace.com
SIC: 3089 2064 Molding primary plastic; candy & other confectionery products

(G-7525)
MATTRESS DEV CO DEL LLC
Also Called: Eclipse International
1375 Jersey Ave (08902-1600)
PHONE......................732 628-0800
Sughra Zaidi, *Controller*
Matt Connolly, *Chief Mktg Ofcr*
Stuart Carlitz,
EMP: 30
SQ FT: 80,000
SALES (est): 61.9K **Privately Held**
SIC: 2515 Mattresses & bedsprings

(G-7526)
MERIAL INC
631 Us Highway 1 (08902-3390)
PHONE......................732 729-5700
Fax: 732 729-5761
Lisa Baker, *Research*
Dave Sirish, *Manager*
EMP: 30
SALES (corp-wide): 21.2B **Privately Held**
SIC: 2834 Pharmaceutical preparations
HQ: Merial, Inc.
    3239 Satellite Blvd
    Duluth GA 30096

(G-7527)
MIDDLESEX PUBLICATIONS
Also Called: Suburban Parent Magazine
850 Us Highway 1 Fl 4 Flr 4 (08902)
PHONE......................732 435-0005
Fax: 732 435-0677
Mark Chelton, *President*
EMP: 10
SALES (est): 1MM **Privately Held**
SIC: 2721 Magazines: publishing only, not printed on site

(G-7528)
MUSEAMI INC
2 King Arthur Ct Ste A (08902-3381)
PHONE......................609 917-3000
Robert Taub, *President*
EMP: 14
SALES (est): 1.4MM **Privately Held**
SIC: 7372 Publishers' computer software

(G-7529)
N&K TRADING INC
1980 Us Highway 1 Bldg 3 (08902-9834)
PHONE......................609 616-3110
▲ EMP: 30
SALES (est): 5.1MM **Privately Held**
SIC: 2371 Fur finishers & liners for the fur goods trade

(G-7530)
NAUTICAL MARINE PAINT CORP (PA)
Also Called: National Paint Supply
1999 Elizabeth St (08902-4905)
PHONE......................732 821-3200
Fax: 732 821-8180
Michael Schnurr, *President*
Donald Schnurr Jr, *Vice Pres*
Donald Schnurr Sr, *Director*
EMP: 25 EST: 1959
SQ FT: 87,000
SALES (est): 7.2MM **Privately Held**
SIC: 2851 5198 Paints & allied products; paints & paint additives; paints

(G-7531)
NOBELUS LLC
1665 Jersey Ave (08902-1448)
PHONE......................800 895-2747
EMP: 4
SALES (corp-wide): 24MM **Privately Held**
SIC: 5112 5084 3081 Blank books; cement making machinery; film base, cellulose acetate or nitrocellulose plastic
PA: Nobelus Llc
    900 Dutch Valley Dr
    Knoxville TN 37918
    865 688-5264

(G-7532)
OHM LABORATORIES INC (DH)
1385 Livingston Ave (08902-1829)
P.O. Box 7587, Princeton (08543-7587)
PHONE......................732 418-2235
Fax: 732 418-7208
Dipak Chattaraj, *President*
Ganpat Desai, *Vice Pres*
Venkatachalam Krishnan, *Vice Pres*
Robert Patton, *Vice Pres*
John Meister, *Engineer*
▲ EMP: 91
SQ FT: 90,000
SALES (est): 34.6MM
SALES (corp-wide): 1.2B **Privately Held**
WEB: www.ranbaxy.com
SIC: 2834 Druggists' preparations (pharmaceuticals)
HQ: Ranbaxy Inc.
    2 Independence Way
    Princeton NJ 08540
    609 720-9200

(G-7533)
PARKWAY-KEW CORPORATION
2095 Excelsior Ave (08902-4431)
PHONE......................732 398-2100
Fax: 732 398-2101
Gene Klein Sr, *President*
Eugene E Klein, *Principal*
Michael Hoffarth, *Vice Pres*
William Sibree, *Vice Pres*
EMP: 15 EST: 1953
SQ FT: 23,000
SALES (est): 3.2MM **Privately Held**
WEB: www.parkwaykew.com
SIC: 3599 8711 Machine shop, jobbing & repair; engineering services

(G-7534)
PHOENICIAN INC
Also Called: Phoenician Bakery, The
608 Georges Rd (08902-3313)
PHONE......................732 545-3915
John Soueid, *President*
Nabil Eid, *Vice Pres*
EMP: 4
SQ FT: 1,800
SALES (est): 358.2K **Privately Held**
SIC: 2051 Breads, rolls & buns

(G-7535)
PRO TAPES & SPECIALTIES INC
621 Us Highway 1 Unit A (08902-6302)
P.O. Box 53026, Newark (07101-5326)
PHONE......................732 346-0900
Arnold S Silver, *CEO*
Ed Miller, *President*
Barry Hart, *COO*
Barney Silver, *Vice Pres*
Russ Hart, *Purchasing*
◆ EMP: 115
SQ FT: 142,000
SALES (est): 82.9MM **Privately Held**
WEB: www.protapes.com
SIC: 5113 2675 Pressure sensitive tape; die-cut paper & board

(G-7536)
QUICK BIAS BNDING TRMMING INDS
9 Creekside Ct (08902-4774)
PHONE......................732 422-0123
Thomas Gagliano, *President*
Lorraine Gagliano, *Shareholder*
EMP: 11 EST: 1965
SQ FT: 15,000
SALES (est): 1MM **Privately Held**
SIC: 2396 Bindings, bias: made from purchased materials; trimming, fabric

(G-7537)
SCALA PASTRY
1896 Us Highway 130 (08902-3038)
PHONE.....................732 398-9808
Paul Scala, *Owner*
EMP: 5 **EST:** 2001
SALES (est): 312.4K **Privately Held**
SIC: 2051 5311 Bread, cake & related
products; department stores

(G-7538)
SOLVAY USA INC
219 Black Horse Ln (08902-4301)
P.O. Box 7500 (08902-7500)
PHONE.....................732 297-0100
Brian Wheeler, *Principal*
EMP: 250
SALES (corp-wide): 10MM **Privately
Held**
WEB: www.food.us.rhodia.com
SIC: 2819 2812 2865 2869 Boric acid;
phosphates, except fertilizers: defluori-
nated & ammoniated; soda ash, sodium
carbonate (anhydrous); phenol, alkylated
& cumene; diphenylamines; isocyanates;
fluorinated hydrocarbon gases; silicones;
plastics materials & resins; flavoring ex-
tracts & syrups
HQ: Solvay Usa Inc.
504 Carnegie Ctr
Princeton NJ 08540
609 860-4000

(G-7539)
SONGBIRD HEARING INC
210 N Center Dr (08902-4246)
PHONE.....................732 422-7203
Thomas E Gaedner, *Ch of Bd*
Thomas E Gardner, *Ch of Bd*
EMP: 46 **EST:** 1997
SQ FT: 20,000
SALES (est): 2.6MM **Privately Held**
SIC: 8731 3842 Medical research, com-
mercial; electronic research; hearing aids

(G-7540)
SPECTRA MATTRESS INC
633 Nassau St (08902-2940)
PHONE.....................732 545-5900
Isaac Srour, *President*
EMP: 4
SQ FT: 50,000
SALES: 1MM **Privately Held**
SIC: 2515 Mattresses & bedsprings

(G-7541)
SUNRISE INTL EDUCATN INC
1542 Edly Cove Ct (08902-3074)
PHONE.....................917 525-0272
Gavin Newton-Taver, *CEO*
EMP: 54
SALES: 4MM **Privately Held**
SIC: 8299 7372 Educational services; ed-
ucational computer software

(G-7542)
**THER-A-PEDIC SLEEP
PRODUCTS (PA)**
Also Called: Bedding Industries of America
1375 Jersey Ave (08902-1600)
PHONE.....................732 628-0800
Fax: 732 628-0803
Stuart Carlitz, *CEO*
Greg Tanis, *Vice Pres*
Mike Campbell, *Opers Staff*
◆ **EMP:** 74 **EST:** 1958
SQ FT: 90,000
SALES: 35MM **Privately Held**
WEB: www.therapedic.com
SIC: 2515 Mattresses, innerspring or box
spring; box springs, assembled

(G-7543)
TIFFANEES TOYS INC
601 Nassau St Ste 593 (08902-2940)
PHONE.....................732 828-6333
Fax: 732 828-4575
Mirta D'Amaro, *President*
Jacqueline Bracero, *Vice Pres*
EMP: 17
SQ FT: 20,000
SALES (est): 2.1MM **Privately Held**
SIC: 3942 Dolls & stuffed toys

(G-7544)
**URIGEN PHARMACEUTICALS
INC**
675 Us Highway 1 Ste 206b (08902-3378)
PHONE.....................732 640-0160
Dan Vickery, *CEO*
EMP: 4
SALES (est): 295K **Privately Held**
SIC: 2834 Pharmaceutical preparations

(G-7545)
VESAG HEALTH INC
675 Us Highway 1 B202c (08902-3378)
PHONE.....................732 333-1876
Rajendra Sadhu, *CEO*
Pradeep Karki, *Vice Pres*
Girija Rupakula, *Vice Pres*
EMP: 18 **EST:** 2011
SQ FT: 2,000
SALES: 200K **Privately Held**
SIC: 8099 3841 Health screening service;
diagnostic apparatus, medical

(G-7546)
VISH LLC
Also Called: Vish Group
1605 Jersey Ave (08902-1448)
PHONE.....................201 529-2900
Shiv Kukreja, *Vice Pres*
Chris Hamilton, *Purch Mgr*
Mike Kukreja, *Sales Mgr*
Paul Hingorani, *Marketing Staff*
Tina Kukreja, *Technology*
◆ **EMP:** 25
SQ FT: 48,000
SALES (est): 18.9MM **Privately Held**
SIC: 3081 Unsupported plastics film &
sheet

North Haledon
Passaic County

(G-7547)
ACEY INDUSTRIES INC
Also Called: Bergen Screen Printing
9 Cranberry Ct (07508-2860)
PHONE.....................973 595-1222
Fax: 973 595-5707
Uday Patel, *President*
EMP: 7 **EST:** 1998
SQ FT: 9,500
SALES: 405.7K **Privately Held**
SIC: 2396 Screen printing on fabric articles

(G-7548)
HOFER CONNECTORS CO INC
126 Linda Vista Ave (07508-2654)
PHONE.....................973 427-1195
Allan P Hofer, *President*
EMP: 20
SALES (est): 2.3MM **Privately Held**
SIC: 5063 3643 Electrical fittings & con-
struction materials; current-carrying wiring
devices

(G-7549)
**HOFER MACHINE & TOOL CO
INC**
126 Linda Vista Ave (07508-2654)
PHONE.....................973 427-1195
Fax: 973 427-6906
Alan P Hofer, *President*
EMP: 19 **EST:** 1947
SQ FT: 10,000
SALES (est): 2.9MM **Privately Held**
SIC: 3643 Connectors & terminals for elec-
trical devices

(G-7550)
**MANNER TEXTILE PROCESSING
INC**
41 Oakdale Ct (07508-2948)
PHONE.....................973 942-8718
Patrick Cupo, *President*
Anthony Cupo, *Treasurer*
EMP: 55 **EST:** 1959
SQ FT: 25,000
SALES (est): 4.9MM **Privately Held**
SIC: 2231 2269 2865 2261 Fabric finish-
ing: wool, mohair or similar fibers; finish-
ing plants; cyclic crudes & intermediates;
finishing plants, cotton

(G-7551)
METAL COMPONENTS INC
92 Marilyn St (07508)
PHONE.....................973 247-1204
Frank Mottola, *President*
Thomas Roskop, *QC Mgr*
Dee Tallaksen, *Office Mgr*
Al Schroeder, *Director*
EMP: 24 **EST:** 1959
SQ FT: 22,000
SALES (est): 2.7MM **Privately Held**
SIC: 3451 Screw machine products

(G-7552)
**MINI FROST FOODS
CORPORATION**
Also Called: Belmont Bakery
23 Willow Brook Ct (07508-2539)
PHONE.....................973 427-4258
Fax: 973 427-0973
Katherine Parsells, *President*
EMP: 20
SQ FT: 5,000
SALES (est): 5.7MM **Privately Held**
SIC: 5142 5461 2052 2051 Bakery prod-
ucts, frozen; bakeries; cookies & crack-
ers; bread, cake & related products

(G-7553)
PHOENIX SYSTEMS
39 Morningside Ave (07508-2507)
PHONE.....................201 788-5511
Andrew Zaccaro, *Owner*
EMP: 3
SALES: 1.4MM **Privately Held**
WEB: www.phoenixsystemsglobal.com
SIC: 3651 Audio electronic systems

(G-7554)
SUN METAL FINISHING INC
5 Sicomac Rd 105 (07508-2972)
PHONE.....................973 684-0119
Fax: 973 684-7866
Michael O'Brien, *President*
EMP: 20
SQ FT: 32,000
SALES (est): 1.4MM **Privately Held**
SIC: 3471 Finishing, metals or formed
products

(G-7555)
**TOTOWA METAL FABRICATORS
INC**
40 Lee Dr (07508-3038)
PHONE.....................973 423-1943
Fax: 973 684-8594
Frank Creegan, *CEO*
EMP: 15
SQ FT: 10,000
SALES (est): 1.2MM **Privately Held**
SIC: 3444 Metal ventilating equipment

North Middletown
Monmouth County

(G-7556)
**ADVANCED MICRO DEVICES
INC**
16 Snyder Dr (07748-5902)
PHONE.....................732 787-2892
Michael Russo, *Manager*
EMP: 131
SALES (corp-wide): 5.3B **Publicly Held**
WEB: www.amd.com
SIC: 3674 Integrated circuits, semiconduc-
tor networks, etc.
PA: Advanced Micro Devices, Inc.
2485 Augustine Dr
Santa Clara CA 95054
408 749-4000

(G-7557)
**GUTTENPLANS FROZEN
DOUGH INC**
100 State Route 36 E (07748-5249)
PHONE.....................732 495-9480
Fax: 732 495-2415
Abe Littenberg, *President*
Jack Guttenplan, *Vice Pres*
Eric Littenberg, *Safety Dir*
Debra Howard, *Accounts Mgr*
Michael Schwartz, *Accounts Mgr*

EMP: 100
SQ FT: 54,000
SALES (est): 63.4MM **Privately Held**
WEB: www.guttenplan.com
SIC: 2041 Doughs, frozen or refrigerated

(G-7558)
QUALITY DIE SHOP INC
17 Argonne Pl (07748-5102)
PHONE.....................732 787-0041
Fax: 732 888-5423
Kirk Harris, *President*
Suzanne Harris, *Vice Pres*
EMP: 7
SQ FT: 11,000
SALES (est): 490K **Privately Held**
SIC: 3544 Dies, steel rule

North Plainfield
Union County

(G-7559)
**GRANITE AND MARBLE ASSOC
INC**
Also Called: American Architectual Stone
310 Tremont Ave (07063-1669)
PHONE.....................908 416-1100
John J Donatelli, *President*
John Donatelli, *President*
▲ **EMP:** 8
SALES (est): 606.4K **Privately Held**
SIC: 3281 Cut stone & stone products

(G-7560)
**ORLANDO SYSTEMS LTD LBLTY
CO**
375 North Dr Apt A10 (07060-3744)
PHONE.....................908 400-5052
Theodor Basch, *President*
▼ **EMP:** 4
SALES: 1.5MM **Privately Held**
WEB: www.orlando-systems.com
SIC: 5065 5049 5047 3829 Electronic
parts & equipment; telephone & telegraphic equipment; laboratory equipment,
except medical or dental; electro-medical
equipment; whole body counters, nuclear;
automobile house trailer chassis; automobile assembly, including specialty automobiles

(G-7561)
RACEWAY PETROLEUM INC
643 Us Highway 22 (07060-3728)
PHONE.....................908 222-2999
Gurbreed Singh, *Branch Mgr*
EMP: 17 **Privately Held**
SIC: 3644 Raceways
PA: Raceway Petroleum Inc
1411 Stelton Rd
Piscataway NJ 08854

Northfield
Atlantic County

(G-7562)
**ADVANCED SHORE IMAGING
ASSOCIA**
2605 Shore Rd (08225-2136)
P.O. Box 6750, Portsmouth NH (03802-
6750)
PHONE.....................732 678-0087
Thomas Yu, *President*
Laura Cougar, *COO*
EMP: 17
SQ FT: 10,500
SALES (est): 1.1MM **Privately Held**
SIC: 3829 Medical diagnostic systems, nu-
clear

(G-7563)
ARTISTIC HARDWARE
430 Tilton Rd Ste 2 (08225-1268)
PHONE.....................609 383-1909
Tom Vassallo, *Opers Staff*
Carol Kelly, *Manager*
Patrick McCarthy,
EMP: 7
SQ FT: 3,800

SALES (est): 1.1MM **Privately Held**
SIC: 5251 3469 3429 1799 Builders'
hardware; kitchen fixtures & equipment;
porcelain enameled; cabinet hardware;
kitchen & bathroom remodeling

(G-7564)
SUPERIOR JEWELRY CO
Also Called: Ocean-Craft International
430 Tilton Rd Ste 1 (08225-1268)
P.O. Box 188 (08225-0188)
PHONE....................................215 677-8100
Howard Wiener, *President*
Barry Wiener, *Corp Secy*
Ruth Wiener, *Vice Pres*
Howard W Pressales, *Manager*
▲ EMP: 11 EST: 1935
SQ FT: 5,000
SALES (est): 2.4MM **Privately Held**
WEB: www.superiorjewelry.com
SIC: 5094 3961 Jewelry; costume jewelry,
ex. precious metal & semiprecious stones

(G-7565)
ZEBRA TECHNOLOGIES CORPORATION
1501 Tilton Rd (08225-1876)
PHONE....................................609 383-8743
Stacey Didonato, *Principal*
EMP: 400
SALES (corp-wide): 3.7B **Publicly Held**
SIC: 3577 Bar code (magnetic ink) printers
PA: Zebra Technologies Corporation
3 Overlook Pt
Lincolnshire IL 60069
847 634-6700

Northvale
Bergen County

(G-7566)
A D M TRONICS UNLIMITED INC (PA)
224 Pegasus Ave Ste A (07647-1921)
PHONE....................................201 767-6040
Fax: 201 784-0620
Andre Dimino, *President*
▲ EMP: 22
SQ FT: 16,000
SALES: 3.7MM **Publicly Held**
WEB: www.admtronics.com
SIC: 2891 2899 3841 2844 Adhesives &
sealants; chemical preparations; surgical
& medical instruments; cosmetic prepara-
tions

(G-7567)
ABON PHARMACEUTICALS LLC
140 Legrand Ave (07647-2403)
PHONE....................................201 367-1702
Salah U Ahmed, *President*
Bruce L Downey, *Chairman*
Jennifer Barr, *QC Dir*
Mahish Patel, *Director*
Yanming Zu, *Director*
EMP: 38
SALES (est): 9.2MM **Privately Held**
SIC: 2834 Pharmaceutical preparations

(G-7568)
ACEDEPOTCOM (PA)
159 Paris Ave (07647-2029)
PHONE....................................800 844-0962
EMP: 11
SALES (est): 2.7MM **Privately Held**
SIC: 3579 5112 5111 Address labeling
machines; marking devices; fine paper

(G-7569)
AIG INDUSTRIAL GROUP INC (HQ)
220 Pegasus Ave (07647-1904)
PHONE....................................201 767-7300
Fax: 201 767-1741
Gerald Anderson, *President*
Melanie Kershaw, *Treasurer*
EMP: 12
SQ FT: 26,000
SALES (est): 5.4MM
SALES (corp-wide): 14.9MM **Privately Held**
SIC: 3829 2819 2843 Gas detectors; in-
dustrial inorganic chemicals; penetrants

PA: Meson Group, Inc
220 Pegasus Ave
Northvale NJ 07647
201 767-7300

(G-7570)
ALCAN BALTEK CORPORATION
108 Fairway Ct (07647-2401)
P.O. Box 16148, High Point NC (27261-6148)
PHONE....................................201 767-1400
Fax: 201 367-1201
Jacques Kohn, *CEO*
▲ EMP: 100
SALES (est): 14.5MM **Privately Held**
SIC: 2493 Reconstituted wood products

(G-7571)
ALEX MACHINE SHOP INC
267 Livingston St (07647-1901)
P.O. Box 268 (07647-0268)
PHONE....................................201 768-9110
Fax: 201 768-9132
EMP: 8
SQ FT: 3,000
SALES (est): 813.1K **Privately Held**
SIC: 3599 Machine Shop

(G-7572)
AMERICAN GAS & CHEMICAL CO LTD
220 Pegasus Ave (07647-1904)
PHONE....................................201 767-7300
Gerald Anderson, *President*
Scott Bruce, *General Mgr*
James Zanosky, *General Mgr*
Melanie Kershaw, *Vice Pres*
Edouard Zuraik, *Technology*
EMP: 30
SQ FT: 26,000
SALES (est): 5.4MM
SALES (corp-wide): 14.9MM **Privately Held**
WEB: www.amgas.com
SIC: 2819 3829 2843 3812 Industrial in-
organic chemicals; measuring & control-
ling devices; penetrants; search &
navigation equipment
HQ: Aig Industrial Group Inc
220 Pegasus Ave
Northvale NJ 07647
201 767-7300

(G-7573)
BARR LABORATORIES INC
265 Livingston St (07647-1901)
PHONE....................................201 767-1589
Peter Stiffel, *Manager*
EMP: 130
SALES (corp-wide): 22.3B **Privately Held**
SIC: 2834 Pharmaceutical preparations
HQ: Barr Laboratories, Inc.
1090 Horsham Rd
North Wales PA 19454
215 591-3000

(G-7574)
BARR LABORATORIES INC
232 Pegasus Ave (07647-1904)
PHONE....................................845 362-1100
David Mendelson, *Branch Mgr*
EMP: 20
SALES (corp-wide): 22.3B **Privately Held**
WEB: www.barrlabs.com
SIC: 2834 Pharmaceutical preparations
HQ: Barr Laboratories, Inc.
1090 Horsham Rd
North Wales PA 19454
215 591-3000

(G-7575)
BIPORE INC
31 Industrial Pkwy (07647-2203)
PHONE....................................201 767-1993
Durmus Koch, *President*
EMP: 16
SQ FT: 7,000
SALES (est): 2.7MM **Privately Held**
SIC: 3841 Catheters

(G-7576)
CELUS FASTENERS MFG INC (PA)
200 Paris Ave (07647-2205)
PHONE....................................800 289-7483
Frank C Lahnston, *President*

▲ EMP: 44
SQ FT: 27,000
SALES (est): 2.2MM **Privately Held**
SIC: 3429 3452 Metal fasteners; rivets,
metal

(G-7577)
DELPHIAN CORPORATION
220 Pegasus Ave (07647-1900)
PHONE....................................201 767-7300
Gerald Anderson, *Ch of Bd*
Sherri Vollmer, *Accountant*
EMP: 145
SQ FT: 26,000
SALES: 9MM
SALES (corp-wide): 14.9MM **Privately Held**
WEB: www.delphian.com
SIC: 3823 3829 On-stream gas/liquid
analysis instruments, industrial; gas de-
tectors
PA: Meson Group, Inc
220 Pegasus Ave
Northvale NJ 07647
201 767-7300

(G-7578)
ELITE LABORATORIES INC
165 Ludlow Ave (07647-2305)
PHONE....................................201 750-2646
Fax: 201 845-0707
Bernard Berk, *CEO*
Mark Gittelman, *Corp Secy*
Doug Plassche, *VP Opers*
EMP: 38
SALES (est): 3.9MM **Publicly Held**
WEB: www.elitepharma.com
SIC: 2834 Pharmaceutical preparations
PA: Elite Pharmaceuticals, Inc.
165 Ludlow Ave
Northvale NJ 07647
201 750-2646

(G-7579)
ELITE PHARMACEUTICALS INC (PA)
165 Ludlow Ave (07647-2305)
PHONE....................................201 750-2755
Nasrat Hakim, *President*
Douglas Plassche, *Exec VP*
Carter J Ward, *CFO*
Peter Kinkel, *Director*
Davis Caskey, *Bd of Directors*
EMP: 30
SQ FT: 15,000
SALES: 3.9MM **Publicly Held**
WEB: www.elitepharma.com
SIC: 2834 Pharmaceutical preparations

(G-7580)
FEI-ELCOM TECH INC
260 Union St (07647-2208)
PHONE....................................201 767-8030
Fax: 201 767-0542
James Davis, *CEO*
Chuck Scheetz, *President*
Joe Milo, *General Mgr*
Cristina Rizzo, *Materials Mgr*
Janice Martini, *Purch Agent*
▲ EMP: 50
SALES (est): 5MM
SALES (corp-wide): 39.4MM **Publicly Held**
WEB: www.elcom-tech.com
SIC: 3663 Microwave communication
equipment
PA: Frequency Electronics, Inc.
55 Charles Lindbergh Blvd # 2
Uniondale NY 11553
516 794-4500

(G-7581)
FILLO FACTORY INC
10 Fairway Ct (07647-2401)
P.O. Box 155, Dumont (07628-0155)
PHONE....................................201 439-1036
Ron Rexroth, *President*
Mike Gillies, *Opers Mgr*
Melissa Rexroth, *Manager*
Phil Digaetano, *Technology*
EMP: 50
SQ FT: 15,000
SALES (est): 12.4MM **Privately Held**
WEB: www.fillofactory.com
SIC: 2041 Doughs & batters

(G-7582)
GLOBTEK INC (PA)
186 Veterans Dr (07647-2303)
PHONE....................................201 784-1000
Fax: 201 784-0111
Anna Kaplan, *CEO*
Gino Cardillo, *Vice Pres*
Cheryl D'Amico, *Purchasing*
Eric Visperas, *Engineer*
Jayson Bandivas, *Project Engr*
▲ EMP: 400
SQ FT: 25,000
SALES (est): 66.1MM **Privately Held**
WEB: www.globtek.com
SIC: 3612 Specialty transformers

(G-7583)
HAUSMANN ENTERPRISES LLC
Also Called: Hausmann Industries
130 Union St (07647-2207)
PHONE....................................201 767-0255
Fax: 201 767-1369
Kelvyn Cullimore, *CEO*
Abhay Jain, *Manager*
◆ EMP: 95 EST: 1955
SQ FT: 60,000
SALES (est): 14.5MM
SALES (corp-wide): 35.7MM **Publicly Held**
WEB: www.hausmann.com
SIC: 2599 2531 Hospital furniture, except
beds; public building & related furniture
PA: Dynatronics Corporation
7030 S Park Centre Dr
Salt Lake City UT 84121
801 568-7000

(G-7584)
INDUSTRIAL RIVET & FASTENER CO (PA)
200 Paris Ave (07647-2205)
PHONE....................................201 750-1040
Fax: 201 750-1050
William Goodman, *President*
Joanne Sherman, *Corp Secy*
▲ EMP: 54
SQ FT: 23,000
SALES (est): 22.9MM **Privately Held**
WEB: www.rivet.com
SIC: 5072 5085 3452 Miscellaneous fas-
teners; bolts; rivets; industrial supplies;
bolts, nuts, rivets & washers

(G-7585)
INRAD OPTICS INC (PA)
181 Legrand Ave (07647-2498)
PHONE....................................201 767-1910
Jan M Winston, *Ch of Bd*
Amy Eskilson, *President*
Thomas A Caughey, *Vice Pres*
Chuck Rogol, *Engineer*
Bill Foote, *CFO*
EMP: 63
SQ FT: 41,935
SALES: 9.8MM **Publicly Held**
WEB: www.ppgrpinc.com
SIC: 3699 3827 Laser systems & equip-
ment; lenses, optical: all types except
ophthalmic

(G-7586)
INTERPLEX NAS INC
232 Pegasus Ave (07647-1904)
PHONE....................................201 367-1300
Fax: 201 768-8988
Jack Seidler, *CEO*
Art Madgwick, *Principal*
▲ EMP: 50
SALES (est): 10.7MM
SALES (corp-wide): 223.2MM **Privately Held**
SIC: 3679 Rheostats, for electronic end
products
HQ: Interplex Industries, Inc.
231 Ferris Ave
Rumford RI 02916
718 961-6212

(G-7587)
JENTEC INC
20 Charles St Ste C (07647-2214)
PHONE....................................201 784-1031
Fax: 201 750-1841
Robert Jensen, *Ch of Bd*
Jarl Jensen, *President*
EMP: 3

▲ = Import ▼=Export
◆ =Import/Export

SQ FT: 2,000
SALES: 1MM **Privately Held**
WEB: www.jentecinc.com
SIC: **8711 3842** Engineering services; surgical appliances & supplies

(G-7588)
JOHN G PAPAILIAS CO INC
Also Called: J G Papailias
245 Pegasus Ave (07647-1903)
PHONE..................................201 767-4027
George Papailias, *President*
▲ EMP: 8
SQ FT: 25,000
SALES (est): 870K **Privately Held**
WEB: www.papailias.com
SIC: **3823 3648** Liquid level instruments, industrial process type; flow instruments, industrial process type; lighting equipment

(G-7589)
LAB TECH INC (PA)
170 Legrand Ave (07647-2407)
PHONE..................................201 767-5613
Michael Pildes, *CEO*
▲ EMP: 8
SALES (est): 680.6K **Privately Held**
SIC: **3851** Lens grinding, except prescription: ophthalmic

(G-7590)
LEXI INDUSTRIES
252 Livingston St (07647-1906)
PHONE..................................201 297-7900
EMP: 9 EST: 2009
SALES (est): 996.4K **Privately Held**
SIC: **3999** Manufacturing industries

(G-7591)
MESON GROUP INC (PA)
220 Pegasus Ave (07647-1904)
PHONE..................................201 767-7300
Gerald Anderson, *President*
Melanie Kershaw, *Vice Pres*
▲ EMP: 30
SQ FT: 26,000
SALES (est): 14.9MM **Privately Held**
WEB: www.mesongroup.com
SIC: **3823 3829 2819 2843** On-stream gas/liquid analysis instruments, industrial; gas detectors; industrial inorganic chemicals; penetrants

(G-7592)
MRC PRECISION METAL OPTICS INC
Also Called: Inrad Optics
181 Legrand Ave (07647-2404)
PHONE..................................941 753-8707
Joe Rutherford, *President*
Joseph J Rutherford, *Vice Pres*
William J Foote, *CFO*
George Murray, *VP Sales*
EMP: 30
SQ FT: 25,000
SALES (est): 3.9MM
SALES (corp-wide): 9.8MM **Publicly Held**
WEB: www.inradoptics.com
SIC: **3577 3827** Optical scanning devices; optical instruments & lenses
PA: Inrad Optics, Inc.
181 Legrand Ave
Northvale NJ 07647
201 767-1910

(G-7593)
MULTIMATIC LLC (PA)
Also Called: Multimatic Dry Cleaning Mch
162 Veterans Dr (07647-2300)
P.O. Box 156 (07647-0156)
PHONE..................................201 767-9660
Fax: 201 767-7037
Ronald Velli,
▲ EMP: 9 EST: 1968
SQ FT: 30,000
SALES (est): 1.4MM **Privately Held**
SIC: **3582** Drycleaning equipment & machinery, commercial

(G-7594)
NAOMI PET INTERNATIONAL INC
20 Charles St Ste D (07647-2214)
PHONE..................................201 660-7918
Sunkyu Lee, *Officer*
EMP: 4

SALES: 500K **Privately Held**
SIC: **3999** Pet supplies

(G-7595)
NEW LIFE PHARMA LTD LBLTY CO
265 Livingston St (07647-1901)
PHONE..................................201 784-7812
Art Leong, *Director*
Danielle Tracy, *Director*
EMP: 4
SQ FT: 8,000
SALES (est): 208.5K **Privately Held**
SIC: **2834** Pharmaceutical preparations

(G-7596)
NEW LIFE RESOURCES INC
153 Walnut St (07647-2107)
PHONE..................................201 750-7880
Fax: 201 750-7885
EMP: 16
SALES (est): 3.8MM **Privately Held**
SIC: **2834 5122** Mfg Pharmaceutical Preparations Whol Drugs/Sundries

(G-7597)
NEW YORK BOTANY INC
20 Charles St Ste B (07647-2214)
PHONE..................................201 564-7444
Younghoon Kim, *Officer*
EMP: 20
SALES: 1.2MM **Privately Held**
SIC: **2844 5122** Cosmetic preparations; cosmetics

(G-7598)
OLYMPIA LIGHTING INC
148 Veterans Dr (07647-2311)
PHONE..................................201 812-7880
Judy Shalvi, *President*
EMP: 5
SALES (est): 280.4K **Privately Held**
SIC: **3648** Lighting equipment

(G-7599)
ORTHOFEET INC
152 Veterans Dr Ste A (07647-2307)
PHONE..................................800 524-2845
Fax: 201 767-6748
Mark Koide, *CEO*
Aharon Bar, *President*
Mike Saccente, *COO*
Michael Bar, *Vice Pres*
Rick Hynes, *CFO*
▲ EMP: 30
SQ FT: 30,000
SALES (est): 5.9MM **Privately Held**
WEB: www.orthofeet.com
SIC: **3842** Foot appliances, orthopedic

(G-7600)
PALM PRESS INC
Also Called: Minuteman Press
202 Livingston St (07647-1710)
PHONE..................................201 767-6504
Margaret Lorenzo, *President*
Vivian Abitabilo, *Treasurer*
EMP: 5 EST: 1980
SQ FT: 1,100
SALES: 650K **Privately Held**
WEB: www.minutemannorthvale.com
SIC: **2752 2791 2789 2759** Commercial printing, offset; typesetting; bookbinding & related work; commercial printing

(G-7601)
PELOTON INTERACTIVE INC
206 Pegasus Ave (07647-1909)
PHONE..................................201 784-9510
EMP: 5
SALES (corp-wide): 28.5MM **Privately Held**
SIC: **3949** Gymnasium equipment
PA: Peloton Interactive, Inc.
125 W 25th St Fl 11
New York NY 10001
866 650-1996

(G-7602)
RAB LIGHTING INC (PA)
170 Ludlow Ave (07647-2305)
P.O. Box 970 (07647-0970)
PHONE..................................201 784-8600
Fax: 201 784-0077
Ross Barna, *Ch of Bd*
Richard A Barna, *President*

Vinny Guercio, *President*
Ravi Parikh, *Business Mgr*
Rich Allis, *Vice Pres*
◆ EMP: 240 EST: 1946
SQ FT: 200,000
SALES (est): 83.8MM **Privately Held**
WEB: www.rabweb.com
SIC: **3625 3648 3646** Electric controls & control accessories, industrial; outdoor lighting equipment; floodlights; commercial indusl & institutional electric lighting fixtures

(G-7603)
RADHA BEAUTY PRODUCTS LLC
100 Stonehurst Ct (07647-2405)
PHONE..................................732 993-6242
Jose Bernardo De La Vega, *CEO*
Rebeka Letch, *Exec VP*
EMP: 7
SALES (est): 204.1K **Privately Held**
SIC: **2844** Perfumes, natural or synthetic

(G-7604)
REMA CORROSION CONTROL
240 Pegasus Ave (07647-1923)
P.O. Box 171 (07647-0171)
PHONE..................................201 256-8400
Charlie Altizer, *President*
Deb Kareha, *Prdtn Mgr*
Chris Balsley, *Sales Staff*
Raj Patel, *Marketing Staff*
Steve Byous, *Manager*
EMP: 10
SALES: 2MM
SALES (corp-wide): 2.5B **Privately Held**
SIC: **2851** Epoxy coatings
HQ: Rema Tip Top/North America, Inc.
240 Pegasus Ave Unit 2
Northvale NJ 07647
201 768-8100

(G-7605)
REMA TIP TOP/NORTH AMERICA INC (HQ)
240 Pegasus Ave Unit 2 (07647-1924)
P.O. Box 76 (07647-0076)
PHONE..................................201 768-8100
Fax: 201 768-0946
Olafur Gunnarsson, *President*
James McFadden, *Regional Mgr*
Kelly Thomas, *Regional Mgr*
Adam Tillery, *Regional Mgr*
Brian Bennett, *Business Mgr*
▲ EMP: 22 EST: 1923
SALES (est): 109MM
SALES (corp-wide): 2.5B **Privately Held**
WEB: www.rema.com
SIC: **5085 3069 5014** Rubber goods, mechanical; liner strips, rubber; tire & tube repair materials
PA: Stahlgruber Otto Gruber Ag
Gruber Str. 65
Poing 85586
812 170-70

(G-7606)
RICH ART COLOR CO INC
202 Pegasus Ave (07647-1904)
P.O. Box 198 (07647-0198)
PHONE..................................201 767-0009
Ben Horwitz, *President*
Mark Morrison, *Vice Pres*
Erika Freed, *Director*
EMP: 10
SQ FT: 30,000
SALES (est): 2.3MM **Privately Held**
WEB: www.richardwimmer.com
SIC: **3952 2851** Artists' materials, except pencils & leads; paints & allied products

(G-7607)
SHADE POWERS CO INC
Also Called: Window Designs By Powers
112 Paris Ave Ste C (07647-1544)
PHONE..................................201 767-3727
Fax: 201 767-3877
Barbara Powers, *President*
Gregory Powers Jr, *Corp Secy*
EMP: 12
SQ FT: 2,500
SALES (est): 1.4MM **Privately Held**
SIC: **5719 3429 2591** Window furnishings; manufactured hardware (general); drapery hardware & blinds & shades

(G-7608)
SONOTRON MEDICAL SYSTEMS INC
Also Called: ADM Tronics
224 Pegasus Ave (07647-1920)
PHONE..................................201 767-6040
Andre Di Mino, *President*
Dominic Albi, *Vice Pres*
Vincent Di Mino, *Vice Pres*
Jenny Dimino, *Info Tech Mgr*
▲ EMP: 8
SQ FT: 8,000
SALES (est): 1.4MM
SALES (corp-wide): 3.7MM **Publicly Held**
WEB: www.admtronics.com
SIC: **3845** Electromedical equipment
PA: A D M Tronics Unlimited, Inc.
224 Pegasus Ave Ste A
Northvale NJ 07647
201 767-6040

(G-7609)
TAKASAGO INTL CORP USA
Also Called: Fragrance Factory
267 Union St (07647-2210)
P.O. Box 932 (07647-0932)
PHONE..................................201 767-9001
Yutaka Okamura, *Human Resources*
Linda Sherwin, *Accounts Mgr*
Sue Harrison, *Mktg Dir*
Ron Rand, *Branch Mgr*
Anthony Budraitis, *Department Mgr*
EMP: 65
SALES (corp-wide): 1.3B **Privately Held**
SIC: **2844** Concentrates, perfume
HQ: Takasago International Corporation (U.S.A)
4 Volvo Dr
Rockleigh NJ 07647
201 767-9001

(G-7610)
UNITED INSTRUMENT COMPANY LLC
207 Washington St Ste A (07647-2045)
PHONE..................................201 767-6000
George Petikas,
▲ EMP: 4
SALES (est): 661.8K **Privately Held**
SIC: **3545 3829** Machine tool accessories; measuring & controlling devices

(G-7611)
VIZ MOLD & DIE LTD
210 Industrial Pkwy (07647-2219)
PHONE..................................201 784-8383
Fax: 201 784-4420
Dimitrios Lymberis, *President*
Georgia Lymberis, *Opers Mgr*
Joan Peters, *Admin Sec*
EMP: 10
SALES (est): 1.5MM **Privately Held**
WEB: www.vizmold.com
SIC: **3089 3544** Molding primary plastic; special dies, tools, jigs & fixtures

(G-7612)
X-FACTOR CMMNCTONS HLDINGS INC (PA)
100 Stonehurst Ct (07647-2405)
PHONE..................................877 741-3727
Fax: 201 440-5805
Charles Saracino, *Ch of Bd*
Michael Piro, *Vice Pres*
Edwin F Heinen, *CFO*
Jeffrey Singman, *Sales Staff*
Brian Watts, *CIO*
EMP: 4
SQ FT: 1,500
SALES (est): 744K **Publicly Held**
SIC: **7372** Prepackaged software; application computer software

(G-7613)
ZENITH LABORATORIES INC
140 Legrand Ave (07647-2403)
PHONE..................................201 767-1700
William Schreck, *President*
EMP: 4
SALES (corp-wide): 22.3B **Privately Held**
SIC: **2834** Pharmaceutical preparations
HQ: Zenith Laboratories, Inc
140 Legrand Ave
Northvale NJ 07647
201 767-1700

(G-7614)
ZENITH LABORATORIES INC (DH)
140 Legrand Ave (07647-2403)
PHONE..............................201 767-1700
Fax: 201 784-1719
William Schreck, *President*
Lenora C Gavalas, *Exec VP*
Veerappan S Sueramanian, *Vice Pres*
Richard H Friedman, *CFO*
Ruth H Wallestad, *Treasurer*
EMP: 245
SQ FT: 81,600
SALES (est): 24.4MM
SALES (corp-wide): 22.3B **Privately Held**
WEB: www.onxol.com
SIC: 2834 Pharmaceutical preparations; drugs acting on the cardiovascular system, except diagnostic; drugs acting on the central nervous system & sense organs; drugs affecting parasitic & infective diseases

Norwood
Bergen County

(G-7615)
ARDE
500 Walnut St (07648-1316)
PHONE..............................201 440-1453
Fax: 201 784-9710
Dennis Ledermam, *QC Mgr*
Scott Roy, *Sales Executive*
EMP: 7
SALES (est): 461.7K **Privately Held**
SIC: 3443 2752 Industrial vessels, tanks & containers; commercial printing, lithographic

(G-7616)
BON-JOUR GROUP LLC
Also Called: Bon Jour Promotions
1100 Blanch Ave (07648-1509)
PHONE..............................201 646-1070
Paul Tchertchian, *President*
Michael Tchertchian, *Vice Pres*
EMP: 12
SQ FT: 20,000
SALES: 1.3MM **Privately Held**
WEB: www.bon-jour.com
SIC: 2395 Embroidery products, except schiffli machine

(G-7617)
C & S SPECIALTY INC
121 Piermont Rd (07648-2317)
PHONE..............................201 750-7740
Soon K Chun, *President*
Seth Atkinson, *Director*
▲ EMP: 5
SALES (est): 1.8MM **Privately Held**
WEB: www.cs-sales.net
SIC: 2899 Chemical preparations

(G-7618)
CHERINGAL ASSOCIATES INC
Also Called: Control Group
500 Walnut St (07648-1316)
PHONE..............................201 784-8721
Lynne Levine, *General Mgr*
William Cheringal, *Co-President*
Jeffrey Levine, *Co-President*
Russel Vizzi, *Vice Pres*
Susan Drennen, *Financial Exec*
▲ EMP: 65
SQ FT: 58,000
SALES (est): 11.1MM **Privately Held**
WEB: www.controlgroupusa.com
SIC: 2759 5999 3672 Flexographic printing; cosmetics; printed circuit boards

(G-7619)
CHIC BTQ DOLL DESIGN CO LLC
331 Piermont Rd Ste 8 (07648-1407)
PHONE..............................201 784-7727
Murray S Bass,
Allen Fu,
Sarah Nguyen,
EMP: 7
SALES (est): 540K **Privately Held**
SIC: 3942 Dolls & doll clothing

(G-7620)
CREATIVE CONCEPTS CORPORATION
70 Oak St Ste 202 (07648-1300)
PHONE..............................201 750-1234
Jean Pierre Subrenat, *President*
Marie Reilly, *Sales Mgr*
EMP: 5 EST: 1990
SQ FT: 3,000
SALES (est): 811.6K **Privately Held**
WEB: www.creaconcepts.com
SIC: 2844 Perfumes & colognes

(G-7621)
EMABOND SOLUTIONS LLC
49 Walnut St Ste 2 (07648-1390)
PHONE..............................201 767-7400
Fax: 201 767-3608
Scott Tedrick, *Sales Dir*
Steve Chookazian, *Mng Member*
Drew Lamarca, *Mng Member*
Randy Reiman, *Manager*
EMP: 25
SQ FT: 26,000
SALES (est): 5.6MM **Privately Held**
SIC: 3548 Welding apparatus

(G-7622)
FLAVOR DEVELOPMENT CORP
388 Chestnut St (07648-2002)
PHONE..............................201 784-8188
Joe Staffieri, *President*
Ned Brennan, *Opers Mgr*
Kathy Shubert, *Purchasing*
Maureen Brown, *Accounts Mgr*
Andrew Marquez, *Technician*
EMP: 10
SQ FT: 10,000
SALES (est): 1.8MM **Privately Held**
WEB: www.flavordev.com
SIC: 2869 Perfumes, flavorings & food additives

(G-7623)
GRUPPO EDITORIALE OGGI INC
Also Called: America Oggi
475 Walnut St (07648-1318)
PHONE..............................201 358-6582
Andrea Mantineo, *President*
Massimo Jaus, *Treasurer*
▲ EMP: 40
SALES (est): 3.2MM **Privately Held**
SIC: 2711 Newspapers: publishing only, not printed on site

(G-7624)
H GALOW CO INC
15 Maple St (07648-2003)
PHONE..............................201 768-0547
Fax: 201 768-2311
Michael Galow, *President*
Robert Galow, *Vice Pres*
Karen Galow, *Manager*
EMP: 42
SALES (est): 8.1MM **Privately Held**
WEB: www.hgalowco.com
SIC: 3812 3841 Aircraft flight instruments; medical instruments & equipment, blood & bone work

(G-7625)
INTAROME FRAGRANCE CORPORATION (PA)
370 Chestnut St (07648-2002)
PHONE..............................201 767-8700
Fax: 201 767-8757
D G Funsch, *CEO*
Ron Benton, *Sales Mgr*
Denise Cable, *Cust Mgr*
Kenneth McAlister, *Director*
EMP: 55 EST: 1969
SQ FT: 40,000
SALES (est): 13.8MM **Privately Held**
SIC: 2844 5122 Cosmetic preparations; perfumes

(G-7626)
J B OFFSET PRINTING CORP
475 Walnut St (07648-1318)
PHONE..............................201 264-4400
Roy Steiger, *Principal*
EMP: 4 EST: 2014
SALES (est): 286.4K **Privately Held**
SIC: 2752 Commercial printing, lithographic

(G-7627)
J MEDIA LLC (PA)
Also Called: Luis Network
55 Walnut St Ste 105a (07648-1348)
PHONE..............................201 600-4573
Luis Jimenez,
Maria Alma-Jimenez,
EMP: 6
SALES: 623K **Privately Held**
SIC: 2741 7929 ; entertainment service

(G-7628)
LEMON INC
72 Mohawk Ave (07648-2417)
PHONE..............................201 417-5412
EMP: 4
SALES (est): 250K **Privately Held**
SIC: 2369 Mfg Girl/Youth Outerwear

(G-7629)
MT EMBROIDERY & PROMOTIONS LLC
Also Called: Bon Jour
1100 Blanch Ave (07648-1509)
PHONE..............................201 646-1070
Michael Tcherchian, *Owner*
Michael Tchectchian, *Mng Member*
EMP: 8
SALES: 750K **Privately Held**
SIC: 2395 2261 Embroidery & art needlework; screen printing of cotton broadwoven fabrics

(G-7630)
NICOMAC SYSTEMS INC
54 Summit St (07648)
PHONE..............................201 871-0916
Paolo Nigris, *President*
EMP: 5
SALES (est): 463.8K **Privately Held**
SIC: 7372 Business oriented computer software

(G-7631)
NICOS GROUP INC
80 Oak St Ste 201 (07648-1342)
PHONE..............................201 768-9501
Francesco Nigris, *President*
Agop Shirinian, *Sales Mgr*
Rosanne Cangialosi, *Manager*
Rosanne Candialosi, *Admin Sec*
▲ EMP: 5
SQ FT: 1,500
SALES: 6.1MM
SALES (corp-wide): 73.7K **Privately Held**
WEB: www.nicomac.com
SIC: 3559 Pharmaceutical machinery; carpentry work
PA: Nicomac Srl
    Via Curiel 12
    Liscate MI
    029 542-041

(G-7632)
NORWOOD PRINTING INC
Also Called: Control Group
530 Walnut St (07648-1343)
PHONE..............................201 784-8721
Fax: 201 784-1527
William Cheringal, *President*
Curtis Burns, *Manager*
Tony Sarno, *Director*
Jeff Levine, *Executive*
Susan Drennen, *Admin Sec*
▲ EMP: 10
SQ FT: 21,000
SALES (est): 1.7MM **Privately Held**
SIC: 2752 Commercial printing, offset

(G-7633)
OGGI MEDIA GROUP LLC
475 Walnut St (07648-1318)
PHONE..............................201 358-6582
Andrea Mantineo,
Massimo Jaus,
EMP: 50
SALES (est): 1.9MM **Privately Held**
SIC: 2711 2741 Newspapers, publishing & printing; miscellaneous publishing

(G-7634)
RAINMEN USA INCORPORATED (PA)
Also Called: AAA Umbrella Co
10 Maple St (07648-2004)
PHONE..............................201 784-3244
Fax: 201 784-3242
Jeffrey Nanus, *President*
Kelly Borre, *Regional Mgr*
Adam Scheps, *Vice Pres*
Lisa Hansell, *CFO*
Emily Nagel, *Regl Sales Mgr*
▲ EMP: 60
SQ FT: 60,000
SALES (est): 13MM **Privately Held**
WEB: www.rainmenusa.com
SIC: 3999 Garden umbrellas

(G-7635)
SOLENIS LLC
Ashland Water Technologies
49 Walnut St (07648-1329)
PHONE..............................201 767-7400
Steve Chookazian, *Manager*
EMP: 20
SALES (corp-wide): 263.6MM **Privately Held**
WEB: www.ashland.com
SIC: 2899 Water treating compounds
HQ: Solenis Llc
    3 Beaver Valley Rd # 500
    Wilmington DE 19803
    866 337-1533

(G-7636)
TELESCRIPT INC (PA)
445 Livingston St (07648-1311)
PHONE..............................201 767-6733
Fax: 201 784-0323
EMP: 8
SQ FT: 3,000
SALES (est): 1MM **Privately Held**
SIC: 3663 Mfg Radio/Tv Communication Equipment

(G-7637)
TRU MFG CORP
40 Oak St Ste 2 (07648-1315)
PHONE..............................201 768-4050
Fax: 201 768-3057
Angela Mastropietro, *President*
Paul Mastropaola, *President*
EMP: 23 EST: 1977
SQ FT: 24,000
SALES (est): 4.2MM **Privately Held**
WEB: www.trumfg.com
SIC: 3599 Machine shop, jobbing & repair

(G-7638)
ZENITH MFG & CHEMICAL CORP
Also Called: Zenith Ultrasonic
85 Oak St (07648-1313)
P.O. Box 412 (07648-0412)
PHONE..............................201 767-1332
Michael Pedzy, *President*
EMP: 15 EST: 1937
SALES: 1.5MM **Privately Held**
WEB: www.zenith-ultrasonics.com
SIC: 3699 Cleaning equipment, ultrasonic, except medical & dental

Nutley
Essex County

(G-7639)
AMERICAN DIAGNSTC IMAGING INC
410 Centre St 2 (07110-1635)
PHONE..............................973 980-1724
Sadia Chaudhry, *President*
Danny Chaudhry, *Vice Pres*
EMP: 15
SALES (est): 1.2MM **Privately Held**
SIC: 3841 Diagnostic apparatus, medical

(G-7640)
AMY PUBLICATIONS LLC
11 Robert St (07110-1330)
PHONE..............................973 235-1800
Larry Mills,
Richard Miller,
EMP: 9

▲ = Import ▼=Export
◆ =Import/Export

SALES: 1MM **Privately Held**
SIC: 2721 Magazines: publishing & printing

(G-7641)
ANADYS PHARMACEUTICALS INC
340 Kingsland St (07110-1150)
PHONE..................................972 235-4295
Douglas D Richman, *Chairman*
James Appleman, *Senior VP*
Kevin L Eastwood, *Senior VP*
James L Freddo MD, *Senior VP*
Elizabeth E Reed, *Senior VP*
EMP: 31
SQ FT: 14,000
SALES (est): 5.4MM
SALES (corp-wide): 53.9B **Publicly Held**
WEB: www.anadyspharma.com
SIC: 2834 8733 Pharmaceutical preparations; drugs affecting parasitic & infective diseases; medical research
HQ: Hoffmann-La Roche Inc.
150 Clove Rd Ste 88th
Little Falls NJ 07424
973 890-2268

(G-7642)
BAUMAR INDUSTRIES INC
29 E Centre St (07110-3409)
PHONE..................................973 667-5490
Fax: 973 667-2552
Arthur Bautis, *President*
Daniel Marfino Jr, *Vice Pres*
EMP: 9
SQ FT: 6,000
SALES (est): 843.9K **Privately Held**
WEB: www.baumar.net
SIC: 2819 Industrial inorganic chemicals

(G-7643)
BSI CORP
52 E Centre St Ste 2 (07110-5406)
PHONE..................................631 589-1118
Jeremy Linder, *President*
◆ EMP: 22
SQ FT: 12,000
SALES: 3.1MM **Privately Held**
WEB: www.blockscientific.com
SIC: 5047 3821 Medical equipment & supplies; laboratory apparatus & furniture

(G-7644)
CELTIC PASSIONS LLC
35 Park Dr (07110-2747)
PHONE..................................973 865-7046
Joanne Manley,
EMP: 10
SALES: 500K **Privately Held**
WEB: www.celticpassions.com
SIC: 2051 Bakery: wholesale or wholesale/retail combined

(G-7645)
COZY FORMAL WEAR INC (PA)
Also Called: Uniforms By Cozy
695 Passaic Ave (07110-1229)
PHONE..................................973 661-9781
Fax: 973 661-1736
Ralph Savastano, *President*
EMP: 9 EST: 1968
SQ FT: 8,250
SALES (est): 1.1MM **Privately Held**
WEB: www.cozytux.com
SIC: 7299 5699 2395 Tuxedo rental; uniforms & work clothing; embroidery products, except schiffli machine

(G-7646)
DIETECH SERVICES LLC
40 Holmes St (07110-2616)
P.O. Box 641 (07110-0641)
PHONE..................................973 667-0798
Robin Rodriguez,
▲ EMP: 4
SQ FT: 3,000
SALES: 350K **Privately Held**
SIC: 3554 Paper industries machinery

(G-7647)
GRIFFITH SHADE COMPANY INC
308 Washington Ave Ste 1 (07110-1985)
PHONE..................................973 667-1474
Fax: 973 667-0496
John Griffith Jr, *President*
Mary Anne Griffith, *Vice Pres*
EMP: 4 EST: 1950

SQ FT: 2,250
SALES (est): 741.4K **Privately Held**
WEB: www.nutley.com
SIC: 2591 5719 Window shades; window shades

(G-7648)
HOFFMANN-LA ROCHE INC
340 Kingsland St (07110-1199)
PHONE..................................973 235-3092
EMP: 61
SALES (corp-wide): 53.9B **Publicly Held**
WEB: www.rocheusa.com
SIC: 2834 Pharmaceutical preparations
HQ: Hoffmann-La Roche Inc.
150 Clove Rd Ste 88th
Little Falls NJ 07424
973 890-2268

(G-7649)
HOFFMANN-LA ROCHE INC
500 Kingsland St (07110-1046)
PHONE..................................973 235-1016
Fax: 973 235-0411
Dianne Keel Atkins, *Branch Mgr*
EMP: 25
SALES (corp-wide): 53.9B **Publicly Held**
WEB: www.rocheusa.com
SIC: 2834 Pharmaceutical preparations
HQ: Hoffmann-La Roche Inc.
150 Clove Rd Ste 88th
Little Falls NJ 07424
973 890-2268

(G-7650)
LANXESS SOLUTIONS US INC
10 Kingsland St (07110-1310)
P.O. Box 610, Birdsboro PA (19508-0610)
PHONE..................................973 235-1800
George Cox, *Manager*
EMP: 150
SALES (corp-wide): 11.4B **Privately Held**
WEB: www.cromptoncorp.com
SIC: 2899 Chemical preparations
HQ: Lanxess Solutions Us Inc.
199 Benson Rd
Middlebury CT 06762
203 573-2000

(G-7651)
MANVA INDUSTRIES INC
Also Called: Printing Techniques
48 Franklin Ave (07110-3225)
PHONE..................................973 667-2606
Fax: 973 667-9517
Joseph Vitiello, *President*
Richard Vitiello, *Vice Pres*
Dan Vitiello, *Admin Sec*
EMP: 12
SQ FT: 3,500
SALES (est): 2MM **Privately Held**
SIC: 2752 Commercial printing, offset

(G-7652)
PNC INC
115 E Centre St (07110-3400)
PHONE..................................973 284-1600
Fax: 973 284-1925
Sam Sangani, *President*
Nisarg Gurjar, *Vice Pres*
Ravin Sangani, *Prdtn Mgr*
Janine Likos, *Purch Agent*
Nicole Hurley, *Purchasing*
▲ EMP: 200
SALES (est): 13.7MM **Privately Held**
WEB: www.pnconline.com
SIC: 3672 Circuit boards, television & radio printed

(G-7653)
SECURITY DEFENSE SYSTEMS CORP
160 Park Ave Ste 1 (07110-2808)
PHONE..................................973 235-0606
Fax: 973 235-0132
Donna L Korkala, *President*
Jasmine Demerjian, *Corp Secy*
Garrett Sollitto, *QC Dir*
EMP: 6
SQ FT: 8,500
SALES (est): 590K **Privately Held**
WEB: www.securitydefense.com
SIC: 3844 X-ray apparatus & tubes

(G-7654)
THOMAS GRECO PUBLISHING INC (PA)
Also Called: New Jersey Automotive Mag
244 Chestnut St Ste 4 (07110-4318)
PHONE..................................973 667-6965
Fax: 973 235-1963
Thomas Greco, *President*
Lea Velocci, *Vice Pres*
Donna Greco, *Office Mgr*
EMP: 10
SALES: 1MM **Privately Held**
WEB: www.nutleychamber.com
SIC: 2721 Magazines: publishing & printing

(G-7655)
THOMSON REUTERS CORPORATION
492 River Rd (07110-3609)
PHONE..................................973 662-3070
Jim McHugh, *Branch Mgr*
EMP: 15
SALES (corp-wide): 3.2B **Publicly Held**
SIC: 2741 8111 7372 7383 Miscellaneous publishing; legal services; prepackaged software; news syndicates
HQ: Thomson Reuters Corporation
3 Times Sq
New York NY 10036
646 223-4000

(G-7656)
UNILITE INCORPORATED
151 River Rd (07110-3513)
PHONE..................................973 667-1674
Fax: 973 667-1728
Michael Foti, *President*
Quinto Foti, *Vice Pres*
Mario Foti, *Treasurer*
EMP: 5
SQ FT: 3,000
SALES (est): 746K **Privately Held**
SIC: 3469 Metal stampings

(G-7657)
WAFFLE WAFFLE LLC (PA)
43 River Rd (07110-3411)
PHONE..................................201 559-1286
Sam Rockwell, *Managing Prtnr*
Gennaro Mirabella, *Vice Pres*
Brian Samuels, *Vice Pres*
Justin Samuels, *Mng Member*
Samuel Rockwell,
EMP: 12
SQ FT: 8,000
SALES (est): 2MM **Privately Held**
SIC: 2038 Breakfasts, frozen & packaged

(G-7658)
ZINICOLA BAKING CO
127 King St (07110-3340)
PHONE..................................973 667-1306
John Zinicola Jr, *President*
EMP: 8
SQ FT: 5,000
SALES (est): 500K **Privately Held**
SIC: 2051 5461 Bread, all types (white, wheat, rye, etc): fresh or frozen; bread

---

Oak Ridge
Passaic County

(G-7659)
A GIMENEZ TRADING LLC
5 Wegmann Way (07438-9600)
PHONE..................................973 697-2240
Fax: 973 697-2249
Melissa Laserna, *Mng Member*
Amy Laserna,
EMP: 8
SALES (est): 830K **Privately Held**
SIC: 2013 Sausages & other prepared meats

(G-7660)
DUNBAR CONCRETE PRODUCTS INC
173 Oak Ridge Rd (07438-8911)
PHONE..................................973 697-2525
Walter M Dunbar, *President*
EMP: 19

SALES (est): 2.2MM **Privately Held**
SIC: 3272 3271 Concrete products, precast; covers, catch basin: concrete; sewer & manhole block, concrete

(G-7661)
DURA-CARB INC
204 Chamberlain Rd (07438-8891)
P.O. Box 407 (07438-0407)
PHONE..................................973 697-6665
Fax: 973 697-0279
Scott Beiermester, *President*
Joann Beiermeister, *Corp Secy*
Scott Beiermeister, *Vice Pres*
EMP: 8 EST: 1975
SQ FT: 5,000
SALES: 1.3MM **Privately Held**
WEB: www.dura-carb.com
SIC: 3544 Special dies & tools

(G-7662)
ESCO PRODUCTS INC
Also Called: Esco Optics
95 Chamberlain Rd (07438-8853)
P.O. Box 308 (07438-0308)
PHONE..................................973 697-3700
Fax: 973 697-3011
Gary Steneken, *President*
Linn Rossi, *Purch Mgr*
Ron Pietranowicz, *CFO*
Jason Wickersham, *Marketing Staff*
Deanna Burd, *Director*
EMP: 45 EST: 1946
SQ FT: 20,000
SALES: 8MM **Privately Held**
WEB: www.escoproducts.com
SIC: 3827 Lenses, optical: all types except ophthalmic; mirrors, optical; prisms, optical

(G-7663)
NORTH CHURCH GRAVEL INC
173 Oak Ridge Rd (07438-8911)
P.O. Box 235 (07438-0235)
PHONE..................................201 796-1556
Anthony Dell, *Principal*
EMP: 6 EST: 2005
SALES (est): 560K **Privately Held**
SIC: 1442 Construction sand & gravel

(G-7664)
RAUE SCREW MACHINE PRODUCTS CO
173 Oak Ridge Rd (07438-8911)
P.O. Box 207 (07438-0207)
PHONE..................................973 697-7500
Fax: 973 697-7010
Carl Raue, *President*
Rod Raue, *Corp Secy*
Guy Raue, *Vice Pres*
EMP: 4
SQ FT: 3,200
SALES (est): 544.5K **Privately Held**
SIC: 3599 Machine shop, jobbing & repair

(G-7665)
ROYAL OAK RAILINGS LLC
3 Field Ct (07438-9129)
PHONE..................................973 208-8900
Ernest Intorrella, *Principal*
EMP: 4
SALES (est): 453.8K **Privately Held**
SIC: 2431 Staircases, stairs & railings

(G-7666)
RUNDING LLC
90 Greendale Dr (07438-8971)
P.O. Box 118 (07438-0118)
PHONE..................................973 277-8775
Glen Deleeuw,
Brittney Deleeuw,
EMP: 7
SQ FT: 2,000
SALES: 1.2MM **Privately Held**
SIC: 3441 Fabricated structural metal

Oakhurst
Monmouth County

(G-7667)
ALKALINE CORPORATION
714 W Park Ave (07755-1014)
P.O. Box 306 (07755-0306)
PHONE.............................732 531-7830
Isadore Bale, *President*
Ron Kay, *Vice Pres*
Gabriella Cantella, *Admin Sec*
EMP: 21
SQ FT: 3,300
SALES (est): 3.8MM Privately Held
WEB: www.allergyhelp.com
SIC: 2819 Elements

(G-7668)
EXHIBIT NETWORK INC
434 Brookside Ave (07755-1402)
PHONE.............................732 751-9600
Linda Merrill, *President*
Sammy Merrill, *Vice Pres*
EMP: 15
SQ FT: 30,000
SALES (est): 1.1MM Privately Held
SIC: 3993 Signs & advertising specialties

(G-7669)
FRIENDS HARDWOOD FLOORS INC
60 Monmouth Rd (07755-1631)
P.O. Box 591 (07755-0591)
PHONE.............................732 859-4019
Demir Santos, *Principal*
EMP: 6 EST: 2009
SALES (est): 818.1K Privately Held
SIC: 2426 1771 1752 Flooring, hardwood; flooring contractor; floor laying & floor work

(G-7670)
KWIK ENTERPRISES LLC
Also Called: Vitamins For Life
1806 Bellmore St (07755-2904)
PHONE.............................732 663-1559
Marcelo Gruberg,
Bernard Gruberg,
▼ EMP: 8
SQ FT: 2,000
SALES (est): 8MM Privately Held
WEB: www.vitaminsforlife.net
SIC: 2834 Vitamin preparations

(G-7671)
OCEAN ENERGY INDUSTRIES INC
715 W Park Ave Unit 1073 (07755-8042)
PHONE.............................954 828-2177
Robert Bado, *Owner*
Artem Madatov, *Owner*
EMP: 10
SALES (est): 419.5K Privately Held
SIC: 1629 3699 3511 Dams, waterways, docks & other marine construction; electrical equipment & supplies; wheels, water

(G-7672)
R & K INDUSTRIES INC
Also Called: Waterloov
259 Overbrook Ave (07755-1505)
PHONE.............................732 531-1123
Richard Kuhns, *President*
EMP: 8
SALES (est): 833K Privately Held
SIC: 7299 3089 Home improvement & renovation contractor agency; gutters (glass fiber reinforced), fiberglass or plastic

(G-7673)
SWEET DELIGHT
65 Monmouth Rd (07755-1667)
PHONE.............................732 263-9100
Frida Fitzgerald, *Owner*
Michael Paolantonio, *Owner*
EMP: 10
SALES (est): 350.6K Privately Held
WEB: www.sweetdelight.com
SIC: 2024 Ice cream & frozen desserts

Oakland
Bergen County

(G-7674)
AMERLUX LLC (PA)
Also Called: Amerlux Lighting Systems
178 Bauer Dr (07436-3105)
PHONE.............................973 882-5010
Fax: 973 882-8970
Chuck Campagna, *CEO*
Ted D Enfants, *President*
Dave Silverman, *President*
Frank Diassi, *Chairman*
Don Knickerbocker, *Vice Pres*
▲ EMP: 200
SQ FT: 45,000
SALES (est): 96.4MM Privately Held
WEB: www.amerlux.com
SIC: 3646 Commercial indusl & institutional electric lighting fixtures

(G-7675)
AZEGO TECHNOLOGY SVCS US INC (PA)
103 Bauer Dr Ste A (07436-3102)
PHONE.............................201 327-7500
Bob Gallagher, *President*
John Byrnes, *Vice Pres*
Bob Reynics, *Vice Pres*
Robert Gallagher, *Sales Executive*
Jackie Cohen, *Admin Sec*
EMP: 8
SQ FT: 8,000
SALES (est): 5MM Privately Held
SIC: 3559 Electronic component making machinery

(G-7676)
BLOOMFIELD MANUFACTURING CO (PA)
29 Crosby Ln (07436-3202)
P.O. Box 1266, Caldwell (07007-1266)
PHONE.............................973 575-8900
Fax: 973 575-8663
Susan Masinda, *President*
Linda Heberling, *Vice Pres*
EMP: 15
SQ FT: 30,000
SALES (est): 2MM Privately Held
WEB: www.bloomfield.com
SIC: 3444 Sheet metalwork

(G-7677)
BROWN CHEMICAL CO INC (PA)
302 W Oakland Ave (07436-1381)
P.O. Box 440 (07436-0440)
PHONE.............................201 337-0900
Fax: 201 337-9026
Douglas A Brown, *CEO*
Patrick Brown, *Vice Pres*
Dave Lyle, *Vice Pres*
Doug Blum, *Human Resources*
Tony Gulli, *Sales Staff*
▲ EMP: 35
SQ FT: 46,000
SALES (est): 21MM Privately Held
WEB: www.brownchem.com
SIC: 5169 2869 Industrial chemicals; accelerators, rubber processing: cyclic or acyclic

(G-7678)
CAPTIVE FASTENERS CORP
19 Thornton Rd (07436-3115)
PHONE.............................201 337-6800
Fax: 201 337-1012
Joseph T Alderisio, *President*
Randy Carbora, *Vice Pres*
Ralph Rosario, *Plant Mgr*
Adam Barbieri, *Accounts Mgr*
Diane Struble, *Office Mgr*
▲ EMP: 310 EST: 1974
SALES (est): 43.1MM Privately Held
WEB: www.captive-fastener.com
SIC: 3965 5085 Fasteners; industrial supplies

(G-7679)
COLLAGEN MATRIX INC (PA)
15 Thornton Rd (07436-3115)
PHONE.............................201 405-1477
Bart J Doedens, *CEO*
Peggy Hansen, *Vice Pres*
Debbie Yuen, *Vice Pres*
Aaron Weiss, *Materials Mgr*
Anthony Mazza, *Facilities Mgr*
EMP: 66
SQ FT: 28,000
SALES (est): 14.3MM Privately Held
WEB: www.collagenmatrix.com
SIC: 3841 8731 Surgical & medical instruments; commercial physical research

(G-7680)
CONCRETE ON DEMAND INC
45 Edison Ave Ste 1 (07436-1308)
PHONE.............................201 337-0005
David Gross, *President*
EMP: 15
SQ FT: 10,000
SALES (est): 3.5MM Privately Held
SIC: 3273 4213 Ready-mixed concrete; building materials transport

(G-7681)
CROWN EQUIPMENT CORPORATION
Also Called: Crown Lift Trucks
104 Bauer Dr (07436-3105)
PHONE.............................201 337-1211
Fax: 201 337-5868
Paul Almeida, *Branch Mgr*
Ray Milano, *Manager*
EMP: 61
SALES (corp-wide): 3.1B Privately Held
SIC: 3537 Lift trucks, industrial: fork, platform, straddle, etc.
PA: Crown Equipment Corporation
44 S Washington St
New Bremen OH 45869
419 629-2311

(G-7682)
CUSTOM CREATIONS (PA)
294 W Oakland Ave (07436-1312)
PHONE.............................201 651-9676
Charles Stoppiello, *Owner*
EMP: 8
SQ FT: 1,800
SALES (est): 770.4K Privately Held
WEB: www.custom-create.com
SIC: 2542 Cabinets: show, display or storage: except wood

(G-7683)
DBMCORP INC
32a Spruce St (07436-1811)
PHONE.............................201 677-0008
Dale Sydnor, *President*
Mike Cagney, *General Mgr*
William Pastor, *Vice Pres*
Michael Cagney, *VP Sls/Mktg*
Steve Dans, *Technology*
EMP: 15
SQ FT: 6,000
SALES (est): 3.2MM Privately Held
WEB: www.dbmcorp.com
SIC: 3825 Test equipment for electronic & electric measurement

(G-7684)
DEWEY ELECTRONICS CORPORATION (PA)
27 Muller Rd (07436-1375)
PHONE.............................201 337-4700
Fax: 201 337-3976
John H D Dewey, *CEO*
Edward L Proskey, *Senior VP*
EMP: 24 EST: 1955
SQ FT: 49,200
SALES: 3.3MM Publicly Held
WEB: www.deweyelectronics.com
SIC: 3621 3699 Motors & generators; electrical equipment & supplies

(G-7685)
DEWEY ELECTRONICS CORPORATION
Pitometer Log Division
27 Muller Rd (07436-1375)
PHONE.............................201 337-4700
John Dewey, *President*
EMP: 25
SALES (corp-wide): 3.3MM Publicly Held
WEB: www.deweyelectronics.com
SIC: 3812 Warfare counter-measure equipment

PA: The Dewey Electronics Corporation
27 Muller Rd
Oakland NJ 07436
201 337-4700

(G-7686)
DRS LEONARDO INC
Also Called: Drs Data & Imaging Systems
133 Bauer Dr (07436-3123)
PHONE.............................201 337-3800
David Stapley, *President*
EMP: 28
SALES (corp-wide): 9.2B Privately Held
SIC: 3812 Navigational systems & instruments
HQ: Leonardo Drs, Inc.
2345 Crystal Dr Ste 1000
Arlington VA 22202
703 416-8000

(G-7687)
ENGINEERING LABORATORIES INC
360 W Oakland Ave (07436-1249)
PHONE.............................201 337-8116
Daniel Mason, *President*
Marjorie Mason, *Corp Secy*
Adam Mason, *Vice Pres*
Jason Mason, *Vice Pres*
▲ EMP: 35 EST: 1935
SQ FT: 34,000
SALES (est): 7.2MM Privately Held
WEB: www.plasticball.com
SIC: 3089 Injection molded finished plastic products

(G-7688)
FIMS MANUFACTURING CORPORATION
8 Allerman Rd (07436-3324)
PHONE.............................201 845-7088
Fax: 201 845-8287
Sergio Facchini, *President*
Michael Facchini, *Vice Pres*
EMP: 24 EST: 1962
SQ FT: 20,000
SALES (est): 4.9MM Privately Held
SIC: 3599 Machine shop, jobbing & repair

(G-7689)
FREEDOM PLASTICS LLC
37 Edison Ave (07436-1301)
PHONE.............................201 337-9450
Charlie Romaniello, *President*
EMP: 12 EST: 2002
SQ FT: 25,000
SALES (est): 2.2MM Privately Held
SIC: 2673 Bags: plastic, laminated & coated

(G-7690)
GOLDSTEIN & BURTON INC
Also Called: Nu Products Seasonings
20 Potash Rd (07436-3100)
PHONE.............................201 440-0065
Henry Goldstein, *President*
▼ EMP: 65 EST: 1949
SALES (est): 8.1MM Privately Held
WEB: www.nuproductsseasoning.com
SIC: 2099 Spices, including grinding; seasonings: dry mixes

(G-7691)
HOLIDAY BOWL INC
29 Spruce St (07436-1810)
PHONE.............................201 337-6516
Fax: 201 337-1891
Ed Dougherty, *President*
Gill Doltoy, *Manager*
EMP: 20
SQ FT: 40,000
SALES (est): 1.4MM Privately Held
WEB: www.holidaybowl.com
SIC: 3949 7933 Bowling alleys & accessories; ten pin center

(G-7692)
ID TECHNOLOGY LLC
48 Spruce St (07436-1830)
PHONE.............................201 405-0767
Robert Zuilhof, *President*
EMP: 45
SALES (corp-wide): 641.6MM Privately Held
SIC: 3565 Labeling machines, industrial

HQ: Id Technology Llc
5051 N Sylvania Ave
Fort Worth TX 76137
817 626-7779

(G-7693)
JOHN R ZABKA ASSOCIATES INC (PA)
Also Called: Hospital & Health Care Compen
3 Post Rd Ste 3 # 3 (07436-1610)
P.O. Box 376 (07436-0376)
PHONE..............................201 405-0075
Fax: 201 405-2110
Thomas Cioffe, *President*
Rosanne Zabka, *General Mgr*
Rosanne Cioffe, *Director*
EMP: 11
SALES: 1,000K **Privately Held**
WEB: www.hhcsinc.com
SIC: 2741 Miscellaneous publishing

(G-7694)
LABELING SYSTEMS LLC
48 Spruce St (07436-1830)
PHONE..............................201 405-0767
Fax: 201 405-1179
Robert Zuilhof, *President*
Jack Roe, *Exec VP*
EMP: 45
SQ FT: 44,000
SALES (est): 8.1MM
SALES (corp-wide): 641.6MM **Privately Held**
WEB: www.labelingsystems.com
SIC: 3565 Labeling machines, industrial
PA: Pro Mach, Inc.
50 E Rivercntr Blvd 180
Covington KY 41011
513 831-8778

(G-7695)
METRONIC ENGINEERING CO INC
32 Iron Horse Rd (07436-1306)
PHONE..............................201 337-1266
Fax: 201 337-1256
D Lindsay Conner Jr, *President*
EMP: 17
SQ FT: 7,500
SALES (est): 1.1MM
SALES (corp-wide): 2.1MM **Privately Held**
WEB: www.tracermed.com
SIC: 3599 Machine shop, jobbing & repair
PA: Tracer Tool & Machine Co Inc
32 Iron Horse Rd
Oakland NJ 07436
201 337-6184

(G-7696)
METROPOLITAN VACUUM CLR CO INC
Also Called: METRO ELECTRIC DUSTER
5 Raritan Rd (07436-2709)
PHONE..............................201 405-2225
Fax: 201 357-1640
Jules Stern, *President*
Karen S Cohen, *VP Finance*
Kenneth Stern, *VP Sales*
David Stern, *VP Mktg*
▲ **EMP:** 70 EST: 1940
SQ FT: 60,000
SALES: 11.4MM **Privately Held**
WEB: www.metrovacworld.com
SIC: 3635 3589 3564 3563 Household vacuum cleaners; vacuum cleaners & sweepers, electric: industrial; blowers & fans; air & gas compressors

(G-7697)
MURRAY ELECTRONICS INC
12 Fox Ct (07436-3204)
PHONE..............................201 405-1158
Harold Murray, *President*
Kelly D Smith, *Treasurer*
EMP: 6
SQ FT: 2,400
SALES (est): 629.2K **Privately Held**
WEB: www.murrayelectronics.com
SIC: 3651 5065 7622 Household video equipment; video equipment, electronic; video repair

(G-7698)
NATIONAL ELECTRONIC ALLOYS INC (PA)
3 Fir Ct (07436-1884)
PHONE..............................201 337-9400
Fax: 201 337-9698
Richard Geoffrion, *President*
Karen Bertalotto, *Natl Sales Mgr*
Denise Vandal, *Sales Staff*
Michael Sancetta, *Marketing Mgr*
Marie Gasser, *Office Mgr*
▲ **EMP:** 28
SQ FT: 20,000
SALES (est): 17.4MM **Privately Held**
WEB: www.nealloys.com
SIC: 5051 3341 3339 Steel; secondary nonferrous metals; primary nonferrous metals

(G-7699)
NICKEL SAVERS
90 Andrew Ave (07436-3802)
PHONE..............................201 405-1153
Robyn Sparacio, *President*
EMP: 6 EST: 2011
SALES (est): 467.8K **Privately Held**
SIC: 3356 Nickel

(G-7700)
P M C DINERS INC
Also Called: Paramount Modular Concepts
56 Spruce St (07436-1830)
PHONE..............................201 337-6146
Herbert G Enyart, *President*
EMP: 12
SQ FT: 30,000
SALES (est): 2MM **Privately Held**
SIC: 3448 Prefabricated metal buildings

(G-7701)
PARK PLUS INC (PA)
Also Called: Romax Parking Solutions
31 Iron Horse Rd Ste 1 (07436-1305)
PHONE..............................201 651-8590
Ronald Astrup, *Ch of Bd*
▲ **EMP:** 7
SQ FT: 2,600
SALES: 10.4MM **Privately Held**
WEB: www.parkplusinc.com
SIC: 3559 Parking facility equipment & supplies

(G-7702)
RCM LTD INC
Also Called: Custom Golf
25 Cardinal Dr (07436-3910)
PHONE..............................201 337-3328
Bob Piccoli, *President*
EMP: 5
SALES: 400K **Privately Held**
SIC: 5941 3949 Golf goods & equipment; shafts, golf club

(G-7703)
REY CONSULTING INC
350 Ramapo Valley Rd (07436-2702)
PHONE..............................201 337-0051
Joe Rey, *President*
EMP: 10
SALES (est): 790K **Privately Held**
SIC: 7372 Prepackaged software

(G-7704)
RFF SERVICES LLC
40 Edison Ave Ste C (07436-1303)
PHONE..............................201 564-0040
Boris Burakov, *Mng Member*
EMP: 18
SQ FT: 3,300
SALES (est): 920K **Privately Held**
SIC: 7641 2512 Furniture repair & maintenance; upholstered household furniture

(G-7705)
ROYAL MASTER GRINDERS INC
143 Bauer Dr (07436-3103)
P.O. Box 630 (07436-0630)
PHONE..............................201 337-8500
Fax: 201 337-2324
John Memmelaar Jr, *President*
Rodney Allen, *Vice Pres*
Matthew Sikel, *Controller*
▲ **EMP:** 51 EST: 1946
SQ FT: 24,000

SALES (est): 21.3MM **Privately Held**
WEB: www.royalmaster.com
SIC: 3541 5084 Grinding machines, metalworking; machine tools & metalworking machinery

(G-7706)
TOPCON AMERICA CORPORATION (HQ)
111 Bauer Dr (07436-3123)
PHONE..............................201 599-5100
David Mudrick, *President*
Michael Burenkov, *Project Mgr*
Kathy Lowery, *Senior Buyer*
Annette Baker, *Purch Agent*
James Bashant, *Sales Dir*
▲ **EMP:** 400
SALES (est): 274.1MM
SALES (corp-wide): 1.3B **Privately Held**
SIC: 3845 Laser systems & equipment, medical
PA: Topcon Corporation
75-1, Hasunumacho
Itabashi-Ku TKY 174-0
339 663-141

(G-7707)
TOPCON MEDICAL SYSTEMS INC (DH)
111 Bauer Dr (07436-3123)
PHONE..............................201 599-5100
Shigehiro Ogino, *President*
David Mudrick, *President*
Alena Acosta, *Vice Pres*
Elena Klyachman, *QA Dir*
Ying Dong, *Research*
▲ **EMP:** 100
SQ FT: 85,000
SALES: 74.1MM
SALES (corp-wide): 1.3B **Privately Held**
SIC: 3841 3826 3827 3829 Surgical & medical instruments; analytical instruments; optical instruments & apparatus; surveying instruments & accessories; ophthalmic goods; scientific instruments; engineers' equipment & supplies; optical goods; surveyors' instruments
HQ: Topcon America Corporation
111 Bauer Dr
Oakland NJ 07436
201 599-5100

(G-7708)
TRACER TOOL & MACHINE CO INC (PA)
32 Iron Horse Rd (07436-1392)
PHONE..............................201 337-6184
Fax: 201 337-3156
D Lindsay Conner Jr, *President*
Tina Tomat, *Sales Mgr*
EMP: 15 EST: 1960
SQ FT: 6,000
SALES (est): 2.1MM **Privately Held**
WEB: www.tracermed.com
SIC: 3599 3841 Machine shop, jobbing & repair; surgical & medical instruments

(G-7709)
V G CONTROLS INC
17 Raritan Rd Ste 2 (07436-2743)
P.O. Box 7010 (07436-7010)
PHONE..............................973 764-6500
Vitaly Gelman, *President*
Elena Bubnova, *Manager*
EMP: 9
SALES (est): 3.1MM **Privately Held**
WEB: www.vgcontrols.com
SIC: 3823 Industrial instrmnts msrmnt display/control process variable; engineering services

(G-7710)
ALLIANCE VINYL WINDOWS CO INC
301 Crescent Blvd (08107)
PHONE..............................856 456-4954
Paul Miraglia, *President*
EMP: 35

SALES (est): 6.9MM **Privately Held**
SIC: 5031 3442 Windows; metal doors, sash & trim

(G-7711)
A C D CUSTOM GRANITE INC
1304 Roller Rd (07712-3904)
PHONE..............................732 695-2400
Fax: 732 695-2401
Cynthia Schomaker, *President*
EMP: 13
SQ FT: 13,000
SALES: 2MM **Privately Held**
SIC: 3281 Curbing, granite or stone

(G-7712)
ACCESS RESPONSE INC
Also Called: Access Publishing Co
3321 Doris Ave (07712-4049)
P.O. Box 379, Asbury Park (07712-0379)
PHONE..............................732 660-0770
Jonathan H Weiss, *President*
EMP: 8
SQ FT: 5,500
SALES: 1.5MM **Privately Held**
SIC: 2741 7331 7311 Miscellaneous publishing; direct mail advertising services; advertising agencies

(G-7713)
ADPRO IMPRINTS
Also Called: Budget Banners
1206 State Route 35 (07712-3515)
PHONE..............................732 531-2133
Fax: 732 531-2142
Peter Demaree, *Owner*
EMP: 6 EST: 1982
SALES (est): 673.1K **Privately Held**
WEB: www.adproimprints.com
SIC: 2759 Screen printing

(G-7714)
AKW INC
Also Called: A W Eurostile
1414 Roller Rd Rear (07712-3427)
PHONE..............................732 493-1883
Fax: 732 493-2905
Elizabeth Wyman, *Branch Mgr*
EMP: 7
SALES (corp-wide): 1.4MM **Privately Held**
WEB: www.aweurostile.com
SIC: 3443 5032 Fabricated plate work (boiler shop); tile & clay products; marble building stone
PA: Akw Inc
41 Newman Springs Rd E
Shrewsbury NJ 07702
732 530-9186

(G-7715)
ANDANTEX U S A INC
1705 Valley Rd (07712-3949)
PHONE..............................732 493-2812
Fax: 732 493-2949
Michael G Munn, *President*
Dave Regiec, *VP Engrg*
John Tashjian, *Engineer*
Mary Ann Bradley, *Treasurer*
Mary Vaccarelli, *VP Finance*
▲ **EMP:** 22
SQ FT: 8,800
SALES (est): 5.8MM **Privately Held**
WEB: www.andantex.com
SIC: 3568 Power transmission equipment

(G-7716)
ASBURY SYRUP COMPANY INC
3504 Rose Ave Ste 3 (07712-3983)
PHONE..............................732 774-5746
Fax: 732 775-8881
Anthony Sammarco Sr, *President*
EMP: 15
SALES (est): 3.5MM **Privately Held**
SIC: 5145 5113 2087 Syrups, fountain; toppings, soda fountain; industrial & personal service paper; flavoring extracts & syrups

GEOGRAPHIC

(G-7717)
ATLANTIC PRTG & GRAPHICS LLC
1301 W Park Ave Ste D (07712-3190)
PHONE..................................732 493-4222
Edward Lawrence,
EMP: 5
SQ FT: 13,000
SALES (est): 532.9K **Privately Held**
SIC: 2752 Offset & photolithographic printing

(G-7718)
CAROL PRODUCTS CO INC
1750 Brielle Ave Ste A1 (07712-3953)
PHONE..................................732 918-0800
Fax: 732 918-9051
Carol Hersh, *President*
David Hersh, *Vice Pres*
EMP: 60
SQ FT: 8,700
SALES (est): 7.4MM **Privately Held**
WEB: www.carolproducts.com
SIC: 3569 Filters

(G-7719)
COOPER POWER SYSTEMS LLC
42 Cindy Ln (07712-7250)
PHONE..................................732 481-4630
Paul Gruenebaum, *Manager*
EMP: 200 **Privately Held**
SIC: 3612 Power transformers, electric
HQ: Cooper Power Systems, Llc
2300 Badger Dr
Waukesha WI 53188
262 896-2400

(G-7720)
CROWN PRODUCTS INC
1302 Roller Rd (07712-3904)
PHONE..................................732 493-0022
Daria Tagliareni, *President*
▲ EMP: 35
SALES (est): 3.1MM **Privately Held**
SIC: 2392 5091 3949 Towels, fabric & nonwoven: made from purchased materials; golf equipment; sporting & athletic goods

(G-7721)
D L IMPRINTS
1701 Valley Rd Ste E (07712-3947)
PHONE..................................732 493-8555
Anthony L Lugo, *President*
Peter Demaree Jr, *Vice Pres*
EMP: 4
SALES: 235K **Privately Held**
SIC: 2759 Screen printing

(G-7722)
E L BAXTER CO INC
1227 Deal Rd (07712-2507)
PHONE..................................732 229-8219
Elwood L Baxter, *CEO*
Ron Eberhardt, *President*
Devra Budzik, *Director*
EMP: 15
SQ FT: 20,000
SALES (est): 2.5MM **Privately Held**
WEB: www.elbaxter.com
SIC: 2441 2653 Boxes, wood; boxes, corrugated: made from purchased materials

(G-7723)
EAGLE SYSTEMS INC
Also Called: Graphic Arts Systems
1310 Roller Rd (07712-3904)
PHONE..................................732 226-2111
Michael King, *CEO*
EMP: 5
SQ FT: 5,000
SALES (est): 988K **Privately Held**
SIC: 7336 2679 3353 3469 Commercial art & graphic design; foil board: made from purchased material; aluminum sheet, plate & foil; metal stampings

(G-7724)
ECLEARVIEW TECHNOLOGIES INC
60 Barberry Dr (07712-8550)
PHONE..................................732 695-6999
Esther Soong, *Principal*
EMP: 6

SQ FT: 100
SALES (est): 599K **Privately Held**
SIC: 3663 3572 7371 7372 Radio & TV communications equipment; computer storage devices; custom computer programming services; prepackaged software; computer integrated systems design; administrative management

(G-7725)
EMC CORPORATION
Also Called: EMC Toy
8 The Fellsway (07712-3207)
PHONE..................................732 922-6353
Rachel Presser, *Branch Mgr*
EMP: 79
SALES (corp-wide): 78.6B **Publicly Held**
SIC: 3572 Computer storage devices
HQ: Emc Corporation
176 South St
Hopkinton MA 01748
508 435-1000

(G-7726)
GARDEN STATE IRON INC
3418 Sunset Ave (07712-3925)
PHONE..................................732 918-0760
Greg Andersen, *President*
EMP: 15
SALES (est): 1.8MM **Privately Held**
SIC: 1791 3446 Structural steel erection; ornamental metalwork

(G-7727)
GARDEN STATE PROSTHETICS
3500 Sunset Ave (07712-3955)
PHONE..................................732 922-6650
Michael Dipersio, *Manager*
EMP: 4
SALES (est): 400K **Privately Held**
SIC: 3842 Prosthetic appliances

(G-7728)
I V MILLER & SONS INC
15 Cindy Ln (07712-7249)
PHONE..................................732 493-4040
Fax: 732 493-4044
George Miller, *President*
Jack Miller, *Vice Pres*
Juni Fraser, *Treasurer*
▲ EMP: 18 EST: 1949
SQ FT: 10,000
SALES (est): 2MM **Privately Held**
WEB: www.finalcut.com
SIC: 3479 Painting, coating & hot dipping

(G-7729)
KINETRON INC
1416 Roller Rd (07712-3496)
PHONE..................................732 918-7777
Fax: 732 493-8277
Judith Labrecque, *President*
James Gogan, *Principal*
Timothy Labrecque, *Principal*
EMP: 15 EST: 1960
SQ FT: 5,000
SALES (est): 1.5MM **Privately Held**
WEB: www.kinetron.com
SIC: 3444 Sheet metal specialties, not stamped

(G-7730)
KMSCO INC
42 Cindy Ln (07712-7250)
PHONE..................................732 238-8666
Paul Van Anda, *President*
Alice Van Anda, *Vice Pres*
Bryan Finley, *Technology*
EMP: 12 EST: 1904
SQ FT: 13,000
SALES: 1.2MM **Privately Held**
WEB: www.logoknits.com
SIC: 2299 Fabrics: linen, jute, hemp, ramie

(G-7731)
LEIBROCK METAL PRODUCTS INC
1800 Brielle Ave (07712-3927)
PHONE..................................732 695-0326
William Vogel, *President*
EMP: 8
SQ FT: 10,000
SALES: 1MM **Privately Held**
SIC: 3469 3444 3316 Electronic enclosures, stamped or pressed metal; sheet metalwork; cold finishing of steel shapes

(G-7732)
ORYCON CONTROL TECHNOLOGY INC
3407 Rose Ave (07712-3968)
PHONE..................................732 922-2400
Salvatore Benenati, *President*
Thomas Miller, *Vice Pres*
Vincent Civale, *Treasurer*
David De Longe, *Admin Sec*
EMP: 26
SQ FT: 10,000
SALES (est): 4MM **Privately Held**
WEB: www.orycon.com
SIC: 3544 3823 Dies, plastics forming; temperature instruments: industrial process type

(G-7733)
PACENT ENGINEERING
3430 Sunset Ave Ste 18 (07712-3918)
PHONE..................................914 390-9150
Paul Pacent, *Owner*
William Pacent, *Co-Owner*
EMP: 4
SALES (est): 133.2K **Privately Held**
SIC: 3999 Manufacturing industries

(G-7734)
PEPSI-COLA METRO BTLG CO INC
3411 Sunset Ave (07712-3911)
PHONE..................................732 922-9000
Fax: 732 922-6030
Roseann Isasi, *Sales/Mktg Mgr*
Paul Porcelli, *Sales Staff*
EMP: 160
SQ FT: 3,096
SALES (corp-wide): 63.5B **Publicly Held**
WEB: www.joy-of-cola.com
SIC: 2086 5149 Soft drinks: packaged in cans, bottles, etc.; soft drinks
HQ: Pepsi-Cola Metropolitan Bottling Company, Inc.
1111 Westchester Ave
White Plains NY 10604
914 767-6000

(G-7735)
PETER L DEMAREE
1206 State Route 35 (07712-3515)
PHONE..................................732 531-2133
Peter Demaree Jr, *Owner*
Adam Kenter, *Co-Owner*
Anthony Lugo, *Co-Owner*
EMP: 8
SQ FT: 4,193
SALES (est): 300K **Privately Held**
SIC: 2261 Printing of cotton broadwoven fabrics

(G-7736)
PHILLIPS ENTERPRISES INC
3600 Sunset Ave (07712-3915)
P.O. Box 2286, Asbury Park (07712-2286)
PHONE..................................732 493-3191
Joseph Phillips, *President*
Paul Phillips, *Vice Pres*
Brian Phillips, *Admin Sec*
EMP: 8
SQ FT: 12,000
SALES (est): 1.1MM **Privately Held**
WEB: www.phillipsentinc.com
SIC: 3315 3496 3469 Wire & fabricated wire products; miscellaneous fabricated wire products; metal stampings

(G-7737)
PHOENIX MANUFACTORING INC
1306 Brielle Ave (07712-3902)
PHONE..................................732 380-1666
Richard Sheridan, *President*
EMP: 9
SALES (est): 890K **Privately Held**
WEB: www.phoenixpvcrails.com
SIC: 2821 Polyvinyl chloride resins (PVC)

(G-7738)
Q P 195 INC
Also Called: Quikie Print & Copy Shop
827 W Park Ave (07712-7205)
PHONE..................................732 531-8860
Francine Goldstein, *President*
Gerald Goldstein, *Corp Secy*
Katherine Bosco, *Manager*
John Thompson, *Manager*

EMP: 10
SQ FT: 3,000
SALES: 600K **Privately Held**
SIC: 2752 Commercial printing, lithographic

(G-7739)
Q P 500 INC
Also Called: Quickie Print & Copy Shop
827 W Park Ave (07712-7205)
PHONE..................................732 531-8860
Francine Goldstein, *President*
Gerald Goldstein, *Corp Secy*
EMP: 4
SALES (est): 573.2K **Privately Held**
SIC: 2752 Commercial printing, offset

(G-7740)
RAGAR CO INC
2106 Kings Hwy (07712-7204)
PHONE..................................732 493-1416
▲ EMP: 5
SALES (est): 360K **Privately Held**
SIC: 2499 Imports Exotic Woods

(G-7741)
RELIABILITY MAINTENANCE SVCS
823 W Park Ave Pmb 245 (07712-7205)
PHONE..................................732 922-8878
Alex B Johnston, *President*
EMP: 6
SALES: 150K **Privately Held**
SIC: 8734 3829 Testing laboratories; vibration meters, analyzers & calibrators

(G-7742)
SADWITH INDUSTRIES CORP
1015 Berkeley Ave (07712-3603)
P.O. Box 506, Matawan (07747-0506)
PHONE..................................732 531-3856
Jeff Sadwith, *President*
EMP: 5
SQ FT: 30,000
SALES (est): 537.1K **Privately Held**
SIC: 3582 Commercial laundry equipment

(G-7743)
SCHALL MANUFACTURING INC
3501 Rose Ave (07712-3907)
PHONE..................................732 918-8800
Fax: 732 918-2318
Martin Schall, *President*
EMP: 6
SALES (est): 480K **Privately Held**
SIC: 3599 8742 Machine shop, jobbing & repair; manufacturing management consultant

(G-7744)
SELECTIVE COATINGS & INKS
Also Called: SCI
1750 Brielle Ave Ste B4 (07712-3953)
PHONE..................................732 493-0707
Fax: 732 493-2555
William Zak, *Branch Mgr*
EMP: 7
SALES (corp-wide): 1.9MM **Privately Held**
WEB: www.sci-inc-usa.com
SIC: 2893 Gravure ink
PA: Selective Coatings & Inks, Inc
5008 Industrial Rd
Wall Township NJ 07727
732 938-7677

(G-7745)
SIERRA PACKAGING INC
2106 Kings Hwy (07712-7204)
PHONE..................................732 571-2900
Paul Dorato, *President*
EMP: 12
SALES (est): 1.3MM **Privately Held**
WEB: www.sierrapackaging.com
SIC: 3086 Packaging & shipping materials, foamed plastic

(G-7746)
SPECIALTY LIGHTING INDS INC
1306 Doris Ave (07712-4041)
PHONE..................................732 517-0800
Ben Solomon, *Founder*
Mary Pate, *Regional Mgr*
Neil Goldstein, *Vice Pres*
Jake Metz, *Vice Pres*
AWI Salomon, *Vice Pres*

▲ **EMP:** 30
SALES (est): 86.8K **Privately Held**
WEB: www.specialtylightingindustries.com
SIC: 3646 Commercial indusl & institutional electric lighting fixtures

(G-7747)
STAMPING COM INC
Also Called: Molnar Tool and Dye
3600 Sunset Ave (07712-3915)
PHONE..................................732 493-4697
Chuck Molnar, *President*
EMP: 5 **EST:** 2009
SALES: 1.2MM **Privately Held**
SIC: 3469 Metal stampings

(G-7748)
UTE MICROWAVE INC
3500 Sunset Ave Ste D1 (07712-3956)
PHONE..................................732 922-1009
Fax: 732 922-1848
Lennart H Nilson, *President*
Andrew Owens, *Chief Engr*
EMP: 20
SQ FT: 15,000
SALES (est): 3.2MM **Privately Held**
WEB: www.utemicrowave.com
SIC: 3679 Microwave components

(G-7749)
YEGHEN COMPUTER SYSTEM
Also Called: Y C S
5 Brook Dr Ste 101 (07712-3611)
PHONE..................................732 996-5500
J Yeghen, *President*
Pj N Yeghen, *President*
EMP: 10
SALES (est): 649K **Privately Held**
SIC: 7372 Prepackaged software

Ocean City
Cape May County

(G-7750)
COFFEE COMPANY LLC (PA)
Also Called: Ocean City Coffee Company
928 Boardwalk (08226-3537)
PHONE..................................609 399-5533
Joan Williamson,
Calvin Corvaia,
EMP: 6
SALES (est): 653.1K **Privately Held**
SIC: 2095 5812 Coffee roasting (except by wholesale grocers); coffee shop

(G-7751)
COFFEE COMPANY LLC
Also Called: Ocean City Coffee Company
917 Asbury Ave (08226-3535)
PHONE..................................609 398-2326
EMP: 7
SALES (est): 493.8K
SALES (corp-wide): 653.1K **Privately Held**
PA: The Coffee Company L L C
928 Boardwalk
Ocean City NJ 08226
609 399-5533

(G-7752)
DAIRY MAID CONFECTIONERY CO
852 Boardwalk (08226-3633)
P.O. Box 899 (08226-0899)
PHONE..................................609 399-0100
Gene Arnone, *Controller*
EMP: 6
SALES (est): 370.3K **Privately Held**
SIC: 2064 Candy & other confectionery products

(G-7753)
M C SIGNS
323 Ocean Ave (08226-4034)
PHONE..................................609 399-7446
Fax: 609 926-8759
Mark Crego, *Owner*
EMP: 4
SQ FT: 4,500

SALES (est): 368.7K **Privately Held**
SIC: 3993 Signs, not made in custom sign painting shops; electric signs

(G-7754)
RAILING DYNAMICS INC (DH)
Also Called: R D I
3814 Waterview Blvd (08226-1836)
P.O. Box 319, Linwood (08221-0319)
PHONE..................................609 601-1300
Fax: 609 601-0180
Chris Terrels, *President*
Jonathan Gronow, *Exec VP*
Jay Penney, *Vice Pres*
Joe Russell, *Vice Pres*
Kirk Evanov, *Regl Sales Mgr*
◆ **EMP:** 15
SQ FT: 22,000
SALES (est): 8MM
SALES (corp-wide): 67.8K **Privately Held**
WEB: www.rdirail.com
SIC: 3315 Fence gates posts & fittings: steel
HQ: Barrette Outdoor Living, Inc.
7830 Freeway Cir
Middleburg Heights OH 44130
440 891-0790

(G-7755)
RAUHAUSERS INC
Also Called: Rauhauser's Own Make Candies
721 Asbury Ave (08226-3720)
PHONE..................................609 399-1465
Fax: 609 399-1465
Nancy Bloomdahl, *President*
Donald Bloomdahl, *Vice Pres*
EMP: 13 **EST:** 1959
SQ FT: 1,500
SALES (est): 300K **Privately Held**
SIC: 2064 5441 Candy & other confectionery products; candy

(G-7756)
ROBERT BROWN
Also Called: Browns Awning Co
1125 West Ave 1 (08226-3350)
PHONE..................................609 398-6262
Fax: 609 398-6264
Robert Brown, *Owner*
EMP: 5
SQ FT: 950
SALES (est): 321.2K **Privately Held**
SIC: 2394 Canvas & related products

(G-7757)
SAMPLE MEDIA INC (PA)
Also Called: Ocean City Sentinel The
112 E 8th St (08226-3736)
P.O. Box 238 (08226-0238)
PHONE..................................609 399-5411
David Nahan, *President*
George Sample III, *Vice Pres*
EMP: 34 **EST:** 1881
SALES (est): 3.9MM **Privately Held**
SIC: 2752 2711 Commercial printing, lithographic; newspapers

(G-7758)
SHRIVERS SALT WTR TAFFY FUDGE
852 Boardwalk (08226-3633)
P.O. Box 899 (08226-0899)
PHONE..................................609 399-0100
Fax: 609 398-2075
Meryl Vangelov, *Principal*
EMP: 8
SALES (est): 752K **Privately Held**
SIC: 2064 5145 5441 Candy & other confectionery products; chewing candy, not chewing gum; candy; candy

(G-7759)
TJS ICE CREAM
Also Called: T J'S Ice Cream Plus
100 E Atlantic Blvd (08226-4511)
PHONE..................................609 398-5055
Salvatore Pepe, *Owner*
EMP: 5
SALES (est): 245.6K **Privately Held**
WEB: www.tjsicecream.com
SIC: 2024 Ice cream & frozen desserts

Ocean Grove
Monmouth County

(G-7760)
COMFORT ZONE
44 Main Ave (07756-1546)
PHONE..................................732 869-9990
Steve Mandeville, *Owner*
EMP: 4 **EST:** 2000
SALES (est): 230K **Privately Held**
WEB: www.comfortzoneoceangrove.com
SIC: 7389 Mounting merchandise on cards; stained glass: made from purchased glass

(G-7761)
FRANKLEN SHEET METAL CO INC
122 S Main St (07756-1014)
PHONE..................................732 988-0808
Fax: 732 774-4285
Steve Smith, *President*
Mindy Rebelo, *Office Mgr*
EMP: 10 **EST:** 1976
SQ FT: 2,000
SALES (est): 2MM **Privately Held**
SIC: 3444 Sheet metal specialties, not stamped

Ocean View
Cape May County

(G-7762)
ACTION SUPPLY INC
1413 Stagecoach Rd (08230-1305)
PHONE..................................609 390-0663
Fax: 609 390-2491
Thomas Tower, *President*
John Cox, *Purch Mgr*
John Fennekohl, *Sales Dir*
EMP: 12
SQ FT: 5,000
SALES (est): 4.3MM **Privately Held**
WEB: www.actionsupplynj.com
SIC: 1442 5032 3273 Construction sand mining; masons' materials; ready-mixed concrete

(G-7763)
EARTHWORK ASSOCIATES INC
477 Corsons Tavern Rd (08230-1670)
PHONE..................................609 624-9395
Fax: 609 624-1212
Janet Ay, *President*
Don Ay, *Treasurer*
EMP: 15 **EST:** 1947
SQ FT: 3,500
SALES (est): 1.4MM **Privately Held**
SIC: 1794 1442 Excavation work; construction sand & gravel

(G-7764)
MAGNETRAN INC
24 Elizabeth Ln (08230-1372)
PHONE..................................856 768-7787
George McCauley, *President*
EMP: 10 **EST:** 1979
SQ FT: 17,750
SALES (est): 890K **Privately Held**
WEB: www.magnetran.com
SIC: 3612 Electronic meter transformers

(G-7765)
OCEANVIEW MARINE WELDING LLC
414 Wodbine Ocean View Rd (08230-1078)
P.O. Box 516, South Seaville (08246-0516)
PHONE..................................609 624-9669
Andrew McDevitt, *Managing Prtnr*
EMP: 4
SALES (est): 334.9K **Privately Held**
SIC: 7692 3429 Welding repair; marine hardware

(G-7766)
SEAVILLE MOTORSPORTS
Also Called: Easydook Midatlantic
3024 N Route 9 (08230-1104)
PHONE..................................609 624-0040

Ray Lepf, *Owner*
EMP: 10
SALES (est): 711.9K **Privately Held**
SIC: 3949 Water sports equipment

Oceanport
Monmouth County

(G-7767)
ROY PRESS INC
Also Called: Roy Press Printers
57 Bridgewaters Dr Apt 17 (07757-1155)
PHONE..................................732 922-9460
Fax: 732 922-6860
Ralph Lawrence, *President*
EMP: 6
SQ FT: 6,000
SALES (est): 694.5K **Privately Held**
SIC: 2752 Commercial printing, lithographic

(G-7768)
SHORE DRILLING INC
23 Branch Ave (07757-1016)
PHONE..................................732 935-1776
Kimberly Young Parent, *President*
Gary Parent, *Vice Pres*
EMP: 5
SALES: 700K **Privately Held**
SIC: 1381 Drilling oil & gas wells

Ogdensburg
Sussex County

(G-7769)
AJ SIRIS PRODUCTS CORP
Also Called: Accessories Plus
150 Main St (07439-1175)
P.O. Box 39 (07439-0039)
PHONE..................................973 823-0050
Fax: 973 684-3251
Donald F Ryan, *President*
John F Woods, *Corp Secy*
▲ **EMP:** 25 **EST:** 1918
SQ FT: 20,000
SALES: 10MM **Privately Held**
SIC: 5122 5199 3089 Cosmetics; bags, baskets & cases; caps, plastic

(G-7770)
CLEAR CONTROL LLC
93 Main St (07439-1236)
P.O. Box 155 (07439-0155)
PHONE..................................973 823-8200
Fax: 201 651-9729
Carl Flar, *Owner*
EMP: 6
SALES (est): 585.5K **Privately Held**
SIC: 2759 Screen printing

(G-7771)
GRAHAM GRAPHIC GROUP INC
8 Main St (07439-1206)
PHONE..................................973 827-6177
Fax: 973 209-8894
Robert Graham Sr, *President*
Robert Graham Jr, *Vice Pres*
EMP: 8
SQ FT: 11,500
SALES: 2MM **Privately Held**
WEB: www.grahamgraphicgroup.com
SIC: 3555 3559 Printing trades machinery; recycling machinery

Old Bridge
Middlesex County

(G-7772)
ACCUMIX PHARMACEUTICALS LLC
42 Morris Dr (08857-3575)
PHONE..................................609 632-2225
Pishbhai Patel, *Managing Dir*
Patrick Patel, *Director*
Sam Patel, *Director*
EMP: 8

SALES: 1MM **Privately Held**
SIC: 2834 8731 Pharmaceutical preparations; proprietary drug products; commercial research laboratory

(G-7773)
ALSTROM ENERGY GROUP LLC
11 Jocama Blvd Ste 11a (08857-3521)
PHONE..................................718 824-4901
EMP: 6
SALES (est): 129.4K **Privately Held**
SIC: 3621 Motors & generators

(G-7774)
BARMENSEN LABS LLC
2685 Hwy 516 (08857-2300)
PHONE..................................732 593-3515
Frank V Barone Jr,
EMP: 5
SALES (est): 575.8K **Privately Held**
SIC: 2844 Cosmetic preparations

(G-7775)
BLONDER TONGUE LABS INC (PA)
1 Jake Brown Rd (08857-1985)
PHONE..................................732 679-4000
Fax: 732 679-4353
Steven L Shea, *Ch of Bd*
Robert J Palle, *President*
Allen Horvath, *VP Mfg*
Eric S Skolnik, *CFO*
Jeffrey Smith, *VP Sales*
EMP: 122 EST: 1950
SQ FT: 130,000
SALES: 23.2MM **Publicly Held**
WEB: www.blondertongue.com
SIC: 3663 3699 Television broadcasting & communications equipment; television antennas (transmitting) & ground equipment; security control equipment & systems; security devices

(G-7776)
DELUXE GOURMET SPC LTD LBLTY
Also Called: Bea's Brooklyn's Best
85 Corona Ct (08857-2854)
PHONE..................................732 485-7519
Beatrissa Namm,
EMP: 14
SALES (est): 2MM **Privately Held**
SIC: 2099 Sauces: gravy, dressing & dip mixes

(G-7777)
EDGE VENTURES INC
24 Front Ct (08857-1942)
P.O. Box 3163, Jersey City (07303-3163)
PHONE..................................877 841-1402
Noelle Mingione, *Vice Pres*
Michael Franklin, *Manager*
EMP: 6
SALES (est): 163.3K **Privately Held**
SIC: 2741

(G-7778)
EDWARD BERGER INC
1510 Farrell Ct (08857-3448)
PHONE..................................609 571-9676
Arnold Turok, *President*
Steve Siegel, *Vice Pres*
EMP: 22
SALES: 2.5MM **Privately Held**
WEB: www.edwardberger.com
SIC: 2396 2353 Veils & veiling: bridal, funeral, etc.; hats, caps & millinery

(G-7779)
FORMAN INDUSTRIES INC
Also Called: F I Companies
3150 Bordentown Ave (08857-9703)
PHONE..................................732 727-8100
Fax: 732 727-1881
Scott Forman, *CEO*
Ronald Sherry, *CFO*
EMP: 100
SQ FT: 39,000
SALES (est): 21.8MM **Privately Held**
WEB: www.ficompanies.com
SIC: 8711 2434 1542 1721 Consulting engineer; wood kitchen cabinets; custom builders, non-residential; interior commercial painting contractor; lighting maintenance service; safety inspection service

(G-7780)
GLOBAL COLORANTS INC
5 Macbeth Dr (08857-2709)
PHONE..................................973 751-2227
Iveth Lozano, *President*
Frank Pentz, *Vice Pres*
EMP: 5
SQ FT: 4,000
SALES: 1.5MM **Privately Held**
SIC: 2087 2816 Colorings, bakers'; inorganic pigments

(G-7781)
GOLDEN CHAMPION NORTH AMERICA
1405 State Route 18 # 205 (08857-3719)
P.O. Box 568, Metuchen (08840-0568)
PHONE..................................732 481-9000
▲ EMP: 8
SALES (est): 803.4K **Privately Held**
SIC: 2591 Window blinds

(G-7782)
JUST A TOUCH OF BAKING LLC
3141 Us Highway 9 (08857-2690)
PHONE..................................732 679-5123
EMP: 4
SALES (est): 269.4K **Privately Held**
SIC: 2051 Bread, cake & related products

(G-7783)
M&L POWER SYSTEMS MAINT INC
109 White Oak Ln Ste 82 (08857-1980)
PHONE..................................732 679-1800
Fax: 732 679-9326
Shriram Bagle, *Ch of Bd*
Milind Bagle, *President*
Lalita Bagle, *Admin Sec*
Cathy Vincent, *Admin Asst*
EMP: 25 EST: 1982
SQ FT: 4,200
SALES: 3.7MM **Privately Held**
WEB: www.mlpower.com
SIC: 1731 3625 7629 3643 Electrical work; industrial electrical relays & switches; electrical equipment repair, high voltage; bus bars (electrical conductors)

(G-7784)
MADISON INDUSTRIES INC
554 Water Works Rd (08857-1731)
PHONE..................................732 727-2225
Fax: 732 727-2653
Bruce Bzura, *President*
Joel Bzura, *Vice Pres*
Wayne Jensen, *Plant Mgr*
EMP: 35 EST: 1963
SQ FT: 15,000
SALES (est): 7.3MM **Privately Held**
SIC: 2819 Zinc chloride; copper compounds or salts, inorganic; iron (ferric/ferrous) compounds or salts

(G-7785)
MIDHATTAN WOODWORKING CORP
3130 Bordentown Ave (08857-9703)
P.O. Box 163 (08857-0163)
PHONE..................................732 727-3020
Edmund Greco Sr, *CEO*
Edmund Greco Jr, *President*
Janine Bird, *Vice Pres*
George Greco, *Vice Pres*
Robert Brig, *Project Mgr*
EMP: 50 EST: 1932
SQ FT: 112,000
SALES (est): 10.5MM **Privately Held**
WEB: www.midhattan.com
SIC: 2431 Woodwork, interior & ornamental

(G-7786)
NJ FUEL HAULERS INC
3617 Us Highway 9 (08857-3517)
PHONE..................................732 740-3681
Grigori Bruselovsky, *Principal*
EMP: 4
SALES (est): 213K **Privately Held**
SIC: 2869 Fuels

(G-7787)
OLD BRIDGE CHEMICALS INC
554 Water Works Rd (08857-1731)
PHONE..................................732 727-2225

Bruce Bzura, *President*
Joel Bzura, *Vice Pres*
Wayne Jensen, *Plant Mgr*
Jill Bzura, *Human Res Dir*
Joel Goldschmidt, *Manager*
◆ EMP: 40 EST: 1968
SQ FT: 55,000
SALES (est): 17.4MM **Privately Held**
SIC: 2819 Industrial inorganic chemicals; copper compounds or salts, inorganic

(G-7788)
PFIZER INC
11 Erin Ln (08857-2756)
PHONE..................................732 591-2106
Subhash Aanda, *Branch Mgr*
EMP: 57
SALES (corp-wide): 52.5B **Publicly Held**
WEB: www.pfizer.com
SIC: 2834 Pharmaceutical preparations
PA: Pfizer Inc.
235 E 42nd St
New York NY 10017
212 733-2323

(G-7789)
PKM PANEL SYSTEMS CORP
4420 Bordentown Ave (08857-1738)
PHONE..................................732 238-6760
Fax: 732 238-4095
Wallace Toto, *President*
EMP: 14 EST: 1971
SQ FT: 8,000
SALES (est): 2.3MM **Privately Held**
SIC: 3613 Control panels, electric

(G-7790)
PRIMARY SYSTEMS INC
30 State Route 18 (08857-1420)
PHONE..................................732 679-2200
Fax: 732 679-4040
Eric Alter, *President*
Scott Alter, *Vice Pres*
EMP: 13
SQ FT: 3,000
SALES (est): 3.2MM **Privately Held**
WEB: www.primarysys.com
SIC: 7373 8711 3699 Computer systems analysis & design; systems integration services; engineering services; electrical equipment & supplies

(G-7791)
QUALITY PLUS ONE CATERING INC (PA)
Also Called: Atlantic U S
10 Kerry Ct (08857-2610)
PHONE..................................732 967-1525
Fax: 732 679-7778
Joe Kowalski, *President*
Scott Kowalski, *Vice Pres*
EMP: 4
SQ FT: 7,600
SALES (est): 600K **Privately Held**
SIC: 7389 3589 Coffee service; water filters & softeners, household type

(G-7792)
REP TRADING ASSOCIATES INC
Also Called: Nifty Packaging
4 Jocama Blvd (08857-3513)
P.O. Box 161, Marlboro (07746-0161)
PHONE..................................732 591-1140
Fax: 732 591-8477
Norman Ferber, *President*
Audrey Tick, *Vice Pres*
Nic Kipke, *Sales Mgr*
Robyn Ferber, *Admin Sec*
▲ EMP: 15
SQ FT: 20,000
SALES (est): 2.5MM **Privately Held**
WEB: www.repmarkassoc.com
SIC: 3086 3842 Packaging & shipping materials, foamed plastic; adhesive tape & plasters, medicated or non-medicated

(G-7793)
SUPERIOR SIGNAL COMPANY LLC
Also Called: Superior Smoke
178 W Greystone Rd (08857-3426)
P.O. Box 96, Spotswood (08884-0096)
PHONE..................................732 251-0800
Fax: 732 251-9442
James Kovacs,
▲ EMP: 18 EST: 1943

SQ FT: 8,100
SALES (est): 3.8MM **Privately Held**
WEB: www.superiorsignal.com
SIC: 3829 7549 Measuring & controlling devices; emissions testing without repairs, automotive

(G-7794)
TRI-STATE GLASS & MIRROR INC (PA)
11a Jocama Blvd (08857-3513)
PHONE..................................732 591-5545
Michael Panebianco, *President*
EMP: 5
SQ FT: 7,100
SALES (est): 679.8K **Privately Held**
SIC: 3211 Flat glass

(G-7795)
YONKERS PLYWOOD MANUFACTURING
3130 Bordentown Ave (08857-9703)
P.O. Box 152 (08857-0152)
PHONE..................................732 727-1200
Edmund J Greco Jr, *President*
George Greco, *Vice Pres*
Eugene Zullo, *Foreman/Supr*
Lito Villegas, *Supervisor*
Steve Goldberg, *Executive*
EMP: 25
SQ FT: 112,000
SALES (est): 2.9MM **Privately Held**
SIC: 2435 Panels, hardwood plywood

Old Tappan
Bergen County

(G-7796)
ABC DIGITAL ELECTRONICS INC
Also Called: Automation Dynamics Systems
44 Country Squire Rd (07675-6837)
PHONE..................................201 666-6888
Benjamin K Cheng, *Ch of Bd*
C H Wu, *President*
Yuk Fung Cheng, *Admin Sec*
EMP: 6 EST: 1973
SQ FT: 10,000
SALES: 1.3MM **Privately Held**
SIC: 3825 7629 Test equipment for electronic & electrical circuits; electrical repair shops

(G-7797)
AMERICAN COMPRESSED GASES INC (PA)
189 Central Ave (07675-7399)
P.O. Box 715 (07675-0715)
PHONE..................................201 767-3200
Fax: 201 767-6554
Ray Konrad, *Ch of Bd*
Arthur F Ramsdell Jr, *President*
Roger Hawkes, *Vice Pres*
Adam Konrad, *Vice Pres*
EMP: 21 EST: 1953
SQ FT: 6,000
SALES (est): 32.1MM **Privately Held**
WEB: www.dryicecorp.com
SIC: 5984 3823 Liquefied petroleum gas dealers; industrial instrmnts msrmnt display/control process variable

(G-7798)
ELYMAT CORP
180 Old Tappan Rd Ste 11 (07675-7048)
PHONE..................................201 767-7105
Robert Gardner, *President*
EMP: 20
SQ FT: 3,500
SALES (est): 3.9MM **Privately Held**
SIC: 3669 Intercommunication systems, electric

(G-7799)
ELYMAT INDUSTRIES INC
180 Old Tappan Rd Ste 3 (07675-7052)
PHONE..................................201 767-7105
Fax: 201 767-8440
Robert Gardner, *President*
Roni Kaye, *Vice Pres*
Joanne Fontana, *Buyer*
Sandi Kohen, *Buyer*
Sandy McGrath, *Buyer*
EMP: 20

SQ FT: 3,500
SALES (est): 5.9MM **Privately Held**
WEB: www.elymat.com
SIC: 3669 Intercommunication systems, electric

(G-7800)
PEARSON TECHNOLOGY CENTRE INC (HQ)
Also Called: Pearson Business Services
200 Old Tappan Rd Ste 1 (07675-7005)
PHONE............................201 767-5000
Gloria Samuels, *CEO*
Helene Avraham, *Editor*
Renee Beach, *Editor*
Michael Gillespie, *Editor*
Jay McElroy, *Editor*
▼ **EMP:** 2
SALES (est): 25.3MM
SALES (corp-wide): 5.9B **Privately Held**
WEB: www.informit.com
SIC: 2731 8732 Textbooks: publishing only, not printed on site; business research service
PA: Pearson Plc
Shell Mex House
London WC2R
207 010-2000

(G-7801)
WOLF FORM CO INC
289 Orangeburgh Rd (07675-7484)
PHONE............................201 567-6556
Bruno Ferri, *President*
Wendell Hunton, *Vice Pres*
Lorraine Hunton, *Treasurer*
EMP: 30
SQ FT: 28,000
SALES (est): 2.5MM **Privately Held**
SIC: 3999 Forms: display, dress & show

(G-7802)
WORLDCAST NETWORK INC
20 Foxwood Sq S (07675-7358)
PHONE............................201 767-2040
George Bukhbinder, *President*
Michael Galperin, *Principal*
EMP: 5
SALES (est): 610.6K **Privately Held**
SIC: 3364 Nonferrous die-castings except aluminum

Oldwick
Hunterdon County

(G-7803)
AM BEST COMPANY INC (PA)
1 Ambest Rd (08858-7000)
PHONE............................908 439-2200
Fax: 908 439-3296
Arthur Snyder, *President*
Douglas Woelfel, *President*
Emmanuel Modu, *Managing Dir*
Kim Bjorheim, *Editor*
John Weber, *Editor*
▲ **EMP:** 525
SQ FT: 200,000
SALES (est): 166.9MM **Privately Held**
WEB: www.bestwire.com
SIC: 2731 2721 2732 7323 Books: publishing only; magazines: publishing only, not printed on site; book printing; credit reporting services

(G-7804)
AM BEST COMPANY INC
Am Best Rd (08858)
PHONE............................908 439-2200
Peter Viscomi, *Assistant VP*
Art Snyder, *Vice Pres*
EMP: 500
SALES (corp-wide): 166.9MM **Privately Held**
WEB: www.bestwire.com
SIC: 2731 2721 Book publishing; periodicals
PA: A.M. Best Company, Inc.
1 Ambest Rd
Oldwick NJ 08858
908 439-2200

Oradell
Bergen County

(G-7805)
CHEMSTAFF INC
640 Iroquois St (07649-1222)
PHONE............................201 265-8655
Donald Staff, *President*
EMP: 4
SALES (est): 234.9K **Privately Held**
SIC: 8748 2819 Business consulting; industrial inorganic chemicals

(G-7806)
CHR INTERNATIONAL INC
296 Kinderkamack Rd # 220 (07649-2147)
PHONE............................201 262-8186
Catherine Huang, *President*
Arthur Rosenberg, *Vice Pres*
▲ **EMP:** 5
SALES (est): 1.9MM **Privately Held**
SIC: 5142 2092 Vegetables, frozen; seafoods, frozen: prepared

(G-7807)
COMPUTECH APPLICATIONS LLC
768 Howard Ct E (07649-2419)
PHONE............................201 261-5251
EMP: 5
SALES (est): 274.6K **Privately Held**
SIC: 7372 Prepackaged Software Services

(G-7808)
EMERSON SPEED PRINTING INC
379 Kinderkamack Rd (07649-2141)
PHONE............................201 265-7977
Fax: 201 265-7397
Herb Kassab, *President*
Jane Lennon, *Department Mgr*
EMP: 4
SQ FT: 3,000
SALES (est): 505.9K **Privately Held**
WEB: www.emersonspeedprinting.com
SIC: 2752 Photo-offset printing; commercial printing, offset

(G-7809)
FULCRUM INC
660 Kinderkamack Rd # 203 (07649-1525)
PHONE............................973 473-6900
Fax: 973 777-8302
James Maloy, *President*
Karl Nowosielski, *Vice Pres*
▲ **EMP:** 8
SQ FT: 3,900
SALES (est): 1.3MM **Privately Held**
WEB: www.fulcruminc.net
SIC: 3545 Scales, measuring (machinists' precision tools)

(G-7810)
GLOBAL BEVERAGE CORPORATION
700 Kinderkamack Rd # 314 (07649-1533)
PHONE............................201 599-5925
Danielle Pessolano, *Vice Pres*
▼ **EMP:** 3
SALES (est): 2MM **Privately Held**
SIC: 2086 Bottled & canned soft drinks

(G-7811)
HEAD PIECE HEAVEN
449 2nd St (07649-1715)
PHONE............................201 262-0788
Fax: 201 262-0788
Marcia Morris, *Owner*
EMP: 5
SALES (est): 420.4K **Privately Held**
SIC: 2335 Wedding gowns & dresses

(G-7812)
R T I INC
Also Called: Rti Computer Services
401 Hasbrouck Blvd (07649-2263)
PHONE............................201 261-5852
Richard Tashjian, *President*
EMP: 25
SQ FT: 4,000

SALES: 1MM **Privately Held**
SIC: 3577 5045 5734 7373 Computer peripheral equipment; computers, peripherals & software; computer & software stores; computer integrated systems design; computer peripheral equipment repair & maintenance; computer related consulting services

(G-7813)
S J T IMAGING INC
475 Kinderkamack Rd Ste 2 (07649-1545)
PHONE............................201 262-7744
Harry J Abrahamsen, *President*
EMP: 92
SQ FT: 14,000
SALES: 25MM **Privately Held**
WEB: www.sjtimaging.com
SIC: 7335 2759 8711 Commercial photography; color separation, photographic & movie film; commercial printing; mechanical engineering

(G-7814)
TROPICAL BOTTLING CORPORATION
700 Kinderkamack Rd (07649-1533)
PHONE............................786 636-6169
Erik Brito, *Branch Mgr*
EMP: 10
SALES (corp-wide): 654K **Privately Held**
SIC: 2086 Bottled & canned soft drinks
PA: Tropical Bottling Corporation
8074 Nw 74th Ave
Medley FL 33166
786 636-6169

(G-7815)
WEBER PACKAGING INC
494 Demarest Ave (07649-1703)
PHONE............................201 262-6022
Lisa Weber, *President*
EMP: 4
SQ FT: 3,500
SALES (est): 589.7K **Privately Held**
WEB: www.webdesign.com
SIC: 2653 5113 7336 Boxes, corrugated: made from purchased materials; corrugated & solid fiber boxes; package design

Orange
Essex County

(G-7816)
AMERICAN FOOD & BEV INDS LLC
50 S Center St Ste 20 (07050-3530)
PHONE............................347 241-9827
Mina Georgy,
EMP: 55
SALES (est): 1.7MM **Privately Held**
SIC: 2037 5149 2099 Fruit juices; juices; seasonings, sauces & extracts; vinegar

(G-7817)
BELLEVILLE SCALE & BALANCE LLC
50 S Center St Ste 13 (07050-3530)
P.O. Box 540 (07051-0540)
PHONE............................973 759-4487
Fax: 973 676-9778
▲ **EMP:** 5
SALES (est): 450K **Privately Held**
SIC: 3545 Mfg Machine Tool Accessories

(G-7818)
BERENNIAL INTERNATIONAL
Also Called: Instant Printing
355 Main St (07050-2703)
PHONE............................973 675-6266
Fax: 973 674-2342
Bharati Tolia, *President*
EMP: 4
SQ FT: 1,000
SALES: 500K **Privately Held**
SIC: 2752 7334 Commercial printing, offset; photocopying & duplicating services

(G-7819)
EAST TRADING WEST INV LLC
Also Called: American Traffic & St Sign Co
200 S Jefferson St (07050-1409)
PHONE............................973 678-0800

Fax: 973 674-4111
M G Khaleeli, *President*
▲ **EMP:** 9
SQ FT: 7,500
SALES: 811.7K **Privately Held**
SIC: 3993 5099 Signs, not made in custom sign painting shops; signs, except electric

(G-7820)
LYCIRET CORP
377 Crane St (07050-2602)
P.O. Box 759 (07051-0759)
PHONE............................973 882-0322
Morris Zelkha, *President*
Benjamin Regev, *CFO*
EMP: 46
SQ FT: 120,000
SALES (est): 4.3MM
SALES (corp-wide): 3.1B **Privately Held**
WEB: www.pharmachem.com
SIC: 5169 2834 Chemicals & allied products; pharmaceutical preparations
HQ: Lycored Ltd
60 Hebron Rd.
Beer Sheba
732 327-323

(G-7821)
LYCORED CORP (DH)
Also Called: Lycored USA
377 Crane St (07050-2602)
P.O. Box 759 (07051-0759)
PHONE............................973 882-0322
Doug Lynch, *President*
Rony Patishi-Chillim, *Chairman*
Morris Zelkha, *Chairman*
Michael Reuben, *Vice Pres*
Zev Ziegler, *Vice Pres*
▲ **EMP:** 49
SALES: 35MM
SALES (corp-wide): 3.1B **Privately Held**
SIC: 2023 Dietary supplements, dairy & non-dairy based
HQ: Lycored Ltd
60 Hebron Rd.
Beer Sheba
732 327-323

(G-7822)
METFAB STEEL WORKS LLC
560 Freeman St (07050-1325)
PHONE............................973 675-7676
Fax: 973 675-7446
Edward Huneke, *Production*
Lorraine Murray,
EMP: 19
SQ FT: 5,000
SALES (est): 3.7MM **Privately Held**
SIC: 3441 Fabricated structural metal

(G-7823)
NEWARK TRADE TYPOGRAPHERS
Also Called: Newark Trade Digital Graphics
177 Oakwood Ave (07050-3911)
PHONE............................973 674-3727
Fax: 973 674-8752
Robert Wislocky, *President*
Bob Wislocky, *COO*
Gary Datrio, *Opers Staff*
Gail Wislocky, *Bookkeeper*
EMP: 18 **EST:** 1938
SQ FT: 12,000
SALES (est): 2.1MM **Privately Held**
WEB: www.newarktrade.com
SIC: 2791 Typographic composition, for the printing trade

(G-7824)
PRISM SHEET METAL INC
50 S Center St Ste 9 (07050-3530)
PHONE............................973 673-0213
Nicholas Catone, *President*
Richard Smith, *Vice Pres*
EMP: 6 **EST:** 1997
SALES: 2MM **Privately Held**
SIC: 3444 Sheet metalwork

(G-7825)
RESOLV CORPORATION
164 Elmwynd Dr (07050-3111)
PHONE............................973 220-5141
Saif Aghi, *President*
Syed A Rizvi, *Vice Pres*
▲ **EMP:** 10 **EST:** 1995

SALES (est): 700K Privately Held
WEB: www.resolvcorp.com
SIC: 3544 Special dies, tools, jigs & fixtures

(G-7826)
SAVIGNANO FOOD CORP
Also Called: Andrea Company
107 S Jefferson St (07050-1512)
PHONE..................................973 673-3355
Fax: 973 673-8231
Michael Savignano, President
▲ EMP: 50
SQ FT: 3,000
SALES (est): 9.4MM Privately Held
WEB: www.andreafoods.com
SIC: 2038 5411 Ethnic foods, frozen; grocery stores, independent

(G-7827)
SERRANIS BAKERY
Also Called: Orange Sanitary
114 S Essex Ave (07050-2612)
PHONE..................................973 678-1777
Fax: 973 325-0789
William Serrani, President
Jeanne Serrani, Vice Pres
EMP: 12
SQ FT: 4,800
SALES (est): 1.6MM Privately Held
SIC: 5149 5461 2051 Bakery products; bread; bread, cake & related products

(G-7828)
SPS ALFACHEM INC (PA)
164 Elmwynd Dr (07050-3111)
PHONE..................................973 676-5141
Syed Rizvi, President
EMP: 7
SALES (est): 795.5K Privately Held
SIC: 8733 5047 2865 8731 Biotechnical research, noncommercial; diagnostic equipment, medical; food dyes or colors, synthetic; biotechnical research, commercial

(G-7829)
SUNSHINE METAL & SIGN INC
Also Called: Sunshine Container
461 Maryland St (07050-1415)
PHONE..................................973 676-4432
Fax: 973 676-7392
Jonathan W White, President
Karen J White, Vice Pres
EMP: 9
SQ FT: 8,500
SALES (est): 1.8MM Privately Held
SIC: 2631 2653 Corrugating medium; corrugated & solid fiber boxes

(G-7830)
T & E INDUSTRIES INC
215 Watchung Ave (07050-1717)
PHONE..................................973 672-5454
Fax: 973 672-0180
Edward McEntee, President
Thomas Vanleet, Manager
▼ EMP: 45 EST: 1961
SQ FT: 30,000
SALES: 6.6MM Privately Held
WEB: www.teindustries.com
SIC: 3679 Hermetic seals for electronic equipment

(G-7831)
TRYCO TOOL & MFG CO INC
363 S Jefferson St (07050-1393)
PHONE..................................973 674-6867
Fax: 973 674-1244
Nelson Melillo Sr, President
Jim Heasty, General Mgr
Arthur Stasiuk, General Mgr
Vera Melillo, Corp Secy
Arthur Melillo, VP Mfg
EMP: 41 EST: 1940
SQ FT: 40,000
SALES (est): 10.6MM Privately Held
WEB: www.trycotool.com
SIC: 3544 3469 Die sets for metal stamping (presses); metal stampings

(G-7832)
UNICORP
291 Cleveland St (07050-2817)
P.O. Box 280 (07051-0280)
PHONE..................................973 674-1700

Fax: 973 674-3803
Steven Mercadante, Owner
Chris Mercadante, General Mgr
▲ EMP: 150
SQ FT: 28,000
SALES (est): 22.3MM Privately Held
WEB: www.unicorpinc.com
SIC: 3678 3429 Electronic connectors; manufactured hardware (general)

Oxford
Warren County

(G-7833)
TILCON NEW YORK INC
Also Called: Oxford Quarry
Mount Pisgah Ave (07863)
P.O. Box 120 (07863-0120)
PHONE..................................800 789-7625
Tim Rooks, Plant Mgr
EMP: 45
SALES (corp-wide): 29.7B Privately Held
WEB: www.tilcon.com
SIC: 1429 Trap rock, crushed & broken-quarrying
HQ: Tilcon New York Inc.
    9 Entin Rd
    Parsippany NJ 07054
    800 789-7625

Palisades Park
Bergen County

(G-7834)
BBM GROUP LLC
280 Broad Ave Fl 3 (07650-1574)
PHONE..................................201 482-6500
Chang Sik Kim, President
Dukwoo Lee, Vice Pres
▲ EMP: 7
SALES (est): 1.3MM Privately Held
SIC: 2342 Bras, girdles & allied garments

(G-7835)
BEAR USA INC (PA)
460 Bergen Blvd Ste 370 (07650-2358)
PHONE..................................201 943-4748
Thomas Hong, President
Albert Hong, Vice Pres
Robert Hong, Vice Pres
▲ EMP: 11
SQ FT: 34,000
SALES (est): 1MM Privately Held
WEB: www.bearusa.com
SIC: 2329 2339 3021 Men's & boys' leather, wool & down-filled outerwear; men's & boys' sportswear & athletic clothing; women's & misses' outerwear; women's & misses' athletic clothing & sportswear; shoes, rubber or plastic molded to fabric

(G-7836)
BSC USA LLC
Also Called: World Impro
111 Grand Ave Ste 220 (07650-1035)
PHONE..................................908 487-4437
Namik Shakhpelangov, Mng Member
Fahad Sheikh, Manager
EMP: 10
SQ FT: 2,500
SALES: 1.2MM Privately Held
SIC: 2033 5141 Fruit juices: packaged in cans, jars, etc.; food brokers

(G-7837)
CHENILLE PRODUCTS INC
30 Henry Ave (07650-1114)
PHONE..................................201 703-1917
Alexander Dimant, President
Joan Dimant, Vice Pres
EMP: 11 EST: 1971
SQ FT: 10,000
SALES: 700K Privately Held
SIC: 2397 2395 Schiffli machine embroideries; emblems, embroidered; embroidery products, except schiffli machine

(G-7838)
DELTA CORRUGATED PPR PDTS CORP
199 W Ruby Ave (07650-1088)
PHONE..................................201 941-1910
Fax: 201 941-9399
Walter Lieb, President
Ira Parker, Vice Pres
Andrew Paer, Info Tech Mgr
John Mulvaney, Maintence Staff
▲ EMP: 190 EST: 1959
SQ FT: 150,000
SALES (est): 45.3MM Privately Held
SIC: 2653 Boxes, corrugated: made from purchased materials; boxes, solid fiber: made from purchased materials; display items, corrugated: made from purchased materials; display items, solid fiber: made from purchased materials

(G-7839)
MICROSIGNALS INC
Also Called: MSI
29 Fairview St Ste 1a (07650-1085)
PHONE..................................800 225-4508
Fax: 201 363-0955
Kevin Kidd, President
EMP: 50
SALES (est): 1.5MM Privately Held
SIC: 3663 3677 3612 Radio & TV communications equipment; electronic coils, transformers & other inductors; transformers, except electric

(G-7840)
NORTH JRSEY PRSTHTICS ORTHTICS
39 Broad Ave (07650-1436)
PHONE..................................201 943-4448
Gary Marano, President
Anthony Marano, Vice Pres
EMP: 6
SALES (est): 640K Privately Held
SIC: 3842 Prosthetic appliances; orthopedic appliances

(G-7841)
PALISADES MAGNOLIA PRPRTS LLC
169 Roosevelt Pl Unit B (07650-1152)
PHONE..................................201 424-7180
Jerry Milsap, Principal
EMP: 4 EST: 2015
SALES (est): 101.4K Privately Held
SIC: 2711 Newspapers

(G-7842)
PRECIOUS METAL PROCESSING CONS
430 Bergen Blvd (07650-2320)
PHONE..................................201 944-8053
Randy Epner, President
EMP: 4
SQ FT: 2,000
SALES (est): 400K Privately Held
WEB: www.preciousmetals-pmpc.com
SIC: 3549 Metalworking machinery

(G-7843)
ROYAL CREST HOME FASHIONS INC
170 Fair St (07650-1222)
PHONE..................................201 461-4600
Ron Haboush, President
▲ EMP: 5
SALES (est): 380K Privately Held
SIC: 2392 Shower curtains: made from purchased materials; tablecloths: made from purchased materials

(G-7844)
SUSHI HOUSE INC
Also Called: Gowasabi
225 Commercial Ave (07650-1109)
PHONE..................................201 482-0609
Alex Kim, Ch of Bd
Sung Choe, Senior VP
EMP: 25
SQ FT: 11,000

SALES: 10MM Privately Held
WEB: www.gowasabi.com
SIC: 2091 2092 5812 Canned & cured fish & seafoods; fresh or frozen packaged fish; caterers

(G-7845)
UNITED POS SOLUTIONS INC
Also Called: Up Solution
535 Broad Ave (07650-1607)
PHONE..................................800 303-2567
Lee Chang, Manager
EMP: 4 Privately Held
SIC: 3578 Cash registers
PA: United Pos Solutions Inc.
    255 Route 17 S
    Hackensack NJ 07601

Palmyra
Burlington County

(G-7846)
ARMOTEK INDUSTRIES INC
1 Roto Ave (08065)
PHONE..................................856 829-4585
John Burgess, Vice Pres
EMP: 48 EST: 1946
SQ FT: 70,000
SALES (est): 4.6MM Privately Held
WEB: www.armotek.com
SIC: 2759 Engraving
PA: Pamarco Technologies Llc
    235 E 11th Ave
    Roselle NJ 07203

(G-7847)
DEVECE & SHAFFER INC
400 Legion Ave (08065-2441)
P.O. Box 201 (08065-0201)
PHONE..................................856 829-7282
Fax: 856 829-1779
William De Vece Jr, President
EMP: 7
SQ FT: 5,000
SALES (est): 1.7MM Privately Held
SIC: 2752 2791 2789 Commercial printing, offset; typesetting; bookbinding & related work

(G-7848)
HERCULES WELDING & MACHINE CO
618 W 5th St (08065-2407)
PHONE..................................856 829-1820
Edward Beddall Jr, President
Francis B Beddall Jr, Vice Pres
Kathleen Beddall, Corp Secy
EMP: 4 EST: 1913
SQ FT: 4,000
SALES: 270K Privately Held
SIC: 3599 Machine & other job shop work

(G-7849)
LYDEM LLC
1 E Broad St (08065-1604)
PHONE..................................856 566-1419
Lily Shekhter, Principal
EMP: 5 EST: 2012
SALES (est): 698.4K Privately Held
SIC: 2834 Solutions, pharmaceutical

(G-7850)
PAMARCO GLOBAL GRAPHICS INC
1 Roto Ave (08065)
PHONE..................................856 829-4585
John Stubblefield, Vice Pres
EMP: 10 Privately Held
SIC: 3555 Printing trades machinery
HQ: Pamarco Global Graphics, Inc.
    235 E 11th Ave
    Roselle NJ 07203
    908 241-1200

(G-7851)
THEODORE E MOZER INC
14 E 4th St (08065-1503)
P.O. Box 25 (08065-0025)
PHONE..................................856 829-1432
Fax: 856 829-1865
Theodore E Mozer Jr, President
Thomas Mozer, Vice Pres
EMP: 20

▲ = Import ▼=Export
◆ =Import/Export

SQ FT: 16,000
SALES (est): 3.1MM **Privately Held**
WEB: www.theodoremozer.com
SIC: 3444 3443 3441 Sheet metal specialties, not stamped; fabricated plate work (boiler shop); fabricated structural metal

Paramus
Bergen County

(G-7852)
ADIDAS NORTH AMERICA INC
1 Garden State Plz (07652-2417)
PHONE..............................201 843-4555
EMP: 4
SALES (corp-wide): 25B **Privately Held**
SIC: 2329 Athletic (warmup, sweat & jogging) suits: men's & boys'
HQ: Adidas North America, Inc.
    5055 N Greeley Ave
    Portland OR 97217
    971 234-2300

(G-7853)
ALTERNATE SIDE STREET SUSPENDE
Also Called: Parking Survival Experts
16 Arcadian Way Ste C1 (07652-1291)
PHONE..............................201 291-7878
Fax: 201 291-1615
Glen Bulofsky, *President*
EMP: 5
SALES (est): 617.2K **Privately Held**
SIC: 2721 Periodicals

(G-7854)
AUSOME LLC
80 E State Rt 4 Ste 290 (07652-2661)
PHONE..............................732 951-8818
David Tsu, *CEO*
▲ **EMP:** 6
SALES (est): 121.5K **Privately Held**
SIC: 2064 Candy & other confectionery products

(G-7855)
AZAR INTERNATIONAL INC (PA)
Also Called: Azar Displays
80 W Century Rd Ste 400 (07652-1467)
P.O. Box 567 (07653-0567)
PHONE..............................845 624-8808
Fax: 845 624-7156
Elazar Cohen, *CEO*
Kellita Weber, *Vice Pres*
Loree Cohen, *Controller*
Deborah Lacorte, *Controller*
Jonathan Friedman, *Sales Mgr*
▲ **EMP:** 50 **EST:** 1975
SALES (est): 8.5MM **Privately Held**
WEB: www.azardisplays.com
SIC: 3993 Displays & cutouts, window & lobby

(G-7856)
B&B IMAGING LLC
Also Called: Cartridge World Paramus
733 Bush Pl (07652-4005)
Rural Route 484 Route (07652)
PHONE..............................201 261-3131
Robert Doyle, *CEO*
Yong Cho, *COO*
EMP: 9
SQ FT: 700
SALES (est): 907.7K **Privately Held**
SIC: 3861 5085 7389 5045 Toners, prepared photographic (not made in chemical plants); ink, printers'; printers' services: folding, collating; printers, computer

(G-7857)
BARRINGTON PRESS INC (PA)
Also Called: PIP Printing
37 Spring Valley Ave (07652-2637)
PHONE..............................201 843-6556
Fax: 201 843-6262
Paul Ramirez, *CEO*
Paul E Ramirez, *President*
Linda Ramirez, *Treasurer*
EMP: 11
SQ FT: 6,000

SALES: 1.9MM **Privately Held**
WEB: www.barringtonpress.com
SIC: 2752 Commercial printing, offset

(G-7858)
BERGEN OPEN MRI
1 W Ridgewood Ave Ste G2 (07652-2359)
PHONE..............................201 652-1213
Fax: 201 652-8765
Kim O'Brien, *Principal*
EMP: 8
SALES (est): 1.1MM **Privately Held**
SIC: 3826 Magnetic resonance imaging apparatus

(G-7859)
BNP MEDIA INC
Also Called: Stone World Magazine
210 E Rte 4 Ste 203 (07652-5103)
PHONE..............................201 291-9001
Alex Bachrach, *Branch Mgr*
Heather Fiore, *Manager*
EMP: 5
SQ FT: 3,700
SALES (corp-wide): 154.9MM **Privately Held**
SIC: 2721 Trade journals: publishing only, not printed on site
PA: Bnp Media, Inc.
    2401 W Big Beaver Rd # 700
    Troy MI 48084
    248 362-3700

(G-7860)
CB MARATHON OPCO LLC
Also Called: Rockport
1 Garden State Plz (07652-2417)
PHONE..............................201 843-5416
EMP: 54 **Privately Held**
SIC: 3143 Men's footwear, except athletic
PA: Cb Marathon Opco, Llc
    200 Clarendon St Fl 54
    Boston MA 02116
    617 619-5400

(G-7861)
COLD STAT REFREGIRATION
Also Called: Csr
60 Eisenhower Dr (07652-1401)
P.O. Box 246 (07653-0246)
PHONE..............................201 251-2203
Ian Sarkisian, *President*
EMP: 15
SALES (est): 1.2MM **Privately Held**
SIC: 3585 Refrigeration equipment, complete

(G-7862)
COMMERCE ENTERPRISES INC
61 S Paramus Rd Ste 135 (07652-1266)
PHONE..............................201 368-2100
John Galandak, *President*
Tony Russo, *Exec VP*
Miles Epstin, *Vice Pres*
EMP: 12
SALES (est): 910K **Privately Held**
SIC: 2721 Magazines: publishing only, not printed on site

(G-7863)
CRANIAL TECHNOLOGIES INC
115 W Century Rd Ste 280 (07652-1459)
PHONE..............................201 265-3993
Fax: 201 265-8142
Jeannie Pomatto, *President*
EMP: 50
SALES (est): 3.5MM **Privately Held**
WEB: www.cranialtechnologies.com
SIC: 2241 3841 Hat band fabrics; surgical & medical instruments
PA: Cranial Technologies, Inc.
    1395 W Auto Dr
    Tempe AZ 85284

(G-7864)
CREAMY CREATION LLC (DH)
61 S Paramus Rd Ste 535 (07652-1257)
PHONE..............................585 344-3300
Diederik C Van Dijk, *CFO*
EMP: 8
SALES (est): 844.3K
SALES (corp-wide): 14.2B **Privately Held**
WEB: www.creamy-creation.com
SIC: 2085 Ethyl alcohol for beverage purposes

HQ: Frieslandcampina Ingredients North America, Inc
    61 S Paramus Rd Ste 535
    Paramus NJ 07652
    201 655-7780

(G-7865)
CURTISS-WRIGHT SURFC TECH LLC (HQ)
80 E Rte 4 Ste 310 (07652-2662)
PHONE..............................201 843-7800
Dan McAllister, *Opers Mgr*
Shawn Owens, *Facilities Mgr*
Rosemarie Finizio, *Human Resources*
Ed Weyand, *Accounts Mgr*
David Rivellini, *Mng Member*
EMP: 10
SQ FT: 7,500
SALES: 300MM
SALES (corp-wide): 2.2B **Publicly Held**
SIC: 3398 Metal heat treating
PA: Curtiss-Wright Corporation
    130 Harbour Place Dr # 300
    Davidson NC 28036
    704 869-4600

(G-7866)
DMV-FNTERRA EXCIPIENTS USA LLC
61 S Paramus Rd (07652-1236)
PHONE..............................609 858-2111
Gerhard Pool, *COO*
Hermans Ermens,
◆ **EMP:** 4
SQ FT: 1,982
SALES (est): 640.3K
SALES (corp-wide): 54.9MM **Privately Held**
SIC: 2834 Pharmaceutical preparations
PA: Dmv-Fonterra Excipients Gmbh & Co. Kg
    Klever Str. 187
    Goch 47574
    282 392-8877

(G-7867)
ESSEXUSA LLC
Also Called: Essex Computers
185 N State Rt 17 (07652-2903)
PHONE..............................201 576-0001
Fax: 973 773-2626
Tom Napolitano, *CFO*
Mudit Gupta,
EMP: 15
SQ FT: 4,500
SALES (est): 8.1MM **Privately Held**
WEB: www.essexusa.com
SIC: 3699 7373 Security control equipment & systems; value-added resellers, computer systems

(G-7868)
EUROPEAN IMPORTS OF LA INC
Also Called: Ebocent
25 Columbine Rd (07652-2144)
PHONE..............................973 536-1823
Jorge E Zuniga, *President*
EMP: 15 **EST:** 2013
SQ FT: 700
SALES (est): 818.6K **Privately Held**
SIC: 3911 Jewelry, precious metal

(G-7869)
FANTASIA INDUSTRIES CORP
20 Park Pl (07652-3674)
PHONE..............................201 261-7070
Fax: 201 261-3060
Paul Bogosian, *Ch of Bd*
Archie Bogosian, *Corp Secy*
Juanita Bogosian, *Vice Pres*
John Perrone, *VP Sales*
EMP: 25
SQ FT: 28,000
SALES (est): 10.1MM **Privately Held**
WEB: www.fantasiahaircare.com
SIC: 2844 Hair coloring preparations

(G-7870)
GANZ BROTHERS INC
12 Mulberry Ct (07652-1350)
PHONE..............................201 820-1975
Christopher Ganz, *President*
Jonathan Ganz, *Vice Pres*
EMP: 14 **EST:** 1895
SQ FT: 20,000

SALES (est): 1MM **Privately Held**
WEB: www.ganzbrothers.com
SIC: 3565 5084 Packaging machinery; industrial machinery & equipment

(G-7871)
GASS CUSTOM WOODWORKING
169 Birchwood Rd (07652-1954)
PHONE..............................201 493-9282
Cynthia V Gass, *Principal*
EMP: 4
SALES (est): 446.3K **Privately Held**
SIC: 2431 Millwork

(G-7872)
GENERAL MCH EXPERIMENTAL WORKS
117 Gertrude Ave Ste 1 (07652-2593)
PHONE..............................201 843-9035
Fax: 201 843-9064
Paul Oelkrug, *President*
Regina Oelkrug, *Vice Pres*
EMP: 5
SQ FT: 3,400
SALES (est): 443.6K **Privately Held**
SIC: 3599 Machine shop, jobbing & repair

(G-7873)
GLOBE SCIENTIFIC INC
610 Winters Ave Ste 1 (07652-3911)
P.O. Box 1625 (07653-1625)
PHONE..............................201 599-1400
Fax: 201 599-1406
Milton Diamond, *President*
Lisa Diamond Berger, *Vice Pres*
Dara Diamond, *Vice Pres*
Beverly Diamond, *Admin Sec*
◆ **EMP:** 36
SQ FT: 40,000
SALES (est): 12.8MM **Privately Held**
WEB: www.globescientific.com
SIC: 5047 3841 Medical laboratory equipment; surgical & medical instruments

(G-7874)
GREAT EASTERN COLOR LITH
210 E State Rt 4 Ste 211 (07652-5103)
PHONE..............................201 843-5656
Fax: 201 843-8775
Lou Peretta, *Manager*
EMP: 7
SALES (corp-wide): 16.1MM **Privately Held**
WEB: www.magnapublishing.com
SIC: 5113 2752 Industrial & personal service paper; commercial printing, lithographic
PA: Great Eastern Color Lithographic Corporation
    46 Violet Ave
    Poughkeepsie NY 12601
    845 454-7420

(G-7875)
HAYMARKET MEDIA INC
140 E Ridgewood Ave 370s (07652-3923)
PHONE..............................201 799-4800
Fax: 201 799-4820
Amey Bordikar, *President*
Nanisico Lee, *Owner*
Gemma Boyd, *General Mgr*
Melissa Foster, *Editor*
Rick Maffei, *Editor*
EMP: 5
SALES (corp-wide): 223.6MM **Privately Held**
SIC: 2721 Magazines: publishing only, not printed on site
HQ: Haymarket Media, Inc.
    275 7th Ave Fl 10
    New York NY 10001
    646 638-6000

(G-7876)
INFORMATION TECHNOLGY CORP
121 Gertrude Ave (07652-2515)
PHONE..............................201 556-1999
Cindy Garcia, *President*
Ryan Karl, *Director*
EMP: 5
SALES (est): 544.7K **Privately Held**
SIC: 3575 Computer terminals

(PA)=Parent Co (HQ)=Headquarters (DH)=Div Headquarters
✿ = New Business established in last 2 years
              2018 Harris New Jersey
              Manufacturers Directory
                                              313

GEOGRAPHIC

(G-7877)
JAY-BEE LAMP & SHADE CO INC
Also Called: Liberty Lamp & Shade
540 Salem St (07652-5659)
PHONE....................................201 265-0762
Louis Schurman, *President*
Robert Schurman, *Asst Sec*
EMP: 5 EST: 1956
SQ FT: 12,000
SALES (est): 618.9K Privately Held
SIC: 3645 5719 Lamp & light shades;
lamps & lamp shades

(G-7878)
JE TAIME SHOES
Garden State Plz Mall (07652)
PHONE....................................201 845-7463
David Vigilance, *Manager*
EMP: 5 EST: 2014
SALES (est): 286.1K Privately Held
SIC: 3144 Dress shoes, women's

(G-7879)
JOURNAL NEWS V INC
424 Acorn Dr (07652-4144)
PHONE....................................201 986-1458
Suresh Patel, *Principal*
EMP: 4
SALES (est): 200.5K Privately Held
SIC: 2711 Newspapers, publishing & print-
ing

(G-7880)
KIEHLS SINCE 1851 INC
355 N Highway 17 (07652)
PHONE....................................201 843-1125
Klaus Heidegger, *Branch Mgr*
EMP: 8
SALES (corp-wide): 4.2B Privately Held
SIC: 2834 Pharmaceutical preparations
HQ: Kiehl's Since 1851, Inc.
435 Hudson St Fl 5
New York NY 10014
917 606-2740

(G-7881)
KINGSTER LLC
618 Mazur Ave (07652-1748)
PHONE....................................310 951-5127
Katie Donnelly, *Vice Pres*
EMP: 4
SALES (est): 126.8K Privately Held
SIC: 7372 Application computer software

(G-7882)
**KOCH MDLAR PROCESS
SYSTEMS LLC (PA)**
45 Eisenhower Dr Ste 350 (07652-1416)
PHONE....................................201 368-2929
Chris Loftus, *Project Mgr*
William Morrocco, *Project Mgr*
Wendy Parker, *Research*
Brendan Cross, *Engineer*
Jim Denoble, *Engineer*
EMP: 70
SQ FT: 24,000
SALES (est): 29MM Privately Held
WEB: www.modularprocess.com
SIC: 3559 8711 Chemical machinery &
equipment; consulting engineer; chemical
engineering

(G-7883)
LD ELECTRIC LLC
300 N Farview Ave (07652-3335)
PHONE....................................201 225-1001
Gino Degennaro, *Principal*
EMP: 4
SALES (est): 426.3K Privately Held
SIC: 3699 Electrical equipment & supplies

(G-7884)
LG&P GROUP LLC
Also Called: LG&p In-Store Agency
650 From Rd Fl 5 (07652-3517)
PHONE....................................201 634-9099
Eileen Ford, *Vice Pres*
Sacha Joseph, *Vice Pres*
Tricia Kerr, *Vice Pres*
Erez Rousseau, *Vice Pres*
Sandy Davidson, *VP Opers*
▲ EMP: 38
SQ FT: 6,000
SALES (est): 10MM Privately Held
SIC: 2542 8742 Fixtures, store: except
wood; fixtures: display, office or store: ex-
cept wood; merchandising consultant

(G-7885)
LUNET INC
Also Called: Sir Speedy
300 N State Rt 17 Ste 3 (07652-2918)
PHONE....................................201 261-3883
Fax: 201 261-7162
Louis Sallemi, *President*
Ron Sallemi, *Vice Pres*
Ronald Sallemi, *Vice Pres*
EMP: 7
SQ FT: 2,000
SALES (est): 933.2K Privately Held
SIC: 2752 2791 2789 Commercial print-
ing, offset; typesetting; bookbinding & re-
lated work

(G-7886)
LUX HOME INC
Also Called: Pella Window Store
483 N Rte 17 (07652-3001)
PHONE....................................845 623-2821
Fax: 201 225-1388
Ellen Harmon, *Manager*
EMP: 7
SALES (corp-wide): 47.9MM Privately
Held
WEB: www.luxhome.com
SIC: 5211 2431 Door & window products;
millwork
PA: Lux Home, Inc.
4 Dedrick Pl
West Caldwell NJ 07006
973 575-0200

(G-7887)
METAL IMPROVEMENT CO INC
80 E Rte 4 Ste 310 (07652-2662)
PHONE....................................253 677-8604
David Adams, *President*
Paul Beeksma, *Sales Mgr*
EMP: 5
SALES (est): 287.5K Privately Held
SIC: 3398 Metal heat treating

(G-7888)
**METAL IMPROVEMENT
COMPANY LLC (HQ)**
Also Called: Curtiss-Wright
80 E Rte 4 Ste 310 (07652-2662)
PHONE....................................201 843-7800
David M Rivellini, *President*
Jay McMurray, *President*
Kevin Kobus, *General Mgr*
William Bauer, *Senior VP*
Helmut Watko, *Senior VP*
▲ EMP: 20
SQ FT: 5,000
SALES (est): 212.2MM
SALES (corp-wide): 2.2B Publicly Held
WEB: www.mic-houston.com
SIC: 3398 Metal heat treating; shot peen-
ing (treating steel to reduce fatigue)
PA: Curtiss-Wright Corporation
130 Harbour Place Dr # 300
Davidson NC 28036
704 869-4600

(G-7889)
**MICROWIZE TECHNOLOGY INC
(PA)**
1 Kalisa Way Ste 104 (07652-3538)
PHONE....................................800 955-0321
Robert Gabriel, *President*
Fred Dawli, *Vice Pres*
EMP: 18 EST: 1997
SALES (est): 3.6MM Privately Held
WEB: www.microwize.com
SIC: 7372 Prepackaged software

(G-7890)
MOVADO GROUP INC (PA)
650 From Rd Ste 375 (07652-3556)
PHONE....................................201 267-8000
Fax: 201 267-8077
Efraim Grinberg, *Ch of Bd*
Alex Grinberg, *Senior VP*
Frank A Morelli, *Senior VP*
Mitchell C Sussis, *Senior VP*
Sallie A Demarsilis, *CFO*
◆ EMP: 271
SQ FT: 98,300

SALES (est): 567.9MM Publicly Held
WEB: www.movado-outlet.com
SIC: 3873 3915 7631 Watches, clocks,
watchcases & parts; jewel preparing: instruments, tools, watches & jewelry;
watch repair

(G-7891)
MOVADO RETAIL GROUP INC
650 From Rd Ste 375 (07652-3551)
PHONE....................................201 267-8000
Efraim Grinberg, *President*
Dana McCarthy, *Senior Mgr*
EMP: 6
SALES (est): 815.5K
SALES (corp-wide): 567.9MM Publicly
Held
SIC: 3873 Watches, clocks, watchcases &
parts
PA: Movado Group, Inc.
650 From Rd Ste 375
Paramus NJ 07652
201 267-8000

(G-7892)
MY HOUSE KITCHEN INC
492 N Rte 17 (07652-3004)
PHONE....................................201 262-9000
Okan Kinaci, *President*
EMP: 4 EST: 2016
SALES (est): 217.7K Privately Held
SIC: 2511 Wood household furniture

(G-7893)
**NASSAUS WINDOW FASHIONS
INC**
799 N State Rt 17 (07652-3112)
PHONE....................................201 689-6030
Fax: 201 261-0030
Lewis Sallemi, *President*
Bruce Heyman, *President*
Robert Mittenmaier, *Treasurer*
EMP: 23
SQ FT: 13,800
SALES (est): 2.3MM Privately Held
SIC: 5714 5719 2591 2391 Curtains;
draperies; bedding (sheets, blankets,
spreads & pillows); drapery hardware &
blinds & shades; curtains & draperies

(G-7894)
NEU HAUS INC
1 Garden State Plz (07652-2417)
PHONE....................................201 845-0040
Jessica Cordero, *General Mgr*
EMP: 4
SALES (est): 178.2K Privately Held
SIC: 2066 Chocolate

(G-7895)
NORMAN WEIL INC
Also Called: Norman Weil Textile
140 E Ridgewood Ave # 415 (07652-3917)
PHONE....................................201 940-7345
Norman Weil III, *President*
▲ EMP: 7
SALES: 5MM Privately Held
SIC: 2299 Batting, wadding, padding & fill-
ings

(G-7896)
PAC TEAM AMERICA INC (PA)
205 Robin Rd Ste 200 (07652-1455)
PHONE....................................201 599-5000
Alain Borle, *CEO*
Eric Zuckerman, *President*
Dieter Pasewaldt, *CFO*
Meg Outerbridge, *Sr Project Mgr*
Lance Arcello, *Director*
▲ EMP: 30
SALES: 25MM Privately Held
SIC: 2541 7336 Store & office display
cases & fixtures; package design

(G-7897)
**POWER PACKAGING SERVICES
CORP**
20 Park Pl (07652-3617)
PHONE....................................201 261-2566
Fax: 201 261-4366
Don Simmons, *CEO*
EMP: 3
SQ FT: 400
SALES: 4MM Privately Held
SIC: 3999 Advertising display products

(G-7898)
RADCOM EQUIPMENT INC
10 Forest Ave (07652-5242)
PHONE....................................201 518-0033
AVI Zamir, *President*
Hilik Itman, *Vice Pres*
Ruti Lavi, *VP Human Res*
Ilan David, *Info Tech Mgr*
Yehiel Keren, *Exec Dir*
EMP: 7
SQ FT: 6,500
SALES (est): 1.3MM
SALES (corp-wide): 8MM Privately Held
WEB: www.radcomusa.com
SIC: 3825 3829 3577 Semiconductor test
equipment; measuring & controlling de-
vices; computer peripheral equipment
PA: Radcom Ltd
24 Wallenberg Raul
Tel Aviv-Jaffa 69719
364 550-55

(G-7899)
RENELL LABEL PRINT INC
15 Sunflower Ave (07652-3701)
P.O. Box 403, Saddle River (07458-0403)
PHONE....................................201 652-6544
W Rene Huber, *President*
David Huber, *Vice Pres*
Melody L Huber, *Treasurer*
EMP: 9
SQ FT: 3,000
SALES (est): 980K Privately Held
WEB: www.renell.com
SIC: 2679 2672 Labels, paper: made from
purchased material; coated & laminated
paper

(G-7900)
ROYALE PIGMENTS & CHEM INC
12 N State Rt 17 Ste 203 (07652-2644)
PHONE....................................201 845-4666
John Logue, *CEO*
Lindsay Logue, *President*
▲ EMP: 9
SQ FT: 4,000
SALES (est): 12.1MM Privately Held
SIC: 5169 2869 Chemicals, industrial &
heavy; industrial organic chemicals

(G-7901)
SIMEX MEDICAL IMAGING INC
68 Alden Rd (07652-3731)
PHONE....................................201 490-0204
Abraham Danan, *President*
EMP: 5
SALES (est): 470K Privately Held
SIC: 3845 Electromedical equipment

(G-7902)
**SONY CORPORATION OF
AMERICA**
115 W Century Rd Ste 250 (07652-1459)
PHONE....................................201 930-1000
Fax: 201 358-4058
Keith Anser, *Manager*
EMP: 300
SALES (corp-wide): 80.1B Privately Held
SIC: 3695 3652 3651 3577 Optical disks
& tape, blank; compact laser discs, prere-
corded; household audio & video equip-
ment; computer peripheral equipment;
computer storage devices
HQ: Sony Corporation Of America
25 Madison Ave Fl 27
New York NY 10010
212 833-8000

(G-7903)
SONY ELECTRONICS INC
Sony Medical Systems
115 W Century Rd Ste 2 (07652-1459)
P.O. Box 407, Fort Lee (07024-0407)
PHONE....................................201 930-7030
Tom Danisiewicz, *Vice Pres*
Rick Blazier, *Manager*
EMP: 159
SALES (corp-wide): 80.1B Privately Held
SIC: 3651 Household audio & video equip-
ment
HQ: Sony Electronics Inc.
16535 Via Esprillo Bldg 1
San Diego CA 92127
858 942-2400

GEOGRAPHIC (side tab)

(G-7904)
SONY ELECTRONICS INC
115 W Century Rd Ste 250 (07652-1459)
PHONE..........................201 930-1000
Fax: 201 358-4977
Alec Shapiro, *Branch Mgr*
EMP: 800
SALES (corp-wide): 80.1B **Privately Held**
SIC: 3651 Household audio & video equipment
HQ: Sony Electronics Inc.
16535 Via Esprillo Bldg 1
San Diego CA 92127
858 942-2400

(G-7905)
SOPHION BIOSCIENCE INC
215 College Rd (07652-1400)
PHONE..........................732 745-0221
Torsten Freltoft, *President*
Chris Mathes, *Vice Pres*
Finn Martensen, *Admin Sec*
EMP: 4
SQ FT: 5,125
SALES (est): 2.4MM
SALES (corp-wide): 68.4K **Privately Held**
SIC: 3826 Mass spectroscopy instrumentation
HQ: Sophion Bioscience A/S
Baltorpvej 154
Ballerup
446 088-00

(G-7906)
STERI-PHARMA LLC (PA)
120 N State Rt 17 (07652-2819)
PHONE..........................201 857-8210
Kyle Bailey, *QC Mgr*
Robert Giordanella,
EMP: 56
SALES (est): 18MM **Privately Held**
SIC: 2834 Pharmaceutical preparations

(G-7907)
SUEZ TREATMENT SOLUTIONS INC (DH)
461 From Rd Ste 400 (07652-3526)
P.O. Box 1129 (07653-1129)
PHONE..........................201 767-9300
Maximilien Pellegrini, *Ch of Bd*
Vernon D Lucy, *Ch of Bd*
Paul G Davia, *Senior VP*
Albert A Pristera, *Vice Pres*
Robert W Winslow, *Treasurer*
▲ EMP: 173
SQ FT: 44,000
SALES (est): 152MM
SALES (corp-wide): 86.1MM **Privately Held**
SIC: 3589 Sewage & water treatment equipment
HQ: Suez Groupe
Tour Cb21
Courbevoie 92400
158 812-000

(G-7908)
SWAROVSKI NORTH AMERICA LTD
700 Paramus Park (07652-3557)
PHONE..........................201 265-4888
Fax: 201 265-4990
EMP: 4
SALES (corp-wide): 3.7B **Privately Held**
SIC: 3961 Costume jewelry
HQ: Swarovski North America Limited
1 Kenney Dr
Cranston RI 02920
401 463-6400

(G-7909)
SYNERON
707 Reeder Rd (07652-3721)
PHONE..........................201 599-9451
Richard Partridge, *President*
EMP: 4
SALES (est): 321K **Privately Held**
SIC: 3845 Electromedical equipment

(G-7910)
TESLA INC
Also Called: Tesla Motors
530 N Rte 17 (07652-3006)
PHONE..........................201 225-2544
EMP: 5

SALES (corp-wide): 11.7B **Publicly Held**
SIC: 3711 3714 Motor vehicles & car bodies; motor vehicle parts & accessories
PA: Tesla, Inc.
3500 Deer Creek Rd
Palo Alto CA 94304
650 681-5000

(G-7911)
TWI PHARMACEUTICALS USA INC
115 W Century Rd Ste 180 (07652-1450)
PHONE..........................201 762-1410
Rick Pallokat, *Exec VP*
Rich Franchi, *Vice Pres*
Linda Nesbitt, *Manager*
Kari Olson, *Manager*
Angel Chiu, *Director*
EMP: 6
SALES (est): 294.2K **Privately Held**
SIC: 2834 Druggists' preparations (pharmaceuticals)

(G-7912)
VERSA PRODUCTS COMPANY INC
22 Spring Valley Rd (07652-4300)
PHONE..........................201 291-0379
Fax: 201 843-2931
Larsson Jan, *CEO*
Karl Larsson, *President*
Gramegna Gerry, *Vice Pres*
▲ EMP: 130 EST: 1949
SQ FT: 52,000
SALES (est): 30.4MM **Privately Held**
WEB: www.versa-valves.com
SIC: 3492 Control valves, fluid power: hydraulic & pneumatic

(G-7913)
WIRED PRODUCTS LLC
49 E Midland Ave Ste 6 (07652-2922)
PHONE..........................551 231-5800
Casey Dent,
Mark Barbalat,
EMP: 12
SALES: 100K **Privately Held**
SIC: 3449 Miscellaneous metalwork

(G-7914)
ZALE DELAWARE INC
Also Called: Silver & Gold Connection 1294
35 Garden State Plz K33 (07652-2404)
PHONE..........................201 291-0690
EMP: 5 **Privately Held**
SIC: 3915 Jewel cutting, drilling, polishing, recutting or setting
HQ: Zale Delaware, Inc.
9797 Rombauer Rd
Coppell TX 75019
972 580-4000

(G-7915)
ZWIVEL LLC
45 Eisenhower Dr Ste 220 (07652-1416)
P.O. Box 97, Glen Rock (07452-0097)
PHONE..........................844 499-4835
Scott Kera, *President*
Elizabeth Spence, *Vice Pres*
Jeffrey Woodrow, *Vice Pres*
EMP: 20
SALES (est): 1.2MM **Privately Held**
SIC: 7372 Application computer software

Park Ridge
Bergen County

(G-7916)
AVIDA INCORPORATED
174 Kinderkamack Rd Ste A (07656-1364)
P.O. Box 2 (07656-0002)
PHONE..........................201 802-0749
Eric Kruegle, *CEO*
Herman Kruegle, *Vice Pres*
EMP: 4
SALES (est): 600K **Privately Held**
WEB: www.avida-sw.com
SIC: 3699 Electrical equipment & supplies

(G-7917)
DECORATING WITH FABRIC INC
1 Broadway (07656-2105)
PHONE..........................845 352-5064

Neil Gordon, *CEO*
Gino Ver Eecke, *Manager*
EMP: 6
SALES: 840K **Privately Held**
SIC: 5714 2261 7389 Draperies; decorative finishing of cotton broadwoven fabrics;

(G-7918)
DREAM MAKERS INC
53 Glendale Rd (07656-2011)
PHONE..........................201 248-5502
Susan Gerace, *President*
Lori Fields, *Vice Pres*
Rosina Hirsh, *CFO*
EMP: 4 EST: 2001
SALES (est): 450.5K **Privately Held**
SIC: 5092 3942 3069 Toys & hobby goods & supplies; dolls & stuffed toys; toys, rubber

(G-7919)
FARBEST-TALLMAN FOODS CORP (PA)
Also Called: Farbest Brands
1 Maynard Dr Ste 3101 (07656-1878)
PHONE..........................714 897-7199
Daniel M Meloro, *President*
Chip Jackson, *Senior VP*
Pam Bryant, *Vice Pres*
Robert W Claire, *Treasurer*
Brent Lambert, *Sales Dir*
▲ EMP: 65
SQ FT: 6,600
SALES (est): 14.3MM **Privately Held**
WEB: www.farbest.com
SIC: 2023 2869 5149 5144 Dietary supplements, dairy & non-dairy based; sweeteners, synthetic; specialty food items; poultry & poultry products; food preparations; flavoring extracts & syrups

(G-7920)
FORINO KITCHEN CABINETS INC
33 S Maple Ave (07656-2146)
PHONE..........................201 573-0990
Fax: 201 573-0208
Charles Forino, *President*
Catherine Forino, *Corp Secy*
EMP: 9
SQ FT: 6,000
SALES: 840K **Privately Held**
SIC: 2499 2511 Woodenware, kitchen & household; kitchen & dining room furniture

(G-7921)
GORALSKI INC
Also Called: Goralski Embroidery
4 Marti Rd (07656-1023)
PHONE..........................201 573-1529
Fax: 201 791-0671
Victor F Goralski Jr, *President*
EMP: 25
SQ FT: 6,000
SALES (est): 1.7MM **Privately Held**
SIC: 2397 2395 Schiffli machine embroideries; pleating & stitching

(G-7922)
HALFWAY HOUNDS
108 E Main St (07656)
P.O. Box 132 (07656-0132)
PHONE..........................201 970-6235
Lynn Gregorski, *Principal*
EMP: 4
SALES (est): 227.5K **Privately Held**
SIC: 3999 Pet supplies

(G-7923)
INTERNATIONAL BUS MCHS CORP
Also Called: IBM
225 Brae Blvd (07656-1870)
PHONE..........................201 307-5136
Vince Ippolito, *Manager*
Lynda E McOwen, *Technology*
EMP: 20
SALES (corp-wide): 79.1B **Publicly Held**
WEB: www.ibm.com
SIC: 7372 Application computer software; operating systems computer software

PA: International Business Machines Corporation
1 New Orchard Rd Ste 1 # 1
Armonk NY 10504
914 499-1900

(G-7924)
LETTIE PRESS INC
1 Evelyn St (07656-1804)
PHONE..........................201 391-6388
Theodore W Lettie, *President*
EMP: 5 EST: 1973
SALES (est): 320K **Privately Held**
WEB: www.lettieprell.com
SIC: 2752 Commercial printing, offset

(G-7925)
LEXMARK INTERNATIONAL INC
1 Maynard Dr Ste 3 (07656-1878)
PHONE..........................201 307-4600
Mindy Schlossman, *Branch Mgr*
Kristen De Steno, *Manager*
EMP: 10
SALES (corp-wide): 3.5B **Privately Held**
WEB: www.lexmark.com
SIC: 3577 Printers, computer
PA: Lexmark International Inc.
740 W New Circle Rd
Lexington KY 40511
859 232-2000

(G-7926)
MILO RUNTAK WELDING MACHINERY
174 Kinderkamack Rd Ste A (07656-1364)
PHONE..........................201 391-0380
Milo Runtak, *Owner*
EMP: 5
SQ FT: 1,700
SALES (est): 280K **Privately Held**
SIC: 3599 Machine shop, jobbing & repair

(G-7927)
PLANET ASSOCIATES INC
24 Wampum Rd (07656-2161)
PHONE..........................201 693-8700
William Spencer, *President*
Fred Schlossberg, *CFO*
Ed Robbins, *Info Tech Dir*
Patrick Thoms, *Info Tech Mgr*
Timothy Brockey, *Technical Staff*
EMP: 25
SQ FT: 3,000
SALES (est): 2.5MM **Privately Held**
WEB: www.planetassoc.com
SIC: 7371 7372 8713 7373 Computer software development; prepackaged software; surveying services; computer systems analysis & design; software training, computer

Parlin
Middlesex County

(G-7928)
ASHLAND LLC
50 S Minnisink Ave Ste 2 (08859-1082)
PHONE..........................732 353-7718
EMP: 75
SALES (corp-wide): 3.2B **Publicly Held**
SIC: 5169 1611 1622 2821 Alkalines & chlorine; alcohols & anti-freeze compounds; noncorrosive products & materials; chemical additives; highway & street construction; surfacing & paving; concrete construction: roads, highways, sidewalks, etc.; general contractor, highway & street construction; bridge construction; plastics materials & resins; ester gum; polyesters; thermoplastic materials; heavy distillates; oils, lubricating
HQ: Ashland Llc
50 E Rivercenter Blvd # 1600
Covington KY 41011
859 815-3333

(G-7929)
ASHLAND SPCALTY INGREDIENTS GP
Ashland Aqlon Fnctnal Ingrdnts
50 S Minnisink Ave Ste 1 (08859-1082)
PHONE..........................732 353-7708
Fax: 732 651-6495

Paul Tuck, *Branch Mgr*
EMP: 50
SALES (corp-wide): 3.2B **Publicly Held**
SIC: 2869 2899 2851 Industrial organic chemicals; chemical preparations; paints & allied products
HQ: Ashland Specialty Ingredients G.P.
8145 Blazer Dr
Wilmington DE 19808
302 594-5000

(G-7930)
E I DU PONT DE NEMOURS & CO
Also Called: Dupont
250 Cheesequake Rd (08859-1080)
PHONE...................................732 257-1579
Fax: 732 613-2032
Lou Perricelli, *Senior Buyer*
Adrian Lungu, *Research*
Charles P Richwine, *Corp Comm Staff*
Toichi Hamajima, *Branch Mgr*
Bob Peyton, *Manager*
EMP: 50
SALES (corp-wide): 62.4B **Publicly Held**
WEB: www.dupont.com
SIC: 2819 2851 2796 Industrial inorganic chemicals; paints & allied products; platemaking services
HQ: E. I. Du Pont De Nemours And Company
974 Centre Rd
Wilmington DE 19805
302 774-1000

(G-7931)
HITACHI CHEM DUPONT MICROSYST (PA)
Also Called: Hd Microsystems
250 Cheesequake Rd (08859-1080)
PHONE...................................732 613-2404
Toichi Hamajima, *President*
Steve Anderson, *Business Mgr*
Ariel Hernandez, *Engineer*
Hitcahi Chemicals,
Dupont Industries,
▲ EMP: 32
SALES (est): 41.7MM **Privately Held**
WEB: www.hdmicrosystems.com
SIC: 2821 Polyimides (skybond, kaplon)

(G-7932)
INDUSTRIAL SUMMIT TECH CORP (HQ)
Also Called: I.S.t
250 Cheesequake Rd (08859-1080)
PHONE...................................732 238-2211
Fax: 732 238-2369
Yoshi Haramo, *CEO*
Baba Mohammed, *Engineer*
▲ EMP: 32
SALES (est): 9.7MM **Privately Held**
SIC: 2899 2851 Chemical preparations; paints & allied products
PA: I.S.T Corporation
5-13-13, Ichiriyama
Otsu SGA
775 432-211

(G-7933)
JOHN E HERBST HEATING & COOLG
Also Called: Herbst John E Heating & Coolg
3143 Bordentown Ave 2b (08859-1163)
PHONE...................................732 721-0088
John E Herbst, *President*
EMP: 4 EST: 1973
SQ FT: 2,000
SALES: 450K **Privately Held**
SIC: 1711 3444 Warm air heating & air conditioning contractor; ventilation & duct work contractor; sheet metalwork

(G-7934)
JOY-REI ENTERPRISES INC
Also Called: Joyrei Enterprises
3143 Bordentown Ave 5b (08859-1163)
P.O. Box 260 (08859-0260)
PHONE...................................732 727-0742
Fax: 732 727-0773
James Reising, *President*
EMP: 9
SQ FT: 10,000
SALES (est): 770K **Privately Held**
SIC: 3542 3469 Mechanical (pneumatic or hydraulic) metal forming machines; machine parts, stamped or pressed metal

(G-7935)
MADISON PARK VOLUNTEER FIRE CO
3011 Cheesequake Rd (08859-1247)
PHONE...................................732 727-1143
Fax: 732 316-2660
Mark Lebowitz, *Principal*
Nicholas Giugno, *Vice Pres*
Jim Ross, *Treasurer*
Anthony Guarnera, *Admin Sec*
EMP: 40
SQ FT: 12,000
SALES: 80.3K **Privately Held**
SIC: 3569 Firefighting apparatus & related equipment

(G-7936)
XCHANGE SOFTWARE INC
499 Ernston Rd Ste A7 (08859-1406)
PHONE...................................732 444-6666
Prabhaka Reddy, *President*
EMP: 42
SQ FT: 2,000
SALES (est): 1.8MM **Privately Held**
SIC: 7372 Application computer software

Parsippany
Morris County

(G-7937)
42 DESIGN SQUARE LLC
350 Parsippany Rd Apt 128 (07054-5162)
PHONE...................................888 272-5979
Sapna Sheth, *Director*
Arpita Sheth,
EMP: 15
SALES: 500K **Privately Held**
SIC: 7336 8742 2721 Commercial art & graphic design; training & development consultant; periodicals

(G-7938)
ACROW CORPORATION OF AMERICA (PA)
181 New Rd Ste 202 (07054-5645)
PHONE...................................973 244-0080
Fax: 973 244-0085
William Killeen, *President*
Mark Joosten, *President*
Kenneth J Scott, *President*
Paul Sullivan, *Senior VP*
Scott Patterson, *Chief Engr*
◆ EMP: 30
SQ FT: 50,000
SALES (est): 39.9MM **Privately Held**
WEB: www.acrowusa.com
SIC: 3441 8711 Fabricated structural metal; construction & civil engineering

(G-7939)
ACTAVIS LABORATORIES FL INC (DH)
400 Interpace Pkwy Ste A1 (07054-1119)
PHONE...................................862 261-7000
Paul Bisaro, *CEO*
David A Buchen, *Senior VP*
Thomas Giordano, *Senior VP*
Todd Joyce, *CFO*
Brett W Hagadorn, *Asst Sec*
EMP: 5 EST: 2002
SALES (est): 39.4MM **Privately Held**
SIC: 2834 Pharmaceutical preparations

(G-7940)
ACTAVIS PHARMA INC (DH)
400 Interpace Pkwy Ste A1 (07054-1119)
PHONE...................................862 261-7000
Paul M Bisaro, *CEO*
Carol Yeomans, *Vice Pres*
Ken Indahl, *QC Mgr*
Scott Sharp, *QC Mgr*
Bassil Bardaghji, *Engineer*
EMP: 102
SALES (est): 1.8B **Privately Held**
SIC: 2834 Pharmaceutical preparations

(G-7941)
ADVANSIX INC (PA)
300 Kimball Dr Ste 101 (07054-2186)
PHONE...................................973 526-1800
Erin N Kane, *President*
Hans Quitmeyer, *Senior VP*

Christopher Gramm, *Vice Pres*
Michael Preston, *CFO*
Darrell Hughes, *Bd of Directors*
EMP: 277
SALES: 1.4B **Publicly Held**
SIC: 2899 2821 5162 Chemical preparations; plastics materials & resins; resins

(G-7942)
ALFRED DUNNER INC
200 Walsh Dr (07054-1044)
PHONE...................................212 944-6660
Fax: 973 331-9629
Mary Givnish, *Production*
Ray Discher, *Manager*
EMP: 100
SQ FT: 90,000
SALES (corp-wide): 70.5MM **Privately Held**
WEB: www.alfreddunner.com
SIC: 4225 2339 General warehousing & storage; women's & misses' outerwear
PA: Alfred Dunner, Inc.
1333 Broadway Fl 11
New York NY 10018
212 478-4300

(G-7943)
ALLERGAN HOLDCO US INC (HQ)
400 Interpace Pkwy Ste D (07054-1118)
PHONE...................................862 261-7000
Stephen M Kaufhold, *Treasurer*
EMP: 0
SALES (est): 24.4MM **Privately Held**
SIC: 6719 3841 Investment holding companies, except banks; surgical & medical instruments

(G-7944)
ALLSTATE CAN CORPORATION
Also Called: Think Tin
1 Woodhollow Rd (07054-2821)
PHONE...................................973 560-9030
Fax: 973 560-9217
David West, *President*
Richard Papera, *President*
Louis Papera, *Vice Pres*
Stan Cherry, *Plant Mgr*
Bob Cucci, *Opers Mgr*
▲ EMP: 86
SQ FT: 135,000
SALES (est): 26MM **Privately Held**
WEB: www.allstatecan.com
SIC: 3411 Food containers, metal

(G-7945)
AMG INTERNATIONAL INC
Also Called: Freeman Products
71 Walsh Dr (07054-1010)
PHONE...................................404 297-9083
Terry Tucker, *Manager*
EMP: 4
SALES (est): 509.1K **Privately Held**
SIC: 3914 Trophies
PA: Amg International Inc
71 Walsh Dr Ste 101
Parsippany NJ 07054

(G-7946)
AMG INTERNATIONAL INC (PA)
Also Called: Freeman Products Worldwide
71 Walsh Dr Ste 101 (07054-1010)
PHONE...................................201 475-4800
Jean F Lefebvre, *CEO*
George Ercolino, *President*
◆ EMP: 78
SALES (est): 12.1MM **Privately Held**
SIC: 3914 Trophies

(G-7947)
APHENA PHRMA SLUTIONS - NJ LLC
2 Cranberry Rd Unit A3 (07054-1053)
PHONE...................................973 947-5441
EMP: 91
SQ FT: 27,680
SALES (est): 3MM **Privately Held**
SIC: 2834 Mfg Pharmaceutical Preparations

(G-7948)
APTALIS PHARMA LLC
400 Interpace Pkwy Ste A1 (07054-1119)
PHONE...................................862 261-7000
Frank Verwiel, *CEO*

EMP: 441 **Privately Held**
SIC: 2834 Pharmaceutical preparations
HQ: Aptalis Pharma, Llc
22 Inverness Center Pkwy # 310
Birmingham AL 35242

(G-7949)
AROUND CLOCK SWEEPING LLC
45 Essex Rd (07054-2662)
PHONE...................................973 887-1144
Ronald A Natoli, *Principal*
EMP: 5
SALES (est): 15K **Privately Held**
SIC: 3991 Street sweeping brooms, hand or machine

(G-7950)
ARTLINE HEAT TRANSFER INC
2 Eastmans Rd (07054-3703)
PHONE...................................973 599-0104
Simone Parisi, *President*
EMP: 10
SALES (est): 930K **Privately Held**
SIC: 3999 Heating pads, nonelectric

(G-7951)
ASCEND LABORATORIES LLC
339 Jefferson Rd Ste 101 (07054-3707)
PHONE...................................201 476-1977
Venkatesh Srinivasan, *President*
Allen Bagatsing, *Principal*
Schuyler Vanwinkle, *Senior VP*
John Dillaway, *Vice Pres*
Peter Licata, *Vice Pres*
EMP: 25
SQ FT: 3,600
SALES (est): 3.1MM
SALES (corp-wide): 667.3MM **Privately Held**
WEB: www.ascendlaboratories.com
SIC: 2834 Pharmaceutical preparations
PA: Alkem Laboratories Limited
Devashish Building, Alkem House
Mumbai MH 40001
223 982-9999

(G-7952)
ASCENSIA DIABETES CARE US INC (DH)
Also Called: Contour Next
5 Woodhollow Rd Ste 3 (07054-2832)
PHONE...................................973 560-6500
Michael Kloss, *CEO*
Tetsuyuki Watanabe, *President*
Steven Lynum, *Vice Pres*
Hiromichi Yoshitake, *Vice Pres*
Masashi Inada, *Treasurer*
EMP: 150 EST: 2016
SALES: 400MM **Publicly Held**
SIC: 5047 2835 3841 Electro-medical equipment; in vitro diagnostics; diagnostic apparatus, medical
HQ: Ascensia Diabetes Care Holdings Ag
Peter Merian-Strasse 90
Basel BS 4052
444 658-355

(G-7953)
ASCO VALVE LLC
7 Eastmans Rd (07054-3702)
PHONE...................................973 386-9000
Robert Rafter, *Principal*
EMP: 25
SALES (corp-wide): 407.8MM **Privately Held**
WEB: www.rapcoassoc.com
SIC: 3443 Fabricated plate work (boiler shop)
PA: Asco Valve, Llc
50-60 Hanover Rd
Florham Park NJ 07932
973 966-2437

(G-7954)
ATLAS COPCO HURRICANE LLC
7 Campus Dr Ste 200 (07054-4413)
PHONE...................................800 754-7408
Ronnie Leten, *CEO*
Annika Berglund, *Senior VP*
Johan Halling, *Senior VP*
Hkan Osvald, *Senior VP*
Mats Rahmstrom, *Senior VP*
◆ EMP: 90

SALES (est): 14.7MM
SALES (corp-wide): 13.8B **Privately Held**
SIC: 3563 Air & gas compressors
HQ: Atlas Copco North America Llc
7 Campus Dr Ste 200
Parsippany NJ 07054
973 397-3400

(G-7955)
ATLAS COPCO NORTH AMERICA LLC (DH)
7 Campus Dr Ste 200 (07054-4413)
PHONE...................973 397-3400
Mark Trent, *Asst Controller*
Eric Moore, *Mng Member*
EMP: 1
SALES (est): 1.5B
SALES (corp-wide): 13.8B **Privately Held**
SIC: 3312 Tool & die steel

(G-7956)
B&G FOODS INC (PA)
4 Gatehall Dr Ste 110 (07054-4522)
PHONE...................973 401-6500
Fax: 973 630-6550
Stephen C Sherrill, *Ch of Bd*
Robert C Cantwell, *President*
Kenneth G Romanzi, *COO*
Brian Spitser, *Counsel*
Eric H Hart, *Exec VP*
EMP: 277 EST: 1996
SALES (est): 1.6B **Publicly Held**
WEB: www.bgfoods.com
SIC: 2013 2032 2033 2035 Canned meats (except baby food) from purchased meat; beans & bean sprouts, canned, jarred, etc.; Mexican foods: packaged in cans, jars, etc.; canned fruits & specialties; pickles, sauces & salad dressings; syrups; seasonings & spices

(G-7957)
B&G FOODS INC
4 Gatehall Dr Ste 110 (07054-4522)
PHONE...................973 401-6500
David L Wenner, *President*
EMP: 256
SALES (corp-wide): 1.6B **Publicly Held**
WEB: www.bgfoods.com
SIC: 2013 2032 2033 2035 Canned meats (except baby food) from purchased meat; beans & bean sprouts, canned, jarred, etc.; Mexican foods: packaged in cans, jars, etc.; canned fruits & specialties; pickles, sauces & salad dressings; syrups; seasonings & spices
PA: B&G Foods, Inc.
4 Gatehall Dr Ste 110
Parsippany NJ 07054
973 401-6500

(G-7958)
B&G FOODS NORTH AMERICA INC (HQ)
4 Gatehall Dr Ste 110 (07054-4522)
PHONE...................973 401-6500
Robert Cantwell, *President*
Thomas Crimmins, *CFO*
EMP: 15
SALES (est): 53.8MM
SALES (corp-wide): 1.6B **Publicly Held**
SIC: 2013 Canned meats (except baby food) from purchased meat
PA: B&G Foods, Inc.
4 Gatehall Dr Ste 110
Parsippany NJ 07054
973 401-6500

(G-7959)
BEDDING SHOPPE INC
811 Route 46 (07054-3405)
PHONE...................973 334-9000
Michael Hatler, *President*
James Mascia, *Vice Pres*
EMP: 7
SQ FT: 12,500
SALES (est): 1.6MM **Privately Held**
WEB: www.beddingshoppe.com
SIC: 5712 7359 2515 Bedding & bedsprings; mattresses; furniture rental; chair beds

(G-7960)
BENCKISER N RECKITT AMER INC
Also Called: RB
399 Interpace Pkwy # 101 (07054-1133)
PHONE...................973 404-2600
Alexander Lacik, *President*
Jiri Kulik, *General Mgr*
Heather Allen, *Exec VP*
Rakesh Kapoor, *Exec VP*
Frank Coughlin, *Vice Pres*
▲ EMP: 1600
SQ FT: 13,000
SALES (est): 115.9K
SALES (corp-wide): 15.2B **Privately Held**
WEB: www.reckittbenckiser.com
SIC: 2035 2842 Pickles, sauces & salad dressings; specialty cleaning, polishes & sanitation goods
HQ: Reckitt Benckiser Holdings (Usa) Limited
103-105 Bath Road
Slough BERKS SL1 3
175 321-7800

(G-7961)
BIRDS EYE FOODS INC
Also Called: Agrilink Foods
399 Jefferson Rd (07054-3707)
PHONE...................920 435-5300
Robb Lillibridge, *Manager*
EMP: 120
SALES (corp-wide): 3.1B **Publicly Held**
WEB: www.agrilinkfoods.com
SIC: 2037 Vegetables, quick frozen & cold pack, excl. potato products
HQ: Birds Eye Foods, Inc.
121 Woodcrest Rd
Cherry Hill NJ 08003
585 383-1850

(G-7962)
BMC SOFTWARE INC
6 Campus Dr Ste 7 (07054-4406)
PHONE...................973 401-7700
Andrew Park, *Branch Mgr*
EMP: 25
SALES (corp-wide): 1.3B **Privately Held**
WEB: www.bmc.com
SIC: 7372 Utility computer software
HQ: Bmc Software, Inc.
2103 Citywest Blvd # 2100
Houston TX 77042
713 918-8800

(G-7963)
BOONTON ELECTRONICS CORP
25 Eastmans Rd (07054-3702)
PHONE...................201 261-8797
Fax: 973 386-9191
EMP: 32
SQ FT: 50,000
SALES (est): 7.6MM
SALES (corp-wide): 46MM **Publicly Held**
WEB: www.boonton.com
SIC: 3825 3829 3621 Microwave test equipment; impedance measuring equipment; test equipment for electronic & electrical circuits; audiometers; measuring & controlling devices; motors & generators
PA: Wireless Telecom Group, Inc.
25 Eastmans Rd
Parsippany NJ 07054
973 386-9696

(G-7964)
CASTLE CREEK PHRMCEUTICALS LLC
6 Century Dr Ste 2 (07054-4611)
PHONE...................862 286-0400
Michael Derby, *CEO*
Amir Tavakkol, *Exec VP*
EMP: 17
SALES (est): 894.8K **Privately Held**
SIC: 2834 Pharmaceutical preparations

(G-7965)
CELLEBRITE INC
7 Campus Dr Ste 210 (07054-4413)
PHONE...................201 848-8552
James H Grady, *CEO*
Chris Shin, *President*
Jennifer Fernandez, *General Mgr*
Derek Brown, *Vice Pres*
Mike Merkle, *Vice Pres*
EMP: 76
SALES (est): 18.4MM **Privately Held**
WEB: www.cellebriteusa.com
SIC: 3663 Cellular radio telephone

(G-7966)
CENTRAL PLASTICS INCORPORATED
Also Called: Plastic Profiles Co Div
333 New Rd Ste 3 (07054-4212)
PHONE...................973 808-0990
Michelle Tripucka, *President*
Frank Tripucka, *Corp Secy*
EMP: 5
SQ FT: 10,000
SALES (est): 896.4K **Privately Held**
SIC: 3081 5162 Polypropylene film & sheet; polyvinyl film & sheet; plastics products; plastics sheets & rods; plastics film

(G-7967)
CEREXA INC
400 Interpace Pkwy Ste A1 (07054-1119)
PHONE...................510 285-9200
Dennis Podlesak, *CEO*
George H Talbot MD, *Exec VP*
James G E MD PHD, *Vice Pres*
Bill Nelson PHD, *Vice Pres*
Stan E Abel, *CFO*
EMP: 22
SALES (est): 4.3MM **Privately Held**
SIC: 2834 Pharmaceutical preparations
HQ: Forest Laboratories, Llc
909 3rd Ave Fl 23
New York NY 10022
212 421-7850

(G-7968)
CHEMTRADE CHEMICALS CORP (DH)
Also Called: General Performance Products
90 E Halsey Rd Ste 301 (07054-3709)
PHONE...................973 515-0900
William E Redmond MD, *CEO*
Greg Gilbert, *Vice Pres*
Douglas J Grierson, *Vice Pres*
James Imbriaco, *Vice Pres*
Douglas Mc Farland, *Vice Pres*
◆ EMP: 80
SQ FT: 50,000
SALES (est): 199.4MM
SALES (corp-wide): 1.1B **Privately Held**
SIC: 2819 Industrial inorganic chemicals
HQ: Chemtrade Gcc Holding Company
90 E Halsey Rd Ste 301
Parsippany NJ 07054
973 515-0900

(G-7969)
CHEMTRADE GCC HOLDING COMPANY (DH)
90 E Halsey Rd Ste 301 (07054-3709)
PHONE...................973 515-0900
William E Redmond Jr, *President*
Douglas Mc Farland, *Vice Pres*
EMP: 2
SALES (est): 112.6MM
SALES (corp-wide): 1.1B **Privately Held**
SIC: 6719 2819 Investment holding companies, except banks; industrial inorganic chemicals
HQ: Chemtrade Water Chemical Inc.
90 E Halsey Rd Ste 301
Parsippany NJ 07054
973 515-0900

(G-7970)
CHEMTRADE SOLUTIONS LLC (DH)
90 E Halsey Rd Ste 301 (07054-3709)
PHONE...................973 515-0900
Vincent J Opalewski,
Douglas Grierson,
◆ EMP: 1
SALES (est): 175.5MM
SALES (corp-wide): 1.1B **Privately Held**
SIC: 5169 2819 Chemicals & allied products; aluminum sulfate

(G-7971)
CHEMTRADE WATER CHEMICAL INC (HQ)
90 E Halsey Rd Ste 301 (07054-3709)
PHONE...................973 515-0900
EMP: 0
SALES (est): 73MM
SALES (corp-wide): 1.1B **Privately Held**
SIC: 6719 2819 Investment holding companies, except banks; industrial inorganic chemicals
PA: Chemtrade Logistics Income Fund
155 Gordon Baker Rd Suite 300
North York ON M2H 3
416 496-5856

(G-7972)
CLASSIC INDUSTRIES INC
50 Us Highway 46 Ste 100 (07054-2395)
PHONE...................973 227-1366
Robert D H Luke, *President*
Ralph Loveys, *Vice Pres*
James Luke, *Treasurer*
EMP: 5
SALES (est): 310K **Privately Held**
SIC: 3444 Sheet metalwork

(G-7973)
CLEAN AIR GROUP
6 Campus Dr Ste 2 (07054-4406)
PHONE...................908 232-4200
Clara Rosales, *Manager*
EMP: 6
SALES (est): 693.6K **Privately Held**
SIC: 3559 Recycling machinery

(G-7974)
COLOR LOGIC INC
8 Woodhollow Rd Ste Pl-3 (07054-2829)
PHONE...................973 515-0099
Fax: 973 515-9610
Joseph Albertini, *President*
EMP: 44
SQ FT: 11,000
SALES (est): 4.3MM **Privately Held**
WEB: www.colorlogic.com
SIC: 2759 Commercial printing

(G-7975)
CONAGRAPHICS INC
Also Called: PIP Printing
1180 Us Highway 46 Ste 2 (07054-2153)
PHONE...................973 331-1113
Fax: 973 331-1288
Martin Contzius, *President*
Janet Contzius, *Vice Pres*
EMP: 4
SQ FT: 1,150
SALES (est): 370K **Privately Held**
SIC: 2752 Commercial printing, offset

(G-7976)
CROLL-REYNOLDS CO INC (PA)
6 Campus Dr Ste 2 (07054-4406)
PHONE...................908 232-4200
Samuel W Croll III, *CEO*
Henry Hage, *COO*
Phillip E Reynolds, *Vice Pres*
◆ EMP: 24 EST: 1917
SQ FT: 5,000
SALES (est): 9.5MM **Privately Held**
WEB: www.croll.com
SIC: 3563 3822 3564 Vacuum (air extraction) systems, industrial; air flow controllers, air conditioning & refrigeration; air cleaning systems

(G-7977)
CRONITE CO INC (PA)
120 E Halsey Rd (07054-3720)
P.O. Box 6330 (07054-7330)
PHONE...................973 887-7900
Roberts Steffens, *Ch of Bd*
Thomas R Ward, *CFO*
▲ EMP: 35 EST: 1886
SQ FT: 30,300
SALES (est): 3.1MM **Privately Held**
WEB: www.cronite.com
SIC: 3555 5169 Engraving machinery & equipment, except plates; chemicals & allied products

(G-7978)
CROSS RIP OCEAN ENGRG LLC
Also Called: Cr Ocean Engineering, LLC
6 Campus Dr (07054-4406)
PHONE....................................973 455-0005
Samuel W Croll III, *CEO*
Nicholas Confuorto, *COO*
EMP: 5
SALES (est): 772.5K Privately Held
SIC: 3564 Purification & dust collection
equipment

(G-7979)
DENTAMACH INC
14 Walsh Dr Ste 102 (07054-1063)
PHONE....................................973 334-2220
Bill Pollack, *Ch of Bd*
Bruce Miller, *President*
EMP: 10
SALES (est): 873.8K Privately Held
SIC: 3843 Dental equipment & supplies;
teeth, artificial (not made in dental labora-
tories)

(G-7980)
**DEPENDABLE PRECISION
PRODUCTS**
42 Schindler Ct (07054-3300)
PHONE....................................973 887-3304
Donald Carlucci, *President*
EMP: 9
SQ FT: 4,800
SALES: 650K Privately Held
SIC: 3544 Industrial molds

(G-7981)
DIALOGIC INC (DH)
4 Gatehall Dr (07054-4518)
PHONE....................................973 967-6000
Fax: 973 967-6006
Bill Crank, *President*
Christian Primeau, *COO*
Anthony Housefather, *Exec VP*
Kevin Gould, *Senior VP*
Jim Machi, *Senior VP*
EMP: 135
SALES (est): 106MM
SALES (corp-wide): 213.4K Privately
Held
WEB: www.dialogic.com
SIC: 3661 3577 7371 Telephone & tele-
graph apparatus; data conversion equip-
ment, media-to-media: computer;
computer software development & appli-
cations
HQ: Groupe Dialogic Inc
375 Boul Roland-Therrien Bureau 210
Longueuil QC J4H 4
450 651-5000

(G-7982)
DIGITAL PRINT SOLUTIONS INC
Also Called: Alphagraphics Printshops of th
5 Eastmans Rd (07054-3721)
PHONE....................................973 263-1890
Fax: 973 263-2054
Joseph Yutsus, *President*
Darin Hicks, *Vice Pres*
Tommy E Auger, *CFO*
Ruth Braid, *Accounts Mgr*
EMP: 10
SQ FT: 7,500
SALES (est): 2MM Privately Held
SIC: 2752 Commercial printing, litho-
graphic

(G-7983)
DISPLAY WORKS LLC (PA)
1 Gatehall Dr Ste 210 (07054-4540)
PHONE....................................201 327-1260
Mike Fernandez, *CEO*
Herb Hite, *Principal*
Mike Bartley, *COO*
Donna Magallones, *Vice Pres*
Matthew Ketsdever, *CFO*
EMP: 110
SQ FT: 205,900
SALES (est): 54MM Privately Held
WEB: www.displayworks.net
SIC: 7389 3999 3993 2542 Trade show
arrangement; advertising display prod-
ucts; signs & advertising specialties; parti-
tions & fixtures, except wood; advertising
agencies

(G-7984)
DONRAY PRINTING INC
2 Eastmans Rd (07054-3703)
PHONE....................................973 515-8100
Fax: 973 515-8102
Art Ferriola, *President*
Ray Ferriola, *Vice Pres*
▲ EMP: 35
SQ FT: 40,000
SALES (est): 6.9MM Privately Held
WEB: www.donrayprinting.com
SIC: 2752 2396 Color lithography; auto-
motive & apparel trimmings

(G-7985)
DPI NEWCO LLC
Also Called: D P X
45 Waterview Blvd (07054-7611)
PHONE....................................973 257-8113
Jenny Tan, *Human Res Mgr*
Jim Mullen, *Mng Member*
EMP: 41 EST: 1994
SALES (est): 72.3MM
SALES (corp-wide): 3.1B Privately Held
SIC: 2834 Pharmaceutical preparations
PA: Gpv Iii, Inc.
245 Park Ave Fl 1601
New York NY 10167
212 286-8600

(G-7986)
**DRS INFRARED TECHNOLOGIES
LP**
5 Sylvan Way Ste 305 (07054-3813)
PHONE....................................973 898-1500
Linda Zerpolo, *COO*
EMP: 5
SALES (est): 374K Privately Held
SIC: 3812 Search & navigation equipment

(G-7987)
DRS LEONARDO INC
5 Sylvan Way (07054-3818)
PHONE....................................973 898-1500
Mark Newman, *CEO*
EMP: 39
SALES (corp-wide): 9.2B Privately Held
SIC: 3812 Navigational systems & instru-
ments
HQ: Leonardo Drs, Inc.
2345 Crystal Dr Ste 1000
Arlington VA 22202
703 416-8000

(G-7988)
DRS LEONARDO INC
Also Called: Drs Srviilance Support Systems
5 Sylvan Way (07054-3818)
PHONE....................................973 898-1500
Michael Hlavaty, *President*
John Riggs, *President*
Richard Danforth, *Principal*
Donald Fairbairn, *Senior VP*
Jason Rinsky, *Senior VP*
EMP: 38
SALES (corp-wide): 9.2B Privately Held
SIC: 3812 Search & navigation equipment
HQ: Leonardo Drs, Inc.
2345 Crystal Dr Ste 1000
Arlington VA 22202
703 416-8000

(G-7989)
**DSM NUTRITIONAL PRODUCTS
LLC (DH)**
Also Called: D S M
45 Waterview Blvd (07054-7611)
PHONE....................................800 526-0189
Richard Polacek, *President*
Patrick Weinberg, *Treasurer*
Joshua De Freitas, *Manager*
◆ EMP: 277
SQ FT: 106,000
SALES (est): 577.5MM
SALES (corp-wide): 10.1B Privately Held
WEB: www.nutraaccess.com
SIC: 2834 2836 Pharmaceutical prepara-
tions; vitamin, nutrient & hematinic prepa-
rations for human use; biological
products, except diagnostic; veterinary bi-
ological products

(G-7990)
DSM SIGHT & LIFE INC
45 Waterview Blvd (07054-7611)
PHONE....................................973 257-8208
Hugh Welsh, *President*
Roberto Boscio, *Principal*
James Hamilton, *Principal*
EMP: 4
SALES: 0
SALES (corp-wide): 10.1B Privately Held
SIC: 8699 2834 Charitable organization;
vitamin preparations
HQ: Dsm Nutritional Products, Llc
45 Waterview Blvd
Parsippany NJ 07054
800 526-0189

(G-7991)
E B R MANUFACTURING INC
10 Woodhaven Rd (07054-1468)
PHONE....................................973 263-8810
Herbert Wolf, *President*
Maxine Wolf, *Admin Sec*
EMP: 25
SQ FT: 42,000
SALES (est): 1.6MM Privately Held
SIC: 2395 Quilting, for the trade

(G-7992)
**EARTH COLOR NEW YORK INC
(HQ)**
249 Pomeroy Rd (07054-3727)
PHONE....................................973 884-1300
Robert Kashan, *CEO*
Jeff Wright, *Vice Pres*
Robert Pagan, *Facilities Mgr*
Dennis Ganzak, *CFO*
EMP: 45
SALES (est): 67.2MM
SALES (corp-wide): 189.9MM Privately
Held
SIC: 2752 7336 2791 Commercial print-
ing, lithographic; graphic arts & related
design; typesetting
PA: Mittera Group, Inc.
1312 Locust St Ste 202
Des Moines IA 50309
515 343-5353

(G-7993)
EARTH THEBAULT INC (DH)
249 Pomeroy Rd (07054-3727)
PHONE....................................973 884-1300
J Brian Thebault, *CEO*
Wes Vanderwende, *President*
Kenneth Marino, *COO*
Don Seitz, *Senior VP*
Jeff Yonkers, *Vice Pres*
▲ EMP: 234 EST: 1930
SQ FT: 93,000
SALES (est): 74.2MM Publicly Held
WEB: www.thebault.com
SIC: 2752 Commercial printing, offset

(G-7994)
EARTHCOLOR INC (HQ)
Also Called: Earth Digital
249 Pomeroy Rd (07054-3727)
PHONE....................................973 884-1300
Robert Kashan, *CEO*
Bruce Wexler, *President*
Cheryl Kahanec, *Exec VP*
Domenic Pizzanelli, *Facilities Mgr*
Dennis Ganzak, *CFO*
EMP: 139
SQ FT: 93,000
SALES (est): 117.8MM Publicly Held
SIC: 2752 2759 Commercial printing, litho-
graphic; business forms: printing; laser
printing

(G-7995)
EBI LLC
Also Called: Biomet Bone Healing Tech
100 Interpace Pkwy (07054-1149)
P.O. Box 346 (07054-0346)
PHONE....................................800 526-2579
Bob Phelp, *President*
Robert Gabriele, *Controller*
Bradley J Tandy, *Mng Member*
Jeffrey R Binder, *Mng Member*
Michael T Hodges, *Mng Member*
▲ EMP: 1504
SQ FT: 125,000
SALES (est): 146.5MM
SALES (corp-wide): 7.8B Publicly Held
WEB: www.ebimedical.com
SIC: 3842 Surgical appliances & supplies
HQ: Biomet, Inc.
345 E Main St
Warsaw IN 46580
574 267-6639

(G-7996)
EBI LP
Also Called: Biomet Spine and Biomet
Trauma
399 Jefferson Rd (07054-3707)
PHONE....................................973 299-9022
Eric Hayes, *Administration*
EMP: 33
SALES (est): 5MM
SALES (corp-wide): 7.8B Publicly Held
WEB: www.biomet.com
SIC: 3842 Surgical appliances & supplies
HQ: Biomet, Inc.
345 E Main St
Warsaw IN 46580
574 267-6639

(G-7997)
EBI MEDICAL SYSTEMS LLC
100 Interpace Pkwy Ste 1 (07054-1149)
PHONE....................................973 299-3330
Fax: 973 299-0913
James Bechtold, *Principal*
EMP: 15
SALES (est): 1.9MM
SALES (corp-wide): 7.8B Publicly Held
WEB: www.biomet.com
SIC: 3842 Surgical appliances & supplies
HQ: Biomet, Inc.
345 E Main St
Warsaw IN 46580
574 267-6639

(G-7998)
**EDENBRIDGE
PHARMACEUTICALS LLC**
169 Lackawanna Ave # 110 (07054-1007)
PHONE....................................201 292-1292
Ryan Collins, *CEO*
Patrick Chu, *President*
EMP: 4
SALES (est): 964.1K Privately Held
SIC: 2834 Pharmaceutical preparations

(G-7999)
EFFICIENT LIGHTING INC
2 Cranberry Rd Ste 5b (07054-1053)
PHONE....................................973 846-8568
David Rivera, *President*
EMP: 16
SALES (est): 2.6MM Privately Held
SIC: 3645 5063 5719 Boudoir lamps;
chandeliers, residential; desk lamps; floor
lamps; lighting fixtures; lighting fixtures
PA: Efficient Lighting, Inc
201 E Center St
Anaheim CA 92805

(G-8000)
ELEVATE HR INC
1055 Parsippany Blvd # 511 (07054-1273)
PHONE....................................973 917-3230
David M Erickson, *President*
EMP: 20
SALES (est): 1.9MM Privately Held
SIC: 7372 8742 Business oriented com-
puter software; human resource consult-
ing services

(G-8001)
EMERSON RADIO CORP (PA)
35 Waterview Blvd (07054-1200)
PHONE....................................973 428-2000
Duncan Hon, *CEO*
Christopher Ho, *Ch of Bd*
Michael Binney, *CFO*
◆ EMP: 12 EST: 1912
SQ FT: 5,541
SALES: 15MM Publicly Held
WEB: www.emersonradio.com
SIC: 3651 Household audio & video equip-
ment

▲ = Import ▼=Export
◆ =Import/Export

(G-8002)
EPOCH EVERLASTING PLAY LLC
Also Called: International Playthings
75d Lackawanna Ave (07054-5700)
PHONE..................................973 316-2500
Fax: 973 316-5883
Rich Driscoll, *Warehouse Mgr*
Stacy Lobosco, *Sales Staff*
Michael Varda,
◆ EMP: 46 EST: 1967
SQ FT: 120,000
SALES (est): 11.9MM
SALES (corp-wide): 182.9MM **Privately Held**
WEB: www.intplay.com
SIC: 3944 5092 Games, toys & children's vehicles; toys & hobby goods & supplies
PA: Epoch Co., Ltd.
2-2-2, Komagata
Taito-Ku TKY 111-0
338 438-812

(G-8003)
EVONIK CORPORATION (DH)
Also Called: Degussa
299 Jefferson Rd (07054-2827)
P.O. Box 677 (07054-0677)
PHONE..................................973 929-8000
Fax: 973 541-8013
John Rolando, *President*
Joe Lally, *General Mgr*
Sabine Fleming, *Business Mgr*
John Tarabocchia, *Business Mgr*
Noah Fisette, *Counsel*
▲ EMP: 400 EST: 1973
SQ FT: 150,500
SALES (est): 1.9B
SALES (corp-wide): 2.4B **Privately Held**
WEB: www.degussa.com
SIC: 2819 2869 2851 2816 Industrial inorganic chemicals; industrial organic chemicals; paints & allied products; inorganic pigments
HQ: Evonik Industries Ag
Rellinghauser Str. 1-11
Essen 45128
201 177-01

(G-8004)
EVONIK CYRO LLC (DH)
Also Called: Rohm America
299 Jefferson Rd (07054-2827)
PHONE..................................973 929-8000
Fax: 973 541-8447
John Rolando, *President*
Mark Steinhauer, *Plant Engr*
Johan Holleman, *Marketing Mgr*
Lisa Langel, *Manager*
◆ EMP: 100
SQ FT: 31,200
SALES (est): 229.8MM
SALES (corp-wide): 2.4B **Privately Held**
SIC: 2821 Plastics materials & resins; acrylic resins; molding compounds, plastics
HQ: Evonik Corporation
299 Jefferson Rd
Parsippany NJ 07054
973 929-8000

(G-8005)
EVONIK FOAMS INC (DH)
299 Jefferson Rd (07054-2827)
PHONE..................................973 929-8000
Alexander Roth, *President*
▼ EMP: 24
SQ FT: 40,000
SALES (est): 4.1MM
SALES (corp-wide): 2.4B **Privately Held**
SIC: 3086 Insulation or cushioning material, foamed plastic
HQ: Evonik Corporation
299 Jefferson Rd
Parsippany NJ 07054
973 929-8000

(G-8006)
EXTREMITY MEDICAL LLC
300 Interpace Pkwy # 410 (07054-1148)
PHONE..................................973 588-8980
James Gannoe, *President*
Matthew Lyons, *President*
Brian Rowan, *Division VP*
Ray Penzimer, *Project Engr*
Brett Verni, *Regl Sales Mgr*

EMP: 14
SALES (est): 1.8MM **Privately Held**
SIC: 3842 Orthopedic appliances

(G-8007)
FAMCAM INC
3 Eastmans Rd (07054-3702)
PHONE..................................973 503-1600
Robert Perna, *President*
EMP: 28
SQ FT: 18,000
SALES: 3.2MM **Privately Held**
SIC: 3679 Electronic circuits

(G-8008)
FARMPLAST LLC
125 E Halsey Rd (07054-3723)
PHONE..................................973 287-6070
Mark Lomak,
◆ EMP: 28
SQ FT: 40,000
SALES (est): 7.2MM **Privately Held**
SIC: 3089 Injection molded finished plastic products

(G-8009)
FERRERO U S A INC (DH)
7 Sylvan Way Fl 4 (07054-3805)
PHONE..................................732 764-9300
Fax: 732 764-2700
Bernard F Kreilmann, *CEO*
Rudy Sequeira, *Managing Dir*
Pietro Ferrero, *Senior VP*
Glenn Lawse, *Vice Pres*
Daniel Degiovanni, *Opers Mgr*
◆ EMP: 160
SQ FT: 150,000
SALES (est): 226.4MM
SALES (corp-wide): 196.9MM **Privately Held**
WEB: www.ferrerousa.com
SIC: 5145 2064 Candy; candy & other confectionery products
HQ: Ferrero Spa
Piazzale Pietro Ferrero 1
Alba CN 12051
017 322-7500

(G-8010)
FERRING PHARMACEUTICALS INC (DH)
100 Interpace Pkwy (07054-1149)
PHONE..................................973 796-1600
Fax: 973 796-1666
Aaron Graff, *President*
Robyn Davis, *Business Mgr*
Per Falk, *Exec VP*
William N Garbarini, *Vice Pres*
Brenda Marczi, *Vice Pres*
▲ EMP: 216
SQ FT: 26,000
SALES (est): 110.5MM **Privately Held**
WEB: www.ferringusa.com
SIC: 2834 5122 Pharmaceutical preparations; pharmaceuticals
HQ: Ferring B.V.
Polarisavenue 144
Hoofddorp 2132
235 680-300

(G-8011)
FERRING PRODUCTION INC
100 Interpace Pkwy (07054-1149)
PHONE..................................973 796-1600
L P Brunse, *President*
Ahluwalia Lalit, *CFO*
L Ahluwalia, *Treasurer*
R Anderson, *Treasurer*
▲ EMP: 50 EST: 2011
SALES (est): 14MM **Privately Held**
SIC: 2834 Pharmaceutical preparations
HQ: Ferring Holding Inc.
100 Interpace Pkwy
Parsippany NJ 07054
973 796-1600

(G-8012)
FINLANDIA CHEESE INC (HQ)
2001 Us Highway 46 # 303 (07054-1315)
PHONE..................................973 316-6699
Fax: 973 316-6609
Emma Aer, *CEO*
Monique Charito, *COO*
Michael Restivo, *CFO*
Patrick Whalen, *Accountant*
Sam Aquino, *Sales Dir*

▲ EMP: 30 EST: 1998
SQ FT: 2,500
SALES (est): 4.1MM **Privately Held**
WEB: www.finlandiacheese.com
SIC: 2022 5143 Natural cheese; dairy products, except dried or canned; cheese
PA: Valio Oy
Meijeritie 6
Helsinki 00370
103 811-21

(G-8013)
FLOWSERVE CORPORATION
333 Littleton Rd Ste 303 (07054-4866)
PHONE..................................973 334-9444
George Georgas, *Branch Mgr*
EMP: 6
SALES (corp-wide): 3.6B **Publicly Held**
SIC: 3561 Pumps & pumping equipment
PA: Flowserve Corporation
5215 N Oconnor Blvd Connor
Irving TX 75039
972 443-5600

(G-8014)
FLUOROTHERM POLYMERS INC
333 New Rd Ste 1 (07054-4212)
PHONE..................................973 575-0760
Prabhat Shukla, *President*
Madhuri Shukla, *Vice Pres*
▲ EMP: 8
SQ FT: 5,000
SALES (est): 1.4MM **Privately Held**
SIC: 3082 3498 3317 3083 Unsupported plastics profile shapes; fabricated pipe & fittings; steel pipe & tubes; laminated plastics plate & sheet; chemical preparations; paints & allied products

(G-8015)
FORESIGHT GROUP LLC
119 Cherry Hill Rd # 230 (07054-1117)
PHONE..................................888 992-8880
Tim Neely, *Managing Dir*
Linda Mier, *Vice Pres*
Janice Scheider, *Mktg Dir*
Gretchen Arndt, *Manager*
Vincent Budhai, *Manager*
EMP: 11 EST: 2006
SALES (est): 1.3MM **Privately Held**
SIC: 2834 8731 Chlorination tablets & kits (water purification); commercial research laboratory

(G-8016)
FOREST PHARMACEUTICALS INC (DH)
400 Interpace Pkwy Ste A1 (07054-1119)
PHONE..................................862 261-7000
Howard Solomon, *Ch of Bd*
Kenneth Goodman, *President*
William B Sparks, *Exec VP*
▲ EMP: 800
SQ FT: 87,000
SALES (est): 153.7MM **Privately Held**
WEB: www.forestpharm.com
SIC: 2834 Pharmaceutical preparations
HQ: Forest Laboratories, Llc
909 3rd Ave Fl 23
New York NY 10022
212 421-7850

(G-8017)
FREEMAN PRODUCTS INC (PA)
71 Walsh Dr Ste 101 (07054-1010)
PHONE..................................201 475-4800
Fax: 201 475-4818
George Ercolino, *President*
Vincent Cariello, *President*
George Ercolino, *CFO*
◆ EMP: 10
SQ FT: 40,000
SALES (est): 23.4MM **Privately Held**
SIC: 3914 Trophies

(G-8018)
FRONTLINE MED CMMNICATIONS INC (HQ)
Also Called: Frontline Med Communications
7 Century Dr Ste 302 (07054-4609)
PHONE..................................973 206-2328
Stephen Stoneburn, *Ch of Bd*
Mary Holeton, *President*
Josh Prizer, *Publisher*
Diana Sabatino, *Publisher*
Alicia Wendt, *Editor*

EMP: 184
SALES (est): 42.8MM **Privately Held**
WEB: www.cosderm.com
SIC: 2721 Trade journals: publishing & printing

(G-8019)
G HOLDINGS INC (PA)
1 Campus Dr (07054-4404)
PHONE..................................973 628-3000
Robert B Tafaro, *CEO*
Adel Collado, *Purchasing*
Joel Chavez, *Manager*
◆ EMP: 1
SALES (est): 1.5B **Privately Held**
SIC: 2869 2843 3295 Solvents, organic; surface active agents; roofing granules

(G-8020)
GANNETT CO INC
Also Called: Daily Record, The
800 Jefferson Rd (07054-3717)
PHONE..................................973 428-6200
Walt Lafferty, *Branch Mgr*
EMP: 4
SALES (corp-wide): 3.1B **Publicly Held**
WEB: www.gannett.com
SIC: 2711 Newspapers
PA: Gannett Co., Inc.
7950 Jones Branch Dr
Mc Lean VA 22102
703 854-6000

(G-8021)
GANNETT STLLITE INFO NTWRK INC
Daily Record, The
800 Jefferson Rd (07054-3717)
PHONE..................................973 428-6200
Fax: 973 428-6666
Walt Lafferty, *Manager*
EMP: 300
SALES (corp-wide): 3.1B **Publicly Held**
WEB: www.usatoday.com
SIC: 2711 Newspapers
HQ: Gannett Satellite Information Network, Llc
7950 Jones Branch Dr
Mc Lean VA 22102
703 854-6000

(G-8022)
GENERAL DYNAMICS GLBL IMG TECH
AST Bearings
222 New Rd Ste 1 (07054-5626)
PHONE..................................973 335-2230
Mitchell L Dutton, *President*
Daniel Fox, *VP Sales*
Dale Kaminski, *Branch Mgr*
EMP: 48
SALES (corp-wide): 30.9B **Publicly Held**
WEB: www.axsys.com
SIC: 3562 Ball & roller bearings
HQ: General Dynamics Global Imaging Technologies, Inc.
24 Simon St
Nashua NH 03060
603 864-6300

(G-8023)
GENERAL ELECTRIC COMPANY
700 Parsippany Rd (07054-3712)
PHONE..................................973 887-6635
Fax: 973 887-1755
Laura Fowler, *General Mgr*
Aaron Arias, *Engineer*
Theodore Wheeler, *Engineer*
Elise Mundrick, *Human Res Dir*
EMP: 270
SALES (corp-wide): 122B **Publicly Held**
SIC: 3599 3541 Machine shop, jobbing & repair; milling machines
PA: General Electric Company
41 Farnsworth St
Boston MA 02210
617 443-3000

(G-8024)
GENTEK INC (PA)
90 E Halsey Rd Ste 301 (07054-3709)
PHONE..................................973 515-0900
Fax: 973 515-1997
William E Redmond Jr, *President*
Douglas J Grierson, *Vice Pres*
James Imbriaco, *Vice Pres*

Jim Mahen, *Vice Pres*
Vincent J Opalewski, *Vice Pres*
◆ **EMP:** 177
SALES (est): 167.2MM **Privately Held**
WEB: www.generalchemical.com/
SIC: 2869 2819 2844 3714 Industrial organic chemicals; industrial inorganic chemicals; toilet preparations; motor vehicle parts & accessories; cable, uninsulated wire: made from purchased wire

(G-8025)
GSK CONSUMER HEALTHCARE
2 Sylvan Way (07054-3809)
PHONE..................................973 539-0645
EMP: 100
SALES (corp-wide): 36B **Privately Held**
SIC: 2834 Mfg Pharmaceutical Preparations
HQ: Gsk Consumer Healthcare
184 Liberty Corner Rd # 78
Warren NJ 07059
973 503-8000

(G-8026)
HAMMER PRESS PRINTERS INC
2 Cranberry Rd Ste 2 # 2 (07054-1053)
PHONE..................................973 334-4500
Fax: 973 404-1777
Susan Hammer, *CEO*
Sidney B Hammer, *President*
Kenneth Hammer, *Vice Pres*
EMP: 85 **EST:** 1929
SALES (est): 8.3MM **Privately Held**
WEB: www.hammerpress.com
SIC: 2752 Commercial printing, lithographic

(G-8027)
HARMS SOFTWARE INC
Also Called: Millennium Systems Intl
28 Eastmans Rd (07054-3703)
PHONE..................................973 402-9500
Fax: 973 402-8812
John Harms, *President*
EMP: 75
SQ FT: 13,000
SALES (est): 14.7MM **Privately Held**
WEB: www.harmssoftware.com
SIC: 7372 Business oriented computer software

(G-8028)
ILLINOIS TOOL WORKS INC
ITW Thielex
6 Ringwood Dr (07054-1617)
PHONE..................................732 968-5300
Fax: 732 873-0015
Roger Cybert, *Manager*
EMP: 60
SQ FT: 45,000
SALES (corp-wide): 14.3B **Publicly Held**
SIC: 3082 5085 Tubes, unsupported plastic; industrial supplies
PA: Illinois Tool Works Inc.
155 Harlem Ave
Glenview IL 60025
847 724-7500

(G-8029)
INDUSTRY PUBLICATIONS INC
Also Called: Spray Tech & Marketing
140 Littleton Rd Ste 320 (07054-1867)
PHONE..................................973 331-9545
Fax: 973 331-9547
Cynthia Vandervoort, *President*
Michael San Giovanni, *President*
Don Farrell, *Vice Pres*
John Abplanalp, *Advisor*
EMP: 10 **EST:** 1922
SALES (est): 950K **Privately Held**
WEB: www.oilheating.com
SIC: 2721 Magazines: publishing only, not printed on site

(G-8030)
INTEGRATION INTERNATIONAL INC (PA)
160 Littleton Rd Ste 106 (07054-1871)
PHONE..................................973 796-2300
Fax: 973 535-3115
Pratap Jaykar, *President*
Suresh Patel, *CFO*
Parshuram Chenna, *Architect*
EMP: 31
SQ FT: 6,500

SALES (est): 14.4MM **Privately Held**
WEB: www.i3intl.com
SIC: 7379 7378 7372 Computer related consulting services; computer maintenance & repair; prepackaged software

(G-8031)
INTEGRATION PARTNERS-NY CORP
1719 State Rt 10 Ste 114 (07054-4537)
PHONE..................................973 871-2100
Richard Schneider, *Manager*
EMP: 257 **EST:** 2008
SALES (est): 12.3MM **Publicly Held**
SIC: 8741 7372 Management services; prepackaged software
PA: Intercloud Systems, Inc.
1030 Broad St Ste 102
Shrewsbury NJ 07702

(G-8032)
INTERNTONAL MED NEWS GROUP LLC (DH)
Also Called: I M N G
7 Century Dr Ste 302 (07054-4609)
PHONE..................................973 290-8237
Fax: 973 290-8250
Alan Imhoff, *President*
Sylvia Reitman, *Vice Pres*
EMP: 16
SQ FT: 6,100
SALES (est): 20.4MM
SALES (corp-wide): 9.7B **Privately Held**
WEB: www.imng.com
SIC: 2721 Magazines: publishing only, not printed on site

(G-8033)
JHP GROUP HOLDINGS INC
1 Upper Pond Rd Ste 4 (07054-1050)
PHONE..................................973 658-3569
Paul Campanelli, *CEO*
EMP: 957
SALES (est): 56.2MM **Privately Held**
SIC: 2834 Pharmaceutical preparations; druggists' preparations (pharmaceuticals); tablets, pharmaceutical; medicines, capsuled or ampuled
HQ: Par Pharmaceutical Companies, Inc.
1 Ram Ridge Rd
Chestnut Ridge NY 10977
845 573-5500

(G-8034)
JNBC ASSOCIATES LLC
100 Jefferson Rd (07054-3708)
PHONE..................................973 560-5518
Gadi Cohen, *Partner*
EMP: 5
SALES (est): 430K **Privately Held**
SIC: 3672 Printed circuit boards

(G-8035)
KABEL N ELETTROTEK AMER INC
2 Cranberry Rd Ste 5a (07054-1053)
PHONE..................................973 265-0850
Nicola Malaguti, *President*
Joseph Basso, *Info Tech Mgr*
▲ **EMP:** 5
SQ FT: 11,000
SALES: 9MM
SALES (corp-wide): 30.9MM **Privately Held**
SIC: 3315 1389 5063 Cable, steel: insulated or armored; oil & gas wells: building, repairing & dismantling; wire & cable
PA: Elettrotek Kabel Spa
Via Imerio Tondelli 10
Bagnolo In Piano RE 42011
052 295-6001

(G-8036)
LAENNEC PUBLISHING INC
4 Woodhollow Rd Ste 1 (07054-2814)
PHONE..................................973 882-9500
David Canfield, *President*
W P Harvey MD, *Vice Pres*
James McCarthy, *Vice Pres*
EMP: 5
SQ FT: 500
SALES: 45K **Privately Held**
SIC: 2741 Miscellaneous publishing

(G-8037)
LAFARGE ROAD MARKING INC
400 Lanidex Plz (07054-2722)
PHONE..................................973 884-0300
Robert A Dirienzo, *President*
Anthony Cipolla, *Vice Pres*
Steve Shinners, *Vice Pres*
EMP: 250
SALES (est): 28.8MM **Privately Held**
SIC: 2851 3953 Paints & allied products; marking devices

(G-8038)
LANGAN ENGINEERING ENVIRONMEN (PA)
300 Kimball Dr Ste 4 (07054-2184)
PHONE..................................973 560-4900
Andrew J Ciancia, *Ch of Bd*
David T Gockel, *President*
Nicholas De Rose, *Principal*
Rudolph P Frizzi, *Principal*
Ronald A Fuerst, *Principal*
EMP: 7 **EST:** 2012
SALES (est): 197.7MM **Privately Held**
SIC: 8711 8748 1389 0781 Consulting engineer; environmental consultant; testing, measuring, surveying & analysis services; landscape architects

(G-8039)
LL BUILDING PRODUCTS INC (DH)
1 Campus Dr (07054-4404)
PHONE..................................973 628-3000
EMP: 13
SALES (est): 12.4MM
SALES (corp-wide): 1.5B **Privately Held**
SIC: 3089 Plastic hardware & building products

(G-8040)
LP THEBAULT CO
249 Pomeroy Rd (07054-3727)
PHONE..................................973 884-1300
Fax: 973 952-8283
Bruce Wexler, *Exec VP*
EMP: 10
SALES (est): 965.6K **Privately Held**
SIC: 2752 Commercial printing, offset

(G-8041)
MATHESON GAS PRODUCTS INC
959 Us Highway 46 (07054-3409)
PHONE..................................201 867-4101
Fax: 973 257-9393
Chuck Beecher, *Production*
Penny Lewis, *Planning Mgr*
Curtis Kraft, *Planning*
EMP: 15 **EST:** 1989
SALES (est): 35.8K **Privately Held**
SIC: 2813 Industrial gases

(G-8042)
MAXIMUM MATERIAL HANDLING LLC
750 Edwards Rd (07054-4265)
P.O. Box 750, Pine Brook (07058-0750)
PHONE..................................973 227-1227
Renee Vecchio, *Office Mgr*
Michael Dal Bon Jr,
EMP: 6
SALES (est): 1.5MM **Privately Held**
SIC: 3536 Hoists, cranes & monorails

(G-8043)
MEDICINES COMPANY (PA)
8 Sylvan Way (07054-3801)
PHONE..................................973 290-6000
Fax: 973 656-9898
Clive A Meanwell, *CEO*
Fredric N Eshelman, *Ch of Bd*
Kevin Siska, *Partner*
Christopher T Cox, *Exec VP*
Jeff Frazier, *Exec VP*
EMP: 170
SQ FT: 173,146
SALES: 44.7MM **Publicly Held**
WEB: www.themedicinescompany.com
SIC: 2834 Pharmaceutical preparations; intravenous solutions

(G-8044)
MEDINOL USA INC
8 Campus Dr Fl 2 (07054-4416)
PHONE..................................201 654-4534
Sachi Gerlitz, *President*
Matt Donnelly, *General Mgr*
Efi Haber Naor, *Vice Pres*
Dafna Perlovitch, *Vice Pres*
Dennis Rodrigues, *Vice Pres*
EMP: 24
SQ FT: 5,000
SALES (est): 6.3MM **Privately Held**
SIC: 3841 Surgical & medical instruments
PA: Medinol Ltd.
8 Street 2184
Tel Aviv-Jaffa
376 790-48

(G-8045)
MEDTRONIC USA INC
300 Interpace Pkwy # 340 (07054-1100)
PHONE..................................973 331-7914
Janet Adamovic, *Principal*
EMP: 11 **Privately Held**
SIC: 3841 Surgical & medical instruments
HQ: Medtronic Usa, Inc.
710 Medtronic Pkwy
Minneapolis MN 55432
763 514-4000

(G-8046)
METO CORP
Also Called: Meto Engineering
29 E Halsey Rd (07054-3704)
PHONE..................................201 405-0311
Helmut Habicht, *CEO*
Mark Habicht, *President*
Rosemarie Habicht, *Corp Secy*
Susan L Haas, *VP Admin*
▲ **EMP:** 14 **EST:** 1969
SQ FT: 11,000
SALES (est): 2.9MM **Privately Held**
WEB: www.metolift.com
SIC: 3537 Cradles, drum

(G-8047)
METO LIFT INC
29 E Halsey Rd (07054-3704)
PHONE..................................201 405-0311
Fax: 201 405-0322
Susan Haas, *Principal*
Susan L Haas, *Principal*
EMP: 12 **EST:** 2012
SALES (est): 238.4K **Privately Held**
SIC: 3537 Cradles, drum
PA: Steinen Holdings Inc.
29 E Halsey Rd
Parsippany NJ 07054

(G-8048)
MICROLAB/FXR
25 Eastmans Rd (07054-3702)
PHONE..................................973 386-9696
Anthony Ramsden, *President*
▲ **EMP:** 106 **EST:** 1950
SQ FT: 45,000
SALES (est): 15.3MM
SALES (corp-wide): 46MM **Publicly Held**
WEB: www.microlab.fxr.com
SIC: 3663 Radio & TV communications equipment
PA: Wireless Telecom Group, Inc.
25 Eastmans Rd
Parsippany NJ 07054
973 386-9696

(G-8049)
MOBILOGY INC (HQ)
7 Campus Dr Ste 210 (07054-4413)
PHONE..................................201 848-8552
Kyle Ford, *President*
Ido Zur, *CFO*
EMP: 10
SALES (est): 221.8K
SALES (corp-wide): 55.9MM **Privately Held**
SIC: 7372 Application computer software
PA: Zephyrtel, Inc.
401 Congress Ave Ste 2650
Austin TX 78701
920 490-7327

(G-8050)
MSI TECHNOLOGIES LLC (PA)
1055 Parsippany Blvd 205a (07054-1394)
PHONE..................................973 263-0080

▲ = Import ▼=Export
◆ =Import/Export

Fax: 973 927-5711
Dale Baver, *Partner*
Jeffrey Herwitt, *Partner*
Darren Pico,
Darren Sammartino,
EMP: 10
SALES: 2.7MM **Privately Held**
WEB: www.msitechnologies.net
SIC: 7373 7372 Computer integrated systems design; business oriented computer software

(G-8051)
OHAUS CORPORATION (DH)
7 Campus Dr Ste 310 (07054-4413)
PHONE................973 377-9000
Ted Xia, *President*
Jean-Yves Chever, *General Mgr*
Sue Fredericks, *Export Mgr*
Paul Lewandowski, *Purchasing*
Marty Colasurdo, *QC Mgr*
▲ **EMP:** 53 **EST:** 1897
SQ FT: 130,000
SALES (est): 10.2MM
SALES (corp-wide): 2.7B **Publicly Held**
WEB: www.ohaus.com
SIC: 3821 3596 3423 Laboratory measuring apparatus; balances, laboratory; industrial scales; hand & edge tools
HQ: Mettler-Toledo, Llc
1900 Polaris Pkwy Fl 6
Columbus OH 43240
614 438-4511

(G-8052)
ONKOS SURGICAL INC
77 E Halsey Rd (07054-3714)
PHONE................973 264-5400
Patrick Treacy, *President*
Gordon Ballard, *Vice Pres*
Charlie Christian, *Vice Pres*
Sean Curry, *Vice Pres*
Jerry Dalessio, *Vice Pres*
EMP: 27
SQ FT: 10,000
SALES: 2.2MM **Privately Held**
SIC: 3842 Implants, surgical

(G-8053)
PACIFICHEALTH LABORATORIES INC (PA)
800 Lanidex Plz Ste 220 (07054-2795)
PHONE................732 739-2900
Fax: 732 739-4360
Fred Duffner, *President*
Stephen P Kuchen, *CFO*
▲ **EMP:** 9
SQ FT: 3,200
SALES: 6.9MM **Publicly Held**
WEB: www.pacifichealthlabs.com
SIC: 2834 2833 Vitamin, nutrient & hematinic preparations for human use; vitamins, natural or synthetic: bulk, uncompounded

(G-8054)
PACIRA PHARMACEUTICALS INC (PA)
5 Sylvan Way Ste 300 (07054-3813)
PHONE................973 254-3560
David Stack, *Ch of Bd*
Scott Braunstein, *COO*
James B Jones, *Senior VP*
Richard Scranton, *Vice Pres*
Charles A Reinhart III, *CFO*
EMP: 487
SQ FT: 42,000
SALES: 286.6MM **Publicly Held**
SIC: 2834 Pharmaceutical preparations

(G-8055)
PBF ENERGY COMPANY
1 Sylvan Way Ste 2 (07054-3879)
PHONE................973 455-7500
Thomas Nimbley, *CEO*
EMP: 5
SALES (est): 553.4K **Privately Held**
SIC: 2911 Petroleum refining

(G-8056)
PBF ENERGY COMPANY LLC (HQ)
Also Called: Pbf Tdo
1 Sylvan Way Ste 2 (07054-3879)
PHONE................973 455-7500

Thomas J Nimbley, *CEO*
Thomas O'Malley, *Ch of Bd*
Michael Gayda, *President*
Jeffrey Dill, *Senior VP*
Matthew Lucey, *CFO*
◆ **EMP:** 80
SALES (est): 21.7B
SALES (corp-wide): 21.7B **Publicly Held**
WEB: www.pbfenergy.com
SIC: 2911 Petroleum refining
PA: Pbf Energy Inc.
1 Sylvan Way Ste 2
Parsippany NJ 07054
973 455-7500

(G-8057)
PBF ENERGY INC (PA)
1 Sylvan Way Ste 2 (07054-3879)
PHONE................973 455-7500
Thomas J Nimbley, *Ch of Bd*
Matthew C Lucey, *President*
Trecia Canty, *Senior VP*
Thomas L O'Connor, *Senior VP*
Herman Seedorf, *Senior VP*
◆ **EMP:** 1714
SQ FT: 58,000
SALES: 21.7B **Publicly Held**
SIC: 2911 Petroleum refining

(G-8058)
PBF HOLDING COMPANY LLC (DH)
Also Called: PBF TDO
1 Sylvan Way Ste 2 (07054-3879)
PHONE................888 661-8949
Thomas J Nimbley, *CEO*
Michael Gayda, *President*
Jeffrey Dill, *Senior VP*
Matthew Lucey, *Vice Pres*
Erik Young, *CFO*
◆ **EMP:** 254
SQ FT: 53,000
SALES: 21.7B
SALES (corp-wide): 21.7B **Publicly Held**
SIC: 2911 2992 Petroleum refining; lubricating oils

(G-8059)
PBF SERVICES COMPANY LLC
1 Sylvan Way Ste 2 (07054-3879)
PHONE................973 455-7500
EMP: 1
SALES (est): 6.8MM
SALES (corp-wide): 21.7B **Publicly Held**
SIC: 2911 Petroleum refining
PA: Pbf Energy Inc.
1 Sylvan Way Ste 2
Parsippany NJ 07054
973 455-7500

(G-8060)
PENSKE TRUCK LEASING CO LP
600 Edwards Rd (07054-4202)
PHONE................973 575-0169
EMP: 30
SALES (corp-wide): 2.8B **Privately Held**
WEB: www.pensketruckleasing.com
SIC: 7513 4213 3519 Truck leasing, without drivers; truck rental, without drivers; contract haulers; diesel engine rebuilding
PA: Penske Truck Leasing Co., L.P.
2675 Morgantown Rd
Reading PA 19607
610 775-6000

(G-8061)
PFIZER INC
400 Webro Rd (07054-2894)
PHONE................973 739-0430
Tom Ladas, *Vice Pres*
Bob Van Andel, *Finance*
Jaymie Carbon, *Manager*
Anthony Corso, *Manager*
EMP: 100
SALES (corp-wide): 52.5B **Publicly Held**
WEB: www.pfizer.com
SIC: 2844 8741 Cosmetic preparations; management services
PA: Pfizer Inc.
235 E 42nd St
New York NY 10017
212 733-2323

(G-8062)
PIERRE FBRE PHRMACEUTICALS INC
8 Campus Dr Ste 2 (07054-4409)
PHONE................973 898-1042
Jean Jacques Bertrand, *Chairman*
EMP: 6
SALES (est): 873.3K **Privately Held**
SIC: 2834 Pharmaceutical preparations
HQ: Pierre Fabre Medicament
Labo Robopharm Pierre Fabre Pharmaceut
Boulogne Billancourt 92100
563 712-125

(G-8063)
PINNACLE FOODS FINANCE LLC (DH)
399 Jefferson Rd (07054-3707)
PHONE................973 541-6620
Robert J Gamgort, *CEO*
John Butler, *Exec VP*
Mary Beth Denooyer, *Exec VP*
Antonio F Fernandez, *Exec VP*
Duncan Hines, *Exec VP*
▲ **EMP:** 108
SALES: 2.4B
SALES (corp-wide): 3.1B **Publicly Held**
SIC: 2038 2092 2099 2045 Frozen specialties; breakfasts, frozen & packaged; pizza, frozen; waffles, frozen; prepared fish or other seafood cakes & sticks; pancake syrup, blended & mixed; cake flour: from purchased flour; pancake mixes, prepared: from purchased flour

(G-8064)
PINNACLE FOODS GROUP LLC (DH)
399 Jefferson Rd (07054-3707)
PHONE................856 969-8238
Robert J Gamgort, *CEO*
Roger Deromedi, *Ch of Bd*
Mark L Schiller, *President*
Marybeth Denooyer, *Exec VP*
Antonio F Fernandez, *Exec VP*
◆ **EMP:** 60
SALES: 796.3MM
SALES (corp-wide): 3.1B **Publicly Held**
WEB: www.aurorafoods.com
SIC: 2038 2092 2099 2045 Frozen specialties; breakfasts, frozen & packaged; pizza, frozen; waffles, frozen; prepared fish or other seafood cakes & sticks; pancake syrup, blended & mixed; cake flour: from purchased flour; bread & bread type roll mixes: from purchased flour; pancake mixes, prepared: from purchased flour

(G-8065)
PINNACLE FOODS INC (PA)
399 Jefferson Rd (07054-3707)
P.O. Box 3900, Peoria IL (61612-3900)
PHONE................973 541-6620
Fax: 856 969-7303
Mark Clouse, *CEO*
Roger Deromedi, *Ch of Bd*
Michael Allen, *President*
Mark Schiller, *President*
Tony Fernandez, *Exec VP*
EMP: 112
SALES: 3.1B **Publicly Held**
SIC: 2038 2035 Frozen specialties; pickles, sauces & salad dressings

(G-8066)
PINSONAULT ASSOCIATES LLC
5 Woodhollow Rd Ste 2 (07054-2832)
PHONE................800 372-9009
Fax: 973 448-1005
Tony Pinsonault, *Mktg Dir*
Christian Pinsonault,
Elizabeth Pinsonault,
EMP: 40
SQ FT: 10,000
SALES (est): 2.9MM
SALES (corp-wide): 502.1MM **Privately Held**
WEB: www.pinsonault.com
SIC: 7372 Business oriented computer software
HQ: Decision Resources, Inc.
100 District Ave Ste 213
Burlington MA 01803
781 993-2500

(G-8067)
PIRATE BRANDS LLC
4 Gatehall Dr Ste 110 (07054-4522)
PHONE................973 401-6500
Mike Repole, *Mng Member*
Mel Ehrlich,
Jorgene Hertzwig,
EMP: 10
SALES (est): 1.3MM
SALES (corp-wide): 1.6B **Publicly Held**
WEB: www.robertsamericangourmet.com
SIC: 2096 Potato chips & similar snacks
HQ: B&G Foods North America, Inc.
4 Gatehall Dr Ste 110
Parsippany NJ 07054
973 401-6500

(G-8068)
PNY TECHNOLOGIES INC (PA)
100 Jefferson Rd (07054-3708)
PHONE................973 515-9700
Fax: 973 560-5283
Gadi Cohen, *Ch of Bd*
John Hughes, *Senior VP*
Robert Stone, *Senior VP*
Alfonso Huaman, *Facilities Mgr*
Mark Ciano, *VP Finance*
▲ **EMP:** 380
SALES (est): 170.1MM **Privately Held**
WEB: Www.pny.com
SIC: 3572 Computer storage devices

(G-8069)
POLARIS PLATING INC
36 Teaneck Rd (07054-3642)
PHONE................973 278-0033
Frank J Zemo, *President*
EMP: 9
SQ FT: 20,000
SALES (est): 86.8K **Privately Held**
SIC: 3471 Electroplating of metals or formed products; finishing, metals or formed products

(G-8070)
PRECISION SPINE INC (PA)
5 Sylvan Way Fl 2 (07054-3818)
PHONE................601 420-4244
James R Pastena, *Ch of Bd*
Rich Dickerson, *President*
Christopher A Denicola, *COO*
Joe Deluca, *Senior VP*
Bob Fruge, *Vice Pres*
EMP: 10 **EST:** 2012
SALES (est): 2MM **Privately Held**
SIC: 3841 Anesthesia apparatus

(G-8071)
PREDICTIVE ANALYTCS DCISION
Also Called: Prads
2001 Route 46 Ste 310 (07054-1315)
PHONE................973 541-7020
Vivek Agarwal, *Exec Dir*
EMP: 2
SALES: 1MM **Privately Held**
SIC: 7372 Prepackaged software
PA: Predictive Analytics Mauritius Holding Limited
C/O Dtos Ltd Raffles Tower, 19
Ebene
404 600-0

(G-8072)
PRINTING INDUSTRIES LLC
Also Called: D R Printing
1543 Us Hwy Rte 46 E (07054)
PHONE................973 334-9775
Deron Baumfeld, *Vice Pres*
Doug Rohlfing,
EMP: 8
SQ FT: 2,000
SALES (est): 450K **Privately Held**
SIC: 2752 Commercial printing, offset

(G-8073)
PRISMACOLOR CORP
Also Called: Colortec Printing Ink
120 E Halsey Rd (07054-3720)
P.O. Box 6330 (07054-7330)
PHONE................973 887-6040
Edward Ranno, *President*
EMP: 7
SALES (est): 860K **Privately Held**
SIC: 5085 2893 Ink, printers'; printing ink

GEOGRAPHIC

(G-8074)
QUADRANT MEDIA CORP INC (PA)
7 Century Dr Ste 302 (07054-4609)
PHONE..................................973 701-8900
Stephen Stoneburn, *President*
EMP: 2
SALES (est): 42.8MM Privately Held
WEB: www.ptmg.com
SIC: 2721 Trade journals: publishing & printing

(G-8075)
RB HEALTH MANUFACTURING US LLC
399 Interpace Pkwy (07054-1133)
PHONE..................................973 404-2600
Nitish Kapoor, *President*
Geoffroy Ribadeau Dumas, *Vice Pres*
Paulo Quirino Dos Reis, *Vice Pres*
Andrew Gilchrist, *VP Mfg*
Gabriel Millan, *Treasurer*
EMP: 331 Privately Held
SIC: 3841 Druggists' preparations (pharmaceuticals)

(G-8076)
RB MANUFACTURING LLC (DH)
399 Interpace Pkwy (07054-1133)
P.O. Box 225 (07054-0225)
PHONE..................................973 404-2600
Alexander Lacik, *President*
Krista Davis, *Vice Pres*
Philippe Escoffier, *Vice Pres*
Kelly M Slavitt, *Vice Pres*
Clayton Thomas, *Warehouse Mgr*
EMP: 248
SALES (est): 358.3MM
SALES (corp-wide): 15.2B Privately Held
SIC: 2035 2842 Mustard, prepared (wet); deodorants, nonpersonal; specialty cleaning preparations; laundry cleaning preparations; disinfectants, household or industrial plant
HQ: Reckitt Benckiser Llc
    399 Interpace Pkwy # 101
    Parsippany NJ 07054
    973 404-2600

(G-8077)
RECKITT BENCKISER LLC (HQ)
399 Interpace Pkwy # 101 (07054-1133)
P.O. Box 225 (07054-0225)
PHONE..................................973 404-2600
Rakesh Kapoor, *CEO*
Alexander Lacik, *President*
Laurent Faracci, *General Mgr*
Chris Tedesco, *General Mgr*
Javed Ahmed, *Principal*
◆ EMP: 400
SQ FT: 139,500
SALES (est): 896.8MM
SALES (corp-wide): 15.2B Privately Held
WEB: www.reckittprofessional.com
SIC: 2035 2842 Mustard, prepared (wet); deodorants, nonpersonal
PA: Reckitt Benckiser Group Plc
    103-105 Bath Road
    Slough BERKS SL1 3
    175 350-6800

(G-8078)
REGENT CABINETS LLC (PA)
1719 State Rt 10 Ste 220 (07054-4537)
PHONE..................................732 363-5630
Reuvan Sternstein, *President*
EMP: 11 EST: 2012
SQ FT: 25,000
SALES (est): 3.6MM Privately Held
SIC: 2434 Wood kitchen cabinets

(G-8079)
RESPIRONICS INC
Also Called: Respironics Healthscan
5 Woodhollow Rd Ste 1 (07054-2832)
PHONE..................................973 581-6000
Fax: 973 599-5646
EMP: 171
SALES (corp-wide): 26B Privately Held
SIC: 3842 3845 3841 3564 Mfg Surgical Appliances Mfg Electromedical Equip Mfg Surgical/Med Instr

HQ: Respironics, Inc.
    1010 Murry Ridge Ln
    Murrysville PA 15668
    724 387-5200

(G-8080)
ROCKWELL AUTOMATION INC
299 Cherry Hill Rd # 200 (07054-1111)
PHONE..................................973 658-1500
Jim Tomamichel, *Branch Mgr*
EMP: 40 Publicly Held
SIC: 3625 Control equipment, electric
PA: Rockwell Automation, Inc.
    1201 S 2nd St
    Milwaukee WI 53204

(G-8081)
ROCKWELL AUTOMATION INC
700 Lanidex Plz Ste 101 (07054-2705)
PHONE..................................973 526-3901
Adam Kirshbaum, *Engineer*
EMP: 9 Publicly Held
SIC: 3625 Relays & industrial controls
PA: Rockwell Automation, Inc.
    1201 S 2nd St
    Milwaukee WI 53204

(G-8082)
ROSEMOUNT INC
1160 Parsippany Blvd # 102 (07054-1811)
PHONE..................................973 257-2300
Fax: 973 257-0539
Doug Viafora, *Manager*
EMP: 12
SALES (corp-wide): 15.2B Publicly Held
WEB: www.rosemount.com
SIC: 3823 Manometers, industrial process type
HQ: Rosemount Inc.
    8200 Market Blvd
    Chanhassen MN 55317
    952 906-8888

(G-8083)
SAYBOLT NORTH AMERICA INC
300 Lanidex Plz (07054-2723)
PHONE..................................973 884-3200
Fax: 201 884-1881
Frerik Pluimer, *President*
David Mead, *Exec VP*
Jan W Heinsbroek, *Vice Pres*
Robert Petoia, *Treasurer*
Joseph Maddaloni Jr, *Admin Sec*
EMP: 500
SQ FT: 15,273
SALES (est): 30.7MM Privately Held
SIC: 1389 Testing, measuring, surveying & analysis services; oil consultants; oil field services

(G-8084)
SENSOREDGE INC
140 Littleton Rd Ste 220 (07054-1896)
PHONE..................................973 975-4163
Igor Ofenbakh, *CEO*
EMP: 7
SALES (est): 785.7K Privately Held
SIC: 2834 Medicines, capsuled or ampuled

(G-8085)
SEVERNA OPERATIONS INC
3 Eastmans Rd (07054-3702)
PHONE..................................973 503-1600
Fax: 973 503-1704
Samir Aboulhosn, *President*
Sharon Lester, *Personnel Exec*
EMP: 28
SALES (est): 5.4MM Privately Held
SIC: 3678 Electronic connectors

(G-8086)
SIGNIFY FINCL SOLUTIONS LLC
300 Interpace Pkwy Bldg A (07054-1100)
PHONE..................................862 930-4682
Jeffrey Oulton, *CEO*
Olga Dovgan, *Business Anlyst*
EMP: 33 EST: 2013
SALES (est): 686.8K Privately Held
SIC: 7372 Publishers' computer software

(G-8087)
SIMON & SCHUSTER INC
1639 State Rt 10 Ste 200 (07054-4506)
PHONE..................................973 656-6000
Dave Upchurch, *Controller*
EMP: 50

SALES (corp-wide): 13.7B Publicly Held
WEB: www.digonsite.com
SIC: 2731 2741 7372 8732 Books: publishing only; textbooks: publishing only, not printed on site; miscellaneous publishing; technical manuals: publishing only, not printed on site; maps: publishing only, not printed on site; atlases: publishing only, not printed on site; business oriented computer software; business research service
HQ: Simon & Schuster, Inc.
    1230 Ave Of The Americas
    New York NY 10020
    212 698-7000

(G-8088)
SKYLINE STEEL CORPORATION
8 Woodhollow Rd Ste 102 (07054-2829)
PHONE..................................973 428-6100
Fax: 973 428-7399
EMP: 500
SALES (est): 76.7K Privately Held
SIC: 2296 Tire cord & fabrics

(G-8089)
SONNEBORN LLC (HQ)
600 Parsippany Rd Ste 100 (07054-3715)
PHONE..................................201 760-2940
Paul Raymond III, *President*
Joe Brignola, *Vice Pres*
John Holloway, *Vice Pres*
Todd Weinblatt, *Vice Pres*
Steve Puskas, *Project Engr*
▼ EMP: 11
SALES (est): 78.9MM
SALES (corp-wide): 2.3B Privately Held
SIC: 2869 Industrial organic chemicals
PA: Oep Capital Advisors, L.P.
    510 Madison Ave Fl 19
    New York NY 10022
    212 277-1552

(G-8090)
SONNEBORN HOLDING LLC
600 Parsippany Rd Ste 100 (07054-3715)
PHONE..................................201 760-2940
Luther Jones, *Vice Pres*
Gregg Kam, *CFO*
Paul C Raymond III, *Mng Member*
James Stiff, *
EMP: 340
SALES (est): 69.6MM Privately Held
WEB: www.sonneborn.com
SIC: 2869 Fluorinated hydrocarbon gases

(G-8091)
SPICE GRILL
111 Us Highway 46 (07054-2300)
PHONE..................................973 882-4646
Raja Jhanji, *Principal*
EMP: 4
SALES (est): 382.4K Privately Held
SIC: 2599 Bar, restaurant & cafeteria furniture

(G-8092)
STANDARD INDUSTRIES INC (DH)
Also Called: Bmca
1 Campus Dr (07054-4404)
PHONE..................................973 628-3000
Robert B Tafaro, *President*
Richard A Nowak, *COO*
Daniel J Goldstein, *Senior VP*
Jan E Jerger-Stevens, *Senior VP*
Matti Kiik, *Senior VP*
◆ EMP: 1000
SALES (est): 1.3B
SALES (corp-wide): 1.5B Privately Held
SIC: 2493 Insulation & roofing material, reconstituted wood
HQ: Bmca Holdings Corporation
    1361 Alps Rd
    Wayne NJ 07470
    973 628-3000

(G-8093)
SUKHADIAS SWEETS & SNACKS
Also Called: Sukhadia's Indian Grill
61 New Rd (07054-4206)
PHONE..................................973 227-6400
Piyush Sukhadia, *President*
EMP: 4

SALES (est): 255.4K Privately Held
SIC: 2051 Cakes, pies & pastries
PA: Sukhadia's Sweets & Snacks Inc
    124 Case Dr
    South Plainfield NJ 07080

(G-8094)
SUN CHEMICAL CORPORATION (HQ)
Also Called: US Advanced Materials Division
35 Waterview Blvd Ste 100 (07054-1285)
P.O. Box 32040, Cincinnati OH (45232-0040)
PHONE..................................973 404-6000
Fax: 973 404-6001
Rudi Lenz, *CEO*
John L McKeown, *Senior VP*
Jeffrey Berger, *Vice Pres*
Raymond Perry, *Vice Pres*
Ken Sexton, *Vice Pres*
◆ EMP: 100
SALES (est): 2.4B
SALES (corp-wide): 7B Privately Held
WEB: www.sunchemical.com
SIC: 2893 2865 Printing ink; color pigments, organic
PA: Dic Corporation
    3-7-20, Nihombashi
    Chuo-Ku TKY 103-0
    367 333-000

(G-8095)
SYBASE INC
400 Interpace Pkwy Ste D1 (07054-1118)
PHONE..................................973 537-5700
EMP: 70
SALES (corp-wide): 22.5B Publicly Held
SIC: 7372 5045 Prepackaged Software Services Whol Computers/Peripherals
HQ: Sybase, Inc.
    1 Sybase Dr
    Dublin CA 94583
    925 236-5000

(G-8096)
TANGOE US INC (HQ)
169 Lackawanna Ave Ste 2b (07054-1007)
PHONE..................................973 257-0300
Robert Irwin, *CEO*
Chris Taylor, *CFO*
Sidra Berman, *Chief Mktg Ofcr*
Mike Sheridan, *Officer*
Eric Wansong, *Officer*
EMP: 120
SQ FT: 66,000
SALES (est): 383.5MM Privately Held
WEB: www.tangoe.com
SIC: 7372 Application computer software
PA: Tangoe, Llc
    6410 Poplar Ave Ste 200
    Memphis TN 38119
    901 752-6200

(G-8097)
TARGANTA THERAPEUTICS CORP (HQ)
8 Sylvan Way (07054-3801)
PHONE..................................973 290-6000
Mark W Leuchtenberger, *President*
Daniel S Char, *Vice Pres*
Roger D Miller, *VP Opers*
George A Eldridge, *CFO*
EMP: 70
SQ FT: 7,839
SALES (est): 4.1MM
SALES (corp-wide): 44.7MM Publicly Held
WEB: www.themedicinescompany.com
SIC: 2834 Pharmaceutical preparations
PA: The Medicines Company
    8 Sylvan Way
    Parsippany NJ 07054
    973 290-6000

(G-8098)
TEVA API INC
400 Interpace Pkwy Ste A1 (07054-1119)
PHONE..................................201 307-6900
Kerri Wood, *President*
Aharon Yaari, *Vice Pres*
Erez Israeli, *Director*
◆ EMP: 23
SQ FT: 4,200

SALES (est): 8.1MM
SALES (corp-wide): 22.3B **Privately Held**
WEB: www.plantexusa.com
SIC: **2834** Pharmaceutical preparations
PA: Teva Pharmaceutical Industries Limited
5 Bazel
Petah Tikva 49510
392 672-67

(G-8099)
TEVA PHARMACEUTICALS
400 Interpace Pkwy Ste A1 (07054-1119)
PHONE..................................888 838-2872
Kare Schultz, *President*
Lisa Pepe, *Senior Mgr*
Jane Frahn, *Associate Dir*
Helke Wright, *Executive Asst*
Susan Overgard, *Admin Asst*
▲ EMP: 13
SALES (est): 2.2MM **Privately Held**
SIC: **5912** 2834 Drug stores & proprietary stores; pharmaceutical preparations

(G-8100)
TEVA PHARMACEUTICALS USA INC
400 Interpace Pkwy Ste A1 (07054-1119)
PHONE..................................845 362-1100
Bruce Downey, *CEO*
EMP: 7
SALES (corp-wide): 22.3B **Privately Held**
SIC: **2834** Pharmaceutical preparations
HQ: Teva Pharmaceuticals Usa, Inc.
1090 Horsham Rd
North Wales PA 19454
215 591-3000

(G-8101)
TILCON NEW YORK INC (DH)
Also Called: Totowa Asphalt
9 Entin Rd (07054-5000)
PHONE..................................800 789-7625
Fax: 845 480-3128
Charles Clifton Morris, *President*
Natalie Lopez, *Business Mgr*
Dan Batelli, *Transptn Dir*
Mel Rodriguez, *Warehouse Mgr*
Dave Buccafusca, *Foreman/Supr*
▲ EMP: 270 EST: 1964
SALES (est): 466MM
SALES (corp-wide): 29.7B **Privately Held**
WEB: www.tilconny.com
SIC: **1429** 5039 Trap rock, crushed & broken-quarrying; dolomitic marble, crushed & broken-quarrying; metal buildings
HQ: Tilcon Inc.
301 Hartford Ave
Newington CT 06111
860 223-3651

(G-8102)
TILCON NEW YORK INC
Also Called: Mount Hope Quarry
9 Entin Rd Ste 12 (07054-5000)
PHONE..................................800 789-7625
EMP: 8
SALES (corp-wide): 29.7B **Privately Held**
SIC: **1429** 2911 Trap rock, crushed & broken-quarrying; asphalt or asphaltic materials, made in refineries
HQ: Tilcon New York Inc.
9 Entin Rd
Parsippany NJ 07054
800 789-7625

(G-8103)
TOYOTA MOTOR SALES
300 Webro Rd (07054-2825)
PHONE..................................973 515-5012
EMP: 12
SALES (est): 862.9K **Privately Held**
SIC: **5511** 5012 3711 Automobiles, new & used; automobile auction; motor vehicles & car bodies

(G-8104)
TSI ACCESSORY GROUP INC (HQ)
Also Called: Roman & Sunstone
141 New Rd Ste 210 (07054-4297)
PHONE..................................847 965-1700
Sally Haigh Alex, *President*
John Burnett, *Finance Dir*
Annette Eckerle, *Admin Sec*
▲ EMP: 95
SQ FT: 95,000

SALES (est): 9.5MM
SALES (corp-wide): 221.8MM **Privately Held**
SIC: **5944** 3961 Jewelry stores; costume jewelry
PA: Tsi Holding Company
999 Exectve Pkwy Dr # 202
Saint Louis MO 63141
314 628-6000

(G-8105)
UA PIPEFITTERS LOCAL 274
205 Jefferson Rd (07054-2827)
PHONE..................................201 943-4700
John R Wende, *Treasurer*
EMP: 7
SALES (est): 883.8K **Privately Held**
SIC: **3089** Fittings for pipe, plastic

(G-8106)
UKRAINIAN NATIONAL ASSOCIATION (PA)
2200 State Rt 10 Ste 201 (07054-5305)
P.O. Box 280 (07054-0280)
PHONE..................................973 292-9800
Fax: 973 292-0900
Stefan Kaczaraj, *President*
Michael Koziupa, *Vice Pres*
Eugene Oscislawski, *Vice Pres*
Myron Groch, *Director*
Christine Kozak, *Admin Sec*
EMP: 41
SALES: 15.5MM **Privately Held**
WEB: www.ukrweekly.com
SIC: **6311** 6512 6513 2711 Fraternal life insurance organizations; commercial & industrial building operation; apartment building operators; newspapers

(G-8107)
VALIDUS PHARMACEUTICALS LLC (PA)
119 Cherry Hill Rd # 310 (07054-1126)
PHONE..................................973 265-2777
Lee Rios, *President*
Richard Post, *Vice Pres*
Gina Walljasper, *Purchasing*
David Paznek, *QC Mgr*
Rick White, *Accountant*
EMP: 13
SALES (est): 3.2MM **Privately Held**
SIC: **2834** Pharmaceutical preparations

(G-8108)
VANDERBILT LLC
Also Called: Vanderbilt Industries
2 Cranberry Rd Ste 3b (07054-1053)
PHONE..................................973 316-3900
Mitchell Kane,
EMP: 35 EST: 2013
SALES (est): 4.7MM
SALES (corp-wide): 4.8MM **Privately Held**
SIC: **7382** 3651 Security systems services; audio electronic systems
PA: A.C.R.E., Llc
300 State St
New London CT 06320
949 637-0423

(G-8109)
VENUS LABORATORIES INC
50 Lackawanna Ave (07054-1008)
PHONE..................................973 257-8983
EMP: 25
SALES (corp-wide): 93.5MM **Privately Held**
SIC: **2842** Mfg Polish/Sanitation Goods
PA: Venus Laboratories, Inc.
111 S Rohlwing Rd
Addison IL 60101
630 595-1900

(G-8110)
WARNER CHILCOTT (US) LLC (DH)
Also Called: Warner Chilcott Laboratories
400 Interpace Pkwy (07054-1120)
PHONE..................................862 261-7000
Roger Boissonneault, *CEO*
Leland Cross, *Senior VP*
Izumi Hara, *Senior VP*
William Poll, *Vice Pres*
John Goll, *CFO*
▲ EMP: 58

SQ FT: 16,000
SALES (est): 100.9MM **Privately Held**
SIC: **2834** Pharmaceutical preparations
HQ: Warner Chilcott Corporation
100 Enterprise Dr Ste 280
Rockaway NJ 07866
862 261-7000

(G-8111)
WATERS TECHNOLOGIES CORP
1259 Route 46 Ste 3 (07054-4913)
PHONE..................................973 394-5660
John Antwerp, *Manager*
EMP: 10 **Publicly Held**
SIC: **3826** Chromatographic equipment, laboratory type
HQ: Waters Technologies Corporation, 34 Maple St
Milford MA 01757
508 478-2000

(G-8112)
WATSON LABORATORIES INC (DH)
Also Called: Allergan Pharmacy
400 Interpace Pkwy (07054-1120)
P.O. Box 1900, Corona CA (92878-1900)
PHONE..................................951 493-5300
Fax: 951 493-5842
Karin Shanahan, *President*
Paul M Bisaro, *Chairman*
Glenn Novick, *Purch Mgr*
Lawrence Ventura, *Director*
▲ EMP: 200
SQ FT: 100,000
SALES (est): 202.1MM **Privately Held**
SIC: **2834** Pharmaceutical preparations

(G-8113)
WINDOW TRENDS
194 Fieldcrest Rd (07054-2415)
PHONE..................................973 887-6676
Mike Ianndone, *Owner*
EMP: 4
SALES (est): 246.4K **Privately Held**
SIC: **2431** Window frames, wood

(G-8114)
WIRELESS TELECOM GROUP INC (PA)
25 Eastmans Rd (07054-3702)
PHONE..................................973 386-9696
Timothy Whelan, *CEO*
Alan L Bazaar, *Ch of Bd*
Michael Kandell, *CFO*
Daniel Monopoli, *CTO*
EMP: 67
SQ FT: 45,700
SALES: 46MM **Publicly Held**
WEB: www.willtek.com
SIC: **3625** 3825 Noise control equipment; microwave test equipment; semiconductor test equipment; volt meters

(G-8115)
WIZDATA SYSTEMS INC
140 Littleton Rd Ste 220 (07054-1896)
PHONE..................................973 975-4113
Igor Ofenbakh, *President*
EMP: 12
SQ FT: 300
SALES: 1.2MM **Privately Held**
WEB: www.wdsystems.com
SIC: **8732** 7372 Business analysis; prepackaged software

(G-8116)
WM STEINEN MFG CO (PA)
29 E Halsey Rd (07054-3704)
PHONE..................................973 887-6400
Fax: 973 887-4632
William Steinen, *CEO*
Thomas Keenan, *Vice Pres*
Sylvia Hunts, *CIO*
John Delaney, *Admin Sec*
EMP: 98 EST: 1907
SQ FT: 40,000
SALES (est): 19.7MM **Privately Held**
WEB: www.steinen.com
SIC: **3494** 3432 3491 Valves & pipe fittings; plumbing & heating valves; plumbing fixture fittings & trim; process control regulator valves

(G-8117)
YUKON GRAPHICS INC
239 New Rd Ste B110 (07054-5614)
PHONE..................................973 575-5700
Fax: 973 575-5795
Alan Verbeke, *President*
Debbie Hanley, *Admin Sec*
EMP: 4
SQ FT: 16,000
SALES (est): 620.3K **Privately Held**
WEB: www.yukongraphics.com
SIC: **2752** Commercial printing, offset

(G-8118)
ZIMMER TRABECULAR MET TECH INC
10 Pomeroy Rd (07054-3722)
PHONE..................................973 576-0032
Fax: 973 884-6084
David Dvorak, *CEO*
Alex Khowaylo, *CEO*
Ajey Atre, *General Mgr*
EMP: 180
SQ FT: 100,000
SALES (est): 35.1MM
SALES (corp-wide): 7.8B **Publicly Held**
WEB: www.implex.com
SIC: **3841** 3842 Veterinarians' instruments & apparatus; implants, surgical
PA: Zimmer Biomet Holdings, Inc.
345 E Main St
Warsaw IN 46580
574 267-6131

(G-8119)
ZOETIS INC (PA)
10 Sylvan Way Ste 105 (07054-3825)
PHONE..................................973 822-7000
Juan Ramon Alaix, *CEO*
Michael B McCallister, *Ch of Bd*
Shirley Thompson, *Business Mgr*
Nicole Werner, *Business Mgr*
Tom White, *Business Mgr*
EMP: 277
SALES: 5.3B **Publicly Held**
SIC: **2834** Pharmaceutical preparations

(G-8120)
ZOETIS LLC (HQ)
10 Sylvan Way Ste 105 (07054-3825)
PHONE..................................973 822-7000
Juan Ramon Alaix, *CEO*
Roxanne Lagano, *Exec VP*
Stefan Weiskopf, *Exec VP*
EMP: 277 EST: 2012
SALES (est): 396.8MM
SALES (corp-wide): 5.3B **Publicly Held**
SIC: **2834** Pharmaceutical preparations
PA: Zoetis Inc.
10 Sylvan Way Ste 105
Parsippany NJ 07054
973 822-7000

Passaic
Passaic County

(G-8121)
3FORTY GROUP INC
90 Dayton Ave Ste 6a (07055-7014)
PHONE..................................973 773-1806
Jason Kin, *President*
EMP: 15
SQ FT: 13,000
SALES: 2.5MM **Privately Held**
SIC: **2253** Shirts (outerwear), knit

(G-8122)
A S A P NAMEPLATE & LABELING
Also Called: ASAP Printed Products
92 1st St (07055-6438)
PHONE..................................973 773-3934
EMP: 10
SALES (est): 690K **Privately Held**
SIC: **3479** 2789 2396 Coating/Engraving Service Bookbinding/Related Work Mfg Auto/Apparel Trimming

(G-8123)
A W ROSS INC
297 Monroe St Ste 1 (07055-5293)
PHONE..................................973 471-5900
Fax: 973 471-5926

Vojtek Rys, *President*
EMP: 14 **EST:** 1968
SQ FT: 28,000
SALES (est): 1.8MM **Privately Held**
SIC: 2541 2434 Counters or counter display cases, wood; wood kitchen cabinets

(G-8124)
ACME ENGRAVING CO INC (PA)
19-37 Delaware Ave (07055-2099)
P.O. Box 1657 (07055-1657)
PHONE................................973 778-0885
Fax: 973 778-1790
Roy Murat, *President*
EMP: 45 **EST:** 1947
SQ FT: 30,000
SALES (est): 4MM **Privately Held**
WEB: www.acmeengraving.com
SIC: 2796 2754 3479 3471 Platemaking services; rotogravure printing; etching & engraving; plating & polishing; printing trades machinery

(G-8125)
ARMADILLO METALWORKS INC
61 Willet St Ste 1 (07055-1971)
PHONE................................973 777-2105
Jesse Krzywon, *President*
EMP: 23
SALES (est): 4.9MM **Privately Held**
SIC: 3479 Sherardizing of metals or metal products

(G-8126)
ATLANTIC MILLS INC
Also Called: Illinois Tools
1 Market St Ste 9 (07055-7364)
PHONE................................973 344-2001
Michael O'Connell, *General Mgr*
▲ **EMP:** 65
SQ FT: 95,000
SALES (est): 6.8MM **Privately Held**
WEB: www.atlanticmills.com
SIC: 2211 Towels, dishcloths & washcloths: cotton

(G-8127)
BEARHANDS LTD
90 Dayton Ave Ste 9 (07055-7016)
PHONE................................201 807-9898
Jeffrey Golden, *President*
Michael Wolinsky, *Vice Pres*
▲ **EMP:** 4
SALES (est): 363.1K **Privately Held**
WEB: www.bearhands.net
SIC: 2399 Hand woven apparel

(G-8128)
BETSY & ADAM LTD
Also Called: London Nite
90 Dayton Ave Ste 36 (07055-7017)
PHONE................................212 302-3750
Fax: 973 594-0198
Michael Sklar, *Manager*
EMP: 15
SALES (corp-wide): 17MM **Privately Held**
WEB: www.betsyandadam.com
SIC: 5621 2335 Women's clothing stores; women's, juniors' & misses' dresses
PA: Betsy & Adam, Ltd.
　525 Fashion Ave Fl 21
　New York NY 10018
　212 302-3750

(G-8129)
CLOTHING EMPORIUM INC
682 Main Ave (07055-5115)
PHONE................................973 773-3250
Park Young, *Officer*
EMP: 14
SALES (corp-wide): 12.8MM **Privately Held**
SIC: 2759 Tickets: printing
PA: Clothing Emporium, Inc.
　375 Chestnut St
　Norwood NJ 07648
　201 843-3116

(G-8130)
COLONIAL - BENDE RIBBONS INC
180 Autumn St (07055-8511)
PHONE................................973 777-8700
Andras Bende, *President*
Rene Rioux, *President*

▲ **EMP:** 7
SQ FT: 10,000
SALES (est): 420K **Privately Held**
SIC: 2396 Ribbons & bows, cut & sewed

(G-8131)
COUNTERTOPS PLUS INC
61 Willet St (07055-1971)
PHONE................................973 365-2232
Fax: 973 365-0960
Leo Sullivan, *President*
EMP: 10
SQ FT: 4,000
SALES (est): 940K **Privately Held**
SIC: 2541 Counter & sink tops

(G-8132)
CROWN PRECISION CORP
61 Willet St Ste 6 (07055-1971)
PHONE................................973 470-0097
Fax: 973 470-9763
Todd W Evans, *President*
Patricia Evans, *Vice Pres*
EMP: 4 **EST:** 1997
SQ FT: 1,800
SALES (est): 330K **Privately Held**
SIC: 3599 Machine & other job shop work

(G-8133)
CUSTOM COUNTERS BY PRECISION
11-17 Linden St (07055-2709)
PHONE................................973 773-0111
Fax: 973 773-8203
William Pruseski, *President*
EMP: 25 **EST:** 1990
SALES (est): 3.9MM **Privately Held**
SIC: 2541 2821 2431 Counter & sink tops; plastics materials & resins; millwork

(G-8134)
DIMILO INDUSTRIES
90 Dayton Ave Ste 38 (07055-7017)
PHONE................................973 955-0460
Fax: 973 955-0464
Richard Krauser, *President*
EMP: 8 **EST:** 2007
SALES (est): 440K **Privately Held**
SIC: 3694 Engine electrical equipment

(G-8135)
DURAN CUTTING CORP
90 Dayton Ave Ste 6 (07055-7014)
PHONE................................973 916-0006
Rafael Duran, *President*
◆ **EMP:** 14
SALES (est): 1.5MM **Privately Held**
SIC: 2335 Bridal & formal gowns

(G-8136)
E5 USA INC
61 Willet St Ste 24 (07055-1950)
PHONE................................973 773-0750
Ron Koch, *President*
EMP: 7
SQ FT: 12,000
SALES (est): 700K **Privately Held**
SIC: 2389 Apparel for handicapped

(G-8137)
EMERALD ELECTRONICS USA INC
Also Called: E and E USA
90 Dayton Ave Ste 50 (07055-7019)
PHONE................................718 872-5544
Elliot Tobal, *CEO*
EMP: 9
SQ FT: 6,500
SALES: 400K **Privately Held**
SIC: 3634 Electric household cooking appliances

(G-8138)
ET MANUFACTURING & SALES INC
Also Called: Ferber Plastics
90 Dayton Ave Ste C5 (07055-7014)
PHONE................................973 777-6662
Michele Albo, *President*
▲ **EMP:** 45 **EST:** 1948
SQ FT: 26,000
SALES (est): 4.2MM **Privately Held**
SIC: 3993 Signs & advertising specialties

(G-8139)
ETHAN ALLEN RETAIL INC
1 Market St Ste 1 # 1 (07055-7364)
PHONE................................973 473-1019
Fax: 973 473-3255
Michael A Caffrey Jr, *Principal*
EMP: 125
SALES (corp-wide): 766.7MM **Publicly Held**
WEB: www.smyrna.ethanallen.com
SIC: 5712 3641 Furniture stores; electric lamps
HQ: Ethan Allen Retail, Inc.
　25 Lake Avenue Ext
　Danbury CT 06811
　203 743-8000

(G-8140)
FALSTROM COMPANY
1 Falstrom Ct (07055)
PHONE................................973 777-0013
Fax: 973 777-6396
Clifford F Lindholm III, *President*
EMP: 100 **EST:** 1870
SQ FT: 120,000
SALES (est): 23.3MM **Privately Held**
WEB: www.falstromcompany.com
SIC: 3441 Fabricated structural metal

(G-8141)
GARYS KIDS
314 Monroe St (07055-8437)
PHONE................................973 458-1818
Belkis D De Leon, *Principal*
EMP: 4
SALES (est): 318.5K **Privately Held**
SIC: 3672 Printed circuit boards

(G-8142)
GEIGER TOOL & MFG CO INC
50 Liberty St (07055-2737)
PHONE................................973 777-2136
Fax: 973 777-1514
James Nogrady, *President*
Josef Schormann, *Vice Pres*
Debrah Heller, *Manager*
Alba Vasquez, *Manager*
EMP: 16
SQ FT: 20,000
SALES: 2MM **Privately Held**
WEB: www.geigertool.com
SIC: 3599 Machine shop, jobbing & repair

(G-8143)
GEIGER TOOL CO INC
Also Called: LPI
50 Liberty St (07055-2737)
PHONE................................973 777-5094
James Nogrady, *President*
Josef Schormann, *Vice Pres*
EMP: 18
SQ FT: 20,000
SALES (est): 1.8MM **Privately Held**
SIC: 3599 Machine shop, jobbing & repair

(G-8144)
GENEVA METAL PRODUCTS CO INC
157 10th St (07055-8316)
PHONE................................973 472-3073
Fax: 973 472-6003
EMP: 14
SQ FT: 15,000
SALES (est): 1.5MM **Privately Held**
SIC: 3441 3469 3444 Structural Metal Fabrication Mfg Metal Stampings Mfg Sheet Metalwork

(G-8145)
GLOBAL WIRE & CABLE INC
61 Willet St Ste 4b (07055-1991)
PHONE................................973 471-1000
George Szakacs, *President*
Leslie Kovach, *Vice Pres*
EMP: 45 **EST:** 1973
SQ FT: 50,000
SALES (est): 886.3K **Privately Held**
SIC: 3315 3357 Wire, steel: insulated or armored; cable, steel: insulated or armored; nonferrous wiredrawing & insulating

(G-8146)
HAMPTON INDUSTRIES INC
1 Market St Ste 13 (07055-7364)
PHONE................................973 574-8900
Fax: 973 574-9042
Carl Streit, *Ch of Bd*
Michael Streit, *President*
EMP: 40
SQ FT: 1,700
SALES: 10MM **Privately Held**
SIC: 2259 Curtains & bedding, knit; bedspreads, knit

(G-8147)
HOUSE OF HERBS INC
Also Called: Prime Choice Foods
38 Ann St (07055-5889)
P.O. Box 178 (07055-0178)
PHONE................................973 779-2422
Fax: 973 779-6809
Paul Fischer, *President*
EMP: 8
SQ FT: 15,000
SALES (est): 550K **Privately Held**
SIC: 2035 Pickles, sauces & salad dressings

(G-8148)
INTERCHANGE EQUIPMENT INC
90 Dayton Ave Ste 120 (07055-7041)
PHONE................................973 473-5005
Fax: 973 473-4485
Marc Herrmann, *President*
▲ **EMP:** 30
SQ FT: 30,000
SALES (est): 9.9MM **Privately Held**
SIC: 5084 3555 Printing trades machinery, equipment & supplies; printing trades machinery

(G-8149)
J G SCHMIDT STEEL
Also Called: J G Schmidt Iron Works
211 Central Ave (07055-8613)
PHONE................................973 473-4822
Fax: 973 473-5031
Raymond C Schlaier Jr, *President*
Robert Schlaier, *Vice Pres*
EMP: 19 **EST:** 1956
SQ FT: 20,000
SALES (est): 5.4MM **Privately Held**
SIC: 3441 3446 Building components, structural steel; architectural metalwork

(G-8150)
JACK GEORGES INC
823 Main Ave (07055-8401)
PHONE................................973 777-6999
Fax: 973 777-6028
Jack Georges, *President*
Frank Georges, *Vice Pres*
Denise Dellavolpe, *Financial Exec*
Brian Cousins, *Sales Staff*
Tom Lambrinides, *Mktg Dir*
▲ **EMP:** 35
SQ FT: 16,000
SALES: 6.6MM **Privately Held**
WEB: www.jackgeorges.com
SIC: 3161 Briefcases

(G-8151)
JACKIE EVANS INC
Also Called: Jackie Evans Fashions
18 3rd St 26 (07055-7310)
PHONE................................973 471-6991
Mario Monaco Sr, *President*
Mario Monaco Jr, *Vice Pres*
Domenick Monaco, *Admin Sec*
EMP: 150
SQ FT: 50,000
SALES (est): 13.2MM **Privately Held**
WEB: www.jackieevans.com
SIC: 2337 Women's & misses' suits & coats

(G-8152)
JRM INDUSTRIES INC (PA)
1 Mattimore St (07055-7009)
PHONE................................973 779-9340
Melvin Siegel, *Ch of Bd*
Lou Simon, *President*
Donna Simon, *Treasurer*
Steven Pearlman, *Controller*
Luke Lawley, *Sales Staff*
▲ **EMP:** 55 **EST:** 1920
SQ FT: 36,000

SALES (est): 8.4MM **Privately Held**
WEB: www.jrm.com
SIC: **2241** 2672 2679 2759 Ribbons; fabric tapes; labels, woven; tape, pressure sensitive: made from purchased materials; tags, paper (unprinted): made from purchased paper; commercial printing; packaging paper & plastics film, coated & laminated; automotive & apparel trimmings

(G-8153)
K & K AUTOMOTIVE INC
979 Main Ave (07055-8620)
PHONE......................973 777-2235
Fax: 973 777-4777
Abe Hazian, *President*
Imran Hazian, *Admin Sec*
EMP: 6 EST: 1966
SQ FT: 8,500
SALES (est): 510K **Privately Held**
WEB: www.kkautomotive.com
SIC: **3714** Motor vehicle engines & parts

(G-8154)
K-D INDUSTRIES INC
18 Falstrom Ct (07055-4465)
P.O. Box 118 (07055-0118)
PHONE......................973 594-4800
Fax: 973 594-4700
Chris D'Alessandro, *President*
Glenn D'Alessandro, *Vice Pres*
Bruce Eklfon, *Bookkeeper*
Ajay Patel, *Manager*
EMP: 52
SQ FT: 12,000
SALES: 2.5MM **Privately Held**
SIC: **3599** Machine shop, jobbing & repair

(G-8155)
KINNERY PRECISION LLC
Also Called: Kinnery Metal
11 Exchange Pl (07055-4904)
PHONE......................973 473-4664
Chaudhari Naresh, *Mng Member*
EMP: 5
SQ FT: 5,000
SALES (est): 410K **Privately Held**
SIC: **3523** Farm machinery & equipment

(G-8156)
LA MILAGROSA
32 Wall St (07055-8320)
PHONE......................973 928-1799
▲ EMP: 4
SALES (est): 497.1K **Privately Held**
SIC: **3429** Keys, locks & related hardware

(G-8157)
LOVELINE INDUSTRIES INC
90 Dayton Ave Ste 33 (07055-7017)
PHONE......................973 928-3427
Martin Goldstein, *President*
Adam Goldstein, *Vice Pres*
Dan Goldstein, *Vice Pres*
▲ EMP: 20 EST: 1955
SQ FT: 10,400
SALES (est): 860K **Privately Held**
SIC: **2326** Work garments, except raincoats: waterproof

(G-8158)
MAJESTIC INDUSTRIES INC
2 Canal St (07055-6402)
PHONE......................973 473-3434
Fax: 973 473-3825
Peter Ferentinos, *President*
Joe Ursini, *COO*
Michael Cattaneo, *Plant Mgr*
Nat Holt, *Sales Staff*
▲ EMP: 45
SQ FT: 100,000
SALES (est): 7.4MM **Privately Held**
SIC: **3944** Baby carriages & restraint seats

(G-8159)
MARTE CABINETS COUNTERTOPS LLC
48 Palmer St Apt 1 (07055-5420)
P.O. Box 1432 (07055-1432)
PHONE......................973 525-9502
EMP: 4
SALES (est): 298.8K **Privately Held**
SIC: **2434** Wood kitchen cabinets

(G-8160)
MARZULLO
55 Passaic St (07055-8326)
PHONE......................973 955-5309
Joseph Marzullo, *President*
EMP: 10
SALES (est): 580K **Privately Held**
SIC: **2411** Logging

(G-8161)
MEGA INDUSTRIES LLC
79 South St (07055-7914)
P.O. Box 1565 (07055-1565)
PHONE......................973 779-8772
Gilberto Estupinan, *Mng Member*
▲ EMP: 6
SQ FT: 4,500
SALES: 2.3MM **Privately Held**
SIC: **2024** Non-dairy based frozen desserts; ices, flavored (frozen dessert); juice pops, frozen

(G-8162)
MERCURY ADHESIVES INC
140 Dayton Ave (07055)
PHONE......................973 472-3307
Joel Zeichner, *President*
EMP: 10
SQ FT: 10,000
SALES (est): 1.5MM **Privately Held**
SIC: **2891** Adhesives

(G-8163)
MERCURY PLASTIC BAG CO INC (PA)
168 7th St (07055-8216)
PHONE......................973 778-7200
Fax: 973 778-0549
Marvin Rosen, *President*
Stuart Rosen, *Vice Pres*
Saundra Rosen, *Admin Sec*
EMP: 20 EST: 1961
SQ FT: 14,000
SALES (est): 1.8MM **Privately Held**
SIC: **2673** Plastic bags: made from purchased materials

(G-8164)
METAL FINISHING CO LLC
25 Prospect St (07055-4914)
PHONE......................973 778-9550
James Hakimi, *Principal*
EMP: 4
SALES (est): 379K **Privately Held**
SIC: **3559** 3471 Metal finishing equipment for plating, etc.; electroplating of metals or formed products

(G-8165)
MIRROTEK INTERNATIONAL LLC
Also Called: Iron Chef
90 Dayton Ave (07055-7035)
PHONE......................973 472-1400
Fax: 973 472-5170
Tamar Bezborodko, *CPA*
Bezzi Boaz, *Info Tech Dir*
Joseph Bezborodko,
EMP: 45
SQ FT: 40,000
SALES: 7MM **Privately Held**
SIC: **3229** 2035 Glass furnishings & accessories; seasonings & sauces, except tomato & dry

(G-8166)
MWT MATERIALS INC
90 Dayton Ave Ste 6e (07055-7035)
PHONE......................973 928-8300
Fax: 973 472-5915
Michael Katz, *President*
Paul Butler, *Vice Pres*
EMP: 12
SALES (est): 1.5MM **Privately Held**
WEB: www.mwt-materials.com
SIC: **3812** 3679 Radar systems & equipment; microwave components

(G-8167)
NORTHEAST PRO-TECH INC (PA)
61 Willet St Bldg L (07055-1971)
PHONE......................973 777-5654
Fax: 973 472-5437
Frank De Work, *President*

Leslie De Work, *Vice Pres*
▲ EMP: 10
SALES: 1.3MM **Privately Held**
SIC: **2824** Organic fibers, noncellulosic

(G-8168)
OLDE GRANDAD INDUSTRIES INC
1 Market St Ste 15 (07055-7364)
PHONE......................201 997-1899
Michael Kostak, *President*
▲ EMP: 6
SALES (est): 620K **Privately Held**
SIC: **3714** Motor vehicle parts & accessories

(G-8169)
PATELLA CONSTRUCTION CORP
Also Called: Patella Woodworking
99 South St (07055-7914)
PHONE......................973 916-0100
Michael Ostroff, *President*
Richard Whitley, *COO*
Jens Sand, *VP Mfg*
Scott Glickman, *CFO*
EMP: 85
SQ FT: 80,000
SALES (est): 11MM **Privately Held**
WEB: www.patellawood.com
SIC: **2431** Interior & ornamental woodwork & trim

(G-8170)
PLASTIC PLUS INC
184 Willet St (07055-1962)
PHONE......................973 614-0271
Vijay Choksi, *President*
Viral Choksi, *Vice Pres*
▲ EMP: 4
SQ FT: 2,000
SALES: 1MM **Privately Held**
SIC: **3086** Plastics foam products

(G-8171)
PREMIUM IMPORTS INC
90 Dayton Ave Ste 98 (07055-7040)
PHONE......................718 486-7125
Edward Fulop, *Ch of Bd*
Eugene Fulop, *CFO*
◆ EMP: 4
SALES (est): 1.9MM **Privately Held**
WEB: www.premiumimportsny.com
SIC: **2389** 5699 Men's miscellaneous accessories; uniforms & work clothing

(G-8172)
PUEBLA FOODS INC (PA)
26 Jefferson St (07055-6506)
PHONE......................973 246-6311
Fax: 973 473-3854
Felix Sanchez, *President*
Carmen Sanchez, *Vice Pres*
EMP: 22
SQ FT: 15,000
SALES (est): 3.4MM **Privately Held**
SIC: **2099** Tortillas, fresh or refrigerated

(G-8173)
PUEBLA FOODS INC
26 Jefferson St (07055-6506)
PHONE......................973 473-4494
Felix Sanchez, *President*
EMP: 10
SALES (corp-wide): 3.4MM **Privately Held**
SIC: **2099** Tortillas, fresh or refrigerated
PA: Puebla Foods Inc
26 Jefferson St
Passaic NJ 07055
973 246-6311

(G-8174)
QUALCO INC
225 Passaic St (07055-6414)
PHONE......................973 473-1222
John Ferentinos, *President*
Ed Solla, *General Mgr*
Thomas Ferentinos, *Vice Pres*
Juan Quintanar, *Opers Mgr*
Juan Quintiar, *Safety Mgr*
▲ EMP: 50
SQ FT: 200,000
SALES (est): 19.9MM **Privately Held**
WEB: www.qualco.com
SIC: **2812** Alkalies & chlorine

(G-8175)
R L R FOIL STAMPING LLC
245 4th St Ste 4 (07055-7840)
PHONE......................973 778-9464
Fax: 973 778-9434
Lawrence Vincent,
Richard Vincent,
EMP: 10
SQ FT: 15,000
SALES (est): 1.4MM **Privately Held**
WEB: www.rlrfoilstamping.com
SIC: **2679** 2752 Paper products, converted; commercial printing, offset

(G-8176)
RENAISSANCE CREATIONS LLC
95 8th St Fl 2 (07055-7905)
PHONE......................551 206-1878
Arkadiusz Such,
EMP: 4 EST: 2011
SALES (est): 426.8K **Privately Held**
SIC: **2521** 2531 2599 2511 Wood office furniture; library furniture; school furniture; bar furniture; kitchen & dining room furniture

(G-8177)
ROSALINDAS DISCOUNT FURNITURE
76 Lexington Ave (07055-5206)
PHONE......................973 928-2838
EMP: 12
SQ FT: 8,000
SALES (est): 860K **Privately Held**
SIC: **2599** Mfg Furniture/Fixtures

(G-8178)
S&P MACHINE COMPANY INC
Also Called: Rehtek Machine Co.
135 Monroe St (07055-6513)
PHONE......................973 365-2101
Fax: 973 365-2174
Stephen K Reh, *President*
Paul Reh, *Vice Pres*
EMP: 12
SQ FT: 9,000
SALES: 1.3MM **Privately Held**
WEB: www.rehtek.com
SIC: **3599** Machine shop, jobbing & repair

(G-8179)
SANDIK MANUFACTURING INC
100 8th St Ste 8 (07055-7980)
PHONE......................973 779-0707
Fax: 973 779-2844
Girish Shah, *President*
Anup Shah, *Vice Pres*
EMP: 5 EST: 1978
SQ FT: 2,500
SALES: 800K **Privately Held**
SIC: **3469** Machine parts, stamped or pressed metal

(G-8180)
SANIT TECHNOLOGIES LLC
Also Called: Durisan
90 Dayton Ave Ste 1811 (07055-7035)
PHONE......................862 238-7555
Arthur Wein, *VP Opers*
Joe Giovanniello, *Mng Member*
EMP: 12 EST: 2014
SQ FT: 20,000
SALES: 80K **Privately Held**
SIC: **2869** 2819 2861 Industrial organic chemicals; industrial inorganic chemicals; gum & wood chemicals

(G-8181)
SIGNMASTERS INC
217 Brook Ave Ste 2 (07055-3300)
PHONE......................973 614-8300
Howard Muser, *CEO*
John Fernandez, *Vice Pres*
EMP: 72 EST: 1978
SQ FT: 75,000
SALES (est): 17.4MM **Privately Held**
SIC: **2759** Promotional printing

(G-8182)
STERLING PRODUCTS INC
90 Dayton Ave Ste 77 (07055-7022)
PHONE......................973 471-2858
Fax: 973 471-2454
Zipora Cartagena, *Principal*
Sharoni Specter, *Vice Pres*

EMP: 14
SALES (est): 1.8MM **Privately Held**
SIC: 3229 Glass lighting equipment parts

(G-8183)
SUNBRITE DYE CO INC (PA)
35 8th St Ste 6 (07055-7900)
P.O. Box 1076 (07055-1076)
PHONE.................................973 777-9830
Fax: 973 777-0678
Anthony Maltese Jr, *President*
EMP: 30 **EST:** 1961
SQ FT: 125,000
SALES (est): 13.5MM **Privately Held**
SIC: 2262 Dyeing: manmade fiber & silk broadwoven fabrics

(G-8184)
TECHNICAL NAMEPLATE CORP
Also Called: ASAP Nameplate and Label Co
92 1st St (07055-6438)
PHONE.................................973 773-4256
Perla Navarro, *President*
Dominic Ciancitto, *General Mgr*
Dom Salvatore, *General Mgr*
Harry Warshaw, *Admin Sec*
EMP: 20 **EST:** 1966
SQ FT: 10,000
SALES: 900K **Privately Held**
WEB: www.technicalnameplate.com
SIC: 3479 3993 2752 Name plates: engraved, etched, etc.; signs & advertising specialties; commercial printing, lithographic

(G-8185)
TUBARI INC
90 Dayton Ave Ste 48 (07055-7018)
PHONE.................................973 779-8693
Fax: 973 779-8663
Michelle Glass, *President*
EMP: 23
SQ FT: 20,000
SALES (est): 1.6MM **Privately Held**
SIC: 3999 2011 Furs; meat packing plants

(G-8186)
V M DISPLAY
90 Dayton Ave Ste 1g (07055-7035)
PHONE.................................973 365-8027
Victor Jimenez, *Owner*
EMP: 10
SQ FT: 5,000
SALES (est): 500K **Privately Held**
SIC: 2542 Stands, merchandise display: except wood

(G-8187)
VALLE PRECISION MACHINE CO
58 Myrtle Ave (07055-3023)
PHONE.................................973 773-3037
Fax: 973 773-8120
Luis Valle, *President*
Carol Valle, *Vice Pres*
EMP: 8
SQ FT: 2,500
SALES: 1MM **Privately Held**
SIC: 3599 Machine shop, jobbing & repair

(G-8188)
VALUEWALK LLC
381 Terhune Ave (07055-2448)
PHONE.................................973 767-2181
Michelle Jones, *Sales Associate*
Jacob Wolinsky,
EMP: 7
SALES (est): 504.9K **Privately Held**
SIC: 2711 Newspapers, publishing & printing

(G-8189)
WEES BEYOND PRODUCTS CORP
1 Market St Ste 6 (07055-7364)
PHONE.................................862 238-8800
Xia Zhou, *President*
William Bai, *Vice Pres*
EMP: 11
SQ FT: 30,000
SALES: 5MM **Privately Held**
SIC: 2499 Woodenware, kitchen & household

(G-8190)
WICK IT LLC
1 Gregory Ave (07055-5715)
P.O. Box 413, Windsor (08561-0413)
PHONE.................................973 249-2970
Joe Blythe, *Mng Member*
Danny Hughes, *Mng Member*
EMP: 8
SALES (est): 1.1MM **Privately Held**
WEB: www.wickit.com
SIC: 3292 Wick, asbestos

Paterson
Passaic County

(G-8191)
A C BAKERY DISTRIBUTORS INC
Also Called: AC Bakery
1 Industrial Plz (07503-2964)
PHONE.................................973 977-2255
Fax: 973 977-2253
Anthony Cipriano, *President*
▲ **EMP:** 10
SQ FT: 5,000
SALES (est): 1.7MM **Privately Held**
SIC: 2051 Bread, cake & related products

(G-8192)
A S 4 PLASTIC INC
116 Getty Ave (07503-2807)
PHONE.................................973 925-5223
EMP: 4
SALES (est): 330.6K **Privately Held**
SIC: 3089 Plastic processing

(G-8193)
A S M TECHNICAL
34 Waite St (07524-1216)
PHONE.................................973 225-0111
EMP: 5
SALES (est): 400K **Privately Held**
SIC: 3559 Mfg Misc Industry Machinery

(G-8194)
A TO Z BOHEMIAN GLASS INC
250 E 17th St (07524-2013)
PHONE.................................212 725-2033
David Dvash, *President*
▲ **EMP:** 36
SQ FT: 15,000
SALES (est): 4.7MM **Privately Held**
WEB: www.cyberbeads.com
SIC: 3961 Costume jewelry, ex. precious metal & semiprecious stones

(G-8195)
ABBA METAL WORKS INC
337 River St (07524-2211)
PHONE.................................973 684-0808
Fax: 201 319-1401
Corrado Abbattista, *President*
Madaline Abbattista, *Vice Pres*
Mark Abbattista, *Project Mgr*
EMP: 7
SQ FT: 3,600
SALES (est): 1.3MM **Privately Held**
SIC: 3446 5719 1799 Stairs, staircases, stair treads: prefabricated metal; metalware; ornamental metal work

(G-8196)
ABCO METAL LLC
138 3rd Ave (07514-1513)
PHONE.................................973 772-8160
Todd Abrams,
EMP: 15
SALES (est): 1.4MM **Privately Held**
SIC: 3444 Sheet metalwork

(G-8197)
ABUELITO CHEESE INC
607 Main St (07503-3025)
PHONE.................................973 345-3503
Miguel Torres, *President*
Carolina Paiz, *General Mgr*
Senen Torres, *Plant Mgr*
EMP: 9
SALES (est): 1MM **Privately Held**
SIC: 2022 Natural cheese

(G-8198)
ACCURATE BRONZE BEARING CO
64 Illinois Ave (07503-1707)
PHONE.................................973 345-2304
Fax: 973 345-2305
Roger Zito, *President*
Nancy Zito, *Corp Secy*
EMP: 5 **EST:** 1953
SQ FT: 4,200
SALES: 500K **Privately Held**
SIC: 3568 5085 Power transmission equipment; bearings

(G-8199)
AEROTECH PROC SOLUTIONS LLC
57 Wood St (07524-1007)
PHONE.................................973 782-4485
Glorianne Zyskowski, *Manager*
EMP: 4
SQ FT: 15,000
SALES (est): 275.7K **Privately Held**
SIC: 3471 Anodizing (plating) of metals or formed products

(G-8200)
AHZANIS CASTLE LLC
134 E Main St (07522-1852)
PHONE.................................973 874-3191
Joseph Torres, *President*
EMP: 6
SALES: 100K **Privately Held**
SIC: 2051 Cakes, bakery: except frozen

(G-8201)
AIRWORLD INC
70 Spruce St (07501-1734)
PHONE.................................973 720-1008
Fax: 973 523-0015
Sam OH, *Owner*
John Rizzuto, *Vice Pres*
Joseph Chung, *Vice Pres*
EMP: 11
SQ FT: 5,000
SALES (est): 800K **Privately Held**
SIC: 3582 Commercial laundry equipment

(G-8202)
ALBEN METAL PRODUCTS INC
Also Called: V A Metal Products
11 Iowa Ave (07503-2516)
PHONE.................................973 279-8891
Fax: 973 279-6529
Benjamin Vollero, *President*
Alexander Vollero, *Treasurer*
EMP: 4 **EST:** 1967
SQ FT: 3,000
SALES: 340K **Privately Held**
SIC: 3599 3541 Machine shop, jobbing & repair; machine tools, metal cutting type

(G-8203)
ALCHEMY BILLBOARDS LLC
125 5th Ave (07524-1204)
PHONE.................................973 977-8828
George Wang,
EMP: 4
SALES (est): 398.5K **Privately Held**
SIC: 2396 Fabric printing & stamping

(G-8204)
ALL IN COLOR INC
132 Beckwith Ave (07503-2815)
PHONE.................................973 626-0987
Daniel Parisi, *CEO*
Christopher Massa, *President*
EMP: 4
SALES: 300K **Privately Held**
SIC: 2732 8742 Book printing; marketing consulting services

(G-8205)
ALLIED PLASTICS NEW JERSEY LLC
155 Sherman Ave (07502-1707)
PHONE.................................973 956-9200
Fax: 973 956-9234
Menash Oratz, *CEO*
EMP: 85
SALES (est): 10MM
SALES (corp-wide): 70K **Privately Held**
WEB: www.alliedextruders.com
SIC: 2673 Bags: plastic, laminated & coated

PA: Allied Plastics Holdings, Llc
560 Ferry St
Newark NJ 07105
718 729-5500

(G-8206)
AMB ENTERPRISES LLC (PA)
Also Called: Baker Adhesives
25 Lake St (07501-1516)
PHONE.................................973 225-1070
Fax: 973 481-6346
Anthony Bucco, *Mng Member*
William Zelman,
EMP: 20
SQ FT: 40,000
SALES (est): 7.2MM **Privately Held**
SIC: 2891 Adhesives

(G-8207)
AMERICAN DRAWTECH COMPANY INC
53 E 34th St (07514-1307)
P.O. Box Ae (07509-0529)
PHONE.................................973 684-1600
Martin Rosen, *President*
William Cohen, *Vice Pres*
Stephen Wener, *Admin Sec*
▲ **EMP:** 50
SALES (est): 3.3MM **Privately Held**
SIC: 2281 Yarn spinning mills

(G-8208)
AMERICAN HOSE HYDRAULIC CO INC (PA)
700 21st Ave (07513-1145)
PHONE.................................973 684-3225
Uri Dobriner, *President*
Jean Gaudino, *Opers Dir*
Danielle Dobriner, *Treasurer*
Idalee Ojeda, *Controller*
Tim Butler, *Branch Mgr*
▲ **EMP:** 30
SALES (est): 25.5MM **Privately Held**
SIC: 5084 7699 3492 Hydraulic systems equipment & supplies; hydraulic equipment repair; hose & tube fittings & assemblies, hydraulic/pneumatic

(G-8209)
AMERICAN REFUSE SUPPLY INC (PA)
700 21st Ave (07513-1145)
PHONE.................................973 684-3225
Fax: 973 684-3789
Uri Dobriner, *President*
Danielle Dobriner, *Treasurer*
EMP: 18
SQ FT: 10,000
SALES (est): 2.1MM **Privately Held**
SIC: 3714 Motor vehicle parts & accessories

(G-8210)
AMERICARE LABORATORIES LTD
Also Called: Ameriderm Laboratories
126 Pennsylvania Ave # 104 (07503-2527)
PHONE.................................973 279-5100
Fax: 973 279-8720
Bernard Elefant, *President*
Phyllis Elefant, *Treasurer*
▲ **EMP:** 20 **EST:** 1998
SQ FT: 15,000
SALES (est): 3.9MM **Privately Held**
WEB: www.ameriderm.com
SIC: 2844 5122 2841 Face creams or lotions; toiletries; soap & other detergents

(G-8211)
AMNEAL PHARMACEUTICALS LLC
209 Mclean Blvd (07504-1005)
PHONE.................................973 357-0222
Mita Patel, *Branch Mgr*
EMP: 41
SALES (corp-wide): 74.4K **Publicly Held**
SIC: 2834 Pharmaceutical preparations
HQ: Amneal Pharmaceuticals Llc
400 Crossing Blvd Fl 3
Bridgewater NJ 08807

(G-8212)
ANDARN ELECTRO SERVICE INC
72 Michigan Ave (07503-1808)
P.O. Box 188 (07543-0188)
PHONE..................................973 523-2220
Fax: 973 523-3140
Raman Patel, *President*
Chandra Patel, *Vice Pres*
Dinesh Patel, *Admin Sec*
EMP: 20
SQ FT: 10,000
SALES (est): 2.2MM **Privately Held**
SIC: 3471 Anodizing (plating) of metals or formed products

(G-8213)
ANNITTI ENTERPRISES INC
Also Called: E & H Laminating & Slitting Co
138 Grand St (07501-2639)
PHONE..................................973 345-1725
Fax: 973 345-3224
Kenneth S Annitti, *President*
Ethel H Annitti, *Chairman*
Kevin W Annitti, *Vice Pres*
▲ EMP: 29
SQ FT: 27,000
SALES (est): 8.5MM **Privately Held**
WEB: www.ehlam.com
SIC: 2891 Adhesives

(G-8214)
ARAB VOICE NEWSPAPER
956 Main St (07503-2307)
PHONE..................................973 523-7815
Fax: 973 523-0351
Walid Rabah, *Owner*
EMP: 8
SALES (est): 389.4K **Privately Held**
SIC: 2711 Newspapers, publishing & printing

(G-8215)
ARROW STEEL INC
629 E 19th St (07514-2800)
PHONE..................................973 523-1122
Fax: 973 977-9490
Frank Tondo, *President*
Gail Tondo, *Treasurer*
EMP: 10
SQ FT: 20,000
SALES: 2MM **Privately Held**
WEB: www.arrowcompactor.com
SIC: 3639 3589 Trash compactors, household; garbage disposers & compactors, commercial

(G-8216)
ASI PLASTIC INC
120 Getty Ave (07503-2807)
PHONE..................................973 332-4720
Bob Halek, *President*
Mike Halek, *Vice Pres*
EMP: 2 EST: 1987
SQ FT: 32,000
SALES (est): 1.5MM **Privately Held**
WEB: www.asiplastic.com
SIC: 3089 Plastic kitchenware, tableware & houseware; clothes hangers, plastic

(G-8217)
ATLANTIC STEEL SOLUTIONS LLC
74 Railroad Ave Bldg 102 (07501-2910)
PHONE..................................973 978-0026
Weverton Palmieri, *Mng Member*
EMP: 10
SQ FT: 10,000
SALES (est): 364K **Privately Held**
SIC: 3462 Iron & steel forgings

(G-8218)
B L WHITE WELDING & STEEL CO
527 E 33rd St (07504-1746)
PHONE..................................973 684-4111
Fax: 973 279-5040
Richard Haddad, *President*
EMP: 6 EST: 1951
SQ FT: 12,000
SALES (est): 778.6K **Privately Held**
SIC: 3441 7692 3446 Fabricated structural metal; welding repair; architectural metalwork

(G-8219)
BAKER/TITAN ADHESIVES
25 Lake St (07501-1516)
PHONE..................................973 225-1070
Tony Bucco, *President*
Morris Gialli, *General Mgr*
Bill Zelman, *Vice Pres*
▼ EMP: 20
SALES: 7MM
SALES (corp-wide): 7.2MM **Privately Held**
SIC: 2891 Adhesives
PA: Amb Enterprises Llc
25 Lake St
Paterson NJ 07501
973 225-1070

(G-8220)
BALTIMORE TRANSFORMER COMPANY
460 Totowa Ave (07522-1513)
PHONE..................................973 942-2222
Alice Glazer, *President*
Martin Gorman, *President*
Frances Cezar, *Administration*
EMP: 38
SALES: 950K **Privately Held**
SIC: 3612 3677 Power transformers, electric; electronic transformers

(G-8221)
BASIC PLASTICS COMPANY INC (PA)
318 Mclean Blvd Bldg 5 (07504-1245)
PHONE..................................973 977-8151
Fax: 973 977-8774
Erol Bulur, *President*
Paul Winakur, *Vice Pres*
EMP: 25
SQ FT: 40,000
SALES (est): 2.5MM **Privately Held**
WEB: www.basicplastics.com
SIC: 2673 2671 Plastic bags: made from purchased materials; plastic film, coated or laminated for packaging

(G-8222)
BERGEN SIGN COMPANY INC (PA)
161 E Railway Ave (07503-2101)
PHONE..................................973 742-7755
Fax: 973 742-0598
Thomas Schneider, *CEO*
Richard Walker, *COO*
Ethel Lewis, *Office Mgr*
EMP: 23
SQ FT: 32,000
SALES: 6.1MM **Privately Held**
WEB: www.bergensign.com
SIC: 1799 3993 Sign installation & maintenance; neon signs

(G-8223)
BEST LINEN FACTORY INC
93 Harrison St Ste 6 (07501-1251)
PHONE..................................973 279-8244
Ahmad Awad, *President*
EMP: 11
SQ FT: 12,000
SALES: 3MM **Privately Held**
SIC: 2391 Curtains, window: made from purchased materials

(G-8224)
BREAD GUY INC
840 E 28th St (07513-1219)
P.O. Box 97 (07543-0097)
PHONE..................................973 881-9002
EMP: 19 EST: 1996
SALES (est): 3MM **Privately Held**
SIC: 2051 5149 Mfg Bread/Related Products Whol Groceries

(G-8225)
BRENTRICK INC
527 E 39th St (07504-1407)
PHONE..................................973 357-3579
Rick Coren, *President*
Brent Kozlowski, *Exec VP*
EMP: 4 EST: 1996
SQ FT: 5,000
SALES: 700K **Privately Held**
WEB: www.brentrick.com
SIC: 3089 Extruded finished plastic products

(G-8226)
BRISAR INDUSTRIES INC
Also Called: Brisar Delvco Packaging Svcs
150 E 7th St (07524-1607)
PHONE..................................973 278-2500
Fax: 973 278-4670
Mark Cohen, *President*
Adel Elsayed, *Vice Pres*
Kate Schultz, *Production*
EMP: 105
SQ FT: 100,000
SALES: 6.2MM **Privately Held**
WEB: www.brisar.com
SIC: 7389 3089 7331 3544 Packaging & labeling services; thermoformed finished plastic products; direct mail advertising services; special dies & tools

(G-8227)
BURLINGTON TEXTILE MACHINERY
Also Called: Btm
39 Mcbride Ave (07501-1715)
PHONE..................................973 279-5900
Tom West, *President*
EMP: 17 EST: 1999
SALES (est): 1.7MM
SALES (corp-wide): 12MM **Privately Held**
WEB: www.glenro.com
SIC: 3552 5084 Textile machinery; textile machinery & equipment
PA: Glenro, Inc.
39 Mcbride Ave
Paterson NJ 07501
973 279-5900

(G-8228)
C & S MACHINERY REBUILDING
636 E 19th St Ste 642 (07514)
PHONE..................................973 742-7302
Fax: 973 742-4034
Cosmo Scardino, *President*
EMP: 4
SQ FT: 3,500
SALES (est): 380K **Privately Held**
SIC: 3542 Rebuilt machine tools, metal forming types

(G-8229)
CACCIOLA IRON WORKS INC
65 N 9th St (07522-1109)
PHONE..................................973 595-0854
Angelo Cacciola, *President*
Sal Cacciola, *Corp Secy*
Joe Cacciola, *Vice Pres*
▲ EMP: 6
SQ FT: 3,000
SALES: 350K **Privately Held**
SIC: 3446 Railings, bannisters, guards, etc.: made from metal pipe

(G-8230)
CAPITAL SOAP PRODUCTS LLC
62 Kearney St (07522-1508)
PHONE..................................973 333-6100
A J Kretz, *President*
Kip Venezia, *Manager*
EMP: 18 EST: 1948
SQ FT: 50,000
SALES (est): 3.6MM **Privately Held**
SIC: 2842 2841 Sweeping compounds, oil or water absorbent, clay or sawdust; soap: granulated, liquid, cake, flaked or chip

(G-8231)
CENTURY SERVICE AFFILIATES INC (PA)
Also Called: Carry Cases Plus
510 E 31st St (07504-2120)
PHONE..................................973 742-3516
Fax: 973 742-1133
Steve Holand, *President*
Lawrence Holand, *Vice Pres*
Alley Trofel, *Manager*
Lizzie R Work, *Manager*
▲ EMP: 30
SQ FT: 24,000
SALES (est): 5.2MM **Privately Held**
WEB: www.carrycasesplus.com
SIC: 3086 Packaging & shipping materials, foamed plastic

(G-8232)
CERESIST INC
176 E 7th St Ste 2 (07524-1600)
P.O. Box 213, Hawthorne (07507-0213)
PHONE..................................973 345-3231
Fax: 973 345-3066
Dino Tsasaris, *President*
◆ EMP: 10
SALES (est): 2.3MM **Privately Held**
WEB: www.ceresist.com
SIC: 3272 Pipe, concrete or lined with concrete

(G-8233)
CHURCH VESTMENT MFG CO INC
41 Paterson Ave Ste 1 (07522-1460)
PHONE..................................973 942-2833
Fax: 973 389-9346
Gerard J Siccardi Jr, *President*
Michelle Siccardi, *Vice Pres*
Gerard J Siccardi Sr, *Treasurer*
EMP: 4 EST: 1955
SQ FT: 1,500
SALES (est): 199.6K **Privately Held**
SIC: 2389 Clergymen's vestments

(G-8234)
CLOVER STAMPING INC
60 Spruce St (07501-1727)
PHONE..................................973 278-4888
Fax: 973 278-0017
Robert Kellenberger, *President*
EMP: 9 EST: 1953
SQ FT: 15,000
SALES: 800K **Privately Held**
WEB: www.cloverstamping.com
SIC: 3469 3544 Stamping metal for the trade; special dies, tools, jigs & fixtures

(G-8235)
COLOR DECOR LTD LIABILITY CO
518 E 36th St (07504-1723)
PHONE..................................973 689-2699
Ed Velky,
EMP: 3
SALES: 3MM **Privately Held**
SIC: 2499 Yard sticks, wood

(G-8236)
COLUMBIAN ORNA IR WORKS INC
332 Vreeland Ave (07513-1014)
PHONE..................................973 697-0927
Fax: 973 684-3509
John Marogi, *President*
EMP: 4
SQ FT: 10,000
SALES (est): 716K **Privately Held**
SIC: 3446 Architectural metalwork

(G-8237)
COMMANDER IMAGING PRODUCTS INC
70 Spruce St Ste 8 (07501-1728)
PHONE..................................973 742-9298
Fax: 973 742-9168
Christine Brady, *President*
Richard A Brady, *Vice Pres*
Jose Marte, *Vice Pres*
Patricia Brady, *Admin Sec*
▲ EMP: 28
SQ FT: 32,000
SALES (est): 4.1MM **Privately Held**
WEB: www.commanderimaging.com
SIC: 3955 5112 Ribbons, inked: typewriter, adding machine, register, etc.; stationery & office supplies

(G-8238)
COMMUNICATION PRODUCTS CO
201 Mclean Blvd (07504-1000)
PHONE..................................973 977-8490
Joan Huang, *Manager*
EMP: 6
SALES (est): 367.9K **Privately Held**
SIC: 3679 Electronic components

GEOGRAPHIC

(G-8239)
**CONDUENT STATE
HEALTHCARE LLC**
Also Called: Mj Family Care
100 Hamilton Plz Ste 400 (07505-2104)
PHONE................................973 754-6134
Naeil Hamdi, *Branch Mgr*
EMP: 5
SALES (corp-wide): 6B **Publicly Held**
SIC: 3577 Computer peripheral equipment
HQ: Conduent State Healthcare, Llc
12410 Milestone Dr Ste 500
Germantown MD 20876
301 820-4200

(G-8240)
CREATING YOUR DESIGN LLC
95 Montgomery St (07501-1117)
PHONE................................973 357-1080
EMP: 6
SQ FT: 6,500
SALES: 578K **Privately Held**
SIC: 2431 7999 7389 Mfg Millwork
Amusement/Recreation Services Business Services

(G-8241)
CROWN ROLL LEAF INC (PA)
91 Illinois Ave (07503-1798)
P.O. Box 2305, Clifton (07015-2305)
PHONE................................973 742-4000
Fax: 973 742-0219
Margaret Waitts, *CEO*
George Waitts, *COO*
James Waitts, *COO*
Manny Cueli, *Vice Pres*
Manuel Cueli, *Vice Pres*
▲ EMP: 147
SQ FT: 150,000
SALES (est): 63.8MM **Privately Held**
WEB: www.crownrollleaf.com
SIC: 3497 Metal foil & leaf

(G-8242)
CROWN ROLL LEAF INC
12 Columbia Ave (07503-1701)
PHONE................................973 684-2600
Maggy Waitts, *Branch Mgr*
EMP: 25
SALES (corp-wide): 63.8MM **Privately Held**
WEB: www.crownrollleaf.com
SIC: 7389 2759 Trading stamp promotion & redemption; commercial printing
PA: Crown Roll Leaf, Inc.
91 Illinois Ave
Paterson NJ 07503
973 742-4000

(G-8243)
CUSTOM LAMINATIONS INC
Also Called: Cli Group, The
932 Market St (07513-1129)
P.O. Box 2066 (07509-2066)
PHONE................................973 279-9174
Fax: 973 689-8050
Daren Silverstein, *President*
Paul Harencak, *Vice Pres*
Jane Silverstein, *VP Sls/Mktg*
Joyce Silverstein, *Admin Sec*
▲ EMP: 25
SQ FT: 50,000
SALES (est): 4.5MM **Privately Held**
WEB: www.customlaminations.com
SIC: 2295 2672 2396 Laminating of fabrics; coated & laminated paper; fabric printing & stamping

(G-8244)
DANIELLE DIE CUT PRODUCTS INC
238 Lindbergh Pl Ste 3 (07503-2823)
PHONE................................973 278-3000
Fax: 973 278-3399
Daniel Dibetitto, *President*
▲ EMP: 32
SALES (est): 5.6MM **Privately Held**
SIC: 3423 2675 Cutting dies, except metal cutting; die-cut paper & board

(G-8245)
DANTCO CORP
Also Called: Dantco Mixers
9 Oak St (07501)
PHONE................................973 278-8776

Fax: 973 278-1538
Michael D Antuono, *President*
Juan Cintron, *Exec Dir*
▲ EMP: 10 EST: 1968
SQ FT: 6,000
SALES (est): 732K **Privately Held**
WEB: www.dantco.com
SIC: 3556 3559 3679 Food products machinery; dairy & milk machinery; pharmaceutical machinery; paint making machinery; electronic circuits

(G-8246)
DE JONG IRON WORKS INC
223 Godwin Ave 231 (07501-1602)
P.O. Box 532, Hawthorne (07507-0532)
PHONE................................973 684-1633
Fax: 973 684-2309
Ed De Jong, *President*
John Sabilio, *Corp Secy*
Mark Boonstra, *Vice Pres*
Jerry De Jong, *Vice Pres*
EMP: 9 EST: 1908
SQ FT: 7,800
SALES (est): 1.2MM **Privately Held**
WEB: www.dejongiron.com
SIC: 3441 Fabricated structural metal

(G-8247)
DE LEON PLASTICS CORP
473 Getty Ave (07503-1815)
PHONE................................973 653-3480
Mike Hamman, *CEO*
Hany Hammam, *President*
Hany Hamman, *President*
EMP: 15
SQ FT: 200
SALES: 1.2MM **Privately Held**
SIC: 3089 Plastic containers, except foam

(G-8248)
**DELUXE FOODS
INTERNATIONAL**
29 E 25th St (07514-1503)
PHONE................................845 825-3442
Elya Kraus, *CEO*
Ervin Silver, *President*
EMP: 5 EST: 2013
SALES: 2.2MM **Privately Held**
SIC: 2099 Food preparations

(G-8249)
DELVCO PHARMA PACKG SVCS INC
Also Called: Brisar Delvco
150 E 7th St (07524-1607)
PHONE................................973 278-2500
Adel Elsayed, *President*
Mark Cohen, *COO*
Raul Martinez, *Info Tech Mgr*
Cristian Lopez, *Administration*
▲ EMP: 74
SALES (est): 9.9MM **Privately Held**
WEB: www.brisar.com
SIC: 3089 2653 Thermoformed finished plastic products; boxes, corrugated: made from purchased materials

(G-8250)
DICAR DIAMOND TOOL CORP
108 Kentucky Ave (07503-2508)
PHONE................................973 684-0949
James Zambrano, *President*
Mark Zambrano, *Vice Pres*
EMP: 11
SALES: 200K **Privately Held**
WEB: www.dicardiamond.com
SIC: 5085 3423 Industrial tools; hand & edge tools

(G-8251)
DILLON YARN CORPORATION (PA)
53 E 34th St (07514-1307)
P.O. Box Ae (07509-0529)
PHONE................................973 684-1600
William Cohen, *CEO*
Mitchel Weinberger, *President*
Michelle Oneill, *Vice Pres*
Alex Vlassis, *Admin Asst*
◆ EMP: 50
SQ FT: 20,000
SALES (est): 22.1MM **Privately Held**
WEB: www.dillonyarn.com
SIC: 2282 Textured yarn

(G-8252)
DYERICH FLOORING DESIGNS LTD
35 Dale Ave (07505-1906)
PHONE................................973 357-0600
Richmond Eshaghoff, *President*
Richmond Eshagoff, *Vice Pres*
▲ EMP: 2
SALES: 4MM **Privately Held**
SIC: 3996 Hard surface floor coverings

(G-8253)
EDI/ECI
15 Jane St (07522-1168)
PHONE................................973 790-9100
EMP: 5
SALES (est): 680.4K **Privately Held**
SIC: 3534 Elevators & equipment

(G-8254)
EDKO ELECTRONICS
460 Totowa Ave (07522-1513)
PHONE................................973 942-2222
Martin Gorman, *Principal*
Dan Cezar, *Sales Mgr*
Cliff Markowitz, *Director*
EMP: 38
SALES: 950K **Privately Held**
SIC: 3612 3677 Transformers, except electric; electronic transformers

(G-8255)
ELECTRONIC TRANSFORMER CORP
460 Totowa Ave (07522-1513)
PHONE................................973 942-2222
Fax: 973 942-9014
Daniel H Cezar, *President*
Daniel Cezar, *President*
EMP: 45 EST: 1961
SQ FT: 37,000
SALES (est): 6.2MM **Privately Held**
WEB: www.electronictransformercorp.com
SIC: 3677 Transformers power supply, electronic type; filtration devices, electronic

(G-8256)
ELEVATOR CABS OF NY INC
Also Called: Elevator Doors-Elevator Cabs
15 Jane St (07522-1197)
PHONE................................973 790-9100
Cheryl Kozlowski, *CEO*
Thomas Aveni, *President*
EMP: 70 EST: 1960
SQ FT: 65,000
SALES (est): 17.6MM **Privately Held**
SIC: 3534 Elevators & equipment

(G-8257)
ELEVATOR DOORS INC
15 Jane St (07522-1197)
PHONE................................973 790-9100
Fax: 973 790-1007
Thomas Aveni, *President*
Juergen Henselmann, *Purchasing*
Onur Cayirli, *Engineer*
Rich Scibor, *Director*
▲ EMP: 110
SQ FT: 60,000
SALES (est): 21MM **Privately Held**
SIC: 3534 Elevators & equipment

(G-8258)
ELEVATOR ENTERANCES NY INC
15 Jane St (07522-1168)
PHONE................................973 790-9100
Thomas Aveni, *President*
EMP: 25
SQ FT: 65,000
SALES (est): 3.3MM **Privately Held**
WEB: www.elevatordoors.com
SIC: 3534 Elevators & equipment

(G-8259)
ELEVATOR ENTRANCE INC
15 Jane St (07522-1168)
PHONE................................973 790-9100
Thomas Aveni, *President*
EMP: 35 EST: 1945
SQ FT: 48,000
SALES (est): 7.9MM **Privately Held**
SIC: 3534 3442 Elevators & equipment; metal doors, sash & trim

(G-8260)
ELEVATOR TECHNOLOGY CORP
337 Market St (07501-2247)
P.O. Box 2753 (07509-2753)
PHONE................................973 523-7760
Fax: 973 523-4075
Shlomo Tagjer, *President*
▲ EMP: 5
SQ FT: 3,500
SALES (est): 869.5K **Privately Held**
SIC: 3534 Elevators & equipment

(G-8261)
EMBROIDERY CONCEPTS
41 Paterson Ave 43 (07522-1460)
P.O. Box 2334 (07509-2334)
PHONE................................973 942-8555
EMP: 4
SALES (est): 150K **Privately Held**
SIC: 2397 Embroidery

(G-8262)
EMPIRE ELECTRONICS INC
70 Spruce St Ste 2 (07501-1728)
P.O. Box U (07509-0319)
PHONE................................973 278-8282
Fax: 973 278-0376
Robert T Banks, *President*
O Ralph Valerio, *Vice Pres*
EMP: 15
SQ FT: 12,000
SALES (est): 1.3MM **Privately Held**
WEB: www.rdrelectronics.com
SIC: 3679 Harness assemblies for electronic use; wire or cable

(G-8263)
EMPIRE INDUSTRIES INC
40 Warren St (07524-2205)
PHONE................................973 279-2050
Fax: 973 279-8987
Jacob Goren, *President*
Bonnie Goren, *Treasurer*
▲ EMP: 52
SQ FT: 94,000
SALES (est): 8MM **Privately Held**
WEB: www.empire-industries.com
SIC: 3431 Bathroom fixtures, including sinks

(G-8264)
ENA MEAT PACKING INC (PA)
240 E 5th St (07524-2109)
PHONE................................973 742-4790
Fax: 973 742-4407
Ali Kucukkarca, *President*
Saffet Kucukkara, *Vice Pres*
Zatibeg Kucukkara, *Admin Sec*
EMP: 21
SQ FT: 100,000
SALES (est): 3.3MM **Privately Held**
SIC: 2011 2015 2013 Beef products from beef slaughtered on site; lamb products from lamb slaughtered on site; poultry slaughtering & processing; sausages & other prepared meats

(G-8265)
EVIVA LLC (PA)
30 Wood St (07524-1008)
PHONE................................973 925-4028
Yahya Mohammad, *Mng Member*
EMP: 7
SQ FT: 20,000
SALES: 2MM **Privately Held**
SIC: 2499 1799 Kitchen, bathroom & household ware: wood; kitchen & bathroom remodeling

(G-8266)
EXALENT PACKAGING INC
55 1st Ave (07514-2035)
PHONE................................973 742-9600
Fax: 973 742-9647
EMP: 22
SQ FT: 22,000
SALES (est): 2.3MM **Privately Held**
SIC: 2652 Mfg Setup Paperboard Boxes

(G-8267)
EXCEL HOBBY BLADES CORP
Also Called: Excel Blades
481 Getty Ave (07503-1313)
PHONE................................973 278-4000
Fax: 973 278-4343
Mike Hamman, *President*

▲ = Import ▼=Export
◆ =Import/Export

Kenda Hammam, *Sales Staff*
▲ **EMP:** 45
SQ FT: 18,000
SALES (est): 6.8MM **Privately Held**
SIC: 3423 3952 Hand & edge tools; lead
pencils & art goods

(G-8268)
F & R MACHINE CORP
41 Bleeker St (07524-1016)
P.O. Box 1262 (07509-1262)
PHONE...................973 684-8139
Fax: 973 684-2651
Jack Liberzon, *President*
◆ **EMP:** 22
SQ FT: 18,000
SALES: 3.5MM **Privately Held**
SIC: 3599 Machine shop, jobbing & repair

(G-8269)
**FABRICOLOR HOLDING INTL
LLC**
24 1/2 Van Houten St (07505-1031)
P.O. Box 1856 (07509-1856)
PHONE...................973 742-5800
Oleg Ponomarev, *Vice Pres*
Miro E Muzik, *Mng Member*
EMP: 5
SQ FT: 10,000
SALES: 2MM **Privately Held**
SIC: 2865 Dyes, synthetic organic

(G-8270)
FAIRFIELD TEXTILES CORP (PA)
Also Called: Paterson Laundry & Die Div
34 Waite St (07524-1216)
PHONE...................973 227-1656
Otto Kuczynski, *President*
▲ **EMP:** 80 **EST:** 1976
SQ FT: 65,000
SALES (est): 14.6MM **Privately Held**
SIC: 2253 Jerseys, knit; dyeing & finishing
knit outerwear, excl. hosiery & glove

(G-8271)
FELCO PRODUCTS LLC
18 Furler St (07512-1802)
PHONE...................973 890-7979
▲ **EMP:** 5
SALES (est): 452.1K **Privately Held**
SIC: 3714 Mfg Motor Vehicle Parts/Acces-
sories

(G-8272)
FLECH PAPER PRODUCTS INC
55 1st Ave Ste 1 (07514-2036)
PHONE...................973 357-8111
Douglas Kandel, *Co-President*
Stephen Echikson, *Co-President*
Charles Benedict, *Plant Mgr*
Doug Kandel, *Office Mgr*
◆ **EMP:** 15
SQ FT: 24,000
SALES: 2MM **Privately Held**
SIC: 2631 Specialty board

(G-8273)
**FREED TRANSFORMER
COMPANY**
460 Totowa Ave (07522-1513)
PHONE...................973 942-2222
Martin Gorman, *President*
EMP: 38
SQ FT: 40,000
SALES (est): 2.8MM **Privately Held**
SIC: 3677 Electronic coils, transformers &
other inductors

(G-8274)
G & H METAL FINISHERS INC
282 Dakota St (07503-2412)
PHONE...................201 909-9808
Fax: 973 523-6256
George Grimm, *President*
Fred Grimm, *Corp Secy*
Henry Kunz, *Vice Pres*
EMP: 6 **EST:** 1956
SQ FT: 11,000
SALES (est): 710K **Privately Held**
SIC: 3471 Electroplating & plating; polish-
ing, metals or formed products

(G-8275)
**GENERAL CARBON
CORPORATION**
33 Paterson St (07501-1015)
PHONE...................973 523-2223
Robert J Muller, *President*
Irwin Benkert, *President*
Rob Murray, *Opers Mgr*
Mike Geiger, *Engineer*
◆ **EMP:** 15
SQ FT: 20,000
SALES (est): 7.2MM **Privately Held**
WEB: www.generalcarbon.com
SIC: 2819 Charcoal (carbon), activated

(G-8276)
GIO VALI HANDBAG CORP
Also Called: Giovali Handbag
463 Grand St (07505-2036)
PHONE...................973 279-3032
ARA Messrobian, *President*
EMP: 8
SQ FT: 7,500
SALES (est): 399.3K **Privately Held**
SIC: 3171 Handbags, women's

(G-8277)
GLENRO INC (PA)
39 Mcbride Ave (07501-1799)
P.O. Box 3052 (07509-3052)
PHONE...................973 279-5900
Fax: 973 279-9103
Gary Van Denend, *President*
Dominic Mirante, *Engineer*
John Rasmussen, *Manager*
▲ **EMP:** 14
SQ FT: 20,000
SALES (est): 12MM **Privately Held**
WEB: www.glenro.com
SIC: 3567 3672 Heating units & devices,
industrial: electric; induction heating
equipment; radiant heating systems, in-
dustrial process; infrared ovens, indus-
trial; printed circuit boards

(G-8278)
GLOBAL INGREDIENTS INC
317 9th Ave (07514-2310)
PHONE...................973 278-6677
Frank Mountain, *President*
Harlie Mountain, *Vice Pres*
James Minella, *Manager*
▲ **EMP:** 8
SQ FT: 15,000
SALES: 3MM **Privately Held**
WEB: www.globalingredients.net
SIC: 2099 Food preparations

(G-8279)
GORMAN INDUSTRIES INC
Also Called: Eagle Products Div
700 21st Ave (07513-1145)
PHONE...................973 345-5424
Uri Dobriner, *President*
Danielle Dobriner, *Corp Secy*
EMP: 29
SQ FT: 10,000
SALES (est): 3.6MM **Privately Held**
SIC: 3714 5013 Motor vehicle parts & ac-
cessories; motor vehicle supplies & new
parts

(G-8280)
**GREAT FALLS METALWORKS
INC**
301 E 22nd St (07514-2220)
PHONE...................973 523-6811
Fax: 973 523-6010
Flora Brothers, *President*
EMP: 6
SQ FT: 12,500
SALES (est): 490K **Privately Held**
SIC: 3911 Jewelry, precious metal

(G-8281)
**GREENBAUM INTERIORS LLC
(PA)**
101 Washington St (07505-1301)
PHONE...................973 279-3000
Fax: 973 279-3006
Joseph Jimmy Greenbaum,
Ellen Greenbaum,
Susan Greenbaum,
▲ **EMP:** 52
SQ FT: 123,000

SALES (est): 11.1MM **Privately Held**
WEB: www.greenbauminteriors.com
SIC: 5712 5021 2511 7389 Furniture
stores; furniture; wood household furniture; interior decorating

(G-8282)
**GRIMALDI DEVELOPMENT
CORP**
65 1st Ave (07514-2000)
PHONE...................973 345-0660
David Grimaldi, *President*
EMP: 5 **EST:** 1998
SQ FT: 6,000
SALES (est): 360K **Privately Held**
SIC: 3599 Machine shop, jobbing & repair

(G-8283)
GRIMCO PNEUMATIC CORP
65 1st Ave (07514-2030)
PHONE...................973 345-0660
Fax: 973 345-0660
David Grimaldi, *President*
▼ **EMP:** 8
SQ FT: 14,000
SALES (est): 700K **Privately Held**
WEB: www.grimcopresses.com
SIC: 3599 Machine shop, jobbing & repair

(G-8284)
GROMMET MART INC
85-99 Hazel St (07503-2462)
PHONE...................973 278-4100
Cilek Seker, *President*
EMP: 10
SALES (est): 1.4MM **Privately Held**
SIC: 3423 Hand & edge tools; hammers
(hand tools); tools or equipment for use
with sporting arms; ironworkers' hand
tools

(G-8285)
**GUERNSEY CREST ICE CREAM
CO**
134 19th Ave (07513-1208)
PHONE...................973 742-4620
Margaret Cornwell, *President*
Joy Cornwell, *Vice Pres*
EMP: 4 **EST:** 1935
SQ FT: 3,200
SALES (est): 240K **Privately Held**
SIC: 2024 5812 Ice cream & frozen
desserts; ice cream stands or dairy bars

(G-8286)
**H C GRAPHICS
SCREENPRINTING**
238 Lindbergh Pl Ste 3 (07503-2823)
PHONE...................973 247-0544
Fax: 973 247-0590
Thomas J Mueller, *President*
Carol Mueller, *Corp Secy*
▲ **EMP:** 8
SQ FT: 4,500
SALES (est): 1.5MM **Privately Held**
WEB: www.hcgraphics.com
SIC: 2759 2752 Screen printing; commer-
cial printing, offset

(G-8287)
HARMONY ELASTOMERS LLC
34 Trenton Ave (07513)
PHONE...................973 340-4000
Arish Kiani, *President*
Sawib Toor, *CFO*
EMP: 20
SQ FT: 10,000
SALES: 5MM **Privately Held**
SIC: 2822 Synthetic rubber

(G-8288)
HARRIS & TIPPOGRAPH INC
93 Harrison St Ste 2 (07501-1251)
PHONE...................973 523-5204
Barbara Jones, *Principal*
EMP: 5
SALES (est): 467.6K **Privately Held**
SIC: 3544 Special dies & tools

(G-8289)
HILL MACHINE INC (PA)
Also Called: Hill Mixers Machine
295 Governor St (07501-1320)
PHONE...................973 684-2808
Fax: 973 345-4080

Robert Brewer, *President*
Robert W Brewer Jr, *Corp Secy*
John Pullos, *Vice Pres*
Mike Titos, *Manager*
EMP: 5 **EST:** 1895
SQ FT: 11,500
SALES (est): 548.6K **Privately Held**
SIC: 3556 Homogenizing machinery: dairy,
fruit, vegetable

(G-8290)
HO-HO-KUS INC
189 Lyon St 201 (07524-2523)
PHONE...................973 278-2274
Fax: 973 278-4805
Tom Nepola, *President*
EMP: 24
SQ FT: 5,300
SALES (est): 4.7MM **Privately Held**
WEB: www.hohokusinc.com
SIC: 3429 3812 3728 Manufactured hard-
ware (general); search & navigation
equipment; aircraft parts & equipment

(G-8291)
HY-TEST PACKAGING CORP
515 E 41st St (07504-1209)
PHONE...................973 754-7000
Fax: 973 754-7020
John S Smith, *President*
Jackalyn Quazza, *Vice Pres*
Ted Smith, *Vice Pres*
EMP: 9
SQ FT: 34,000
SALES (est): 700K **Privately Held**
WEB: www.hy-testpackaging.com
SIC: 7389 2844 2841 Packaging & label-
ing services; toilet preparations; soap &
other detergents

(G-8292)
**IDEAL PLATING & POLISHING
CO**
107 Alabama Ave (07503-2108)
PHONE...................973 759-5559
Fax: 973 759-0277
Ronald F Knigge, *President*
Constance Knigge, *Corp Secy*
Derek Thompson, *Admin Sec*
EMP: 10
SQ FT: 18,000
SALES (est): 1.1MM **Privately Held**
SIC: 3471 Electroplating of metals or
formed products

(G-8293)
**INDEPENDENCE PLATING CORP
(PA)**
Also Called: Ideal Plating
107 Alabama Ave (07503-2199)
PHONE...................973 523-1776
Fax: 973 279-1274
Ronald F Knigge, *President*
EMP: 18
SQ FT: 28,000
SALES (est): 1.3MM **Privately Held**
WEB: www.independenceplating.com
SIC: 3471 Anodizing (plating) of metals or
formed products; electroplating of metals
or formed products

(G-8294)
INDUSTRIAL MACHINE CORP
44 Lehigh Ave (07503-1729)
PHONE...................973 345-1800
Fax: 973 345-7545
Sam Szewzcyk, *President*
EMP: 9
SQ FT: 9,000
SALES: 750K **Privately Held**
SIC: 3599 Machine shop, jobbing & repair

(G-8295)
**INTERNTNAL PHARMA
REMEDIES INC**
244 Dixon Ave (07501-3308)
PHONE...................201 417-3891
Nelson Herreira, *CEO*
EMP: 6
SALES (est): 477.8K **Privately Held**
SIC: 2834 Pharmaceutical preparations

(PA)=Parent Co (HQ)=Headquarters (DH)=Div Headquarters
✪ = New Business established in last 2 years

2018 Harris New Jersey
Manufacturers Directory

329

GEOGRAPHIC

(G-8296)
J KAUFMAN IRON WORKS INC
217 Godwin Ave (07501-1695)
P.O. Box 213, Elmwood Park (07407-0213)
PHONE..................................973 925-9972
Fax: 973 893-7168
Larry Kaufman, *President*
Joseph Kaufman, *Admin Sec*
EMP: 17
SALES (est): 3.1MM **Privately Held**
WEB: www.kaufmaniron.com
SIC: 3446 Gates, ornamental metal

(G-8297)
J V Q INC
245 E 17th St (07524-2012)
P.O. Box 2070, West Paterson (07424-7070)
PHONE..................................973 523-8806
Vic Amati, *President*
Quintin Amati, *Vice Pres*
Jim Reese, *Treasurer*
EMP: 14
SQ FT: 4,000
SALES (est): 900K **Privately Held**
WEB: www.jvq.com
SIC: 3544 Special dies, tools, jigs & fixtures

(G-8298)
JACHTS - COLUMBIA CAN LLC
90 6th Ave (07524-1406)
PHONE..................................973 925-8020
Darren Jachts, *CEO*
Eric Hammesfahr, *Regl Sales Mgr*
Teresa Zatorski, *Supervisor*
EMP: 17
SALES (est): 12.6MM **Privately Held**
SIC: 2655 Fiber cans, drums & containers

(G-8299)
JC PALLETS INC
354 Marshall St (07503-3123)
PHONE..................................973 345-1102
Jose Cruz, *President*
EMP: 13
SALES (est): 1.4MM **Privately Held**
SIC: 2448 Pallets, wood & wood with metal

(G-8300)
JC PRINTING & ADVERTISING INC
168 8th Ave (07514-2218)
PHONE..................................973 881-8612
Fax: 973 881-9406
James Chappell, *President*
Cheryl Chappell, *Director*
Carlos Moscoso, *Graphic Designe*
EMP: 5
SQ FT: 2,000
SALES (est): 837.5K **Privately Held**
WEB: www.jcprintinginc.com
SIC: 2752 Commercial printing, offset

(G-8301)
JCC MILITARY SUPPLY LLC
125 5th Ave (07524-1204)
P.O. Box 1370, Twp Washinton (07676-1370)
PHONE..................................973 341-1314
Michael Cavallo,
▲ **EMP:** 5
SALES: 225K **Privately Held**
SIC: 3496 Miscellaneous fabricated wire products

(G-8302)
JEFFREY DANEE INC
372 E 23rd St (07514-2315)
P.O. Box 1547, Wayne (07474-1547)
PHONE..................................973 872-9388
David Amoscato, *President*
EMP: 4
SQ FT: 7,000
SALES: 300K **Privately Held**
SIC: 2431 Woodwork, interior & ornamental

(G-8303)
JIT MANUFACTURING INC
50 Peel St (07524-1004)
PHONE..................................973 247-7300
Fax: 973 247-7304
John Norton, *President*
Andrew Graziano, *Vice Pres*

EMP: 12
SQ FT: 12,000
SALES (est): 2.4MM **Privately Held**
SIC: 2631 2675 Packaging board; die-cut paper & board

(G-8304)
JK INGREDIENTS INC
Also Called: J&K Ingredients
160 E 5th St (07524-1603)
PHONE..................................973 340-8700
James K Sausville, *President*
Andy Madacsi, *Controller*
Fred Denman, *Human Res Mgr*
◆ **EMP:** 85
SQ FT: 37,000
SALES (est): 20.5MM **Privately Held**
WEB: www.jkingredients.net
SIC: 2087 2099 Flavoring extracts & syrups; powders, flavoring (except drink); food preparations; pie fillings, except fruit, meat & vegetable

(G-8305)
JOHN ANTHONY BREAD DISTRIBUTOR
298 21st Ave (07501-3521)
PHONE..................................973 523-9258
John Imparato, *Owner*
Donna Imparato, *Partner*
EMP: 4
SALES (est): 260K **Privately Held**
SIC: 2051 Bread, cake & related products

(G-8306)
JOSEPH MONGA JR
Also Called: Decorative Iron Works
7383 Belmont Ave (07522)
PHONE..................................973 595-8517
Fax: 973 627-6529
Joseph Monga, *Owner*
EMP: 5
SALES (est): 569.2K
SALES (corp-wide): 570.3K **Privately Held**
SIC: 3446 Stairs, fire escapes, balconies, railings & ladders; stairs, staircases, stair treads: prefabricated metal
PA: Joseph Monga Jr
　　300 Main St
　　Little Ferry NJ 07643
　　201 641-2431

(G-8307)
KB FOOD ENTERPRISES INC
19 E 5th St (07524)
PHONE..................................973 278-2800
Rick Paulso, *President*
EMP: 12
SQ FT: 14,500
SALES (est): 920K **Privately Held**
SIC: 2051 Bread, cake & related products

(G-8308)
KENNETEX INC
53 E 34th St (07514-1307)
P.O. Box 6356 (07509-6356)
PHONE..................................610 444-0600
Martin Rosen, *President*
Arthur Rosen, *Vice Pres*
▲ **EMP:** 57
SQ FT: 45,000
SALES (est): 5.7MM **Privately Held**
WEB: www.kennetex.com
SIC: 2281 2269 5949 Yarn spinning mills; finishing plants; sewing, needlework & piece goods

(G-8309)
KESSLER INDUSTRIES
40 Warren St (07524-2205)
PHONE..................................973 279-1417
Fax: 973 684-1139
EMP: 4
SALES (est): 700.2K **Privately Held**
SIC: 5074 3432 Whol Plumbing Equipment/Supplies Mfg Plumbing Fixture Fittings

(G-8310)
KLEIN RIBBON CORP
Also Called: Jeffrey Klein Ribbon Designs
176 E 7th St Ste 2 (07524-1600)
P.O. Box 540 (07543-0540)
PHONE..................................973 684-4671
Fax: 973 684-1136

Raymond Klein, *President*
EMP: 36 **EST:** 1925
SQ FT: 25,000
SALES (est): 3.6MM **Privately Held**
WEB: www.myownribbon.com
SIC: 2241 2396 2297 Ribbons; automotive & apparel trimmings; nonwoven fabrics

(G-8311)
KOHLER INDUSTRIES INC
Also Called: Interfoam
155 Mcbride Ave Ste 1 (07501-2663)
PHONE..................................336 545-3289
Ronald Kohler, *President*
EMP: 5
SQ FT: 20,000
SALES (est): 478.4K **Privately Held**
SIC: 3086 Insulation or cushioning material, foamed plastic

(G-8312)
L & F GRAPHICS LTD LBLTY CO
Also Called: Lf Graphics
207 E 15th St (07524-2018)
PHONE..................................973 240-7033
Lenaure Foxworth, *Managing Prtnr*
Lenaure Foxworth Jr,
EMP: 5
SQ FT: 2,900
SALES: 735K **Privately Held**
SIC: 3953 7336 7389 3993 Screens, textile printing; commercial art & graphic design; embroidering of advertising on shirts, etc.; signs & advertising specialties

(G-8313)
L & M MACHINE & TOOL CO INC
105 Lehigh Ave (07503-1218)
PHONE..................................973 523-5288
Francisco Moran, *President*
EMP: 5 **EST:** 1959
SQ FT: 5,500
SALES: 200K **Privately Held**
SIC: 3541 5084 3599 Machine tools, metal cutting type; metalworking tools (such as drills, taps, dies, files); machine shop, jobbing & repair

(G-8314)
L ARDEN CORP
72 Putnam St (07524-2206)
PHONE..................................973 523-6400
Luis Alvarez, *Owner*
EMP: 8
SALES: 750K **Privately Held**
SIC: 3531 Dozers, tractor mounted: material moving

(G-8315)
L D L TECHNOLOGY INC
137 Pennsylvania Ave (07503)
PHONE..................................973 345-9111
Fax: 973 345-3984
Daniel Laufer, *President*
Eleonore Tarricone, *Admin Sec*
EMP: 6
SQ FT: 5,000
SALES (est): 510K **Privately Held**
SIC: 3339 Zinc refining (primary), including slabs & dust; zinc smelting (primary), including zinc residue

(G-8316)
LA FAVORITE INDUSTRIES INC
33 Shady St (07524-1014)
PHONE..................................973 279-1266
Thomas Mastin, *President*
Eric Hague, *Vice Pres*
Linda Zisa, *Controller*
EMP: 14
SALES: 2MM **Privately Held**
WEB: www.lafavorite.com
SIC: 3069 2891 Expansion joints, rubber; sealing compounds, synthetic rubber or plastic

(G-8317)
LANCO-YORK INC (PA)
Also Called: Lanco Container
864 E 25th St (07513-1202)
PHONE..................................973 278-7400
Fax: 973 278-8883
Mitchell Leibowitz, *President*
Rochelle Leibowitz, *Corp Secy*
Chris Panza, *Vice Pres*

Joshua Karlin, *Sales Mgr*
▲ **EMP:** 22 **EST:** 1942
SQ FT: 50,000
SALES (est): 7.9MM **Privately Held**
SIC: 2653 Boxes, corrugated: made from purchased materials

(G-8318)
LBU INC
7 4th Ave 33 (07524-1202)
PHONE..................................973 773-4800
Fax: 973 773-6005
Jeffrey Mayer, *President*
Brian Seltzer, *VP Opers*
Jerry Cong, *CFO*
Jim Black, *Financial Exec*
Fred King, *Office Mgr*
▲ **EMP:** 30
SQ FT: 30,000
SALES (est): 5MM **Privately Held**
WEB: www.lbuinc.com
SIC: 2393 2392 3161 Textile bags; knapsacks, canvas: made from purchased materials; bags, laundry: made from purchased materials; ironing board pads: made from purchased materials; luggage

(G-8319)
LEVINE INDUSTRIES INC (PA)
Also Called: Levine Packaging Co
70 Levine St (07503-2734)
PHONE..................................973 742-1000
Fax: 973 742-0588
Jeff Levine, *President*
Alan Levine, *President*
Theodore R Levine, *Vice Pres*
EMP: 35
SQ FT: 90,000
SALES (est): 9MM **Privately Held**
WEB: www.levineind.com
SIC: 2653 5113 Boxes, corrugated: made from purchased materials; shipping supplies

(G-8320)
LIBERTY ENVELOPE INC
45 E 5th St (07524-1101)
PHONE..................................973 546-5600
Ligia Guarderas, *President*
Kevin Guarderas, *CFO*
EMP: 16
SQ FT: 40,000
SALES (est): 1.9MM **Privately Held**
WEB: www.libertyenv.com
SIC: 2752 2759 7331 Commercial printing, offset; envelopes: printing; mailing service

(G-8321)
LINDSTROM & KING CO INC
108 Mclean Blvd (07514-1114)
PHONE..................................973 279-2511
Fax: 973 279-9650
Peter M Madsen, *President*
EMP: 5 **EST:** 1939
SQ FT: 6,000
SALES (est): 624.2K **Privately Held**
WEB: www.lindstromking.com
SIC: 3494 Valves & pipe fittings

(G-8322)
LINEN FOR TABLES
407 20th Ave (07513-1544)
PHONE..................................973 345-8472
Herbert Allen Jr, *Partner*
Victoria Allen, *Partner*
Wanda Vazquez, *Human Resources*
Margarita Diaz, *Admin Asst*
EMP: 7
SQ FT: 3,000
SALES (est): 440K **Privately Held**
WEB: www.allenlinen.com
SIC: 2392 5131 Napkins, fabric & nonwoven: made from purchased materials; tablecloths: made from purchased materials; linen piece goods, woven

(G-8323)
LITTLE FALLS ALLOYS INC (PA)
171-191 Caldwell Ave (07501)
PHONE..................................973 278-1666
Fax: 973 278-7345
Don Fellman, *President*
Donald P Fellman, *President*
Orlando Veltri, *Vice Pres*
Fred Walter, *Vice Pres*

▲ **EMP**: 32 **EST**: 1945
SQ FT: 30,000
SALES (est): 7.2MM **Privately Held**
WEB: www.lfa-wire.com
SIC: 3351 Wire, copper & copper alloy

(G-8324)
LMC-HB CORP
Also Called: Les Metalliers Champenois
23 27 East 23rd St (07514)
PHONE.............................862 239-9814
Samuel Bonnet, *Director*
EMP: 21
SALES: 12.7MM **Privately Held**
SIC: 8712 3442 3446 Architectural services; metal doors, sash & trim; architectural metalwork

(G-8325)
LO PRESTI & SONS LLC
Also Called: Giannella Deli
298 21st Ave (07501-3521)
PHONE.............................973 523-9258
Fax: 973 523-5857
▲ **EMP**: 34
SQ FT: 12,500
SALES (est): 1.5MM **Privately Held**
SIC: 5812 5149 5411 2052 Eating Place
Whol Groceries Ret Groceries Mfg Cookies/Crackers Mfg Bread/Related Prdts

(G-8326)
LOTITO FOODS INC
510 E 35th St (07504-1720)
P.O. Box 39 (07543-0039)
PHONE.............................973 684-2900
Michael Gali, *Manager*
EMP: 16
SALES (corp-wide): 44MM **Privately Held**
WEB: www.lotitofoods.com
SIC: 2022 Cheese, natural & processed
PA: Lotito Foods Inc.
240 Carter Dr
Edison NJ 08817
732 248-0222

(G-8327)
M & S MACHINE & TOOL CORP
108 Maryland Ave (07503-2113)
PHONE.............................973 345-5847
Nazim Sylejmanovski, *President*
Maksut Vebi, *Vice Pres*
EMP: 10
SALES (est): 1.8MM **Privately Held**
WEB: www.mandsmachine.com
SIC: 3599 3552 Machine shop, jobbing & repair; textile machinery

(G-8328)
MAB ENTERPRISES INC
Also Called: Vibration Isolation Co
225 Grand St (07501-2725)
PHONE.............................973 345-8282
Fax: 973 345-8285
Marlene Bennett, *President*
EMP: 15
SQ FT: 12,500
SALES (est): 1.4MM **Privately Held**
WEB: www.vibrationiso.com
SIC: 3829 Measuring & controlling devices; vibration meters, analyzers & calibrators

(G-8329)
MAJKA RAILING INC
125 Mcbride Ave (07501-2606)
PHONE.............................973 247-7603
Fax: 973 247-7605
Mary Majka, *President*
Keith Majka, *Purch Dir*
EMP: 7
SALES: 250K **Privately Held**
SIC: 3446 1799 Railings, bannisters, guards, etc.: made from metal pipe; railings, prefabricated metal; home/office interiors finishing, furnishing & remodeling

(G-8330)
MANHATTAN SIGNS & DESIGNS LTD
130 Beckwith Ave Ste 2b (07503-2819)
PHONE.............................973 278-3603
Eugene Nifenecker, *President*
EMP: 20

SALES (corp-wide): 2.4MM **Privately Held**
SIC: 3993 Signs & advertising specialties
PA: Manhattan Signs & Designs, Ltd.
224 W 30th St
New York NY 10001
212 564-4400

(G-8331)
MAR MACHINE KEN MANUFACTURING
Also Called: Maria
477 E 30th St (07504-2110)
PHONE.............................973 278-5827
Fax: 973 278-7658
Kenneth A Walder, *President*
Ewald Schlosser, *Vice Pres*
▲ **EMP**: 26 **EST**: 1940
SQ FT: 17,000
SALES (est): 3.9MM **Privately Held**
WEB: www.ken-mar-machine.com
SIC: 3842 Prosthetic appliances

(G-8332)
MARDON ASSOCIATES INC
Also Called: Bakers Puff Pastry
1 Industrial Plz (07503-2964)
PHONE.............................973 977-2251
Anthony Cipriano, *President*
Orlie Parker, *Vice Pres*
Wolfgang Rathmann, *Vice Pres*
EMP: 11
SQ FT: 4,800
SALES (est): 1.1MM **Privately Held**
SIC: 2053 Frozen bakery products, except bread; pastries (danish): frozen

(G-8333)
MASTER METAL POLISHING CORP
Also Called: Master Metal Finishers
57 Wood St (07524-1007)
PHONE.............................973 684-0119
Gerardo Almeyda, *Ch of Bd*
Jeffrey Almeyda, *President*
Kevin Almeyda, *Vice Pres*
EMP: 20 **EST**: 1962
SQ FT: 7,000
SALES: 2.5MM **Privately Held**
WEB: www.mastermetal.com
SIC: 3471 Anodizing (plating) of metals or formed products; polishing, metals or formed products; coloring & finishing of aluminum or formed products

(G-8334)
MEDICI INTERNATIONAL INC
85 5th Ave Build18 (07524-1110)
PHONE.............................973 684-6084
Fax: 973 684-6069
Pierre Dabagh, *President*
EMP: 5
SALES (est): 744.3K **Privately Held**
SIC: 3171 8011 Women's handbags & purses; offices & clinics of medical doctors

(G-8335)
MENDELS MUFFINS AND STUFF INC
53 Jersey St (07501-1701)
PHONE.............................973 881-9900
Mendel Neustadt, *Owner*
EMP: 6
SALES (est): 814.5K **Privately Held**
SIC: 2051 Bread, cake & related products

(G-8336)
MENDLES JUST BREAD INC
53 Jersey St (07501-1701)
PHONE.............................973 881-9900
Mendle Nuestadt, *President*
EMP: 8
SALES (est): 239.7K **Privately Held**
SIC: 2051 Pies, bakery: except frozen

(G-8337)
METRO MILLS INC
Also Called: Fashion Windows Etc
151 Linwood Ave (07502-1895)
P.O. Box 247, Totowa (07511-0247)
PHONE.............................973 942-6034
Fax: 973 942-4109
Donald Kapit, *President*
Fred Pepe, *Treasurer*

EMP: 20
SQ FT: 17,000
SALES: 1.2MM **Privately Held**
SIC: 2391 2591 2211 Draperies, plastic & textile: from purchased materials; blinds vertical; window shades; bedspreads, cotton

(G-8338)
MICROSEAL INDUSTRIES INC
610 E 36th St (07513-1167)
P.O. Box 3054 (07509-3054)
PHONE.............................973 523-0704
Michael Silverstein, *President*
Ken Lutz, *Controller*
Sheldon Silverstein, *Mktg Dir*
▲ **EMP**: 17
SQ FT: 25,000
SALES (est): 4.5MM **Privately Held**
WEB: www.microseal.com
SIC: 2672 Tape, pressure sensitive: made from purchased materials; coated paper, except photographic, carbon or abrasive

(G-8339)
MICROWAVE CONSULTING CORP
Also Called: McC Norsal
150 Railroad Ave (07501-2943)
P.O. Box 6040 (07509-6040)
PHONE.............................973 523-6700
Scott Warner, *President*
EMP: 6
SALES: 350K **Privately Held**
SIC: 3679 Microwave components

(G-8340)
MIDLAND FARMS INC
845 E 25th St (07513-1201)
PHONE.............................800 749-6455
Demetrios Haseotes, *Branch Mgr*
EMP: 24
SALES (corp-wide): 14.5MM **Privately Held**
SIC: 2026 Milk processing (pasteurizing, homogenizing, bottling)
PA: Midland Farms, Inc.
375 Broadway
Menands NY 12204
518 436-7038

(G-8341)
MOCOCO PARTNERS CORP
439 E 22nd St (07514-2321)
PHONE.............................862 204-3461
Daysi Duverge, *Principal*
EMP: 4 **EST**: 2016
SALES (est): 195.6K **Privately Held**
SIC: 2086 Bottled & canned soft drinks

(G-8342)
MP PLASTIC LLC
14 Florida Ave (07503-2115)
PHONE.............................973 279-9300
Maher Muheisen,
EMP: 25
SALES (est): 3.3MM **Privately Held**
SIC: 2673 Plastic & pliofilm bags

(G-8343)
MPT DELIVERY SYSTEMS INC
Also Called: Pharmachem Laboratories
95 Prince St (07501-2905)
PHONE.............................973 278-0283
Roger Herrell, *Principal*
▲ **EMP**: 6
SALES (est): 595.6K **Privately Held**
SIC: 2834 Pharmaceutical preparations

(G-8344)
MPT DELIVERY SYSTEMS INC
95 Prince St (07501-2905)
PHONE.............................973 279-4132
David Holmes, *President*
Colin Mac Intyre, *Vice Pres*
Andrea Bauer, *Treasurer*
Catherine Holmes, *Admin Sec*
▲ **EMP**: 60
SQ FT: 26,000
SALES (est): 7.9MM
SALES (corp-wide): 3.2B **Publicly Held**
SIC: 2833 Vitamins, natural or synthetic: bulk, uncompounded

HQ: Pharmachem Laboratories, Llc
265 Harrison Tpke
Kearny NJ 07032
201 246-1000

(G-8345)
MS SIGNS INC
6 Morris St (07501-1706)
PHONE.............................973 569-1111
MO Ladak, *President*
Salma Ladak, *Corp Secy*
Kevin Cherashore, *Vice Pres*
▲ **EMP**: 7
SQ FT: 6,000
SALES (est): 1.4MM **Privately Held**
WEB: www.stgcorp.com
SIC: 3993 Signs & advertising specialties

(G-8346)
NABLUS PASTRY & SWEETS
1050 Main St Fl 1 (07503-2212)
PHONE.............................973 881-8003
Shar Abedravvo, *Owner*
▲ **EMP**: 5 **EST**: 1997
SALES (est): 292.4K **Privately Held**
SIC: 2051 Bakery: wholesale or wholesale/retail combined

(G-8347)
NEW ERA CONVERTING MACHINERY
235 Rt 20 N (07504)
P.O. Box 377, Hawthorne (07507-0377)
PHONE.............................201 670-4848
Fax: 201 670-8867
Frank P Lembo, *CEO*
Robert Pasquale, *President*
John Pasquale, *Vice Pres*
▲ **EMP**: 40
SQ FT: 25,000
SALES (est): 11.3MM **Privately Held**
WEB: www.neweraconverting.com
SIC: 3599 Custom machinery

(G-8348)
NEW JERSEY BALANCING SVC INC
138 Michigan Ave Ste 40 (07503-1709)
PHONE.............................973 278-5106
Fax: 973 278-5851
Francis Kennedy, *President*
EMP: 6
SQ FT: 5,000
SALES (est): 500K **Privately Held**
WEB: www.njbalancinginc.com
SIC: 3599 Machine shop, jobbing & repair

(G-8349)
NEW JERSEY DIAMOND PRODUCTS CO
108 Kentucky Ave (07503-2508)
PHONE.............................973 684-0949
Fax: 973 684-3716
Mark Zambrano, *President*
James G Zambrano, *Vice Pres*
EMP: 10 **EST**: 1966
SQ FT: 5,000
SALES (est): 1.5MM **Privately Held**
WEB: www.njdp.com
SIC: 3545 3291 Diamond cutting tools for turning, boring, burnishing, etc.; abrasive products

(G-8350)
NEW WORLD INTERNATIONAL INC
46 Lewis St (07501-3607)
PHONE.............................973 881-8100
Carmen Bires, *President*
John J Bires, *Vice Pres*
▼ **EMP**: 10
SQ FT: 47,000
SALES: 2MM **Privately Held**
SIC: 2844 Toilet preparations; cosmetic preparations

(G-8351)
NEXTWAVE WEB LLC
229 Marshall St (07503-3121)
PHONE.............................973 742-4339
Yashoda Annirood, *Project Mgr*
Samy Suqi, *Technology*
ISA Suqi,
Ana De La Rosa, *Graphic Designe*
Alia Suqi,

GEOGRAPHIC

EMP: 11
SQ FT: 7,500
SALES (est): 2MM **Privately Held**
SIC: 2752 2741 Commercial printing, lithographic; miscellaneous publishing

(G-8352)
NORTH JERSEY SKEIN DYEING CO
Also Called: Hoof Fe Dye Works
152 Putnam St (07524-1913)
P.O. Box 319 (07544-0319)
PHONE.............................201 247-4202
Fax: 973 345-7455
Dominick H Aldi Sr, *President*
EMP: 8 **EST:** 1962
SQ FT: 5,000
SALES (est): 490K **Privately Held**
SIC: 2262 Dyeing: manmade fiber & silk broadwoven fabrics

(G-8353)
NORTHEAST TOMATO COMPANY INC
4 22 Erie St (07524)
PHONE.............................973 684-4890
Gerald Pfund, *President*
EMP: 10
SALES (est): 147.1K **Privately Held**
SIC: 2033 Vegetable pastes: packaged in cans, jars, etc.

(G-8354)
NORTHERN STATE PERIODICALS LLC
251 Vreeland Ave Ste B (07504-1736)
PHONE.............................973 782-6100
Juan J Santos, *CEO*
EMP: 7
SALES: 200K **Privately Held**
SIC: 2741 Miscellaneous publishing

(G-8355)
OKONITE COMPANY
959 Market St (07513-1196)
PHONE.............................201 825-0300
Fax: 973 684-7307
David Mitchell, *Treasurer*
Thomas Scanlon, *Manager*
EMP: 85
SALES (corp-wide): 413.7MM **Privately Held**
WEB: www.okonite.com
SIC: 3357 Nonferrous wiredrawing & insulating
PA: The Okonite Company
102 Hilltop Rd
Ramsey NJ 07446
201 825-0300

(G-8356)
ORIGINAL MIAMI ONION ROLL INC
111 Berkshire Ave (07502-1812)
PHONE.............................973 389-2202
Fax: 973 389-2206
Harriet Davis, *President*
Don Rossi, *Corp Secy*
Jacqueline Rossi, *Executive Asst*
EMP: 40
SQ FT: 20,000
SALES (est): 8.5MM **Privately Held**
SIC: 2051 Breads, rolls & buns

(G-8357)
ORTHO-DYNAMICS INC
210 E 16th St (07524-2009)
PHONE.............................973 742-4390
Fax: 973 742-4556
Steve Tushingham, *President*
EMP: 9
SQ FT: 5,000
SALES (est): 730K **Privately Held**
WEB: www.ortho-dynamics.com
SIC: 3842 Foot appliances, orthopedic

(G-8358)
P & S BLIZZARD CORPORATION
Also Called: Blizzard Parts & Service
722 Madison Ave (07501-2407)
PHONE.............................973 523-1700
Fax: 973 523-6221
Paul Kostovski, *President*
EMP: 6

SALES (est): 410K **Privately Held**
SIC: 2499 7699 7538 Snow fence, wood; recreational sporting equipment repair services; industrial equipment services; general automotive repair shops

(G-8359)
PAPER TUBES CORES & BOXES INC
Also Called: Paper Tube and Core
239 Lindbergh Pl (07503-2821)
PHONE.............................973 977-8823
Fax: 973 977-8668
Russ Panzer, *President*
Howard Panzer, *Chairman*
Jeff Schindle, *Vice Pres*
▼ **EMP:** 14
SQ FT: 16,000
SALES (est): 3.6MM **Privately Held**
SIC: 2655 Fiber cans, drums & containers

(G-8360)
PARISER INDUSTRIES INC (PA)
91 Michigan Ave (07503-1807)
PHONE.............................973 569-9090
Fax: 973 569-9101
Albert Pariser, *President*
Craig Moser, *Regional Mgr*
Stephen Staum, *Regional Mgr*
Bill Little, *District Mgr*
Victor Naumenko, *District Mgr*
◆ **EMP:** 27
SQ FT: 7,500
SALES (est): 11.1MM **Privately Held**
WEB: www.pariserchem.com
SIC: 2843 2899 Textile finishing agents; water treating compounds

(G-8361)
PATERSON BLEACHERY INC (PA)
207 E 15th St 219 (07524-2018)
PHONE.............................973 684-1034
Antonio Armenante, *President*
George Armenante, *Vice Pres*
EMP: 15 **EST:** 1940
SQ FT: 35,000
SALES (est): 961.5K **Privately Held**
SIC: 2231 2241 2221 Broadwoven fabric mills, wool; fabric, animal fiber: narrow woven; broadwoven fabric mills, manmade

(G-8362)
PECATA ENTERPRISES INC
Also Called: Ultimate Textile
18 Market St (07501-1721)
PHONE.............................973 523-9498
Fax: 973 523-5457
Roger Glickman, *President*
Stella Garzon, *Office Mgr*
◆ **EMP:** 50
SQ FT: 30,000
SALES (est): 8.4MM **Privately Held**
WEB: www.pecata.com
SIC: 2759 3552 Screen printing; textile machinery

(G-8363)
PERAGALLO ORGAN COMPANY OF NJ
Also Called: Peragallo Pipe Organ
306 Buffalo Ave (07503-1103)
PHONE.............................973 684-3414
Fax: 973 684-2237
John Peragallo Jr, *President*
Frank Peragallo, *Vice Pres*
John Peragallo III, *Vice Pres*
EMP: 16 **EST:** 1918
SQ FT: 2,500
SALES (est): 2.1MM **Privately Held**
WEB: www.peragallo.com
SIC: 3931 7699 Organs, all types: pipe, reed, hand, electronic, etc.; synthesizers, music; organ tuning & repair; musical instrument repair services

(G-8364)
PETER GARAFANO & SON INC
Also Called: Garafano Tank Service
500 Marshall St (07503-2927)
PHONE.............................973 278-0350
Fax: 973 345-7633
Peter Garafano, *President*
Mary Cunningham, *Bookkeeper*

Daniel Garafano, *Admin Sec*
EMP: 24
SQ FT: 18,000
SALES (est): 8.2MM **Privately Held**
WEB: www.garafanotankservice.com
SIC: 5012 3441 7692 3713 Trailers for trucks, new & used; fabricated structural metal; welding repair; dump truck bodies

(G-8365)
PROMOTIONAL GRAPHICS INC
81 E 26th St (07514-1615)
PHONE.............................973 423-3900
Fax: 201 423-3989
Diane Dopp, *President*
Wayne Dopp, *VP Prdtn*
Rodney Dopp, *CFO*
EMP: 16
SQ FT: 6,500
SALES (est): 1.6MM **Privately Held**
SIC: 2759 Labels & seals: printing

(G-8366)
QUALITY REMANUFACTURING INC
565 E 37th St (07504)
PHONE.............................973 523-8800
Rick Waghorne, *President*
Brooks Reed, *Vice Pres*
EMP: 15
SQ FT: 15,000
SALES (est): 150.1K **Privately Held**
SIC: 3714 Transmission housings or parts, motor vehicle

(G-8367)
R A O CONTRACT SALES NY INC
Also Called: R A O Contract Sales
94 Fulton St Ste 4 (07501-1200)
PHONE.............................201 652-1500
Fax: 973 279-6448
Brian Bergman, *President*
Brian B Bergman, *President*
Seth C Bergman, *Vice Pres*
Bruce E Bergman, *Treasurer*
Allison Ehrlich, *Office Mgr*
EMP: 9
SQ FT: 20,000
SALES (est): 1.2MM **Privately Held**
WEB: www.rao.com
SIC: 2499 3499 2493 3231 Picture & mirror frames, wood; picture frames, metal; bulletin boards, cork; bulletin boards, wood; mirrored glass

(G-8368)
RENTALIFT INC
Also Called: Jersey Lift Truck
48 Alabama Ave (07503-2107)
PHONE.............................973 684-6111
Edward Gerena, *President*
EMP: 11
SALES (est): 2.9MM **Privately Held**
SIC: 3537 Forklift trucks

(G-8369)
RICO FOODS INC
Also Called: Rico Products
527 E 18th St (07514-2611)
PHONE.............................973 278-0589
Fax: 973 278-0378
Emilio Hernandez, *President*
Lazara Fernandez, *Vice Pres*
Christine Hernandez, *Prdtn Mgr*
EMP: 41
SQ FT: 2,600
SALES (est): 9MM **Privately Held**
SIC: 2038 5999 Frozen specialties; packaging materials: boxes, padding, etc.

(G-8370)
RIGO INDUSTRIES INC
50 California Ave (07503-2518)
PHONE.............................973 881-1780
Fax: 973 881-0906
Isaac Gorovitz, *President*
Zelieg Rivkin, *Vice Pres*
Mendel Karp, *Project Mgr*
Ed Schwartz, *Natl Sales Mgr*
Rachel Brook, *Admin Sec*
EMP: 40
SQ FT: 45,000
SALES (est): 8.7MM **Privately Held**
WEB: www.rigowall.com
SIC: 2621 Wallpaper (hanging paper)

(G-8371)
ROCCO PRESS ADVG TYPOGRAPHY
171 Walnut St (07522-1425)
P.O. Box 1457, Wayne (07474-1457)
PHONE.............................973 790-4000
Fax: 973 790-4086
Louis Rocco, *President*
EMP: 12
SQ FT: 15,000
SALES (est): 3.6MM **Privately Held**
WEB: www.roccopress.com
SIC: 2759 2752 Letterpress printing; commercial printing, lithographic

(G-8372)
ROYCE ASSOCIATES A LTD PARTNR
Also Called: Passaic Color & Chemical
28 Paterson St (07501-1016)
PHONE.............................973 279-0400
Fax: 973 279-3175
Adams Rice, *Manager*
EMP: 25
SALES (est): 5.7MM
SALES (corp-wide): 18.3MM **Privately Held**
SIC: 2865 Cyclic crudes & intermediates
PA: Royce Associates, A Limited Partnership
35 Carlton Ave
East Rutherford NJ 07073
201 438-5200

(G-8373)
SABRE DIE CUTTING CO INC
68 Mill St (07501-1825)
PHONE.............................973 357-9800
Michaqel Culver, *President*
Michael Culver, *President*
Elizabeth Flores, *Vice Pres*
Patrick Cammarata, *Prdtn Mgr*
EMP: 30
SQ FT: 35,000
SALES (est): 3.8MM **Privately Held**
SIC: 2675 7389 Paper die-cutting; packaging & labeling services

(G-8374)
SAHARA TEXTILE INC
52 Courtland St (07503-2947)
PHONE.............................973 247-9900
Fax: 973 247-0247
Othman Jabbar, *President*
Nizar Jabbar, *Vice Pres*
▲ **EMP:** 20 **EST:** 1997
SQ FT: 90,000
SALES (est): 1.4MM **Privately Held**
SIC: 2392 Comforters & quilts: made from purchased materials

(G-8375)
SAMNA CNSTRCTN & STEEL FABRCTN
75 Dale Ave (07501-2903)
PHONE.............................973 977-8400
Salem El Samna, *President*
EMP: 10
SALES (est): 1.1MM **Privately Held**
SIC: 3441 Fabricated structural metal

(G-8376)
SAMSTUBEND INC
31 Maryland Ave (07503-2110)
PHONE.............................973 278-2555
Fax: 973 278-2664
Steve Baresse, *President*
Sam Ajadi, *COO*
Arnold Virula, *Plant Mgr*
EMP: 12
SQ FT: 7,000
SALES (est): 3.1MM **Privately Held**
SIC: 3498 5074 Tube fabricating (contract bending & shaping); plumbing & hydronic heating supplies

(G-8377)
SAMUELSON FURNITURE INC
11-13 Maryland Ave (07503-2110)
PHONE.............................973 278-4372
Fax: 973 333-6086
Lawrence Chaflin, *President*
Michael Chalfin, *Vice Pres*
Brittany Larusso, *Project Mgr*
Marianne San George, *Controller*

2018 Harris New Jersey
Manufacturers Directory

▲ = Import ▼=Export
◆ =Import/Export

Mina Sandoval, *Receptionist*
▲ **EMP:** 15
SALES (est): 3.5MM **Privately Held**
WEB: www.samuelsonfurniture.com
SIC: 3553 Furniture makers' machinery, woodworking

(G-8378)
SANITARY SOAP COMPANY
81 Dale Ave (07501-2903)
PHONE...................973 279-8500
Fax: 973 278-9424
Paul Yankner, *President*
Felicia Yankner, *Admin Sec*
EMP: 25 **EST:** 1937
SQ FT: 30,000
SALES (est): 3.2MM **Privately Held**
SIC: 2841 Soap & other detergents

(G-8379)
SAPPHIRE BATH INC
93 Harrison St Ste 5 (07501-1251)
PHONE...................718 215-1262
Josh Leser, *CEO*
EMP: 5
SQ FT: 11,000
SALES: 1MM **Privately Held**
SIC: 3431 Bathroom fixtures, including sinks

(G-8380)
SEABOARD PAPER AND TWINE LLC
37 E 6th St (07524-1173)
PHONE...................973 413-8100
Mike Fiore, *Mng Member*
Robert Baretz,
Bill Mulligan,
▲ **EMP:** 26
SQ FT: 52,000
SALES (est): 4.2MM **Privately Held**
WEB: www.seaboardpaperandtwine.com
SIC: 2298 2679 3589 Twine; filter paper: made from purchased material; paperboard products, converted; commercial cleaning equipment

(G-8381)
SEALY MATTRESS CO N J INC
Also Called: Sealy Paterson
697 River St (07524-1538)
PHONE...................973 345-8800
Fax: 973 345-7124
David Hertz, *President*
◆ **EMP:** 250 **EST:** 1907
SQ FT: 131,000
SALES: 100MM **Privately Held**
WEB: www.sealy.com
SIC: 2515 3493 Mattresses & foundations; steel springs, except wire

(G-8382)
SENAT POULTRY LLC
28 Warren St (07524-2104)
PHONE...................973 742-9316
Atabey Kucukkarca, *President*
EMP: 35
SALES (est): 4.7MM **Privately Held**
SIC: 2015 Poultry slaughtering & processing

(G-8383)
SKORR PRODUCTS LLC
90 George St (07503-2319)
P.O. Box 723, Butler (07405-0723)
PHONE...................973 523-2606
Fax: 973 523-3009
Robert Skvorecz, *Mng Member*
▲ **EMP:** 15
SALES (est): 2.5MM **Privately Held**
WEB: www.skorrproducts.com
SIC: 5051 3496 Metal wires, ties, cables & screening; miscellaneous fabricated wire products

(G-8384)
STEPHCO SALES INC
238 Lindbergh Pl Ste 3 (07503-2823)
PHONE...................973 278-5454
Danny Dibetitto, *President*
Carmen Orasco, *Admin Sec*
▲ **EMP:** 32

SALES (est): 4.3MM **Privately Held**
SIC: 5087 3089 2675 Carpet & rug cleaning equipment & supplies, commercial; plastic containers, except foam; die-cut paper & board

(G-8385)
STEPHEN DOUGLAS PLASTICS INC
22 Green St 36 (07501-2825)
P.O. Box 2775 (07509-2775)
PHONE...................973 523-3030
Fax: 973 523-0643
Stewart Graff, *President*
Miriam Graff, *Corp Secy*
Douglas Graff, *Vice Pres*
Beshaw Paul, *CFO*
Carla Ferrentino, *Controller*
◆ **EMP:** 135
SQ FT: 79,000
SALES (est): 38.7MM **Privately Held**
WEB: www.douglasstephen.com
SIC: 3089 Plastic containers, except foam; plastic kitchenware, tableware & houseware

(G-8386)
STONEBRIDGE PAPER LLC
Also Called: Converting Resources
37 E 6th St (07524-1173)
P.O. Box 2571, Wayne (07474-2571)
PHONE...................973 413-8100
Robert Baretz,
▲ **EMP:** 12
SQ FT: 42,000
SALES: 2MM **Privately Held**
SIC: 2679 Paper products, converted

(G-8387)
SUNGLO FABRICS INC
50 California Ave (07503-2503)
PHONE...................201 935-0830
Larry B Weissenberg, *President*
Chris Biviano, *Sales Engr*
Casey Hepler, *Sales Staff*
◆ **EMP:** 10 **EST:** 1932
SQ FT: 23,000
SALES (est): 1.6MM **Privately Held**
WEB: www.sunglofabrics.com
SIC: 2759 Screen printing

(G-8388)
SUNRISE SNACKS ROCKLAND INC
787 E 27th St (07504-2019)
PHONE...................845 352-2676
Simon Singer, *Branch Mgr*
EMP: 15
SALES (corp-wide): 1.4MM **Privately Held**
SIC: 2099 Food preparations
PA: Sunrise Snacks Of Rockland, Inc.
3 Sunrise Dr
Monsey NY 10952
845 352-2676

(G-8389)
SUPERTEX INC
860 Market St (07513-1127)
PHONE...................973 345-1000
Edward W Cumins, *President*
Howard Cumins, *Vice Pres*
Cheryl Severson,
EMP: 40
SQ FT: 30,000
SALES (est): 3.7MM **Privately Held**
WEB: www.meshtruckcovers.com
SIC: 2253 T-shirts & tops, knit

(G-8390)
SUPPLY PLUS NJ INC
3 E 26th St (07514-1505)
PHONE...................973 782-5930
Issac Greensfeld, *President*
▲ **EMP:** 40
SQ FT: 10,000
SALES (est): 9.7MM **Privately Held**
SIC: 3069 Sponge rubber & sponge rubber products

(G-8391)
SUPPLY PLUS NY INC
3 E 26th St (07514-1505)
PHONE...................973 481-4800
Fax: 973 782-5931
Sam Neustein, *Ch of Bd*

Samuel Neustein Jr, *President*
Alex Neustein, *Vice Pres*
Murray Neustein, *Treasurer*
Hanna Neustein, *Admin Sec*
▲ **EMP:** 26
SQ FT: 66,000
SALES (est): 4.6MM **Privately Held**
SIC: 3291 5199 Pads, scouring: soap impregnated; sponges, scouring: metallic; foam rubber

(G-8392)
SUPPLYONE NEW YORK INC
143 Getty Ave (07503-2806)
PHONE...................718 392-7400
William T Leith, *Ch of Bd*
Jerry Gitelli, *President*
Dennis Francy, *Warehouse Mgr*
Jason Fuller, *CFO*
▲ **EMP:** 30 **EST:** 1934
SQ FT: 70,000
SALES (est): 16.2MM
SALES (corp-wide): 488.7MM **Privately Held**
SIC: 3565 Carton packing machines
PA: Supplyone Holdings Company, Inc.
11 Campus Blvd Ste 150
Newtown Square PA 19073
484 582-5005

(G-8393)
SWEET POTATO PIE INC
140 Auburn St (07501-2035)
PHONE...................973 279-3405
Fax: 973 279-1436
Edgar Ramsey, *President*
Gwendolyn Ramsey, *Treasurer*
EMP: 40
SQ FT: 6,500
SALES (est): 4.7MM **Privately Held**
WEB: www.classicpies.com
SIC: 2051 Pies, bakery: except frozen

(G-8394)
SYNERGY MICROWAVE CORP (PA)
201 Mclean Blvd (07504-1138)
PHONE...................973 881-8800
Ulrich L Rohde, *Ch of Bd*
Meta Rohde, *President*
Susan McIntosh-James, *Purch Agent*
Ronnie Sorrin, *Purchasing*
Clark Heber, *QC Mgr*
▲ **EMP:** 100
SQ FT: 22,000
SALES (est): 15.7MM **Privately Held**
WEB: www.synergymwave.com
SIC: 3679 Microwave components

(G-8395)
T & T CABINET WORKS INC
388 River St (07524-2217)
PHONE...................973 279-0909
Fax: 973 279-0909
Anthony Cercone, *President*
EMP: 5
SQ FT: 5,000
SALES: 200K **Privately Held**
SIC: 2434 Wood kitchen cabinets

(G-8396)
TABLECLOTH CO INC
514 Totowa Ave (07522-1541)
PHONE...................973 942-1555
Fax: 973 942-3092
Judith Metzger, *President*
Michael Kramer, *Exec VP*
Bernie Kramer, *Vice Pres*
▼ **EMP:** 50
SQ FT: 18,000
SALES (est): 5MM **Privately Held**
WEB: www.tablecloth.com
SIC: 2392 5949 Tablecloths: made from purchased materials; sewing, needlework & piece goods

(G-8397)
TEC INSTALLATIONS INC
375 E 22nd St (07514-2312)
PHONE...................973 684-0503
Fax: 973 684-0710
Scott Crance, *President*
EMP: 10
SQ FT: 20,000

SALES (est): 2MM **Privately Held**
SIC: 3535 Conveyors & conveying equipment

(G-8398)
TECHNICAL PROCESSING INC
81 Dale Ave (07501-2903)
PHONE...................973 278-4950
Paul R Yankner, *President*
▼ **EMP:** 12
SQ FT: 30,000
SALES (est): 1.8MM **Privately Held**
SIC: 2869 Industrial organic chemicals

(G-8399)
THEBGB INC (PA) ✪
840 E 28th St (07513-1219)
PHONE...................917 749-5309
Jessica Sillaro, *President*
EMP: 1 **EST:** 2017
SQ FT: 10,000
SALES: 3MM **Privately Held**
SIC: 2051 Bread, cake & related products

(G-8400)
THERMA-TECH CORPORATION
300 Dakota St Ste 1 (07503-2448)
PHONE...................973 345-0076
Fax: 973 345-3228
Yonina Papka, *President*
Benjamin Papka, *Treasurer*
EMP: 10
SALES: 1.1MM **Privately Held**
SIC: 3567 Infrared ovens, industrial

(G-8401)
TRB ELECTRO CORP
6 Morris St (07501-1706)
P.O. Box 840 (07543-0840)
PHONE...................973 278-9014
Fax: 973 278-5124
Raman Patel, *Owner*
Dan Patel, *Corp Secy*
Chandra Patel, *Vice Pres*
EMP: 30
SQ FT: 4,000
SALES (est): 3.4MM **Privately Held**
SIC: 3471 Anodizing (plating) of metals or formed products

(G-8402)
TRINITY PRESS INC
655 Market St (07513-1228)
PHONE...................973 881-0690
Fax: 973 881-0696
Kevin Barnes, *President*
EMP: 40
SQ FT: 23,500
SALES (est): 9.2MM **Privately Held**
WEB: www.kevinbarnes.com
SIC: 2752 Commercial printing, offset

(G-8403)
TRISTATE CRATING PALLET CO INC
85 Fulton St (07501-1208)
PHONE...................973 357-8293
Fax: 973 357-8296
Marc Ellison, *President*
Maria Ellison, *President*
▲ **EMP:** 35
SQ FT: 30,000
SALES (est): 7.4MM **Privately Held**
WEB: www.tristatecrating.com
SIC: 2448 Pallets, wood

(G-8404)
UNITED MACHINE INC
239 Lindbergh Pl Ste 2a (07503-2821)
PHONE...................973 345-4505
Yakov Opatzevfky, *President*
EMP: 4
SQ FT: 10,000
SALES: 200K **Privately Held**
SIC: 3599 Water leak detectors; weather vanes

(G-8405)
UNIX CABINETRY INC
468 Totowa Ave Ste 2 (07522-1573)
PHONE...................201 995-6969
Sabahattin Sungu, *President*
EMP: 5
SQ FT: 1,000
SALES (est): 146.4K **Privately Held**
SIC: 2431 Millwork

(G-8406)
URBAN MILLWORK & SUPPLY CORP
90 2nd Ave (07514-2025)
PHONE................................973 278-7072
Fax: 973 278-0754
Sheer Stundell, *President*
Brett Stundell, *Vice Pres*
EMP: 2 EST: 1964
SQ FT: 17,500
SALES: 1.3MM **Privately Held**
SIC: 2431 5211 Staircases & stairs, wood; doors, storm: wood or metal

(G-8407)
VACS BANDAGE COMPANY INC
163 Pennsylvania Ave (07503-2122)
PHONE................................973 345-3355
Fax: 973 345-8311
Anthony Vacca, *President*
EMP: 12
SQ FT: 7,000
SALES: 806.7K **Privately Held**
SIC: 2211 Bandage cloths, cotton

(G-8408)
VISION LIGHTING INC
48 N 2nd St (07522-1705)
PHONE................................973 720-1200
Fax: 973 720-9470
Barry Mabery, *President*
Frank Giarratana, *Vice Pres*
EMP: 5
SQ FT: 5,000
SALES (est): 490K **Privately Held**
WEB: www.fxlight.com
SIC: 3646 Commercial indusl & institutional electric lighting fixtures

(G-8409)
ZENEX PRECISION PRODUCTS CORP
69 George St (07503-2318)
PHONE................................973 523-6910
Zenon Wronski, *President*
Robert Wronski, *Vice Pres*
EMP: 10
SALES (est): 950K **Privately Held**
WEB: www.zenexprecision.com
SIC: 3599 Machine shop, jobbing & repair

(G-8410)
ZULU FIRE DOORS LTD LBLTY CO
923 Market St (07513-1128)
PHONE................................973 569-9858
Harpal Singh Rai, *Mng Member*
EMP: 9
SALES (est): 1.1MM **Privately Held**
SIC: 3442 Metal doors, sash & trim

Paulsboro
Gloucester County

(G-8411)
AAA PHARMACEUTICAL INC
157-160 W Jefferson St (08066)
PHONE................................856 423-2700
Tejash Sheth, *Vice Pres*
EMP: 15
SALES (corp-wide): 20MM **Privately Held**
SIC: 2834 Pharmaceutical preparations
PA: Aaa Pharmaceutical
    681 Main St
    Lumberton NJ 08048
    609 288-6060

(G-8412)
ACTIVE CONTROLS LLC
1501 Grandview Ave # 400 (08066-1865)
PHONE................................856 669-0940
Michael Flowers, *President*
Jordan Flowers, *COO*
Russ Rolt, *Vice Pres*
▲ EMP: 4
SALES (est): 630.4K **Privately Held**
SIC: 3629 Electrical industrial apparatus

(G-8413)
ASTRAL DIAGNOSTICS INC
1224 Forest Pkwy Ste 200 (08066-1722)
PHONE................................856 224-0900
Fax: 856 224-9466
Edward McCaffrey, *President*
EMP: 5
SQ FT: 8,000
SALES (est): 949.6K
SALES (corp-wide): 71.2MM **Privately Held**
WEB: www.astraldiagnostics.com
SIC: 2835 In vitro & in vivo diagnostic substances
PA: Polysciences, Inc.
    400 Valley Rd
    Warrington PA 18976
    215 343-6484

(G-8414)
BOSTIK INC
2000 Nolte Dr (08066-1700)
PHONE................................856 848-8669
Theresa Honeycut, *Branch Mgr*
Paul Dollard, *Planning*
EMP: 70
SALES (corp-wide): 77.8MM **Privately Held**
WEB: www.bostik-us.com
SIC: 2891 2899 Adhesives; chemical preparations
HQ: Bostik, Inc.
    11320 W Wtertown Plank Rd
    Wauwatosa WI 53226
    414 774-2250

(G-8415)
COIM USA INC
Also Called: Air Products
675 Billingsport Rd (08066-1037)
PHONE................................856 224-1668
Cathy Myers, *Principal*
EMP: 30
SQ FT: 20,000
SALES (corp-wide): 401.9MM **Privately Held**
WEB: www.airproducts.com
SIC: 2813 2869 2819 Industrial gases; industrial organic chemicals; industrial inorganic chemicals
HQ: Coim Usa Inc.
    286 Mantua Grove Rd # 1
    West Deptford NJ 08066
    856 224-8560

(G-8416)
CPI OPERATIONS LLC
4 Paradise Rd (08066-1740)
PHONE................................856 423-5400
EMP: 49
SALES (corp-wide): 425.8MM **Privately Held**
SIC: 2911 Petroleum Refiner
HQ: Cpi Operations Llc
    750 Wshngton Blvd Ste 600
    Stamford CT 06901

(G-8417)
INTELCO
1927 Nolte Dr (08066-1727)
PHONE................................856 384-8562
Grant Wells, *Branch Mgr*
EMP: 28 **Privately Held**
SIC: 2541 1799 2434 Table or counter tops, plastic laminated; counter top installation; vanities, bathroom: wood
PA: Intelco
    250 Harvard Ave
    Westville NJ 08093

(G-8418)
LAMATEK INC (PA)
1226 Forest Pkwy (08066-1728)
PHONE................................856 599-6000
G Robert Carlson, *CEO*
Laura Basara, *Vice Pres*
Fernando Gisone, *Buyer*
Terri Chicosky, *QC Mgr*
Christine Ronkin, *Controller*
▼ EMP: 30
SQ FT: 13,000
SALES (est): 6.4MM **Privately Held**
SIC: 3069 3053 Weather strip, sponge rubber; gaskets, packing & sealing devices

(G-8419)
MATTHEY JOHNSON INC
2003 Nolte Dr (08066-1727)
PHONE................................856 384-7022
Fax: 856 384-7217
Anita Sargable, *Safety Mgr*
William Dennys, *Purch Mgr*
Rachel Beatrice, *Buyer*
Frank Lord, *Buyer*
Dieter Blank, *Engineer*
EMP: 131
SALES (corp-wide): 15B **Privately Held**
SIC: 3341 Platinum group metals, smelting & refining (secondary)
HQ: Matthey Johnson Inc
    435 Devon Park Dr Ste 600
    Wayne PA 19087
    610 971-3000

(G-8420)
MCGRORY GLASS INC
1400 Grandview Ave (08066-1801)
PHONE................................856 579-3200
Fax: 856 579-3232
Christopher McGrory, *President*
Gary McGrory, *Corp Secy*
Charles McGrory, *Vice Pres*
▲ EMP: 60
SQ FT: 108,000
SALES (est): 17MM **Privately Held**
WEB: www.mcgrory-glass.com
SIC: 3211 5039 3231 3229 Construction glass; glass construction materials; products of purchased glass; pressed & blown glass; laminated plastics plate & sheet

(G-8421)
MOBIL RESEARCH AND DEV CORP
600 Billingsport Rd (08066-1034)
PHONE................................856 224-2134
Fax: 856 224-3602
J E Crawford, *President*
R H Gardner, *Vice Pres*
J R Green, *Vice Pres*
J R Katzer, *Vice Pres*
K D Kroupa, *Vice Pres*
◆ EMP: 2300
SALES (est): 207MM
SALES (corp-wide): 244.3B **Publicly Held**
SIC: 2911 Petroleum refining
HQ: Exxonmobil Oil Corporation
    2805 Sycamore St
    Beaumont TX 77701
    409 757-3763

(G-8422)
OIL TECHNOLOGIES SERVICES INC (PA)
Also Called: Seahawk Services
1501 Grandview Ave Ste 1 (08066-1865)
PHONE................................856 845-4142
Fax: 856 845-3650
Wajdi Abdmessih, *President*
Fabiola Abdmessih, *Vice Pres*
EMP: 6
SQ FT: 5,000
SALES: 1MM **Privately Held**
SIC: 1389 5551 Testing, measuring, surveying & analysis services; oil consultants; marine supplies & equipment

(G-8423)
OIL TECHNOLOGIES SERVICES INC
Also Called: Seahawk Services
1501 Grandview Ave Ste 1 (08066-1865)
PHONE................................856 845-4142
Wajdi Abdmessih, *President*
Fabiola Abdmessih, *Vice Pres*
EMP: 6
SQ FT: 5,000
SALES: 1MM **Privately Held**
SIC: 1389 5551 Testing, measuring, surveying & analysis services; oil consultants; marine supplies & equipment

(G-8424)
PAULSBORO REFINING COMPANY LLC
Also Called: Pbf Energy
800 Billingsport Rd (08066-1035)
PHONE................................973 455-7500
Thomas J Nimbley, *CEO*

Michael D Gayda, *President*
Donald F Lucey, *Exec VP*
Matthew C Lucey, *Exec VP*
Jeffrey Dill, *Senior VP*
▲ EMP: 1500
SALES (est): 19B
SALES (corp-wide): 21.7B **Publicly Held**
SIC: 2911 Oils, partly refined: sold for rerunning
HQ: Pbf Holding Company Llc
    1 Sylvan Way Ste 2
    Parsippany NJ 07054

(G-8425)
PENNZOIL-QUAKER STATE COMPANY
1224 Forest Pkwy Ste 100 (08066-1722)
PHONE................................856 423-1388
Ed Barney, *Manager*
EMP: 4
SALES (corp-wide): 305.1B **Privately Held**
WEB: www.pzl.com
SIC: 2911 Petroleum refining
HQ: Pennzoil-Quaker State Company
    150 N Dairy Ashford Rd
    Houston TX 77079
    713 245-4800

(G-8426)
STETSERS JD CANVAS PDTS INC
644 Billings Ave (08066-1213)
PHONE................................856 423-4901
Fax: 856 423-4904
Patricia Stetser, *President*
Donald Stetser, *Vice Pres*
EMP: 6
SQ FT: 8,000
SALES: 320K **Privately Held**
WEB: www.stetserscanvas.net
SIC: 2394 Awnings, fabric: made from purchased materials

(G-8427)
TRIANGLE TUBE/PHASE III CO INC
1240 Forest Pkwy Ste 100 (08066-1719)
PHONE................................856 228-9940
Fax: 856 228-3584
Daniel Lasserre, *Ch of Bd*
Jack Weaver, *President*
Douglas Dodds, *VP Sales*
◆ EMP: 51
SQ FT: 50,000
SALES (est): 11.6MM
SALES (corp-wide): 65.4MM **Privately Held**
WEB: www.triangletube.com
SIC: 3433 3639 3621 3443 Heating equipment, except electric; hot water heaters, household; motors & generators; fabricated plate work (boiler shop)
PA: Acv International Nv
    Oude Vijverweg 6
    Beersel 1653
    233 482-40

(G-8428)
VALERO REF COMPANY-NEW JERSEY
800 Billingsport Rd (08066)
PHONE................................856 224-6000
Fax: 856 224-6681
Paul Borbhu, *Manager*
EMP: 550
SALES (corp-wide): 93.9B **Publicly Held**
SIC: 2911 Petroleum refining
HQ: Valero Refining Company-New Jersey
    1 Valero Way
    San Antonio TX 78249
    210 345-2000

Peapack
Somerset County

(G-8429)
PFIZER INC
100 Rte 206 N (07977)
P.O. Box 800 (07977-0800)
PHONE................................908 901-8000
Juan C Perez, *Manager*
Mark Pohan, *Manager*

Tina Lawrence, *Senior Mgr*
EMP: 146
SALES (corp-wide): 52.5B **Publicly Held**
WEB: www.pfizer.com
SIC: 2834 Antibiotics, packaged
PA: Pfizer Inc.
235 E 42nd St
New York NY 10017
212 733-2323

(G-8430)
PHARMACIA & UPJOHN INC (HQ)
100 Route 206 N (07977)
PHONE..........................908 901-8000
Goran A Ando, *Exec VP*
Christopher J Coughlin, *CFO*
▲ **EMP:** 400
SALES (est): 825.6MM
SALES (corp-wide): 52.5B **Publicly Held**
WEB: www.pharmaciaupjohn.com
SIC: 2834 2833 Pharmaceutical preparations; medicinal chemicals
PA: Pfizer Inc.
235 E 42nd St
New York NY 10017
212 733-2323

(G-8431)
PHARMACIA & UPJOHN COMPANY LLC (HQ)
Also Called: Pfizer
100 Rte 206 N (07977)
PHONE..........................908 901-8000
Ley S Smith, *President*
Carla Wright, *Engineer*
Michael Lantigua, *Business Anlyst*
Marty Brown, *Manager*
Don Dibenedetto, *Manager*
◆ **EMP:** 274 **EST:** 2005
SQ FT: 300,000
SALES (corp-wide): 52.5B **Publicly Held**
SIC: 2834 2833 2048 Pharmaceutical preparations; druggists' preparations (pharmaceuticals); drugs acting on the central nervous system & sense organs; analgesics; medicinal chemicals; organic medicinal chemicals: bulk, uncompounded; alkaloids & other botanical based products; agar-agar (ground); feed supplements
PA: Pfizer Inc.
235 E 42nd St
New York NY 10017
212 733-2323

(G-8432)
R P R GRAPHICS INC
87 Main St (07977-9801)
P.O. Box 118 (07977-0118)
PHONE..........................908 654-8080
Fax: 908 654-0713
Richard P Ruocco, *President*
Laura J Ruocco, *President*
Luis Velez, *President*
Susan J Arlington, *COO*
Frances Ruocco, *Treasurer*
EMP: 50
SQ FT: 12,000
SALES (est): 6.2MM **Privately Held**
WEB: www.rprgraphicsinc.com
SIC: 3663 2796 Digital encoders; color separations for printing

Pedricktown
Salem County

(G-8433)
CMI-PROMEX INC
7 Benjamin Green Rd (08067-3502)
PHONE..........................856 351-1000
Fax: 856 351-1659
Wayne Ligato, *President*
Michele S Barbara, *General Mgr*
Andrew Corlett, *Engineer*
Richard Cavalier, *VP Finance*
Bob Frawley, *Sales Dir*
EMP: 19
SQ FT: 10,000

SALES (est): 4.4MM **Privately Held**
WEB: www.cmi-promex.com
SIC: 3312 4013 7692 Tool & die steel; switching & terminal services; welding repair

(G-8434)
CST PAVERS
345 Route 130 (08067-3617)
PHONE..........................856 299-5339
David Guidi, *Principal*
EMP: 11
SALES (est): 1.4MM **Privately Held**
SIC: 3272 Concrete products

(G-8435)
DOCK RESINS CORPORATION
76 Porcupine Rd (08067-3509)
PHONE..........................908 862-2351
Howard Burke, *President*
James Robinson III, *Exec VP*
Joe Barbanel, *Senior VP*
A Warman, *Production*
▲ **EMP:** 46 **EST:** 1947
SQ FT: 24,000
SALES (est): 9.3MM
SALES (corp-wide): 242.1B **Publicly Held**
WEB: www.lubrizol.com
SIC: 2821 Plastics materials & resins
HQ: The Lubrizol Corporation
29400 Lakeland Blvd
Wickliffe OH 44092
440 943-4200

(G-8436)
JE BERKOWITZ LP
1 Gateway Blvd (08067-3629)
P.O. Box 427 (08067-0427)
PHONE..........................856 456-7800
Fax: 856 299-4970
Chris Lewandowski, *President*
Arthur M Berkowitz, *Partner*
Alan Berkowitz, *Partner*
Edwin J Berkowitz, *Partner*
David B Byruch, *Partner*
▲ **EMP:** 200 **EST:** 1920
SQ FT: 200,000
SALES (est): 80.3MM **Privately Held**
WEB: www.jeberkowitz.com
SIC: 3231 3211 Insulating glass: made from purchased glass; tempered glass: made from purchased glass; laminated glass

(G-8437)
LETTERING PLUS SIGN COMPANY
438 Perkintown Rd (08067-3106)
PHONE..........................856 299-0404
Bill Stouch, *President*
Sandra Stouch, *Treasurer*
EMP: 4
SALES (est): 392.3K **Privately Held**
SIC: 3993 7389 Signs, not made in custom sign painting shops; lettering & sign painting services

(G-8438)
LUBRIZOL ADVANCED MTLS INC
Also Called: B F Goodrich Performance Mtls
76 Porcupine Rd (08067-3509)
PHONE..........................856 299-3764
Fax: 856 351-2128
Joseph Lazevnick, *Manager*
EMP: 39
SALES (corp-wide): 242.1B **Publicly Held**
WEB: www.pharma.noveoninc.com
SIC: 2899 3087 Chemical preparations; custom compound purchased resins
HQ: Lubrizol Advanced Materials Inc.
9911 Brecksville Rd
Brecksville OH 44141
216 447-5000

(G-8439)
PALLET SERVICES INC
66 Pennsgrve Pedrcktwn Rd (08067)
P.O. Box 9, Swedesboro (08085-0009)
PHONE..........................856 514-3908
Steve Sorbello Jr, *President*
EMP: 4
SALES (est): 680.4K **Privately Held**
SIC: 2448 Pallets, wood

(G-8440)
SALEM OAK VINEYARDS LTD LBLTY
62 N Railroad Ave (08067-3524)
PHONE..........................856 889-2121
Mandi Cassidy,
EMP: 5
SALES (est): 376.7K **Privately Held**
SIC: 2084 Wines

(G-8441)
WJV MATERIALS LLC
93 Pennsgrve Pedrcktwn (08067)
PHONE..........................856 299-8244
Dan Federanko,
EMP: 20
SALES (est): 2MM **Privately Held**
SIC: 3273 Ready-mixed concrete

Pemberton
Burlington County

(G-8442)
AZTECH MFG INC
147 W Hampton St (08068-1012)
PHONE..........................609 726-1212
Daniel R Murphy, *President*
EMP: 10
SALES (est): 962.3K **Privately Held**
SIC: 3599 Machine shop, jobbing & repair

(G-8443)
TOTALLY T SHIRTS & MORE INC
201 W Hampton St (08068-1014)
PHONE..........................609 894-0011
Tony Miraglia, *President*
EMP: 5
SQ FT: 1,000
SALES (est): 611.7K **Privately Held**
SIC: 2759 Screen printing

Pennington
Mercer County

(G-8444)
BRISTOL-MYERS SQUIBB COMPANY
311 Pnnington Rocky HI Rd (08534-2130)
PHONE..........................212 546-4000
Fax: 609 818-4035
Chandra Shukla, *Manager*
EMP: 40
SALES (corp-wide): 20.7B **Publicly Held**
WEB: www.bms.com
SIC: 2834 Pills, pharmaceutical
PA: Bristol-Myers Squibb Company
430 E 29th St Fl 14
New York NY 10016
212 546-4000

(G-8445)
CERCIS INC
25 Route 31 S Ste C2030 (08534-2511)
PHONE..........................609 737-5120
Karen Kinsman, *Corp Secy*
EMP: 6
SQ FT: 1,500
SALES (est): 710K **Privately Held**
WEB: www.cercis.com
SIC: 3827 Light sources, standard

(G-8446)
CHRISTENSEN MANUFACTURING
11 Moores Mill Mt Rose Rd (08534-1840)
P.O. Box 592 (08534-0592)
PHONE..........................609 466-9700
Dave Christensen, *President*
John Healy, *Vice Pres*
EMP: 17
SQ FT: 6,000
SALES (est): 4.9MM **Privately Held**
WEB: www.christensenmfg.com
SIC: 3537 3713 Trucks, tractors, loaders, carriers & similar equipment; truck & bus bodies

(G-8447)
COMMERCIAL PDTS SVCS GROUP INC (PA)
Also Called: Green Building Solutions
1580 Reed Rd (08534-5000)
PHONE..........................609 730-4111
Robert A Rosenthal, *CEO*
Elizabeth Rosenthal, *President*
EMP: 8
SALES (est): 1.4MM **Privately Held**
SIC: 3699 Electrical equipment & supplies

(G-8448)
DARWIN PRESS INC
280 N Main St (08534-2275)
P.O. Box 2202, Princeton (08543-2202)
PHONE..........................609 737-1349
Fax: 609 737-0929
Ed Breisacher, *President*
▲ **EMP:** 4
SQ FT: 1,500
SALES (est): 279.4K **Privately Held**
WEB: www.darwinpress.com
SIC: 2731 Books: publishing only

(G-8449)
DIVERSATECH INC
1584 Reed Rd (08534-5003)
PHONE..........................609 730-9668
Haskel Zeloof, *President*
Sam Zeloof, *Maintence Staff*
EMP: 8
SQ FT: 4,000
SALES (est): 907.5K **Privately Held**
WEB: www.diversatech.com
SIC: 3599 Machine shop, jobbing & repair

(G-8450)
ELECTROCHEMICAL SOCIETY INC
Also Called: E C S
65 S Main St (08534-2827)
PHONE..........................609 737-1902
Fax: 609 737-2743
Paul Natishan, *President*
Becca J Compton, *General Mgr*
Linda Cannon, *Finance*
Rob Gerth, *Mktg Dir*
Logan Streu, *Publications*
EMP: 20
SQ FT: 6,000
SALES: 7.4MM **Privately Held**
WEB: www.electrochem.org
SIC: 8621 2741 Scientific membership association; miscellaneous publishing

(G-8451)
GENERAL SULLIVAN GROUP INC (PA)
Also Called: Sullivan Steel Service
85 Route 31 N (08534-3601)
PHONE..........................609 745-5004
Fax: 609 745-5012
Philip Trainer Jr, *Ch of Bd*
Alfred Deblasio Jr, *President*
◆ **EMP:** 26
SQ FT: 40,000
SALES: 19MM **Privately Held**
WEB: www.usatolerancerings.com
SIC: 5051 3316 Steel; corrugating iron & steel, cold-rolled

(G-8452)
GENERAL SULLIVAN GROUP INC
USA Tolerance Rings
85 Route 31 N (08534-3601)
PHONE..........................609 745-5000
Joseph Trainer, *Manager*
EMP: 18
SALES (corp-wide): 19MM **Privately Held**
SIC: 5051 3429 3452 Steel; metal fasteners; bolts, metal
PA: General Sullivan Group, Inc.
85 Route 31 N
Pennington NJ 08534
609 745-5004

(G-8453)
HOPEWELL VALLEY VINEYARDS LLC
46 Yard Rd (08534-3905)
PHONE..........................609 737-4465

Fax: 609 537-0061
Serjio Neri, *Mng Member*
Liz Radzki, *Manager*
Violeta Neri,
▲ **EMP:** 20
SALES (est): 3MM **Privately Held**
SIC: 2084 Wines

(G-8454)
JL PACKAGING GROUP CORP (PA)
2 Birch St (08534-3304)
PHONE................................609 610-0286
Judy Chen, *CEO*
Kevin Chen, *Vice Pres*
Rachelle Blue, *Director*
▲ **EMP:** 4
SALES: 9MM **Privately Held**
SIC: 3411 7389 Tin cans;

(G-8455)
KOOLTRONIC INC (PA)
30 Pennington Hopewell Rd (08534-3612)
PHONE................................609 466-3400
Anne L Freedman, *CEO*
Barry J Freedman, *President*
Steve Coulton, *Business Mgr*
Deborah S Freedman, *Vice Pres*
Bill Green, *Opers Mgr*
▲ **EMP:** 120
SQ FT: 170,000
SALES (est): 35MM **Privately Held**
WEB: www.kooltronic.com
SIC: 3585 3564 3559 3443 Air condition-ing equipment, complete; air conditioning units, complete: domestic or industrial; blowers & fans; blowing fans: industrial or commercial; recycling machinery; heat exchangers: coolers (after, inter), con-densers, etc.

(G-8456)
LORNAN LITHO INC
130 Route 31 N Ste E (08534-3620)
PHONE................................609 818-1198
Ronald Shankoff, *President*
Michael Shankoff, *Vice Pres*
Mike Shankoff, *Treasurer*
EMP: 10
SQ FT: 8,500
SALES (est): 118.3K **Privately Held**
SIC: 2759 Commercial printing

(G-8457)
PENNINGTON FURNACE SUPPLY INC
6 Brookside Ave (08534-2209)
P.O. Box 218 (08534-0218)
PHONE................................609 737-2500
Mark E Blackwell, *President*
Sarah Bregenzer, *Admin Sec*
EMP: 4 EST: 1960
SQ FT: 15,000
SALES (est): 429.4K **Privately Held**
SIC: 5075 1711 3567 Furnaces, warm air; heating systems repair & maintenance; induction heating equipment

(G-8458)
RLCT INDUSTRIES LLC ♦
Also Called: Nanodesal
2 E Acres Dr (08534-2101)
PHONE................................609 712-1318
Salatore Gaglio, *Mng Member*
EMP: 5 EST: 2017
SQ FT: 1,500
SALES (est): 317.5K **Privately Held**
SIC: 3589 2819 Commercial cooking & foodwarming equipment; elements

(G-8459)
ROLL TECH INDUSTRIES
55 Route 31 S Ste A (08534-2579)
PHONE................................609 730-9500
John King, *Owner*
Meredith Murphy, *Office Mgr*
EMP: 18
SALES: 7MM **Privately Held**
SIC: 3315 Steel wire & related products

(G-8460)
TKG COMPONENTS LLC
55 Route 31 S (08534-2513)
PHONE................................609 730-1501
Kevin Dougherty, *Owner*
Robert Kaplan, *Principal*

EMP: 6
SALES (est): 394.2K **Privately Held**
SIC: 3679 Electronic components

(G-8461)
TRAP ROCK INDUSTRIES INC
Pennington Hwy Rr 31 (08534)
P.O. Box 419, Kingston (08528-0419)
PHONE................................609 924-0300
Mickey Stavola, *Principal*
EMP: 18
SALES (corp-wide): 131.7MM **Privately Held**
WEB: www.traprock.com
SIC: 1429 Igneous rock, crushed & bro-ken-quarrying
PA: Trap Rock Industries, Inc.
460 River Rd
Kingston NJ 08528
609 924-0300

(G-8462)
UNCLE EDS CREAMERY
155 W Delaware Ave (08534-1602)
PHONE................................609 818-0100
Edward P Gola, *Principal*
EMP: 5 EST: 2010
SALES (est): 375.7K **Privately Held**
SIC: 2024 Ice cream, bulk

(G-8463)
ZYDUS PHARMACEUTICALS USA INC
73 Route 31 N (08534-3601)
PHONE................................609 730-1900
Fax: 609 730-1998
Joseph D Renner, *CEO*
Michael Keenley, *President*
Ravi Yadavar, *CFO*
▲ **EMP:** 31
SQ FT: 18,870
SALES: 466.3MM
SALES (corp-wide): 865MM **Privately Held**
WEB: www.zydususa.com
SIC: 2834 Pills, pharmaceutical
PA: Cadila Healthcare Limited
Zydus Tower, Satellite Cross Road
Ahmedabad GJ 38001
792 686-8100

Penns Grove
Salem County

(G-8464)
CST PRODUCTS LLC
345 Route 130 (08069)
PHONE................................856 299-5339
Laurie Christy, *Sales Associate*
Ronald Krueger,
▲ **EMP:** 20
SALES (est): 2.9MM **Privately Held**
SIC: 3272 Paving materials, prefabricated concrete

(G-8465)
EMPIRE SCALE & BALANCE
35 S Broad St Ste D (08069-1653)
PHONE................................856 299-1651
Margery Deneis, *President*
EMP: 5 EST: 1990
SALES (est): 329.1K **Privately Held**
WEB: www.empirescalecorp.com
SIC: 3596 5046 Industrial scales; scales, except laboratory

(G-8466)
U P N PALLET CO INC
305 N Virginia Ave (08069-1126)
PHONE................................856 299-1192
Fax: 856 299-5824
Greg Massari, *President*
EMP: 10 EST: 1969
SQ FT: 6,000
SALES (est): 1MM **Privately Held**
SIC: 2448 Pallets, wood

Pennsauken
Camden County

(G-8467)
175 DEROUSSE LLC
175 Derousse Ave (08110-3851)
PHONE................................856 662-0100
EMP: 4
SALES (est): 305.9K **Privately Held**
SIC: 3554 Mfg Paper Industrial Machinery

(G-8468)
ABB MOTORS AND MECHANICAL INC
103 Central Ave 400 B (08110)
PHONE................................856 661-1442
Craig Childs, *Branch Mgr*
EMP: 17
SALES (corp-wide): 34.3B **Privately Held**
SIC: 3621 Armatures, industrial
HQ: Abb Motors And Mechanical Inc.
5711 Rs Boreham Jr St
Fort Smith AR 72901
479 646-4711

(G-8469)
ABC SIGN SYSTEMS INC
7970 National Hwy (08110-1412)
P.O. Box 622 (08110-0622)
PHONE................................856 665-0950
Patrick Trifiletti, *President*
Joan Reily, *Business Mgr*
Dave Trifiletti, *Vice Pres*
Stephen Trifiletti, *Vice Pres*
Michael Fulforth, *Purchasing*
EMP: 15 EST: 1952
SQ FT: 22,000
SALES (est): 2.3MM **Privately Held**
WEB: www.abcsignsystems.com
SIC: 3993 Electric signs

(G-8470)
ACRO DISPLAY INC (PA)
2250 Sherman Ave Unit A1 (08110-1539)
PHONE................................215 229-1100
Fax: 215 227-2586
Paul Berenato Sr, *President*
EMP: 50
SQ FT: 150,000
SALES (est): 6.7MM **Privately Held**
WEB: www.acrodisplay.com
SIC: 2541 2542 Display fixtures, wood; partitions & fixtures, except wood

(G-8471)
ADVANCED ABRASIVES CORPORATION
7980 National Hwy (08110-1412)
PHONE................................856 665-9300
Matthew Bees, *President*
Hodge Jones, *Marketing Staff*
Delia Caban, *Office Mgr*
Bryan Bees, *Administration*
▲ **EMP:** 15
SQ FT: 10,200
SALES (est): 1.7MM **Privately Held**
WEB: www.advancedabrasives.com
SIC: 3291 Abrasive products

(G-8472)
AFFORDABLE OFFSET PRINTING INC
Also Called: Affordable Roofing
809 Hylton Rd Ste 11 (08110-1335)
PHONE................................856 661-0722
Fax: 856 661-0922
Gary Coates, *CEO*
EMP: 6
SQ FT: 4,000
SALES (est): 961.1K **Privately Held**
WEB: www.affordableoffset.com
SIC: 2752 Commercial printing, offset

(G-8473)
AIRBORNE SYSTEMS N AMER INC (HQ)
Also Called: Airborne Systems NA
5800 Magnolia Ave (08109-1309)
PHONE................................856 663-1275
Fax: 856 663-8159
Elek Puskas, *CEO*
Vicki Panhuise, *President*

Brad Pedersen, *President*
JC Berland, *Exec VP*
Mike Garten, *Exec VP*
EMP: 5
SALES (est): 83.1MM
SALES (corp-wide): 3.5B **Publicly Held**
SIC: 2426 3429 Textile machinery acces-sories, hardwood; parachute hardware
PA: Transdigm Group Incorporated
1301 E 9th St Ste 3000
Cleveland OH 44114
216 706-2960

(G-8474)
AIRBORNE SYSTEMS N AMER NJ INC
5800 Magnolia Ave (08109-1309)
PHONE................................856 663-1275
Bryce Wiedeman, *President*
▼ **EMP:** 170
SQ FT: 44,400
SALES (est): 31.6MM
SALES (corp-wide): 3.5B **Publicly Held**
WEB: www.paraflite.com
SIC: 2399 Parachutes
HQ: Airborne Systems North America Inc.
5800 Magnolia Ave
Pennsauken NJ 08109
856 663-1275

(G-8475)
ALUMINUM SHAPES INC
9000 River Rd (08110-3296)
PHONE................................856 662-5500
Fax: 856 662-5605
Christopher V Boland, *Principal*
▲ **EMP:** 26
SALES (est): 6.8MM **Privately Held**
SIC: 3354 Aluminum extruded products

(G-8476)
AMER-RAC LLC
8128 River Rd (08110-2437)
PHONE................................856 488-6210
Fax: 856 488-6271
Steven Shore,
EMP: 12
SQ FT: 15,000
SALES (est): 1.3MM **Privately Held**
WEB: www.amer-rac.com
SIC: 3317 Steel pipe & tubes

(G-8477)
AMERICAN ALUMINUM ALLOYS LLC
701 N 36th St (08110-3700)
PHONE................................717 417-5966
David Feinstein, *Mng Member*
EMP: 30
SQ FT: 6,000
SALES: 6MM **Privately Held**
SIC: 3341 Aluminum smelting & refining (secondary)

(G-8478)
APOLLO EAST LLC
7895 Airport Hwy (08109-4322)
PHONE................................856 486-1882
Dora Ngan,
EMP: 50 EST: 2005
SQ FT: 70,000
SALES (est): 6MM
SALES (corp-wide): 5.7MM **Privately Held**
WEB: www.apolloemb.com
SIC: 2395 8743 Embroidery products, ex-cept schiffli machine; promotion service
PA: National Premium Merchandising Inc
1650 W Artesia Blvd
Gardena CA 90248
310 217-2700

(G-8479)
APTAPHARMA CORPORATION
1533 Union Ave (08110-2489)
PHONE................................856 665-0025
Ishwar Chauhan, *President*
Rakesh Lad, *Vice Pres*
Sivaramakrishna Nutalapati, *Treasurer*
EMP: 30
SQ FT: 30,000
SALES: 4MM **Privately Held**
SIC: 2834 Druggists' preparations (phar-maceuticals)

(G-8480)
ARROW INFORMATION PACKAGIG LLC
7100 Westfield Ave (08110-4021)
PHONE..................................856 317-9000
Margaret A Cassano,
EMP: 6
SALES (est): 1.4MM Privately Held
SIC: 2449 3086 2541 Rectangular boxes
& crates, wood; packaging & shipping
materials, foamed plastic; wood partitions
& fixtures

(G-8481)
ATLANTIC ASSOCIATES INTL INC
Also Called: Hibrett Puratex
7001 Westfield Ave (08110-2633)
PHONE..................................856 662-1717
Fax: 856 662-0550
John P J Madden, President
Marc Palmer, Sales Staff
EMP: 15 EST: 1959
SALES (est): 3.9MM Privately Held
SIC: 2842 2841 2819 Cleaning or polish-
ing preparations; soap & other deter-
gents; industrial inorganic chemicals

(G-8482)
AUDIO AND VIDEO LABS INC (HQ)
Also Called: Avl Digital Group
7905 N Crescent Blvd (08110-1402)
PHONE..................................856 663-9030
Fax: 856 661-3458
Tony Van Veen, CEO
Morris Ballen, Ch of Bd
Brian Felsen, President
Jeff Hurst, Editor
John Healy, Business Mgr
◆ EMP: 310
SQ FT: 120,000
SALES (est): 158.5MM Privately Held
SIC: 3652 5099 7389 3651 Compact
laser discs, prerecorded; compact discs;
music copying service; packaging & label-
ing services; music distribution apparatus

(G-8483)
BARRY CALLEBAUT USA LLC
1500 Suckle Hwy (08110-1423)
PHONE..................................856 663-2260
Magdalini Fliska, Engineer
Amy Heitkamp, Controller
Michelle Smith, Human Res Mgr
Benson Jung, Mktg Dir
Michelle Trembley, Manager
EMP: 37
SALES (corp-wide): 45.9MM Privately
Held
SIC: 2066 2099 Chocolate; cocoa & cocoa
products; food preparations
HQ: Barry Callebaut U.S.A. Llc
600 W Chicago Ave Ste 860
Chicago IL 60654

(G-8484)
BARRY CALLEBAUT USA LLC
1600 Suckle Hwy (08110-1444)
PHONE..................................856 663-2260
Ted Bertran, Manager
EMP: 92
SALES (corp-wide): 45.9MM Privately
Held
SIC: 2066 Chocolate; cocoa & cocoa prod-
ucts
HQ: Barry Callebaut U.S.A. Llc
600 W Chicago Ave Ste 860
Chicago IL 60654

(G-8485)
BEEF INTERNATIONAL INC
Also Called: B.I. Foods
7010 Central Hwy (08109-4367)
PHONE..................................856 663-6763
Fax: 856 663-1006
Biagio De Mento, President
Robert De Mento, Corp Secy
Steve Pepitone, Engineer
Connie Jackson, Manager
Tom McMille, Planning
EMP: 60
SQ FT: 35,000

SALES (est): 12.3MM Privately Held
SIC: 2011 Beef products from beef slaughtered on site

(G-8486)
BELL SUPPLY CO (PA)
7221 N Crescent Blvd (08110-1597)
PHONE..................................856 663-3900
Fax: 856 665-2196
Dominick Vittese, President
Carl Zuccarelli, Opers Mgr
Chase Campbell, Purchasing
Dorothy Vittese, Treasurer
Matthew Parkhill, Marketing Staff
EMP: 25 EST: 1946
SQ FT: 5,000
SALES (est): 13.8MM Privately Held
WEB: www.bellsupplyinc.com
SIC: 1742 3271 Drywall; blocks, concrete
or cinder: standard

(G-8487)
BON ARCHITECTUAL MILL WORK LLC
9120 Pennsauken Hwy (08110-1206)
PHONE..................................856 320-2872
EMP: 4
SALES (est): 335.9K Privately Held
SIC: 2431 Millwork

(G-8488)
BRAVO PACK INC
90 Twinbridge Dr (08110-4200)
PHONE..................................856 872-2937
Aibek Hakimov, CEO
▲ EMP: 4 EST: 2013
SALES (est): 944.9K Privately Held
SIC: 2677 5112 Envelopes; envelopes

(G-8489)
CAMPBELL HAUSFELD LLC
8550 Remington Ave (08110-1336)
PHONE..................................856 661-1800
Fax: 856 661-1882
Roy Raider, Principal
EMP: 134
SALES (corp-wide): 242.1B Publicly
Held
SIC: 3563 Air & gas compressors including
vacuum pumps
HQ: Campbell Hausfeld, Llc
100 Production Dr
Harrison OH 45030
513 367-4811

(G-8490)
CELOTEX
1500 John Tipton Blvd (08110-2397)
PHONE..................................856 663-2626
Fax: 856 663-1198
Walt Geery, President
EMP: 5
SALES (est): 396.2K Privately Held
SIC: 3089 Plastics products

(G-8491)
CETYLITE INDUSTRIES INC
9051 River Rd (08110-3293)
PHONE..................................856 665-6111
Fax: 856 665-5408
Stanley L Wachman, Ch of Bd
Keith Henry, Prdtn Mgr
Bruce Epley, Safety Mgr
Denise Lamack, Purch Mgr
Sue Wong, Mktg Dir
▲ EMP: 28
SQ FT: 22,400
SALES (est): 7.6MM Privately Held
WEB: www.cetylite.com
SIC: 2834 Pharmaceutical preparations

(G-8492)
CGS SALES AND SERVICE LLC
6950 River Rd (08110-2611)
PHONE..................................856 665-6154
Tony Pernicello, Technical Staff
Anthony W Pernicello,
▲ EMP: 5
SALES (est): 675.8K Privately Held
SIC: 2759 Screen printing

(G-8493)
CLARITY IMAGING TECH INC
4350 Haddonfield Rd # 300 (08109-3387)
PHONE..................................413 693-1234
Mark Bridge, Manager

EMP: 50
SALES (corp-wide): 439.3K Privately
Held
WEB: www.clarityimaging.com
SIC: 3555 3861 Printing trade parts & at-
tachments; photographic equipment &
supplies
HQ: Clarity Imaging Technologies, Inc.
4350 Haddonfield Rd # 300
Pennsauken NJ 08109

(G-8494)
CLARITY IMAGING TECH INC (DH)
4350 Haddonfield Rd # 300 (08109-3387)
PHONE..................................877 272-4362
Peter Corritori, CEO
Claire Walter, CFO
David Mac Isaac, Bd of Directors
▲ EMP: 6
SQ FT: 2,000
SALES (est): 11.1MM
SALES (corp-wide): 439.3K Privately
Held
WEB: www.clarityimaging.com
SIC: 3555 Printing trade parts & attach-
ments
HQ: Turbon Usa, Inc.
4350 Haddonfield Rd # 300
Pennsauken NJ 08109
856 665-6650

(G-8495)
COLORSOURCE INC
7025 Central Hwy (08109-4312)
PHONE..................................856 488-8100
Fax: 856 488-9181
Alfred Demarco, President
Murray Ellis, President
EMP: 8
SQ FT: 15,000
SALES (est): 3.1MM Privately Held
WEB: www.colorsource.com
SIC: 2752 Color lithography

(G-8496)
COMMERCIAL COMPOSITION & PRTG
1601 Sherman Ave Ste B (08110-2632)
PHONE..................................856 662-0557
EMP: 5 EST: 1983
SQ FT: 12,000
SALES (est): 230K Privately Held
SIC: 2791 Typesetting & Lithographic Print-
ing

(G-8497)
COMPOSING ROOM INC (PA)
Also Called: Crw Graphics
9100 Pennsauken Hwy (08110-1206)
PHONE..................................856 662-9111
Harriet Weiss, CEO
Mark Weiss, President
Jon Conant, General Mgr
Scott Lang, General Mgr
Elizabeth Lott, Business Mgr
EMP: 125 EST: 1978
SQ FT: 47,000
SALES (est): 31MM Privately Held
SIC: 2759 Screen printing

(G-8498)
CONNECTOR PRODUCTS INC
1300 John Tipton Blvd (08110-2315)
P.O. Box 2516, Cinnaminson (08077-4916)
PHONE..................................856 829-9190
Fax: 856 829-9195
Mario Polidori, CEO
Thomas Polidori, President
Jessica Polidori, Treasurer
EMP: 13
SQ FT: 11,400
SALES (est): 3.4MM Privately Held
WEB: www.connectorproducts.com
SIC: 3643 Connectors, electric cord; rail
bonds, electric: for propulsion & signal cir-
cuits

(G-8499)
CSL SERVICES INC
7905 Browning Rd Ste 316 (08109-4321)
PHONE..................................856 755-9440
Fax: 856 755-9445
Bruce Cohen, President
Alyson Lee, Business Mgr
Bill Dawson, Vice Pres

Harry Clark, Opers Mgr
Shari Snyder, Accountant
EMP: 14
SQ FT: 1,000
SALES (est): 3.5MM Privately Held
SIC: 3613 Metering panels, electric

(G-8500)
DATWYLER PHARMA PACKAGING
9012 Pennsauken Hwy (08110-1204)
PHONE..................................856 663-2202
Fax: 609 386-3594
Richard Gardner, Director
EMP: 50
SALES (corp-wide): 1.3B Privately Held
SIC: 3069 8731 3053 Druggists' rubber
sundries; commercial physical research;
gaskets, packing & sealing devices
HQ: Datwyler Pharma Packaging Usa Re-
alty Inc.
9012 Pennsauken Hwy
Pennsauken NJ 08110
856 663-2202

(G-8501)
DAYSEQUERRA CORPORATION
7209 Browning Rd (08109-4602)
P.O. Box 1530, Voorhees (08043-7530)
PHONE..................................856 719-9900
David Day, President
John Instone, Vice Pres
Sandy Martin, Opers Mgr
Cynthia Henderson, Sales Staff
Cliff Gano, Director
EMP: 11
SQ FT: 4,000
SALES (est): 2.1MM Privately Held
WEB: www.daysequerra.com
SIC: 3663 Radio & TV communications
equipment

(G-8502)
DELAIR LLC
Also Called: Delgard Premier Alum Fencing
9000 River Rd (08110-3204)
PHONE..................................856 663-2900
David Stewart, CEO
◆ EMP: 75
SQ FT: 400,000
SALES (est): 5.9MM Privately Held
SIC: 3949 3446 3496 3444 Swimming
pools, except plastic; fences, gates, posts
& flagpoles; miscellaneous fabricated wire
products; sheet metalwork
PA: Shapes/Arch Holdings Llc
9000 River Rd
Delair NJ 08110

(G-8503)
DICAPERL MINERALS CORP
9111 River Rd (08110-3205)
PHONE..................................856 320-2919
EMP: 5
SALES (est): 486.6K Privately Held
SIC: 3295 2821 Diatomaceous earth,
ground or otherwise treated; cellulose de-
rivative materials
PA: Dicaperl Minerals Corp.
1 Bala Ave Ste 310
Bala Cynwyd PA 19004

(G-8504)
DISC MAKERS INC
7905 N Crescent Blvd (08110-1402)
PHONE..................................800 468-9353
Fax: 856 661-3455
Tony Van Veen, President
◆ EMP: 300
SALES (est): 2.2MM Privately Held
SIC: 3652 Compact laser discs, prere-
corded
HQ: Audio And Video Labs Inc.
7905 N Crescent Blvd
Pennsauken NJ 08110
856 663-9030

(G-8505)
DISPLAY IMPRESSIONS
9265 Commerce Hwy (08110-1201)
PHONE..................................856 488-1777
EMP: 11
SALES (est): 1.4MM Privately Held
SIC: 2759 Commercial printing

(G-8506)
DOW CHEMICAL COMPANY
1500 John Tipton Blvd (08110-2304)
PHONE..................856 663-2627
Walt Geery, *Branch Mgr*
EMP: 40
SALES (corp-wide): 62.4B **Publicly Held**
WEB: www.dow.com
SIC: 2869 Industrial organic chemicals
HQ: The Dow Chemical Company
　　2030 Dow Ctr
　　Midland MI 48674
　　989 636-1000

(G-8507)
E P R INDUSTRIES INC
Also Called: Dental Manufacturing
4576 S Crescent Blvd (08109-1828)
PHONE..................856 488-1120
Robert Cherkas, *President*
Paul Cherkas, *Vice Pres*
EMP: 15 **EST:** 1976
SQ FT: 11,000
SALES (est): 2.4MM **Privately Held**
SIC: 3843 Dental materials; compounds, dental

(G-8508)
ENERTIA LLC
10471049 Thomas Busch (08110)
PHONE..................856 330-4767
Eric Rivera,
EMP: 9
SALES (est): 849.2K **Privately Held**
SIC: 7372 7352 7371 7319 Application computer software; medical equipment rental; computer software development & applications; distribution of advertising material or sample services

(G-8509)
EVERITE MACHINE PRODUCTS CO (PA)
1555 Route 73 (08110-1325)
PHONE..................856 330-6700
Daniel Stern, *CEO*
Mergenthal Bruce, *President*
Chris Zhu, *General Mgr*
Larry Lewandowski, *QC Mgr*
Amy Zhang, *QC Mgr*
▲ **EMP:** 50 **EST:** 1950
SQ FT: 68,000
SALES (est): 12.7MM **Privately Held**
WEB: www.everite.net
SIC: 3541 3599 3613 Grinding machines, metalworking; machine shop, jobbing & repair; control panels, electric

(G-8510)
FLUIDYNE CORP
9100 Collins Ave (08110-1037)
PHONE..................856 663-1818
Fax: 856 662-5158
William M Bloemker, *President*
EMP: 25
SQ FT: 15,000
SALES (est): 5.7MM **Privately Held**
WEB: www.fluidynecorp.com
SIC: 3494 Valves & pipe fittings

(G-8511)
FOULKROD ASSOCIATES
Also Called: Canada Dry of Delaware Valley
8275 N Crescent Blvd (08110-1435)
PHONE..................856 662-6767
Harold Honickman, *Chairman*
John Taglienti, *Sales Executive*
EMP: 600
SALES (est): 92.5MM **Privately Held**
SIC: 3411 5149 Beverage cans, metal: except beer; groceries & related products

(G-8512)
FRANBETH INC
Also Called: Sir Speedy
5505 N Crescent Blvd (08110-1803)
PHONE..................856 488-1480
Francis Gavin, *President*
EMP: 5
SQ FT: 3,000
SALES: 685K **Privately Held**
SIC: 7336 7334 2752 3993 Graphic arts & related design; photocopying & duplicating services; commercial printing, lithographic; signs & advertising specialties

(G-8513)
GAMBAY INC
1545 Route 73 (08110-1325)
PHONE..................856 330-4397
Marc Kaufer, *President*
Kelli Kearney, *Vice Pres*
EMP: 9
SALES: 500K **Privately Held**
SIC: 2434 Wood kitchen cabinets

(G-8514)
GARDEN STATE MGNTIC IMAGING PC
6027 S Crescent Blvd (08110-6401)
PHONE..................609 581-2727
Fax: 609 581-3772
Faizah Zuberi MD, *President*
EMP: 11
SQ FT: 5,000
SALES (est): 1.6MM **Privately Held**
SIC: 3826 Magnetic resonance imaging apparatus

(G-8515)
GARRISON PRINTING COMPANY INC
7155 Airport Hwy (08109-4301)
PHONE..................856 488-1900
Fax: 856 488-6191
Jack Garrison, *CEO*
Jake Garrison III, *President*
William Fynes, *Vice Pres*
Daniel C Garrison, *Vice Pres*
Barbara Garrison, *Treasurer*
EMP: 32
SQ FT: 22,000
SALES: 5.5MM **Privately Held**
SIC: 2796 2752 Platemaking services; commercial printing, lithographic

(G-8516)
GOLDEN RULE INC
7150 N Park Dr Ste 620 (08109-4203)
PHONE..................856 663-3074
Fax: 856 486-3537
John Liberto, *President*
EMP: 4
SQ FT: 1,800
SALES (est): 305.5K **Privately Held**
SIC: 3544 Special dies & tools

(G-8517)
GRAND DISPLAYS INC (PA)
1700 Suckle Hwy (08110-1427)
PHONE..................201 994-1500
George Gross, *CEO*
Marjorie Sacino, *COO*
EMP: 33
SALES (est): 7.6MM **Privately Held**
SIC: 2675 Die-cut paper & board

(G-8518)
GREAT SOCKS LLC (PA)
Also Called: Standard Merchandising
7001 N Park Dr (08109-4399)
PHONE..................856 964-9700
Fax: 856 964-9135
Leilani Kane, *Opers Mgr*
Jennifer Noon, *Prdtn Mgr*
Donna Rogers, *Office Mgr*
Robyn Mohr, *Director*
Jordan Baatable,
▲ **EMP:** 50
SQ FT: 4,902
SALES (est): 28.2MM **Privately Held**
SIC: 3949 2252 2339 2251 Sporting & athletic goods; hosiery; women's & misses' outerwear; women's hosiery, except socks

(G-8519)
GSC IMAGING LLC
7150 N Park Dr Ste 540 (08109-4203)
PHONE..................856 317-9301
Fax: 856 317-9302
Ron Coutta, *Vice Pres*
Robert Sinatra, *Vice Pres*
William Gallagher, *Mng Member*
▲ **EMP:** 15
SQ FT: 16,000
SALES (est): 3.5MM **Privately Held**
WEB: www.gscimaging.com
SIC: 3955 5112 Print cartridges for laser & other computer printers; inked ribbons

(G-8520)
H & H INDUSTRIES INC
7612 N Crescent Blvd (08110-2594)
PHONE..................856 663-4444
Fax: 856 663-4446
Gertrude Hajduk, *President*
Maryann Hajduk, *Vice Pres*
Walter Hajduk III, *Vice Pres*
EMP: 42 **EST:** 1950
SQ FT: 47,000
SALES (est): 7.8MM **Privately Held**
SIC: 3444 Sheet metalwork

(G-8521)
HAYS SHEET METAL INC
Also Called: H M Hays Sheet Metal Co
7070 Bldg B Kaighns Ave (08109)
PHONE..................856 662-7722
Fax: 856 662-2665
Herbert M Hays, *President*
Michael Hays, *President*
EMP: 50
SQ FT: 9,000
SALES (est): 10MM **Privately Held**
SIC: 3444 Metal ventilating equipment

(G-8522)
HOLMAN ENTERPRISES INC
R M P Delaware Valley
9040 Burrough Dover Ln (08110-1033)
P.O. Box 615 (08110-0615)
PHONE..................856 532-2410
Fax: 856 663-1745
Frank Lepore, *MIS Dir*
Lance Lewis, *Administration*
EMP: 196
SALES (corp-wide): 1.7B **Privately Held**
WEB: www.holmanenterprises.com
SIC: 3714 5013 Motor vehicle engines & parts; motor vehicle supplies & new parts
PA: Holman Enterprises Inc.
　　244 E Kings Hwy
　　Maple Shade NJ 08052
　　856 663-5200

(G-8523)
HOSOKAWA MICRON INTERNATIONAL
Also Called: Menardi-Criswell
751 Hylton Rd (08110-1357)
PHONE..................866 507-4974
Fax: 856 661-0471
Alan Furraro, *Manager*
EMP: 17
SALES (corp-wide): 444.6MM **Privately Held**
WEB: www.hosokawa.com
SIC: 3559 Chemical machinery & equipment
HQ: Hosokawa Micron International, Inc
　　10 Chatham Rd
　　Summit NJ 07901
　　908 273-6360

(G-8524)
HOUSE OF GOLD INC
1505 Suckle Hwy (08110-1468)
PHONE..................856 665-0020
Fax: 856 665-6270
Leonard Solomon, *President*
EMP: 50
SQ FT: 23,000
SALES (est): 9MM **Privately Held**
WEB: www.houseofgold.com
SIC: 3469 Ash trays, stamped metal

(G-8525)
I ASSOCIATES LLC
9255 Commerce Hwy (08110-1201)
PHONE..................215 262-7754
Jim Wolstenholme, *Principal*
EMP: 6
SALES (est): 390K **Privately Held**
SIC: 3993 Advertising artwork

(G-8526)
INCREASE BEVERAGE INTL INC
7250 Westfield Ave Ste M (08110-4093)
P.O. Box 5, Palmyra (08065-0005)
PHONE..................609 303-3117
Joseph Roberts Jr, *President*
Daniel P Wergin, *Treasurer*
Terence P Fox, *Admin Sec*
◆ **EMP:** 15

SALES (est): 3.1MM **Privately Held**
SIC: 5149 2086 Soft drinks; bottled & canned soft drinks

(G-8527)
INNOVATIVE POWDER COATINGS LLC
9105 Burrough Dover Ln (08110-1003)
PHONE..................856 661-0086
David Mac William,
Timothy Hhyde,
▲ **EMP:** 7
SQ FT: 20,000
SALES (est): 1.1MM **Privately Held**
SIC: 3479 Coating of metals & formed products

(G-8528)
INSERTS EAST INCORPORATED
Also Called: G & F Graphic Services
7045 Central Hwy (08109-4312)
PHONE..................856 663-8181
Nick Maiale, *Principal*
Andy Kavulic, *CFO*
Andy Kavulich, *CFO*
Carla Bogart, *Human Res Mgr*
Michelle Baxter, *Manager*
EMP: 125
SQ FT: 104,000
SALES (est): 62.5MM **Privately Held**
WEB: www.gfgraphics.com
SIC: 5043 8742 2791 2752 Photographic equipment & supplies; printing apparatus, photographic; management consulting services; business planning & organizing services; typesetting; commercial printing, lithographic

(G-8529)
INTERIOR SPECIALTIES LLC
6006 S Crescent Blvd (08109-1512)
PHONE..................856 663-1700
Joseph Wood,
EMP: 12
SQ FT: 6,000
SALES (est): 1.4MM **Privately Held**
WEB: www.interior-specialties.com
SIC: 3231 3229 5719 Mirrored glass; doors, glass: made from purchased glass; glass furnishings & accessories; closet organizers & shelving units

(G-8530)
INTERNATIONAL PROCESS EQP CO
Also Called: Ipec
9300 N Crescent Blvd (08110-1303)
PHONE..................856 665-4007
Ronald Miller, *President*
EMP: 5
SQ FT: 14,000
SALES (est): 955.6K **Privately Held**
WEB: www.rotormill.com
SIC: 3532 Mining machinery

(G-8531)
J & J SNACK FOODS CORP (PA)
6000 Central Hwy (08109-4672)
PHONE..................856 665-9533
Fax: 856 665-6359
Gerald B Shreiber, *Ch of Bd*
Alan Murphy, *General Mgr*
Robert M Radano, *COO*
Gerard G Law, *Senior VP*
Robert J Pape, *Senior VP*
EMP: 300 **EST:** 1971
SQ FT: 70,000
SALES: 1B **Publicly Held**
WEB: www.jjsnack.com
SIC: 2053 2087 2086 2024 Frozen bakery products, except bread; doughnuts, frozen; syrups, drink; mineral water, carbonated: packaged in cans, bottles, etc.; ices, flavored (frozen dessert); juice pops, frozen; cookies; bread, cake & related products

(G-8532)
J & J SNACK FOODS CORP PA (HQ)
6000 Central Hwy (08109-4672)
PHONE..................856 665-9533
Gerald B Shreiber, *President*
Robert M Radano, *COO*
Dennis G Moore, *Vice Pres*

▲ = Import ▼=Export
◆ =Import/Export

Bill Dougherty, *Director*
EMP: 5
SQ FT: 70,000
SALES (est): 3MM
SALES (corp-wide): 1B **Publicly Held**
WEB: www.icee.net
SIC: 5145 2052 Pretzels; pretzels
PA: J & J Snack Foods Corp.
    6000 Central Hwy
    Pennsauken NJ 08109
    856 665-9533

(G-8533)
J AND M PRECISION INC
Also Called: Jig Grinding Specialists
8103 River Rd (08110-2436)
PHONE.................................856 661-9595
Martin Moskag, *President*
Joseph H Gaynor, *Vice Pres*
EMP: 4
SQ FT: 1,600
SALES: 371.5K **Privately Held**
SIC: 3541 Jig boring & grinding machines

(G-8534)
J D CREW INC
Also Called: Krimstock Enterprises
1426 Union Ave (08110-2459)
PHONE.................................856 665-3676
Joseph Crew, *President*
Christina Crew, *Vice Pres*
EMP: 5 **EST:** 1945
SQ FT: 7,000
SALES: 500K **Privately Held**
SIC: 3993 3953 Signs & advertising specialties; displays & cutouts, window & lobby; marking devices

(G-8535)
JARVIS ELECTRIC MOTORS INC
6001 S Crescent Blvd (08110-6401)
PHONE.................................856 662-7710
Fax: 856 662-7971
Carl Barner, *President*
Mariana Barner, *Admin Sec*
EMP: 5 **EST:** 1944
SQ FT: 2,500
SALES: 1MM **Privately Held**
SIC: 7694 5251 Electric motor repair; tools, power

(G-8536)
JERSEY CAST STONE LTD LBLTY CO
6845 Westfield Ave (08110-1527)
PHONE.................................856 333-6900
Anthony Ruggiero, *President*
Luis Rodriguez, *Vice Pres*
EMP: 11
SQ FT: 15,000
SALES: 2MM **Privately Held**
SIC: 3272 Stone, cast concrete

(G-8537)
JERSEY SPECIALTY CO INC
Also Called: Jsc Wire & Cable
7861 Airport Hwy (08109-4322)
P.O. Box 248, East Longmeadow MA
(01028-0248)
PHONE.................................413 525-2292
R D Foster, *CEO*
Jim Foster, *President*
▲ **EMP:** 20 **EST:** 1932
SQ FT: 40,000
SALES: 10MM **Privately Held**
WEB: www.jscwire.com
SIC: 3315 Steel wire & related products

(G-8538)
JULIALI WOODWORK
1700 Admiral Wilson Blvd (08109-3988)
PHONE.................................856 225-0772
Fax: 856 225-0773
Dennis Valenti, *Owner*
EMP: 5
SQ FT: 6,000
SALES (est): 385.5K **Privately Held**
SIC: 2431 Woodwork, interior & ornamental

(G-8539)
KEYSTONE ADJUSTABLE CAP CO INC
1591 Hylton Rd Ste B (08110-1338)
PHONE.................................856 356-2809
Fax: 856 663-6075

Andrew Feinstein, *CEO*
Malcolm W George, *President*
Vicki Metzger, *COO*
Jay Rigberg, *CFO*
Neal Woods, *VP Sales*
▲ **EMP:** 45 **EST:** 1925
SQ FT: 90,000
SALES (est): 12MM **Privately Held**
WEB: www.keystonecap.com
SIC: 2676 2389 Sanitary paper products; disposable garments & accessories

(G-8540)
KOHLDER MANUFACTURING INC
Also Called: Bush Refrigeration
1700 Admiral Wilson Blvd (08109-3988)
PHONE.................................856 963-1801
Fax: 856 963-0770
Jeffrey Bush, *CEO*
Jeffrey Kerber, *Vice Pres*
EMP: 5
SQ FT: 40,000
SALES (est): 881.1K **Privately Held**
WEB: www.bushrefrigeration.com
SIC: 3585 Refrigeration equipment, complete

(G-8541)
KUSHNER DRAPERIES MFG LLC
5305 Marlton Pike (08109-4749)
PHONE.................................856 317-9696
Fax: 856 317-9096
Arthur Kushner, *Mng Member*
Boonie Kushner,
Carla Moore,
EMP: 30
SQ FT: 16,000
SALES: 2.1MM **Privately Held**
SIC: 2391 5023 7641 Draperies, plastic & textile: from purchased materials; curtains; draperies; slip covers (furniture); upholstery work

(G-8542)
LATTICE INCORPORATED (PA)
7150 N Park Dr Ste 500 (08109-4203)
P.O. Box 536, Collingswood (08108-0536)
PHONE.................................856 910-1166
Paul Burgess, *Ch of Bd*
Joe Noto, *CFO*
EMP: 12
SQ FT: 4,000
SALES: 7.5MM **Publicly Held**
WEB: www.scidyn.com
SIC: 3661 8711 8742 7372 Telephone & telegraph apparatus; engineering services; management consulting services; application computer software

(G-8543)
LIDESTRI FOODS INC
Also Called: Lidestri Foods of New Jersey
1550 John Tipton Blvd (08110-2304)
PHONE.................................856 661-3218
Jim Clavin, *QC Mgr*
Bud Heckler, *Manager*
EMP: 80
SALES (corp-wide): 247.9MM **Privately Held**
WEB: www.francescorinaldi.com
SIC: 2033 Spaghetti & other pasta sauce: packaged in cans, jars, etc.
PA: Lidestri Foods, Inc.
    815 Whitney Rd W
    Fairport NY 14450
    585 377-7700

(G-8544)
MARSDEN INC
6800 Westfield Ave (08110-1532)
PHONE.................................856 663-2227
Fax: 856 663-2137
Thomas Smith, *President*
Suzanne Longacre, *Principal*
Melissa Lucidi, *Admin Sec*
EMP: 20
SQ FT: 20,000
SALES (est): 3.9MM **Privately Held**
WEB: www.marsdeninc.com
SIC: 3567 Driers & redriers, industrial process

(G-8545)
MASTERWORK RECORDING INC
7503 Baxter Ave (08109-3229)
PHONE.................................267 731-7031
Peter Humphreys, *President*
Albert Oon, *Vice Pres*
EMP: 5
SQ FT: 3,000
SALES (est): 705K **Privately Held**
WEB: www.masterworkrecording.com
SIC: 3652 Master records or tapes, preparation of

(G-8546)
MCALLISTER SERVICE COMPANY (PA)
Also Called: Honeywell Authorized Dealer
7116 Park Ave (08109-3055)
P.O. Box 1327, Merchantville (08109-0327)
PHONE.................................856 665-4545
Fax: 856 488-2129
George McAllister, *CEO*
James McAllister, *President*
Donald McAllister, *Exec VP*
John Hammond, *Vice Pres*
Thomas McAllister, *Vice Pres*
EMP: 21
SQ FT: 2,000
SALES (est): 9.7MM **Privately Held**
SIC: 5983 7629 7623 1711 Fuel oil dealers; electrical repair shops; refrigeration service & repair; heating & air conditioning contractors; petroleum refining

(G-8547)
MCCORMICKS BINDERY INC
5815 Magnolia Ave (08109-1308)
PHONE.................................856 663-8035
Dan McCormick, *President*
Dan Mc Cormick, *President*
Rod Mc Cormick, *Vice Pres*
Rod McCormick, *Vice Pres*
EMP: 42
SALES: 3MM **Privately Held**
SIC: 2789 Pamphlets, binding

(G-8548)
MCKELLA 2-8-0 INC
Also Called: McKella 280
7025 Central Hwy (08109-4312)
PHONE.................................856 813-1153
Joseph Lagrossa, *President*
Rose M Balcavage, *Vice Pres*
Ronald Etter, *Vice Pres*
Bill Coll, *Plant Mgr*
Rose Balcabage, *CFO*
EMP: 85 **EST:** 1977
SQ FT: 45,000
SALES (est): 28.9MM **Privately Held**
WEB: www.citationgraphics.net
SIC: 2752 2791 7336 Commercial printing, offset; typesetting; commercial art & graphic design

(G-8549)
MCLEAN PACKAGING CORPORATION
Also Called: Mc Lean Corrugated Containers
1000 Thomas Busch Mem Hwy
(08110-2313)
PHONE.................................856 359-2600
Stuart Fenkel, *Principal*
Carol Skinner, *CFO*
EMP: 75
SQ FT: 4,500
SALES (corp-wide): 82MM **Privately Held**
SIC: 2652 2653 Setup paperboard boxes; boxes, corrugated: made from purchased materials
PA: Mclean Packaging Corporation
    1504 Glen Ave
    Moorestown NJ 08057
    856 359-2600

(G-8550)
MENU EXPRESS
1053 Thomas Busch Mem Hwy
(08110-2312)
PHONE.................................856 216-7777
EMP: 11
SALES (est): 1.4MM **Privately Held**
SIC: 2759 Commercial printing

(G-8551)
MOD-TEK CONVERTING LLC
2550 Haddonfield Rd Ste E (08110-1152)
PHONE.................................856 662-6884
Vicki Wilkinson,
Shawn Borman,
EMP: 16
SQ FT: 3,000
SALES: 3.2MM **Privately Held**
SIC: 2679 Tags & labels, paper

(G-8552)
MONARCH COLOR CORPORATION
7247 Browning Rd (08109-4602)
PHONE.................................215 923-2235
Fax: 856 662-0130
Bruce Gill, *Manager*
EMP: 10
SQ FT: 5,000
SALES (corp-wide): 14.5MM **Privately Held**
WEB: www.monarchcolor.com
SIC: 2893 Printing ink
PA: Monarch Color Corporation
    5327 Brookshire Blvd
    Charlotte NC 28216
    704 394-4626

(G-8553)
NATIONAL DISPLAY GROUP INC
6850 River Rd (08110-2609)
PHONE.................................856 661-1212
Fax: 856 661-1233
Gene Gold, *Mng Member*
EMP: 20
SALES (est): 2.8MM **Privately Held**
WEB: www.nationaldisplaygroup.com
SIC: 2542 Office & store showcases & display fixtures

(G-8554)
NEWTON TOOL & MFG INC
7249b Browning Rd (08109-4602)
PHONE.................................856 241-1500
Kurt Joerger, *CEO*
Otto J Del Prado, *President*
▲ **EMP:** 90 **EST:** 1970
SQ FT: 61,400
SALES (est): 8.8MM **Privately Held**
SIC: 3053 3569 3586 3544 Gaskets, packing & sealing devices; filters, general line: industrial; gasoline pumps, measuring or dispensing; special dies, tools, jigs & fixtures

(G-8555)
NOVELTY CONE CO INC
807 Sherman Ave (08110-2684)
PHONE.................................856 665-9525
Fax: 856 665-0216
Steven Marinucci, *President*
Ron Marinucci, *Vice Pres*
John Marshall, *Warehouse Mgr*
Steve Marinucci, *Executive*
▲ **EMP:** 23 **EST:** 1902
SQ FT: 14,500
SALES (est): 4.8MM **Privately Held**
WEB: www.noveltycone.com
SIC: 2052 Cones, ice cream

(G-8556)
PARK PRINTING SERVICES INC
7300 N Crescent Blvd # 21 (08110-1542)
PHONE.................................856 675-1600
Donald G Reed Sr, *President*
Margaret Reed, *Vice Pres*
Bob Bonsall, *Manager*
EMP: 11 **EST:** 1934
SQ FT: 4,500
SALES (est): 2MM **Privately Held**
WEB: www.parkprintingco.co
SIC: 2752 Commercial printing, offset

(G-8557)
PENNOCK COMPANY
Also Called: Pennock Floral Co
7135 Colonial Ln (08109-4314)
PHONE.................................215 492-7900
Robert Billings, *President*
Kareem Jones, *Sales Staff*
Michelle Morgan, *Sales Staff*
David Sherfey, *Department Mgr*
EMP: 25

SALES (corp-wide): 77.5MM Privately Held
SIC: **5992** 3999 Flowers, fresh; artificial trees & flowers
PA: Pennock Company
5060 W Chester Pike
Edgemont PA 19028
215 492-7900

(G-8558)
PEPSI-COLA NAT BRND BEVS LTD (PA)
8275 N Crescent Blvd (08110-1435)
PHONE.................................856 665-6200
Fax: 856 663-6737
Jeff Honickman, *CEO*
Harold Honickman, *Ch of Bd*
Marvin Goldstein, *Vice Ch Bd*
Gwen Dolceamore, *President*
Walter Wilkinson, *CFO*
EMP: 300 EST: 1956
SQ FT: 90,000
SALES (est): **182MM Privately Held**
SIC: **2086** Soft drinks: packaged in cans, bottles, etc.

(G-8559)
PEPSICO INC
8275 N Route 130 (08110-1435)
PHONE.................................856 661-4604
Robert Brockway, *Branch Mgr*
EMP: 50
SALES (corp-wide): **63.5B Publicly Held**
WEB: www.pepsico.com
SIC: **2086** Carbonated soft drinks, bottled & canned
PA: Pepsico, Inc.
700 Anderson Hill Rd
Purchase NY 10577
914 253-2000

(G-8560)
PERMALITH PLASTICS LLC
6901 N Crescent Blvd (08110-1513)
PHONE.................................215 925-5659
Fax: 856 488-2455
Joe Schaeffer, *Manager*
William Callanan,
Thomas Leonard,
Robert O'Leary,
▲ EMP: 55 EST: 1956
SQ FT: 63,000
SALES (est): **13.7MM Privately Held**
WEB: www.permalith.com
SIC: **3089** 3993 Laminating of plastic; signs & advertising specialties

(G-8561)
PPG IND INC
Also Called: PPG Auto Glass
75 Twinbridge Dr Ste C (08110-4205)
PHONE.................................856 662-9323
Cliff Nelson, *Principal*
EMP: 5
SALES (est): **419.9K Privately Held**
SIC: **3211** 5013 Plate & sheet glass; automobile glass

(G-8562)
PREFERRED PLASTICS INC
6512 Park Ave (08109-2430)
PHONE.................................856 662-6250
Bob Gillon, *President*
Joseph Flood, *Treasurer*
EMP: 5 EST: 1996
SQ FT: 4,500
SALES: **400K Privately Held**
SIC: **3089** Injection molding of plastics

(G-8563)
PREMIER DISP & EXHIBITS INC
7070 Colonial Hwy (08109-4306)
PHONE.................................856 382-7497
Christopher J Bullard, *Branch Mgr*
EMP: 16
SALES (corp-wide): **25.7MM Privately Held**
SIC: **3993** Displays & cutouts, window & lobby
PA: Premier Displays & Exhibits, Inc.
11261 Warland Dr
Cypress CA 90630
562 431-2731

(G-8564)
PREMIER PRESS INC
7120 Airport Hwy (08109-4302)
PHONE.................................856 665-0722
Joseph Shipton, *President*
Mary Shipton, *Treasurer*
EMP: 12
SQ FT: 10,000
SALES (est): **2.1MM Privately Held**
WEB: www.premierpress.net
SIC: **2759** Commercial printing

(G-8565)
PRINCETON TECTONICS (PA)
1777 Hylton Rd (08110-1315)
P.O. Box 8057, Trenton (08650-0057)
PHONE.................................609 298-9331
Fax: 609 298-9601
William Stephens, *President*
Brad Strahm, *Division Mgr*
David Cozzone, *Vice Pres*
Richard Shenowski, *Vice Pres*
Mark Buehler, *Purch Mgr*
▲ EMP: 120
SQ FT: 80,000
SALES: **20MM Privately Held**
WEB: www.princetontec.com
SIC: **3648** 3089 Flashlights; injection molding of plastics

(G-8566)
PRINT MAIL COMMUNICATIONS LLC (PA)
7025 Colonial Hwy Ste 2 (08109-4309)
PHONE.................................856 488-0345
Fax: 856 488-0346
Julie Geary, *Production*
Paul Pollastrelli, *Sales Executive*
Scott Spruill, *Mng Member*
Ed Adair, *Manager*
EMP: 22
SALES (est): **5MM Privately Held**
WEB: www.printnmail.net
SIC: **2752** 2759 Commercial printing, lithographic; commercial printing

(G-8567)
PRO WORLD
961 Bethel Ave (08110-2607)
PHONE.................................856 406-1020
Debbie Dill, *Principal*
◆ EMP: 6
SALES (est): **350K Privately Held**
SIC: **2326** Industrial garments, men's & boys'

(G-8568)
PURATOS CORPORATION
8030 National Hwy (08110-1414)
PHONE.................................856 266-1736
Fax: 856 665-0005
Heinc Wiechmann, *General Mgr*
EMP: 20 **Privately Held**
WEB: www.puratos.com
SIC: **2099** Food preparations
HQ: Puratos Corporation
1941 Old Cuthbert Rd
Cherry Hill NJ 08034

(G-8569)
RBS INTRNTONAL DIRECT MKTG LLC (PA)
825 Hylton Rd (08110-1307)
PHONE.................................856 663-2500
Anna Garcia, *Account Dir*
Eric Price, *Account Dir*
EMP: 4
SALES (est): **3.8MM Privately Held**
SIC: **7372** 8743 Prepackaged software; public relations services

(G-8570)
REBUILT PARTS CO LLC
Also Called: RPC Driveline Service
7929 River Rd (08110-2434)
PHONE.................................856 662-3252
Fax: 856 662-8731
Henry Matznic, *Owner*
EMP: 12
SQ FT: 6,500
SALES (est): **1.3MM Privately Held**
SIC: **5015** 3714 Automotive parts & supplies, used; motor vehicle parts & accessories; automotive accessories; automotive parts

(G-8571)
REDHAWK DISTRIBUTION INC
6835 Westfield Ave (08110-1527)
PHONE.................................516 884-9911
Arvind Choudhary, *President*
Taram Singh, *Vice Pres*
EMP: 15
SALES (est): **1MM Privately Held**
SIC: **2392** Cushions & pillows

(G-8572)
RELIANCE ELECTRIC COMPANY
1035 Thomas Busch Mem Hwy (08110-2312)
PHONE.................................856 661-1442
Adres Hernandez, *Branch Mgr*
EMP: 20
SQ FT: 13,600
SALES (corp-wide): **34.3B Privately Held**
SIC: **3621** 3625 Electric motor & generator parts; relays & industrial controls
HQ: Reliance Electric Company
6040 Ponders Ct
Greenville SC 29615
864 297-4800

(G-8573)
RHOADS METAL WORKS INC
1551 John Tipton Blvd (08110-2303)
PHONE.................................856 486-1551
Fax: 856 486-1710
William Rhoads, *President*
EMP: 30
SQ FT: 36,000
SALES (est): **7MM Privately Held**
WEB: www.rhoadsmetalworks.com
SIC: **3444** Sheet metal specialties, not stamped

(G-8574)
RICHMOND STEEL RULE DIES INC
Also Called: Clearcut New Jersey
1416 Union Ave (08110-2459)
PHONE.................................856 661-0900
Dave Zingaro, *Branch Mgr*
EMP: 9
SALES (est): **1.7MM Privately Held**
SIC: **3544** Dies, steel rule
PA: Richmond Steel Rule Dies, Inc.
3721 Goodell Rd
Richmond VA

(G-8575)
ROYER GROUP INC
7120 Airport Hwy (08109-4302)
PHONE.................................856 324-0171
Amanda Schwartz, *CEO*
Michael Schwartz, *Production*
EMP: 20
SQ FT: 12,000
SALES (est): **3.8MM Privately Held**
SIC: **2759** 2789 2752 Commercial printing; bookbinding & related work; commercial printing, lithographic

(G-8576)
S & S PRECISION COMPANY INC
Also Called: S&S Precision
2205 Sherman Ave (08110-1530)
PHONE.................................856 662-0006
Gerald Spiece, *President*
EMP: 5
SQ FT: 5,000
SALES (est): **512.9K Privately Held**
SIC: **3599** Machine shop, jobbing & repair

(G-8577)
SEMINOLE WIRE & CABLE CO INC
Also Called: Seminole Wire Products
7861 Airport Hwy (08109-4322)
PHONE.................................856 324-2929
Fax: 856 438-6875
George H Genzel, *President*
Michael Genzel, *Vice Pres*
Janice Genzel, *Treasurer*
EMP: 18 EST: 1962
SQ FT: 7,800

SALES (est): 2.5MM Privately Held
SIC: **3357** 3699 3496 Nonferrous wire-drawing & insulating; aircraft wire & cable, nonferrous; automotive wire & cable, except ignition sets: nonferrous; lead-in wires, electric lamp; miscellaneous fabricated wire products

(G-8578)
SIMMONS PET FOOD NJ INC
Also Called: Menu Foods Inc
9130 Griffith Morgan Ln (08110-3211)
PHONE.................................856 662-7412
Fax: 856 662-4673
Jason Godsey, *President*
Jennifer Ponticiello, *Human Res Mgr*
◆ EMP: 285
SQ FT: 195,000
SALES: 152.5MM
SALES (corp-wide): **600MM Privately Held**
WEB: www.menufoods.com
SIC: **2047** Dog food; cat food
PA: Simmons Pet Food, Inc.
601 N Hico St
Siloam Springs AR 72761
479 524-8151

(G-8579)
SISCO MANUFACTURING CO INC
7930 National Hwy (08110-1462)
PHONE.................................856 486-7550
Ken Smith, *CEO*
▲ EMP: 14
SALES (est): **2.2MM Privately Held**
SIC: **3822** Hydronic pressure or temperature controls

(G-8580)
SOLIDSURFACE DESIGNS INC
1651 Sherman Ave (08110-2624)
PHONE.................................856 910-7720
Matthew Baiada, *CEO*
EMP: 26
SQ FT: 13,200
SALES (est): **3.7MM Privately Held**
WEB: www.solidsurfacedesigns.com
SIC: **2821** 5211 3281 1743 Plastics materials & resins; counter tops; marble, building: cut & shaped; granite, cut & shaped; marble installation, interior

(G-8581)
SPECTRUM NEON SIGN GROUP LLC
9130 Pennsauken Hwy Ste B (08110-1285)
PHONE.................................856 317-9223
Theresa String, *Principal*
EMP: 4
SQ FT: 4,000
SALES (est): **240.9K Privately Held**
SIC: **3993** Neon signs; letters for signs, metal; signs, not made in custom sign painting shops

(G-8582)
TABLOID GRAPHIC SERVICES INC
7101 Westfield Ave (08110-4001)
PHONE.................................856 486-0410
Fax: 856 486-0033
Steve Brosious, *President*
Thomas Lynch, *Vice Pres*
Tom Lynch, *Vice Pres*
Ken Koruba, *Manager*
EMP: 55
SQ FT: 28,000
SALES (est): **8.2MM Privately Held**
SIC: **2752** Commercial printing, offset

(G-8583)
TAYLOR MADE CUSTOM CABINETRY
7035 Central Hwy 200 (08109-4312)
PHONE.................................856 786-5433
Fax: 856 786-5435
Jay Taylor, *Owner*
EMP: 13

SALES: 1.2MM **Privately Held**
WEB: www.tmcc-inc.com
SIC: 1521 1751 7389 2499 Single-family home remodeling, additions & repairs; cabinet building & installation; exhibit construction by industrial contractors; decorative wood & woodwork

(G-8584)
THANKS FOR BEING GREEN LLC
Also Called: Magnum Computer Recycling
5070b Central Hwy (08109-4606)
PHONE..........................856 333-0991
Nicole Martorano, *General Mgr*
John Martorano Jr, *Principal*
EMP: 20
SQ FT: 28,000
SALES: 440K **Privately Held**
SIC: 3559 Recycling machinery

(G-8585)
THE CREATIVE PRINT GROUP INC
7905 Browning Rd Ste 112 (08109-4319)
PHONE..........................856 486-1700
Howard Friedman, *President*
Joel Mordecai, *Vice Pres*
Stuart Franks, *Sales Mgr*
EMP: 16
SQ FT: 3,800
SALES (est): 3MM **Privately Held**
WEB: www.creativeprintgroup.com
SIC: 2752 7374 8743 8742 Commercial printing, offset; data processing & preparation; public relations services; marketing consulting services

(G-8586)
TPG GRAPHICS LLC
Also Called: Clinton Envelope
9130 Pennsauken Hwy Ste C
(08110-1285)
PHONE..........................856 314-0117
Fax: 856 314-0121
Robert Donner,
EMP: 9
SALES (est): 1MM **Privately Held**
WEB: www.tpggraphics.com
SIC: 2677 Envelopes

(G-8587)
TURBO SOLUTIONS LLC (PA)
8500 Remington Ave Unit 1 (08110-1398)
PHONE..........................856 209-6900
Chris Marino, *Controller*
Warren Klein, *Mng Member*
EMP: 11 EST: 2015
SALES (est): 1.5MM **Privately Held**
SIC: 3714 Axles, motor vehicle

(G-8588)
WERKO MACHINE CO
9200 Collins Ave (08110-1039)
PHONE..........................856 662-0669
Fax: 856 662-7305
Robert Paul Mueller Jr, *Engineer*
Barbara Mueller, *Admin Sec*
EMP: 14 EST: 1946
SQ FT: 12,000
SALES (est): 2.5MM **Privately Held**
WEB: www.werkomachine.com
SIC: 3599 3549 Machine shop, jobbing & repair; metalworking machinery

(G-8589)
WINDMILL PRESS INC
1051 Thomas Busch Mem Hwy
(08110-2312)
PHONE..........................856 663-8990
Burton Hurff, *President*
Helen Hurff, *Vice Pres*
EMP: 6
SALES: 450K **Privately Held**
SIC: 2789 7389 Bookbinding & related work; document embossing

(G-8590)
WURZ SIGNSYSTEMS LLC
2600 Haddonfield Rd (08110-1133)
PHONE..........................856 461-4397
Robert Wurz, *Owner*
EMP: 4
SALES: 950K **Privately Held**
SIC: 3993 Electric signs

(G-8591)
ZIN-TECH INC (PA)
Also Called: Z-Tech
1416 Union Ave (08110-2459)
PHONE..........................856 661-0900
Joseph Zingaro, *President*
Sylvester Rossi, *Vice Pres*
EMP: 22
SQ FT: 11,000
SALES (est): 3.2MM **Privately Held**
SIC: 3544 Dies, steel rule

Pennsville
Salem County

(G-8592)
JLB HAULING LTD LIABILITY CO
90 Dolbow Ave (08070-1706)
PHONE..........................856 514-2771
John Bruno Jr, *President*
Laird Bruno, *Vice Pres*
EMP: 6
SALES (est): 264.3K **Privately Held**
SIC: 4212 1481 Light haulage & cartage, local; mine & quarry services, nonmetallic minerals

(G-8593)
QUANTUM RENOVATIONS
8 Meghans Way (08070-9653)
PHONE..........................856 278-0176
EMP: 5
SALES (est): 590.3K **Privately Held**
SIC: 3572 Computer storage devices

(G-8594)
SIEGFRIED USA HOLDING INC (HQ)
33 Industrial Park Rd (08070-3244)
PHONE..........................856 678-3601
Michael Husler, *Chairman*
Bryan Jackson, *Opers Staff*
John Keenan, *Opers Staff*
Christopher Hood, *Mfg Staff*
Robert Nilsen, *Finance*
▲ **EMP:** 43
SALES (est): 185MM
SALES (corp-wide): 759MM **Privately Held**
SIC: 2834 Druggists' preparations (pharmaceuticals)
PA: Siegfried Holding Ag
Untere Bruhlstrasse 4
Zofingen AG 4800
627 461-111

(G-8595)
SIEGFRIED USA LLC (DH)
33 Industrial Park Rd (08070-3244)
PHONE..........................856 678-3601
Rudolf Hanko, *CEO*
Shane Brown, *Business Mgr*
Ed Lefler, *Business Mgr*
Aaron Mercier, *Business Mgr*
Walter Kittl, *Senior VP*
◆ **EMP:** 140 EST: 1928
SALES: 52MM
SALES (corp-wide): 759MM **Privately Held**
WEB: www.siegfried-usa.com
SIC: 2834 Pharmaceutical preparations
HQ: Siegfried Usa Holding , Inc.
33 Industrial Park Rd
Pennsville NJ 08070
856 678-3601

Pequannock
Morris County

(G-8596)
ALLEN CABINETS AND MILLWORK
60 Newark Pompton Tpke (07440-1624)
PHONE..........................973 694-0665
Fax: 973 694-0245
Len Vanderstad, *President*
EMP: 9
SQ FT: 2,500

SALES (est): 1.1MM **Privately Held**
WEB: www.allencabinets.com
SIC: 2434 Wood kitchen cabinets

(G-8597)
AMBRO INC
303 Newark Pompton Tpke (07440-1333)
PHONE..........................201 818-9717
Fax: 201 818-9672
Andrew Yu, *President*
Angela Yu, *Vice Pres*
▲ **EMP:** 34
SALES (est): 4.3MM **Privately Held**
SIC: 5065 5169 3357 Communication equipment; chemicals & allied products; nonferrous wiredrawing & insulating

(G-8598)
ANELLO FENCE LLC
50 State Rt 23 (07440-1433)
PHONE..........................973 692-9200
Steven Anello,
▲ **EMP:** 25
SALES (est): 5.1MM **Privately Held**
SIC: 3312 Fence posts, iron & steel

(G-8599)
FLUENT DIAGNOSTICS
22 W Parkway (07440-1710)
PHONE..........................201 414-4516
Terence Sullivan, *Principal*
Daniel Tanis,
Sheryl Carlson,
Stephen Morrison,
Paul Sullivan,
EMP: 4
SALES (est): 213.4K **Privately Held**
SIC: 3845 8082 Electromedical apparatus; respiratory analysis equipment, electromedical; home health care services

(G-8600)
FREEDOM VINYL SYSTEMS INC
67 2nd St (07440-1215)
PHONE..........................973 692-0332
Salvatore Anello, *President*
EMP: 5
SALES (est): 385.9K **Privately Held**
SIC: 3089 Fences, gates & accessories: plastic

(G-8601)
REEVES INTERNATIONAL INC (PA)
14 Industrial Rd (07440-1991)
PHONE..........................973 694-5006
Fax: 973 694-5213
Anthony Fleischmann, *President*
Kathleen Fallon, *Vice Pres*
Sandra Huber, *Purch Agent*
Arthur Minnocci, *CFO*
Diane Wheeler, *HR Admin*
▲ **EMP:** 50
SQ FT: 53,000
SALES (est): 26.8MM **Privately Held**
WEB: www.breyerhorses.com
SIC: 5092 5199 3942 Dolls; gift baskets; stuffed toys, including animals

Perrineville
Monmouth County

(G-8602)
RDL MARKETING GROUP LLC
352a Sweetmans Ln (08535-1216)
PHONE..........................732 446-0817
Bob Levine,
EMP: 5
SALES (est): 400K **Privately Held**
SIC: 2741 Catalogs: publishing & printing

(G-8603)
SUCCESS PUBLISHERS LLC
29 Hampton Hollow Dr (08535-1004)
PHONE..........................609 443-0792
John F Abate, *Owner*
EMP: 6
SALES (est): 530K **Privately Held**
SIC: 2741 Miscellaneous publishing

Perth Amboy
Middlesex County

(G-8604)
ACE SIGN COMPANY INC
419 Summit Ave (08861-2016)
P.O. Box 66 (08862-0066)
PHONE..........................732 826-3858
Fax: 732 826-2612
Philip Smith, *President*
Patricia Smith, *Corp Secy*
EMP: 7
SQ FT: 5,000
SALES (est): 925.8K **Privately Held**
SIC: 3993 7389 Electric signs; sign painting & lettering shop

(G-8605)
ACOLYTE TECHNOLOGIES CORP
1000 Amboy Ave (08861-1916)
PHONE..........................212 629-3239
EMP: 4
SALES (est): 255.1K **Privately Held**
SIC: 3674 Light emitting diodes

(G-8606)
ALL MECHANICAL SERVICES INC
430 High St (08861-3504)
P.O. Box 110 (08862-0110)
PHONE..........................732 442-8292
Fax: 732 442-0736
Joe Auriemma, *President*
Greg Huhn, *Vice Pres*
Jeff Shelters, *Shareholder*
EMP: 13
SQ FT: 10,000
SALES (est): 1.9MM **Privately Held**
SIC: 3599 Machine shop, jobbing & repair

(G-8607)
AMT STITCH INC
257 New Brunswick Ave (08861-4024)
PHONE..........................732 376-0009
Fax: 732 376-0616
Miladys Gomez, *President*
◆ **EMP:** 8
SALES (est): 844.1K **Privately Held**
SIC: 2211 Decorative trim & specialty fabrics, including twist weave

(G-8608)
CARDINAL FIBREGLASS INDUSTRIES
1050 State St (08861-2002)
PHONE..........................718 625-4350
William J Weidmann, *President*
Mary Ellen Snow, *President*
EMP: 4
SQ FT: 17,000
SALES (est): 320K **Privately Held**
SIC: 3089 Plastic & fiberglass tanks

(G-8609)
CHEVRON PHILLIPS CHEM CO LP
1200 State St (08861-2003)
PHONE..........................732 738-2000
Fax: 732 738-2045
Joe F Bromiley, *Branch Mgr*
EMP: 20
SALES (corp-wide): 9.6B **Privately Held**
WEB: www.cpchem.com
SIC: 2821 Plastics materials & resins
HQ: Chevron Phillips Chemical Company Lp
10001 Six Pines Dr
The Woodlands TX 77380
832 813-4100

(G-8610)
CHEVRON USA INC
1200 State St (08861-2003)
PHONE..........................732 738-2000
Fax: 732 738-2028
Scott Wooten, *Manager*
Bob Mancini, *Manager*
Kevin McMahon, *Manager*
EMP: 100

SALES (corp-wide): 141.7B **Publicly Held**
SIC: 5541 2951 Filling stations, gasoline; asphalt paving mixtures & blocks
HQ: Chevron U.S.A. Inc.
　　6001 Bollinger Canyon Rd D1248
　　San Ramon CA 94583
　　925 842-1000

(G-8611)
CROMPTON CORP
1000 Convery Blvd (08861-1932)
PHONE.................................732 826-6600
Nick Lettieri, *Principal*
EMP: 5
SALES (est): 862.2K **Privately Held**
SIC: 2869 Industrial organic chemicals

(G-8612)
ENGLERT INC (PA)
1200 Amboy Ave (08861-1956)
PHONE.................................800 364-5378
Fax: 732 826-8865
Debra Harnett, *CEO*
Joseph Turovach, *Vice Pres*
Tom Harnett, *Plant Mgr*
Steven Del Popolo, *Manager*
◆ EMP: 150 EST: 1966
SQ FT: 176,000
SALES (est): 92.5MM **Privately Held**
WEB: www.englertinc.com
SIC: 3444 5033 Gutters, sheet metal; siding, sheet metal; roof deck, sheet metal; roofing, siding & insulation

(G-8613)
EVANS MACHINE & TOOL CO
410 Summit Ave (08861-2017)
PHONE.................................732 442-1144
Thomas Geslak, *Owner*
▲ EMP: 7
SQ FT: 10,000
SALES: 520K **Privately Held**
SIC: 3599 5051 Machine shop, jobbing & repair; steel

(G-8614)
FERRARA BAKERY & CAFE INC
915 Amboy Ave (08861-1921)
PHONE.................................732 826-8700
Peter Lepore, *Branch Mgr*
EMP: 15
SALES (corp-wide): 10.8MM **Privately Held**
SIC: 2051 Bakery products, partially cooked (except frozen)
PA: Ferrara Bakery & Cafe Inc.
　　195 Grand St
　　New York NY 10013
　　212 226-6150

(G-8615)
GOODLITE PRODUCTS INC
500 Division St (08861-3530)
PHONE.................................718 697-7502
Nathan Meisels, *President*
▲ EMP: 10
SQ FT: 20,000
SALES (est): 2MM **Privately Held**
SIC: 3229 Bulbs for electric lights

(G-8616)
GRIMES MANUFACTURING INC
599 State St (08861-3542)
PHONE.................................732 442-4572
Christopher Grimes, *President*
Mark Grimes, *Treasurer*
EMP: 6
SQ FT: 4,000
SALES (est): 660K **Privately Held**
WEB: www.grimesmanufacturing.com
SIC: 3599 Machine shop, jobbing & repair

(G-8617)
HOSEPHARM LTD LIABILITY CO
351 Smith St (08861-3921)
PHONE.................................732 376-0044
EMP: 4
SALES (est): 312.4K **Privately Held**
SIC: 3052 Mfg Rubber/Plastic Hose/Belting

(G-8618)
HOT DIP GALVANIZING
1190 Amboy Ave (08861-1920)
PHONE.................................732 442-7555
Fax: 732 442-5560

EMP: 9
SALES (est): 1MM **Privately Held**
SIC: 3479 Galvanizing of iron, steel or end-formed products

(G-8619)
INTERNATIONAL PROCESSING CORP
1250 Amboy Ave (08861-1920)
PHONE.................................732 826-4240
John Hawrylko, *President*
EMP: 14
SALES (est): 2.5MM **Privately Held**
SIC: 2048 Livestock feeds

(G-8620)
LANXESS SOLUTIONS US INC
1000 Coventry Blvd (08861)
PHONE.................................732 826-1018
Rich Lissenden, *Manager*
EMP: 150
SQ FT: 50,000
SALES (corp-wide): 11.4B **Privately Held**
WEB: www.cromptoncorp.com
SIC: 2869 2821 Industrial organic chemicals; plastics materials & resins
HQ: Lanxess Solutions Us Inc.
　　199 Benson Rd
　　Middlebury CT 06762
　　203 573-2000

(G-8621)
LINCOLN SIGNS & AWNINGS INC
895 State St (08861-2042)
PHONE.................................732 442-3151
Julio Hernandez, *President*
Narda Hernandez, *Vice Pres*
EMP: 9
SQ FT: 2,000
SALES (est): 1.7MM **Privately Held**
SIC: 3993 Signs, not made in custom sign painting shops

(G-8622)
MAYAB HAPPY TACOS INC
450 Florida Grove Rd (08861-3729)
PHONE.................................732 293-0400
Jorge W Alamilla, *President*
Anna Alamilla, *Corp Secy*
Jorge M Alamilla, *Vice Pres*
EMP: 28
SQ FT: 10,000
SALES (est): 5.4MM **Privately Held**
SIC: 2041 2096 2032 Flour & other grain mill products; potato chips & similar snacks; Mexican foods: packaged in cans, jars, etc.

(G-8623)
MENDEZ DAIRY CO INC
450 Fayette St (08861-3805)
P.O. Box 1357 (08862-1357)
PHONE.................................732 442-6337
Rafael Mendez, *President*
Michelle Farkas, *Admin Sec*
EMP: 100
SQ FT: 15,000
SALES (est): 9.4MM **Privately Held**
SIC: 2022 Cheese, natural & processed

(G-8624)
MONOGRAM CENTER INC
437 Amboy Ave (08861-3141)
PHONE.................................732 442-1800
Fax: 732 442-1501
Bill Kraemer, *President*
Michael Kraemer, *Vice Pres*
EMP: 35
SQ FT: 14,000
SALES (est): 6.8MM **Privately Held**
WEB: www.monogramcenter.com
SIC: 5136 5137 7389 7336 Sportswear, men's & boys'; sportswear, women's & children's; lettering service; silk screen design; automotive & apparel trimmings; pleating & stitching

(G-8625)
MORTON SALT INC
920 State St (08861-2091)
P.O. Box 909 (08862-0909)
PHONE.................................732 826-8414
Fax: 732 826-3599
Bill White, *Branch Mgr*
EMP: 14
SQ FT: 45,000

SALES (corp-wide): 4.2B **Privately Held**
SIC: 1479 2819 Salt & sulfur mining; industrial inorganic chemicals
HQ: Morton Salt, Inc.
　　444 W Lake St Ste 3000
　　Chicago IL 60606

(G-8626)
POWER MAGNE-TECH CORP
Also Called: Power Magnetic
653 Sayre Ave (08861-3612)
PHONE.................................732 826-4700
Fax: 732 826-4706
Leon Zelcer, *President*
Harold Tischler, *Sales Executive*
▲ EMP: 20
SQ FT: 11,000
SALES (est): 3.8MM **Privately Held**
WEB: www.quantummarketing.net
SIC: 3612 3621 Tripping transformers; inverters, rotating: electrical

(G-8627)
RECONSERVE INC
1250 Amboy Ave (08861-1920)
PHONE.................................732 826-4240
Rick Brown, *Branch Mgr*
EMP: 6
SALES (corp-wide): 203.7MM **Privately Held**
SIC: 2048 Livestock feeds
HQ: Reconserve, Inc.
　　2811 Wilshire Blvd # 410
　　Santa Monica CA 90403
　　310 458-1574

(G-8628)
RIVERDALE COLOR MFG INC (PA)
1 Walnut St (08861-4531)
PHONE.................................732 376-9300
Fax: 732 376-9394
Paul Maguire, *President*
Charles Irish, *Vice Pres*
Steve Maguire, *Vice Pres*
Mendez Denise, *Purchasing*
Pilar Jimenez, *Cust Mgr*
▼ EMP: 33
SQ FT: 60,000
SALES (est): 4.4MM **Privately Held**
WEB: www.riverdalecolor.com
SIC: 2865 2816 Dyes & pigments; color pigments

(G-8629)
SHIVA FUEL INC
737 New Brunswick Ave (08861-3649)
PHONE.................................732 826-3228
EMP: 4
SALES (est): 218.9K **Privately Held**
SIC: 2869 Fuels

(G-8630)
SHOP RITE SUPERMARKETS INC
Also Called: Shoprite
Convery Blvd Fayette (08861)
PHONE.................................732 442-1717
Fax: 732 442-3133
Arthur Hardardt, *Manager*
EMP: 150
SALES (corp-wide): 12.5B **Privately Held**
SIC: 5411 5912 2051 Supermarkets, chain; drug stores & proprietary stores; bread, cake & related products
HQ: Shop Rite Supermarkets, Inc.
　　5000 Riverside Dr
　　Keasbey NJ 08832
　　908 527-3300

(G-8631)
SKYCAM TECHNOLOGIES LLC
235 Kearny Ave (08861-4403)
PHONE.................................908 205-5548
Arlen Encarnacion, *Mng Member*
EMP: 5
SALES: 500K **Privately Held**
SIC: 3699 Security devices

(G-8632)
SUPREME GRAPHICS AND PRTG INC
1027 State St (08861)
PHONE.................................718 989-9817
Abraham Greenwald, *CEO*

EMP: 1
SQ FT: 2,000
SALES: 1MM **Privately Held**
SIC: 2752 Commercial printing, lithographic

(G-8633)
TOM JAMES COMPANY
Also Called: Tom James of Perth Amboy 2
581 Cortlandt St (08861-3354)
PHONE.................................732 826-8400
Ames Turner, *Branch Mgr*
EMP: 20
SALES (corp-wide): 562.5MM **Privately Held**
WEB: www.englishamericanco.com
SIC: 2311 Suits, men's & boys': made from purchased materials
PA: Tom James Company
　　263 Seaboard Ln
　　Franklin TN 37067
　　615 771-1122

(G-8634)
TROPICAL CHEESE INDUSTRIES (PA)
452 Fayette St (08861-3805)
P.O. Box 1357 (08862-1357)
PHONE.................................732 442-4898
Fax: 732 442-8227
Rafael Mendez, *President*
Sonal Patel, *General Mgr*
Carlos Torres, *General Mgr*
Alex Lopez, *Vice Pres*
Luis Mendez, *Vice Pres*
▲ EMP: 320 EST: 1982
SQ FT: 73,000
SALES (est): 150.6MM **Privately Held**
SIC: 2022 5143 Natural cheese; cheese

(G-8635)
VIRA MANUFACTURING INC
1 Buckingham Ave (08861-3532)
PHONE.................................732 771-8269
Sam Grow, *Vice Pres*
Kenny Viviano, *Facilities Mgr*
Luis E Torres, *Mfg Staff*
Kevin Esposito, *Finance*
Richard Walsh, *Sales Dir*
EMP: 28
SALES (est): 4.4MM **Privately Held**
SIC: 3999 Manufacturing industries

(G-8636)
VOIGT & SCHWEITZER LLC
Also Called: V & S Perth Amboy
1190 Amboy Ave (08861-1920)
PHONE.................................732 442-7555
Tammy Short, *Controller*
John Feeman, *Sales Staff*
Carl Fristick, *Marketing Staff*
Robert Messler, *Manager*
EMP: 60
SALES (corp-wide): 773.1MM **Privately Held**
WEB: www.hotdipgalvanizing.com
SIC: 3479 Galvanizing of iron, steel or end-formed products
HQ: Voigt & Schweitzer Llc
　　987 Buckeye Park Rd
　　Columbus OH 43207
　　614 449-8281

(G-8637)
WIKSTROM MACHINES INC
412 Summit Ave (08861-2017)
PHONE.................................732 826-4800
Walter Geslak, *President*
EMP: 10
SQ FT: 14,000
SALES (est): 850K **Privately Held**
SIC: 3548 Electric welding equipment

Phillipsburg
Warren County

(G-8638)
ACCURATUS CERAMIC CORP
35 Howard St (08865-3060)
PHONE.................................908 213-7070
Fax: 908 213-7069
Raymond Tsao, *President*
Stephen Zelnick, *Admin Sec*

GEOGRAPHIC (vertical tab)

▼ EMP: 20
SQ FT: 20,000
SALES: 3MM **Privately Held**
WEB: www.accuratus.com
SIC: 3545 3823 Diamond cutting tools for turning, boring, burnishing, etc.; industrial instrmnts msrmnt display/control process variable

(G-8639)
ARCHITCTRAL CBINETRY MLLWK LLC
1425 3rd Ave (08865-4605)
PHONE....................908 213-2001
Cheryl Fortner,
EMP: 6
SALES: 400K **Privately Held**
SIC: 2431 Millwork

(G-8640)
AVANTOR PERFORMANCE MTLS LLC
Also Called: J T Baker Chemical Co
600 N Broad St (08865-1271)
PHONE....................908 859-2151
Fax: 908 859-9318
Craig Romanelli, *Manager*
EMP: 300
SALES (corp-wide): 574.8MM **Privately Held**
SIC: 2879 2899 2869 2819 Trace elements (agricultural chemicals); chemical preparations; industrial organic chemicals; industrial inorganic chemicals
HQ: Avantor Performance Materials, Llc
100 W Matsonford Rd # 1
Radnor PA 19087
610 573-2600

(G-8641)
BAER AGGREGATES INC
454 River Rd (08865-7513)
PHONE....................908 454-4412
Fax: 908 454-9370
Lou Mitschele, *President*
EMP: 13
SQ FT: 2,400
SALES (est): 1.3MM **Privately Held**
SIC: 1442 Construction sand & gravel

(G-8642)
BERRY GLOBAL INC
190 Strykers Rd (08865-9775)
PHONE....................980 689-1660
EMP: 8 **Publicly Held**
SIC: 3089 Plastic containers, except foam
HQ: Berry Global, Inc.
101 Oakley St
Evansville IN 47710
812 424-2904

(G-8643)
BERRY GLOBAL INC
190 Strykers Rd (08865-9775)
PHONE....................908 454-0900
Mark Selz, *Branch Mgr*
EMP: 50 **Publicly Held**
WEB: www.captiveplastics.com
SIC: 3089 3081 Bottle caps, molded plastic; unsupported plastics film & sheet
HQ: Berry Global, Inc.
101 Oakley St
Evansville IN 47710
812 424-2904

(G-8644)
BIHLER OF AMERICA INC
85 Industrial Rd Bldg B (08865-4080)
PHONE....................908 213-9001
Fax: 908 329-9111
Maxine Nordmeyer, *CEO*
Mathias Bihler, *President*
Barry Littlewood, *Vice Pres*
Dana Mallen, *QC Mgr*
Vulgen Schoen, *Shareholder*
▲ EMP: 190
SQ FT: 200,000
SALES (est): 80.7MM **Privately Held**
WEB: www.bihler.de
SIC: 3679 5084 3544 Electronic circuits; metalworking machinery; special dies & tools

(G-8645)
CAPTIVE PLASTICS INC
190 Strykers Rd (08865-9775)
PHONE....................812 424-2904
Fax: 908 454-0976
Scott Bungert, *Branch Mgr*
EMP: 101 **Publicly Held**
SIC: 3089 Bottle caps, molded plastic
HQ: Captive Plastics, Inc.
101 Oakley St
Evansville IN 47710
812 424-2904

(G-8646)
DAVID SISCO JR
Also Called: Treasure Hunt
1223 S Main St (08865-3730)
PHONE....................908 454-0880
Fax: 908 859-5152
David Sisco Jr, *Owner*
EMP: 7
SQ FT: 800
SALES (est): 490.1K **Privately Held**
SIC: 7319 7313 2711 Transit advertising services; newspaper advertising representative; newspapers

(G-8647)
FERGUSON CONTAINERS CO INC
16 Industrial Rd (08865-4081)
P.O. Box 42 (08865-0042)
PHONE....................908 454-9755
Fax: 908 454-7144
Derek Klingel, *Sales Staff*
Kevin Ferguson, *Shareholder*
Scott Ferguson, *Shareholder*
Chris Ferguson, *Admin Sec*
EMP: 25 **EST:** 1960
SQ FT: 20,000
SALES (est): 5.5MM **Privately Held**
WEB: www.fergusoncontainers.com
SIC: 2653 Boxes, corrugated: made from purchased materials; boxes, solid fiber: made from purchased materials

(G-8648)
FLOWSERVE CORPORATION
222 Cameron Dr Ste 200 (08865-2777)
PHONE....................908 859-7000
Fax: 908 859-7482
Robert Rajeski, *Principal*
Michael Radio, *Cust Mgr*
Jim Parker, *Manager*
EMP: 200
SALES (corp-wide): 3.6B **Publicly Held**
SIC: 3561 Industrial pumps & parts
PA: Flowserve Corporation
5215 N Oconnor Blvd Connor
Irving TX 75039
972 443-6500

(G-8649)
G J OLIVER INC
50 Industrial Rd (08865-4083)
PHONE....................908 454-9743
Fax: 908 454-0927
John G Oliver, *CEO*
Charles A Parker, *President*
Charles Parker, *Vice Pres*
Chuck Conroy, *Project Mgr*
Kevin Dishinger, *Project Mgr*
▲ EMP: 80 **EST:** 1960
SQ FT: 120,000
SALES: 17MM **Privately Held**
WEB: www.gjoliver.com
SIC: 3441 3443 Fabricated structural metal; vessels, process or storage (from boiler shops): metal plate

(G-8650)
GRAPHIC ACTION INC
296 S Main St (08865-2825)
PHONE....................908 213-0055
Frank T Geraghty, *President*
EMP: 6
SQ FT: 600
SALES: 350K **Privately Held**
SIC: 2752 7334 7336 Commercial printing, offset; photocopying & duplicating services; commercial art & graphic design

(G-8651)
GULCO INC
1 Riverside Way (08865-2340)
PHONE....................908 238-2030

Fax: 908 454-4133
Donald Gulbrandsen, *President*
Jim Kane, *Business Mgr*
Ray Freaney, *Plant Mgr*
Edgar Mejias, *Plant Mgr*
Robert Mikovitch, *Safety Mgr*
◆ EMP: 39
SQ FT: 20,000
SALES (est): 8.4MM **Privately Held**
SIC: 2819 2899 Aluminum chloride; chemical preparations
PA: Gulbrandsen Technologies Inc.
2 Main St
Clinton NJ 08809

(G-8652)
HARMONY SAND & GRAVEL INC
County Rd 519 (08865)
PHONE....................908 475-4690
Fax: 908 475-5760
Richard L Hummer Jr, *President*
EMP: 30
SQ FT: 5,000
SALES (est): 6.3MM **Privately Held**
SIC: 1442 Construction sand & gravel

(G-8653)
J H M COMMUNICATIONS INC
Also Called: JHM Signs
1593 Springtown Rd (08865-4629)
PHONE....................908 859-6668
Fax: 908 859-6698
John Maxman, *President*
Brenda Maxman, *Corp Secy*
EMP: 12
SALES: 1MM **Privately Held**
WEB: www.jhmsigns.com
SIC: 3993 2759 Signs & advertising specialties; promotional printing; circulars: printing

(G-8654)
JERSEY STRAND & CABLE INC
259 Center St Ste 3 (08865-3328)
PHONE....................908 213-9350
Fax: 908 213-2203
Alfred Pratt Jr, *President*
Diane Pratt, *Vice Pres*
George Mazur, *Sales Mgr*
Michelle Johnson, *Payroll Mgr*
▲ EMP: 65 **EST:** 1978
SQ FT: 417
SALES (est): 12.7MM **Privately Held**
WEB: www.jerseystrandandcable.com
SIC: 3496 Cable, uninsulated wire: made from purchased wire

(G-8655)
KEYSTONE PACKAGING SERVICE
555 Warren St (08865-3230)
PHONE....................908 454-8567
Fax: 908 454-7173
John R Schoeneck, *President*
Enoch Schoeneck, *Treasurer*
Norman Peil Jr, *Admin Sec*
EMP: 4 **EST:** 1937
SQ FT: 63,000
SALES: 400K **Privately Held**
SIC: 2673 Bags: plastic, laminated & coated

(G-8656)
LINDE GAS NORTH AMERICA LLC
225 Strykers Rd (08865-9486)
PHONE....................908 777-9125
Dr Wolfgang Reitzle, *CEO*
EMP: 6
SALES (corp-wide): 20.1B **Privately Held**
SIC: 2813 Industrial gases
HQ: Linde Gas North America Llc
200 Somerset Corp Blvd # 7000
Bridgewater NJ 08807

(G-8657)
MAGNETIKA INC
Also Called: Manufacturing Branch
300 Red School Ln (08865-2233)
PHONE....................908 454-2600
Ameet Butala, *Opers Dir*
Hernando Ortega, *Engineer*
Paul Suborits, *Engineer*
Mark Vandoren, *Engineer*
Sheryl Furst, *Controller*
EMP: 40

SALES (corp-wide): 40.4MM **Privately Held**
SIC: 3612 Ballasts for lighting fixtures; power transformers, electric
PA: Magnetika, Inc.
2041 W 139th St
Gardena CA 90249
310 527-8100

(G-8658)
MCWANE INC
Atlantic States Cast Iron Pipe
183 Sitgreaves St (08865-3052)
PHONE....................908 454-1161
Fax: 908 454-1026
David Hiestand, *Vice Pres*
Joe Carter, *Plant Mgr*
Shannon Brunner, *Safety Mgr*
Eladio Quinones, *Safety Mgr*
Randy Hanks, *Foreman/Supr*
EMP: 300
SALES (corp-wide): 1.3B **Privately Held**
WEB: www.mcwane.com
SIC: 3321 Pressure pipe & fittings, cast iron
PA: Mcwane, Inc.
2900 Highway 280 S # 300
Birmingham AL 35223
205 414-3100

(G-8659)
MED CONNECTION LLC
65 Howard St (08865-3101)
PHONE....................908 213-7012
Robert K Kolonia, *President*
Glen Hanson, *Project Mgr*
EMP: 4
SALES: 310K **Privately Held**
WEB: www.micromoldinginc.com
SIC: 2821 Molding compounds, plastics

(G-8660)
MOSER JEWEL COMPANY
518 State Route 57 (08865-9484)
PHONE....................908 454-1155
Fax: 908 454-1199
Sharon L Duffield, *CEO*
Alexandre La Roche, *President*
EMP: 7 **EST:** 1941
SQ FT: 6,300
SALES (est): 1MM **Privately Held**
WEB: www.mosercompany.com
SIC: 3915 3674 3568 Jewel bearings, synthetic; semiconductors & related devices; power transmission equipment

(G-8661)
N E R ASSOCIATES INC
Also Called: General Machine Kraft
45 Howard St (08865-3060)
PHONE....................908 454-5955
Gene Cancelliere, *President*
Douglas Cancelliere, *Admin Sec*
EMP: 8
SQ FT: 4,000
SALES (est): 1.4MM **Privately Held**
SIC: 3449 Miscellaneous metalwork

(G-8662)
PHARM OPS INC
101 Broad St (08865-1208)
PHONE....................908 454-7733
Shankar Musunuri, *Managing Dir*
Khurshid Iqbal, *Managing Dir*
EMP: 5
SALES (est): 723K **Privately Held**
SIC: 2834 Pharmaceutical preparations

(G-8663)
PHILIP MAMRAK
Also Called: P M Construction Co
531 Victory Ave (08865-3826)
PHONE....................908 454-6089
Philip Mamrak, *Owner*
EMP: 8
SQ FT: 3,800
SALES (est): 514.9K **Privately Held**
WEB: www.pmconstructionco.com
SIC: 1623 1794 1611 2851 Water & sewer line construction; excavation work; highway & street paving contractor; epoxy coatings

(G-8664)
PHILLIPSBURG MARBLE CO INC
1 Marble Hill Rd (08865-9331)
P.O. Box 172 (08865-0172)
PHONE....................................908 859-3435
Fax: 908 859-2706
Robert S Barron, *President*
▲ EMP: 22
SQ FT: 32,000
SALES (est): 4.4MM **Privately Held**
WEB: www.pburgmarble.com
SIC: 5032 3281 Marble building stone;
marble, building: cut & shaped

(G-8665)
**PRECAST MANUFACTURING CO
LLC**
187 Strykers Rd (08865-9776)
PHONE....................................908 454-2122
Fax: 908 454-0512
Gregory P Fisher, *President*
Raymond M Fisher, *Vice Pres*
Vilma Delva, *Plant Mgr*
Dean Kloiber, *QC Mgr*
Barry Lauritano, *Sales Staff*
EMP: 36
SQ FT: 10,000
SALES (est): 6.2MM **Privately Held**
WEB: www.precastmfgco.com
SIC: 3272 Concrete products, precast

(G-8666)
**PRESBYTERIAN REFORMED
PUBG CO**
Also Called: P & R PUBLISHING
1102 Marble Hill Rd (08865)
P.O. Box 817 (08865-0817)
PHONE....................................908 454-0505
Fax: 908 859-2390
Bryce Craig, *President*
Virginia Horridge, *Vice Pres*
Robert Den Dulk, *Treasurer*
Ron Evans, *Human Res Dir*
Aaron Gottier, *Sr Project Mgr*
▲ EMP: 17 EST: 1930
SQ FT: 12,000
SALES: 1.4MM **Privately Held**
WEB: www.prpbooks.com
SIC: 2731 Books: publishing only

(G-8667)
R & H CO INC
Also Called: Metal Fabricators
1286 Strykers Rd (08865-9204)
PHONE....................................610 258-3177
William Kowalchuk Jr, *President*
EMP: 5
SQ FT: 6,000
SALES (est): 647.8K **Privately Held**
SIC: 3545 Machine tool attachments & ac-
cessories

(G-8668)
RON BANAFATO INC
Also Called: Rbi Toys
1161 3rd Ave (08865-4708)
P.O. Box 288, Pluckemin (07978-0288)
PHONE....................................908 685-9447
Ron Banafato, *President*
▲ EMP: 8
SQ FT: 8,000
SALES (est): 1.1MM **Privately Held**
SIC: 3942 Stuffed toys, including animals

(G-8669)
RUTLER SCREEN PRINTING INC
169 Belview Rd (08865-2120)
PHONE....................................908 859-3327
Fax: 908 859-2138
John Shubert, *President*
Shauna Mackerer, *Sales Dir*
Tara Carson, *Sales Staff*
EMP: 13
SALES: 500K **Privately Held**
WEB: www.rutler.com
SIC: 2759 Screen printing; automo-
tive & apparel trimmings

(G-8670)
SCC CONCRETE INC
1051 River Rd (08865-8112)
P.O. Box 47 (08865-0047)
PHONE....................................908 859-2172
Fax: 908 859-1720
Richard Cornely, *President*

Patricia Cornely, *Corp Secy*
Francis Stine, *Vice Pres*
EMP: 13
SQ FT: 1,820
SALES (est): 2MM **Privately Held**
SIC: 3273 Ready-mixed concrete

(G-8671)
**STARLIGHT ELECTRO-OPTICS
INC**
660 Hrmony Brass Cstle Rd (08865-9356)
PHONE....................................908 859-1362
Peter Curreri, *President*
EMP: 5
SALES (est): 610.9K **Privately Held**
SIC: 3699 3559 Laser systems & equip-
ment; semiconductor manufacturing ma-
chinery

(G-8672)
STATELINE FABRICATORS LLC
100 Foul Rift Rd (08865-9533)
PHONE....................................908 387-8800
Edward Esposito, *President*
Frank Impeciati,
EMP: 40
SALES: 12MM **Privately Held**
SIC: 3441 5051 Building components,
structural steel; structural shapes, iron or
steel

(G-8673)
TITANIUM SMOKING KINGS LLC
509 March Blvd (08865-3908)
PHONE....................................908 339-8876
Robert William Ingraham Jr, *Principal*
EMP: 7
SALES (est): 146.3K **Privately Held**
SIC: 3356 Titanium

(G-8674)
TKL SPECIALTY PIPING INC
175 Broad St (08865-1208)
PHONE....................................908 454-0030
EMP: 5
SQ FT: 6,000
SALES: 1MM **Privately Held**
SIC: 3494 Valves And Pipe Fittings, Nec

(G-8675)
**VILLA MILAGRO VINEYARDS
LLC**
33 Warren Glen Rd (08865)
PHONE....................................908 995-2072
Steve Gambino,
Audrey Gambino,
EMP: 4
SALES (est): 449.5K **Privately Held**
SIC: 0721 2084 Vines, cultivation of;
wines

Pilesgrove
Salem County

(G-8676)
**RICHARD E PIERSON MTLS
CORP (PA)**
Also Called: R E Pierson Materials
426 Swedesboro Rd (08098-2534)
P.O. Box 430, Woodstown (08098-0430)
PHONE....................................856 467-4199
Fax: 856 467-5360
Richard E Pierson, *President*
EMP: 110
SALES (est): 36.9MM **Privately Held**
SIC: 2951 1611 1771 Asphalt paving mix-
tures & blocks; highway & street construc-
tion; concrete work

(G-8677)
TRIM FACTORY INC
1210 Route 40 (08098-3107)
PHONE....................................856 769-8746
Fax: 856 769-0100
Peggy Yurgin, *President*
Ida Yurgin, *Principal*
Phillip Yurgin, *Principal*
EMP: 6
SALES (est): 731.9K **Privately Held**
SIC: 2431 Exterior & ornamental wood-
work & trim

Pine Beach
Ocean County

(G-8678)
**CASTLE WOODCRAFT ASSOC
LLC**
161 Atlantic City Blvd (08741)
PHONE....................................732 349-1519
Ernest Guenzburger, *Mng Member*
Gerhart Frenz,
EMP: 15
SQ FT: 10,000
SALES: 1.5MM **Privately Held**
SIC: 2431 2434 5712 Millwork; wood
kitchen cabinets; cabinet work, custom

Pine Brook
Morris County

(G-8679)
ABOX AUTOMATION CORP
45 Us Highway 46 Ste 606 (07058-9390)
PHONE....................................973 659-9611
Harish Tailor, *President*
David Pfaff, *Vice Pres*
Steve Kanthan, *Treasurer*
Sean Keogh, *Admin Sec*
EMP: 4
SQ FT: 4,000
SALES (est): 1.7MM **Privately Held**
WEB: www.aboxautomation.com
SIC: 5084 3821 Packaging machinery &
equipment; laboratory apparatus & furni-
ture

(G-8680)
ADHESIVE FILMS INC (PA)
4 Barnet Rd (07058-9504)
P.O. Box 651 (07058-0651)
PHONE....................................973 882-4944
Fax: 973 882-2817
John Farr, *President*
Bryan Stauff, *Vice Pres*
Michael Carbonare, *VP Opers*
Brian F Stauff, *VP Opers*
Adam Hackett, *Executive*
◆ EMP: 14
SQ FT: 37,000
SALES (est): 2.2MM **Privately Held**
WEB: www.adhesivefilms.com
SIC: 2672 Adhesive backed films, foams &
foils

(G-8681)
AGSCO CORPORATION
60 Chapin Rd (07058-9216)
P.O. Box 669 (07058-0669)
PHONE....................................973 244-0005
Edward Plonsker, *Branch Mgr*
EMP: 23
SALES (corp-wide): 22.4MM **Privately
Held**
SIC: 5085 3291 Bottler supplies; rouge,
polishing: abrasive
PA: Agsco Corporation
160 W Hintz Rd
Wheeling IL 60090
847 520-4455

(G-8682)
ALMATICA PHARMA INC
10 Bloomfield Ave B (07058-9743)
PHONE....................................877 447-7979
Douglas Drysdale, *CEO*
Robert Wessman, *Ch of Bd*
Kevin Dain, *CFO*
EMP: 21
SQ FT: 10,000
SALES (est): 3.5MM **Privately Held**
SIC: 2834 Pharmaceutical preparations
PA: Alvogen Group, Inc.
10 Bloomfield Ave
Pine Brook NJ 07058

(G-8683)
ALVOGEN GROUP INC (PA)
10 Bloomfield Ave (07058-9743)
PHONE....................................973 796-3400
Robert Wessman, *CEO*
Darren Alkins, *President*

Elin Gabriel, *COO*
Lisa Graver, *Exec VP*
Georg Ingram, *Exec VP*
EMP: 42
SQ FT: 17,000
SALES (est): 365MM **Privately Held**
SIC: 2834 Pharmaceutical preparations

(G-8684)
ALVOGEN INC
10 Bloomfield Ave Ste 3 (07058-9743)
PHONE....................................973 796-3400
Lisa Graver, *Exec VP*
Kevin Bain, *CFO*
EMP: 110 EST: 2009
SQ FT: 43,000
SALES: 250MM **Privately Held**
SIC: 2834 Pharmaceutical preparations
PA: Alvogen Group, Inc.
10 Bloomfield Ave
Pine Brook NJ 07058

(G-8685)
ALVOGEN PHARMA US INC
10 Bloomfield Ave (07058-9743)
PHONE....................................973 796-3400
Robert Wessman, *CEO*
Lisa Graver, *President*
Graham Baker, *CFO*
EMP: 1652
SALES (est): 253.1K **Privately Held**
SIC: 3559 Pharmaceutical machinery
PA: Alvogen Group, Inc.
10 Bloomfield Ave
Pine Brook NJ 07058

(G-8686)
**AMERICAN AERONAUTIC MFG
CO**
45 Us Highway 46 Ste 606 (07058-9390)
PHONE....................................973 442-8138
Wassim Ezzeddine, *Owner*
EMP: 5
SALES (est): 547.1K **Privately Held**
SIC: 3545 Machine tool attachments & ac-
cessories

(G-8687)
**AMERICAN GARVENS
CORPORATION**
19a Chapin Rd (07058-9204)
PHONE....................................973 276-1093
Thomas Dudutis, *Vice Pres*
Thomas J Dudutis, *Vice Pres*
EMP: 4
SALES (est): 283.7K
SALES (corp-wide): 2.7B **Publicly Held**
WEB: www.mt.com
SIC: 3596 Scales & balances, except labo-
ratory
PA: Mettler-Toledo International Inc.
1900 Polaris Pkwy Fl 6
Columbus OH 43240
614 438-4511

(G-8688)
**BELL-MARK SALES CO INC
(PA)**
331 Changebridge Rd Ste 1 (07058-9180)
P.O. Box 2007 (07058-2007)
PHONE....................................973 882-0202
Fax: 973 808-4616
John Marozzi, *President*
Bob Batesko, *Vice Pres*
Robert Batesko, *Vice Pres*
Thomas Pugh III, *Vice Pres*
Wayne Becker, *Engineer*
▲ EMP: 20
SQ FT: 8,000
SALES (est): 17MM **Privately Held**
WEB: www.bell-mark.com
SIC: 3555 Printing trades machinery

(G-8689)
BGA CONSTRUCTION INC (PA)
321 Changebridge Rd (07058-9583)
PHONE....................................973 809-9745
Benjamin Gaudiosi, *President*
Hobart Carlton Price, *Opers Mgr*
▲ EMP: 55
SQ FT: 20,000
SALES: 12MM **Privately Held**
WEB: www.bgaconstruction.com
SIC: 2541 Garment racks, wood

▲ = Import ▼=Export
◆ =Import/Export

(G-8690)
CANVAS 4 LIFE INC
30 Chapin Rd Ste 1210 (07058-8902)
P.O. Box 216 (07058-0216)
PHONE................................973 276-3200
Cheryl Stoyle, *Principal*
▲ EMP: 4
SALES (est): 437.3K **Privately Held**
SIC: 2211 Canvas

(G-8691)
CHIRAL PHOTONICS INC
26 Chapin Rd Ste 1104 (07058-8802)
P.O. Box 694 (07058-0694)
PHONE................................973 732-0030
Dan Neugroschl, *President*
Azriel Genack, *CTO*
▲ EMP: 10
SALES (est): 2.4MM **Privately Held**
WEB: www.chiralphotonics.com
SIC: 3577 Optical scanning devices

(G-8692)
CHIRAL PHOTONICS INC
26 Chapin Rd Ste 1104 (07058-8802)
P.O. Box 694 (07058-0694)
PHONE................................973 732-0030
Dan Neugroschl, *President*
Zhou Shi, *Research*
Jonathan Singer, *Engineer*
Victor Kopp, *Director*
EMP: 15
SALES (est): 1.4MM **Privately Held**
SIC: 3827 Optical instruments & lenses

(G-8693)
CHRISTINE VALMY INC (PA)
285 Changebridge Rd Ste 1 (07058-9599)
PHONE................................973 575-1050
Peter De Haydu, *President*
Christine Valmy, *Chairman*
Marina Dehaydu, *Vice Pres*
Martin Seminario, *Research*
Thomas J Fellig, *Admin Sec*
▲ EMP: 21 EST: 1965
SQ FT: 20,000
SALES (est): 7MM **Privately Held**
WEB: www.christinevalmy.com
SIC: 2844 7231 Cosmetic preparations;
cosmetology school

(G-8694)
CLARK EQUIPMENT COMPANY
Also Called: Doosan Machine Tools
19a Chapin Rd (07058-9204)
PHONE................................973 618-2500
EMP: 3281
SALES (corp-wide): 2.4B **Privately Held**
SIC: 3531 Construction machinery
HQ: Clark Equipment Company
250 E Beaton Dr
West Fargo ND 58078
701 241-8700

(G-8695)
**COUNTY LINE
PHRMACEUTICALS LLC**
10 Bloomfield Ave Ste 3 (07058-9743)
PHONE................................262 439-8109
Richard Losiniecki, *CEO*
Lisa Schumacher, *General Mgr*
Jeff Rumler,
Jon Thiel,
EMP: 9
SQ FT: 2,800
SALES (est): 3.4MM **Privately Held**
SIC: 2834 Pharmaceutical preparations

(G-8696)
CROWN TROPHY
101 Us Highway 46 Ste 136 (07058-9608)
PHONE................................973 808-8400
Fax: 973 808-0404
Patricia May, *Owner*
EMP: 4
SQ FT: 1,400
SALES (est): 190K **Privately Held**
SIC: 5999 2499 2759 Trophies & plaques;
trophy bases, wood; engraving

(G-8697)
DICAR INC (DH)
30 Chapin Rd (07058-9392)
P.O. Box 643 (07058-0643)
PHONE................................973 575-1377

Fax: 973 575-1455
Steve Warll, *President*
Daniel Freifeld, *President*
Marcel Tigchelaar, *General Mgr*
Ron Warll, *Principal*
Stephen Warll, *Principal*
◆ EMP: 50
SQ FT: 25,000
SALES (est): 45.7MM
SALES (corp-wide): 2.9MM **Privately
Held**
SIC: 2822 3081 Synthetic rubber; plastic
film & sheet
HQ: Dicar B.V.
De Boeg 8
Drachten 9206
512 582-682

(G-8698)
DICAR INC
5 Bader Rd (07058-9814)
P.O. Box 643 (07058-0643)
PHONE................................973 575-4220
Fax: 973 575-8122
Dan Freifeld, *President*
Marina Sadikoska, *Prgrmr*
EMP: 72
SALES (corp-wide): 2.9MM **Privately
Held**
SIC: 2822 Synthetic rubber
HQ: Dicar, Inc.
30 Chapin Rd
Pine Brook NJ 07058
973 575-1377

(G-8699)
DIOPSYS INC
16 Chapin Rd Ste 912 (07058-8900)
P.O. Box 672 (07058-0672)
PHONE................................973 244-0622
Alberto Gonzlez Garcia, *Ch of Bd*
Matt Emmer, *President*
Joseph Fontanetta, *President*
Tibor Szoke, *General Mgr*
John Siegfried, *Principal*
▼ EMP: 39
SQ FT: 4,800
SALES (est): 12.4MM **Privately Held**
WEB: www.diopsys.com
SIC: 3841 Surgical & medical instruments

(G-8700)
**DOOSAN MACHINE TOOLS
AMER CORP (HQ)**
19a Chapin Rd (07058-9204)
PHONE................................973 618-2500
Hyeong Joo Kim, *CEO*
Michael P Stanley, *President*
David Barber, *General Mgr*
Kim Parkinson, *COO*
John Howard, *Vice Pres*
◆ EMP: 60
SALES: 179.7MM
SALES (corp-wide): 2.4B **Privately Held**
WEB: www.doosanlift.com
SIC: 5084 5082 3545 Machine tools & ac-
cessories; lift trucks & parts; construction
& mining machinery; machine tool acces-
sories
PA: Doosan Infracore Co., Ltd.
489 Injung-Ro, Dong-Gu
Incheon 22502
106 862-1223

(G-8701)
ELUSYS THERAPEUTICS INC
25 Riverside Dr Ste 1 (07058-9391)
PHONE................................973 808-0222
Fax: 973 808-0322
Elizabeth Posillico, *President*
Leslie Casey, *Vice Pres*
Stephen Haworth, *Vice Pres*
Jeremy Middleton, *Vice Pres*
James Porter, *Vice Pres*
EMP: 25
SQ FT: 13,000
SALES (est): 6MM **Privately Held**
WEB: www.elusys.com
SIC: 2834 Pharmaceutical preparations

(G-8702)
**FORD ATLANTIC FASTENER
CORP**
Also Called: Ford Atlanic
341 Changebridge Rd (07058-9717)
P.O. Box 733 (07058-0733)
PHONE................................973 882-1191
Tony Innamarato, *President*
Glenn Ehrhardt, *Vice Pres*
Anthony Innamarato, *Plant Mgr*
Ed Duncza, *Sales Staff*
Joann Dura,
▲ EMP: 27 EST: 1982
SQ FT: 15,000
SALES (est): 11.5MM **Privately Held**
SIC: 5072 3452 Bolts, nuts & screws;
bolts, nuts, rivets & washers

(G-8703)
I & J FISNAR INC
19 Chapin Rd Bldg C (07058-9385)
PHONE................................973 646-5044
David Woloszyk, *CFO*
▲ EMP: 16
SALES (est): 4.7MM **Privately Held**
WEB: www.ijfisnar.com
SIC: 3569 Liquid automation machinery &
equipment

(G-8704)
II-VI INCORPORATED
Also Called: Ii-VI Advanced Materials Sic S
20 Chapin Rd Ste 1007 (07058-9272)
P.O. Box 840 (07058-0840)
PHONE................................973 227-1551
Carl Johnson, *President*
EMP: 13
SALES (corp-wide): 972MM **Publicly
Held**
SIC: 3674 Silicon wafers, chemically
doped
PA: Ii-Vi Incorporated
375 Saxonburg Blvd
Saxonburg PA 16056
724 352-4455

(G-8705)
II-VI WIDE BAND GAP INC
20 Chapin Rd Ste 1005 (07058-9393)
P.O. Box 840 (07058-0840)
PHONE................................973 227-1551
Fax: 973 227-8658
Fran Kramer, *President*
Craig Creaturo, *Treasurer*
EMP: 4
SALES (est): 340.4K
SALES (corp-wide): 972MM **Publicly
Held**
SIC: 3827 Optical instruments & lenses
PA: Ii-Vi Incorporated
375 Saxonburg Blvd
Saxonburg PA 16056
724 352-4455

(G-8706)
INGERSOLL-RAND COMPANY
26 Chapin Rd Ste 1107 (07058-8802)
PHONE................................973 882-0924
EMP: 7 **Privately Held**
SIC: 3131 Rands
HQ: Ingersoll-Rand Company
800 Beaty St Ste B
Davidson NC 28036
704 655-4000

(G-8707)
**INTERNATIONAL BEAUTY
PRODUCTS**
Also Called: Mauden International
26 Chapin Rd Ste 1108 (07058-8802)
P.O. Box 708 (07058-0708)
PHONE................................973 575-6400
Henry Cho, *President*
Anthony Sehnaoui, *Vice Pres*
▲ EMP: 11 EST: 1989
SQ FT: 20,000
SALES (est): 2.5MM **Privately Held**
SIC: 2844 Toilet preparations

(G-8708)
JIAHERB INC (HQ)
1 Chapin Rd Ste 1 # 1 (07058-9221)
PHONE................................973 439-6869
Ying Chen, *President*
Chris Oesterheld, *Exec VP*

Scott Chen, *Vice Pres*
Guillaume Gigot, *Accounts Mgr*
Stephanie Jimenez, *Accounts Mgr*
▲ EMP: 22
SALES: 3.6MM
SALES (corp-wide): 96.4MM **Privately
Held**
SIC: 2833 Medicinals & botanicals
PA: Shaanxi Jiahe Phytochem Co., Ltd.
A-6th Floor, No.66 Jinye 1st Road, Hi-
Tech Park
Xian 71007
298 834-8327

(G-8709)
**MECHANICAL TECHNOLOGIES
LLC**
10 Bloomfield Ave Ste 6 (07058-9743)
PHONE................................973 616-3800
Chris Panza, *President*
Rich Fembleaux, *Vice Pres*
Lawrence Bovich, *Mng Member*
EMP: 38
SALES (est): 11.2MM **Privately Held**
SIC: 3585 Air conditioning equipment,
complete; heating equipment, complete

(G-8710)
NATIONAL FUEL LLC
287 Changebridge Rd (07058-9560)
PHONE................................973 227-4549
EMP: 5
SALES (est): 196.9K **Privately Held**
SIC: 2869 Fuels

(G-8711)
NEWARK MORNING LEDGER CO
Also Called: Star Ledger
26 Riverside Dr (07058-9758)
PHONE................................973 882-6120
Bob Jared, *Manager*
Peter Finella, *Director*
EMP: 149
SALES (corp-wide): 217.5MM **Privately
Held**
SIC: 2782 2711 Ledgers & ledger sheets;
newspapers, publishing & printing
PA: Newark Morning Ledger Co.
1 Gateway Ctr Ste 1100
Newark NJ 07102
973 392-4141

(G-8712)
**PARKER-HANNIFIN
CORPORATION**
Also Called: Pneutronics Division
45 Us Highway 46 Ste 602 (07058-9390)
P.O. Box 778 (07058-0778)
PHONE................................973 575-4844
Donald Washkewicz, *President*
John Pollara, *QC Mgr*
Harry Wang, *Engineer*
EMP: 50
SALES (corp-wide): 12B **Publicly Held**
WEB: www.parker.com
SIC: 3491 3492 Solenoid valves; fluid
power valves & hose fittings
PA: Parker-Hannifin Corporation
6035 Parkland Blvd
Cleveland OH 44124
216 896-3000

(G-8713)
PCR TECHNOLOGIES INC
26 Chapin Rd Ste 1111 (07058-9211)
P.O. Box 868 (07058-0868)
PHONE................................973 882-0017
Mark Vanzini, *President*
Peter Lemma, *Vice Pres*
EMP: 8
SQ FT: 7,000
SALES: 1.7MM **Privately Held**
WEB: www.pcrouting.com
SIC: 3672 3679 3444 3469 Circuit
boards, television & radio printed; elec-
tronic circuits; microwave components;
sheet metalwork; metal stampings; vul-
canized fiber plates, sheets, rods or tubes

(G-8714)
**PURE SOCCER ACADEMY LTD
LBLTY**
330 Changebridge Rd # 101 (07058-9839)
PHONE................................877 945-6423
Nigel J W Nicholls, *President*

Ben Manning, *Director*
Joe Owen, *Director*
EMP: 5
SALES (est): 267.3K **Privately Held**
SIC: 3949 Sporting & athletic goods

(G-8715)
REFINE TECHNOLOGY LLC
26 Chapin Rd Ste 1107 (07058-8802)
P.O. Box 691 (07058-0691)
PHONE..........................973 952-0002
Sol Genauer, *CEO*
Jerry Shevitz, *President*
Edi Eliezer, *Vice Pres*
Bradley Maykow, *QC Mgr*
John B Carter, *VP Sales*
EMP: 18
SALES (est): 45.1K **Privately Held**
SIC: 3845 Laser systems & equipment, medical

(G-8716)
SATO LBLING SOLUTIONS AMER INC
30 Chapin Rd Ste 1201 (07058-9398)
P.O. Box 777 (07058-0777)
PHONE..........................973 287-3641
Joseph Podsedly, *Branch Mgr*
EMP: 94
SALES (corp-wide): 20.3MM **Privately Held**
SIC: 2759 Labels & seals: printing
PA: Sato Labeling Solutions America, Inc.
1140 Windham Pkwy
Romeoville IL 60446
630 771-4200

(G-8717)
SIGNATURE MARKETING GROUP LTD (PA)
25 Riverside Dr Ste 4 (07058-9391)
PHONE..........................973 575-7785
Thomas J Cioletti, *President*
Danielle Umstead, *Treasurer*
William Becher, *Accounts Mgr*
Luke Tuske, *Manager*
▲ **EMP:** 15
SQ FT: 24,000
SALES (est): 3MM **Privately Held**
WEB: www.signaturegroupltd.net
SIC: 3631 Household cooking equipment

(G-8718)
TRANE US INC
26 Chapin Rd Ste 1103 (07058-8802)
P.O. Box 154 (07058-0154)
PHONE..........................973 882-3220
Fax: 973 882-5592
Walter Macko, *Branch Mgr*
Bruce Hanna, *Manager*
EMP: 6 **Privately Held**
SIC: 3585 Refrigeration & heating equipment
HQ: Trane U.S. Inc.
3600 Pammel Creek Rd
La Crosse WI 54601
608 787-2000

(G-8719)
VOLTA BELTING USA INC
60 Chapin Rd Ste 3 (07058-9217)
PHONE..........................973 276-7905
Zvika Avidan, *President*
▲ **EMP:** 17
SALES (est): 4.2MM **Privately Held**
SIC: 3535 Belt conveyor systems, general industrial use

(G-8720)
WEXCO INDUSTRIES INC
3 Barnet Rd (07058-9505)
PHONE..........................973 244-5777
Fax: 973 244-9179
Paula Lombard, *President*
Steve Schwartz, *COO*
Mike Parmelee, *Vice Pres*
Bill Stahl, *Opers Mgr*
Jeff Forbes, *VP Bus Dvlpt*
▲ **EMP:** 20
SQ FT: 35,000
SALES (est): 9MM **Privately Held**
SIC: 5013 3714 Automotive supplies & parts; wipers, windshield, motor vehicle

Pine Hill
Camden County

(G-8721)
BRUCE MCCOY SR
Also Called: Wilcoy Press
5402 Tall Pnes (08021-7627)
PHONE..........................609 217-6153
Rema McCoy, *Vice Pres*
EMP: 6 EST: 2006
SALES (est): 350K **Privately Held**
SIC: 2752 Commercial printing, lithographic

(G-8722)
PINE HILL PRINTING INC
200 Erial Rd (08021-6212)
PHONE..........................856 346-2915
Fax: 856 783-6633
Edith Mc Cusker, *President*
Peter A Mc Cusker, *Vice Pres*
Peter A McCusker, *Vice Pres*
EMP: 9
SQ FT: 9,000
SALES: 1.5MM **Privately Held**
SIC: 2752 Commercial printing, offset

Piscataway
Middlesex County

(G-8723)
ABOUT OUR TOWN INC
2 Lakeview Ave Ste 312 (08854-2750)
PHONE..........................732 968-1615
Fax: 732 968-2205
Ronald Chilson, *President*
EMP: 6
SALES (est): 250K **Privately Held**
WEB: www.aboutourtown.com
SIC: 2711 7331 Newspapers, publishing & printing; direct mail advertising services

(G-8724)
ACG NORTH AMERICA LLC
262 Old New Brunswick Rd A (08854-3756)
PHONE..........................908 757-3425
Ajit Singh, *President*
Nikunj Desai, *General Mgr*
Hemant Mhatre, *General Mgr*
Ganesh Shenoy, *Business Mgr*
Ilesh Desai, *Vice Pres*
▲ **EMP:** 25
SQ FT: 10,000
SALES (est): 3.1MM **Privately Held**
WEB: www.ucllc.net
SIC: 2834 Pharmaceutical preparations

(G-8725)
ADELLO BIOLOGICS LLC (PA)
20 New England Ave (08854-4101)
PHONE..........................312 620-1500
Chintu Patel, *CEO*
Sarfaraz Niazi,
Robert A Salcedo,
▲ **EMP:** 25
SQ FT: 30,822
SALES (est): 11.8MM **Privately Held**
SIC: 2834 Pharmaceutical preparations

(G-8726)
AFH INDUSTRIES LLC
141 Ethel Rd W (08854-5928)
PHONE..........................917 407-6866
Isaac Saideh, *Principal*
EMP: 4
SALES (est): 171.9K
SALES (corp-wide): 20MM **Privately Held**
SIC: 3999 Atomizers, toiletry
PA: A.J. Facts Inc.
110 W 34th St Fl 7
New York NY
212 967-4430

(G-8727)
AFLEX EXTRUSION TECHNOLOGIES
240b N Randolphville Rd (08854-3127)
PHONE..........................732 752-0048

Fax: 732 752-3795
Daryl Little, *President*
▲ **EMP:** 21
SQ FT: 12,500
SALES (est): 4.1MM **Privately Held**
SIC: 3089 Extruded finished plastic products; plastic processing

(G-8728)
AGILEX FLAVORS FRAGRANCES INC (HQ)
140 Centennial Ave (08854-3908)
PHONE..........................732 885-0702
Fax: 201 236-8154
Raymond J Hughes, *CEO*
Gail Guilbert, *Vice Pres*
Bill Nelson, *Vice Pres*
Alice Rebeck, *Vice Pres*
Randall Richards, *Vice Pres*
◆ **EMP:** 3
SALES (est): 61.5MM
SALES (corp-wide): 3.1B **Privately Held**
SIC: 2844 Perfumes & colognes
PA: Firmenich International Sa
Route Des Jeunes 1
Les Acacias GE 1227
227 802-211

(G-8729)
AIRBRASIVE JET TECH LLC
151 Old New Brunswick Rd (08854-3708)
PHONE..........................201 725-7340
Joel Levine, *Managing Dir*
Bruce Berger,
Nat Wasserstein,
EMP: 5
SQ FT: 2,500
SALES (est): 700.8K **Privately Held**
SIC: 3545 Dressers, abrasive wheel: diamond point or other

(G-8730)
ALL AMERICAN POLY CORP (PA)
40 Turner Pl (08854-3839)
P.O. Box 10148, New Brunswick (08906-0148)
PHONE..........................732 752-3200
Jack Klein, *President*
Joe Friedman, *Senior VP*
Neil Koenig, *Vice Pres*
Leon Ortega, *Plant Mgr*
Warren Maruca, *Opers Staff*
▼ **EMP:** 250
SQ FT: 160,000
SALES (est): 75.8MM **Privately Held**
WEB: www.allampoly.com
SIC: 3081 2673 Unsupported plastics film & sheet; plastic bags: made from purchased materials

(G-8731)
AMERICAN HOME MFG LLC
4 Corporate Pl (08854-4120)
PHONE..........................732 465-1530
EMP: 10
SALES (corp-wide): 104.4MM **Privately Held**
SIC: 2299 Pillow fillings: curled hair, cotton waste, moss, hemp tow
HQ: American Home Manufacturing Llc
302 5th Ave
New York NY 10001
212 643-0680

(G-8732)
AMERICAN PHARMACEUTICAL LLC
1 New England Ave (08854-4128)
PHONE..........................732 645-3030
Ken Cappel, *Manager*
EMP: 6
SALES (est): 634.7K **Privately Held**
SIC: 2834 Pharmaceutical preparations

(G-8733)
AMERICAN STANDARD INTL INC
1 Centennial Ave Ste 101 (08854-3921)
P.O. Box 6820 (08855-6820)
PHONE..........................732 652-7100
Jay D Gould, *CEO*
Carol Houlik, *Director*
EMP: 25

SALES (est): 4.8MM **Privately Held**
SIC: 2499 Kitchen, bathroom & household ware: wood
HQ: Trane U.S. Inc.
3600 Pammel Creek Rd
La Crosse WI 54601
608 787-2000

(G-8734)
AMNEAL PHARMACEUTICALS LLC
1 New England Ave Bldg A (08854-4128)
PHONE..........................908 947-3120
Ken Cappel, *Branch Mgr*
EMP: 17
SALES (corp-wide): 74.4K **Publicly Held**
SIC: 5122 2834 Pharmaceuticals; pharmaceutical preparations
HQ: Amneal Pharmaceuticals Llc
400 Crossing Blvd Fl 3
Bridgewater NJ 08807

(G-8735)
AMNEAL PHARMACEUTICALS LLC
47 Colonial Dr Bldg B (08854-4113)
PHONE..........................908 947-3120
Alpesh Patel, *Manager*
EMP: 14
SALES (corp-wide): 74.4K **Publicly Held**
SIC: 2834 Pharmaceutical preparations
HQ: Amneal Pharmaceuticals Llc
400 Crossing Blvd Fl 3
Bridgewater NJ 08807

(G-8736)
APPCO PHARMA LLC
262 Old New Brunswick Rd (08854-3756)
PHONE..........................732 271-8300
Nagaraju Kanchanapalli, *Branch Mgr*
EMP: 35
SALES (est): 3.6MM
SALES (corp-wide): 8.2MM **Privately Held**
SIC: 2834 Pharmaceutical preparations
PA: Appco Pharma Llc
120 Belmont Dr
Somerset NJ 08873
732 271-8300

(G-8737)
AROMATIC TECHNOLOGIES INC
Also Called: Aromatech
140 Centennial Ave (08854-3908)
PHONE..........................732 393-7300
Raymond Hughes, *CEO*
Kevin M Gilbert, *Senior VP*
Natalie L Hinden-Kuhles, *Senior VP*
Tony Trinco, *Senior VP*
Dan Freimuth, *Vice Pres*
▲ **EMP:** 80
SQ FT: 60,000
SALES (est): 21.3MM
SALES (corp-wide): 1B **Privately Held**
WEB: www.aromatec.com
SIC: 2869 Perfumes, flavorings & food additives
PA: Midocean Us Advisor, L.P.
320 Park Ave Fl 16
New York NY 10022
212 497-1400

(G-8738)
AS AMERICA INC (DH)
Also Called: American Standard Brands
1 Centennial Ave Ste 101 (08854-3921)
P.O. Box 6820 (08855-6820)
PHONE..........................732 980-3000
Fax: 732 980-6130
Steve Delarge, *President*
Richard Kealty, *Regional Mgr*
Jean L'Henaff, *Vice Pres*
Dan Harvey, *Opers Mgr*
Kathy Bowman, *Opers Staff*
◆ **EMP:** 200
SALES (est): 2.1B
SALES (corp-wide): 15.6B **Privately Held**
SIC: 3261 3432 Vitreous plumbing fixtures; plumbing fixture fittings & trim
HQ: Lixil Corporation
3-2-5, Kasumigaseki
Chiyoda-Ku TKY 100-0
362 733-601

▲ = Import ▼=Export
◆ =Import/Export

(G-8739)
ASD HOLDING CORP
Also Called: American Standard
1 Centennial Ave (08854-3921)
P.O. Box 6820 (08855-6820)
PHONE....................................800 442-1902
Steven P Delarge, *President*
EMP: 7
SALES (est): 518.3K
SALES (corp-wide): 15.6B **Privately Held**
SIC: 3431 5047 Bathtubs: enameled iron,
cast iron or pressed metal; bathroom fix-
tures, including sinks; plumbing fixtures:
enameled iron cast iron or pressed metal;
baths, whirlpool
HQ: Lixil Corporation
3-2-5, Kasumigaseki
Chiyoda-Ku TKY 100-0
362 733-601

(G-8740)
BCC (USA) INC
Also Called: Bearing Castings USA
143 Ethel Rd W (08854-5928)
PHONE....................................732 572-5450
Jimmy Chu, *President*
Andrew Doong, *General Mgr*
Marquis Yeh, *Treasurer*
▲ EMP: 5
SQ FT: 13,700
SALES (est): 450K **Privately Held**
SIC: 3568 5085 5045 Bearings, plain;
bearings; computer peripheral equipment

(G-8741)
BEAUTY-PACK LLC
170 Circle Dr N (08854-3703)
P.O. Box 610, Gladstone (07934-0610)
PHONE....................................732 802-8200
Gregory Harmon,
EMP: 10 EST: 2013
SQ FT: 110,000
SALES (est): 670.2K **Privately Held**
SIC: 7389 2631 5084 Cosmetic kits, as-
sembling & packaging; container, packag-
ing & boxboard; processing & packaging
equipment

(G-8742)
CAMBER PHARMACEUTICALS INC
1031 Centennial Ave (08854-4125)
PHONE....................................732 529-0430
Konstantin Ostaficiuk, *President*
Kon Ostaficiuk, *Vice Pres*
Ashish Patel, *Purch Agent*
Kirk Hessels, *Finance Dir*
Pravin Pillai, *Finance*
▲ EMP: 47
SQ FT: 66,000
SALES: 30.8MM
SALES (corp-wide): 215.1MM **Privately Held**
SIC: 5122 2834 Pharmaceuticals; medi-
cines, capsuled or ampuled
PA: Hetero Drugs Limited
7-2-A2, Hetero Corporate,
Hyderabad TS 50001
402 370-7744

(G-8743)
CAPTIVE PLASTICS INC
251 Circle Dr N (08854-3759)
PHONE....................................732 469-7900
Fax: 732 271-5205
R Beeler, *President*
EMP: 101 **Publicly Held**
SIC: 3089 Plastic containers, except foam
HQ: Captive Plastics, Inc.
101 Oakley St
Evansville IN 47710
812 424-2904

(G-8744)
CATCHING ZZZ LLC
Also Called: Tanda Sleep
91 New England Ave (08854-4142)
PHONE....................................888 339-1604
Venkata Chinni, *Mng Member*
Janice Yates, *Director*
EMP: 6
SALES (est): 227.6K **Privately Held**
SIC: 2515 Mattresses & bedsprings

(G-8745)
CAVALLI CABINETS INC
1531 S Washington Ave # 1 (08854-6701)
PHONE....................................201 528-7070
Tom Yu, *President*
▲ EMP: 6
SALES (est): 126.3K **Privately Held**
SIC: 2434 Wood kitchen cabinets

(G-8746)
CENTURY PRINTING CORP
10 New England Ave (08854-4101)
PHONE....................................732 981-0544
Guy T Greck, *President*
Michael Maroney, *Corp Secy*
EMP: 4
SQ FT: 2,000
SALES: 350K **Privately Held**
SIC: 2752 Commercial printing, litho-
graphic

(G-8747)
CERAMI WOOD PRODUCTS INC
154 12th St (08854-1934)
PHONE....................................732 968-7222
Fax: 732 968-7227
EMP: 12 EST: 1979
SQ FT: 10,500
SALES: 1.5MM **Privately Held**
SIC: 2511 2431 Mfg Wood Household Fur-
niture Mfg Millwork

(G-8748)
CHANEL INC
876 Centennial Ave Ste 1 (08854-3937)
P.O. Box 308 (08855-0308)
PHONE....................................732 885-5500
Fax: 732 980-2070
Pamela Tapia, *Regional Mgr*
Zvi Eiref, *Vice Pres*
Anthony Arroyo, *Vice Pres*
Jeffrey Barth, *Vice Pres*
Ken Ellmer, *Vice Pres*
EMP: 750 **Privately Held**
WEB: www.chanel.com
SIC: 2844 Cosmetic preparations
HQ: Chanel, Inc.
9 W 57th St Bsmt 2b
New York NY 10019
212 688-5055

(G-8749)
CLASSIC PRINTERS & CONVERTERS
140 Ethel Rd W Ste K (08854-5951)
PHONE....................................732 985-1100
Fax: 732 985-1560
Sat Khurana, *President*
Rachna Khurana, *Vice Pres*
Raj Kumar, *Vice Pres*
EMP: 6
SQ FT: 4,500
SALES (est): 939.2K **Privately Held**
WEB: www.tapesandlabels.com
SIC: 2759 Labels & seals: printing

(G-8750)
CLEMS ORNEMENTAL IRON WORKS
Also Called: Clem's
110 11th St (08854-1508)
PHONE....................................732 968-7200
Fax: 732 968-0105
Clement L Carfaro Jr, *President*
Clem Carfaro III, *Vice Pres*
Nancy Pittson, *Director*
▼ EMP: 60
SQ FT: 20,500
SALES (est): 10.4MM **Privately Held**
WEB: www.clemsironworks.com
SIC: 3446 Architectural metalwork

(G-8751)
COLGATE-PALMOLIVE COMPANY
909 River Rd (08854-5596)
P.O. Box 1343 (08855-1343)
PHONE....................................732 878-7500
Fax: 732 878-7443
Craig Buehner, *Purch Mgr*
Roger Lim, *Technical Mgr*
Tracey Aldrich, *Research*
Isabel Diaz, *Research*
Julia Dugdale, *Research*
EMP: 750

SALES (corp-wide): 15.4B **Publicly Held**
WEB: www.colgate.com
SIC: 2844 Toothpastes or powders, denti-
frices
PA: Colgate-Palmolive Company
300 Park Ave Fl 3
New York NY 10022
212 310-2000

(G-8752)
CONTINENTAL PRECISION CORP (PA)
Also Called: Montrose Molders
25 Howard St (08854-1435)
PHONE....................................908 754-3030
Judith Wilson, *Corp Secy*
William H Wilson, *Vice Pres*
▲ EMP: 195 EST: 1966
SQ FT: 940,000
SALES (est): 23.2MM **Privately Held**
WEB: www.montrosemolders.com
SIC: 3089 3544 Injection molding of plas-
tics; forms (molds), for foundry & plastics
working machinery

(G-8753)
DAQ ELECTRONICS LLC
262 Old New Brunswick Rd B
(08854-3756)
PHONE....................................732 981-0050
Fax: 732 981-0058
David Green, *President*
Robert Musumeci, *VP Opers*
Maira Medina, *Purch Agent*
Robert Kukoly, *QC Mgr*
Mike Schwartz, *Controller*
▼ EMP: 28
SQ FT: 25,000
SALES: 8MM **Privately Held**
WEB: www.daq.net
SIC: 3699 3823 Security control equip-
ment & systems; telemetering instru-
ments, industrial process type; data
loggers, industrial process type

(G-8754)
DATAPRO INTERNATIONAL INC
Also Called: Keydata International
201 Circle Dr N Ste 101 (08854-3723)
P.O. Box 1267, South Plainfield (07080-
9267)
PHONE....................................732 868-0588
Fax: 732 868-6356
George Wu, *President*
▲ EMP: 36
SQ FT: 24,000
SALES (est): 4.5MM **Privately Held**
WEB: www.dataprocorp.com
SIC: 5045 5961 7373 7379 Computers,
peripherals & software; computers & pe-
ripheral equipment, mail order; computer
integrated systems design; computer re-
lated consulting services; electronic com-
puters

(G-8755)
DEOSEN USA INC
1140 Stelton Rd Ste 205 (08854-5291)
PHONE....................................908 382-6518
Lawrence Herbolsheimer, *CEO*
▲ EMP: 6
SQ FT: 1,500
SALES: 575.7K
SALES (corp-wide): 105.1MM **Privately Held**
SIC: 2099 Food preparations
PA: Deosen Biochemical Science And
Technology Ltd.
No.89, An'ping Road, Linzi District
Zibo 25543
533 721-1374

(G-8756)
DESIGN & MOLDING SERVICES INC
25 Howard St (08854-1496)
PHONE....................................732 752-0300
Fax: 732 752-9672
John L Fontenelli, *Senior Partner*
Jerry Fontenelli, *Principal*
Robert Malenchek, *Principal*
EMP: 150 EST: 1968
SQ FT: 73,000

SALES (est): 15.5MM **Privately Held**
WEB: www.designmold.com
SIC: 3089 Injection molding of plastics;
molding primary plastic

(G-8757)
DFI-ITOX LLC
15 Corporate Pl S Ste 201 (08854-6107)
PHONE....................................732 562-0693
Ping Liu, *President*
Gavin Chan, *General Mgr*
David Lu, *General Mgr*
Eric Oo, *Engineer*
Leo Martin, *Sales Staff*
▲ EMP: 40
SQ FT: 82,000
SALES (est): 13.3MM **Privately Held**
WEB: www.itox.com
SIC: 5045 3571 Computer peripheral
equipment; electronic computers

(G-8758)
DIABETO INC
200 Centennial Ave # 200 (08854-3950)
PHONE....................................646 397-3175
Shreekant Pawar, *CEO*
Hemanshu Jain, *COO*
Kirk Treasure, *Sales Staff*
EMP: 5
SQ FT: 100
SALES (est): 351.4K **Privately Held**
SIC: 3841 3845 7371 Diagnostic appara-
tus, medical; electromedical equipment;
computer software development & appli-
cations
PA: Livongo Health, Inc.
444 N Michigan Ave # 2880
Chicago IL 60611

(G-8759)
DPK CONSULTING LLC
220 Old New Brunswick Rd # 201
(08854-3757)
PHONE....................................732 764-0100
Steven Parents, *Owner*
Judi Skalak, *Opers Staff*
Steven D Parent, *Mng Member*
Jonathan Stuhl, *Manager*
EMP: 13
SQ FT: 900
SALES (est): 1.3MM **Privately Held**
SIC: 8713 1389 Photogrammetric engi-
neering; testing, measuring, surveying &
analysis services

(G-8760)
DREAM ON ME INDUSTRIES INC (PA)
1532 S Washington Ave # 1 (08854-3947)
PHONE....................................732 752-7220
Mark Serure, *Ch of Bd*
Shareva Bacchus, *Opers Mgr*
Morris Srour, *Prdtn Mgr*
Charles Plittman, *CFO*
Robert Omansky, *VP Sales*
▲ EMP: 100
SQ FT: 150,000
SALES (est): 28.8MM **Privately Held**
WEB: www.babieskingdom.com
SIC: 2511 Children's wood furniture

(G-8761)
DYNAMIC METALS INC
1713 S 2nd St (08854-1741)
PHONE....................................908 769-0522
Fax: 908 769-5057
Michael Wright, *CEO*
Larry Parish, *President*
James R Moore, *Vice Pres*
Douglas D Parsons, *Vice Pres*
Robert Paxson, *Vice Pres*
EMP: 25
SQ FT: 125,000
SALES (est): 28.4MM **Privately Held**
SIC: 5051 3914 Metals service centers &
offices; steel; stainless steel ware

(G-8762)
ELVI PHARMA LLC
60 Ethel Rd W Ste 1 (08854-5995)
PHONE....................................732 640-2707
Yovanny Garcia, *Mng Member*
EMP: 10
SALES: 1.5MM **Privately Held**
SIC: 2834 Pharmaceutical preparations

(G-8763)
EMC PAVING LLC
57 Justice St (08854-5425)
PHONE..................................908 636-1054
John J Hanrahan, *Principal*
EMP: 7
SALES (est): 152.3K Privately Held
SIC: 3572 Computer storage devices

(G-8764)
EVONIK CORPORATION
2 Turner Pl (08854-3839)
PHONE..................................732 981-5000
Marnie Phillips, *Export Mgr*
Ashish Guha, *Research*
Janice Whitmore, *Empl Benefits*
Helen Liao, *Sales Staff*
Ahmed Nousser, *Sales Staff*
EMP: 61
SALES (corp-wide): 2.4B Privately Held
SIC: 2869 Industrial organic chemicals
HQ: Evonik Corporation
299 Jefferson Rd
Parsippany NJ 07054
973 929-8000

(G-8765)
EVONIK CORPORATION
2 Turner Pl (08854-3839)
PHONE..................................503 907-1210
Burkhard Zoller, *Branch Mgr*
EMP: 22
SALES (corp-wide): 2.4B Privately Held
SIC: 2819 Silica compounds
HQ: Evonik Corporation
299 Jefferson Rd
Parsippany NJ 07054
973 929-8000

(G-8766)
EXHIBIT CO INC
239 Old New Brunswick Rd (08854-3712)
PHONE..................................732 465-1070
Francesco Geraci, *President*
▲ EMP: 26
SQ FT: 60,000
SALES (est): 3.9MM Privately Held
WEB: www.exhibitcompanyinc.com
SIC: 3993 Signs & advertising specialties

(G-8767)
FLAVOR SOLUTIONS INC
120 New England Ave (08854-4127)
PHONE..................................732 354-1931
William May, *President*
EMP: 5
SQ FT: 40,000
SALES (est): 1.1MM Privately Held
SIC: 2087 Extracts, flavoring

(G-8768)
G & W LABORATORIES INC
Also Called: G W Laboratories
1551 S Washington Ave (08854-6700)
PHONE..................................732 474-0729
EMP: 85
SALES (corp-wide): 269.7MM Privately
Held
SIC: 2834 Pharmaceutical preparations
PA: G & W Laboratories, Inc.
111 Coolidge St
South Plainfield NJ 07080
908 753-2000

(G-8769)
GOLD SIGNATURE
INCORPORATED
1260 Stelton Rd (08854-5282)
PHONE..................................732 777-9170
Raymond Morris, *President*
Gloria Morris, *Corp Secy*
EMP: 6
SALES (est): 490K Privately Held
SIC: 3911 5094 Jewelry, precious metal;
jewelry

(G-8770)
GORGIAS PRESS
46 Orris Ave (08854-5710)
PHONE..................................732 699-0343
George A Kiraz, *Partner*
▲ EMP: 6
SALES (est): 489.6K Privately Held
WEB: www.gorgiaspress.com
SIC: 2741 Miscellaneous publishing

(G-8771)
GRAPHIC PRESENTATIONS
SYSTEMS
Also Called: Graphic Systems
262 Old New Brnswk Rd F (08854-3756)
PHONE..................................732 981-1120
Fax: 732 981-1540
Kevin Keizer, *President*
Michael Williams, *Prdtn Mgr*
Kris Harrison, *Manager*
Michael Yannotta, *Manager*
Kenneth Haus, *Administration*
EMP: 19
SQ FT: 28,000
SALES (est): 2.4MM Privately Held
WEB: www.gpsinj.com
SIC: 3993 Displays & cutouts, window &
lobby

(G-8772)
HEALTH AND NATURAL BEAUTY
USA
Also Called: Health & Natural Beauty
140 Ethel Rd W Ste W (08854-5951)
PHONE..................................732 640-1830
Sayed Ibrahim, *President*
Russ Pritchard, *Chief Mktg Ofcr*
EMP: 12
SALES: 5MM Privately Held
SIC: 5999 2844 Toiletries, cosmetics &
perfumes; oral preparations

(G-8773)
HERBAKRAFT INCORPORATED
121 Ethel Rd W Ste 6 (08854-5952)
PHONE..................................732 463-1000
Fax: 732 463-3336
Nisha Khanijow, *President*
Denis Semana, *Business Mgr*
Vinod Khanijow, *Exec VP*
Lissett Jaquez, *Vice Pres*
Terumi Nishiyama, *Vice Pres*
▲ EMP: 11
SQ FT: 6,000
SALES (est): 2.3MM Privately Held
SIC: 2833 Drugs & herbs: grading, grinding
& milling

(G-8774)
HOMECO LLC
739 South Ave (08854-1472)
PHONE..................................732 802-7733
Schmiley Schick, *Mng Member*
Aaron Kedz,
◆ EMP: 22
SQ FT: 43,000
SALES: 17MM Privately Held
SIC: 3942 3634 Housewares, excluding
cooking appliances & utensils; dolls &
stuffed toys

(G-8775)
HORIBA INSTRUMENTS INC
Spex Forensics Group
20 Knightsbridge Rd (08854-3913)
PHONE..................................732 623-8335
Eric Teboul, *Branch Mgr*
EMP: 50
SALES (corp-wide): 1.7B Privately Held
SIC: 3641 Ultraviolet lamps
HQ: Horiba Instruments Incorporated
9755 Research Dr
Irvine CA 92618
949 250-4811

(G-8776)
HORIBA INSTRUMENTS INC
Also Called: Horiba Scientific
20 Knightsbridge Rd (08854-3913)
PHONE..................................732 494-8660
Fax: 732 494-8705
▲ EMP: 198
SQ FT: 49,000
SALES: 45.5MM
SALES (corp-wide): 1.7B Privately Held
WEB: www.horiba.com
SIC: 3826 Mfg Analytical Instruments
HQ: Horiba Instruments Incorporated
9755 Research Dr
Irvine CA 92618
949 250-4811

(G-8777)
HUMANSCALE CORPORATION
220 Circle Dr N (08854-3705)
PHONE..................................732 537-2944
Geraint Phillips, *Vice Pres*
Michele Gerards, *Manager*
EMP: 220
SALES (corp-wide): 140.8MM Privately
Held
SIC: 3577 Computer peripheral equipment
PA: Humanscale Corporation
11 E 26th St Fl 7
New York NY 10010
212 725-4749

(G-8778)
INGERSOLL-RAND INTL INC
1 Centennial Ave Ste 101 (08854-3921)
PHONE..................................559 271-4625
Angie Paine, *Credit Mgr*
Melisa Mohn, *Sales Mgr*
James Wood, *Sr Project Mgr*
Jeffrey Armstrong, *Manager*
Paul Syers, *Manager*
EMP: 66
SALES (est): 1.1MM Privately Held
SIC: 3531 Construction machinery

(G-8779)
INGERSOLL-RAND US TRANE
(HQ)
1 Centennial Ave Ste 101 (08854-3921)
P.O. Box 6820 (08855-6820)
PHONE..................................732 652-7100
Michael W Lamach, *CEO*
Steven R Shawley, *CFO*
◆ EMP: 83
SALES (est): 13B Privately Held
SIC: 3585 Refrigeration & heating equip-
ment

(G-8780)
INNO PHARMA LLC
860 Centennial Ave (08854-3918)
PHONE..................................732 885-2939
Fax: 732 885-1248
Roger Smith, *CFO*
EMP: 10
SALES (est): 809.1K Privately Held
SIC: 2834 Medicines, capsuled or ampuled

(G-8781)
INNOVANCE INC
Also Called: Innovance Networks
15 Corporate Pl S Ste 101 (08854-6107)
PHONE..................................732 529-2300
EMP: 0 EST: 2000
SALES (est): 6.5MM Privately Held
SIC: 3661 Fiber Optic Communications

(G-8782)
INTELLECT DESIGN ARENA INC
(HQ)
Also Called: INTELLECT SEEC
20 Corporate Pl S (08854-6144)
PHONE..................................732 769-1037
Pranav Pasricha, *CEO*
Ravindra Koka, *President*
Keith Keir, *Partner*
Uppili Srinivasan, *COO*
EMP: 18
SQ FT: 8,000
SALES: 12.5MM
SALES (corp-wide): 225.8MM Privately
Held
SIC: 7372 Prepackaged software
PA: Polaris Consulting & Services Limited
Foundation, 34, It Highway
Chennai TN 60310
443 987-4000

(G-8783)
INTERNTONAL FRAGRANCE
TECH INC
Also Called: I F T
140 Centennial Ave (08854-3908)
PHONE..................................770 345-3079
Fax: 770 345-3086
Stuart Zlotnik, *President*
EMP: 34
SQ FT: 25,000

SALES (est): 5MM
SALES (corp-wide): 3.1B Privately Held
WEB: www.agilexfandf.com
SIC: 2869 2844 Perfumes, flavorings &
food additives; toilet preparations
HQ: Agilex Flavors & Fragrances, Inc.
140 Centennial Ave
Piscataway NJ 08854
732 885-0702

(G-8784)
JC MACELROY CO INC (PA)
91 Ethel Rd W (08854-5955)
P.O. Box 850 (08855-0850)
PHONE..................................732 572-7100
Fax: 732 572-7112
Scott J Spota, *President*
Douglas Steiner, *General Mgr*
Jeffrey Spota, *Vice Pres*
Justin Chirdon, *Project Mgr*
Thomas Normant, *Purchasing*
◆ EMP: 55 EST: 1932
SQ FT: 17,000
SALES (est): 29.9MM Privately Held
WEB: www.macelroy.com
SIC: 3441 5088 3452 3564 Fabricated
structural metal; marine crafts & supplies;
bolts, metal; blowers & fans; manufac-
tured hardware (general)

(G-8785)
JOHNSON & JOHNSON
35 Azalea Pl (08854-7500)
PHONE..................................732 524-0400
EMP: 80
SALES (corp-wide): 76.4B Publicly Held
SIC: 2676 Feminine hygiene paper prod-
ucts
PA: Johnson & Johnson
1 Johnson And Johnson Plz
New Brunswick NJ 08933
732 524-0400

(G-8786)
LOG STORM SECURITY INC
1551 S Washington Ave # 401
(08854-6700)
PHONE..................................732 393-6000
Andy Gleason, *Manager*
Denae Dalia, *Info Tech Mgr*
Shelley Lamberta, *Director*
EMP: 30 EST: 2013
SALES: 3MM Privately Held
SIC: 7372 Application computer software

(G-8787)
LUBRIZOL CORPORATION
377 Hoes Ln Ste 210 (08854-4153)
PHONE..................................732 981-0149
Jean Bryant, *CEO*
EMP: 7
SALES (corp-wide): 242.1B Publicly
Held
SIC: 2899 Chemical preparations
HQ: The Lubrizol Corporation
29400 Lakeland Blvd
Wickliffe OH 44092
440 943-4200

(G-8788)
MACHINE ATOMATED CTRL
TECH LLC
1308 Centennial Ave # 109 (08854-4324)
PHONE..................................732 921-8935
Carl Macalalad,
EMP: 4
SALES: 250K Privately Held
SIC: 7373 7372 Computer-aided engi-
neering (CAE) systems service; business
oriented computer software

(G-8789)
MANDIP INC
240 Woodrow Ave W (08854-2903)
PHONE..................................732 752-4875
Dipak Patel, *Principal*
EMP: 5 EST: 2010
SALES (est): 168.2K Privately Held
SIC: 2711 Newspapers

(G-8790)
MARK ALAN PRINTING &
GRAPHICS
Also Called: Sir Speedy
1032 Stelton Rd Ste 2 (08854-4333)
PHONE..................................732 981-9011

▲ = Import ▼=Export
◆ =Import/Export

Fax: 732 981-1121
Mark Yanofsky, *President*
EMP: 4
SQ FT: 1,250
SALES (est): 584.8K **Privately Held**
SIC: 2752 Commercial printing, litho-graphic

(G-8791)
MICHAEL ANTHONY SIGN DSIGN INC
Also Called: Michael Anthony Sign & Awng Co
250 Stelton Rd Ste 1 (08854-3285)
PHONE..........................732 453-6120
Michael Bradley, *President*
EMP: 25
SQ FT: 44,000
SALES (est): 4MM **Privately Held**
WEB: www.masign.com
SIC: 3993 3444 Electric signs; awnings & canopies

(G-8792)
MILLSON PRECISION MACHINING
145 11th St (08854-1954)
PHONE..........................732 424-1700
Fax: 732 424-0808
Bryan Miller Sr, *President*
Bryan Miller Jr, *Vice Pres*
EMP: 6
SQ FT: 3,600
SALES (est): 500K **Privately Held**
WEB: www.mastercamedu.com
SIC: 3599 Machine shop, jobbing & repair

(G-8793)
MONTROSE MOLDERS CORPORATION
25 Howard St (08854-1435)
PHONE..........................908 754-3030
William Wilson, *Principal*
Lori Guarino, *Project Mgr*
EMP: 28 EST: 2013
SALES (est): 6.7MM **Privately Held**
SIC: 3089 Molding primary plastic

(G-8794)
MSN PHARMACEUTICALS INC
20 Duke Rd (08854-3714)
PHONE..........................908 360-1500
Bharat Chintapathy, *President*
Steven Beagle, *Admin Sec*
▲ **EMP:** 6
SQ FT: 1,679
SALES (est): 874.6K **Privately Held**
SIC: 2834 Druggists' preparations (pharmaceuticals)
PA: Msn Laboratories Private Limited
Msn House, Plot No. C-24
Hyderabad TS 50001

(G-8795)
NETWORK TYPESETTING INC
1637 Stelton Rd Ste B4 (08854-5961)
PHONE..........................732 819-0949
Marty Perzan, *President*
EMP: 4
SALES (est): 220K **Privately Held**
SIC: 2791 Typesetting

(G-8796)
NEWARK MORNING LEDGER CO
Also Called: Star Ledger
20 Duke Rd (08854-3714)
PHONE..........................732 560-1560
Fax: 732 560-0230
Jay Lustig, *Editor*
Tara Oliver, *Editor*
Joe Maker, *Manager*
Anthony Venutolo, *Director*
EMP: 200
SALES (corp-wide): 217.5MM **Privately Held**
SIC: 2711 Newspapers, publishing & printing
PA: Newark Morning Ledger Co.
1 Gateway Ctr Ste 1100
Newark NJ 07102
973 392-4141

(G-8797)
NGENIOUS SOLUTIONS INC
30 Knightsbridge Rd # 525 (08854-3948)
PHONE..........................732 873-3385
Nilesh Mehta, *CEO*
EMP: 7 EST: 2005
SQ FT: 100
SALES (est): 230.5K **Privately Held**
SIC: 7371 7372 Computer software development & applications; computer software systems analysis & design, custom; computer software development; software programming applications; application computer software

(G-8798)
PARKWAY PLASTICS INC
561 Stelton Rd (08854-3868)
PHONE..........................732 752-3636
Fax: 732 752-2192
Ed Rowan, *CEO*
Edward W Rowan III, *President*
Shirley Alvarez, *QC Mgr*
Kirstin Rowan Kelly, *Treasurer*
Ned Rowan, *Marketing Mgr*
◆ **EMP:** 48 EST: 1954
SQ FT: 30,000
SALES (est): 6.2MM **Privately Held**
WEB: www.parkwayjars.com
SIC: 3089 Jars, plastic

(G-8799)
PEPSI-COLA METRO BTLG CO INC
Also Called: Pepsico
2200 New Brunswick Ave (08854-2746)
PHONE..........................732 424-3000
Fax: 732 424-3259
Mark Opdyke, *General Mgr*
Tim McCormick, *Sales Staff*
William Warren, *Marketing Staff*
Lou Allegretto, *Manager*
Cathy Bodnar, *Director*
EMP: 400
SALES (corp-wide): 63.5B **Publicly Held**
WEB: www.pbg.com
SIC: 2086 Carbonated soft drinks, bottled & canned
HQ: Pepsi-Cola Metropolitan Bottling Company, Inc.
1111 Westchester Ave
White Plains NY 10604
914 767-6000

(G-8800)
PHARMASOURCE INTERNATIONAL LLC
1090 Stelton Rd (08854-5201)
PHONE..........................732 985-6182
EMP: 6
SALES (est): 510K **Privately Held**
SIC: 2834 3841 Mfg Pharmaceutical Preparations Mfg Surgical/Medical Instruments

(G-8801)
POLONICA INC
147 Ethel Rd W (08854-5928)
PHONE..........................732 855-0008
Fax: 732 855-9436
Marek Pyrycz, *President*
▲ **EMP:** 5
SQ FT: 18,000
SALES (est): 2.1MM **Privately Held**
SIC: 2033 Fruit juices: packaged in cans, jars, etc.

(G-8802)
PREMIERE RACEWAY SYS LLC
230 Saint Nicholas Ave (08854)
PHONE..........................732 629-7715
William Wilson, *CEO*
Michael Sweeney, *COO*
Susan Linder,
James Williams,
EMP: 5
SALES (est): 410K **Privately Held**
SIC: 3089 Plastic hardware & building products

(G-8803)
PROSPECT GROUP LLC
Also Called: Yes Pac
260 Centennial Ave (08854-2947)
PHONE..........................718 635-4007

Eli Weinfeld,
EMP: 12 EST: 2005
SALES (est): 1.3MM **Privately Held**
SIC: 2656 Cups, paper: made from purchased material

(G-8804)
QUALITY SHEET METAL & WLDG INC
23 Clawson St (08854-2116)
PHONE..........................732 469-7111
Fax: 732 752-2266
Raymond Kavanagh, *President*
Ed Eager, *Vice Pres*
David Doll, *Manager*
EMP: 16 EST: 1997
SQ FT: 8,600
SALES (est): 3.9MM **Privately Held**
SIC: 3444 Sheet metal specialties, not stamped

(G-8805)
RESEARCH & EDUCATION ASSN
61 Ethel Rd W (08854-5969)
PHONE..........................732 819-8880
Fax: 732 819-8808
Carl M Fuchs, *President*
Everett Scherrer, *President*
John Cording, *Vice Pres*
Larry Kling, *Vice Pres*
Pamela Weston, *Vice Pres*
EMP: 30
SQ FT: 40,000
SALES (est): 3.2MM
SALES (corp-wide): 3.6B **Publicly Held**
WEB: www.rea.com
SIC: 2731 Book publishing
HQ: Courier Communications Llc
15 Wellman Ave
North Chelmsford MA 01863
978 251-6000

(G-8806)
ROBERTET FLAVORS INC
Also Called: Robertet Flavors & Fragrances
10 Colonial Dr (08854-4114)
PHONE..........................732 271-1804
Bob Murphy, *Manager*
Lisa Drake, *Commercial*
EMP: 10
SALES (corp-wide): 273.9MM **Privately Held**
SIC: 2087 2023 Powders, flavoring (except drink); dry, condensed, evaporated dairy products
HQ: Robertet Flavors, Inc.
10 Colonial Dr
Piscataway NJ 08854
732 981-8300

(G-8807)
SATURN BEAUTY GROUP LLC
140 Ethel Rd W Ste G (08854-5951)
P.O. Box 683, Edison (08818-0683)
PHONE..........................908 561-5000
Ravi Verg, *CEO*
Mira Verg, *Mng Member*
EMP: 4
SQ FT: 3,500
SALES (est): 12MM **Privately Held**
SIC: 2844 Toilet preparations

(G-8808)
SCALABLE SYSTEMS INC
15 Corporate Pl S Ste 222 (08854-6107)
PHONE..........................732 993-4320
Sam Biswal, *President*
Jack Francis, *Vice Pres*
Suman Biswal, *Manager*
EMP: 30
SALES (est): 3.4MM **Privately Held**
WEB: www.scalable-systems.com
SIC: 7372 8748 Application computer software; systems analysis & engineering consulting services

(G-8809)
SHANGHAI FREEMEN AMERICAS LLC (HQ)
377 Hoes Ln Ste 240 (08854-4138)
PHONE..........................732 981-1288
Oyang Li, *CEO*
Hanks Li, *President*
Andrew Falocco, *Marketing Mgr*
▲ **EMP:** 20
SQ FT: 2,000

SALES (est): 2.1MM
SALES (corp-wide): 46.8MM **Privately Held**
SIC: 2833 Vitamins, natural or synthetic: bulk, uncompounded
PA: Shanghai Freemen Lifescience Co., Ltd.
No.19 Building, 2500 Lane,Xiupu Rd.,Pudong New Area
Shanghai 20131
216 118-3110

(G-8810)
SHASUN USA INC
15 Corporate Pl S Ste 222 (08854-6107)
PHONE..........................732 465-0700
Fax: 732 668-0320
Abhaya Kumar Shankarlal, *CEO*
N Govindarajan, *CEO*
Jitesh Devendra, *President*
Michel Spagnol, *President*
▲ **EMP:** 13 EST: 1999
SALES (est): 2.2MM **Privately Held**
WEB: www.shasun.com
SIC: 2834 Pharmaceutical preparations

(G-8811)
SIVANTOS INC (DH)
10 Constitution Ave (08854-6145)
PHONE..........................732 562-6600
Steve Mahon, *CEO*
Brian Kinnerk, *CEO*
Marie Hepola, *Vice Pres*
Naahid Kajiji, *Financial Analy*
Johnathan Davis, *Sales Mgr*
▲ **EMP:** 357
SQ FT: 83,000
SALES (est): 306.9MM **Privately Held**
WEB: www.siemens-hearing.com
SIC: 3842 Orthopedic appliances; hearing aids
HQ: Sivantos Pte. Ltd.
18 Tai Seng Street
Singapore 53977
637 096-66

(G-8812)
SNACK INNOVATIONS INC (PA)
Also Called: Gourmet Basics
41 Ethel Rd W (08854-5969)
PHONE..........................718 509-9366
Allen Benz, *CEO*
Jack Benz, *Vice Pres*
▲ **EMP:** 20
SQ FT: 30,000
SALES (est): 4.6MM **Privately Held**
SIC: 2096 Potato chips & similar snacks

(G-8813)
SOLIDIA TECHNOLOGIES INC
11 Colonial Dr (08854-4113)
PHONE..........................908 315-5901
Thomas Schuler, *CEO*
Bo Boylan, *Vice Pres*
Dhamo Srinivasan, *Vice Pres*
Stephen Blackman, *Engineer*
Daniel Gonzalez, *Manager*
▲ **EMP:** 29
SALES (est): 10MM **Privately Held**
SIC: 3531 Construction machinery

(G-8814)
SOZIO INC
51 Ethel Rd W (08854-5969)
PHONE..........................732 572-5600
Fax: 908 755-6006
Arnaud Moor, *President*
Dominique Bouley, *COO*
Christophe Politi, *Plant Mgr*
Melanie Ritter, *Purch Mgr*
Jack Stanaszek, *Natl Sales Mgr*
◆ **EMP:** 60
SQ FT: 20,000
SALES (est): 17.4MM
SALES (corp-wide): 9.5MM **Privately Held**
WEB: www.jesozio.com
SIC: 2844 Cosmetic preparations
HQ: Sozio J Et E -Descollonges
6 Rue Barbes
Levallois Perret 92300
181 930-072

GEOGRAPHIC

(G-8815)
SPECTRUM PLASTICS
250 Circle Dr N (08854-3705)
PHONE..............................732 564-1899
Ben Tran, *Owner*
EMP: 5
SALES (est): 881.7K Privately Held
SIC: 2673 Plastic bags: made from purchased materials

(G-8816)
SPEM CORPORATION
403 Bell St (08854-2349)
PHONE..............................732 356-3366
Fax: 732 356-5922
Satish Patel, *President*
John Seto, *Vice Pres*
Paul Ruggierio, *Admin Sec*
EMP: 23
SQ FT: 17,500
SALES (est): 1.7MM Privately Held
SIC: 3672 3679 3931 Printed circuit boards; harness assemblies for electronic use: wire or cable; synthesizers, music

(G-8817)
STAR CREATIONS INC (PA)
Also Called: Sumangel Jewellers
1506 Stelton Rd (08854-5915)
PHONE..............................212 221-3570
Kavita Khandelwal, *President*
Rekha Kenoongo, *Vice Pres*
EMP: 2
SQ FT: 2,500
SALES (est): 10MM Privately Held
WEB: www.starcreation.com
SIC: 1499 Gemstone & industrial diamond mining

(G-8818)
STRATO INC
100 New England Ave Ste 1 (08854-4144)
PHONE..............................732 981-1515
Michael J Foxx, *CEO*
Steven Foxx, *Corp Secy*
Michael Corridon, *CFO*
Sarika Russo, *Financial Analy*
Dorothy Putyrske, *Administration*
▲ EMP: 100
SQ FT: 100,000
SALES (est): 42.5MM Privately Held
WEB: www.stratoinc.com
SIC: 3743 Railroad equipment

(G-8819)
SWAPSHUB COMPANY INC
15 Corporate Pl S Ste 130 (08854-6117)
PHONE..............................732 529-4813
Mani Pillai, *President*
Jamal Mohamed, *Info Tech Mgr*
EMP: 6
SALES (est): 273.3K Privately Held
SIC: 7372 Business oriented computer software

(G-8820)
T & P MACHINE SHOP INC
600 Prospect Ave Ste E (08854-1414)
PHONE..............................732 424-9141
Tony Pasquale, *President*
EMP: 5
SALES (est): 550K Privately Held
SIC: 3599 Machine shop, jobbing & repair

(G-8821)
TECOGEN INC
417 Bell St (08854-2349)
PHONE..............................732 356-5601
EMP: 28
SALES (corp-wide): 33.2MM Publicly Held
SIC: 3585 Air conditioning units, complete: domestic or industrial
PA: Tecogen Inc.
   45 1st Ave
   Waltham MA 02451
   781 622-6400

(G-8822)
TEKLTD (PA)
95 Mitchell Ave (08854-5556)
PHONE..............................732 463-2100
John C Lee, *President*
EMP: 8

SALES: 4MM Privately Held
WEB: www.tekltd.com
SIC: 3714 Motor vehicle parts & accessories

(G-8823)
THALES AVIONICS INC (HQ)
140 Centennial Ave (08854-3908)
PHONE..............................732 242-6300
Alan Pellegrini, *President*
Kenneth Coleman, *General Mgr*
Donna Makara-Diaz, *Project Mgr*
Ludovic Chouasne, *Finance Dir*
Wayne Zsamba, *Manager*
▲ EMP: 168 EST: 1977
SQ FT: 61,000
SALES (est): 88.3MM
SALES (corp-wide): 305.4MM Privately Held
SIC: 7699 3728 8711 Aircraft & heavy equipment repair services; aircraft parts & equipment; aviation &/or aeronautical engineering
PA: Thales
   Carpe Diem Esplanade Nord Tour Aig
   Courbevoie 92400
   157 778-000

(G-8824)
THERAPEUTIC PROTEINS INC
20 New England Ave (08854-4101)
PHONE..............................312 620-1500
Peter F Moesta, *CEO*
Zafeer Ahmad, *CEO*
Thomas L Flynn III, *President*
Sarfaraz K Niazi PHD, *Chairman*
Michael W Washabaugh, *Security Dir*
▲ EMP: 19
SALES (est): 6.8MM Privately Held
WEB: www.theraproteins.com
SIC: 2834 Pharmaceutical preparations

(G-8825)
TINGLEY RUBBER CORPORATION (PA)
1551 S Washington Ave # 403 (08854-6700)
PHONE..............................800 631-5498
Fax: 908 757-9239
William McCollum, *CEO*
Michael S Zedalis, *President*
Michael Zedalis, *COO*
Roger Brewer, *CFO*
Brad Domagala, *Sales Mgr*
▲ EMP: 32 EST: 1929
SQ FT: 17,000
SALES (est): 10.7MM Privately Held
WEB: www.tingleyrubber.com
SIC: 3021 3069 Protective footwear, rubber or plastic; rubber coated fabrics & clothing

(G-8826)
TMG ENTERPRISES INC (PA)
200 Circle Dr N (08854-3705)
PHONE..............................732 469-2900
Dermot Murphy, *CEO*
Charles Zammit, *Vice Pres*
Letty Murphy, *Admin Sec*
EMP: 30
SQ FT: 11,300
SALES (est): 24.7MM Privately Held
WEB: www.tmg4mail.com
SIC: 7331 8744 2752 Mailing service; facilities support services; commercial printing, offset

(G-8827)
TOLLGRADE COMMUNICATIONS INC
30 Knightsbridge Rd # 602 (08854-3948)
PHONE..............................732 743-6720
Fax: 732 743-0284
EMP: 5
SALES (corp-wide): 262.6MM Privately Held
SIC: 3661 Telephone central office equipment, dial or manual
HQ: Tollgrade Communications, Inc.
   260 Executive Dr 150
   Cranberry Township PA 16066
   724 720-1400

(G-8828)
TRANE INC (DH)
1 Centennial Ave Ste 101 (08854-3921)
P.O. Box 6820 (08855-6820)
PHONE..............................732 652-7100
Michael W Lamach, *CEO*
Jeff Billingsley, *Partner*
Tom Callahan, *Area Mgr*
Willis Lovejoy, *Area Mgr*
Trent Speers, *Area Mgr*
▲ EMP: 238
SALES (est): 13B Privately Held
WEB: www.trane.com
SIC: 3585 Refrigeration & heating equipment

(G-8829)
TRANE US INC
1 Centennial Ave Ste 101 (08854-3921)
PHONE..............................732 652-7100
Christopher Coperchio, *Principal*
Clifford L Tomei, *Principal*
EMP: 140 Privately Held
SIC: 3585 Refrigeration & heating equipment
HQ: Trane U.S. Inc.
   3600 Pammel Creek Rd
   La Crosse WI 54601
   608 787-2000

(G-8830)
TRANSACTION PUBLISHERS INC (PA)
Also Called: Society Trnsaction Periodicals
10 Corporate Pl S Ste 102 (08854-6148)
P.O. Box 383, Rocky Hill (08553-0383)
PHONE..............................732 445-2280
Mary Curtis, *President*
Scott Bramson, *President*
Frank Novak, *Vice Pres*
Michael Celletto, *Accounts Mgr*
Nancy Conine, *Cust Mgr*
◆ EMP: 19 EST: 1963
SQ FT: 5,000
SALES (est): 3.3MM Privately Held
WEB: www.transactionpub.com
SIC: 2721 2731 Periodicals: publishing only; book publishing

(G-8831)
TURQUOISE CHEMISTRY INC
537 New Durham Rd (08854-5314)
PHONE..............................908 561-0002
Teoman Mutlu, *President*
▲ EMP: 10
SALES (est): 1.3MM Privately Held
SIC: 2851 Removers & cleaners

(G-8832)
VALUEMOMENTUM INC (HQ)
220 Old New Brunswick Rd # 100 (08854-3757)
PHONE..............................908 755-0025
Fax: 908 755-0393
Kalyan Kodali, *CEO*
Ravi RAO, *Managing Dir*
Gopimaniraju Samanthapudi, *Chairman*
Swarup Ghosh, *COO*
James Carlucci, *Vice Pres*
EMP: 60
SQ FT: 20,000
SALES (est): 76.5MM Privately Held
WEB: www.valuemomentum.com
SIC: 7373 7371 7372 Systems software development services; computer software development & applications; business oriented computer software

(G-8833)
VASCULOGIC LLC
37 E Burgess Dr (08854-6658)
PHONE..............................908 278-3573
Tim Maguire, *President*
EMP: 5
SALES (est): 360K Privately Held
SIC: 3845 Electromedical equipment

(G-8834)
VASWANI INC
201 Circle Dr N Ste 114 (08854-3723)
PHONE..............................732 377-9794
Ishwar Vaswani, *Branch Mgr*
EMP: 10

SALES (corp-wide): 27MM Privately Held
WEB: www.vaswani.com
SIC: 2521 5021 Chairs, office: padded, upholstered or plain: wood; office & public building furniture
PA: Vaswani, Inc.
   75 Carter Dr Ste 1
   Edison NJ 08817
   877 376-4425

(G-8835)
VIRA INSIGHT LLC
100 Ethel Rd W (08854-5967)
PHONE..............................732 442-6756
Jeff Jones, *CEO*
EMP: 117
SALES (corp-wide): 37.6MM Privately Held
SIC: 2542 Fixtures, store: except wood; office & store showcases & display fixtures
PA: Vira Insight, Llc
   120 Dividend Dr 100
   Coppell TX 75019
   800 366-2345

(G-8836)
WILLIAM KENYON & SONS INC (HQ)
90 Ethel Rd W (08854-5929)
PHONE..............................732 985-8980
Christopher C Kenyon, *Ch of Bd*
William D Clark, *President*
Mike Wheaton, *COO*
Michael Wheaton, *Vice Pres*
▼ EMP: 20 EST: 1937
SQ FT: 42,000
SALES (est): 3MM
SALES (corp-wide): 17.7MM Privately Held
WEB: www.william-kenyon.com
SIC: 3599 2298 3829 3674 Custom machinery; rope, except asbestos & wire; measuring & controlling devices; semiconductors & related devices; miscellaneous fabricated wire products; chemical preparations
PA: William Kenyon & Sons Limited
   Chapel Field Works
   Hyde SK14
   161 308-6030

(G-8837)
YC CABLE (EAST) INC
240 Circle Dr N (08854-3705)
PHONE..............................732 868-0800
Fax: 732 650-9885
Kai Cheng Hsu, *President*
James Hsu, *President*
Jean Shao, *General Mgr*
Bruce Wilson, *Sales Staff*
▲ EMP: 20
SQ FT: 15,000
SALES (est): 6.4MM Privately Held
WEB: www.yceast.com
SIC: 3679 5065 5063 Harness assemblies for electronic use: wire or cable; electronic parts & equipment; electrical apparatus & equipment

(G-8838)
ZIEGLER CHEM & MINERAL CORP (PA)
600 Prospect Ave Ste A (08854-1414)
PHONE..............................732 752-4111
Fax: 732 752-9477
Gordon S Ziegler Jr, *Ch of Bd*
James Febo, *Vice Pres*
William Hyland, *Vice Pres*
Gordon S Ziegler III, *CFO*
Kathy Malanga, *Sales Staff*
▼ EMP: 14 EST: 1962
SQ FT: 3,000
SALES (est): 20.5MM Privately Held
WEB: www.zieglerchemical.com
SIC: 2911 1499 Asphalt or asphaltic materials, made in refineries; gilsonite mining

(G-8839)
ZIEGLER CHEM & MINERAL CORP
Also Called: Allied Asphalt Division
600 Prospect Ave Ste 1 (08854-1414)
PHONE..............................732 752-4111
Paul Gordman, *Plant Mgr*
Jim Febo, *Sales Executive*

▲ = Import ▼=Export
◆ =Import/Export

Paul Gorman, *Branch Mgr*
EMP: 30
SALES (corp-wide): 20.5MM **Privately Held**
WEB: www.zieglerchemical.com
SIC: 1499 2951 Asphalt (native) mining; gilsonite mining; asphalt paving mixtures & blocks
PA: Ziegler Chemical & Mineral Corp.
600 Prospect Ave Ste A
Piscataway NJ 08854
732 752-4111

Pitman
Gloucester County

(G-8840)
COMET TOOL COMPANY INC
651 Lambs Rd (08071-2042)
PHONE..................856 256-1070
Fax: 856 256-1005
Frank L Maatje, *President*
Griff Noon, *Vice Pres*
EMP: 78 EST: 1973
SQ FT: 73,000
SALES (est): 26.7MM **Privately Held**
WEB: www.comet-tool.com
SIC: 3089 Injection molding of plastics

(G-8841)
CROSS MEDICAL SPECIALTIES INC
450 Andbro Dr Unit 7 (08071-1274)
PHONE..................856 589-3288
EMP: 15
SQ FT: 1,200
SALES (est): 1.4MM **Privately Held**
SIC: 7699 3841 Repair Services Mfg Surgical/Medical Instruments

(G-8842)
INOX COMPONENTS
And 553 Rr 55 (08071)
PHONE..................856 256-0800
Fax: 856 256-0736
Michael Duffy, *President*
EMP: 10
SQ FT: 10,000
SALES (est): 1.1MM **Privately Held**
SIC: 3444 Sheet metalwork

(G-8843)
KANE WOOD FUEL
512 Cedar Ave (08071-1815)
PHONE..................856 589-3292
Frank Kane, *Owner*
Marguerite Kane, *Co-Owner*
EMP: 4
SALES (est): 520.8K **Privately Held**
SIC: 2411 5099 Logging; firewood

(G-8844)
REVIEW PRINTING INC
53 E Holly Ave 55 (08071-1198)
PHONE..................856 589-7200
Fax: 856 589-7443
Douglas K Peterson, *President*
Carol Peterson, *Admin Sec*
EMP: 5 EST: 1898
SQ FT: 5,200
SALES (est): 380K **Privately Held**
SIC: 2752 Commercial printing, offset

(G-8845)
SALMON SIGNS
478 W Holly Ave (08071-1302)
PHONE..................856 589-5600
Fax: 856 589-5188
Richard Salmon, *Owner*
EMP: 7 EST: 1960
SQ FT: 15,000
SALES (est): 488K **Privately Held**
WEB: www.richardsalmon.com
SIC: 7389 3993 Sign painting & lettering shop; signs & advertising specialties

(G-8846)
SHERIDAN OPTICAL CO INC
Also Called: Sheridan Optical Lab
108 Clinton Ave (08071-1209)
P.O. Box 8 (08071-0008)
PHONE..................856 582-0963
Fax: 856 582-1970

Edward F Sheridan, *President*
EMP: 21
SQ FT: 2,000
SALES (est): 2.9MM **Privately Held**
SIC: 3827 Optical instruments & lenses

Pittsgrove
Salem County

(G-8847)
PHOENIX GLASS LLC
615 Alvine Rd (08318-4128)
PHONE..................856 692-0100
Fax: 856 696-5155
Charles R Everham, *Owner*
◆ EMP: 47
SALES (est): 7MM **Privately Held**
SIC: 5231 2396 Glass; automotive & apparel trimmings

Pittstown
Hunterdon County

(G-8848)
AJG PACKAGING LLC
10 Northwood Dr (08867-5130)
PHONE..................908 528-6052
Matthew Grimaldi, *Mng Member*
EMP: 5 EST: 2011
SALES: 3.2MM **Privately Held**
SIC: 3565 5084 7389 Bottling machinery: filling, capping, labeling; packaging machinery & equipment;

(G-8849)
BENEDUCE VINEYARD
1 Jeremiah Ln (08867-5168)
PHONE..................908 996-3823
Mike Beneduce Jr, *Principal*
Jen Pollard, *Manager*
EMP: 4 EST: 2011
SALES (est): 332.6K **Privately Held**
SIC: 2084 Wines

(G-8850)
EUROPEAN COUNTRY KITCHENS INC
Also Called: Peer & Picone Woodworking
272 Pittstown Rd (08867-4156)
PHONE..................908 735-6659
David Peer, *President*
EMP: 54
SQ FT: 50,000
SALES (est): 2.9MM **Privately Held**
SIC: 2434 5211 1751 Wood kitchen cabinets; cabinets, kitchen; cabinet & finish carpentry

(G-8851)
SMITTYS DOOR SERVICE INC
170 Oak Grove Rd (08867-4006)
PHONE..................908 284-0506
Tim Smith, *President*
Gwen Smith, *Admin Sec*
EMP: 8
SQ FT: 3,000
SALES (est): 1.5MM **Privately Held**
SIC: 2431 Doors, wood

Plainfield
Union County

(G-8852)
A N LAGGREN AWNGS CANVAS MFG
Also Called: Mark I Interiors
1414 South Ave (07062-1941)
PHONE..................908 756-1948
Fax: 908 756-7560
David Lasser, *President*
Estelle Lasser, *Admin Sec*
EMP: 15
SQ FT: 6,000
SALES (est): 1.9MM **Privately Held**
SIC: 2591 Drapery hardware & blinds & shades

(G-8853)
AMERICAN CODING AND MKG INK CO
1220 North Ave (07062-1796)
PHONE..................908 756-0373
Thomas Sweet, *President*
Jamie Pedinoff, *Admin Sec*
EMP: 7
SQ FT: 5,000
SALES: 980K **Privately Held**
WEB: www.americancoding.com
SIC: 2893 Printing ink

(G-8854)
ARCHITECTURAL IRON DESIGNS
Also Called: Duragates
950 S 2nd St (07063-1302)
PHONE..................908 757-2323
Fax: 908 757-3439
Jayesh Shah, *President*
Allan R Papp, *Chairman*
Joseph Alves, *Sales Mgr*
▲ EMP: 6
SQ FT: 7,000
SALES (est): 1.3MM **Privately Held**
WEB: www.archirondesign.com
SIC: 3446 Architectural metalwork

(G-8855)
ARROW PAPER COMPANY INC (PA)
633 North Ave (07060-1418)
P.O. Box 147, Millburn (07041-0147)
PHONE..................908 756-1111
Fax: 908 756-1131
Jay Gutkin, *President*
Evelyn Gutkin, *Corp Secy*
Daniel Gutkin, *Vice Pres*
EMP: 9
SQ FT: 150,000
SALES (est): 702.6K **Privately Held**
SIC: 2679 5112 Paper products, converted; stationery & office supplies

(G-8856)
CAPITAL CONTRACTING & DESIGN (PA)
640 North Ave (07060-1419)
P.O. Box 1333 (07061-1333)
PHONE..................908 561-8411
Fax: 908 753-2979
Donald W Finley, *President*
Mark McQuillan, *Vice Pres*
Scott Angelica, *Sales Executive*
Michele Reese, *Office Mgr*
EMP: 26
SQ FT: 60,000
SALES: 3MM **Privately Held**
WEB: www.captlfix.com
SIC: 2541 2542 Display fixtures, wood; fixtures: display, office or store: except wood

(G-8857)
DEK TRON INTERNATIONAL CORP
244 E 3rd St (07060-1848)
PHONE..................908 226-1777
Salvador Diespensiera, *President*
Hector Vargas, *Principal*
EMP: 25
SQ FT: 12,000
SALES (est): 3.2MM **Privately Held**
WEB: www.dektroncorp.com
SIC: 3821 Laboratory measuring apparatus

(G-8858)
DUCTWORKS INC
434 W Front St (07060-1122)
P.O. Box 7031, Watchung (07069-0799)
PHONE..................908 754-8190
Fax: 908 754-5773
Dianne Rocco, *Manager*
EMP: 12
SALES (est): 1.3MM **Privately Held**
SIC: 3444 Metal ventilating equipment

(G-8859)
EDWARD P PAUL & CO INC (PA)
525 South Ave (07060-1998)
PHONE..................908 757-4212
Arthur Arditti, *Ch of Bd*
Andrew Arditi, *President*

EMP: 7
SQ FT: 100,000
SALES (est): 559K **Privately Held**
SIC: 2512 5023 Upholstered household furniture; lamps: floor, boudoir, desk

(G-8860)
EDWIN LEONEL RAMIREZ
Also Called: Pin Express
918 Putnam Ave (07060-1842)
PHONE..................732 648-5587
Edwin L Ramirez, *Principal*
EMP: 4
SALES (est): 251.9K **Privately Held**
SIC: 3452 Pins

(G-8861)
F & C PROF ALUM RAILINGS CORP
1149 W Front St (07063-1130)
PHONE..................908 753-8886
Fax: 908 753-8448
Segundo A Flores, *President*
Segundo B Flores, *Vice Pres*
EMP: 25
SALES (est): 5.9MM **Privately Held**
SIC: 3446 Architectural metalwork

(G-8862)
FLECK KNITWEAR CO INC
400 Leland Ave (07062-1606)
PHONE..................908 754-8888
Peter Fleck, *President*
Heinz Fleck, *President*
Ursula Fleck, *Corp Secy*
EMP: 25
SQ FT: 30,000
SALES: 1MM **Privately Held**
SIC: 2253 Sweaters & sweater coats, knit; collar & cuff sets, knit

(G-8863)
H & S FUEL INC
1100 South Ave (07062-1918)
PHONE..................908 769-1362
EMP: 5 EST: 2009
SALES (est): 233.5K **Privately Held**
SIC: 2869 Mfg Industrial Organic Chemicals

(G-8864)
HARSCO CORPORATION
709 Loretta Ter (07062-2104)
PHONE..................908 454-7169
Jim Cook, *Branch Mgr*
EMP: 40
SQ FT: 500
SALES (corp-wide): 1.6B **Publicly Held**
WEB: www.ikgindustries.com
SIC: 5051 3446 Steel; architectural metalwork
PA: Harsco Corporation
350 Poplar Church Rd
Camp Hill PA 17011
717 763-7064

(G-8865)
INJECTRON CORPORATION
Also Called: Detailed Designs
1000 S 2nd St (07063-1306)
P.O. Box 3012 (07063-0012)
PHONE..................908 753-1990
Fax: 908 769-7599
Lou Pollak, *President*
Vincent Robinson, *COO*
Marvin Kaplan, *Vice Pres*
Craig Ford, *QC Mgr*
Larry Kettner, *Info Tech Dir*
▲ EMP: 300 EST: 1959
SQ FT: 300,000
SALES (est): 56.4MM **Privately Held**
SIC: 3089 Injection molding of plastics

(G-8866)
LOB-STER INC
Also Called: Lobster Sports
1118 North Ave (07062-1633)
PHONE..................818 764-6000
Fax: 908 764-6061
Leilani Makuakane, *Manager*
EMP: 5
SALES (est): 267.6K
SALES (corp-wide): 1.6MM **Privately Held**
WEB: www.lobstersports.com
SIC: 3949 Tennis equipment & supplies

PA: Lob-Ster, Inc.
7340 Fulton Ave
North Hollywood CA 91605
818 764-6000

(G-8867)
NEUMANN SHEET METAL INC
759 North Ave (07062-1616)
PHONE..................................908 756-0415
William J McLean, *President*
Lora McLean, *Admin Sec*
EMP: 6
SQ FT: 5,200
SALES (est): 1.1MM **Privately Held**
SIC: 3444 Sheet metal specialties, not
stamped

(G-8868)
NEW INDUSTRIAL FOAM CORP
1355 W Front St Ste 3 (07063-1151)
P.O. Box 3120 (07063-0120)
PHONE..................................908 561-4010
Fax: 908 561-4022
Michael Weisman, *President*
Russell Kussner, *General Mgr*
Robert Weisman, *Corp Secy*
Bruce Klein, *Director*
EMP: 7 EST: 1960
SQ FT: 50,000
SALES (est): 980K **Privately Held**
SIC: 3086 Packaging & shipping materials,
foamed plastic

(G-8869)
NEW JERSEY HARDWOODS INC
1340 W Front St (07063-1127)
PHONE..................................908 754-0990
Ollie Herttua, *President*
Paula Herttua, *General Mgr*
EMP: 30 EST: 1981
SQ FT: 26,000
SALES (est): 5.6MM **Privately Held**
SIC: 5211 2431 Millwork & lumber; mill-
work

(G-8870)
O K TOOL CORPORATION
1233 North Ave (07062-1724)
PHONE..................................908 561-9920
Eric Kiesel, *President*
Theresa Kiesel, *Corp Secy*
Glen Kiesel, *Vice Pres*
▲ **EMP:** 5
SQ FT: 4,000
SALES (est): 410K **Privately Held**
WEB: www.glenmartech.com
SIC: 3599 Machine shop, jobbing & repair

(G-8871)
PAPP IRON WORKS INC
950 S 2nd St (07063-1302)
P.O. Box 3149 (07063-0149)
PHONE..................................908 731-1000
Fax: 908 757-3567
Allan Papp, *President*
Chris Wrobel, *Plant Mgr*
Ken Casale, *Project Mgr*
Thomas Hale, *Project Mgr*
EMP: 70 EST: 1948
SQ FT: 40,000
SALES (est): 17.3MM **Privately Held**
WEB: www.pappironworks.com
SIC: 3446 Architectural metalwork

(G-8872)
RAK FOAM SALES INC
1355 W Front St Ste 2 (07063-1151)
P.O. Box 3248 (07063-0248)
PHONE..................................908 668-1122
Robert Kussner, *President*
Russel Kussner, *Vice Pres*
EMP: 8
SQ FT: 3,000
SALES: 1MM **Privately Held**
SIC: 3069 Weather strip, sponge rubber

(G-8873)
REINCO INC
520 North Ave (07060-1417)
P.O. Box 512 (07061-0512)
PHONE..................................908 755-0921
Erich Reinecker, *President*
Walter Reinecker, *Chairman*
George Braun, *Vice Pres*
▼ **EMP:** 12 EST: 1958
SQ FT: 8,000

SALES (est): 2.4MM **Privately Held**
WEB: www.reinco.com
SIC: 3531 Construction machinery

(G-8874)
UNITED BEDDING INDUSTRIES LLC
Also Called: Ubi
300 W 4th St (07060-4233)
PHONE..................................908 668-0220
Fax: 908 668-4870
Jose Furman,
EMP: 25
SQ FT: 60,000
SALES (est): 3.4MM **Privately Held**
SIC: 2392 Blankets, comforters & beddings

Plainsboro
Middlesex County

(G-8875)
BAGEL STREET
660 Plainsboro Rd Ste 18 (08536-3002)
PHONE..................................609 936-1755
Fax: 609 936-7332
James Rohr, *Owner*
Doug Rohr, *Co-Owner*
EMP: 25
SALES (est): 734.4K **Privately Held**
SIC: 5461 5812 2051 Bagels; eating
places; bread, cake & related products

(G-8876)
BIOPHORE LLC
4510 Quail Ridge Dr (08536-4227)
PHONE..................................609 275-3713
EMP: 2
SALES: 3MM **Privately Held**
SIC: 8731 2834 8748 Coml Physical Re-
search Mfg Pharmaceutical Preps Busi-
ness Consulting Svcs

(G-8877)
BRISTOL-MYERS SQUIBB COMPANY
777 Scudders Mill Rd (08536-1615)
PHONE..................................609 897-3771
Fax: 609 897-6117
Angie Bernstein, *Finance*
James Cline, *Sales Staff*
Susan Sweeney, *Marketing Staff*
Kristian Hubbard, *Manager*
Ramesh Modali, *Manager*
EMP: 34
SALES (corp-wide): 20.7B **Publicly Held**
SIC: 2834 Pharmaceutical preparations
PA: Bristol-Myers Squibb Company
430 E 29th St Fl 14
New York NY 10016
212 546-4000

(G-8878)
COMMEATUS LLC
5216 Fox Run Dr (08536-3467)
PHONE..................................847 772-5314
Sibtain Shabbir, *CEO*
EMP: 10
SALES (est): 400.4K **Privately Held**
SIC: 3429 7389 Manufactured hardware
(general);

(G-8879)
CSONKA WORLDWIDE
501 Plainsboro Rd Ph (08536-2070)
PHONE..................................609 514-2766
Fax: 609 514-7329
Michael Chunko, *President*
▲ **EMP:** 30 EST: 1996
SQ FT: 4,000
SALES (est): 4.2MM **Privately Held**
WEB: www.csonka.com
SIC: 5075 2121 5194 3564 Dehumidi-
fiers, except portable; cigars; cigars; air
purification equipment; humidifiers & de-
humidifiers

(G-8880)
DERMA SCIENCES INC (HQ)
Also Called: Integra
311 Enterprise Dr (08536-3344)
PHONE..................................609 514-4744
Fax: 609 514-0502
Stephen T Wills, *CEO*

Marideth Wolf, *Partner*
Frederic Eigner, *Exec VP*
Les Burrows, *Vice Pres*
Ron Ingram, *Vice Pres*
▲ **EMP:** 117
SQ FT: 15,065
SALES: 84.4MM **Publicly Held**
WEB: www.dermasciences.com
SIC: 3842 2211 2834 Surgical appliances
& supplies; bandages & dressings; band-
ages, gauzes & surgical fabrics, cotton;
pharmaceutical preparations; ointments

(G-8881)
FEHU JEWEL LLC
2912 Quail Ridge Dr (08536-4070)
PHONE..................................609 297-5491
Jigar Narola,
EMP: 150
SALES (est): 3.7MM **Privately Held**
SIC: 3911 Jewelry, precious metal

(G-8882)
G S BABU & CO
57 Woodland Dr (08536-2053)
PHONE..................................732 939-5190
Prem Babu, *Owner*
Jayanthi Haribabu, *Mktg Dir*
EMP: 10
SALES (est): 370K **Privately Held**
SIC: 3199 Leggings or chaps, canvas or
leather

(G-8883)
GADDE PHARMA LLC
41 Madison Dr (08536-2320)
PHONE..................................609 651-7772
Vijaya Gadde, *Principal*
EMP: 5
SALES (est): 325K **Privately Held**
SIC: 2834 Pharmaceutical preparations

(G-8884)
GLYSORTIA LLC
281 Hampshire Dr (08536-4336)
P.O. Box 708, Hudson WI (54016-0708)
PHONE..................................715 426-5358
Rick Beardmore,
◆ **EMP:** 4
SALES (est): 690.2K **Privately Held**
SIC: 2879 Fungicides, herbicides

(G-8885)
INDOTRONIX INTERNATIONAL CORP
101 Morgan Ln Ste 210 (08536-3345)
PHONE..................................609 750-0700
Fax: 609 750-1212
Venkat Mantha, *Branch Mgr*
EMP: 4
SALES (corp-wide): 20.6MM **Privately
Held**
WEB: www.iic.com
SIC: 7379 7371 7372 Computer related
consulting services; custom computer
programming services; computer software
development; prepackaged software
HQ: Indotronix International Corp
687 Lee Rd Ste 250
Rochester NY 14606
845 473-1137

(G-8886)
INPHOT INC
13 Blossom Hill Dr (08536-3122)
PHONE..................................609 799-7172
Krishna Linga, *CEO*
EMP: 4
SALES (est): 462.5K **Privately Held**
SIC: 3674 Semiconductors & related de-
vices

(G-8887)
INTEGRA LFSCNCES HOLDINGS CORP (PA)
311 Enterprise Dr (08536-3344)
PHONE..................................609 275-0500
Fax: 609 936-2263
Stuart M Essig, *Ch of Bd*
Peter J Arduini, *President*
Robert T Davis Jr, *President*
Jerry Klawitter, *President*
Mari Klaseen, *Business Mgr*
▼ **EMP:** 200

SALES: 1.1B **Publicly Held**
WEB: www.integra-ls.com
SIC: 3841 2836 3842 Surgical & medical
instruments; biological products, except
diagnostic; surgical appliances & supplies; implants, surgical

(G-8888)
INTEGRA LIFESCIENCES CORP (HQ)
Also Called: Jarit
311 Enterprise Dr (08536-3344)
P.O. Box 639 (08536-0639)
PHONE..................................609 275-2700
Peter Arduini, *CEO*
Stuart M Essig, *President*
Ray Petersen, *President*
Tracy Sterling, *District Mgr*
John Mooradian, *Senior VP*
EMP: 200 EST: 1994
SALES (est): 350MM **Publicly Held**
SIC: 3841 Surgical & medical instruments

(G-8889)
INTEGRA LIFESCIENCES CORP
Integra Neurosciences
311 Enterprise Dr (08536-3344)
PHONE..................................609 275-0500
John Henneman, *Manager*
EMP: 80 **Publicly Held**
SIC: 2834 3841 2836 Pharmaceutical
preparations; surgical & medical instru-
ments; biological products, except diag-
nostic
HQ: Integra Lifesciences Corporation
311 Enterprise Dr
Plainsboro NJ 08536
609 275-2700

(G-8890)
INTEGRA LIFESCIENCES CORP
105 Morgan Ln (08536-3339)
PHONE..................................609 275-2700
Jeremy Howe-Smith, *Manager*
EMP: 20 **Publicly Held**
SIC: 3841 Surgical & medical instruments
HQ: Integra Lifesciences Corporation
311 Enterprise Dr
Plainsboro NJ 08536
609 275-2700

(G-8891)
INTEGRA LIFESCIENCES SALES LLC
311 Enterprise Dr (08536-3344)
PHONE..................................609 275-0500
Peter J Arduini, *CEO*
Deborah Leonetti, *Senior VP*
Joanne Harla, *Vice Pres*
Linda Littlejohns, *Vice Pres*
Bill Weber, *Vice Pres*
EMP: 300
SALES: 50.9MM **Publicly Held**
SIC: 3841 Surgical & medical instruments
HQ: Integra Lifesciences Corporation
311 Enterprise Dr
Plainsboro NJ 08536
609 275-2700

(G-8892)
INTELLISPHERE LLC (HQ)
Also Called: Targeted Healthcare
666 Plainsboro Rd Ste 300 (08536-3000)
PHONE..................................609 716-7777
Fax: 609 716-4747
Michael Hennessy,
EMP: 21
SALES (est): 4MM
SALES (corp-wide): 5.6MM **Privately
Held**
WEB: www.mdnetguide.com
SIC: 2721 Trade journals: publishing &
printing
PA: Michael J. Hennessy And Associates
Inc.
666 Plainsboro Rd Ste 300
Plainsboro NJ 08536
609 716-7777

(G-8893)
MACLEODS PHARMA USA INC
666 Plainsboro Rd Ste 230 (08536-0009)
PHONE..................................609 269-5250
Pat O'Malley, *VP Opers*
▲ **EMP:** 13

▲ = Import ▼=Export
◆ =Import/Export

SALES (est): 2MM **Privately Held**
SIC: 2834 Pharmaceutical preparations
PA: Macleods Pharmaceuticals Limited
304, Atlanta Arcade, Marol Church
Road
Mumbai MH 40005

(G-8894)
NOVO NORDISK INC (HQ)
800 Scudders Mill Rd (08536-1606)
PHONE..........................609 987-5800
Doug Langa, *President*
Jesper Hiland, *President*
Martin Soeters, *President*
Amy R Bryson, *Partner*
Frank Bigley, *Principal*
◆ **EMP:** 277
SALES: 8B
SALES (corp-wide): 17.7B **Privately Held**
WEB: www.innolet-us.com
SIC: 2834 Pharmaceutical preparations
PA: Novo Nordisk A/S
Novo Alle 1
BagsvArd 2880
444 488-88

(G-8895)
PHYSICANS EDUCATN RESOURCE LLC
666 Plainsboro Rd Ste 300 (08536-3000)
PHONE..........................609 378-3701
Neil Glasser, *Partner*
Leah Babitz, *Partner*
EMP: 8
SALES (est): 673.8K **Privately Held**
SIC: 2721 Trade journals: publishing only,
not printed on site

(G-8896)
PRINCTON SATELLITE SYSTEMS INC
6 Market St Ste 926 (08536-2096)
PHONE..........................609 275-9606
Fax: 609 275-9609
Michael Paluszek, *President*
Carl Van Dyke, *Treasurer*
Paul Griesemer, *VP Sales*
Marilyn Ham, *Admin Sec*
EMP: 8
SQ FT: 1,100
SALES (est): 1.6MM **Privately Held**
WEB: www.psatellite.com
SIC: 3812 7371 7379 Acceleration indica-
tors & systems components, aerospace;
computer software development & appli-
cations; computer related consulting serv-
ices; solar cells

(G-8897)
QUANTUM INTEGRATORS GROUP LLC
8 Madison Dr (08536-2315)
PHONE..........................609 632-0621
EMP: 55
SALES (corp-wide): 2.9MM **Privately Held**
SIC: 3572 Computer storage devices
PA: Quantum Integrators Group Llc
186 Princeton Hightstown
Princeton Junction NJ 08550
609 632-0621

(G-8898)
QUGEN INC
666 Plainsboro Rd Ste 215 (08536-3071)
PHONE..........................609 716-6300
Shirka Jain, *President*
Varun Suri, *Vice Pres*
▲ **EMP:** 3
SQ FT: 500
SALES (est): 6.7MM **Privately Held**
SIC: 2834 Pharmaceutical preparations

(G-8899)
ROSEMONT PUBLISHING & PRINTING
Also Called: Associated University Presses
10 Schalks Crossing Rd (08536-1612)
PHONE..........................609 269-8094
Fax: 609 655-8366
Julien Yoseloff, *President*
Darlene Yoseloff, *Vice Pres*
EMP: 10
SQ FT: 2,900

SALES (est): 610K **Privately Held**
SIC: 2731 Books: publishing only

(G-8900)
SPHINX SOFTWARE INC
2 Red Oak Dr (08536-3704)
PHONE..........................609 275-5085
Fax: 609 799-0063
Tariq Malik, *President*
Munazzah Malik, *CFO*
Darik Malik, *Treasurer*
EMP: 8
SQ FT: 1,500
SALES: 500K **Privately Held**
SIC: 7372 Prepackaged software

(G-8901)
T N T INFORMATION SYSTEMS
666 Plainsboro Rd Ste 100 (08536-3030)
PHONE..........................609 799-9488
Eali Pao, *Partner*
Yichun Zhang, *Partner*
EMP: 4
SQ FT: 1,000
SALES: 300K **Privately Held**
WEB: www.tntinfo.com
SIC: 7372 Application computer software

Pleasantville
Atlantic County

(G-8902)
ATLANTIC CITY WEEK
Also Called: Whoot Newspaper
8025 Black Horse Pike # 350 (08232-2900)
PHONE..........................609 646-4848
Fax: 609 646-7338
Lewis B Steiner, *President*
Christine Steiner, *Admin Sec*
EMP: 15 **EST:** 1974
SQ FT: 500
SALES (est): 737.6K **Privately Held**
WEB: www.whoot.com
SIC: 2711 5812 Newspapers: publishing
only, not printed on site; eating places

(G-8903)
C & D SALES
Also Called: Screen Printing & Embroidery
73 E West Jersey Ave (08232-2753)
P.O. Box 1489 (08232-6489)
PHONE..........................609 383-9292
Fax: 609 383-1769
Catherine Carber, *Owner*
EMP: 6
SQ FT: 7,000
SALES (est): 495K **Privately Held**
SIC: 2759 2395 Screen printing; embroi-
dery & art needlework

(G-8904)
C G I CSTM FIBERGLAS & DECKING
48 S Main St (08232-2728)
PHONE..........................609 646-5302
Gregory Fiore, *Owner*
EMP: 10
SALES (est): 675.6K **Privately Held**
SIC: 3089 1521 Plastics products; single-
family home remodeling, additions & re-
pairs

(G-8905)
COLONIAL UPHL & WIN TREATMENTS
425 S Main St (08232-3031)
PHONE..........................609 641-3124
Linda Tuccinardi, *Owner*
Lorenzo Tuccinardi, *Vice Pres*
EMP: 5
SQ FT: 4,800
SALES (est): 220K **Privately Held**
WEB: www.interiordesign-concepts.com
SIC: 7641 2391 2392 Reupholstery & fur-
niture repair; curtains & draperies; blan-
kets, comforters & beddings

(G-8906)
CURRENT NEWSPAPER LLC
Also Called: Catamaran Media
1000 W Washington Ave (08232-3861)
PHONE..........................609 383-8994
Stacy Wagner, *Sales Associate*

Richard Travers,
EMP: 25
SALES (est): 1MM **Privately Held**
SIC: 2711 Newspapers: publishing only,
not printed on site

(G-8907)
DAVIDMARK LLC
711 N Main St Ste 7 (08232-1590)
PHONE..........................609 277-7361
Mark Stubblefield,
EMP: 5
SALES (est): 225.3K **Privately Held**
SIC: 2339 Women's & misses' accessories

(G-8908)
FRANK & JIMS INC
Also Called: Frank Jims Storm Windows
Doors
711 N Main St Ste 3 (08232-1590)
PHONE..........................609 646-1655
Fax: 609 641-6126
Michael Quinn, *President*
David Magill, *Vice Pres*
EMP: 4
SQ FT: 1,500
SALES (est): 520K **Privately Held**
SIC: 5211 1751 7699 2541 Door & win-
dow products; window & door installation
& erection; door & window repair; shelv-
ing, office & store, wood

(G-8909)
HAYES MINDISH INC
1401 N Main St Ste 7 (08232-1096)
PHONE..........................609 641-9880
Fax: 609 272-9222
Sally Hayes, *President*
Michael Mindish, *Vice Pres*
EMP: 4
SALES: 600K **Privately Held**
SIC: 2759 Commercial printing

(G-8910)
ITS THE PITTS INC
Also Called: Lucky Dog Custom Apparel
619 Church St (08232-4208)
PHONE..........................609 645-7319
Fax: 609 645-7319
Richard Pitts, *President*
Cindy Pitts, *Vice Pres*
EMP: 8
SQ FT: 6,000
SALES (est): 519.5K **Privately Held**
SIC: 5699 2395 T-shirts, custom printed;
emblems, embroidered

(G-8911)
JEWISH TIMES OF SOUTH JERSEY
21 W Delilah Rd (08232-1403)
PHONE..........................609 646-2063
Fax: 609 407-0999
Shy Kramer, *President*
EMP: 5
SALES (est): 230K **Privately Held**
WEB: www.jewishtimes-sj.com
SIC: 2711 Newspapers, publishing & print-
ing

(G-8912)
MAINLAND PLATE GLASS COMPANY
53 E West Jersey Ave (08232-2753)
PHONE..........................609 277-2938
Richard Bozzelli, *President*
EMP: 10
SQ FT: 8,000
SALES (est): 960K **Privately Held**
SIC: 1793 3449 Glass & glazing work;
miscellaneous metalwork

(G-8913)
SALAD CHEF INC
Also Called: Green Fresh Fruit Salad
125 Shadeland Ave (08232-3623)
P.O. Box 244 (08232-0244)
PHONE..........................609 641-5455
Fax: 609 641-5795
Francis Green, *President*
Richard Green, *Vice Pres*
EMP: 11
SQ FT: 1,500
SALES: 300K **Privately Held**
SIC: 2099 5149 Salads, fresh or refriger-
ated; groceries & related products

(G-8914)
SEABOARD INSTRUMENT CO
4 N 1st St (08232-2604)
PHONE..........................609 641-5300
Fax: 609 641-7786
Thomas R Higbee, *President*
EMP: 5
SQ FT: 12,000
SALES: 250K **Privately Held**
SIC: 3825 Measuring instruments & me-
ters, electric; tachometer generators; time
code generators

(G-8915)
SHY KRAMER & ASSOCIATES
Also Called: Distributors Buying Service
21 W Delilah Rd (08232-1403)
PHONE..........................609 646-2063
Fax: 609 646-1519
Charles L Kramer, *Owner*
EMP: 10
SQ FT: 1,400
SALES (est): 954.6K **Privately Held**
SIC: 2731 5199 8742 Pamphlets: publish-
ing only, not printed on site; general mer-
chandise, non-durable; sales (including
sales management) consultant

(G-8916)
SOUTH JERSEY PUBLISHING CO (DH)
Also Called: Press of Atlantic City, The
1000 W Washington Ave (08232-3861)
P.O. Box 3100 (08232-0039)
PHONE..........................609 272-7000
Fax: 609 272-7224
Charles W Bitzer, *President*
Owen Gallagher, *Editor*
Paula Gillis, *Editor*
Becky Hendricks, *Editor*
Linda Hildebrand, *Editor*
EMP: 335
SQ FT: 30,000
SALES (est): 50.3MM
SALES (corp-wide): 361.4MM **Privately
Held**
WEB: www.pressofac.com
SIC: 2711 Newspapers: publishing only,
not printed on site; newspapers, publish-
ing & printing
HQ: Wilmington Trust Sp Services
1105 N Market St Ste 1300
Wilmington DE 19801
302 427-7650

(G-8917)
TRIBUNA HISPANA
1614 Dolphin Ave (08232-4657)
PHONE..........................609 646-9167
Jose Polo, *Owner*
EMP: 9
SALES (est): 280K **Privately Held**
SIC: 2711 Newspapers: publishing only,
not printed on site

(G-8918)
WILMINGTON TRUST SP SERVICES
Also Called: Press of Atlantic City, The
1000 W Washington Ave (08232-3861)
PHONE..........................609 272-7000
Mark Blum, *Publisher*
Edward Steiger, *HR Admin*
Paul Merkoski, *Manager*
Sherry Page, *Admin Asst*
EMP: 175
SALES (corp-wide): 361.4MM **Privately
Held**
SIC: 2759 2711 2752 Commercial print-
ing; newspapers; commercial printing,
lithographic
HQ: Wilmington Trust Sp Services
1105 N Market St Ste 1300
Wilmington DE 19801
302 427-7650

GEOGRAPHIC

Pluckemin
Somerset County

(G-8919)
FRANKS CABINET SHOP INC
Also Called: Gbd Cabinet Shop
1992 Burnt Mills Rd (07978)
P.O. Box 78 (07978-0078)
PHONE....................................908 658-4396
Fax: 908 658-9112
John Darrow, *President*
Frank Klausz, *President*
Doug Boom,
EMP: 7
SQ FT: 4,000
SALES: 500K **Privately Held**
SIC: 2434 Wood kitchen cabinets

Point Pleasant Beach
Ocean County

(G-8920)
JUMP START PRESS
802 Cedar Ave (08742-2508)
PHONE....................................732 892-4994
Mary Pearce, *President*
Tiffany Gaestel, *Assoc Editor*
Gari Fairweather, *Web Dvlpr*
EMP: 6
SALES (est): 172.5K **Privately Held**
SIC: 2731 Books: publishing only

(G-8921)
KEEFE PRINTING INC
501 Atlantic Ave (08742-3077)
PHONE....................................732 295-2099
Kevin Keefe, *President*
Christopher Ehrhardt, *Vice Pres*
EMP: 6
SQ FT: 1,500
SALES (est): 480K **Privately Held**
WEB: www.kprint.com
SIC: 2759 Commercial printing

(G-8922)
LAURELTON WELDING SERVICE INC
117 Channel Dr (08742-2619)
PHONE....................................732 899-6348
Fax: 732 892-9121
Thomas Gallagher, *President*
Shelia Crane, *Admin Sec*
EMP: 7
SQ FT: 6,500
SALES (est): 470K **Privately Held**
SIC: 7692 Welding repair

(G-8923)
MCBRIDE AWNING CO
304 Richmond Ave (08742-2547)
PHONE....................................732 892-6256
Kerry Mc Bride, *Partner*
Brian Mc Bride, *Partner*
John Mc Bride, *Partner*
Kerry McBride, *Partner*
EMP: 5
SQ FT: 2,200
SALES (est): 709.1K **Privately Held**
SIC: 3089 1799 Awnings, fiberglass & plastic combination; awning installation

(G-8924)
NORMA K CORPORATION
Also Called: Pleasant
30 Broadway (08742-2679)
PHONE....................................732 477-6441
Norma E Keller, *President*
Kenneth Keller, *Corp Secy*
John G Kennell, *Vice Pres*
Sharon Keller Hawryluk, *Admin Sec*
EMP: 5
SALES: 200K **Privately Held**
WEB: www.pleasant.com
SIC: 4493 3732 Marinas; fishing boats: lobster, crab, oyster, etc.: small

(G-8925)
OCEAN STAR
421 River Ave (08742-2569)
PHONE....................................732 899-7606
Fax: 732 899-9778
Jim Manser, *Owner*
EMP: 6
SALES (est): 172.8K **Privately Held**
SIC: 2711 Newspapers: publishing only, not printed on site

(G-8926)
POINT LOBSTER COMPANY INC
1 Saint Louis Ave (08742-2651)
PHONE....................................732 892-1718
Fax: 732 892-3928
EMP: 10
SALES (est): 1MM **Privately Held**
SIC: 2091 Mfg Canned/Cured Fish/Seafood

(G-8927)
TBS INDUSTRIAL FLOORING PDTS
300 New Jersey Ave (08742-3328)
PHONE....................................732 899-1486
Thomas Brennan, *President*
EMP: 5
SALES (est): 400K **Privately Held**
SIC: 3996 1752 Hard surface floor coverings; floor laying & floor work

(G-8928)
WOODHAVEN LUMBER & MILLWORK
1303 Richmond Ave (08742-3099)
PHONE....................................732 295-8800
Fax: 732 295-4935
Chuck Hessenaemter, *Manager*
EMP: 20
SALES (corp-wide): 48.5MM **Privately Held**
WEB: www.woodhavenlumber.com
SIC: 5251 2431 5211 Hardware; millwork; lumber products
PA: Woodhaven Lumber & Millwork Inc
200 James St
Lakewood NJ 08701
732 901-0030

(G-8929)
YO GOT IT
606 Arnold Ave (08742-2531)
PHONE....................................732 475-7913
Scott Mizrahi, *Principal*
EMP: 4
SALES (est): 256.8K **Privately Held**
SIC: 2026 Yogurt

Point Pleasant Boro
Ocean County

(G-8930)
ALL SURFACE ASPHALT PAVING
528 Hardenberg Ave (08742-2827)
PHONE....................................732 295-3800
Lori Coe, *President*
EMP: 7
SQ FT: 650
SALES: 1MM **Privately Held**
SIC: 2951 Asphalt paving mixtures & blocks

(G-8931)
ARNOLDS YACHT BASIN INC (PA)
1671 Beaver Dam Rd Ste 1 (08742-5161)
PHONE....................................732 892-3000
Arnold Dambrosa, *President*
David Dambrosa, *Vice Pres*
EMP: 6
SQ FT: 32,000
SALES: 490K **Privately Held**
SIC: 4493 5551 2759 Yacht basins; motor boat dealers; marine supplies; screen printing

(G-8932)
ATLAS RECORDING MACHINES CORP
2140 Bridge Ave (08742-4916)
PHONE....................................732 295-3663
Fax: 732 899-8306
Anthony Hopcroft, *President*
Mary Hopcroft, *Corp Secy*
EMP: 8

SQ FT: 8,000
SALES: 172K **Privately Held**
SIC: 3599 Machine & other job shop work

(G-8933)
BLAZING VISUALS
2138 Bridge Ave (08742-4916)
PHONE....................................732 781-1401
EMP: 6 EST: 2013
SALES (est): 438.3K **Privately Held**
SIC: 3993 Signs & advertising specialties

(G-8934)
CARVER BOAT SALES INC
714 Canal St (08742-4509)
PHONE....................................732 892-0328
Christopher Carver, *Corp Secy*
EMP: 4 EST: 1947
SALES (est): 290K **Privately Held**
SIC: 3732 5551 Boat building & repairing; boat dealers

(G-8935)
COLIE SAIL MAKERS INC
1649 Bay Ave (08742-4501)
PHONE....................................732 892-4344
Fax: 732 899-8965
Dev Colie, *President*
Stephanie Colie, *Corp Secy*
EMP: 7
SQ FT: 6,500
SALES (est): 658.5K **Privately Held**
WEB: www.coliesail.com
SIC: 2394 5551 Canvas & related products; sailboats & equipment

(G-8936)
COURTNEY BOATLIFTS INC
Also Called: Atlantic Boatlifts
1209 Bay Ave (08742-4017)
P.O. Box 4381, Brick (08723-1581)
PHONE....................................732 892-8900
James R Courtney, *President*
EMP: 4
SALES (est): 410K **Privately Held**
SIC: 1629 3536 Dams, waterways, docks & other marine construction; boat lifts

(G-8937)
DAIRY QUEEN
2506 Bridge Ave (08742-4259)
PHONE....................................732 892-5700
Alex Zicelli, *Owner*
EMP: 16
SALES (est): 289.7K **Privately Held**
SIC: 5812 5143 2024 Ice cream stands or dairy bars; frozen dairy desserts; ice cream & frozen desserts

(G-8938)
DELICIOUS BAGELS INC (PA)
2259 Bridge Ave (08742-4920)
PHONE....................................732 892-9265
Fax: 732 892-7244
Tony Pontecorvo, *President*
Florence Pontecorvo, *Vice Pres*
EMP: 4
SQ FT: 1,800
SALES (est): 871.9K **Privately Held**
SIC: 2051 5461 Bagels, fresh or frozen; bagels

(G-8939)
EAGLE ENGINEERING & AUTOMATION
Also Called: Eagle Drives & Controls
2111 Herbertsville Rd (08742-2255)
P.O. Box 924 (08742-0924)
PHONE....................................732 899-2292
Robert M Ryan, *President*
Maureen Akersten, *Controller*
EMP: 4
SQ FT: 8,000
SALES: 900K **Privately Held**
WEB: www.walker-eagle.com
SIC: 3621 3613 Motors, electric; control panels, electric

(G-8940)
SHORE SOFTWARE INC
1102 Arnold Ave (08742-2311)
PHONE....................................732 899-6878
John Barone, *President*
Terry Biundo, *Vice Pres*
EMP: 5

SALES: 500K **Privately Held**
WEB: www.shoresoftware.com
SIC: 7372 Prepackaged software

(G-8941)
TROPICAL EXPRESSIONS INC
2127 Bridge Ave (08742-4959)
PHONE....................................732 899-8680
Jack Lathrop McGuire, *President*
EMP: 4
SQ FT: 1,000
SALES: 250K **Privately Held**
WEB: www.tropicalislandimports.com
SIC: 3999 Lawn ornaments

(G-8942)
VASCURE NATURAL LLC
3828 River Rd (08742-2054)
PHONE....................................732 528-6492
Thomas McCrink, *Principal*
EMP: 4
SALES (est): 399.6K **Privately Held**
SIC: 2834 Druggists' preparations (pharmaceuticals)

(G-8943)
WALKER ENGINEERING INC
2111 Herbertsville Rd (08742-2255)
P.O. Box 924 (08742-0924)
PHONE....................................732 899-2550
Jillian Leinen, *President*
Robert Ryan, *Vice Pres*
Maureen Akersten, *Office Mgr*
Susan Butler, *Admin Asst*
EMP: 11
SQ FT: 8,000
SALES (est): 3.3MM **Privately Held**
SIC: 5063 3625 Motors, electric; control equipment, electric

Pomona
Atlantic County

(G-8944)
ARGO CORP
Richard Stockton College (08240)
PHONE....................................609 652-4560
Dan Grote, *Principal*
EMP: 15
SALES: 53.8K **Privately Held**
WEB: www.argocorp.com
SIC: 2711 Newspapers, publishing & printing

(G-8945)
SIGHT2SITE MEDIA LLC
269 W White Horse Pike (08240-1103)
PHONE....................................856 637-2479
EMP: 5 EST: 2011
SALES (est): 290K **Privately Held**
SIC: 2741 7389 Internet Publishing And Broadcasting

Pompton Lakes
Passaic County

(G-8946)
AUTO TIG WELDING FABRICATING
88 Cannonball Rd Ste B (07442-1775)
PHONE....................................973 839-8877
John Pajenski, *Principal*
EMP: 4
SQ FT: 3,000
SALES: 300K **Privately Held**
SIC: 7692 Welding repair

(G-8947)
GABRIEL SOUND LTD LIABILITY CO
138 Cannonball Rd (07442-1708)
P.O. Box 287 (07442-0287)
PHONE....................................973 831-7800
Erick Wain,
EMP: 7
SALES (est): 739.5K **Privately Held**
SIC: 3651 Speaker systems

2018 Harris New Jersey
Manufacturers Directory

▲ = Import ▼=Export
◆ =Import/Export

GEOGRAPHIC

(G-8948)
SOLAR PRODUCTS INC
228 Wanaque Ave (07442-2131)
PHONE....................................973 248-9370
Richard Eck, *Ch of Bd*
David Eck, *President*
Susan Robertson, *Corp Secy*
Tim Robertson, *Vice Pres*
John Schafer, *Vice Pres*
▲ EMP: 37
SQ FT: 30,000
SALES (est): 8.7MM **Privately Held**
WEB: www.solarproducts.com
SIC: 3567 3679 Heating units & devices,
industrial: electric; quartz crystals, for
electronic application

(G-8949)
**TANDEM COLOR IMAGING
GRAPHICS (PA)**
Also Called: Tandem Graphics
207 Wanaque Ave (07442-2103)
PHONE....................................973 513-9779
Michael Nass, *President*
EMP: 6
SQ FT: 4,500
SALES (est): 1.2MM **Privately Held**
WEB: www.tandemgraphics.net
SIC: 7336 2752 Film strip, slide & still film
production; commercial printing, litho-
graphic

(G-8950)
TILCON NEW YORK INC
Also Called: Pompton Lakes Quarry
Foot Of Broad St (07442)
PHONE....................................800 789-7625
Frank Jaluski, *Branch Mgr*
EMP: 27
SALES (corp-wide): 29.7B **Privately Held**
SIC: 1429 Trap rock, crushed & broken-
quarrying
HQ: Tilcon New York Inc.
9 Entin Rd
Parsippany NJ 07054
800 789-7625

Pompton Plains
Morris County

(G-8951)
**ALADDIN MANUFACTURING
CORP**
100 Alexander Ave (07444-1847)
PHONE....................................973 616-4600
Jeff Labinski, *Branch Mgr*
EMP: 260
SALES (corp-wide): 9.4B **Publicly Held**
SIC: 2273 5032 5023 Carpets, textile
fiber; brick, stone & related material;
home furnishings
HQ: Aladdin Manufacturing Corporation
160 S Industrial Blvd
Calhoun GA 30701
706 629-7721

(G-8952)
AMMARK CORPORATION
230 W Parkway Ste 12 (07444-1060)
P.O. Box 519, Boonton (07005-0519)
PHONE....................................973 616-2555
Fax: 973 616-0246
John T Ford, *President*
Veronica Ford, *Vice Pres*
▲ EMP: 4 EST: 1966
SALES (est): 515.4K **Privately Held**
WEB: www.ammarkcorp.com
SIC: 3494 3822 Valves & pipe fittings; air
flow controllers, air conditioning & refrig-
eration

(G-8953)
AR2 PRODUCTS LLC
Also Called: Gopole
210 W Parkway Ste 9 (07444-1000)
PHONE....................................800 667-1263
Russell Van Zile, *CEO*
Ryan Vosburg, *Vice Pres*
Anthony Anari,
▲ EMP: 6
SQ FT: 5,000

(G-8954)
ASHLEY NORTON INC
210 W Parkway Ste 1 (07444-1000)
P.O. Box 374 (07444-0374)
PHONE....................................973 835-4027
Narendra Karnani, *President*
Ashish Karnani, *Vice Pres*
◆ EMP: 15
SQ FT: 18,000
SALES (est): 3.2MM **Privately Held**
SIC: 3429 Manufactured hardware (gen-
eral)

(G-8955)
BAYVIEW ENTERTAINMENT LLC
210 W Parkway Ste 7 (07444-1000)
PHONE....................................201 880-5331
Fax: 201 488-6112
Seth Goldstein,
Peter Castro,
Sam Napolitano,
▲ EMP: 20
SALES (est): 3.2MM **Privately Held**
WEB: www.bayviewent.com
SIC: 3651 Household audio & video equip-
ment

(G-8956)
CHILLER SOLUTIONS LLC
Also Called: Edwards Engineering
101 Alexander Ave Unit 3 (07444-1854)
PHONE....................................973 835-2800
Fax: 973 835-2805
Dorothy Luzzi, *Manager*
Ala Uddin, *Manager*
Thomas Dellinger, *Bd of Directors*
Gene A Passaro,
EMP: 32
SALES (est): 7.4MM **Privately Held**
WEB: www.chillersolutions.com
SIC: 3585 Heating equipment, complete

(G-8957)
DEVON PRODUCTS
230 W Parkway Ste 3 (07444-1065)
PHONE....................................732 438-3855
EMP: 4
SALES: 300K **Privately Held**
SIC: 2844 Services-Misc

(G-8958)
EDWARDS COILS CORP
101 Alexander Ave Unit 3 (07444-1854)
P.O. Box 181, Hampton Falls NH (03844-
0181)
PHONE....................................973 835-2800
Ernest M Cherry, *President*
Jose Mercedes, *Manager*
▲ EMP: 17
SQ FT: 35,000
SALES (est): 3.7MM **Privately Held**
SIC: 3443 Heat exchangers, condensers &
components

(G-8959)
FRAGRANCE FACTORY INC
12 Peck Ave (07444-1429)
PHONE....................................973 835-2002
Robert Scherr, *Manager*
EMP: 4
SALES: 330K **Privately Held**
WEB: www.fragrancefactory.com
SIC: 2844 Perfumes & colognes

(G-8960)
**GLOBAL BUSINESS
DIMENSIONS INC (PA)**
220 W Parkway Ste 8 (07444-1048)
PHONE....................................973 831-5866
Fax: 201 831-0867
Sanjay Prasad, *President*
Sam Phillips, *Vice Pres*
Lynn Rin, *Vice Pres*
Pacelli Sequeria, *Vice Pres*
Sarika Singh, *Human Resources*
EMP: 26
SQ FT: 11,000
SALES (est): 4.1MM **Privately Held**
WEB: www.globalbd.com
SIC: 3571 5063 Electronic computers;
electrical supplies

(G-8961)
M C TECHNOLOGIES INC
4 Kinney Pl (07444-1608)
PHONE....................................973 839-2779
John M Chizacky, *President*
Melanie Chizacky, *Vice Pres*
EMP: 24
SALES: 2.1MM **Privately Held**
SIC: 3559 8731 8711 Automotive related
machinery; engineering laboratory, except
testing; consulting engineer

(G-8962)
**MEDALLION INTERNATIONAL
INC**
233 W Parkway (07444-1028)
PHONE....................................973 616-3401
Michael Boudjouk, *President*
Paula Boudjouk, *President*
◆ EMP: 15
SALES (est): 3MM **Privately Held**
SIC: 2087 2844 Extracts, flavoring; toilet
preparations

(G-8963)
MORRIS INDUSTRIES INC (PA)
777 State Rt 23 (07444-1498)
P.O. Box 278 (07444-0278)
PHONE....................................973 835-6600
Fax: 973 835-7414
Robert Nochenson, *President*
▲ EMP: 42
SQ FT: 30,000
SALES (est): 37.1MM **Privately Held**
WEB: www.morrispipe.com
SIC: 5051 5084 5074 3317 Pipe & tub-
ing, steel; drilling equipment, excluding
bits; drilling bits; pumps & pumping equip-
ment; pipes & fittings, plastic; steel pipe &
tubes; well casing, wrought: welded, lock
joint or heavy riveted; service establish-
ment equipment

(G-8964)
PENN ELCOM INC
232 W Parkway (07444-1029)
PHONE....................................973 839-7777
Fax: 973 839-2277
Helen Stratford, *Accounts Mgr*
Shawn Anderson, *Marketing Staff*
Richard Stratford, *Branch Mgr*
EMP: 10 **Privately Held**
WEB: www.elcomhardware.com
SIC: 3429 5072 Manufactured hardware
(general); hardware
HQ: Penn Elcom, Inc.
7465 Lampson Ave
Garden Grove CA 92841

(G-8965)
PHT AEROSPACE LLC (PA)
230 W Parkway Ste 2 (07444-1065)
PHONE....................................973 831-1230
Joe Wall, *General Mgr*
David Sanborn, *Production*
Iris Castello, *Purch Agent*
Dan Stanions, *QC Mgr*
John Tobak, *Engineer*
▲ EMP: 15
SQ FT: 5,000
SALES (est): 3.1MM **Privately Held**
SIC: 3621 Motors & generators

(G-8966)
TRICOMP INC
230 W Parkway Ste 14 (07444-1060)
PHONE....................................973 835-1110
Fax: 973 835-5015
Thomas P Lospinoso, *President*
Joan L Graff, *Vice Pres*
EMP: 120
SQ FT: 5,000
SALES (est): 14.1MM **Privately Held**
WEB: www.tricomp.com
SIC: 3082 3061 3499 3053 Unsupported
plastics profile shapes; mechanical rubber
goods; magnets, permanent: metallic;
gaskets, all materials; weather strip,
metal; weather strip, sponge rubber

(G-8967)
TRIFORM PRODUCTS INC
164 W Parkway (07444-1255)
PHONE....................................973 278-2042
Doug Troast, *President*
David Troast, *Vice Pres*

EMP: 35
SQ FT: 17,500
SALES (est): 4MM **Privately Held**
SIC: 3469 Metal stampings

(G-8968)
**WATER WORKS SUPPLY
COMPANY (PA)**
660 State Rt 23 (07444-1422)
P.O. Box 306 (07444-0306)
PHONE....................................973 835-2153
Fax: 973 835-8743
James C Schmutz, *President*
Craig Connolly, *Sales Staff*
Dave Galvao, *Sales Associate*
John Mastrogiovanni, *Sales Associate*
Susan Schmutz, *Admin Sec*
EMP: 15
SQ FT: 7,000
SALES (est): 14.1MM **Privately Held**
SIC: 5051 3321 Cast iron pipe; cast iron
pipe & fittings

(G-8969)
ZAXCOM INC
Also Called: Zaxcom Video
230 W Parkway Ste 9 (07444-1060)
PHONE....................................973 835-5000
Fax: 973 835-6633
Glen Sanders, *President*
Lisa Apriceno, *Finance Mgr*
Colleen Goodsir, *Manager*
Eric Lane, *Technician*
EMP: 10
SQ FT: 6,700
SALES (est): 2.1MM **Privately Held**
WEB: www.zaxcom.com
SIC: 3663 Television broadcasting & com-
munications equipment

(G-8970)
ZODIAC PAINTBALL INC
4 Sage Way (07444-1473)
PHONE....................................973 616-7230
Kenneth Hefferle, *Principal*
EMP: 4
SALES (est): 293.4K **Privately Held**
SIC: 3499 Nozzles, spray: aerosol, paint or
insecticide

Port Elizabeth
Cumberland County

(G-8971)
WHIBCO INC
377 Port Commerland Rd (08348)
PHONE....................................856 825-5200
Fax: 856 825-4743
Marvin Blechen, *Manager*
EMP: 30
SALES (corp-wide): 16.5MM **Privately
Held**
WEB: www.whibco.com
SIC: 3299 Insulsleeves (foundry materials)
PA: Whibco, Inc.
87 E Commerce St
Bridgeton NJ 08302
856 455-9200

(G-8972)
WHIBCO OF NEW JERSEY INC
377 Port Cumberland Rd (08348)
PHONE....................................856 455-9200
Wade R Sjogren, *President*
Walter R Sjogren Jr, *Vice Pres*
Jane Sorgren, *Admin Sec*
EMP: 25
SALES (est): 2.1MM
SALES (corp-wide): 16.5MM **Privately
Held**
SIC: 1446 1442 Industrial sand; sand min-
ing
PA: Whibco, Inc.
87 E Commerce St
Bridgeton NJ 08302
856 455-9200

Port Monmouth
Monmouth County

(G-8973)
PHOENIX ALLIANCE GROUP LLC
337 State Route 36 (07758-1367)
PHONE................................732 495-4800
Rodney Cocuzza, *Mng Member*
EMP: 14
SQ FT: 1,000
SALES (est): 847.9K **Privately Held**
WEB: www.phoenixalliancegroup.net
SIC: 2759 Commercial printing

Port Murray
Warren County

(G-8974)
AMERICAN PROCESS SYSTEMS
131 Cherry Tree Bend Rd (07865-4112)
PHONE................................908 216-6781
Carl Anderson, *Owner*
EMP: 8
SALES: 850K **Privately Held**
SIC: 5084 3999 Controlling instruments & accessories; dock equipment & supplies, industrial

(G-8975)
ANDREX SYSTEMS INC
17 Karrville Rd (07865-4118)
P.O. Box 115 (07865-0115)
PHONE................................908 835-1720
William T Pote, *President*
Thomas Pote, *Vice Pres*
Bill Bright, *Project Engr*
Rodger Johasen, *Product Mgr*
EMP: 8
SALES (est): 1.1MM **Privately Held**
WEB: www.andrex-sys.com
SIC: 3679 Harness assemblies for electronic use: wire or cable

(G-8976)
BOREALIS COMPOUNDS INC
176 Thomas Rd (07865-4014)
PHONE................................908 850-6200
Fax: 908 850-1236
Kenneth Wiecoreck, *President*
Ernst Buchner, *General Mgr*
Nicholas Kolesch, *General Mgr*
Vladan Popovic, *General Mgr*
Willy Raymaekers, *Managing Dir*
◆ EMP: 112
SQ FT: 10,000
SALES (est): 62.8MM **Privately Held**
SIC: 3087 Custom compound purchased resins
HQ: Borealis Ag
Wagramer StraBe 17-19
Wien 1220
122 400-300

(G-8977)
FLEXCO MICROWAVE INC
17 Karrville Rd (07865-4118)
P.O. Box 115 (07865-0115)
PHONE................................908 835-1720
Fax: 908 835-0002
William T Pote, *President*
Thomas W Pote, *Vice Pres*
Colene Thomas, *Vice Pres*
Jeremy Medina, *Controller*
Kathleen Medina, *Admin Sec*
▲ EMP: 35
SQ FT: 18,200
SALES (est): 7.5MM **Privately Held**
WEB: www.flexcomw.com
SIC: 3357 Coaxial cable, nonferrous

(G-8978)
LENNOX INDUSTRIES INC
555 Route 57 (07865-4335)
PHONE................................908 223-6002
EMP: 4
SALES (corp-wide): 3.8B **Publicly Held**
SIC: 3585 Furnaces, warm air: electric; air conditioning units, complete: domestic or industrial

HQ: Lennox Industries Inc.
2100 Lake Park Blvd
Richardson TX 75080
972 497-5000

Port Norris
Cumberland County

(G-8979)
BIVALVE PACKING INC (HQ)
6957 Miller Ave (08349-3167)
P.O. Box 336 (08349-0336)
PHONE................................856 785-0270
Fax: 856 785-1406
Steve Fleetwood, *President*
Steeve Fleetwood, *President*
EMP: 4
SQ FT: 3,000
SALES (est): 2MM
SALES (corp-wide): 5.9MM **Privately Held**
SIC: 2092 Shellfish, fresh: shucked & packed in nonsealed containers

(G-8980)
HILLARD BLOOM PACKING CO INC
2601 Ogden Ave (08349-3141)
PHONE................................856 785-0120
Hillard Bloom, *President*
Lena Hughes, *Corp Secy*
Harold Bickings, *Vice Pres*
EMP: 9
SQ FT: 5,000
SALES (est): 968.7K
SALES (corp-wide): 5.9MM **Privately Held**
WEB: www.bloombrothers.com
SIC: 2091 2092 Oysters: packaged in cans, jars, etc.; fresh or frozen packaged fish
PA: Tallmadge Bros Incorporated
132 Water St
Norwalk CT

(G-8981)
MILLER BERRY & SONS INC
2615 Robinstown Rd (08349)
P.O. Box 174 (08349-0174)
PHONE................................856 785-1420
Fax: 856 785-2638
Dean Berry, *President*
Barbara Moore, *Corp Secy*
EMP: 11
SQ FT: 45,000
SALES: 1.3MM **Privately Held**
SIC: 2515 0139 Mattresses, containing felt, foam rubber, urethane, etc.; mattresses, innerspring or box spring; hay farm

(G-8982)
RICCI BROS SAND COMPANY INC
Also Called: Ricci Brothers Sand
2099 Dragston Rd (08349)
P.O. Box 664 (08349-0664)
PHONE................................856 785-0166
Fax: 856 785-8126
Samuel J Ricci Sr, *President*
EMP: 24
SQ FT: 7,750
SALES (est): 6.3MM **Privately Held**
WEB: www.riccisand.com
SIC: 1442 Construction sand mining; gravel mining

(G-8983)
SURFSIDE FOODS LLC
Also Called: Surfside Products
1733 Main St (08349-3340)
P.O. Box 692 (08349-0692)
PHONE................................856 785-2115
EMP: 7
SALES (est): 100.4K **Privately Held**
SIC: 2099 3556 Food preparations; food products machinery

Port Reading
Middlesex County

(G-8984)
A & D INDUS & MAR REPR INC
900 Port Reading Ave B2 (07064-1044)
PHONE................................732 541-1481
Maryann Bryant, *Principal*
EMP: 21
SALES (est): 3.7MM **Privately Held**
SIC: 3732 3089 Boat building & repairing; plastic boats & other marine equipment

(G-8985)
ACME MANUFACTURING CO
900 Port Reading Ave A2 (07064-1044)
P.O. Box 70 (07064-0070)
PHONE................................732 541-2800
Richard Morrone, *Partner*
Paul Morrone, *Partner*
EMP: 5
SQ FT: 6,000
SALES (est): 634K **Privately Held**
WEB: www.acmecoating.com
SIC: 2542 Office & store showcases & display fixtures

(G-8986)
ALLIED OLD ENGLISH INC
100 Markley St (07064-1897)
PHONE................................732 636-2060
Fax: 732 636-2538
Fred Ross, *Ch of Bd*
Sean Colon, *COO*
Mike Golden, *Warehouse Mgr*
Rick McGlynn, *Plant Engr*
Frank Gatti, *CFO*
◆ EMP: 45 EST: 1951
SQ FT: 63,000
SALES: 18MM **Privately Held**
WEB: www.alliedoldenglish.com
SIC: 2099 Food preparations; sauces; gravy, dressing & dip mixes; syrups; jelly, corncob (gelatin)

(G-8987)
DURABOND DIVISION US GYPSUM
300 Markley St (07064-1819)
PHONE................................732 636-7900
James Wilson, *Principal*
▲ EMP: 11 EST: 2007
SALES (est): 2.5MM **Privately Held**
SIC: 3275 Gypsum products

(G-8988)
NASCO STONE AND TILE LLC
200 Markley St (07064-1820)
PHONE................................732 634-0589
Sammy Tawil, *Vice Pres*
Dianne Bailey, *Controller*
Jerry Miller, *Sales Staff*
Ellen Schaed, *Sales Associate*
▲ EMP: 30
SALES (est): 4.2MM **Privately Held**
SIC: 3253 Ceramic wall & floor tile

(G-8989)
RS MARBLE AND GRANITE INC
900 Port Reading Ave B3 (07064-1044)
PHONE................................732 802-9220
Dicky Kochhar, *President*
Kelvin Kochhar, *Admin Sec*
▲ EMP: 5
SQ FT: 10,000
SALES (est): 389.7K **Privately Held**
SIC: 3253 Ceramic wall & floor tile

(G-8990)
SPEEDWAY LLC
750 Cliff Rd (07064-2201)
PHONE................................732 750-7800
Darryl Harris, *Manager*
EMP: 300 **Publicly Held**
WEB: www.hess.com
SIC: 1311 2911 5172 Crude petroleum production; natural gas production; petroleum refining; petroleum products
HQ: Speedway Llc
500 Speedway Dr
Enon OH 45323
937 864-3000

(G-8991)
UNITED STATES GYPSUM COMPANY
300 Markley St (07064-1895)
PHONE................................732 636-7900
Fax: 732 636-6097
Jordan Egg, *Production*
Peter Geedman, *Purch Mgr*
Michael Sencic, *Engineer*
Bill Elser, *Plant Engr*
James Wilson, *Manager*
EMP: 81
SALES (corp-wide): 3.2B **Publicly Held**
WEB: www.usg.com
SIC: 3275 Gypsum products
HQ: United States Gypsum Company Inc
550 W Adams St Ste 1300
Chicago IL 60661
312 606-4000

Princeton
Mercer County

(G-8992)
ABBOTT LABORATORIES
400 College Rd E (08540-6607)
PHONE................................609 443-9300
Fax: 609 443-9310
Barry Bass, *Branch Mgr*
EMP: 21
SALES (corp-wide): 27.3B **Publicly Held**
SIC: 2834 Pharmaceutical preparations
PA: Abbott Laboratories
100 Abbott Park Rd
Abbott Park IL 60064
224 667-6100

(G-8993)
ABBOTT POINT OF CARE INC (HQ)
400 College Rd E (08540-6607)
PHONE................................609 454-9000
William P Moffitt, *President*
Sharon Bracken, *President*
Claudia Moreno, *Engineer*
Lisa Siko, *Manager*
Chad Montgomery, *Info Tech Mgr*
EMP: 240
SALES (est): 197.7MM
SALES (corp-wide): 27.3B **Publicly Held**
SIC: 3841 Diagnostic apparatus, medical
PA: Abbott Laboratories
100 Abbott Park Rd
Abbott Park IL 60064
224 667-6100

(G-8994)
ACCELERATED TECHNOLOGIES INC
Also Called: Damco
2 Research Way Fl 2 # 2 (08540-6628)
PHONE................................609 632-0350
Ranjan Chattopadhyay, *President*
Brahm Sharma, *CFO*
EMP: 4
SQ FT: 1,700
SALES (est): 174.8K **Privately Held**
SIC: 7372 Prepackaged software
PA: Damco Solutions Private Limited
No.108, Hsidc Industrial Estate,
Faridabad HR 12100

(G-8995)
ACQUEON TECHNOLOGIES INC
100 Overlook Ctr Fl 2 (08540-7814)
PHONE................................609 945-3139
David Sokoler, *Vice Pres*
Parthasarathy Balasubramanian, *Technical Mgr*
Baskar Subramanian, *Branch Mgr*
EMP: 4
SALES (corp-wide): 263.9K **Privately Held**
WEB: www.acqueon.com
SIC: 7372 Prepackaged software
PA: Acqueon Technologies, Inc.
14785 Preston Rd Ste 550
Dallas TX 75254
888 946-6878

2018 Harris New Jersey
Manufacturers Directory

▲ = Import ▼=Export
◆ =Import/Export

(G-8996)
ADVAXIS INC (PA)
305 College Rd E (08540-6608)
PHONE.................................609 452-9813
Fax: 732 545-1084
Anthony Lombardi, *CEO*
David Sidransky, *Ch of Bd*
Kenneth A Berlin, *President*
Robert G Petit, *Exec VP*
Thomas Hare, *Vice Pres*
EMP: 108
SQ FT: 48,500
SALES: 12MM **Publicly Held**
WEB: www.advaxis.com
SIC: 2834 Pharmaceutical preparations

(G-8997)
AGILE THERAPEUTICS INC
101 Poor Farm Rd (08540-1941)
PHONE.................................609 683-1880
Fax: 609 683-1855
Al Altomari, *Ch of Bd*
Scott M Coiante, *CFO*
Joe D'Urso, *Controller*
Renee Selman, *Ch Credit Ofcr*
Elizabeth Garner, *Chief Mktg Ofcr*
EMP: 16
SQ FT: 7,000
SALES (est): 2.4MM **Privately Held**
WEB: www.agiletherapeutics.com
SIC: 2834 8733 Pharmaceutical prepara-
tions; medical research

(G-8998)
AICUMEN TECHNOLOGIES INC
11 Nestlewood Way (08540-6132)
PHONE.................................732 668-4204
Anantha Krishnan, *CEO*
EMP: 5 **Privately Held**
SIC: 3571 Computers, digital, analog or
hybrid

(G-8999)
AKILA HOLDINGS INC
Also Called: AKILA HOLDINGS INC LLC
12 Hampstead Ct (08540-7074)
PHONE.................................609 454-5034
EMP: 4 EST: 2002
SALES: 13.2MM
SALES (corp-wide): 5.5MM **Privately
Held**
SIC: 2099 5153 Sugar; grain & field beans
PA: Akila Trading Private Limited
S-9, 2nd Floor,
New Delhi DL 11001
112 647-2642

(G-9000)
**AL TAYYAR ENRGY- PRINCETON
LLC**
63 Moran Ave Ste B (08542-3815)
P.O. Box 6289, Washington DC (20015-
0289)
PHONE.................................609 479-8603
Dr Granville Smith, *CEO*
EMP: 4
SALES (est): 321.9K **Privately Held**
SIC: 6799 3621 Investors; electric motor &
generator parts
PA: Al Tayyar Energy
Al Khalidiah Area
Abu Dhabi

(G-9001)
ALAN PAUL ACCESSORIES INC
Also Called: Alan Paul Neckware
66 Witherspoon St # 3300 (08542-3239)
PHONE.................................609 924-4022
Alan Paul Spielholz, *President*
Amparo Spielholz, *Manager*
EMP: 5
SQ FT: 1,500
SALES (est): 331K **Privately Held**
SIC: 2253 Knit outerwear mills

(G-9002)
ALK TECHNOLOGIES INC (HQ)
1 Independence Way # 400 (08540-6662)
PHONE.................................609 683-0220
Katherine Kornhauser, *President*
Michael Kornhauser, *President*
Dave Ward, *Partner*
Michalela Washington, *General Mgr*
Mike Bodden, *Senior VP*
EMP: 147
SQ FT: 12,000

SALES (est): 29.5MM
SALES (corp-wide): 2.6B **Publicly Held**
SIC: 3812 7372 Search & navigation
equipment; prepackaged software
PA: Trimble Inc.
935 Stewart Dr
Sunnyvale CA 94085
408 481-8000

(G-9003)
ALLOS THERAPEUTICS INC
302 Carnegie Ctr Ste 200 (08540-6376)
PHONE.................................609 936-3760
Mary McCalister, *Branch Mgr*
EMP: 4 **Publicly Held**
SIC: 2834 Pharmaceutical preparations
HQ: Allos Therapeutics, Inc.
11000 Westmoor Cir # 150
Westminster CO 80021

(G-9004)
**APPEX INNOVATION
SOLUTIONS LLC**
103 Carnegie Ctr (08540-6235)
PHONE.................................215 313-3332
Pooja Vora, *President*
Manoj Vora, *Vice Pres*
Ankur Vora,
EMP: 5 EST: 2013
SALES (est): 129.8K **Privately Held**
SIC: 7379 7372 7371 7373 ; application
computer software; computer software
systems analysis & design, custom; sys-
tems software development services

(G-9005)
APPLE TREE
47 Hulfish St Ste 441 (08542-3713)
PHONE.................................609 751-5375
Seth Harrison, *Principal*
Maja Nowak CPA, *Accounting Mgr*
EMP: 5
SALES (est): 756.9K **Privately Held**
SIC: 3571 Personal computers (microcom-
puters)

(G-9006)
**ARALEZ PHARMACEUTICALS
MGT INC**
Also Called: Aralez Management
400 Alexander Park (08540-6539)
PHONE.................................609 917-9330
Adrian Adams, *CEO*
EMP: 4
SALES (est): 135.6K
SALES (corp-wide): 105.9MM **Privately
Held**
SIC: 2834 Pharmaceutical preparations
PA: Aralez Pharmaceuticals Inc
7100 W Credit Ave Suite 101
Mississauga ON L5N 0
905 876-1118

(G-9007)
**ARALEZ PHARMACEUTICALS
US INC**
400 Alexander Park (08540-6539)
PHONE.................................609 917-9330
Scott Charles, *CFO*
Jason Aryeh, *Bd of Directors*
Neal Fowler, *Bd of Directors*
Robert Harris, *Bd of Directors*
Arthur Kirsch, *Bd of Directors*
EMP: 10
SALES (est): 2.9MM **Privately Held**
SIC: 2834 Pharmaceutical preparations

(G-9008)
ARGYLE INTERNATIONAL INC
254 Wall St (08540-1511)
PHONE.................................609 924-9484
Fax: 609 924-2679
Arthur Gillman, *President*
Lian Shentu, *Vice Pres*
EMP: 7
SQ FT: 2,000
SALES (est): 590K **Privately Held**
WEB: www.argyleint.com
SIC: 3827 Optical instruments & lenses

(G-9009)
**ARM & HAMMER ANIMAL NTRTN
LLC (HQ)**
Also Called: Arm & Hammer Animal & Fd
Prod
469 N Harrison St (08540-3510)
PHONE.................................800 526-3563
Matthew Farrell, *CEO*
EMP: 5 EST: 2014
SALES (est): 207.2K
SALES (corp-wide): 3.7B **Publicly Held**
SIC: 3556 Dairy & milk machinery
PA: Church & Dwight Co., Inc.
500 Charles Ewing Blvd
Ewing NJ 08628
609 806-1200

(G-9010)
ARMKEL LLC (HQ)
469 N Harrison St (08540-3510)
PHONE.................................609 683-5900
Robert A Davies III,
Bradley A Casper,
Zvi Eiref,
Adrian Huns,
Maureen K Usifer,
▲ EMP: 650
SALES (est): 76.8MM
SALES (corp-wide): 3.7B **Publicly Held**
WEB: www.naircare.com
SIC: 2844 2835 Toilet preparations; de-
pilatories (cosmetic); pregnancy test kits
PA: Church & Dwight Co., Inc.
500 Charles Ewing Blvd
Ewing NJ 08628
609 806-1200

(G-9011)
ARTEZIO LLC
195 Nassau St Rear 32 (08542-7004)
PHONE.................................609 786-2435
Pavel Adylin, *CEO*
Alexander Izosenkov, *Manager*
EMP: 4
SALES: 4.8MM
SALES (corp-wide): 6.4MM **Privately
Held**
SIC: 7371 7379 7372 Computer software
development & applications; ; business
oriented computer software
PA: Artezio, Ooo
D. 36 Korp. 1, Shosse Pyatnitskoe
Moscow 12343
495 232-2683

(G-9012)
AVEBE NORTH AMERICA INC
4 Independence Way (08540-6634)
PHONE.................................609 520-1400
Bernard Palowitch Jr, *President*
▲ EMP: 10
SALES (est): 1.1MM **Privately Held**
SIC: 2819 2833 Chemicals, high purity: re-
fined from technical grade; medicinal
chemicals

(G-9013)
BATALLURE BEAUTY LLC (PA)
104 Carnegie Ctr Ste 202 (08540-6232)
PHONE.................................609 716-1200
Robin Burns McNeil, *Ch of Bd*
Loren Zachau, *Purchasing*
Ann Speranza, *Human Resources*
Jeff Ghusson, *Marketing Mgr*
Amy Schinoff, *Marketing Mgr*
▲ EMP: 40
SQ FT: 4,000
SALES (est): 12.9MM **Privately Held**
WEB: www.batallure.com
SIC: 2844 Perfumes & colognes

(G-9014)
**BERLITZ LANGUAGES US INC
(DH)**
7 Roszel Rd Fl 3 (08540-6257)
PHONE.................................609 759-5371
Yukako Uchinaga, *CEO*
Paul Weinstein, *Vice Pres*
Alistair Gatoff, *VP Finance*
Allison Raets, *Sales Staff*
EMP: 65
SQ FT: 62,275

SALES (est): 113MM
SALES (corp-wide): 4B **Privately Held**
WEB: www.berlitz.us
SIC: 8299 7389 2731 Language school;
translation services; books: publishing
only
HQ: Berlitz Corporation
7 Roszel Rd Fl 3
Princeton NJ 08540
207 828-3768

(G-9015)
**BERLITZ PUBLISHING
COMPANY INC**
7 Roszel Rd (08540-6287)
PHONE.................................609 514-9650
Soichiro Fukutake, *Ch of Bd*
Ellen Adler, *Vice Pres*
EMP: 33
SALES (est): 2MM
SALES (corp-wide): 4B **Privately Held**
SIC: 2731 2741 Books: publishing only;
miscellaneous publishing
HQ: Berlitz Languages (United States), Inc.
7 Roszel Rd Fl 3
Princeton NJ 08540
609 759-5371

(G-9016)
BIONPHARMA INC
600 Alexander Rd Ste 2-4b (08540-6013)
PHONE.................................609 380-3313
Venkat Krishman, *CEO*
Bill Winter, *Senior VP*
EMP: 5 EST: 2014
SALES (est): 523K **Privately Held**
SIC: 2834 Pharmaceutical preparations

(G-9017)
BLUECLONE NETWORKS LLC
103 Carnegie Ctr Ste 300 (08540-6235)
P.O. Box 241, Princeton Junction (08550-
0241)
PHONE.................................609 944-8433
Fax: 609 944-8433
Milan Baria, *CEO*
EMP: 8
SQ FT: 10,000
SALES (est): 980K **Privately Held**
SIC: 3572 4813 7376 7373 Computer
storage devices; voice telephone commu-
nications; computer facilities manage-
ment; systems integration services;
computer maintenance & repair

(G-9018)
**BRISTOL-MYERS SQUIBB
COMPANY**
100 Nassau Park Blvd # 200 (08540-5997)
PHONE.................................609 419-5000
Richard Wyzga, *Project Mgr*
Dadong LI, *Director*
Sujit Srivastava, *Associate Dir*
EMP: 5
SALES (corp-wide): 20.7B **Publicly Held**
WEB: www.bms.com
SIC: 2834 Pharmaceutical preparations
PA: Bristol-Myers Squibb Company
430 E 29th St Fl 14
New York NY 10016
212 546-4000

(G-9019)
**BRISTOL-MYERS SQUIBB
COMPANY**
Province Line Rd Rr 206 (08540)
P.O. Box 5200 (08543-5200)
PHONE.................................609 252-4875
Leon Rosenberg, *Principal*
EMP: 4
SALES (corp-wide): 20.7B **Publicly Held**
SIC: 8731 2834 Commercial physical re-
search; pharmaceutical preparations
PA: Bristol-Myers Squibb Company
430 E 29th St Fl 14
New York NY 10016
212 546-4000

(G-9020)
**CALYPTUS PHARMACEUTICALS
INC ✪**
174 Nassau St Ste 364 (08542-7005)
PHONE.................................908 720-6049
Sujeet Singh, *CEO*
EMP: 10 EST: 2017

SALES (est): 508.3K **Privately Held**
SIC: 2834 Pharmaceutical preparations

(G-9021)
CHEMICAL RESOURCES INC (PA)
Also Called: Chemres
103 Carnegie Ctr Ste 100 (08540-6235)
PHONE..............................609 520-0000
Paul Keimig, *Owner*
Jim Couture, *Vice Pres*
Bob Hamilton, *Vice Pres*
◆ EMP: 35
SQ FT: 5,000
SALES (est): 99.2MM **Privately Held**
WEB: www.chemicalresourcesinc.com
SIC: 5162 5169 2865 Plastics materials & basic shapes; chemicals & allied products; cyclic crudes & intermediates

(G-9022)
CHRYSLIS DATA SLTONS SVCS CORP (PA)
Also Called: Cdss
100 Overlook Ctr Fl 2 (08540-7814)
PHONE..............................609 375-2000
Subramani Somasundaram, *Ch of Bd*
Seethalakshmi Vaidyanathan, *Admin Sec*
EMP: 5
SALES (est): 219.8K **Privately Held**
SIC: 7374 2741 7371 Data processing & preparation; ; computer software development & applications

(G-9023)
CHURCH & DWIGHT CO INC
Arm & Hammer
101 Thanet Cir Ste 1 (08540-3675)
PHONE..............................609 683-8021
Steven Kugini, *Branch Mgr*
EMP: 9
SALES (corp-wide): 3.7B **Publicly Held**
WEB: www.churchdwight.com
SIC: 2812 Sodium bicarbonate
PA: Church & Dwight Co., Inc.
500 Charles Ewing Blvd
Ewing NJ 08628
609 806-1200

(G-9024)
CURRAN & CONNORS INC
5 Independence Way # 300 (08540-6627)
PHONE..............................609 514-0104
Fax: 609 514-0108
Shelley Feder, *Regional Mgr*
EMP: 5
SALES (corp-wide): 15.4MM **Privately Held**
SIC: 2721 Periodicals
PA: Curran & Connors, Inc.
140 Adams Ave Ste C20
Hauppauge NY 11788
631 435-0400

(G-9025)
CYBAGE SOFTWARE INC
500 College Rd E Ste 203 (08540-6635)
PHONE..............................848 219-1221
Mahesh Kumar, *Publisher*
Gurvinder S Chhatwal, *Principal*
Himanshu Patel, *Project Mgr*
Nitin Soni, *Project Mgr*
Rohit Deshpande, *Engineer*
EMP: 5 **Privately Held**
SIC: 7372 Prepackaged software
HQ: Cybage Software, Inc.
4058 148th Ave Ne 1d
Redmond WA 98052
425 861-9190

(G-9026)
CYTEC INDUSTRIES INC
504 Carnegie Ctr (08540-6241)
PHONE..............................877 463-7645
EMP: 8
SALES (corp-wide): 10MM **Privately Held**
SIC: 2899 Chemical preparations
HQ: Cytec Industries Inc.
250 Pehle Ave Ste 306
Saddle Brook NJ 07663

(G-9027)
DAILY PLAN IT EXECUTIVE CENTER
707 Alexander Rd Ste 208 (08540-6331)
PHONE..............................609 514-9494
Fax: 609 243-0045
Michelle Stemmer, *Principal*
EMP: 4
SALES (est): 173K **Privately Held**
SIC: 2711 Newspapers, publishing & printing

(G-9028)
DATARAM MEMORY
777 Alexander Rd Ste 100 (08540-6300)
PHONE..............................609 799-0071
David A Moylan, *President*
Anthony M Lougee, *CFO*
EMP: 40
SALES: 17MM
SALES (corp-wide): 28MM **Privately Held**
SIC: 3572 Computer storage devices
PA: Leading Testing Laboratories Llc
20823 Park Row Dr Ste 28c
Katy TX 77449
281 600-8227

(G-9029)
DIVERSITYINC MEDIA LLC
100 Overlook Ctr Fl 2 (08540-7814)
P.O. Box 348 (08542-0348)
PHONE..............................973 494-0539
Carolynn Johnson, *COO*
Lucas J Visconti, *Mng Member*
EMP: 19
SQ FT: 5,500
SALES (est): 946.4K **Privately Held**
WEB: www.diversityinc.com
SIC: 2721 Magazines: publishing only, not printed on site

(G-9030)
DOLAN LLC
Also Called: Virginia Lawyers Weekly
421 Executive Dr (08540-1526)
PHONE..............................800 451-9998
EMP: 4
SALES (corp-wide): 483MM **Privately Held**
SIC: 2711 Newspapers
HQ: Dolan Llc
222 S 9th St Ste 2300
Minneapolis MN 55402

(G-9031)
DOLCE TECHNOLOGIES LLC
90 Nassau St Fl 4 (08542-4529)
PHONE..............................609 497-7319
Fax: 609 497-7363
John C Dries,
Marshall Cohen,
John Dries,
Michael Ettenberg,
Michael Lange,
EMP: 4
SALES (est): 311.3K **Privately Held**
SIC: 3826 Mass spectroscopy instrumentation

(G-9032)
DR REDDYS LABORATORIES INC (HQ)
107 College Rd E (08540-6623)
PHONE..............................609 375-9900
Fax: 908 203-4970
Alok Sonig, *President*
Swaninathan Chandrasekaran, *Corp Secy*
Sunil Kumar Chebrolu, *Finance*
◆ EMP: 38
SQ FT: 1,742,400
SALES (est): 54.2MM **Privately Held**
SIC: 3089 5122 Cases, plastic; pharmaceuticals

(G-9033)
DVX LLC
31 Airpark Rd Ste 2 (08540-1533)
PHONE..............................609 924-3590
Fax: 609 651-4422
David Vilkomerson,
EMP: 4
SQ FT: 5,000

SALES: 500K **Privately Held**
WEB: www.dvx.com
SIC: 3845 Ultrasonic medical equipment, except cleaning

(G-9034)
E R SQUIBB & SONS INTER-AM (HQ)
Also Called: Bristol-Myers Squibb
3551 Lawrenceville Rd (08540-4715)
P.O. Box 4000 (08543-4000)
PHONE..............................609 252-4111
Fax: 609 252-6703
Lamberto Andreotti, *CEO*
Quintan Oswald, *President*
James M Cornelius, *Chairman*
Rebecca Prince, *Counsel*
Donald Hayden, *Senior VP*
▲ EMP: 1
SQ FT: 735,000
SALES (est): 84.9MM
SALES (corp-wide): 20.7B **Publicly Held**
WEB: www.unitedinpurpose.com
SIC: 2834 Pharmaceutical preparations
PA: Bristol-Myers Squibb Company
430 E 29th St Fl 14
New York NY 10016
212 546-4000

(G-9035)
ECO LLC
344 Nassau St Ste F (08540-4622)
PHONE..............................609 683-9030
Kevin Stockdale,
EMP: 4
SALES (est): 333K **Privately Held**
SIC: 2834 Veterinary pharmaceutical preparations

(G-9036)
EDDA TECHNOLOGY INC
5 Independence Way # 210 (08540-6627)
PHONE..............................609 919-9889
Jian-Zhong Qian, *President*
LI Fan, *COO*
EMP: 12
SALES (est): 1.7MM **Privately Held**
SIC: 3841 Diagnostic apparatus, medical

(G-9037)
ELECTEDFACE LLC
26 Snowden Ln (08540-3916)
PHONE..............................609 924-3636
Richard H Glanton,
Richard Glanton,
EMP: 32 EST: 2010
SALES (est): 1.6MM **Privately Held**
SIC: 2741

(G-9038)
EMPTY WALLS INC
Also Called: Framesmith Gallery, The
3495 Us Highway 1 Ste 21 (08540-5933)
PHONE..............................609 452-8488
Paul Smith, *President*
Lisa Schwartz, *Vice Pres*
EMP: 5
SQ FT: 1,600
SALES: 300K **Privately Held**
SIC: 5999 3952 Art dealers; frames for artists' canvases

(G-9039)
ENTERPRISE SERVICES LLC
989 Lenox Dr (08544-0001)
PHONE..............................609 259-9400
Larry Consalvoas, *Branch Mgr*
EMP: 53
SALES (corp-wide): 13.4B **Publicly Held**
WEB: www.eds.com
SIC: 7372 Prepackaged software
HQ: Enterprise Services Llc
5400 Legacy Dr
Plano TX 75024
703 245-9675

(G-9040)
EON LABS INC
506 Carnegie Ctr Ste 400 (08540-6243)
PHONE..............................609 627-8600
Bernhard Hampl, *President*
▲ EMP: 525
SQ FT: 20,000
SALES (est): 55.8MM **Privately Held**
WEB: www.eonlabs.com
SIC: 2834 Pharmaceutical preparations

(G-9041)
EVENUS PHARMACEUTICAL LABS INC
506 Carnegie Ctr Ste 100 (08540-6243)
PHONE..............................609 395-8625
Jack Zheng, *CEO*
▲ EMP: 8
SQ FT: 5,732
SALES (est): 630K **Privately Held**
SIC: 2834 Pharmaceutical preparations

(G-9042)
EVEX ANALYTICAL INSTRUMENTS
Also Called: Evex Instruments
857 State Rd (08540-1415)
P.O. Box 8439 (08543-8439)
PHONE..............................609 252-9192
Peter Tarquinio, *President*
EMP: 14
SQ FT: 15,000
SALES (est): 1.5MM **Privately Held**
WEB: www.evex.com
SIC: 3826 Analytical instruments

(G-9043)
EXCELL BRANDS LTD LIABILITY CO
3 Independence Way # 114 (08540-6626)
PHONE..............................908 561-1130
EMP: 5
SALES (est): 658.3K **Privately Held**
SIC: 2844 5149 Perfumes & colognes; flavourings & fragrances

(G-9044)
FELLOWSHIP IN PRAYER INC
291 Witherspoon St (08542-3227)
PHONE..............................609 924-6863
Howard Ende, *President*
EMP: 4
SALES: 57.2K **Privately Held**
SIC: 2721 Trade journals: publishing only, not printed on site

(G-9045)
FINEX TRADE
315 Riverside Dr (08540-5429)
PHONE..............................609 921-2747
Cuneyt Buyukucak, *Owner*
▲ EMP: 1
SQ FT: 2,500
SALES (est): 5.7MM **Privately Held**
WEB: www.finextrade.com
SIC: 2079 1799 Olive oil; athletic & recreation facilities construction

(G-9046)
FOUNDATION FOR STUDENT COMM
Also Called: BUSINESS TODAY
48 University Pl Ste 305 (08540-5116)
PHONE..............................609 258-1111
Fax: 609 258-1222
Carol Klein, *President*
Jonathan Hastings, *President*
David Green, *Editor*
Amit Mukherjee, *Trustee*
Jack Jundanian, *Manager*
EMP: 50
SALES: 1.2MM **Privately Held**
SIC: 2721 7389 Periodicals: publishing only; convention & show services

(G-9047)
FRAUSCHER SENSOR TECH USA INC
300 Carnegie Ctr Ste 320 (08540-6255)
PHONE..............................609 285-5492
Vivek Caroli, *Director*
EMP: 10 EST: 2015
SALES (est): 193K **Privately Held**
SIC: 3674 Radiation sensors
HQ: Frauscher Sensortechnik Gmbh
GewerbestraBe 1
St. Marienkirchen 4774
771 129-200

(G-9048)
FREYR INC
150 College Rd W Ste 102 (08540-6659)
PHONE..............................908 483-7958
Srinivasa Sadhu, *President*
Marc Adams, *Sr Associate*

▲ = Import ▼=Export
◆ =Import/Export

EMP: 150 EST: 2011
SALES: 6.5MM **Privately Held**
SIC: 7372 5045 Prepackaged software;
computer software

(G-9049)
GEISTLICH PHARMA NORTH AMERICA
202 Carnegie Ctr Ste 103 (08540-6239)
PHONE................................609 779-6560
Andreas Geistlich PHD, *CEO*
David Swanson, *General Mgr*
Maria Nyholm, *Sales Staff*
Alexandra Rodriguez, *Marketing Mgr*
Karen Benson, *Corp Comm Staff*
EMP: 39
SQ FT: 3,500
SALES (est): 24.1MM **Privately Held**
SIC: 3843 Dental equipment & supplies
HQ: Geistlich Pharma Ag
    Bahnhofstrasse 40
    Wolhusen LU
    414 925-555

(G-9050)
GLOBAL IDS INC
182 Nassau St Ste 202 (08542-7000)
PHONE................................609 683-1066
Arka Mukherjee, *CEO*
EMP: 100
SALES (est): 4.9MM **Privately Held**
SIC: 7372 Prepackaged software

(G-9051)
GUERBET LLC
821 Alexander Rd Ste 204 (08540-6352)
PHONE................................812 333-0059
Fax: 812 333-0084
Massimo Carrara, *Mng Member*
▲ EMP: 21
SALES (est): 6.4MM
SALES (corp-wide): 550.5MM **Privately Held**
WEB: www.guerbet-us.com
SIC: 2833 5122 Medicinals & botanicals;
drugs, proprietaries & sundries
PA: Guerbet
    Roissy Cdg Cedex
    Villepinte 93420
    145 915-000

(G-9052)
HALO PUB ICE CREAM
9 Hulfish St (08542-3709)
PHONE................................609 921-1710
Jerry Reilly, *Owner*
EMP: 17
SALES (est): 992.8K **Privately Held**
SIC: 2024 Ice cream, bulk

(G-9053)
HALTON LABORATORIES LLC
400 Alexander Park (08540-6539)
PHONE................................609 917-9330
Andrew Kovan, *President*
Scott J Charles, *Treasurer*
Alan Sokaler, *Asst Treas*
Eric Trachtenberg, *Admin Sec*
EMP: 4
SALES (est): 408.9K
SALES (corp-wide): 105.9MM **Privately Held**
SIC: 2834 Pharmaceutical preparations
PA: Aralez Pharmaceuticals Inc
    7100 W Credit Ave Suite 101
    Mississauga ON L5N 0
    905 876-1118

(G-9054)
HEALTHPER INC (PA)
124 Brookstone Dr (08540-2404)
P.O. Box 110005, Trumbull CT (06611-0005)
PHONE................................888 257-1804
David Lenihan, *Ch of Bd*
Narinder Makin, *Vice Pres*
EMP: 1
SALES: 1MM **Privately Held**
SIC: 7372 Application computer software

(G-9055)
HENGRUI THERAPEUTICS INC
506 Carnegie Ctr Ste 102 (08540-6243)
PHONE................................609 423-2155
EMP: 4

SALES (est): 90K **Privately Held**
SIC: 2834 Pharmaceutical preparations

(G-9056)
I-EXCEED TECH SOLUTIONS INC
103 Carnegie Ctr Ste 300 (08540-6235)
PHONE................................917 693-3207
EMP: 4 EST: 2011
SALES: 1.5MM **Privately Held**
SIC: 7372 7371 Prepackaged Software
Services Custom Computer Programing

(G-9057)
INDO-US MIM TEC PRIVATE LTD
214 Carnegie Ctr Ste 104 (08540-6244)
PHONE................................734 327-9842
Param Gutti, *Manager*
EMP: 5 **Privately Held**
SIC: 3545 3544 3423 Machine tool accessories; special dies, tools, jigs & fixtures; hand & edge tools
PA: Indo-Mim Private Limited
    No 45, (P) Kiadb Industrial Area
    Bengaluru KA 56211

(G-9058)
INFINIX CORP
4390 Us Highway 1 Ste 213 (08540-5747)
PHONE................................609 936-0101
Uday Nadkarni, *President*
EMP: 30
SQ FT: 2,500
SALES (est): 2MM **Privately Held**
WEB: www.infinixcorp.com
SIC: 7372 Prepackaged software

(G-9059)
INTELLIGENT MTL SOLUTIONS INC
Also Called: IMS
201 Washington Rd (08540-6449)
PHONE................................609 514-4031
Howard Bell, *President*
Joe Dempsey, *CFO*
Josh Collins, *CTO*
EMP: 15
SQ FT: 12,000
SALES (est): 3.6MM **Privately Held**
SIC: 2819 Industrial inorganic chemicals

(G-9060)
IRON4U INC
5 Independence Way # 300 (08540-6627)
PHONE................................609 514-5163
Odd Vaage-Nilsen, *President*
Lars Peitersen, *Vice Pres*
Christian Rode, *CFO*
EMP: 5
SALES (est): 303.3K **Privately Held**
SIC: 2834 Veterinary pharmaceutical preparations

(G-9061)
JB ELECTRONICS
101 Wall St (08540-1522)
PHONE................................609 497-2952
EMP: 10
SALES (est): 660K **Privately Held**
SIC: 3679 Design & Assemble Electronic Circuits

(G-9062)
JIANGSU HENGRUI MEDICINE CO
506 Carnegie Ctr (08540-6243)
PHONE................................609 395-8625
EMP: 6
SALES (est): 823.8K **Privately Held**
SIC: 2834 Pharmaceutical preparations

(G-9063)
JOHNSON & JOHNSON
51 Pettit Pl (08540-7645)
PHONE................................732 524-0400
EMP: 80
SALES (corp-wide): 76.4B **Publicly Held**
SIC: 2676 Feminine hygiene paper products
PA: Johnson & Johnson
    1 Johnson And Johnson Plz
    New Brunswick NJ 08933
    732 524-0400

(G-9064)
KOAMTAC INC
116 Village Blvd Ste 305 (08540-5721)
PHONE................................609 734-4335
Hanjin Lee, *President*
Terence Brown, *Sales Mgr*
Clara Lee, *Sales Mgr*
Kevin Conabree, *Director*
EMP: 8
SQ FT: 1,200
SALES (est): 1.1MM **Privately Held**
SIC: 3679 Electronic circuits

(G-9065)
KYOWA HAKKO KIRIN CAL INC
212 Carnegie Ctr Ste 101 (08540-6236)
PHONE................................609 580-7400
Kazuyoshi Tachibana, *President*
Licat Lavake Lisa, *Project Mgr*
Tom Lauterio, *Director*
EMP: 5
SALES (corp-wide): 16.6B **Privately Held**
SIC: 2834 Pharmaceutical preparations
HQ: Kyowa Hakko Kirin California, Inc.
    9420 Athena Cir
    La Jolla CA 92037

(G-9066)
LDM INC
Also Called: Ivy Inn
248 Nassau St (08542-4623)
PHONE................................609 921-8555
Richard Ryan, *President*
EMP: 15
SQ FT: 2,700
SALES (est): 757.4K **Privately Held**
SIC: 5813 2599 Tavern (drinking places);
bar, restaurant & cafeteria furniture

(G-9067)
LIGHTSCAPE MATERIALS INC
201 Washington Rd (08540-6449)
PHONE................................609 734-2224
Gerard Frederickson, *CEO*
Jennifer Downes, *Office Mgr*
▲ EMP: 6
SALES: 950K **Privately Held**
SIC: 2816 Inorganic pigments

(G-9068)
LRK INC
Also Called: Lucy's Ravioli Kitchen
830 State Rd Ste 3 (08540-1443)
PHONE................................609 924-6881
Caron Wendell, *President*
Joseph McLaughlin, *Vice Pres*
EMP: 14
SALES (est): 2MM **Privately Held**
SIC: 2099 5812 Pasta, uncooked: packaged with other ingredients; eating places

(G-9069)
LUYE PHARMA USA LTD
502 Carnegie Ctr Ste 103 (08540-6289)
PHONE................................609 799-7600
Liu Dian-Bo, *Chairman*
EMP: 23 EST: 2015
SALES (est): 4.2MM **Privately Held**
SIC: 2834 Druggists' preparations (pharmaceuticals)

(G-9070)
MARKUS WIENER PUBLISHERS INC
231 Nassau St (08542-4601)
PHONE................................609 921-1141
Fax: 609 921-1140
Markus Wiener, *President*
Shelley Frisch, *Vice Pres*
EMP: 6
SALES: 1MM **Privately Held**
WEB: www.markuswiener.com
SIC: 2731 Books: publishing only

(G-9071)
MAYFAIR TECH LTD LBLTY CO
Also Called: Pendotech
66 Witherspoon St (08542-3239)
PHONE................................609 802-1262
James Furey,
EMP: 10
SALES: 2MM **Privately Held**
WEB: www.pendotech.com
SIC: 3823 Industrial instrmnts msrmnt display/control process variable

(G-9072)
MEGALITH PHARMACEUTICALS INC
302 Carnegie Ctr (08540-6374)
PHONE................................877 436-7220
EMP: 4
SALES (est): 189.4K **Privately Held**
SIC: 2834 Pharmaceutical preparations

(G-9073)
METAL POWDER INDS FEDERATION
105 College Rd E Ste 101 (08540-6622)
PHONE................................609 452-7700
C James Trambino, *CEO*
Jillaine K Regan, *Vice Pres*
EMP: 16
SQ FT: 7,100
SALES: 4.5MM **Privately Held**
SIC: 8611 2731 Trade associations; book publishing

(G-9074)
MIKROS SYSTEMS CORPORATION (PA)
707 Alexander Rd (08540-6331)
P.O. Box 7189 (08543-7189)
PHONE................................609 987-1513
Thomas J Meaney, *CEO*
Paul G Casner, *Ch of Bd*
Walter T Bristow, *COO*
Walter Bristow, *COO*
Thomas Meaney, *CFO*
EMP: 2
SALES: 7.2MM **Publicly Held**
SIC: 3571 7371 8731 Personal computers (microcomputers); computer software development; computer (hardware) development

(G-9075)
MILLENNIUM INFO TECH INC
4390 Us Highway 1 Ste 121 (08540-5747)
PHONE................................609 750-7120
Ramana Krosuri, *President*
Sunita Krosuri, *CFO*
EMP: 95
SQ FT: 2,000
SALES: 6MM **Privately Held**
WEB: www.mitiweb.com
SIC: 7372 Prepackaged software

(G-9076)
MMTC INC
12 Roszel Rd Ste A203 (08540-6286)
PHONE................................609 520-9699
Fax: 609 520-9859
Fred Sterzer, *President*
EMP: 6
SALES (est): 470K **Privately Held**
SIC: 3825 Microwave test equipment

(G-9077)
MORE THAN A NOTION FABRICS LTD
4437 Route 27 (08540-8715)
PHONE................................732 821-5580
Valerie T Thomas, *Managing Prtnr*
EMP: 5
SALES (est): 279.4K **Privately Held**
SIC: 2335 Wedding gowns & dresses

(G-9078)
MORSE METAL PRODUCTS CO INC (PA)
1 Hunters Run (08540-8646)
PHONE................................732 422-3676
Carl H Geisler, *President*
Ceasar Leiva, *Manager*
EMP: 6 EST: 1945
SALES (est): 705.1K **Privately Held**
SIC: 3537 Industrial trucks & tractors

(G-9079)
MULTIFORCE SYSTEMS CORPORATION
101 Wall St (08540-1522)
PHONE................................609 683-4242
Fax: 609 497-2953
Thomas Bates, *President*
W K Griesinger, *Chairman*
G Hallman, *Shareholder*
▼ EMP: 19 EST: 1981
SQ FT: 10,400

SALES (est): 4.4MM **Privately Held**
WEB: www.fuelforce.com
SIC: 3823 8748 7373 Gas flow computers, industrial process type; business consulting; computer systems analysis &
design

(G-9080)
NEWCARDIO INC
103 Carnegie Ctr Ste 300 (08540-6235)
PHONE.............................877 332-4324
Dr Jess Emery Jones, *CEO*
Michael E Hanson, *Principal*
James A Heisch, *Principal*
Greg Sadowski, *COO*
EMP: 11
SQ FT: 2,000
SALES (est): 838.1K **Privately Held**
SIC: 3845 Electromedical equipment

(G-9081)
NIKSUN INC (PA)
457 N Harrison St (08540-3510)
PHONE.............................609 936-9999
Parag Pruthi, *CEO*
Satish C Pruthi, *President*
Andrew Heybey, *Chief*
Ted Galletta, *Vice Pres*
Korwin Lee, *Vice Pres*
EMP: 200 EST: 1997
SQ FT: 30,616
SALES (est): 38.2MM **Privately Held**
WEB: www.niksun.com
SIC: 7373 3571 Computer integrated sys-
tems design; electronic computers

(G-9082)
NONZERO FOUNDATION INC
321 Prospect Ave (08540-5330)
PHONE.............................609 688-0793
Robert Wright, *President*
Paul Glastris, *Trustee*
Jacqueline Shire, *Trustee*
EMP: 5
SALES (est): 282.1K **Privately Held**
SIC: 2741

(G-9083)
NOVO NORDISK INC
1100 Camput Rd (08540)
PHONE.............................609 987-5800
EMP: 6
SALES (corp-wide): 17.7B **Privately Held**
SIC: 2834 Pharmaceutical preparations
HQ: Novo Nordisk Inc.
800 Scudders Mill Rd
Plainsboro NJ 08536
609 987-5800

(G-9084)
**OAVCO LTD LIABILITY
COMPANY (PA)**
Also Called: Oav Air Bearing
103 Carnegie Ctr (08540-6235)
P.O. Box 7421 (08543-7421)
PHONE.............................855 535-4227
Murat Erturk, *Principal*
EMP: 10
SQ FT: 10,000
SALES (est): 2MM **Privately Held**
SIC: 3812 Omnibearing indicators

(G-9085)
OAVIATION CORPORATION
103 Carnegie Ctr Ste 212 (08540-6235)
PHONE.............................609 619-3060
Murat Erturk, *President*
EMP: 25
SQ FT: 25,000
SALES (est): 4.1MM **Privately Held**
SIC: 3812 Search & navigation equipment

(G-9086)
OHM LABORATORIES INC
Also Called: Ranbaxy Pharmaceuticals
2 Independence Way (08540-6620)
P.O. Box 8208 (08543-8208)
PHONE.............................609 720-9200
Lavesh Samtani, *Vice Pres*
Bob Patton, *Plant Mgr*
Kishore Durga, *Opers Staff*
Debbie Stryker, *Buyer*
Jane Edwards, *Accounting Dir*
EMP: 100

SALES (corp-wide): 1.2B **Privately Held**
WEB: www.ranbaxy.com
SIC: 2834 Pharmaceutical preparations
HQ: Ohm Laboratories Inc.
1385 Livingston Ave
North Brunswick NJ 08902
732 418-2235

(G-9087)
**OMTHERA PHARMACEUTICALS
INC**
Also Called: (A DEVELOPMENT-STAGE
COMPANY)
707 State Rd Ste 206 (08540-1437)
PHONE.............................908 741-4399
Fax: 908 741-6524
Gerald Wisler, *President*
Bernardus N Machielse, *COO*
Ramona M Lloyd, *Vice Pres*
Timothy J Maines, *Vice Pres*
Christian S Schade, *CFO*
EMP: 14
SALES (est): 1.9MM
SALES (corp-wide): 22.4B **Privately Held**
SIC: 2834 Pharmaceutical preparations
HQ: Astrazeneca Pharmaceuticals Lp
1 Medimmune Way
Gaithersburg MD 20878

(G-9088)
**ORCHID PHARMACEUTICALS
INC**
Also Called: Orchid Chemicals
116 Village Blvd Ste 200 (08540-5700)
PHONE.............................609 951-2209
Satish Srinivasan, *President*
▲ EMP: 4
SALES (est): 324K **Privately Held**
SIC: 2834 Pharmaceutical preparations

(G-9089)
PATHEON BIOLOGICS (NJ) LLC
201 College Rd E (08540-6610)
PHONE.............................609 919-3300
Mark R Bamforth, *CEO*
Robert J Broeze, *Senior VP*
Steven H Kasok, *CFO*
Vincent Matonti, *Manager*
▲ EMP: 86
SQ FT: 60,000
SALES (est): 33.6MM **Privately Held**
WEB: www.laureatepharma.com
SIC: 5122 2834 Pharmaceuticals; phar-
maceutical preparations
HQ: Patheon Biologics Llc
4766 Laguardia Dr
Saint Louis MO 63134

(G-9090)
PATHEON BIOLOGICS LLC
201 College Rd E (08540-6610)
PHONE.............................609 919-3300
Kim Hodges, *Production*
Robert Welch, *Production*
Michael Cola, *Branch Mgr*
Jacqueline Ramos, *Admin Asst*
EMP: 86 **Privately Held**
SIC: 2834 5122 Pharmaceutical prepara-
tions; pharmaceuticals
HQ: Patheon Biologics Llc
4766 Laguardia Dr
Saint Louis MO 63134

(G-9091)
**PHARMACEUTICAL
REGULATORY SVCS (PA)**
Also Called: P R S
58 Fairway Dr (08540-2408)
PHONE.............................609 497-9694
Jurij Petrin, *President*
Vilma Petrin, *Vice Pres*
EMP: 6
SALES (est): 955.6K **Privately Held**
WEB: www.pharmregservices.com
SIC: 2834 Pharmaceutical preparations

(G-9092)
PHILIP LIEF GROUP INC
371 Sayre Dr (08540-5860)
PHONE.............................609 430-1000
Fax: 609 430-0300
Philip Lief, *President*
EMP: 4
SQ FT: 2,500

SALES (est): 180K **Privately Held**
WEB: www.philliefgroup.com
SIC: 2731 Book publishing

(G-9093)
**POLYMATHES HOLDINGS I LLC
(PA)**
20 Nassau St Ste M (08542-4536)
PHONE.............................609 945-1690
Greg Amato, *CEO*
Murray S Cohen, *Ch of Bd*
James Ivchenko, *President*
EMP: 7 EST: 2012
SALES (est): 1.5MM **Privately Held**
SIC: 2865 6512 Dyes & pigments; nonres-
idential building operators

(G-9094)
**PRINCETON BIOPHARMA
STRATEGIES**
660 Pretty Brook Rd (08540-7510)
PHONE.............................609 203-5303
Fax: 609 688-8405
Mark Altmeyer, *Principal*
EMP: 4
SALES (est): 319.4K **Privately Held**
SIC: 2834 Pharmaceutical preparations

(G-9095)
**PRINCETON INFORMATION
CENTER**
Also Called: Applied Psychological Services
330 N Harrison St Ste 6 (08540-3500)
PHONE.............................609 924-7019
Robert Karlin, *President*
Barbara Scanna, *Business Mgr*
EMP: 4
SALES: 400K **Privately Held**
SIC: 2741 8999 Miscellaneous publishing;
psychological consultant

(G-9096)
**PRINCETON KEYNES GROUP
INC (PA)**
116 Village Blvd Ste 200 (08540-5700)
PHONE.............................609 951-2239
Douglas Stewart, *CEO*
▼ EMP: 13
SQ FT: 25,000
SALES (est): 1.6MM **Privately Held**
WEB: www.princetonkeynes.com
SIC: 2891 8711 Adhesives & sealants; en-
gineering services

(G-9097)
PRINCETON PACKET INC (HQ)
Also Called: Packet Publications
300 Witherspoon St (08542-3497)
P.O. Box 350 (08542-0350)
PHONE.............................609 924-3244
Fax: 609 924-3842
James B Kilgore, *President*
June Vogel, *Corp Secy*
Peg Gerke, *CFO*
Joan White, *Accounts Exec*
EMP: 169
SQ FT: 21,000
SALES (est): 41.7MM **Privately Held**
WEB: www.packetmediaguide.com
SIC: 2711 3993 Commercial printing &
newspaper publishing combined; signs &
advertising specialties
PA: Packet Media, Llc
198 Us Highway 9 Ste 100
Englishtown NJ 07726
856 779-3800

(G-9098)
PRINCETON PLASMA PHYSICS
100 Stellarator Rd (08540-6655)
PHONE.............................609 243-2000
Fax: 609 243-2751
Adam Cohen, *Principal*
Manfred Bitter, *Research*
Michio Okabayashi, *Research*
Kristen Fischer, *CFO*
Arturo Dominguez, *Senior Mgr*
EMP: 19 EST: 2011
SALES (est): 10.9MM **Privately Held**
SIC: 2836 Plasmas

(G-9099)
**PRINCETON PUBLISHING
GROUP**
650 Rosedale Rd (08540-2218)
PHONE.............................609 577-0693
Adam Drake Baer, *President*
EMP: 5
SALES (est): 304.9K **Privately Held**
SIC: 2731 Book publishing

(G-9100)
**PRINCETON QUADRANGLE
CLUB**
33 Prospect Ave (08540-5210)
PHONE.............................609 258-0376
Dinesh Maneyapanda, *Exec Dir*
Mary Eklund, *Admin Sec*
EMP: 7
SALES (est): 920.1K **Privately Held**
SIC: 8322 2099 Meal delivery program;
food preparations

(G-9101)
**PRINCETON RESEARCH
INSTRUMENTS**
Also Called: P R I
42 Cherry Valley Rd (08540-7640)
PHONE.............................609 924-0570
Charles A Crider, *President*
EMP: 4
SQ FT: 2,000
SALES (est): 320K **Privately Held**
WEB: www.prileeduhv.com
SIC: 3826 Analytical instruments

(G-9102)
PRINCETON SUPPLY CORP
301 N Harrison St Ste 473 (08540-3527)
PHONE.............................609 683-9100
John Astrab, *Principal*
EMP: 9
SALES (est): 2MM **Privately Held**
SIC: 2679 Paper products, converted

(G-9103)
**PRINCETON TRADE AND
TECHNOLOGY**
1 Wall St (08540)
PHONE.............................609 683-0215
Mohammed Labib, *President*
EMP: 10
SQ FT: 4,000
SALES (est): 942.9K **Privately Held**
SIC: 3845 Medical cleaning equipment, ul-
trasonic

(G-9104)
**PRINCETON UNIVERSITY PRESS
(PA)**
41 William St Ste 1 (08540-5223)
PHONE.............................609 258-4900
Fax: 609 258-4900
Harold T Shapiro, *President*
Anne Savarese, *Editor*
Peter J Dougherty, *Director*
Eric Crahan, *Senior Editor*
Alison Kalett, *Senior Editor*
▲ EMP: 99 EST: 1910
SQ FT: 26,000
SALES (est): 23.2MM **Privately Held**
WEB: www.pupress.princeton.edu
SIC: 2731 2741 Book publishing; miscella-
neous publishing

(G-9105)
**PRINCTON ALMNI PBLICATIONS
INC**
Also Called: Princeton Alumni Weekly
194 Nassau St Ste 38 (08542-7003)
PHONE.............................609 258-4885
Fax: 609 258-2247
Marilyn Mark, *President*
John I Merritt III, *President*
Nancy S Macmillan, *Admin Sec*
EMP: 8
SALES (est): 816.1K **Privately Held**
SIC: 2721 Magazines: publishing & printing

(G-9106)
PROMIA INCORPORATED
322 Commons Way (08540-1510)
PHONE.............................609 252-1850
Fax: 609 252-1855
Amy Reynolds, *Branch Mgr*

EMP: 5 **Privately Held**
SIC: **5734** 7379 7371 7372 Computer software & accessories; computer related consulting services; computer software development; prepackaged software
PA: Promia Incorporated
802 Chamberlain Ct
Mill Valley CA

(G-9107)
PROMIUS PHARMA LLC
107 College Rd E Ste 100 (08540-6623)
PHONE...............................609 282-1400
Anil Namboodiripad, *President*
Swaninathan Chandrasekaran, *Corp Secy*
Sunil Kumar Chebrolu, *Finance*
▲ EMP: 87
SALES (est): 24MM **Privately Held**
SIC: **2834** Pharmaceutical preparations
PA: Dr Reddy's Laboratories Limited
Door No. 8-2-337, Road No. 3
Hyderabad TS 50003

(G-9108)
QUANTUM SECURITY SYSTEMS INC
124 Fairfield Rd (08540-9579)
PHONE...............................609 252-0505
Harry Krotowski, *President*
EMP: 5
SALES (est): 693.7K **Privately Held**
SIC: **3699** Security control equipment & systems

(G-9109)
RANBAXY USA INC
2 Independence Way (08540-6620)
PHONE...............................609 720-9200
EMP: 25
SALES (est): 3.5MM
SALES (corp-wide): 1.2B **Privately Held**
SIC: **2834** 5122 Mfg Pharmaceutical Preparations Whol Drugs/Sundries
PA: Sun Pharmaceutical Industries Limited
Sun House, Cts No. 201 B/1,
Mumbai MH 40006
224 324-4324

(G-9110)
REFFERALS ONLY INC
Also Called: Roi Rnovations
3321 Lawrenceville Rd (08540-4719)
PHONE...............................609 921-1033
Linda Fahmie, *President*
EMP: 5
SALES (est): 432.4K **Privately Held**
SIC: **1389** Construction, repair & dismantling services

(G-9111)
REGENTREE LLC
116 Village Blvd Ste 200 (08540-5700)
PHONE...............................609 734-4328
Sunny Kim, *Manager*
EMP: 4
SALES (est): 194.1K **Privately Held**
SIC: **2834** Pharmaceutical preparations

(G-9112)
REPORTE HISPANO
42 Dorann Ave (08540-3906)
PHONE...............................609 933-1400
Fax: 609 924-5392
Kleibeel Sanandoval, *Principal*
EMP: 4
SALES (est): 278.7K **Privately Held**
SIC: **2711** Newspapers

(G-9113)
ROCKWOOD HOLDINGS INC (HQ)
100 Overlook Ctr Ste 101 (08540-7814)
PHONE...............................609 514-0300
Seifi Ghasemi, *CEO*
Monika Engel-Bader, *President*
Andrew M Ross, *President*
Thomas J Riordan, *Exec VP*
Robert J Zatta, *CFO*
◆ EMP: 35
SALES (est): 1.3B **Publicly Held**
SIC: **2819** 2816 Industrial inorganic chemicals; iron oxide pigments (ochers, siennas, umbers)

(G-9114)
ROCKWOOD SPECIALTIES GROUP INC (DH)
100 Overlook Ctr Ste 101 (08540-7814)
PHONE...............................609 514-0300
Fax: 609 514-8720
Seifi Ghasemi, *CEO*
Bob Zatta, *CFO*
◆ EMP: 10
SALES (est): 342.5MM **Publicly Held**
WEB: www.rockwoodadditives.com
SIC: **5169** 2899 Industrial chemicals; chemical preparations
HQ: Rockwood Holdings, Inc.
100 Overlook Ctr Ste 101
Princeton NJ 08540
609 514-0300

(G-9115)
SANDOZ INC (HQ)
100 College Rd W (08540-6604)
PHONE...............................609 627-8500
Benhard Hamel, *President*
Don Degolyer, *President*
Peter Goldschmidt, *President*
Robin Adelstein, *Vice Pres*
Mark Boehmer, *Vice Pres*
▲ EMP: 140 EST: 1963
SQ FT: 240,000
SALES (est): 519.3MM
SALES (corp-wide): 49.1B **Privately Held**
WEB: www.sandoz.com
SIC: **2834** 5122 Tablets, pharmaceutical; pills, pharmaceutical; pharmaceuticals
PA: Novartis Ag
Lichtstrasse 35
Basel BS 4056
613 241-111

(G-9116)
SENSORS UNLIMITED INC
330 Carter Rd Ste 100 (08540-7438)
PHONE...............................609 333-8000
Fax: 609 520-1663
John Trezza, *Principal*
Scott Divine, *Accounts Mgr*
Robert Freeman,
▲ EMP: 64
SQ FT: 41,000
SALES (est): 17MM
SALES (corp-wide): 59.8B **Publicly Held**
WEB: www.sensorsinc.com
SIC: **3357** 3663 3229 Fiber optic cable (insulated); electronic research; pressed & blown glass
HQ: Goodrich Corporation
2730 W Tyvola Rd
Charlotte NC 28217
704 423-7000

(G-9117)
SES ENGINEERING (US) INC
4 Research Way (08540-6707)
PHONE...............................609 987-4000
Michael Rist, *President*
Win Caldwell, *General Mgr*
Doug Clayton, *Senior VP*
Deepak Mathur, *Vice Pres*
John Matlaga, *Vice Pres*
EMP: 99
SALES (est): 27.6MM **Privately Held**
SIC: **3663** Satellites, communications
PA: Ses Sa
Chateau De Betzdorf
Betzdorf
710 725-

(G-9118)
SIGHTLOGIX INC
745 Alexander Rd Ste 5 (08540-6343)
PHONE...............................609 951-0008
Fax: 609 951-0024
Jim Hahn, *Ch of Bd*
John Romanowich, *President*
James Hahn, *Chairman*
Frank De Fina, *Exec VP*
Gabe Barbaro, *Mfg Dir*
EMP: 21
SQ FT: 5,000
SALES (est): 3.2MM **Privately Held**
WEB: www.sightlogix.com
SIC: **7382** 7373 3669 Protective devices, security; computer-aided manufacturing (CAM) systems service; visual communication systems

(G-9119)
SNOWDON INC
66 Maybury Hill Rd (08540-3617)
PHONE...............................732 230-3796
Fax: 732 235-3475
William J Welsh, *Principal*
EMP: 4
SALES (est): 250K **Privately Held**
SIC: **2834** Pharmaceutical preparations

(G-9120)
SOLIGENIX INC (PA)
29 Emmons Dr Ste B10 (08540-5950)
PHONE...............................609 538-8200
Fax: 609 538-8205
Christopher J Schaber, *Ch of Bd*
Oreola Donini, *Senior VP*
Karen Krumeich, *CFO*
Richard Straube, *Chief Mktg Ofcr*
Marco Brughera, *Bd of Directors*
EMP: 18
SQ FT: 6,200
SALES: 5.4MM **Publicly Held**
WEB: www.dorbiopharma.com
SIC: **8731** 2834 2836 Biological research; biotechnical research, commercial; pharmaceutical preparations; biological products, except diagnostic; vaccines

(G-9121)
SOLVAY HOLDING INC
Also Called: Rhodia
504 Carnegie Ctr (08540-6241)
P.O. Box 5203 (08543-5203)
PHONE...............................609 860-4000
James Harton, *President*
Jean Pierre Clamadieu, *Chairman*
John P Donahue, *Senior VP*
Karim Hajjar, *CFO*
Michel Defourny, *Admin Sec*
◆ EMP: 12825
SALES (est): 228.8MM
SALES (corp-wide): 10MM **Privately Held**
WEB: www.us.rhodia.com
SIC: **2819** 2812 2865 2869 Boric acid; phosphates, except fertilizers: defluorinated & ammoniated; soda ash, sodium carbonate (anhydrous); phenol, alkylated & cumene; diphenylamines; isocyanates; fluorinated hydrocarbon gases; silicones
HQ: Rhodia Holdings Limited
Oak House
Watford HERTS WD24

(G-9122)
SOLVAY USA INC (HQ)
504 Carnegie Ctr (08540-6241)
P.O. Box 477, Jersey City (07303-0477)
PHONE...............................609 860-2250
Fax: 609 860-2250
Michael Lacey, *President*
John P Donahue, *Vice Pres*
Mark Dahlinger, *CFO*
Anthony Saviano, *Admin Sec*
◆ EMP: 350 EST: 1995
SQ FT: 94,500
SALES (est): 954.8MM
SALES (corp-wide): 10MM **Privately Held**
WEB: www.food.us.rhodia.com
SIC: **2899** 2869 2821 2087 Chemical preparations; fluorinated hydrocarbon gases; silicones; plastics materials & resins; flavoring extracts & syrups; phenol, alkylated & cumene; diphenylamines; isocyanates
PA: Solvay Sa
Rue De Ransbeek 310
Bruxelles 1120
226 421-11

(G-9123)
SONDPEX CORP AMERICA LLC
Also Called: Sondpex Electronics
4185 Route 27 (08540-8704)
PHONE...............................732 940-4430
Fax: 732 940-4424
Katie Wu,
Chuck Chen,
▲ EMP: 8
SQ FT: 6,500
SALES (est): 4.5MM **Privately Held**
WEB: www.sondpex.com
SIC: **3651** Audio electronic systems

(G-9124)
SPACETOUCH INC
34 Chambers St (08542-3739)
PHONE...............................609 712-6572
Yingzhe Hu, *CEO*
EMP: 5 EST: 2015
SQ FT: 5,000
SALES: 50K **Privately Held**
SIC: **3571** Electronic computers

(G-9125)
STEWARD LLC
Also Called: Steward Mag
345 Witherspoon St (08542-3405)
PHONE...............................609 816-8825
EMP: 5
SALES (est): 242.5K **Privately Held**
SIC: **7371** 2721 Custom Computer Programing Periodicals-Publishing/Printing

(G-9126)
SUN PHARMACEUTICAL INDS INC
2 Independence Way (08540-6620)
PHONE...............................313 871-8400
Subramanian Kalyanasundaram, *CEO*
Robert Leahey, *Director*
EMP: 30
SALES (corp-wide): 1.2B **Privately Held**
SIC: **2834** Pharmaceutical preparations
HQ: Sun Pharmaceutical Industries, Inc.
270 Prospect Plains Rd
Cranbury NJ 08512
609 495-2800

(G-9127)
SUREWAY PRTG & GRAPHICS LLC
338 Wall St (08540-1518)
P.O. Box 2213 (08543-2213)
PHONE...............................609 430-4333
George Bilgrav, *Sales Staff*
Christopher Sustak,
Pam Sustak,
EMP: 5
SALES (est): 627.6K **Privately Held**
SIC: **2752** Commercial printing, offset

(G-9128)
TAG OPTICS INC
200 N Harrison St (08540-3507)
P.O. Box 1572 (08542-1572)
PHONE...............................609 356-2142
Christian Theriault, *CEO*
EMP: 4
SALES (est): 433.6K **Privately Held**
SIC: **3827** Optical instruments & lenses

(G-9129)
TAREE PHARMA LLC
342 Herrontown Rd (08540-2931)
PHONE...............................609 252-9596
Scheire Raymond, *Principal*
EMP: 4
SALES (est): 219.4K **Privately Held**
SIC: **2834** Pharmaceutical preparations

(G-9130)
TRAC INTERMODAL LLC (HQ)
750 College Rd E (08540-6646)
PHONE...............................609 452-8900
Val T Noel, *COO*
Rodney Goderwis, *COO*
Gregg Carpene, *Exec VP*
Inbal Arie, *Vice Pres*
Rich Hediger, *Vice Pres*
EMP: 5 EST: 2012
SALES (est): 69.6MM **Privately Held**
SIC: **7359** 3715 5012 Equipment rental & leasing; truck trailers; trailers for passenger vehicles

(G-9131)
TRAC INTERSTAR LLC (DH)
750 College Rd E (08540-6646)
PHONE...............................609 452-8900
EMP: 9 EST: 2016
SALES (est): 22.9MM **Privately Held**
SIC: **7359** 3715 5012 Equipment rental & leasing; truck trailers; trailers for passenger vehicles
HQ: Trac Intermodal Llc
750 College Rd E
Princeton NJ 08540
609 452-8900

GEOGRAPHIC

(G-9132)
TRENDMARK LLC
465 Meadow Rd Apt 10207 (08540-6366)
PHONE..............................551 226-7973
Tejas Vora, *CEO*
EMP: 4
SQ FT: 1,000
SALES (est): 148.7K **Privately Held**
SIC: 7372 Business oriented computer
software

(G-9133)
**TYCO INTERNATIONAL MGT CO
LLC (DH)**
9 Roszel Rd Ste 2 (08540-6205)
PHONE..............................609 720-4200
Fax: 609 720-4208
George R Oliver, *CEO*
Edward D Breen, *President*
Paul Fitzhenry, *President*
Tammy Brettell, *General Mgr*
Dana S Deasy, *Principal*
◆ **EMP:** 40 **EST:** 1962
SALES (est): 14.9B **Privately Held**
SIC: 3999 1711 1731 3669 Fire extin-
guishers, portable; fire sprinkler system
installation; safety & security specializa-
tion; fire detection & burglar alarm sys-
tems specialization; fire detection
systems, electric; smoke detectors; fire
alarm apparatus, electric; industrial
valves; automatic regulating & control
valves
HQ: Johnson Controls, Inc.
5757 N Green Bay Ave
Milwaukee WI 53209
414 524-1200

(G-9134)
UNISTAR INC
Also Called: Unistar Creations
61 Castleton Rd (08540-1644)
PHONE..............................212 840-2100
Peter Nukala, *President*
EMP: 4
SQ FT: 7,800
SALES: 1.5MM **Privately Held**
WEB: www.unistarcreations.com
SIC: 5094 3911 Jewelry & precious
stones; jewelry, precious metal

(G-9135)
**VENSUN PHARMACEUTICALS
INC**
103 Carnegie Ctr Ste 300 (08540-6235)
PHONE..............................908 278-8386
George Sager, *Opers Staff*
EMP: 18
SALES (est): 1.1MM
SALES (corp-wide): 10MM **Privately
Held**
SIC: 2834 Pharmaceutical preparations
PA: Vensun Pharmaceuticals, Inc.
790 Towns Line Rd Ste 250
Yardley PA 19067
215 809-2015

(G-9136)
VENTURE INFO NETWORK
Also Called: The Vine
226 Linden Ln (08540-3449)
PHONE..............................609 279-0777
Fax: 609 924-3936
Micky Morgan, *Agent*
EMP: 5
SALES (est): 262.5K **Privately Held**
SIC: 2711 Newspapers

(G-9137)
**VGYAAN PHARMACEUTICALS
LLC**
100 Overlook Ctr Fl 2 (08540-7814)
PHONE..............................609 452-2770
Nailesh Bhatt, *CEO*
Nimisha Bhatt, *COO*
EMP: 4 **EST:** 2014
SALES (est): 400.1K **Privately Held**
SIC: 2834 5122 Pharmaceutical prepara-
tions; pharmaceuticals

(G-9138)
**WESTERN DIGITAL
CORPORATION**
116 Village Blvd Ste 200 (08540-5700)
PHONE..............................609 734-7479

Fax: 609 734-7489
Tom Everett, *Manager*
EMP: 8
SALES (corp-wide): 19B **Publicly Held**
WEB: www.wdc.com
SIC: 3572 Disk drives, computer
PA: Western Digital Corporation
5601 Great Oaks Pkwy
San Jose CA 95119
408 717-6000

(G-9139)
WILSHIRE TECHNOLOGIES INC
318 Wall St (08540-1515)
PHONE..............................609 683-1117
Joe San Filippo, *CEO*
Anthony Gargano, *Assistant*
▲ **EMP:** 5
SQ FT: 600
SALES (est): 618.6K **Privately Held**
WEB: www.wilshiretechnologies.com
SIC: 8748 2899 Business consulting;
chemical preparations

(G-9140)
**WONG ROBINSON & CO INC
(PA)**
Also Called: Pequod Communications
743 Alexander Rd Ste 15 (08540-6328)
PHONE..............................609 951-0300
Fax: 609 951-0352
James Robertson, *President*
Andre Liu, *Vice Pres*
Ron Cohen, *Director*
▲ **EMP:** 20
SQ FT: 15,000
SALES (est): 3.1MM **Privately Held**
SIC: 2752 Commercial printing, offset

(G-9141)
XEROX CORPORATION
100 Overlook Ctr Ste 310 (08540-7814)
PHONE..............................609 987-5500
Fax: 609 987-5654
Brennan Fusco, *General Mgr*
Jill Piecko, *Marketing Mgr*
George Walton, *Manager*
EMP: 450
SALES (corp-wide): 10.2B **Publicly Held**
WEB: www.xerox.com
SIC: 3861 Photographic equipment & sup-
plies
PA: Xerox Corporation
201 Merritt 7
Norwalk CT 06851
203 968-3000

(G-9142)
ZULTNER & COMPANY
12 Wallingford Dr (08540-6428)
PHONE..............................609 452-0216
Richard Zultner, *Owner*
EMP: 10
SQ FT: 2,500
SALES (est): 640.2K **Privately Held**
WEB: www.zultner.com
SIC: 7372 Operating systems computer
software

(G-9143)
ZYCUS INC (HQ)
103 Carnegie Ctr Ste 201 (08540-6235)
PHONE..............................609 799-5664
Aatish Dedhia, *President*
Chiranjib Guha, *Senior VP*
Dixit Jasani, *Vice Pres*
Richard Fernandez, *Project Mgr*
Shibu Nair, *Project Mgr*
EMP: 37
SQ FT: 3,353
SALES: 9MM **Privately Held**
WEB: www.zycus.com
SIC: 7372 Prepackaged software

Princeton Junction
Mercer County

(G-9144)
AEON CORPORATION
186 Princeton Hightstown (08550-1668)
PHONE..............................609 275-9003
Leo Spiekman, *Principal*
EMP: 9

SALES (est): 985.8K **Privately Held**
SIC: 3674 Semiconductors & related devices

(G-9145)
AI TECHNOLOGY INC
Also Called: A I T
70 Washington Rd (08550-1012)
PHONE..............................609 799-9388
Kevin Chung, *CEO*
V Cirincione, *Principal*
EMP: 40
SALES (est): 8.1MM **Privately Held**
SIC: 3678 Electronic connectors

(G-9146)
AIBENS IMORT
7 York Rd (08550-3273)
PHONE..............................609 902-9953
Tanmay Trivedi, *Owner*
EMP: 5
SALES (est): 238.2K **Privately Held**
SIC: 3312 Blast furnaces & steel mills

(G-9147)
AMERASIA INTL TECH INC
Also Called: A I T
70 Washington Rd (08550-1012)
P.O. Box 3081, Princeton (08543-3081)
PHONE..............................609 799-9388
Kevin Chung, *President*
Cynthia Chu, *Exec VP*
Robinson Salguero, *Project Engr*
Ben Jakubovic, *Accountant*
Yulin Huang, *Sr Software Eng*
EMP: 41
SQ FT: 52,000
SALES: 2.9MM **Privately Held**
WEB: www.aitechnology.com
SIC: 2891 Adhesives; sealants

(G-9148)
AMERITEX INDUSTRIES CORP
39 Everett Dr Ste 2 (08550-5393)
PHONE..............................609 502-0123
Richard Tuscano, *President*
EMP: 13
SALES (est): 1.2MM **Privately Held**
SIC: 3999 Barber & beauty shop equip-
ment

(G-9149)
**AVANTE INTERNATIONAL TECH
INC**
70 Washington Rd (08550-1012)
PHONE..............................609 799-9388
Fax: 609 799-9308
Kevin Chung, *CEO*
Cynthia Chu, *Exec VP*
Albert Chung, *Vice Pres*
Jeffery Douglass, *Project Mgr*
Michael Caracciolo, *Research*
EMP: 40
SQ FT: 35,000
SALES (est): 7.1MM **Privately Held**
WEB: www.avantetech.com
SIC: 3579 Voting machines

(G-9150)
**COMMUNITY PRIDE
PUBLICATIONS**
55 Prnceton Hightstown Rd (08550-1110)
PHONE..............................609 921-8760
EMP: 10
SQ FT: 1,800
SALES (est): 690K **Privately Held**
SIC: 2741 Misc Publishing

(G-9151)
CURA BIOMED INC
103 S Longfellow Dr (08550-2237)
PHONE..............................609 647-1474
Jayasimha Raju, *Officer*
EMP: 4
SALES (est): 149.2K **Privately Held**
SIC: 3841 5047 Surgical & medical instru-
ments; medical equipment & supplies

(G-9152)
ENGILITY LLC
15 Roszel Rd (08550)
PHONE..............................703 633-8300
Anthony Smeraglinolo, *CEO*
Edward P Boykin, *Principal*
Darryll J Pines, *Principal*

Anthony Principi, *Principal*
Charles S Ream, *Principal*
EMP: 14 **Publicly Held**
SIC: 3663 8733 Radio & TV communica-
tions equipment; noncommercial research
organizations
HQ: Engility Llc
4803 Stonecroft Blvd
Chantilly VA 20151
703 708-1400

(G-9153)
ENTOURAGE IMAGING INC
Also Called: Entourage Yearbooks
39 Everett Dr Ste 1-2 (08550-5393)
PHONE..............................888 926-6571
Elias Jo, *President*
Edward Jo, *COO*
Tianna Ellerbee, *Accounting Mgr*
Kelsey Charzewski, *Accounts Mgr*
Lauren Karol, *Accounts Mgr*
EMP: 28 **EST:** 2005
SQ FT: 4,000
SALES (est): 4.1MM **Privately Held**
SIC: 2741 Miscellaneous publishing; direc-
tories: publishing & printing; yearbooks:
publishing & printing

(G-9154)
EXCEL INDUSTRIAL CO INC
17 Huntington Dr (08550-2126)
PHONE..............................609 275-1748
Ben C Sun, *President*
EMP: 5
SALES: 100K **Privately Held**
WEB: www.excel-uae.com
SIC: 3552 Textile machinery

(G-9155)
FUCELTECH INC
11 Glengarry Way (08550-3033)
PHONE..............................609 275-0070
Chuni Ghosh, *CEO*
EMP: 4
SQ FT: 1,000
SALES: 10K **Privately Held**
SIC: 3674 Fuel cells, solid state

(G-9156)
FUNNIBONZ LLC
3 Lake View Ct (08550-4915)
PHONE..............................609 915-3685
James H Barbour, *Mng Member*
James Barbour,
Fredrick Kurtz,
Ryan Marrone,
EMP: 5
SALES (est): 360K **Privately Held**
SIC: 2033 Barbecue sauce: packaged in
cans, jars, etc.

(G-9157)
**HAIGHTS CROSS
CMMNICATIONS INC (PA)**
295 Prncton Hightstown Rd (08550-3123)
PHONE..............................212 209-0500
Fax: 212 209-0501
Rick Noble, *CEO*
Kevin R Brueggeman, *President*
Rich Freese, *President*
Julie Latzer, *Senior VP*
Diane Q Curtin, *Vice Pres*
▲ **EMP:** 41
SQ FT: 35,000
SALES (est): 83.8MM **Privately Held**
WEB: www.haightscross.com
SIC: 2731 Books: publishing only

(G-9158)
INNOLUTIONS INC
4 Wellesley Ct (08550-1829)
PHONE..............................609 490-9799
Fax: 609 490-9788
Manoj Kumar-Patel, *President*
Piyushkumar Patel, *Vice Pres*
Michael Friedman, *Software Engr*
Smita Patel, *Admin Sec*
EMP: 9
SQ FT: 3,000
SALES: 2MM **Privately Held**
WEB: www.innoinc.com
SIC: 3625 Control equipment, electric

▲ = Import ▼=Export
◆ =Import/Export

(G-9159)
MISTRAS GROUP INC (PA)
195 Clarksville Rd Ste 2 (08550-5392)
PHONE.............................609 716-4000
Sotirios J Vahaviolos, *Ch of Bd*
Michael J Lange, *Vice Ch Bd*
Dennis Bertolotti, *President*
Jonathan H Wolk, *COO*
Michael C Keefe, *Exec VP*
EMP: 135
SALES: 700.9MM **Publicly Held**
WEB: www.mistrasgroup.com
SIC: 8711 7372 3829 3825 Engineering
services; prepackaged software; measur-
ing & controlling devices; instruments to
measure electricity

(G-9160)
P S I CEMENT INC
12 Robert Dr (08550-3021)
PHONE.............................609 716-1515
Mike Ekladous, *President*
Samia Ekladous, *Vice Pres*
Mina Ekladous, *Admin Sec*
EMP: 6
SQ FT: 3,600
SALES (est): 1MM **Privately Held**
WEB: www.psicement.com
SIC: 5084 2674 Cement making machin-
ery; cement bags: made from purchased
materials

(G-9161)
PBA OF WEST WINDSOR
376 N Post Rd (08550-1325)
PHONE.............................609 799-6535
Keith Hillman, *Principal*
EMP: 40
SALES (est): 2.3MM **Privately Held**
SIC: 2499 Policemen's clubs, wood

(G-9162)
**PHYSICAL ACOUSTICS
CORPORATION**
Also Called: Vibra-Metrics
195 Clarksville Rd (08550-5392)
PHONE.............................609 716-4000
Fax: 609 716-0706
Sotirios Vahaviolos, *President*
Mark Carlos, *Exec VP*
Theron Shoemaker, *QC Mgr*
David Carlson, *Engineer*
Peter Banakiewicz, *Electrical Engi*
EMP: 135
SQ FT: 50,000
SALES (est): 23.6MM **Publicly Held**
WEB: www.pacndt.com
SIC: 3829 Measuring & controlling devices
PA: Mistras Group, Inc.
195 Clarksville Rd Ste 2
Princeton Junction NJ 08550

(G-9163)
**SCHLUMBERGER
TECHNOLOGY CORP**
Also Called: E M R Photoelectric Div
20 Wallace Rd (08550-1008)
P.O. Box 44 (08550-0044)
PHONE.............................609 275-3815
Patrice Ligneul, *Principal*
EMP: 115 **Publicly Held**
SIC: 1389 Oil field services
HQ: Schlumberger Technology Corp
100 Gillingham Ln
Sugar Land TX 77478
281 285-8500

(G-9164)
**SWEETLY SPIRITED CUPCAKES
LTD**
10 Newport Dr (08550-2224)
PHONE.............................917 846-4238
Cheryl G Ojeda, *Administration*
EMP: 7
SALES (est): 341.9K **Privately Held**
SIC: 2051 Bread, cake & related products

(G-9165)
VIBGYOR SOLUTIONS INC
14 Washington Rd Ste 623 (08550-1028)
PHONE.............................609 750-9158
Chandra Karnei, *President*
EMP: 6

SALES (est): 470K **Privately Held**
WEB: www.vibgyorsolutions.com
SIC: 7372 Prepackaged software

(G-9166)
WIZCOM CORPORATION
19 Washington Rd Ste D (08550-1030)
PHONE.............................609 750-0601
Fax: 609 750-0603
Nagarjuna Thota, *President*
Sonai Chatterjee, *Manager*
Deepak Kotte, *Software Dev*
Aditya Pandiri, *Software Dev*
EMP: 20
SQ FT: 900
SALES: 10MM **Privately Held**
WEB: www.wizcomcorp.com
SIC: 7371 7372 Computer software devel-
opment; business oriented computer soft-
ware

(G-9167)
YOGO MIX
44 Normandy Dr (08550-3275)
PHONE.............................609 897-1379
Carlo Pugliese, *Principal*
EMP: 5
SALES (est): 524.2K **Privately Held**
SIC: 3273 Ready-mixed concrete

Prospect Park
Passaic County

(G-9168)
ADVANCED BREWING SYS LLC
91 Savoy Pl (07508-2228)
PHONE.............................973 633-1777
Vincent Fulco, *Principal*
▲ EMP: 7
SALES (est): 595.6K **Privately Held**
SIC: 2082 Malt beverages

(G-9169)
**ENVELOPES & PRINTED PDTS
INC**
135 Fairview Ave (07508-1923)
PHONE.............................973 942-1232
William F Higgins, *President*
Christoper Higgins, *Admin Sec*
EMP: 9
SQ FT: 2,000
SALES (est): 1.1MM **Privately Held**
WEB: www.specialtyprinting.com
SIC: 2759 Invitation & stationery printing &
engraving

(G-9170)
MICHELEX CORPORATION (PA)
204 Haledon Ave (07508-2023)
PHONE.............................201 977-1177
Albert Lacle, *President*
Venkat Kakani, *President*
EMP: 3
SALES (est): 2.4MM **Privately Held**
SIC: 7389 2834 Financial services; drug-
gists' preparations (pharmaceuticals)

Rahway
Union County

(G-9171)
A AFFORDABLE SIGN
1053 Madison Ave (07065-1802)
PHONE.............................732 287-0446
Michael Miczewski, *Owner*
▲ EMP: 15
SALES (est): 2.2MM **Privately Held**
WEB: www.a-affordablesign.com
SIC: 3993 Signs, not made in custom sign
painting shops

(G-9172)
AIRTEC INC
Also Called: Airtec-Unique
17 W Scott Ave (07065-4529)
P.O. Box 1181 (07065-1181)
PHONE.............................732 382-3700
Joseph M Niemczyk, *President*
EMP: 8 EST: 1967
SQ FT: 20,000

SALES (est): 830K **Privately Held**
SIC: 3444 Sheet metalwork

(G-9173)
**AISHA&ANNA NATION OF
TRENDS**
2 Park Sq Apt 2210 (07065-4061)
PHONE.............................201 951-8197
Aisha Hale, *Principal*
▼ EMP: 4
SALES (est): 159.4K **Privately Held**
SIC: 2844 Toilet preparations

(G-9174)
API AMERICAS INC
329 New Brunswick Ave (07065-2928)
PHONE.............................732 382-6800
Fax: 732 382-6800
David A Walton, *President*
Robert Kirkpatrick, *Business Mgr*
Scott Lewis, *Vice Pres*
Jeff Pendleton, *Opers Mgr*
Mark Thomason, *Technical Mgr*
EMP: 60 **Privately Held**
WEB: www.apifoils.com
SIC: 3497 2891 Metal foil & leaf; adhe-
sives & sealants
HQ: Api Americas Inc.
3841 Greenway Cir
Lawrence KS 66046

(G-9175)
**ARTISTIC BIAS PRODUCTS CO
INC**
1905 Elizabeth Ave (07065-4534)
PHONE.............................732 382-4141
Fax: 732 382-2471
Daniel Berg, *President*
▲ EMP: 50 EST: 1938
SALES (est): 5.1MM **Privately Held**
SIC: 2396 5131 2891 Trimming, fabric;
piece goods & notions; adhesives &
sealants

(G-9176)
ASSOCIATED PLASTICS INC
179 E Inman Ave (07065-4709)
PHONE.............................732 574-2800
Richard W Fisher Jr, *President*
Bruce Fisher, *Vice Pres*
EMP: 12 EST: 1962
SQ FT: 11,000
SALES (est): 1.7MM **Privately Held**
SIC: 3357 3089 Nonferrous wiredrawing &
insulating; closures, plastic

(G-9177)
**ASTRO TOOL & MACHINE CO
INC**
810 Martin St (07065-5410)
P.O. Box 1264 (07065-1264)
PHONE.............................732 382-2454
Fax: 732 382-6394
Gary Price, *President*
EMP: 26 EST: 1964
SQ FT: 20,000
SALES (est): 4.5MM **Privately Held**
WEB: www.astrotoolco.com
SIC: 3545 Machine tool accessories

(G-9178)
**ATLANTIC AIR ENTERPRISES
INC**
856 Elston St (07065-5408)
PHONE.............................732 381-4000
Darin Severino, *President*
EMP: 19 EST: 1941
SQ FT: 11,400
SALES (est): 3.9MM **Privately Held**
WEB: www.atlanticairent.com
SIC: 1761 3444 Sheet metalwork; sheet
metalwork

(G-9179)
**BARLICS MANUFACTURING CO
INC**
Also Called: Innan Molding
815 Martin St (07065-5409)
P.O. Box 1143 (07065-1143)
PHONE.............................732 381-6229
Fax: 732 574-3604
Glen Barlics, *President*
Mark Barlics, *Vice Pres*
EMP: 4

SALES: 1MM **Privately Held**
SIC: 5162 3544 Plastics products; special
dies, tools, jigs & fixtures

(G-9180)
CAMEO METAL PRODUCTS INC
Also Called: Cameo Metal Forms
1745 Elizabeth Ave (07065-4532)
PHONE.............................732 388-4000
Fax: 732 388-4799
EMP: 12
SQ FT: 5,000
SALES (est): 870K **Privately Held**
SIC: 3471 Plating/Polishing Service

(G-9181)
CARBOLINE COMPANY
Also Called: Car Boline
842 Elston St (07065-5408)
PHONE.............................732 388-2912
EMP: 23
SALES (corp-wide): 5.3B **Publicly Held**
SIC: 2851 Lacquers, varnishes, enamels &
other coatings
HQ: Carboline Company
2150 Schuetz Rd Fl 1
Saint Louis MO 63146
314 644-1000

(G-9182)
CLASSIC COOKING LLC
1600 St Grges Ave Ste 301 (07065)
PHONE.............................718 439-0200
Andy Reichgut, *President*
Anthony Minuto, *QA Dir*
William Martz, *Cust Mgr*
Julie Gould, *Marketing Staff*
Karen Velazquez, *Office Mgr*
▲ EMP: 100
SQ FT: 40,000
SALES: 15.8MM **Privately Held**
SIC: 2035 2037 2038 Pickles, sauces &
salad dressings; vegetables, quick frozen
& cold pack, excl. potato products; soups,
frozen

(G-9183)
**DASON STAINLESS PRODUCTS
CO**
1773 Elizabeth Ave (07065-4532)
PHONE.............................732 382-7272
Fax: 732 382-7145
William Thompson Jr, *President*
Rose Cummings, *Office Mgr*
EMP: 12 EST: 1961
SQ FT: 7,000
SALES (est): 1.6MM **Privately Held**
SIC: 3494 Pipe fittings

(G-9184)
DPJ INC
245 E Inman Ave (07065-4704)
PHONE.............................732 499-8600
Derek Delhoyo, *President*
Jim Tozer, *Admin Sec*
EMP: 13
SQ FT: 6,500
SALES (est): 1.2MM **Privately Held**
SIC: 3993 Signs & advertising specialties

(G-9185)
**ELECTRONIC MARINE SYSTEMS
INC (PA)**
Also Called: Engine Efficiency Associates
800 Ferndale Pl (07065-4909)
PHONE.............................732 680-4120
Fax: 908 388-5111
Thomas J Priola, *President*
▲ EMP: 15
SQ FT: 10,000
SALES: 4MM **Privately Held**
WEB: www.emsmarcon.com
SIC: 3669 Intercommunication systems,
electric; fire alarm apparatus, electric;
burglar alarm apparatus, electric

(G-9186)
ELECTRUM INC
Also Called: Electrum Recovery Works
827 Martin St (07065-5409)
PHONE.............................732 396-1616
Matthew Douglas, *President*
John A Silva Jr, *Vice Pres*
Donna Helm, *Regl Sales Mgr*
Alicia Kehler, *Regl Sales Mgr*
Adam Napell, *Regl Sales Mgr*

GEOGRAPHIC

◆ **EMP:** 14
SQ FT: 20,000
SALES (est): 2.8MM **Privately Held**
WEB: www.electruminc.com
SIC: 3339 Precious metals

(G-9187)
ELIXENS AMERICA INC
1443 Pinewood St Bldg 4u (07065-5503)
PHONE..................................732 388-3555
Adrian America, *Chairman*
▲ **EMP:** 3
SALES (est): 2.6MM
SALES (corp-wide): 1.2MM **Privately Held**
WEB: www.elixensamerica.com
SIC: 5122 2899 Perfumes; oils & essential oils
HQ: Elixens
83 85
Paris 75013
156 617-280

(G-9188)
EXTRA OFFICE INC
580 Leesville Ave (07065-4822)
PHONE..................................732 381-9774
Fax: 732 381-9753
Louis Prince Jr, *President*
Louis Prince Sr, *Vice Pres*
EMP: 12
SQ FT: 16,000
SALES (est): 1.6MM **Privately Held**
WEB: www.extraoffice.net
SIC: 2522 1799 5046 7641 Office chairs, benches & stools, except wood; office bookcases, wallcases & partitions, except wood; office cabinets & filing drawers: except wood; office desks & tables: except wood; office furniture installation; partitions; office furniture repair & maintenance

(G-9189)
FORTUNE RVRSIDE AUTO PARTS INC (PA)
Also Called: Fortune Metal Recycling
900 Leesville Ave (07065-4828)
PHONE..................................732 381-3355
Fax: 732 381-7919
Norman Ng, *CEO*
Chris Lam, *Vice Pres*
John Paik, *Vice Pres*
Simon Wong, *Vice Pres*
▼ **EMP:** 43
SQ FT: 12,000
SALES (est): 8.5MM **Privately Held**
WEB: www.fortuneriverside.com
SIC: 3324 Steel investment foundries

(G-9190)
FRANK B ROSS CO INC (PA)
970 New Brunswick Ave H (07065-3814)
PHONE..................................732 669-0810
Larry Powell, *President*
Donald Ayerlee, *Vice Pres*
Carmen Mangan, *Vice Pres*
Maryanne Willemsen, *Admin Sec*
▼ **EMP:** 15 **EST:** 1902
SQ FT: 77,000
SALES (est): 1.6MM **Privately Held**
WEB: www.rosswaxes.com
SIC: 2842 Beeswax, processing of; waxes for wood, leather & other materials

(G-9191)
FROST TECH INC
830 Elston St (07065-5408)
P.O. Box Ag (07065-0290)
PHONE..................................732 396-0071
Fax: 732 396-8323
Dennis P Berthiaame, *President*
EMP: 15
SALES (est): 1.2MM **Privately Held**
SIC: 1793 3211 Glass & glazing work; flat glass

(G-9192)
FUGLE-MILLER LABORATORIES INC
1401 Witherspoon St Ste 1 (07065-5523)
PHONE..................................732 574-3121
John Dobracki, *President*
EMP: 28 **EST:** 1963
SQ FT: 12,000

SALES (est): 2.6MM **Privately Held**
SIC: 3679 3677 Electronic circuits; electronic coils, transformers & other inductors

(G-9193)
GENERAL ELECTRONIC ENGINEERING (PA)
132 W Main St (07065-4106)
PHONE..................................732 381-1144
William A Piegari, *President*
Ralph Eisenberge, *Vice Pres*
EMP: 12
SQ FT: 4,000
SALES (est): 1.3MM **Privately Held**
WEB: www.genelectronic.com
SIC: 3625 Electric controls & control accessories, industrial

(G-9194)
GRIGNARD COMPANY LLC
505 Capobianco Plz (07065-5401)
P.O. Box 1535 (07065-7535)
PHONE..................................732 340-1111
Kelly A Grignard, *Mng Member*
Etienne Grignard,
▲ **EMP:** 25
SQ FT: 40,000
SALES: 10MM **Privately Held**
WEB: www.grignard.com
SIC: 2899 4225 6519 Chemical preparations; general warehousing & storage; real property lessors

(G-9195)
HARBISONWALKER INTL INC
868 Elston St (07065-5408)
PHONE..................................732 388-4011
Ralph Turano, *Manager*
EMP: 8
SALES (corp-wide): 923MM **Privately Held**
SIC: 3255 Clay refractories
HQ: Harbisonwalker International, Inc.
1305 Cherrington Pkwy # 100
Moon Township PA 15108

(G-9196)
HARRISON ELECTRO MECHANICAL
1607 Coach St (07065-4103)
PHONE..................................732 382-6008
William Piegari, *President*
Arlene Piegari, *Corp Secy*
EMP: 12
SQ FT: 4,800
SALES (est): 2.1MM
SALES (corp-wide): 1.3MM **Privately Held**
WEB: www.harrisonelectro.com
SIC: 3674 3672 3625 3357 Semiconductor diodes & rectifiers; circuit boards, television & radio printed; relays & industrial controls; nonferrous wiredrawing & insulating
PA: General Electronic Engineering Inc
132 W Main St
Rahway NJ 07065
732 381-1144

(G-9197)
HONE-A-MATIC TOOL & CUTTER CO
187 Wescott Dr (07065-4706)
PHONE..................................732 382-6000
Fax: 732 382-9732
Anthony R Lamastra, *President*
Ken Lamastra, *Vice Pres*
EMP: 5
SQ FT: 8,000
SALES (est): 567.3K **Privately Held**
SIC: 3541 3542 5084 Machine tools, metal cutting type; machine tools, metal forming type; metalworking tools (such as drills, taps, dies, files)

(G-9198)
INMAN MOLD MANUFACTURING INC (PA)
815 Martin St (07065-5409)
PHONE..................................732 381-3033
Glen Barlics, *President*
Mark Barlics, *Treasurer*
EMP: 9
SQ FT: 12,000

SALES (est): 1MM **Privately Held**
SIC: 3089 3999 Injection molding of plastics; novelties, bric-a-brac & hobby kits

(G-9199)
INMAN MOLD MANUFACTURING INC
273 E Inman Ave (07065-4704)
P.O. Box 1143 (07065-1143)
PHONE..................................732 381-3033
Glen Barlics, *President*
EMP: 8
SALES (corp-wide): 1MM **Privately Held**
SIC: 3089 Injection molding of plastics
PA: Inman Mold Manufacturing, Inc.
815 Martin St
Rahway NJ 07065
732 381-3033

(G-9200)
INSTRUMENTATION TECHNOLOGY SLS
205 E Inman Ave (07065-4700)
PHONE..................................732 388-0866
Anna Sadowska, *President*
Stanley Lewand, *Vice Pres*
EMP: 7
SQ FT: 3,500
SALES (est): 760K **Privately Held**
SIC: 3625 Relays & industrial controls

(G-9201)
J C CONTRACTING INC
681 Mill St (07065-4812)
PHONE..................................973 748-5600
EMP: 16 **EST:** 2000
SQ FT: 20,000
SALES (est): 3MM **Privately Held**
SIC: 3661 3669 Mfg Telephone/Telegraph Apparatus Mfg Communications Equipment

(G-9202)
J VITALE SIGN CO INC
2204 Elizabeth Ave Ste 1 (07065-4601)
PHONE..................................732 388-8401
Fax: 732 388-0908
Joseph Frank Vitale, *President*
EMP: 6 **EST:** 1951
SQ FT: 2,000
SALES (est): 500K **Privately Held**
SIC: 7389 3993 Sign painting & lettering shop; lettering service; signs & advertising specialties

(G-9203)
JASON METAL PRODUCTS CORP
1072 Randolph Ave (07065-5526)
PHONE..................................732 396-1132
Fax: 732 396-1712
Richard Jaszyn, *President*
Chris Jaszyn, *Vice Pres*
EMP: 7 **EST:** 1979
SQ FT: 16,000
SALES (est): 1MM **Privately Held**
SIC: 3469 Stamping metal for the trade

(G-9204)
JM AHLE CO INC
625 Leesville Ave (07065-4821)
PHONE..................................732 388-5507
J Formisano, *General Mgr*
EMP: 4
SALES (corp-wide): 63.1MM **Publicly Held**
SIC: 3272 Building materials, except block or brick: concrete
HQ: J.M. Ahle Co., Inc.
190 William St Ste 2d
South River NJ 08882
732 238-1700

(G-9205)
JOSEPH BBINEC SHTMTL WORKS INC
774 Martin St (07065-5410)
PHONE..................................732 388-0155
Fax: 732 382-2018
Joseph T Babinec, *CEO*
Jason Babinec, *President*
Desiree Latorre, *Vice Pres*
EMP: 37
SQ FT: 45,000

SALES (est): 7.3MM **Privately Held**
SIC: 1761 3444 Sheet metalwork; sheet metalwork

(G-9206)
KAUFMAN STAIRS INC (PA)
150 E Inman Ave (07065-4702)
PHONE..................................908 862-3579
Alan Kaufman, *President*
Barbara Simon, *Vice Pres*
EMP: 34 **EST:** 1962
SQ FT: 17,000
SALES (est): 5.3MM **Privately Held**
WEB: www.kaufmanstairs.com
SIC: 2431 3446 Staircases & stairs, wood; architectural metalwork

(G-9207)
KIDDESIGNS INC
1299 Main St (07065-5024)
PHONE..................................732 574-9000
Suzanne Fellows, *CEO*
Isaac E Ashkenazi, *President*
Edward Blanco, *Vice Pres*
Sean Chraime, *Vice Pres*
Isaac H Franco, *Vice Pres*
▲ **EMP:** 24
SQ FT: 55,000
SALES (est): 12.3MM **Privately Held**
WEB: www.kiddirect.com
SIC: 5092 3944 Toys & games; electronic toys

(G-9208)
LIEBERFARB INC
2100 Felver Ct (07065-5721)
PHONE..................................973 676-9090
Fax: 973 676-9488
Mark Schonwetter, *President*
Ann S Arnold, *Vice Pres*
Isabella Schonwetter, *Vice Pres*
Luba Schonwetter, *Vice Pres*
EMP: 18
SQ FT: 2,400
SALES (est): 2.4MM **Privately Held**
WEB: www.lieberfarb.com
SIC: 3911 Rings, finger: precious metal

(G-9209)
LINDEN MOLD AND TOOL CORP
155 Wescott Dr (07065-4710)
P.O. Box C (07065-1215)
PHONE..................................732 381-1411
Fax: 732 381-8770
Vincent M Illuzzi, *President*
Steve Guzik, *Manager*
▲ **EMP:** 45
SQ FT: 15,000
SALES (est): 7.3MM **Privately Held**
WEB: www.lindenmold.com
SIC: 3544 3089 Industrial molds; injection molding of plastics

(G-9210)
LM AIR TECHNOLOGY INC
1467 Pinewood St (07065-5503)
PHONE..................................732 381-8200
Peter Daniele, *President*
Myron Szewczuk, *Vice Pres*
Susan Szewczuk, *Administration*
EMP: 20
SQ FT: 5,000
SALES (est): 4.7MM **Privately Held**
WEB: www.lmairtech.com
SIC: 3564 3821 Air purification equipment; laboratory apparatus & furniture

(G-9211)
M RAFI SONS GARMENT INDUSTRIES
1463 Pinewood St (07065-5503)
PHONE..................................732 381-7660
Zaheed Rafi, *Owner*
▲ **EMP:** 5
SALES (est): 450K **Privately Held**
SIC: 2326 Work garments, except raincoats: waterproof
PA: M. Rafi Sons Garments Industries (Pvt) Ltd.
'plot 10-A, Block-1,'
Lahore
427 466-988

(G-9212)
MERCK & CO INC
126 E Lincoln Ave (07065-4646)
P.O. Box 2000 (07065-0900)
PHONE..................................908 740-4000
Fax: 732 594-8170
Lori Bash, *Business Mgr*
John Hladick, *Technical Staff*
EMP: 100
SALES (corp-wide): 40.1B **Publicly Held**
SIC: 2834 2836 2844 5122 Pharmaceutical preparations; druggists' preparations (pharmaceuticals); drugs acting on the respiratory system; drugs affecting parasitic & infective diseases; vaccines; veterinary biological products; suntan lotions & oils; animal medicines
PA: Merck & Co., Inc.
2000 Galloping Hill Rd
Kenilworth NJ 07033
908 740-4000

(G-9213)
MERCK RESEARCH LABORATORIES
126 E Lincoln Ave (07065-4607)
P.O. Box 100, Whitehouse Station (08889-0100)
PHONE..................................732 594-4000
Fax: 732 594-4465
Leslie A Brun, *CEO*
Roger Perlmutter MD PHD, *President*
Kenneth C Frazier, *President*
David Lashen, *Production*
Thomas Zakszewski, *Buyer*
EMP: 91
SALES (est): 58.2MM **Privately Held**
SIC: 2834 Pharmaceutical preparations

(G-9214)
MERCK SHARP & DOHME CORP
126 E Lincoln Ave (07065-4607)
P.O. Box 2000 (07065-0900)
PHONE..................................732 594-4000
Fax: 732 594-3925
Ron Maturo, *Manager*
EMP: 100
SALES (corp-wide): 40.1B **Publicly Held**
SIC: 2834 Pharmaceutical preparations
HQ: Merck Sharp & Dohme Corp.
2000 Galloping Hill Rd
Kenilworth NJ 07033
908 740-4000

(G-9215)
MIGHTY MUG INCORPORATED
665 Martin St (07065-5409)
PHONE..................................732 382-3911
James Smaldone, *President*
Say Smaldone, *Vice Pres*
Danielle Vinci, *Sales Staff*
Valerie Skaggs, *Administration*
▲ EMP: 4
SALES: 15MM **Privately Held**
SIC: 3089 5085 Plastic kitchenware, tableware & houseware; plastic bottles

(G-9216)
OLD FASHION WOODWORKING INC
273 E Inman Ave (07065-4704)
PHONE..................................973 808-9663
Dorothy Bonanno, *Principal*
EMP: 15
SALES (est): 2.4MM **Privately Held**
SIC: 2431 Millwork

(G-9217)
POLMAR IRON WORK INC
673 New Brunswick Ave (07065-3817)
PHONE..................................732 882-0900
Marek Wresilo, *President*
EMP: 12
SALES (est): 2.2MM **Privately Held**
SIC: 3325 Steel foundries

(G-9218)
PREMAC INC
167 Wescott Dr (07065-4710)
P.O. Box 9 (07065-0009)
PHONE..................................732 381-7550
Fax: 732 381-2184
Edward H Schenker Sr, *President*
Eric L Schenker, *Vice Pres*
Fred Schenker, *Vice Pres*

Frieda Schenker, *Admin Sec*
EMP: 15 EST: 1950
SQ FT: 4,000
SALES (est): 2.1MM **Privately Held**
SIC: 3812 Instrument landing systems (ILS), airborne or ground

(G-9219)
R&R COSMETICS LLC
1140 Randolph Ave (07065-5507)
P.O. Box 1211 (07065-1211)
PHONE..................................732 340-1000
Fax: 732 340-1030
Musthafa E Kamal, *General Mgr*
EMP: 7
SALES (est): 1.1MM **Privately Held**
SIC: 2844 Face creams or lotions

(G-9220)
ROBERT MANSE DESIGNS LLC
Also Called: Bali Designs
2100 Felver Ct (07065-5721)
PHONE..................................732 428-8305
Robert Manse, *President*
EMP: 38
SQ FT: 24,000
SALES (est): 1.5MM **Privately Held**
SIC: 3911 Jewelry, precious metal

(G-9221)
ROYAL LACE CO INC
902 E Hazelwood Ave (07065-5608)
PHONE..................................718 495-9327
Moises Guttman, *Ch of Bd*
Aaron Guttman, *President*
Nathan Green, *Admin Sec*
▲ EMP: 25
SQ FT: 20,000
SALES (est): 4MM **Privately Held**
SIC: 2258 5131 Lace, knit; lace fabrics

(G-9222)
RSR ELECTRONICS INC
Also Called: Electronix Express
900 Hart St (07065-5630)
PHONE..................................732 381-8777
Fax: 732 381-1572
Eli Rosenbaum, *President*
Ajit Gulati, *Vice Pres*
Hitesh Vyas, *CFO*
Sol Kaye, *Marketing Mgr*
Victor Neumark, *Marketing Mgr*
▲ EMP: 45
SQ FT: 32,750
SALES (est): 7.8MM **Privately Held**
WEB: www.rsrelectronics.com
SIC: 3999 5065 3825 3577 Education aids, devices & supplies; electronic parts & equipment; instruments to measure electricity; computer peripheral equipment

(G-9223)
SDI TECHNOLOGIES INC (PA)
1299 Main St (07065-5024)
PHONE..................................732 574-9000
Fax: 732 574-1486
Isaac Ashkenazi, *Ch of Bd*
Ezra S Ashkenazi, *President*
Mark Chraime, *Senior VP*
Sean Chraime, *Vice Pres*
Christopher Boczkus, *Facilities Mgr*
◆ EMP: 98 EST: 1956
SQ FT: 40,000
SALES (est): 35.1MM **Privately Held**
WEB: www.sdiworld.com
SIC: 3651 Sound reproducing equipment; tape recorders: cassette, cartridge or reel: household use; radio receiving sets

(G-9224)
SUNRISE PHARMACEUTICAL INC
665 E Lincoln Ave (07065-5711)
PHONE..................................732 382-6085
Fax: 732 382-6880
Utpal Patel, *CEO*
Jayanti Patel, *President*
▲ EMP: 25
SQ FT: 33,000
SALES (est): 6.4MM **Privately Held**
SIC: 2834 Pharmaceutical preparations

(G-9225)
TRUCKEROS NEWS LLC
1720 Lawrence St (07065-5110)
P.O. Box 1646 (07065-7646)
PHONE..................................732 340-1043
Cesar Vargas, *Owner*
EMP: 10
SALES (est): 738.9K **Privately Held**
SIC: 2731 Books: publishing & printing

(G-9226)
UNIQUE METAL PRODUCTS
17 W Scott Ave (07065-4529)
P.O. Box 1181 (07065-1181)
PHONE..................................732 388-1888
Fax: 732 388-0084
Joseph Niemczyk Jr, *President*
EMP: 11
SQ FT: 30,000
SALES (est): 1.2MM **Privately Held**
SIC: 3444 Sheet metal specialties, not stamped

(G-9227)
UNIQUE PRECISION CO INC
2095 Elizabeth Ave (07065-4624)
PHONE..................................732 382-8699
Fax: 732 382-7991
Anthony Bobkoskie, *President*
Anthony Bobkowskie, *President*
EMP: 6
SQ FT: 3,200
SALES (est): 510K **Privately Held**
SIC: 3541 3599 Lapping machines; grinding castings for the trade

(G-9228)
WYTECH INDUSTRIES INC (PA)
960 E Hazelwood Ave (07065-5635)
PHONE..................................732 396-3900
Fax: 732 396-4943
Anthony J Casalino, *CEO*
Michael Casalino, *President*
Bob Roche, *COO*
Arthur Barry, *Vice Pres*
Michael Brown, *Vice Pres*
EMP: 65
SQ FT: 23,000
SALES (est): 24.9MM **Privately Held**
WEB: www.wytech.com
SIC: 3496 3315 Miscellaneous fabricated wire products; wire products, ferrous/iron: made in wiredrawing plants

---

Ramsey
Bergen County

(G-9229)
ACHILLES PROSTHETCS & ORTHOTCS
503 N Franklin Tpke # 12 (07446-1166)
PHONE..................................201 785-9944
Peter R Buffington, *Principal*
EMP: 4
SALES (est): 345.9K **Privately Held**
SIC: 3842 Orthopedic appliances

(G-9230)
ADMA BIOLOGICS INC (PA)
465 State Rt 17 (07446-2049)
PHONE..................................201 478-5552
Steven A Elms, *Ch of Bd*
Jerrold B Grossman, *Vice Ch Bd*
Adam S Grossman, *President*
Brian Lenz, *CFO*
James Mond, *Chief Mktg Ofcr*
EMP: 58
SQ FT: 4,200
SALES: 22.7MM **Publicly Held**
SIC: 2836 Biological products, except diagnostic

(G-9231)
AERO TEC LABORATORIES INC (PA)
Also Called: A T L
45 Spear Rd (07446-1221)
PHONE..................................201 825-1400
Fax: 201 825-1962
Peter J Regna, *President*
David Dack, *Vice Pres*
▼ EMP: 34
SQ FT: 70,000

SALES (est): 13.1MM **Privately Held**
WEB: www.atlinc.com
SIC: 3069 8731 Rubber automotive products; commercial physical research

(G-9232)
ALTEON
170 Williams Dr (07446-2907)
PHONE..................................201 934-1624
Fax: 201 934-8880
Marilyn Breslow, *Principal*
EMP: 5
SALES (est): 628.5K **Privately Held**
SIC: 2834 8731 Vitamin preparations; commercial physical research

(G-9233)
ANGELOS ITALIAN ICES ICECREAM
96 E Main St (07446-1925)
PHONE..................................201 962-7575
Angelo Onello, *Owner*
EMP: 4
SALES (est): 213.4K **Privately Held**
SIC: 2024 Dairy based frozen desserts

(G-9234)
APOGEE SOUND INTERNATIONAL LLC
50 Spring St Ste 1 (07446-1131)
PHONE..................................201 934-8500
Jonathan Guss, *CEO*
Maureen Flotard, *CFO*
EMP: 40
SALES (est): 5MM **Publicly Held**
WEB: www.apogeesound.com
SIC: 3651 Speaker systems
PA: Bogen Communications International, Inc.
1200 Macarthur Blvd # 303
Mahwah NJ 07430

(G-9235)
ATL
45 Spear Rd (07446-1221)
PHONE..................................201 825-1400
Peter Regna, *President*
EMP: 6 EST: 1975
SQ FT: 70,000
SALES (est): 596.2K
SALES (corp-wide): 13.1MM **Privately Held**
WEB: www.atlinc.com
SIC: 2869 Industrial organic chemicals
PA: Aero Tec Laboratories Inc.
45 Spear Rd
Ramsey NJ 07446
201 825-1400

(G-9236)
AYDIN JEWELRY MENUFECTURING
119 E Main St (07446-1926)
PHONE..................................201 818-1002
Rick Aydin, *Principal*
EMP: 4
SALES (est): 285.7K **Privately Held**
SIC: 3911 Jewelry, precious metal

(G-9237)
BOGEN CORPORATION (PA)
50 Spring St Ste 1 (07446-1131)
PHONE..................................201 934-8500
Johnathan Guss, *CEO*
Michael P Fleischer, *President*
Maureen A Flotard, *CFO*
EMP: 1
SQ FT: 70,000
SALES (est): 23.4MM **Privately Held**
SIC: 3651 3661 3663 3669 Amplifiers: radio, public address or musical instrument; audio electronic systems; telephone & telegraph apparatus; telephones & telephone apparatus; radio broadcasting & communications equipment; intercommunication systems, electric

(G-9238)
COMPTIME INC
Also Called: Comptime Print & Copy Center
385 N Franklin Tpke Ste 6 (07446-2820)
PHONE..................................201 760-2400
Fax: 201 760-9140
Christopher Tausch, *President*
David Santulli, *Corp Secy*

EMP: 6
SQ FT: 1,250
SALES (est): 778.4K **Privately Held**
WEB: www.comptime.net
SIC: 7334 2791 Blueprinting service; type-setting

(G-9239)
DTROVISION LLC
Also Called: Purelink
535 E Crescent Ave Ste 1 (07446-2922)
PHONE..............................201 488-3232
Minsoo Park, *President*
Howard Schilling, *Sales Dir*
Christine Park, *Marketing Staff*
Keith Frey, *Manager*
Jake Kim, *Manager*
EMP: 25
SQ FT: 9,000
SALES: 4.1MM **Privately Held**
WEB: www.dtrovision.com
SIC: 3651 Audio electronic systems

(G-9240)
FRELL CORP
Also Called: Buono Bagel-To The Max
885 State Rt 17 Ste 5 (07446-1654)
PHONE..............................201 825-2500
Fred Greenberg, *President*
EMP: 10
SQ FT: 3,000
SALES (est): 430K **Privately Held**
SIC: 2051 5461 Bagels, fresh or frozen;
bagels

(G-9241)
GENESIS BPS LLC
465 Route 17 S (07446-2012)
P.O. Box 331 (07446-0331)
PHONE..............................201 708-1400
Fax: 201 488-3968
Jerrold Grossman, *Mng Member*
▲ EMP: 25
SQ FT: 30,000
SALES (est): 4.9MM **Privately Held**
WEB: www.genesisbps.com
SIC: 3841 Medical instruments & equip-ment, blood & bone work
PA: Genesis Bps International Sarl
C/O Harmannus Koeneman
Arnex-Sur-Nyon VD
223 631-816

(G-9242)
GLEBAR OPERATING LLC
Also Called: Glebar Company
565 E Crescent Ave (07446-1219)
P.O. Box 623, Franklin Lakes (07417-0623)
PHONE..............................201 337-1500
Fax: 201 337-6848
Adam Cook, *CEO*
John Bannayan, *President*
Mark Bannayan, *Vice Pres*
Robert Gleason, *Vice Pres*
Mark Scanel, *Vice Pres*
▼ EMP: 61
SQ FT: 40,000
SALES (est): 20.5MM **Privately Held**
WEB: www.glebar.com
SIC: 3541 Grinding machines, metalwork-ing

(G-9243)
INGUI DESIGN LLC
Also Called: Aurorae
46 N Central Ave (07446-1808)
PHONE..............................201 264-9126
Dennis Ingui,
Valerie Ingui,
EMP: 4
SQ FT: 3,000
SALES: 2MM **Privately Held**
SIC: 3949 Exercise equipment

(G-9244)
INNOVATIVE ART CONCEPTS LLC
Also Called: Cutting Edge Stencils
630 Swan St (07446-1014)
PHONE..............................201 828-9146
John G Swisher, *Mng Member*
Michelle Zakko, *Manager*
Janna Makaeva,
Harris M Recht,
EMP: 12 EST: 2009

SALES: 2.5MM **Privately Held**
SIC: 3953 Stencils, painting & marking

(G-9245)
LIQUID-SOLIDS SEPARATION CORP (HQ)
25 Arrow Rd (07446-1204)
PHONE..............................201 236-4833
David J Painter, *President*
R Donald Peterson, *Treasurer*
Mary Zielinski, *Office Mgr*
Clemente Rivera, *Officer*
EMP: 40
SQ FT: 24,000
SALES (est): 9.7MM **Privately Held**
WEB: www.leemlssfiltration.com
SIC: 3569 3089 5074 Filters, general line:
industrial; plastic containers, except foam;
water purification equipment

(G-9246)
LONGO ASSOCIATES INC
100 Hilltop Rd (07446-1119)
PHONE..............................201 825-1500
Nat Longo, *President*
Anthony Stellatos, *Marketing Mgr*
◆ EMP: 13
SQ FT: 4,200
SALES (est): 2.6MM **Privately Held**
WEB: www.longoschools.com
SIC: 2531 Public building & related furni-ture; school furniture; library furniture

(G-9247)
MER MADE FILTER
25 Arrow Rd (07446-1204)
PHONE..............................201 236-0217
Dave Painter, *President*
EMP: 5
SALES: 320K **Privately Held**
SIC: 5085 3564 Filters, industrial; blowers
& fans

(G-9248)
MODEL ELECTRONICS INC (PA)
615 E Crescent Ave (07446-1220)
PHONE..............................201 961-9200
Matthew Sasso, *President*
Peter Maroccia, *President*
Thomas Churchill, *Vice Pres*
Elizabeth Schwartz, *Accounts Mgr*
EMP: 73
SALES (est): 22MM **Privately Held**
WEB: www.modelelectronicsinc.com
SIC: 3679 5064 5731 Recording & play-back apparatus, including phonograph;
radios; sound equipment, automotive

(G-9249)
MODEL ELECTRONICS INC
526 State Rt 17 (07446-2015)
PHONE..............................201 961-1717
EMP: 34
SALES (corp-wide): 22MM **Privately Held**
SIC: 3679 Recording & playback appara-tus, including phonograph
PA: Model Electronics, Inc.
615 E Crescent Ave
Ramsey NJ 07446
201 961-9200

(G-9250)
OKONITE COMPANY (PA)
102 Hilltop Rd (07446-1171)
P.O. Box 340 (07446-0340)
PHONE..............................201 825-0300
Fax: 201 825-9026
Victor A Viggiano, *Ch of Bd*
A C Coppola, *President*
Eric Canning, *District Mgr*
Patrick Nash, *District Mgr*
Jeff Page, *District Mgr*
◆ EMP: 200 EST: 1878
SQ FT: 70,000
SALES (est): 413.7MM **Privately Held**
WEB: www.okonite.com
SIC: 3357 3315 3355 Nonferrous wire-drawing & insulating; cable, steel: insu-lated or armored; aluminum wire & cable

(G-9251)
PRONTO PRINTING & COPYING CTR
630 Swan St (07446-1014)
PHONE..............................201 426-0009

John Cortes, *President*
EMP: 6 EST: 1974
SQ FT: 3,000
SALES: 808K **Privately Held**
SIC: 2752 Commercial printing, litho-graphic

(G-9252)
TAURUS INTERNATIONAL CORP
275 N Franklin Tpke Ste 3 (07446-2812)
PHONE..............................201 825-2420
William J Coleman, *President*
Richard E Toth, *Vice Pres*
Jasen Toth, *VP Opers*
Sam Latkovic, *Engineer*
Lynette Castaldo, *Manager*
▲ EMP: 20
SQ FT: 5,000
SALES (est): 6.5MM **Privately Held**
WEB: www.taurusinternational.com
SIC: 5013 5082 5088 3462 Motor vehicle
supplies & new parts; construction & min-ing machinery; transportation equipment
& supplies; automotive & internal com-bustion engine forgings; automotive
stampings

(G-9253)
TOILETTREE PRODUCTS INC
41 Orchard St Ste 1 (07446-1158)
PHONE..............................845 358-5316
Gary Parisi, *CEO*
Steve Parisi, *President*
Paul Parisi, *CFO*
▲ EMP: 6
SQ FT: 1,000
SALES (est): 4MM **Privately Held**
SIC: 5211 3261 Bathroom fixtures, equip-ment & supplies; bathroom
accessories/fittings, vitreous china or
earthenware

(G-9254)
TRI STATE ATHC FIELD SVCS SUPS
145 N Franklin Tpke # 109 (07446-1602)
P.O. Box 72, Allendale (07401-0072)
PHONE..............................201 760-9700
Robert Buono, *President*
Tom Bruno, *Manager*
EMP: 4 EST: 1998
SQ FT: 200
SALES (est): 370K **Privately Held**
SIC: 3949 Track & field athletic equipment

(G-9255)
WALDEN MOTT CORP
225 N Franklin Tpke Ste 1 (07446-1600)
PHONE..............................201 962-3704
Fax: 201 818-8720
Alfred F Walden, *President*
Charles Walden, *Exec VP*
EMP: 5
SQ FT: 4,000
SALES: 425K **Privately Held**
WEB: www.papercatalog.com
SIC: 2721 2741 2711 Magazines: publish-ing only, not printed on site; directories:
publishing only, not printed on site; news-papers: publishing only, not printed on
site

Rancocas
Burlington County

(G-9256)
CONSARC CORPORATION (DH)
100 Indel Ave (08073)
P.O. Box 156 (08073-0156)
PHONE..............................609 267-8000
Fax: 609 267-6264
William J Marino, *President*
James Molloy, *Vice Pres*
Raymond J Roberts, *Vice Pres*
Lewis Jones, *VP Opers*
Gus John, *Plant Mgr*
◆ EMP: 50 EST: 1962
SQ FT: 62,000

SALES (est): 19.7MM
SALES (corp-wide): 930.4MM **Privately Held**
WEB: www.consarc.com
SIC: 3567 Metal melting furnaces, indus-trial: electric; metal melting furnaces, in-dustrial: fuel-fired; induction heating
equipment
HQ: Indel, Inc.
10 Indel Ave
Rancocas NJ 08073
609 267-9000

(G-9257)
ELECTRO-STEAM GENERATOR CORP
50 Indel Ave (08073)
P.O. Box 438 (08073-0438)
PHONE..............................609 288-9071
Fax: 609 288-9078
Robert A Murnane Jr, *President*
Brad Weigle, *Vice Pres*
EMP: 479
SALES (est): 60.5MM
SALES (corp-wide): 930.4MM **Privately Held**
WEB: www.indelinc.com
SIC: 3621 Generators & sets, electric
HQ: Indel, Inc.
10 Indel Ave
Rancocas NJ 08073
609 267-9000

(G-9258)
INDUCTOTHERM CORPORATION (HQ)
10 Indel Ave (08073)
P.O. Box 157 (08073-0157)
PHONE..............................609 267-9000
Fax: 609 267-3537
Satyen N Prabhu, *President*
Paul C Webber, *General Mgr*
Trevor Heilman, *District Mgr*
Bill Newbold, *District Mgr*
Virginia R Smith, *Vice Pres*
◆ EMP: 180
SQ FT: 155,000
SALES (est): 46.2MM
SALES (corp-wide): 930.4MM **Privately Held**
WEB: www.inductotherm.com
SIC: 3567 Induction heating equipment
PA: Rowan Technologies, Inc.
10 Indel Ave
Rancocas NJ 08073
609 267-9000

(G-9259)
INDUCTOTHERM TECHNOLOGIES INC (HQ)
Also Called: Inductotherm Group
10 Indel Ave (08073)
PHONE..............................609 267-9000
Virginia Rowan Smith, *Vice Pres*
EMP: 7
SALES (est): 1.6MM
SALES (corp-wide): 930.4MM **Privately Held**
SIC: 3449 Miscellaneous metalwork; bars,
concrete reinforcing: fabricated steel
PA: Rowan Technologies, Inc.
10 Indel Ave
Rancocas NJ 08073
609 267-9000

(G-9260)
PEMBERTON FABRICATORS INC
Also Called: Pemfab
30 Indel Ave (08073)
P.O. Box 227 (08073-0227)
PHONE..............................609 267-0922
Fax: 800 373-6322
Robert Murnane, *President*
Cheryl Parker, *Admin Sec*
◆ EMP: 2101 EST: 1962
SQ FT: 75,000
SALES: 11.3MM
SALES (corp-wide): 930.4MM **Privately Held**
WEB: www.pemfab.com
SIC: 3444 3824 Sheet metal specialties,
not stamped; fluid meters & counting de-vices

GEOGRAPHIC

HQ: Indel, Inc.
    10 Indel Ave
    Rancocas NJ 08073
    609 267-9000

(G-9261)
PV/T INC
100 Indel Ave (08073)
P.O. Box 156 (08073-0156)
PHONE.........................609 267-3933
Brett Wenger, *Manager*
EMP: 4
SQ FT: 75,000
SALES (est): 442.7K
SALES (corp-wide): 930.4MM **Privately
Held**
WEB: www.pvt-vf.com
SIC: 3567 Heating units & devices, indus-
    trial: electric
HQ: Consarc Corporation
    100 Indel Ave
    Rancocas NJ 08073
    609 267-8000

(G-9262)
**ROWAN TECHNOLOGIES INC
(PA)**
10 Indel Ave (08073)
P.O. Box 157 (08073-0157)
PHONE.........................609 267-9000
Virginia Rowan Smith, *President*
Manning J Smith, *Vice Pres*
Francis D Manley, *Treasurer*
◆ **EMP:** 100
SALES (est): 930.4MM **Privately Held**
SIC: 3567 3548 3822 3541 Metal melting
    furnaces, industrial: fuel-fired; induction
    heating equipment; vacuum furnaces &
    ovens; welding & cutting apparatus & ac-
    cessories; temperature controls, auto-
    matic; saws & sawing machines

(G-9263)
SQN PERIPHERALS INC (DH)
Also Called: Sqn Banking Systems
65 Indel Ave (08073)
P.O. Box 423 (08073-0423)
PHONE.........................609 261-5500
Fax: 609 265-9517
Joseph Uhland Jr, *President*
Jim Matusko, *Treasurer*
Martin Flynn, *Sales Mgr*
Lawrence A Krupnick, *Admin Sec*
EMP: 30
SQ FT: 5,000
SALES (est): 3.9MM
SALES (corp-wide): 930.4MM **Privately
Held**
WEB: www.sqnbankingsystems.com
SIC: 3577 Optical scanning devices
HQ: Indel, Inc.
    10 Indel Ave
    Rancocas NJ 08073
    609 267-9000

(G-9264)
TELEGENIX INC
71 Indel Ave (08073)
PHONE.........................609 265-3910
Fax: 609 265-3920
Henry M Rowan Jr, *Ch of Bd*
Joseph J Miller, *President*
Michael Gleeson, *Treasurer*
EMP: 16
SQ FT: 7,000
SALES (est): 3.1MM
SALES (corp-wide): 930.4MM **Privately
Held**
WEB: www.telegenix.com
SIC: 3669 3577 Transportation signaling
    devices; computer peripheral equipment
PA: Rowan Technologies, Inc.
    10 Indel Ave
    Rancocas NJ 08073
    609 267-9000

(G-9265)
WEL-FAB INC
50 Indel Ave (08073)
P.O. Box 86, Lumberton (08048-0086)
PHONE.........................609 261-1393
Fax: 609 261-7336
Dan O'Connor, *President*
Pj Elstone, *General Mgr*
Paul Elstone, *Vice Pres*
Bobby Clark, *VP Sales*

Charlie Branstetter, *Director*
EMP: 20
SQ FT: 4,875
SALES (est): 4MM **Privately Held**
WEB: www.wel-fab.com
SIC: 1799 7692 Welding on site; welding
    repair

Randolph
Morris County

(G-9266)
A & R SPORTS LLC
10 Middlebury Blvd Ste 1 (07869-1126)
PHONE.........................201 941-8875
Steve Armstrong, *President*
Cathy Lum, *Design Engr*
Russell Grodin, *VP Mktg*
▲ **EMP:** 25
SQ FT: 40,000
SALES (est): 3.5MM **Privately Held**
SIC: 3949 Team sports equipment

(G-9267)
**ADI AMERICAN DISTRIBUTORS
LLC (PA)**
2 Emery Ave Ste 1 (07869-1368)
PHONE.........................973 328-1181
Fax: 973 328-2302
David Beck, *CEO*
Steve Pela, *Buyer*
Christopher Fuente, *QA Dir*
Bart Mallory, *QC Mgr*
Melissa Rudyk, *QC Mgr*
▲ **EMP:** 56
SQ FT: 28,000
SALES (est): 49MM **Privately Held**
WEB: www.americandistr.com
SIC: 5065 3679 3621 3672 Electronic
    parts & equipment; power supplies, all
    types: static; frequency converters (elec-
    tric generators); printed circuit boards

(G-9268)
AFK MACHINE INC (PA)
50 High Ridge Rd (07869-4569)
PHONE.........................973 539-1329
John Klein, *Principal*
EMP: 4
SALES (est): 370K **Privately Held**
SIC: 3599 Machine shop, jobbing & repair

(G-9269)
**AMERICAN MCH TOOL RPR
RBLDG CO**
12 Middlebury Blvd (07869-1111)
PHONE.........................973 927-0820
Alex Karoly, *President*
Olga Karoly, *Admin Sec*
EMP: 9
SALES (est): 1.2MM **Privately Held**
SIC: 3541 7699 Machine tool replacement
    & repair parts, metal cutting types; indus-
    trial machinery & equipment repair

(G-9270)
ARPAC TECHNOLOGY
45 Park Ave (07869-1705)
PHONE.........................973 252-0012
Pete Capra, *Principal*
EMP: 9
SALES (est): 1.2MM **Privately Held**
SIC: 3089 Plastic processing

(G-9271)
**ARTISAN CONTROLS
CORPORATION (PA)**
111 Canfield Ave Ste B-18 (07869-1127)
PHONE.........................973 598-9400
Fax: 973 598-9410
John D Murray, *President*
Danielle Murray, *General Mgr*
Leigh Ann Stevens, *Vice Pres*
Denise Maas, *Treasurer*
Deniese Moss, *Finance*
EMP: 21
SQ FT: 10,000
SALES (est): 3.2MM **Privately Held**
WEB: www.artisancontrols.com
SIC: 3625 Timing devices, electronic

(G-9272)
**CHEN BROTHERS MACHINERY
CO**
Also Called: C.B.M. Co.
503 State Route 10 (07869-2152)
PHONE.........................973 328-0086
Kevin Chen, *Partner*
EMP: 5
SQ FT: 1,000
SALES (est): 137.2K **Privately Held**
SIC: 7699 3589 5087 Industrial equip-
    ment cleaning; car washing machinery;
    carwash equipment & supplies; laundry
    equipment & supplies

(G-9273)
DIBELLO USA INC
41 Forrest Rd (07869-4329)
PHONE.........................212 279-9099
Nick Xhumba, *CEO*
EMP: 2
SALES (est): 100MM **Privately Held**
SIC: 3199 7389 Leather garments;

(G-9274)
**DOUGLAS ELEC COMPONENTS
INC**
5 Middlebury Blvd (07869-1112)
PHONE.........................973 627-8230
Edward W Douglas, *President*
Karen Humphreys, *Materials Mgr*
Chuck Dean, *CFO*
Kim Tucci, *Human Res Mgr*
Joe Cowin, *Sales Staff*
▲ **EMP:** 60 **EST:** 1945
SALES (est): 14.4MM **Privately Held**
WEB: www.douglaselectrical.com
SIC: 3679 3699 Electronic circuits; electri-
    cal equipment & supplies

(G-9275)
ENVIROSIGHT LLC (PA)
Also Called: Pipeline Renewal Technologies
111 Canfield Ave Ste B-3 (07869-1129)
PHONE.........................973 970-9284
Richard Lindner, *President*
Jim Adams, *Opers Staff*
Marie Weinberg, *Opers Staff*
Tammy Smith, *Production*
Douglas Ehrlich, *Asst Controller*
EMP: 27
SQ FT: 2,800
SALES (est): 9MM **Privately Held**
WEB: www.envirosight.com
SIC: 5084 5046 3577 Industrial machin-
    ery & equipment; commercial equipment;
    computer peripheral equipment

(G-9276)
EUGENE KOZAK
Also Called: Kozak Precision Products
193 Franklin Rd (07869-1612)
PHONE.........................973 442-1001
Eugene Kozak, *Owner*
EMP: 4
SALES (est): 300K **Privately Held**
SIC: 3599 Machine shop, jobbing & repair

(G-9277)
FIRST JUICE INC
19 Tulip Ln (07869-4773)
PHONE.........................973 895-3085
David Glasser, *President*
Robert J Klausner, *VP Finance*
Cheryl Thomas, *VP Mktg*
Allan Carlin, *Admin Sec*
EMP: 9
SQ FT: 1,400
SALES (est): 630K **Privately Held**
WEB: www.tastebudtraining.com
SIC: 2086 Fruit drinks (less than 100%
    juice): packaged in cans, etc.

(G-9278)
**GENERAL WIRE & STAMPING
CO**
1 Emery Ave Ste 3 (07869-1387)
PHONE.........................973 366-8080
Fax: 973 366-3982
Kenneth J Kelly, *President*
Judy Kelly, *General Mgr*
Patrick Egan, *Vice Pres*
EMP: 10
SQ FT: 12,000

SALES: 1.3MM **Privately Held**
WEB: www.generalwire.com
SIC: 3496 3469 Miscellaneous fabricated
    wire products; metal stampings

(G-9279)
**GLENBROOK TECHNOLOGIES
INC**
11 Emery Ave (07869-1308)
PHONE.........................973 361-8866
Gilbert Zweig, *President*
Daxesh Patel, *General Mgr*
Claire Zweig, *Exec VP*
Donna Miller, *Accounting Mgr*
Steven Zweig, *VP Sales*
▼ **EMP:** 15
SQ FT: 13,300
SALES (est): 3.3MM **Privately Held**
WEB: www.glenbrooktech.com
SIC: 3844 X-ray apparatus & tubes; fluoro-
    scopic X-ray apparatus & tubes

(G-9280)
**GRANVILLE CONCRETE
PRODUCTS**
1076 State Route 10 (07869-1803)
PHONE.........................973 584-6653
Brian Peach, *President*
Bernard Peach, *Corp Secy*
Kevin Peach, *Vice Pres*
EMP: 4
SQ FT: 6,000
SALES: 900K **Privately Held**
SIC: 3272 Septic tanks, concrete

(G-9281)
GRAPHICS DEPOT INC
Also Called: Copy Depot, The
11 Middlebury Blvd Ste 4 (07869-1119)
PHONE.........................973 927-8200
Fax: 973 927-8253
David Bernstein, *President*
Joseph Taliercio, *General Mgr*
Robert Donohue, *Admin Sec*
EMP: 15
SALES (est): 1.7MM **Privately Held**
SIC: 2752 7334 Commercial printing, off-
    set; photocopying & duplicating services

(G-9282)
GT MICROWAVE INC
2 Emery Ave Ste 2 # 2 (07869-1368)
PHONE.........................973 361-5700
Fax: 973 361-5722
Antonio C Baliotis, *President*
George Apsley, *Vice Pres*
Todd Zaleski, *Engineer*
Ellen Baliotas, *CFO*
Ellen Baliotis, *Admin Sec*
EMP: 20
SQ FT: 5,000
SALES: 4.1MM **Privately Held**
WEB: www.gtmicrowave.com
SIC: 3679 5199 Microwave components;
    packaging materials

(G-9283)
HAWK GRAPHICS INC
1248 Sussex Tpke (07869-2908)
P.O. Box 308, Mount Freedom (07970-
0308)
PHONE.........................973 895-5569
Fax: 973 895-7258
Nicholas J Battaglino, *President*
Dorothy Battaglino, *Vice Pres*
Lorane Killer, *Administration*
EMP: 20
SQ FT: 20,000
SALES: 3MM **Privately Held**
SIC: 2752 Commercial printing, offset

(G-9284)
IMPERIAL COPY PRODUCTS INC
961 State Route 10 1ee (07869-1905)
PHONE.........................973 927-5500
Fax: 973 584-3410
Brian Abrams, *President*
David Abrams, *Vice Pres*
▲ **EMP:** 20
SQ FT: 20,000

SALES (est): 3.3MM **Privately Held**
WEB: www.imperialcopy.com
SIC: **5999** 7699 5734 3674 Photocopy machines; photocopy machine repair; printers & plotters: computers; light emitting diodes; duplicating machines; office forms & supplies

(G-9285)
JAYGO INCORPORATED
7 Emery Ave (07869-1308)
PHONE..................................908 688-3600
Fax: 908 688-6060
John R Hayday, *President*
Joris Banning, *Vice Pres*
Jason Hayday, *Vice Pres*
Lauren Laverso, *Bookkeeper*
▲ EMP: 7
SQ FT: 35,000
SALES: 3MM **Privately Held**
WEB: www.jaygoinc.com
SIC: **3559** Chemical machinery & equipment; pharmaceutical machinery

(G-9286)
LANDICE INCORPORATED
Also Called: Landice Treadmills
111 Canfield Ave Ste A-1 (07869-1130)
PHONE..................................973 927-9010
Fax: 973 927-0630
Greg Savettiere, *President*
Andrew Taitel, *Vice Pres*
◆ EMP: 30
SQ FT: 22,000
SALES (est): 5.7MM **Privately Held**
WEB: www.landice.com
SIC: **3949** Treadmills

(G-9287)
LAROSE INDUSTRIES LLC (PA)
Also Called: Pen Master
1578 Sussex Tpke (07869-1833)
PHONE..................................973 543-2037
Joe Nardozza, *President*
Randall Tarino, *COO*
Vito Amato, *Vice Pres*
Parviz Daftari, *Vice Pres*
Rich Ginelli, *Vice Pres*
◆ EMP: 90
SQ FT: 125,000
SALES (est): 51.1MM **Privately Held**
SIC: **5092** 3269 3944 Arts & crafts equipment & supplies; stationery articles, pottery; craft & hobby kits & sets

(G-9288)
MASTERCOOL USA INC (PA)
1 Aspen Dr Ste 1 (07869-1123)
PHONE..................................973 252-9119
Fax: 973 252-2455
Kia Nili, *President*
Michael Barjesteh, *Principal*
Bob Cacciabeve, *Vice Pres*
Steven Gillespie, *Engineer*
Chris Carroll, *Sales Staff*
◆ EMP: 45
SALES (est): 4.9MM **Privately Held**
WEB: www.mastercool.com
SIC: **3423** Hand & edge tools

(G-9289)
METRIE INC
1578 Sussex Tpke Ste 300 (07869-1833)
PHONE..................................973 584-0040
Bill Cody, *Branch Mgr*
EMP: 10
SALES (corp-wide): 92.2MM **Privately Held**
SIC: **3089** Molding primary plastic
HQ: Metrie Inc.
2200 140th Ave E Ste 600
Sumner WA 98390
253 470-5050

(G-9290)
NEWTYPE INC
447 State Route 10 Ste 14 (07869-2132)
PHONE..................................973 361-6000
Fax: 973 361-6005
Jo Ann Porto, *CEO*
Mark F Porto, *President*
EMP: 12
SALES: 720K **Privately Held**
WEB: www.newtypeinc.com
SIC: **7389** 2791 Translation services; typesetting

(G-9291)
NORWALT DESIGN INC
961 Route 10 E Ste 2a (07869-1921)
PHONE..................................973 927-3200
Fax: 973 927-2841
Walter McDonald, *President*
Michael Seitel, *COO*
Norbert Seitel, *Vice Pres*
Herbie Hoos, *Project Mgr*
Lee Reilly, *Purchasing*
▼ EMP: 54
SQ FT: 40,000
SALES (est): 12.5MM **Privately Held**
WEB: www.norwalt.com
SIC: **3599** Custom machinery

(G-9292)
NYMAR MANUFACTURING COMPANY
215 State Route 10 2-4 (07869-2413)
PHONE..................................973 366-7265
Fax: 973 366-4687
Gerald Hughes, *President*
EMP: 15 EST: 1967
SQ FT: 7,500
SALES (est): 1.4MM **Privately Held**
WEB: www.nymar.com
SIC: **3599** Machine shop, jobbing & repair

(G-9293)
OMEGA SHIELDING PRODUCTS INC
9 Emery Ave (07869-1308)
PHONE..................................973 366-0080
Leon Komsa, *President*
Andy Morris, *QC Mgr*
Chiungyao Chen, *Info Tech Dir*
Laurence R Niebling, *Admin Sec*
EMP: 12
SQ FT: 20,000
SALES (est): 2.3MM **Privately Held**
SIC: **3053** Gaskets, all materials

(G-9294)
PARTY CITY CORPORATION
477 State Route 10 # 102 (07869-2143)
PHONE..................................973 537-1707
Fax: 973 983-4500
Gordon Vanderhoff, *Manager*
EMP: 10
SALES (corp-wide): 2.3B **Publicly Held**
WEB: www.partycity.com
SIC: **5947** 5199 7299 2759 Party favors; party favors; balloons, hats, etc.; costume rental; invitation & stationery printing & engraving
HQ: Party City Corporation
25 Green Pond Rd Ste 1
Rockaway NJ 07866

(G-9295)
RAME-HART INC
5 Emery Ave Ste 1 (07869-1300)
PHONE..................................973 335-0560
Fax: 973 335-2920
Thor Stadil, *CEO*
Ken Christiansen, *President*
Samuel Rich, *Treasurer*
EMP: 25 EST: 1961
SQ FT: 17,500
SALES: 9MM **Privately Held**
WEB: www.ramehart.com
SIC: **3826** Analytical instruments

(G-9296)
SCREENTEK MANUFACTURING CO LLC
220 Franklin Rd B (07869-1605)
PHONE..................................973 328-2121
James Rodimer,
▲ EMP: 15
SQ FT: 8,000
SALES (est): 2.7MM **Privately Held**
SIC: **5063** 3315 Wire & cable; wire & fabricated wire products

(G-9297)
SERVOLIFT LLC
35 Righter Rd Ste A (07869-1707)
PHONE..................................973 442-7878
Fax: 973 442-1874
Marc Kaufman, *President*
Joachim Litterst, *Vice Pres*
Joe Litterst, *VP Opers*
Seth Ruckel, *Project Mgr*

Kim Pavone, *Purch Mgr*
◆ EMP: 35
SQ FT: 15,000
SALES (est): 7MM **Privately Held**
WEB: www.servo-lift.com
SIC: **3821** 5084 Chemical laboratory apparatus; chemical process equipment

(G-9298)
SOURCE MICRO LLC
5 Rolling Ridge Rd (07869-4506)
PHONE..................................973 328-1749
Curtis Tarvin, *VP Sls/Mktg*
Robert Schaffer,
EMP: 10
SQ FT: 3,000
SALES: 5.1MM **Privately Held**
WEB: www.sourcemicro.com
SIC: **3577** Computer peripheral equipment

(G-9299)
SSI NORTH AMERICA INC
961 State Route 10 Ste 2i (07869-1927)
PHONE..................................973 598-0152
G Thomas Ennis, *CEO*
Lucas Lowenstein, *President*
Dennis Leberecht, *Vice Pres*
▲ EMP: 9
SALES (est): 8.8MM **Privately Held**
WEB: www.ssinorthamerica.com
SIC: **3081** Plastic film & sheet

(G-9300)
SURFACE SOURCE INTL INC
Also Called: Ssi North America
961 State Route 10 Ste 2i (07869-1927)
PHONE..................................973 598-0152
Lucas Marcus Lowenstein, *President*
Dennis Leberecht, *Vice Pres*
EMP: 12 EST: 2004
SQ FT: 20,000
SALES (est): 10MM **Privately Held**
SIC: **2821** Polyvinyl chloride resins (PVC)

(G-9301)
TECHNOLOGY REVIEWS INC
Also Called: Technovations
14 Red Barn Ln (07869-3816)
PHONE..................................973 537-9511
Jaidev S Talwar, *President*
Robert Berger, *Principal*
Ramon Talwar, *Vice Pres*
EMP: 5
SALES (est): 720.2K **Privately Held**
SIC: **2821** 8742 Plasticizer/additive based plastic materials; industry specialist consultants

(G-9302)
TROLEX CORPORATION
Also Called: Zone First
6 Aspen Dr (07869-1103)
PHONE..................................201 794-8004
Richard N Foster Jr, *President*
Joe Romyns, *General Mgr*
Amanda Delgado, *Vice Pres*
Frank Artim, *Manager*
Lori Vanderkooy, *Manager*
EMP: 40
SQ FT: 16,000
SALES (est): 8.2MM **Privately Held**
WEB: www.trolexcorp.com
SIC: **3822** Auto controls regulating residntl & coml environmt & applncs

(G-9303)
ULTRAFLEX SYSTEMS FLORIDA INC
1578 Sussex Tpke Ste 400 (07869-1833)
PHONE..................................973 627-8608
John Schleicher, *President*
EMP: 37
SALES (est): 7.1MM
SALES (corp-wide): 14.7MM **Privately Held**
SIC: **2221** Manmade & synthetic broadwoven fabrics
PA: Ultraflex Systems Of Florida, Inc.
6333 Pelican Creek Cir
Riverview FL 33578
973 664-6739

(G-9304)
UNETTE CORPORATION
1578 Sussex Tpke Ste 5 (07869-1833)
PHONE..................................973 328-6800

Fax: 973 537-1010
Joseph Hark, *President*
Carol Ann Hark, *Vice Pres*
Chris Doscher, *VP Finance*
Anthony Nugent, *VP Sales*
Tony Nugent, *VP Sales*
▲ EMP: 65
SQ FT: 115,000
SALES (est): 15MM **Privately Held**
WEB: www.unette.com
SIC: **3089** 3085 Plastic containers, except foam; plastics bottles

(G-9305)
VALLEY DIE CUTTING INC
100 Washington St (07869-1633)
PHONE..................................973 731-8884
Harold Lohse, *Manager*
EMP: 8
SALES (est): 821.3K
SALES (corp-wide): 8.2MM **Privately Held**
WEB: www.reel-parts.com
SIC: **4225** 3544 General warehousing & storage; special dies, tools, jigs & fixtures
PA: Valley Die Cutting, Inc
10 Park Ave
West Orange NJ
973 731-8884

(G-9306)
WRITE ELEMENT LLC
14 James Rd (07869-2728)
PHONE..................................973 584-0373
Stacy White, *Principal*
EMP: 4
SALES (est): 98.5K **Privately Held**
SIC: **2819** Elements

Raritan
Somerset County

(G-9307)
BBK TECHNOLOGIES INC
Also Called: Fastsigns
13 Rte 206 S (08869)
PHONE..................................908 231-0306
Elizabeth Bowater, *President*
EMP: 7
SQ FT: 1,800
SALES (est): 736.9K **Privately Held**
SIC: **3993** Signs & advertising specialties

(G-9308)
D S F INC
Also Called: D S F Millwork
401 Us Highway 202 (08869-1529)
PHONE..................................908 218-5153
Simon Degirolamo, *President*
Janet Degirolamo, *Corp Secy*
EMP: 20
SALES (est): 2.9MM **Privately Held**
SIC: **2541** Wood partitions & fixtures

(G-9309)
JANSSEN GLOBAL SERVICES LLC
700 Route 202 (08869-1422)
PHONE..................................908 704-4000
EMP: 10
SALES (est): 1.3MM
SALES (corp-wide): 76.4B **Publicly Held**
SIC: **2834** 8731 Pharmaceutical preparations; commercial physical research
PA: Johnson & Johnson
1 Johnson And Johnson Plz
New Brunswick NJ 08933
732 524-0400

(G-9310)
JANSSEN RESEARCH & DEV LLC (HQ)
920 Us Highway 202 (08869-1420)
P.O. Box 300 (08869-0602)
PHONE..................................908 704-4000
Fax: 908 722-5867
P A Paterson MD, *Chairman*
Nicholas C Dracopoli, *Vice Pres*
Yusri A Elsayed, *Vice Pres*
Joseph Erhardt, *Vice Pres*
Michael Heftonrr MBA, *Vice Pres*
EMP: 1800

▲ = Import ▼=Export
◆ =Import/Export

SALES (est): 647.5MM
SALES (corp-wide): 76.4B Publicly Held
WEB: www.jnjpharmarnd.com
SIC: 2834 8731 Pharmaceutical preparations; commercial physical research
PA: Johnson & Johnson
1 Johnson And Johnson Plz
New Brunswick NJ 08933
732 524-0400

(G-9311)
JOHNSON & JOHNSON
1000 Rte 202 (08869-1425)
P.O. Box 300 (08869-0602)
PHONE...................................908 722-9319
Fax: 908 253-9787
Michelle Tomsho, *Project Mgr*
Jill Lavitsky, *Opers Mgr*
Erin Broderick, *Research*
Sarah Lazzaro, *Finance*
Julie Reynolds, *Train & Dev Mgr*
EMP: 5
SALES (corp-wide): 76.4B Publicly Held
WEB: www.jnj.com
SIC: 3842 3841 2834 2844 Surgical appliances & supplies; ligatures, medical; sutures, absorbable & non-absorbable; dressings, surgical; surgical & medical instruments; surgical instruments & apparatus; diagnostic apparatus, medical; ophthalmic instruments & apparatus; pharmaceutical preparations; drugs acting on the central nervous system & sense organs; dermatologicals; drugs affecting parasitic & infective diseases; toilet preparations; oral preparations; toilet preparations; powder: baby, face, talcum or toilet; feminine hygiene paper products; napkins, sanitary: made from purchased paper; panty liners: made from purchased paper; infant & baby paper products
PA: Johnson & Johnson
1 Johnson And Johnson Plz
New Brunswick NJ 08933
732 524-0400

(G-9312)
JOHNSON & JOHNSON
1101 Us Highway 202 (08869-1426)
PHONE...................................908 704-6809
Elliot Millenson, *President*
Robert Boland, *Manager*
EMP: 79
SALES (corp-wide): 76.4B Publicly Held
WEB: www.jnj.com
SIC: 2834 Pharmaceutical preparations
PA: Johnson & Johnson
1 Johnson And Johnson Plz
New Brunswick NJ 08933
732 524-0400

(G-9313)
JOHNSON & JOHNSON
1003 Us Highway 202 P (08869-1424)
PHONE...................................908 526-5425
Fax: 908 685-1860
Kathy Schnur, *Manager*
Adnan Siddiqui, *Manager*
Renee Woods, *Manager*
Mike Horn-Mitchem, *Info Tech Dir*
Christopher Flotta, *Info Tech Mgr*
EMP: 47
SALES (corp-wide): 76.4B Publicly Held
SIC: 2834 Pharmaceutical preparations
PA: Johnson & Johnson
1 Johnson And Johnson Plz
New Brunswick NJ 08933
732 524-0400

(G-9314)
ORTHO-CLINICAL DIAGNOSTICS INC (PA)
1001 Us Highway 202 (08869-1424)
P.O. Box 350 (08869-0606)
PHONE...................................908 218-8000
Fax: 908 218-8649
Dr Martin D Madaus, *Ch of Bd*
Michael Beckstead, *Regional Mgr*
Robert Yates, *COO*
Lujean Bonham, *Buyer*
Ana Saravia, *Business Anlyst*
▲ EMP: 1000 EST: 1994
SQ FT: 335,000

SALES (est): 707.3MM Privately Held
WEB: www.orthoclinical.com
SIC: 2835 2834 Blood derivative diagnostic agents; pharmaceutical preparations

(G-9315)
ORTHO-MCNEIL PHRM LLC (HQ)
Also Called: Ortho-Mcneil Phrm Inc
1000 Rte 202 (08869-1425)
P.O. Box 300 (08869-0602)
PHONE...................................908 203-4090
Fax: 908 218-9032
Seth Fischer, *President*
Michelle Van Nest, *Production*
Joseph Bondi, *CFO*
MBA Lesley Kraut, *Director*
◆ EMP: 25
SALES (est): 29.7MM
SALES (corp-wide): 76.4B Publicly Held
WEB: www.ortho-mcneil.com
SIC: 2833 2834 Medicinals & botanicals; pharmaceutical preparations
PA: Johnson & Johnson
1 Johnson And Johnson Plz
New Brunswick NJ 08933
732 524-0400

(G-9316)
SOMERSET WOOD PRODUCTS CO
1 Johnson Dr (08869-1661)
PHONE...................................908 526-0030
Dorothy Bloch, *Ch of Bd*
Lester Bloch, *President*
EMP: 20
SQ FT: 16,500
SALES (est): 3.5MM Privately Held
SIC: 2431 Millwork; interior & ornamental woodwork & trim

Red Bank
Monmouth County

(G-9317)
A S MILL PRODUCTS INC
280 State Route 35 # 104 (07701-5940)
PHONE...................................212 695-2244
Andrew Hewson, *President*
▲ EMP: 4
SALES (est): 895K Privately Held
WEB: www.asmillproducts.com
SIC: 3353 Aluminum sheet, plate & foil
HQ: Aluminium Silicon Mill Products Gmbh
Baarerstrasse 94
Zug ZG 6300
417 261-212

(G-9318)
ALL AMERICAN PRINT & COPY CTR
500 State Route 35 (07701-5038)
PHONE...................................732 758-6200
Fax: 732 758-9686
Ralph Cucinelli, *Vice Pres*
EMP: 4
SALES (est): 386.4K Privately Held
SIC: 2752 7334 4822 Commercial printing, offset; blueprinting service; facsimile transmission services

(G-9319)
ANCHOR CONCRETE PRODUCTS INC (DH)
331 Newman Springs Rd # 236 (07701-5688)
PHONE...................................732 842-5010
Fax: 732 292-2650
Michael P O'Neill, *President*
John K O'Neill, *Vice Pres*
▲ EMP: 20 EST: 1955
SQ FT: 9,000
SALES (est): 40.7MM
SALES (corp-wide): 29.7B Privately Held
SIC: 3271 5032 Blocks, concrete or cinder: standard; masons' materials
HQ: Oldcastle Architectural, Inc.
3 Glenlake Pkwy
Atlanta GA 30328
770 804-3363

(G-9320)
ANSELL INC
Also Called: Ansell Red Bank,
200 Schult Dr Ste 2 (07701-6745)
PHONE...................................732 345-5400
Harry Boon, *CEO*
EMP: 100
SALES (corp-wide): 1.3B Privately Held
SIC: 3069 8742 Latex, foamed; management consulting services
HQ: Ansell Inc.
1635 Industrial Rd
Dothan AL 36303
334 794-4231

(G-9321)
ASTRIX SOFTWARE TECHNOLOGY (PA)
Also Called: Astrix Technology Group
125 Half Mile Rd Ste 200 (07701-6749)
PHONE...................................732 661-0400
Richard Albert, *CEO*
Robert Walla, *President*
Dr Larry Hacker, *Vice Pres*
Michael Zachowski, *Vice Pres*
Brent Chyna, *Personnel*
EMP: 125
SQ FT: 2,000
SALES (est): 8.6MM Privately Held
SIC: 7363 7372 Temporary help service; prepackaged software

(G-9322)
B & C CUSTOM WD HANDRAIL CORP
Also Called: Stairshop
26 Sunset Ave (07701)
P.O. Box 2008 (07701-0901)
PHONE...................................732 530-6640
Christopher Kalkucki, *President*
Joyce Kalkucki, *Corp Secy*
EMP: 5
SQ FT: 5,000
SALES (est): 741.7K Privately Held
SIC: 2431 Woodwork, interior & ornamental

(G-9323)
CRH AMERICAS INC
Also Called: Anchor
331 Newman Springs Rd (07701-5688)
PHONE...................................732 292-2500
Matt Lynch, *President*
EMP: 20
SALES (corp-wide): 29.7B Privately Held
SIC: 3271 Concrete block & brick
HQ: Crh Americas, Inc.
3 Glenlake Pkwy Ste 12
Sandy Springs GA 30328
770 804-3363

(G-9324)
D & S VENTURES INC
Also Called: AlphaGraphics
68 White St Ste 4 (07701-1649)
PHONE...................................732 758-0095
Fax: 732 758-0098
Dom Pellegrino, *President*
Sharon Pellegrino, *Vice Pres*
EMP: 8
SALES (est): 1.3MM Privately Held
SIC: 2752 Commercial printing, lithographic

(G-9325)
DAB DESIGN INC
331 Newman Springs Rd # 143 (07701-6767)
PHONE...................................732 224-8686
Dana Barone, *President*
Neil Barone, *Vice Pres*
EMP: 5
SQ FT: 1,200
SALES (est): 359.8K Privately Held
SIC: 2511 Wood household furniture

(G-9326)
DENALI COMPANY LLC (PA)
211 Broad St (07701-2009)
PHONE...................................732 219-7771
Kenneth A Lindemann,
Sholom Goldfeder,
Keith Hawkins,
EMP: 20 EST: 1997

SALES (est): 2.2MM Privately Held
WEB: www.denalico.com
SIC: 2241 5699 Ribbons; marine apparel

(G-9327)
DEVOTION SPIRITS INC
Also Called: Devotion Vodka
566b Hwy 35 (07701-5066)
PHONE...................................877 415-3190
Drew Adelman, *CEO*
Michael Calleja, *COO*
EMP: 5
SALES (est): 388.1K Privately Held
SIC: 2085 2084 Vodka (alcoholic beverage); wines, brandy & brandy spirits

(G-9328)
DYER COMMUNICATIONS INC
Also Called: Two River Times
75 W Front St Ste 2 (07701-1660)
PHONE...................................732 219-5788
Fax: 732 747-7213
Jody Calendar, *Principal*
Domenic Di Piero, *Principal*
Lynette Wojcik, *VP Opers*
Peggy Ierardi, *Sales Staff*
EMP: 25
SQ FT: 2,400
SALES (est): 1.7MM Privately Held
WEB: www.tworivertimes.com
SIC: 2711 Newspapers: publishing only, not printed on site

(G-9329)
ES INDUSTRIAL
10 Mechanic St Ste 200 (07701-1855)
P.O. Box 843 (07701-0843)
PHONE...................................732 842-5600
Joe Alonzo, *Owner*
EMP: 53
SALES (est): 3.2MM Privately Held
SIC: 3589 Commercial cleaning equipment

(G-9330)
F T MILLWORK INC
Also Called: Custom Woodwork
9 Catherine St (07701-1205)
PHONE...................................732 741-1216
Frank Thomas, *President*
▲ EMP: 4 EST: 1982
SQ FT: 1,800
SALES (est): 340K Privately Held
SIC: 2431 Millwork

(G-9331)
INNOCOR INC (HQ)
Also Called: Sleep Innovations
200 Schulz Dr Ste 2 (07701-6745)
PHONE...................................732 945-6222
Fax: 732 263-0900
Carol S Eicher, *President*
Nitin Chadda, *Exec VP*
Allen Knight, *Plant Mgr*
Doug Vaughan, *CFO*
Mary Anne Spencer, *VP Human Res*
◆ EMP: 197
SQ FT: 28,000
SALES (est): 1B
SALES (corp-wide): 209.9MM Privately Held
WEB: www.sleepinnovations.com
SIC: 2515 2392 3069 Mattresses & foundations; cushions & pillows; bathmats, rubber
PA: Comfort Holding, Llc
187 Rte 36 Ste 101
West Long Branch NJ 07764
732 263-0800

(G-9332)
INNOCOR FOAM TECH - ACP INC (DH)
Also Called: Flexible Foam
200 Schulz Dr Ste 2 (07701-6745)
PHONE...................................732 945-6222
Carol Eicher, *CEO*
Doug Vaughan, *CFO*
EMP: 90
SALES (est): 41.1MM
SALES (corp-wide): 209.9MM Privately Held
SIC: 2515 2392 3069 Mattresses & foundations; cushions & pillows; bathmats, rubber

---

(G-9333)
INNOCOR FOAM TECHNOLOGIES LLC (DH)
200 Schulz Dr Ste 2 (07701-6745)
PHONE.....................844 824-9348
Carol S Eicher, *CEO*
Rachel Levy, *Vice Pres*
Nitin Chadda, *VP Prdtn*
Justin Gazi, *Marketing Staff*
Nancy Sattan, *Manager*
EMP: 181
SQ FT: 27,611
SALES (est): 220.9MM
SALES (corp-wide): 209.9MM **Privately Held**
SIC: 3086 Plastics foam products; carpet & rug cushions, foamed plastic; insulation or cushioning material, foamed plastic; padding, foamed plastic

(G-9334)
KULTUR INTERNATIONAL FILMS LTD
Also Called: Kultur Video
2 Bridge Ave Ste 633 (07701-4606)
PHONE.....................732 229-2343
Fax: 732 229-0066
Pearl Lee, *Principal*
Dennis Hedlund, *Chairman*
EMP: 25
SQ FT: 10,000
SALES (est): 2.9MM **Privately Held**
SIC: 5099 3651 7812 Video cassettes, accessories & supplies; household video equipment; video tape production

(G-9335)
MAVERICK OIL CO
9 Central Ave (07701-1509)
PHONE.....................732 747-8637
Pat Mazuca, *Owner*
EMP: 26
SALES (est): 721K **Privately Held**
SIC: 1381 Drilling oil & gas wells

(G-9336)
MCGINNIS PRINTING
20 Monmouth St (07701-1614)
PHONE.....................732 758-0060
Fax: 732 758-0070
Dennis Mc Ginnis, *Owner*
EMP: 4
SQ FT: 1,000
SALES (est): 240K **Privately Held**
WEB: www.jasonsdreamsforkids.com
SIC: 2752 Commercial printing, offset

(G-9337)
MEDIA VISTA INC
Also Called: Mediavista News
60 Broad St Ste 100 (07701-1937)
PHONE.....................732 747-8060
Fax: 732 747-8955
Barry Weisbord, *CEO*
Sue Finley, *Vice Pres*
EMP: 8
SALES (est): 797.1K **Privately Held**
SIC: 2741 Miscellaneous publishing

(G-9338)
MONMOUTH JOURNAL
212 Maple Ave Ste 1 (07701-1758)
PHONE.....................732 747-7007
Gary Chapman, *Partner*
EMP: 5
SALES (est): 426.8K **Privately Held**
WEB: www.themonmouthjournal.com
SIC: 2711 Newspapers, publishing & printing

(G-9339)
PACIFIC DNLOP HOLDINGS USA LLC (DH)
200 Schulz Dr (07701-6776)
PHONE.....................732 345-5400
Doug Tough, *CEO*
Phil Corke, *Senior VP*
William Reed, *Senior VP*
Rustom Jilla, *Treasurer*
William Reilly Jr, *Admin Sec*
EMP: 7

SALES (est): 211.7MM
SALES (corp-wide): 1.3B **Privately Held**
SIC: 3069 3691 Balloons, advertising & toy: rubber; birth control devices, rubber; finger cots, rubber; storage batteries
HQ: Pacific Dunlop Investments (Usa) Inc
    200 Schulz Dr
    Red Bank NJ 07701
    732 345-5400

(G-9340)
PACIFIC DUNLOP INVESTMENTS USA (HQ)
200 Schulz Dr (07701-6776)
PHONE.....................732 345-5400
Doug Tough, *President*
William Reed, *Vice Pres*
Rustom Jilla, *Treasurer*
William G Reilly Jr, *Admin Sec*
◆ EMP: 12
SALES (est): 217.6MM
SALES (corp-wide): 1.3B **Privately Held**
WEB: www.ap.ansell.com
SIC: 3069 3842 Rubber coated fabrics & clothing; gloves, safety
PA: Ansell Limited
    L3 678 Victoria St
    Richmond VIC 3121
    392 707-270

(G-9341)
QSA GLOBAL NATIONAL CORP
Also Called: Qsa National
331 Newman Springs Rd (07701-5688)
PHONE.....................865 888-6798
Leonard Becker, *President*
Jesse Telesz, *Vice Pres*
EMP: 3
SQ FT: 400
SALES (est): 2MM **Privately Held**
SIC: 8741 3699 7382 5043 Management services; security control equipment & systems; protective devices, security; identity recorders for photographing checks or fingerprints

(G-9342)
RED BANK GSTRNTROLOGY ASSOC PA
365 Broad St Ste 2e (07701-2151)
PHONE.....................732 842-4294
Fax: 732 842-3854
Brian Boyle MD, *President*
Howard Hampel, *Med Doctor*
EMP: 40
SALES (est): 4.7MM **Privately Held**
WEB: www.rbgastro.com
SIC: 8011 2711 Gastronomist; newspapers

(G-9343)
SEALS-EASTERN INCORPORATED
134 Pearl St (07701-1525)
P.O. Box 520 (07701-0520)
PHONE.....................732 747-9200
Daniel Hertz III, *President*
Daniel L Hertz, *Vice Pres*
James M Weil Jr, *Treasurer*
▲ EMP: 150 EST: 1960
SQ FT: 60,000
SALES: 15.6MM **Privately Held**
WEB: www.sealseastern.com
SIC: 3053 Gaskets, all materials

(G-9344)
SIC-NAICS LLC
Also Called: Siccode
331 Newman Springs Rd (07701-5688)
P.O. Box 25, Sea Girt (08750-0025)
PHONE.....................929 344-2633
Brian Kelly, *Director*
EMP: 5
SALES (est): 183.9K **Privately Held**
SIC: 2741 Telephone & other directory publishing

(G-9345)
STONEWORLD AT REDBANK INC
247 Cooper Rd (07701-6007)
PHONE.....................732 383-5110
Luis Pereira, *President*
EMP: 4

SALES: 1.2MM **Privately Held**
SIC: 3281 5999 Granite, cut & shaped; rock & stone specimens

(G-9346)
SUGARUSH
37 E Front St (07701-1822)
PHONE.....................732 414-9044
Mildred Hulsart, *Principal*
EMP: 6 EST: 2011
SALES (est): 318.7K **Privately Held**
SIC: 2053 Cakes, bakery: frozen

(G-9347)
TOMMAX INC
65 Mechanic St Ste 205 (07701-1852)
PHONE.....................732 224-1046
Fax: 732 224-1047
Max Braverman, *Ch of Bd*
Thomas Langan, *President*
EMP: 7
SQ FT: 2,200
SALES: 1.7MM **Privately Held**
SIC: 2741 2721 5085 Catalogs: publishing & printing; magazines: publishing only, not printed on site; industrial supplies

(G-9348)
ULTRA CHEMICAL INC (PA)
2 Bridge Ave Ste 631 (07701-4606)
PHONE.....................732 224-0200
Fax: 732 224-0017
Arthur J Lynch, *President*
Laura Anderson, *Sales Staff*
Brian Lynch, *Director*
Bryan Brown, *Admin Dir*
EMP: 14
SALES: 14MM **Privately Held**
SIC: 2869 5169 High purity grade chemicals, organic; organic chemicals, synthetic

---
Richland
Atlantic County

(G-9349)
BLUE CLAW MFG & SUPPLY COMPANY
118 Clover Ln (08350-2438)
PHONE.....................856 696-4366
Leonard Streeper, *President*
EMP: 7
SALES (est): 560K **Privately Held**
SIC: 3496 5091 Traps, animal & fish

Ridgefield
Bergen County

(G-9350)
BASHIAN BROS INC (PA)
Also Called: Bashian Rugs
65 Railroad Ave Ste 8 (07657-2130)
PHONE.....................201 330-1001
Fax: 201 330-1001
George G Bashian Jr, *Ch of Bd*
Garo Bashian, *Vice Pres*
Michael Keleshian, *CFO*
Malcolm Samad, *Treasurer*
Avinash Bawa, *Manager*
▲ EMP: 29 EST: 1959
SQ FT: 18,000
SALES (est): 4.8MM **Privately Held**
WEB: www.bashianrug.com
SIC: 2273 Carpets & rugs

(G-9351)
BERGEN INSTANT PRINTING INC
350 Broad Ave (07657-2325)
PHONE.....................201 945-7303
Bill Ackerman, *President*
William Ackerman, *Vice Pres*
Louise Perlstein, *Office Mgr*
EMP: 6
SQ FT: 2,000
SALES (est): 737.1K **Privately Held**
SIC: 2752 Commercial printing, offset

(G-9352)
BIAZZO DAIRY PRODUCTS INC
1145 Edgewater Ave (07657-2102)
PHONE.....................201 941-8579
Fax: 201 941-4151
John Iapichino Sr, *President*
Ann Iapichino, *Corp Secy*
John Iapichino Jr, *Vice Pres*
Angel Mendez, *Buyer*
Mariela Dilev, *Human Res Mgr*
▲ EMP: 50 EST: 1940
SQ FT: 58,000
SALES (est): 11.7MM **Privately Held**
WEB: www.biazzo.com
SIC: 2022 Natural cheese

(G-9353)
BRUDERER MACHINERY INC (PA)
1200 Hendricks Cswy (07657-2106)
PHONE.....................201 941-2121
Fax: 201 886-2010
Alois Rupp, *CEO*
Alois J Rupp, *President*
Anneli Martin, *Opers Mgr*
Sean Tucker, *Chief Engr*
ADI Kutz, *Sales Engr*
▲ EMP: 26
SQ FT: 29,000
SALES (est): 8.7MM **Privately Held**
WEB: www.bruderer.com
SIC: 3542 Punching & shearing machines

(G-9354)
CAROLACE EMBROIDERY CO INC (PA)
65 Railroad Ave Ste 3 (07657-2130)
PHONE.....................201 945-2151
Howard Mann, *President*
David Mann, *Chairman*
▲ EMP: 80 EST: 1951
SQ FT: 15,000
SALES (est): 54MM **Privately Held**
SIC: 2397 2395 2241 Schiffli machine embroideries; lace, burnt-out, for the trade; braids, textile

(G-9355)
COLORITE PLASTICS COMPANY (DH)
101 Railroad Ave (07657-2312)
PHONE.....................201 941-2900
Fax: 201 941-0308
Miguel Nistal, *Vice Pres*
Barbara O'Connell, *Purchasing*
Thomas V Gilboy, *CFO*
◆ EMP: 36
SALES (est): 14MM
SALES (corp-wide): 1B **Privately Held**
SIC: 3089 Blister or bubble formed packaging, plastic

(G-9356)
COLORITE POLYMERS
101 Railroad Ave (07657-2312)
PHONE.....................800 631-1577
David Katz, *Principal*
◆ EMP: 12
SALES (est): 1.7MM
SALES (corp-wide): 1B **Privately Held**
SIC: 3052 Rubber & plastics hose & beltings
PA: Tekni-Plex, Inc.
    460 E Swedesford Rd # 3000
    Wayne PA 19087
    484 690-1520

(G-9357)
COSMETIC ESSENCE LLC
Also Called: C E I
1135 Pleasantview Ter (07657-2310)
PHONE.....................201 941-9800
Fax: 201 278-5051
Andy Catenzaro, *Branch Mgr*
EMP: 100
SALES (corp-wide): 265.8MM **Privately Held**
WEB: www.ceidistribution.com
SIC: 2844 Cosmetic preparations
HQ: Cosmetic Essence, Llc
    2182 Hwy 35
    Holmdel NJ 07733
    732 888-7788

▲ = Import ▼=Export
◆ =Import/Export

(G-9358)
DOLCO PACKAGING CORP (HQ)
101 Railroad Ave (07657-2312)
PHONE..............................201 941-2900
EMP: 50
SALES (est): 14.5MM
SALES (corp-wide): 1B **Privately Held**
SIC: 3089 Blister or bubble formed packaging, plastic
PA: Tekni-Plex, Inc.
460 E Swedesford Rd # 3000
Wayne PA 19087
484 690-1520

(G-9359)
EYELET EMBROIDERIES INC
65 Railroad Ave Ste 3 (07657-2130)
PHONE..............................201 945-2151
EMP: 60
SQ FT: 15,000
SALES (est): 2.6MM
SALES (corp-wide): 54MM **Privately Held**
SIC: 2397 Mfg Schiffli Embroidery
PA: Carolace Embroidery Co, Inc.
65 Railroad Ave Ste 3
Ridgefield NJ 07657
201 945-2151

(G-9360)
FIS DATA SYSTEMS INC
1008 Virgil Ave (07657-1602)
PHONE..............................201 945-1774
Dan Liu, *Vice Pres*
EMP: 30
SALES (corp-wide): 9.1B **Publicly Held**
WEB: www.sungard.com
SIC: 7374 7372 Data processing service; prepackaged software
HQ: Fis Data Systems Inc.
200 Campus Dr
Collegeville PA 19426
484 582-2000

(G-9361)
GARDEN STATE PRECISION INC
510 Church St (07657-2131)
P.O. Box 921 (07657-0921)
PHONE..............................201 945-6410
Fax: 201 945-3695
Joseph Molino, *President*
EMP: 8
SQ FT: 5,000
SALES (est): 1.2MM **Privately Held**
WEB: www.gardenstateprecision.com
SIC: 3544 Special dies & tools

(G-9362)
GENZYME CORPORATION
Also Called: Genzyme Biosurgery
1125 Pleasantview Ter (07657-2310)
PHONE..............................201 313-9660
Fax: 201 313-8808
Don Woodhouse, *Vice Pres*
Keith Green, *Mfg Staff*
Maritza Garcia, *Purch Mgr*
Ardis Thompson, *QC Mgr*
David Armistead, *Engineer*
EMP: 115
SALES (corp-wide): 609.6MM **Privately Held**
WEB: www.genzyme.com
SIC: 2834 Pharmaceutical preparations
HQ: Genzyme Corporation
50 Binney St
Cambridge MA 02142
617 252-7500

(G-9363)
GROW COMPANY INC
Also Called: Vol Employees Beneficiary Assn
55 Railroad Ave (07657-2109)
PHONE..............................201 941-8777
Andrew Szalay, *CEO*
Magda Peck, *President*
Massoud Arvanaghi, *Vice Pres*
EMP: 20
SQ FT: 40,000
SALES (est): 3.3MM
SALES (corp-wide): 1.3B **Privately Held**
SIC: 2023 2834 2844 2087 Dietary supplements, dairy & non-dairy based; pharmaceutical preparations; cosmetic preparations; food colorings

PA: Frutarom Industries Ltd
25 Hashaish
Haifa 26291
996 038-00

(G-9364)
HITRONS TECH INC
1 Remsen Pl Ste 107 (07657-2321)
PHONE..............................201 941-0024
Serom Park, *Principal*
EMP: 5
SALES (est): 172.2K **Privately Held**
SIC: 3699 Electrical equipment & supplies

(G-9365)
HOLOGRAPHIC FINISHING INC
501 Hendricks Cswy (07657-2116)
P.O. Box 597 (07657-0597)
PHONE..............................201 941-4651
Fax: 201 941-4453
Michael Vulcano, *President*
Mariann Vulcano, *Corp Secy*
Charles Vulcano, *Vice Pres*
EMP: 13
SQ FT: 14,457
SALES: 1MM **Privately Held**
WEB: www.holographicfinishing.com
SIC: 3554 2752 2789 Die cutting & stamping machinery, paper converting; commercial printing, lithographic; bookbinding & related work

(G-9366)
HR INDUSTRIES INC
605 Broad Ave Ste 102 (07657-1628)
PHONE..............................201 941-8000
Fax: 201 941-8253
Sylvia Siegal, *President*
Howard Rothbein, *Vice Pres*
EMP: 10
SQ FT: 1,800
SALES (est): 4MM **Privately Held**
SIC: 2653 Boxes, corrugated: made from purchased materials

(G-9367)
INTERNTNAL FOLDING PPR BOX SLS
1039 Hoyt Ave (07657-1507)
PHONE..............................201 941-3100
Stanley Shapiro, *Mng Member*
EMP: 26
SQ FT: 1,000
SALES (est): 3.2MM **Privately Held**
SIC: 5113 2657 Folding paperboard boxes; folding paperboard boxes

(G-9368)
JOHNSON & JOHNSON
472 Chestnut St (07657-2640)
PHONE..............................917 573-8007
John Yoon, *Branch Mgr*
EMP: 80
SALES (corp-wide): 76.4B **Publicly Held**
SIC: 2676 Feminine hygiene paper products
PA: Johnson & Johnson
1 Johnson And Johnson Plz
New Brunswick NJ 08933
732 524-0400

(G-9369)
K RON ART & MIRRORS INC
395 Broad Ave (07657-2333)
PHONE..............................201 313-7080
Albert Choi, *President*
EMP: 4
SQ FT: 14,500
SALES: 700K **Privately Held**
SIC: 5023 2499 Frames & framing, picture & mirror; picture & mirror frames, wood

(G-9370)
LASERCAM LLC (PA)
1039 Hoyt Ave (07657-1507)
PHONE..............................201 941-1262
Karl Koether, *General Mgr*
Maryellen Alesso, *Controller*
Greg Orlik, *Sales Staff*
George Fee, *Manager*
David Shapiro,
▲ EMP: 40
SQ FT: 12,000
SALES (est): 6.5MM **Privately Held**
WEB: www.lasercam.com
SIC: 3544 Dies, steel rule

(G-9371)
LES TOUT PETITE INC
600 Grand Ave (07657-1516)
PHONE..............................201 941-8675
Fax: 201 941-3711
Lois Letzt, *President*
Daniel Letzt, *Vice Pres*
EMP: 9
SQ FT: 8,000
SALES (est): 1.1MM **Privately Held**
SIC: 2369 2339 Girls' & children's outerwear; sportswear, women's

(G-9372)
LYNN AMIEE INC
Also Called: Amiee Lynn Accessories
65 Railroad Ave Ste 209 (07657-2130)
PHONE..............................201 840-6766
Fax: 201 840-8743
Steven Spolansky, *Principal*
Kayla Coppola, *Production*
Stephanie Murphy, *Accounts Exec*
Peggy Freedman, *Director*
EMP: 50 **Privately Held**
SIC: 2389 4213 Handkerchiefs, except paper; heavy machinery transport
PA: Lynn Amiee Inc
366 5th Ave Fl 11
New York NY 10001

(G-9373)
MDVIANI DESIGNS INC
724 Bergen Blvd Ste 2 (07657-1442)
PHONE..............................201 840-5410
Nelly Minassian, *Principal*
EMP: 4
SALES (est): 290K **Privately Held**
SIC: 3911 3915 Jewelry, precious metal; jewel settings & mountings, precious metal; gems, real & imitation: preparation for settings

(G-9374)
MISCHIEF INTERNATIONAL INC
501 Broad Ave Ste 12 (07657-2348)
PHONE..............................201 840-6888
Max Bhavnani, *President*
▲ EMP: 5
SALES: 5MM **Privately Held**
SIC: 2326 Men's & boys' work clothing

(G-9375)
MONTENA TARANTO FOODS INC
400 Victoria Ter (07657-2113)
PHONE..............................201 943-8484
Fax: 201 943-6037
Wade Montena, *President*
Joe Taranto, *Vice Pres*
▲ EMP: 20
SALES (est): 5.8MM **Privately Held**
WEB: www.montitrentini.com
SIC: 2022 Natural cheese

(G-9376)
MORSEMERE IRON WORKS INC
1085 Linden Ave Ste 2 (07657-1013)
PHONE..............................201 941-1133
Fax: 201 941-7745
Mark Candelitti, *President*
EMP: 10
SQ FT: 5,000
SALES: 1.1MM **Privately Held**
SIC: 3446 3449 Architectural metalwork; miscellaneous metalwork

(G-9377)
NES LIGHT INC
1179 Edgewater Ave (07657-2102)
PHONE..............................201 840-0400
Daniel Shin, *Manager*
EMP: 6 EST: 2012
SQ FT: 1,500
SALES (est): 577.3K **Privately Held**
SIC: 3993 Electric signs

(G-9378)
NEW LIFE COLOR REPRODUCTIONS
610 Broad Ave (07657-1626)
PHONE..............................201 943-7005
Fax: 201 943-7010
Dragomir Zivkovich, *President*
Kova Zivkovich, *Admin Sec*
EMP: 4

SQ FT: 12,000
SALES (est): 346.1K **Privately Held**
SIC: 7384 2752 Photographic services; commercial printing, offset

(G-9379)
PC MARKETING INC (PA)
Also Called: Montego Bay
1040 Wilt Ave (07657-1512)
PHONE..............................201 943-6100
Fax: 201 943-4234
Susan Miller, *President*
Eric Haynes, *Vice Pres*
Bruce Williams, *Vice Pres*
Alicia Acevedo, *Executive*
Jessica Castillo, *Executive Asst*
▲ EMP: 44
SQ FT: 27,000
SALES (est): 18.5MM **Privately Held**
SIC: 5099 3639 Tanning salon equipment & supplies; major kitchen appliances, except refrigerators & stoves

(G-9380)
PLASTIC SPECIALTIES & TECH INC (HQ)
101 Railroad Ave (07657-2312)
PHONE..............................201 941-2900
David Katz, *President*
Kenneth Baker, *CFO*
◆ EMP: 140
SQ FT: 9,900
SALES (est): 56.6MM
SALES (corp-wide): 1B **Privately Held**
WEB: www.coloritepolymers.tekni-plex.com
SIC: 3052 3082 2821 4953 Garden hose, plastic; tubes, unsupported plastic; thermoplastic materials; polyvinyl chloride resins (PVC); recycling, waste materials; paints & allied products
PA: Tekni-Plex, Inc.
460 E Swedesford Rd # 3000
Wayne PA 19087
484 690-1520

(G-9381)
PURE TEC CORPORATION (HQ)
101 Railroad Ave (07657-2312)
PHONE..............................201 941-2900
EMP: 4
SALES (est): 14MM
SALES (corp-wide): 1B **Privately Held**
SIC: 3089 Blister or bubble formed packaging, plastic
PA: Tekni-Plex, Inc.
460 E Swedesford Rd # 3000
Wayne PA 19087
484 690-1520

(G-9382)
RAYBEAM MANUFACTURING CORP
700 Grand Ave Ste 5 (07657-1527)
P.O. Box 538 (07657-0538)
PHONE..............................201 941-4529
Larry Muhlberg, *President*
Rose Wurst, *Corp Secy*
EMP: 3
SQ FT: 1,000
SALES: 1MM **Privately Held**
SIC: 2842 5169 Cleaning or polishing preparations; industrial chemicals

(G-9383)
RQ FLOORS CORP (PA)
425 Victoria Ter (07657-2112)
PHONE..............................201 654-3587
Leon Shekhets, *President*
Vera Shekhets, *Vice Pres*
Jan Maczuga, *Manager*
EMP: 27
SQ FT: 30,000
SALES: 7MM **Privately Held**
SIC: 2491 Flooring, treated wood block

(G-9384)
SAPORITO INC
959 Edgewater Ave (07657-2438)
PHONE..............................201 265-8212
Caren Zahn, *President*
EMP: 5
SQ FT: 10,000
SALES: 500K **Privately Held**
SIC: 2022 Cheese, natural & processed

(G-9385)
STANDARD COATING CORPORATION
461 Broad Ave (07657-2391)
PHONE...................................201 945-5058
David Roogh, *Manager*
Bernard Katz, *Admin Sec*
▲ **EMP: 4 EST:** 1937
SQ FT: 11,250
SALES (est): 692.7K **Privately Held**
WEB: www.nitrostan.com
SIC: 2851 Lacquer: bases, dopes, thinner; enamels; coating, air curing

(G-9386)
TONE LAYOUT LLC
Also Called: Koomus
1015 Hudson Ave (07657-2316)
PHONE...................................201 438-1746
Jong Hyuk Lee, *CEO*
EMP: 5
SQ FT: 5,000
SALES (est): 2.3MM **Privately Held**
SIC: 3663 Mobile communication equipment

(G-9387)
TOTAL IMAGE AND SIGN
719 Grand Ave Ste 1 (07657-1049)
PHONE...................................201 941-2307
Seung Hee Kim, *President*
EMP: 7
SALES (est): 732.1K **Privately Held**
SIC: 3993 Signs & advertising specialties

(G-9388)
TOUFAYAN BAKERY INC (PA)
Also Called: Toufayan Bakeries
175 Railroad Ave (07657-2312)
PHONE...................................201 861-4131
Fax: 201 941-7988
Harry Toufayan, *President*
Tony Fortunato, *Regional Mgr*
Sean Clark, *Plant Mgr*
Anthony Damiano, *Production*
Todd Germick, *Purchasing*
▼ **EMP:** 135
SALES (est): 40.1MM **Privately Held**
SIC: 2051 Bakery: wholesale or wholesale/retail combined

(G-9389)
TREND PRINTING/INTL LABEL
1183 Edgewater Ave (07657-2102)
PHONE...................................201 941-6611
Fax: 201 941-6307
David Fishbein, *President*
Arlene Fishbein, *Vice Pres*
EMP: 10
SQ FT: 10,000
SALES (est): 1.5MM **Privately Held**
SIC: 2759 Flexographic printing

(G-9390)
UNION CITY FILAMENT CORP
1039 Hoyt Ave A (07657-1507)
P.O. Box 777 (07657-0777)
PHONE...................................201 945-3366
Fax: 201 945-6634
Joseph Celia Jr, *President*
Constance Celia, *Vice Pres*
EMP: 40 **EST:** 1950
SQ FT: 11,000
SALES (est): 9MM **Privately Held**
WEB: www.ucfilament.com
SIC: 3356 3641 3671 Tungsten, basic shapes; filaments, for electric lamps; electron tubes

(G-9391)
UNITED CITY ICE CUBE CO INC
695 Elm Ave (07657-1229)
PHONE...................................201 945-8387
Salvina Palmadessa, *Principal*
EMP: 5 **EST:** 2008
SALES (est): 264.1K **Privately Held**
SIC: 2097 Ice cubes

(G-9392)
UNITED ENVELOPE LLC (PA)
65 Railroad Ave (07657-2140)
PHONE...................................201 699-5800
Kenneth Bernstein, *President*
EMP: 116
SQ FT: 30,000

SALES (est): 107.4MM **Privately Held**
SIC: 2759 2677 Envelopes: printing; envelopes

(G-9393)
WATERDOCTOR INC
734 Grand Ave Unit E (07657-1042)
PHONE...................................732 972-4510
Joseph Lee, *CEO*
Thomas Lee, *COO*
Elizabeth Lee, *CFO*
▲ **EMP:** 16
SALES (est): 1.8MM **Privately Held**
WEB: www.waterdoctorusa.com
SIC: 3589 Water treatment equipment, industrial

(G-9394)
WESTCHESTER DENIM BROTHERS INC
736 Slocum Ave (07657-1838)
PHONE...................................203 260-1629
Mourad Elayan, *Principal*
EMP: 8
SALES (est): 598K **Privately Held**
SIC: 2211 Denims

Ridgefield Park
Bergen County

(G-9395)
ADVERTISERS SERVICE GROUP INC
65 Railroad Ave (07660-1321)
PHONE...................................201 440-5577
Fax: 201 440-5134
Edward F Kelly, *President*
Patricia Kelly, *Corp Secy*
EMP: 12 **EST:** 1961
SQ FT: 15,000
SALES: 1MM **Privately Held**
WEB: www.advertisersservices.com
SIC: 7336 7311 2752 2796 Graphic arts & related design; advertising agencies; commercial printing, lithographic; commercial printing, offset; platemaking services

(G-9396)
ALL NU TROPHY & SCREEN PRTG
243 Teaneck Rd (07660-2013)
PHONE...................................201 807-0808
Alan Jones, *Owner*
EMP: 13
SQ FT: 5,000
SALES: 700K **Privately Held**
SIC: 5999 2759 3993 2396 Trophies & plaques; screen printing; signs & advertising specialties; automotive & apparel trimmings

(G-9397)
ALPINE CORRUGATED MCHY INC
100 Challenger Rd Ste 304 (07660-2119)
PHONE...................................201 440-3030
Linda Katsigeorgis, *President*
▼ **EMP:** 3
SQ FT: 30,000
SALES (est): 6.5MM **Privately Held**
WEB: www.alpinemachinery.com
SIC: 3554 Corrugating machines, paper

(G-9398)
BETTER FOODS JEYER LLC
185 Industrial Ave (07660-1333)
P.O. Box 30, Fair Lawn (07410-0030)
PHONE...................................888 717-6412
Yaniv Mazor, *President*
EMP: 4 **EST:** 2015
SALES (est): 123K **Privately Held**
SIC: 2041 Flour

(G-9399)
CAOLION BNC CO LTD
65 Challenger Rd Ste 44 (07660-2103)
PHONE...................................201 641-4709
James Jang, *CEO*
EMP: 146
SQ FT: 2,436

SALES (est): 4MM **Privately Held**
SIC: 2844 Cosmetic preparations

(G-9400)
CEDGE INDUSTRIES INC (PA)
Also Called: Edgeco
71 Preston St (07660-1507)
P.O. Box 338, Little Ferry (07643-0338)
PHONE...................................201 641-3222
Fax: 201 641-7349
C James Esposito, *President*
Rena Esposito, *Vice Pres*
EMP: 18
SALES (est): 2.1MM **Privately Held**
WEB: www.edgeoamerica.com
SIC: 3841 Surgical & medical instruments

(G-9401)
CONSOLIDATED PACKG GROUP INC
30 Bergen Tpke (07660-2383)
P.O. Box 261 (07660-0261)
PHONE...................................201 440-4240
William Kaufman, *CEO*
Chaim Kaufman, *President*
Ben Kaufman, *Vice Pres*
EMP: 150
SQ FT: 120,000
SALES (est): 27MM **Privately Held**
SIC: 2673 2671 Plastic bags: made from purchased materials; plastic film, coated or laminated for packaging

(G-9402)
DATA COMMUNIQUE INC
65 Challenger Rd Fl 4 (07660-2103)
PHONE...................................201 508-6000
Richard Plotka, *CEO*
Brian Essman, *CEO*
Ethan Kende, *President*
Gary Polanco, *President*
John Closson, *Principal*
EMP: 45
SQ FT: 7,500
SALES: 12MM
SALES (corp-wide): 78.4MM **Privately Held**
SIC: 7313 8741 2791 2759 Radio, television, publisher representatives; management services; typesetting; financial note & certificate printing & engraving; computer software development
HQ: Havas
29 30
Puteaux 92800
158 478-000

(G-9403)
DATA COMMUNIQUE INTL INC
65 Challenger Rd Ste 400 (07660-2122)
PHONE...................................201 508-6000
Richard Posen, *Principal*
Sean Heffernan, *Vice Pres*
EMP: 45
SALES (est): 2.2MM
SALES (corp-wide): 78.4MM **Privately Held**
SIC: 2759 2752 Commercial printing; commercial printing, lithographic
HQ: Havas
29 30
Puteaux 92800
158 478-000

(G-9404)
DMG AMERICA LLC
Also Called: Goldsmith & Revere
65 Challenger Rd Ste 340 (07660-2122)
PHONE...................................201 894-5500
Celia Basile, *Finance*
George Wolfe, *Mng Member*
▲ **EMP:** 30
SQ FT: 10,000
SALES (est): 5.5MM **Privately Held**
WEB: www.zenithdmg.com
SIC: 3843 5047 Dental equipment & supplies; medical & hospital equipment

(G-9405)
EQUIPMENT DISTRIBUTING CORP (PA)
3 Eucker St (07660-2335)
PHONE...................................201 641-8414
Antonio S Limbardo, *President*
EMP: 7
SQ FT: 1,200

SALES (est): 1.1MM **Privately Held**
SIC: 3312 3441 Wire products, steel or iron; fabricated structural metal

(G-9406)
FLIR SECURITY INC
65 Challenger Rd (07660-2103)
PHONE...................................201 368-9700
Andrew C Teich, *President*
Todd M Duchene, *Senior VP*
Jeffrey D Frank, *Senior VP*
Shane R Harrison, *Senior VP*
Travis D Merrill, *Senior VP*
EMP: 5
SALES (est): 278.2K
SALES (corp-wide): 1.8B **Publicly Held**
SIC: 3663 5731 Digital encoders; video cameras & accessories
PA: Flir Systems, Inc.
27700 Sw Parkway Ave
Wilsonville OR 97070
503 498-3547

(G-9407)
HOSPITALITY GL BRANDS USA INC
185 Industrial Ave (07660-1333)
PHONE...................................800 869-5258
▲ **EMP:** 15
SALES (est): 1.9MM **Privately Held**
SIC: 3229 Novelty glassware

(G-9408)
KIRKWOOD NJ GLOBE ACQSTION LLC
1 Teaneck Rd (07660-2360)
PHONE...................................201 440-0800
Bob Coppinger, *CEO*
Stephan A Duncan, *President*
Eddie Kelley, *COO*
Christopher Noble, *Senior VP*
Craig Wenrich, *Vice Pres*
EMP: 5
SALES (est): 378K **Privately Held**
SIC: 3555 Printing presses

(G-9409)
KOLON USA INCORPORATED
Also Called: Scen'a Video Tape
65 Challenger Rd (07660-2103)
PHONE...................................201 641-5800
Fax: 973 575-1332
Edward Kang, *President*
Bruce Lee, *General Mgr*
Ivan Park, *General Mgr*
Jeffrey Hong, *Treasurer*
Debbie Hanlon, *Manager*
▲ **EMP:** 19
SQ FT: 58,000
SALES (est): 4.6MM
SALES (corp-wide): 2.9B **Privately Held**
WEB: www.kolonscena.com
SIC: 5199 3081 Packaging materials; unsupported plastics film & sheet
PA: Kolon Industries, Inc.
110 Magokdong-Ro, Gangseo-Gu
Seoul 07793
822 367-7602

(G-9410)
KUPELIAN FOODS INC
146 Bergen Tpke (07660-2323)
PHONE...................................201 440-8055
Edward Kupelian, *President*
EMP: 5
SQ FT: 1,500
SALES (est): 440K **Privately Held**
SIC: 2013 Sausages & other prepared meats

(G-9411)
OE SOLUTIONS AMERICA INC
Also Called: Moon
65 Challenger Rd Ste 240 (07660-2122)
PHONE...................................201 568-1188
Yong Kwan Park, *President*
Moonsoo Park, *Vice Pres*
Chuck Sinha, *VP Bus Dvlpt*
Christopher Kim, *Sales Mgr*
Richard Burroughs, *Manager*
EMP: 15
SALES (est): 3MM
SALES (corp-wide): 70MM **Privately Held**
SIC: 3661 Fiber optics communications equipment

PA: Oe Solutions Co., Ltd.
53 Cheomdanyeonsin-Ro 30beon-Gil,
Buk-Gu
Gwangju 61080
826 296-0525

(G-9412)
OUTPUT SERVICES GROUP INC (PA)
Also Called: OSG Billing Services
100 Challenger Rd Ste 303 (07660-2119)
PHONE..................................201 871-1100
Scott W Bernstein, *CEO*
John Springthorpe III, *President*
Alan Connolly, *Exec VP*
John Delaney, *Exec VP*
Neil Metviner, *Exec VP*
EMP: 34
SQ FT: 10,000
SALES (est): 128.2MM **Privately Held**
WEB: www.osgbilling.com
SIC: 7372 Business oriented computer
software

(G-9413)
SAMSUNG SDS GLOBL SCL AMER INC (HQ)
100 Challenger Rd Ste 601 (07660-2121)
PHONE..................................201 229-4456
Sean Seung Gyo Kae, *CEO*
Ki Hyung Cho, *President*
Jong Moo Bae, *CFO*
Ryan Park, *Manager*
Yoon Chul Shin, *Manager*
EMP: 20
SALES (est): 214.2MM
SALES (corp-wide): 4.1B **Privately Held**
WEB: www.samsungsdsa.com
SIC: 7372 7371 Prepackaged software;
computer software development
PA: Samsung Sds Co., Ltd.
125 Olympic-Ro 35-Gil, Songpa-Gu
Seoul 05510
822 615-5311

(G-9414)
SOFIELD MANUFACTURING CO INC
2 Main St (07660-2213)
PHONE..................................201 931-1530
EMP: 4
SQ FT: 5,000
SALES (est): 420K **Privately Held**
SIC: 3469 Mfg Metal Stampings

(G-9415)
SONOCO DISPLAY & PACKAGING LLC
Also Called: Sonoco Corrflex
55 Challenger Rd Ste 500 (07660-2107)
PHONE..................................201 612-4008
EMP: 8
SALES (corp-wide): 5B **Publicly Held**
SIC: 3086 Packaging & shipping materials,
foamed plastic
HQ: Sonoco Display & Packaging, Llc
555 Aureole St
Winston Salem NC 27107

(G-9416)
STAR SOAP/STAR CANDLE/PRAYER C
Also Called: Star Candle Company
300 Industrial Ave (07660-1346)
PHONE..................................201 690-9090
Stanley Gurewitsch, *Mng Member*
Arnie Gurewitsch,
Steven Gurewitsch,
Sam Schwartz,
▲ EMP: 200 EST: 1939
SQ FT: 150,000
SALES (est): 38.2MM **Privately Held**
WEB: www.starcandle.com
SIC: 3999 Candles

(G-9417)
VITEX LLC
105 Challenger Rd Ste 401 (07660-2101)
PHONE..................................201 296-0145
Amit Bose, *Sales Engr*
Michael Ko,
EMP: 7
SQ FT: 1,500

SALES: 8MM **Privately Held**
WEB: www.vitextech.com
SIC: 5065 3661 Communication equipment; fiber optics communications equipment

(G-9418)
WEILING YANG
65 Challenger Rd (07660-2103)
PHONE..................................201 440-5329
Te Zhong, *President*
EMP: 6 EST: 2015
SALES (est): 148.1K **Privately Held**
SIC: 5499 2836 Spices & herbs; extracts

(G-9419)
ZIREX INC
Also Called: Samsung Pleomax America
105 Challenger Rd Fl 1 (07660-2100)
PHONE..................................201 807-6401
Andew Pilho Kang, *President*
Bono Choi, *COO*
IL Moon Hwang, *Admin Sec*
▲ EMP: 5
SQ FT: 1,000
SALES (est): 756.1K **Privately Held**
SIC: 3572 Magnetic storage devices, com-
puter

Ridgewood
Bergen County

(G-9420)
ARAYA INC
Also Called: Araya Rebirth
10 Garber Sq Ste A (07450-3129)
PHONE..................................201 445-7005
Danella Musano, *President*
EMP: 5
SALES (est): 611.3K **Privately Held**
WEB: www.araya.com
SIC: 3842 Cosmetic restorations

(G-9421)
CIMWARE USA INC
226 Brookside Ave (07450-4631)
PHONE..................................201 493-0521
Martha Ranky, *President*
Marti Ranky, *Principal*
EMP: 4
SALES (est): 190K **Privately Held**
WEB: www.cimwareukandusa.com
SIC: 2741 Miscellaneous publishing

(G-9422)
CUPCAKES BY CAROUSEL (PA)
192 E Ridgewood Ave (07450-3848)
PHONE..................................201 389-3090
EMP: 4 EST: 2009
SALES (est): 217.7K **Privately Held**
SIC: 2051 Bakery: wholesale or whole-
sale/retail combined

(G-9423)
DOUGLAS LIVA MD
Also Called: Liva Eye Center
625 Franklin Tpke (07450-1913)
PHONE..................................201 444-7770
Fax: 201 447-9338
Douglas Liva, *Owner*
Douglas S Liva, *Office Mgr*
EMP: 7
SQ FT: 80,000
SALES (est): 795K **Privately Held**
WEB: www.eyemd.com
SIC: 3851 8011 Protectors, eye; ophthal-
mologist

(G-9424)
ERJ BAKING LLC
235 N Pleasant Ave (07450-2834)
PHONE..................................201 906-1300
Jeffrey Jayson, *Principal*
EMP: 4
SALES (est): 270.6K **Privately Held**
SIC: 2051 Bread, cake & related products

(G-9425)
HORIZON PRODUCTS NJ LLC
40 W Ridgewood Ave (07450-3136)
P.O. Box 1209, Fair Lawn (07410-8209)
PHONE..................................201 773-7015
Don Turner, *General Mgr*

EMP: 6
SALES (est): 1.4MM **Privately Held**
SIC: 2842 Degreasing solvent

(G-9426)
INTEGRATE TECH INC
778 E Ridgewood Ave (07450-3924)
PHONE..................................201 693-5625
Maxwell Witt, *CEO*
Kevin Celisca, *CFO*
EMP: 4
SALES (est): 98.3K **Privately Held**
SIC: 7372 Educational computer software

(G-9427)
NUTRA NUTS INC (PA)
Also Called: Grandpa Po's Nutra Nuts
247 Emmett Pl (07450-2803)
PHONE..................................323 260-7457
Mark Porro, *President*
Michael Porro, *CFO*
EMP: 4
SQ FT: 3,300
SALES: 200K **Privately Held**
WEB: www.nutranuts.com
SIC: 2064 Popcorn balls or other treated
popcorn products

(G-9428)
PUBLISHERS PARTNERSHIP CO
23 N Pleasant Ave (07450-3920)
PHONE..................................201 689-1613
Molly Ledwith, *Partner*
EMP: 99
SALES (est): 2.8MM **Privately Held**
SIC: 2741 5942 Miscellaneous publishing;
book stores

(G-9429)
QUALITY PRINT SOLUTIONS
589 Franklin Tpke (07450-1989)
PHONE..................................888 679-7237
Steve Fischgrund, *Partner*
EMP: 4
SALES: 350K **Privately Held**
SIC: 2752 Commercial printing, litho-
graphic

(G-9430)
RIDGEWOOD PRESS INC
609 Franklin Tpke (07450-1913)
PHONE..................................201 670-9797
Fax: 201 670-9799
Robert Modelski, *President*
John Pagluica, *Co-President*
Susan Burke, *Cust Mgr*
Michele Phalon, *Consultant*
EMP: 12
SALES (est): 2.1MM **Privately Held**
WEB: www.rpress.com
SIC: 2752 7334 7336 Commercial print-
ing, offset; photocopying & duplicating
services; commercial art & graphic design

(G-9431)
SUDARSHAN NORTH AMERICA INC
76 N Walnut St (07450-3224)
PHONE..................................201 652-2046
Rajesh Rathi, *CEO*
William Baker, *President*
▲ EMP: 7
SALES: 610MM
SALES (corp-wide): 201.5MM **Privately
Held**
WEB: www.sudarshan.com
SIC: 2816 Color pigments
PA: Sudarshan Chemical Industries Limited
No-162, Wellesley Road
Pune MH 41100
202 605-8888

(G-9432)
SVTC PHARMA INC
60 E Ridgewood Ave (07450-3810)
PHONE..................................201 652-0013
Purnachandra RAO Akkineni, *Principal*
EMP: 7 EST: 2011
SALES (est): 827.9K **Privately Held**
SIC: 2834 Pharmaceutical preparations

(G-9433)
T AND C NEUROMAX LLC
106 Prospect St (07450-4433)
PHONE..................................201 447-2020
John J Herr, *Owner*

EMP: 6
SALES (est): 728.3K **Privately Held**
SIC: 2834 Druggists' preparations (phar-
maceuticals)

(G-9434)
UBERTESTERS INC
72 S Maple Ave (07450-4542)
PHONE..................................201 203-7903
Ran Rachlin, *CEO*
Viktor Dmytrenko, *Marketing Mgr*
Alexey Taran, *Manager*
EMP: 14
SQ FT: 1,000
SALES (est): 349.8K **Privately Held**
SIC: 7372 Business oriented computer
software

Ringoes
Hunterdon County

(G-9435)
ARGUS INTERNATIONAL INC (PA)
424 Route 31 N (08551-1409)
P.O. Box 559 (08551-0559)
PHONE..................................609 466-1677
Bernard J Costello, *President*
Maryellen Costello, *Executive*
EMP: 20
SQ FT: 25,000
SALES (est): 4.1MM **Privately Held**
WEB: www.argus-international.com
SIC: 3567 3672 3625 3563 Heating units
& devices, industrial: electric; printed cir-
cuit boards; relays & industrial controls;
air & gas compressors

(G-9436)
CATERING BY MADDALENAS INC
415 Route 31 N (08551-1408)
P.O. Box 681 (08551-0681)
PHONE..................................609 466-7510
Janet Maddalena, *President*
Eugene Maddalena, *Vice Pres*
EMP: 5
SQ FT: 5,000
SALES (est): 270K **Privately Held**
WEB: www.maddalenascatering.com
SIC: 5812 2051 Caterers; cakes, pies &
pastries; bakery products; bakeries

(G-9437)
HED INTERNATIONAL INC
Also Called: Unique/Pereny
449 Route 31 N (08551-1408)
P.O. Box 246 (08551-0246)
PHONE..................................609 466-1900
Fax: 609 466-3608
James Dennis, *President*
John S Dennis, *CFO*
Terrance Dennis, *Mktg Dir*
EMP: 15
SQ FT: 25,000
SALES (est): 4.3MM **Privately Held**
WEB: www.hed.com
SIC: 3567 Heating units & devices, indus-
trial: electric; ceramic kilns & furnaces

(G-9438)
INENERGY INC
293 Wertsville Rd (08551-1701)
PHONE..................................609 466-2512
Michael Kurtis, *President*
Mark Kurtz, *Vice Pres*
EMP: 25
SALES (est): 4MM **Privately Held**
SIC: 3433 Solar heaters & collectors

(G-9439)
JAY JARIWALA
Also Called: Dunkin' Donuts
1019 Us Highway 202 (08551-1049)
PHONE..................................908 806-8266
Fax: 908 806-0521
Jay Jariwala, *Owner*
EMP: 15
SALES (est): 304.1K **Privately Held**
SIC: 5461 2051 Doughnuts; doughnuts,
except frozen

(G-9440)
MATTHEW WARREN INC
Also Called: Atlantic Spring
137 Us Highway 202 (08551-1909)
P.O. Box 650, Flemington (08822-0650)
PHONE....................908 788-5800
Fax: 908 788-0511
Scott Solomon, *Exec VP*
Christine Ruffolo, *Purchasing*
EMP: 10
SALES (corp-wide): 169MM **Privately Held**
SIC: 3493 3495 Steel springs, except wire; wire springs
HQ: Matthew Warren, Inc.
9501 Tech Blvd Ste 401
Rosemont IL 60018
847 349-5760

(G-9441)
OLD YORK CELLARS
80 Old York Rd (08551-1309)
PHONE....................908 284-9463
David Wolin, *Owner*
Jennifer Tanner, *Sales Mgr*
Loren Dorman, *Manager*
Narendra Haynes, *Director*
Austin White, *Planning*
EMP: 6
SALES (est): 386.2K **Privately Held**
SIC: 2084 Wines

(G-9442)
REAGENT CHEMICAL & RES INC
115 Us Highway 202 Ste E (08551-1913)
PHONE....................908 284-2800
Fax: 732 469-1074
Brian Finney, *Vice Pres*
Steve Khan, *Vice Pres*
Russell Straz, *Project Engr*
Mike Devore, *Sales Mgr*
Robert Erwood, *Sales Mgr*
EMP: 50
SALES (corp-wide): 375MM **Privately Held**
WEB: www.biotarget.com
SIC: 2819 3949 Sulfur, recovered or refined, incl. from sour natural gas; targets, archery & rifle shooting
PA: Reagent Chemical & Research, Inc.
115 Rte 202
Ringoes NJ 08551
908 284-2800

(G-9443)
UNIONVILLE VINEYARDS LLC
9 Rocktown Rd (08551-1214)
PHONE....................908 788-0400
Fax: 908 806-4692
Patricia Galloway, *Partner*
Kris Nielsen, *Partner*
John Cifelli, *General Mgr*
Tiffany Baldino, *Manager*
EMP: 8
SALES (est): 949.6K **Privately Held**
WEB: www.unionvillevineyards.com
SIC: 2084 0172 Wines; grapes

Ringwood
Passaic County

(G-9444)
BACH TOOL PRECISION INC
51 Executive Pkwy (07456-1429)
PHONE....................973 962-6224
Richard Ebersbach, *President*
Jane Ebersbach, *Office Admin*
EMP: 6
SALES (est): 590K **Privately Held**
WEB: www.bachtoolprecision.com
SIC: 3544 3545 Special dies & tools; precision tools, machinists'

(G-9445)
CIRCONIX TECHNOLOGIES LLC (DH)
29 Executive Pkwy (07456-1429)
PHONE....................973 962-6160
Andre Icso, *President*
▲ EMP: 14
SQ FT: 15,000

SALES (est): 3.5MM **Privately Held**
WEB: www.circonix.com
SIC: 3613 7373 3823 Switchgear & switchboard apparatus; computer-aided engineering (CAE) systems service; industrial instrmnts msrmnt display/control process variable

(G-9446)
CROWN FASTENER & SUPPLY CORP
Also Called: Kingline
8 Industrial Pkwy Ste 3 (07456-1441)
PHONE....................845 268-5150
Loren Ware, *Mng Member*
Marilyn Ware,
▲ EMP: 6
SALES: 2.7MM **Privately Held**
SIC: 5085 3965 5051 Staplers & tackers; fasteners; nails

(G-9447)
GB INDUSTRIES II INC
341 Margaret King Ave (07456-1415)
PHONE....................973 728-5900
Fax: 973 728-1267
Gerard Barrere, *President*
John Barrere, *Vice Pres*
EMP: 6
SQ FT: 9,100
SALES: 1.2MM **Privately Held**
WEB: www.gbindustriesii.com
SIC: 3599 Machine shop, jobbing & repair

(G-9448)
HALL MANUFACTURING CORP
297 Margaret King Ave (07456-1423)
PHONE....................973 962-6022
Fax: 973 962-7652
Michael Goceljak, *President*
EMP: 24 EST: 1946
SQ FT: 21,000
SALES (est): 4MM **Privately Held**
SIC: 3089 Extruded finished plastic products; plastic processing

(G-9449)
ILL EAGLE ENTERPRISES LTD
Also Called: Ill-Eagle Enterprises
101 Miller Ln (07456-1208)
PHONE....................973 237-1111
Fax: 973 237-1112
Darryl Sgroi, *President*
▲ EMP: 32
SQ FT: 20,000
SALES (est): 6MM **Privately Held**
WEB: www.illeagle.com
SIC: 3499 3914 2499 Novelties & giftware, including trophies; trophies, plated (all metals); picture frame molding, finished

(G-9450)
INOPAK LTD
24 Executive Pkwy (07456-1430)
PHONE....................973 962-1121
Fax: 973 962-0811
John Polite, *President*
David Polite, *Corp Secy*
Nick Disarro, *Exec VP*
Monica Garcia, *QA Dir*
▲ EMP: 17
SQ FT: 17,500
SALES (est): 3.9MM **Privately Held**
WEB: www.inopak.com
SIC: 2841 3999 Soap & other detergents; soap dispensers

(G-9451)
MEMBRANES INTERNATIONAL INC
219 Margaret King Ave # 2 (07456-1440)
P.O. Box 219 (07456-0219)
PHONE....................973 998-5530
Dwight Loren, *CEO*
Jack Loren, *President*
EMP: 4
SALES (est): 857.4K **Privately Held**
WEB: www.membranesinternational.com
SIC: 3569 Filters

(G-9452)
MICROMAT CO
1165 Greenwood Lake Tpke E (07456-1416)
PHONE....................201 529-3738

Fax: 201 529-5942
Erwin Eibert, *President*
EMP: 7 EST: 1963
SQ FT: 5,000
SALES (est): 1.1MM **Privately Held**
WEB: www.micromat.com
SIC: 3491 Industrial valves; pressure valves & regulators, industrial

(G-9453)
PRO-PAC SERVICE INC
15 Van Natta Dr (07456-1412)
PHONE....................973 962-8080
Fax: 973 962-8010
Brian Douglas, *President*
▲ EMP: 12
SQ FT: 10,000
SALES (est): 2.4MM **Privately Held**
SIC: 3565 Packaging machinery

(G-9454)
PROGRESSIVE RUESCH INC
21 Van Natta Dr (07456-1412)
P.O. Box 325 (07456-0325)
PHONE....................973 962-7700
Stephen Honezarenko, *President*
▲ EMP: 30
SQ FT: 22,000
SALES: 7MM **Privately Held**
WEB: www.rueschmachinery.com
SIC: 3549 5084 Rotary slitters (metalworking machines); industrial machinery & equipment

(G-9455)
ROBERT NICHOLS CONTRACTING
407 Conklintown Rd (07456-2415)
PHONE....................973 902-2632
EMP: 10
SALES (est): 900K **Privately Held**
SIC: 2899 Mfg Chemical Preparations

(G-9456)
SUSAN R BAUER INC
Also Called: Bauer Enterprises
427 Margaret King Ave (07456-1438)
PHONE....................973 657-1590
Susan R Bauer, *President*
Mary Ellen Gutowski, *Manager*
Richard Bauer, *Admin Sec*
EMP: 8
SQ FT: 24,000
SALES (est): 950K **Privately Held**
SIC: 3441 Fabricated structural metal for bridges; expansion joints (structural shapes), iron or steel

(G-9457)
TERHUNE BROS WOODWORKING
58 Bearfort Ter (07456-2943)
PHONE....................973 962-6686
Michael Terhune, *Principal*
EMP: 4
SALES (est): 324.6K **Privately Held**
SIC: 2431 Millwork

Rio Grande
Cape May County

(G-9458)
HANGER PRSTHETCS & ORTHO INC
1 Secluded Ln (08242-1546)
PHONE....................609 889-8447
Virginia Millar, *Principal*
EMP: 7
SALES (corp-wide): 1B **Publicly Held**
SIC: 3842 Surgical appliances & supplies
HQ: Hanger Prosthetics & Orthotics, Inc.
10910 Domain Dr Ste 300
Austin TX 78758
512 777-3800

(G-9459)
HANSEN AWNING CO
18 Church Rd (08242-1902)
PHONE....................609 886-1685
Lillian McGill, *Partner*
Patricia Reed, *Partner*
EMP: 4

SALES: 90K **Privately Held**
SIC: 3444 Awnings & canopies

(G-9460)
MICHAELS CABINET CONNECTION
1054 Route 47 S (08242-1506)
PHONE....................609 889-6611
Michael Snow, *CEO*
EMP: 5
SQ FT: 5,000
SALES: 170K **Privately Held**
SIC: 2434 Wood kitchen cabinets

(G-9461)
RESDEL CORPORATION (PA)
Industrial Park (08242)
PHONE....................609 886-1111
Fax: 609 886-6329
Nicholas Calio, *President*
Dave Beckas, *Prdtn Mgr*
Debbie Fazen, *Office Admin*
Charles Mannella, *Admin Sec*
EMP: 20 EST: 1957
SQ FT: 10,000
SALES (est): 2.3MM **Privately Held**
SIC: 3082 Tubes, unsupported plastic

(G-9462)
SEAWAVE CORP
Also Called: Cape May County Herald
1508 Route 47 (08242-1413)
PHONE....................609 886-8600
Fax: 609 886-1879
Arthur R Hall, *President*
Patricia Hall, *Admin Sec*
EMP: 29
SQ FT: 4,000
SALES (est): 2MM **Privately Held**
WEB: www.cmcherald.com
SIC: 2711 8611 Newspapers, publishing & printing; business associations

River Edge
Bergen County

(G-9463)
COLEMAX GROUP LLC (PA)
41 Grand Ave Ste 103 (07661-1947)
P.O. Box 103, Glen Rock (07452-0103)
PHONE....................201 489-1080
Louie Valenti, *Accounts Mgr*
Richard Flashenberg,
▲ EMP: 5
SQ FT: 3,000
SALES (est): 4.4MM **Privately Held**
WEB: www.colemaxgroup.com
SIC: 3172 Cases, glasses

(G-9464)
CONTEMPOCORK LLC
175 Dorchester Rd (07661-1224)
PHONE....................201 262-7738
EMP: 5
SALES (est): 380K **Privately Held**
SIC: 1752 2499 Floor Contractor

(G-9465)
FEDEX CORPORATION
Also Called: Fedex Offic 5720
1071 Main St (07661-2011)
PHONE....................201 525-5070
EMP: 5
SALES (corp-wide): 65.4B **Publicly Held**
SIC: 2752 Commercial printing, lithographic
PA: Fedex Corporation
942 Shady Grove Rd S
Memphis TN 38120
901 818-7500

(G-9466)
KELLOGG COMPANY
164 Monroe Ave (07661-2113)
PHONE....................201 634-9140
J Volmar, *Principal*
EMP: 29
SALES (corp-wide): 12.9B **Publicly Held**
WEB: www.kelloggs.com
SIC: 2043 Cereal breakfast foods

PA: Kellogg Company
1 Kellogg Sq
Battle Creek MI 49017
269 961-2000

(G-9467)
P & P EQUIPMENT CORPORATION
286 Kinderkamack Rd (07661-1825)
PHONE..............................201 489-0050
Harvey S Levine, *President*
Vivian Levine, *Corp Secy*
EMP: 10
SQ FT: 20,000
SALES (est): 1.4MM **Privately Held**
SIC: 5084 3559 Metalworking machinery; metalworking tools (such as drills, taps, dies, files); metal finishing equipment for plating, etc.

(G-9468)
ZSOMBOR ANTAL DESIGNS INC
Also Called: Best Cast
822 Kinderkamack Rd (07661-2324)
PHONE..............................201 225-1750
Zsombor Antal, *President*
Laura Antal, *Vice Pres*
▲ **EMP:** 4
SQ FT: 4,000
SALES (est): 1.6MM **Privately Held**
WEB: www.best-cast.com
SIC: 3471 3911 Decorative plating & finishing of formed products; gold plating; jewelry, precious metal

River Vale
Bergen County

(G-9469)
DOORTEC ARCHTCTURAL MET GL LLC (PA)
303 Martin St (07675-5610)
PHONE..............................201 497-5056
Jeffrey Bentzen,
Boris Barskiy,
EMP: 1
SALES: 4.8MM **Privately Held**
SIC: 3446 Architectural metalwork

(G-9470)
INTERTAPE POLYMER CORP
648 Athlone Ter (07675-6548)
PHONE..............................201 391-3315
EMP: 135
SALES (corp-wide): 898.1MM **Privately Held**
SIC: 2672 Tape, pressure sensitive: made from purchased materials
HQ: Intertape Polymer Corp.
100 Paramount Dr Ste 300
Sarasota FL 34232
888 898-7834

(G-9471)
JOY JEWELERY AMERICA INC
228 Rivervale Rd Ste A (07675-6216)
PHONE..............................201 689-1150
Keith Lesser, *Principal*
EMP: 4
SALES (est): 400.7K **Privately Held**
SIC: 3911 Jewelry, precious metal

(G-9472)
UMBRELLAS UNLIMITED
808 Rivervale Rd (07675-6122)
PHONE..............................201 476-1011
Robert S Reiss, *Ch of Bd*
Ron Goldstein, *President*
Angela Sanfilippo, *Manager*
Raymond Lo, *Shareholder*
EMP: 2
SALES: 1.6MM **Privately Held**
SIC: 2211 Umbrella cloth, cotton

Riverdale
Morris County

(G-9473)
A & A CONCRETE PRODUCTS INC
2 S Corporate Dr (07457-1721)
P.O. Box 108 (07457-0108)
PHONE..............................973 835-2239
Fax: 973 835-3095
Sandra Alway, *President*
Dan Jiles, *Foreman/Supr*
EMP: 5
SQ FT: 6,000
SALES: 325K **Privately Held**
SIC: 5082 5039 3272 Concrete processing equipment; septic tanks; concrete products

(G-9474)
ALEXAM RIVERDALE
4000 Riverdale Rd (07457-1729)
PHONE..............................973 831-0065
EMP: 4
SALES (est): 433.7K **Privately Held**
SIC: 3713 Automobile wrecker truck bodies

(G-9475)
BER PLASTICS INC
5 Curtis St (07457-1113)
P.O. Box 2 (07457-0002)
PHONE..............................973 839-2100
Fax: 973 839-7929
Edward Ringley, *Ch of Bd*
Bernard Ewasko, *President*
Bernie A Ewasko, *Sales Executive*
EMP: 24 **EST:** 1965
SQ FT: 17,000
SALES (est): 3.6MM **Privately Held**
SIC: 3082 3081 Tubes, unsupported plastic; plastic film & sheet

(G-9476)
CAMFIL USA INC (HQ)
1 N Corporate Dr (07457-1715)
PHONE..............................973 616-7300
Armando Brunetti, *President*
Carl Larochelle, *General Mgr*
Charles Seyffer, *General Mgr*
Paul Cleveland, *Managing Dir*
Rhys Anderson, *Area Mgr*
◆ **EMP:** 180
SQ FT: 106,000
SALES (est): 271.3MM
SALES (corp-wide): 864.2MM **Privately Held**
SIC: 3564 3569 Purification & dust collection equipment; filters, air: furnaces, air conditioning equipment, etc.; air purification equipment; dust or fume collecting equipment, industrial; filters; filters, general line: industrial
PA: Camfil Ab
Sveavagen 56e
Stockholm 111 3
854 512-500

(G-9477)
CARL STAHL SAVA INDUSTRIES INC (HQ)
4 N Corporate Dr (07457-1715)
P.O. Box 30 (07457-0030)
PHONE..............................973 835-0882
Fax: 973 835-0877
Zdenek A Fremund, *CEO*
Marc E Alterman, *President*
Gregory Soja, *Vice Pres*
Bruce R Staubitz, *Vice Pres*
Carl Stahl, *Controller*
▲ **EMP:** 85
SQ FT: 70,000
SALES: 17.1MM
SALES (corp-wide): 273.6MM **Privately Held**
WEB: www.savacable.com
SIC: 3496 Miscellaneous fabricated wire products
PA: Carl Stahl Gmbh
Tobelstr. 2
SuBen 73079
716 240-070

(G-9478)
CVE INC
5 N Corporate Dr (07457-1715)
PHONE..............................201 770-0005
Fax: 201 770-1313
Kyu Taek Cho, *President*
Jae Joon, *General Mgr*
▲ **EMP:** 100
SQ FT: 63,000
SALES (est): 30.6MM **Privately Held**
WEB: www.cveusa.com
SIC: 3651 Household audio & video equipment

(G-9479)
DIVERSITECH INC
Also Called: K & E Components
18 Hamburg Tpke (07457-1116)
PHONE..............................973 835-2900
Keith Wolos, *President*
James Schmieder, *President*
EMP: 28 **EST:** 1965
SQ FT: 27,000
SALES (est): 4.9MM **Privately Held**
WEB: www.sierrakd.com
SIC: 3599 Machine shop, jobbing & repair

(G-9480)
EVS INTERACTIVE INC
Also Called: Redyref
100 Riverdale Rd (07457-1700)
PHONE..............................718 784-3690
Scott Berkowitz, *President*
Joseph Amico, *Vice Pres*
David Falco, *Opers Staff*
Fred Ravo, *Design Engr*
EMP: 15
SALES (est): 1MM **Privately Held**
SIC: 3444 Sheet metalwork

(G-9481)
GLASS CYCLE SYSTEMS INC
5 Mathews Ave (07457-1010)
P.O. Box 816, Butler (07405-0816)
PHONE..............................973 838-0034
David Bowlby, *President*
EMP: 4
SQ FT: 2,200
SALES: 150K **Privately Held**
SIC: 3559 4953 Recycling machinery; recycling, waste materials

(G-9482)
INDEPENDENT SHEET METAL CO INC
2 N Corporate Dr 2 # 2 (07457-1715)
PHONE..............................973 423-1150
Edward Rebenack, *President*
Stephen Pucilowski, *Vice Pres*
Andrew Borbely, *Manager*
Jim Boniface, *Info Tech Mgr*
Thomas Boniface, *Admin Sec*
EMP: 100
SQ FT: 40,000
SALES (est): 24.4MM **Privately Held**
WEB: www.indsm.com
SIC: 3444 1761 Sheet metalwork; sheet metalwork

(G-9483)
PROMET INC
8220 Sanctuary Blvd (07457-1640)
PHONE..............................303 371-2300
▲ **EMP:** 4 **EST:** 2011
SALES (est): 318.1K **Privately Held**
SIC: 3542 Bending machines

(G-9484)
RAINBOW METAL UNITS CORP
Also Called: Dawnex Industries
1 Kenner Ct (07457-1500)
PHONE..............................718 784-3690
William Pymm, *President*
Edward Pymm, *Vice Pres*
EMP: 20
SQ FT: 30,000
SALES (est): 2.9MM **Privately Held**
WEB: www.redyref.com
SIC: 3444 Sheet metalwork

(G-9485)
RIVERDALE QUARRY LLC
125 Hamburg Tpke (07457-1000)
PHONE..............................973 835-0028
Fax: 973 835-0582

Gary Mahan, *General Mgr*
Charles Highler, *Manager*
EMP: 50
SALES (est): 2.1MM **Privately Held**
SIC: 1429 2951 Igneous rock, crushed & broken-quarrying; asphalt & asphaltic paving mixtures (not from refineries)

(G-9486)
SENTRY WATER MANAGEMENT
35 Newark Pompton Tpke (07457-1144)
PHONE..............................973 616-9000
Fax: 973 616-9919
Matt Copley, *General Mgr*
EMP: 40
SALES (est): 3.9MM **Privately Held**
SIC: 2899 Water treating compounds

(G-9487)
SETCON INDUSTRIES INC
5 Mathews Ave Ste 7 (07457-1034)
PHONE..............................973 283-0500
Fax: 973 283-0301
Glen Azzolino, *President*
Joseph Azzolino, *President*
Robert Azzolino, *Vice Pres*
EMP: 10
SQ FT: 4,000
SALES (est): 1.1MM **Privately Held**
WEB: www.setconindustries.com
SIC: 2819 Industrial inorganic chemicals; calcium chloride & hypochlorite

(G-9488)
SIGMA-NETICS INC
2 N Corporate Dr (07457-1715)
PHONE..............................973 227-6372
Alan Glanzman, *CEO*
Claudio Dacal, *Vice Pres*
Roseann Nestor, *Buyer*
Avinash Patel, *Engineer*
Igor Kitanovski, *Project Engr*
▲ **EMP:** 35 **EST:** 1965
SQ FT: 55,000
SALES: 8MM **Privately Held**
WEB: www.sigmanetics.com
SIC: 3829 3625 3822 3613 Measuring & controlling devices; switches, electric power; auto controls regulating residntl & coml environmt & applncs; power switching equipment

(G-9489)
SPECIALIZED FIRE & SEC INC
20 Cotluss Rd Ste 9 (07457-1400)
P.O. Box 110 (07457-0110)
PHONE..............................212 255-1010
Chris Kelly, *President*
Jack McHugh, *VP Opers*
Joe Branco, *Project Mgr*
Mike Fischer, *Project Mgr*
Andy Takach, *Project Mgr*
EMP: 20 **EST:** 1991
SQ FT: 5,500
SALES (est): 6MM **Privately Held**
SIC: 3699 Security control equipment & systems

(G-9490)
TILCON NEW YORK INC
Also Called: Riverdale Quarry
125 Hamburg Tpke (07457-1003)
PHONE..............................973 835-0028
Fax: 973 616-4785
Frank Gelewski, *Manager*
EMP: 60
SALES (corp-wide): 29.7B **Privately Held**
WEB: www.tilconny.com
SIC: 2951 Asphalt paving mixtures & blocks
HQ: Tilcon New York Inc.
9 Entin Rd
Parsippany NJ 07054
800 789-7625

(G-9491)
TTSS INTERACTIVE PRODUCTS INC
100 Riverdale Rd (07457-1700)
PHONE..............................301 230-1464
William Pymm, *President*
EMP: 20
SALES (est): 1.7MM **Privately Held**
SIC: 3679 Electronic circuits

Riverside
Burlington County

(G-9492)
ALLISON SYSTEMS CORPORATION
220 Adams St (08075-3150)
PHONE................................856 461-9111
Fax: 856 461-9373
Thomas K Allison Jr, *Principal*
Bill Warner, *Vice Pres*
Eve Allison, *Opers Mgr*
Tim Main, *Technology*
Marion Bobo, *Technical Staff*
▲ EMP: 18 EST: 1968
SQ FT: 10,000
SALES (est): 3.9MM **Privately Held**
WEB: www.allisonblades.com
SIC: 3555 Presses, gravure

(G-9493)
BEVERLY MANUFACTURING CO INC
Also Called: Beverly Transformers
63 Webster St (08075-3642)
PHONE................................856 764-7898
Fax: 856 461-9238
Tony Cruz, *President*
Sonia Cruz, *Manager*
Filipe Cruz, *Info Tech Mgr*
EMP: 7
SALES (est): 847K **Privately Held**
WEB: www.beverlytransformers.com
SIC: 3612 Specialty transformers

(G-9494)
C & C TOOL AND MACHINE CO LLC
38 W Scott St (08075-3602)
P.O. Box 407 (08075-7407)
PHONE................................856 764-0911
Fax: 856 764-6106
Frank Canduci,
Nunzio Canduci,
EMP: 5 EST: 1973
SQ FT: 4,500
SALES: 1.2MM **Privately Held**
SIC: 3599 Machine shop, jobbing & repair

(G-9495)
CINDERELLA CHEESECAKE CO INC
Also Called: Cinderella Cheese Cake
208 N Fairview St (08075-3113)
P.O. Box 36 (08075-0036)
PHONE................................856 461-6302
Joseph Makin, *President*
Bernadette Makin, *Corp Secy*
Alfred Rezende, *Vice Pres*
EMP: 15 EST: 1958
SQ FT: 20,000
SALES (est): 1.6MM **Privately Held**
SIC: 2053 2051 Cakes, bakery: frozen; bread, cake & related products

(G-9496)
DEL BAKERS INC
Also Called: Delucca's Bakery
412 Kossuth St (08075-3234)
PHONE................................856 461-0089
Fax: 856 461-4552
Nicola De Lucca, *President*
EMP: 20
SQ FT: 3,500
SALES (est): 2.4MM **Privately Held**
SIC: 2051 5149 Bread, cake & related products; bakery products

(G-9497)
DRINK A TOAST COMPANY INC
Also Called: Boost Company, The
603 Harrison St (08075-3399)
P.O. Box 204 (08075-0204)
PHONE................................856 461-1000
Fax: 856 461-5964
Daniel P McDonough, *President*
Nancy J Faunce, *President*
Daniel McDonough, *General Mgr*
Karen C Rogers, *Vice Pres*
Richard W Stockton, *Vice Pres*
EMP: 10
SQ FT: 18,000

SALES (est): 1.3MM **Privately Held**
WEB: www.boostevents.com
SIC: 2087 Syrups, drink

(G-9498)
GOOD IMPRESSIONS INC
Also Called: G I Trade Copy
28 E Scott St (08075-3616)
P.O. Box 409 (08075-7409)
PHONE................................856 461-3232
Fax: 856 461-3290
Robert F Price, *President*
EMP: 7
SQ FT: 7,000
SALES (est): 1MM **Privately Held**
SIC: 2752 2759 7334 7389 Commercial printing, offset; letterpress printing; photocopying & duplicating services; interior designer; binding only: books, pamphlets, magazines, etc.

(G-9499)
HOWARD LIPPINCOTT
Also Called: Lippincott Marine
74 Norman Ave (08075-1004)
PHONE................................856 764-8282
Howard Lippincott, *Owner*
EMP: 4
SALES (est): 213.1K **Privately Held**
SIC: 5199 2394 2392 Canvas products; canvas & related products; household furnishings

(G-9500)
HUN MACHINE WORKS INC
Also Called: Wrought Metal Products Div
51 Whittaker St (08075-1499)
P.O. Box 189 (08075-0189)
PHONE................................856 461-6911
Fax: 856 461-8612
Shirley Kiss, *President*
Emery Kiss, *Vice Pres*
EMP: 12
SQ FT: 6,000
SALES (est): 1.3MM **Privately Held**
WEB: www.hunmachine.com
SIC: 3599 Machine shop, jobbing & repair

(G-9501)
M & D PRCSION CNTRLESS GRNDING
120 Kossuth St (08075-3228)
PHONE................................856 764-1616
Fax: 856 764-7444
Dave Speegle, *Owner*
EMP: 5
SALES (est): 195K **Privately Held**
SIC: 7389 3599 Grinding, precision: commercial or industrial; machine shop, jobbing & repair

(G-9502)
M AND D PRECISION GRINDING
120 Kossuth St (08075-3228)
PHONE................................856 764-1616
Dave Speegle, *President*
Denise Daziani, *Corp Secy*
Frank Grasso, *Vice Pres*
EMP: 5
SQ FT: 6,700
SALES (est): 563.6K **Privately Held**
SIC: 3599 Grinding castings for the trade

(G-9503)
MELVILLE INDUSTRIES INC
Also Called: Cleardrain
219 Saint Mihiel Dr Ste 2 (08075-3028)
P.O. Box 555, Willingboro (08046-0555)
PHONE................................856 461-0091
Fax: 856 461-0092
Frank Chille, *President*
John Middleton, *Marketing Staff*
EMP: 9 EST: 2010
SALES (est): 1MM **Privately Held**
SIC: 3561 Pumps & pumping equipment

(G-9504)
PER-FIL INDUSTRIES INC
407 Adams St (08075-3098)
P.O. Box 9 (08075-0009)
PHONE................................856 461-5700
Horst E Boellmann, *Ch of Bd*
Shari Becker, *President*
Charlotte Boellmann, *Principal*
◆ EMP: 25
SQ FT: 20,000

SALES (est): 3.2MM **Privately Held**
WEB: www.per-fil.com
SIC: 3565 Packaging machinery

(G-9505)
RICH PRODUCTS CORPORATION
100 American Legion Dr (08075-3054)
PHONE................................800 356-7094
EMP: 750
SALES (corp-wide): 4.1B **Privately Held**
SIC: 2053 Frozen bakery products, except bread
PA: Rich Products Corporation
1 Robert Rich Way
Buffalo NY 14213
716 878-8000

(G-9506)
RIVERSIDE MARINA YACHT SLS LLC
74 Norman Ave Ste 1 (08075-1097)
PHONE................................856 461-1077
Fax: 856 461-7261
Glenn Winter, *President*
Rebecca Winter, *Marketing Staff*
Nancy Balliet, *Manager*
Bruce Woodington, *Director*
EMP: 15
SQ FT: 30,000
SALES (est): 1.6MM **Privately Held**
WEB: www.riversideys.com
SIC: 4493 7699 3441 5551 Boat yards, storage & incidental repair; boat repair; boat & barge sections, prefabricated metal; marine supplies

(G-9507)
US PIPE FABRICATION LLC
200 Rhawn St (08075-4680)
PHONE................................856 461-3000
EMP: 19
SALES (corp-wide): 39.7MM **Privately Held**
SIC: 3312 Blast Furnace- Steel Works
HQ: Us Pipe Fabrication, Llc
2 Chase Corporate Dr # 200
Hoover AL 35244
205 263-8540

Riverton
Burlington County

(G-9508)
NICHOLAS LONGO SR
Also Called: Family House of Lamps
205 2nd St (08077-1170)
PHONE................................856 642-1971
Nicholas Longo Sr, *Owner*
EMP: 4
SQ FT: 2,500
SALES (est): 251.6K **Privately Held**
WEB: www.nicholaslongo.com
SIC: 5719 3645 Lamps & lamp shades; lighting, lamps & accessories; lamp & light shades

(G-9509)
ZENAS PATISSERIE
308 Broad St (08077-1304)
PHONE................................856 303-8700
Zena Denirceeiren, *Owner*
EMP: 8
SALES (est): 568.1K **Privately Held**
SIC: 2051 5812 Bread, cake & related products; coffee shop

Robbinsville
Mercer County

(G-9510)
AMERICAN BANK NOTE HOLOGRAPHIC (HQ)
2 Applegate Dr (08691-2342)
PHONE................................609 208-0591
Fax: 609 632-0850
Salvatore D'Amato, *Ch of Bd*
Kenneth H Traub, *President*
John Hynes, *Vice Pres*
Mark J Bonney, *CFO*

Michael T Banahan, *VP Sales*
▲ EMP: 100
SQ FT: 134,000
SALES (est): 4.9MM
SALES (corp-wide): 811.4MM **Publicly Held**
WEB: www.abnh.com
SIC: 2759 Laser printing
PA: Viavi Solutions Inc.
6001 America Center Dr # 6
San Jose CA 95002
408 404-3600

(G-9511)
BIND-RITE ROBBINSVILLE LLC
1 Applegate Dr (08691-2341)
PHONE................................609 208-1917
Paul Frontczak, *Vice Pres*
Tim Marsden, *Manager*
Harry Scharle, *Technology*
Rick Sommers, *Technology*
Steven Merson,
▲ EMP: 95
SALES (est): 19.1MM **Privately Held**
SIC: 2752 Commercial printing, offset

(G-9512)
CCL LABEL INC
104 N Gold Dr (08691-1602)
PHONE................................609 586-1332
Fax: 609 631-9137
Christie Bailey, *Branch Mgr*
EMP: 190
SALES (corp-wide): 3.7B **Privately Held**
SIC: 2759 2679 Labels & seals: printing; labels, paper: made from purchased material
HQ: Ccl Label, Inc.
161 Worcester Rd Ste 504
Framingham MA 01701
508 872-4511

(G-9513)
CJ TMI MANUFACTURING AMER LLC
2 Applegate Dr (08691-2342)
PHONE................................609 669-0100
Feongjin Hwang,
EMP: 150
SALES (est): 234.9K
SALES (corp-wide): 4.8B **Privately Held**
SIC: 2099 Noodles, fried (Chinese)
HQ: Tmi Trading Corp.
7 Bushwick Pl
Brooklyn NY 11206

(G-9514)
DAILY DOG WALKER LLC
4 Chestnut Dr (08691-3600)
PHONE................................609 755-5364
EMP: 4 EST: 2015
SALES (est): 115.8K **Privately Held**
SIC: 2711 Apartment locating service

(G-9515)
ECLECTICISM PUBLISHING LLC
33 Stanwyck Ct (08691-3018)
PHONE................................212 714-4714
Joseph A Halsey, *Principal*
EMP: 4 EST: 2013
SALES (est): 222.7K **Privately Held**
SIC: 2741 Miscellaneous publishing

(G-9516)
GAUM INC (PA)
1080 Us Highway 130 (08691-1717)
P.O. Box 485, Trenton (08691-0485)
PHONE................................609 586-0132
Fax: 609 586-9748
Robert E Gaum, *President*
Tom Weiss, *Vice Pres*
Cheryl Gaum, *Admin Sec*
EMP: 33 EST: 1945
SQ FT: 11,000
SALES (est): 6.2MM **Privately Held**
WEB: www.gauminc.com
SIC: 3599 3544 Machine shop, jobbing & repair; special dies, tools, jigs & fixtures

(G-9517)
HARRISON HOSE AND TUBING INC
2705 Kuser Rd (08691-1807)
P.O. Box 9386, Trenton (08650-1386)
PHONE................................609 631-8804
Fax: 609 631-8796

▲ = Import ▼=Export
◆ =Import/Export

James Logue, *President*
EMP: 20 **EST:** 1997
SQ FT: 12,000
SALES (est): 3.7MM **Privately Held**
WEB: www.harrisonhose.com
SIC: 3052 Plastic hose

(G-9518)
MOBILE SOLUTIONS INTL LLC
26 Wildflower Trl (08691-2517)
PHONE..................................609 448-3089
Keith Johnson, *Partner*
Patricia Johnson, *Partner*
EMP: 5
SALES (est): 304K **Privately Held**
SIC: 2393 Textile bags

(G-9519)
NORDSON EFD LLC
8 Applegate Dr (08691-2342)
PHONE..................................609 259-9222
Jeff Pembroke, *President*
Curt Metzbower, *Opers Mgr*
Paul Bannwart, *Purchasing*
Anil Thakker, *Manager*
EMP: 180
SALES (corp-wide): 2B **Publicly Held**
SIC: 3089 Injection molded finished plastic
products
HQ: Nordson Efd Llc
40 Catamore Blvd
East Providence RI 02914
401 434-1680

(G-9520)
NOVACYL INC
1 Union St Ste 108 (08691-4219)
PHONE..................................609 259-0444
Kimberly Jones, *President*
Carolyn Nicholas, *Vice Pres*
Robert Dollinger, *Treasurer*
▲ **EMP:** 9
SQ FT: 1,900
SALES (est): 1.4MM **Privately Held**
SIC: 2834 Pharmaceutical preparations
HQ: Novacap
21 Ecully Parc
Ecully 69130

(G-9521)
RAS PROCESS EQUIPMENT
324 Meadowbrook Rd (08691-2503)
PHONE..................................609 371-1000
Fax: 609 371-1200
John Bonacorda, *Owner*
Pat Horne, *Purchasing*
Dave Risoldi, *QC Mgr*
EMP: 26
SQ FT: 52,000
SALES (est): 5.2MM **Privately Held**
WEB: www.ras-inc.com
SIC: 3443 Reactor containment vessels,
metal plate; heat exchangers, condensers
& components; vessels, process or stor-
age (from boiler shops): metal plate

(G-9522)
THOMAS A CASERTA INC
11 S Gold Dr Ste E (08691)
PHONE..................................609 586-2807
Clifford Cicogna, *President*
Stanley P Rette, *Shareholder*
EMP: 14
SQ FT: 10,000
SALES (est): 2MM **Privately Held**
WEB: www.casertainc.com
SIC: 3069 3053 Washers, rubber; gaskets,
packing & sealing devices

(G-9523)
**TRI-STATE KNIFE GRINDING
CORP**
3 S Gold Dr (08691-1606)
PHONE..................................609 890-4989
Fax: 201 523-6060
Scott Peterson, *President*
EMP: 20 **EST:** 2001
SALES (est): 2.2MM
SALES (corp-wide): 21.3MM **Privately
Held**
WEB: www.colterpeterson.com
SIC: 7389 7699 3554 Grinding, precision:
commercial or industrial; knife, saw & tool
sharpening & repair; paper industries ma-
chinery

PA: Colter & Peterson, Inc.
19 Fairfield Pl
West Caldwell NJ 07006
973 684-0901

(G-9524)
WEBTECH INC
108 N Gold Dr (08691-1602)
PHONE..................................609 259-2800
Fax: 609 259-9311
Art Maynard, *Corp Secy*
Stacy Evgeniadis, *Office Mgr*
EMP: 25
SQ FT: 30,000
SALES (est): 5MM **Privately Held**
WEB: www.webtech-hts.com
SIC: 2679 Insulating paper: batts, fills &
blankets

Rochelle Park
Bergen County

(G-9525)
ADD ROB LITHO LLC
11 W Passaic St Ste 1 (07662-3225)
PHONE..................................201 556-0700
Harvey Ginsberg,
EMP: 5
SALES (est): 703.2K **Privately Held**
WEB: www.addroblitho.com
SIC: 2752 Commercial printing, offset

(G-9526)
ATLANTIC WASTE SERVICES
28 North Dr (07662-3602)
PHONE..................................201 368-0428
William Covino, *Owner*
EMP: 14
SALES (est): 1.5MM **Privately Held**
SIC: 2655 Wastebaskets, fiber: made from
purchased material

(G-9527)
DELL SOFTWARE INC
80 Parkway (07662-4204)
PHONE..................................201 556-4600
Fax: 201 527-4699
EMP: 30
SALES (corp-wide): 23.2B **Publicly Held**
SIC: 7372 Prepackaged Software Services
HQ: Dell Software, Inc.
5 Polaris Way
Aliso Viejo CA 92656
949 754-8000

(G-9528)
FUTUREX INC
114 Essex St Ste 100 (07662-4348)
PHONE..................................201 933-3943
Affonso Ze Aquino, *CEO*
Luiz Felipe Ze Aquino, *President*
Ninon Sanguesa, *Manager*
EMP: 11
SALES (est): 1.6MM **Privately Held**
SIC: 3821 Laboratory equipment: fume
hoods, distillation racks, etc.

(G-9529)
INSTAPAK CORP SEALED AIR
80 Parker Ave Fl 2 (07662-3409)
PHONE..................................201 791-7600
William Hickey, *President*
EMP: 60
SALES (est): 7.6MM
SALES (corp-wide): 4.4B **Publicly Held**
WEB: www.sealedair.com
SIC: 3086 Plastics foam products
PA: Sealed Air Corporation
2415 Cascade Pointe Blvd
Charlotte NC 28208
980 221-3235

(G-9530)
**JMK TOOL DIE AND MFG CO INC
(PA)**
19 W Passaic St (07662-3213)
PHONE..................................201 845-4710
Fax: 201 845-0240
John Kristofich, *President*
Mary Kristofich, *Corp Secy*
Robert Kristofich, *Vice Pres*
EMP: 7
SQ FT: 17,500

SALES (est): 1.8MM **Privately Held**
WEB: www.jmktool.com
SIC: 3469 3544 Stamping metal for the
trade; special dies & tools

(G-9531)
LABEL SOLUTIONS INC
151 W Passaic St 2 (07662-3105)
PHONE..................................201 599-0909
Fax: 201 599-9888
Ilana Weiss, *President*
EMP: 3
SQ FT: 700
SALES: 1MM **Privately Held**
WEB: www.labelsolutions.com
SIC: 2752 2759 Commercial printing, litho-
graphic; labels & seals: printing

(G-9532)
ORBCOMM LLC (HQ)
395 W Passaic St Ste 3 (07662-3016)
PHONE..................................703 433-6300
Jerome Eisenberg, *CEO*
John J Stolte, *Exec VP*
John Stolte Jr, *Exec VP*
Guido Alcantara, *Manager*
Marc Desrosiers, *Director*
EMP: 21
SALES (est): 15.5MM
SALES (corp-wide): 254.2MM **Publicly
Held**
SIC: 3663 Satellites, communications
PA: Orbcomm Inc.
395 W Passaic St Ste 325
Rochelle Park NJ 07662
703 433-6361

(G-9533)
**PANOS HOLDING COMPANY
(HQ)**
395 W Passaic St Ste 2 (07662-3016)
PHONE..................................201 843-8900
Steven Grossman, *CEO*
EMP: 1
SALES (est): 9.2MM **Privately Held**
SIC: 5141 2099 Groceries, general line;
food preparations

(G-9534)
REDFIELD CORPORATION
336 W Passaic St Ste 3 (07662-3027)
PHONE..................................201 845-3990
Fax: 201 845-3993
Andrew Gould, *CEO*
EMP: 4
SQ FT: 2,600
SALES: 2.5MM **Privately Held**
WEB: www.redfieldcorp.com
SIC: 5047 3841 Medical equipment & sup-
plies; surgical & medical instruments

(G-9535)
REMPAC FOAM CORP
370 W Passaic St (07662-3009)
PHONE..................................973 881-8880
Fax: 973 881-9368
William Martin, *President*
Peter Pankiw, *CFO*
Steve Sobel, *HR Admin*
◆ **EMP:** 13
SALES (est): 2MM **Privately Held**
SIC: 3086 Plastics foam products

(G-9536)
REMPAC LLC (PA)
Also Called: Tek-Pak Div
370 W Passaic St (07662-3009)
PHONE..................................201 843-4585
William Salomon, *COO*
Peter Pankiw, *CFO*
Ralph Gallucio, *Sales Staff*
Alan Bushell,
Marc Bushell,
▲ **EMP:** 125
SQ FT: 10,000
SALES (est): 49.1MM **Privately Held**
WEB: www.memoryfoamfactory.com
SIC: 3086 3053 3061 Plastics foam prod-
ucts; gaskets, packing & sealing devices;
mechanical rubber goods

(G-9537)
**SPRINGFELD PRCISION INSTRS
INC**
114 Essex St (07662-4335)
PHONE..................................866 843-3905

Steve Lattman, *President*
Robert Kulkusky, *Vice Pres*
▲ **EMP:** 50
SQ FT: 103,148
SALES (est): 4.2MM **Privately Held**
WEB: www.springfieldprecision.com
SIC: 3823 3873 3829 Industrial instrmnts
msrmnt display/control process variable;
watches, clocks, watchcases & parts;
measuring & controlling devices
HQ: Taylor Precision Products, Inc.
2311 W 22nd St Ste 200
Oak Brook IL 60523
630 954-1250

(G-9538)
**THAT 10 MINUTE OIL CHANGE
PL**
257 Rochelle Ave (07662-3914)
PHONE..................................201 587-0220
John Mitchell, *Owner*
EMP: 5
SALES (est): 260K **Privately Held**
SIC: 1389 Construction, repair & disman-
tling services

(G-9539)
TRADE THERMOGRAPHERS INC
82 Chestnut Ave (07662-3821)
PHONE..................................201 489-2060
Fax: 201 489-6680
Raymond Gramaglia, *President*
EMP: 15
SQ FT: 2,000
SALES (est): 850K **Privately Held**
SIC: 2759 2791 2752 Thermography;
typesetting; commercial printing, litho-
graphic

Rockaway
Morris County

(G-9540)
ABC PRINTING
20 Wall St Ste C (07866-2900)
PHONE..................................973 664-1160
Yvonne Cook, *Owner*
EMP: 4
SALES: 100K **Privately Held**
SIC: 2752 Commercial printing, litho-
graphic

(G-9541)
ABLE GEAR & MACHINE CO
91 Stickle Ave (07866-3127)
PHONE..................................973 983-8055
Fax: 973 983-8750
Robert Hebrank, *Owner*
EMP: 5
SALES: 240K **Privately Held**
WEB: www.ablegear.com
SIC: 3599 3462 3566 Amusement park
equipment; gear & chain forgings; speed
changers, drives & gears

(G-9542)
ACCLIVITY LLC
300 Round Hill Dr Ste 2 (07866-1227)
PHONE..................................973 586-2200
Scott Davisson, *Managing Prtnr*
Annette Brooks, *Engineer*
Melissa Thornley, *Mktg Coord*
Ed Sherry, *Marketing Staff*
Mike McGowan, *Manager*
EMP: 45
SQ FT: 10,000
SALES (est): 3.2MM **Privately Held**
SIC: 7372 Business oriented computer
software
HQ: Priority-Software U.S. Llc
300 Round Hill Dr Ste 2
Rockaway NJ 07866
973 586-2200

(G-9543)
ADMIRAL FILTER COMPANY LLC
18 Green Pond Rd Ste 3 (07866-2054)
PHONE..................................973 664-0400
Brian Hoffmann, *President*
Ira J Perlmuter,
EMP: 10
SQ FT: 10,000

SALES (est): 2.5MM **Privately Held**
SIC: 3569 Filters, general line: industrial

(G-9544)
ADMIRAL TECHNOLOGY LLC
18 Green Pond Rd Ste 3 (07866-2054)
PHONE..............................973 698-5920
Ira Perlmuter, *Mng Member*
EMP: 38
SALES (est): 1.7MM **Privately Held**
SIC: 3491 Industrial valves

(G-9545)
ADVANCED PAVEMENT TECHNOLOGIES
195 Green Pond Rd (07866-1216)
PHONE..............................973 366-8044
Ted Wilson, *Partner*
Andrew Muller, *Partner*
EMP: 12
SALES (est): 729K **Privately Held**
SIC: 1799 1794 3272 Parking lot mainte-
nance; excavation & grading, building
construction; paving materials, prefabri-
cated concrete

(G-9546)
ADVANCED TECHNOLOGY GROUP INC
Also Called: Atg
101 Round Hill Dr Ste 3 (07866-1214)
PHONE..............................973 627-6955
Fax: 973 627-5980
Ll Tao, *President*
Faithann M Hanus, *Vice Pres*
Eric Maier, *Vice Pres*
Faithann McIver-Hanus, *Vice Pres*
EMP: 30
SQ FT: 12,000
SALES (est): 4.3MM **Privately Held**
WEB: www.advtechgr.com
SIC: 3679 Electronic circuits

(G-9547)
ADVANTAGE BUSINESS MEDIA LLC (PA)
100 Enterprise Dr Ste 600 (07866-2129)
P.O. Box 912 (07866-0912)
PHONE..............................973 920-7000
George Fox, *President*
Margie Rogers, *President*
Ryan Bushey, *Editor*
Meagan Parrish, *Editor*
Tim B Besecker, *Vice Pres*
EMP: 99
SQ FT: 38,000
SALES (est): 32.1MM **Privately Held**
SIC: 2721 Magazines: publishing & printing

(G-9548)
AGILIS CHEMICALS INC
100 Enterprise Dr Ste 301 (07866-2129)
PHONE..............................973 910-2424
Jay Bhatia, *CEO*
EMP: 9
SALES: 15MM **Privately Held**
SIC: 2869 2819 2899 2843 Industrial organic chemicals; industrial inorganic
chemicals; antifreeze compounds; surface active agents; vitamin preparations;
agricultural chemicals

(G-9549)
ALLIED CONCRETE CO INC (PA)
205 Franklin Ave (07866-3409)
PHONE..............................973 627-6150
Kathryn Gallo, *President*
Michael C Gallo III, *Corp Secy*
EMP: 4 EST: 1951
SALES (est): 1.1MM **Privately Held**
SIC: 3273 Ready-mixed concrete

(G-9550)
ALLIED CONCRETE CO INC
205 Franklin Ave (07866-3409)
PHONE..............................973 627-6150
Michael Gallo III, *Manager*
EMP: 6
SQ FT: 500
SALES (corp-wide): 1.1MM **Privately
Held**
SIC: 3273 Ready-mixed concrete

PA: Allied Concrete Co Inc
205 Franklin Ave
Rockaway NJ 07866
973 627-6150

(G-9551)
AMSCAN INC
25 Green Pond Rd (07866-2047)
PHONE..............................973 983-0888
Lisa Laube, *Manager*
EMP: 52
SALES (corp-wide): 2.3B **Publicly Held**
SIC: 2656 Sanitary food containers
HQ: Amscan Inc.
80 Grasslands Rd Ste 3
Elmsford NY 10523
914 345-2020

(G-9552)
ATLANTIC INTERNATIONAL TECH
114 Beach St Ste 3 (07866-3529)
PHONE..............................973 625-0053
Fax: 973 625-1215
Robert Campbell, *CEO*
EMP: 15
SALES: 2MM **Privately Held**
SIC: 3231 Products of purchased glass

(G-9553)
BAKERS PERFECTION INC
198 Green Pond Rd Ste 5 (07866-1219)
PHONE..............................973 983-0700
Patrick S Amello Sr, *President*
EMP: 41
SQ FT: 11,200
SALES (est): 7.6MM **Privately Held**
WEB: www.bakersperfection.com
SIC: 2051 2052 2032 Cakes, pies & pas-
tries; cookies & crackers; canned special-
ties

(G-9554)
BRUCE KINDBERG
Also Called: Bmk Enterprises
305 Us Highway 46 (07866-3833)
PHONE..............................973 664-0195
Fax: 973 664-0194
Bruce Kindberg, *Owner*
EMP: 5
SQ FT: 8,000
SALES: 2.7MM **Privately Held**
SIC: 3711 3714 3993 5531 Automobile
assembly, including specialty automo-
biles; motor vehicle parts & accessories;
electric signs; speed shops, including
race car supplies; automotive parts; auto-
motive repair shops; radiator repair shop,
automotive; radiators

(G-9555)
BTECH INC
Also Called: B Tech
10 Astro Pl Ste A (07866-4052)
PHONE..............................973 983-1120
Fax: 973 983-1125
Manfred Laidig, *CEO*
Thomas Leonard, *President*
George Petersen, *Business Mgr*
◆ EMP: 23
SQ FT: 18,000
SALES (est): 6.8MM **Privately Held**
WEB: www.btechinc.com
SIC: 3825 3823 5063 Battery testers,
electrical; industrial instrmnts msrmnt dis-
play/control process variable; batteries

(G-9556)
CARSON & GEBEL RIBBON CO LLC
17 Green Pond Rd (07866-2001)
PHONE..............................973 627-4200
Fax: 973 627-1175
Henry Gebel,
Richard Gebel,
▲ EMP: 40 EST: 1923
SQ FT: 50,000
SALES (est): 4.4MM
SALES (corp-wide): 361.9MM **Publicly
Held**
SIC: 5131 2241 Ribbons; ribbons
HQ: Berwick Offray Llc
2015 W Front St
Berwick PA 18603
570 752-5934

(G-9557)
CBT SUPPLY INC
Also Called: Smart Desks
83 Jacobs Rd (07866-4603)
P.O. Box 391, Hibernia (07842-0391)
PHONE..............................973 586-2783
Jeffery Korber, *President*
EMP: 7
SALES (est): 810K **Privately Held**
SIC: 2521 Wood office furniture

(G-9558)
CREATIVE PATTERNS & MFG
114 Beach St Ste 4 (07866-3529)
P.O. Box 159 (07866-0159)
PHONE..............................973 589-1391
David J Cummins, *President*
James Generoso, *Vice Pres*
EMP: 7
SQ FT: 5,400
SALES (est): 46.3MM **Privately Held**
SIC: 3543 Industrial patterns

(G-9559)
CSUS LLC
300 Forge Way Ste 3 (07866-2056)
PHONE..............................973 298-8599
Juan Paez,
EMP: 6
SALES: 950K **Privately Held**
SIC: 3842 Surgical appliances & supplies

(G-9560)
CUTTING TECHNIQUES INC
18 Green Pond Rd Ste 1 (07866-2054)
PHONE..............................201 438-2222
EMP: 7
SQ FT: 7,600
SALES (est): 842.3K **Privately Held**
SIC: 3599 Mfg Industrial Machinery

(G-9561)
DMG MORI USA INC
Also Called: Dmg Mori Seiki
400 Commons Way Ste A (07866-2030)
PHONE..............................973 257-9620
Masaki Sasaki, *General Mgr*
EMP: 7
SALES (corp-wide): 3.9B **Privately Held**
SIC: 3545 Measuring tools & machines,
machinists' metalworking type
HQ: Dmg Mori Usa, Inc.
2400 Huntington Blvd
Hoffman Estates IL 60192
847 593-5400

(G-9562)
EAST COAST SECURITY PRODUCTS
53 Green Pond Rd Ste 1 (07866-2044)
PHONE..............................973 625-3277
Fax: 973 586-4090
William R Vogt, *President*
EMP: 11
SQ FT: 8,083
SALES (est): 2.2MM **Privately Held**
WEB: www.ecspi.com
SIC: 3699 Security control equipment &
systems

(G-9563)
EMC SQUARED LLC
30 Rolling Ridge Dr (07866-4315)
PHONE..............................973 586-8854
Ed Morgan, *Principal*
EMP: 5
SALES (est): 389.6K **Privately Held**
SIC: 3572 Computer storage devices

(G-9564)
ENDOT INDUSTRIES INC (PA)
60 Green Pond Rd (07866-2002)
PHONE..............................973 625-8500
Gary Wellmann, *Ch of Bd*
Jennifer Wellmann Marin, *President*
Todne Wellmann, *Vice Pres*
EMP: 65
SQ FT: 52,000
SALES (est): 18MM **Privately Held**
SIC: 3084 3089 2823 Plastics pipe; duct-
ing, plastic; cellulosic manmade fibers

(G-9565)
F G CLOVER COMPANY INC
40 Stickle Ave (07866-3128)
PHONE..............................973 627-1160
Norman Iversen, *President*
EMP: 9 EST: 1879
SQ FT: 14,000
SALES (est): 660K **Privately Held**
SIC: 3999 3469 Badges, metal: police-
men, firemen, etc.; identification tags, ex-
cept paper; spinning metal for the trade

(G-9566)
FABER PRECISION INC
198 Green Pond Rd Ste 6 (07866-1219)
PHONE..............................973 983-1844
Kevin Faber, *President*
Stacey Faber, *Corp Secy*
EMP: 6
SQ FT: 8,400
SALES: 800K **Privately Held**
SIC: 3312 Stainless steel

(G-9567)
FETTE COMPACTING AMERICA INC
400 Forge Way (07866-2033)
PHONE..............................973 586-8722
Fax: 973 586-0450
Olaf Mueller, *President*
Anna Dewald, *Human Resources*
▲ EMP: 30
SQ FT: 28,000
SALES (est): 10.4MM
SALES (corp-wide): 394.9MM **Privately
Held**
WEB: www.lmtfette.com
SIC: 5084 3559 Pharmaceutical machin-
ery; industrial machinery & equipment
HQ: Lmt Usa, Inc.
1081 S Northpoint Blvd
Waukegan IL 60085
630 693-3270

(G-9568)
FIREFREEZE WORLDWIDE INC
272 Us Highway 46 (07866-3826)
PHONE..............................973 627-0722
Evelyn Geisler, *President*
▲ EMP: 20
SALES (est): 4.2MM **Privately Held**
SIC: 2869 Hydraulic fluids, synthetic base

(G-9569)
FOOD MFG
100 Enterprise Dr (07866-2116)
PHONE..............................973 920-7000
EMP: 200
SALES (est): 7MM **Privately Held**
SIC: 2754 Gravure Commercial Printing

(G-9570)
GLITTERWRAP INC (DH)
701 Ford Rd Ste 1 (07866-2053)
PHONE..............................800 745-4883
Fax: 973 625-3757
Alfred Scott, *CEO*
Melinda Scott, *President*
▲ EMP: 55
SQ FT: 81,000
SALES (est): 5.3MM
SALES (corp-wide): 458.8MM **Privately
Held**
SIC: 2679 Gift wrap & novelties, paper
HQ: Ig Design Group Americas, Inc.
338 Industrial Blvd
Midway GA 31320
912 884-9727

(G-9571)
GLOBAL SEVEN INC
198 Green Pond Rd Ste 4 (07866-1219)
P.O. Box 367, Franklin (07416-0367)
PHONE..............................973 209-7474
Jonathan Dean, *President*
EMP: 25
SQ FT: 100,000
SALES (est): 3.7MM **Privately Held**
SIC: 2899 Chemical preparations

(G-9572)
HTP CONNECTIVITY LLC
300 Round Hill Dr Ste 4 (07866-1227)
PHONE..............................973 586-2286
▲ EMP: 4

2018 Harris New Jersey
Manufacturers Directory

▲ = Import ▼=Export
◆ =Import/Export

SALES (est): 392.8K **Privately Held**
SIC: 3559 Electronic component making machinery

(G-9573)
IN THE SPOTLIGHTS
301 Mount Hope Ave # 2091 (07866-2130)
PHONE..................................973 361-7768
EMP: 4
SALES (est): 480.2K **Privately Held**
SIC: 3648 Mfg Lighting Equipment

(G-9574)
INDUSTRIAL SERVICES ENTPS INC
Industrial Services Entps
159 Us Highway 46 Ste 1 (07866-4062)
P.O. Box 218, Dover (07802-0218)
PHONE..................................973 361-6780
Kevin Donnelly, *Manager*
EMP: 35
SALES (est): 5.3MM
SALES (corp-wide): 6.1MM **Privately Held**
SIC: 3441 Fabricated structural metal
PA: Industrial Services Enterprises Incorporated
159 Route 46
Rockaway NJ
973 366-3939

(G-9575)
INTERNET-SALES USA CORPORATION
Also Called: Greenproducts.info
65 Fleetwood Dr (07866-2220)
PHONE..................................775 468-8379
Samantha Schnurman, *Publisher*
David Schnurman, *Vice Pres*
Arianne Schnurman, *Vice Pres*
Jordan Schnurman, *Project Mgr*
Michael Schnurman, *Finance Dir*
EMP: 6
SALES (est): 458.2K **Privately Held**
SIC: 1542 0139 0191 3444 Greenhouse construction; farm building construction; food crops; general farms, primarily crop; sheet metalwork;

(G-9576)
IONNI SIGN INC (PA)
14 White Meadow Ave (07866-2610)
P.O. Box 437 (07866-0437)
PHONE..................................973 625-3815
Fax: 973 625-3955
Joseph Ionni Jr, *President*
EMP: 5
SQ FT: 3,200
SALES (est): 937.7K **Privately Held**
WEB: www.ionnisign.com
SIC: 1799 3993 Sign installation & maintenance; signs & advertising specialties

(G-9577)
J & W SERVO SYSTEMS COMPANY
53 Green Pond Rd Ste 2 (07866-2044)
P.O. Box 97, Montville (07045-0097)
PHONE..................................973 335-1007
Fax: 973 335-1661
Anthony Villano, *President*
Phil Marshall, *Vice Pres*
Philip Gunn-Russell, *Sales Associate*
EMP: 17
SQ FT: 30,000
SALES (est): 6.4MM **Privately Held**
WEB: www.servosystems.com
SIC: 5065 3823 Electronic parts & equipment; industrial instrmnts msrmnt display/control process variable

(G-9578)
J HEBRANK INC
Also Called: Linker Machines
20 Pine St (07866-3131)
PHONE..................................973 983-0001
Fax: 973 983-0011
Jean Hebrank, *President*
Robert Hebrank Sr, *Vice Pres*
Michael Hebrank, *Finance Mgr*
EMP: 13 EST: 1939
SALES (est): 1.6MM **Privately Held**
WEB: www.linkermachines.com
SIC: 3556 Food products machinery

(G-9579)
JASON EQUIPMENT CORP
164 Franklin Ave (07866-3408)
P.O. Box 695 (07866-0695)
PHONE..................................973 983-7212
John Tolta, *President*
EMP: 21
SALES (est): 2.1MM **Privately Held**
SIC: 3559 Pharmaceutical machinery

(G-9580)
KESTREL CLOSETS LLC
29 Hillside Rd (07866-4404)
PHONE..................................973 586-1144
Craig Holzhauer, *Principal*
EMP: 7
SALES (est): 854.1K **Privately Held**
SIC: 2673 Wardrobe bags (closet accessories): from purchased materials

(G-9581)
KG SQUARED LLC
Also Called: Apw Company
5 Astro Pl Ste B (07866-4053)
PHONE..................................973 627-0643
Jason Kellenberger,
▼ EMP: 13
SQ FT: 5,000
SALES: 1MM **Privately Held**
SIC: 3679 3677 3612 Cores, magnetic; coil windings, electronic; transformers, except electric

(G-9582)
KOP-COAT INC
Kop-Coat Marine Group
36 Pine St (07866-3131)
PHONE..................................800 221-4466
Fax: 973 625-8303
James Mc Carthy, *Technical Mgr*
Linda Smith, *Branch Mgr*
EMP: 50
SALES (corp-wide): 5.3B **Publicly Held**
WEB: www.kop-coat.com
SIC: 2851 2891 5198 Paints & paint additives; adhesives & sealants; paints
HQ: Kop-Coat, Inc.
3040 William Pitt Way
Pittsburgh PA 15238
412 227-2426

(G-9583)
L3 MOBILE-VISION INC
Also Called: L-3 Cmmnctons Mbile-Vision Inc
400 Commons Way Ste F (07866-2030)
PHONE..................................973 263-1090
Fax: 973 257-3024
Leo Lorenzetti, *President*
Chief Mike Burridge, *Vice Pres*
Chris Kadoch, *Vice Pres*
Kurt Kessel, *Vice Pres*
▲ EMP: 99
SQ FT: 20,000
SALES (est): 56.5MM
SALES (corp-wide): 9.5B **Publicly Held**
WEB: www.mobile-vision.com
SIC: 5065 3663 Closed circuit television; television closed circuit equipment
PA: L3 Technologies, Inc.
600 3rd Ave Fl 34
New York NY 10016
212 697-1111

(G-9584)
LINK BIO INC
101 Round Hill Dr Ste 7 (07866-1214)
PHONE..................................973 625-1333
Massimo Calafiore, *President*
Roslyn Kirschner, *Executive*
Michele Rencis, *Admin Sec*
▲ EMP: 9
SALES (est): 1.2MM
SALES (corp-wide): 165.9MM **Privately Held**
SIC: 3842 Implants, surgical
HQ: Deru Gmbh
Oststr. 4-10
Norderstedt 22844
405 544-5880

(G-9585)
LMT USA INC
Also Called: Fette-America
400 Forge Way (07866-2033)
PHONE..................................973 586-8722
Philip Meyers, *Branch Mgr*

EMP: 6
SALES (corp-wide): 394.9MM **Privately Held**
WEB: www.lmtfette.com
SIC: 5084 3559 Machine tools & metalworking machinery; pharmaceutical machinery
HQ: Lmt Usa, Inc.
1081 S Northpoint Blvd
Waukegan IL 60085
630 693-3270

(G-9586)
MCWILLIAMS FORGE COMPANY (DH)
387 Franklin Ave (07866-4014)
PHONE..................................973 627-0200
Fax: 973 625-9316
Alexander M Mc Williams, *President*
Timothy C McWilliams, *Exec VP*
▲ EMP: 79 EST: 1945
SQ FT: 125,000
SALES: 60MM
SALES (corp-wide): 242.1B **Publicly Held**
WEB: www.mcwilliamsforge.com
SIC: 3462 3769 3463 Nuclear power plant forgings, ferrous; machinery forgings, ferrous; pump & compressor forgings, ferrous; aircraft forgings, ferrous; guided missile & space vehicle parts & auxiliary equipment; nonferrous forgings
HQ: Precision Castparts Corp.
4650 Sw Mcdam Ave Ste 300
Portland OR 97239
503 946-4800

(G-9587)
MODULAR PACKAGING SYSTEMS INC
385 Franklin Ave Ste C (07866-4037)
PHONE..................................973 970-9393
Clifford Smith, *President*
Bradford Smith, *Vice Pres*
EMP: 10
SQ FT: 15,000
SALES: 4.1MM **Privately Held**
WEB: www.modularpackaging.com
SIC: 5084 3599 Packaging machinery & equipment; amusement park equipment

(G-9588)
MONSTER COATINGS INC
12 Midway Ct (07866-1619)
PHONE..................................973 983-7662
Denise B Tomahatsch, *President*
EMP: 4 EST: 2002
SALES: 400K **Privately Held**
SIC: 2631 Coated & treated board

(G-9589)
NICKEL ARTISTIC SERVICES LLC
39 Us Highway 46 (07866-4105)
PHONE..................................973 627-0390
Brett Nickel, *Mng Member*
Brian Nickel, *Mng Member*
Denise Nickel, *Mng Member*
Ken Nickel,
EMP: 4 EST: 2000
SALES (est): 340K **Privately Held**
SIC: 3993 Signs, not made in custom sign painting shops

(G-9590)
NOVA PRECISION PRODUCTS INC
160 Franklin Ave (07866-3429)
PHONE..................................973 625-1586
Fax: 973 586-2434
Chester Suhoski, *President*
Iris Suhoski, *Vice Pres*
EMP: 110
SQ FT: 6,500
SALES (est): 14MM **Privately Held**
WEB: www.novaprecisionproducts.com
SIC: 3451 3541 Screw machine products; machine tools, metal cutting type

(G-9591)
NUCLEAR DIAGNOSTIC PDTS INC (PA)
101 Round Hill Dr Ste 4 (07866-1214)
PHONE..................................973 664-9696
Fax: 973 664-9699

Frank Ruddy, *President*
Rodney Prosser, *Vice Pres*
EMP: 2
SQ FT: 10,000
SALES (est): 2.2MM **Privately Held**
SIC: 2834 Pharmaceutical preparations

(G-9592)
O O M INC
Also Called: Dunkin' Donuts
387 Us Highway 46 (07866-3806)
PHONE..................................973 328-9408
Dipak Patel, *President*
EMP: 6
SQ FT: 1,000
SALES (est): 215.6K **Privately Held**
SIC: 5461 2051 Doughnuts; doughnuts, except frozen

(G-9593)
PACKAGE DEVELOPMENT CO INC
100 Round Hill Dr Ste 8 (07866-1220)
PHONE..................................973 983-8500
Fax: 973 983-8666
Charles Schwester, *President*
Roberta Schwester, *Corp Secy*
Rick Folbrecht, *Senior VP*
Summer Schwester, *Plant Mgr*
Ron Sosna, *Opers Staff*
▼ EMP: 50
SQ FT: 55,000
SALES: 10MM **Privately Held**
WEB: www.pkgdev.com
SIC: 3081 4783 2653 Packing materials, plastic sheet; packing goods for shipping; display items, corrugated: made from purchased materials; display items, solid fiber: made from purchased materials

(G-9594)
PATRIOT AMERICAN SOLUTIONS LLC
5 Astro Pl (07866-4053)
PHONE..................................862 209-4772
William O'Cconnor, *President*
Richard Ferri, *Exec VP*
Jay Marantz, *Controller*
EMP: 61
SQ FT: 35,000
SALES: 7MM **Privately Held**
SIC: 3679 8711 Antennas, receiving; electrical or electronic engineering

(G-9595)
PHOENIX COLOR CORP
Also Called: Lehigh Phoenis
40 Green Pond Rd (07866-2002)
PHONE..................................800 632-4111
Fax: 973 983-7660
Sandy Damato, *Vice Pres*
Marie Van Strander, *Financial Exec*
Rosa Dominguez, *Human Res Dir*
Mitchell Weiss, *Branch Mgr*
EMP: 30 **Publicly Held**
WEB: www.phoenixcolor.com
SIC: 2732 Books: printing only
HQ: Phoenix Color Corp.
18249 Phoenix Rd
Hagerstown MD 21742
301 733-0018

(G-9596)
PIERSON INDUSTRIES INC
7 Astro Pl (07866-4022)
PHONE..................................973 627-7945
Fax: 973 627-1638
Ted Pierson, *President*
Rich Carle, *Principal*
Maria Pierson, *Vice Pres*
Fred Smith, *Plant Mgr*
Richard Caryle, *Plant Engr*
▲ EMP: 145
SQ FT: 42,000
SALES (est): 35.3MM **Privately Held**
WEB: www.piersonindustries.com
SIC: 3089 Injection molding of plastics; molding primary plastic

(G-9597)
PLASTIFORM PACKAGING INC
114 Beach St Ste 6 (07866-3529)
P.O. Box 186 (07866-0186)
PHONE..................................973 983-8900
Fax: 973 983-8989
George Smith, *President*

Kathleen Smith, *Vice Pres*
EMP: 26
SQ FT: 21,000
SALES (est): 6MM **Privately Held**
SIC: 3089 Blister or bubble formed packaging, plastic

(G-9598)
POLYFIL CORPORATION
74 Green Pond Rd (07866-2002)
P.O. Box 130 (07866-0130)
PHONE....................................973 627-4070
Fax: 973 627-7344
Gerald Fabiano, *President*
Juan Castaneda, *Plant Mgr*
Linda Conrad, *Opers-Prdtn-Mfg*
Abraham Tanenbaum, *Treasurer*
Brenda Isherwood, *Financial Exec*
EMP: 27
SQ FT: 60,000
SALES (est): 7.6MM **Privately Held**
WEB: www.polyfilcorp.com
SIC: 2821 Polyethylene resins

(G-9599)
POWER HAWK TECHNOLOGIES INC
300 Forge Way Ste 2 (07866-2056)
PHONE....................................973 627-4646
William R Hickerson, *President*
Dosha Hebron, *General Mgr*
Lisa More, *General Mgr*
John McCarthy, *Vice Pres*
Ed Kulahli, *Mfg Staff*
▲ **EMP:** 17
SQ FT: 5,000
SALES: 2.1MM **Privately Held**
WEB: www.powerhawk.com
SIC: 3423 5099 Hand & edge tools; safety equipment & supplies

(G-9600)
PRIORITY-SOFTWARE US LLC (DH)
300 Round Hill Dr Ste 2 (07866-1227)
PHONE....................................973 586-2200
Andres Richter, *CEO*
Scott Davisson, *Managing Dir*
EMP: 3
SALES (est): 3.2MM **Privately Held**
SIC: 7372 Business oriented computer software
HQ: Priority Software Ltd
　　12 Amal
　　Rosh Haayin
　　392 510-00

(G-9601)
PRODUCT CLUB CORP
41 Pine St Ste 15 (07866-3139)
PHONE....................................973 664-0565
Fax: 973 983-5687
Eric B Polesuk, *President*
Kevin Palmquist, *VP Sales*
Mary Albanese, *VP Mktg*
Kristina Schulman, *Education*
▲ **EMP:** 10
SQ FT: 15,000
SALES (est): 1.3MM
SALES (corp-wide): 91.9MM **Privately Held**
WEB: www.productclub.com
SIC: 2844 Hair coloring preparations
PA: The Burmax Company Inc
　　28 Barretts Ave
　　Holtsville NY 11742
　　631 447-8700

(G-9602)
PURE RUBBER PRODUCTS CO
300 Round Hill Dr Ste 5 (07866-1227)
PHONE....................................973 784-3690
Fax: 973 808-0246
William McCrink, *President*
Frank McCrink, *Principal*
Virginia McCrink, *Manager*
EMP: 8 EST: 1935
SQ FT: 5,090
SALES (est): 740K **Privately Held**
WEB: www.purerubber.com
SIC: 3069 Molded rubber products

(G-9603)
RICCARR DISPLAYS INC
52 Green Pond Rd (07866-2002)
PHONE....................................973 983-6701

Paul Carr, *CEO*
Marc Niderman, *President*
EMP: 50
SQ FT: 100,000
SALES (est): 5.6MM **Privately Held**
WEB: www.tmird.com
SIC: 3993 Displays & cutouts, window & lobby; displays, paint process

(G-9604)
RIDGE MANUFACTURING CORP
5 Astro Pl Ste A (07866-4053)
PHONE....................................973 586-2717
Richard Ferri, *President*
Kevin Garvin, *Vice Pres*
EMP: 75
SALES (est): 16.8MM **Privately Held**
SIC: 3559 Electronic component making machinery

(G-9605)
RIVERSTONE INDUSTRIES CORP
65 Fleetwood Dr Ste 200 (07866-2220)
PHONE....................................973 586-2564
David Schnurman, *Vice Pres*
▲ **EMP:** 7 EST: 2010
SALES (est): 8.1MM **Privately Held**
SIC: 3999 Atomizers, toiletry

(G-9606)
ROYSONS CORPORATION
Also Called: Roysons Wall Covering
40 Vanderhoof Ave (07866-3138)
PHONE....................................973 625-5570
Fax: 973 625-5917
Roy Ritchie, *President*
Omega Larue, *COO*
Allison Testa, *Project Mgr*
Curt Hammaren, *Engineer*
Peter Cohan, *CFO*
◆ **EMP:** 100
SQ FT: 110,000
SALES (est): 27.4MM **Privately Held**
WEB: www.roysons.com
SIC: 3083 Plastic finished products, laminated

(G-9607)
SAVIT CORPORATION
400 Commons Way Ste D (07866-2030)
PHONE....................................862 209-4516
Anthony Fabiano, *President*
EMP: 11
SQ FT: 7,000
SALES (est): 1.2MM **Privately Held**
WEB: www.savitcorporation.com
SIC: 3795 3761 Specialized tank components, military; guided missiles & space vehicles

(G-9608)
SERVICE METAL FABRICATING INC (PA)
10 Stickle Ave (07866-3114)
PHONE....................................973 625-8882
Fax: 973 625-0694
Joseph Moretti Sr, *President*
David Lewin, *Opers Mgr*
Doug Reeve, *Engineer*
Colleen Reardon, *Receptionist*
◆ **EMP:** 78
SQ FT: 22,000
SALES (est): 20.6MM **Privately Held**
WEB: www.servicemetal.com
SIC: 3444 Sheet metal specialties, not stamped

(G-9609)
STAPLING MACHINES INC (PA)
41 Pine St Ste 101 (07866-3139)
PHONE....................................973 627-4400
Fax: 973 627-5355
Wade Howle, *President*
Doug Halkenhauser, *President*
Michael Bell, *Vice Pres*
Timothy Catton, *Vice Pres*
EMP: 30
SQ FT: 66,000
SALES (est): 3.2MM **Privately Held**
WEB: www.smcllc.com
SIC: 3553 Box making machines, for wooden boxes

(G-9610)
STILES ENTERPRISES INC
114 Beach St (07866-3529)
P.O. Box 92 (07866-0092)
PHONE....................................973 625-9660
Fax: 973 625-9346
Richard Stiles, *President*
Diane Killiam, *Vice Pres*
Nancy Stiles, *Vice Pres*
▲ **EMP:** 10 EST: 1934
SQ FT: 10,000
SALES (est): 2.9MM **Privately Held**
SIC: 5085 3061 3053 3052 Rubber goods, mechanical; mechanical rubber goods; gaskets, packing & sealing devices; rubber & plastics hose & beltings; synthetic rubber; carpets & rugs

(G-9611)
SUPERMATIC CORP
27 Old Beach Glen Rd (07866-1313)
PHONE....................................973 627-4433
Fax: 973 627-7464
Ted Kobrynowicz, *President*
Irene Kobrynowicz, *Vice Pres*
Maria Kobrynowicz, *Admin Sec*
EMP: 10 EST: 1969
SQ FT: 6,000
SALES (est): 1.4MM **Privately Held**
WEB: www.supermaticnc.com
SIC: 3451 Screw machine products

(G-9612)
THERMO COTE INC
198 Green Pond Rd Ste 5 (07866-1219)
PHONE....................................973 464-3575
Chris Cordero, *Principal*
EMP: 4 EST: 2008
SALES (est): 434.1K **Privately Held**
SIC: 2851 Vinyl coatings, strippable

(G-9613)
TITANIUM INDUSTRIES INC (PA)
18 Green Pond Rd Ste 1 (07866-2054)
PHONE....................................973 983-1185
Brett S Paddock, *President*
Dan Dinapoli, *General Mgr*
Debby Hazen, *General Mgr*
Craig Simpson, *Managing Dir*
Jay Pudlock, *Regional Mgr*
▲ **EMP:** 45
SALES (est): 76.6MM **Privately Held**
SIC: 5051 3542 3462 Iron & steel (ferrous) products; metal deposit forming machines; flange, valve & pipe fitting forgings, ferrous

(G-9614)
TOCAD AMERICA INC (DH)
Also Called: Sunpak Division
53 Green Pond Rd Ste 4 (07866-2044)
PHONE....................................973 627-9600
Fax: 973 664-2438
Takeshi Fujikawa, *President*
Richard Darrow, *President*
Mitsuhiro Matsumoto, *CFO*
▲ **EMP:** 41
SQ FT: 35,000
SALES (est): 8.7MM **Privately Held**
WEB: www.tocad.com
SIC: 5043 3691 5063 Photographic equipment & supplies; photographic cameras, projectors, equipment & supplies; storage batteries; batteries
HQ: Tocad Energy Co., Ltd.
　　1-4-6, Kitasenzoku
　　Ota-Ku TKY 145-0
　　357 011-111

(G-9615)
TOLAN MACHINERY COMPANY INC
164 Franklin Ave (07866-3408)
P.O. Box 695 (07866-0695)
PHONE....................................973 983-7212
Fax: 973 983-7217
John Tolpa, *Owner*
Bill Ebbinghouser, *Principal*
John Staiber, *Principal*
Stephen Tolpa, *Principal*
Jeff Stoppelkamp, *Vice Pres*
EMP: 21 EST: 1945
SALES (est): 4.4MM **Privately Held**
SIC: 3443 Tanks, standard or custom fabricated: metal plate

(G-9616)
TOLAN MACHINERY POLISHING CO
164 Franklin Ave (07866-3408)
P.O. Box 695 (07866-0695)
PHONE....................................973 983-7212
John M Tolpa Jr, *President*
Stephen Tolpa, *Vice Pres*
Harsh Patel, *Engineer*
Christina Candelaria, *Office Mgr*
EMP: 50
SQ FT: 90,000
SALES (est): 11MM **Privately Held**
WEB: www.tolanmachinery.com
SIC: 3443 Plate work for the metalworking trade

(G-9617)
TOLAN POLISHING CORP
164 Franklin Ave (07866-3408)
P.O. Box 695 (07866-0695)
PHONE....................................973 983-7212
John M Tolpa Jr, *President*
Michael Tolpa, *Corp Secy*
EMP: 11 EST: 1974
SQ FT: 40,000
SALES: 2MM **Privately Held**
SIC: 3471 Polishing, metals or formed products

(G-9618)
TOM PONTE MODEL MAKERS INC
25 Pine St Ste 2 (07866-3143)
PHONE....................................973 627-5906
Mike Leone, *President*
Matt Malajko, *Vice Pres*
EMP: 5
SQ FT: 2,800
SALES (est): 525.7K **Privately Held**
WEB: www.pontemodels.com
SIC: 3999 Novelties, bric-a-brac & hobby kits

(G-9619)
TRIPACK INDUSTRIAL USA LLC
52 Green Pond Rd (07866-2002)
PHONE....................................973 627-8350
Greg Colaccitti,
EMP: 9
SALES (est): 2.7MM **Privately Held**
SIC: 3089 Injection molding of plastics

(G-9620)
UNITAO NUTRACEUTICALS LLC
6 Reservoir Pl (07866-1605)
P.O. Box 679 (07866-0679)
PHONE....................................973 983-1121
Robert Colon, *Manager*
EMP: 2
SALES: 7.5MM **Privately Held**
SIC: 2834 Vitamin preparations

(G-9621)
VAPOR LOUNGE LLC
15 Van Duyne Ave (07866-4102)
PHONE....................................973 627-1277
Timothy Braun, *CEO*
Eric Totten, *CEO*
EMP: 6
SQ FT: 1,600
SALES (est): 651.3K **Privately Held**
SIC: 3634 Cigar lighters, electric

(G-9622)
VINTAGE VIBE LTD LIABILITY CO
114 Beach St (07866-3529)
PHONE....................................973 989-2178
Chris Carroll,
▲ **EMP:** 8
SQ FT: 6,500
SALES (est): 600K **Privately Held**
WEB: www.vintagevibe.com
SIC: 3931 Pianos, all types: vertical, grand, spinet, player, etc.

(G-9623)
WARNER CHILCOTT CORPORATION (HQ)
100 Enterprise Dr Ste 280 (07866-2198)
PHONE....................................862 261-7000
Fax: 973 442-3346
EMP: 22

▲ = Import ▼=Export
◆ =Import/Export

SALES (est): 100.9MM **Privately Held**
SIC: **2834 6719** Mfg Pharmaceutical
Preparations

(G-9624)
WELDON ASPHALT CORP
311 W Main St Ste 1 (07866-3317)
PHONE..................................973 627-7500
Fax: 973 627-5387
Bob Weldon, *President*
EMP: 10
SALES (corp-wide): 6.7MM **Privately
Held**
SIC: **2951** Asphalt paving mixtures &
blocks
PA: Weldon Asphalt Corp
141 Central Ave
Westfield NJ
908 233-4444

(G-9625)
WIDE BAND SYSTEMS INC
389 Franklin Ave (07866-4014)
P.O. Box 289 (07866-0289)
PHONE..................................973 586-6500
Fax: 973 627-9190
Frank Padula, *President*
Kevin Burns, *General Mgr*
Andrew Prezuhy, *Prdtn Mgr*
Debbie Shapiro, *Purch Agent*
Mark Stanley, *Engineer*
▼ EMP: 15
SQ FT: 9,300
SALES (est): 3.4MM **Privately Held**
WEB: www.widebandsystems.com
SIC: **3663** Microwave communication
equipment

(G-9626)
**WYMAN-GORDON FORGINGS
INC**
387 Franklin Ave (07866-4014)
PHONE..................................973 627-0200
Karen Norlin, *Manager*
EMP: 33
SALES (corp-wide): 242.1B **Publicly
Held**
SIC: **3462** Iron & steel forgings; missile
forgings, ferrous; nuclear power plant
forgings, ferrous
HQ: Wyman-Gordon Forgings, Inc.
10825 Telge Rd
Houston TX 77095
281 897-2400

Rockleigh
Bergen County

(G-9627)
CARLEE CORPORATION
28 Piermont Rd (07647-2797)
PHONE..................................201 768-6800
Fax: 201 768-7614
Bruce A Burgermaster, *President*
Reggie Gencer, *General Mgr*
EMP: 25 EST: 1950
SQ FT: 47,000
SALES (est): 8.4MM **Privately Held**
WEB: www.carlee.com
SIC: **2824** Polyester fibers

(G-9628)
**CRESTRON ELECTRONICS INC
(PA)**
15 Volvo Dr (07647-2507)
PHONE..................................201 767-3400
Fax: 201 767-7576
Randy Klein, *President*
Paul Riley, *Regional Mgr*
Scott Smith, *Regional Mgr*
Dan Feldstein, *COO*
David Hakula, *Exec VP*
◆ EMP: 200 EST: 1971
SALES: 500MM **Privately Held**
SIC: **3571 3651 1731 3663** Minicomput-
ers; household audio & video equipment;
electrical work; radio & TV communica-
tions equipment; fire- or burglary-resistive
products; intercommunication systems,
electric

(G-9629)
**FRESENIUS MED CARE
HLDINGS INC**
Fresenius Med Care - N Amer
22 Paris Ave (07647-2600)
PHONE..................................201 767-7700
Gene Sullivan, *Vice Pres*
Margaret Austria, *Officer*
EMP: 4
SALES (corp-wide): 20.9B **Privately Held**
SIC: **5047 3841 8071** Medical equipment
& supplies; surgical & medical instru-
ments; medical laboratories
HQ: Fresenius Medical Care Holdings, Inc.
920 Winter St
Waltham MA 02451

(G-9630)
HBC SOLUTIONS INC
Also Called: Harris Broadcast
22 Paris Ave Ste 110 (07647-2600)
PHONE..................................973 267-5990
EMP: 4
SALES (corp-wide): 2.2B **Privately Held**
SIC: **3663** Wholesales Electronic Parts
And Equipment
HQ: Hbc Solutions, Inc.
9800 S Meridian Blvd
Englewood CO 75034
303 476-4590

(G-9631)
IMAGE ACCESS CORP (PA)
22 Paris Ave Ste 210 (07647-2600)
PHONE..................................201 342-7878
Fax: 201 487-3456
Robert Feulner, *President*
William Bresnak Jr, *Vice Pres*
Claire Feulner, *Vice Pres*
Marilyn Bresnak, *Treasurer*
Joseph Chmielewski, *Accounts Mgr*
▼ EMP: 30
SQ FT: 4,000
SALES (est): 22.7MM **Privately Held**
WEB: www.imageaccesscorp.com
SIC: **5044 7389 7371 7372** Microfilm
equipment; micrographic equipment; mi-
crofilm recording & developing service;
computer software development & appli-
cations; prepackaged software; computer
peripheral equipment repair & mainte-
nance

(G-9632)
NEWARK FIBERS INC (PA)
28 Piermont Rd (07647-2712)
PHONE..................................201 768-6800
Bruce A Burgermaster, *President*
EMP: 1
SQ FT: 18,000
SALES (est): 1.2MM **Privately Held**
SIC: **2299 2823** Batting, wadding, padding
& fillings; cellulosic manmade fibers

(G-9633)
**ROYAL SOVEREIGN INTL INC
(PA)**
2 Volvo Dr (07647-2508)
PHONE..................................800 397-1025
Fax: 201 750-1022
T K Lim, *CEO*
Keung S Lim, *President*
◆ EMP: 45
SQ FT: 68,000
SALES (est): 13.7MM **Privately Held**
WEB: www.royalsovereign.com
SIC: **5044 3639 3083** Office equipment;
major kitchen appliances, except refriger-
ators & stoves; laminated plastics plate &
sheet

(G-9634)
**TAKASAGO INTL CORP USA
(HQ)**
4 Volvo Dr (07647-2508)
P.O. Box 932 (07647-0932)
PHONE..................................201 767-9001
Fax: 201 784-7277
Ritaro Igaki, *CEO*
Sean G Traynor, *Ch of Bd*
Michelle Stangl, *President*
Miriam Almazora, *General Mgr*
Paul Ireland, *General Mgr*
◆ EMP: 170 EST: 1968
SQ FT: 50,000

SALES (est): 169.3MM
SALES (corp-wide): 1.3B **Privately Held**
SIC: **2844** Concentrates, perfume
PA: Takasago International Corporation
5-37-1, Kamata
Ota-Ku TKY 144-0
357 440-511

(G-9635)
TIBURON LOCKERS INC
22 Paris Ave Ste 106 (07647-2600)
PHONE..................................201 750-4960
Jared Lowenthal, *CEO*
Carlos Rodriguez, *Project Mgr*
Steve Shipp, *Opers Mgr*
Steve Perdue, *Opers Spvr*
Michael Kreie, *Accounts Mgr*
EMP: 9
SALES (est): 174.5K **Privately Held**
SIC: **3429** Locks or lock sets

(G-9636)
**VOLVO CAR NORTH AMERICA
LLC (DH)**
1 Volvo Dr (07647-2507)
PHONE..................................201 768-7300
Fax: 201 767-4816
Victor H Doolan, *President*
Rick Copley, *District Mgr*
Alain Delisle, *District Mgr*
John Johnston, *Business Mgr*
Curtis Puterbaugh, *Business Mgr*
◆ EMP: 300 EST: 1957
SQ FT: 289,000
SALES (est): 442.2MM
SALES (corp-wide): 42B **Privately Held**
WEB: www.volvocars.com
SIC: **5511 5013 6159 7515** Automobiles,
new & used; automotive supplies & parts;
automobile finance leasing; passenger
car leasing; motor vehicle parts & acces-
sories
HQ: Volvo Personvagnar Ab
Volvo Torslandaverken
Goteborg 405 3
315 900-00

Rocky Hill
Somerset County

(G-9637)
**ENVIRNMNTAL DYNAMICS
GROUP INC (PA)**
5 Crscent Ave (08553)
PHONE..................................609 924-4489
Fax: 609 924-8524
Duke Wiser, *President*
Martin Cummins, *Vice Pres*
Ronald Knight, *Vice Pres*
EMP: 13
SQ FT: 5,000
SALES (est): 2.1MM **Privately Held**
WEB: www.environmentaldynamics.com
SIC: **3564** Filters, air: furnaces, air condi-
tioning equipment, etc.

Roebling
Burlington County

(G-9638)
**MAGNATROL VALVE
CORPORATION**
Also Called: Clark Cooper
941 Hamilton Ave (08554-1707)
PHONE..................................856 829-4580
Fax: 856 829-7303
Chryssa Wilson, *General Mgr*
Dave Decaro, *Buyer*
John Busch, *Branch Mgr*
EMP: 15
SALES (corp-wide): 14.2MM **Privately
Held**
WEB: www.magnatrol.com
SIC: **3561 3491** Pumps & pumping equip-
ment; solenoid valves
PA: Magnatrol Valve Corporation
67 5th Ave
Hawthorne NJ 07506
973 427-4341

Roosevelt
Monmouth County

(G-9639)
**ACTION PACKAGING
AUTOMATION**
Also Called: A P A I
15 Oscar Dr (08555-7010)
P.O. Box 190 (08555-0190)
PHONE..................................609 448-9210
Fax: 609 448-8116
John Wojnicki, *President*
P J Wojnicki, *Corp Secy*
Robin Carroll, *Mktg Dir*
▲ EMP: 8
SQ FT: 18,000
SALES (est): 1.5MM **Privately Held**
WEB: www.apai-usa.com
SIC: **3565 3824 3542** Packaging machin-
ery; fluid meters & counting devices; ma-
chine tools, metal forming type

(G-9640)
DIAMOND MACHINE CO INC
30 N Valley Rd (08555-7017)
P.O. Box 420 (08555-0420)
PHONE..................................609 490-8940
George Pall, *President*
Ilona Pall, *Admin Sec*
EMP: 8
SALES (est): 665.5K **Privately Held**
SIC: **3599** Machine shop, jobbing & repair

(G-9641)
ICY COOLS INC
15 Oscar Dr (08555-7010)
P.O. Box 686 (08555-0686)
PHONE..................................609 448-0172
Paul Wojnicki, *President*
▲ EMP: 5
SQ FT: 10,000
SALES (est): 352K **Privately Held**
WEB: www.icycools.com
SIC: **3585 5078** Room coolers, portable;
refrigeration equipment & supplies

Roseland
Essex County

(G-9642)
**AMANO CINCINNATI
INCORPORATED (DH)**
Also Called: Amano Cincinnati Distributor
140 Harrison Ave (07068-1239)
PHONE..................................973 403-1900
Fax: 973 364-1086
Michael Lee, *President*
Osamu Okagaki, *President*
Kaushal Gokli, *Vice Pres*
Sabi Olyaie, *Warehouse Mgr*
Jodie Dooley, *Mfg Spvr*
◆ EMP: 100
SQ FT: 20,000
SALES (est): 39.1MM
SALES (corp-wide): 1.1B **Privately Held**
SIC: **3579 3559** Time clocks & time
recording devices; parking facility equip-
ment & supplies
HQ: Amano Usa Holdings, Inc.
140 Harrison Ave
Roseland NJ 07068
973 403-1900

(G-9643)
**AMANO USA HOLDINGS INC
(HQ)**
140 Harrison Ave (07068-1239)
PHONE..................................973 403-1900
Tomoaki Hashimoto, *President*
Thomas M Benton, *President*
Yoshio Misumi, *Vice Pres*
Chun Tang, *Business Anlyst*
Hiroaki Yamagishi, *Manager*
◆ EMP: 2
SQ FT: 20,000

GEOGRAPHIC

SALES (est): 107.6MM
SALES (corp-wide): 1.1B **Privately Held**
SIC: 3589 2842 3579 3559 Floor washing & polishing machines, commercial;
cleaning or polishing preparations; time
clocks & time recording devices; parking
facility equipment & supplies; industrial
chemicals; floor machinery, maintenance
PA: Amano Corporation
　　275, Mamedocho, Kohoku-Ku
　　Yokohama KNG 222-0
　　454 011-441

(G-9644)
ANNIN & CO (PA)
Also Called: Annin Flag Makers
105 Eisenhower Pkwy # 203 (07068-1640)
PHONE..............................973 228-9400
Fax: 973 228-4905
Carter Beard, *CEO*
Lindley Scarlett, *Exec VP*
Joe Brennan, *Vice Pres*
Sandra Van Lieu, *Vice Pres*
Rich Caramanga, *VP Opers*
▲ EMP: 50 EST: 1847
SALES (est): 165.1MM **Privately Held**
WEB: www.annin.com
SIC: 2399 Flags, fabric; banners, made
from fabric; pennants

(G-9645)
ARLO CORPORATION
119 Harrison Ave (07068)
PHONE..............................973 618-0030
Fax: 973 618-1144
Alan Aranowitz, *President*
EMP: 9
SQ FT: 5,000
SALES (est): 1.7MM **Privately Held**
SIC: 3965 5085 Fasteners; fasteners &
fastening equipment

(G-9646)
B&G FOODS INC
Also Called: Roseland Manufacturing
426 Eagle Rock Ave (07068-1719)
PHONE..............................973 403-6795
Ed Snook, *Plant Mgr*
Dennis Leo, *Warehouse Mgr*
Florina Raro, *Manager*
EMP: 150
SALES (corp-wide): 1.6B **Publicly Held**
WEB: www.bgfoods.com
SIC: 2033 Jams, including imitation: pack-
aged in cans, jars, etc.; jellies, edible, in-
cluding imitation: in cans, jars, etc.
PA: B&G Foods, Inc.
　　4 Gatehall Dr Ste 110
　　Parsippany NJ 07054
　　973 401-6500

(G-9647)
**BARRETT PAVING MATERIALS
INC (DH)**
3 Becker Farm Rd Ste 307 (07068-1726)
PHONE..............................973 533-1001
Fax: 973 533-1020
Robert Doucet, *President*
Michael Abbondandolo, *General Mgr*
Jim M Meckstroth, *Regional Mgr*
Ron Albers, *Vice Pres*
Dennis Luba, *Vice Pres*
◆ EMP: 20
SQ FT: 8,500
SALES (est): 209.5MM
SALES (corp-wide): 95.5MM **Privately
Held**
WEB: www.barrettpaving.com
SIC: 1611 2951 4213 1799 Highway &
street paving contractor; road materials,
bituminous (not from refineries); trucking,
except local; building site preparation; ex-
cavation work
HQ: Barrett Industries Corporation
　　73 Headquarters Plz
　　Morristown NJ 07960
　　973 533-1001

(G-9648)
BROTHERS SHEET METAL INC
15 Grand (07068)
PHONE..............................973 228-3221
Traci Dube, *President*
EMP: 14
SALES (est): 1.3MM **Privately Held**
SIC: 3444 Sheet metalwork

(G-9649)
**EMISPHERE TECHNOLOGIES
INC**
4 Becker Farm Rd Ste 103 (07068-1734)
PHONE..............................973 532-8000
Fax: 973 532-8121
Timothy G Rothwell, *Ch of Bd*
Alan L Rubino, *President*
Alan Gallantar, *CFO*
John Harkey, *Bd of Directors*
Timothy McInerney, *Bd of Directors*
EMP: 10
SQ FT: 4,100
SALES (est): 1.2MM **Privately Held**
WEB: www.emisphere.com
SIC: 2834 8731 Pharmaceutical prepara-
tions; biological research

(G-9650)
**GLOBAL ECOLOGY
CORPORATION (PA)**
101 Eisenhower Pkwy # 300 (07068-1054)
PHONE..............................973 655-9001
Joseph Battiato, *Ch of Bd*
Peter Ubaldi, *President*
EMP: 4
SQ FT: 1,000
SALES (est): 63.1K **Privately Held**
WEB: www.hsni.us
SIC: 3589 Water treatment equipment, in-
dustrial

(G-9651)
GRANCO GROUP LLC
Also Called: Portable Container Services
101 Eisenhower Pkwy # 300 (07068-1032)
PHONE..............................973 515-4721
Walter Granco,
◆ EMP: 4
SQ FT: 1,000
SALES (est): 858.7K **Privately Held**
SIC: 3715 5085 5999 2448 Demountable
cargo containers; commercial containers;
packaging materials: boxes, padding,
etc.; cargo containers, wood & wood with
metal; milk (fluid) shipping containers,
metal; trucks, tractors & trailers: new &
used

(G-9652)
**HAAS ENVIRONMENTAL INC
(PA)**
75 Eisenhower Pkwy # 200 (07068-1600)
PHONE..............................609 859-3100
Eugene Haas, *President*
Gene Haas, *President*
Wayne Muir, *Senior VP*
Chris Hall, *Vice Pres*
Michael Hopkins, *CFO*
EMP: 12
SQ FT: 4,000
SALES (est): 38.3MM **Privately Held**
SIC: 3312 Blast furnaces & steel mills

(G-9653)
**KNOW AMERICA MEDIA LLC
(PA)**
Also Called: Diversity In Action
157 Eagle Rock Ave (07068-1353)
PHONE..............................770 650-1102
Larry Lebovitz, *CEO*
John Hanna, *Treasurer*
Marilyn Walker, *Comptroller*
Adrienne Lewin, *Manager*
EMP: 7
SQ FT: 3,495
SALES (est): 559K **Privately Held**
SIC: 2721 Magazines: publishing only, not
printed on site

(G-9654)
OUTSOURCING TODAY LLC
103 Eisenhower Pkwy # 206 (07068-1031)
PHONE..............................973 439-0060
Fax: 973 439-0061
Jay Whitehead,
Harry Feinberg,
EMP: 10
SALES (est): 1.1MM **Privately Held**
SIC: 7319 2721 Media buying service;
magazines: publishing & printing

(G-9655)
PAR CODE SYMBOLOGY INC
119 Harrison Ave (07068-1218)
P.O. Box 87 (07068-0087)
PHONE..............................973 918-0550
Fax: 973 618-9901
David Aranowitz, *President*
Frankie Palmer, *Sales Dir*
EMP: 12
SQ FT: 8,000
SALES: 1.8MM **Privately Held**
WEB: www.parcode.com
SIC: 2672 5046 Coated & laminated
paper; commercial equipment

(G-9656)
TDK ASSOCIATES CORP
Also Called: Signarama Roseland
12 Eisenhower Pkwy Ste 9 (07068-1638)
PHONE..............................862 210-8085
Tarek Eldakak, *President*
Joan Eldakak, *Vice Pres*
EMP: 5
SQ FT: 2,000
SALES: 300K **Privately Held**
SIC: 1799 5046 3993 Sign installation &
maintenance; signs, electrical; signs &
advertising specialties

(G-9657)
WELDON CONCRETE CORP
Also Called: Asphalt Plant
1 Eisenhower Pkwy (07068-1607)
PHONE..............................973 228-7473
Joe Keppler, *Branch Mgr*
EMP: 4
SALES (corp-wide): 2.7MM **Privately
Held**
SIC: 3531 Asphalt plant, including gravel-
mix type
PA: Weldon Concrete Corp
　　141 Central Ave
　　Westfield NJ
　　908 233-4444

(G-9658)
ZC UTILITY SERVICES LLC
Also Called: Carner Bros
10 Steel Ct (07068-1236)
P.O. Box 116 (07068-0116)
PHONE..............................973 226-1840
Kevin Corb, *Vice Pres*
Todd Zartman,
EMP: 8 EST: 2015
SALES: 1MM **Privately Held**
SIC: 1389 7389 Excavating slush pits &
cellars; automobile recovery service

┌─────────────────────────┐
│　　　　**Roselle**　　　　│
│　　　*Union County*　　　│
└─────────────────────────┘

(G-9659)
**ADVANCED CUTTING SERVICES
LLC**
169 E Highland Pkwy (07203-2643)
PHONE..............................908 241-5332
Fax: 908 241-5592
Bob Valchunnis,
EMP: 5
SALES (est): 728.4K **Privately Held**
WEB: www.acswaterjet.com
SIC: 3545 Cutting tools for machine tools

(G-9660)
**AMERICAN RIGGING & REPAIR
INC**
Also Called: Metro Industrial Supply
356 W 1st Ave (07203-1001)
PHONE..............................866 478-7129
Robert Banks, *President*
Tom Banks, *Treasurer*
▼ EMP: 10 EST: 1998
SQ FT: 12,000
SALES: 1.5MM **Privately Held**
SIC: 3731 Marine rigging

(G-9661)
**ART MOLD & POLISHING CO
INC**
220 Columbus Ave (07203-2018)
PHONE..............................908 518-9191
Fax: 908 241-1254

Michael Dellapia, *President*
Daniel Notarnicola, *Vice Pres*
EMP: 10
SQ FT: 10,000
SALES (est): 1.3MM **Privately Held**
SIC: 3544 3471 Industrial molds; polish-
ing, metals or formed products

(G-9662)
BINDGRAPHICS INC
490 W 1st Ave (07203-1041)
PHONE..............................908 245-1110
Fax: 908 245-0159
Eugene Trunzo, *President*
EMP: 22
SQ FT: 20,000
SALES (est): 3.4MM **Privately Held**
SIC: 2789 Binding only: books, pamphlets,
magazines, etc.

(G-9663)
**BODYCOTE THERMAL PROC
INC**
304 Cox St (07203-1704)
PHONE..............................908 245-0717
Bobby Lebell, *Manager*
EMP: 25
SALES (corp-wide): 911.9MM **Privately
Held**
WEB: www.mic-houston.com
SIC: 3398 Metal heat treating
HQ: Bodycote Thermal Processing, Inc.
　　12700 Park Central Dr # 700
　　Dallas TX 75251
　　214 904-2420

(G-9664)
**BODYCOTE THERMAL
PROCESSING**
304 Cox St (07203-1704)
PHONE..............................908 245-0717
Robert Lobell, *President*
Robert J Lobell, *President*
John S Ross, *President*
George Johnson, *Manager*
Bob Lobell, *Manager*
EMP: 30 EST: 1944
SQ FT: 12,000
SALES (est): 5.1MM **Privately Held**
WEB: www.metall.com
SIC: 3398 Metal heat treating

(G-9665)
CLENESCO PRODUCTS CORP
298 Cox St (07203-1704)
PHONE..............................908 245-5255
Ronald Globerman, *President*
Neil Salerno, *Admin Sec*
EMP: 12
SQ FT: 8,000
SALES (est): 1.5MM
SALES (corp-wide): 14.8MM **Privately
Held**
WEB: www.rmsllc.net
SIC: 2842 Specialty cleaning preparations
PA: Ronell Industries Inc
　　298 Cox St
　　Roselle NJ 07203
　　908 245-5255

(G-9666)
COMFORTFIT LABS INC
246 Columbus Ave (07203-2018)
PHONE..............................908 259-9100
Fax: 908 259-9105
Howell Schorr, *President*
Thomas J Calagna, *Vice Pres*
Gwenn Smith,
EMP: 50
SALES (est): 7.6MM **Privately Held**
SIC: 3559 Sewing machines & hat & zipper
making machinery

(G-9667)
**COMMERCE FINANCIAL PRTRS
CORP**
Also Called: Register & Transfer
305 Cox St (07203-1703)
PHONE..............................908 241-9880
Fax: 908 241-5653
William T Saeger, *Ch of Bd*
Thomas L Montrone, *President*
Richard Brostowski, *Vice Pres*
EMP: 35
SQ FT: 6,000

SALES (est): 5.2MM **Privately Held**
WEB: www.cfpprint.com
SIC: 2752 2791 2789 2759 Commercial printing, offset; typesetting; bookbinding & related work; commercial printing

(G-9668)
CUSTOM ROLLER INC (PA)
240b Columbus Ave (07203-2088)
PHONE..................................908 298-7797
Fax: 908 298-7797
Elaine Ambrosio, *President*
Paul Materia, *Owner*
EMP: 8
SQ FT: 5,000
SALES (est): 1.1MM **Privately Held**
SIC: 3555 Printing trades machinery

(G-9669)
FARRELL EQP & CONTRLS INC
Also Called: Assured Automtn Flow Solutions
263 Cox St (07203-1703)
PHONE..................................732 770-4142
William Farrell, *President*
Brian Booth, *Vice Pres*
Mike O'Neill, *VP Sales*
Judith Farrell, *Admin Sec*
▲ EMP: 15
SQ FT: 10,000
SALES (est): 10.8MM **Privately Held**
WEB: www.flows.com
SIC: 5085 3491 Valves & fittings; industrial valves

(G-9670)
FORMIA MARBLE & STONE INC
219 E 11th Ave (07203-2015)
PHONE..................................908 259-0606
Filippo Berta, *President*
Ennio Grignolo, *Project Mgr*
Roy Ramotaur, *Project Mgr*
Melissa Knight, *Manager*
Philip Berta, *Supervisor*
◆ EMP: 18
SALES (est): 2.5MM **Privately Held**
SIC: 3281 Table tops, marble

(G-9671)
GIANT STL FABRICATORS ERECTORS
197 E Highland Pkwy (07203-2643)
PHONE..................................908 241-6766
John J Sorber Jr, *President*
Thomas A Fischetti, *Manager*
EMP: 4
SQ FT: 10,000
SALES (est): 399.1K **Privately Held**
SIC: 3441 3444 Fabricated structural metal; sheet metalwork

(G-9672)
HILLSIDE CANDY LLC
1112 Walnut St (07203-2024)
PHONE..................................908 241-4747
Henry Adamkowski, *Branch Mgr*
William Young, *Web Dvlpr*
EMP: 25
SALES (corp-wide): 6MM **Privately Held**
WEB: www.hillsidecandy.com
SIC: 5441 2064 Candy; candy & other confectionery products
PA: Hillside Candy Llc
35 Hillside Ave
Hillside NJ 07205
973 926-2300

(G-9673)
HOWARD PRESS INC
Also Called: Fedex Office Commercial Press
450 W 1st Ave (07203-1095)
P.O. Box 379 (07203-0379)
PHONE..................................908 245-4400
Scott B Porter, *General Mgr*
Gordon E Eitel Jr, *Exec VP*
Robert Porter, *MIS Dir*
▲ EMP: 60
SQ FT: 65,000
SALES (est): 10.3MM
SALES (corp-wide): 65.4B **Publicly Held**
WEB: www.howardpress.com
SIC: 2754 2752 2796 2759 Letter, circular & form: gravure printing; commercial printing, offset; platemaking services; commercial printing; book printing; book publishing

HQ: Fedex Office And Print Services, Inc.
7900 Legacy Dr
Plano TX 75024
214 550-7000

(G-9674)
KRAFTWARE CORPORATION (PA)
270 Cox St (07203-1704)
PHONE..................................732 345-7091
Donald R Grant, *Ch of Bd*
D Rustin Grant, *President*
L Ripley Grant, *Exec VP*
▲ EMP: 25 EST: 1947
SQ FT: 30,000
SALES (est): 4.9MM **Privately Held**
WEB: www.kraftwareonline.com
SIC: 3499 3229 5023 3914 Metal household articles; glassware, art or decorative; kitchen tools & utensils; silverware & plated ware; metal barrels, drums & pails

(G-9675)
MATERIALS RESEARCH GROUP INC
244 W 1st Ave (07203-1102)
PHONE..................................908 245-3301
Walt Reed, *President*
Sharon Reed, *Vice Pres*
▲ EMP: 7
SQ FT: 8,000
SALES (est): 710K **Privately Held**
WEB: www.materialsresearchgroup.com
SIC: 3229 Pressed & blown glass

(G-9676)
MECHANITRON CORPORATION INC
Also Called: Mechanictron
310 W 1st Ave (07203-1001)
PHONE..................................908 620-1001
Dave Newman, *President*
EMP: 8
SQ FT: 3,000
SALES (est): 760K **Privately Held**
SIC: 3599 3452 Machine shop, jobbing & repair; bolts, nuts, rivets & washers

(G-9677)
MICHELLER & SON HYDRAULICS INC
534 W 1st Ave Ste 540 (07203-1028)
PHONE..................................908 687-1545
Birgetta Micheller, *Corp Secy*
John Micheller, *Vice Pres*
Patricia Waznica, *Office Mgr*
EMP: 10
SQ FT: 6,000
SALES: 1MM **Privately Held**
SIC: 3511 5084 7699 3599 Hydraulic turbines; hydraulic systems equipment & supplies; hydraulic equipment repair; machine shop, jobbing & repair; welding repair

(G-9678)
OILTEST INC
109 Aldene Rd Ste 4 (07203-1093)
PHONE..................................908 245-9330
Fax: 908 245-8972
EMP: 5
SALES (est): 616.8K **Privately Held**
SIC: 1389 Oil/Gas Field Services

(G-9679)
PAMARCO GLOBAL GRAPHICS INC (HQ)
Also Called: Memco
235 E 11th Ave (07203-2090)
PHONE..................................908 241-1200
Fax: 908 241-4009
Terry Ford, *President*
David Burgess, *Vice Pres*
◆ EMP: 50 EST: 1946
SQ FT: 110,000
SALES (est): 32.3MM **Privately Held**
SIC: 3555 Printing trades machinery

(G-9680)
PAMARCO TECHNOLOGIES LLC (PA)
235 E 11th Ave (07203-2090)
PHONE..................................908 241-1200
Fax: 908 665-8501

Terrence W Ford, *CEO*
Nick Walker, *General Mgr*
Martin Winnicki, *Plant Mgr*
John Rastetter, *VP Sls/Mktg*
Doug Johnson, *CFO*
▲ EMP: 36
SALES (est): 104.5MM **Privately Held**
WEB: www.armotek.com
SIC: 3555 Printing trades machinery

(G-9681)
PAR SHEET METAL INC
220 W 1st Ave (07203-1102)
PHONE..................................908 241-2477
Anthony Costa, *President*
Andy Costa, *Vice Pres*
EMP: 10
SQ FT: 5,000
SALES (est): 650K **Privately Held**
SIC: 3444 Sheet metalwork

(G-9682)
RONELL INDUSTRIES INC (PA)
298 Cox St (07203-1798)
PHONE..................................908 245-5255
Fax: 908 241-4244
Ronald Globerman, *President*
Neil Salerno, *Vice Pres*
EMP: 482
SQ FT: 10,000
SALES (est): 14.8MM **Privately Held**
WEB: www.rmsllc.net
SIC: 7349 2842 Janitorial service, contract basis; specialty cleaning preparations

(G-9683)
STAMPLUS MANUFACTURING INC
654 W 1st Ave (07203-1026)
PHONE..................................908 241-8844
Fax: 908 241-6634
Jaromir Batka, *President*
EMP: 15
SQ FT: 19,000
SALES (est): 3.3MM **Privately Held**
SIC: 3469 Electronic enclosures, stamped or pressed metal

(G-9684)
SUPERFINE ONLINE INC
205 E 11th Ave (07203-2015)
PHONE..................................212 827-0063
EMP: 8
SQ FT: 4,000
SALES (est): 30.6K **Privately Held**
SIC: 2752 Lithographic Commercial Printing

(G-9685)
VICTORY BOX CORP
645 W 1st Ave (07203-1049)
P.O. Box 842, Cranford (07016-0842)
PHONE..................................908 245-5100
Alex Landy, *President*
Paul Bell, *Vice Pres*
Michael Radin, *Vice Pres*
Seymour Cohen, *Admin Sec*
EMP: 6 EST: 1996
SQ FT: 120,000
SALES (est): 810K **Privately Held**
SIC: 2653 Boxes, corrugated: made from purchased materials

(G-9686)
VITA-PURE INC (PA)
410 W 1st Ave (07203-1047)
PHONE..................................908 245-1212
Fax: 908 245-1999
Achyut Sahasra, *President*
▲ EMP: 25
SQ FT: 17,500
SALES (est): 8.4MM **Privately Held**
SIC: 2833 2834 Vitamins, natural or synthetic: bulk, uncompounded; pharmaceutical preparations

(G-9687)
ACCURATE MACHINE & TOOL CO
135 W Clay Ave (07204-1946)
P.O. Box 187 (07204-0187)
PHONE..................................908 245-5545
Jeral Diehl, *President*
EMP: 6
SQ FT: 5,000
SALES: 350K **Privately Held**
SIC: 3544 Special dies & tools

(G-9688)
AYR COMPOSITION INC
320 Chestnut St (07204-1904)
PHONE..................................908 241-8118
Fax: 908 241-7590
Carl Gamba, *President*
Jeanette Gamba, *President*
John Gamba, *Vice Pres*
Nick Gamba, *Vice Pres*
EMP: 6
SQ FT: 2,800
SALES (est): 616.7K **Privately Held**
SIC: 2759 2791 Commercial printing; typesetting

(G-9689)
AYR GRAPHICS & PRINTING INC
Also Called: Proforma Ayr Graphics & Prtg
320 Chestnut St (07204-1904)
PHONE..................................908 241-8118
Carl Gamba, *President*
Melissa Carle, *Manager*
Jennefer Chatman, *Admin Sec*
EMP: 6
SALES (est): 811.4K **Privately Held**
SIC: 2752 Commercial printing, lithographic

(G-9690)
CASAS NEWS PUBLISHING CO
325 E Westfield Ave (07204-2317)
PHONE..................................908 245-6767
George Castro, *President*
EMP: 30
SALES (est): 1.7MM **Privately Held**
SIC: 2711 Newspapers, publishing & printing

(G-9691)
CROSSFIELD PRODUCTS CORP
Also Called: Dex-O-Tex Floor Coverings
140 Valley Rd (07204-1402)
P.O. Box 125 (07204-0125)
PHONE..................................908 245-2801
Fax: 908 245-0659
Charles R Watt, *Branch Mgr*
EMP: 75
SQ FT: 35,000
SALES (est): 14.8MM
SALES (corp-wide): 28.8MM **Privately Held**
WEB: www.crossfieldproducts.com
SIC: 2821 3272 3089 Plastics materials & resins; concrete products; floor coverings, plastic
PA: Crossfield Products Corp.
3000 E Harcourt St
Compton CA 90221
310 886-9100

(G-9692)
CUSUMANO PERMA-RAIL CO
213 W Westfield Ave (07204-1894)
PHONE..................................908 245-9281
Fax: 908 245-7696
Vincent Cusumano, *Ch of Bd*
Jeffrey Cusumano, *President*
Joan Cusumano, *Treasurer*
EMP: 8 EST: 1952
SQ FT: 5,000
SALES (est): 1.1MM **Privately Held**
WEB: www.cusumanorailings.com
SIC: 3446 5211 Architectural metalwork; lumber & other building materials

(G-9693)
**D K TOOL & DIE WELDING
GROUP (PA)**
Also Called: D-K Tool & Die Welding
181 W Clay Ave (07204-1946)
PHONE..............................908 241-7600
Fax: 908 241-1513
Stanley W Dickerson, *President*
EMP: 20
SQ FT: 16,000
SALES (est): 1.1MM **Privately Held**
WEB: www.d-kwelding.com
SIC: 7692 Welding repair

(G-9694)
DELICIOUS FRESH PIEROGI INC
594 Chestnut St (07204-1320)
P.O. Box 109 (07204-0109)
PHONE..............................908 245-0550
Fax: 908 245-8868
Richard Jackiewicz, *President*
EMP: 17
SALES (est): 1.7MM **Privately Held**
SIC: 2038 5149 5499 Ethnic foods,
frozen; specialty food items; gourmet food
stores

(G-9695)
**EXTRUDERS INTERNATIONAL
INC**
181 W Clay Ave (07204-1946)
PHONE..............................908 241-7750
Stanley W Dickerson, *President*
EMP: 5
SQ FT: 5,000
SALES (est): 420K **Privately Held**
SIC: 3469 Machine parts, stamped or
pressed metal

(G-9696)
G CATALANO INC
222 Valley Rd (07204-1404)
PHONE..............................908 241-6333
Fax: 908 241-1138
Giordano Catalano, *President*
Catherine Catalano, *Admin Sec*
EMP: 4
SQ FT: 1,521
SALES: 150K **Privately Held**
SIC: 3599 Machine shop, jobbing & repair

(G-9697)
**HEXACON ELECTRIC COMPANY
INC**
161 W Clay Ave (07204-1946)
PHONE..............................908 245-6200
Fax: 908 245-6176
Kathryn J Schwaiger, *President*
Rashonda Aiken, *Administration*
EMP: 50 EST: 1932
SQ FT: 70,844
SALES (est): 8.4MM **Privately Held**
WEB: www.hexaconelectric.com
SIC: 3423 3548 Soldering guns or tools,
hand: electric; soldering equipment, ex-
cept hand soldering irons

(G-9698)
INDUSTL ENVRNMNTL POLLUTN
176 W Westfield Ave (07204-1817)
PHONE..............................908 241-3830
Michael Mouracade, *President*
Alexander Mouracade, *Vice Pres*
EMP: 28
SQ FT: 15,000
SALES (est): 3.3MM **Privately Held**
SIC: 3556 Food products machinery

(G-9699)
**MONTE PRINTING & GRAPHICS
INC**
225 W Clay Ave (07204-1909)
P.O. Box 293 (07204-0293)
PHONE..............................908 241-6600
Philip A Montalto, *President*
EMP: 5
SQ FT: 2,300
SALES: 650K **Privately Held**
SIC: 2752 7336 Commercial printing, off-
set; commercial art & graphic design

(G-9700)
MYLES F KELLY INC
210 W Westfield Ave (07204-1819)
PHONE..............................908 245-2033

Fax: 908 241-3441
Frank Barreira, *Sales Staff*
Michael Oroake, *Manager*
EMP: 15 **Privately Held**
SIC: 5033 3353 Roofing & siding materi-
als; roofing, asphalt & sheet metal; siding,
except wood; aluminum sheet, plate & foil
HQ: Myles F. Kelly, Inc.
43 Harrison Ave Ste 57
Harrison NJ 07029

(G-9701)
PRINTSMITH
253 W Westfield Ave (07204-1824)
PHONE..............................908 245-3000
Ray Smith, *Owner*
EMP: 4
SALES (est): 227.2K **Privately Held**
SIC: 2759 Screen printing

(G-9702)
R W WHEATON CO
215 W Clay Ave (07204-1909)
P.O. Box 4017 (07204-0517)
PHONE..............................908 241-4955
Christopher E Kern, *President*
Wendy W Kern, *Treasurer*
EMP: 5
SQ FT: 1,900
SALES: 2.7MM **Privately Held**
SIC: 3324 Commercial investment cast-
ings, ferrous

(G-9703)
**SQUILLACE STL FABRICATORS
LLC**
240 W Westfield Ave (07204-1819)
PHONE..............................908 241-6424
Rick Squillace, *President*
EMP: 5
SALES (est): 592.9K **Privately Held**
SIC: 3441 Fabricated structural metal
PA: Squillace Steel Fabricators Llc
771 Amsterdam Ave
Roselle NJ 07203

Rosemont
Hunterdon County

(G-9704)
FREDERICKS MACHINE INC
99 Kingwood Stockton Rd (08556-9990)
P.O. Box 247 (08556-0247)
PHONE..............................609 397-4991
Peter Frederiks, *President*
Pete Frederiks, *President*
EMP: 5
SALES (est): 472.6K **Privately Held**
SIC: 3599 Machine shop, jobbing & repair

(G-9705)
MAGNETICS & CONTROLS INC
99 Kingwood Stockton Rd (08556-9990)
P.O. Box 127 (08556-0127)
PHONE..............................609 397-8203
Fax: 609 397-0202
Jonathan C Lamson, *President*
Charlene E Lamson, *Corp Secy*
EMP: 17
SQ FT: 7,500
SALES (est): 1.4MM **Privately Held**
WEB: www.magcon.com
SIC: 3679 Cores, magnetic

Rosenhayn
Cumberland County

(G-9706)
CUMBERLAND DAIRY INC (PA)
899 Landis Ave (08352)
P.O. Box 308 (08352-0308)
PHONE..............................800 257-8484
Fax: 856 453-9334
Carmine C Catalana IV, *President*
Frank Catalana, *COO*
David A Catalana, *Vice Pres*
Frank J Catalana, *Vice Pres*
▲ EMP: 110 EST: 1962
SQ FT: 24,000
SALES (est): 26MM **Privately Held**
SIC: 2026 Milk drinks, flavored; yogurt

(G-9707)
F&S PRODUCE COMPANY INC
913 Bridgeton Ave (08352)
P.O. Box 17 (08352-0017)
PHONE..............................856 453-0316
Fax: 856 453-0494
Salvatore Pipitone Jr, *President*
Bryan Hunsberger, *Maintenance Dir*
Colin Turner, *Plant Mgr*
▲ EMP: 35
SQ FT: 85,000
SALES: 111.4MM **Privately Held**
WEB: www.freshcutproduce.com
SIC: 0723 2099 2032 0181 Vegetable
crops market preparation services; veg-
etable packing services; vegetables,
peeled for the trade; canned specialties;
ornamental nursery products

(G-9708)
QIS INC
778 Vineland Ave (08352)
P.O. Box 517 (08352-0517)
PHONE..............................856 455-3736
Fax: 856 455-3894
Diane Rizzo Lodge, *President*
▲ EMP: 10
SQ FT: 5,000
SALES (est): 1.3MM **Privately Held**
SIC: 3229 Pressed & blown glass

(G-9709)
QUARK ENTERPRISES INC
320 Morton Ave (08352)
P.O. Box 2396, Vineland (08362-2396)
PHONE..............................856 455-0376
Fax: 856 455-3373
Doug Riley, *President*
Pearl Riley, *Corp Secy*
Susan Burt, *Vice Pres*
EMP: 23
SQ FT: 10,000
SALES (est): 2.6MM **Privately Held**
WEB: www.quarkglass.com
SIC: 3229 3231 Scientific glassware; nov-
elty glassware; products of purchased
glass

(G-9710)
**UNITED FARM PROCESSING
CORP**
458 Garrison Rd (08352)
P.O. Box 355 (08352-0355)
PHONE..............................856 451-4612
Fax: 856 451-4690
EMP: 10 **Privately Held**
SIC: 2035 Mfg Pickles/Sauces/Dressing
PA: United Farm Processing Corp
4366 Park Ave
Bronx NY 10457

Roxbury Township
Morris County

(G-9711)
**CLASSIC MARKING PRODUCTS
INC**
3 Gold Mine Rd Ste 104 (07836-0579)
PHONE..............................973 383-2223
Fred Thornton, *President*
EMP: 6
SALES (est): 680.2K **Privately Held**
WEB: www.classicmarking.com
SIC: 3953 Marking devices

(G-9712)
**PHOENIX MACHINE
REBUILDERS INC**
4 Gold Mine Rd (07836-9122)
PHONE..............................973 691-8029
Fax: 973 691-8939
Michael Coulson, *President*
EMP: 10
SQ FT: 6,000
SALES (est): 820K **Privately Held**
SIC: 3599 Machine & other job shop work

Rumson
Monmouth County

(G-9713)
J NELSON PRESS INC
111 E River Rd (07760-1699)
PHONE..............................732 747-0330
Fax: 732 520-8567
Scott Thompsen, *President*
EMP: 5 EST: 1933
SQ FT: 3,750
SALES: 510K **Privately Held**
WEB: www.nelsonpress.net
SIC: 3555 Printing presses

(G-9714)
REISS CORPORATION (PA)
Also Called: Reiss Manufacturing
36 Bingham Ave (07760-1535)
P.O. Box 159 (07760-0159)
PHONE..............................732 446-6100
Carl Reiss, *President*
Charles Stegura, *Controller*
William Bryan, *Manager*
▲ EMP: 125 EST: 1896
SQ FT: 135,000
SALES (est): 27.8MM **Privately Held**
WEB: www.reissmfg.com
SIC: 3061 Mechanical rubber goods

(G-9715)
**REISS MANUFACTURING INC
(HQ)**
Also Called: Ronsil Silicone Rubber Div
36 Bingham Ave (07760-1535)
P.O. Box 159 (07760-0159)
PHONE..............................732 446-6100
Carl Reiss, *President*
Wayne Ruotolo, *Opers Staff*
Caron Figgatt, *Production*
Eduardo Ponte, *Production*
Robert Geist, *Engineer*
◆ EMP: 125
SQ FT: 135,000
SALES (est): 34MM
SALES (corp-wide): 27.8MM **Privately
Held**
WEB: www.reissmfg.com
SIC: 2822 Silicone rubbers
PA: Reiss Corporation
36 Bingham Ave
Rumson NJ 07760
732 446-6100

(G-9716)
RUMSONS KITCHENS INC
103 E River Rd (07760-1611)
PHONE..............................732 842-1810
Louis Gualtieri, *President*
Elizabeth Gualtieri, *Vice Pres*
EMP: 5
SQ FT: 2,500
SALES (est): 430K **Privately Held**
SIC: 2514 1521 Kitchen cabinets: metal;
general remodeling, single-family houses

Runnemede
Camden County

(G-9717)
**CAPITAL GASKET AND RUBBER
INC**
325 E Clements Bridge Rd (08078-1404)
P.O. Box 141, Glendora (08029-0141)
PHONE..............................856 939-3670
Dennis Iocono, *President*
EMP: 5
SQ FT: 2,990
SALES: 400K **Privately Held**
SIC: 3053 5199 5085 Gasket materials;
packaging materials; gaskets

(G-9718)
**DELAWARE VALLEY
INSTALLATION**
200 Evergreen Rd (08078)
PHONE..............................856 546-0097
Jo Ann Brooks, *President*
EMP: 7
SQ FT: 1,500

▲ = Import ▼=Export
◆ =Import/Export

SALES (est): 621.7K **Privately Held**
SIC: 2541 Cabinets, lockers & shelving

(G-9719)
GENERAL CIVIL COMPANY INC
710 Irish Hill Rd (08078-1474)
P.O. Box 72592, Thorndale PA (19372-0592)
PHONE..................866 435-1200
George Detore, *Principal*
Giglio Dibattista, *Vice Pres*
Lawrence McLaughlin, *Admin Sec*
EMP: 10
SALES: 740K **Privately Held**
SIC: 1541 8744 1389 1799 Industrial buildings & warehouses; industrial buildings, new construction; ; oil & gas wells: building, repairing & dismantling; building site preparation; concrete block masonry laying; plumbing, heating, air-conditioning contractors

(G-9720)
RAPID MODELS & PROTOTYPES INC
101 C Rose Ave (08078)
PHONE..................856 933-2929
Angela Pizzo, *President*
Joseph Pizzo, *Vice Pres*
EMP: 4
SQ FT: 7,000
SALES: 350K **Privately Held**
WEB: www.rapidmodels.net
SIC: 8711 3999 Industrial engineers; models, general, except toy

(G-9721)
RISSE & RISSE GRAPHICS INC
901 E Clements Bridge Rd # 3 (08078-2000)
PHONE..................856 751-7671
Rich Risse, *President*
Rob Risse, *Vice Pres*
EMP: 40
SALES: 5MM **Privately Held**
SIC: 2395 Embroidery & art needlework

(G-9722)
RUOFF & SONS INC
1030 Rose Ave (08078-1088)
P.O. Box 320 (08078-0320)
PHONE..................856 931-2064
Fax: 856 931-0539
Steve Ruoff, *President*
Victor Norbuts, *Manager*
Steffanie Smith, *Manager*
EMP: 30 EST: 1950
SQ FT: 27,000
SALES (est): 7MM **Privately Held**
SIC: 3599 Machine shop, jobbing & repair

(G-9723)
SILVERTOP ASSOCIATES INC (PA)
Also Called: Rasta Imposta
600 E Clements Bridge Rd (08078-1453)
P.O. Box 7 (08078-0007)
PHONE..................856 939-9599
Fax: 856 939-5990
Robert Berman, *President*
Jodi Berman, *COO*
Tom Matthews, *Controller*
Tina Berman, *Ch Credit Ofcr*
▲ EMP: 35
SQ FT: 16,000
SALES: 14MM **Privately Held**
WEB: www.rastaimposta.com
SIC: 2389 2353 Costumes; hats, caps & millinery

(G-9724)
STRYKER
165 E 9th Ave Unit F (08078-1162)
PHONE..................856 312-0046
Patti Coulter, *Principal*
EMP: 7
SALES (est): 1.1MM **Privately Held**
SIC: 3841 Surgical & medical instruments

Rutherford
Bergen County

(G-9725)
APPLE AIR COMPRESSOR CORP (PA)
Also Called: Airtech Vacuum
301 Veterans Blvd (07070-2564)
PHONE..................888 222-9940
Fax: 201 569-1696
Tom Latsos, *President*
Chris Latsos, *Corp Secy*
Andriy Yakymenko, *Prdtn Mgr*
Elias Rontogiannis, *Buyer*
Dorian Simonetti, *Purchasing*
▲ EMP: 13
SQ FT: 20,000
SALES (est): 7.4MM **Privately Held**
SIC: 5084 3561 Pumps & pumping equipment; pumps & pumping equipment

(G-9726)
ARCHITECTURAL WINDOW MFG CORP
359 Veterans Blvd (07070-2564)
PHONE..................201 933-5094
Anthony M Laino Jr, *President*
Michael A Laino, *Vice Pres*
Ken Thompson, *Vice Pres*
Paul Laino, *CFO*
Harold Delmastro, *Finance Dir*
EMP: 200
SQ FT: 170,000
SALES: 44.3MM **Privately Held**
SIC: 3442 1751 Sash, door or window: metal; window & door (prefabricated) installation

(G-9727)
BEBUS CABINETRY LLC
12 Ames Ave (07070-1702)
PHONE..................201 729-9300
Raul A Garcia, *Administration*
EMP: 4
SALES (est): 171.2K **Privately Held**
SIC: 2434 Wood kitchen cabinets

(G-9728)
CHERISHMET INC
301 State Rt 17 Ste 800 (07070-2581)
P.O. Box 1652 (07070-0652)
PHONE..................201 842-7612
Adam Wang, *President*
▲ EMP: 10
SALES (est): 3.6MM **Privately Held**
WEB: www.cherishmet.com
SIC: 5051 1446 Ferroalloys; filtration sand mining

(G-9729)
DAIRY DELIGHT LLC
1 Industrial Dr (07070-2523)
PHONE..................201 939-7878
Fax: 201 939-2888
Shulim Ostreicher, *Programmer Anys*
Victor Ostreicher,
Joe Sptizer,
▲ EMP: 10
SALES (est): 4.3MM **Privately Held**
SIC: 5084 2023 5149 Dairy products manufacturing machinery; dry, condensed, evaporated dairy products; milk, canned or dried

(G-9730)
EAGLETREE-PUMP AQUISITON CORP ✪
301 Veterans Blvd (07070-2564)
PHONE..................201 569-1173
Robert Fogelson, *President*
Nitin Singhal, *Admin Sec*
EMP: 85 EST: 2017
SALES (est): 3MM **Privately Held**
SIC: 3563 Vacuum pumps, except laboratory

(G-9731)
EBSCO INDUSTRIES INC
Also Called: Vulcan Information Packaging
201 Highway 17 Ste 300 (07070-2583)
PHONE..................201 933-1800
Marie Curcio, *Branch Mgr*

EMP: 15
SALES (corp-wide): 2.8B **Privately Held**
WEB: www.ebscoind.com
SIC: 2782 Blankbooks & looseleaf binders; looseleaf binders & devices
PA: Ebsco Industries, Inc.
5724 Highway 280 E
Birmingham AL 35242
205 991-6600

(G-9732)
FUNAI CORPORATION INC (HQ)
201 Route 17 Ste 903 (07070-2635)
PHONE..................201 806-7635
Ryo Fukuda, *President*
George Kanazawa, *CFO*
▲ EMP: 25
SALES (est): 16.5MM
SALES (corp-wide): 1.2B **Privately Held**
SIC: 3651 Household audio & video equipment
PA: Funai Electric Co., Ltd.
7-7-1, Nakagaito
Daito OSK 574-0
728 704-303

(G-9733)
GZGN INC
Also Called: Vrpark
301 Nj 17 Ste 800 (07070)
PHONE..................201 842-7622
Mehmet Aksakal, *Founder*
EMP: 15
SQ FT: 1,000
SALES (est): 568K **Privately Held**
SIC: 3651 Home entertainment equipment, electronic

(G-9734)
HIGHPONT CORPORATION
Also Called: Pierrepont & Co
63 E Pierrepont Ave (07070-2330)
P.O. Box 35, Lyndhurst (07071-0035)
PHONE..................201 460-1364
Peter Paluch, *President*
EMP: 9
SALES (est): 560K **Privately Held**
SIC: 2013 Sausages from purchased meat

(G-9735)
JOHANSEN BOOK BINDERY INC
71 E Van Ness Ave (07070-2738)
PHONE..................201 438-4263
Richard Johansen, *President*
Beverly Johansen, *Corp Secy*
Walter Johansen, *Vice Pres*
EMP: 4 EST: 1943
SQ FT: 4,000
SALES (est): 323.1K **Privately Held**
SIC: 2789 Binding only: books, pamphlets, magazines, etc.

(G-9736)
JORY ENGRAVERS INC
23 W Erie Ave (07070-1299)
PHONE..................201 939-1546
Fax: 201 939-2952
Gary Gagliardi, *President*
EMP: 5
SQ FT: 3,500
SALES (est): 814.7K **Privately Held**
SIC: 2752 7389 Commercial printing, lithographic; engraving service

(G-9737)
JUNGANEW LLC
1 Orient Way Ste F104 (07070-2524)
PHONE..................201 832-0892
Esther Giordano, *Mng Member*
EMP: 6
SALES (est): 334.1K **Privately Held**
SIC: 7372 Prepackaged software; application computer software; educational computer software

(G-9738)
L-E-M PLASTICS AND SUPPLIES
255 Highland Cross Ste 4 (07070-2594)
PHONE..................201 933-9150
Thomas Pietrowitz, *Principal*
Sally Burns, *Business Mgr*
EMP: 5
SALES (est): 1.4MM **Privately Held**
SIC: 5162 3089 Plastics sheets & rods; air mattresses, plastic

(G-9739)
MAGPIE MARKETING INC
194 Woodland Ave (07070-2839)
PHONE..................201 507-9155
Peter Hollingsworth, *President*
Laura White, *Vice Pres*
▲ EMP: 2
SQ FT: 3,000
SALES: 1.5MM **Privately Held**
WEB: www.magpiemarketing.com
SIC: 3251 Ceramic glazed brick, clay

(G-9740)
METAWATER USA INC (PA)
301 State Rt 17 Ste 504 (07070-2580)
PHONE..................201 935-3436
Fax: 201 935-3439
Ken Akikawa, *CEO*
Ichiro Fukushima, *CEO*
EMP: 2
SALES (est): 67.7MM **Privately Held**
SIC: 3589 Water treatment equipment, industrial

(G-9741)
NORTH JERSEY MEDIA GROUP INC
Also Called: South Bergenite Editorial
9 Lincoln Ave (07070-2112)
P.O. Box 471, Little Falls (07424-0471)
PHONE..................201 933-1166
Fax: 201 933-9247
Terri Dockray, *Sales Staff*
Jaime Winters, *Director*
EMP: 5
SALES (corp-wide): 173.6MM **Privately Held**
WEB: www.njmg.com
SIC: 2711 Newspapers, publishing & printing
HQ: North Jersey Media Group Inc.
1 Garret Mountain Plz # 201
Woodland Park NJ 07424
201 646-4000

(G-9742)
ORION MACHINERY CO LTD
301 Veterans Blvd (07070-2564)
PHONE..................201 569-3220
Fax: 201 569-7654
Thomas Latsos, *President*
▲ EMP: 24
SQ FT: 20,000
SALES (est): 3.1MM **Privately Held**
WEB: www.orionmach.net
SIC: 3563 5084 3561 Vacuum pumps, except laboratory; industrial machinery & equipment; pumps & pumping equipment

(G-9743)
PEARL BAUMELL COMPANY INC
201 State Rt 17 Ste 302 (07070-2583)
PHONE..................415 421-2113
Fax: 415 421-2753
Isaac Baum, *President*
Evelyn Baum, *Vice Pres*
EMP: 8
SQ FT: 1,500
SALES (est): 1.5MM **Privately Held**
SIC: 5094 3911 Pearls; precious stones (gems); jewelry, precious metal

(G-9744)
SI PACKAGING LLC
1 Orient Way Ste F191 (07070-2524)
PHONE..................973 869-9920
Peter S Rodriguez, *Mng Member*
EMP: 10 EST: 2013
SQ FT: 30,000
SALES: 8MM **Privately Held**
SIC: 2879 5169 2841 Exterminating products, for household or industrial use; chemicals & allied products; detergents & soaps, except specialty cleaning; soap & other detergents

(G-9745)
SONY MUSIC HOLDINGS INC
Also Called: Bmg Entertainment
301 State Rte Hwy (07070)
PHONE..................201 777-3933
Fax: 201 460-5567
Andrew Lack, *Manager*
EMP: 400

SALES (corp-wide): 80.1B **Privately Held**
SIC: 3652 8721 7929 5735 Pre-recorded records & tapes; auditing services; entertainers & entertainment groups; record & prerecorded tape stores
HQ: Sony Music Holdings Inc.
25 Madison Ave Fl 26
New York NY 10010
212 833-8000

(G-9746)
WORLD PLASTIC EXTRUDERS INC
41 Park Ave (07070-1713)
PHONE..............................201 933-2915
Charles Bierds, *President*
EMP: 75
SQ FT: 31,500
SALES (est): 6.3MM
SALES (corp-wide): 434.6MM **Privately Held**
WEB: www.alhyde.com
SIC: 3089 Extruded finished plastic products
HQ: Ensinger Grenloch, Inc.
1 Main St
Grenloch NJ 08032

Saddle Brook
Bergen County

(G-9747)
A A A STAMP AND SEAL MFG CO
361 N Midland Ave (07663-5701)
PHONE..............................201 796-1500
Fax: 201 796-5675
Barry Goldman, *President*
EMP: 5
SQ FT: 1,800
SALES (est): 560.5K **Privately Held**
WEB: www.aaastamp.com
SIC: 3953 5999 Embossing seals & hand stamps; rubber stamps

(G-9748)
AA GRAPHICS INC
431 N Midland Ave (07663-5527)
PHONE..............................201 398-0710
Fax: 201 398-0925
Anthony Acocella, *President*
Francine Acocella, *Vice Pres*
EMP: 5
SQ FT: 4,000
SALES (est): 500K **Privately Held**
WEB: www.aagraphics.com
SIC: 2752 Commercial printing, lithographic

(G-9749)
AARUBCO RUBBER CO INC
259 2nd St (07663-6201)
P.O. Box 8028 (07663-8028)
PHONE..............................973 772-8177
Fax: 973 772-4902
Stephen Wharton, *President*
Ruth Wharton, *Vice Pres*
Amber Wharton, *Technical Mgr*
Paul Dec, *Sales Staff*
Patrick Kelly, *Sales Staff*
EMP: 32
SQ FT: 33,000
SALES (est): 7MM **Privately Held**
WEB: www.aarubco.com
SIC: 3052 3061 Rubber belting; mechanical rubber goods

(G-9750)
ACETRIS HEALTH LLC
Park 80 West Plz 1 (07663)
PHONE..............................201 961-9000
Salvatore Guccion, *CEO*
EMP: 5
SALES (est): 2.3MM
SALES (corp-wide): 638.3MM **Publicly Held**
SIC: 2834 5122 Pharmaceutical preparations; drugs & drug proprietaries
HQ: Rising Pharmaceuticals, Inc.
Park 80 W Plz 1 250 Pehle
Saddle Brook NJ 07663

(G-9751)
ALLIED ELASTIC BRAID INC
280 N Midland Ave Bldg C1 (07663-5708)
PHONE..............................201 941-8875
Fax: 201 941-8879
Ira Grodin, *President*
EMP: 20 **EST:** 1951
SQ FT: 17,000
SALES (est): 2.3MM **Privately Held**
SIC: 2241 2396 Narrow fabric mills; automotive & apparel trimmings

(G-9752)
ARROW FASTENER CO LLC
271 Mayhill St (07663-5395)
PHONE..............................201 843-6900
Gary Duboff, *President*
Ted Shapiro, *Controller*
▲ **EMP:** 280 **EST:** 2009
SQ FT: 250,000
SALES (est): 111.7MM
SALES (corp-wide): 646MM **Privately Held**
WEB: www.arrowfastener.com
SIC: 3579 3315 3452 3542 Stapling machines (hand or power); staples, steel: wire or cut; rivets, metal; riveting machines
PA: Hangzhou Greatstar Industrial Co., Ltd.
No.35 Jiuhuan Road, Jianggan District
Hangzhou 31001
571 816-0107

(G-9753)
ATLANTIC WOODWORKING INC
280 N Midland Ave Ste 230 (07663-5717)
PHONE..............................201 773-9277
James A Portelli, *President*
EMP: 6
SQ FT: 2,500
SALES: 800K **Privately Held**
WEB: www.atlanticwood.net
SIC: 2511 Wood household furniture

(G-9754)
B&M TECHNOLOGIES INC
109 5th St Ste 1 (07663-6157)
PHONE..............................201 291-8505
Brian Cho, *President*
EMP: 12
SQ FT: 5,000
SALES (est): 120.9K **Privately Held**
SIC: 2759 Laser printing

(G-9755)
BLUE GAUNTLET FENCING GEAR INC
Also Called: Blue Gauntlet Fencing Co
280 N Midland Ave Bldg W (07663-5708)
PHONE..............................201 797-3332
Fax: 201 797-9190
Jing Xi Chen, *President*
▲ **EMP:** 10
SQ FT: 3,600
SALES (est): 1.1MM **Privately Held**
WEB: www.blue-gauntlet.com
SIC: 3315 5039 5211 Fencing made in wiredrawing plants; wire fence, gates & accessories; fencing

(G-9756)
BLUE MONKEY INC
Also Called: Speed Center USA
456b Sylvan St (07663-6107)
PHONE..............................201 805-0055
Joseph Saade, *President*
EMP: 4
SQ FT: 5,000
SALES (est): 300K **Privately Held**
WEB: www.speedcenterusa.com
SIC: 2211 Denims

(G-9757)
CHEFLER FOODS LLC
400 Lyster Ave (07663-5910)
PHONE..............................201 596-3710
Michael Leffler, *CEO*
Michael Kurland, *CFO*
EMP: 10 **EST:** 2016
SQ FT: 92,000
SALES (est): 583.5K **Privately Held**
SIC: 2833 3089 Vegetable oils; medicinal grade: refined or concentrated; tubs, plastic (containers)

(G-9758)
CHEMAID LABORATORIES INC (DH)
100 Mayhill St (07663-5302)
P.O. Box 888 (07663-0888)
PHONE..............................201 843-3300
Fax: 201 843-5579
Roy Reiner, *President*
Marc Reiner, *Vice Pres*
▲ **EMP:** 102
SQ FT: 75,000
SALES (est): 30.4MM
SALES (corp-wide): 91.8MM **Privately Held**
WEB: www.chemaidlabs.com
SIC: 2844 Cosmetic preparations

(G-9759)
CLARITY IMAGING TECH INC
250 Pehle Ave Ste 402 (07663-5832)
PHONE..............................877 272-4362
EMP: 28
SALES (corp-wide): 439.3K **Privately Held**
SIC: 3555 Printing trade parts & attachments
HQ: Clarity Imaging Technologies, Inc.
4350 Haddonfield Rd # 300
Pennsauken NJ 08109

(G-9760)
CRESSI SUB USA
3 Rosol Ln (07663-5501)
PHONE..............................201 594-1450
Antonio Cressi, *President*
Robert Cooper, *Manager*
◆ **EMP:** 5
SALES (est): 717.1K
SALES (corp-wide): 34MM **Privately Held**
SIC: 3949 Sporting & athletic goods
PA: Cressi Sub Spa
Via Gelasio Adamoli 501
Genova GE 16165
010 830-791

(G-9761)
CYTEC INDUSTRIES INC (HQ)
Also Called: Cytec Solvay Group
250 Pehle Ave Ste 306 (07663-5837)
P.O. Box 376, Little Falls (07424-0376)
PHONE..............................973 357-3100
Fax: 973 357-3050
Shane D Fleming, *Ch of Bd*
Frank Aranzana, *President*
Andrew Burke, *Vice Pres*
Roy D Smith, *Vice Pres*
Ying Meng Song, *Vice Pres*
▼ **EMP:** 250
SALES (est): 2B
SALES (corp-wide): 10MM **Privately Held**
SIC: 2899 2821 2672 2851 Chemical preparations; water treating compounds; plastics materials & resins; adhesive backed films, foams & foils; paints & allied products; cellulosic manmade fibers; industrial inorganic chemicals
PA: Solvay Sa
Rue De Ransbeek 310
Bruxelles 1120
226 421-11

(G-9762)
DIAZ FOODS
4 Rosol Ln (07663-5503)
P.O. Box 870 (07663-0870)
PHONE..............................404 629-3616
Rene M Diaz, *CEO*
Marsh Selaya, *Vice Chairman*
EMP: 100
SQ FT: 2,000
SALES: 200MM **Privately Held**
SIC: 2038 Frozen specialties

(G-9763)
EASTERN CONCRETE MATERIALS INC (HQ)
Also Called: Nyc Concrete Materials
250 Pehle Ave Ste 503 (07663-5832)
PHONE..............................201 797-7979
Michael K Gentoso, *President*
William Steele, *Vice Pres*
EMP: 106

SALES (est): 54MM
SALES (corp-wide): 1.3B **Publicly Held**
SIC: 3273 1429 1442 Ready-mixed concrete; trap rock, crushed & broken-quarrying; construction sand mining; gravel mining
PA: U.S. Concrete, Inc.
331 N Main St
Euless TX 76039
817 835-4105

(G-9764)
ENTERPRISE CONTAINER LLC (PA)
575 N Midland Ave (07663-5505)
PHONE..............................201 797-7200
Jim Breit, *COO*
Gary Berkowitz,
Edward Berkowitz,
Rochelle Berkowitz,
EMP: 11
SALES (est): 2.4MM **Privately Held**
SIC: 2653 Boxes, corrugated: made from purchased materials; pads, solid fiber: made from purchased materials

(G-9765)
FASTPULSE TECHNOLOGY INC
Also Called: Lasermetrics Division
220 Midland Ave (07663-6404)
PHONE..............................973 478-5757
Fax: 201 478-6115
Robert Goldstein, *Ch of Bd*
Steven Goldstein, *President*
Mark Percevault, *Manager*
Marion Goldstein, *Admin Sec*
EMP: 14
SQ FT: 5,000
SALES: 1.5MM **Privately Held**
WEB: www.fastpulse.com
SIC: 3699 Laser systems & equipment

(G-9766)
GEL UNITED LTD LIABILITY CO
635 N Midland Ave 3184 (07663-5523)
PHONE..............................855 435-8683
Emad William Awadalla, *CEO*
EMP: 4
SALES (est): 226K **Privately Held**
SIC: 2822 Synthetic rubber

(G-9767)
GRATEFUL PED INC
Also Called: Levy & Rappel
339 10th St (07663-6315)
PHONE..............................973 478-6511
Fax: 973 478-1760
Robert Kramer, *President*
EMP: 16
SQ FT: 5,500
SALES: 1MM **Privately Held**
WEB: www.levyandrappel.com
SIC: 3842 8011 Orthopedic appliances; offices & clinics of medical doctors

(G-9768)
HISPANIC OUTLOOK IN HIGHER
299 Market St Ste 140 (07663-5312)
P.O. Box 68, Paramus (07653-0068)
PHONE..............................201 587-8800
Fax: 201 587-9105
Jose Lopez ISA, *President*
Nicole Lopez ISA, *Vice Pres*
EMP: 7
SQ FT: 28,000
SALES: 728.9K **Privately Held**
SIC: 2731 Book publishing

(G-9769)
INTERNATIONAL CHEFS INC
33 Bella Vista Ave (07663-4803)
PHONE..............................917 645-2900
Mike Khalil, *President*
Joseph Khalil, *Vice Pres*
EMP: 15 **EST:** 1970
SQ FT: 20,000
SALES: 8.5MM **Privately Held**
SIC: 2099 Ready-to-eat meals, salads & sandwiches

(G-9770)
INTERNATIONAL MOLASSES CORP
88 Market St Fl 2 (07663-4830)
PHONE..............................201 368-8036
Ronald Targan, *President*

▲ = Import ▼=Export
◆ =Import/Export

Thomas McNiellie, *Vice Pres*
John Johansen, *Manager*
EMP: 20
SALES (est): 1.7MM **Privately Held**
SIC: 5149 2083 2061 Molasses, industrial; malt; raw cane sugar

(G-9771)
KAY WINDOW FASHIONS INC
271 2nd St (07663-6201)
PHONE..................862 591-1554
Fax: 862 591-1557
Jeffrey Kleinstein, *CEO*
Sol Kleinstein, *President*
Joseph Kleinstein, *Vice Pres*
EMP: 10
SALES (est): 910K **Privately Held**
SIC: 2591 Window shades; blinds vertical

(G-9772)
MALT PRODUCTS CORPORATION (PA)
88 Market St (07663-4830)
P.O. Box 898 (07663-0898)
PHONE..................201 845-4420
Amy Targen, *President*
Ronald G Targen, *President*
Joe Hickenbottom, *Vice Pres*
Nathan Mandelbaum, *Treasurer*
David Mandelbaum, *Admin Sec*
▼ **EMP:** 35
SALES (est): 182MM **Privately Held**
SIC: 2083 2087 Malt; malt byproducts; flavoring extracts & syrups

(G-9773)
MALT PRODUCTS CORPORATION
88 Market St (07663-4830)
PHONE..................201 845-9106
Chuck Stewart, *Superintendent*
EMP: 30
SALES (corp-wide): 182MM **Privately Held**
SIC: 2083 2087 Malt; malt byproducts; flavoring extracts & syrups
PA: Malt Products Corporation
88 Market St
Saddle Brook NJ 07663
201 845-4420

(G-9774)
MEESE INC (HQ)
Also Called: Modroto
535 N Midland Ave (07663-5505)
PHONE..................201 796-4490
William J Tingue, *Ch of Bd*
Ryan, *President*
Karla Renecker, *Opers Staff*
John H Hurst, *CFO*
John Hurst, *CFO*
▼ **EMP:** 35 **EST:** 1931
SQ FT: 35,000
SALES (est): 7.3MM
SALES (corp-wide): 107.8MM **Privately Held**
WEB: www.modroto.com
SIC: 3089 2394 3443 Plastic containers, except foam; canvas & related products; containers, shipping (bombs, etc.): metal plate
PA: Tingue, Brown & Co.
535 N Midland Ave
Saddle Brook NJ 07663
201 796-4490

(G-9775)
MIDLAND SCREEN PRINTING INC
280 N Midland Ave Ste 218 (07663-5708)
PHONE..................201 703-0066
Fax: 201 703-8238
Robert Witrak, *President*
EMP: 15
SALES: 710K **Privately Held**
SIC: 2759 2395 Screen printing; embroidery products, except schiffli machine

(G-9776)
MJSE LLC
Also Called: Fairfield Stamping
374 N Midland Ave (07663-5702)
P.O. Box 8358 (07663-8358)
PHONE..................201 791-9888
Steve Orkenyi,

Micheal Rebuth,
John Ross,
EMP: 10 **EST:** 1976
SQ FT: 5,500
SALES: 1MM **Privately Held**
WEB: www.fairfieldstamping.com
SIC: 3469 Metal stampings

(G-9777)
MUELLER DIE CUT SOLUTIONS INC
150 N Midland Ave (07663-5926)
P.O. Box 510 (07663-0510)
PHONE..................201 791-5000
Pete Futia, *General Mgr*
EMP: 50
SALES (corp-wide): 19.7MM **Privately Held**
SIC: 3053 Gaskets, packing & sealing devices
PA: Mueller Die Cut Solutions, Inc.
10415 Westlake Dr
Charlotte NC 28273
704 588-3900

(G-9778)
NTT ELECTRONICS AMERICA INC
250 Pehle Ave Ste 706 (07663-5832)
PHONE..................201 556-1770
Keiichi Kurakazu, *President*
Leonardo Castro, *Engineer*
Keigo Matsumura, *Treasurer*
Paul Chalifour, *Director*
EMP: 10
SQ FT: 2,500
SALES: 25MM
SALES (corp-wide): 110.7B **Privately Held**
WEB: www.nel-world.com
SIC: 3661 Switchboards, telephone or telegraph
HQ: Ntt Electronics Corporation
1-1-32, Shin-Urashimacho, Kanagawa-Ku
Yokohama KNG 221-0
454 149-700

(G-9779)
PAM INTERNATIONAL CO INC (PA)
45 Mayhill St (07663-5301)
P.O. Box 741, Hackettstown (07840-0741)
PHONE..................201 291-1200
Fax: 732 291-0021
Don E Kreiter, *Ch of Bd*
Karen Scholz, *President*
Deborah Kreiter, *Vice Pres*
▲ **EMP:** 90
SQ FT: 205,000
SALES (est): 5.4MM **Privately Held**
WEB: www.pamint.com
SIC: 2541 2542 Store & office display cases & fixtures; store fixtures, wood; office & store showcases & display fixtures; fixtures, store: except wood

(G-9780)
PARADIGM PACKAGING EAST LLC (DH)
141 5th St (07663-6125)
PHONE..................201 909-3400
Fax: 201 291-3855
Robert Donnahoo, *President*
▼ **EMP:** 200 **EST:** 1995
SALES (est): 64.4MM
SALES (corp-wide): 12.9MM **Privately Held**
WEB: www.paradigmpackaging.com
SIC: 3053 Packing materials
HQ: Comar, Llc
220 Laurel Rd Fl 2
Voorhees NJ 08043
856 692-6100

(G-9781)
PEOPLES EDUCTL HOLDINGS INC (PA)
Also Called: Mastery Education
299 Market St Ste 240 (07663-5312)
P.O. Box 513 (07663-0513)
PHONE..................201 712-0090
James J Peoples, *Ch of Bd*
Brian T Beckwith, *President*
Michael L Demarco, *CFO*

EMP: 195
SQ FT: 23,000
SALES (est): 25.6MM **Publicly Held**
WEB: www.peoplespublishing.com
SIC: 2731 Books: publishing & printing

(G-9782)
PETER THOMAS ROTH LABS LLC
45 Mayhill St (07663-5301)
PHONE..................201 329-9100
Fax: 201 329-9440
Barbara Hubbard, *Research*
June Jacobs, *Manager*
EMP: 110
SALES (corp-wide): 28.2MM **Privately Held**
SIC: 2844 Cosmetic preparations
PA: Peter Thomas Roth Labs Llc
460 Park Ave Fl 16
New York NY 10022
212 581-5800

(G-9783)
POSTCARD PRESS INC
435 N Midland Ave (07663-5527)
PHONE..................310 747-3878
EMP: 31
SALES (corp-wide): 9.5MM **Privately Held**
SIC: 2759 Visiting cards (including business): printing
PA: Postcard Press, Inc.
8000 Haskell Ave
Van Nuys CA 91406
310 747-3800

(G-9784)
PRIME INGREDIENTS INC
280 N Midland Ave Ste 340 (07663-5721)
PHONE..................201 791-6655
Fax: 201 791-4244
James Walsh, *President*
Tim Walsh, *Prdtn Mgr*
Walter Maurer, *Accounts Exec*
Robin Tecchio, *Sales Mgr*
Sandy Williams, *Sales Associate*
EMP: 9
SQ FT: 17,000
SALES (est): 1.3MM **Privately Held**
WEB: www.primeingredients.com
SIC: 2087 Food colorings; extracts, flavoring

(G-9785)
RFS COMMERCIAL
Also Called: Master Craft Interiors
280 N Midland Ave Bldg M (07663-5708)
PHONE..................201 796-0006
Fax: 201 440-5597
Anthony Pizzuto, *President*
Robert Pizzuto, *VP Opers*
Michael Pizzuto, *Sales Staff*
EMP: 24
SQ FT: 7,500
SALES: 4MM **Privately Held**
WEB: www.rugandfloors.com
SIC: 5021 2591 1771 2531 Furniture; window shades; concrete repair; flooring contractor; school furniture; library furniture

(G-9786)
RIBBLE COMPANY INC
Also Called: Saddle Brook Controls
280 N Midland Ave Ste 380 (07663-5719)
P.O. Box 881 (07663-0881)
PHONE..................201 475-1812
Fax: 201 791-0393
Gary F Laurita, *President*
Mark Bastinck, *Vice Pres*
Alan Kowal, *Vice Pres*
Michael Montalbano, *Treasurer*
Mike Montalbano, *Manager*
EMP: 19 **EST:** 1933
SQ FT: 10,700
SALES: 18MM **Privately Held**
WEB: www.saddlebrookcontrols.com
SIC: 5065 3823 Electronic parts & equipment; computer interface equipment for industrial process control

(G-9787)
RISING HEALTH LLC
Park 80 W Plz (07663)
PHONE..................201 961-9000

Walter Kaczmarek, *COO*
Steven S Rogers,
EMP: 50 **EST:** 2016
SQ FT: 4,000
SALES (est): 2.2MM
SALES (corp-wide): 638.3MM **Publicly Held**
SIC: 2834 5122 Pharmaceutical preparations; drugs & drug proprietaries
HQ: Rising Pharmaceuticals, Inc.
Park 80 W Plz I 250 Pehle
Saddle Brook NJ 07663

(G-9788)
RISING PHARMACEUTICALS INC (HQ)
Park 80 W Plz I 250 Pehle (07663)
PHONE..................201 961-9000
Fax: 201 961-1234
Albert L Eilender, *CEO*
Douglas Roth, *CFO*
EMP: 50
SALES (est): 11.4MM
SALES (corp-wide): 638.3MM **Publicly Held**
SIC: 2834 5122 Pharmaceutical preparations; drugs & drug proprietaries
PA: Aceto Corporation
4 Tri Harbor Ct
Port Washington NY 11050
516 627-6000

(G-9789)
SALERNOS KITCHEN CABINETS
Also Called: Salerno's Custom Cabinetry
599 N Midland Ave (07663-5505)
PHONE..................201 794-1990
Fax: 201 794-6992
Luciano Salerno, *President*
Peter Salerno, *Vice Pres*
EMP: 32
SQ FT: 4,000
SALES (est): 4.3MM **Privately Held**
WEB: www.salernos.com
SIC: 2511 2434 2431 Wood household furniture; wood kitchen cabinets; millwork

(G-9790)
SCHEINERT & SONS INC
Also Called: Sidney Scheinert & Son
404 N Midland Ave 2 (07663-5707)
P.O. Box 527 (07663-0527)
PHONE..................201 791-4600
Fax: 201 791-8551
Richard P Scheinert, *President*
Irwin Scheinert, *Vice Pres*
Margaret Scheinert, *Treasurer*
Barbara Scheinert, *Admin Sec*
▲ **EMP:** 25 **EST:** 1902
SQ FT: 75,000
SALES (est): 6.8MM **Privately Held**
SIC: 5085 5072 3452 Fasteners, industrial: nuts, bolts, screws, etc.; bolts, nuts & screws; bolts, nuts, rivets & washers

(G-9791)
SCODIX INC
250 Pehle Ave Ste 101 (07663-5833)
PHONE..................855 726-3491
Kobi Bar, *CEO*
Roy Porat, *CEO*
Yaron Hermeche, *CFO*
Atara Lev, *Human Resources*
Amit Shvartz, *VP Mktg*
◆ **EMP:** 10
SALES (est): 70.9K **Privately Held**
SIC: 2752 Commercial printing, offset

(G-9792)
SEALED AIR CORPORATION
301 Mayhill St (07663-5303)
PHONE..................201 712-7000
Fax: 201 712-1265
Richard Shanley, *Principal*
Rohn Shellenberger, *Business Mgr*
Diane Johansson, *Transptn Dir*
Margie Dorazio, *Plant Mgr*
Ed Ackershoek, *Opers Mgr*
EMP: 150
SALES (corp-wide): 4.4B **Publicly Held**
WEB: www.sealedair.com
SIC: 3086 Packaging & shipping materials, foamed plastic

PA: Sealed Air Corporation
2415 Cascade Pointe Blvd
Charlotte NC 28208
980 221-3235

(G-9793)
SEALED AIR CORPORATION
301 Mayhill St (07663-5303)
PHONE.............................973 890-4735
Wayne Sweet, *Branch Mgr*
EMP: 75
SALES (corp-wide): 4.4B Publicly Held
WEB: www.sealedair.com
SIC: 3086 Packaging & shipping materials,
foamed plastic
PA: Sealed Air Corporation
2415 Cascade Pointe Blvd
Charlotte NC 28208
980 221-3235

(G-9794)
SKW QUAB CHEMICALS INC
250 Pehle Ave Ste 403 (07663-5832)
PHONE.............................201 556-0300
Harold Feigenbaum, *President*
Karen Oneill, *Marketing Staff*
Karen O'Neill, *Director*
◆ EMP: 19
SQ FT: 2,700
SALES (est): 25MM
SALES (corp-wide): 241.5MM Privately
Held
SIC: 2899 Chemical preparations
PA: Skw Stahl-Metallurgie Holding Ag
Prinzregentenstr. 68
Munchen 81675
895 998-9230

(G-9795)
SYMRISE INC
250 Pehle Ave Ste 207 (07663-5832)
PHONE.............................201 288-3200
EMP: 5
SALES (corp-wide): 3.5B Privately Held
SIC: 2869 Perfume materials, synthetic;
flavors or flavoring materials, synthetic
HQ: Symrise Inc.
300 North St
Teterboro NJ 07608
201 288-3200

(G-9796)
TE WIRE & CABLE LLC
Also Called: PMC Thermocouple Division
107 5th St (07663-6125)
PHONE.............................201 845-9400
Fax: 201 291-1190
Robert M Canny, *Principal*
Pat Durkin, *Vice Pres*
Michael Mescall, *CFO*
▲ EMP: 120
SQ FT: 84,000
SALES: 48MM
SALES (corp-wide): 242.1B Publicly
Held
SIC: 3357 Nonferrous wiredrawing & insu-
lating
HQ: Marmon Holdings, Inc.
181 W Madison St Ste 2600
Chicago IL 60602
312 372-9500

(G-9797)
TOPPAN VINTAGE INC
109 5th St (07663-6157)
PHONE.............................201 226-9220
Bob Cesarano, *Branch Mgr*
EMP: 35
SALES (corp-wide): 21MM Privately
Held
SIC: 8732 2759 Merger, acquisition & re-
organization research; commercial print-
ing; financial note & certificate printing &
engraving; security certificates: engraved
PA: Toppan Vintage Inc.
747 3rd Ave Fl 7
New York NY 10017
212 596-7747

(G-9798)
UNILUX INC (HQ)
59 5th St (07663-6113)
PHONE.............................201 712-1266
Fax: 201 712-1366
Steven A Hirsh, *Ch of Bd*
Steven Hirsh, *Ch of Bd*

Michael P Simonis, *President*
John Banek, *Vice Pres*
Tom Herold, *Vice Pres*
▼ EMP: 28 EST: 1972
SQ FT: 20,000
SALES (est): 6.6MM
SALES (corp-wide): 3.6MM Privately
Held
WEB: www.unilux.com
SIC: 3648 Lighting equipment
PA: Astro Communications, Inc
630 Dundee Rd Ste 345
Northbrook IL
847 236-4121

(G-9799)
VIZIFLEX SEELS INC
406 N Midland Ave (07663-5707)
PHONE.............................201 488-3446
Sergio Gonzalez, *President*
Devin Gonzalez, *Vice Pres*
Loretta Afif,
EMP: 15
SQ FT: 20,000
SALES (est): 3MM Privately Held
WEB: www.viziflex.com
SIC: 3053 Gaskets, packing & sealing de-
vices

(G-9800)
WESTLOCK CONTROLS
CORPORATION (HQ)
280 N Midland Ave Ste 232 (07663-5717)
PHONE.............................201 794-7650
Ronald Bozzo, *President*
Joel Wittkamp, *Purch Mgr*
Alan Kerstner, *Engineer*
Ron Bozzo, *VP Finance*
Bill Jones, *Sales Mgr*
▲ EMP: 120
SQ FT: 46,000
SALES (est): 33.7MM
SALES (corp-wide): 2.7B Publicly Held
WEB: www.westlockcontrols.com
SIC: 3492 Control valves, fluid power: hy-
draulic & pneumatic
PA: Crane Co.
100 1st Stamford Pl # 300
Stamford CT 06902
203 363-7300

(G-9801)
WISCO PROMO & UNIFORM INC
160 Us Highway 46 (07663-6228)
PHONE.............................973 767-2022
Charlotte Yeon, *CEO*
▲ EMP: 5
SALES: 928.2K Privately Held
SIC: 2759 Screen printing

Saddle River
Bergen County

(G-9802)
ALLIANCE CORRUGATED BOX
INC
10 E Saddle River Rd (07458-3205)
P.O. Box 1471, Secaucus (07096-1471)
PHONE.............................877 525-5269
Eric Levine, *President*
EMP: 20 EST: 2015
SQ FT: 110,000
SALES (est): 333.8K Privately Held
SIC: 2653 5113 3086 5199 Boxes, corru-
gated: made from purchased materials;
corrugated & solid fiber boxes; packaging
& shipping materials, foamed plastic;
packaging materials

Salem
Salem County

(G-9803)
BLACKHAWK CRE
CORPORATION (PA)
25 New Market St (08079-1408)
PHONE.............................856 887-0162
Don Zappley, *President*
Robert Keonopka, *Vice Pres*
John Scott, *CFO*

EMP: 10
SQ FT: 12,000
SALES: 5.6MM Privately Held
SIC: 3444 5013 3613 Sheet metalwork;
automotive servicing equipment;
switchgear & switchboard apparatus

(G-9804)
COOPER INTERCONNECT
23 S Front St (08079-1342)
PHONE.............................856 935-7560
Curt Andersson, *President*
EMP: 5 EST: 2013
SALES (est): 417.1K Privately Held
SIC: 3646 3679 Commercial indusl & insti-
tutional electric lighting fixtures; electronic
loads & power supplies

(G-9805)
D AND M DISCOUNT FUELS
383 E Broadway (08079-1146)
PHONE.............................856 935-0919
Dean Wood, *Principal*
EMP: 7 EST: 2011
SALES (est): 739.8K Privately Held
SIC: 2869 Fuels

(G-9806)
MANNINGTON MILLS INC (PA)
Also Called: Mannington Rsilient Floors Div
75 Mannington Mills Rd (08079-2009)
P.O. Box 30 (08079-0030)
PHONE.............................856 935-3000
Fax: 856 339-5910
Russel Grizzel, *CEO*
Keith S Campbell, *Ch of Bd*
Thomas S Davis, *President*
Dennis Bradway, *General Mgr*
Kim Speakman, *General Mgr*
◆ EMP: 600 EST: 1915
SQ FT: 1,000,000
SALES (est): 774.9MM Privately Held
WEB: www.mannington.com
SIC: 3996 3253 2273 2435 Hard surface
floor coverings; wall tile, ceramic; floor
tile, ceramic; rugs, tufted; carpets, hand &
machine made; veneer stock, hardwood;
hardwood plywood, prefinished; panels,
hardwood plywood; plywood, hardwood
or hardwood faced

(G-9807)
MEDIANEWS GROUP INC
Also Called: Evening News, The
93 5th St (08079-1041)
P.O. Box 596, Bridgeton (08302-0490)
PHONE.............................856 451-1000
Frank Gargano, *President*
EMP: 85
SALES (corp-wide): 4.3B Privately Held
SIC: 2711 Newspapers: publishing only,
not printed on site
HQ: Medianews Group, Inc.
101 W Colfax Ave Ste 1100
Denver CO 80202

(G-9808)
PRINTERS OF SALEM COUNTY
LLC
38 Market St (08079-1902)
PHONE.............................856 935-5032
Eric Pankok, *Owner*
EMP: 5
SALES (est): 602.5K Privately Held
SIC: 2752 Commercial printing, offset

(G-9809)
SALEM PACKING CO
705 Salem Quinton Rd (08079-1288)
P.O. Box 131 (08079-0131)
PHONE.............................856 878-0002
Fax: 856 935-2481
Josephine Bonaccurso, *President*
Samuel Bonaccurso, *Vice Pres*
Anthony Bonaccurso, *Manager*
EMP: 20
SQ FT: 3,000
SALES (est): 2.6MM Privately Held
SIC: 2011 Meat packing plants

(G-9810)
WIRE-PRO INC (DH)
Also Called: Wpi-Salem Division
90 W Broadway (08079-1301)
PHONE.............................856 935-7560
Fax: 856 935-7555

Henry J Barbera, *President*
Gerald Eddis, *President*
Robert A Barbera, *Vice Pres*
Robert Oldstein, *CFO*
◆ EMP: 140 EST: 1971
SQ FT: 7,500
SALES (est): 36.2MM Privately Held
WEB: www.wpi-interconnect.com
SIC: 3678 3679 Electronic connectors;
harness assemblies for electronic use:
wire or cable
HQ: Cooper Crouse-Hinds, Llc
1201 Wolf St
Syracuse NY 13208
866 764-5454

Sandyston
Sussex County

(G-9811)
CUSTOM DOCKS INC
Also Called: Bob's Custom Docks
234 Us Highway 206 N (07826-8000)
PHONE.............................973 948-3732
Fax: 973 948-2729
Robert Putera, *President*
EMP: 10
SQ FT: 12,000
SALES (est): 896.5K Privately Held
WEB: www.customdocks.net
SIC: 3999 5551 Dock equipment & sup-
plies, industrial; boat dealers

Sayreville
Middlesex County

(G-9812)
AKAY USA LLC
500 Hartle St (08872-2770)
PHONE.............................732 254-7177
Rajive Joseph, *General Mgr*
Shaji Vilson,
▲ EMP: 2
SALES: 8.5MM Privately Held
SIC: 2087 Powders, flavoring (except
drink)

(G-9813)
ALL NATURAL PRODUCTS
4000 Bordentown Ave # 20 (08872-2752)
PHONE.............................212 391-2870
Gene Davidovich, *Owner*
EMP: 10
SALES: 950K Privately Held
SIC: 2051 Bread, cake & related products

(G-9814)
ALZO INTERNATIONAL INC
650 Jernee Mill Rd (08872-1755)
PHONE.............................732 254-1901
Albert A Zofchak, *President*
Joyce Zofchak, *Vice Pres*
▲ EMP: 30
SQ FT: 71,000
SALES (est): 13.3MM Privately Held
WEB: www.alzointernational.com
SIC: 2869 Perfume materials, synthetic

(G-9815)
BENCHMARK SCIENTIFIC INC
2600a Main St (08872-1462)
P.O. Box 709, Edison (08818-0709)
PHONE.............................908 769-5555
Tony Damsia, *President*
▲ EMP: 50
SALES (est): 6.1MM Privately Held
SIC: 3821 Autoclaves, laboratory

(G-9816)
CHARIOT COURIER & TRANS
SVCS
7 Parr Dr (08872-1084)
PHONE.............................888 532-9125
Tina Marshall, *VP Opers*
Keith Marshall,
EMP: 10
SALES (est): 318.2K Privately Held
SIC: 4213 2759 7389 Automobiles, trans-
port & delivery; contract haulers; heavy
hauling; schedules, transportation: print-
ing;

(G-9817)
CHEMO DYNAMICS INC
3 Crossman Rd S (08872-1404)
PHONE.................................732 721-4700
Fax: 732 721-6835
Subir Chakraborty, *President*
Sunder N Bharathi, *Vice Pres*
Tao Jiang, *Research*
EMP: 10
SQ FT: 16,000
SALES (est): 1.9MM **Privately Held**
WEB: www.chemodynamics.com
SIC: 2869 8734 Perfumes, flavorings &
food additives; food testing service

(G-9818)
**COAST TO COAST LEA & VINYL
INC (PA)**
1 Crossman Rd S (08872-1404)
PHONE.................................732 525-8877
Fax: 732 525-2726
Pamela Ross, *President*
Michael Ross, *Vice Pres*
▲ **EMP:** 9
SQ FT: 10,000
SALES (est): 2MM **Privately Held**
WEB: www.coast2coastleather.com
SIC: 3111 Mechanical leather

(G-9819)
CRA-Z WORKS CO INC
Also Called: East Coast Custom
242 Main St (08872-1190)
PHONE.................................732 390-8238
Fax: 732 390-1651
Benjamin Pendleton, *President*
EMP: 6
SQ FT: 1,000
SALES (est): 849.8K **Privately Held**
SIC: 2329 5699 Athletic (warmup, sweat &
jogging) suits: men's & boys'; sports ap-
parel

(G-9820)
DMJ AND ASSOCIATES INC
27 William St (08872-1144)
PHONE.................................732 613-7867
Daniel Vitti, *President*
James Morris, *Vice Pres*
EMP: 20
SALES (est): 2.2MM **Privately Held**
SIC: 4841 3663 1623 1711 Direct broadcast satellite services (DBS); multipoint
distribution systems services (MDS);
satellite master antenna systems services
(SMATV); television broadcasting & communications equipment; water & sewer
line construction; plumbing, heating, air-
conditioning contractors; installing building equipment; electrical apparatus &
equipment; electronic wire & cable; electrical construction materials

(G-9821)
**GERDAU AMRSTEEL
SAYREVILLE INC**
N Crossman Rd (08872)
P.O. Box 249 (08871-0249)
PHONE.................................732 721-6600
Peter Campo, *President*
Zilmar Cardoso, *General Mgr*
Carl Czarnik, *Vice Pres*
Jim Kerkvliet, *Vice Pres*
Andre Pires, *Vice Pres*
▲ **EMP:** 45000
SALES (est): 228.8MM **Privately Held**
SIC: 3312 Blast furnaces & steel mills;
bars & bar shapes, steel, hot-rolled
HQ: Gerdau Usa Inc.
4221 W Boy Scout Blvd
Tampa FL 33607
813 286-8383

(G-9822)
GREATER MEDIA NEWSPAPERS
201 Hartle St Ste B (08872-1883)
PHONE.................................732 254-7004
Kevin Whitman, *Branch Mgr*
EMP: 4
SALES (corp-wide): 232.1MM **Publicly
Held**
SIC: 2711 Newspapers, publishing & print-
ing

HQ: Greater Media Newspapers
198 Us Highway 9 Ste 100
Englishtown NJ 07726
732 358-5200

(G-9823)
HOMESPUN GLOBAL LLC
4000 Bordentown Ave # 18 (08872-2752)
PHONE.................................917 674-9684
Neeraj Jalan, *President*
Manoj Purohit, *Vice Pres*
Rajat Srivastava,
EMP: 5
SQ FT: 1,000
SALES (est): 15MM **Privately Held**
SIC: 5719 5023 2211 Bedding (sheets,
blankets, spreads & pillows); towels;
sheets, textile; linens & towels; towels;
sheets & sheetings, cotton

(G-9824)
INTEGRITY IRONWORKS CORP
33 Brookside Ave (08872-1236)
P.O. Box 129 (08871-0129)
PHONE.................................732 254-2200
James Zagata, *President*
EMP: 5
SALES (est): 1.1MM **Privately Held**
SIC: 3446 Architectural metalwork

(G-9825)
JAY FRANCO & SONS INC
115 Kennedy Dr (08872-1459)
PHONE.................................732 721-0022
Paul Weldler, *VP Opers*
Sam Sutton, *Branch Mgr*
EMP: 100
SALES (corp-wide): 147.1MM **Privately
Held**
SIC: 2211 5023 Towels & toweling, cotton;
towels
PA: Jay Franco & Sons, Inc.
295 5th Ave Ste 312
New York NY 10016
212 679-3022

(G-9826)
KELKEN-GOLD INC
Also Called: Kelken Construction Systems
550 Hartle St Ste C (08872-2771)
PHONE.................................732 416-6730
Ken Ginsky, *President*
Richard Gonzalez, *Vice Pres*
Peter Coutin, *Treasurer*
EMP: 5
SQ FT: 4,000
SALES: 1.2MM **Privately Held**
WEB: www.kelken.com
SIC: 3272 Concrete products

(G-9827)
LCI GRAPHICS INC
2400 Main St Ste 8 (08872-1474)
PHONE.................................973 893-2913
Fax: 973 893-8214
Dan Seratelli Sr, *President*
Dan Seratelli Jr, *Exec VP*
Danielle Ross, *Manager*
EMP: 16
SQ FT: 5,000
SALES (est): 1.6MM **Privately Held**
WEB: www.lcigraphics.com
SIC: 2752 Commercial printing, offset

(G-9828)
LEETS STEEL INC
495 Raritan St (08872-1466)
PHONE.................................917 416-7977
John Miranda, *President*
EMP: 6
SALES (est): 245.2K **Privately Held**
SIC: 3446 3441 1791 Ornamental metal-
work; fabricated structural metal; struc-
tural steel erection

(G-9829)
LIPPMAN ENTERPRISES LLC
250 Kennedy Dr Fl 2 (08872-1468)
PHONE.................................732 316-4946
Deborah Lippman, *Mng Member*
EMP: 21
SALES (est): 2.1MM **Privately Held**
SIC: 2844 Cosmetic preparations

(G-9830)
LIVING FASHIONS LLC
602 Hartle St (08872)
PHONE.................................732 626-5200
Yousuf Admani,
EMP: 10
SALES (est): 383.1K **Privately Held**
SIC: 5023 2392 2252 Linens & towels;
table mats, plastic & textile; men's, boys'
& girls' hosiery

(G-9831)
LUNAR AUDIO VIDEO LLC
701 Hartle St Unit 703 (08872-2774)
P.O. Box 58, Pequannock (07440-0058)
PHONE.................................973 233-7700
Chris Young, *Owner*
John Remelgado, *Project Mgr*
▲ **EMP:** 8
SALES (est): 1.1MM **Privately Held**
SIC: 3651 Household audio & video equip-
ment

(G-9832)
MACTEC PACKAGING TECH LLC
550 Hartle St Ste A (08872-2771)
PHONE.................................732 343-1607
Michael Castaldo, *Mng Member*
Daniel Luna,
EMP: 4
SQ FT: 5,000
SALES: 1MM **Privately Held**
SIC: 3565 Packaging machinery

(G-9833)
**MAIN STREET AUTO & FUEL
LLC**
227 Main St (08872-1171)
PHONE.................................732 238-0044
▲ **EMP:** 7
SALES (est): 798.5K **Privately Held**
SIC: 2869 Mfg Industrial Organic Chemi-
cals

(G-9834)
OEG BUILDING MATERIALS INC
6001 Bordentown Ave (08872)
PHONE.................................732 667-3636
Oscar Rosner, *President*
Asher Engel, *CFO*
EMP: 25
SALES (est): 17.3MM **Privately Held**
SIC: 3444 3441 Sheet metalwork; fabri-
cated structural metal

(G-9835)
**PHARMETIC MFG COMPANY
LLC**
650 Jernee Mill Rd (08872-1755)
PHONE.................................732 254-1901
Albert A Zofchak,
Joyce Zofchak,
▲ **EMP:** 6
SALES (est): 850K **Privately Held**
SIC: 2869 Perfume materials, synthetic

(G-9836)
**PREMIER PRINTING SOLUTIONS
LLC**
508 Raritan St Ste D (08872-1429)
PHONE.................................732 525-0740
Carol Ciak, *Owner*
Edward Ciak, *Vice Pres*
Kevin Ciak, *Treasurer*
EMP: 5
SALES (est): 150K **Privately Held**
SIC: 2752 7338 2261 2789 Commercial
printing, offset; secretarial & typing serv-
ice; printing of cotton broadwoven fabrics;
bookbinding & related work

(G-9837)
SABERT CORPORATION (PA)
2288 Main St (08872-1476)
PHONE.................................800 722-3781
Fax: 732 721-0622
Albert Salama, *President*
◆ **EMP:** 200
SQ FT: 250,000
SALES (est): 161.6MM **Privately Held**
WEB: www.sabert.com
SIC: 3089 Trays, plastic; plates, plastic;
food casings, plastic

(G-9838)
SABERT CORPORATION
879 Main St Ste 899 (08872-1463)
PHONE.................................732 721-5544
Fax: 732 721-0567
Albert Salama, *Branch Mgr*
EMP: 42
SALES (corp-wide): 161.6MM **Privately
Held**
SIC: 3089 Trays, plastic; plates, plastic;
food casings, plastic
PA: Sabert Corporation
2288 Main St
Sayreville NJ 08872
800 722-3781

(G-9839)
SKAFFLES GROUP LLC (PA)
115 Kennedy Dr (08872-1459)
PHONE.................................732 721-0022
Steven Shwekey, *Mng Member*
EMP: 2
SALES (est): 2.6MM **Privately Held**
SIC: 3999 Pet supplies

(G-9840)
STEIMLING & SON INC
7 Nickel Ave (08872-1717)
P.O. Box 283 (08871-0283)
PHONE.................................732 613-1550
Fax: 732 390-3317
Linda Steimling, *President*
EMP: 11
SQ FT: 15,000
SALES (est): 1.8MM **Privately Held**
SIC: 3599 Machine shop, jobbing & repair

(G-9841)
TMS INTERNATIONAL LLC
1 Crossman Rd N (08872-1402)
PHONE.................................732 721-7477
EMP: 5 **Privately Held**
SIC: 3312 Blast furnaces & steel mills
HQ: Tms International, Llc
12 Monongahela Ave
Glassport PA 15045
412 678-6141

(G-9842)
TURN-KEY TECHNOLOGIES INC
2400 Main St Ste 11 (08872-1474)
PHONE.................................732 553-9100
Craig Badrick, *President*
Stephen Murray, *Vice Pres*
Steve Badrick, *Exec Dir*
EMP: 18
SQ FT: 6,000
SALES (est): 22.4MM **Privately Held**
WEB: www.turn-keytechnologies.com
SIC: 5065 7622 3663 Paging & signaling
equipment; radio repair shop; radio & TV
communications equipment

(G-9843)
ZOOMESSENCE INC
550 Hartle St Ste B (08872-2771)
PHONE.................................732 416-6638
Bruce Leskanic, *Branch Mgr*
EMP: 7
SALES (corp-wide): 5.5MM **Privately
Held**
SIC: 2899 2869 Chemical preparations;
flavors or flavoring materials, synthetic
PA: Zoomessence, Inc.
1131 Victory Pl
Hebron KY 41048
859 534-5974

Scotch Plains
Union County

(G-9844)
ALL ENVMTL & TANK SVCS LLC
2560 Us Highway 22 346 (07076-1529)
PHONE.................................908 755-2962
EMP: 13
SALES (est): 2.4MM **Privately Held**
SIC: 3795 Tanks & tank components

(G-9845)
ANDERSON PUBLISHING LTD
180 Glenside Ave (07076-1518)
PHONE.................................908 301-1995

Fax: 908 301-1997
Oliver Anderson, *President*
Brenda Anderson, *Vice Pres*
Michael T Hearney, *Controller*
EMP: 6
SALES (est): 700K **Privately Held**
WEB: www.appliedradiology.com
SIC: 2721 Trade journals: publishing only, not printed on site

(G-9846)
ART DMENSIONS
1998 Us Highway 22 (07076-1014)
PHONE......................908 322-8488
Bernice Pulido, *Owner*
EMP: 8
SALES (est): 847.4K **Privately Held**
WEB: www.artdmensions.com
SIC: 3993 Signs, not made in custom sign painting shops

(G-9847)
BE CU MANUFACTURING CO INC (PA)
2347 Beryllium Rd (07076-2194)
PHONE......................908 233-3342
Stephan Hoeckele, *President*
John Oshea, *Controller*
Tim Hoeckele, *Manager*
EMP: 25 **EST:** 1942
SQ FT: 18,000
SALES: 2.2MM **Privately Held**
SIC: 3469 Metal stampings

(G-9848)
CPL AROMAS INC
1812 Front St (07076-1103)
PHONE......................732 469-0680
Fax: 732 868-8332
Chris Pickthall, *CEO*
Clive Munday, *General Mgr*
Thomas Wan, *Managing Dir*
Angus McJannet, *Accounts Mgr*
Caryn Wolak, *Accounts Exec*
▲ **EMP:** 19
SALES (est): 3.7MM
SALES (corp-wide): 106MM **Privately Held**
WEB: www.cplaromas.com
SIC: 2844 Perfumes & colognes; cosmetic preparations
HQ: Cpl Aromas Limited
Innovation House
Bishop's Stortford HERTS CM23
127 950-2300

(G-9849)
GLEICHER MANUFACTURING CORP
851 Jerusalem Rd (07076-2039)
PHONE......................908 233-2211
Fax: 800 233-2292
Charles Gleicher, *President*
Chick Gleicher, *President*
Maxine Gleicher, *Corp Secy*
EMP: 25 **EST:** 1937
SQ FT: 22,000
SALES (est): 7.9MM **Privately Held**
WEB: www.gleicher.com
SIC: 2675 2672 2671 2295 Die-cut paper & board; coated & laminated paper; packaging paper & plastics film, coated & laminated; coated fabrics, not rubberized

(G-9850)
HNT INDUSTRIES INC
Also Called: Westbrook Industries
233 Union Ave (07076-1254)
PHONE......................908 322-0414
Kathleen Holmes, *CEO*
Mike Tatsch, *President*
EMP: 5 **EST:** 1945
SQ FT: 14,000
SALES: 500K **Privately Held**
SIC: 3469 Ornamental metal stampings

(G-9851)
HOBBY BLADE SPECIALTY INC
725 Jerusalem Rd (07076-2029)
PHONE......................908 317-9306
Mike Torres, *President*
Ada Falcon, *Vice Pres*
EMP: 4
SALES (est): 505K **Privately Held**
SIC: 3421 Razor blades & razors

(G-9852)
NATURES BEAUTY MARBLE & GRAN
2476 Plainfield Ave (07076-2057)
PHONE......................908 233-5300
Thelma Carinhas, *Owner*
EMP: 12
SALES (est): 1.1MM **Privately Held**
SIC: 5032 3281 Granite building stone; marble building stone; table tops, marble

(G-9853)
NEW SATELLITE NETWORK LLC
1942 Sunset Pl (07076-1207)
PHONE......................908 922-0967
Vladimir Makarenko, *Principal*
EMP: 4
SALES (est): 165.3K **Privately Held**
SIC: 2711 Newspapers

(G-9854)
SALESCASTER DISPLAYS CORP
2095 Portland Ave (07076-1849)
P.O. Box 247 (07076-0247)
PHONE......................908 322-3046
Dennis Tort, *President*
Mark Tort, *Vice Pres*
EMP: 5 **EST:** 1950
SQ FT: 10,000
SALES (est): 640K **Privately Held**
WEB: www.salescaster.com
SIC: 5046 3577 5063 Display equipment, except refrigerated; computer peripheral equipment; signaling equipment, electrical

(G-9855)
SECORD INC
1812 Front St (07076-1103)
PHONE......................908 754-2147
Ria Williams, *President*
EMP: 10
SALES (est): 1.1MM **Privately Held**
SIC: 2834 Pharmaceutical preparations

(G-9856)
SHOOTING STAR INC
2500 Plainfield Ave (07076-2057)
PHONE......................908 789-2500
Fax: 908 789-3356
Fred Andreae Jr, *President*
EMP: 4
SQ FT: 3,000
SALES (est): 527.4K **Privately Held**
WEB: www.shootingstar.net
SIC: 3999 Coin-operated amusement machines

(G-9857)
STRAHAN CONSULTING GROUP LLC
1290 Martine Ave (07076-2515)
PHONE......................908 790-0873
Paul Strahan, *Owner*
EMP: 4
SALES: 500K **Privately Held**
SIC: 7379 3571 7374 4813 Computer related consulting services; electronic computers; computer graphics service;

(G-9858)
SYNTHETIC SURFACES INC (PA)
2450 Plainfield Ave (07076-2042)
P.O. Box 241 (07076-0241)
PHONE......................908 233-6803
Norris Legue, *President*
Dorothy Legue, *Vice Pres*
Patricia Dicarlo, *Manager*
EMP: 4
SQ FT: 1,700
SALES: 2MM **Privately Held**
WEB: www.syntheticsurfacesinc.com
SIC: 2891 2851 8742 Adhesives; epoxy adhesives; lacquers, varnishes, enamels & other coatings; industrial consultant

Sea Bright
Monmouth County

(G-9859)
BIOXYGEN DISTRIBUTION CORP
370 Ocean Ave (07760-2112)
PHONE......................732 212-1799
Christopher Cappillo, *President*
Kevin Delgaudio, *VP Sales*
EMP: 4
SQ FT: 4,600
SALES (est): 308.6K **Privately Held**
SIC: 2813 Oxygen, compressed or liquefied

Sea Girt
Monmouth County

(G-9860)
140 MAIN STREET CORP
Also Called: Campbell's Pharmacy
2175 Highway 35 Ste 13 (08750-1009)
PHONE......................732 974-2929
Fax: 732 974-2644
Dennis Campbell, *President*
EMP: 10
SQ FT: 1,200
SALES (est): 2MM **Privately Held**
WEB: www.campbellspharmacy.com
SIC: 2834 5912 Pharmaceutical preparations; drug stores

(G-9861)
ADVANTAGE MOLDING PRODUCTS
2106 Highway 35 (08750-1002)
PHONE......................732 303-8667
Jacqueline Cassidy, *President*
Jackie Cassidy, *Opers Staff*
◆ **EMP:** 12
SQ FT: 5,000
SALES (est): 1.1MM **Privately Held**
SIC: 3089 Molding primary plastic

(G-9862)
ROCK SOLID WOODWORKING LLC
508 Washington Blvd Apt A (08750-2992)
PHONE......................732 974-1261
Marie Marrone, *Principal*
EMP: 4
SALES (est): 334.9K **Privately Held**
SIC: 2431 Millwork

Sea Isle City
Cape May County

(G-9863)
LARSEN MARINE SERVICES LLC
333 45th Pl (08243-1847)
P.O. Box 12 (08243-0012)
PHONE......................609 408-3564
Brian Larsen, *Mng Member*
Andrew Larsen,
EMP: 7
SALES: 800K **Privately Held**
SIC: 2499 Fencing, docks & other outdoor wood structural products

(G-9864)
SEA ISLE ICE CO INC (PA)
230 42nd St (08243-1952)
PHONE......................609 263-8748
Fax: 609 263-7775
Sue Ann Romano, *Vice Pres*
Joseph A Romano Sr, *Treasurer*
EMP: 25 **EST:** 1960
SQ FT: 8,000
SALES: 950K **Privately Held**
SIC: 2097 Manufactured ice

Secaucus
Hudson County

(G-9865)
ACME COSMETIC COMPONENTS LLC
80 Seaview Dr Ste 1 (07094-1828)
P.O. Box 449, Woodside NY (11377)
PHONE......................718 335-3000
Michael Roughton, *President*
David Wood,
▼ **EMP:** 39
SQ FT: 40,000
SALES (est): 9.3MM **Privately Held**
WEB: www.acmepans.com
SIC: 3469 Stamping metal for the trade

(G-9866)
AXG CORPORATION
700 Plaza Dr Ste 204 (07094-3604)
PHONE......................212 213-3313
Vince Di Mattia, *President*
EMP: 5
SALES (est): 37.8MM **Privately Held**
SIC: 2542 Office & store showcases & display fixtures

(G-9867)
BEACHCARTS USA
296 Julianne Ter (07094-4013)
PHONE......................201 319-0091
◆ **EMP:** 4
SALES (est): 266.5K **Privately Held**
SIC: 3949 Sporting & athletic goods

(G-9868)
BIGFLYSPORTS INC
Also Called: Bigflysports Com
60 Metro Way Ste 2 (07094-1913)
PHONE......................201 653-4414
Chris Maillet, *President*
Donja Bryan, *Accounts Mgr*
Marc Weinman, *Mng Member*
Harran Holmes, *Associate*
▲ **EMP:** 7 **EST:** 2008
SALES (est): 6.9MM **Privately Held**
SIC: 5941 4783 3999 Team sports equipment; water sport equipment; containerization of goods for shipping; barrettes

(G-9869)
BIND-RITE GRAPHICS INC
100 Castle Rd (07094-1602)
P.O. Box 2399 (07096-2399)
PHONE......................201 863-8100
Alan Mirson, *President*
Elliot Ward, *Vice Pres*
EMP: 35
SQ FT: 47,000
SALES (est): 6MM **Privately Held**
SIC: 2789 2678 Binding only: books, pamphlets, magazines, etc.; binding & repair of books, magazines & pamphlets; stationery products

(G-9870)
CALIGOR RX INC
801 Penhorn Ave Ste 4 (07094-2150)
PHONE......................212 988-0590
Fax: 212 879-8415
Tammy Bishop, *CEO*
EMP: 32 **EST:** 2011
SALES (est): 6.6MM **Privately Held**
SIC: 2834 Pharmaceutical preparations

(G-9871)
CAMEO CHINA INC
Also Called: Cameo China East
501 Penhorn Ave Ste 12 (07094-2136)
PHONE......................201 865-7650
Fax: 201 865-6068
Eric Lin, *Manager*
EMP: 5 **Privately Held**
WEB: www.cameochina.com
SIC: 3269 Figures: pottery, china, earthenware & stoneware
PA: Cameo China, Inc.
1938 Chico Ave
South El Monte CA 91733

(G-9872)
CLEVE SHIRTMAKERS INC
200 Meadowlands Pkwy # 2 (07094-2312)
P.O. Box 678, Saddle River (07458-0678)
PHONE....................................201 825-6122
David Stich, *President*
▲ EMP: 5
SALES (est): 390K **Privately Held**
WEB: www.cleveshirt.com
SIC: 2321 2331 Men's & boys' furnishings;
women's & misses' blouses & shirts

(G-9873)
COMMAND WEB OFFSET
COMPANY INC (PA)
100 Castle Rd (07094-1602)
P.O. Box 2399 (07096-2399)
PHONE....................................201 863-8100
Fax: 201 863-5443
Andrew Merson, *Ch of Bd*
Chris Huckleberry, *General Mgr*
Paul Frontczak, *Exec VP*
Charles B Gardner, *Exec VP*
Steven Merson, *Vice Pres*
EMP: 151 EST: 1946
SALES (est): 108.8MM **Privately Held**
WEB: www.commandweb.com
SIC: 2752 2732 Lithographing on metal;
books: printing only

(G-9874)
CR LAURENCE CO INC
70 Seaview Dr (07094-1807)
PHONE....................................201 770-1077
Peter Ascherl, *Branch Mgr*
EMP: 12
SALES (corp-wide): 29.7B **Privately Held**
WEB: www.crlaurence.com
SIC: 3231 Products of purchased glass
HQ: C.R. Laurence Co., Inc.
2503 E Vernon Ave
Vernon CA 90058
323 588-1281

(G-9875)
CREATIONS BY STEFANO INC
1261 Paterson Plank Rd (07094-3229)
PHONE....................................201 863-8337
Stefano Simone, *President*
EMP: 4
SALES (est): 340K **Privately Held**
SIC: 3911 Jewel settings & mountings, pre-
cious metal

(G-9876)
DELTA GALIL USA INC (HQ)
1 Harmon Plz Fl 5 (07094-2800)
PHONE....................................201 902-0055
Fax: 201 348-3624
Isaac Dabah, *CEO*
Colette Mynes, *President*
Noam Lautman, *Chairman*
Itzhak Weinstock, *COO*
Steven Mastrotietro, *Senior VP*
▲ EMP: 100
SQ FT: 22,000
SALES: 700MM
SALES (corp-wide): 1.3B **Privately Held**
SIC: 2341 Women's & children's undergar-
ments; women's & children's nightwear
PA: Delta Galil Industries Ltd.
45 Haeshel
Caesarea 30889
768 177-229

(G-9877)
DESIGNCORE LTD
585 Windsor Dr Ste 1 (07094-2759)
PHONE....................................718 499-0337
Joseph F Ianno, *President*
▲ EMP: 70
SQ FT: 100,000
SALES (est): 14.4MM **Privately Held**
SIC: 2541 2431 2521 Wood partitions &
fixtures; interior & ornamental woodwork
& trim; wood office furniture

(G-9878)
EMPORIUM LEATHER COMPANY
INC
Also Called: Royce Leather
501 Penhorn Ave Ste 9 (07094-2136)
PHONE....................................201 330-7720
Fax: 201 330-7660
Kathy Bauer, *President*

Harold Bauer, *Vice Pres*
Mark Tessler, *Controller*
Jean Saltos, *Cust Mgr*
Maria Izurieta, *Sales Executive*
◆ EMP: 20
SQ FT: 7,500
SALES: 5.3MM **Privately Held**
WEB: www.royceleathergifts.com
SIC: 3199 Equestrian related leather arti-
cles

(G-9879)
ESCADA US SUBCO LLC
55 Hartz Way Ste 17 (07094-2415)
PHONE....................................201 865-5200
Monica Arden, *Manager*
EMP: 318 **Privately Held**
SIC: 2339 Service apparel, wash-
able: women's; Army-Navy goods
PA: Escada America Llc
26 Main St
Chatham NJ 07928

(G-9880)
EUROPEAN AMRCN FOODS
GROUP INC
425 Route 3 (07094-3737)
P.O. Box 2427 (07096-2427)
PHONE....................................201 583-1101
Antonio R Fasolino, *CEO*
EMP: 265
SALES (corp-wide): 33.1MM **Privately**
Held
SIC: 2099 2079 Pasta, uncooked: pack-
aged with other ingredients; edible oil
products, except corn oil
PA: European American Foods Group
Company Inc.
698 Kennedy Blvd
Bayonne NJ 07002
201 436-6106

(G-9881)
EVENING JOURNAL
ASSOCIATION (HQ)
Also Called: Jersey Journal
1 Harmon Plz Ste 1000 (07094-2806)
PHONE....................................201 653-1000
Fax: 201 217-2459
Samuel Newhouse III, *President*
Lois Ditommaso, *Editor*
Ron Zeitlinger, *Editor*
Harvey Zucker, *Editor*
Denise Copeland, *COO*
▲ EMP: 15
SQ FT: 100,000
SALES (est): 6.1MM
SALES (corp-wide): 1.4B **Privately Held**
WEB: www.jjournal.com
SIC: 2711 Job printing & newspaper pub-
lishing combined
PA: Advance Digital Inc.
3100 Harborside Fincl 3
Jersey City NJ 07311
201 459-2808

(G-9882)
FAST-PAK TRADING INC
375 County Ave Ste 2 (07094-2618)
PHONE....................................201 293-4757
Ivanco Ivanovski, *Owner*
Kiro Ivanovski, *Co-Owner*
▲ EMP: 8
SQ FT: 75,000
SALES: 2.5MM **Privately Held**
WEB: www.fastpakstore.com
SIC: 5145 2032 2038 5149 Snack foods;
ethnic foods: canned, jarred, etc.; ethnic
foods, frozen; health foods

(G-9883)
FH GROUP INTERNATIONAL INC
265 Secaucus Rd (07094-2117)
PHONE....................................201 210-2426
Jin Hao, *Vice Pres*
Samantha Fang, *Vice Pres*
Linda Jiang, *Manager*
▲ EMP: 30
SQ FT: 60,000
SALES (est): 4.3MM **Privately Held**
SIC: 2273 2211 Aircraft & automobile floor
coverings; seat cover cloth, automobile:
cotton

(G-9884)
FRESHPET INC (PA)
400 Plaza Dr Fl 1 (07094-3605)
P.O. Box 2157 (07096-2157)
PHONE....................................201 520-4000
William B Cyr, *CEO*
Charles A Norris, *Ch of Bd*
Scott Morris, *President*
Justin Joyner, *Business Mgr*
Stephen Weise, *Exec VP*
EMP: 28
SQ FT: 20,000
SALES: 156.3MM **Publicly Held**
SIC: 2047 Dog & cat food

(G-9885)
FURNITURE OF AMERICA NJ
50 Enterprise Ave N (07094-2525)
PHONE....................................201 605-8200
David Lin, *President*
◆ EMP: 36
SQ FT: 250,000
SALES (est): 200MM **Privately Held**
SIC: 5712 2512 Furniture stores; uphol-
stered household furniture

(G-9886)
GEISLER GANZ CORP
505 Windsor Dr (07094-2708)
PHONE....................................201 223-1200
Bernard Chalfin, *President*
▲ EMP: 9 EST: 1946
SQ FT: 15,000
SALES (est): 1.1MM **Privately Held**
SIC: 3965 3999 2353 Buckles & buckle
parts; hair & hair-based products; beads,
unassembled; hats, caps & millinery

(G-9887)
GENERAL GLASS INTL CORP
Also Called: GCI
101 Venture Way (07094-1825)
PHONE....................................201 553-1850
Fax: 201 553-1851
Arthur Balik, *Ch of Bd*
Albert S Balik, *Vice Ch Bd*
David D Balik, *President*
Carol Balik, *Vice Pres*
Richard Balik, *Vice Pres*
▲ EMP: 125
SQ FT: 14,000
SALES (est): 8.9MM **Privately Held**
WEB: www.generalglass.com
SIC: 3211 3231 5039 Flat glass; mirrored
glass; glass construction materials

(G-9888)
GENERAL TOOLS & INSTRS CO
LLC (PA)
75 Seaview Dr (07094-1806)
PHONE....................................212 431-6100
Ralph Mallozzi, *President*
▲ EMP: 41
SQ FT: 40,000
SALES (est): 7.2MM **Privately Held**
WEB: www.generaltools.com
SIC: 3423 Hand & edge tools

(G-9889)
GENERAL TOOLS MFG CO LLC
75 Seaview Dr (07094-1806)
PHONE....................................201 770-1380
Gerry Weinstein, *Chairman*
▲ EMP: 6
SALES (est): 364K **Privately Held**
SIC: 3999 Manufacturing industries

(G-9890)
GOYA FOODS INC
100 Seaview Dr (07094-1887)
PHONE....................................201 348-4900
Robert Unanue, *President*
EMP: 314
SALES (corp-wide): 953.8MM **Privately**
Held
SIC: 2032 Canned specialties
PA: Goya Foods, Inc.
350 County Rd
Jersey City NJ 07307
201 348-4900

(G-9891)
GOYA FOODS INC
650 New County Rd (07094-1624)
PHONE....................................201 865-3470

Nelson Perez, *Branch Mgr*
EMP: 50
SALES (corp-wide): 953.8MM **Privately**
Held
SIC: 2032 Beans & bean sprouts, canned,
jarred, etc.; beans, baked with meat:
packaged in cans, jars, etc.
PA: Goya Foods, Inc.
350 County Rd
Jersey City NJ 07307
201 348-4900

(G-9892)
GRAMERCY PRODUCTS INC
600 Mdwlands Pkwy Ste 131 (07094-1637)
PHONE....................................212 868-2559
Rishi Gupta, *CEO*
Daniel R Troiano, *President*
▲ EMP: 20 EST: 2013
SALES: 3MM **Privately Held**
SIC: 3999 Pet supplies

(G-9893)
GREEN DISTRIBUTION LLC
565 Windsor Dr Ste 1 (07094-2716)
PHONE....................................201 293-4381
Robert Butters, *CEO*
▼ EMP: 85
SQ FT: 52,000
SALES (est): 14.4MM **Privately Held**
SIC: 2211 2396 5131 Apparel & outer-
wear fabrics, cotton; apparel findings &
trimmings; trimmings, apparel
PA: Falfurrias Capital Partners, L.P.
100 N Tryon St Ste 4100
Charlotte NC 28202

(G-9894)
HARTZ MOUNTAIN
CORPORATION (HQ)
400 Plaza Dr Ste 400 # 400 (07094-3688)
P.O. Box 2488 (07096-2488)
PHONE....................................800 275-1414
Fax: 201 271-0068
Tatsuya Suto, *President*
Gumpei Futagami, *President*
Jason Fales, *Maint Spvr*
Rebecca Senkiw, *Production*
John Ramsden, *Senior Buyer*
◆ EMP: 250
SQ FT: 100,000
SALES (est): 728.9MM
SALES (corp-wide): 5.7B **Privately Held**
SIC: 5199 3999 Pet supplies; pet supplies
PA: Unicharm Corporation
3-5-27, Mita
Minato-Ku TKY 108-0
334 515-111

(G-9895)
HOUSE OF KALON NEW YORK
2 Radio Ave Apt C24 (07094-3851)
PHONE....................................786 259-0786
Aj Sharma, *Partner*
EMP: 15 EST: 2016
SALES: 100K **Privately Held**
SIC: 5023 3229 Decorative home furnish-
ings & supplies; glassware, art or decora-
tive

(G-9896)
HYGRADE BUSINESS GROUP
INC (PA)
30 Seaview Dr (07094-1826)
PHONE....................................800 836-7714
Fax: 973 249-6109
Victor Albetta, *President*
Joseph Molanelli, *COO*
Lewis Murilli, *COO*
Bob Isola, *Vice Pres*
Phil Masiell, *Vice Pres*
EMP: 30
SQ FT: 40,000
SALES: 20MM **Privately Held**
WEB: www.hygradebusiness.com
SIC: 2761 2759 Manifold business forms;
promotional printing

(G-9897)
JACMEL JEWELRY INC
401 Penhorn Ave Ste 1 (07094-2142)
PHONE....................................201 223-0435
Mark Clemente, *Branch Mgr*
EMP: 7

SALES (est): 777.4K
SALES (corp-wide): 100MM **Privately Held**
SIC: 3961 Costume jewelry
PA: Jacmel Jewelry Inc.
 1385 Broadway Fl 8
 New York NY 10018
 718 349-4300

(G-9898)
KASHEE & SONS INC (PA)
600 Meadowlands Pkwy 21b (07094-1633)
PHONE..................................201 867-6900
Kashee Aslam, *President*
▲ **EMP:** 11 **EST:** 2011
SALES (est): 6.7MM **Privately Held**
SIC: 2273 Carpets & rugs

(G-9899)
KEURIG DR PEPPER INC
100 Electric Ave (07094-2616)
PHONE..................................201 832-0695
Mary Pepper, *Branch Mgr*
EMP: 99 **Publicly Held**
SIC: 2086 Soft drinks: packaged in cans, bottles, etc.
PA: Keurig Dr Pepper Inc.
 5301 Legacy Dr
 Plano TX 75024

(G-9900)
KYNC DESIGN LLC
701 Penhorn Ave Ste 1 (07094-2132)
PHONE..................................201 293-4677
Mehmet Tutuncu, *CEO*
Devi Shaheed, *President*
Isra Erbas, *Admin Sec*
EMP: 6
SALES (est): 854.1K **Privately Held**
SIC: 2273 5023 2841 2281 Carpets, hand & machine made; carpets; soap & other detergents; crochet yarn, spun

(G-9901)
L J LOEFFLER SYSTEMS INC
95 Centre Ave (07094-3250)
PHONE..................................212 924-7597
Jeanette Pioppi, *President*
John Pioppi, *Vice Pres*
Dominick Pioppi, *Treasurer*
EMP: 8 **EST:** 1977
SQ FT: 3,000
SALES: 650K **Privately Held**
SIC: 5065 3669 Intercommunication equipment, electronic; intercommunication systems, electric

(G-9902)
LITTLEGIFTS INC
600 Mdwlands Pkwy Ste 131 (07094-1637)
PHONE..................................212 868-2559
Rishi Gupta, *CEO*
Daniel R Troiano, *President*
▲ **EMP:** 10
SALES (est): 2.5MM **Privately Held**
WEB: www.littlegifts.com
SIC: 3961 3911 3999 Costume jewelry; jewelry, precious metal; pet supplies

(G-9903)
MAINETTI AMERICAS INC (PA)
115 Enterprise Ave S (07094-1912)
PHONE..................................201 215-2900
Roberto Peruzzo, *President*
Steve Regino, *Co-President*
▲ **EMP:** 4
SALES (est): 12.5MM **Privately Held**
SIC: 2759 3089 Bag, wrapper & seal printing & engraving; clothes hangers, plastic

(G-9904)
MG DECOR LLC
2 Radio Ave Apt C24 (07094-3851)
PHONE..................................201 923-5493
Madz Gill, *Mng Member*
Ajeeth Sharma,
▲ **EMP:** 11 **EST:** 2015
SQ FT: 10,000
SALES (est): 739.1K **Privately Held**
SIC: 3229 Christmas tree ornaments, from glass produced on-site

(G-9905)
MOOSAVI RUGS INC
Also Called: Moosavi Oriental Rugs
 100 Park Plaza Dr 208n (07094-3635)
PHONE..................................201 617-9500
▲ **EMP:** 5
SQ FT: 5,500
SALES (est): 380K **Privately Held**
SIC: 2273 Mfg Carpets/Rugs

(G-9906)
MYX BEVERAGE LLC
Also Called: Myx Fusions
 424 W 33rd St Ste 520 (07094)
PHONE..................................585 978-3542
Peter Reaske, *CEO*
▼ **EMP:** 13
SQ FT: 600
SALES: 12MM **Privately Held**
SIC: 2087 Beverage bases

(G-9907)
NORTHSTAR TRAVEL MEDIA LLC (PA)
100 Lighting Way Ste 200 (07094-3681)
PHONE..................................201 902-2000
Fax: 201 902-2045
Tom Kemp, *CEO*
Vincent Alonzo, *Editor*
Michael Baker, *Editor*
Josh Lieberman, *Editor*
Adetola Popoola, *Editor*
EMP: 215
SQ FT: 32,000
SALES (est): 296.9MM **Privately Held**
WEB: www.northstartravelmedia.com
SIC: 2721 4789 4724 Magazines: publishing only, not printed on site; cargo loading & unloading services; travel agencies

(G-9908)
ORANGEHRM INC
538 Teal Plz (07094-2218)
PHONE..................................914 458-4254
Sujee Saparamadu, *President*
Brendan Callaghan, *Sales Dir*
Alex Chiru, *Sales Staff*
Glenn Bouchard, *Sales Associate*
Shaun Bradley, *Manager*
EMP: 50
SALES (est): 5MM **Privately Held**
SIC: 7372 Prepackaged software

(G-9909)
PENN JERSEY ADVANCE INC
Also Called: Penn Jersey Advance Centl Svcs
 1 Harmon Plz Fl 9 (07094-2804)
PHONE..................................201 775-6610
Richard Diamond, *Branch Mgr*
EMP: 100 **Privately Held**
SIC: 2711 Newspapers
PA: Penn Jersey Advance Inc.
 18 Centre Sq
 Easton PA 18042

(G-9910)
PERFORMANCE ALLOYS & MATERIALS
462 Dunlin Plz (07094-2202)
P.O. Box 1191 (07096-1191)
PHONE..................................201 865-5268
Tatiana Svyadoz, *President*
Dove Goldman, *Vice Pres*
EMP: 4
SQ FT: 1,000
SALES: 100K **Privately Held**
SIC: 8711 3399 Engineering services; metal powders, pastes & flakes

(G-9911)
PLASTIC PLUS GROUP LLC
600 Mdwlands Pkwy Ste 134 (07094-1637)
PHONE..................................201 561-0405
Joe Waldman, *Mng Member*
AVI Berg,
▲ **EMP:** 25
SQ FT: 20,000
SALES: 10MM **Privately Held**
WEB: www.plasticplusgroup.com
SIC: 3081 Unsupported plastics film & sheet

(G-9912)
PREMIUM DISTRIBUTION CORP
401 Penhorn Ave Ste 2 (07094-2142)
PHONE..................................212 533-1100
Oksana Sabo, *President*
EMP: 4
SALES (est): 301.3K
SALES (corp-wide): 42MM **Privately Held**
SIC: 3651 Electronic kits for home assembly: radio, TV, phonograph; home entertainment equipment, electronic
PA: Premium Distribution Corp.
 130 7th Ave Ste 218
 New York NY 10011
 212 533-1100

(G-9913)
PRG GROUP INC
915 Secaucus Rd (07094-2409)
PHONE..................................201 758-4000
Jeremiah Harris, *Ch of Bd*
Blair Lacorte, *President*
Nicole Scano-Schwiebert, *Exec VP*
Scott Hansen, *CFO*
EMP: 8
SALES (est): 1.1MM **Privately Held**
SIC: 3646 1731 Commercial indusl & institutional electric lighting fixtures; lighting contractor

(G-9914)
PROFORM ACOUSTIC SURFACES LLC
307 Julianne Ter (07094-4012)
PHONE..................................201 553-9614
Anna Porcelli,
EMP: 5
SALES (est): 675.3K **Privately Held**
SIC: 3275 Acoustical plaster, gypsum

(G-9915)
QUEST DIAGNOSTICS INCORPORATED (PA)
500 Plaza Dr Ste G (07094-3656)
PHONE..................................973 520-2700
Stephen H Rusckowski, *Ch of Bd*
Everett V Cunningham, *Senior VP*
Everett Cunningham, *Senior VP*
Catherine T Doherty, *Senior VP*
Lidia Fonseca, *Senior VP*
▲ **EMP:** 2800
SALES: 7.7B **Publicly Held**
WEB: www.questdiagnostics.com
SIC: 8071 2835 Testing laboratories; in vitro & in vivo diagnostic substances

(G-9916)
RANDY HANGERS LLC
115 Enterprise Ave S (07094-1912)
PHONE..................................201 215-2900
Ellen Stein, *Mng Member*
Andy Rupp,
▲ **EMP:** 9 **EST:** 1982
SQ FT: 600,000
SALES (est): 851.2K
SALES (corp-wide): 12.5MM **Privately Held**
SIC: 3089 Clothes hangers, plastic
HQ: Mainetti Usa Inc.
 300 Mac Ln
 Keasbey NJ 08832
 201 215-2900

(G-9917)
RELATIONAL SECURITY CORP
Also Called: Relsec
 1 Harmon Plz Ste 700 (07094-2803)
PHONE..................................201 867-1330
Vivek Shivananda, *CEO*
Jim Curham, *Senior VP*
Smitha Murthy, *Senior VP*
Gary Napotnik, *Senior VP*
Gowri Sankar Sivaprasad, *Senior VP*
EMP: 42
SQ FT: 3,000
SALES (est): 9.4MM **Privately Held**
WEB: www.relsec.com
SIC: 7372 Application computer software

(G-9918)
ROSE BRAND WIPERS INC (PA)
Also Called: Rose Brand East
 4 Emerson Ln (07094-2504)
 P.O. Box 1536 (07096-1536)
PHONE..................................201 809-1730
George M Jacobstein, *President*
Bertrand Bob, *General Mgr*
Tina Carlin, *General Mgr*
Rita Shapiro, *Vice Pres*
Tori Oggioni, *Production*
▲ **EMP:** 239 **EST:** 1921
SQ FT: 13,000
SALES (est): 135.2MM **Privately Held**
SIC: 5049 2399 Theatrical equipment & supplies; emblems, badges & insignia

(G-9919)
ROSE BRAND WIPERS INC
4 Emerson Ln (07094-2504)
PHONE..................................201 770-1441
EMP: 150
SQ FT: 145,000
SALES (est): 13.7MM **Privately Held**
SIC: 2399 Mfg Fabricated Textile Products

(G-9920)
SANDER SALES ENTERPRISES LTD
Also Called: Cozy Home Fashions
 200 Seaview Dr Fl 2 (07094-1830)
PHONE..................................201 808-6705
Aron Weiss, *President*
Ronald J Aronne, *Controller*
▲ **EMP:** 30
SQ FT: 143,000
SALES (est): 4.9MM **Privately Held**
WEB: www.sandersales.net
SIC: 2299 Linen fabrics

(G-9921)
SARKLI-REPECHAGE LTD
300 Castle Rd (07094-1600)
PHONE..................................201 549-4200
Fax: 201 549-4240
Lydia Sarfati, *President*
David Sarfati, *COO*
Shiri Sarfati, *Vice Pres*
Theresa Zazzera, *Opers Staff*
Narda Galvez, *Buyer*
▲ **EMP:** 55 **EST:** 1980
SQ FT: 50,000
SALES (est): 13.9MM **Privately Held**
WEB: www.repechage.com
SIC: 2844 Cosmetic preparations

(G-9922)
SCHNEDER ELC BLDNGS AMRCAS INC
210 Meadowlands Pkwy (07094-2311)
PHONE..................................201 348-9240
Joe Darrigo, *Regional Mgr*
Ann Patten, *Engineer*
Sam Belbina, *Manager*
Ann Titone, *Officer*
EMP: 36
SALES (corp-wide): 200.4K **Privately Held**
SIC: 5084 3823 3822 Instruments & control equipment; industrial instrmnts msrmnt display/control process variable; auto controls regulating residntl & coml environmt & applncs
HQ: Schneider Electric Buildings Americas, Inc.
 1650 W Crosby Rd
 Carrollton TX 75006
 972 323-1111

(G-9923)
SCHOLASTIC INC
100 Plaza Dr Fl 4 (07094-3677)
PHONE..................................201 633-2400
David Walsh, *President*
Vincent Lucinese, *Vice Pres*
Fouad Sarkardei, *Project Mgr*
Yuriy Denysov, *Engineer*
Carlos Jimenez, *Engineer*
EMP: 6 **EST:** 2015
SALES (est): 53.7K **Privately Held**
SIC: 2731 Books: publishing only

(G-9924)
SCHOLASTIC UK GROUP LLC
Also Called: Scholastic National Field Off
100 Plaza Dr Fl 4 (07094-3677)
PHONE..................................201 633-2400
Richard Robinson, *President*
Kevin Mc Enery, *President*
David J Walsh, *President*
Andrew Hedden, *Exec VP*
Maureen O'Connell, *Exec VP*
▲ **EMP:** 200
SALES (est): 39.1MM
SALES (corp-wide): 1.6B **Publicly Held**
WEB: www.scholastic.com
SIC: 2721 Magazines: publishing only, not printed on site
PA: Scholastic Corporation
    557 Broadway Lbby 1
    New York NY 10012
    212 343-6100

(G-9925)
SCOTT KAY INC
55 Hartz Way Ste 1 (07094-2425)
PHONE..................................201 287-0100
David Minster, *CEO*
Scott Kay, *President*
Jeffrey Simon, *CFO*
Elaine Ye, *Controller*
EMP: 120
SQ FT: 12,000
SALES (est): 16.7MM **Privately Held**
WEB: www.scottkay.com
SIC: 3911 5944 Jewelry, precious metal; jewelry stores

(G-9926)
SCOTT KAY STERLING LLC
55 Hartz Way Ste 1 (07094-2425)
PHONE..................................201 287-0100
Scott Kay, *CEO*
Jeffrey Somon, *COO*
EMP: 9
SQ FT: 4,000
SALES (est): 904K **Privately Held**
SIC: 5094 3911 Jewelry; jewelry, precious metal

(G-9927)
SEKISUI AMERICA CORPORATION (HQ)
Also Called: Voltek Division
333 Meadowlands Pkwy (07094-1804)
PHONE..................................201 423-7960
Fax: 201 423-7979
Naofumi Negishi, *President*
Noritake Yoshimizu, *Vice Pres*
Hirmuo Mitsui, *Treasurer*
◆ **EMP:** 13
SQ FT: 4,400
SALES (est): 517.7MM
SALES (corp-wide): 10.3B **Privately Held**
SIC: 3086 Plastics foam products
PA: Sekisui Chemical Co., Ltd.
    2-4-4, Nishitemma, Kita-Ku
    Osaka OSK 530-0
    663 654-122

(G-9928)
SIGN UP INC
Also Called: Fastsigns
255 State Rt 3 Ste 104a (07094-3857)
PHONE..................................201 902-8640
Fax: 201 902-8645
Elizabeth Selbach, *President*
Rose Conklin, *Vice Pres*
EMP: 5
SQ FT: 2,600
SALES (est): 460K **Privately Held**
SIC: 3993 7532 Signs & advertising specialties; truck painting & lettering

(G-9929)
SMITH OPTICS INC
300 Lighting Way Ste 400 (07094-3672)
PHONE..................................208 726-4477
Scott Macguffie, *Vice Pres*
EMP: 5 EST: 2016
SALES (est): 103K **Privately Held**
SIC: 3851 Ophthalmic goods

(G-9930)
SONATA GRAPHICS INC
Also Called: Minuteman Press
1247 Paterson Plank Rd # 65 (07094-3229)
PHONE..................................201 866-0186
Fax: 201 866-1886
Tal Goldgraber, *President*
Brosh Goldgraber, *COO*
EMP: 5
SQ FT: 3,000
SALES (est): 713.7K **Privately Held**
WEB: www.sonatagraphics.com
SIC: 2752 2741 2789 2791 Commercial printing, offset; art copy & poster publishing; bookbinding & related work; typesetting

(G-9931)
SPRINGER SCNCE + BUS MEDIA LLC
333 Mdwlands Pkwy Fl 2 (07094-1814)
PHONE..................................201 348-4033
Fax: 201 348-4505
Christian Staral, *Production*
Dennis Looney, *CFO*
Acasia Dalmau, *Manager*
Minerva Rodriguez, *Manager*
EMP: 60
SALES (corp-wide): 1.7B **Privately Held**
SIC: 2721 2731 Trade journals: publishing only, not printed on site; books: publishing only
HQ: Springer Science + Business Media, Llc
    233 Spring St Fl 6
    New York NY 10013
    212 460-1500

(G-9932)
ST JUDE MEDICAL LLC
333 Mdwlands Pkwy Ste 502 (07094-1822)
PHONE..................................800 645-5368
Peter L Spadaro, *Vice Pres*
Frank Sorrentino, *Sales Staff*
Bob Marchetti, *Branch Mgr*
EMP: 43
SALES (corp-wide): 27.3B **Publicly Held**
WEB: www.sjm.com
SIC: 3845 Pacemaker, cardiac
HQ: St. Jude Medical, Llc
    1 Saint Jude Medical Dr
    Saint Paul MN 55117
    651 756-2000

(G-9933)
STRATEGIC CONTENT IMAGING
100 Castle Rd (07094-1602)
P.O. Box 2399 (07096-2399)
PHONE..................................201 863-8100
Fax: 201 935-1493
Steven Murson, *Vice Pres*
EMP: 180 EST: 2001
SALES (est): 43MM **Privately Held**
WEB: www.sciimage.com
SIC: 7334 7379 2752 7389 Photocopying & duplicating services; ; commercial printing, lithographic; printers' services: folding, collating

(G-9934)
THERMAL CONDUCTION ENGINEERING
Also Called: T C E
865 Roosevelt Ave (07094-3535)
P.O. Box 1371 (07096-1371)
PHONE..................................201 865-1084
Jay Corrigan, *President*
Edward Perry, *President*
EMP: 9 EST: 1960
SQ FT: 9,000
SALES (est): 970K **Privately Held**
SIC: 3567 Induction heating equipment

(G-9935)
TOSCANA CHEESE COMPANY INC
575 Windsor Dr (07094-2746)
PHONE..................................201 617-1500
Victor J Paparazzo, *President*
▲ **EMP:** 45
SQ FT: 42,500
SALES (est): 18MM **Privately Held**
WEB: www.toscanacheese.com
SIC: 2022 Natural cheese

(G-9936)
TRAVEL WEEKLY
100 Lighting Way Ste 200 (07094-3681)
PHONE..................................201 902-1931
Dennis Schaal, *Principal*
Harvey Chipkin, *Editor*
Daisy Ouyang, *Editor*
Robert Silk, *Editor*
Wang Xinsheng, *Editor*
EMP: 8
SALES (est): 812K **Privately Held**
SIC: 2759 Commercial printing

(G-9937)
US DISPLAY GROUP INC
100 Electric Ave (07094-2616)
PHONE..................................931 455-9585
Al Rossi, *General Mgr*
EMP: 11
SALES (corp-wide): 113.2MM **Privately Held**
WEB: www.usdisplaygroup.com
SIC: 2653 Boxes, corrugated: made from purchased materials
HQ: U.S. Display Group, Inc.
    810 S Washington St
    Tullahoma TN 37388
    931 455-9585

(G-9938)
VITEC VIDEOCOM INC
700 Penhorn Ave Ste 1 (07094-2158)
PHONE..................................908 852-3700
Alan Hollis, *Senior VP*
Paul Weiser, *Vice Pres*
Robert Putkowski, *Purch Agent*
Simon Rose, *Finance Dir*
Fiorella Quiroz, *Hum Res Coord*
▲ **EMP:** 20
SALES (est): 2MM **Privately Held**
SIC: 3663 Microwave communication equipment

(G-9939)
WILENTA CARTING INC
46 Henry St (07094-2104)
P.O. Box 2596 (07096-2596)
PHONE..................................201 325-0044
Peter Wilenta, *President*
Michael Wilenta, *COO*
EMP: 13
SQ FT: 1,700
SALES (est): 4.4MM **Privately Held**
SIC: 3555 5191 4953 Bronzing or dusting machines for the printing trade; animal feeds; recycling, waste materials

(G-9940)
WILENTA FEED INC
46 Henry St (07094-2104)
P.O. Box 2596 (07096-2596)
PHONE..................................201 325-0044
Peter Wilenta, *President*
Michael Wilenta, *COO*
Jack Caffrey, *Manager*
Jennifer Garcia, *Manager*
◆ **EMP:** 13
SQ FT: 1,700
SALES (est): 2.2MM **Privately Held**
SIC: 3556 5191 4953 Bakery machinery; animal feeds; recycling, waste materials

(G-9941)
ZOLLANVARI LTD
600 Mdwlands Pkwy Ste 130 (07094-1637)
PHONE..................................201 330-3344
Fax: 201 330-7728
Reza Zollanvari, *President*
▲ **EMP:** 11
SQ FT: 11,527
SALES (est): 1.4MM **Privately Held**
WEB: www.zollanvari.com
SIC: 2273 Carpets & rugs

(G-9942)
ZT SYSTEMS
333 Meadowlands Pkwy Fl 2 (07094-1814)
PHONE..................................201 559-1000
EMP: 5
SALES (est): 374.5K **Privately Held**
SIC: 3571 Electronic computers

Sewaren
Middlesex County

(G-9943)
AUTOMATED MEDICAL PDTS CORP
440 Cliff Rd (07077-1408)
PHONE..................................732 602-7717
Janice Brown, *President*
EMP: 7
SQ FT: 2,000
SALES (est): 1.1MM **Privately Held**
WEB: www.ironintern.com
SIC: 3841 Surgical instruments & apparatus

Sewell
Gloucester County

(G-9944)
ACE RESTORATION
24 Mariner Dr (08080-1946)
PHONE..................................267 897-2384
Matthew Gibson, *Owner*
EMP: 4 EST: 2016
SALES (est): 154.7K **Privately Held**
SIC: 3088 Plastics plumbing fixtures

(G-9945)
CONCORD PRODUCTS COMPANY INC
360 Columbia Dr (08080-4578)
PHONE..................................856 933-3000
Fax: 856 933-9339
Erik Anthonsen, *Vice Pres*
Jeff Latvenas, *Sales Mgr*
◆ **EMP:** 47
SQ FT: 65,000
SALES (est): 8.5MM **Privately Held**
SIC: 2522 Office furniture, except wood

(G-9946)
COPERION CORPORATION (HQ)
590 Woodbury Glassboro Rd (08080-4558)
PHONE..................................201 327-6300
Thomas Kehl, *President*
Peter Hoffmann, *General Mgr*
Werner Strauch, *General Mgr*
Axel K Kiefer, *Managing Dir*
Steve Broes, *Business Mgr*
◆ **EMP:** 110
SQ FT: 89,000
SALES (est): 55.7MM **Publicly Held**
SIC: 3559 8711 3535 8734 Plastics working machinery; rubber working machinery, including tires; structural engineering; bulk handling conveyor systems; testing laboratories

(G-9947)
COPERION K-TRON PITMAN INC (DH)
590 Woodbury Glassboro Rd (08080-4558)
PHONE..................................856 589-0500
Fax: 856 256-3281
Kevin C Bowen, *President*
Robert Barnett, *Vice Pres*
Brandon Dohn, *Engineer*
Tom Leaf, *Engineer*
Robert Wisniewski, *CFO*
▲ **EMP:** 10
SQ FT: 92,000
SALES (est): 20MM **Publicly Held**
SIC: 3823 3829 3596 3535 Industrial process control instruments; measuring & controlling devices; scales & balances, except laboratory; conveyors & conveying equipment

(G-9948)
COUNTY CONSERVATION CO INC
212 Blckwood Barnsboro Rd (08080-4202)
PHONE..................................856 227-6900
Fax: 856 228-9600
Francis Petrongolo Jr, *President*
John Petrongolo, *Owner*
Jeffrey Petrongolo, *Treasurer*
EMP: 13

GEOGRAPHIC

SALES (est): 3.7MM **Privately Held**
SIC: 3559 Recycling machinery

(G-9949)
CREATIVE COMPETITIONS INC
Also Called: Odyssey of The Mind
406 Ganttown Rd (08080-1862)
PHONE..............................856 256-2797
Samuel Micklus, *President*
Cheryl Micklus, *Treasurer*
EMP: 11
SQ FT: 4,000
SALES: 400K **Privately Held**
WEB: www.odysseyofthemind.com
SIC: 2731 Books: publishing only

(G-9950)
DELSEA PIPE INC
445 Delsea Dr (08080-9337)
PHONE..............................856 589-9374
Nick Bozine, *President*
EMP: 25
SQ FT: 8,000
SALES (est): 3.1MM **Privately Held**
SIC: 3317 Steel pipe & tubes

(G-9951)
EDWARD KURTH AND SON INC
220 Blckwood Barnsboro Rd (08080-4202)
PHONE..............................856 227-5252
Fax: 856 227-9394
Edward Kurth Jr, *President*
Andrew Kurth, *Vice Pres*
Robert B Kurth, *Admin Sec*
EMP: 30
SQ FT: 28,000
SALES (est): 4.4MM **Privately Held**
WEB: www.edkurth.com
SIC: 7692 7699 Welding repair; boiler repair shop

(G-9952)
EDWIN R BURGER & SON INC
732 Main St (08080-4546)
P.O. Box 184 (08080-0184)
PHONE..............................856 468-2300
Mark Burger, *President*
EMP: 30 **EST:** 1953
SQ FT: 8,000
SALES (est): 1.6MM **Privately Held**
SIC: 1799 3496 Fence construction; miscellaneous fabricated wire products

(G-9953)
EKS PARTS INC
220 Blckwood Barnsboro Rd (08080-4202)
PHONE..............................856 227-8811
Edward F Kurth Jr, *Owner*
Robert B Kurth, *Corp Secy*
Andrew L Kurth, *Vice Pres*
EMP: 4
SALES (est): 390K **Privately Held**
SIC: 3443 Boiler shop products: boilers, smokestacks, steel tanks

(G-9954)
ELECTRIC MOBILITY CORPORATION (PA)
Also Called: Rascal Company, The
591 Mantua Blvd (08080-1032)
P.O. Box 36000, Louisville KY (40233-6000)
PHONE..............................856 468-1000
Michael Flowers, *Ch of Bd*
Sanford Pearl, *COO*
Susan Flowers, *Treasurer*
Jordan Flowers, *Admin Sec*
▲ **EMP:** 110
SQ FT: 50,000
SALES (est): 34MM **Privately Held**
WEB: www.electricmobility.com
SIC: 5047 3842 Medical equipment & supplies; wheelchairs

(G-9955)
ELECTRIC MOBILITY CORPORATION
Also Called: Rascal Company, The
599 Mantua Blvd (08080-1016)
PHONE..............................856 468-1000
Michael Flowers, *Manager*
EMP: 200

SALES (corp-wide): 34MM **Privately Held**
WEB: www.electricmobility.com
SIC: 3751 5999 Motor scooters & parts; medical apparatus & supplies
PA: Electric Mobility Corporation
591 Mantua Blvd
Sewell NJ 08080
856 468-1000

(G-9956)
HUTCHINSON CABINETS
244 Bark Bridge Rd (08080-4612)
PHONE..............................856 468-5500
Fax: 856 468-4857
Etta Hutchinson, *Opers-Prdtn-Mfg*
Edward Hufnell, *Purch Mgr*
George Hutchinson,
Lorrie Hutchinson, *Assistant*
EMP: 45 **EST:** 1976
SQ FT: 35,000
SALES (est): 4.9MM **Privately Held**
WEB: www.hutchinsoncabinets.com
SIC: 2434 2431 Wood kitchen cabinets; millwork

(G-9957)
IMPRESSIONS UNLIMITED PRTG LLC
638 Delsea Dr (08080-9399)
P.O. Box 386 (08080-0386)
PHONE..............................856 256-0200
Fax: 856 256-0005
Joseph G Layton, *Mng Member*
EMP: 4
SALES (est): 250K **Privately Held**
WEB: www.iuprint.com
SIC: 2752 Commercial printing, offset

(G-9958)
IRON ASYLUM INCORPORATED
233 Delsea Dr (08080-9401)
PHONE..............................856 228-2700
EMP: 14 **EST:** 2010
SQ FT: 1,000
SALES: 2MM **Privately Held**
SIC: 3441 Structural Metal Fabrication

(G-9959)
J & J MARINE INC
Also Called: J & J Tool & Die
1596 Hurffville Rd (08080-4270)
PHONE..............................856 228-4744
Fax: 856 228-8993
James Clauss, *President*
EMP: 14
SALES (est): 1.2MM **Privately Held**
SIC: 3544 1629 Special dies, tools, jigs & fixtures; marine construction

(G-9960)
JANNETTI PUBLICATIONS
200 E Holly Ave (08080-2641)
P.O. Box 56, Pitman (08071-0056)
PHONE..............................856 256-2300
Anthony J Jannetti, *Owner*
Charlene Fuhrer, *Manager*
EMP: 53
SALES (est): 3MM **Privately Held**
WEB: www.medsurgnursing.net
SIC: 2721 8299 Periodicals: publishing only; educational service, nondegree granting: continuing educ.

(G-9961)
JVS COPY SERVICES INC
460 Main St (08080-4316)
PHONE..............................856 415-9090
Fax: 856 415-0323
Anthony Di Sciascio, *President*
Beverly Di Sciascio, *Vice Pres*
EMP: 10
SQ FT: 10,000
SALES: 1.5MM **Privately Held**
WEB: www.jvscopy.com
SIC: 7334 2752 Photocopying & duplicating services; commercial printing, lithographic

(G-9962)
K-TRON INTERNATIONAL INC (HQ)
Also Called: Pennsylvania Crusher
590 Woodbury Glassboro Rd (08080-4558)
PHONE..............................856 589-0500
Fax: 856 589-8113

Edward B Cloues II, *Ch of Bd*
Kevin Buchler, *General Mgr*
Kevin C Bowen, *Senior VP*
Lukas Guenthardt, *Senior VP*
Donald W Melchiorre, *Senior VP*
◆ **EMP:** 66
SQ FT: 92,000
SALES (est): 125.1MM **Publicly Held**
WEB: www.ktron.com
SIC: 3532 3535 Feeders, ore & aggregate; conveyors & conveying equipment

(G-9963)
OMEGA TOOL DIE
Also Called: International Roll Forms
8 International Ave (08080)
P.O. Box 5426, Deptford (08096-0426)
PHONE..............................856 228-7100
Jack Bosbikian, *President*
EMP: 8
SALES (est): 560K **Privately Held**
SIC: 3544 Special dies & tools

(G-9964)
PAONE FABRICATION INC
345 Chapel Heights Rd (08080-1871)
PHONE..............................856 589-3821
Edward Paone, *President*
EMP: 5
SALES (est): 511.7K **Privately Held**
SIC: 3441 Fabricated structural metal

(G-9965)
PASTARAMA DISTRIBUTORS INC
164 Center St (08080-1359)
PHONE..............................609 847-0378
Nicholas Z Pellicciotti, *President*
Barbara Pellicciotti, *Corp Secy*
EMP: 4
SQ FT: 150
SALES (est): 240K **Privately Held**
SIC: 2099 Pasta, uncooked: packaged with other ingredients

(G-9966)
TREC ELECTRIC
11 Kensington Ct (08080-3627)
PHONE..............................856 374-3433
Thomas Redman, *Owner*
EMP: 5
SALES (est): 714.7K **Privately Held**
SIC: 3699 Electrical equipment & supplies

(G-9967)
YASHEEL INC
Also Called: Sir Speedy
11 Samantha Ct (08080-3151)
PHONE..............................856 275-6812
Shila Gohil, *President*
EMP: 4
SALES (est): 270K **Privately Held**
SIC: 2752 3993 2789 Commercial printing, offset; signs & advertising specialties; bookbinding & related work

---

Shamong
Burlington County

(G-9968)
BROOK SADDLE RIDGE EQUEST
Also Called: Saddlebrook Ridge Equest Ctr
10 Saddle Brook Ct (08088-8225)
PHONE..............................609 953-1600
Gail Pratt, *Owner*
EMP: 10
SALES (est): 851K **Privately Held**
SIC: 3199 Equestrian related leather articles

(G-9969)
GLOW TUBE INC
83 Springers Brook Rd (08088-9567)
P.O. Box 725, Medford (08055-0725)
PHONE..............................609 268-7707
C W Keith, *President*
Dorthy Keith, *Treasurer*
Marique Keith, *Admin Sec*
EMP: 5
SALES: 150K **Privately Held**
SIC: 3825 Energy measuring equipment, electrical

(G-9970)
HARRY SHAW MODEL MAKER INC
401 Stokes Rd (08088-8954)
P.O. Box 2087, Medford (08055-7087)
PHONE..............................609 268-0647
Fax: 609 268-8796
John W Kerby, *President*
William Jackman, *Corp Secy*
EMP: 4 **EST:** 1952
SQ FT: 7,500
SALES: 700K **Privately Held**
WEB: www.harryshawmodel.com
SIC: 3999 Models, general, except toy

(G-9971)
SHAMONG MANUFACTURING COMPANY
33 Bunker Hill Rd (08088-8990)
PHONE..............................609 654-2549
Fax: 609 953-0217
Donald Autio, *President*
EMP: 34
SQ FT: 20,000
SALES (est): 6.6MM **Privately Held**
WEB: www.shamongmfg.com
SIC: 3444 Sheet metal specialties, not stamped

(G-9972)
VALENZANO WINERY
1090 Route 206 (08088-9599)
PHONE..............................856 701-7871
EMP: 5
SALES (est): 641.1K **Privately Held**
SIC: 2084 Wines

Ship Bottom
Ocean County

(G-9973)
RON JON SURF SHOP FLA INC
201 W 9th St (08008-4614)
PHONE..............................609 494-8844
Fax: 609 494-6811
Patty Gawronski, *Branch Mgr*
EMP: 14
SALES (corp-wide): 35.1MM **Privately Held**
WEB: www.rjss.com
SIC: 3949 5941 Surfboards; surfing equipment & supplies
PA: Ron Jon Surf Shop Of Fla., Inc.
4151 N Atlantic Ave
Cocoa Beach FL 32931
321 799-8888

Short Hills
Essex County

(G-9974)
AB SCIENCE USA LLC
51 John F Kennedy Pkwy (07102-2704)
PHONE..............................973 218-2437
Alain Moussy, *Mng Member*
Katelynn Dulinsky, *Manager*
Albert Ahn,
EMP: 6
SQ FT: 1,500
SALES (est): 543.3K
SALES (corp-wide): 2MM **Privately Held**
SIC: 2834 Pharmaceutical preparations
PA: Ab Science
3 Avenue George V
Paris 75008
472 330-246

(G-9975)
CAVALIER CHEMICAL CO INC
42 Colonial Way (07078-1813)
PHONE..............................908 558-0110
Norman Lubin, *President*
Mark Sherman, *Vice Pres*
EMP: 30
SQ FT: 52,000
SALES (est): 5.6MM **Privately Held**
WEB: www.cavalierchem.com
SIC: 2842 2841 Cleaning or polishing preparations; dishwashing compounds

(G-9976)
CHEESECAKE FACTORY INC
Also Called: Cheesecake Factory, The
1200 Morris Tpke Ste D103 (07078-0319)
PHONE..............................973 921-0930
EMP: 6 Publicly Held
SIC: 5812 2051 American restaurant;
cakes, bakery: except frozen
PA: The Cheesecake Factory Incorporated
26901 Malibu Hills Rd
Calabasas Hills CA 91301

(G-9977)
DUN & BRADSTREET INC
Also Called: D&B
103 John F Kennedy Pkwy (07078-2708)
PHONE..............................973 921-5500
Mike Grossman, Manager
EMP: 50 Publicly Held
SIC: 7372 Business oriented computer
software
HQ: Dun & Bradstreet, Inc
103 Jfk Pkwy
Short Hills NJ 07078
973 921-5500

(G-9978)
GOLF ODYSSEY LLC
60 Woodcrest Ave (07078-2124)
PHONE..............................973 564-6223
David Baum, Owner
EMP: 4
SALES (est): 263.4K Privately Held
SIC: 2721 Magazines: publishing only, not
printed on site

(G-9979)
JAMES COLUCCI ENTERPRISES LLC
150 Jfk Pkwy (07078-2703)
P.O. Box 1345, Summit (07902-1345)
PHONE..............................877 403-4900
James Colucci, Principal
EMP: 29
SALES: 11.5MM Privately Held
SIC: 3861 7371 Developers, photographic
(not made in chemical plants); software
programming applications

(G-9980)
M BLAUSTEIN INC (PA)
Also Called: Blaustein M Furs
516 Millburn Ave (07078-2523)
PHONE..............................973 379-1080
Fax: 973 376-6550
Lloyd Perkel, CEO
Julius Blaustein, Ch of Bd
Irene Blaustein, Vice Pres
Lauren Perkel, Treasurer
EMP: 4
SQ FT: 6,000
SALES (est): 458.7K Privately Held
SIC: 5632 2371 Furriers; fur apparel,
made to custom order; apparel acces-
sories; fur goods; coats, fur

(G-9981)
MALCAM US
51 John F Kennedy Pkwy (07078-2704)
PHONE..............................973 218-2461
Danny Moshe, President
EMP: 4
SALES (est): 205.6K Privately Held
SIC: 3823 Industrial process measurement
equipment

(G-9982)
MORGAN CYCLE LLC
227 Old Short Hills Rd (07078-2133)
PHONE..............................973 218-9233
John Yen, Mng Member
▲ EMP: 2
SQ FT: 10,000
SALES: 1.2MM Privately Held
SIC: 3944 Wagons: coaster, express &
play: children's

(G-9983)
PIKE MACHINE PRODUCTS INC
17 Clive Hills Rd (07078-1314)
PHONE..............................973 379-9128
Morton Weisman, President
Russell Weisman, Vice Pres
EMP: 100
SQ FT: 76,000

SALES (est): 11.7MM
SALES (corp-wide): 7.8B Publicly Held
WEB: www.pikedoors.com
SIC: 3231 Doors, glass: made from pur-
chased glass
HQ: Anthony Doors, Inc.
12391 Montero Ave
Sylmar CA 91342
818 365-9451

(G-9984)
RELATNSHIP CAPITL PARTNERS INC
51 Jfk Pkwy Fl 1 (07078-2713)
PHONE..............................908 962-4881
Martin Wise, CEO
Robert Summers, Vice Pres
EMP: 14
SQ FT: 1,000
SALES (est): 906.4K Privately Held
SIC: 7372 Application computer software

(G-9985)
RELPRO INC
51 Jfk Pkwy Fl 1w (07078-2702)
PHONE..............................908 962-4881
Martin Wise, CEO
EMP: 8
SQ FT: 1,000
SALES (est): 186.1K Privately Held
SIC: 7372 Application computer software

(G-9986)
TRUE RELIGION APPAREL INC
Also Called: True Religion Brand Jeans
1200 Morris Tpke Ste D107 (07078-0408)
PHONE..............................973 564-9030
EMP: 5
SALES (corp-wide): 350MM Privately
Held
SIC: 2331 Women's & misses' blouses &
shirts
HQ: True Religion Apparel, Inc.
1888 Rosecrans Ave # 1000
Manhattan Beach CA 90266
323 266-3072

(G-9987)
VIATAR CTC SOLUTIONS INC
29 Clive Hills Rd (07078-1314)
PHONE..............................617 299-6590
Ilan K Reich, CEO
EMP: 5 EST: 2007
SALES (est): 278.6K Privately Held
SIC: 3841 Surgical & medical instruments

Shrewsbury
Monmouth County

(G-9988)
AKW INC (PA)
Also Called: A W Eurostile
41 Newman Springs Rd E (07702-4038)
PHONE..............................732 530-9186
Fax: 732 530-0372
Andrea Wyman, President
Elizabeth Wyman, Corp Secy
Michele Wyman, Shareholder
▲ EMP: 5
SQ FT: 30,000
SALES (est): 1.4MM Privately Held
WEB: www.aweurostile.com
SIC: 3443 5032 5211 Fabricated plate
work (boiler shop); tile & clay products;
marble building stone; tile, ceramic; ma-
sonry materials & supplies

(G-9989)
AMERTECH TOWERSERVICES LLC
149 Avenue At The Cmn (07702-4577)
PHONE..............................732 389-2200
Fax: 732 345-9366
Mark Gaeta, President
Robert Canino, Partner
David Marquez, Regl Sales Mgr
EMP: 30
SQ FT: 5,000
SALES (est): 2.1MM Privately Held
SIC: 2499 Cooling towers, wood or wood &
sheet metal combination

(G-9990)
ATHLETES ALLEY
Also Called: Imprint Ink
483 Broad St (07702-4003)
PHONE..............................732 842-1127
Fax: 732 842-9473
Nicholas Ford Jr, Partner
Greg Ford, Partner
EMP: 10 EST: 1976
SQ FT: 1,290
SALES (est): 1MM Privately Held
WEB: www.athletesalley.com
SIC: 5941 5699 2284 2893 Sporting
goods & bicycle shops; sports apparel;
embroidery thread; printing ink

(G-9991)
BEDROCK GRANITE INC
803 Shrewsbury Ave (07702-4307)
PHONE..............................732 741-0010
Fax: 732 985-4351
Joseph Iacono, President
Philip Vivolo, Admin Sec
EMP: 24
SQ FT: 12,000
SALES (est): 3.8MM Privately Held
WEB: www.bedrockgranite.net
SIC: 3281 1411 Granite, cut & shaped; di-
mension stone

(G-9992)
CEMP INC
Also Called: Detail Doctor
479 Broad St (07702-4003)
PHONE..............................732 933-1000
Sean Gatta, President
Matthew Cop, Manager
EMP: 13
SALES: 500K Privately Held
WEB: www.cemp.com
SIC: 3471 5511 Cleaning, polishing & fin-
ishing; new & used car dealers

(G-9993)
CHARTER FINCL PUBG NETWRK INC
Also Called: Financial Advisor Magazine
499 Broad St (07702-4043)
P.O. Box 7550 (07702-7550)
PHONE..............................732 450-8866
Fax: 732 450-8877
Charlie Stroller, CEO
EMP: 30
SQ FT: 4,000
SALES (est): 4.5MM Privately Held
WEB: www.financialadvisormagazine.com
SIC: 2721 Magazines: publishing & print-
ing; magazines: publishing only, not
printed on site

(G-9994)
CHISHOLM TECHNOLOGIES INC
450 Shrewsbury Plz # 301 (07702-4325)
PHONE..............................732 859-5578
Agnes Chisholm, President
Rosena Murray, Vice Pres
EMP: 4
SALES (est): 202.1K Privately Held
WEB: www.chisholmtech.com
SIC: 7372 Application computer software

(G-9995)
COUTURE EXCHANGE
691 Broad St (07702-4201)
PHONE..............................732 933-1123
Richard Patrick, Owner
Jennifer Patrick, Co-Owner
EMP: 5
SALES (est): 366.2K Privately Held
WEB: www.thecoutureexchange.com
SIC: 2389 Apparel & accessories

(G-9996)
DCG PRINTING INC
Also Called: Omega Graphics
661 State Rte 35 (07702)
PHONE..............................732 530-4441
Douglas Godfrey, President
Stephanie Godfrey, Admin Sec
EMP: 4
SALES: 500K Privately Held
SIC: 2752 Commercial printing, offset

(G-9997)
DJEET
637 Broad St (07702-4150)
PHONE..............................732 224-8887
Fax: 732 224-8987
Casey Pesce, Owner
EMP: 6
SALES (est): 538.8K Privately Held
SIC: 2099 Food preparations

(G-9998)
EBSCO INDUSTRIES INC
Also Called: Ebsco Information Services
1151 Broad St Ste 212 (07702-4328)
P.O. Box 830625, Birmingham AL (35283-
0625)
PHONE..............................732 542-8600
Fax: 732 544-9777
Stanley Terry, General Mgr
Oliver Kim, Sales Mgr
Leslie Sierra, Senior Mgr
Hyun Lee, Administration
EMP: 50
SALES (corp-wide): 2.8B Privately Held
WEB: www.ebscoind.com
SIC: 2741 Miscellaneous publishing
PA: Ebsco Industries, Inc.
5724 Highway 280 E
Birmingham AL 35242
205 991-6600

(G-9999)
GAIL GERSONS WINE & DINE RESTA
812 Broad St (07702-4214)
PHONE..............................732 758-0888
Gail Gerson, Principal
EMP: 4
SALES (est): 232.7K Privately Held
SIC: 2711 7311 Newspapers, publishing &
printing; advertising agencies

(G-10000)
HYDRO MILLING GROUP INC
20 Thomas Ave (07702-4022)
PHONE..............................732 450-2488
Carlo J Montisano, President
Milo Leach, Vice Pres
EMP: 8
SALES: 500K Privately Held
SIC: 2046 Pipeline construction

(G-10001)
INK ON PAPER COMMUNICATIONS (PA)
Also Called: Iop Communications
450 Shrewsbury Plz # 372 (07702-4325)
PHONE..............................732 758-6280
Gail De Nofa, President
Gail Denofa, President
Micheal E De Nofa Jr, Vice Pres
EMP: 2
SALES: 1MM Privately Held
WEB: www.iopcomm.com
SIC: 2759 Commercial printing

(G-10002)
MECHANICAL INGENUITY CORP
61 Riordan Pl (07702-4305)
PHONE..............................732 842-8889
Fax: 732 842-9454
Peter Manning, CEO
Howard Beckerman, Vice Pres
◆ EMP: 20
SQ FT: 6,000
SALES (est): 3.6MM Privately Held
WEB: www.mechanicalingenuity.com
SIC: 3679 Electronic circuits

(G-10003)
METALLIX DIRECT GOLD LLC
59 Avenue At The Cmn # 201
(07702-4806)
PHONE..............................732 544-0891
Pamela Rollins, Principal
EMP: 8
SALES (est): 873K Privately Held
SIC: 3339 Precious metals

(G-10004)
METALLIX REFINING INC (PA)
59 Avenue At The Cmn # 201
(07702-4806)
PHONE..............................732 936-0050
Eric Leiner, President

GEOGRAPHIC

Maria Piastre, *President*
Dimitri Fiodorov, *Buyer*
Lynn Falk, *CFO*
▲ **EMP:** 12 **EST:** 1970
SQ FT: 3,000
SALES (est): 12.7MM **Privately Held**
WEB: www.metallixrefining.com
SIC: 3339 Precious metals; gold refining (primary); platinum group metal refining (primary)

(G-10005)
MICHAEL DURU CLOTHIERS LLC
Also Called: Executive Clothiers
801 Broad St (07702-4201)
PHONE..................................732 741-1999
Michael Duru, *President*
Murat M Duru,
EMP: 7
SQ FT: 3,900
SALES (est): 1.1MM **Privately Held**
SIC: 2311 Tailored suits & formal jackets

(G-10006)
MISTER GOOD LUBE INC
Also Called: Mr Good Lube
473 Broad St (07702-4003)
PHONE..................................732 842-3266
Harideshi Kudo, *Manager*
EMP: 5
SALES (corp-wide): 2.5MM **Privately Held**
SIC: 1389 Construction, repair & dismantling services
PA: Mister Good Lube Inc
3411 Us Highway 9
Freehold NJ 07728
732 308-1111

(G-10007)
MONMOUTH TRUCK RAM DIV LLC
Also Called: Monmouth Hose & Hydraulics
799 Shrewsbury Ave (07702-4306)
PHONE..................................732 741-5001
Michele S Margiotta, *Mng Member*
EMP: 7
SALES (est): 176.6K **Privately Held**
SIC: 3599 Machine shop, jobbing & repair

(G-10008)
POLARIS PLATE HEAT EXCHNGERS L
Also Called: Polaris Thermal
1151 Broad St Ste 218 (07702-4328)
PHONE..................................732 345-7188
Jason Ryan, *Principal*
Barbara Blauth,
Steve Weintraub,
▼ **EMP:** 4
SQ FT: 1,400
SALES (est): 713.2K
SALES (corp-wide): 6.8B **Privately Held**
SIC: 3443 1711 Heat exchangers, condensers & components; plumbing, heating, air-conditioning contractors
HQ: Danfoss A/S
Nordborgvej 81
Nordborg 6430
748 822-22

(G-10009)
RAM HYDRAULICS INC
745 Shrewsbury Ave (07702-4306)
PHONE..................................732 237-0904
Michael Mattei, *President*
EMP: 5
SQ FT: 6,200
SALES (est): 729.2K **Privately Held**
SIC: 3714 7538 Cylinder heads, motor vehicle; general truck repair

(G-10010)
RELAXZEN INC
621 Shrewsbury Ave (07702-4153)
PHONE..................................732 936-1500
▼ **EMP:** 10
SQ FT: 900
SALES (est): 690K **Privately Held**
SIC: 2086 Energy Drink Manufacturer

(G-10011)
STANGER ROBERT A & CO LP
1129 Broad St Fl 2 (07702-4333)
PHONE..................................732 389-3600
Keith D Allaire, *Principal*
Robert A Stanger, *Chairman*
Kevin Gannon, *Director*
EMP: 20
SALES (est): 2.2MM **Privately Held**
WEB: www.rastanger.com
SIC: 6726 6211 2741 Investment offices; security brokers & dealers; miscellaneous publishing

(G-10012)
SUPPLY CHAIN TECHNOLOGIES LLC
Also Called: Sct Software
1161 Broad St Ste 312 (07702-4362)
PHONE..................................856 206-9849
David Henig, *CEO*
Rahul Agarwal, *President*
EMP: 6
SALES (est): 325.6K **Privately Held**
SIC: 7372 Business oriented computer software

(G-10013)
VERTICAL PROTECTIVE AP LLC
830 Broad St Ste 3 (07702-4216)
PHONE..................................203 904-6099
Christopher Neary,
Phyllis Fee, *Administration*
EMP: 1
SQ FT: 1,000
SALES: 10MM **Privately Held**
SIC: 2326 Men's & boys' work clothing

(G-10014)
ZOONO USA LLC
1151 Broad St Ste 115 (07702-4312)
PHONE..................................732 722-8757
Tom French, *President*
David Broadhead, *Prdtn Mgr*
Paul Ravlich, *CFO*
EMP: 4
SALES (est): 472.3K **Privately Held**
SIC: 2842 Sanitation preparations, disinfectants & deodorants

---
Sicklerville
Camden County

(G-10015)
7TH SEVENTH DAY WELLNESS CTR
Also Called: Over The Rainbow Bridge Crysta
6 Sherwick Ct (08081-1317)
PHONE..................................856 308-0991
Lisa M Dottoli, *Owner*
EMP: 6
SALES: 150K **Privately Held**
SIC: 2833 Medicinals & botanicals

(G-10016)
ANVIL IRON WORKS INC
Little Mill Rd (08081)
PHONE..................................856 783-5959
William C Natoli Jr, *President*
EMP: 5
SALES (corp-wide): 1MM **Privately Held**
SIC: 3446 Architectural metalwork
PA: Anvil Iron Works Inc
1022 Washington Ave 26
Philadelphia PA 19147
215 468-8300

(G-10017)
AUTOACCESS LLC
451 Church Rd (08081-1772)
P.O. Box 529 (08081-0529)
PHONE..................................908 240-5919
Tunji Olabode, *CEO*
Olaide Olabode, *Vice Pres*
Olarenwaju Olabode, *Vice Pres*
EMP: 10
SALES (est): 447.9K **Privately Held**
SIC: 3711 5012 Motor vehicles & car bodies; automobiles & other motor vehicles

(G-10018)
ESI
Also Called: Electronic Assemblies, Inc Esi
1541 New Broklyn Erial Rd (08081-3294)
PHONE..................................856 629-2492
Christine J Cunningham, *President*
James Cunningham, *Vice Pres*
EMP: 25
SQ FT: 5,000
SALES: 1.2MM **Privately Held**
SIC: 3643 3679 3672 3357 Power line cable; harness assemblies for electronic use: wire or cable; printed circuit boards; nonferrous wiredrawing & insulating

(G-10019)
GARY R MARZILI
Also Called: GM Precision Machine
840 Jarvis Rd (08081-2132)
PHONE..................................856 782-1546
Gary R Marzili, *Owner*
EMP: 4
SALES (est): 280K **Privately Held**
SIC: 3541 Machine tools, metal cutting type

(G-10020)
J & M CSTM SHTMTL LTD LBLTY CO
1331 New Broklyn Erial Rd (08081-3292)
PHONE..................................856 627-6252
Janet Monitzer,
EMP: 9
SALES: 700K **Privately Held**
SIC: 3441 Fabricated structural metal

(G-10021)
NATIONAL COLOR GRAPHICS
1755 Wlliamstown Erial Rd (08081-1238)
PHONE..................................856 435-6800
Fax: 856 435-0503
Jeffrey Hughes, *President*
Joseph Hughes, *Corp Secy*
EMP: 10
SQ FT: 5,000
SALES (est): 943.1K **Privately Held**
SIC: 7336 2759 Graphic arts & related design; commercial printing

(G-10022)
NICKOS CONSTRUCTION INC
17 Arcadian Dr (08081-3811)
PHONE..................................267 240-3997
Alex Nikolaenko, *President*
EMP: 17
SALES: 3.3MM **Privately Held**
SIC: 1389 7389 Construction, repair & dismantling services;

(G-10023)
PRO-MOTION INDUSTRIES LLC
102 Allied Pkwy (08081-9738)
PHONE..................................856 809-0040
Fax: 856 809-0041
Kelly Cone,
Erica Newsham, *Admin Asst*
▲ **EMP:** 10
SQ FT: 20,000
SALES (est): 3MM **Privately Held**
WEB: www.contractlabeling.com
SIC: 3565 Packaging machinery

(G-10024)
RAYS SEAMLESS RAIN GUTTERS
Also Called: Gutter Cleaning
33 Hawthorne Rd (08081-2530)
PHONE..................................856 629-8407
Ray Thies, *Owner*
EMP: 4
SALES: 340K **Privately Held**
SIC: 3444 Gutters, sheet metal

(G-10025)
RIO SUPPLY
100 Allied Pkwy (08081-9738)
PHONE..................................856 719-0081
Renee Hastings, *Principal*
Dave Linden, *Area Mgr*
EMP: 7
SALES (est): 600K **Privately Held**
SIC: 3824 Fluid meters & counting devices

(G-10026)
SPARK HOLLAND INC
Also Called: Ichrom Solutions
542 Berlin Cross Keys Rd 3-376 (08081-4367)
PHONE..................................609 799-7250
John Crutchfield, *President*
Key Contacts Crutchfield, *General Mgr*
Stella Schindler, *Engineer*
Gert Schuurman, *Sales Engr*
Tjipke Beer, *Systs Prg Mgr*
EMP: 4
SALES: 1.8MM **Privately Held**
WEB: www.ichrom.com
SIC: 3821 3826 Laboratory equipment: fume hoods, distillation racks, etc.; analytical instruments; liquid testing apparatus; liquid chromatographic instruments; environmental testing equipment

(G-10027)
STORM CITY ENTERTAINMENT INC
700 Liberty Pl (08081-5715)
PHONE..................................856 885-6902
Susan Kain Jurgensen, *CEO*
Steve Newton, *President*
Raymond Pierce, *CFO*
EMP: 10
SQ FT: 3,300
SALES: 8MM **Privately Held**
SIC: 7372 Home entertainment computer software

(G-10028)
WASTEQUIP MANUFACTURING CO
1031 Hickstown Rd (08081-1091)
PHONE..................................856 784-5500
Andrew De Stefano, *President*
EMP: 100
SALES (corp-wide): 574.7MM **Privately Held**
WEB: www.rayfo.com
SIC: 3443 Dumpsters, garbage
HQ: Wastequip Manufacturing Company Llc
1901 Roxborough Rd # 300
Charlotte NC 28211

Skillman
Somerset County

(G-10029)
CONNECTING PRODUCTS INC
186 Tamarack Cir (08558-2021)
PHONE..................................609 512-1121
Anthony Freakes, *President*
EMP: 10
SALES (est): 600.9K **Privately Held**
SIC: 8711 3699 Mechanical engineering; electrical equipment & supplies

(G-10030)
CONNECTING PRODUCTS INC
194 Tamarack Cir Ste 1 (08558-2076)
PHONE..................................609 688-1808
▲ **EMP:** 7
SQ FT: 4,000
SALES (est): 2.4MM **Privately Held**
SIC: 3599 Mfg Industrial Machinery

(G-10031)
FORGE AHEAD LLC
1800 Route 206 (08558-1915)
PHONE..................................908 346-4794
Benton Camper, *CEO*
EMP: 4
SQ FT: 100
SALES (est): 98.3K **Privately Held**
SIC: 7372 Prepackaged software

(G-10032)
JOHNSON & JOHNSON CONSUMER INC (HQ)
199 Grandview Rd (08558-1303)
PHONE..................................908 874-1000
Fax: 908 874-1191
Kathleen Widmer, *President*
Rebecca Tillet, *President*
Michelle M Freyre, *Vice Pres*
Christopher Picariello, *Treasurer*

Alberto Guerrero, *Manager*
◆ **EMP:** 900 **EST:** 1879
SQ FT: 200,000
SALES (est): 465.2MM
SALES (corp-wide): 76.4B **Publicly Held**
SIC: 2834 Pharmaceutical preparations
PA: Johnson & Johnson
   1 Johnson And Johnson Plz
   New Brunswick NJ 08933
   732 524-0400

(G-10033)
MIDLANTIC MEDICAL SYSTEMS INC
61 Fieldstone Rd (08558-1642)
PHONE...............................908 432-4599
Tom Devine, *President*
EMP: 3
SALES: 3MM **Privately Held**
SIC: 8099 3842 Medical services organization; implants, surgical

(G-10034)
MONTGOMERY NEWS
88 Orchard Rd Ste 10 (08558-2642)
PHONE...............................908 874-0020
Cliff Moore, *Owner*
EMP: 4
SALES (est): 308.8K **Privately Held**
WEB: www.montgomerynewsonline.com
SIC: 2711 Newspapers, publishing & printing

(G-10035)
PERIBU GLOBAL SOURCING
Also Called: Peribu Collections LLC
5 Brookside Dr (08558-2104)
P.O. Box 130 (08558-0130)
PHONE...............................704 560-2035
Jessica Fogg, *Principal*
EMP: 10
SALES (est): 349.4K **Privately Held**
SIC: 2299 Textile goods

(G-10036)
PRINCETON BIOMEDITECH CORP
75 Orchard Rd (08558-2609)
PHONE...............................908 281-0112
Caroline Christopher, *Branch Mgr*
EMP: 20
SALES (corp-wide): 18.3MM **Privately Held**
SIC: 2835 In vitro diagnostics
PA: Princeton Biomeditech Corp
   4242 Us Highway 1
   Monmouth Junction NJ 08852
   732 274-1000

(G-10037)
VISIONWARE SYSTEMS INC
174 Tamarack Cir (08558-2021)
PHONE...............................609 924-0800
Fax: 609 924-1003
Larry Fridkis, *President*
Christopher Barranco, *Opers Staff*
EMP: 10
SQ FT: 1,700
SALES (est): 857.5K **Privately Held**
SIC: 7372 7335 Prepackaged software; commercial photography

Somerdale
Camden County

(G-10038)
ACCURATE MOLD INC
900 Chestnut Ave Ste G (08083-1457)
PHONE...............................856 784-8484
Fax: 856 784-9476
Willard Miller, *President*
EMP: 32
SALES (est): 2.8MM **Privately Held**
WEB: www.accuratemold.net
SIC: 3089 3544 Injection molding of plastics; special dies, tools, jigs & fixtures

(G-10039)
BISAGA INC
Also Called: Technique Precision
212 Ashland Ave (08083-1044)
PHONE...............................856 784-7966
Fax: 856 784-7974

Robert E Bisaga, *President*
Elizabeth J Bisaga, *Treasurer*
Carole Ritz, *Controller*
EMP: 12
SQ FT: 14,000
SALES (est): 1.2MM **Privately Held**
WEB: www.techniqueprecision.com
SIC: 3599 Machine shop, jobbing & repair

(G-10040)
FIORE SKYLIGHTS INC
700 Grace St (08083-1446)
P.O. Box 160 (08083-0160)
PHONE...............................856 346-0118
Fax: 856 346-9332
Richard Materio, *President*
John Kennedy, *Treasurer*
EMP: 18
SQ FT: 10,000
SALES (est): 2.8MM **Privately Held**
WEB: www.fioreskylights.com
SIC: 3444 Skylights, sheet metal

(G-10041)
LINTHICUM SAILS
607 Grace St (08083-1435)
PHONE...............................856 783-4288
Bradford Linthicum, *Owner*
EMP: 5
SQ FT: 2,800
SALES (est): 230K **Privately Held**
SIC: 2394 Sails: made from purchased materials

(G-10042)
PEPCO MANUFACTURING CO (PA)
210 E Evergreen Ave (08083-1014)
P.O. Box 160 (08083-0160)
PHONE...............................856 783-3700
Fax: 856 783-8098
John M Kennedy, *CEO*
Frank A Reiss, *President*
Mark Berwick, *Purch Agent*
Al Coughlin, *QC Mgr*
Beverly Winter, *CFO*
EMP: 85
SQ FT: 82,000
SALES: 7.5MM **Privately Held**
WEB: www.pepcosheetmetal.com
SIC: 3444 3469 Sheet metalwork; electronic enclosures, stamped or pressed metal

(G-10043)
SANDOVAL GRAPHICS & PRINTING
Also Called: Sandoval Graphic Co
9 Minnetonka Rd (08083-2718)
PHONE...............................856 435-7320
Fax: 856 435-7507
Gilbert Sandoval, *Partner*
Anthony Sandoval, *Partner*
Chris Sandoval, *Partner*
EMP: 6 **EST:** 1968
SQ FT: 6,000
SALES: 300K **Privately Held**
WEB: www.sandovalgraphics.com
SIC: 2791 2752 7336 Typesetting; commercial printing, lithographic; commercial printing, offset; graphic arts & related design

(G-10044)
STAINES INC
Also Called: S & S Printing
610 S White Horse Pike (08083-1246)
PHONE...............................856 784-2718
Fax: 856 783-7653
Carolann Staines, *President*
William Staines, *Corp Secy*
EMP: 12
SQ FT: 5,000
SALES (est): 1.9MM **Privately Held**
SIC: 2752 2796 2791 Commercial printing, lithographic; platemaking services; typesetting

Somers Point
Atlantic County

(G-10045)
BHAVIKA FUEL LLC
45 W Laurel Dr (08244-1249)
PHONE...............................609 926-4500
EMP: 6
SALES (est): 753.7K **Privately Held**
SIC: 2869 Fuels

(G-10046)
ERCO CEILINGS SOMERS POINT INC
5 Chestnut St (08244-1130)
PHONE...............................609 517-2531
Ronald Meischker, *General Mgr*
Esther Sykora, *Principal*
EMP: 30
SALES (est): 1.3MM **Privately Held**
SIC: 2591 Drapery hardware & blinds & shades

(G-10047)
MOONBABIES LLC
505 New Rd Ste 7 (08244-2049)
PHONE...............................609 926-0201
Fax: 609 926-0957
EMP: 4
SALES (est): 230K **Privately Held**
SIC: 3911 Whole/Mfg Jewelry

(G-10048)
UNIVERSAL TAPE SUPPLY CORP (PA)
110 W New Jersey Ave (08244-1765)
PHONE...............................609 653-3191
Fax: 609 653-3184
Joseph V Curcio, *President*
Mario Curcio, *Vice Pres*
Bob Semet, *Manager*
▲ **EMP:** 12
SQ FT: 2,000
SALES (est): 2.4MM **Privately Held**
WEB: www.universaltape.com
SIC: 2672 5113 3842 2891 Tape, pressure sensitive: made from purchased materials; pressure sensitive tape; surgical appliances & supplies; adhesives & sealants

Somerset
Somerset County

(G-10049)
ADVANCED FOOD SYSTEMS INC
21 Roosevelt Ave (08873-5030)
PHONE...............................732 873-6776
Fax: 732 828-5938
Yongkeun Joh, *President*
Sun P Joh, *Corp Secy*
Sunny Joh, *Vice Pres*
Shakirah Dickens, *Opers Staff*
Mark Purpura, *Technical Mgr*
EMP: 50
SQ FT: 26,800
SALES (est): 13.5MM **Privately Held**
SIC: 2087 8742 Flavoring extracts & syrups; food & beverage consultant

(G-10050)
AEON INDUSTRIES INC
76 Veronica Ave (08873-3417)
PHONE...............................732 246-3224
Fax: 732 828-4884
John Baumann, *President*
Louis Bonapace, *Principal*
EMP: 5
SALES (est): 1.1MM **Privately Held**
SIC: 2679 2671 Labels, paper: made from purchased material; packaging paper & plastics film, coated & laminated

(G-10051)
AEP NETWORKS INC
Also Called: 100 Owned By Ultra Elec Uk
347 Elizabeth Ave Ste 100 (08873-1123)
PHONE...............................732 652-5200
Fax: 732 764-8862

Pat Donnellan, *CEO*
Peter Van De Geest, *Managing Dir*
Kathryn M Kinnamon, *CFO*
EMP: 90 **EST:** 2000
SQ FT: 5,200
SALES (est): 11.9MM
SALES (corp-wide): 1B **Privately Held**
WEB: www.aepnetworks.com
SIC: 3577 Computer peripheral equipment
HQ: Aep Networks Limited
   Bray Business Park
   Bray

(G-10052)
AI-LOGIX INC
27 Worlds Fair Dr Ste 2 (08873-1353)
PHONE...............................732 469-0880
Fax: 732 469-2298
Moshe Tal, *President*
Mark Ringel, *CFO*
▲ **EMP:** 47
SQ FT: 19,500
SALES (est): 6.2MM
SALES (corp-wide): 145.5MM **Privately Held**
SIC: 3672 Circuit boards, television & radio printed
HQ: Audiocodes, Inc.
   27 Worlds Fair Dr Ste 2
   Somerset NJ 08873
   732 469-0880

(G-10053)
AKORN INC
72 Veronica Ave Ste 6 (08873-3426)
PHONE...............................732 659-6443
EMP: 60
SALES (corp-wide): 841MM **Publicly Held**
SIC: 2834 5047 Pharmaceutical Preparations
PA: Akorn, Inc.
   1925 W Field Ct Ste 300
   Lake Forest IL 60045
   847 279-6100

(G-10054)
ALPHA ASSEMBLY SOLUTIONS INC (DH)
Also Called: Alpha Advanced Materials
300 Atrium Dr Fl 3 (08873-4160)
P.O. Box 206703, Dallas TX (75320-6703)
PHONE...............................908 791-3000
Rick Ertmann, *CEO*
▲ **EMP:** 22
SALES: 102MM
SALES (corp-wide): 3.7B **Publicly Held**
WEB: www.alphametals.com
SIC: 3356 3341 3313 3339 Solder: wire, bar, acid core, & rosin core; lead smelting & refining (secondary); tin smelting & refining (secondary); alloys, additive, except copper: not made in blast furnaces; lead smelting & refining (primary); tin refining (primary); fluxes: brazing, soldering, galvanizing & welding
HQ: Macdermid, Incorporated
   245 Freight St
   Waterbury CT 06702
   203 575-5700

(G-10055)
ALTERA CORPORATION
106 Charles St (08873-2706)
PHONE...............................732 649-3477
John P Daane, *Branch Mgr*
EMP: 8
SALES (corp-wide): 62.7B **Publicly Held**
SIC: 3674 Semiconductors & related devices
HQ: Altera Corporation
   101 Innovation Dr
   San Jose CA 95134
   408 544-7000

(G-10056)
AMERICAN FIBERTEK INC
Also Called: Afi
120 Belmont Dr (08873-4243)
PHONE...............................732 302-0660
Fax: 732 302-0667
Jack Fernandes, *President*
Edward Davis, *Vice Pres*
EMP: 50
SQ FT: 10,800

GEOGRAPHIC

SALES (est): 11MM **Privately Held**
WEB: www.americanfibertek.com
SIC: 3679 3577 Electronic circuits;
input/output equipment, computer

(G-10057)
AMERICAN POWER CORD CORP
4 Smalley Ave (08873)
PHONE..............................973 574-8301
Makil A Simon, *President*
EMP: 5 EST: 1994
SALES (est): 177.6K **Privately Held**
SIC: 2298 Twine, cord & cordage

(G-10058)
ANALOG DEVICES INC
285 Davidson Ave Ste 402 (08873-4153)
PHONE..............................732 868-7100
Fax: 732 868-7101
John Kenney, *Manager*
EMP: 45
SALES (corp-wide): 5.1B **Publicly Held**
WEB: www.analog.com
SIC: 3674 Integrated circuits, semiconduc-
tor networks, etc.; hybrid integrated cir-
cuits
PA: Analog Devices, Inc.
1 Technology Way
Norwood MA 02062
781 329-4700

(G-10059)
API NANOFABRICATION & RES CORP
Also Called: Nanoopto
1600 Cottontail Ln Ste 1 (08873-5106)
PHONE..............................732 627-0808
EMP: 17
SALES (est): 1.8MM
SALES (corp-wide): 333.6MM **Privately Held**
SIC: 3827 Mfg Optical Instruments/Lenses
HQ: Api Technologies Corp.
400 Nickerson Rd
Marlborough MA 01752

(G-10060)
APICORE LLC (HQ)
49 Napoleon Ct Ste 1 (08873-9800)
PHONE..............................732 748-8882
Ravishanker Kovi, *President*
Sanjay Bhargav, *Opers Staff*
EMP: 40
SALES (est): 9.1MM
SALES (corp-wide): 21.2MM **Privately Held**
SIC: 2834 Pharmaceutical preparations;
solutions, pharmaceutical; powders, phar-
maceutical; proprietary drug products
PA: Medicure Inc
1250 Waverley St Suite 2
Winnipeg MB R3T 6
204 487-7412

(G-10061)
APICORE US LLC
49 Napoleon Ct (08873-1392)
PHONE..............................732 748-8882
Ravishinka Kovi, *Mng Member*
EMP: 40
SALES (est): 7.9MM **Privately Held**
SIC: 2834 Pharmaceutical preparations

(G-10062)
APPCO PHARMA LLC (PA)
Also Called: Appco Pharmaceuticals Corp.
120 Belmont Dr (08873-4243)
PHONE..............................732 271-8300
Rajendra P Appalaneni, *President*
Nagaraju Kanchanapali, *General Mgr*
Mahender Korapati, *COO*
EMP: 39 EST: 2009
SQ FT: 25,000
SALES (est): 8.2MM **Privately Held**
SIC: 2834 Pharmaceutical preparations

(G-10063)
APPCO PHARMA LLC
120 Belmont Dr (08873-4243)
PHONE..............................732 271-8300
Nagaraju Kanchanapalli, *Branch Mgr*
EMP: 35
SALES (corp-wide): 8.2MM **Privately Held**
SIC: 2834 Pharmaceutical preparations

PA: Appco Pharma Llc
120 Belmont Dr
Somerset NJ 08873
732 271-8300

(G-10064)
ASCENTTA INC
370 Campus Dr Ste 105 (08873-1128)
PHONE..............................732 868-1766
Shao H Liang, *Ch of Bd*
Jennifer Ke, *Vice Pres*
Anna Rooney, *Sales Staff*
EMP: 15
SALES (est): 2MM **Privately Held**
WEB: www.ascentta.com
SIC: 3357 Fiber optic cable (insulated)

(G-10065)
ASPIRE PHARMACEUTICALS INC (PA)
41 Veronica Ave (08873-6800)
PHONE..............................732 447-1444
Madhav Pai, *CEO*
Greg Szabo, *President*
Bhargav Bhatt, *Vice Pres*
Sonali Pai, *Vice Pres*
Oscar Martinez, *Facilities Mgr*
▲ EMP: 77
SQ FT: 38,000
SALES (est): 24.3MM **Privately Held**
SIC: 2834 Pharmaceutical preparations

(G-10066)
AUDIOCODES INC
27 Worlds Fair Dr Ste 2 (08873-1353)
PHONE..............................732 469-0880
Ben Rabinowitz, *Vice Pres*
EMP: 8
SALES (corp-wide): 145.5MM **Privately Held**
SIC: 3823 7371 Transmitters of process
variables, stand. signal conversion; com-
puter software development
HQ: Audiocodes, Inc.
27 Worlds Fair Dr Ste 2
Somerset NJ 08873
732 469-0880

(G-10067)
AUDIOCODES INC (HQ)
27 Worlds Fair Dr Ste 2 (08873-1353)
PHONE..............................732 469-0880
Shabtai Adlersberg, *President*
Bruce Gellman, *President*
Yossi Zilberfarb, *President*
Guy Avidan, *Vice Pres*
Nimrod Borovsky, *Vice Pres*
▲ EMP: 15
SQ FT: 3,000
SALES (est): 49.7MM
SALES (corp-wide): 145.5MM **Privately Held**
SIC: 3823 7371 Transmitters of process
variables, stand. signal conversion; com-
puter software development
PA: Audiocodes Ltd
1 Hayarden
Airport City 70199
397 640-00

(G-10068)
AUTOMANN INC (PA)
Also Called: Automann USA
850 Randolph Rd (08873-1288)
P.O. Box 6327 (08875-6327)
PHONE..............................201 529-4996
Thanwant Khanduja, *President*
John Younger, *General Mgr*
Chiranjeev Khanduja, *Vice Pres*
CJ Khanduja, *Vice Pres*
Jeev Khanduja, *Vice Pres*
◆ EMP: 83
SQ FT: 80,000
SALES (est): 91.5MM **Privately Held**
WEB: www.automann.com
SIC: 5013 3715 Truck parts & acces-
sories; truck trailer chassis

(G-10069)
BERNAFON LLC
2501 Cottontail Ln # 102 (08873-5125)
PHONE..............................888 941-4203
Fax: 732 560-4877
Joseph Lugara, *President*
EMP: 4

SALES (est): 500.3K **Privately Held**
SIC: 3841 Surgical & medical instruments
HQ: William Demant Holding A/S
Kongebakken 9
SmOrum 2765
391 771-00

(G-10070)
BLUE RIBBON AWARDS INC
12 Worlds Fair Dr Ste J (08873-1361)
PHONE..............................732 560-0046
Raymond F Zwigard, *President*
EMP: 4
SQ FT: 5,000
SALES (est): 420K **Privately Held**
SIC: 5999 2759 Trophies & plaques; en-
graving

(G-10071)
BUSINESS SOFTWARE APPLICATIONS
Also Called: Bsa Consulting
6 Sunny Ct (08873-5224)
PHONE..............................908 500-9980
Syed A Rahman, *President*
Khursheed Rahman, *Vice Pres*
EMP: 2
SALES: 1.2MM **Privately Held**
SIC: 7372 Prepackaged software

(G-10072)
CAMBRDGE INDS FOR VSLLY IMPRED
1230 Hamilton St (08873-3343)
PHONE..............................732 247-6668
Ben Tabatchnick, *Principal*
EMP: 8
SALES (est): 370.6K **Privately Held**
SIC: 3999 Manufacturing industries

(G-10073)
CARDINAL HEALTH SYSTEMS INC (HQ)
14 Schoolhouse Rd (08873-1213)
PHONE..............................732 537-6544
Jeff Henderson, *President*
Ivelisse Rivera, *Cust Mgr*
Bhupinder Thomas, *Manager*
Christy Albertson, *Director*
Rodney O'Gorman, *Director*
EMP: 300 EST: 1988
SALES (est): 114.9MM
SALES (corp-wide): 129.9B **Publicly Held**
WEB: www.cardinal.com
SIC: 7372 2834 Prepackaged software;
pharmaceutical preparations
PA: Cardinal Health, Inc.
7000 Cardinal Pl
Dublin OH 43017
614 757-5000

(G-10074)
CARTERET DIE-CASTING CORP
74 Veronica Ave (08873-3417)
P.O. Box 5610 (08875-5610)
PHONE..............................732 246-0070
Fax: 732 246-0196
John Burk, *President*
Gary Vogt, *Plant Mgr*
Mark Sirinathsingh, *Project Mgr*
John Mudrak, *VP Sales*
Paula Sirinathsingh, *Officer*
▲ EMP: 32 EST: 1960
SQ FT: 21,000
SALES (est): 8MM **Privately Held**
WEB: www.carteretdiecasting.com
SIC: 3364 Zinc & zinc-base alloy die-cast-
ings

(G-10075)
CATALENT INC (PA)
14 Schoolhouse Rd (08873-1213)
PHONE..............................732 537-6200
John R Chiminski, *President*
Aristippos Gennadios, *President*
Wetteny Joseph, *President*
Barry Littlejohns, *President*
Stephen Vanni, *General Mgr*
EMP: 88
SQ FT: 265,000
SALES: 2B **Publicly Held**
SIC: 2834 Pharmaceutical preparations

(G-10076)
CATALENT CTS KANSAS CITY LLC
14 Schoolhouse Rd (08873-1213)
PHONE..............................732 537-6200
Scott Houlton, *Principal*
EMP: 4
SALES (est): 768.6K **Publicly Held**
SIC: 2834 Pharmaceutical preparations
PA: Catalent, Inc.
14 Schoolhouse Rd
Somerset NJ 08873

(G-10077)
CATALENT PHARMA SOLUTIONS LLC (HQ)
14 Schoolhouse Rd (08873-1213)
P.O. Box 982106, El Paso TX (79998-
2106)
PHONE..............................732 537-6200
Cornell Stamoran,
▲ EMP: 75
SALES (est): 34.7MM **Publicly Held**
SIC: 2834 Pharmaceutical preparations

(G-10078)
CATALENT PHARMA SOLUTIONS INC (HQ)
14 Schoolhouse Rd (08873-1213)
PHONE..............................732 537-6200
Fax: 732 537-5932
John R Chiminski, *President*
Matthew Mollan, *General Mgr*
Dan Novin, *COO*
Michael Del Priore, *Senior VP*
Stephen Leonard, *Senior VP*
▲ EMP: 377
SQ FT: 265,000
SALES (est): 1.8B **Publicly Held**
SIC: 2834 3841 Pharmaceutical prepara-
tions; medical instruments & equipment,
blood & bone work

(G-10079)
CATALENT US HOLDING I LLC
14 Schoolhouse Rd (08873-1213)
PHONE..............................877 587-1835
EMP: 5
SALES (est): 127.3K **Publicly Held**
SIC: 2834 Pharmaceutical preparations
PA: Catalent, Inc.
14 Schoolhouse Rd
Somerset NJ 08873

(G-10080)
CAVAGNA NORTH AMERICA INC
50 Napoleon Ct (08873-1347)
PHONE..............................732 469-2100
Fax: 732 469-3344
Richard Darche, *Vice Pres*
Federico Bruschi, *Sales Mgr*
Nishant Patel, *Accounts Mgr*
Tom Biedebach, *Sales Staff*
Lynette Walcott, *Office Mgr*
▲ EMP: 35
SQ FT: 27,000
SALES (est): 7.8MM
SALES (corp-wide): 2.6MM **Privately Held**
SIC: 3491 Gas valves & parts, industrial
HQ: Cavagna Group Spa
Via Statale 11/13
Calcinato BS 25011
030 966-3111

(G-10081)
CEDAR HILL LANDSCAPING
Also Called: Cedar Hill Topsoil
127 Cedar Grove Ln (08873-4718)
PHONE..............................732 469-1400
Fax: 732 469-3252
John E Janho Jr, *President*
Nancy White, *Bookkeeper*
Kelly Janho, *Office Mgr*
Diana Lentzsch, *Admin Asst*
EMP: 20
SQ FT: 4,700
SALES (est): 3.4MM **Privately Held**
SIC: 4212 5261 1794 1429 Dump truck
haulage; top soil; excavation work; trap
rock, crushed & broken-quarrying

(G-10082)
CHROMAK RESEARCH INC
350 Campus Dr (08873-1126)
PHONE.....................................732 560-1366
Onkar Tomer, *President*
EMP: 4
SALES: 750K **Privately Held**
SIC: **8731** 8734 8331 7363 Medical research, commercial; product testing laboratories; vocational training agency; medical help service; medicinal chemicals

(G-10083)
COMPOSECURE LLC
309 Pierce St (08873-1229)
PHONE.....................................908 518-0500
Michele Logan, *Mng Member*
EMP: 250 **Privately Held**
SIC: **2821** Plasticizer/additive based plastic materials
PA: Composecure L.L.C.
500 Memorial Dr Ste 4
Somerset NJ 08873

(G-10084)
COMPOSECURE LLC (PA)
500 Memorial Dr Ste 4 (08873-1383)
PHONE.....................................908 518-0500
Dan Dundon, *Senior VP*
Luis Dasilva, *Vice Pres*
Justin D'Angelo, *VP Opers*
Justin Dangelo, *VP Opers*
Vincent Lombardo, *Mfg Mgr*
▲ EMP: 200
SQ FT: 10,000
SALES (est): 123.5MM **Privately Held**
SIC: **2821** Plasticizer/additive based plastic materials

(G-10085)
CONSUMER GRAPHICS INC
18 Fordham Rd (08873-1064)
PHONE.....................................732 469-4699
Ann Marie Dilorenzo, *President*
Mark Herzog, *Vice Pres*
EMP: 9
SQ FT: 7,500
SALES: 1.5MM **Privately Held**
SIC: **2741** 2791 Miscellaneous publishing; typesetting

(G-10086)
COZZOLI MACHINE COMPANY (PA)
50 Schoolhouse Rd (08873-1289)
PHONE.....................................732 564-0400
Fax: 732 564-0444
Joan Cozzoli Rooney, *President*
Michael Schuhlein, *Engineer*
Pat Belefronte, *Human Res Mgr*
Jasmine Chow, *Administration*
▲ EMP: 90 EST: 1919
SQ FT: 100,000
SALES (est): 17.1MM **Privately Held**
WEB: www.cozzoli.com
SIC: **3565** 3542 Packaging machinery; bottle washing & sterilizing machines; bottling machinery: filling, capping, labeling; marking machines

(G-10087)
CSF CORPORATION (PA)
285 Davidson Ave Ste 103 (08873-4142)
PHONE.....................................732 302-2222
Rich Scanlon, *President*
Melissa Spinola, *Business Mgr*
Frank Lauria, *Exec VP*
Ashley Kaplan, *Marketing Mgr*
EMP: 50
SALES (est): 3.4MM **Privately Held**
SIC: **7372** Operating systems computer software

(G-10088)
CUSTOM ESSENCE
53 Veronica Ave (08873-3448)
PHONE.....................................732 249-6405
Fax: 732 249-8528
Felix Buccellato, *President*
Christian Buccellato, *Exec VP*
Malini Amin, *Vice Pres*
Bob Diakon, *Vice Pres*
Raman Patel, *Vice Pres*
▼ EMP: 16
SQ FT: 5,000

SALES (est): 5.7MM **Privately Held**
WEB: www.customessence.com
SIC: **2844** Perfumes, natural or synthetic

(G-10089)
DAVIS-STANDARD LLC
220 Davidson Ave Ste 401 (08873-4146)
PHONE.....................................908 722-6000
Fax: 732 722-6444
Frank Kennedy, *Branch Mgr*
EMP: 42 **Privately Held**
SIC: **3561** Pumps & pumping equipment
HQ: Davis-Standard, Llc
1 Extrusion Dr
Pawcatuck CT 06379

(G-10090)
DOW CHEMICAL COMPANY
1 Riverview Dr (08873-1139)
PHONE.....................................800 258-2436
EMP: 71
SALES (corp-wide): 62.4B **Publicly Held**
SIC: **2821** 3081 Thermoplastic materials; plastic film & sheet
HQ: The Dow Chemical Company
2030 Dow Ctr
Midland MI 48674
989 636-1000

(G-10091)
DYNAMIC SAFETY USA LLC
Also Called: Dynamic Safety International
400 Apgar Dr Ste H (08873-1154)
PHONE.....................................844 378-7200
Rajeev S Emany,
EMP: 4
SALES (est): 504K **Privately Held**
SIC: **3842** Personal safety equipment

(G-10092)
EFFEXOFT INC
1553 State Route 27 # 1100 (08873-3980)
PHONE.....................................732 221-3642
Prasad Kunisetty, *President*
EMP: 5 EST: 2007
SALES: 1MM **Privately Held**
SIC: **7372** 7389 Business oriented computer software;

(G-10093)
EMMCO DEVELOPMENT CORP
243 Belmont Dr (08873-1286)
PHONE.....................................732 469-6464
Fax: 732 469-9180
Linda Degaeta, *Vice Pres*
EMP: 15 EST: 1954
SQ FT: 16,000
SALES (est): 2.1MM **Privately Held**
SIC: **3562** 3568 Ball bearings & parts; pivots, power transmission

(G-10094)
ENERSYS
80 Veronica Ave Ste 1 (08873-3498)
PHONE.....................................800 719-7887
Fred Weber, *Branch Mgr*
EMP: 88
SALES (corp-wide): 2.5B **Publicly Held**
SIC: **3691** 5063 Storage batteries; batteries
PA: Enersys
2366 Bernville Rd
Reading PA 19605
610 208-1991

(G-10095)
ENVIGO CRS INC (DH)
100 Mettlers Rd (08873-7378)
P.O. Box 2360, East Millstone (08875-2360)
PHONE.....................................732 873-2550
Fax: 732 790-7330
Brian Cass, *CEO*
Michael Caulfield, *General Mgr*
Lisa Craig, *Top Exec*
Joe Bedford, *Exec VP*
Carl John Michael Berg, *Vice Pres*
EMP: 300
SQ FT: 200,000
SALES (est): 78.2MM **Privately Held**
WEB: www.huntingdon.com
SIC: **2834** Pharmaceutical preparations
HQ: Life Sciences Research, Inc.
Mettlers Rd
East Millstone NJ 08875
732 649-9961

(G-10096)
EPIC MILLWORK LLC
1022 Hamilton St Ste J (08873-3387)
PHONE.....................................732 296-0273
Fax: 732 448-9400
Robert Epifano Jr, *Mng Member*
Michael Minetti, *Sr Project Mgr*
John Epifano,
EMP: 40 EST: 2001
SALES: 2.8MM **Privately Held**
SIC: **1751** 2431 Cabinet building & installation; millwork

(G-10097)
EQUIPMENT ERECTORS INC
15 Veronica Ave (08873-3489)
PHONE.....................................732 846-1212
Fax: 732 846-0833
George Anderson, *President*
Rob Anderson, *Vice Pres*
Robert Anderson, *Vice Pres*
Michelle Anderson, *Director*
EMP: 50
SQ FT: 32,000
SALES (est): 9.9MM **Privately Held**
WEB: www.equipmenterectors.com
SIC: **3535** 1796 Conveyors & conveying equipment; machinery installation

(G-10098)
EURODIA INDUSTRIE SA
Ameridia Div Eurodia Industrie
20 Worlds Fair Dr Ste F (08873-1362)
PHONE.....................................732 805-4001
Daniel H Bar, *Vice Pres*
EMP: 4 **Privately Held**
WEB: www.ameridia.com
SIC: **7389** 3569 Design, commercial & industrial; sifting & screening machines
HQ: Eurodia Industrie
Eurodia Oenodia Saint Martin
Pertuis 84120
490 087-500

(G-10099)
F WALTHER ELECTRIC CORP
12 Worlds Fair Dr Ste F (08873-1361)
PHONE.....................................732 537-9201
Fax: 732 537-9209
Kai Kalthoff, *President*
EMP: 5
SQ FT: 25,000
SALES (est): 1.3MM
SALES (corp-wide): 30.7MM **Privately Held**
SIC: **3699** Electrical equipment & supplies
PA: Walther-Werke Ferdinand Walther Gmbh
Ramsener Str. 6
Eisenberg (Pfalz) 67304
635 147-50

(G-10100)
FALCON INDUSTRIES INC
371 Campus Dr (08873-1125)
PHONE.....................................732 563-9889
Fax: 732 563-0899
Zig Michalski, *President*
Jim Harabedian, *Vice Pres*
Michael Miller, *Vice Pres*
Milosz Szpakowski, *Project Mgr*
Henny Hadjar, *Purch Mgr*
EMP: 60
SQ FT: 50,000
SALES (est): 12.4MM **Privately Held**
SIC: **3444** Sheet metalwork

(G-10101)
FANCYHEAT CORPORATION
40 Veronica Ave (08873-3417)
PHONE.....................................973 589-1450
Fiore Masci, *President*
Robert Masci, *Vice Pres*
▲ EMP: 16
SQ FT: 4,500
SALES (est): 4MM **Privately Held**
WEB: www.fancyheat.com
SIC: **2869** Fuels

(G-10102)
FLAVOR AND FD INGREDIENTS INC (PA)
Also Called: Summit Hill Flavors
21 Worlds Fair Dr (08873-1344)
PHONE.....................................732 805-0335
Fax: 732 805-1994

Dwight Grenawalt, *Vice Pres*
▲ EMP: 37
SQ FT: 10,000
SALES (est): 7.6MM **Privately Held**
WEB: www.summithillflavors.com
SIC: **2087** Flavoring extracts & syrups

(G-10103)
G J CHEMICAL CO (PA)
40 Veronica Ave (08873-3417)
PHONE.....................................973 589-1450
Diane Colonna, *President*
Arnold Colonna, *Purch Agent*
Gina Lopez, *Human Resources*
Gary Wagman, *Manager*
Nicolas Colonna, *Info Tech Mgr*
▲ EMP: 50
SQ FT: 45,000
SALES (est): 14.2MM **Privately Held**
SIC: **2819** 5169 Industrial inorganic chemicals; chemicals, reagent grade: refined from technical grade; industrial chemicals

(G-10104)
GENLYTE THOMAS GROUP LLC (DH)
Also Called: Philips Entertainment Lighting
200 Franklin Square Dr (08873-4181)
PHONE.....................................800 825-5844
Bruno Biasiotta, *Mng Member*
Paul Cavanaugh, *Mng Member*
David A Dripchak, *Mng Member*
James Galeese, *Mng Member*
Joseph E Innamorati, *Mng Member*
◆ EMP: 30 EST: 1998
SQ FT: 15,000
SALES (est): 201.5MM
SALES (corp-wide): 20.9B **Privately Held**
WEB: www.lightguard.com
SIC: **3646** Commercial indusl & institutional electric lighting fixtures; ceiling systems, luminous; ornamental lighting fixtures, commercial; fluorescent lighting fixtures, commercial
HQ: Philips Lighting North America Corporation
3 Burlington Woods Dr # 4
Burlington MA 01803
617 423-9999

(G-10105)
GERICKE USA INC
14 Worlds Fair Dr Ste C (08873-1365)
PHONE.....................................855 888-0088
Markus Gericke, *President*
Alberto Rodriguez, *Senior VP*
Alex Bickel, *Admin Sec*
◆ EMP: 4
SALES (est): 208.2K **Privately Held**
SIC: **3556** Dehydrating equipment, food processing

(G-10106)
GO FOTON CORPORATION (PA)
28 Worlds Fair Dr (08873-1391)
PHONE.....................................732 412-7375
Simin Cai, *President*
Feng Tian, *Vice Pres*
Michael Zammit, *Vice Pres*
Qin Zhang, *Vice Pres*
Hisao Nagata, *Research*
▲ EMP: 16 EST: 1983
SQ FT: 49,000
SALES (est): 2.5MM **Privately Held**
WEB: www.nsgamerica.com
SIC: **3229** Fiber optics strands

(G-10107)
HERR FOODS INCORPORATED
790 New Brunswick Rd (08873-5220)
PHONE.....................................732 356-1295
Fax: 732 356-2722
Billy Esolda, *Branch Mgr*
Billy Esolida, *Manager*
EMP: 45
SQ FT: 10,000
SALES (corp-wide): 448.6MM **Privately Held**
WEB: www.herrs.com
SIC: **2096** Potato chips & similar snacks
PA: Herr Foods Incorporated
20 Herr Dr
Nottingham PA 19362
610 932-9330

(G-10108)
HOUSE FOODS AMERICA CORP
801 Randolph Rd (08873-1224)
PHONE......................................732 537-9500
Fax: 732 537-0500
Tomio Uehara, *Manager*
EMP: 70
SALES (corp-wide): 2.5B Privately Held
WEB: www.house-foods.com
SIC: 2075 Soybean oil, cake or meal
HQ: House Foods America Corporation
　　7351 Orangewood Ave
　　Garden Grove CA 92841
　　714 901-4350

(G-10109)
HOUSE OF CUPCAKES LLC
51 Suydam Rd (08873-7306)
PHONE......................................908 413-3076
Ruth Bzdewka, *Principal*
EMP: 8
SALES (est): 590.2K Privately Held
SIC: 2051 Bread, cake & related products

(G-10110)
HYDRATIGHT OPERATIONS INC
Also Called: Biach
12 Worlds Fair Dr Ste A (08873-1348)
PHONE......................................732 271-4100
Robert Boychuk, *General Mgr*
Paulette Weiss, *Vice Pres*
Richard Hill, *Branch Mgr*
Ginger Gromadski, *Manager*
EMP: 17
SALES (corp-wide): 1.1B Publicly Held
SIC: 3599 Machine & other job shop work
HQ: Hydratight Operations, Inc.
　　1102 Hall Ct
　　Deer Park TX 77536
　　713 860-4200

(G-10111)
INDUSTRIAL COMBUSTION ASSN
20 Worlds Fair Dr Ste C (08873-1362)
PHONE......................................732 271-0300
Robert Peles, *President*
Regina Peles, *Corp Secy*
EMP: 11 EST: 1938
SQ FT: 5,600
SALES (est): 3.5MM Privately Held
WEB: www.icanj.com
SIC: 5074 5075 3594 Oil burners; warm
　　air heating equipment & supplies; fluid
　　power pumps & motors

(G-10112)
INVADERM CORPORATION
25 Worlds Fair Dr (08873-1344)
PHONE......................................973 572-5676
Dilip Solanki, *Director*
EMP: 6
SALES: 2MM Privately Held
SIC: 2834 Pharmaceutical preparations

(G-10113)
IQE RF LLC
394 Elizabeth Ave Ste 1 (08873-5117)
PHONE......................................732 271-5990
Alex Ceruzzi, *Mng Member*
William Kurtz,
◆ EMP: 71
SALES (est): 11.1MM
SALES (corp-wide): 204.1MM Privately
Held
SIC: 3679 Electronic circuits
PA: Iqe Plc
　　Pascal Close
　　Cardiff S GLAM CF3 0
　　292 083-9400

(G-10114)
IVOCLAR VIVADENT MFG INC
500 Memorial Dr (08873-1383)
PHONE......................................732 563-4755
Paul Panzera, *General Mgr*
Lou Alcuri, *Project Mgr*
Adam Pasierski, *Production*
Harry Mullaney, *Finance Dir*
Luciana Celeste, *Director*
▲ EMP: 80 EST: 1961
SQ FT: 17,000

SALES (est): 16.4MM
SALES (corp-wide): 818.2MM Privately
Held
WEB: www.ivoclarna.com
SIC: 3843 Dental materials
HQ: Ivoclar Vivadent, Inc.
　　175 Pineview Dr
　　Amherst NY 14228
　　716 691-0010

(G-10115)
JACQUELINE MAZZA LLC
6 Saw Mill Dr (08873-7363)
PHONE......................................732 718-2944
Jacqueline Mazza, *Principal*
EMP: 4
SALES (est): 238.6K Privately Held
SIC: 2051 Bread, cake & related products

(G-10116)
JANSSEN PHARMACEUTICALS INC
1 Cottontail Ln (08873-1135)
P.O. Box 300, Raritan (08869-0602)
PHONE......................................908 218-7701
Fax: 908 469-8535
George Weaver, *Director*
EMP: 80
SALES (corp-wide): 76.4B Publicly Held
WEB: www.ortho-mcneil.com
SIC: 2833 Medicinals & botanicals
HQ: Ortho-Mcneil Pharmaceutical, Llc
　　1000 Rte 202
　　Raritan NJ 08869
　　908 203-4090

(G-10117)
JERSEY METAL WORKS LLC
1022 Hamilton St Untid (08873)
PHONE......................................732 565-1313
Robert Epifano Jr, *Mng Member*
John Epifano, *Mng Member*
EMP: 8
SALES (est): 1.2MM Privately Held
SIC: 3441 Fabricated structural metal

(G-10118)
KAS ORIENTAL RUGS INC (PA)
62 Veronica Ave Ste A (08873-3484)
PHONE......................................732 545-1900
Fax: 732 545-5836
Prasadarao B Yarlagadda, *President*
Prasadarao Yarlagadda, *Principal*
Santhi Yarlagadda, *Vice Pres*
Ellen Demeo, *Credit Staff*
Brianne Coradini, *Marketing Staff*
▲ EMP: 27
SQ FT: 100,000
SALES (est): 5.8MM Privately Held
WEB: www.kasrugs.com
SIC: 2392 2273 Cushions & pillows; carpets & rugs

(G-10119)
KRAUS & NAIMER INC (PA)
760 New Brunswick Rd (08873-5299)
PHONE......................................732 560-1240
Joachim Laurenz Naimer, *President*
Mark Farrell, *Managing Dir*
Wang David, *Vice Pres*
Ray Paella, *Vice Pres*
Ray Parello, *Vice Pres*
EMP: 40 EST: 1950
SQ FT: 45,000
SALES (est): 15.8MM Privately Held
WEB: www.krausnaimer.com
SIC: 5063 3678 3643 Electrical supplies;
　　electronic connectors; current-carrying
　　wiring devices

(G-10120)
LA CASA DE TORTILLA
2017 State Route 27 (08873-3838)
PHONE......................................732 398-0660
Peter Chan, *Owner*
EMP: 6
SALES (est): 336.7K Privately Held
SIC: 2099 Tortillas, fresh or refrigerated

(G-10121)
LABVANTAGE SOLUTIONS INC (DH)
265 Davidson Ave Ste 220 (08873-4120)
PHONE......................................908 707-4100
John Hesier, *President*
William Musil, *Technical Mgr*

Shweta Grover, *Manager*
Mark Hill, *Technology*
EMP: 50
SQ FT: 15,000
SALES (est): 38.4MM Privately Held
WEB: www.labvantage.com
SIC: 7372 Prepackaged software

(G-10122)
LEAD BEAD PUBLISHING COMPANY
46 Shelly Dr (08873-1806)
PHONE......................................732 246-0410
James H Wiggins III, *Owner*
EMP: 4
SALES (est): 119.2K Privately Held
SIC: 2741 Music book & sheet music publishing

(G-10123)
LEVOMED INC
2 Rue Matisse (08873-4890)
PHONE......................................908 359-4804
Mohan Devineni, *President*
◆ EMP: 2
SALES: 1.5MM Privately Held
SIC: 2834 7389 Pills, pharmaceutical;

(G-10124)
LEWIS SCHELLER PRINTING CORP
Also Called: Scheller, Lewis Printing
1723 Hwy 27 (08873)
PHONE......................................732 843-5050
Fax: 732 843-5535
Lewis Scheller, *President*
Peggy Scheller, *Principal*
EMP: 6
SQ FT: 1,800
SALES (est): 94K Privately Held
WEB: www.lewprint.com
SIC: 2752 7334 Commercial printing, offset; photocopying & duplicating services

(G-10125)
LOGAN INSTRUMENTS CORPORATION
19c Schoolhouse Rd Ste C (08873)
P.O. Box 5785 (08875-5785)
PHONE......................................732 302-9888
Fax: 732 302-9898
Luke Lee, *President*
Vivian Lee, *Admin Sec*
◆ EMP: 17
SQ FT: 8,000
SALES: 30K Privately Held
SIC: 3559 Pharmaceutical machinery

(G-10126)
LUMETA CORPORATION (PA)
300 Atrium Dr Ste 300 # 300 (08873-4160)
P.O. Box 822043, Philadelphia PA (19182-2043)
PHONE......................................732 357-3500
Fax: 732 564-0731
Michael Markulec, *President*
Ana Paula Sebastiao, *General Mgr*
George Budd, *Principal*
Valerie Clayton, *Principal*
Constantine Malaxos, *Principal*
EMP: 25
SQ FT: 14,000
SALES (est): 3.7MM Privately Held
WEB: www.lumeta.com
SIC: 7372 Business oriented computer
　　software

(G-10127)
LUPIN PHARMACEUTICALS INC
390 Campus Dr (08873-1102)
PHONE......................................908 603-6075
EMP: 4
SALES (est): 328.7K Privately Held
SIC: 2834 Pharmaceutical preparations

(G-10128)
LUPIN PHARMACEUTICALS INC ✪
400 Campus Dr (08873-1145)
PHONE......................................908 603-6000
EMP: 6 EST: 2017
SALES (est): 691.6K Privately Held
SIC: 2834 Pharmaceutical preparations

(G-10129)
MARIANO PRESS LLC
14 Veronica Ave (08873-3417)
PHONE......................................732 247-3659
Fax: 732 214-1383
Jerry Mariano, *Partner*
Joe Mariano, *Partner*
▲ EMP: 12
SQ FT: 10,000
SALES: 2.3MM Privately Held
WEB: www.marianopress.com
SIC: 2752 2796 2789 2759 Commercial
　　printing, offset; platemaking services;
　　bookbinding & related work; commercial
　　printing

(G-10130)
MARMO ENTERPRISES INC
468 Elizabeth Ave (08873-5200)
PHONE......................................732 649-3011
Fax: 732 649-3072
Matthew Partsinevelos, *President*
EMP: 9
SQ FT: 9,400
SALES (est): 1.4MM Privately Held
WEB: www.marmoenterprises.com
SIC: 3281 Granite, cut & shaped

(G-10131)
MATERIALS TECHNOLOGY INC
Also Called: MTI Solar
220 Churchill Ave (08873-3441)
PHONE......................................732 246-1000
Sheldon L Soskin, *President*
Martin Stanko, *Vice Pres*
▲ EMP: 6
SQ FT: 26,800
SALES (est): 887.3K Privately Held
WEB: www.mtisolar.com
SIC: 3497 Copper foil
PA: Marshel Associates Inc
　　220 Churchill Ave
　　Somerset NJ 08873
　　732 246-1000

(G-10132)
MATRIX CONTROLS COMPANY INC
330 Elizabeth Ave (08873-7018)
PHONE......................................732 469-5551
Fax: 732 469-7299
Robert Lindeman, *Vice Pres*
Eduardo Planchon, *Design Engr*
EMP: 15 EST: 1958
SQ FT: 1,800
SALES (est): 1.9MM Privately Held
SIC: 3823 Controllers for process variables, all types

(G-10133)
MEDICAL TRANSCRIPTION BILLING (PA)
Also Called: MTBC
7 Clyde Rd (08873-5049)
PHONE......................................732 873-5133
Fax: 732 873-6858
Stephen A Snyder, *CEO*
A Hadi Chaudhry, *President*
Mahmud Haq, *Chairman*
Bill Korn, *CFO*
Norman Roth,
EMP: 10
SQ FT: 2,400
SALES: 31.8MM Publicly Held
WEB: www.mtbc.com
SIC: 7372 Prepackaged software

(G-10134)
MEGAWATT MACHINE SERVICES LLC
417 Elizabeth Ave (08873-1292)
PHONE......................................732 805-4000
Andre Balogh, *Vice Pres*
Istvan Balogh Jr, *Vice Pres*
Steven Balogh, *VP Sales*
Pauline Balogh,
EMP: 25
SQ FT: 30,000
SALES (est): 6.3MM Privately Held
SIC: 3599 Machine shop, jobbing & repair

(G-10135)
MELILLO CONSULTING INC (PA)
285 Davidson Ave Ste 202 (08873-4153)
PHONE......................................732 563-8400

Fax: 732 563-8450
Mark J Melillo, *CEO*
Karen L Melillo, *Vice Pres*
Karen Melillo, *Vice Pres*
Joe Staiber, *Vice Pres*
Dan Sytsma, *Vice Pres*
EMP: 40
SQ FT: 21,000
SALES (est): 20.9MM **Privately Held**
WEB: www.mjm.com
SIC: 7371 7373 7372 5045 Computer
software development & applications;
computer integrated systems design;
prepackaged software; computers, pe-
ripherals & software

(G-10136)
MELLON D P M L L C (HQ)
2 Worlds Fair Dr Ste 310 (08873-1372)
PHONE...................................732 563-0030
Robert M Aaron, *President*
Steve R Diemer, *Vice Pres*
Guy Castranova, *CFO*
Charles Crow, *Asst Sec*
EMP: 5
SQ FT: 20,000
SALES (est): 30MM
SALES (corp-wide): 15.5B **Publicly Held**
SIC: 2421 Sawmills & planing mills, gen-
eral
PA: The Bank Of New York Mellon Corpora-
tion
240 Greenwich St
New York NY 10286
212 495-1784

(G-10137)
MERCK SHARP & DOHME
EUROPE INC (DH)
300 Franklin Square Dr (08873-4187)
PHONE...................................908 423-1000
Fax: 732 868-2510
Greg Warner, *President*
Judy Lewent, *Vice Pres*
Francis Spiegel, *Vice Pres*
M Tarnow, *Vice Pres*
EMP: 10
SALES (est): 5.5MM
SALES (corp-wide): 40.1B **Publicly Held**
SIC: 2834 Pharmaceutical preparations
HQ: Merck Sharp & Dohme Corp.
2000 Galloping Hill Rd
Kenilworth NJ 07033
908 740-4000

(G-10138)
MICRO STAMPING
CORPORATION (PA)
Also Called: Micro Medical Technologies
140 Belmont Dr (08873-5113)
PHONE...................................732 302-0800
Fax: 732 302-0436
Brian Semcer, *President*
Frank J Semcer, *Chairman*
Steve Santoro, *Exec VP*
Charles Edwards, *Vice Pres*
Carl Savage, *Vice Pres*
▲ EMP: 240 EST: 1945
SQ FT: 68,000
SALES (est): 51.2MM **Privately Held**
WEB: www.microstamping.com
SIC: 3841 3469 Surgical & medical instru-
ments; metal stampings

(G-10139)
MODULATION SCIENCES INC
12 Worlds Fair Dr Ste A (08873-1348)
PHONE...................................732 302-3090
Fax: 732 302-0206
Eric Small, *CEO*
EMP: 14
SQ FT: 7,500
SALES (est): 2.4MM **Privately Held**
WEB: www.modsci.com
SIC: 3663 Satellites, communications

(G-10140)
MTBC HEALTH INC (HQ)
7 Clyde Rd (08873-5049)
PHONE...................................732 873-5133
Stephen Snyder, *CEO*
Bill Korn, *CFO*
EMP: 2

SALES (est): 3.4MM
SALES (corp-wide): 31.8MM **Publicly**
Held
SIC: 7372 Prepackaged software
PA: Medical Transcription Billing, Corp.
7 Clyde Rd
Somerset NJ 08873
732 873-5133

(G-10141)
MTBC PRACTICE MANAGEMENT
CORP
7 Clyde Rd (08873-5049)
PHONE...................................732 873-5133
Stephen Snyder, *CEO*
Bill Korn, *CFO*
EMP: 120
SALES (est): 1.5MM
SALES (corp-wide): 31.8MM **Publicly**
Held
SIC: 7372 Prepackaged software
HQ: Mtbc Health, Inc.
7 Clyde Rd
Somerset NJ 08873
732 873-5133

(G-10142)
MULTILINK TECHNOLOGY CORP
300 Atrium Dr Fl 2 (08873-4160)
PHONE...................................732 805-9355
Richard Nottenburg PHD, *Ch of Bd*
John Soenksen, *CFO*
Scott Schaeffer, *Architect*
EMP: 45
SQ FT: 36,000
SALES (est): 3MM
SALES (corp-wide): 3.9B **Publicly Held**
WEB: www.mltc.com
SIC: 3674 Semiconductors & related de-
vices
HQ: Microsemi Communications, Inc.
4721 Calle Carga
Camarillo CA 93012
805 388-3700

(G-10143)
NANOOPTO CORPORATION
1600 Cottontail Ln Ste 1 (08873-5106)
PHONE...................................732 627-0808
Fax: 732 627-9886
EMP: 31
SALES (est): 4.7MM **Privately Held**
SIC: 3827 Mfg Optical Instruments/Lenses

(G-10144)
NEW WORLD STAINLESS LLC
100 Randolph Rd Ste 5 (08873-1384)
PHONE...................................732 412-7137
Bob Zagari, *Facilities Mgr*
Harry Stamateris, *Marketing Staff*
J Cameron Zielinskie,
EMP: 40
SALES (est): 14.6MM **Privately Held**
SIC: 3312 Blast furnaces & steel mills

(G-10145)
NOVEL LABORATORIES INC
400 Campus Dr (08873-1145)
PHONE...................................908 603-6000
Veerappan Subramanian, *President*
Prasad Uv, *Opers Staff*
Rakesh Jambudi, *Production*
Venu Padmanabhan, *Production*
Devraj Swaminarayan, *Production*
▲ EMP: 175
SQ FT: 90,000
SALES (est): 74.9MM
SALES (corp-wide): 1.5B **Privately Held**
WEB: www.novellabs.net
SIC: 2834 Pharmaceutical preparations
HQ: Lupin Pharmaceuticals, Inc.
111 S Calvert St Fl 21
Baltimore MD 21202
410 576-2000

(G-10146)
OGURA INDUSTRIAL CORP (HQ)
100 Randolph Rd (08873-1384)
P.O. Box 5790 (08875-5790)
PHONE...................................586 749-1900
Yasihero Ogura, *CEO*
Frank J Flemming, *President*
Mike Garvey, *Regional Mgr*
Junichi Ebisawa, *Treasurer*
Brian Mather, *Sales Mgr*
▲ EMP: 13 EST: 1997

SALES (est): 1.9MM
SALES (corp-wide): 333MM **Privately**
Held
WEB: www.oguraclutch.com
SIC: 3714 Motor vehicle parts & acces-
sories
PA: Ogura Clutch Co., Ltd.
2-678, Aioicho
Kiryu GNM 376-0
277 547-101

(G-10147)
ORION PRECISION INDUSTRIES
8 Veronica Ave (08873-3400)
PHONE...................................732 247-9704
Fax: 732 828-8878
John Sztankovits, *President*
Edith Sztankovits, *Vice Pres*
Paul Murcavage, *Plant Mgr*
Steve Foulon, *VP Sls/Mktg*
Olivia Paladi, *Regl Sales Mgr*
EMP: 25
SQ FT: 8,000
SALES (est): 5.5MM **Privately Held**
WEB: www.orionprecision.com
SIC: 3451 Screw machine products

(G-10148)
OTICON INC (DH)
580 Howard Ave (08873-1136)
P.O. Box 6724 (08875-6724)
PHONE...................................732 560-1220
Fax: 732 560-0029
Niels Jacobsen, *CEO*
Svend Thomsen, *CFO*
Robert Buchas, *Admin Sec*
▲ EMP: 145
SQ FT: 25,000
SALES (est): 30.5MM **Privately Held**
WEB: www.oticonus.com
SIC: 3842 5047 Hearing aids; hearing aids
HQ: William Demant Holding A/S
Kongebakken 9
SmOrum 2765
391 771-00

(G-10149)
OTICON MEDICAL LLC
580 Howard Ave (08873-1136)
PHONE...................................732 560-0727
Curt Gorman, *President*
John Sparacio, *President*
Cathy Van Evra, *QC Mgr*
▲ EMP: 23
SQ FT: 3,000
SALES (est): 2.8MM **Privately Held**
SIC: 3842 Implants, surgical
HQ: Oticon Medical Ab
Datavagen 37b
Askim 436 3
317 486-100

(G-10150)
P & R CASTINGS LLC
325 Pierce St (08873-1229)
PHONE...................................732 302-3600
Brian H Margulies,
Benjamin S Margulies,
▲ EMP: 25
SQ FT: 53,000
SALES (est): 2.9MM **Privately Held**
SIC: 3297 Castable refractories, nonclay

(G-10151)
P & R FASTENERS INC (PA)
325 Pierce St (08873-1229)
PHONE...................................732 302-3600
Fax: 732 302-3636
Benjamin S Margulies, *President*
Brian Isaacson, *VP Sales*
Ana Lynch, *Sales Staff*
Carmen Perez, *Sales Staff*
Ron Chomsky, *Info Tech Dir*
▲ EMP: 65 EST: 1970
SQ FT: 103,000
SALES (est): 32.4MM **Privately Held**
WEB: www.prfast.com
SIC: 5085 3452 Fasteners, industrial:
nuts, bolts, screws, etc.; screws, metal

(G-10152)
PACON MANUFACTURING CORP
Also Called: Baumgartner Associates
400 Pierce St (08873)
PHONE...................................732 764-9070
Fax: 732 754-1728

Dorothy H Shannon, *Ch of Bd*
A Vernon Shannon III, *President*
Micheal Shannon, *President*
Lawrence H Shannon, *Vice Pres*
▲ EMP: 125
SQ FT: 168,000
SALES (est): 45.5MM **Privately Held**
WEB: www.paconmfg.com
SIC: 2676 3821 3842 Sanitary paper
products; incubators, laboratory; surgical
appliances & supplies

(G-10153)
PERMABOND LLC (PA)
223 Churchill Ave (08873-3487)
PHONE...................................610 323-5003
Fax: 732 868-0267
Attilio Grossi, *CEO*
Amy Sutryn,
▲ EMP: 6
SALES (est): 3.6MM **Privately Held**
WEB: www.permabond.com
SIC: 2891 Adhesives & sealants

(G-10154)
PHILIPS LIGHTING N AMER
CORP
200 Franklin Square Dr (08873-4181)
PHONE...................................732 563-3000
Erik Bouts, *President*
EMP: 280
SQ FT: 200,000
SALES (corp-wide): 20.9B **Privately Held**
WEB: www.usa.philips.com
SIC: 3641 Electric light bulbs, complete
HQ: Philips Lighting North America Corpo-
ration
3 Burlington Woods Dr # 4
Burlington MA 01803
617 423-9999

(G-10155)
PIM BRANDS LLC
500 Pierce St (08873-1270)
P.O. Box 8, Allentown (08501-0008)
PHONE...................................732 560-8300
Michael Rosenberg, *CEO*
Kevin Walsh, *President*
▲ EMP: 89
SQ FT: 180,000
SALES (est): 23MM **Privately Held**
WEB: www.promotioninmotion.com
SIC: 2064 Candy & other confectionery
products

(G-10156)
POWER CONTAINER CORP
Also Called: PCC
33 Schoolhouse Rd Ste 2 (08873-1386)
PHONE...................................732 560-3655
Pittheus Molemans, *President*
Rigel Millan, *General Mgr*
Brian Bartle, *Prdtn Mgr*
Michael Ochieng, *Engineer*
Richard Tomasco, *Engineer*
▲ EMP: 32
SQ FT: 40,000
SALES (est): 6.4MM **Privately Held**
WEB: www.powercontainer.com
SIC: 3589 Commercial cooking & food-
warming equipment

(G-10157)
PRESPERSE CORPORATION
(HQ)
19 Schoolhouse Rd (08873-1385)
PHONE...................................732 356-5200
Fax: 732 356-3533
Paulo Rodrigues, *President*
Kathleen Niemann, *Purch Mgr*
Joseph Macri, *CFO*
Tim Phillip, *Controller*
Heidi Lebel, *Mktg Dir*
▲ EMP: 20
SALES: 43.3MM
SALES (corp-wide): 45.3B **Privately Held**
WEB: www.presperse.com
SIC: 2844 Cosmetic preparations
PA: Sumitomo Corporation
1-8-11, Harumi
Chuo-Ku TKY 104-0
351 665-000

G
E
O
G
R
A
P
H
I
C

(G-10158)
PRESTIGE CAMERA LLC
245 Belmont Dr (08873-1217)
PHONE..............................718 257-5888
Albert Houllou,
Frieda Stern,
▼ EMP: 50
SALES (est): 2.9MM Privately Held
SIC: 3861 Cameras & related equipment

(G-10159)
PROMOTION IN MOTION INC
500 Pierce St (08873-1270)
PHONE..............................732 560-8300
Frank McSorley, Branch Mgr
Susan O'Donnell, Director
EMP: 30
SALES (corp-wide): 179.3MM Privately
Held
WEB: www.promotioninmotion.com
SIC: 2064 Candy & other confectionery
products
PA: Promotion In Motion, Inc
25 Commerce Dr
Allendale NJ 07401
201 962-8530

(G-10160)
**PTS INTERMEDIATE HOLDINGS
LLC**
14 Schoolhouse Rd (08873-1213)
PHONE..............................732 537-6200
EMP: 3000
SALES (est): 576.5MM Publicly Held
SIC: 2834 Pharmaceutical preparations
PA: Catalent, Inc.
14 Schoolhouse Rd
Somerset NJ 08873

(G-10161)
QUAD/GRAPHICS INC
13 Jensen Dr Ste 100 (08873-1393)
PHONE..............................732 469-0189
EMP: 50
SALES (corp-wide): 4.3B Publicly Held
SIC: 2752 Lithographic Commercial Print-
ing
PA: Quad/Graphics Inc.
N61w23044 Harrys Way
Sussex WI 53089
414 566-6000

(G-10162)
RARITAN INC (DH)
400 Cottontail Ln (08873-1238)
PHONE..............................732 764-8886
Doug Fikse, President
Ashley Fox, Vice Pres
Henry Hsu, Vice Pres
Andy Schreiber, Opers Staff
Lori Cartaciano, Purchasing
▲ EMP: 40
SALES (est): 93.1MM
SALES (corp-wide): 20.7MM Privately
Held
SIC: 3612 3577 Transformers, except
electric; computer peripheral equipment
HQ: Legrand North America, Llc
60 Woodlawn St
West Hartford CT 06110
860 233-6251

(G-10163)
RARITAN AMERICAS INC (DH)
Also Called: Raritan Computer
400 Cottontail Ln (08873-1238)
PHONE..............................732 764-8886
Fax: 732 764-8887
Ching-I Hsu, President
Stephen Gagliardo, Technical Mgr
Huimin Cao, Engineer
Bob Dennerlein, CFO
Seth Feldman, Sales Staff
▲ EMP: 110
SQ FT: 55,000
SALES (est): 48.6MM
SALES (corp-wide): 20.7MM Privately
Held
WEB: www.raritan.com
SIC: 3577 Computer peripheral equipment

(G-10164)
RED SQUARE FOODS INC
62 Berry St (08873-3505)
PHONE..............................732 846-0190
Boris Rapoport, President

Yuri Muzykozsky, Vice Pres
EMP: 12
SQ FT: 3,500
SALES (est): 2MM Privately Held
SIC: 2013 Head cheese from purchased
meat products

(G-10165)
RENDAS TOOL & DIE INC
417 Elizabeth Ave (08873-1292)
P.O. Box 49, Martinsville (08836-0049)
PHONE..............................732 469-4670
Fax: 732 469-6171
Laszlo Rendas, President
Mary Ellen Rendas, Admin Sec
EMP: 25
SQ FT: 30,000
SALES (est): 1.6MM Privately Held
SIC: 3599 Machine shop, jobbing & repair

(G-10166)
REVENT INCORPORATED
22 Roosevelt Ave (08873-5031)
PHONE..............................732 777-5187
Daniel Lago, CEO
Charles Rampersaud, Co-Owner
Stefan Fallgren, Vice Pres
Stuart Hendry, Vice Pres
Michael Rekuc, Accounting Mgr
◆ EMP: 40
SQ FT: 50,000
SALES: 18.6MM
SALES (corp-wide): 33.6MM Privately
Held
WEB: www.revent.com
SIC: 3556 Ovens, bakery
PA: Revent International Ab
Ekebyvagen 18ekeby Gard
Upplands Vasby 194 9
859 000-600

(G-10167)
ROSENWACH TANK CO LLC
Also Called: Rosenwach Group
1100 Randolph Rd (08873-1291)
PHONE..............................732 563-4900
Andrew Rosenwach,
EMP: 30
SALES (est): 333.1K Privately Held
SIC: 3443 1711 Water tanks, metal plate;
heating & air conditioning contractors

(G-10168)
ROTOR CLIP COMPANY INC (PA)
Also Called: Rotor Clamp
187 Davidson Ave (08873-4192)
PHONE..............................732 469-7707
Fax: 732 469-7898
Robert Slass, President
Jon Coiro, General Mgr
Craig Slass, Vice Pres
Henry Yates, Vice Pres
Jeff Van Arsdale, Warehouse Mgr
▲ EMP: 290
SQ FT: 50,000
SALES (est): 74.4MM Privately Held
WEB: www.rotorclip.com
SIC: 3429 Metal fasteners; clamps & cou-
plings, hose

(G-10169)
RUST-OLEUM CORPORATION
323 Campus Dr (08873-1138)
PHONE..............................732 469-8100
Rebecca Spencer, Branch Mgr
EMP: 30
SALES (corp-wide): 5.3B Publicly Held
WEB: www.zinsser.com
SIC: 2851 2821 Shellac (protective coat-
ing); plastics materials & resins
HQ: Rust-Oleum Corporation
11 E Hawthorn Pkwy
Vernon Hills IL 60061
847 367-7700

(G-10170)
**SAINT-GOBAIN PRFMCE PLAS
CORP**
Also Called: Flexible Components
1600 Cottontail Ln (08873-5106)
PHONE..............................732 652-0910
George Carpenter, Manager
EMP: 75

SALES (corp-wide): 213.5MM Privately
Held
SIC: 3599 3429 2891 2851 Flexible
metal hose, tubing & bellows; manufactured hardware (general); adhesives &
sealants; paints & allied products
HQ: Saint-Gobain Performance Plastics
Corporation
31500 Solon Rd
Solon OH 44139
440 836-6900

(G-10171)
**SATURN OVERHEAD
EQUIPMENT LLC**
100 Apgar Dr (08873-1146)
PHONE..............................732 560-7210
Fax: 973 465-4219
Steven Gordan,
Eugenio Moutela,
▲ EMP: 11
SQ FT: 15,000
SALES (est): 3.5MM Privately Held
WEB: www.saturneng.com
SIC: 3537 3536 Industrial trucks & trac-
tors; hoists

(G-10172)
**SOMERSET OUTPATIENT
SURGERY**
100 Franklin Square Dr # 100
(08873-4109)
PHONE..............................781 635-2807
Sharon Bowen, Principal
EMP: 4
SALES (est): 310K Privately Held
SIC: 3841 Surgical & medical instruments

(G-10173)
SONIC INNOVATIONS INC
2501 Cottontail Ln (08873-5125)
P.O. Box 6779 (08875-6779)
PHONE..............................888 423-7834
Joseph A Lugara, President
EMP: 8
SALES (est): 1.3MM Privately Held
SIC: 3842 Hearing aids
PA: Sonic Ag
Morgenstrasse 131b
Bern BE 3018
315 602-121

(G-10174)
**STUART STEEL PROTECTION
CORP**
411 Elizabeth Ave (08873-1292)
P.O. Box 476, South Bound Brook (08880-
0476)
PHONE..............................732 469-5544
Fax: 732 469-9270
Gordon Stuart, President
◆ EMP: 20 EST: 1952
SALES: 14MM Privately Held
WEB: www.stusteel.com
SIC: 3599 3292 2899 Custom machinery;
pipe covering (heat insulating material);
except felt; chemical preparations

(G-10175)
STULL TECHNOLOGIES LLC
17 Veronica Ave (08873-3514)
PHONE..............................732 873-5000
Fax: 732 873-7131
Gene Stull, CEO
Vicky Clark, Production
Sanket Khandelwal, Engineer
Joe Sebastian, Engineer
Dan Fay, Sr Project Mgr
▲ EMP: 95 EST: 1986
SQ FT: 189,000
SALES (est): 33.3MM Privately Held
WEB: www.stulltech.com
SIC: 3089 Closures, plastic
HQ: Mold-Rite Plastics, Llc
30 N La Salle St Ste 2425
Chicago IL 60602
518 561-1812

(G-10176)
SUNBIRD SOFTWARE INC
200 Cottontail Ln B106e (08873-1231)
PHONE..............................732 993-4476
Herman Chan, President
EMP: 60 EST: 2015
SQ FT: 4,350

SALES (est): 6.9MM Privately Held
SIC: 7372 7371 Business oriented computer software; computer software development

(G-10177)
**SYSCO GUEST SUPPLY LLC
(HQ)**
Also Called: Int'l Purchasing Exchange
300 Davidson Ave (08873-4175)
P.O. Box 6782 (08875-6782)
PHONE..............................732 537-2297
Fax: 609 514-2692
Tom McDonald, Managing Dir
Dave M Shattuck, Vice Pres
◆ EMP: 125
SALES (est): 1.4B
SALES (corp-wide): 55.3B Publicly Held
SIC: 5122 2844 5131 5139 Toilet soap;
druggists' sundries; shampoos, rinses,
conditioners: hair; toilet preparations;
mouthwashes; sewing accessories; hair
accessories; shoe accessories; hotels;
casino hotel; hotel or motel management
PA: Sysco Corporation
1390 Enclave Pkwy
Houston TX 77077
281 584-1390

(G-10178)
**T C P RELIABLE
MANUFACTURING**
Also Called: Tcp/Reliable
285 Davidson Ave Ste 303 (08873-4153)
PHONE..............................732 346-9200
Maurice Barakat, President
Anthony Spina, Treasurer
▲ EMP: 45
SQ FT: 63,000
SALES (est): 7MM
SALES (corp-wide): 33.8MM Privately
Held
WEB: www.tcpreliable.com
SIC: 3086 Plastics foam products
PA: Tcp Reliable Inc.
551 Raritan Center Pkwy
Edison NJ 08837
848 229-2466

(G-10179)
**TAKARA BELMONT USA INC
(HQ)**
101 Belmont Dr (08873-1293)
PHONE..............................732 469-5000
Fax: 732 280-7504
Hidetaka Yoshikawa, CEO
Kunifousa Yashikawa, Ch of Bd
Toshi Hiraoka, Exec VP
Masahiro Kanaya, Exec VP
Pam Oldewurtel, Production
▲ EMP: 60
SQ FT: 100,000
SALES (est): 30.9MM
SALES (corp-wide): 483.2MM Privately
Held
WEB: www.belmontequip.com
SIC: 3843 3999 Dental chairs; barber &
beauty shop equipment
PA: Takara Belmont Corporation
2-1-1, Higashishinsaibashi, Chuo-Ku
Osaka OSK 542-0
662 112-831

(G-10180)
TAKARA BELMONT USA INC
Belmont Equipment Company
101 Belmont Dr (08873-1293)
PHONE..............................732 469-5000
Fax: 732 469-9430
Belmont Takara, Branch Mgr
EMP: 50
SALES (corp-wide): 483.2MM Privately
Held
WEB: www.belmontequip.com
SIC: 3843 Dental equipment
HQ: Takara Belmont Usa, Inc.
101 Belmont Dr
Somerset NJ 08873
732 469-5000

(G-10181)
TAYLOR COMMUNICATIONS INC
625 Pierce St Ste A (08873-1267)
PHONE..............................732 560-3410
Fax: 732 560-4648
Peter Vanderzee, Manager

EMP: 55
SALES (corp-wide): 3.5B **Privately Held**
WEB: www.stdreg.com
SIC: 2761 Manifold business forms
HQ: Taylor Communications, Inc.
    4205 S 96th St
    Omaha NE 68127
    402 898-6422

(G-10182)
TEAM NISCA
100 Randolph Rd (08873-1384)
PHONE..................................732 271-7367
Andrew Peterson, *Natl Sales Mgr*
Rob Miskelly, *Manager*
Tom Hudson, *Director*
EMP: 5
SALES (est): 411K **Privately Held**
SIC: 3089 Identification cards, plastic

(G-10183)
TECH BRAINS SOLUTIONS INC
Also Called: It Talent
220 Davidson Ave Ste 303 (08873-4144)
PHONE..................................732 952-0552
Dheerta Kapoor, *President*
EMP: 40 EST: 2014
SALES: 6.6MM **Privately Held**
SIC: 7372 Application computer software

(G-10184)
TERUMO AMERICAS HOLDING INC (HQ)
2101 Cottontail Ln (08873-5115)
PHONE..................................732 302-4900
Yutaro Shintaku, *CEO*
Hiroshi Matsumura, *Vice Pres*
Emily Miner, *Vice Pres*
Phil Lester, *Production*
Brian Hubis, *Senior Buyer*
▲ EMP: 75
SQ FT: 100,000
SALES (est): 862.3MM
SALES (corp-wide): 5.5B **Privately Held**
WEB: www.terumomedical.com
SIC: 3841 Surgical & medical instruments;
    needles, suture; catheters
PA: Terumo Corporation
    2-44-1, Hatagaya
    Shibuya-Ku TKY 151-0
    333 748-111

(G-10185)
TERUMO MEDICAL CORPORATION (DH)
2101 Cottontail Ln (08873-5115)
PHONE..................................732 302-4900
Fax: 732 302-3083
Jim Takeuchi, *President*
William Cahill, *Principal*
Ryota Sugimoto, *Business Mgr*
Bruce Canter, *Vice Pres*
Nagai Hirofumi, *Vice Pres*
▲ EMP: 160
SALES (est): 55.9MM
SALES (corp-wide): 5.5B **Privately Held**
SIC: 3841 Surgical & medical instruments;
    needles, suture; catheters
HQ: Terumo Americas Holding, Inc.
    2101 Cottontail Ln
    Somerset NJ 08873
    732 302-4900

(G-10186)
TEVA WOMENS HEALTH INC
400 Campus Dr (08873-1145)
PHONE..................................201 930-3300
Larry Downey, *Branch Mgr*
EMP: 5
SALES (corp-wide): 22.3B **Privately Held**
SIC: 2834 Pharmaceutical preparations
HQ: Teva Women's Health, Inc.
    5040 Duramed Rd
    Cincinnati OH 45213
    513 731-9900

(G-10187)
THERMO FISHER SCIENTIFIC INC
265 Davidson Ave Ste 101 (08873-4120)
PHONE..................................732 627-0220
Herb Kenny, *Vice Pres*
EMP: 15

SALES (corp-wide): 20.9B **Publicly Held**
WEB: www.thermo.com
SIC: 3826 Analytical instruments
PA: Thermo Fisher Scientific Inc.
    168 3rd Ave
    Waltham MA 02451
    781 622-1000

(G-10188)
TOPPAN PRINTING CO AMER INC
Also Called: Peeq Media
1100 Randolph Rd (08873-5114)
PHONE..................................732 469-8400
Shingo Ohkado, *President*
Phil Candura, *Vice Pres*
Jeffrey Snyder, *Vice Pres*
Carol Houlik, *Sls & Mktg Exec*
Toshiro Masuda, *Financial Exec*
EMP: 125
SALES (corp-wide): 13.6B **Privately Held**
WEB: www.toppan.com
SIC: 2759 7336 2796 2789 Commercial
    printing; commercial art & graphic design;
    platemaking services; bookbinding & re-
    lated work; commercial printing, litho-
    graphic; automotive & apparel trimmings
HQ: Toppan Printing Company (America),
    Inc.
    2175 Greenhill Dr
    Round Rock TX 78664
    512 310-6212

(G-10189)
TRODAT USA INC (DH)
48 Heller Park Ln (08873-1206)
PHONE..................................732 529-8500
Paul Demartini, *CEO*
Tim Snell, *Sales Mgr*
Shawn Chunn,
EMP: 11
SALES (est): 12.7MM **Privately Held**
SIC: 3953 Marking devices
HQ: Trodat Gmbh
    Linzer StraBe 156
    Wels 4600
    724 223-90

(G-10190)
TRODAT USA LLC
48 Heller Park Ln (08873-1206)
PHONE..................................732 562-9500
Paul Demartini, *President*
Saurabh Gupta, *Managing Dir*
Manfred Prinz, *Exec VP*
Chris Boyle, *Vice Pres*
Nalini Shukla, *Asst Controller*
▲ EMP: 61
SALES (est): 12.7MM **Privately Held**
SIC: 3953 Embossing seals & hand
    stamps
HQ: Trodat Usa, Inc.
    48 Heller Park Ln
    Somerset NJ 08873

(G-10191)
UNITED PLASTICS GROUP INC
30 Commerce Dr (08873-3468)
PHONE..................................732 873-8777
Fax: 732 873-5611
Chihming Wong, *President*
▲ EMP: 44
SQ FT: 45,000
SALES (est): 9.4MM **Privately Held**
SIC: 2656 Sanitary food containers

(G-10192)
VEECO
Also Called: Mocvd Systems
394 Elizabeth Ave (08873-5117)
PHONE..................................732 560-5300
Fax: 732 560-5301
John Peeler, *CEO*
David Glass, *Exec VP*
Bill Miller, *Exec VP*
Nino Federico, *Senior VP*
Ken Macwilliams, *Senior VP*
EMP: 21 EST: 2013
SALES (est): 3.9MM **Privately Held**
SIC: 3559 Semiconductor manufacturing
    machinery

(G-10193)
VEECO INSTRUMENTS INC
394 Elizabeth Ave (08873-5117)
PHONE..................................732 560-5300

Herman Itzkowitz, *Senior VP*
Susan Stapleton, *Vice Pres*
Bruce Cowper, *Project Mgr*
Krauss Jay, *Production*
Paul Wraga, *Research*
EMP: 34
SALES (corp-wide): 484.7MM **Publicly Held**
SIC: 3559 3572 3827 Semiconductor
    manufacturing machinery; computer stor-
    age devices; optical instruments & lenses;
    microscopes, except electron, proton &
    corneal
PA: Veeco Instruments Inc.
    1 Terminal Dr
    Plainview NY 11803
    516 677-0200

(G-10194)
VEECO PROCESS EQUIPMENT INC
394 Elizabeth Ave (08873-5117)
PHONE..................................732 560-5300
Malden Braun, *Branch Mgr*
EMP: 115
SQ FT: 5,600
SALES (corp-wide): 484.7MM **Publicly Held**
SIC: 3826 Analytical instruments
HQ: Veeco Process Equipment Inc.
    1 Terminal Dr
    Plainview NY 11803

(G-10195)
VENKATESHWARA INC
Also Called: Femto Calibrations
285 Davidson Ave Ste 100 (08873-4153)
PHONE..................................908 964-4777
Fax: 908 964-0970
Sanjay Saxena, *President*
Madhu Saxena, *Admin Sec*
EMP: 10 EST: 1991
SQ FT: 2,000
SALES: 750K **Privately Held**
SIC: 3829 Measuring & controlling devices

(G-10196)
W A CLEARY PRODUCTS INC
Also Called: W.A. Cleary Products
1049 Somerset St (08873-5014)
PHONE..................................732 246-2829
John Christman, *President*
EMP: 15
SALES (est): 2.1MM
SALES (corp-wide): 6MM **Privately Held**
WEB: www.wacleary products.com
SIC: 2076 Vegetable oil mills
PA: W.A. Cleary Corporation
    1049 Somerset St
    Somerset NJ 08873
    732 247-8000

(G-10197)
W R GRACE & CO-CONN
8 Heller Park Ln (08873-1206)
PHONE..................................732 868-6914
Bruce Robertson, *Manager*
EMP: 35
SALES (corp-wide): 1.7B **Publicly Held**
WEB: www.grace.com
SIC: 2899 Concrete curing & hardening
    compounds
HQ: W. R. Grace & Co.-Conn.
    7500 Grace Dr
    Columbia MD 21044
    410 531-4000

Somerville
Somerset County

(G-10198)
A R BOTHERS WOODWORKING INC
236 Dukes Pkwy E (08876)
P.O. Box 127 (08876-0127)
PHONE..................................908 725-2891
Fax: 908 707-1062
Charles A Bothers, *President*
Evelyn Bothers, *Corp Secy*
Ron Bothers, *Vice Pres*
EMP: 20
SQ FT: 20,000

SALES (est): 2MM **Privately Held**
SIC: 2434 Wood kitchen cabinets; vanities,
    bathroom: wood

(G-10199)
ADIANT (PA)
92 E Main St Ste 405 (08876-2319)
PHONE..................................800 264-8303
Ash Nashed, *CEO*
Ian Kane, *Publisher*
Anton Kashcheyev, *Publisher*
Jon Carmen, *Senior VP*
Rafael Cosentino, *Senior VP*
EMP: 12
SALES (est): 3.1MM **Privately Held**
SIC: 3993 Advertising artwork

(G-10200)
AGFA CORPORATION
1318 State Hwy 31 (08876)
PHONE..................................908 231-5000
Fax: 908 231-5210
Perry Premdas, *Branch Mgr*
EMP: 5
SQ FT: 200,000
SALES (corp-wide): 526.3MM **Privately Held**
SIC: 2796 2893 Lithographic plates, posi-
    tives or negatives; printing ink
HQ: Agfa Corporation
    611 River Dr Ste 305
    Elmwood Park NJ 07407
    800 540-2432

(G-10201)
ALLIANCE SAND CO INC (PA)
51 Tannery Rd (08876-6040)
PHONE..................................908 534-4116
Ernest Renda, *President*
EMP: 3
SQ FT: 4,000
SALES (est): 1.8MM **Privately Held**
WEB: www.allpoconos.com
SIC: 1442 Common sand mining; construc-
    tion sand mining; gravel mining

(G-10202)
BLUE CHIP INDUSTRIES INC
50 Old Camplain Rd (08876)
PHONE..................................908 704-1466
Fax: 908 704-1467
Carl A Inhoff, *President*
EMP: 6 EST: 1965
SQ FT: 4,500
SALES (est): 613.1K **Privately Held**
SIC: 3599 Machine shop, jobbing & repair

(G-10203)
BRUNSWICK WASTE SYSTEM
Beekman Ln (08876)
PHONE..................................908 369-2223
Dave Byerley, *Owner*
EMP: 5
SQ FT: 14,000
SALES (est): 431.3K **Privately Held**
SIC: 5084 7699 3441 Industrial machin-
    ery & equipment; industrial machinery &
    equipment repair; fabricated structural
    metal

(G-10204)
CENTURY TUBE CORP
22 Tannery Rd (08876-6000)
PHONE..................................908 534-2001
Fax: 908 534-4030
Dominick De Angelo, *President*
Nick De Angelo, *Vice Pres*
▲ EMP: 40
SQ FT: 28,000
SALES (est): 14.8MM **Privately Held**
SIC: 3312 3317 3498 Tubes, steel & iron;
    steel pipe & tubes; tube fabricating (con-
    tract bending & shaping)

(G-10205)
CHOICE CABINETRY LLC
61 5th St (08876-3260)
PHONE..................................908 707-8801
Norman Pollock, *Mng Member*
▲ EMP: 50
SALES (est): 8MM **Privately Held**
SIC: 2434 Wood kitchen cabinets

(G-10206)
DEMAND LLC
36 S Adamsville Rd 1 (08876)
PHONE..................................908 526-2020
Fax: 908 526-8012
Joseph Kafara, *Mng Member*
EMP: 19
SALES (est): 3.5MM **Privately Held**
SIC: 3444 Sheet metalwork

(G-10207)
ETHICON INC (HQ)
Us Route 22 (08876)
P.O. Box 151 (08876-0151)
PHONE..................................732 524-0400
Fax: 908 218-2471
Steven Henn, *President*
Sarah G Brennan, *Vice Pres*
Robert J Decker, *Treasurer*
Harish Potharaju, *Information Mgr*
Veera Rastogi, *Admin Sec*
◆ EMP: 2500 EST: 1945
SQ FT: 772,000
SALES (est): 1.3B
SALES (corp-wide): 76.4B **Publicly Held**
WEB: www.ethiconinc.com
SIC: 3842 Sutures, absorbable & non-absorbable; ligatures, medical
PA: Johnson & Johnson
    1 Johnson And Johnson Plz
    New Brunswick NJ 08933
    732 524-0400

(G-10208)
ETHICON LLC (HQ)
Rr 22 Box W (08876)
P.O. Box 16571, New Brunswick (08906-6571)
PHONE..................................908 218-3195
Fax: 908 218-3518
Clifford Holland, *President*
Louis Rivera, *Project Mgr*
Sunil Bhutani, *Engineer*
Dan Cahill, *Sales Staff*
Janet Garcia, *Sales Staff*
EMP: 55
SALES (est): 35.9MM
SALES (corp-wide): 76.4B **Publicly Held**
SIC: 3845 Endoscopic equipment, electromedical
PA: Johnson & Johnson
    1 Johnson And Johnson Plz
    New Brunswick NJ 08933
    732 524-0400

(G-10209)
G & B MACHINE INC
35 N Middaugh St Ste B (08876-1827)
PHONE..................................908 707-1181
Fax: 908 722-2215
Gary Boccadutre, *President*
EMP: 5
SQ FT: 4,000
SALES (est): 500K **Privately Held**
WEB: www.gbmachineinc.com
SIC: 3599 Machine shop, jobbing & repair

(G-10210)
GALEN PUBLISHING LLC
Also Called: Advanced Studies In Medicine
166 W Main St (08876-2204)
PHONE..................................908 253-9001
Fax: 908 253-9002
John A Flynn, *Editor*
Paul J Scheel, *Chief*
Gourley Dick, *Dean*
Bobby Thomas, *Dean*
Mary Camillo, *Production*
EMP: 25
SALES (est): 2.1MM **Privately Held**
SIC: 8011 2721 Offices & clinics of medical doctors; periodicals

(G-10211)
GANNETT CO INC
Also Called: Courier News
92 E Main St Ste 202 (08876-2319)
PHONE..................................908 243-6953
Michael Deak, *Manager*
EMP: 77
SALES (corp-wide): 3.1B **Publicly Held**
SIC: 2711 Newspapers, publishing & printing

PA: Gannett Co., Inc.
    7950 Jones Branch Dr
    Mc Lean VA 22102
    703 854-6000

(G-10212)
GLENTECH INC
46 4th St (08876-3206)
P.O. Box 7617, Hillsborough (08844-7617)
PHONE..................................908 685-2205
Fax: 908 685-1626
Scott Gordon, *President*
James Gordon, *Vice Pres*
Gregory Para, *Shareholder*
EMP: 12
SQ FT: 9,000
SALES (est): 1.6MM **Privately Held**
SIC: 3441 Fabricated structural metal

(G-10213)
HAMON CORPORATION (DH)
58 E Main St (08876-2312)
P.O. Box 1500 (08876-1251)
PHONE..................................908 333-2000
William P Dillon, *CEO*
Victor Bochicchio, *President*
Oliver Acheson, *COO*
Don Kawecki, *Exec VP*
H James Peters, *Exec VP*
▲ EMP: 95
SQ FT: 33,000
SALES (est): 113.1MM
SALES (corp-wide): 156.5K **Privately Held**
WEB: www.hamonusa.com
SIC: 1629 3564 3499 5084 Industrial plant construction; blowers & fans; friction material, made from powdered metal; industrial machinery & equipment
HQ: Hamon & Cie (International) Sa
    Rue Emile Francqui 2
    Mont-Saint-Guibert 1435
    103 904-00

(G-10214)
HOME NEWS TRIBUNE
92 E Main St Ste 202 (08876-2319)
PHONE..................................908 243-6600
EMP: 20
SALES (est): 347.8K **Privately Held**
SIC: 2711 Newspapers, publishing & printing

(G-10215)
INDEPENDENCE TECHNOLOGY LLC
W Ethicon Bldg Rr 22 (08876)
PHONE..................................908 722-3767
Sandra Denarski, *CFO*
Kenneth Giason,
EMP: 12
SALES (est): 1.5MM
SALES (corp-wide): 76.4B **Publicly Held**
WEB: www.indetech.com
SIC: 3842 Wheelchairs
PA: Johnson & Johnson
    1 Johnson And Johnson Plz
    New Brunswick NJ 08933
    732 524-0400

(G-10216)
INTERNATIONAL SHTMTL PLATE MFG
112 Veterans Mem Dr E (08876-2911)
P.O. Box 506 (08876-0506)
PHONE..................................908 722-6614
Fax: 908 722-4039
John Novak III, *President*
Andrew Novak, *Vice Pres*
Michelle Novak, *Office Mgr*
EMP: 32
SQ FT: 7,500
SALES (est): 8.2MM **Privately Held**
WEB: www.internationalsheetmetal.com
SIC: 3444 Sheet metal specialties, not stamped

(G-10217)
J & M AIR INC
189 S Bridge St (08876-3217)
PHONE..................................908 707-4040
Fax: 908 707-0447
Michael Favreau, *President*
Jamie Favreau, *Vice Pres*
EMP: 20
SQ FT: 5,000

SALES (est): 3MM **Privately Held**
SIC: 3589 5046 3444 Commercial cooking & foodwarming equipment; commercial cooking & food service equipment; sheet metalwork

(G-10218)
JOHNSON & JOHNSON
51 Chubb Way (08876)
P.O. Box 151 (08876-0151)
PHONE..................................908 725-7256
Gerrie Canfield Johnson, *Branch Mgr*
EMP: 79
SALES (corp-wide): 76.4B **Publicly Held**
WEB: www.jnj.com
SIC: 2834 Pharmaceutical preparations
PA: Johnson & Johnson
    1 Johnson And Johnson Plz
    New Brunswick NJ 08933
    732 524-0400

(G-10219)
JOHNSON & JOHNSON MEDICAL INC (DH)
Us Rt 22 (08876)
PHONE..................................908 218-0707
William Clarke, *President*
EMP: 700 EST: 1949
SQ FT: 1,000,000
SALES (est): 169.4MM
SALES (corp-wide): 76.4B **Publicly Held**
SIC: 3842 Surgical appliances & supplies; drapes, surgical (cotton)
HQ: Ethicon Inc.
    Us Route 22
    Somerville NJ 08876
    732 524-0400

(G-10220)
KOMPAC TECHNOLOGIES LLC
7 Commerce St Ste 1 (08876-6039)
PHONE..................................908 534-8411
Fax: 973 227-7532
Colin Hayes, *Electrical Engi*
Thomas Hayes, *Mng Member*
Michael Pek,
▲ EMP: 22 EST: 2006
SQ FT: 13,000
SALES (est): 5.7MM **Privately Held**
SIC: 3565 Labeling machines, industrial

(G-10221)
NEW JERSEY ELECTRIC MOTORS
84 Somerset St Ste A (08876-2842)
PHONE..................................908 526-5225
Fax: 908 704-1440
Salvatore Gambino, *President*
EMP: 6 EST: 1978
SQ FT: 800
SALES (est): 1MM **Privately Held**
SIC: 5999 7694 Motors, electric; electric motor repair

(G-10222)
NEXIRA INC
15 Somerset St (08876-2828)
PHONE..................................908 704-7480
Stephane Dondain, *President*
Teresa Yazbek, *Vice Pres*
Niall McStay, *Accounts Mgr*
◆ EMP: 10
SQ FT: 6,000
SALES (est): 22.5MM
SALES (corp-wide): 115.4MM **Privately Held**
WEB: www.cniworld.com
SIC: 2051 5145 2099 Bakery: wholesale or wholesale/retail combined; confectionery; emulsifiers, food
PA: Nexira
    129 Chemin De Croisset
    Rouen 76000
    232 831-818

(G-10223)
PHILDESCO INC
50 Division St Ste 207 (08876-2943)
PHONE..................................732 937-6560
Juan Quimson, *CEO*
Augusto S Santos, *CFO*
Anna Maria Decastro, *Admin Sec*
▲ EMP: 5
SALES (est): 22.1K **Privately Held**
SIC: 2099 Coconut, desiccated & shredded

(G-10224)
PLATINUM DESIGNS LLC
87 W Main St (08876-2243)
P.O. Box 232, Flemington (08822-0232)
PHONE..................................908 782-4010
Robin Cairl, *Finance*
Ian G Cairl,
EMP: 8
SQ FT: 2,000
SALES: 1.5MM **Privately Held**
SIC: 2434 Wood kitchen cabinets

(G-10225)
POWERSPEC INC
25 4th St (08876-3205)
PHONE..................................732 494-9490
Fax: 732 494-9494
Laurie Elkoury, *President*
Peter Elkoury, *Vice Pres*
Peter E Koury, *Manager*
EMP: 30
SQ FT: 10,000
SALES (est): 3.5MM **Privately Held**
SIC: 6221 5084 3629 Commodity contracts brokers, dealers; industrial machinery & equipment; power conversion units, a.c. to d.c.: static-electric

(G-10226)
ROAN PRINTING INC
Also Called: Minuteman Press
4 E Main St (08876-2308)
PHONE..................................908 526-5990
Fax: 908 526-4958
Sherman Feuer, *President*
Carole Feuer, *Vice Pres*
EMP: 10 EST: 1979
SQ FT: 3,750
SALES (est): 1.6MM **Privately Held**
WEB: www.mmpprinting.com
SIC: 2752 2791 7334 2789 Commercial printing, offset; typesetting; photocopying & duplicating services; bookbinding & related work; commercial printing

(G-10227)
SYMBOLOGY ENTERPRISES INC (PA)
50 Division St Ste 203 (08876-2943)
PHONE..................................908 725-1699
Gail Mc Inerney, *President*
Gail McInerney, *President*
Thomas McInerney, *Vice Pres*
Shaun McInerney, *Technology*
EMP: 10
SQ FT: 5,000
SALES: 3MM **Privately Held**
WEB: www.symbology.net
SIC: 3577 Verifiers, punch card; magnetic ink recognition devices

(G-10228)
THERMAL TRANSFER CORP
58 E Main St (08876-2312)
PHONE..................................412 460-4004
Raymond T Betler, *President*
EMP: 4
SALES (est): 198K
SALES (corp-wide): 3.8B **Publicly Held**
SIC: 3433 Heating equipment, except electric
PA: Westinghouse Air Brake Technologies Corporation
    1001 Airbrake Ave
    Wilmerding PA 15148
    412 825-1000

(G-10229)
TOP KNOBS USA INC (DH)
3 Millennium Way (08876-3876)
P.O. Box 779, Belle Mead (08502-0779)
PHONE..................................908 359-6174
Greg Gotleib, *CEO*
Mike Denvir, *Ch of Bd*
Warren Ramsland, *President*
Peter Suffredini, *Corp Secy*
Rick Yancey, *CFO*
▲ EMP: 50
SQ FT: 30,000
SALES (est): 6.3MM
SALES (corp-wide): 1.3B **Privately Held**
WEB: www.topknobsusa.com
SIC: 3264 Porcelain electrical supplies

HQ: Dimora Brands, Inc.
170 Township Line Rd
Hillsborough NJ 08844
908 359-6174

(G-10230)
TOWNE TECHNOLOGIES INC
6-10 Bell Ave (08876-1802)
P.O. Box 460 (08876-0460)
PHONE..............................908 722-9500
Fax: 908 722-8394
Dr Hercharan Dhillon, *President*
Daniel J Hughes, *Vice Pres*
Sal Losardo, *Sales Executive*
Kuldip Dhillon, *Admin Sec*
▲ EMP: 15
SQ FT: 44,000
SALES: 1.5MM **Privately Held**
WEB: www.townetech.com
SIC: 3861 Photographic equipment & supplies

(G-10231)
TRUCKFORM INC
50 James St (08876-3015)
PHONE..............................908 526-5443
Fax: 908 526-9202
Jules Tischler, *President*
EMP: 14 EST: 1968
SQ FT: 25,000
SALES (est): 2MM **Privately Held**
WEB: www.truckform.com
SIC: 3429 3441 Manufactured hardware (general); fabricated structural metal

(G-10232)
WHITEHOUSE MACHINE & MFG CO
3585 Us Highway 22 (08876-3437)
PHONE..............................908 534-4722
Fax: 908 534-9662
Samuel Kessel, *President*
Mark Kessel, *Vice Pres*
Matthew Kessel, *Treasurer*
EMP: 7
SQ FT: 3,500
SALES: 400K **Privately Held**
SIC: 3599 Machine shop, jobbing & repair

South Amboy
Middlesex County

(G-10233)
ACE MOUNTINGS CO INC (PA)
11 Cross Ave (08879-1024)
PHONE..............................732 721-6200
Albert Chiang, *President*
Cindy Chiang, *Vice Pres*
Ll Liou, *Marketing Staff*
▲ EMP: 14
SQ FT: 5,000
SALES (est): 2.6MM **Privately Held**
WEB: www.acemount.com
SIC: 3674 Optical isolators

(G-10234)
ALL STATE PLASTICS INC
237 Raritan St (08879-1379)
PHONE..............................732 654-5054
Fax: 732 727-4182
John Vaccaro, *President*
Greg Vaccaro, *Vice Pres*
▲ EMP: 40
SQ FT: 25,000
SALES (est): 7.9MM **Privately Held**
WEB: www.allstateplastics.com
SIC: 3082 Unsupported plastics profile shapes

(G-10235)
COMPLETE FILTER
3 Donamar Ln (08879-2900)
PHONE..............................732 441-0321
EMP: 4
SALES (est): 463.3K **Privately Held**
SIC: 3569 Filters

(G-10236)
COPYSHOP
921 Us Highway 9 (08879-1485)
PHONE..............................732 721-5700
Fax: 732 721-9441
Scott Restiano, *Mng Member*

EMP: 5
SALES (est): 310K **Privately Held**
SIC: 3993 Signs & advertising specialties; commercial printing, lithographic

(G-10237)
CYPRA WALLCOVERINGS INC
32 Merritt Ave (08879-1957)
PHONE..............................732 525-0340
Curtis Cypra, *President*
James Parse, *Vice Pres*
EMP: 4
SALES (est): 325K **Privately Held**
SIC: 2221 Upholstery, tapestry & wall covering fabrics

(G-10238)
GARDEN STATE TOOL & MOLD CORP
501 Bordentown Ave (08879-1500)
PHONE..............................908 245-2041
Fax: 908 245-3464
Thomas Dziedzic, *President*
EMP: 5
SQ FT: 2,100
SALES (est): 380K **Privately Held**
SIC: 3544 Industrial molds

(G-10239)
I-YELL-O FOODS INC
603 Washington Ave (08879-1263)
PHONE..............................732 525-2201
Alfonso Aiello, *President*
EMP: 5
SQ FT: 10,000
SALES: 2MM **Privately Held**
WEB: www.brooklyncannoli.com
SIC: 2053 Frozen bakery products, except bread

(G-10240)
KICKSONFIRECOM LLC
28 Lighthouse Dr (08879-3435)
PHONE..............................718 753-4248
Furqan Khan,
EMP: 5
SALES: 300K **Privately Held**
SIC: 2721 7371 Magazines: publishing & printing; computer software development & applications

(G-10241)
LOCKWOOD BOAT WORKS INC
1825 State Route 35 (08879-2525)
PHONE..............................732 721-1605
Fax: 732 525-8209
William Lockwood, *President*
William L Lockwood, *President*
Mary Lockwood, *Corp Secy*
Theresa Lockwood, *Manager*
EMP: 25
SQ FT: 13,000
SALES (est): 7.6MM **Privately Held**
WEB: www.lockwoodboatworks.com
SIC: 5551 4493 4226 3732 Marine supplies; marinas; special warehousing & storage; boat building & repairing

(G-10242)
METALINE PRODUCTS COMPANY INC
101 N Feltus St (08879-1529)
PHONE..............................732 721-1373
Fax: 732 727-0272
Dolores Zilincar, *CEO*
August Zilincar III, *President*
▲ EMP: 25
SQ FT: 25,000
SALES (est): 5.2MM **Privately Held**
SIC: 2542 3993 Stands, merchandise display: except wood; signs & advertising specialties

(G-10243)
MORGAN PRINTING SERVICE INC
333 S Pine Ave (08879)
PHONE..............................732 721-2959
Fax: 732 721-5610
Robert Dein, *President*
Jason Madden, *Marketing Staff*
▲ EMP: 10
SQ FT: 4,500

SALES (est): 1.8MM **Privately Held**
SIC: 2752 2791 Commercial printing, offset; typesetting

(G-10244)
ROBOKILLER LLC
101 S Broadway (08879-1707)
PHONE..............................723 838-1901
Meir Cohen, *CEO*
EMP: 40
SALES: 658.8K **Privately Held**
SIC: 7372 7371 Application computer software; computer software development & applications
PA: Teltech Systems, Inc.
101 S Broadway
South Amboy NJ 08879

(G-10245)
SOUTH AMBOY DESIGNER T SHIRT L
603 Washington Ave Ste 5b (08879-1263)
PHONE..............................732 456-2594
Daniel Castillo,
EMP: 6
SALES (est): 339.9K **Privately Held**
SIC: 2752 2395 Commercial printing, lithographic; embroidery products, except schiffli machine

(G-10246)
VENETIAN CARE AND REHABLITATN
275 John T Oleary Blvd (08879)
PHONE..............................732 721-8200
Fax: 201 881-1195
Hayman Jacobs, *CEO*
EMP: 9
SALES (est): 80.6K **Privately Held**
SIC: 8093 8322 3845 Nursing home, except skilled & intermediate care facility

(G-10247)
WHITE CASTLE
987 Us Highway 9 (08879-3302)
PHONE..............................732 721-3565
Janet Boehm, *Principal*
EMP: 25
SALES (est): 1.4MM **Privately Held**
SIC: 2085 Distilled & blended liquors

South Bound Brook
Somerset County

(G-10248)
CLEARY MACHINERY CO INC
24 Cedar St (08880-1352)
PHONE..............................732 560-3200
Fax: 732 757-2825
Gerard V Cleary, *President*
James A Cleary, *Vice Pres*
▲ EMP: 4
SQ FT: 4,200
SALES (est): 1.1MM **Privately Held**
WEB: www.clearymachinery.com
SIC: 5082 3699 7699 General construction machinery & equipment; tractor-mounting equipment; laser systems & equipment; construction equipment repair

(G-10249)
TRI TECH TOOL & DESIGN CO INC
30 Cherry St (08880-1321)
PHONE..............................732 469-5433
Fax: 732 469-1595
Arthur Weber, *President*
Jason Weber, *Vice Pres*
EMP: 27 EST: 1978
SQ FT: 7,500
SALES: 6.5MM **Privately Held**
SIC: 3089 Injection molding of plastics

South Hackensack
Bergen County

(G-10250)
A-1 TABLECLOTH CO INC
450 Huyler St Ste 102 (07606-1563)
PHONE..............................201 727-4364

Fax: 201 727-8988
Robert Fox, *President*
▼ EMP: 150
SQ FT: 45,000
SALES (est): 8.5MM **Privately Held**
SIC: 7218 2392 Industrial launderers; tablecloths & table settings

(G-10251)
ADCOMM INC
Also Called: Adcomm Government Systems
89 Leuning St Ste 9 (07606-1335)
PHONE..............................201 342-3338
Dennis Nathan, *President*
Allen Cohen, *COO*
Eddie Boock, *Purchasing*
Roger Alexander, *QC Mgr*
Joe Chen, *Info Tech Mgr*
EMP: 125
SQ FT: 60,000
SALES (est): 20.9MM **Privately Held**
SIC: 3679 Electronic circuits

(G-10252)
AEROSMITH
176 Saddle River Ave B (07606-1902)
PHONE..............................973 614-9392
David Lakin, *Owner*
Tim Lakin, *Owner*
EMP: 5 EST: 1999
SALES (est): 510.1K **Privately Held**
SIC: 3444 Sheet metalwork

(G-10253)
AFRICA IMPORTS INC
240 S Main St Ste A (07606-1458)
PHONE..............................201 457-1995
Fax: 201 457-1910
Wayne Kiltz, *CEO*
Jason Sonnichsen, *Sales Staff*
Samuel Kiltz, *Director*
◆ EMP: 20
SALES (est): 2.5MM **Privately Held**
WEB: www.africaimports.com
SIC: 2499 Carved & turned wood

(G-10254)
ALPRO INC
50 Romanelli Ave (07606-1424)
PHONE..............................201 342-4498
Girish Desai, *President*
EMP: 7
SALES (est): 620K **Privately Held**
SIC: 2834 Vitamin, nutrient & hematinic preparations for human use

(G-10255)
BIND-RITE SERVICES INC
16 Horizon Blvd (07606-1804)
PHONE..............................201 440-5585
Fax: 201 440-7973
Elliott Ward, *President*
Andrew Ward, *Principal*
Maria Ward, *Corp Secy*
Mike Bell, *Safety Mgr*
Rick Decker, *Info Tech Mgr*
EMP: 150
SQ FT: 70,000
SALES (est): 20.9MM **Privately Held**
SIC: 2789 Binding only: books, pamphlets, magazines, etc.

(G-10256)
C W BRABENDER INSTRS INC
50 E Wesley St (07606-1416)
P.O. Box 2127 (07606-0727)
PHONE..............................201 343-8425
Fax: 201 343-0608
Richard Thoma, *President*
Ewald Heckmann, *Vice Pres*
Sirkka Vanderer, *Admin Sec*
▲ EMP: 28 EST: 1922
SQ FT: 20,000
SALES (est): 7.2MM **Privately Held**
WEB: www.cwbrabender.com
SIC: 3829 8734 3826 3821 Measuring & controlling devices; testing laboratories; analytical instruments; laboratory apparatus & furniture
HQ: C.W. Brabender Gesellschaft Mit Beschränkter Haftung
Kulturstr. 49-51
Duisburg
203 778-8100

(G-10257)
CASE MEDICAL INC
19 Empire Blvd (07606-1805)
P.O. Box 5069 (07606-4269)
PHONE......................................201 313-1999
Marcia Frieze, *CEO*
Allan Frieze, *President*
Sandy Swerdloff, *General Mgr*
Paulina Pelaez, *Prdtn Mgr*
Steve Meredith, *Opers Staff*
▲ EMP: 40 EST: 1943
SQ FT: 34,000
SALES (est): 29MM **Privately Held**
WEB: www.casemed.com
SIC: 5047 3469 Medical equipment & supplies; boxes, stamped metal

(G-10258)
CLEMENTS INDUSTRIES INC
Also Called: Tach-It
50 Ruta Ct (07606-1709)
PHONE......................................201 440-5500
Fax: 201 440-1455
Alan Clements, *President*
Stanley Clements, *Vice Pres*
Steven Clements, *Treasurer*
Arlene Peconio, *Credit Staff*
Jim Lyon, *Natl Sales Mgr*
◆ EMP: 25
SQ FT: 15,000
SALES (est): 5.7MM **Privately Held**
WEB: www.clementsindustries.com
SIC: 3565 3599 5113 3552 Labeling machines, industrial; bread wrapping machinery; ties, form: metal; shipping supplies; textile machinery; miscellaneous fabricated wire products

(G-10259)
DANMAR PRESS INC
24 E Wesley St (07606-1416)
PHONE......................................201 487-4400
Fax: 201 487-1555
Danieal Stenchever, *President*
EMP: 12 EST: 1981
SQ FT: 4,050
SALES (est): 1.3MM **Privately Held**
SIC: 2752 Commercial printing, offset

(G-10260)
DIAMOND SYSTEMS USA CORP
176 Saddle River Ave C (07606-1958)
PHONE......................................973 777-9075
Donna Lobe, *Exec VP*
EMP: 5
SQ FT: 2,100
SALES (est): 654.2K **Privately Held**
SIC: 2834 Digitalis pharmaceutical preparations

(G-10261)
E & E GROUP CORP
7 Maple Ave 2 (07606-1605)
P.O. Box 1521 (07606-0121)
PHONE......................................201 814-0414
Fax: 201 814-9004
Hae K Cho, *Owner*
EMP: 4 EST: 1997
SALES (est): 567.6K **Privately Held**
SIC: 2671 Paper coated or laminated for packaging

(G-10262)
ECO LIGHTING USA LTD LBLTY CO
217 Huyler St (07606-1302)
PHONE......................................201 621-5661
Sean Blackman, *Mng Member*
◆ EMP: 8
SALES: 728K **Privately Held**
SIC: 3648 5063 Lighting equipment; lighting fixtures, commercial & industrial; lighting fixtures, residential

(G-10263)
EJZ FOODS LLC
21 Empire Blvd (07606-1805)
PHONE......................................201 229-0500
Matthew Berger, *Mng Member*
◆ EMP: 5
SALES (est): 139.9K
SALES (corp-wide): 145.2MM **Privately Held**
SIC: 2037 Fruit juices

PA: Dora's Naturals, Inc
21 Empire Blvd
South Hackensack NJ 07606
201 229-0500

(G-10264)
ENCORE ENTERPRISES INC (PA)
Also Called: Creative Safety Products
57 Leuning St (07606-1307)
PHONE......................................201 489-5044
Fax: 201 489-0735
Angelo C Congello Sr, *President*
Angelo Congelo Jr, *President*
EMP: 5
SQ FT: 14,200
SALES (est): 1.2MM **Privately Held**
WEB: www.officerphil.com
SIC: 8299 7336 2752 Educational service, nondegree granting: continuing educ.; graphic arts & related design; commercial printing, lithographic

(G-10265)
ESSENTIAL DENTAL SYSTEMS INC
Also Called: EDS
89 Leuning St Ste 8 (07606-1334)
PHONE......................................201 487-9090
Fax: 201 487-5120
Dr Barry Musikant, *President*
Dr Allen Deutsch, *Exec VP*
Kishwar Hoque, *Research*
Mary Allaire, *Human Res Mgr*
Tom Dammeyer, *Sales Mgr*
▲ EMP: 25
SQ FT: 10,000
SALES (est): 3.6MM **Privately Held**
WEB: www.edsdental.com
SIC: 3843 Dental materials; cement, dental; compounds, dental

(G-10266)
EUROPEAN STONE ART LLC
208 Huyler St (07606-1303)
PHONE......................................201 441-9116
Hiedi J Saville, *Mng Member*
Gary Saville,
EMP: 11
SALES (est): 1.4MM **Privately Held**
WEB: www.europeanstoneart.com
SIC: 3272 Concrete products

(G-10267)
F P SCHMIDT MANUFACTURING CO
143 Leuning St (07606-1385)
PHONE......................................201 343-4241
Fax: 201 343-0372
Robert F Schmidt, *Managing Prtnr*
Elizabeth L Butz, *Partner*
William P Schmidt, *Partner*
EMP: 15 EST: 1947
SQ FT: 20,000
SALES: 1MM **Privately Held**
SIC: 3451 Screw machine products

(G-10268)
FINE MANUFACTURING INC
80 Wesley St (07606-1510)
PHONE......................................201 880-9136
Fax: 973 340-0998
Harry Epstin, *President*
Daniel Nelson, *Vice Pres*
EMP: 18
SQ FT: 10,000
SALES (est): 3.6MM **Privately Held**
WEB: www.finemanufacturing.com
SIC: 3469 Machine parts, stamped or pressed metal

(G-10269)
G-WAY MICROWAVE INC
38 Leuning St (07606-1318)
PHONE......................................201 343-6388
Fax: 201 343-6390
Greg David, *President*
Eduard Segal, *Manager*
Sharon David, *Assistant*
▲ EMP: 19
SQ FT: 4,400
SALES (est): 4MM **Privately Held**
WEB: www.gwaymicrowave.com
SIC: 3679 Microwave components

(G-10270)
IMAGINE GOLD LLC
60 Romanelli Ave (07606-1424)
PHONE......................................201 488-5988
Joe Curran, *President*
Karen Windfuhr,
◆ EMP: 20 EST: 1953
SQ FT: 22,000
SALES (est): 3.3MM **Privately Held**
WEB: www.imaginegold.com
SIC: 5199 3085 Pet supplies; plastics bottles

(G-10271)
J JOSEPHSON INC (HQ)
35 Horizon Blvd (07606-1804)
PHONE......................................201 440-7000
Fax: 201 440-7109
Mark Goodman, *President*
Luis Abreu, *Warehouse Mgr*
Efrain Nieves, *Engineer*
Teresa Messineo, *Finance Mgr*
Arabelis Mendoza, *Hum Res Coord*
◆ EMP: 122 EST: 1962
SQ FT: 160,000
SALES (est): 94.4MM
SALES (corp-wide): 10MM **Privately Held**
WEB: www.jjosephson.com
SIC: 2679 Wallpaper, embossed plastic: made on textile backing
PA: Coronet Wallpapers (Ontario) Limited
88 Ronson Dr
Etobicoke ON M9W 1
416 245-2900

(G-10272)
J JOSEPHSON INC
35 Empire Blvd (07606-1896)
PHONE......................................201 440-7000
Kin Bogg, *Manager*
EMP: 150
SALES (corp-wide): 10MM **Privately Held**
WEB: www.jjosephson.com
SIC: 2679 Wallpaper, embossed plastic: made on textile backing
HQ: J. Josephson, Inc.
35 Horizon Blvd
South Hackensack NJ 07606
201 440-7000

(G-10273)
J JOSEPHSON INC
14 Central Blvd (07606-1802)
PHONE......................................201 426-2646
Paola Cruz, *Admin Asst*
EMP: 150
SALES (corp-wide): 10MM **Privately Held**
SIC: 2679 Wallpaper, embossed plastic: made on textile backing
HQ: J. Josephson, Inc.
35 Horizon Blvd
South Hackensack NJ 07606
201 440-7000

(G-10274)
KDF REPROGRAPHICS INC
65 Worth St (07606-1422)
PHONE......................................201 784-9991
Fax: 201 784-9955
Stephen Hoey, *President*
Brian Hamilton, *Business Mgr*
John Dickson, *Corp Secy*
Kurt Flechsig, *Exec VP*
Radim Horak, *Prdtn Mgr*
EMP: 10
SQ FT: 33,000
SALES (est): 1.5MM **Privately Held**
WEB: www.kdf-comp.com
SIC: 2759 3993 7922 7389 Commercial printing; electric signs; scenery design, theatrical; lettering & sign painting services; sign installation & maintenance

(G-10275)
LA FORGE DE STYLE LLC
57 Romanelli Ave (07606-1427)
PHONE......................................201 488-1955
Franck Chartrain,
David Gore,
EMP: 8
SQ FT: 8,000
SALES (est): 1.5MM **Privately Held**
SIC: 3446 Ornamental metalwork

(G-10276)
LYDON BROS CORP
254 Green St (07606-1429)
P.O. Box 708, Hackensack (07602-0708)
PHONE......................................201 343-4334
Fax: 201 343-7335
Timothy Mc Bride, *President*
S Mc Bride, *Vice Pres*
EMP: 22
SQ FT: 3,000
SALES (est): 2.3MM **Privately Held**
WEB: www.lydonoven.com
SIC: 3567 Driers & redriers, industrial process; enameling ovens

(G-10277)
M H OPTICAL SUPPLIES INC
Also Called: Quality Eyework
128 Leuning St (07606-1317)
PHONE......................................800 445-3090
Fax: 201 489-0999
Mitchel Hirsch, *President*
▲ EMP: 32
SQ FT: 20,000
SALES (est): 6.2MM **Privately Held**
SIC: 3827 Optical instruments & lenses

(G-10278)
MARINE ELECTRIC SYSTEMS INC
Also Called: Mesys
80 Wesley St (07606-1510)
PHONE......................................201 531-8600
Harry Epstein, *CEO*
Michael Epstein, *Chairman*
Mario Luba, *Opers Staff*
Carolyn Gould, *Purch Mgr*
Caroline I Woelber, *VP Sales*
EMP: 21 EST: 1940
SQ FT: 25,000
SALES (est): 6.5MM **Privately Held**
WEB: www.marineelectricsystems.com
SIC: 3825 3823 3643 3613 Test equipment for electronic & electric measurement; industrial instrmnts msrmnt display/control process variable; current-carrying wiring devices; switchgear & switchboard apparatus

(G-10279)
NAPOLEON SPRING WORKS INC
Also Called: Lynx USA
25 Empire Blvd (07606-1807)
PHONE......................................973 278-5588
Fax: 973 742-9832
Jack Schram, *Regl Sales Mgr*
Robert Schram, *Branch Mgr*
EMP: 25
SQ FT: 33,000
SALES (corp-wide): 8.8MM **Privately Held**
SIC: 3678 Electronic connectors
HQ: Spring Napoleon Works Inc
111 Weires Dr
Archbold OH 43502
419 445-1010

(G-10280)
NATUREX HOLDINGS INC (HQ)
375 Huyler St (07606-1532)
PHONE......................................201 440-5000
Olivier Rigaud, *Ch of Bd*
Gaetan Sourceau, *CFO*
EMP: 3
SALES (est): 237.7MM **Privately Held**
SIC: 2833 6719 Botanical products, medicinal: ground, graded or milled; investment holding companies, except banks

(G-10281)
NATUREX INC
125 Phillips Ave (07606-1585)
PHONE......................................201 440-5000
Thierry Lambert, *President*
EMP: 6 **Privately Held**
SIC: 2833 Botanical products, medicinal: ground, graded or milled
HQ: Naturex Inc.
375 Huyler St
South Hackensack NJ 07606
201 440-5000

(G-10282)
NATUREX INC (DH)
375 Huyler St (07606-1532)
PHONE..........................201 440-5000
Olivier Rigaud, *Ch of Bd*
Mary Clarke, *Senior VP*
Gaetan Sourceau, *CFO*
Jean-Noel Lorenzoni, *Admin Sec*
◆ **EMP:** 200
SALES: 234.7MM **Privately Held**
SIC: 2833 Botanical products, medicinal:
ground, graded or milled
HQ: Naturex Holdings Inc.
375 Huyler St
South Hackensack NJ 07606
201 440-5000

(G-10283)
NEW JERSEY LABEL LLC
30 Wesley St Unit 7 (07606-1509)
PHONE..........................201 880-5102
Steven Haedrich,
EMP: 12 **EST:** 1995
SALES (est): 1.2MM **Privately Held**
SIC: 2752 2791 2759 Commercial print-
ing, lithographic; typesetting; commercial
printing

(G-10284)
NO FIRE TECHNOLOGIES INC
5 James St (07606-1438)
PHONE..........................201 818-1616
Sam Oolie, *Ch of Bd*
Samuel Gottfried, *President*
◆ **EMP:** 7
SQ FT: 8,000
SALES (est): 1.1MM **Privately Held**
WEB: www.nofire.net
SIC: 2899 Fire retardant chemicals

(G-10285)
ON SITE COMMUNICATION
Also Called: Ess
15 Worth St (07606-1313)
P.O. Box 4103 (07606-4103)
PHONE..........................201 488-4123
T H Betz, *Partner*
Robert Dale, *Partner*
William Park, *Partner*
EMP: 50
SALES (est): 4.7MM **Privately Held**
SIC: 3663 Radio broadcasting & communi-
cations equipment

(G-10286)
OVERDRIVE HOLDINGS INC
540 Huyler St (07606-1544)
PHONE..........................201 440-1911
Ralph Guadagno, *Branch Mgr*
EMP: 12
SALES (corp-wide): 23.4MM **Privately
Held**
SIC: 5013 3714 Trailer parts & acces-
sories; automotive brakes; truck parts &
accessories; wheels, motor vehicle; trans-
missions, motor vehicle; differentials &
parts, motor vehicle
PA: Overdrive Holdings, Inc.
2501 Route 73
Cinnaminson NJ
856 665-4445

(G-10287)
PAINTING INC
60 Leuning St (07606-1317)
PHONE..........................201 489-6565
Lee Bronster, *CEO*
Wilson Richardson, *President*
EMP: 14
SQ FT: 5,000
SALES: 1.2MM **Privately Held**
SIC: 7532 2396 Lettering & painting serv-
ices; automotive & apparel trimmings

(G-10288)
**PHARMACHEM LABORATORIES
INC**
130 Wesley St (07606-1510)
PHONE..........................201 343-3611
Fax: 201 343-5807
Andrea Bauer, *Branch Mgr*
EMP: 30
SALES (corp-wide): 3.2B **Publicly Held**
SIC: 2099 2834 Food preparations; phar-
maceutical preparations

HQ: Pharmachem Laboratories, Llc
265 Harrison Tpke
Kearny NJ 07032
201 246-1000

(G-10289)
PIONEER EMBROIDERY CO
Also Called: Fabric Bee
31 Saddle River Ave (07606)
PHONE..........................973 777-6418
EMP: 4
SQ FT: 1,200
SALES (est): 170K **Privately Held**
SIC: 2395 5949 Pleating/Stitching Serv-
ices Ret Sewing Supplies/Fabrics

(G-10290)
PRINT GROUP INC
Also Called: Print Group The
24 E Wesley St (07606-1416)
PHONE..........................201 487-4400
Fax: 201 489-4349
Michael De Stefan, *President*
Anne De Stefan, *Admin Sec*
EMP: 10 **EST:** 1953
SALES (est): 1.7MM **Privately Held**
SIC: 2752 Photo-offset printing

(G-10291)
**PROCESS SUPPLY COMPANY
INC**
Also Called: Naz-Dar/East
208 Huyler St (07606-1303)
P.O. Box 1568 (07606-0168)
PHONE..........................201 487-1616
David Cordell, *Branch Mgr*
EMP: 11
SALES (corp-wide): 187MM **Privately
Held**
SIC: 2759 Screen printing
HQ: Process Supply Company, Inc
1087 N North Branch St
Chicago IL 60642
312 943-8338

(G-10292)
REFUEL INC
150 Wesley St (07606-1510)
PHONE..........................917 645-2974
SRI Kasa, *Branch Mgr*
EMP: 4
SALES (corp-wide): 4MM **Privately Held**
SIC: 5091 5699 2211 Sporting & recre-
ation goods; sports apparel; apparel &
outerwear fabrics, cotton
PA: Refuel Inc
1384 Broadway Rm 608
New York NY 10018
917 645-2974

(G-10293)
ROBERT J SMITH
Also Called: Mastercrafts
152 Louis St (07606-1721)
PHONE..........................201 641-6555
Robert J Smith, *Owner*
EMP: 6
SQ FT: 5,000
SALES: 500K **Privately Held**
SIC: 2521 2511 Wood office furniture;
wood household furniture

(G-10294)
RQ FLOORS CORP
550 Huyler St (07606-1544)
PHONE..........................201 654-3587
Leon Shekhets, *President*
EMP: 14
SALES (corp-wide): 7MM **Privately Held**
SIC: 2491 Flooring, treated wood block
PA: Rq Floors Corp
425 Victoria Ter
Ridgefield NJ 07657
201 654-3587

(G-10295)
SALON INTERIORS INC
62 Leuning St (07606-1317)
PHONE..........................201 488-7888
Fax: 201 488-0051
Walter Siegordner, *President*
Keith Cauwenberghs, *Foreman/Supr*
Milton Santos, *Design Engr*
Marilyn Murphy, *CFO*
Dawn Rodriguez, *Mktg Dir*
▲ **EMP:** 28 **EST:** 1979

SQ FT: 35,000
SALES (est): 6.1MM **Privately Held**
WEB: www.saloninteriors.com
SIC: 1542 5087 2541 Commercial & office building contractors; beauty parlor
equipment & supplies; store & office display cases & fixtures

(G-10296)
SONDRA ROBERTS INC
3 Empire Blvd (07606-1806)
PHONE..........................212 684-3344
George Altirs, *CEO*
EMP: 20
SALES (est): 615.4K **Privately Held**
SIC: 2339 Women's & misses' accessories

(G-10297)
**SPRING TIME MATTRESS MFG
CORP (PA)**
Also Called: Springtime Bedding
25 Saddle River Ave (07606-1922)
P.O. Box 4157 (07606-4157)
PHONE..........................973 473-5400
Isaac Jakobovits, *CEO*
Joel Wieder, *CFO*
EMP: 69
SALES (est): 12.1MM **Privately Held**
SIC: 2515 Mattresses & bedsprings

(G-10298)
TORQUE GUN COMPANY LLC
Also Called: Torque Gun Co, The
120 Wesley St (07606-1510)
PHONE..........................201 512-9800
EMP: 20
SALES (est): 2MM **Privately Held**
SIC: 3621 Torque motors, electric

(G-10299)
**WELTER & KREUTZ PRINTING
CO**
51 Worth St (07606-1422)
PHONE..........................201 489-9098
Fax: 201 489-2125
Robert Kreutz, *President*
Barry R Kreutz, *Vice Pres*
EMP: 5
SQ FT: 3,000
SALES (est): 470K **Privately Held**
SIC: 2752 Commercial printing, offset

(G-10300)
**YOUNIVERSAL LABORTORIES
(PA)**
Also Called: USA Head Office & Warehouse
100 Louis St (07606-1723)
PHONE..........................201 807-9000
Emir Agbas, *Owner*
▲ **EMP:** 5
SALES (est): 280.5K **Privately Held**
SIC: 2819 Industrial inorganic chemicals

South Orange
Essex County

(G-10301)
**BIERMAN-EVERETT FOUNDRY
CO**
7 Speir Dr (07079-1023)
P.O. Box 1023 (07079-7023)
PHONE..........................973 373-8800
Fax: 973 373-3949
Robert Julius, *President*
Theresa Notoli, *Vice Pres*
EMP: 8 **EST:** 1913
SQ FT: 36,000
SALES (est): 1.1MM **Privately Held**
SIC: 3321 3363 3366 3365 Gray iron
castings; ductile iron castings; aluminum
die-castings; copper foundries; aluminum
foundries

(G-10302)
DANMOLA LARA
Also Called: Laras Designs
524 N Wyoming Ave (07079-1653)
P.O. Box 984 (07079-0984)
PHONE..........................973 762-7581
Lara Danmola, *Owner*
EMP: 5

SALES (est): 270K **Privately Held**
WEB: www.larasdesigns.com
SIC: 3911 Jewelry, precious metal

(G-10303)
DIVERSITY PLUS MAGAZINE
Also Called: American & Hispanic Bus Journa
111 S Orange Ave Ste 28 (07079-1931)
P.O. Box 178 (07079-0178)
PHONE..........................973 275-1405
Paul Lachhau, *President*
EMP: 20
SQ FT: 2,200
SALES (est): 1.9MM **Privately Held**
WEB: www.diversityplus.com
SIC: 2721 Periodicals

(G-10304)
ENDOTEC INC (PA)
20 Valley St Ste 210 (07079-2881)
PHONE..........................973 762-6100
Michael Pappas, *President*
Fred Buechel, *Vice Pres*
Stan Matlak, *VP Sales*
EMP: 15
SQ FT: 3,000
SALES (est): 1.2MM **Privately Held**
WEB: www.endotec.com
SIC: 3842 8011 Implants, surgical; offices
& clinics of medical doctors

(G-10305)
FAN OF WORD
249 Waverly Pl (07079-2124)
PHONE..........................201 341-5474
Joseph Oniyama, *Partner*
EMP: 4
SALES (est): 224.5K **Privately Held**
SIC: 3499 7389 Novelties & giftware, in-
cluding trophies;

(G-10306)
FLEET PACKAGING INC
75 S Orange Ave Ste 216 (07079-1743)
PHONE..........................866 302-0340
Gary Shippy, *President*
EMP: 4
SQ FT: 400
SALES: 5.4MM **Privately Held**
SIC: 7389 3053 5199 Design services;
packing materials; packaging materials

(G-10307)
G & R GRAPHICS INC
303 Irvington Ave (07079-2510)
P.O. Box 7095, West Orange (07052-7095)
PHONE..........................973 731-7438
Fax: 973 313-2211
David Gonzales, *President*
Luis Gonzales, *Vice Pres*
Anibal Gonzalez, *Admin Sec*
EMP: 6
SQ FT: 1,500
SALES: 350K **Privately Held**
SIC: 3953 2796 3993 Marking devices;
platemaking services; signs & advertising
specialties

(G-10308)
**JEFFERSON PROSTHETIC
ORTHOTIC**
120 Prospect St Ste B (07079-2103)
PHONE..........................973 762-0780
Simon Chang, *President*
EMP: 5
SQ FT: 1,400
SALES (est): 340K **Privately Held**
SIC: 3842 Limbs, artificial; braces, ortho-
pedic

(G-10309)
LEVEL DESIGNS GROUP LLC
495 W South Orange Ave (07079-1200)
PHONE..........................973 761-1675
Altair H Marques, *Mng Member*
EMP: 5
SALES: 700K **Privately Held**
SIC: 7389 2653 2541 Design services;
display items, solid fiber: made from pur-
chased materials; display fixtures, wood

(G-10310)
MYERS GROUP LLC
Also Called: New World Leather
74 Blanchard Rd (07079-1341)
P.O. Box 1162, Maplewood (07040-0453)
PHONE.............................973 761-6414
Jay Myers, *Branch Mgr*
EMP: 7
SALES (corp-wide): 87MM **Privately Held**
SIC: 3111 Tanneries, leather
PA: The Myers Group Llc
    257 W 38th St
    New York NY 10018
    973 761-6414

(G-10311)
MYLAN LABORATORIES INC
76 S Orange Ave Ste 301 (07079-1923)
PHONE.............................973 761-1600
Steven Schneider, *Vice Pres*
▲ EMP: 6
SQ FT: 7,500
SALES: 20MM **Privately Held**
SIC: 2834 Pharmaceutical preparations
HQ: Mylan Laboratories Limited
    Plot No.564/A/22, Road No.92,
    Hyderabad TS 50009
    403 086-6088

(G-10312)
NEPHROS INC (PA)
380 Lackawanna Pl (07079-1704)
PHONE.............................201 343-5202
Fax: 201 343-5207
Daron Evans, *President*
Gregory Collins, *Vice Pres*
Allen Jayaraj, *Engineer*
Andrew Astor, *CFO*
Andy Astor, *CFO*
◆ EMP: 5
SQ FT: 4,688
SALES: 3.8MM **Publicly Held**
WEB: www.nephros.com
SIC: 3841 8731 Surgical & medical instru-
    ments; medical research, commercial

(G-10313)
PATHMARK STORES INC
407 Valley St (07079-2807)
PHONE.............................973 762-5044
Fax: 973 378-3449
Susan Ristovski, *Manager*
EMP: 250
SALES (corp-wide): 2B **Privately Held**
WEB: www.pathmark.com
SIC: 5411 5912 5992 2051 Supermar-
    kets, chain; drug stores; florists; bread,
    cake & related products
PA: Pathmark Stores, Inc.
    2 Paragon Dr
    Montvale NJ 07645
    866 443-7374

(G-10314)
ROCKET SHIP & PRINT INC
71 S Orange Ave (07079-1715)
PHONE.............................973 275-1144
Jim Gordon, *Manager*
EMP: 4
SALES (est): 253K **Privately Held**
SIC: 2752 Commercial printing, litho-
    graphic

(G-10315)
SNOTEX USA INC
116 Irvington Ave Apt 2f (07079-1973)
PHONE.............................973 762-0358
Fax: 973 762-9880
Kermit Lin, *President*
▲ EMP: 4
SALES: 1.2MM **Privately Held**
SIC: 2339 Women's & misses' outerwear

(G-10316)
TOTAL COVER IT LLC
223 Waverly Pl (07079-2124)
PHONE.............................973 342-4623
David G Quick,
EMP: 4
SALES (est): 121.2K **Privately Held**
SIC: 7372 Application computer software

(G-10317)
WORLD CONFECTIONS INC
14 S Orange Ave Ste A (07079-1754)
PHONE.............................718 768-8100
Matthew Cohen, *President*
Drew Cohen, *Vice Pres*
▲ EMP: 60
SQ FT: 20,000
SALES (est): 9.9MM **Privately Held**
SIC: 2064 5145 Candy & other confec-
    tionery products; candy

South Plainfield
Middlesex County

(G-10318)
A FRIERI MACHINE TOOL INC
1112 Belmont Ave (07080-4303)
PHONE.............................908 753-7555
Andrew Frieri, *President*
EMP: 6
SQ FT: 12,500
SALES: 650K **Privately Held**
SIC: 3599 3544 Machine shop, jobbing &
    repair; special dies, tools, jigs & fixtures

(G-10319)
A&A COMPANY INC
Also Called: A & A Coating
2700 S Clinton Ave (07080-1428)
PHONE.............................908 561-2378
Fax: 908 753-9225
R Stewart Brunhouse Jr, *President*
Riken Patel, *Engineer*
Richard Brunhouse, *Sales Mgr*
Robert Rigney, *CTO*
EMP: 22 EST: 1944
SQ FT: 22,000
SALES (est): 4.2MM **Privately Held**
SIC: 3471 Plating & polishing

(G-10320)
ACCELERATED CNC LLC
2500 S Clinton Ave (07080-1414)
PHONE.............................908 561-8875
John Kologe, *Mng Member*
William Ehling,
EMP: 6
SQ FT: 100
SALES: 840K **Privately Held**
SIC: 3599 Machine shop, jobbing & repair

(G-10321)
ADMERA HEALTH LLC
126 Corporate Blvd (07080-2411)
PHONE.............................908 222-0533
Steve Sun, *CEO*
Guanghui Hu, *President*
Ling Zhang, *Sales Staff*
Arthur Bolbirer, *Manager*
Brendan Dermody, *Manager*
EMP: 1
SALES (est): 1MM
SALES (corp-wide): 45.1MM **Privately
Held**
SIC: 2835 8731 In vitro & in vivo diagnos-
    tic substances; commercial physical re-
    search
PA: Genewiz, Llc
    115 Corporate Blvd
    South Plainfield NJ 07080
    908 222-0711

(G-10322)
AIRGAS USA LLC
2330 Hamilton Blvd (07080-3104)
PHONE.............................908 754-7700
David Ludwig, *Vice Pres*
Carl Wiley, *Branch Mgr*
Jeff Roberts, *Maintence Staff*
EMP: 12
SALES (corp-wide): 164.2MM **Privately
Held**
WEB: www.asgemail.com
SIC: 2813 Industrial gases
HQ: Airgas Usa, Llc
    259 N Radnor Chester Rd # 100
    Radnor PA 19087
    610 687-5253

(G-10323)
ALLEN FLAVORS INC
220 Saint Nicholas Ave (07080-1810)
PHONE.............................908 753-0544
Joseph Allen, *Manager*
EMP: 12
SALES (est): 2.3MM
SALES (corp-wide): 29.3MM **Privately
Held**
SIC: 2087 Extracts, flavoring; beverage
    bases, concentrates, syrups, powders &
    mixes
PA: Allen Flavors, Inc.
    23 Progress St
    Edison NJ 08820
    908 561-5995

(G-10324)
ALLIED TILE MFG CORP
631 Montrose Ave (07080-2601)
PHONE.............................718 647-2200
G Peter Gregor, *President*
▲ EMP: 9
SQ FT: 10,000
SALES (est): 1.3MM **Privately Held**
WEB: www.alliedtile.com
SIC: 3292 Tile, vinyl asbestos

(G-10325)
**ALPHA ASSEMBLY SOLUTIONS
INC**
109 Corporate Blvd (07080-2409)
PHONE.............................908 561-5170
EMP: 41
SALES (corp-wide): 3.7B **Publicly Held**
SIC: 3356 3341 3313 3339 Solder: wire,
    bar, acid core, & rosin core; lead smelting
    & refining (secondary); tin smelting & re-
    fining (secondary); alloys, additive, except
    copper: not made in blast furnaces; lead
    smelting & refining (primary); tin refining
    (primary); fluxes: brazing, soldering, gal-
    vanizing & welding
HQ: Alpha Assembly Solutions Inc.
    300 Atrium Dr Fl 3
    Somerset NJ 08873
    908 791-3000

(G-10326)
**AMERICAN HOME ESSENTIALS
INC**
600 Mont Rose Ave (07080)
PHONE.............................908 561-3200
Fax: 732 568-9799
Sohail Bari, *President*
Rashad H Hassan, *Vice Pres*
EMP: 8
SQ FT: 23,000
SALES: 5MM **Privately Held**
SIC: 2299 Linen fabrics

(G-10327)
**AMERICAN STRIP STEEL INC
(HQ)**
400 Metuchen Rd (07080-4807)
PHONE.............................800 526-1216
Le Roy Schecter, *President*
Lori Hagedorn, *CFO*
EMP: 16 EST: 1951
SQ FT: 90,000
SALES (est): 30.3MM
SALES (corp-wide): 163.5MM **Privately
Held**
SIC: 5051 3441 3316 Steel; fabricated
    structural metal; cold finishing of steel
    shapes
PA: Ware Industries Inc.
    400 Metuchen Rd
    South Plainfield NJ 07080
    908 757-9000

(G-10328)
AMERIFAST CORP
104 Sylvania Pl (07080-1448)
PHONE.............................908 668-1959
Fax: 908 668-1959
James Peightel, *President*
▲ EMP: 10
SQ FT: 24,000
SALES (est): 1.7MM **Privately Held**
SIC: 3452 Nuts, metal

(G-10329)
ARCH CHEMICALS INC
70 Tyler Pl (07080-1210)
PHONE.............................908 561-5200
Bob Koroshitz, *Branch Mgr*
EMP: 75
SALES (corp-wide): 5.1B **Privately Held**
SIC: 2819 Industrial inorganic chemicals
HQ: Arch Chemicals, Inc.
    1200 Bluegrass Lakes Pkwy
    Alpharetta GA 30004
    678 624-5800

(G-10330)
**ARCH PERSONAL CARE
PRODUCTS LP**
70 Tyler Pl (07080-1210)
PHONE.............................908 226-9329
Joseph Shaulson, *President*
Lisa Bouldin, *Vice Pres*
Steve Giuliano, *Vice Pres*
▼ EMP: 45
SQ FT: 30,000
SALES (est): 5.9MM
SALES (corp-wide): 5.1B **Privately Held**
WEB: www.archchemicals.com
SIC: 2844 Depilatories (cosmetic)
HQ: Arch Chemicals, Inc.
    1200 Bluegrass Lakes Pkwy
    Alpharetta GA 30004
    678 624-5800

(G-10331)
ARIEL LABORATORIES LP
31 Davis St (07080-1429)
PHONE.............................908 755-4080
Peter Bohm, *Partner*
Ronni Bohm, *Partner*
Imperial Cosmetics, *General Ptnr*
Vincent Brindisi, *Production*
Judith Amman, *Admin Asst*
▲ EMP: 6
SQ FT: 30,000
SALES (est): 1.3MM **Privately Held**
WEB: www.ariellabs.com
SIC: 2844 Cosmetic preparations; lipsticks;
    face creams or lotions

(G-10332)
ASCENT AROMATICS INC
120 Case Dr (07080-5109)
PHONE.............................908 755-0120
John Pascame, *President*
Jem Unanth, *Vice Pres*
EMP: 5
SALES (est): 1MM **Privately Held**
SIC: 2844 Perfumes & colognes

(G-10333)
ATLAS ENTERPRISE
Also Called: Atlas Welders & Fabricators
2505 S Clinton Ave (07080-1425)
PHONE.............................908 561-1144
Fax: 908 561-9205
Ronald Eodice, *President*
Charles Percevault, *Corp Secy*
Joseph Novakowski, *Vice Pres*
EMP: 15 EST: 1977
SQ FT: 5,000
SALES (est): 1.6MM **Privately Held**
SIC: 7692 3441 Welding repair; fabricated
    structural metal

(G-10334)
BANKER STEEL NJ LLC
1640 New Market Ave (07080-1641)
PHONE.............................732 968-6061
Donald Banker, *CEO*
EMP: 70
SQ FT: 34,300
SALES (est): 2MM
SALES (corp-wide): 2.2B **Privately Held**
SIC: 1791 3441 Structural steel erection;
    fabricated structural metal
HQ: Banker Steel Co., L.L.C.
    1619 Wythe Rd Ste B
    Lynchburg VA 24501
    434 847-4575

(G-10335)
BCSMACHINE & MFG CORP
3575 Kennedy Rd (07080-1996)
PHONE.............................908 561-1656
Fax: 908 753-2076
Salvatore Capparelli, *President*
Cynthia Bolesta, *Corp Secy*

Frank M Capparelli, *Vice Pres*
Debra Capparelli, *Shareholder*
Maria Farrell, *Shareholder*
EMP: 9 **EST:** 1964
SQ FT: 8,200
SALES (est): 870K **Privately Held**
SIC: 3599 3444 Machine shop, jobbing & repair; sheet metalwork

(G-10336)
BEATRICE HOME FASHIONS INC (PA)
151 Helen St (07080-3806)
P.O. Box 86 (07080-0086)
PHONE....................908 561-7370
Fax: 908 757-9629
Sam Gindi, *President*
Sam N Gindi, *President*
▲ **EMP:** 20
SQ FT: 45,000
SALES (est): 5.6MM **Privately Held**
SIC: 2392 2391 Bedspreads & bed sets: made from purchased materials; draperies, plastic & textile: from purchased materials

(G-10337)
BIOACTIVE RESOURCES LLC
138 Sylvania Pl (07080-1448)
PHONE....................908 561-3114
Divya Desai, *CEO*
Mayur Desai,
▲ **EMP:** 13
SQ FT: 150,000
SALES (est): 4.3MM **Privately Held**
WEB: www.bioactiveresources.com
SIC: 2834 Vitamin preparations

(G-10338)
BRACO MANUFACTURING INC
4031b New Brunswick Ave (07080)
PHONE....................732 752-7777
Jack Braha, *President*
Paul Clark, *COO*
Elliott Braha, *Vice Pres*
▲ **EMP:** 28
SQ FT: 40,000
SALES (est): 6.6MM **Privately Held**
WEB: www.bracomanufacturing.com
SIC: 2676 Diapers, paper (disposable): made from purchased paper; napkins, sanitary: made from purchased paper

(G-10339)
BRENNTAG SPECIALTIES INC (DH)
1 Cragwood Rd Ste 302 (07080-2416)
PHONE....................800 732-0562
Steve Brauer, *President*
Brendan Cullinan, *Vice Pres*
Bob Przybylowski, *Vice Pres*
Brad Owens, *Treasurer*
John Down, *Manager*
◆ **EMP:** 60 **EST:** 2003
SQ FT: 110,000
SALES (est): 277.7MM
SALES (corp-wide): 13.8B **Privately Held**
WEB: www.mpsi-sw.com
SIC: 5169 2816 2899 Industrial chemicals; color pigments; chemical preparations
HQ: Brenntag North America, Inc.
5083 Pottsville Pike
Reading PA 19605
610 926-6100

(G-10340)
BUSHWICK METALS LLC
1641 New Market Ave (07080-1634)
PHONE....................908 604-1450
Dan De Silva, *General Mgr*
EMP: 5
SALES (corp-wide): 242.1B **Publicly Held**
SIC: 3315 Steel wire & related products
HQ: Bushwick Metals, Llc
560 N Washington Ave # 2
Bridgeport CT 06604
888 399-4070

(G-10341)
BUSHWICK METALS LLC
Also Called: Azco Steel Company
1641 New Market Ave (07080-1634)
PHONE....................908 754-8700
Fax: 908 754-8728

Roy Strandberg, *Branch Mgr*
EMP: 30
SALES (corp-wide): 242.1B **Publicly Held**
WEB: www.bushwickmetals.com
SIC: 5064 5051 3312 Irons; steel; pipes, iron & steel
HQ: Bushwick Metals, Llc
560 N Washington Ave # 2
Bridgeport CT 06604
888 399-4070

(G-10342)
C M C STEEL FABRICATORS INC
Also Called: CMC Joist & Deck
14 Harmich Rd (07080-4804)
PHONE....................908 561-3484
Keven Gennarelli, *Principal*
Mike Polesky, *Branch Mgr*
EMP: 140
SQ FT: 125,000
SALES (corp-wide): 4.5B **Publicly Held**
WEB: www.cmcsg.com
SIC: 3444 3441 Roof deck, sheet metal; fabricated structural metal
HQ: C M C Steel Fabricators, Inc.
1 Steel Mill Dr
Seguin TX 78155
830 372-8200

(G-10343)
CANDELA CORPORATION
Also Called: Applied Optronics
111 Corporate Blvd Ste I (07080-2480)
PHONE....................908 753-6300
Fax: 908 753-4041
Bob Sellers, *General Mgr*
EMP: 12 **Privately Held**
WEB: www.candelalaser.com
SIC: 3674 3699 Integrated circuits, semiconductor networks, etc.; laser systems & equipment
HQ: Candela Corporation
530 Boston Post Rd
Wayland MA 01778
949 716-6670

(G-10344)
CAST TECHNOLOGY INC
161 West St (07080-3812)
PHONE....................908 753-5155
Kenneth Shilay Sr, *President*
Margaret Shilay, *Admin Sec*
EMP: 5
SALES: 700K **Privately Held**
WEB: www.castechnology.com
SIC: 3519 Diesel engine rebuilding

(G-10345)
CHATHAM BRASS CO INC
1253 New Market Ave Ste D (07080-2033)
PHONE....................908 668-0500
Allen Leighton, *President*
Gene Adamusik, *Vice Pres*
▲ **EMP:** 7 **EST:** 1956
SQ FT: 9,500
SALES: 1.6MM **Privately Held**
SIC: 3432 Plumbing fixture fittings & trim

(G-10346)
CHEMMARK DEVELOPMENT INC
70 Tyler Pl (07080-1210)
PHONE....................908 561-0923
Robert C Mc Manus, *President*
Geoffrey Brooks, *Shareholder*
Ivar Malmstrom, *Shareholder*
EMP: 3
SQ FT: 200
SALES: 2.2MM **Privately Held**
WEB: www.cosmeticindex.com
SIC: 2869 Industrial organic chemicals

(G-10347)
COLOR TECHNIQUES INC
260 Ryan St (07080-4208)
PHONE....................908 412-9292
Fax: 908 412-9339
Joseph Bolitsky, *President*
Jennifer Bolitsky, *Vice Pres*
Carol Edridge, *VP Mktg*
◆ **EMP:** 12
SQ FT: 20,000

SALES (est): 1.8MM **Privately Held**
WEB: www.color-techniques.com
SIC: 2865 2816 Color pigments, organic; inorganic pigments

(G-10348)
COLORFUL STORY BOOKS INC
4301 New Brunswick Ave (07080-1205)
PHONE....................908 561-3333
Fax: 908 561-3810
John J Blewitt III, *President*
EMP: 30
SQ FT: 34,000
SALES: 1.5MM **Privately Held**
SIC: 2789 Binding only: books, pamphlets, magazines, etc.

(G-10349)
CONFIRES FIRE PRTCTION SVC LLC
910 Oak Tree Ave (07080-5142)
PHONE....................908 822-2700
Fax: 908 824-3134
Mark Calleo,
EMP: 13
SALES (est): 2.1MM **Privately Held**
SIC: 5087 3569 3429 3669 Service establishment equipment; sprinkler systems, fire: automatic; nozzles, fire fighting; emergency alarms

(G-10350)
CONVERSION TECHNOLOGY CO INC
4301 New Brunswick Ave A (07080-1205)
PHONE....................732 752-5660
Fax: 732 752-5944
Karel Choteborsky, *General Mgr*
EMP: 10 **Privately Held**
WEB: www.fluidink.com
SIC: 2899 Ink or writing fluids
PA: Conversion Technology Co., Inc.
5360 N Commerce Ave
Moorpark CA 93021

(G-10351)
CULTECH INC
3500 Hadley Rd (07080-1152)
PHONE....................732 225-2722
Isao Aiba, *President*
Jean-Christophe Duchamp, *Principal*
◆ **EMP:** 130 **EST:** 1990
SQ FT: 140,000
SALES (est): 30.4MM **Privately Held**
WEB: www.cultech.com
SIC: 2657 Folding paperboard boxes

(G-10352)
DANMARK ENTERPRISES INC (PA)
Also Called: Designer Bagel
692 Oak Tree Ave (07080-5122)
PHONE....................732 321-3366
Milton Celko, *President*
Linda Celko, *Treasurer*
EMP: 5
SQ FT: 2,500
SALES (est): 401.6K **Privately Held**
SIC: 2051 5461 Bagels, fresh or frozen; bagels

(G-10353)
DEER OUT ANIMAL REPELLANT LLC
3651 S Clinton Ave (07080-1322)
P.O. Box 290 (07080-0290)
PHONE....................908 769-4242
Gregg Latorre, *Mng Member*
EMP: 3
SALES: 10MM **Privately Held**
WEB: www.deerout.com
SIC: 2879 Insecticides & pesticides

(G-10354)
DEFENSE PHOTONICS GROUP INC
126 Corporate Blvd Ste A (07080-2411)
PHONE....................908 822-1075
John Husaim, *CEO*
▼ **EMP:** 18 **EST:** 2003
SQ FT: 7,500
SALES: 2MM **Privately Held**
SIC: 3721 5088 Aircraft; transportation equipment & supplies

(G-10355)
ENGO CO
128 Case Dr (07080-5199)
PHONE....................908 754-6600
Fax: 908 754-6605
Robert Engo, *President*
Richard Engo, *Admin Sec*
▲ **EMP:** 35
SQ FT: 60,000
SALES (est): 5.4MM **Privately Held**
WEB: www.engo.com
SIC: 2542 Partitions & fixtures, except wood

(G-10356)
ENZON PHARMACEUTICALS INC
300 Corporate Ct Ste C (07080-2415)
PHONE....................732 980-4500
Fax: 908 668-5997
Christopher Phillip, *Manager*
EMP: 95
SALES (corp-wide): 8.3MM **Publicly Held**
WEB: www.enzon.com
SIC: 2834 Pharmaceutical preparations
PA: Enzon Pharmaceuticals, Inc.
20 Commerce Dr Ste 135
Cranford NJ 07016
732 980-4500

(G-10357)
EPOCH TIMES
50 Cragwood Rd Ste 305 (07080-2436)
PHONE....................908 548-8026
Guangxun LI, *Principal*
Vanessa Rios, *Editor*
▲ **EMP:** 3 **EST:** 2013
SALES: 2MM **Privately Held**
SIC: 2711 Newspapers

(G-10358)
EVERGARD STEEL CORP
3313 Revere Rd (07080-5120)
PHONE....................908 925-6800
Fax: 908 925-6802
Connie Macellara, *President*
Catherine Smith, *Vice Pres*
EMP: 10 **EST:** 1961
SQ FT: 10,000
SALES (est): 1.3MM **Privately Held**
SIC: 3315 3496 Wire products, ferrous/iron: made in wiredrawing plants; miscellaneous fabricated wire products

(G-10359)
EVERLASTING VALVE COMPANY INC
108 Somogyi Ct (07080-4897)
PHONE....................908 769-0700
Fax: 908 769-8697
Richard G Base, *President*
Frank Hawley, *Vice Pres*
Roger Jensen, *VP Mfg*
Oscar Turk, *Buyer*
Jim Wilson, *VP Engrg*
▼ **EMP:** 30 **EST:** 1906
SQ FT: 28,000
SALES: 11.2MM
SALES (corp-wide): 105MM **Privately Held**
WEB: www.everlastingvalve.com
SIC: 3494 Valves & pipe fittings
PA: Armstrong International, Inc.
816 Maple St
Three Rivers MI 49093
269 273-1415

(G-10360)
EXACTAL TOOL LTD INC
Also Called: Exactal Tool & Die
3586 Kennedy Rd Ste 3 (07080-1997)
PHONE....................908 561-1177
Scott Kaese, *President*
EMP: 5
SQ FT: 4,500
SALES: 250K **Privately Held**
SIC: 3599 Machine shop, jobbing & repair

(G-10361)
EXCELHIGH INC
910 Oak Tree Ave Ste H (07080-5137)
PHONE....................212 947-8543
Roshini Soysa, *Branch Mgr*
EMP: 4 **Privately Held**

SIC: 2655 Fiber cans, drums & similar
products
PA: Excelhigh Inc.
20 Secatogue Ave
Farmingdale NY 11735

(G-10362)
F AND M EQUIPMENT LTD
Also Called: Komatsu Northeast
2820 Hamilton Blvd (07080-2518)
Rural Route 73 (07080)
PHONE..................................215 822-0145
Ben Norris, President
EMP: 100
SALES (est): 115.6K
SALES (corp-wide): 23.4B Privately Held
SIC: 3537 3531 Lift trucks, industrial: fork,
platform, straddle, etc.; construction ma-
chinery
HQ: Komatsu America Corp.
1701 Golf Rd Ste 1-100
Rolling Meadows IL 60008
847 437-5800

(G-10363)
FEDERAL METALS & ALLOYS CO
Also Called: Federal Reclamation Center
4216 S Clinton Ave (07080-1316)
PHONE..................................908 756-0900
Fax: 908 756-9201
Mark Scoda, President
Thomas C Dietz, President
Walter Adamczyk, Corp Secy
EMP: 9 EST: 1974
SALES (est): 1.4MM Privately Held
SIC: 3341 4953 Secondary nonferrous
metals; metal scrap & waste materials

(G-10364)
FERRO CORPORATION
2501 S Clinton Ave (07080-1425)
PHONE..................................908 226-2148
Carl Vogelzang, Manager
EMP: 4
SALES (corp-wide): 1.4B Publicly Held
SIC: 3479 Coating of metals & formed
products
PA: Ferro Corporation
6060 Parkland Blvd # 250
Mayfield Heights OH 44124
216 875-5600

(G-10365)
FINANCIAL INFORMATION INC
1 Cragwood Rd Ste 2 (07080-2448)
PHONE..................................908 222-5300
Fax: 908 222-5396
Elizabeth Kappel, President
Wayne Meszaros, CFO
Ivette Vazquez, Manager
Elaine Villani, Manager
Christy Deloatch, Supervisor
EMP: 40
SQ FT: 7,500
SALES (est): 3.1MM Privately Held
WEB: www.fiinet.com
SIC: 2711 2741 Newspapers, publishing &
printing; miscellaneous publishing

(G-10366)
FLAVOR DYNAMICS INC
640 Montrose Ave (07080-2602)
PHONE..................................888 271-8424
Fax: 908 822-8547
Dolf De Rovira, President
Sandy Biedermann, Sales Mgr
Ken Warren, Manager
EMP: 24
SQ FT: 29,000
SALES (est): 4.2MM Privately Held
WEB: www.flavordynamics.com
SIC: 2087 Extracts, flavoring

(G-10367)
FOURSCONSULTING LTD LBLTY CO
295 Durham Ave Ste 206 (07080-2548)
PHONE..................................732 599-4324
Renuka Balaji, Manager
Ashish Kumar, Technical Staff
Soruba Subramanian, Administration
Suraj Desai, Tech Recruiter
Abhilash Nair, Tech Recruiter
EMP: 6 EST: 2006

SALES (est): 418.9K Privately Held
SIC: 7372 Application computer software;
business oriented computer software

(G-10368)
FRAGRANCE SOLUTIONS CORP
3357 S Clinton Ave (07080-1303)
PHONE..................................732 832-7800
John Yorey, President
▼ EMP: 7 EST: 2011
SQ FT: 4,500
SALES (est): 542.6K Privately Held
SIC: 2844 Perfumes & colognes

(G-10369)
G & W LABORATORIES INC (PA)
111 Coolidge St (07080-3801)
PHONE..................................908 753-2000
Fax: 908 753-9264
Ronald Greenblatt, CEO
Jay Galeota, President
Kurt Orlofski, President
Michael Pavlak, President
James Coy, Vice Pres
▲ EMP: 300
SQ FT: 140,000
SALES (est): 269.7MM Privately Held
WEB: www.gwlabs.com
SIC: 2834 Suppositories; ointments

(G-10370)
G & W LABORATORIES INC
101 Coolidge St (07080-3801)
PHONE..................................908 753-2000
EMP: 85
SALES (corp-wide): 269.7MM Privately
Held
SIC: 2834 Suppositories; ointments
PA: G & W Laboratories, Inc.
111 Coolidge St
South Plainfield NJ 07080
908 753-2000

(G-10371)
G&W PA LABORATORIES LLC
111 Coolidge St (07080-3801)
PHONE..................................908 753-2000
Ronald Greenblatt, Mng Member
EMP: 9
SALES (corp-wide): 269.7MM Privately
Held
SIC: 2834 Pharmaceutical preparations
HQ: G&W Pa Laboratories, Llc
650 Cathill Rd
Sellersville PA 18960
215 799-5333

(G-10372)
GE HEALTHCARE INC
Also Called: Medi-Physics
900 Durham Ave (07080-2402)
PHONE..................................908 757-0500
Albert Vallejos, Project Mgr
Simon Steingart, Opers Mgr
Simon Eingart, Manager
Frank Mastromonica, Manager
EMP: 40
SALES (corp-wide): 122B Publicly Held
SIC: 2834 Pharmaceutical preparations
HQ: Ge Healthcare Inc.
100 Results Way
Marlborough MA 01752
800 292-8514

(G-10373)
GLOPAK CORP
132 Case Dr (07080-5109)
PHONE..................................908 753-8735
Fax: 973 344-0265
Cydnee Martin, CEO
Robert Macdougall, General Mgr
Barbara Martin, Principal
Harold Martin Jr, Vice Pres
EMP: 30
SQ FT: 100,000
SALES (est): 7.5MM Privately Held
SIC: 3069 3081 3086 2821 Bags, rubber
or rubberized fabric; polyethylene film;
plastics foam products; plastics materials
& resins

(G-10374)
GOLDEN W PPR CONVERTING CORP
121 Helen St (07080-3806)
PHONE..................................908 412-8889

Fax: 908 769-8860
David Hooi, Manager
EMP: 20
SALES (corp-wide): 24.3MM Privately
Held
SIC: 3565 Carton packing machines
PA: Golden West Paper Converting Corpo-
ration
16500 Worthley Dr
San Lorenzo CA 94580
510 317-0646

(G-10375)
GREETINGTAP
Also Called: Tap For Message
832 Spicer Ave (07080-3949)
PHONE..................................347 731-4263
Kadeer Beg,
Ahmer Beg,
EMP: 6
SALES (est): 338.4K Privately Held
SIC: 2741 5045 2771 ; computers, pe-
ripherals & software; greeting cards

(G-10376)
GULTON G I D
116 Corporate Blvd Ste A (07080-2437)
PHONE..................................908 791-4622
Joan Srivastava, Principal
EMP: 5
SALES (est): 608.3K Privately Held
SIC: 3679 5065 Antennas, receiving; elec-
tronic parts & equipment

(G-10377)
GULTON INCORPORATED
116 Corporate Blvd Ste A (07080-2437)
PHONE..................................908 791-4622
Om Srivastava, President
Dennis Flanagan, Vice Pres
Joan Srivastava, Vice Pres
Thomas Michalski, CFO
Dave Van Saun, Accounts Mgr
EMP: 20
SQ FT: 13,000
SALES (est): 4.8MM Privately Held
WEB: www.gulton.com
SIC: 3577 Printers & plotters

(G-10378)
HARRIS STRUCTURAL STEEL CO INC (PA)
1640 New Market Ave (07080-1641)
PHONE..................................732 752-6070
Fax: 732 752-1158
Thomas Harris Jr, Ch of Bd
Marvin Strauss, Exec VP
Bill Butrico, Engineer
John Brunetto, Branch Mgr
EMP: 40 EST: 1910
SQ FT: 100,000
SALES (est): 6.2MM Privately Held
SIC: 3441 Fabricated structural metal

(G-10379)
HARRIS STRUCTURAL STEEL CO INC
1640 New Market Ave (07080-1641)
PHONE..................................732 752-6070
John Brunetto, Branch Mgr
EMP: 6
SALES (corp-wide): 6.2MM Privately
Held
SIC: 3441 1791 Fabricated structural
metal; structural steel erection
PA: Harris Structural Steel Co., Inc.
1640 New Market Ave
South Plainfield NJ 07080
732 752-6070

(G-10380)
HONEYWELL INTERNATIONAL INC
107 Corporate Blvd (07080-2482)
PHONE..................................908 561-1888
Joseph Maselli, Manager
EMP: 6
SALES (corp-wide): 40.5B Publicly Held
WEB: www.honeywell.com
SIC: 3724 Aircraft engines & engine parts
PA: Honeywell International Inc.
115 Tabor Rd
Morris Plains NJ 07950
973 455-2000

(G-10381)
HUMMEL CROTON INC
Also Called: Hummel Chemical
10 Harmich Rd (07080-4899)
PHONE..................................908 754-1800
Fax: 908 754-1815
Bernard F Schoen, President
Mark Dugan, Vice Pres
Michael Richard, Opers Staff
Eileen Gryszel, Sales Associate
◆ EMP: 15
SQ FT: 20,000
SALES (est): 4MM Privately Held
WEB: www.hummelcroton.com
SIC: 2819 5169 Barium compounds; in-
dustrial chemicals

(G-10382)
IGI CORP
6 Ingersoll Rd (07080-1306)
PHONE..................................908 753-5570
Bud Philbrook, President
EMP: 5
SALES (est): 549.5K Privately Held
SIC: 2672 Coated & laminated paper

(G-10383)
ILEOS OF AMERICA INC
Also Called: Flexpaq
550 Hadley Rd (07080-2426)
PHONE..................................908 753-7300
Fax: 908 753-7959
Mark Andrei, President
▲ EMP: 200 EST: 1997
SQ FT: 150,000
SALES (est): 29MM Privately Held
WEB: www.flexpaq.com
SIC: 3559 2671 Semiconductor manufac-
turing machinery; packaging paper &
plastics film, coated & laminated
HQ: Ileos
Tour Montparnasse Batiment A
Paris 75015

(G-10384)
INNOVATIVE DISPOSABLES LLC
3611 Kennedy Rd (07080-1801)
PHONE..................................908 222-7111
Fax: 908 222-7113
Neal Schramm, Mng Member
Michael Schramm,
◆ EMP: 45 EST: 2000
SQ FT: 22,000
SALES (est): 15.3MM Privately Held
SIC: 2676 Diapers, paper (disposable):
made from purchased paper

(G-10385)
INTELLGENT TRFFIC SUP PDTS LLC
Also Called: I T S Products
3005 Hadley Rd Ste 5 (07080-1108)
PHONE..................................908 791-1200
Kevin Flynn,
EMP: 5
SALES (est): 1.8MM Privately Held
WEB: www.its-products.com
SIC: 5063 3669 5085 Signaling equip-
ment, electrical; traffic signals, electric; in-
dustrial supplies

(G-10386)
INTERNATIONAL GRAPHICS INC
6 Ingersoll Rd (07080-1306)
PHONE..................................908 753-5570
Bud Philbrook, President
EMP: 165
SQ FT: 50,000
SALES (est): 12.4MM Privately Held
SIC: 2672 Coated & laminated paper

(G-10387)
J R S TOOL & METAL FINISHING
Also Called: J R S Mch & Tl Sls Corp Ameri
107 Borman Rd (07080-2928)
P.O. Box 52 (07080-0052)
PHONE..................................908 753-2050
John Stopherd, President
Linda Stopherd, Vice Pres
EMP: 4
SQ FT: 6,000

GEOGRAPHIC (vertical side tab)

SALES: 199K **Privately Held**
SIC: **3599** 5084 7375 3471 Machine shop, jobbing & repair; machine tools & accessories; information retrieval services; plating & polishing; hand & edge tools; paints & allied products

(G-10388)
JERSEY TANK FABRICATORS INC
1271 New Market Ave Ste D (07080-2034)
P.O. Box 257, Cream Ridge (08514-0257)
PHONE..................................609 758-7670
Fax: 908 758-7988
Eric Turinsky, *Ch of Bd*
Arlene Turinsky, *Corp Secy*
Stacy Nownes, *Finance Mgr*
▲ EMP: 30
SALES (est): 5.1MM **Privately Held**
WEB: www.jerseytank.com
SIC: **1791** 7699 3443 Storage tanks, metal; erection; tank repair; fabricated plate work (boiler shop)

(G-10389)
JORDACHE LTD
200 Helen St (07080-3800)
PHONE..................................908 226-4930
Scott Reichert, *Manager*
▲ EMP: 11
SALES (est): 1.1MM
SALES (corp-wide): 1.4B **Privately Held**
SIC: **2325** 2339 2369 Jeans: men's, youths' & boys'; men's & boys' jeans & dungarees; jeans: women's, misses' & juniors'; jeans: girls', children's & infants'
PA: Jordache Enterprises Inc.
    1400 Broadway Rm 1404b
    New York NY 10018
    212 643-8400

(G-10390)
K & A INDUSTRIES INC
51 Cragwood Rd Ste 204 (07080-2405)
PHONE..................................908 226-7000
Fax: 908 226-7007
George Keelty, *President*
Robert Aitkens, *Vice Pres*
Leon Deane, *Vice Pres*
EMP: 6
SQ FT: 2,500
SALES (est): 720K **Privately Held**
WEB: www.kaindustries.com
SIC: **3699** Security control equipment & systems

(G-10391)
KADAKIA INTERNATIONAL INC
Also Called: Kadakia International Group
669 Montrose Ave (07080-2601)
PHONE..................................908 754-4445
Sailesh Kadakia, *President*
Prital Kadakia, *Vice Pres*
Priti Kadakia, *Vice Pres*
▲ EMP: 6
SQ FT: 8,000
SALES (est): 2.1MM **Privately Held**
SIC: **5162** 2851 Plastics film; enamels

(G-10392)
KEYSTONE PLASTICS INC
3451 S Clinton Ave (07080-1303)
PHONE..................................908 561-1300
Fax: 908 561-3404
Marvin J Naftal, *President*
Frances Gould-Naftal, *Corp Secy*
Michael Naftal, *Vice Pres*
Orlando Rios, *Manager*
Rita Bongiovi, *Receptionist*
◆ EMP: 60
SQ FT: 62,000
SALES (est): 14.5MM **Privately Held**
SIC: **3082** 3991 Unsupported plastics profile shapes; brooms & brushes

(G-10393)
KOBO PRODUCTS INC (PA)
3474 S Clinton Ave (07080-1320)
P.O. Box 36079, Newark (07188-6006)
PHONE..................................908 757-0033
Fax: 908 757-0905
David Schlossman, *President*
Oreste Nuzzo, *Warehouse Mgr*
April Vandunk, *Export Mgr*
Kathy X Sun, *Research*
Vince Mondano, *Engineer*

◆ EMP: 35
SQ FT: 11,000
SALES (est): 115.3MM **Privately Held**
WEB: www.koboproductsinc.com
SIC: **5122** 2844 Cosmetics; cosmetic preparations

(G-10394)
KOBO PRODUCTS INC
690 Montrose Ave (07080-2602)
P.O. Box 767 (07080-0767)
PHONE..................................908 941-3406
Sadi Benzemma, *Plant Mgr*
Ashley Bishop, *Buyer*
Julian Navarro, *Branch Mgr*
EMP: 25
SALES (corp-wide): 115.3MM **Privately Held**
SIC: **2844** Cosmetic preparations
PA: Kobo Products, Inc.
    3474 S Clinton Ave
    South Plainfield NJ 07080
    908 757-0033

(G-10395)
KOBO PRODUCTS INC
234 Saint Nicholas Ave (07080-1810)
P.O. Box 767, Short Hills (07078-0767)
PHONE..................................908 757-0033
Yun Shao, *Vice Pres*
Elsie Ruiz-Alvarado, *QC Mgr*
Denise Fishman, *Research*
Mark Sine, *Accounts Mgr*
Danielle Kennedy, *Director*
EMP: 30
SALES (corp-wide): 115.3MM **Privately Held**
SIC: **2844** Cosmetic preparations
PA: Kobo Products, Inc.
    3474 S Clinton Ave
    South Plainfield NJ 07080
    908 757-0033

(G-10396)
LE PAPILLON LTD
Also Called: Le Papillon of New Jersey
500 Hadley Rd (07080-2426)
PHONE..................................908 753-7300
Fax: 732 843-6118
Watson Warriner, *President*
Mark Rosso, *Vice Pres*
▲ EMP: 15
SQ FT: 4,000
SALES (est): 3.4MM **Privately Held**
WEB: www.lepapillon.com
SIC: **3221** Bottles for packing, bottling & canning: glass
HQ: Ileos
    Tour Montparnasse Batiment A
    Paris 75015

(G-10397)
LEHIGH UTILITY ASSOCIATES INC
1300 New Market Ave (07080-1452)
P.O. Box 398 (07080-0398)
PHONE..................................908 561-5252
Fax: 908 668-7959
Frank J Butrico, *President*
William A Butrico, *Vice Pres*
William Butrico, *Vice Pres*
Florence Volosin, *Director*
EMP: 16
SQ FT: 32,000
SALES (est): 4.3MM **Privately Held**
WEB: www.lehighutility.com
SIC: **3441** Fabricated structural metal

(G-10398)
LELAND LIMITED INC
2614 S Clinton Ave (07080-1427)
P.O. Box 466 (07080-0466)
PHONE..................................908 561-2000
Leland C Stanford, *President*
Dawn Klinger, *Vice Pres*
◆ EMP: 13
SQ FT: 10,000
SALES (est): 4MM **Privately Held**
WEB: www.lelandltd.com
SIC: **3443** 3069 5063 Tanks, standard or custom fabricated: metal plate; life jackets, inflatable: rubberized fabric; lighting fixtures, commercial & industrial

(G-10399)
M & M INTERNATIONAL
3619 Kennedy Rd Ste A (07080-1891)
PHONE..................................908 412-8300
Min Lim, *Owner*
◆ EMP: 10
SALES (est): 940.2K **Privately Held**
WEB: www.mminternational.net
SIC: **3317** Steel pipe & tubes

(G-10400)
MADHU B GOYAL MD
908 Oak Tree Ave Ste C (07080-5100)
PHONE..................................908 769-0307
Fax: 908 757-3317
Madhu B Goyal, *Owner*
Madhu Goyal, *Med Doctor*
EMP: 4
SALES (est): 266.3K **Privately Held**
SIC: **8011** 7631 3444 1711 Geriatric specialist, physician/surgeon; watch repair; sheet metalwork; ventilation & duct work contractor; malpractice & negligence law

(G-10401)
MARBURN STORES INC
4975 Stelton Rd (07080-1113)
PHONE..................................908 412-1962
Ed Hund, *Branch Mgr*
EMP: 7
SALES (corp-wide): 33.5MM **Privately Held**
SIC: **2391** Curtains & draperies
PA: Marburn Stores, Inc.
    13a Division St
    Fairview NJ 07022
    201 943-0222

(G-10402)
MARDEE COMPANY INC
Also Called: Mardee Video Company
242 Saint Nicholas Ave (07080-1810)
PHONE..................................908 753-4343
Fax: 908 753-2319
Mariano De Santis, *President*
Steve Saunders, *Client Mgr*
Andres Torres, *Art Dir*
▲ EMP: 50
SQ FT: 31,000
SALES (est): 7.8MM **Privately Held**
WEB: www.mardee.com
SIC: **3651** 5099 Household audio & video equipment; video & audio equipment

(G-10403)
MARINO BUILDING SYSTEMS CORP
Also Called: American Panel TEC
1640 New Market Ave 1a (07080-1641)
P.O. Box 70 (07080-0070)
PHONE..................................732 968-0555
Fax: 732 968-4777
John A Marino, *Ch of Bd*
John Marino, *Ch of Bd*
John Lanzilotta, *President*
Keith Sherman, *Plant Mgr*
Matthew Folkerts, *Project Mgr*
EMP: 125
SQ FT: 90,000
SALES (est): 21MM **Privately Held**
WEB: www.americanpaneltec.com
SIC: **3448** Trusses & framing: prefabricated metal

(G-10404)
MARINO INTERNATIONAL CORP
1640 New Market Ave (07080-1641)
P.O. Box 178 (07080-0178)
PHONE..................................732 752-5100
Fax: 732 752-6252
John A Marino, *Chairman*
Tatyana Marino, *Vice Pres*
EMP: 2
SQ FT: 60,000
SALES: 1.2MM **Privately Held**
SIC: **2439** 3444 3441 2452 Structural wood members; sheet metalwork; fabricated structural metal; prefabricated wood buildings

(G-10405)
MEDPLAST MEDICAL INC (DH)
6 Century Ln (07080-1323)
PHONE..................................908 561-0717
Dan Croteau, *CEO*
Brett Williams, *President*

Michael Hoch, *General Mgr*
Alberto Meseguer, *General Mgr*
Katie Karmelek, *Business Mgr*
◆ EMP: 172
SQ FT: 40,000
SALES: 271.2MM
SALES (corp-wide): 189.2MM **Privately Held**
WEB: www.medtech-grp.com
SIC: **3841** Surgical & medical instruments

(G-10406)
MICRODATA INSTRUMENT INC
1207 Hogan Dr (07080-2474)
PHONE..................................908 222-1717
George Cai, *President*
EMP: 10
SQ FT: 2,000
SALES (est): 850K **Privately Held**
WEB: www.microdatamdi.com
SIC: **3821** Laboratory apparatus, except heating & measuring

(G-10407)
MILLCO CUSTOM FABRICATORS INC
601 Montrose Ave (07080-2601)
PHONE..................................908 756-3640
Fax: 908 756-3467
Jim Curcio, *President*
Thomas Eads, *Vice Pres*
Jill Indyk, *Vice Pres*
EMP: 5
SQ FT: 5,000
SALES (est): 674.9K **Privately Held**
WEB: www.millco.com
SIC: **3444** Sheet metalwork

(G-10408)
MOBILE MINI INC
2400 Roosevelt Ave (07080-1468)
PHONE..................................908 561-5033
Barry McElyea, *Manager*
EMP: 20
SALES (corp-wide): 533.5MM **Publicly Held**
WEB: www.mobilemini.com
SIC: **3448** Buildings, portable: prefabricated metal
PA: Mobile Mini, Inc.
    4646 E Van Buren St # 400
    Phoenix AZ 85008
    480 894-6311

(G-10409)
MONARCH TOWEL COMPANY INC (PA)
Also Called: Monarch Robe and Towel Company
301 Hollywood Ave (07080-4201)
PHONE..................................800 729-7623
Fax: 732 442-0419
Ashley Chadowitz, *President*
Myron Chadowitz, *General Mgr*
Hillary Flaim, *Vice Pres*
Marilyn Robillard, *Cust Mgr*
▲ EMP: 25
SQ FT: 40,000
SALES: 15MM **Privately Held**
WEB: www.kfn.com
SIC: **2384** Bathrobes, men's & women's: made from purchased materials

(G-10410)
MONTROSE MOLDERS CORPORATION
230 Saint Nicholas Ave (07080-1810)
PHONE..................................908 754-3030
William H Wilson, *President*
Judith Wilson, *Corp Secy*
EMP: 120
SQ FT: 76,000
SALES (est): 8.1MM
SALES (corp-wide): 23.2MM **Privately Held**
WEB: www.montrosemolders.com
SIC: **3081** Unsupported plastics film & sheet
PA: Continental Precision Corp
    25 Howard St
    Piscataway NJ 08854
    908 754-3030

(G-10411)
MULTI PACKAGING SOLUTIONS INC
901 Durham Ave (07080-2401)
PHONE..............................908 757-6000
Jack Frank, *Prdtn Mgr*
Bob S Pierre, *CFO*
John Weir, *Manager*
Bill Van Jura, *Director*
EMP: 200
SALES (corp-wide): 14.8B Publicly Held
SIC: 2631 2752 2671 2657 Folding boxboard; commercial printing, lithographic; packaging paper & plastics film, coated & laminated; folding paperboard boxes
HQ: Multi Packaging Solutions, Inc.
150 E 52nd St Ste 2800
New York NY 10022

(G-10412)
NEW JERSEY BINDERY SVCS LLC
4301 New Brunswick Ave (07080-1205)
PHONE..............................732 200-8024
EMP: 4
SALES (est): 129.1K Privately Held
SIC: 2789 Bookbinding & related work

(G-10413)
NMR MANUFACTURING LLC
25 Davis St (07080-1429)
PHONE..............................908 769-3234
Mary Rinaldi, *Principal*
▲ EMP: 4 EST: 2002
SALES (est): 220K Privately Held
SIC: 2844 Toilet preparations

(G-10414)
NOODLE GOGO
4811 Stelton Rd (07080-1194)
PHONE..............................908 222-8898
Phillip LI, *President*
EMP: 4
SALES (est): 241.9K Privately Held
SIC: 2098 Noodles (e.g. egg, plain & water), dry

(G-10415)
NU-MEAT TECHNOLOGY INC
601 Hadley Rd (07080-2403)
P.O. Box 897 (07080-0897)
PHONE..............................908 754-3400
Fax: 908 754-3401
John Sbraga, *CEO*
Manfred Unfried, *Ch of Bd*
Brian Dowd, *President*
Josep Lagares, *General Mgr*
Gary Raines, *Treasurer*
▲ EMP: 20
SQ FT: 6,532
SALES (est): 11MM Privately Held
WEB: www.nu-meat.com
SIC: 5147 2011 Meats & meat products; meat packing plants

(G-10416)
NUTRO LABORATORIES INC
650 Hadley Rd Ste C (07080-2477)
PHONE..............................908 755-7984
Fax: 908 754-5640
Michael Slade, *President*
▲ EMP: 210
SQ FT: 85,000
SALES (est): 32.2MM Publicly Held
WEB: www.nbty.com
SIC: 2834 Vitamin preparations; analgesics; antiseptics, medicinal; laxatives
HQ: The Nature's Bounty Co
2100 Smithtown Ave
Ronkonkoma NY 11779
631 200-2000

(G-10417)
NYLTITE CORP OF AMERICA
3451 S Clinton Ave (07080-1303)
PHONE..............................908 561-1300
Frances Gould, *President*
Charna Gould, *Corp Secy*
EMP: 10
SQ FT: 67,000
SALES: 600K Privately Held
WEB: www.nyltite.com
SIC: 3965 2221 Fasteners; broadwoven fabric mills, manmade

(G-10418)
OMG ELECTRONIC CHEMICALS INC
Also Called: Fidelity Chemical Products Div
400 Corporate Ct Ste A (07080-2414)
PHONE..............................908 222-5800
Chris Vidoli, *Vice Pres*
Chris Bidoli, *Vice Pres*
Joseph Simioni, *Vice Pres*
▼ EMP: 205 EST: 1969
SQ FT: 15,000
SALES (est): 26.8MM
SALES (corp-wide): 2B Privately Held
SIC: 2899 2819 3339 Plating compounds; nickel compounds or salts, inorganic; zinc chloride; primary nonferrous metals
PA: Vectra Co.
120 S Central Ave Ste 200
Saint Louis MO 63105
314 797-8600

(G-10419)
PETRA SYSTEMS INC
Also Called: Petra Solar
1 Cragwood Rd Ste 303 (07080-2416)
PHONE..............................908 462-5200
Fax: 908 755-0369
Shihab Kuran, *CEO*
Imran A Bhutta, *President*
Dan Brdar, *COO*
Imran Bhutta, *Vice Pres*
Mary Grikas, *Vice Pres*
EMP: 116
SALES (est): 98.5MM Privately Held
SIC: 5074 3671 Heating equipment & panels, solar; light sensing & emitting tubes

(G-10420)
PETRO INC
40 Cragwood Rd Ste D (07080-2440)
PHONE..............................877 745-7687
Daniel P Donovan, *President*
EMP: 6 Publicly Held
SIC: 1311 Crude petroleum & natural gas
HQ: Petro, Inc.
9 W Broad St Ste 430
Stamford CT 06902
203 325-5400

(G-10421)
POLYMER DYNAMIX LLC
Also Called: Poly-Dyn International
238 Saint Nicholas Ave (07080-1810)
PHONE..............................732 381-1600
Lou Rey, *QC Mgr*
Zheng Qian, *Research*
Veerag Mehta, *Mng Member*
Viggy Mehta,
Vikas Mehta,
▲ EMP: 15
SQ FT: 6,000
SALES (est): 3.6MM Privately Held
WEB: www.polymerdynamix.com
SIC: 3089 Plastic containers, except foam

(G-10422)
PORTON USA LLC (HQ)
3001 Hadley Rd Ste 1-4 (07080-1134)
PHONE..............................908 791-9100
Bruce Jiang,
EMP: 30 EST: 2015
SALES (est): 4MM
SALES (corp-wide): 178.7MM Privately Held
SIC: 2834 Pharmaceutical preparations

(G-10423)
POWERHUSE FRMLTONS LTD LABILIT
150 Maple Ave Ste 216 (07080-3407)
PHONE..............................888 666-7715
EMP: 4 EST: 2009
SQ FT: 600
SALES (est): 350K Privately Held
SIC: 2834 Mfg Natural Food Supplements

(G-10424)
PRESTO PRINTING SERVICE INC
19 S Plainfield Ave (07080-3408)
PHONE..............................908 756-5337
Richard Depinto, *President*
Richard De Pinto, *President*
EMP: 4
SQ FT: 1,200

SALES (est): 330K Privately Held
SIC: 2752 Commercial printing, offset

(G-10425)
PTC THERAPEUTICS INC
100 Corporate Ct (07080-2400)
PHONE..............................908 222-7000
Fax: 908 222-7231
Stuart W Peltz, *CEO*
Michael Schmertzler, *Ch of Bd*
Marcio Souza, *COO*
John Babiak, *Vice Pres*
Ernest Dietel, *Vice Pres*
EMP: 373
SALES: 194.3MM Privately Held
WEB: www.ptcbio.com
SIC: 2834 8731 Pharmaceutical preparations; biotechnical research, commercial

(G-10426)
QUALIS PACKAGING INC (PA)
550 Hadley Rd (07080-2426)
PHONE..............................908 782-0305
Julie Vandoren, *Vice Pres*
EMP: 10 EST: 2008
SQ FT: 50,000
SALES (est): 3.2MM Privately Held
SIC: 2844 Perfumes & colognes

(G-10427)
QUALITY COSMETICS MFG
4455 S Clinton Ave (07080-1213)
PHONE..............................908 755-9588
Fax: 908 545-4379
Anthony Richard Persaud, *President*
Teresa Persaud, *Vice Pres*
Christina Persaud,
▲ EMP: 40
SQ FT: 33,000
SALES (est): 8.4MM Privately Held
WEB: www.qualitycosmetics.com
SIC: 2844 Cosmetic preparations

(G-10428)
QUALITY GLASS INC
2300 S Clinton Ave Ste C (07080-1498)
PHONE..............................908 754-2652
Ronald Morris, *President*
Karen Morris, *Vice Pres*
EMP: 12
SALES (est): 1.7MM Privately Held
SIC: 7536 7699 3231 Automotive glass replacement shops; china & glass repair; door & window repair; products of purchased glass

(G-10429)
QUALTEQ INC
Also Called: Vct - Qualteq
800 Montrose Ave Cn1037 (07080-1804)
PHONE..............................908 668-0999
Merrill J Martin, *COO*
Anu Veluchamy, *Vice Pres*
◆ EMP: 130
SQ FT: 65,000
SALES (est): 13.6MM
SALES (corp-wide): 57.2MM Privately Held
WEB: www.vct-nj.co m
SIC: 3089 Aquarium accessories, plastic
PA: Versatile Card Technology, Inc.
5200 Thatcher Rd
Downers Grove IL 60515
630 852-5600

(G-10430)
R & D CIRCUITS INC (PA)
Also Called: R&D Altanova
3601 S Clinton Ave (07080-1322)
PHONE..............................732 549-4554
Seyed Paransun, *President*
Grace Micu, *Materials Mgr*
Faisal Azeem, *Engineer*
Jeff Bavaro, *Engineer*
Tony Serafino, *Engineer*
▲ EMP: 150 EST: 1971
SQ FT: 270,000
SALES (est): 33.4MM Privately Held
WEB: www.rdcircuits.com
SIC: 3672 Printed circuit boards

(G-10431)
R TAPE CORPORATION (DH)
6 Ingersoll Rd (07080-1306)
PHONE..............................908 753-5570
Fax: 908 753-5014

Paul Charapata, *CEO*
Scott Bell, *Business Mgr*
Ramiro Diaz, *Prdtn Mgr*
Tom Kennedy, *CFO*
Tim Reimer, *Controller*
◆ EMP: 125
SQ FT: 53,000
SALES (est): 32.3MM Privately Held
WEB: www.rtape.com
SIC: 2671 2241 Plastic film, coated or laminated for packaging; fabric tapes
HQ: Nekoosa Coated Products, Llc
841 Market St
Nekoosa WI 54457
800 826-4886

(G-10432)
RADIANT COMMUNICATIONS CORP (PA)
5001 Hadley Rd (07080-1128)
P.O. Box 867 (07080-0867)
PHONE..............................908 757-7444
Fax: 908 757-8666
Tom Lewis, *President*
David Mandell, *Corp Secy*
Mike Whalen, *Prdtn Mgr*
Lyubomir Trayanov, *Engineer*
Marlene Swist, *Accounting Dir*
▲ EMP: 41
SQ FT: 10,000
SALES (est): 7.6MM Privately Held
WEB: www.rccfiber.com
SIC: 3229 Fiber optics strands

(G-10433)
RECYCLE INC
20a Harmich Rd (07080-4824)
P.O. Box 340 (07080-0340)
PHONE..............................908 756-2200
Fax: 908 757-2211
Jeffrey Bey, *President*
Stanley Bey, *Chairman*
Jeanine Rutar, *CFO*
Glenn Richard, *Manager*
▲ EMP: 60
SQ FT: 85,000
SALES (est): 12.3MM Privately Held
SIC: 4953 3087 Recycling, waste materials; custom compound purchased resins

(G-10434)
RECYCLE INC EAST
20a Harmich Rd (07080-4824)
P.O. Box 340 (07080-0340)
PHONE..............................908 756-2200
Jeff Bey, *President*
EMP: 90
SQ FT: 80,000
SALES (est): 22.4MM Privately Held
SIC: 2655 3412 2821 Fiber cans, drums & containers; drums, fiber: made from purchased material; metal barrels, drums & pails; drums, shipping: metal; polyethylene resins
HQ: National Container Group, Llc
3620 W 38th St
Chicago IL 60632

(G-10435)
SENSIENT TECHNOLOGIES CORP
Also Called: Sensient Cosmetics Technology
107 Wade Ave (07080-1311)
P.O. Box 705 (07080-0705)
PHONE..............................908 757-4500
Debby Keyes, *Mktg Coord*
Gregg White, *Manager*
Jennifer Lee, *Manager*
EMP: 46
SQ FT: 18,000
SALES (corp-wide): 1.3B Publicly Held
WEB: www.sensient-tech.com
SIC: 2087 2099 2816 Flavoring extracts & syrups; beverage bases; food colorings; yeast; seasonings & spices; chili pepper or powder; seasonings: dry mixes; inorganic pigments
PA: Sensient Technologies Corporation
777 E Wisconsin Ave # 1100
Milwaukee WI 53202
414 271-6755

(G-10436)
SUKHADIAS SWEETS & SNACKS (PA)
Also Called: India Cafe
124 Case Dr (07080-5109)
PHONE..................................908 222-0069
Piyush Sukhadia, *President*
Jay Sukhadia, *Vice Pres*
Bindu Sukhadia, *Admin Sec*
▲ EMP: 15
SQ FT: 6,000
SALES (est): 2.1MM **Privately Held**
SIC: 2051 Cakes, pies & pastries

(G-10437)
SUPERSEAL MANUFACTURING CO INC (DH)
125 Helen St (07080-3806)
P.O. Box 795 (07080-0795)
PHONE..................................908 561-5910
Fax: 908 561-7885
Joseph Vespa Jr, *President*
Ronald A Vespa, *Vice Pres*
EMP: 21 EST: 1980
SQ FT: 128,000
SALES (est): 9.3MM
SALES (corp-wide): 1.2B **Privately Held**
SIC: 3089 Window frames & sash, plastic
HQ: Hwd Acquisition, Inc.
575 S Whelen Ave
Medford WI 54451
800 433-4873

(G-10438)
TECHNICK PRODUCTS INC
238 Saint Nicholas Ave (07080-1810)
PHONE..................................908 791-0400
Amita Mehta, *President*
Veerag Mehta, *Vice Pres*
Vaibhav Desai, *Research*
Carlos Technick, *Technician*
▲ EMP: 12
SQ FT: 12,000
SALES (est): 4.4MM **Privately Held**
WEB: www.technickproducts.com
SIC: 2821 2841 Plastics materials & resins; soap & other detergents

(G-10439)
TEVCO ENTERPRISES INC
110 Pomponio Ave (07080-1900)
PHONE..................................908 754-7306
Fax: 908 756-0934
Marc Bergschneider, *President*
Jim Joyce, *President*
◆ EMP: 55 EST: 1987
SALES (est): 11MM
SALES (corp-wide): 5.3B **Publicly Held**
WEB: www.tevco.com
SIC: 2851 Enamels; lacquer: bases, dopes, thinner; removers & cleaners
PA: Rpm International Inc.
2628 Pearl Rd
Medina OH 44256
330 273-5090

(G-10440)
TOUCH DYNAMIC INC (PA)
121 Corporate Blvd (07080-2409)
PHONE..................................732 382-5701
Craig Paritz, *President*
▲ EMP: 68
SQ FT: 40,000
SALES (est): 16.8MM **Privately Held**
WEB: www.touchdynamic.com
SIC: 3575 3571 Computer terminals, monitors & components; personal computers (microcomputers)

(G-10441)
TRAFFIC SAFETY SERVICE LLC
601 Hadley Rd (07080-2403)
P.O. Box 615 (07080-0615)
PHONE..................................908 561-4800
Fax: 908 561-3800
Theodore Pecararo, *CEO*
Theodore Pecararo, *CEO*
John McCormick, *General Mgr*
Michael Pecoraro, *COO*
Skylar Bastedo, *Opers Staff*
▲ EMP: 47
SQ FT: 20,000

SALES (est): 22.3MM **Privately Held**
WEB: www.trafficsafetyservice.com
SIC: 5099 3993 7359 Reflective road markers; signs & advertising specialties; equipment rental & leasing

(G-10442)
TUMI HOLDINGS INC (DH)
1001 Durham Ave Ste 1b (07080-2300)
PHONE..................................908 756-4400
Jerome S Griffith, *President*
Peter L Gray, *Exec VP*
Michael J Mardy, *CFO*
EMP: 66
SQ FT: 47,905
SALES: 547.6MM **Privately Held**
SIC: 3161 3172 5948 Traveling bags; clothing & apparel carrying cases; satchels; card cases; wallets; luggage & leather goods stores
HQ: Samsonite International S.A.
25/F The Gateway Harbour City Twr 2
Tsim Sha Tsui KLN
242 226-11

(G-10443)
TWO RIVERS COFFEE LLC
Also Called: Brooklyn Bean Roastery
101 Kentile Rd Unit 13 (07080-4805)
P.O. Box 527 (07080-0527)
PHONE..................................908 205-0018
Steven Schreiber,
Mayer Koenig,
EMP: 5
SQ FT: 100,000
SALES (est): 1MM **Privately Held**
SIC: 2095 Coffee roasting (except by wholesale grocers)

(G-10444)
UMICORE PRECIOUS METALS NJ LLC
3950 S Clinton Ave (07080-1316)
PHONE..................................908 222-5006
Fax: 908 561-3945
Rick Holt, *Vice Pres*
Stephan Marczinkowski, *Vice Pres*
▲ EMP: 25
SALES (est): 9.4MM
SALES (corp-wide): 3.3B **Privately Held**
SIC: 3339 2869 Precious metals; industrial organic chemicals
PA: Umicore Sa
Rue Du Marais 31
Bruxelles 1000
222 771-11

(G-10445)
UMICORE USA INC
3900 S Clinton Ave (07080-1316)
PHONE..................................908 226-2053
Gregory Hedden, *Branch Mgr*
EMP: 19
SALES (corp-wide): 3.3B **Privately Held**
SIC: 3339 Precious metals
HQ: Umicore Usa Inc.
3600 Glenwood Ave Ste 250
Raleigh NC 27612

(G-10446)
US PLASTIC SALES LLC
651 Metuchen Rd (07080-4820)
P.O. Box 617 (07080-0617)
PHONE..................................908 754-9404
Fax: 908 754-9221
Raphael Bilia,
▲ EMP: 5
SQ FT: 50,000
SALES: 6MM **Privately Held**
SIC: 3081 Unsupported plastics film & sheet

(G-10447)
US SOFTWARE GROUP INC
Also Called: Ussg
1550 Park Ave Ste 202 (07080-5565)
P.O. Box 854, Edison (08818-0854)
PHONE..................................732 361-4636
Jake Kris, *Director*
EMP: 50
SALES (est): 4.8MM **Privately Held**
SIC: 7379 7372 4813 ; application computer software;

(G-10448)
VAN HYDRAULICS INC
110 Snyder Rd (07080-1915)
P.O. Box 320, Keasbey (08832-0320)
PHONE..................................732 442-5500
Fax: 732 442-5443
Arthur Fernandez Jr, *President*
Karen Fernandez, *Corp Secy*
EMP: 40
SQ FT: 5,000
SALES (est): 7.1MM **Privately Held**
WEB: www.vanhydraulics.com
SIC: 3593 5084 7699 Fluid power cylinders & actuators; hydraulic systems equipment & supplies; hydraulic equipment repair

(G-10449)
VAN-NICK PALLET INC
104 Snyder Rd (07080-1915)
PHONE..................................908 753-1800
Bobby Ducalo, *Owner*
EMP: 8
SALES (est): 1.2MM **Privately Held**
SIC: 2448 Pallets, wood & wood with metal

(G-10450)
VANGUARD RESEARCH INDUSTRIES
239 Saint Nicholas Ave (07080-1809)
PHONE..................................908 753-2770
Fax: 908 753-6540
Harry F Sica Jr, *CEO*
Peter Costa, *President*
David Chester, *Production*
EMP: 23
SQ FT: 35,000
SALES (est): 3.1MM **Privately Held**
WEB: www.vanguardholdings.com
SIC: 3471 Electroplating of metals or formed products

(G-10451)
VISUAL ARCHITECTURAL DESIGNS
Also Called: V A Design
15 Harmich Rd (07080-4804)
PHONE..................................908 754-3000
Fax: 732 769-6636
Sara Chrysanthopoulos, *CEO*
Michael Chrysanthopoulo, *Project Mgr*
Frank Nieves, *Sales Staff*
Paul Christman, *Sales Executive*
EMP: 19
SALES (est): 3.2MM **Privately Held**
SIC: 2541 2434 2531 2431 Store & office display cases & fixtures; wood kitchen cabinets; school furniture; vehicle furniture; millwork

(G-10452)
VITACARE PHARMA LLC
111 Skyline Dr (07080-1806)
PHONE..................................908 754-1792
Manav Shah,
Amrita Gupta,
Harendra Gupta,
EMP: 5
SALES (est): 1.1MM **Privately Held**
SIC: 2834 Pharmaceutical preparations

(G-10453)
WALL STREET GROUP INC
2 Hollywood Ct B (07080-4204)
PHONE..................................201 333-4784
Fax: 201 332-1597
Philip J Mc Gee, *President*
Alfred J Basile, *Vice Pres*
Charles Basile, *Vice Pres*
Mark Gorenstein, *Vice Pres*
Julie McGee Verbaro, *Vice Pres*
EMP: 60
SQ FT: 35,000
SALES (est): 12.3MM **Privately Held**
WEB: www.wallstreetgroup.com
SIC: 2759 Commercial printing

(G-10454)
WARE INDUSTRIES INC (PA)
Also Called: Marino Ware Division
400 Metuchen Ave (07080-4807)
P.O. Box 467 (07080-0467)
PHONE..................................908 757-9000
Fax: 908 753-8786
Leroy Schecter, *Ch of Bd*

Chip Gardner, *President*
Richard Dargel, *COO*
Dave Sirlouis, *VP Opers*
Edgar Pardo, *Mfg Dir*
◆ EMP: 68 EST: 1972
SQ FT: 100,000
SALES (est): 163.5MM **Privately Held**
WEB: www.marinoware.com
SIC: 3444 Sheet metalwork

(G-10455)
XBOX EXCLUSIVE
111 Eleanor St (07080-4705)
PHONE..................................908 756-3731
Steven Melanson, *Owner*
EMP: 7
SALES (est): 381.7K **Privately Held**
WEB: www.xboxexclusive.com
SIC: 3651 7993 Household audio & video equipment; video game arcade

South River
Middlesex County

(G-10456)
A-1 SPECIALIZED SVCS & SUPS
369 Whitehead Ave (08882-2534)
P.O. Box 173 (08882-0173)
PHONE..................................732 238-2900
Suresh Khosla, *President*
EMP: 40
SQ FT: 40,000
SALES (est): 3.6MM **Privately Held**
SIC: 5015 3714 Motor vehicle parts, used; motor vehicle parts & accessories

(G-10457)
ABINGTON RELDAN METALS LLC
Also Called: Reldan Metals Company
395-402 Whitehead (08882)
PHONE..................................732 238-8550
Alan Nadler, *Branch Mgr*
EMP: 9 **Privately Held**
SIC: 3339 Precious metals
PA: Abington Reldan Metals, Llc
550 Old Bordentown Rd
Fairless Hills PA 19030

(G-10458)
ALLTITE GASKET CO
323 William St (08882-1077)
PHONE..................................732 254-2154
Fax: 732 254-7150
Ronald Dreger, *President*
John Graney, *Vice Pres*
EMP: 10 EST: 1947
SQ FT: 5,000
SALES (est): 1.2MM **Privately Held**
SIC: 3053 Gaskets, all materials

(G-10459)
BUCATI LEATHER INC
427 Whitehead Ave Ste 2 (08882-2595)
PHONE..................................732 254-0480
▲ EMP: 8 EST: 1993
SQ FT: 8,000
SALES (est): 2MM **Privately Held**
SIC: 3199 5199 Mfg Leather Goods Whol Nondurable Goods

(G-10460)
DA-GREEN ELECTRONICS LTD
37 Main St (08882-1224)
P.O. Box 267 (08882-0267)
PHONE..................................732 254-2735
Fax: 732 254-9172
Marc Gable, *Partner*
Barry Greenberg, *Principal*
Ellen Gable, *Shareholder*
Arline Kane, *Shareholder*
Lillian Moore, *Shareholder*
EMP: 25
SQ FT: 37,000
SALES: 3MM **Privately Held**
WEB: www.dgecorp.com
SIC: 3679 5065 3678 Harness assemblies for electronic use: wire or cable; connectors, electronic; electronic connectors

(G-10461)
ENVIROCHEM INC
425 Whitehead Ave (08882-2536)
PHONE.............................732 238-6700
Fax: 732 238-5590
Deborah Gildersleeve, *President*
David Gershman, *Vice Pres*
Sidney Fleisher, *Controller*
Ed Castans, *Regl Sales Mgr*
Bob Imparato, *Manager*
◆ EMP: 48 EST: 1975
SQ FT: 90,000
SALES: 15MM Privately Held
SIC: 2842 7389 Cleaning or polishing
preparations; packaging & labeling serv-
ices

(G-10462)
KYOSIS LLC
148 Whitehead Ave Ste 1 (08882-1735)
PHONE.............................908 202-8894
Rupesh Patel,
EMP: 6
SQ FT: 1,000
SALES (est): 192.8K Privately Held
SIC: 7379 1799 7521 3559 Computer re-
lated maintenance services; parking facil-
ity equipment & maintenance; parking
facility equipment installation; parking
garage; parking structure; parking facility
equipment & supplies

(G-10463)
MILLWOOD INC
7 Brick Plant Rd Ste C (08882-1145)
PHONE.............................732 967-8818
Fax: 732 967-8839
Chris Verbosky, *Manager*
EMP: 70 Privately Held
WEB: www.millwoodinc.com
SIC: 2448 Pallets, wood; skids, wood
PA: Millwood, Inc.
3708 International Blvd
Vienna OH 44473

(G-10464)
RELDAN METALS INC (PA)
396 Whitehead Ave 402 (08882-2900)
PHONE.............................732 238-8550
Fax: 732 238-8595
Alan Nadler, *President*
Howard Steinberg, *Senior VP*
Kathleen Whitaker, *Project Mgr*
EMP: 20
SALES (est): 12MM Privately Held
SIC: 3341 Gold smelting & refining (sec-
ondary)

(G-10465)
RELDAN METALS INC
396 Whitehead Ave 402 (08882-2900)
PHONE.............................732 238-8550
Kathleen Heiss, *Branch Mgr*
EMP: 180
SALES (corp-wide): 12MM Privately
Held
SIC: 3341 Gold smelting & refining (sec-
ondary)
PA: Reldan Metals Inc.
396 Whitehead Ave 402
South River NJ 08882
732 238-8550

(G-10466)
**SERIOUS WELDING & MECH
LLC**
427 Whitehead Ave Ste 3 (08882-2595)
P.O. Box 5241, Somerset (08875-5241)
PHONE.............................732 698-7478
Paul Bari, *President*
Paul Stevens, *Vice Pres*
EMP: 13
SQ FT: 2,000
SALES: 1.5MM Privately Held
SIC: 7699 7692 Mechanical instrument re-
pair; welding repair

(G-10467)
SPORTSTAR WORLD WIDE INC
19 Thomas St (08882-1142)
PHONE.............................732 254-9214
Fax: 732 432-0306
Steve Kumar, *President*
Roger Thacar, *Owner*
EMP: 17

SALES: 1.1MM Privately Held
SIC: 2329 Athletic (warmup, sweat & jogging) suits: men's & boys'

(G-10468)
THIND FUEL SERVICE LLC
178 Hillside Ave (08882-1957)
PHONE.............................732 613-1808
EMP: 5
SALES (est): 207.9K Privately Held
SIC: 2869 Mfg Industrial Organic Chemi-
cals

Southampton
Burlington County

(G-10469)
ALPHA 1 STUDIO INC
3 Linda Ln (08088-9174)
PHONE.............................609 859-2200
Fax: 609 859-4010
Ray Witthauer, *President*
Michele Stow, *Director*
EMP: 8
SALES (est): 902K Privately Held
WEB: www.signstudio.com
SIC: 3993 7336 Signs & advertising spe-
cialties; commercial art & graphic design

(G-10470)
BENJAMIN BOOTH COMPANY
523 Meadowyck Ln (08088-9110)
PHONE.............................609 859-1995
David Frey, *President*
O Paul Frey, *Vice Pres*
Shirley Frey, *Treasurer*
▲ EMP: 12
SQ FT: 25,000
SALES (est): 1.3MM Privately Held
SIC: 3552 3991 Card clothing, textile ma-
chinery; brushes, household or industrial

(G-10471)
ESS GROUP INC
129 Eayrestown Rd (08088-9122)
PHONE.............................609 755-3139
Steven Szafara, *CEO*
EMP: 7
SALES (corp-wide): 35.9MM Privately
Held
SIC: 2835 Electrolyte diagnostic agents
PA: The Ess Group Inc
78 Carranza Rd
Tabernacle NJ 08088
609 268-1200

(G-10472)
EVERLAST ASSOCIATES INC
Also Called: Everlast Sheds
203 Route 530 (08088-1645)
PHONE.............................609 261-1888
Fax: 609 261-1546
Daniel Capocci, *President*
Daniel I Capocci, *President*
EMP: 8
SALES (est): 1.1MM Privately Held
WEB: www.everlastsheds.net
SIC: 3448 5211 5039 Buildings, portable;
prefabricated metal; lumber products; pre-
fabricated structures

(G-10473)
GENIE HOUSE CORP (PA)
139 Red Lion Rd (08088-8893)
P.O. Box 2478, Vincentown (08088-2478)
PHONE.............................609 859-0600
Fax: 609 859-0565
Lloyd Williams Jr, *President*
Deborah Ware, *General Mgr*
◆ EMP: 28 EST: 1967
SQ FT: 12,000
SALES (est): 5.2MM Privately Held
WEB: www.geniehouse.com
SIC: 3645 5719 Wall lamps; desk lamps;
floor lamps; lighting fixtures

(G-10474)
GMP PUBLICATIONS INC
4 Linda Ln Ste B (08088-9178)
P.O. Box 335, Medford (08055-0335)
PHONE.............................609 859-3400
Fax: 609 654-5992
John Cuspilich, *Principal*

Michael Van Horn, *Principal*
EMP: 4
SQ FT: 1,100
SALES (est): 489.3K Privately Held
WEB: www.pharmarecruiters.com
SIC: 2741 Miscellaneous publishing

(G-10475)
**IMAGES COSTUME
PRODUCTIONS**
881 Westminster Dr N (08088-1037)
PHONE.............................609 859-7372
Charles Veasey, *President*
Annette Veasey, *Vice Pres*
EMP: 5 EST: 1980
SALES: 500K Privately Held
SIC: 7922 2389 Costume & scenery de-
sign services; masquerade costumes

(G-10476)
JKA SPECIALTIES MFR INC
Also Called: J K A Specialties
157 Eayrestown Rd (08088-9122)
PHONE.............................609 859-2090
Fax: 609 859-3896
James F Young Sr, *President*
Kimnberly Brown, *President*
EMP: 15
SQ FT: 7,500
SALES (est): 2.3MM Privately Held
SIC: 2297 3999 3993 Nonwoven fabrics;
badges, metal: policemen, firemen, etc.;
signs & advertising specialties

(G-10477)
L & L REDI-MIX INC (PA)
1939 Route 206 (08088-9593)
PHONE.............................609 859-2271
Linwood C Gerber, *President*
Larry Gerber, *Vice Pres*
Geoff Warren, *Sales Staff*
Jim Gerber, *Manager*
EMP: 42
SQ FT: 9,000
SALES (est): 12.5MM Privately Held
WEB: www.llredimix.com
SIC: 3273 Ready-mixed concrete

(G-10478)
MCW PRECISION
137 Eayrestown Rd (08088-9122)
P.O. Box 2513, Vincentown (08088-2513)
PHONE.............................609 859-4400
Michael Wolfrom, *Owner*
Beth Wolfrom, *Office Mgr*
EMP: 10
SALES (est): 1.3MM Privately Held
SIC: 3399 Primary metal products

(G-10479)
**MEDFORD CEDAR PRODUCTS
INC**
59 Old Red Lion Rd (08088-2811)
PHONE.............................609 859-1400
Fax: 609 859-2778
Charline Scheibner, *CEO*
Albin E Scheibner Jr, *President*
EMP: 5
SQ FT: 5,000
SALES: 1MM Privately Held
WEB: www.medfordcedar.com
SIC: 5211 2499 5712 Planing mill prod-
ucts & lumber; flooring, wood; fencing,
docks & other outdoor wood structural
products; outdoor & garden furniture

(G-10480)
RCC FABRICATORS INC
2035 Route 206 (08088-3530)
PHONE.............................609 859-9350
Alfonso Daloisio Jr, *President*
EMP: 25
SALES (est): 6.4MM
SALES (corp-wide): 70.8MM Privately
Held
WEB: www.railroadconstruction.com
SIC: 3441 Building components, structural
steel
PA: Railroad Construction Company, Inc.
75-77 Grove St
Paterson NJ 07503
973 684-0362

(G-10481)
SAFETY-KLEEN SYSTEMS INC
123 Red Lion Rd (08088-8830)
PHONE.............................609 859-2049
Fax: 609 859-1740
Keith Wilson, *Manager*
EMP: 19
SALES (corp-wide): 2.9B Publicly Held
SIC: 7359 4212 3559 4953 Equipment
rental & leasing; hazardous waste trans-
port; degreasing machines, automotive &
industrial; refuse systems
HQ: Safety-Kleen Systems, Inc.
2600 N Central Expy # 400
Richardson TX 75080
972 265-2000

(G-10482)
**SAU-SEA SWIMMING POOL
PRODUCTS**
Also Called: Sausea Swimming Pool Enamels
1855 Route 206 (08088-3528)
P.O. Box 1419, Medford (08055-6419)
PHONE.............................609 859-8500
Fax: 609 859-1500
Mary Hunter, *President*
Steven Hunter, *Principal*
Thelma H Hunter, *Shareholder*
EMP: 12 EST: 1976
SQ FT: 5,000
SALES: 1MM Privately Held
WEB: www.sau-sea.com
SIC: 2851 5169 Paints, waterproof; chemi-
cals & allied products

(G-10483)
TRIPLE D ENTERPRISES INC
135 Eayrestown Rd (08088-9122)
PHONE.............................609 859-3000
Ira Feingold, *Human Resources*
David J Helgeson, *Director*
EMP: 6
SALES (est): 750K Privately Held
SIC: 3531 Plows: construction, excavating
& grading

(G-10484)
WOOD PRODUCTS INC
34 Allentown Rd (08088-8835)
PHONE.............................609 859-0303
John Taylor, *President*
Ronald G Taylor, *Vice Pres*
EMP: 5
SQ FT: 3,200
SALES (est): 450K Privately Held
SIC: 2431 Staircases & stairs, wood

Sparta
Sussex County

(G-10485)
ADVANCED PRECISION INC
Also Called: API
15 Wilson Dr Ste B (07871-4409)
PHONE.............................800 788-9473
Fax: 973 383-3774
Vincent Fay, *CEO*
Hugo Papa, *CFO*
EMP: 25
SQ FT: 8,500
SALES (est): 4.9MM Privately Held
WEB: www.advancedprecision.com
SIC: 3841 Surgical & medical instruments

(G-10486)
AEROSPACE INDUSTRIES LLC
520 Lafayette Rd (07871-3447)
PHONE.............................973 383-9307
Fax: 973 383-1606
Robert J Lesko,
EMP: 5
SQ FT: 1,200
SALES: 500K Privately Held
SIC: 3724 5088 Aircraft engines & engine
parts; aircraft & parts

(G-10487)
ALPINE CREAMERY
14 White Deer Plz (07871-1858)
PHONE.............................973 726-0777
John Tulp, *Owner*
EMP: 4

2018 Harris New Jersey
Manufacturers Directory

▲ = Import ▼=Export
◆ =Import/Export

SALES (est): 226.1K **Privately Held**
SIC: 2024 Ice cream, bulk

(G-10488)
ALTAFLO LLC
23 Wilson Dr Ste 1 (07871-4410)
PHONE...................973 300-3344
Mary Hyde, *Mng Member*
Donald C Bishop,
EMP: 10
SQ FT: 15,000
SALES (est): 1.8MM **Privately Held**
WEB: www.altaflo.com
SIC: 2821 Plastics materials & resins

(G-10489)
AUTHENTICITY BREWING LLC
23 Kroghs Ln (07871-3444)
PHONE...................862 432-9622
Aaron Buch,
EMP: 5
SALES (est): 150.7K **Privately Held**
SIC: 3999 Manufacturing industries

(G-10490)
B & W PLASTICS INC
20 Wilson Dr (07871-3400)
PHONE...................973 383-0020
Fax: 973 579-5304
William Post, *President*
Louise Post, *VP Finance*
Christina Lordy, *VP Sales*
EMP: 7
SQ FT: 12,000
SALES (est): 1.3MM **Privately Held**
SIC: 3089 Injection molding of plastics

(G-10491)
CARL BUCK CORPORATION
14 Park Lake Rd Ste 3 (07871-3257)
PHONE...................973 300-5575
Peter Gennaro, *President*
Cynthia Gennaro, *Vice Pres*
▼ EMP: 8 EST: 1946
SQ FT: 12,500
SALES (est): 1.5MM **Privately Held**
WEB: www.camacindustries.com
SIC: 3559 Metal finishing equipment for plating, etc.; chemical machinery & equipment

(G-10492)
COLINEAR MACHINE & DESIGN INC
7 Wilson Dr (07871-3427)
PHONE...................973 300-1681
Fax: 973 300-1683
John T San Giacomo Jr, *President*
John T S Giacomo Jr, *President*
Jae Castellana, *Opers Mgr*
Michelle S Giacomo, *CFO*
EMP: 19
SQ FT: 13,000
SALES: 2.2MM **Privately Held**
WEB: www.colinearmachine.com
SIC: 3599 Machine shop, jobbing & repair

(G-10493)
COMPACT FLUORESCENT SYSTEMS
Also Called: CFS
463 Stanhope Rd (07871-2816)
PHONE...................908 475-8991
Gary Broyer, *President*
Dory Broyer, *Vice Pres*
▲ EMP: 6
SALES (est): 120K **Privately Held**
SIC: 3646 Commercial indusl & institutional electric lighting fixtures

(G-10494)
COUNTRY CLUB ICE CREAM
4 Tyler St (07871-2717)
P.O. Box 77 (07871-0077)
PHONE...................973 729-5570
Maria E Rodriguez, *Director*
EMP: 7
SALES (est): 118.8K **Privately Held**
SIC: 5812 2024 Ice cream stands or dairy bars; ice cream & frozen desserts

(G-10495)
CREATIVE METAL WORKS INC
22b Gail Ct (07871-3439)
P.O. Box 1068 (07871-5068)
PHONE...................973 579-3717
Zoran Grubic, *President*
EMP: 10
SALES (est): 1.5MM **Privately Held**
SIC: 3446 Architectural metalwork

(G-10496)
DEW ASSOCIATES INC (PA)
48 Woodport Rd (07871-2424)
PHONE...................973 702-0545
Paulajean V Waldron-Mego, *CEO*
Christopher B Waldron, *Exec VP*
Timothey J Waldron, *Exec VP*
Dennis Waldron, *CFO*
EMP: 400 EST: 1978
SQ FT: 33,500
SALES: 7.8MM **Privately Held**
WEB: www.dewassoc.com
SIC: 3577 7371 Computer peripheral equipment; custom computer programming services

(G-10497)
DIAMOND CHIP REALTY LLC
Also Called: Diamond Sand & Gravel
33 Demarest Rd (07871-3441)
PHONE...................973 383-4651
Frank Hunklene, *Mng Member*
EMP: 30
SALES (est): 1.1MM **Privately Held**
SIC: 3272 3273 Building stone, artificial; concrete; ready-mixed concrete

(G-10498)
ELITE PRINTING SERVICE
30 Heritage Dr (07871-2541)
PHONE...................973 729-0366
Alicson Marcinkowski, *Owner*
EMP: 4
SALES (est): 307K **Privately Held**
SIC: 2759 Commercial printing

(G-10499)
FIREFIGHTER ONE LTD LBLTY CO
Also Called: Ff1 Professional Safety Svcs
34 Wilson Dr (07871-3400)
PHONE...................973 940-3061
Jonathon Van Norman, *President*
Brian Kredatus, *Accounts Mgr*
Bryan Crawford, *Mktg Dir*
Stephen Spotts, *Mktg Coord*
Todd Rudloff, *Manager*
EMP: 6 EST: 2005
SALES (est): 1.6MM **Privately Held**
SIC: 2311 2899 3052 3429 Firemen's uniforms: made from purchased materials; fire extinguisher charges; fire hose, rubber; nozzles, fire fighting; fire hydrant valves

(G-10500)
GATE TECHNOLOGIES INC
Also Called: Cds.
27 Wilson Dr Unit C (07871-3484)
PHONE...................973 300-0090
Fax: 973 300-0061
Robert Zaruba, *President*
Stephen Gough, *Manager*
▲ EMP: 6
SQ FT: 5,300
SALES (est): 1.2MM **Privately Held**
WEB: www.cdsindexers.com
SIC: 3443 3568 Heat exchangers, condensers & components; power transmission equipment

(G-10501)
GRINNELL CON PAVINGSTONES INC
482 Houses Corner Rd (07871-3404)
PHONE...................973 383-9300
Margaret A Cofrancesco, *CEO*
Craig Austin, *President*
Jason N Cofrancesco, *Vice Pres*
Lauren Berg, *Credit Mgr*
Jarrod C Cofrancesco, *Admin Sec*
▼ EMP: 100 EST: 1986
SQ FT: 10,000

SALES (est): 20.3MM **Privately Held**
WEB: www.grinnellpavers.com
SIC: 3272 Stone, cast concrete

(G-10502)
H & H PRODUCTION MACHINING
Also Called: H & H Sheet Metal & Machining
30 White Lake Rd (07871-3249)
PHONE...................973 383-6880
Fax: 973 383-6650
Eric Hohmann, *President*
David Hohmann, *President*
EMP: 6
SQ FT: 15,000
SALES (est): 1.9MM **Privately Held**
WEB: www.hhsmm.com
SIC: 3599 Machine shop, jobbing & repair

(G-10503)
H I D SYSTEMS INC
520 Lafayette Rd (07871-3447)
PHONE...................973 383-8535
Robert J Lesko, *President*
EMP: 7
SQ FT: 5,500
SALES (est): 861K **Privately Held**
WEB: www.hid.com
SIC: 3699 5063 Electrical equipment & supplies; electrical apparatus & equipment

(G-10504)
HCH INCORPORATED
99 Demarest Rd Ste 4 (07871-3489)
PHONE...................973 300-4551
Fax: 973 300-4751
Gene Cinotti, *President*
EMP: 6
SQ FT: 3,000
SALES (est): 904.1K **Privately Held**
SIC: 5046 3556 Restaurant equipment & supplies; food products machinery

(G-10505)
HID ULTRAVIOLET LLC
520 Lafayette Rd (07871-3447)
PHONE...................973 383-8535
Robert Lesko, *President*
EMP: 11
SALES (est): 1MM **Privately Held**
SIC: 3641 Ultraviolet lamps

(G-10506)
ISTEC CORPORATION
Also Called: Istec Flow Measurement & Ctrl
5 Park Lake Rd Ste 6 (07871-3247)
PHONE...................973 383-9888
Fax: 973 383-9088
Peter Johnson, *President*
Edward Bullis, *Vice Pres*
Justin Johnson, *Opers Mgr*
▲ EMP: 10
SQ FT: 6,000
SALES (est): 1.2MM **Privately Held**
SIC: 3823 Industrial instrmnts msrmnt display/control process variable

(G-10507)
KOMLINE-SANDERSON ENGRG CORP
34 White Lake Rd Ste C (07871-3233)
PHONE...................973 579-0090
James Schutte, *CEO*
EMP: 5
SALES (corp-wide): 47.5MM **Privately Held**
SIC: 3356 Battery metal
PA: Komline-Sanderson Corporation
12 Holland Ave
Peapack NJ 07977
908 234-1000

(G-10508)
LANTEK CORPORATION
29 Brookfield Dr (07871-3212)
PHONE...................973 579-8100
Daniel Yodaiken, *President*
▲ EMP: 15
SQ FT: 3,000
SALES (est): 6.1MM **Privately Held**
WEB: www.lantekcorp.com
SIC: 3679 Electronic circuits

(G-10509)
LEHIGH CEMENT COMPANY
66 Demarest Rd (07871-3440)
PHONE...................973 579-2111
Fax: 973 579-5069
Dan Harrington, *President*
Joe Lanardo, *Vice Pres*
James Ethridge, *Buyer*
Mike Kreimer, *Accountant*
Johnny Elrod, *Sales Associate*
EMP: 8
SQ FT: 19,200
SALES (est): 1.7MM
SALES (corp-wide): 20.3B **Privately Held**
WEB: www.lehighcement.com
SIC: 5032 3241 Cement; cement, hydraulic
HQ: Lehigh Cement Company Llc
300 E John Carpenter Fwy
Irving TX 75062
877 534-4442

(G-10510)
LINDE LLC
Also Called: Boc Gases
20 Demarest Rd (07871-3440)
PHONE...................973 579-2065
Michael Stevenson, *Branch Mgr*
EMP: 6
SALES (corp-wide): 20.1B **Privately Held**
SIC: 2813 3569 3561 3511 Oxygen, compressed or liquefied; nitrogen; argon; hydrogen; gas separators (machinery); pumps & pumping equipment; turbines & turbine generator sets; industrial flow & liquid measuring instruments; anesthetics, in bulk form
HQ: Linde Llc
200 Somerset Corporate Bl
Bridgewater NJ 08807
908 464-8100

(G-10511)
MEGA MEDIA CONCEPTS LTD LBLTY
26 Gail Ct Ste 1 (07871-3487)
PHONE...................973 919-5661
Anthony Senatora, *Vice Pres*
Amy Pink,
▼ EMP: 4
SALES: 1MM **Privately Held**
WEB: www.megamediaconcepts.com
SIC: 3993 2759 8412 Signs & advertising specialties; commercial printing; museums & art galleries

(G-10512)
MP PRODUCTION
Also Called: Applied Microphone Technology
104 Hillside Rd (07871-2015)
PHONE...................973 729-9333
Martin Paglione, *Owner*
Ron Oswanski, *Executive*
▲ EMP: 15
SQ FT: 2,500
SALES (est): 1.4MM **Privately Held**
SIC: 3651 Microphones

(G-10513)
NATURES CHOICE CORPORATION (PA)
482 Houses Corner Rd (07871-3404)
PHONE...................973 969-3299
Fax: 201 333-4135
James Schafle, *CEO*
James Panzini, *President*
EMP: 15
SQ FT: 6,000
SALES (est): 44.2MM **Privately Held**
WEB: www.enatureschoice.com
SIC: 4953 2824 Recycling, waste materials; acrylic fibers

(G-10514)
NEWTON MEMORIAL HOSPITAL INC
89 Sparta Ave Ste 210 (07871-1792)
PHONE...................973 726-0904
Michael Gallagher, *Branch Mgr*
EMP: 7 **Privately Held**
SIC: 3841 8062 Diagnostic apparatus, medical; general medical & surgical hospitals

HQ: Newton Memorial Hospital (Inc)
175 High St
Newton NJ 07860
973 383-2121

(G-10515)
NORTH AMERICA PRINTING
156 Woodport Rd (07871-2331)
PHONE..................................973 726-7713
EMP: 5 EST: 1998
SALES (est): 250K Privately Held
SIC: 2759 Commercial Printing

(G-10516)
NOVA CHEMICALS INC
56 Castlewood Trl (07871-3704)
PHONE..................................973 726-0056
Aroustamian Jean, Branch Mgr
EMP: 4 Privately Held
SIC: 2819 Industrial inorganic chemicals
HQ: Nova Chemicals Inc.
1555 Coraopolis Hts Rd
Moon Township PA 15108
412 490-4000

(G-10517)
PDS CONSULTANTS INC
22 Rainbow Trl (07871-1723)
PHONE..................................201 970-2313
Richard Murray, President
EMP: 20 EST: 2006
SALES (est): 1MM Privately Held
SIC: 8742 3851 Management consulting
services; ophthalmic goods

(G-10518)
PRINTING CENTER INC
1 White Lake Rd (07871-3206)
PHONE..................................973 383-6362
Vince Perrella, President
Steve Guido, President
Mike Whitaker, President
Donna Fern, General Mgr
Rick Breakstone, Vice Pres
EMP: 38 EST: 1971
SALES (est): 7.9MM Privately Held
WEB: www.printcenter.com
SIC: 2752 Commercial printing, offset

(G-10519)
QUANTUM PHARMACEUTICALS INC
3 Arielle Way (07871-3449)
P.O. Box 244, Ogdensburg (07439-0244)
PHONE..................................973 222-6485
EMP: 4 EST: 2006
SALES: 20K Privately Held
SIC: 2834 7389 Manufactures Develop
And Makrkets Otc / Rx Drugs Business
Services At Non-Commercial Site

(G-10520)
R D ASSOCIATES
97 Warren Rd (07871-2720)
PHONE..................................973 729-7944
Robert Dippel, Owner
EMP: 4
SALES (est): 183.3K Privately Held
SIC: 3545 Precision tools, machinists'

(G-10521)
SUMMERLANDS INC
Also Called: Krogh's Restaurant
23 White Deer Plz (07871-1823)
PHONE..................................973 729-8428
Fax: 973 729-1556
Robert Fuchs, President
EMP: 50
SQ FT: 2,500
SALES (est): 1.9MM Privately Held
WEB: www.kroghs.com
SIC: 5812 5813 2082 American restaurant; tavern (drinking places); malt beverages

(G-10522)
TECHFLEX INC (HQ)
104 Demarest Rd Ste 1 (07871-4407)
P.O. Box 119 (07871-0119)
PHONE..................................973 300-9242
Fax: 973 729-9320
William Dermody III, President
Vicki Greene, General Mgr
Mike Ballard, Vice Pres
Julie Seames, Accountant
Driscoll Bowlby, Sales Staff

EMP: 35
SQ FT: 40,000
SALES (est): 7.9MM
SALES (corp-wide): 7MM Privately Held
WEB: www.techflex.com
SIC: 3089 3663 3651 Plastic containers,
except foam; radio broadcasting & communications equipment; household audio
& video equipment
PA: Dermody Associates Inc
104 Demarest Rd Ste 1
Sparta NJ
973 300-9242

(G-10523)
TESA RENTALS LLC
286 Houses Corner Rd (07871-4400)
PHONE..................................973 300-0913
Christopher M Tiso,
EMP: 10
SQ FT: 3,000
SALES (est): 500K Privately Held
SIC: 3822 Auto controls regulating residntl
& coml environmt & applncs

(G-10524)
THERMOPLASTICS BIO-LOGICS LLC
Also Called: Tbl Performance Plastics
18 White Lake Rd (07871-3200)
PHONE..................................973 383-2834
Robert Dupont, Partner
Diane Dupont, Accounts Mgr
EMP: 10
SALES (est): 2.6MM Privately Held
SIC: 3089 Extruded finished plastic products; plastic processing

(G-10525)
TIFFANY PACKAGING
270 Sparta Ave (07871-1122)
PHONE..................................973 726-8130
Sharon Willms, Owner
EMP: 8 EST: 1982
SALES (est): 754.7K Privately Held
SIC: 2673 Plastic & pliofilm bags

(G-10526)
TRI-COR FLEXIBLE PACKAGING INC
27 Brookfield Dr (07871-3212)
PHONE..................................973 940-1500
Guy Zimmermann, President
Donna Zimmermann, Admin Sec
▲ EMP: 24
SQ FT: 9,000
SALES (est): 14MM Privately Held
WEB: www.tri-cor.com
SIC: 3081 Polyethylene film

Spotswood
Middlesex County

(G-10527)
BP MACHINE CO INC
10 American Way Ste 3 (08884-1262)
PHONE..................................732 251-0449
Fax: 732 251-0440
Robert Provell, President
Steven Spennato, Vice Pres
EMP: 4
SQ FT: 1,500
SALES (est): 400K Privately Held
SIC: 3599 Machine shop, jobbing & repair

(G-10528)
INTERNATIONAL PAPER COMPANY
140 Summerhill Rd (08884-1235)
PHONE..................................732 251-2000
Margaret Guiliano, Manager
Gary Melbaurn, Manager
EMP: 163
SALES (corp-wide): 21.7B Publicly Held
SIC: 2631 Paperboard mills
PA: International Paper Company
6400 Poplar Ave
Memphis TN 38197
901 419-9000

(G-10529)
MJS OF SPOTSWOOD LLC
Also Called: Mjs Pizza Bar & Grill
19 Summerhill Rd (08884-1251)
PHONE..................................732 251-7400
EMP: 8 EST: 2015
SALES (est): 391.1K Privately Held
SIC: 2038 2045 Pizza, frozen; pizza
mixes: from purchased flour

(G-10530)
SCHWEITZER-MAUDUIT INTL INC
85 Main St (08884-1212)
PHONE..................................732 723-6100
Fax: 732 251-7437
Kevin Boland, Manager
EMP: 500 Publicly Held
SIC: 2141 2621 Tobacco stemming &
redrying; paper mills
PA: Schweitzer-Mauduit International, Inc.
100 N Point Ctr E Ste 600
Alpharetta GA 30022

(G-10531)
SURATI NJ LLC
15 American Way (08884-1254)
PHONE..................................732 251-3404
Yashvantrai Sheth, Principal
▲ EMP: 13
SALES (est): 2MM Privately Held
SIC: 2035 Pickles, sauces & salad dressings

Spring Lake
Monmouth County

(G-10532)
BOZAK INC
204 State Route 71 Ste B1 (07762-1882)
PHONE..................................732 282-1556
Kenneth Bozak, President
EMP: 3 EST: 1980
SALES: 8MM Privately Held
WEB: www.bozak.com
SIC: 3399 Laminating steel

(G-10533)
H T HALL INC (PA)
Also Called: Rock of Ages Monuments
1716 State Route 71 Ste 1 (07762-3225)
PHONE..................................732 449-3441
Fax: 732 449-3447
Harold T Hall Jr, President
Joan Hall, Vice Pres
Harold Hall III, Admin Sec
EMP: 16
SQ FT: 20,000
SALES (est): 1.4MM Privately Held
WEB: www.hthall.com
SIC: 3272 3281 Monuments & grave
markers, except terrazo; tombstones, precast terrazzo or concrete; concrete products, precast; cut stone & stone products

(G-10534)
MATRIX SALES GROUP LLC
Also Called: Matrix Apparel
309 Morris Ave Ste E (07762-1359)
PHONE..................................908 461-4148
Anthony Pristo, Mng Member
John Cottingham,
Dina Johannemann,
EMP: 80
SALES (est): 5.2MM Privately Held
SIC: 2326 2339 Men's & boys' work clothing; women's & misses' athletic clothing &
sportswear

(G-10535)
THIRD AVE CHOCOLATE SHOPPE
1118 3rd Ave (07762-1329)
PHONE..................................732 449-7535
Matthew Magyar, Owner
EMP: 6
SALES (est): 210K Privately Held
SIC: 2066 5149 Chocolate; chocolate

Springfield
Union County

(G-10536)
ALLMARK DOOR COMPANY LLC (PA)
15 Stern Ave (07081-2904)
PHONE..................................610 358-9800
Andrew Markham, Vice Pres
Ralph Markham, Vice Pres
Eric Weinstein, Controller
Meghan King, Accountant
Randall Emtage, Regl Sales Mgr
▲ EMP: 13
SQ FT: 8,000
SALES (est): 7MM Privately Held
SIC: 5031 3442 Doors; fire doors, metal

(G-10537)
APPLES & HONEY PRESS LLC
11 Edison Pl (07081-1310)
PHONE..................................973 379-7200
David Behrman, President
EMP: 17
SALES (est): 682.5K Privately Held
SIC: 2731 5942 Book publishing; children's books

(G-10538)
ATCO PRODUCTS INC
115 Victory Rd (07081-1314)
PHONE..................................973 379-3171
Fax: 862 763-5033
Martin Gornstein, President
Alan Gornstein, Vice Pres
Jill Larsen, Info Tech Dir
▲ EMP: 50 EST: 1938
SQ FT: 28,800
SALES (est): 4.6MM Privately Held
WEB: www.atcoproducts.com
SIC: 3429 3312 3161 Luggage hardware;
tool & die steel & alloys; luggage

(G-10539)
ATLAS MARBLE & GRANITE LLC
44 Fadem Rd (07081-3116)
PHONE..................................973 491-5454
Fax: 973 491-2654
Marco Duran,
Elizabeth Gmyrek,
EMP: 12
SALES (est): 1.2MM Privately Held
WEB: www.atlasmarbleandgranite.com
SIC: 3281 Cut stone & stone products

(G-10540)
AZTEC SOFTWARE ASSOCIATES INC
51 Commerce St (07081-3014)
PHONE..................................973 258-0011
Fax: 973 258-0010
Jonathan Blitt, CEO
Michael Kheyfets, President
Phyllis Schwartz, President
Geraldine Kaplan, Vice Pres
Raeann Sereno, Accounts Mgr
EMP: 27
SQ FT: 3,500
SALES (est): 1.1MM Privately Held
SIC: 7371 7372 5045 Computer software
development; prepackaged software;
computer software

(G-10541)
BARWORTH INC
Also Called: General Hydraulics
673 Morris Tpke (07081-1596)
PHONE..................................973 376-4883
Fax: 973 376-5041
Robert Swatsworth, President
John C Swathworth Jr, Corp Secy
EMP: 4 EST: 1953
SQ FT: 2,200
SALES: 1MM Privately Held
WEB: www.barworthinc.com
SIC: 3491 Industrial valves; gas valves &
parts, industrial

▲ = Import ▼=Export
◆ =Import/Export

(G-10542)
BELAIR INSTRUMENT COMPANY LLC (PA)
Also Called: AVANTIK
36 Commerce St (07081-3004)
P.O. Box 619 (07081-0619)
PHONE..........................973 912-8900
Fax: 973 232-0077
David L Patterson, *President*
Andrew Storr, *Opers Staff*
Riki Amin, *Controller*
Margaret J Patterson, *Admin Sec*
▲ **EMP:** 38
SQ FT: 4,000
SALES: 33.1MM **Privately Held**
SIC: 3826 3841 3842 5047 Analytical instruments; surgical & medical instruments; surgical appliances & supplies; medical & hospital equipment

(G-10543)
BIGELOW COMPONENTS CORP
74 Diamond Rd (07081)
PHONE..........................973 467-1200
Fax: 973 467-9397
Brett Harman, *President*
David Harman, *President*
EMP: 30
SQ FT: 15,000
SALES (est): 5.4MM **Privately Held**
SIC: 3452 3469 3316 Pins; rivets, metal; metal stampings; cold finishing of steel shapes

(G-10544)
BONNEY-VEHSLAGE TOOL CO
3 Dundar Rd (07081-3516)
PHONE..........................973 589-6975
Fax: 973 589-0038
Ramsay W Vehslage, *President*
Joseph R Krehel, *Vice Pres*
Ann B Vehslage, *Admin Sec*
EMP: 13
SQ FT: 6,000
SALES (est): 1.8MM **Privately Held**
WEB: www.bvtoolco.com
SIC: 3544 Punches, forming & stamping

(G-10545)
BRIGHTON AIR
21 Springfield Ave (07081-1312)
P.O. Box 1834, Cranford (07016-5834)
PHONE..........................973 258-1500
Daniel Ghanime, *Principal*
EMP: 8
SALES (est): 1.4MM **Privately Held**
SIC: 3822 Water heater controls

(G-10546)
CG AUTOMATION SOLUTIONS USA (PA)
60 Fadem Rd (07081-3116)
PHONE..........................973 379-7400
Fax: 973 379-2138
Stephen Dalyai, *President*
Normand Lavoie, *President*
Phong Lieu, *Managing Prtnr*
James Link, *Vice Pres*
Norm Lavoie, *Opers Mgr*
▼ **EMP:** 50 **EST:** 1975
SQ FT: 45,000
SALES (est): 7.8MM **Privately Held**
WEB: www.qeiinc.com
SIC: 3823 Telemetering instruments, industrial process type; controllers for process variables, all types; computer interface equipment for industrial process control

(G-10547)
CINCINNATI THERMAL SPRAY INC
80 Fadem Rd (07081-3116)
PHONE..........................973 379-0003
Fax: 973 379-4066
Scot Crabtree, *Branch Mgr*
EMP: 25 **Privately Held**
SIC: 3479 3469 Coating of metals & formed products; machine parts, stamped or pressed metal
PA: Cincinnati Thermal Spray, Inc.
10904 Deerfield Rd
Blue Ash OH 45242

(G-10548)
COMTRON INC
12 Commerce St (07081-2903)
PHONE..........................732 446-7571
Guenther Wackerman, *President*
EMP: 15
SQ FT: 10,000
SALES (est): 3.2MM **Privately Held**
SIC: 3663 Radio broadcasting & communications equipment

(G-10549)
CORNELL MACHINE CO INC
45 Brown Ave (07081-2901)
PHONE..........................973 379-6860
Martin M Huska, *President*
Allan Huska, *Corp Secy*
Alan Huska,
EMP: 6
SQ FT: 7,400
SALES (est): 1MM **Privately Held**
WEB: www.cornellmachine.com
SIC: 3556 Mixers, commercial, food; homogenizing machinery: dairy, fruit, vegetable

(G-10550)
DANLINE INC
Also Called: Danline Quality Brushes
1 Silver Ct (07081-3113)
PHONE..........................973 376-1000
Fax: 973 376-9888
Suresh Seth, *President*
Brain Oleary, *Vice Pres*
Usha Seth, *Vice Pres*
▲ **EMP:** 30
SQ FT: 53,000
SALES (est): 3.5MM **Privately Held**
WEB: www.danlinebrushes.com
SIC: 3991 Brushes, household or industrial

(G-10551)
DRG INTERNATIONAL INC (PA)
841 Mountain Ave (07081-3437)
PHONE..........................973 564-7555
Fax: 908 233-0758
Cyril Geacintov, *President*
Gustavo Ruales, *Area Mgr*
Eric Van Bladel, *COO*
Elke Geacintov, *VP Admin*
Sheila Dawson, *Sales Dir*
▲ **EMP:** 25
SQ FT: 7,500
SALES (est): 30.8MM **Privately Held**
WEB: www.drg-international.com
SIC: 5047 8071 3829 Medical equipment & supplies; diagnostic equipment, medical; medical laboratories; measuring & controlling devices

(G-10552)
EASY UNDIES LLC
Also Called: Easylving Brand, The
23 Springfield Ave (07081-1312)
P.O. Box 1311 (07081-5311)
PHONE..........................201 715-4909
Rochelle Denning,
EMP: 4 **EST:** 2000
SALES (est): 494.5K **Privately Held**
SIC: 5047 2211 Incontinent care products & supplies; underwear fabrics, cotton

(G-10553)
ELKAY PRODUCTS CO INC
35 Brown Ave (07081-2982)
P.O. Box 149 (07081-0149)
PHONE..........................973 376-7550
Fax: 973 912-0418
Steven Piller, *President*
EMP: 10 **EST:** 1929
SQ FT: 25,000
SALES (est): 1.7MM **Privately Held**
SIC: 2299 5084 Padding & wadding, textile; materials handling machinery

(G-10554)
F AND L MACHINERY
48 Commerce St (07081-3004)
PHONE..........................973 218-6216
Fred Villaverde, *Owner*
EMP: 5
SALES (est): 767.8K **Privately Held**
SIC: 5084 3599 Industrial machinery & equipment; machine shop, jobbing & repair

(G-10555)
FEDEX OFFICE & PRINT SVCS INC
55 Route 22 (07081-3128)
PHONE..........................973 376-3966
Jose Carrillo, *Manager*
EMP: 5
SALES (corp-wide): 65.4B **Publicly Held**
WEB: www.kinkos.com
SIC: 7334 2791 Photocopying & duplicating services; typesetting
HQ: Fedex Office And Print Services, Inc.
7900 Legacy Dr
Plano TX 75024
214 550-7000

(G-10556)
HUDSON ROBOTICS INC
10 Stern Ave (07081-2905)
PHONE..........................973 376-7400
Philip J Farrelly, *President*
Philip Farrelly, *General Mgr*
Debbie Peterson, *General Mgr*
John Celecki, *Prdtn Mgr*
Ron Majewski, *Design Engr*
EMP: 17
SQ FT: 12,000
SALES (est): 4.4MM **Privately Held**
WEB: www.hudsoncontrol.com
SIC: 3826 Analytical instruments

(G-10557)
i4 SUSTAINABILITY LLC
Also Called: Omniflow USA
140 Mountain Ave Ste 303 (07081-1725)
PHONE..........................732 618-3310
Luis Barros, *Mng Member*
EMP: 5
SQ FT: 5,000
SALES: 175K **Privately Held**
SIC: 5063 5074 3511 Lighting fixtures, commercial & industrial; heating equipment & panels, solar; turbines & turbine generator sets

(G-10558)
J OBRIEN CO INC
40 Commerce St (07081-3004)
PHONE..........................973 379-8844
Fax: 973 379-8373
Sharmay O'Brien, *President*
Diane R O'Brien, *Corp Secy*
Christopher Droussiotis, *Technical Mgr*
Michael Piana, *Sales Staff*
Wes Winters, *Info Tech Mgr*
▲ **EMP:** 20
SQ FT: 64,000
SALES (est): 5.1MM **Privately Held**
WEB: www.jobrien.com
SIC: 3089 5084 Plastic containers, except foam; identification cards, plastic; industrial machinery & equipment

(G-10559)
JEN ELECTRIC INC
631 Morris Ave (07081-1511)
PHONE..........................973 467-4901
Jennifer Daidone, *CEO*
John Daidone, *Vice Pres*
Frank Dobiszewski, *Chief Engr*
Jorge Doig, *Sales Staff*
EMP: 10
SQ FT: 2,800
SALES (est): 2MM **Privately Held**
SIC: 3669 Traffic signals, electric

(G-10560)
JURY VRDICT RVIEW PUBLICATIONS
Also Called: New Jersey Jury
45 Springfield Ave Ste 2 (07081-1316)
PHONE..........................973 376-9002
Fax: 973 376-1775
Ira Zarin, *President*
Gary Zarin, *Partner*
Meredith Whelan, *General Mgr*
Cristina Hyde, *Editor*
Jed Zarin, *Vice Pres*
EMP: 4
SQ FT: 5,000
SALES (est): 810K **Privately Held**
WEB: www.jvra.com
SIC: 2721 Magazines: publishing only, not printed on site

(G-10561)
KEMPAK INDUSTRIES
33 Fernhill Rd (07081-3708)
P.O. Box 2073, Union (07083-2073)
PHONE..........................908 687-4188
Joel Sacher, *President*
Susan Sacher, *Corp Secy*
EMP: 10 **EST:** 1970
SALES (est): 1.9MM **Privately Held**
SIC: 2841 Soap & other detergents

(G-10562)
KG SYSTEMS INC
765 Mountain Ave Ste 120 (07081-3231)
PHONE..........................973 515-4664
Fax: 973 515-1033
Daniel R Garlen, *CEO*
Marilyn K Garlen, *Treasurer*
Jean R Kardux, *Admin Sec*
EMP: 5
SQ FT: 3,000
SALES (est): 1MM **Privately Held**
WEB: www.kgsystems.com
SIC: 3545 Scales, measuring (machinists' precision tools)

(G-10563)
KREMENTZ & CO (PA)
Also Called: Krementz Gemstones
51 Commerce St (07081-3014)
P.O. Box 55, Ho Ho Kus (07423-0055)
PHONE..........................973 621-8300
Richard Krementz Jr, *Ch of Bd*
EMP: 10
SQ FT: 160,000
SALES (est): 1.2MM **Privately Held**
SIC: 3911 Jewelry, precious metal

(G-10564)
LIFE SKILLS EDUCATION INC
51 Commerce St (07081-3014)
PHONE..........................507 645-2994
Fax: 507 645-2995
Robert Cierna, *President*
Suzannah Cierna, *Manager*
EMP: 6
SQ FT: 2,500
SALES (est): 1.1MM **Privately Held**
WEB: www.lifeskillsed.com
SIC: 2731 8322 Pamphlets: publishing & printing; individual & family services

(G-10565)
MIRANDA MTI INC
195 Mountain Ave (07081-1755)
PHONE..........................973 376-4275
Strath Goodship, *CEO*
EMP: 15
SALES (est): 1.9MM **Privately Held**
SIC: 3663 Television broadcasting & communications equipment

(G-10566)
NAAVA INC (PA)
21 Fadem Rd Ste 7 (07081-3136)
PHONE..........................844 666-2282
Aki Soudunsaari, *CEO*
Niko Jarvinen, *President*
Jason Kahn, *Manager*
EMP: 4
SQ FT: 30,000
SALES: 1.5MM **Privately Held**
SIC: 8742 3564 New products & services consultants; air purification equipment

(G-10567)
NARVA INC
Also Called: New York Kitchen Specialist
101 Victory Rd (07081-1314)
PHONE..........................973 218-1200
Alex Morizou, *President*
EMP: 6
SQ FT: 10,000
SALES: 1.4MM **Privately Held**
WEB: www.narvakitchens.com
SIC: 5722 2499 1799 1751 Kitchens, complete (sinks, cabinets, etc.); decorative wood & woodwork; counter top installation; cabinet & finish carpentry

(G-10568)
NEWARK BRUSH COMPANY LLC
1 Silver Ct (07081-3113)
PHONE..........................973 376-1000

Jeremy Glick, *Principal*
Brian O'Leary, *Exec VP*
Brian Oleary, *Exec VP*
Ramon Matti, *Controller*
Matthew Stewart, *Sales Staff*
▲ **EMP:** 18
SALES (est): 3.4MM **Privately Held**
SIC: 3991 Brooms & brushes; street sweeping brooms, hand or machine; brushes, household or industrial

(G-10569)
PACKAGED GAS SYSTEMS INC (PA)
18 Stern Ave (07081-2905)
PHONE..................................908 755-2780
Anthony Etimiraos, *President*
Catherine Atimiraos, *Corp Secy*
EMP: 5
SQ FT: 800
SALES (est): 253K **Privately Held**
WEB: www.packagedgassystems.com
SIC: 3826 Gas analyzing equipment

(G-10570)
PAYLOCITY HOLDING CORPORATION
21 Fadem Rd Ste 10 (07081-3136)
PHONE..................................908 917-3027
EMP: 300
SALES (corp-wide): 300MM **Publicly Held**
SIC: 7372 Prepackaged software
PA: Paylocity Holding Corporation
1400 American Ln
Schaumburg IL 60173
847 463-3200

(G-10571)
PEMCO DENTAL CORPORATION
35 Stern Ave (07081-2904)
P.O. Box 249 (07081-0249)
PHONE..................................800 526-4170
Richard Balfour, *President*
Elizabeth Balfour, *Vice Pres*
Lawrence Balfour, *Vice Pres*
Liz Balfour, *Human Res Dir*
EMP: 35
SQ FT: 36,000
SALES: 6.4MM **Privately Held**
SIC: 5047 2521 Dental equipment & supplies; cabinets, office: wood

(G-10572)
PRINT MEDIA LLC
232 Morris Ave (07081-1212)
PHONE..................................973 467-0007
Robert Wallick, *Partner*
Sandy Walsh, *Partner*
EMP: 7 **EST:** 1999
SALES (est): 809.7K **Privately Held**
SIC: 2759 Commercial printing

(G-10573)
PRINT TECH LLC (PA)
49 Fadem Rd (07081-3115)
PHONE..................................908 232-2287
Russell F Evans, *CEO*
Frances Angiola, *Editor*
Gary Aleisso, *Sales Executive*
Enrico Dinardo, *Manager*
Shirley Schroeder, *Technology*
▼ **EMP:** 70 **EST:** 2001
SQ FT: 18,100
SALES (est): 13.3MM **Privately Held**
SIC: 2752 Commercial printing, offset

(G-10574)
RAGS INTERNATIONAL INC
15 Tooker Ave (07081-1703)
PHONE..................................787 632-8447
Carlos Rivera, *CEO*
EMP: 8
SALES (est): 340.6K **Privately Held**
SIC: 3949 5661 Sporting & athletic goods; team sports equipment; footwear, athletic

(G-10575)
RAMSEY MACHINE & TOOL CO INC
60 Tooker Ave (07081-1704)
PHONE..................................973 376-7404
Ronald A Majewski Jr, *President*
EMP: 8 **EST:** 1950
SQ FT: 6,500

SALES (est): 600K **Privately Held**
SIC: 3599 Machine shop, jobbing & repair

(G-10576)
RENARD COMMUMICATIONS INC
Also Called: Diversity/Careers In Enginrng
197 Mountain Ave (07081-1755)
P.O. Box 557 (07081-0557)
PHONE..................................973 912-8550
Fax: 973 912-8599
Roberta Renard, *President*
Jeff Wiener, *Vice Pres*
EMP: 32
SQ FT: 5,500
SALES: 6.4MM **Privately Held**
WEB: www.diversitycareers.com
SIC: 2721 Magazines: publishing & printing

(G-10577)
RING CONTAINER TECH LLC
50 Fadem Rd (07081-3116)
PHONE..................................973 258-0707
Fax: 908 851-9366
John Redman, *Branch Mgr*
EMP: 18
SALES (corp-wide): 295MM **Privately Held**
WEB: www.ringcontainer.com
SIC: 3089 Plastic containers, except foam
PA: Ring Container Technologies, Llc.
1 Industrial Park
Oakland TN 38060
800 280-7464

(G-10578)
SPRINGFIELD METAL PDTS CO INC
8 Commerce St (07081-2903)
PHONE..................................973 379-4600
Fax: 973 379-7314
John D Sommer, *President*
Lori M Perrine, *Treasurer*
Lori Sommer, *Treasurer*
Irene G Powell, *Admin Sec*
EMP: 10
SQ FT: 6,600
SALES (est): 1.3MM **Privately Held**
SIC: 3444 3443 3441 Sheet metal specialties, not stamped; fabricated plate work (boiler shop); fabricated structural metal

(G-10579)
TAYLOR COMMUNICATIONS INC
899 Mountain Ave Ste 2f (07081-3403)
PHONE..................................973 467-8259
EMP: 17
SALES (corp-wide): 3.5B **Privately Held**
SIC: 2754 Commercial printing, gravure
HQ: Taylor Communications, Inc.
4205 S 96th St
Omaha NE 68127
402 898-6422

(G-10580)
TROPAION INC
955 S Springfield Ave C302 (07081-3570)
PHONE..................................908 654-3870
Fax: 908 654-3871
Bruce Meyer, *President*
Elitza Meyer, *Vice Pres*
EMP: 4
SQ FT: 1,000
SALES: 300K **Privately Held**
WEB: www.tropaion.com
SIC: 8243 7372 7379 Software training, computer; prepackaged software; computer related consulting services

(G-10581)
UNITED WINDOW & DOOR MFG INC (PA)
24 Fadem Rd 36 (07081-3116)
PHONE..................................973 912-0600
Howard Rose, *President*
Nick Derrico, *Vice Pres*
Chris Kanipe, *Vice Pres*
Gregg Proscia, *Vice Pres*
Alan Schulman, *Vice Pres*
EMP: 30
SQ FT: 110,000
SALES (est): 52.3MM **Privately Held**
SIC: 3089 Windows, plastic

(G-10582)
UNIVERSAL TOOLS & MFG CO
115 Victory Rd (07081-1376)
PHONE..................................973 379-4193
Dorothy Principe, *President*
Robin McElwee, *COO*
Helder Ruivo, *Plant Mgr*
Jessi McElwee, *Web Dvlpr*
▲ **EMP:** 27
SQ FT: 12,000
SALES (est): 4.2MM **Privately Held**
WEB: www.utmfg.com
SIC: 3469 3544 Stamping metal for the trade; special dies, tools, jigs & fixtures

(G-10583)
VALCOR ENGINEERING CORPORATION (PA)
2 Lawrence Rd (07081-3165)
PHONE..................................973 467-8400
Fax: 973 467-8382
Jody K Friedman, *Ch of Bd*
Lori K Klinghoffer, *Ch of Bd*
Robin K Walters, *Ch of Bd*
Tom Iervolino, *Vice Pres*
Fran Lucano, *Vice Pres*
▲ **EMP:** 220
SQ FT: 176,000
SALES (est): 33.7MM **Privately Held**
WEB: www.valcor.com
SIC: 3492 3561 Fluid power valves & hose fittings; pumps & pumping equipment

(G-10584)
VALCOR ENGINEERING CORPORATION
Also Called: Electroid Co Div
2 Lawrence Rd (07081-3165)
PHONE..................................973 467-8100
Steve Etter, *Branch Mgr*
EMP: 50
SALES (corp-wide): 33.7MM **Privately Held**
WEB: www.valcor.com
SIC: 3621 3714 3568 Control equipment for buses or trucks, electric; motor vehicle parts & accessories; power transmission equipment
PA: Valcor Engineering Corporation
2 Lawrence Rd
Springfield NJ 07081
973 467-8400

(G-10585)
VALCOR ENGINEERING CORPORATION
Electroid Company
2 Lawrence Rd (07081-3165)
PHONE..................................973 467-8400
EMP: 40
SALES (corp-wide): 33.7MM **Privately Held**
SIC: 3625 Actuators, industrial
PA: Valcor Engineering Corporation
2 Lawrence Rd
Springfield NJ 07081
973 467-8400

(G-10586)
WPI COMMUNICATIONS INC
Also Called: Atrium Publishing
55 Morris Ave Ste 312 (07081-1496)
PHONE..................................973 467-8700
Fax: 800 677-9742
Steven H Klinghoffer, *President*
Steve Klinghoffer, *Founder*
Lori K Klinghoffer, *Exec VP*
EMP: 15
SQ FT: 3,500
SALES (est): 1.5MM **Privately Held**
SIC: 2741 Newsletter publishing

```
Stanhope
Sussex County
```

(G-10587)
ALL IN ICING
24 Woods Edge Rd (07874-3242)
PHONE..................................973 896-5990
Donna Infantolino, *Owner*
EMP: 4

SALES (est): 282K **Privately Held**
SIC: 2051 Bread, cake & related products

(G-10588)
NEW YORK FOLDING BOX CO INC
20 Continental Dr (07874-2658)
PHONE..................................973 347-6932
Ken Kaplan, *Vice Pres*
Gregg Kaplan, *Vice Pres*
Mike Fiscella, *Controller*
EMP: 22
SQ FT: 100,000
SALES (est): 5.2MM **Privately Held**
SIC: 2657 2653 Folding paperboard boxes; corrugated & solid fiber boxes

(G-10589)
PANEL COMPONENTS & SYSTEMS (PA)
Also Called: PC & S
149 Main St (07874-2667)
PHONE..................................973 448-9400
Fax: 973 448-1674
Tanja Lewit, *President*
Joseph Knolmayer, *Vice Pres*
Marty Leichtman, *Regl Sales Mgr*
EMP: 17
SQ FT: 6,000
SALES (est): 4.1MM **Privately Held**
WEB: www.pc-s.com
SIC: 5063 5084 3825 Electrical supplies; instruments & control equipment; instruments to measure electricity

(G-10590)
TILCON NEW YORK INC
11 Lackawanna Dr (07874-3114)
PHONE..................................973 347-2405
John Brownell, *Manager*
EMP: 12
SALES (corp-wide): 29.7B **Privately Held**
WEB: www.tilconny.com
SIC: 1429 Crushed/Broken Stone
HQ: Tilcon New York Inc.
9 Entin Rd
Parsippany NJ 07054
800 789-7625

(G-10591)
UNITED STATES MINERAL PDTS CO (HQ)
Also Called: US Minerals
41 Furnace St (07874-2624)
PHONE..................................973 347-1200
Fax: 973 347-5131
Giovanni C Pacheco, *CEO*
Russell Harvey, *District Mgr*
Rudolph Sanson, *Counsel*
Rob Nicholoff, *Plant Mgr*
Noah Pnce, *Safety Mgr*
◆ **EMP:** 65 **EST:** 1875
SQ FT: 50,000
SALES (est): 48.1MM **Privately Held**
WEB: www.cafco.com
SIC: 3296 Mineral wool insulation products

(G-10592)
WAGNER INDUSTRIES INC
51 Sparta Rd (07874-2881)
PHONE..................................973 347-0800
Fax: 973 347-0885
William S Wagner Sr, *President*
Michael Slavescu, *Engineer*
▼ **EMP:** 15
SQ FT: 10,000
SALES (est): 1MM **Privately Held**
WEB: www.wagner-industries.com
SIC: 3565 5084 3599 Packaging machinery; industrial machinery & equipment; machine shop, jobbing & repair

```
Stewartsville
Warren County
```

(G-10593)
D & H CUTOFF CO
2600 State Route 57 (08886-3158)
PHONE..................................908 454-4961
Fax: 908 832-9619
Eric Smith, *President*
Art Desaules, *President*
EMP: 7 **EST:** 1930

▲ = Import ▼ =Export
◆ =Import/Export

SQ FT: 4,000
SALES (est): 1MM **Privately Held**
WEB: www.dandhcutoff.com
SIC: 3599 Machine shop, jobbing & repair

(G-10594)
DAROS GROUP
200 Arbor Dr (08886-2322)
PHONE..........................908 454-7811
Thomas Daros, *Principal*
EMP: 4 EST: 1999
SALES (est): 259.1K **Privately Held**
SIC: 2869 Fuels

(G-10595)
EAGLE STEEL & IRON LLC
102 Willever Way (08886-2011)
PHONE..........................908 587-1025
Karol Kulik,
EMP: 6
SALES (est): 545.6K **Privately Held**
SIC: 3441 3449 7389 Fabricated structural metal; bars, concrete reinforcing: fabricated steel;

(G-10596)
LINDE GAS NORTH AMERICA LLC
1 Greenwich St (08886-2020)
PHONE..........................908 329-9300
Robert White, *General Mgr*
Rebecca Dabkowski, *Manager*
EMP: 35
SALES (corp-wide): 20.1B **Privately Held**
SIC: 2813 Oxygen, compressed or liquefied
HQ: Linde Gas North America Llc
200 Somerset Corp Blvd # 7000
Bridgewater NJ 08807

(G-10597)
LINDE LLC
1 Greenwich St Ste 200 (08886-2020)
PHONE..........................908 329-9619
Mark McGough, *Technical Mgr*
Roxanne Bailey, *Branch Mgr*
Allen Russell, *CTO*
Elaine Bradford, *Analyst*
EMP: 22
SALES (corp-wide): 20.1B **Privately Held**
SIC: 2813 Nitrogen
HQ: Linde Llc
200 Somerset Corporate Bl
Bridgewater NJ 08807
908 464-8100

(G-10598)
T & M PALLET CO INC
116 Edison Rd (08886-3123)
P.O. Box 177 (08886-0177)
PHONE..........................908 454-3042
Fax: 908 454-5959
Amos Tigar, *President*
Randy Tigar, *Treasurer*
EMP: 20
SQ FT: 4,305
SALES (est): 2.8MM **Privately Held**
SIC: 2448 7699 2441 Pallets, wood; pallet repair; nailed wood boxes & shook

Stirling
Morris County

(G-10599)
ENGINEERED PLASTIC PDTS INC (PA)
269 Mercer St (07980-1418)
P.O. Box 196 (07980-0196)
PHONE..........................908 647-3500
Fax: 908 647-1868
Chris Ratti, *President*
▲ EMP: 22
SQ FT: 25,000
SALES (est): 3.2MM **Privately Held**
WEB: www.engineeredplastic.com
SIC: 3089 Injection molding of plastics; plastic processing

(G-10600)
FIBERGUIDE INDUSTRIES INC (HQ)
1 Bay St Ste 1 # 1 (07980-1529)
PHONE..........................908 647-6601

Fax: 908 647-8464
Patricia Seniw, *President*
Mac He, *Business Mgr*
Ernest J Rich, *Corp Secy*
William Bozarth, *Vice Pres*
Bess Dibben, *Purchasing*
▼ EMP: 23
SQ FT: 13,500
SALES (est): 8MM
SALES (corp-wide): 1.5B **Privately Held**
WEB: www.fiberguide.com
SIC: 3229 Fiber optics strands
PA: Halma Public Limited Company
Misbourne Court
Amersham BUCKS HP7 0
149 472-1111

(G-10601)
INTERTEK LABORATORIES INC
340 Union St (07980-1312)
PHONE..........................908 903-1800
Fax: 908 903-1866
Denis R Rybkiewicz, *President*
Timmy Cutugno, *Technology*
Alan Scerri, *Technology*
EMP: 30
SQ FT: 6,000
SALES (est): 6.7MM **Privately Held**
WEB: www.interteklabsinc.com
SIC: 3812 3823 3825 8711 Search & navigation equipment; industrial instrmnts msrmnt display/control process variable; instruments to measure electricity; electrical or electronic engineering; electronic research

(G-10602)
ISOLANTITE MANUFACTURING CO
337 Warren Ave (07980-1443)
PHONE..........................908 647-3333
Fax: 908 580-0936
George W Lumpe, *President*
Mary Lou Hall, *VP Sales*
EMP: 30
SQ FT: 25,000
SALES (est): 4.3MM **Privately Held**
WEB: www.isolantite.com
SIC: 3264 Porcelain electrical supplies; insulators, electrical: porcelain

(G-10603)
M & M WELDING & STEEL FABG
Also Called: M & M Welding & Machine
344 Essex St (07980-1342)
PHONE..........................908 647-6060
Oldrich Masek, *President*
Marie Masek, *Vice Pres*
EMP: 5
SQ FT: 6,000
SALES (est): 380K **Privately Held**
SIC: 7692 3599 Welding repair; machine shop, jobbing & repair

(G-10604)
P M Z TOOL INC
321 Warren Ave (07980-1442)
P.O. Box 201 (07980-0201)
PHONE..........................908 647-2125
Paul M Zuzak, *President*
EMP: 7
SQ FT: 3,400
SALES (est): 1.1MM **Privately Held**
SIC: 5084 3599 Machine tools & metalworking machinery; machine shop, jobbing & repair

(G-10605)
RECORDER PUBLISHING CO
Also Called: Recorder Newspaper
254 Mercer St (07980-1487)
PHONE..........................908 647-1180
Fax: 908 647-7679
EMP: 20
SALES (corp-wide): 15.4MM **Privately Held**
SIC: 2752 2711 Lithographic Commercial Printing Newspapers-Publishing/Printing
PA: Recorder Publishing Co
17 Morristown Rd
Bernardsville NJ 07981
908 766-3900

(G-10606)
SECURE SYSTEM INC
Also Called: Personal Secure
320 Essex St Ste 3 (07980-1339)
PHONE..........................732 922-3609
Fax: 732 922-2221
Gregory Lawson, *President*
Donald Ullery, *Vice Pres*
Stephen E Roman Jr, *CFO*
EMP: 25
SQ FT: 9,000
SALES: 4MM **Privately Held**
WEB: www.securesysteminc.com
SIC: 7382 3699 Protective devices, security; security control equipment & systems

(G-10607)
SUMAN REALTY LLC
103 Saint Josephs Dr (07980-1250)
PHONE..........................908 350-8039
Suman L Singh, *Principal*
EMP: 4
SALES (est): 271.9K **Privately Held**
SIC: 2869 Fuels

(G-10608)
TPI PARTNERS INC
Also Called: Thermoplastic Processes
1268 Valley Rd (07980-1425)
PHONE..........................908 561-3000
Fax: 908 753-6749
Lynn Kinney, *Administration*
EMP: 6
SALES (est): 566.4K
SALES (corp-wide): 17.2MM **Privately Held**
SIC: 3082 Tubes, unsupported plastic; rods, unsupported plastic
PA: Tpi Partners, Inc.
21649 Cedar Creek Ave
Georgetown DE 19947
302 855-0139

(G-10609)
WORLD OF COFFEE INC
Also Called: World of Tea
328 Essex St (07980-1302)
PHONE..........................908 647-1218
Fax: 908 647-7827
Charles Newman, *President*
▲ EMP: 9 EST: 1975
SQ FT: 7,500
SALES (est): 1.4MM **Privately Held**
SIC: 2095 Coffee roasting (except by wholesale grocers)

Stockholm
Sussex County

(G-10610)
RJTICECO LLC
Also Called: Crush Rite
4 Northwoods Trl (07460-1124)
P.O. Box 645 (07460-0645)
PHONE..........................973 697-0156
Bob Tice,
Jeanne Tice,
EMP: 4
SALES (est): 472.7K **Privately Held**
SIC: 3634 Ice crushers, electric

Stockton
Hunterdon County

(G-10611)
GREEN LAND & LOGGING LLC
328 Rosemont Ringoes Rd (08559-1514)
PHONE..........................908 894-2361
Scott Green, *Principal*
EMP: 6
SALES (est): 434.8K **Privately Held**
SIC: 2411 Logging

(G-10612)
ROBERT WALLACE
Also Called: Lucid Lighting
811 Rosemont Ringoes Rd (08559-1610)
PHONE..........................609 649-0596
Robert Wallace, *Owner*
EMP: 5
SQ FT: 900

SALES (est): 146.4K **Privately Held**
WEB: www.lucidlighting.com
SIC: 3645 3646 5719 5063 Residential lighting fixtures; commercial indusl & institutional electric lighting fixtures; lighting fixtures; lighting fixtures

Stone Harbor
Cape May County

(G-10613)
CAMP MARINE SERVICES INC
1000 Stone Harbor Blvd (08247-1423)
P.O. Box 35 (08247-0035)
PHONE..........................609 368-1777
Barry Camp, *President*
EMP: 4
SALES (est): 2MM **Privately Held**
SIC: 3732 5551 4493 Yachts, building & repairing; marine supplies; marinas

(G-10614)
CES IMPORTS LLC
252 93rd St (08247-2030)
PHONE..........................610 299-7930
Robert Ernst, *Mng Member*
Greg Ernst,
EMP: 4
SALES (est): 149.2K **Privately Held**
SIC: 3842 Clothing, fire resistant & protective

Stratford
Camden County

(G-10615)
CYPHER INSURANCE SOFTWARE
32 Sunnybrook Rd (08084-1650)
P.O. Box 433 (08084-0433)
PHONE..........................856 216-0575
EMP: 4
SALES: 118K **Privately Held**
SIC: 7372 Prepackaged Software Services

(G-10616)
PENNY PRESS
908 N White Horse Pike (08084-1002)
PHONE..........................856 547-1991
Joe Skeggs, *Partner*
Charlotte Skeggs, *Partner*
EMP: 7
SALES (est): 993.1K **Privately Held**
SIC: 2752 5199 7334 Commercial printing, offset; advertising specialties; photocopying & duplicating services

(G-10617)
SOUTH JERSEY PRETZEL INC
912 N White Horse Pike A (08084-1017)
PHONE..........................856 435-5055
Fax: 856 627-2810
George W Dudley, *President*
Robin Williams, *Manager*
EMP: 12
SALES (est): 1.3MM **Privately Held**
SIC: 2052 5142 5461 2024 Pretzels; poultry, frozen: packaged; pretzels; ices, flavored (frozen dessert); ice cream & ices; ice cream, soft drink & soda fountain stands

Succasunna
Morris County

(G-10618)
50 PLUS MONTHLY INC
5 Clearfield Rd (07876-1531)
P.O. Box 28, Nassau DE (19969-0028)
PHONE..........................973 584-7911
Lorraine Cintron, *President*
EMP: 5
SALES (est): 200K **Privately Held**
SIC: 2711 Newspapers

(G-10619)
C & N TOOLING & GRINDING INC
19 State Route 10 E # 14 (07876-1749)
PHONE......................................973 598-8411
Neil Rambaldi, *President*
Elmira Rambaldi, *Corp Secy*
EMP: 10
SQ FT: 3,000
SALES (est): 1.8MM **Privately Held**
SIC: 3599 7699 Machine shop, jobbing & repair; knife, saw & tool sharpening & repair

(G-10620)
COLFAJAS INC
5 West St (07876-1620)
PHONE......................................973 727-4813
Albeiro Ramirez, *President*
EMP: 4 EST: 2010
SALES (est): 304.5K **Privately Held**
SIC: 2342 Bras, girdles & allied garments

(G-10621)
D & F WICKER IMPORT CO INC (PA)
295 State Route 10 E (07876-1321)
P.O. Box 430, Ledgewood (07852-0430)
PHONE......................................973 736-5861
David Gruber, *President*
Jeffrey Gruber, *Vice Pres*
Frances Gruber, *Treasurer*
▲ EMP: 31
SQ FT: 40,000
SALES (est): 10MM **Privately Held**
WEB: www.dfwicker.com
SIC: 5021 2519 Household furniture; wicker & rattan furniture

(G-10622)
DAVIS CENTER INC
19 State Route 10 E # 25 (07876-1750)
PHONE......................................862 251-4637
Dorinne S Davis, *President*
EMP: 5
SALES (est): 450K **Privately Held**
WEB: www.thedaviscenter.com
SIC: 3845 8049 8299 5999 Audiological equipment, electromedical; audiologist; speech specialist; tutoring school; hearing aids

(G-10623)
HOLLAND MANUFACTURING CO INC (PA)
15 Main St (07876-1747)
P.O. Box 404 (07876-0404)
PHONE......................................973 584-8141
Fax: 973 584-6845
Jack Holland, *CEO*
Michael Pallante, *Vice Pres*
Brian Allanson, *Opers Mgr*
Chase Holland, *Purch Dir*
Ron Soares, *Engineer*
◆ EMP: 128
SQ FT: 150,000
SALES (est): 26.9MM **Privately Held**
WEB: www.hollandmfg.com
SIC: 2672 2621 2671 Gummed tape, cloth or paper base: from purchased materials; gummed paper: made from purchased materials; coated paper, except photographic, carbon or abrasive; specialty or chemically treated papers; building paper & felts; packaging paper & plastics film, coated & laminated

(G-10624)
JOSTENS INC
86 Roseville Rd (07876)
PHONE......................................973 584-5843
Fax: 973 347-5893
Lou Esposito, *General Mgr*
EMP: 6
SALES (corp-wide): 14.7B **Publicly Held**
WEB: www.jostens.com
SIC: 3911 Rings, finger: precious metal
HQ: Jostens, Inc.
7760 France Ave S Ste 400
Minneapolis MN 55435
952 830-3300

(G-10625)
MRI OF WEST MORRIS PA
66 Sunset Strip Ste 105 (07876-1362)
PHONE......................................973 927-1010

Fax: 973 927-7273
Michelle Dunn, *Manager*
Jeff Dunn, *Manager*
EMP: 11
SALES (est): 890K **Privately Held**
WEB: www.mriwestmorris.com
SIC: 3861 8011 X-ray film; radiologist

(G-10626)
PUSH BEVERAGES LLC
7 Longfellow Dr (07876-1165)
P.O. Box 343 (07876-0343)
PHONE......................................973 766-2663
Laurel Whitney, *Principal*
EMP: 4
SALES (est): 139.4K **Privately Held**
SIC: 2086 Bottled & canned soft drinks

(G-10627)
R P SMITH & SON INC
199 Main St (07876-1335)
P.O. Box 209 (07876-0209)
PHONE......................................973 584-4063
Robert P Smith, *President*
EMP: 10
SALES (est): 1.5MM **Privately Held**
SIC: 3271 Blocks, concrete or cinder: standard

(G-10628)
RAME-HART INSTRUMENT CO LLC
Also Called: Rame Hart Instrument
19 State Route 10 E # 11 (07876-1749)
P.O. Box 400, Netcong (07857-0400)
PHONE......................................973 448-0305
Carl Clegg, *Mng Member*
Ken Christiansen,
Rolf Pfeil,
EMP: 8
SALES: 2MM **Privately Held**
SIC: 3826 Analytical instruments

(G-10629)
S V O INC
Also Called: Single Vender Outsource
28 State Route 10 W (07876-1724)
PHONE......................................973 983-8380
Richard Spender, *President*
EMP: 4
SQ FT: 1,000
SALES (est): 535.4K **Privately Held**
SIC: 2759 Commercial printing

Summit
Union County

(G-10630)
ABRAXIS BIOSCIENCE INC (HQ)
86 Morris Ave (07901-3915)
PHONE......................................908 673-9000
Lonnie Moulder, *President*
Mitchell Fogelman, *CFO*
Karen Legge, *Manager*
Aaron Fobes, *Associate Dir*
EMP: 100
SQ FT: 60,900
SALES (est): 108.2MM
SALES (corp-wide): 13B **Publicly Held**
SIC: 2834 Pharmaceutical preparations
PA: Celgene Corporation
86 Morris Ave
Summit NJ 07901
908 673-9000

(G-10631)
ABRAXIS BIOSCIENCE INC
86 Morris Ave (07901-3915)
PHONE......................................908 673-9000
Marie Benedicto, *Treasurer*
EMP: 100
SALES (corp-wide): 13B **Publicly Held**
SIC: 2834 Pharmaceutical preparations
HQ: Abraxis Bioscience, Inc.
86 Morris Ave
Summit NJ 07901

(G-10632)
ACETYLON PHARMACEUTICALS INC (HQ)
86 Morris Ave (07901-3915)
PHONE......................................908 673-9000
Mark Alles, *President*

Marc A Cohen, *Corp Secy*
John H Vanduzer, *Vice Pres*
Catherine A Wheeler, *Vice Pres*
David Tamang, *Research*
EMP: 10
SALES (est): 848.3K
SALES (corp-wide): 13B **Publicly Held**
SIC: 2834 Pharmaceutical preparations
PA: Celgene Corporation
86 Morris Ave
Summit NJ 07901
908 673-9000

(G-10633)
AHS HOSPITAL CORP
Also Called: Overlook Hospital, Summit Mri
99 Beauvoir Ave (07901-3533)
P.O. Box 220 (07902-0220)
PHONE......................................908 522-2000
Cathy Wasck, *Manager*
Rajesh Kumari, *Manager*
Patricia Gazzola, *Nurse Practr*
EMP: 35
SQ FT: 2,392 **Privately Held**
WEB: www.atlantichealth.org
SIC: 3845 3842 8062 Magnetic resonance imaging device, nuclear; surgical appliances & supplies; general medical & surgical hospitals
PA: Ahs Hospital Corp.
465 South St
Morristown NJ 07960

(G-10634)
AMERICAN ESTATES WINES INC
19 Hillside Ave (07901-1904)
PHONE......................................908 273-5060
Fax: 908 273-5068
George G Galey, *President*
Angie Kristic, *District Mgr*
Tom Jackson, *Sales Staff*
▲ EMP: 7
SALES (est): 470K **Privately Held**
SIC: 2084 Wines

(G-10635)
ARTMOLDS JOURNAL LLC
18 Bank St Ste 1 (07901-3659)
PHONE......................................908 273-5600
Edmund McCormick,
EMP: 4
SALES (est): 210.6K **Privately Held**
SIC: 2621 Catalog, magazine & newsprint papers

(G-10636)
ASSOCIATE FIREPLACE BUILDERS
Also Called: Fireplace Place Summit, The
331 Springfield Ave (07901-3626)
PHONE......................................908 273-5900
Fax: 908 273-5557
John Vierra, *President*
Dennis Miller, *Exec VP*
EMP: 7
SALES (est): 1MM **Privately Held**
SIC: 3272 5023 Fireplace & chimney material: concrete; fireplace equipment & accessories

(G-10637)
BOURAS INDUSTRIES INC (PA)
25 Deforest Ave Ste 100 (07901-2140)
PHONE......................................908 918-9400
Nicholas J Bouras, *President*
Carl Koehler, *Exec VP*
Gary Ruckelshaus, *Vice Pres*
EMP: 650
SALES (est): 78MM **Privately Held**
WEB: www.bourasind.com
SIC: 5051 3444 4212 4214 Steel; roof deck, sheet metal; flooring, cellular steel; siding, sheet metal; local trucking, without storage; local trucking with storage; fabricated structural metal

(G-10638)
CELGENE CORPORATION
Also Called: US NJ Summit West
556 Morris Ave (07901-1330)
PHONE......................................908 897-4603
EMP: 22
SALES (corp-wide): 13B **Publicly Held**
SIC: 2834 Pharmaceutical preparations

PA: Celgene Corporation
86 Morris Ave
Summit NJ 07901
908 673-9000

(G-10639)
CELGENE CORPORATION (PA)
86 Morris Ave (07901-3915)
P.O. Box 421248, Indianapolis IN (46242-1248)
PHONE......................................908 673-9000
Fax: 908 673-9001
Mark J Alles, *Ch of Bd*
Ailyn Abin, *Counsel*
Teresia Bost, *Counsel*
Gerald F Masoudi, *Exec VP*
Jennifer Dudinak, *Senior VP*
EMP: 211
SALES: 13B **Publicly Held**
WEB: www.celgene.com
SIC: 2834 Pharmaceutical preparations

(G-10640)
COLTON INDUSTRIES INC
117 Colt Rd (07901-3039)
PHONE......................................908 277-2040
B G Colton, *CEO*
Brenda Colton, *Ch of Bd*
Stefanie Colton, *President*
EMP: 4
SALES: 6MM **Privately Held**
SIC: 2231 Fabric finishing: wool, mohair or similar fibers

(G-10641)
ENVIRONMOLDS LLC
18 Bank St Ste 1 (07901-3659)
PHONE......................................908 273-5401
Ed McCormick, *Mng Member*
Hong Zhang,
▲ EMP: 10
SQ FT: 3,000
SALES (est): 710K **Privately Held**
SIC: 3299 5092 5999 Art goods: plaster of paris, papier mache & scagliola; arts & crafts equipment & supplies; art dealers

(G-10642)
GALLERY OF RUGS INC
447 Springfield Ave (07901-2615)
PHONE......................................908 934-0040
EMP: 5 EST: 2000
SALES (est): 460K **Privately Held**
SIC: 2273 Mfg Carpets/Rugs

(G-10643)
GSI
12 Princeton St (07901-4208)
PHONE......................................908 608-1325
Genevieve Spielberg, *Principal*
Toni Rhatican, *Office Mgr*
EMP: 4
SALES (est): 499.2K **Privately Held**
SIC: 3699 Laser systems & equipment

(G-10644)
HOSOKAWA MICRON INTERNATIONAL
Also Called: Hosokawa Tech
10 Chatham Rd (07901-1310)
PHONE......................................908 273-6360
Bill Manzini, *Manager*
EMP: 150
SALES (corp-wide): 444.6MM **Privately Held**
WEB: www.hosokawa.com
SIC: 8711 8721 3532 Engineering services; accounting, auditing & bookkeeping; mining machinery
HQ: Hosokawa Micron International, Inc
10 Chatham Rd
Summit NJ 07901
908 273-6360

(G-10645)
HOSOKAWA MICRON INTERNATIONAL
Also Called: Hosokawa Micron Powder Systems
10 Chatham Rd (07901-1310)
PHONE......................................908 273-6360
Rob Coorhees, *Branch Mgr*
EMP: 67

SALES (corp-wide): 444.6MM **Privately Held**
SIC: 3559 Chemical machinery & equipment; plastics working machinery
HQ: Hosokawa Micron International, Inc
10 Chatham Rd
Summit NJ 07901
908 273-6360

(G-10646)
HOSOKAWA MICRON INTERNATIONAL
Also Called: Micron Powder Systems
10 Chatham Rd (07901-1310)
PHONE..........................908 273-6360
Rob Voorhes, *Vice Pres*
EMP: 60
SALES (corp-wide): 444.6MM **Privately Held**
WEB: www.hosokawa.com
SIC: 3559 Chemical machinery & equipment; plastics working machinery
HQ: Hosokawa Micron International, Inc
10 Chatham Rd
Summit NJ 07901
908 273-6360

(G-10647)
HOSOKAWA MICRON INTERNATIONAL (HQ)
Also Called: Hosokawa Micron Powder Systems
10 Chatham Rd (07901-1310)
PHONE..........................908 273-6360
Fax: 908 273-6344
Isao Sato, *President*
Rob Boorhees, *President*
Yoshio Hosokawa, *Exec VP*
Jodi Levine, *Purch Agent*
Judi Macgregor, *CFO*
◆ **EMP:** 70
SQ FT: 195,000
SALES (est): 67.3MM
SALES (corp-wide): 444.6MM **Privately Held**
WEB: www.hosokawa.com
SIC: 3559 Chemical machinery & equipment; plastics working machinery
PA: Hosokawa Micron Corporation
1-9, Tajika, Shodai
Hirakata OSK 573-1
728 552-226

(G-10648)
I T C PRINTING PROMOTION
24 Beechwood Rd (07901-2516)
PHONE..........................908 918-1122
Larry Manshel, *President*
Roger Manshel, *President*
Keith Simpson, *Sales Associate*
EMP: 8
SALES (est): 555.2K **Privately Held**
SIC: 2752 8742 Commercial printing, lithographic; marketing consulting services

(G-10649)
MARKOV PROCESSES INTERNATIONAL
475 Sprngfeld Ave Ste 401 (07901)
PHONE..........................908 608-1558
Fax: 908 608-1601
Michael Markov, *Ch of Bd*
EMP: 35 **EST:** 1992
SALES (est): 4.2MM **Privately Held**
SIC: 7372 Business oriented computer software

(G-10650)
MERCK & CO INC
566 Morris Ave (07901-1311)
PHONE..........................908 298-4000
EMP: 48
SALES (corp-wide): 40.1B **Publicly Held**
SIC: 2834 Mfg Pharmaceutical Preparations
PA: Merck & Co., Inc.
2000 Galloping Hill Rd
Kenilworth NJ 07033
908 740-4000

(G-10651)
MYSUPERFOODS LTD LIABILITY CO
371 Springfield Ave Ste 2 (07901-2708)
PHONE..........................646 283-7455

Katie Jesionowski, *President*
Silvia Gianni, *President*
Kelly Cavanaugh, *Business Dir*
EMP: 10
SALES (est): 1.2MM **Privately Held**
SIC: 2032 Baby foods, including meats: packaged in cans, jars, etc.

(G-10652)
OPTIONS EDGE LLC
53 Division Ave Apt 12 (07901-2350)
PHONE..........................973 701-0051
Mark Guthner,
EMP: 4
SALES (est): 162K **Privately Held**
SIC: 2721 Periodicals

(G-10653)
PHARMION CORPORATION (HQ)
86 Morris Ave (07901-3915)
PHONE..........................908 673-9000
M James Barrett, *Ch of Bd*
Patrick J Mahaffy, *President*
Michael Cosgrave, *Exec VP*
Steven N Dupont, *Vice Pres*
Erle T Mast, *CFO*
EMP: 35
SQ FT: 29,000
SALES (est): 24.2MM
SALES (corp-wide): 13B **Publicly Held**
WEB: www.pharmion.com
SIC: 2834 Drugs affecting neoplasms & endocrine systems
PA: Celgene Corporation
86 Morris Ave
Summit NJ 07901
908 673-9000

(G-10654)
SAFETY POWER INC
Also Called: SPI
55 Union Pl Ste 178 (07901-2563)
PHONE..........................908 277-1826
Robert Desnoyers, *President*
Bob Stelzer, *Chairman*
Randy Sadler, *VP Sls/Mktg*
EMP: 5
SQ FT: 200
SALES: 10MM
SALES (corp-wide): 2.1MM **Privately Held**
SIC: 3564 Air purification equipment
PA: Safety Power Inc
1200 Aerowood Dr Suite 1
Mississauga ON L4W 2
416 477-2709

(G-10655)
SEQIRUS USA INC
25 Deforest Ave (07901-2140)
PHONE..........................908 739-0200
Brent Macgregor, *President*
Richard Culbert, *Treasurer*
John Minardo, *Admin Sec*
EMP: 10
SALES (est): 2.3MM
SALES (corp-wide): 6.9B **Privately Held**
SIC: 2836 Biological products, except diagnostic
PA: Csl Limited
45 Poplar Rd
Parkville VIC 3052
393 891-911

(G-10656)
SERVICE DATA CORP INC
Also Called: Service Data Forms
265 Oak Ridge Ave (07901-3258)
PHONE..........................908 522-0020
Fax: 908 522-1888
Ross Wagner, *President*
Katherine Wagner, *Corp Secy*
EMP: 6
SALES (est): 770K **Privately Held**
SIC: 5112 2732 2752 Business forms; book printing; commercial printing, lithographic

(G-10657)
SILICON PRESS INC
25 Beverly Rd (07901-1619)
PHONE..........................908 273-8919
Fax: 908 273-6149
Narain Gehani, *CEO*
Indu Gehani, *President*
EMP: 5

SALES (est): 370K **Privately Held**
WEB: www.silicon-press.com
SIC: 2731 5192 Book publishing; books, periodicals & newspapers

(G-10658)
SOFTWARE PRACTICES AND TECH
73 Stone Ridge Rd (07901-4156)
PHONE..........................908 464-2923
EMP: 6
SALES (est): 460K **Privately Held**
SIC: 7371 7372 Custom Computer Programing Prepackaged Software Services

(G-10659)
STESSL & NEUGEBAUER INC
9 Industrial Pl (07901-3512)
PHONE..........................908 277-3340
Fax: 908 277-0833
Wilfred Stessl, *President*
Carole Stessl, *Corp Secy*
EMP: 15
SALES (est): 1.8MM **Privately Held**
SIC: 2391 7641 Draperies, plastic & textile: from purchased materials; reupholstery

(G-10660)
SUMMIT MILLWORK & SUPPLY INC
235 Morris Ave (07901-5501)
P.O. Box 373 (07902-0373)
PHONE..........................908 273-1486
Aldo Curiale, *President*
Irene Curiale, *Admin Sec*
EMP: 4
SQ FT: 5,000
SALES (est): 664.3K **Privately Held**
SIC: 2431 Millwork

(G-10661)
SUMMIT TRUCK BODY INC (PA)
50 Franklin Pl (07901-3684)
PHONE..........................908 277-4342
Fax: 908 277-4015
Timothy Erday, *President*
EMP: 14 **EST:** 1953
SQ FT: 12,000
SALES (est): 1.6MM **Privately Held**
WEB: www.summittruckbody.com
SIC: 7538 3713 7532 General automotive repair shops; general truck repair; truck bodies & parts; top & body repair & paint shops

(G-10662)
SWEET ORANGE LLC
545 Morris Ave (07901-1325)
PHONE..........................908 522-0011
Dina Kim, *Principal*
EMP: 5
SALES (est): 250.6K **Privately Held**
SIC: 2024 Ice cream, bulk

(G-10663)
VENTURE APP LLC ✪
12 Aubrey St (07901-1464)
PHONE..........................908 644-3985
Leonel Ayala,
EMP: 4 **EST:** 2017
SALES (est): 98.3K **Privately Held**
SIC: 7372 7389 Prepackaged software;

Surf City
Ocean County

(G-10664)
AMERICAN DIRECTORY PUBLISHING
Also Called: Regional Directory
1816 Long Beach Blvd (08008-5461)
PHONE..........................609 494-4055
Michael Paul, *President*
EMP: 8
SQ FT: 1,000
SALES (est): 530K **Privately Held**
SIC: 2741 Miscellaneous publishing

(G-10665)
JERSEY SHORE NEWS MGAZINES INC (PA)
Also Called: Beachcomber, The
1816 Long Beach Blvd (08008-5461)
PHONE..........................609 494-5900
Fax: 609 494-1437
Curt Travers, *President*
Juliet Kaszas-Hoch, *Technical Staff*
EMP: 30
SQ FT: 5,000
SALES (est): 2.9MM **Privately Held**
WEB: www.thesandpaper.net
SIC: 2711 2741 Newspapers, publishing & printing; miscellaneous publishing

---

Sussex
Sussex County

(G-10666)
ANNETTE & JIM DIZENZO SLS LLC (PA)
Also Called: Kristino Handbags & ACC
6 Glenview Ln (07461-4848)
PHONE..........................973 875-0895
Jim Dizenzo, *Mng Member*
Annette Dizenzo,
EMP: 4
SQ FT: 1,605
SALES (est): 384.7K **Privately Held**
SIC: 3171 Handbags, women's

(G-10667)
CAROL HEALEY
Also Called: Dcw Packaging
14 Bantry Ter (07461-2617)
PHONE..........................973 875-1990
Carol Healey, *Owner*
David Healey, *Co-Owner*
EMP: 4
SALES (est): 192.6K **Privately Held**
SIC: 2671 Packaging paper & plastics film, coated & laminated

(G-10668)
DEW ASSOCIATES INC
7 Armstrong Rd (07461-3005)
PHONE..........................973 702-0545
Charles Mego, *COO*
EMP: 47
SALES (corp-wide): 7.8MM **Privately Held**
WEB: www.dewassoc.com
SIC: 3577 Computer peripheral equipment
PA: Dew Associates Inc
48 Woodport Rd
Sparta NJ 07871
973 702-0545

(G-10669)
DOLAN ASSOC INC
71 Holland Rd A (07461-2838)
PHONE..........................973 875-6408
Margaret Dolan, *President*
EMP: 5
SALES (est): 728K **Privately Held**
SIC: 3585 Heating & air conditioning combination units

(G-10670)
EASTERN CONCRETE MATERIALS INC
80 Estate Dr 23n (07461)
PHONE..........................973 702-7866
Dave Besaw, *Manager*
EMP: 7
SALES (corp-wide): 1.3B **Publicly Held**
SIC: 1499 Asphalt mining & bituminous stone quarrying
HQ: Eastern Concrete Materials, Inc.
250 Pehle Ave Ste 503
Saddle Brook NJ 07663
201 797-7979

(G-10671)
GLASPLEX LLC
8 Estate Dr (07461-2710)
PHONE..........................973 940-8940
Tiffany D'Angelo, *Office Mgr*
EMP: 6 **EST:** 2013
SALES (est): 415.8K **Privately Held**
SIC: 3089 Air mattresses, plastic

GEOGRAPHIC

(G-10672)
HIGH POINT PRECISION PRODUCTS
1 First St (07461-2509)
PHONE..................................973 875-6229
Fax: 973 875-1116
Charles Stipo, *President*
Marilyn Stipo, *Treasurer*
Marie O'Connor, *Human Resources*
Bill Janos, *Manager*
EMP: 20 EST: 1971
SQ FT: 10,000
SALES (est): 3.7MM **Privately Held**
SIC: 3541 Screw machines, automatic

(G-10673)
INDUSTRIAL PROCESS & EQP INC
Also Called: Ipe
803 State Rt 23 (07461-3333)
P.O. Box 7068 (07461-7068)
PHONE..................................973 702-0330
Fax: 973 702-0669
John Stearns, *President*
EMP: 18
SQ FT: 400
SALES (est): 4.1MM **Privately Held**
SIC: 1711 1796 3444 Process piping contractor; machine moving & rigging; machinery installation; millwright; pipe, sheet metal

(G-10674)
J PAUL ALLEN INC
127 Sally Harden Rd (07461-3831)
P.O. Box 270, Sparta (07871-0270)
PHONE..................................973 702-1174
Jon Baker, *President*
EMP: 4
SALES (est): 246.8K **Privately Held**
SIC: 3546 Drills & drilling tools

(G-10675)
NEW HEAVEN CHEMICALS IOWA LLC
18 Jenny Ln (07461-4550)
PHONE..................................201 506-9109
Ross N Cohen, *Principal*
EMP: 6
SALES (est): 374.5K **Privately Held**
SIC: 2819 Industrial inorganic chemicals

(G-10676)
RS PHILLIPS STEEL LLC
128 Lake Pochung Rd (07461-4127)
PHONE..................................973 827-6464
Fax: 973 827-2323
Joseph Thomas, *General Mgr*
Mark Vanderwerf, *Business Mgr*
Bruce Russell, *Sales Associate*
Neil Phillips, *Mng Member*
Scott Phillips,
EMP: 25
SQ FT: 8,000
SALES: 8.5MM **Privately Held**
SIC: 1791 3441 3449 5051 Structural steel erection; fabricated structural metal; miscellaneous metalwork; metals service centers & offices

(G-10677)
TAMARAS EUROPEAN AMERICAN DELI
13 Essex Rd (07461-1109)
PHONE..................................973 875-5461
Richard Stuckey, *Principal*
EMP: 6
SALES (est): 210K **Privately Held**
SIC: 2099 Food preparations

(G-10678)
TEK MOLDING
1440 County Rd 565 (07461-3135)
P.O. Box 735, Vernon (07462-0735)
PHONE..................................973 702-0450
Tim Tanney, *Owner*
EMP: 6
SALES (est): 448.1K **Privately Held**
SIC: 3089 Molding primary plastic

(G-10679)
TIMPLEX CORP
1370 State Rt 23 (07461-3605)
PHONE..................................973 875-5500
Fax: 973 875-6732

Ronald Slate, *President*
Marilyn Slate, *Corp Secy*
EMP: 18
SQ FT: 18,000
SALES (est): 3.1MM **Privately Held**
SIC: 2439 5211 Structural wood members; lumber & other building materials

(G-10680)
US OUTWORKERS LLC
6 Hunter Ridge Rd (07461-4600)
P.O. Box 453, Glenwood (07418-0453)
PHONE..................................973 362-1458
Ryan Williams,
Robert Quaranta,
▲ EMP: 5
SALES (est): 585.2K **Privately Held**
SIC: 4959 3531 5033 Snowplowing; pavers; roofing, asphalt & sheet metal

---

Swedesboro
Gloucester County

(G-10681)
AMERICAN RENOLIT CORP LA
301 Berkeley Dr B (08085-1255)
PHONE..................................856 241-4901
Fred Breidenbach, *General Mgr*
Pieter De Graaff, *Sales Staff*
EMP: 7
SALES (corp-wide): 1.9B **Privately Held**
SIC: 3081 Vinyl film & sheet
HQ: Solvay Draka, Inc.
6900 Elm St
Commerce CA 90040
323 725-7010

(G-10682)
ARTHUR H THOMAS COMPANY (PA)
Also Called: Thomas Scientific
1654 High Hill Rd (08085-1780)
P.O. Box 99 (08085-6099)
PHONE..................................856 467-2000
Fax: 856 467-3087
Edward B Patterson Jr, *Principal*
Robert D Patterson, *Chairman*
Paul F Seliskar, *COO*
Lee Smith, *COO*
Robin Carroll, *Vice Pres*
◆ EMP: 277 EST: 1900
SQ FT: 140,000
SALES (est): 104.7MM **Privately Held**
SIC: 3821 5049 Laboratory equipment: fume hoods, distillation racks, etc.; scientific & engineering equipment & supplies

(G-10683)
BIOCHEMICAL SCIENCES INC
200 Commodore Dr (08085-1270)
PHONE..................................856 467-1813
Doug Dowd, *General Mgr*
EMP: 4
SALES (est): 296.1K **Privately Held**
SIC: 2819 Industrial inorganic chemicals

(G-10684)
BOEING COMPANY
800 Arlington Blvd (08085-2502)
PHONE..................................610 591-1978
EMP: 996
SALES (corp-wide): 93.3B **Publicly Held**
SIC: 3721 Airplanes, fixed or rotary wing
PA: The Boeing Company
100 N Riverside Plz
Chicago IL 60606
312 544-2000

(G-10685)
BRASSCRAFT MANUFACTURING CO
Cobra Products
1 Warner Ct (08085-1743)
PHONE..................................856 241-7700
Paul Sanderson, *CEO*
EMP: 6
SALES (corp-wide): 7.6B **Publicly Held**
SIC: 3423 2842 Hand & edge tools; drain pipe solvents or cleaners
HQ: Brasscraft Manufacturing Company
39600 Orchard Hill Pl
Novi MI 48375
248 305-6000

(G-10686)
CADDY CORPORATION OF AMERICA
509 Sharptown Rd (08085-3163)
P.O. Box 345, Bridgeport (08014-0345)
PHONE..................................856 467-4222
Fax: 856 467-5511
Craig Cohen, *CEO*
Harry Schmidt, *President*
Dave Euler, *Engineer*
EMP: 52
SQ FT: 71,000
SALES (est): 16.6MM **Privately Held**
WEB: www.caddycorp.com
SIC: 3556 Food products machinery

(G-10687)
CENTRAL INK CORPORATION
2085 Center Square Rd A (08085-1790)
PHONE..................................856 467-5562
Stephen Corson, *Branch Mgr*
Bruce Gill, *Manager*
EMP: 9
SALES (corp-wide): 34.4MM **Privately Held**
WEB: www.cicink.com
SIC: 2893 Letterpress or offset ink
PA: Central Ink Corporation
1100 Harvester Rd
West Chicago IL 60185
630 231-6500

(G-10688)
COBRA PRODUCTS INC
Also Called: Speedway
1 Warner Ct (08085-1743)
PHONE..................................856 241-7700
Don Woody, *President*
▲ EMP: 77
SQ FT: 175,000
SALES (est): 12.7MM
SALES (corp-wide): 7.6B **Publicly Held**
WEB: www.cobraus.com
SIC: 1711 2842 Plumbing contractors; drain pipe solvents or cleaners
PA: Masco Corporation
17450 College Pkwy
Livonia MI 48152
313 274-7400

(G-10689)
DAIMLER TRUCKS NORTH AMER LLC
Also Called: Bridgeport Parts Dist Ctr
1140 Commerce Blvd (08085-1772)
PHONE..................................856 467-6000
Susan Garozzo, *Human Res Mgr*
Millie Perez, *Human Res Mgr*
EMP: 9
SALES (corp-wide): 193.7B **Privately Held**
SIC: 3711 Truck tractors for highway use, assembly of
HQ: Daimler Trucks North America Llc
4555 N Channel Ave
Portland OR 97217
503 745-8000

(G-10690)
DAMASK KANDIES
Also Called: Damask Candies
2255 Route 322 (08085-3633)
PHONE..................................856 467-1661
Douglas Damask, *Owner*
EMP: 6
SALES (est): 445.4K **Privately Held**
SIC: 2064 5145 5441 Candy & other confectionery products; candy; candy

(G-10691)
DESIGN ASSISTANCE CORPORATION
3 Killdeer Ct Ste 301 (08085-1753)
P.O. Box 215 (08085-0215)
PHONE..................................856 241-9500
Fax: 856 241-9545
Glenn Woerner, *President*
John Clements, *Division Mgr*
Mary Phelps, *Mfg Mgr*
Kristina Bateman, *Sales Staff*
Harold Sheppard, *Sales Staff*
▼ EMP: 16
SALES (est): 3.6MM **Privately Held**
WEB: www.dac-3d.com
SIC: 3699 Electronic training devices

(G-10692)
DIGITAL PRODUCTIONS INC
100 Berkeley Dr (08085-9710)
PHONE..................................856 224-1111
Fax: 856 848-9255
Charles Budd, *President*
Ron Bruno, *Vice Pres*
Juli Gioia, *Director*
EMP: 12
SALES (est): 3.3MM **Privately Held**
SIC: 2752 Commercial printing, lithographic

(G-10693)
DIVERSIFIED FOAM PRODUCTS INC
Also Called: Diversified Industries
121 High Hill Rd (08085-1777)
PHONE..................................856 662-1981
David Hoyt, *CEO*
Matthew Harris, *CEO*
Bruce Castor, *President*
Edward Janes, *Vice Pres*
Craig Kene, *Vice Pres*
◆ EMP: 60
SQ FT: 105,000
SALES (est): 24.5MM **Privately Held**
WEB: www.diversifiedindustries.com
SIC: 3069 Foam rubber

(G-10694)
DR SCHAR USA INC
305 Heron Dr (08085-1773)
PHONE..................................856 803-5100
Martin Ziegler, *Manager*
EMP: 35
SALES (corp-wide): 181.3MM **Privately Held**
SIC: 2051 Bakery: wholesale or wholesale/retail combined
HQ: Dr. Schar Usa, Inc.
125 Chubb Ave Ste 1a
Lyndhurst NJ 07071

(G-10695)
EAGLEBURGMANN INDUSTRIES LP
614 Heron Dr Ste 8 (08085-1846)
PHONE..................................856 241-7300
Fax: 856 241-0033
Patrick McCann, *General Mgr*
EMP: 10
SALES (corp-wide): 8.3B **Privately Held**
SIC: 3053 Gaskets, packing & sealing devices
HQ: Eagleburgmann Industries Lp
10035 Brookriver Dr
Houston TX 77040
713 939-9515

(G-10696)
ETHYLENE ATLANTIC CORP
136 Church St (08085-1123)
P.O. Box 1273, Kitty Hawk NC (27949-1273)
PHONE..................................856 467-0010
Fax: 856 467-0610
Michael P Johnston, *President*
James Monaghan, *Corp Secy*
Barbara Johnston, *Vice Pres*
EMP: 25
SQ FT: 7,200
SALES (est): 2.6MM **Privately Held**
WEB: www.ethyleneatlantic.com
SIC: 3599 Machine shop, jobbing & repair

(G-10697)
FIOPLEX
49 Fredrick Blvd (08085-4245)
PHONE..................................856 689-7213
Ronald Guittar, *President*
EMP: 4
SALES (est): 207K **Privately Held**
SIC: 3993 7389 Signs & advertising specialties

(G-10698)
GEORGE H BUCHANAN COMPANY
Also Called: George H Buchanan Printing
2 Mallard Ct (08085-1727)
P.O. Box 788 (08085-0788)
PHONE..................................856 241-3960
Carl J Zweigle III, *President*
Gregory R Zweigle, *Treasurer*

▲ **EMP: 22 EST:** 1886
SQ FT: 40,000
SALES (corp-wide): 4.1MM **Privately Held**
WEB: www.ghbuchanan.com
SIC: 2752 Commercial printing, offset

(G-10699)
GINSEY INDUSTRIES INC
2078 Center Square Rd (08085-1703)
PHONE.................................856 933-1300
Fax: 856 933-2342
Herbert Briggs, *CEO*
George Valletti, *CFO*
▲ **EMP:** 75
SQ FT: 150,000
SALES (est): 24MM **Privately Held**
WEB: www.ginsey.com
SIC: 3261 Bathroom accessories/fittings,
vitreous china or earthenware

(G-10700)
GREAT NORTHERN CORPORATION
500a Pedricktown Rd (08085-1729)
PHONE.................................856 241-0080
Mark Van, *Vice Pres*
Phil Brooks, *Manager*
Daniel Snyder, *Maintence Staff*
EMP: 8
SALES (corp-wide): 392.5MM **Privately
Held**
SIC: 2653 Boxes, corrugated: made from
purchased materials
PA: Great Northern Corporation
395 Stroebe Rd
Appleton WI 54914
920 739-3671

(G-10701)
HEINKEL FILTERING SYSTEMS INC
520 Sharptown Rd (08085-3161)
PHONE.................................856 467-3399
Fax: 856 467-1010
Allen Ferraro, *President*
Eckenroad Gary, *Vice Pres*
Dave Altum, *Engineer*
Sam An, *Project Engr*
Josephine Hubbs, *Controller*
▲ **EMP:** 10
SQ FT: 20,000
SALES (est): 2.7MM **Privately Held**
WEB: www.heinkelusa.com
SIC: 3569 Centrifuges, industrial
HQ: Heinkel Process Technology Gmbh
Ferdinand-Porsche-Str. 8
Besigheim
714 396-920

(G-10702)
HERITAGE BAG COMPANY
2123 High Hill Rd (08085)
PHONE.................................856 467-2247
Fax: 856 467-5591
Carl Allen, *President*
Donna Hubbard, *Vice Pres*
Gary Pennington, *Executive*
Bob Seidl, *Executive*
EMP: 70
SQ FT: 50,000
SALES (corp-wide): 2.9B **Privately Held**
WEB: www.heritage-bag.com
SIC: 2673 3081 Plastic bags: made from
purchased materials; unsupported plas-
tics film & sheet
HQ: Heritage Bag Company
501 Gateway Pkwy
Roanoke TX 76262
972 241-5525

(G-10703)
INTRA PAC SWEDESBORO (HQ)
20 Ashton Ave (08085-1117)
PHONE.................................856 467-0485
Dick Derosa, *Vice Pres*
Robert Blankenheim, *Vice Pres*
Thelma Collins, *Director*
◆ **EMP:** 80
SQ FT: 40,000
SALES (est): 5.6MM
SALES (corp-wide): 282.7MM **Privately
Held**
SIC: 3312 2821 Pipes & tubes; plastics
materials & resins

(G-10704)
KENRIC INC
110 Richardson Ave (08085-1149)
P.O. Box 203 (08085-0203)
PHONE.................................856 294-9161
Kennard J Sharr, *President*
Lisa M Scharr, *Admin Sec*
EMP: 5
SQ FT: 10,000
SALES (est): 1.8MM **Privately Held**
SIC: 3449 Bars, concrete reinforcing: fabri-
cated steel

(G-10705)
L & L KILN MFG INC
505 Sharptown Rd (08085-3163)
P.O. Box 1898, Boothwyn PA (19061-7898)
PHONE.................................856 294-0077
Stephen J Lewicki, *President*
Gregory D Lewicki, *Vice Pres*
◆ **EMP:** 20 **EST:** 1945
SQ FT: 28,000
SALES (est): 5MM **Privately Held**
WEB: www.hotkilns.com
SIC: 3567 Industrial furnaces & ovens

(G-10706)
LEWIS-GOETZ AND COMPANY INC
Also Called: Philadelphia Division
1 Killdeer Ct Ste 4 (08085-1845)
PHONE.................................856 579-1421
Fax: 856 579-1429
Rick Keller, *Branch Mgr*
EMP: 14 **Privately Held**
WEB: www.lewis-goetz.com
SIC: 3052 Air line or air brake hose, rubber
or rubberized fabric
HQ: Eriks North America, Inc.
650 Washington Rd Ste 500
Pittsburgh PA 15228
800 937-9070

(G-10707)
MAPEI CORPORATION
2155 High Hill Rd (08085-4529)
PHONE.................................732 254-4830
Fax: 732 254-2693
Eddie Dilaurenzio, *Branch Mgr*
EMP: 40 **Privately Held**
SIC: 3531 2899 2891 Concrete grouting
equipment; chemical preparations; adhe-
sives & sealants
HQ: Mapei Corporation
1144 E Newport Center Dr
Deerfield Beach FL 33442
954 246-8888

(G-10708)
MAPEI CORPORATION
2155 High Hill Rd (08085-4529)
PHONE.................................732 254-4830
John Zimmerman, *Branch Mgr*
EMP: 12 **Privately Held**
SIC: 2891 Adhesives & sealants
HQ: Mapei Corporation
1144 E Newport Center Dr
Deerfield Beach FL 33442
954 246-8888

(G-10709)
MATTHIAS PAPER CORPORATION (PA)
301 Arlington Blvd (08085-1370)
P.O. Box 130 (08085-0130)
PHONE.................................856 467-6970
Fax: 856 467-6991
John R Matthias, *CEO*
Mark Sekel, *General Mgr*
Warren E Storck, *Vice Pres*
Michael D'Alessandro, *Opers Mgr*
John R Matthias Jr, *Admin Sec*
◆ **EMP:** 28 **EST:** 1915
SQ FT: 46,000
SALES (est): 25.1MM **Privately Held**
WEB: www.matthiaspaper.com
SIC: 5113 2679 Paper & products, wrap-
ping or coarse; paper products, converted

(G-10710)
MEDTRONIC INC
1130 Commerce Blvd # 100 (08085-1439)
PHONE.................................908 289-5969
Tim Ward, *District Mgr*
EMP: 173 **Privately Held**

SIC: 3845 Electromedical equipment
HQ: Medtronic, Inc.
710 Medtronic Pkwy
Minneapolis MN 55432
763 514-4000

(G-10711)
MISSA BAY CITRUS COMPANY
101 Arlington Blvd (08085-1265)
PHONE.................................856 241-0900
Fax: 856 241-0020
Frank C Pollera, *President*
EMP: 19
SALES (est): 2.9MM **Privately Held**
SIC: 2099 Food preparations

(G-10712)
MISSA BAY LLC (DH)
101 Arlington Blvd (08085-1265)
PHONE.................................856 241-0900
Frank C Pollera, *President*
Dennis Gertmenian,
Salvatore Tedesco,
▲ **EMP:** 51
SQ FT: 96,000
SALES (est): 39.1MM **Privately Held**
WEB: www.missabay.com
SIC: 2099 5142 Food preparations; pack-
aged frozen goods
HQ: Ready Pac Foods, Inc.
4401 Foxdale St
Irwindale CA 91706
626 856-8686

(G-10713)
MULTI-PLASTICS INC
210 Commodore Dr (08085-1292)
PHONE.................................856 241-9014
Fax: 856 241-1904
Mike Budd, *COO*
Robert Parsio, *Branch Mgr*
Mark Hess, *Manager*
EMP: 30
SALES (corp-wide): 220MM **Privately
Held**
WEB: www.multi-plastics.com
SIC: 5162 3089 Plastics materials; plastic
processing
PA: Multi-Plastics, Inc.
7770 N Central Dr
Lewis Center OH 43035
740 548-4894

(G-10714)
NEW ENGLAND WOOD CRAFTERS
226 Spruce Trl (08085-4008)
PHONE.................................856 241-9270
Robert Faulkner, *Principal*
EMP: 5
SALES (est): 188.8K **Privately Held**
SIC: 2491 Wood products, creosoted

(G-10715)
NP BIO FUELS LLC
18 Reisling Pl (08085-1313)
PHONE.................................856 467-2273
Adam Paolino, *Principal*
EMP: 4
SALES (est): 217K **Privately Held**
SIC: 2869 Fuels

(G-10716)
OMEGA ENGINEERING INC
1 Killdeer Ct (08085-1845)
PHONE.................................856 467-4200
Jim Ferguson, *President*
EMP: 14
SALES (corp-wide): 2B **Privately Held**
SIC: 3823 Industrial instrmnts msrmnt dis-
play/control process variable
HQ: Omega Engineering, Inc.
800 Connecticut Ave 5n01
Norwalk CT 06854
203 359-1660

(G-10717)
PENNSYLVANIA MACHINE WORKS INC
U S Drop Forge Division
Rr 551 (08085)
P.O. Box 131 (08085-0131)
PHONE.................................856 467-0500
Fax: 856 467-4598
Charles J Lafferty, *Manager*
EMP: 50

SALES (corp-wide): 37.6MM Privately
Held
SIC: 3462 3494 Iron & steel forgings; pipe
fittings
PA: Pennsylvania Machine Works, Inc.
201 Bethel Ave
Upper Chichester PA 19014
610 497-3300

(G-10718)
PHARMA SYNERGY LLC
103 Somerfield Rd (08085-2505)
PHONE.................................856 241-2316
Antonio J Petillo, *Principal*
EMP: 4
SALES (est): 239.1K **Privately Held**
SIC: 2834 Pharmaceutical preparations

(G-10719)
POLYMER ADDITIVES INC
Also Called: Valtris Specialty Chemicals
170 Us 130 (08085)
PHONE.................................856 467-8220
Bob Natan, *Plant Mgr*
EMP: 80
SALES (corp-wide): 271.6MM **Privately
Held**
SIC: 2899 Chemical preparations; fire re-
tardant chemicals
HQ: Polymer Additives, Inc.
7500 E Pleasant Valley Rd
Independence OH 44131
216 875-7200

(G-10720)
PRECISE TECHNOLOGY INC
406 Heron Dr Ste A (08085-1755)
PHONE.................................856 241-1760
Fax: 856 241-1740
William Finkley, *Branch Mgr*
EMP: 42 **Privately Held**
SIC: 3089 Injection molding of plastics
HQ: Rexam Limited
4 Millbank
London SW1P
158 240-8999

(G-10721)
RADIO SYSTEMS DESIGN INC
601 Heron Dr (08085-1741)
PHONE.................................856 467-8000
Daniel J Braverman, *President*
Gerrett Conover, *CFO*
Dennis Greben, *Treasurer*
EMP: 23
SQ FT: 13,000
SALES: 2.4MM **Privately Held**
SIC: 3663 Radio & TV communications
equipment

(G-10722)
RAJYSAN INCORPORATED
3 Hawk Ct (08085-1724)
PHONE.................................800 433-1382
EMP: 23
SALES (corp-wide): 49.5MM **Privately
Held**
SIC: 5084 5082 3621 Whol Industrial
Equipment Whol Construction/Mining
Equipment Mfg Motors/Generators
PA: Rajysan, Incorporated
4175 Guardian St
Simi Valley CA 93063
661 775-4920

(G-10723)
RAMSEY CHARLES COMPANY
617 Heron Dr (08085-1741)
PHONE.................................845 338-1464
Fax: 845 338-5751
▲ **EMP:** 12
SQ FT: 12,000
SALES: 1.5MM **Privately Held**
SIC: 3441 Metal Fabrication

(G-10724)
RASTELLI BROTHERS INC (PA)
Also Called: Rastelli's Foods
300 Heron Dr (08085-1707)
PHONE.................................856 803-1100
Fax: 856 803-1115
Ray Rastelli, *President*
Fabio Capone, *General Mgr*
Anthony Rastelli, *Exec VP*
Patrick Ternyila, *Vice Pres*
Joseph Cangemi, *Facilities Mgr*

▼ **EMP:** 75
SQ FT: 40,000
SALES (est): 117MM **Privately Held**
WEB: www.rastellis.com
SIC: 5147 5421 2011 Meats, fresh; meat markets, including freezer provisioners; canned meats (except baby food), meat slaughtered on site

(G-10725)
RASTELLI FOODS GROUP INC
300 Heron Dr (08085-1707)
PHONE..................856 803-1100
Ray Rastelli III, *President*
Paul Zaun, *CFO*
Mark Broccoli, *Director*
▲ **EMP:** 11
SALES (est): 5.4MM **Privately Held**
SIC: 5147 5421 2011 Meats, fresh; meat markets, including freezer provisioners; canned meats (except baby food), meat slaughtered on site

(G-10726)
READY PAC FODS - SWEDESBORO NJ
101 Arlington Blvd (08085-1265)
PHONE..................609 360-0953
EMP: 10
SALES (est): 1.3MM **Privately Held**
SIC: 2099 Food preparations

(G-10727)
SAVITA NATURALS LTD
617 Heron Dr (08085-1741)
PHONE..................856 467-4949
Richard Trout, *President*
Michael Trout, *Opers Staff*
Joe Roy, *Executive*
EMP: 20 **EST:** 1997
SQ FT: 380,000
SALES (est): 1.3MM **Privately Held**
SIC: 2066 Chocolate & cocoa products

(G-10728)
STANDARD INDUSTRIES INC
700 2nd St Ste C&D (08085-1138)
PHONE..................856 241-0241
EMP: 119
SALES (corp-wide): 1.5B **Privately Held**
SIC: 2493 Insulation & roofing material, reconstituted wood
HQ: Standard Industries Inc.
1 Campus Dr
Parsippany NJ 07054

(G-10729)
STECHER DAVE WELDING & FABG SP
1040 Township Line Rd (08085-1786)
PHONE..................856 467-3558
Dave Stecher, *Owner*
EMP: 5
SQ FT: 4,000
SALES (est): 393.1K **Privately Held**
SIC: 7692 Welding repair

(G-10730)
STERIGENICS US LLC
303 Heron Dr (08085-1773)
PHONE..................856 241-8880
Shaun Baburam, *Branch Mgr*
EMP: 9
SALES (corp-wide): 699.9MM **Privately Held**
SIC: 2842 Disinfectants, household or industrial plant
HQ: Sterigenics U.S., Llc
2015 Spring Rd Ste 650
Oak Brook IL 60523
630 928-1700

(G-10731)
SUPERIOR MARINE CANVAS
75 Belfiore Dr (08085-3613)
PHONE..................856 241-1724
Brian Reed, *Owner*
EMP: 5
SALES (est): 257.8K **Privately Held**
WEB: www.superiorcanvas.com
SIC: 2394 Canvas & related products

(G-10732)
TAYLOR FARMS NEW JERSEY INC
406 Heron Dr Ste A (08085-1755)
PHONE..................856 241-0097
Bruce Taylor, *CEO*
Dana Coughlin, *Production*
Marie Butler, *QA Dir*
Ilya Sidorochev, *Project Engr*
Tom Bryan, *CFO*
◆ **EMP:** 28
SALES (est): 12.2MM **Privately Held**
SIC: 2099 Food preparations
PA: Taylor Fresh Foods, Inc
150 Main St Ste 400
Salinas CA 93901

(G-10733)
THOMAS SCIENTIFIC INC
1654 High Hill Rd (08085-1780)
P.O. Box 99 (08085-6099)
PHONE..................800 345-2100
Richard Drew, *President*
Edward B Patterson Jr, *Principal*
Robert D Patterson, *Chairman*
Paul F Seliskar, *COO*
Craig D Kingery, *CFO*
EMP: 300
SQ FT: 140,000
SALES (est): 22.6MM
SALES (corp-wide): 104.7MM **Privately Held**
SIC: 5049 3821 Scientific & engineering equipment & supplies; laboratory equipment: fume hoods, distillation racks, etc.
PA: Arthur H Thomas Company
1654 High Hill Rd
Swedesboro NJ 08085
856 467-2000

(G-10734)
THOMAS SCIENTIFIC LLC (HQ)
1654 High Hill Rd (08085-1780)
PHONE..................800 345-2100
Charles Simmons, *CEO*
Robin Carroll, *Vice Pres*
Kevin Lannan, *CFO*
Elizabeth Nolan, *Human Res Dir*
Noelle Albertson, *Accounts Mgr*
EMP: 2
SQ FT: 200,000
SALES: 100MM
SALES (corp-wide): 3.6B **Publicly Held**
SIC: 5049 3821 Scientific & engineering equipment & supplies; laboratory equipment: fume hoods, distillation racks, etc.
PA: The Carlyle Group L P
1001 Pennsylvania Ave Nw 220s
Washington DC 20004
202 729-5626

(G-10735)
UNIVEG LOGISTICS AMERICA INC
100 Dartmouth Dr Ste 400 (08085-2008)
PHONE..................856 241-0097
Mayda Sotomayer, *President*
Vitor Figuiredo, *CFO*
Cordlee Penebad, *Admin Sec*
EMP: 9
SALES (est): 1.1MM **Privately Held**
SIC: 3086 Packaging & shipping materials, foamed plastic

(G-10736)
WAGONHOUSE WINERY LLC
1401 State Highway 45 (08085-1657)
PHONE..................609 780-8019
Wagonhouse Winery, *Principal*
EMP: 5
SALES (est): 679.2K **Privately Held**
SIC: 2084 Wines

Tabernacle
Burlington County

(G-10737)
CONTE FARMS
299 Flyatt Rd (08088-9307)
PHONE..................609 268-0513
Fax: 609 268-8048
Joseph Conte Jr, *Owner*
EMP: 12

SALES (est): 794.8K **Privately Held**
WEB: www.contefarms.com
SIC: 0161 0175 2051 Vegetables & melons; deciduous tree fruits; bread, cake & related products

(G-10738)
JASCO SPECIALTIES AND FORMS
Also Called: Jasco Printing
86 Patty Bowker Rd (08088-9363)
PHONE..................856 627-5511
EMP: 7
SALES (est): 700K **Privately Held**
SIC: 7336 2752 Commercial Art/Graphic Design Lithographic Commercial Printing

(G-10739)
WATER RESOURCES NEW JERSEY LLC
Also Called: Water Resources of New Jersey
1609 Route 206 (08088-8837)
P.O. Box 2172, Vincentown (08088-2172)
PHONE..................609 268-7965
Craig Cocco, *Mng Member*
Chris Cocco, *Manager*
EMP: 5
SALES (est): 500K **Privately Held**
WEB: www.waterresourcesnj.com
SIC: 3589 Sewage & water treatment equipment; water treatment equipment, industrial

Teaneck
Bergen County

(G-10740)
ADVANCING OPPORTUNITIES INC
Also Called: United Crbral Plsy Bldg Blocks
639 Teaneck Rd (07666-4258)
PHONE..................201 907-0200
Fax: 201 907-0400
Lisa Camberery, *Branch Mgr*
EMP: 8
SALES (corp-wide): 11.6MM **Privately Held**
WEB: www.cpofnj.com
SIC: 3577 Computer peripheral equipment
PA: Advancing Opportunities, Inc.
1005 Whitehead Road Ext 1a
Ewing NJ 08638
609 882-4182

(G-10741)
AETREX WORLDWIDE INC (PA)
414 Alfred Ave (07666-5756)
PHONE..................201 833-2700
Fax: 201 833-1485
Larry Schwartz, *CEO*
Dan Grskovic, *President*
Evan Schwartz, *President*
Richard B Schwartz, *Chairman*
Matthew Schwartz, *Exec VP*
▲ **EMP:** 136
SQ FT: 72,000
SALES (est): 25.8MM **Privately Held**
WEB: www.apexfoot.com
SIC: 3842 Foot appliances, orthopedic

(G-10742)
ASSOCIATED CLEANING SYSTEMS
569 Oritani Pl (07666-1664)
PHONE..................201 530-9197
Elizio Portes, *President*
Lourdes Mendoza-Portes, *Vice Pres*
EMP: 8
SALES: 400K **Privately Held**
SIC: 7699 2842 Cleaning services; specialty cleaning preparations

(G-10743)
AVACYN PHARMACEUTICALS INC
719 Downing St (07666-2220)
PHONE..................201 836-2599
Allan Goldberg, *President*
EMP: 6
SALES (est): 344.2K **Privately Held**
SIC: 2834 Pharmaceutical preparations

(G-10744)
BETTER LISTEN LLC
492c Cedar Ln (07666-1713)
PHONE..................917 623-9834
Steve Stein,
EMP: 8
SALES: 250K **Privately Held**
SIC: 2741 7389 Miscellaneous publishing;

(G-10745)
CIRCULITE INC
500 F W Burr Blvd Ste 40 (07666)
PHONE..................201 478-7575
Eric Rose, *Ch of Bd*
Paul Southworth, *President*
Peter Pfreundschuh, *CFO*
EMP: 13
SALES (est): 1.3MM **Privately Held**
WEB: www.circulite.net
SIC: 3845 Electromedical equipment
HQ: Heartware International, Inc.
500 Old Connecticut Path
Framingham MA 01701

(G-10746)
COGNIZANT TECH SOLUTIONS CORP (PA)
500 Frank W Burr Blvd (07666-6804)
PHONE..................201 801-0233
Francisco D'Souza, *CEO*
Michael Patsalos-Fox, *Ch of Bd*
Debashis Chatterjee, *President*
Ramakrishna Prasad Chintamanen, *President*
Sumithra Gomatam, *President*
EMP: 80
SQ FT: 100,000
SALES: 14.8B **Publicly Held**
WEB: www.cognizant.com
SIC: 7371 7379 7372 Computer software development & applications; computer related consulting services; business oriented computer software

(G-10747)
DBC INC
Also Called: Photoscribe
300 Frank W Burr Blvd # 56 (07666-6704)
PHONE..................212 819-1177
David Benderly, *President*
Carroll Dounn, *Vice Pres*
EMP: 60
SQ FT: 20,000
SALES (est): 7.8MM **Privately Held**
WEB: www.photoscribe.com
SIC: 3911 5944 Jewelry, precious metal; jewelry stores

(G-10748)
DIAGNOSTIX PLUS INC
811 Queen Anne Rd (07666-4643)
PHONE..................201 530-5505
Fax: 201 608-4556
Donald Bogustski, *President*
▲ **EMP:** 8
SQ FT: 500
SALES: 2MM **Privately Held**
WEB: www.diagplus.com
SIC: 5047 3841 Medical equipment & supplies; diagnostic apparatus, medical

(G-10749)
DISCOUNT PACKAGING CORPORATION
200 Chadwick Rd (07666-4252)
PHONE..................201 836-0521
Howard Alt, *President*
Nina Gonzalez, *Manager*
EMP: 30
SQ FT: 40,000
SALES (est): 3.9MM **Privately Held**
SIC: 2655 Fiber cans, drums & similar products

(G-10750)
DUNKIN DONUTS BASKIN ROBBINS
Also Called: Baskin-Robbins
332 Cedar Ln (07666-3418)
PHONE..................201 692-1900
Mahdi Naeb, *General Mgr*
EMP: 4
SALES (est): 264.9K **Privately Held**
SIC: 2024 5461 5812 Ice cream, bulk; bakeries; ice cream stands or dairy bars

(G-10751)
DYNA-SEA GROUP INC
765 Carroll Pl (07666-3303)
PHONE....................................201 928-0133
Daniel Berlin, *President*
▲ EMP: 6
SALES (est): 947.7K **Privately Held**
WEB: www.dyna-disk.com
SIC: 2099 Food preparations

(G-10752)
EMBROIDERIES UNLIMITED INC
532 Wyndham Rd (07666-2612)
PHONE....................................201 692-1560
Bruce Prince, *President*
EMP: 7
SQ FT: 3,500
SALES: 950K **Privately Held**
SIC: 2395 Embroidery products, except
schiffli machine

(G-10753)
EVANS CHEMETICS LP (PA)
Glenpointe Center West 4 (07666)
PHONE....................................201 992-3100
Jelle Westra, *CEO*
Detlaf Schmidt, *General Ptnr*
Anthony Moschetti, *CFO*
▲ EMP: 68
SQ FT: 2,500
SALES: 29.7MM **Privately Held**
WEB: www.evanschemetics.com
SIC: 2899 Acids

(G-10754)
GENESIS MARKETING GROUP INC
269 Edgemont Ter (07666-3405)
PHONE....................................201 836-1392
William Straus, *President*
EMP: 5
SQ FT: 1,800
SALES (est): 450K **Privately Held**
WEB: www.genesismkting.com
SIC: 3993 5199 8742 Signs & advertising
specialties; advertising specialties; incen-
tive or award program consultant

(G-10755)
GREENER CORNERS LTD LBLTY CO
1178 W Laurelton Pkwy (07666-2749)
PHONE....................................201 638-2218
Aaron Klein, *Principal*
EMP: 5 EST: 2009
SALES (est): 376.9K **Privately Held**
SIC: 2833 Botanical products, medicinal;
ground, graded or milled

(G-10756)
H LAUZON FURNITURE CO INC
1098 Decatur Ave (07666-5709)
PHONE....................................201 837-7598
Francis Lauzon, *President*
Kenneth V Lauzon, *Corp Secy*
EMP: 12 EST: 1935
SQ FT: 12,500
SALES: 500K **Privately Held**
SIC: 2512 7641 5712 Chairs: upholstered
on wood frames; couches, sofas & daven-
ports: upholstered on wood frames; living
room furniture: upholstered on wood
frames; reupholstery; furniture stores

(G-10757)
JA HEILFERTY LLC
Also Called: Primepak Company
133 Cedar Ln (07666-4416)
PHONE....................................201 836-5060
Fax: 201 836-3275
John Verrier, *Partner*
William G Poppe Jr, *Principal*
William Poppe Jr, *Principal*
Christopher J Poppe, *COO*
EMP: 31
SQ FT: 2,000
SALES: 36MM **Privately Held**
WEB: www.primepakcompany.com
SIC: 5162 3081 Plastics products; unsup-
ported plastics film & sheet

(G-10758)
JEWISH STANDARD INC
Also Called: Jewish Media Group
1086 Teaneck Rd Ste 2f (07666-4839)
PHONE....................................201 837-8818
Fax: 201 833-4959
James Janoff, *Publisher*
Peggy Elias, *Accounts Exec*
Brenda Sutcliffe, *Accounts Exec*
Jane Carr, *Advt Staff*
Larry Yudelson, *Assoc Editor*
EMP: 15
SALES (est): 842.8K **Privately Held**
SIC: 2711 Newspapers, publishing & print-
ing

(G-10759)
LA MART MANUFACTURING CORP
Also Called: Lamart Manufacturing Co
1465 Palisade Ave (07666-3624)
PHONE....................................718 384-6917
Louis Spitzer, *President*
▲ EMP: 8 EST: 1989
SQ FT: 3,000
SALES (est): 1.5MM **Privately Held**
WEB: www.coverus.com
SIC: 3083 Plastic finished products, lami-
nated

(G-10760)
LEEWARD INTERNATIONAL INC
400 Frank W Burr Blvd # 68 (07666-6841)
PHONE....................................201 836-8830
Byungkuk Lee, *Ch of Bd*
▲ EMP: 11
SQ FT: 5,100
SALES: 7.5MM **Privately Held**
WEB: www.leewardinc.com
SIC: 5137 2339 2329 2369 Sportswear,
women's & children's; nightwear:
women's, children's & infants'; sports-
wear, women's; men's & boys' sportswear
& athletic clothing; bathing suits &
swimwear: girls', children's & infants'

(G-10761)
LUST FOR LIFE FOOTWEAR LLC
1086 Teaneck Rd Ste 3d (07666-4858)
PHONE....................................631 327-2811
Steven Berend,
David Berend,
Karen Berend,
▲ EMP: 10
SQ FT: 2,500
SALES (est): 802.4K **Privately Held**
SIC: 3021 5139 Protective footwear, rub-
ber or plastic; footwear

(G-10762)
NIPPON PAINT (USA) INC (HQ)
Also Called: Nippon Paint America
300 Frank W Burr Blvd # 10 (07666-6726)
PHONE....................................201 692-1111
Fax: 201 692-0555
Hiroaki Ueno, *CEO*
Hidefumi Morita, *President*
Joan P Daniels, *CFO*
▲ EMP: 10
SALES (est): 202.7MM
SALES (corp-wide): 5.4B **Privately Held**
SIC: 2851 Paints & allied products
PA: Nippon Paint Holdings Co., Ltd.
2-1-2, Oyodokita, Kita-Ku
Osaka OSK 531-0
664 581-111

(G-10763)
NITTO AMERICAS INC
300 Frank W Burr Blvd (07666-6704)
PHONE....................................201 645-4950
Fax: 201 645-4951
Keiko Iwabuchi, *Manager*
Yumiko Nagahama, *Manager*
EMP: 16
SALES (corp-wide): 8B **Privately Held**
SIC: 2672 3589 5162 5065 Tape, pres-
sure sensitive: made from purchased ma-
terials; water treatment equipment,
industrial; plastics products; electronic
parts

HQ: Nitto Americas, Inc.
48500 Fremont Blvd
Fremont CA 94538
510 445-5400

(G-10764)
OCTAL CORPORATION
125 Galway Pl Ste B (07666-3633)
PHONE....................................201 862-1010
Dani Bar David, *President*
Danielle Nir, *Project Mgr*
Zvi Davidzon, *Opers Mgr*
Tony Dimitrov, *Engineer*
▲ EMP: 24
SQ FT: 1,500
SALES (est): 5.6MM **Privately Held**
WEB: www.octalcorporation.com
SIC: 3824 Mechanical & electromechanical
counters & devices

(G-10765)
PHIBRO ANIMAL HEALTH CORP (HQ)
300 Frank W Burr Blvd (07666-6704)
PHONE....................................201 329-7300
Fax: 201 329-7070
Jack C Bendheim, *Ch of Bd*
Dean J Warras, *President*
Larry L Miller, *COO*
Daniel M Bendheim, *Exec VP*
Thomas G Dagger, *Senior VP*
◆ EMP: 90 EST: 1946
SALES: 764.2MM **Publicly Held**
WEB: www.pahc.com
SIC: 2834 Veterinary pharmaceutical
preparations
PA: Bfi Co., Llc
300 Frank W Burr Blvd # 21
Teaneck NJ 07666
201 329-7300

(G-10766)
PHIBRO ANMAL HLTH HOLDINGS INC (PA)
300 Frank W Burr Blvd (07666-6704)
PHONE....................................201 329-7300
Larry Miller, *President*
Jennifer Cohen, *Manager*
EMP: 4
SALES (est): 2.2MM **Privately Held**
SIC: 2047 5191 Dog & cat food; animal
feeds

(G-10767)
PHIBRO-TECH INC (DH)
Also Called: Phibro Animal Health Holdings
300 Frank W Burr Blvd # 21 (07666-6704)
PHONE....................................201 329-7300
Fax: 201 329-7034
Jack C Bendheim, *Ch of Bd*
W Dwight Glover, *President*
Gerald Carlson, *COO*
Daniel Welch, *Senior VP*
Richard Johnson, *CFO*
▲ EMP: 25
SQ FT: 23,000
SALES (est): 17.5MM
SALES (corp-wide): 764.2MM **Publicly Held**
WEB: www.phibrochem.com
SIC: 2819 4953 Industrial inorganic chem-
icals; nickel compounds or salts, inor-
ganic; copper compounds or salts,
inorganic; chemical detoxification
HQ: C P Chemicals, Inc.
65 Challenger Rd
Ridgefield Park NJ
201 329-7300

(G-10768)
PHIBROCHEM INC
300 Frank W Burr Blvd # 21 (07666-6704)
PHONE....................................201 329-7300
Jack Bendheim, *President*
Gerald Carlson, *COO*
David Storbeck, *Vice Pres*
Daniel Welch, *Vice Pres*
Richard Johnson, *CFO*
▲ EMP: 5
SALES (est): 216.1K
SALES (corp-wide): 764.2MM **Publicly Held**
SIC: 2819 Industrial inorganic chemicals

HQ: Phibro Animal Health Corporation
300 Frank W Burr Blvd
Teaneck NJ 07666
201 329-7300

(G-10769)
POLARIS COMMUNICATIONS INC
1300 Wellington Ave (07666-2109)
PHONE....................................201 928-0780
Fax: 201 836-2134
Harry Schipper, *President*
Camilla Marstrand, *Vice Pres*
Felicia Schipper, *Vice Pres*
EMP: 14 EST: 1968
SQ FT: 2,000
SALES: 1.9MM **Privately Held**
SIC: 7311 7336 2759 Advertising agen-
cies; graphic arts & related design; cata-
logs: printing

(G-10770)
PRINCE AGRI PRODUCTS INC (DH)
300 Frank W Burr Blvd (07666-6704)
PHONE....................................201 329-7300
Jack Bendheim, *Ch of Bd*
Dean J Warras, *Division Pres*
Daniel Welch, *Senior VP*
Clayton Lamkin, *Vice Pres*
Richard Johnson, *CFO*
◆ EMP: 35
SALES (est): 79.3MM
SALES (corp-wide): 764.2MM **Publicly Held**
WEB: www.princeagri.com
SIC: 2048 Feed supplements
HQ: Phibro Animal Health Corporation
300 Frank W Burr Blvd
Teaneck NJ 07666
201 329-7300

(G-10771)
RSD AMERICA INC
Also Called: Roger Software Distribution
300 Frank W Burr Blvd # 54 (07666-6713)
PHONE....................................201 996-1000
Fax: 201 996-1001
Pierre Van Beneden, *President*
Louis Pierre Roger, *Vice Pres*
Mark Wurtzbacher, *Engineer*
Serge Quiniou, *Treasurer*
Byron Maynard, *Manager*
EMP: 18
SQ FT: 7,000
SALES: 5MM **Privately Held**
WEB: www.rsd-intl.com
SIC: 5045 7372 7379 Computer software;
prepackaged software; computer related
consulting services

(G-10772)
SAMSUNG OPT-LCTRONICS AMER INC
Also Called: HANWHA TECHWIN AMERICA
500 Frank W Burr Blvd # 43 (07666-6804)
PHONE....................................201 325-2612
Ki Chul Kim, *President*
Lloyd Taylor, *Regl Sales Mgr*
◆ EMP: 150
SQ FT: 8,610
SALES: 193.4MM
SALES (corp-wide): 1.7B **Privately Held**
WEB: www.samsungcamerausa.com
SIC: 5043 7699 3861 Photographic cam-
eras, projectors, equipment & supplies;
photographic & optical goods equipment
repair services; photographic instruments,
electronic
PA: Hanwha Aerospace Co., Ltd.
1204 Changwon-Daero, Seongsan-Gu
Changwon 51542
825 526-0211

(G-10773)
SCJ GROUP LLC
492 Cedar Ln Ste 102c (07666-1713)
PHONE....................................201 289-5841
Sam Roney, *Mng Member*
EMP: 4
SALES (est): 330K **Privately Held**
SIC: 3651 Audio electronic systems

(G-10774)
SMARTEKG LLC
287 Rutland Ave (07666-2843)
PHONE.....................................201 376-4556
Benjamin Strauss,
Lawrence Baruch,
Eric Forkosh,
Kalman Katlowitz,
EMP: 4
SALES (est): 235.6K Privately Held
SIC: 3841 Diagnostic apparatus, medical

(G-10775)
TROPHY KING INC
309 Queen Anne Rd (07666-3242)
PHONE.....................................201 836-1482
Fax: 201 836-6763
James Walsh, President
Lorraine Walsh, Treasurer
EMP: 6
SALES: 525K Privately Held
WEB: www.trophyking.net
SIC: 3914 5999 5947 Trophies; trophies
& plaques; gift shop

(G-10776)
VACUUM SOLUTIONS GROUP INC
555 Cedar Ln Ste 1 (07666-1743)
P.O. Box 2136 (07666-1536)
PHONE.....................................781 762-0414
Robert Flynn, President
Lawrence Gilbert, Treasurer
EMP: 3
SQ FT: 200
SALES: 7MM Privately Held
WEB: www.vacuumsolutions.com
SIC: 3565 Vacuum packaging machinery

(G-10777)
WORLDWIDE PT SL LTD LBLTY CO
Also Called: International Point of Sale
555 Cedar Ln Ste 7 (07666-1743)
PHONE.....................................201 928-0222
Ed Levin,
EMP: 11
SALES (est): 1.3MM Privately Held
SIC: 3578 7371 Accounting machines &
cash registers; computer software devel-
opment & applications

(G-10778)
WORLDWIDE SAFETY SYSTEMS LLC
Also Called: Durabak Depot
1297 Sussex Rd (07666-2805)
PHONE.....................................888 613-4501
Aliza P Strauss,
Jacob Y Strauss,
EMP: 4
SALES (est): 814.7K Privately Held
SIC: 5169 2851 5198 2899 Polyurethane
products; polyurethane coatings; paints,
varnishes & supplies; chemical prepara-
tions

(G-10779)
ZESTOS FOODS LLC
1297 Sussex Rd (07666-2805)
PHONE.....................................888 407-5852
AVI Aviner, CEO
Jacob Strauss, President
EMP: 4
SALES: 200K Privately Held
SIC: 5141 5145 5149 2096 Groceries,
general line; snack foods; health foods;
dried or canned foods; potato chips &
similar snacks;

Tenafly
Bergen County

(G-10780)
ALL AMERICAN METAL FABRICATORS
34 Harold St (07670-1820)
PHONE.....................................201 567-2898
Fax: 201 567-4661
Robert Leopold, President
EMP: 6
SQ FT: 2,500
SALES: 650K Privately Held
SIC: 3446 1799 3441 Stairs, staircases,
stair treads: prefabricated metal; welding
on site; fabricated structural metal

(G-10781)
ALPEX WHEEL CO INC (PA)
29 Atwood Ave (07670-1011)
P.O. Box 280 (07670-0280)
PHONE.....................................201 871-1700
Fax: 201 871-1521
Richard S Baum, President
Charles Jonathan, Vice Pres
Barbara Baum, Treasurer
Robert Grayson, Human Res Mgr
Jonathan Baum, VP Sales
▲ EMP: 16
SQ FT: 14,000
SALES (est): 3.7MM Privately Held
WEB: www.alpexwheel.com
SIC: 3291 3545 Wheels, abrasive; ma-
chine tool accessories

(G-10782)
BITWINE INC
4 Thatcher Rd (07670-3030)
PHONE.....................................888 866-9435
Alon Cohen, Principal
EMP: 14
SALES (est): 902.4K Privately Held
SIC: 2741

(G-10783)
CHIC BEBE INC
53 Howard Park Dr (07670-2936)
PHONE.....................................201 941-5414
Caren Karpik, President
EMP: 8
SQ FT: 1,600
SALES (est): 500K Privately Held
WEB: www.bebechic.com
SIC: 2392 2211 2221 Blankets, com-
forters & beddings; sheets, bedding &
table cloths: cotton; bedding, manmade or
silk fabric

(G-10784)
EXCITE VIEW LLC
4 Thatcher Rd Ste 2001 (07670-3030)
PHONE.....................................201 227-7075
Alon Cohen,
Rafi Maslaton,
EMP: 50
SALES (est): 4.7MM Privately Held
SIC: 3651 Home entertainment equipment,
electronic

(G-10785)
MATHEMATICS LEAGUE INC
Also Called: Math League Press
17 Lancaster Rd (07670-2307)
P.O. Box 17 (07670-0017)
PHONE.....................................201 568-6328
Daniel R Flegler, President
Steven R Conrad, Vice Pres
EMP: 4
SALES: 800K Privately Held
SIC: 2731 Book publishing

(G-10786)
PROGRAMATIC PLATERS INC
32 Laurel Ave (07670-2128)
PHONE.....................................718 721-4330
Arnold Abbey, President
EMP: 12
SQ FT: 15,000
SALES (est): 1MM Privately Held
SIC: 3471 Plating of metals or formed
products; electroplating of metals or
formed products

(G-10787)
TIN CAN LIDS LLC
48 Lylewood Dr (07670-1909)
PHONE.....................................201 503-0677
Nissim Gershon, Owner
EMP: 6
SALES (est): 260.7K Privately Held
SIC: 3411 Tin cans

(G-10788)
V AND S WOODWORKS INC
105 Piermont Rd (07670-1023)
PHONE.....................................201 568-0659
Vincent Scroufari, President
Richard Vallejo, Vice Pres
EMP: 4
SQ FT: 2,500
SALES: 150K Privately Held
SIC: 2511 Wood household furniture

(G-10789)
VICOR INDUSTRIES INC
225 County Rd (07670-1872)
PHONE.....................................201 569-1947
Fax: 201 569-4666
Isaac Gershoni, President
Jose Liz, Technical Staff
EMP: 15
SQ FT: 7,500
SALES (est): 3.9MM Privately Held
WEB: www.vicorind.com
SIC: 3674 Semiconductors & related de-
vices

Tennent
Monmouth County

(G-10790)
REED & PERRINE INC
396 Main St (07763)
PHONE.....................................732 446-6363
Fax: 732 446-1344
Virginia Bulkowski, CEO
Ginny Bulkowski, President
Bob Bulkowski, Vice Pres
Robert Bulkowski, Vice Pres
▼ EMP: 23
SQ FT: 100,000
SALES (est): 5.9MM Privately Held
SIC: 2873 2875 Fertilizers: natural (or-
ganic), except compost; fertilizers, mixing
only

(G-10791)
REED & PERRINE SALES INC
396 Main St (07763)
PHONE.....................................732 446-6363
Virginia Bulkowski, CEO
Ginny Bulkowski, President
Tammy Smith, Principal
Bob Bulkowski, Vice Pres
Keith Haines, Marketing Staff
EMP: 24 EST: 1983
SQ FT: 100,000
SALES: 18.7MM Privately Held
SIC: 2873 Fertilizers: natural (organic), ex-
cept compost

Teterboro
Bergen County

(G-10792)
E & T PLASTIC MFG CO INC
200 Green St (07608-1208)
PHONE.....................................201 596-5017
Peter Scala, Sales Staff
Ron Chiosse, Manager
EMP: 40
SALES (corp-wide): 27.4MM Privately
Held
SIC: 3089 Extruded finished plastic prod-
ucts
PA: E & T Plastic Manufacturing Co., Inc.
4545 37th St
Long Island City NY 11101
718 729-6226

(G-10793)
E WORTMANN MACHINE WORKS INC
50 Hollister Rd (07608-1117)
PHONE.....................................201 288-1654
Fax: 201 288-5242
Raymond Rogers, President
George Rogers Sr, Principal
EMP: 14 EST: 1937
SQ FT: 20,000
SALES (est): 2.8MM Privately Held
SIC: 3561 Pumps & pumping equipment

(G-10794)
EBIN NEW YORK INC
506 Us Highway 46 (07608-1104)
PHONE.....................................201 288-8887
Joon Park, Principal
▲ EMP: 20 EST: 2014
SALES (est): 4.6MM Privately Held
SIC: 2844 Toilet preparations

(G-10795)
FOOD & BEVERAGE INC
Also Called: Chris's Cookies
100 Hollister Rd Unit C-1 (07608-1148)
PHONE.....................................201 288-8881
Manish Wadia, CEO
Betty Osmanoglu, Exec VP
Christian Gargiulo, Vice Pres
EMP: 100
SQ FT: 40,000
SALES: 12MM Privately Held
WEB: www.chriscookies.com
SIC: 2052 5149 Cookies; crackers, cook-
ies & bakery products

(G-10796)
FOOD INGREDIENT SOLUTIONS LLC (PA)
10 Malcolm Ave Ste 1 (07608-1054)
PHONE.....................................201 440-4377
Jeff Greaves, President
Helen Greaves, Vice Pres
Sandeep Kulshrestha, Project Mgr
Ray Haywood, Prdtn Mgr
Patrick Troutman, Accounts Exec
▲ EMP: 9
SQ FT: 9,200
SALES (est): 7.6MM Privately Held
SIC: 2099 Food preparations

(G-10797)
GALVES AUTO PRICE LIST INC
430 Industrial Ave Ste 3 (07608-1046)
PHONE.....................................201 393-0051
Fax: 201 393-0508
Paul Younger, President
Paul RAD, Sls & Mktg Exec
EMP: 12 EST: 1957
SQ FT: 10,000
SALES (est): 1.5MM Privately Held
WEB: www.galves.com
SIC: 2731 2741 Books: publishing only;
miscellaneous publishing

(G-10798)
GOTHAM INK OF NEW ENGLAND INC (HQ)
100 North St (07608-1202)
PHONE.....................................201 478-5600
Jeffrey Simons, CEO
Harvey R Brice, President
EMP: 9 EST: 1948
SQ FT: 50,000
SALES (est): 1.3MM
SALES (corp-wide): 117.1MM Privately
Held
SIC: 2893 Printing ink; gravure ink
PA: Superior Printing Ink Co Inc
100 North St
Teterboro NJ 07608
201 478-5600

(G-10799)
INTERFASHION COSMETICS CORP
32 Henry St (07608-1102)
PHONE.....................................201 288-5858
James Chang, President
Wendy Chang, Vice Pres
Jimmy Chang, Opers Staff
▲ EMP: 50
SALES (est): 9.8MM Privately Held
WEB: www.ifcosmetics.com
SIC: 2844 Cosmetic preparations

(G-10800)
JET AVIATION ST LOUIS INC
Also Called: Jet Aviation Aircraft Maint
113 Chrles A Lindbergh Dr (07608-1009)
PHONE.....................................201 462-4026
Michele Mizeski, President
John Paterson, Chief
Gary Dolski, Vice Pres
Don Haloburdo, Vice Pres
Nina Serrano, Buyer
EMP: 22
SALES (corp-wide): 30.9B Publicly Held
SIC: 4581 5172 3721 5088 Aircraft main-
tenance & repair services; petroleum
products; aircraft; transportation equip-
ment & supplies

▲ = Import ▼=Export
◆ =Import/Export

HQ: Jet Aviation St. Louis, Inc.
6400 Curtiss Steinberg Dr
Cahokia IL 62206
618 646-8000

(G-10801)
JOHN S SWIFT COMPANY INC
375 North St Ste N (07608-1200)
PHONE..................................201 935-2002
Douglas Wilhelmy, *Vice Pres*
Rick Frydrych, *Purch Agent*
EMP: 6
SALES (corp-wide): 15.7MM **Privately
Held**
WEB: www.jssco.com
SIC: 2752 2791 2789 Commercial print-
ing, offset; typesetting; bookbinding & re-
lated work
PA: John S Swift Company Incorporated
999 Commerce Ct
Buffalo Grove IL 60089
847 465-3300

(G-10802)
JOHN S SWIFT PRINT OF NJ INC
Also Called: John S Swift Co
375 North St Ste N (07608-1200)
PHONE..................................201 678-3232
John S Swift III, *President*
EMP: 5
SQ FT: 5,400
SALES: 1.5MM **Privately Held**
SIC: 2752 Commercial printing, offset

(G-10803)
JOLT COMPANY INC (PA)
Also Called: Wet Planet Beverages
100 Hollister Rd Unit 1 (07608-1139)
PHONE..................................201 288-0535
C J Rapp, *President*
Lowell Patric, *CFO*
▲ EMP: 31
SQ FT: 4,000
SALES (est): 4.6MM **Privately Held**
WEB: www.wetplanet.com
SIC: 2086 Carbonated beverages, nonal-
coholic; bottled & canned

(G-10804)
KERRY INC
Also Called: Kerry Ingredients and Flavours
546 Us Highway 46 (07608-1104)
PHONE..................................201 373-1111
Fax: 201 288-5104
Steve Raphel, *Manager*
EMP: 65 **Privately Held**
WEB: www.kerryingredients.com
SIC: 2023 Dry, condensed, evaporated
dairy products
HQ: Kerry Inc.
3330 Millington Rd
Beloit WI 53511
608 363-1200

(G-10805)
MASTERTASTE INC
Also Called: Flavor and Fragrance Division
546 Us Highway 46 (07608-1104)
PHONE..................................201 373-1111
Fax: 201 288-8389
Edmond Scanlon, *Branch Mgr*
EMP: 10 **Privately Held**
WEB: www.mastertaste.com
SIC: 2087 2844 Extracts, flavoring; per-
fumes, natural or synthetic
HQ: Mastertaste, Inc.
160 Terminal Ave
Clark NJ 07066
732 882-0202

(G-10806)
MICROFOLD INC
375 North St Ste C (07608-1200)
PHONE..................................201 641-5052
Paul Perna, *President*
EMP: 4
SALES (est): 415.1K **Privately Held**
SIC: 3554 Folding machines, paper

(G-10807)
**NORTHERN ARCHITECTURAL
SYSTEMS (PA)**
111 Central Ave (07608-1123)
PHONE..................................201 943-6400
Robert Pecorella, *President*
Grace Piccini, *Buyer*

Bipin Patel, *Engineer*
Michael McKee, *Controller*
Stacey Shubsda, *Office Mgr*
▲ EMP: 68
SQ FT: 127,000
SALES (est): 24.7MM **Privately Held**
WEB: www.northernwindow.com
SIC: 3442 Window & door frames

(G-10808)
PANTINA COSMETICS INC
30 Henry St (07608-1102)
PHONE..................................201 288-7767
Fax: 201 288-9466
Morris Chang, *Manager*
◆ EMP: 25
SQ FT: 22,000
SALES (est): 3.6MM **Privately Held**
SIC: 2844 Cosmetic preparations

(G-10809)
ROYLE SYSTEMS GROUP LLC
375 North St Ste M (07608-1200)
PHONE..................................201 644-0345
Fax: 201 644-0346
Gregory J Ramsey, *CEO*
John C Ramsey, *Ch of Bd*
Navtej Khurana, *General Mgr*
Paulson Kunjukunju, *General Mgr*
Peter Ramsey, *General Mgr*
◆ EMP: 20
SQ FT: 85,000
SALES (est): 3.7MM **Privately Held**
WEB: www.roylesystems.com
SIC: 3542 Machine tools, metal forming
type

(G-10810)
**SUPERIOR PRINTING INK CO
INC (PA)**
100 North St (07608-1202)
PHONE..................................201 478-5600
Fax: 201 478-5650
Jeffrey Simons, *President*
▲ EMP: 175 EST: 1918
SALES (est): 117.1MM **Privately Held**
SIC: 2893 2851 Printing ink; gravure ink;
varnishes

(G-10811)
**SUPERIOR PRINTING INK CO
INC**
100 North St (07608-1202)
PHONE..................................716 685-6763
EMP: 5
SALES (corp-wide): 117.1MM **Privately
Held**
SIC: 2893 Printing ink
PA: Superior Printing Ink Co Inc
100 North St
Teterboro NJ 07608
201 478-5600

(G-10812)
**SUPERIOR PRINTING INK CO
INC**
100 North St (07608-1202)
PHONE..................................716 685-6763
Dennis Kuenzi, *Manager*
EMP: 4
SALES (corp-wide): 117.1MM **Privately
Held**
SIC: 2893 Printing ink
PA: Superior Printing Ink Co Inc
100 North St
Teterboro NJ 07608
201 478-5600

(G-10813)
SYMRISE INC (HQ)
300 North St (07608-1204)
PHONE..................................201 288-3200
Fax: 201 462-2200
Achim Daub, *CEO*
Mike Cavender, *President*
Natalia Khashkovskaya, *Business Mgr*
Kari Arienti, *Vice Pres*
Dirk Bennwitz, *Vice Pres*
◆ EMP: 320 EST: 1994
SQ FT: 125
SALES (est): 352.4MM
SALES (corp-wide): 3.5B **Privately Held**
WEB: www.symriseinc.com
SIC: 2869 Perfume materials, synthetic;
flavors or flavoring materials, synthetic

PA: Symrise Ag
Muhlenfeldstr. 1
Holzminden 37603
553 190-0

(G-10814)
TAKASAGO INTL CORP USA
Also Called: TAKASAGO INTERNATIONAL
CORPORATION (U.S.A.)
100 Green St (07608-1207)
PHONE..................................201 727-4200
Fax: 201 727-4240
Frank Jones, *General Mgr*
Nancy Escalante, *Purch Agent*
Deborah Rech, *Manager*
David Picardi, *Technician*
EMP: 45
SALES (corp-wide): 1.3B **Privately Held**
SIC: 3996 2087 Hard surface floor cover-
ings; flavoring extracts & syrups
HQ: Takasago International Corporation
(U.S.A)
4 Volvo Dr
Rockleigh NJ 07647
201 767-9001

(G-10815)
TAPIA ACCESSORY GROUP INC
Also Called: Tag
370 North St Ste 2 (07608-1213)
PHONE..................................201 393-0028
George Tapia, *President*
EMP: 50
SALES (est): 4.3MM **Privately Held**
SIC: 3911 3961 Jewelry, precious metal;
costume jewelry

(G-10816)
TRANSCORE LP
25 Central Ave (07608-1154)
PHONE..................................201 329-9200
George Sheppard, *Branch Mgr*
EMP: 13
SALES (corp-wide): 4.6B **Publicly Held**
WEB: www.transcore.com
SIC: 7373 7622 3661 5065 Computer in-
tegrated systems design; communication
equipment repair; toll switching equip-
ment, telephone; communication equip-
ment
HQ: Transcore, Lp
150 4th Ave N Ste 1200
Nashville TN 37219
615 988-8962

(G-10817)
TRUCKPRO LLC
Also Called: Truckpro 192
150 Central Ave (07608-1116)
PHONE..................................201 229-0599
Fax: 201 288-0121
Rich Poskorka, *Branch Mgr*
EMP: 20
SALES (corp-wide): 1.8B **Privately Held**
WEB: www.lightruck.com
SIC: 3714 Transmissions, motor vehicle
HQ: Truckpro, Llc
1900 Charles Bryan Rd
Cordova TN 38016
901 252-4200

Thorofare
Gloucester County

(G-10818)
ACCU-COTE INC
Also Called: Automatic Plating-Accu-Cote
3410 Jessup Rd (08086)
PHONE..................................856 845-7323
Fax: 856 848-8639
Ralph Dreyfuss, *President*
Edith Dreyfuss, *Treasurer*
EMP: 9
SQ FT: 15,750
SALES (est): 701K **Privately Held**
SIC: 3471 Electroplating of metals or
formed products

(G-10819)
GARLOCK BEARINGS INC
700 Mid Atlantic Pkwy (08086)
PHONE..................................856 848-3200
Fax: 856 848-4552
Al Lenac, *CEO*

EMP: 18
SALES (est): 3.3MM **Privately Held**
SIC: 3568 Power transmission equipment

(G-10820)
GEISLERS LIQUOR STORE
195 Crown Point Rd (08086)
PHONE..................................856 845-0482
Fax: 856 384-2802
Grace Geisler, *Owner*
EMP: 14
SQ FT: 2,500
SALES (est): 1.5MM **Privately Held**
SIC: 2082 5921 7299 Ale (alcoholic bev-
erage); liquor stores; beer (packaged);
wine;

(G-10821)
GGB NORTH AMERICA LLC (HQ)
700 Mid Atlantic Pkwy (08086)
P.O. Box 189 (08086-0189)
PHONE..................................856 848-3200
Susan Sweeney, *President*
Kenneth Walker, *General Mgr*
E Joseph Fults, *Vice Pres*
John Pacana, *Electrical Engi*
Jill Burggraf, *Sales Engr*
◆ EMP: 178
SQ FT: 120,000
SALES (est): 82.3MM
SALES (corp-wide): 1.3B **Publicly Held**
WEB: www.ggbearings.com
SIC: 3568 Bearings, bushings & blocks
PA: Enpro Industries, Inc.
5605 Carnegie Blvd # 500
Charlotte NC 28209
704 731-1500

Three Bridges
Hunterdon County

(G-10822)
**ENGINEERED COMPONENTS
INC**
546 Old York Rd (08887-2308)
P.O. Box 360 (08887-0360)
PHONE..................................908 788-8393
John M Liggett, *President*
Kevin McBrearty, *Vice Pres*
▲ EMP: 15
SQ FT: 14,000
SALES (est): 4.5MM **Privately Held**
WEB: www.engrcomp.com
SIC: 5084 3545 Industrial machine parts;
machine tool attachments & accessories

Tinton Falls
Monmouth County

(G-10823)
ADIDAS NORTH AMERICA INC
Also Called: Adidas Outlet Store Tinton FLS
1 Premium Outlet Blvd (07753-7469)
PHONE..................................732 695-0085
EMP: 9
SALES (corp-wide): 25B **Privately Held**
SIC: 2329 Athletic (warmup, sweat & jog-
ging) suits: men's & boys'; men's & boys'
athletic uniforms; knickers, dress (sepa-
rate): men's & boys'
HQ: Adidas North America, Inc.
5055 N Greeley Ave
Portland OR 97217
971 234-2300

(G-10824)
**BIOPHARMA RESEARCH
COUNCIL**
1 Sheila Dr (07724-2658)
PHONE..................................732 403-3137
EMP: 4
SALES (est): 317.9K **Privately Held**
SIC: 2834 Mfg Pharmaceutical Prepara-
tions

(G-10825)
C W GRIMMER & SONS INC
75 W Gilbert St (07701-4919)
PHONE..................................732 741-2189
Fax: 732 741-6210

GEOGRAPHIC

William D Grimmer, *President*
Fulton W Hallowell III, *Vice Pres*
Arline Kinscherf, *Treasurer*
EMP: 10 **EST:** 1927
SQ FT: 10,000
SALES (est): 1.4MM **Privately Held**
SIC: 3446 3441 Fire escapes, metal; railings, bannisters, guards, etc.: made from metal pipe; fabricated structural metal

(G-10826)
CLAYTON BLOCK COMPANY INC
100 Commerce Dr (07753)
PHONE 732 905-3234
Bill Grace, *Manager*
EMP: 13
SALES (corp-wide): 44.5MM **Privately Held**
WEB: www.claytononline.com
SIC: 3271 Blocks, concrete or cinder: standard
PA: Clayton Block Company, Inc.
1355 Campus Pkwy Ste 200
Wall Township NJ 07753
732 363-1995

(G-10827)
COMMVAULT AMERICAS INC
Also Called: Tinton Falls Systems
1 Commvault Way (07724-3096)
PHONE 888 746-3849
Robert Hammer, *President*
Jeff Gusky, *Partner*
Edgar Arevalo, *Engineer*
Matt Jaquillard, *Engineer*
Michael Klose, *Engineer*
EMP: 5
SALES (est): 198.2K **Privately Held**
SIC: 7372 Prepackaged software

(G-10828)
COMMVAULT SYSTEMS INC (PA)
1 Commvault Way (07724-3096)
PHONE 732 870-4000
Fax: 732 870-4524
N Robert Hammer, *Ch of Bd*
Jacqueline Barrientos, *Partner*
Ray Eckenrode, *Partner*
Corey Wilensky, *Superintendent*
Jeremy Allen, *Principal*
EMP: 250
SALES: 699.3MM **Publicly Held**
WEB: www.commvault.com
SIC: 7373 7372 7376 Computer integrated systems design; prepackaged software; computer facilities management

(G-10829)
CURVON CORPORATION
34 Apple St (07724-2600)
PHONE 732 747-3832
Fax: 732 747-5491
Blake G Banta, *President*
▲ **EMP:** 20 **EST:** 1891
SQ FT: 16,350
SALES (est): 2.1MM **Privately Held**
WEB: www.curvon.com
SIC: 2399 Horse blankets

(G-10830)
DIGITAL OUTDOOR ADVG LLC
788 Shrewsbury Ave Ste 22 (07724-3080)
PHONE 732 616-2232
Christine Lanziano,
EMP: 7
SALES (est): 434.4K **Privately Held**
SIC: 3999 5199 7311 Advertising display products; advertising specialties; advertising consultant

(G-10831)
DIRECT DEVELOPMENT LLC
Also Called: Monitor Newspaper
97 Apple St 2 (07724-2637)
PHONE 732 739-8890
Clifford Moore, *Mng Member*
Lori Donnelly, *Creative Dir*
Vinod Gopal,
EMP: 8
SALES: 250K **Privately Held**
SIC: 2711 Newspapers, publishing & printing

(G-10832)
EAST COAST PANELBOARD INC
Also Called: East Coast Power Systems
101 Tornillo Way (07712-7521)
PHONE 732 739-6400
Fax: 732 739-6482
Salvatore Rinaldi, *President*
Mary Rinaldi, *Controller*
EMP: 40
SQ FT: 110,000
SALES (est): 22.2MM **Privately Held**
SIC: 5063 3699 Panelboards; electrical equipment & supplies

(G-10833)
EATON FILTRATION LLC
44 Apple St Ste 3 (07724-2672)
PHONE 732 767-4200
Craig Arnold, *COO*
Thomas S Gross, *COO*
Richard H Fearon, *CFO*
Hans Pedersen, *Sales Staff*
Alexander M Cutler,
▲ **EMP:** 350
SALES (est): 57.8MM **Privately Held**
WEB: www.eaton.com
SIC: 3569 Filters & strainers, pipeline
HQ: Eaton Corporation
1000 Eaton Blvd
Cleveland OH 44122
440 523-5000

(G-10834)
EATON HYDRAULICS LLC
44 Apple St (07724-2671)
PHONE 732 212-4700
Mary Jo, *Vice Pres*
Jose Davila, *Plant Mgr*
Scott Bailey, *Opers Staff*
Andreas Staudt-Schnicks, *Pub Rel Mgr*
Kurian Pulikot, *Finance Mgr*
EMP: 50
SALES (est): 6.4MM **Privately Held**
SIC: 3625 Motor controls & accessories
HQ: Eaton Corporation
1000 Eaton Blvd
Cleveland OH 44122
440 523-5000

(G-10835)
EBSCO INDUSTRIES INC
30 Park Rd Ste 2 (07724-9794)
PHONE 201 569-2500
Alan Block, *Vice Pres*
Christina Braun, *Manager*
EMP: 75
SALES (corp-wide): 2.8B **Privately Held**
WEB: www.ebscoind.com
SIC: 2741 Miscellaneous publishing
PA: Ebsco Industries, Inc.
5724 Highway 280 E
Birmingham AL 35242
205 991-6600

(G-10836)
ELITE STONE IMPORTERS LLC
45 Park Rd (07724-9716)
PHONE 732 542-7900
Courtney Larsen, *Sales Staff*
Chelsea Jorgenson, *Marketing Staff*
Michael Johnson, *Mng Member*
▲ **EMP:** 8
SALES (est): 1.2MM **Privately Held**
SIC: 3281 Cut stone & stone products

(G-10837)
FIS AVANTGARD LLC
106 Apple St Ste 110 (07724-2670)
PHONE 732 530-9303
Samuel Fensterstock, *Director*
EMP: 4
SALES (corp-wide): 9.1B **Publicly Held**
SIC: 7372 7378 7379 Business oriented computer software; computer maintenance & repair; computer related consulting services
HQ: Fis Avantgard Llc
680 E Swedesford Rd
Wayne PA 19087
800 468-7483

(G-10838)
HATTERAS PRESS INC
56 Park Rd (07724-9715)
PHONE 732 935-9800
Fax: 732 223-1232

Bill Duerr, *President*
Scott Duerr, *President*
Charles F Duerr, *Owner*
Richard Lanza, *General Mgr*
Richard McKenna, *Senior VP*
EMP: 260
SQ FT: 30,000
SALES (est): 93.2MM **Privately Held**
WEB: www.hatteraspress.com
SIC: 2752 2796 Commercial printing, offset; platemaking services

(G-10839)
JSM CO
1052 Wayside Rd (07712-3146)
PHONE 732 695-9577
David J Paraskevas, *Owner*
EMP: 5
SQ FT: 3,000
SALES (est): 250K **Privately Held**
WEB: www.jerseyspeedskiffs.com
SIC: 3599 Machine & other job shop work; custom machinery

(G-10840)
KENNETH ASMAR CUSTOM INTERIORS
Also Called: Red Bank Cabinet
548 Shrewsbury Ave (07701-4907)
PHONE 732 544-6137
Kenneth Asmar, *President*
Christine Asmar, *Vice Pres*
EMP: 6
SALES (est): 460K **Privately Held**
SIC: 2431 Woodwork, interior & ornamental

(G-10841)
LEVI STRAUSS & CO
1 Premium Outlet Blvd (07753-7469)
PHONE 732 493-4595
Stacy Blumenthal, *Branch Mgr*
EMP: 19
SALES (corp-wide): 4.9B **Privately Held**
SIC: 2325 Jeans: men's, youths' & boys'
PA: Levi Strauss & Co.
1155 Battery St
San Francisco CA 94111
415 501-6000

(G-10842)
NIKE INC
1 Premium Outlet Blvd # 699 (07753-7479)
PHONE 732 695-0108
EMP: 38
SALES (corp-wide): 36.4B **Publicly Held**
SIC: 3021 Rubber & plastics footwear
PA: Nike, Inc.
1 Sw Bowerman Dr
Beaverton OR 97005
503 671-6453

(G-10843)
PERFUMANIA INC
1 Premium Outlet Blvd # 269 (07753-7473)
PHONE 732 493-4116
EMP: 4
SALES (corp-wide): 468.8MM **Privately Held**
SIC: 2844 Perfumes & colognes
HQ: Perfumania, Inc.
35 Sawgrass Dr Ste 2
Bellport NY 11713

(G-10844)
RANGER INDUSTRIES INC (PA)
15 Park Rd (07724-9716)
PHONE 732 389-3535
Fax: 732 389-1102
Loretta Berry, *President*
Patricia Behan, *Mktg Coord*
Eldeen Jones, *Supervisor*
▲ **EMP:** 40
SQ FT: 17,000
SALES (est): 10.1MM **Privately Held**
SIC: 3953 2893 Pads, inking & stamping; printing ink

(G-10845)
SAMSONITE LLC
1 Premium Outlet Blvd # 825 (07753-7485)
PHONE 732 493-5146
EMP: 3335 **Privately Held**
WEB: www.samsonite.com
SIC: 3161 Luggage

HQ: Samsonite Llc
575 West St Ste 110
Mansfield MA 02048
508 851-1400

(G-10846)
SCHELLMARK INC
Also Called: Schellmark Interactive
7 Thistledown St (07753-7589)
PHONE 732 345-7143
Bill Scheller, *President*
EMP: 5
SQ FT: 4,500
SALES: 500K **Privately Held**
WEB: www.comicgallery.com
SIC: 7311 2752 Advertising agencies; calendars, lithographed; cards, lithographed; post cards, picture: lithographed

(G-10847)
SENOR LOPEZ (PA)
15 Spring Ct (07724-3278)
PHONE 732 229-7622
Kim Lopez, *Partner*
Joseph Lopez, *Partner*
EMP: 1
SALES: 1.5MM **Privately Held**
WEB: www.senorlopez.com
SIC: 2329 Men's & boys' sportswear & athletic clothing

(G-10848)
STAVOLA ASPHALT COMPANY INC (PA)
Also Called: Stavola Paving Company
175 Drift Rd (07724-9701)
P.O. Box 482, Red Bank (07701-0482)
PHONE 732 542-2328
John Stavola, *President*
Joseph C Stavola, *Vice Pres*
Joseph Stavola, *Vice Pres*
Richard Stavola, *Vice Pres*
Karen Dunn, *Office Mgr*
EMP: 22
SALES (est): 17.1MM **Privately Held**
SIC: 5033 2951 1611 Roofing & siding materials; asphalt paving mixtures & blocks; highway & street construction

(G-10849)
STAVOLA CONSTRUCTION MTLS INC (PA)
175 Drift Rd (07724-9701)
P.O. Box 482, Red Bank (07701-0482)
PHONE 732 542-2328
Fax: 732 389-5372
John Stavola Jr, *President*
Frank Stavola Jr, *Vice Pres*
Joseph Stavola III, *Treasurer*
James Stavola Jr, *Admin Sec*
EMP: 49
SQ FT: 5,000
SALES (est): 9.3MM **Privately Held**
WEB: www.stavola.com
SIC: 3281 Stone, quarrying & processing of own stone products

(G-10850)
STAVOLA HOLDING CORPORATION
175 Drift Rd (07724-9701)
P.O. Box 482, Red Bank (07701-0482)
PHONE 732 542-2328
Joseph C Stavola III, *President*
John Stavola, *Principal*
Richard Stavola, *Vice Pres*
Joseph Stavola III, *Treasurer*
James Stavola Jr, *Admin Sec*
EMP: 250
SALES: 11.6MM **Privately Held**
SIC: 1611 2951 General contractor, highway & street construction; paving mixtures; paving blocks

(G-10851)
TRF MUSIC INC
Also Called: Trf Production Music Libraries
106 Apple St Ste 302 (07724-2670)
PHONE 201 335-0005
Michael Nurko, *President*
Ann Marie Van Denheuvel, *Office Mgr*
EMP: 11
SQ FT: 3,000

▲ = Import ▼=Export
◆ =Import/Export

SALES (est): 940K **Privately Held**
SIC: **2741** 5736 Music, sheet: publishing only, not printed on site; musical instrument stores

(G-10852)
UNDER ARMOUR INC
1 Premium Outlet Blvd # 101 (07753-7469)
PHONE..................................732 493-2444
EMP: 50
SALES (corp-wide): 4.9B **Publicly Held**
SIC: **2353** Hats, caps & millinery
PA: Under Armour, Inc.
 1020 Hull St Ste 300
 Baltimore MD 21230
 410 454-6428

(G-10853)
VANS INC
1 Premium Outlet Blvd # 815 (07753-7484)
PHONE..................................732 493-1516
Jeff Traub, *Branch Mgr*
EMP: 10
SALES (corp-wide): 11.8B **Publicly Held**
SIC: **3021** Canvas shoes, rubber soled
HQ: Vans, Inc.
 1588 S Coast Dr
 Costa Mesa CA 92626
 855 909-8267

(G-10854)
WEBB-MASON INC
628 Shrewsbury Ave Ste G (07701-4912)
PHONE..................................732 747-6585
Fax: 732 212-8380
Kevin Brennan, *Manager*
EMP: 4
SALES (corp-wide): 113.5MM **Privately Held**
SIC: **2752** 8742 8732 Business form & card printing, lithographic; marketing consulting services; market analysis or research
PA: Webb-Mason, Inc.
 10830 Gilroy Rd
 Hunt Valley MD 21031
 410 785-1111

Titusville
Mercer County

(G-10855)
JANSSEN PHARMACEUTICALS INC (HQ)
1125 Trnton Harbourton Rd (08560-1499)
P.O. Box 200 (08560-1002)
PHONE..................................609 730-2000
Fax: 609 730-2029
Jennifer Taubert, *President*
Michael Yang, *Vice Pres*
Steve Bariahtaris, *Treasurer*
Linda Kapp, *Manager*
Vincent Ranieri, *Manager*
▲ EMP: 1100
SQ FT: 20,000
SALES (est): 591.5MM
SALES (corp-wide): 76.4B **Publicly Held**
WEB: www.janau.jnj.com
SIC: **2833** 2834 Anesthetics, in bulk form; antihistamine preparations; astringents, medicinal
PA: Johnson & Johnson
 1 Johnson And Johnson Plz
 New Brunswick NJ 08933
 732 524-0400

(G-10856)
SPECTARE SYSTEMS INC
17 Independence Way (08560-1522)
PHONE..................................609 303-0957
Christopher Near, *Chief Engr*
EMP: 9 EST: 2007
SALES (est): 247K **Privately Held**
SIC: **7372** Business oriented computer software

(G-10857)
TRAP ROCK INDUSTRIES INC
Rr 29 (08560)
P.O. Box 419, Kingston (08528-0419)
PHONE..................................609 924-0300
Michael Stavola, *General Mgr*
EMP: 35

SALES (corp-wide): 131.7MM **Privately Held**
WEB: www.traprock.com
SIC: **1429** 1442 Grits mining (crushed stone); gravel mining
PA: Trap Rock Industries, Inc.
 460 River Rd
 Kingston NJ 08528
 609 924-0300

Toms River
Ocean County

(G-10858)
ABB LIGHTING INC
1501 Industrial Way (08755-4955)
PHONE..................................866 222-8866
Guy Esposito, *President*
EMP: 4 EST: 2015
SQ FT: 12,000
SALES (est): 273.1K **Privately Held**
SIC: **3648** Public lighting fixtures

(G-10859)
ABOVE REST GLASS
2345 Route 9 Ste 31 (08755-0994)
PHONE..................................732 370-1616
William Mackay, *Owner*
EMP: 4
SALES (est): 170K **Privately Held**
SIC: **3231** 1793 Products of purchased glass; glass & glazing work

(G-10860)
ALEX REAL LLC
Also Called: Superior Promotional Bags
1876 Lakewood Rd (08755-1210)
PHONE..................................732 730-8770
Alexander Vorhand,
▲ EMP: 11 EST: 2007
SALES (est): 1.6MM **Privately Held**
SIC: **2759** 5199 Screen printing; bags, textile

(G-10861)
ALL AMERICAN POWDERCOATING LLC
2002 Route 9 (08755-1214)
PHONE..................................732 349-7001
John Ciccone, *Principal*
EMP: 4
SALES (est): 342.8K **Privately Held**
SIC: **3479** Metal coating & allied service

(G-10862)
ALTANTIC PRINTING AND DESIGN
467 Lakehurst Rd (08755-6342)
PHONE..................................732 557-9600
Jovi Flores, *President*
EMP: 17
SALES (est): 117K **Privately Held**
SIC: **2759** Commercial printing

(G-10863)
ANDREVIN INC
Also Called: Ideal Tile Company Toms River
792 Fischer Blvd (08753-4667)
PHONE..................................732 270-2794
Vincent Elardo, *President*
Dianne Elardo, *Manager*
EMP: 8
SQ FT: 3,000
SALES (est): 680K **Privately Held**
SIC: **3253** Ceramic wall & floor tile

(G-10864)
ARTS WINDOWS INC
154537 W Unit 1 St 37 (08755)
PHONE..................................732 905-9595
Fax: 732 367-5177
Arthur Engel, *President*
Ronnie Engel, *Vice Pres*
EMP: 5
SQ FT: 12,000
SALES (est): 1MM **Privately Held**
WEB: www.artswindows.com
SIC: **2591** 5719 5023 Window shade rollers & fittings; vertical blinds; vertical blinds

(G-10865)
AUTOSHRED LLC
1358 Hooper Ave (08753-2882)
PHONE..................................732 244-0950
Peter Levitt, *General Mgr*
C Bruce Rush,
EMP: 4 EST: 2008
SALES (est): 430K **Privately Held**
SIC: **3589** Shredders, industrial & commercial

(G-10866)
BAMBOO & RATTAN WORKS INC
1931 Silverton Rd (08753-1414)
PHONE..................................732 255-4239
Fax: 732 905-8386
Arthur L Maison, *President*
Suzanne Maison, *Vice Pres*
▲ EMP: 7 EST: 1880
SQ FT: 22,500
SALES (est): 1.6MM **Privately Held**
WEB: www.bambooandrattan.com
SIC: **5031** 2541 3993 3496 Lumber, plywood & millwork; wood partitions & fixtures; signs & advertising specialties; miscellaneous fabricated wire products; logging; carpets & rugs

(G-10867)
BANQUET SERVICES INTERNATIONAL
2214 Route 37 E Ste 1 (08753-6047)
PHONE..................................732 270-1188
Rosemarie Hansen, *President*
EMP: 5
SQ FT: 2,500
SALES (est): 411.5K **Privately Held**
SIC: **2731** Pamphlets: publishing only, not printed on site

(G-10868)
BARRY URNER PUBLICATIONS INC
1001 Corporate Cir (08755-4815)
P.O. Box 389 (08754-0389)
PHONE..................................732 240-5330
Paul B Brown Jr, *President*
Richard Brown, *Vice Pres*
Richard A Brown, *Treasurer*
Brian W Quigley, *Controller*
Michael W O'Shaughnessy, *Admin Sec*
EMP: 63 EST: 1858
SQ FT: 16,000
SALES (est): 10.9MM **Privately Held**
WEB: www.urnerbarry.com
SIC: **2721** Trade journals: publishing & printing

(G-10869)
BASF CORPORATION
227 Oak Ridge Pkwy (08755-4107)
PHONE..................................848 221-2786
Ken Dupuis, *Manager*
EMP: 25
SALES (corp-wide): 76B **Privately Held**
WEB: www.cibasc.com
SIC: **2869** Industrial organic chemicals
HQ: Basf Corporation
 100 Park Ave
 Florham Park NJ 07932
 973 245-6000

(G-10870)
BAYSIDE ORTHOPEDICS LLC
780 Route 37 W Ste 330 (08755-5064)
PHONE..................................732 691-4898
Erik S Larsen,
EMP: 8
SALES (est): 1MM **Privately Held**
SIC: **3842** Orthopedic appliances

(G-10871)
CICCONE INC
Also Called: Ciccone Brothers
2002 Route 9 (08755-1214)
PHONE..................................732 349-7071
Robyn Ciccone, *President*
John Ciccone, *Principal*
EMP: 6
SQ FT: 3,000
SALES: 500K **Privately Held**
SIC: **3446** Architectural metalwork

(G-10872)
CLAYTON BLOCK COMPANY INC
Also Called: Jersey Concrete
194 Chestnut St (08753-5321)
P.O. Box 3015, Lakewood (08701-9015)
PHONE..................................732 349-3700
Fax: 732 349-3472
Jack Lally, *Plant Mgr*
Faith Skizewski, *Manager*
EMP: 18
SQ FT: 2,000
SALES (corp-wide): 44.5MM **Privately Held**
WEB: www.claytononline.com
SIC: **3273** 3271 Ready-mixed concrete; concrete block & brick
PA: Clayton Block Company, Inc.
 1355 Campus Pkwy Ste 200
 Wall Township NJ 07753
 732 363-1995

(G-10873)
COTTRELL GRAPHICS & ADVG SPC
2121 Route 9 (08755-1215)
PHONE..................................732 349-7430
Fax: 732 349-2920
David Cottrell, *President*
EMP: 7
SQ FT: 4,800
SALES (est): 453.7K **Privately Held**
SIC: **2752** Commercial printing, offset

(G-10874)
ENAILSUPPLY CORPORATION
Also Called: 911 Tatical Direct
2161 Whitesville Rd Ste C (08755-1478)
PHONE..................................909 725-1698
Sudeep Arya, *President*
EMP: 6
SALES (est): 432.1K **Privately Held**
SIC: **2326** Work uniforms

(G-10875)
FERMAG TECHNOLOGIES INC
146 Village Rd (08755-0904)
P.O. Box 1364, Edison (08818-1364)
PHONE..................................732 985-7300
Fax: 732 985-7566
John Perkins, *President*
Peter Leddy, *Corp Secy*
▲ EMP: 8 EST: 1946
SQ FT: 30,000
SALES: 1.6MM **Privately Held**
WEB: www.fermagtechnologies.com
SIC: **3264** Ferrite & ferrite parts

(G-10876)
FIBER-SPAN INC
670 Commons Way (08755-6431)
PHONE..................................908 253-9080
Fax: 908 253-9086
Hal Halpern, *CEO*
Henry Wojtunik, *President*
EMP: 40
SQ FT: 15,000
SALES (est): 10.5MM **Privately Held**
WEB: www.fiber-span.com
SIC: **3663** 3661 Amplifiers, RF power & IF; fiber optics communications equipment

(G-10877)
FIRST NATIONAL SERVICING & DEV
102 Starc Rd (08755-1329)
PHONE..................................732 341-5409
Bryan Grodzinski, *President*
EMP: 25
SQ FT: 6,000
SALES (est): 1.3MM **Privately Held**
SIC: **2834** 5047 8071 Pharmaceutical preparations; medical & hospital equipment; medical laboratories

(G-10878)
FIX IT GUY
2562 Balfrey Dr (08753-4607)
PHONE..................................732 278-9000
Al Pinerta, *Principal*
EMP: 4
SALES (est): 545K **Privately Held**
SIC: **3553** Cabinet makers' machinery

(G-10879)
FUEL MANAGEMENT SERVICES INC
13 Main Bayway (08753-7019)
PHONE................................732 929-1964
Mark Stellmach, *President*
Mary Kitchen, *Corp Secy*
EMP: 3
SALES (est): 1.5MM **Privately Held**
WEB: www.fuelmanagementservices.com
SIC: 5169 2899 Chemicals & allied products; chemical preparations

(G-10880)
GEORGE CIOCHER INC
1241 Birmingham Ave (08757-1532)
PHONE................................732 818-3495
Fax: 201 861-0027
George Ciocher, *President*
EMP: 7 EST: 1992
SALES (est): 671.4K **Privately Held**
SIC: 3446 1542 Architectural metalwork; religious building construction

(G-10881)
GOOD AS GOLD JEWELERS INC
226 Route 37 W Ste 9 (08755-8047)
PHONE................................732 286-1111
Robert Teufel, *President*
Todd Teufel, *Vice Pres*
EMP: 4
SQ FT: 980
SALES (est): 300K **Privately Held**
SIC: 5944 7631 5932 3915 Jewelry, precious stones & precious metals; jewelry repair services; used merchandise stores; jewel cutting, drilling, polishing, recutting or setting

(G-10882)
HANSEN LITHOGRAPHY LTD
2214 Route 37 E Ste 1 (08753-6047)
PHONE................................732 270-1188
Rose Hansen,
EMP: 5
SQ FT: 2,400
SALES (est): 325.4K **Privately Held**
SIC: 2752 Publication printing, lithographic

(G-10883)
HENRY DUDLEY
Also Called: Dudley Lab
1508 Wellington Ave (08757-1602)
PHONE................................732 240-6895
Henry Dudley, *Owner*
EMP: 4 EST: 1970
SALES (est): 330K **Privately Held**
WEB: www.henfrocks.com
SIC: 3559 Electronic component making machinery

(G-10884)
HEYCO MOLDED PRODUCTS INC (DH)
1800 Industrial Way (08755-4809)
P.O. Box 517 (08754-0517)
PHONE................................732 286-4336
William H Jemison, *Ch of Bd*
William D Jemison, *President*
◆ EMP: 19
SALES (est): 10MM
SALES (corp-wide): 483.7MM **Privately Held**
SIC: 3089 3469 3644 Injection molding of plastics; metal stampings; noncurrent-carrying wiring services

(G-10885)
HEYCO PRODUCTS CORP (DH)
1800 Industrial Way (08755-4809)
P.O. Box 517 (08754-0517)
PHONE................................732 286-1800
William Jemison, *President*
EMP: 5
SQ FT: 250,000
SALES (est): 18.1MM
SALES (corp-wide): 483.7MM **Privately Held**
SIC: 3351 3679 Copper rolling & drawing; commutators, electronic
HQ: Penn Engineering & Manufacturing Corp.
　　5190 Old Easton Rd
　　Danboro PA 18916
　　215 766-8853

(G-10886)
HEYCO STAMPED PRODUCTS
1800 Industrial Way (08755-4809)
P.O. Box 517 (08754-0517)
PHONE................................732 286-4336
Fax: 732 244-8843
Vincent L Fevola, *President*
Charles Lusk, *Treasurer*
EMP: 65
SQ FT: 40,000
SALES (est): 7.8MM
SALES (corp-wide): 483.7MM **Privately Held**
WEB: www.heyco.com
SIC: 3469 Stamping metal for the trade
HQ: Heyco Products Corp.
　　1800 Industrial Way
　　Toms River NJ 08755

(G-10887)
HUDSON VALLEY ENVIROMENTAL INC
Also Called: Hve
2063 Basswood Ct (08755-1391)
PHONE................................732 967-0060
Fax: 732 967-0062
Frank Pasalano, *CEO*
Vincent Mastria, *Vice Pres*
EMP: 40 EST: 1995
SQ FT: 500
SALES: 7.6MM **Privately Held**
WEB: www.hvenvironmentalservices.com
SIC: 1389 1795 1794 1629 Derrick building, repairing & dismantling; wrecking & demolition work; demolition, buildings & other structures; excavation work; timber removal

(G-10888)
INSULITE INC
1890 Church Rd (08753-1499)
PHONE................................732 255-1700
B Albert Horn, *President*
Shari Stein, *Finance Mgr*
EMP: 14 EST: 1960
SQ FT: 22,000
SALES: 1MM **Privately Held**
SIC: 3231 Insulating glass: made from purchased glass

(G-10889)
JERSEY COVER CORP
1746 Route 9 (08755-1208)
PHONE................................732 286-6300
Kathleen Stern, *President*
Kathleen Ferraro, *Accountant*
EMP: 10
SQ FT: 5,000
SALES (est): 1.3MM **Privately Held**
SIC: 3949 Water sports equipment

(G-10890)
KITCHEN KING INC (PA)
1561 Route 9 Ste 9 (08755-3284)
PHONE................................732 341-9660
Fax: 732 341-3445
Terry Barth, *President*
EMP: 19
SQ FT: 10,000
SALES (est): 1.4MM **Privately Held**
WEB: www.kitchenking.net
SIC: 2434 Wood kitchen cabinets

(G-10891)
KITCHENS BY FRANK INC
2345 Route 9 Ste 5 (08755-0966)
PHONE................................732 364-1343
Fax: 732 364-1477
Frank Duelly, *President*
EMP: 5
SQ FT: 12,780
SALES (est): 1.5MM **Privately Held**
SIC: 2521 Cabinets, office: wood

(G-10892)
KUFALL PRINTING
4 Oak Ridge Pkwy (08755-8002)
PHONE................................732 505-9847
Charles Kufall, *Partner*
Herbert Kufall, *Partner*
EMP: 6
SALES (est): 343.1K **Privately Held**
SIC: 2752 Commercial printing, offset; lithographing on metal

(G-10893)
LE-ED CONSTRUCTION INC
Also Called: Le-Ed Concrete & Supply Co
1609 Route 9 (08755-1205)
PHONE................................732 341-4546
Fax: 732 505-4914
Edward Steitz, *President*
EMP: 20
SQ FT: 3,500
SALES (est): 8.5MM **Privately Held**
SIC: 5191 3273 Farm supplies; ready-mixed concrete

(G-10894)
M E C TECHNOLOGIES INC
2200 Industrial Way S (08755-4945)
PHONE................................732 505-0308
Fax: 732 505-2151
Richard Kulkaski, *CEO*
EMP: 48
SQ FT: 21,000
SALES (est): 7.2MM **Privately Held**
WEB: www.mectech.com
SIC: 3674 Semiconductor circuit networks

(G-10895)
MAX FLIGHT CORP
7 Executive Dr (08755-4947)
PHONE................................732 281-2007
Fax: 732 281-2009
Frank McClintic, *President*
Bill Francovitch, *Purchasing*
Lou Calao, *CFO*
Jan McClintic, *Info Tech Dir*
Carol Siracusa, *Admin Asst*
EMP: 50
SQ FT: 30,000
SALES: 7MM **Privately Held**
WEB: www.maxflight.com
SIC: 3699 Flight simulators (training aids), electronic

(G-10896)
MECHANICAL COMPONENTS CORP
1 Executive Dr Unit B (08755-4947)
PHONE................................732 938-3737
Fax: 732 938-3372
Ronald Fisher, *Vice Pres*
EMP: 4
SQ FT: 3,500
SALES: 320K **Privately Held**
SIC: 3469 Machine parts, stamped or pressed metal

(G-10897)
MULE ROAD PHARMACY
600 Mule Rd (08757-6460)
PHONE................................732 244-3737
Guiyan Jiang, *Principal*
EMP: 8
SALES (est): 770.3K **Privately Held**
SIC: 2834 5912 Pharmaceutical preparations; drug stores & proprietary stores

(G-10898)
MULTICOMM SOLUTIONS INC
1285 Rolls Ct (08755-1349)
PHONE................................877 796-8480
Solomon Erenthal, *President*
EMP: 6
SALES (est): 943.6K **Privately Held**
SIC: 3699 Security control equipment & systems

(G-10899)
PAINTMASTER AUTO BODY
1920 Route 37 E Ste 1 (08755-8298)
PHONE................................732 270-1700
Edward Jacobson, *President*
Ellen Jacobson, *Admin Sec*
EMP: 16
SQ FT: 37,500
SALES (est): 3MM **Privately Held**
SIC: 3714 Motor vehicle parts & accessories

(G-10900)
PATHMARK STORES INC
1256 Indian Head Rd # 35 (08755-4075)
PHONE................................732 505-6440
Fax: 732 349-6318
William Koczan, *Manager*
EMP: 200
SALES (corp-wide): 2B **Privately Held**
WEB: www.pathmark.com
SIC: 5411 5912 2051 Supermarkets, chain; drug stores; bread, cake & related products
PA: Pathmark Stores, Inc.
　　2 Paragon Dr
　　Montvale NJ 07645
　　866 443-7374

(G-10901)
PENTACLE PUBLISHING CORP
Also Called: New Jersey 50 Plus
1830 Route 9 Ste 1 (08755-1487)
PHONE................................732 240-3000
Patricia Jasin, *President*
EMP: 23
SQ FT: 2,800
SALES (est): 2MM **Privately Held**
SIC: 2721 7929 Periodicals: publishing only; entertainment service

(G-10902)
PHILIP PAPALIA
Also Called: CCA/Custom Change Aprons
21 Dugan Ln (08755-4025)
PHONE................................732 349-5530
Philip Papalia, *Owner*
EMP: 15
SQ FT: 500
SALES (est): 880K **Privately Held**
SIC: 2339 2389 2393 Aprons, except rubber or plastic: women's, misses', juniors'; men's miscellaneous accessories; bags & containers, except sleeping bags: textile

(G-10903)
PRESSTO GRAPHICS
109 Foxwood Ter (08755-7327)
P.O. Box 64 (08754-0064)
PHONE................................732 286-9300
Fax: 732 286-9030
Bill Debernardis, *President*
EMP: 10
SALES (est): 908.3K **Privately Held**
WEB: www.presstographics.com
SIC: 2759 2752 Commercial printing; commercial printing, lithographic

(G-10904)
PRIMAK PLUMBING & HEATING INC
904 Dorset Psge (08753-4019)
PHONE................................732 270-6282
Michael Primak, *President*
EMP: 7
SALES (est): 1MM **Privately Held**
SIC: 3494 Plumbing & heating valves

(G-10905)
R V LIVOLSI INCORPORATED (PA)
Also Called: Triangle Reprocenter
20 E Water St (08753-7627)
PHONE................................732 286-2200
Fax: 732 286-0012
Robert Livolsi, *President*
EMP: 5
SALES (est): 802K **Privately Held**
SIC: 7334 2752 Photocopying & duplicating services; blueprinting service; commercial printing, offset

(G-10906)
RAPID MANUFACTURING CO INC
25 Bay Point Dr (08753-2405)
PHONE................................732 279-1252
Dante Cannella, *President*
Robert Gualtier, *Vice Pres*
Allen Cannella, *Treasurer*
EMP: 30 EST: 1955
SQ FT: 45,000
SALES (est): 3.8MM **Privately Held**
SIC: 3089 3469 Injection molding of plastics; stamping metal for the trade

(G-10907)
S D L POWDER COATING INC
1591 Route 37 W Ste E4 (08755-4808)
PHONE................................732 473-0800
Louis Russo, *Owner*
Louis Rossio, *Owner*
EMP: 5

▲ = Import ▼=Export
◆ =Import/Export

SALES (est): 335.4K **Privately Held**
SIC: **3479** Coating of metals & formed products; painting, coating & hot dipping

(G-10908)
S L P ENGINEERING INC
Also Called: Slp Performance
1501 Industrial Way (08755-4955)
PHONE................................732 240-3696
Fax: 732 341-6084
Edward Hamburger, *President*
EMP: 65
SALES (est): 11.1MM **Privately Held**
SIC: **3711 8711 3714** Automobile assembly, including specialty automobiles; engineering services; motor vehicle parts & accessories

(G-10909)
SANTON INC
Also Called: Wasmund Bindery
128 Grand View Dr (08753-2018)
PHONE................................201 444-9080
Fax: 201 444-5306
Anthony Prestifilippo, *President*
Lorraine Whalen, *Treasurer*
Sandra Prestifilippo, *Admin Sec*
EMP: 27
SQ FT: 8,000
SALES (est): 1.5MM **Privately Held**
WEB: www.wasmundbindery.com
SIC: **2789 7334** Bookbinding & repairing: trade, edition, library, etc.; photocopying & duplicating services

(G-10910)
SHORE PRECISION MFG INC
1000 Industrial Way Ste D (08755-5057)
PHONE................................732 914-0949
Fax: 732 914-0566
Wayne Cornwell, *President*
EMP: 10
SQ FT: 4,000
SALES (est): 1MM **Privately Held**
SIC: **3599** Machine shop, jobbing & repair

(G-10911)
SHOWCASE PUBLICATIONS INC (PA)
Also Called: Auto Shopper
90 Irons St (08753-6534)
PHONE................................732 349-1134
Fax: 732 349-9020
Bob Draper, *President*
Donald F Hulucha, *Corp Secy*
April Ottaviani, *Accounting Mgr*
Randy Moniz, *Sales Mgr*
Peggy Hickman, *Accounts Exec*
EMP: 10
SQ FT: 5,000
SALES (est): 7.7MM **Privately Held**
WEB: www.showpubs.org
SIC: **2721** Trade journals: publishing & printing

(G-10912)
SIGNATURE AUDIO VIDEO SYSTEMS
164 Kettle Creek Rd (08753-1858)
PHONE................................732 864-1039
Howard Cohen, *President*
Angela Marquini, *Vice Pres*
EMP: 4
SALES: 320K **Privately Held**
SIC: **3651** Household audio & video equipment

(G-10913)
SPECIALTY SYSTEMS INC (PA)
1451 Route 37 W Ste 1 (08755-4969)
PHONE................................732 341-1011
Fax: 732 341-0655
Emil Kaunitz, *President*
William Cabey, *Vice Pres*
Vincent Cervellieri, *Vice Pres*
George Galler, *Engineer*
Amanda Douglas, *CFO*
EMP: 36 EST: 1978
SQ FT: 9,000
SALES: 5.3MM **Privately Held**
WEB: www.specialtysystems.com
SIC: **7371 7379 7372 7373** Computer software development; computer related consulting services; prepackaged software; computer integrated systems design; engineering services

(G-10914)
STEEL RISER CORP
402 Marc Dr (08753-4228)
PHONE................................732 341-7031
Shawn Maguira, *President*
Charles Becella, *Vice Pres*
EMP: 5
SALES (est): 560K **Privately Held**
SIC: **3291** Grit, steel

(G-10915)
SUFFOLK COUNTY CONTRACTORS
Also Called: Suffolk Recycling
242 Dover Rd Unit 2 (08757-5157)
PHONE................................732 349-7726
William Major, *President*
Bill Clark, *Manager*
EMP: 30
SQ FT: 1,500
SALES (est): 3.9MM **Privately Held**
SIC: **1623 1611 3273** Sewer line construction; highway & street paving contractor; grading; ready-mixed concrete

(G-10916)
T L C SPECIALTIES INC
Also Called: TLC Signs & Banners
188 Walnut St (08753-5451)
PHONE................................732 244-4225
Fax: 732 244-3699
Timothy Snover, *President*
Cheryl Snover, *Vice Pres*
EMP: 18
SQ FT: 3,000
SALES (est): 2.1MM **Privately Held**
WEB: www.tlcsignandbanner.com
SIC: **5999 3993** Banners, flags, decals & posters; signs & advertising specialties

(G-10917)
TECHNIDYNE CORPORATION
2190 Route 9 Ste 9 (08755-0970)
PHONE................................732 363-1055
Fax: 732 901-0307
Frank Jehn, *President*
EMP: 8
SQ FT: 4,400
SALES (est): 700K **Privately Held**
WEB: www.technivet.com
SIC: **3596 7352** Scales & balances, except laboratory; medical equipment rental

(G-10918)
TRADEWINDS MARINE SERVICE
122 Eton Ct (08757-4447)
PHONE................................848 448-6888
Darrin Gordon, *Principal*
EMP: 8 EST: 2016
SALES (est): 362.1K **Privately Held**
SIC: **3732** Boat building & repairing

(G-10919)
UNIVERSAL INTERLOCK CORP
Also Called: Kitchenexpo
910 Hooper Ave (08753-8365)
PHONE................................732 818-8484
Fax: 732 818-8488
Brian Gordon, *President*
EMP: 4
SALES (est): 277K
SALES (corp-wide): 12.9MM **Privately Held**
WEB: www.gotokitchenexpo.com
SIC: **2599 5812** Cabinets, factory; eating places
PA: Universal Interlock Corporation
950 New Durham Rd
Edison NJ 08817
732 650-9700

(G-10920)
WANASAVEALOTCOM LLC
524 Fielders Ln (08755-2146)
PHONE................................732 286-6956
Scott Gussin,
◆ EMP: 14
SQ FT: 15,000
SALES: 8.6MM **Privately Held**
WEB: www.wanasavealot.com
SIC: **5023 5064 3634 3639** Home furnishings; electrical appliances, television & radio; electric household cooking appliances; major kitchen appliances, except refrigerators & stoves

(G-10921)
WHE RESEARCH INC
Also Called: Atlantic Protective Pouches
1545 Route 37 W Ste 6 (08755-4985)
P.O. Box 1191 (08754-1191)
PHONE................................732 240-3871
Walter A Haine, *President*
Lorraine R Haine, *Vice Pres*
EMP: 5
SQ FT: 3,000
SALES (est): 340K **Privately Held**
WEB: www.wheresearch.com
SIC: **3089** Plastic processing

(G-10922)
WIRELESS EXPERIENCE OF PA INC (PA)
Also Called: Wireless Experience, The
1451 Rte 37 W A (08755-4969)
PHONE................................732 552-0050
Brian Wainwright, *President*
Robert Shaver, *CFO*
Matt Mott, *Human Resources*
Chris Bulmer, *Manager*
Matt Langford, *Director*
EMP: 8 EST: 2008
SALES (est): 30.9MM **Privately Held**
SIC: **2451 1731 4812** Mobile homes; telephone & telephone equipment installation; cellular telephone services

(G-10923)
WIZARD TECHNOLOGY INC
2165 Route 9 (08755-1215)
PHONE................................732 730-0800
Anthony Hesse, *President*
▼ EMP: 10
SALES (est): 880K **Privately Held**
SIC: **3552** Dyeing, drying & finishing machinery & equipment

(G-10924)
ZYCAL BIOCEUTICALS MFG LLC (PA)
5a Executive Dr (08755-4947)
PHONE................................888 779-9225
James J Scaffidi, *CEO*
EMP: 8 EST: 2013
SALES (est): 817K **Privately Held**
SIC: **3999** Barber & beauty shop equipment

Totowa
Passaic County

(G-10925)
ACCENT PRESS INC
132 Winifred Dr (07512-1144)
PHONE................................973 785-3127
Fax: 973 338-2878
Thomas Mostello, *President*
EMP: 5
SQ FT: 2,500
SALES (est): 604.2K **Privately Held**
SIC: **2752** Commercial printing, lithographic

(G-10926)
ADVANCED BIOTECH OVERSEAS LLC (PA)
Also Called: A B T
10 Taft Rd (07512-1006)
PHONE................................973 339-6242
James Mulligan, *Principal*
EMP: 4
SALES (est): 634.3K **Privately Held**
SIC: **5149 8731 2869** Flavourings & fragrances; biotechnical research, commercial; perfumes, flavorings & food additives

(G-10927)
ALLIANCE DESIGN INC
Also Called: Alliance Design Group
434 Union Blvd (07512-2562)
PHONE................................973 904-9450
Fax: 973 904-9666
William Ng, *President*
Ej Davis, *VP Sales*
Susan Kluhspies, *Creative Dir*
Debra Faust, *Graphic Designe*
EMP: 12
SQ FT: 2,500

SALES (est): 1.3MM **Privately Held**
SIC: **7336 2759** Graphic arts & related design; commercial printing

(G-10928)
ALLOY STAINLESS PRODUCTS CO
611 Union Blvd (07512-2402)
PHONE................................973 256-1616
Annemarie Appleton, *President*
J Albert Dimauro, *President*
EMP: 100 EST: 1946
SQ FT: 14,000
SALES (est): 8.1MM
SALES (corp-wide): 16.4MM **Privately Held**
WEB: www.aspfitting.com
SIC: **3312 5051** Stainless steel; metals service centers & offices
PA: Knickerbocker Machine Shop Inc.
611 Union Blvd
Totowa NJ 07512
973 256-1616

(G-10929)
AMERICAN TIRE DISTRIBUTORS
50 Us Highway 46 (07512-2302)
PHONE................................973 646-5600
William Berry, *President*
EMP: 9
SALES (est): 1MM **Privately Held**
SIC: **5531 3011** Automotive tires; tires & inner tubes
HQ: American Tire Distributors, Inc.
12200 Herbert Wayne Ct # 150
Huntersville NC 28078
704 992-2000

(G-10930)
AMISH DAIRY PRODUCTS LLC
41 Vreeland Ave Ste 208 (07512-1120)
PHONE................................973 256-7676
Kenneth Tensen,
EMP: 7 EST: 1996
SALES (est): 816.7K **Privately Held**
SIC: **2023** Dietary supplements, dairy & non-dairy based

(G-10931)
APB-DYNASONICS INC
145 Shepherds Ln (07512-2130)
PHONE................................973 785-1101
Peter Patel, *President*
John Lee, *Managing Dir*
Charles Augustowski, *Principal*
▲ EMP: 6
SQ FT: 25,000
SALES (est): 1.5MM **Privately Held**
WEB: www.apbdynasonics.com
SIC: **3651** Audio electronic systems

(G-10932)
ATLANTIC INERTIAL SYSTEMS INC
20f Commerce Way (07512-3111)
PHONE................................973 237-2713
Gerry Cordone, *Principal*
EMP: 315
SALES (corp-wide): 59.8B **Publicly Held**
WEB: www.condorpacific.com
SIC: **3812** Gyroscopes; navigational systems & instruments
HQ: Atlantic Inertial Systems Inc.
250 Knotter Dr
Cheshire CT 06410
203 250-3500

(G-10933)
BAE SYSTEMS INFO & ELEC SYS
100 Campus Rd Ste 1 (07512-1212)
PHONE................................603 885-4321
Ray Sookhoo, *Principal*
Zev Fixler, *Engrg Dir*
Nissan Clark, *Engineer*
Keen Lee, *Engineer*
John Pezzulo, *Engineer*
EMP: 400
SALES (corp-wide): 24.2B **Privately Held**
WEB: www.iesi.na.baesystems.com
SIC: **3812** Search & navigation equipment

HQ: Bae Systems Information And Electronic Systems Integration Inc.
65 Spit Brook Rd
Nashua NH 03060
603 885-4321

(G-10934)
BALLET MAKERS INC (PA)
Also Called: Capezio
1 Campus Rd (07512-1296)
PHONE...................................973 595-9000
Fax: 973 595-1767
Lynn Shanahan, *CEO*
Donald Terlizzi, *Ch of Bd*
Anthony Giacoio, *Vice Ch Bd*
Nicholas Terlizzi Jr, *Vice Ch Bd*
Marc Terlizzi, *COO*
◆ EMP: 413
SQ FT: 80,000
SALES (est): 71.8MM **Privately Held**
SIC: 5661 3149 2389 5137 Shoe stores; ballet slippers; theatrical costumes; women's & children's sportswear & swimsuits; footwear, athletic; dancewear

(G-10935)
BEZERRA CORPORATION
232 Union Blvd (07512-2670)
PHONE...................................973 595-7775
Wilson Bezerra, *CEO*
Silvana A Bezerra, *President*
EMP: 6
SALES (est): 429.1K **Privately Held**
SIC: 3751 Motorcycles, bicycles & parts

(G-10936)
BIMBO BAKERIES USA INC
930 Riverview Dr Ste 100 (07512-1156)
PHONE...................................973 256-8200
John Coster, *Principal*
EMP: 175 **Privately Held**
WEB: www.gwbakeries.com
SIC: 2079 5149 Margarine, including imitation; groceries & related products
HQ: Bimbo Bakeries Usa, Inc
255 Business Center Dr # 200
Horsham PA 19044
215 347-5500

(G-10937)
CARAVAN INGREDIENTS INC
100 Adams Dr (07512-2200)
P.O. Box 1004 (07511-1004)
PHONE...................................973 256-8886
John Stone, *Branch Mgr*
EMP: 153
SALES (corp-wide): 12.9MM **Privately Held**
SIC: 2045 Bread & bread type roll mixes: from purchased flour; blended flour: from purchased flour
HQ: Caravan Ingredients Inc.
7905 Quivira Rd
Lenexa KS 66215
913 890-5500

(G-10938)
CENTROME INC
Also Called: Advanced Biotech
10 Taft Rd (07512-1006)
PHONE...................................973 339-6242
Fax: 973 357-0644
Augustin Isernia, *President*
Adam Arteaga, *Production*
Paolo Camara, *Production*
Yuri Moreno, *Purch Agent*
Dasia McKenzie, *Purchasing*
▲ EMP: 40
SQ FT: 40,000
SALES (est): 10.2MM **Privately Held**
WEB: www.adv-bio.com
SIC: 2087 Flavoring extracts & syrups

(G-10939)
CLEANERS CHOICE INC
999 Riverview Dr Ste 201 (07512-1165)
PHONE...................................800 652-2533
Jack Belluscio, *CEO*
EMP: 10 EST: 2010
SQ FT: 15,000
SALES: 10MM **Privately Held**
SIC: 2899 Chemical preparations

(G-10940)
CORBION GROUP
100 Adams Dr (07512-2202)
PHONE...................................973 256-0198
EMP: 8
SALES (est): 1.1MM **Privately Held**
SIC: 2869 2499 3556 Perfumes, flavorings & food additives; bakers' equipment, wood; food products machinery

(G-10941)
CORONET INC
Also Called: Coronet Led
55 Shepherds Ln (07512-2130)
PHONE...................................973 345-7660
Fax: 973 345-8705
Russel Osur, *CEO*
Steven Klauber, *COO*
Matthew Grasso, *Vice Pres*
John Duarte, *Senior Engr*
Jim Linsalata, *CFO*
▲ EMP: 130 EST: 1946
SQ FT: 90,000
SALES (est): 18.9MM **Privately Held**
SIC: 3646 Fluorescent lighting fixtures, commercial

(G-10942)
ECI TECHNOLOGY INC
60 Gordon Dr (07512-2204)
PHONE...................................973 773-8686
Marianna Rabinovitch, *CEO*
Vinh Nguyen, *President*
Lyor Kogan, *COO*
Peter Bratin, *Vice Pres*
Edward Rabinovitch, *Vice Pres*
▲ EMP: 175
SQ FT: 45,800
SALES (est): 30MM **Privately Held**
WEB: www.ecitechnology.com
SIC: 3826 Automatic chemical analyzers

(G-10943)
ELEGANT USA LLC
Also Called: Saddleman Elegant
100 Bomont Pl (07512-2326)
P.O. Box 438 (07511-0438)
PHONE...................................973 812-8820
Isaac Aframian, *Vice Pres*
Yohanon Hartog, *Mng Member*
◆ EMP: 90 EST: 1997
SALES (est): 8.6MM **Privately Held**
WEB: www.elegantusa.com
SIC: 2396 2399 3714 Automotive & apparel trimmings; seat covers, automobile; motor vehicle parts & accessories

(G-10944)
FABULOUS FABRICATORS LLC
Also Called: Source One
11 Jackson Rd (07512-1001)
PHONE...................................973 779-2400
Jay Schainholz,
▼ EMP: 50
SQ FT: 78,000
SALES (est): 6.7MM **Privately Held**
SIC: 3444 Sheet metalwork

(G-10945)
GABHEN INC (PA)
Also Called: Spiral James Burn
1 Maltese Dr (07512-1402)
P.O. Box 286 (07511-0286)
PHONE...................................800 631-3572
Fax: 973 256-5981
◆ EMP: 150 EST: 1932
SQ FT: 75,000
SALES (est): 70MM **Privately Held**
WEB: www.spiralbinding.com
SIC: 2789 3083 5112 2891 Bookbinding/Related Work Mfg Lamnatd Plstc Plates Whol Stationery/Offc Sup Mfg Adhesives/Sealants

(G-10946)
GABHEN INC
1 Maltese Dr (07512-1402)
PHONE...................................973 256-0666
EMP: 5
SALES (corp-wide): 70MM **Privately Held**
SIC: 3496 Mfg Mechanical Binding Wire
PA: Gabhen, Inc.
1 Maltese Dr
Totowa NJ 07512
800 631-3572

(G-10947)
GBW MANUFACTURING INC
20 W End Rd (07512-1406)
PHONE...................................973 279-0077
Ernest Relyea, *President*
EMP: 40
SQ FT: 25,000
SALES (est): 4.1MM **Privately Held**
SIC: 3229 3499 3231 Glass furnishings & accessories; metal household articles; novelties & specialties, metal; products of purchased glass

(G-10948)
GENZYME CORPORATION
25 Madison Rd (07512-1003)
PHONE...................................973 256-2106
EMP: 6
SALES (corp-wide): 609.6MM **Privately Held**
SIC: 2835 2834 8071 3842 Enzyme & isoenzyme diagnostic agents; in vitro diagnostics; pharmaceutical preparations; biological laboratory; surgical appliances & supplies; biological products, except diagnostic; drugs & drug proprietaries
HQ: Genzyme Corporation
50 Binney St
Cambridge MA 02142
617 252-7500

(G-10949)
GOODRICH CORPORATION
20 Commerce Way (07512-1154)
PHONE...................................973 237-2700
Fax: 973 734-1982
Calvin Purdin, *Branch Mgr*
EMP: 227
SALES (corp-wide): 59.8B **Publicly Held**
WEB: www.bfgoodrich.com
SIC: 3728 Aircraft parts & equipment
HQ: Goodrich Corporation
2730 W Tyvola Rd
Charlotte NC 28217
704 423-7000

(G-10950)
GRANDVIEW PRINTING CO INC
33 W End Rd (07512-1405)
PHONE...................................973 890-0006
Fax: 973 890-0081
Lewis De Marco, *President*
Jeffrey De Marco, *Vice Pres*
EMP: 10
SQ FT: 13,000
SALES (est): 1.6MM **Privately Held**
SIC: 2789 2796 2752 Bookbinding & related work; platemaking services; commercial printing, offset

(G-10951)
HOFFMANN-LA ROCHE INC
701 Union Blvd (07512-2207)
PHONE...................................973 235-8216
John Hemerick, *Branch Mgr*
EMP: 11
SALES (corp-wide): 53.9B **Publicly Held**
WEB: www.rocheusa.com
SIC: 2834 Pharmaceutical preparations
HQ: Hoffmann-La Roche Inc.
150 Clove Rd Ste 88th
Little Falls NJ 07424
973 890-2268

(G-10952)
JEN MAR GRAPHICS INC
60 Commerce Way Ste A (07512-1154)
PHONE...................................973 256-6622
Joseph Russo, *President*
EMP: 40
SALES (est): 2.8MM **Privately Held**
WEB: www.jenmar.com
SIC: 2741 Miscellaneous publishing

(G-10953)
KNICKERBOCKER MACHINE SHOP INC (PA)
Also Called: Alloy Stainless Products Co
611 Union Blvd (07512-2402)
PHONE...................................973 256-1616
Fax: 973 256-5256
John Simonelli, *President*
Flavian Simonelli, *Exec VP*
Anthony P Auferio, *Vice Pres*
Annemarie Appleton, *VP Mfg*
Angel Caradonna, *Purch Agent*

EMP: 58 EST: 1944
SQ FT: 22,000
SALES (est): 16.4MM **Privately Held**
WEB: www.alloystainless.com
SIC: 3494 3432 Valves & pipe fittings; plumbing fixture fittings & trim

(G-10954)
LIGHTNING PRESS INC
140 Furler St (07512-1825)
PHONE...................................973 890-4422
Fax: 973 890-4414
Ron Balinski, *President*
Dana Balinski, *Vice Pres*
EMP: 12
SQ FT: 6,500
SALES (est): 1.9MM **Privately Held**
WEB: www.lightningpress.com
SIC: 2752 Commercial printing, offset

(G-10955)
MEDIN TECHNOLOGIES INC
11 Jackson Rd (07512-1001)
PHONE...................................973 779-2400
Bill Donaldson, *CEO*
Carol Bishop, *Asst Controller*
▲ EMP: 101
SALES (est): 31MM **Privately Held**
WEB: www.medin.com
SIC: 3841 3914 3411 Surgical & medical instruments; surgical instruments & apparatus; silverware & plated ware; metal cans

(G-10956)
MORENG METAL PRODUCTS INC
100 W End Rd (07512-1407)
P.O. Box 185 (07511-0185)
PHONE...................................973 256-2001
Fax: 973 256-1803
James R Moreng, *CEO*
Joseph H Moreng Jr, *Vice Pres*
EMP: 85
SQ FT: 45,000
SALES (est): 23.3MM **Privately Held**
WEB: www.morengmetal.com
SIC: 3444 3644 Sheet metal specialties, not stamped; noncurrent-carrying wiring services

(G-10957)
NATIONAL PLASTIC PRINTING
130 Furler St (07512-1825)
PHONE...................................973 785-1460
Richard Ullman, *President*
Kenneth D Ullman, *Vice Pres*
EMP: 30
SQ FT: 13,000
SALES (est): 3.5MM **Privately Held**
SIC: 3089 2759 Laminating of plastic; commercial printing

(G-10958)
O T D INC
Also Called: Unipro
18 Furler St (07512-1802)
PHONE...................................973 890-7979
Fax: 973 890-4898
▲ EMP: 8
SQ FT: 12,000
SALES (est): 690K **Privately Held**
SIC: 3714 Mfg Motor Vehicle Parts & Accessories

(G-10959)
OMEGA PACKAGING CORP
55 Kings Rd (07512-2205)
PHONE...................................973 890-9505
Larry Kalb, *President*
Bill Carr, *Vice Pres*
W M Prosser, *Vice Pres*
Jennifer Hartle, *Executive*
▲ EMP: 70
SQ FT: 40,000
SALES (est): 12.7MM **Privately Held**
SIC: 2844 2099 Cosmetic preparations; food preparations; spices, including grinding

(G-10960)
ORGANICS CORPORATION AMERICA
Also Called: Ambix Laboratories
55 W End Rd (07512-1405)
PHONE...................................973 890-9002

▲ = Import ▼=Export
◆ =Import/Export

Fax: 973 939-7090
Elkin Serna, *President*
Alvin J Goren, *Chairman*
Michael Chanin, *Vice Pres*
▲ EMP: 40
SQ FT: 50,000
SALES (est): 11.3MM **Privately Held**
WEB: www.ambixlabs.com
SIC: 2844 2834 Cosmetic preparations; vitamin, nutrient & hematinic preparations for human use

(G-10961)
PCC ASIA LLC (PA)
200 Maltese Dr (07512-1404)
PHONE..................................973 890-3873
Peter Longo, *Mng Member*
Garrett Graven, *Manager*
▲ EMP: 5
SALES (est): 1.3MM **Privately Held**
SIC: 2295 Coated fabrics, not rubberized

(G-10962)
PHARMACHEM LABORATORIES INC
15 Adams Dr (07512-2201)
PHONE..................................973 256-1340
Andrea Bauer, *Branch Mgr*
EMP: 30
SALES (corp-wide): 3.2B **Publicly Held**
SIC: 2099 2834 Food preparations; pharmaceutical preparations
HQ: Pharmachem Laboratories, Llc
265 Harrison Tpke
Kearny NJ 07032
201 246-1000

(G-10963)
PHOENIX DOWN CORPORATION
85 Route 46 (07512-2301)
PHONE..................................973 812-8100
Fax: 973 812-9077
John Facatselis, *President*
Josie Molina, *Accountant*
Kevin Miller, *Mktg Dir*
▼ EMP: 130
SQ FT: 60,000
SALES (est): 15.2MM **Privately Held**
WEB: www.phoenixdown.com
SIC: 2392 Pillows, bed: made from purchased materials; comforters & quilts: made from purchased materials

(G-10964)
PNC ELECTRONICS INC
20 W End Rd (07512-1406)
PHONE..................................973 237-0400
Fax: 973 237-0401
Peter Patel, *President*
Ila Sheh, *Corp Secy*
Sam Sangani, *Vice Pres*
▲ EMP: 30
SALES (est): 5.5MM **Privately Held**
SIC: 3577 Computer peripheral equipment

(G-10965)
PRATT INDUSTRIES USA INC
Also Called: Pratt Displays
11 Commerce Way Unit C (07512-1154)
PHONE..................................973 774-4680
EMP: 7
SALES (corp-wide): 2.1B **Privately Held**
SIC: 3999 Barber & beauty shop equipment
PA: Pratt Industries, Inc.
1800 Sarasota Busin Ste C
Conyers GA 30013
770 918-5678

(G-10966)
PRECISION CUSTOM COATINGS LLC (PA)
Also Called: P C C
200 Maltese Dr (07512-1404)
PHONE..................................973 890-3873
Fax: 973 785-8180
Aneta Konior, *Research*
Jack Higgins, *Controller*
Keith Martin, *Sales Mgr*
Kristen Lopresti, *Sales Staff*
Gerry Welkley, *Sales Staff*
◆ EMP: 430
SQ FT: 210,000
SALES (est): 126.6MM **Privately Held**
WEB: www.pcc-usa.com
SIC: 2295 Coated fabrics, not rubberized

(G-10967)
PROTAMEEN CHEMICALS INC (PA)
375 Minnisink Rd (07512-1804)
P.O. Box 166 (07511-0166)
PHONE..................................973 256-4374
Fax: 973 256-6764
Emmanuel Balsamides Jr, *President*
Thomas Balsamides, *Vice Pres*
▲ EMP: 40
SQ FT: 40,000
SALES (est): 10.4MM **Privately Held**
WEB: www.protameen.com
SIC: 2819 7231 2869 Industrial inorganic chemicals; beauty shops; industrial organic chemicals

(G-10968)
REDHEDINK LLC
135 Minnisink Rd (07512-1945)
PHONE..................................973 890-2320
Diane Byrne, *Principal*
EMP: 4
SALES (est): 209.4K **Privately Held**
SIC: 2711 Newspapers, publishing & printing

(G-10969)
RELIANCE ELECTRONICS INC
145 Shepherds Ln (07512-2130)
PHONE..................................973 237-0400
Mamta Narkhede, *President*
Ramila Patel, *General Mgr*
Paresh Patel, *Vice Pres*
Yogesh Patel, *Treasurer*
Angela Carbone, *Sales Staff*
▲ EMP: 24
SALES (est): 6MM **Privately Held**
SIC: 3571 Electronic computers

(G-10970)
SANDVIK PROCESS SYSTEMS INC
21 Campus Rd (07512-1211)
PHONE..................................973 720-7000
Fax: 973 790-9247
Walter Miller, *President*
Henrik Furhoff, *President*
Brian J Knowles, *Vice Pres*
Joann Mitchell, *Project Engr*
Paul Hodgen, *Treasurer*
◆ EMP: 50
SQ FT: 50,000
SALES (est): 11MM
SALES (corp-wide): 10.7B **Privately Held**
SIC: 3823 3535 Industrial process measurement equipment; conveyors & conveying equipment
HQ: Sandvik, Inc.
17-02 Nevins Rd
Fair Lawn NJ 07410
201 794-5000

(G-10971)
SE TYLOS USA
140 Commerce Way (07512-1158)
PHONE..................................973 837-8001
EMP: 4 EST: 2013
SALES (est): 321.4K **Privately Held**
SIC: 2869 Industrial organic chemicals

(G-10972)
SK CUSTOM CREATIONS INC
Also Called: S K
50 Furler St (07512-1802)
PHONE..................................973 754-9261
Fax: 973 754-9267
Ivan Acapana, *President*
Bov Radeliffe, *Vice Pres*
EMP: 50
SQ FT: 32,000
SALES (est): 8.2MM **Privately Held**
SIC: 2542 Office & store showcases & display fixtures

(G-10973)
SPIRAL BINDING LLC (PA) ✪
1 Maltese Dr (07512-1413)
P.O. Box 286 (07511-0286)
PHONE..................................973 256-0666
Rob Roth, *CEO*
Matt Roth, *President*
Kevin Dalton, *Sales Staff*
▲ EMP: 150 EST: 2017
SQ FT: 75,000

(G-10974)
T F S INC
Also Called: United Federated Systems
40 Vreeland Ave Ste 101 (07512-1169)
PHONE..................................973 890-7651
Cathy Mostyn, *President*
Alan Rendfrey, *Controller*
Angle Ortiz, *Manager*
EMP: 29
SALES (est): 4.9MM **Privately Held**
SIC: 3699 7382 Security control equipment & systems; security systems services

(G-10975)
TOTOWA KICKBOXING LTD LBLTY CO
Also Called: Cko Kickboxing
1 Us Highway 46 (07512-2333)
PHONE..................................973 507-9106
Mauricio Barriga,
EMP: 18
SQ FT: 7,850
SALES (est): 467K **Privately Held**
SIC: 7941 3949 7991 Sports clubs, managers & promoters; gloves, sport & athletic: boxing, handball, etc.; physical fitness facilities

(G-10976)
TOTOWA PRECISION TOOLING INC
442 Riverview Dr (07512-2319)
PHONE..................................973 256-2283
Fax: 973 256-6891
George Bondarenko, *President*
Maria Bondarenko, *Admin Sec*
EMP: 14 EST: 1974
SQ FT: 5,000
SALES (est): 2.8MM **Privately Held**
WEB: www.totowaprecision.com
SIC: 2865 3545 3599 3544 Dyes & pigments; machine tool attachments & accessories; machine shop, jobbing & repair; special dies, tools, jigs & fixtures

(G-10977)
VECTRACOR INC
785 Totowa Rd Ste 100 (07512-1500)
PHONE..................................973 904-0444
EMP: 10 EST: 2010
SALES (est): 838.2K **Privately Held**
SIC: 3845 Mfg Electromedical Equipment

(G-10978)
VECTRACOR INC
785 Totowa Rd Ste 100 (07512-1500)
PHONE..................................973 768-0402
Brad S Schreck, *President*
Michael Andrias, *Sales Staff*
EMP: 11
SQ FT: 3,000
SALES (est): 840K **Privately Held**
SIC: 3845 Electromedical equipment

(G-10979)
VERSABAR CORPORATION
100 Maltese Dr (07512-1403)
PHONE..................................973 279-8400
Fax: 973 942-8282
William E Taylor, *President*
Sarah Taylor, *Treasurer*
▲ EMP: 15 EST: 1945
SQ FT: 22,000
SALES (est): 3.1MM **Privately Held**
WEB: www.versabar.com
SIC: 3499 3429 Strapping, metal; manufactured hardware (general)

(G-10980)
VIBRA SCREW INC
755 Union Blvd (07512-2207)
P.O. Box 229 (07511-0229)
PHONE..................................973 256-7410
Fax: 973 256-7567
Eugene A Wahl Sr, *President*
Richard C Wahl, *Exec VP*
Joanne Young, *Purch Mgr*
Ellen Wahl Skibiak, *Treasurer*
Edward Giacobbe, *Regl Sales Mgr*
EMP: 40
SQ FT: 50,000
SALES: 10MM **Privately Held**
WEB: www.vibrascrew.com
SIC: 3535 3559 Conveyors & conveying equipment

(G-10981)
VIGOR INC
45 Frances St (07512-2471)
PHONE..................................973 851-9539
Victor Melnychuk, *Owner*
EMP: 4 EST: 2010
SALES: 140K **Privately Held**
SIC: 2431 Interior & ornamental woodwork & trim

(G-10982)
VISKAL PRINTING LLC
Also Called: AlphaGraphics
40e Commerce Way (07512-3110)
PHONE..................................973 812-6600
Krishnan Thampi, *President*
EMP: 7
SALES (est): 1.1MM **Privately Held**
SIC: 2752 Commercial printing, offset

(G-10983)
WESTROCK RKT COMPANY
29g Commerce Way (07512-3112)
PHONE..................................973 594-6000
EMP: 183
SALES (corp-wide): 14.8B **Publicly Held**
SIC: 2657 Folding paperboard boxes
HQ: Westrock Rkt Company
1000 Abernathy Rd Ste 125
Atlanta GA 30328
770 448-2193

(G-10984)
WESTROCK RKT COMPANY
Also Called: Alliance Display
1 Center Ct Unit Ab (07512-1170)
PHONE..................................973 237-9570
Bob Pasante, *Manager*
EMP: 40
SALES (corp-wide): 14.8B **Publicly Held**
WEB: www.rocktenn.com
SIC: 2631 Paperboard mills
HQ: Westrock Rkt Company
1000 Abernathy Rd Ste 125
Atlanta GA 30328
770 448-2193

(G-10985)
WG PRODUCTS INC
70 Maltese Dr (07512-1403)
P.O. Box 695 (07511-0695)
PHONE..................................973 256-5999
Kevin Cooney, *President*
▲ EMP: 8
SALES (est): 1.2MM **Privately Held**
SIC: 3999 Chairs, hydraulic, barber & beauty shop

(G-10986)
WINDTREE THERAPEUTICS INC
710 Union Blvd (07512-2210)
PHONE..................................973 339-2889
Fax: 973 256-5257
Ernest Tyler, *Branch Mgr*
EMP: 10
SALES (corp-wide): 1.4MM **Publicly Held**
WEB: www.discoverylabs.com
SIC: 2834 5122 Pharmaceutical preparations; pharmaceuticals
PA: Windtree Therapeutics, Inc.
2600 Kelly Rd Ste 100
Warrington PA 18976
215 488-9300

Towaco
Morris County

(G-10987)
APOGEE TECHNOLOGIES LLC
Also Called: R&L Sheet Metal
3 Cole Rd (07082)
PHONE..................................973 575-8448
Jerry Grieco,
EMP: 10

SALES (est): 862.7K **Privately Held**
SIC: 3499 Fabricated metal products

(G-10988)
BAUMER OF AMERICA INC
425 Main Rd (07082-1201)
P.O. Box 18 (07082-0018)
PHONE......................................973 263-1569
Fax: 973 299-8587
Philipp Schuster, *General Mgr*
Jesse Collinson, *General Mgr*
▲ EMP: 12
SQ FT: 10,000
SALES (est): 2.6MM
SALES (corp-wide): 69.1MM **Privately
Held**
WEB: www.baumerofamerica.com
SIC: 3423 Knives, agricultural or industrial;
cutting dies, except metal cutting
PA: Albrecht Baumer Gmbh & Co. Kg
Spezialmaschinenfabrik
Asdorfer Str. 96-106
Freudenberg 57258
273 428-90

(G-10989)
BOARDS AND BEAMS CO LLC
1275 Blmfield Ave Bldg 10 (07082)
PHONE......................................973 299-6100
Steve Djurasek,
EMP: 5
SALES (est): 585K **Privately Held**
SIC: 2421 Sawmills & planing mills, gen-
eral

(G-10990)
BOSCO PRODUCTS INC
441 Main Rd (07082-1201)
PHONE......................................973 334-7534
Steven Sanders, *President*
▼ EMP: 5
SQ FT: 40,000
SALES (est): 455K **Privately Held**
SIC: 2066 Chocolate

(G-10991)
CRAFT-PAK INC
1 Ashley Pl (07082-1447)
PHONE......................................718 763-0700
Anthony De Biasi, *President*
Vincent Tomaselli, *Vice Pres*
EMP: 16
SQ FT: 13,000
SALES (est): 2MM **Privately Held**
SIC: 2673 Plastic bags: made from pur-
chased materials

(G-10992)
DELMHORST INSTRUMENT COMPANY
51 Indian Ln E (07082-1025)
PHONE......................................973 334-2557
Fax: 973 334-2657
Aristide Laurenzi, *Ch of Bd*
Thomas Laurenzi, *President*
Clay Corbett, *Accounts Mgr*
Paul Laurenzi, *Chief Mktg Ofcr*
▲ EMP: 28 EST: 1946
SQ FT: 13,970
SALES (est): 5.8MM **Privately Held**
WEB: www.delmhorst.com
SIC: 3829 Measuring & controlling devices

(G-10993)
DIVERSIFIED HEAT TRANSFER INC
439 Main Rd (07082-1369)
PHONE......................................800 221-1522
Norman Goldberg, *CEO*
James Colwell, *Vice Pres*
Thomas Francullo, *Vice Pres*
Jake Goldberg, *Vice Pres*
Jonathan Goldberg, *Vice Pres*
◆ EMP: 75 EST: 1932
SQ FT: 100,000
SALES (est): 27.7MM **Privately Held**
WEB: www.dhtnet.com
SIC: 3585 Evaporative condensers, heat
transfer equipment

(G-10994)
DROM INTERNATIONAL INC
Also Called: Inc Drom International
5 Jacksonville Rd (07082-1125)
PHONE......................................973 316-8400
Fax: 973 316-9039

Bruno Storp PHD, *Ch of Bd*
Andrew O Shea, *President*
Richard Rude, *COO*
Robert Astapf, *Vice Pres*
Donald H Latici, *Vice Pres*
▲ EMP: 33
SQ FT: 22,000
SALES (est): 9.3MM
SALES (corp-wide): 105.8MM **Privately
Held**
SIC: 2844 Toilet preparations
PA: Drom Fragrances Gmbh & Co. Kg
Oberdiller Str. 18
Baierbrunn 82065
897 442-50

(G-10995)
ENGINEERED SECURITY SYSTEMS (PA)
Also Called: E S S
1 Indian Ln E (07082-1025)
PHONE......................................973 257-0555
Fax: 973 257-0550
Laurice R George, *CEO*
David R George, *President*
Angelo George, *Chairman*
EMP: 40 EST: 1971
SQ FT: 9,000
SALES (est): 8.6MM **Privately Held**
WEB: www.essi.net
SIC: 7382 3699 Burglar alarm mainte-
nance & monitoring; fire alarm mainte-
nance & monitoring; security control
equipment & systems

(G-10996)
GLOBAL GRAPHICS INTERGRATION
14 Willard Ln (07082-1517)
PHONE......................................973 334-9653
Julia Murray, *CEO*
EMP: 16
SQ FT: 60,000
SALES (est): 966.2K **Privately Held**
SIC: 2759 7311 8742 Commercial print-
ing; advertising agencies; marketing con-
sulting services

(G-10997)
JENISSE LEISURE PRODUCTS INC
5 Van Duyne Ct (07082-1439)
PHONE......................................973 331-1177
Richard Dehart, *President*
EMP: 10
SALES (est): 1.2MM **Privately Held**
SIC: 2899 Chemical preparations

(G-10998)
M D CARBIDE TOOL CORP
19 Old Jacksonville Rd (07082-1013)
PHONE......................................973 263-0104
Marian Depczynski, *President*
EMP: 21 EST: 1964
SALES (est): 85K **Privately Held**
SIC: 3599 3545 3369 Machine shop, job-
bing & repair; machine tool accessories;
nonferrous foundries

(G-10999)
MULTIPOWER INTERNATIONAL INC
7 Woodshire Ter (07082-1457)
P.O. Box 187 (07082-0187)
PHONE......................................973 727-0327
Qiang GE, *President*
▲ EMP: 7
SALES (est): 200K **Privately Held**
SIC: 3743 Engines, steam (locomotive)

(G-11000)
PANOVA INC
33 Jacksonville Rd Ste 2 (07082-1100)
PHONE......................................973 263-1700
Ehren A Dimitry, *CEO*
Ronald C Knauf, *President*
Deborah Ceglarski, *Controller*
Carl Grossi, *Mktg Dir*
Frieda Dimitry, *Admin Sec*
▲ EMP: 35
SQ FT: 12,500
SALES (est): 6MM **Privately Held**
WEB: www.amecorporation.com
SIC: 3069 3061 Molded rubber products;
mechanical rubber goods

(G-11001)
PLASTINETICS INC
439 Main Rd (07082-1369)
P.O. Box 322 (07082-0322)
PHONE......................................818 364-1611
Fax: 973 316-0300
Edward J Batta, *President*
EMP: 7
SQ FT: 6,500
SALES (est): 6.5MM **Privately Held**
WEB: www.plastinetics.com
SIC: 3089 Plastic containers, except foam;
plastic kitchenware, tableware & house-
ware; plastic hardware & building prod-
ucts; boot or shoe products, plastic

(G-11002)
Q GLASS COMPANY INC
624 Rte 202 (07082)
PHONE......................................973 335-5191
Fax: 973 335-2057
Daniel J Dotterweich Jr, *President*
Daniel Seme, *Sales Staff*
EMP: 7 EST: 1947
SQ FT: 8,000
SALES (est): 745.3K **Privately Held**
WEB: www.qglass.com
SIC: 3229 Glassware, industrial

(G-11003)
SEA BREEZE FRUIT FLAVORS INC
441 Main Rd (07082-1298)
PHONE......................................973 334-7777
Fax: 973 334-2617
Steven Sanders, *President*
Josh Sanders, *Vice Pres*
Tim Kachur, *Purch Agent*
Peter Hope, *Purchasing*
Shawn Gray, *QC Mgr*
EMP: 70 EST: 1925
SQ FT: 40,000
SALES (est): 17.8MM **Privately Held**
SIC: 2087 5046 Syrups, drink; commercial
equipment

(G-11004)
TELEDYNAMICS LLC
45 Indian Ln E Ste 1 (07082-1025)
PHONE......................................973 248-3360
Eric Witt, *Manager*
▼ EMP: 25
SQ FT: 18,000
SALES (est): 6.5MM **Privately Held**
SIC: 3536 Monorail systems

(G-11005)
TROY HILLS MANUFACTURING INC
2 Como Ct (07082-1128)
P.O. Box 98 (07082-0098)
PHONE......................................973 263-1885
Brian Melgaard, *President*
▲ EMP: 6
SALES (est): 908.4K **Privately Held**
SIC: 3632 3061 Freezers, home & farm;
mechanical rubber goods

(G-11006)
UHLMANN PACKAGING SYSTEMS LP
44 Indian Ln E (07082-1032)
PHONE......................................973 402-8855
Fax: 973 402-2144
Markus Leuprecht, *Project Mgr*
Maria Bumpus, *Purchasing*
Chris Mentone, *Engineer*
Bogdan Nitulescu, *Engineer*
Abdon Villa, *Engineer*
▲ EMP: 75
SQ FT: 50,000
SALES (est): 18.7MM
SALES (corp-wide): 366.4MM **Privately
Held**
WEB: www.uhlmann-usa.com
SIC: 3541 5084 Machine tool replacement
& repair parts, metal cutting types; ma-
chine tools & metalworking machinery; in-
struments & control equipment
PA: Uhlmann Pac-Systeme Gmbh & Co. Kg
Uhlmannstr. 14-18
Laupheim 88471
739 270-20

(G-11007)
WHITE MARINE INC
7 Old Jacksonville Rd (07082-1013)
PHONE......................................732 826-4491
Fax: 732 826-4478
Jennifer Billand, *President*
EMP: 17
SQ FT: 25,000
SALES: 5MM **Privately Held**
WEB: www.whitemarineinc.com
SIC: 7699 3731 Industrial machinery &
equipment repair; shipbuilding & repairing

Tranquility
Sussex County

(G-11008)
TECHNODIAMANT USA INC
35a Kennedy Rd (07879)
P.O. Box 398 (07879-0398)
PHONE......................................908 850-8505
David Slaperud, *President*
EMP: 2
SQ FT: 1,000
SALES: 1.2MM
SALES (corp-wide): 41.1K **Privately Held**
WEB: www.technodiamant.com
SIC: 3545 5085 Diamond cutting tools for
turning, boring, burnishing, etc.; dressers,
abrasive wheel: diamond point or other;
wheel turning equipment, diamond point
or other; industrial supplies
HQ: Technodiamant Almere B.V.
De Vest 1 C
Valkenswaard

Trenton
Mercer County

(G-11009)
21ST CENTURY MEDIA NEWSPPR LLC (HQ)
Also Called: Journal Register Company
600 Perry St (08618-3934)
PHONE......................................215 504-4200
John Paton, *CEO*
Jeff Bairstow, *President*
Madeline Wood, *CTO*
EMP: 53
SALES (est): 18.2MM
SALES (corp-wide): 4.3B **Privately Held**
SIC: 2711 Newspapers
PA: Digital First Media, Llc
101 W Colfax Ave Fl 11
Denver CO 80202
212 257-7212

(G-11010)
A M GATTI INC
524 Tindall Ave (08610-5399)
PHONE......................................609 396-1577
Fax: 609 695-4339
Anthony Ursic, *Principal*
Chris Warner, *Manager*
Gina Soyka, *Office Admin*
EMP: 19
SALES (est): 4.1MM **Privately Held**
SIC: 3568 Power transmission equipment

(G-11011)
A R J CUSTOM FABRICATION INC
151 Taylor St (08638-4320)
PHONE......................................609 695-6227
Fax: 609 695-6136
Anthony R Jones, *President*
Barbara Jones, *Treasurer*
EMP: 12
SQ FT: 15,000
SALES (est): 2.3MM **Privately Held**
SIC: 3444 Sheet metalwork

(G-11012)
A SIGN COMPANY
258 Old York Rd (08620)
PHONE......................................609 298-3388
EMP: 6
SQ FT: 9,000

SALES (est): 250K **Privately Held**
SIC: 3993 Mfg Signs/Advertising Specialties

(G-11013)
A STITCH AHEAD
448 Whitehead Rd Ste 3 (08619-3282)
PHONE..................................609 586-1068
Fax: 609 586-2443
Glenn Mangee, *Owner*
EMP: 10
SALES (est): 622K **Privately Held**
WEB: www.astitchahead.com
SIC: 2395 Embroidery products, except schiffli machine

(G-11014)
ALIGN SOURCING LTD LBLTY CO
46 Doe Dr (08620-1326)
P.O. Box 8482, Hamilton (08650-0482)
PHONE..................................609 375-8550
James Karas, *Mng Member*
EMP: 2
SALES (est): 1MM **Privately Held**
SIC: 3823 7389 Thermal conductivity instruments, industrial process type;

(G-11015)
ALL COUNTY RECYCLING INC
391 Enterprise Ave (08638-4413)
PHONE..................................609 393-6445
Mark Barretti, *CEO*
EMP: 10 EST: 2007
SQ FT: 600
SALES (est): 1.8MM **Privately Held**
SIC: 4953 2631 Recycling, waste materials; cardboard

(G-11016)
ALLIANCE FOOD EQUIPMENT
Also Called: Gram Equipment
1 S Gold Dr (08691-1606)
P.O. Box 236, Northvale (07647-0236)
PHONE..................................201 784-1101
Fax: 201 784-1116
Neal E White, *President*
Jakob Hansen, *Principal*
EMP: 15
SQ FT: 28,000
SALES (est): 4.6MM **Privately Held**
SIC: 3565 Packaging machinery

(G-11017)
ANA DESIGN CORP
1 Ott St (08638-5196)
PHONE..................................609 394-0300
Fax: 609 394-5030
Fred Cohen, *CEO*
Donald Weeden, *Ch of Bd*
Frank Weeden, *President*
Elizabeth Barek, *Treasurer*
EMP: 12
SALES (est): 1.1MM **Privately Held**
WEB: www.anadesigncorp.com
SIC: 3999 Candles

(G-11018)
ANDREA AROMATICS INC
150 Enterprise Ave (08638-4404)
P.O. Box 3091, Princeton (08543-3091)
PHONE..................................609 695-7710
Fax: 609 392-8914
Michael D'Andrea, *President*
Janine Riggs, *Treasurer*
Susan D'Andrea, *Admin Sec*
▲ EMP: 20
SQ FT: 21,000
SALES: 7MM **Privately Held**
SIC: 2844 Toilet preparations

(G-11019)
AREA AUTO RACING NEWS INC
2831 S Broad St (08610-3603)
P.O. Box 8547 (08650-0547)
PHONE..................................609 888-3618
Fax: 609 888-2538
Leonard Sammons, *President*
EMP: 6
SQ FT: 3,000
SALES: 570K **Privately Held**
WEB: www.aarn.com
SIC: 2711 2721 Newspapers, publishing & printing; magazines: publishing & printing; periodicals: publishing & printing

(G-11020)
ARM NATIONAL FOOD INC
539 Chestnut Ave (08611-1233)
PHONE..................................609 695-4911
Fax: 609 695-4919
Armando Rienzi, *Manager*
EMP: 5
SALES (corp-wide): 14MM **Privately Held**
SIC: 5141 5421 5147 5142 Groceries, general line; meat & fish markets; meats & meat products; packaged frozen goods; sausages & other prepared meats; meat packing plants
PA: Arm National Food, Inc.
1546 Lamberton Rd
Trenton NJ 08611
609 394-0431

(G-11021)
AVANZATO JEWELERS LLC
2440 Whthrse Hmlton Sq Rd (08690-2820)
PHONE..................................609 890-0500
Raymond Whitehouse, *General Mgr*
Tom Avanzato, *Mng Member*
EMP: 7
SQ FT: 1,000
SALES (est): 722.1K **Privately Held**
SIC: 5944 3911 Jewelry, precious stones & precious metals; jewelry, precious metal

(G-11022)
AVONY ENTERPRISES INC ✪
39 Meade St Ste 122 (08638-4321)
PHONE..................................212 242-8144
Jack Colon, *Principal*
EMP: 35 EST: 2017
SALES (est): 1.1MM **Privately Held**
SIC: 3599 Tubing, flexible metallic

(G-11023)
AZTEC GRAPHICS INC
420 Whitehead Rd (08619-3255)
PHONE..................................609 587-1000
Fax: 609 587-9117
Ronald Balerno, *President*
Keith Balerno, *Marketing Staff*
Eric Bonczkiewicz, *Graphic Designe*
EMP: 15
SQ FT: 9,500
SALES (est): 2.1MM **Privately Held**
WEB: www.aztecgraphics.com
SIC: 2261 2791 2396 2395 Screen printing of cotton broadwoven fabrics; typesetting; automotive & apparel trimmings; pleating & stitching

(G-11024)
B & R PRINTING INC
Also Called: B & R Bindery Division
84 Hummingbird Dr (08690-3544)
PHONE..................................609 448-3328
Fax: 609 882-9280
James Buckley Jr, *President*
EMP: 7
SQ FT: 9,500
SALES (est): 1MM **Privately Held**
SIC: 2752 2789 Commercial printing, offset; photo-offset printing; binding only: books, pamphlets, magazines, etc.

(G-11025)
BARTLEY CRUCIBLE REFRACTORIES
15 Muirhead Ave (08638-5110)
P.O. Box 5464 (08638-0464)
PHONE..................................609 393-0066
Dan Mischel, *President*
David Mischel, *Vice Pres*
▲ EMP: 13
SQ FT: 40,000
SALES (est): 1.8MM **Privately Held**
SIC: 3297 Crucibles: graphite, magnesite, chrome, silica, etc.

(G-11026)
BENTON GRAPHICS INC
3 Industrial Dr (08619-3244)
PHONE..................................609 587-4000
Fax: 609 587-9890
Mary A Benton, *President*
Margaret Linico, *Vice Pres*
EMP: 38
SQ FT: 22,500

SALES (est): 8.4MM **Privately Held**
WEB: www.bentongraphics.com
SIC: 3555 3542 Printing trades machinery; machine tools, metal forming type

(G-11027)
BILLS PRINTING SERVICE INC
2829 S Broad St (08610-3603)
PHONE..................................609 888-1841
Fax: 609 888-4424
William Mason, *President*
Patricia Mason, *Corp Secy*
EMP: 9
SQ FT: 4,000
SALES (est): 1.5MM **Privately Held**
SIC: 2752 Commercial printing, offset

(G-11028)
BLACK LAGOON INC
78 Orourke Dr (08691-3913)
P.O. Box 9031, Hamilton (08650-1031)
PHONE..................................609 815-1654
Chris Borek, *President*
EMP: 5 EST: 2008
SALES (est): 270K **Privately Held**
SIC: 2782 Blankbooks & looseleaf binders

(G-11029)
BOLT WELDING & IRON WORKS
78 Wall St (08609-1106)
PHONE..................................609 393-3993
Christopher Hiltey, *Owner*
EMP: 5
SQ FT: 1,500
SALES (est): 569.1K **Privately Held**
SIC: 3446 3449 Architectural metalwork; stairs, fire escapes, balconies, railings & ladders; open flooring & grating for construction; fences, gates, posts & flagpoles; miscellaneous metalwork

(G-11030)
BUNN INDUSTRIES INCORPORATED (PA)
Also Called: Delaware Valley Box & Lbr Co
2651 E State Street Ext (08619-3319)
PHONE..................................609 890-2900
Fax: 609 890-8241
Charles C Gould, *President*
EMP: 10
SQ FT: 15,000
SALES (est): 3.7MM **Privately Held**
SIC: 2653 2441 2448 Boxes, corrugated: made from purchased materials; boxes, wood; wood pallets & skids

(G-11031)
BWAY CORPORATION
6 Litho Rd (08648-3304)
PHONE..................................609 883-4300
Fax: 732 997-4055
Rich Charlton, *Opers Mgr*
Aren Millan, *Prdtn Mgr*
Berrdi James, *Branch Mgr*
Rich Shenowski, *Manager*
EMP: 17
SALES (corp-wide): 787.1MM **Privately Held**
SIC: 3399 Metal powders, pastes & flakes
HQ: Bway Corporation
8607 Roberts Dr Ste 250
Atlanta GA 30350

(G-11032)
CAPITOL STEEL INC
Also Called: Capitol Steel Products
10 Escher St (08609-1018)
PHONE..................................609 538-9313
Sal Borgese, *President*
EMP: 11
SQ FT: 2,000
SALES (est): 2.3MM **Privately Held**
SIC: 3441 Building components, structural steel

(G-11033)
CARFARO INC
2075 E State Street Ext (08619-3323)
PHONE..................................609 890-6600
Joseph Carfaro, *President*
Gayle L Carfaro, *Corp Secy*
Maria R Carfaro, *Vice Pres*
Charles Tilton, *Technology*
EMP: 50
SQ FT: 25,000

SALES (est): 16.8MM **Privately Held**
WEB: www.carfaro.com
SIC: 3446 Architectural metalwork

(G-11034)
CARPENTER LLC
Also Called: Carpenter Emergency Lighting
2 Marlen Dr (08691-1601)
PHONE..................................609 689-3090
Avinash Diwan,
▲ EMP: 14
SALES (est): 2.9MM **Privately Held**
SIC: 3571 3993 3648 Computers, digital, analog or hybrid; signs & advertising specialties; lighting equipment

(G-11035)
CASE PORK ROLL CO INC
644 Washington St (08611-3682)
P.O. Box 33019 (08629-3019)
PHONE..................................609 396-8171
Fax: 609 396-4444
Thomas Grieb, *CEO*
Thomas Dolan, *President*
Richard Clem, *Corp Secy*
Tom Dolan, *Vice Pres*
Arlene Greib, *Vice Pres*
EMP: 25 EST: 1950
SQ FT: 6,000
SALES (est): 4.9MM **Privately Held**
WEB: www.caseporkrollstore.com
SIC: 2013 Pork, cured: from purchased meat

(G-11036)
CB&I LLC
200 Horizon Center Blvd (08691-1904)
PHONE..................................856 482-3000
EMP: 240
SALES (corp-wide): 2.9B **Publicly Held**
SIC: 1791 3443 3312 Structural steel erection; storage tanks, metal: erection; fabricated plate work (boiler shop); blast furnaces & steel mills
HQ: Cb&I Llc
2103 Research Forest Dr
The Woodlands TX 77380
281 870-5000

(G-11037)
CCL LABEL (DELAWARE) INC
104 N Gold Dr (08691-1602)
PHONE..................................609 259-1055
Craig Groendyk, *General Mgr*
EMP: 150
SALES (corp-wide): 3.7B **Privately Held**
SIC: 2759 2672 Flexographic printing; letterpress printing; coated & laminated paper
HQ: Ccl Label (Delaware), Inc.
15 Controls Dr
Shelton CT 06484
203 926-1253

(G-11038)
CENTRAL RECORD PUBLICATIONS
Also Called: Ad Lines
600 Perry St (08618-3934)
PHONE..................................609 654-5000
Pat Haughey, *Manager*
EMP: 30 EST: 1896
SQ FT: 2,500
SALES (est): 1.3MM **Privately Held**
SIC: 2711 2741 2721 Commercial printing & newspaper publishing combined; miscellaneous publishing; periodicals

(G-11039)
CHENEY FLASHING COMPANY LLC
623 Prospect St (08618-3108)
P.O. Box 1083, Langhorne PA (19047-6083)
PHONE..................................609 394-8175
Fax: 609 394-8891
Richard Levine, *President*
Sarah Rowland, *Office Mgr*
Cindy Carlson, *Manager*
Harry Levine, *Vice Pres*
EMP: 16
SQ FT: 20,000
SALES (est): 3.8MM **Privately Held**
WEB: www.cheneyflashing.com
SIC: 3444 Sheet metal specialties, not stamped

(G-11040)
CIAO CUPCAKE
7 Wycklow Dr (08691-1204)
PHONE..................................609 964-6167
Natalie Catalano, *Principal*
EMP: 4
SALES (est): 214.1K Privately Held
SIC: 2051 Bread, cake & related products

(G-11041)
CLARICI GRAPHICS INC
88 Youngs Rd (08619-1013)
PHONE..................................609 587-7204
Fax: 609 587-5932
Eugene S Clarici Sr, *President*
Eugene S Clarici Jr, *Vice Pres*
EMP: 20 EST: 1923
SQ FT: 2,000
SALES (est): 2.2MM Privately Held
WEB: www.clarici.com
SIC: 7336 2396 Silk screen design; automotive & apparel trimmings

(G-11042)
CLEAN-TEX SERVICES INC
198 Reservoir St (08618-3604)
PHONE..................................908 912-2700
David Zahler, *CEO*
Jacob Zahler, *President*
EMP: 350 EST: 1995
SALES (est): 2.6MM Privately Held
SIC: 7231 7212 2299 Cosmetology & personal hygiene salons; pickup station, laundry & drycleaning; truck route, laundry & drycleaning; retail agent, laundry & drycleaning; crash, linen; towels & towelings, linen & linen-and-cotton mixtures

(G-11043)
COCCO ENTERPRISES INC (PA)
3575 Quakerbridge Rd # 204 (08619-1271)
PHONE..................................609 393-5939
Fax: 609 393-5924
Jan Saunders, *President*
Vicky Romanoski, *Vice Pres*
Rebecca Irish, *Director*
EMP: 15
SQ FT: 3,000
SALES (est): 1.4MM Privately Held
WEB: www.cocco-ent.com
SIC: 3842 Orthopedic appliances; prosthetic appliances

(G-11044)
CONGOLEUM CORPORATION (PA)
3500 Quakerbridge Rd (08619-1206)
P.O. Box 3127 (08619-0127)
PHONE..................................609 584-3000
Fax: 609 584-3555
Christopher Oconnor, *President*
Roy Parpart, *District Mgr*
Chris O'Connor, *COO*
Kurt Denman, *Senior VP*
Merrill Smith, *Vice Pres*
◆ EMP: 36
SQ FT: 36,000
SALES (est): 117.8MM Privately Held
WEB: www.congoleum.com
SIC: 3081 Floor or wall covering, unsupported plastic; tile, unsupported plastic

(G-11045)
CONGOLEUM CORPORATION
3705 Quakerbridge Rd # 211 (08619-1288)
P.O. Box 3127 (08619-0127)
PHONE..................................609 584-3601
Fax: 609 584-3518
Bob Agada, *Manager*
Allan Carrigan, *Database Admin*
EMP: 100
SALES (corp-wide): 117.8MM Privately Held
SIC: 7389 3081 3996 3253 Purchasing service; vinyl film & sheet; hard surface floor coverings; ceramic wall & floor tile
PA: Congoleum Corporation
3500 Quakerbridge Rd
Trenton NJ 08619
609 584-3000

(G-11046)
CONGOLEUM CORPORATION
1945 E State Street Ext (08619-3305)
P.O. Box 3127 (08619-0127)
PHONE..................................609 584-3000

L Novak, *Engineer*
Wayne Neville, *Manager*
EMP: 313
SALES (corp-wide): 117.8MM Privately Held
WEB: www.congoleum.com
SIC: 3081 Floor or wall covering, unsupported plastic
PA: Congoleum Corporation
3500 Quakerbridge Rd
Trenton NJ 08619
609 584-3000

(G-11047)
CRAZY STEVES CONCOCTIONS LLC
Also Called: Crazy Steve's Pickles & Salsa
38 Herbert Rd (08691-2901)
PHONE..................................908 787-2089
Steve Zielinski, *CEO*
EMP: 5 EST: 2009
SALES (est): 263.4K Privately Held
SIC: 2035 Pickled fruits & vegetables

(G-11048)
CREATIVE MACHINING SYSTEMS
124 Youngs Rd (08619-1097)
PHONE..................................609 586-3932
Fax: 609 586-5633
Victor Scharko, *President*
Antonina Scharko, *Vice Pres*
EMP: 12
SQ FT: 13,000
SALES (est): 2.4MM Privately Held
WEB: www.creativemachining.com
SIC: 3599 7692 Machine shop, jobbing & repair; welding repair

(G-11049)
CREST GROUP INC (HQ)
Also Called: Cresttek
Scotch Trenton Mercer Air (08628)
P.O. Box 7266 (08628-0266)
PHONE..................................609 883-4000
J Michael Goodson, *CEO*
EMP: 10
SQ FT: 45,000
SALES (est): 4.1MM
SALES (corp-wide): 41.3MM Privately Held
WEB: www.thecrestgroup.com
SIC: 3699 Cleaning equipment, ultrasonic, except medical & dental
PA: Crestek, Inc.
18 Graphics Dr
Ewing NJ 08628
609 883-4000

(G-11050)
CYTOTHERM LP
110 Sewell Ave (08610-6059)
PHONE..................................609 396-1456
Fax: 609 396-9395
Roman Kuzyk, *Partner*
EMP: 6
SQ FT: 2,000
SALES: 1.5MM Privately Held
WEB: www.cytotherm.com
SIC: 3861 Processing equipment, photographic

(G-11051)
CZAR INDUSTRIES INC
Also Called: Rjd Machine Products
1424-1426 Heath Ave (08638)
PHONE..................................609 392-1515
Curtis P Duval, *President*
EMP: 9
SALES (est): 357.3K Privately Held
SIC: 3399 Primary metal products

(G-11052)
D A K OFFICE SERVICES INC
Also Called: Sir Speedy
3100 Quakerbridge Rd (08619-1658)
PHONE..................................609 586-8222
Fax: 609 586-8512
David A Kaplan, *President*
Joanne Kaplan, *Treasurer*
EMP: 8
SQ FT: 5,000
SALES (est): 1.4MM Privately Held
SIC: 2752 2791 2789 Commercial printing, offset; typesetting; bookbinding & related work

(G-11053)
DENAKA PARTNERS LP
Also Called: Home Rubber Company
31 Wolverton St 35 (08611-2429)
P.O. Box 878 (08605-0878)
PHONE..................................609 394-1176
Fax: 609 396-1985
Richard Balka, *Partner*
Richard Dobuski, *Partner*
Greg Piegaro, *Partner*
Norman Ziegler, *Partner*
EMP: 44
SQ FT: 62,000
SALES (est): 9.1MM Privately Held
WEB: www.homerubber.com
SIC: 3061 Mechanical rubber goods

(G-11054)
DEVATAL INC
644 Newkirk Ave (08610-4448)
PHONE..................................609 586-1575
Yair Devash, *Principal*
EMP: 4
SALES (est): 542.3K Privately Held
SIC: 2836 Biological products, except diagnostic

(G-11055)
DIGITAL ATELIER LLC
60 Sculptors Way Ste A (08619-3428)
PHONE..................................609 890-6666
Jon E Lash, *Mng Member*
EMP: 6
SALES: 867.3K Privately Held
SIC: 7336 3299 Art design services; art goods: plaster of paris, papier mache & scagliola

(G-11056)
E R SQUIBB & SONS INTER-AM
Also Called: Bristol-Myers Squibb
3 Hamilton Health Pl (08690-3542)
PHONE..................................609 818-3715
Pam Kagil, *Manager*
EMP: 7
SALES (corp-wide): 20.7B Publicly Held
WEB: www.unitedinpurpose.com
SIC: 2834 Pharmaceutical preparations
HQ: E. R. Squibb & Sons Inter-American Corporation
3551 Lawrenceville Rd
Princeton NJ 08540
609 252-4111

(G-11057)
EAST WEST SERVICE CO INC
2 Marlen Dr (08691-1601)
PHONE..................................609 631-9000
Fax: 609 689-3091
Avinash Diwan, *President*
▲ EMP: 25
SQ FT: 4,000
SALES (est): 3.3MM Privately Held
SIC: 3699 5065 Electrical equipment & supplies; electronic parts & equipment

(G-11058)
ELECTRICAL MOTOR REPR CO OF NJ
809 E State St (08609-1411)
P.O. Box 3787 (08629-0787)
PHONE..................................609 392-6149
Fax: 609 392-6117
Paul Doran, *President*
Joseph Castiglione, *Vice Pres*
EMP: 19
SQ FT: 3,800
SALES: 4MM Privately Held
WEB: www.elevatormotor.com
SIC: 7694 5063 Electric motor repair; motors, electric

(G-11059)
FAIRWAY BUILDING PRODUCTS LLC
Also Called: Carfaro
2075 E State Street Ext (08619-3323)
PHONE..................................609 890-6600
Fax: 609 890-7522
Joseph Carfaro, *Manager*
EMP: 50
SALES (corp-wide): 31.8MM Privately Held
SIC: 3446 Architectural metalwork

PA: Fairway Building Products, Llc
53 Eby Chiques Rd
Mount Joy PA 17552
717 653-6777

(G-11060)
GREATER NEW YORK BOX CO INC
1400 E State St (08609-1714)
PHONE..................................609 631-7900
Frederick Edelman, *President*
EMP: 4
SALES (est): 226.2K Privately Held
SIC: 2653 Corrugated & solid fiber boxes

(G-11061)
GRIFFITH ELECTRIC SUP CO INC (PA)
5 2nd St (08611-2293)
PHONE..................................609 695-6121
Fax: 609 695-3217
Meta Griffith, *President*
William Goodwin, *Principal*
Margaret Kline, *Exec VP*
Jack V Bok, *Marketing Staff*
EMP: 56
SQ FT: 65,000
SALES (est): 22.6MM Privately Held
WEB: www.griffithelec.com
SIC: 8711 3999 Electrical or electronic engineering; atomizers; toiletry

(G-11062)
HALO PUB INC
4617 Nottingham Way (08690-3819)
PHONE..................................609 586-1811
Jerry Reolie, *President*
EMP: 10
SALES (est): 590.8K Privately Held
SIC: 2024 Ice cream, bulk

(G-11063)
HODA INC
Also Called: Suburban Fence Company
532 Mulberry St (08638-3304)
PHONE..................................609 695-3000
Fax: 609 695-4035
David Solomon, *President*
Shirley Solomon, *Corp Secy*
EMP: 12
SQ FT: 3,500
SALES: 1MM Privately Held
WEB: www.hoda.com
SIC: 5031 5211 2499 Fencing, wood; trim, sheet metal; fencing; fencing, wood

(G-11064)
HUTCHINSON INDUSTRIES INC
251 Southard St (08609)
PHONE..................................609 394-1010
Bill Murray, *Branch Mgr*
EMP: 15
SALES (corp-wide): 8.3B Publicly Held
WEB: www.hutchinsoninc.com
SIC: 3069 3444 Rubber automotive products; sheet metalwork
HQ: Hutchinson Industries, Inc.
460 Southard St
Trenton NJ 08638
609 394-1010

(G-11065)
HUTCHINSON INDUSTRIES INC (DH)
460 Southard St (08638-4224)
PHONE..................................609 394-1010
Fax: 609 394-2031
Bob Graefe, *Opers Staff*
Glen Weisman, *Purch Mgr*
Mike Finsterbusch, *QC Mgr*
Thomas Marple, *QC Mgr*
Andrew Morrison, *Engineer*
◆ EMP: 150
SQ FT: 300,000
SALES (est): 168.3MM
SALES (corp-wide): 8.3B Publicly Held
WEB: www.hutchinsoninc.com
SIC: 3069 Rubber automotive products
HQ: Hutchinson Corporation
460 Fuller Ave Ne
Grand Rapids MI 49503
616 459-4541

▲ = Import ▼=Export
◆ =Import/Export

(G-11066)
HUTCHINSON INDUSTRIES INC
84 Parker Ave Ste 86 (08609-1624)
PHONE..................................609 394-1010
George Thomas, *Branch Mgr*
EMP: 14
SALES (corp-wide): 8.3B **Publicly Held**
WEB: www.hutchinsoninc.com
SIC: 3069 Rubber automotive products
HQ: Hutchinson Industries, Inc.
460 Southard St
Trenton NJ 08638
609 394-1010

(G-11067)
HUTCHINSON INDUSTRIES INC
106 108 Mulberry St (08609)
PHONE..................................609 394-1010
EMP: 4
SALES (corp-wide): 8.3B **Publicly Held**
SIC: 3999 Barber & beauty shop equipment
HQ: Hutchinson Industries, Inc.
460 Southard St
Trenton NJ 08638
609 394-1010

(G-11068)
INDUSTRIAL WATER INSTITUTE
33 Maitland Rd (08620-1014)
P.O. Box 1389, Hightstown (08520-0975)
PHONE..................................609 585-4880
Fax: 609 585-6477
Ray Kerollis, *President*
Joanne Taussig, *Vice Pres*
Eugene Sarafin, *Admin Sec*
EMP: 6
SALES: 275K **Privately Held**
SIC: 3999 Atomizers, toiletry

(G-11069)
INTERSTATE PANEL LLC (PA)
67 Benson Ave (08610-4407)
PHONE..................................609 586-4411
Fax: 609 586-4422
Jerry Turner, *COO*
Dorothy White, *Sales Mgr*
Mark Berube, *Manager*
Donald J Anderson,
Jerry R Turner,
EMP: 10
SQ FT: 9,000
SALES: 3.6MM **Privately Held**
SIC: 3446 Architectural metalwork

(G-11070)
JERSEY PRECAST CORPORATION INC
853 Nottingham Way (08638-4447)
PHONE..................................609 689-3700
M Amir Ulislam, *Ch of Bd*
Khwaja Abbas, *General Mgr*
Jeff Weachock, *Plant Supt*
Ray Chavez, *Director*
▲ EMP: 160
SQ FT: 250,000
SALES (est): 33.5MM **Privately Held**
WEB: www.jerseyprecast.com
SIC: 3272 Concrete products, precast

(G-11071)
JOHNSON & JOHNSON
205 Waverly Ct (08691-3033)
PHONE..................................732 524-0400
Michael Ferrio, *Master*
EMP: 80
SALES (corp-wide): 76.4B **Publicly Held**
SIC: 2676 Feminine hygiene paper products
PA: Johnson & Johnson
1 Johnson And Johnson Plz
New Brunswick NJ 08933
732 524-0400

(G-11072)
JPC MERGER SUB LLC
Also Called: Jersey Precast
853 Nottingham Way (08638-4447)
PHONE..................................609 890-4343
M Amir Ulislam, *Mng Member*
EMP: 131
SQ FT: 185,000
SALES: 37.4MM **Privately Held**
SIC: 3272 Concrete products, precast

(G-11073)
KAYLINE PROCESSING INC (PA)
31 Coates St (08611-2903)
PHONE..................................609 695-1449
Fax: 609 989-1094
Michael J Lebwohl, *President*
Rob Lebwohl, *Exec VP*
Ed Lieb, *Plant Mgr*
Tom Spinner, *Purchasing*
Pete Burns, *Engineer*
▲ EMP: 34 EST: 1972
SQ FT: 4,000
SALES: 5.8MM **Privately Held**
WEB: www.kayline.com
SIC: 3081 Polyvinyl film & sheet; vinyl film & sheet; plastic film & sheet

(G-11074)
KNF NEUBERGER INC (DH)
2 Black Forest Rd (08691-1810)
PHONE..................................609 890-8889
Fax: 609 890-8323
Martin Becker, *Principal*
Eric Wilson, *Production*
Monica Heidenhofer, *Purch Mgr*
Thomas Rank, *Buyer*
Gerald Giraldi, *Engineer*
EMP: 100 EST: 1977
SQ FT: 40,000
SALES (est): 20.1MM
SALES (corp-wide): 108.3MM **Privately Held**
WEB: www.knf.com
SIC: 3821 3563 Vacuum pumps, laboratory; air & gas compressors including vacuum pumps
HQ: Knf Neuberger Gmbh
Alter Weg 3
Freiburg Im Breisgau 79112
766 459-090

(G-11075)
LENAPE PRODUCTS INC
610 Plum St (08638-3349)
PHONE..................................609 394-5376
Stephen M Bielawski, *President*
Thomas E Wenczel Jr, *Corp Secy*
Donald Bielawski, *Vice Pres*
◆ EMP: 50
SQ FT: 40,000
SALES: 5MM
SALES (corp-wide): 15.7MM **Privately Held**
WEB: www.lenapebath.com
SIC: 3261 Bathroom accessories/fittings, vitreous china or earthenware
PA: New Jersey Porcelain Co Inc
600 Plum St
Trenton NJ 08638
609 394-5376

(G-11076)
LINSEIS INC
109 N Gold Dr (08691)
PHONE..................................609 223-2070
Claus Linseis, *President*
Robert Ansel, *General Mgr*
Annellore Linseis, *Treasurer*
EMP: 5 EST: 1978
SQ FT: 6,000
SALES (est): 1.3MM **Privately Held**
WEB: www.linseis.net
SIC: 3825 Analyzers for testing electrical characteristics

(G-11077)
LOCKWOODS ELECTRIC MOTOR SVC
2239 Nottingham Way (08619-3047)
PHONE..................................609 587-2333
Fax: 609 587-5018
Richard L Dey, *President*
Joanne Dey, *Corp Secy*
Kathleen Dey, *Corp Secy*
EMP: 34
SQ FT: 20,000
SALES (est): 5.7MM **Privately Held**
WEB: www.lockwoodselectricmotor.com
SIC: 7694 5999 Electric motor repair; motors, electric; electronic parts & equipment

(G-11078)
MAN-HOW INC
Also Called: Style Plus
1150 Southard St Ste 3 (08638-5042)
P.O. Box 2705 (08607-2705)
PHONE..................................609 392-4895
Fax: 609 392-0194
Glen F Mangee, *President*
Jim Letton, *Accountant*
▲ EMP: 9
SQ FT: 35,000
SALES (est): 4.3MM **Privately Held**
SIC: 5139 2385 Footwear; raincoats, except vulcanized rubber: purchased materials

(G-11079)
MARSHALL MAINTENANCE (PA)
Also Called: Marshall Industrial Tech
529 S Clinton Ave (08611-1809)
PHONE..................................609 394-7153
Fax: 609 396-8884
John Mako, *President*
Joe Caranci, *Project Mgr*
Jim Milligan, *Project Mgr*
Ed Sauer, *Foreman/Supr*
Ed Sour, *CFO*
EMP: 136 EST: 1951
SQ FT: 35,000
SALES (est): 34MM **Privately Held**
WEB: www.marshallindtech.com
SIC: 1796 1731 1711 3599 Machinery installation; electrical work; heating & air conditioning contractors; machine shop, jobbing & repair

(G-11080)
MERCER MACHINE & TOOL PRODUCTS
332 Darcy Ave (08629-1313)
PHONE..................................609 587-1106
Fax: 609 587-1239
Tom Erni, *President*
EMP: 4 EST: 1945
SQ FT: 2,400
SALES (est): 545.5K **Privately Held**
SIC: 3599 Machine shop, jobbing & repair

(G-11081)
MILLNER KITCHENS INC
Also Called: Millner Lumber Co
200 Whitehead Rd Ste 108 (08619-3278)
PHONE..................................609 890-7300
John Millner, *President*
EMP: 8
SALES (est): 850K **Privately Held**
SIC: 2541 5211 Counters or counter display cases, wood; cabinets, kitchen

(G-11082)
MUIRHEAD RINGOES NJ INC
1040 Pennsylvania Ave (08638-3345)
PHONE..................................609 695-7803
Edward Simpson, *President*
Doris Simpson, *Vice Pres*
EMP: 9
SQ FT: 2,500
SALES (est): 450.8K **Privately Held**
WEB: www.muirheadfoods.com
SIC: 5812 2099 Eating places; dressings, salad: dry mixes

(G-11083)
NEW HORIZON GRAPHICS INC
2 Christine Ave (08619-2906)
PHONE..................................609 584-1301
Fax: 609 587-4059
Lyn Marlin, *President*
Richard Marlin, *Vice Pres*
EMP: 4
SALES: 125K **Privately Held**
SIC: 2752 Commercial printing, lithographic

(G-11084)
NEW JERSEY BUS & INDUST ASSN (PA)
Also Called: Njbia
10 W Lafayette St (08608-2002)
PHONE..................................609 393-7707
Fax: 609 695-9597
Philip Kirschner, *President*
Steve Wilson, *President*
Stefanie Riehl, *Assistant VP*
Robin Taylor, *Assistant VP*
Betty Boros, *Vice Pres*
EMP: 57
SQ FT: 15,000
SALES (est): 9.2MM **Privately Held**
WEB: www.njbia.net
SIC: 8611 2721 Trade associations; magazines: publishing only, not printed on site

(G-11085)
NEW JERSEY DEPARTMENT TREASURY
Also Called: Print Shop
101 Carroll St (08609-1009)
P.O. Box 30 (08625-0030)
PHONE..................................609 292-5133
Sandy Gallino, *Manager*
EMP: 25 **Privately Held**
WEB: www.tax.state.nj.us
SIC: 2754 9311 Commercial printing, gravure; finance, taxation & monetary policy;
HQ: New Jersey Department Of Treasury
125 W State St
Trenton NJ 08608

(G-11086)
NEW JERSEY PORCELAIN CO INC (PA)
600 Plum St (08638-3349)
PHONE..................................609 394-5376
Fax: 609 394-0929
Stephen M Bielawski, *President*
Thomas E Wenczel Jr, *Corp Secy*
Donald A Bielawski, *Vice Pres*
◆ EMP: 15 EST: 1920
SQ FT: 100,000
SALES (est): 15.7MM **Privately Held**
SIC: 3261 3264 Plumbing fixtures, vitreous china; insulators, electrical: porcelain

(G-11087)
NEW JRSEY STATE LEAG MNCPLTIES
222 W State St (08608-1000)
PHONE..................................609 695-3481
Fax: 609 695-0151
William G Dressel Jr, *Principal*
Brian Leszczak, *Info Tech Mgr*
Michael Darcy, *Asst Director*
EMP: 19
SQ FT: 3,000
SALES: 4.1MM **Privately Held**
SIC: 8641 2721 Civic social & fraternal associations; magazines: publishing only, not printed on site

(G-11088)
NEWFUTUREVEST TWO LLC (PA)
17a Marlen Dr (08691-1648)
PHONE..................................609 586-8004
Seth Harmening, *CFO*
Ron Gale,
Jan Gale,
EMP: 2
SALES (est): 1MM **Privately Held**
SIC: 2819 Industrial inorganic chemicals

(G-11089)
NEWMARKET PHARMACEUTICALS LLC
4 Pitcairn Ave (08628-1317)
PHONE..................................609 252-9600
Mark Ridall, *CEO*
Brian McDonald, *President*
EMP: 4
SALES (est): 381.2K **Privately Held**
SIC: 2834 Veterinary pharmaceutical preparations

(G-11090)
NINI DISPOSAL
410 Whitehead Rd (08619-3255)
PHONE..................................609 587-2411
Sebastiano Nini, *Principal*
EMP: 7
SALES (est): 665.7K **Privately Held**
SIC: 3089 Garbage containers, plastic

(G-11091)
NORTH EASTERN BUSINESS FORMS
Also Called: Harrison Press
1111 Chestnut Ave (08611-2011)
PHONE................................609 392-1161
George Demeter, *Owner*
EMP: 5 EST: 1953
SALES (est): 313.5K Privately Held
SIC: 2761 2759 Manifold business forms; commercial printing

(G-11092)
OLD BARRACKS ASSOCIATION INC
Also Called: OLD BARRACKS MUSEUM
101 Barrack St (08608-2007)
PHONE................................609 396-1776
Fax: 609 777-4000
Richard Patterson, *Exec Dir*
Howard E Mitchell Jr,
EMP: 14
SQ FT: 15,000
SALES: 692.1K Privately Held
SIC: 8412 2741 Museum; newsletter publishing

(G-11093)
OMAHA STANDARD INC TR NJ
572 Whitehead Rd (08619-4804)
PHONE................................609 588-5400
EMP: 6
SALES (est): 456.3K Privately Held
SIC: 3965 Hooks, crochet

(G-11094)
PAHCO MACHINE INC (PA)
572 Whitehead Rd Ste 101 (08619-4804)
PHONE................................609 587-1188
Fax: 609 587-3463
Peter A Horvath Jr, *President*
Peter A Horvath Sr, *Chairman*
Judy Horvath, *Corp Secy*
EMP: 7
SQ FT: 8,000
SALES (est): 705.1K Privately Held
SIC: 3599 3544 Machine shop, jobbing & repair; industrial molds

(G-11095)
PALFINGER NORTH AMERICA
Also Called: Omaha Standards
572 Whitehead Rd Ste 301 (08619-4804)
P.O. Box 5757 (08638-0757)
PHONE................................609 588-5400
Warren Kimble, *General Mgr*
Lazar Marmur, *Engineer*
Ken Bailey, *Design Engr*
Sam Matino, *Sales Staff*
Michael Kanter, *Manager*
◆ EMP: 80
SALES (est): 22.5MM Privately Held
SIC: 3536 3537 Hoists, cranes & monorails; industrial trucks & tractors

(G-11096)
PERFORMANCE INDUSTRIES INC
Also Called: Davy Jnes Swmming Pool Pnt Div
51 Tucker St (08618-4705)
PHONE................................609 392-1450
Stewart Azarchi, *President*
Ginger Azarchi, *Treasurer*
EMP: 30 EST: 1946
SQ FT: 20,000
SALES (est): 2MM Privately Held
WEB: www.performanceindustries.com
SIC: 2851 Paints, waterproof

(G-11097)
PHOENIX CONTAINER INC
6 Litho Rd (08648-3304)
PHONE................................732 247-3931
Ken Sokoloff, *President*
Barry Zankel, *VP Finance*
▲ EMP: 110
SQ FT: 106,000
SALES (est): 10.8MM
SALES (corp-wide): 787.1MM Privately Held
SIC: 3411 Pails, except shipping: metal
HQ: Bway Corporation
8607 Roberts Dr Ste 250
Atlanta GA 30350

(G-11098)
PHOTO OFFSET PRTG & PUBG CO
536 Highway 33 (08619-4406)
PHONE................................609 587-4900
Fax: 609 587-4907
Robert A Perilli, *President*
EMP: 5
SQ FT: 18,000
SALES (est): 674.8K Privately Held
SIC: 2752 Photo-offset printing

(G-11099)
PMP COMPOSITES CORPORATION
572 Whitehead Rd Ste 101 (08619-4804)
PHONE................................609 587-1188
Peter A Horvath Sr, *Chairman*
EMP: 30
SALES (est): 4.4MM Privately Held
SIC: 3089 Injection molded finished plastic products; plastic processing

(G-11100)
PORFIRIO FOODS INC
320 Anderson St (08611-1106)
PHONE................................609 393-4116
Robert Calabro, *President*
Anthony Calabro, *Vice Pres*
EMP: 5 EST: 1965
SQ FT: 3,000
SALES (est): 516.3K Privately Held
SIC: 5411 2098 Grocery stores; macaroni products (e.g. alphabets, rings & shells), dry

(G-11101)
POWER MAGNETICS INC (PA)
377 Reservoir St (08618-3641)
PHONE................................609 695-1170
Fax: 609 695-5907
Ilene Pearl Bannwart, *CEO*
Carl A Bannwart, *President*
Maria Buono, *Finance*
Travis Harper, *Supervisor*
▲ EMP: 20
SQ FT: 17,000
SALES: 4MM Privately Held
WEB: www.powermagneticsinc.com
SIC: 3612 3621 Power transformers, electric; phase or rotary converters (electrical equipment)

(G-11102)
POWER PRODUCTS AND ENGRG LLC
Also Called: Ppe
324 Meadowbrook Rd (08691-2503)
PHONE................................855 769-3751
Joe Polizzi, *Principal*
EMP: 30
SQ FT: 52,000
SALES (est): 1.3MM Privately Held
SIC: 3443 Condensers, steam; heat exchangers: coolers (after, inter), condensers, etc.; economizers (boilers); industrial vessels, tanks & containers

(G-11103)
PRESCRIPTION PODIATRY LABS
826 S Broad St (08611-1904)
PHONE................................609 695-1221
Robert Pagono, *President*
EMP: 6
SQ FT: 2,000
SALES (est): 300K Privately Held
SIC: 3842 Surgical appliances & supplies

(G-11104)
PRESS ROOM INC
100 Youngs Rd Ste 2 (08619-1025)
PHONE................................609 689-3817
Fax: 609 689-1166
Ted Altomari, *President*
EMP: 10
SALES (est): 1.3MM Privately Held
SIC: 2759 7334 Commercial printing; photocopying & duplicating services

(G-11105)
PRESTIGE ASSOCIATES INC
39 Meade St (08638-4321)
P.O. Box 3873 (08629-0873)
PHONE................................609 393-1509
Fax: 609 393-9211

Robert McGuire, *President*
EMP: 50
SQ FT: 25,000
SALES (est): 8.7MM Privately Held
SIC: 2675 3081 Die-cut paper & board; floor or wall covering, unsupported plastic

(G-11106)
PRINCETON INSTRUMENTS INC
3660 Quakerbridge Rd (08619-1208)
PHONE................................609 587-9797
William Asher, *President*
Ravi Guntupalli, *Vice Pres*
Robert Hyland, *Vice Pres*
Maureen Kettner, *Opers Mgr*
Sathish Kuruvilla, *Manager*
EMP: 4 EST: 2014
SALES (est): 205.3K Privately Held
SIC: 3827 Optical instruments & lenses

(G-11107)
PRINCETON MICROWAVE TECHNOLOGY
5 Nami Ln Ste 1 (08619-1261)
PHONE................................609 586-8140
Fax: 609 586-1231
Amar Kaur, *President*
Sarijt Singh, *Corp Secy*
EMP: 7
SQ FT: 2,500
SALES: 1.4MM Privately Held
WEB: www.princetonmicrowave.com
SIC: 3679 Microwave components; oscillators; passive repeaters

(G-11108)
PRINCETON OPTRONICS INC
1 Electronics Dr (08619-2054)
PHONE................................609 584-9696
Fax: 609 584-2448
Chuni Ghosh, *President*
Dr Chuni L Ghosh, *President*
Carl Wessendorf, *Engineer*
Jim Lucas, *Marketing Staff*
Robert Leeuwen, *Manager*
EMP: 33
SQ FT: 26,200
SALES: 8.9MM Privately Held
WEB: www.princetonoptronics.com
SIC: 3229 3679 Fiber optics strands; electronic loads & power supplies

(G-11109)
PRO-DECK SUPPLY
3 Pembroke Ct (08648-2008)
PHONE................................609 771-1100
Chad Mickley, *Manager*
EMP: 8 Privately Held
SIC: 3444 Roof deck, sheet metal
PA: Pro-Deck Supply
1608 5th St
Ewing NJ 08638

(G-11110)
R J D MACHINE PRODUCTS INC
1424-1428 Heath Ave (08638)
PHONE................................609 392-1515
Fax: 609 392-1098
Richard Roslowski, *President*
Deborah Roslowski, *Corp Secy*
Julie Roslowski, *Purch Dir*
EMP: 11
SQ FT: 10,000
SALES (est): 1.6MM Privately Held
WEB: www.rjdmachineproducts.com
SIC: 3599 Machine shop, jobbing & repair

(G-11111)
RALPH CLAYTON & SONS LLC
Also Called: Clayton Block
1144 New York Ave (08638-3308)
P.O. Box 3015, Lakewood (08701-9015)
PHONE................................609 695-0767
Earl Brown, *Principal*
Joe Sweeney, *Manager*
EMP: 30
SALES (corp-wide): 96.7MM Privately Held
WEB: www.claytonco.com
SIC: 5032 3273 Concrete mixtures; gravel; sand, construction; ready-mixed concrete
PA: Ralph Clayton & Sons L.L.C.
1355 Campus Pkwy
Wall Township NJ 07753
732 363-1995

(G-11112)
RICZTONE INC
Also Called: Future Signs
19 Bow Hill Ave (08610-6509)
PHONE................................609 695-6263
Rich Rutzler, *President*
Kimberly Arena, *Chairman*
EMP: 4
SQ FT: 2,200
SALES (est): 530.8K Privately Held
SIC: 3993 Signs, not made in custom sign painting shops

(G-11113)
ROCK DREAMS ELECTRONICS LLC
362 State Highway 33 (08619-4402)
PHONE................................609 890-0808
EMP: 5
SQ FT: 8,000
SALES (est): 530K Privately Held
SIC: 3651 Home entertainment equipment, electronic

(G-11114)
ROPER SCIENTIFIC INC (HQ)
Also Called: Princeton Instruments
3660 Quakerbridge Rd (08619-1208)
PHONE................................520 889-9933
Fax: 609 587-1970
Susan Carter, *General Mgr*
Francine Lucier, *General Mgr*
Michael Case, *Exec VP*
Bill Asher, *Vice Pres*
Dana Kelly, *Vice Pres*
EMP: 100
SQ FT: 20,000
SALES (est): 43.9MM
SALES (corp-wide): 4.6B Publicly Held
WEB: www.roperscientific.com
SIC: 3827 3861 8748 3829 Optical instruments & lenses; cameras & related equipment; systems analysis or design; measuring & controlling devices
PA: Roper Technologies, Inc.
6901 Prof Pkwy E Ste 200
Sarasota FL 34240
941 556-2601

(G-11115)
SCHOOL SPIRIT PROMOTIONS
3 Ely Ct (08690-2203)
PHONE................................609 588-6902
Ron Thomson, *Principal*
EMP: 8
SALES (est): 583.1K Privately Held
SIC: 2389 Apparel & accessories

(G-11116)
SGW FUEL DELIVERY
353 Churchill Ave (08610-3220)
PHONE................................609 209-8773
Scott M White, *Principal*
EMP: 4
SALES (est): 473.6K Privately Held
SIC: 2869 Fuels

(G-11117)
STEVEN MADOLA
Also Called: Park Ave Printing
2001 S Broad St (08610-6005)
PHONE................................609 989-8022
Steven Madola, *Owner*
James Madola, *Exec Dir*
EMP: 9
SQ FT: 3,000
SALES: 400K Privately Held
SIC: 2752 Commercial printing, lithographic

(G-11118)
STONITE COIL CORPORATION
476 Route 156 (08620-9701)
P.O. Box 11036 (08620-0036)
PHONE................................609 585-6600
Fax: 609 585-6603
William G Engel, *President*
Scott Root, *Vice Pres*
Rob Hamilton, *Purch Agent*
Kimberley Cotner, *Accountant*
Carol Engel, *VP Human Res*
▲ EMP: 26 EST: 1950
SQ FT: 25,000

SALES (est): 8MM **Privately Held**
WEB: www.stonitecoil.com
SIC: **3677** Electronic coils, transformers & other inductors

(G-11119)
SWITLIK PARACHUTE COMPANY INC
Lalor & Hancock Sts (08609)
P.O. Box 1328 (08607-1328)
PHONE.................................609 587-3300
Richard Switlik, *Vice Pres*
Phuok Tran, *MIS Mgr*
EMP: 10
SALES (corp-wide): 20.5MM **Privately Held**
SIC: **3069** 2399 3842 2326 Life jackets, inflatable: rubberized fabric; life rafts, rubber; parachutes; surgical appliances & supplies; men's & boys' clothing
PA: Switlik Parachute Company, Inc.
1325 E State St
Trenton NJ 08609
609 587-3300

(G-11120)
TEKTITE INDUSTRIES INC
Also Called: Tektite Mfg Division
309 N Clinton Ave (08638-5122)
PHONE.................................609 656-0600
Scott Mele, *President*
Richard Saint Cyr, *Vice Pres*
Wayne Fowler, *Site Mgr*
▲ EMP: 9
SQ FT: 10,000
SALES (est): 1.5MM **Privately Held**
WEB: www.tek-tite.com
SIC: **3648** 3089 3646 Lighting equipment; injection molding of plastics; commercial indusl & institutional electric lighting fixtures

(G-11121)
TIMES OF TRENTON PUBG CORP
413 River View Plz (08611-3427)
PHONE.................................609 989-5454
Fax: 609 695-8665
Richard Bilotti, *President*
Tony Hagen, *Editor*
Richard Diamond, *Vice Pres*
Martin Stewart, *Treasurer*
Sheila Montone, *Advt Staff*
EMP: 735 EST: 1882
SQ FT: 50,000
SALES (est): 29.2MM **Privately Held**
WEB: www.njtimes.com
SIC: **7313** 2711 Newspaper advertising representative; newspapers

(G-11122)
TIMOTHY P BRYAN ELC CO INC
Also Called: T.P. Bryan Electric
1926 Chestnut Ave (08611-2704)
PHONE.................................609 393-8325
Fax: 609 393-7931
Timothy P Bryan, *President*
Timothy Bryan Jr, *Vice Pres*
EMP: 9
SQ FT: 1,500
SALES (est): 1.5MM **Privately Held**
WEB: www.bryanelectricco.com
SIC: **1731** 3629 General electrical contractor; battery chargers, rectifying or non-rotating

(G-11123)
TRANE US INC
2231 E State Street Ext (08619-3311)
PHONE.................................609 587-3400
Fax: 609 588-4208
Andy Stevenson, *General Mgr*
EMP: 61 **Privately Held**
SIC: **3585** Refrigeration & heating equipment
HQ: Trane U.S. Inc.
3600 Pammel Creek Rd
La Crosse WI 54601
608 787-2000

(G-11124)
TRENT BOX MANUFACTURING CO
1384 Yardville Ham Rd (08691-3343)
P.O. Box 2650 (08690-0150)
PHONE.................................609 587-7515
Carl A Angelini, *President*
Joyce Angelini, *Admin Sec*
EMP: 20 EST: 1959
SQ FT: 30,000
SALES (est): 4.3MM **Privately Held**
WEB: www.trent.com
SIC: **2653** Boxes, corrugated: made from purchased materials; boxes, solid fiber: made from purchased materials

(G-11125)
TRENTON PRINTING LLC
1150 Southard St Ste 2 (08638-5099)
PHONE.................................609 695-6485
Fax: 609 695-8897
Lucille Raymond, *CFO*
Steve Sadiwnyk, *Sales Mgr*
David Nugent, *Mng Member*
Bill Nugent, *Mng Member*
Bob Lennon, *Manager*
EMP: 17 EST: 1929
SQ FT: 17,500
SALES (est): 3.5MM **Privately Held**
WEB: www.trentonprinting.com
SIC: **2752** 7331 Commercial printing, offset; mailing service

(G-11126)
TRENTON SHEET METAL INC
30 Adam Ave (08618-4108)
P.O. Box 1121 (08606-1121)
PHONE.................................609 695-6328
Fax: 609 695-1929
Robert Somogyi, *President*
Bob Somogyi, *President*
Marilyn Somogyi, *Corp Secy*
EMP: 30
SQ FT: 25,000
SALES (est): 5.3MM **Privately Held**
WEB: www.trentonsheetmetal.com
SIC: **3444** Sheet metal specialties, not stamped

(G-11127)
TRI-STEEL FABRICATORS INC
501 Prospect St (08618-3640)
P.O. Box 5756 (08638-0756)
PHONE.................................609 392-8660
James Werosta, *President*
Karl Werosta, *Principal*
EMP: 26 EST: 1949
SALES (est): 5.9MM **Privately Held**
SIC: **3441** 1791 Fabricated structural metal; structural steel erection

(G-11128)
TRIEFELDT STUDIOS INC
1115 Hamilton Ave (08629-1910)
PHONE.................................609 656-2380
Lauri Triefeldt, *President*
Wayne Triefeldt, *Corp Secy*
EMP: 4
SALES: 50K **Privately Held**
SIC: **2741** Directories: publishing & printing

(G-11129)
TUERFF SZIBER CAPITOL COPY SVC
116 W State St (08608-1102)
P.O. Box 72, Titusville (08560-0072)
PHONE.................................609 989-8776
Fax: 609 989-9570
Raymond Sziber, *President*
EMP: 7
SQ FT: 1,500
SALES (est): 852.2K **Privately Held**
WEB: www.capitol-copy.com
SIC: **2752** Commercial printing, offset

(G-11130)
UTHE TECHNOLOGY INC (HQ)
Scotch Rd (08628)
P.O. Box 7266 (08628-0266)
PHONE.................................609 883-4000
J Michael Goodson, *President*
EMP: 1 EST: 1966
SQ FT: 10,000

SALES (est): 1.8MM
SALES (corp-wide): 41.3MM **Privately Held**
SIC: **3679** Power supplies, all types: static
PA: Crestek, Inc.
18 Graphics Dr
Ewing NJ 08628
609 883-4000

(G-11131)
VIAVI SOLUTIONS INC
2 Applegate Dr (08691-2342)
PHONE.................................609 632-0800
John Hynes, *Manager*
Sam Jhaveri, *Manager*
Adam Scheer, *Manager*
EMP: 129
SALES (corp-wide): 811.4MM **Publicly Held**
WEB: www.jdsuniphase.com
SIC: **3674** Semiconductors & related devices
PA: Viavi Solutions Inc.
6001 America Center Dr # 6
San Jose CA 95002
408 404-3600

(G-11132)
WHITE EAGLE PRINTING CO INC
2550 Kuser Rd (08691-3499)
PHONE.................................609 586-2032
Eric Bielawski, *President*
A Thad Bielawski Jr, *President*
Edward Krupa Jr, *Principal*
Lorretta Daunis, *Treasurer*
EMP: 25 EST: 1933
SQ FT: 1,500
SALES (est): 4.6MM **Privately Held**
WEB: www.whiteeagledistribution.co.uk
SIC: **2752** Commercial printing, offset

(G-11133)
WOODLAND MANUFACTURING COMPANY
1936 E State Street Ext (08619-3306)
P.O. Box 8094 (08650-0094)
PHONE.................................609 587-4180
Fax: 609 587-1880
Lawrence A Marcinkus Jr, *President*
Joseph Sciacca, *Accounts Mgr*
EMP: 15
SQ FT: 110,000
SALES (est): 4.3MM **Privately Held**
WEB: www.woodlandmfg.com
SIC: **2653** Boxes, solid fiber: made from purchased materials

(G-11134)
WORD CENTER PRINTING
1905 Highway 33 Ste 10 (08690-1742)
PHONE.................................609 586-5825
Fax: 609 586-5835
Jerry Silverman, *Owner*
Marilyn Silverman, *Co-Owner*
Diane Heinz, *Sales Mgr*
EMP: 4
SQ FT: 1,500
SALES: 300K **Privately Held**
WEB: www.wordcenterprinting.com
SIC: **7338** 2791 7334 Word processing service; hand composition typesetting; photocopying & duplicating services

(G-11135)
WT MEDIA LLC
4 Applegate Dr (08691-2342)
PHONE.................................609 921-3490
James Frintner, *Mng Member*
EMP: 17
SQ FT: 20,000
SALES (est): 1.8MM **Privately Held**
SIC: **2731** 7311 Books: publishing & printing; advertising agencies

Tuckahoe
Cape May County

(G-11136)
MAUND ENTERPRISES INC
112 Buckhill Rd (08250)
P.O. Box 561 (08250-0561)
PHONE.................................609 628-2475

Keith Maund II, *President*
EMP: 5
SALES (est): 627.6K **Privately Held**
SIC: **3272** Burial vaults, concrete or precast terrazzo

(G-11137)
PIPE DREAMS MARINE LLC
251 Mill Rd (08250)
PHONE.................................609 628-9353
Donald Battin,
EMP: 4
SALES (est): 482K **Privately Held**
SIC: **3499** Marine horns, compressed air or steam

(G-11138)
SUNSPLASH MARINA LLC
5 Mosquito Landing Rd (08250)
PHONE.................................609 628-4445
John Yank,
EMP: 7
SALES (est): 732.4K **Privately Held**
SIC: **3732** Boat building & repairing

(G-11139)
TUCKAHOE SAND & GRAVEL CO INC
And Sharp Rd Rr 610 (08250)
P.O. Box 991, Pleasantville (08232-0991)
PHONE.................................609 861-2082
Fax: 609 861-3671
James E Johnston Jr, *President*
Ron Carusi, *Sales Mgr*
EMP: 35 EST: 1952
SQ FT: 4,750
SALES (est): 7.5MM **Privately Held**
WEB: www.tuckahoesand-gravel.com
SIC: **1442** Gravel & pebble mining; gravel mining

(G-11140)
YANK MARINE INC
Mosquito Landing Rd (08250)
P.O. Box 569 (08250-0569)
PHONE.................................609 628-2928
Fax: 609 628-2628
John Yank, *President*
▲ EMP: 25
SQ FT: 10,000
SALES (est): 5.5MM **Privately Held**
SIC: **3732** Boat building & repairing

Turnersville
Camden County

(G-11141)
CDM ELECTRONICS INC (PA)
130 American Blvd (08012-1735)
PHONE.................................856 740-1200
Fax: 856 740-0500
Carmen De Leo, *President*
Christina Harrison, *Sales Staff*
Brian Kudlicki, *Sales Staff*
EMP: 108
SQ FT: 16,000
SALES (est): 72.6MM **Privately Held**
WEB: www.cdmelec.com
SIC: **5065** 3357 Aircraft wire & cable, non-ferrous

Twp Washinton
Bergen County

(G-11142)
FLUIDSENS INTERNATIONAL INC
703 Beechwood Dr (07676-3802)
PHONE.................................914 338-3932
Arnon Scheflan, *CEO*
Irit Scheflan, *COO*
Gideon Vardi, *Vice Pres*
Alex Keinan, *Engineer*
Josef More, *CFO*
EMP: 5
SALES (est): 340K **Privately Held**
SIC: **3822** Auto controls regulating residntl & coml environmt & applncs

(G-11143)
NANO-OPTIC DEVICES LLC
280 S Chestnut St (07676-4916)
PHONE..................................201 594-0226
Vladimir Yankov,
Victor Yanin,
EMP: 10
SALES (est): 1.2MM **Privately Held**
SIC: 3827 Optical instruments & lenses

(G-11144)
TRILEX LTD
Also Called: Trilex Cleaners
50 Hemlock Dr (07676-5105)
PHONE..................................201 664-5576
Fax: 973 471-7676
David Kornhauser, *President*
EMP: 30
SALES (est): 1.8MM **Privately Held**
WEB: www.trilexcleanfiregear.com
SIC: 2311 7211 5136 2326 Firemen's
uniforms: made from purchased materi-
als; power laundries, family & commer-
cial; men's & boys' clothing; men's &
boys' work clothing

Union
Union County

(G-11145)
360 MEDIA INNOVATIONS LLC
1511a Stuyvesant Ave (07083)
PHONE..................................201 228-0941
Chima Gale, *President*
Jovita Gale, *Principal*
Abiose Gale,
EMP: 6
SQ FT: 900
SALES (est): 750K **Privately Held**
SIC: 3651 5065 4813 Household audio &
video equipment; audio electronic sys-
tems; communication equipment; tele-
phone communication, except radio

(G-11146)
**ACUPOWDER INTERNATIONAL
LLC (DH)**
901 Lehigh Ave (07083-7632)
PHONE..................................908 851-4500
Rober Dothan, *General Mgr*
Edul Daver,
EMP: 7
SALES (est): 1.2MM **Privately Held**
WEB: www.acupowder.com
SIC: 3399 Powder, metal

(G-11147)
ADAM TECH ASIA LLC (HQ)
909 Rahway Ave (07083-6549)
PHONE..................................908 687-5000
Vincent Devito, *CEO*
EMP: 3
SALES (est): 1.2MM
SALES (corp-wide): 8MM **Privately Held**
SIC: 3678 Electronic connectors
PA: Adam Technologies Inc.
909 Rahway Ave
Union NJ
908 687-5000

(G-11148)
ALL TOOL COMPANY INC
899 Rahway Ave (07083-6699)
PHONE..................................908 687-3636
John Vinciguerra, *President*
Scott Daniels, *General Mgr*
Dominick Rose, *Purch Agent*
Roselin Mutek, *Controller*
EMP: 11 **EST:** 1941
SQ FT: 15,000
SALES (est): 1.8MM **Privately Held**
SIC: 3599 Machine shop, jobbing & repair

(G-11149)
ALLARY CORPORATION
2204 Morris Ave Ste 209 (07083-5914)
P.O. Box 693, Livingston (07039-0693)
PHONE..................................908 851-0077
Fax: 908 851-9229
Alan B Sorrell, *President*
Larry Self, *Exec VP*
Lisa Gittleman, *Vice Pres*
Anita D Sorrell, *Vice Pres*

Jaina Naik, *Bookkeeper*
◆ **EMP:** 14
SQ FT: 3,000
SALES (est): 2.7MM **Privately Held**
SIC: 3965 Buckles & buckle parts; tape,
hook-and-eye & snap fastener

(G-11150)
**AMERICAN BRASS AND
CRYSTAL INC**
835 Lehigh Ave (07083-7631)
PHONE..................................908 688-8611
Ross Kirshenbaum, *President*
Lori Kirshenbaum, *Vice Pres*
▲ **EMP:** 20
SQ FT: 20,000
SALES (est): 3.5MM **Privately Held**
SIC: 3645 3646 Residential lighting fix-
tures; commercial indusl & institutional
electric lighting fixtures

(G-11151)
**AMERICAN INTR RESOURCES
INC**
Also Called: Locker Lady, The
1206 Francyne Way (07083-5800)
P.O. Box 3656 (07083-1894)
PHONE..................................908 851-0014
Fax: 908 851-0485
Alwine Schooff, *President*
EMP: 4
SALES (est): 799.3K **Privately Held**
SIC: 7389 2541 5021 Interior design serv-
ices; cabinets, lockers & shelving; lockers

(G-11152)
**AMERICAN PRODUCTS
COMPANY INC**
610 Rahway Ave Ste 1 (07083-6696)
PHONE..................................908 687-4100
Fax: 908 687-0037
Richard Picut, *President*
Christopher Walsh, *President*
Russell Picut, *Vice Pres*
Bruno Garcia, *Production*
Mike Lysak, *Production*
EMP: 95
SQ FT: 70,000
SALES (est): 16.7MM **Privately Held**
WEB: www.amerprod.com
SIC: 3491 Industrial valves; steam traps
PA: Picut Industries Inc
140 Mount Bethel Rd
Warren NJ 07059

(G-11153)
ANISHA ENTERPRISES INC
Also Called: Axiam Printing
2165 Morris Ave Ste 1 (07083-5913)
PHONE..................................908 964-3380
Nisha Jhawar, *President*
Dan Maheshwari, *Exec VP*
Purushottam Jhawar, *Vice Pres*
Shakuntala Maheshwari, *Vice Pres*
EMP: 7
SQ FT: 4,000
SALES (est): 1MM **Privately Held**
WEB: www.axiamprinting.com
SIC: 2752 Commercial printing, offset

(G-11154)
ARMORPOXY INC
805 Lehigh Ave (07083-7626)
PHONE..................................908 810-9613
Fax: 908 810-9612
Daniel Blum, *President*
Elisabeth Speckhart, *Mktg Dir*
▲ **EMP:** 18
SALES (est): 5.6MM **Privately Held**
WEB: www.armorpoxy.com
SIC: 2851 5033 5023 5713 Epoxy coat-
ings; roofing & siding materials; floor cov-
erings; floor covering stores; floor laying &
floor work

(G-11155)
B & G PLASTICS INC (PA)
Also Called: B & G International
1085 Morris Ave Ste 5d (07083-7136)
PHONE..................................973 824-9220
Chet Kolton, *President*
Michael Norman, *Exec VP*
▲ **EMP:** 45
SQ FT: 80,000

SALES (est): 5.6MM **Privately Held**
WEB: www.bgplastics.com
SIC: 3089 2679 Clothes hangers, plastic;
paper products, converted

(G-11156)
BASF CORPORATION
2655 Route 22 W (07083-8505)
PHONE..................................732 205-2700
Thomas Anderson, *Branch Mgr*
EMP: 157
SALES (corp-wide): 76B **Privately Held**
SIC: 2869 Industrial organic chemicals
HQ: Basf Corporation
100 Park Ave
Florham Park NJ 07932
973 245-6000

(G-11157)
BEAUTY WOOD DESIGNS
284 Concord Ave (07083-4219)
PHONE..................................908 687-9697
Charles Potzer, *Owner*
EMP: 5
SQ FT: 2,500
SALES (est): 250K **Privately Held**
SIC: 2759 Engraving

(G-11158)
**BELTING INDUSTRIES GROUP
LLC (HQ)**
1090 Lousons Rd (07083-5030)
P.O. Box 310, Kenilworth (07033-0310)
PHONE..................................908 272-8591
Fax: 908 272-3825
Webb Scott Cooper, *President*
Gene Hobson, *COO*
Paul West, *CFO*
▲ **EMP:** 50
SQ FT: 33,000
SALES (est): 23.4MM **Privately Held**
WEB: www.beltingindustries.com
SIC: 5085 3052 2399 Hose, belting &
packing; rubber belting; plastic belting;
belting, fabric: made from purchased ma-
terials
PA: Passaic Rubber Co.
45 Demarest Dr
Wayne NJ 07470
973 696-9500

(G-11159)
**BHAMRA CHAIN
MANUFACTURING**
1020 Springfield Rd (07083-8160)
PHONE..................................908 686-4555
Fax: 908 686-4556
Ajit Bhamra, *President*
Varmeet Bhamra, *Vice Pres*
EMP: 4
SQ FT: 2,500
SALES (est): 330K **Privately Held**
SIC: 3911 Necklaces, precious metal

(G-11160)
BUTTERFLY BOW TIES LLC
911 Garden St (07083-6557)
PHONE..................................973 626-2536
Edward Armah, *Owner*
EMP: 8
SQ FT: 5,000
SALES (est): 322.1K **Privately Held**
SIC: 2389 Men's miscellaneous acces-
sories

(G-11161)
BUY BUY BABY INC (HQ)
650 Liberty Ave (07083-8107)
PHONE..................................908 688-0888
Steven H Temares, *CEO*
Vickie Bingle, *Buyer*
Chrissy Dibella, *Buyer*
Lilly Duryee, *Buyer*
Doug Zindulka, *Buyer*
◆ **EMP:** 15
SQ FT: 5,000
SALES (est): 99.2MM
SALES (corp-wide): 12.3B **Publicly Held**
SIC: 5641 5999 2023 Children's wear; in-
fants' wear; baby carriages & strollers;
high chairs; baby formulas
PA: Bed Bath & Beyond Inc.
650 Liberty Ave
Union NJ 07083
908 688-0888

(G-11162)
**CARDAN MEDICAL PRODUCTS
INC**
1060 Commerce Ave (07083-5026)
PHONE..................................908 964-0800
Thomas George, *Principal*
EMP: 5
SALES (est): 667.9K **Privately Held**
SIC: 3841 Surgical & medical instruments

(G-11163)
CASE PRINCETON CO INC
1119 Morris Ave (07083-3305)
PHONE..................................908 687-1750
Steve Parker, *President*
Steven Parker Jr, *Exec VP*
◆ **EMP:** 20 **EST:** 1964
SQ FT: 30,000
SALES (est): 1.4MM **Privately Held**
WEB: www.princetoncase.com
SIC: 3089 3161 Cases, plastic; luggage

(G-11164)
CE DE CANDY INC (PA)
Also Called: Smarties
1091 Lousons Rd (07083-5097)
PHONE..................................908 964-0660
Fax: 908 964-0911
Edward Dee, *Ch of Bd*
Jonathan Dee, *President*
Michael Dee, *Vice Pres*
▲ **EMP:** 150 **EST:** 1949
SQ FT: 82,000
SALES (est): 59.3MM **Privately Held**
SIC: 2064 Candy & other confectionery
products

(G-11165)
**COMPREHENSIVE MKTG
SYSTEMS**
Also Called: Comprehensive Mktg Systems
850 Springfield Rd # 353 (07083-8614)
PHONE..................................908 810-9778
Carl Fazio, *President*
Sanford Greenman, *Vice Pres*
EMP: 5
SALES (est): 450K **Privately Held**
WEB: www.compmark.com
SIC: 7331 2752 Direct mail advertising
services; commercial printing, offset

(G-11166)
**CONTINNTAL CONCESSION
SUPS INC**
1135 Springfield Rd (07083-8120)
PHONE..................................516 629-4906
Reggie Leary, *Branch Mgr*
EMP: 25
SALES (corp-wide): 17.6B **Publicly Held**
WEB: www.ccsicandy.com
SIC: 5145 5113 2086 2096 Popcorn &
supplies; candy; cups, disposable plastic
& paper; napkins, paper; tea, iced: pack-
aged in cans, bottles, etc.; fruit drinks
(less than 100% juice): packaged in cans,
etc.; popcorn, already popped (except
candy covered)
HQ: Continental Concession Supplies, Inc.
575 Jericho Tpke Ste 300
Jericho NY 11753
516 739-8777

(G-11167)
CORONATION SHEET METAL CO
2198 Stanley Ter (07083-4315)
PHONE..................................908 686-0930
Fax: 908 686-1534
Joseph Cafiero, *President*
Stephen C Cafiero, *Treasurer*
Helene Albright, *Office Mgr*
EMP: 9
SQ FT: 10,000
SALES: 1.1MM **Privately Held**
SIC: 3444 Sheet metal specialties, not
stamped; ducts, sheet metal; ventilators,
sheet metal

(G-11168)
CP EQUIPMENT SALES CO
1504 Oakland Ave (07083-5468)
P.O. Box 3723 (07083-1892)
PHONE..................................908 687-9621
Thomas J Kazalski, *President*
Susan Rice, *Treasurer*
EMP: 12

▲ = Import ▼=Export
◆ =Import/Export

SALES (est): 1.1MM **Privately Held**
WEB: www.cpequip.com
SIC: **3589** Water treatment equipment, industrial

(G-11169)
D & D TECHNOLOGY INC
254 Elmwood Ave (07083-6775)
P.O. Box 3636 (07083-1894)
PHONE..............................908 688-5154
Fax: 908 688-5184
Roberta Varga, *CEO*
Ed G Varga, *President*
EMP: 9
SQ FT: 1,700
SALES (est): 3.5MM **Privately Held**
SIC: **5162 3544** Plastics materials & basic shapes; special dies, tools, jigs & fixtures

(G-11170)
DARTAGNAN INC (PA)
600 Green Ln (07083-8074)
PHONE..............................973 344-0565
Fax: 973 465-1870
Ariane Daguin, *President*
Andy Wertheim, *President*
Kirk Eilers, *General Mgr*
Padraic Doherty, *Vice Pres*
Christopher Hantis, *Opers Staff*
▲ EMP: 81
SQ FT: 36,000
SALES (est): 80.4MM **Privately Held**
WEB: www.dartagnan.com
SIC: **5147 5148 5149 2011** Meats, fresh; vegetables; natural & organic foods; canned meats (except baby food), meat slaughtered on site

(G-11171)
DEEP FOODS INC (PA)
Also Called: Inter Trend
1090 Springfield Rd Ste 1 (07083-8147)
PHONE..............................908 810-7500
Fax: 908 810-8482
Arvind Amin, *President*
Jeffrey Comitz, *Engineer*
Peter Duffy, *Sales Staff*
Tanya Sones, *Technical Staff*
Jackie Henning, *Assistant*
◆ EMP: 150 **EST: 1977**
SQ FT: 60,000
SALES (est): 45.4MM **Privately Held**
WEB: www.deepfoods.com
SIC: **2038 2052 2024 5141** Dinners, frozen & packaged; bakery products, dry; ice milk, bulk; groceries, general line

(G-11172)
DORAN LLC
Also Called: Doran Company
599 Green Ln (07083-7701)
PHONE..............................908 289-9200
Fax: 908 289-9202
Randy Wojcik,
EMP: 4
SQ FT: 20,000
SALES (est): 350K **Privately Held**
SIC: **3542** Machine tools, metal forming type

(G-11173)
DUERR TOOL & DIE CO INC (PA)
1135 Springfield Rd (07083-8120)
PHONE..............................908 810-9035
Karl Duerr, *President*
Walter Duerr, *Corp Secy*
Jens Duerr, *Exec VP*
▲ EMP: 17 **EST: 1945**
SQ FT: 125,000
SALES (est): 6.1MM **Privately Held**
WEB: www.duerrinc.com
SIC: **3089 3544** Injection molding of plastics; special dies & tools

(G-11174)
DUREX INC (PA)
Also Called: Creative Serving
5 Stahuber Ave (07083-5086)
PHONE..............................908 688-0800
Fax: 908 688-0718
Robert Denholtz, *CEO*
Jimy Castiglione, *Mfg Mgr*
Mike Danniballe, *Engineer*
Ryan Gatarz, *Design Engr*
Kevin McGrath, *Natl Sales Mgr*
▲ EMP: 150

SQ FT: 120,000
SALES (est): 37.5MM **Privately Held**
WEB: www.durexinc.com
SIC: **3469 3471 3444** Stamping metal for the trade; finishing, metals or formed products; sheet metalwork; metal housings, enclosures, casings & other containers

(G-11175)
DURO MANUFACTURING COMPANY
5 Stahuber Ave (07083-5037)
P.O. Box 1771 (07083-1771)
PHONE..............................908 810-9588
Robert Failla, *President*
Ann Marie Failla, *Corp Secy*
▲ EMP: 6
SQ FT: 8,000
SALES: 550K **Privately Held**
SIC: **3451** Screw machine products

(G-11176)
DYNA-LITE INC
1050 Commerce Ave Ste 2 (07083-5081)
PHONE..............................908 687-8800
Fax: 908 686-6682
Peter Poremba, *President*
Johnathan Prazeres, *Cust Svc Dir*
▲ EMP: 18
SQ FT: 12,000
SALES (est): 3.3MM **Privately Held**
WEB: www.dynalite.com
SIC: **3861** Flashlight apparatus for photographers, except bulbs

(G-11177)
EASY STREET PUBLICATIONS INC
1473 Ridgeway St (07083-5127)
P.O. Box 138, Vauxhall (07088-0138)
PHONE..............................917 699-7820
▲ EMP: 9
SQ FT: 2,000
SALES (est): 2.4MM **Privately Held**
SIC: **2771** Publishes Greeting Cards

(G-11178)
ECHO MOLDING INC
911 Springfield Rd Ste 1 (07083-8600)
PHONE..............................908 688-0099
Fax: 908 688-0529
Dieter Hekler, *President*
Gerhard Schlotterbeck, *Corp Secy*
▲ EMP: 38
SQ FT: 60,000
SALES (est): 9.3MM **Privately Held**
WEB: www.echomolding.com
SIC: **3089** Injection molding of plastics

(G-11179)
EDU-MET INTERACTIVE SYSTEMS CO
407 Chestnut St (07083-9305)
PHONE..............................908 851-9394
Fax: 908 851-2031
John Panichi, *President*
Gail A Panichi, *Vice Pres*
Anthony Panichi, *Treasurer*
EMP: 14
SQ FT: 5,200
SALES (est): 1.1MM **Privately Held**
WEB: www.edumet.com
SIC: **7372 7373** Educational computer software; utility computer software; systems integration services

(G-11180)
EL BATAL CORPORATION
Also Called: Grip Tight Tools
1060 Commerce Ave (07083-5026)
PHONE..............................908 964-3427
Walid Nakhla, *CEO*
▲ EMP: 18
SQ FT: 30,000
SALES (est): 2.2MM **Privately Held**
WEB: www.griptighttools.com
SIC: **5072 5032 3432** Hand tools; security devices, locks; building stone; granite building stone; plumbers' brass goods: drain cocks, faucets, spigots, etc.

(G-11181)
ELEMENTAL CONTAINER INC
860 Springfield Rd (07083-8614)
PHONE..............................908 687-7720
Luc Tournaire, *President*
Madelyn Cicalese, *General Mgr*
Ashley Force, *Opers Mgr*
Patricia Cataldo, *Accounts Mgr*
Henry Colmenares, *Technical Staff*
▲ EMP: 7
SQ FT: 22,000
SALES: 6MM **Privately Held**
WEB: www.elementalcontainer.com
SIC: **3411** Metal cans

(G-11182)
ERNEST SCHAEFER INC
731 Lehigh Ave (07083-7626)
PHONE..............................908 964-1280
Fax: 908 964-6787
Ernest Schaeffer III, *President*
EMP: 6 **EST: 1922**
SQ FT: 10,000
SALES: 1MM **Privately Held**
SIC: **5084 3555** Printing trades machinery, equipment & supplies; type, foundry (for printing)

(G-11183)
EVOQUA WATER TECHNOLOGIES LLC
Also Called: Electric Catalytic Pdts Group
2 Milltown Ct (07083-8108)
PHONE..............................908 851-4250
John Martin, *Manager*
EMP: 85
SALES (corp-wide): 1.1B **Publicly Held**
SIC: **3589** Water treatment equipment, industrial
HQ: Evoqua Water Technologies Llc
210 6th Ave Ste 3300
Pittsburgh PA 15222
724 772-0044

(G-11184)
FLOW-TURN INC
1050 Commerce Ave (07083-5087)
PHONE..............................908 687-3225
Hermann Miedel, *President*
Dennis Arroyo, *Project Mgr*
Dan Otero, *Opers Mgr*
Young Ran Miedel, *Director*
EMP: 25
SQ FT: 36,000
SALES: 2.5MM **Privately Held**
WEB: www.flow-turn.com
SIC: **3535** Belt conveyor systems, general industrial use

(G-11185)
FOREMOST MANUFACTURING CO INC
941 Ball Ave (07083-8799)
PHONE..............................908 687-4646
Fax: 908 687-8821
Herbert S Schiller, *CEO*
Patrick Curtin, *COO*
Michael Franciosa, *Sales Executive*
Joan Schiller, *Admin Sec*
▲ EMP: 70 **EST: 1957**
SQ FT: 52,000
SALES (est): 11.7MM **Privately Held**
SIC: **3471** Finishing, metals or formed products

(G-11186)
FOWLER ROUTE CO INC (PA)
565 Rahway Ave (07083-6690)
PHONE..............................908 686-3400
Fax: 908 686-8756
Douglas Fowler, *President*
Thomas Schmidt, *Exec VP*
EMP: 48
SALES (est): 5.9MM **Privately Held**
SIC: **3582** Commercial laundry equipment

(G-11187)
GAISERS ERPEAN STYLE PROVS INC
2019 Morris Ave (07083-6013)
PHONE..............................908 686-3421
Fax: 908 686-7131
Boris Vadrar, *President*
Jeff Rebrlov, *Vice Pres*
EMP: 13

SALES (est): 1.8MM **Privately Held**
SIC: **2013** Sausages & other prepared meats

(G-11188)
GAVAN GRAHAM ELEC PDTS CORP (PA)
751 Rahway Ave (07083-6689)
PHONE..............................908 729-9000
Fax: 908 736-9939
Ron Regan, *President*
John Robak, *VP Opers*
Jaime Mendez, *Controller*
Mike Donohue, *Sales Mgr*
Christina Dobosiewicz, *Office Mgr*
EMP: 30
SQ FT: 42,000
SALES (est): 12MM **Privately Held**
WEB: www.gavangraham.com
SIC: **3441** Fabricated structural metal

(G-11189)
GEORGE J BENDER INC
Also Called: Bender Enterprises
1 Milltown Ct (07083-8108)
PHONE..............................908 687-0081
John Appicie, *President*
Brenda Keith, *Purch Mgr*
EMP: 35 **EST: 1935**
SQ FT: 6,700
SALES (est): 3.3MM **Privately Held**
SIC: **7694 5063 1731** Motor repair services; motors, electric; generators; electrical work

(G-11190)
GOLDSTEIN SETTING CO INC
Also Called: Dan Mar Jewelers
2464 Morris Ave (07083-5705)
PHONE..............................908 964-1034
Fax: 908 964-1254
Joseph Goldstein, *President*
Myrna Goldstein, *Admin Sec*
EMP: 12
SQ FT: 3,000
SALES: 460K **Privately Held**
SIC: **3911 5944** Jewel settings & mountings, precious metal; jewelry, precious stones & precious metals

(G-11191)
HASSELBLAD INC
Also Called: Hasselblad Bron Incorporated
1080a Garden State Rd (07083-8102)
PHONE..............................800 456-0203
Michael Hejtmanek, *President*
▲ EMP: 21
SALES (est): 3MM **Privately Held**
SIC: **3861** Photographic equipment & supplies
PA: Hasselblad Ab

Goteborg

(G-11192)
HATHAWAY PLASTIC
911 Springfield Rd Ste 1 (07083-8600)
PHONE..............................908 688-9494
Robert Daniel, *Principal*
EMP: 7
SALES (est): 690.6K **Privately Held**
SIC: **3089** Injection molding of plastics

(G-11193)
HUMMEL DISTRIBUTING CORP (PA)
850 Springfield Rd (07083-8614)
PHONE..............................908 688-5300
Fax: 908 688-6020
John Hummel, *President*
Lorraine Hummel, *Corp Secy*
Herbert Hummel Jr, *Vice Pres*
Mark Hurwitz, *VP Sales*
▲ EMP: 30
SQ FT: 33,000
SALES: 4.4MM **Privately Held**
WEB: www.hummelprintmail.com
SIC: **2759 7331** Commercial printing; mailing service

(G-11194)
HUMMEL PRINTING INC
850 Springfield Rd (07083-8614)
PHONE..............................908 688-5300
John Hummel, *President*
Lorraine Hummel, *Corp Secy*

Herbert Hummel Jr, *Vice Pres*
EMP: 30
SALES (est): 4.4MM **Privately Held**
SIC: 2759 7331 Commercial printing; mailing service
PA: Hummel Distributing Corp
　　850 Springfield Rd
　　Union NJ 07083
　　908 688-5300

(G-11195)
INSTRU-MET CORPORATION
931 Lehigh Ave (07083-7632)
PHONE..............................908 851-0700
Fax: 908 686-1688
Paul Metzger, *President*
Ward Ruoff, *Vice Pres*
Maria Silva, *Sales Mgr*
Maria Silvia, *Admin Sec*
EMP: 8
SQ FT: 4,500
SALES (est): 860K **Privately Held**
WEB: www.instrumet.com
SIC: 3824 7629 3829 3825 Mechanical & electromechanical counters & devices; electronic equipment repair; testing equipment: abrasion, shearing strength, etc.; instruments to measure electricity

(G-11196)
JAY-BEE OIL & GAS INC (PA)
Also Called: Jay Bee Oil & Gas Company
1720 Us Highway 22 E # 1 (07083-6126)
PHONE..............................908 686-1493
Fax: 908 688-4380
Randy Broda, *President*
Deborah B Morgan, *Vice Pres*
Shane Dowell, *Office Mgr*
Brian Paugh, *Manager*
EMP: 75 **EST:** 1989
SQ FT: 1,000
SALES (est): 57.6MM **Privately Held**
SIC: 1381 Directional drilling oil & gas wells

(G-11197)
JERSEY BOUND LATINO LLC
Also Called: Jersey Bound Latino Magazine
841 Hueston St (07083-7104)
P.O. Box 1230 (07083-1230)
PHONE..............................908 591-2830
Victor Nichols, *CEO*
Marlene Jauregui, *President*
EMP: 6
SALES (est): 259.1K **Privately Held**
SIC: 7389 8742 2741 5192 Subscription fulfillment services: magazine, newspaper, etc.; marketing consulting services; ; books, periodicals & newspapers; survey service: marketing, location, etc.

(G-11198)
JOHN CANARY CUSTOM WDWKG INC
Also Called: Canary' Closets & Cabinetry
697 Rahway Ave (07083-6683)
PHONE..............................908 851-2894
John Canary, *President*
Steve Seibert, *General Mgr*
Karol Weiland, *Bookkeeper*
Wayne Coe, *Sales Associate*
EMP: 18
SALES (est): 2MM **Privately Held**
WEB: www.canarycustom.com
SIC: 2434 Wood kitchen cabinets

(G-11199)
JOHNSON CONTROLS INC
50 Progress St (07083-8123)
P.O. Box 327 (07083-0327)
PHONE..............................732 752-2395
Joseph Ott, *Manager*
EMP: 49 **Privately Held**
SIC: 3822 Building services monitoring controls, automatic
HQ: Johnson Controls, Inc.
　　5757 N Green Bay Ave
　　Milwaukee WI 53209
　　414 524-1200

(G-11200)
KALUSTYAN CORPORATION
855 Rahway Ave (07083-6633)
PHONE..............................908 688-0853
Errol Karakash, *CEO*
John O Bas, *President*

Savas Ovan, *General Mgr*
Greg Lightfoot, *Business Mgr*
Luis Ortriz, *Warehouse Mgr*
◆ **EMP:** 80
SQ FT: 110,500
SALES (est): 27.9MM **Privately Held**
WEB: www.kalustyan.com
SIC: 2099 5149 5159 5153 Seasonings & spices; spices, including grinding; spices & seasonings; fruits, dried; nuts & nut by-products; beans, dry: bulk

(G-11201)
LINCOLN ELECTRIC PDTS CO INC
947 Lehigh Ave (07083-7632)
PHONE..............................908 688-2900
Fax: 908 688-8549
Bruce Leff, *President*
Peter Vallone, *Project Mgr*
David Bairamian, *Design Engr*
Vincent Abenanti, *Sales Engr*
Jay Patel, *Sales Engr*
EMP: 35 **EST:** 1949
SQ FT: 50,000
SALES (est): 15.4MM **Privately Held**
WEB: www.leproduct.com
SIC: 3613 Panelboards & distribution boards, electric; switchboards & parts, power

(G-11202)
LIONI LATTICINI INC (PA)
555 Lehigh Ave (07083-7976)
PHONE..............................908 686-6061
Giuseppe Salzarulo, *President*
Sal Salzarulo, *Vice Pres*
Mike Virga, *VP Opers*
Charles Disalvo, *VP Sales*
Michelina Salzarulo, *Sales Mgr*
◆ **EMP:** 58
SALES (est): 12.9MM **Privately Held**
SIC: 2022 Cheese, natural & processed

(G-11203)
LIONI MOZZARELLA & SPECIALTY
Also Called: Lioni Specialty Foods
555 Lehigh Ave (07083-7976)
PHONE..............................908 624-9450
Guiseppe Salzarulo, *President*
Charlie Disalvo, *Vice Pres*
Neil Aurilia, *CFO*
Lenny Frazzano, *Sales Mgr*
Lori Church, *Marketing Staff*
▲ **EMP:** 39
SALES (est): 4.9MM **Privately Held**
SIC: 2022 5143 Cheese spreads, dips, pastes & other cheese products; cheese
PA: Lioni Latticini, Inc
　　555 Lehigh Ave
　　Union NJ 07083

(G-11204)
MAJOR PRINTING CO INC
934 Savitt Pl (07083-6759)
P.O. Box 1356 (07083-1356)
PHONE..............................908 686-7296
Fax: 908 686-9229
Joseph Stampone, *President*
John Stampone, *Vice Pres*
EMP: 4
SQ FT: 6,000
SALES: 600K **Privately Held**
WEB: www.majorprinting.com
SIC: 2752 Commercial printing, offset

(G-11205)
MANNING & LEWIS ENGRG CO INC
675 Rahway Ave Ste 1 (07083-6695)
PHONE..............................908 687-2400
Fax: 908 687-2404
Kurt Nelson, *President*
John R Hayday, *Vice Pres*
Alvin Matt, *Vice Pres*
▲ **EMP:** 60
SQ FT: 40,000
SALES (est): 7.1MM **Privately Held**
WEB: www.manninglewis.com
SIC: 3443 3559 Heat exchangers: coolers (after, inter), condensers, etc.; chemical machinery & equipment

(G-11206)
MARVIC CORP
Also Called: Marvic Formica In Design
2450 Iorio Ct (07083-8105)
PHONE..............................908 686-4340
Fax: 908 686-9085
Alfred D'Alessandro, *President*
Victoria D'Alessandro, *Corp Secy*
Mildred Carbone, *Vice Pres*
Al Dalessandro, *VP Opers*
Ivan Marinov, *Software Dev*
EMP: 50 **EST:** 1961
SQ FT: 10,000
SALES (est): 7.4MM **Privately Held**
SIC: 2541 3281 Counter & sink tops; cut stone & stone products

(G-11207)
MERRILL CORPORATION
649 Rahway Ave (07083-6683)
PHONE..............................908 810-3740
Fax: 908 688-1983
Tom Arnold, *President*
EMP: 100
SALES (corp-wide): 566.6MM **Privately Held**
WEB: www.merrillcorp.com
SIC: 2752 2759 Commercial printing, lithographic; business form & card printing, lithographic; commercial printing
PA: Merrill Corporation
　　1 Merrill Cir
　　Saint Paul MN 55108
　　651 646-4501

(G-11208)
MORRE-TEC INDUSTRIES INC
Also Called: Extracts and Ingredients
1 Gary Rd (07083-5527)
PHONE..............................908 688-9009
Leonard Glass, *President*
Estelle Glass, *Admin Sec*
◆ **EMP:** 24
SQ FT: 20,000
SALES (est): 13.5MM **Privately Held**
WEB: www.morretec.com
SIC: 5169 2819 Industrial chemicals; industrial inorganic chemicals

(G-11209)
MR QUICKLY INC
Also Called: Quickly Printing
1965 Morris Ave (07083)
PHONE..............................908 687-6000
Fax: 908 687-6006
Larry Kovacs, *President*
EMP: 4
SQ FT: 1,000
SALES: 400K **Privately Held**
SIC: 2752 7334 Commercial printing, offset; photocopying & duplicating services

(G-11210)
MULBERRY METAL PRODUCTS INC (PA)
2199 Stanley Ter (07083-4399)
PHONE..............................908 688-8850
Fax: 908 688-7294
Richard Horn, *President*
Richard E Mueller, *Exec VP*
Kristina Hom, *Vice Pres*
Inge Horn, *Admin Sec*
EMP: 90 **EST:** 1927
SQ FT: 135,000
SALES: 24MM **Privately Held**
WEB: www.mulberrymetal.com
SIC: 3644 5065 Face plates (wiring devices); semiconductor devices

(G-11211)
NATIONAL WOODWORKING CO
985 Tinkettle Turn (07083-3499)
PHONE..............................908 851-9316
Fax: 908 688-7188
Richard Weber, *President*
Evelyn Weber, *Vice Pres*
EMP: 4
SQ FT: 7,500
SALES: 450K **Privately Held**
SIC: 2431 2511 Woodwork, interior & ornamental; wood household furniture

(G-11212)
PAIGE ELECTRIC COMPANY LP (PA)
1160 Springfield Rd (07083-8121)
P.O. Box 368 (07083-0368)
PHONE..............................908 687-7810
Fax: 908 687-2722
James Coleman, *CEO*
Jim Cichy, *General Mgr*
David Coleman, *Vice Pres*
Marty Fox, *Vice Pres*
Vince Nolletti, *Vice Pres*
◆ **EMP:** 47
SQ FT: 47,000
SALES: 132.5MM **Privately Held**
WEB: www.paigewire.com
SIC: 5063 3699 Electronic wire & cable; electrical equipment & supplies

(G-11213)
PALMAROZZO BINDERY
850 Springfield Rd (07083-8614)
PHONE..............................908 688-5300
Tina Palmarozzo, *Owner*
EMP: 4
SALES (est): 150K **Privately Held**
SIC: 2789 Bookbinding & related work

(G-11214)
PATEL PRINTING PLUS CORP
1036 Commerce Ave (07083-5026)
PHONE..............................908 964-6422
Jawahar C Patel, *President*
Sharon Patel, *Vice Pres*
EMP: 10
SQ FT: 6,000
SALES (est): 1.2MM **Privately Held**
WEB: www.patelprintingplus.com
SIC: 2752 2791 Commercial printing, offset; typesetting

(G-11215)
PHILIP CRETER INC
20 Monroe St (07083-8192)
PHONE..............................908 686-2910
Fax: 908 687-1853
Doris Logan, *President*
Bruce Logan, *Vice Pres*
EMP: 6 **EST:** 1941
SQ FT: 10,000
SALES (est): 430K **Privately Held**
SIC: 3544 3599 3469 Special dies & tools; machine & other job shop work; machine parts, stamped or pressed metal

(G-11216)
PREMESCO INC
Also Called: Premesco Seamless Ring Co Div
2389 Vauxhall Rd (07083-5036)
PHONE..............................908 686-0513
Mark Tessler, *President*
EMP: 300
SQ FT: 40,000
SALES: 42.3MM **Privately Held**
SIC: 3911 3339 Rings, finger: precious metal; precious metals

(G-11217)
QUALITY INDEXING LLC
939 Lehigh Ave (07083-7632)
PHONE..............................908 810-0200
Fax: 908 810-9610
Daniel Blum, *Owner*
William E Ulrich, *Consultant*
EMP: 45 **EST:** 1920
SALES (est): 5.3MM **Privately Held**
SIC: 2675 Index cards, die-cut: made from purchased materials

(G-11218)
R M F ASSOCIATES INC
202 Carolyn Rd (07083-9403)
PHONE..............................908 687-9355
Roger M Furiness, *President*
Michael Rogers, *Vice Pres*
EMP: 140
SQ FT: 11,000
SALES: 10MM **Privately Held**
SIC: 3469 3444 Metal stampings; sheet metalwork

(G-11219)
ROCKWOOD CORPORATION
Also Called: Speedwell Targets
410 Clermont Ter Ste D (07083-8000)
PHONE......................908 355-8600
Michael Panos, *President*
EMP: 8
SQ FT: 12,000
SALES: 5MM **Privately Held**
WEB: www.speedwelltargets.com
SIC: 5941 2741 Sporting goods & bicycle shops; miscellaneous publishing

(G-11220)
S AND D FUEL LLC
1351 Magie Ave (07083-8070)
PHONE......................908 248-8188
EMP: 4
SALES (est): 32.6K **Privately Held**
SIC: 2869 Fuels

(G-11221)
SATEC INC
10 Milltown Ct (07083-8108)
PHONE......................908 258-0924
Ed Hoinowski, *President*
Esli Latorre, *General Mgr*
Rodny Jean-Charles, *Project Engr*
Christia Laborde, *Sales Mgr*
Bill McCormack, *Manager*
▲ EMP: 23
SALES (est): 5.2MM **Privately Held**
WEB: www.oksatec.com
SIC: 3825 Meters, power factor & phase angle

(G-11222)
SCHOTT NYC CORP
735 Rahway Ave (07083-6689)
PHONE......................800 631-5407
Steven Colin, *CEO*
Walter Reed, *General Mgr*
Roslyn Schott, *Corp Secy*
David Colin, *Vice Pres*
Maryann Schumacher, *Controller*
▲ EMP: 100
SALES (est): 12MM
SALES (corp-wide): 12.2MM **Privately Held**
WEB: www.schottnyc.com
SIC: 2386 2329 Coats & jackets, leather & sheep-lined; garments, leather; down-filled clothing: men's & boys'
PA: Schott Bros, Inc.
735 Rahway Ave
Union NJ 07083
908 527-0011

(G-11223)
SHAFFER PRODUCTS INC
20 Milltown Rd (07083-8110)
P.O. Box 427 (07083-0427)
PHONE......................908 206-1980
Fax: 908 206-1975
H Sabet, *Ch of Bd*
James K Shahidi, *President*
EMP: 25 EST: 1951
SQ FT: 10,000
SALES (est): 1.9MM **Privately Held**
WEB: www.shafferproducts.com
SIC: 2393 Bags & containers, except sleeping bags: textile

(G-11224)
SPINAL KINETICS LLC (PA)
950 W Chestnut St (07083-6966)
PHONE......................908 687-2552
Steven Brownstein MD, *Partner*
Steven P Brownstein MD, *Partner*
Joseph Cioffi, *Opers Staff*
Donald Cioffi DC, *Mktg Dir*
EMP: 4 EST: 2008
SALES (est): 428.7K **Privately Held**
SIC: 8041 3842 8011 Offices & clinics of chiropractors; trusses, orthopedic & surgical; neurosurgeon

(G-11225)
STERNVENT CO INC
No5 Stahuber Ave (07083)
PHONE......................908 688-0807
Philip Feiner, *President*
Gerson Feiner, *Vice Pres*
Penni Feiner, *Treasurer*
EMP: 35
SQ FT: 42,000
SALES (est): 6.2MM
SALES (corp-wide): 37.5MM **Privately Held**
WEB: www.sternvent.com
SIC: 3564 Dust or fume collecting equipment, industrial
PA: Durex Inc.
5 Stahuber Ave
Union NJ 07083
908 688-0800

(G-11226)
SUMMIT FILTER CORP
20 Milltown Rd (07083-8110)
P.O. Box 427 (07083-0427)
PHONE......................908 687-3500
Fax: 908 687-4202
James K Shahidi, *President*
Lois Gloss, *Vice Pres*
Cathy Maher, *Executive*
EMP: 30
SQ FT: 25,000
SALES (est): 6.1MM **Privately Held**
WEB: www.summitfilter.com
SIC: 3569 3564 2674 Filters, general line: industrial; blowers & fans; bags: uncoated paper & multiwall

(G-11227)
TARLTON C & T CO INC (PA)
Also Called: Nedco Conveyor Technology
967 Lehigh Ave (07083-7632)
PHONE......................908 964-9400
Fax: 908 964-9411
Curtis Tarlton, *President*
Theresa Tarlton, *Corp Secy*
Dan Oliva, *Manager*
EMP: 40 EST: 1961
SQ FT: 23,000
SALES (est): 10MM **Privately Held**
SIC: 3535 Conveyors & conveying equipment

(G-11228)
TESSLER & WEISS/PREMESCO INC
2389 Vauxhall Rd (07083-5091)
PHONE......................800 535-3501
Mark Tessler, *President*
Esther Tessler, *Corp Secy*
EMP: 175 EST: 1936
SQ FT: 40,000
SALES (est): 19.8MM **Privately Held**
SIC: 3911 3915 Rings, finger: precious metal; jewelers' materials & lapidary work

(G-11229)
THERMO PLASTIC TECH INC
1119 Morris Ave (07083-3305)
PHONE......................908 687-4833
Fax: 908 687-5829
Tino Quintanilla, *President*
Flor Quint, *Vice Pres*
▲ EMP: 30
SQ FT: 18,000
SALES (est): 5.5MM **Privately Held**
SIC: 3089 Molding primary plastic; plastic processing

(G-11230)
TRIPLE S EXPRESS
1991 William St (07083-4503)
PHONE......................908 686-0557
Robert Seidenschwarz, *Principal*
EMP: 4
SALES (est): 273.2K **Privately Held**
SIC: 2741 Miscellaneous publishing

(G-11231)
UNION CASTING INDUSTRIES INC (PA)
Also Called: Industrial Ferguson Foundry
2365 Us Highway 22 W (07083-8517)
P.O. Box 531 (07083-0531)
PHONE......................908 686-8888
Fax: 908 908-8891
Harvey Gross, *President*
Ken Kartodich, *Vice Pres*
Sally Lim, *Export Mgr*
EMP: 17

SALES (est): 3.2MM Privately Held
WEB: www.industrialferguson.com
SIC: 3364 3365 3366 Brass & bronze die-castings; copper & copper alloy die-castings; zinc & zinc-base alloy die-castings; aluminum & aluminum-based alloy castings; castings (except die): copper & copper-base alloy

(G-11232)
VALCONN ELECTRONICS INC
909 Rahway Ave (07083-6549)
PHONE......................908 687-1600
Fax: 908 687-8599
Vince Devito, *CEO*
Joel Cohn, *President*
▲ EMP: 20
SQ FT: 16,000
SALES (est): 1.8MM **Privately Held**
SIC: 3679 3678 Harness assemblies for electronic use: wire or cable; electronic connectors

(G-11233)
VULCAN TOOL COMPANY INC
1080 Garden State Rd # 1 (07083-8181)
PHONE......................908 686-0550
Fax: 908 686-8522
Anton Heldmann, *President*
EMP: 17 EST: 1967
SQ FT: 15,000
SALES (est): 3.9MM **Privately Held**
WEB: www.vulcantool.com
SIC: 3469 Machine parts, stamped or pressed metal

(G-11234)
WET-N-STICK LLC
Also Called: Duratape International
2816 Morris Ave Ste 21 (07083-4869)
P.O. Box 1266, Maplewood (07040-0455)
PHONE......................908 687-8273
Lee Goldman, *President*
▲ EMP: 7
SQ FT: 19,000
SALES (est): 938.4K **Privately Held**
WEB: www.duratape.com
SIC: 2672 Adhesive papers, labels or tapes: from purchased material

(G-11235)
WILLIAM T HUTCHINSON COMPANY
453 Lehigh Ave (07083-7926)
PHONE......................908 688-0533
Fax: 908 688-8296
Dean Roth, *President*
Jen Tara, *Office Mgr*
EMP: 13
SQ FT: 5,000
SALES (est): 1.8MM **Privately Held**
WEB: www.hssblanks.com
SIC: 3545 3546 Drilling machine attachments & accessories; power-driven hand-tools

Union Beach
Monmouth County

(G-11236)
INTERNTNAL FLVORS FRGRNCES INC
800 Rose Ln (07735-3550)
PHONE......................732 264-4500
Fax: 732 335-2254
Clint Brooks, *Manager*
Neil Da Costa, *Associate*
EMP: 250
SALES (corp-wide): 3.4B **Publicly Held**
SIC: 2844 Toilet preparations
PA: International Flavors & Fragrances Inc.
521 W 57th St
New York NY 10019
212 765-5500

(G-11237)
INTERNTNAL FLVORS FRGRNCES INC
800 Rose Ln (07735-3550)
PHONE......................732 264-4500
Jane Fujimoto, *Engineer*
Clint Brooks, *Manager*
EMP: 126

SALES (corp-wide): 3.4B **Publicly Held**
WEB: www.iff.com
SIC: 2869 Flavoring materials, synthetic
PA: International Flavors & Fragrances Inc.
521 W 57th St
New York NY 10019
212 765-5500

(G-11238)
J R M PRODUCTS INC
701 Locust St (07735-1750)
PHONE......................732 203-0200
Fax: 732 495-1144
Marianne Wichowski, *Branch Mgr*
EMP: 4
SALES (corp-wide): 320K **Privately Held**
SIC: 3469 Stamping metal for the trade
PA: J R M Products Inc
15 Phillips Mills Dr
North Middletown NJ 07748
732 495-3092

Union City
Hudson County

(G-11239)
ALPINE BAKERY INC
521-523 30th St (07087-3863)
PHONE......................201 902-0605
Fax: 201 902-0281
Danilo Torres, *President*
EMP: 8
SALES (est): 480K **Privately Held**
SIC: 2051 Bread, cake & related products

(G-11240)
AMALIA CARRARA INC
2111 Kerrigan Ave (07087-2122)
PHONE......................201 348-4500
Eve Muscio, *President*
EMP: 50 EST: 2001
SALES (est): 1.7MM **Privately Held**
WEB: www.amaliacarrara.com
SIC: 2335 Bridal & formal gowns

(G-11241)
ANDY GRAPHICS SERVICE BUREAU
3711 Park Ave (07087-6021)
PHONE......................201 866-9407
Andy Nazarian, *Owner*
EMP: 4
SALES (est): 190K **Privately Held**
SIC: 2759 Commercial printing

(G-11242)
APHELION ORBITALS INC
540 39th St Ste 40 (07087-2500)
PHONE......................321 289-0872
Matthew B Travis, *President*
Matthew Travis, *President*
Connor Givans, *Vice Pres*
Sihao Huang, *Vice Pres*
David Nagy, *Vice Pres*
EMP: 4
SALES (est): 197.4K **Privately Held**
SIC: 3663 2899 5088 3764 Space satellite communications equipment; pyrotechnic ammunition: flares, signals, rockets, etc.; guided missiles & space vehicles; guided missile & space vehicle engines, research & devel.; propulsion units for guided missiles & space vehicles

(G-11243)
ATARA LLC
4315 Park Ave Apt 2i (07087-6566)
PHONE......................916 765-2217
Kostyantyn Beynars, *Principal*
EMP: 4 EST: 2012
SALES (est): 220K **Privately Held**
SIC: 2844 7389 Shampoos, rinses, conditioners: hair;

(G-11244)
CUNY & GUERBER INC
Also Called: C G Automation Group
2100 Kerrigan Ave (07087-2123)
P.O. Box 1192 (07087-1192)
PHONE......................201 617-5800
Fax: 201 617-5557
David Matthews, *President*

GEOGRAPHIC

Ray Cuny, *Vice Pres*
David B Matthews Sr, *Vice Pres*
David B Matthews Jr, *Vice Pres*
Steve Matthews, *Vice Pres*
EMP: 25
SQ FT: 22,500
SALES (est): 33.2MM **Privately Held**
WEB: www.cuny.biz
SIC: 5063 4783 3699 Lighting fixtures;
  containerization of goods for shipping;
  electrical equipment & supplies

(G-11245)
**DENGEN SCIENTIFIC
CORPORATION**
315 4th St (07087-4006)
PHONE....................................201 687-2983
Ysabel Depaul, *CFO*
EMP: 25
SALES (est): 903.2K **Privately Held**
SIC: 8711 8731 3812 3629 Engineering
  services; commercial physical research;
  defense systems & equipment; battery
  chargers, rectifying or nonrotating; prod-
  uct testing laboratories;

(G-11246)
GROSS BROS PRINTING CO INC
3125 Summit Ave (07087-2430)
PHONE....................................201 865-4606
▲ **EMP:** 25
SQ FT: 36,000
SALES (est): 1.9MM **Privately Held**
SIC: 2752 2789 Lithographic Commercial
  Printing Bookbinding/Related Work

(G-11247)
**HAMILTON EMBROIDERY CO
INC**
907 21st St (07087-2104)
PHONE....................................201 867-4084
Fax: 201 867-2066
Frank Blaso Sr, *President*
Frank Blaso Jr, *Vice Pres*
▲ **EMP:** 17
SQ FT: 25,000
SALES: 3.4MM **Privately Held**
WEB: www.hamiltonembroidery.com
SIC: 2397 2241 Schiffli machine embroi-
  deries; narrow fabric mills

(G-11248)
**IMAGERY EMBROIDARY
CORPORATION**
2907 Jeannette St 2911 (07087-2333)
PHONE....................................201 343-9333
Edison Cruz, *President*
EMP: 10
SQ FT: 4,500
SALES: 250K **Privately Held**
SIC: 2759 2395 Screen printing; embroi-
  dery & art needlework

(G-11249)
J & T EMBROIDERY INC
646 36th St (07087-2511)
PHONE....................................201 867-4897
Thomas Betancourt, *President*
EMP: 5
SALES (est): 300K **Privately Held**
SIC: 2395 Embroidery products, except
  schiffli machine

(G-11250)
JARCO U S CASTING CORP
4407 Park Ave (07087-6345)
PHONE....................................201 271-0003
Mario Herrera, *President*
Felix Disla, *Vice Pres*
▲ **EMP:** 45 **EST:** 1981
SQ FT: 14,000
SALES: 3MM **Privately Held**
WEB: www.jarcousa.com
SIC: 3993 3369 3272 Signs & advertising
  specialties; castings, except die-castings,
  precision; cast stone, concrete

(G-11251)
JCT DESIGN ENTERPRISES INC
1701 Summit Ave (07087-2020)
PHONE....................................212 629-7412
Carlos Tapia, *President*
EMP: 25
SALES: 1.3MM **Privately Held**
SIC: 3911 Jewelry, precious metal

(G-11252)
KALEIDOSCOPE SOUND
514 Monastery Pl (07087-3389)
PHONE....................................201 223-2868
Randy Craftone, *Owner*
EMP: 4
SALES (est): 363.2K **Privately Held**
SIC: 3663 Studio equipment, radio & tele-
  vision broadcasting

(G-11253)
LA TRIBUNA PUBLICATION INC
300 36th St Apt 1 (07087-4724)
P.O. Box 805 (07087-0805)
PHONE....................................201 617-1360
Ruth M Molenaar, *President*
Soraya Molenaar, *Vice Pres*
EMP: 37 **EST:** 1988
SALES (est): 1.5MM **Privately Held**
SIC: 2711 8661 Newspapers: publishing
  only, not printed on site; religious organi-
  zations

(G-11254)
LICINI BROTHERS INC
Also Called: Licini Bros Provision
907 West St (07087-3007)
PHONE....................................201 865-1130
Andrew Licini, *President*
Daniel Licini, *Corp Secy*
EMP: 9
SQ FT: 5,700
SALES (est): 925.8K **Privately Held**
SIC: 2013 5147 5421 Sausages & other
  prepared meats; meats, fresh; meat & fish
  markets

(G-11255)
LUSTERLINE INC
501 30th St Ste 1a (07087-3876)
PHONE....................................201 758-5148
Devyani V Patel, *President*
Namesh Patel, *Vice Pres*
◆ **EMP:** 5
SQ FT: 1,200
SALES (est): 1.4MM **Privately Held**
SIC: 3911 Jewelry, precious metal

(G-11256)
MAXSYL LEATHER CO LLC
131 35th St (07087-5911)
PHONE....................................201 864-0579
Walter Martillo Jr, *President*
John Bryant, *General Mgr*
EMP: 90
SALES (est): 5.4MM **Privately Held**
SIC: 3172 3111 Personal leather goods;
  leather processing

(G-11257)
MILADY BRIDALS INC
Also Called: Eve of Milady
2111 Kerrigan Ave (07087-2122)
PHONE....................................201 348-4500
Fax: 201 865-6366
Eve Muscio, *President*
EMP: 25
SQ FT: 3,000
SALES (est): 7MM **Privately Held**
WEB: www.eveofmiladybridals.com
SIC: 2335 Women's, juniors' & misses'
  dresses; gowns, formal; wedding gowns
  & dresses

(G-11258)
MSJ UNLIMITED SERVICES
519 35th St (07087-2501)
PHONE....................................201 617-0764
Ruben Cruz, *Owner*
EMP: 5
SALES (est): 380.7K **Privately Held**
SIC: 3822 1711 Air conditioning & refriger-
  ation controls; plumbing, heating, air-con-
  ditioning contractors

(G-11259)
**MUSINGS PRESS LTD LIABILITY
CO**
1013 Palisade Ave Apt B1 (07087-4171)
PHONE....................................347 210-8820
Benjamin Hinson-Ekong, *Owner*
EMP: 10

SALES: 2K **Privately Held**
SIC: 5065 2732 7313 2211 Electronic
  parts & equipment; book printing; electronic media advertising representatives;
  printed media advertising representatives;
  print cloths, cotton

(G-11260)
NICOLOSI FOODS INC
2214 Summit Ave (07087-2129)
PHONE....................................201 624-1702
Fax: 201 331-2924
Robert Nicolosi, *President*
EMP: 9
SALES (est): 1.6MM **Privately Held**
SIC: 0751 2013 Slaughtering: custom live-
  stock services; sausages & other pre-
  pared meats

(G-11261)
NOBLEWORKS INC
500 Paterson Plank Rd (07087-3416)
PHONE....................................201 420-0095
Ron Kanfi, *President*
▲ **EMP:** 12
SQ FT: 8,000
SALES: 1.6MM **Privately Held**
WEB: www.nobleworksinc.com
SIC: 2771 5112 Greeting cards; greeting
  cards

(G-11262)
**NORTH JERSEY PAPER
PRODUCTS**
625 18th St (07087-2054)
PHONE....................................973 372-4646
Frank Capozzi, *President*
Robert Goch, *Treasurer*
EMP: 10
SALES (est): 999.2K **Privately Held**
SIC: 2652 5113 2653 Setup paperboard
  boxes; industrial & personal service
  paper; corrugated & solid fiber boxes

(G-11263)
PUEBLO LATINO LAUNDRY LLC
1717 Bergenline Ave (07087-3232)
PHONE....................................201 864-1666
EMP: 7
SQ FT: 1,800
SALES (est): 660K **Privately Held**
SIC: 2211 7215 Cotton Broadwoven Fab-
  ric Mill Coin-Operated Laundry

(G-11264)
R & R FUEL INC
3205 Hudson Ave (07087-5803)
PHONE....................................201 223-0786
Mussarat Shaheen, *Principal*
EMP: 5
SALES (est): 416.6K **Privately Held**
SIC: 2869 Fuels

(G-11265)
**S JARCO-U CASTINGS
CORPORATION**
109 45th St (07087-6311)
PHONE....................................201 271-0003
Fax: 201 271-0009
Mario A Herrera, *President*
▲ **EMP:** 7
SALES (est): 851.1K **Privately Held**
SIC: 3369 Nonferrous foundries

(G-11266)
SOCIO PRODUCE INC
Also Called: City Fresh Market
518 32nd St (07087-3911)
PHONE....................................201 348-3660
EMP: 4
SALES (est): 212.4K **Privately Held**
SIC: 2038 5411 Ethnic foods, frozen; gro-
  cery stores; supermarkets

(G-11267)
**SOCKS 47 LTD LIABILITY
COMPANY**
4620 Bergenline Ave (07087-5126)
PHONE....................................201 866-2222
Abdulnaser Daaboul, *Principal*
EMP: 5
SALES (est): 107.4K **Privately Held**
SIC: 2252 Socks

(G-11268)
SONIA FASHION INC
422 11th St (07087-4260)
P.O. Box 8146 (07087-1846)
PHONE....................................201 864-3483
Fax: 201 864-2169
Louis Taupier Jr, *President*
Lisa Taupier, *Vice Pres*
▲ **EMP:** 4
SQ FT: 10,500
SALES (est): 482.8K **Privately Held**
WEB: www.soniafashion.com
SIC: 2339 Jeans: women's, misses' & jun-
  iors'

(G-11269)
U S A DISTRIBUTORS INC
Also Called: El Estelcil
3510 Bergenline Ave Ste 4 (07087-4775)
PHONE....................................201 348-1959
Anthony Ibarria, *President*
EMP: 50
SQ FT: 7,000
SALES (est): 2.4MM **Privately Held**
SIC: 2711 Newspapers: publishing only,
  not printed on site

(G-11270)
**UNION CITY MIRROR & TABLE
CO**
129 34th St (07087-5902)
P.O. Box 825 (07087-0825)
PHONE....................................201 867-0050
Fax: 201 867-2552
Lisa Russo, *Corp Secy*
Thomas Russo, *Vice Pres*
Gene Russo, *Vice Pres*
EMP: 48 **EST:** 1921
SQ FT: 55,000
SALES (est): 6.5MM **Privately Held**
SIC: 2511 3231 Tables, household: wood;
  mirrored glass

(G-11271)
**UNION CITY WHIRLPOOL
REPAIR**
507 43rd St (07087-2611)
PHONE....................................908 428-9146
Hilton Lehmann, *Principal*
EMP: 8 **EST:** 2016
SALES (est): 88.7K **Privately Held**
SIC: 7692 Welding repair

(G-11272)
**UNIQUE IMPRESSIONS LTD
LBLTY**
718 25th St (07087-2257)
PHONE....................................201 751-4088
Frank Corbiserie,
EMP: 5
SALES (est): 301.3K **Privately Held**
SIC: 2759 Bag, wrapper & seal printing &
  engraving

Upper Saddle River
Bergen County

(G-11273)
ATLANTIC EQP ENGINEERS INC
24 Industrial Ave (07458-2302)
P.O. Box 181 (07458-0181)
PHONE....................................201 828-9400
Fax: 201 387-0291
Alan M Kessler, *President*
Barry E Kessler, *Vice Pres*
Barry Kessler, *Vice Pres*
EMP: 11 **EST:** 1963
SQ FT: 12,000
SALES: 6MM **Privately Held**
WEB: www.metal-powders.com
SIC: 3399 3324 3479 Powder, metal;
  aerospace investment castings, ferrous;
  coating of metals & formed products

(G-11274)
**BERGEN DIGITAL GRAPHICS
LLC**
Also Called: Fastsigns
346 State Rt 17 (07458-2308)
PHONE....................................201 825-0011
Fax: 201 825-4556
William Miller,

Kevin Miller,
EMP: 4
SQ FT: 2,500
SALES (est): 623.6K **Privately Held**
SIC: 3993 Signs & advertising specialties

(G-11275)
BUSINESS CARDS TOMORROW
Also Called: B C T
11 Industrial Ave (07458-2301)
PHONE.....................201 236-0088
Fax: 201 236-9010
John Cerdendino, *Owner*
Sue Negrin, *Vice Pres*
EMP: 20
SALES (est): 1.7MM **Privately Held**
SIC: 2752 Commercial printing, lithographic

(G-11276)
CAPUANO PLUMBING INC
327 W Saddle River Rd (07458-2146)
PHONE.....................201 327-0676
Louis Capuano, *President*
Karen C Capuano, *Admin Sec*
EMP: 6
SALES (est): 918.6K **Privately Held**
SIC: 1711 3533 Plumbing contractors; heating & air conditioning contractors; water well drilling equipment

(G-11277)
CUSTOM LINERS INC
345 State Rt 17 (07458-2307)
PHONE.....................732 940-0084
John Boag, *Principal*
EMP: 4
SALES (est): 553.5K **Privately Held**
SIC: 2844 Toilet preparations

(G-11278)
DIHCO INC
612 E Crescent Ave Ste A (07458-1859)
PHONE.....................201 327-0518
Fax: 201 327-8759
Gus Hess, *President*
Peter Diamandea, *Vice Pres*
EMP: 4
SQ FT: 10,000
SALES: 700K **Privately Held**
SIC: 3599 Machine shop, jobbing & repair

(G-11279)
HOFMANN TOOL & DIE CORPORATION
356 State Rt 17 (07458-2308)
PHONE.....................201 327-0226
Charles Franco, *President*
EMP: 6
SQ FT: 5,000
SALES (est): 580K **Privately Held**
SIC: 3544 Special dies & tools

(G-11280)
MINWAX GROUP (INC)
10 Montinview Rd Ste N300 (07458)
PHONE.....................201 818-7500
Fax: 201 818-7610
Peter Black, *President*
Stewart D Bill, *President*
Ridgely W Harrison III, *President*
Ann Allard, *Vice Pres*
Paul Gaynor, *Vice Pres*
EMP: 990
SALES (est): 113.5MM **Privately Held**
SIC: 2851 Stains: varnish, oil or wax

(G-11281)
MORE COPY PRINTING SERVICE
302 State Rt 17 (07458-2308)
PHONE.....................201 327-1106
Felix Gomez, *Owner*
EMP: 4
SALES (est): 240K **Privately Held**
SIC: 2752 Commercial printing, lithographic

(G-11282)
PEARSON INC
1 Lake St (07458-1813)
PHONE.....................201 236-7000
Leeanne Fisher, *President*
Wendy Craven, *Editor*
Anton Yakovlev, *Editor*
Stephen Olson, *District Mgr*
Katherine Rosenthal, *District Mgr*

EMP: 22
SALES (corp-wide): 5.9B **Privately Held**
SIC: 2731 Books: publishing & printing; textbooks: publishing & printing
HQ: Pearson Inc.
1330 Hudson St
New York NY 10013
212 641-2400

(G-11283)
PERKINS PLUMBING & HEATING
89 Fawnhill Rd (07458-1518)
PHONE.....................201 327-2736
Fax: 201 327-5688
James Redmond, *President*
EMP: 4
SALES (est): 390.1K **Privately Held**
SIC: 1711 1389 Plumbing contractors; bailing, cleaning, swabbing & treating of wells

(G-11284)
RED LETTER PRESS INC
16 Deerhorn Trl (07458-1131)
P.O. Box 393, Saddle River (07458-0393)
PHONE.....................609 597-5257
Jack Kreismer, *President*
Robin Kreismer, *Admin Sec*
EMP: 3
SALES: 1.5MM **Privately Held**
SIC: 2759 2679 Letterpress printing; novelties, paper: made from purchased material

(G-11285)
SOLAR TURBINES INCORPORATED
600 E Crescent Ave # 305 (07458-1858)
PHONE.....................201 825-8200
Alex Munoz, *Mfg Spvr*
Mark Fitzgerald, *Manager*
Mohamed Seddik, *Supervisor*
Patricia Laughlin, *Administration*
Enrique Rodriguez, *Technician*
EMP: 11
SALES (corp-wide): 45.4B **Publicly Held**
WEB: www.esolar.cat.com
SIC: 3511 Gas turbine generator set units, complete
HQ: Solar Turbines Incorporated
2200 Pacific Hwy
San Diego CA 92101
619 544-5000

(G-11286)
TRIANGLE MANUFACTURING CO
116 Pleasant Ave (07458-2396)
PHONE.....................201 962-7433
Fax: 201 825-0402
EMP: 8
SALES (est): 790K **Privately Held**
SIC: 3999 Mfg Misc Products

(G-11287)
TRIANGLE MANUFACTURING CO INC
120 Pleasant Ave (07458-2304)
PHONE.....................201 825-1212
Neal Strohmeyer, *Branch Mgr*
EMP: 60
SALES (corp-wide): 45MM **Privately Held**
WEB: www.cyclonewinder.com
SIC: 3599 Machine & other job shop work; machine shop, jobbing & repair
PA: Triangle Manufacturing Co Inc
25 Park Way
Upper Saddle River NJ 07458
201 825-1212

(G-11288)
WORLD PAC PAPER LLC
600 E Crescent Ave # 301 (07458-1842)
PHONE.....................877 837-2737
Edgar L Smith Jr, *CEO*
EMP: 4 **EST:** 2004
SALES (est): 759K **Privately Held**
SIC: 2621 Book, bond & printing papers

(G-11289)
XTREME POWERTECH LLC
123 Pleasant Ave (07458-2303)
PHONE.....................201 791-5050
Fax: 201 791-5805

Paul Hilfer, *Managing Prtnr*
Marty Lanning,
EMP: 11
SQ FT: 20,000
SALES (est): 1.7MM **Privately Held**
SIC: 3674 Semiconductor circuit networks; transistors

Ventnor City
Atlantic County

(G-11290)
CAR WASH PARTS INC
6927 Atlantic Ave (08406-2504)
PHONE.....................215 633-9250
Edward Eckelman, *President*
Ruth Eckelman, *Vice Pres*
Steven Krevitz, *Treasurer*
EMP: 4
SQ FT: 25,000
SALES (est): 671.4K **Privately Held**
SIC: 3589 5087 Car washing machinery; carwash equipment & supplies

(G-11291)
FRENCH CREEK SHEEP & WOOL CO
5000 Boardwalk Apt 1717 (08406-2923)
PHONE.....................610 286-5700
Fax: 610 286-0324
Jean S Flaxenburg, *President*
Eric M Flaxenburg, *Principal*
EMP: 20
SQ FT: 6,500
SALES (est): 1.8MM **Privately Held**
WEB: www.frenchcreeksw.com
SIC: 2386 2253 2231 Garments, leather; sweaters & sweater coats, knit; broadwoven fabric mills, wool

(G-11292)
GPSCHARTSCOM
5021 Winchester Ave (08406-2459)
PHONE.....................609 226-8842
Craig Bates, *Owner*
EMP: 4
SALES (est): 241K **Privately Held**
SIC: 2782 7389 Chart & graph paper, ruled;

(G-11293)
PHILDELPHIA-NEWSPAPERS-LLC
Also Called: Atlantic City News
109 S Dorset Ave (08406-2835)
PHONE.....................609 823-0453
Stephanie Arnold, *Editor*
Brian Tierney, *Branch Mgr*
Jeanine Reilly, *Director*
Bentley Alberts, *Executive*
EMP: 1001
SALES (corp-wide): 232.9MM **Privately Held**
SIC: 2711 Newspapers, publishing & printing
PA: Phildelphia-Newspapers-Llc
801 Market St Ste 300
Philadelphia PA 19107
215 854-2000

(G-11294)
VOICINGS PUBLICATION INC
Also Called: Preachers Illustration Service
3 S Weymouth Ave Ste 2 (08406-2980)
PHONE.....................609 822-9401
Fax: 609 822-1638
James Colainni Sr, *President*
James Colaianni Sr, *President*
Patricia Colaianni, *Vice Pres*
EMP: 5
SALES (est): 360K **Privately Held**
WEB: www.voicings.com
SIC: 2721 Periodicals: publishing only

Vernon
Sussex County

(G-11295)
ABOVE ENVIRONMENTAL SERVICES
57 Vernon Crossing Rd (07462-3209)
P.O. Box 801 (07462-0801)
PHONE.....................973 702-7021
Fax: 973 764-9082
Thomas Bove, *President*
EMP: 5
SALES (est): 520.1K **Privately Held**
SIC: 1389 Oil field services

(G-11296)
BLISSFUL BITES
36 Butternut Dr (07462-3301)
PHONE.....................973 670-6928
Dawn Mele, *Principal*
EMP: 4
SALES (est): 196K **Privately Held**
SIC: 2051 Bread, cake & related products

(G-11297)
CONGRUENT MACHINE CO INC
107 Maple Grange Rd (07462-3211)
P.O. Box 888 (07462-0888)
PHONE.....................973 764-6767
Fax: 973 764-6718
Gerald Caiafa, *President*
EMP: 5
SQ FT: 12,000
SALES (est): 1MM **Privately Held**
SIC: 3599 3545 3952 3546 Machine shop, jobbing & repair; precision tools, machinists'; lead pencils & art goods; power-driven handtools; screw machine products

(G-11298)
INDEMAX INC
1 Industrial Dr (07462-3466)
PHONE.....................973 209-2424
Alphonse Infurna, *President*
Patricia Infurna, *Vice Pres*
EMP: 7
SALES (est): 1.2MM **Privately Held**
WEB: www.indemax.com
SIC: 3547 Finishing equipment, rolling mill

(G-11299)
METALFAB INC
Prices Switch Rd (07462)
P.O. Box 9 (07462-0009)
PHONE.....................973 764-2000
Fax: 973 764-0272
William Westdyk, *President*
Tony Manno, *Regional Mgr*
Michael Randazzo, *COO*
Anthony R Bartello, *Vice Pres*
Cornelius De Bonte Jr, *Vice Pres*
▼ **EMP:** 30
SQ FT: 30,000
SALES (est): 7.2MM **Privately Held**
WEB: www.metalfabinc.com
SIC: 3444 3535 Sheet metal specialties, not stamped; conveyors & conveying equipment

(G-11300)
METALFAB MTL HDLG SYSTEMS LLC
11 Prices Switch Rd (07462-3311)
PHONE.....................973 764-2000
Tony Manno,
Mike McMahon,
EMP: 30
SALES: 6MM **Privately Held**
SIC: 3535 Conveyors & conveying equipment

(G-11301)
NORTHWIND VENTURES INC
39 Woodland Dr (07462-3510)
PHONE.....................917 509-1964
William Duffy, *President*
EMP: 4
SALES (est): 221.1K **Privately Held**
SIC: 7372 Prepackaged software

(G-11302)
TEO FABRICATIONS INC
95 Maple Grange Rd (07462-3206)
P.O. Box 232 (07462-0232)
PHONE..............................973 764-5500
Fax: 973 764-5510
Robert Hearn, *President*
Elizabeth Hearn, *Vice Pres*
EMP: 4
SQ FT: 2,400
SALES (est): 580.6K **Privately Held**
WEB: www.teopro.com
SIC: 3711 Automobile assembly, including specialty automobiles

---

Verona
Essex County

(G-11303)
ANNIN & CO
163 Bloomfield Ave (07044-2702)
PHONE..............................973 239-9000
Fax: 973 228-1633
Joe Vallone, *Manager*
EMP: 230
SALES (corp-wide): 165.1MM **Privately Held**
WEB: www.annin.com
SIC: 2399 Flags, fabric
PA: Annin & Co.
    105 Eisenhower Pkwy # 203
    Roseland NJ 07068
    973 228-9400

(G-11304)
CAMECO INC
100 Pine St (07044-1346)
P.O. Box 209 (07044-0209)
PHONE..............................973 239-2845
Fax: 973 239-5392
Jerome Perl, *CEO*
Richard Perl, *Corp Secy*
EMP: 70 EST: 1944
SQ FT: 25,000
SALES (est): 46MM **Privately Held**
SIC: 5147 5149 2011 2033 Meats, fresh; canned goods: fruit, vegetables, seafood, meats, etc.; meat packing plants; fruits & fruit products in cans, jars, etc.

(G-11305)
ELECTION GRAPHICS INC
15 Rockland Ter (07044-1607)
PHONE..............................201 758-9966
Fax: 201 758-9946
Adam Perna, *President*
Louis Gelormini, *Vice Pres*
John Hollop, *Vice Pres*
EMP: 16
SQ FT: 2,700
SALES (est): 1.4MM **Privately Held**
SIC: 2752 Commercial printing, offset

(G-11306)
FERRANTE PRESS INC
Also Called: NJ Memorial Art
516 Bloomfield Ave (07044-2001)
PHONE..............................609 239-4257
Fax: 973 239-4806
Vincent J Ferrante, *President*
Vincent Ferrante, *Manager*
EMP: 4
SQ FT: 2,600
SALES: 280K **Privately Held**
SIC: 2759 Letterpress printing

(G-11307)
M + P INTERNATIONAL INC
271 Grove Ave Ste G (07044-1729)
PHONE..............................973 239-3005
Fax: 973 239-2858
Jim Churchill, *Area Mgr*
Guido Bossaert, *Vice Pres*
Dale Schick, *Opers Mgr*
Chris Wilcox, *Manager*
Irene Kennedy, *Officer*
EMP: 35
SALES (est): 5.3MM **Privately Held**
WEB: www.mpihome.com
SIC: 7373 7372 Computer integrated systems design; prepackaged software

(G-11308)
OZONE CONFECTIONERS BAKERS SUP
27 W Lincoln St (07044-1511)
PHONE..............................201 791-4444
Patrick Lapone, *President*
Salvatore Lapone, *Corp Secy*
Louis Lapone, *Vice Pres*
EMP: 13 EST: 1947
SQ FT: 4,200
SALES (est): 1.5MM **Privately Held**
SIC: 2064 Candy & other confectionery products

(G-11309)
PROCLEAN SERVICES INC
Also Called: New Jersey Drapery Service
150 Linden Ave (07044-2204)
PHONE..............................973 857-5408
Robert Saeed, *President*
Patricia Bailey, *Vice Pres*
EMP: 11
SQ FT: 2,200
SALES: 900K **Privately Held**
SIC: 7216 2211 5719 1799 Drycleaning plants, except rugs; curtain cleaning & repair; draperies & drapery fabrics, cotton; window furnishings; window treatment installation

(G-11310)
RELIANCE GRAPHICS INC (PA)
80 Pompton Ave Ste 1 (07044-2913)
PHONE..............................973 239-5411
Robert Fetterly, *President*
EMP: 4
SQ FT: 1,000
SALES (est): 543.6K **Privately Held**
WEB: www.relianceballots.com
SIC: 2752 Commercial printing, offset

(G-11311)
SUBITO MUSIC SERVICE INC
60 Depot St (07044-1338)
PHONE..............................973 857-3440
Stephen Culbertson, *President*
Christopher Haught, *Marketing Staff*
Brian Vandenberge, *Manager*
▲ EMP: 7
SQ FT: 3,000
SALES: 450K **Privately Held**
WEB: www.subitomusic.com
SIC: 2741 Music book & sheet music publishing; music books: publishing only, not printed on site; music, sheet: publishing only, not printed on site

(G-11312)
VERONA ALUMINUM PRODUCTS INC
320 Bloomfield Ave (07044-2497)
PHONE..............................973 857-4809
Fax: 973 857-7530
Christopher Cetruller, *President*
Joseph Cetruller, *Treasurer*
EMP: 6
SALES (est): 592.2K **Privately Held**
SIC: 1751 1796 3442 Window & door (prefabricated) installation; installing building equipment; screens, window, metal; sash, door or window: metal

---

Villas
Cape May County

(G-11313)
BEACH NUTTS MEDIA INC
Also Called: Shoppe
2503 Bayshore Rd (08251-1412)
PHONE..............................609 886-4113
Otto Jensch, *President*
Gene Nachel, *Manager*
EMP: 9
SALES (est): 660K **Privately Held**
SIC: 2621 Newsprint paper

(G-11314)
MAJEWSKI PLUMBING & HTG LLC
14 E Miami Ave (08251-3115)
PHONE..............................609 374-6001
Michelle Cooper,
EMP: 5
SALES (est): 600K **Privately Held**
SIC: 3432 Plastic plumbing fixture fittings, assembly

(G-11315)
RYDER TECHNOLOGY
Also Called: Ryder Global
36 E Drumbed Rd (08251-1907)
PHONE..............................215 817-7868
Ernest Ryder, *Owner*
▼ EMP: 5
SALES: 200K **Privately Held**
WEB: www.rydertechnology.com
SIC: 3585 Refrigeration & heating equipment

(G-11316)
SHOPPE CMC SHOPPERS GUIDE (PA)
2503 Bayshore Rd (08251-1412)
PHONE..............................609 886-4112
Fax: 609 889-1756
Gerry Jensch, *President*
Otto Jensch, *Publisher*
EMP: 6
SALES (est): 874.8K **Privately Held**
SIC: 7319 2741 Shopping news, advertising & distributing service; miscellaneous publishing

---

Vincentown
Burlington County

(G-11317)
JAMES D MORRISSEY INC
Also Called: Ward Sand & Material
223 Sooy Place Rd (08088-6901)
PHONE..............................609 859-2860
Fax: 609 859-4294
Al Synder, *Office Mgr*
EMP: 12
SALES (corp-wide): 46.5MM **Privately Held**
WEB: www.jdm-inc.com
SIC: 1446 Silica mining
PA: James D. Morrissey Inc.
    9119 Frankford Ave
    Philadelphia PA 19114
    215 708-8420

Vineland
Cumberland County

(G-11318)
A M K GLASS INC
2880 Industrial Way (08360-1514)
PHONE..............................856 692-1488
Fax: 856 691-5084
Michael Kousmine, *President*
Kristine Kousmine, *President*
Marc Kousmine, *Vice Pres*
Mike Kousmine, *Vice Pres*
EMP: 8
SQ FT: 10,000
SALES (est): 1MM **Privately Held**
WEB: www.amkglass.com
SIC: 3231 8734 Medical & laboratory glassware: made from purchased glass; testing laboratories

(G-11319)
ACE GLASS INCORPORATED (HQ)
Also Called: A C E
1430 N West Blvd (08360-2299)
P.O. Box 688 (08362-0688)
PHONE..............................856 692-3333
Fax: 856 692-8919
Richard Kramme, *President*
Kristi Donoflio, *General Mgr*
Darryl Hill, *Plant Mgr*
Suzette Rodriguez, *Export Mgr*
Mimi Suprun, *Purch Mgr*
EMP: 95 EST: 1936
SALES: 13.3MM
SALES (corp-wide): 19.4MM **Privately Held**
WEB: www.aceglass.com
SIC: 3231 Laboratory glassware

PA: Kramme Consolidated Inc
    Main St
    Monroeville NJ 08343
    856 358-8151

(G-11320)
AGC ACQUISITION LLC
Also Called: Andrews Glass Company
3740 N West Blvd (08360-1653)
PHONE..............................856 692-4435
Paul Dejuliis, *CEO*
Wayne Downs, *Vice Pres*
Jay Wilson, *Materials Mgr*
Peggy Scarpa, *CFO*
Peggy McMahon, *Controller*
EMP: 38
SQ FT: 32,000
SALES: 4.6MM **Privately Held**
WEB: www.andrews-glass.com
SIC: 3229 Scientific glassware

(G-11321)
ALLIED SPECIALTY FOODS INC
Also Called: Allied Steaks
1585 W Forest Grove Rd (08360-1570)
PHONE..............................856 507-1100
Fax: 856 507-0540
Paul Litten, *President*
EMP: 85
SQ FT: 20,000
SALES (est): 22.5MM
SALES (corp-wide): 38.2B **Publicly Held**
WEB: www.alliedsteaks.com
SIC: 2013 Sausages & other prepared meats
HQ: Advancepierre Foods, Inc.
    9987 Carver Rd Ste 500
    Blue Ash OH 45242
    513 874-8741

(G-11322)
ALUSEAL LLC
1649 Castpa Pl (08360-3411)
PHONE..............................856 692-3355
Donald Bayer, *Owner*
▲ EMP: 4
SQ FT: 38,000
SALES (est): 572.1K **Privately Held**
SIC: 3354 Bars, extruded, aluminum

(G-11323)
ASSEM - PAK INC
1649 Castpa Pl (08360-3411)
PHONE..............................856 692-3355
Don Bayer Jr, *President*
Roseann Bayer, *Vice Pres*
▲ EMP: 140 EST: 2000
SQ FT: 40,000
SALES (est): 19.2MM **Privately Held**
SIC: 3221 2891 7389 Bottles for packing, bottling & canning: glass; sealing compounds, synthetic rubber or plastic; packaging & labeling services

(G-11324)
ATCO RUBBER PRODUCTS INC
1480 N West Blvd (08360-2202)
PHONE..............................856 794-3393
Fax: 856 794-3397
Ray Savingel, *Manager*
EMP: 50
SALES (corp-wide): 2.2B **Publicly Held**
SIC: 3444 Metal ventilating equipment
HQ: Atco Rubber Products, Inc.
    7101 Atco Dr
    Fort Worth TX 76118
    817 595-2894

(G-11325)
AUNT KITTYS FOODS INC
270 N Mill Rd (08360-3437)
P.O. Box 334, Hanover PA (17331-0334)
PHONE..............................856 691-2100
Gary Knisely, *Vice Pres*
Peitro Giraffa, *Vice Pres*
Pete Giraffa, *Vice Pres*
Steve Robertson, *Treasurer*
▲ EMP: 100
SQ FT: 100,000
SALES (est): 17.1MM
SALES (corp-wide): 686.6MM **Publicly Held**
WEB: www.auntkittys.com
SIC: 2032 Soups & broths: canned, jarred, etc.

▲ = Import ▼=Export
◆ =Import/Export

PA: Hanover Foods Corporation
1486 York St
Hanover PA 17331
717 632-6000

(G-11326)
BABBITT MFG CO INC
719 E Park Ave (08360-3290)
PHONE.............................856 692-3245
Fax: 856 692-4404
Lois Gavigan, *President*
Steven Gavigan, *Vice Pres*
Brian G Gavigan, *Treasurer*
Mary Gavigan, *Office Admin*
Ronald Gavigan, *Admin Sec*
EMP: 15
SQ FT: 19,400
SALES (est): 3.1MM **Privately Held**
SIC: 3444 5039 5031 5033 Sheet metal-work; awnings; doors & windows; siding, except wood; roofing, siding & sheet metal work

(G-11327)
BARUFFI BROS INC (PA)
907 N Main Rd Bldg D (08360-8200)
PHONE.............................856 692-6400
Leonard Gagliarti Jr, *Ch of Bd*
Dominick Baruffi II, *President*
Michael J Jelinek, *General Mgr*
Micheal Jelinek, *General Mgr*
Art Baruffi, *Vice Pres*
EMP: 18
SALES: 984.8K **Privately Held**
SIC: 3275 Wallboard, gypsum

(G-11328)
BELLCO GLASS INC
340 Edrudo Rd (08360-3416)
P.O. Box 869 (08362-0869)
PHONE.............................800 257-7043
Fax: 856 691-3247
Steven Harker, *CEO*
Penny Taylor, *Sales Staff*
EMP: 85 **EST:** 1940
SQ FT: 55,000
SALES (est): 21.7MM **Privately Held**
SIC: 3821 3231 5047 Laboratory equipment: fume hoods, distillation racks, etc.; medical & laboratory glassware: made from purchased glass; medical equipment & supplies

(G-11329)
BEREZIN NILOLAI
402 E Wheat Rd (08360-2183)
PHONE.............................856 692-6191
Nilolai Berezin, *Owner*
EMP: 6
SALES (est): 250K **Privately Held**
SIC: 3599 Machine shop, jobbing & repair

(G-11330)
BERRY BLAST SMOOTHIES LLC
1194 Sharp Rd (08360-2460)
PHONE.............................856 692-6174
Brian M Buglio, *Principal*
EMP: 4
SALES (est): 191.1K **Privately Held**
SIC: 2037 Frozen fruits & vegetables

(G-11331)
BIE REAL ESTATE HOLDINGS LLC
3539 Reilly Ct (08360-1500)
PHONE.............................856 691-9765
Alan Bierig, *Mng Member*
Daniel Bierig,
David Bierig,
Jacob Bierig,
EMP: 7
SQ FT: 100,000
SALES (est): 309.9K **Privately Held**
SIC: 2011 Meat packing plants

(G-11332)
BK MACHINE SHOP
586 N West Blvd (08360-2742)
PHONE.............................856 457-7150
EMP: 4
SALES (est): 208.2K **Privately Held**
SIC: 3599 Machine shop, jobbing & repair

(G-11333)
BRIDOR USA INC
2260 Industrial Way (08360-1517)
PHONE.............................856 691-8000
Jean-Franois Duquesne, *CEO*
Jean-Pierre Hyacinthe, *VP Opers*
Anthony Lefevre, *Plant Mgr*
Robert Duba, *Research*
Karolyn Ager, *CFO*
◆ **EMP:** 59
SALES (est): 18.3MM
SALES (corp-wide): 67.8K **Privately Held**
SIC: 2051 Bakery: wholesale or wholesale/retail combined
HQ: Bridor Inc
1370 Rue Graham-Bell
Boucherville QC J4B 6
450 641-1265

(G-11334)
CASA DI BERTACCHI CORPORATION
1910 Gallagher Dr (08360-1545)
P.O. Box 245, Buffalo NY (14240-0245)
PHONE.............................856 696-5600
Fax: 856 696-3341
Robert E Rich Jr, *President*
Basilio Gomez, *Production*
John Dougherty, *Treasurer*
EMP: 209
SQ FT: 100,000
SALES (est): 27.5MM
SALES (corp-wide): 4.1B **Privately Held**
WEB: www.casadibertacchi.com
SIC: 2013 2098 Sausages from purchased meat; macaroni & spaghetti
PA: Rich Products Corporation
1 Robert Rich Way
Buffalo NY 14213
716 878-8000

(G-11335)
CERVINIS INC
Also Called: Cervini's Auto Design
3656 N Mill Rd (08360-1528)
PHONE.............................856 691-1744
Fax: 856 691-5331
Danny Cervini, *President*
Lou Fava, *Mfg Staff*
Judy Coulter, *Human Res Dir*
John Landicini, *Supervisor*
▲ **EMP:** 10
SQ FT: 15,000
SALES (est): 1.9MM **Privately Held**
WEB: www.cervinis.com
SIC: 3714 5531 Motor vehicle body components & frame; automotive & home supply stores

(G-11336)
CHEMGLASS INC
3800 N Mill Rd (08360-1528)
PHONE.............................856 696-0014
Fax: 856 696-9102
Walter E Surdam, *CEO*
Steve Ware, *President*
David Surdam, *Vice Pres*
Philip Surdam, *Vice Pres*
Nancy Dillahey, *Purch Agent*
▲ **EMP:** 225
SQ FT: 30,000
SALES (est): 22.9MM **Privately Held**
WEB: www.chemglass.com
SIC: 3231 Products of purchased glass; laboratory glassware; scientific & technical glassware: from purchased glass

(G-11337)
COMAR LLC
3100 N Mill Rd (08360-1524)
PHONE.............................856 507-5483
Fax: 856 794-2162
Don Hutchinson, *Branch Mgr*
EMP: 200
SALES (corp-wide): 12.9MM **Privately Held**
SIC: 3231 Products of purchased glass
HQ: Comar, Llc
220 Laurel Rd Fl 2
Voorhees NJ 08043
856 692-6100

(G-11338)
COMFORTAIRE LTD LIABILITY CO
Also Called: Comfortaire Htg & A Conditio
1435 E Sherman Ave (08361-7161)
P.O. Box 180 (08362-0180)
PHONE.............................856 692-5000
Robert Pizzo,
EMP: 4
SALES: 300K **Privately Held**
SIC: 3585 Refrigeration & heating equipment

(G-11339)
COMPASS WIRE CLOTH &
1942 N Mill Rd (08360-2030)
PHONE.............................856 853-7616
Mike McGrath Sr, *President*
Michael McGrath, *Vice Pres*
Chris Toppi, *Vice Pres*
Steve Elliott, *Finance*
EMP: 40
SQ FT: 65,000
SALES (est): 6.4MM **Privately Held**
SIC: 3496 Miscellaneous fabricated wire products

(G-11340)
COMPASS WIRE CLOTH CORP
1942 N Mill Rd (08360-2030)
PHONE.............................856 853-7616
Fax: 856 853-1387
Michael Mc Grath, *President*
Bob Abate, *Vice Pres*
Robert Abate, *Vice Pres*
Chris Toppi, *Vice Pres*
Christopher Toppi, *Vice Pres*
▲ **EMP:** 32
SQ FT: 30,000
SALES (est): 8.5MM **Privately Held**
WEB: www.compasswire.com
SIC: 3496 Miscellaneous fabricated wire products; screening, woven wire: made from purchased wire

(G-11341)
CONTES PASTA COMPANY INC
310 Wheat Rd (08360-9627)
PHONE.............................856 697-3400
Michael Conte, *President*
Judy Sabella, *Vice Pres*
Tony Napoleon, *Research*
▲ **EMP:** 35
SQ FT: 28,000
SALES (est): 7MM **Privately Held**
WEB: www.contespasta.com
SIC: 2099 Pasta, uncooked: packaged with other ingredients

(G-11342)
CORNING PHARMACEUTICAL GL LLC
563 Crystal Ave (08360-3238)
PHONE.............................856 794-7100
Wendell P Weeks, *Mng Member*
EMP: 5 **EST:** 2015
SALES (est): 83.3K
SALES (corp-wide): 10.1B **Publicly Held**
SIC: 3229 Tubing, glass
PA: Corning Incorporated
1 Riverfront Plz
Corning NY 14831
607 974-9000

(G-11343)
CROWN CLOTHING CO
609 Paul St (08360-5699)
PHONE.............................856 691-0343
Fax: 856 691-1771
Howard Levin, *President*
Marsha Levin, *Corp Secy*
EMP: 152
SQ FT: 30,000
SALES (est): 13.6MM **Privately Held**
WEB: www.crownclothing.com
SIC: 2311 Military uniforms, men's & youths': purchased materials

(G-11344)
CUMBERLAND MARBLE & MONUMENT
Also Called: C M M Rentals
2858 S West Blvd (08360-7022)
PHONE.............................856 691-3334
Fax: 856 691-5997

Paul Presgrave III, *President*
Kim Presgraves, *Partner*
EMP: 4
SQ FT: 2,400
SALES (est): 511.2K **Privately Held**
WEB: www.indiadairy.com
SIC: 3272 7336 Art marble, concrete; silk screen design

(G-11345)
CUMBERLAND NEWS INC
603 E Landis Ave (08360-8004)
PHONE.............................856 691-2244
Paul DOE, *President*
Peter DOE, *Vice Pres*
Maribel Echevarria, *Officer*
EMP: 4
SALES (est): 350K **Privately Held**
SIC: 2711 Newspapers: publishing only, not printed on site

(G-11346)
CUMBERLAND VACUUM PRODUCTS INC
Also Called: C V P
720 S West Blvd (08360-5510)
PHONE.............................856 691-9155
Fax: 856 692-8114
Lloyd Ronchetti, *President*
▼ **EMP:** 5
SQ FT: 5,000
SALES (est): 800.1K **Privately Held**
WEB: www.cumberlandvacuum.com
SIC: 2992 Oils & greases, blending & compounding

(G-11347)
CUSTOM GRAPHICS OF VINELAND
71 W Landis Ave (08360-8122)
PHONE.............................856 691-7858
Fax: 856 691-0190
James Mc Mahon, *President*
Russell Hull, *Corp Secy*
EMP: 27
SQ FT: 17,000
SALES (est): 3.1MM **Privately Held**
SIC: 2759 3993 2396 Screen printing; signs & advertising specialties; automotive & apparel trimmings

(G-11348)
D ELECTRIC MOTORS INC
94 W Sherman Ave (08360-7011)
P.O. Box 2367 (08362-2367)
PHONE.............................856 696-5959
Fax: 856 692-2505
Anthony L Desiere, *President*
Devin K Desiere, *Treasurer*
EMP: 9
SQ FT: 10,000
SALES (est): 2.3MM **Privately Held**
SIC: 7694 5063 Electric motor repair; electrical apparatus & equipment

(G-11349)
DDM STEEL CNSTR LTD LBLTY CO
3659 N Delsea Dr (08360-1664)
PHONE.............................856 794-9400
Rich Muckenfuss, *Mng Member*
EMP: 10
SALES (est): 2.1MM **Privately Held**
SIC: 3441 Building components, structural steel

(G-11350)
DDM STEEL SERVICES INC
3659 N Delsea Dr (08360-1664)
PHONE.............................856 794-1931
Rich Muckenfuss, *President*
EMP: 12
SQ FT: 2,500
SALES (est): 1.1MM **Privately Held**
SIC: 3441 Building components, structural steel

(G-11351)
DE ROSSI & SON CO INC
411 S 6th St (08360-4628)
PHONE.............................856 691-0061
Fax: 856 691-5342
Donald De Rossi, *President*
EMP: 170 **EST:** 1925
SQ FT: 50,000

SALES (est): 16.4MM **Privately Held**
SIC: 2311 Military uniforms, men's & youths': purchased materials

(G-11352)
DESIGNS BY JAMES
892 N Delsea Dr (08360-2744)
PHONE..............................856 692-1316
Fax: 856 692-7194
James J Crescenzeo, *Owner*
EMP: 4
SALES (est): 242K **Privately Held**
WEB: www.designsbyjames.com
SIC: 2396 2211 3993 Screen printing on fabric articles; print cloths, cotton; signs & advertising specialties

(G-11353)
DUN-RITE SAND & GRAVEL CO (PA)
573 E Grant Ave (08360-7109)
PHONE..............................856 692-2520
Fax: 856 692-1105
Peter Galetto, *President*
EMP: 32
SQ FT: 1,500
SALES: 10.2MM **Privately Held**
SIC: 1442 1411 Sand mining; gravel mining; dimension stone

(G-11354)
DUTRA SHEET METAL CO
1940 S West Blvd Ste E (08360-7088)
P.O. Box 2265 (08362-2265)
PHONE..............................856 692-8058
Fax: 856 692-4472
D'Lee Dutra, *President*
EMP: 9
SQ FT: 6,600
SALES: 1.5MM **Privately Held**
WEB: www.dutrasheetmetal.com
SIC: 3444 Sheet metalwork

(G-11355)
EATEM CORPORATION
Also Called: Eatem Foods
1829 Gallagher Dr (08360-1548)
PHONE..............................856 692-1663
Fax: 856 692-0847
Ron Savelli, *President*
Jerry Santos, *Plant Mgr*
Jimmy Cruz, *Warehouse Mgr*
Carlos Rosa, *Production*
Amy Rivera, *Purchasing*
◆ **EMP:** 80
SQ FT: 55,600
SALES (est): 25.3MM
SALES (corp-wide): 60.8B **Publicly Held**
WEB: www.eatemfoods.com
SIC: 2099 Food preparations
PA: Archer-Daniels-Midland Company
77 W Wacker Dr Ste 4600
Chicago IL 60601
312 634-8100

(G-11356)
FRANK E GANTER INC
Also Called: R-Way Tooling Co
224 S Lincoln Ave (08361-7803)
P.O. Box 236 (08362-0236)
PHONE..............................856 692-2218
Fax: 856 692-5952
Frank E Ganter, *President*
Irene Ganter, *Vice Pres*
EMP: 8 EST: 1960
SQ FT: 6,500
SALES (est): 1.2MM **Privately Held**
SIC: 3599 5169 5084 7692 Machine shop, jobbing & repair; industrial gases; welding machinery & equipment; welding repair

(G-11357)
GANNETT STLLITE INFO NTWRK INC
Daily Journal, The
891 E Oak Rd (08360-2311)
PHONE..............................856 691-5000
Fax: 856 691-6535
Nancy Monaghan, *President*
EMP: 175
SALES (corp-wide): 3.1B **Publicly Held**
WEB: www.usatoday.com
SIC: 2711 2752 8741 Newspapers; commercial printing, offset; management services

HQ: Gannett Satellite Information Network, Llc
7950 Jones Branch Dr
Mc Lean VA 22102
703 854-6000

(G-11358)
GANNETT STLLITE INFO NTWRK LLC
Also Called: Hammonton News, The
891 E Oak Rd Unit A (08360-2311)
PHONE..............................609 561-2300
Hushan Leiser, *Sales/Mktg Mgr*
EMP: 13
SALES (corp-wide): 3.1B **Publicly Held**
WEB: www.usatoday.com
SIC: 2711 Newspapers: publishing only, not printed on site
HQ: Gannett Satellite Information Network, Llc
7950 Jones Branch Dr
Mc Lean VA 22102
703 854-6000

(G-11359)
GARDELLAS RVIOLI ITLN DELI LLC
527 S Brewster Rd (08360-9621)
PHONE..............................856 697-3509
Diane Martine, *Mng Member*
EMP: 10 EST: 2005
SQ FT: 1,800
SALES (est): 954.8K **Privately Held**
SIC: 2098 Macaroni & spaghetti

(G-11360)
GERRESHEIMER GLASS INC (DH)
537 Crystal Ave (08360-3238)
PHONE..............................856 692-3600
Uwe Rohrhoff, *CEO*
Axel Herberg, *Chairman*
Franck Langet, *Business Mgr*
Erica Solin, *Production*
Charlie Rogers, *Purchasing*
▲ **EMP:** 350
SQ FT: 200,000
SALES: 500MM
SALES (corp-wide): 1.5B **Privately Held**
WEB: www.kimblescience.com
SIC: 3221 Medicine bottles, glass
HQ: Gerresheimer Glas Gmbh
Klaus-Bungert-Str. 4
Dusseldorf 40468
211 618-100

(G-11361)
GERRESHEIMER GLASS INC
91 W Forest Grove Rd (08360-2016)
PHONE..............................856 507-5852
Axel Herberg, *Chairman*
EMP: 350
SALES (corp-wide): 1.5B **Privately Held**
SIC: 3231 Products of purchased glass
HQ: Gerresheimer Glass Inc.
537 Crystal Ave
Vineland NJ 08360
856 692-3600

(G-11362)
GLASS DYNAMICS LLC
2662 Hance Bridge Rd (08361-7560)
PHONE..............................856 205-1503
Sharon Scudstill,
Kimberly Lawson,
▲ **EMP:** 6
SALES (est): 292.8K **Privately Held**
WEB: www.marketingtipsinprint.com
SIC: 3231 Stained glass: made from purchased glass

(G-11363)
GLASTRON INC
510 N West Blvd (08360-2896)
P.O. Box 687 (08362-0687)
PHONE..............................856 692-0500
Fax: 856 692-0340
Rex Gary, *Ch of Bd*
Bryan Wolcott, *President*
Alden Kille, *Corp Secy*
Ed Rohland, *Vice Pres*
Lynn Weiner, *Vice Pres*
EMP: 40
SQ FT: 12,000

SALES (est): 5.2MM **Privately Held**
WEB: www.glastroninc.com
SIC: 3231 3841 Products of purchased glass; surgical & medical instruments

(G-11364)
GRAPHICOLOR CORPORATION
1370 S Main Rd (08360-6501)
PHONE..............................856 691-2507
Fax: 856 696-3229
Robert W Stenger Jr, *President*
Hollie Biggs, *Admin Sec*
EMP: 22 EST: 1919
SQ FT: 10,000
SALES: 4.3MM **Privately Held**
WEB: www.graphicolorcorp.com
SIC: 2752 7336 Commercial printing, offset; chart & graph design

(G-11365)
GROVE SUPPLY INC
144 W Forest Grove Rd (08360-2017)
PHONE..............................856 205-0687
Fax: 856 205-1033
Matthew Grodsky, *Director*
EMP: 22
SALES (corp-wide): 71.2MM **Privately Held**
SIC: 3432 5074 Plumbing fixture fittings & trim; plumbing fittings & supplies
PA: Grove Supply, Inc.
106 Steamboat Dr
Warminster PA 18974
215 672-8666

(G-11366)
GS FRESH BEETS INCORPORATED
Also Called: Love Beets
2321 Industrial Way (08360-1551)
PHONE..............................856 692-1740
George Shropshire, *President*
Huw Griffith, *Vice Pres*
▲ **EMP:** 10
SALES (est): 725.8K
SALES (corp-wide): 620.7MM **Privately Held**
SIC: 2099 Food preparations
HQ: G's Fresh Limited
Hainey Farm
Ely CAMBS CB7 5
135 372-7200

(G-11367)
H P MACHINE SHOP INC
415 Oxford St (08360-2794)
PHONE..............................856 692-1192
John Petyan, *President*
Shirley Horvath, *Manager*
EMP: 9 EST: 1964
SQ FT: 7,000
SALES (est): 525K **Privately Held**
WEB: www.hp-machine.com
SIC: 3599 Machine shop, jobbing & repair

(G-11368)
H S MARTIN COMPANY INC
1149 S East Blvd (08360-6493)
P.O. Box 661 (08362-0661)
PHONE..............................856 692-8700
Fax: 856 692-3805
Nontas Kontes, *President*
John Trieres, *Vice Pres*
James E Kontes, *Treasurer*
Robert Ciesla, *Controller*
EMP: 15
SQ FT: 15,000
SALES (est): 2.4MM **Privately Held**
WEB: www.hsmartin.com
SIC: 3231 3829 Scientific & technical glassware: from purchased glass; medical & laboratory glassware: made from purchased glass; measuring & controlling devices

(G-11369)
HARRY J LAWALL & SON INC
3071 E Chestnut Ave C9 (08361-7847)
PHONE..............................856 691-7764
Harry Lawall, *Manager*
EMP: 7
SALES (corp-wide): 16.8MM **Privately Held**
SIC: 3842 5999 Limbs, artificial; artificial limbs

PA: Harry J. Lawall & Son, Inc.
8028 Frankford Ave
Philadelphia PA 19136
215 338-6611

(G-11370)
HONEYWELL INTERNATIONAL INC
2658 N West Blvd (08360-2057)
PHONE..............................856 691-5111
EMP: 673
SALES (corp-wide): 40.5B **Publicly Held**
SIC: 3724 Aircraft engines & engine parts
PA: Honeywell International Inc.
115 Tabor Rd
Morris Plains NJ 07950
973 455-2000

(G-11371)
HOWES STANDARD PUBLISHING CO
1980 S West Blvd (08360-7018)
PHONE..............................856 691-2000
Fax: 856 692-4399
Barry Opromollo, *President*
EMP: 35 EST: 1892
SQ FT: 12,500
SALES (est): 5MM **Privately Held**
WEB: www.standard-publishing.com
SIC: 2752 2759 Commercial printing, offset; letterpress printing

(G-11372)
I S PARTS INTERNATIONAL INC
Also Called: Lattimer
3603 N Mill Rd (08360-1595)
PHONE..............................856 691-2203
Fax: 856 691-5509
Stephen Abernathy, *President*
Walter Martin, *CFO*
▼ **EMP:** 36
SQ FT: 24,374
SALES (est): 7.6MM
SALES (corp-wide): 13.8MM **Privately Held**
WEB: www.lattimer.com
SIC: 3443 3565 Metal parts; packaging machinery
HQ: Lattimer Holdings Limited
79-83 Shakespeare Street
Southport PR8 5
170 453-5040

(G-11373)
INNOVA GROUP INC
327 Tuckahoe Rd (08360-9243)
PHONE..............................856 696-1053
John Tombleson, *President*
EMP: 4
SQ FT: 2,000
SALES (est): 460K **Privately Held**
SIC: 3089 Doors, folding: plastic or plastic coated fabric

(G-11374)
J D MACHINE PARTS INC
158 W Weymouth Rd (08360-1630)
PHONE..............................856 691-8430
Fax: 856 692-9444
Joseph D Mento, *President*
EMP: 11
SQ FT: 25,000
SALES (est): 600K **Privately Held**
WEB: www.jdmachineparts.com
SIC: 3599 7692 Machine shop, jobbing & repair; welding repair

(G-11375)
J F GILLESPIE INC
2547 Brunetta Dr (08360-7028)
PHONE..............................856 692-2233
Fax: 856 692-5457
Jerome F Gillespie, *President*
Dolores Gillespie, *Admin Sec*
EMP: 40 EST: 1949
SQ FT: 10,000
SALES (est): 4.9MM **Privately Held**
WEB: www.jfgillespieinc.com
SIC: 3272 Concrete products

▲ = Import ▼=Export
◆ =Import/Export

(G-11376)
JOFFE LUMBER & SUPPLY CO INC
Also Called: Joffe Millwork & Supply
18 Burns Ave (08360-7799)
P.O. Box 2309 (08362-2309)
PHONE..................................856 825-9550
Fax: 856 327-0798
Michael Bergen, *President*
EMP: 75 **EST:** 1933
SQ FT: 133,000
SALES (est): 34.1MM **Privately Held**
WEB: www.joffemillwork.com
SIC: 5031 2431 Lumber, plywood & millwork; doors & door parts & trim, wood

(G-11377)
KASHMIR
3926 N Delsea Dr (08360-1686)
PHONE..................................856 691-8969
Michael Radie, *Principal*
EMP: 4
SALES (est): 261.7K **Privately Held**
SIC: 2599 Bar, restaurant & cafeteria furniture

(G-11378)
KENNEDY CONCRETE INC
1969 S East Ave (08360-7141)
PHONE..................................856 692-8650
Fax: 856 692-6677
Thomas Towers, *President*
Tom Tower, *Vice Pres*
EMP: 50
SQ FT: 1,000
SALES (est): 8MM **Privately Held**
WEB: www.kennedyconcrete.com
SIC: 3273 Ready-mixed concrete

(G-11379)
LEAK DETECTION ASSOCIATES
3003 N Mill Rd 1a (08360-1523)
PHONE..................................856 401-7718
Fax: 856 401-7720
Darrell R Morrow, *Ch of Bd*
Jeffrey Lucas, *President*
Leslie D Morrow, *Vice Pres*
Jeffrey Morrow-Lucas, *Vice Pres*
EMP: 9
SQ FT: 16,000
SALES (est): 1.2MM **Privately Held**
SIC: 3829 Measuring & controlling devices

(G-11380)
LIMPERT BROTHERS INC
200 N West Blvd (08360-3794)
P.O. Box 1480 (08362-1480)
PHONE..................................856 691-1353
Fax: 856 794-8968
Pearl Giordano, *President*
Ruth Dawson, *General Mgr*
Jeanna Whittick, *Purch Mgr*
Ruth Keller, *Manager*
EMP: 24 **EST:** 1902
SQ FT: 70,000
SALES (est): 1.2MM **Privately Held**
WEB: www.limpertbrothers.com
SIC: 5812 2087 Eating places; fruits, crushed: for fountain use

(G-11381)
LT CHINI INC
Also Called: Gorgo Pallet Company
646 S Delsea Dr (08360-4459)
PHONE..................................856 692-0303
Fax: 856 692-2499
Louis Chini, *President*
Nick Biagi, *Vice Pres*
EMP: 9
SQ FT: 5,000
SALES (est): 1.8MM **Privately Held**
SIC: 2448 7699 Pallets, wood; pallet repair

(G-11382)
N B & SONS LLC
402 E Wheat Rd (08360-2183)
PHONE..................................856 692-6191
Fax: 856 692-0299
Maria Berezin, *Partner*
Nikolai Berezin Mg Mem, *Principal*
Annette Berezin,
EMP: 6
SQ FT: 2,500

SALES (est): 430K **Privately Held**
WEB: www.nbsons.com
SIC: 3599 Machine shop, jobbing & repair

(G-11383)
NARDELLI BROS INC
1145 N Main Rd (08360-2538)
PHONE..................................856 692-0723
Richard Simpson, *Manager*
EMP: 6
SALES (corp-wide): 14.7MM **Privately Held**
SIC: 3537 Loading docks: portable, adjustable & hydraulic
PA: Nardelli Bros. Inc.
54 Main St
Cedarville NJ 08311
856 447-4000

(G-11384)
NATURE LABS LLC
46 N West Ave Ste B (08360-3611)
PHONE..................................856 839-0400
Louis Rivers, *CEO*
EMP: 7
SALES (est): 489.8K **Privately Held**
SIC: 2844 Toilet preparations

(G-11385)
NDS TECHNOLOGIES INC
891 E Oak Rd Unit B (08360-2311)
PHONE..................................856 691-0330
Fax: 856 696-3533
Norman Neill, *President*
Helene Miller, *Project Mgr*
Margaret Mays, *Production*
Keith Cooney, *Engineer*
Robert Degrazia, *Treasurer*
EMP: 35
SQ FT: 6,000
SALES (est): 6.1MM **Privately Held**
WEB: www.ndstechnologiesinc.com
SIC: 3229 Scientific glassware

(G-11386)
OMNI BAKING COMPANY LLC
2621 Freddy Ln Bldg 7 (08360-1559)
PHONE..................................856 205-1485
Fax: 856 205-1735
Lenny Amorso Jr, *Partner*
Daniel Amoroso Jr, *Partner*
Lenny Amoroso Jr, *Partner*
John V Mulloy Sr, *Partner*
Daniel Mulloy, *CFO*
EMP: 500
SQ FT: 55,000
SALES (est): 139MM **Privately Held**
WEB: www.omnibaking.com
SIC: 2051 Bakery: wholesale or wholesale/retail combined

(G-11387)
P J GILLESPIE INC
Also Called: Gillespie Industries
2565 Brunetta Dr (08360-7028)
PHONE..................................856 327-2993
Fax: 856 825-3894
Paul J Gillespie Sr, *President*
Brigita Gillespie, *Vice Pres*
Donna Ruberti, *Vice Pres*
EMP: 20
SQ FT: 750
SALES (est): 3.3MM **Privately Held**
SIC: 3272 Concrete products; septic tanks, concrete; manhole covers or frames, concrete

(G-11388)
PACKAGING CORPORATION AMERICA
Also Called: PCA/Supply Services 302a
46 N West Ave Ste A (08360-3611)
PHONE..................................856 696-0114
Ron Capriotti, *Manager*
EMP: 4
SALES (corp-wide): 6.4B **Publicly Held**
SIC: 2653 Corrugated & solid fiber boxes
PA: Packaging Corporation Of America
1955 W Field Ct
Lake Forest IL 60045
847 482-3000

(G-11389)
PARRISH SIGN CO INC
2242 S Delsea Dr (08360-7094)
PHONE..................................856 696-4040

Fax: 856 692-0606
Charles Parrish, *CEO*
Charles R Parrish Sr, *President*
Craig Parrish, *General Mgr*
Charles R Parrish Jr, *Vice Pres*
Craig S Parrish, *Treasurer*
EMP: 8
SQ FT: 10,000
SALES (est): 1.2MM
SALES (corp-wide): 1.6MM **Privately Held**
WEB: www.parrishsign.com
SIC: 3993 Signs, not made in custom sign painting shops
PA: Charles R Parrish Inc
2242 S Delsea Dr
Vineland NJ 08360
856 691-4080

(G-11390)
PHIL DESIERE ELECTRIC MTR SVC
Also Called: Desiere Electric Motor Service
1338 Almond Rd (08360-2682)
PHONE..................................856 692-8442
Fax: 856 692-0342
Eugene Boston, *President*
Lucinda Adams, *Corp Secy*
Paul Cascia, *Vice Pres*
EMP: 10
SQ FT: 11,000
SALES (est): 750K **Privately Held**
SIC: 7694 5063 Electric motor repair; motors, electric

(G-11391)
PHILCORR LLC
2317 Almond Rd (08360-3486)
PHONE..................................856 205-0557
Fax: 856 205-0539
Tom Fitzpatrick,
Peter Cadwallader,
Vernon Litzinger,
Mario Russo,
Ted Sidenburgh,
▲ **EMP:** 61
SALES (est): 14.6MM **Privately Held**
WEB: www.philcorr.com
SIC: 3089 Corrugated panels, plastic

(G-11392)
PHOENIX BUSINESS FORMS INC
2231 N East Blvd (08360-2174)
PHONE..................................856 691-2266
Fax: 856 691-1532
Joanne Buckalew, *President*
EMP: 5 **EST:** 1977
SQ FT: 5,500
SALES (est): 510K **Privately Held**
SIC: 2752 7389 Commercial printing, offset; advertising, promotional & trade show services

(G-11393)
PRECISION ELECTRONIC GLASS INC
Also Called: P E G
1013 Hendee Rd (08360-3295)
PHONE..................................856 691-2234
Fax: 856 691-3090
Phillip Rossi, *President*
Domenic Ciancarelli, *Vice Pres*
Max Kirsch, *Production*
▲ **EMP:** 75
SQ FT: 48,000
SALES (est): 12.6MM **Privately Held**
WEB: www.pegglass.com
SIC: 3231 Products of purchased glass

(G-11394)
R WAY TOOLING & MET WORKS LLC
Also Called: R-Way Machine and Fabrication
224 S Lincoln Ave (08361-7803)
PHONE..................................856 692-2218
James M Preziosi,
EMP: 14
SALES (est): 2MM **Privately Held**
SIC: 3599 3441 Machine shop, jobbing & repair; fabricated structural metal

(G-11395)
RENNOC CORPORATION
1450 E Chestnut Ave Ste B (08361-8467)
PHONE..................................856 327-5400

Michael Bruzzese, *President*
Richard W Conner, *Shareholder*
▲ **EMP:** 90 **EST:** 1954
SQ FT: 215,000
SALES (est): 7.9MM **Privately Held**
WEB: www.rennoc.com
SIC: 2329 Men's & boys' athletic uniforms

(G-11396)
RFC CONTAINER LLC (PA)
Also Called: RFC CONTAINER COMPANY
2066 S East Ave (08360-7129)
PHONE..................................856 692-0404
Mario Russo, *President*
Thomas Russo, *Vice Pres*
EMP: 74
SQ FT: 125,000
SALES (est): 18.4MM **Privately Held**
WEB: www.rfccontainer.com
SIC: 2653 Boxes, corrugated: made from purchased materials

(G-11397)
RHOADS OHARA ARCHITECTURAL
3690 N West Blvd (08360-1653)
P.O. Box 783, Newfield (08344-0783)
PHONE..................................856 692-4100
Fax: 856 692-4220
Lance Rhoads, *Mng Member*
Robert O'Hara,
EMP: 9
SQ FT: 10,000
SALES (est): 2MM **Privately Held**
SIC: 2435 Hardwood veneer & plywood; hardwood plywood, prefinished; panels, hardwood plywood; plywood, hardwood or hardwood faced

(G-11398)
RICH PRODUCTS CORPORATION
1910 Gallagher Dr (08360-1545)
PHONE..................................856 696-5600
Tony Nardello, *Maint Spvr*
Robert Ponist, *Human Resources*
Sandeep Raut, *Sales Executive*
Brad Bisbing, *Pub Rel Dir*
Sarah Burke, *Marketing Staff*
EMP: 5
SALES (corp-wide): 4.1B **Privately Held**
SIC: 2038 Frozen specialties
PA: Rich Products Corporation
1 Robert Rich Way
Buffalo NY 14213
716 878-8000

(G-11399)
RICHARD E PIERSON MTLS CORP
Also Called: R E Pierson Materials
184 W Sherman Ave (08360-7011)
PHONE..................................856 691-0083
Richard E Pierson, *President*
EMP: 6 **Privately Held**
SIC: 2951 1611 1771 Asphalt paving mixtures & blocks; highway & street construction; concrete work
PA: Richard E. Pierson Materials Corp.
426 Swedesboro Rd
Pilesgrove NJ 08098

(G-11400)
RUDCO PRODUCTS INC (PA)
114 E Oak Rd (08360-2991)
P.O. Box 705 (08362-0705)
PHONE..................................856 691-0800
Fax: 856 696-0084
Robert A Rudolph, *President*
Loretta Duus, *Purch Mgr*
Justin Johnson, *Parts Mgr*
Deborah M Rudolph, *CFO*
Matt Stien, *Manager*
EMP: 85 **EST:** 1964
SQ FT: 25,000
SALES (est): 22.8MM **Privately Held**
SIC: 3443 3536 Dumpsters, garbage; hoists

(G-11401)
S P INDUSTRIES INC
AB Glass
1172 N West Blvd (08360-2201)
PHONE..................................856 691-3200
Bill Downs, *CEO*

Cloud Volpe, *Branch Mgr*
EMP: 79
SALES (corp-wide): 1.4B **Privately Held**
WEB: www.virtis.com
SIC: 3231 Products of purchased glass
HQ: S P Industries, Inc.
　　935 Mearns Rd
　　Warminster PA 18974
　　215 672-7800

(G-11402)
SEREN INC
Also Called: Seren Industrial Power Systems
1670 Gallagher Dr (08360-1561)
PHONE..............................856 205-1131
Lawrence Hooper, *President*
EMP: 25
SQ FT: 10,000
SALES (est): 3.8MM **Privately Held**
SIC: 3825 Radio frequency measuring equipment

(G-11403)
SEREN INDUSTRIAL POWER SYSTEMS
1670 Gallagher Dr (08360-1561)
PHONE..............................856 205-1131
Larry Hooper, *President*
EMP: 13
SQ FT: 10,000
SALES: 3MM **Privately Held**
WEB: www.serenips.com
SIC: 3679 Electronic circuits

(G-11404)
SEREN IPS INC
1670 Gallagher Dr (08360-1561)
PHONE..............................856 205-1131
Fax: 856 205-1141
Lawrence Hooper, *President*
EMP: 55
SALES (est): 16.8MM **Privately Held**
SIC: 3699 Generators, ultrasonic

(G-11405)
SOUTH JERSEY PRECISION TL MOLD
4375 S Lincoln Ave (08361-7757)
PHONE..............................856 327-0500
Fax: 856 327-9442
Victor Rone, *President*
Robert G Rone, *Vice Pres*
Wyne Reeves, *Admin Sec*
EMP: 14
SQ FT: 9,000
SALES: 1.1MM **Privately Held**
WEB: www.southjerseyprecision.com
SIC: 3544 Special dies, tools, jigs & fixtures

(G-11406)
SOUTH JERSEY PUBLISHING CO
Also Called: Press of Atlantic City
22 W Landis Ave (08360-8134)
PHONE..............................856 692-0455
Fax: 856 794-5101
Gary Campbell, *Manager*
EMP: 15
SALES (corp-wide): 361.4MM **Privately Held**
WEB: www.pressofac.com
SIC: 2711 2741 Commercial printing & newspaper publishing combined; miscellaneous publishing
HQ: South Jersey Publishing Company
　　1000 W Washington Ave
　　Pleasantville NJ 08232
　　609 272-7000

(G-11407)
SOUTHERN NEW JERSEY STL CO INC (PA)
Also Called: Southern NJ Steel
2591 N East Blvd (08360-1771)
PHONE..............................856 696-1612
Hugh Mc Caffrey, *President*
Carlo Gentilitti Sr, *President*
John Mosley, *Prdtn Mgr*
Sue Dodds, *Admin Sec*
EMP: 50
SQ FT: 25,000
SALES (est): 10.3MM **Privately Held**
SIC: 3441 Fabricated structural metal

(G-11408)
TECTUBES USA INC
1299 W Forest Grove Rd (08360-1513)
PHONE..............................856 589-1250
Steven Wargo, *President*
▲ **EMP:** 35
SQ FT: 29,000
SALES (est): 4.1MM
SALES (corp-wide): 376.2MM **Privately Held**
WEB: www.norden.com
SIC: 2759 2752 Screen printing; commercial printing, lithographic
HQ: Emballator Tectubes Sweden Ab
　　Tubgatan 2
　　Hjo 544 5
　　503 326-00

(G-11409)
TJK MACHINE LLC
870 E Elmer Rd (08360-6466)
PHONE..............................856 691-7811
Fax: 856 691-7255
Nancy Parkin,
Jeffery Parkin,
EMP: 4
SALES: 300K **Privately Held**
SIC: 3599 Machine shop, jobbing & repair

(G-11410)
TUCKAHOE MANUFACTURING INC
327 Tuckahoe Rd (08360-9243)
PHONE..............................856 696-4100
John Tombleson, *President*
Robert Meighan, *Sales Mgr*
EMP: 6
SQ FT: 3,000
SALES (est): 700.1K **Privately Held**
SIC: 3442 Metal doors, sash & trim

(G-11411)
UGSI CHEMICAL FEED INC
Also Called: Ugsi Chemfeed, Inc.
1901 W Garden Rd (08360-1530)
PHONE..............................856 896-2160
Andrew Seidel, *President*
Joe Millen, *Chairman*
Rajesh Patel, *Vice Pres*
EMP: 40
SQ FT: 40,000
SALES (est): 9.6MM
SALES (corp-wide): 1.3B **Publicly Held**
SIC: 3589 Sewage & water treatment equipment
HQ: Underground Solutions, Inc.
　　13135 Danielson St # 201
　　Poway CA 92064

(G-11412)
UNIVERSAL MOLD & TOOL INC
1200 S West Blvd Ste 4e (08360-6472)
PHONE..............................856 563-0488
Fax: 856 563-0079
Mile Kznaric, *President*
David Rainear, *Corp Secy*
Micheal Mitros, *Vice Pres*
EMP: 16
SQ FT: 6,000
SALES (est): 2MM **Privately Held**
SIC: 3544 Industrial molds

(G-11413)
URBAN SIGN & CRANE INC
527 E Chestnut Ave (08360-5620)
P.O. Box 640 (08362-0640)
PHONE..............................856 691-8388
Seth Davis, *President*
Maryann Gonyea, *Vice Pres*
EMP: 9
SALES (est): 1.5MM **Privately Held**
WEB: www.urbansigncompany.com
SIC: 3993 Electric signs

(G-11414)
V M GLASS CO
3231 N Mill Rd (08360-1525)
PHONE..............................856 794-9333
Fax: 856 794-9695
Michael Greico, *Owner*
EMP: 7
SQ FT: 5,000
SALES (est): 300K **Privately Held**
WEB: www.vmglass.com
SIC: 3231 Scientific & technical glassware: from purchased glass

(G-11415)
VINELAND KOSHER POULTRY INC (PA)
1050 S Mill Rd (08360-4376)
PHONE..............................856 692-1871
Fax: 856 794-8031
Israel Leifer, *President*
EMP: 160 **EST:** 1967
SQ FT: 30,000
SALES (est): 19.3MM **Privately Held**
WEB: www.vinelandkosherpoultry.com
SIC: 2015 Poultry slaughtering & processing

(G-11416)
VINELAND PACKAGING CORP
3602 N Mill Rd (08360-1508)
PHONE..............................856 794-3300
Joseph D Alessandro Jr, *President*
David D Alessandro, *Vice Pres*
Mike D'Alessandro, *Vice Pres*
EMP: 30
SQ FT: 33,000
SALES (est): 8.7MM **Privately Held**
WEB: www.vpcbox.com
SIC: 2653 Boxes, corrugated: made from purchased materials

(G-11417)
VINELAND SYRUP INC
723 S East Blvd (08360-5679)
P.O. Box 1326 (08362-1326)
PHONE..............................856 691-5772
Fax: 856 691-0359
Meilech Kornbluh, *President*
EMP: 32
SQ FT: 30,000
SALES (est): 6MM **Privately Held**
WEB: www.vinelandsyrup.com
SIC: 2087 7359 Flavoring extracts & syrups; equipment rental & leasing

(G-11418)
WORLDWIDE GLASS RESOURCES INC
1022 Spruce St (08360-2841)
PHONE..............................856 205-1508
Fax: 856 205-1607
James O Crawford, *President*
Edward Poisker, *Corp Secy*
Dave Fordham, *Sales Executive*
▲ **EMP:** 25 **EST:** 2001
SQ FT: 6,000
SALES (est): 4.6MM **Privately Held**
WEB: www.wwglassresource.com
SIC: 3221 Vials, glass

Voorhees
Camden County

(G-11419)
ADVANCED ENERGY VOORHEES INC
1007 Laurel Oak Rd (08043-3515)
PHONE..............................856 627-1287
William A Ruff, *President*
Richard Beck, *Principal*
Doug Schatz, *Principal*
EMP: 90 **EST:** 1981
SQ FT: 78,000
SALES (est): 8.1MM
SALES (corp-wide): 671MM **Publicly Held**
WEB: www.advanced-energy.com
SIC: 3679 Power supplies, all types: static
PA: Advanced Energy Industries, Inc.
　　1625 Sharp Point Dr
　　Fort Collins CO 80525
　　970 221-4670

(G-11420)
ALLSTATE CONVEYOR SERVICE
256 Terrace Blvd (08043-4211)
P.O. Box 308, Medford (08055-0308)
PHONE..............................856 768-6566
Karla Porter, *President*
William J Porter, *Vice Pres*
EMP: 21
SALES (est): 5.2MM **Privately Held**
SIC: 3535 Conveyors & conveying equipment

(G-11421)
AMERICAN WATER - PRIDESA LLC (PA)
1025 Laurel Oak Rd (08043-3506)
PHONE..............................856 435-7711
Eric Sabolsice,
▲ **EMP:** 5
SALES (est): 883.2K **Privately Held**
SIC: 2899 Desalter kits, sea water

(G-11422)
AUNTIE ANNES HMDE SFT PRTZLS
1337 Voorhees Town Ctr (08043)
PHONE..............................856 772-3737
Fax: 856 772-3737
EMP: 15
SALES: 400K **Privately Held**
SIC: 5461 2052 5812 2096 Mfg Cookies/Crackers Retail Bakery Eating Place Mfg Potato Chips/Snacks Mfg Bread/Related Prdts

(G-11423)
BROOKDALE SENIOR LIVING INC
207 Laurel Rd (08043-2317)
PHONE..............................856 772-9400
EMP: 12
SALES (corp-wide): 4.7B **Publicly Held**
SIC: 3825 Network analyzers
PA: Brookdale Senior Living
　　111 Westwood Pl Ste 400
　　Brentwood TN 37027
　　615 221-2250

(G-11424)
BURNS LINK MANUFACTURING CO
253 American Way (08043-1114)
P.O. Box 811, Cherry Hill (08003-0811)
PHONE..............................856 429-6844
Fax: 856 429-3734
Daniel Zoltowski, *President*
Stephen Zoltowski, *Vice Pres*
Darcy Veiock, *Bookkeeper*
Bob Knorr, *Sales Executive*
EMP: 16 **EST:** 1957
SQ FT: 20,000
SALES (est): 3.8MM **Privately Held**
WEB: www.linkburns.com
SIC: 3444 Sheet metal specialties, not stamped

(G-11425)
COMAR INC (PA)
Also Called: Comar Glass
201 Laurel Rd Fl 2 (08043-2329)
PHONE..............................856 692-6100
Fax: 856 692-9190
Mike Ruggieri, *CEO*
Dan Mullock, *President*
Bill Hughes, *COO*
Mike Rozgony, *Vice Pres*
Jeff Schempp, *CFO*
◆ **EMP:** 25
SQ FT: 7,000
SALES (est): 77.9MM **Privately Held**
SIC: 3089 3231 Plastic containers, except foam; products of purchased glass

(G-11426)
COMAR INC
Also Called: Innovation Design Center
201 Laurel Rd Fl 2 (08043-2329)
PHONE..............................856 507-5461
John Deli, *Manager*
EMP: 15
SALES (corp-wide): 77.9MM **Privately Held**
SIC: 2671 Plastic film, coated or laminated for packaging
PA: Comar, Inc.
　　201 Laurel Rd Fl 2
　　Voorhees NJ 08043
　　856 692-6100

(G-11427)
COMAR LLC (HQ)
Also Called: Comar Plastics
220 Laurel Rd Fl 2 (08043-2362)
P.O. Box 786776, Philadelphia PA (19178-6776)
PHONE..............................856 692-6100
Mike Ruggieri, *Mng Member*

Bob Boyce, *Maintence Staff*
◆ **EMP:** 260
SQ FT: 107,000
SALES (est): 99.3MM
SALES (corp-wide): 12.9MM **Privately Held**
SIC: 3089 3231 Plastic containers, except foam; products of purchased glass
PA: Comar Holding Company, Llc
220 Laurel Rd Fl 2
Voorhees NJ 08043
856 692-6100

(G-11428)
DAVID MITCHELL INC
210 Park Dr (08043-1130)
PHONE..................856 429-2610
Fax: 856 429-8058
David Mitchell, *President*
Edith Mitchell, *Admin Sec*
EMP: 20 **EST:** 1973
SQ FT: 8,000
SALES (est): 3.3MM **Privately Held**
WEB: www.rmit.edu.au
SIC: 5144 2015 Poultry products; poultry slaughtering & processing

(G-11429)
EL JAY POULTRY CORP (PA)
1010 Hddonfield Berlin Rd (08043-3514)
P.O. Box 778 (08043-0778)
PHONE..................856 435-0900
Fax: 856 435-3019
Leo Rubin, *President*
Art Nogram, *Principal*
Arthur Milgrim, *Vice Pres*
Bruce Utain, *Vice Pres*
EMP: 19
SQ FT: 3,800
SALES (est): 15.3MM **Privately Held**
SIC: 8741 2015 Administrative management; turkey, slaughtered & dressed

(G-11430)
FIS FINANCIAL SYSTEMS LLC
Also Called: Sungard
600 Laurel Oak Rd (08043-4456)
PHONE..................856 784-7230
Charles Miller, *Branch Mgr*
EMP: 51
SALES (corp-wide): 9.1B **Publicly Held**
SIC: 7374 7372 Data processing service; business oriented computer software
HQ: Fis Financial Systems Llc
601 Riverside Ave
Jacksonville FL 32204
904 438-6000

(G-11431)
GOOD TO GO INC
Also Called: Sweet Eats Bakery
310 S Burnt Mill Rd (08043-1107)
PHONE..................856 627-8241
EMP: 20
SQ FT: 3,000
SALES (est): 1.9MM **Privately Held**
SIC: 2051 Whol & Ret Bakery

(G-11432)
GREENBUILT INTL BLDG CO
1081 Pndleton Ct Voorhees (08043)
P.O. Box 1361, Camden (08105-0361)
PHONE..................609 300-9091
Dean Kriner, *President*
EMP: 124
SQ FT: 130,000
SALES: 22MM **Privately Held**
SIC: 1521 1522 2493 5031 Single-family housing construction; residential construction; multi-family dwelling construction; reconstituted wood products; building materials, exterior; building materials, interior; strawboard

(G-11433)
I SEE OPTICAL LABORATORIES
312 W Somerdale Rd (08043-2237)
PHONE..................856 795-6435
Irv Palkovicz, *Branch Mgr*
EMP: 6
SALES (corp-wide): 1.2MM **Privately Held**
SIC: 3851 Eyeglasses, lenses & frames

PA: I See Optical Laboratories Inc
44 W Church St
Blackwood NJ 08012
856 227-9300

(G-11434)
ITALIAN TREASURES
1020 Voorhees Town Ctr (08043-1940)
PHONE..................856 770-9188
Celeste J Cinalli, *Owner*
EMP: 4
SQ FT: 1,000
SALES (est): 100K **Privately Held**
SIC: 5947 2759 5099 Gift, novelty & souvenir shop; souvenir cards: printing; souvenirs

(G-11435)
MANTECH SYSTEMS ENGRG CORP
1000 Haddonfield Berlin R (08043-3520)
PHONE..................856 566-9155
Gene Kiernan, *Manager*
EMP: 7
SALES (corp-wide): 1.7B **Publicly Held**
SIC: 3812 Defense systems & equipment
HQ: Mantech Systems Engineering Corporation
12015 Lee Jackson Hwy # 110
Fairfax VA 22033
703 218-6000

(G-11436)
PRODUCTIVE INDUSTRIAL FINSHG
103 American Way (08043-1112)
PHONE..................856 427-9646
Fax: 856 427-0042
Diane Stoelker-Stern, *President*
Kevin Stern, *Vice Pres*
EMP: 7
SQ FT: 7,000
SALES (est): 462.2K **Privately Held**
WEB: www.xyzfinishing.com
SIC: 3479 3471 Painting of metal products; plating & polishing

(G-11437)
SENTRIMED LTD LIABILITY CO
49 Holly Oak Dr (08043-1511)
PHONE..................914 582-8631
Ellen Marks, *President*
EMP: 5
SALES (est): 479.5K **Privately Held**
SIC: 2834 Pharmaceutical preparations

(G-11438)
SULLIVAN-CARSON INC (PA)
1010 Hddonfield Berlin Rd (08043-3514)
PHONE..................856 566-1400
Fax: 856 784-1151
James B Carson, *Ch of Bd*
James B Carson Sr, *Ch of Bd*
Paul Klapach, *Vice Pres*
EMP: 3 **EST:** 1853
SQ FT: 1,800
SALES (est): 4.9MM **Privately Held**
SIC: 2241 Elastic narrow fabrics, woven or braided; fabric tapes; webbing, woven

(G-11439)
TEMPTROL CORP
242 Terrace Blvd Ste E (08043-4209)
PHONE..................856 461-7977
Fax: 856 461-7813
Robert R Schweder, *President*
Robin Nosari, *Vice Pres*
EMP: 21 **EST:** 1972
SQ FT: 4,000
SALES: 2.2MM **Privately Held**
SIC: 1711 3443 Warm air heating & air conditioning contractor; heat exchangers, condensers & components

(G-11440)
TOUCH OF CLASS PROMOTIONS LLC
19 Festival Dr (08043-4325)
PHONE..................267 994-0860
Tammy Freedman, *President*
Stephen Kornfeld, *Officer*
EMP: 4
SALES: 600K **Privately Held**
SIC: 3993 3951 5199 Advertising novelties; ball point pens & parts; badges

Waldwick
Bergen County

(G-11441)
BERTONE AROMATICS
26 Dora Ave (07463-2006)
P.O. Box 46, West Stockbridge MA (01266-0046)
PHONE..................201 444-9821
Alan Birnbaum, *Owner*
EMP: 1
SALES: 2MM **Privately Held**
SIC: 2911 Aromatic chemical products

(G-11442)
CARTER PUMP INC
152d Franklin Tpke (07463-1802)
PHONE..................201 568-9798
Fax: 201 568-1313
Kevin Powers, *President*
John McCarty, *Chairman*
EMP: 3
SQ FT: 35,000
SALES (est): 1.6MM
SALES (corp-wide): 10.6MM **Privately Held**
SIC: 3561 5084 Pumps, domestic: water or sump; industrial machinery & equipment
HQ: Coffin Turbo Pump, Inc.
326 S Dean St
Englewood NJ 07631
201 568-4700

(G-11443)
CORBETT INDUSTRIES INC
39 Hewson Ave Ste B (07463-1827)
P.O. Box 212 (07463-0212)
PHONE..................201 445-6311
Richard Geier, *President*
Justin Krouse, *Vice Pres*
William Carman, *Treasurer*
Diane Procino, *Controller*
EMP: 11 **EST:** 1951
SQ FT: 10,000
SALES (est): 2.6MM **Privately Held**
WEB: www.corbettind.com
SIC: 7699 3567 Industrial machinery & equipment repair; heating units & devices, industrial: electric

(G-11444)
DESIGN PRODUCTIONS INC
9 Industrial Park (07463-1512)
PHONE..................201 447-5656
Fax: 201 447-5858
Thomas Murphy, *President*
Terence J Murphy, *Sales Executive*
▲ **EMP:** 9
SQ FT: 15,000
SALES (est): 1.8MM **Privately Held**
WEB: www.designproductionsinc.com
SIC: 3993 Signs & advertising specialties

(G-11445)
DNP FOODS AMERICA LTD LBLTY CO
2 Dipippo Ct (07463-1025)
P.O. Box 128, Montvale (07645-0128)
PHONE..................201 654-5581
Larry Mattessich, *Managing Dir*
EMP: 5
SALES (est): 266.9K **Privately Held**
SIC: 2844 3999 Toilet preparations; flowers, artificial & preserved

(G-11446)
EM ORTHODONTIC LABS INC
6 Lafayette Pl (07463-1711)
P.O. Box 112 (07463-0112)
PHONE..................201 652-4411
Eva Macz, *President*
EMP: 8
SALES: 240K **Privately Held**
SIC: 3843 8072 Orthodontic appliances; orthodontic appliance production

(G-11447)
KOELLMANN GEAR CORPORATION
8 Industrial Park (07463-1512)
PHONE..................201 447-0200
Fax: 201 447-6595

Michael Rasovic, *CEO*
▲ **EMP:** 250 **EST:** 1974
SQ FT: 15,000
SALES (est): 36.9MM **Privately Held**
WEB: www.koellmann.com
SIC: 3566 Gears, power transmission, except automotive; reduction gears & gear units for turbines, except automotive

(G-11448)
MENSHEN PACKAGING USA INC
21 Industrial Park (07463-1512)
PHONE..................201 445-7436
Fax: 201 445-3473
Susan Kobernick, *Principal*
Jeff Dugal, *VP Opers*
George Flores, *Prdtn Mgr*
Ryan Frankle, *Mfg Mgr*
Darrin Taynor, *Safety Mgr*
▲ **EMP:** 98
SALES (est): 30MM
SALES (corp-wide): 471MM **Privately Held**
SIC: 2842 Industrial plant disinfectants or deodorants
HQ: Georg Menshen Gmbh & Co. Kg
Industriestr. 26
Finnentrop 57413
272 151-80

(G-11449)
MINERVA CUSTOM PRODUCTS LLC
49 Lockwood Dr (07463-1018)
PHONE..................201 447-4731
Deborah Dellavechia, *Principal*
EMP: 5
SALES (est): 334K **Privately Held**
SIC: 2441 2449 2542 7336 Cases, wood; shipping cases, wood: nailed or lock corner; shipping cases, wood: wirebound; counters or counter display cases: except wood; art design services

(G-11450)
MOSSTYPE CORPORATION
150 Franklin Tpke (07463-1897)
PHONE..................201 444-8000
Fax: 201 444-0095
Lester Moss, *President*
Richard Moss, *Vice Pres*
Bruce Anderson, *Manager*
EMP: 4
SALES (est): 762.3K **Privately Held**
SIC: 3555 Printing plates

(G-11451)
MOSSTYPE HOLDING CORP (PA)
150 Franklin Tpke (07463-1802)
PHONE..................201 444-8000
Lester Moss, *President*
Richard Moss, *Vice Pres*
EMP: 50 **EST:** 1896
SQ FT: 80,000
SALES (est): 4.7MM **Privately Held**
WEB: www.mosstype.com
SIC: 3555 2796 Printing plates; engraving machinery & equipment, except plates; platemaking services

(G-11452)
NEXTPHASE MEDICAL DEVICES LLC (PA)
Also Called: Meditron Devices
150 Hopper Ave (07463-1513)
PHONE..................201 968-9400
Milton Frank, *President*
Russ Van Zile, *Opers Staff*
▲ **EMP:** 30
SQ FT: 10,100
SALES (est): 5.8MM **Privately Held**
WEB: www.nexcoretech.com
SIC: 3845 Electromedical apparatus

(G-11453)
STAUFF CORPORATION (DH)
7 William Demarest Pl (07463-1511)
PHONE..................201 444-7800
Knut Menshen, *Ch of Bd*
Jeffrey Behlinger, *President*
Denise Schock, *Asst Controller*
Peter Koch, *Manager*
Ellen Von Weisenstein, *Executive Asst*
▲ **EMP:** 48

SQ FT: 40,000
SALES: 25MM
SALES (corp-wide): 471MM Privately Held
SIC: 3569 Liquid automation machinery & equipment
HQ: Walter Stauffenberg Gmbh & Co Kg
Im Ehrenfeld 4
Werdohl 58791
239 291-60

(G-11454)
SUPERIOR TRADEMARK INC
Also Called: Samson Sign Company
45 Zazzetti St (07463-1618)
P.O. Box 35 (07463-0035)
PHONE.............................201 652-1900
Fax: 201 447-8867
Gordon D Mc Intire, *President*
Leslie Becher, *General Mgr*
Sue Mc Intire, *Admin Sec*
EMP: 8 EST: 1929
SQ FT: 6,000
SALES (est): 1.9MM Privately Held
SIC: 5084 2752 Printing trades machinery, equipment & supplies; transfers, decalcomania or dry: lithographed

(G-11455)
WALDWICK PLASTICS CORP
21 Industrial Park (07463-1512)
PHONE.............................201 445-7436
Fax: 201 444-2839
George Flores, *Plant Mgr*
Anthony Vicale, *Treasurer*
◆ **EMP: 6 EST:** 2010
SALES (est): 723.1K Privately Held
SIC: 3089 Injection molding of plastics

(G-11456)
WALDWICK PRINTING CO
1 Harrison Ave (07463-1708)
PHONE.............................201 652-5848
Fax: 201 652-3120
William R Cook, *Owner*
EMP: 4 EST: 1953
SQ FT: 2,700
SALES: 300K Privately Held
SIC: 2752 Commercial printing, offset

(G-11457)
WALDWICK VOL AMB CORPS INC
20 Whites Ln (07463-1716)
P.O. Box 244 (07463-0244)
PHONE.............................201 445-8772
Samuel Ramirez,
EMP: 25
SALES: 75.7K Privately Held
SIC: 3713 Ambulance bodies

Wall
Monmouth County

(G-11458)
AMERICAN PLUS PRINTERS INC
2604 Atlantic Ave Ste 300 (07719-9757)
PHONE.............................732 528-2170
Fax: 732 528-2174
Dianne Strohmenger, *President*
Michelle Coty, *Vice Pres*
Mark Velazquez, *Sales Staff*
Sharon Boyhan, *Admin Sec*
EMP: 28
SQ FT: 26,000
SALES (est): 4MM Privately Held
WEB: www.americanplusprinters.com
SIC: 2752 Commercial printing, offset

Wall Township
Monmouth County

(G-11459)
A&E ADVNCED CLSURE SYSTEMS LLC ✪
5206 Asbury Rd (07727-3609)
PHONE.............................732 938-2266
Michael T Wojciechowicz, *President*
EMP: 50 **EST:** 2017

SQ FT: 55K
SALES (corp-wide): 12.1MM Privately Held
SIC: 3841 Surgical & medical instruments
HQ: A & E Medical Corporation
5206 Asbury Rd
Wall Township NJ 07727
732 938-2266

(G-11460)
AIR CRUISERS COMPANY LLC (DH)
1747 State Route 34 (07727-3935)
PHONE.............................732 681-3527
Fax: 732 681-9163
Kelly Svihla, *General Mgr*
T Webb, *Vice Pres*
William Najd, *Engineer*
Shirley Robbins, *Personnel*
John Hendricksen, *Manager*
◆ **EMP:** 223
SQ FT: 37,500
SALES (est): 497.4MM
SALES (corp-wide): 650.9MM Privately Held
WEB: www.aircruisers.com
SIC: 2531 3069 3728 2399 Seats, aircraft; air-supported rubber structures; fuel tanks, aircraft; parachutes
HQ: Zodiac Us Corporation
1747 State Route 34
Wall Township NJ 07727
732 681-3527

(G-11461)
ALTO DEVELOPMENT CORP (PA)
Also Called: A&E Medical
5206 Asbury Rd (07727-3609)
P.O. Box 758, Farmingdale (07727-0758)
PHONE.............................732 938-2266
Fax: 732 938-2399
Eric Sklar, *CEO*
Michael Wojciechowicz, *President*
EMP: 62 **EST:** 1967
SQ FT: 25,000
SALES (est): 12.1MM Privately Held
WEB: www.aemedical.com
SIC: 3841 Surgical & medical instruments

(G-11462)
AP GLOBAL ENTERPRISES INC
Also Called: AP International
5044 Industrial Rd (07727-3629)
P.O. Box 601, Oakhurst (07755-0601)
PHONE.............................732 919-6200
Andy Papiccio, *CEO*
EMP: 8 **EST:** 2010
SALES (est): 532K Privately Held
SIC: 3931 5099 Musical instruments; musical instruments parts & accessories

(G-11463)
APPLICAD INC
Also Called: Aci
5029 Industrial Rd (07727-3651)
PHONE.............................732 751-2555
Fax: 732 919-3467
Paul Macmillan, *CEO*
John Macmillan, *President*
John Vowteras, *Vice Pres*
Erin Macmillan, *Production*
Erin Drumm, *Purch Mgr*
▲ **EMP:** 45
SQ FT: 20,000
SALES (est): 13.7MM Privately Held
WEB: www.aci-applicad.com
SIC: 3672 8711 Circuit boards, television & radio printed; engineering services

(G-11464)
ATLANTIS AROMATICS INC
5047 Industrial Rd Ste 4 (07727-4026)
PHONE.............................732 919-1112
Phillip Abbot, *President*
EMP: 6
SQ FT: 6,000
SALES (est): 1MM Privately Held
WEB: www.atlantisaromatics.com
SIC: 2844 Perfumes & colognes

(G-11465)
BEL-RAY COMPANY INC (HQ)
1201 Bowman Ave (07727-3910)
P.O. Box 526, Farmingdale (07727-0526)
PHONE.............................732 378-4000

Fax: 732 938-4232
Daryl Brosnan, *CEO*
Jim Self, *General Mgr*
Chris McAvoy, *Regional Mgr*
Cody Wolf, *Regional Mgr*
Jennifer Liquori, *COO*
◆ **EMP:** 100 **EST:** 1946
SQ FT: 80,000
SALES (est): 22.5MM
SALES (corp-wide): 3.7B Publicly Held
WEB: www.belray.com
SIC: 2992 Re-refining lubricating oils & greases; rust arresting compounds, animal or vegetable oil base
PA: Calumet Specialty Products Partners Lp
2780 Waterfront Pkwy
Indianapolis IN 46214
317 328-5660

(G-11466)
BEVERAGE WORKS NJ INC (PA)
1800 State Route 34 # 203 (07719-9145)
PHONE.............................732 938-7600
Gerald Ponsiglione, *President*
Sabato Satucci, *Vice Pres*
James Amberg, *VP Sales*
Chris Ustick, *VP Sales*
Rob Felicito, *Sales Mgr*
EMP: 350
SALES (est): 56MM Privately Held
WEB: www.beverageworks.com
SIC: 2086 Bottled & canned soft drinks

(G-11467)
BIO-KEY INTERNATIONAL INC (PA)
3349 Hwy 138 Ste E (07719-9671)
PHONE.............................732 359-1100
Michael W Depasquale, *Ch of Bd*
Barbara Rivera, *COO*
James Sullivan, *Senior VP*
Scott Mahnken, *Vice Pres*
Renat Zhdanov, *Vice Pres*
EMP: 21
SQ FT: 4,517
SALES: 6.3MM Publicly Held
WEB: www.bio-key.com
SIC: 3699 3999 7372 7375 Electrical equipment & supplies; security control equipment & systems; fingerprint equipment; prepackaged software; information retrieval services

(G-11468)
CHAVANT INC
5043 Industrial Rd (07727-3651)
PHONE.............................732 751-0003
Fax: 732 751-1982
Jack North, *President*
▲ **EMP:** 10 **EST:** 1870
SQ FT: 12,000
SALES (est): 1.8MM Privately Held
WEB: www.chavant.com
SIC: 3952 Modeling clay

(G-11469)
CHRISTIAN MSSONS IN MANY LANDS
Also Called: Cmml
2751 18th Ave (07719-9550)
P.O. Box 13, Spring Lake (07762-0013)
PHONE.............................732 449-8880
Fax: 732 974-0888
Samuel E Robinson, *President*
Thomas J Turner, *President*
Christian Elliott, *Editor*
Paul Gilkensen, *Vice Pres*
Tom Turner, *Vice Pres*
EMP: 6
SQ FT: 20,300
SALES (est): 15.8MM Privately Held
WEB: www.cmmlusa.org
SIC: 8661 2721 Non-church religious organizations; magazines: publishing only, not printed on site

(G-11470)
CLAYTON BLOCK COMPANY INC (PA)
1355 Campus Pkwy Ste 200 (07753-6832)
P.O. Box 3015, Lakewood (08701-9015)
PHONE.............................732 363-1995
Fax: 732 905-7863
William R Clayton, *President*
Daniel Clayton, *Vice Pres*

Douglas Clayton, *Vice Pres*
Joe Forestieri, *CFO*
Cole Fischer, *Sales Mgr*
◆ **EMP:** 30
SALES (est): 44.5MM Privately Held
WEB: www.claytononline.com
SIC: 3271 Tool rental

(G-11471)
CLAYTON BLOCK COMPANY INC
1601 18th Ave (07719-3783)
PHONE.............................732 681-0186
Fax: 732 681-5103
Toni Sabatani, *Manager*
EMP: 26
SALES (corp-wide): 44.5MM Privately Held
WEB: www.claytononline.com
SIC: 3271 5211 5032 3272 Blocks, concrete or cinder: standard; concrete & cinder block; concrete & cinder block; concrete products
PA: Clayton Block Company, Inc.
1355 Campus Pkwy Ste 200
Wall Township NJ 07753
732 363-1995

(G-11472)
COATES INTERNATIONAL LTD (PA)
2100 Highway 34 (07719-9110)
PHONE.............................732 449-7717
Fax: 732 449-9372
George J Coates, *Ch of Bd*
Barry C Kaye, *CFO*
Gregory Coates, *Admin Sec*
EMP: 5
SQ FT: 29,000
SALES: 19.2K Publicly Held
WEB: www.coatesengine.com
SIC: 3519 Parts & accessories, internal combustion engines

(G-11473)
COATES PRECISION ENGINEERING
2100 State Route 34 (07719-9110)
PHONE.............................732 449-9382
George Coates, *President*
Gregory Coates, *Vice Pres*
EMP: 6
SALES (est): 407.7K
SALES (corp-wide): 19.2K Publicly Held
WEB: www.coatesengine.com
SIC: 3599 Machine shop, jobbing & repair
PA: Coates International Ltd.
2100 Highway 34
Wall Township NJ 07719
732 449-7717

(G-11474)
COLUMBIA FUEL SERVICES INC
1717 Highway 34 (07727-3989)
PHONE.............................732 751-0044
Fax: 732 751-0199
Dave Oaks, *Manager*
EMP: 10
SALES (corp-wide): 9.1MM Privately Held
SIC: 2911 5084 Jet fuels; industrial machinery & equipment
PA: Columbia Fuel Services, Inc.
175 Tower Ave
Groton CT 06340
860 449-1400

(G-11475)
CONCEPT PROFESSIONAL SYSTEMS
5005 Belmar Blvd Ste B1 (07727-4020)
PHONE.............................732 938-5321
Donald C Gspann, *President*
Jeff Etten, *Vice Pres*
George Bachar, *VP Bus Dvlpt*
EMP: 4
SQ FT: 1,800
SALES (est): 350K Privately Held
SIC: 3651 Audio electronic systems

(G-11476)
D & A ELECTRONICS MFG
5303 Asbury Rd (07727-3612)
PHONE.............................732 938-7400
Demetrios Tsoutsas, *President*

▲ = Import ▼=Export
◆ =Import/Export

EMP: 12
SQ FT: 22,000
SALES (est): 980K **Privately Held**
SIC: 3822 Temperature controls, automatic

(G-11477)
DIALIGHT CORPORATION (DH)
1501 State Route 34 (07727-3932)
PHONE................................732 919-3119
Fax: 732 751-5779
Roy Burton, *CEO*
Bill Ronald, *Chairman*
Gareth Eaton, *Vice Pres*
Dennis Geary, *Plant Mgr*
Joe Chambers, *Facilities Mgr*
▲ EMP: 80
SQ FT: 35,000
SALES (est): 297.3MM
SALES (corp-wide): 239.1MM **Privately Held**
WEB: www.dialight.com
SIC: 3679 3674 Liquid crystal displays (LCD); electronic circuits; semiconductors & related devices
HQ: Roxboro Holdings Inc
1501 State Route 34
Wall Township NJ 07727
732 919-3119

(G-11478)
EARLE THE WALTER R CORP (PA)
1800 State Route 34 # 205 (07719-9168)
P.O. Box 556, Farmingdale (07727-0556)
PHONE................................732 308-1113
Fax: 732 462-9626
Walter R Earle, *President*
Marianne Earle, *Vice Pres*
▲ EMP: 1
SQ FT: 2,500
SALES (est): 3.8MM **Privately Held**
WEB: www.theearlecompanies.com
SIC: 2951 Concrete, bituminous

(G-11479)
EARLE ASPHALT COMPANY (PA)
Also Called: Earle Companies, The
1800 State Route 34 # 205 (07719-9168)
P.O. Box 556, Farmingdale (07727-0556)
PHONE................................732 308-1113
Walter R Earle, *President*
Walter R Earle II, *President*
Marianne Earle, *Vice Pres*
Thomas J Earle, *Vice Pres*
William Mead, *Project Mgr*
EMP: 122 EST: 1968
SQ FT: 1,500
SALES (est): 40.5MM **Privately Held**
SIC: 2951 Asphalt paving mixtures & blocks

(G-11480)
EXALENZ BIOSCIENCE INC
1712 M St (07719-3452)
PHONE................................732 232-4393
Lawrence Cohen, *CEO*
Dennis Boyle, *Principal*
Gavin Doree, *VP Sales*
EMP: 30
SALES (est): 3.2MM **Privately Held**
SIC: 3841 Diagnostic apparatus, medical

(G-11481)
FERMATEX VASCULAR TECH LLC
Also Called: Adam Spence Vascular Tech
1746 Rte 34 (07727-3937)
PHONE................................732 681-7070
Mike Janish, *CEO*
EMP: 10
SALES (est): 93.7K
SALES (corp-wide): 5.7B **Privately Held**
SIC: 3061 Medical & surgical rubber tubing (extruded & lathe-cut)
HQ: Pexco Llc
2500 Northwinds Pkwy # 472
Alpharetta GA 30009
404 564-8560

(G-11482)
FIVE ELEMENTS ROBOTICS LLC
Also Called: 5 Elements Robotics
1333 Campus Pkwy (07753-6815)
PHONE................................800 681-8514
Wendy Roberts, *CEO*
EMP: 6 EST: 2012

SQ FT: 1,000
SALES: 800K **Privately Held**
SIC: 3571 5099 5045 Minicomputers; robots, service or novelty; computer software

(G-11483)
FIZZICS GROUP LLC
1775 State Route 34 D14 (07727-3961)
PHONE................................917 545-4533
Philip Petracca, *CEO*
Roger An, *Principal*
Courtney Baldwin, *Principal*
Greg Taylor, *Principal*
Steve Balog, *CFO*
EMP: 7
SALES (est): 283.8K **Privately Held**
SIC: 2082 Beer (alcoholic beverage)

(G-11484)
FRED MCDOWELL INC
34 St Hwy (07753)
PHONE................................732 681-5000
Fred Mc Dowell Jr, *President*
Frank Fine, *Vice Pres*
Jean Mc Dowell, *Treasurer*
EMP: 6 EST: 1929
SQ FT: 2,000
SALES: 853.7K **Privately Held**
SIC: 3531 Asphalt plant, including gravel-mix type

(G-11485)
GARDEN STATE PRECAST INC
1630 Wyckoff Rd (07727-3921)
P.O. Box 702, Farmingdale (07727-0702)
PHONE................................732 938-4436
Fax: 732 938-7296
J Kirby O Malley, *President*
Dan Morris, *Vice Pres*
Daniel Morris, *Vice Pres*
Michael Vergona, *Production*
Billy Morris, *Sales Staff*
EMP: 70
SQ FT: 871,200
SALES: 12.5MM **Privately Held**
WEB: www.gardenstateprecast.com
SIC: 3272 Concrete products

(G-11486)
HANGER PRSTHETCS & ORTHO INC
5100 Belmar Blvd (07727-4027)
PHONE................................732 919-7774
Fax: 732 919-0188
Sheryl Price, *Principal*
Brian Kleiberg, *Manager*
EMP: 5
SALES (corp-wide): 1B **Publicly Held**
SIC: 3842 Surgical appliances & supplies
HQ: Hanger Prosthetics & Orthotics, Inc.
10910 Domain Dr Ste 300
Austin TX 78758
512 777-3800

(G-11487)
HANSON AGGREGATES WRP INC (DH)
Also Called: Western Rock Products
1333 Campus Pkwy (07753-6815)
PHONE................................972 653-5500
Alan Murray, *President*
EMP: 34
SALES (est): 16.7MM
SALES (corp-wide): 20.3B **Privately Held**
SIC: 3281 3272 2951 1442 Cut stone & stone products; concrete products; asphalt paving mixtures & blocks; construction sand & gravel

(G-11488)
HONEYWELL INTERNATIONAL INC
5047 Industrial Rd Ste 2 (07727-4026)
PHONE................................732 919-0010
Tom McMann, *Manager*
EMP: 657
SALES (corp-wide): 40.5B **Publicly Held**
WEB: www.honeywell.com
SIC: 3724 Aircraft engines & engine parts
PA: Honeywell International Inc.
115 Tabor Rd
Morris Plains NJ 07950
973 455-2000

(G-11489)
HUECK FOILS HOLDING CO (DH)
1955 State Route 34 3c (07719-9735)
PHONE................................732 974-4100
Fax: 732 974-4111
Dietmar Wohlfart, *President*
Herbert Schwemmer, *Treasurer*
▲ EMP: 5
SALES (est): 82.7MM **Privately Held**
WEB: www.hueckfoils.com
SIC: 3497 Zinc foil
HQ: Hc Beteiligungsges. Mbh
Pirkmuhle 14-16
Pirk
961 870-

(G-11490)
I 2 R CORP (PA)
Also Called: EMC Technologists
5033 Industrial Rd Ste 6 (07727-3946)
PHONE................................732 919-1100
James Watts, *President*
William Watts, *President*
Dave Guzman, *Sales Engr*
Steve Rust, *Sales Staff*
Jeanne Sass, *Sales Associate*
▲ EMP: 4
SQ FT: 5,000
SALES (est): 851.3K **Privately Held**
WEB: www.emceupen.com
SIC: 3699 8748 Electrical equipment & supplies; environmental consultant; consulting engineer; electrical supplies

(G-11491)
ICE COLD NOVELTY PRODUCTS INC
5005 Belmar Blvd Ste B2 (07727-4020)
PHONE................................732 751-0011
Kevin Enright, *CEO*
Chris Ulrich, *President*
EMP: 7
SQ FT: 4,500
SALES: 966.2K **Privately Held**
SIC: 5046 2024 Commercial equipment; non-dairy based frozen desserts

(G-11492)
KAVON FILTER PRODUCTS CO
5022 Industrial Rd (07727-3650)
P.O. Box 1166 (07719-1166)
PHONE................................732 938-3135
Douglas Von Bulow, *President*
Francis Cavanaugh, *Vice Pres*
Michael Cavanaugh, *Vice Pres*
Linda Von Bulow, *Exec Dir*
▼ EMP: 13 EST: 1962
SQ FT: 11,000
SALES (est): 2.8MM **Privately Held**
WEB: www.kavonfilter.com
SIC: 3599 3569 Machine & other job shop work; filters, general line: industrial

(G-11493)
KEMPTON WOOD PRODUCTS
2800 Ridgewood Rd (07719-9644)
PHONE................................732 449-8673
Kevin Kempton, *Mng Member*
William Smith,
EMP: 5
SQ FT: 3,000
SALES (est): 1.3MM **Privately Held**
WEB: www.kemptonwoodproducts.com
SIC: 5211 2431 Millwork & lumber; millwork

(G-11494)
KEY SOFTWARE SYSTEMS LLC
5100 Belmar Blvd Ste 8 (07727-4028)
PHONE................................732 409-6068
Charles Pisciotta,
EMP: 12
SALES (est): 1.6MM **Privately Held**
WEB: www.keysoftwaresystems.com
SIC: 7372 Prepackaged software

(G-11495)
LEES WOODWORKING INC
726 Walling Ave (07719-3064)
PHONE................................732 681-1002
Minh Lee, *Owner*
EMP: 4
SALES (est): 290K **Privately Held**
SIC: 2431 Millwork

(G-11496)
MACLEARIE PRINTING LLC
917 18th Ave (07719-3260)
PHONE................................732 681-2772
Fax: 732 681-2775
James Maclearie, *Mng Member*
EMP: 6
SALES (est): 628.8K **Privately Held**
WEB: www.maclearie.com
SIC: 2759 Screen printing

(G-11497)
MELSTROM MANUFACTURING CORP
5303 Asbury Rd (07727-3612)
PHONE................................732 938-7400
Fax: 732 938-2765
Demitrios Tsoutsas, *President*
EMP: 55
SQ FT: 25,000
SALES (est): 7.4MM **Privately Held**
SIC: 3679 Harness assemblies for electronic use: wire or cable

(G-11498)
MUSCO SPORTS LIGHTING LLC
Also Called: Musco Lighting
5146 W Hurley Pond Rd # 1 (07727-1622)
PHONE................................732 751-9114
Fax: 732 751-9115
Dan Shalloo, *Sales Staff*
EMP: 7
SALES (corp-wide): 161MM **Privately Held**
SIC: 3648 Lighting equipment
HQ: Musco Sports Lighting, Llc
100 1st Ave W
Oskaloosa IA 52577
641 673-0410

(G-11499)
NICHOLAS OLIVER LLC
Also Called: BO&nic
1933 State Route 35 (07719-3502)
PHONE................................732 690-7144
Nicholas Solazzo, *President*
Connie Dean Taylor, *Vice Pres*
Nicholas Oliver,
EMP: 6
SALES (est): 520K **Privately Held**
SIC: 2331 2335 Blouses, women's & juniors': made from purchased material; women's, juniors' & misses' dresses

(G-11500)
ONCO INC
1451 State Route 34 # 302 (07727-1615)
PHONE................................732 292-7460
James Hendrickson, *President*
EMP: 15
SALES (est): 1.3MM **Privately Held**
SIC: 7372 7371 Business oriented computer software; custom computer programming services

(G-11501)
OPDYKE AWNINGS INC
2036 State Route 35 (07719-3529)
PHONE................................732 449-5940
James Opdyke, *President*
Andrew Opdyke, *Vice Pres*
EMP: 15
SALES (est): 1.2MM **Privately Held**
SIC: 2394 3993 Awnings, fabric: made from purchased materials; signs & advertising specialties

(G-11502)
PALUMBO MILLWORK INC
5033 Industrial Rd Ste 8 (07727-3946)
PHONE................................732 938-3266
Nick Palumbo, *President*
EMP: 4
SQ FT: 5,000
SALES (est): 330K **Privately Held**
SIC: 2434 2431 Wood kitchen cabinets; millwork

(G-11503)
PLASTI-CLAD METAL PRODUCTS INC
2601 Ridgewood Rd (07719-9641)
P.O. Box 440, Allenwood (08720-0440)
PHONE................................732 449-2665
Mark Matthews, *President*

GEOGRAPHIC

Cyril Matthews, *Principal*
Scott Matthews, *Corp Secy*
▲ **EMP:** 13 **EST:** 1951
SQ FT: 20,000
SALES (est): 2.2MM **Privately Held**
WEB: www.plasti-clad.com
SIC: 3315 3496 Wire, steel: insulated or armored; miscellaneous fabricated wire products

(G-11504)
R & H SPRING & TRUCK REPAIR
4806 W Hurley Pond Rd (07719-9633)
PHONE..................................732 681-9000
Fax: 732 681-5887
Frank Todero, *President*
Elizabeth Todero, *Vice Pres*
Paul Botticelli, *Parts Mgr*
EMP: 10
SQ FT: 8,000
SALES: 1.5MM **Privately Held**
SIC: 7538 3531 3711 General truck repair; blades for graders, scrapers, dozers & snow plows; snow plow attachments; snow plows (motor vehicles), assembly of

(G-11505)
R T KUNTZ CO
5146 W Hurley Pond Rd # 2 (07727-1622)
PHONE..................................732 751-1770
Rod Kuntz, *President*
Adam Cocuzza, *Accounts Exec*
Nina Levenstein, *Office Mgr*
EMP: 12
SALES (est): 2.1MM **Privately Held**
SIC: 3559 Plastics working machinery

(G-11506)
ROXBORO HOLDINGS INC (HQ)
1501 State Route 34 (07727-3932)
PHONE..................................732 919-3119
Roy Burton, *President*
Nick Gallogly, *Vice Pres*
▲ **EMP:** 100
SQ FT: 35,000
SALES (est): 298.2MM
SALES (corp-wide): 239.1MM **Privately Held**
SIC: 3643 3679 3993 3823 Current-carrying wiring devices; electronic circuits; signs & advertising specialties; industrial instrmnts msrmnt display/control process variable; semiconductors & related devices
PA: Dialight Plc
Leaf C Level 36 Tower 42
London EC2N
203 058-3540

(G-11507)
SCREEN PRINTING & EMBROIDERY
5005 Belmar Blvd Ste B6 (07727-4020)
PHONE..................................732 256-9610
Timothy Dubrow, *Mng Member*
EMP: 4
SALES (est): 350.6K **Privately Held**
SIC: 2752 Commercial printing, lithographic

(G-11508)
SELECTIVE COATINGS & INKS (PA)
Also Called: SCI
5008 Industrial Rd (07727-3650)
PHONE..................................732 938-7677
Fax: 732 938-2719
William Zak, *President*
Joseph Bernardo, *Vice Pres*
Scott Beriont, *Director*
Joan Zak, *Admin Sec*
▲ **EMP:** 15
SQ FT: 5,000
SALES (est): 1.9MM **Privately Held**
WEB: www.sci-inc-usa.com
SIC: 2893 Gravure ink

(G-11509)
SHORE AWNING CO
1933 State Route 35 # 126 (07719-3553)
PHONE..................................732 775-3351
Fax: 732 578-1885
Michael Mc Clellan, *President*
Larry Gray, *Vice Pres*
EMP: 8 **EST:** 1946
SQ FT: 4,000

SALES: 965.4K **Privately Held**
SIC: 2394 Awnings, fabric: made from purchased materials

(G-11510)
SIMA S ENTERPRISES LLC
Also Called: Sima Enterprises
1298 Evans Rd (07719-4018)
PHONE..................................877 223-7639
Mordy Naftaly, *Mng Member*
▲ **EMP:** 5
SALES (est): 390.5K **Privately Held**
SIC: 2741 7389 ;

(G-11511)
STONE GRAPHICS
5020 Industrial Rd (07727-3650)
PHONE..................................732 919-1111
Fax: 732 919-7888
Raymond C Stone Jr, *President*
▲ **EMP:** 13
SQ FT: 7,200
SALES (est): 600K **Privately Held**
WEB: www.signsbystone.com
SIC: 3993 2396 Signs, not made in custom sign painting shops; automotive & apparel trimmings

(G-11512)
SURE DESIGN
5027 Industrial Rd Ste 3 (07727-4040)
PHONE..................................732 919-3066
Fax: 732 919-3071
Ken Thomas, *Managing Prtnr*
EMP: 15
SALES (est): 2.5MM **Privately Held**
WEB: www.sure-design.com
SIC: 3672 Printed circuit boards

(G-11513)
SYNTIRO DYNAMICS LLC
1606 Cammar Dr (07719-4704)
PHONE..................................732 377-3307
EMP: 6
SALES (est): 583K **Privately Held**
SIC: 3494 Pipe fittings

(G-11514)
THORTEL FIREPROOF FABRICS INC
Also Called: Interspec
5025 Industrial Rd (07727-3651)
P.O. Box 705, Allenwood (08720-0705)
PHONE..................................732 938-4114
Richard Deacon, *President*
John Hearn, *Mng Member*
▲ **EMP:** 12
SQ FT: 12,000
SALES (est): 1.9MM **Privately Held**
SIC: 2391 Curtains & draperies

(G-11515)
TOTAL GARAGE SOLUTIONS LLC
1709 State Route 34 Ste 2 (07727-4036)
PHONE..................................732 749-3993
Annette Yodice, *Marketing Mgr*
Tara McSherry, *Office Mgr*
Tracy Yodice, *Manager*
EMP: 10
SALES (est): 1.3MM **Privately Held**
SIC: 2431 3699 Garage doors, overhead: wood; door opening & closing devices, electrical

(G-11516)
TRINITY HEATING & AIR INC (PA)
Also Called: Trinity Solar Systems
2211 Allenwood Rd (07719-9692)
PHONE..................................732 780-3779
Fax: 732 780-6671
Tom Pollock, *President*
Bill Condit, *General Mgr*
James Bradshaw, *District Mgr*
Kristian Calibuso, *District Mgr*
Craig Groenewold, *District Mgr*
▲ **EMP:** 65
SQ FT: 145,000
SALES (est): 66.8MM **Privately Held**
WEB: www.trinityheatingandair.com
SIC: 3433 1731 1711 Solar heaters & collectors; electrical work; solar energy contractor

(G-11517)
VERNI VITO
Also Called: Minuteman Press
1818 State Route 35 Ste 8 (07719-3540)
PHONE..................................732 449-1760
Fax: 732 449-0841
Vito Verni, *Owner*
Detria Gallenger, *Bookkeeper*
EMP: 5
SQ FT: 1,500
SALES: 400K **Privately Held**
SIC: 2752 2791 2789 Commercial printing, offset; typesetting; bookbinding & related work

(G-11518)
VERSO PAPER MANAGEMENT LP
5100 Belmar Blvd Ste 7 (07727-4028)
PHONE..................................732 938-3167
EMP: 773 **Privately Held**
SIC: 2621 Paper mills
PA: Verso Paper Management Lp
60 W 42nd Ste 1942
New York NY 10165

(G-11519)
WILLIAM OPDYKE AWNINGS INC (PA)
2036 State Route 35 (07719-3529)
PHONE..................................732 449-5940
James Opdyke, *President*
▲ **EMP:** 8
SQ FT: 18,000
SALES (est): 1.7MM **Privately Held**
SIC: 5999 5712 2394 Awnings; furniture stores; canvas & related products

(G-11520)
ZODIAC US CORPORATION (DH)
Also Called: Zodiac Aerosystems
1747 State Route 34 (07727-3935)
PHONE..................................732 681-3527
Jean-Louis Gerondeau, *CEO*
Jean-Jacques Jegou, *COO*
Neil Cavaleri, *Vice Pres*
Mark Jeffers, *Vice Pres*
Robert Schalhoub, *Vice Pres*
▲ **EMP:** 584
SALES (est): 2.4B
SALES (corp-wide): 650.9MM **Privately Held**
SIC: 3728 Aircraft landing assemblies & brakes
HQ: Zodiac Aerospace
Cs20001
Plaisir 78370
161 342-323

┌─────────────────────────┐
│   **Wallington**   │
│   *Bergen County*   │
└─────────────────────────┘

(G-11521)
AEROSPACE MANUFACTURING INC
80 Van Winkle Ave (07057-1148)
P.O. Box 3398 (07057-0398)
PHONE..................................973 472-9888
Fax: 973 472-4120
Al Shafa, *President*
Lester Paszkowski, *Mfg Staff*
James Hakimi, *Shareholder*
Vivian Hakimi, *Shareholder*
EMP: 50
SQ FT: 30,000
SALES (est): 7.9MM **Privately Held**
WEB: www.aero-space.us
SIC: 3728 Aircraft parts & equipment

(G-11522)
ALLIED WASTE PRODUCTS INC
61 Midland Ave Ste 61-71 (07057-1715)
PHONE..................................973 473-7638
John Macchiarelli, *President*
Mario Macchiarelli, *Treasurer*
EMP: 6 **EST:** 1950
SQ FT: 8,000
SALES (est): 590K **Privately Held**
SIC: 3559 Recycling machinery; boots, shoes & leather working machinery

(G-11523)
BRENNER METAL PRODUCTS (PA)
16 Main Ave (07057-1106)
P.O. Box 3517 (07057-0517)
PHONE..................................973 778-2466
Christine Brenner, *President*
EMP: 30
SQ FT: 18,000
SALES (est): 5.1MM **Privately Held**
SIC: 3842 5047 Surgical appliances & supplies; medical & hospital equipment

(G-11524)
BRENNER METAL PRODUCTS
51 Paterson Ave (07057-1115)
PHONE..................................973 778-2466
Fax: 973 778-8780
Christine Brenner, *President*
EMP: 20
SALES (est): 1.2MM
SALES (corp-wide): 5.1MM **Privately Held**
SIC: 3599 Machine & other job shop work
PA: Brenner Metal Products (Inc)
16 Main Ave
Wallington NJ 07057
973 778-2466

(G-11525)
DIJON ENTERPRISES LLC
Also Called: Make Wine With US
21 Curie Ave (07057-2233)
PHONE..................................201 876-9463
Fax: 201 804-0007
John Gizzi,
Dianne Greco,
EMP: 5
SQ FT: 12,000
SALES (est): 412.5K **Privately Held**
WEB: www.makewinewithus.com
SIC: 2084 Wines

(G-11526)
GARFIELD MOLDING CO INC
10 Midland Ave (07057-1795)
PHONE..................................973 777-5700
Charles Murray, *President*
EMP: 28 **EST:** 1908
SQ FT: 65,000
SALES (est): 4.6MM **Privately Held**
SIC: 3089 Molding primary plastic

(G-11527)
HYGLOSS PRODUCTS INC
45 Hathaway St (07057-1008)
PHONE..................................973 458-1700
Moshe Neurath, *President*
Mordy Schiller, *Manager*
▲ **EMP:** 25
SQ FT: 19,000
SALES (est): 4.6MM **Privately Held**
WEB: www.hygloss.com
SIC: 3944 3999 5092 Craft & hobby kits & sets; education aids, devices & supplies; arts & crafts equipment & supplies

(G-11528)
MERCHANTS ALARM SYSTEMS INC
203 Paterson Ave Ste 5 (07057-1344)
PHONE..................................973 779-1296
Fax: 973 779-7010
Walter Wargacki, *President*
Elizabeth Wargacki, *Vice Pres*
EMP: 30
SQ FT: 10,000
SALES (est): 3.3MM **Privately Held**
SIC: 1731 7381 3669 Fire detection & burglar alarm systems specialization; burglary protection service; burglar alarm apparatus, electric

(G-11529)
R S RUBBER CORP
55 Paterson Ave (07057-1115)
P.O. Box 3400 (07057-0400)
PHONE..................................973 777-2200
Robert Buschgans, *President*
EMP: 10
SQ FT: 15,000
SALES (est): 1.8MM **Privately Held**
SIC: 3053 5085 Gaskets, all materials; gaskets

(G-11530)
TRIANGLE INK CO INC (PA)
53-57 Van Dyke St (07057)
PHONE..................................201 935-2777
Fax: 201 935-5961
Chester Bartolomei, *President*
EMP: 19 EST: 1978
SQ FT: 14,000
SALES (est): 4.5MM Privately Held
WEB: www.triangleink.com
SIC: 2893 Screen process ink

Wanaque
Passaic County

(G-11531)
BKH ELECTRONICS
9j Brookside Hts (07465-1620)
P.O. Box 247 (07465-0247)
PHONE..................................210 410-2757
Georgina Fabian, *Owner*
EMP: 4
SALES (est): 300K Privately Held
SIC: 3679 Electronic circuits

Waretown
Ocean County

(G-11532)
AMERILUBES LLC
5 Mantoloking Ln (08758-2354)
PHONE..................................704 399-7701
▼ EMP: 2
SALES: 5MM Privately Held
SIC: 3569 Mfg General Industrial Machinery

Warren
Somerset County

(G-11533)
21ST CENTURY OPTICS INC
Also Called: S & G Optical
5 Powderhorn Dr (07059-5105)
PHONE..................................808 935-1119
Edward Glassheim, *Branch Mgr*
EMP: 7 Privately Held
SIC: 3827 Lenses, optical: all types except ophthalmic
HQ: 21st Century Optics Inc.
4700 33rd St Ste 1r
Long Island City NY 11101
347 527-1079

(G-11534)
3SHAPE INC
10 Independence Blvd # 150 (07059-2730)
PHONE..................................908 219-4641
Flemming Thorup, *President*
Michael Maccaquano, *Sales Mgr*
Danny Caro, *Sales Staff*
Sara Lelchuk, *Manager*
John Nabors, *Manager*
EMP: 9
SALES (est): 69.5K Privately Held
SIC: 3845 5045 CAT scanner (Computerized Axial Tomography) apparatus; computer software

(G-11535)
ACRELIC INTERACTIVE LLC (PA)
16 Mount Bethel Rd (07059-5604)
PHONE..................................908 222-2900
David A Rosen, *President*
Gordon S Smith, *President*
Garth A Rose, *COO*
Pamela M Hakim, *Director*
EMP: 4
SALES (est): 1.6MM Privately Held
WEB: www.acrelic.com
SIC: 7372 Business oriented computer software

(G-11536)
AETERNA ZENTARIS INC
20 Independence Blvd # 401 (07059-2737)
PHONE..................................908 626-5428

Juergen Engel, *CEO*
David Mazzo, *President*
Ellen McDonald, *Vice Pres*
Mario Paradis, *Vice Pres*
Nicholas Pelliccione, *Vice Pres*
EMP: 8
SQ FT: 9,000
SALES (est): 2.3MM
SALES (corp-wide): 911K Privately Held
WEB: www.aeternazentaris.com
SIC: 5122 2834 Pharmaceuticals; pharmaceutical preparations
PA: Aeterna Zentaris Inc
1 Place Ville-Marie Bureau 2500
Montreal QC H3B 1

(G-11537)
AQUESTIVE THERAPEUTICS INC (PA)
30 Technology Dr (07059-5166)
PHONE..................................908 941-1900
Santo Costa, *Ch of Bd*
Keith J Kendall, *President*
Daniel Barber, *Senior VP*
Peter Boyd, *Senior VP*
Lori J Braender, *Senior VP*
EMP: 10
SQ FT: 16,454
SALES: 66.9MM Publicly Held
SIC: 2834 Pharmaceutical preparations

(G-11538)
BALLARD COLLECTION INC
Also Called: Karen Lee Ballard
221 Stirling Rd (07059-5238)
PHONE..................................908 604-0082
Fax: 908 931-9222
Karen Lee Engemann, *CEO*
Becky Sooy, *Vice Pres*
EMP: 7
SALES (est): 560K Privately Held
WEB: www.karenleeballard.com
SIC: 2392 Tablecloths & table settings

(G-11539)
BELLEROPHON THERAPEUTICS INC
184 Liberty Corner Rd # 302 (07059-6868)
PHONE..................................908 574-4770
Fabian Tenenbaum, *CEO*
Jonathan M Peacock, *Ch of Bd*
Martin Dekker, *Vice Pres*
Amy Edmonds, *Vice Pres*
Parag Shah, *Vice Pres*
EMP: 20 EST: 2009
SQ FT: 22,000
SALES (est): 6.6MM Privately Held
SIC: 2834 Pharmaceutical preparations

(G-11540)
C S L WATER TREATMENT INC
Also Called: C S L Water Quality
156 Mount Bethel Rd (07059-5147)
P.O. Box 4246 (07059-0246)
PHONE..................................908 647-1400
Fax: 908 647-1080
John Truglio, *President*
Bernadette Truglio, *Admin Sec*
EMP: 12 EST: 1930
SQ FT: 8,000
SALES (est): 1.4MM Privately Held
WEB: www.cslwater.com
SIC: 2899 Water treating compounds

(G-11541)
CELGENE CORPORATION
Also Called: Celgene Cellular Therapeutics
7 Powderhorn Dr (07059-5190)
PHONE..................................732 271-1001
Fax: 732 805-3931
Kathy Davis, *General Mgr*
Jonathan Biller, *Vice Pres*
Timothy Polson, *Production*
Linda Jensen, *Purchasing*
Shan Shao, *Research*
EMP: 30
SALES (corp-wide): 13B Publicly Held
SIC: 2834 Pharmaceutical preparations
PA: Celgene Corporation
86 Morris Ave
Summit NJ 07901
908 673-9000

(G-11542)
CHEMBIOPOWER INC
211 Warren St Ste 503 (07059)
PHONE..................................908 209-5595
Jeremiah Sullivan, *CFO*
EMP: 4
SALES (est): 156.7K Privately Held
SIC: 2869 Industrial organic chemicals

(G-11543)
CHROMIS FIBEROPTICS INC
6 Powderhorn Dr (07059-5105)
PHONE..................................732 764-0900
Fax: 732 764-0933
Frank Graziano, *President*
Miri Park, *COO*
Michael Bohrer, *Vice Pres*
Lee Plyler, *CTO*
Whitney White, *Officer*
▲ EMP: 10
SQ FT: 12,100
SALES (est): 2.2MM Privately Held
WEB: www.chromisfiber.com
SIC: 3661 Fiber optics communications equipment

(G-11544)
DEALAMAN ENTERPRISES INC
214 Mountainview Rd (07059-5037)
PHONE..................................908 647-5533
Fax: 908 604-8030
George Dealaman, *President*
George Dealaman Jr, *Vice Pres*
Bruce Dealaman, *Treasurer*
Elizabeth Dealaman, *Admin Sec*
EMP: 30 EST: 1944
SQ FT: 1,751
SALES (est): 2.9MM Privately Held
SIC: 2011 4151 Pork products from pork slaughtered on site; school buses

(G-11545)
ELGEE MANUFACTURING COMPANY
Also Called: Elgee Power Vac Sweeper
225 Stirling Rd (07059-5238)
PHONE..................................908 647-4100
Stephen Heinle, *President*
Rosie Uride, *Partner*
Will Winton, *Manager*
EMP: 8 EST: 1960
SQ FT: 10,000
SALES (est): 500K Privately Held
WEB: www.elgee.com
SIC: 3589 3444 Dirt sweeping units, industrial; roof deck, sheet metal

(G-11546)
EMERSON PROCESS MANAGEMENT
20 Independence Blvd (07059-2731)
PHONE..................................908 605-4551
EMP: 7
SALES (corp-wide): 15.2B Publicly Held
SIC: 3823 Industrial instrmnts msrmnt display/control process variable
HQ: Emerson Process Management Power & Water Solutions, Inc.
200 Beta Dr
Pittsburgh PA 15238
412 963-4000

(G-11547)
ESSILOR LABORATORIES AMER INC
Also Called: Eloa - New Jersey
5 Powderhorn Dr (07059-5105)
PHONE..................................732 563-9884
Fax: 732 563-1342
Debra Case, *General Mgr*
Elaine Ellis, *Manager*
EMP: 15 Privately Held
WEB: www.crizal.com
SIC: 3851 Eyeglasses, lenses & frames
HQ: Essilor Laboratories Of America, Inc.
13515 N Stemmons Fwy
Dallas TX 75234
972 241-4141

(G-11548)
FRANK FERREIRA CAB & MILL WORK
74 King George Rd (07059-6959)
PHONE..................................732 564-1499
EMP: 4 EST: 2009

SALES (est): 288.8K Privately Held
SIC: 2434 Wood kitchen cabinets

(G-11549)
GLAXOSMITHKLINE CONSUMER (DH)
184 Libery Corner Rd (07059)
PHONE..................................251 591-4188
Colin Mackenzie, *President*
Sherri Von Stein, *Human Res Mgr*
Tom Leeker, *Director*
◆ EMP: 400
SQ FT: 200,000
SALES (est): 418.3MM
SALES (corp-wide): 39.8B Privately Held
SIC: 2834 Pharmaceutical preparations
HQ: Glaxosmithkline Llc
5 Crescent Dr
Philadelphia PA 19112
215 751-4000

(G-11550)
GLAXOSMITHKLINE CONSUMER HLTH (DH)
184 Liberty Corner Rd (07059-6796)
PHONE..................................215 751-5046
William Mosher, *Director*
EMP: 9 EST: 2015
SALES (est): 61.2MM
SALES (corp-wide): 39.8B Privately Held
SIC: 2834 Druggists' preparations (pharmaceuticals)

(G-11551)
GSK CONSUMER HEALTH INC (HQ)
184 Liberty Corner Rd # 78 (07059-6796)
PHONE..................................919 269-5000
Fax: 973 503-8450
Joseph Jimenez, *CEO*
John McKenna, *CFO*
Matthias Vogt, *Treasurer*
◆ EMP: 300
SALES (est): 332.9MM
SALES (corp-wide): 39.8B Privately Held
SIC: 2834 Pharmaceutical preparations
PA: Glaxosmithkline Plc
980 Great West Road
Brentford MIDDX TW8 9
208 047-5000

(G-11552)
HILLARYS FASHION BOUTIQUE LLC
Also Called: Hillary's Fashions
177 Washington Valley Rd (07059-7210)
PHONE..................................732 667-7733
Fax: 732 667-7734
Hillary Scharf,
EMP: 11
SALES (est): 825K Privately Held
SIC: 5621 5632 2335 Boutiques; women's accessory & specialty stores; women's, juniors' & misses' dresses

(G-11553)
HORIZON GROUP USA INC (PA)
45 Technology Dr (07059-5184)
PHONE..................................908 810-1111
Roshan Wijerama, *CEO*
Evan Buzzerio, *President*
Deb Derby, *President*
Michael Heyer, *President*
Marla Canfield, *Vice Pres*
◆ EMP: 150 EST: 2000
SQ FT: 50,000
SALES: 200MM Privately Held
WEB: www.horizongroupusa.com
SIC: 3944 Games, toys & children's vehicles

(G-11554)
HUBER+SUHNER ASTROLAB INC
4 Powderhorn Dr (07059-5105)
PHONE..................................732 560-3800
Andrew Weirback, *CEO*
Lisa Kiernan, *Controller*
EMP: 46
SQ FT: 21,000
SALES (est): 12.1MM
SALES (corp-wide): 782.8MM Privately Held
SIC: 2298 3678 Cable, fiber; electronic connectors

HQ: Huber + Suhner (North America) Corporation
8530 Steele Creek Pl
Charlotte NC 28273
704 790-7300

(G-11555)
II-VI OPTOELECTRONIC DVCS INC (HQ)
141 Mount Bethel Rd (07059-5128)
PHONE..............................908 668-5000
Fax: 908 412-5942
Giovanni Barbarossa, *President*
Gary Ruland, *General Mgr*
Bob Cameron, *Engineer*
Tom Czirok, *Engineer*
Rajat Jain, *Engineer*
▲ EMP: 277
SQ FT: 150,000
SALES (est): 64.5MM
SALES (corp-wide): 972MM **Publicly Held**
WEB: www.anadigics.com
SIC: 3674 Semiconductors & related devices; integrated circuits, semiconductor networks, etc.
PA: Ii-Vi Incorporated
375 Saxonburg Blvd
Saxonburg PA 16056
724 352-4455

(G-11556)
INLC TECHNOLOGY CORPORATION
30 Technology Dr Ste 1d (07059-5177)
PHONE..............................908 834-8390
Clarel Thevenot, *Manager*
Seong W Suh,
EMP: 15
SQ FT: 1,400
SALES (est): 1.1MM **Privately Held**
SIC: 3827 3661 Polarizers; telephone & telegraph apparatus

(G-11557)
JENCKS SIGNS CORP
16 Geiger Ln (07059-5620)
PHONE..............................908 542-1400
Fax: 908 963-5656
Patricia Herman, *President*
Barry Herman, *Admin Sec*
EMP: 4
SQ FT: 5,000
SALES (est): 360K **Privately Held**
SIC: 3993 Electric signs; signs, not made in custom sign painting shops

(G-11558)
LINCOLN MOLD & DIE CORP
13 Deerwood Trl (07059-5562)
PHONE..............................908 241-3344
Vincent Comitini, *President*
Edward Drozd, *President*
John Raymonds, *Chairman*
Catherine Raymonds, *Corp Secy*
EMP: 55 EST: 1954
SQ FT: 25,000
SALES (est): 6.1MM **Privately Held**
WEB: www.lmold.com
SIC: 3544 Forms (molds), for foundry & plastics working machinery

(G-11559)
MEGAPLEX SOFTWARE INC
21 Broadway Rd (07059-5055)
PHONE..............................908 647-3273
Dhiraj Sharma, *President*
EMP: 5
SALES (est): 1MM **Privately Held**
SIC: 7372 7379 Prepackaged software; data processing consultant

(G-11560)
MOLNAR TOOLS INC
3 Stoningham Dr (07059-6740)
PHONE..............................908 580-0671
Charles Molnar, *President*
Sophia Molnar, *Treasurer*
Charles Molnar Jr, *Admin Sec*
EMP: 11
SQ FT: 12,000
SALES (est): 1.6MM **Privately Held**
SIC: 3469 5251 Metal stampings; tools

(G-11561)
MOUNTAIN MILLWORK
142 Mountain Ave (07059-5260)
PHONE..............................908 647-1100
Tom Guarino, *Principal*
EMP: 4
SALES (est): 522.7K **Privately Held**
SIC: 2431 Millwork

(G-11562)
PICUT INDUSTRIES INC (PA)
140 Mount Bethel Rd (07059-5147)
PHONE..............................908 754-1333
Richard Picut, *President*
Ray Mattes, *Vice Pres*
Frederick Picut, *Executive*
EMP: 70
SQ FT: 170,000
SALES (est): 67.3MM **Privately Held**
SIC: 3491 Industrial valves; steam traps

(G-11563)
PICUT MFG CO INC
140 Mount Bethel Rd (07059-5147)
PHONE..............................908 754-1333
Fax: 908 754-3280
Frederick R Picut, *President*
Walter Ryder, *Corp Secy*
Richard Picut, *Vice Pres*
Russell Picut, *Vice Pres*
Cheryl Lloyd, *Controller*
▲ EMP: 95
SQ FT: 50,000
SALES (est): 19.5MM **Privately Held**
WEB: www.picut.com
SIC: 3541 Drilling & boring machines

(G-11564)
PITNEY BOWES INC
15 Mountainview Rd (07059-6711)
PHONE..............................908 903-2870
Scott Powley, *Manager*
EMP: 13
SALES (corp-wide): 3.5B **Publicly Held**
SIC: 3579 7359 Postage meters; business machine & electronic equipment rental services
PA: Pitney Bowes Inc.
3001 Summer St Ste 3
Stamford CT 06905
203 356-5000

(G-11565)
REDPURO LLC
Also Called: Redpuro Import
106 Mount Horeb Rd Apt 8b (07059-5566)
PHONE..............................908 370-4460
Alejandro Flores, *Owner*
EMP: 4
SQ FT: 900
SALES (est): 90K **Privately Held**
SIC: 2084 Wines

(G-11566)
SHERRY INTERNATIONAL INC
31 Mountain Blvd Bldg M (07059-5647)
PHONE..............................908 279-7255
Leilei Wang, *CEO*
Weixing Wang, *President*
▲ EMP: 10
SALES (est): 1.2MM **Privately Held**
SIC: 3825 Frequency meters: electrical, mechanical & electronic

(G-11567)
SIEMENS INDUSTRY INC
163 Washington Valley Rd (07059-7180)
PHONE..............................732 302-1686
David B Blum, *Branch Mgr*
EMP: 4
SALES (corp-wide): 97.7B **Privately Held**
SIC: 3823 Electrodes used in industrial process measurement
HQ: Siemens Industry, Inc.
100 Technology Dr
Alpharetta GA 30005
770 740-3000

(G-11568)
SUPERIOR CUSTOM KITCHENS LLC
126 Mount Bethel Rd (07059-5129)
PHONE..............................908 753-6005
John A Barna,
Joseph Borin,

EMP: 27
SQ FT: 4,000
SALES (est): 3.3MM **Privately Held**
WEB: www.superiorcustomkitchens.com
SIC: 5712 5211 2434 Cabinet work, custom; lumber & other building materials; wood kitchen cabinets

(G-11569)
UNIVERSAL PALLET INC
118 Smoke Rise Dr (07059-6821)
PHONE..............................732 356-2624
Michael Dinardi, *Principal*
EMP: 7
SALES (est): 49.7K **Privately Held**
SIC: 2448 Pallets, wood & wood with metal

(G-11570)
VANTAGE SPCLTY INGREDIENTS INC (DH)
150 Mount Bethel Rd (07059-5192)
PHONE..............................973 345-8600
Julian Steinberg, *CEO*
Diana Tang, *General Mgr*
Christopher Huberstone, *Exec VP*
Anthony Vicale, *Controller*
Cherylin Hynes, *Accounts Mgr*
▲ EMP: 103
SQ FT: 120,000
SALES (est): 31.9MM
SALES (corp-wide): 1.3B **Privately Held**
WEB: www.lipochemicals.com
SIC: 2899 5169 Chemical preparations; chemicals & allied products; adhesives, chemical; aromatic chemicals; chemical bulk station & terminal
HQ: Vantage Specialty Chemicals, Inc.
4650 S Racine Ave
Chicago IL 60609
800 833-2864

(G-11571)
VANTAGE TOOL & MFG INC
223 Stirling Rd (07059-5238)
PHONE..............................908 647-1010
Fax: 908 647-4242
Stephen Heinle, *President*
Nancy D Heinle, *Vice Pres*
EMP: 4
SQ FT: 5,000
SALES (est): 300K **Privately Held**
SIC: 3544 3542 Special dies & tools; machine tools, metal forming type

(G-11572)
WARREN CAPITAL INC
6 Westwood Ct (07059-2704)
PHONE..............................732 910-8134
Wendy Wu, *Principal*
EMP: 4
SALES (est): 250.7K **Privately Held**
SIC: 3442 Metal doors, sash & trim

Washington
Warren County

(G-11573)
ALBEA AMERICAS INC (DH)
191 State Route 31 N (07882-1529)
PHONE..............................908 689-3000
Francois Luscan, *President*
Franois Tassart, *Exec VP*
Jose Filipe, *Vice Pres*
Herv Marion, *Vice Pres*
Douglas Jerman, *Plant Mgr*
◆ EMP: 250
SALES (est): 167.2MM **Privately Held**
SIC: 3312 Pipes & tubes
HQ: Albea Services
Zac Des Barbanniers Le Signac
Gennevilliers 92230
181 932-000

(G-11574)
ARCTIC FOODS INC
Also Called: Jmee Financial Division
251 E Washington Ave (07882-2405)
PHONE..............................908 689-0590
Fax: 908 689-1260
Mark Rossi, *President*
Ezio Rossi, *Chairman*
Joseph Claps, *Vice Pres*
Amanda Rossi, *Sales Staff*

EMP: 24 EST: 1959
SQ FT: 15,000
SALES (est): 2.4MM **Privately Held**
WEB: www.arcticfoods.com
SIC: 5421 5722 5147 5142 Meat markets, including freezer provisioners; food & freezer plans, meat; freezer provisioners, meat; household appliance stores; meats & meat products; packaged frozen goods; frozen specialties

(G-11575)
ARMIN KOSOSKI
Also Called: All Sports Stadium
297 State Route 31 S (07882-4068)
PHONE..............................908 689-0411
Fax: 908 689-4701
Armin Kososki, *Owner*
Lisa Lacey, *Manager*
EMP: 7
SQ FT: 2,100
SALES (est): 1.2MM **Privately Held**
SIC: 5091 5941 5699 5999 Sporting & recreation goods; sporting goods & bicycle shops; sports apparel; trophies & plaques; screen printing

(G-11576)
BASF CORPORATION
Washington New Jersey Site
2 Pleasant View Ave (07882-2320)
PHONE..............................908 689-2500
Martha Brabston, *Branch Mgr*
EMP: 62
SALES (corp-wide): 76B **Privately Held**
WEB: www.basf.com
SIC: 2869 2843 Industrial organic chemicals; surface active agents
HQ: Basf Corporation
100 Park Ave
Florham Park NJ 07932
973 245-6000

(G-11577)
BEMIS COMPANY INC
31 State St (07882)
PHONE..............................908 689-3000
Eduardo Posada, *Business Mgr*
Angela Lowe, *Plant Mgr*
Daniel Duggan, *Prdtn Mgr*
Eric Mann, *Production*
Liliana Garcia, *Buyer*
EMP: 450
SALES (corp-wide): 4B **Publicly Held**
WEB: www.pechineyplasticpackaging.com
SIC: 3498 Fabricated pipe & fittings
PA: Bemis Company, Inc.
2301 Industrial Dr
Neenah WI 54956
920 527-5000

(G-11578)
BIG BUCKS ENTERPRISES INC
Also Called: Massina Wildlife Management
55 Willow St (07882-2138)
P.O. Box 122, Chester (07930-0122)
PHONE..............................908 320-7009
James Messina, *Vice Pres*
▲ EMP: 20
SALES (est): 193K **Privately Held**
SIC: 5191 2879 Fertilizer & fertilizer materials; fungicides, herbicides

(G-11579)
CANDLE ARTISANS INCORPORATED
253 E Washington Ave (07882-2405)
P.O. Box 190 (07882-0190)
PHONE..............................908 689-2000
Fax: 908 689-2387
Robert Rumfield, *President*
▲ EMP: 20
SQ FT: 36,000
SALES (est): 2.4MM **Privately Held**
WEB: www.candleartisans.com
SIC: 3999 Candles

(G-11580)
CAPRA CUSTOM CABINETRY
259 E Washington Ave (07882-2405)
PHONE..............................908 797-9848
John Capra, *Principal*
EMP: 4
SALES (est): 220K **Privately Held**
SIC: 2434 Wood kitchen cabinets

▲ = Import ▼=Export
◆ =Import/Export

(G-11581)
GOOD IMPRESSIONS INC (PA)
325 W Washington Ave (07882-2153)
PHONE.....................................908 689-3071
Marian Kennedy, *President*
Bonnie Groff, *Accounts Mgr*
Jennifer Bellis, *Graphic Designe*
EMP: 10
SQ FT: 2,500
SALES (est): 1.1MM **Privately Held**
WEB: www.good-impressions.com
SIC: 2752 7334 Commercial printing, off-
set; photocopying & duplicating services

(G-11582)
HAZ LABORATORIES
39 Hartmans Corner Rd (07882-4378)
PHONE.....................................908 453-3300
Fax: 908 453-3310
Henry Zajac Jr, *Owner*
EMP: 12
SQ FT: 10,000
SALES (est): 1.3MM **Privately Held**
WEB: www.mu-tron.com
SIC: 3679 3625 3841 Electronic circuits;
industrial controls: push button, selector
switches, pilot; surgical & medical instru-
ments

(G-11583)
HERBALIST & ALCHEMIST INC
51 S Wandling Ave (07882-2192)
PHONE.....................................908 689-9020
Beth Lambert, *CEO*
David Winston, *President*
Elizabeth Lambert, *Treasurer*
Russell Chell, *Shareholder*
EMP: 10
SQ FT: 9,000
SALES (est): 1.4MM **Privately Held**
WEB: www.herbalist-alchemist.com
SIC: 2833 Medicinals & botanicals

(G-11584)
JOST BROTHERS JEWELRY MFG CORP
295 Jost Dr (07882)
PHONE.....................................908 453-2266
Stephen Jost, *President*
Charles Jost, *Vice Pres*
EMP: 13 **EST:** 1935
SALES (est): 1.7MM **Privately Held**
SIC: 3911 Jewelry, precious metal

(G-11585)
MYSTIC TIMBER LLC
95 Youmans Ave (07882-1807)
PHONE.....................................908 223-7878
Bruce Jorgensen,
Deb Jorgensen,
EMP: 4 **EST:** 2010
SALES (est): 325.4K **Privately Held**
SIC: 3443 Boiler shop products: boilers,
smokestacks, steel tanks

(G-11586)
RDO INDUCTION LTD LIABILITY CO
2170 State Route 57 W (07882-3523)
PHONE.....................................908 835-7222
Robert Okner, *Principal*
◆ EMP: 6
SALES (est): 8.1K **Privately Held**
SIC: 3999 Heating pads, nonelectric

(G-11587)
SCHNEIDERS KITCHENS INC
252 State Route 31 N (07882-1550)
PHONE.....................................908 689-5649
Fax: 908 689-8537
Walter Schneider, *President*
Silvia Winiger, *Vice Pres*
Adolph Schneider, *Treasurer*
EMP: 7
SQ FT: 9,000
SALES (est): 910.8K **Privately Held**
SIC: 5712 2511 Cabinet work, custom;
wood household furniture

(G-11588)
STEPHEN SWINTON STUDIO INC
49 New Hampton Rd (07882-4003)
PHONE.....................................908 537-9135
Stephen Swinton, *President*
EMP: 5

SALES: 275K **Privately Held**
WEB: www.swintonstudio.com
SIC: 7336 7374 7312 3993 Graphic arts
& related design; service bureau, computer; poster advertising, outdoor; signs &
advertising specialties; commercial photography; custom computer programming
services

(G-11589)
T M BAXTER SERVICES LLC
1307 Washington Gdns (07882-2174)
PHONE.....................................908 500-9065
Thomas Zuchowski, *President*
EMP: 25
SQ FT: 2,500
SALES (est): 3.1MM **Privately Held**
SIC: 2499 1741 Veneer work, inlaid; ma-
sonry & other stonework

(G-11590)
WITTE CO INC
507 Rte 31 S (07882)
P.O. Box 47 (07882-0047)
PHONE.....................................908 689-6500
Fax: 908 537-6806
Richard B Witte, *CEO*
Tyson B Witte, *President*
▲ EMP: 41
SQ FT: 5,600
SALES: 7.3MM **Privately Held**
WEB: www.witte.com
SIC: 3559 Chemical machinery & equip-
ment; plastics working machinery

Watchung
Somerset County

(G-11591)
FANWOOD CRUSHED STONE COMPANY
Also Called: Welding Materials
1 New Providence Rd (07069-5015)
PHONE.....................................908 322-7840
Fax: 908 233-9440
Chuck Valley, *Manager*
EMP: 70
SALES (corp-wide): 34.9MM **Privately Held**
SIC: 1411 5032 Granite, dimension-quar-
rying; stone, crushed or broken
PA: Fanwood Crushed Stone Company Inc
141 Central Ave
Westfield NJ
908 233-4444

(G-11592)
L & Z TOOL AND ENGINEERING INC
Also Called: La Marca Industries
1691 Us Highway 22 (07069-6501)
PHONE.....................................908 322-2220
Fax: 908 322-6163
Thomas Lamarca, *President*
Lena Lamarca, *Corp Secy*
Lance Lamonte, *Vice Pres*
Frank Cooper, *Mktg Dir*
Thomas La Marca, *Director*
EMP: 32
SQ FT: 20,000
SALES (est): 5.5MM **Privately Held**
WEB: www.lztool.com
SIC: 3544 Special dies & tools

(G-11593)
MEDISCOPE MANUFACTURING INC (PA)
744 Mountain Blvd Fl 2w (07069-6297)
PHONE.....................................908 756-2411
Dan Helme, *President*
Daniel Helme, *COO*
EMP: 7
SQ FT: 2,000
SALES (est): 5MM **Privately Held**
WEB: www.mediscope-mfg.com
SIC: 3841 Surgical & medical instruments

(G-11594)
STANDARD TILE WATCHUNG CORP
1515 Us Highway 22 Ste 24 (07069-6516)
PHONE.....................................908 754-4200

Fax: 908 754-4403
Bill Spina, *President*
▲ EMP: 5 **EST:** 1942
SALES (est): 450K **Privately Held**
SIC: 3253 Ceramic wall & floor tile

(G-11595)
SUN PLASTICS CO INC
35 Blue Wolf Trl (07069-5425)
PHONE.....................................908 490-0870
Victoria Salerno, *President*
Jerry R Salerno, *Vice Pres*
EMP: 15
SQ FT: 13,000
SALES (est): 980K **Privately Held**
SIC: 3652 Phonograph record blanks;
phonograph records, prerecorded

(G-11596)
SUPPLIES-SUPPLIES INC
85 Maple St (07069-6311)
PHONE.....................................908 272-5100
Fax: 908 272-5192
Carl Streko, *President*
Bette Jo Streko, *Director*
EMP: 16
SQ FT: 2,300
SALES (est): 4MM **Privately Held**
WEB: www.ssofficesupplies.com
SIC: 5021 5112 5943 2752 Office furni-
ture; school desks; stationery & office
supplies; office forms & supplies; busi-
ness form & card printing, lithographic

(G-11597)
WELDON ASPHALT CORP
1 New Providence Rd (07069-5015)
PHONE.....................................908 322-7840
Fax: 908 322-4198
Dick Meyers, *Manager*
EMP: 25
SALES (corp-wide): 6.7MM **Privately Held**
SIC: 2951 Asphalt paving mixtures &
blocks
PA: Weldon Asphalt Corp
141 Central Ave
Westfield NJ
908 233-4444

Waterford Works
Camden County

(G-11598)
JAMES R MACAULEY INC
1 Industrial Dr (08089)
PHONE.....................................856 767-3474
George Macauley, *President*
EMP: 1
SQ FT: 13,000
SALES: 2MM **Privately Held**
SIC: 4953 5085 2842 Recycling, waste
materials; commercial containers; spe-
cialty cleaning, polishes & sanitation
goods

Wayne
Passaic County

(G-11599)
202 SMOOTHIE LLC
11 Danielle Dr (07470-2538)
PHONE.....................................973 985-4973
Koushby Majagah, *Principal*
EMP: 5
SALES (est): 235.2K **Privately Held**
SIC: 2037 Frozen fruits & vegetables

(G-11600)
AARISSE HEALTH CARE PRODUCTS
11 Robin Hood Way (07470-5427)
PHONE.....................................973 686-1811
Jeff Behr, *Manager*
EMP: 6
SALES (est): 210.5K **Privately Held**
WEB: www.aarisse.com
SIC: 8082 3841 Home health care serv-
ices; surgical & medical instruments

(G-11601)
ACCELEDEV CHEMICAL LLC (PA)
18 Apple Ln (07470-1964)
P.O. Box 3431 (07474-3431)
PHONE.....................................862 239-1524
Charles Lewis, *President*
EMP: 5
SALES (est): 613K **Privately Held**
SIC: 8999 2899 Chemical consultant;
chemical preparations

(G-11602)
ALAN CHEMICAL CORPORATION INC
573 Valley Rd Ste 1 (07470-3552)
PHONE.....................................973 628-7777
Fax: 973 628-8309
Alan Braxton, *President*
EMP: 8
SALES (est): 1.1MM **Privately Held**
SIC: 2891 Adhesives & sealants

(G-11603)
ALL AMERICAN OIL RECOVERY CO
1067 State Route 23 (07470-6649)
PHONE.....................................973 628-9278
Roy R Vanvarick, *President*
Robert Vanvarick, *Treasurer*
Ann Billack, *Admin Sec*
EMP: 20
SALES (est): 3.3MM **Privately Held**
WEB: www.vanvarickandsons.com
SIC: 1382 4959 Oil & gas exploration
services; sanitary services

(G-11604)
AMERICAN RENOLIT CORPORATION
1310 Hamburg Tpke Ste 5 (07470-4064)
PHONE.....................................973 706-6912
EMP: 5
SALES (corp-wide): 1.9B **Privately Held**
SIC: 3081 5162 Plastic film & sheet; plas-
tics film
HQ: American Renolit Corporation
1207 E Lincolnway
La Porte IN 46350
219 324-6886

(G-11605)
ANODIZING CORPORATION
Also Called: J E B Urban Renewal Associates
10 Legrande Ter (07470-6029)
PHONE.....................................973 694-6449
Jack Lavorgna, *President*
EMP: 8 **EST:** 1974
SQ FT: 16,800
SALES (est): 460K **Privately Held**
SIC: 3471 Anodizing (plating) of metals or
formed products

(G-11606)
ATLANTIC EXTERIOR WALL SYSTEMS
25 Mansard Ct (07470-6040)
PHONE.....................................973 646-8200
Joseph Farina, *President*
Nicholas D'Albo, *Vice Pres*
Salvatore D'Albo, *Vice Pres*
▲ EMP: 55
SQ FT: 35,000
SALES (est): 11.5MM **Privately Held**
SIC: 2439 1791 Trusses, except roof: lam-
inated lumber; exterior wall system instal-
lation

(G-11607)
BAE SYSTEMS INFO & ELEC SYS
164 Totowa Rd (07470-3118)
PHONE.....................................973 633-6000
Ronald Day, *General Mgr*
Carlo Lisica, *Engineer*
Roger E Johnson, *Branch Mgr*
EMP: 750
SALES (corp-wide): 24.2B **Privately Held**
WEB: www.iesi.na.baesystems.com
SIC: 3812 Aircraft/aerospace flight instru-
ments & guidance systems; defense sys-
tems & equipment

HQ: Bae Systems Information And Electronic Systems Integration Inc.
65 Spit Brook Rd
Nashua NH 03060
603 885-4321

(G-11608)
BEL-ART PRODUCTS INC (DH)
661 Rte 23 (07470-6814)
PHONE....................................973 694-0500
David Landsberger, *President*
Brad Mahood, *COO*
John Denkler, *Vice Pres*
Anthony Chiarella, *Purch Mgr*
Carl Sisco, *QC Mgr*
◆ EMP: 40 EST: 1945
SQ FT: 62,000
SALES: 30MM
SALES (corp-wide): 1.4B **Privately Held**
WEB: www.nutechmfg.com
SIC: 3089 3479 Trays, plastic; coating of metals with plastic or resins
HQ: S P Industries, Inc.
935 Mearns Rd
Warminster PA 18974
215 672-7800

(G-11609)
BIMBO BAKERIES USA INC
100 Riverview Dr (07470-3104)
PHONE....................................973 872-6167
EMP: 24 **Privately Held**
SIC: 2051 Bakery: wholesale or wholesale/retail combined
HQ: Bimbo Bakeries Usa, Inc
255 Business Center Dr # 200
Horsham PA 19044
215 347-5500

(G-11610)
BMCA HOLDINGS CORPORATION (DH)
Also Called: Building Materials Corp Amer
1361 Alps Rd (07470-3700)
PHONE....................................973 628-3000
Fax: 973 628-3335
Robert Tasaro, *Ch of Bd*
Daniel Goldstein, *Senior VP*
Adam Panick, *Senior VP*
Dave Rueter, *Senior VP*
Dawn Skare, *Senior VP*
EMP: 44
SALES (est): 1.3B
SALES (corp-wide): 1.5B **Privately Held**
SIC: 2493 Insulation & roofing material, reconstituted wood
HQ: G-I Holdings Inc.
1361 Alps Rd
Wayne NJ 07470
973 628-3000

(G-11611)
BONLAND INDUSTRIES INC (PA)
50 Newark Pompton Tpke (07470-6698)
P.O. Box 200 (07474-0200)
PHONE....................................973 694-3211
Fax: 973 628-1120
William Boniface, *CEO*
Andrew Boniface, *President*
Linda West, *Exec VP*
Ken Crowley, *Project Mgr*
Jeff Miller, *Project Mgr*
EMP: 99
SQ FT: 30,000
SALES (est): 70.5MM **Privately Held**
WEB: www.bonlandhvac.com
SIC: 1711 3444 Ventilation & duct work contractor; warm air heating & air conditioning contractor; mechanical contractor; ventilators, sheet metal

(G-11612)
BOSTON SCIENTIFIC CORPORATION
45 Barbour Pond Dr (07470-2094)
PHONE....................................973 709-7000
Fax: 973 709-6502
Paul Southworth, *President*
Faythe Williams, *Marketing Staff*
EMP: 40
SALES (corp-wide): 9B **Publicly Held**
WEB: www.bsci.com
SIC: 3841 3842 Surgical & medical instruments; surgical appliances & supplies

PA: Boston Scientific Corporation
300 Boston Scientific Way
Marlborough MA 01752
508 683-4000

(G-11613)
BP CORPORATION NORTH AMER INC
1500 Valley Rd (07470-2040)
PHONE....................................973 633-2200
Rodger Harris, *Manager*
EMP: 8
SALES (corp-wide): 240.2B **Privately Held**
WEB: www.bpamoco.com
SIC: 2911 Petroleum refining
HQ: Bp Corporation North America Inc.
501 Westlake Park Blvd
Houston TX 77079
281 366-2000

(G-11614)
BP LUBRICANTS USA INC (DH)
Also Called: B P
1500 Valley Rd (07470-2040)
PHONE....................................973 633-2200
Fax: 973 633-9867
Marci Brand, *CEO*
Robert Meyers, *General Mgr*
Marianne Geuss, *Vice Pres*
Donna Young, *Vice Pres*
Emiliano Pasini, *Project Mgr*
◆ EMP: 300
SQ FT: 90,000
SALES (est): 380.8MM
SALES (corp-wide): 240.2B **Privately Held**
WEB: www.castrolna.com
SIC: 2992 Lubricating oils & greases
HQ: Bp America Inc
4101 Winfield Rd Ste 200
Warrenville IL 60555
630 420-5111

(G-11615)
BROOKLINE CHEMICAL CORP
26 Hanes Dr (07470-4722)
PHONE....................................301 767-1177
Steve Hoh, *Branch Mgr*
EMP: 22
SALES (corp-wide): 6MM **Privately Held**
WEB: www.brookline-chem.com
SIC: 2261 Chemical coating or treating of cotton broadwoven fabrics
PA: Brookline Chemical Corp.
9817 Inglemere Dr
Bethesda MD 20817
301 767-1177

(G-11616)
BUILDING MATERIALS MFG CORP
1361 Alps Rd (07470-3700)
PHONE....................................973 628-3000
Richard A Nowak, *President*
EMP: 1
SALES (est): 7.7MM
SALES (corp-wide): 1.5B **Privately Held**
SIC: 2493 Reconstituted wood products
HQ: Standard Industries Inc.
1 Campus Dr
Parsippany NJ 07054

(G-11617)
C & N PACKAGING INC
Also Called: Suffolk Molds
155 Us Highway 46 Ste 200 (07470-6819)
PHONE....................................631 491-1400
Alain Mutschler, *CEO*
▲ EMP: 79
SQ FT: 32,000
SALES (est): 14.8MM
SALES (corp-wide): 7.3MM **Privately Held**
WEB: www.cnpkg.com
SIC: 3089 Closures, plastic
HQ: Mar-Lee Companies, Inc.
180 Authority Dr
Fitchburg MA 01420
978 343-9600

(G-11618)
CARDINAL INTERNATIONAL INC
30 Corporate Dr (07470-3113)
P.O. Box 897, Pine Brook (07058-0897)
PHONE....................................973 628-0900

Fax: 973 628-7639
Bryan Ovouke, *President*
Nichole Vanderhoof, *Mktg Coord*
EMP: 18
SALES (est): 2.4MM
SALES (corp-wide): 4.9MM **Privately Held**
SIC: 3229 Pressed & blown glass
PA: Arc Holdings
104 Avenue Du General De Gaulle
Arques 62510
321 954-647

(G-11619)
CLIFTON ADHESIVE INC
48 Burgess Pl (07470-6734)
PHONE....................................973 694-0845
Fax: 973 694-5678
Robert A Lefelar, *President*
Dan Higgins, *Engineer*
Rosemary Conklin, *Administration*
◆ EMP: 25
SQ FT: 22,000
SALES (est): 5.4MM **Privately Held**
WEB: www.cliftonadhesive.com
SIC: 2891 Adhesives, plastic

(G-11620)
COCO INTERNATIONAL INC
6 Highpoint Dr (07470-7423)
PHONE....................................973 694-1200
Don Lee, *CEO*
Michael Kim, *Accounts Mgr*
Bud Reisman, *Accounts Mgr*
▲ EMP: 20 EST: 2008
SALES (est): 3.5MM **Privately Held**
SIC: 2041 5149 Grain cereals, cracked; breakfast cereals

(G-11621)
CREATIVE INDUSTRIAL KITCHENS
8 Leo Pl (07470-7272)
PHONE....................................973 633-0420
Fax: 973 633-7022
Tom Walsh, *Owner*
EMP: 5
SQ FT: 5,000
SALES: 500K **Privately Held**
SIC: 3564 1711 Blowers & fans; ventilation & duct work contractor

(G-11622)
CYBEREXTRUDERCOM INC
1401 Valley Rd Ste 208 (07470-2074)
PHONE....................................973 623-7900
Fax: 973 623-8900
John Ives, *President*
EMP: 4
SALES: 1MM **Privately Held**
WEB: www.cyberextruder.com
SIC: 7372 7371 7373 Prepackaged software; custom computer programming services; computer integrated systems design

(G-11623)
DI-FERRARO INC
Also Called: Mead Wilbert
28 Burgess Pl (07470-6734)
PHONE....................................973 694-7200
Fax: 973 694-4313
Mario Ferraro Sr, *President*
Mario Ferraro Jr, *President*
Anna Ferraro, *Vice Pres*
EMP: 40 EST: 1937
SQ FT: 20,000
SALES (est): 7.7MM **Privately Held**
SIC: 3272 Burial vaults, concrete or precast terrazzo

(G-11624)
DMJ INDUSTRIAL SERVICES LLC
1 Hilltop Ter (07470-5807)
PHONE....................................973 692-8406
Stephen Sangle, *Owner*
EMP: 7
SALES: 120K **Privately Held**
SIC: 3441 Fabricated structural metal

(G-11625)
DOLAN & TRAYNOR INC
32 Riverview Dr (07470-3102)
PHONE....................................973 696-8700
Fax: 973 696-8282

Timothy J Traynor, *President*
B Michael Dolan, *Exec VP*
Tim Dolan, *Vice Pres*
Stephen G Wilkinson, *Vice Pres*
Gary Mastrache, *CFO*
EMP: 36
SQ FT: 40,000
SALES: 20MM **Privately Held**
WEB: www.dolan-traynor.com
SIC: 2421 5032 Building & structural materials, wood; marble building stone

(G-11626)
DONNELLY INDUSTRIES INC
Also Called: Donnelly Construction
557 Rte 23 (07470-6818)
PHONE....................................973 672-1800
Rod Donnelly, *CEO*
Gerard J Donnelly Jr, *President*
Chris Powers, *President*
Shahzad Khan, *COO*
Irshad Khan, *Vice Pres*
▲ EMP: 95
SQ FT: 32,000
SALES: 41.7MM **Privately Held**
WEB: www.donnellyind.com
SIC: 1542 2431 Commercial & office buildings, renovation & repair; millwork

(G-11627)
ENCORE LED LTG LTD LBLTY CO
155 Us Highway 46 (07470-6831)
PHONE....................................866 694-4533
William Dato,
EMP: 8
SALES (est): 644.5K **Privately Held**
SIC: 3646 3645 3648 Commercial indusl & institutional electric lighting fixtures; garden, patio, walkway & yard lighting fixtures: electric; decorative area lighting fixtures; street lighting fixtures

(G-11628)
EPOCH PRESS INC
7 Highpoint Dr (07470-7432)
PHONE....................................973 357-0080
Fax: 973 357-0080
Eva Werthen, *President*
Paulina Werthen, *Principal*
▲ EMP: 24
SALES (est): 4MM **Privately Held**
SIC: 2741 Miscellaneous publishing

(G-11629)
ESPERTECH INC
26 Hamilton Ave (07470-3059)
P.O. Box 3129 (07474-3129)
PHONE....................................973 577-6406
Thomas Bernhardt, *CTO*
EMP: 11
SALES (est): 637.9K **Privately Held**
SIC: 7372 Utility computer software

(G-11630)
EVA MARIA WOLFE
6 Westbelt (07470-6810)
PHONE....................................412 777-2000
Bayer Healthcare Phrm, *Principal*
EMP: 6
SALES (est): 659.5K **Privately Held**
SIC: 2834 Pharmaceutical preparations

(G-11631)
EZ GENERAL CONSTRUCTION CORP
Also Called: Marble and Granite
155 Webster Dr (07470-5449)
PHONE....................................201 223-1101
Julio C Bonilla, *President*
Arturo Bonilla, *Vice Pres*
EMP: 6
SALES (est): 560.9K **Privately Held**
SIC: 3281 1522 1521 Cut stone & stone products; residential construction; single-family home remodeling, additions & repairs

(G-11632)
FIDELITY INDUSTRIES INC (PA)
Also Called: Fidelity Wallcoverings
559 Rte 23 (07470-6832)
PHONE....................................973 696-9120
Fax: 973 696-4123
Dvosia Rivkin, *President*
Samuel Brook, *Vice Pres*

◆ **EMP:** 40 **EST:** 1974
SQ FT: 20,000
SALES (est): 17.5MM **Privately Held**
WEB: www.fidelitywall.com
SIC: 3069 Wallcoverings, rubber

(G-11633)
FILTREX INC
450 Hamburg Tpke Ste 2 (07470-8485)
P.O. Box 2273 (07474-2273)
PHONE..................973 595-0400
Fax: 973 595-6506
Ken Bergstrom, *President*
Trish Koberowski, *Corp Secy*
EMP: 10
SQ FT: 8,000
SALES (est): 1.5MM **Privately Held**
SIC: 3589 Swimming pool filter & water conditioning systems; water treatment equipment, industrial

(G-11634)
FIN-TEK CORPORATION (PA)
Also Called: Fin-Tek Ozone
6 Leo Pl (07470-7272)
PHONE..................973 628-2988
Donald Finnegan, *President*
Mary Finnegan, *Vice Pres*
Paul Finnegan, *Treasurer*
EMP: 7
SQ FT: 5,000
SALES (est): 1.8MM **Privately Held**
WEB: www.fin-tek.com
SIC: 8711 3589 Engineering services; sewage & water treatment equipment

(G-11635)
FOREMOST CORP
2025 Hamburg Tpke Ste A (07470-6250)
PHONE..................973 839-3360
Fax: 973 839-5926
William F Formosa Jr, *President*
Doris Formosa, *Corp Secy*
EMP: 3
SQ FT: 750
SALES (est): 1MM **Privately Held**
SIC: 5065 3679 Electronic parts; electronic circuits

(G-11636)
FOUR WAY ENTERPRISES INC
Also Called: Butler Sign Co.
582 Fairfield Rd (07470-7354)
PHONE..................973 633-5757
Fax: 973 633-7449
John Janis Jr, *President*
Brenda Janis, *Treasurer*
Brian Travers, *Marketing Staff*
EMP: 16
SQ FT: 6,500
SALES (est): 2.1MM **Privately Held**
WEB: www.butlersignco.com
SIC: 3993 Electric signs; neon signs

(G-11637)
G T ASSOCIATES
440 Indian Rd (07470-4914)
P.O. Box 2005 (07474-2005)
PHONE..................973 694-6040
Fax: 973 694-6493
Arthur L Tambe, *President*
Sam Giovino, *Admin Sec*
EMP: 8
SALES (est): 650K **Privately Held**
SIC: 3674 Semiconductors & related devices

(G-11638)
G-I HOLDINGS INC (HQ)
Also Called: G A F
1361 Alps Rd (07470-3700)
PHONE..................973 628-3000
Fax: 973 628-3865
Robert B Tafaro, *CEO*
Peter Ganz, *President*
Susan Yoss, *President*
Joe Gregory, *General Mgr*
John M Sergey, *Exec VP*
▲ **EMP:** 5
SALES (est): 1.4B
SALES (corp-wide): 1.5B **Privately Held**
SIC: 2869 2843 3295 Solvents, organic; surface active agents; roofing granules

PA: G Holdings Inc.
1 Campus Dr
Parsippany NJ 07054
973 628-3000

(G-11639)
GAF ELK MATERIALS CORPORATION
1361 Alps Rd (07470-3700)
P.O. Box 402, Broadway (08808-0402)
PHONE..................973 628-4083
Robert B Tafaro, *CEO*
Janssen Hunter, *Purch Mgr*
Tony Vallance, *Sales Staff*
Karl Luechau, *Manager*
Matthew Martin, *Manager*
▲ **EMP:** 137
SALES (est): 57.6MM **Privately Held**
SIC: 3271 3272 3444 Roof ballast block, concrete; roofing tile & slabs, concrete; metal roofing & roof drainage equipment; roof deck, sheet metal

(G-11640)
GETINGE GROUP LOGISTICS AMERIC
45 Barbour Pond Dr (07470-2094)
PHONE..................973 709-6000
Victor Guzman,
EMP: 40
SALES (est): 1.2MM **Privately Held**
SIC: 3841 3845 Surgical & medical instruments; medical cleaning equipment, ultrasonic

(G-11641)
GILL ASSOCIATES LLC
Also Called: Gill Assoc Idntfcation Systems
2025 Hamburg Tpke Ste M (07470-6250)
PHONE..................973 835-5456
Fax: 973 835-3235
Alicia Zagorski, *Sales Executive*
John D Gill,
Nemesio Torres, *Administration*
EMP: 6
SQ FT: 1,500
SALES (est): 825K **Privately Held**
SIC: 5043 3089 5946 Photographic equipment & supplies; laminating of plastic; photographic supplies

(G-11642)
GRAPHIC PACKAGING INTL INC
5 Haul Rd (07470-6624)
PHONE..................973 709-9100
EMP: 6 **Publicly Held**
SIC: 2631 Container, packaging & boxboard
HQ: Graphic Packaging International, Llc
1500 Riveredge Pkwy # 100
Atlanta GA 30328

(G-11643)
GRAPHIC PACKAGING INTL LLC
Also Called: Altivity Packaging
5 Haul Rd (07470-6624)
PHONE..................732 424-2100
Anthony Kolenski, *Manager*
EMP: 200 **Publicly Held**
SIC: 2631 Folding boxboard
HQ: Graphic Packaging International, Llc
1500 Riveredge Pkwy # 100
Atlanta GA 30328

(G-11644)
GRIMBILAS ENTERPRISES CORP
Also Called: Tornqvist Div
29 Hanes Dr (07470-4721)
PHONE..................973 686-5999
John Grimbilas, *President*
Kenneth Grimbilas, *Vice Pres*
Peter Grimbilas, *Vice Pres*
Robert Grimbilas, *Vice Pres*
EMP: 20
SQ FT: 28,000
SALES (est): 2.8MM **Privately Held**
SIC: 3441 Fabricated structural metal; building components, structural steel

(G-11645)
HAIER APPLIANCE PRODUCTS LP (DH)
Also Called: GE Appliances
1800 Valley Rd (07470-2047)
PHONE..................973 617-1800
Charles Blankenship, *Partner*
▲ **EMP:** 1
SALES (est): 6.2MM
SALES (corp-wide): 24B **Privately Held**
SIC: 3491 Boiler gauge cocks
HQ: Haier Us Appliance Solutions, Inc.
4000 Buechel Bank Rd
Louisville KY 40225
502 452-4666

(G-11646)
HAYDON CORPORATION (PA)
415 Hamburg Tpke Ste 1 (07470-2164)
PHONE..................973 904-0800
Doug H Hillman, *President*
Giuseppe Testa, *Vice Pres*
Richard Phelan, *VP Opers*
Edward Quist, *Transportation*
Kathy Passaro, *Purch Mgr*
▲ **EMP:** 90
SQ FT: 105,000
SALES (est): 63MM **Privately Held**
WEB: www.2haydon.com
SIC: 3449 3634 3567 Miscellaneous metalwork; heating units, electric (radiant heat): baseboard or wall; industrial furnaces & ovens

(G-11647)
HERBERT J HINCHMAN & SON INC
26 Pike Dr (07470-2493)
PHONE..................973 942-2063
Fax: 973 942-9319
Donald H Hinchman, *President*
Donald J Hinchman, *President*
EMP: 20
SQ FT: 7,500
SALES (est): 3.2MM **Privately Held**
SIC: 3273 5032 Ready-mixed concrete; gravel

(G-11648)
HEROS SALUTE AWARDS CO
1875 State Route 23 Ste 1 (07470-7528)
PHONE..................973 696-5085
Fax: 973 696-9114
Robert Terry, *President*
EMP: 6
SQ FT: 1,125
SALES (est): 826.8K **Privately Held**
WEB: www.herossalute.com
SIC: 5999 3479 3993 Trophies & plaques; engraving jewelry silverware, or metal; signs & advertising specialties

(G-11649)
IMAGE MAKERS INSTANT PRINTING
1581 State Route 23 (07470-7506)
PHONE..................973 633-1771
Fax: 973 628-8238
Gino Nuzzo, *President*
EMP: 5
SALES: 450K **Privately Held**
SIC: 2752 Commercial printing, offset

(G-11650)
INDUSTRIAL HABONIM VALVES & AC
22 Riverview Dr Ste 103 (07470-3100)
PHONE..................201 820-3184
Josef Dotan, *President*
▲ **EMP:** 10 **EST:** 2008
SALES (est): 1.9MM **Privately Held**
SIC: 3491 3593 5085 Industrial valves; fluid power cylinders & actuators; valves, pistons & fittings

(G-11651)
INNOVATIVE RESIN SYSTEMS INC (PA)
70 Verkade Dr (07470-8215)
PHONE..................973 465-6887
Pinakin Patel, *President*
John Khosdeghian, *CFO*
▲ **EMP:** 20
SQ FT: 3,500

SALES: 6.1MM **Privately Held**
WEB: www.innovativeresinsystems.com
SIC: 2821 Epoxy resins

(G-11652)
INNOVATIVE RESIN SYSTEMS INC
70 Verkade Dr (07470-8215)
PHONE..................973 633-5342
Pinakin Patel, *President*
EMP: 15
SALES (corp-wide): 6.1MM **Privately Held**
WEB: www.innovativeresinsystems.com
SIC: 2821 Epoxy resins
PA: Innovative Resin Systems, Inc.
70 Verkade Dr
Wayne NJ 07470
973 465-6887

(G-11653)
INTERNTONAL SPECIALTY PDTS INC (DH)
Also Called: Ashland
1361 Alps Rd (07470-3700)
PHONE..................859 815-3333
Fax: 973 628-3432
Sunil Kumar, *CEO*
Douglas Vaughan, *CFO*
Susan B Yoss, *Treasurer*
Pierre Varin, *Sales Dir*
Gil Nollora, *Manager*
◆ **EMP:** 725
SQ FT: 100,000
SALES (est): 511.5MM
SALES (corp-wide): 3.2B **Publicly Held**
WEB: www.ispcorp.com
SIC: 2869 2821 2843 2842 Amines, acids, salts, esters; plastics materials & resins; surface active agents; specialty cleaning, polishes & sanitation goods; chemical preparations
HQ: Ashland Llc
50 E Rivercenter Blvd # 1600
Covington KY 41011
859 815-3333

(G-11654)
ISP CHEMCO LLC (PA)
1361 Alps Rd (07470-3700)
PHONE..................973 628-4000
Sunil Kumar, *CEO*
EMP: 2
SALES (est): 150.8MM **Privately Held**
SIC: 2869 Industrial organic chemicals

(G-11655)
ISP GLOBAL TECHNOLOGIES INC (DH)
1361 Alps Rd (07470-3700)
PHONE..................973 628-4000
Sunil Kamar, *President*
Richard Weinberg, *Exec VP*
Susan Yoss, *Treasurer*
EMP: 10
SQ FT: 100,000
SALES (est): 916.4MM
SALES (corp-wide): 3.2B **Publicly Held**
SIC: 3295 2869 Minerals, ground or treated; industrial organic chemicals
HQ: Ashland Llc
50 E Rivercenter Blvd # 1600
Covington KY 41011
859 815-3333

(G-11656)
ISP GLOBAL TECHNOLOGIES LLC (DH)
1361 Alps Rd (07470-3700)
PHONE..................973 628-4000
Sunil Kamar, *CEO*
EMP: 3
SALES (est): 1.9MM
SALES (corp-wide): 3.2B **Publicly Held**
SIC: 3295 2869 Minerals, ground or treated; industrial organic chemicals

(G-11657)
JVC INDUSTRIAL AMERICA INC (DH)
1700 Valley Rd Ste 1 (07470-2045)
PHONE..................800 247-3608
Fax: 973 317-5010
Fuji Sawa, *President*
Gregory Cameron, *Vice Pres*

Matt Parkinson, *Engineer*
Taka Nami, *Treasurer*
▼ **EMP:** 45 **EST:** 1996
SALES (est): 5.8MM
SALES (corp-wide): 2.8B **Privately Held**
SIC: 3651 8741 Television receiving sets; management services
HQ: Jvckenwood Usa Corporation
　　2201 E Dominguez St
　　Long Beach CA 90810
　　310 639-9000

(G-11658)
JVCKENWOOD USA CORPORATION
1700 Valley Rd (07470-2045)
PHONE..................................973 317-5000
Kazuhiro Aigami, *CEO*
Takeshi Yamasaki, *Engineer*
Jamie Pasley, *Marketing Mgr*
Michele Porter, *Administration*
EMP: 29
SALES (corp-wide): 2.8B **Privately Held**
SIC: 3651 Home entertainment equipment, electronic
HQ: Jvckenwood Usa Corporation
　　2201 E Dominguez St
　　Long Beach CA 90810
　　310 639-9000

(G-11659)
KOP MARBLE GRANITE INC
155 Lions Head Dr W (07470-4002)
PHONE..................................973 283-8000
EMP: 5
SALES (est): 246K **Privately Held**
SIC: 1423 Diorite, crushed & broken-quarrying

(G-11660)
KROWNE METAL CORP
100 Haul Rd (07470-6616)
PHONE..................................973 305-3300
Roger Forman, *President*
Frank Bastante, *Exec VP*
Paul Cali, *Sales Mgr*
Lauren Lomoriello, *Executive Asst*
Pete Chritis,
▲ **EMP:** 50 **EST:** 1948
SQ FT: 80,000
SALES (est): 13.1MM **Privately Held**
WEB: www.krowne.com
SIC: 3585 Soda fountain & beverage dispensing equipment & parts

(G-11661)
MADDAK INC (DH)
661 State Route 23 (07470-6814)
PHONE..................................973 628-7600
Kurt Landsberger, *Ch of Bd*
David Landsberger, *President*
Anny Landsberger, *Admin Sec*
▲ **EMP:** 4
SQ FT: 35,000
SALES: 4.2MM
SALES (corp-wide): 1.4B **Privately Held**
WEB: www.maddak.com
SIC: 5047 3841 Medical equipment & supplies; surgical & medical instruments
HQ: Bel-Art Products, Inc.
　　661 Rte 23
　　Wayne NJ 07470
　　973 694-0500

(G-11662)
MANE USA INC (DH)
60 Demarest Dr (07470-6702)
PHONE..................................973 633-5533
Fax: 973 633-5538
Michel Mane, *President*
Bob Bagnato, *Vice Pres*
Jason Boland, *Vice Pres*
Wendy Diamond, *Vice Pres*
Debrah Knight, *Human Res Mgr*
▲ **EMP:** 120
SQ FT: 65,000
SALES (est): 166.4MM **Privately Held**
SIC: 2869 Perfumes, flavorings & food additives
HQ: V. Mane Fils
　　Quartier Notre Dame
　　Le Bar Sur Loup 06620
　　493 425-425

(G-11663)
MAQUET CARDIOVASCULAR LLC
45 Barbour Pond Dr (07470-2094)
PHONE..................................973 709-7000
Fax: 732 667-1901
Raoul Quintero, *CEO*
Julien Bergmans, *Managing Dir*
Philip Freed, *Senior VP*
Jeff Harris, *Vice Pres*
Joseph Knight, *Vice Pres*
▲ **EMP:** 58
SALES (est): 18.1MM **Privately Held**
SIC: 3829 Medical diagnostic systems, nuclear

(G-11664)
MARTIN SPROCKET & GEAR INC
7 Highpoint Dr (07470-7432)
PHONE..................................973 633-5700
Fax: 973 633-7196
EMP: 10
SALES (corp-wide): 284.2MM **Privately Held**
SIC: 3566 3568 Mfg Speed Changers/Drives Mfg Power Transmission Equipment
PA: Martin Sprocket & Gear, Inc.
　　3100 Sprocket Dr
　　Arlington TX 76015
　　817 258-3000

(G-11665)
MICROSOFT CORPORATION
1400 Willowbrook Mall (07470-6905)
PHONE..................................973 785-0982
EMP: 5
SALES (corp-wide): 110.3B **Publicly Held**
SIC: 7372 Prepackaged software
PA: Microsoft Corporation
　　1 Microsoft Way
　　Redmond WA 98052
　　425 882-8080

(G-11666)
MP CUSTOM FL LLC
Also Called: Mp Millwork
624 Alps Rd (07470-3904)
PHONE..................................973 417-2288
Marek Pochwatka,
EMP: 10
SALES (est): 1MM **Privately Held**
SIC: 2431 2521 2599 2434 Planing mill, millwork; wood office furniture; hotel furniture; hospital furniture, except beds; wood kitchen cabinets

(G-11667)
NORTH JERSEY METAL FABRICATORS
130 Ryerson Ave Ste 107 (07470-8137)
PHONE..................................973 305-9830
Bela Ecker, *President*
EMP: 4
SQ FT: 5,000
SALES (est): 694.2K **Privately Held**
SIC: 3446 Railings, prefabricated metal

(G-11668)
ORSILLO & COMPANY
Also Called: Construction Services
189 Berdan Ave (07470-3233)
PHONE..................................973 248-1833
Pat Orsillo, *President*
EMP: 7 **EST:** 2013
SALES: 900K **Privately Held**
SIC: 1442 Construction sand & gravel

(G-11669)
PAGE 2 LLC
508 Hamburg Tpke Ste 108 (07470-8482)
PHONE..................................862 239-9830
Robert Richman,
Andrea Richman,
EMP: 6
SALES (est): 454.1K **Privately Held**
SIC: 2759 Advertising literature: printing

(G-11670)
PASSAIC COUNTY WELDERS INC
100 Parish Dr (07470-6099)
PHONE..................................973 696-1200
Robert Grimbilas, *Vice Pres*

Peter Grimbilas, *Vice Pres*
EMP: 30 **EST:** 1933
SQ FT: 24,000
SALES (est): 6.9MM **Privately Held**
WEB: www.passaiccountynj.org
SIC: 3441 Building components, structural steel

(G-11671)
PASSAIC RUBBER CO (PA)
45 Demarest Dr (07470-6747)
P.O. Box 505 (07474-0505)
PHONE..................................973 696-9500
Fax: 973 696-0686
John Mathey, *President*
Jeffrey Leach, *COO*
▲ **EMP:** 93 **EST:** 1919
SQ FT: 70,000
SALES (est): 23.4MM **Privately Held**
WEB: www.passaic.com
SIC: 3061 3052 3069 2296 Mechanical rubber goods; rubber belting; rolls, solid or covered rubber; tire cord & fabrics

(G-11672)
PATRIOT PICKLE INC
20 Edison Dr (07470-4713)
PHONE..................................973 709-9487
Fax: 973 709-0995
William McEntee Jr, *President*
Bob Rento, *Vice Pres*
Neil Harth, *Sales Mgr*
EMP: 60
SALES (est): 12.8MM **Privately Held**
SIC: 2035 Pickles, sauces & salad dressings

(G-11673)
PHOTOGRAPHIC ANALYSIS COMPANY (PA)
190 Parish Dr (07470-4633)
PHONE..................................973 696-1000
Fax: 973 696-8589
Constance Mc Guire, *President*
L Arthur Jantzen, *Vice Pres*
Charles A Jantzen, *Treasurer*
EMP: 5
SQ FT: 1,500
SALES (est): 655.8K **Privately Held**
SIC: 3861 7699 Cameras & related equipment; photographic equipment repair

(G-11674)
POLYMERIC RESOURCES CORP (PA)
Also Called: A LM
55 Haul Rd Ste A (07470-6613)
P.O. Box 4237 (07474-4237)
PHONE..................................973 694-4141
Fax: 973 694-3549
Solomon Schlesinger, *President*
Moses Friedman, *COO*
Shiraz Meghji, *Vice Pres*
Charlie Cook, *QC Mgr*
Arthur Quint, *CFO*
▲ **EMP:** 45
SQ FT: 200,000
SALES (est): 24.4MM **Privately Held**
WEB: www.polyconverting.com
SIC: 2821 3087 Plastics materials & resins; custom compound purchased resins

(G-11675)
PR PRODUCTS DISTRIBUTORS INC
189 Berdan Ave Ste 281 (07470-3233)
PHONE..................................973 928-1120
Fernando Badillo, *President*
EMP: 7
SALES (est): 751.4K **Privately Held**
SIC: 2064 5145 Candy & other confectionery products; confectionery

(G-11676)
QUARTER SPOT
145 Us Highway 46 Fl 3 (07470-6830)
PHONE..................................917 647-9170
Adam Cohen, *Owner*
EMP: 10
SALES (est): 668.7K **Privately Held**
SIC: 7372 Prepackaged software

(G-11677)
REED-LANE INC
359 Newark Pompton Tpke (07470-6642)
PHONE..................................973 709-1090
Fax: 973 709-1091
Frederick Clauss, *Ch of Bd*
Patricia Elvin, *President*
EMP: 125
SQ FT: 135,000
SALES (est): 19.9MM **Privately Held**
WEB: www.reedlane.com
SIC: 7389 2834 Packaging & labeling services; pharmaceutical preparations

(G-11678)
REEVES INTERNATIONAL INC
Also Called: Breyer Manufacturing
34 Owens Dr (07470-2341)
PHONE..................................973 956-9555
Bill Rausch, *Managing Dir*
Frank Casamento, *Branch Mgr*
EMP: 30
SALES (est): 3.5MM
SALES (corp-wide): 26.8MM **Privately Held**
WEB: www.breyerhorses.com
SIC: 3944 Games, toys & children's vehicles
PA: Reeves International Inc.
　　14 Industrial Rd
　　Pequannock NJ 07440
　　973 694-5006

(G-11679)
REGAL CROWN FD SVC SPECIALIST
20 Edison Dr (07470-4713)
PHONE..................................508 752-2679
Fax: 508 831-0775
Douglas Freund, *President*
EMP: 9
SQ FT: 20,000
SALES (est): 1MM **Privately Held**
SIC: 2035 Pickles, vinegar

(G-11680)
ROYAL ADHESIVES & SEALANTS LLC
Also Called: Clifton Adhesives
48 Burgess Pl (07470-6734)
PHONE..................................973 694-0845
Ken Vara, *Opers Staff*
Dan Higgins, *Engineer*
Chris Bond, *VP Sales*
Karl Huelsenbeck, *Branch Mgr*
James Fahey, *Manager*
EMP: 30
SALES (corp-wide): 2.3B **Publicly Held**
SIC: 2891 Sealants
HQ: Royal Adhesives And Sealants Llc
　　2001 W Washington St
　　South Bend IN 46628
　　574 246-5000

(G-11681)
SAINT-GOBAIN PRFMCE PLAS CORP
150 Dey Rd (07470-4670)
PHONE..................................973 696-4700
Rene Sarmiento, *Branch Mgr*
EMP: 162
SALES (corp-wide): 213.5MM **Privately Held**
SIC: 2821 Plastics materials & resins
HQ: Saint-Gobain Performance Plastics Corporation
　　31500 Solon Rd
　　Solon OH 44139
　　440 836-6900

(G-11682)
SALOMONE RD-MIX LTD LIABITLITY
17 Demarest Dr (07470-6701)
PHONE..................................973 305-0022
Joseph Salomone, *President*
EMP: 16
SALES (est): 2MM **Privately Held**
SIC: 3273 Ready-mixed concrete

(G-11683)
SCREENS INCORPORATED
130 Ryerson Ave Ste 219 (07470-8138)
P.O. Box 383, Pequannock (07440-0383)
PHONE..................................973 633-8558

Robert Vorndran, *President*
EMP: 4
SQ FT: 3,500
SALES (est): 320K **Privately Held**
WEB: www.screens-inc.com
SIC: 2431 Window screens, wood frame

(G-11684)
T V L ASSOCIATES INC
3 Donna Ln (07470-2710)
PHONE..................973 790-6766
EMP: 1
SALES: 1.4MM **Privately Held**
SIC: 4841 5051 3672 Cable/Pay Television Service Metals Service Center Mfg Printed Circuit Boards

(G-11685)
TOSHIBA AMER CONSMR PDTS INC
82 Totowa Rd (07470-3114)
PHONE..................973 628-8000
Akio Ozaka, *CEO*
Tetsuya Sakaguchi, *Vice Pres*
Takahiro Nishio, *Sales Staff*
EMP: 215
SQ FT: 100,000
SALES (est): 34.1K
SALES (corp-wide): 37B **Privately Held**
SIC: 3651 Television receiving sets; video camera-audio recorders, household use
HQ: Toshiba America Inc
1251 Ave Of Ameri
New York NY 10020
212 596-0600

(G-11686)
TOYSRUSCOM INC
Also Called: Toys "R" Us
1 Geoffrey Way (07470-2066)
PHONE..................973 617-3500
Antonio Urcelay, *CEO*
Wolfgang Link, *President*
Monika Merz, *President*
Richard Barry, *Exec VP*
Deborah Derby, *Exec VP*
EMP: 102
SALES (est): 51.5MM
SALES (corp-wide): 11.5B **Privately Held**
SIC: 3944 Electronic toys; blocks, toy
PA: Toys "r" Us, Inc.
1 Geoffrey Way
Wayne NJ 07470
973 617-3500

(G-11687)
TURBINE TEK INC
130 Ryerson Ave Ste 303 (07470-8139)
PHONE..................973 872-0903
James Scageline, *Owner*
EMP: 6 **EST:** 2013
SALES (est): 175.1K **Privately Held**
SIC: 3714 Motor vehicle parts & accessories

(G-11688)
UNIVERSAL METALCRAFT INC
24 Burgess Pl (07470-6734)
PHONE..................973 345-3284
Fax: 973 345-7648
Viktor Wenstrom, *Ch of Bd*
Eric Wenstrom, *President*
Marlene Wenstrom, *Corp Secy*
Marc Wenstrom, *Vice Pres*
▲ **EMP:** 22
SQ FT: 42,000
SALES (est): 4.1MM **Privately Held**
WEB: www.umcraft.com
SIC: 3599 3452 3545 Machine shop, jobbing & repair; bolts, nuts, rivets & washers; precision tools, machinists'

(G-11689)
US SIGN AND LIGHTING SVC LLC
105 Dorsa Ave (07470-8107)
PHONE..................973 305-8900
John Kelley, *Manager*
Michael P Kelly,
EMP: 7
SQ FT: 3,000
SALES: 430K **Privately Held**
SIC: 3993 Electric signs

(G-11690)
VACUMET CORP
22 Riverview Dr Ste 101 (07470-3115)
PHONE..................973 628-0405
Robert T Korowicki, *CEO*
EMP: 4
SALES (est): 289.9K **Privately Held**
SIC: 3089 Plastics products

(G-11691)
VISION RESEARCH INC (HQ)
100 Dey Rd (07470-4604)
PHONE..................973 696-4500
Fax: 973 696-0560
Charles A Jantzen, *President*
Jay Sepleton, *General Mgr*
Maurice Mevissen, *Vice Pres*
Pat Pellicano, *Vice Pres*
Mark Pellicano, *Purch Mgr*
EMP: 93
SALES (est): 23.6MM
SALES (corp-wide): 4.3B **Publicly Held**
WEB: www.visionresearch.com
SIC: 3861 Cameras, still & motion picture (all types)
PA: Ametek, Inc.
1100 Cassatt Rd
Berwyn PA 19312
610 647-2121

(G-11692)
WAYNE MOTORS INC
Also Called: Lincoln Mercury of Wayne
1910 State Route 23 (07470-6577)
PHONE..................973 696-9710
Fax: 973 696-3677
Peter Spina, *President*
Gaspar J Spina, *Chairman*
Rona Spina, *Corp Secy*
Robert Spina, *Vice Pres*
EMP: 90 **EST:** 1968
SQ FT: 9,700
SALES (est): 40.6MM **Privately Held**
WEB: www.waynelincolnmercury.com
SIC: 5511 7532 7538 3714 Automobiles, new & used; body shop, automotive; general automotive repair shops; motor vehicle parts & accessories

(G-11693)
WILLOWBROOK GOLF CENTER LLC
366 Us Highway 46 (07470-4822)
PHONE..................973 256-6922
Fax: 973 256-0936
Song Hong,
EMP: 10
SALES (est): 935.1K **Privately Held**
WEB: www.willowbrookgolfcenter.com
SIC: 3949 Driving ranges, golf, electronic

(G-11694)
Z FAB LLC
24 Bodie Rd (07470-6102)
PHONE..................973 248-0686
Scott Silodor,
EMP: 6
SALES (est): 298.9K **Privately Held**
SIC: 2759 Commercial printing

Weehawken
Hudson County

(G-11695)
HANOVER DIRECT INC (PA)
Also Called: Hanover Direct Operating Group
1500 Harbor Blvd Ste 3 (07086-6782)
PHONE..................201 863-7300
Fax: 201 392-5035
Don Kelley, *President*
Pete Van Donk, *Info Tech Mgr*
▲ **EMP:** 340
SQ FT: 56,700
SALES (est): 214.7MM **Privately Held**
WEB: www.hanoverdirect.com
SIC: 7389 2221 5712 2211 Telemarketing services; comforters & quilts, manmade fiber & silk; bedding & bedsprings; pillow tubing; catalog & mail-order houses

(G-11696)
HUDSON CAKERY
1816 Willow Ave (07086-6622)
PHONE..................201 319-0363
Jennifer Bunce, *Owner*
EMP: 7
SALES (est): 474.3K **Privately Held**
SIC: 2053 Cakes, bakery: frozen

(G-11697)
JERSEY BEAT
3726 Park Ave Apt E2 (07086-8905)
PHONE..................201 864-9054
Jim Testa, *Principal*
EMP: 4
SALES (est): 193.7K **Privately Held**
SIC: 2711 Newspapers

(G-11698)
MARKO ENGRAVING & ART CORP (PA)
19 Baldwin Ave (07086)
PHONE..................201 864-6500
Marko Melnitschenko, *President*
Ljubow Melnitschenko, *Corp Secy*
EMP: 15
SQ FT: 5,000
SALES (est): 1.2MM **Privately Held**
SIC: 3555 2796 Printing plates; platemaking services

(G-11699)
SWATCH GROUP LES BTQUES US INC
1200 Harbor Blvd (07086-6762)
PHONE..................201 271-1400
Caroline Faivet, *President*
Joseph Mella, *Vice Pres*
Joseph Panetta, *VP Corp Comm*
Peter Mager, *Info Tech Dir*
Hanspeter Rentsch, *Admin Sec*
EMP: 1
SALES (est): 4.7MM
SALES (corp-wide): 8B **Privately Held**
SIC: 3625 5094 3873 Timing devices, electronic; clocks, watches & parts; watches, clocks, watchcases & parts
HQ: The Swatch Group U S Inc
703 Nw 62nd Ave Ste 450
Miami FL 33126
201 271-1400

(G-11700)
UNITED CABINET WORKS LLC
9 Bonn Pl Apt 2 (07086-6942)
PHONE..................917 686-3395
Nick Roccaforte, *Mng Member*
EMP: 3
SALES: 2.6MM **Privately Held**
SIC: 2434 7389 Wood kitchen cabinets;

Wenonah
Gloucester County

(G-11701)
51MAPS INC
500 E Mantua Ave (08090-2015)
PHONE..................800 927-5181
EMP: 7
SALES (est): 362K **Privately Held**
SIC: 7372 Prepackaged Software Services

(G-11702)
ALETE PRINTING LLC
722 Dartmouth Ct (08090-1003)
P.O. Box 371 (08090-0371)
PHONE..................856 468-3536
Patricia Koskinen, *President*
John Koskinen, *Vice Pres*
EMP: 4
SALES (est): 486.2K **Privately Held**
WEB: www.aleteprinting.com
SIC: 2752 Commercial printing, offset

(G-11703)
COTTERMAN INC
100 Hayes Ave (08090)
P.O. Box 278 (08090-0278)
PHONE..................856 415-0800
Fax: 856 464-6930
William M Thomas, *President*
Robert Flasher, *Vice Pres*

Michael Bonaventure, *Treasurer*
EMP: 15 **EST:** 1999
SALES (est): 2.3MM **Privately Held**
WEB: www.cottermaninc.com
SIC: 3548 Welding & cutting apparatus & accessories

West Berlin
Camden County

(G-11704)
ARTISTIC GLASS & DOORS INC
Also Called: Stained Glass Overlay
154 Cooper Rd Ste 201 (08091-9105)
PHONE..................856 768-1414
Michael Baron, *President*
EMP: 8
SQ FT: 2,200
SALES (est): 780K **Privately Held**
WEB: www.artisticglassanddoors.com
SIC: 5231 3231 5211 Glass, leaded or stained; stained glass: made from purchased glass; door & window products

(G-11705)
ASCALON STUDIOS INC
Also Called: Ascalon Art Studios
430 Cooper Rd (08091-3843)
PHONE..................856 768-3779
Fax: 856 768-3902
David Ascalon, *President*
Eric Ascalon, *Vice Pres*
EMP: 12
SQ FT: 3,000
SALES (est): 1.2MM **Privately Held**
WEB: www.ascalonstudios.com
SIC: 3231 Stained glass: made from purchased glass

(G-11706)
CAROLINA FLUID HANDLING INC
140 Bradford Dr (08091-9216)
PHONE..................248 228-8900
Fred Giuliano, *Director*
▲ **EMP:** 610
SALES (est): 55MM
SALES (corp-wide): 13.3B **Privately Held**
WEB: www.daycoinc.com
SIC: 3714 Fuel systems & parts, motor vehicle
PA: Sun Capital Partners, Inc.
5200 Town Center Cir # 400
Boca Raton FL 33486
561 962-3400

(G-11707)
CHAMPION OPCO LLC
Also Called: Champion Window Delaware Vly
414 Bloomfield Dr Ste 1 (08091-2416)
PHONE..................856 662-3400
Bruce Greenberg, *Manager*
EMP: 16
SALES (corp-wide): 515.7MM **Privately Held**
SIC: 3442 Window & door frames
PA: Champion Opco, Llc
12121 Champion Way
Cincinnati OH 45241
513 924-4858

(G-11708)
CHICK CAPOLI SALES
420 Commerce Ln Ste 7 (08091-9278)
PHONE..................856 768-4500
Chick Capoli, *Owner*
EMP: 20
SALES (est): 2.3MM **Privately Held**
SIC: 3714 Motor vehicle parts & accessories

(G-11709)
COLORTEC PRINTING AND MAILING
424 Kelley Dr Ste A (08091-9285)
PHONE..................856 767-0108
Fax: 856 767-1975
Wayne Farlow, *Owner*
EMP: 5
SALES (est): 337K **Privately Held**
SIC: 2759 4731 Commercial printing; freight transportation arrangement

(G-11710)
COMPEX CORPORATION
439 Commerce Ln Ste 1 (08091-9206)
PHONE..........................856 719-8657
Fax: 856 335-7223
David Gordon, *President*
▲ EMP: 30 EST: 1976
SQ FT: 5,000
SALES (est): 6.5MM **Privately Held**
WEB: www.compexcorp.com
SIC: 3679 Microwave components

(G-11711)
CONCEPT GROUP INC (PA)
380 Cooper Rd (08091-9203)
PHONE..........................856 767-5506
Fax: 856 768-3981
Aarne Reid, *CEO*
David Reid, *President*
Jim Dugan, *Manager*
John S Boyer,
EMP: 25
SQ FT: 13,000
SALES (est): 20MM **Privately Held**
WEB: www.conceptgroupinc.com
SIC: 3679 3599 Hermetic seals for electronic equipment; machine shop, jobbing & repair

(G-11712)
COOPER POWER SYSTEMS LLC
402 Bloomfield Dr Ste 1 (08091-2405)
PHONE..........................856 719-1100
EMP: 200 **Privately Held**
SIC: 3612 Power transformers, electric
HQ: Cooper Power Systems, Llc
2300 Badger Dr
Waukesha WI 53188
262 896-2400

(G-11713)
CROWFOOT ASSOCIATES INC
Also Called: Crowfoot Asphalt
Winslow Township (08091)
PHONE..........................609 561-0107
Dennis E Powell, *President*
EMP: 8
SQ FT: 40,000
SALES (est): 1.1MM **Privately Held**
SIC: 2951 Asphalt paving mixtures & blocks

(G-11714)
DANIEL MAGUIRE
Also Called: Dan Maguire Electrical Contr
140 Collings Ave (08091-9121)
PHONE..........................856 767-8443
Daniel Maguire, *Owner*
EMP: 23
SALES (est): 1.7MM **Privately Held**
SIC: 3699 Electrical equipment & supplies

(G-11715)
DV8 ENTERPRISES LLC
151 Cooper Rd (08091-9244)
PHONE..........................201 507-6288
Robert Virella, *COO*
Michael Mozeika, *Mng Member*
EMP: 12
SQ FT: 35,000
SALES (est): 1.6MM **Privately Held**
SIC: 3086 Plastics foam products

(G-11716)
DYNASIL CORPORATION AMERICA
385 Cooper Rd (08091-9145)
PHONE..........................856 767-4600
Fax: 856 767-6813
Craig Dunham, *President*
▲ EMP: 4
SALES (est): 636.4K **Privately Held**
SIC: 3841 Surgical & medical instruments

(G-11717)
E S INDUSTRIES INC
701 S Route 73 A (08091-2603)
PHONE..........................856 753-8400
David A Kohler, *President*
EMP: 7
SQ FT: 8,500

WEB: www.esind.com
SIC: 3826 Chromatographic equipment, laboratory type

(G-11718)
EAST COAST PLASTICS INC
427 Commerce Ln Ste 7 (08091-9212)
PHONE..........................856 768-8700
Fax: 856 768-8282
David Lorenz, *President*
EMP: 9
SQ FT: 8,400
SALES (est): 1.3MM **Privately Held**
SIC: 3089 Molding primary plastic

(G-11719)
ELECTRO PARTS INC
465 E Taunton Ave Ste 201 (08091-3847)
PHONE..........................856 767-5923
Fax: 856 767-5924
Esteban Sobrado, *President*
EMP: 7
SQ FT: 2,600
SALES: 900K **Privately Held**
WEB: www.electropartsinc.com
SIC: 5072 3312 Hardware; bar, rod & wire products

(G-11720)
FOODLINE PIPING PRODUCTS CO
225 Edgewood Ave (08091-2615)
PHONE..........................856 767-1177
Daniel Diadul, *President*
▼ EMP: 5
SALES (est): 635.5K **Privately Held**
SIC: 3498 Pipe sections fabricated from purchased pipe

(G-11721)
FOTOBRIDGE
154 Cooper Rd Ste 203 (08091-9105)
PHONE..........................856 809-9400
Paul Cooper, *Owner*
EMP: 5 EST: 2008
SALES (est): 667.4K **Privately Held**
SIC: 3577 Magnetic ink & optical scanning devices

(G-11722)
GALAXY TRANS & MAGNETICS LLC
386 Cooper Rd (08091-9203)
P.O. Box 27, Atco (08004-0027)
PHONE..........................856 753-4546
Will Curry, *Sales Staff*
James R Nancy Curry,
James R Curry,
Nancy Curry,
▲ EMP: 12 EST: 1998
SQ FT: 4,500
SALES (est): 1.9MM **Privately Held**
WEB: www.galaxytransformers.com
SIC: 3612 Power transformers, electric

(G-11723)
GARY R BANKS INDUSTRIAL GROUP
575 N Route 73 Ste C6 (08091-9292)
PHONE..........................856 687-2227
Gary Banks, *Mng Member*
EMP: 19
SALES (est): 397.9K **Privately Held**
SIC: 8748 1742 3479 Business consulting; plastering, drywall & insulation; coating, rust preventive

(G-11724)
GENERAL SIGN CO INC
105 Chestnut Ave (08091-3801)
PHONE..........................856 753-3535
Louis Brocco, *President*
Steven Brocco, *Vice Pres*
EMP: 7
SALES: 700K **Privately Held**
SIC: 3993 1799 Signs & advertising specialties; sign installation & maintenance

(G-11725)
HORIZON LABEL LLC
1049 Industrial Dr (08091-9136)
PHONE..........................856 767-0777
Ron Davis, *General Mgr*
August Roderick, *Sales Staff*

Tom Koslowsky, *Director*
Paul Falkowski,
EMP: 16
SQ FT: 15,000
SALES (est): 2.8MM **Privately Held**
SIC: 2759 2672 Flexographic printing; coated & laminated paper

(G-11726)
JMJ PROFILE INC
154 Cooper Rd Ste 1303 (08091-9122)
PHONE..........................856 767-3930
Fax: 856 767-3931
Joseph M Colachi, *President*
Joseph A Colachi, *Vice Pres*
EMP: 7 EST: 1992
SALES (est): 1MM **Privately Held**
WEB: www.jmjprofile.com
SIC: 3083 Laminated plastic sheets

(G-11727)
JOHN B HORAY WELDING
399 Blaine Ave (08091-2131)
PHONE..........................856 336-2154
John B Horay Sr, *Owner*
Peter Horay, *Owner*
EMP: 5
SALES (est): 250K **Privately Held**
SIC: 7692 Welding repair

(G-11728)
KESSLER STEEL RULE DIE INC
Also Called: Dennis Kessler Steel Rule Die
1004 Industrial Dr Ste 10 (08091-9189)
PHONE..........................856 767-0231
Dennis Kessler, *President*
EMP: 6
SALES (est): 651.2K **Privately Held**
SIC: 3544 Dies, steel rule; special dies & tools

(G-11729)
LIGHTNING PRVNTION SYSTEMS INC
154 Cooper Rd Ste 1201 (08091-9116)
P.O. Box 353 (08091-0353)
PHONE..........................856 767-7806
Fax: 856 767-7547
Patricia McLaughlin, *CEO*
Ian Fawthrop, *President*
Jessica Jones, *Vice Pres*
EMP: 8
SQ FT: 2,500
SALES: 1.3MM **Privately Held**
WEB: www.lpsnet.com
SIC: 3643 3663 Lightning protection equipment; antennas, transmitting & communications

(G-11730)
LIQUID IRON INDUSTRIES INC
150 Cooper Rd Ste B4 (08091-9257)
PHONE..........................856 336-2639
EMP: 4
SALES (est): 265.8K **Privately Held**
SIC: 3999 Manufacturing industries

(G-11731)
LONGRUN PRESS INC
1002 Industrial Dr (08091-9164)
P.O. Box 1536, Cherry Hill (08034-0069)
PHONE..........................856 719-9202
Fax: 856 719-9203
Carl J Buehler III, *President*
Mary Beth Buehler, *Vice Pres*
EMP: 10
SQ FT: 12,000
SALES (est): 880K **Privately Held**
SIC: 2752 7389 Commercial printing, lithographic; offset & photolithographic printing; printing broker

(G-11732)
M C CUSTOM SHTMTL FABRICATION
215 Old Egg Harbor Rd C (08091-1653)
PHONE..........................856 767-9509
Fax: 856 767-3826
Michael Carr Sr, *President*
Michael Carr Jr, *Vice Pres*
Shawn Carr, *Treasurer*
April Carr, *Admin Sec*
EMP: 6 EST: 1982
SALES (est): 690K **Privately Held**
SIC: 3444 Ducts, sheet metal

(G-11733)
MEDPLAST WEST BERLIN INC (DH)
225 Old Egg Harbor Rd (08091-1602)
PHONE..........................856 753-7600
Harold Faig, *CEO*
Carl Dedtens, *President*
Robert D Piccoli, *Vice Pres*
Mike Torti, *Vice Pres*
Doug Cain, *Engineer*
▲ EMP: 49
SQ FT: 65,000
SALES (est): 13MM
SALES (corp-wide): 189.2MM **Privately Held**
WEB: www.medplastgroup.com
SIC: 3089 Injection molding of plastics

(G-11734)
MOD-U-KRAF HOMES LLC (DH)
140 Bradford Dr Ste A (08091-9216)
PHONE..........................540 482-0273
Jeffery Powell,
EMP: 33
SQ FT: 104,000
SALES (est): 27.9MM **Privately Held**
WEB: www.mod-u-kraf.com
SIC: 2452 1521 Prefabricated wood buildings; modular homes, prefabricated, wood; single-family housing construction
HQ: All American Group, Inc.
2831 Dexter Dr
Elkhart IN 46514
574 262-0123

(G-11735)
MODERN PRECISION TECH INC
225 Old Egg Harbor Rd (08091-1602)
PHONE..........................856 335-9303
Joe Lovallo, *CEO*
Douglas Cain, *Engineer*
EMP: 12
SALES (est): 435.7K **Privately Held**
SIC: 3599 Machine shop, jobbing & repair

(G-11736)
NEW DIMENSIONS INDUSTRIES LLC
151 Cooper Rd (08091-9244)
PHONE..........................201 531-1010
Fax: 201 641-3468
Michael Mozeika Jr, *President*
Robert Virella, *COO*
Judith Mozeika, *Admin Sec*
▲ EMP: 8
SQ FT: 40,000
SALES (est): 1.4MM **Privately Held**
WEB: www.newdimension-inc.com
SIC: 3086 Plastics foam products

(G-11737)
NOVA FLEX GROUP
1024 Industrial Dr (08091-9164)
PHONE..........................856 768-2275
Jerry McCool, *Manager*
EMP: 10
SALES (corp-wide): 22.8MM **Privately Held**
WEB: www.novaflexgroup.com
SIC: 3443 Ducting, metal plate
HQ: Nova Flex Group
1024 Industrial Dr
West Berlin NJ 08091

(G-11738)
NOVA FLEX GROUP (DH)
1024 Industrial Dr (08091-9164)
PHONE..........................856 768-2275
Fax: 856 768-2385
Ian Donnelly, *President*
Jeffrey Green, *Sales Associate*
Michael Sloan, *Manager*
Danielle Shaw, *Admin Asst*
▲ EMP: 10
SQ FT: 21,000
SALES (est): 4.3MM
SALES (corp-wide): 22.8MM **Privately Held**
WEB: www.novaflexgroup.com
SIC: 3443 Fabricated plate work (boiler shop)

▲ = Import ▼=Export
◆ =Import/Export

(G-11739)
NOVAFLEX INDUSTRIES INC
1024 Industrial Dr (08091-9164)
PHONE...................................856 768-2275
Melinda Donnelly, *President*
Kevin Donnelly, *Vice Pres*
Claire R Howard, *Admin Sec*
EMP: 11
SALES (est): 1.9MM **Privately Held**
SIC: 3492 3052 Hose & tube couplings, hydraulic/pneumatic; rubber & plastics hose & beltings

(G-11740)
OWENS FASTENERS INC
154 Cooper Rd Ste 101 (08091-9100)
PHONE...................................856 768-6580
Fax: 856 753-8217
Ana Cabalceta, *President*
EMP: 7
SALES (est): 1.2MM **Privately Held**
WEB: www.owenfasteners.com
SIC: 3429 Manufactured hardware (general)

(G-11741)
PACKAGING GRAPHICS INC
435 Commerce Ln (08091-9254)
P.O. Box 160 (08091-0160)
PHONE...................................856 767-9000
Fax: 856 767-2759
Eileen Koff, *President*
Jason Clark, *President*
EMP: 28
SQ FT: 14,000
SALES (est): 4.8MM **Privately Held**
WEB: www.packaginggraphics.net
SIC: 3555 Printing plates

(G-11742)
PHOENIX TOOL & MACHINE INC
1044 Industrial Dr Ste 5 (08091-9104)
PHONE...................................856 753-5565
Fax: 856 753-9755
John R Dusak, *President*
EMP: 7 **EST:** 1997
SQ FT: 3,000
SALES (est): 750K **Privately Held**
SIC: 3599 Machine shop, jobbing & repair

(G-11743)
PRINCETON TECTONICS
110 Collings Ave (08091-9121)
P.O. Box 8057, Trenton (08650-0057)
PHONE...................................609 298-9331
Richard Shenowski, *Branch Mgr*
EMP: 45
SALES (corp-wide): 20MM **Privately Held**
SIC: 3648 Outdoor lighting equipment
PA: Princeton Tectonics
1777 Hylton Rd
Pennsauken NJ 08110
609 298-9331

(G-11744)
PRINTING PLUS OF SOUTH JERSEY
406 N Route 73 (08091-2520)
PHONE...................................856 767-3941
Fax: 856 767-3976
Robert Behnke, *President*
EMP: 8
SQ FT: 3,500
SALES: 810.5K **Privately Held**
SIC: 2752 Commercial printing, offset

(G-11745)
PRO-FIT LLC
215 Edgewood Ave (08091-2615)
PHONE...................................856 809-9910
Fax: 856 809-9945
Tammy Linden, *Principal*
Thomas Dalsey,
EMP: 17
SALES (est): 2.5MM **Privately Held**
SIC: 3842 Limbs, artificial

(G-11746)
RECYCLING N HENSEL AMER INC
1003 Industrial Dr (08091-9136)
PHONE...................................856 753-7614
Peter Lenz, *President*
Frank Rettinger, *Managing Dir*

Jason Tang, *Managing Dir*
Peter Ursprung, *Managing Dir*
Bob Henning, *Principal*
◆ **EMP:** 36
SALES (est): 10.2MM **Privately Held**
SIC: 3341 8742 Recovery & refining of nonferrous metals; business consultant
PA: Hensel Recycling International Gmbh
Muhlweg 10
Aschaffenburg
602 812-090

(G-11747)
RESINTECH INC (PA)
160 Cooper Rd (08091-9258)
PHONE...................................856 768-9600
Fax: 856 768-9601
Michael C Gottlieb, *President*
Frank Firicano, *President*
Jeffrey H Gottlieb, *Vice Pres*
Lawrence Gottlieb, *Vice Pres*
Lynne Gottlieb, *Vice Pres*
▲ **EMP:** 120
SQ FT: 60,000
SALES (est): 83.3MM **Privately Held**
SIC: 5162 2819 3624 Resins; industrial inorganic chemicals; carbon & graphite products

(G-11748)
RUSSELL CAST STONE INC
Also Called: Continental Cast Stone East
400 Cooper Rd (08091-3843)
PHONE...................................856 753-4000
William Russell III, *CEO*
Bill Russell, *Manager*
EMP: 58
SQ FT: 50,000
SALES (est): 6.4MM **Privately Held**
SIC: 3272 Concrete products

(G-11749)
SIGCO TOOL & MFG CO INC
110 Collings Ave (08091-9121)
PHONE...................................856 753-6565
Fax: 856 753-5102
Alfred Signor, *President*
Mark Cohen, *Corp Secy*
EMP: 26
SALES (est): 4.2MM **Privately Held**
WEB: www.sigcotool.com
SIC: 3544 Forms (molds), for foundry & plastics working machinery

(G-11750)
SOUTH JERSEY COUNTERTOP CO
1044 Industrial Dr Ste 12 (08091-9126)
PHONE...................................856 768-7960
Ed Bader, *President*
EMP: 4
SALES (est): 256.6K **Privately Held**
SIC: 2541 1799 Counter & sink tops; counter top installation

(G-11751)
SPAGHETTI ENGINEERING CORP
Also Called: Digitails
150 Cooper Rd Ste C7 (08091-9223)
PHONE...................................856 719-9989
Michael Muhlbaier, *President*
Sbastian Clicharz, *Principal*
EMP: 11
SALES (est): 1.6MM **Privately Held**
SIC: 3647 Automotive lighting fixtures

(G-11752)
SULZER CHEMTECH USA INC
1008 Industrial Dr Ste F (08091-9190)
PHONE...................................856 768-2165
Kelvin Johnson, *Manager*
EMP: 180
SALES (corp-wide): 3B **Privately Held**
SIC: 3822 Electric air cleaner controls, automatic
HQ: Sulzer Chemtech Usa Inc.
8505 E North Belt
Humble TX 77396
281 441-5200

(G-11753)
TAUNTON GRAPHICS INC
1049 Industrial Dr (08091-9136)
PHONE...................................856 719-8084
Fax: 856 719-8086

Paul Falkowski, *President*
EMP: 10
SALES (est): 990.6K **Privately Held**
WEB: www.horizonlabel.com
SIC: 2759 Labels & seals: printing

(G-11754)
TECHNITOOL INC
1028 Industrial Dr (08091-9164)
PHONE...................................856 768-2707
Fax: 856 768-2807
Sal Russomanno, *President*
Peter J Welding, *Vice Pres*
EMP: 30
SQ FT: 20,000
SALES (est): 6.1MM **Privately Held**
WEB: www.technitool.com
SIC: 3089 Injection molding of plastics

(G-11755)
TECHNOBOX INC
154 Cooper Rd Ste 901 (08091-9112)
PHONE...................................856 809-2306
Fax: 609 261-1011
Joseph P Norris, *President*
EMP: 8
SALES (est): 1.5MM **Privately Held**
WEB: www.technobox.com
SIC: 3577 Computer peripheral equipment

(G-11756)
TELECOM ASSISTANCE GROUP INC
Also Called: T A G
150 Cooper Rd Ste F15 (08091-9265)
PHONE...................................856 753-8585
Fax: 856 768-7645
John Humes, *Vice Pres*
Murray Kaplan, *Vice Pres*
EMP: 30
SQ FT: 5,500
SALES (est): 5.5MM **Privately Held**
WEB: www.tagcords.com
SIC: 3661 8748 Telephone & telegraph apparatus; communications consulting

(G-11757)
THWING-ALBERT INSTRUMENT CO
14 W Collings Ave (08091-9134)
PHONE...................................856 767-1000
Fax: 856 767-2615
Scott M Raab, *CEO*
Joseph Raab, *CFO*
Sandra Raab, *Admin Sec*
EMP: 55 **EST:** 1899
SALES (est): 14.1MM **Privately Held**
WEB: www.thwingalbert.com
SIC: 3829 Physical property testing equipment

(G-11758)
TOOL SHOP INC
335 Chestnut Ave (08091-9138)
P.O. Box 36 (08091-0036)
PHONE...................................856 767-8077
Fax: 856 767-8103
Paul Brunninghaus, *President*
EMP: 7
SQ FT: 4,000
SALES (est): 1.1MM **Privately Held**
WEB: www.toolshopinc.com
SIC: 3545 3541 3451 Cutting tools for machine tools; machine tools, metal cutting type; screw machine products

(G-11759)
TRIPLE-T CUTTING TOOLS INC
135 Edgewood Ave Ste A (08091-2601)
PHONE...................................856 768-0800
Fax: 856 768-3773
Steve Thomas, *President*
Mike Thomas, *Corp Secy*
Donna Gauntt, *QC Mgr*
Donna Scullin, *QC Mgr*
Matt Berghof, *Engineer*
EMP: 12
SQ FT: 2,000
SALES: 1.8MM **Privately Held**
WEB: www.triple-t.com
SIC: 3541 Machine tools, metal cutting type

(G-11760)
WESTAR TOOL LLC
427 Commerce Ln Ste 7 (08091-9212)
PHONE...................................856 507-8852
Fax: 856 507-8853
Robert Mason,
Edward Steafankiewick,
EMP: 4
SQ FT: 2,400
SALES: 300K **Privately Held**
SIC: 3089 Injection molding of plastics

(G-11761)
WIRELESS ELECTRONICS INC
Also Called: Wireless Communications & Elec
153 Cooper Rd (08091-9244)
PHONE...................................856 768-4310
Glen Faust, *Sales Staff*
Mike Travassos, *Branch Mgr*
Richard Goldberg, *Manager*
Tim McGeary, *Manager*
Toni Schober, *Associate*
EMP: 20 **Privately Held**
WEB: www.wirelessce.com
SIC: 7622 3663 Communication equipment repair; radio broadcasting & communications equipment
PA: Wireless Electronics Inc
2905 Southampton Rd
Philadelphia PA 19154

West Caldwell
Essex County

(G-11762)
ADHISA MOLDING
11 Patton Dr (07006-6404)
PHONE...................................862 324-5222
Carl Hurowitz, *President*
EMP: 4
SALES (est): 240K **Privately Held**
SIC: 2431 Moldings, wood: unfinished & prefinished

(G-11763)
ALFA WASSERMANN INC (PA)
Also Called: Schiapparelli Biosystems
4 Henderson Dr (07006-6608)
PHONE...................................973 882-8630
Irva Nordlicht, *President*
Mark Gnagy, *Vice Pres*
Peter Natoli, *Vice Pres*
Fernando Garcia, *Engineer*
James McClain, *VP Sales*
▲ **EMP:** 159
SQ FT: 50,000
SALES (est): 33MM **Privately Held**
WEB: www.awst.com
SIC: 3841 Diagnostic apparatus, medical

(G-11764)
ALFA WSSRMANN DAGNSTC TECH LLC
4 Henderson Dr (07006-6608)
PHONE...................................800 220-4488
Irva Nordlicht, *CEO*
EMP: 12
SALES (est): 1.7MM **Privately Held**
SIC: 3841 Diagnostic apparatus, medical
PA: Alfa Wassermann, Inc.
4 Henderson Dr
West Caldwell NJ 07006

(G-11765)
ALL MADINA INC
Also Called: Dunkin' Donuts
592 Passaic Ave (07006-6714)
PHONE...................................973 226-7772
Steven Huff, *Branch Mgr*
EMP: 10
SALES (est): 260.1K **Privately Held**
SIC: 5461 5499 2045 Doughnuts; coffee; doughnut mixes, prepared: from purchased flour
PA: All Madina Inc
199 Littleton Rd
Parsippany NJ 07054

(G-11766)
ATLANTIC ZEISER INC
15 Patton Dr (07006-6404)
PHONE...................................973 228-0800
Fax: 973 228-9064

Tom Coco, *CEO*
Jeff Veksler, *President*
Rick Vandervliet, *General Mgr*
Joseph Weber, *Vice Pres*
Josef Gergen, *Engineer*
▲ EMP: 50
SQ FT: 45,000
SALES (est): 11.2MM
SALES (corp-wide): 294.3MM Privately Held
WEB: www.atlanticzeiser.com
SIC: 3578 5046 3555 Calculating & accounting equipment; commercial equipment; printing trades machinery
HQ: Atlantic Zeiser Gmbh
    Bogenstr. 6-8
    Emmingen-Liptingen 78576
    746 529-10

(G-11767)
AYERSPACE INC
25 Fairfield Ave (07006-7603)
PHONE....................................212 582-8410
Robert Ayers, *President*
EMP: 7 EST: 2001
SQ FT: 11,035
SALES (est): 450.2K Privately Held
SIC: 2515 6513 Spring cushions; apartment building operators

(G-11768)
BISHOP ASCENDANT INC
1083 Bloomfield Ave (07006-7105)
PHONE....................................973 210-5298
Justin Bishop, *CEO*
EMP: 5
SQ FT: 2,000
SALES (est): 51.9K Privately Held
SIC: 8999 8711 1629 3731 Inventor; engineering services; construction & civil engineering; dams, waterways, docks & other marine construction; submersible marine robots, manned or unmanned

(G-11769)
BLOOMFIELD NEWS LLC
172 Orton Rd (07006-8251)
PHONE....................................973 226-2127
Louis Venezia, *Principal*
EMP: 4
SALES (est): 97.7K Privately Held
SIC: 2711 Newspapers

(G-11770)
CENTRAL LETTER SHOP INC
14 Henderson Dr (07006-6608)
PHONE....................................973 808-9595
Fax: 973 808-8339
Benedict Bataglino, *President*
Samuel Bataglino Jr, *Vice Pres*
EMP: 39 EST: 1919
SQ FT: 33,000
SALES (est): 6.9MM Privately Held
WEB: www.centrallettershop.com
SIC: 2752 7331 Commercial printing, offset; direct mail advertising services

(G-11771)
COLTER & PETERSON INC (PA)
19 Fairfield Pl (07006-6206)
PHONE....................................973 684-0901
James Colter, *Ch of Bd*
Bruce Peterson, *President*
Andrew Shields, *Exec VP*
Don Shields, *Exec VP*
Donald Sheilds, *Vice Pres*
◆ EMP: 45
SQ FT: 32,000
SALES (est): 21.3MM Privately Held
WEB: www.colter-peterson.com
SIC: 5084 3554 Printing trades machinery, equipment & supplies; paper industries machinery; cutting machines, paper

(G-11772)
CORPORATE MAILINGS INC (PA)
Also Called: Ccg Marketing Solutions
14 Henderson Dr (07006-6608)
PHONE....................................973 439-1168
Fax: 973 808-9739
Lois M Pinkin, *President*
Jeffrey T Lawshe, *Senior VP*
Jeffrey S Pinkin, *Senior VP*
Heather Pinkin, *Vice Pres*
James E Pinkin, *Vice Pres*

▲ EMP: 178
SQ FT: 375,000
SALES (est): 58.1MM Privately Held
WEB: www.corpcomm.com
SIC: 2752 7311 7331 7374 Promotional printing, lithographic; advertising agencies; mailing service; data processing service

(G-11773)
DIRECT PRTG IMPRESSIONS INC
Also Called: D P I
33 Fairfield Pl (07006-6206)
PHONE....................................973 227-6111
Fax: 973 227-6655
Rich Luggiero, *President*
Rosa Luggiero, *Vice Pres*
Mike Smith, *Production*
Dennis Pikaard, *Human Resources*
Frank Aresta, *Sales Staff*
EMP: 18
SQ FT: 20,000
SALES (est): 3.9MM Privately Held
WEB: www.dpiprints.com
SIC: 2752 Commercial printing, offset

(G-11774)
DONNELLEY FINANCIAL LLC
5 Henderson Dr (07006-6607)
PHONE....................................973 882-7000
Fax: 973 882-1689
Russell Radil, *Manager*
CHI Siu, *Manager*
EMP: 13
SALES (corp-wide): 1B Publicly Held
WEB: www.bowne.com
SIC: 2752 Commercial printing, offset
HQ: Donnelley Financial, Llc
    55 Water St Fl 11
    New York NY 10041
    212 425-0298

(G-11775)
ESSEX RISE CONVEYOR CORP
4 Fairfield Cres (07006-6205)
PHONE....................................973 575-7483
Fax: 973 575-0576
Charles V Wampler, *CEO*
Scott Swander, *Vice Pres*
Patty Spina, *Purch Agent*
EMP: 6
SQ FT: 25,000
SALES (est): 640K Privately Held
WEB: www.essexrise.com
SIC: 3535 Conveyors & conveying equipment

(G-11776)
FANCORT INDUSTRIES INC
31 Fairfield Pl (07006-6286)
P.O. Box 565, Caldwell (07007-0565)
PHONE....................................973 575-0610
Fax: 973 575-9234
Ronald J Corey, *President*
Robert Antonelli, *Vice Pres*
Diane Buchanan, *Buyer*
Michael Bachman, *Sales Staff*
Lee Boki, *Sales Staff*
▲ EMP: 17 EST: 1973
SQ FT: 12,000
SALES (est): 4.5MM Privately Held
WEB: www.fancort.com
SIC: 3544 Special dies, tools, jigs & fixtures

(G-11777)
GIA-TEK LLC
66 Westover Ave (07006-7723)
PHONE....................................973 228-0875
Robert Giannetti, *Principal*
EMP: 5
SALES (est): 414K Privately Held
SIC: 3567 Heating units & devices, industrial: electric

(G-11778)
HOPE ELECTRICAL PRODUCTS CO
3 Fairfield Cres (07006-6204)
PHONE....................................973 882-7400
Margaret Hutchinson, *President*
Travis Hutchinson, *Vice Pres*
EMP: 8 EST: 1933
SQ FT: 16,000

SALES (est): 1.3MM Privately Held
WEB: www.hopeelectricalproducts.com
SIC: 3644 Fuse boxes, electric

(G-11779)
IMPACT INSTRUMENTATION INC
Also Called: Impact Medical
27 Fairfield Pl (07006-6206)
P.O. Box 508, Caldwell (07007-0508)
PHONE....................................973 882-1212
Fax: 973 882-4993
Leslie H Sherman, *President*
Mel Chettum, *Corp Secy*
▲ EMP: 150
SQ FT: 22,000
SALES (est): 29.8MM Privately Held
SIC: 3845 Respiratory analysis equipment, electromedical

(G-11780)
J R E INC
22 Fairfield Pl (07006-6207)
PHONE....................................973 808-0055
Fax: 973 808-7196
James Tuscano Jr, *Vice Pres*
Natalie Tuscano, *Vice Pres*
Terry Tuscano, *Vice Pres*
Patricia Morales, *Prdtn Mgr*
Joshua James, *Purch Agent*
EMP: 32
SQ FT: 5,400
SALES (est): 5.8MM Privately Held
WEB: www.jreinc.com
SIC: 3672 Printed circuit boards

(G-11781)
JAK DIVERSIFIED II INC
Also Called: Multi-Pak Packaging
241 Clinton Rd (07006-6603)
PHONE....................................973 439-1182
Fax: 973 439-1235
John Culligan, *President*
Deborah Culligan, *COO*
Allyson Culligan, *Exec VP*
▲ EMP: 75
SQ FT: 55,000
SALES (est): 19MM Privately Held
SIC: 2834 Pharmaceutical preparations

(G-11782)
JAY GERISH COMPANY
2 York Ave (07006-6407)
PHONE....................................973 403-0655
Fax: 973 403-3449
Jay Gerish, *President*
Joan Gerish, *Corp Secy*
Joseph Gerish, *Vice Pres*
Kathleen Gerish Rieckert, *Vice Pres*
Kathy Gerish, *Finance*
▲ EMP: 8
SQ FT: 42,000
SALES (est): 1.1MM Privately Held
WEB: www.jaygerish.com
SIC: 2353 Hats & caps

(G-11783)
LTS LHMANN THRAPY SYSTEMS CORP
21 Henderson Dr (07006-6607)
PHONE....................................973 575-5170
Fax: 973 575-5174
Wolfgang Hartwig, *CEO*
Stephanie Satz, *Counsel*
Rick Chan, *Vice Pres*
Kenneth Rogers, *Vice Pres*
Dave Sacks, *Vice Pres*
▲ EMP: 1000
SQ FT: 150,000
SALES (est): 228.8MM
SALES (corp-wide): 577.3K Privately Held
WEB: www.ltslohmann.com
SIC: 2834 Pharmaceutical preparations
HQ: Lts Lohmann Therapie-Systeme Ag
    Lohmannstr. 2
    Andernach 56626
    263 299-0

(G-11784)
LUMENARC INC
37 Fairfield Pl (07006-6206)
PHONE....................................973 882-5918
Fax: 973 227-3942
Harminder Bhalla, *President*
Ranbir Bhalla, *Vice Pres*
▲ EMP: 10

SQ FT: 25,000
SALES (est): 1.5MM Privately Held
SIC: 3643 Current-carrying wiring devices

(G-11785)
MARMAXX OPERATING CORP
Also Called: Marshalls
901 Bloomfield Ave (07006-7128)
PHONE....................................973 575-7910
Gwen O'Conner, *Manager*
EMP: 60
SALES (corp-wide): 35.8B Publicly Held
WEB: www.marshallsonline.com
SIC: 5311 5651 5641 2339 Department stores, discount; family clothing stores; children's & infants' wear stores; women's & misses' outerwear
HQ: Marmaxx Operating Corp.
    770 Cochituate Rd
    Framingham MA 01701

(G-11786)
MAXIMUM HUMN PRFMCE HLDNGS LLC (PA)
165 Clinton Rd (07006-6605)
PHONE....................................973 785-9055
Gerald Dente, *CEO*
EMP: 23 EST: 2010
SALES (est): 2.9MM Privately Held
SIC: 2834 Vitamin, nutrient & hematinic preparations for human use

(G-11787)
MAXLITE INC
10 York Ave (07006-6411)
PHONE....................................800 555-5629
EMP: 6 Privately Held
SIC: 3648 Arc lighting fixtures
PA: Maxlite, Inc.
    12 York Ave
    West Caldwell NJ 07006

(G-11788)
MAXLITE INC (PA)
12 York Ave (07006-6411)
PHONE....................................973 244-7300
Yon W Sung, *President*
Greg Galluccio, *President*
Richard Matthews, *President*
Todd Kim, *General Mgr*
Jay Lee, *General Mgr*
◆ EMP: 150
SQ FT: 100,000
SALES (est): 57.6MM Privately Held
WEB: www.maxlite.com
SIC: 3699 5044 3641 5063 Electrical equipment & supplies; office equipment; electric lamps; electrical apparatus & equipment

(G-11789)
MERCURY SYSTEMS INC
2 Henderson Dr Ste B (07006-6608)
PHONE....................................973 244-1040
Fax: 973 244-1188
Ken Hermanny, *CEO*
EMP: 36
SALES (corp-wide): 493.1MM Publicly Held
SIC: 3672 Printed circuit boards
PA: Mercury Systems, Inc.
    50 Minuteman Rd
    Andover MA 01810
    978 256-1300

(G-11790)
MERRIMAC INDUSTRIES INC (HQ)
41 Fairfield Pl (07006-6287)
PHONE....................................973 575-1300
Fax: 973 575-1734
Bob Tavares, *President*
Tom Braviak, *General Mgr*
Greg Shaffer, *General Mgr*
Brendan Curran, *Principal*
Reynold K Green, *COO*
▲ EMP: 100 EST: 1954
SQ FT: 71,200
SALES (est): 28.7MM
SALES (corp-wide): 2.7B Publicly Held
WEB: www.merrimacind.com
SIC: 3679 3663 3264 Microwave components; microwave communication equipment; amplifiers, RF power & IF; space satellite communications equipment; ferrite & ferrite parts

PA: Crane Co.
100 1st Stamford Pl # 300
Stamford CT 06902
203 363-7300

(G-11791)
MICROGEN INC
33 Clinton Rd Ste 102 (07006-6790)
PHONE..............................973 575-9025
Robert G Prince, *President*
EMP: 5
SQ FT: 1,400
SALES: 2MM **Privately Held**
WEB: www.microgeninc.com
SIC: 2842 5169 Sanitation preparations,
disinfectants & deodorants; specialty
cleaning & sanitation preparations

(G-11792)
NEPTUNE RESEARCH &
DEVELOPMENT
Also Called: N Research
267 Fairfield Ave (07006-6203)
PHONE..............................973 808-8811
Fax: 973 808-0086
Akos Sule, *President*
EMP: 20
SQ FT: 23,000
SALES (est): 3.7MM **Privately Held**
WEB: www.nresearch.com
SIC: 3491 Solenoid valves

(G-11793)
OCEAN POWER & EQUIPMENT
CO
1140 Bloomfield Ave # 107 (07006-7126)
PHONE..............................973 575-5775
Richard A Russell, *President*
◆ EMP: 5
SQ FT: 1,000
SALES (est): 967.2K **Privately Held**
WEB: www.ocean-power.us
SIC: 5088 3519 3731 Marine propulsion
machinery & equipment; diesel, semi-
diesel or duel-fuel engines, including ma-
rine; commercial cargo ships, building &
repairing; commercial passenger ships,
building & repairing

(G-11794)
ORIGINAL BAGEL & BIALY CO
INC
2 Fairfield Cres (07006-6205)
PHONE..............................973 227-5777
Fax: 973 227-5767
Bruce Levenbrook, *CEO*
Dave Harris, *President*
Bill Lasek, *COO*
Garrett Levenbrook, *Exec VP*
Ronald Harris, *QC Mgr*
EMP: 43
SQ FT: 30,000
SALES (est): 16.2MM **Privately Held**
WEB: www.originalbagel.com
SIC: 2051 Bagels, fresh or frozen

(G-11795)
OSULLIVAN COMMUNICATIONS
CORP (PA)
1 Fairfield Cres (07006-6204)
PHONE..............................973 227-5112
Elizabeth O'Sullivan, *Exec VP*
Joseph Bonis, *Senior VP*
Paul Fuzzi, *Vice Pres*
Cynthia Araujo, *Project Mgr*
Cristina Sake, *Human Res Mgr*
▼ EMP: 23
SALES (est): 12.1MM **Privately Held**
SIC: 2752 Commercial printing, litho-
graphic

(G-11796)
PCI INC
185 Fairfield Ave Ste 4c (07006-6417)
PHONE..............................973 226-8007
William J Murphy, *President*
Jack O'Dea, *Vice Pres*
EMP: 8
SQ FT: 3,000
SALES (est): 634.7K
SALES (corp-wide): 7.9MM **Privately Held**
WEB: www.advancedhorizons.com
SIC: 6531 3699 Rental agent, real estate;
electrical equipment & supplies

PA: Advanced Horizons, Inc.
185 Fairfield Ave Ste 4c
West Caldwell NJ 07006
973 226-8007

(G-11797)
PLASTINETICS INC
195 Fairfield Ave (07006-6424)
PHONE..............................973 618-9090
Ed Batta, *Principal*
EMP: 4
SALES (est): 288.9K **Privately Held**
SIC: 3083 Plastic finished products, lami-
nated

(G-11798)
POTDEVIN MACHINE CO
26 Fairfield Pl (07006-6207)
P.O. Box 1409, Caldwell (07007-1409)
PHONE..............................973 227-8828
Robert S Potdevin, *President*
Barbara Brose, *Bookkeeper*
Dominick Gagliano, *Sales Mgr*
EMP: 10
SQ FT: 25,000
SALES (est): 1.9MM **Privately Held**
WEB: www.potdevin.com
SIC: 3565 Packaging machinery

(G-11799)
QUAGEN PHARMACEUTICALS
LLC (PA)
11 Patton Dr (07006-6404)
PHONE..............................973 228-9600
Ashish Shah, *President*
EMP: 15
SALES: 789K **Privately Held**
SIC: 2834 Druggists' preparations (phar-
maceuticals)

(G-11800)
QUAGEN PHARMACEUTICALS
LLC
34 Fairfield Pl (07006-6209)
PHONE..............................973 228-9600
Ashish Shah, *President*
EMP: 10
SALES (corp-wide): 789K **Privately Held**
SIC: 2834 Pharmaceutical preparations
PA: Quagen Pharmaceuticals Llc
11 Patton Dr
West Caldwell NJ 07006
973 228-9600

(G-11801)
R R DONNELLEY & SONS
COMPANY
5 Henderson Dr (07006-6607)
PHONE..............................973 439-8321
Russell Radil, *Branch Mgr*
Christine Urbanski, *Executive*
EMP: 200
SALES (corp-wide): 6.9B **Publicly Held**
WEB: www.rrdonnelley.com
SIC: 2754 Catalogs: gravure printing, not
published on site
PA: R. R. Donnelley & Sons Company
35 W Wacker Dr Ste 3650
Chicago IL 60601
312 326-8000

(G-11802)
REGI US INC
8 Fairfield Cres Unit 1 (07006-6205)
PHONE..............................862 702-3901
Terry Gretsas, *Director*
EMP: 4
SQ FT: 35,000
SALES (est): 252.3K **Privately Held**
SIC: 2844 Toilet preparations

(G-11803)
REVERE SURVIVAL PRODUCTS
INC
3 Fairfield Cres (07006-6204)
PHONE..............................973 575-8811
Fax: 973 575-1788
Howard Koffman, *President*
◆ EMP: 10
SALES (est): 651.1K **Privately Held**
SIC: 3429 Manufactured hardware (gen-
eral)

(G-11804)
RISE CORPORATION
Also Called: Richards Industries
4 Fairfield Cres (07006-6205)
PHONE..............................973 575-7480
Fax: 973 575-6783
Chester V Wampler II, *CEO*
Robert B Taylor, *President*
Carl Bondorff, *CFO*
Chuck Bechtel, *Info Tech Dir*
EMP: 20
SQ FT: 25,000
SALES (est): 3.8MM **Privately Held**
SIC: 3499 3537 Fire- or burglary-resistive
products; pallets, metal; dollies (hand or
power trucks), industrial except mining;
skids, metal

(G-11805)
SCHIFF & CO
1120 Bloomfield Ave # 103 (07006-7131)
PHONE..............................973 227-1830
Fax: 973 227-5330
Robert Schiff, *President*
Mary Ann Weinberg, *General Mgr*
Joann Schiff, *Vice Pres*
Hannah Lewis, *Executive Asst*
EMP: 13 EST: 1982
SALES (est): 1.5MM **Privately Held**
WEB: www.schiffco.com
SIC: 8742 2721 Management consulting
services; auditing services

(G-11806)
TIMELINE PROMOTIONS INC
19 Aldrin Dr (07006-7201)
PHONE..............................973 226-1512
Kim Meth, *President*
EMP: 4
SALES (est): 560K **Privately Held**
WEB: www.timelinepromotions.com
SIC: 8743 2759 Promotion service; com-
mercial printing

(G-11807)
VITAQUEST INTERNATIONAL
LLC (PA)
8 Henderson Dr (07006-6608)
PHONE..............................973 575-9200
Keith Frankel, *Ch of Bd*
Angela Vanhouten, *General Mgr*
David P Illingworth, *COO*
Yvonne York, *Wholesale*
Angela Van Houten, *Manager*
▲ EMP: 500
SQ FT: 150,000
SALES (est): 162.5MM **Privately Held**
WEB: www.gardenstatenutritionals.com
SIC: 2834 5149 5122 8742 Vitamin
preparations; health foods; vitamins &
minerals; marketing consulting services

West Cape May
Cape May County

(G-11808)
FLYING FISH STUDIO
130 Park Blvd (08204-1239)
PHONE..............................609 884-2760
Fax: 609 884-5744
Susan B Lotozo, *Owner*
EMP: 5
SQ FT: 1,200
SALES: 350K **Privately Held**
WEB: www.flyingfishstudio.com
SIC: 7336 5947 5699 2326 Silk screen
design; souvenirs; customized clothing &
apparel; work apparel, except uniforms;
service apparel (baker, barber, lab, etc.),
washable: men's

West Creek
Ocean County

(G-11809)
BARNEGAT LIGHT FIBRGLS
SUP LLC
304 Forge Rd Unit 12 (08092-3219)
PHONE..............................609 294-8870
Norma Bunkelberger, *Principal*

Thomas L Maher,
EMP: 3
SQ FT: 1,200
SALES (est): 2MM **Privately Held**
SIC: 5169 3732 3083 Chemicals & allied
products; boat building & repairing; lami-
nated plastics plate & sheet

(G-11810)
DOWN SHORE PUBLISHING
CORP
638 Teal St (08092)
P.O. Box 100 (08092-0100)
PHONE..............................609 978-1233
Raymond G Fisk, *President*
▲ EMP: 6
SALES (est): 660.4K **Privately Held**
WEB: www.down-the-shore.com
SIC: 2741 Miscellaneous publishing

(G-11811)
HORSETRACS
99 Oak Ave (08092-2816)
PHONE..............................732 228-7646
Barbara Frayman, *Owner*
EMP: 4
SALES (est): 210.6K **Privately Held**
SIC: 2399 Horse harnesses & riding crops,
etc.: non-leather

(G-11812)
WOODWARD WOOD PRODUCTS
DESIGN
Also Called: Handmade Furniture
612 Main St (08092-9757)
PHONE..............................609 597-2708
Fax: 609 978-0636
Richard Woodward, *President*
EMP: 15
SQ FT: 8,000
SALES: 2MM **Privately Held**
SIC: 2499 2512 Kitchen, bathroom &
household ware: wood; wood upholstered
chairs & couches

West Deptford
Gloucester County

(G-11813)
ACC FOODS LTD LIABILITY CO
280 Jessup Rd (08086-2128)
PHONE..............................856 848-8877
John D Ong, *Opers Mgr*
Dong John, *Sales Staff*
Hing Kong,
Kuang M Kwok,
Kai Chuen Wong,
◆ EMP: 106
SALES: 12.5MM **Privately Held**
SIC: 2099 Food preparations

(G-11814)
AKERS BIOSCIENCES INC
201 Grove Rd (08086-2231)
PHONE..............................856 848-8698
Howard R Yeaton, *CEO*
Raymond F Akers Jr, *Ch of Bd*
Doug Carrara, *Vice Pres*
Nicolas Daurel, *Vice Pres*
Richard McKee, *Engineer*
EMP: 32
SQ FT: 12,500
SALES: 3.3MM **Privately Held**
WEB: www.akersbiosciences.com
SIC: 2835 3829 In vitro diagnostics; meas-
uring & controlling devices; medical diag-
nostic systems, nuclear

(G-11815)
ANDREW B DUFFY INC
322 Crown Point Rd (08086-2120)
P.O. Box 569, Thorofare (08086-0569)
PHONE..............................856 845-4900
Fax: 856 845-3921
Brian M Duffy, *President*
Sherri Veacock, *Office Mgr*
William Harle, *Manager*
EMP: 15 EST: 1951
SQ FT: 12,000

GEOGRAPHIC

SALES (est): 3.2MM **Privately Held**
WEB: www.abduffy.com
SIC: 3443 3444 3441 3412 Industrial vessels, tanks & containers; sheet metalwork; fabricated structural metal; metal barrels, drums & pails

(G-11816)
AQUATROLS CORP OF AMERICA
Also Called: Aqua Controls
1273 Imperial Way (08066-1808)
PHONE..............................856 537-6003
Tracy Jarman, *CEO*
Ryan Lebon, *CFO*
Andy Moore, *Sales Dir*
Dan Macias, *Sales Mgr*
Darlene Dipaolo, *Office Mgr*
◆ **EMP:** 34
SQ FT: 64,000
SALES (est): 11.5MM **Privately Held**
WEB: www.aquatrols.com
SIC: 2879 Agricultural chemicals

(G-11817)
ASSOCIATED ASPHALT MKTG LLC
400 Grove Rd (08066-1844)
PHONE..............................210 249-9988
Carol Streeper, *Branch Mgr*
EMP: 25 **Privately Held**
SIC: 1311 Crude petroleum & natural gas
PA: Associated Asphalt Partners, Llc
110 Franklin Rd Sw Fl 9
Roanoke VA 24011

(G-11818)
BOYLE TOOL & DIE CO INC
135 Crown Point Rd (08086-2173)
PHONE..............................856 853-1819
Fax: 856 848-2418
Thomas J Boyle, *President*
Steve Boyle, *Vice Pres*
EMP: 10
SQ FT: 10,000
SALES (est): 878.4K **Privately Held**
SIC: 3544 3469 3496 3315 Special dies & tools; metal stampings; miscellaneous fabricated wire products; steel wire & related products

(G-11819)
BUMPER SPECIALTIES INC
1607 Imperial Way (08066-1816)
PHONE..............................856 345-7650
Fax: 856 345-7690
Leon Braunstein, *President*
Robert Steers, *Controller*
EMP: 149
SQ FT: 80,000
SALES (est): 25.8MM **Privately Held**
WEB: www.bumperspecialties.com
SIC: 3069 Hard rubber products

(G-11820)
CHECKPOINT SECURITY SYSTEMS GR
101 Wolf Dr (08086-2243)
PHONE..............................952 933-8858
George Off, *CEO*
Steve Champeau, *Vice Pres*
EMP: 125
SQ FT: 12,000
SALES (est): 8.4MM
SALES (corp-wide): 3.7B **Privately Held**
SIC: 1731 7382 3829 Fire detection & burglar alarm systems specialization; closed circuit television installation; fire alarm maintenance & monitoring; burglar alarm maintenance & monitoring; protective devices, security; measuring & controlling devices
HQ: Checkpoint Systems, Inc.
101 Wolf Dr
West Deptford NJ 08086
800 257-5540

(G-11821)
CHECKPOINT SYSTEMS INC (HQ)
101 Wolf Dr (08086-2243)
P.O. Box 188, Thorofare (08086-0188)
PHONE..............................800 257-5540
Fax: 856 848-0937
George Babich Jr, *President*

David Murrihy, *Business Mgr*
Birgitta Pettersson, *Business Mgr*
James Wrigley, *COO*
Bernard Gremillet, *Exec VP*
◆ **EMP:** 104
SALES: 587.1MM
SALES (corp-wide): 3.7B **Privately Held**
WEB: www.checkpointsystems.com
SIC: 3699 3812 3663 Security control equipment & systems; detection apparatus: electronic/magnetic field, light/heat; television closed circuit equipment
PA: Ccl Industries Inc
111 Gordon Baker Rd Suite 801
Toronto ON M2H 3
416 756-8500

(G-11822)
CHECKPOINT SYSTEMS INC
101 Wolf Dr (08086-2243)
PHONE..............................856 848-1800
George Babich Jr, *Branch Mgr*
John Watson, *Administration*
EMP: 114
SALES (corp-wide): 3.7B **Privately Held**
SIC: 3699 3812 3663 Security control equipment & systems; detection apparatus: electronic/magnetic field, light/heat; television closed circuit equipment
HQ: Checkpoint Systems, Inc.
101 Wolf Dr
West Deptford NJ 08086
800 257-5540

(G-11823)
CHECKPOINT SYSTEMS INC
101 Wolf Dr (08086-2243)
PHONE..............................952 933-8858
Nick Khalil, *President*
EMP: 125
SALES (corp-wide): 3.7B **Privately Held**
WEB: www.checkpointsystems.com
SIC: 1731 7382 3829 Fire detection & burglar alarm systems specialization; closed circuit television installation; fire alarm maintenance & monitoring; burglar alarm maintenance & monitoring; protective devices, security; measuring & controlling devices
HQ: Checkpoint Systems, Inc.
101 Wolf Dr
West Deptford NJ 08086
800 257-5540

(G-11824)
CHECKPOINT SYSTEMS INC
101 Wolf Dr (08086-2243)
PHONE..............................856 848-1800
Michael Smith, *Branch Mgr*
EMP: 175
SALES (corp-wide): 3.7B **Privately Held**
SIC: 3699 Security control equipment & systems
HQ: Checkpoint Systems, Inc.
101 Wolf Dr
West Deptford NJ 08086
800 257-5540

(G-11825)
COIM USA INC (HQ)
Also Called: Novacote Flexpack
286 Mantua Grove Rd # 1 (08066-1738)
PHONE..............................856 224-8560
Lucio Siano, *CEO*
Michelangelo Cavallo, *President*
Angelo Macchi, *Principal*
Dale Richmond, *Business Mgr*
Ashim Parmar, *Plant Engr*
◆ **EMP:** 84
SALES (est): 34.1MM
SALES (corp-wide): 401.9MM **Privately Held**
WEB: www.us.coimgroup.com
SIC: 2891 2821 Adhesives; polyesters; elastomers, nonvulcanizable (plastics)
PA: C.O.I.M. Spa Chimica Organica Industriale Milanese
Via Alessandro Manzoni 28
Settimo Milanese MI 20019
023 350-51

(G-11826)
EDWARDS BROTHERS INC
1301 Metropolitan Ave # 300 (08066-1862)
PHONE..............................856 848-6900
EMP: 5

SALES (corp-wide): 308.1MM **Privately Held**
SIC: 2752 Lithographic Commercial Printing
HQ: Edwards Brothers, Inc.
5411 Jackson Rd
Ann Arbor MI 48103
800 722-3231

(G-11827)
HANGSTERFERS LABORATORIES (PA)
175 Ogden Rd (08051-1615)
PHONE..............................856 468-0216
Fax: 856 468-0200
Ann Jones, *CEO*
Edward Jones, *COO*
Pat Brewer, *Human Res Mgr*
Skip Wolford, *Sales Mgr*
Barry Gall, *Manager*
◆ **EMP:** 30 **EST:** 1946
SQ FT: 30,000
SALES (est): 4.5MM **Privately Held**
WEB: www.hangsterfers.com
SIC: 2992 7389 Oils & greases, blending & compounding;

(G-11828)
HUSSMANN CORPORATION
Also Called: Convenience Works
875 Kings Hwy Ste 205 (08096-3165)
PHONE..............................800 320-3510
Tim Lowery, *Manager*
EMP: 20
SALES (corp-wide): 74.9B **Privately Held**
WEB: www.hussmann.com
SIC: 3585 Refrigeration & heating equipment
HQ: Hussmann Corporation
12999 St Charles Rock Rd
Bridgeton MO 63044
314 291-2000

(G-11829)
ICS CORPORATION
100 Friars Blvd (08086-2141)
PHONE..............................215 427-3355
Fax: 215 634-1522
Richard Bastian, *President*
Matthew I Bastian, *President*
Patrick Bailey, *Exec VP*
Richard Prendergast, *Vice Pres*
Fran King, *Materials Mgr*
EMP: 225
SQ FT: 100,000
SALES (est): 34.2MM **Privately Held**
WEB: www.ics-corporation.com
SIC: 7374 2759 7331 Data processing & preparation; commercial printing; direct mail advertising services

(G-11830)
INTERNATIONAL PAPER COMPANY
33 Phoenix Dr (08086-2156)
PHONE..............................856 853-7000
Rich Rosenbach, *President*
EMP: 21
SALES (corp-wide): 21.7B **Publicly Held**
WEB: www.internationalpaper.com
SIC: 2621 Paper mills
PA: International Paper Company
6400 Poplar Ave
Memphis TN 38197
901 419-9000

(G-11831)
JEROME GROUP INC
Also Called: Jerome Medical
1414 Metropolitan Ave (08066-1869)
PHONE..............................856 234-8600
Ronald S Kowalski, *President*
Anthony H Martinez, *Vice Pres*
Karen L Smith, *Vice Pres*
▲ **EMP:** 55 **EST:** 1947
SQ FT: 15,000
SALES (est): 5.5MM
SALES (corp-wide): 520.9MM **Privately Held**
WEB: www.miamij.com
SIC: 3842 Splints, pneumatic & wood; supports: abdominal, ankle, arch, kneecap, etc.

HQ: Ossur Americas, Inc.
27051 Towne Centre Dr
Foothill Ranch CA 92610
949 362-3883

(G-11832)
JOHNSON MATTHEY INC
Also Called: Catalyst Chemicals and Ref Div
2001 Nolte Dr (08066-1795)
PHONE..............................856 384-7000
David Frew, *Production*
Clem Vanzelst, *Purch Mgr*
John Hunt, *Engineer*
Shane Yeh, *Engineer*
Martin D Turney, *Branch Mgr*
EMP: 235
SALES (corp-wide): 15B **Privately Held**
SIC: 3341 Secondary nonferrous metals
HQ: Matthey Johnson Inc
435 Devon Park Dr Ste 600
Wayne PA 19087
610 971-3000

(G-11833)
KEYSTONE AUTOMOTIVE INDS INC
39 Phoenix Dr (08086-2156)
PHONE..............................856 829-4700
Mike Grisko, *Manager*
EMP: 20
SALES (corp-wide): 9.7B **Publicly Held**
WEB: www.kool-vue.com
SIC: 3714 Motor vehicle parts & accessories
HQ: Keystone Automotive Industries, Inc.
655 Grassmere Park
Nashville TN 37211
615 781-5200

(G-11834)
LACROSSE REPUBLIC
711 Mantua Pike Ste 2 (08096-3357)
PHONE..............................856 853-8787
Bill Keane, *Owner*
EMP: 4
SALES (est): 364.4K **Privately Held**
SIC: 3949 Sporting & athletic goods

(G-11835)
MATTHEY JOHNSON INC
Also Called: Catalyst Chemicals and Ref Div
2001 Nolte Dr (08066-1727)
PHONE..............................856 384-7132
Bruce Kubat, *Maint Spvr*
Brent Hackette, *Branch Mgr*
EMP: 230
SALES (corp-wide): 15B **Privately Held**
SIC: 3341 3339 3356 2834 Platinum group metals, smelting & refining (secondary); gold smelting & refining (secondary); silver smelting & refining (secondary); platinum group metal refining (primary); gold refining (primary); silver refining (primary); precious metals; platinum group metals: rolling, drawing or extruding; gold & gold alloy: rolling, drawing or extruding; powders, pharmaceutical; metal powders, pastes & flakes; paste, metal; exhaust systems & parts, motor vehicle
HQ: Matthey Johnson Inc
435 Devon Park Dr Ste 600
Wayne PA 19087
610 971-3000

(G-11836)
MATTHEY JOHNSON INC
Also Called: Johnson Matthey Phrm Mtls
2003 Nolte Dr (08066-1727)
PHONE..............................856 384-7001
Fax: 856 384-7276
Joe Moy, *Sales Staff*
John Fowler, *Branch Mgr*
William Tamblyn, *Director*
EMP: 43
SALES (corp-wide): 15B **Privately Held**
SIC: 2834 Pharmaceutical preparations
HQ: Matthey Johnson Inc
435 Devon Park Dr Ste 600
Wayne PA 19087
610 971-3000

(G-11837)
OSSUR AMERICAS INC
680 Grove Rd (08086-2232)
PHONE..............................856 345-6000

▲ = Import ▼=Export
◆ =Import/Export

Ron Kowalski, *Branch Mgr*
EMP: 4
SALES (corp-wide): 520.9MM **Privately Held**
SIC: 3842 Prosthetic appliances
HQ: Ossur Americas, Inc.
27051 Towne Centre Dr
Foothill Ranch CA 92610
949 362-3883

(G-11838)
P W B OMNI INC
1319 Vallee Dr (08096-3139)
PHONE..................................856 384-1300
Fax: 856 384-0260
Elizabeth Foradori, *President*
EMP: 3
SALES (est): 5MM **Privately Held**
WEB: www.omnipwb.com
SIC: 5065 3672 Electronic parts & equipment; wiring boards

(G-11839)
PRECISION ORTHOTIC LAB OF NJ
1595 Imperial Way Ste 103 (08066-1864)
PHONE..................................856 848-6226
Fax: 856 848-7944
Aron Adams, *President*
EMP: 15
SQ FT: 1,500
SALES (est): 1.1MM **Privately Held**
WEB: www.precisionorthotic.com
SIC: 3842 Orthopedic appliances

(G-11840)
PUBLISHERS INC
Also Called: Fort Nassau Graphics
1757 Imperial Way (08066-1818)
PHONE..................................856 853-2800
Paul F Cipolone, *President*
Brian Francis, *Vice Pres*
Lorraine Gabbett, *Vice Pres*
EMP: 40 EST: 1957
SQ FT: 20,000
SALES (est): 10.7MM **Privately Held**
WEB: www.publishers.com
SIC: 2752 Commercial printing, offset

(G-11841)
SOLVAY SPCLTY POLYMERS USA LLC
10 Leonard Ln (08086-2150)
PHONE..................................856 853-8119
Justin Gattuso, *Business Mgr*
Mahesh Padigala, *Engineer*
James Ford, *Controller*
Joseph Martin, *Natl Sales Mgr*
Charles Jones, *Branch Mgr*
EMP: 150
SQ FT: 5,000
SALES (corp-wide): 10MM **Privately Held**
SIC: 2819 Industrial inorganic chemicals
HQ: Solvay Specialty Polymers Usa, L.L.C.
4500 Mcginnis Ferry Rd
Alpharetta GA 30005
770 772-8200

(G-11842)
USA WOOD DOOR INC
1475 Imperial Way (08066-1812)
P.O. Box 116, Thorofare (08086-0116)
PHONE..................................856 384-9663
Fax: 856 384-7444
John Krause, *President*
EMP: 50
SQ FT: 17,000
SALES (est): 7.6MM
SALES (corp-wide): 2B **Publicly Held**
WEB: www.usawooddoor.com
SIC: 2431 5211 Door frames, wood; door sashes, wood; door trim, wood; doors & door parts & trim, wood; door & window products; doors, wood or metal, except storm
PA: Masonite International Corporation
201 N Franklin St Ste 300
Tampa FL 33602
813 877-2726

West Long Branch
Monmouth County

(G-11843)
ARTS EMBROIDERY LLC
175 Monmouth Rd (07764-1028)
PHONE..................................732 870-2400
Art Kraucis,
INA Kraucis,
EMP: 4
SALES (est): 231.2K **Privately Held**
SIC: 2395 2759 Embroidery & art needlework; screen printing

(G-11844)
BORO PRINTING INC
813 Broadway (07764-1542)
PHONE..................................732 229-1899
Fax: 732 222-6809
Gary Delatush, *President*
Evelyn Delatush, *President*
EMP: 5
SQ FT: 3,500
SALES: 300K **Privately Held**
WEB: www.boroprinting.com
SIC: 2621 2752 Printing paper; commercial printing, offset

(G-11845)
COMFORT RVOLUTION HOLDINGS LLC
187 Rte 36 Ste 205 (07764-1306)
P.O. Box 1290, Eatontown (07724-5290)
PHONE..................................732 272-9111
Michael Fux, *CEO*
Thomas Bruno, *CFO*
Dan Lufkin,
◆ EMP: 15
SALES (est): 4.5MM **Privately Held**
SIC: 2515 Mattresses & bedsprings; box springs, assembled; mattresses, waterbed flotation

(G-11846)
SHREM CONSULTING LTD LBLTY CO
Also Called: Nexxbrands
457 Monmouth Rd (07764-1263)
PHONE..................................917 371-0581
Abraham Shrem,
Talia Shrem,
EMP: 2
SALES: 1MM **Privately Held**
SIC: 2085 2086 5149 5182 Cocktails, alcoholic; mineral water, carbonated: packaged in cans, bottles, etc.; mineral or spring water bottling; cocktails, alcoholic: premixed;

(G-11847)
SMB INTERNATIONAL LLC
121 State Route 36 # 180 (07764-1436)
PHONE..................................732 222-4888
Scott Margulis, *COO*
Barry Margulis,
▼ EMP: 15
SALES (est): 4.8MM **Privately Held**
SIC: 2992 Lubricating oils

(G-11848)
SPECIALTY PRODUCTS PLUS
215 Locust Ave (07764-1112)
PHONE..................................732 380-1188
Don Baldwin, *Owner*
EMP: 5
SALES (est): 535.9K **Privately Held**
SIC: 3432 Plumbing fixture fittings & trim

West Milford
Passaic County

(G-11849)
ALMOND BRANCH INC
Also Called: Agape Child Care Center
184 Marshall Hill Rd (07480-3512)
PHONE..................................973 728-3479
Fax: 973 728-5257
Cindy Palazzolo, *Pastor*
Rich Palazzolo, *Pastor*
Nicholas J Padovani, *Sr Pastor*

Alene Rhinesmith, *Office Admin*
Nancy Carhart, *Director*
EMP: 25
SQ FT: 5,000
SALES: 700K **Privately Held**
WEB: www.agapechildcarecenter.com
SIC: 8661 8351 7372 Assembly of God Church; preschool center; application computer software

(G-11850)
ANCHOR SALES & MARKETING INC
Also Called: Anchor Home Products
755 Macopin Rd 1 (07480-2608)
PHONE..................................973 545-2277
Fax: 201 493-0016
Frank G Petronzio, *President*
Linda Petronzio, *Vice Pres*
EMP: 13
SQ FT: 10,000
SALES (est): 1.3MM **Privately Held**
SIC: 2392 5023 Towels, fabric & nonwoven: made from purchased materials; tablecloths: made from purchased materials; slip covers & pads; linens & towels; linens, table; towels

(G-11851)
BEL-TECH STAMPING INC
26 Industrial Rd Ste A (07480-4600)
PHONE..................................973 728-8229
Jim Beloch, *President*
EMP: 13
SQ FT: 4,500
SALES: 500K **Privately Held**
SIC: 3469 Metal stampings

(G-11852)
HYDRAULIC MANIFOLDS USA LLC
Also Called: Selling Precision
264 Marshall Hill Rd (07480-3511)
PHONE..................................973 728-1214
Nimit Patel, *Mng Member*
EMP: 30
SALES (est): 999.3K **Privately Held**
SIC: 3674 Integrated circuits, semiconductor networks, etc.

(G-11853)
LA DUCA TECHNICAL SERVICES LLC
51 Shadowy Ln (07480-1458)
PHONE..................................570 309-4009
Brian Laduca,
EMP: 1
SALES: 120K **Privately Held**
SIC: 3571 Electronic computers

(G-11854)
MARGARITAVILLE INC
Also Called: Pressure Wash
129 Lincoln Ave (07480-2136)
P.O. Box 371 (07480-0371)
PHONE..................................973 728-7562
Eric Hasting, *President*
EMP: 6
SALES: 300K **Privately Held**
SIC: 3589 High pressure cleaning equipment

(G-11855)
NEXTGEN EDGE INC
50 Beacon Hill Rd Apt A (07480-1255)
PHONE..................................610 507-6904
William Furniss, *CEO*
David Booth, *CFO*
EMP: 4
SQ FT: 1,500
SALES (est): 235.2K **Privately Held**
SIC: 3841 Surgical & medical instruments; surgical knife blades & handles

(G-11856)
SELLING PRECISION INC
264 Marshall Hill Rd (07480-3511)
PHONE..................................973 728-1214
William Calcagno Jr, *President*
Kenneth Calcagno, *Vice Pres*
Luis Granizo, *Design Engr*
EMP: 35
SQ FT: 9,000

SALES (est): 8MM **Privately Held**
WEB: www.sellingprecision.com
SIC: 3498 Manifolds, pipe: fabricated from purchased pipe

(G-11857)
SYMCON INC
Also Called: Symcon Controls
47 Cedar Ln (07480-2391)
PHONE..................................973 728-8661
Fax: 973 728-8680
Stella Scilingo, *President*
Michael Scilingo, *Vice Pres*
EMP: 4 EST: 1970
SALES: 27K **Privately Held**
SIC: 3613 3498 3494 Panelboards & distribution boards, electric; fabricated pipe & fittings; valves & pipe fittings

(G-11858)
WALGREEN EASTERN CO INC
Also Called: Walgreens
1502 Union Valley Rd (07480-1354)
PHONE..................................973 728-3172
Fax: 973 728-3176
EMP: 30
SALES (corp-wide): 118.2B **Publicly Held**
SIC: 5912 2834 Drug stores; pharmaceutical preparations
HQ: Walgreen Eastern Co., Inc.
200 Wilmot Rd
Deerfield IL 60015
847 940-2500

(G-11859)
WOODS INDUSTRIAL LLC
Also Called: Wood's Industrial Services
81 Hudson Dr (07480-4216)
PHONE..................................973 208-0664
Meredith Wood, *Managing Prtnr*
Robert J Wood, *Partner*
EMP: 10
SALES (est): 760K **Privately Held**
SIC: 3599 1799 1796 Machine & other job shop work; welding on site; machine moving & rigging

---

West New York
Hudson County

(G-11860)
AIRCHARTERCOM LLC
6515 Kennedy Blvd E (07093-4231)
PHONE..................................212 999-4926
John Harrison, *CEO*
Imane Echouafni, *CFO*
Narjis Oughla, *Mng Member*
EMP: 42
SQ FT: 1,500
SALES (est): 5MM **Privately Held**
SIC: 7372 4522 Application computer software; flying charter service

(G-11861)
CABIO NEWSPAPER
604 56th St (07093-1236)
PHONE..................................201 902-0811
Yamile Camacho, *Principal*
EMP: 5 EST: 2010
SALES (est): 160.2K **Privately Held**
SIC: 2711 Newspapers: publishing only, not printed on site

(G-11862)
CHRISTIAN ART
567 52nd St Ste 15 (07093-5623)
PHONE..................................201 867-8096
Anthony Ferrer, *Owner*
EMP: 5
SALES (est): 522.5K **Privately Held**
SIC: 2531 3911 Church furniture; rosaries or other small religious articles, precious metal

(G-11863)
DANIEL FASHIONS INC
Also Called: Danielle Fashion
6108 Hudson Ave (07093-2902)
PHONE..................................201 869-1008
Nagy Garas, *President*
EMP: 7

GEOGRAPHIC

SALES (est): 730K **Privately Held**
SIC: 2331 Blouses, women's & juniors':
made from purchased material

(G-11864)
DU-MATT CORPORATION
12 65th St (07093-4104)
PHONE..........................201 861-4271
Adolpho Mattiello, *President*
Delia Mattiello, *Vice Pres*
J Sander, *Finance Dir*
EMP: 6
SQ FT: 6,000
SALES (est): 798.5K **Privately Held**
WEB: www.dumatt.com
SIC: 3423 Jewelers' hand tools

(G-11865)
ENTERPRISE SOLUTION PRODUCTS
28 Av At Pt Imperial 23 (07093)
PHONE..........................201 678-9200
Wayne Corion, *President*
EMP: 4
SQ FT: 1,800
SALES: 2.5MM **Privately Held**
SIC: 5112 3861 Photocopying supplies;
photocopy machines

(G-11866)
HILL CROSS CO INC
543 56th St (07093-8401)
P.O. Box 60 (07093-0060)
PHONE..........................201 864-3393
Christopher Hammer, *President*
Donald Rosegren, *Vice Pres*
EMP: 7
SQ FT: 18,000
SALES (est): 932.3K **Privately Held**
SIC: 3471 Electroplating of metals or
formed products

(G-11867)
IMPERIAL DRUG & SPICE CORP
5620 Kennedy Blvd W (07093-1208)
P.O. Box 8624, Woodcliff Lake (07677-8624)
PHONE..........................201 348-1551
Francisco Gil, *President*
EMP: 5
SALES (est): 633.1K **Privately Held**
SIC: 2844 Hair preparations, including
shampoos

(G-11868)
J & S FINISHING INC
443 62nd St Fl 1 (07093-2326)
PHONE..........................201 854-0338
Fax: 201 854-0420
Pedro A Calvo, *President*
EMP: 5
SALES (est): 363K **Privately Held**
SIC: 2395 Embroidery products, except
schiffli machine; embroidery & art needle-
work

(G-11869)
JAV LATIN AMERICA EXPRESS
6321 Bergenline Ave (07093-1606)
PHONE..........................201 868-5004
Filomena Zaino, *Owner*
EMP: 4
SALES (est): 289.4K **Privately Held**
SIC: 2741 Miscellaneous publishing

(G-11870)
JID TRANSPORTATION LLC
158 61st St Apt 2 (07093-2925)
PHONE..........................201 362-0841
Jaile Luis Diaz, *Principal*
EMP: 1
SALES: 85MM **Privately Held**
SIC: 3713 4212 7363 Truck cabs for
motor vehicles; truck rental with drivers;
truck driver services

(G-11871)
LENS LAB EXPRESS
5917 Bergenline Ave (07093-1306)
PHONE..........................201 861-0016
Howard Halle, *President*
EMP: 7
SALES (est): 861.7K **Privately Held**
SIC: 3851 5995 5049 Ophthalmic goods;
opticians; optical goods

(G-11872)
M & Z INTERNATIONAL INC
358 Oswego Ct (07093-8315)
PHONE..........................201 864-3331
Yuqiong Zhao, *President*
Liyu MA, *Director*
EMP: 5
SALES: 1MM **Privately Held**
WEB: www.mzinternational.com
SIC: 3699 Security devices

(G-11873)
MARLENE EMBROIDERY INC (PA)
6805 Madison St (07093-1818)
PHONE..........................201 868-1682
Ernest Hepperle, *President*
Marlene Hepperle, *Corp Secy*
James Hepperle, *Vice Pres*
EMP: 3
SQ FT: 5,000
SALES (est): 2.4MM **Privately Held**
SIC: 2397 Schiffli machine embroideries

(G-11874)
MASHAL SIGNS CO INC
568 55th St (07093-4625)
PHONE..........................201 348-8500
Alai Mashal, *CEO*
EMP: 6
SALES (est): 717.2K **Privately Held**
SIC: 3993 Signs & advertising specialties

(G-11875)
NESS PLASTICS INC
6040 Kennedy Blvd E 22f (07093-3825)
PHONE..........................201 854-4072
EMP: 10
SQ FT: 3,400
SALES (est): 590K **Privately Held**
SIC: 3069 8711 Mfg Fabricated Rubber
Products Engineering Services

(G-11876)
PRIAMO DESIGNS LTD
6614 Broadway (07093-3298)
PHONE..........................201 861-8808
Fax: 201 861-0170
Priamo Espaillat, *President*
▲ EMP: 7
SQ FT: 7,750
SALES: 600K **Privately Held**
SIC: 2341 Nightgowns & negligees:
women's & children's

(G-11877)
PRINTING LAB LTD LIABILITY CO
609 55th St (07093-4636)
PHONE..........................201 305-0404
Julian Ospina,
Louis Ospina,
EMP: 15
SALES: 1.2MM **Privately Held**
SIC: 3993 Signs & advertising specialties

(G-11878)
PROMEKO INC
543 59th St (07093-1317)
PHONE..........................201 861-9446
Fax: 201 861-5245
Edalio Rondon, *President*
Ylia Rondon, *Corp Secy*
EMP: 8
SQ FT: 15,000
SALES (est): 660K **Privately Held**
WEB: www.promekoinc.com
SIC: 2844 Cosmetic preparations

(G-11879)
QUADELLE TEXTILE CORP
573 56th St (07093-1233)
PHONE..........................201 865-1112
Rose Lenson, *President*
Harry Lenson, *Corp Secy*
EMP: 10 EST: 1957
SQ FT: 10,000
SALES: 110K **Privately Held**
SIC: 2397 2395 Schiffli machine embroi-
deries; pleating & stitching

(G-11880)
ROYAL PRINTING SERVICE
441 51st St (07093-1903)
P.O. Box 1000 (07093-1000)
PHONE..........................201 863-3131
Fax: 201 867-4437
Ralph S Passante Sr, *President*
Kevin Passante, *Vice Pres*
David Passante, *Admin Sec*
Christopher Holmes, *Graphic Designe*
EMP: 43
SQ FT: 20,000
SALES (est): 7.4MM **Privately Held**
WEB: www.royalprintingnj.com
SIC: 2752 Commercial printing, offset

(G-11881)
SAUD & SON JEWELRY INC
Also Called: Saud Jewelry
441 60th St (07093-2211)
PHONE..........................201 866-4445
Jose Saud, *President*
EMP: 7
SQ FT: 2,000
SALES (est): 733.8K **Privately Held**
SIC: 5944 7631 3911 5094 Jewelry, pre-
cious stones & precious metals; jewelry
repair services; jewelry, precious metal;
jewelry

(G-11882)
SWISSTEX COMPANY
220 61st St Ste 2 (07093-2931)
PHONE..........................201 861-8000
Fax: 201 861-8001
Robert Wolfe, *Owner*
EMP: 20 EST: 1934
SQ FT: 10,000
SALES (est): 950K **Privately Held**
SIC: 2339 2341 2251 Sportswear,
women's; bathing suits: women's, misses'
& juniors'; women's & children's night-
wear; women's hosiery, except socks

(G-11883)
WEBER & DOEBRICH INC
Also Called: Wedo
119 61st St (07093-2909)
PHONE..........................201 868-6122
Fax: 201 854-5564
Jane Zellweger, *President*
EMP: 9
SALES: 400K **Privately Held**
SIC: 2397 Schiffli machine embroideries

West Orange
Essex County

(G-11884)
A & F ELECTROPLATING INC
106 Ashland Ave (07052-5401)
PHONE..........................973 983-2459
Fax: 973 736-1718
Frank Chabala, *President*
Lucille Chabala, *Corp Secy*
Barry Chabala, *Vice Pres*
EMP: 4 EST: 1968
SQ FT: 6,000
SALES: 600K **Privately Held**
SIC: 3471 Electroplating of metals or
formed products

(G-11885)
ALL-STATE FENCE INC
347 Mount Pleasant Ave # 300
(07052-2730)
PHONE..........................732 431-4944
Fax: 732 431-9352
Scott Skrable, *President*
Michael Skrable, *Vice Pres*
EMP: 35
SQ FT: 3,000
SALES (est): 6.2MM **Privately Held**
WEB: www.allstatefence.com
SIC: 5031 5211 1799 2499 Fencing,
wood; fencing; fence construction; fenc-
ing, wood

(G-11886)
ASAP CONTAINERS NJ NY CORP
25 Mountain Dr (07052-4016)
PHONE..........................732 659-4402

Ronen Barak, *President*
EMP: 10
SALES: 1MM **Privately Held**
SIC: 3715 Demountable cargo containers

(G-11887)
AURAPLAYER USA INC
21 Dale Dr (07052-2005)
PHONE..........................617 879-9013
Mia Urman, *President*
Gwen Edwards, *Exec VP*
Yossi Nakash, *CTO*
EMP: 11
SQ FT: 550
SALES: 146K **Privately Held**
SIC: 7372 7379 Business oriented com-
puter software; computer related consult-
ing services
PA: Auraplayer Ltd
13 Kehilat Zhytomyr
Tel Aviv-Jaffa
522 934-361

(G-11888)
B T O INDUSTRIES INC
11 Lenox Ter (07052-2623)
P.O. Box 1845, Bloomfield (07003-1845)
PHONE..........................973 243-0011
Bruce Osborne, *President*
EMP: 9
SQ FT: 500
SALES (est): 1.1MM **Privately Held**
SIC: 7311 8748 2721 Advertising agen-
cies; publishing consultant; magazines:
publishing only, not printed on site

(G-11889)
BILDISCO MFG INC
Also Called: Bildisco Door Mfg
21 Central Ave (07052-5298)
PHONE..........................973 673-2400
Fax: 973 673-2236
Salvatore Valente, *President*
EMP: 15
SQ FT: 25,000
SALES (est): 2.8MM **Privately Held**
SIC: 3442 2431 3429 Metal doors; doors,
wood; door locks, bolts & checks

(G-11890)
COR PRODUCTS INC
20 Standish Ave (07052-5519)
PHONE..........................973 731-4952
Cindy Douglas, *Principal*
EMP: 5
SALES (est): 522.5K **Privately Held**
SIC: 2542 Fixtures, office: except wood

(G-11891)
COZZOLINO INC
20 Standish Ave (07052-5519)
PHONE..........................973 731-9292
Fax: 973 731-0190
Michael Cozzolino, *President*
Steven Cozzolino, *Vice Pres*
EMP: 38
SQ FT: 22,000
SALES (est): 5.9MM **Privately Held**
WEB: www.cozzolino.com
SIC: 5712 2521 2511 2431 Cabinet work,
custom; custom made furniture, except
cabinets; wood office furniture; wood
household furniture; millwork

(G-11892)
D2CF LLC (PA)
108 Coccio Dr (07052-4119)
PHONE..........................973 699-4111
Amanda Zazoff, *Principal*
EMP: 2 EST: 2015
SALES (est): 1.3MM **Publicly Held**
SIC: 3669 Emergency alarms

(G-11893)
DATALINK SOLUTIONS INC
27 Fundus Rd (07052-3510)
PHONE..........................973 731-9373
Lenny Jacobs, *Manager*
EMP: 10
SALES (est): 935.6K **Privately Held**
SIC: 3825 Network analyzers

(G-11894)
FIRST MOUNTAIN CONSULTING
Also Called: Mostly Software Development
3 Colony Ct (07052-4613)
PHONE................................973 325-8480
Simeon Berman MD, *President*
Rose Hutter, *Corp Secy*
Carol Berman, *Vice Pres*
Carol Bromberg, *Vice Pres*
EMP: 4
SQ FT: 4,000
SALES: 450K **Privately Held**
SIC: 7372 Prepackaged software

(G-11895)
GENOMESAFE LLC
4 Linden Ave (07052-4721)
PHONE................................203 676-3752
Kurt Rohloff,
EMP: 4
SALES (est): 91.3K **Privately Held**
SIC: 8748 7371 7372 Systems engineer-
ing consultant, ex. computer or profes-
sional; computer software systems
analysis & design, custom; utility com-
puter software

(G-11896)
HAMMER TOO LLC
Also Called: Cartridge World of Union
623 Eagle Rock Ave (07052-2948)
PHONE................................908 688-5601
Rod Young, *Chairman*
Alexander Martello,
EMP: 4
SQ FT: 1,000
SALES: 180K **Privately Held**
SIC: 3955 Print cartridges for laser & other
computer printers

(G-11897)
**HANGER PRSTHETCS & ORTHO
INC**
59 Main St Ste 111 (07052-5333)
PHONE................................973 736-0628
Fax: 973 736-1640
Thomas P Kirk, *Principal*
EMP: 7
SALES (corp-wide): 1B **Publicly Held**
SIC: 3842 Limbs, artificial
HQ: Hanger Prosthetics & Orthotics, Inc.
10910 Domain Dr Ste 300
Austin TX 78758
512 777-3800

(G-11898)
MDR LLC
401 Pleasant Valley Way # 2 (07052-2951)
PHONE................................973 731-7100
Richard Heyderman, *Managing Prtnr*
Cecelia Rampolla, *Admin Asst*
EMP: 4
SALES (est): 717.7K **Privately Held**
SIC: 2541 Store & office display cases &
fixtures

(G-11899)
**MEASUREMENT CONTROL
CORP**
Also Called: Measurement & Computing Co
9 Cummings Cir (07052-2255)
PHONE................................800 504-9010
Robert Friedman, *CEO*
Michael Levin, *General Mgr*
EMP: 4
SALES (est): 739.3K **Privately Held**
SIC: 3823 Industrial process measurement
equipment

(G-11900)
METRO TAG & LABEL INC
24 Park Ave 2 (07052-5553)
PHONE................................201 845-4747
Philp Glassman, *President*
EMP: 3
SQ FT: 1,200
SALES: 3MM **Privately Held**
SIC: 2754 Labels: gravure printing

(G-11901)
**NATIONAL COMMUNICATIONS
INC**
69 Washington St (07052-5538)
PHONE................................973 325-3151
Fax: 973 325-2690

Andy Brooke, *President*
Glen Kaufman, *Office Mgr*
EMP: 30
SQ FT: 22,000
SALES (est): 5MM **Privately Held**
WEB: www.trynci.com
SIC: 5065 5045 3357 Telephone equip-
ment; terminals, computer; nonferrous
wiredrawing & insulating

(G-11902)
**OMEGA HEAT TRANSFER CO
INC**
36 Rock Spring Ave (07052-2633)
PHONE................................732 340-0023
Steven Simon, *Owner*
▲ EMP: 18
SALES (est): 3.4MM **Privately Held**
SIC: 2672 Adhesive papers, labels or
tapes: from purchased material

(G-11903)
**PACKAGING MACHINERY & EQP
CO**
181 Watson Ave (07052-6050)
PHONE................................973 325-2418
Fax: 973 325-6937
James Lyle Clark, *President*
Mary Cameron, *Admin Sec*
EMP: 6
SQ FT: 6,000
SALES (est): 1.3MM **Privately Held**
SIC: 3565 Packaging machinery

(G-11904)
PANTHER PRINTING INC
29 Northfield Ave (07052-5358)
PHONE................................239 542-1050
Thomas Cusmano, *President*
Anthony Cusmano, *Vice Pres*
Donald Cusmano, *Treasurer*
EMP: 5 EST: 1994
SQ FT: 3,000
SALES: 500K **Privately Held**
SIC: 2752 Commercial printing, offset

(G-11905)
**PROGRESSIVE 4 COLOR LTD
LBLTY**
24 Park Ave (07052-5553)
Rural Route 24 Park Ave (07052)
PHONE................................973 736-5800
Andrea Risoli,
Michael Risoli,
EMP: 5
SQ FT: 5,000
SALES (est): 1MM **Privately Held**
WEB: www.progressiveprintingcorp.com
SIC: 2752 Commercial printing, offset

(G-11906)
TELUCA INC
414 Eagle Rock Ave (07052-4229)
PHONE................................973 232-0002
Karen Celleri, *President*
Albert Celleri, *COO*
▲ EMP: 5
SALES (est): 684.8K **Privately Held**
SIC: 3999 Hair & hair-based products

(G-11907)
UMC INC
24 Burnett Ter (07052-3810)
P.O. Box 21268, Sarasota FL (34276-4268)
PHONE................................973 325-0031
Arthur Burgess, *President*
EMP: 5
SALES (est): 251.7K **Privately Held**
SIC: 2322 Underwear, men's & boys':
made from purchased materials

(G-11908)
URSO FUEL CORP
10 Rollinson St (07052-4602)
PHONE................................973 325-3324
Janet Urso, *Principal*
EMP: 4
SALES (est): 271.5K **Privately Held**
SIC: 2869 Fuels

West Windsor
Mercer County

(G-11909)
ORGANICA WATER INC (PA)
61 Prnceton Hightstown Rd (08550-1120)
PHONE................................609 651-8885
ARI Raivetz, *CEO*
Robert Freudenberg, *COO*
Attila Bodnr, *Vice Pres*
Robert Jaworski, *CFO*
EMP: 15 EST: 2013
SQ FT: 2,000
SALES (est): 8.9MM **Privately Held**
SIC: 3589 4953 Water treatment equip-
ment, industrial;

Westampton
Burlington County

(G-11910)
ALCON PRODUCTS INC
161 Burrs Rd (08060-5507)
PHONE................................609 267-3898
Joseph F Matarese Jr, *President*
Joseph Matrese Jr, *Vice Pres*
EMP: 12
SQ FT: 8,000
SALES (est): 1.3MM **Privately Held**
SIC: 3354 Aluminum extruded products

(G-11911)
ATLANTIC CAN COMPANY
1200 Highland Dr (08060-5118)
PHONE................................609 518-9950
EMP: 5 EST: 2011
SALES (est): 461.8K **Privately Held**
SIC: 3086 Packaging & shipping materials,
foamed plastic

(G-11912)
DIANE MATSON INC
Also Called: Heidelberg Press
49 Brighton Rd (08060-2326)
PHONE................................609 288-6833
Ray Vozdovic, *President*
Diane Vozdovic, *Treasurer*
EMP: 10 EST: 1958
SQ FT: 8,000
SALES: 800K **Privately Held**
SIC: 2752 Commercial printing, offset; off-
set & photolithographic printing

(G-11913)
JERSEY ORDNANCE INC
600 Highland Dr Ste 602 (08060-5124)
PHONE................................609 267-2112
Frank S Key, *President*
EMP: 6
SALES (corp-wide): 1.9MM **Privately
Held**
WEB: www.purestcolloids.com
SIC: 2023 Dietary supplements, dairy &
non-dairy based
PA: Jersey Ordnance Inc
600 Highland Dr Ste 602
Westampton NJ 08060
609 267-2112

(G-11914)
**PARIS CORPORATION NEW
JERSEY (PA)**
800 Highland Dr (08060-5109)
PHONE................................609 265-9200
Fax: 609 261-4853
Gerard Toscani, *Principal*
Sharon Hennelly, *Principal*
John Murray, *Principal*
Don Showmaker, *Principal*
Bob Fredericks, *Maint Spvr*
▲ EMP: 80 EST: 1994
SQ FT: 130,000
SALES (est): 104MM **Privately Held**
SIC: 5112 2752 5063 Computer paper;
business forms, lithographed; commercial
printing, offset; batteries

(G-11915)
PRIMEPOINT LLC
2 Springside Rd (08060-5644)
PHONE................................609 298-7373
Jim Jacob, *President*
Scott Schroeder, *President*
Irma Fahy, *Opers Mgr*
Jon Hoffman, *Opers Mgr*
Patrick Toner, *Engineer*
EMP: 21
SALES (est): 2.7MM **Privately Held**
WEB: www.eprimepoint.com
SIC: 7372 8721 Prepackaged software;
accounting, auditing & bookkeeping

(G-11916)
PROTOFORM INC
112 Burrs Rd (08060-4405)
PHONE................................609 261-6920
Fax: 609 261-6921
Jeffrey Gazzara, *President*
EMP: 5
SQ FT: 8,000
SALES: 1MM **Privately Held**
SIC: 2834 Pharmaceutical preparations

(G-11917)
QUAD/GRAPHICS INC
80 Stemmers Ln (08060-5652)
PHONE................................609 534-7308
Jim Coss, *Director*
EMP: 50
SALES (corp-wide): 4.1B **Publicly Held**
SIC: 2752 Commercial printing, offset
PA: Quad/Graphics Inc.
N61w23044 Harrys Way
Sussex WI 53089
414 566-6000

(G-11918)
SUN BASKET INC
600 Highland Dr Ste 614 (08060-5124)
PHONE................................408 669-4418
Todd Smith, *Branch Mgr*
EMP: 175
SALES (corp-wide): 100MM **Privately
Held**
SIC: 2099 Almond pastes
PA: Sun Basket, Inc.
1170 Olinder Ct
San Jose CA 95122
408 669-4418

Westfield
Union County

(G-11919)
AMANTE INTERNATIONAL LTD
510 Codding Rd (07090-4100)
PHONE................................908 518-1688
LI Chen Fu, *President*
Grace Lee, *Vice Pres*
▼ EMP: 10
SALES (est): 581.1K **Privately Held**
SIC: 2329 2339 Men's & boys' sportswear
& athletic clothing; women's & misses'
athletic clothing & sportswear

(G-11920)
ANCOL
860 Bradford Ave (07090-3007)
PHONE................................908 233-8907
Ann Quirk, *Owner*
Joseph Quirk, *Co-Owner*
EMP: 4
SALES: 5MM **Privately Held**
WEB: www.ancol.com
SIC: 3571 Personal computers (microcom-
puters)

(G-11921)
ARNHEM INC
Also Called: Arnhem Group, The
1 Elm St Ste 1 # 1 (07090-2194)
PHONE................................908 709-4045
Fax: 908 709-9221
Michael Bonner, *President*
▲ EMP: 9
SALES (est): 1.2MM **Privately Held**
WEB: www.arnhemgroup.com
SIC: 2087 Flavoring extracts & syrups

GEOGRAPHIC

(G-11922)
BRUNSWICK HOT MIX CORP
Also Called: Weldon Asphalt Division
141 Central Ave (07090-2149)
PHONE.............................908 233-4444
Richard Weldon, *President*
William Weldon, *Vice Pres*
Robert Weldon III, *Treasurer*
Richard Myers, *Admin Sec*
EMP: 80
SALES (est): 4.3MM **Privately Held**
SIC: 1611 7513 2951 Surfacing & paving;
truck rental & leasing, no drivers; asphalt
paving mixtures & blocks

(G-11923)
CARBOLINE COMPANY
449 South Ave E (07090-1468)
PHONE.............................908 233-3150
Richard French, *Opers-Prdtn-Mfg*
EMP: 15
SALES (corp-wide): 5.3B **Publicly Held**
SIC: 2851 Paints & allied products
HQ: Carboline Company
2150 Schuetz Rd Fl 1
Saint Louis MO 63146
314 644-1000

(G-11924)
FOLDTEX II LTD
Also Called: Artistic Creations
705 E Broad St (07090-2001)
PHONE.............................908 928-0919
Fax: 908 241-0739
Bernard Formal, *President*
▲ EMP: 20
SQ FT: 61,000
SALES: 700K **Privately Held**
SIC: 3999 5131 Christmas trees, artificial;
novelties, bric-a-brac & hobby kits; piece
goods & notions

(G-11925)
GEORGE BRUMMER
Also Called: Brummer's Chocolates
125 E Broad St (07090-2275)
PHONE.............................908 232-1904
George Brummer, *Owner*
EMP: 4 EST: 1989
SQ FT: 2,000
SALES (est): 306K **Privately Held**
SIC: 2066 5441 Chocolate candy, solid;
confectionery produced for direct sale on
the premises

(G-11926)
**HANDLER MANUFACTURING
COMPANY**
612 North Ave E (07090-1400)
P.O. Box 520 (07091-0520)
PHONE.............................908 233-7796
William A Lehman, *CEO*
Lorraine Lehman, *Corp Secy*
▲ EMP: 26 EST: 1920
SQ FT: 36,000
SALES (est): 5.8MM **Privately Held**
WEB: www.handlermfg.com
SIC: 3843 3545 3564 3821 Dental labo-
ratory equipment; machine tool acces-
sories; purification & dust collection
equipment; laboratory apparatus & furni-
ture

(G-11927)
HEARD WOODWORKING LLC
31 Normandy Dr (07090-3431)
PHONE.............................908 232-3978
Russell Heard, *President*
Annemarie Heard, *Partner*
EMP: 7
SALES (est): 591K **Privately Held**
SIC: 2434 Wood kitchen cabinets

(G-11928)
PRINT TECH LLC
Also Called: Sign Tech
349 South Ave E (07090-1465)
PHONE.............................908 232-0767
Fax: 908 232-1076
John Szalkowski, *Manager*
EMP: 4
SALES (corp-wide): 13.3MM **Privately
Held**
SIC: 2752 Commercial printing, offset

PA: Print Tech Llc
49 Fadem Rd
Springfield NJ 07081
908 232-2287

(G-11929)
**ROMARK LOGISTICS CES LLC
(PA)**
Also Called: Jtp Romark Logistics
822 South Ave W (07090-1460)
PHONE.............................908 789-2800
Marc D Lebovitz, *President*
Marc Lebovitz, *Principal*
Amy S Lebovitz, *Exec VP*
Rob Benz, *Transptn Dir*
Howard Berlly, *CFO*
EMP: 26
SALES (est): 88MM **Privately Held**
SIC: 4225 4789 2631 General warehous-
ing; cargo loading & unloading services;
container, packaging & boxboard

(G-11930)
S M Z ENTERPRISES INC
Also Called: Bagel Chateau
223 South Ave E (07090-1456)
PHONE.............................908 232-1921
Fax: 908 232-4770
Scott Zilberberg, *President*
Mara Zilberberg, *Admin Sec*
EMP: 10 EST: 1980
SQ FT: 2,500
SALES: 530K **Privately Held**
SIC: 5812 2051 5461 American restau-
rant; bagels, fresh or frozen; bagels

(G-11931)
SECOND SKIN LLC
935 Sedgewick Ct (07090-3751)
PHONE.............................212 931-0621
▲ EMP: 14
SQ FT: 6,500
SALES (est): 1.5MM **Privately Held**
SIC: 2331 2339 2335 Mfg
Women's/Misses' Blouses Mfg
Women's/Misses' Outerwear Mfg
Women's/Misses' Dresses

(G-11932)
UNIVERSAL VENDING MGT LLC
425 North Ave E Ste 2 (07090-1537)
P.O. Box 130 (07091-0130)
PHONE.............................908 233-4373
Fax: 908 233-4898
Bruce Lipkin, *President*
Rudy Marano, *COO*
Robert Katz, *Exec VP*
Len Krieger, *CFO*
Janet Cullen, *Accounts Exec*
EMP: 18
SQ FT: 5,000
SALES: 13MM **Privately Held**
WEB: www.uvmweb.com
SIC: 8741 3581 Management services;
automatic vending machines

(G-11933)
**WATTHUNG COMMUNICATIONS
INC**
Also Called: The Westfield Leader
251 North Ave W Ste 7 (07090-1499)
P.O. Box 250 (07091-0250)
PHONE.............................908 232-4407
Fax: 908 232-0473
Horace R Corbin, *President*
Rob Connelly, *General Mgr*
David Corbin, *Sls & Mktg Exec*
EMP: 10
SQ FT: 2,000
SALES (est): 470K **Privately Held**
WEB: www.letitrip.org
SIC: 2711 Newspapers: publishing only,
not printed on site

(G-11934)
WELDON MATERIALS INC (PA)
Also Called: Weldon Concrete Co.
141 Central Ave (07090-2189)
PHONE.............................908 233-4444
Richard T Weldon, *President*
William Weldon, *Vice Pres*
Robert Whaley, *Purchasing*
Peter Kochek, *Manager*
Dominick Mileto, *Director*
EMP: 40
SQ FT: 3,000

SALES (est): 33.5MM **Privately Held**
WEB: www.weldonmaterials.com
SIC: 3273 Ready-mixed concrete

(G-11935)
WEST DRY INDUSTRIES INC
755 W Broad St (07090-4464)
P.O. Box 2595, Plainfield (07060-0595)
PHONE.............................908 757-4400
Fax: 908 757-1010
John Onacki, *President*
▲ EMP: 4
SALES (est): 560K **Privately Held**
SIC: 2819 Catalysts, chemical

Westville
Gloucester County

(G-11936)
ARTEX KNITTING MILLS INC
300 Harvard Ave (08093-1445)
P.O. Box 183 (08093-0183)
PHONE.............................856 456-2800
Fax: 856 456-4111
Arthur Pottash, *President*
Bernard Gerbarg, *Vice Pres*
◆ EMP: 80 EST: 1923
SQ FT: 80,000
SALES (est): 15.5MM **Privately Held**
WEB: www.artexknit.com
SIC: 2253 Hats & headwear, knit; scarves
& mufflers, knit; neckties, knit

(G-11937)
CORNELL CRANE MFG LTD
224 Llenroc Ln (08093-1433)
P.O. Box 807 (08093)
PHONE.............................609 742-1900
Fax: 856 742-8676
Dolores Cornell, *President*
Thomas Kanzler, *Vice Pres*
Kevin Brockway, *Treasurer*
EMP: 10
SQ FT: 5,000
SALES: 1MM **Privately Held**
SIC: 3531 Cranes

(G-11938)
**EAST COAST RUBBER
PRODUCTS**
1000 Delsea Dr Ste D2 (08093-1506)
PHONE.............................856 384-2747
John McDermott, *President*
EMP: 4
SQ FT: 2,400
SALES: 400K **Privately Held**
SIC: 3053 Oil seals, rubber

(G-11939)
EDGAR C BARCUS CO INC
416 Gateway Blvd (08093-1370)
PHONE.............................856 456-0204
Fax: 856 456-5970
Leo Laskowski, *President*
Regina Laskowski, *Treasurer*
Lauren Laskowski, *Admin Sec*
EMP: 17 EST: 1949
SQ FT: 5,000
SALES (est): 1.7MM **Privately Held**
SIC: 3544 Dies, steel rule

(G-11940)
ENERGY COMPANY INC
Also Called: Energy Combustion Systems
50 Cutler Ave Ste 6 (08093-1577)
P.O. Box 68 (08093-0068)
PHONE.............................856 742-1916
Fax: 856 742-8015
Martin E Mittleman, *CEO*
Martin L Mittleman, *President*
Robert Smith, *Corp Secy*
Vincent Santangelo, *Vice Pres*
Tom Fleming, *Project Mgr*
EMP: 20
SALES: 3.7MM **Privately Held**
WEB: www.energycombustionsystems.com
SIC: 1799 3433 1711 Welding on site;
burners, furnaces, boilers & stokers;
boiler maintenance contractor; boiler set-
ting contractor

(G-11941)
FORCE SYSTEMS
29 Hayes Ave (08093-1669)
PHONE.............................856 848-8026
Pat Force, *Owner*
EMP: 10
SALES: 790K **Privately Held**
SIC: 3443 Chambers & caissons

(G-11942)
**HERITAGE SERVICE
SOLUTIONS LLC**
Also Called: Hawks and Co
1000 Delsea Dr Ste A1 (08093-1506)
PHONE.............................856 845-7311
Fax: 856 845-7244
Martin A Rosica, *Mng Member*
Dona Dymon,
EMP: 15 EST: 2005
SALES (est): 3.9MM **Privately Held**
WEB: www.hawksandco.com
SIC: 3585 Refrigeration & heating equip-
ment

(G-11943)
**HYDRO-MECHANICAL SYSTEMS
INC**
1030 Delsea Dr Unit 8 (08093-1590)
P.O. Box 87 (08093-0087)
PHONE.............................856 848-8888
Fax: 856 848-6071
Howard Rosenbloom, *President*
Mario Eisenbacher, *President*
Anita Carney, *General Mgr*
Steve Rosenbloom, *General Mgr*
Nathan Goodman, *Treasurer*
▲ EMP: 17
SQ FT: 20,000
SALES (est): 4MM **Privately Held**
WEB: www.hydromechanical.com
SIC: 3292 3621 3568 3511 Clutch fac-
ings, asbestos; motors & generators;
power transmission equipment; turbines &
turbine generator set units, complete

(G-11944)
INTELCO (PA)
Also Called: Barkercraft
250 Harvard Ave (08093-1443)
P.O. Box 9 (08093-0009)
PHONE.............................856 456-6755
Fax: 856 456-6755
Michael E Wells, *President*
EMP: 69
SQ FT: 25,000
SALES (est): 20.2MM **Privately Held**
WEB: www.intelcousa.com
SIC: 2499 2821 2541 Kitchen, bathroom
& household ware: wood; plastics materi-
als & resins; wood partitions & fixtures

(G-11945)
LAWN MEDIC INC
Also Called: Lawn Medic of Delaware Valley
512 River Dr (08093-1024)
P.O. Box 310, Haddon Heights (08035-
0310)
PHONE.............................856 742-1111
Peter Galantic, *Manager*
EMP: 4
SALES: 248.1K
SALES (corp-wide): 1.8MM **Privately
Held**
WEB: www.lawnmedic.com
SIC: 0782 3524 2752 Lawn care services;
lawn & garden equipment; commercial
printing, offset
PA: Lawn Medic Inc
10 Gates St
Bergen NY 14416
585 494-1462

(G-11946)
MALCO ELECTRIC LLC
602 Ryan Ave (08093-1583)
PHONE.............................856 202-5503
Mark Lamarra Jr, *President*
EMP: 8
SALES (est): 575.4K **Privately Held**
SIC: 3699 Electrical equipment & supplies

▲ = Import ▼=Export
◆ =Import/Export

(G-11947)
RELIABLE WOOD PRODUCTS LLC
145 Broadway (08093-1148)
PHONE..................856 456-6300
EMP: 79
SALES (corp-wide): 11MM **Privately Held**
WEB: www.reliablewoodproducts.com
SIC: 2611 Pulp manufactured from waste or recycled paper
PA: Reliable Wood Products, Llc
   482 Houses Corner Rd
   Sparta NJ 07871
   201 333-5244

(G-11948)
ROYALTY PRESS INC
Also Called: Royalty Press Group
165 Broadway (08093-1148)
PHONE..................856 663-2288
Scott Lang, *President*
Mike Kravitz, *Vice Pres*
EMP: 35
SALES (est): 5.3MM **Privately Held**
WEB: www.royaltypress.com
SIC: 2759 Commercial printing

(G-11949)
TECHNOL INC
1030 Delsea Dr Unit 8e (08093-1590)
P.O. Box 87 (08093-0087)
PHONE..................856 848-5480
Fax: 856 848-0024
Howard Rosenbloom, *President*
Nathan Goodman, *Treasurer*
EMP: 18
SQ FT: 10,000
SALES (est): 2.3MM **Privately Held**
SIC: 3594 5084 Fluid power pumps & motors; hydraulic systems equipment & supplies

(G-11950)
THERMAL CHEK INC
912 Broadway (08093-1435)
PHONE..................856 742-1200
Fax: 856 742-1199
Joseph E Heaton Sr, *President*
Joseph E Heaton Jr, *Vice Pres*
EMP: 24
SQ FT: 55,500
SALES (est): 4.2MM **Privately Held**
SIC: 3089 5031 Windows, plastic; fences, gates & accessories: plastic; lumber, plywood & millwork

(G-11951)
VINELAND SPECIALTY FOODS L L C
201 Harvard Ave (08093-1444)
P.O. Box 187 (08093-0187)
PHONE..................856 742-5001
Marvin Raab, *Principal*
EMP: 6
SQ FT: 19,300
SALES: 1.5MM **Privately Held**
SIC: 2038 Ethnic foods, frozen

Westwood
Bergen County

(G-11952)
ALLIANCE HAND & PHYSICAL
24 Booker St Ste 3 (07675-2632)
PHONE..................201 822-0100
Pam Muscara, *President*
EMP: 16
SALES (est): 2.9MM **Privately Held**
SIC: 3842 Whirlpool baths, hydrotherapy equipment; hydrotherapy equipment

(G-11953)
ALPINE MACHINE & TOOL CORP
42 Bergenline Ave (07675-3115)
PHONE..................201 666-0959
Fax: 201 666-2569
Thomas Wanner, *President*
EMP: 10
SQ FT: 3,000
SALES (est): 1.5MM **Privately Held**
SIC: 3728 3965 Aircraft parts & equipment; airframe assemblies, except for guided missiles; fasteners

(G-11954)
AMERICAN MACHINE SPC NJ LLC
51 Bergenline Ave (07675-3105)
PHONE..................201 664-0006
Brian Peltier,
EMP: 25
SALES (est): 4.4MM **Privately Held**
SIC: 3599 Machine shop, jobbing & repair

(G-11955)
ASIAMERICA GROUP INC
245 Old Hook Rd (07675-3172)
PHONE..................201 497-5993
Yumin Zhang, *Principal*
EMP: 6
SALES (est): 108.9K **Privately Held**
SIC: 2834 Vitamin, nutrient & hematinic preparations for human use

(G-11956)
AUTO-STAK SYSTEMS INC (PA)
49 Old Hook Rd (07675-2406)
PHONE..................201 358-9070
Fax: 201 358-8328
Mark Ritz, *President*
EMP: 5
SQ FT: 600
SALES (est): 520.9K **Privately Held**
WEB: www.autostak.com
SIC: 2542 Racks, merchandise display or storage: except wood

(G-11957)
CH TECHNOLOGIES USA INC
778 Carver Ave (07675-2605)
PHONE..................201 666-2335
Rudolph Jaeger, *President*
Janet Squilanti, *CFO*
EMP: 9 EST: 1987
SQ FT: 500
SALES (est): 998.2K **Privately Held**
WEB: www.toxics.com
SIC: 3841 8748 0782 Surgical & medical instruments; business consulting; landscape contractors

(G-11958)
D R HANDMADE STRINGS INC
Also Called: D R Music
40 Carver Ave (07675-3205)
PHONE..................201 599-3113
Mark Dronge, *Managing Prtnr*
▲ EMP: 70
SQ FT: 8,500
SALES (est): 6.2MM **Privately Held**
SIC: 3931 Guitars & parts, electric & non-electric

(G-11959)
E-VENTS REGISTRATION LLC
40 Tillman St (07675-2611)
PHONE..................201 722-9221
Vanessa Gollaher, *Sales Dir*
Jason Brookins, *Software Dev*
Jeffrey Posner,
EMP: 10
SQ FT: 2,000
SALES: 1.2MM **Privately Held**
SIC: 3999 Identification badges & insignia

(G-11960)
FRANKLIN GRAPHICS INC
Also Called: Franklin Press
60 Brickell Ave (07675-2044)
PHONE..................201 935-5900
Fax: 201 991-3754
Stanley Baguchinsky, *President*
EMP: 6
SALES (est): 708.7K **Privately Held**
SIC: 2752 Commercial printing, offset

(G-11961)
KRISTINE DEER INC
Also Called: K-Deer
174 Westwood Ave (07675-1708)
PHONE..................201 497-3333
Kristine Deer, *President*
EMP: 5
SALES (est): 222.9K **Privately Held**
SIC: 7999 2389 Yoga instruction; men's miscellaneous accessories

(G-11962)
LIETH HOLDINGS LLC (PA)
Also Called: Westwood Sleep Centers
30 Westwood Ave Ste A (07675-1756)
PHONE..................201 358-8282
Dion Vonderlieth, *Mng Member*
Leslie Vonderlieth, *Mng Member*
EMP: 9
SALES (est): 1.1MM **Privately Held**
SIC: 5712 2515 Mattresses; sleep furniture

(G-11963)
OBERG & LINDQUIST CORP (PA)
671 Broadway (07675-1695)
PHONE..................201 664-1300
Fax: 201 664-8974
John Oberg, *President*
Michelle Skura, *Sales Mgr*
Billy Volz, *Sales Mgr*
Debra A Oberg, *Admin Sec*
EMP: 25 EST: 1945
SQ FT: 14,000
SALES (est): 2.6MM **Privately Held**
WEB: www.obergandlindquist.com
SIC: 2434 5722 Wood kitchen cabinets; household appliance stores

(G-11964)
PACKETSTORM COMMUNICATIONS INC
6 Sullivan St (07675-3171)
P.O. Box 18162, Sarasota FL (34276-1162)
PHONE..................732 840-3871
Fax: 732 544-2437
Bill Luthy, *President*
Donald Ziliotto, *Sr Software Eng*
EMP: 10
SQ FT: 5,000
SALES (est): 4.3MM **Privately Held**
WEB: www.packetstorm.com
SIC: 3661 Telephone & telegraph apparatus

(G-11965)
PASCACK PRESS
69 Woodland Ave (07675-3114)
PHONE..................201 664-2105
Fax: 201 664-2109
George Harcher, *President*
EMP: 7
SALES (est): 351.6K **Privately Held**
SIC: 2711 Newspapers, publishing & printing

(G-11966)
PASCACK VALLEY COPY CENTER
Also Called: Valley Prtg & Graphic Design
69 Woodland Ave (07675-3114)
PHONE..................201 664-1917
Fax: 201 664-5758
Shawn Jeffas, *President*
EMP: 6
SQ FT: 1,300
SALES: 480K **Privately Held**
SIC: 2752 Commercial printing, offset

(G-11967)
QUANTUM VECTOR CORP
700 Broadway (07675-1683)
PHONE..................201 870-1782
Isidor Farish, *President*
EMP: 4
SQ FT: 4,000
SALES (est): 280K **Privately Held**
SIC: 3572 2211 3873 Computer storage devices; apparel & outerwear fabrics, cotton; watches, clocks, watchcases & parts

(G-11968)
RE SYSTEMS GROUP INC
700 Broadway Ste 204 (07675-1674)
PHONE..................201 883-1572
Ira Gidon, *Treasurer*
EMP: 5
SQ FT: 4,000
SALES (est): 972K **Privately Held**
WEB: www.resystemsgroup.com
SIC: 7372 7379 Prepackaged software; computer related consulting services

(G-11969)
REVELATION TECHNOLOGIES INC (HQ)
Also Called: Revelation Software
99 Kinderkamack Rd # 109 (07675-3020)
PHONE..................201 594-1422
Michael Ruane, *President*
Robert Catalano, *Sales Dir*
Bryan Shumsky, *Software Dev*
Nancy Ruane, *Admin Sec*
EMP: 17
SQ FT: 6,000
SALES: 3MM
SALES (corp-wide): 3.4MM **Privately Held**
SIC: 7372 Application computer software
PA: Win Win Solutions Inc
   99 Kinderkamack Rd # 109
   Westwood NJ 07675
   201 722-9814

(G-11970)
RINGFEDER PWR TRANSM USA CORP
165 Carver Ave (07675-2604)
PHONE..................201 666-3320
Fax: 201 664-6053
Ross Rivard, *President*
Gordon Raspe, *CFO*
▲ EMP: 23
SQ FT: 15,840
SALES (est): 13.3MM
SALES (corp-wide): 355.7MM **Privately Held**
WEB: www.ringfeder.com
SIC: 5084 3545 Industrial machinery & equipment; machine tool attachments & accessories
HQ: Ringfeder Power-Transmission Gmbh
   Werner-Heisenberg-Str. 18
   GroB-Umstadt 64823
   607 893-850

(G-11971)
SCANTRON CORPORATION
99 Kinderkamack Rd # 211 (07675-3012)
PHONE..................201 666-7009
Bill Looney, *Principal*
EMP: 6 **Privately Held**
WEB: www.scantron.com
SIC: 3577 Optical scanning devices
HQ: Scantron Corporation
   1313 Lone Oak Rd
   Eagan MN 55121
   651 683-6000

(G-11972)
SOCK COMPANY INC (PA)
40 Carver Ave (07675-3205)
P.O. Box 5122, Clinton (08809-0122)
PHONE..................201 307-0675
Eileen J Tabano, *President*
Richard V Tabano, *Corp Secy*
Jennifer E Seamans, *Vice Pres*
James R Tabano, *Vice Pres*
Vincent R Tabano, *Vice Pres*
EMP: 24
SQ FT: 8,500
SALES (est): 4.8MM **Privately Held**
WEB: www.amerisox.com
SIC: 5632 5611 5621 5641 Dancewear; hosiery; lingerie (outerwear); lingerie & corsets (underwear); men's & boys' clothing stores; clothing, sportswear, men's & boys'; women's sportswear; children's & infants' wear stores; stockings: men's, women's & children's; hosiery

(G-11973)
TONI EMBROIDERY
475 Broadway (07675-1720)
PHONE..................201 664-6909
Tom Cornicelli, *Partner*
Louis Cornicelli, *Partner*
EMP: 5
SQ FT: 1,600
SALES (est): 270K **Privately Held**
SIC: 2395 Embroidery products, except schiffli machine

(G-11974)
US AIR POWER SYSTEMS
56 Otoole St (07675-3435)
PHONE..................201 892-5235
Vijay Trivedi, *Principal*

EMP: 4
SALES (est): 522.5K **Privately Held**
SIC: 3822 Pressure controllers, air-conditioning system type

(G-11975)
VERIZON COMMUNICATIONS INC
285 Old Hook Rd (07675-3102)
PHONE....................................201 666-9934
John Eric, *Branch Mgr*
EMP: 45
SALES (corp-wide): 126B **Publicly Held**
WEB: www.verizon.com
SIC: 4813 4812 2741 8721 Data telephone communications; local telephone communications; voice telephone communications; cellular telephone services; directories, telephone: publishing only, not printed on site; billing & bookkeeping service; computer integrated systems design
PA: Verizon Communications Inc.
　　1095 Ave Of The Americas
　　New York NY 10036
　　212 395-1000

(G-11976)
YOURE SO INVITED LLC
260 Westwood Ave (07675-1716)
PHONE....................................201 664-8600
Linda Del Santo, *Owner*
EMP: 4 **EST:** 2009
SALES (est): 397.2K **Privately Held**
SIC: 2754 Stationery & invitation printing, gravure

(G-11977)
ZEKELMAN INDUSTRIES INC
Also Called: Wheatland Tube Co
90 Hurlbut St (07675-2915)
PHONE....................................724 342-6851
Fax: 201 666-1265
Bob Bussiere, *General Mgr*
Pat Shovlin, *Manager*
David Hoffman, *Manager*
EMP: 77 **Privately Held**
SIC: 3317 Steel pipe & tubes
PA: Zekelman Industries, Inc.
　　227 W Monroe St Ste 2600
　　Chicago IL 60606

Wharton
Morris County

(G-11978)
AMS PRODUCTS LLC
Also Called: Object Design
105 W Dewey Ave Ste 305 (07885-1659)
PHONE....................................973 442-5790
Amy Kim,
Mungjung Kim,
▲ **EMP:** 10
SQ FT: 14,000
SALES: 2MM **Privately Held**
WEB: www.laundrybagsny.com
SIC: 2393 2392 Textile bags; pillows; bed: made from purchased materials

(G-11979)
AMS TOY INTL INC
105 W Dewey Ave (07885-1660)
PHONE....................................973 442-5790
Amy Kim, *President*
Mong Jung Kim, *Vice Pres*
▲ **EMP:** 30
SQ FT: 12,000
SALES (est): 2.2MM **Privately Held**
WEB: www.amstoy.com
SIC: 2392 5092 Cushions & pillows; toys & hobby goods & supplies

(G-11980)
APPLIED RESOURCES CORP (PA)
105 W Dewey Ave Ste 311 (07885-1659)
PHONE....................................973 328-3882
Fax: 973 328-3885
Matthew Colello, *President*
Paul Potts, *Manager*
▼ **EMP:** 20
SQ FT: 6,500

SALES: 3MM **Privately Held**
WEB: www.appliedresource.com
SIC: 3679 3825 3549 Electronic circuits; test equipment for electronic & electrical circuits; metalworking machinery

(G-11981)
BOLTTECH MANNINGS INC
Also Called: Bolttech-Mannings
321 Richard Mine Rd Ste 1 (07885-1838)
PHONE....................................973 537-1576
Peter Smith, *Branch Mgr*
EMP: 55
SALES (corp-wide): 460.4MM **Privately Held**
SIC: 3585 Heating equipment, complete
HQ: Bolttech Mannings, Inc.
　　501 Mosside Blvd
　　North Versailles PA 15137
　　724 872-4873

(G-11982)
CONVERTECH INC
353 Richard Mine Rd Ste 4 (07885-1800)
PHONE....................................973 328-1850
Larry Taitel, *President*
Robert Gensheimer, *General Mgr*
Frank D'Olivera, *Engineer*
Frank Dolivera, *Engineer*
Lisa Chen, *Controller*
▲ **EMP:** 38
SQ FT: 27,000
SALES (est): 10.3MM **Privately Held**
WEB: www.convertech.com
SIC: 3555 Printing trades machinery

(G-11983)
DAILY DISH
915 Berkshire Valley Rd (07885-1515)
PHONE....................................973 537-9700
Theodore Stanko, *COO*
EMP: 5
SALES (est): 157.4K **Privately Held**
SIC: 2711 Newspapers, publishing & printing

(G-11984)
DEFINED PRO MACHINING LLC
105 W Dewey Ave Ste 419 (07885-1669)
PHONE....................................973 891-1038
Henrietta Fidler,
Mikheil Fidler,
EMP: 5
SQ FT: 4,000
SALES: 400K **Privately Held**
SIC: 3545 7389 Precision tools, machinists';

(G-11985)
DEZINE LINE INC
17 Robert St Ste B2 (07885-1922)
PHONE....................................973 989-1009
Fax: 973 989-1150
Steve Mattero, *President*
EMP: 10
SQ FT: 3,000
SALES: 593.6K **Privately Held**
WEB: www.dezineline.com
SIC: 2759 5699 2395 Screen printing; customized clothing & apparel; embroidery products, except schiffli machine

(G-11986)
EB MACHINE CORP
Also Called: Ebmachine
320 Richard Mine Rd (07885-1802)
PHONE....................................973 442-7729
Emil Boller, *President*
EMP: 7
SALES (est): 873.8K **Privately Held**
SIC: 3544 Industrial molds

(G-11987)
FOSSIL FUEL
105 W Dewey Ave (07885-1640)
PHONE....................................973 366-9111
Stephen Porcello, *Principal*
EMP: 5
SALES (est): 370.4K **Privately Held**
SIC: 2869 Fuels

(G-11988)
GAS DRYING INC
355 Richard Mine Rd (07885-1305)
P.O. Box 504 (07885-0504)
PHONE....................................973 361-2212

Fax: 973 361-4215
Gary Behrens, *President*
EMP: 10 **EST:** 1957
SQ FT: 25,000
SALES (est): 1.2MM **Privately Held**
WEB: www.gasdrying.com
SIC: 3563 5084 Air & gas compressors including vacuum pumps; industrial machinery & equipment

(G-11989)
INDEPENDENT WELDING CO
Also Called: Independent Enclosures
105 W Dewey Ave Ste 307 (07885-1659)
P.O. Box 404 (07885-0404)
PHONE....................................973 361-9731
Fax: 973 361-3817
Nelson Guevara, *President*
EMP: 15
SQ FT: 25,000
SALES (est): 1.8MM **Privately Held**
WEB: www.ienclosure.com
SIC: 2542 1799 Telephone booths: except wood; welding on site

(G-11990)
JAMES A STANLICK JR
Also Called: Precision Welding
845 Berkshire Valley Rd (07885-1525)
PHONE....................................973 366-7316
James Stanlick, *Owner*
Rich Campanella, *Manager*
Barbara Jacobson, *Manager*
EMP: 5
SQ FT: 6,500
SALES: 900K **Privately Held**
SIC: 3444 3446 1799 Sheet metalwork; stairs, staircases, stair treads: prefabricated metal; welding on site

(G-11991)
LONGO ELCTRICAL-MECHANICAL INC (PA)
Also Called: Longo Industries
1 Harry Shupe Blvd (07885-1646)
P.O. Box 511 (07885-0511)
PHONE....................................973 537-0400
Fax: 973 537-0404
Joseph M Longo, *Ch of Bd*
Richard Dewalk, *Treasurer*
Pam Longo, *Admin Sec*
▲ **EMP:** 98
SQ FT: 60,000
SALES: 21MM **Privately Held**
WEB: www.longo-ind.com
SIC: 5063 5084 7694 Electrical supplies; generators; motors, electric; pumps & pumping equipment; armature rewinding shops

(G-11992)
MARTIN TOOL COMPANY INC
60 State Route 15 S (07885-1227)
PHONE....................................973 361-9212
Fax: 973 361-8711
Lewis Martin, *President*
EMP: 12
SQ FT: 14,000
SALES (est): 1.6MM **Privately Held**
SIC: 3545 Precision tools, machinists'

(G-11993)
NATIONAL FLAG & DISPLAY CO INC
Also Called: Metro Flag Co
353 Richard Mine Rd Ste 5 (07885-1800)
PHONE....................................973 366-1776
Fax: 973 366-0956
Donald Bornstein, *Vice Pres*
EMP: 32
SALES (corp-wide): 7.4MM **Privately Held**
WEB: www.nationalflag.com
SIC: 2399 Flags, fabric
PA: National Flag & Display Co., Inc.
　　30 E 21st St Apt 2b
　　New York NY 10010
　　212 228-6600

(G-11994)
NOWAK INC
17 Robert St (07885-1922)
PHONE....................................973 366-7208
Fax: 973 366-8445
Mark Nowak, *President*
EMP: 15

SQ FT: 5,000
SALES (est): 3.4MM **Privately Held**
SIC: 3556 3599 Food products machinery; machine shop, jobbing & repair

(G-11995)
ODYSSEY AUTO SPECIALTY INC
317 Richard Mine Rd (07885-1837)
PHONE....................................973 328-2667
Fax: 973 328-2639
Laurence J Kahan, *President*
▲ **EMP:** 34
SQ FT: 19,000
SALES (est): 8MM **Privately Held**
WEB: www.odysseyauto.com
SIC: 3711 Automobile assembly, including specialty automobiles

(G-11996)
PEACE MEDICAL INC
105 W Dewey Ave Unit 1-2 (07885-1643)
PHONE....................................800 537-9564
Fax: 973 672-3404
Tim Fegan, *President*
Jennifer Nunez, *Office Mgr*
▲ **EMP:** 10
SQ FT: 10,000
SALES (est): 2MM **Privately Held**
WEB: www.peacemedical.com
SIC: 3842 Surgical appliances & supplies

(G-11997)
PHOENIX INDUSTRIES LLC
105 W Dewey Ave Ste 204 (07885-1642)
P.O. Box 416 (07885-0416)
PHONE....................................973 366-4199
Brent Norcia, *Accounts Mgr*
Judith Morris, *Office Mgr*
Vincent Norcia,
Brent Noccria,
EMP: 5
SQ FT: 3,000
SALES: 1MM **Privately Held**
SIC: 2821 Plastics materials & resins

(G-11998)
REFRESCO US INC
92 N Main St (07885-1607)
PHONE....................................973 361-9794
Fax: 973 361-2202
David Alexander, *Manager*
EMP: 100
SALES (corp-wide): 58.5K **Privately Held**
SIC: 2033 7389 Fruit juices: packaged in cans, jars, etc.; packaging & labeling services
HQ: Refresco Us, Inc.
　　6655 S Lewis Ave
　　Tulsa OK 74136
　　918 524-4029

(G-11999)
SAFE-STRAP COMPANY INC
105 W Dewey Ave Ste 410 (07885-1669)
PHONE....................................973 442-4623
Paul F Giampavolo, *President*
Ray Buonomo, *Vice Pres*
Raymond J Buonomo, *Vice Pres*
Jeff Kagan, *VP Sales*
Renee Kenney, *Mktg Coord*
▲ **EMP:** 50
SALES (est): 8.9MM **Privately Held**
WEB: www.safestrap.com
SIC: 3199 Safety belts, leather

(G-12000)
SUNSET PRINTING AND ENGRV CORP
Also Called: Sunset Stationers
10 Kice Ave (07885-2217)
PHONE....................................973 537-9600
Mitchel Wainer, *Ch of Bd*
Deron Wainer, *Principal*
Jared Wainer, *Principal*
Ted Wainer, *Chairman*
Robert Wainer, *Corp Secy*
EMP: 49 **EST:** 1945
SQ FT: 24,000
SALES (est): 7MM **Privately Held**
WEB: www.sunsetcorpid.com
SIC: 2759 2752 Engraving; commercial printing, lithographic

(G-12001)
TREASURE CHEST CORP
10 N Main St Ste 1 (07885-2248)
PHONE..................................973 328-7747
Curtis P Morgan, *President*
James Harmke, *Vice Pres*
EMP: 4
SALES (est): 338.6K **Privately Held**
SIC: 2741 Miscellaneous publishing

(G-12002)
TRIANGLE AUTOMATIC INC
105 W Dewey Ave Ste 305 (07885-1659)
PHONE..................................973 625-3830
Fax: 973 625-7649
Zbigniew Rossa, *President*
EMP: 4
SQ FT: 2,000
SALES (est): 400K **Privately Held**
SIC: 3599 Machine shop, jobbing & repair

(G-12003)
TURUL BOOKBINDERY INC
60 State Route 15 S (07885-1227)
PHONE..................................973 361-2810
Fax: 973 361-6762
Margit Rahill, *President*
Michael Rahill, *Purch Mgr*
EMP: 5 EST: 1932
SQ FT: 3,800
SALES: 220K **Privately Held**
WEB: www.thebookbindery.com
SIC: 2789 2759 3469 3544 Bookbinding
& repairing: trade, edition, library, etc.;
embossing on paper; metal stampings;
paper cutting dies

Whippany
Morris County

(G-12004)
3M COMPANY
140 Algonquin Pkwy (07981-1633)
PHONE..................................973 884-2500
Vic Ison, *Plant Mgr*
Julie Joy, *Branch Mgr*
EMP: 324
SALES (corp-wide): 31.6B **Publicly Held**
SIC: 3841 3842 3291 2842 Surgical instruments & apparatus; bandages &
dressings; bandages: plastic, muslin,
plaster of paris, etc.; dressings, surgical;
gauze, surgical; abrasive products;
coated abrasive products; pads, scouring:
soap impregnated; specialty cleaning,
polishes & sanitation goods
PA: 3m Company
3m Center
Saint Paul MN 55144
651 733-1110

(G-12005)
**ABBOTT LABORATORIES
PARSIPANNY**
30 N Jefferson Rd (07981-1030)
PHONE..................................973 428-4000
Fax: 973 428-4100
Clive Bennett, *Principal*
◆ EMP: 5
SALES (est): 424.9K **Privately Held**
SIC: 2834 Pharmaceutical preparations

(G-12006)
AGWAY ENERGY SERVICES LLC
240 State Route 10 (07981-2105)
PHONE..................................973 887-5300
EMP: 28
SQ FT: 86,000
SALES (est): 2.2MM **Publicly Held**
WEB: www.hometownhearthandgrill.com
SIC: 1311 5261 Natural gas production;
nurseries & garden centers
HQ: Gas Connection, Llc
9801 Se 82nd Ave
Portland OR 97086

(G-12007)
BAYER CORPORATION (HQ)
100 Bayer Blvd (07981-1544)
P.O. Box 135, Pittsburgh PA (15230-0135)
PHONE..................................412 777-2000
Fax: 412 777-4889
Klaus H Risse, *President*

Patrick Lockwood-Taylor, *President*
Bruce Benda, *Principal*
Angie Toriggino, *Business Mgr*
Antje Woodman, *Business Mgr*
◆ EMP: 1900
SALES (est): 3.6B
SALES (corp-wide): 41.2B **Privately Held**
SIC: 2821 2879 2819 2834 Polypropy-
lene resins; pesticides, agricultural or
household; industrial inorganic chemicals;
pharmaceutical preparations; surgical &
medical instruments
PA: Bayer Ag
Kaiser-Wilhelm-Allee 1
Leverkusen 51373
214 301-

(G-12008)
BAYER HEALTHCARE LLC (DH)
100 Bayer Blvd (07981-1544)
P.O. Box 915 (07981-0915)
PHONE..................................862 404-3000
Gregory S Babe, *CEO*
Erica L Mann, *President*
Joerg Ohle, *President*
Mark Trudeau, *President*
Solvejg Nasert, *Principal*
◆ EMP: 800
SALES (est): 1.9B
SALES (corp-wide): 41.2B **Privately Held**
WEB: www.bayerhealthcare.com
SIC: 2834 8731 3845 3841 Pharmaceuti-
cal preparations; commercial physical re-
search; electromedical equipment;
surgical & medical instruments
HQ: Bayer Corporation
100 Bayer Blvd
Whippany NJ 07981
412 777-2000

(G-12009)
**BAYER HLTHCARE
PHRMCTICALS INC**
Also Called: Bayer Hcp Inc For FDA Pur-
poses
100 Bayer Blvd (07981-1544)
P.O. Box 915 (07981-0915)
PHONE..................................862 404-3000
Marcus Bruner, *Sales Staff*
Leslie Perrell, *Senior Mgr*
Willy Scherf, *Director*
Jennifer Korch, *Deputy Dir*
EMP: 773
SALES (corp-wide): 41.2B **Privately Held**
SIC: 2834 Drugs affecting neoplasms &
endrocrine systems
HQ: Bayer Healthcare Pharmaceuticals Inc.
100 Bayer Blvd
Whippany NJ 07981
862 404-3000

(G-12010)
**BAYER HLTHCARE
PHRMCTICALS INC**
100 Bayer Blvd (07981-1544)
PHONE..................................973 709-3545
Fax: 973 305-5489
Andrew Colbourn, *Sales Staff*
Richard Nieman, *Manager*
EMP: 23
SALES (corp-wide): 41.2B **Privately Held**
SIC: 2834 3841 Drugs affecting neo-
plasms & endrocrine systems; drugs act-
ing on the central nervous system &
sense organs; drugs acting on the cardio-
vascular system, except diagnostic; surgi-
cal & medical instruments
HQ: Bayer Healthcare Pharmaceuticals Inc.
100 Bayer Blvd
Whippany NJ 07981
862 404-3000

(G-12011)
**BAYER HLTHCARE
PHRMCTICALS INC (DH)**
100 Bayer Blvd (07981-1544)
P.O. Box 915 (07981-0915)
PHONE..................................862 404-3000
Daniel Apel, *President*
Habib Dable, *Principal*
Richard K Heller, *Vice Pres*
Jon Stelzmiller, *Vice Pres*
Darara Dibabu, *Research*
▲ EMP: 773

SALES (est): 574.7MM
SALES (corp-wide): 41.2B **Privately Held**
SIC: 2834 Drugs affecting neoplasms & endrocrine systems; drugs acting on the central nervous system &
sense organs; drugs acting on the cardiovascular system, except diagnostic; surgical & medical instruments
HQ: Berlin Schering Inc
100 Bayer Blvd
Whippany NJ 07981
862 404-3000

(G-12012)
BIOMEDTRIX LLC
9 Whippany Rd Bldg B2-7 (07981-1530)
PHONE..................................973 331-7800
Christopher Sidebotham, *Mng Member*
Joseph Pych,
EMP: 17
SQ FT: 15,000
SALES: 6MM **Privately Held**
SIC: 5047 2835 Veterinarians' equipment
& supplies; veterinary diagnostic sub-
stances

(G-12013)
BLISPAK ACQUISITION CORP
1 Apollo Dr Ste 3 (07981-1424)
PHONE..................................973 884-4141
Fax: 973 884-4162
James Horan, *President*
EMP: 55
SQ FT: 20,000
SALES: 4MM **Privately Held**
WEB: www.blispakinc.com
SIC: 2671 5084 Plastic film, coated or
laminated for packaging; processing &
packaging equipment

(G-12014)
BREEZE-EASTERN LLC (HQ)
35 Melanie Ln (07981-1638)
PHONE..................................973 602-1001
Fax: 973 739-9334
Rodger Hahneman, *President*
Gary Olson, *Vice Pres*
John McKinley, *Opers Mgr*
John Thompson, *Opers Staff*
Lisa Ardino, *Purch Mgr*
▲ EMP: 6
SQ FT: 115,335
SALES: 89.7MM
SALES (corp-wide): 3.5B **Publicly Held**
WEB: www.transtechnology.com
SIC: 3728 3563 3531 Aircraft parts &
equipment; aircraft armament, except
guns; air & gas compressors including
vacuum pumps; winches
PA: Transdigm Group Incorporated
1301 E 9th St Ste 3000
Cleveland OH 44114
216 706-2960

(G-12015)
BREEZE-EASTERN LLC
35 Melanie Ln (07981-1638)
PHONE..................................973 602-1001
Rodger Hahneman, *Manager*
EMP: 100
SALES (corp-wide): 3.5B **Publicly Held**
WEB: www.transtechnology.com
SIC: 3728 3769 3536 3531 Aircraft parts
& equipment; guided missile & space ve-
hicle parts & auxiliary equipment; hoists,
cranes & monorails; construction machin-
ery
HQ: Breeze-Eastern Llc
35 Melanie Ln
Whippany NJ 07981
973 602-1001

(G-12016)
CHAMBERLAIN GROUP INC
35 Melanie Ln (07981-1638)
PHONE..................................201 472-4200
Mike Bado, *Principal*
EMP: 8
SALES (corp-wide): 1.4B **Privately Held**
SIC: 3699 Door opening & closing devices,
electrical
HQ: The Chamberlain Group Inc
300 Windsor Dr
Oak Brook IL 60523
630 279-3600

(G-12017)
CORPORATE MAILINGS INC
Also Called: United Shippers Associates
26 Parsippany Rd (07981-1447)
PHONE..................................973 808-0009
Fax: 973 386-1079
Jim Pinkin, *Branch Mgr*
EMP: 100
SALES (corp-wide): 58.1MM **Privately
Held**
WEB: www.corpcomm.com
SIC: 7331 7311 7374 2752 Mailing serv-
ice; advertising agencies; data processing
service; promotional printing, lithographic
PA: Corporate Mailings, Inc.
14 Henderson Dr
West Caldwell NJ 07006
973 439-1168

(G-12018)
**DOSCH-KING COMPANY INC
(PA)**
Also Called: Dosch-King Emulsions
16 Troy Hills Rd (07981-1529)
PHONE..................................973 887-0145
David J King, *President*
Jeffrey King, *Treasurer*
EMP: 15
SQ FT: 3,500
SALES (est): 7.2MM **Privately Held**
SIC: 1611 2951 Highway & street paving
contractor; asphalt & asphaltic paving
mixtures (not from refineries)

(G-12019)
ESSEX MORRIS SIGN CO
30 Troy Rd Ste 2 (07981-1641)
PHONE..................................973 386-1755
Fax: 973 386-5878
Michael Hoehn, *Partner*
Christopher Hoehn, *Partner*
EMP: 8
SQ FT: 2,000
SALES (est): 1.1MM **Privately Held**
SIC: 3993 7532 Signs, not made in cus-
tom sign painting shops; truck painting &
lettering

(G-12020)
FOODTEK INC (PA)
9 Whippany Rd Bldg C-2 (07981-1530)
PHONE..................................973 257-4000
Fax: 973 257-5555
Victor Davila, *President*
Gilbert Finkel, *President*
Millicent Finkel, *Admin Sec*
EMP: 13 EST: 1972
SQ FT: 5,000
SALES (est): 2.4MM **Privately Held**
WEB: www.food-tek.com
SIC: 2045 2099 Prepared flour mixes &
doughs; food preparations

(G-12021)
GE AVIATION SYSTEMS LLC
110 Algonquin Pkwy (07981-1602)
PHONE..................................973 428-9898
Paul Hemingway, *Director*
EMP: 150
SALES (corp-wide): 122B **Publicly Held**
SIC: 4581 3812 3593 Aircraft mainte-
nance & repair services; search & naviga-
tion equipment; fluid power cylinders &
actuators
HQ: Ge Aviation Systems Llc
1 Neumann Way
Cincinnati OH 45215
937 898-9600

(G-12022)
GEL CONCEPTS LLC
30 Leslie Ct (07981-1635)
PHONE..................................973 884-8995
Larry Kersen, *Manager*
Bob Gould,
Lawrence Kersen,
▲ EMP: 25
SALES (est): 2.8MM **Privately Held**
WEB: www.gelconcepts.com
SIC: 2844 Cosmetic preparations

(G-12023)
HALO PHARMACEUTICAL INC (HQ)
30 N Jefferson Rd (07981-1030)
PHONE.............................973 428-4000
Lee Karras, *CEO*
Clive V Bennett, *President*
Mohd Asif, *CFO*
▲ EMP: 100
SQ FT: 240,000
SALES (est): 26.9MM **Privately Held**
SIC: 2834 Pharmaceutical preparations

(G-12024)
HERLEY INDUSTRIES INC
9 Whippany Rd (07981-1540)
PHONE.............................973 884-2580
Lloyd Kuhnle, *Engineer*
Earl Granville, *Administration*
EMP: 65
SALES (corp-wide): 1B **Privately Held**
SIC: 3679 Microwave components
HQ: Herley Industries, Inc.
    3061 Industry Dr
    Lancaster PA 17603
    717 397-2777

(G-12025)
HERLEY-CTI INC (DH)
Also Called: Ultra Electronics Herley
9 Whippany Rd (07981-1540)
PHONE.............................973 884-2580
Deanna Lund, *CEO*
Eric Demarco, *President*
Michael Fink, *Vice Pres*
Mark Peterson, *Buyer*
Laura Siegal, *Treasurer*
EMP: 10
SQ FT: 22,000
SALES (est): 98.2MM
SALES (corp-wide): 1B **Privately Held**
WEB: www.cti-inc.com
SIC: 3679 Microwave components; oscillators
HQ: Herley Industries, Inc.
    3061 Industry Dr
    Lancaster PA 17603
    717 397-2777

(G-12026)
MARK/TRECE INC
160 Algonquin Pkwy Ste 1 (07981-1691)
PHONE.............................973 884-1005
Fax: 973 884-2938
Paul Rachanow, *Manager*
EMP: 45
SALES (corp-wide): 41.5MM **Privately Held**
SIC: 3555 2796 Printing plates; platemaking services
PA: Mark/Trece, Inc.
    2001 Stockton Rd
    Joppa MD 21085
    410 879-0060

(G-12027)
NEW JERSEY JEWISH NEWS (PA)
Also Called: Metrowest Jewish News
901 State Route 10 (07981-1105)
PHONE.............................973 887-3900
Fax: 973 887-4152
Murray Laulicht, *President*
Gabe Kahn, *Editor*
Nancy Karpf, *Accounts Exec*
Lauri Sirois, *Supervisor*
Howard Rabner, *Director*
EMP: 28
SQ FT: 110,000
SALES (est): 18.6MM **Privately Held**
WEB: www.jhsmw.org
SIC: 8399 2711 Fund raising organization, non-fee basis; newspapers

(G-12028)
NUTRA-MED PACKAGING INC
118 Algonquin Pkwy (07981-1602)
PHONE.............................973 625-2274
Fax: 973 625-1219
Mahesh Gupta, *Principal*
Kunal Gupta, *Vice Pres*
Sagar Chokshi, *Project Mgr*
Julie Callahan, *QA Dir*
Harish Sanghvi, *QA Dir*
▲ EMP: 90

SQ FT: 100,000
SALES (est): 25.5MM **Privately Held**
WEB: www.nutra-med.com
SIC: 2834 7389 Pharmaceutical preparations; packaging & labeling services

(G-12029)
ONE-SOURCE COMMUNICATIONS
9 Whippany Rd Bldg C-4 (07981-1530)
PHONE.............................973 463-0250
Fax: 973 463-0254
Tom Coultas, *President*
Wayne Coultas, *Vice Pres*
William Crammer, *Opers Staff*
Marc Frederick, *CIO*
Lisa Brown, *Officer*
EMP: 21
SQ FT: 12,000
SALES (est): 4.9MM **Privately Held**
SIC: 2752 Lithographic Commercial Printing

(G-12030)
P-AMERICAS LLC
Also Called: Pepsico
15 Melanie Ln (07981-1652)
PHONE.............................973 739-4900
Fax: 973 739-9504
Mike Vanklingeren, *Safety Mgr*
Mark Optyke, *Manager*
Renee Ferguson, *Admin Asst*
EMP: 165
SALES (corp-wide): 63.5B **Publicly Held**
SIC: 2086 Carbonated soft drinks, bottled & canned
HQ: P-Americas Llc
    1 Pepsi Way
    Somers NY 10589
    336 896-5740

(G-12031)
PALMA INC
628 State Route 10 Ste 2 (07981-1522)
PHONE.............................973 429-1490
Fax: 973 429-2149
Federico Palma, *President*
Gregory Manton, *Vice Pres*
Fred Palma III, *Treasurer*
Laurie Henle, *Bookkeeper*
Michael Palma, *Admin Sec*
EMP: 15
SQ FT: 6,000
SALES (est): 2.5MM **Privately Held**
WEB: www.palmainc.com
SIC: 1752 2821 2851 Resilient floor laying; plastics materials & resins; epoxy coatings

(G-12032)
PDR EQUITY LLC (PA)
Also Called: Pdr Network
200 Jefferson Park (07981-1069)
PHONE.............................201 358-7200
Mark Heinold, *CEO*
Ruth Williams, *Senior VP*
Mike Burnett, *CFO*
Salvatore Volpe, *Chief Mktg Ofcr*
David Cheng, *CTO*
EMP: 81
SQ FT: 42,000
SALES (est): 22.3MM **Privately Held**
SIC: 2834 5912 Pharmaceutical preparations; drug stores

(G-12033)
PERLIN CONVERTING LLC
Also Called: Perlen Packaging
135 Algonquin Pkwy (07981-1601)
PHONE.............................973 887-0257
Douglas Voreis, *General Mgr*
Fredy Brunner, *Sales Staff*
Spencer Dixon, *Sales Staff*
Douglas Vories, *Mng Member*
▲ EMP: 15
SALES (est): 2.8MM
SALES (corp-wide): 475.1MM **Privately Held**
SIC: 3081 Plastic film & sheet
HQ: Perlen Converting Ag
    Perlenring 3
    Perlen LU 6035
    414 558-800

(G-12034)
POLY-GEL LLC
30 Leslie Ct (07981-1635)
PHONE.............................973 884-3300
Fax: 973 884-1331
Larry Kersen, *CEO*
Marty Vogel, *Vice Pres*
Mary Nimon, *Mktg Coord*
Gina Reda, *Technology*
Donna Rubin, *Admin Asst*
▲ EMP: 28
SALES (est): 4.2MM **Privately Held**
WEB: www.polygel.com
SIC: 2099 Gelatin dessert preparations

(G-12035)
POR-15 INC
Also Called: Restomotive Laboratories
64 S Jefferson Rd Ste 2 (07981-1014)
PHONE.............................973 887-1999
Fax: 973 887-8007
Tom Slutsker, *President*
Marion L Bechler, *Vice Pres*
EMP: 25 EST: 1975
SQ FT: 25,000
SALES (est): 4.2MM **Privately Held**
WEB: www.por15.com
SIC: 2899 5169 Rust resisting compounds; rustproofing chemicals

(G-12036)
POWER DYNAMICS INC
145 Algonquin Pkwy Ste 2 (07981-1645)
PHONE.............................973 560-0019
Fax: 973 560-0076
James Papianni, *President*
Edward Grayson, *Chairman*
Frank W Petrillo, *Natl Sales Mgr*
Dave Budge, *Sales Mgr*
Margaret Wojtala, *Sales Mgr*
▲ EMP: 50
SQ FT: 25,000
SALES (est): 9.3MM **Privately Held**
WEB: www.powerdynamics.com
SIC: 3629 5065 Electronic generation equipment; electronic parts

(G-12037)
RECORDER PUBLISHING CO INC (PA)
Also Called: Parker Publications Corporated
100 S Jefferson Rd # 104 (07981-1009)
PHONE.............................908 766-3900
Stephen Parker, *President*
Christine Lee, *Editor*
Robert Corio, *Accounts Exec*
Linda Proctor, *Sales Staff*
Terry Earle, *Sales Executive*
EMP: 60 EST: 1896
SQ FT: 5,000
SALES (est): 17.9MM **Privately Held**
WEB: www.recordernewspapers.com
SIC: 2711 Commercial printing & newspaper publishing combined

(G-12038)
SCHERING BERLIN INC (DH)
100 Bayer Blvd (07981-1544)
PHONE.............................862 404-3000
Daniel Apel, *Officer*
▲ EMP: 1 EST: 1986
SALES (est): 965MM
SALES (corp-wide): 41.2B **Privately Held**
SIC: 2834 3841 Drugs affecting neoplasms & endrocrine systems; drugs acting on the central nervous system & sense organs; drugs acting on the cardiovascular system, except diagnostic; surgical & medical instruments
HQ: Bayer Healthcare Llc
    100 Bayer Blvd
    Whippany NJ 07981
    862 404-3000

(G-12039)
SNO SKINS INC
622 State Route 10 Ste 19 (07981-1543)
PHONE.............................973 884-8801
Steve Weiss, *President*
Janine Weiss, *Vice Pres*
▲ EMP: 6
SALES (est): 884.5K **Privately Held**
WEB: www.snoskins.com
SIC: 2339 Women's & misses' athletic clothing & sportswear

(G-12040)
STEPHEN GOULD CORPORATION (PA)
35 S Jefferson Rd (07981-1043)
PHONE.............................973 428-1500
Fax: 973 428-1610
Michael Golden, *CEO*
John Golden, *President*
Justin Golden, *President*
Peter V Slyke, *Vice Pres*
Alan Ng, *Project Dir*
◆ EMP: 100 EST: 1939
SQ FT: 42,000
SALES: 678.7MM **Privately Held**
WEB: www.stephengould.com
SIC: 2631 2759 Container, packaging & boxboard; labels & seals: printing

(G-12041)
V L V ASSOCIATES
34 Troy Rd (07981-1639)
PHONE.............................973 428-2884
Michael Vaillancourt, *President*
Danielle Quinn, *QC Mgr*
Steve Slater, *Engineer*
Gregory Dwyer, *Manager*
Michael Pfefferkorn, *Manager*
EMP: 12
SQ FT: 10,000
SALES (est): 2.4MM **Privately Held**
WEB: www.vlvassociates.com
SIC: 3845 Ultrasonic scanning devices, medical

(G-12042)
WATER DYNAMICS INCORPORATED
9 Valley Forge Dr (07981-2214)
PHONE.............................973 428-8330
Kim Dwyer, *CEO*
Gregory Dwyer, *President*
EMP: 4 EST: 1999
SALES: 375K **Privately Held**
SIC: 2899 Water treating compounds

(G-12043)
WHIPPANY ACTUATION SYSTEMS LLC
110 Algonquin Pkwy (07981-1602)
PHONE.............................973 428-9898
Gary Corde, *Business Mgr*
Marc Mastrangelo, *Opers Mgr*
Fred Stokes, *Opers Mgr*
Carmine Cameroni, *Materials Mgr*
Michael Robbins, *Opers Staff*
EMP: 236
SALES (est): 86.4MM
SALES (corp-wide): 3.5B **Publicly Held**
SIC: 3625 3728 Actuators, industrial; aircraft parts & equipment
PA: Transdigm Group Incorporated
    1301 E 9th St Ste 3000
    Cleveland OH 44114
    216 706-2960

(G-12044)
WHIPTAIL TECHNOLOGIES LLC
Also Called: Whiptail Technologies Inc.
9 Whippany Rd Ste 67 (07981-1540)
PHONE.............................973 585-6375
Daniel Crain, *CEO*
Cristobal Conde, *Ch of Bd*
Cameron Pforr, *President*
Erik Hardy, *Exec VP*
EMP: 72
SQ FT: 12,000
SALES (est): 10.9MM
SALES (corp-wide): 48B **Publicly Held**
WEB: www.whiptailtech.com
SIC: 3572 Computer storage devices
PA: Cisco Systems, Inc.
    170 W Tasman Dr
    San Jose CA 95134
    408 526-4000

Whitehouse
Hunterdon County

(G-12045)
DALLAS GROUP OF AMERICA INC (PA)
374 Rte 22 (08888)
P.O. Box 489 (08888-0489)
PHONE..............................908 534-7800
Fax: 908 534-0084
David Dallas, *CEO*
Robert Dallas II, *President*
Jesse Jenkins, *District Mgr*
Rick Perez, *District Mgr*
Clair Conzelman, *Business Mgr*
◆ EMP: 250
SQ FT: 12,000
SALES (est): 122.3MM **Privately Held**
SIC: 3339 2819 Primary nonferrous metals; industrial inorganic chemicals

(G-12046)
LARUE MANUFACTURING CORP
Also Called: American Display
Salem Indstrl Park 8 (08888)
P.O. Box 244 (08888-0244)
PHONE..............................908 534-2700
Fax: 908 534-6966
Keith Larue, *President*
Anita Thompson, *Vice Pres*
EMP: 12
SQ FT: 10,000
SALES: 1.5MM **Privately Held**
WEB: www.americandisplayusa.com
SIC: 3993 7336 7319 Signs & advertising specialties; commercial art & graphic design; display advertising service

(G-12047)
NAHALLAC LLC
6 Carman Ln (08888)
PHONE..............................908 635-0999
Dwayne Looney, *Principal*
Bruce Callahan, *Principal*
John Callahan, *Principal*
EMP: 7
SALES (est): 400K **Privately Held**
SIC: 3842 Sponges, surgical

(G-12048)
READINGTON FARMS INC (HQ)
12 Mill Rd (08888)
PHONE..............................908 534-2121
Dominick V Romano, *Ch of Bd*
Donald Merrigan, *President*
Barry S Snyder, *Vice Pres*
Michelle West, *Sls & Mktg Exec*
Ned Gladstein, *Admin Sec*
EMP: 87
SQ FT: 20,000
SALES: 190MM
SALES (corp-wide): 12.5B **Privately Held**
WEB: www.readingtonfarms.com
SIC: 2026 Milk processing (pasteurizing, homogenizing, bottling)
PA: Wakefern Food Corp.
5000 Riverside Dr
Keasbey NJ 08832
908 527-3300

Whitehouse Station
Hunterdon County

(G-12049)
ALPHA SCIENTIFIC CORPORATION
442 Rt 202 206n Pmb 435 (08889)
PHONE..............................908 534-9941
Bronson Crouch, *Branch Mgr*
EMP: 6
SALES (est): 714.8K **Privately Held**
WEB: www.alphascientificinc.com
SIC: 3825 Test equipment for electronic & electric measurement
PA: Alpha Scientific Corporation
820 Springdale Dr
Exton PA 19341

(G-12050)
CE TECH LLC
8 Fairway Dr (08889-3369)
PHONE..............................908 229-3803
Tim Dywer, *President*
Todd Henderckson, *VP Sales*
EMP: 8
SALES (est): 186.1K **Privately Held**
SIC: 7372 7379 Prepackaged software; computer related consulting services

(G-12051)
HUNTERDON BREWING COMPANY LLC
12 Coddington Rd (08889-3629)
P.O. Box 1050 (08889-1050)
PHONE..............................908 454-7445
Fax: 908 454-5921
Lyle Smith, *Manager*
Dave Masterson,
▲ EMP: 97 EST: 1996
SQ FT: 4,000
SALES (est): 16.6MM **Privately Held**
WEB: www.hunterdonbrewing.com
SIC: 2082 2084 Beer (alcoholic beverage); wines; wine coolers (beverages)

(G-12052)
INSPIRE PHARMACEUTICALS INC
1 Merck Dr (08889-3400)
PHONE..............................908 423-1000
John Canan, *President*
Mark McDonough, *Treasurer*
EMP: 240
SQ FT: 43,278
SALES (est): 18.2MM
SALES (corp-wide): 841MM **Publicly Held**
WEB: www.inspirepharm.com
SIC: 2836 Biological products, except diagnostic
HQ: Oak Pharmaceuticals, Inc.
1925 W Field Ct Ste 300
Lake Forest IL 60045

(G-12053)
MASTER MARTINI USA INC
460 Route 22 W (08889)
PHONE..............................908 455-4434
Joseph Campbell, *President*
▲ EMP: 5
SALES (est): 377.8K **Privately Held**
SIC: 2066 Baking chocolate

(G-12054)
MERCK HOLDINGS LLC (DH)
1 Merck Dr (08889-3497)
PHONE..............................908 423-1000
Richard Henriques, *President*
Richard T Clark, *President*
Judy Lewent, *Senior VP*
Caroline Dorsa, *Treasurer*
Michael Hacker, *Asst Treas*
EMP: 10
SQ FT: 100,000
SALES (est): 269.7MM
SALES (corp-wide): 40.1B **Publicly Held**
SIC: 2834 6712 Proprietary drug products; bank holding companies
HQ: Merck Sharp & Dohme Corp.
2000 Galloping Hill Rd
Kenilworth NJ 07033
908 740-4000

(G-12055)
MERCK RESOURCE MANAGEMENT INC
1 Merck Dr (08889-3497)
P.O. Box 100 (08889-0100)
PHONE..............................908 423-1000
W Merck, *President*
EMP: 5
SALES (est): 598.3K **Privately Held**
SIC: 2834 Pharmaceutical preparations

(G-12056)
MERCK SHARP & DOHME CORP
2 Merck Dr (08889-3436)
PHONE..............................908 423-3000
Roschelle Jackson, *Senior Engr*
Joel Krikston, *Branch Mgr*
Kelly Lazicky, *Admin Asst*
EMP: 33

SALES (corp-wide): 40.1B **Publicly Held**
SIC: 2834 Pharmaceutical preparations
HQ: Merck & Dohme Corp.
2000 Galloping Hill Rd
Kenilworth NJ 07033
908 740-4000

(G-12057)
MERCK SHARPE & DOHME DE PR INC
1 Merck Dr (08889-3497)
P.O. Box 100 (08889-0100)
PHONE..............................908 423-1000
Kenneth C Frazier, *CEO*
Bruce N Kuhlik, *Exec VP*
Leslie Brun, *Director*
Maria Hoffman, *Director*
Theresa M Lane, *Director*
▲ EMP: 5
SALES (est): 377K
SALES (corp-wide): 40.1B **Publicly Held**
SIC: 2834 Pharmaceutical preparations
HQ: Merck Sharp & Dohme Corp.
2000 Galloping Hill Rd
Kenilworth NJ 07033
908 740-4000

(G-12058)
MINALEX CORPORATION
25 Coddington Rd (08889-3630)
P.O. Box 247 (08889-0247)
PHONE..............................908 534-4044
Fax: 908 534-6788
James J Casey, *President*
Christopher Casey, *General Mgr*
James P Kowalski, *Vice Pres*
Ron Allen, *QC Mgr*
Robert Handel, *Manager*
EMP: 36 EST: 1965
SQ FT: 25,000
SALES (est): 9.6MM **Privately Held**
WEB: www.minalex.com
SIC: 3354 Aluminum extruded products

(G-12059)
ORGANON USA INC
1 Merck Dr (08889-3400)
PHONE..............................908 423-1000
Joanne Bollman, *Principal*
EMP: 6 EST: 2013
SALES (est): 595.6K
SALES (corp-wide): 40.1B **Publicly Held**
SIC: 2834 2836 Pharmaceutical preparations; druggists' preparations (pharmaceuticals); drugs acting on the respiratory system; drugs affecting parasitic & infective diseases; vaccines; veterinary biological products
PA: Merck & Co., Inc.
2000 Galloping Hill Rd
Kenilworth NJ 07033
908 740-4000

(G-12060)
PALUMBO ASSOCIATES INC
27 Ridge Rd (08889-3641)
PHONE..............................908 534-2142
Gary Palumbo, *President*
Josh Mertz, *Graphic Designe*
EMP: 13
SQ FT: 5,000
SALES (est): 1.2MM **Privately Held**
SIC: 7389 3999 Exhibit construction by industrial contractors; preparation of slides & exhibits

(G-12061)
PHOENIX INDUSTRIAL LLC
531 Route 22 E 194 (08889)
PHONE..............................908 955-0114
ARI Falk, *Owner*
EMP: 5
SQ FT: 5,000
SALES (est): 313.1K **Privately Held**
SIC: 3423 Hand & edge tools

(G-12062)
SATELLITE PROS INC
148 Main St (08889-3692)
PHONE..............................908 823-9500
Andrew Hoffman, *President*
EMP: 7
SALES: 1.5MM **Privately Held**
SIC: 3663 Satellites, communications

(G-12063)
SCHERNG-PLOUGH PDTS CARIBE INC
1 Merck Dr (08889-3400)
PHONE..............................908 423-1000
Scott Grandville, *Principal*
Gregory Hood, *Director*
Rochelle Wills, *Assistant*
EMP: 9 EST: 2014
SALES (est): 959.5K **Privately Held**
SIC: 2834 Pharmaceutical preparations

(G-12064)
VALLEY TECH INC
295 Us Highway 22 E 201w (08889-3429)
P.O. Box 124 (08889-0124)
PHONE..............................908 534-5565
Fax: 908 534-5765
Richard A Schulley, *President*
Bill Linney, *Vice Pres*
EMP: 5
SQ FT: 1,000
SALES (est): 766.7K **Privately Held**
WEB: www.valleytechinc.com
SIC: 3561 7389 Pumps & pumping equipment; air pollution measuring service

Whiting
Ocean County

(G-12065)
BIG EYE LAMP INC
870 Route 530 Ste 2 (08759-3546)
PHONE..............................732 557-9400
EMP: 6
SQ FT: 3,000
SALES: 300K **Privately Held**
SIC: 3645 Mfg High Intensity Magnifying Lamps

(G-12066)
CMC COMPOSITES LLC
870 Route 530 Ste 12 (08759-3546)
PHONE..............................732 505-9400
Nicholas Taaffe, *Mng Member*
EMP: 20 EST: 2007
SQ FT: 2,500
SALES (est): 1.5MM **Privately Held**
SIC: 3353 Aluminum sheet, plate & foil

(G-12067)
JARAHIAN MILLWORK INC
870 Route 530 Ste 4 (08759-3546)
PHONE..............................732 240-5151
Harold Jarahian, *President*
EMP: 4
SQ FT: 5,000
SALES: 1MM **Privately Held**
SIC: 2431 Door trim, wood; moldings, wood: unfinished & prefinished

(G-12068)
LOGPOWERCOM LLC
47 Lacey Rd (08759-4439)
PHONE..............................732 350-9663
Todd Cooper, *President*
Marchia Ammons, *Vice Pres*
EMP: 5
SALES (est): 324.7K **Privately Held**
SIC: 3553 2421 Woodworking machinery; custom sawmill

Wildwood
Cape May County

(G-12069)
A B S SIGN COMPANY INC
3008 Park Blvd (08260-2496)
PHONE..............................609 522-6833
Fax: 609 522-0680
Randy Hentges, *President*
EMP: 7 EST: 1964
SQ FT: 2,750
SALES: 300K **Privately Held**
SIC: 3993 Neon signs

(G-12070)
CANTOL INC (HQ)
4701 Mediterranean Ave (08260-1651)
PHONE..............................609 846-7912

GEOGRAPHIC

Elmer E Snethen, *President*
Richard Petsche, *Vice Pres*
Edward Berger, *Admin Sec*
EMP: 42
SQ FT: 40,000
SALES (est): 3.7MM
SALES (corp-wide): 5.1MM **Privately Held**
WEB: www.cantol.com
SIC: 2842 2899 2841 Cleaning or polishing preparations; chemical preparations; soap & other detergents
PA: Cantol Corp
　199 Steelcase Rd W
　Markham ON L3R 2
　905 475-6141

(G-12071)
CUSTOM CABINETS BY JIM BUCKO
135 W Burk Ave (08260-1617)
PHONE..............................609 522-6646
Fax: 609 889-7613
James Bucko, *President*
EMP: 6
SALES: 900K **Privately Held**
SIC: 2434 Wood kitchen cabinets

(G-12072)
HALLCO INC
Also Called: Leader Printers
5914 New Jersey Ave (08260-1346)
PHONE..............................609 729-0161
Fax: 609 523-0464
Dennis O Hall, *President*
Arthur Hall, *Vice Pres*
Terri Hall, *Treasurer*
EMP: 6
SQ FT: 3,750
SALES (est): 440K **Privately Held**
SIC: 2752 Commercial printing, offset

(G-12073)
INDOOR ENTERTAINMENT OF NJ
5301 Ocean Ave (08260-4463)
P.O. Box 4 (08260-0004)
PHONE..............................609 522-6700
Fax: 609 522-6738
Richard Ramagosa, *President*
EMP: 20
SALES (est): 300K **Privately Held**
SIC: 3599 7999 3559 Carousels (merry-go-rounds); amusement & recreation; special industry machinery

(G-12074)
M S BROWN MFG JEWELERS (PA)
Also Called: M S Brown Jewelers
3304 Pacific Ave (08260-4824)
PHONE..............................609 522-7604
Fax: 609 522-0657
Gail Brown, *President*
Michael Brown, *Treasurer*
EMP: 4
SQ FT: 2,000
SALES (est): 452.6K **Privately Held**
WEB: www.msbrownjewelers.com
SIC: 5944 3911 Jewelry, precious stones & precious metals; jewelry, precious metal

(G-12075)
WALGREEN EASTERN CO INC
Also Called: Walgreens
5000 Park Blvd (08260-1428)
PHONE..............................609 522-1291
Fax: 609 522-1394
EMP: 30
SALES (corp-wide): 118.2B **Publicly Held**
SIC: 5912 2834 Drug stores; pharmaceutical preparations
HQ: Walgreen Eastern Co., Inc.
　200 Wilmot Rd
　Deerfield IL 60015
　847 940-2500

Wildwood Crest
Cape May County

(G-12076)
NEDOHON INC (PA)
302 E Newark Ave (08260-3423)
PHONE..............................302 533-5512
Donna J Nedohon, *President*
Richard Nedohon, *Vice Pres*
EMP: 2 **EST:** 1963
SQ FT: 40,000
SALES (est): 2.2MM **Privately Held**
SIC: 5085 5051 3341 Valves & fittings; nonferrous metal sheets, bars, rods, etc.; secondary nonferrous metals

---

Williamstown
Gloucester County

(G-12077)
A-WIT TECHNOLOGIES INC
656 Ironwood Dr (08094-1686)
PHONE..............................800 985-2948
Orlando Hernadez, *President*
EMP: 7
SALES: 200K **Privately Held**
SIC: 3999 Education aids, devices & supplies

(G-12078)
AMCOR PHRM PACKG USA INC
918 E Malaga Rd (08094-3610)
P.O. Box 448 (08094-0448)
PHONE..............................856 728-9300
Ed Walsh, *Principal*
William Taylor, *Manager*
EMP: 120
SALES (corp-wide): 9.1B **Privately Held**
WEB: www.alcanpackaging.com
SIC: 3221 2396 Cosmetic jars, glass; automotive & apparel trimmings
HQ: Amcor Pharmaceutical Packaging Usa, Llc
　625 Sharp St N
　Millville NJ 08332
　856 327-1540

(G-12079)
APPLIED THERMAL SOLUTIONS INC
93 Eldridge Ave (08094-1343)
PHONE..............................856 818-8194
Jeffrey Bailey, *President*
Matt Dawkins, *Principal*
EMP: 5
SALES: 138K **Privately Held**
SIC: 3433 Heating equipment, except electric; burners, furnaces, boilers & stokers; furnaces, domestic steam or hot water

(G-12080)
BETTER IMAGE GRAPHICS INC
1041 Glassboro Rd Ste E6 (08094-3545)
PHONE..............................856 262-0735
Lawrence E Faragalli, *President*
Prilscilla Faragalli, *Vice Pres*
Pat Preston, *Treasurer*
EMP: 6
SQ FT: 2,500
SALES: 300K **Privately Held**
SIC: 2752 Commercial printing, lithographic

(G-12081)
BLUE LIGHT WELDING & FABG LLC
2164 Grant Ave (08094-6132)
PHONE..............................856 629-5891
Vicky Hargesheimer, *Mng Member*
Michael Hargesheimer,
EMP: 7
SALES (est): 1.6MM **Privately Held**
WEB: www.bluelightwelding.com
SIC: 7692 Welding repair

(G-12082)
CADPRO INC
431 S Main St (08094-1728)
P.O. Box 1209, Waterford Works (08089-0209)
PHONE..............................856 435-0050
Fax: 856 435-0060
EMP: 10
SQ FT: 9,000
SALES: 1.3MM **Privately Held**
SIC: 3599 Mfg Industrial Machinery

(G-12083)
COLOR COMP INC
1041 Glassboro Rd Ste E5 (08094-3545)
PHONE..............................856 262-3040
Fax: 856 262-7710
William Shisler, *President*
Donna Shisler, *Vice Pres*
Bill Shisler, *Manager*
EMP: 6
SALES (est): 731.8K **Privately Held**
WEB: www.colorcomp.net
SIC: 7336 2396 Graphic arts & related design; automotive & apparel trimmings

(G-12084)
COSMIC CUSTOM SCREEN PRINTING (PA)
935 S Black Horse Pike (08094-1900)
PHONE..............................856 629-8337
Debbie Bochaud,
EMP: 4
SALES: 250K **Privately Held**
SIC: 2759 Screen printing

(G-12085)
CREATIVE CMPT CONCEPTS LLC
2030 N Black Horse Pike (08094-9132)
PHONE..............................877 919-7988
Francis Peirce,
Raymond Nicloud,
EMP: 5
SALES: 125K **Privately Held**
SIC: 7373 7378 7371 5961 Systems software development services; local area network (LAN) systems integrator; computer maintenance & repair; computer software systems analysis & design, custom; computer equipment & electronics, mail order; computer installation; computer auxiliary storage units

(G-12086)
F P DEVELOPMENTS INC
402 S Main St (08094-1729)
PHONE..............................856 875-7100
Fax: 856 875-6717
Frederick W Pfleger Jr, *President*
Frederick W Pfleger Sr, *Chairman*
David Pfleger, *COO*
William Pfleger, *Treasurer*
Mary Pfleger, *Admin Sec*
EMP: 37 **EST:** 1963
SQ FT: 24,000
SALES (est): 9.5MM **Privately Held**
WEB: www.fpdevelopments.com
SIC: 3559 3565 Pharmaceutical machinery; packaging machinery

(G-12087)
FORMS & FLYERS OF NEW JERSEY
102 Sicklerville Rd (08094-1472)
PHONE..............................856 629-0718
Fax: 856 629-9214
Deborah Evangelista, *Owner*
Harry Evangelista, *Owner*
EMP: 4
SALES: 200K **Privately Held**
SIC: 2759 5943 Commercial printing; office forms & supplies

(G-12088)
GRAPHIC IMAGE
1401 N Blck Horse Pike A (08094-9164)
PHONE..............................856 262-8900
James McGhee Jr, *Partner*
Tim Geist, *Partner*
EMP: 5
SQ FT: 2,000
SALES: 260K **Privately Held**
SIC: 2759 Screen printing

(G-12089)
GREAT RAILING INC
1086 N Black Horse Pike (08094-9143)
PHONE..............................856 875-0050
Mario Conlin, *President*
Great Railing, *Principal*
EMP: 15
SQ FT: 12,200
SALES: 5MM **Privately Held**
SIC: 3444 5051 5211 Roof deck, sheet metal; steel decking; fencing

(G-12090)
INTERCOASTAL FABRICATORS INC
300 Thomas Ave Ste 301 (08094-3442)
PHONE..............................856 629-4105
Paul Daiber, *President*
EMP: 4
SALES: 250K **Privately Held**
SIC: 3444 Sheet metalwork

(G-12091)
JUST GLASS & MIRROR INC
1250 N Black Horse Pike (08094-2834)
PHONE..............................856 728-8383
Fax: 856 728-1992
Al Pfafman, *President*
EMP: 12
SQ FT: 2,000
SALES (est): 1.6MM **Privately Held**
WEB: www.justglassandmirror.net
SIC: 3211 5719 Insulating glass, sealed units; mirrors

(G-12092)
MONROE TOOL & DIE INC
197 Sharp Rd (08094-7446)
PHONE..............................856 629-5164
Fax: 856 875-8868
Steven Kennedy, *President*
EMP: 5 **EST:** 1964
SQ FT: 4,400
SALES (est): 761.4K **Privately Held**
SIC: 3544 3469 Dies & die holders for metal cutting, forming, die casting; metal stampings

(G-12093)
MTS SYSTEMS CORPORATION
745 Debra Dr (08094-1641)
PHONE..............................856 875-4478
Chip Emery, *Manager*
EMP: 1000
SALES (corp-wide): 787.9MM **Publicly Held**
WEB: www.mts.com
SIC: 8711 7699 3699 3577 Engineering services; hydraulic equipment repair; electrical equipment & supplies; computer peripheral equipment
PA: Mts Systems Corporation
　14000 Technology Dr
　Eden Prairie MN 55344
　952 937-4000

(G-12094)
OK TOOL & DIE COMPANY INC
603 Blue Bell Rd (08094-1710)
PHONE..............................856 629-5757
Fax: 856 629-1028
Kenneth C Ostapovich, *President*
Judy Ostapovich, *Vice Pres*
EMP: 20
SQ FT: 10,000
SALES: 1MM **Privately Held**
SIC: 3089 3599 Injection molding of plastics; machine shop, jobbing & repair

(G-12095)
PACE TARGET BROKERAGE INC
716 Clayton Rd (08094-3530)
P.O. Box 337 (08094-0337)
PHONE..............................856 629-2551
Fax: 856 629-8546
Joseph J Pace Jr, *President*
Regina Pace, *Vice Pres*
Nicholas Pace, *Treasurer*
Joe Pace III, *Admin Sec*
EMP: 25
SQ FT: 2,800
SALES (est): 3.5MM **Privately Held**
WEB: www.pacetarget.com
SIC: 2052 5145 Bakery products, dry; snack foods; candy; pretzels; potato chips

(G-12096)
PIPING SUPPLIES INC
18 E Black Horse Pike (08094-2613)
PHONE..................................609 561-9323
Nancy Walker, *President*
▲ EMP: 7
SQ FT: 79,500
SALES (est): 1.1MM **Privately Held**
SIC: 3494 3462 3463 Pipe fittings; flange, valve & pipe fitting forgings, ferrous; flange, valve or pipe fitting forgings, non-ferrous

(G-12097)
PIRAMAL GLASS - USA INC
918 E Malaga Rd (08094-3610)
PHONE..................................856 728-9300
Charles Macho, *Principal*
EMP: 130
SALES (corp-wide): 186.3MM **Privately Held**
SIC: 3221 Glass containers
HQ: Piramal Glass - Usa, Inc.
329 Herrod Blvd
Dayton NJ 08810
856 293-6400

(G-12098)
PIRAMAL GLASS - USA INC
Also Called: Decoration Operations
918 E Malaga Rd (08094-3610)
PHONE..................................856 293-6400
Charlie Macho, *Manager*
EMP: 365
SALES (corp-wide): 186.3MM **Privately Held**
SIC: 3221 Glass containers
HQ: Piramal Glass - Usa, Inc.
329 Herrod Blvd
Dayton NJ 08810
856 293-6400

(G-12099)
PRECISION BALL SPECIALTIES
1451 Glassboro Rd (08094-3300)
P.O. Box 132 (08094-0132)
PHONE..................................856 881-5646
Fax: 856 881-5789
John Williams, *President*
EMP: 10
SQ FT: 6,000
SALES (est): 1.4MM **Privately Held**
WEB: www.precisionballspecialties.com
SIC: 3545 3544 3496 Precision tools, machinists'; special dies, tools, jigs & fixtures; miscellaneous fabricated wire products

(G-12100)
PRECISION METALCRAFTERS INC
17 Filbert St (08094-1897)
PHONE..................................856 629-1020
Fax: 856 875-8658
Frank Falconi, *President*
Louise Falconi, *Admin Sec*
EMP: 25
SQ FT: 22,500
SALES (est): 4.3MM **Privately Held**
WEB: www.precisionmetalcrafters.net
SIC: 3599 3444 3441 Machine shop, jobbing & repair; sheet metalwork; fabricated structural metal

(G-12101)
PREMIER ASSET LOGISTICS NETWOR (PA)
Also Called: Palnet
100 N Black Horse Pike # 100 (08094-1483)
PHONE..................................877 725-6381
Jorge Aguilar, *Opers Mgr*
Michael L Smith, *Mng Member*
Bernie Bartley,
Darren Bronco,
Sean Crowe,
EMP: 14
SALES (est): 2.6MM **Privately Held**
SIC: 2448 Pallets, wood

(G-12102)
RESPONSE TIME INCORPORATED
1 Fiber Optic Ln (08094-4051)
PHONE..................................856 875-0025

Fax: 856 875-0074
Catrina Lancour Hahn, *CEO*
Frank Ross, *Opers Mgr*
EMP: 25
SALES (est): 3MM **Privately Held**
SIC: 3661 Fiber optics communications equipment

(G-12103)
RICHARD E PIERSON MTLS CORP
Also Called: R E Pierson Materials
151 Industrial Dr (08094-7543)
PHONE..................................856 740-2400
Fax: 856 740-4200
Brian Hart, *Branch Mgr*
EMP: 6 **Privately Held**
SIC: 2951 1611 1771 Asphalt paving mixtures & blocks; highway & street construction; concrete work
PA: Richard E. Pierson Materials Corp.
426 Swedesboro Rd
Pilesgrove NJ 08098

(G-12104)
ROBERT J DONALDSON INC
1287 Glassboro Rd (08094-3507)
PHONE..................................856 629-2737
Fax: 856 629-1956
Douglas A Donaldson, *President*
W Scott Donaldson, *Vice Pres*
Benita Donaldson, *Shareholder*
Charles K Donaldson, *Shareholder*
Harold Oneio, *Shareholder*
EMP: 12
SQ FT: 10,000
SALES: 1.8MM **Privately Held**
WEB: www.donaldsonwire.com
SIC: 3496 3446 Miscellaneous fabricated wire products; gates, ornamental metal

(G-12105)
SCHUSTERS SHOES INC
1122 Rembrandt Way 1 (08094-6340)
PHONE..................................856 885-4551
Fax: 856 767-5977
Bill Nims, *President*
Joseph Watson, *Vice Pres*
EMP: 9 EST: 1958
SQ FT: 5,800
SALES (est): 1.2MM **Privately Held**
WEB: www.schustershoes.com
SIC: 5661 3144 Footwear, athletic; orthopedic shoes, women's

(G-12106)
SNAP SET SPECIALISTS INC
300 Thomas Ave Bldg 6 (08094-3442)
P.O. Box 8074, Blackwood (08012-8074)
PHONE..................................856 629-9552
EMP: 4 EST: 1982
SQ FT: 2,500
SALES (est): 250K **Privately Held**
SIC: 2761 Mfg Manifold Business Forms

(G-12107)
SOUTH STATE INC
1340 Glassboro Rd (08094-8925)
PHONE..................................856 881-6030
EMP: 20
SALES (corp-wide): 12.3MM **Privately Held**
SIC: 2951 5032 1611 Mfg Asphalt Mixtures/Blocks Whol Brick/Stone Material Highway/Street Construction
PA: South State Inc
202 Reeves Rd
Bridgeton NJ
856 451-5300

(G-12108)
SPECTACLE SHOPPE
Also Called: Precision Optical Lab
202 Dickens Ct (08094-1962)
PHONE..................................856 875-5046
George E Du Bois, *Owner*
EMP: 4 EST: 1976
SALES: 200K **Privately Held**
SIC: 5995 3851 Opticians; ophthalmic goods

(G-12109)
TOMWAR CORP
413 Paradise Rd (08094-3071)
PHONE 856 740-0111
Frances B Wark, *President*

Barbara Horn, *Vice Pres*
EMP: 20
SQ FT: 25,000
SALES (est): 963K **Privately Held**
SIC: 2782 Sample books

(G-12110)
TUBE CRAFT OF AMERICA INC
667 Lebanon Ave (08094-4003)
PHONE..................................856 629-5626
George Taniewski, *Vice Pres*
Diane Marino, *Office Mgr*
Ivan Taniewiski, *Admin Sec*
EMP: 4
SALES (est): 370K **Privately Held**
WEB: www.tubecraftflange.com
SIC: 3498 Fabricated pipe & fittings

(G-12111)
UNIVERSITY FASHIONS BY JANET
1888 Winslow Rd Bldg B (08094-4026)
PHONE..................................856 228-1615
Fax: 856 228-3131
Janet James, *Owner*
Ulysses James, *Co-Owner*
EMP: 7
SALES: 545K **Privately Held**
WEB: www.universityfashions.com
SIC: 2395 7336 Embroidery & art needlework; silk screen design

(G-12112)
VECTOR PRECISION MACHINING
1558 Janvier Rd (08094-3972)
PHONE..................................856 740-5131
Pawel Les, *President*
EMP: 5
SALES (est): 557.2K **Privately Held**
SIC: 3599 Machine shop, jobbing & repair

(G-12113)
VFI FABRICATORS INC
Also Called: V F I Fabricators
300 Thomas Ave Ste 101 (08094-3442)
P.O. Box 263 (08094-0263)
PHONE..................................856 629-8786
Alfred E Fabrico Sr, *President*
Alfred E Fabrico Jr, *Vice Pres*
Danielle Wilder, *Admin Sec*
EMP: 30
SQ FT: 15,000
SALES (est): 6.5MM **Privately Held**
WEB: www.vfifab.com
SIC: 3444 Sheet metal specialties, not stamped

(G-12114)
WASTEQUIP MANUFACTURING CO LLC
New Brooklyn & Filbert St (08094)
PHONE..................................856 629-9222
Andrew Stesanio, *Branch Mgr*
EMP: 49
SALES (corp-wide): 574.7MM **Privately Held**
WEB: www.rayfo.com
SIC: 3443 Dumpsters, garbage
HQ: Wastequip Manufacturing Company Llc
1901 Roxborough Rd # 300
Charlotte NC 28211

(G-12115)
WOOD WORKS
1111 N Black Horse Pike (08094-2838)
PHONE..................................856 728-4520
Fax: 856 875-1428
Robert B Bartling, *Partner*
Carol A Bartling, *Partner*
EMP: 8
SQ FT: 7,500
SALES: 1MM **Privately Held**
SIC: 2431 5031 5211 Millwork; millwork; millwork & lumber

(G-12116)
ALTERNATIVE AIR LLC (PA)
Also Called: Alternative Air Fixture
30 Echo Ln (08046-2247)
PHONE..................................609 261-5870
Jim Lunstead, *Partner*
Mike Banks, *Partner*
EMP: 5 EST: 1994
SALES (est): 646K **Privately Held**
WEB: www.airalternative.com
SIC: 2542 Fixtures, store: except wood

(G-12117)
BURLINGTON TIMES INC (HQ)
Also Called: Burlington County Times
4284 Route 130 (08046-2027)
PHONE..................................609 871-8000
Fax: 609 871-0490
Grover J Friend, *President*
Sandy V Fischer, *Purch Mgr*
Edward J Birch, *Treasurer*
EMP: 350 EST: 1958
SALES (est): 48.9MM
SALES (corp-wide): 1.3B **Publicly Held**
SIC: 2711 Commercial printing & newspaper publishing combined; newspapers, publishing & printing
PA: New Media Investment Group Inc.
1345 Avenue Of The Americ
New York NY 10105
212 479-3160

(G-12118)
COUNTER-FIT INC
1 Ironside Ct (08046-2533)
PHONE..................................609 871-8888
Michael Macaluso, *President*
Andrea Greerly, *Payroll Mgr*
▲ EMP: 135
SQ FT: 28,000
SALES (est): 11.5MM **Privately Held**
WEB: www.counter-fit.com
SIC: 2339 2337 3281 Sportswear, women's; women's & misses' suits & coats; cut stone & stone products

(G-12119)
HERMAN EICKHOFF
Also Called: Kennedy Shop N Bag
400 John F Kennedy Way (08046-2121)
PHONE..................................609 871-1809
Herman Eickhoff, *President*
Richard Eickhoff, *Vice Pres*
Karl Eickhoff, *Treasurer*
Pam Stein, *Human Res Dir*
Bill Andrews, *Manager*
EMP: 104
SQ FT: 35,000
SALES (est): 6.8MM **Privately Held**
SIC: 5411 2051 Supermarkets, chain; bread, cake & related products

(G-12120)
MAXTER CORPORATION
18 Chalford Ln (08046-3402)
PHONE..................................609 877-9700
John Mughal, *President*
Saida Mughal, *Vice Pres*
Rick Ruggerio, *Manager*
EMP: 4
SALES: 250K **Privately Held**
SIC: 3841 Surgical & medical instruments

(G-12121)
NATHJI PLUS INC
1 Rose St (08046-2537)
PHONE..................................609 877-7600
Hiren M Patel, *Principal*
EMP: 5
SALES (est): 668.1K **Privately Held**
SIC: 2836 Vaccines & other immunizing products

(G-12122)
PARADISE PUBLISHING GROUP LLC
25 Middlebury Ln Ste 3b (08046-2931)
PHONE..................................609 227-7642
Shema'yah Bey, *Principal*
EMP: 4

SALES (est): 83.8K **Privately Held**
SIC: 2711 Newspapers

(G-12123)
WHOLE STONES LLC
1 Ironside Ct (08046-2533)
PHONE..............................856 266-0091
Mehmet Kahyaoglu,
EMP: 6
SALES (est): 343.4K **Privately Held**
SIC: 5032 3281 1743 Granite building
stone; granite, cut & shaped; marble in-
stallation, interior

Windsor
Mercer County

(G-12124)
**ASSA ABLOY ENTRANCE
SYSTEMS US**
Besam Entrance Solutions
92 N Main St Unit A (08561-3209)
P.O. Box 519 (08561-0519)
PHONE..............................609 443-5800
Fax: 609 443-7597
Michael McCaslin, *Branch Mgr*
EMP: 50
SALES (corp-wide): 9B **Privately Held**
SIC: 3699 1796 3442 Door opening &
closing devices, electrical; installing build-
ing equipment; metal doors
HQ: Assa Abloy Entrance Systems Us Inc.
1900 Airport Rd
Monroe NC 28110
704 290-5520

(G-12125)
**DAVID BRADLEY CHOCOLATIER
INC (PA)**
92 N Main St Bldg 19 (08561-3209)
PHONE..............................609 443-4747
David Bradley, *Principal*
Mary Hicks, *Executive*
EMP: 14
SALES (est): 2.2MM **Privately Held**
SIC: 2066 2064 Chocolate & cocoa prod-
ucts; candy & other confectionery prod-
ucts

(G-12126)
GRIFFITH ELECTRIC SUPPLY CO
1381 Route 130 N (08561)
PHONE..............................609 632-0253
Derek Davidson, *Branch Mgr*
EMP: 4
SALES (corp-wide): 22.6MM **Privately
Held**
SIC: 3699 Electrical equipment & supplies
PA: Griffith Electric Supply Co., Inc.
5 2nd St
Trenton NJ 08611
609 695-6121

(G-12127)
HARWILL CORPORATION
Also Called: Harwill Express Press
92 N Main St (08561-3209)
P.O. Box 1645, East Windsor (08520-8945)
PHONE..............................609 895-1955
Fax: 609 896-3322
Steven Portrude, *President*
Norma Smith, *Accounts Exec*
Harriet Portrude, *Admin Sec*
EMP: 7
SALES (est): 1.2MM **Privately Held**
WEB: www.harwill.net
SIC: 2759 7389 7336 Promotional print-
ing; advertising literature: printing; adver-
tising, promotional & trade show services;
commercial art & graphic design; art de-
sign services; creative services to adver-
tisers, except writers

(G-12128)
**PYROMETER INSTRUMENT CO
INC**
92 N Main St Bldg 18d (08561-3209)
P.O. Box 479 (08561-0479)
PHONE..............................609 443-5522
Fax: 609 443-5590
EMP: 24 EST: 1928
SQ FT: 7,500

SALES (est): 4.4MM **Privately Held**
SIC: 3823 Mfg Process Control Instruments

(G-12129)
SILVER BRUSH LIMITED
92 N Main St Ste 19-I (08561-3209)
P.O. Box 414 (08561-0414)
PHONE..............................609 443-4900
Fax: 609 443-4888
Deirdra Silver, *President*
Edward Flax, *Corp Secy*
Ed Flax, *CFO*
▲ EMP: 5
SQ FT: 2,500
SALES (est): 972K **Privately Held**
WEB: www.silverbrush.com
SIC: 5199 3991 Artists' materials; paint
brushes

(G-12130)
SPEC STEEL RULE DIES INC
92 N Main St Bldg 1b (08561-3209)
P.O. Box 33 (08561-0033)
PHONE..............................609 443-4435
Fax: 609 443-9230
John Nagy, *President*
Robert Margon, *Vice Pres*
Jessica Brown, *Admin Sec*
▲ EMP: 30
SQ FT: 7,000
SALES (est): 4.9MM **Privately Held**
WEB: www.specdies.com
SIC: 3544 Dies, steel rule

Winfield Park
Union County

(G-12131)
AK CONTRACTING LLC
32b Seafoam Ave (07036-7542)
PHONE..............................908 220-8527
Lori S Viola,
EMP: 7
SALES: 100K **Privately Held**
SIC: 7299 1389 Home improvement &
renovation contractor agency; construc-
tion, repair & dismantling services

Winslow
Camden County

(G-12132)
GLOBAL TEAK INC
530 S Rte 73 (08095)
PHONE..............................609 208-2854
Ravi Gadiraju, *President*
Michael Whitelock, *Vice Pres*
◆ EMP: 17
SQ FT: 5,000
SALES (est): 1.6MM **Privately Held**
WEB: www.globalteak.com
SIC: 2421 Building & structural materials,
wood

Wood Ridge
Bergen County

(G-12133)
ACADEMIA FURNITURE LLC
Also Called: Academia Furniture Industries
74 Passaic St (07075-1004)
PHONE..............................973 472-0100
Fax: 973 472-8444
Isaac Wagner, *CEO*
▲ EMP: 40
SQ FT: 140,000
SALES (est): 6.5MM **Privately Held**
SIC: 2531 5021 School furniture; office &
public building furniture

(G-12134)
APPLE CORRUGATED BOX LTD
1 Passaic St Unit 76 (07075-1004)
PHONE..............................201 635-1269
Paul Belfiore, *Partner*
EMP: 16

SALES (est): 4.5MM **Privately Held**
SIC: 2653 Corrugated & solid fiber boxes

(G-12135)
CERTECH INC (DH)
Also Called: Morgan Technical Ceramics
1 Park Pl W (07075-2498)
PHONE..............................201 842-6800
Fax: 201 939-1423
John Stang, *CEO*
James McRickard, *President*
Christopher Donovan, *General Mgr*
Ross Johnson, *Vice Pres*
Gilbert Carrasquillo, *Research*
▲ EMP: 104
SALES (est): 93.7MM
SALES (corp-wide): 1.3B **Privately Held**
SIC: 3364 Nonferrous die-castings except
aluminum
HQ: Morganite Industries Inc.
4000 Westchase Blvd # 170
Raleigh NC 27607
919 821-1253

(G-12136)
CON CAP SPORTS WEAR
Also Called: Continental Cap & Import
64 Passaic St (07075-1004)
PHONE..............................973 778-2628
Fax: 973 778-2583
Tina Ng, *President*
Perry Ng, *VP Sales*
▲ EMP: 15
SQ FT: 15,000
SALES (est): 2MM **Privately Held**
SIC: 2353 Baseball caps

(G-12137)
KASANOVA INC
175 State Rt 17 (07075-2435)
PHONE..............................201 368-8400
Fax: 201 368-8409
Kathleen Campbell, *President*
▲ EMP: 6
SALES (est): 550K **Privately Held**
WEB: www.kasanova.com
SIC: 2434 Wood kitchen cabinets

(G-12138)
SKYLINE WINDOWS LLC
210 Park Pl E (07075-1808)
PHONE..............................201 531-9600
Fax: 201 896-4166
David Kraus, *President*
EMP: 45
SALES (corp-wide): 54.7MM **Privately
Held**
SIC: 2431 3442 Windows & window parts
& trim, wood; metal doors, sash & trim
PA: Skyline Windows, Llc
220 E 138th St
Bronx NY 10451
646 273-1492

(G-12139)
STARFIRE LIGHTING INC
7 Donna Dr (07075-1915)
PHONE..............................201 438-9540
Fax: 201 438-9541
Zachary Gomes, *President*
Phyllis Eckstein, *Project Mgr*
Craig Newman, *Treasurer*
Tante Rivera, *Controller*
Maggie Wisse, *Admin Asst*
▲ EMP: 50 EST: 1980
SQ FT: 50,000
SALES: 15.5MM **Privately Held**
WEB: www.starfirelighting.com
SIC: 3646 3645 Commercial indusl & insti-
tutional electric lighting fixtures; residen-
tial lighting fixtures

(G-12140)
TECH-PAK INC
3 Ethel Blvd (07075-2431)
PHONE..............................201 935-3800
Marvin Grossbard, *President*
EMP: 12
SALES (est): 1.4MM **Privately Held**
SIC: 3086 4226 3993 2672 Packaging &
shipping materials, foamed plastic; spe-
cial warehousing & storage; signs & ad-
vertising specialties; coated & laminated
paper; bookbinding & related work

Woodbine
Cape May County

(G-12141)
BELLEPLAIN SUPPLY CO INC
Also Called: Belleplain Supply Gun Center
346 Hands Mill Rd (08270-3938)
PHONE..............................609 861-2345
Nicholas Germanio, *President*
Lou Ann Germanio, *Admin Sec*
EMP: 4 EST: 1967
SQ FT: 15,000
SALES (est): 595.6K **Privately Held**
WEB: www.browningguncenter.com
SIC: 3949 5699 Cases, gun & rod (sport-
ing equipment); fishing equipment; sports
apparel

(G-12142)
G & J SOLUTIONS INC
Also Called: Bill's Canvas Shop
419 Madison Ave (08270-2314)
PHONE..............................609 861-9838
Fax: 609 861-9840
John Dipompeo, *President*
Grace Dipompeo, *Corp Secy*
Yvonne Szafranski, *Marketing Staff*
EMP: 13 EST: 1971
SQ FT: 7,300
SALES (est): 980K **Privately Held**
WEB: www.billscanvasshop.com
SIC: 2394 Awnings, fabric: made from pur-
chased materials

(G-12143)
JMM STUDIOS
1524 Dehirsch Ave (08270-2412)
PHONE..............................609 861-3094
James Melonic, *Owner*
Adam Melonic, *Project Mgr*
EMP: 4
SALES (est): 250K **Privately Held**
SIC: 2531 Public building & related furni-
ture

Woodbridge
Middlesex County

(G-12144)
35 FOOD CORP
Also Called: Antonio's Pasta
545 Us Highway 9 N (07095-1002)
PHONE..............................732 442-1640
Fax: 732 442-4033
Barbara Winant, *President*
Richard Winant, *Vice Pres*
EMP: 8
SQ FT: 3,800
SALES (est): 1MM **Privately Held**
SIC: 2099 5143 5149 Pasta, uncooked:
packaged with other ingredients; cheese;
pasta & rice

(G-12145)
**ASCO POWER TECHNOLOGIES
LP**
1460 Us Highway 9 N # 209 (07095-1408)
PHONE..............................732 596-1733
Fax: 732 596-0150
Don Bachman, *Branch Mgr*
EMP: 11
SALES (corp-wide): 200.4K **Privately
Held**
SIC: 3699 5063 Electrical equipment &
supplies; electrical apparatus & equip-
ment
HQ: Asco Power Technologies, L.P.
160 Park Ave
Florham Park NJ 07932

(G-12146)
AUTOMATIC SWITCH COMPANY
1460 Us Highway 9 N # 209 (07095-1408)
PHONE..............................732 596-1731
Ken Martin, *Manager*
EMP: 10
SALES (corp-wide): 15.2B **Publicly Held**
SIC: 3491 Solenoid valves

HQ: Automatic Switch Company
50-60 Hanover Rd
Florham Park NJ 07932
973 966-2000

(G-12147)
BOOKCODE CORP
2312 Plaza Dr (07095-1132)
PHONE..................................732 742-0481
Alok Mahapatra, *Director*
EMP: 9
SALES: 100K **Privately Held**
SIC: 2731 Book publishing

(G-12148)
FIBRENETICS INC
2 Cutters Dock Rd (07095-2701)
P.O. Box 632 (07095-0632)
PHONE..................................732 636-5670
Fax: 732 636-6624
Herbert T Segars, *President*
Tom Segars, *Vice Pres*
Chris St Leon, *Manager*
Tim Englehardt, *Technology*
EMP: 10
SQ FT: 12,000
SALES (est): 1.4MM **Privately Held**
WEB: www.fibglass.com
SIC: 3089 Plastic containers, except foam

(G-12149)
GARDEN ST CHASIS REMANUF
1 Pennville Rd (07095)
PHONE..................................732 283-1910
Joseph Perez, *President*
Sabato Catucci, *Vice Pres*
Ronald Catucci, *Treasurer*
EMP: 50
SQ FT: 60,000
SALES (est): 6.4MM **Privately Held**
SIC: 3713 3711 Truck bodies (motor vehicles); chassis, motor vehicle

(G-12150)
HARY MANUFACTURING INC
210 Grove Ave (07095-2337)
P.O. Box 187 (07095-0187)
PHONE..................................908 722-7100
Paul Hary, *President*
EMP: 10 EST: 2010
SQ FT: 10,000
SALES (est): 1.4MM **Privately Held**
SIC: 2759 3567 Screen printing; driers &
redriers, industrial process

(G-12151)
MAUSER USA LLC
14 Convery Blvd (07095-2649)
PHONE..................................732 634-6000
Giovanni Balsano, *Plant Supt*
Monica McGrath, *Purch Mgr*
Herman Graff, *Branch Mgr*
Musy Abraham, *Manager*
Dennis Platek, *Director*
EMP: 150 **Privately Held**
WEB: www.mausergroup.com
SIC: 3412 Metal barrels, drums & pails
HQ: Mauser Usa, Llc
2 Tower Center Blvd 20-1
East Brunswick NJ 08816
732 353-7100

(G-12152)
RCLC INC (PA)
Also Called: Ra Liquidating
1480 Us Highway 9 N # 301 (07095-1407)
PHONE..................................732 877-1788
Louis V Aronson II, *President*
Daryl K Holcomb, *CFO*
Erwin M Ganz, *Treasurer*
Justin P Walder, *Admin Sec*
EMP: 18 EST: 1928
SALES (est): 4.6MM **Privately Held**
WEB: www.ronsoncorp.com
SIC: 3999 2899 3728 7363 Cigarette
lighters, except precious metal; cigarette
lighter flints; lighter fluid; aircraft parts &
equipment; pilot service, aviation

(G-12153)
SNEAKER SWARM LLC
581 Main St Ste 640 (07095-1196)
PHONE..................................908 693-9262
Raheem Hardy, *Mng Member*
EMP: 11
SQ FT: 200,000

SALES (est): 350.1K **Privately Held**
SIC: 2721 Magazines: publishing & printing

(G-12154)
STONE MOUNTAIN PRINTING INC
Also Called: A-1 Thrifty Centers
74 Main St Fl 1 (07095-2963)
PHONE..................................732 636-8450
Fax: 732 634-4415
Steven Steinberg, *President*
Hank Steinberg, *Corp Secy*
EMP: 8
SQ FT: 24,000
SALES (est): 810K **Privately Held**
WEB: www.stonemountainprinting.com
SIC: 2752 Commercial printing, offset

(G-12155)
TRANSPORTATION TECH SVCS INC
Also Called: Tandem Technologies
1480 Us Highway 9 N # 204 (07095-1407)
PHONE..................................732 326-0700
Tim Rose, *CEO*
EMP: 28
SALES (est): 498.8K **Privately Held**
SIC: 7372 Application computer software

(G-12156)
WOODBRIDGE MACHINE & TOOL CO
259 Bergen St (07095-1829)
PHONE..................................732 634-0179
Fax: 732 602-0922
Steve J Sepa, *President*
Irma Sepa, *Corp Secy*
EMP: 7
SQ FT: 2,500
SALES (est): 1MM **Privately Held**
SIC: 3599 Machine shop, jobbing & repair

Woodbury
Gloucester County

(G-12157)
AUNTIE ANNES SOFT PRETZELS
1750 Deptford Center Rd # 2086
(08096-5222)
PHONE..................................856 845-3667
Jane Hanson, *Manager*
Christine Aquelino, *Manager*
Melvin Sickler, *Admin Sec*
EMP: 35
SALES (est): 900.8K **Privately Held**
SIC: 5461 2052 Pretzels; pretzels

(G-12158)
BELLIA & SONS
1047 N Broad St (08096-3565)
PHONE..................................856 845-2234
Fax: 856 845-1180
Tom Bellia, *Owner*
Anthony Bellia, *Owner*
Carmen Dominguez, *Project Mgr*
Janet Santoro, *Accounts Exec*
EMP: 30
SQ FT: 3,000
SALES (est): 4.1MM **Privately Held**
SIC: 6513 7334 5943 5712 Apartment
hotel operation; blueprinting service; office forms & supplies; office furniture; invitation & stationery printing & engraving

(G-12159)
DEWECHTER INC
Also Called: Constitution Co
58 S Broad St (08096-4629)
P.O. Box 358 (08096-7358)
PHONE..................................856 845-0225
Fax: 856 845-5496
Daniel Dewechter, *President*
EMP: 4 EST: 1946
SQ FT: 3,000
SALES (est): 360.3K **Privately Held**
SIC: 2759 Letterpress printing

(G-12160)
EP HENRY CORPORATION (PA)
201 Park Ave (08096-3599)
P.O. Box 615 (08096-7615)
PHONE..................................856 845-6200
Fax: 856 845-0023
James C Henry III, *CEO*
James C Henry Jr, *CEO*
Shafer Henry, *Vice Pres*
John Poignard, *Vice Pres*
James Nash, *Treasurer*
▲ EMP: 100
SALES (est): 27.8MM **Privately Held**
WEB: www.ephenry.com
SIC: 3271 3281 5072 Blocks, concrete or
cinder: standard; paving blocks, cut
stone; builders' hardware

(G-12161)
FERRETT PRINTING INC
468 Warwick Rd (08096-6018)
PHONE..................................856 686-4896
Nicholas Ferrett, *President*
EMP: 5
SALES (est): 625.8K **Privately Held**
SIC: 2752 Commercial printing, offset

(G-12162)
GLOUCESTER COUNTY TIMES
309 S Broad St (08096-2406)
PHONE..................................856 845-7484
Fax: 856 845-5480
Frank Gargano, *President*
EMP: 5
SALES (est): 83.8K **Privately Held**
SIC: 2711 Newspapers, publishing & printing

(G-12163)
GTM MARKETING INC
1960 Harris Dr (08096-3863)
PHONE..................................856 227-2333
Fax: 856 227-8886
Karl R Baker, *President*
EMP: 6
SALES (est): 604.1K **Privately Held**
SIC: 2759 Screen printing

(G-12164)
MAJE SYSTEMS INC
45 Delaware St Ste 1 (08096-5931)
PHONE..................................856 845-5363
William J Sandoz, *President*
Dean Macris, *Vice Pres*
Maria Sandoz, *Shareholder*
EMP: 4
SQ FT: 600
SALES: 700K **Privately Held**
SIC: 2844 Hair coloring preparations

(G-12165)
NJ DEPT MILITARY VTRANS
Also Called: New Jersey National Guard
658 N Evergreen Ave (08096-3512)
PHONE..................................856 384-8831
EMP: 4 **Privately Held**
SIC: 9711 2731 National Security BooksPublishing/Printing
HQ: New Jersey Department Of Military
And Veterans Affairs
101 Eggerts Crossing Rd
Lawrenceville NJ
609 530-6957

(G-12166)
ONE TWO THREE INC
537 Mantua Pike Ste B (08096-3257)
P.O. Box 123 (08096-7123)
PHONE..................................856 251-1238
Randy Rigley, *President*
EMP: 13
SALES (est): 1.7MM **Privately Held**
SIC: 2752 5199 Commercial printing, lithographic; advertising specialties

(G-12167)
PATHMARK STORES INC
1450 Clements Bridge Rd (08096-3067)
PHONE..................................856 853-5533
Fax: 856 853-6293
EMP: 200
SALES (corp-wide): 2B **Privately Held**
SIC: 5411 5912 2051 Ret Groceries Ret
Drugs/Sundries Mfg Bread/Related Products

PA: Pathmark Stores, Inc.
2 Paragon Dr
Montvale NJ 07645
866 443-7374

(G-12168)
PAUL FAGO CABINET MAKING INC
425 S Columbia St (08096-5733)
PHONE..................................856 384-0496
Susan Fago, *Executive*
EMP: 8
SALES (est): 704.6K **Privately Held**
SIC: 2434 Wood kitchen cabinets

(G-12169)
SECURITY 21 LLC
119 Steeplechase Ct (08096-6801)
PHONE..................................856 384-7474
Vince Reilly,
EMP: 6
SALES (est): 757.7K **Privately Held**
SIC: 3699 Security control equipment &
systems

(G-12170)
SIGN SHOPPE INC
370 Glassboro Rd (08097-1009)
PHONE..................................856 384-2937
Fax: 856 384-2881
Janet Philphs, *President*
EMP: 5
SALES (est): 416K **Privately Held**
SIC: 3993 1799 7532 Signs & advertising
specialties; sign installation & maintenance; truck painting & lettering

(G-12171)
SPECIALTY CASTING INC
42 Curtis Ave (08096-4636)
PHONE..................................856 845-3105
Fax: 856 848-3185
John F Cowgill, *President*
Daniel Cowgill, *Vice Pres*
EMP: 4
SQ FT: 5,000
SALES (est): 270K **Privately Held**
WEB: www.specialtycasting.com
SIC: 2821 Plastics materials & resins

(G-12172)
WORK N GEAR LLC
Also Called: Work'n Gear 8047
1692 Clements Bridge Rd H (08096-3028)
PHONE..................................856 848-7676
Lisa Grasso, *Manager*
EMP: 7
SALES (corp-wide): 53.5MM **Privately
Held**
WEB: www.workngear.com
SIC: 5961 2759 Catalog & mail-order
houses; screen printing
PA: Work 'n Gear, Llc
2300 Crown Colony Dr # 301
Quincy MA 02169
781 746-0100

Woodbury Heights
Gloucester County

(G-12173)
431 CONVERTERS INC
Also Called: Converter Company, The
230 Glassboro Rd (08097-1013)
PHONE..................................856 848-8949
Fax: 856 456-8651
Austin Bombaro, *President*
Ted Reinder, *Treasurer*
EMP: 6
SALES (est): 975.9K **Privately Held**
SIC: 3566 Torque converters, except automotive

(G-12174)
BILL CHAMBERS SHEET METAL
371 Glassboro Rd Ste 5 (08097-1026)
P.O. Box 172 (08097-0172)
PHONE..................................856 848-4774
Fax: 856 845-5166
William Chambers III, *Owner*
EMP: 3
SQ FT: 3,600

(PA)=Parent Co (HQ)=Headquarters (DH)=Div Headquarters
✪ = New Business established in last 2 years

2018 Harris New Jersey
Manufacturers Directory

479

G E O G R A P H I C

SALES: 1.5MM **Privately Held**
SIC: 3444 Sheet metalwork

(G-12175)
ELLENBY TECHNOLOGIES INC
412 Grandview Ave (08097-1556)
PHONE..................................856 848-2020
Fax: 856 848-7080
Bob Dobbins, *CEO*
Doug Padula, *Opers Mgr*
Marco Polit, *Purch Mgr*
Rick Morgan, *Purchasing*
Tom Carullo, *Engineer*
▲ **EMP:** 45
SQ FT: 50,000
SALES (est): 9.1MM **Privately Held**
WEB: www.ellenbytech.com
SIC: 3699 8711 5063 Electrical equipment & supplies; consulting engineer; electrical apparatus & equipment

(G-12176)
EVERGREEN DENTAL
549 S Evergreen Ave (08097-1004)
PHONE..................................856 845-3299
Sandy Moran, *Manager*
Richard D Ruden, *Fmly & Gen Dent*
EMP: 4 **EST:** 2008
SALES (est): 539.7K **Privately Held**
SIC: 3843 Enamels, dentists'

(G-12177)
EXCEL COLOR GRAPHICS INC
207 W Jersey Ave (08097-1035)
PHONE..................................856 848-3345
Fax: 856 848-3233
Jean-Paul Bonnette, *President*
Linda S Bonnette, *Corp Secy*
EMP: 6
SQ FT: 7,500
SALES: 650K **Privately Held**
SIC: 2752 Commercial printing, offset

(G-12178)
WOODBURY ROOF TRUSS INC
Also Called: Concord Truss Co
692 S Evergreen Ave (08097-1021)
PHONE..................................856 845-3848
Fax: 856 845-0831
Richard Phalines, *President*
John Gligor Sr, *Corp Secy*
EMP: 85
SQ FT: 40,000
SALES (est): 19.7MM **Privately Held**
SIC: 2439 Trusses, wooden roof; trusses, except roof: laminated lumber

---

Woodcliff Lake
Bergen County

(G-12179)
AMERICAN AUTO CARRIERS INC
188 Broadway Ste 1 (07677-8072)
PHONE..................................201 573-0371
Ray Ebeling, *President*
Arlen F Henock, *CFO*
EMP: 4
SALES (est): 298.3K
SALES (corp-wide): 191.4MM **Privately Held**
WEB: www.walleniuslines.com
SIC: 3443 Industrial vessels, tanks & containers
HQ: Wallenius Lines Holding, Inc.
　188 Broadway Ste 1
　Woodcliff Lake NJ 07677

(G-12180)
AMERICAN LOGISTICS NETWORK LLC
Also Called: Aln
188 Broadway Ste 1 (07677-8072)
PHONE..................................201 391-1054
Jhon Igltsias, *Principal*
Robin Tarantino, *Director*
EMP: 8
SALES (est): 820K **Privately Held**
SIC: 3423 Jewelers' hand tools

(G-12181)
ATLANTEX INSTRUMENTS INC
7 Reeds Ln (07677-8348)
PHONE..................................201 391-5148
Hatcho A Fendian, *President*
EMP: 5
SALES (est): 736.3K **Privately Held**
SIC: 3699 Photographic control systems, electronic

(G-12182)
BMC SOFTWARE INC
50 Tice Blvd (07677-7654)
PHONE..................................703 761-0400
John Beischer, *Manager*
EMP: 8
SALES (corp-wide): 1.3B **Privately Held**
WEB: www.bmc.com
SIC: 7372 Prepackaged software
HQ: Bmc Software, Inc.
　2103 Citywest Blvd # 2100
　Houston TX 77042
　713 918-8800

(G-12183)
BMW OF NORTH AMERICA LLC (DH)
Also Called: BMW Group
300 Chestnut Ridge Rd (07677-7731)
P.O. Box 1227, Westwood (07675-1227)
PHONE..................................201 307-4000
Fax: 201 307-0880
Ludwig Willisch, *CEO*
Craig Helsing, *President*
Stefan Borbe, *General Mgr*
Markus Seidel, *General Mgr*
Joachim Steinle, *General Mgr*
◆ **EMP:** 700
SQ FT: 200,000
SALES (est): 1.7B
SALES (corp-wide): 116.3B **Privately Held**
WEB: www.detroitbmw.com
SIC: 5013 3751 5012 3711 Automotive supplies & parts; motorcycles, bicycles & parts; automobiles; motor vehicles & car bodies
HQ: Bmw (Us) Holding Corp.
　300 Chestnut Ridge Rd
　Woodcliff Lake NJ 07677
　201 307-4000

(G-12184)
BUTTONWOOD ENTERPRISES LLC
52 Winding Way (07677-7930)
PHONE..................................201 505-1901
Andrew Groh, *Mng Member*
Alan Edelman,
▲ **EMP:** 4
SALES: 500K **Privately Held**
SIC: 3825 7389 Internal combustion engine analyzers, to test electronics;

(G-12185)
CAST INC
Also Called: Computer Aided Software Tech
11 Stonewall Ct (07677-8412)
PHONE..................................201 391-8300
Nikolaos Zervas, *CEO*
Stephen Pollock, *President*
Juliani Sendjaja, *General Mgr*
Harold Barbour, *Chairman*
Bill Finch, *Exec VP*
EMP: 9
SALES: 4MM **Privately Held**
WEB: www.cast-inc.com
SIC: 3674 Semiconductors & related devices

(G-12186)
CATALOGIC SOFTWARE INC
50 Tice Blvd Ste 110 (07677-7654)
PHONE..................................201 249-8980
Ken Barth, *President*
Ira Goodman, *Vice Pres*
Mike Kuehn, *Vice Pres*
CHI S Chang, *Engineer*
Tom Amato, *Sales Staff*
EMP: 120
SALES (est): 17.6MM **Privately Held**
SIC: 7372 Business oriented computer software

(G-12187)
CLIC TIME LLC
50 Tice Blvd Ste 340 (07677-7681)
PHONE..................................201 497-6743
James Richardson, *Managing Dir*
Mark Shell, *Mng Member*
◆ **EMP:** 22
SQ FT: 2,600
SALES: 14.9MM
SALES (corp-wide): 23.5MM **Privately Held**
SIC: 3873 5094 Watches, clocks, watchcases & parts; clocks, watches & parts
PA: Clic Time Holdings Limited
　Unit 4, Meadowfield Court
　Newcastle-Upon-Tyne NE20

(G-12188)
EAGLE PHARMACEUTICALS INC (PA)
50 Tice Blvd Ste 315 (07677-7637)
PHONE..................................201 326-5300
Scott Tarriff, *CEO*
Michael Graves, *Ch of Bd*
David Pernock, *President*
Pete A Meyers, *CFO*
David E Riggs, *CFO*
▲ **EMP:** 43
SQ FT: 20,497
SALES (est): 236.7MM **Publicly Held**
SIC: 2834 Druggists' preparations (pharmaceuticals)

(G-12189)
EISAI INC (DH)
100 Tice Blvd (07677-8404)
PHONE..................................201 692-1100
Cynthia Schwalm, *President*
Alex Scott, *President*
Lihua Yu, *President*
Colleen Lynch, *District Mgr*
Hideo Dan, *Senior VP*
▲ **EMP:** 150
SALES (est): 173.6MM
SALES (corp-wide): 5.6B **Privately Held**
WEB: www.aciphex.com
SIC: 2834 Pharmaceutical preparations

(G-12190)
ESCO INDUSTRIAL CORPORATION
30 Stonewall Ct (07677-8413)
PHONE..................................973 478-5888
Jack Shu, *President*
▲ **EMP:** 7
SALES (est): 614.4K **Privately Held**
SIC: 3089 Fittings for pipe, plastic

(G-12191)
ESCO INDUSTRIES CORP
30 Stonewall Ct (07677-8413)
PHONE..................................973 478-5888
Fax: 973 478-3288
Leo Hsu, *President*
James Hsu, *General Mgr*
Jack Hsu, *Vice Pres*
Kathy Hsu, *Admin Sec*
▲ **EMP:** 25
SQ FT: 40,000
SALES (est): 5.3MM **Privately Held**
SIC: 3498 Fabricated pipe & fittings

(G-12192)
FIDELIO LIMITED PARTNERSHIP
188 Broadway Ste 1 (07677-8072)
PHONE..................................201 307-1626
Ray Ebeling, *Partner*
John Ridlon, *Partner*
Jim Wells, *Partner*
Arlen F Henock, *CFO*
EMP: 4
SALES (est): 318.5K
SALES (corp-wide): 191.4MM **Privately Held**
WEB: www.walleniuslines.com
SIC: 3443 Industrial vessels, tanks & containers
HQ: Wallenius Lines Holding, Inc.
　188 Broadway Ste 1
　Woodcliff Lake NJ 07677

(G-12193)
ID SYSTEMS INC (PA)
123 Tice Blvd (07677-7670)
PHONE..................................201 996-9000

Fax: 201 996-9144
Chris Wolfe, *CEO*
Jason Schilb, *Partner*
Matt Murillo, *Business Mgr*
Norman L Ellis, *COO*
Joey Pinzon, *Vice Pres*
▲ **EMP:** 101
SQ FT: 21,400
SALES: 40.9MM **Publicly Held**
WEB: www.id-systems.com
SIC: 3663 4812 ; radio telephone communication; cellular telephone services

(G-12194)
IHS INC
Also Called: Automotive Database Marketing
50 Tice Blvd Ste 130 (07677-7666)
PHONE..................................201 391-0084
Jeffery Martini, *Branch Mgr*
EMP: 8 **Privately Held**
SIC: 7331 8732 2741 Mailing service; commercial nonphysical research; miscellaneous publishing
HQ: Ihs Inc.
　15 Inverness Way E
　Englewood CO 80112
　303 790-0600

(G-12195)
IVAX PHARMACEUTICALS LLC
400 Chestnut Ridge Rd (07677-7604)
PHONE..................................201 767-1700
Eric Mittleberg, *Branch Mgr*
EMP: 5
SALES (corp-wide): 22.3B **Privately Held**
WEB: www.ivaxpharmaceuticals.com
SIC: 2834 Pharmaceutical preparations
HQ: Ivax Pharmaceuticals, Llc
　74 Nw 176th St
　Miami FL 33169

(G-12196)
J&N PHARMA LLC
50 Tice Blvd Ste 340 (07677-7681)
PHONE..................................201 391-3139
Nicholas Dimaio, *Principal*
EMP: 4
SALES (est): 290.5K **Privately Held**
SIC: 2834 Pharmaceutical preparations

(G-12197)
OPPENHEIM PLASTICS CO INC
90 Broadway (07677-8005)
P.O. Box 310, Saddle River (07458-0310)
PHONE..................................201 995-9595
Florence Oppenheim, *President*
Susan Mandell, *Treasurer*
EMP: 35 **EST:** 1951
SQ FT: 1,000
SALES (est): 3.5MM **Privately Held**
SIC: 3089 Plastic containers, except foam

(G-12198)
PATAGONIA PHARMACEUTICALS LLC
50 Tice Blvd Ste A26 (07677-7682)
PHONE..................................201 264-7866
Rome Joshua, *Principal*
Zachary Rome, *Exec VP*
EMP: 5
SALES (est): 422.7K **Privately Held**
SIC: 2834 Pharmaceutical preparations

(G-12199)
PERFECT CLICKS LLC
172 Broadway Rear Bldg (07677-8077)
PHONE..................................845 323-6116
Chad Agrawal,
EMP: 4
SALES: 500K **Privately Held**
SIC: 2741

(G-12200)
ROLLS-ROYCE MOTOR CARS NA LLC
300 Chestnut Ridge Rd (07677-7739)
P.O. Box 1227, Westwood (07675-1227)
PHONE..................................201 307-4117
Pedro Moto, *President*
Joshua Dobbins, *Opers Mgr*
Katie Todora, *Purch Agent*
Andrew Vandussen, *Engineer*
Julia Petrini, *Analyst*
◆ **EMP:** 4293

▲ = Import ▼=Export
◆ =Import/Export

SALES (est): 228.8MM
SALES (corp-wide): 116.3B Privately Held
SIC: 3711 Motor vehicles & car bodies
HQ: Bmw (Us) Holding Corp.
300 Chestnut Ridge Rd
Woodcliff Lake NJ 07677
201 307-4000

(G-12201)
SKY GROWTH INTERMEDIATE
300 Tice Blvd (07677-8406)
PHONE................................201 802-4000
Paul V Campanelli, CEO
Mike Burton, President
Scott Koenig, Vice Pres
John Tableriou, Plant Mgr
George Hernandez, Accounting Mgr
EMP: 350
SQ FT: 61,000
SALES (est): 25.5MM Privately Held
SIC: 2834 Pharmaceutical preparations;
druggists' preparations (pharmaceuticals);
tablets, pharmaceutical; medicines, cap-
suled or ampuled
HQ: Par Pharmaceutical, Inc.
1 Ram Ridge Rd
Chestnut Ridge NY 10977
845 573-5500

(G-12202)
SONY CORPORATION OF AMERICA
123 Tice Blvd (07677-7670)
PHONE................................201 930-1000
Jerry Kaplan, Branch Mgr
EMP: 15
SALES (corp-wide): 80.1B Privately Held
WEB: www.sony.com
SIC: 7812 7832 5064 3559 Motion picture production & distribution; motion picture production & distribution, television;
motion picture theaters, except drive-in;
television sets; radios; video cassette
recorders & accessories; tape players &
recorders; metal finishing equipment for
plating, etc.; household audio equipment;
household video equipment; software,
computer games
HQ: Sony Corporation Of America
25 Madison Ave Fl 27
New York NY 10010
212 833-8000

(G-12203)
SONY ELECTRONICS INC
123 Tice Blvd (07677-7670)
PHONE................................201 930-1000
Fax: 201 358-4621
Bill Hackett, Manager
EMP: 700
SALES (corp-wide): 80.1B Privately Held
SIC: 3652 Pre-recorded records & tapes
HQ: Sony Electronics Inc.
16535 Via Esprillo Bldg 1
San Diego CA 92127
858 942-2400

(G-12204)
SYS-CON PUBLICATIONS INC
Also Called: Java Developer's Journal
577 Chestnut Ridge Rd # 6 (07677-8400)
PHONE................................201 802-3000
Fax: 201 782-9601
Fuat Kircaali, President
▲ EMP: 40
SQ FT: 9,000
SALES (est): 4.3MM Privately Held
WEB: www.sys-con.com
SIC: 2721 Trade journals: publishing &
printing

(G-12205)
TAB NETWORKS
50 Tice Blvd Ste 365 (07677-7673)
PHONE................................201 746-0067
Thomas Plaut, President
Karen Richardson, Accountant
EMP: 5
SALES (est): 630.8K Privately Held
SIC: 7372 Prepackaged software

(G-12206)
UNIPORT INDUSTRIES CORPORATION
Also Called: Image Builder Appliques
23 Campbell Ave (07677-8061)
P.O. Box 8642 (07677-8642)
PHONE................................201 391-7676
Fax: 201 391-0729
Diane Anderson, President
Harry Anderson, Vice Pres
EMP: 6
SQ FT: 2,000
SALES (est): 640K Privately Held
WEB: www.uniportind.com
SIC: 5131 2395 Piece goods & notions;
emblems, embroidered

Woodland Park
Passaic County

(G-12207)
ACE METAL KRAFT CO INC
815 Mcbride Ave (07424-2892)
PHONE................................973 278-6605
Richard Zega, President
John Lamanna, Vice Pres
EMP: 21
SQ FT: 6,400
SALES (est): 3.8MM Privately Held
SIC: 3599 Machine shop, jobbing & repair

(G-12208)
ADVANCED SEWER
10 Memorial Dr (07424-2515)
P.O. Box 2056, West Paterson (07424-7056)
PHONE................................973 278-1948
Fax: 973 742-7705
Barbra Denora, President
EMP: 15
SALES (est): 1MM Privately Held
SIC: 1711 2842 Plumbing contractors;
drain pipe solvents or cleaners

(G-12209)
AMIT FUEL COMPANY
703 Mcbride Ave (07424-2819)
PHONE................................973 684-9409
EMP: 5
SALES (est): 426.5K Privately Held
SIC: 2869 Fuels

(G-12210)
AUTOPLAST SYSTEMS INC
Also Called: Asi
256 Bergen Blvd (07424-2502)
P.O. Box 312, Closter (07624-0312)
PHONE................................973 785-8333
Elias Haber, President
EMP: 4
SALES (est): 428.9K Privately Held
SIC: 3559 Plastics working machinery

(G-12211)
BMB MACHINING LLC
86 Lackawanna Ave 208b (07424-2565)
PHONE................................973 256-4010
Lawrence H Malone, Owner
Gennaro Minichino, Owner
EMP: 4
SALES (est): 155.1K Privately Held
SIC: 3451 Screw machine products

(G-12212)
BROMILOWS CANDY CO (PA)
350 Rifle Camp Rd (07424-2726)
PHONE................................973 684-1496
Fax: 973 345-0564
Thomas Stewart, President
Virginia R Monk, General Mgr
Ida Bromilow Stewart, Vice Pres
EMP: 6 EST: 1940
SQ FT: 5,000
SALES (est): 1.4MM Privately Held
WEB: www.bromilow.com
SIC: 5441 2064 2066 Candy; chocolate
candy, except solid chocolate; chocolate
& cocoa products

(G-12213)
CAMEO METAL FORMS INC
12 Andrews Dr (07424-2640)
PHONE................................718 788-1106

Antonio Di Maio, President
Vito Di Maio, Vice Pres
EMP: 10
SALES (est): 780K Privately Held
SIC: 3951 3221 Ball point pens & parts;
cosmetic jars, glass

(G-12214)
CENTURY BATHWORKS INC (PA)
Also Called: Century Shower Door
250 Lackawanna Ave Ste 2 (07424-2962)
PHONE................................973 785-4290
Fax: 973 785-0777
Michael Macmillan, President
Mark Smerak, Purchasing
Rosa Jurewicz, Cust Mgr
David Dixon, Marketing Staff
Ben Peschler, Manager
▲ EMP: 95 EST: 1946
SQ FT: 75,000
SALES (est): 22.1MM Privately Held
WEB: www.centuryshowerdoor-usa.com
SIC: 3231 3442 Doors, glass: made from
purchased glass; screen doors, metal

(G-12215)
CENTURY BATHWORKS INC
Also Called: Screens & Fabricated Metals
250 Lackawanna Ave Ste 1 (07424-2962)
P.O. Box 647, West Paterson (07424-2962)
PHONE................................201 785-1414
Fax: 973 785-0378
Phillip Bolchune, Manager
EMP: 30
SQ FT: 30,000
SALES (corp-wide): 22.1MM Privately
Held
WEB: www.centuryshowerdoor-usa.com
SIC: 3442 3231 Metal doors; products of
purchased glass
PA: Century Bathworks, Inc.
250 Lackawanna Ave Ste 2
Woodland Park NJ 07424
973 785-4290

(G-12216)
CONTACT UNTD TL & STAMPING CO
6 Andrews Dr (07424-2640)
PHONE................................973 256-7171
John Giarrusso, Vice Pres
EMP: 60
SQ FT: 32,000
SALES (est): 5.6MM Privately Held
WEB: www.eunitedtool.com
SIC: 3469 Metal stampings
PA: United Industries Inc
6 Andrews Dr
Woodland Park NJ 07424

(G-12217)
ELAINE INC
Also Called: Motomco
1 Hazel St (07424-3203)
PHONE................................973 345-6200
Fax: 973 297-5758
Anthony Abbate, President
Elaine Abbate, Admin Sec
EMP: 6
SQ FT: 8,000
SALES: 500K Privately Held
WEB: www.njmeter.com
SIC: 5075 3823 Air filters; moisture me-
ters, industrial process type

(G-12218)
F S R INC
244 Bergen Blvd (07424-2502)
PHONE................................973 785-4347
Janice Sandri, President
William Fitzsimmons, Chairman
Frank Van Morrelgem, Vice Pres
Tom Damiano, Purch Agent
Frank Velardo, QC Mgr
◆ EMP: 85
SQ FT: 27,000
SALES (est): 16.9MM Privately Held
SIC: 3663 3624 Radio & television switch-
ing equipment; electric carbons

(G-12219)
FMC CORPORATION
1130 Mcbride Ave (07424-3806)
PHONE................................973 256-0768
Claire Sasak, Branch Mgr

EMP: 61
SALES (corp-wide): 2.8B Publicly Held
SIC: 2812 Soda ash, sodium carbonate
(anhydrous)
PA: Fmc Corporation
2929 Walnut St
Philadelphia PA 19104
215 299-6000

(G-12220)
G & Y SPECIALTY FOODS LLC
2 Andrews Dr Ste 5 (07424-2604)
PHONE................................956 821-9652
Jose Yvan Vazquez, Mng Member
Yusleidy Diaz, Mng Member
EMP: 8
SALES (est): 247.3K Privately Held
SIC: 5149 2037 Groceries & related prod-
ucts; fruit juices

(G-12221)
HERALD NEWS (PA)
Also Called: North Jersey Com. Newspaper
1 Garret Mountain Plz # 201 (07424-3398)
PHONE................................973 569-7000
Fax: 973 569-7129
Malcom Borg, Publisher
Young West III, Principal
Eric Rivas, Prdtn Mgr
Gail Carlin, Payroll Mgr
EMP: 5
SALES (est): 2.3MM Privately Held
SIC: 2711 5521 2752 Newspapers, pub-
lishing & printing; used car dealers; com-
mercial printing, lithographic

(G-12222)
IFORTRESS
228 Lackawanna Ave (07424-2996)
PHONE................................973 812-6400
Karen Loughran, Principal
Douglas Tarnopoll, VP Sales
Jack Pero, Manager
EMP: 4
SALES (est): 230K Privately Held
SIC: 3699 Security control equipment &
systems

(G-12223)
KEARFOTT CORPORATION (HQ)
1150 Mcbride Ave Ste 1 (07424-2564)
PHONE................................973 785-6000
Fax: 973 785-6025
Ronald E Zelazo, President
Middleton John, General Mgr
Natasha McLucas, General Mgr
Peter Boyfield, Business Mgr
Jeff Brown, Business Mgr
EMP: 220
SQ FT: 1,000,000
SALES (est): 196.8MM
SALES (corp-wide): 396.4MM Privately
Held
WEB: www.ashfield.kearfott.com
SIC: 3812 Search & navigation equipment
PA: Astronautics Corporation Of America
4115 N Teutonia Ave
Milwaukee WI 53209
414 449-4000

(G-12224)
MAXELL CORPORATION OF AMERICA (HQ)
3 Garret Mountain Plz # 300 (07424-3352)
PHONE................................973 653-2400
Fax: 973 653-2450
Steven Wafhio, President
Len Haine, Vice Pres
Kyoko Murakami, Export Mgr
Robert Meadows, Natl Sales Mgr
Bruce Francisco, Sales Mgr
▲ EMP: 30
SQ FT: 28,000
SALES (est): 840MM
SALES (corp-wide): 1.3B Privately Held
WEB: www.maxell.com
SIC: 3691 3652 3679 Storage batteries;
pre-recorded records & tapes; head-
phones, radio
PA: Maxell Holdings, Ltd.
2-16-2, Konan
Minato-Ku TKY 108-0
357 157-037

(G-12225)
NORTH JERSEY MEDIA GROUP INC (HQ)
Also Called: NORTH JERSEY MEDIA GROUP FOUNDATION
1 Garret Mountain Plz # 201 (07424-3318)
P.O. Box 471 (07424-0471)
PHONE..........................201 646-4000
Fax: 201 569-7766
Malcolm A Borg, Ch of Bd
Stephen A Borg, President
John Cichowski, Editor
Alfred Doblin, Editor
Kelly Nicholaides, Editor
▲ EMP: 1301 EST: 1964
SQ FT: 360,000
SALES: 247K
SALES (corp-wide): 173.6MM Privately Held
WEB: www.njmg.com
SIC: 2711 4813 Newspapers, publishing & printing;
PA: Macromedia Incorporated
150 River St
Hackensack NJ 07601
201 646-4000

(G-12226)
NORTH JERSEY MEDIA GROUP INC
Also Called: Herald News
1 Garret Mountain Plz # 201 (07424-3318)
P.O. Box 471, West Paterson (07424-0471)
PHONE..........................973 569-7100
James Toolen, Manager
EMP: 40
SALES (corp-wide): 173.6MM Privately Held
WEB: www.njmg.com
SIC: 2711 2741 Newspapers; miscellaneous publishing
HQ: North Jersey Media Group Inc.
1 Garret Mountain Plz # 201
Woodland Park NJ 07424
201 646-4000

(G-12227)
OKONITE COMPANY
3 Garret Mountain Plz # 304 (07424-3352)
PHONE..........................212 239-0660
Hubert Mack, Foreman/Supr
Justin Frakes, Engineer
Michael Cronk, Sales Staff
John Macko, Manager
EMP: 5
SALES (corp-wide): 413.7MM Privately Held
WEB: www.okonite.com
SIC: 3357 Nonferrous wiredrawing & insulating
PA: The Okonite Company
102 Hilltop Rd
Ramsey NJ 07446
201 825-0300

(G-12228)
POCHET OF AMERICA INC
Also Called: Art-Deco Division
1 Garret Mountain Plz # 502 (07424-3320)
PHONE..........................973 942-4923
Fax: 973 942-5364
Jean Claude Moreau, President
▲ EMP: 150
SQ FT: 73,000
SALES (est): 19.9MM
SALES (corp-wide): 28.8MM Privately Held
WEB: www.pochet.org
SIC: 3221 2759 Glass containers; engraving
HQ: Pochet Du Courval
44 46
Clichy 92110
964 439-556

(G-12229)
PREMIER COMPACTION SYSTEMS
264 Lackawanna Ave Ste 1 (07424-2959)
PHONE..........................718 328-5990
Robert Frustaci, Mng Member
EMP: 10 EST: 2013

SALES (est): 1.9MM Privately Held
SIC: 5084 3589 Compaction equipment; garbage disposers & compactors, commercial

(G-12230)
QUALIPAC AMERICA CORP
1 Garret Mountain Plz # 502 (07424-3312)
PHONE..........................973 754-9920
Herve Robine, President
▲ EMP: 17
SQ FT: 30,000
SALES (est): 3MM
SALES (corp-wide): 28.8MM Privately Held
SIC: 3089 3085 Cases, plastic; bottle caps, molded plastic; closures, plastic; plastics bottles
HQ: Qualipac
44 46
Clichy 92110

(G-12231)
RBC DAIN RAUSCHER
3 Garret Mountain Plz # 201 (07424-3352)
PHONE..........................973 778-7300
Stan Golderberg, Principal
EMP: 15
SALES (est): 1.9MM Privately Held
SIC: 3324 Steel investment foundries

(G-12232)
RELX INC
1167 Mcbride Ave Ste 3 (07424-2543)
PHONE..........................973 812-1900
Robert Sikora, Research
EMP: 60
SALES (corp-wide): 9.7B Privately Held
WEB: www.lexis-nexis.com
SIC: 2721 Periodicals
HQ: Relx Inc.
230 Park Ave Ste 700
New York NY 10169
212 309-8100

(G-12233)
SKS FUEL INC
941 Mcbride Ave (07424-2618)
PHONE..........................973 200-0796
EMP: 4
SALES (est): 210.2K Privately Held
SIC: 2869 Fuels

(G-12234)
TECHNIQUES INC
14 Alexandria Ct (07424-3410)
PHONE..........................973 256-0947
Arvind Patel, President
EMP: 29 EST: 1955
SQ FT: 15,000
SALES: 1.7MM Privately Held
SIC: 3672 3613 Printed circuit boards; time switches, electrical switchgear apparatus

(G-12235)
TOMCEL MACHINE INC
86 Lackawanna Ave Ste 301 (07424-3805)
PHONE..........................973 256-8257
Frederick Foy, President
EMP: 5
SQ FT: 2,100
SALES: 250K Privately Held
SIC: 3599 Machine & other job shop work

(G-12236)
UNITED INDUSTRIES INC (PA)
Also Called: United Tool & Stamping Co
6 Andrews Dr (07424-2640)
PHONE..........................973 256-7171
Fax: 973 256-5139
John R Giarrusso, President
EMP: 60
SQ FT: 32,000
SALES (est): 9MM Privately Held
SIC: 3469 Metal stampings

Woodstown
Salem County

(G-12237)
A1 CUSTOM COUNTERTOPS INC
20 Old Salem Rd (08098-9474)
PHONE..........................856 200-3596
Thomas Matteo, President
Steve Matteo, Vice Pres
Elaine Matteo, Treasurer
Everett Matteo, Admin Sec
EMP: 10
SALES (est): 603.8K Privately Held
SIC: 2541 Counter & sink tops

(G-12238)
HAIR QUARTERS
221 Borton Dr (08098-1209)
PHONE..........................856 624-4072
Paula Brickner, Principal
EMP: 4
SALES (est): 378.7K Privately Held
SIC: 3131 Quarters

(G-12239)
P W PERKINS CO INC
221 Commissioners Pike (08098-2032)
PHONE..........................856 769-3525
Charles B Perkins III, CEO
EMP: 7
SQ FT: 2,500
SALES (est): 831.8K Privately Held
WEB: www.pwperkins.com
SIC: 2819 Industrial inorganic chemicals

(G-12240)
SOUTH JERSEY FARMERS EXCHANGE
101 East Ave (08098-1318)
PHONE..........................856 769-0062
Fax: 856 769-0343
Lee C Williams Jr, President
Sara Williams, Corp Secy
EMP: 7
SQ FT: 35,000
SALES (est): 1MM Privately Held
SIC: 2873 3523 Fertilizers: natural (organic), except compost; turf equipment, commercial

Woolwich Township
Gloucester County

(G-12241)
SHANI AUTO FUEL CORP
541 Kings Hwy (08085-5057)
PHONE..........................856 241-9767
EMP: 4
SALES (est): 309K Privately Held
SIC: 2869 Fuels

Wrightstown
Burlington County

(G-12242)
MARANATHA CERAMIC TILE & MARBL
Also Called: Maranatha Stairs
253 Cokstown New Egypt Rd (08562-1722)
PHONE..........................609 758-1168
Thomas Raab, President
Patricia Raab, Treasurer
EMP: 20
SQ FT: 12,000
SALES (est): 4.7MM Privately Held
WEB: www.maranathastairs.net
SIC: 5211 1743 1799 2431 Tile, ceramic; tile installation, ceramic; home/office interiors finishing, furnishing & remodeling; staircases & stairs, wood

(G-12243)
SPECIALTY FABRICATORS LLC
118 Meany Rd (08562-1612)
PHONE..........................609 758-6995

Fax: 609 758-8130
Buddy Wilkins, Purch Mgr
Nicole Stewart, Sales Staff
Robert Varra, Marketing Staff
Ed Symbouras, Mng Member
Ross Varra, Manager
EMP: 40
SQ FT: 20,000
SALES (est): 9.1MM Privately Held
WEB: www.specialtyfabricators.com
SIC: 3585 Office & store showcases & display fixtures

Wyckoff
Bergen County

(G-12244)
AIR & HYDRAULIC POWER INC
555 Goffle Rd (07481-2937)
P.O. Box 159 (07481-0159)
PHONE..........................201 447-1589
Fax: 201 447-0302
Robert A Main Jr, President
Susan Main, Corp Secy
Timothy Den Bleyker, Vice Pres
Bill Main, Vice Pres
William Main, Vice Pres
EMP: 8
SQ FT: 32,000
SALES: 550K
SALES (corp-wide): 28.7MM Privately Held
SIC: 3492 Valves, hydraulic, aircraft
PA: Main, Robert A & Sons Holding Company Inc
555 Goffle Rd
Wyckoff NJ 07481
201 447-3700

(G-12245)
ALADEN ATHLETIC WEAR LLC
465 W Main St Ste 5 (07481-1452)
PHONE..........................973 838-2425
Fax: 973 838-3336
Ron L Blaustein, President
Carlos A Arco, Vice Pres
Rafael A Arco,
EMP: 25
SQ FT: 11,000
SALES (est): 1.5MM Privately Held
SIC: 2329 Men's & boys' sportswear & athletic clothing

(G-12246)
BUTTERFLY BAKERY INC
615 Bridle Path (07481-2928)
PHONE..........................973 815-1501
Fax: 201 847-8520
Brenda Isaacs, President
EMP: 22
SALES (est): 3.3MM Privately Held
WEB: www.butterfly-bakery.com
SIC: 2052 Bakery products, dry

(G-12247)
C J ELECTRIC
327 Franklin Ave (07481-2041)
PHONE..........................201 891-0739
EMP: 5
SALES (est): 92.4K Privately Held
SIC: 4911 3699 1731 Electric services; electrical equipment & supplies; electrical work

(G-12248)
CORDES PRINTING INC
460 Braen Ave (07481-2949)
PHONE..........................201 652-7272
Mark Cordes, President
Linda March, Technology
EMP: 6
SALES (est): 1MM Privately Held
WEB: www.cordesprinting.com
SIC: 2752 2791 Commercial printing, offset; typesetting

(G-12249)
DAF PRODUCTS INC
Also Called: D A F
420 Braen Ave (07481-2949)
PHONE..........................201 251-1222
Fax: 201 251-1221
Thomas P Palmer, President
Mario Fusco, Vice Pres

▲ = Import ▼=Export
◆ =Import/Export

Karen Kliemisch, *Sales Staff*
Larry Delesio, *Technology*
▲ **EMP:** 18
SALES: 15MM **Privately Held**
SIC: 2295 3552 Laminating of fabrics; textile machinery

(G-12250)
DLITE PRODUCTS INC
540 Ravine Ct (07481-2921)
PHONE..................................201 444-0822
Bill Hennessy, *President*
Roger Mayfarth, *Vice Pres*
▲ **EMP:** 6
SALES (est): 338.7K **Privately Held**
WEB: www.dlite.com
SIC: 3999 Magic equipment, supplies & props

(G-12251)
DMA DATA INDUSTRIES INC
479 Goffle Rd (07481-3003)
PHONE..................................201 444-5733
Louis Ciarlo, *President*
EMP: 5
SQ FT: 2,000
SALES (est): 540K **Privately Held**
SIC: 7372 Prepackaged software

(G-12252)
FACTONOMY INC
459 Oldwoods Rd (07481-1448)
P.O. Box 14 Wall St, New York NY (10005)
PHONE..................................201 848-7812
Philip Rugani, *CEO*
Neil Jordan, *COO*
EMP: 11
SQ FT: 4,500
SALES (est): 525.2K **Privately Held**
SIC: 7371 7372 Computer software development & applications; application computer software

(G-12253)
GARDEN STATE IRRIGATION
500 W Main St Ste 5 (07481-1406)
PHONE..................................201 848-1300
Fax: 201 848-0120
Mark Nidowizz, *Owner*
EMP: 15
SALES (est): 2.6MM **Privately Held**
WEB: www.gardenstateirrigation.com
SIC: 3648 Outdoor lighting equipment

(G-12254)
ICEBOXX LLC
600 Braen Ave (07481-2914)
PHONE..................................201 857-0404
Kevin Schimidt,
EMP: 6
SALES (est): 790K **Privately Held**
SIC: 3585 Ice making machinery

(G-12255)
KEL INSTRUMENTS CO INC
471 Clinton Ave (07481-1403)
P.O. Box 54 (07481-0054)
PHONE..................................201 847-8353
Jeanne Rothman, *President*
David Keller, *Vice Pres*
Barbara Keller, *Admin Sec*
▲ **EMP:** 4
SALES (est): 610K **Privately Held**
SIC: 5169 3824 Air, water or soil test kits; pedometers

(G-12256)
M B R ORTHOTICS INC
579 Goffle Rd (07481-2946)
PHONE..................................201 444-7750
Michael Rebarber, *President*
EMP: 4
SQ FT: 800
SALES (est): 554.4K **Privately Held**
SIC: 3842 Orthopedic appliances

(G-12257)
M K ENTERPRISES INC
Also Called: Van Grouw Welding & Fabg
430 W Main St (07481-1420)
PHONE..................................201 891-4199
Fax: 201 847-0132
Mark Pouzzuli, *President*
Ken Vandenberg, *Admin Sec*
EMP: 4
SQ FT: 6,000

SALES (est): 564K **Privately Held**
SIC: 3441 7699 Fabricated structural metal; welding equipment repair

(G-12258)
MAIN ROBERT A & SONS HOLDG CO (PA)
555 Goffle Rd (07481-2937)
P.O. Box 159 (07481-0159)
PHONE..................................201 447-3700
Robert A Main Jr, *Principal*
Susan Main, *Corp Secy*
William Main, *Vice Pres*
EMP: 27
SQ FT: 29,000
SALES (est): 28.7MM **Privately Held**
SIC: 3496 3535 3443 3441 Miscellaneous fabricated wire products; conveyors & conveying equipment; cylinders, pressure: metal plate; tower sections, radio & television transmission; screw machine products; metal stampings

(G-12259)
MARKBILT INC
308 Canterbury Ln (07481-2304)
P.O. Box 32, Hawthorne (07507-0032)
PHONE..................................201 891-7842
Plutarco Leyva, *General Mgr*
EMP: 55
SALES (corp-wide): 4.4MM **Privately Held**
SIC: 2259 Convertors, knit goods
PA: Markbilt Inc
55 Thomas Rd N
Hawthorne NJ
973 423-0556

(G-12260)
PRO PACK INC
Also Called: Dynaclear Packaging
500 W Main St Ste 12 (07481-1406)
PHONE..................................201 485-7587
Piero Quercia, *CEO*
Barbara Kaywork, *CFO*
▲ **EMP:** 18
SQ FT: 1,000
SALES (est): 8MM **Privately Held**
WEB: www.shrinkfilm.com
SIC: 5084 5199 3565 Packaging machinery & equipment; packaging materials; packing & wrapping machinery

(G-12261)
RADIATION SYSTEMS INC
455 W Main St (07481-1419)
PHONE..................................201 891-7515
Fax: 201 891-4407
Richard Ver Hage, *President*
Glenn Ver Hage, *Vice Pres*
Henry Ver Hage, *Vice Pres*
William Van Dyke Jr, *Vice Pres*
EMP: 7
SQ FT: 9,000
SALES (est): 740K **Privately Held**
WEB: www.radiationsystems.com
SIC: 3567 3444 Infrared ovens, industrial; sheet metal specialties, not stamped

(G-12262)
RICHARD J BELL CO INC
Also Called: Rjb Design Group Co.
465 W Main St (07481-1453)
PHONE..................................201 847-0887
Fax: 201 847-0886
Richard J Bell, *President*
EMP: 10
SQ FT: 10,000
SALES (est): 1.2MM **Privately Held**
SIC: 2542 Counters or counter display cases: except wood

(G-12263)
RONY INC
393 Crescent Ave Ste 12 (07481-2837)
PHONE..................................201 891-2551
Fax: 201 891-1713
Manuel Pires, *CEO*
Ronald Pires, *President*
▼ **EMP:** 5
SQ FT: 5,000
SALES (est): 807.2K **Privately Held**
WEB: www.rony.com
SIC: 3714 5013 Motor vehicle parts & accessories; motor vehicle supplies & new parts

(G-12264)
STRAPS MANUFACTURING NJ INC
Also Called: Titan Trading Co
480 Braen Ave (07481-2949)
PHONE..................................201 368-5201
Fax: 201 368-5207
Joel Rothstein, *President*
EMP: 16
SQ FT: 12,000
SALES (est): 1.3MM **Privately Held**
WEB: www.titan-trading.com
SIC: 2387 3965 Apparel belts; fasteners

(G-12265)
SUMMIT INTL FILTRATION SYSTEMS
500 W Main St Ste 10 (07481-1406)
PHONE..................................201 847-2370
Charles Cole, *President*
David Koontz, *Vice Pres*
Rick Koontz, *Vice Pres*
Brian Cole, *Treasurer*
EMP: 7
SQ FT: 20,000
SALES (est): 570K **Privately Held**
WEB: www.summitfiltration.com
SIC: 3677 Filtration devices, electronic

(G-12266)
TRAP-ZAP ENVIRONMENTAL SYSTEMS
255 Braen Ave (07481-2948)
PHONE..................................201 251-9970
Fax: 201 251-0903
Robert Belle, *President*
EMP: 40
SQ FT: 3,000
SALES (est): 8MM **Privately Held**
WEB: www.trapzap.com
SIC: 3272 2842 Grease traps, concrete; specialty cleaning, polishes & sanitation goods

(G-12267)
TYPELINE
506 Spencer Dr (07481-2925)
PHONE..................................201 251-2201
Fax: 201 836-8337
EMP: 10
SQ FT: 2,000
SALES: 500K **Privately Held**
SIC: 2791 7336 2759 2752 Typesetting Services Coml Art/Graphic Design Commercial Printing Lithographic Coml Print

(G-12268)
U S LASER CORP
825 Windham Ct N Ste 2 (07481-3470)
PHONE..................................201 848-9200
Fax: 201 848-9006
Robert Regna, *President*
Eric Fink, *Manager*
EMP: 20
SQ FT: 18,000
SALES (est): 3.6MM **Privately Held**
WEB: www.uslasercorp.com
SIC: 3699 Laser systems & equipment

(G-12269)
VICTORY IRON WORKS INC
780 Mountain Ave (07481-1098)
PHONE..................................201 485-7181
Fax: 201 848-7875
Theresa Edson, *President*
Mae Marchese, *Vice Pres*
EMP: 6 **EST:** 1926
SQ FT: 5,000
SALES (est): 823.4K **Privately Held**
SIC: 3441 Fabricated structural metal

Zarephath
Somerset County

(G-12270)
PILLAR OF FIRE (PA)
10 Chapel Dr (08890)
PHONE..................................732 356-0102
Robert Dallenbach, *President*
Joseph Gross, *Exec VP*
Lois R Stewart, *Treasurer*
S Rey Crawford, *Admin Sec*

EMP: 80
SALES (est): 26.8MM **Privately Held**
WEB: www.almaheights.org
SIC: 4832 8211 2721 8221 Religious; preparatory school; magazines: publishing only, not printed on site; theological seminary; group day care center

Standard Industrial Classification Alphabetical Index

SIC NO	PRODUCT

A

3291 Abrasive Prdts
2891 Adhesives & Sealants
3563 Air & Gas Compressors
3585 Air Conditioning & Heating Eqpt
3721 Aircraft
3724 Aircraft Engines & Engine Parts
3728 Aircraft Parts & Eqpt, NEC
2812 Alkalies & Chlorine
3363 Aluminum Die Castings
3354 Aluminum Extruded Prdts
3365 Aluminum Foundries
3355 Aluminum Rolling & Drawing, NEC
3353 Aluminum Sheet, Plate & Foil
3483 Ammunition, Large
3826 Analytical Instruments
2077 Animal, Marine Fats & Oils
2389 Apparel & Accessories, NEC
2387 Apparel Belts
3446 Architectural & Ornamental Metal Work
7694 Armature Rewinding Shops
3292 Asbestos products
2952 Asphalt Felts & Coatings
3822 Automatic Temperature Controls
3581 Automatic Vending Machines
3465 Automotive Stampings
2396 Automotive Trimmings, Apparel Findings, Related Prdts

B

2673 Bags: Plastics, Laminated & Coated
2674 Bags: Uncoated Paper & Multiwall
3562 Ball & Roller Bearings
2836 Biological Prdts, Exc Diagnostic Substances
2782 Blankbooks & Looseleaf Binders
3312 Blast Furnaces, Coke Ovens, Steel & Rolling Mills
3564 Blowers & Fans
3732 Boat Building & Repairing
3452 Bolts, Nuts, Screws, Rivets & Washers
2732 Book Printing, Not Publishing
2789 Bookbinding
2731 Books: Publishing & Printing
3131 Boot & Shoe Cut Stock & Findings
2342 Brassieres, Girdles & Garments
2051 Bread, Bakery Prdts Exc Cookies & Crackers
3251 Brick & Structural Clay Tile
3991 Brooms & Brushes
3995 Burial Caskets
2021 Butter

C

3578 Calculating & Accounting Eqpt
2064 Candy & Confectionery Prdts
2033 Canned Fruits, Vegetables & Preserves
2032 Canned Specialties
2394 Canvas Prdts
3624 Carbon & Graphite Prdts
2895 Carbon Black
3955 Carbon Paper & Inked Ribbons
3592 Carburetors, Pistons, Rings & Valves
2273 Carpets & Rugs
2823 Cellulosic Man-Made Fibers
3241 Cement, Hydraulic
3253 Ceramic Tile
2043 Cereal Breakfast Foods
2022 Cheese
1479 Chemical & Fertilizer Mining
2899 Chemical Preparations, NEC
2067 Chewing Gum
2361 Children's & Infants' Dresses & Blouses
3261 China Plumbing Fixtures & Fittings
3262 China, Table & Kitchen Articles
2066 Chocolate & Cocoa Prdts
2111 Cigarettes
2121 Cigars
2257 Circular Knit Fabric Mills
3255 Clay Refractories
1459 Clay, Ceramic & Refractory Minerals, NEC
1241 Coal Mining Svcs
3479 Coating & Engraving, NEC
2095 Coffee
3316 Cold Rolled Steel Sheet, Strip & Bars
3582 Commercial Laundry, Dry Clean & Pressing Mchs
2759 Commercial Printing

2754 Commercial Printing: Gravure
2752 Commercial Printing: Lithographic
3646 Commercial, Indl & Institutional Lighting Fixtures
3669 Communications Eqpt, NEC
3577 Computer Peripheral Eqpt, NEC
3572 Computer Storage Devices
3575 Computer Terminals
3271 Concrete Block & Brick
3272 Concrete Prdts
3531 Construction Machinery & Eqpt
1442 Construction Sand & Gravel
2679 Converted Paper Prdts, NEC
3535 Conveyors & Eqpt
2052 Cookies & Crackers
3366 Copper Foundries
1021 Copper Ores
2298 Cordage & Twine
2653 Corrugated & Solid Fiber Boxes
3961 Costume Jewelry & Novelties
2261 Cotton Fabric Finishers
2211 Cotton, Woven Fabric
3466 Crowns & Closures
1311 Crude Petroleum & Natural Gas
1423 Crushed & Broken Granite
1422 Crushed & Broken Limestone
1429 Crushed & Broken Stone, NEC
3643 Current-Carrying Wiring Devices
2391 Curtains & Draperies
3087 Custom Compounding Of Purchased Plastic Resins
3281 Cut Stone Prdts
3421 Cutlery
2865 Cyclic-Crudes, Intermediates, Dyes & Org Pigments

D

3843 Dental Eqpt & Splys
2835 Diagnostic Substances
2675 Die-Cut Paper & Board
3544 Dies, Tools, Jigs, Fixtures & Indl Molds
1411 Dimension Stone
2047 Dog & Cat Food
3942 Dolls & Stuffed Toys
2591 Drapery Hardware, Window Blinds & Shades
2381 Dress & Work Gloves
2034 Dried Fruits, Vegetables & Soup
1381 Drilling Oil & Gas Wells

E

3263 Earthenware, Whiteware, Table & Kitchen Articles
3634 Electric Household Appliances
3641 Electric Lamps
3694 Electrical Eqpt For Internal Combustion Engines
3629 Electrical Indl Apparatus, NEC
3699 Electrical Machinery, Eqpt & Splys, NEC
3845 Electromedical & Electrotherapeutic Apparatus
3313 Electrometallurgical Prdts
3675 Electronic Capacitors
3677 Electronic Coils & Transformers
3679 Electronic Components, NEC
3571 Electronic Computers
3678 Electronic Connectors
3676 Electronic Resistors
3471 Electroplating, Plating, Polishing, Anodizing & Coloring
3534 Elevators & Moving Stairways
3431 Enameled Iron & Metal Sanitary Ware
2677 Envelopes
2892 Explosives

F

2241 Fabric Mills, Cotton, Wool, Silk & Man-Made
3499 Fabricated Metal Prdts, NEC
3498 Fabricated Pipe & Pipe Fittings
3443 Fabricated Plate Work
3069 Fabricated Rubber Prdts, NEC
3441 Fabricated Structural Steel
2399 Fabricated Textile Prdts, NEC
2295 Fabrics Coated Not Rubberized
2297 Fabrics, Nonwoven
3523 Farm Machinery & Eqpt
3965 Fasteners, Buttons, Needles & Pins
2875 Fertilizers, Mixing Only
2655 Fiber Cans, Tubes & Drums
2091 Fish & Seafoods, Canned & Cured
2092 Fish & Seafoods, Fresh & Frozen
3211 Flat Glass

2087 Flavoring Extracts & Syrups
2045 Flour, Blended & Prepared
2041 Flour, Grain Milling
3824 Fluid Meters & Counters
3593 Fluid Power Cylinders & Actuators
3594 Fluid Power Pumps & Motors
3492 Fluid Power Valves & Hose Fittings
2657 Folding Paperboard Boxes
3556 Food Prdts Machinery
2099 Food Preparations, NEC
3149 Footwear, NEC
2053 Frozen Bakery Prdts
2037 Frozen Fruits, Juices & Vegetables
2038 Frozen Specialties
2371 Fur Goods
2599 Furniture & Fixtures, NEC

G

3944 Games, Toys & Children's Vehicles
3524 Garden, Lawn Tractors & Eqpt
3053 Gaskets, Packing & Sealing Devices
2369 Girls' & Infants' Outerwear, NEC
3221 Glass Containers
3231 Glass Prdts Made Of Purchased Glass
1041 Gold Ores
3321 Gray Iron Foundries
2771 Greeting Card Publishing
3769 Guided Missile/Space Vehicle Parts & Eqpt, NEC
3764 Guided Missile/Space Vehicle Propulsion Units & parts
3761 Guided Missiles & Space Vehicles
2861 Gum & Wood Chemicals
3275 Gypsum Prdts

H

3423 Hand & Edge Tools
3425 Hand Saws & Saw Blades
3171 Handbags & Purses
3429 Hardware, NEC
2426 Hardwood Dimension & Flooring Mills
2435 Hardwood Veneer & Plywood
2353 Hats, Caps & Millinery
3433 Heating Eqpt
3536 Hoists, Cranes & Monorails
2252 Hosiery, Except Women's
2251 Hosiery, Women's Full & Knee Length
2392 House furnishings: Textile
3142 House Slippers
3639 Household Appliances, NEC
3651 Household Audio & Video Eqpt
3631 Household Cooking Eqpt
2519 Household Furniture, NEC
3632 Household Refrigerators & Freezers
3635 Household Vacuum Cleaners

I

2097 Ice
2024 Ice Cream
2819 Indl Inorganic Chemicals, NEC
3823 Indl Instruments For Meas, Display & Control
3569 Indl Machinery & Eqpt, NEC
3567 Indl Process Furnaces & Ovens
3537 Indl Trucks, Tractors, Trailers & Stackers
2813 Industrial Gases
2869 Industrial Organic Chemicals, NEC
3543 Industrial Patterns
1446 Industrial Sand
3491 Industrial Valves
2816 Inorganic Pigments
3825 Instrs For Measuring & Testing Electricity
3519 Internal Combustion Engines, NEC
3462 Iron & Steel Forgings

J

3915 Jewelers Findings & Lapidary Work
3911 Jewelry: Precious Metal

K

1455 Kaolin & Ball Clay
2253 Knit Outerwear Mills
2254 Knit Underwear Mills
2259 Knitting Mills, NEC

L

3821 Laboratory Apparatus & Furniture
2258 Lace & Warp Knit Fabric Mills

SIC

SIC NO	PRODUCT
3952	Lead Pencils, Crayons & Artist's Mtrls
2386	Leather & Sheep Lined Clothing
3151	Leather Gloves & Mittens
3199	Leather Goods, NEC
3111	Leather Tanning & Finishing
3648	Lighting Eqpt, NEC
3274	Lime
3996	Linoleum & Hard Surface Floor Coverings, NEC
2085	Liquors, Distilled, Rectified & Blended
2411	Logging
2992	Lubricating Oils & Greases
3161	Luggage

M

SIC NO	PRODUCT
2098	Macaroni, Spaghetti & Noodles
3545	Machine Tool Access
3541	Machine Tools: Cutting
3542	Machine Tools: Forming
3599	Machinery & Eqpt, Indl & Commercial, NEC
3322	Malleable Iron Foundries
2083	Malt
2082	Malt Beverages
2761	Manifold Business Forms
3999	Manufacturing Industries, NEC
3953	Marking Devices
2515	Mattresses & Bedsprings
3829	Measuring & Controlling Devices, NEC
3586	Measuring & Dispensing Pumps
2011	Meat Packing Plants
3568	Mechanical Power Transmission Eqpt, NEC
2833	Medicinal Chemicals & Botanical Prdts
2329	Men's & Boys' Clothing, NEC
2323	Men's & Boys' Neckwear
2325	Men's & Boys' Separate Trousers & Casual Slacks
2321	Men's & Boys' Shirts
2311	Men's & Boys' Suits, Coats & Overcoats
2322	Men's & Boys' Underwear & Nightwear
2326	Men's & Boys' Work Clothing
3143	Men's Footwear, Exc Athletic
3412	Metal Barrels, Drums, Kegs & Pails
3411	Metal Cans
3442	Metal Doors, Sash, Frames, Molding & Trim
3497	Metal Foil & Leaf
3398	Metal Heat Treating
2514	Metal Household Furniture
1081	Metal Mining Svcs
3469	Metal Stampings, NEC
3549	Metalworking Machinery, NEC
2026	Milk
2023	Milk, Condensed & Evaporated
2431	Millwork
3296	Mineral Wool
3295	Minerals & Earths: Ground Or Treated
3532	Mining Machinery & Eqpt
3496	Misc Fabricated Wire Prdts
2741	Misc Publishing
3449	Misc Structural Metal Work
1499	Miscellaneous Nonmetallic Mining
2451	Mobile Homes
3061	Molded, Extruded & Lathe-Cut Rubber Mechanical Goods
3714	Motor Vehicle Parts & Access
3711	Motor Vehicles & Car Bodies
3751	Motorcycles, Bicycles & Parts
3621	Motors & Generators
3931	Musical Instruments

N

SIC NO	PRODUCT
1321	Natural Gas Liquids
2711	Newspapers: Publishing & Printing
2873	Nitrogenous Fertilizers
3297	Nonclay Refractories
3644	Noncurrent-Carrying Wiring Devices
3364	Nonferrous Die Castings, Exc Aluminum
3463	Nonferrous Forgings
3369	Nonferrous Foundries: Castings, NEC
3357	Nonferrous Wire Drawing
3299	Nonmetallic Mineral Prdts, NEC
1481	Nonmetallic Minerals Svcs, Except Fuels

O

SIC NO	PRODUCT
2522	Office Furniture, Except Wood
3579	Office Machines, NEC
1382	Oil & Gas Field Exploration Svcs
1389	Oil & Gas Field Svcs, NEC
3533	Oil Field Machinery & Eqpt
3851	Ophthalmic Goods
3827	Optical Instruments
3489	Ordnance & Access, NEC
3842	Orthopedic, Prosthetic & Surgical Appliances/Splys

P

SIC NO	PRODUCT
3565	Packaging Machinery
2851	Paints, Varnishes, Lacquers, Enamels
2671	Paper Coating & Laminating for Packaging
2672	Paper Coating & Laminating, Exc for Packaging
3554	Paper Inds Machinery
2621	Paper Mills
2631	Paperboard Mills
2542	Partitions & Fixtures, Except Wood
2951	Paving Mixtures & Blocks
3951	Pens & Mechanical Pencils
2844	Perfumes, Cosmetics & Toilet Preparations
2721	Periodicals: Publishing & Printing
3172	Personal Leather Goods
2879	Pesticides & Agricultural Chemicals, NEC
2911	Petroleum Refining
2834	Pharmaceuticals
3652	Phonograph Records & Magnetic Tape
2874	Phosphatic Fertilizers
3861	Photographic Eqpt & Splys
2035	Pickled Fruits, Vegetables, Sauces & Dressings
3085	Plastic Bottles
3086	Plastic Foam Prdts
3083	Plastic Laminated Plate & Sheet
3084	Plastic Pipe
3088	Plastic Plumbing Fixtures
3089	Plastic Prdts
3082	Plastic Unsupported Profile Shapes
3081	Plastic Unsupported Sheet & Film
2821	Plastics, Mtrls & Nonvulcanizable Elastomers
2796	Platemaking & Related Svcs
2395	Pleating & Stitching For The Trade
3432	Plumbing Fixture Fittings & Trim, Brass
3264	Porcelain Electrical Splys
2096	Potato Chips & Similar Prdts
3269	Pottery Prdts, NEC
2015	Poultry Slaughtering, Dressing & Processing
3546	Power Hand Tools
3612	Power, Distribution & Specialty Transformers
3448	Prefabricated Metal Buildings & Cmpnts
2452	Prefabricated Wood Buildings & Cmpnts
7372	Prepackaged Software
2048	Prepared Feeds For Animals & Fowls
3229	Pressed & Blown Glassware, NEC
3692	Primary Batteries: Dry & Wet
3399	Primary Metal Prdts, NEC
3339	Primary Nonferrous Metals, NEC
3334	Primary Production Of Aluminum
3331	Primary Smelting & Refining Of Copper
3672	Printed Circuit Boards
2893	Printing Ink
3555	Printing Trades Machinery & Eqpt
2999	Products Of Petroleum & Coal, NEC
2531	Public Building & Related Furniture
2611	Pulp Mills
3561	Pumps & Pumping Eqpt

R

SIC NO	PRODUCT
3663	Radio & T V Communications, Systs & Eqpt, Broadcast/Studio
3671	Radio & T V Receiving Electron Tubes
3743	Railroad Eqpt
3273	Ready-Mixed Concrete
2493	Reconstituted Wood Prdts
3695	Recording Media
3625	Relays & Indl Controls
3645	Residential Lighting Fixtures
2044	Rice Milling
2384	Robes & Dressing Gowns
3547	Rolling Mill Machinery & Eqpt
3351	Rolling, Drawing & Extruding Of Copper
3356	Rolling, Drawing-Extruding Of Nonferrous Metals
3021	Rubber & Plastic Footwear
3052	Rubber & Plastic Hose & Belting

S

SIC NO	PRODUCT
2068	Salted & Roasted Nuts & Seeds
2656	Sanitary Food Containers
2676	Sanitary Paper Prdts
2013	Sausages & Meat Prdts
2421	Saw & Planing Mills
3596	Scales & Balances, Exc Laboratory
2397	Schiffli Machine Embroideries
3451	Screw Machine Prdts
3812	Search, Detection, Navigation & Guidance Systs & Instrs
3341	Secondary Smelting & Refining Of Nonferrous Metals
3674	Semiconductors
3589	Service Ind Machines, NEC
2652	Set-Up Paperboard Boxes
3444	Sheet Metal Work

SIC NO	PRODUCT
3731	Shipbuilding & Repairing
2079	Shortening, Oils & Margarine
3993	Signs & Advertising Displays
2262	Silk & Man-Made Fabric Finishers
2221	Silk & Man-Made Fiber
1044	Silver Ores
3914	Silverware, Plated & Stainless Steel Ware
3484	Small Arms
3482	Small Arms Ammunition
2841	Soap & Detergents
2086	Soft Drinks
2075	Soybean Oil Mills
2842	Spec Cleaning, Polishing & Sanitation Preparations
3559	Special Ind Machinery, NEC
3566	Speed Changers, Drives & Gears
3949	Sporting & Athletic Goods, NEC
2678	Stationery Prdts
3511	Steam, Gas & Hydraulic Turbines & Engines
3325	Steel Foundries, NEC
3324	Steel Investment Foundries
3317	Steel Pipe & Tubes
3493	Steel Springs, Except Wire
3315	Steel Wire Drawing & Nails & Spikes
3691	Storage Batteries
3259	Structural Clay Prdts, NEC
2439	Structural Wood Members, NEC
2061	Sugar, Cane
2062	Sugar, Cane Refining
2843	Surface Active & Finishing Agents, Sulfonated Oils
3841	Surgical & Medical Instrs & Apparatus
3613	Switchgear & Switchboard Apparatus
2824	Synthetic Organic Fibers, Exc Cellulosic
2822	Synthetic Rubber (Vulcanizable Elastomers)

T

SIC NO	PRODUCT
3795	Tanks & Tank Components
3661	Telephone & Telegraph Apparatus
2393	Textile Bags
2269	Textile Finishers, NEC
2299	Textile Goods, NEC
3552	Textile Machinery
2284	Thread Mills
2296	Tire Cord & Fabric
3011	Tires & Inner Tubes
2141	Tobacco Stemming & Redrying
3799	Transportation Eqpt, NEC
3792	Travel Trailers & Campers
3713	Truck & Bus Bodies
3715	Truck Trailers
2791	Typesetting

V

SIC NO	PRODUCT
3494	Valves & Pipe Fittings, NEC
2076	Vegetable Oil Mills
3647	Vehicular Lighting Eqpt

W

SIC NO	PRODUCT
3873	Watch & Clock Devices & Parts
2385	Waterproof Outerwear
3548	Welding Apparatus
7692	Welding Repair
2046	Wet Corn Milling
2084	Wine & Brandy
3495	Wire Springs
2331	Women's & Misses' Blouses
2335	Women's & Misses' Dresses
2339	Women's & Misses' Outerwear, NEC
2337	Women's & Misses' Suits, Coats & Skirts
3144	Women's Footwear, Exc Athletic
2341	Women's, Misses' & Children's Underwear & Nightwear
2441	Wood Boxes
2449	Wood Containers, NEC
2511	Wood Household Furniture
2512	Wood Household Furniture, Upholstered
2434	Wood Kitchen Cabinets
2521	Wood Office Furniture
2448	Wood Pallets & Skids
2499	Wood Prdts, NEC
2491	Wood Preserving
2517	Wood T V, Radio, Phono & Sewing Cabinets
2541	Wood, Office & Store Fixtures
3553	Woodworking Machinery
2231	Wool, Woven Fabric

X

SIC NO	PRODUCT
3844	X-ray Apparatus & Tubes

Y

SIC NO	PRODUCT
2281	Yarn Spinning Mills
2282	Yarn Texturizing, Throwing, Twisting & Winding Mills

SIC INDEX

SIC NO	PRODUCT

10 METAL MINING
1021 Copper Ores
1041 Gold Ores
1044 Silver Ores
1081 Metal Mining Svcs

12 COAL MINING
1241 Coal Mining Svcs

13 OIL AND GAS EXTRACTION
1311 Crude Petroleum & Natural Gas
1321 Natural Gas Liquids
1381 Drilling Oil & Gas Wells
1382 Oil & Gas Field Exploration Svcs
1389 Oil & Gas Field Svcs, NEC

14 MINING AND QUARRYING OF NONMETALLIC MINERALS, EXCEPT FUELS
1411 Dimension Stone
1422 Crushed & Broken Limestone
1423 Crushed & Broken Granite
1429 Crushed & Broken Stone, NEC
1442 Construction Sand & Gravel
1446 Industrial Sand
1455 Kaolin & Ball Clay
1459 Clay, Ceramic & Refractory Minerals, NEC
1479 Chemical & Fertilizer Mining
1481 Nonmetallic Minerals Svcs, Except Fuels
1499 Miscellaneous Nonmetallic Mining

20 FOOD AND KINDRED PRODUCTS
2011 Meat Packing Plants
2013 Sausages & Meat Prdts
2015 Poultry Slaughtering, Dressing & Processing
2021 Butter
2022 Cheese
2023 Milk, Condensed & Evaporated
2024 Ice Cream
2026 Milk
2032 Canned Specialties
2033 Canned Fruits, Vegetables & Preserves
2034 Dried Fruits, Vegetables & Soup
2035 Pickled Fruits, Vegetables, Sauces & Dressings
2037 Frozen Fruits, Juices & Vegetables
2038 Frozen Specialties
2041 Flour, Grain Milling
2043 Cereal Breakfast Foods
2044 Rice Milling
2045 Flour, Blended & Prepared
2046 Wet Corn Milling
2047 Dog & Cat Food
2048 Prepared Feeds For Animals & Fowls
2051 Bread, Bakery Prdts Exc Cookies & Crackers
2052 Cookies & Crackers
2053 Frozen Bakery Prdts
2061 Sugar, Cane
2062 Sugar, Cane Refining
2064 Candy & Confectionery Prdts
2066 Chocolate & Cocoa Prdts
2067 Chewing Gum
2068 Salted & Roasted Nuts & Seeds
2075 Soybean Oil Mills
2076 Vegetable Oil Mills
2077 Animal, Marine Fats & Oils
2079 Shortening, Oils & Margarine
2082 Malt Beverages
2083 Malt
2084 Wine & Brandy
2085 Liquors, Distilled, Rectified & Blended
2086 Soft Drinks
2087 Flavoring Extracts & Syrups
2091 Fish & Seafoods, Canned & Cured
2092 Fish & Seafoods, Fresh & Frozen
2095 Coffee
2096 Potato Chips & Similar Prdts
2097 Ice
2098 Macaroni, Spaghetti & Noodles
2099 Food Preparations, NEC

21 TOBACCO PRODUCTS
2111 Cigarettes
2121 Cigars
2141 Tobacco Stemming & Redrying

22 TEXTILE MILL PRODUCTS
2211 Cotton, Woven Fabric
2221 Silk & Man-Made Fiber
2231 Wool, Woven Fabric
2241 Fabric Mills, Cotton, Wool, Silk & Man-Made
2251 Hosiery, Women's Full & Knee Length
2252 Hosiery, Except Women's
2253 Knit Outerwear Mills
2254 Knit Underwear Mills
2257 Circular Knit Fabric Mills
2258 Lace & Warp Knit Fabric Mills
2259 Knitting Mills, NEC
2261 Cotton Fabric Finishers
2262 Silk & Man-Made Fabric Finishers
2269 Textile Finishers, NEC
2273 Carpets & Rugs
2281 Yarn Spinning Mills
2282 Yarn Texturizing, Throwing, Twisting & Winding Mills
2284 Thread Mills
2295 Fabrics Coated Not Rubberized
2296 Tire Cord & Fabric
2297 Fabrics, Nonwoven
2298 Cordage & Twine
2299 Textile Goods, NEC

23 APPAREL AND OTHER FINISHED PRODUCTS MADE FROM FABRICS AND SIMILAR MATERIAL
2311 Men's & Boys' Suits, Coats & Overcoats
2321 Men's & Boys' Shirts
2322 Men's & Boys' Underwear & Nightwear
2323 Men's & Boys' Neckwear
2325 Men's & Boys' Separate Trousers & Casual Slacks
2326 Men's & Boys' Work Clothing
2329 Men's & Boys' Clothing, NEC
2331 Women's & Misses' Blouses
2335 Women's & Misses' Dresses
2337 Women's & Misses' Suits, Coats & Skirts
2339 Women's & Misses' Outerwear, NEC
2341 Women's, Misses' & Children's Underwear & Nightwear
2342 Brassieres, Girdles & Garments
2353 Hats, Caps & Millinery
2361 Children's & Infants' Dresses & Blouses
2369 Girls' & Infants' Outerwear, NEC
2371 Fur Goods
2381 Dress & Work Gloves
2384 Robes & Dressing Gowns
2385 Waterproof Outerwear
2386 Leather & Sheep Lined Clothing
2387 Apparel Belts
2389 Apparel & Accessories, NEC
2391 Curtains & Draperies
2392 House furnishings: Textile
2393 Textile Bags
2394 Canvas Prdts
2395 Pleating & Stitching For The Trade
2396 Automotive Trimmings, Apparel Findings, Related Prdts
2397 Schiffli Machine Embroideries
2399 Fabricated Textile Prdts, NEC

24 LUMBER AND WOOD PRODUCTS, EXCEPT FURNITURE
2411 Logging
2421 Saw & Planing Mills
2426 Hardwood Dimension & Flooring Mills
2431 Millwork
2434 Wood Kitchen Cabinets
2435 Hardwood Veneer & Plywood
2439 Structural Wood Members, NEC
2441 Wood Boxes
2448 Wood Pallets & Skids
2449 Wood Containers, NEC
2451 Mobile Homes
2452 Prefabricated Wood Buildings & Cmpnts
2491 Wood Preserving
2493 Reconstituted Wood Prdts
2499 Wood Prdts, NEC

25 FURNITURE AND FIXTURES
2511 Wood Household Furniture
2512 Wood Household Furniture, Upholstered
2514 Metal Household Furniture
2515 Mattresses & Bedsprings
2517 Wood T V, Radio, Phono & Sewing Cabinets
2519 Household Furniture, NEC
2521 Wood Office Furniture
2522 Office Furniture, Except Wood
2531 Public Building & Related Furniture
2541 Wood, Office & Store Fixtures
2542 Partitions & Fixtures, Except Wood
2591 Drapery Hardware, Window Blinds & Shades
2599 Furniture & Fixtures, NEC

26 PAPER AND ALLIED PRODUCTS
2611 Pulp Mills
2621 Paper Mills
2631 Paperboard Mills
2652 Set-Up Paperboard Boxes
2653 Corrugated & Solid Fiber Boxes
2655 Fiber Cans, Tubes & Drums
2656 Sanitary Food Containers
2657 Folding Paperboard Boxes
2671 Paper Coating & Laminating for Packaging
2672 Paper Coating & Laminating, Exc for Packaging
2673 Bags: Plastics, Laminated & Coated
2674 Bags: Uncoated Paper & Multiwall
2675 Die-Cut Paper & Board
2676 Sanitary Paper Prdts
2677 Envelopes
2678 Stationery Prdts
2679 Converted Paper Prdts, NEC

27 PRINTING, PUBLISHING, AND ALLIED INDUSTRIES
2711 Newspapers: Publishing & Printing
2721 Periodicals: Publishing & Printing
2731 Books: Publishing & Printing
2732 Book Printing, Not Publishing
2741 Misc Publishing
2752 Commercial Printing: Lithographic
2754 Commercial Printing: Gravure
2759 Commercial Printing
2761 Manifold Business Forms
2771 Greeting Card Publishing
2782 Blankbooks & Looseleaf Binders
2789 Bookbinding
2791 Typesetting
2796 Platemaking & Related Svcs

28 CHEMICALS AND ALLIED PRODUCTS
2812 Alkalies & Chlorine
2813 Industrial Gases
2816 Inorganic Pigments
2819 Indl Inorganic Chemicals, NEC
2821 Plastics, Mtrls & Nonvulcanizable Elastomers
2822 Synthetic Rubber (Vulcanizable Elastomers)
2823 Cellulosic Man-Made Fibers
2824 Synthetic Organic Fibers, Exc Cellulosic
2833 Medicinal Chemicals & Botanical Prdts
2834 Pharmaceuticals
2835 Diagnostic Substances
2836 Biological Prdts, Exc Diagnostic Substances
2841 Soap & Detergents
2842 Spec Cleaning, Polishing & Sanitation Preparations
2843 Surface Active & Finishing Agents, Sulfonated Oils
2844 Perfumes, Cosmetics & Toilet Preparations
2851 Paints, Varnishes, Lacquers, Enamels
2861 Gum & Wood Chemicals
2865 Cyclic-Crudes, Intermediates, Dyes & Org Pigments
2869 Industrial Organic Chemicals, NEC
2873 Nitrogenous Fertilizers
2874 Phosphatic Fertilizers
2875 Fertilizers, Mixing Only
2879 Pesticides & Agricultural Chemicals, NEC
2891 Adhesives & Sealants
2892 Explosives
2893 Printing Ink
2895 Carbon Black
2899 Chemical Preparations, NEC

29 PETROLEUM REFINING AND RELATED INDUSTRIES
2911 Petroleum Refining
2951 Paving Mixtures & Blocks
2952 Asphalt Felts & Coatings
2992 Lubricating Oils & Greases
2999 Products Of Petroleum & Coal, NEC

30 RUBBER AND MISCELLANEOUS PLASTICS PRODUCTS
3011 Tires & Inner Tubes
3021 Rubber & Plastic Footwear
3052 Rubber & Plastic Hose & Belting
3053 Gaskets, Packing & Sealing Devices
3061 Molded, Extruded & Lathe-Cut Rubber Mechanical Goods
3069 Fabricated Rubber Prdts, NEC
3081 Plastic Unsupported Sheet & Film
3082 Plastic Unsupported Profile Shapes

S I C

SIC NO	PRODUCT
3083	Plastic Laminated Plate & Sheet
3084	Plastic Pipe
3085	Plastic Bottles
3086	Plastic Foam Prdts
3087	Custom Compounding Of Purchased Plastic Resins
3088	Plastic Plumbing Fixtures
3089	Plastic Prdts

31 LEATHER AND LEATHER PRODUCTS

SIC NO	PRODUCT
3111	Leather Tanning & Finishing
3131	Boot & Shoe Cut Stock & Findings
3142	House Slippers
3143	Men's Footwear, Exc Athletic
3144	Women's Footwear, Exc Athletic
3149	Footwear, NEC
3151	Leather Gloves & Mittens
3161	Luggage
3171	Handbags & Purses
3172	Personal Leather Goods
3199	Leather Goods, NEC

32 STONE, CLAY, GLASS, AND CONCRETE PRODUCTS

SIC NO	PRODUCT
3211	Flat Glass
3221	Glass Containers
3229	Pressed & Blown Glassware, NEC
3231	Glass Prdts Made Of Purchased Glass
3241	Cement, Hydraulic
3251	Brick & Structural Clay Tile
3253	Ceramic Tile
3255	Clay Refractories
3259	Structural Clay Prdts, NEC
3261	China Plumbing Fixtures & Fittings
3262	China, Table & Kitchen Articles
3263	Earthenware, Whiteware, Table & Kitchen Articles
3264	Porcelain Electrical Splys
3269	Pottery Prdts, NEC
3271	Concrete Block & Brick
3272	Concrete Prdts
3273	Ready-Mixed Concrete
3274	Lime
3275	Gypsum Prdts
3281	Cut Stone Prdts
3291	Abrasive Prdts
3292	Asbestos products
3295	Minerals & Earths: Ground Or Treated
3296	Mineral Wool
3297	Nonclay Refractories
3299	Nonmetallic Mineral Prdts, NEC

33 PRIMARY METAL INDUSTRIES

SIC NO	PRODUCT
3312	Blast Furnaces, Coke Ovens, Steel & Rolling Mills
3313	Electrometallurgical Prdts
3315	Steel Wire Drawing & Nails & Spikes
3316	Cold Rolled Steel Sheet, Strip & Bars
3317	Steel Pipe & Tubes
3321	Gray Iron Foundries
3322	Malleable Iron Foundries
3324	Steel Investment Foundries
3325	Steel Foundries, NEC
3331	Primary Smelting & Refining Of Copper
3334	Primary Production Of Aluminum
3339	Primary Nonferrous Metals, NEC
3341	Secondary Smelting & Refining Of Nonferrous Metals
3351	Rolling, Drawing & Extruding Of Copper
3353	Aluminum Sheet, Plate & Foil
3354	Aluminum Extruded Prdts
3355	Aluminum Rolling & Drawing, NEC
3356	Rolling, Drawing-Extruding Of Nonferrous Metals
3357	Nonferrous Wire Drawing
3363	Aluminum Die Castings
3364	Nonferrous Die Castings, Exc Aluminum
3365	Aluminum Foundries
3366	Copper Foundries
3369	Nonferrous Foundries: Castings, NEC
3398	Metal Heat Treating
3399	Primary Metal Prdts, NEC

34 FABRICATED METAL PRODUCTS, EXCEPT MACHINERY AND TRANSPORTATION EQUIPMENT

SIC NO	PRODUCT
3411	Metal Cans
3412	Metal Barrels, Drums, Kegs & Pails
3421	Cutlery
3423	Hand & Edge Tools
3425	Hand Saws & Saw Blades
3429	Hardware, NEC
3431	Enameled Iron & Metal Sanitary Ware
3432	Plumbing Fixture Fittings & Trim, Brass
3433	Heating Eqpt
3441	Fabricated Structural Steel
3442	Metal Doors, Sash, Frames, Molding & Trim
3443	Fabricated Plate Work
3444	Sheet Metal Work

SIC NO	PRODUCT
3446	Architectural & Ornamental Metal Work
3448	Prefabricated Metal Buildings & Cmpnts
3449	Misc Structural Metal Work
3451	Screw Machine Prdts
3452	Bolts, Nuts, Screws, Rivets & Washers
3462	Iron & Steel Forgings
3463	Nonferrous Forgings
3465	Automotive Stampings
3466	Crowns & Closures
3469	Metal Stampings, NEC
3471	Electroplating, Plating, Polishing, Anodizing & Coloring
3479	Coating & Engraving, NEC
3482	Small Arms Ammunition
3483	Ammunition, Large
3484	Small Arms
3489	Ordnance & Access, NEC
3491	Industrial Valves
3492	Fluid Power Valves & Hose Fittings
3493	Steel Springs, Except Wire
3494	Valves & Pipe Fittings, NEC
3495	Wire Springs
3496	Misc Fabricated Wire Prdts
3497	Metal Foil & Leaf
3498	Fabricated Pipe & Pipe Fittings
3499	Fabricated Metal Prdts, NEC

35 INDUSTRIAL AND COMMERCIAL MACHINERY AND COMPUTER EQUIPMENT

SIC NO	PRODUCT
3511	Steam, Gas & Hydraulic Turbines & Engines
3519	Internal Combustion Engines, NEC
3523	Farm Machinery & Eqpt
3524	Garden, Lawn Tractors & Eqpt
3531	Construction Machinery & Eqpt
3532	Mining Machinery & Eqpt
3533	Oil Field Machinery & Eqpt
3534	Elevators & Moving Stairways
3535	Conveyors & Eqpt
3536	Hoists, Cranes & Monorails
3537	Indl Trucks, Tractors, Trailers & Stackers
3541	Machine Tools: Cutting
3542	Machine Tools: Forming
3543	Industrial Patterns
3544	Dies, Tools, Jigs, Fixtures & Indl Molds
3545	Machine Tool Access
3546	Power Hand Tools
3547	Rolling Mill Machinery & Eqpt
3548	Welding Apparatus
3549	Metalworking Machinery, NEC
3552	Textile Machinery
3553	Woodworking Machinery
3554	Paper Inds Machinery
3555	Printing Trades Machinery & Eqpt
3556	Food Prdts Machinery
3559	Special Ind Machinery, NEC
3561	Pumps & Pumping Eqpt
3562	Ball & Roller Bearings
3563	Air & Gas Compressors
3564	Blowers & Fans
3565	Packaging Machinery
3566	Speed Changers, Drives & Gears
3567	Indl Process Furnaces & Ovens
3568	Mechanical Power Transmission Eqpt, NEC
3569	Indl Machinery & Eqpt, NEC
3571	Electronic Computers
3572	Computer Storage Devices
3575	Computer Terminals
3577	Computer Peripheral Eqpt, NEC
3578	Calculating & Accounting Eqpt
3579	Office Machines, NEC
3581	Automatic Vending Machines
3582	Commercial Laundry, Dry Clean & Pressing Mchs
3585	Air Conditioning & Heating Eqpt
3586	Measuring & Dispensing Pumps
3589	Service Ind Machines, NEC
3592	Carburetors, Pistons, Rings & Valves
3593	Fluid Power Cylinders & Actuators
3594	Fluid Power Pumps & Motors
3596	Scales & Balances, Exc Laboratory
3599	Machinery & Eqpt, Indl & Commercial, NEC

36 ELECTRONIC AND OTHER ELECTRICAL EQUIPMENT AND COMPONENTS, EXCEPT COMPUTER

SIC NO	PRODUCT
3612	Power, Distribution & Specialty Transformers
3613	Switchgear & Switchboard Apparatus
3621	Motors & Generators
3624	Carbon & Graphite Prdts
3625	Relays & Indl Controls
3629	Electrical Indl Apparatus, NEC
3631	Household Cooking Eqpt
3632	Household Refrigerators & Freezers
3634	Electric Household Appliances
3635	Household Vacuum Cleaners

SIC NO	PRODUCT
3639	Household Appliances, NEC
3641	Electric Lamps
3643	Current-Carrying Wiring Devices
3644	Noncurrent-Carrying Wiring Devices
3645	Residential Lighting Fixtures
3646	Commercial, Indl & Institutional Lighting Fixtures
3647	Vehicular Lighting Eqpt
3648	Lighting Eqpt, NEC
3651	Household Audio & Video Eqpt
3652	Phonograph Records & Magnetic Tape
3661	Telephone & Telegraph Apparatus
3663	Radio & T V Communications, Systs & Eqpt, Broadcast/Studio
3669	Communications Eqpt, NEC
3671	Radio & T V Receiving Electron Tubes
3672	Printed Circuit Boards
3674	Semiconductors
3675	Electronic Capacitors
3676	Electronic Resistors
3677	Electronic Coils & Transformers
3678	Electronic Connectors
3679	Electronic Components, NEC
3691	Storage Batteries
3692	Primary Batteries: Dry & Wet
3694	Electrical Eqpt For Internal Combustion Engines
3695	Recording Media
3699	Electrical Machinery, Eqpt & Splys, NEC

37 TRANSPORTATION EQUIPMENT

SIC NO	PRODUCT
3711	Motor Vehicles & Car Bodies
3713	Truck & Bus Bodies
3714	Motor Vehicle Parts & Access
3715	Truck Trailers
3721	Aircraft
3724	Aircraft Engines & Engine Parts
3728	Aircraft Parts & Eqpt, NEC
3731	Shipbuilding & Repairing
3732	Boat Building & Repairing
3743	Railroad Eqpt
3751	Motorcycles, Bicycles & Parts
3761	Guided Missiles & Space Vehicles
3764	Guided Missile/Space Vehicle Propulsion Units & parts
3769	Guided Missile/Space Vehicle Parts & Eqpt, NEC
3792	Travel Trailers & Campers
3795	Tanks & Tank Components
3799	Transportation Eqpt, NEC

38 MEASURING, ANALYZING AND CONTROLLING INSTRUMENTS; PHOTOGRAPHIC, MEDICAL AN

SIC NO	PRODUCT
3812	Search, Detection, Navigation & Guidance Systs & Instrs
3821	Laboratory Apparatus & Furniture
3822	Automatic Temperature Controls
3823	Indl Instruments For Meas, Display & Control
3824	Fluid Meters & Counters
3825	Instrs For Measuring & Testing Electricity
3826	Analytical Instruments
3827	Optical Instruments
3829	Measuring & Controlling Devices, NEC
3841	Surgical & Medical Instrs & Apparatus
3842	Orthopedic, Prosthetic & Surgical Appliances/Splys
3843	Dental Eqpt & Splys
3844	X-ray Apparatus & Tubes
3845	Electromedical & Electrotherapeutic Apparatus
3851	Ophthalmic Goods
3861	Photographic Eqpt & Splys
3873	Watch & Clock Devices & Parts

39 MISCELLANEOUS MANUFACTURING INDUSTRIES

SIC NO	PRODUCT
3911	Jewelry: Precious Metal
3914	Silverware, Plated & Stainless Steel Ware
3915	Jewelers Findings & Lapidary Work
3931	Musical Instruments
3942	Dolls & Stuffed Toys
3944	Games, Toys & Children's Vehicles
3949	Sporting & Athletic Goods, NEC
3951	Pens & Mechanical Pencils
3952	Lead Pencils, Crayons & Artist's Mtrls
3953	Marking Devices
3955	Carbon Paper & Inked Ribbons
3961	Costume Jewelry & Novelties
3965	Fasteners, Buttons, Needles & Pins
3991	Brooms & Brushes
3993	Signs & Advertising Displays
3995	Burial Caskets
3996	Linoleum & Hard Surface Floor Coverings, NEC
3999	Manufacturing Industries, NEC

73 BUSINESS SERVICES

SIC NO	PRODUCT
7372	Prepackaged Software

76 MISCELLANEOUS REPAIR SERVICES

SIC NO	PRODUCT
7692	Welding Repair
7694	Armature Rewinding Shops

SIC SECTION

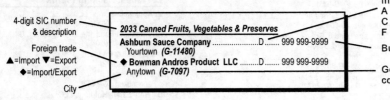

4-digit SIC number & description

Foreign trade
▲=Import ▼=Export
◆=Import/Export
City

2033 Canned Fruits, Vegetables & Preserves
Ashburn Sauce Company ....D...... 999 999-9999
Yourtown *(G-11480)*
◆ **Bowman Andros Product LLC** ....D...... 999 999-9999
Anytown *(G-7097)*

Indicates approximate employment figure
A = Over 500 employees, B = 251-500
C = 101-250, D = 51-100, E = 20-50
F = 10-19, G = 4-9

Business phone

Geographic Section entry number where full company information appears.

See footnotes for symbols and codes identification.

- The SIC codes in this section are from the latest Standard Industrial Classification manual published by the U.S. Government's Office of Management and Budget. For more information regarding SICs, see the Explanatory Notes.
- Companies may be listed under multiple classifications.

10 METAL MINING

1021 Copper Ores
Freeport-Mcmoran Inc ....G...... 908 558-4361
Elizabeth *(G-2735)*

1041 Gold Ores
Freeport-Mcmoran Inc ....G...... 908 558-4361
Elizabeth *(G-2735)*

1044 Silver Ores
Freeport-Mcmoran Inc ....G...... 908 558-4361
Elizabeth *(G-2735)*

1081 Metal Mining Svcs
Coastal Metal Recycling Corp ....G...... 732 738-6000
Keasbey *(G-4927)*
◆ **Connell Mining Products LLC** ....D...... 908 673-3700
Berkeley Heights *(G-406)*
Demaio Inc ....E...... 609 965-4094
Egg Harbor City *(G-2661)*
Industrial Stl & Fastener Corp ....G...... 610 667-2220
Cherry Hill *(G-1380)*

12 COAL MINING

1241 Coal Mining Svcs
◆ **Asbury Carbons Inc** ....G...... 908 537-2155
Asbury *(G-66)*
Starfuels Inc ....G...... 201 685-0400
Englewood *(G-2934)*

13 OIL AND GAS EXTRACTION

1311 Crude Petroleum & Natural Gas
Agway Energy Services LLC ....E...... 973 887-5300
Whippany *(G-12006)*
Associated Asphalt Mktg LLC ....E...... 210 249-9988
West Deptford *(G-11817)*
◆ **JM Huber Corporation** ....D...... 732 603-3630
Edison *(G-2546)*
MRC Global (us) Inc ....F...... 732 225-4005
East Brunswick *(G-2168)*
Njr Clean Energy Ventures Corp ....B...... 732 938-1000
Belmar *(G-360)*
Petro Inc ....G...... 877 745-7687
South Plainfield *(G-10420)*
Phoenix National Petroleum Co ....G...... 201 568-5568
Cresskill *(G-1947)*
Speedway LLC ....B...... 732 750-7800
Port Reading *(G-8990)*
Zenith Energy US LP ....G...... 732 515-7410
Metuchen *(G-6135)*

1321 Natural Gas Liquids
M G S ....G...... 609 698-7000
Barnegat *(G-163)*
Pipeline Eqp Resources Co LLC ....G...... 888 232-7372
Boonton *(G-579)*

1381 Drilling Oil & Gas Wells
Foundation Monitoring ....G...... 856 829-0410
Cinnaminson *(G-1462)*
Jay-Bee Oil & Gas Inc ....D...... 908 686-1493
Union *(G-11196)*

Maverick Oil Co ....E...... 732 747-8637
Red Bank *(G-9335)*
Shore Drilling Inc ....G...... 732 935-1776
Oceanport *(G-7768)*
UNI-Tech Drilling Company Inc ....E...... 856 694-4200
Franklinville *(G-3633)*

1382 Oil & Gas Field Exploration Svcs
All American Oil Recovery Co ....E...... 973 628-9278
Wayne *(G-11603)*
American Shale Oil LLC ....G...... 973 438-3500
Newark *(G-7083)*
Core Laboratories LP ....F...... 609 896-2673
Lawrenceville *(G-5255)*
Foresight Enviroprobe Inc ....G...... 609 259-1244
Clarksburg *(G-1519)*
Hess Corporation ....G...... 609 882-8477
Ewing *(G-3023)*
Masouleh Corp ....E...... 973 470-8900
Clifton *(G-1668)*
Mep Alaska LLC ....G...... 646 535-9005
Livingston *(G-5543)*
Ridgewood Energy S Fund LLC ....G...... 201 307-0470
Montvale *(G-6473)*
Ridgewood Energy T Fund LLC ....G...... 800 942-5550
Montvale *(G-6474)*
Ridgewood Energy U Fund LLC ....G...... 201 447-9000
Montvale *(G-6475)*
Ridgewood Energy V Fund LLC ....G...... 800 942-5550
Montvale *(G-6476)*
Ridgewood Energy Y Fund LLC ....G...... 201 447-9000
Montvale *(G-6477)*

1389 Oil & Gas Field Svcs, NEC
A H Hoffmann LLC ....G...... 732 988-6000
Neptune *(G-6897)*
Above Environmental Services ....G...... 973 702-7021
Vernon *(G-11295)*
AK Contracting LLC ....G...... 908 220-8527
Winfield Park *(G-12131)*
All Seasons Construction Inc ....G...... 908 852-0955
Long Valley *(G-5634)*
Conti-Robert and Co JV ....D...... 732 520-5000
Edison *(G-2489)*
Creamer Glass LLC ....G...... 856 327-2023
Millville *(G-6295)*
Dematte Oil Service Inc ....G...... 856 692-9125
Millville *(G-6298)*
Dpk Consulting LLC ....F...... 732 764-0100
Piscataway *(G-8759)*
Environmental Technical Drlg ....G...... 732 938-3222
Farmingdale *(G-3385)*
Garden State Fuel ....G...... 856 442-0061
Monroeville *(G-6399)*
Gateway Property Solutions Ltd ....E...... 732 901-9700
Lakewood *(G-5128)*
General Civil Company Inc ....F...... 866 435-1200
Runnemede *(G-9719)*
Hudson Valley Enviromental Inc ....E...... 732 967-0060
Toms River *(G-10887)*
▲ **Kabel N Elettrotek Amer Inc** ....G...... 973 265-0850
Parsippany *(G-8035)*
Langan Engineering Environmen ....G...... 973 560-4900
Parsippany *(G-8038)*
Mep Alaska LLC ....G...... 646 535-9005
Livingston *(G-5543)*
Mine Hill Spartan ....G...... 973 442-2280
Mine Hill *(G-6328)*
Mister Good Lube Inc ....G...... 732 842-3266
Shrewsbury *(G-10006)*

Nickos Construction Inc ....F...... 267 240-3997
Sicklerville *(G-10022)*
Oil Technologies Services Inc ....G...... 856 845-4142
Paulsboro *(G-8422)*
Oil Technologies Services Inc ....G...... 856 845-4142
Paulsboro *(G-8423)*
Oil Technologies Services Inc ....G...... 856 845-4142
Linden *(G-5422)*
Oiltest Inc ....G...... 908 245-9330
Roselle *(G-9678)*
Perkins Plumbing & Heating ....G...... 201 327-2736
Upper Saddle River *(G-11283)*
Petroleum Trends International ....G...... 732 494-0405
Metuchen *(G-6117)*
Refferals Only Inc ....G...... 609 921-1033
Princeton *(G-9110)*
Region Oil ....C...... 973 366-3100
Dover *(G-2107)*
Ridgewood Energy O Fund LLC ....G...... 201 447-9000
Montvale *(G-6472)*
Robert Weidener ....G...... 201 703-5700
Fair Lawn *(G-3111)*
Saybolt LP ....G...... 908 523-2000
Linden *(G-5438)*
Saybolt North America Inc ....B...... 973 884-3200
Parsippany *(G-8083)*
Schlumberger Technology Corp ....C...... 609 275-3815
Princeton Junction *(G-9163)*
Shelby Mechanical Inc ....E...... 856 665-4540
Cinnaminson *(G-1487)*
That 10 Minute Oil Change Pl ....G...... 201 587-0220
Rochelle Park *(G-9538)*
Vet Construction Inc ....F...... 732 987-4922
Jackson *(G-4682)*
Zc Utility Services LLC ....G...... 973 226-1840
Roseland *(G-9658)*
Zion Industries Inc ....E...... 973 998-0162
Morris Plains *(G-6682)*

14 MINING AND QUARRYING OF NONMETALLIC MINERALS, EXCEPT FUELS

1411 Dimension Stone
▲ **Ankur International Inc** ....F...... 609 409-6009
Cranbury *(G-1812)*
Bedrock Granite Inc ....E...... 732 741-0010
Shrewsbury *(G-9991)*
Dun-Rite Sand & Gravel Co ....E...... 856 692-2520
Vineland *(G-11353)*
Eastern Concrete Materials Inc ....E...... 973 827-7625
Hamburg *(G-4091)*
Eastern Concrete Materials Inc ....G...... 908 537-2135
Glen Gardner *(G-3814)*
Fanwood Crushed Stone Company ....D...... 908 322-7840
Watchung *(G-11591)*
Morelli Contracting LLC ....G...... 732 356-8800
Middlesex *(G-6181)*
S J Quarry Materials Inc ....D...... 856 691-3133
Elmer *(G-2797)*
▲ **Stone Surfaces Inc** ....G...... 201 935-8803
East Rutherford *(G-2328)*

1422 Crushed & Broken Limestone
Legacy Vulcan LLC ....E...... 973 253-8828
Clifton *(G-1659)*
Limecrest Quarry Developer LLC ....F...... 973 383-7100
Lafayette *(G-5050)*

S I C

1423 Crushed & Broken Granite

Kop Marble Granite Inc...............G...... 973 283-8000
Wayne *(G-11659)*

Stone Industries Inc.....................D...... 973 595-6250
Haledon *(G-4085)*

1429 Crushed & Broken Stone, NEC

A E Stone Inc.................................E...... 609 641-2781
Egg Harbor Township *(G-2675)*

Cedar Hill Landscaping...............E...... 732 469-1400
Somerset *(G-10081)*

Eastern Concrete Materials Inc ......C...... 201 797-7979
Saddle Brook *(G-9763)*

Emil Dipalma Inc..........................G...... 973 477-2766
Hackettstown *(G-4004)*

Joseph and William Stavola........E...... 609 924-0300
Kingston *(G-5028)*

Millington Quarry Inc ....D...... 908 542-0055
Basking Ridge *(G-199)*

R B Badat Landscaping Inc ....E...... 609 877-7138
Mount Holly *(G-6776)*

Riverdale Quarry LLC ....F...... 973 835-0028
Riverdale *(G-9485)*

▲ Stone Surfaces Inc...................D...... 201 935-8803
East Rutherford *(G-2328)*

▲ Tilcon New York Inc ....B...... 800 789-7625
Parsippany *(G-8101)*

Tilcon New York Inc ....E...... 800 789-7625
Pompton Lakes *(G-8950)*

Tilcon New York Inc ....B...... 800 789-7625
Kearny *(G-4917)*

Tilcon New York Inc ....G...... 800 789-7625
Parsippany *(G-8102)*

Tilcon New York Inc ....F...... 800 789-7625
Oxford *(G-7833)*

Tilcon New York Inc ....F...... 973 347-2405
Stanhope *(G-10590)*

Trap Rock Industries Inc ....F...... 609 924-0300
Pennington *(G-8461)*

Trap Rock Industries Inc ....E...... 609 924-0300
Titusville *(G-10857)*

Trap Rock Industries Inc ....B...... 609 924-0300
Kingston *(G-5030)*

Trap Rock Industries LLC ....E...... 609 924-0300
Kingston *(G-5031)*

1442 Construction Sand & Gravel

Action Supply Inc.........................F...... 609 390-0663
Ocean View *(G-7762)*

Alliance Sand Co Inc....................G...... 908 534-4116
Somerville *(G-10201)*

Baer Aggregates Inc ....F...... 908 454-4412
Phillipsburg *(G-8641)*

Control Industries Inc ....F...... 201 437-3826
Bayonne *(G-221)*

County Concrete Corporation ......F...... 973 538-3113
Morristown *(G-6702)*

Dun-Rite Sand & Gravel Co ....E...... 856 692-2520
Vineland *(G-11353)*

Earthwork Associates Inc ....F...... 609 624-9395
Ocean View *(G-7763)*

Eastern Concrete Materials Inc .....C...... 201 797-7979
Saddle Brook *(G-9763)*

Eastern Concrete Materials Inc .....E...... 973 827-7625
Hamburg *(G-4091)*

F W Bennett & Son Inc ....G...... 973 383-4050
Lafayette *(G-5046)*

Hanson Aggregates Wrp Inc ....E...... 972 653-5500
Wall Township *(G-11487)*

Harmony Sand & Gravel Inc.........E...... 908 475-4690
Phillipsburg *(G-8652)*

Intelligentproject LLC ....G...... 732 928-3421
Jackson *(G-4669)*

J Gennaro Trucking ....F...... 973 773-0805
Garfield *(G-3740)*

Mays Landing Sand & Gravel Co ......G...... 856 447-4294
Newport *(G-7377)*

New Jersey Pulverizing Co Inc .....F...... 732 269-1400
Bayville *(G-259)*

North Church Gravel Inc ....G...... 201 796-1556
Oak Ridge *(G-7663)*

Orsillo & Company ....G...... 973 248-1833
Wayne *(G-11668)*

Partac Peat Corp ....F...... 908 637-4191
Great Meadows *(G-3850)*

Pinnacle Materials Inc ....F...... 732 254-7676
East Brunswick *(G-2173)*

Pioneer Concrete Corp ....E...... 609 693-6151
Forked River *(G-3539)*

Ricci Bros Sand Company Inc........E...... 856 785-0166
Port Norris *(G-8982)*

Saxton Falls Sand & Gravel Co ......E...... 908 852-0121
Budd Lake *(G-943)*

Trap Rock Industries Inc ....E...... 609 924-0300
Titusville *(G-10857)*

Tuckahoe Sand & Gravel Co Inc ......E...... 609 861-2082
Tuckahoe *(G-11139)*

Whibco Inc ....F...... 856 455-9200
Bridgeton *(G-804)*

Whibco of New Jersey Inc ....E...... 856 455-9200
Port Elizabeth *(G-8972)*

1446 Industrial Sand

▲ Cherishmet Inc..........................F...... 201 842-7612
Rutherford *(G-9728)*

Covia Holdings Corporation ....E...... 856 785-2700
Dividing Creek *(G-2071)*

Covia Holdings Corporation ....E...... 856 451-6400
Bridgeton *(G-782)*

▲ Inversand Company Inc ....F...... 856 881-2345
Clayton *(G-1525)*

James D Morrissey Inc ....F...... 609 859-2860
Vincentown *(G-11317)*

New Jersey Pulverizing Co Inc .....F...... 732 269-1400
Bayville *(G-259)*

U S Silica Company ....E...... 856 785-0720
Mauricetown *(G-6035)*

Whibco Inc ....F...... 856 455-9200
Bridgeton *(G-804)*

Whibco of New Jersey Inc ....E...... 856 455-9200
Port Elizabeth *(G-8972)*

1455 Kaolin & Ball Clay

◆ JM Huber Corporation ....D...... 732 603-3630
Edison *(G-2546)*

1459 Clay, Ceramic & Refractory Minerals, NEC

▼ Eaglevision Usa LLC ....G...... 908 322-1892
Fanwood *(G-3372)*

Partac Peat Corp ....F...... 908 637-4191
Great Meadows *(G-3850)*

1479 Chemical & Fertilizer Mining

Axiom Ingredients LLC ....F...... 732 669-2458
Iselin *(G-4615)*

Morton Salt Inc ....F...... 732 826-8414
Perth Amboy *(G-8625)*

1481 Nonmetallic Minerals Svcs, Except Fuels

Jersey Boring & Drlg Co Inc ....E...... 973 242-3800
Fairfield *(G-3235)*

Jlb Hauling Ltd Liability Co ....G...... 856 514-2771
Pennsville *(G-8592)*

Tag Minerals Inc ....G...... 732 252-5146
Freehold *(G-3689)*

1499 Miscellaneous Nonmetallic Mining

◆ Asbury Carbons Inc ....G...... 908 537-2155
Asbury *(G-66)*

▲ Diamond Wholesale Co ....E...... 201 727-9595
Moonachie *(G-6514)*

Eastern Concrete Materials Inc ......G...... 973 702-7866
Sussex *(G-10670)*

▼ Hungerford & Terry Inc ....E...... 856 881-3200
Clayton *(G-1524)*

Innovative Cutng Concepts LLC ......G...... 609 484-9960
Egg Harbor Township *(G-2685)*

Mteixeira Soapstone VA LLC ....G...... 201 757-8608
Fort Lee *(G-3570)*

Partac Peat Corp ....F...... 908 637-4191
Great Meadows *(G-3850)*

Partac Peat Corporation ....F...... 908 637-4631
Great Meadows *(G-3851)*

Star Creations Inc ....G...... 212 221-3570
Piscataway *(G-8817)*

Sussex Humus & Supply Inc ....G...... 973 779-8812
Clifton *(G-1732)*

Titan America LLC ....G...... 973 690-5896
Newark *(G-7344)*

Ziegler Chem & Mineral Corp........E...... 732 752-4111
Piscataway *(G-8839)*

▼ Ziegler Chem & Mineral Corp......F...... 732 752-4111
Piscataway *(G-8838)*

20 FOOD AND KINDRED PRODUCTS

2011 Meat Packing Plants

▲ Applegate Farms LLC ....C...... 908 725-2768
Bridgewater *(G-812)*

Arm National Food Inc..................G...... 609 695-4911
Trenton *(G-11020)*

B & B Poultry Co Inc ....C...... 856 692-8893
Norma *(G-7412)*

Beef International Inc ....D...... 856 663-6763
Pennsauken *(G-8485)*

Bie Real Estate Holdings LLC ....G...... 856 691-9765
Vineland *(G-11331)*

Bringhurst Bros Inc ....E...... 856 767-0110
Berlin *(G-429)*

Buckhead Meat Company ....C...... 732 661-4900
Edison *(G-2476)*

▲ Burger Maker Inc ....E...... 201 939-4747
Carlstadt *(G-1134)*

Cameco Inc ....D...... 973 239-2845
Verona *(G-11304)*

Carl Streit & Son Co.....................E...... 732 775-0803
Neptune *(G-6903)*

Carnegie Deli Inc ....D...... 201 507-5557
Carlstadt *(G-1138)*

Comarco Products Inc ....E...... 856 342-7557
Camden *(G-1054)*

▲ DArtagnan Inc ....D...... 973 344-0565
Union *(G-11170)*

Dealaman Enterprises Inc ....E...... 908 647-5533
Warren *(G-11544)*

Dorzar Corporation ....E...... 973 589-6363
Newark *(G-7141)*

Ena Meat Packing Inc ....E...... 973 742-4790
Paterson *(G-8264)*

Katzs Delicatessen Mfg ....E...... 212 254-2246
Carlstadt *(G-1177)*

Kleemeyer & Merkel Inc...............F...... 973 377-0875
Green Village *(G-3865)*

Mamamancinis Holdings Inc ....G...... 201 531-1212
East Rutherford *(G-2307)*

▲ Nourhan Trading Group Inc ......G...... 732 381-8110
Avenel *(G-144)*

▲ Nu-Meat Technology Inc ....E...... 908 754-3400
South Plainfield *(G-10415)*

▲ Premio Foods Inc ....C...... 800 864-7622
Hawthorne *(G-4255)*

Pulaski Meat Products Co ....E...... 908 925-5380
Linden *(G-5432)*

▼ Rastelli Brothers Inc ....D...... 856 803-1100
Swedesboro *(G-10724)*

▲ Rastelli Foods Group Inc ....F...... 856 803-1100
Swedesboro *(G-10725)*

Salem Packing Co ....E...... 856 878-0002
Salem *(G-9809)*

Seabrite Corp ....E...... 973 491-0399
Newark *(G-7305)*

Tubari Inc ....E...... 973 779-8693
Passaic *(G-8185)*

Veroni Usa Inc ....E...... 609 970-0320
Logan Township *(G-5616)*

York Street Caterers Inc ....C...... 201 868-9088
Englewood *(G-2945)*

2013 Sausages & Meat Prdts

A Gimenez Trading LLC ....E...... 973 697-2240
Oak Ridge *(G-7659)*

◆ Al and John Inc ....B...... 973 742-4990
Caldwell *(G-1024)*

Allied Specialty Foods Inc ....D...... 856 507-1100
Vineland *(G-11321)*

Appetito Provisions Company.......E...... 201 864-3410
Harrington Park *(G-4170)*

▲ Applegate Farms LLC ....C...... 908 725-2768
Bridgewater *(G-812)*

Arm National Food Inc..................G...... 609 695-4911
Trenton *(G-11020)*

B&G Foods Inc ....B...... 973 401-6500
Parsippany *(G-7956)*

B&G Foods Inc ....B...... 973 401-6500
Parsippany *(G-7957)*

B&G Foods North America Inc ......F...... 973 401-6500
Parsippany *(G-7958)*

Best Provision Co Inc ....D...... 973 242-5000
Newark *(G-7107)*

Bringhurst Bros Inc ....E...... 856 767-0110
Berlin *(G-429)*

Buckhead Meat Company ....C...... 732 661-4900
Edison *(G-2476)*

◆ **Campbell Soup Supply Co LLC**..........G....... 856 342-4800
Camden *(G-1050)*
Casa Di Bertacchi Corporation............C....... 856 696-5600
Vineland *(G-11334)*
Case Pork Roll Co Inc...........................E....... 609 396-8171
Trenton *(G-11035)*
CW Brown Foods Inc...........................E....... 856 423-3700
Mount Royal *(G-6850)*
CW Brown Foods Inc...........................E....... 856 423-3700
Mount Royal *(G-6851)*
Dubon Corp...G....... 212 812-2171
Elizabeth *(G-2726)*
Ena Meat Packing Inc..........................E....... 973 742-4790
Paterson *(G-8264)*
▲ **Fratelli Beretta Usa Inc**...................D....... 201 438-0723
Budd Lake *(G-929)*
Gaisers Erpean Style Provs Inc............F....... 908 686-3421
Union *(G-11187)*
Groezinger Provisions Inc...................F....... 732 775-3220
Neptune *(G-6917)*
Highpont Corporation..........................G....... 201 460-1364
Rutherford *(G-9734)*
Kupelian Foods Inc..............................G....... 201 440-8055
Ridgefield Park *(G-9410)*
Lawless Jerky LLC................................G....... 310 869-5733
Marlton *(G-5981)*
Licini Brothers Inc...............................G....... 201 865-1130
Union City *(G-11254)*
Lopes Sausage Co.................................G....... 973 344-3063
Newark *(G-7225)*
Mamamancinis Holdings Inc................G....... 201 531-1212
East Rutherford *(G-2307)*
▲ **Marathon Enterprises Inc**.................F....... 201 935-3330
Englewood *(G-2912)*
Martins Specialty Sausage Co..............F....... 856 423-4000
Mickleton *(G-6137)*
Mayabeque Products Inc......................G....... 201 869-0531
North Bergen *(G-7466)*
Nicolosi Foods Inc................................G....... 201 624-1702
Union City *(G-11260)*
▲ **Nitta Casings Inc**...............................C....... 908 218-4400
Bridgewater *(G-866)*
▲ **Premio Foods Inc**................................C....... 800 864-7622
Hawthorne *(G-4255)*
Pulaski Meat Products Co....................E....... 908 925-5380
Linden *(G-5432)*
Rajbhog Foods(nj) Inc..........................C....... 551 222-4700
Jersey City *(G-4814)*
Real Kosher LLC....................................G....... 973 690-5394
Newark *(G-7286)*
Red Square Foods Inc...........................F....... 732 846-0190
Somerset *(G-10164)*
Shahnawaz Food LLC............................F....... 908 413-4206
Edison *(G-2615)*
Smithfield Packaged Meats Corp..........E....... 908 354-2674
Elizabeth *(G-2774)*
Thumann Incorporated..........................C....... 201 935-3636
Carlstadt *(G-1230)*
Wagner Provision Co Inc.......................F....... 856 423-1630
Gibbstown *(G-3793)*

2015 Poultry Slaughtering, Dressing & Processing

B & B Poultry Co Inc.............................C....... 856 692-8893
Norma *(G-7412)*
Carl Streit & Son Co..............................G....... 732 775-0803
Neptune *(G-6903)*
David Mitchell Inc..................................E....... 856 429-2610
Voorhees *(G-11428)*
◆ **Deb El Food Products LLC**..................G....... 908 282-0120
Newark *(G-7136)*
◆ **Deb-El Foods Corporation**..................C....... 908 351-0330
Newark *(G-7137)*
El Jay Poultry Corp................................F....... 856 435-0900
Voorhees *(G-11429)*
Ena Meat Packing Inc.............................E....... 973 742-4790
Paterson *(G-8264)*
▲ **Golden Platter Foods Inc**....................E....... 973 344-8770
Newark *(G-7175)*
Hinck Turkey Farm Inc...........................G....... 732 681-0508
Neptune *(G-6918)*
Mamamancinis Holdings Inc.................G....... 201 531-1212
East Rutherford *(G-2307)*
▲ **Nema Food Distribution Inc**...............G....... 973 256-4415
Fairfield *(G-3267)*
▼ **Papettis Hygrade Egg Pdts Inc**...........A....... 908 282-7900
Elizabethport *(G-2786)*
Perdue Farms Inc...................................G....... 609 298-4100
Bordentown *(G-608)*
Senat Poultry LLC..................................E....... 973 742-9316
Paterson *(G-8382)*
Vineland Kosher Poultry Inc..................C....... 856 692-1871
Vineland *(G-11415)*

2021 Butter

Cookman Creamery LLC........................G....... 732 361-5215
Brielle *(G-911)*

2022 Cheese

Abuelito Cheese Inc...............................G....... 973 345-3503
Paterson *(G-8197)*
◆ **Arthur Schuman Inc**............................D....... 973 227-0030
Fairfield *(G-3139)*
▲ **Biazzo Dairy Products Inc**..................E....... 201 941-8579
Ridgefield *(G-9352)*
Capital Foods Inc...................................E....... 908 587-9050
Linden *(G-5355)*
▲ **Cognati Cheese Company Inc**............E....... 201 807-9100
Moonachie *(G-6513)*
▲ **Colonna Brothers Inc**..........................D....... 800 626-8384
North Bergen *(G-7443)*
ECB USA Inc...G....... 973 575-3226
Fairfield *(G-3181)*
▲ **Finlandia Cheese Inc**...........................E....... 973 316-6699
Parsippany *(G-8012)*
Hawk Dairy Inc..G....... 973 466-9030
Newark *(G-7187)*
Home and Garden Kraft LLC..................G....... 908 995-9355
Milford *(G-6246)*
Jvm Sales Corp.......................................D....... 908 862-4866
Linden *(G-5394)*
Lebanon Cheese Company Inc..............G....... 908 236-2611
Lebanon *(G-5295)*
◆ **Lioni Latticini Inc**..................................D....... 908 686-6061
Union *(G-11202)*
▲ **Lioni Mozzarella & Specialty**...............E....... 908 624-9450
Union *(G-11203)*
▲ **Losurdo Foods Inc**..............................E....... 201 343-6680
Hackensack *(G-3940)*
Lotito Foods Inc......................................F....... 973 684-2900
Paterson *(G-8326)*
Mendez Dairy Co Inc..............................D....... 732 442-6337
Perth Amboy *(G-8623)*
Mondelez International Inc....................E....... 973 503-2000
East Hanover *(G-2228)*
▲ **Montena Taranto Foods Inc**................E....... 201 943-8484
Ridgefield *(G-9375)*
Saporito Inc...G....... 201 265-8212
Ridgefield *(G-9384)*
Saputo Cheese USA Inc..........................E....... 201 508-6400
Carlstadt *(G-1213)*
Schratter Foods Incorporated................G....... 973 575-3226
Moonachie *(G-6541)*
South American Imports Corp...............G....... 201 941-2020
Cliffside Park *(G-1545)*
▲ **Tipico Products Co Inc**........................D....... 732 942-8820
Lakewood *(G-5195)*
Tone Kraft Inc..G....... 856 283-8043
Cinnaminson *(G-1494)*
▲ **Toscana Cheese Company Inc**...........E....... 201 617-1500
Secaucus *(G-9935)*
▲ **Tropical Cheese Industries**.................B....... 732 442-4898
Perth Amboy *(G-8634)*

2023 Milk, Condensed & Evaporated

▼ **Allegro Nutrition Inc**.............................E....... 732 364-3777
Neptune *(G-6899)*
▲ **American Casein Company**..................E....... 609 387-2988
Burlington *(G-954)*
▲ **American Custom Drying Co**...............E....... 609 387-3933
Burlington *(G-955)*
Amish Dairy Products LLC......................G....... 973 256-7676
Totowa *(G-10930)*
Arla Foods Ingredients N Amer..............F....... 908 604-8551
Basking Ridge *(G-180)*
Ben & Jerrys of Hoboken........................F....... 201 792-1966
Hoboken *(G-4459)*
Body Boost Labs Ltd Lblty Co...............F....... 609 519-1070
Laurel Springs *(G-5232)*
◆ **Buy Buy Baby Inc**..................................F....... 908 688-0888
Union *(G-11161)*
▲ **Dairy Delight LLC**..................................F....... 201 939-7878
Rutherford *(G-9729)*
▲ **Farbest-Tallman Foods Corp**...............D....... 714 897-7199
Park Ridge *(G-7919)*
Food Sciences Corp..................................C....... 856 778-4192
Mount Laurel *(G-6798)*
▲ **Gerber Products Company**.................C....... 973 593-7500
Florham Park *(G-3504)*
Gold Star Distribution LLC......................F....... 973 882-5300
East Hanover *(G-2223)*
Grow Company Inc..................................E....... 201 941-8777
Ridgefield *(G-9363)*
Horphag Research (usa) Inc...................G....... 201 459-0300
Hoboken *(G-4475)*
▲ **Icelandirect Inc**......................................F....... 800 763-4690
Clifton *(G-1645)*
Jersey Ordnance Inc................................G....... 609 267-2112
Westampton *(G-11913)*
Kerry Inc..D....... 201 373-1111
Teterboro *(G-10804)*
▲ **Lycored Corp**...E....... 973 882-0322
Orange *(G-7821)*
Nestle Usa Inc..C....... 973 390-9555
Keasbey *(G-4929)*
▲ **Nutri Sport Pharmacal Inc**...................F....... 973 827-9287
Franklin *(G-3604)*
▲ **Orcas International Inc**.........................F....... 973 448-2801
Landing *(G-5225)*
Panos Brands LLC....................................E....... 800 229-1706
Linden *(G-5423)*
Robertet Flavors Inc................................F....... 732 271-1804
Piscataway *(G-8806)*
▼ **Syncom Pharmaceuticals Inc**..............E....... 973 787-2405
Fairfield *(G-3318)*
Unique Encapsulation Tech LLC............E....... 973 448-2801
Landing *(G-5228)*
▲ **V E N Inc**...C....... 973 786-7862
Andover *(G-55)*

2024 Ice Cream

Agape Inc..F....... 973 923-7625
Irvington *(G-4570)*
Alpine Creamery.......................................G....... 973 726-0777
Sparta *(G-10487)*
Angelos Italian Ices Icecream................G....... 201 962-7575
Ramsey *(G-9233)*
Applegate Farm Homemade Ice Cr........F....... 973 744-5900
Montclair *(G-6406)*
Arctic Products Co Inc.............................F....... 609 393-4264
Ewing *(G-3004)*
Bergenline Gelato LLC............................G....... 201 861-1100
North Bergen *(G-7435)*
Bertolotti LLC...F....... 201 941-3116
Fairview *(G-3358)*
Best of Farms LLC....................................G....... 201 512-8400
Fair Lawn *(G-3083)*
◆ **Bindi North America Inc**......................E....... 973 812-8118
Kearny *(G-4865)*
Cielito Lindo...G....... 580 286-1127
New Brunswick *(G-6952)*
Confectionately Yours LLC.....................E....... 732 821-6863
Franklin Park *(G-3626)*
Conopco Inc..C....... 920 499-2509
Englewood Cliffs *(G-2955)*
Country Club Ice Cream..........................G....... 973 729-5570
Sparta *(G-10494)*
Cumberland Dairy Inc..............................E....... 856 451-1300
Bridgeton *(G-783)*
Dairy Queen..F....... 732 892-5700
Point Pleasant Boro *(G-8937)*
◆ **Deep Foods Inc**.....................................C....... 908 810-7500
Union *(G-11171)*
Dunkin Donuts Baskin Robbins..............G....... 201 692-1900
Teaneck *(G-10750)*
Elegant Desserts Inc................................F....... 201 933-7309
Lyndhurst *(G-5679)*
Evereast Trading Inc................................G....... 201 944-6484
Fort Lee *(G-3553)*
Gelotti Confections LLC...........................G....... 973 403-9968
Caldwell *(G-1029)*
Guernsey Crest Ice Cream Co.................G....... 973 742-4620
Paterson *(G-8285)*
Halo Pub Ice Cream.................................F....... 609 921-1710
Princeton *(G-9052)*
Halo Pub Inc..F....... 609 586-1811
Trenton *(G-11062)*
Heavenly Havens Creamery LLC............G....... 609 259-6600
Allentown *(G-31)*
Ice Cold Novelty Products Inc..................G....... 732 751-0011
Wall Township *(G-11491)*
Icykidz..G....... 973 342-9665
Irvington *(G-4590)*
J & J Snack Foods Corp...........................B....... 856 665-9533
Pennsauken *(G-8531)*
J & J Snack Foods Corp...........................D....... 856 467-9552
Bridgeport *(G-767)*
Kwality Foods Ltd Liability Co.................G....... 732 906-1941
Edison *(G-2554)*

S I C

Leos Ice Cream Company ....G...... 856 797-8771
Medford (G-6076)
Magliones Italian Ices LLC ....F...... 732 283-0705
Iselin (G-4631)
Marks Ice Cream ....G...... 201 861-5099
North Bergen (G-7463)
Mars Incorporated ....F...... 973 691-3500
Budd Lake (G-936)
▲ Mega Industries LLC ....G...... 973 779-8772
Passaic (G-8161)
◆ Mister Cookie Face Inc ....C...... 732 370-5533
Lakewood (G-5161)
Mr Green Tea Ice Cream Corp ....E...... 732 446-9800
Keyport (G-5021)
Mr Green Tea Ice Cream Corp ....F...... 732 446-9800
Keyport (G-5022)
Piemonte & Liebhauser LLC ....F...... 973 937-6200
Florham Park (G-3514)
Rajbhog Foods(nj) Inc ....C...... 551 222-4700
Jersey City (G-4814)
Rolo Systems ....E...... 973 627-4214
Denville (G-2056)
Rw Delights Inc ....G...... 718 683-1038
Millington (G-6261)
South Jersey Pretzel Inc ....F...... 856 435-5055
Stratford (G-10617)
Sweet Delight ....F...... 732 263-9100
Oakhurst (G-7673)
Sweet Orange LLC ....G...... 908 522-0011
Summit (G-10662)
Talenti Gelato LLC ....E...... 800 298-4020
Englewood Cliffs (G-2980)
▲ Taylor Products Inc ....E...... 732 225-4620
Edison (G-2637)
Tjs Ice Cream ....G...... 609 398-5055
Ocean City (G-7759)
▼ Tofutti Brands Inc ....G...... 908 272-2400
Cranford (G-1928)
Uncle Eds Creamery ....G...... 609 818-0100
Pennington (G-8462)
▲ Unilever United States Inc ....A...... 201 894-4000
Englewood Cliffs (G-2986)

2026 Milk

▲ Cumberland Dairy Inc ....C...... 800 257-8484
Rosenhayn (G-9706)
Cumberland Dairy Inc ....E...... 856 451-1300
Bridgeton (G-783)
Frozen Falls LLC ....G...... 908 350-3939
Basking Ridge (G-188)
Garelick Farms LLC ....C...... 609 499-2600
Burlington (G-975)
Georges Wine and Spirits Galle ......G...... 973 948-9950
Branchville (G-730)
Halo Farm Inc ....L...... 609 695-3311
Lawrenceville (G-5257)
▲ Johanna Foods Inc ....B...... 908 788-2200
Flemington (G-3452)
Midland Farms Inc ....E...... 800 749-6455
Paterson (G-8340)
Mualema LLC ....G...... 609 820-6098
Lawrence Township (G-5244)
Readington Farms Inc ....D...... 908 534-2121
Whitehouse (G-12048)
Tuscan/Lehigh Dairies Inc ....D...... 570 385-1884
Burlington (G-992)
▼ Vitamia Pasta Boy Inc ....F...... 973 546-1140
Lodi (G-5608)
Wakefern Food Corp ....B...... 732 819-0140
Edison (G-2649)
◆ Wakefern Food Corp ....B...... 908 527-3300
Keasbey (G-4932)
Wwf Operating Company ....F...... 856 459-3890
Bridgeton (G-805)
Yamate Chocolatier Inc ....G...... 732 249-4847
Highland Park (G-4306)
Yo Got It ....E...... 732 475-7913
Point Pleasant Beach (G-8929)
Yogurt Paradise LLC ....G...... 732 534-6395
Jackson (G-4683)

2032 Canned Specialties

◆ Antonio Mozzarella Factory Inc......F...... 973 353-9411
Newark (G-7087)
Antonio Mozzarella Factory Inc ......E...... 973 353-9411
Newark (G-7088)
▲ Aunt Kittys Foods Inc ....D...... 856 691-2100
Vineland (G-11325)
B&G Foods Inc ....B...... 973 401-6500
Parsippany (G-7956)

B&G Foods Inc ....B...... 973 401-6500
Parsippany (G-7957)
Bakers Perfection Inc ....E...... 973 983-0700
Rockaway (G-9553)
▲ Bono USA Inc ....B...... 973 978-7361
Fairfield (G-3151)
Campbell Soup Company ....A...... 856 342-4800
Camden (G-1049)
◆ Campbell Soup Supply Co LLC......G...... 856 342-4800
Camden (G-1050)
Crave Foods LLC ....F...... 973 233-1220
Montclair (G-6409)
CSC Brands LP ....F...... 800 257-8443
Camden (G-1057)
▲ F&S Produce Company Inc ....E...... 856 453-0316
Rosenhayn (G-9707)
▲ Fast-Pak Trading Inc ....G...... 201 293-4757
Secaucus (G-9882)
Goya Foods Inc ....B...... 201 348-4900
Secaucus (G-9890)
Goya Foods Inc ....B...... 201 865-3470
Secaucus (G-9891)
◆ Manischewitz Company ....D...... 201 553-1100
Newark (G-7235)
Mayab Happy Tacos Inc ....E...... 732 293-0400
Perth Amboy (G-8622)
▲ Mrs Mazzulas Food Products ....G...... 732 248-0555
Edison (G-2577)
▲ Mushroom Wisdom Inc ....F...... 973 470-0010
East Rutherford (G-2312)
Mysuperfoods Ltd Liability Co ....F...... 646 283-7455
Summit (G-10651)
▲ Nema Food Distribution Inc ....G...... 973 256-4415
Fairfield (G-3267)
◆ Nestle Healthcare Nutrtn Inc ....C...... 952 848-6000
Bridgewater (G-863)
◆ Novartis Corporation ....E...... 212 307-1122
East Hanover (G-2232)
Project Feed Usa Inc ....F...... 201 443-7143
Jersey City (G-4807)
▲ Sanket Corporation ....F...... 732 287-0201
Edison (G-2611)
Tuscany Especially Itln Foods ....F...... 732 308-1118
Marlboro (G-5962)
▼ Universal Prtein Spplmnts Corp .....D...... 732 545-3130
New Brunswick (G-7010)

2033 Canned Fruits, Vegetables & Preserves

B&G Foods Inc ....C...... 973 403-6795
Roseland (G-9646)
B&G Foods Inc ....B...... 973 401-6500
Parsippany (G-7956)
B&G Foods Inc ....B...... 973 401-6500
Parsippany (G-7957)
BSC USA LLC ....F...... 908 487-4437
Palisades Park (G-7836)
▼ C & E Canners Inc ....F...... 609 561-1078
Hammonton (G-4135)
Cameco Inc ....D...... 973 239-2845
Verona (G-11304)
Campbell Soup Company ....A...... 856 342-4800
Camden (G-1049)
▲ European Amrcn Foods Group Inc ..E...... 201 436-6106
Bayonne (G-224)
Funnibonz LLC ....G...... 609 915-3685
Princeton Junction (G-9156)
▲ Gardner Resources Inc ....G...... 732 872-0755
Highlands (G-4309)
Garelick Farms LLC ....C...... 609 499-2600
Burlington (G-975)
Halo Farm Inc ....L...... 609 695-3311
Lawrenceville (G-5257)
▲ Johanna Foods Inc ....B...... 908 788-2200
Flemington (G-3452)
▲ Lassonde Pappas and Co Inc ....E...... 856 455-1000
Carneys Point (G-1245)
Lassonde Pappas and Co Inc ....E...... 856 455-1001
Bridgeton (G-788)
Lidestri Foods Inc ....E...... 856 661-3218
Pennsauken (G-8543)
▲ Losurdo Foods Inc ....E...... 201 343-6680
Hackensack (G-3940)
Northeast Tomato Company Inc ......F...... 973 684-4890
Paterson (G-8353)
Pappas Lassonde Holdings Inc ....E...... 856 455-1000
Carneys Point (G-1246)
▲ Polonica Inc ....G...... 732 855-0008
Piscataway (G-8801)
▲ Pomi USA Inc ....F...... 732 541-4115
Matawan (G-6029)

Refresco Us Inc ....D...... 973 361-9794
Wharton (G-11998)
Wayne County Foods Inc ....E...... 973 399-0101
Irvington (G-4607)

2034 Dried Fruits, Vegetables & Soup

▲ Cibo Vita Inc ....C...... 201 773-4873
Fair Lawn (G-3087)
Elaine K Josephson Inc ....G...... 609 259-2256
New Brunswick (G-6958)
◆ Fornazor International Inc ....E...... 201 664-4000
Hillsdale (G-4382)
◆ International Foodsource LLC ....D...... 973 361-7044
Dover (G-2094)
▲ JF Braun & Sons Inc ....B...... 908 393-7400
Elizabeth (G-2750)
▲ Joyce Food LLC ....C...... 973 491-9696
Newark (G-7209)
▲ Major Products Co Inc ....E...... 201 641-5555
Little Ferry (G-5512)
▲ Mrs Mazzulas Food Products ....G...... 732 248-0555
Edison (G-2577)
▲ Osem USA Inc ....G...... 201 871-4433
Englewood Cliffs (G-2976)
◆ Unilever Bestfoods North Amer .....F...... 201 894-4000
Englewood Cliffs (G-2985)

2035 Pickled Fruits, Vegetables, Sauces & Dressings

B&G Foods Inc ....B...... 973 401-6500
Parsippany (G-7956)
B&G Foods Inc ....B...... 973 401-6500
Parsippany (G-7957)
▲ Benckiser N Reckitt Amer Inc ....A...... 973 404-2600
Parsippany (G-7960)
◆ Birds Eye Foods Inc ....C...... 585 383-1850
Cherry Hill (G-1350)
▼ Chelten House Products Inc ....C...... 856 467-1600
Bridgeport (G-762)
▲ Classic Cooking LLC ....D...... 718 439-0200
Rahway (G-9182)
Conopco Inc ....G...... 201 894-7760
Englewood Cliffs (G-2954)
◆ Cosmopolitan Food Group Inc ....G...... 908 998-1818
Hoboken (G-4466)
Crazy Steves Concoctions LLC ....G...... 908 787-2089
Trenton (G-11047)
▼ Dee & L LLC ....F...... 201 858-0138
Bayonne (G-222)
▼ Edsall Group USA Inc ....D...... 908 874-6953
Hillsborough (G-4330)
House of Herbs Inc ....G...... 973 779-2422
Passaic (G-8147)
Jjs Own Ltd Liability Company ....G...... 551 486-8510
Little Ferry (G-5510)
Kaplan & Zubrin ....E...... 856 964-1083
Camden (G-1073)
Mamamancinis Holdings Inc ....G...... 201 531-1212
East Rutherford (G-2307)
Mirrotek International LLC ....E...... 973 472-1400
Passaic (G-8165)
◆ Oasis Trading Co Inc ....C...... 908 964-0477
Hillside (G-4433)
Panos Brands LLC ....E...... 800 229-1706
Linden (G-5423)
Patriot Pickle Inc ....D...... 973 709-9487
Wayne (G-11672)
Pinnacle Foods Inc ....C...... 973 541-6620
Parsippany (G-8065)
R C Fine Foods Inc ....D...... 908 359-5500
Hillsborough (G-4366)
RB Manufacturing LLC ....C...... 908 533-2000
Hillsborough (G-4367)
RB Manufacturing LLC ....C...... 973 404-2600
Parsippany (G-8076)
◆ Reckitt Benckiser LLC ....B...... 973 404-2600
Parsippany (G-8077)
Reckitt Benckiser LLC ....C...... 973 404-2600
Montvale (G-6471)
Regal Crown Fd Svc Specialist ....G...... 508 752-2679
Wayne (G-11679)
◆ Silver Palate Kitchens Inc ....E...... 201 568-0110
Cresskill (G-1948)
▲ Surati NJ LLC ....F...... 732 251-3404
Spotswood (G-10531)
Technical Oil Products Co Inc ....G...... 973 940-8920
Newton (G-7408)
◆ Unilever Bestfoods North Amer .....F...... 201 894-4000
Englewood Cliffs (G-2985)

▲ **Unilever United States Inc** ....A 201 894-4000
Englewood Cliffs *(G-2986)*
Unilever United States Inc ....G 800 298-5018
Englewood Cliffs *(G-2987)*
United Farm Processing Corp ....F 856 451-4612
Rosenhayn *(G-9710)*
▲ **Vitamia Pasta Boy Inc** ....F 973 546-1140
Lodi *(G-5608)*
▲ **Yipin Food Products Inc** ....F 718 788-3059
Edison *(G-2652)*

2037 Frozen Fruits, Juices & Vegetables

202 Smoothie LLC ....G 973 985-4973
Wayne *(G-11599)*
American Food & Bev Inds LLC ....D 347 241-9827
Orange *(G-7816)*
Berry Blast Smoothies LLC ....G 856 692-6174
Vineland *(G-11330)*
◆ **Birds Eye Foods Inc** ....C 585 383-1850
Cherry Hill *(G-1350)*
Birds Eye Foods Inc ....C 920 435-5300
Parsippany *(G-7961)*
▲ **Classic Cooking LLC** ....D 718 439-0200
Rahway *(G-9182)*
◆ **Ejz Foods LLC** ....G 201 229-0500
South Hackensack *(G-10263)*
G & Y Specialty Foods LLC ....G 956 821-9652
Woodland Park *(G-12220)*
▲ **Gerber Products Company** ....C 973 593-7500
Florham Park *(G-3504)*
Mojo Organics Inc ....G 201 633-6519
Jersey City *(G-4785)*
▲ **Seabrook Brothers & Sons Inc** ......C 856 455-8080
Bridgeton *(G-796)*

2038 Frozen Specialties

Amys Omelette Hse Burlington ....F 609 386-4800
Burlington *(G-956)*
Appetizers Made Easy Inc ....E 201 531-1212
East Rutherford *(G-2277)*
Arctic Foods Inc ....E 908 689-0590
Washington *(G-11574)*
Battistini Foods ....G 609 476-2184
Egg Harbor Township *(G-2682)*
◆ **Birds Eye Foods Inc** ....C 585 383-1850
Cherry Hill *(G-1350)*
▲ **Caesars Pasta LLC** ....E 856 227-2585
Blackwood *(G-474)*
Campbell Soup Company ....A 856 342-4800
Camden *(G-1049)*
▲ **Classic Cooking LLC** ....D 718 439-0200
Rahway *(G-9182)*
Cuisine Innvtons Unlimited LLC ....C 732 730-9310
Lakewood *(G-5101)*
◆ **Deep Foods Inc** ....C 908 810-7500
Union *(G-11171)*
Delicious Fresh Pierogi Inc ....F 908 245-0550
Roselle Park *(G-9694)*
Dewy Meadow Farms Inc ....F 908 218-5655
Bridgewater *(G-834)*
Diaz Foods ....D 404 629-3616
Saddle Brook *(G-9762)*
DO Productions LLC ....D 856 866-3566
Lodi *(G-5582)*
▲ **Dr Pregers Sensible Foods Inc** ......D 201 703-1300
Elmwood Park *(G-2817)*
▲ **Fast-Pak Trading Inc** ....G 201 293-4757
Secaucus *(G-9882)*
▲ **Group Martin LLC Jj** ....F 862 240-1813
Newark *(G-7180)*
L E Rosellis Food Specialties ....F 609 654-4816
Medford *(G-6074)*
McCain Ellios Foods Inc ....C 201 368-0600
Lodi *(G-5595)*
Mjs of Spotswood LLC ....G 732 251-7400
Spotswood *(G-10529)*
▲ **Old Fashion Kitchen Inc** ....D 732 364-4100
Lakewood *(G-5168)*
Peak Finance Holdings LLC ....G 856 969-7100
Cherry Hill *(G-1411)*
Pinnacle Food Group Inc ....E 856 969-7100
Cherry Hill *(G-1414)*
▲ **Pinnacle Foods Finance LLC** ....C 973 541-6620
Parsippany *(G-8063)*
◆ **Pinnacle Foods Group LLC** ....D 856 969-8238
Parsippany *(G-8064)*
Pinnacle Foods Inc ....C 973 541-6620
Parsippany *(G-8065)*
Rajbhog Foods(nj) Inc ....C 551 222-4700
Jersey City *(G-4814)*

Rich Products Corporation ....G 856 696-5600
Vineland *(G-11398)*
Rico Foods Inc ....E 973 278-0589
Paterson *(G-8369)*
▲ **Savignano Food Corp** ....E 973 673-3355
Orange *(G-7826)*
Severino Pasta Mfg Co Inc ....E 856 854-3716
Collingswood *(G-1773)*
Seviroli Foods Inc ....G 856 931-1900
Bellmawr *(G-351)*
Socio Produce Inc ....G 201 348-3660
Union City *(G-11266)*
▲ **Tovli Inc** ....E 718 417-6677
Newark *(G-7346)*
▲ **Unilever United States Inc** ....A 201 894-4000
Englewood Cliffs *(G-2986)*
Vineland Specialty Foods L L C ....G 856 742-5001
Westville *(G-11951)*
Waffle Waffle LLC ....F 201 559-1286
Nutley *(G-7657)*

2041 Flour, Grain Milling

A & S Frozen Inc ....E 201 672-0510
East Rutherford *(G-2274)*
Bay State Milling Company ....D 973 772-3400
Clifton *(G-1573)*
Better Foods Jeyer LLC ....G 888 717-6412
Ridgefield Park *(G-9398)*
▲ **Cibo Vita Inc** ....C 201 773-4873
Fair Lawn *(G-3087)*
▲ **Coco International Inc** ....E 973 694-1200
Wayne *(G-11620)*
Fillo Factory Inc ....E 201 439-1036
Northvale *(G-7581)*
Frewitt USA Inc ....E 908 829-5245
Hillsborough *(G-4333)*
Guttenplans Frozen Dough Inc ....D 732 495-9480
North Middletown *(G-7557)*
J Spinelli & Sons Inc ....E 856 691-3133
Elmer *(G-2793)*
Mayab Happy Tacos Inc ....E 732 293-0400
Perth Amboy *(G-8622)*

2043 Cereal Breakfast Foods

Dim Inc ....F 908 925-2043
Linden *(G-5369)*
▲ **Gerber Products Company** ....C 973 593-7500
Florham Park *(G-3504)*
Kellogg Company ....E 201 634-9140
River Edge *(G-9466)*
Kellogg Company ....D 609 567-1688
Hammonton *(G-4141)*
▲ **Mm Packaging Group LLC** ....G 908 759-0101
Linden *(G-5411)*
◆ **Silver Palate Kitchens Inc** ....E 201 568-0110
Cresskill *(G-1948)*
Simi Granola LLC ....F 848 459-5619
Jackson *(G-4678)*
Vivis Life LLC ....G 201 798-1938
Jersey City *(G-4844)*

2044 Rice Milling

▲ **Diamond Foods USA Inc** ....G 732 543-2186
North Brunswick *(G-7515)*
◆ **Fornazor International Inc** ....E 201 664-4000
Hillsdale *(G-4382)*

2045 Flour, Blended & Prepared

All Madina Inc ....F 973 226-7772
West Caldwell *(G-11765)*
Caravan Ingredients Inc ....C 973 256-8886
Totowa *(G-10937)*
Foodtek Inc ....F 973 257-4000
Whippany *(G-12020)*
◆ **Fornazor International Inc** ....E 201 664-4000
Hillsdale *(G-4382)*
Jimmys Cookies LLC ....C 973 779-8500
Clifton *(G-1653)*
▲ **Joyce Food LLC** ....C 973 491-9696
Newark *(G-7209)*
▲ **Losurdo Foods Inc** ....E 201 343-6680
Hackensack *(G-3940)*
◆ **Manischewitz Company** ....D 201 553-1100
Newark *(G-7235)*
Mjs of Spotswood LLC ....G 732 251-7400
Spotswood *(G-10529)*
Nijama Corporation ....G 973 272-3223
Clifton *(G-1684)*

Peak Finance Holdings LLC ....G 856 969-7100
Cherry Hill *(G-1411)*
▲ **Pinnacle Foods Finance LLC** ....C 973 541-6620
Parsippany *(G-8063)*
◆ **Pinnacle Foods Group LLC** ....D 856 969-8238
Parsippany *(G-8064)*
Procter & Gamble Mfg Co ....D 732 602-4500
Avenel *(G-148)*
R C Fine Foods Inc ....D 908 359-5500
Hillsborough *(G-4366)*
◆ **Slt Foods Inc** ....F 732 661-1030
Dayton *(G-1987)*
William R Tatz Industries ....G 973 751-0720
Belleville *(G-328)*

2046 Wet Corn Milling

Hydro Milling Group Inc ....G 732 450-2488
Shrewsbury *(G-10000)*
Ingredion Incorporated ....D 908 685-5000
Bridgewater *(G-846)*
▼ **National Strch Chem Holdg Corp** ....A 908 685-5000
Bridgewater *(G-861)*
◆ **Unilever Bestfoods North Amer** ......F 201 894-4000
Englewood Cliffs *(G-2985)*

2047 Dog & Cat Food

Freshpet Inc ....E 201 520-4000
Secaucus *(G-9884)*
Gwenstone Inc ....G 732 785-2600
Lakewood *(G-5131)*
Mars Incorporated ....F 973 691-3500
Budd Lake *(G-936)*
Mars Food Us LLC ....F 908 852-1000
Hackettstown *(G-4024)*
Phibro Anmal Hlth Holdings Inc ....G 201 329-7300
Teaneck *(G-10766)*
◆ **Simmons Pet Food Nj Inc** ....B 856 662-7412
Pennsauken *(G-8578)*

2048 Prepared Feeds For Animals & Fowls

Buckhead Meat Company ....C 732 661-4900
Edison *(G-2476)*
Darling Ingredients Inc ....C 973 465-1900
Newark *(G-7133)*
Glenburnie Feed & Grain ....G 856 986-8128
Mount Laurel *(G-6800)*
International Processing Corp ....F 732 826-4240
Perth Amboy *(G-8619)*
Microfeed LLC ....G 201 886-9200
Fort Lee *(G-3568)*
New York Poultry Co ....F 908 523-1600
Linden *(G-5419)*
Pet Devices LLC ....G 929 244-0012
Livingston *(G-5555)*
◆ **Pharmacia & Upjohn Company LLC** ..B 908 901-8000
Peapack *(G-8431)*
◆ **Prince Agri Products Inc** ....E 201 329-7300
Teaneck *(G-10770)*
R World Enterprises ....G 201 795-2428
Jersey City *(G-4811)*
Reconserve Inc ....G 732 826-4240
Perth Amboy *(G-8627)*

2051 Bread, Bakery Prdts Exc Cookies & Crackers

9001 Corporation ....E 201 963-2233
Jersey City *(G-4693)*
9002 Corporation ....E 201 792-9595
Jersey City *(G-4694)*
▲ **A C Bakery Distributors Inc** ....F 973 977-2255
Paterson *(G-8191)*
Ability2work A NJ Nnprfit Corp ....F 908 782-3458
Flemington *(G-3423)*
Acme Markets Inc ....E 609 884-7217
Cape May *(G-1090)*
Advisory Dumas Group LLC ....F 850 778-1624
Lawrence Township *(G-5239)*
Ahzanis Castle LLC ....G 973 874-3191
Paterson *(G-8200)*
All In Icing ....G 973 896-5990
Stanhope *(G-10587)*
All Natural Products ....F 212 391-2870
Sayreville *(G-9813)*
Alpine Bakery Inc ....G 201 902-0605
Union City *(G-11239)*
American Harvest Baking Co Inc ....E 856 642-9955
Mount Laurel *(G-6778)*
▼ **Amorosos Baking Co** ....B 215 471-4740
Bellmawr *(G-331)*

Angelo Bakery Corp ....G.... 973 537-7220
Dover (G-2076)

Angelos Panetteria Inc ....G.... 201 435-4659
Jersey City (G-4706)

Angels Bakery USA LLC ....E.... 718 389-1400
Carteret (G-1248)

▲ Anthony & Sons Bakery Itln Bky ......D.... 973 625-2323
Denville (G-2031)

Antique Bakery & Pizzeria ....G.... 201 714-9323
Hoboken (G-4457)

Artisan Oven Inc ....G.... 201 488-6261
Hackensack (G-3875)

Auntie Annes Hmde Sft Prtzls ....F.... 856 772-3737
Voorhees (G-11422)

Auntie Annes Soft Pretzels ....E.... 856 722-0433
Moorestown (G-6561)

Aversas Italian Bakery Inc ....E.... 856 227-8005
Blackwood (G-472)

Bagel Club ....F.... 908 806-6022
Flemington (G-3429)

Bagel Street ....E.... 609 936-1755
Plainsboro (G-8875)

Bakers Perfection Inc ....E.... 973 983-0700
Rockaway (G-9553)

Barbeitos Inc ....G.... 732 726-9543
Avenel (G-127)

Bella Palermo Pastry Shop ....G.... 908 931-0298
Kenilworth (G-4943)

Berat Corporation ....C.... 609 953-7700
Medford (G-6065)

Bimbo Bakeries Usa Inc ....G.... 732 886-1881
Lakewood (G-5085)

Bimbo Bakeries Usa Inc ....D.... 732 390-7715
East Brunswick (G-2138)

Bimbo Bakeries Usa Inc ....E.... 856 435-0500
Clementon (G-1530)

Bimbo Bakeries Usa Inc ....E.... 973 872-6167
Wayne (G-11609)

Blissful Bites ....G.... 973 670-6928
Vernon (G-11296)

Branchville Bagels Inc ....G.... 973 948-7077
Branchville (G-727)

Bread & Bagels ....F.... 856 667-2333
Cherry Hill (G-1353)

Bread Guy Inc ....F.... 973 881-9002
Paterson (G-8224)

◆ Bridor USA Inc ....D.... 856 691-8000
Vineland (G-11333)

Cake Specialty Inc ....F.... 973 238-0500
Hawthorne (G-4224)

Calandra Italian & French Bky ....D.... 973 484-5598
Newark (G-7118)

Cambridge Bagels Inc ....F.... 973 743-5683
Bloomfield (G-505)

Campbell Soup Company ....A.... 856 342-4800
Camden (G-1049)

Carnegie Deli Inc ....D.... 201 507-5557
Carlstadt (G-1138)

Catering By Maddalenas Inc ....G.... 609 466-7510
Ringoes (G-9436)

Celtic Passions LLC ....F.... 973 865-7046
Nutley (G-7644)

Cheesecake Factory Inc ....G.... 973 921-0930
Short Hills (G-9976)

Chocolate Face Cupcake ....G.... 609 624-2253
Cape May Court House (G-1112)

Ciao Cupcake ....G.... 609 964-6167
Trenton (G-11040)

Cinderella Cheesecake Co Inc ....F.... 856 461-6302
Riverside (G-9495)

Conte Farms ....F.... 609 268-0513
Tabernacle (G-10737)

Cravings...F.... 732 531-7122
Allenhurst (G-25)

Creative Desserts ....G.... 732 477-0808
Brick (G-740)

Crijuodama Baking Corp T.....................G.... 732 451-1250
Lakewood (G-5100)

Crust and Crumb Bakery ....G.... 609 492-4966
Beach Haven (G-264)

Cupcake Celebrations ....G.... 973 885-0826
Columbus (G-1802)

Cupcake Kitschen ....G.... 862 221-8872
Mahwah (G-5761)

Cupcakes By Carousel ....G.... 201 389-3090
Ridgewood (G-9422)

▼ Damascus Bakery NJ LLC ....D.... 718 855-1456
Newark (G-7132)

Danmark Enterprises Inc ....G.... 732 321-3366
South Plainfield (G-10352)

Del Bakers Inc ....E.... 856 461-0089
Riverside (G-9496)

Del Buono Bakery Inc ....E.... 856 546-9585
Haddon Heights (G-4047)

Delicious Bagels Inc ....G.... 732 892-9265
Point Pleasant Boro (G-8938)

Dell Aquila Baking Company ....G.... 201 886-0613
Englewood (G-2886)

Dina Hernandez ....G.... 973 772-8883
Lodi (G-5581)

Doms Bakery Grand Inc ....G.... 201 653-1948
Hoboken (G-4469)

Dr Schar Usa Inc ....G.... 856 803-5100
Swedesboro (G-10694)

Ecce Panis Inc ....G.... 877 706-0510
Carlstadt (G-1159)

Elis Hot Bagels Inc ....E.... 732 566-4523
Matawan (G-6020)

Erj Baking LLC ....G.... 201 906-1300
Ridgewood (G-9424)

Excellence In Baking Inc ....G.... 732 287-1313
Edison (G-2516)

Feed Your Soul Ltd Lblty Co ....G.... 201 204-0720
Kearny (G-4873)

Ferrara Bakery & Cafe Inc ....F.... 732 826-8700
Perth Amboy (G-8614)

Food Circus Super Markets Inc ....D.... 732 291-4079
Atlantic Highlands (G-111)

Formica Bros Bakery ....F.... 609 348-8934
Atlantic City (G-96)

Fragales Bakery Inc ....F.... 973 546-0327
Garfield (G-3735)

Frell Corp ....F.... 201 825-2500
Ramsey (G-9240)

G N J Inc ....F.... 856 786-1127
Cinnaminson (G-1463)

Good To Go Inc ....E.... 856 627-8241
Voorhees (G-11431)

Herman Eickhoff ....C.... 609 871-1809
Willingboro (G-12119)

House of Cupcakes ....G.... 862 225-9536
Clifton (G-1642)

House of Cupcakes LLC ....G.... 908 413-3076
Somerset (G-10109)

▲ International Delights LLC ....C.... 973 928-5431
Clifton (G-1648)

J & J Snack Foods Corp ....C.... 856 933-3597
Bellmawr (G-344)

J & J Snack Foods Corp ....B.... 856 665-9533
Pennsauken (G-8531)

J & J Snack Foods Corp ....D.... 856 467-9552
Bridgeport (G-767)

J K P Donuts Inc ....G.... 856 234-9844
Mount Laurel (G-6809)

Jacqueline Mazza LLC ....G.... 732 718-2944
Somerset (G-10115)

Jad Bagels LLC ....G.... 201 567-4500
Englewood (G-2906)

Jay Jariwala ....F.... 908 806-8266
Ringoes (G-9439)

John Anthony Bread Distributor ....G.... 973 523-9258
Paterson (G-8305)

Just A Touch of Baking LLC ....G.... 732 679-5123
Old Bridge (G-7782)

▲ Kashmir Crown Baking LLC ....E.... 908 474-1470
Linden (G-5396)

Katis Kupcakes ....G.... 609 332-2172
Moorestown (G-6589)

KB Food Enterprises Inc ....F.... 973 278-2800
Paterson (G-8307)

Kohouts Bakery ....G.... 973 772-7270
Garfield (G-3741)

Lithuanian Bakery T J Inc ....F.... 908 354-0970
Elizabeth (G-2752)

Little Falls Shop Rite Super ....B.... 973 256-0909
Little Falls (G-5481)

Little Miss Cupcake LLC ....G.... 732 370-3083
Lakewood (G-5149)

Livingston Bagel Warren Inc ....G.... 973 994-1915
Livingston (G-5540)

▲ Lo Presti & Sons LLC ....G.... 973 523-9258
Paterson (G-8325)

Local Baking Products Inc ....E.... 973 482-1400
Newark (G-7223)

Lodi Cml Cooperative LLC ....G.... 201 820-2380
Lodi (G-5593)

Luccas Bakery Inc ....G.... 609 561-5558
Hammonton (G-4142)

Mendels Muffins and Stuff Inc ....G.... 973 881-9900
Paterson (G-8335)

Mendles Just Bread Inc ....G.... 973 881-9900
Paterson (G-8336)

Mfb Soft Pretzels Inc ....G.... 609 953-6773
Medford (G-6077)

Millburn Bagel Company ....E.... 973 258-1334
Millburn (G-6258)

Minardi Baking Co Inc ....E.... 973 742-1107
Denville (G-2050)

Mini Frost Foods Corporation ....E.... 973 427-4258
North Haledon (G-7552)

Mondelez Global LLC ....A.... 201 794-4000
Fair Lawn (G-3103)

Mrs Sullivans Inc ....G.... 908 246-8937
Martinsville (G-6010)

▲ Nablus Pastry & Sweets ....G.... 973 881-8003
Paterson (G-8346)

Nan Bread Distribution ....G.... 201 475-9311
Elmwood Park (G-2838)

◆ Nexira Inc ....F.... 908 704-7480
Somerville (G-10222)

Northeast Foods Inc ....D.... 732 549-2243
Edison (G-2584)

Nuchas Tsq LLC ....F.... 212 913-9682
North Bergen (G-7472)

O O M Inc ....G.... 973 328-9408
Rockaway (G-9592)

Omni Baking Company LLC ....B.... 856 205-1485
Vineland (G-11386)

Original Bagel & Bialy Co Inc ....E.... 973 227-5777
West Caldwell (G-11794)

Original Miami Onion Roll Inc ....E.... 973 389-2202
Paterson (G-8356)

Orthodox Baking Co Inc ....E.... 973 844-9393
Belleville (G-309)

Pao Ba Avo LLC ....G.... 908 962-9090
Elizabeth (G-2765)

▲ Paramount Bakeries Inc ....G.... 973 482-6638
Newark (G-7263)

Paramount Bakeries Inc ....G.... 973 482-6638
East Orange (G-2263)

Paramount Bakeries Inc ....E.... 973 481-4763
Newark (G-7264)

Pathmark Stores Inc ....C.... 856 853-5533
Woodbury (G-12167)

Pathmark Stores Inc ....C.... 732 505-6440
Toms River (G-10900)

Pathmark Stores Inc ....C.... 973 762-5044
South Orange (G-10313)

Pechters Southern NJ LLC ....E.... 856 786-8000
Cinnaminson (G-1483)

Perk & Pantry ....G.... 856 451-4333
Bridgeton (G-794)

Phoenician Inc ....G.... 732 545-3915
North Brunswick (G-7534)

◆ Prestige Bread Jersey Cy Inc ....D.... 201 422-7900
North Bergen (G-7476)

Pretty Lil Cupcakes ....G.... 201 256-1205
Harrison (G-4188)

Provence LLC ....C.... 201 503-9717
Englewood (G-2926)

R P Baking LLC ....E.... 973 483-3374
Harrison (G-4189)

Rombiolo LLC ....G.... 973 680-0405
Bloomfield (G-529)

▲ Royal Baking Co Inc ....D.... 201 296-0888
Moonachie (G-6540)

S M Z Enterprises Inc ....G.... 908 232-1921
Westfield (G-11930)

Scala Pastry ....G.... 732 398-9808
North Brunswick (G-7537)

Schripps European Bread Inc ....E.... 201 867-0909
North Bergen (G-7485)

Serranis Bakery ....F.... 973 678-1777
Orange (G-7537)

Shop Rite Supermarkets Inc ....C.... 732 442-1717
Perth Amboy (G-8630)

Shop Rite Supermarkets Inc ....C.... 732 775-4250
Neptune (G-6932)

Shop-Rite Supermarkets Inc ....C.... 609 646-2448
Absecon (G-4)

Sibi Distributors ....G.... 908 658-4448
Basking Ridge (G-205)

Spindlers Bake Shop ....G.... 201 288-1345
Hasbrouck Heights (G-4198)

Springdale Farm Market Inc ....E.... 856 424-8674
Cherry Hill (G-1421)

Sukhadias Sweets & Snacks ....G.... 973 227-6400
Parsippany (G-8093)

▲ Sukhadias Sweets & Snacks ....F.... 908 222-0069
South Plainfield (G-10436)

Sweet Potato Pie Inc............................E....... 973 279-3405
  Paterson (G-8393)
Sweetly Spirited Cupcakes Ltd.............G..... 917 846-4238
  Princeton Junction (G-9164)
▲ Symphony Inc..................................F....... 856 727-9596
  Moorestown (G-6626)
Tasty Baking Company ....G..... 609 641-8588
  Egg Harbor Township (G-2697)
Tasty Cake South Jersey....................G..... 856 428-8414
  Cherry Hill (G-1427)
▲ Tbb Inc..G..... 973 589-8875
  Newark (G-7337)
Terrignos Bakery...............................E....... 856 451-6368
  Bridgeton (G-799)
Thebgb Inc...G..... 917 749-5309
  Paterson (G-8399)
▼ Toufayan Bakery Inc ....C....... 201 861-4131
  Ridgefield (G-9388)
Tri-State Buns LLC.............................E....... 973 418-8323
  Harrison (G-4190)
◆ Unilever Bestfoods North Amer.......F....... 201 894-4000
  Englewood Cliffs (G-2985)
Uptown Bakeries ....C....... 856 467-9552
  Logan Township (G-5615)
◆ Vieiras Bakery Inc............................D..... 973 589-7719
  Newark (G-7357)
▲ Vitamia Pasta Boy Inc ....F....... 973 546-1140
  Lodi (G-5608)
Wenner Bread Products Inc ....D..... 631 563-6262
  New Brunswick (G-7012)
Y & J Bakers Inc ....E....... 732 363-3636
  Lakewood (G-5208)
Zaiya Inc..E....... 201 343-3988
  Hackensack (G-3993)
Zenas Patisserie................................G..... 856 303-8700
  Riverton (G-9509)
Zinicola Baking Co.............................G..... 973 667-1306
  Nutley (G-7658)

2052 Cookies & Crackers

A & A Soft Pretzel Company ....G..... 856 338-0208
  Camden (G-1039)
Arysta LLC...G..... 856 417-8100
  Logan Township (G-5611)
Auntie Annes Hmde Sft Prtzls ....F....... 856 772-3737
  Voorhees (G-11422)
Auntie Annes Soft Pretzels ....E....... 856 845-3667
  Woodbury (G-12157)
Bakers Perfection Inc ....E....... 973 983-0700
  Rockaway (G-9553)
◆ Birds Eye Foods Inc ....C....... 585 383-1850
  Cherry Hill (G-1350)
Butterfly Bakery Inc ....E....... 973 815-1501
  Wyckoff (G-12246)
Caliz - Malko LLC...............................G..... 973 207-5200
  Fairfield (G-3154)
Campbell Soup Company ....A..... 856 342-4800
  Camden (G-1049)
Chips Ice Cream LLC..........................G..... 732 840-6332
  Howell (G-4548)
Continental Cookies Inc ....F....... 201 498-1966
  Hackensack (G-3899)
◆ Deep Foods Inc.................................C....... 908 810-7500
  Union (G-11171)
Direct Sales and Services Inc ....E....... 973 340-4480
  Garfield (G-3730)
European Pretzel One LLC..................F....... 201 867-6117
  North Bergen (G-7451)
◆ Fairfield Gourmet Food Corp ....D..... 973 575-4365
  Cedar Grove (G-1283)
Federal Pretzel Baking Co..................E....... 215 467-0505
  Bridgeport (G-764)
Food & Beverage Inc ....D..... 201 288-8881
  Teterboro (G-10795)
▲ Gerber Products Company ....C....... 973 593-7500
  Florham Park (G-3504)
Grab Em Snacks Ltd Lblty Co ....G..... 908 333-3229
  Hillsborough (G-4337)
Interntnal Bscits Cnfctons Inc ....G..... 856 813-1008
  Marlton (G-5979)
J & J Snack Foods Corp......................C....... 856 933-3597
  Bellmawr (G-344)
J & J Snack Foods Corp......................B....... 856 665-9533
  Pennsauken (G-8531)
J & J Snack Foods Corp......................D..... 856 467-9552
  Bridgeport (G-767)
J & J Snack Foods Corp PA.................B....... 856 665-9533
  Pennsauken (G-8532)
Jassmine Corp...................................G..... 848 565-0515
  Clifton (G-1652)

Jimmys Cookies LLC..........................C....... 973 779-8500
  Clifton (G-1653)
▲ John Wm Macy Cheesesticks Inc.....D..... 201 791-8036
  Elmwood Park (G-2827)
▲ Joyce Food LLC ....C....... 973 491-9696
  Newark (G-7209)
Kitchen Table Bakers Inc ....E....... 516 931-5113
  Fairfield (G-3243)
Little Falls Shop Rite Super ....B....... 973 256-0909
  Little Falls (G-5481)
▲ Lo Presti & Sons LLC ....E....... 973 523-9258
  Paterson (G-8325)
Local Baking Products Inc ....E....... 973 482-1400
  Newark (G-7223)
◆ Manischewitz Company ....D..... 201 553-1100
  Newark (G-7235)
Medford Soft Pretzels Inc...................G..... 856 662-8792
  Marlton (G-5987)
Meltdown ....G..... 609 207-0527
  Long Beach Township (G-5617)
Millstone Dq Inc ....G..... 609 259-6733
  Clarksburg (G-1521)
Mini Frost Foods Corporation ....E....... 973 427-4258
  North Haledon (G-7552)
Mondelez Global LLC ....A..... 201 794-4000
  Fair Lawn (G-3103)
Mondelez Global LLC ....A..... 201 794-4080
  Fair Lawn (G-3104)
Nabisco Royal Argentina Inc ....G..... 973 503-2000
  East Hanover (G-2230)
▲ Novelty Cone Co Inc ....E....... 856 665-9525
  Pennsauken (G-8555)
Oven Art LLC ....E....... 973 910-2266
  Hackensack (G-3958)
Pace Target Brokerage Inc ....E....... 856 629-2551
  Williamstown (G-12095)
▲ Royal Baking Co Inc ....D..... 201 296-0888
  Moonachie (G-6540)
South Jersey Pretzel Inc ....F....... 856 435-5055
  Stratford (G-10617)

2053 Frozen Bakery Prdts

A & S Frozen Inc ....E....... 201 672-0510
  East Rutherford (G-2274)
Aiva Naturals LLC ....G..... 201 825-0749
  Newark (G-7075)
Cinderella Cheesecake Co Inc.............F....... 856 461-6302
  Riverside (G-9495)
Country Home Bakers LLC - GA..........C....... 856 931-7052
  Bellmawr (G-335)
Country Oven ....G..... 732 494-4838
  Iselin (G-4622)
Hudson Cakery ....G..... 201 319-0363
  Weehawken (G-11696)
I-Yell-O Foods Inc..............................G..... 732 525-2201
  South Amboy (G-10239)
J & J Snack Foods Corp......................B....... 856 665-9533
  Pennsauken (G-8531)
J & J Snack Foods Corp......................D..... 856 467-9552
  Bridgeport (G-767)
J & J Snack Foods Corp......................C....... 856 933-3597
  Bellmawr (G-344)
Mardon Associates Inc ....F....... 973 977-2251
  Paterson (G-8332)
▲ Nema Food Distribution Inc ....G..... 973 256-4415
  Fairfield (G-3267)
Rich Products Corporation ....A..... 800 356-7094
  Riverside (G-9505)
▲ Royal Baking Co Inc ....D..... 201 296-0888
  Moonachie (G-6540)
Sugar & Plumm Upper West LLC ....D..... 201 334-1600
  Moonachie (G-6544)
Sugar and Plumm LLC ....G..... 201 334-1600
  Moonachie (G-6545)
Sugarush ....G..... 732 414-9044
  Red Bank (G-9346)
Wenner Bread Products Inc ....D..... 631 563-6262
  New Brunswick (G-7012)

2061 Sugar, Cane

Global Commodities Exportacao ....G..... 201 613-1532
  Newark (G-7171)
International Molasses Corp................E....... 201 368-8036
  Saddle Brook (G-9770)

2062 Sugar, Cane Refining

▼ Domino Foods Inc ....E....... 732 590-1173
  Iselin (G-4623)
International Molasses Corp................E....... 201 368-8036
  Maywood (G-6051)

2064 Candy & Confectionery Prdts

Al Richrds Homemade Chocolates ......F....... 201 436-0915
  Bayonne (G-210)
Amys Omelette Hse Burlington ....F....... 609 386-4800
  Burlington (G-956)
Ann Hemyng Candy Inc.......................G..... 215 536-7004
  Bridgewater (G-811)
◆ Astor Chocolate Corp ....C....... 732 901-1000
  Lakewood (G-5077)
▲ Ausome LLC ....G..... 732 951-8818
  Paramus (G-7854)
▲ Bergen Marzipan & Chocolate ....G..... 201 385-8343
  Bergenfield (G-383)
Bromilows Candy Co ....G..... 973 684-1496
  Woodland Park (G-12212)
▲ Cadbury Adams USA LLC..................E....... 973 503-2000
  East Hanover (G-2203)
▲ Candy Treasure LLC ....G..... 201 830-3600
  Lebanon (G-5279)
Capco Enterprises Inc ....F....... 973 884-0044
  East Hanover (G-2206)
▲ Ce De Candy Inc ....C....... 908 964-0660
  Union (G-11164)
▲ Cns Confectionery Products LLC .....D..... 201 823-1400
  Bayonne (G-220)
Dairy Maid Confectionery Co ....G..... 609 399-0100
  Ocean City (G-7752)
Damask Kandies ....G..... 856 467-1661
  Swedesboro (G-10690)
David Bradley Chocolatier Inc ....G..... 609 443-4747
  Windsor (G-12125)
David Bradley Chocolatier Inc ....G..... 732 536-7719
  Englishtown (G-2991)
Enjou Chocolat Morristown Inc ....G..... 973 993-9090
  Morristown (G-6707)
▲ Ensign Overseas (usa) Ltd................G..... 201 662-7150
  North Bergen (G-7450)
◆ Ferrero U S A Inc ....C....... 732 764-9300
  Parsippany (G-8009)
Fralingers Inc ....G..... 609 345-2177
  Atlantic City (G-98)
Fralingers Inc ....E....... 609 345-2177
  Atlantic City (G-97)
Genevieves Inc...................................F....... 973 772-8816
  Garfield (G-3737)
Giambris Quality Sweets Inc ....G..... 856 783-1099
  Clementon (G-1532)
◆ Guylian USA Inc ....G..... 201 871-4144
  Englewood Cliffs (G-2962)
▼ Hillside Candy LLC ....F....... 973 926-2300
  Hillside (G-4413)
Hillside Candy LLC ....E....... 908 241-4747
  Roselle (G-9672)
▲ James Candy Company ....D..... 609 344-1519
  Atlantic City (G-101)
Joy Snacks LLC..................................F....... 732 272-0707
  Avenel (G-136)
▲ Koppers Chocolate LLC ....D..... 212 243-0220
  Cranford (G-1912)
Krauses Homemade Candy Inc ....F....... 201 943-4790
  Fairview (G-3364)
▲ Life of Party LLC ....E....... 732 828-0886
  North Brunswick (G-7524)
Lucas World Inc ....G..... 832 293-3770
  Budd Lake (G-933)
◆ Mafco Worldwide Corporation ....C....... 856 964-8840
  Camden (G-1075)
Marlow Candy & Nut Co Inc ....E....... 201 569-7606
  Englewood (G-2913)
Mars Incorporated ....A..... 908 852-1000
  Hackettstown (G-4020)
Mars Incorporated ....D..... 908 850-2420
  Hackettstown (G-4021)
◆ Mars Chocolate North Amer LLC ......A..... 908 852-1000
  Hackettstown (G-4022)
Mars Chocolate North Amer LLC ....A..... 908 979-5070
  Hackettstown (G-4023)
Mars Wrigley Conf US LLC ....G..... 908 852-1000
  Hackettstown (G-4025)
Minhura Inc..G..... 862 763-4078
  North Arlington (G-7421)
Naturee Nuts Inc ....F....... 732 786-4663
  Kenilworth (G-4979)
Nutra Nuts Inc ....G..... 323 260-7457
  Ridgewood (G-9427)
Old Monmouth Peanut Brittle Co ....G..... 732 462-1311
  Freehold (G-3674)
▲ Oral Fixation LLC ....G..... 609 937-9972
  Hopewell (G-4543)

Ozone Confectioners Bakers Sup ....F 201 791-4444
  Verona *(G-11308)*

Packom LLC ....F 201 378-8382
  Little Falls *(G-5484)*

▲ Pim Brands LLC ....D 732 560-8300
  Somerset *(G-10155)*

PR Products Distributors Inc ....G 973 928-1120
  Wayne *(G-11675)*

▲ Promotion In Motion Inc ....D 201 962-8530
  Allendale *(G-16)*

Promotion In Motion Inc ....E 732 560-8300
  Somerset *(G-10159)*

Rauhausers Inc ....F 609 399-1465
  Ocean City *(G-7755)*

Rayge Candy Co ....F 732 458-2179
  Brick *(G-756)*

Reilys Candy Inc ....F 609 953-0040
  Medford *(G-6079)*

Sherwood Brands Corporation.............F 973 249-8200
  New Brunswick *(G-7003)*

Shrivers Salt Wtr Taffy Fudge ....G 609 399-0100
  Ocean City *(G-7758)*

Sims Lee Inc ....G 201 433-1308
  Jersey City *(G-4828)*

▲ U I S Industries Inc ....A 201 946-2600
  Jersey City *(G-4839)*

Webers Candy Store ....G 856 455-8277
  Bridgeton *(G-803)*

William R Tatz Industries ....G 973 751-0720
  Belleville *(G-328)*

▲ World Confections Inc ....D 718 768-8100
  South Orange *(G-10317)*

▲ Yolo Candy LLC ....G 201 252-8765
  Mahwah *(G-5825)*

2066 Chocolate & Cocoa Prdts

Barry Callebaut USA LLC ....E 856 663-2260
  Pennsauken *(G-8483)*

Barry Callebaut USA LLC ....D 856 663-2260
  Pennsauken *(G-8484)*

▲ Bergen Marzipan & Chocolate ....G 201 385-8343
  Bergenfield *(G-383)*

Birnn Chocolates Inc ....G 732 214-8680
  Highland Park *(G-4301)*

▼ Bosco Products Inc ....G 973 334-7534
  Towaco *(G-10990)*

Bromilows Candy Co ....G 973 684-1496
  Woodland Park *(G-12212)*

▲ Candy Treasure LLC ....G 201 830-3600
  Lebanon *(G-5279)*

▲ Chocmod USA Inc ....E 201 585-8730
  Fort Lee *(G-3549)*

Cocoa Processing Corp ....G 908 688-0415
  Jersey City *(G-4729)*

Cocoa Services Inc ....F 856 234-1700
  Moorestown *(G-6568)*

David Bradley Chocolatier Inc ....F 609 443-4747
  Windsor *(G-12125)*

David Bradley Chocolatier Inc ....E 732 536-7719
  Englishtown *(G-2991)*

Dove Chocolate Discoveries LLC ....E 866 922-3683
  Mount Arlington *(G-6753)*

Forget ME Not Chocolates By NA ....G 856 753-8916
  Atco *(G-89)*

Fralingers Inc ....F 609 345-2177
  Atlantic City *(G-97)*

Genevieves Inc ....F 973 772-8816
  Garfield *(G-3737)*

George Brummer ....G 908 232-1904
  Westfield *(G-11925)*

K K S Criterion Chocolates ....E 732 542-7847
  Eatontown *(G-2409)*

▲ Koppers Chocolate LLC ....D 212 243-0220
  Cranford *(G-1912)*

Mack Trading LLC ....G 973 794-4904
  Hewitt *(G-4290)*

Mars Incorporated ....D 908 850-2420
  Hackettstown *(G-4021)*

Mars Incorporated ....A 908 852-1000
  Hackettstown *(G-4020)*

Mars Incorporated ....F 973 691-3500
  Budd Lake *(G-936)*

◆ Mars Chocolate North Amer LLC .....A 908 852-1000
  Hackettstown *(G-4022)*

Mars Retail Group Inc ....E 973 398-2078
  Mount Arlington *(G-6757)*

▲ Master Martini USA Inc ....G 908 455-4434
  Whitehouse Station *(G-12053)*

Matisse Chocolatier Inc ....G 201 568-2288
  Englewood *(G-2914)*

Neu Haus Inc ....G 201 845-0040
  Paramus *(G-7894)*

Nouveautes Inc ....F 973 882-8850
  Fairfield *(G-3274)*

▲ Promotion In Motion Inc ....D 201 962-8530
  Allendale *(G-16)*

Savita Naturals Ltd ....E 856 467-4949
  Swedesboro *(G-10727)*

Third Ave Chocolate Shoppe ....G 732 449-7535
  Spring Lake *(G-10535)*

Transmar Group LLC ....G 973 359-4040
  Morristown *(G-6745)*

2067 Chewing Gum

▲ Gum Runners LLC ....F 201 333-0756
  Jersey City *(G-4763)*

▲ L A Dreyfus Co ....C 732 549-1600
  Edison *(G-2555)*

2068 Salted & Roasted Nuts & Seeds

▲ Cibo Vita Inc ....C 201 773-4873
  Fair Lawn *(G-3087)*

▲ Cns Confectionery Products LLC .....F 201 823-1400
  Bayonne *(G-220)*

Naturee Nuts Inc ....F 732 786-4663
  Kenilworth *(G-4979)*

▲ Nutsco Inc ....F 856 966-6400
  Camden *(G-1080)*

◆ Star Snacks Co LLC ....B 201 200-9820
  Jersey City *(G-4832)*

2075 Soybean Oil Mills

◆ Fornazor International Inc ....E 201 664-4000
  Hillsdale *(G-4382)*

House Foods America Corp ....D 732 537-9500
  Somerset *(G-10108)*

2076 Vegetable Oil Mills

Romulus Emprises Inc ....G 609 683-4549
  Hightstown *(G-4314)*

Textron Inc ....E 201 945-1500
  Edgewater *(G-2442)*

W A Cleary Products Inc ....F 732 246-2829
  Somerset *(G-10196)*

2077 Animal, Marine Fats & Oils

Bringhurst Bros Inc ....E 856 767-0110
  Berlin *(G-429)*

Darling Ingredients Inc ....C 973 465-1900
  Newark *(G-7133)*

Daybrook Holdings Inc ....G 973 538-6766
  Morristown *(G-6705)*

Epicore Networks USA Inc ....E 609 267-9118
  Mount Holly *(G-6770)*

2079 Shortening, Oils & Margarine

▲ Aak USA Inc ....D 973 344-1300
  Edison *(G-2446)*

▲ Aarhuskarlshamn USA Inc ....G 973 344-1300
  Newark *(G-7068)*

Bimbo Bakeries USA Inc ....C 973 256-8200
  Totowa *(G-10936)*

◆ Cosmopolitan Food Group Inc ....G 908 998-1818
  Hoboken *(G-4466)*

Edesia Oil LLC ....F 732 851-7979
  Manalapan *(G-5843)*

▲ European Amrcn Foods Group Inc ...E 201 436-6106
  Bayonne *(G-224)*

European Amrcn Foods Group Inc ....B 201 583-1101
  Secaucus *(G-9880)*

▲ Finex Trade ....G 609 921-2747
  Princeton *(G-9045)*

▲ Hojiblanca USA Inc ....G 201 384-3007
  Dumont *(G-2118)*

International Olive Oil Inc ....C 732 612-3338
  Manasquan *(G-5871)*

◆ Oasis Trading Co Inc ....C 908 964-0477
  Hillside *(G-4433)*

▲ Olivos USA Inc ....G 201 893-0142
  Fort Lee *(G-3576)*

Procter & Gamble Mfg Co ....D 732 602-4500
  Avenel *(G-148)*

Technical Oil Products Co Inc ....G 973 940-8920
  Newton *(G-7408)*

Western Pacific Foods Inc ....F 908 838-0186
  Kearny *(G-4921)*

2082 Malt Beverages

▲ Advanced Brewing Sys LLC ....G 973 633-1777
  Prospect Park *(G-9168)*

Anheuser-Busch LLC ....C 973 645-7700
  Jersey City *(G-4707)*

Brix City Brewing ....G 201 440-0865
  Little Ferry *(G-5495)*

Bucks County Brewing Co Inc ....G 609 929-0148
  Lambertville *(G-5211)*

Cape May Brewing Ltd Lblty Co ....F 609 849-9933
  Cape May *(G-1092)*

Cape May Brewing Ltd Lblty Co ....E 609 849-9933
  Cape May *(G-1093)*

▲ Carton Brewing Company LLC ....G 732 654-2337
  Atlantic Highlands *(G-110)*

Coors Brewing Company ....E 732 767-3300
  Edison *(G-2491)*

Core 3 Brewery Ltd Lblty Co ....G 856 562-0386
  Franklinville *(G-3629)*

Fizzics Group LLC ....G 917 545-4533
  Wall Township *(G-11483)*

Geislers Liquor Store ....F 856 845-0482
  Thorofare *(G-10820)*

▲ Group Martin LLC Jj ....F 862 240-1813
  Newark *(G-7180)*

Headquarters Pub LLC ....G 609 347-2579
  Atlantic City *(G-100)*

▲ High Point Brewing Co Inc ....G 973 838-7400
  Butler *(G-1007)*

▲ Hunterdon Brewing Company LLC ..D 908 454-7445
  Whitehouse Station *(G-12051)*

Jersey Girl Brewing Company ....G 908 269-5523
  Hackettstown *(G-4014)*

Pinelands Brewing Ltd Lblty Co ....F 609 296-6169
  Ltl Egg Hbr *(G-5646)*

Proximo Distillers LLC ....D 201 204-1718
  Jersey City *(G-4809)*

River Horse Brewery Co Inc ....F 609 883-0890
  Ewing *(G-3053)*

▲ Shore Point Distrg Co Inc ....C 732 308-3334
  Freehold *(G-3688)*

Summerlands Inc ....G 973 729-8428
  Sparta *(G-10521)*

Triumph Brewing of Princeton ....G 609 773-0111
  Lambertville *(G-5222)*

Tuckahoe Brewing Company LLC ....F 609 645-2739
  Egg Harbor Twp *(G-2701)*

2083 Malt

International Molasses Corp ....E 201 368-8036
  Saddle Brook *(G-9770)*

▼ Malt Products Corporation ....E 201 845-4420
  Saddle Brook *(G-9772)*

Malt Products Corporation ....E 201 845-9106
  Saddle Brook *(G-9773)*

2084 Wine & Brandy

▲ American Estates Wines Inc ....G 908 273-5060
  Summit *(G-10634)*

Bellview Farms Inc ....G 856 697-7172
  Landisville *(G-5230)*

Beneduce Vineyard ....G 908 996-3823
  Pittstown *(G-8849)*

Brook Hollow Winery LLC ....G 908 496-8200
  Columbia *(G-1796)*

▲ Cava Winery and Vineyard Inc ....F 973 823-9463
  Hamburg *(G-4089)*

Cream Ridge Winery ....G 609 259-9797
  Cream Ridge *(G-1933)*

Devotion Spirits Inc ....G 877 415-3190
  Red Bank *(G-9327)*

Dijon Enterprises LLC ....G 201 876-9463
  Wallington *(G-11525)*

E & J Gallo Winery ....G 973 877-0118
  Newark *(G-7148)*

GP Wine Works LLC ....G 201 997-6055
  Bayonne *(G-230)*

Grape Bginnings Handson Winery ....G 732 380-7356
  Eatontown *(G-2397)*

▲ Hojiblanca USA Inc ....G 201 384-3007
  Dumont *(G-2118)*

▲ Hopewell Valley Vineyards LLC ....E 609 737-4465
  Pennington *(G-8453)*

▲ Hunterdon Brewing Company LLC ..D 908 454-7445
  Whitehouse Station *(G-12051)*

Jersey Cider Works LLC ....G 917 604-0067
  Montclair *(G-6420)*

Jersey Cider Works LLC ....G 908 940-4115
  Asbury *(G-71)*

◆ Laird & Company.................E....... 732 542-0312
Eatontown *(G-2411)*

Michelle Ste Wine Estates Ltd..........G....... 973 770-8100
Mount Arlington *(G-6758)*

Monroeville Vineyard & Winery..........F....... 856 521-0523
Monroeville *(G-6401)*

Natali Vineyards LLC.............G....... 609 465-0075
Cape May Court House *(G-1116)*

◆ Oasis Trading Co Inc............C....... 908 964-0477
Hillside *(G-4433)*

Old York Cellars.............G....... 908 284-9463
Ringoes *(G-9441)*

▲ Opici Import Co Inc............E....... 201 689-3256
Glen Rock *(G-3827)*

▲ Petit Pois Corp.............G....... 856 608-9644
Moorestown *(G-6612)*

Plagidos Winery LLC............G....... 609 567-4633
Hammonton *(G-4146)*

Redpuro LLC.............G....... 908 370-4460
Warren *(G-11565)*

▲ Renault Winery Inc............E....... 609 965-2111
Egg Harbor City *(G-2669)*

Ripe Life Wines LLC............G....... 201 560-3233
Franklin Lakes *(G-3623)*

◆ Royal Wine Corporation............C....... 718 384-2400
Bayonne *(G-243)*

Royal Wine Corporation............C....... 201 535-9006
Bayonne *(G-244)*

Salem Oak Vineyards Ltd Lblty............G....... 856 889-2121
Pedricktown *(G-8440)*

Sharrott Wine.............G....... 609 567-9463
Hammonton *(G-4148)*

Southwind Equestrian.............G....... 856 364-9690
Millville *(G-6325)*

▲ Tomasello Winery Inc............F....... 609 561-0567
Hammonton *(G-4151)*

Unionville Vineyards LLC.............G....... 908 788-0400
Ringoes *(G-9443)*

Valenzano Winery.............G....... 856 701-7871
Shamong *(G-9972)*

Villa Milagro Vineyards LLC.............G....... 908 995-2072
Phillipsburg *(G-8675)*

W J R B Inc.............G....... 609 884-1169
Cape May *(G-1107)*

Wagonhouse Winery LLC.............G....... 609 780-8019
Swedesboro *(G-10736)*

Willow Creek Winery Inc.............G....... 609 770-8782
Cape May *(G-1108)*

Winery Pak LLC.............G....... 800 434-4599
Cedar Knolls *(G-1323)*

2085 Liquors, Distilled, Rectified & Blended

Claremont Distilled Spirits.................F....... 973 227-7027
Fairfield *(G-3160)*

Corgi Spirits LLC.............G....... 862 219-3114
Jersey City *(G-4734)*

Creamy Creation LLC.............G....... 585 344-3300
Paramus *(G-7864)*

Devotion Spirits Inc.............G....... 877 415-3190
Red Bank *(G-9327)*

Hoboken Mary Ltd Liability Co............G....... 201 234-9910
Hoboken *(G-4474)*

▲ Prince Black Distillery Inc............E....... 212 695-6187
Clifton *(G-1704)*

Shrem Consulting Ltd Lblty Co............G....... 917 371-0581
West Long Branch *(G-11846)*

White Castle.............E....... 732 721-3565
South Amboy *(G-10247)*

2086 Soft Drinks

▼ 3rd Generation Enterprises.................F....... 201 528-7274
Carlstadt *(G-1119)*

B-Tea Beverage LLC.............E....... 201 512-8400
Fair Lawn *(G-3081)*

Beverage Works Nj Inc.............F....... 973 439-5700
Fairfield *(G-3149)*

Beverage Works Nj Inc.............B....... 732 938-7600
Wall Township *(G-11466)*

▲ Boston Tea Company LLC............G....... 201 440-3004
Hackensack *(G-3884)*

Bot LLC.............G....... 609 439-1537
Lawrenceville *(G-5251)*

Briars Usa.............G....... 732 821-7600
Monmouth Junction *(G-6332)*

Canada Dry Bottling Co NY LP............E....... 201 489-6600
Hackensack *(G-3893)*

Ccbcc Operations LLC.............D....... 609 324-7424
Bordentown *(G-594)*

Coca Cola Bottling Co Mid Amer..........F....... 732 398-4800
Monmouth Junction *(G-6337)*

Coca-Cola Refreshments USA Inc ......F....... 732 398-4800
Monmouth Junction *(G-6338)*

Coca-Cola Refreshments USA Inc ......B....... 201 635-6300
Carlstadt *(G-1147)*

◆ Continental Food & Bev Inc............F....... 973 815-1600
Clifton *(G-1589)*

Continntal Concession Sups Inc............E....... 516 629-4906
Union *(G-11166)*

Crescent Bottling Co Inc.............G....... 856 964-2268
Camden *(G-1056)*

▲ Crystal Beverage Corporation............C....... 201 991-2342
Kearny *(G-4869)*

Evereast Trading Inc.............E....... 201 944-6484
Fort Lee *(G-3553)*

Ferolito Vultaggio & Sons.............E....... 908 282-4480
Elizabeth *(G-2732)*

First Juice Inc.............G....... 973 895-3085
Randolph *(G-9277)*

Garden State Btlg Ltd Lblty Co............F....... 201 991-2342
Kearny *(G-4877)*

▲ Gerber Products Company............G....... 973 593-7500
Florham Park *(G-3504)*

▼ Global Beverage Corporation..........G....... 201 599-5925
Oradell *(G-7810)*

Hillside Bottling Corp.............G....... 908 353-6773
Hillside *(G-4412)*

Iceberg Coffee LLC.............G....... 908 675-6972
Freehold *(G-3660)*

◆ Increase Beverage Intl Inc............F....... 609 303-3117
Pennsauken *(G-8526)*

J & J Snack Foods Corp.............B....... 856 665-9533
Pennsauken *(G-8531)*

J & J Snack Foods Corp.............D....... 856 467-9552
Bridgeport *(G-767)*

▲ Jolt Company Inc.............E....... 201 288-0535
Teterboro *(G-10803)*

Keurig Dr Pepper Inc.............D....... 908 684-4400
Andover *(G-52)*

Keurig Dr Pepper Inc.............E....... 732 969-1600
Carteret *(G-1261)*

Keurig Dr Pepper Inc.............D....... 201 933-0070
Carlstadt *(G-1178)*

Keurig Dr Pepper Inc.............D....... 201 832-0695
Secaucus *(G-9899)*

Keurig Dr Pepper Inc.............D....... 732 388-5545
Avenel *(G-138)*

Liberty Coca-Cola Bevs LLC............D....... 215 427-4500
Moorestown *(G-6593)*

Liberty Coca-Cola Bevs LLC............E....... 856 988-3844
Marlton *(G-5982)*

▼ Maplewood Beverage Packers LLC .C....... 973 416-4582
Maplewood *(G-5923)*

Mococo Partners Corp.............G....... 862 204-3461
Paterson *(G-8341)*

Mosse Beverage Industries LLC............G....... 732 977-5558
Bayville *(G-258)*

▲ Nirwana Foods LLC.............F....... 201 659-2200
Jersey City *(G-4791)*

P-Americas LLC.............C....... 973 739-4900
Whippany *(G-12030)*

Pepsi.............G....... 732 238-1598
East Brunswick *(G-2171)*

Pepsi-Cola Metro Btlg Co Inc............G....... 201 955-2691
Kearny *(G-4905)*

Pepsi-Cola Metro Btlg Co Inc............D....... 732 922-9000
Ocean *(G-7734)*

Pepsi-Cola Metro Btlg Co Inc............B....... 732 424-3000
Piscataway *(G-8799)*

Pepsi-Cola Nat Brnd Bevs Ltd............B....... 856 665-6200
Pennsauken *(G-8558)*

Pepsico Inc.............B....... 856 661-4604
Pennsauken *(G-8559)*

Push Beverages LLC.............G....... 973 766-2663
Succasunna *(G-10626)*

▼ Relaxzen Inc.............F....... 732 936-1500
Shrewsbury *(G-10010)*

Shabazz Fruit Cola Company LLC ....G....... 973 230-4641
Newark *(G-7308)*

Shrem Consulting Ltd Lblty Co............G....... 917 371-0581
West Long Branch *(G-11846)*

Snapple Beverage Corp (del)..........D....... 201 933-0070
Carlstadt *(G-1219)*

▲ Snapple Distributors Inc............E....... 732 815-2800
Avenel *(G-151)*

◆ Supreme Manufacturing Co Inc............E....... 732 254-0087
East Brunswick *(G-2190)*

Tropical Bottling Corporation............F....... 786 636-6169
Oradell *(G-7814)*

Tuscan/Lehigh Dairies Inc............D....... 570 385-1884
Burlington *(G-992)*

▲ Unilever United States Inc............A....... 201 894-4000
Englewood Cliffs *(G-2986)*

◆ Union Beverage Packers LLC..........C....... 908 206-9111
Hillside *(G-4446)*

▲ V E N Inc.............C....... 973 786-7862
Andover *(G-55)*

Water On Time Bottled.............G....... 862 252-9798
East Orange *(G-2273)*

2087 Flavoring Extracts & Syrups

▼ 201 Food Packing Inc.............F....... 973 463-0777
East Hanover *(G-2198)*

◆ A A Sayia & Company Inc............G....... 201 659-1179
Hoboken *(G-4455)*

Adron Inc.............E....... 973 334-1600
Boonton *(G-551)*

Advanced Food Systems Inc............E....... 732 873-6776
Somerset *(G-10049)*

Akay USA LLC.............G....... 732 254-7177
Sayreville *(G-9812)*

Allen Flavors Inc.............C....... 908 561-5995
Edison *(G-2456)*

Allen Flavors Inc.............F....... 908 753-0544
South Plainfield *(G-10323)*

▲ Arnhem Inc.............G....... 908 709-4045
Westfield *(G-11921)*

Asbury Syrup Company Inc............F....... 732 774-5746
Ocean *(G-7716)*

Bluewater Inc.............F....... 973 532-1225
Millington *(G-6260)*

▲ Brand Aromatics Intl Inc............D....... 732 363-1204
Lakewood *(G-5088)*

Briars Usa.............G....... 732 821-7600
Monmouth Junction *(G-6332)*

Cargill Incorporated.............G....... 908 820-9800
Elizabeth *(G-2717)*

▲ Centrome Inc.............E....... 973 339-6242
Totowa *(G-10938)*

◆ Citroil Enterprises Inc............F....... 201 933-8405
Carlstadt *(G-1142)*

◆ Citromax Flavors Inc............G....... 201 933-8405
Carlstadt *(G-1143)*

Citromax Usa Inc.............G....... 201 933-8405
Carlstadt *(G-1144)*

Drink A Toast Company Inc............F....... 856 461-1000
Riverside *(G-9497)*

▲ Elan Inc.............D....... 973 344-8014
Newark *(G-7150)*

▲ Farbest-Tallman Foods Corp..........D....... 714 897-7199
Park Ridge *(G-7919)*

▲ Flavor & Fragrance Spc Inc............C....... 201 828-9400
Mahwah *(G-5773)*

Flavor and Fd Ingredients Inc............E....... 201 298-6964
Middlesex *(G-6166)*

▲ Flavor and Fd Ingredients Inc............E....... 732 805-0335
Somerset *(G-10102)*

Flavor Associates Inc.............F....... 973 238-9300
Hawthorne *(G-4236)*

Flavor Dynamics Inc.............E....... 888 271-8424
South Plainfield *(G-10366)*

Flavor Solutions Inc.............G....... 732 354-1931
Piscataway *(G-8767)*

Flavors of Origin Inc.............G....... 201 460-8306
Carlstadt *(G-1161)*

◆ Flavors of Origin Inc............E....... 732 499-9700
Avenel *(G-131)*

Givaudan Flavors Corporation..........D....... 609 409-6200
Cranbury *(G-1835)*

Givaudan Flavors Corporation..........C....... 973 386-9800
East Hanover *(G-2219)*

Givaudan Fragrances Corp..........C....... 973 386-9900
East Hanover *(G-2220)*

Global Colorants Inc.............G....... 973 751-2227
Old Bridge *(G-7780)*

Grow Company Inc.............E....... 201 941-8777
Ridgefield *(G-9363)*

Ifc Products Inc.............F....... 908 587-1221
Linden *(G-5384)*

▼ Ifc Solutions Inc.............G....... 908 862-8810
Linden *(G-5385)*

Interbahm International Inc............E....... 732 499-9700
Avenel *(G-135)*

Interntnal Flvors Frgrnces Inc..........D....... 732 329-4600
Dayton *(G-1972)*

J & J Snack Foods Corp.............B....... 856 665-9533
Pennsauken *(G-8531)*

J & J Snack Foods Corp.............D....... 856 467-9552
Bridgeport *(G-767)*

◆ Jk Ingredients Inc.............D....... 973 340-8700
Paterson *(G-8304)*

Kerry Flavor Systems Us LLC ....C....... 513 771-4682
Clark *(G-1504)*
Kerry Inc ....D....... 908 237-1595
Flemington *(G-3453)*
Limpert Brothers Inc ....E....... 856 691-1353
Vineland *(G-11380)*
▼ **Malt Products Corporation** ....E....... 201 845-4420
Saddle Brook *(G-9772)*
Malt Products Corporation ....E....... 201 845-9106
Saddle Brook *(G-9773)*
◆ **Mastertaste Inc** ....C....... 732 882-0202
Clark *(G-1508)*
Mastertaste Inc ....F....... 201 373-1111
Teterboro *(G-10805)*
◆ **Medallion International Inc** ....F....... 973 616-3401
Pompton Plains *(G-8962)*
▼ **Myx Beverage LLC** ....F....... 585 978-3542
Secaucus *(G-9906)*
▲ **Natural Flavors Inc** ....E....... 973 589-1230
Newark *(G-7248)*
Novel Ingredient Services LLC ....G....... 973 808-5900
East Hanover *(G-2238)*
◆ **Penta International Corp** ....D....... 973 740-2300
Livingston *(G-5554)*
▲ **Premier Specialties Inc** ....F....... 732 469-6615
Middlesex *(G-6190)*
Prime Ingredients Inc ....G....... 201 791-6655
Saddle Brook *(G-9784)*
R C Fine Foods Inc ....D....... 908 359-5500
Hillsborough *(G-4366)*
▼ **Reeves Enterprises Inc** ....G....... 800 883-6752
New Providence *(G-7052)*
▲ **Robertet Inc** ....E....... 201 337-7100
Budd Lake *(G-939)*
Robertet Flavors Inc ....F....... 732 271-1804
Piscataway *(G-8806)*
Sapphire Flvors Fragrances LLC ....F....... 973 200-8849
Fairfield *(G-3300)*
▲ **Savoury Systems Intl Inc** ....F....... 908 526-2524
Branchburg *(G-702)*
Sea Breeze Fruit Flavors Inc ....D....... 973 334-7777
Towaco *(G-11003)*
Sensient Technologies Corp ....E....... 908 757-4500
South Plainfield *(G-10435)*
▲ **Sentrex Ingredients LLC** ....G....... 908 862-4440
Linden *(G-5440)*
▲ **Sodastream USA Inc** ....D....... 856 755-3400
Mount Laurel *(G-6843)*
◆ **Solvay USA Inc** ....B....... 609 860-4000
Princeton *(G-9122)*
Solvay USA Inc ....C....... 732 297-0100
North Brunswick *(G-7538)*
Takasago Intl Corp USA ....E....... 201 727-4200
Teterboro *(G-10814)*
Vineland Syrup Inc ....E....... 856 691-5772
Vineland *(G-11417)*
Whittle & Mutch Inc ....F....... 856 235-1165
Mount Laurel *(G-6846)*
Wild Flavors Inc ....F....... 908 820-9800
Elizabeth *(G-2782)*

2091 Fish & Seafoods, Canned & Cured

Bumble Bee Foods LLC ....C....... 609 884-0440
Cape May *(G-1091)*
Cape May Foods LLC ....E....... 856 825-8111
Millville *(G-6292)*
▲ **Gerber Products Company** ....C....... 973 593-7500
Florham Park *(G-3504)*
Hillard Bloom Packing Co Inc ....G....... 856 785-0120
Port Norris *(G-8980)*
▲ **Lamonica Fine Foods LLC** ....C....... 856 776-2126
Millville *(G-6311)*
◆ **Manischewitz Company** ....D....... 201 553-1100
Newark *(G-7235)*
Point Lobster Company Inc ....F....... 732 892-1718
Point Pleasant Beach *(G-8926)*
Sea Harvest Inc ....E....... 609 884-3000
Cape May *(G-1105)*
Sushi House Inc ....E....... 201 482-0609
Palisades Park *(G-7844)*

2092 Fish & Seafoods, Fresh & Frozen

Azuma Foods Intl Inc USA ....F....... 201 372-1112
East Rutherford *(G-2282)*
Bivalve Packing Inc ....G....... 856 785-0270
Port Norris *(G-8979)*
Black Sea Fisheries ....G....... 973 553-1580
Fort Lee *(G-3548)*
Certified Clam Corp ....F....... 732 872-6650
Highlands *(G-4307)*
▲ **CHR International Inc** ....G....... 201 262-8186
Oradell *(G-7806)*
◆ **Delight Foods USA LLC** ....F....... 201 369-1199
Jersey City *(G-4738)*
▲ **Golden Tropics Ltd** ....E....... 973 484-0202
Newark *(G-7176)*
Hillard Bloom Packing Co Inc ....G....... 856 785-0120
Port Norris *(G-8980)*
J & R Foods Inc ....F....... 732 229-4020
Long Branch *(G-5625)*
▲ **Lamonica Fine Foods LLC** ....C....... 856 776-2126
Millville *(G-6311)*
▲ **Lm Foods LLC** ....D....... 732 855-9500
Carteret *(G-1262)*
◆ **Lunds Fisheries Inc** ....D....... 609 884-7600
Cape May *(G-1102)*
New Jrsey Sfood Mktg Group LLC ....G....... 609 296-7026
Egg Harbor City *(G-2668)*
Peak Finance Holdings LLC ....G....... 856 969-7100
Cherry Hill *(G-1411)*
▲ **Pinnacle Foods Finance LLC** ....C....... 973 541-6620
Parsippany *(G-8063)*
◆ **Pinnacle Foods Group LLC** ....D....... 856 969-8238
Parsippany *(G-8064)*
◆ **Ruggiero Sea Food Inc** ....D....... 973 589-0524
Newark *(G-7294)*
Ruggiero Sea Food Inc ....G....... 973 589-0524
Newark *(G-7295)*
Sushi House Inc ....E....... 201 482-0609
Palisades Park *(G-7844)*

2095 Coffee

26 Flavors LLC ....G....... 855 662-7299
Newark *(G-7063)*
◆ **Adagio Teas Inc** ....G....... 973 253-7400
Elmwood Park *(G-2801)*
Arias Mountain-Coffee LLC ....G....... 973 927-9595
Dover *(G-2077)*
▼ **Coffee Associates Inc** ....E....... 201 945-1060
Edgewater *(G-2436)*
Coffee Company LLC ....G....... 609 399-5533
Ocean City *(G-7750)*
Coffee Company LLC ....G....... 609 398-2326
Ocean City *(G-7751)*
▲ **Corim International Coffee Imp** ....D....... 800 942-4201
Brick *(G-739)*
Counting Sheep Coffee Inc ....G....... 973 589-4104
Newark *(G-7128)*
Eight OClock Coffee Company ....D....... 201 571-9214
Montvale *(G-6455)*
◆ **European Coffee Classics Inc** ....E....... 856 428-7202
Cherry Hill *(G-1363)*
Greene Bros Spclty Cof Rasters ....F....... 908 979-0022
Hackettstown *(G-4009)*
Longview Coffee Co NJ Inc ....E....... 908 788-4186
Frenchtown *(G-3703)*
▲ **Massimo Zanetti Beverage USA** ....F....... 201 440-1700
Moonachie *(G-6530)*
Melitta Usa Inc ....E....... 856 428-7202
Cherry Hill *(G-1399)*
▲ **Mire Enterprises LLC** ....G....... 732 882-1010
Linden *(G-5410)*
Nestle Usa Inc ....C....... 732 462-1300
Freehold *(G-3673)*
Orens Daily Roast Inc ....F....... 201 432-2008
Jersey City *(G-4795)*
Pan American Coffee Company ....E....... 201 963-2329
Hoboken *(G-4489)*
Socafe LLC ....F....... 973 589-4104
Newark *(G-7318)*
Two Rivers Coffee LLC ....G....... 908 205-0018
South Plainfield *(G-10443)*
United Mijovi Amer Ltd Lblty ....F....... 732 718-1001
New Brunswick *(G-7008)*
▲ **World of Coffee Inc** ....G....... 908 647-1218
Stirling *(G-10609)*

2096 Potato Chips & Similar Prdts

Auntie Annes Hmde Sft Prtzls ....F....... 856 772-3737
Voorhees *(G-11422)*
Auntie Annes Soft Pretzels ....E....... 856 722-0433
Moorestown *(G-6561)*
◆ **Birds Eye Foods Inc** ....C....... 585 383-1850
Cherry Hill *(G-1350)*
Campbell Soup Company ....A....... 856 342-4800
Camden *(G-1049)*
Continntal Concession Sups Inc ....E....... 516 629-4906
Union *(G-11166)*
▲ **Golden Fluff Inc** ....F....... 732 367-5448
Lakewood *(G-5130)*
Grab Em Snacks Ltd Lblty Co ....G....... 908 333-3229
Hillsborough *(G-4337)*
Hain Celestial Group Inc ....E....... 201 935-4500
Moonachie *(G-6520)*
Herr Foods Incorporated ....E....... 732 356-1295
Somerset *(G-10107)*
Herr Foods Incorporated ....E....... 732 905-1600
Lakewood *(G-5134)*
Ktb Acquisition Sub Inc ....G....... 973 240-0200
Fairfield *(G-3244)*
Mayab Happy Tacos Inc ....E....... 732 293-0400
Perth Amboy *(G-8622)*
Pirate Brands LLC ....F....... 973 401-6500
Parsippany *(G-8067)*
Planet Popcorn LLC ....G....... 732 294-8680
Freehold *(G-3677)*
Rajbhog Foods(nj) Inc ....C....... 551 222-4700
Jersey City *(G-4814)*
▲ **Snack Innovations Inc** ....E....... 718 509-9366
Piscataway *(G-8812)*
Wise Foods Inc ....G....... 201 440-2876
Moonachie *(G-6552)*
Zestos Foods LLC ....G....... 888 407-5852
Teaneck *(G-10779)*
Ziggy Snack Foods LLC ....E....... 917 662-6038
Clifton *(G-1747)*

2097 Ice

Arctic Glacier USA Inc ....F....... 973 771-3391
Montclair *(G-6407)*
Artic Ice Manufacturing Co ....G....... 973 772-7000
Garfield *(G-3718)*
Cold Spring Ice Inc ....G....... 609 884-3405
Cape May *(G-1096)*
Sea Isle Ice Co Inc ....E....... 609 263-8748
Sea Isle City *(G-9864)*
United City Ice Cube Co Inc ....G....... 201 945-8387
Ridgefield *(G-9391)*
◆ **United States Cold Storage Inc** ....B....... 856 354-8181
Camden *(G-1088)*

2098 Macaroni, Spaghetti & Noodles

◆ **A Zeregas Sons Inc** ....C....... 201 797-1400
Fair Lawn *(G-3072)*
Casa Di Bertacchi Corporation ....C....... 856 696-5600
Vineland *(G-11334)*
Gardellas Rvioli Itln Deli LLC ....F....... 856 697-3509
Vineland *(G-11359)*
L E Rosellis Food Specialties ....F....... 609 654-4816
Medford *(G-6074)*
Noodle Fan ....G....... 732 446-2820
Monroe Township *(G-6385)*
Noodle Gogo ....G....... 908 222-8898
South Plainfield *(G-10414)*
Porfirio Foods Inc ....G....... 609 393-4116
Trenton *(G-11100)*
Raffettos Corp ....F....... 201 372-1222
Moonachie *(G-6538)*
Severino Pasta Mfg Co Inc ....E....... 856 854-3716
Collingswood *(G-1773)*
◆ **Silver Palate Kitchens Inc** ....E....... 201 568-0110
Cresskill *(G-1948)*
Star Ravioli Manufacturing Co ....F....... 201 933-6427
Moonachie *(G-6543)*
▲ **Sun Noodle New Jersey LLC** ....G....... 201 530-1100
Carlstadt *(G-1225)*
◆ **Unilever Bestfoods North Amer** ....F....... 201 894-4000
Englewood Cliffs *(G-2985)*
▲ **Vitamia Pasta Boy Inc** ....F....... 973 546-1140
Lodi *(G-5608)*

2099 Food Preparations, NEC

35 Food Corp ....G....... 732 442-1640
Woodbridge *(G-12144)*
▲ **A Cheerful Giver Inc** ....F....... 856 358-4438
Elmer *(G-2787)*
◆ **ACC Foods Ltd Liability Co** ....C....... 856 848-8877
West Deptford *(G-11813)*
Akila Holdings Inc ....G....... 609 454-5034
Princeton *(G-8999)*
◆ **Allied Old English Inc** ....E....... 732 636-2060
Port Reading *(G-8986)*
▲ **American Custom Drying Co** ....E....... 609 387-3933
Burlington *(G-955)*
American Food & Bev Inds LLC ....D....... 347 241-9827
Orange *(G-7816)*
Applied Nutrition Corp ....E....... 973 734-0023
Cedar Knolls *(G-1307)*
▲ **Arome America LLC** ....G....... 908 806-7003
Neshanic Station *(G-6938)*

B&G Foods Inc ....B...... 973 401-6500
Parsippany (G-7956)
B&G Foods Inc ....B...... 973 401-6500
Parsippany (G-7957)
Barry Callebaut USA LLC ....E...... 856 663-2260
Pennsauken (G-8483)
Boulevard Lunch Service Inc..........F...... 732 381-5772
Clark (G-1498)
▼ Bylada Foods LLC ....G...... 201 933-7474
Moonachie (G-6510)
Caravan Ingredients Inc ....E...... 201 672-0510
East Rutherford (G-2292)
CJ TMI Manufacturing Amer LLC ....C...... 609 669-0100
Robbinsville (G-9513)
▲ Colonna Brothers Inc ....D...... 800 626-8384
North Bergen (G-7443)
▲ Contes Pasta Company Inc ....E...... 856 697-3400
Vineland (G-11341)
◆ Cosmopolitan Food Group Inc ......G...... 908 998-1818
Hoboken (G-4466)
▲ Crispy Green Inc ....F...... 973 679-4515
Fairfield (G-3169)
Croces Pasta Poducts ....G...... 856 795-6000
Cherry Hill (G-1358)
Daves Salad House Inc ....G...... 908 965-0773
Elizabeth (G-2722)
Deluxe Foods International ....G...... 845 825-3442
Paterson (G-8248)
Deluxe Gourmet Spc Ltd Lblty ....F...... 732 485-7519
Old Bridge (G-7776)
▲ Deosen Usa Inc ....G...... 908 382-6518
Piscataway (G-8755)
Dipietro Foods Inc ....G...... 973 762-4077
Maplewood (G-5918)
DJeet ....G...... 732 224-8887
Shrewsbury (G-9997)
DOrazio Foods Inc ....D...... 856 931-1900
Bellmawr (G-337)
Dulce A Dessert Bar LLC ....G...... 908 461-2418
Matawan (G-6018)
▲ Dyna-Sea Group Inc ....G...... 201 928-0133
Teaneck (G-10751)
◆ Eatem Corporation ....D...... 856 692-1663
Vineland (G-11355)
▼ Edsall Group USA Inc ....D...... 908 874-6953
Hillsborough (G-4330)
▲ Empire Specialty Foods Inc ....G...... 646 773-2630
East Brunswick (G-2153)
▲ Empirical Group LLC ....E...... 201 571-0300
Montvale (G-6456)
▲ European Amrcn Foods Group Inc ..E...... 201 436-6106
Bayonne (G-224)
European Amrcn Foods Group Inc ......B...... 201 583-1101
Secaucus (G-9880)
◆ Excellentia Flavours LLC ....F...... 732 749-9840
Fairfield (G-3190)
▲ F&S Produce Company Inc ....E...... 856 453-0316
Rosenhayn (G-9707)
▲ Farbest-Tallman Foods Corp ....D...... 714 897-7199
Park Ridge (G-7919)
▲ Firma Foods USA Corporation ....G...... 201 794-1181
Englewood (G-2896)
Flavour Tee International LLC ....G...... 201 440-3281
Little Ferry (G-5505)
◆ Food Ingredient Solutions LLC ......G...... 201 440-4377
Teterboro (G-10796)
Foodtek Inc ....F...... 973 257-4000
Whippany (G-12020)
◆ Gel Spice Co Inc ....B...... 201 339-0700
Bayonne (G-227)
Gel Spice Co LLC ....C...... 201 339-0700
Bayonne (G-228)
▲ Global Ingredients Inc ....G...... 973 278-6677
Paterson (G-8278)
▲ Golden Tropics Ltd ....G...... 973 484-0202
Newark (G-7176)
▼ Goldstein & Burton Inc ....D...... 201 440-0065
Oakland (G-7690)
◆ Good Earth Teas Inc ....G...... 831 423-7913
Montvale (G-6457)
▲ Gourmet Kitchen LLC ....C...... 732 775-5222
Neptune (G-6916)
Green Labs LLC ....G...... 862 220-4845
Newark (G-7178)
▲ GS Fresh Beets Incorporated ....F...... 856 692-1740
Vineland (G-11366)
Harris Freeman & Co Inc ....D...... 856 787-9026
Moorestown (G-6583)
▲ Hojiblanca USA Inc ....G...... 201 384-3007
Dumont (G-2118)

Iam International Inc ....G...... 908 713-9651
Lebanon (G-5289)
International Chefs Inc ....F...... 917 645-2900
Saddle Brook (G-9769)
▲ International Coconut Corp ....F...... 908 289-1555
Elizabeth (G-2748)
International Olive Oil Inc ....G...... 732 612-3338
Manasquan (G-5871)
Interntnal Ingrdent Sltons Inc ....E...... 856 778-6623
Mount Laurel (G-6806)
J & J Snack Foods Corp ....C...... 856 933-3597
Bellmawr (G-344)
◆ Jk Ingredients Inc ....D...... 973 340-8700
Paterson (G-8304)
▲ Joyce Food LLC ....G...... 973 491-9696
Newark (G-7209)
◆ Kalustyan Corporation ....D...... 908 688-0853
Union (G-11200)
Knight Foods LLC ....G...... 973 385-1230
Cedar Grove (G-1287)
L and Ds Sapore Ravioli Cheese ....F...... 732 563-9190
Middlesex (G-6175)
L E Rosellis Food Specialties ....F...... 609 654-4816
Medford (G-6074)
La Casa De Tortilla ....G...... 732 398-0660
Somerset (G-10120)
▲ La Pace Imports Inc ....F...... 973 895-5420
Morristown (G-6720)
Le Bon Magot Ltd Liability Co ....G...... 609 895-0211
Lawrenceville (G-5261)
▲ Leng-Dor USA Inc ....F...... 732 254-4300
Cranbury (G-1854)
Longview Coffee Co NJ Inc ....E...... 908 788-4186
Frenchtown (G-3703)
Lrk Inc ....F...... 609 924-6881
Princeton (G-9068)
Maverick Caterers LLC ....E...... 718 433-3776
Hackensack (G-3944)
MCI Service Parts ....G...... 732 967-9081
East Brunswick (G-2166)
▲ Mediterranean Chef Inc ....F...... 855 628-0903
Lincoln Park (G-5329)
◆ Megas Yeeros LLC ....E...... 212 777-6342
Lyndhurst (G-5692)
▲ Melissa Spice Trading Corp ....F...... 862 262-7773
Glen Rock (G-3826)
▲ Metropolitan Foods Inc ....C...... 973 672-9400
Clifton (G-1673)
▲ Mincing Trading Corporation ....E...... 732 355-9944
Dayton (G-1980)
Missa Bay Citrus Company ....F...... 856 241-0900
Swedesboro (G-10711)
▲ Missa Bay LLC ....B...... 856 241-0900
Swedesboro (G-10712)
Muirhead Ringoes NJ Inc ....G...... 609 695-7803
Trenton (G-11082)
▲ Mushroom Wisdom Inc ....G...... 973 470-0010
East Rutherford (G-2312)
▲ National Lecithim Inc ....G...... 973 940-8920
Newton (G-7398)
Nestle Usa Inc ....C...... 732 462-1300
Freehold (G-3673)
◆ Nexira Inc ....F...... 908 704-7480
Somerville (G-10222)
▲ Omega Packaging Corp ....D...... 973 890-9505
Totowa (G-10959)
Organica Aromatics Corp ....G...... 609 443-3333
East Windsor (G-2364)
▲ Palsgaard Incorporated ....F...... 973 998-7951
Morris Plains (G-6677)
Panos Holding Company ....G...... 201 843-8900
Rochelle Park (G-9533)
◆ Papa Johns New Jersey ....D...... 609 395-0045
Cranbury (G-1867)
Pastarama Distributors Inc ....G...... 609 847-0378
Sewell (G-9965)
▲ Paulaur Corporation ....D...... 609 395-8844
Cranbury (G-1868)
▲ PDM Packaging Inc ....F...... 201 864-1115
North Bergen (G-7474)
Peak Finance Holdings LLC ....G...... 856 969-7100
Cherry Hill (G-1411)
Pennant Ingredients Inc ....G...... 856 428-4300
Cherry Hill (G-1412)
Perfecto Foods LLC ....G...... 201 889-5328
Kearny (G-4907)
Pharmachem Laboratories Inc ....E...... 973 256-1340
Totowa (G-10962)
Pharmachem Laboratories Inc ....E...... 201 343-3611
South Hackensack (G-10288)

◆ Pharmachem Laboratories LLC ......D...... 201 246-1000
Kearny (G-4908)
▲ Phildesco Inc ....G...... 732 937-6560
Somerville (G-10223)
▲ Pinnacle Foods Finance LLC ....C...... 973 541-6620
Parsippany (G-8063)
◆ Pinnacle Foods Group LLC ....D...... 856 969-8238
Parsippany (G-8064)
▲ Poly-Gel LLC ....E...... 973 884-3300
Whippany (G-12034)
Prince Chikovani Inc ....G...... 347 622-2789
Bayonne (G-242)
Princeton Quadrangle Club ....G...... 609 258-0376
Princeton (G-914)
Procter & Gamble Mfg Co ....D...... 732 602-4500
Avenel (G-148)
Puebla Foods Inc ....E...... 973 246-6311
Passaic (G-8172)
Puebla Foods Inc ....G...... 973 473-4494
Passaic (G-8173)
Puratos Corporation ....E...... 856 266-1736
Pennsauken (G-8568)
◆ Puratos Corporation ....C...... 856 428-4300
Cherry Hill (G-1417)
Pyramid Food Services Corp ....G...... 973 900-6513
Newark (G-7280)
Quality Ingredients Corp ....F...... 908 879-2227
Chester (G-1439)
R C Fine Foods Inc ....D...... 908 359-5500
Hillsborough (G-4366)
Ready Pac Fods - Swedesboro NJ .....F...... 609 360-0953
Swedesboro (G-10726)
Ready Pac Produce Inc ....D...... 609 499-1900
Florence (G-3480)
▲ Regina Wine Co ....G...... 973 589-6911
Newark (G-7288)
Rex Wine Vinegar Company ....G...... 973 589-6911
Newark (G-7289)
Saker Shoprites Inc ....F...... 908 925-1550
Linden (G-5437)
Salad Chef Inc ....F...... 609 641-5455
Pleasantville (G-8913)
▲ Sam Hak Food Corp ....G...... 908 688-4993
Hillside (G-4439)
▲ Sebastian & King Ltd Lblty Co .....F...... 908 874-6953
Hillsborough (G-4371)
Sensient Technologies Corp ....E...... 908 757-4500
South Plainfield (G-10435)
Sheris Cookery Inc ....F...... 973 589-2060
Newark (G-7311)
◆ Silver Palate Kitchens Inc ....E...... 201 568-0110
Cresskill (G-1948)
▲ Spice Chain Corporation ....C...... 732 518-1100
East Brunswick (G-2185)
Sultan Foods Inc ....F...... 908 874-6953
Hillsborough (G-4374)
Sun Basket Inc ....G...... 408 669-4418
Westampton (G-11918)
Sunrise Snacks Rockland Inc ....F...... 845 352-2676
Paterson (G-8388)
Surfside Foods LLC ....G...... 856 785-2115
Port Norris (G-8983)
▲ Suruchi Foods LLC ....G...... 201 432-2201
Jersey City (G-4836)
Tamaras European American Deli ....G...... 973 875-5461
Sussex (G-10677)
▲ Taste It Presents Inc ....D...... 908 241-9191
Kenilworth (G-4999)
Taste Italy Manufacturing LLC ....G...... 856 223-0707
Egg Harbor City (G-2671)
◆ Taylor Farms New Jersey Inc ....E...... 856 241-0097
Swedesboro (G-10732)
▲ Tetley USA Inc ....E...... 800 728-0084
New Providence (G-7058)
Tin Man Snacks LLC ....G...... 732 329-9100
Dayton (G-1991)
▼ Tofutti Brands Inc ....G...... 908 272-2400
Cranford (G-1928)
◆ Unilever Bestfoods North Amer ....F...... 201 894-4000
Englewood Cliffs (G-2985)
◆ United Natural Trading Co ....D...... 732 650-9905
Edison (G-2640)
Venetian Corp ....F...... 973 546-2250
Garfield (G-3771)
Vine Hill Farm ....G...... 973 383-0100
Newton (G-7411)
▲ Vitamia Pasta Boy Inc ....F...... 973 546-1140
Lodi (G-5608)
Zinas Salads Inc ....E...... 973 428-0660
East Hanover (G-2252)

21 TOBACCO PRODUCTS

2111 Cigarettes

Philip Morris USA Inc ....F 908 781-6400
Bedminster *(G-282)*

Sherman Group Holdings ....G 201 735-9000
Fort Lee *(G-3582)*

◆ **Sherman Nat Inc** ....E 201 735-9000
Englewood *(G-2930)*

Shermans 1400 Brdway N Y C Ltd ...D 201 735-9000
Englewood *(G-2931)*

Urban State ....G 646 836-4311
Hillside *(G-4449)*

2121 Cigars

▲ **Csonka Worldwide** ....E 609 514-2766
Plainsboro *(G-8879)*

Itg Brands LLC ....G 973 386-9087
East Hanover *(G-2225)*

◆ **Sherman Nat Inc** ....E 201 735-9000
Englewood *(G-2930)*

2141 Tobacco Stemming & Redrying

Schweitzer-Mauduit Intl Inc ....B 732 723-6100
Spotswood *(G-10530)*

22 TEXTILE MILL PRODUCTS

2211 Cotton, Woven Fabric

▲ **Absecon Mills Inc** ....C 609 965-5373
Cologne *(G-1775)*

▲ **Allison Corp** ....G 973 992-3800
Livingston *(G-5523)*

◆ **Amt Stitch Inc** ....G 732 376-0009
Perth Amboy *(G-8607)*

▲ **Atlantic Mills Inc** ....D 973 344-2001
Passaic *(G-8126)*

Aurora Apparel Inc ....G 201 646-4590
Hackensack *(G-3876)*

Avail Inc ....G 732 560-2222
Bridgewater *(G-817)*

Bai Lar Interior Services Inc ....G 732 738-0350
Fords *(G-3527)*

Blue Monkey Inc ....G 201 805-0055
Saddle Brook *(G-9756)*

▲ **Canvas 4 Life Inc** ....G 973 276-3200
Pine Brook *(G-8690)*

Chic Bebe Inc ....G 201 941-5414
Tenafly *(G-10783)*

▲ **Derma Sciences Inc** ....C 609 514-4744
Plainsboro *(G-8880)*

Designs By James ....G 856 692-1316
Vineland *(G-11352)*

Easy Undies LLC ....G 201 715-4909
Springfield *(G-10552)*

▲ **Fh Group International Inc** ....E 201 210-2426
Secaucus *(G-9883)*

◆ **Franco Manufacturing Co Inc** ......C 732 494-0500
Metuchen *(G-6104)*

Gene Mignola Inc ....G 732 775-9291
Asbury Park *(G-78)*

▼ **Green Distribution LLC** ....D 201 293-4381
Secaucus *(G-9893)*

▲ **Hanover Direct Inc** ....B 201 863-7300
Weehawken *(G-11695)*

Homespun Global LLC ....G 917 674-9684
Sayreville *(G-9823)*

Integrity Medical Devices Del ......D 609 567-8175
Hammonton *(G-4139)*

▲ **Jacquard Fabrics Inc** ....E 732 905-4545
Lakewood *(G-5138)*

Jay Franco & Sons Inc ....D 732 721-0022
Sayreville *(G-9825)*

Leggs Hns Bli Plytx Fctry Outl ......G 908 289-7262
Elizabeth *(G-2751)*

▼ **Marcotex International Inc** ....E 201 991-8200
Kearny *(G-4898)*

▲ **Material Imports** ....G 201 229-1180
Moonachie *(G-6531)*

▲ **Meadowgate Farm Alpacas** ....G 609 219-0529
Lawrenceville *(G-5262)*

Medical Scrubs Collectn NJ LLC ....G 732 719-8600
Lakewood *(G-5158)*

Metro Mills Inc ....E 973 942-6034
Paterson *(G-8337)*

Musings Press Ltd Liability Co ......F 347 210-8820
Union City *(G-11259)*

Picture Knits Inc ....E 973 340-3131
Clifton *(G-1696)*

Proclean Services Inc ....F 973 857-5408
Verona *(G-11309)*

Pueblo Latino Laundry LLC ....G 201 864-1666
Union City *(G-11263)*

Quantum Vector Corp ....G 201 870-1782
Westwood *(G-11967)*

Refuel Inc ....G 917 645-2974
South Hackensack *(G-10292)*

Sensible Collection Inc ....E 201 831-1063
Hackensack *(G-3972)*

▲ **Stanbee Company Inc** ....E 201 933-9666
Carlstadt *(G-1222)*

▲ **Stanek Netting Co Inc** ....G 973 680-1616
Bloomfield *(G-531)*

Teefx Screen Printing LLC ....G 973 942-6800
Haledon *(G-4086)*

▲ **Tex Gul Inc** ....G 973 857-3200
Cedar Grove *(G-1301)*

Trimtex Company Inc ....D 201 945-2151
Englewood Cliffs *(G-2984)*

Umbrellas Unlimited ....G 201 476-1011
River Vale *(G-9472)*

Vacs Bandage Company Inc ....F 973 345-3355
Paterson *(G-8407)*

Westchester Denim Brothers Inc ....G 203 260-1629
Ridgefield *(G-9394)*

2221 Silk & Man-Made Fiber

▲ **Absecon Mills Inc** ....C 609 965-5373
Cologne *(G-1775)*

▲ **Alex Silk Co Inc** ....G 973 427-0499
Hawthorne *(G-4217)*

▲ **Allison Corp** ....G 973 992-3800
Livingston *(G-5523)*

Chic Bebe Inc ....G 201 941-5414
Tenafly *(G-10783)*

Cypra Wallcoverings Inc ....G 732 525-0340
South Amboy *(G-10237)*

▲ **Fablok Mills Inc** ....E 908 464-1950
New Providence *(G-7034)*

▲ **Hanover Direct Inc** ....B 201 863-7300
Weehawken *(G-11695)*

Invitation Studio ....G 732 740-5558
Morganville *(G-6645)*

▲ **Kt America Corp** ....E 609 655-5333
Cranbury *(G-1850)*

◆ **L&M Architectural Graphics Inc** ....F 973 575-7665
Fairfield *(G-3245)*

New Community Corp ....E 973 643-5300
Newark *(G-7249)*

Nyltite Corp of America ....F 908 561-1300
South Plainfield *(G-10417)*

▲ **Nyp Corp (frmr Ny-Pters Corp)** ....D 908 351-6550
Elizabeth *(G-2761)*

Paterson Bleachery Inc ....F 973 684-1034
Paterson *(G-8361)*

Picture Knits Inc ....E 973 340-3131
Clifton *(G-1696)*

▼ **Satex Fabrics Ltd** ....G 212 221-5555
North Bergen *(G-7484)*

◆ **Star Binding & Trimming LLC** ......E 201 864-2220
Lodi *(G-5601)*

Tex-Net Inc ....E 609 499-9111
Florence *(G-3481)*

Thomas Clark Fiberglass LLC ......G 609 492-9257
Barnegat *(G-167)*

Ultraflex Systems Florida Inc ......E 973 627-8608
Randolph *(G-9303)*

United Eqp Fabricators LLC ....G 973 242-2737
Newark *(G-7353)*

▲ **Wearbest Sil-Tex Mills Ltd** ....G 973 340-8844
Garfield *(G-3772)*

2231 Wool, Woven Fabric

Alma Park Alpacas ....G 732 620-1052
Jobstown *(G-4853)*

▲ **C3 Concepts Inc** ....E 212 840-1116
North Bergen *(G-7437)*

Colton Industries Inc ....G 908 277-2040
Summit *(G-10640)*

▲ **Dollfus Mieg Company Inc** ....C 732 662-1005
Edison *(G-2502)*

French Creek Sheep & Wool Co ....E 610 286-5700
Ventnor City *(G-11291)*

Manner Textile Processing Inc ......D 973 942-8718
North Haledon *(G-7550)*

Paterson Bleachery Inc ....F 973 684-1034
Paterson *(G-8361)*

Soh LLC ....E 646 943-4066
Jersey City *(G-4830)*

2241 Fabric Mills, Cotton, Wool, Silk & Man-Made

▲ **Allied Bias Products Corp** ....F 201 432-6050
Jersey City *(G-4702)*

Allied Elastic Braid Inc ....E 201 941-8875
Saddle Brook *(G-9751)*

▲ **Avitex Co Inc** ....E 973 242-2410
Newark *(G-7101)*

Avitex Co Inc ....G 973 242-2410
Newark *(G-7102)*

Beau Label ....D 973 318-7800
Hillside *(G-4396)*

Brian Lenhart Interactive LLC .....G 610 737-5314
Berkeley Heights *(G-402)*

▲ **Carolace Embroidery Co Inc** ......D 201 945-2151
Ridgefield *(G-9354)*

▲ **Carson & Gebel Ribbon Co LLC** ...E 973 627-4200
Rockaway *(G-9556)*

▲ **Cottage Lace and Ribbon Co Inc** ...G 732 776-9353
Neptune *(G-6905)*

Cranial Technologies Inc ....E 201 265-3993
Paramus *(G-7863)*

Denali Company LLC ....E 732 219-7771
Red Bank *(G-9326)*

▲ **Hamilton Embroidery Co Inc** ....F 201 867-4084
Union City *(G-11247)*

▲ **Jrm Industries Inc** ....D 973 779-9340
Passaic *(G-8152)*

Klein Ribbon Corp ....E 973 684-4671
Paterson *(G-8310)*

Marlene Trimmings LLC ....E 201 926-3108
North Bergen *(G-7464)*

▲ **Otex Specialty Narrow Fabrics** .....G 908 879-3636
Bernardsville *(G-452)*

Paterson Bleachery Inc ....F 973 684-1034
Paterson *(G-8361)*

◆ **R Tape Corporation** ....E 908 753-5570
South Plainfield *(G-10431)*

▲ **Reddaway Manufacturing Co Inc** ...F 973 589-1410
Newark *(G-7287)*

▲ **Snapco Manufacturing Corp** ....E 973 282-0300
Hillside *(G-4441)*

◆ **Star Binding & Trimming LLC** ......E 201 864-2220
Lodi *(G-5601)*

Sullivan-Carson Inc ....G 856 566-1400
Voorhees *(G-11438)*

▲ **Textol Systems Inc** ....E 800 624-8746
Carlstadt *(G-1228)*

Trimtex Company Inc ....D 201 945-2151
Englewood Cliffs *(G-2984)*

Wingold Embroidery LLC ....G 732 845-9802
Freehold *(G-3693)*

2251 Hosiery, Women's Full & Knee Length

▲ **Great Socks LLC** ....E 856 964-9700
Pennsauken *(G-8518)*

Swisstex Company ....E 201 861-8000
West New York *(G-11882)*

2252 Hosiery, Except Women's

▲ **Great Socks LLC** ....E 856 964-9700
Pennsauken *(G-8518)*

J T Murdoch Shoes ....G 973 748-6484
Bloomfield *(G-514)*

Living Fashions Llc ....F 732 626-5200
Sayreville *(G-9830)*

Sock Company Inc ....E 201 307-0675
Westwood *(G-11972)*

Socks 47 Ltd Liability Company .....G 201 866-2222
Union City *(G-11267)*

2253 Knit Outerwear Mills

3forty Group Inc ....F 973 773-1806
Passaic *(G-8121)*

Alan Paul Accessories Inc ....G 609 924-4022
Princeton *(G-9001)*

◆ **Artex Knitting Mills Inc** ....D 856 456-2800
Westville *(G-11936)*

Chiha Inc ....F 201 861-2000
North Bergen *(G-7440)*

D & G LLC ....G 201 289-5750
Hackensack *(G-3902)*

D L V Lounge Inc ....G 973 783-6988
Montclair *(G-6410)*

▲ **Elegant Headwear Co Inc** ....C 908 558-1200
Elizabeth *(G-2728)*

▲ **Fairfield Textiles Corp** ....D 973 227-1656
Paterson *(G-8270)*

Fleck Knitwear Co Inc ....E 908 754-8888
Plainfield (G-8862)

Flemington Knitting Mills ....F 908 995-9590
Milford (G-6244)

French Creek Sheep & Wool Co ....E 610 286-5700
Ventnor City (G-11291)

Jtwo Inc ....G 201 410-1616
Kinnelon (G-5037)

Ralph Lauren Corporation ....D 201 531-6000
Lyndhurst (G-5704)

Sophies Fashions ....G 973 272-8321
Garfield (G-3763)

Supertex Inc ....E 973 345-1000
Paterson (G-8389)

▲ Triumph Knitting Machine Svc ....E 201 646-0022
Hackensack (G-3986)

2254 Knit Underwear Mills

Komar Intimates LLC ....F 212 725-1500
Jersey City (G-4773)

▲ Komar Kids LLC ....F 212 725-1500
Jersey City (G-4774)

William Carter Company ....G 201 313-1783
Edgewater (G-2443)

2257 Circular Knit Fabric Mills

Meadows Knitting Corp ....E 973 482-6400
Newark (G-7238)

▲ Susan Mills Inc ....F 908 355-1400
Hillside (G-4443)

Trimtex Company Inc ....D 201 945-2151
Englewood Cliffs (G-2984)

2258 Lace & Warp Knit Fabric Mills

All-Lace Processing Corp ....F 201 867-1974
North Bergen (G-7427)

▲ Endurance Net Inc ....F 609 499-3450
Florence (G-3478)

▲ Fablok Mills Inc ....E 908 464-1950
New Providence (G-7034)

◆ Jason Mills LLC ....G 732 651-7200
Milltown (G-6269)

▲ Keystone Dyeing and Finishing ......G 718 482-7780
Dayton (G-1975)

Ques Aprv A R Knitwear Inc ....G 201 869-1333
North Bergen (G-7477)

Rebtex Inc ....C 908 722-3549
Branchburg (G-698)

▲ Royal Lace Co Inc ....E 718 495-9327
Rahway (G-9221)

▲ Stern Knit Inc ....G 732 364-8055
Lakewood (G-5192)

▲ Westchester Lace & Textiles ....C 201 864-2150
North Bergen (G-7495)

World Class Marketing Corp ....E 201 313-0022
Fort Lee (G-3591)

2259 Knitting Mills, NEC

Curtain Care Plus Inc ....G 800 845-6155
Clifton (G-1595)

D Kwitman & Son Inc ....F 201 798-5511
Hoboken (G-4468)

▲ Dollfus Mieg Company Inc ....C 732 662-1005
Edison (G-2502)

Hampton Industries Inc ....E 973 574-8900
Passaic (G-8146)

Markbilt Inc ....D 201 891-7842
Wyckoff (G-12259)

2261 Cotton Fabric Finishers

Anne Alanna Inc ....G 609 465-3787
Cape May Court House (G-1109)

Aztec Graphics Inc ....F 609 587-1000
Trenton (G-11023)

Brookline Chemical Corp ....E 301 767-1177
Wayne (G-11615)

Chartwell Promotions Ltd Inc ....G 732 780-6900
Freehold (G-3646)

Decorating With Fabric Inc ....G 845 352-5064
Park Ridge (G-7917)

E & W Piece Dye Works ....E 973 942-8718
Haledon (G-4082)

▲ Finn & Emma LLC ....G 973 227-7770
Fairfield (G-3195)

▲ Hanes Companies - NJ LLC ....F 201 729-9100
Edison (G-2532)

▲ Keystone Dyeing and Finishing ......G 718 482-7780
Dayton (G-1975)

▲ Lacoa Inc ....G 973 754-1000
Elmwood Park (G-2831)

Manner Textile Processing Inc ....D 973 942-8718
North Haledon (G-7550)

Martin Corporation ....F 856 451-0900
Bridgeton (G-790)

Mt Embroidery & Promotions LLC ....G 201 646-1070
Norwood (G-7629)

Paul Dyeing Company ....F 973 484-1121
Newark (G-7266)

Peter L Demaree ....G 732 531-2133
Ocean (G-7735)

Premier Printing Solutions LLC ....G 732 525-0740
Sayreville (G-9836)

Rebtex Inc ....C 908 722-3549
Branchburg (G-698)

Rolferrys Specialties Inc ....G 856 456-2999
Brooklawn (G-921)

Safer Textile Processing Corp ....B 973 482-6400
Newark (G-7300)

Screened Images Inc ....E 732 651-8181
East Brunswick (G-2182)

Unique Screen Printing Corp ....E 908 925-3773
Linden (G-5456)

2262 Silk & Man-Made Fabric Finishers

Chartwell Promotions Ltd Inc ....G 732 780-6900
Freehold (G-3646)

Design N Stitch Inc ....G 201 488-1314
Hackensack (G-3904)

Dye Into Print Inc ....D 973 772-8019
Clifton (G-1606)

Gilbert Storms Jr ....G 973 835-5729
Haskell (G-4207)

▲ Keystone Dyeing and Finishing ......G 718 482-7780
Dayton (G-1975)

Life Liners Inc ....G 973 635-9234
Chatham (G-1333)

Marijon Dyeing & Finishing Co ....C 201 933-9770
East Rutherford (G-2308)

Martin Corporation ....F 856 451-0900
Bridgeton (G-790)

North Jersey Skein Dyeing Co ....G 201 247-4202
Paterson (G-8352)

Screened Images Inc ....E 732 651-8181
East Brunswick (G-2182)

▲ Stefan Enterprises Inc ....E 973 253-6005
Garfield (G-3765)

Sunbrite Dye Co Inc ....E 973 777-9830
Passaic (G-8183)

Unique Screen Printing Corp ....E 908 925-3773
Linden (G-5456)

2269 Textile Finishers, NEC

◆ Asha44 LLC ....E 201 306-3600
Fairfield (G-3140)

Dye Into Print Inc ....D 973 772-8019
Clifton (G-1606)

◆ Franco Manufacturing Co Inc ....C 732 494-0500
Metuchen (G-6104)

▲ Kennetex Inc ....D 610 444-0600
Paterson (G-8308)

Manner Textile Processing Inc ....D 973 942-8718
North Haledon (G-7550)

▲ Multi-Tex Products Corp ....E 201 991-7262
Kearny (G-4902)

▲ Star Narrow Fabrics Inc ....G 973 778-8600
Lodi (G-5602)

2273 Carpets & Rugs

A & J Carpets Inc ....G 856 227-1753
Blackwood (G-469)

Aladdin Manufacturing Corp ....B 973 616-4600
Pompton Plains (G-8951)

▲ Amici Imports Inc ....F 908 272-8300
Cranford (G-1896)

▲ Bamboo & Rattan Works Inc ....G 732 255-4239
Toms River (G-10866)

▲ Bashian Bros Inc ....E 201 330-1001
Ridgefield (G-9350)

▲ Ben Aharon & Son Inc ....G 201 541-2388
Englewood (G-2875)

Cno Corporation ....G 732 785-5799
Brick (G-737)

▲ Fh Group International Inc ....E 201 210-2426
Secaucus (G-9883)

Gallery of Rugs Inc ....G 908 934-0040
Summit (G-10642)

Hakakian Behzad ....E 973 267-2506
Cedar Knolls (G-1313)

▲ Kas Oriental Rugs Inc ....E 732 545-1900
Somerset (G-10118)

▲ Kashee & Sons Inc ....F 201 867-6900
Secaucus (G-9898)

Kync Design LLC ....G 201 293-4677
Secaucus (G-9900)

La Forchetta ....G 973 304-4797
Hawthorne (G-4245)

◆ Mannington Mills Inc ....A 856 935-3000
Salem (G-9806)

Mohawk Industries ....G 973 982-6200
Kearny (G-4901)

▲ Moosavi Rugs Inc ....G 201 617-9500
Secaucus (G-9905)

Newark Auto Top Co Inc ....F 973 677-9935
East Orange (G-2262)

▲ Samad Brothers Inc ....G 201 372-0909
East Rutherford (G-2325)

▲ Seldom Seen Designs LLC ....G 973 535-8805
Livingston (G-5559)

Shaw Industries Inc ....B 609 655-8300
Cranbury (G-1880)

▲ SNS Oriental Rugs LLC ....G 201 355-8786
Carlstadt (G-1220)

▲ Stiles Enterprises Inc ....F 973 625-9660
Rockaway (G-9610)

▲ Worldwide Whl Flr Cvg Inc ....D 732 906-1400
Edison (G-2651)

▲ Zollanvari Ltd ....F 201 330-3344
Secaucus (G-9941)

2281 Yarn Spinning Mills

▲ American Drawtech Company Inc ......E 973 684-1600
Paterson (G-8207)

▲ Kennetex Inc ....D 610 444-0600
Paterson (G-8308)

Kync Design LLC ....G 201 293-4677
Secaucus (G-9900)

▲ Multi-Tex Products Corp ....E 201 991-7262
Kearny (G-4902)

World Class Marketing Corp ....E 201 313-0022
Fort Lee (G-3591)

2282 Yarn Texturizing, Throwing, Twisting & Winding Mills

◆ Brawer Bros Inc ....C 973 238-0163
Hawthorne (G-4222)

◆ Dillon Yarn Corporation ....E 973 684-1600
Paterson (G-8251)

Family Screen Printing Inc ....F 856 933-2780
Bellmawr (G-340)

Kairos Enterprises LLC ....F 201 731-3181
Englewood Cliffs (G-2969)

▲ Middleburg Yarn Processing Co ......E 973 238-1800
Hawthorne (G-4248)

▲ Safer Holding Corp ....A 973 485-1458
Newark (G-7299)

▲ Star Narrow Fabrics Inc ....G 973 778-8600
Lodi (G-5602)

▲ Warp Processing Inc ....G 973 238-1800
Hawthorne (G-4266)

2284 Thread Mills

▲ 5 Kids Group Ltd Liability Co ......F 732 774-5331
Neptune (G-6896)

Athletes Alley ....F 732 842-1127
Shrewsbury (G-9990)

◆ Cobyco Inc ....G 732 446-4448
Manalapan (G-5841)

2295 Fabrics Coated Not Rubberized

AK Associates LLC ....G 732 786-0002
Jackson (G-4652)

Alpha Associates Inc ....E 732 730-1800
Lakewood (G-5067)

◆ Alpha Engneered Composites LLC .....C 732 634-5700
Lakewood (G-5068)

◆ Butler Prtg & Laminating Inc ....G 973 838-8550
Butler (G-999)

Commercial Products Co Inc ....F 973 427-6887
Hawthorne (G-4227)

▲ Custom Laminations Inc ....G 973 279-9174
Paterson (G-8243)

▲ Daf Products Inc ....F 201 251-1222
Wyckoff (G-12249)

DMS Inc ....G 973 928-3040
Cedar Grove (G-1279)

▲ Ferland Industries Inc ....G 732 246-3200
Colts Neck (G-1784)

Gleicher Manufacturing Corp ....E 908 233-2211
Scotch Plains (G-9849)
Interplast Universal Inds ....E 973 471-4100
Lodi (G-5589)
Laboratory Diagnostics Co Inc ....F 732 536-6300
Morganville (G-6646)
▲ PCC Asia LLC 973 890-3873
Totowa (G-10961)
Plastic By All LLC 732 785-5900
Brick (G-755)
◆ Precision Custom Coatings LLC .....B 973 890-3873
Totowa (G-10966)
Safer Textile Processing Corp ....B 973 482-6400
Newark (G-7300)
▲ W C Omni Incorporated ....E 732 248-0999
Edison (G-2648)

2296 Tire Cord & Fabric

◆ Jomel Industries Inc....................F 973 282-0300
Hillside (G-4421)
Jomel Seams Reasonable LLC ....G 973 282-0300
Hillside (G-4422)
▲ Passaic Rubber Co ....D 973 696-9500
Wayne (G-11671)
Skyline Steel Corporation ....B 973 428-6100
Parsippany (G-8088)

2297 Fabrics, Nonwoven

◆ Fabrictex LLC ....G 732 225-3990
Edison (G-2518)
▲ Fibertech Group Inc ....C 856 697-1600
Landisville (G-5231)
JKA Specialties Mfr Inc ....F 609 859-2090
Southampton (G-10476)
Klein Ribbon Corp ....E 973 684-4671
Paterson (G-8310)

2298 Cordage & Twine

American Power Cord Corp ....G 973 574-8301
Somerset (G-10057)
Contemporary Cabling Company ......G 732 382-5064
Clark (G-1499)
Dun-Rite Communications Inc ....G 201 444-0080
Mahwah (G-5767)
Egg Harbor Rope Products Inc ....G 609 965-2435
Egg Harbor City (G-2663)
French Textile Co Inc ....F 973 471-5000
Clifton (G-1623)
Huber+suhner Astrolab Inc ....E 732 560-3800
Warren (G-11554)
▲ Motion Control Tech Inc ....F 973 361-2226
Dover (G-2101)
Newtech Group Corp ....G 732 355-0392
Kendall Park (G-4935)
Richard Andrus ....G 856 825-1782
Millville (G-6323)
▲ Seaboard Paper and Twine LLC .....E 973 413-8100
Paterson (G-8380)
▲ Steelstran Industries Inc ....E 732 574-0700
Avenel (G-152)
Sterling Net & Twine Co Inc ....F 973 783-9800
Montclair (G-6436)
▼ William Kenyon & Sons Inc ....E 732 985-8980
Piscataway (G-8836)

2299 Textile Goods, NEC

▲ AMD Fine Linens LLC ....G 201 568-5255
Englewood (G-2868)
American Dawn Inc ....G 856 467-9211
Bridgeport (G-761)
American Home Essentials Inc ....G 908 561-3200
South Plainfield (G-10326)
American Home Mfg LLC ....F 732 465-1530
Piscataway (G-8731)
Classic Silks Com I ....G 908 204-0940
Bernardsville (G-449)
Clean-Tex Services Inc ....G 908 912-2700
Trenton (G-11042)
Crescent Uniforms LLC ....F 732 398-1866
Franklin Park (G-3627)
▼ Douglass Industries Inc ....E 609 804-6040
Egg Harbor City (G-2662)
Elkay Products Co Inc ....F 973 376-7550
Springfield (G-10553)
◆ Halsted Corporation ....E 201 333-0670
Cranbury (G-1836)
Jubili Bead & Yarn Shoppe ....G 856 858-7844
Collingswood (G-1771)

Kmsco Inc ....F 732 238-8666
Ocean (G-7730)
M Chasen & Son Inc ....F 973 374-8956
Irvington (G-4596)
▲ Material Imports ....G 201 229-1180
Moonachie (G-6531)
▲ Multi-Tex Products Corp ....G 201 991-7262
Kearny (G-4902)
Newark Fibers Inc ....G 201 768-6800
Rockleigh (G-9632)
▲ Norman Weil Inc ....G 201 940-7345
Paramus (G-7895)
Peribu Global Sourcing ....G 704 560-2035
Skillman (G-10035)
▲ Sander Sales Enterprises Ltd ....E 201 808-6705
Secaucus (G-9920)
◆ Something Different Linen Inc ....C 973 272-0601
Clifton (G-1728)
★ Star Linen Inc ....E 800 782-7999
Moorestown (G-6623)
▼ Texx Team LLC ....E 201 289-1039
Hillsdale (G-4387)

23 APPAREL AND OTHER FINISHED PRODUCTS MADE FROM FABRICS AND SIMILAR MATERIAL

2311 Men's & Boys' Suits, Coats & Overcoats

▲ Alpine Trading Company Inc ....E 201 871-6111
Englewood (G-2867)
▼ Bimini Bay Outfitters Ltd ....F 201 529-3550
Mahwah (G-5752)
Burlington Coat Factory ....D 908 994-9562
Elizabeth (G-2716)
Crown Clothing Co ....C 856 691-0343
Vineland (G-11343)
De Rossi & Son Co Inc ....C 856 691-0061
Vineland (G-11351)
▲ Fabian Couture Group Intl Inc ....F 800 367-6251
Lyndhurst (G-5681)
▲ Fabian Formals Inc ....E 201 460-7776
Lyndhurst (G-5682)
Firefighter One Ltd Lblty Co ....G 973 940-3061
Sparta (G-10499)
Fordham Inc ....E 973 575-7840
Fairfield (G-3199)
Harve Benard Ltd ....C 973 249-1230
Clifton (G-1638)
Michael Duru Clothiers LLC ....G 732 741-1999
Shrewsbury (G-10005)
New Community Corp ....E 973 643-5300
Newark (G-7249)
Stretch-O-Rama Inc ....E 732 855-1400
Avenel (G-153)
Tom James Company ....G 732 826-8400
Perth Amboy (G-8633)
Trilex Ltd ....E 201 664-5576
Twp Washinton (G-11144)

2321 Men's & Boys' Shirts

▼ Bimini Bay Outfitters Ltd ....F 201 529-3550
Mahwah (G-5752)
◆ Central Mills Inc ....C 732 329-2009
Dayton (G-1961)
▲ Cleve Shirtmakers Inc ....G 201 825-6122
Secaucus (G-9872)
Drifire LLC ....E 866 266-4035
East Brunswick (G-2146)
Gambert Shirt Corp ....E 973 424-9105
Newark (G-7168)
◆ Jade Eastern Trading Inc ....F 201 440-8500
Moonachie (G-6524)
L Gambert LLC ....D 973 344-3440
Newark (G-7215)
New Community Corp ....E 973 643-5300
Newark (G-7249)
▲ New Jersey Headwear Corp ....C 973 497-0102
Newark (G-7250)
◆ New Top Inc ....E 201 438-3990
Carlstadt (G-1193)
Pvh Corp ....G 908 685-0050
Elizabeth (G-2769)
Pvh Corp ....G 609 344-6273
Atlantic City (G-106)
Pvh Corp ....G 732 833-9602
Jackson (G-4676)
Pvh Corp ....G 908 685-0050
Bridgewater (G-880)

Pvh Corp ....G 908 685-0148
Bridgewater (G-881)
Pvh Corp ....G 908 788-5880
Flemington (G-3464)
Pvh Corp ....G 908 685-0050
Bridgewater (G-879)
Ralph Lauren Corporation ....D 201 531-6000
Lyndhurst (G-5704)
Saad Collection Inc ....G 732 763-4015
Edison (G-2610)
Skip Gambert & Associates Inc ....C 973 344-3373
Newark (G-7317)

2322 Men's & Boys' Underwear & Nightwear

Basic Solutions Ltd ....G 201 978-7691
Manalapan (G-5839)
◆ Central Mills Inc ....C 732 329-2009
Dayton (G-1961)
D & G LLC ....G 201 289-5750
Hackensack (G-3902)
◆ Sgi Apparel Ltd ....G 201 342-1200
Hackensack (G-3974)
Umc Inc ....G 973 325-0031
West Orange (G-11907)

2323 Men's & Boys' Neckwear

Albert Forte Neckwear Co Inc ....G 856 423-2342
Mullica Hill (G-6891)
HRA International Inc ....G 609 395-0939
Monroe (G-6374)
▲ Robert Stewart Inc ....G 973 751-5151
Belleville (G-316)

2325 Men's & Boys' Separate Trousers & Casual Slacks

▲ Eddie Domani ....G 908 469-8863
Elizabethport (G-2783)
Guess Inc ....E 201 941-3683
Edgewater (G-2440)
Harve Benard Ltd ....C 973 249-1230
Clifton (G-1638)
▲ Jordache Ltd ....F 908 226-4930
South Plainfield (G-10389)
Levi Strauss & Co ....F 732 493-4595
Tinton Falls (G-10841)
Ralph Lauren Corporation ....D 201 531-6000
Lyndhurst (G-5704)
Spirit Tex LLC ....G 201 440-1113
Little Ferry (G-5518)

2326 Men's & Boys' Work Clothing

◆ Ansell Healthcare Products LLC ......C 732 345-5400
Iselin (G-4611)
▲ B2x Corporation ....G 201 714-2373
Jersey City (G-4712)
Bestwork Inds For The Blind ....D 856 424-2510
Cherry Hill (G-1349)
▲ Bethel Industries Inc ....C 201 656-8222
Jersey City (G-4717)
Db Designs Inc ....G 732 616-5018
Marlboro (G-5937)
◆ Eagle Work Clothes Inc ....E 908 964-8888
Florham Park (G-3499)
Enailsupply Corporation ....G 909 725-1698
Toms River (G-10874)
Flying Fish Studio ....G 609 884-2760
West Cape May (G-11808)
Galvanic LLC ....G 609 600-2604
Cape May (G-1100)
▼ Happy Chef Inc ....E 973 492-2525
Butler (G-1006)
Janet Shops Inc ....F 973 748-4992
Bloomfield (G-515)
▲ Loveline Industries Inc ....E 973 928-3427
Passaic (G-8157)
Luxury and Trash Ltd Lblty Co ....G 201 315-4018
Closter (G-1763)
▲ M Rafi Sons Garment Industries ......G 732 381-7660
Rahway (G-9211)
Matrix Sales Group LLC ....D 908 461-4148
Spring Lake (G-10534)
▲ Mischief International Inc ....G 201 840-6888
Ridgefield (G-9374)
New Community Corp ....E 973 643-5300
Newark (G-7249)
◆ Pro World ....G 856 406-1020
Pennsauken (G-8567)
◆ Red The Uniform Tailor Inc ....E 848 299-0100
Lakewood (G-5176)

Ronald Perry..........................F...... 201 702-2407
Jersey City (G-4820)
▲ Somes Uniforms Inc................F...... 201 843-1199
Hackensack (G-3977)
Switlik Parachute Company Inc......F...... 609 587-3300
Trenton (G-11119)
Tellas Ltd...............................E...... 201 399-8888
Englewood Cliffs (G-2981)
▲ Todd Shelton LLC.................G...... 844 626-6355
East Rutherford (G-2333)
Trilex Ltd...............................E...... 201 664-5576
Twp Washinton (G-11144)
Vertical Protective AP LLC..........G...... 203 904-6099
Shrewsbury (G-10013)

2329 Men's & Boys' Clothing, NEC

Adidas North America Inc...........G...... 201 843-4555
Paramus (G-7852)
Adidas North America Inc...........G...... 732 695-0085
Tinton Falls (G-10823)
Aladen Athletic Wear LLC...........E...... 973 838-2425
Wyckoff (G-12245)
▼ Amante International Ltd..........F...... 908 518-1688
Westfield (G-11919)
▲ Bear USa Inc.....................F...... 201 943-4748
Palisades Park (G-7835)
▼ Bimini Bay Outfitters Ltd........F...... 201 529-3550
Mahwah (G-5752)
Brisco Apparel Co Inc...............E...... 718 715-7110
Lakewood (G-5090)
Central Mills Inc....................G...... 732 329-2009
Dayton (G-1960)
◆ Central Mills Inc.................C...... 732 329-2009
Dayton (G-1961)
CRA-Z Works Co Inc.................G...... 732 390-8238
Sayreville (G-9819)
▲ Daman International Inc..........G...... 917 945-9708
Cherry Hill (G-1359)
Evh LLC................................F...... 973 257-0076
Boonton (G-568)
▲ Finn & Emma LLC.................G...... 973 227-7770
Fairfield (G-3195)
H & A Global Enterprises Inc.......G...... 732 318-2587
Edison (G-2530)
▼ House Pearl Fashions (us) Ltd...F...... 973 778-7551
Lodi (G-5588)
J Harris Company....................G...... 917 731-5080
Madison (G-5726)
Kmba Fashions Inc..................G...... 973 789-1652
East Orange (G-2259)
▲ Leeward International Inc........F...... 201 836-8830
Teaneck (G-10760)
▲ Merc USA Inc.....................F...... 201 489-3527
Hackensack (G-3947)
MISS Sportswear Inc................G...... 212 391-2535
New Brunswick (G-6982)
▲ Moldworks Worldwide LLC........G...... 908 474-8082
Linden (G-5413)
Nautica Retail USA..................G...... 212 541-5757
Jersey City (G-4787)
▲ Onwards Inc......................G...... 732 309-7348
Manalapan (G-5859)
▲ Rennoc Corporation..............D...... 856 327-5400
Vineland (G-11395)
▲ Safire Silk Inc...................G...... 201 636-4061
Carlstadt (G-1212)
▲ Schott Nyc Corp..................D...... 800 631-5407
Union (G-11222)
Selfmade LLC.........................G...... 201 792-8968
Jersey City (G-4826)
Senor Lopez..........................G...... 732 229-7622
Tinton Falls (G-10847)
Sinai Manufacturing Corp...........G...... 973 522-1003
Newark (G-7314)
Sportstar World Wide Inc...........F...... 732 254-9214
South River (G-10467)
SR Shirts & Stuff LLC...............G...... 973 335-3086
Montville (G-6495)
▲ Tony Jones Apparel Inc..........G...... 973 773-6200
Lodi (G-5606)
What A Tee 2 Inc.....................F...... 201 457-0060
Hackensack (G-3991)

2331 Women's & Misses' Blouses

▲ Chic LLC...........................G...... 732 354-0035
East Brunswick (G-2141)
▲ Cleve Shirtmakers Inc............G...... 201 825-6122
Secaucus (G-9872)
Daniel Fashions Inc..................G...... 201 869-1008
West New York (G-11863)

▲ Elie Tahari Ltd....................C...... 973 671-6300
Millburn (G-6249)
Gambert Shirt Corp..................E...... 973 424-9105
Newark (G-7168)
Harve Benard Ltd....................C...... 973 249-1230
Clifton (G-1638)
Luxury and Trash Ltd Lblty Co......G...... 201 315-4018
Closter (G-1763)
▲ Metropolitan Manufacturing Inc..D...... 201 933-8111
East Rutherford (G-2310)
▲ New Jersey Headwear Corp.......C...... 973 497-0102
Newark (G-7250)
Nicholas Oliver LLC..................G...... 732 690-7144
Wall Township (G-11499)
Saad Collection Inc..................G...... 732 763-4015
Edison (G-2610)
▲ Second Skin LLC..................F...... 212 931-0621
Westfield (G-11931)
Spirit Tex LLC.........................G...... 201 440-1113
Little Ferry (G-5518)
◆ Suuchi Inc.........................C...... 201 284-0789
North Bergen (G-7488)
▲ Tahari ASL LLC....................E...... 888 734-7459
Millburn (G-6259)
True Religion Apparel Inc............G...... 973 564-9030
Short Hills (G-9986)

2335 Women's & Misses' Dresses

Amalia Carrara Inc...................E...... 201 348-4500
Union City (G-11240)
Augenbrauns Bridal Passaic LLC....G...... 845 425-3439
Lakewood (G-5078)
Betsy & Adam Ltd....................E...... 212 302-3750
Passaic (G-8128)
▲ Cs Apparel Inc....................G...... 732 906-9666
Edison (G-2498)
Donna Karan International Inc.......G...... 609 345-3402
Atlantic City (G-95)
◆ Duran Cutting Corp...............F...... 973 916-0006
Passaic (G-8135)
▲ Elie Tahari Ltd....................C...... 973 671-6300
Millburn (G-6249)
Head Piece Heaven...................G...... 201 262-0788
Oradell (G-7811)
Hillarys Fashion Boutique LLC.......F...... 732 667-7733
Warren (G-11552)
Kate Spade & Company..............E...... 201 295-7569
North Bergen (G-7460)
Kate Spade & Company..............E...... 609 395-3109
Dayton (G-1974)
▲ Kidcuteture LLC...................G...... 609 532-0149
Lawrenceville (G-5259)
▲ Liz Fields Llc.....................G...... 201 408-5640
Englewood (G-2910)
▲ Metropolitan Manufacturing Inc..D...... 201 933-8111
East Rutherford (G-2310)
Milady Bridals Inc...................E...... 201 348-4500
Union City (G-11257)
More Than A Notion Fabrics Ltd......G...... 732 821-5580
Princeton (G-9077)
Nicholas Oliver LLC..................G...... 732 690-7144
Wall Township (G-11499)
▲ Perceptions Inc...................E...... 973 344-5333
Kearny (G-4906)
▲ Printmaker International Ltd......G...... 212 629-9260
Irvington (G-4601)
▲ Second Skin LLC..................F...... 212 931-0621
Westfield (G-11931)
Sophies Fashions...................G...... 973 272-8321
Garfield (G-3763)
Success Sewing Inc.................G...... 973 622-0328
Newark (G-7333)
▲ Tahari ASL LLC....................E...... 888 734-7459
Millburn (G-6259)

2337 Women's & Misses' Suits, Coats & Skirts

▲ Chic LLC...........................G...... 732 354-0035
East Brunswick (G-2141)
▲ Counter-Fit Inc....................C...... 609 871-8888
Willingboro (G-12118)
E-Lo Sportswear LLC.................F...... 862 902-5220
Harrison (G-4179)
◆ Eagle Work Clothes Inc...........E...... 908 964-8888
Florham Park (G-3499)
▲ Elie Tahari Ltd....................C...... 973 671-6300
Millburn (G-6249)
Fordham Inc..........................E...... 973 575-7840
Fairfield (G-3199)

Fyi Marketing Inc.....................G...... 646 546-5226
Englewood Cliffs (G-2960)
▼ Happy Chef Inc....................E...... 973 492-2525
Butler (G-1006)
Harve Benard Ltd....................C...... 973 249-1230
Clifton (G-1638)
Jackie Evans Inc......................C...... 973 471-6991
Passaic (G-8151)
▲ Metropolitan Manufacturing Inc..D...... 201 933-8111
East Rutherford (G-2310)
Nana Creations Inc...................F...... 201 263-1112
Fort Lee (G-3573)
New Community Corp.................E...... 973 643-5300
Newark (G-7249)
Nine West Holdings Inc..............G...... 908 354-8895
Elizabeth (G-2758)
Nine West Holdings Inc..............G...... 201 541-7004
Englewood (G-2919)
Success Sewing Inc.................G...... 973 622-0328
Newark (G-7333)

2339 Women's & Misses' Outerwear, NEC

Alfred Dunner Inc....................D...... 212 944-6660
Parsippany (G-7942)
▼ Amante International Ltd..........F...... 908 518-1688
Westfield (G-11919)
▲ Attitudes In Dressing Inc.........B...... 908 354-7218
Elizabeth (G-2711)
▲ Bear USa Inc.....................F...... 201 943-4748
Palisades Park (G-7835)
Bestwork Inds For The Blind........D...... 856 424-2510
Cherry Hill (G-1349)
Blue Fish Clothing Inc...............C...... 908 996-3720
Frenchtown (G-3697)
▲ BT Industries Inc.................D...... 201 866-0201
North Bergen (G-7436)
◆ Central Mills Inc.................C...... 732 329-2009
Dayton (G-1961)
▲ Chic LLC...........................G...... 732 354-0035
East Brunswick (G-2141)
▲ City Design Group Inc.............G...... 201 329-7711
Little Ferry (G-5497)
Collection Xiix Ltd...................C...... 201 854-7740
North Bergen (G-7441)
▲ Counter-Fit Inc....................C...... 609 871-8888
Willingboro (G-12118)
Davidmark LLC.......................G...... 609 277-7361
Pleasantville (G-8907)
▲ Elie Tahari Ltd....................C...... 973 671-6300
Millburn (G-6249)
Escada US Subco LLC...............B...... 201 865-5200
Secaucus (G-9879)
Evigto Inc.............................G...... 201 951-2187
Edgewater (G-2438)
Fordham Inc..........................E...... 973 575-7840
Fairfield (G-3199)
Fyi Marketing Inc.....................G...... 646 546-5226
Englewood Cliffs (G-2960)
Garylin Togs.........................D...... 908 354-7218
Elizabeth (G-2737)
▲ Great Socks LLC..................E...... 856 964-9700
Pennsauken (G-8518)
▼ Happy Chef Inc....................E...... 973 492-2525
Butler (G-1006)
Harve Benard Ltd....................C...... 973 249-1230
Clifton (G-1638)
▲ Hedaya Home Fashions Inc........C...... 908 352-0808
Elizabeth (G-2745)
Helen Morley LLC....................E...... 201 348-6459
Cresskill (G-1945)
▼ House Pearl Fashions (us) Ltd...F...... 973 778-7551
Lodi (G-5588)
▲ Jordache Ltd......................E...... 908 226-4930
South Plainfield (G-10389)
Kmba Fashions Inc..................G...... 973 789-1652
East Orange (G-2259)
▲ Leeward International Inc........F...... 201 836-8830
Teaneck (G-10760)
Les Tout Petite Inc...................G...... 201 941-8675
Ridgefield (G-9371)
Marmaxx Operating Corp............D...... 973 575-7910
West Caldwell (G-11785)
Matrix Sales Group LLC.............D...... 908 461-4148
Spring Lake (G-10534)
▲ Metropolitan Manufacturing Inc..D...... 201 933-8111
East Rutherford (G-2310)
New Community Corp.................E...... 973 643-5300
Newark (G-7249)
Nine West Holdings Inc..............E...... 908 647-6168
Gillette (G-3796)

◆ Ocean Drive Inc ....G 908 964-2591
　Kenilworth (G-4983)

Philip Papalia ....F 732 349-5530
　Toms River (G-10902)

▲ Printmaker International Ltd ....G 212 629-9260
　Irvington (G-4601)

◆ Red The Uniform Tailor Inc ....E 848 299-0100
　Lakewood (G-5176)

▲ Second Skin LLC ....G 212 931-0621
　Westfield (G-11931)

▲ Sno Skins Inc ....G 973 884-8801
　Whippany (G-12039)

▲ Snotex USA Inc ....G 973 762-0358
　South Orange (G-10315)

Sondra Roberts Inc ....E 212 684-3344
　South Hackensack (G-10296)

▲ Sonia Fashion Inc ....G 201 864-3483
　Union City (G-11268)

Spirit Tex LLC ....G 201 440-1113
　Little Ferry (G-5518)

Swisstex Company ....E 201 861-8000
　West New York (G-11882)

▲ Tahari ASL LLC ....E 888 734-7459
　Millburn (G-6259)

Tellas Ltd ....E 201 399-8888
　Englewood Cliffs (G-2981)

▲ Tripp Nyc Inc ....G 201 520-0420
　North Bergen (G-7490)

What A Tee 2 Inc ....F 201 457-0060
　Hackensack (G-3991)

2341 Women's, Misses' & Children's Underwear & Nightwear

▲ Carole Hchman Design Group Inc....C 866 267-3945
　Jersey City (G-4724)

◆ Central Mills Inc ....C 732 329-2009
　Dayton (G-1961)

◆ Charles Komar & Sons Inc ....B 212 725-1500
　Jersey City (G-4726)

D & G LLC ....G 201 289-5750
　Hackensack (G-3902)

▲ Delta Galil USA Inc ....D 201 902-0055
　Secaucus (G-9876)

◆ Dolce Vita Intimates LLC ....D 973 482-8400
　Harrison (G-4178)

▲ Fashion Central LLC ....G 732 887-7683
　Lakewood (G-5121)

Komar Intimates LLC ....F 212 725-1500
　Jersey City (G-4773)

▲ Maidenform ....A 732 621-2216
　Iselin (G-4632)

▲ Maidenform Brands Inc ....E 888 573-0299
　Iselin (G-4633)

▲ Priamo Designs Ltd ....G 201 861-8808
　West New York (G-11876)

◆ Sgi Apparel Ltd ....G 201 342-1200
　Hackensack (G-3974)

Swisstex Company ....E 201 861-8000
　West New York (G-11882)

◆ Wacoal America Inc ....C 201 933-8400
　Lyndhurst (G-5713)

◆ Wacoal International Corp ....G 201 933-8400
　Lyndhurst (G-5714)

2342 Brassieres, Girdles & Garments

▲ Bbm Group LLC ....E 201 482-6500
　Palisades Park (G-7834)

▲ Carole Hchman Design Group Inc....C 866 267-3945
　Jersey City (G-4724)

Colfajas Inc ....G 973 727-4813
　Succasunna (G-10620)

◆ Dolce Vita Intimates LLC ....D 973 482-8400
　Harrison (G-4178)

▲ Maidenform Brands Inc ....E 888 573-0299
　Iselin (G-4633)

◆ Wacoal America Inc ....C 201 933-8400
　Lyndhurst (G-5713)

2353 Hats, Caps & Millinery

▲ Alboum W Hat Company Inc ....E 201 399-4110
　Irvington (G-4572)

American Baby Headwear Co Inc ....D 908 558-0017
　Elizabeth (G-2709)

Castellane Manufacturing Co ....G 609 625-3427
　Mays Landing (G-6038)

▲ Con Cap Sports Wear ....F 973 778-2628
　Wood Ridge (G-12136)

Edward Berger Inc ....E 609 571-9676
　Old Bridge (G-7778)

▲ Geisler Ganz Corp ....G 201 223-1200
　Secaucus (G-9886)

Headwear Creations Inc ....E 973 622-1144
　Newark (G-7188)

▲ Impact Design Inc ....E 908 289-2900
　Elizabethport (G-2785)

▲ Jay Gerish Company ....G 973 403-0655
　West Caldwell (G-11782)

John B Stetson Company ....E 212 563-1848
　Hoboken (G-4478)

▲ Kathy Gibson Designs Inc ....F 201 420-0088
　North Bergen (G-7461)

▲ Kathy Jeanne Inc ....G 973 575-9898
　Fairfield (G-3239)

Nes Enterprises Inc ....G 201 964-1400
　Carlstadt (G-1192)

▲ New Jersey Headwear Corp ....G 973 497-0102
　Newark (G-7250)

Serratelli Hat Company Inc ....G 973 623-4133
　Newark (G-7307)

▲ Silvertop Associates Inc ....G 856 939-9599
　Runnemede (G-9723)

Under Armour Inc ....E 732 493-2444
　Tinton Falls (G-10852)

2361 Children's & Infants' Dresses & Blouses

▲ Jasper Fashion Ltd Lblty Co ....F 917 561-4533
　Elizabeth (G-2749)

Lollytogs Ltd ....F 732 438-5500
　Dayton (G-1978)

▲ Sally Miller LLC ....G 732 729-4840
　Milltown (G-6271)

2369 Girls' & Infants' Outerwear, NEC

American Baby Headwear Co Inc ....D 908 558-0017
　Elizabeth (G-2709)

▲ Attitudes In Dressing Inc ....G 908 354-7218
　Elizabeth (G-2711)

Bib and Tucker Inc ....G 201 489-9600
　Hackensack (G-3881)

Blue Fish Clothing Inc ....G 908 996-3720
　Frenchtown (G-3697)

◆ Central Mills Inc ....C 732 329-2009
　Dayton (G-1961)

Frenchtoastcom LLC ....F 732 438-5500
　Dayton (G-1964)

Garylin Togs ....D 908 354-7218
　Elizabeth (G-2737)

In Mocean Group LLC ....G 732 960-2415
　North Brunswick (G-7519)

◆ Jordache Ltd ....F 908 226-4930
　South Plainfield (G-10389)

JP Group International LLC ....G 201 820-1444
　Maywood (G-6057)

◆ Leeward International Inc ....G 201 836-8830
　Teaneck (G-10760)

Lemon Inc ....G 201 417-5412
　Norwood (G-7628)

Les Tout Petite Inc ....G 201 941-8675
　Ridgefield (G-9371)

Lollytogs Ltd ....D 732 438-5500
　Dayton (G-1979)

Lollytogs Ltd ....F 732 438-5500
　Dayton (G-1978)

Spirit Tex LLC ....G 201 440-1113
　Little Ferry (G-5518)

2371 Fur Goods

▲ American Fur Felt LLC ....F 973 344-3026
　Newark (G-7082)

M Blaustein Inc ....G 973 379-1080
　Short Hills (G-9980)

▲ N&K Trading Inc ....E 609 616-3110
　North Brunswick (G-7529)

S & H R Inc ....G 908 925-3797
　Linden (G-5436)

2381 Dress & Work Gloves

American Baby Headwear Co Inc ....D 908 558-0017
　Elizabeth (G-2709)

▲ George Glove Company Inc ....G 201 251-1200
　Midland Park (G-6226)

2384 Robes & Dressing Gowns

▲ Carole Hchman Design Group Inc....C 866 267-3945
　Jersey City (G-4724)

◆ Charles Komar & Sons Inc ....B 212 725-1500
　Jersey City (G-4726)

Chiha Inc ....F 201 861-2000
　North Bergen (G-7440)

▲ Monarch Towel Company Inc ....G 800 729-7623
　South Plainfield (G-10409)

2385 Waterproof Outerwear

A J P Scientific Inc ....G 973 472-7200
　Clifton (G-1552)

▲ Man-How Inc ....G 609 392-4895
　Trenton (G-11078)

2386 Leather & Sheep Lined Clothing

Cockpit Usa Inc ....F 212 575-1616
　Elizabeth (G-2719)

French Creek Sheep & Wool Co ....E 610 286-5700
　Ventnor City (G-11291)

G-III Apparel Group Ltd ....D 732 438-0209
　Dayton (G-1965)

G-III Leather Fashions Inc ....D 212 403-0500
　Dayton (G-1966)

▲ Prime Fur & Leather Inc ....F 201 941-9600
　Fairview (G-3369)

▲ Schott Nyc Corp ....G 800 631-5407
　Union (G-11222)

2387 Apparel Belts

Josemi Inc ....G 917 710-2110
　Hoboken (G-4481)

Straps Manufacturing NJ Inc ....F 201 368-5201
　Wyckoff (G-12264)

Two 12 Fashion LLC ....G 848 222-1562
　Lakewood (G-5198)

2389 Apparel & Accessories, NEC

Apparel Strgc Alliances LLC ....F 732 833-7771
　Jackson (G-4654)

◆ Ballet Makers Inc ....B 973 595-9000
　Totowa (G-10934)

Better Team USA Corporation ....E 973 365-0947
　Clifton (G-1575)

Blu-J2 LLC ....G 201 750-1407
　Demarest (G-2026)

Butterfly Bow Ties LLC ....G 973 626-2536
　Union (G-11160)

Church Vestment Mfg Co Inc ....G 973 942-2833
　Paterson (G-8233)

▲ Costume Gallery Inc ....E 609 386-6601
　Delanco (G-2005)

Couture Exchange ....G 732 933-1123
　Shrewsbury (G-9995)

E5 Usa Inc ....G 973 773-0750
　Passaic (G-8136)

Evigto Inc ....G 201 951-2187
　Edgewater (G-2438)

Fine Wear U S A ....G 201 313-3777
　Fort Lee (G-3554)

Global Manufacturing LLC ....G 973 494-5413
　Newark (G-7172)

Handcraft Manufacturing Corp ....E 973 565-0077
　Newark (G-7185)

Hat Box ....E 732 961-2262
　Lakewood (G-5133)

Images Costume Productions ....G 609 859-7372
　Southampton (G-10475)

Jaclyn Inc ....F 201 909-6000
　Maywood (G-6052)

▲ Jese Apparel LLC ....F 732 969-3200
　Dayton (G-1973)

▲ Keystone Adjustable Cap Co Inc ......E 856 356-2809
　Pennsauken (G-8539)

Kristine Deer Inc ....G 201 497-3333
　Westwood (G-11961)

Lion Sales Corp ....G 732 417-9363
　Edison (G-2557)

Lynn Amiee Inc ....E 201 840-6766
　Ridgefield (G-9372)

▲ New York Popular Inc ....D 718 499-2020
　Carteret (G-1263)

Paradise ....G 973 425-0505
　Morristown (G-6732)

Personality Handkerchiefs Inc ....E 973 565-0077
　Newark (G-7269)

Philip Papalia ....F 732 349-5530
　Toms River (G-10902)

◆ Premium Imports Inc ....G 718 486-7125
　Passaic (G-8171)

▲ Robert Gaiser Inc ....F 973 838-9254
　Butler (G-1017)

School Spirit Promotions................G...... 609 588-6902
  Trenton (G-11115)
▲ Silvertop Associates Inc.............E...... 856 939-9599
  Runnemede (G-9723)
Steps Clothing Inc ....E...... 201 420-1496
  Jersey City (G-4834)
Stylus Custom Apparel Inc ....G...... 908 587-0800
  Linden (G-5450)
Too Cool of Ocean City ....G...... 908 810-6363
  Kenilworth (G-5000)
Xcessory LLC ....G...... 917 647-7523
  North Bergen (G-7497)

2391 Curtains & Draperies

▲ Ackerson Drapery Decorator Svc......G...... 732 797-1967
  Lakewood (G-5065)
▲ Beatrice Home Fashions Inc...........E...... 908 561-7370
  South Plainfield (G-10336)
Beltor Manufacturing Corp ....G...... 856 768-5570
  Berlin (G-426)
Best Linen Factory Inc ....F...... 973 279-8244
  Paterson (G-8223)
Bloomfield Drapery Co Inc ....F...... 973 777-3566
  East Rutherford (G-2287)
Colonial Uphl & Win Treatments ......G...... 609 641-3124
  Pleasantville (G-8905)
▲ D Kwitman & Son Inc ....F...... 201 798-5511
  Hoboken (G-4467)
D Kwitman & Son Inc ....E...... 201 798-5511
  Hoboken (G-4468)
Dons Drapery Manufacturing............F...... 973 751-1544
  Belleville (G-300)
Drapery & More Inc ....G...... 201 271-9661
  North Bergen (G-7447)
◆ Dru Whitacre Media Svcs Ltd ....D...... 201 770-9950
  North Bergen (G-7448)
Forsters Cleaning & Tailoring ....G...... 201 659-4411
  Jersey City (G-4757)
Franks Upholstery & Draperies ....G...... 856 779-8585
  Maple Shade (G-5902)
Gordon Frgson Intr Dsigns Svcs.......G...... 973 378-2330
  Maplewood (G-5920)
Interior Art & Design Inc ....E...... 201 488-8855
  Hackensack (G-3930)
▲ Iweiss Inc ....E...... 201 402-6500
  Fairview (G-3362)
Kushner Draperies Mfg LLC ....E...... 856 317-9696
  Pennsauken (G-8541)
Lawrence Custom Drapery Shop ....F...... 609 882-4007
  Ewing (G-3034)
Marburn Stores Inc ....G...... 908 412-1962
  South Plainfield (G-10401)
Master Drapery Workroom Inc ....F...... 908 272-4404
  Kenilworth (G-4973)
Metro Mills Inc ....E...... 973 942-6034
  Paterson (G-8337)
Nassaus Window Fashions Inc...........E...... 201 689-6030
  Paramus (G-7893)
Stessl & Neugebauer Inc.................F...... 908 277-3340
  Summit (G-10659)
▲ Thortel Fireproof Fabrics Inc ....F...... 732 938-4114
  Wall Township (G-11514)
▲ W Gerriets International Inc ....G...... 609 771-8111
  Ewing (G-3068)

2392 House furnishings: Textile

A & R Sewing Company Inc ....F...... 201 332-0622
  Jersey City (G-4695)
▼ A-1 Tablecloth Co Inc...................C...... 201 727-4364
  South Hackensack (G-10250)
▲ Ackerson Drapery Decorator Svc...G...... 732 797-1967
  Lakewood (G-5065)
American Dawn Inc ....G...... 856 467-9211
  Bridgeport (G-761)
▲ AMS Products LLC ....F...... 973 442-5790
  Wharton (G-11978)
▲ AMS Toy Intl Inc ....E...... 973 442-5790
  Wharton (G-11979)
Anchor Sales & Marketing Inc ....F...... 973 545-2277
  West Milford (G-11850)
▲ Asbury Towel Company Inc ....F...... 732 370-3908
  Lakewood (G-5076)
B T Partners Inc ....G...... 609 652-6511
  Galloway (G-3709)
Ballard Collection Inc ....G...... 908 604-0082
  Warren (G-11538)
▲ Beatrice Home Fashions Inc..........E...... 908 561-7370
  South Plainfield (G-10336)
▲ Better Sleep Inc ....F...... 908 464-2200
  Branchburg (G-643)

Carlyle Custom Convertibles............D...... 973 546-4502
  Moonachie (G-6511)
Chic Bebe Inc ....G...... 201 941-5414
  Tenafly (G-10783)
Colonial Uphl & Win Treatments ....G...... 609 641-3124
  Pleasantville (G-8905)
▲ Crown Products Inc ....E...... 732 493-0022
  Ocean (G-7720)
Custom Alley ....G...... 609 294-1875
  Ltl Egg Hbr (G-5643)
▲ D Kwitman & Son Inc ....F...... 201 798-5511
  Hoboken (G-4467)
▲ Drake Corp ....G...... 732 254-1530
  East Brunswick (G-2145)
Fine Linen Inc ....F...... 908 469-3634
  Elizabeth (G-2733)
◆ Franco Manufacturing Co Inc ....G...... 732 494-0500
  Metuchen (G-6104)
Global Weavers Corp ....G...... 973 824-5500
  Newark (G-7173)
▲ Hedaya Home Fashions Inc ....C...... 908 352-0808
  Elizabeth (G-2745)
Howard Lippincott ....G...... 856 764-8282
  Riverside (G-9499)
◆ Innocor Inc ....C...... 732 945-6222
  Red Bank (G-9331)
Innocor Foam Tech - Acp Inc ....D...... 732 945-6222
  Red Bank (G-9332)
Interior Art & Design Inc ....E...... 201 488-8855
  Hackensack (G-3930)
◆ J&S Houseware Corp ....G...... 973 824-5500
  Newark (G-7204)
▲ Janico Inc ....F...... 732 370-2223
  Freehold (G-3662)
▲ Kas Oriental Rugs Inc ....E...... 732 545-1900
  Somerset (G-10118)
▲ Lbu Inc ....E...... 973 773-4800
  Paterson (G-8318)
Leggett & Platt Incorporated.............D...... 904 786-0750
  Brick (G-750)
Linen For Tables ....G...... 973 345-8472
  Paterson (G-8322)
Living Fashions Llc ....F...... 732 626-5200
  Sayreville (G-9830)
Marketing Administration Assoc ....G...... 732 840-3021
  Brick (G-752)
▲ Orient Originals Inc ....E...... 201 332-5005
  Jersey City (G-4796)
◆ Pegasus Home Fashions Inc...........D...... 908 965-1919
  Elizabeth (G-2766)
▼ Phoenix Down Corporation ....C...... 973 812-8100
  Totowa (G-10963)
▲ R L Plastics Inc ....G...... 732 340-1100
  Avenel (G-149)
Redhawk Distribution Inc................F...... 516 884-9911
  Pennsauken (G-8571)
▲ Royal Crest Home Fashions Inc .....G...... 201 461-4600
  Palisades Park (G-7843)
▲ Sahara Textile Inc ....G...... 973 247-9900
  Paterson (G-8374)
▲ Sheex Inc ....E...... 856 334-3021
  Marlton (G-5999)
Stanlar Enterprises Inc..................E...... 973 680-4488
  Bloomfield (G-532)
◆ Star Linen Inc..............................E...... 800 782-7999
  Moorestown (G-6623)
Sunham Home Fashions LLC ....D...... 908 363-1100
  New Providence (G-7055)
▼ Tablecloth Co Inc ....E...... 973 942-1555
  Paterson (G-8396)
▲ Tatara Group Inc ....G...... 732 231-6031
  Avenel (G-155)
Tex Spar Co Inc ....C...... 732 367-9439
  Lakewood (G-5194)
▲ Triangle Home Fashions LLC ....G...... 732 355-9800
  Dayton (G-1993)
United Bedding Industries LLC ....E...... 908 668-0220
  Plainfield (G-8874)
White Lotus Home Ltd Lblty Co ....F...... 732 828-2111
  New Brunswick (G-7013)

2393 Textile Bags

Ace Bag & Burlap Company Inc ....F...... 973 242-2200
  Newark (G-7071)
▲ ADM Corporation ....D...... 732 469-0900
  Middlesex (G-6143)
American Dawn Inc ....G...... 856 467-9211
  Bridgeport (G-761)
▲ AMS Products LLC ....F...... 973 442-5790
  Wharton (G-11978)

▲ Elements Accessories Inc..............G...... 646 801-5187
  Maplewood (G-5919)
◆ Halsted Corporation ....E...... 201 333-0670
  Cranbury (G-1836)
▲ Kt America Corp ....F...... 609 655-5333
  Cranbury (G-1850)
▲ Lbu Inc ....E...... 973 773-4800
  Paterson (G-8318)
Mobile Solutions Intl LLC ....G...... 609 448-3089
  Robbinsville (G-9518)
▲ Nyp Corp (frmr Ny-Pters Corp) ......D...... 908 351-6550
  Elizabeth (G-2761)
Philip Papalia ....F...... 732 349-5530
  Toms River (G-10902)
Shaffer Products Inc.......................E...... 908 206-1980
  Union (G-11223)

2394 Canvas Prdts

Beachwood Canvas Works LLC ....F...... 732 929-1783
  Island Heights (G-4651)
Blacher Canvas Products Inc ....G...... 732 968-3666
  Dunellen (G-2128)
▲ Canvas Creations ....G...... 609 465-8428
  Cape May Court House (G-1111)
Colie Sail Makers Inc......................G...... 732 892-4344
  Point Pleasant Boro (G-8935)
Costa Mar Cnvas Enclosures LLC .....F...... 609 965-1538
  Egg Harbor City (G-2660)
Fisher Canvas Products Inc ....G...... 609 239-2733
  Burlington (G-972)
G & J Solutions Inc ....G...... 609 861-9838
  Woodbine (G-12142)
Harold F Fisher & Sons Inc ....G...... 800 624-2868
  Delanco (G-2006)
Howard Lippincott ....G...... 856 764-8282
  Riverside (G-9499)
Hudson Awning Co Inc ....E...... 201 339-7171
  Bayonne (G-232)
▼ Kerry Wilkens Inc ....G...... 732 787-0070
  Belford (G-288)
Linthicum Sails ....G...... 856 783-4288
  Somerdale (G-10041)
Lloyds of Millville Inc......................F...... 856 825-0345
  Millville (G-6312)
▼ Meese Inc ....E...... 201 796-4490
  Saddle Brook (G-9774)
North Sales ....G...... 732 528-8899
  Manasquan (G-5876)
Opdyke Awnings Inc ....F...... 732 449-5940
  Wall Township (G-11501)
Polyair Inter Pack Inc ....D...... 201 804-1700
  Carlstadt (G-1205)
Pv Deroche LLC ....G...... 908 475-2266
  Belvidere (G-374)
Revere Plastics Inc ....G...... 201 641-0777
  Little Ferry (G-5514)
Robert Brown ....G...... 609 398-6262
  Ocean City (G-7756)
Sconda Canvas Products Inc ....E...... 732 225-3500
  Edison (G-2612)
Shore Awning Co ....G...... 732 775-3351
  Wall Township (G-11509)
Stetsers JD Canvas Pdts Inc ....G...... 856 423-4901
  Paulsboro (G-8426)
Superior Marine Canvas ....G...... 856 241-1724
  Swedesboro (G-10731)
Texas Canvas Co Inc ....G...... 973 278-3802
  Fairfield (G-3324)
▲ William Opdyke Awnings Inc ....G...... 732 449-5940
  Wall Township (G-11519)

2395 Pleating & Stitching For The Trade

A Stitch Ahead ....F...... 609 586-1068
  Trenton (G-11013)
Advantage Ds LLC ....E...... 856 307-9600
  Glassboro (G-3800)
Ambro Manufacturing Inc ....F...... 908 806-8337
  Flemington (G-3425)
Apollo East LLC ....G...... 856 486-1882
  Pennsauken (G-8478)
Arts Embroidery LLC ....G...... 732 870-2400
  West Long Branch (G-11843)
◆ Avanti Linens Inc ....F...... 201 641-7766
  Moonachie (G-6506)
Aztec Graphics Inc ....F...... 609 587-1000
  Trenton (G-11023)
Bauer Sport Shop ....G...... 201 384-6522
  Dumont (G-2115)
Bon-Jour Group LLC ....F...... 201 646-1070
  Norwood (G-7616)

S
I
C

C & D Sales....G....609 383-9292
Pleasantville (G-8903)
▲ Carolace Embroidery Co Inc....D....201 945-2151
Ridgefield (G-9354)
CDK Industries LLC....G....856 488-5456
Cherry Hill (G-1356)
▲ Central Safety Equipment Co....E....609 386-6448
Burlington (G-963)
Chenille Products Inc....F....201 703-1917
Palisades Park (G-7837)
Cozy Formal Wear Inc....G....973 661-9781
Nutley (G-7645)
Craig Fabrics Inc....F....201 869-9126
Guttenberg (G-3868)
Creative Embroidery Corp....E....973 497-5700
Newark (G-7130)
Deerbrook Fabrics....F....201 945-4141
Guttenberg (G-3869)
Design N Stitch Inc....G....201 488-1314
Hackensack (G-3904)
Dezine Line Inc....F....973 989-1009
Wharton (G-11985)
E B R Manufacturing Inc....E....973 263-8810
Parsippany (G-7991)
Embroideries Unlimited Inc....G....201 692-1560
Teaneck (G-10752)
Embroidery In Stitches Inc....F....732 460-2660
Morganville (G-6641)
Family Screen Printing Inc....F....856 933-2780
Bellmawr (G-340)
Gilbert Storms Jr....G....973 835-5729
Haskell (G-4207)
Golden Rule Creations Inc....G....201 337-4050
Franklin Lakes (G-3619)
Goralski Inc....E....201 573-1529
Park Ridge (G-7921)
Imagery Embroidary Corporation....F....201 343-9333
Union City (G-11248)
▲ Innovative Design Inc....G....201 227-2555
Cresskill (G-1946)
Its The Pitts Inc....G....609 645-7319
Pleasantville (G-8910)
J & S Finishing Inc....G....201 854-0338
West New York (G-11868)
J & T Embroidery Inc....G....201 867-4897
Union City (G-11249)
J and S Sporting Apparel LLC....G....732 787-5500
Keansburg (G-4856)
Mary Bridget Enterprises....E....609 267-4830
Cinnaminson (G-1475)
Midland Screen Printing Inc....F....201 703-0066
Saddle Brook (G-9775)
Monogram Center Inc....E....732 442-1800
Perth Amboy (G-8624)
Mt Embroidery & Promotions LLC....G....201 646-1070
Norwood (G-7629)
NJ Logo Wear LLC....G....609 597-9400
Manahawkin (G-5832)
O Stitch Matic Inc....G....201 861-3045
Guttenberg (G-3870)
Patchworks Co Inc....G....973 627-2002
Dover (G-2106)
Pioneer Embroidery Co....G....973 777-6418
South Hackensack (G-10289)
Pro Image Promotions Inc....G....973 252-8000
Kenvil (G-5013)
Quadelle Textile Corp....F....201 865-1112
West New York (G-11879)
Red Diamond Company....G....973 759-2005
Belleville (G-314)
Risse & Risse Graphics Inc....E....856 751-7671
Runnemede (G-9721)
Semels Embroidery Inc....F....973 473-6868
Clifton (G-1719)
Sequins of Distinction Inc....G....201 348-8111
North Bergen (G-7486)
Sgh Inc....G....609 698-8868
Barnegat (G-165)
Sniderman John....F....201 569-5482
Englewood (G-2932)
South Amboy Designer T Shirt L....G....732 456-2594
South Amboy (G-10245)
▲ Star Embroidery Corp....E....973 481-4300
Newark (G-7328)
▲ Tone Embroidery Corp....E....201 943-1082
Fairview (G-3371)
Toni Embroidery....G....201 664-6909
Westwood (G-11973)
Uniport Industries Corporation....G....201 391-7676
Woodcliff Lake (G-12206)
Unique Embroidery Inc....F....201 943-9191
Elmwood Park (G-2853)
University Fashions By Janet....G....856 228-1615
Williamstown (G-12111)
Walker Eight Corp....G....201 861-4208
North Bergen (G-7494)
Wally Enterprises Inc....F....732 329-2613
Monmouth Junction (G-6371)
William Cromley....G....856 881-6019
Clayton (G-1529)
World Class Marketing Corp....E....201 313-0022
Fort Lee (G-3591)
Wostbrock Embroidery Inc....G....201 445-3074
Midland Park (G-6243)

2396 Automotive Trimmings, Apparel Findings, Related Prdts

A S A P Nameplate & Labeling....F....973 773-3934
Passaic (G-8122)
Acey Industries Inc....G....973 595-1222
North Haledon (G-7547)
Alchemy Billboards LLC....G....973 977-8828
Paterson (G-8203)
Alco Trimming....G....201 854-8608
North Bergen (G-7426)
All Nu Trophy & Screen Prtg....F....201 807-0808
Ridgefield Park (G-9396)
Allied Elastic Braid Inc....E....201 941-8875
Saddle Brook (G-9751)
Ambro Manufacturing Inc....F....908 806-8337
Flemington (G-3425)
Amcor Phrm Packg USA Inc....C....856 728-9300
Williamstown (G-12078)
Art Flag Co Inc....F....212 334-1890
Fair Haven (G-3070)
Art Guild Inc....F....732 390-5300
East Brunswick (G-2135)
▲ Artistic Bias Products Co Inc....E....732 382-4141
Rahway (G-9175)
▲ Associated Fabrics Corporation....G....201 300-6053
Fair Lawn (G-3078)
Aztec Graphics Inc....F....609 587-1000
Trenton (G-11023)
Budget Print Center....G....973 743-0073
Bloomfield (G-503)
C Q Corporation....F....201 935-8488
East Rutherford (G-2289)
C S Hot Stamping....G....201 840-4004
Edgewater (G-2435)
◆ Circle Visual Inc....E....212 719-5153
Carlstadt (G-1141)
Clarici Graphics Inc....E....609 587-7204
Trenton (G-11041)
▲ Colonial - Bende Ribbons Inc....G....973 777-8700
Passaic (G-8130)
Color Comp Inc....G....856 262-3040
Williamstown (G-12083)
Cox Stationers and Printers....E....908 928-1010
Linden (G-5363)
Creative Embroidery Corp....E....973 497-5700
Newark (G-7130)
Custom Graphics of Vineland....E....856 691-7858
Vineland (G-11347)
▲ Custom Laminations Inc....E....973 279-9174
Paterson (G-8243)
Designs By James....G....856 692-1316
Vineland (G-11352)
▲ Donray Printing Inc....E....973 515-8100
Parsippany (G-7984)
Edward Berger Inc....E....609 571-9676
Old Bridge (G-7778)
◆ Elegant USA LLC....D....973 812-8820
Totowa (G-10943)
Family Screen Printing Inc....F....856 933-2780
Bellmawr (G-340)
French Textile Co Inc....F....973 471-5000
Clifton (G-1623)
▼ Green Distribution LLC....D....201 293-4381
Secaucus (G-9893)
Image Point....G....908 684-1768
Newton (G-7392)
James Smith....G....732 229-8273
Long Branch (G-5626)
▲ Jrm Industries Inc....D....973 779-9340
Passaic (G-8152)
Klein Ribbon Corp....E....973 684-4671
Paterson (G-8310)
Lukoil N Arlington Ltd Lblty....E....856 722-6425
Moorestown (G-6599)
Mail Direct Paper Company LLC....F....201 933-2782
Lyndhurst (G-5689)
Mar-Kal Products Corp....E....973 783-7155
Carlstadt (G-1187)
McLain Studios Inc....G....732 775-0271
Asbury Park (G-81)
Monogram Center Inc....E....732 442-1800
Perth Amboy (G-8624)
Nes Enterprises Inc....G....201 964-1400
Carlstadt (G-1192)
Newark Auto Top Co Inc....F....973 677-9935
East Orange (G-2262)
Painting Inc....F....201 489-6565
South Hackensack (G-10287)
▲ Papillon Ribbon & Bow Inc....E....973 928-6128
Clifton (G-1689)
◆ Phoenix Glass LLC....E....856 692-0100
Pittsgrove (G-8847)
Premier Ribbon Company....G....973 589-2600
Newark (G-7273)
▲ Prismatix Decal Inc....G....201 525-2800
Hackensack (G-3965)
Quick Bias Bnding Trmming Inds....F....732 422-0123
North Brunswick (G-7536)
R & B Printing Inc....G....908 766-4073
Bernardsville (G-454)
Red Diamond Company....G....973 759-2005
Belleville (G-314)
Rutler Screen Printing Inc....F....908 859-3327
Phillipsburg (G-8669)
Safer Textile Processing Corp....B....973 482-6400
Newark (G-7300)
▲ Scher Fabrics Inc....F....212 382-2266
Freehold (G-3687)
Screened Images Inc....E....732 651-8181
East Brunswick (G-2182)
Semels Embroidery Inc....F....973 473-6868
Clifton (G-1719)
Sniderman John....F....201 569-5482
Englewood (G-2932)
◆ Star Binding & Trimming LLC....E....201 864-2220
Lodi (G-5601)
▲ Stefan Enterprises Inc....E....973 253-6005
Garfield (G-3765)
▲ Stone Graphics....F....732 919-1111
Wall Township (G-11511)
Suzie Mac Specialties Inc....E....732 238-3500
East Brunswick (G-2191)
Tarma Sales....G....732 969-3318
Carteret (G-1268)
Toppan Printing Co Amer Inc....C....732 469-8400
Somerset (G-10188)
Total Ink Solutions LLC....F....201 487-9600
Hackensack (G-3985)
◆ U S Screening Corp....C....973 242-1110
Newark (G-7350)
Unique Screen Printing Corp....E....908 925-3773
Linden (G-5456)
Wally Enterprises Inc....F....732 329-2613
Monmouth Junction (G-6371)
Z Line Beachwear....G....732 793-1234
Lavallette (G-5238)
Zone Two Inc....F....732 237-0766
Bayville (G-263)

2397 Schiffli Machine Embroideries

▲ Carolace Embroidery Co Inc....D....201 945-2151
Ridgefield (G-9354)
Chenille Products Inc....F....201 703-1917
Palisades Park (G-7837)
Embroidery Concepts....G....973 942-8555
Paterson (G-8261)
Eyelet Embroideries Inc....D....201 945-2151
Ridgefield (G-9359)
Goralski Inc....E....201 573-1529
Park Ridge (G-7921)
▲ Hamilton Embroidery Co Inc....F....201 867-4084
Union City (G-11247)
Jacqueline Embroidery Co....G....732 278-8121
Hackensack (G-3932)
John M Sniderman Inc....G....201 450-4291
Fairview (G-3363)
Marlene Embroidery Inc....G....201 868-1682
West New York (G-11873)
O Stitch Matic Inc....G....201 861-3045
Guttenberg (G-3870)
Quadelle Textile Corp....F....201 865-1112
West New York (G-11879)
▲ Tone Embroidery Corp....E....201 943-1082
Fairview (G-3371)

Tri-Chem Inc ....F 973 751-9200
  Belleville (G-320)
Weber & Doebrich Inc.........................G..... 201 868-6122
  West New York (G-11883)

2399 Fabricated Textile Prdts, NEC

◆ Air Cruisers Company LLC.............C..... 732 681-3527
  Wall Township (G-11460)
▼ Airborne Systems N Amer NJ Inc.....C..... 856 663-1275
  Pennsauken (G-8474)
▲ Annin & Co ....E..... 973 228-9400
  Roseland (G-9644)
Annin & Co ....C..... 973 239-9000
  Verona (G-11303)
Art Flag Co Inc ....F..... 212 334-1890
  Fair Haven (G-3070)
Atlas Auto Trim Inc ....G..... 732 985-6800
  Edison (G-2468)
▲ Bearhands Ltd ....G..... 201 807-9898
  Passaic (G-8127)
▲ Belting Industries Group LLC ....E..... 908 272-8591
  Union (G-11158)
▲ Bright Ideas Usa LLC ....G..... 732 886-8865
  Lakewood (G-5089)
Clothes Horse International ....F..... 856 829-8460
  Cinnaminson (G-1451)
Covalnce Spcialty Coatings LLC........D..... 732 356-2870
  Middlesex (G-6159)
▲ Curvon Corporation ....E..... 732 747-3832
  Tinton Falls (G-10829)
◆ Elegant USA LLC ....D..... 973 812-8820
  Totowa (G-10943)
Horsetracs ....G..... 732 228-7646
  West Creek (G-11811)
National Flag & Display Co Inc ....E..... 973 366-1776
  Wharton (G-11993)
▲ Northcott Silk USA Inc ....G..... 201 672-9600
  Lyndhurst (G-5696)
Patchworks Co Inc ....G..... 973 627-2002
  Dover (G-2106)
Rapid Transfer Co Inc ....F..... 201 529-0002
  Mahwah (G-5807)
Rose Brand Wipers Inc ....C..... 201 770-1441
  Secaucus (G-9919)
▲ Rose Brand Wipers Inc ....G..... 201 809-1730
  Secaucus (G-9918)
Sterling Net & Twine Co Inc ....G..... 973 783-9800
  Montclair (G-6436)
Stewart-Morris Inc ....G..... 973 822-2777
  Madison (G-5736)
Switlik Parachute Company Inc ....F..... 609 587-3300
  Trenton (G-11119)
Tri G Manufacturing LLC ....F..... 732 460-1881
  Colts Neck (G-1793)
Tuff Mutters LLC ....G..... 973 291-6679
  Kinnelon (G-5041)
▲ Union Hill Corp ....G..... 732 786-9422
  Englishtown (G-2999)
▲ Weatherbeeta USA Inc ....E..... 732 287-1182
  Edison (G-2650)

24 LUMBER AND WOOD PRODUCTS, EXCEPT FURNITURE

2411 Logging

▲ Bamboo & Rattan Works Inc.............G..... 732 255-4239
  Toms River (G-10866)
Green Land & Logging LLC ....G..... 908 894-2361
  Stockton (G-10611)
Kane Wood Fuel ....G..... 856 589-3292
  Pitman (G-8843)
Marzullo ....F..... 973 955-5309
  Passaic (G-8160)
Mountain Top Logging LLC ....G..... 908 413-2982
  Lebanon (G-5298)
New Jersey Fence & Guardrail ....F..... 973 786-5400
  Andover (G-53)
Railing Dynamics Inc ....G..... 609 593-5400
  Millville (G-6321)

2421 Saw & Planing Mills

Boards and Beams Co LLC..................G..... 973 299-6100
  Towaco (G-10989)
Dolan & Traynor Inc ....E..... 973 696-8700
  Wayne (G-11625)
Empire Lumber & Millwork Co ....E..... 973 242-2700
  Newark (G-7153)
◆ Global Teak Inc ....F..... 609 208-2854
  Winslow (G-12132)

John H Abbott Inc ....G..... 609 561-0303
  Hammonton (G-4140)
Landew Sawdust Co Inc ....F..... 973 344-5255
  Newark (G-7216)
Logpowercom LLC ....G..... 732 350-9663
  Whiting (G-12068)
Mellon D P M L L C ....G..... 732 563-0030
  Somerset (G-10136)
P J Murphy Forest Pdts Corp ....G..... 973 316-0800
  Montville (G-6491)
Rex Lumber Company ....D..... 732 446-4200
  Manalapan (G-5861)
Riephoff Saw Mill Inc ....F..... 609 259-7265
  Allentown (G-34)
Sawdust Depot LLC ....F..... 973 344-5255
  Howell (G-4565)
Schairer Brothers ....G..... 609 965-0996
  Egg Harbor City (G-2670)
Thomas Cobb & Sons ....G..... 856 451-0671
  Bridgeton (G-800)
Ufp Berlin LLC ....C..... 856 767-0596
  Berlin (G-443)

2426 Hardwood Dimension & Flooring Mills

Airborne Systems N Amer Inc ....G..... 856 663-1275
  Pennsauken (G-8473)
Alpine Custom Floors ....F..... 201 533-0100
  Jersey City (G-4703)
Atlantic Flooring LLC ....F..... 609 296-7700
  Ltl Egg Hbr (G-5641)
Continental Woodworking Co ....G..... 609 654-0820
  Medford (G-6067)
Eppley Building & Design Inc ....E..... 973 636-9499
  Hawthorne (G-4232)
Flooring Concepts NJ LLC ....F..... 732 409-7600
  Manalapan (G-5848)
▲ Floors For Less Corporation ....G..... 201 933-9663
  East Rutherford (G-2296)
Friends Hardwood Floors Inc ....F..... 732 859-4019
  Oakhurst (G-7669)
Gwynn-E Co ....G..... 215 423-6400
  Moorestown (G-6581)

2431 Millwork

Abatetech Inc ....E..... 609 265-2107
  Lumberton (G-5650)
Adhisa Molding ....G..... 862 324-5222
  West Caldwell (G-11762)
▲ All Seasons Door & Window Inc .....E..... 732 238-7100
  East Brunswick (G-2131)
Alvaro Stairs LLC ....G..... 201 864-6754
  North Bergen (G-7429)
AM Wood Inc ....G..... 732 246-1506
  East Brunswick (G-2133)
American Stairs Inc ....F..... 732 363-3734
  Lakewood (G-5070)
Architctral Cbinetry Mllwk LLC ....G..... 908 213-2001
  Phillipsburg (G-8639)
Architectural Wdwkg Assoc ....G..... 908 996-7866
  Frenchtown (G-3696)
▲ Artistic Doors and Windows Inc .....E..... 732 726-9400
  Avenel (G-125)
B & B Millwork & Doors Inc..................G..... 973 249-0300
  Kenilworth (G-4939)
B & C Custom WD Handrail Corp ....G..... 732 530-6640
  Red Bank (G-9322)
Bell arte Inc ....F..... 908 355-1199
  Elizabeth (G-2713)
Bestmark National LLC ....E..... 862 772-4863
  Irvington (G-4578)
Bildisco Mfg Inc ....F..... 973 673-2400
  West Orange (G-11889)
Bon Architectual Mill Work LLC ....G..... 856 320-2872
  Pennsauken (G-8487)
▲ Bridgewater Wholesalers Inc ....C..... 908 526-7555
  Branchburg (G-645)
Cabinet Tronics Inc ....F..... 609 267-2625
  Birmingham (G-466)
Castle Woodcraft Assoc LLC ....F..... 732 349-1519
  Pine Beach (G-8678)
Caw LLC ....F..... 973 429-7004
  Bloomfield (G-506)
Cerami Wood Products Inc ....F..... 732 968-7222
  Piscataway (G-8747)
Classic Designer Woodwork Inc ....G..... 201 280-3711
  Glen Rock (G-3823)
Clear Cut Window Distrs of NJ ....G..... 201 512-1804
  Mahwah (G-5759)
Cozzolino Inc ....E..... 973 731-9292
  West Orange (G-11891)

Creating Your Design LLC ....G..... 973 357-1080
  Paterson (G-8240)
Creative Concepts of NJ LLC ....G..... 732 833-1776
  Jackson (G-4659)
Creative Wood Products Inc ....F..... 732 370-0051
  Jackson (G-4660)
Crincoli Woodwork Co Inc ....G..... 908 352-9332
  Elizabeth (G-2721)
Custom Counters By Precision ....E..... 973 773-0111
  Passaic (G-8133)
Custom Wood Furniture Inc ....F..... 973 579-4880
  Newton (G-7385)
Cwi Architectural Millwork LLC ....G..... 856 307-7900
  Glassboro (G-3802)
Dans Woodwork ....G..... 973 751-4506
  Belleville (G-299)
▲ Design of Tomorrow Inc ....F..... 973 227-1000
  Fairfield (G-3177)
▲ Designcore Ltd ....D..... 718 499-0337
  Secaucus (G-9877)
DMD Stairs & Rails LLC ....F..... 732 901-0102
  Jackson (G-4664)
▲ Donnelly Industries Inc ....D..... 973 672-1800
  Wayne (G-11626)
Door Stop LLC ....F..... 718 599-5112
  Carlstadt (G-1157)
Dor-Win Manufacturing Co ....E..... 201 796-4300
  Elmwood Park (G-2815)
Dreamstar Construction LLC ....G..... 732 393-2572
  Middletown (G-6213)
Empire Lumber & Millwork Co ....E..... 973 242-2700
  Newark (G-7153)
Epic Millwork LLC ....G..... 732 296-0273
  Somerset (G-10096)
Evertlast Interiors ....G..... 732 252-9965
  Manalapan (G-5845)
F L Feldman Associates ....F..... 732 776-8544
  Asbury Park (G-77)
▲ F T Millwork Inc ....G..... 732 741-1216
  Red Bank (G-9330)
Filipe Custom Woodwork ....E..... 908 486-0033
  Linden (G-5375)
Gass Custom Woodworking ....G..... 201 493-9282
  Paramus (G-7871)
Glen Rock Stair Corp ....E..... 201 337-9595
  Franklin Lakes (G-3618)
Greenbrook Stairs Inc ....G..... 908 221-9145
  Bernardsville (G-450)
Hahns Woodworking ....F..... 908 722-2742
  Branchburg (G-664)
Hutchinson Cabinets ....E..... 856 468-5500
  Sewell (G-9956)
Iacovelli Stairs Incorporated ....F..... 609 693-3476
  Forked River (G-3538)
▲ Ideal Jacobs Corporation ....E..... 973 275-5100
  Maplewood (G-5922)
▼ Infinite Mfg Group Inc ....G..... 973 649-9950
  Kearny (G-4885)
Intex Millwork Solutions LLC ....E..... 856 293-4100
  Mays Landing (G-6039)
Jarahian Millwork Inc ....G..... 732 240-5151
  Whiting (G-12067)
Jeffrey Danee Inc ....G..... 973 872-9388
  Paterson (G-8302)
Joffe Lumber & Supply Co Inc ....D..... 856 825-9550
  Vineland (G-11376)
Joseph Naticchia ....F..... 609 882-7709
  Ewing (G-3028)
Juliali Woodwork ....G..... 856 225-0772
  Pennsauken (G-8538)
K2 Millwork Ltd Liability Co ....G..... 609 379-6411
  Columbus (G-1804)
Katadin Inc ....G..... 908 526-0166
  Branchburg (G-671)
Kaufman Stairs Inc ....E..... 908 862-3579
  Rahway (G-9206)
Kempton Wood Products ....G..... 732 449-8673
  Wall Township (G-11493)
Kenneth Asmar Custom Interiors ....G..... 732 544-6137
  Tinton Falls (G-10840)
Lauderdale Millwork Inc ....F..... 908 508-9550
  Berkeley Heights (G-417)
Lees Woodworking Inc ....G..... 732 681-1002
  Wall Township (G-11495)
Lukach Interiors Inc ....F..... 973 777-1499
  Clifton (G-1666)
Lux Home Inc ....G..... 845 623-2821
  Paramus (G-7886)
M K Woodworking Inc ....G..... 609 771-1350
  Ewing (G-3036)

S
I
C

M R C Millwork & Trim Inc......G...... 201 954-2176
Franklin Lakes *(G-3620)*
Manhattan Door Corp......D...... 718 963-1111
Carlstadt *(G-1186)*
Maranatha Ceramic Tile & Marbl......E...... 609 758-1168
Wrightstown *(G-12242)*
Marty Anderson & Assoc Inc......G...... 201 798-0507
North Bergen *(G-7465)*
Midhattan Woodworking Corp......E...... 732 727-3020
Old Bridge *(G-7785)*
ML Woodwork Inc......G...... 201 953-2175
Elmwood Park *(G-2837)*
Mountain Millwork......G...... 908 647-1100
Warren *(G-11561)*
Mp Custom FL LLC......F...... 973 417-2288
Wayne *(G-11666)*
National Woodworking Co......G...... 908 851-9316
Union *(G-11211)*
New Jersey Hardwoods Inc......E...... 908 754-0990
Plainfield *(G-8869)*
Nyc Woodworking Inc......G...... 718 222-1221
Marlboro *(G-5950)*
Old Fashion Woodworking Inc......F...... 973 808-9663
Rahway *(G-9216)*
Ornate Millwork LLC......G...... 866 464-5596
Lakewood *(G-5169)*
Palisade Lumber & Supply Inc......G...... 201 656-4400
Jersey City *(G-4797)*
Palumbo Millwork Inc......G...... 732 938-3266
Wall Township *(G-11502)*
Patella Construction Corp......D...... 973 916-0100
Passaic *(G-8169)*
Pkc Finewoodworking LLC......G...... 201 951-8880
Montville *(G-6492)*
Precision Dealer Services Inc......E...... 908 237-1100
Flemington *(G-3460)*
▲ **Prestige Millwork LLC**......E...... 908 526-5100
Bridgewater *(G-876)*
Progress Woodwork......G...... 732 906-8680
Edison *(G-2598)*
▲ **R & M Manufacturing Inc**......E...... 609 495-8032
Monroe Township *(G-6390)*
R J Hoppe Store Construction......G...... 973 485-5665
Newark *(G-7283)*
▲ **Randall Mfg Co Inc**......E...... 973 482-8603
Newark *(G-7284)*
Rex Lumber Company......D...... 732 446-4200
Manalapan *(G-5861)*
Rock Solid Woodworking LLC......G...... 732 974-1261
Sea Girt *(G-9862)*
Royal Oak Railings LLC......G...... 973 208-8900
Oak Ridge *(G-7665)*
▲ **RPI Industries Inc**......D...... 609 714-2330
Medford *(G-6080)*
▲ **RSI Woodworking Products Co**......D...... 609 484-1600
Egg Harbor Township *(G-2694)*
RSI Woodworking Products Co......E...... 609 645-9777
Egg Harbor Township *(G-2695)*
Salernos Kitchen Cabinets......E...... 201 794-1990
Saddle Brook *(G-9789)*
Sandkamp Woodworks LLC......G...... 201 200-0101
Jersey City *(G-4822)*
Screens Incorporated......G...... 973 633-8558
Wayne *(G-11683)*
Skyline Windows LLC......E...... 201 531-9600
Wood Ridge *(G-12138)*
Smittys Door Service Inc......G...... 908 284-0506
Pittstown *(G-8851)*
Somerset Wood Products Co......E...... 908 526-0030
Raritan *(G-9316)*
Sourland Mountain Wdwkg LLC T......G...... 908 806-7661
Neshanic Station *(G-6939)*
Stairworks Inc......G...... 908 276-2829
Cranford *(G-1927)*
Summit Millwork & Supply Inc......G...... 908 273-1486
Summit *(G-10660)*
Tea Elle Woodworks......G...... 732 938-9660
Farmingdale *(G-3395)*
Terhune Bros Woodworking......G...... 973 962-6686
Ringwood *(G-9457)*
Total Garage Solutions LLC......F...... 732 749-3993
Wall Township *(G-11515)*
▲ **Trim and Tassels LLC**......G...... 973 808-1566
Fairfield *(G-3331)*
Trim Factory Inc......G...... 856 769-8746
Pilesgrove *(G-8677)*
Unix Cabinetry Inc......G...... 201 995-6969
Paterson *(G-8405)*
Urban Millwork & Supply Corp......G...... 973 278-7072
Paterson *(G-8406)*
USA Wood Door Inc......E...... 856 384-9663
West Deptford *(G-11842)*
V Custom Millwork Inc......F...... 732 469-9600
Bridgewater *(G-907)*
Vanco Millwork Inc......F...... 973 992-3061
Livingston *(G-5568)*
Vigor Inc......G...... 973 851-9539
Totowa *(G-10981)*
Visual Architectural Designs......F...... 908 754-3000
South Plainfield *(G-10451)*
W F Sherman & Son Inc......F...... 732 223-1505
Manasquan *(G-5883)*
West Hudson Lumber & Mllwk Co......G...... 201 991-7191
Kearny *(G-4920)*
Window Factory Inc......E...... 856 546-5050
Mount Ephraim *(G-6765)*
Window Trends......G...... 973 887-6676
Parsippany *(G-8113)*
Wohners......G...... 201 568-7307
Englewood *(G-2944)*
Wood Products Inc......G...... 609 859-0303
Southampton *(G-10484)*
Wood Works......G...... 856 728-4520
Williamstown *(G-12115)*
▲ **Woodhaven Lumber & Millwork**......C...... 732 901-0030
Lakewood *(G-5206)*
Woodhaven Lumber & Millwork......E...... 732 295-8800
Point Pleasant Beach *(G-8928)*
Woodtec Inc......G...... 908 979-0180
Hackettstown *(G-4043)*
Woodworking Inc Corporate......E...... 973 227-2211
Fairfield *(G-3354)*
Zone Defense Inc......F...... 973 328-0436
Hackettstown *(G-4044)*

2434 Wood Kitchen Cabinets

▲ **10-31 Incorporated**......E...... 908 496-4946
Columbia *(G-1795)*
A & J Carpets Inc......G...... 856 227-1753
Blackwood *(G-469)*
A R Bothers Woodworking Inc......E...... 908 725-2891
Somerville *(G-10198)*
A W Ross Inc......F...... 973 471-5900
Passaic *(G-8123)*
Allen Cabinets and Millwork......G...... 973 694-0665
Pequannock *(G-8596)*
◆ **Bcg Marble Gran Fabricators Co**......F...... 201 343-8487
Hackensack *(G-3879)*
Bebus Cabinetry LLC......G...... 201 729-9300
Rutherford *(G-9727)*
Bennett Cabinets......G...... 732 548-1616
Edison *(G-2471)*
Bernard Miller Fabricators......G...... 856 541-9499
Camden *(G-1043)*
Capra Custom Cabinetry......G...... 908 797-9848
Washington *(G-11580)*
Castle Woodcraft Assoc LLC......F...... 732 349-1519
Pine Beach *(G-8678)*
▲ **Cavalli Cabinets Inc**......G...... 201 528-7070
Piscataway *(G-8745)*
Certified Cabinet Corp......G...... 732 741-0755
Marlboro *(G-5936)*
▲ **Choice Cabinetry LLC**......E...... 908 707-8801
Somerville *(G-10205)*
CPB Inc......E...... 856 697-2700
Buena *(G-946)*
Custom Cabinets By Jim Bucko......G...... 609 522-6646
Wildwood *(G-12071)*
David Leiz Custom Woodwork......G...... 908 486-1533
Linden *(G-5368)*
Designer Kitchens......F...... 732 370-5500
Jackson *(G-4663)*
Elite Cabinetry Corp......G...... 973 583-0194
Newark *(G-7152)*
▲ **Euro Kraft Group LLC**......E...... 856 451-7450
Bridgeton *(G-784)*
European Country Kitchens Inc......D...... 908 735-6659
Pittstown *(G-8850)*
F L Feldman Associates......F...... 732 776-8544
Asbury Park *(G-77)*
◆ **Fabuwood Cabinetry Corp**......B...... 201 432-6555
Jersey City *(G-4751)*
Fernandes Custom Cabinets......G...... 732 446-2829
Manalapan *(G-5847)*
Foley-Waite Associates Inc......F...... 908 298-0700
Kenilworth *(G-4957)*
Forman Industries Inc......D...... 732 727-8100
Old Bridge *(G-7779)*
Frank Burton & Sons Inc......G...... 856 455-1202
Bridgeton *(G-785)*
Frank Ferreira Cab & Mill Work......G...... 732 564-1499
Warren *(G-11548)*
Franks Cabinet Shop Inc......G...... 908 658-4396
Pluckemin *(G-8919)*
G & M Custom Formica Work......G...... 732 888-0360
Keyport *(G-5019)*
Gambay Inc......G...... 856 330-4397
Pennsauken *(G-8513)*
Gemcraft Inc......G...... 732 449-8944
Belmar *(G-358)*
Hanssem......G...... 732 425-7695
Edison *(G-2533)*
▲ **Hanssem Corporation**......D...... 908 754-4949
Edison *(G-2534)*
Heard Woodworking LLC......G...... 908 232-3978
Westfield *(G-11927)*
Hutchinson Cabinets......E...... 856 468-5500
Sewell *(G-9956)*
Intelco......E...... 856 384-8562
Paulsboro *(G-8417)*
J & R Custom Woodworking Inc......G...... 973 625-4114
Denville *(G-2043)*
John Canary Custom Wdwkg Inc......F...... 908 851-2894
Union *(G-11198)*
▲ **Kasanova Inc**......G...... 201 368-8400
Wood Ridge *(G-12137)*
Ken Bauer Inc......E...... 201 664-6881
Hillsdale *(G-4385)*
Kerk Cabinetry LLC......G...... 856 881-4213
Glassboro *(G-3807)*
Kinzee Industries Inc......F...... 201 408-4301
Englewood *(G-2907)*
Kitchen Cabinet......G...... 856 228-8989
Blackwood *(G-487)*
Kitchen Crafters Plus......G...... 732 566-7995
Matawan *(G-6023)*
Kitchen King Inc......F...... 732 341-9660
Toms River *(G-10890)*
Kobolak & Son Inc......G...... 856 829-6106
Cinnaminson *(G-1472)*
L&W Audio/Video Inc......G...... 212 980-2862
Hoboken *(G-4483)*
Lexora Inc......G...... 855 453-9672
Newark *(G-7218)*
M K Woodworking Inc......G...... 609 771-1350
Ewing *(G-3036)*
Marte Cabinets Countertops LLC......G...... 973 525-9502
Passaic *(G-8159)*
Masterpiece Kitchens Inc......G...... 609 518-7887
Cherry Hill *(G-1396)*
Michael Lubrich......G...... 732 223-4235
Manasquan *(G-5874)*
Michaels Cabinet Connection......G...... 609 889-6611
Rio Grande *(G-9460)*
Millner Kitchens Inc......G...... 609 890-7300
Hamilton *(G-4118)*
▲ **Mk Wood Inc**......G...... 973 450-5110
Belleville *(G-308)*
Mp Custom FL LLC......F...... 973 417-2288
Wayne *(G-11666)*
▲ **Mr Pauls Custom Cabinets**......G...... 732 528-9427
Manasquan *(G-5875)*
Nmn Closet Inc......E...... 201 438-2462
Carlstadt *(G-1194)*
Oberg & Lindquist Corp......E...... 201 664-1300
Westwood *(G-11963)*
Palumbo Millwork Inc......G...... 732 938-3266
Wall Township *(G-11502)*
Parsons Cabinets Inc......G...... 973 279-4954
Montclair *(G-6430)*
Paul Burkhardt & Sons Inc......G...... 856 435-2020
Lindenwold *(G-5462)*
Paul Fago Cabinet Making Inc......G...... 856 384-0496
Woodbury *(G-12168)*
Pine Park Kitchens Inc......G...... 732 987-6520
Lakewood *(G-5171)*
Platinum Designs LLC......G...... 908 782-4010
Somerville *(G-10224)*
▲ **Platon Interiors**......G...... 201 567-5533
Englewood *(G-2922)*
▲ **R & M Manufacturing Inc**......E...... 609 495-8032
Monroe Township *(G-6390)*
Regency Cabinetry LLC......G...... 732 363-5630
Lakewood *(G-5178)*
▲ **Regency Cabinetry LLC**......F...... 732 363-5630
Lakewood *(G-5179)*
Regent Cabinets LLC......F...... 732 363-5630
Parsippany *(G-8078)*
Royal Cabinet Company Inc......E...... 908 203-8000
Bound Brook *(G-622)*

Salernos Kitchen Cabinets ....E 201 794-1990
Saddle Brook (G-9789)

Shearman Cabinets ....G 973 677-0071
East Orange (G-2269)

▲ Shekia Group LLC ....E 732 372-7666
Edison (G-2616)

St Martin Cabinetry Inc ....E 732 902-6020
Edison (G-2626)

Studio L Contracting LLC ....G 201 837-1650
Hackensack (G-3982)

Superior Custom Kitchens LLC ....E 908 753-6005
Warren (G-11568)

T & T Cabinet Works Inc ....G 973 279-0909
Paterson (G-8395)

United Cabinet Works LLC ....G 917 686-3395
Weehawken (G-11700)

Visual Architectural Designs ....F 908 754-3000
South Plainfield (G-10451)

Vitillo & Sons Inc ....F 732 886-1393
Lakewood (G-5201)

2435 Hardwood Veneer & Plywood

▲ Essex Coatings LLC ....F 732 855-9400
Avenel (G-130)

◆ Mannington Mills Inc ....A 856 935-3000
Salem (G-9806)

Rhoads OHara Architectural ....G 856 692-4100
Vineland (G-11397)

Woodhut LLC ....F 732 414-6440
Freehold (G-3694)

Yonkers Plywood Manufacturing ....E 732 727-1200
Old Bridge (G-7795)

2439 Structural Wood Members, NEC

Arnold Steel Co Inc ....D 732 363-1079
Howell (G-4546)

▲ Atlantic Exterior Wall Systems ....D 973 646-8200
Wayne (G-11606)

Marino International Corp ....G 732 752-5100
South Plainfield (G-10404)

Thomas Smock Woodworking ....G 732 542-9167
Eatontown (G-2426)

Timplex Corp ....F 973 875-5500
Sussex (G-10679)

Truss Engineering ....G 201 871-4800
Englewood (G-2938)

Woodbury Roof Truss Inc ....D 856 845-3848
Woodbury Heights (G-12178)

2441 Wood Boxes

Boxworks Inc ....G 856 456-9030
Bellmawr (G-332)

Bunn Industries Incorporated ....F 609 890-2900
Trenton (G-11030)

Cutler Bros Box & Lumber Co ....E 201 943-2535
Fairview (G-3360)

E L Baxter Co Inc ....F 732 229-8219
Ocean (G-7722)

Minerva Custom Products LLC ....G 201 447-4731
Waldwick (G-11449)

T & M Pallet Co Inc ....E 908 454-3042
Stewartsville (G-10598)

2448 Wood Pallets & Skids

Atco Pallet Company ....E 856 461-8141
Delanco (G-2003)

Atlantic Indus WD Pdts LLC ....G 609 965-4555
Egg Harbor City (G-2656)

Avenel Pallet Co Inc ....F 732 752-0500
Dunellen (G-2126)

Bunn Industries Incorporated ....F 609 890-2900
Trenton (G-11030)

Cutler Bros Box & Lumber Co ....E 201 943-2535
Fairview (G-3360)

D & H Pallets LLC ....G 973 481-2981
Newark (G-1064)

▼ Delisa Pallet Corp ....G 732 667-7070
Middlesex (G-6161)

East Coast Pallets LLC ....G 732 308-3616
Manalapan (G-5842)

Extreme Pallet Inc ....G 973 286-1717
Newark (G-7159)

F & R Pallets Inc ....E 856 964-8516
Camden (G-1064)

General Pallet LLC ....G 732 549-1000
Flemington (G-3445)

Global Direct Marketing Group ....G 856 427-6116
Haddonfield (G-4060)

◆ Granco Group LLC ....G 973 515-4721
Roseland (G-9651)

Greenway Products & Svcs LLC ....C 732 442-0200
New Brunswick (G-6965)

Isco ....G 856 672-9182
Barrington (G-179)

JC Pallets Inc ....F 973 345-1102
Paterson (G-8299)

Jimenez Pallets LLC ....G 862 267-3900
Kearny (G-4889)

Lawrence M Gichan Incorporated ......F 201 330-3222
North Bergen (G-7462)

Love Pallet LLC ....G 908 964-3385
Hillside (G-4426)

Lt Chini Inc ....G 856 692-0303
Vineland (G-11381)

M Hand Pallets ....G 908 887-2100
Elizabeth (G-2753)

Millwood Inc ....D 732 967-8818
South River (G-10463)

North Eastern Pallet Exchange ....E 908 289-0018
Elizabeth (G-2759)

Notie Corp ....G 609 259-3477
Allentown (G-32)

Pallet Services Inc ....G 856 514-3908
Pedricktown (G-8439)

Pedestal Pallet Inc ....G 732 968-7488
Dunellen (G-2129)

Petro Pallet LLC ....E 732 230-3287
Monmouth Junction (G-6354)

Poor Boy Pallet LLC ....G 856 451-3771
Bridgeton (G-795)

Premier Asset Logistics Networ ....F 877 725-6381
Williamstown (G-12101)

Reliable Pallet Services LLC ....G 973 900-2260
Hillside (G-4438)

Reliable Pallet Services LLC ....G 732 243-9642
Metuchen (G-6118)

Riephoff Saw Mill Inc ....F 609 259-7265
Allentown (G-34)

Royal Pallet Inc ....G 973 299-0445
Boonton (G-581)

Select Enterprises Inc ....E 732 287-8622
Edison (G-2613)

T & M Pallet Co Inc ....E 908 454-3042
Stewartsville (G-10598)

Tommys Pallet Yard LLC ....G 609 424-3996
Bordentown (G-612)

▲ Tristate Crating Pallet Co Inc ....E 973 357-8293
Paterson (G-8403)

U P N Pallet Co Inc ....F 856 299-1192
Penns Grove (G-8466)

Universal Pallet Inc ....G 732 356-2624
Warren (G-11569)

Van-Nick Pallet Inc ....G 908 753-1800
South Plainfield (G-10449)

Warren Pallet Company Inc ....F 908 995-7172
Bloomsbury (G-547)

Wm Leiber Inc ....G 732 938-2080
Farmingdale (G-3397)

2449 Wood Containers, NEC

Arrow Information Packagig LLC ....G 856 317-9000
Pennsauken (G-8480)

B Spinelli Farm Containers ....G 732 566-5619
Matawan (G-6013)

Boxworks Inc ....G 856 456-9030
Bellmawr (G-332)

Builders Firstsource Inc ....E 856 767-3153
Berlin (G-430)

Caudalie Usa Inc ....G 201 939-4969
Carlstadt (G-1139)

Cutler Bros Box & Lumber Co ....E 201 943-2535
Fairview (G-3360)

Jan Packaging Inc ....D 973 361-7200
Dover (G-2095)

Minerva Custom Products LLC ....G 201 447-4731
Waldwick (G-11449)

Vandereems Manufacturing Co ....F 973 427-2355
Hawthorne (G-4263)

2451 Mobile Homes

Acton Mobile Industries Inc ....G 610 485-5100
Burlington (G-953)

Wireless Experience of PA Inc ....G 732 552-0050
Toms River (G-10922)

2452 Prefabricated Wood Buildings & Cmpnts

All Structures LLC ....G 732 233-7071
Little Silver (G-5519)

Laraccas Manufacturing Inc ....E 973 571-1452
Cedar Grove (G-1288)

Marino International Corp ....G 732 752-5100
South Plainfield (G-10404)

Mdb Construction ....G 908 628-8010
Lebanon (G-5296)

Mod-U-Kraf Homes LLC ....E 540 482-0273
West Berlin (G-11734)

R H Vassallo Inc ....G 856 358-8841
Malaga (G-5827)

Sustanble Bldg Innovations Inc ....G 800 560-4143
Manasquan (G-2548)

Walpole Woodworkers Inc ....E 973 539-3555
Morris Plains (G-6681)

2491 Wood Preserving

Atlantic Wood Industries Inc ....F 609 267-4700
Hainesport (G-4070)

New England Wood Crafters ....G 856 241-9270
Swedesboro (G-10714)

Rq Floors Corp ....E 201 654-3587
Ridgefield (G-9383)

Rq Floors Corp ....E 201 654-3587
South Hackensack (G-10294)

2493 Reconstituted Wood Prdts

▲ Alcan Baltek Corporation ....D 201 767-1400
Northvale (G-7570)

AMP Custom Rubber Inc ....F 732 888-2714
Keyport (G-5015)

Bmca Holdings Corporation ....E 973 628-3000
Wayne (G-11610)

Building Materials Mfg Corp ....G 973 628-3000
Wayne (G-11616)

Eagle Fabrication Inc ....E 732 739-5300
Ltl Egg Hbr (G-5644)

Greenbuilt Intl Bldg Co ....C 609 300-9091
Voorhees (G-11432)

Homasote Company ....C 609 883-3300
Ewing (G-3024)

Homestyle Kitchens & Baths LLC ....G 908 979-9000
Hackettstown (G-4011)

◆ JM Huber Corporation ....D 732 603-3630
Edison (G-2546)

Johns Manville Corporation ....E 732 225-9190
Edison (G-2548)

New York Blackboard of NJ Inc ....G 973 926-1600
Hillside (G-4432)

R A O Contract Sales NY Inc ....G 201 652-1500
Paterson (G-8367)

Shelan Chemical Company Inc ....G 732 796-1003
Monroe Township (G-6392)

Standard Industries Inc ....G 856 241-0241
Swedesboro (G-10728)

◆ Standard Industries Inc ....A 973 628-3000
Parsippany (G-8092)

2499 Wood Prdts, NEC

◆ Africa Imports Inc ....E 201 457-1995
South Hackensack (G-10253)

All-State Fence Inc ....G 732 431-4944
West Orange (G-11885)

American Standard Intl Inc ....E 732 652-7100
Piscataway (G-8733)

Amertech Towerservices LLC ....G 732 389-2200
Shrewsbury (G-9989)

AMP Custom Rubber Inc ....F 732 888-2714
Keyport (G-5015)

Anthony Excavating & Dem ....G 609 926-8804
Egg Harbor Township (G-2678)

Architectural Wdwkg Assoc ....G 908 996-7866
Frenchtown (G-3696)

▲ Atlantic Coolg Tech & Svcs LLC ......E 201 939-0900
Carlstadt (G-1129)

Atlas Woodwork Inc ....F 973 621-9595
Newark (G-7097)

Bathware House Ltd Lblty Co ....G 732 546-3220
Linden (G-5352)

Best Value Rugs & Carpets Inc ....G 732 752-3528
Dunellen (G-2127)

Canac Kitchens of NJ Inc ....F 201 567-9585
Englewood (G-2881)

Color Decor Ltd Liability Co ....G 973 689-2699
Paterson (G-8235)

S I C

Comprelli Equipment and Svc ....G...... 973 428-8687
East Hanover *(G-2208)*
Contempocork LLC ....G...... 201 262-7738
River Edge *(G-9464)*
Corbion Group ....G...... 973 256-0198
Totowa *(G-10940)*
Crown Trophy ....G...... 973 808-8400
Pine Brook *(G-8696)*
Denby USA Limited ....G...... 800 374-6479
Bridgewater *(G-833)*
Distinctive Wdwrk By Rob Hoffm ....G...... 609 877-8122
Beverly *(G-462)*
Distinctive Woodwork Inc ....G...... 609 714-8505
Lumberton *(G-5656)*
Doerre Fence Co LLC ....F 732 751-9700
Farmingdale *(G-3384)*
Don Shrts Pcture Frmes Molding ....G...... 732 363-1323
Howell *(G-4552)*
Edison Finishing ....G...... 732 287-6660
Edison *(G-2509)*
Eviva LLC ....G...... 973 925-4028
Paterson *(G-8265)*
Forino Kitchen Cabinets Inc ....G...... 201 573-0990
Park Ridge *(G-7920)*
Frameco Inc ....E 973 989-1424
Dover *(G-2087)*
◆ **Frameware Inc** ....F 800 582-5608
Fairfield *(G-3201)*
▲ **General Metal Manufacturing Co** .....E 973 386-1818
East Hanover *(G-2218)*
Greenway Products & Svcs LLC ....C...... 732 442-0200
New Brunswick *(G-6965)*
▲ **HB Technik USA Ltd Lblty Prtnr** ......G...... 973 875-8688
Branchville *(G-731)*
Hoboken Executive Art Inc ....G...... 201 420-8262
Hoboken *(G-4473)*
Hoda Inc ....F 609 695-3000
Trenton *(G-11063)*
Howell Township Police ....D...... 732 919-2805
Howell *(G-4556)*
▲ **III Eagle Enterprises Ltd** ....E 973 237-1111
Ringwood *(G-9449)*
Intelco ....D...... 856 456-6755
Westville *(G-11944)*
Jorgensen Carr Ltd ....G...... 201 792-2278
East Orange *(G-2257)*
K Ron Art & Mirrors Inc ....G...... 201 313-7080
Ridgefield *(G-9369)*
Krfc Custom Woodworking Inc ....G...... 732 363-0522
Lakewood *(G-5143)*
Lardieri Custom Woodworking ....F 732 905-6334
Lakewood *(G-5145)*
Larsen Marine Services LLC ....G...... 609 408-3564
Sea Isle City *(G-9863)*
Larson-Juhl US LLC ....E 973 439-1801
Caldwell *(G-1030)*
Lexora Inc ....G...... 855 453-9672
Newark *(G-7218)*
M and R Manufacturing ....G...... 732 905-1061
Lakewood *(G-5150)*
Medford Cedar Products Inc ....G...... 609 859-1400
Southampton *(G-10479)*
Metroplex Products Company Inc ....G...... 732 249-0653
Monroe Township *(G-6384)*
Narva Inc ....G...... 973 218-1200
Springfield *(G-10567)*
▲ **National Fence Systems Inc** ....D...... 732 636-5600
Avenel *(G-143)*
P & S Blizzard Corporation ....G...... 973 523-1700
Paterson *(G-8358)*
Pba of West Windsor ....E 609 799-6535
Princeton Junction *(G-9161)*
Perk & Pantry ....G...... 856 451-4333
Bridgeton *(G-794)*
R A O Contract Sales NY Inc ....G...... 201 652-1500
Paterson *(G-8367)*
▲ **Ragar Co Inc** ....G...... 732 493-1416
Ocean *(G-7740)*
Randells Cstm Fniture Kitchens ....F 856 216-9400
Cherry Hill *(G-1418)*
Restortions By Peter Schichtel ....G...... 973 605-8818
Morristown *(G-6739)*
Revelation Gallery Inc ....G...... 973 627-6558
Denville *(G-2054)*
Roma Moulding Inc ....F 732 346-0999
Edison *(G-2607)*
Steelstran Industries Inc ....G...... 732 566-5040
Matawan *(G-6033)*
Studio L Contracting LLC ....G...... 201 837-1650
Hackensack *(G-3982)*

Swiss Madison LLC ....F 434 623-4766
Dayton *(G-1990)*
T M Baxter Services LLC ....E 908 500-9065
Washington *(G-11589)*
Taylor Made Custom Cabinetry ....F 856 786-5433
Pennsauken *(G-8583)*
▼ **Tlw Bath Ltd Liability Company** ......E 732 942-7117
Lakewood *(G-5196)*
◆ **Vaswani Inc** ....D...... 877 376-4425
Edison *(G-2641)*
Walpole Woodworkers Inc ....E 973 539-3555
Morris Plains *(G-6681)*
Wardale Corp ....E 800 813-4050
Lakewood *(G-5204)*
Wees Beyond Products Corp ....F 862 238-8800
Passaic *(G-8189)*
Woodward Wood Products Design ....F 609 597-2708
West Creek *(G-11812)*

25 FURNITURE AND FIXTURES

2511 Wood Household Furniture

▲ **10-31 Incorporated** ....E 908 496-4946
Columbia *(G-1795)*
Atlantic Woodworking Inc ....G...... 201 773-9277
Saddle Brook *(G-9753)*
Bau-Lo Wooden Furniture Inc ....G...... 212 664-9188
Mays Landing *(G-6037)*
◆ **Bcg Marble Gran Fabricators Co** .....F 201 343-8487
Hackensack *(G-3879)*
▲ **Berg East Imports Inc** ....D...... 908 354-5252
Barrington *(G-172)*
Bernard Miller Fabricators ....G...... 856 541-9499
Camden *(G-1043)*
Bng Industries LLC ....F 862 229-2414
Harrison *(G-4173)*
Bozzone Custom Woodwork Inc ....G...... 973 334-5598
Montville *(G-6484)*
▲ **Central Shippee Inc** ....E 973 838-1100
Bloomingdale *(G-541)*
Cerami Wood Products Inc ....F 732 968-7222
Piscataway *(G-8747)*
Cozzolino Inc ....G...... 973 731-9292
West Orange *(G-11891)*
Creative Cabinet Designs Inc ....F 973 402-5886
Boonton *(G-561)*
Dab Design Inc ....G...... 732 224-8686
Red Bank *(G-9325)*
Designer Kitchens ....G...... 732 370-5500
Jackson *(G-4663)*
▲ **Dream On ME Industries Inc** ....D...... 732 752-7220
Piscataway *(G-8760)*
Foley-Waite Associates Inc ....F 908 298-0700
Kenilworth *(G-4957)*
Forino Kitchen Cabinets Inc ....G...... 201 573-0990
Park Ridge *(G-7920)*
▲ **Greenbaum Interiors LLC** ....G...... 973 279-3000
Paterson *(G-8281)*
Interchange Group Inc ....F 973 783-7032
Montclair *(G-6418)*
L&W Audio/Video Inc ....G...... 212 980-2862
Hoboken *(G-4483)*
Mango Custom Cabinets Inc ....G...... 908 813-3077
Hackettstown *(G-4019)*
My House Kitchen Inc ....G...... 201 262-9000
Paramus *(G-7892)*
National Woodworking Co ....G...... 908 851-9316
Union *(G-11211)*
R H Vassallo Inc ....G...... 856 358-8841
Malaga *(G-5827)*
Rainbow Closets Inc ....G...... 973 882-3800
Fairfield *(G-3289)*
Renaissance Creations LLC ....G...... 551 206-1878
Passaic *(G-8176)*
Robert J Smith ....G...... 201 641-6555
South Hackensack *(G-10293)*
Salernos Kitchen Cabinets ....G...... 201 794-1990
Saddle Brook *(G-9789)*
Sawitz Studios Inc ....G...... 201 842-9444
Carlstadt *(G-1214)*
Schneiders Kitchens Inc ....G...... 908 689-5649
Washington *(G-11587)*
Starphil Inc ....G...... 908 353-8943
Elizabeth *(G-2775)*
Union City Mirror & Table Co ....E 201 867-0050
Union City *(G-11270)*
V and S Woodworks Inc ....G...... 201 568-0659
Tenafly *(G-10788)*
Vine Hill Farm ....G...... 973 383-0100
Newton *(G-7411)*

Walpole Woodworkers Inc ....E 973 539-3555
Morris Plains *(G-6681)*
▲ **Woodline Works Corporation** ....E 732 828-9100
New Brunswick *(G-7014)*
▲ **Woodpeckers Inc** ....E 973 751-4744
Belleville *(G-329)*

2512 Wood Household Furniture, Upholstered

Carlyle Custom Convertibles ....D...... 973 546-4502
Moonachie *(G-6511)*
Custom Decorators Service ....G...... 973 625-0516
Denville *(G-2034)*
Edward P Paul & Co Inc ....G...... 908 757-4212
Plainfield *(G-8859)*
◆ **Furniture of America NJ** ....E 201 605-8200
Secaucus *(G-9885)*
H Lauzon Furniture Co Inc ....E 201 837-7598
Teaneck *(G-10756)*
Masters Interiors Inc ....E 973 253-0784
Clifton *(G-1669)*
Rff Services LLC ....F 201 564-0040
Oakland *(G-7704)*
Sofa Doctor Inc ....G...... 718 292-6300
Guttenberg *(G-3871)*
Woodward Wood Products Design ....F 609 597-2708
West Creek *(G-11812)*

2514 Metal Household Furniture

Avantegarde Image LLC ....F 732 363-8701
Lakewood *(G-5079)*
Christopher Szuco ....G...... 732 684-7643
Millstone Twp *(G-6266)*
▲ **De Saussure Equipment Co Inc** ....E 201 845-6517
Maywood *(G-6047)*
▼ **Knickerbocker Bed Company** ....E 201 933-3100
Carlstadt *(G-1180)*
◆ **NPS Public Furniture Corp** ....D...... 973 594-1100
Clifton *(G-1685)*
Rumsons Kitchens Inc ....G...... 732 842-1810
Rumson *(G-9716)*
South Jersey Metal Inc ....E 856 228-0642
Deptford *(G-2067)*
Taylor Made Cabinets Inc ....E 609 978-6900
Manahawkin *(G-5834)*

2515 Mattresses & Bedsprings

Ayerspace Inc ....G...... 212 582-8410
West Caldwell *(G-11767)*
Bedding Shoppe Inc ....G...... 973 334-9000
Parsippany *(G-7959)*
Carlyle Custom Convertibles ....D...... 973 546-4502
Moonachie *(G-6511)*
Catching Zzz LLC ....G...... 888 339-1604
Piscataway *(G-8744)*
◆ **Comfort Rvolution Holdings LLC** ....F 732 272-9111
West Long Branch *(G-11845)*
Custom Bedding Co ....G...... 973 761-1100
Maplewood *(G-5917)*
▲ **Dream Well Collection Inc** ....F 732 545-5900
New Brunswick *(G-6956)*
Eclipse Sleep Products LLC ....D...... 732 628-0002
New Brunswick *(G-6957)*
Grand Life Inc ....G...... 201 556-8975
Carlstadt *(G-1164)*
◆ **Innocor Inc** ....C...... 732 945-6222
Red Bank *(G-9331)*
Innocor Foam Tech - Acp Inc ....C...... 732 945-6222
Red Bank *(G-9332)*
J P Egan Industries Inc ....G...... 973 642-1500
Newark *(G-7203)*
◆ **Jomel Industries Inc** ....F 973 282-0300
Hillside *(G-4421)*
Jomel Seams Reasonable LLC ....G...... 973 282-0300
Hillside *(G-4422)*
Leggett & Platt Incorporated ....D...... 732 225-2440
Edison *(G-2556)*
Leggett & Platt Incorporated ....D...... 904 786-0750
Brick *(G-750)*
Lieth Holdings LLC ....G...... 201 358-8282
Westwood *(G-11962)*
Mattress Dev Co Del LLC ....E 732 628-0800
North Brunswick *(G-7525)*
Miller Berry & Sons Inc ....G...... 856 785-1420
Port Norris *(G-8981)*
New England Bedding Trnspt Inc ....G...... 631 484-0147
Kearny *(G-4903)*
◆ **Sealy Mattress Co N J Inc** ....C...... 973 345-8800
Paterson *(G-8381)*

▲ Sheex Inc ....E 856 334-3021
Marlton (G-5999)
Spectra Mattress Inc ....G 732 545-5900
North Brunswick (G-7540)
Spring Time Mattress Mfg Corp..........D 973 473-5400
South Hackensack (G-10297)
◆ Ther-A-Pedic Sleep Products .....E 732 628-0800
North Brunswick (G-7542)
White Lotus Home Ltd Lblty Co ....F 732 828-2111
New Brunswick (G-7013)

2517 Wood T V, Radio, Phono & Sewing Cabinets

Bernard Miller Fabricators ....G 856 541-9499
Camden (G-1043)
Imagine Audio LLC ....G 856 488-1466
Cherry Hill (G-1378)
L&W Audio/Video Inc ....G 212 980-2862
Hoboken (G-4483)
Parsons Cabinets Inc ....G 973 279-4954
Montclair (G-6430)
Silverthorne Furniture Corp ....G 908 689-6969
Asbury (G-73)

2519 Household Furniture, NEC

▲ D & F Wicker Import Co Inc ....E 973 736-5861
Succasunna (G-10621)
Gendell Assoicates PA ....G 201 656-4498
Hoboken (G-4471)
Scott W Springman ....G 856 751-2411
Cherry Hill (G-1419)
South Brunswick Furniture Inc..........C 732 658-8850
Linden (G-5446)

2521 Wood Office Furniture

Arnold Desks Inc ....E 908 686-5656
Irvington (G-4574)
Arnold Furniture Mfrs Inc ....F 973 399-0505
Irvington (G-4575)
Arnold Kolax Furniture Inc ....E 973 375-3344
Irvington (G-4576)
▲ Arnold Reception Desks Inc ....E 973 375-8101
Irvington (G-4577)
Atlantic Coast Woodwork Inc ....G 609 294-2478
Ltl Egg Hbr (G-5640)
Cbt Supply Inc ....G 973 586-2783
Rockaway (G-9557)
Cozzolino Inc ....E 973 731-9292
West Orange (G-11891)
▲ Designcore Ltd ....D 718 499-0337
Secaucus (G-9877)
◆ Fu WEI Inc ....G 732 937-8388
East Brunswick (G-2156)
◆ G & A Coml Seating Pdts Corp.......G 908 233-8000
Mountainside (G-6882)
Gordon International Inc ....F 732 431-3361
Freehold (G-3658)
Kitchens By Frank Inc ....G 732 364-1343
Toms River (G-10891)
La Cour Inc ....E 973 227-3300
Fairfield (G-3246)
M2 Electric LLC ....F 973 770-4596
Mine Hill (G-6327)
Mbs Installations Inc ....F 888 446-9135
Jackson (G-4672)
Mp Custom FL LLC ....F 973 417-2288
Wayne (G-11666)
Pemco Dental Corporation ....E 800 526-4170
Springfield (G-10571)
R J Hoppe Store Construction ....G 973 485-5665
Newark (G-7283)
Reda Furniture LLC ....F 732 948-1703
Manasquan (G-5878)
Renaissance Creations LLC ....G 551 206-1878
Passaic (G-8176)
Robert J Smith ....G 201 641-6555
South Hackensack (G-10293)
▼ Seating Expert Inc ....E 201 299-9109
Kenilworth (G-4995)
Vaswani Inc ....F 877 376-4425
Edison (G-2642)
Vaswani Inc ....F 732 377-9794
Piscataway (G-8834)
Vinos Custom Mllwk & Finshg............F..... 732 356-1147
Middlesex (G-6209)

2522 Office Furniture, Except Wood

◆ Concord Products Company Inc......E 856 933-3000
Sewell (G-9945)

Creative Innovations Inc ....F 973 636-9060
Fair Lawn (G-3088)
▲ Daco Limited Partnership ....D 973 263-1100
Boonton (G-562)
Denmatt Industries LLC ....F 609 689-0099
Hamilton (G-4106)
Extra Office Inc ....E 732 381-9774
Rahway (G-9188)
Fehlberg Mfg Inc ....E 973 399-1905
Irvington (G-4585)
Gaw Associates Inc ....F 856 608-1428
Cherry Hill (G-1370)
◆ Global Industries Inc ....E 856 596-3390
Marlton (G-5977)
La Cour Inc ....E 973 227-3300
Fairfield (G-3246)
◆ Stylex Inc ....C 856 461-5600
Delanco (G-2008)
Top Line Seating Inc ....F 908 241-9051
Kenilworth (G-5001)

2531 Public Building & Related Furniture

▲ Academia Furniture LLC ....E 973 472-0100
Wood Ridge (G-12133)
▲ Air Cruisers Company LLC ....C 732 681-3527
Wall Township (G-11460)
Archer Plastics Inc ....G 856 692-0242
Elmer (G-2789)
Christian Art ....G 201 867-8096
West New York (G-11862)
▲ Drake Corp ....G 732 254-1530
East Brunswick (G-2145)
Fortune Brands Home & SEC Inc ....A 973 402-6440
Boonton (G-570)
◆ Hausmann Enterprises LLC ....G 201 767-0255
Northvale (G-7583)
Jcdecaux Mallscape LLC ....G 201 288-2024
Hasbrouck Heights (G-4195)
Jmm Studios ....G 609 861-3094
Woodbine (G-12143)
Johnson Controls Inc ....E 856 245-9977
Blackwood (G-484)
◆ Longo Associates Inc ....F 201 825-1500
Ramsey (G-9246)
Renaissance Creations LLC ....G 551 206-1878
Passaic (G-8176)
RFS Commercial ....E 201 796-0006
Saddle Brook (G-9785)
▼ Suburban Auto Seat Co Inc ....G 973 778-9227
Lodi (G-5603)
Union County Seating & Sup Co ....E 908 241-4949
Kenilworth (G-5002)
Visual Architectural Designs ....F 908 754-3000
South Plainfield (G-10451)

2541 Wood, Office & Store Fixtures

▲ 10-31 Incorporated ....E 908 496-4946
Columbia (G-1795)
A W Ross Inc ....F 973 471-5900
Passaic (G-8123)
A1 Custom Countertops Inc ....F 856 200-3596
Woodstown (G-12237)
Acro Display Inc ....E 215 229-1100
Pennsauken (G-8470)
Allure Box & Display Co ....F 212 807-7070
Hackensack (G-3873)
American Intr Resources Inc ....G 908 851-0014
Union (G-11151)
▲ Amko Displays Corporation ....E 201 460-7199
Moonachie (G-6505)
Arrow Information Packagig LLC ....G 856 317-9000
Pennsauken (G-8480)
▲ Bamboo & Rattan Works Inc ....G 732 255-4239
Toms River (G-10866)
Banner Design Inc ....E 908 687-5335
Hillside (G-4395)
Bernard Miller Fabricators ....G 856 541-9499
Camden (G-1043)
▲ Bga Construction Inc ....D 973 809-9745
Pine Brook (G-8689)
Bossen Architectural Millwork ....F 856 786-1100
Cinnaminson (G-1449)
Bozzone Custom Woodwork Inc ....G 973 334-5598
Montville (G-6484)
Capital Contracting & Design ....E 908 561-8411
Plainfield (G-8856)
Costa Custom Cabinets Inc ....F 973 429-7004
Bloomfield (G-510)
Counter Efx Inc ....G 908 203-0155
Hillsborough (G-4326)

Countertops Plus Inc...................F 973 365-2232
Passaic (G-8131)
CPB Inc ....E 856 697-2700
Buena (G-946)
Cronos-Prim Colorado LLC ....G 303 369-7477
Lodi (G-5580)
Custom Counters By Precision ....E 973 773-0111
Passaic (G-8133)
D S F Inc ....E 908 218-5153
Raritan (G-9308)
Delaware Valley Installation ....G 856 546-0097
Runnemede (G-9718)
▲ Design Display Group Inc ....C 201 438-6000
Carlstadt (G-1154)
▲ Designcore Ltd ....D 718 499-0337
Secaucus (G-9877)
Dubell Lumber Co ....G 609 654-4143
Medford (G-6068)
E Berkowitz & Co Inc ....G 856 608-1118
Mount Laurel (G-6794)
Eagle Fabrication Inc ....E 732 739-5300
Ltl Egg Hbr (G-5644)
East Coast Storage Eqp Co Inc ....E 732 451-1316
Brick (G-742)
Form Tops Lminators of Trenton ....G 609 409-4357
Jamesburg (G-4685)
Frank & Jims Inc ....G 609 646-1655
Pleasantville (G-8908)
Garley Inc ....G 215 788-5756
Burlington (G-976)
▼ Handy Store Fixtures Inc ....D 973 242-1600
Newark (G-7186)
Hawthorne Kitchens Inc ....F 973 427-9010
Hawthorne (G-4238)
▲ Impact Unlimited Inc ....C 732 274-2000
Dayton (G-1970)
Intelco ....E 856 384-8562
Paulsboro (G-8417)
Intelco ....D 856 456-6755
Westville (G-11944)
Ken Bauer Inc ....E 201 664-6881
Hillsdale (G-4385)
◆ Kubik Maltbie Inc ....E 856 234-0052
Mount Laurel (G-6811)
Laminetics Inc ....G 732 367-1116
Lakewood (G-5144)
Level Designs Group LLC ....E 973 761-1675
South Orange (G-10309)
Lyle/Carlstrom Associates Inc..........E 908 526-2270
Branchburg (G-677)
Marvic Corp ....E 908 686-4340
Union (G-11206)
Masco Cabinetry LLC ....E 732 363-3797
Lakewood (G-5153)
Masco Cabinetry LLC ....E 732 942-5138
Lakewood (G-5154)
Mdr LLC ....E 973 731-7100
West Orange (G-11898)
▲ Medlaurel Inc ....E 856 461-6600
Delanco (G-2007)
Millner Kitchens Inc ....E 609 890-7300
Trenton (G-11081)
Obare Services Ltd Lblty Co ....G 908 456-1887
Elizabeth (G-2762)
▲ Pac Team America Inc ....E 201 599-5000
Paramus (G-7896)
▲ Pam International Co Inc ....D 201 291-1200
Saddle Brook (G-9779)
Paramount Fixture Corporation ....E 973 485-1585
Newark (G-7265)
Parsons Cabinets Inc ....G 973 279-4954
Montclair (G-6430)
Precision Dealer Services Inc ....E 908 237-1100
Flemington (G-3460)
Quality Solid Surface Inc ....G 973 772-8600
Garfield (G-3755)
R J Hoppe Store Construction ....G 973 485-5665
Newark (G-7283)
S L Enterprises Inc ....G 908 272-8145
Ewing (G-3054)
▲ Salon Interiors Inc ....E 201 488-7888
South Hackensack (G-10295)
Sawitz Studios Inc ....E 201 842-9444
Carlstadt (G-1214)
Showtech Inc ....E 973 249-6336
Clifton (G-1723)
South Jersey Countertop Co ....G 856 768-7960
West Berlin (G-11750)
▲ Trinity Manufacturing LLC ....C 732 549-2866
Metuchen (G-6129)

S I C

Universal Systems Installers ....E 732 656-9002
  Monroe *(G-6375)*

Visual Architectural Designs ....F 908 754-3000
  South Plainfield *(G-10451)*

Wagner Rack Inc ....G 973 278-6966
  Clifton *(G-1741)*

Warehouse Solutions Inc ....F 201 880-1110
  Fair Lawn *(G-3123)*

Wilsonart LLC ....F 800 822-7613
  Moorestown *(G-6633)*

2542 Partitions & Fixtures, Except Wood

Acme Manufacturing Co.....................G 732 541-2800
  Port Reading *(G-8985)*

Acro Display Inc.................................E 215 229-1100
  Pennsauken *(G-8470)*

All Racks Industries Inc ....G 212 244-1069
  Linden *(G-5346)*

Alternative Air LLC ....G 609 261-5870
  Willingboro *(G-12116)*

Atlantic Coast Woodwork Inc ....G 609 294-2478
  Ltl Egg Hbr *(G-5640)*

Auto-Stak Systems Inc ....G 201 358-9070
  Westwood *(G-11956)*

Axg Corporation................................G 212 213-3313
  Secaucus *(G-9866)*

Benco Inc ....F 973 575-4440
  Fairfield *(G-3146)*

Capital Contracting & Design ....E 908 561-8411
  Plainfield *(G-8856)*

Carib-Display Co ....G 732 583-1648
  Matawan *(G-6014)*

▲ Clip Strip Corp...............................E 201 342-9155
  Hackensack *(G-3897)*

Cor Products Inc ....G 973 731-4952
  West Orange *(G-11890)*

Custom Creations...............................G 201 651-9676
  Oakland *(G-7682)*

Display Equation LLC ....G 201 343-4135
  Hackensack *(G-3906)*

Display Works LLC ....C 201 327-1260
  Parsippany *(G-7983)*

E J M Store Fixtures Inc ....G 973 372-7907
  Irvington *(G-4582)*

East Coast Storage Eqp Co Inc ....E 732 451-1316
  Brick *(G-742)*

▲ Engo Co ....G 908 754-6600
  South Plainfield *(G-10355)*

▼ Frazier Industrial Company ....E 908 876-3001
  Long Valley *(G-5637)*

Gauer Metal Products Co Inc ....E 908 241-4080
  Kenilworth *(G-4958)*

▼ Handy Store Fixtures Inc ....D 973 242-1600
  Newark *(G-7186)*

▲ High Tech Manufacturing Inc ....G 973 372-7907
  Irvington *(G-4589)*

Imperial Design ....G 856 742-8480
  Gloucester City *(G-3839)*

Independent Welding Co ....F 973 361-9731
  Wharton *(G-11989)*

Infinite Mfg Group Inc......................G 973 649-9950
  Kearny *(G-4884)*

Insign Inc ....E 856 424-1161
  Cherry Hill *(G-1381)*

Leo Prager Inc ....G 201 266-8888
  Englewood *(G-2909)*

▲ LG&p Group LLC ....E 201 634-9099
  Paramus *(G-7884)*

Lyle/Carlstrom Associates Inc ....E 908 526-2270
  Branchburg *(G-677)*

M P M Display Inc.............................F 973 374-3477
  Irvington *(G-4597)*

▲ Metaline Products Company Inc .....E 732 721-1373
  South Amboy *(G-10242)*

Minerva Custom Products LLC ....G 201 447-4731
  Waldwick *(G-11449)*

▲ Modern Showcase Inc ....F 201 935-2929
  Carlstadt *(G-1190)*

Modern Store Equipment ....F 609 241-7438
  Burlington *(G-985)*

National Display Group Inc ....E 856 661-1212
  Pennsauken *(G-8553)*

▲ Ner Data Products Inc ....E 888 637-3282
  Glassboro *(G-3810)*

Nicks Workshop Inc..........................G 856 784-6097
  Gibbsboro *(G-3788)*

North Bergen Marble & Granite ....G 201 945-9988
  Cliffside Park *(G-1544)*

▲ Pam International Co Inc ....D 201 291-1200
  Saddle Brook *(G-9779)*

▲ Pool Tables Plus Inc ....G 732 968-8228
  Green Brook *(G-3862)*

Rbdel Inc ....G 609 324-0040
  Bordentown *(G-610)*

Richard J Bell Co Inc ....F 201 847-0887
  Wyckoff *(G-12262)*

S L Enterprises Inc ....G 908 272-8145
  Ewing *(G-3054)*

Sk Custom Creations Inc ....G 973 754-9261
  Totowa *(G-10972)*

Spark Wire Products Co Inc ....G 973 773-6945
  Clifton *(G-1729)*

Ted-Steel Industries Ltd ....G 212 279-3878
  Linden *(G-5452)*

▲ Testrite Instrument Co Inc ....C 201 543-0240
  Hackensack *(G-3984)*

Toltec Products LLC ....G 908 832-2131
  Califon *(G-1037)*

V M Display..F 973 365-8027
  Passaic *(G-8186)*

Vira Insight LLC ....G 732 442-6756
  Piscataway *(G-8835)*

Vitillo & Sons Inc..............................F 732 886-1393
  Lakewood *(G-5201)*

2591 Drapery Hardware, Window Blinds & Shades

A N Laggren Awngs Canvas Mfg.........F 908 756-1948
  Plainfield *(G-8852)*

A Plus Installs LLC ....G 201 255-4412
  Bloomfield *(G-499)*

▲ Ackerson Drapery Decorator Svc...G 732 797-1967
  Lakewood *(G-5065)*

▲ Acme Drapemaster America Inc .....G 732 512-0613
  Edison *(G-2449)*

Arts Windows Inc ....G 732 905-9595
  Toms River *(G-10864)*

Best Draperies Inc ....G 856 429-5453
  Cherry Hill *(G-1347)*

Best Drapery Inc ....G 856 429-2242
  Cherry Hill *(G-1348)*

C & M Shade Corp.............................E 201 807-1200
  Fairfield *(G-3152)*

Erco Ceilings Somers Point Inc ....E 609 517-2531
  Somers Point *(G-10046)*

Glasscare Inc....................................F 201 943-1122
  Cliffside Park *(G-1540)*

▲ Golden Champion North America ...G 732 481-9000
  Old Bridge *(G-7781)*

Griffith Shade Company Inc ....G 973 667-1474
  Nutley *(G-7647)*

Hudson & Bergen Company ....G 201 991-4900
  Kearny *(G-4881)*

Kay Window Fashions Inc ....F 862 591-1554
  Saddle Brook *(G-9771)*

Metro Mills Inc ....E 973 942-6034
  Paterson *(G-8337)*

Nassaus Window Fashions Inc ....E 201 689-6030
  Paramus *(G-7893)*

▲ Newell Brands Inc ....B 201 610-6600
  Hoboken *(G-4486)*

RFS Commercial................................E 201 796-0006
  Saddle Brook *(G-9785)*

SF Lutz LLC ....F 609 646-9490
  Egg Harbor Township *(G-2696)*

Shade Powers Co Inc ....E 201 767-3727
  Northvale *(G-7607)*

Spotless Venetian Blind Servic ....G 732 548-1711
  Edison *(G-2625)*

Vertical Group Inc ....F 908 277-3737
  Basking Ridge *(G-208)*

▲ Worldwide Whl Flr Cvg Inc ....D 732 906-1400
  Edison *(G-2651)*

2599 Furniture & Fixtures, NEC

Acorn Industry Inc ....F 732 536-6256
  Englishtown *(G-2989)*

Atlantic Coast Woodwork Inc ....G 609 294-2478
  Ltl Egg Hbr *(G-5640)*

Best American Hands ....B 203 247-2028
  Hillside *(G-4398)*

▼ Custom Sales & Service Inc ....E 800 257-7855
  Hammonton *(G-4136)*

G & H Sheet Metal Works Inc ....F 973 923-1100
  Hillside *(G-4408)*

◆ Hausmann Enterprises LLC ....D 201 767-0255
  Northvale *(G-7583)*

Hill-Rom Holdings Inc ....E 856 486-2117
  Moorestown *(G-6584)*

▼ Infinite Mfg Group Inc....................E 973 649-9950
  Kearny *(G-4885)*

Kashmir ....G 856 691-8969
  Vineland *(G-11377)*

Lbd Corp ....E 201 541-6760
  Englewood *(G-2908)*

Ldm Inc ....F 609 921-8555
  Princeton *(G-9066)*

▲ M Deitz & Sons Inc ....E 908 686-8800
  Hillside *(G-4427)*

Marlo Manufacturing Co Inc..............E 973 423-0226
  Boonton *(G-575)*

Modernlinefurniture Inc ....E 908 486-0200
  Linden *(G-5412)*

Mp Custom FL LLC ....F 973 417-2288
  Wayne *(G-11666)*

▲ Organize It All Inc ....E 201 488-0808
  Bogota *(G-549)*

◆ Outwater Plstcs/Industries Inc ......D 201 498-8750
  Bogota *(G-550)*

Renaissance Creations LLC ....G 551 206-1878
  Passaic *(G-8176)*

Rosalindas Discount Furniture...........F 973 928-2838
  Passaic *(G-8177)*

Spice Grill ....G 973 882-4646
  Parsippany *(G-8091)*

Universal Interlock Corp ....E 732 818-8484
  Toms River *(G-10919)*

West Hudson Lumber & Mllwk Co........E 201 991-7191
  Kearny *(G-4920)*

▲ Wood Textures ....F 732 230-5005
  Dayton *(G-1996)*

26 PAPER AND ALLIED PRODUCTS

2611 Pulp Mills

All Amrcan Recycl Corp Clifton...........C 201 656-3363
  Jersey City *(G-4701)*

County of Somerset ....C 732 469-3363
  Bridgewater *(G-830)*

Garden State Recycl Edison LLC ....F 732 393-0200
  Edison *(G-2526)*

▲ Laminated Industries Inc...............E 908 862-5995
  Linden *(G-5400)*

▼ Reliable Paper Recycling Inc ....C 201 333-5244
  Jersey City *(G-4819)*

Reliable Wood Products LLC ....D 856 456-6300
  Westville *(G-11947)*

2621 Paper Mills

Allure Box & Display Co ....F 212 807-7070
  Hackensack *(G-3873)*

Amcor Flexibles LLC ....C 856 825-1400
  Millville *(G-6275)*

◆ American Banknote Corporation ....G 203 941-4090
  Fort Lee *(G-3543)*

Arthur A Kaplan Co Inc ....E 201 806-2100
  East Rutherford *(G-2279)*

Artmolds Journal LLC ....G 908 273-5600
  Summit *(G-10635)*

Beach Nutts Media Inc......................E 609 886-4113
  Villas *(G-11313)*

▲ Borak Group Inc ....D 718 665-8500
  Jersey City *(G-4720)*

Boro Printing Inc ....G 732 229-1899
  West Long Branch *(G-11844)*

▲ Case It Inc ....G 800 441-4710
  Lyndhurst *(G-5675)*

Cell Distributors Inc ....E 718 473-0162
  Dayton *(G-1959)*

City Envelope Inc ....E 201 792-9292
  Jersey City *(G-4727)*

◆ Cw International Sales LLC ....G 732 367-4444
  Lakewood *(G-5103)*

Daily News LP ....F 212 210-2100
  Jersey City *(G-4736)*

Delta Paper Corporation ....E 856 532-0333
  Burlington *(G-968)*

▲ Flexo-Craft Prints Inc ....G 973 482-7200
  Harrison *(G-4183)*

◆ G R Impex Ltd Liability Co..............F 732 931-7001
  Avenel *(G-133)*

Glue Fold Inc ....D 973 575-8400
  Clifton *(G-1628)*

◆ Holland Manufacturing Co Inc........G 973 584-6141
  Succasunna *(G-10623)*

Institutional Edge LLC ....G 201 944-5447
  Englewood Cliffs *(G-2966)*

International Paper Company ....E 856 853-7000
  West Deptford *(G-11830)*

International Paper Company ....C 856 931-8000
Bellmawr (G-343)

International Paper Company ....C 856 546-7000
Barrington (G-178)

International Paper Company ....G 973 405-2400
Clifton (G-1649)

▲ IW Tremont Co Inc ....E 973 427-3800
Hawthorne (G-4242)

Lodor Offset Corporation ....F 201 935-7100
Carlstadt (G-1184)

◆ Lps Industries Inc ....C 201 438-3515
Moonachie (G-6529)

Peter Morley LLC ....G 732 264-0010
Hazlet (G-4282)

Popnfold Papers Inc ....G 201 933-2015
Lyndhurst (G-5702)

Printwrap Corporation ....G 973 239-1144
Cedar Grove (G-1297)

Retrographics Publishing Inc ....G 201 501-0505
Closter (G-1765)

Rigo Industries Inc ....E 973 881-1780
Paterson (G-8370)

Schweitzer-Mauduit Intl Inc ....B 732 723-6100
Spotswood (G-10530)

Screen Reproductions Co Inc ....G 201 935-0830
Carlstadt (G-1215)

Sealed Air Holdings ....G 201 791-7600
Elmwood Park (G-2849)

Sre Ventures LLC ....G 973 785-0099
Little Falls (G-5489)

▲ Steiner Paper Corp ....G 732 651-6009
Manalapan (G-5863)

Verso Paper Management LP ....A 732 938-3167
Wall Township (G-11518)

Victor Securities Inc ....G 646 481-4835
Englewood (G-2942)

World Pac Paper LLC ....G 877 837-2737
Upper Saddle River (G-11288)

2631 Paperboard Mills

All County Recycling Inc ....F 609 393-6445
Trenton (G-11015)

Allure Box & Display Co ....F 212 807-7070
Hackensack (G-3873)

Beauty-Pack LLC ....F 732 802-8200
Piscataway (G-8741)

Caraustar Industries Inc ....G 908 782-0505
Frenchtown (G-3698)

◆ Flech Paper Products Inc ....F 973 357-8111
Paterson (G-8272)

Four Star Reproductions Inc ....E 862 268-8200
Newton (G-7388)

Graphic Packaging Intl Inc ....G 973 709-9100
Wayne (G-11642)

Graphic Packaging Intl LLC ....C 732 424-2100
Wayne (G-11643)

Greenbuilt Intl Bldg Co ....F 609 300-9091
Voorhees (G-11432)

International Paper Company ....C 732 251-2000
Spotswood (G-10528)

JIT Manufacturing Inc ....F 973 247-7300
Paterson (G-8303)

▲ Lamitech Inc ....E 609 860-8037
Cranbury (G-1851)

M S C Paper Products Corp ....F 908 686-2200
Hillside (G-4428)

Monster Coatings Inc ....C 973 983-7662
Rockaway (G-9588)

Multi Packaging Solutions Inc ....C 908 757-6000
South Plainfield (G-10411)

Nu-EZ Custom Bindery LLC ....E 201 488-4140
Hackensack (G-3955)

Packageman ....G 201 898-1922
Belleville (G-310)

▲ Pinnacle Cosmetic Packg LLC ....F 908 241-7777
Kenilworth (G-4988)

▲ Qualserv Imports Inc ....G 973 620-9234
Denville (G-2052)

Romark Logistics CES LLC ....E 908 789-2800
Westfield (G-11929)

▲ Shell Packaging Corporation ....E 908 871-7000
Berkeley Heights (G-422)

Shure-Pak Corporation ....G 856 825-0808
Millville (G-6324)

Sonoco Products Company ....D 908 713-6900
Annandale (G-60)

◆ Stephen Gould Corporation ....D 973 428-1500
Whippany (G-12040)

Sunshine Metal & Sign Inc ....G 973 676-4432
Orange (G-7829)

Tekni-Plex Inc ....D 908 782-4000
Flemington (G-3471)

Union Container Corp ....E 973 242-3600
Newark (G-7351)

▼ United States Box Corp ....E 973 481-2000
Fairfield (G-3335)

Vanguard Packaging Corp ....G 973 391-9200
Livingston (G-5569)

Westrock CP LLC ....D 732 866-1890
Colts Neck (G-1794)

Westrock CP LLC ....G 973 594-6000
Clifton (G-1743)

Westrock Rkt Company ....G 973 237-9570
Totowa (G-10984)

Wjj and Company LLC ....F 973 246-7480
Garfield (G-3773)

2652 Set-Up Paperboard Boxes

Capitol Box Corp ....E 201 867-6018
North Bergen (G-7438)

Cross Country Box Co Inc ....F 973 673-8349
Clifton (G-1593)

Exalent Packaging Inc ....E 973 742-9600
Paterson (G-8266)

Global Direct Marketing Group ....G 856 427-6116
Haddonfield (G-4060)

Granite Packaging Supply Co ....D 856 727-1010
Moorestown (G-6579)

▲ McLean Packaging Corporation ....B 856 359-2600
Moorestown (G-6600)

McLean Packaging Corporation ....D 856 359-2600
Pennsauken (G-8549)

North Jersey Paper Products ....F 973 372-4646
Union City (G-11262)

Ruffino Paper Box Mfg Co ....F 201 487-1260
Hackensack (G-3968)

Shure-Pak Corporation ....G 856 825-0808
Millville (G-6324)

▼ United States Box Corp ....E 973 481-2000
Fairfield (G-3335)

2653 Corrugated & Solid Fiber Boxes

Ace Box Landau Co Inc ....G 201 871-4776
Englewood Cliffs (G-2946)

Albert Paper Products Company ....E 973 373-0330
Irvington (G-4571)

▲ Algar/Display Connection Corp ....D 201 438-1000
Moonachie (G-6501)

Alliance Corrugated Box Inc ....E 877 525-5269
Saddle River (G-9802)

◆ Allstate Paper Box Co Inc ....D 973 589-2600
Newark (G-7079)

Apple Corrugated Box Ltd ....F 201 635-1269
Wood Ridge (G-12134)

B Spinelli Farm Containers ....G 732 566-5619
Matawan (G-6013)

▲ Bell Container Corp ....C 973 344-4400
Newark (G-7104)

Boxworks Inc ....G 856 456-9030
Bellmawr (G-332)

Bradley Corrugated Box Co Inc ....G 973 483-0505
Harrison (G-4174)

Bunn Industries Incorporated ....F 609 890-2900
Trenton (G-11030)

▲ Cases By Source Inc ....E 201 831-0005
Mahwah (G-5756)

Creoh Usa LLC ....G 718 821-0570
Lakewood (G-5099)

Dauson Corrugated Container ....F 973 827-1494
Hamburg (G-4090)

▲ Delta Corrugated Ppr Pdts Corp ....C 201 941-1910
Palisades Park (G-7838)

▲ Delvco Pharma Packg Svcs Inc ....D 973 278-2500
Paterson (G-8249)

Diamex International Corp ....G 973 838-8844
Kinnelon (G-5034)

E L Baxter Co Inc ....F 732 229-8219
Ocean (G-7722)

Enterprise Container LLC ....F 201 797-7200
Saddle Brook (G-9764)

Ferguson Containers Co Inc ....E 908 454-9755
Phillipsburg (G-8647)

Georgia-Pacific LLC ....C 908 995-2228
Milford (G-6245)

Global Direct Marketing Group ....G 856 427-6116
Haddonfield (G-4060)

Graphcorr LLC ....F 732 355-0088
Dayton (G-1967)

Great Northern Corporation ....G 856 241-0080
Swedesboro (G-10700)

Greater New York Box Co Inc ....G 609 631-7900
Trenton (G-11060)

Holly Packaging Inc ....E 856 327-8281
Millville (G-6308)

HR Industries Inc ....F 201 941-8000
Ridgefield (G-9366)

International Container Co ....E 201 440-1600
Hackensack (G-3931)

International Paper Company ....D 732 828-1700
Milltown (G-6268)

Kampack Inc ....C 973 589-7400
Newark (G-7210)

Kampack Inc ....C 973 589-7400
Newark (G-7211)

▲ Lanco-York Inc ....E 973 278-7400
Paterson (G-8317)

Level Designs Group LLC ....G 973 761-1675
South Orange (G-10309)

Levine Industries Inc ....G 973 742-1000
Paterson (G-8319)

Levine Packaging Supply Corp ....E 973 575-3456
Fairfield (G-3251)

▲ McLean Packaging Corporation ....B 856 359-2600
Moorestown (G-6600)

McLean Packaging Corporation ....D 856 359-2600
Pennsauken (G-8549)

Menasha Packaging Company LLC ......C 973 893-1300
Lyndhurst (G-5693)

Menasha Packaging Company LLC ......C 732 985-0800
Edison (G-2568)

New York Folding Box Co Inc ....E 973 347-6932
Stanhope (G-10588)

North Jersey Paper Products ....F 973 372-4646
Union City (G-11262)

Orora Packaging Solutions ....E 609 249-5200
Cranbury (G-1865)

▼ Package Development Co Inc ....E 973 983-8500
Rockaway (G-9593)

Packaging Corporation America ....G 856 596-5020
Marlton (G-5992)

Packaging Corporation America ....G 908 452-9271
Hackettstown (G-4031)

Packaging Corporation America ....G 856 696-0114
Vineland (G-11388)

▼ Paige Company Containers Inc ....E 201 461-7800
Elmwood Park (G-2840)

Pin Point Container Corp ....G 856 848-2115
Deptford (G-2066)

Pratt Industries USA Inc ....D 201 934-1900
Allendale (G-15)

▲ President Cont Group II LLC ....B 201 933-7500
Moonachie (G-6536)

Raritan Packaging Industries ....E 732 246-7200
New Brunswick (G-6999)

Rectico Inc ....F 973 575-0009
Fairfield (G-3290)

Rfc Container LLC ....C 856 692-0404
Vineland (G-11396)

RTS Packaging LLC ....D 908 782-0505
Frenchtown (G-3706)

SA Richards Inc ....G 201 947-3850
Fort Lee (G-3580)

Schiffenhaus Industries Inc ....C 973 484-5000
Newark (G-7303)

Squire Corrugated Cont Corp ....D 908 862-9111
Basking Ridge (G-206)

Sunshine Metal & Sign Inc ....G 973 676-4432
Orange (G-7829)

Sutherland Packaging Inc ....D 973 786-5141
Andover (G-54)

Trent Box Manufacturing Co ....G 609 587-7515
Trenton (G-11124)

Trenton Corrugated Products ....E 609 695-0808
Ewing (G-3061)

US Display Group Inc ....F 931 455-9585
Secaucus (G-9937)

Victory Box Corp ....G 908 245-5100
Roselle (G-9685)

Vineland Packaging Corp ....E 856 794-3300
Vineland (G-11416)

Weber Packaging Inc ....G 201 262-6022
Oradell (G-7815)

Westrock Rkt Company ....D 732 274-2500
Dayton (G-1994)

Westrock Rkt Company ....C 856 596-8604
Marlton (G-6004)

Westrock Rkt Company ....G 973 484-5000
Newark (G-7359)

Woodland Manufacturing Company ......F 609 587-4180
Trenton (G-11133)

S I C

2655 Fiber Cans, Tubes & Drums

Alvaro P Escandon Inc..........G....... 973 274-1040
Newark *(G-7081)*
Atlantic Waste Services..........F....... 201 368-0428
Rochelle Park *(G-9526)*
Discount Packaging Corporation..........E....... 201 836-0521
Teaneck *(G-10749)*
Excelhigh Inc..........G....... 212 947-8543
South Plainfield *(G-10361)*
Greif Inc..........E....... 609 448-5300
Millstone Township *(G-6264)*
▲ **Hicube Coating LLC**..........G....... 973 883-7404
Clifton *(G-1640)*
Ironbound Express Inc..........G....... 973 491-5151
Newark *(G-7198)*
Ironbound Intermodal Inds Inc..........F....... 973 491-5151
Newark *(G-7199)*
Jachts - Columbia Can LLC..........F....... 973 925-8020
Paterson *(G-8298)*
John J Chando Jr Inc..........F....... 732 793-2122
Mantoloking *(G-5890)*
▲ **JRC Web Accessories**..........F....... 973 625-3888
Fairfield *(G-3238)*
◆ **Mauser Usa LLC**..........E....... 732 353-7100
East Brunswick *(G-2165)*
▼ **Paper Tubes Cores & Boxes Inc**..........F....... 973 977-8823
Paterson *(G-8359)*
Recycle Inc East..........D....... 908 756-2200
South Plainfield *(G-10434)*
▲ **Schutz Container Systems Inc**..........D....... 908 429-1637
Branchburg *(G-703)*
◆ **Schutz Corp**..........D....... 908 526-6161
Branchburg *(G-704)*
Slys Express LLC..........G....... 908 787-7516
Linden *(G-5443)*
Sonoco Products Company..........D....... 609 655-0300
Dayton *(G-1988)*
▲ **Tunnel Barrel & Drum Co Inc**..........E....... 201 933-1444
Carlstadt *(G-1235)*
Union Container Corp..........E....... 973 242-3600
Newark *(G-7351)*

2656 Sanitary Food Containers

◆ **American International Cont**..........F....... 973 917-3331
Boonton *(G-554)*
Amscan Inc..........D....... 973 983-0888
Rockaway *(G-9551)*
◆ **Cw International Sales LLC**..........E....... 732 367-4444
Lakewood *(G-5103)*
Heavenly Havens Creamery LLC..........G....... 609 259-6600
Allentown *(G-31)*
Prospect Group LLC..........F....... 718 635-4007
Piscataway *(G-8803)*
▲ **Round Cups LLC**..........G....... 732 734-0244
Linden *(G-5435)*
▲ **Soundview Paper Holdings LLC**..........A....... 201 796-4000
Elmwood Park *(G-2850)*
▲ **United Plastics Group Inc**..........E....... 732 873-8777
Somerset *(G-10191)*

2657 Folding Paperboard Boxes

Albert Paper Products Company..........E....... 973 373-0330
Irvington *(G-4571)*
Contemprary Grphics Bndery Inc..........C....... 856 663-7277
Camden *(G-1055)*
◆ **Cultech Inc**..........C....... 732 225-2722
South Plainfield *(G-10351)*
Global Direct Marketing Group..........G....... 856 427-6116
Haddonfield *(G-4060)*
International Container Co..........E....... 201 440-1600
Hackensack *(G-3931)*
Interntnal Folding Ppr Box Sls..........E....... 201 941-3100
Ridgefield *(G-9367)*
Keystone Folding Box Company..........D....... 973 483-1054
Newark *(G-7212)*
▲ **McLean Packaging Corporation**..........B....... 856 359-2600
Moorestown *(G-6600)*
Multi Packaging Solutions Inc..........C....... 908 757-6000
South Plainfield *(G-10411)*
New York Folding Box Co Inc..........E....... 973 347-6932
Stanhope *(G-10588)*
R J Blen Grphic Arts Cnverting..........E....... 732 545-3501
New Brunswick *(G-6998)*
Westrock Rkt Company..........C....... 973 594-6000
Totowa *(G-10983)*

2671 Paper Coating & Laminating for Packaging

Aeon Industries Inc..........G....... 732 246-3224
Somerset *(G-10050)*
Allure Box & Display Co..........F....... 212 807-7070
Hackensack *(G-3873)*
Amcor Flexibles Inc..........E....... 609 267-5900
Mount Holly *(G-6766)*
Amcor Flexibles LLC..........C....... 856 825-1400
Millville *(G-6275)*
▲ **ANS Plastics Corporation**..........F....... 732 247-2776
New Brunswick *(G-6944)*
◆ **Arch Crown Inc**..........E....... 973 731-6300
Hillside *(G-4390)*
Basic Plastics Company Inc..........E....... 973 977-8151
Paterson *(G-8221)*
Blispak Acquisition Corp..........D....... 973 884-4141
Whippany *(G-12013)*
Carol Healey..........G....... 973 875-1990
Sussex *(G-10667)*
Comar Inc..........F....... 856 507-5461
Voorhees *(G-11426)*
Consolidated Packg Group Inc..........C....... 201 440-4240
Ridgefield Park *(G-9401)*
Delta Paper Corporation..........E....... 856 532-0333
Burlington *(G-968)*
E & E Group Corp..........G....... 201 814-0414
South Hackensack *(G-10261)*
Employment Horizons Inc..........B....... 973 538-8822
Cedar Knolls *(G-1311)*
▲ **Forem Packaging Inc**..........F....... 973 589-0402
Newark *(G-7164)*
Gleicher Manufacturing Corp..........E....... 908 233-2211
Scotch Plains *(G-9849)*
◆ **Holland Manufacturing Co Inc**..........C....... 973 584-8141
Succasunna *(G-10623)*
Homasote Company..........C....... 609 883-3300
Ewing *(G-3024)*
▲ **Ileos of America Inc**..........C....... 908 753-7300
South Plainfield *(G-10383)*
▲ **Jrm Industries Inc**..........D....... 973 779-9340
Passaic *(G-8152)*
Kansas City Design Inc..........G....... 609 460-4629
Lambertville *(G-5216)*
▲ **Lally-Pak Inc**..........D....... 908 351-4141
Hillside *(G-4424)*
◆ **Lps Industries Inc**..........C....... 201 438-3515
Moonachie *(G-6529)*
LV Adhesive Inc..........E....... 201 507-0080
Carlstadt *(G-1185)*
MSC Marketing & Technology..........E....... 201 507-9100
Lyndhurst *(G-5694)*
Multi Packaging Solutions Inc..........C....... 908 757-6000
South Plainfield *(G-10411)*
▲ **Norpak Corporation**..........E....... 973 589-4200
Newark *(G-7260)*
Polyair Inter Pack Inc..........D....... 201 804-1725
Carlstadt *(G-1204)*
◆ **Princeton Corp Graphics Inc**..........D....... 732 545-6163
New Brunswick *(G-6995)*
◆ **R Tape Corporation**..........C....... 908 753-5570
South Plainfield *(G-10431)*
Tekni-Plex Inc..........D....... 908 782-4000
Flemington *(G-3471)*
▼ **US Magic Box Inc**..........G....... 973 772-2070
Garfield *(G-3770)*

2672 Paper Coating & Laminating, Exc for Packaging

◆ **Adhesive Films Inc**..........F....... 973 882-4944
Pine Brook *(G-8680)*
American Biltrite Inc..........C....... 856 778-0700
Moorestown *(G-6557)*
Avery Dennison Corporation..........G....... 201 956-6100
Fair Lawn *(G-3080)*
Capital Label and Affixing Co..........G....... 856 786-1700
Cinnaminson *(G-1450)*
CCL Label Inc..........D....... 609 443-3700
Hightstown *(G-4311)*
CCL Label (delaware) Inc..........C....... 609 259-1055
Trenton *(G-11037)*
▲ **Custom Laminations Inc**..........E....... 973 279-9174
Paterson *(G-8243)*
▼ **Cytec Industries Inc**..........C....... 973 357-3100
Saddle Brook *(G-9761)*
▲ **Dikeman Laminating Corporation**..........E....... 973 473-5696
Clifton *(G-1599)*
Fedex Office & Print Svcs Inc..........E....... 856 427-0099
Cherry Hill *(G-1364)*
Gleicher Manufacturing Corp..........E....... 908 233-2211
Scotch Plains *(G-9849)*
Graphic Express Menu Co Inc..........E....... 973 685-0022
Clifton *(G-1630)*
◆ **Holland Manufacturing Co Inc**..........C....... 973 584-8141
Succasunna *(G-10623)*
Horizon Label LLC..........F....... 856 767-0777
West Berlin *(G-11725)*
Igi Corp..........G....... 908 753-5570
South Plainfield *(G-10382)*
International Graphics Inc..........C....... 908 753-5570
South Plainfield *(G-10386)*
Intertape Polymer Corp..........C....... 201 391-3315
River Vale *(G-9470)*
▲ **Jrm Industries Inc**..........D....... 973 779-9340
Passaic *(G-8152)*
▲ **Kraemer Properties Inc**..........E....... 732 886-6557
Lakewood *(G-5142)*
▲ **Label Graphics Mfg Inc**..........E....... 973 890-5665
Little Falls *(G-5480)*
Label Graphics Mfg Inc..........G....... 973 276-1555
Fairfield *(G-3248)*
Label Master Inc..........G....... 973 546-3110
Lodi *(G-5591)*
▲ **Lacoa Inc**..........G....... 973 754-1000
Elmwood Park *(G-2831)*
◆ **Lamart Corporation**..........C....... 973 772-6262
Clifton *(G-1657)*
LV Adhesive Inc..........E....... 201 507-0080
Carlstadt *(G-1185)*
◆ **Main Tape Company Inc**..........C....... 609 395-1704
Cranbury *(G-1859)*
▲ **Microseal Industries Inc**..........F....... 973 523-0704
Paterson *(G-8338)*
Nitto Americas Inc..........F....... 732 901-7905
Lakewood *(G-5165)*
Nitto Americas Inc..........F....... 201 645-4950
Teaneck *(G-10763)*
Nitto Inc..........G....... 732 901-0035
Lakewood *(G-5166)*
▲ **Norco Inc**..........E....... 908 789-1550
Garwood *(G-3781)*
▲ **Omega Heat Transfer Co Inc**..........F....... 732 340-0023
West Orange *(G-11902)*
Par Code Symbology Inc..........F....... 973 918-0550
Roseland *(G-9655)*
◆ **Plus Packaging Inc**..........G....... 973 538-2216
Morristown *(G-6736)*
Renell Label Print Inc..........G....... 201 652-6544
Paramus *(G-7899)*
Tech-Pak Inc..........F....... 201 935-3800
Wood Ridge *(G-12140)*
Thermwell Products Co Inc..........G....... 201 684-4400
Mahwah *(G-5821)*
▲ **Trek Inc**..........G....... 732 269-6300
Bayville *(G-261)*
▲ **Unifoil Corporation**..........D....... 973 244-9900
Fairfield *(G-3334)*
United Label Corp..........F....... 973 589-6500
Newark *(G-7354)*
▲ **Universal Tape Supply Corp**..........F....... 609 653-3191
Somers Point *(G-10048)*
▲ **Web-Cote Ltd**..........F....... 973 827-2299
Hamburg *(G-4099)*
▲ **Wet-N-Stick LLC**..........G....... 908 687-8273
Union *(G-11234)*

2673 Bags: Plastics, Laminated & Coated

▲ **A-1 Plastic Bags Inc**..........D....... 973 344-4441
Newark *(G-7067)*
Ace Box Landau Co Inc..........G....... 201 871-4776
Englewood Cliffs *(G-2946)*
▼ **All American Poly Corp**..........C....... 732 752-3200
Piscataway *(G-8730)*
Allied Plastics New Jersey LLC..........D....... 973 956-9200
Paterson *(G-8205)*
▲ **Alpha Industries MGT Inc**..........C....... 201 933-6000
Lyndhurst *(G-5667)*
American Transparent Plastic..........E....... 732 287-3000
Edison *(G-2459)*
▲ **ANS Plastics Corporation**..........F....... 732 247-2776
New Brunswick *(G-6944)*
Apco Extruders Inc..........E....... 732 287-3000
Edison *(G-2462)*
▲ **Basic Ltd**..........E....... 718 871-6106
Lakewood *(G-5081)*
Basic Plastics Company Inc..........E....... 973 977-8151
Paterson *(G-8221)*
Beta Plastics..........C....... 201 933-1400
Carlstadt *(G-1131)*

CCL Label Inc ....D...... 609 443-3700
Hightstown (G-4311)

Central Poly-Bag Corp ....F...... 908 862-7570
Linden (G-5358)

Consolidated Packg Group Inc ....C...... 201 440-4240
Ridgefield Park (G-9401)

Craft-Pak Inc ....F...... 718 763-0700
Towaco (G-10991)

Dana Poly Corp ....E...... 800 474-1020
Dover (G-2085)

Encore Poly ....G...... 201 845-4510
Maywood (G-6050)

Essentra Packaging US Inc ....G...... 856 439-1700
Moorestown (G-6577)

Ez-Dumpster LLC ....G...... 908 752-2787
Bridgewater (G-839)

Flexbiosys Inc ....F...... 908 300-3244
Lebanon (G-5286)

Freedom Plastics LLC ....F...... 201 337-9450
Oakland (G-7689)

Gemini Plastic Films Corp ....E...... 973 340-0700
Garfield (G-3736)

General Film Products Inc ....E...... 908 351-0454
Elizabeth (G-2738)

Global Direct Marketing Group ....G...... 856 427-6116
Haddonfield (G-4060)

Goetz & Ruschmann Inc ....E...... 973 383-9270
Newton (G-7391)

◆ Halsted Corporation ....E...... 201 333-0670
Cranbury (G-1836)

Harris Freeman & Co Inc ....D...... 856 787-9026
Moorestown (G-6583)

Heritage Bag Company ....D...... 856 467-2247
Swedesboro (G-10702)

Hershey Industries Inc ....F...... 908 353-3344
Hillside (G-4411)

◆ Inteplast Group Corporation ....B...... 973 994-8000
Livingston (G-5535)

Katies Closets ....G...... 973 300-4007
Newton (G-7394)

Kestrel Closets LLC ....G...... 973 586-1144
Rockaway (G-9580)

Keystone Packaging Service ....G...... 908 454-8567
Phillipsburg (G-8655)

◆ Lps Industries Inc ....C...... 201 438-3515
Moonachie (G-6529)

◆ M & E Packaging Corp ....G...... 201 635-1381
Lyndhurst (G-5688)

M S Plastics and Packg Co ....F...... 973 492-2400
Butler (G-1011)

Mercury Plastic Bag Co Inc ....E...... 973 778-7200
Passaic (G-8163)

MP Plastic Llc ....E...... 973 279-9300
Paterson (G-8342)

▼ Nexus Plastics Incorporated ....D...... 973 427-3311
Hawthorne (G-4249)

▲ Omega Plastics Corp ....D...... 201 507-9100
Lyndhurst (G-5697)

◆ Plus Packaging Inc ....G...... 973 538-2216
Morristown (G-6736)

Potti-Bags Inc ....G...... 201 796-5555
Elmwood Park (G-2845)

Power Bag and Film LLC ....G...... 908 832-6648
Califon (G-1035)

Refrig-It Warehouse ....E...... 973 344-4545
Kearny (G-4912)

◆ Sigma Extruding Corp ....D...... 201 933-5353
Lyndhurst (G-5707)

▲ Source Direct Inc ....F...... 856 768-7445
Cinnaminson (G-1488)

Spectrum Plastics ....G...... 732 564-1899
Piscataway (G-8815)

Tiffany Packaging ....G...... 973 726-8130
Sparta (G-10525)

▲ Trinity Plastics Inc ....C...... 973 994-8018
Livingston (G-5566)

▲ X-L Plastics Inc ....C...... 973 777-9400
Clifton (G-1745)

2674 Bags: Uncoated Paper & Multiwall

Duro Bag Manufacturing Company ......C...... 908 351-2400
Elizabeth (G-2727)

▲ Flexo-Craft Prints Inc ....E...... 973 482-7200
Harrison (G-4183)

P S I Cement Inc ....G...... 609 716-1515
Princeton Junction (G-9160)

Summit Filter Corp ....E...... 908 687-3500
Union (G-11226)

2675 Die-Cut Paper & Board

American Bindery Depot Inc ....C...... 732 287-2370
Edison (G-2457)

▲ Custom Converters Inc ....E...... 201 994-9000
Livingston (G-5527)

▲ Danielle Die Cut Products Inc ....E...... 973 278-3000
Paterson (G-8244)

Dynamic Die Cutting & Finshg ....F...... 973 589-8338
Newark (G-7147)

Gleicher Manufacturing Corp ....E...... 908 233-2211
Scotch Plains (G-9849)

▲ Globe Die-Cutting Products Inc ....E...... 732 494-7744
Metuchen (G-6105)

Goetz & Ruschmann Inc ....E...... 973 383-9270
Newton (G-7391)

Grand Displays Inc ....F...... 201 994-1500
North Bergen (G-7455)

Grand Displays Inc ....G...... 201 994-1500
Pennsauken (G-8517)

JIT Manufacturing Inc ....F...... 973 247-7300
Paterson (G-8303)

Prestige Associates Inc ....E...... 609 393-1509
Trenton (G-11105)

◆ Pro Tapes & Specialties Inc ....C...... 732 346-0900
North Brunswick (G-7535)

Quality Indexing LLC ....E...... 908 810-0200
Union (G-11217)

R J Blen Grphic Arts Cnverting ....E...... 732 545-3501
New Brunswick (G-6998)

Recycled Pprbd Inc Clifton ....E...... 201 768-7468
Clifton (G-1711)

Red Wallet Connection Inc ....D...... 201 223-2644
Manchester (G-5889)

Sabre Die Cutting Co Inc ....E...... 973 357-9800
Paterson (G-8373)

▲ Stephco Sales Inc ....E...... 973 278-5454
Paterson (G-8384)

Vmc Die Cutting Corp ....F...... 973 450-4655
Belleville (G-326)

2676 Sanitary Paper Prdts

▲ Arquest Inc ....B...... 609 395-9500
Millstone Township (G-6262)

▲ Braco Manufacturing Inc ....E...... 732 752-7777
South Plainfield (G-10338)

Federal Equipment & Mfg Co Inc ....G...... 973 340-7600
Lodi (G-5584)

◆ Innovative Disposables LLC ....E...... 908 222-7111
South Plainfield (G-10384)

▲ Interganic Fzco LLC ....G...... 224 436-0372
Hillsborough (G-4350)

Jnj International Inv LLC ....G...... 732 524-0400
New Brunswick (G-6973)

Johnson & Johnson ....D...... 732 524-0400
Piscataway (G-8785)

Johnson & Johnson ....D...... 732 524-0400
Princeton (G-9063)

Johnson & Johnson ....D...... 917 573-8007
Ridgefield (G-9368)

Johnson & Johnson ....D...... 732 524-0400
Lambertville (G-5214)

Johnson & Johnson ....D...... 732 524-0400
Branchburg (G-670)

Johnson & Johnson ....D...... 732 524-0400
Trenton (G-11071)

Johnson & Johnson ....D...... 732 422-5000
North Brunswick (G-7522)

◆ Johnson & Johnson ....A...... 732 524-0400
New Brunswick (G-6974)

Johnson & Johnson ....G...... 908 722-9319
Raritan (G-9311)

Johnson & Johnson ....C...... 908 874-1000
Morris Plains (G-6673)

Johnson & Johnson ....C...... 732 524-0400
New Brunswick (G-6975)

▲ Keystone Adjustable Cap Co Inc ....E...... 856 356-2809
Pennsauken (G-8539)

◆ Marcal Manufacturing LLC ....G...... 201 703-6225
Elmwood Park (G-2833)

Marcal Paper Mills LLC ....A...... 800 631-8451
Elmwood Park (G-2834)

▲ Pacon Manufacturing Corp ....C...... 732 764-9070
Somerset (G-10152)

▲ Soundview Paper Holdings LLC ....A...... 201 796-4000
Elmwood Park (G-2850)

2677 Envelopes

▲ Bravo Pack Inc ....G...... 856 872-2937
Pennsauken (G-8488)

Cenveo Inc ....D...... 201 434-2100
Jersey City (G-4725)

Corporate Envelope & Prtg Co ....G...... 732 752-4333
Green Brook (G-3855)

Red Wallet Connection Inc ....D...... 201 223-2644
Manchester (G-5889)

Tpg Graphics LLC ....G...... 856 314-0117
Pennsauken (G-8586)

United Envelope LLC ....C...... 201 699-5800
Ridgefield (G-9392)

Washington Stamp Exchange Inc ....F...... 973 966-0001
Florham Park (G-3523)

Watonka Printing Inc ....G...... 732 974-8878
Belmar (G-365)

2678 Stationery Prdts

▲ Adler International Ltd ....G...... 201 843-4525
Maywood (G-6045)

▲ ADM Corporation ....D...... 732 469-0900
Middlesex (G-6143)

Arna Marketing Group Inc ....D...... 908 625-7395
Branchburg (G-638)

Bind-Rite Graphics Inc ....E...... 201 863-8100
Secaucus (G-9869)

▲ Officemate International Corp ....D...... 732 225-7422
Edison (G-2587)

Yerg Inc ....G...... 973 759-4041
Lakehurst (G-5060)

2679 Converted Paper Prdts, NEC

Aeon Industries Inc ....G...... 732 246-3224
Somerset (G-10050)

▲ Allied Group Inc ....D...... 973 543-4994
Mendham (G-6086)

◆ Arch Crown Inc ....E...... 973 731-6300
Hillside (G-4390)

Arrow Paper Company Inc ....G...... 908 756-1111
Plainfield (G-8855)

▲ B & G Plastics Inc ....E...... 973 824-9220
Union (G-11155)

Burlington Design Center Inc ....F...... 856 778-7772
Mount Laurel (G-6785)

Caraustar Clifton Primary Pack ....C...... 973 472-4900
Clifton (G-1580)

▼ Cartolith Group ....G...... 908 624-9833
Hillside (G-4401)

CCL Label Inc ....D...... 609 443-3700
Hightstown (G-4311)

CCL Label Inc ....C...... 609 586-1332
Robbinsville (G-9512)

Cenveo Inc ....D...... 201 434-2100
Jersey City (G-4725)

Collins and Company LLC ....G...... 973 427-4068
Hawthorne (G-4226)

Custom Quick Label Inc ....G...... 856 596-7555
Marlton (G-5969)

Eagle Systems Inc ....G...... 732 226-2111
Ocean (G-7723)

▲ Flexo-Craft Prints Inc ....E...... 973 482-7200
Harrison (G-4183)

Georgia-Pacific LLC ....C...... 908 995-2228
Milford (G-6245)

▲ Glitterwrap Inc ....D...... 800 745-4883
Rockaway (G-9570)

Goetz & Ruschmann Inc ....E...... 973 383-9270
Newton (G-7391)

▲ Icup Inc ....E...... 856 751-2045
Cherry Hill (G-1376)

◆ J Josephson Inc ....C...... 201 440-7000
South Hackensack (G-10271)

J Josephson Inc ....G...... 201 440-7000
South Hackensack (G-10272)

J Josephson Inc ....D...... 201 426-2646
South Hackensack (G-10273)

Johnson & Mayer Inc ....F...... 201 646-1717
Hackensack (G-3934)

▲ Jrm Industries Inc ....D...... 973 779-9340
Passaic (G-8152)

▲ Laminated Industries Inc ....E...... 908 862-5995
Linden (G-5400)

Laminated Paperboard Corp ....G...... 908 862-5995
Linden (G-5401)

▲ Legacy Converting Inc ....E...... 609 642-7020
Cranbury (G-1853)

M S C Paper Products Corp ....G...... 908 686-2200
Hillside (G-4428)

Magnetic Ticket & Label Corp ....E...... 973 759-6500
Belleville (G-305)

◆ Matthias Paper Corporation ....E...... 856 467-6970
Swedesboro (G-10709)

S I C

Mod-Tek Converting LLC ....F 856 662-6884
  Pennsauken (G-8551)
Princeton Supply Corp.........................G 609 683-9100
  Princeton (G-9102)
R L R Foil Stamping LLC.......................F 973 778-9464
  Passaic (G-8175)
Red Letter Press Inc ....G 609 597-5257
  Upper Saddle River (G-11284)
Renell Label Print Inc ....G 201 652-6544
  Paramus (G-7899)
Rockline Industries Inc ....C 973 257-2884
  Montville (G-6493)
Schiffenhaus Industries Inc ....C 973 484-5000
  Newark (G-7303)
Schurman Fine Papers........................E 856 985-1776
  Marlton (G-5998)
▲ Seaboard Paper and Twine LLC ....E 973 413-8100
  Paterson (G-8380)
▲ Steiner Paper Corp ....G 732 651-6009
  Manalapan (G-5863)
▲ Stonebridge Paper LLC ....E 973 413-8100
  Paterson (G-8386)
◆ Tekkote Corporation........................D 201 585-1708
  Leonia (G-5321)
Tekni-Plex Inc ....C 908 575-7661
  Branchburg (G-710)
United Label Corp ....F 973 589-6500
  Newark (G-7354)
Webtech Inc ....E 609 259-2800
  Robbinsville (G-9524)

27 PRINTING, PUBLISHING, AND ALLIED INDUSTRIES

2711 Newspapers: Publishing & Printing

10x Daily LLC ....G 732 276-6407
  Lakewood (G-5061)
21st Century Media Newsppr LLC.........D 215 504-4200
  Trenton (G-11009)
24 Horas Inc ....F 973 817-7400
  Newark (G-7062)
50 Plus Monthly Inc ....G 973 584-7911
  Succasunna (G-10618)
About Our Town Inc............................G 732 968-1615
  Piscataway (G-8723)
Achievement Journal LLC...................G 732 297-1570
  North Brunswick (G-7501)
Advocate Publishing Corp ....E 973 497-4200
  Newark (G-7073)
African Telecom Inc ....G 973 675-9919
  East Orange (G-2254)
Ainsworth Media ....G 856 854-1400
  Collingswood (G-1769)
Alm Media LLC ....E 973 642-0075
  Newark (G-7080)
Andis Inc ....G 973 627-0400
  Denville (G-2030)
Arab Voice Newspaper ....G 973 523-7815
  Paterson (G-8214)
Area Auto Racing News Inc ....G 609 888-3618
  Trenton (G-11019)
Argo Corp ....F 609 652-4560
  Pomona (G-8944)
Arts Weekly Inc ....E 973 812-6766
  Little Falls (G-5470)
▲ Asbury Park Press Inc ....A 732 922-6000
  Neptune (G-6900)
Atlantic City Week ....F 609 646-4848
  Pleasantville (G-8902)
Aus Inc ....G 856 234-9200
  Mount Laurel (G-6779)
Bay Shore Press Inc ....E 732 957-0070
  Middletown (G-6211)
Bayonne Community News ....E 201 437-2460
  Bayonne (G-214)
Bernardsville News ....G 908 766-3900
  Bernardsville (G-448)
Binding Products Inc ....F 212 947-1192
  Jersey City (G-4719)
Bloomfield Life Inc ....F 973 233-5001
  Cedar Grove (G-1273)
Bloomfield News LLC.........................G 973 226-2127
  West Caldwell (G-11769)
Borton Enterprises ....F 856 453-9221
  Bridgeton (G-778)
Brazilian Press & Advertising.............F 973 344-4555
  Newark (G-7112)
Brazilian Voice...................................G 973 491-6200
  Newark (G-7113)

Bright Hrzons Fmly Sltions LLC...........E 609 520-7501
  Monmouth Junction (G-6333)
Burlington Times Inc ....B 609 871-8000
  Willingboro (G-12117)
Cabio Newspaper ....G 201 902-0811
  West New York (G-11861)
Casas News Publishing Co ....G 908 245-6767
  Roselle Park (G-9690)
Catholic Star Herald..........................G 856 583-6142
  Camden (G-1051)
Central Record Publications ....E 609 654-5000
  Trenton (G-11038)
Cgw News LLC....................................G 973 473-3972
  Clifton (G-1581)
Coast Star ....G 732 223-0076
  Manasquan (G-5869)
Coaster Inc ....F 732 775-3010
  Asbury Park (G-75)
Community News Network Inc ....G 856 428-3399
  Haddonfield (G-4058)
Community News Service LLC ....G 609 396-1511
  Lawrenceville (G-5254)
Convention News Company Inc ....F 201 444-5075
  Midland Park (G-6224)
Cumberland News Inc ....G 856 691-2244
  Vineland (G-11345)
Current Newspaper LLC.....................G 609 383-8994
  Pleasantville (G-8906)
Daily Dish..G 973 537-9700
  Wharton (G-11983)
Daily Dog Walker LLC ....G 609 755-5364
  Robbinsville (G-9514)
Daily Dollar LLC ....G 732 236-9709
  Monroe Township (G-6381)
Daily News LP ....F 212 210-2100
  Jersey City (G-4736)
Daily Plan It Executive Center ....G 609 514-9494
  Princeton (G-9027)
David Sisco Jr ....G 908 454-0880
  Phillipsburg (G-8646)
Diocese of Camden New Jersey ....A 856 756-7900
  Camden (G-1059)
Diocese of Paterson ....F 973 279-8845
  Clifton (G-1600)
Direct Development LLC ....G 732 739-8890
  Tinton Falls (G-10831)
Dolan LLC ....G 800 451-9998
  Princeton (G-9030)
Dorf Feature Service Inc ....G 908 518-1802
  Mountainside (G-6878)
Dow Jones & Company Inc ....F 609 520-4000
  Cranbury (G-1829)
Dow Jones & Company Inc ....D 609 520-5238
  Monmouth Junction (G-6341)
Dyer Communications Inc...................E 732 219-5788
  Red Bank (G-9328)
Elmer Times Co Inc............................G 856 358-6171
  Elmer (G-2791)
▲ Epoch Times ....G 908 548-8026
  South Plainfield (G-10357)
▲ Evening Journal Association ....F 201 653-1000
  Secaucus (G-9881)
Evergreen Information Svcs Inc ....F 973 339-9672
  Little Falls (G-5475)
Financial Information Inc ....G 908 222-5300
  South Plainfield (G-10365)
First Friday Global Inc ....G 201 776-6709
  Newark (G-7162)
Gail Gersons Wine & Dine Resta.........G 732 758-0888
  Shrewsbury (G-9999)
Gannett Co Inc ....D 908 243-6953
  Somerville (G-10211)
Gannett Co Inc ....G 973 428-6200
  Parsippany (G-8020)
Gannett Stllite Info Ntwrk Inc.............B 973 428-6200
  Parsippany (G-8021)
Gannett Stllite Info Ntwrk Inc ....G 856 691-5000
  Vineland (G-11357)
Gannett Stllite Info Ntwrk LLC ....F 609 561-2300
  Vineland (G-11358)
Gannett Stllite Info Ntwrk LLC ....D 856 663-6000
  Cherry Hill (G-1369)
Gatehuse Media PA Holdings Inc ....G 732 246-7677
  New Brunswick (G-6961)
Glassboro News & Food Store ....G 856 881-1181
  Glassboro (G-3806)
Gloucester County Times ....G 856 845-7484
  Woodbury (G-12162)
Greater Media Newspapers ....E 732 358-5200
  Englishtown (G-2993)

Greater Media Newspapers..................G 732 254-7004
  Sayreville (G-9822)
▲ Gruppo Editoriale Oggi Inc ....E 201 358-6582
  Norwood (G-7623)
Halsey News ....G 973 645-0017
  Newark (G-7184)
Hawthorne Press.................................F 973 427-3330
  Hawthorne (G-4239)
Herald News ....G 973 569-7000
  Woodland Park (G-12221)
Hoboken Reporter...............................G 201 553-0130
  North Bergen (G-7457)
Home News Tribune ....G 908 243-6600
  Somerville (G-10214)
Hudson West Publishing Co ....F 201 991-1600
  Kearny (G-4882)
Hunterdon County Democrat Inc........D 908 782-4747
  Flemington (G-3448)
Hunterdon County Democrat Inc.........D 908 996-4047
  Frenchtown (G-3701)
James Kinkade....................................F 856 451-1177
  Bridgeton (G-787)
Jersey Beat ....G 201 864-9054
  Weehawken (G-11697)
Jersey Shore News Mgazines Inc........E 609 494-5900
  Surf City (G-10665)
Jewish Standard Inc ....F 201 837-8818
  Teaneck (G-10758)
Jewish Times of South Jersey ....G 609 646-2063
  Pleasantville (G-8911)
Jose Moreira ....G 201 991-9001
  Kearny (G-4890)
Journal News V Inc ....G 201 986-1458
  Paramus (G-7879)
Korean Bergen News Inc.....................F 201 894-9061
  Englewood Cliffs (G-2971)
La Tribuna Publication Inc ....G 201 617-1360
  Union City (G-11253)
Latino U S A ....G 732 870-1475
  Long Branch (G-5628)
Leader Newsgroup LLC ....E 201 438-6801
  Lyndhurst (G-5685)
Levy Innovation ....G 908 303-4492
  Morristown (G-6722)
Link News ....G 732 222-4300
  Long Branch (G-5629)
Luso Americano ....G 973 344-3200
  Newark (G-7227)
Luso-Americano Co Inc ....G 973 344-3200
  Newark (G-7229)
Macromedia Incorporated ....E 201 646-4000
  Hackensack (G-3942)
Mandip Inc ....G 732 752-4875
  Piscataway (G-8789)
Medianews Group Inc.........................D 856 451-1000
  Salem (G-9807)
Medieval Times USA Inc ....C 201 933-2220
  Lyndhurst (G-5691)
Micro Media Publications Inc.............G 732 657-7344
  Lakehurst (G-5059)
Monmouth Journal ....G 732 747-7007
  Red Bank (G-9338)
Montclair Local News LLC ....G 973 744-6243
  Montclair (G-6423)
Montgomery News ....G 908 874-0020
  Skillman (G-10034)
Muse Monthly LLC ....G 609 443-3509
  East Windsor (G-2362)
New Jersey Herald ....C 973 383-1500
  Newton (G-7399)
New Jersey Jewish News ....E 973 887-3900
  Whippany (G-12027)
New Satellite Network LLC..................G 908 922-0967
  Scotch Plains (G-9853)
New View Media ....E 973 691-3002
  Budd Lake (G-938)
Newark Morning Ledger Co ....B 973 392-4141
  Newark (G-7257)
Newark Morning Ledger Co ....C 732 560-1560
  Piscataway (G-8796)
Newark Morning Ledger Co ....C 973 882-6120
  Pine Brook (G-8711)
News Inc Gloucester City ....G 856 456-1199
  Gloucester City (G-3841)
Newspaper Media Group LLC ....E 856 779-3800
  Cherry Hill (G-1404)
Newspaper Media Group LLC ....E 201 798-7800
  Bayonne (G-239)
NJ Advance Media LLC ....D 732 902-4300
  Edison (G-2582)

NJ Press Media ....G...... 732 643-3604
   Neptune *(G-6926)*

▲ North Jersey Media Group Inc ....A..... 201 646-4000
   Woodland Park *(G-12225)*

North Jersey Media Group Inc ....G...... 201 933-1166
   Rutherford *(G-9741)*

North Jersey Media Group Inc ....E...... 973 233-5000
   Montclair *(G-6426)*

North Jersey Media Group Inc ....E...... 973 569-7100
   Woodland Park *(G-12226)*

North Jersey Media Group Inc ....C...... 201 485-7800
   Mahwah *(G-5798)*

Observer Park ....F...... 201 798-7007
   Hoboken *(G-4488)*

Ocean Star ....G...... 732 899-7606
   Point Pleasant Beach *(G-8925)*

Oggi Media Group LLC ....E...... 201 358-6582
   Norwood *(G-7633)*

Packet Media LLC ....G...... 856 779-3800
   Englishtown *(G-2996)*

Palisades Magnolia Prpts LLC ....G...... 201 424-7180
   Palisades Park *(G-7841)*

Paper Dove Press LLC ....G...... 201 641-7938
   Little Ferry *(G-5513)*

Paradise Publishing Group LLC ....G...... 609 227-7642
   Willingboro *(G-12122)*

Parker Publications ....F...... 908 766-3900
   Madison *(G-5730)*

Parker Publications Inc ....E...... 908 766-3900
   Bernardsville *(G-453)*

Pascack Press ....G...... 201 664-2105
   Westwood *(G-11965)*

Penn Jersey Advance Inc ....D...... 201 775-6610
   Secaucus *(G-9909)*

Philadelphia Inquirer ....G...... 856 779-3840
   Cherry Hill *(G-1413)*

Phildelphia-Newspapers-Llc ....A...... 609 823-0453
   Ventnor City *(G-11293)*

Princeton Packet Inc ....C...... 609 924-3244
   Princeton *(G-9097)*

Publishing Technology Inc ....G...... 732 563-9292
   New Brunswick *(G-6997)*

Recorder Newspaper ....G...... 973 226-4000
   Caldwell *(G-1033)*

Recorder Publishing Co ....E...... 908 647-1180
   Stirling *(G-10605)*

Recorder Publishing Co Inc ....D...... 908 766-3900
   Whippany *(G-12037)*

Red Bank Gstrntrology Assoc PA ....E...... 732 842-4294
   Red Bank *(G-9342)*

Redhedink LLC ....G...... 973 890-2320
   Totowa *(G-10968)*

Reminder Newspaper ....F...... 856 825-8811
   Millville *(G-6322)*

Reporte Hispano ....G...... 609 933-1400
   Princeton *(G-9112)*

Richard Rein ....F...... 609 452-7000
   Lawrence Township *(G-5247)*

Riverbend Advertiser ....G...... 908 475-3431
   Belvidere *(G-375)*

Sample Media Inc ....G...... 609 884-2021
   Cape May *(G-1104)*

Sample Media Inc ....E...... 609 399-5411
   Ocean City *(G-7757)*

School Publications Co Inc ....E...... 732 988-1100
   Neptune *(G-6929)*

Seawave Corp ....E...... 609 886-8600
   Rio Grande *(G-9462)*

South Jersey Publishing Co ....B...... 609 272-7000
   Pleasantville *(G-8916)*

South Jersey Publishing Co ....F...... 856 692-0455
   Vineland *(G-11406)*

Str8line Publishing Company ....G...... 919 717-6740
   Newark *(G-7331)*

Summit Professional Networks ....E...... 201 526-1230
   Hoboken *(G-4499)*

Tapintonet ....G...... 908 279-0303
   New Providence *(G-7057)*

Targum Publishing Company ....E...... 732 247-1286
   New Brunswick *(G-7006)*

Teg New Jersey Inc ....A...... 973 776-8660
   Newark *(G-7338)*

Times of Trenton Pubg Corp ....A...... 609 989-5454
   Trenton *(G-11121)*

Times The Villadom Inc ....F...... 201 652-0744
   Midland Park *(G-6240)*

Tribuna Hispana ....G...... 609 646-9167
   Pleasantville *(G-8917)*

U S A Distributors Inc ....E...... 201 348-1959
   Union City *(G-11269)*

Ukrainian National Association ....E...... 973 292-9800
   Parsippany *(G-8106)*

Valuewalk LLC ....G...... 973 767-2181
   Passaic *(G-8188)*

Venture Info Network ....G...... 609 279-0777
   Princeton *(G-9136)*

Vicinity Media Group Inc ....F...... 973 276-1688
   Fairfield *(G-3342)*

Walden Mott Corp ....G...... 201 962-3704
   Ramsey *(G-9255)*

Wall Street Journal ....G...... 609 520-4000
   Monmouth Junction *(G-6370)*

Watthung Communications Inc ....F...... 908 232-4407
   Westfield *(G-11933)*

West Essex Tribune Inc ....F...... 973 992-1771
   Livingston *(G-5571)*

Wilmington Trust Sp Services ....G...... 609 272-7000
   Pleasantville *(G-8918)*

World Journal LLC ....F...... 732 632-8890
   Metuchen *(G-6134)*

Worrall Community Newspapers ....G...... 973 743-4040
   Bloomfield *(G-537)*

2721 Periodicals: Publishing & Printing

42 Design Square LLC ....F...... 888 272-5979
   Parsippany *(G-7937)*

Advanstar Communications Inc ....E...... 973 944-7777
   Montvale *(G-6441)*

Advanstar Communications Inc ....E...... 732 596-0276
   Iselin *(G-4608)*

Advantage Business Media LLC ....D...... 973 920-7000
   Rockaway *(G-9547)*

▲ Airbrush Action Inc ....G...... 732 223-7878
   Barnegat *(G-160)*

Alexander Communications Group ....F...... 973 265-2300
   Mountain Lakes *(G-6854)*

Alternate Side Street Suspende ....G...... 201 291-7878
   Paramus *(G-7853)*

▲ AM Best Company Inc ....A...... 908 439-2200
   Oldwick *(G-7803)*

AM Best Company Inc ....B...... 908 439-2200
   Oldwick *(G-7804)*

American Foreclosures Inc ....F...... 201 501-0200
   Bergenfield *(G-380)*

Amy Publications LLC ....G...... 973 235-1800
   Nutley *(G-7640)*

Anderson Publishing Ltd ....G...... 908 301-1995
   Scotch Plains *(G-9845)*

Area Auto Racing News Inc ....G...... 609 888-3618
   Trenton *(G-11019)*

Arts Weekly Inc ....E...... 973 812-6766
   Little Falls *(G-5470)*

B T O Industries Inc ....G...... 973 243-0011
   West Orange *(G-11888)*

Backroads Inc ....G...... 973 948-4176
   Newton *(G-7381)*

Barry Urner Publications Inc ....D...... 732 240-5330
   Toms River *(G-10868)*

▲ Bauer Publishing Company LP ....G...... 201 569-6699
   Englewood Cliffs *(G-2950)*

BNP Media Inc ....G...... 201 291-9001
   Paramus *(G-7859)*

Bobit Business Media Inc ....G...... 856 596-0999
   Marlton *(G-5965)*

Bondi Digital Publishing LLC ....G...... 212 405-1655
   Edgewater *(G-2434)*

Carstens Publications Inc ....E...... 973 383-3355
   Newton *(G-7384)*

Casino Player Publishing LLC ....E...... 609 404-0600
   Galloway *(G-3710)*

Central Record Publications ....E...... 609 654-5000
   Trenton *(G-11038)*

Charter Fincl Pubg Netwrk Inc ....E...... 732 450-8866
   Shrewsbury *(G-9993)*

Christian Mssons In Many Lands ....G...... 732 449-8880
   Wall Township *(G-11469)*

Civic Research Institute Inc ....G...... 609 683-4450
   Kingston *(G-5027)*

Commerce Enterprises Inc ....E...... 201 368-2100
   Paramus *(G-7862)*

Convention News Company Inc ....F...... 201 444-5075
   Midland Park *(G-6224)*

Curran & Connors Inc ....G...... 609 514-0104
   Princeton *(G-9024)*

Data Cntrum Communications Inc ....F...... 201 391-1911
   Montvale *(G-6452)*

Dentistry Today Inc ....E...... 973 882-4700
   Fairfield *(G-3176)*

Diversity Plus Magazine ....E...... 973 275-1405
   South Orange *(G-10303)*

Diversityinc Media LLC ....F...... 973 494-0539
   Princeton *(G-9029)*

Dowden Health Media Inc ....D...... 201 740-6100
   Montvale *(G-6453)*

Drug Delivery Technology LLC ....E...... 973 299-1200
   Montville *(G-6487)*

E W Williams Publications ....F...... 201 592-7007
   Fort Lee *(G-3552)*

Ensembleiq Inc ....D...... 973 252-0100
   Newark *(G-7155)*

Evergreen Information Svcs Inc ....F...... 973 339-9672
   Little Falls *(G-5475)*

Excerpta Medica Inc ....D...... 908 547-2100
   Bridgewater *(G-837)*

Fellowship In Prayer Inc ....E...... 609 924-6863
   Princeton *(G-9044)*

Foundation For Student Comm ....E...... 609 258-1111
   Princeton *(G-9046)*

Friday Morning Quarterback ....E...... 856 424-6873
   Cherry Hill *(G-1366)*

Frontline Med Cmmnications Inc ....C...... 973 206-2328
   Parsippany *(G-8018)*

Galen Publishing LLC ....E...... 908 253-9001
   Somerville *(G-10210)*

Garden State Woman Mag LLC ....G...... 908 879-7143
   Long Valley *(G-5638)*

General Commis Archives & Hstr ....G...... 973 408-3189
   Madison *(G-5723)*

Global Strategy Institute A ....G...... 973 615-7447
   Bloomfield *(G-513)*

Golf Odyssey LLC ....G...... 973 564-6223
   Short Hills *(G-9978)*

Hammonton Gazette Inc ....G...... 609 704-1939
   Hammonton *(G-4138)*

Haymarket Media Inc ....G...... 201 799-4800
   Paramus *(G-7875)*

Heinrich Bauer Publishing LP ....F...... 201 569-6699
   Englewood *(G-2902)*

Heinrich Bauer Verlag ....E...... 201 569-0006
   Englewood Cliffs *(G-2963)*

▲ Hobby Publications Inc ....E...... 732 536-5160
   Freehold *(G-3659)*

Houses Magazine Inc ....F...... 973 605-1877
   Morris Plains *(G-6669)*

Hsh Assoc Financial Publishers ....G...... 973 838-3330
   Butler *(G-1008)*

Hyp Hair Inc ....E...... 201 843-4004
   Montclair *(G-6416)*

Industry Publications Inc ....F...... 973 331-9545
   Parsippany *(G-8029)*

Information Today Inc ....E...... 609 654-6266
   Medford *(G-6071)*

Innovation In Medtech LLC ....G...... 888 202-5939
   Chatham *(G-1328)*

Intellisphere LLC ....E...... 609 716-7777
   Plainsboro *(G-8892)*

International Data Group Inc ....F...... 732 460-9404
   Eatontown *(G-2408)*

Interntonal Med News Group LLC ....F...... 973 290-8237
   Parsippany *(G-8032)*

Investment Casting Institute ....G...... 201 573-9770
   Montvale *(G-6460)*

Jannetti Publications ....D...... 856 256-2300
   Sewell *(G-9960)*

◆ John Wiley & Sons Inc ....D...... 201 748-6000
   Hoboken *(G-4479)*

Jonas Media Group Inc ....F...... 973 438-1900
   Newark *(G-7208)*

JS Paluch Co Inc ....F...... 732 516-1900
   Edison *(G-2550)*

Jury Vrdict Rview Publications ....G...... 973 376-9002
   Springfield *(G-10560)*

Keypoint Intelligence LLC ....G...... 201 489-6439
   Hackensack *(G-3936)*

Keypoint Intelligence LLC ....E...... 973 797-2100
   Fairfield *(G-3240)*

Kicksonfirecom LLC ....G...... 718 753-4248
   South Amboy *(G-10240)*

Know America Media LLC ....G...... 770 650-1102
   Roseland *(G-9653)*

Krystal Clear Media Group LLC ....G...... 302 715-1069
   Bloomfield *(G-517)*

Lawyers Diary and Manual LLC ....E...... 973 642-1440
   New Providence *(G-7041)*

Lead Conversion Plus ....F...... 802 497-1557
   Manalapan *(G-5853)*

Lont & Overkamp Pubg Co Inc ....E...... 973 942-2243
   Clifton *(G-1664)*

M2 Communications Inc ....E...... 201 433-1746
   Jersey City *(G-4781)*

Macromedia Incorporated ....E 201 646-4000
Hackensack (G-3942)

McMunn Associates ....E 856 858-3440
Collingswood (G-1772)

Medical Strategic Planning Inc ....G 732 219-5090
Lincroft (G-5339)

Middlesex Publications ....F 732 435-0005
North Brunswick (G-7527)

Mindwise Media LLC ....G 973 701-0685
Chatham (G-1334)

Missionary Society of St Paul ....E 201 825-7300
Mahwah (G-5792)

Mod Media Ltd Liability Co ....G 973 249-6157
Fairfield (G-3262)

Modern Drummer Publications ....F 973 239-4140
Fairfield (G-3263)

Montage Media Corporation ....E 201 891-3200
Mahwah (G-5793)

Music Trades Corp ....G 201 871-1965
Englewood (G-2918)

▼ N J W Magazine ....F 201 886-2185
Fort Lee (G-3571)

National Housing Institute ....G 973 509-1600
Montclair (G-6424)

Neighborhood Shoppers ....G 856 988-7722
Marlton (G-5989)

New Jersey Bus & Indust Assn ....D 609 393-7707
Trenton (G-11084)

New Jersey Business Magazine ....G 973 882-5004
Fairfield (G-3269)

New Jersey Monthly LLC ....E 973 539-8230
Morristown (G-6730)

New Jrsey State Leag Mncplties ....F 609 695-3481
Trenton (G-11087)

Northstar Travel Media LLC ....C 201 902-2000
Secaucus (G-9907)

Npt Publishing Group Inc ....F 973 401-0202
Morris Plains (G-6675)

Nsgv Inc ....F 212 620-2200
Jersey City (G-4793)

Options Edge LLC ....G 973 701-0051
Summit (G-10652)

Outsourcing Today LLC ....F 973 439-0060
Roseland (G-9654)

P D Salco Inc ....F 973 716-0517
Livingston (G-5553)

Pentacle Publishing Corp ....E 732 240-3000
Toms River (G-10901)

Physicans Educatn Resource LLC ....G 609 378-3701
Plainsboro (G-8895)

Pillar of Fire ....D 732 356-0102
Zarephath (G-12270)

Pioneer Associates Inc ....E 201 592-7007
Fort Lee (G-3577)

▲ Plexus Publishing Inc ....E 609 654-6500
Medford (G-6078)

Princton Almni Pblications Inc ....G 609 258-4885
Princeton (G-9105)

Quadrant Media Corp Inc ....G 973 701-8900
Parsippany (G-8074)

▲ Quick Frozen Foods Intl ....E 201 592-7007
Fort Lee (G-3579)

Recruit Co Ltd ....D 201 216-0600
Jersey City (G-4816)

Relx Inc ....D 973 812-1900
Woodland Park (G-12232)

Renard Communmications Inc ....E 973 912-8550
Springfield (G-10576)

Retail Management Pubg Inc ....F 212 981-0217
Montclair (G-6434)

Rodman Media Corp ....E 201 825-2552
Montvale (G-6478)

Rvs Publishing Inc ....F 856 810-7743
Marlton (G-5997)

Schiff & Co ....F 973 227-1830
West Caldwell (G-11805)

▲ Scholastic Uk Group LLC ....C 201 633-2400
Secaucus (G-9924)

School Publications Co Inc ....E 732 988-1100
Neptune (G-6929)

Showcase Publications Inc ....F 732 349-1134
Toms River (G-10911)

Sino Monthly New Jersey Inc ....F 732 650-0688
Edison (G-2619)

Sj Magazine ....F 856 722-9300
Maple Shade (G-5908)

Skinder-Strauss LLC ....E 973 642-1440
New Providence (G-7054)

SMR Research Corporation ....G 908 852-7677
Hackettstown (G-4037)

Sneaker Swarm LLC ....F 908 693-9262
Woodbridge (G-12153)

Sports Impact Inc ....G 732 257-1451
East Brunswick (G-2186)

Springer Scnce + Bus Media LLC ....D 201 348-4033
Secaucus (G-9931)

Steppin Out Magazine ....G 201 703-0911
Fair Lawn (G-3115)

Steward LLC ....G 609 816-8825
Princeton (G-9125)

▲ Sys-Con Publications Inc ....E 201 802-3000
Woodcliff Lake (G-12204)

Teg New Jersey Inc ....A 973 776-8660
Newark (G-7338)

Thomas Greco Publishing Inc ....F 973 667-6965
Nutley (G-7654)

Thomas Publishing Company LLC ....E 973 543-4994
Chester (G-1440)

Tommax Inc ....G 732 224-1046
Red Bank (G-9347)

◆ Transaction Publishers Inc ....F 732 445-2280
Piscataway (G-8830)

Union Institute Inc ....G 800 914-8138
Mahwah (G-5823)

Unisphere Media LLC ....F 908 795-3701
New Providence (G-7059)

US News & World Report Inc ....F 212 716-6800
Jersey City (G-4841)

Vicinity Publications Inc ....G 973 276-1688
Fairfield (G-3343)

Visual Impact Advertising Inc ....F 973 763-4900
Maplewood (G-5932)

Vitamin Retailer Magazine Inc ....G 732 432-9600
East Brunswick (G-2197)

Voicings Publication Inc ....G 609 822-9401
Ventnor City (G-11294)

Walden Mott Corp ....G 201 962-3704
Ramsey (G-9255)

Webannuitiescom Inc ....G 732 521-5110
Monroe (G-6376)

2731 Books: Publishing & Printing

Africa World Press ....G 609 695-3200
Ewing (G-3002)

Alexander Communications Group ....F 973 265-2300
Mountain Lakes (G-6854)

▲ AM Best Company Inc ....A 908 439-2200
Oldwick (G-7803)

AM Best Company Inc ....B 908 439-2200
Oldwick (G-7804)

Apples & Honey Press LLC ....F 973 379-7200
Springfield (G-10537)

Avstar Publishing Corp ....G 908 236-6210
Lebanon (G-5277)

Banquet Services International ....G 732 270-1188
Toms River (G-10867)

Barnes & Noble Booksellers Inc ....E 201 272-3635
Lyndhurst (G-5671)

▲ Behrman House Inc ....F 973 379-7200
Millburn (G-6248)

Berlitz Languages US Inc ....D 609 759-5371
Princeton (G-9014)

Berlitz Publishing Company Inc ....E 609 514-9650
Princeton (G-9015)

▲ Blue Apple Books LLC ....G 973 763-8191
Maplewood (G-5915)

Blue Dome Inc ....G 646 415-9331
Clifton (G-1577)

Bon Venture Services LLC ....D 973 584-5699
Flanders (G-3402)

Bookcode Corp ....G 732 742-0481
Woodbridge (G-12147)

Carstens Publications Inc ....E 973 383-3355
Newton (G-7384)

Chatham Bookseller Inc ....G 973 822-1361
Madison (G-5720)

Childrens Research & Dev Co ....G 856 546-8814
Haddon Heights (G-4046)

CNG Publishing Company ....G 973 768-0978
Burlington (G-964)

Colt Media Inc ....G 732 946-3276
Colts Neck (G-1782)

Comex Systems Inc ....G 800 543-6959
Chester (G-1435)

Creative Competitions Inc ....F 856 256-2797
Sewell (G-9949)

▲ Darwin Press Inc ....G 609 737-1349
Pennington (G-8448)

Dawn Bible Students Assn ....G 201 438-6421
East Rutherford (G-2293)

Evergreen Information Svcs Inc ....F 973 339-9672
Little Falls (G-5475)

Excerpta Medica Inc ....D 908 547-2100
Bridgewater (G-837)

▲ Franklin Electronic Publs Inc ....D 609 386-2500
Burlington (G-974)

◆ Franklin Mint LLC ....E 800 843-6468
Fort Lee (G-3555)

Galves Auto Price List Inc ....G 201 393-0051
Teterboro (G-10797)

Gann Law Books Inc ....F 973 268-1200
Newark (G-7169)

▲ Haights Cross Cmmnications Inc .....E 212 209-0500
Princeton Junction (G-9157)

Hispanic Outlook In Higher ....G 201 587-8800
Saddle Brook (G-9768)

Hispanic Outlook-12 Mag Inc ....G 201 587-8800
Fair Lawn (G-3095)

▲ Howard Press Inc ....D 908 245-4400
Roselle (G-9673)

▲ Hudson Group (hg) Inc ....B 201 939-5050
East Rutherford (G-2300)

J S Paluch Co Inc ....E 732 238-2412
East Brunswick (G-2163)

◆ John Wiley & Sons Inc ....D 201 748-6000
Hoboken (G-4479)

John Wiley & Sons Inc ....D 732 302-2265
Edison (G-2547)

John Wiley & Sons Inc ....D 201 748-6000
Hoboken (G-4480)

JS Paluch Co Inc ....E 732 516-1900
Edison (G-2550)

Jump Start Press ....G 732 892-4994
Point Pleasant Beach (G-8920)

▲ Just US Books Inc ....G 973 672-7701
East Orange (G-2258)

Learning Links-Usa Inc ....G 516 437-9071
Cranbury (G-1852)

Life Skills Education Inc ....G 507 645-2994
Springfield (G-10564)

▲ Manning Publication Co ....G 856 375-2597
Cherry Hill (G-1394)

Markus Wiener Publishers Inc ....G 609 921-1141
Princeton (G-9070)

Mathematics League Inc ....G 201 568-6328
Tenafly (G-10785)

Matthew Bender & Company Inc ....E 518 487-3000
Newark (G-7237)

McGraw-Hill Glbl Edctn Hldngs ....D 609 371-8301
East Windsor (G-2361)

Metal Powder Inds Federation ....F 609 452-7700
Princeton (G-9073)

Missionary Society of St Paul ....E 201 825-7300
Mahwah (G-5792)

Modern Drummer Publications ....F 973 239-4140
Fairfield (G-3263)

New Horizon Press Publishers ....G 908 604-6311
Liberty Corner (G-5323)

New York-NJ Trail Conference ....F 201 512-9348
Mahwah (G-5795)

NJ Dept Military Vtrans ....G 856 384-8831
Woodbury (G-12165)

Patterson Smith Publishing ....G 973 744-3291
Montclair (G-6431)

▲ Paulist Press Inc ....G 201 825-7300
Mahwah (G-5800)

◆ Pearson Education Inc ....A 201 236-7000
Hoboken (G-4490)

Pearson Education Inc ....E 609 395-6000
Cranbury (G-1869)

Pearson Education Inc ....F 201 785-2721
Hoboken (G-4492)

Pearson Inc ....E 201 236-7000
Upper Saddle River (G-11282)

▼ Pearson Technology Centre Inc ....G 201 767-5000
Old Tappan (G-7800)

Pegasus Group Publishing Inc ....F 973 884-9100
East Hanover (G-2239)

▲ Peoples Education Inc ....C 201 712-0090
Montvale (G-6469)

Peoples Eductl Holdings Inc ....C 201 712-0090
Saddle Brook (G-9781)

Philip Lief Group Inc ....G 609 430-1000
Princeton (G-9092)

▲ Plexus Publishing Inc ....G 609 654-6500
Medford (G-6078)

▲ Presbyterian Reformed Pubg Co ....F 908 454-0505
Phillipsburg (G-8666)

Princeton Publishing Group ....G 609 577-0693
Princeton (G-9099)

▲ Princeton University Press ....D 609 258-4900
Princeton **(G-9104)**

Railpace Co Inc ....G 732 388-4984
Clark **(G-1514)**

Red Sea Press Inc ....G 609 695-3200
Ewing **(G-3049)**

▲ Renaissance House ....G 201 408-4048
Englewood **(G-2928)**

Research & Education Assn ....E 732 819-8880
Piscataway **(G-8805)**

Rosemont Publishing & Printing ....F 609 269-8094
Plainsboro **(G-8899)**

RR Bowker LLC ....C 908 286-1090
New Providence **(G-7053)**

Scholastic Inc ....G 201 633-2400
Secaucus **(G-9923)**

School Publications Co Inc ....E 732 988-1100
Neptune **(G-6929)**

Shy Kramer & Associates ....F 609 646-2063
Pleasantville **(G-8915)**

Silicon Press Inc ....G 908 273-8919
Summit **(G-10657)**

Simon & Schuster Inc ....E 973 656-6000
Parsippany **(G-8087)**

Springer Scnce + Bus Media LLC ....D 201 348-4033
Secaucus **(G-9931)**

Sterling Publishing Co Inc ....E 732 248-6563
Monroe Township **(G-6395)**

Stevens Publishing Co ....G 908 284-9326
Flemington **(G-3468)**

Taryag Legacy Foundation Inc ....G 732 569-2467
Lakewood **(G-5193)**

Techsetters Inc ....E 856 240-7905
Collingswood **(G-1774)**

TFH Publications Inc ....D 732 897-6860
Neptune **(G-6934)**

TFH Publications Inc ....E 732 988-8400
Neptune **(G-6935)**

Thomson Reuters (markets) LLC .....G 973 286-7200
Newark **(G-7342)**

Thomson Reuters Corporation ....B 212 337-4281
Newark **(G-7343)**

◆ Transaction Publishers Inc ....F 732 445-2280
Piscataway **(G-8830)**

Trilogy Publications LLC ....G 201 816-1211
Englewood Cliffs **(G-2983)**

Truckeros News LLC ....F 732 340-1043
Rahway **(G-9225)**

W G I Corp ....F 732 370-2900
Lakewood **(G-5203)**

▲ Wiley Publishing LLC ....B 201 748-6000
Hoboken **(G-4504)**

Wiley Subscription Services ....F 201 748-6000
Hoboken **(G-4505)**

Wordmasters ....G 201 327-4201
Allendale **(G-23)**

▲ World Scientific Publishing Co .....F 201 487-9655
Hackensack **(G-3992)**

Writers & Poets ....G 908 233-2399
Mountainside **(G-6890)**

Wt Media LLC ....F 609 921-3490
Trenton **(G-11135)**

2732 Book Printing, Not Publishing

All In Color Inc ....G 973 626-0987
Paterson **(G-8204)**

▲ AM Best Company Inc ....A 908 439-2200
Oldwick **(G-7803)**

Aramani Inc ....G 201 945-1160
Fairview **(G-3357)**

Athletic Organizational Aids ....E 201 652-1485
Midland Park **(G-6221)**

Binding Products Inc ....E 212 947-1192
Jersey City **(G-4719)**

Command Web Offset Company Inc ...C 201 863-8100
Secaucus **(G-9873)**

Extreme Digital Graphics Inc ....F 973 227-5599
Fairfield **(G-3192)**

Forbes Media LLC ....D 212 620-2200
Jersey City **(G-4754)**

▲ G & H Soho Inc ....F 201 216-9400
Elmwood Park **(G-2820)**

▲ Howard Press Inc ....D 908 245-4400
Roselle **(G-9673)**

Musings Press Ltd Liability Co ....F 347 210-8820
Union City **(G-11259)**

NJ Copy Center LLC ....G 973 788-1600
Fairfield **(G-3272)**

Oceanic Graphic Intl Inc ....F 201 883-1816
Hackensack **(G-3956)**

Phoenix Color Corp ....E 800 632-4111
Rockaway **(G-9595)**

Rush Index Tabs Inc ....E 201 531-1555
East Rutherford **(G-2324)**

School Publications Co Inc ....E 732 988-1100
Neptune **(G-6929)**

Service Data Corp Inc ....G 908 522-0020
Summit **(G-10656)**

Starnet Printing Inc ....E 201 760-2600
Mahwah **(G-5815)**

Surviving Life Corp ....G 973 543-3370
Mendham **(G-6092)**

◆ Wellspring Info Inc ....G 800 268-3682
Montclair **(G-6439)**

Wheal-Grace Corp ....E 973 450-8100
Belleville **(G-327)**

2741 Misc Publishing

Access Response Inc ....G 732 660-0770
Ocean **(G-7712)**

Action Press Park Slope ....G 718 624-3457
Holmdel **(G-4507)**

American Directory Publishing ....G 609 494-4055
Surf City **(G-10664)**

American Soc of Mech Engineers ....D 973 244-2282
Little Falls **(G-5468)**

Arthur A Kaplan Co Inc ....E 201 806-2100
East Rutherford **(G-2279)**

Berlitz Publishing Company Inc ......E 609 514-9650
Princeton **(G-9015)**

Beterrific Corp ....G 201 735-7711
Fort Lee **(G-3546)**

Better Listen LLC ....G 917 623-9834
Teaneck **(G-10744)**

Bitwine Inc ....F 888 866-9435
Tenafly **(G-10782)**

◆ Bookazine Co Inc ....D 201 339-7777
Bayonne **(G-216)**

Brogan Tennyson Group Inc ....F 732 355-0700
Dayton **(G-1956)**

Bruce Teleky Inc ....G 718 965-9694
Jersey City **(G-4721)**

Cape Publishing Inc ....G 609 898-4500
Cape May **(G-1094)**

Captivate Internationallc ....G 732 734-0403
Edison **(G-2478)**

Cariletha Company Inc ....F 609 222-3055
Mount Laurel **(G-6786)**

Catalogue Publishers Inc ....F 973 423-3600
Fair Lawn **(G-3086)**

Central Record Publications ....E 609 654-5000
Trenton **(G-11038)**

Charles Kerr Enterprises Inc ....G 732 738-6500
Edison **(G-2482)**

Chryslis Data Sltons Svcs Corp ......G 609 375-2000
Princeton **(G-9022)**

Cimware USA Inc ....G 201 493-0521
Ridgewood **(G-9421)**

City Master Barbers Inc ....G 732 536-6400
Morganville **(G-6640)**

Clyde Otis Music Group ....G 845 425-8198
Englewood **(G-2884)**

Cohansey Cove ....G 609 884-7726
Cape May **(G-1095)**

College Spun Media Inc ....G 973 945-5040
Hoboken **(G-4465)**

Columbia Marketing Corp ....G 973 275-1700
Maplewood **(G-5916)**

Commerce Register Inc ....E 201 445-3000
Midland Park **(G-6223)**

Community Pride Publications ....F 609 921-8760
Princeton Junction **(G-9150)**

Consumer Graphics Inc ....G 732 469-4699
Somerset **(G-10085)**

Creationsrewards Net LLC ....C 908 526-3127
Manville **(G-5893)**

Criterion Publishing Co ....G 732 548-8300
Metuchen **(G-6101)**

Crossfire Publications ....G 516 352-9087
Caldwell **(G-1025)**

Dex Media Inc ....F 908 237-0956
Flemington **(G-3434)**

Dex Media Inc ....E 856 988-2700
Marlton **(G-5972)**

Door Center Enterprises Inc ....G 609 333-1233
Hopewell **(G-4541)**

Dorado Systems LLC ....F 856 354-0048
Haddonfield **(G-4059)**

▲ Down Shore Publishing Corp ......G 609 978-1233
West Creek **(G-11810)**

Dune Grass Publishing LLC ....G 609 774-6562
Blackwood **(G-476)**

Eastside Express Corporation ....G 908 486-3300
Linden **(G-5370)**

Ebsco Industries Inc ....E 732 542-8600
Shrewsbury **(G-9998)**

Ebsco Industries Inc ....D 201 569-2500
Tinton Falls **(G-10835)**

Ebsco Publishing Inc ....G 201 968-9899
Hackensack **(G-3908)**

Eclecticism Publishing LLC ....G 212 714-4714
Robbinsville **(G-9515)**

Edge Ventures Inc ....G 877 841-1402
Old Bridge **(G-7777)**

Electedface LLC ....E 609 924-3636
Princeton **(G-9037)**

Electrochemical Society Inc ....E 609 737-1902
Pennington **(G-8450)**

Entourage Imaging Inc ....G 888 926-6571
Princeton Junction **(G-9153)**

▲ Epoch Press Inc ....G 973 357-0080
Wayne **(G-11628)**

Excerpta Medica Inc ....D 908 547-2100
Bridgewater **(G-837)**

Exit Zero Cookhouse Inc ....G 609 770-8479
Cape May **(G-1098)**

Faulkner Information Svcs LLC ....D 856 662-2070
Medford **(G-6069)**

Financial Information Inc ....E 908 222-5300
South Plainfield **(G-10365)**

Florentine Press Inc ....G 201 386-9200
Jersey City **(G-4753)**

▲ Form Lectro Inc ....E 973 777-0621
Hackensack **(G-3917)**

▲ Franklin Electronic Publs Inc ......C 609 386-2500
Burlington **(G-974)**

Friday Morning Quarterback ....E 856 424-6873
Cherry Hill **(G-1366)**

Galves Auto Price List Inc ....F 201 393-0051
Teterboro **(G-10797)**

Geolytics Inc ....G 908 707-1505
Branchburg **(G-663)**

Gmp Publications Inc ....G 609 859-3400
Southampton **(G-10474)**

Go Waddle Inc ....G 301 452-5084
Berkeley Heights **(G-411)**

▲ Gorgias Press ....G 732 699-0343
Piscataway **(G-8770)**

Grafwed Internet Media Studios .....G 201 632-1771
Midland Park **(G-6227)**

Greetingtap ....G 347 731-4263
South Plainfield **(G-10375)**

Grey House Publishing Inc ....G 201 968-0500
Hackensack **(G-3924)**

Hal Leonard LLC ....C 973 337-5034
Montclair **(G-6415)**

Harrison Scott Pblications Inc ....E 201 659-1700
Hoboken **(G-4472)**

Heritage Publishing ....G 732 747-7770
Colts Neck **(G-1788)**

Hudson West Publishing Co ....F 201 991-1600
Kearny **(G-4882)**

Hyman W Fisher Inc ....G 973 992-9155
Livingston **(G-5534)**

Ihs Inc ....G 201 391-0084
Woodcliff Lake **(G-12194)**

Information Today Inc ....F 908 219-0279
New Providence **(G-7040)**

Iws License Corp ....F 732 872-0014
Atlantic Highlands **(G-112)**

J D M Associates Inc ....G 973 773-8699
Lodi **(G-5590)**

J Media LLC ....G 201 600-4573
Norwood **(G-7627)**

J S Paluch Co Inc ....E 732 238-2412
East Brunswick **(G-2163)**

Jav Latin America Express ....G 201 868-5004
West New York **(G-11869)**

Jem Printing Inc ....G 908 782-9986
Flemington **(G-3450)**

Jen Mar Graphics Inc ....E 973 256-6622
Totowa **(G-10952)**

Jersey Bound Latino LLC ....G 908 591-2830
Union **(G-11197)**

Jersey Job Guide Inc ....G 732 263-9675
Long Branch **(G-5627)**

Jersey Shore News Mgazines Inc ....E 609 494-5900
Surf City **(G-10665)**

Jersey Shore Publications ....G 732 892-1276
Brick **(G-748)**

▲ **Jigsaw Publishing LLC** G 973 838-4838
Butler *(G-1010)*

John Patrick Publishing LLC D 609 883-2700
Ewing *(G-3027)*

John R Zabka Associates Inc F 201 405-0075
Oakland *(G-7693)*

Jonas Media Group Inc F 973 438-1900
Newark *(G-7208)*

JS Paluch Co Inc F 732 516-1900
Edison *(G-2550)*

Kabab & Curry Express G 732 416-6560
Edison *(G-2551)*

Laennec Publishing Inc G 973 882-9500
Parsippany *(G-8036)*

Lead Bead Publishing Company G 732 246-0410
Somerset *(G-10122)*

▲ **Light Inc** G 973 777-2704
Clifton *(G-1662)*

Little Fox Inc G 609 919-9691
Englewood Cliffs *(G-2975)*

▲ **Lympha Press USA** G 732 792-9677
Freehold *(G-3669)*

M J Powers & Co Publishers G 973 898-1200
Morristown *(G-6724)*

M/C Communications LLC F 908 766-0402
Basking Ridge *(G-193)*

M/C Communications LLC E 609 838-7952
Hamilton *(G-4112)*

▲ **Macie Publishing Company** F 973 983-8700
Mendham *(G-6088)*

Magazinexperts LLC G 973 383-0888
Newton *(G-7395)*

Manna Group LLC F 856 881-7650
Mount Laurel *(G-6816)*

Marquis - Whos Who Inc D 908 673-1006
New Providence *(G-7047)*

Media Vista Inc G 732 747-8060
Red Bank *(G-9337)*

Micro Logic Inc F 201 962-7510
Mahwah *(G-5790)*

Moscova Enterprises Inc F 848 628-4873
Jersey City *(G-4786)*

Nanking Express G 732 549-7788
Iselin *(G-4635)*

National Home Planning Service G 973 376-3200
Chatham *(G-1335)*

New York-NJ Trail Conference F 201 512-9348
Mahwah *(G-5795)*

Nextwave Web LLC F 973 742-4339
Paterson *(G-8351)*

Nighthawk Interactive LLC G 732 243-9922
Edison *(G-2581)*

Nonzero Foundation Inc G 609 688-0793
Princeton *(G-9082)*

North Jersey Media Group Inc E 973 569-7100
Woodland Park *(G-12226)*

Northern State Periodicals LLC G 973 782-6100
Paterson *(G-8354)*

Oasis Entertainment Group G 973 256-7077
Cedar Grove *(G-1294)*

Oggi Media Group LLC E 201 358-6582
Norwood *(G-7633)*

Old Barracks Association Inc F 609 396-1776
Trenton *(G-11092)*

P O V Incorporated F 914 258-4361
Montclair *(G-6428)*

Pavexpress G 201 330-8300
Clifton *(G-1692)*

Perfect Clicks LLC G 845 323-6116
Woodcliff Lake *(G-12199)*

Physicians Weekly LLC G 609 981-7354
Basking Ridge *(G-202)*

Physicians Weekly LLC E 908 766-0421
Basking Ridge *(G-203)*

Princeton Information Center G 609 924-7019
Princeton *(G-9095)*

▲ **Princeton University Press** D 609 258-4900
Princeton *(G-9104)*

Publishers Partnership Co D 201 689-1613
Ridgewood *(G-9428)*

Raphel Marketing Inc G 609 348-6646
Atlantic City *(G-107)*

Rdl Marketing Group LLC G 732 446-0817
Perrineville *(G-8602)*

Review and Judge LLC G 732 987-3905
Lakewood *(G-5183)*

Rockwood Corporation G 908 355-8600
Union *(G-11219)*

▲ **Scafa-Tornabene Art Pubg Co** E 201 842-8500
Lyndhurst *(G-5706)*

Scholastic Book Fairs Inc G 609 578-4142
Cranbury *(G-1878)*

School Publications Co Inc E 732 988-1100
Neptune *(G-6929)*

Sepers Countryside Nursery LLC G 856 451-0719
Bridgeton *(G-797)*

Seven Mile Pubg & Creative F 609 967-7707
Avalon *(G-120)*

Sheridan Printing Company Inc E 908 454-0700
Alpha *(G-46)*

Shoppe CMC Shoppers Guide G 609 886-4112
Villas *(G-11316)*

Sic-Naics LLC G 929 344-2633
Red Bank *(G-9344)*

Sight2site Media LLC G 856 637-2479
Pomona *(G-8945)*

▲ **Sima S Enterprises LLC** G 877 223-7639
Wall Township *(G-11510)*

Simon & Schuster Inc B 856 461-6500
Delran *(G-2022)*

Simon & Schuster Inc E 973 656-6000
Parsippany *(G-8087)*

Sonata Graphics Inc G 201 866-0186
Secaucus *(G-9930)*

South Jersey Publishing Co F 856 692-0455
Vineland *(G-11406)*

Squash Beef LLC G 917 577-8723
Colts Neck *(G-1792)*

Stanger Robert A & Co LP E 732 389-3600
Shrewsbury *(G-10011)*

Starnet Printing Inc G 201 760-2600
Mahwah *(G-5815)*

Steven Orros G 732 972-1104
Monroe Township *(G-6396)*

▲ **Subito Music Service Inc** G 973 857-3440
Verona *(G-11311)*

Success Publishers LLC G 609 443-0792
Perrineville *(G-8603)*

▲ **Sueta Music Ed Publications** F 888 725-2333
Mendham *(G-6091)*

Supermedia LLC B 973 649-9900
Maplewood *(G-5927)*

Tap Into LLC G 908 370-1158
New Providence *(G-7056)*

Teckchek G 919 497-0136
East Brunswick *(G-2193)*

Thepositive Press G 856 266-8765
Cinnaminson *(G-1492)*

Thomas Publishing Company LLC E 973 543-4994
Chester *(G-1440)*

Thomsom Health Care Inc C 201 358-7300
Montvale *(G-6481)*

Thomson Reuters Corporation F 973 662-3070
Nutley *(G-7655)*

Token Torch Ltd Liability Co F 973 629-1805
East Orange *(G-2272)*

Tommax Inc G 732 224-1046
Red Bank *(G-9347)*

Tonymacx86 LLC G 973 584-5273
Ledgewood *(G-5312)*

Treasure Chest Corp G 973 328-7747
Wharton *(G-12001)*

Trf Music Inc F 201 335-0005
Tinton Falls *(G-10851)*

Triefeldt Studios Inc G 609 656-2380
Trenton *(G-11128)*

Triple S Express G 908 686-0557
Union *(G-11230)*

Verizon Communications Inc E 201 666-9934
Westwood *(G-11975)*

Verizon Communications Inc D 609 646-9939
Egg Harbor Township *(G-2698)*

Victory Press G 201 729-1007
Moonachie *(G-6551)*

Walden Mott Corp G 201 962-3704
Ramsey *(G-9255)*

Wcd Enterprises Inc G 732 888-4422
Keyport *(G-5026)*

Wpi Communications Inc F 973 467-8700
Springfield *(G-10586)*

2752 Commercial Printing: Lithographic

A M Graphics Inc G 201 767-5320
Harrington Park *(G-4169)*

A To Z Printing & Promotion G 973 916-9995
Clifton *(G-1553)*

A&E Promotions LLC G 732 382-2300
Holmdel *(G-4506)*

A&R Printing Corporation G 732 886-0505
Lakewood *(G-5062)*

AA Graphics Inc G 201 398-0710
Saddle Brook *(G-9748)*

ABC Printing G 973 664-1160
Rockaway *(G-9540)*

Aboudi Printing LLC G 732 542-2929
Eatontown *(G-2377)*

Absolute Business Services Inc G 856 265-9447
Millville *(G-6273)*

Accent Press Inc G 973 785-3127
Totowa *(G-10925)*

Accucolor LLC G 732 870-1999
Long Branch *(G-5620)*

▲ **Accurate Plastic Printers LLC** E 973 591-0180
Clifton *(G-1555)*

Ace Lthgraphers of Morris Cnty F 973 428-4911
Berkeley Heights *(G-398)*

Action Copy Centers Inc G 973 744-5520
Montclair *(G-6404)*

Action Graphics Inc E 973 633-6500
Lincoln Park *(G-5325)*

Adams Bill Printing & Graphics G 856 455-7177
Bridgeton *(G-776)*

Add Rob Litho LLC G 201 556-0700
Rochelle Park *(G-9525)*

Advertisers Service Group Inc F 201 440-5577
Ridgefield Park *(G-9395)*

AE Litho Offset Printers Inc D 800 235-8888
Beverly *(G-456)*

AE Litho Offset Printers Inc G 609 239-0700
Beverly *(G-457)*

Affordable Offset Printing Inc G 856 661-0722
Pennsauken *(G-8472)*

Agau Inc G 732 583-4343
Matawan *(G-6012)*

AGFA Corporation E 201 440-0111
Carlstadt *(G-1121)*

AGFA Corporation E 201 288-4101
Carlstadt *(G-1122)*

Aladdin Color Inc G 609 518-9858
Moorestown *(G-6556)*

Alan Duffy Printing G 856 768-1046
Atco *(G-88)*

Alete Printing LLC G 856 468-3536
Wenonah *(G-11702)*

All American Print & Copy Ctr G 732 758-6200
Red Bank *(G-9318)*

All Print Resources Group Inc G 201 994-0600
Mountainside *(G-6867)*

Allegro Printing Corporation G 609 641-7060
Galloway *(G-3708)*

▲ **Allied Envelope Co Inc** E 201 440-2000
Carlstadt *(G-1124)*

Allied Printing-Graphics Inc G 973 227-0520
Fairfield *(G-3132)*

AlphaGraphics G 201 327-2200
Mahwah *(G-5746)*

AlphaGraphics F 856 761-8000
Cherry Hill *(G-1343)*

AlphaGraphics Printshops of Th G 973 984-0066
Morristown *(G-6686)*

◆ **American Banknote Corporation** G 203 941-4090
Fort Lee *(G-3543)*

American Graphic Systems Inc G 201 796-0666
Fair Lawn *(G-3076)*

American Plus Printers Inc E 732 528-2170
Wall *(G-11458)*

AMF Graphics Inc F 201 994-1500
Moonachie *(G-6504)*

▲ **Ancraft Press Corp** F 201 792-9200
Jersey City *(G-4705)*

Andrew P Mc Hugh Inc G 856 547-8953
Barrington *(G-171)*

Anisha Enterprises Inc G 908 964-3380
Union *(G-11153)*

Anuco Inc F 973 887-9465
East Hanover *(G-2200)*

Arde G 201 440-1453
Norwood *(G-7615)*

Arglen Industries Inc F 732 888-8100
Hazlet *(G-4269)*

Arna Marketing Group Inc D 908 625-7395
Branchburg *(G-638)*

Artale Graphics F 212 868-0015
Linden *(G-5350)*

▲ **Asbury Park Press Inc** A 732 922-6000
Neptune *(G-6900)*

◆ **Asha44 LLC** E 201 306-3600
Fairfield *(G-3140)*

Atlantic Prtg & Graphics LLC G 732 493-4222
Ocean *(G-7717)*

Aus Inc ....G...... 856 234-9200
  Mount Laurel *(G-6779)*

Ayr Graphics & Printing Inc ....G...... 908 241-8118
  Roselle Park *(G-9689)*

B & B Press Inc ....G...... 908 840-4093
  Lebanon *(G-5278)*

B & R Printing Inc ....G...... 609 448-3328
  Trenton *(G-11024)*

B and W Printing Company Inc ....G...... 908 241-3060
  Kenilworth *(G-4941)*

Bab Printing Jan Service ....G...... 908 272-6224
  Cranford *(G-1897)*

Bannon Group Ltd ....G...... 201 451-6500
  Jersey City *(G-4714)*

Bar Lan Inc ....G...... 856 596-2330
  Brigantine *(G-917)*

Barrington Press Inc ....F...... 201 843-6556
  Paramus *(G-7857)*

Bartlett Printing & Graphic ....G...... 609 386-1525
  Burlington *(G-958)*

Barton & Cooney LLC ....D...... 609 747-9300
  Burlington *(G-959)*

Bassano Prtrs & Lithographers .....E...... 973 423-1400
  Hawthorne *(G-4220)*

Beacon Offset Printing LLC ....G...... 201 488-4241
  Hackensack *(G-3880)*

Berennial International ....G...... 973 675-6266
  Orange *(G-7818)*

Bergen Instant Printing Inc ....G...... 201 945-7303
  Ridgefield *(G-9351)*

Berry Business Procedure Co ....G...... 908 272-6464
  Cranford *(G-1899)*

Better Image Graphics Inc ....G...... 856 262-0735
  Williamstown *(G-12080)*

Big Red Pin LLC ....G...... 732 993-9765
  Edison *(G-2473)*

Bills Printing Service Inc ....G...... 609 888-1841
  Trenton *(G-11027)*

▲ Bind-Rite Robbinsville LLC ....D...... 609 208-1917
  Robbinsville *(G-9511)*

Bittner Industries Inc ....G...... 856 817-8400
  Cherry Hill *(G-1351)*

Boro Printing Inc ....G...... 732 229-1899
  West Long Branch *(G-11844)*

Bowmar Enterprises Inc ....G...... 908 277-3000
  New Providence *(G-7031)*

BP Print Group Inc ....D...... 732 905-9830
  Lakewood *(G-5087)*

Bruce McCoy Sr ....G...... 609 217-6153
  Pine Hill *(G-8721)*

Budget Print Center ....G...... 973 743-0073
  Bloomfield *(G-503)*

Burdol Inc ....G...... 856 453-0336
  Bridgeton *(G-781)*

Burlington Press Corporation ....F...... 609 387-0030
  Burlington *(G-960)*

Business Cards Tomorrow ....E...... 201 236-0088
  Upper Saddle River *(G-11275)*

Business Cards Tomorrow Inc ....F...... 609 965-0808
  Egg Harbor City *(G-2658)*

C Harry Marean Printing ....G...... 609 965-4708
  Egg Harbor City *(G-2659)*

C Jackson Associates Inc ....E...... 856 761-8000
  Cherry Hill *(G-1355)*

Cantone Press Inc ....E...... 201 569-3435
  Englewood *(G-2882)*

Capital Printing Corporation ....D...... 732 560-1515
  Middlesex *(G-6153)*

Carl A Venable Inc ....G...... 732 985-6677
  North Brunswick *(G-7510)*

Catholic Star Herald ....G...... 856 583-6142
  Camden *(G-1051)*

Central Letter Shop Inc ....E...... 973 808-9595
  West Caldwell *(G-11770)*

Century Printing Corp ....G...... 732 981-0544
  Piscataway *(G-8746)*

▲ Challenge Printing Co Inc ....C...... 973 471-4700
  Clifton *(G-1582)*

CIC Letter Service Inc ....D...... 201 896-1900
  Carlstadt *(G-1140)*

Clark Printing Inc ....E...... 201 845-4888
  Fairfield *(G-3161)*

Classic Graphic Inc ....G...... 856 753-0055
  Berlin *(G-431)*

Classic Impressions ....G...... 908 689-3137
  Great Meadows *(G-3848)*

Cmyk Printing Inc ....F...... 201 458-1300
  Carlstadt *(G-1146)*

Coast Star ....E...... 732 223-0076
  Manasquan *(G-5869)*

Color Coded LLC ....G...... 718 482-1063
  Jersey City *(G-4730)*

Colorsource Inc ....G...... 856 488-8100
  Pennsauken *(G-8495)*

Columbia Press Inc ....E...... 973 575-6535
  Fairfield *(G-3163)*

Command Web Offset Company Inc ....C...... 201 863-8100
  Secaucus *(G-9873)*

Commerce Financial Prtrs Corp ....E...... 908 241-9880
  Roselle *(G-9667)*

Comprehensive Mktg Systems ....G...... 908 810-9778
  Union *(G-11165)*

Conagraphics Inc ....G...... 973 331-1113
  Parsippany *(G-7975)*

Contemprary Grphics Bndery Inc .....C...... 856 663-7277
  Camden *(G-1055)*

Copy-Rite Printing ....G...... 609 597-9182
  Manahawkin *(G-5830)*

Corbi Printing Co Inc ....G...... 856 547-2444
  Audubon *(G-116)*

Cordes Printing Inc ....G...... 201 652-7272
  Wyckoff *(G-12248)*

Cornerstone Prints Imaging LLC ......G...... 908 782-7966
  Flemington *(G-3431)*

▲ Corporate Mailings Inc ....C...... 973 439-1168
  West Caldwell *(G-11772)*

Corporate Mailings Inc ....D...... 973 808-0009
  Whippany *(G-12017)*

Cottrell Graphics & Advg Spc ....G...... 732 349-7430
  Toms River *(G-10873)*

County Graphics Forms MGT LLC .....E...... 908 474-9797
  Linden *(G-5362)*

Coventry of New Jersey Inc ....G...... 856 988-5521
  Marlton *(G-5968)*

Craftmaster Printing Inc ....G...... 732 775-0011
  Neptune *(G-6906)*

Craftsmen Photo Lithographers .....E...... 973 316-5791
  East Hanover *(G-2211)*

Creative Color Lithographers ....E...... 908 789-2295
  Garwood *(G-3777)*

Crt International Inc ....F...... 973 887-7737
  Middlesex *(G-6160)*

Custom Book Bindery Inc ....F...... 973 815-1400
  Clifton *(G-1596)*

D & I Printing Co Inc ....F...... 201 871-3620
  Englewood *(G-2885)*

D & S Ventures Inc ....G...... 732 758-0095
  Red Bank *(G-9324)*

D A K Office Services Inc ....G...... 609 586-8222
  Trenton *(G-11052)*

D L Printing Co Inc ....G...... 732 750-1917
  Avenel *(G-129)*

Danmar Press Inc ....F...... 201 487-4400
  South Hackensack *(G-10259)*

Darby Litho Inc ....F...... 908 231-8883
  Manville *(G-5894)*

Data Communique Intl Inc ....E...... 201 508-6000
  Ridgefield Park *(G-9403)*

▲ Datascan Graphics Inc ....E...... 973 543-4803
  Morristown *(G-6704)*

▲ Dato Company Inc ....G...... 732 225-2272
  Cranbury *(G-1828)*

Dcg Printing Inc ....G...... 732 530-4441
  Shrewsbury *(G-9996)*

Dee Jay Printing Inc ....G...... 973 227-7787
  Fairfield *(G-3174)*

Delgen Press Inc ....G...... 973 472-2266
  Clifton *(G-1598)*

Design Factory Nj Inc ....G...... 908 964-8833
  Hillside *(G-4404)*

Devece & Shaffer Inc ....G...... 856 829-7282
  Palmyra *(G-7847)*

Dg3 Group America Inc ....G...... 201 793-5000
  Jersey City *(G-4739)*

Dg3 Holdings LLC ....G...... 201 793-5000
  Jersey City *(G-4740)*

Dg3 North America Inc ....B...... 201 793-5000
  Jersey City *(G-4741)*

Diane Matson Inc ....F...... 609 288-6833
  Westampton *(G-11912)*

Digital Print Solutions Inc ....F...... 973 263-1890
  Parsippany *(G-7982)*

Digital Productions Inc ....F...... 856 224-1111
  Swedesboro *(G-10692)*

Digital Xpress LLC ....G...... 973 627-2609
  Denville *(G-2037)*

▲ Diligaf Enterprises Inc ....E...... 201 684-0900
  Mahwah *(G-5765)*

Direct Prtg Impressions Inc ....F...... 973 227-6111
  West Caldwell *(G-11773)*

Discount Digital Print LLC ....F...... 201 659-9600
  Jersey City *(G-4744)*

Diversified Impressions Inc ....G...... 973 399-9041
  Irvington *(G-4581)*

Divine Printing ....G...... 732 632-8800
  Metuchen *(G-6102)*

Dohrman Printing Co Inc ....G...... 201 933-0346
  Carlstadt *(G-1156)*

Dolce Brothers Printing Inc ....E...... 201 843-0400
  Maywood *(G-6048)*

Dolce Printing ....F...... 201 843-0400
  Maywood *(G-6049)*

Donnelley Financial LLC ....F...... 973 882-7000
  West Caldwell *(G-11774)*

▲ Donray Printing Inc ....E...... 973 515-8100
  Parsippany *(G-7984)*

Douglas Maybury Assoc ....G...... 908 879-5878
  Chester *(G-1436)*

Downtown Printing Center Inc ....F...... 732 246-7990
  New Brunswick *(G-6955)*

Dpi Copies Prtg & Graphics Inc ....F...... 856 874-1355
  Cherry Hill *(G-1360)*

Dynamic Printing & Graphics ....F...... 973 473-7177
  Clifton *(G-1608)*

E Nevin Miller Inc ....F...... 201 444-5784
  Hawthorne *(G-4230)*

Earth Color New York Inc ....E...... 973 884-1300
  Parsippany *(G-7992)*

▲ Earth Thebault Inc ....C...... 973 884-1300
  Parsippany *(G-7993)*

Earthcolor Inc ....C...... 973 884-1300
  Parsippany *(G-7994)*

▲ East Coast Media LLC ....E...... 908 575-9700
  Hillsborough *(G-4329)*

▲ Edison Lithog & Prtg Corp ....D...... 201 902-9191
  North Bergen *(G-7449)*

Edwards Brothers Inc ....G...... 856 848-6900
  West Deptford *(G-11826)*

Elbee Litho Inc ....G...... 732 698-7738
  East Brunswick *(G-2149)*

Election Graphics Inc ....F...... 201 758-9966
  Verona *(G-11305)*

Elite Graphix LLC ....F...... 732 274-2356
  Monmouth Junction *(G-6343)*

Elmwood Press Inc ....F...... 201 794-6273
  Elmwood Park *(G-2818)*

Emerson Speed Printing Inc ....G...... 201 265-7977
  Oradell *(G-7808)*

Encore Enterprises Inc ....G...... 201 489-5044
  South Hackensack *(G-10264)*

Esquire Business Forms ....G...... 609 883-1155
  Ewing *(G-3016)*

Excel Color Graphics Inc ....G...... 856 848-3345
  Woodbury Heights *(G-12177)*

Excellent Prtg & Graphics LLC ....F...... 973 773-6661
  Clifton *(G-1616)*

Express Printing Inc ....G...... 908 925-6300
  Linden *(G-5372)*

Express Printing Services Inc ....G...... 973 585-7355
  Fairfield *(G-3191)*

Falcon Graphics Inc ....G...... 908 232-1991
  Clark *(G-1500)*

Falcon Printing & Graphics ....G...... 732 462-6862
  Freehold *(G-3655)*

Fast Copy Printing Center ....F...... 732 739-4646
  Keyport *(G-5017)*

Fedex Corporation ....G...... 201 525-5070
  River Edge *(G-9465)*

Ferrett Printing Inc ....G...... 856 686-4896
  Woodbury *(G-12161)*

FLM Graphics Corporation ....D...... 973 575-9450
  Fairfield *(G-3196)*

Flortek Corporation ....E...... 201 436-7700
  Bayonne *(G-225)*

Forbes Media LLC ....D...... 212 620-2200
  Jersey City *(G-4754)*

Four Star Reproductions Inc ....E...... 862 268-8200
  Newton *(G-7388)*

Franbeth Inc ....G...... 856 488-1480
  Pennsauken *(G-8512)*

Franklin Graphics Inc ....G...... 201 935-5900
  Westwood *(G-11960)*

Fulfillment Printing and Mail ....G...... 609 953-9500
  Medford Lakes *(G-6085)*

Full House Printing Inc ....G...... 201 798-7073
  Hoboken *(G-4470)*

Full Service Mailers Inc ....E...... 973 478-8813
  Hackensack *(G-3919)*

G J Haerer Co Inc ....D...... 973 614-8090
  Glen Ridge *(G-3818)*

S
I
C

Galvanic Prtg & Plate Co Inc ....E 201 939-3600
Moonachie (G-6518)

Gangi Graphics Inc ....G 732 840-8680
Brick (G-744)

Gannett Stllite Info Ntwrk Inc ....C 856 691-5000
Vineland (G-11357)

Garrison Printing Company Inc ....E 856 488-1900
Pennsauken (G-8515)

Genua & Mulligan Printing ....E 973 894-1500
Clifton (G-1626)

▲ George H Buchanan Company ....E 856 241-3960
Swedesboro (G-10698)

Gerardi Press Inc ....E 973 627-2600
Denville (G-2041)

Gmpc Printing ....G 973 546-6060
Clifton (G-1629)

Gms Litho Corp ....G 973 575-9400
Fairfield (G-3211)

Goffco Industries LLC ....G 973 492-0150
Butler (G-1005)

Good Impressions Inc ....G 856 461-3232
Riverside (G-9498)

Good Impressions Inc ....F 908 689-3071
Washington (G-11581)

Grandview Printing Co Inc ....F 973 890-0006
Totowa (G-10950)

Graph Tech Sales & Service ....E 201 218-1749
Fairfield (G-3213)

Graphic Action Inc ....G 908 213-0055
Phillipsburg (G-8650)

▲ Graphic Impressions Inc ....E 201 487-8788
Hackensack (G-3921)

Graphic Impressions Prtg Co ....G 856 728-2266
Blackwood (G-480)

Graphic Management ....E 908 654-8400
Kearny (G-4879)

Graphicolor Corporation ....E 856 691-2507
Vineland (G-11364)

Graphics Depot Inc ....F 973 927-8200
Randolph (G-9281)

Graytor Printing Company Inc ....E 201 933-0100
Lyndhurst (G-5684)

Great Eastern Color Lith ....G 201 843-5656
Paramus (G-7874)

Great Northern Commercial Svcs .....G 908 475-8855
Belvidere (G-373)

▲ Green Horse Media LLC ....C 856 933-0222
Bellmawr (G-341)

Gregory Press Inc ....F 908 686-6473
Kenilworth (G-4960)

▲ Gross Bros Printing Co Inc ....E 201 865-4606
Union City (G-11246)

Gross Printing Associates Inc ....F 718 832-1110
Clifton (G-1631)

▲ H C Graphics Screenprinting ....G 973 247-0544
Paterson (G-8286)

Hallco Inc ....G 609 729-0161
Wildwood (G-12072)

Hammer Press Printers Inc ....D 973 334-4500
Parsippany (G-8026)

Hansen Lithography Ltd ....G 732 270-1188
Toms River (G-10882)

Happle Printing ....G 609 476-0100
Dorothy (G-2073)

Harvard Printing Group ....D 973 672-0800
Fairfield (G-3216)

Hatteras Press Inc ....B 732 935-9800
Tinton Falls (G-10838)

Hawk Graphics Inc ....E 973 895-5569
Randolph (G-9283)

Herald News ....G 973 569-7000
Woodland Park (G-12221)

Hermitage Press of New Jersey ....D 609 882-3600
Ewing (G-3022)

Highroad Press LLC ....E 201 708-6900
Moonachie (G-6521)

Holographic Finishing Inc ....F 201 941-4651
Ridgefield (G-9365)

Hometown Office Sups & Prtg Co ......G 609 298-9020
Bordentown (G-598)

▲ Howard Press Inc ....D 908 245-4400
Roselle (G-9673)

Howes Standard Publishing Co ....E 856 691-2000
Vineland (G-11371)

Hub Print & Copy Center LLC ....G 201 585-7887
Fort Lee (G-3558)

I Print Nb ....G 201 662-1133
North Bergen (G-7458)

I T C Printing Promotion ....G 908 918-1122
Summit (G-10648)

Image Makers Instant Printing ....G 973 633-1771
Wayne (G-11649)

Imagine Screen Prtg & Prod LLC ....C 732 329-2009
Dayton (G-1969)

Impact Printing ....G 862 225-9167
Little Ferry (G-5508)

Impressions Unlimited Prtg LLC ....G 856 256-0200
Sewell (G-9957)

Ink Well Printers LLC ....G 908 272-8090
Kenilworth (G-4963)

Inserts East Incorporated ....C 856 663-8181
Pennsauken (G-8528)

Instant Imprints ....G 973 252-9500
Flanders (G-3411)

Instant Printing of Dover Inc ....G 973 366-6855
Dover (G-2093)

J B Offset Printing Corp ....G 201 264-4400
Norwood (G-7626)

J D M Associates Inc ....G 973 773-8699
Lodi (G-5590)

Jasco Specialties and Forms ....G 856 627-5511
Tabernacle (G-10738)

JC Printing & Advertising Inc ....G 973 881-8612
Paterson (G-8300)

Jem Printing Inc ....G 908 782-9986
Flemington (G-3450)

Jersey Printing Associates Inc ....E 732 872-9654
Atlantic Highlands (G-113)

Jli Marketing & Printing Corp ....F 732 828-8877
Cranbury (G-1845)

Jmc Design & Graphics Inc ....G 973 276-9033
Fairfield (G-3236)

Jmp Press Inc ....G 201 444-0236
Ho Ho Kus (G-4454)

John S Swift Company Inc ....G 201 935-2002
Teterboro (G-10801)

John S Swift Print of NJ Inc ....G 201 678-3232
Teterboro (G-10802)

Johnston Letter Co Inc ....G 973 482-7535
Flanders (G-3412)

Jon-Da Printing Co Inc ....F 201 653-6200
Jersey City (G-4769)

Jory Engravers Inc ....E 201 939-1546
Rutherford (G-9736)

Joseph Burns Inc ....G 732 356-8355
Bound Brook (G-619)

Jvs Copy Services Inc ....F 856 415-9090
Sewell (G-9961)

K R B Printing For Business ....G 856 751-5200
Cherry Hill (G-1385)

Kay Printing & Envelope Co Inc ....E 973 330-3000
Clifton (G-1655)

Keskes Printing LLC ....G 856 767-4733
Berlin (G-437)

Keystone Printing Inc ....E 201 387-7252
Dumont (G-2119)

Killian Graphics ....G 973 635-5844
Chatham (G-1332)

Kirms Printing Co Inc ....E 732 774-8000
Neptune (G-6920)

Knock Out Graphics Inc ....F 732 774-3331
Asbury Park (G-79)

Kufall Printing ....G 732 505-9847
Toms River (G-10892)

L A S Printing Co ....D 201 991-5362
Jersey City (G-4775)

▲ L L Teach Inc ....E 732 223-1605
Brielle (G-912)

Label Solutions Inc ....G 201 599-0909
Rochelle Park (G-9531)

Lamb Printing Inc ....G 908 852-0837
Hackettstown (G-4016)

Laser Dim Graphics & Prtg Inc ....F 732 821-9000
Colts Neck (G-1789)

Latta Graphics Inc ....E 201 440-4040
Carlstadt (G-1183)

Laureate Press ....G 609 646-1545
Egg Harbor City (G-2666)

Lawn Medic Inc ....G 856 742-1111
Westville (G-11945)

LCI Graphics Inc ....F 973 893-2913
Sayreville (G-9827)

Lettie Press Inc ....G 201 391-6388
Park Ridge (G-7924)

Lewis Scheller Printing Corp ....G 732 843-5050
Somerset (G-10124)

Lexington Graphics Corp ....G 973 345-2493
Clifton (G-1661)

Liberty Envelope Inc ....F 973 546-5600
Paterson (G-8320)

Lightning Press Inc ....F 973 890-4422
Totowa (G-10954)

Linder & Company Inc ....F 201 386-8788
Jersey City (G-4777)

Lithos Estiatorio Ltd Lblty Co ....G 973 758-1111
Livingston (G-5539)

Lmp Printing Corp ....G 973 428-1987
Clifton (G-1663)

Longrun Press Inc ....F 856 719-9202
West Berlin (G-11731)

Lont & Overkamp Pubg Co Inc ....E 973 942-2243
Clifton (G-1664)

LP Thebault Co ....F 973 884-1300
Parsippany (G-8040)

Lunet Inc ....G 201 261-3883
Paramus (G-7885)

M & M Printing Corp ....G 201 288-7787
Hasbrouck Heights (G-4196)

M G X Inc ....F 732 329-0088
Monmouth Junction (G-6350)

Major Printing Co Inc ....G 908 686-7296
Union (G-11204)

Manva Industries Inc ....F 973 667-2606
Nutley (G-7651)

Manzi Printing ....G 732 542-1927
Eatontown (G-2412)

▲ Mariano Press LLC ....G 732 247-3659
Somerset (G-10129)

Mark Alan Printing & Graphics ....G 732 981-9011
Piscataway (G-8790)

Mark Lithography Inc ....G 973 538-5557
Cedar Knolls (G-1316)

Marks Management Systems Inc ....G 856 866-0588
Maple Shade (G-5906)

Master Printing Inc ....E 201 842-9100
Carlstadt (G-1188)

Master Repro Inc ....G 201 447-4800
Midland Park (G-6231)

McGinnis Printing ....G 732 758-0060
Red Bank (G-9336)

McKella 2-8-0 Inc ....D 856 813-1153
Pennsauken (G-8548)

Mercer C AlphaGraphics ....G 609 921-0959
Hamilton (G-4116)

Mercer Digital Printing LLC ....G 609 919-9190
Lawrenceville (G-5263)

Merrill Corporation ....D 908 810-3740
Union (G-11207)

Metro Prtg & Promotions LLC ....F 973 316-1600
Boonton (G-578)

Metro Seliger Industries Inc ....C 201 438-4530
Carlstadt (G-1189)

Metro Web Corp ....E 201 553-0700
North Bergen (G-7467)

Michael Graphics Inc ....E 732 846-8680
Branchburg (G-680)

Mid Atlantic Graphixinc ....G 609 569-9990
Egg Harbor Township (G-2690)

Mint Printing LLC ....G 973 546-2060
Lodi (G-5596)

Minuteman Press ....G 973 403-0146
Caldwell (G-1031)

Minuteman Press ....G 732 536-8788
Manalapan (G-5854)

Monte Printing & Graphics Inc ....G 908 241-6600
Roselle Park (G-9699)

More Copy Printing Service ....G 201 327-1106
Upper Saddle River (G-11281)

▲ Morgan Printing Service Inc ....F 732 721-2959
South Amboy (G-10243)

◆ Morris County Duplicating ....D 973 993-8484
Cedar Knolls (G-1317)

Morris Plains Pip Inc ....G 973 533-9330
Livingston (G-5548)

Morrison Press Inc ....F 201 488-4848
Closter (G-1764)

▲ Mountain Printing Company Inc ......E 856 767-7600
Berlin (G-438)

Mr Quickly Inc ....G 908 687-6000
Union (G-11209)

Multi Packaging Solutions Inc ....G 908 757-6000
South Plainfield (G-10411)

My Way Prints Inc ....G 973 492-1212
Butler (G-1014)

Nassau Communications Inc ....F 609 208-9099
Lawrence Township (G-5245)

National Certified Printing ....G 609 443-6323
Hightstown (G-4313)

Nema Associates Inc ....F 973 274-0052
Linden (G-5418)

New Horizon Graphics Inc ....G..... 609 584-1301
  Trenton (G-11083)
New Jersey Label LLC ....F..... 201 880-5102
  South Hackensack (G-10283)
New Jersey Reprographics Inc...........G..... 908 789-1616
  Garwood (G-3780)
New Life Color Reproductions ....G..... 201 943-7005
  Ridgefield (G-9378)
New Standard Printing Corp ....G..... 973 366-0006
  Dover (G-2104)
▲ Newline Prtg & Tech Solutions ....F..... 973 405-6133
  Mountainside (G-6884)
Nextwave Web LLC ....F..... 973 742-4339
  Paterson (G-8351)
Nitka Graphics Inc ....G..... 201 797-3000
  Fair Lawn (G-3106)
Noble Metals Corp ....G..... 908 925-6300
  Linden (G-5420)
▲ Norwood Printing Inc ....F..... 201 784-8721
  Norwood (G-7632)
Nu-Plan Business Systems Inc ....G..... 732 231-6944
  Clark (G-1510)
Ocsidot Inc ....F..... 908 789-3300
  Garwood (G-3782)
Old Hights Print Shop Inc ....G..... 609 443-4700
  Jackson (G-4674)
On Demand Print Group ....G..... 201 636-2270
  Lyndhurst (G-5698)
One Two Three Inc ....F..... 856 251-1238
  Woodbury (G-12166)
One-Source Communications ....E..... 973 463-0250
  Whippany (G-12029)
Orora Visual LLC ....G..... 973 916-2804
  Clifton (G-1687)
OShea Services Inc ....G..... 201 343-8668
  Hackensack (G-3957)
▼ OSullivan Communications Corp......E..... 973 227-5112
  West Caldwell (G-11795)
Otis Graphics Inc ....E..... 201 438-7120
  Lyndhurst (G-5700)
Pace Press Incorporated ....D..... 201 935-7711
  Moonachie (G-6534)
Pad and Publ Assembly Corp ....E..... 856 424-0158
  Cherry Hill (G-1409)
Palm Press Inc ....G..... 201 767-6504
  Northvale (G-7600)
Panther Printing Inc ....G..... 239 542-1050
  West Orange (G-11904)
▲ Paravista Inc ....E..... 732 752-1222
  Fairfield (G-3281)
▲ Paris Corporation New Jersey ....D..... 609 265-9200
  Westampton (G-11914)
Park Printing Services Inc..................F..... 856 675-1600
  Pennsauken (G-8556)
Parkway Printing Inc ....G..... 732 308-0300
  Marlboro (G-5951)
Parsells Printing Inc ....G..... 973 473-2700
  Maywood (G-6059)
Parth Enterprises Inc ....G..... 732 404-0665
  Iselin (G-4640)
Pascack Valley Copy Center ....G..... 201 664-1917
  Westwood (G-11966)
Patel Printing Plus Corp ....F..... 908 964-6422
  Union (G-11214)
PDM Litho Inc ....E..... 718 301-1740
  Clifton (G-1693)
PDQ Print & Copy Inc ....F..... 201 569-2288
  Englewood (G-2921)
Peacock Communications Inc ....G..... 973 763-3311
  Maplewood (G-5924)
Penn Jersey Press Inc ....G..... 856 627-2200
  Gibbsboro (G-3789)
Penny Press ....G..... 856 547-1991
  Stratford (G-10616)
Pentagraphix Offset Prtg Inc ....F..... 201 526-9300
  Jersey City (G-4800)
Perfect Printing Inc ....E..... 856 787-1877
  Moorestown (G-6611)
Permagraphics Inc ....F..... 201 814-1200
  Moonachie (G-6535)
▲ Pharmaceutic Litho Label Inc ....C..... 336 785-4000
  Cranford (G-1923)
Philip Holzer and Assoc LLC ....E..... 212 691-9500
  Carlstadt (G-1202)
Phillip Balderose ....G..... 732 574-1330
  Clark (G-1512)
Phoenix Business Forms Inc ....G..... 856 691-2266
  Vineland (G-11392)
Photo Offset Prtg & Pubg Co.............G..... 609 587-4900
  Trenton (G-11098)

Pica Printings Inc ....G..... 973 540-0420
  Morristown (G-6735)
Pine Hill Printing Inc ....G..... 856 346-2915
  Pine Hill (G-8722)
Pinnacle Press Inc ....G..... 201 652-0500
  Midland Park (G-6234)
Pinto Printing ....G..... 856 232-2550
  Blackwood (G-489)
Pirolli Printing Co Inc ....F..... 856 933-1285
  Bellmawr (G-349)
Precision Printing Group Inc ....E..... 856 753-0900
  Mount Laurel (G-6831)
Premier Graphics Inc ....E..... 732 872-9933
  Atlantic Highlands (G-115)
Premier Printing Solutions LLC.........G..... 732 525-0740
  Sayreville (G-9836)
Premium Service Printing ....G..... 908 707-1311
  Hillsborough (G-4363)
Pressto Graphics ....F..... 732 286-9300
  Toms River (G-10903)
Presto Printing Service Inc ....G..... 908 756-5337
  South Plainfield (G-10424)
Princetonian Graphics Inc ....F..... 732 329-8282
  Monmouth Junction (G-6359)
Print Factory Ltd Liability Co.............G..... 973 866-5230
  Clifton (G-1705)
Print Group Inc ....F..... 201 487-4400
  South Hackensack (G-10290)
Print Mail Communications LLC.........E..... 856 488-0345
  Pennsauken (G-8566)
Print Peel ....E..... 201 507-0080
  Carlstadt (G-1209)
Print Post ....G..... 973 732-0950
  Newark (G-7275)
Print Shoppe Inc ....G..... 908 782-9213
  Flemington (G-3462)
▼ Print Tech LLC...............................D..... 908 232-2287
  Springfield (G-10573)
Print Tech LLC ....G..... 908 232-0767
  Westfield (G-11928)
Printers of Salem County LLC............G..... 856 935-5032
  Salem (G-9808)
Printers Place Inc ....G..... 973 744-8889
  Montclair (G-6432)
Printing Center Inc ....E..... 973 383-6362
  Sparta (G-10518)
Printing Craftsman Inc ....F..... 201 943-0276
  Fairview (G-3370)
Printing Delite Inc ....G..... 973 676-3033
  East Orange (G-2266)
Printing Industries LLC ....G..... 973 334-9775
  Parsippany (G-8072)
Printing Plus of South Jersey ....G..... 856 767-3941
  West Berlin (G-11744)
Printwrap Corporation ....F..... 973 239-1144
  Cedar Grove (G-1297)
Prisco Digital Ltd Lblty Co ....F..... 973 589-7800
  Newark (G-7277)
Prism Color Corporation ....D..... 856 234-7515
  Moorestown (G-6615)
Prism Dgtal Communications LLC......F..... 973 232-5038
  Mountainside (G-6886)
Pro Screen Printing Inc ....G..... 201 246-7600
  Kearny (G-4910)
Product Identification Co Inc ....F..... 973 227-7770
  Garfield (G-3754)
Professional Printing Services ....G..... 856 428-6300
  Haddonfield (G-4063)
Professional Reproductions Inc..........F..... 212 268-1222
  Marlboro (G-5954)
Progress Printing Co ....F..... 201 433-3133
  Jersey City (G-4806)
Progressive 4 Color Ltd Lblty ....G..... 973 736-5800
  West Orange (G-11905)
Progressive Offset Inc ....E..... 201 569-3900
  Englewood (G-2925)
Prohaska & Co Inc ....G..... 732 238-3420
  East Brunswick (G-2176)
Pronto Printing & Copying Ctr............G..... 201 426-0009
  Ramsey (G-9251)
Publishers Inc ....E..... 856 853-2800
  West Deptford (G-11840)
Puent-Romer Communications Inc......G..... 973 509-7591
  Montclair (G-6433)
Q P 195 Inc ....F..... 732 531-8860
  Ocean (G-7738)
Q P 500 Inc ....G..... 732 531-8860
  Ocean (G-7739)
Quad/Graphics Inc ....E..... 609 534-7308
  Westampton (G-11917)

Quad/Graphics Inc.............................E..... 732 469-0189
  Somerset (G-10161)
Quality Print Solutions ....G..... 888 679-7237
  Ridgewood (G-9429)
R & B Printing Inc ....G..... 908 766-4073
  Bernardsville (G-454)
R L R Foil Stamping LLC ....F..... 973 778-9464
  Passaic (G-8175)
R V Livolsi Incorporated ....G..... 732 286-2200
  Toms River (G-10905)
Rays Reproduction Inc ....G..... 201 666-5650
  Emerson (G-2862)
Recorder Publishing Co ....E..... 908 647-1180
  Stirling (G-10605)
Redmond Bcms Inc ....D..... 973 664-2000
  Denville (G-2053)
Regal Litho Prtrs Ltd Lblty Co............G..... 732 901-1500
  Lakewood (G-5177)
Register Lithographers Ltd ....D..... 973 916-2804
  Clifton (G-1712)
Reliable Envelope and Graphics ....E..... 201 794-7756
  Elmwood Park (G-2848)
Reliance Graphics Inc ....G..... 973 239-5411
  Verona (G-11310)
Remco Press Inc ....E..... 201 751-5703
  North Bergen (G-7479)
Repro Tronics Inc ....G..... 201 722-1880
  Ltl Egg Hbr (G-5647)
Repromatic Printing Inc ....G..... 973 239-7610
  Cedar Grove (G-1299)
Review Printing Inc............................G..... 856 589-7200
  Pitman (G-8844)
Rfm Printing Inc ....F..... 732 938-4400
  Belmar (G-362)
Ridgewood Press Inc ....F..... 201 670-9797
  Ridgewood (G-9430)
Riegel Holding Company Inc ....D..... 609 771-0361
  Ewing (G-3052)
Roan Printing Inc ....F..... 908 526-5990
  Somerville (G-10226)
Rocco Press Advg Typography ....F..... 973 790-4000
  Paterson (G-8371)
Rocket Ship & Print Inc ....G..... 973 275-1144
  South Orange (G-10314)
▲ Roelynn Litho Inc ....F..... 732 942-9650
  Lakewood (G-5185)
Rolls Offset Group Inc ....E..... 201 727-1110
  Lyndhurst (G-5705)
Roned Printing & Reproduction ....G..... 973 386-1848
  East Hanover (G-2241)
Roy D Smith Inc ....G..... 201 384-4163
  Bergenfield (G-393)
Roy Press Inc ....G..... 732 922-9460
  Oceanport (G-7767)
Royal Printing Service ....E..... 201 863-3131
  West New York (G-11880)
Royer Graphics Inc ....G..... 856 344-7935
  Clementon (G-1535)
Royer Group Inc ....E..... 856 324-0171
  Pennsauken (G-8575)
Rush Graphics Inc ....E..... 973 427-9393
  Hawthorne (G-4257)
Rush Index Tabs Inc ....E..... 201 531-1555
  East Rutherford (G-2324)
S & M Press Inc ....F..... 973 546-6111
  Garfield (G-3760)
SAM Graphics Inc ....E..... 732 431-0440
  Marlboro (G-5956)
Sample Media Inc ....E..... 609 399-5411
  Ocean City (G-7757)
Sandoval Graphics & Printing ....G..... 856 435-7320
  Somerdale (G-10043)
◆ Sandy Alexander Inc ....C..... 973 470-8100
  Clifton (G-1715)
Santangelo Printing Co Inc ....F..... 973 779-5880
  Lodi (G-5599)
Sapphire Envelope & Graphics ....E..... 856 782-2227
  Magnolia (G-5742)
Scarlet Printing ....G..... 732 560-1415
  Middlesex (G-6193)
Schellmark Inc ....G..... 732 345-7143
  Tinton Falls (G-10846)
School Publications Co Inc ....E..... 732 988-1100
  Neptune (G-6929)
Schuyler Printing Inc ....G..... 201 997-8083
  Kearny (G-4913)
◆ Scodix Inc ....F..... 855 726-3491
  Saddle Brook (G-9791)
Scott Graphics Printing Co Inc...........G..... 201 262-0473
  New Milford (G-7025)

S
I
C

Screen Printing & Embroidery ....G...... 732 256-9610
Wall Township *(G-11507)*

Service Data Corp Inc ....G...... 908 522-0020
Summit *(G-10656)*

Sherman Printing Co Inc ....G...... 973 345-2493
Clifton *(G-1721)*

Sheroy Printing Inc ....F...... 973 242-4040
Newark *(G-7312)*

Shindo International Inc ....G...... 973 470-8100
Clifton *(G-1722)*

Showcase Printing of Iselin ....G...... 732 283-0438
Iselin *(G-4644)*

Shree Ji Printing Corporation ......E...... 201 842-9500
Carlstadt *(G-1217)*

Signs of Security Inc ....E...... 973 340-8404
Garfield *(G-3762)*

Solid Color Inc ....G...... 212 239-3930
Kearny *(G-4915)*

Sonata Graphics Inc ....E...... 201 866-0186
Secaucus *(G-9930)*

South Amboy Designer T Shirt L .....G...... 732 456-2594
South Amboy *(G-10245)*

Staines Inc ....F...... 856 784-2718
Somerdale *(G-10044)*

Standard Prtg & Mail Svcs Inc ......F...... 973 790-3333
Fairfield *(G-3311)*

Star Litho Inc ....G...... 973 641-1603
Fairfield *(G-3312)*

Star Promotions Inc ....F...... 732 356-5959
Bound Brook *(G-624)*

Stauts Printing & Graphics ....G...... 609 654-5382
Medford *(G-6083)*

Steb Inc ....G...... 973 584-0990
Ledgewood *(G-5310)*

Steb Inc ....F...... 973 584-0990
Ledgewood *(G-5311)*

Steven Madola ....G...... 609 989-8022
Trenton *(G-11117)*

Stobbs Printing Co Inc ....G...... 973 748-4441
Bloomfield *(G-533)*

Stone Mountain Printing Inc ....G...... 732 636-8450
Woodbridge *(G-12154)*

Strategic Content Imaging ....C...... 201 863-8100
Secaucus *(G-9933)*

Stuyvesant Press Inc ....F...... 973 399-3880
Irvington *(G-4605)*

Sunset Printing and Engrv Corp .....E...... 973 537-9600
Wharton *(G-12000)*

Superfine Online Inc ....G...... 212 827-0063
Roselle *(G-9684)*

Superior Trademark Inc ....G...... 201 652-1900
Waldwick *(G-11454)*

Supplies-Supplies Inc ....F...... 908 272-5100
Watchung *(G-11596)*

Supreme Graphics and Prtg Inc .....G...... 718 989-9817
Perth Amboy *(G-8632)*

Supreme Ink Corp ....F...... 973 344-2922
Newark *(G-7335)*

Sureway Prtg & Graphics LLC ....G...... 609 430-4333
Princeton *(G-9127)*

Suzie Mac Specialties Inc ....E...... 732 238-3500
East Brunswick *(G-2191)*

Tabloid Graphic Services Inc ....D...... 856 486-0410
Pennsauken *(G-8582)*

Tandem Color Imaging Graphics .....G...... 973 513-9779
Pompton Lakes *(G-8949)*

Tangent Graphics Inc ....G...... 201 488-2840
Englewood *(G-2936)*

Tanter Inc ....G...... 732 382-3555
Clark *(G-1516)*

Tanzola Printing Inc ....G...... 973 779-0858
Clifton *(G-1734)*

Tape Graphics ....G...... 201 393-9500
Hasbrouck Heights *(G-4199)*

Technical Nameplate Corp ....E...... 973 773-4256
Passaic *(G-8184)*

▲ Tectubes USA Inc ....E...... 856 589-1250
Vineland *(G-11408)*

Tedco Inc ....G...... 609 883-0799
Ewing *(G-3060)*

▲ Tex Print USA LLC ....E...... 201 773-6531
Fair Lawn *(G-3121)*

The Creative Print Group Inc ....F...... 856 486-1700
Pennsauken *(G-8585)*

Thermo X-Press Printing LLC ....G...... 973 585-6505
East Hanover *(G-2245)*

▲ Thermo-Graphics Inc ....G...... 908 486-0100
Avenel *(G-156)*

Thewal Inc ....F...... 973 635-1880
Chatham *(G-1338)*

Thomas H Cox & Son Inc ....E...... 908 928-1010
Linden *(G-5453)*

Tmg Enterprises Inc ....F...... 732 469-2900
Piscataway *(G-8826)*

Toms River Printing Corp ....G...... 732 240-2033
Brielle *(G-915)*

Toppan Printing Co Amer Inc ....C...... 732 469-8400
Somerset *(G-10188)*

Trade Thermographers Inc ....F...... 201 489-2060
Rochelle Park *(G-9539)*

Tremont Printing Co ....G...... 973 227-0742
Fairfield *(G-3330)*

Trenton Printing LLC ....G...... 609 695-6485
Trenton *(G-11125)*

Trentypo Inc ....F...... 609 883-5971
Ewing *(G-3062)*

Tretina Printing Inc ....E...... 732 264-2324
Hazlet *(G-4285)*

Trinity Press Inc ....E...... 973 881-0690
Paterson *(G-8402)*

Trukmanns Inc ....E...... 973 538-7718
Cedar Knolls *(G-1321)*

Tuerff Sziber Capitol Copy Svc .....F...... 609 989-8776
Trenton *(G-11129)*

Twill Inc ....F...... 908 665-1700
Berkeley Heights *(G-423)*

Typeline ....E...... 201 251-2201
Wyckoff *(G-12267)*

Typestyle Inc ....G...... 201 343-3343
Hackensack *(G-3987)*

Unity Graphics & Engraving Co ......E...... 201 541-5462
Englewood *(G-2940)*

Vanguard Printing ....G...... 856 358-2665
Elmer *(G-2800)*

Verni Vito ....G...... 732 449-1760
Wall Township *(G-11517)*

Vernw Printing Company ....G...... 973 751-6462
Belleville *(G-324)*

Vestal Publishing Co Inc ....G...... 732 583-3232
Cliffwood *(G-1550)*

▲ Vintage Print Gallery ....G...... 201 501-0505
Closter *(G-1768)*

Viskal Printing LLC ....G...... 973 812-6600
Totowa *(G-10982)*

Visual Engineering Group Inc ....G...... 908 479-1893
Bloomsbury *(G-546)*

W B Mason Co Inc ....D...... 888 926-2766
Bellmawr *(G-354)*

W B Mason Co Inc ....G...... 888 926-2766
Egg Harbor Township *(G-2699)*

W B Mason Co Inc ....E...... 888 926-2766
Cranbury *(G-1890)*

W G I Corp ....F...... 732 370-2900
Lakewood *(G-5203)*

Waldwick Printing Co ....G...... 201 652-5848
Waldwick *(G-11456)*

Washington Stamp Exchange Inc .....F...... 973 966-0001
Florham Park *(G-3523)*

Watonka Printing Inc ....G...... 732 974-8878
Belmar *(G-365)*

Webb Press ....G...... 609 386-0100
Burlington *(G-995)*

Webb-Mason Inc ....G...... 732 747-6585
Tinton Falls *(G-10854)*

Welter & Kreutz Printing Co ....G...... 201 489-9098
South Hackensack *(G-10299)*

Westbury Press Inc ....D...... 201 894-0444
Englewood *(G-2943)*

White Eagle Printing Co Inc ....E...... 609 586-2032
Trenton *(G-11132)*

Wilcox Press ....G...... 973 827-7474
Hamburg *(G-4100)*

Wilker Graphics LLC ....G...... 201 447-4800
Midland Park *(G-6242)*

William Robert Graphics Inc ....E...... 201 239-7400
Jersey City *(G-4848)*

Wilmington Trust Sp Services ....F...... 609 272-7000
Pleasantville *(G-8918)*

▲ Wong Robinson & Co Inc ....E...... 609 951-0300
Princeton *(G-9140)*

Yasheel Inc ....G...... 856 275-6812
Sewell *(G-9967)*

Your Printer V20 Ltd ....E...... 609 771-4000
Cranbury *(G-1893)*

Yukon Graphics Inc ....G...... 973 575-5700
Parsippany *(G-8117)*

Zippityprint LLC ....F...... 216 438-0001
Mullica Hill *(G-6894)*

Zwier Corp ....G...... 973 748-4009
Bloomfield *(G-539)*

2754 Commercial Printing: Gravure

Acme Engraving Co Inc ....E...... 973 778-0885
Passaic *(G-8124)*

▲ All-State International Inc ....C...... 908 272-0800
Cranford *(G-1895)*

American Business Paper Inc ....F...... 732 363-5788
Lakewood *(G-5069)*

Arna Marketing ....E...... 908 231-1100
Branchburg *(G-639)*

▲ Challenge Printing Co Inc ....C...... 973 471-4700
Clifton *(G-1582)*

Constant Services Inc ....E...... 973 227-2990
Fairfield *(G-3165)*

East Coast Distributors Inc ....F...... 732 223-5995
Eatontown *(G-2391)*

Five Macs Inc ....E...... 856 596-3150
Marlton *(G-5975)*

Food Mfg ....G...... 973 920-7000
Rockaway *(G-9569)*

▲ Howard Press Inc ....D...... 908 245-4400
Roselle *(G-9673)*

Label Master Inc ....G...... 973 546-3110
Lodi *(G-5591)*

▲ Link Color NA Inc ....G...... 201 438-8222
East Rutherford *(G-2303)*

◆ Lps Industries Inc ....C...... 201 438-3515
Moonachie *(G-6529)*

Lrp and P Graphics ....E...... 856 424-0158
Cherry Hill *(G-1391)*

Metro Tag & Label Inc ....E...... 201 845-4747
West Orange *(G-11900)*

New Jersey Department Treasury .....E...... 609 292-5133
Trenton *(G-11085)*

Pad and Publ Assembly Corp ....E...... 856 424-0158
Cherry Hill *(G-1409)*

R R Donnelley & Sons Company .....G...... 973 439-8321
West Caldwell *(G-11801)*

▲ Tadbik NJ Inc ....E...... 973 882-9595
Fairfield *(G-3319)*

Taylor Communications Inc ....E...... 732 561-8210
Monroe Township *(G-6397)*

Taylor Communications Inc ....F...... 973 467-8259
Springfield *(G-10579)*

Wheal-Grace Corp ....E...... 973 450-8100
Belleville *(G-327)*

Winemiller Press Inc ....G...... 732 223-0100
Manasquan *(G-5884)*

Youre So Invited LLC ....G...... 201 664-8600
Westwood *(G-11976)*

2759 Commercial Printing

4 Over Inc ....F...... 201 440-1656
Moonachie *(G-6498)*

▲ A B Tees LLC ....G...... 201 239-0022
Jersey City *(G-4696)*

Abbott Artkives LLC ....G...... 201 232-9477
Belleville *(G-293)*

Action Graphics Inc ....G...... 856 783-1825
Lindenwold *(G-5460)*

Active Learning Associates ....G...... 908 284-0404
Flemington *(G-3424)*

Adpro Imprints ....G...... 732 531-2133
Ocean *(G-7713)*

Advantage Ds LLC ....F...... 856 307-9600
Glassboro *(G-3800)*

Ahern Blueprinting Inc ....F...... 732 223-1476
Manasquan *(G-5865)*

Alcop Adhesive Label Co ....G...... 609 871-4400
Beverly *(G-458)*

▲ Alex Real LLC ....F...... 732 730-8770
Toms River *(G-10860)*

Alfred Sports Inc ....F...... 973 822-8891
Madison *(G-5717)*

All Colors Screen Printing LLC ....G...... 732 777-6033
Highland Park *(G-4300)*

All Nu Trophy & Screen Prtg ....F...... 201 807-0808
Ridgefield Park *(G-9396)*

▲ All-State International Inc ....C...... 908 272-0800
Cranford *(G-1895)*

Allegro Printing Corporation ....E...... 609 641-7060
Galloway *(G-3708)*

Alliance Design Inc ....F...... 973 904-9450
Totowa *(G-10927)*

AlphaGraphics Printshops of Th .....G...... 973 984-0066
Morristown *(G-6686)*

Altantic Printing and Design ....F...... 732 557-9600
Toms River *(G-10862)*

▲ American Bank Note Holographic .....D...... 609 208-0591
Robbinsville *(G-9510)*

◆ **American Banknote Corporation** ......G....... 203 941-4090
Fort Lee *(G-3543)*
▲ **American Envelope** ......G....... 908 241-9900
Linden *(G-5348)*
American Graphic Systems Inc ......G....... 201 796-0666
Fair Lawn *(G-3076)*
American Youth Enterprises Inc ......G....... 609 909-1900
Mays Landing *(G-6036)*
Andy Graphics Service Bureau ......G....... 201 866-9407
Union City *(G-11241)*
Applied Image Inc ......E....... 732 410-2444
Freehold *(G-3638)*
Armin Kososki ......G....... 908 689-0411
Washington *(G-11575)*
Armotek Industries Inc ......E....... 856 829-4585
Palmyra *(G-7846)*
Arnolds Yacht Basin Inc ......G....... 732 892-3000
Point Pleasant Boro *(G-8931)*
Art Guild Inc ......F....... 732 390-5300
East Brunswick *(G-2135)*
Artistic Typography Corp ......G....... 845 783-1990
Englewood *(G-2872)*
Arts Embroidery LLC ......G....... 732 870-2400
West Long Branch *(G-11843)*
ASAP Postal Printing ......G....... 609 597-7421
Manahawkin *(G-5828)*
Avail Inc ......G....... 732 560-2222
Bridgewater *(G-817)*
Ayr Composition Inc ......G....... 908 241-8118
Roselle Park *(G-9688)*
B & H Printers Inc ......G....... 908 688-6990
Hackettstown *(G-3999)*
B and W Printing Company Inc ......G....... 908 241-3060
Kenilworth *(G-4941)*
B P Graphics Inc ......E....... 732 942-2315
Lakewood *(G-5080)*
B&M Technologies Inc ......F....... 201 291-8505
Saddle Brook *(G-9754)*
Bankers Pen Inc ......E....... 800 499-7367
Garfield *(G-3721)*
Bassano Prtrs & Lithographers ......E....... 973 423-1400
Hawthorne *(G-4220)*
Beauty Wood Designs ......G....... 908 687-9697
Union *(G-11157)*
Belle Printing Group LLC ......G....... 856 235-5151
Mount Laurel *(G-6782)*
Bellia & Sons ......E....... 856 845-2234
Woodbury *(G-12158)*
Bistis Press Printing Co ......G....... 973 373-8033
Irvington *(G-4579)*
Blue Ribbon Awards Inc ......G....... 732 560-0046
Somerset *(G-10070)*
Branded Screen Printing ......G....... 908 879-7411
Chester *(G-1434)*
Brimar Industries Inc ......E....... 973 340-7889
Garfield *(G-3724)*
Brite Concepts Inc ......G....... 201 270-8544
Englewood *(G-2878)*
Burdol Inc ......G....... 856 453-0336
Bridgeton *(G-781)*
◆ **Butler Prtg & Laminating Inc** ......C....... 973 838-8550
Butler *(G-999)*
C & D Sales ......G....... 609 383-9292
Pleasantville *(G-8903)*
C and R Printing Corporation ......F....... 201 528-8912
Carlstadt *(G-1135)*
C Harry Marean Printing ......G....... 609 965-4708
Egg Harbor City *(G-2659)*
C2 Imaging LLC ......E....... 646 557-6300
Jersey City *(G-4722)*
Campbell Converting Corp ......G....... 609 835-2720
Beverly *(G-460)*
Campus Coordinates LLC ......G....... 732 866-6060
Freehold *(G-3643)*
CCL Label Inc ......C....... 609 586-1332
Robbinsville *(G-9512)*
CCL Label Inc ......E....... 856 273-0700
Lumberton *(G-5653)*
CCL Label (delaware) Inc ......C....... 609 259-1055
Trenton *(G-11037)*
Central Mills Inc ......G....... 732 329-2009
Dayton *(G-1960)*
▲ **Cgs Sales and Service LLC** ......G....... 856 665-6154
Pennsauken *(G-8492)*
▲ **Chambord Prints Inc** ......E....... 201 795-2007
Hoboken *(G-4464)*
Chariot Courier & Trans Svcs ......F....... 888 532-9125
Sayreville *(G-9816)*
▲ **Cheringal Associates Inc** ......D....... 201 784-8721
Norwood *(G-7618)*
Circa Promotions Inc ......G....... 732 264-1200
Hazlet *(G-4273)*
Classic Printers & Converters ......G....... 732 985-1100
Piscataway *(G-8749)*
Clear Control LLC ......G....... 973 823-8200
Ogdensburg *(G-7770)*
Clothing Emporium Inc ......F....... 973 773-3250
Passaic *(G-8129)*
Color Logic Inc ......E....... 973 515-0099
Parsippany *(G-7974)*
▲ **Color Screen Pros Inc** ......F....... 973 268-5080
Newark *(G-7125)*
Colorcraft Sign Co ......F....... 609 386-1115
Beverly *(G-461)*
Colortec Printing and Mailing ......G....... 856 767-0108
West Berlin *(G-11709)*
Commerce Financial Prtrs Corp ......E....... 908 241-9880
Roselle *(G-9667)*
Composing Room Inc ......C....... 856 662-9111
Pennsauken *(G-8497)*
Cosmic Custom Screen Printing ......G....... 856 629-8337
Williamstown *(G-12084)*
Coventry of New Jersey Inc ......E....... 856 988-5521
Marlton *(G-5968)*
Creative Color Lithographers ......F....... 908 789-2295
Garwood *(G-3777)*
Crown Roll Leaf Inc ......E....... 973 684-2600
Paterson *(G-8242)*
Crown Trophy ......G....... 973 808-8400
Pine Brook *(G-8696)*
Custom Graphics of Vineland ......E....... 856 691-7858
Vineland *(G-11347)*
Custom Labels Inc ......G....... 973 473-1934
Fairfield *(G-3170)*
D L Imprints ......G....... 732 493-8555
Ocean *(G-7721)*
Daily News LP ......F....... 212 210-2100
Jersey City *(G-4736)*
Data Communique Inc ......E....... 201 508-6000
Ridgefield Park *(G-9402)*
Data Communique Intl Inc ......E....... 201 508-6000
Ridgefield Park *(G-9403)*
Deans Graphics ......G....... 609 261-8817
Mount Holly *(G-6767)*
Delgen Press Inc ......G....... 973 472-2266
Clifton *(G-1598)*
Dewechter Inc ......G....... 856 845-0225
Woodbury *(G-12159)*
Dezine Line Inc ......F....... 973 989-1009
Wharton *(G-11985)*
Digital Color Concepts Inc ......D....... 908 264-0504
Mountainside *(G-6877)*
Digital Xpress LLC ......G....... 973 627-2609
Denville *(G-2037)*
▲ **Diligaf Enterprises Inc** ......E....... 201 684-0900
Mahwah *(G-5765)*
Display Impressions ......F....... 856 488-1777
Pennsauken *(G-8505)*
Distributor Label Products ......E....... 908 704-9997
Hillsborough *(G-4327)*
DOT Graphix Inc ......F....... 609 994-3416
Barnegat *(G-162)*
Downtown Printing Center Inc ......F....... 732 246-7990
New Brunswick *(G-6955)*
Driscoll Label Company Inc ......F....... 973 585-7291
East Hanover *(G-2213)*
Dye Into Print Inc ......D....... 973 772-8019
Clifton *(G-1606)*
E C D Ventures Inc ......G....... 856 875-1100
Blackwood *(G-477)*
Earthcolor Inc ......C....... 973 884-1300
Parsippany *(G-7994)*
Elite Printing Service ......G....... 973 729-0366
Sparta *(G-10498)*
Engraved Images Ltd ......G....... 908 234-0323
Far Hills *(G-3375)*
▲ **Enterprise Press Inc** ......E....... 212 741-2111
Englewood *(G-2893)*
Envelopes & Printed Pdts Inc ......G....... 973 942-1232
Prospect Park *(G-9169)*
Envirnmntal Dsign Grphic Entps ......G....... 973 361-1829
Dover *(G-2086)*
F S T Printing Inc ......G....... 732 560-3749
Middlesex *(G-6165)*
Fedex Office & Print Svcs Inc ......G....... 201 672-0508
East Rutherford *(G-2295)*
Fedex Office & Print Svcs Inc ......E....... 732 636-3580
Iselin *(G-4627)*
Ferrante Press Inc ......G....... 609 239-4257
Verona *(G-11306)*
Fischlers Dawnpoint ......G....... 856 428-2092
Cherry Hill *(G-1365)*
Fit Graphix ......G....... 201 488-4670
Hackensack *(G-3912)*
Five Macs Inc ......E....... 856 596-3150
Marlton *(G-5975)*
▲ **Flanagan Holdings Inc** ......D....... 201 512-3338
Mahwah *(G-5772)*
Flexi Printing Plate Co Inc ......F....... 201 939-3600
Moonachie *(G-6517)*
▲ **Flexo-Craft Prints Inc** ......E....... 973 482-7200
Harrison *(G-4183)*
Fordham Inc ......E....... 973 575-7840
Fairfield *(G-3199)*
Forms & Flyers of New Jersey ......G....... 856 629-0718
Williamstown *(G-12087)*
Foto Fantasy ......G....... 732 548-8446
Edison *(G-2521)*
Frank J Zechman ......G....... 732 495-0077
Belford *(G-287)*
Frontend Graphics Inc ......G....... 856 547-1600
Cherry Hill *(G-1367)*
▲ **Fu WEI Inc** ......G....... 732 937-8388
East Brunswick *(G-2156)*
G & M Printwear ......F....... 856 742-5551
Gloucester City *(G-3836)*
Gator Communications Group LLC ......E....... 973 233-6700
Fairfield *(G-3208)*
Global Graphics Intergration ......F....... 973 334-9653
Towaco *(G-10996)*
Good Impressions Inc ......G....... 856 461-3232
Riverside *(G-9498)*
Graphic Arts Printing ......G....... 201 343-6554
Hawthorne *(G-4237)*
Graphic Image ......G....... 856 262-8900
Williamstown *(G-12088)*
Graphic Imagery Inc ......F....... 908 755-2882
New Providence *(G-7038)*
GTM Marketing Inc ......G....... 856 227-2333
Woodbury *(G-12163)*
H & H Graphic Printing Inc ......G....... 201 369-9700
Carlstadt *(G-1166)*
H & L Printing Co ......G....... 201 288-0877
Hasbrouck Heights *(G-4194)*
▲ **H C Graphics Screenprinting** ......G....... 973 247-0544
Paterson *(G-8286)*
Harwill Corporation ......G....... 609 895-1955
Windsor *(G-12127)*
Hary Manufacturing Inc ......F....... 908 722-7100
Woodbridge *(G-12150)*
Hayes Mindish Inc ......G....... 609 641-9880
Pleasantville *(G-8909)*
Heritage Inc ......G....... 201 447-2600
Midland Park *(G-6229)*
▲ **Hit Promo LLC** ......C....... 856 739-4474
Bellmawr *(G-342)*
Horizon Label LLC ......F....... 856 767-0777
West Berlin *(G-11725)*
▲ **Howard Press Inc** ......D....... 908 245-4400
Roselle *(G-9673)*
Howes Standard Publishing Co ......E....... 856 691-2000
Vineland *(G-11371)*
▲ **Hummel Distributing Corp** ......E....... 908 688-5300
Union *(G-11193)*
Hummel Printing Inc ......E....... 908 688-5300
Union *(G-11194)*
Hygrade Business Group Inc ......E....... 800 836-7714
Secaucus *(G-9896)*
Ics Corporation ......C....... 215 427-3355
West Deptford *(G-11829)*
▲ **Ideal Jacobs Corporation** ......E....... 973 275-5100
Maplewood *(G-5922)*
Illinois Tool Works Inc ......E....... 609 395-5600
Cranbury *(G-1837)*
Image Screen Printing Inc ......G....... 732 560-1817
Middlesex *(G-6170)*
Imagery Embroidary Corporation ......F....... 201 343-9333
Union City *(G-11248)*
Important Papers Inc ......G....... 856 751-4544
Cherry Hill *(G-1379)*
Imprintz Cstm Printed Graphics ......G....... 609 386-5673
Lumberton *(G-5660)*
Industrial Lbeling Systems Inc ......E....... 973 808-8188
Fairfield *(G-3230)*
Ink On Paper Communications ......G....... 732 758-6280
Shrewsbury *(G-10001)*
Instant Printing of Dover Inc ......G....... 973 366-6855
Dover *(G-2093)*
Inter City Press Inc ......E....... 908 236-9911
Lebanon *(G-5290)*

S I C

Italian Treasures..................G...... 856 770-9188
Voorhees (G-11434)

J & G Graphics Inc.................G...... 732 223-6660
Manasquan (G-5872)

J and S Sporting Apparel LLC.......G...... 732 787-5500
Keansburg (G-4856)

J F I Printing......................G...... 973 759-3444
Belleville (G-304)

J H M Communications Inc............F...... 908 859-6668
Phillipsburg (G-8653)

J&E Business Services LLC...........G...... 973 984-8444
Morris Plains (G-6672)

James Howard Inc....................F...... 973 928-1560
Clifton (G-1651)

Jefferson Printing Serivce..........F...... 973 491-0019
Newark (G-7206)

Jimcam Publishing Inc...............G...... 201 843-5700
Maywood (G-6055)

John Patrick Publishing LLC.........D...... 609 883-2700
Ewing (G-3027)

▲ Jrm Industries Inc................D...... 973 779-9340
Passaic (G-8152)

▲ Judith Roth Studio Collection.....G...... 973 543-4455
Mendham (G-6087)

K M Media Group LLC.................G...... 973 330-3000
Clifton (G-1654)

Kdf Reprographics Inc...............F...... 201 784-9991
South Hackensack (G-10274)

Keefe Printing Inc..................G...... 732 295-2099
Point Pleasant Beach (G-8921)

Keskes Printing LLC.................G...... 856 767-4733
Berlin (G-437)

Koday Press Inc.....................F...... 201 387-0001
Dumont (G-2121)

Kraftape Printers Inc...............G...... 973 824-3005
Newark (G-7214)

Kraftwork Custom Design.............F...... 609 883-8444
Ewing (G-3033)

Label Solutions Inc.................G...... 201 599-0909
Rochelle Park (G-9531)

▲ Lacoa Inc.........................G...... 973 754-1000
Elmwood Park (G-2831)

▲ Lally-Pak Inc.....................D...... 908 351-4141
Hillside (G-4424)

Lamb Printing Inc...................G...... 908 852-0837
Hackettstown (G-4016)

▲ Laser Xpressions Inc..............F...... 732 303-9530
Freehold (G-3665)

▲ Laserwave Graphics Inc............F...... 732 745-7764
New Brunswick (G-6977)

Latta Graphics Inc..................E...... 201 440-4040
Carlstadt (G-1183)

Liberty Envelope Inc................F...... 973 546-5600
Paterson (G-8320)

Licensee Services Inc...............F...... 609 465-2003
Cape May Court House (G-1115)

▲ Lizard Label Co...................F...... 973 808-3322
Fairfield (G-3254)

Logomania Inc.......................G...... 201 798-0531
Jersey City (G-4778)

Lont & Overkamp Pubg Co Inc.........E...... 973 942-2243
Clifton (G-1664)

Lornan Litho Inc....................F...... 609 818-1198
Pennington (G-8456)

M & M Printing Corp.................G...... 201 288-7787
Hasbrouck Heights (G-4196)

Maclearie Printing LLC..............G...... 732 681-2772
Wall Township (G-11496)

Maggio Printing LLC.................E...... 856 931-7805
Bellmawr (G-346)

Magic Printing Corp.................F...... 732 726-0620
Avenel (G-139)

Main Street Graphics Inc............G...... 856 755-3523
Maple Shade (G-5905)

▲ Mainetti Americas Inc.............G...... 201 215-2900
Secaucus (G-9903)

▲ Mariano Press LLC.................F...... 732 247-3659
Somerset (G-10129)

▲ Marlo Plastic Products Inc........E...... 732 792-1988
Neptune (G-6923)

Mary Bridget Enterprises............G...... 609 267-4830
Cinnaminson (G-1475)

Med-Con Tech Ltd Lblty Co...........G...... 888 654-0856
Clinton (G-1752)

▼ Mega Media Concepts Ltd Lblty.....G...... 973 919-5661
Sparta (G-10511)

Menu Express........................F...... 856 216-7777
Pennsauken (G-8550)

◆ Menu Solutions Inc................D...... 718 575-5160
Belleville (G-306)

Mercer C AlphaGraphics..............G...... 609 921-0959
Hamilton (G-4116)

Merrill Corporation.................D...... 973 643-4403
Newark (G-7240)

Merrill Corporation.................D...... 908 810-3740
Union (G-11207)

Michael Graphics Inc................E...... 732 846-8680
Branchburg (G-680)

Midland Screen Printing Inc.........F...... 201 703-0066
Saddle Brook (G-9775)

Midlantic Color Graphics LLC........G...... 856 786-3113
Cinnaminson (G-1478)

Mike Dolly Screen Printing..........F...... 732 294-8979
Freehold (G-3670)

Mimeocom Inc........................F...... 973 286-2901
Newark (G-7242)

▲ Mj Corporate Sales Inc............E...... 856 778-0055
Mount Laurel (G-6819)

Monarch Art Plastics Co LLC.........E...... 856 235-5151
Mount Laurel (G-6821)

National Color Graphics.............F...... 856 435-6800
Sicklerville (G-10021)

National Plastic Printing...........F...... 973 785-1460
Totowa (G-10957)

National Reprographics Inc..........F...... 609 896-4100
Lawrenceville (G-5265)

New Jersey Label LLC................F...... 201 880-5102
South Hackensack (G-10283)

New Jersey Tech Group LLC...........G...... 609 301-6405
Lumberton (G-5661)

New Line Prtg & Tech Solutions......F...... 973 405-6133
Clifton (G-1682)

Newton Screen Printing Co...........G...... 973 827-0486
Franklin (G-3602)

NJ Logo Wear LLC....................G...... 609 597-9400
Manahawkin (G-5832)

Njiw Limited Liability Company......F...... 201 355-2955
Hackensack (G-3954)

North America Printing..............G...... 973 726-7713
Sparta (G-10515)

North Eastern Business Forms........G...... 609 392-1161
Trenton (G-11091)

O Berk Company LLC..................E...... 201 941-1610
Fairview (G-3367)

Ocsidot Inc.........................F...... 908 789-3300
Garwood (G-3782)

Office Needs Inc....................G...... 732 381-7770
Clark (G-1511)

OShea Services Inc..................G...... 201 343-8668
Hackensack (G-3957)

Outfront Media LLC..................D...... 973 575-6900
Fairfield (G-3278)

Page 2 LLC..........................G...... 862 239-9830
Wayne (G-11669)

Page Stamp LLC......................G...... 732 390-1700
Monroe Township (G-6389)

Palm Press Inc......................G...... 201 767-6504
Northvale (G-7600)

Paper Clip Communication Inc........F...... 973 256-1333
Little Falls (G-5485)

Papery of Marlton LLC...............F...... 856 985-1776
Marlton (G-5993)

Party City Corporation..............F...... 973 537-1707
Randolph (G-9294)

Party City of North Bergen..........F...... 201 865-0040
North Bergen (G-7473)

Patchworks Co Inc...................G...... 973 627-2002
Dover (G-2106)

▲ Peacock Products Inc..............F...... 201 385-5585
Bergenfield (G-392)

◆ Pecata Enterprises Inc............E...... 973 523-9498
Paterson (G-8362)

Penn Jersey Press Inc...............G...... 856 627-2200
Gibbsboro (G-3789)

Penta Digital Incorporated..........G...... 201 839-5392
Jersey City (G-4799)

Perco Inc...........................F...... 908 464-3000
Berkeley Heights (G-420)

▲ Pharmaceutic Litho Label Inc......G...... 336 785-4000
Cranford (G-1923)

Phoenix Alliance Group LLC..........F...... 732 495-4800
Port Monmouth (G-8973)

Platypus Print Productions LLC......G...... 732 772-1212
Morganville (G-6651)

▲ Pochet of America Inc.............C...... 973 942-4923
Woodland Park (G-12228)

Polaris Communications Inc..........F...... 201 928-0780
Teaneck (G-10769)

Postcard Press Inc..................E...... 310 747-3878
Saddle Brook (G-9783)

Precise Corporate Printing Inc......E...... 973 350-0330
Harrison (G-4187)

Premier Press Inc...................F...... 856 665-0722
Pennsauken (G-8564)

Premium Color Group LLC.............E...... 973 472-7007
Carlstadt (G-1208)

Press Room Inc......................F...... 609 689-3817
Trenton (G-11104)

Pressto Graphics...................F...... 732 286-9300
Toms River (G-10903)

▲ Pressworks........................G...... 856 427-9001
Cherry Hill (G-1416)

◆ Princeton Corp Graphics Inc.......D...... 732 545-6163
New Brunswick (G-6995)

Print Communications Group Inc......D...... 973 882-9444
Fairfield (G-3287)

Print Mail Communications LLC.......E...... 856 488-0345
Pennsauken (G-8566)

Print Media LLC.....................G...... 973 467-0007
Springfield (G-10572)

Print Solutions LLC.................F...... 201 567-9622
Englewood (G-2924)

Printing & Signs Express Inc........G...... 201 368-1255
Mahwah (G-5803)

Printing Craftsman Inc..............F...... 201 943-0276
Fairview (G-3370)

Printology.........................G...... 201 345-4632
Midland Park (G-6238)

Printsmith.........................G...... 908 245-3000
Roselle Park (G-9701)

Process Supply Company Inc..........F...... 201 487-1616
South Hackensack (G-10291)

Product Identification Co Inc.......F...... 973 227-7770
Garfield (G-3754)

Promo Graphic Inc...................G...... 732 629-7300
Middlesex (G-6191)

Promotional Graphics Inc............F...... 973 423-3900
Paterson (G-8365)

R & R Printing & Copy Center........G...... 732 249-9450
Hillsborough (G-4365)

Ramsey Graphics and Printing........G...... 201 300-2912
Elmwood Park (G-2846)

Red Diamond Company.................G...... 973 759-2005
Belleville (G-314)

Red Letter Press Inc................E...... 609 597-5257
Upper Saddle River (G-11284)

Redmond Bcms Inc....................D...... 973 664-2000
Denville (G-2053)

Reliable Envelope and Graphics......E...... 201 794-7756
Elmwood Park (G-2848)

Remco Press Inc.....................G...... 201 751-5703
North Bergen (G-7479)

▼ Riegel Cmmunications Group Inc....E...... 609 771-0555
Ewing (G-3051)

Roan Printing Inc...................F...... 908 526-5990
Somerville (G-10226)

Rocco Press Advg Typography.........F...... 973 790-4000
Paterson (G-8371)

Rolferrys Specialties Inc...........G...... 856 456-2999
Brooklawn (G-921)

Royalty Press Inc...................E...... 856 663-2288
Westville (G-11948)

Royer Group Inc.....................E...... 856 324-0171
Pennsauken (G-8575)

Rutler Screen Printing Inc..........F...... 908 859-3327
Phillipsburg (G-8669)

S & M Press Inc.....................F...... 973 546-6111
Garfield (G-3760)

S J T Imaging Inc...................D...... 201 262-7744
Oradell (G-7813)

S V O Inc...........................G...... 973 983-8380
Succasunna (G-10629)

Samuel Elliott Inc..................E...... 856 773-6000
Cinnaminson (G-1486)

Santangelo Printing Co Inc..........F...... 973 779-5880
Lodi (G-5599)

Sapphire Envelope & Graphics........E...... 856 782-2227
Magnolia (G-5742)

Sato Lbling Solutions Amer Inc......D...... 973 287-3641
Pine Brook (G-8716)

▲ Scorpio Posters Inc...............E...... 718 499-2001
Marlboro (G-5957)

Screen Play Inc.....................G...... 973 227-9014
Fairfield (G-3304)

▲ Screen Tech Inc of New Jersey.....D...... 908 862-8000
Linden (G-5439)

Screen-Trans Development Corp.......E...... 201 933-7800
Moonachie (G-6542)

Semels Embroidery Inc...............F...... 973 473-6868
Clifton (G-1719)

Sharp Impressions Inc .... G 201 573-4943
Garfield *(G-3761)*
Sherman Printing Co Inc .... G 973 345-2493
Clifton *(G-1721)*
Signmasters Inc .... D 973 614-8300
Passaic *(G-8181)*
Silver Edmar .... G 973 817-7483
Newark *(G-7313)*
Sjshore Marketing Ltd Lblty Co .... F 609 390-1400
Marmora *(G-6006)*
Skylands Press .... G 973 383-5006
Newton *(G-7404)*
Smith Enterprises .... G 215 416-9881
Mount Laurel *(G-6842)*
Sports Stop Inc .... F 856 881-2763
Glassboro *(G-3812)*
▲ **Star Narrow Fabrics Inc** .... G 973 778-8600
Lodi *(G-5602)*
Starnet Business Solutions .... E 201 252-2863
Mahwah *(G-5814)*
◆ **Stephen Gould Corporation** .... D 973 428-1500
Whippany *(G-12040)*
Stewart Business Forms Inc .... F 856 768-2011
Blackwood *(G-493)*
Stuyvesant Press Inc .... F 973 399-3880
Irvington *(G-4605)*
◆ **Sunglo Fabrics Inc** .... F 201 935-0830
Paterson *(G-8387)*
Sunset Printing and Engrv Corp .... E 973 537-9600
Wharton *(G-12000)*
T G Type-O-Graphics Inc .... G 973 253-3333
Fair Lawn *(G-3118)*
Taunton Graphics Inc .... F 856 719-8084
West Berlin *(G-11753)*
Tbc Color Imaging Inc .... E 973 470-8100
Clifton *(G-1736)*
▲ **Tectubes USA Inc** .... E 856 589-1250
Vineland *(G-11408)*
Tekno Inc .... G 973 423-2004
Hawthorne *(G-4260)*
Terminal Printing Co .... G 201 659-5924
Belleville *(G-319)*
Timeline Promotions Inc .... G 973 226-1512
West Caldwell *(G-11806)*
Tko Visual Communications .... F 610 770-7700
Newark *(G-7345)*
Toppan Printing Co Amer Inc .... C 732 469-8400
Somerset *(G-10188)*
Toppan Vintage Inc .... E 201 226-9220
Saddle Brook *(G-9797)*
Totally T Shirts & More Inc .... G 609 894-0011
Pemberton *(G-8443)*
Trade Thermographers Inc .... F 201 489-2060
Rochelle Park *(G-9539)*
Travel Weekly .... G 201 902-1931
Secaucus *(G-9936)*
Tremont Printing Co .... G 973 227-0742
Fairfield *(G-3330)*
Trend Printing/Intl Label .... F 201 941-6611
Ridgefield *(G-9389)*
Trentypo Inc .... F 609 883-5971
Ewing *(G-3062)*
Trico Web LLC .... G 201 438-3860
Carlstadt *(G-1234)*
Trukmanns Inc .... E 973 538-7718
Cedar Knolls *(G-1321)*
Turul Bookbindery Inc .... G 973 361-2810
Wharton *(G-12003)*
Typecom LLC .... G 201 969-1901
Fort Lee *(G-3586)*
Typeline .... F 201 251-2201
Wyckoff *(G-12267)*
◆ **U S Screening Corp** .... C 973 242-1110
Newark *(G-7350)*
▲ **Unimac Graphics LLC** .... C 201 372-1000
Carlstadt *(G-1236)*
Unique Impressions Ltd Lblty .... G 201 751-4088
Union City *(G-11272)*
United Envelope LLC .... C 201 699-5800
Ridgefield *(G-9392)*
United Forms Finishing Corp .... F 908 687-0494
Hillside *(G-4448)*
United Label Corp .... F 973 589-6500
Newark *(G-7354)*
University Publications Inc .... G 212 268-4222
Belford *(G-289)*
Unlimited Silk Screen Products .... G 609 882-0653
Ewing *(G-3066)*
Vernon Display Graphics Inc .... E 201 935-7117
Carlstadt *(G-1238)*
Vernw Printing Company .... G 973 751-6462
Belleville *(G-324)*
Vertis Inc .... D 215 781-1668
Mount Holly *(G-6777)*
Wagner Foto Screen Process .... G 908 624-0800
Kenilworth *(G-5005)*
Wall Street Group Inc .... D 201 333-4784
South Plainfield *(G-10453)*
Watonka Printing Inc .... G 732 974-8878
Belmar *(G-365)*
Whitehouse Prtg & Labeling LLC .... G 973 521-7648
Fairfield *(G-3352)*
Wilcox Press .... G 973 827-7474
Hamburg *(G-4100)*
Wilmington Trust Sp Services .... C 609 272-7000
Pleasantville *(G-8918)*
Winemiller Press Inc .... G 732 223-0100
Manasquan *(G-5884)*
▲ **Winsome Digital Inc** .... F 609 645-2211
Egg Harbor Township *(G-2700)*
▲ **Wisco Promo & Uniform Inc** .... G 973 767-2022
Saddle Brook *(G-9801)*
Work n Gear LLC .... G 856 848-7676
Woodbury *(G-12172)*
Z Fab LLC .... G 973 248-0686
Wayne *(G-11694)*
Zeeks Tees .... F 732 291-2700
Belford *(G-290)*
Zone Two Inc .... F 732 237-0766
Bayville *(G-263)*
Zwier Corp .... G 973 748-4009
Bloomfield *(G-539)*

2761 Manifold Business Forms

▲ **All-State International Inc** .... C 908 272-0800
Cranford *(G-1895)*
▼ **Degree Day Systems Inc** .... G 973 627-7959
Cedar Grove *(G-1277)*
▲ **Drew & Rogers Inc** .... E 973 575-6210
Fairfield *(G-3179)*
Hygrade Business Group Inc .... E 800 836-7714
Secaucus *(G-9896)*
◆ **Infoseal LLC** .... D 201 569-4500
Englewood *(G-2905)*
North Eastern Business Forms .... G 609 392-1161
Trenton *(G-11091)*
Snap Set Specialists Inc .... G 856 629-9552
Williamstown *(G-12106)*
Stewart Business Forms Inc .... F 856 768-2011
Blackwood *(G-493)*
Stuyvesant Press Inc .... F 973 399-3880
Irvington *(G-4605)*
Taylor Communications Inc .... D 732 560-3410
Somerset *(G-10181)*
Watonka Printing Inc .... G 732 974-8878
Belmar *(G-365)*

2771 Greeting Card Publishing

▲ **Amaryllis Inc** .... G 973 635-0500
Chatham *(G-1325)*
▲ **Easy Street Publications Inc** .... G 917 699-7820
Union *(G-11177)*
Greetingtap .... G 347 731-4263
South Plainfield *(G-10375)*
Magnetic Ticket & Label Corp .... E 973 759-6500
Belleville *(G-305)*
▲ **Nobleworks Inc** .... F 201 420-0095
Union City *(G-11261)*
Prudent Publishing Co Inc .... E 973 347-4554
Landing *(G-5227)*
Saint La Salle Auxiliary Inc .... G 732 842-4359
Lincroft *(G-5341)*
Schurman Fine Papers .... E 856 985-1776
Marlton *(G-5998)*

2782 Blankbooks & Looseleaf Binders

Black Lagoon Inc .... G 609 815-1654
Trenton *(G-11028)*
Cutting Records Inc .... G 201 488-8444
Hackensack *(G-3901)*
Deluxe Corporation .... C 973 334-8000
Mountain Lakes *(G-6857)*
Ebsco Industries Inc .... F 201 933-1800
Rutherford *(G-9731)*
Flortek Corporation .... E 201 436-7700
Bayonne *(G-225)*
Gpschartscom .... G 609 226-8842
Ventnor City *(G-11292)*
Johnthan Leasing Corp .... E 908 226-3434
Lebanon *(G-5293)*
Newark Morning Ledger Co .... C 973 882-6120
Pine Brook *(G-8711)*
Reed Presentations Inc .... G 908 832-0007
Lebanon *(G-5301)*
Star Bindery Inc .... E 609 519-5732
Franklinville *(G-3632)*
Tomwar Corp .... E 856 740-0111
Williamstown *(G-12109)*
Walden Lang In-Pak Service .... E 973 595-5250
Clifton *(G-1742)*

2789 Bookbinding

A S A P Nameplate & Labeling .... F 973 773-3934
Passaic *(G-8122)*
Abby Bindery Co Inc .... E 973 690-5509
Newark *(G-7069)*
Action Copy Centers Inc .... G 973 744-5520
Montclair *(G-6404)*
Allegro Printing Corporation .... G 609 641-7060
Galloway *(G-3708)*
American Bindery Depot Inc .... C 732 287-2370
Edison *(G-2457)*
American Graphic Systems Inc .... G 201 796-0666
Fair Lawn *(G-3076)*
▲ **Ancraft Press Corp** .... F 201 792-9200
Jersey City *(G-4705)*
B & R Printing Inc .... G 609 448-3328
Trenton *(G-11024)*
Bar Lan Inc .... G 856 596-2330
Brigantine *(G-917)*
Bassil Bookbinding Company Inc .... E 201 440-4925
Hackensack *(G-3878)*
Benton Bindery Inc .... F 732 431-9064
Freehold *(G-3642)*
Berk Gold Stamping Corporation .... E 973 786-6052
Andover *(G-49)*
Bethel Bindery .... F 609 296-5043
Ltl Egg Hbr *(G-5642)*
Bind-Rite Graphics Inc .... E 201 863-8100
Secaucus *(G-9869)*
Bind-Rite Services Inc .... C 201 440-5585
South Hackensack *(G-10255)*
Bindgraphics Inc .... E 908 245-1110
Roselle *(G-9662)*
Binding Products Inc .... E 212 947-1192
Jersey City *(G-4719)*
Budget Print Center .... G 973 743-0073
Bloomfield *(G-503)*
C Jackson Associates Inc .... E 856 761-8000
Cherry Hill *(G-1355)*
Capitol Bindery Inc .... G 609 883-5971
Ewing *(G-3006)*
Colorful Story Books Inc .... E 908 561-3333
South Plainfield *(G-10348)*
Commerce Financial Prtrs Corp .... E 908 241-9880
Roselle *(G-9667)*
Cornerstone Prints Imaging LLC .... G 908 782-7966
Flemington *(G-3431)*
Craftsmen Photo Lithographers .... E 973 316-5791
East Hanover *(G-2211)*
Creative Color Lithographers .... F 908 789-2295
Garwood *(G-3777)*
Custom Book Bindery Inc .... F 973 815-1400
Clifton *(G-1596)*
D & I Printing Co Inc .... F 201 871-3620
Englewood *(G-2885)*
D A K Office Services Inc .... G 609 586-8222
Trenton *(G-11052)*
Devece & Shaffer Inc .... G 856 829-7282
Palmyra *(G-7847)*
Dm Graphic Center LLC .... F 973 882-8990
Fairfield *(G-3178)*
E & M Bindery Inc .... C 973 777-9300
Clifton *(G-1609)*
E Nevin Miller Inc .... F 201 444-5784
Hawthorne *(G-4230)*
Fedex Office & Print Svcs Inc .... F 732 249-9222
New Brunswick *(G-6960)*
Fedex Office & Print Svcs Inc .... F 856 273-5959
Mount Laurel *(G-6797)*
Fedex Office & Print Svcs Inc .... E 856 427-0099
Cherry Hill *(G-1364)*
◆ **Gabhen Inc** .... C 800 631-3572
Totowa *(G-10945)*
Good Impressions Inc .... G 856 461-3232
Riverside *(G-9498)*
Grandview Printing Co Inc .... F 973 890-0006
Totowa *(G-10950)*
▲ **Gross Bros Printing Co Inc** .... E 201 865-4606
Union City *(G-11246)*

S I C

Holographic Finishing Inc.....................F..... 201 941-4651
Ridgefield (G-9365)

Hub Print & Copy Center LLC...............G..... 201 585-7887
Fort Lee (G-3558)

Instant Printing of Dover Inc................G..... 973 366-6855
Dover (G-2093)

Jersey Printing Associates Inc.............E..... 732 872-9654
Atlantic Highlands (G-113)

Jmp Press Inc.....................................G..... 201 444-0236
Ho Ho Kus (G-4454)

Johansen Book Bindery Inc..................G..... 201 438-4263
Rutherford (G-9735)

John S Swift Company Inc....................G..... 201 935-2002
Teterboro (G-10801)

Johnston Letter Co Inc........................G..... 973 482-7535
Flanders (G-3412)

Laser Dim Graphics & Prtg Inc............F..... 732 821-9000
Colts Neck (G-1789)

Latta Graphics Inc..............................E..... 201 440-4040
Carlstadt (G-1183)

▲ Lb Book Bindery LLC.......................F..... 973 244-0442
Fairfield (G-3249)

Lo Gatto Bookbinding..........................G..... 201 438-4344
East Rutherford (G-2305)

Lunet Inc...G..... 201 261-3883
Paramus (G-7885)

Marco Book Co Inc.............................G..... 973 458-0485
Lodi (G-5594)

▲ Mariano Press LLC.........................F..... 732 247-3659
Somerset (G-10129)

Marks Management Systems Inc..........G..... 856 866-0588
Maple Shade (G-5906)

McCormicks Bindery Inc......................E..... 856 663-8035
Pennsauken (G-8547)

Meadowlands Bindery Inc....................E..... 201 935-6161
Moonachie (G-6532)

Mid State Bindery...............................G..... 908 755-9388
Middlesex (G-6180)

Miniature Folding Inc..........................F..... 201 773-6477
Elmwood Park (G-2836)

Morris Plains Pip Inc..........................G..... 973 533-9330
Livingston (G-5548)

Myriams Dream Book Bindery...............G..... 609 345-5555
Atlantic City (G-104)

▲ Nb Bookbinding Inc........................G..... 973 247-1200
Clifton (G-1679)

New Jersey Bindery Svcs LLC.............G..... 732 200-8024
South Plainfield (G-10412)

Northeast Bindery Inc.........................F..... 908 436-3737
Elizabeth (G-2760)

Ont Sutter...G..... 201 265-0262
Emerson (G-2861)

OShea Services Inc............................G..... 201 343-8668
Hackensack (G-3957)

Pad and Publ Assembly Corp...............E..... 856 424-0158
Cherry Hill (G-1409)

Palm Press Inc..................................F..... 201 767-6504
Northvale (G-7600)

Palmarozzo Bindery............................G..... 908 688-5300
Union (G-11213)

Permagraphics Inc.............................F..... 201 814-1200
Moonachie (G-6535)

Philip Holzer and Assoc LLC................E..... 212 691-9500
Carlstadt (G-1202)

▲ Poplar Bindery Inc.........................F..... 856 727-8030
Moorestown (G-6614)

Premier Printing Solutions LLC............G..... 732 525-0740
Sayreville (G-9836)

Printing Craftsman Inc........................F..... 201 943-0276
Fairview (G-3370)

Puent-Romer Communications Inc........G..... 973 509-7591
Montclair (G-6433)

R & B Printing Inc..............................G..... 908 766-4073
Bernardsville (G-454)

Redmond Bcms Inc.............................D..... 973 664-2000
Denville (G-2053)

Roan Printing Inc...............................F..... 908 526-5990
Somerville (G-10226)

Robert A Eick Qlty Bookbinding.............F..... 973 822-2100
Madison (G-5733)

Royer Group Inc.................................E..... 856 324-0171
Pennsauken (G-8575)

S & M Press Inc.................................F..... 973 546-6111
Garfield (G-3760)

Santon Inc..E..... 201 444-9080
Toms River (G-10909)

Scarlet Printing.................................G..... 732 560-1415
Middlesex (G-6193)

Scott Graphics Printing Co Inc.............G..... 201 262-0473
New Milford (G-7025)

Sheroy Printing Inc............................F..... 973 242-4040
Newark (G-7312)

Sonata Graphics Inc...........................G..... 201 866-0186
Secaucus (G-9930)

▲ Spiral Binding LLC..........................C..... 973 256-0666
Totowa (G-10973)

Standard Prtg & Mail Svcs Inc.............F..... 973 790-3333
Fairfield (G-3311)

Star Promotions Inc............................F..... 732 356-5959
Bound Brook (G-624)

Steb Inc..G..... 973 584-0990
Ledgewood (G-5310)

Tanter Inc...G..... 732 382-3555
Clark (G-1516)

Tanzola Printing Inc............................G..... 973 779-0858
Clifton (G-1734)

Tech-Pak Inc.....................................F..... 201 935-3800
Wood Ridge (G-12140)

Tedco Inc..G..... 609 883-0799
Ewing (G-3060)

Thewal Inc...F..... 973 635-1880
Chatham (G-1338)

Toppan Printing Co Amer Inc................C..... 732 469-8400
Somerset (G-10188)

Turul Bookbindery Inc.........................G..... 973 361-2810
Wharton (G-12003)

Verni Vito...G..... 732 449-1760
Wall Township (G-11517)

Washington Stamp Exchange Inc.........F..... 973 966-0001
Florham Park (G-3523)

Westbury Press Inc............................G..... 201 894-0444
Englewood (G-2943)

Wilker Graphics LLC...........................G..... 201 447-4800
Midland Park (G-6242)

Windmill Press Inc.............................G..... 856 663-8990
Pennsauken (G-8589)

Yasheel Inc.......................................G..... 856 275-6812
Sewell (G-9967)

2791 Typesetting

A M Graphics Inc................................G..... 201 767-5320
Harrington Park (G-4169)

Action Copy Centers Inc.....................G..... 973 744-5520
Montclair (G-6404)

Allegro Printing Corporation.................G..... 609 641-7060
Galloway (G-3708)

American Graphic Systems Inc............G..... 201 796-0666
Fair Lawn (G-3076)

◆ Arch Crown Inc..............................E..... 973 731-6300
Hillside (G-4390)

Ayr Composition Inc...........................G..... 908 241-8118
Roselle Park (G-9688)

Aztec Graphics Inc.............................F..... 609 587-1000
Trenton (G-11023)

B & B Press Inc.................................G..... 908 840-4093
Lebanon (G-5278)

Bar Lan Inc.......................................G..... 856 596-2330
Brigantine (G-917)

Bartlett Printing & Graphic..................G..... 609 386-1525
Burlington (G-958)

Bowmar Enterprises Inc......................G..... 908 277-3000
New Providence (G-7031)

Budget Print Center............................G..... 973 743-0073
Bloomfield (G-503)

Commerce Financial Prtrs Corp...........E..... 908 241-9880
Roselle (G-9667)

Commercial Composition & Prtg...........G..... 856 662-0557
Pennsauken (G-8496)

Comptime Inc....................................G..... 201 760-2400
Ramsey (G-9238)

Consumer Graphics Inc.......................G..... 732 469-4699
Somerset (G-10085)

Copy-Rite Printing..............................G..... 609 597-9182
Manahawkin (G-5830)

Cordes Printing Inc............................G..... 201 652-7272
Wyckoff (G-12248)

Cornerstone Prints Imaging LLC...........G..... 908 782-7966
Flemington (G-3431)

Craftsmen Photo Lithographers............E..... 973 316-5791
East Hanover (G-2211)

Creative Color Lithographers...............F..... 908 789-2295
Garwood (G-3777)

D A K Office Services Inc....................G..... 609 586-8222
Trenton (G-11052)

Data Communique Inc.........................E..... 201 508-6000
Ridgefield Park (G-9402)

Devece & Shaffer Inc.........................G..... 856 829-7282
Palmyra (G-7847)

Downtown Printing Center Inc..............F..... 732 246-7990
New Brunswick (G-6955)

E Nevin Miller Inc..............................F..... 201 444-5784
Hawthorne (G-4230)

Earth Color New York Inc....................F..... 973 884-1300
Parsippany (G-7992)

Fedex Office & Print Svcs Inc..............F..... 732 249-9222
New Brunswick (G-6960)

Fedex Office & Print Svcs Inc..............F..... 856 273-5959
Mount Laurel (G-6797)

Fedex Office & Print Svcs Inc..............G..... 973 376-3966
Springfield (G-10555)

Fedex Office & Print Svcs Inc..............E..... 856 427-0099
Cherry Hill (G-1364)

Gangi Graphics Inc............................G..... 732 840-8680
Brick (G-744)

Hub Print & Copy Center LLC...............G..... 201 585-7887
Fort Lee (G-3558)

Inserts East Incorporated....................C..... 856 663-8181
Pennsauken (G-8528)

Instant Printing of Dover Inc................G..... 973 366-6855
Dover (G-2093)

J K Design Inc...................................E..... 908 428-4700
Hillsborough (G-4351)

Jem Printing Inc................................G..... 908 782-9986
Flemington (G-3450)

Jmp Press Inc...................................G..... 201 444-0236
Ho Ho Kus (G-4454)

John S Swift Company Inc....................G..... 201 935-2002
Teterboro (G-10801)

Johnston Letter Co Inc........................G..... 973 482-7535
Flanders (G-3412)

Kirms Printing Co Inc..........................E..... 732 774-8000
Neptune (G-6920)

L A S Printing Co...............................G..... 201 991-5362
Jersey City (G-4775)

Laser Dim Graphics & Prtg Inc............F..... 732 821-9000
Colts Neck (G-1789)

▲ Laserwave Graphics Inc..................F..... 732 745-7764
New Brunswick (G-6977)

Lont & Overkamp Pubg Co Inc.............E..... 973 942-2243
Clifton (G-1664)

Lunet Inc..G..... 201 261-3883
Paramus (G-7885)

Marks Management Systems Inc..........G..... 856 866-0588
Maple Shade (G-5906)

McKella 2-8-0 Inc..............................D..... 856 813-1153
Pennsauken (G-8548)

Metro Publishing Group Inc.................F..... 201 385-2000
New Milford (G-7023)

Michael Graphics Inc..........................G..... 732 846-8680
Branchburg (G-680)

▲ Morgan Printing Service Inc.............F..... 732 721-2959
South Amboy (G-10243)

Morris Plains Pip Inc..........................G..... 973 533-9330
Livingston (G-5548)

Nassau Communications Inc................F..... 609 208-9099
Lawrence Township (G-5245)

Network Typesetting Inc.....................G..... 732 819-0949
Piscataway (G-8795)

New Jersey Label LLC........................E..... 201 880-5102
South Hackensack (G-10283)

Newark Trade Typographers................F..... 973 674-3727
Orange (G-7823)

Newtype Inc......................................F..... 973 361-6000
Randolph (G-9290)

Old Hights Print Shop Inc....................G..... 609 443-4700
Jackson (G-4674)

OShea Services Inc............................G..... 201 343-8668
Hackensack (G-3957)

Otis Graphics Inc...............................F..... 201 438-7120
Lyndhurst (G-5700)

Pad and Publ Assembly Corp...............E..... 856 424-0158
Cherry Hill (G-1409)

Painton Studios Inc............................G..... 732 752-8842
Green Brook (G-3861)

Palm Press Inc..................................G..... 201 767-6504
Northvale (G-7600)

Patel Printing Plus Corp......................F..... 908 964-6422
Union (G-11214)

Permagraphics Inc.............................F..... 201 814-1200
Moonachie (G-6535)

Philip Holzer and Assoc LLC................E..... 212 691-9500
Carlstadt (G-1202)

Printing Craftsman Inc........................F..... 201 943-0276
Fairview (G-3370)

Printing Delite Inc.............................G..... 973 676-3033
East Orange (G-2266)

Puent-Romer Communications Inc........G..... 973 509-7591
Montclair (G-6433)

Redmond Bcms Inc.............................D..... 973 664-2000
Denville (G-2053)

Roan Printing Inc ....F 908 526-5990
Somerville (G-10226)

S & M Press Inc ....F 973 546-6111
Garfield (G-3760)

Sandoval Graphics & Printing ....G 856 435-7320
Somerdale (G-10043)

Scarlet Printing ....G 732 560-1415
Middlesex (G-6193)

Scott Graphics Printing Co Inc ....G 201 262-0473
New Milford (G-7025)

Sheroy Printing Inc ....F 973 242-4040
Newark (G-7312)

Sign On Inc ....G 201 384-7714
Dumont (G-2124)

Sonata Graphics Inc ....G 201 866-0186
Secaucus (G-9930)

Staines Inc ....F 856 784-2718
Somerdale (G-10044)

Standard Prtg & Mail Svcs Inc ....F 973 790-3333
Fairfield (G-3311)

Star Promotions Inc ....F 732 356-5959
Bound Brook (G-624)

Steb Inc ....G 973 584-0990
Ledgewood (G-5310)

Tangent Graphics Inc ....G 201 488-2840
Englewood (G-2936)

Tanter Inc ....G 732 382-3555
Clark (G-1516)

Techsetters Inc ....E 856 240-7905
Collingswood (G-1774)

Tedco Inc ....G 609 883-0799
Ewing (G-3060)

Thewal Inc ....F 973 635-1880
Chatham (G-1338)

Trade Thermographers Inc ....F 201 489-2060
Rochelle Park (G-9539)

Trentypo Inc ....F 609 883-5971
Ewing (G-3062)

Typeline ....F 201 251-2201
Wyckoff (G-12267)

Typen Graphics Inc ....G 973 838-6544
Kinnelon (G-5042)

Verni Vito ....G 732 449-1760
Wall Township (G-11517)

Wilker Graphics LLC ....G 201 447-4800
Midland Park (G-6242)

Word Center Printing ....G 609 586-5825
Trenton (G-11134)

Zwier Corp ....G 973 748-4009
Bloomfield (G-539)

2796 Platemaking & Related Svcs

Acme Engraving Co Inc ....E 973 778-0885
Passaic (G-8124)

Advertisers Service Group Inc ....F 201 440-5577
Ridgefield Park (G-9395)

AGFA Corporation ....G 908 231-5000
Somerville (G-10200)

Caporale Engraving Co Inc ....E 201 569-8711
Englewood Cliffs (G-2951)

Celebration (us) Inc ....C 609 261-5200
Lumberton (G-5654)

Container Graphics Corp ....E 732 922-1180
Neptune (G-6904)

Downtown Printing Center Inc ....F 732 246-7990
New Brunswick (G-6955)

E I Du Pont De Nemours & Co ....F 732 257-1579
Parlin (G-7930)

Essex West Graphics Inc ....F 973 227-2400
Fairfield (G-3185)

G & R Graphics Inc ....G 973 731-7438
South Orange (G-10307)

Garrison Printing Company Inc ....E 856 488-1900
Pennsauken (G-8515)

Globe Photo Engraving Co LLC ....E 201 489-2300
Little Ferry (G-5506)

Globe Photo Engraving Corp ....F 201 489-2300
Little Ferry (G-5507)

Grandview Printing Co Inc ....F 973 890-0006
Totowa (G-10950)

Hatteras Press Inc ....B 732 935-9800
Tinton Falls (G-10838)

▲ Howard Press Inc ....D 908 245-4400
Roselle (G-9673)

▲ Lacoa Inc ....G 973 754-1000
Elmwood Park (G-2831)

▲ Mariano Press LLC ....F 732 247-3659
Somerset (G-10129)

Mark/Trece Inc ....E 973 884-1005
Whippany (G-12026)

Marko Engraving & Art Corp ....F 201 864-6500
Weehawken (G-11698)

Marko Engraving & Art Corp ....F 201 945-6555
Fairview (G-3365)

Mosstype Holding Corp ....E 201 444-8000
Waldwick (G-11451)

Nassau Communications Inc ....F 609 208-9099
Lawrence Township (G-5245)

Pan Graphics Inc ....D 973 478-2100
Garfield (G-3745)

R P R Graphics Inc ....F 908 654-8080
Peapack (G-8432)

Staines Inc ....F 856 784-2718
Somerdale (G-10044)

Standard Embossing Plate Mfg ....G 973 344-6670
Newark (G-7327)

Tangent Graphics Inc ....G 201 488-2840
Englewood (G-2936)

Tech-Ni Fold Usa Inc ....G 973 383-6691
Lafayette (G-5053)

Toppan Printing Co Amer Inc ....C 732 469-8400
Somerset (G-10188)

Unity Graphics & Engraving Co ....E 201 541-5462
Englewood (G-2940)

28 CHEMICALS AND ALLIED PRODUCTS

2812 Alkalies & Chlorine

Church & Dwight Co Inc ....F 732 730-3100
Lakewood (G-5093)

Church & Dwight Co Inc ....F 609 655-6101
Cranbury (G-1821)

Church & Dwight Co Inc ....G 609 683-8021
Princeton (G-9023)

◆ Church & Dwight Co Inc ....B 609 806-1200
Ewing (G-3009)

FMC Corporation ....D 973 256-0768
Woodland Park (G-12219)

FMC Corporation ....D 732 541-3000
Carteret (G-1257)

◆ Formosa Plastics Corp USA ....B 973 992-2090
Livingston (G-5530)

◆ Kuehne Chemical Company Inc ....E 973 589-0700
Kearny (G-4893)

◆ PMC Group Inc ....F 856 533-1866
Mount Laurel (G-6828)

▲ Qualco Inc ....E 973 473-1222
Passaic (G-8174)

◆ Solvay Holding Inc ....A 609 860-4000
Princeton (G-9121)

Solvay USA Inc ....C 732 297-0100
North Brunswick (G-7538)

2813 Industrial Gases

Air Liquide Advanced Materials ....F 908 231-9060
Branchburg (G-629)

Air Products and Chemicals Inc ....E 732 446-5676
Manalapan (G-5837)

Airgas Usa LLC ....E 908 754-7700
South Plainfield (G-10322)

Airgas Usa LLC ....F 856 933-0544
Bellmawr (G-330)

Airgas Usa LLC ....F 609 685-4241
Cherry Hill (G-1342)

Airgas Usa LLC ....E 856 829-7878
Cinnaminson (G-1445)

American Spraytech LLC ....E 908 725-6060
Branchburg (G-634)

Bioxygen Distribution Corp ....G 732 212-1799
Sea Bright (G-9859)

▲ Boc Group Inc ....A 908 665-2400
New Providence (G-7030)

Coim USA Inc ....E 856 224-1668
Paulsboro (G-8415)

◆ Concorde Specialty Gases Inc ....E 732 544-9899
Eatontown (G-2388)

Linde Gas North America LLC ....E 908 329-9300
Stewartsville (G-10596)

Linde Gas North America LLC ....G 908 777-9125
Phillipsburg (G-8656)

Linde Gas North America LLC ....F 732 438-9977
Dayton (G-1977)

◆ Linde Gas North America LLC ....A 800 932-0803
Bridgewater (G-853)

◆ Linde Gas USA LLC ....C 908 464-8100
Bridgewater (G-854)

▲ Linde Global Helium Inc ....B 908 464-8100
New Providence (G-7042)

◆ Linde LLC ....C 908 464-8100
Bridgewater (G-855)

Linde LLC ....E 908 329-9619
Stewartsville (G-10597)

Linde LLC ....B 512 330-0153
Bridgewater (G-856)

Linde LLC ....E 908 464-8100
New Providence (G-7043)

Linde LLC ....G 973 579-2065
Sparta (G-10510)

Linde Merchant Production Inc ....F 908 464-8100
New Providence (G-7044)

Linde North America Inc ....D 908 464-8100
New Providence (G-7045)

▼ Linde North America Inc ....B 908 464-8100
Bridgewater (G-857)

Linde North America Inc ....F 908 454-7455
Alpha (G-43)

Matheson Gas Products Inc ....F 201 867-4101
Parsippany (G-8041)

Matheson Tri-Gas Inc ....F 908 991-9200
Basking Ridge (G-194)

◆ Matheson Tri-Gas Inc ....D 908 991-9200
Basking Ridge (G-195)

Matheson Tri-Gas Inc ....F 908 991-9200
Basking Ridge (G-196)

Praxair Inc ....F 732 738-4150
Keasbey (G-4930)

▲ Praxair Cryomag Services Inc ....F 732 738-4000
Keasbey (G-4931)

Praxair Distribution Inc ....F 908 862-7200
Linden (G-5430)

Praxair Distribution Inc ....E 973 589-7895
Newark (G-7272)

2816 Inorganic Pigments

◆ BASF Catalysts LLC ....D 732 205-5000
Iselin (G-4616)

◆ Breen Color Concentrates LLC ....F 609 397-8200
Lambertville (G-5210)

◆ Brenntag Specialties Inc ....D 800 732-0562
South Plainfield (G-10339)

◆ Color Techniques Inc ....F 908 412-9292
South Plainfield (G-10347)

Custom Chemicals Corp ....A 201 791-5100
Elmwood Park (G-2814)

Dispersion Technology Inc ....F 732 364-4488
Lakewood (G-5109)

Elementis Specialties Inc ....E 201 432-0800
East Windsor (G-2375)

◆ Elementis Specialties Inc ....C 609 443-2000
East Windsor (G-2374)

▲ Evonik Corporation ....B 973 929-8000
Parsippany (G-8003)

Ferro Corporation ....E 732 287-4925
Edison (G-2519)

▲ French Color Fragrance Co Inc ....E 201 567-6883
Englewood (G-2898)

Global Colorants Inc ....G 973 751-2227
Old Bridge (G-7780)

Kronos Worldwide Inc ....E 609 860-6200
Cranbury (G-1849)

◆ Kvk Usa Inc ....F 732 846-2355
New Brunswick (G-6976)

▲ Lightscape Materials Inc ....G 609 734-2224
Princeton (G-9067)

▼ Riverdale Color Mfg Inc ....E 732 376-9300
Perth Amboy (G-8628)

◆ Rockwood Holdings Inc ....E 609 514-0300
Princeton (G-9113)

Sensient Technologies Corp ....E 908 757-4500
South Plainfield (G-10435)

▲ Sudarshan North America Inc ....G 201 652-2046
Ridgewood (G-9431)

Vivitone Inc ....F 973 427-8114
Hawthorne (G-4264)

Welsch Metal Products Inc ....G 908 782-5996
Flemington (G-3475)

2819 Indl Inorganic Chemicals, NEC

Acnd Partners Inc ....G 848 200-7460
Metuchen (G-6094)

Affinity Chemical Woodbine LLC ....F 973 873-4070
Flanders (G-3399)

Agilis Chemicals Inc ....G 973 910-2424
Rockaway (G-9548)

AIG Industrial Group Inc ....F 201 767-7300
Northvale (G-7569)

Airgas Usa LLC ....F 609 685-4241
Cherry Hill (G-1342)

S
I
C

Airgas Usa LLC ....E 856 829-7878
Cinnaminson (G-1445)

Akzo Nobel Chemicals LLC ....D 732 985-6262
Edison (G-2454)

Alkaline Corporation ....E 732 531-7830
Oakhurst (G-7667)

Allied Specialty Group Inc ....F 201 223-4600
North Bergen (G-7428)

American Gas & Chemical Co Ltd ......E 201 767-7300
Northvale (G-7572)

Arch Chemicals Inc ....D 908 561-5200
South Plainfield (G-10329)

Atlantic Associates Intl Inc ....F 856 662-1717
Pennsauken (G-8481)

▲ Augmentus LLC ....G 855 240-1100
Hoboken (G-4458)

Avantor Performance Mtls LLC ....B 908 859-2151
Phillipsburg (G-8640)

▲ Avebe North America Inc ....F 609 520-1400
Princeton (G-9012)

◆ BASF Catalysts LLC ....D 732 205-5000
Iselin (G-4616)

◆ BASF Corporation ....B 973 245-6000
Florham Park (G-3492)

▲ Basfin Corporation ....A 973 245-6000
Florham Park (G-3493)

Baumar Industries Inc ....G 973 667-5490
Nutley (G-7642)

◆ Bayer Corporation ....A 412 777-2000
Whippany (G-12007)

Bd Biscnces Systems Rgents Inc ......G 201 847-6800
Franklin Lakes (G-3608)

Biochemical Sciences Inc ....G 856 467-1813
Swedesboro (G-10683)

Caribe Express Associates Inc ....G 201 869-2822
Guttenberg (G-3867)

▲ Chem-Is-Try Inc ....G 732 372-7311
Metuchen (G-6100)

Chemstaff Inc ....G 201 265-8655
Oradell (G-7805)

◆ Chemtrade Chemicals Corp ....D 973 515-0900
Parsippany (G-7968)

Chemtrade Gcc Holding Company ......G 973 515-0900
Parsippany (G-7969)

Chemtrade Solutions LLC ....F 908 464-1500
Berkeley Heights (G-405)

◆ Chemtrade Solutions LLC ....G 973 515-0900
Parsippany (G-7970)

Chemtrade Water Chemical Inc ....G 973 515-0900
Parsippany (G-7971)

Chessco Industries Inc ....E 609 882-0400
Ewing (G-3008)

◆ Church & Dwight Co Inc ....B 609 806-1200
Ewing (G-3009)

Citi-Chem Inc ....E 609 231-6655
Maple Shade (G-5900)

CMS Technology Inc ....E 512 913-1898
Bridgewater (G-828)

Coim USA Inc ....E 856 224-1668
Paulsboro (G-8415)

▼ Cytec Industries Inc ....C 973 357-3100
Saddle Brook (G-9761)

◆ Dallas Group of America Inc ....C 908 534-7800
Whitehouse (G-12045)

E I Du Pont De Nemours & Co ....E 732 257-1579
Parlin (G-7930)

Elemental Interiors ....G 646 861-3596
Montclair (G-6412)

Elementis Chromium Inc ....C 609 443-2000
East Windsor (G-2372)

▲ Elements Global Group LLC ....G 908 468-8407
Gillette (G-3794)

Elements Truffles LLC ....G 908 731-2088
Jersey City (G-4748)

◆ Elkem Silicones USA Corp ....E 732 227-2060
East Brunswick (G-2151)

Engelhard Corporation ....F 732 205-5000
Iselin (G-4625)

▲ Evonik Corporation ....B 973 929-8000
Parsippany (G-8003)

Evonik Corporation ....E 503 907-1210
Piscataway (G-8765)

Evoqua Water Technologies LLC ......F 908 353-7400
Elizabeth (G-2729)

Foster and Company Inc ....E 973 267-4100
Cedar Knolls (G-1312)

▲ Futurrex Inc ....F 973 209-1563
Franklin (G-3599)

▲ G J Chemical Co ....E 973 589-1450
Somerset (G-10103)

◆ General Carbon Corporation ....F 973 523-2223
Paterson (G-8275)

◆ Gentek Inc ....C 973 515-0900
Parsippany (G-8024)

◆ Gulco Inc ....E 908 238-2030
Phillipsburg (G-8651)

Holtec International ....B 856 797-0900
Camden (G-1069)

Honeywell International Inc ....C 973 455-2000
Morris Plains (G-6668)

◆ Hummel Croton Inc ....F 908 754-1800
South Plainfield (G-10381)

Innophos Inc ....G 973 587-8735
Cranbury (G-1838)

Innophos Holdings Inc ....D 609 495-2495
Cranbury (G-1839)

◆ Innophos Inc ....A 609 495-2495
Cranbury (G-1840)

Innophos Investments II Inc ....G 609 495-2495
Cranbury (G-1841)

Innophos Invstmnts Hldings Inc ......G 609 495-2495
Cranbury (G-1842)

Intelligent Mtl Solutions Inc ....F 609 514-4031
Princeton (G-9059)

◆ JM Huber Corporation ....D 732 603-3630
Edison (G-2546)

◆ Kuehne Chemical Company Inc ......G 973 589-0700
Kearny (G-4893)

Ligno Tech USA Inc ....G 908 429-6660
Bridgewater (G-852)

Liquid Elements ....G 856 321-7646
Maple Shade (G-5904)

◆ Lonza Inc ....D 201 316-9200
Allendale (G-13)

Madison Industries Inc ....E 732 727-2225
Old Bridge (G-7784)

Mateson Chemical Corporation ....G 215 423-3200
Cinnaminson (G-1476)

▲ Mel Chemicals Inc ....C 908 782-5800
Flemington (G-3456)

▲ Meson Group Inc ....E 201 767-7300
Northvale (G-7591)

◆ Morre-TEC Industries Inc ....E 908 688-9009
Union (G-11208)

Morton Salt Inc ....G 732 826-8414
Perth Amboy (G-8625)

▲ Munzing North America LP ....E 973 279-1306
Bloomfield (G-523)

New Heaven Chemicals Iowa LLC ......G 201 506-9109
Sussex (G-10675)

Newfuturevest Two LLC ....G 609 586-8004
Trenton (G-11088)

▲ Northeast Chemicals Inc ....E 732 238-9980
East Brunswick (G-2170)

Nova Chemicals Inc ....G 973 726-0056
Sparta (G-10516)

◆ Old Bridge Chemicals Inc ....E 732 727-2225
Old Bridge (G-7787)

▼ Omg Electronic Chemicals Inc ......C 908 222-5800
South Plainfield (G-10418)

P W Perkins Co Inc ....E 856 769-3525
Woodstown (G-12239)

Perimeter Solutions LP ....C 732 541-3000
Carteret (G-1266)

▲ Phibro-Tech Inc ....E 201 329-7300
Teaneck (G-10767)

▲ Phibrochem Inc ....G 201 329-7300
Teaneck (G-10768)

PQ Corporation ....G 732 750-9040
Avenel (G-146)

▲ Protameen Chemicals Inc ....E 973 256-4374
Totowa (G-10967)

▲ R & M Chemical Technologies ......F 908 537-9516
Hampton (G-4166)

◆ Reade Manufacturing Company ......E 732 657-6451
Manchester (G-5888)

Reagent Chemical & RES Inc ....E 908 284-2800
Ringoes (G-9442)

▲ Resintech Inc ....E 856 768-9600
West Berlin (G-11747)

Rive Technology Inc ....E 732 329-4441
Monmouth Junction (G-6361)

Rlct Industries LLC ....G 609 712-1318
Pennington (G-8458)

◆ Rockwood Holdings Inc ....E 609 514-0300
Princeton (G-9113)

Sanit Technologies LLC ....F 862 238-7555
Passaic (G-8180)

Scientific Design Company ....C 201 641-0500
Little Ferry (G-5516)

Setcon Industries Inc ....F 973 283-0500
Riverdale (G-9487)

◆ Solvay Holding Inc ....A 609 860-4000
Princeton (G-9121)

Solvay Spclty Polymers USA LLC ......C 856 853-8119
West Deptford (G-11841)

Solvay USA Inc ....C 732 297-0100
North Brunswick (G-7538)

Solvay USA Inc ....D 609 860-4000
Cranbury (G-1881)

◆ Somerville Acquisitions Co Inc ......F 908 782-9500
Flemington (G-3467)

Southwest Stainless LP ....G 732 961-1520
Howell (G-4567)

Spectrum Laboratory Pdts Inc ....E 732 214-1300
New Brunswick (G-7005)

Spex Certprep Group LLC ....C 732 549-7144
Metuchen (G-6123)

▼ Summit Research Laboratory ....E 908 782-9500
Flemington (G-3469)

▲ Synasia Inc ....C 732 205-9880
Metuchen (G-6126)

Totalcat Group Inc ....G 908 497-9610
Cranford (G-1929)

Tri-State Alum & Stainless Inc ....C 908 693-7337
Bridgewater (G-903)

United Silicon Carbide Inc ....C 732 565-9500
New Brunswick (G-7009)

▲ Water Mark Technologies Inc ....G 973 663-3438
Lake Hopatcong (G-5058)

◆ West Dry Industries Inc ....E 908 757-4400
Westfield (G-11935)

Write Element LLC ....G 973 584-0373
Randolph (G-9306)

▲ Youniversal Labortories ....G 201 807-9000
South Hackensack (G-10300)

2821 Plastics, Mtrls & Nonvulcanizable Elastomers

◆ A&C Catalysts Inc ....E 908 474-9393
Linden (G-5342)

Adco Chemical Company Inc ....E 973 589-0880
Newark (G-7072)

Advansix Inc ....B 973 526-1800
Parsippany (G-7941)

Akzo Nobel Chemicals LLC ....D 732 985-6262
Edison (G-2454)

Allied-Signal China Ltd ....E 973 455-2000
Morristown (G-6685)

Alpine Group Inc ....F 201 549-4400
East Rutherford (G-2275)

Altaflo LLC ....F 973 300-3344
Sparta (G-10488)

Amcor Flexibles LLC ....C 856 825-1400
Millville (G-6275)

American Plastic Works Inc ....E 800 494-7326
Moorestown (G-6559)

Anhydrides & Chemicals Inc ....G 973 465-0077
Newark (G-7086)

▼ Anti Hydro International Inc ....F 908 284-9000
Flemington (G-3427)

▲ ARC International N Amer LLC ....C 856 825-5620
Millville (G-6284)

Ashland LLC ....G 908 243-3500
Bridgewater (G-815)

Ashland LLC ....D 732 353-7718
Parlin (G-7928)

Atlantic Lining Co Inc ....E 609 723-2400
Jobstown (G-4854)

◆ Bayer Corporation ....A 412 777-2000
Whippany (G-12007)

Bergen Manufacturing & Supply ....E 201 854-3461
North Bergen (G-7434)

▼ Berry Global Films LLC ....C 201 641-6600
Montvale (G-6446)

◆ Breen Color Concentrates LLC ......F 609 397-8200
Lambertville (G-5210)

Cain Machine Inc ....F 856 825-7225
Millville (G-6291)

◆ Cary Compounds LLC ....C 732 274-2626
Dayton (G-1958)

Chevron Phillips Chem Co LP ....E 732 738-2000
Perth Amboy (G-8609)

Clausen Company Inc ....F 732 738-1165
Fords (G-3528)

◆ Coim USA Inc ....D 856 224-8560
West Deptford (G-11825)

Composecure LLC ....C 908 518-0500
Somerset (G-10083)

▲ Composecure LLC ....C 908 518-0500
Somerset *(G-10084)*

Covalnce Spcialty Coatings LLC ....D 732 356-2870
Middlesex *(G-6159)*

Crossfield Products Corp ....D 908 245-2801
Roselle Park *(G-9691)*

Custom Counters By Precision ....E 973 773-0111
Passaic *(G-8133)*

Custom Molders Group LLC ....G 908 218-7997
Branchburg *(G-654)*

▼ Cvc Specialty Chemicals Inc ....F 856 533-3000
Moorestown *(G-6571)*

▼ Cytec Industries Inc..................C 973 357-3100
Saddle Brook *(G-9761)*

▲ Deltech Resins Co ....E 973 589-0880
Newark *(G-7140)*

Dicaperl Minerals Corp ....G 856 320-2919
Pennsauken *(G-8503)*

▲ Dock Resins Corporation ....E 908 862-2351
Pedricktown *(G-8435)*

Dow Chemical Company ....D 800 258-2436
Somerset *(G-10090)*

E-Beam Services Inc...................E 513 933-0031
Cranbury *(G-1830)*

Eagle Fabrication Inc ....E 732 739-5300
Ltl Egg Hbr *(G-5644)*

Epsilon Plastics Inc ....D 201 933-6000
Lyndhurst *(G-5680)*

◆ Evonik Cyro LLC ....G 973 929-8000
Parsippany *(G-8004)*

Exxon Mobil Corporation ....E 732 321-6100
Linden *(G-5373)*

▲ Federal Plastics Corporation ....E 908 272-5800
Cranford *(G-1907)*

Flex Moulding Inc ....G 201 487-8080
Hackensack *(G-3914)*

Foam Rubber Fabricators Inc ....E 973 751-1445
Belleville *(G-303)*

◆ Formosa Plastics Corp USA ....B 973 992-2090
Livingston *(G-5530)*

Glopak Corp ....E 908 753-8735
South Plainfield *(G-10373)*

▲ Hitachi Chem Dupont Microsyst......E 732 613-2404
Parlin *(G-7931)*

◆ Honeywell International Inc ....A 973 455-2000
Morris Plains *(G-6666)*

Illinois Tool Works Inc ....E 609 395-5600
Cranbury *(G-1837)*

▲ Infinity Compounding LLC............E 856 467-3030
Logan Township *(G-5614)*

Innovative Resin Systems Inc ....G 973 465-6887
Newark *(G-7197)*

▲ Innovative Resin Systems Inc ....E 973 465-6887
Wayne *(G-11651)*

Innovative Resin Systems Inc ....F 973 633-5342
Wayne *(G-11652)*

Intelco ....D 856 456-6755
Westville *(G-11944)*

◆ Interntonal Specialty Pdts Inc ....A 859 815-3333
Wayne *(G-11653)*

◆ Interplast Inc ....F 609 386-4990
Burlington *(G-980)*

◆ Intra Pac Swedesboro ....D 856 467-0485
Swedesboro *(G-10703)*

Ip Moulding Inc.......................G 574 825-6554
Livingston *(G-5537)*

J-M Manufacturing Company Inc ....D 800 621-4404
Livingston *(G-5538)*

Kairos Enterprises LLC ....F 201 731-3181
Englewood Cliffs *(G-2969)*

Lanxess Solutions US Inc ....C 732 826-1018
Perth Amboy *(G-8620)*

Louis A Nelson Inc ....F 973 743-7404
Bloomfield *(G-518)*

Med Connection LLC ....G 908 213-7012
Phillipsburg *(G-8659)*

Multi-Plastics Extrusions Inc ....F 732 388-2300
Avenel *(G-142)*

North American Composites Co ....F 609 625-8101
Mays Landing *(G-6041)*

Palma Inc ....F 973 429-1490
Whippany *(G-12031)*

Petro Packaging Co Inc ....E 908 272-4054
Cranford *(G-1922)*

Phoenix Industries LLC ....G 973 366-4199
Wharton *(G-11997)*

Phoenix Manufacturing Inc ....G 732 380-1666
Ocean *(G-7737)*

Phoenix Resins Inc ....F 888 627-3769
Cinnaminson *(G-1485)*

◆ Plastic Specialties & Tech Inc ....C 201 941-2900
Ridgefield *(G-9380)*

Polyfil Corporation ....E 973 627-4070
Rockaway *(G-9598)*

▲ Polymer Technologies Inc ....D 973 778-9100
Clifton *(G-1700)*

▲ Polymeric Resources Corp ....E 973 694-4141
Wayne *(G-11674)*

▼ Polyvel Inc ....E 609 567-0080
Hammonton *(G-4147)*

▲ Pure Tech International Inc ....G 908 722-4800
Branchburg *(G-696)*

Recycle Inc East.......................D 908 756-2200
South Plainfield *(G-10434)*

▲ Rimtec Enterprises Inc ....C 609 387-0011
Burlington *(G-989)*

Rust-Oleum Corporation ....E 732 469-8100
Somerset *(G-10169)*

▲ Safas Corporation ....E 973 772-5252
Clifton *(G-1714)*

Saint-Gobain Prfmce Plas Corp..........C 973 696-4700
Wayne *(G-11681)*

Sika Corporation ....E 856 298-2313
Audubon *(G-118)*

Sika Corporation ....E 201 933-8800
Lyndhurst *(G-5709)*

◆ Sika Corporation ....B 201 933-8800
Lyndhurst *(G-5708)*

Solidsurface Designs Inc ....E 856 910-7720
Pennsauken *(G-8580)*

◆ Solvay USA Inc ....B 609 860-4000
Princeton *(G-9122)*

Solvay USA Inc ....C 732 297-0100
North Brunswick *(G-7538)*

Spartech LLC ....E 201 489-4000
Hackensack *(G-3979)*

Spartech LLC ....G 973 344-2700
Newark *(G-7322)*

Specialty Casting Inc ....G 856 845-3105
Woodbury *(G-12171)*

Surface Source Intl Inc ....F 973 598-0152
Randolph *(G-9300)*

▲ Synray Corporation ....G 908 245-2600
Kenilworth *(G-4998)*

▲ Technick Products Inc ....F 908 791-0400
South Plainfield *(G-10438)*

Technology Reviews Inc ....G 973 537-9511
Randolph *(G-9301)*

Thibaut & Walker Co Inc...............G 973 589-3331
Newark *(G-7340)*

Trademark Plastics Corporation..........E 908 925-5900
Newark *(G-7347)*

United Resin Inc.......................F 856 358-2574
Elmer *(G-2799)*

Uvitec Printing Ink Co Inc ....E 973 778-0737
Lodi *(G-5607)*

Weavers Fiberglass ....G 609 597-4324
Manahawkin *(G-5835)*

▲ Wexford International Inc ....G 908 781-7200
Gladstone *(G-3799)*

Wilsonart LLC ....F 800 822-7613
Moorestown *(G-6633)*

Zahk Sales Inc ....G 516 633-9179
Branchburg *(G-720)*

2822 Synthetic Rubber (Vulcanizable Elastomers)

◆ Ansell Healthcare Products LLC ....C 732 345-5400
Iselin *(G-4611)*

Bezwada Biomedical LLC ....G 908 281-7529
Hillsborough *(G-4320)*

◆ Dicar Inc ....E 973 575-1377
Pine Brook *(G-8697)*

Dicar Inc..............................D 973 575-4220
Pine Brook *(G-8698)*

Gel United Ltd Liability Co ....G 855 435-8683
Saddle Brook *(G-9766)*

Harmony Elastomers LLC ....G 973 340-4000
Paterson *(G-8287)*

Kelleigh USA Inc ....G 732 248-1161
Ewing *(G-3029)*

Kini Products Inc ....G 732 299-5555
New Egypt *(G-7016)*

Lyondell Chemical Company ....G 973 578-2200
Newark *(G-7232)*

Newark Auto Top Co Inc ....F 973 677-9935
East Orange *(G-2262)*

Nova Polymers Inc.....................F 973 227-6695
Fairfield *(G-3275)*

Paul Englehardt........................G 908 637-4556
Great Meadows *(G-3852)*

Pierce-Roberts Rubber Company ....F 609 394-5245
Ewing *(G-3043)*

◆ Reiss Manufacturing Inc ....C 732 446-6100
Rumson *(G-9715)*

▲ Stiles Enterprises Inc ....F 973 625-9660
Rockaway *(G-9610)*

2823 Cellulosic Man-Made Fibers

▼ Cytec Industries Inc ....C 973 357-3100
Saddle Brook *(G-9761)*

Endot Industries Inc ....D 973 625-8500
Rockaway *(G-9564)*

Newark Fibers Inc ....C 201 768-6800
Rockleigh *(G-9632)*

▲ Steiner Paper Corp ....G 732 651-6009
Manalapan *(G-5863)*

2824 Synthetic Organic Fibers, Exc Cellulosic

Allied-Signal China Ltd................E 973 455-2000
Morristown *(G-6685)*

Carlee Corporation ....E 201 768-6800
Rockleigh *(G-9627)*

◆ Honeywell International Inc ....A 973 455-2000
Morris Plains *(G-6666)*

Jaclyn Holdings Parent LLC ....G 201 909-6000
Maywood *(G-6053)*

▲ Jaclyn LLC ....D 201 909-6000
Maywood *(G-6054)*

◆ Nan Ya Plastics Corp America ....E 973 992-1775
Livingston *(G-5549)*

Natures Choice Corporation ....F 973 969-3299
Sparta *(G-10513)*

▲ Northeast Pro-Tech Inc ....F 973 777-5654
Passaic *(G-8167)*

Solutia Inc.............................C 908 862-0278
Linden *(G-5445)*

2833 Medicinal Chemicals & Botanical Prdts

7th Seventh Day Wellness Ctr ....G 856 308-0991
Sicklerville *(G-10015)*

◆ Abrazil LLC ....G 732 658-5191
Kendall Park *(G-4933)*

Akzo Nobel Chemicals LLC ....D 732 985-6262
Edison *(G-2454)*

American Ingredients Inc ....F 714 630-6000
Kearny *(G-4860)*

Aromac Inc ....F 973 365-1090
Clifton *(G-1566)*

▲ Avebe North America Inc.............F 609 520-1400
Princeton *(G-9012)*

Bodybio Inc ....E 856 825-8338
Millville *(G-6289)*

Certified Processing Corp..............F 973 923-5200
Hillside *(G-4402)*

Chefler Foods LLC ....F 201 596-3710
Saddle Brook *(G-9757)*

▲ Chem-Is-Try Inc ....G 732 372-7311
Metuchen *(G-6100)*

Chromak Research Inc ....G 732 560-1366
Somerset *(G-10082)*

▲ Cyalume Specialty Products Inc ......E 732 469-7760
Bound Brook *(G-617)*

D & A Granulation LLC ....G 732 994-7480
Lakewood *(G-5104)*

Eleison Pharmaceuticals Inc ....G 215 416-7620
Bordentown *(G-595)*

Fisher Scientific Company LLC..........B 201 796-7100
Fair Lawn *(G-3093)*

Greener Corners Ltd Lblty Co ....G 201 638-2218
Teaneck *(G-10755)*

▲ Guerbet LLC ....E 812 333-0059
Princeton *(G-9051)*

▲ Herbakraft Incorporated ....F 732 463-1000
Piscataway *(G-8773)*

Herbalist & Alchemist Inc ....F 908 689-9020
Washington *(G-11583)*

Herborium Group Inc..................G 201 849-4431
Fort Lee *(G-3556)*

Ipsen Biopharmaceuticals Inc ....C 908 275-6300
Basking Ridge *(G-191)*

Ivy-Dry Inc............................G 973 575-1992
Fairfield *(G-3234)*

Janssen Pharmaceuticals Inc............D 908 218-7701
Somerset *(G-10116)*

▲ Janssen Pharmaceuticals Inc........A 609 730-2000
Titusville *(G-10855)*

▲ Jiaherb Inc ....E 973 439-6869
  Pine Brook (G-8708)
Life Science Labs Mfg LLC ....F 732 367-9937
  Lakewood (G-5147)
Linde LLC ....G 973 579-2065
  Sparta (G-10510)
Mallinckrodt LLC ....F 908 238-6600
  Hampton (G-4164)
Matinas Biopharma Holdings Inc ....F 908 443-1860
  Bedminster (G-278)
▲ Mpt Delivery Systems Inc ....D 973 279-4132
  Paterson (G-8344)
Naturex Holdings Inc ....G 201 440-5000
  South Hackensack (G-10280)
Naturex Inc ....G 201 440-5000
  South Hackensack (G-10281)
◆ Naturex Inc ....G 201 440-5000
  South Hackensack (G-10282)
▲ Navinta LLC ....F 609 883-1135
  Ewing (G-3039)
◆ Ortho-Mcneil Phrm LLC ....E 908 203-4090
  Raritan (G-9315)
▲ Pacifichealth Laboratories Inc ....G 732 739-2900
  Parsippany (G-8053)
Pfizer Inc ....F 973 660-5000
  Madison (G-5731)
Pfizer Inc ....C 212 733-2323
  Bridgewater (G-872)
▲ Pharmacia & Upjohn Inc ....B 908 901-8000
  Peapack (G-8430)
◆ Pharmacia & Upjohn Company LLC .B 908 901-8000
  Peapack (G-8431)
Prime Coding Services LLC ....G 732 254-3036
  East Brunswick (G-2175)
Purevolution ....F 973 919-4047
  Kinnelon (G-5040)
Sanherb Biotech Inc ....G 347 946-5896
  Belle Mead (G-292)
Savient Pharmaceuticals Inc ....F 732 418-9300
  Bridgewater (G-892)
▲ Shanghai Freemen Americas LLC ...E 732 981-1288
  Piscataway (G-8809)
▲ Sk Life Science Inc ....E 201 421-3800
  Fair Lawn (G-3114)
◆ Solgar Inc ....F 201 944-2311
  Leonia (G-5319)
Specialty Measurements Inc ....F 908 534-1500
  Lebanon (G-5302)
Sunflower Seed ....G 908 735-3822
  Clinton (G-1755)
◆ Sytheon Ltd ....G 973 988-1075
  Boonton (G-584)
▲ Toll Compaction Service Inc ....E 732 776-8225
  Neptune (G-6936)
▲ Vita-Pure Inc ....E 908 245-1212
  Roselle (G-9686)
Vitamin Shoppe Industries Inc ....A 201 868-5959
  North Bergen (G-7491)
◆ Zoetis Products LLC ....C 973 660-5000
  Florham Park (G-3525)

2834 Pharmaceuticals

140 Main Street Corp ....F 732 974-2929
  Sea Girt (G-9860)
3r Biopharma LLC ....G 914 486-1898
  North Brunswick (G-7499)
A and P Pharmacy ....G 908 850-7640
  Hackettstown (G-3994)
AAA Pharmaceutical ....D 609 288-6060
  Lumberton (G-5649)
AAA Pharmaceutical Inc ....F 856 423-2700
  Paulsboro (G-8411)
AB Science Usa LLC ....G 973 218-2437
  Short Hills (G-9974)
Abbott Laboratories ....G 732 346-6649
  Edison (G-2447)
Abbott Laboratories ....E 609 443-9300
  Princeton (G-8992)
Abbott Laboratories ....F 856 988-5572
  Marlton (G-5963)
◆ Abbott Laboratories Parsippany ....G 973 428-4000
  Whippany (G-12005)
ABG Lab LLC ....G 973 559-5663
  Fair Lawn (G-3073)
Abon Pharmaceuticals LLC ....E 201 367-1702
  Northvale (G-7567)
Abraxis Bioscience Inc ....D 908 673-9000
  Summit (G-10630)
Abraxis Bioscience Inc ....D 908 673-9000
  Summit (G-10631)

Accelrx Labs LLC ....G 609 301-6446
  East Brunswick (G-2340)
Accumix Pharmaceuticals LLC ......G 609 632-2225
  Old Bridge (G-7772)
Acetris Health LLC ....G 201 961-9000
  Saddle Brook (G-9750)
Acetylon Pharmaceuticals Inc ....F 908 673-9000
  Summit (G-10632)
▲ Acg North America LLC ....E 908 757-3425
  Piscataway (G-8724)
Acino Products Ltd Lblty Co ....F 609 695-4300
  Hamilton (G-4101)
▲ Actavis Elizabeth LLC ....G 908 527-9100
  Elizabeth (G-2704)
Actavis Elizabeth LLC ....C 908 527-9100
  Fort Lee (G-3541)
Actavis Elizabeth LLC ....C 973 442-3200
  Madison (G-5716)
Actavis Laboratories Fl Inc ....G 862 261-7000
  Parsippany (G-7939)
Actavis LLC ....G 800 272-5525
  Morristown (G-6683)
Actavis LLC ....G 732 843-4904
  North Brunswick (G-7502)
Actavis LLC ....D 732 947-5300
  Edison (G-2450)
Actavis Pharma Inc ....C 862 261-7000
  Parsippany (G-7940)
▲ Adello Biologics LLC ....E 312 620-1500
  Piscataway (G-8725)
Advaxis Inc ....G 609 452-9813
  Princeton (G-8996)
Aeterna Zentaris Inc ....G 908 626-5428
  Warren (G-11536)
▲ AF Pharma LLC ....G 908 769-7040
  Hoboken (G-4456)
Aflag Pharmaceuticals LLC ....G 732 609-4139
  Edison (G-2452)
Agile Therapeutics Inc ....G 609 683-1880
  Princeton (G-8997)
Agilis Chemicals Inc ....G 973 910-2424
  Rockaway (G-9548)
Agno Pharma ....G 609 223-0638
  Allentown (G-27)
Ajj Powernutrition LLC ....G 908 452-5164
  Hackettstown (G-3995)
Akorn Inc ....E 609 662-9100
  Cranbury (G-1809)
Akorn Inc ....D 732 659-6443
  Somerset (G-10053)
▼ Akrimax Pharmaceuticals LLC ......D 908 372-0506
  Cranford (G-1894)
Aks Pharma Inc ....G 856 521-0710
  Elmer (G-2788)
Alcami New Jersey Corporation ......D 732 346-5100
  Edison (G-2465)
Alembic Pharmaceuticals Inc ....F 908 393-9604
  Bridgewater (G-807)
Alere Inc ....B 732 620-4244
  Freehold (G-3636)
▲ Align Pharmaceuticals LLC ....G 908 834-0960
  Berkeley Heights (G-399)
Allergan Inc ....D 908 306-0374
  Bedminster (G-265)
Allergan Inc ....G 862 261-7000
  Morristown (G-6684)
▲ Allergan Inc ....A 862 261-7000
  Madison (G-5718)
Allied Pharma Inc ....G 732 738-3295
  Fords (G-3526)
Allos Therapeutics Inc ....G 609 936-3760
  Princeton (G-9003)
Almatica Pharma Inc ....E 877 447-7979
  Pine Brook (G-8682)
▲ Alpharma US Inc ....E 201 228-5090
  Bridgewater (G-808)
Alpro Inc ....G 201 342-4498
  South Hackensack (G-10254)
Alteon ....G 201 934-1624
  Ramsey (G-9232)
Altima Innovations Inc ....G 732 474-1500
  Branchburg (G-632)
Alvogen Group Inc ....E 973 796-3400
  Pine Brook (G-8683)
Alvogen Inc ....G 973 796-3400
  Pine Brook (G-8684)
Amarin Corporation PLC ....E 908 719-1315
  Bedminster (G-266)
American Pharmaceutical LLC ......G 732 645-3030
  Piscataway (G-8732)

Amerigen Pharmaceuticals Ltd ......F 732 993-9826
  East Brunswick (G-2134)
Amicus Therapeutics Inc ....C 609 662-2000
  Cranbury (G-1811)
Amneal Pharmaceuticals LLC ....F 908 947-3120
  Piscataway (G-8735)
Amneal Pharmaceuticals LLC ....G 908 409-6823
  Branchburg (G-635)
▲ Amneal Pharmaceuticals LLC ....F 908 947-3120
  Bridgewater (G-809)
Amneal Pharmaceuticals LLC ....G 908 231-1911
  Branchburg (G-636)
Amneal Pharmaceuticals LLC ....G 973 357-0222
  Paterson (G-8211)
Amneal Pharmaceuticals LLC ....F 908 947-3120
  Piscataway (G-8734)
Amneal-Agila LLC ....F 908 947-3120
  Bridgewater (G-810)
Anadys Pharmaceuticals Inc ....E 972 235-4295
  Nutley (G-7641)
Ans Nutrition Inc ....E 212 235-5205
  Farmingdale (G-3377)
Antares Pharma Inc ....C 609 359-3020
  Ewing (G-3003)
Aphena Phrma Slutions - NJ LLC ...D 973 947-5441
  Parsippany (G-7947)
API Inc ....F 973 227-9335
  Fairfield (G-3137)
Apicore LLC ....E 732 748-8882
  Somerset (G-10060)
Apicore US LLC ....E 732 748-8882
  Somerset (G-10061)
Appco Pharma LLC ....E 732 271-8300
  Somerset (G-10062)
Appco Pharma LLC ....G 732 271-8300
  Piscataway (G-8736)
Appco Pharma LLC ....E 732 271-8300
  Somerset (G-10063)
Applechem Inc ....G 862 210-8344
  Newark (G-7089)
Aprecia Pharmaceuticals Co ....E 215 359-3300
  East Windsor (G-2342)
Aptalis Pharma LLC ....B 862 261-7000
  Parsippany (G-7948)
Aptapharma Corporation ....E 856 665-0025
  Pennsauken (G-8479)
Aquarius Biotechnologies Inc ....G 908 443-1860
  Bedminster (G-267)
Aquestive Therapeutics Inc ....F 908 941-1900
  Warren (G-11537)
Aralez Pharmaceuticals MGT Inc .....G 609 917-9330
  Princeton (G-9006)
Aralez Pharmaceuticals US Inc ....F 609 917-9330
  Princeton (G-9007)
▲ Archon Vitamin LLC ....D 732 537-1220
  Edison (G-2464)
Archon Vitamin LLC ....G 973 371-1700
  Edison (G-2465)
Arisaph Pharmaceuticals Inc ....C 617 986-4500
  Newark (G-7092)
Arno Therapeutics Inc ....C 862 703-7170
  Flemington (G-3428)
Aromac Inc ....G 973 365-1090
  Clifton (G-1566)
Ascend Laboratories LLC ....E 201 476-1977
  Parsippany (G-7951)
Ascendia Pharmaceuticals LLC ......G 732 638-4028
  North Brunswick (G-7505)
▲ Ash Ingredients Inc ....G 201 689-1322
  Glen Rock (G-3821)
Asiamerica Group Inc ....G 201 497-5993
  Westwood (G-11955)
▲ Aspire Pharmaceuticals Inc ....D 732 447-1444
  Somerset (G-10065)
Astrazeneca Pharmaceuticals LP ....F 973 975-0324
  Morristown (G-6688)
Aurex Labs Ltd Lblty Co ....F 609 308-2304
  East Windsor (G-2343)
Auro Health LLC ....G 732 839-9400
  Lawrence Township (G-5240)
Aurobindo Pharma ....G 732 839-9400
  East Windsor (G-2344)
Aurobindo Pharma USA Inc ....G 732 839-9402
  East Windsor (G-2345)
Aurobindo Pharma USA Inc ....G 732 839-9400
  Dayton (G-1953)
▲ Aurobindo Pharma USA Inc ....E 732 839-9400
  East Windsor (G-2346)
Aurobindo Pharma USA Inc ....G 609 409-6774
  East Windsor (G-2347)

Aurobindo Pharma USA LLC ....E 732 839-9400
East Windsor *(G-2348)*
Aurolife Pharma LLC ....E 732 839-9746
Dayton *(G-1954)*
Aurolife Pharma LLC ....G 732 839-9408
East Windsor *(G-2349)*
▲ Aurolife Pharma LLC ....C 732 839-4377
Dayton *(G-1955)*
Auromedics Pharma LLC ....F 732 823-4122
East Windsor *(G-2350)*
▲ Auromedics Pharma LLC ....E 732 839-9400
East Windsor *(G-2351)*
◆ Austarpharma LLC ....D 732 225-2930
Edison *(G-2469)*
Avacyn Pharmaceuticals Inc ....G 201 836-2599
Teaneck *(G-10743)*
▲ Aventis Inc ....A 800 981-2491
Bridgewater *(G-818)*
Aventis Phrmcticals Foundation ....E 908 981-5000
Bridgewater *(G-819)*
Barr Laboratories Inc ....C 201 767-1589
Northvale *(G-7573)*
Barr Laboratories Inc ....E 845 362-1100
Northvale *(G-7574)*
◆ BASF Corporation ....B 973 245-6000
Florham Park *(G-3492)*
▲ Basfin Corporation ....A 973 245-6000
Florham Park *(G-3493)*
▲ Bausch Health Companies Inc ....B 908 927-1400
Bridgewater *(G-821)*
Bayer Consumer Care Inc ....A 973 267-6198
Morristown *(G-6693)*
◆ Bayer Corporation ....A 412 777-2000
Whippany *(G-12007)*
Bayer Healthcare LLC ....F 973 254-5000
Morristown *(G-6694)*
◆ Bayer Healthcare LLC ....A 862 404-3000
Whippany *(G-12008)*
Bayer Hlthcare Phrmcticals Inc ....A 862 404-3000
Whippany *(G-12009)*
Bayer Hlthcare Phrmcticals Inc ....E 973 709-3545
Whippany *(G-12010)*
▲ Bayer Hlthcare Phrmcticals Inc ....A 862 404-3000
Whippany *(G-12011)*
Becton Dickinson Re Inc ....F 201 847-6800
Franklin Lakes *(G-3611)*
Bellerophon Therapeutics Inc ....E 908 574-4770
Warren *(G-11539)*
▲ Bioactive Resources LLC ....F 908 561-3114
South Plainfield *(G-10337)*
Bionpharma Inc ....G 609 380-3313
Princeton *(G-9016)*
Biopharma Research Council ....G 732 403-3137
Tinton Falls *(G-10824)*
Biophore LLC ....G 609 275-3713
Plainsboro *(G-8876)*
Biovail Distribution Company ....G 908 927-1400
Bridgewater *(G-822)*
Blue Ocean Pharma LLC ....G 908 428-4668
Annandale *(G-57)*
Boyds Pharmacy Inc ....F 609 499-0100
Florence *(G-3476)*
Bracco Research USA Inc ....E 609 514-2517
Cranbury *(G-1815)*
▲ Bristol-Myers Squibb Company ....G 800 332-2056
New Brunswick *(G-6948)*
Bristol-Myers Squibb Company ....E 609 897-3771
Plainsboro *(G-8877)*
Bristol-Myers Squibb Company ....G 609 419-5000
Princeton *(G-9018)*
Bristol-Myers Squibb Company ....E 212 546-4000
Pennington *(G-8444)*
Bristol-Myers Squibb Company ....B 908 218-3700
Bridgewater *(G-824)*
Bristol-Myers Squibb Company ....E 212 546-4000
Hillside *(G-4399)*
Bristol-Myers Squibb Company ....A 609 302-3000
Lawrenceville *(G-5252)*
Bristol-Myers Squibb Company ....G 609 252-4875
Princeton *(G-9019)*
Caligor Rx Inc ....E 212 988-0590
Secaucus *(G-9870)*
Calyptus Pharmaceuticals Inc ....F 908 720-6049
Princeton *(G-9020)*
▲ Camber Pharmaceuticals Inc ....E 732 529-0430
Piscataway *(G-8742)*
◆ Cambrex Corporation ....D 201 804-3000
East Rutherford *(G-2290)*
Cambridge Therapeutic Tech LLC ....G 914 420-5555
Hackensack *(G-3892)*

▲ Capsugel Inc ....D 862 242-1700
Morristown *(G-6696)*
Capsugel Holdings Us Inc ....G 862 242-1700
Morristown *(G-6697)*
Capsugel Us LLC ....B 862 242-1700
Morristown *(G-6698)*
Caraco Pharmaceutical Labs ....G 609 819-8200
Cranbury *(G-1820)*
Cardinal Health Systems Inc ....B 732 537-6544
Somerset *(G-10073)*
Carnegie Pharmaceuticals LLC ....G 732 783-7010
Delran *(G-2014)*
Carwin Phrm Assoc LLC ....G 732 344-6987
Hazlet *(G-4272)*
Castle Creek Phrmceuticals LLC ....F 862 286-0400
Parsippany *(G-7964)*
Catalent Inc ....D 732 537-6200
Somerset *(G-10075)*
Catalent Cts LLC ....C 201 785-0275
Allendale *(G-6)*
Catalent CTS Kansas City LLC ....G 732 537-6200
Somerset *(G-10076)*
▲ Catalent Pharma Solutions LLC ....D 732 537-6200
Somerset *(G-10077)*
▲ Catalent Pharma Solutions Inc ....B 732 537-6200
Somerset *(G-10078)*
Catalent US Holding I LLC ....G 877 587-1835
Somerset *(G-10079)*
Celator Pharmaceuticals Inc ....E 609 243-0123
Ewing *(G-3007)*
Celgene Cellular ....A 908 673-9000
Cedar Knolls *(G-1309)*
Celgene Corporation ....F 908 464-8101
Berkeley Heights *(G-403)*
Celgene Corporation ....E 732 271-1001
Warren *(G-11541)*
Celgene Corporation ....F 908 967-1432
Berkeley Heights *(G-404)*
Celgene Corporation ....E 908 897-4603
Summit *(G-10638)*
Celgene Corporation ....C 908 673-9000
Summit *(G-10639)*
Celgene Corporation ....G 908 673-9000
Basking Ridge *(G-182)*
Celimmune ....G 908 399-2954
Lebanon *(G-5280)*
Celldex Therapeutics Inc ....C 908 200-7500
Hampton *(G-4155)*
Cellular Sciences Inc ....G 908 237-1561
Flemington *(G-3430)*
Celsion Corporation ....F 609 896-9100
Lawrenceville *(G-5253)*
Central Admxture Phrm Svcs Inc ....E 201 541-0080
Englewood *(G-2883)*
Cerexa Inc ....E 510 285-9200
Parsippany *(G-7967)*
▲ Cetylite Industries Inc ....B 856 665-6111
Pennsauken *(G-8491)*
Champions Oncology Inc ....D 201 808-8400
Hackensack *(G-3896)*
Chandler Pharmacy LLC ....G 732 543-1568
New Brunswick *(G-6951)*
Chemtract LLC ....G 732 820-0427
Martinsville *(G-6008)*
Cherokee Pharma Llc ....G 732 422-7800
Jamesburg *(G-4684)*
Chromocell Corporation ....D 732 565-1113
North Brunswick *(G-7512)*
▲ Cispharma Inc ....F 609 235-9807
Cranbury *(G-1822)*
Citius Pharmaceuticals Inc ....G 978 938-0338
Cranford *(G-1900)*
Cmic Cmo USA Corporation ....E 609 395-9700
Cranbury *(G-1824)*
▲ Command Nutritionals LLC ....E 973 227-8210
Fairfield *(G-3164)*
Contract Coatings Inc ....F 201 343-3131
Hackensack *(G-3900)*
Contravir Pharmaceuticals Inc ....E 732 902-4000
Edison *(G-2490)*
Core Acquisition LLC ....G 732 983-6025
Middlesex *(G-6156)*
Core Tech Solutions Inc ....F 609 443-1400
East Windsor *(G-2355)*
▲ Corepharma LLC ....G 732 983-6025
Middlesex *(G-6157)*
Cormedix Inc ....G 908 517-9500
Berkeley Heights *(G-407)*
Corrigan Center For Integrativ ....G 973 239-0700
Cedar Grove *(G-1276)*

County Line Phrmaceuticals LLC ....G 262 439-8109
Pine Brook *(G-8695)*
◆ Cubist Pharmaceuticals LLC ....C 908 740-4000
Kenilworth *(G-4949)*
▲ Cyalume Specialty Products Inc ......E 732 469-7760
Bound Brook *(G-617)*
Cyclacel Pharmaceuticals Inc ....F 908 517-7330
Berkeley Heights *(G-408)*
Cyclase Dynamics Inc ....G 973 420-3259
Barnegat Light *(G-169)*
Cypress Pharmaceuticals Inc ....C 601 856-4393
Morristown *(G-6703)*
D&E Nutraceuticals Inc ....E 212 235-5200
Farmingdale *(G-3383)*
Daiichi Sankyo Inc ....F 908 992-6400
Basking Ridge *(G-183)*
▲ Dainippon Sumitomo Pharma Amer.E 201 592-2050
Fort Lee *(G-3550)*
▲ Derma Sciences Inc ....C 609 514-4744
Plainsboro *(G-8880)*
◆ Dermarite Industries LLC ....C 973 247-3491
North Bergen *(G-7446)*
Dermatological Soc of NJ Inc ....G 856 546-5600
Barrington *(G-176)*
Dermatology & Laser Center PA ....G 732 222-8323
Long Branch *(G-5623)*
Diamond Systems USA Corp ....G 973 777-9075
South Hackensack *(G-10260)*
Difco Laboratories Inc ....G 410 316-4113
Franklin Lakes *(G-3613)*
▲ Dishman Usa Inc ....F 732 560-4300
Middlesex *(G-6162)*
◆ Dmv-Fnterra Excipients USA LLC .....G 609 858-2111
Paramus *(G-7866)*
Dpi Newco LLC ....E 973 257-8113
Parsippany *(G-7985)*
▲ Dse Healthcare Solutions LLC ....G 732 417-1870
Edison *(G-2504)*
DSM Nutritional Products LLC ....C 908 475-7093
Belvidere *(G-369)*
DSM Nutritional Products LLC ....B 908 475-0150
Belvidere *(G-370)*
DSM Nutritional Products LLC ....C 908 475-5300
Belvidere *(G-371)*
DSM Nutritional Products LLC ....C 908 475-5300
Belvidere *(G-372)*
◆ DSM Nutritional Products LLC ....B 800 526-0189
Parsippany *(G-7989)*
DSM Sight & Life Inc ....G 973 257-8208
Parsippany *(G-7990)*
E R Squibb & Sons LLC ....G 732 246-3195
East Brunswick *(G-2147)*
E R Squibb & Sons Inter-AM ....G 609 818-3715
Trenton *(G-11056)*
▲ E R Squibb & Sons Inter-AM ....G 609 252-4111
Princeton *(G-9034)*
▲ Eagle Pharmaceuticals Inc ....E 201 326-5300
Woodcliff Lake *(G-12188)*
Ebelle Debelle Phrm Inc ....F 973 823-0665
Hamburg *(G-4093)*
Eco LLC ....G 609 683-9030
Princeton *(G-9035)*
Edenbridge Pharmaceuticals LLC ....G 201 292-1292
Parsippany *(G-7998)*
Edge Therapeutics Inc ....E 800 208-3343
Berkeley Heights *(G-410)*
Edgemont Pharmaceuticals LLC ....G 908 375-8039
Far Hills *(G-3374)*
▲ Eisai Inc ....C 201 692-1100
Woodcliff Lake *(G-12189)*
Ekr Therapeutics Incorporated ....C 877 435-2524
Bedminster *(G-271)*
Eli Lilly and Company ....E 908 704-1807
Branchburg *(G-656)*
Elite Laboratories Inc ....G 201 750-2646
Northvale *(G-7578)*
Elite Pharmaceuticals Inc ....G 201 750-2646
Northvale *(G-7579)*
Elusys Therapeutics Inc ....E 973 808-0222
Pine Brook *(G-8701)*
Elvi Pharma LLC ....F 732 640-2707
Piscataway *(G-8762)*
Emisphere Technologies Inc ....F 973 532-8000
Roseland *(G-9649)*
Encore Pharmaceutical Inc ....G 973 267-9331
Morris Plains *(G-6661)*
Endo Phrmaceuticals Valera Inc ....F 609 235-3230
Cranbury *(G-1831)*
Enteris Biopharma Inc ....G 973 453-3518
Boonton *(G-566)*

Envigo Crs Inc ....B 732 873-2550
Somerset *(G-10095)*

▲ Enzon Pharmaceuticals Inc ....G 732 980-4500
Cranford *(G-1905)*

Enzon Pharmaceuticals Inc ....D 732 980-4500
South Plainfield *(G-10356)*

▲ Eon Labs Inc ....A 609 627-8600
Princeton *(G-9040)*

Esjay Pharma LLC ....G 609 469-5920
East Windsor *(G-2357)*

Esjay Pharma LLC ....F 732 438-1816
Allentown *(G-30)*

Eva Maria Wolfe ....G 412 777-2000
Wayne *(G-11630)*

▲ Evenus Pharmaceutical Labs Inc .....G 609 395-8625
Princeton *(G-9041)*

▲ Exeltis Usa Inc ....D 973 324-0200
Florham Park *(G-3500)*

Exeltis USA Dermatology LLC ....E 973 805-4060
Florham Park *(G-3501)*

Exemplify Biopharma Inc ....G 732 500-3208
Cranbury *(G-1832)*

Eyetech Inc ....F 646 454-1779
Bridgewater *(G-838)*

▲ Faubel Pharma Services ....G 908 730-7563
Bordentown *(G-596)*

Faulding Holdings Inc ....C 908 527-9100
Elizabeth *(G-2730)*

▲ Ferring Pharmaceuticals Inc ....C 973 796-1600
Parsippany *(G-8010)*

▲ Ferring Production Inc ....E 973 796-1600
Parsippany *(G-8011)*

First National Servicing & Dev ....E 732 341-5409
Toms River *(G-10877)*

▲ Five Star Supplies NJ Corp ....E 908 862-8801
Linden *(G-5376)*

Fordoz Pharma Corp ....F 609 469-5949
East Windsor *(G-2358)*

Foresight Group LLC ....F 888 992-8880
Parsippany *(G-8015)*

Forest Laboratories LLC ....F 631 436-4534
Jersey City *(G-4755)*

Forest Laboratories LLC ....E 631 501-5399
Jersey City *(G-4756)*

▲ Forest Pharmaceuticals Inc ....A 862 261-7000
Parsippany *(G-8016)*

Fougera Pharmaceuticals Inc ....E 973 514-4241
East Hanover *(G-2217)*

Fractal Solutions Corp ....G 201 608-6828
Edgewater *(G-2439)*

▲ G & W Laboratories Inc ....B 908 753-2000
South Plainfield *(G-10369)*

G & W Laboratories Inc ....D 732 474-0729
Piscataway *(G-8768)*

G & W Laboratories Inc ....D 908 753-2000
South Plainfield *(G-10370)*

G&W PA Laboratories LLC ....G 908 753-2000
South Plainfield *(G-10371)*

Gadde Pharma LLC ....G 609 651-7772
Plainsboro *(G-8883)*

GE Healthcare Inc ....E 908 757-0500
South Plainfield *(G-10372)*

Genavite LLC ....F 973 779-1532
Clifton *(G-1625)*

Genzyme Corporation ....C 201 313-9660
Ridgefield *(G-9362)*

Genzyme Corporation ....G 973 256-2106
Totowa *(G-10948)*

◆ Glaxosmithkline Consumer ....B 251 591-4188
Warren *(G-11549)*

Glaxosmithkline Consumer Hlth ....G 215 751-5046
Warren *(G-11550)*

Glaxosmithkline LLC ....E 856 952-6023
Collingswood *(G-1770)*

Glaxosmithkline LLC ....E 609 472-8175
Cherry Hill *(G-1371)*

◆ Glenmark Phrmceuticals Inc USA ...D 201 684-8000
Mahwah *(G-5777)*

Glenmark Therapeutics Inc USA ....A 201 684-8000
Mahwah *(G-5778)*

▲ Glenwood LLC ....C 201 569-0050
Englewood *(G-2901)*

▲ Globe Pharma Inc ....G 732 296-9700
New Brunswick *(G-6963)*

Grant Industries Inc ....D 201 791-8700
Elmwood Park *(G-2822)*

▲ Grant Industries Inc ....D 201 791-6700
Elmwood Park *(G-2823)*

Grant Industries Inc ....F 201 791-6700
Elmwood Park *(G-2824)*

Granulation Technology Inc ....F 973 276-0740
Fairfield *(G-3212)*

Grow Company Inc ....E 201 941-8777
Ridgefield *(G-9363)*

◆ Gsk Consumer Health Inc ....B 919 269-5000
Warren *(G-11551)*

Gsk Consumer Healthcare ....D 973 539-0645
Parsippany *(G-8025)*

▲ Guardian Drug Company Inc ....C 609 860-2600
Dayton *(G-1968)*

▲ Halo Pharmaceutical Inc ....D 973 428-4000
Whippany *(G-12023)*

Halton Laboratories LLC ....E 609 917-9330
Princeton *(G-9053)*

Health Science Funding LLC ....F 973 984-6159
Morristown *(G-6713)*

Helsinn Therapeutics US Inc ....E 908 231-1435
Iselin *(G-4628)*

Hengrui Therapeutics Inc ....E 609 423-2155
Princeton *(G-9055)*

Heritage Pharma Holdings Inc ....C 732 429-1000
East Brunswick *(G-2157)*

Heritage Pharma Labs Inc ....F 732 238-7880
East Brunswick *(G-2158)*

▲ Heritage Pharma Labs Inc ....C 732 238-7880
East Brunswick *(G-2159)*

▲ Heritage Pharmaceuticals Inc ....E 732 429-1000
East Brunswick *(G-2160)*

Hikma Injectables USA Inc ....G 732 542-1191
Eatontown *(G-2401)*

◆ Hikma Pharmaceuticals USA Inc ......B 732 542-1191
Eatontown *(G-2402)*

Hikma Pharmaceuticals USA Inc ....G 732 542-1191
Eatontown *(G-2403)*

Hikma Pharmaceuticals USA Inc ....C 856 424-3700
Cherry Hill *(G-1375)*

▲ Hill Pharma Inc ....F 973 521-7400
Fairfield *(G-3222)*

Hisamitsu Phrm Co Inc ....F 973 765-0122
Florham Park *(G-3506)*

Hobart Group Holdings LLC ....C 908 470-1780
Gladstone *(G-3798)*

◆ Hoffmann-La Roche Inc ....A 973 890-2268
Little Falls *(G-5476)*

Hoffmann-La Roche Inc ....F 973 235-8216
Totowa *(G-10951)*

Hoffmann-La Roche Inc ....D 973 235-3092
Nutley *(G-7648)*

Hoffmann-La Roche Inc ....E 973 235-1016
Nutley *(G-7649)*

Holmdel Acpnctr & Ntrl Med Ctr ....G 732 888-4910
Holmdel *(G-4517)*

▲ Hovione LLC ....D 609 918-2600
East Windsor *(G-2359)*

HRP Capital Inc ....G 201 242-4938
Fort Lee *(G-3557)*

I Fcb Holdings Inc ....G 201 934-2000
Mahwah *(G-5784)*

IBC Pharmaceuticals Inc ....F 973 540-9595
Morris Plains *(G-6670)*

Ikaria Therapeutics LLC ....G 908 238-6600
Hampton *(G-4160)*

Imclone Systems LLC ....G 908 541-8100
Branchburg *(G-668)*

◆ Imclone Systems LLC ....C 908 541-8000
Bridgewater *(G-844)*

Imclone Systems LLC ....G 908 218-0147
Branchburg *(G-667)*

Immtech Pharmaceuticals Inc ....E 212 791-2911
Montclair *(G-6417)*

Immune Pharmaceuticals Inc ....F 201 464-2677
Englewood Cliffs *(G-2965)*

▲ Immunomedics Inc ....C 973 605-8200
Morris Plains *(G-6671)*

▼ INB Manhattan Drug Company Inc ....D 973 926-0816
Hillside *(G-4415)*

INB Manhattan Drug Company Inc ......D 973 926-0816
Hillside *(G-4416)*

INB Manhattan Drug Company Inc ......E 973 926-0816
Hillside *(G-4417)*

Indampharm Inc ....F 732 970-0002
Morganville *(G-6644)*

Inno Pharma LLC ....F 732 885-2939
Piscataway *(G-8780)*

◆ Ino Therapeutics LLC ....D 908 238-6600
Bedminster *(G-274)*

Insmed Incorporated ....C 908 977-9900
Bridgewater *(G-847)*

Integra Lifesciences Corp ....D 609 275-0500
Plainsboro *(G-8889)*

Integrated Biopharma Inc ....E 888 319-6962
Hillside *(G-4418)*

Intellect Neurosciences Inc ....G 201 608-5101
Englewood Cliffs *(G-2968)*

International Vitamin Corp ....C 973 371-4400
Irvington *(G-4592)*

International Vitamin Corp ....G 973 416-2000
Irvington *(G-4593)*

Interntnal Pharma Remedies Inc ....G 201 417-3891
Paterson *(G-8295)*

Invaderm Corporation ....G 973 572-5676
Somerset *(G-10112)*

Inventiv Health Clinical LLC ....G 973 348-1000
Basking Ridge *(G-190)*

Ipsen Biopharmaceuticals Inc ....C 908 275-6300
Basking Ridge *(G-191)*

Iron4u Inc ....G 609 514-5163
Princeton *(G-9060)*

Isdin Corp ....E 862 242-8129
Morristown *(G-6718)*

Ivax Pharmaceuticals LLC ....G 201 767-1700
Woodcliff Lake *(G-12195)*

J&N Pharma LLC ....G 201 391-3139
Woodcliff Lake *(G-12196)*

▲ Jak Diversified II Inc ....D 973 439-1182
West Caldwell *(G-11781)*

Jamol Laboratories Inc ....G 201 262-6363
Emerson *(G-2859)*

Janssen Global Services LLC ....F 908 704-4000
Raritan *(G-9309)*

▲ Janssen Pharmaceuticals Inc ....A 609 730-2000
Titusville *(G-10855)*

Janssen Research & Dev LLC ....A 908 704-4000
Raritan *(G-9310)*

Jems Pharma LLC ....G 609 386-0141
Burlington *(G-981)*

Jhp Group Holdings Inc ....A 973 658-3569
Parsippany *(G-8033)*

Jiangsu Hengrui Medicine Co ....G 609 395-8625
Princeton *(G-9062)*

Jnj International Inv LLC ....G 732 524-0400
New Brunswick *(G-6973)*

◆ Johnson & Johnson ....A 732 524-0400
New Brunswick *(G-6974)*

Johnson & Johnson ....D 908 704-6809
Raritan *(G-9312)*

Johnson & Johnson ....E 908 526-5425
Raritan *(G-9313)*

Johnson & Johnson ....D 908 725-7256
Somerville *(G-10218)*

Johnson & Johnson ....D 732 422-5000
North Brunswick *(G-7522)*

Johnson & Johnson ....D 908 722-9319
Raritan *(G-9311)*

Johnson & Johnson ....C 908 874-1000
Morris Plains *(G-6673)*

Johnson & Johnson ....C 732 524-0400
New Brunswick *(G-6975)*

◆ Johnson & Johnson Consumer Inc ...A 908 874-1000
Skillman *(G-10032)*

Juventio LLC ....G 973 908-8097
Chatham *(G-1331)*

Kamat Pharmatech LLC ....G 732 406-6421
North Brunswick *(G-7523)*

Kiehls Since 1851 Inc ....G 201 843-1125
Paramus *(G-7880)*

Klus Pharma Inc ....F 609 651-4466
Cranbury *(G-1847)*

▲ Kos Pharmaceuticals Inc ....F 609 495-0500
Cranbury *(G-1848)*

▼ Kwik Enterprises LLC ....G 732 663-1559
Oakhurst *(G-7670)*

Kyowa Hakko Kirin Cal Inc ....G 609 580-7400
Princeton *(G-9065)*

Kyowa Kirin Inc ....D 908 234-1096
Bedminster *(G-275)*

▲ Lab Express Inc ....F 973 227-1700
Fairfield *(G-3247)*

Lautus Phrmceuticals Ltd Lblty ....G 908 273-2777
Morristown *(G-6721)*

Leading Pharma LLC ....E 201 746-9160
Fairfield *(G-3250)*

Leading Pharma LLC ....E 201 746-9160
Montvale *(G-6465)*

▲ Leo Pharma Inc ....B 973 637-1690
Madison *(G-5728)*

◆ Levomed Inc ....G 908 359-4804
Somerset *(G-10123)*

Lexicon Pharmaceuticals Inc ....F 609 466-5500
Basking Ridge *(G-192)*

Life Science Laboratories LLC G 732 367-1900
Lakewood *(G-5146)*
Life Scnce Labs Spplements LLC F 732 367-1749
Lakewood *(G-5148)*
▼ **Lipoid LLC** G 973 735-2692
Newark *(G-7221)*
LLC Dunn Meadow G 201 297-4603
Fort Lee *(G-3565)*
Lonza Biologics Inc D 603 610-4809
Allendale *(G-12)*
Loving Care Pharmacy G 732 832-2862
Edison *(G-2559)*
▲ **LTS Lhmann Thrapy Systems Corp** A 973 575-5170
West Caldwell *(G-11783)*
Lupin Pharmaceuticals Inc G 908 603-6075
Somerset *(G-10127)*
Lupin Pharmaceuticals Inc G 908 603-6000
Somerset *(G-10128)*
Luye Pharma USA Ltd E 609 799-7600
Princeton *(G-9069)*
Lyciret Corp E 973 882-0322
Orange *(G-7820)*
Lydem LLC G 856 566-1419
Palmyra *(G-7849)*
▲ **Macleods Pharma Usa Inc** F 609 269-5250
Plainsboro *(G-8893)*
▲ **Magnifica Inc** G 323 202-0386
Cranbury *(G-1858)*
Mallinckrodt Ard Inc G 510 400-0700
Bedminster *(G-276)*
Mallinckrodt Ard Inc G 908 238-6600
Bedminster *(G-277)*
Mallinckrodt LLC F 908 238-6600
Hampton *(G-4164)*
Matinas Biopharma Holdings Inc F 908 443-1860
Bedminster *(G-279)*
Matrixx Initiatives Inc E 877 942-2626
Bridgewater *(G-859)*
Matthey Johnson Inc E 856 384-7001
West Deptford *(G-11836)*
Matthey Johnson Inc C 856 384-7132
West Deptford *(G-11835)*
Maximum Humn Prfmce Hldngs LLC E 973 785-9055
West Caldwell *(G-11786)*
Medavante Inc G 609 528-9400
Hamilton *(G-4113)*
Medicines Company C 973 290-6000
Parsippany *(G-8043)*
◆ **Medicis Pharmaceutical Corp** F 866 246-8245
Bridgewater *(G-860)*
Medicon Inc G 201 669-7456
Allendale *(G-14)*
Medimtriks Pharmaceuticals Inc E 973 882-7512
Fairfield *(G-3256)*
Megalith Pharmaceuticals Inc G 877 436-7220
Princeton *(G-9072)*
Merck & Co Inc B 908 740-4000
Kenilworth *(G-4974)*
Merck & Co Inc E 908 740-4000
Kenilworth *(G-4975)*
Merck & Co Inc E 800 224-5318
Madison *(G-5729)*
Merck & Co Inc D 908 298-4000
Kenilworth *(G-4976)*
Merck & Co Inc E 908 298-4000
Summit *(G-10650)*
Merck & Co Inc D 908 740-4000
Rahway *(G-9212)*
Merck Holdings LLC F 908 423-1000
Whitehouse Station *(G-12054)*
Merck Research Laboratories D 732 594-4000
Rahway *(G-9213)*
Merck Resource Management Inc G 908 423-1000
Whitehouse Station *(G-12055)*
◆ **Merck Sharp & Dohme Corp** A 908 740-4000
Kenilworth *(G-4977)*
Merck Sharp & Dohme Corp B 908 423-1000
Kenilworth *(G-4978)*
Merck Sharp & Dohme Corp E 908 423-3000
Whitehouse Station *(G-12056)*
Merck Sharp & Dohme Corp D 732 594-4000
Rahway *(G-9214)*
Merck Sharp & Dohme Corp G 908 685-3892
Branchburg *(G-679)*
Merck Sharp & Dohme Europe Inc F 908 423-1000
Somerset *(G-10137)*
▲ **Merck Sharpe & Dohme De PR Inc** G 908 423-1000
Whitehouse Station *(G-12057)*
Merial Inc E 732 729-5700
North Brunswick *(G-7526)*

Michelex Corporation G 201 977-1177
Prospect Park *(G-9170)*
Mitsubishi Tanabe Pharma E 908 607-1950
Jersey City *(G-4784)*
▲ **Mpt Delivery Systems Inc** G 973 278-0283
Paterson *(G-8343)*
▲ **Msn Pharmaceuticals Inc** G 908 360-1500
Piscataway *(G-8794)*
Mule Road Pharmacy G 732 244-3737
Toms River *(G-10897)*
▲ **Mylan Laboratories Inc** G 973 761-1600
South Orange *(G-10311)*
Myos Rens Technology Inc G 973 509-0444
Cedar Knolls *(G-1318)*
Natures Rule LLC F 888 819-4220
Hillside *(G-4431)*
Nautilus Neurosciences Inc G 908 437-1320
Bedminster *(G-281)*
New Life Pharma Ltd Lblty Co G 201 784-7812
Northvale *(G-7595)*
New Life Resources Inc F 201 750-7880
Northvale *(G-7596)*
Newmarket Pharmaceuticals LLC G 609 252-9600
Trenton *(G-11089)*
Newton Biopharma Solutions LLC G 908 874-7145
Hillsborough *(G-4358)*
▲ **Nextron Medical Tech Inc** D 973 575-0614
Fairfield *(G-3270)*
Njs Associates Company G 973 960-8688
Bridgewater *(G-867)*
▲ **Novacyl Inc** G 609 259-0444
Robbinsville *(G-9520)*
◆ **Novartis Corporation** E 212 307-1122
East Hanover *(G-2232)*
Novartis Corporation D 862 778-8300
East Hanover *(G-2233)*
Novartis Corporation B 973 503-7488
East Hanover *(G-2234)*
Novartis Corporation C 973 377-4794
Florham Park *(G-3512)*
◆ **Novartis Pharmaceuticals Corp** A 862 778-8300
East Hanover *(G-2235)*
Novartis Pharmaceuticals Corp F 973 538-1296
Morris Plains *(G-6674)*
Novartis Pharmaceuticals Corp G 862 778-8300
East Hanover *(G-2237)*
Novartis Pharmaceuticals Corp G 862 778-8300
East Hanover *(G-2236)*
▲ **Novel Laboratories Inc** C 908 603-6000
Somerset *(G-10145)*
Novitium Pharma LLC G 609 469-5920
East Windsor *(G-2363)*
◆ **Novo Nordisk Inc** B 609 987-5800
Plainsboro *(G-8894)*
Novo Nordisk Inc G 609 987-5800
Princeton *(G-9083)*
Novotec Pharma LLC G 609 632-2239
Monroe Township *(G-6386)*
Nuclear Diagnostic Pdts Inc F 856 489-5733
Cherry Hill *(G-1406)*
Nuclear Diagnostic Pdts Inc G 973 664-9696
Rockaway *(G-9591)*
▲ **Nutra-Med Packaging Inc** D 973 625-2274
Whippany *(G-12028)*
▲ **Nutri Sport Pharmacal Inc** F 973 827-9287
Franklin *(G-3604)*
Nutri-Pet Research Inc G 732 786-8822
Manalapan *(G-5857)*
▲ **Nutro Laboratories Inc** C 908 755-7984
South Plainfield *(G-10416)*
▲ **OHM Laboratories Inc** D 732 418-2235
North Brunswick *(G-7532)*
OHM Laboratories Inc D 609 720-9200
Princeton *(G-9086)*
OHM Laboratories Inc D 732 514-1072
New Brunswick *(G-6989)*
▲ **Omniactive Hlth Tchnlogies Inc** E 866 588-3629
Morristown *(G-6731)*
Omthera Pharmaceuticals Inc F 908 741-4399
Princeton *(G-9087)*
Oncobiologics Inc D 609 619-3990
Cranbury *(G-1864)*
Onpharma Inc G 408 335-6850
Bridgewater *(G-868)*
Optimer Pharmaceuticals LLC B 858 909-0736
Kenilworth *(G-4984)*
▲ **Orchid Pharmaceuticals Inc** G 609 951-2209
Princeton *(G-9088)*
▲ **Organics Corporation America** E 973 890-9002
Totowa *(G-10960)*

Organon USA Inc G 908 423-1000
Whitehouse Station *(G-12059)*
Ortho Biotech Products LP D 908 541-4000
Bridgewater *(G-871)*
▲ **Ortho-Clinical Diagnostics Inc** A 908 218-8000
Raritan *(G-9314)*
◆ **Ortho-Mcneil Phrm LLC** E 908 203-4090
Raritan *(G-9315)*
Ossb and L Pharma LLC G 732 940-8701
Milltown *(G-6270)*
▲ **Pacifichealth Laboratories Inc** G 732 739-2900
Parsippany *(G-8053)*
Pacira Pharmaceuticals Inc B 973 254-3560
Parsippany *(G-8054)*
Palatin Technologies Inc E 609 495-2200
Cranbury *(G-1866)*
Parker Labs G 973 276-9500
Fairfield *(G-3282)*
Patagonia Pharmaceuticals LLC G 201 264-7866
Woodcliff Lake *(G-12198)*
▲ **Patheon Biologics (nj) LLC** D 609 919-3300
Princeton *(G-9089)*
Patheon Biologics LLC D 609 919-3300
Princeton *(G-9090)*
Pdr Equity LLC D 201 358-7200
Whippany *(G-12032)*
Penick Corporation G 856 678-3601
Newark *(G-7268)*
Pernix Therapeutics LLC E 800 793-2145
Morristown *(G-6733)*
Pernix Thrpeutics Holdings Inc D 800 793-2145
Morristown *(G-6734)*
Pfizer Inc D 732 591-2106
Old Bridge *(G-7788)*
Pfizer Inc C 973 993-0977
Morris Plains *(G-6678)*
Pfizer Inc C 201 294-8060
North Bergen *(G-7475)*
Pfizer Inc C 908 251-5685
Dunellen *(G-2130)*
Pfizer Inc F 973 660-5000
Madison *(G-5731)*
Pfizer Inc E 609 434-4920
Ewing *(G-3041)*
Pfizer Inc C 908 901-8000
Peapack *(G-8429)*
Pfizer Inc C 212 733-2323
Bridgewater *(G-872)*
Pharm Ops Inc G 908 454-7733
Phillipsburg *(G-8662)*
▲ **Pharm-Rx Chemical Corporation** G 973 917-1400
Clifton *(G-1694)*
Pharma Synergy LLC G 856 241-2316
Swedesboro *(G-10718)*
▲ **Pharmaceutical Innovations** E 973 242-2900
Newark *(G-7270)*
Pharmaceutical Regulatory Svcs G 609 497-9694
Princeton *(G-9091)*
Pharmachem Laboratories Inc E 973 256-1340
Totowa *(G-10962)*
Pharmachem Laboratories Inc E 201 343-3611
South Hackensack *(G-10288)*
◆ **Pharmachem Laboratories LLC** D 201 246-1000
Kearny *(G-4908)*
▲ **Pharmacia & Upjohn Inc** B 908 901-8000
Peapack *(G-8430)*
◆ **Pharmacia & Upjohn Company LLC** B 908 901-8000
Peapack *(G-8431)*
Pharmasource International LLC G 732 985-6182
Piscataway *(G-8800)*
Pharmatech International Inc F 973 244-0393
Fairfield *(G-3283)*
Pharmedium Services LLC E 847 457-2362
Dayton *(G-1982)*
Pharming Healthcare Inc G 908 376-3058
Bridgewater *(G-873)*
Pharmion Corporation E 908 673-9000
Summit *(G-10653)*
◆ **Phibro Animal Health Corp** D 201 329-7300
Teaneck *(G-10765)*
▲ **Phytoceuticals Inc** G 201 791-2255
Elmwood Park *(G-2844)*
Pierre Fbre Phrmaceuticals Inc G 973 898-1042
Parsippany *(G-8062)*
Plantfusion G 732 537-1220
Edison *(G-2595)*
Pmv Pharmaceuticals Inc G 650 241-2822
Cranbury *(G-1871)*
Porton Usa LLC E 908 791-9100
South Plainfield *(G-10422)*

Powerhuse Frmltons Ltd Labilit ....G...... 888 666-7715
South Plainfield (G-10423)
Prescription Dynamics Inc ....F...... 201 746-6262
Mahwah (G-5802)
Prince Sterilization Svcs LLC ....E...... 973 227-6882
Fairfield (G-3286)
Princeton Biopharma Strategies ....G...... 609 203-5303
Princeton (G-9094)
Princeton Enduring Biotech Inc ....G...... 732 406-3041
Monmouth Junction (G-6357)
Princeton Enduring Biotech Inc ....G...... 732 406-3041
Monmouth Junction (G-6358)
▲ Promius Pharma LLC ....D...... 609 282-1400
Princeton (G-9107)
▲ Prosweetz Ingredients Inc ....E...... 732 512-0886
Edison (G-2599)
Protoform Inc ....G...... 609 261-6920
Westampton (G-11916)
Ptc Therapeutics Inc ....B...... 908 222-7000
South Plainfield (G-10425)
Pts Intermediate Holdings LLC ....A...... 732 537-6200
Somerset (G-10160)
Purdue Pharma LP ....C...... 203 588-8000
Ewing (G-3046)
Q&Q Pharma Research Company ....G...... 973 267-0160
Morris Plains (G-6679)
Quagen Pharmaceuticals LLC ....F...... 973 228-9600
West Caldwell (G-11799)
Quagen Pharmaceuticals LLC ....F...... 973 228-9600
West Caldwell (G-11800)
Quantum Pharmaceuticals Inc ....G...... 973 222-6485
Sparta (G-10519)
Quatrx Pharmaceuticals Company ......D...... 734 913-9900
Florham Park (G-3517)
▲ Qugen Inc ....G...... 609 716-6300
Plainsboro (G-8898)
Quinnova Pharmaceuticals Inc ....E...... 877 660-6263
Chatham (G-1337)
Rafael Pharmaceuticals Inc ....F...... 609 409-7050
Cranbury (G-1874)
Ranbaxy USA Inc ....E...... 609 720-9200
Princeton (G-9109)
Ranx Pharmaceuticals Inc ....G...... 571 214-8989
Jamesburg (G-4689)
▲ Raritan Phrmctcals Incoporated ......C...... 732 238-1685
East Brunswick (G-2180)
▲ Rasi Laboratories Inc ....D...... 732 873-8500
Cranbury (G-1876)
Reed-Lane Inc ....C...... 973 709-1090
Wayne (G-11677)
Regado Biosciences Inc ....G...... 908 580-2109
Basking Ridge (G-204)
Regentree LLC ....G...... 609 734-4328
Princeton (G-9111)
Reliance Vitamin LLC ....C...... 732 537-1220
Edison (G-2603)
▲ Renaissance Lakewood LLC ....F...... 732 901-2052
Lakewood (G-5181)
Renaissance Lakewood LLC ....B...... 732 367-9000
Lakewood (G-5182)
Respirerx Pharmaceuticals Inc ....G...... 201 444-4947
Glen Rock (G-3828)
Riconpharma LLC ....E...... 973 627-4685
Denville (G-2055)
Rising Health LLC ....E...... 201 961-9000
Saddle Brook (G-9787)
Rising Pharmaceuticals Inc ....E...... 201 961-9000
Saddle Brook (G-9788)
Rotta Pharmaceuticals Inc ....G...... 732 751-9020
Freehold (G-3686)
Rouses Pt Pharmaceuticals LLC ....G...... 239 390-1495
Cranford (G-1926)
Royal Pharmaceuticals LLC ....G...... 732 292-2661
Manasquan (G-5879)
▲ Salix Pharmaceuticals Ltd ....C...... 866 246-8245
Bridgewater (G-886)
▲ Salus Pharma LLC ....F...... 732 329-8089
Monmouth Junction (G-6362)
▲ Sandoz Inc ....C...... 609 627-8500
Princeton (G-9115)
Sandoz Inc ....A...... 862 778-8300
East Hanover (G-2242)
Sanofi Inc ....B...... 800 981-2491
Bridgewater (G-887)
▲ Sanofi US Services Inc ....A...... 336 407-4994
Bridgewater (G-888)
Sanofi US Services Inc ....E...... 908 231-4000
Bridgewater (G-889)
Sanofi US Services Inc ....F...... 908 231-4000
Bridgewater (G-890)

Sanofi-Synthelabo Inc ....A...... 908 231-2000
Bridgewater (G-891)
Saxa Pharmaceuticals LLC ....G...... 862 571-7630
Holmdel (G-4529)
▲ Schering Berlin Inc ....G...... 862 404-3000
Whippany (G-12038)
Scherng-Plough Pdts Caribe Inc ....G...... 908 423-1000
Whitehouse Station (G-12063)
▲ Sciecure Pharma Inc ....E...... 732 329-8089
Monmouth Junction (G-6363)
Scynexis Inc ....F...... 201 884-5485
Jersey City (G-4825)
Secord Inc ....F...... 908 754-2147
Scotch Plains (G-9855)
Sensoredge Inc ....G...... 973 975-4163
Parsippany (G-8084)
Sentrimed Ltd Liability Co ....G...... 914 582-8631
Voorhees (G-11437)
Sharmatek Inc ....G...... 908 852-5087
Hackettstown (G-4036)
▲ Shasun USA Inc ....E...... 732 465-0700
Piscataway (G-8810)
▲ Siegfried USA Holding Inc ....E...... 856 678-3601
Pennsville (G-8594)
◆ Siegfried USA LLC ....C...... 856 678-3601
Pennsville (G-8595)
▲ Silab Inc ....E...... 732 335-1030
Hazlet (G-4283)
Sky Growth Intermediate ....B...... 201 802-4000
Woodcliff Lake (G-12201)
Snowdon Inc ....G...... 732 230-3796
Princeton (G-9119)
Solaris Pharma Corporation ....G...... 908 864-0404
Bridgewater (G-897)
Solgen Pharmaceuticals Inc ....E...... 732 983-6025
Edison (G-2624)
Soligenix Inc ....F...... 609 538-8200
Princeton (G-9120)
Soma Labs Inc ....F...... 732 271-3444
Middlesex (G-6199)
Spray-Tek Inc ....E...... 732 469-0050
Middlesex (G-6201)
Star Pharma Inc ....G...... 718 466-1790
East Brunswick (G-2187)
Steri-Pharma Inc ....D...... 201 857-8210
Paramus (G-7906)
Strides Pharma Inc ....G...... 609 773-5000
East Brunswick (G-2188)
Strive Pharmaceuticals Inc ....G...... 609 269-2001
East Brunswick (G-2189)
Sun Pharmaceutical Inds Inc ....E...... 313 871-8400
Princeton (G-9126)
Sun Pharmaceutical Inds Inc ....F...... 609 495-2800
Cranbury (G-1882)
▲ Sun Pharmaceutical Inds Inc ....B...... 609 495-2800
Cranbury (G-1883)
Sunovion Pharmaceuticals Inc ....D...... 201 592-2050
Fort Lee (G-3584)
▲ Sunrise Pharmaceutical Inc ....G...... 732 382-6085
Rahway (G-9224)
Sv Pharma Inc ....G...... 732 651-1336
East Brunswick (G-2192)
Svtc Pharma Inc ....G...... 201 652-0013
Ridgewood (G-9432)
Symbiomix Therapeutics LLC ....F...... 609 722-7250
Newark (G-7336)
▲ Synergetica International Inc ....G...... 732 780-5865
Marlboro (G-5960)
T and C Neuromax LLC ....G...... 201 447-2020
Ridgewood (G-9433)
Tap Pharmaceutical Products ....G...... 908 470-9700
Bedminster (G-285)
Taree Pharma LLC ....G...... 609 252-9596
Princeton (G-9129)
Targanta Therapeutics Corp ....D...... 973 290-6000
Parsippany (G-8097)
Taro Pharmaceuticals USA Inc ....E...... 609 655-9002
Cranbury (G-1884)
Teligent Inc ....C...... 856 697-1441
Buena (G-949)
Teligent Inc ....F...... 856 697-1441
Buena (G-950)
◆ Teva Api Inc ....E...... 201 307-6900
Parsippany (G-8098)
▲ Teva Pharmaceuticals ....F...... 888 838-2872
Parsippany (G-8099)
Teva Pharmaceuticals Usa Inc ....G...... 845 362-1100
Parsippany (G-8100)
Teva Pharmaceuticals Usa Inc ....C...... 973 575-2775
Fairfield (G-3323)

Teva Womens Health Inc ....G...... 201 930-3300
Somerset (G-10186)
▲ Therapeutic Proteins Inc ....F...... 312 620-1500
Piscataway (G-8824)
Thrombogenics Inc ....E...... 732 590-2900
Iselin (G-4649)
Topifram Laboratories Inc ....E...... 201 894-9020
Englewood Cliffs (G-2982)
Torrent Pharma Inc ....F...... 269 544-2299
Basking Ridge (G-207)
Tri-State Pharmaceutical LLC ....G...... 732 905-7592
Lakewood (G-5197)
Triarco Industries LLC ....E...... 973 942-5100
Cranbury (G-1885)
▲ Trigen Laboratories LLC ....A...... 732 721-0070
Bridgewater (G-904)
Tris Pharma Inc ....D...... 732 940-0358
Monmouth Junction (G-6365)
Tris Pharma Inc ....C...... 732 940-2800
Monmouth Junction (G-6366)
▲ Tulex Pharmaceuticals Inc ....F...... 609 619-3098
Cranbury (G-1888)
TWI Pharmaceuticals Usa Inc ....G...... 201 762-1410
Paramus (G-7911)
Unipack Inc ....F...... 973 450-9880
Belleville (G-321)
Unitao Nutraceuticals LLC ....G...... 973 983-1121
Rockaway (G-9620)
▼ Universal Prtein Spplmnts Corp ......D...... 732 545-3130
New Brunswick (G-7010)
Urigen Pharmaceuticals Inc ....G...... 732 640-0160
North Brunswick (G-7544)
Valeant Phrmctcals N Amer LLC ....E...... 908 927-1400
Bridgewater (G-908)
Valeritas Holdings Inc ....G...... 908 927-9920
Bridgewater (G-909)
Validus Pharmaceuticals LLC ....F...... 973 265-2777
Parsippany (G-8107)
Vascure Natural LLC ....G...... 732 528-6492
Point Pleasant Boro (G-8942)
Vensun Pharmaceuticals Inc ....F...... 908 278-8386
Princeton (G-9135)
Vermeer Pharma LLC ....G...... 973 270-0073
Morristown (G-6748)
Vertice Pharma LLC ....C...... 877 530-1633
New Providence (G-7060)
Vgyaan Pharmaceuticals LLC ....G...... 609 452-2770
Princeton (G-9137)
Vistapharm Inc ....G...... 908 376-1622
New Providence (G-7061)
▲ Vita-Pure Inc ....E...... 908 245-1212
Roselle (G-9686)
Vitacare Pharma LLC ....G...... 908 754-1792
South Plainfield (G-10452)
Vitaquest International LLC ....F...... 973 575-9200
Fairfield (G-3344)
▲ Vitaquest International LLC ....B...... 973 575-9200
West Caldwell (G-11807)
Vs Hercules LLC ....G...... 201 868-5959
North Bergen (G-7492)
Walgreen Eastern Co Inc ....E...... 973 728-3172
West Milford (G-11858)
Walgreen Eastern Co Inc ....E...... 609 522-1291
Wildwood (G-12075)
Warner Chilcott (us) LLC ....G...... 973 442-3200
Morristown (G-6750)
▲ Warner Chilcott (us) LLC ....D...... 862 261-7000
Parsippany (G-8110)
Warner Chilcott Corporation ....E...... 862 261-7000
Rockaway (G-9623)
▲ Watson Laboratories Inc ....C...... 951 493-5300
Parsippany (G-8112)
Windsor Labs LLC ....G...... 609 301-6446
East Windsor (G-2370)
Windtree Therapeutics Inc ....F...... 973 339-2889
Totowa (G-10986)
▲ Wyeth Holdings LLC ....E...... 973 660-5000
Madison (G-5737)
Wyeth LLC ....B...... 973 660-5000
Madison (G-5738)
Wyeth-Ayerst (asia) Ltd ....G...... 973 660-5500
Madison (G-5739)
Wyeth-Ayerst Pharmaceutical ....F...... 732 274-4221
Monmouth Junction (G-6372)
Wynnpharm Inc ....G...... 732 409-1005
Freehold (G-3695)
Zenia Pharma LLC ....G...... 973 246-9718
Clifton (G-1746)
Zenith Laboratories Inc ....G...... 201 767-1700
Northvale (G-7613)

Zenith Laboratories Inc ....C .. 201 767-1700
Northvale **(G-7614)**

Zoetis Inc ....B .. 973 822-7000
Parsippany **(G-8119)**

Zoetis LLC ....B .. 973 822-7000
Parsippany **(G-8120)**

◆ Zoetis Products LLC ....C .. 973 660-5000
Florham Park **(G-3525)**

Zoetis Products LLC ....F .. 973 660-5000
Bridgewater **(G-910)**

▲ Zydus Pharmaceuticals USA Inc ...E .. 609 730-1900
Pennington **(G-8463)**

2835 Diagnostic Substances

Admera Health LLC ....G .. 908 222-0533
South Plainfield **(G-10321)**

Akers Biosciences Inc ....E .. 856 848-8698
West Deptford **(G-11814)**

Alere Inc ....B .. 732 620-4244
Freehold **(G-3636)**

Alere Inc ....B .. 732 358-5921
Freehold **(G-3637)**

▲ Armkel LLC ....A .. 609 683-5900
Princeton **(G-9010)**

Arthur A Topilow William Lrner ....E .. 732 528-0760
Manasquan **(G-5868)**

Ascensia Diabetes Care US Inc ......C .. 973 560-6500
Parsippany **(G-7952)**

Astral Diagnostics Inc ....G .. 856 224-0900
Paulsboro **(G-8413)**

Baxter Healthcare Corporation ......C .. 732 225-4700
Edison **(G-2470)**

Biomedtrix LLC ....G .. 973 331-7800
Boonton **(G-558)**

Biomedtrix LLC ....F .. 973 331-7800
Whippany **(G-12012)**

▲ Biotech Atlantic Inc ....F .. 732 389-4789
Eatontown **(G-2385)**

▲ Bracco Diagnostics Inc ....C .. 609 514-2200
Monroe Township **(G-6378)**

▲ Bracco USA Inc ....C .. 609 514-2200
Monroe Township **(G-6379)**

Cenogenics Corporation ....G .. 732 536-6457
Morganville **(G-6638)**

DMS Laboratories Inc ....G .. 908 782-3353
Flemington **(G-3436)**

Dpc Cirrus ....F .. 973 927-2828
Flanders **(G-3405)**

▲ Dsrv Inc ....F .. 973 631-1200
Budd Lake **(G-927)**

Ess Group Inc ....G .. 609 755-3139
Southampton **(G-10471)**

Fluoropharma Medical Inc ....G .. 973 744-1565
Montclair **(G-6414)**

Foundation For Embryonic ....G .. 973 656-2847
Basking Ridge **(G-187)**

Genzyme Corporation ....G .. 973 256-2106
Totowa **(G-10948)**

▲ Immunomedics Inc ....C .. 973 605-8200
Morris Plains **(G-6671)**

Laboratory Diagnostics Co Inc ......F .. 732 536-6300
Morganville **(G-6646)**

◆ Mindray Ds Usa Inc ....A .. 201 995-8000
Mahwah **(G-5791)**

▲ Ortho-Clinical Diagnostics Inc ......A .. 908 218-8000
Raritan **(G-9314)**

Petnet Solutions Inc ....G .. 865 218-2000
Hackensack **(G-3962)**

▲ Pharmaseq Inc ....G .. 732 355-0100
Monmouth Junction **(G-6355)**

Princeton Biomeditech Corp ....E .. 908 281-0112
Skillman **(G-10036)**

▲ Princeton Biomeditech Corp ....D .. 732 274-1000
Monmouth Junction **(G-6356)**

▲ Quest Diagnostics Incorporated ......A .. 973 520-2700
Secaucus **(G-9915)**

▲ Recombine LLC ....G .. 646 470-7422
Livingston **(G-5557)**

Sensonics Inc ....F .. 856 547-7702
Haddon Heights **(G-4051)**

Worthington Biochemical Corp ....E .. 732 942-1660
Lakewood **(G-5207)**

2836 Biological Prdts, Exc Diagnostic Substances

A J P Scientific Inc ....G .. 973 472-7200
Clifton **(G-1552)**

Adma Biologics Inc ....D .. 201 478-5552
Ramsey **(G-9230)**

Brainstorm Cell Thrpeutics Inc ......E .. 201 488-0460
Hackensack **(G-3885)**

Devatal Inc ....G .. 609 586-1575
Trenton **(G-11054)**

Difco Laboratories Inc ....G .. 410 316-4113
Franklin Lakes **(G-3613)**

DSM Nutritional Products LLC ......C .. 908 475-7093
Belvidere **(G-369)**

◆ DSM Nutritional Products LLC ....B .. 800 526-0189
Parsippany **(G-7989)**

Eli Lilly and Company ....E .. 908 704-1807
Branchburg **(G-656)**

Epicore Networks USA Inc ....E .. 609 267-9118
Mount Holly **(G-6770)**

Genzyme Corporation ....G .. 973 256-2106
Totowa **(G-10948)**

Imclone LLC ....F .. 908 218-9588
Branchburg **(G-666)**

◆ Imclone Systems LLC ....C .. 908 541-8000
Bridgewater **(G-844)**

Imclone Systems LLC ....D .. 908 218-0147
Branchburg **(G-667)**

Inspire Pharmaceuticals Inc ....C .. 908 423-1000
Whitehouse Station **(G-12052)**

▼ Integra Lfscnces Holdings Corp ....C .. 609 275-0500
Plainsboro **(G-8887)**

Integra Lifesciences Corp ....D .. 609 275-0500
Plainsboro **(G-8889)**

Intervet Inc ....G .. 908 423-6273
Madison **(G-5725)**

Kedrion Biopharma Inc ....D .. 201 242-8900
Fort Lee **(G-3563)**

Lifecell Corporation ....G .. 908 947-1100
Branchburg **(G-674)**

▲ Lifecell Corporation ....G .. 908 947-1100
Branchburg **(G-675)**

Medchem Express LLC ....G .. 732 783-7915
Monmouth Junction **(G-6351)**

Merck & Co Inc ....B .. 908 740-4000
Kenilworth **(G-4974)**

Merck & Co Inc ....D .. 908 740-4000
Rahway **(G-9212)**

Monmouth Bioproducts LLC ....G .. 732 863-0300
Freehold **(G-3671)**

Nathji Plus Inc ....G .. 609 877-7600
Willingboro **(G-12121)**

Novaera Solutions Inc ....D .. 732 452-3605
Iselin **(G-4637)**

Organon USA Inc ....G .. 908 423-1000
Whitehouse Station **(G-12059)**

Princeton Enduring Biotech Inc ....G .. 732 406-3041
Monmouth Junction **(G-6358)**

Princeton Enduring Biotech Inc ....G .. 732 406-3041
Monmouth Junction **(G-6357)**

Princeton Plasma Physics ....F .. 609 243-2000
Princeton **(G-9098)**

Seqirus USA Inc ....F .. 908 739-0200
Summit **(G-10655)**

Soligenix Inc ....F .. 609 538-8200
Princeton **(G-9120)**

Teligent Inc ....F .. 856 697-1441
Buena **(G-950)**

Weiling Yang ....G .. 201 440-5329
Ridgefield Park **(G-9418)**

Worthington Biochemical Corp ....E .. 732 942-1660
Lakewood **(G-5207)**

▲ Wyeth Holdings LLC ....E .. 973 660-5000
Madison **(G-5737)**

Zymes LLC ....F .. 201 727-1520
Hasbrouck Heights **(G-4204)**

2841 Soap & Detergents

▲ Americare Laboratories Ltd ....E .. 973 279-5100
Paterson **(G-8210)**

Ardmore Inc ....G .. 973 481-2406
Newark **(G-7091)**

Arol Chemical Products Co ....G .. 973 344-1510
Newark **(G-7094)**

Atlantic Associates Intl Inc ....F .. 856 662-1717
Pennsauken **(G-8481)**

Aura Detergent LLC ....E .. 718 824-2162
Newark **(G-7099)**

Cantol Inc ....E .. 609 846-7912
Wildwood **(G-12070)**

Capital Soap Products LLC ....F .. 973 333-6100
Paterson **(G-8230)**

Cavalier Chemical Co Inc ....E .. 908 558-0110
Short Hills **(G-9975)**

◆ Church & Dwight Co Inc ....B .. 609 806-1200
Ewing **(G-3009)**

◆ Dermarite Industries LLC ....C .. 973 247-3491
North Bergen **(G-7446)**

Detergent 20 LLC ....F .. 732 545-0200
New Brunswick **(G-6954)**

Dynamic Blending Company Inc ....F .. 856 541-6626
Camden **(G-1060)**

Ecolab Inc ....C .. 856 596-4845
Moorestown **(G-6574)**

Epic Holding Inc ....E .. 732 249-6867
Morristown **(G-6708)**

▲ Fiabila USA Inc ....E .. 973 659-9510
Mine Hill **(G-6326)**

Hy-Test Packaging Corp ....G .. 973 754-7000
Paterson **(G-8291)**

▲ Inopak Ltd ....F .. 973 962-1121
Ringwood **(G-9450)**

Interntional Cnsld Chemex Corp ......E .. 732 828-7676
New Brunswick **(G-6969)**

Inventek Colloidal Clrs LLC ....E .. 856 206-0058
Mount Laurel **(G-6808)**

Kempak Industries ....F .. 908 687-4188
Springfield **(G-10561)**

Kync Design LLC ....G .. 201 293-4677
Secaucus **(G-9900)**

Made Solutions LLC ....G .. 201 254-3693
Fair Lawn **(G-3101)**

Magnuson Products ....F .. 973 472-9292
Clifton **(G-1667)**

Pilot Chemical Company Ohio ....F .. 732 634-6613
Avenel **(G-145)**

Procter & Gamble Mfg Co ....D .. 732 602-4500
Avenel **(G-148)**

S W I International Inc ....G .. 973 334-2525
Boonton **(G-582)**

Sanitary Soap Company ....G .. 973 279-8500
Paterson **(G-8378)**

Si Packaging LLC ....F .. 973 869-9920
Rutherford **(G-9744)**

Stanson Corporation ....D .. 973 344-8666
Kearny **(G-4916)**

▲ Technick Products Inc ....F .. 908 791-0400
South Plainfield **(G-10438)**

▲ Unilever United States Inc ....A .. 201 894-4000
Englewood Cliffs **(G-2986)**

Univerclean Ltd ....G .. 201 674-1563
Fair Lawn **(G-3122)**

2842 Spec Cleaning, Polishing & Sanitation Preparations

3M Company ....B .. 973 884-2500
Whippany **(G-12004)**

▼ A L Wilson Chemical Co ....F .. 201 997-3300
Kearny **(G-4857)**

Advanced Sewer ....F .. 973 278-1948
Woodland Park **(G-12208)**

▲ Agate Lacquer Tri-Nat LLC ....G .. 732 968-1080
Middlesex **(G-6145)**

▲ Allison Corp ....G .. 973 992-3800
Livingston **(G-5523)**

◆ Amano USA Holdings Inc ....G .. 973 403-1900
Roseland **(G-9643)**

Americhem Enterprises Inc ....G .. 732 363-4840
Lakewood **(G-5072)**

▼ Aqua Products Inc ....E .. 856 829-8444
Cinnaminson **(G-1446)**

Arol Chemical Products Co ....G .. 973 344-1510
Newark **(G-7094)**

Associated Cleaning Systems ....G .. 201 530-9197
Teaneck **(G-10742)**

Astra Cleaners of Hazlet ....G .. 732 264-4144
Hazlet **(G-4270)**

Atlantic Associates Intl Inc ....F .. 856 662-1717
Pennsauken **(G-8481)**

▲ Benckiser N Reckitt Amer Inc ....A .. 973 404-2600
Parsippany **(G-7960)**

Brasscraft Manufacturing Co ....G .. 856 241-7700
Swedesboro **(G-10685)**

Cantol Inc ....E .. 609 846-7912
Wildwood **(G-12070)**

Capital Soap Products LLC ....F .. 973 333-6100
Paterson **(G-8230)**

Cavalier Chemical Co Inc ....E .. 908 558-0110
Short Hills **(G-9975)**

◆ Chemetall US Inc ....D .. 908 464-6900
New Providence **(G-7033)**

◆ Church & Dwight Co Inc ....B .. 609 806-1200
Ewing **(G-3009)**

Clenesco Products Corp ....F .. 908 245-5255
Roselle **(G-9665)**

SIC

▲ Cobra Products Inc ....D 856 241-7700
  Swedesboro *(G-10688)*
Edwards Creative Products Inc ....F 856 665-3200
  Cherry Hill *(G-1361)*
◆ Envirochem Inc ....E 732 238-6700
  South River *(G-10461)*
Ep Systems Inc ....G 570 424-0581
  Hackettstown *(G-4005)*
Epic Holding Inc ....G 732 249-6867
  Morristown *(G-6708)*
Fabric Chemical Corporation ....G 201 432-0440
  Jersey City *(G-4750)*
Fine Organics Corporation ....F 973 478-7690
  Clifton *(G-1620)*
▼ Frank B Ross Co Inc ....F 732 669-0810
  Rahway *(G-9190)*
◆ Global Spclty Products-Usa Inc ....F 609 518-7577
  Mount Holly *(G-6771)*
Green Power Chemical LLC ....F 973 770-5600
  Hopatcong *(G-4536)*
Harvester Inc ....E 201 445-1122
  Irvington *(G-4588)*
Horizon Products NJ LLC ....G 201 773-7015
  Ridgewood *(G-9425)*
Houghton Chemical Corporation ......F 201 460-8071
  Carlstadt *(G-1170)*
International Products Corp ....F 609 386-8770
  Burlington *(G-979)*
Interntional Cnsld Chemex Corp .....E 732 828-7676
  New Brunswick *(G-6969)*
◆ Interntional Specialty Pdts Inc ....A 859 815-3333
  Wayne *(G-11653)*
James R Macauley Inc ....G 856 767-3474
  Waterford Works *(G-11598)*
Jobe Industries Inc ....G 908 862-0400
  Linden *(G-5392)*
◆ L & R Manufacturing Co Inc ....D 201 991-5330
  Kearny *(G-4894)*
Made Solutions LLC ....G 201 254-3693
  Fair Lawn *(G-3101)*
Magnuson Products ....F 973 472-9292
  Clifton *(G-1667)*
Matchless United Companies ....G 908 862-7300
  Linden *(G-5406)*
▲ Mennen Company ....B 973 630-1500
  Morristown *(G-6726)*
▲ Menshen Packaging USA Inc ....D 201 445-7436
  Waldwick *(G-11448)*
Microgen Inc ....G 973 575-9025
  West Caldwell *(G-11791)*
National Auto Detailing Netwrk ......E 856 931-5529
  Bellmawr *(G-348)*
Penetone Corporation ....E 201 567-3000
  Carlstadt *(G-1199)*
PQ Corporation ....E 732 750-9040
  Avenel *(G-146)*
▲ Prestige Laboratories Inc ....E 973 772-8922
  East Rutherford *(G-2318)*
Q-Pak Corporation ....E 973 483-4404
  Newark *(G-7281)*
Ramblewood Cleaners Inc ....G 856 235-6051
  Mount Laurel *(G-6834)*
Raybeam Manufacturing Corp ......E 201 941-4529
  Ridgefield *(G-9382)*
RB Manufacturing LLC ....C 908 533-2000
  Hillsborough *(G-4367)*
RB Manufacturing LLC ....C 973 404-2600
  Parsippany *(G-8076)*
Reckitt Benckiser LLC ....C 973 404-2600
  Montvale *(G-6471)*
◆ Reckitt Benckiser LLC ....B 973 404-2600
  Parsippany *(G-8077)*
Ronell Industries Inc ....B 908 245-5255
  Roselle *(G-9682)*
▲ Royce Associates A Ltd Partnr ......D 201 438-5200
  East Rutherford *(G-2322)*
Schulke Inc ....G 973 521-7163
  Fairfield *(G-3303)*
Stanson Corporation ....G 973 344-8666
  Kearny *(G-4916)*
Stepan Company ....D 201 845-3030
  Maywood *(G-6061)*
Stepan Company ....D 609 298-1222
  Bordentown *(G-611)*
Sterigenics US LLC ....G 856 241-8880
  Swedesboro *(G-10730)*
Trap-Zap Environmental Systems ....E 201 251-9970
  Wyckoff *(G-12266)*
Trim Brush Company Inc ....G 973 887-2525
  East Hanover *(G-2247)*

Venus Laboratories Inc ....E 973 257-8983
  Parsippany *(G-8109)*
Zoono USA LLC ....G 732 722-8757
  Shrewsbury *(G-10014)*

2843 Surface Active & Finishing Agents, Sulfonated Oils

Agilis Chemicals Inc ....G 973 910-2424
  Rockaway *(G-9548)*
AIG Industrial Group Inc ....F 201 767-7300
  Northvale *(G-7569)*
American Gas & Chemical Co Ltd ....E 201 767-7300
  Northvale *(G-7572)*
Arol Chemical Products Co ....G 973 344-1510
  Newark *(G-7094)*
Aromac Inc ....G 973 365-1090
  Clifton *(G-1566)*
▲ Atlas Refinery Inc ....E 973 589-2002
  Newark *(G-7096)*
BASF Corporation ....D 908 689-2500
  Washington *(G-11576)*
◆ BASF Corporation ....B 973 245-6000
  Florham Park *(G-3492)*
▲ Basfin Corporation ....A 973 245-6000
  Florham Park *(G-3493)*
Commercial Products Co Inc ....F 973 427-6887
  Hawthorne *(G-4227)*
◆ G Holdings Inc ....G 973 628-3000
  Parsippany *(G-8019)*
◆ G-I Holdings Inc ....G 973 628-3000
  Wayne *(G-11638)*
◆ Interntional Specialty Pdts Inc ......A 859 815-3333
  Wayne *(G-11653)*
◆ Lanxess Sybron Chemicals Inc .....C 609 893-1100
  Birmingham *(G-468)*
▲ Meson Group Inc ....E 201 767-7300
  Northvale *(G-7591)*
Nutech Corp ....G 908 707-2097
  Franklin Lakes *(G-3622)*
◆ Pariser Industries Inc ....E 973 569-9090
  Paterson *(G-8360)*
▲ Pflaumer Brothers Inc ....E 609 883-4610
  Ewing *(G-3042)*
Solv-TEC Incorporated ....E 609 261-4242
  Medford *(G-6082)*
Stepan Company ....D 609 298-1222
  Bordentown *(G-611)*

2844 Perfumes, Cosmetics & Toilet Preparations

▲ A D M Tronics Unlimited Inc ....E 201 767-6040
  Northvale *(G-7566)*
ABG Lab LLC ....G 973 559-5663
  Fair Lawn *(G-3073)*
Acupac Packaging Inc ....C 201 529-3434
  Mahwah *(G-5743)*
Adorage Inc ....G 201 886-7000
  Edgewater *(G-2431)*
Adron Inc ....G 973 334-1600
  Boonton *(G-551)*
◆ ADS Sales Co Inc ....E 732 591-0500
  Morganville *(G-6635)*
◆ Agilex Flavors Fragrances Inc ....G 732 885-0702
  Piscataway *(G-8728)*
▼ AlSha&anna Nation of Trends ......G 201 951-8197
  Rahway *(G-9173)*
Alkaline Corporation ....G 732 531-7830
  Eatontown *(G-2380)*
Aloe Science Inc ....E 908 231-8888
  Branchburg *(G-631)*
American Prvate Label Pdts LLC ....G 845 733-8151
  Franklin *(G-3594)*
American Spraytech LLC ....G 908 725-6060
  Branchburg *(G-634)*
▲ Americare Laboratories Ltd ....E 973 279-5100
  Paterson *(G-8210)*
Anatolian Naturals Inc ....G 201 893-0142
  Fort Lee *(G-3544)*
▲ Andrea Aromatics Inc ....E 609 695-7710
  Trenton *(G-11018)*
▲ AP Deauville LLC ....E 732 545-0200
  New Brunswick *(G-6945)*
▼ Arch Personal Care Products LP ....E 908 226-9329
  South Plainfield *(G-10330)*
▲ Ariel Laboratories LP ....G 908 755-4080
  South Plainfield *(G-10331)*
▲ Armkel LLC ....A 609 683-5900
  Princeton *(G-9010)*

Art of Shaving - Fl LLC ....G 732 410-2520
  Freehold *(G-3639)*
Ascent Aromatics Inc ....G 908 755-0120
  South Plainfield *(G-10332)*
Atara LLC ....G 916 765-2217
  Union City *(G-11243)*
Atlantis Aromatics Inc ....G 732 919-1112
  Wall Township *(G-11464)*
Avon Products Inc ....G 973 779-5590
  Clifton *(G-1570)*
B Witching Bath Company LLC ......G 973 423-1820
  Hawthorne *(G-4219)*
Barmensen Labs LLC ....G 732 593-3515
  Old Bridge *(G-7774)*
▲ Batallure Beauty LLC ....G 609 716-1200
  Princeton *(G-9013)*
▲ Beilis Development LLC ....F 862 203-3650
  Fair Lawn *(G-3082)*
Bellevue Parfums USA LLC ....F 908 262-7774
  Hillsborough *(G-4319)*
Bellwood Aeromatics Inc ....G 201 670-4617
  Fairfield *(G-3145)*
▲ Bentley Laboratories LLC ....C 732 512-0200
  Edison *(G-2472)*
▼ Bio-Nature Labs Ltd Lblty Co ......E 732 738-5550
  Edison *(G-2474)*
▲ Biogenesis Inc ....F 201 678-1992
  Hackensack *(G-3882)*
Bristol-Myers Squibb Company ......E 212 546-4000
  Hillside *(G-4399)*
▲ Caboki LLC ....G 609 642-2108
  Cranbury *(G-1819)*
▲ Cadbury Adams USA LLC ....E 973 503-2000
  East Hanover *(G-2203)*
▲ Cadence Distributors LLC ....G 646 808-3031
  Hackensack *(G-3889)*
Caolion BNC Co Ltd ....C 201 641-4709
  Ridgefield Park *(G-9399)*
Caret Corporation ....G 973 423-5999
  Little Falls *(G-5472)*
▲ Carole Cosmetics LLC ....E 973 283-2893
  Butler *(G-1000)*
CCA Industries Inc ....E 201 935-3232
  Lyndhurst *(G-5676)*
▲ Cei Holdings Inc ....E 732 888-7788
  Holmdel *(G-4511)*
Chanel Inc ....A 732 885-5500
  Piscataway *(G-8748)*
▲ Charabot & Co Inc ....F 201 812-2762
  Budd Lake *(G-926)*
▲ Chemaid Laboratories Inc ....C 201 843-3300
  Saddle Brook *(G-9758)*
Cherri Stone Interactive LLC ....G 844 843-7765
  Lakewood *(G-5092)*
Cheveux Cosmetics Corporation ....D 732 446-7516
  Englishtown *(G-2990)*
▲ Christine Valmy Inc ....E 973 575-1050
  Pine Brook *(G-8693)*
◆ Church & Dwight Co Inc ....B 609 806-1200
  Ewing *(G-3009)*
Cococare Products Inc ....G 973 989-8880
  Dover *(G-2081)*
Colgate-Palmolive Company ....B 732 878-6062
  Highland Park *(G-4302)*
Colgate-Palmolive Company ....A 732 878-7500
  Piscataway *(G-8751)*
Colgate-Palmolive Company ....E 609 239-6001
  Burlington *(G-966)*
Conair Corporation ....C 609 426-1300
  East Windsor *(G-2354)*
Conopco Inc ....E 856 722-1664
  Mount Laurel *(G-6790)*
Continental Aromatics ....E 973 238-9300
  Hawthorne *(G-4229)*
▲ Contract Filling Inc ....C 973 433-0053
  Cedar Grove *(G-1275)*
Cosmetic Coatings Inc ....E 201 438-7150
  Carlstadt *(G-1150)*
▲ Cosmetic Concepts Inc ....C 973 546-1234
  Garfield *(G-3727)*
▲ Cosmetic Essence LLC ....C 732 888-7788
  Holmdel *(G-4512)*
Cosmetic Essence LLC ....D 201 941-9800
  Ridgefield *(G-9357)*
Cosmetic Essence Inc ....C 732 888-7788
  Holmdel *(G-4513)*
▲ Cosrich Group Inc ....E 866 771-7473
  Bloomfield *(G-509)*
Coty US LLC ....D 973 490-8700
  Morris Plains *(G-6658)*

Company	Code	Phone
▲ Cpl Aromas Inc	F	732 469-0680
Scotch Plains *(G-9848)*		
Creative Concepts Corporation	G	201 750-1234
Norwood *(G-7620)*		
▼ Custom Essence	F	732 249-6405
Somerset *(G-10088)*		
Custom Liners Inc	G	732 940-0084
Upper Saddle River *(G-11277)*		
◆ Davion Inc	E	973 485-0793
North Brunswick *(G-7514)*		
▲ Davlyn Industries Inc	C	609 655-5974
East Windsor *(G-2356)*		
Devon Products	G	732 438-3855
Pompton Plains *(G-8957)*		
◆ Disposable Hygiene LLC	G	973 779-1982
Clifton *(G-1601)*		
Dnp Foods America Ltd Lblty Co	G	201 654-5581
Waldwick *(G-11445)*		
▲ Dosis Fragrance LLC	G	718 874-0074
Newark *(G-7142)*		
▲ Drom International Inc	E	973 316-8400
Towaco *(G-10994)*		
▲ Ebin New York Inc	E	201 288-8887
Teterboro *(G-10794)*		
Edgewell Personal Care LLC	E	973 753-3000
Cedar Knolls *(G-1310)*		
Edgewell Personal Care LLC	C	201 785-8000
Allendale *(G-9)*		
▲ Encore International LLC	F	973 423-3880
Hawthorne *(G-4231)*		
▲ Englewood Lab LLC	C	201 567-2267
Englewood *(G-2891)*		
◆ ET Browne Drug Co Inc	D	201 894-9020
Englewood Cliffs *(G-2959)*		
Excell Brands Ltd Liability Co	G	908 561-1130
Princeton *(G-9043)*		
Fantasia Industries Corp	E	201 261-7070
Paramus *(G-7869)*		
▲ Flavor & Fragrance Spc Inc	D	201 828-9400
Mahwah *(G-5773)*		
▲ Fragrance Exchange Inc	G	732 641-2210
Monroe Township *(G-6382)*		
Fragrance Factory Inc	G	973 835-2002
Pompton Plains *(G-8959)*		
◆ Fragrance Resources Inc	F	973 777-2979
Hazlet *(G-4274)*		
Fragrance Resources Inc	D	973 458-5231
Keyport *(G-5018)*		
▼ Fragrance Solutions Corp	G	732 832-7800
South Plainfield *(G-10368)*		
▲ French Color Fragrance Co Inc	E	201 567-6883
Englewood *(G-2898)*		
Gallant Laboratories Inc	G	609 654-4146
Marlton *(G-5976)*		
▲ Gel Concepts LLC	E	973 884-8995
Whippany *(G-12022)*		
◆ Gentek Inc	C	973 515-0900
Parsippany *(G-8024)*		
Givaudan Fragrances Corp	C	973 448-6500
Budd Lake *(G-930)*		
Grenade Supply Co	G	267 968-3115
Lambertville *(G-5213)*		
Grow Company Inc	E	201 941-8777
Ridgefield *(G-9363)*		
▲ Hair Systems Inc	D	732 446-2202
Englishtown *(G-2994)*		
Health and Natural Beauty USA	F	732 640-1830
Piscataway *(G-8772)*		
Hudson Cosmetic Mfg Corp	D	973 472-2323
Clifton *(G-1644)*		
Hy-Test Packaging Corp	G	973 754-7000
Paterson *(G-8291)*		
Imaan Trading Inc	G	201 779-2062
Jersey City *(G-4767)*		
▼ Imperial Dax Co Inc	E	973 227-6105
Fairfield *(G-3226)*		
Imperial Drug & Spice Corp	G	201 348-1551
West New York *(G-11867)*		
▲ Innovative Cosmtc Concepts LLC	F	212 391-8110
Edison *(G-2541)*		
▲ Innovative Cosmtc Concepts LLC	D	973 225-0264
Clifton *(G-1647)*		
Intarome Fragrance Corporation	D	201 767-8700
Norwood *(G-7625)*		
Inter Parfums Inc	E	609 860-1967
Dayton *(G-1971)*		
▲ Interfashion Cosmetics Corp	E	201 288-5858
Teterboro *(G-10799)*		
International Aromatics Inc	F	201 964-0900
Moonachie *(G-6523)*		
▲ International Beauty Products	F	973 575-6400
Pine Brook *(G-8707)*		
Interntnal Flvors Frgrnces Inc	C	732 264-4500
Union Beach *(G-11236)*		
Interntnal Flvors Frgrnces Inc	C	732 264-4500
Hazlet *(G-4276)*		
Interntonal Fragrance Tech Inc	E	770 345-3079
Piscataway *(G-8783)*		
Isp Chemicals LLC	E	973 635-1551
Chatham *(G-1330)*		
Jersey Shore Cosmetics LLC	G	908 500-9954
Flemington *(G-3451)*		
Jnj International Inv LLC	G	732 524-0400
New Brunswick *(G-6973)*		
Johnson & Johnson	D	732 422-5000
North Brunswick *(G-7522)*		
◆ Johnson & Johnson	A	732 524-0400
New Brunswick *(G-6974)*		
Johnson & Johnson	C	908 722-9319
Raritan *(G-9311)*		
Johnson & Johnson	C	908 874-1000
Morris Plains *(G-6673)*		
Johnson & Johnson	C	732 524-0400
New Brunswick *(G-6975)*		
▲ June Jacobs Labs LLC	E	201 329-9100
Moonachie *(G-6526)*		
Klabin Fragrances Inc	F	973 857-3600
Cedar Grove *(G-1286)*		
Kobo Products Inc	E	908 941-3406
South Plainfield *(G-10394)*		
Kobo Products Inc	E	908 757-0033
South Plainfield *(G-10395)*		
◆ Kobo Products Inc	E	908 757-0033
South Plainfield *(G-10393)*		
Lippman Enterprises LLC	E	732 316-4946
Sayreville *(G-9829)*		
LOreal Usa Inc	C	732 499-6617
Clark *(G-1505)*		
LOreal Usa Inc	D	212 818-1500
Clark *(G-1506)*		
LOreal Usa Inc	D	732 499-6690
Clark *(G-1507)*		
LOreal Usa Inc	A	609 860-7500
Cranbury *(G-1855)*		
LOreal USA Products Inc	G	732 873-3520
Jersey City *(G-4779)*		
Lvmh Fragrance Brands US LLC	G	212 931-2668
Edison *(G-2561)*		
MAC Cosmetics Inc	F	856 661-9024
Cherry Hill *(G-1393)*		
Maje Systems Inc	G	856 845-5363
Woodbury *(G-12164)*		
Mastertaste Inc	F	201 373-1111
Teterboro *(G-10805)*		
◆ Medallion International Inc	F	973 616-3401
Pompton Plains *(G-8962)*		
▲ Mennen Company	B	973 630-1500
Morristown *(G-6726)*		
Merck & Co Inc	B	908 740-4000
Kenilworth *(G-4974)*		
Merck & Co Inc	D	908 740-4000
Rahway *(G-9212)*		
Mid Ocean Partners	D	908 707-0100
Branchburg *(G-681)*		
▲ Millennium Research LLC	G	908 867-7646
Long Valley *(G-5639)*		
▲ Mycone Dental Supply Co Inc	C	856 663-4700
Gibbstown *(G-3792)*		
Nature Labs LLC	G	856 839-0400
Vineland *(G-11384)*		
Nellsam Group Inc	G	201 951-9459
Cliffside Park *(G-1543)*		
New Manna Inc	G	973 675-8561
East Orange *(G-2261)*		
▼ New World International Inc	F	973 881-8100
Paterson *(G-8350)*		
New York Botany Inc	E	201 564-7444
Northvale *(G-7597)*		
▲ Nmr Manufacturing LLC	G	908 769-3234
South Plainfield *(G-10413)*		
▲ Novapac Laboratories Inc	F	973 414-8800
Lincoln Park *(G-5331)*		
▲ Nu-World Corporation	C	732 541-6300
Carteret *(G-1264)*		
Nu-World Corporation	G	732 541-6300
Edison *(G-2586)*		
▲ Omega Packaging Corp	D	973 890-9505
Totowa *(G-10959)*		
▲ Organics Corporation America	E	973 890-9002
Totowa *(G-10960)*		
◆ Pantina Cosmetics Inc	E	201 288-7767
Teterboro *(G-10808)*		
▲ Paramount Cosmetics Inc	D	973 472-2323
Clifton *(G-1690)*		
Perfumania Inc	G	732 493-4116
Tinton Falls *(G-10843)*		
Peter Thomas Roth Labs LLC	C	201 329-9100
Saddle Brook *(G-9782)*		
Pfizer Inc	D	973 739-0430
Parsippany *(G-8061)*		
▲ Precious Cosmetics Packaging	F	973 478-4633
Lodi *(G-5597)*		
Premier Consumer Products Inc	G	201 568-9700
Englewood *(G-2923)*		
▲ Premier Specialties Inc	E	732 469-6615
Middlesex *(G-6190)*		
▲ Presperse Corporation	E	732 356-5200
Somerset *(G-10157)*		
Procter & Gamble Mfg Co	D	732 602-4500
Avenel *(G-148)*		
▲ Product Club Corp	F	973 664-0565
Rockaway *(G-9601)*		
Promeko Inc	G	201 861-9446
West New York *(G-11878)*		
Qualis Packaging Inc	G	908 782-0305
South Plainfield *(G-10426)*		
▲ Quality Cosmetics Mfg	E	908 755-9588
South Plainfield *(G-10427)*		
▼ Quest Intl Flvors Frgrnces Inc	B	973 576-9500
East Hanover *(G-2240)*		
R&R Cosmetics LLC	G	732 340-1000
Rahway *(G-9219)*		
Radha Beauty Products LLC	G	732 993-6242
Northvale *(G-7603)*		
Regi US Inc	G	862 702-3901
West Caldwell *(G-11802)*		
Reviva Labs Inc	E	856 428-3885
Haddonfield *(G-4064)*		
Revlon Inc	E	732 287-1400
Edison *(G-2605)*		
Revlon Consumer Products Corp	D	732 287-1400
Edison *(G-2606)*		
▲ Robertet Inc	E	201 337-7100
Budd Lake *(G-939)*		
▲ Robertet Fragrances Inc	E	201 405-1000
Budd Lake *(G-940)*		
Robertet Fragrances Inc	E	973 575-4550
Fairfield *(G-3295)*		
▲ Rossow Cosmetiques - Usa Inc	G	732 872-1464
Matawan *(G-6031)*		
▲ Royal Cosmetics Corporation	F	732 246-7275
New Brunswick *(G-7002)*		
Rubigo Cosmetics	G	973 636-6573
Little Falls *(G-5487)*		
▼ Sahar USA Inc	E	201 868-4900
North Bergen *(G-7482)*		
▲ Sarkli-Repechage Ltd	D	201 549-4200
Secaucus *(G-9921)*		
Saturn Beauty Group LLC	G	908 561-5000
Piscataway *(G-8807)*		
Scories Inc	F	973 923-1372
Newark *(G-7304)*		
SGB Packaging Group Inc	G	201 488-3030
Hackensack *(G-3973)*		
▲ Shiseido America Inc	E	609 371-5800
East Windsor *(G-2366)*		
Shiseido Americas Corporation	G	609 371-5800
East Windsor *(G-2367)*		
▲ Siloa Inc	G	908 234-9040
Bedminster *(G-284)*		
◆ Sozio Inc	D	732 572-5600
Piscataway *(G-8814)*		
Suite K Value Added Svcs LLC	F	732 590-0647
Edison *(G-2629)*		
Suite K Value Added Svcs LLC	F	609 655-6890
Edison *(G-2630)*		
▲ Suite K Value Added Svcs LLC	D	609 655-6890
Edison *(G-2631)*		
Sunrise Glamour LLC	G	800 960-2426
Iselin *(G-4646)*		
◆ Sysco Guest Supply LLC	C	732 537-2297
Somerset *(G-10177)*		
▲ Takasago Intl Corp USA	E	201 767-9001
Rockleigh *(G-9634)*		
Takasago Intl Corp USA	D	201 767-9001
Northvale *(G-7609)*		
Topaz Skin Care Inc	G	201 489-0686
Fort Lee *(G-3585)*		
Topifram Laboratories Inc	E	201 894-9020
Englewood Cliffs *(G-2982)*		

S
I
C

▲ Unilever United States Inc..............A 201 894-4000
  Englewood Cliffs (G-2986)
◆ Victory International USA LLC ....F 732 417-5900
  Eatontown (G-2429)
▲ Vsar Resources LLC........................F 973 233-6000
  Monroe Township (G-6398)
▲ World Wide Packaging LLC ....D 973 805-6500
  Florham Park (G-3524)
Yankee Tool Inc...............................F 973 664-0878
  Denville (G-2062)

2851 Paints, Varnishes, Lacquers, Enamels

ACC Coatings LLC.............................F 732 469-8600
  Middlesex (G-6142)
▼ Actega North America Inc ....C 856 829-6300
  Delran (G-2009)
Actega North America Inc ....F 856 829-6300
  Cinnaminson (G-1444)
▼ Advanced Protective Products ....F 201 794-2000
  Fair Lawn (G-3074)
Affordable Lead Solutions LLC ....E 856 207-1348
  Bridgeton (G-777)
▲ Agate Lacquer Tri-Nat LLC ....G 732 968-1080
  Middlesex (G-6145)
American Chemical & Coating Co......G 908 353-2260
  Elizabeth (G-2710)
◆ Andek Corporation ....F 856 866-7600
  Moorestown (G-6560)
▲ Armorpoxy Inc ....F 908 810-9613
  Union (G-11154)
Ashland LLC.....................................G 908 243-3500
  Bridgewater (G-815)
Ashland Spcalty Ingredients GP ....E 732 353-7708
  Parlin (G-7929)
◆ Benjamin Moore & Co ....E 201 573-9600
  Montvale (G-6444)
Benjamin Moore & Co........................C 973 344-1200
  Newark (G-7105)
Benjamin Moore & Co........................D 973 569-5000
  Clifton (G-1574)
Benjamin Moore & Co........................D 201 573-9600
  Montvale (G-6445)
◆ Breen Color Concentrates LLC ....F 609 397-8200
  Lambertville (G-5210)
▲ Broadview Technologies Inc ....E 973 465-0077
  Newark (G-7116)
Carboline Company ....G 908 233-3150
  Westfield (G-11923)
Carboline Company ....E 732 388-2912
  Rahway (G-9181)
◆ Chemetall US Inc ....D 908 464-6900
  New Providence (G-7033)
Clausen Company Inc ....F 732 738-1165
  Fords (G-3528)
Colorflo Inc ....G 908 862-3010
  Linden (G-5360)
Columbia Paint Lab Inc ....E 201 435-4884
  Jersey City (G-4731)
Covalnce Spcialty Coatings LLC........D 732 356-2870
  Middlesex (G-6159)
Custom Chemicals Corp ....A 201 791-5100
  Elmwood Park (G-2814)
▼ Cytec Industries Inc ....C 973 357-3100
  Saddle Brook (G-9761)
Dunbar Sales Company Inc ....G 201 437-6500
  Bayonne (G-223)
Duraamen Engineered Pdts Inc ....G 973 230-1301
  Newark (G-7144)
Dux Paint LLC ....F 973 473-2376
  Lodi (G-5583)
E I Du Pont De Nemours & Co ....E 732 257-1579
  Parlin (G-7930)
◆ Elementis Specialties Inc ....C 609 443-2000
  East Windsor (G-2374)
Elementis Specialties Inc ....E 201 432-0800
  East Windsor (G-2375)
Environmental Coatings & Cnstr........F 973 509-9456
  Montclair (G-6413)
▲ Evonik Corporation ....B 973 929-8000
  Parsippany (G-8003)
Ferro Corporation ....E 732 287-4925
  Edison (G-2519)
▼ Flexabar Corporation ....E 732 901-6500
  Lakewood (G-5123)
Flexdell Corp ....G 732 901-7771
  Lakewood (G-5124)
▲ Fluorotherm Polymers Inc ....G 973 575-0760
  Parsippany (G-8014)
◆ Fti Inc ....G 973 443-0004
  Florham Park (G-3503)

◆ Gdb International Inc ....D 732 246-3001
  New Brunswick (G-6962)
General Plastics Group ....E 973 748-5500
  Bloomfield (G-512)
Hartin Paint & Filler Corp ....E 201 438-3300
  Carlstadt (G-1168)
Hawthorne Paint Company Inc ....G 973 423-2335
  Lodi (G-5586)
Hempel (usa) Inc ....E 201 939-2801
  Clifton (G-1639)
Hood Products LLC ....E 201 426-0700
  Lodi (G-5587)
▲ Industrial Summit Tech Corp ....E 732 238-2211
  Parlin (G-7932)
J R S Tool & Metal Finishing..............G 908 753-2050
  South Plainfield (G-10387)
▲ Kadakia International Inc ....G 908 754-4445
  South Plainfield (G-10391)
Kop-Coat Inc ....E 800 221-4466
  Rockaway (G-9582)
Lafarge Road Marking Inc ....G 973 884-0300
  Parsippany (G-8037)
▲ Master Bond Inc ....E 201 343-8983
  Hackensack (G-3943)
▲ Milspray LLC ....E 732 886-2223
  Lakewood (G-5159)
Minwax Group (inc) ....A 201 818-7500
  Upper Saddle River (G-11280)
◆ Muralo Company Inc ....C 201 437-0770
  Bayonne (G-238)
Nautical Marine Paint Corp ....E 732 821-3200
  North Brunswick (G-7530)
Newage Painting Corporation ....G 908 547-4734
  Newark (G-7252)
▲ Nippon Paint (usa) Inc ....F 201 692-1111
  Teaneck (G-10762)
Noopys Research Inc ....G 856 358-6001
  Newfield (G-7369)
North Jersey Specialists Inc ....G 973 927-1616
  Flanders (G-3413)
Palma Inc ....F 973 429-1490
  Whippany (G-12031)
Penn Metal Finishing Co Inc ....G 609 387-3400
  Burlington (G-987)
Performance Industries Inc ....E 609 392-1450
  Trenton (G-11096)
Philip Mamrak ....G 908 454-6089
  Phillipsburg (G-8663)
◆ Plastic Specialties & Tech Inc ....C 201 941-2900
  Ridgefield (G-9380)
PPG Industries Inc ....E 856 273-7870
  Mount Laurel (G-6830)
Prem-Khichi Enterprises Inc ....F 973 242-0300
  East Brunswick (G-2174)
▲ Protech Powder Coatings Inc ....D 973 276-1292
  Fairfield (G-3288)
Rema Corrosion Control ....E 201 256-8400
  Northvale (G-7604)
Rich Art Color Co Inc ....F 201 767-0009
  Northvale (G-7606)
Ricks Cleanouts Inc ....E 973 340-7454
  Garfield (G-3756)
▲ Royce Associates A Ltd Partnr.........D 201 438-5200
  East Rutherford (G-2322)
RPM Prfrmnce Catings Group Inc ......E 888 788-4323
  Long Branch (G-5631)
Rust-Oleum Corporation ....E 732 469-8100
  Somerset (G-10169)
Saint-Gobain Prfmce Plas Corp.........D 732 652-0910
  Somerset (G-10170)
◆ Samax Enterprise Inc ....F 973 350-9400
  Newark (G-7301)
Sau-Sea Swimming Pool Products ......F 609 859-8500
  Southampton (G-10482)
▲ Seagrave Coatings Corp ....G 201 933-1000
  Kenilworth (G-4994)
◆ Sika Corporation ....B 201 933-8800
  Lyndhurst (G-5708)
Sika Corporation ....B 201 933-8800
  Lyndhurst (G-5709)
▲ Standard Coating Corporation ....G 201 945-5058
  Ridgefield (G-9385)
Steven Industries Inc ....E 201 437-6500
  Bayonne (G-245)
◆ Stoncor Group Inc ....G 800 257-7953
  Maple Shade (G-5909)
▲ Superior Printing Ink Co Inc ....G 201 478-5600
  Teterboro (G-10810)
Synthetic Surfaces Inc ....G 908 233-6803
  Scotch Plains (G-9858)

▼ Target Coatings Inc ....G 800 752-9922
  Fair Lawn (G-3120)
Technical Coatings Co ....E 973 927-8600
  Flanders (G-3419)
Tenax Finishing Products Co ....F 973 589-9000
  Newark (G-7339)
◆ Tevco Enterprises Inc ....D 908 754-7306
  South Plainfield (G-10439)
Thermo Cote Inc................................G 973 464-3575
  Rockaway (G-9612)
▲ Tq3 north America Inc ....G 973 882-7900
  Fairfield (G-3329)
▲ Turquoise Chemistry Inc ....G 908 561-0002
  Piscataway (G-8831)
◆ Ultra Additives LLC ....G 973 279-1306
  Bloomfield (G-536)
Uvitec Printing Ink Co Inc ....G 973 778-0737
  Lodi (G-5607)
Worldwide Safety Systems LLC ....G 888 613-4501
  Teaneck (G-10778)

2861 Gum & Wood Chemicals

◆ Importers Service Corp ....E 732 248-1946
  Edison (G-2540)
Sanit Technologies LLC ....G 862 238-7555
  Passaic (G-8180)

2865 Cyclic-Crudes, Intermediates, Dyes & Org Pigments

American Chemical & Coating Co........G 908 353-2260
  Elizabeth (G-2710)
Carib Chemical Co Inc ....F 201 791-6700
  Elmwood Park (G-2808)
▲ Carib Chemical Co Inc ....F 201 791-6700
  Elmwood Park (G-2809)
▲ Chem-Is-Try Inc ....G 732 372-7311
  Metuchen (G-6100)
◆ Chemical Resources Inc ....E 609 520-0000
  Princeton (G-9021)
◆ Color Techniques Inc ....F 908 412-9292
  South Plainfield (G-10347)
Coloron Plastics Corporation ....E 908 685-1210
  Branchburg (G-649)
▲ Dominion Colour Corp USA ....F 973 279-9591
  Clifton (G-1604)
◆ Elementis Specialties Inc ....C 609 443-2000
  East Windsor (G-2374)
▲ Epolin Chemical LLC ....G 973 465-9495
  Newark (G-7157)
Fabricolor Holding Intl LLC ....G 973 742-5800
  Paterson (G-8269)
Ferro Corporation ....C 856 467-3000
  Bridgeport (G-765)
Ferro Corporation ....E 732 287-4925
  Edison (G-2519)
▲ French Color Fragrance Co Inc ....E 201 567-6883
  Englewood (G-2898)
◆ Honeyware Inc ....D 201 997-5900
  Kearny (G-4880)
Magruder Color Company Inc ....C 817 837-3293
  Holmdel (G-4521)
Manner Textile Processing Inc ....G 973 942-8718
  North Haledon (G-7550)
◆ Novartis Corporation ....E 212 307-1122
  East Hanover (G-2232)
▲ Orient Corporation of America ....G 908 298-0990
  Cranford (G-1919)
Penn Color Inc ....C 201 791-5100
  Elmwood Park (G-2842)
Polymathes Holdings I LLC ....F 609 945-1690
  Princeton (G-9093)
Primex Color Compounding ....G 800 282-7933
  Garfield (G-3750)
▼ Riverdale Color Mfg Inc ....G 732 376-9300
  Perth Amboy (G-8628)
Royce Associates A Ltd Partnr ....E 973 279-0400
  Paterson (G-8372)
Shelan Chemical Company Inc ....G 732 796-1003
  Monroe Township (G-6392)
◆ Solvay Holding Inc ....A 609 860-4000
  Princeton (G-9121)
Solvay USA Inc ....G 732 297-0100
  North Brunswick (G-7538)
◆ Solvay USA Inc ....G 609 860-4000
  Princeton (G-9122)
SPS Alfachem Inc ....G 973 676-5141
  Orange (G-7828)
◆ Sun Chemical Corporation ....D 973 404-6000
  Parsippany (G-8094)

Totowa Precision Tooling Inc ....F 973 256-2283
Totowa (G-10976)

William R Tatz Industries...................G 973 751-0720
Belleville (G-328)

2869 Industrial Organic Chemicals, NEC

Acceledev Chemical LLC ....G 732 274-1451
Monmouth Junction (G-6330)

Adron Inc ....E 973 334-1600
Boonton (G-551)

Advanced Biotech Overseas LLC ....G 973 339-6242
Totowa (G-10926)

Agilis Chemicals Inc ....G 973 910-2424
Rockaway (G-9548)

◆ Akcros Chemicals Inc ....D 800 500-7890
New Brunswick (G-6943)

▲ Alzo International Inc ....E 732 254-1901
Sayreville (G-9814)

▲ American Beryllia Inc ....E 973 248-8080
Haskell (G-4205)

Amit Fuel Company ....G 973 684-9409
Woodland Park (G-12209)

▲ Aromatic Technologies Inc ....D 732 393-7300
Piscataway (G-8737)

▲ Aromiens Inc ....G 732 225-8689
Edison (G-2466)

Ashland Spcalty Ingredients GP ....C 908 243-3500
Bridgewater (G-816)

Ashland Spcalty Ingredients GP ....E 732 353-7708
Parlin (G-7929)

ATL ....G 201 825-1400
Ramsey (G-9235)

Avantor Performance Mtls LLC ....B 908 859-2151
Phillipsburg (G-8640)

Bal-Edge Corporation ....G 973 895-8826
Eatontown (G-2384)

▲ Barnet Products Corporation ....F 201 346-4620
Englewood Cliffs (G-2949)

BASF Catalysts LLC ....C 732 205-5000
Carteret (G-1252)

◆ BASF Corporation ....B 973 245-6000
Florham Park (G-3492)

BASF Corporation..............................D 908 689-2500
Washington (G-11576)

BASF Corporation..............................E 848 221-2786
Toms River (G-10869)

BASF Corporation..............................C 732 205-5086
Iselin (G-4617)

BASF Corporation..............................C 732 205-2700
Union (G-11156)

BASF Corporation..............................E 973 426-5429
Budd Lake (G-925)

▲ Basfin Corporation ....A 973 245-6000
Florham Park (G-3493)

◆ Berje Incorporated ....G 973 748-8980
Carteret (G-1253)

Bhavika Fuel LLC ....G 609 926-4500
Somers Point (G-10045)

Biotech Support Group LLC ....G 732 613-1967
East Brunswick (G-2139)

▲ Brown Chemical Co Inc ....E 201 337-0900
Oakland (G-7677)

Cambridge Industries Co Inc ....G 973 465-4565
Newark (G-7119)

▼ Chem-Fleur Inc ....D 973 589-4266
Newark (G-7121)

▲ Chem-Is-Try Inc ....G 732 372-7311
Metuchen (G-6100)

Chembiopower Inc ....G 908 209-5595
Warren (G-11542)

Chemmark Development Inc................G 908 561-0923
South Plainfield (G-10346)

Chemo Dynamics Inc ....F 732 721-4700
Sayreville (G-9817)

Coim USA Inc ....E 856 224-1668
Paulsboro (G-8415)

Colibri Scentique Ltd Lblty Co ....G 201 445-5715
Glen Rock (G-3824)

Corbion Group ....G 973 256-0198
Totowa (G-10940)

Crompton Corp ....G 732 826-6600
Perth Amboy (G-8611)

▼ Cvc Specialty Chemicals Inc ....F 856 533-3000
Moorestown (G-6571)

D and M Discount Fuels ....G 856 935-0919
Salem (G-9805)

Daros Group ....G 908 454-7811
Stewartsville (G-10594)

◆ Deleet Merchandising Corp ....E 212 962-6565
Newark (G-7139)

Dow Chemical Company ....E 856 663-2627
Pennsauken (G-8506)

Dow Chemical Company ....D 732 969-5723
Carteret (G-1255)

Easy Stop Food & Fuel Corp ....G 973 517-0478
Hamburg (G-4092)

Elan Food Laboratories Inc ....F 973 344-8014
Newark (G-7149)

▲ Elan Inc ....D 973 344-8014
Newark (G-7150)

▲ Energy Chem America Inc ....D 201 816-2307
Englewood Cliffs (G-2958)

Engineered Silicone Pdts LLC ....G 973 300-5120
Newton (G-7387)

Epic Holding Inc ....E 732 249-6867
Morristown (G-6708)

Evonik Corporation............................D 732 981-5000
Piscataway (G-8764)

▲ Evonik Corporation ....B 973 929-8000
Parsippany (G-8003)

▲ Fancyheat Corporation ....G 973 589-1450
Somerset (G-10101)

▲ Farbest-Tallman Foods Corp ....D 714 897-7199
Park Ridge (G-7919)

▲ Firefreeze Worldwide Inc ....E 973 627-0722
Rockaway (G-9568)

▲ Firmenich ....G 609 580-4498
Monmouth Junction (G-6345)

▲ Flavor & Fragrance Spc Inc ....D 201 828-9400
Mahwah (G-5773)

Flavor Development Corp ....F 201 784-8188
Norwood (G-7622)

FMC Corporation...............................C 609 963-6200
Ewing (G-3018)

Fossil Fuel ....G 973 366-9111
Wharton (G-11987)

Fuel One Inc ....G 732 726-9500
Avenel (G-132)

G & R Fuel Corp ....G 973 732-0530
Newark (G-7166)

◆ G Holdings Inc ....G 973 628-3000
Parsippany (G-8019)

▲ G-I Holdings Inc ....G 973 628-3000
Wayne (G-11638)

◆ Gentek Inc ....C 973 515-0900
Parsippany (G-8024)

Givaudan Flavors Corporation ....G 973 463-8192
Cranbury (G-1834)

Givaudan Flavors Corporation ....C 973 386-9800
East Hanover (G-2219)

Givaudan Fragrances Corp ....C 973 576-9500
East Hanover (G-2221)

Givaudan Fragrances Corp ....C 973 560-1939
East Hanover (G-2222)

Givaudan Fragrances Corp ....C 973 448-6500
Budd Lake (G-930)

Glamorous Glo ....G 732 361-3235
Eatontown (G-2396)

▲ GP Chemicals Inc ....G 201 869-2200
North Bergen (G-7454)

H & S Fuel Inc ....G 908 769-1362
Plainfield (G-8863)

Honig Chemical & Proc Corp ....E 973 344-0881
Newark (G-7192)

Hopatcong Fuel On You LLC ....G 973 770-0854
Hopatcong (G-4537)

Interntnal Flvors Frgrnces Inc ....C 732 264-4500
Union Beach (G-11237)

Interntnal Flvors Frgrnces Inc ....C 732 264-4500
Hazlet (G-4276)

Interntonal Fragrance Tech Inc............E 770 345-3079
Piscataway (G-8780)

◆ Interntonal Specialty Pdts Inc ....A 859 815-3333
Wayne (G-11653)

Isp Chemco LLC ....G 973 628-4000
Wayne (G-11654)

Isp Chemicals LLC ....E 973 635-1551
Chatham (G-1330)

Isp Global Technologies Inc ....G 973 628-4000
Wayne (G-11655)

Isp Global Technologies LLC ....G 973 628-4000
Wayne (G-11656)

Jacquar Fuel ....G 732 441-0700
Manalapan (G-5851)

Jai Ganesh Fuel LLC ....G 201 246-8995
Kearny (G-4888)

Jarchem Industries Inc ....F 973 344-0600
Newark (G-7205)

Jt Fuels LLC ....G 973 527-4470
Ledgewood (G-5306)

▲ Just In Time Chemical Sales & ......G 908 862-7726
Linden (G-5393)

Karebay Biochem Inc ....G 732 823-1545
Monmouth Junction (G-6349)

▲ Kenrich Petrochemicals Inc ....E 201 823-9000
Bayonne (G-235)

Kp Fuel Corporation ....G 973 350-1202
Newark (G-7213)

Lanxess Solutions US Inc ....C 732 826-1018
Perth Amboy (G-8620)

Lanxess Solutions US Inc ....C 973 887-7411
East Hanover (G-2227)

Lanxess Solutions US Inc ....C 732 738-1000
Fords (G-3530)

Ligno Tech USA Inc ....G 908 429-6660
Bridgewater (G-852)

◆ Lonza Inc ....D 201 316-9200
Allendale (G-13)

Lubrizol Advanced Mtls Inc ....F 973 471-1300
Clifton (G-1665)

Lyondell Chemical Company ....G 973 578-2200
Newark (G-7232)

Lyondellbasell ....F 732 985-6262
Edison (G-2562)

Main Fuel LLC ....G 201 941-2707
Cliffside Park (G-1542)

▲ Main Street Auto & Fuel LLC...........G 732 238-0044
Sayreville (G-9833)

▲ Mane USA Inc ....C 973 633-5533
Wayne (G-11662)

Modern Fuel Inc ....G 973 471-1501
Clifton (G-1675)

Montclair Fuel LLC ....G 973 744-4300
Montclair (G-6422)

◆ Nan Ya Plastics Corp America ....E 973 992-1775
Livingston (G-5549)

National Fuel LLC ....G 973 227-4549
Pine Brook (G-8710)

▼ National Strch Chem Holdg Corp .....A 908 685-5000
Bridgewater (G-861)

NJ Fuel Haulers Inc...........................G 732 740-3681
Old Bridge (G-7786)

▲ Northeast Chemicals Inc ....E 732 238-9980
East Brunswick (G-2170)

NP Bio Fuels LLC ....G 856 467-2273
Swedesboro (G-10715)

▲ Pharmetic Mfg Company LLC ....G 732 254-1901
Sayreville (G-9835)

▲ Phoenix Chemical Inc ....F 908 707-0232
Branchburg (G-689)

Pilot Chemical Company Ohio..............F 732 634-6613
Avenel (G-145)

Prospect Transportation Inc ....G 201 933-9999
Carlstadt (G-1210)

▲ Protameen Chemicals Inc ....E 973 256-4374
Totowa (G-10967)

Quality Sweets ....G 732 283-3799
Iselin (G-4641)

R & R Fuel Inc ....G 201 223-0786
Union City (G-11264)

Route 22 Fuel Inc ....G 908 526-5270
Bridgewater (G-884)

▲ Royale Pigments & Chem Inc ....G 201 845-4666
Paramus (G-7900)

▲ Royce Associates A Ltd Partnr ....D 201 438-5200
East Rutherford (G-2322)

Royce International Corp ....G 201 438-5200
East Rutherford (G-2323)

S and D Fuel LLC ....G 908 248-8188
Union (G-11220)

Sanit Technologies LLC ....F 862 238-7555
Passaic (G-8180)

Scher Chemicals Inc ....A 973 471-1300
Clifton (G-1716)

SE Tylos USA ....G 973 837-8001
Totowa (G-10971)

Sgw Fuel Delivery ....G 609 209-8773
Trenton (G-11116)

Shani Auto Fuel Corp ....G 856 241-9767
Woolwich Township (G-12241)

Shiva Fuel Inc ....G 732 826-3228
Perth Amboy (G-8629)

Sks Fuel Inc ....G 973 200-0796
Woodland Park (G-12233)

▲ Small Molecules Inc ....G 201 918-4664
Hoboken (G-4498)

▲ Solvay Holding Inc ....A 609 860-4000
Princeton (G-9121)

◆ Solvay USA Inc ....B 609 860-4000
Princeton (G-9122)

Solvay USA Inc ....C 732 297-0100
North Brunswick (G-7538)
▼ Sonneborn LLC ....F 201 760-2940
Parsippany (G-8089)
Sonneborn Holding LLC ....B 201 760-2940
Parsippany (G-8090)
◆ Spectrum Laboratory Pdts Inc ....C 732 214-1300
New Brunswick (G-7004)
Spectrum Laboratory Pdts Inc ....E 732 214-1300
New Brunswick (G-7005)
Stepan Company ....D 609 298-1222
Bordentown (G-611)
Suman Realty LLC ....G 908 350-8039
Stirling (G-10607)
Surface Technology Inc ....F 609 259-0099
Ewing (G-3058)
▲ Sweet Solutions Inc ....G 732 512-0777
Edison (G-2635)
◆ Symrise Inc ....B 201 288-3200
Teterboro (G-10813)
Symrise Inc ....G 201 288-3200
Saddle Brook (G-9795)
Symrise Inc ....D 908 429-6824
Branchburg (G-707)
Talent Investment LLC ....G 732 931-0088
Hazlet (G-4284)
Techenzyme Inc ....G 732 632-8600
Iselin (G-4648)
Technical Oil Products Co Inc ....G 973 940-8920
Newton (G-7408)
▼ Technical Processing Inc ....F 973 278-4950
Paterson (G-8398)
Thind Fuel Service LLC ....G 732 613-1808
South River (G-10468)
◆ Troy Corporation ....D 973 443-4200
Florham Park (G-3521)
Ultra Chemical Inc ....F 732 224-0200
Red Bank (G-9348)
▲ Umicore Precious Metals NJ LLC ....E 908 222-5006
South Plainfield (G-10444)
▲ Unitex International Inc ....G 856 786-5000
Cinnaminson (G-1497)
Urso Fuel Corp ....G 973 325-3324
West Orange (G-11908)
Veolia Es ....E 732 469-5100
Middlesex (G-6208)
Viva Chemical Corporation ....G 201 461-5281
Fort Lee (G-3589)
Zoomessence Inc ....G 732 416-6638
Sayreville (G-9843)

2873 Nitrogenous Fertilizers

Agrium Advanced Tech US Inc ....F 732 296-8448
North Brunswick (G-7503)
Andritz Separation Inc ....G 732 269-5305
Bayville (G-249)
Growmark Fs LLC ....F 609 267-7054
Eastampton (G-2376)
▼ Miracle Verde Group LLC ....G 201 399-2222
Kearny (G-4900)
▼ Plant Food Company Inc ....E 609 448-0935
Cranbury (G-1870)
▼ Reed & Perrine Inc ....E 732 446-6363
Tennent (G-10790)
Reed & Perrine Sales Inc ....E 732 446-6363
Tennent (G-10791)
Scotts Company LLC ....F 201 246-0180
North Arlington (G-7424)
South Jersey Farmers Exchange ....G 856 769-0062
Woodstown (G-12240)

2874 Phosphatic Fertilizers

Growmark Fs LLC ....F 609 267-7054
Eastampton (G-2376)
Innophos Inc ....G 973 587-8735
Cranbury (G-1838)
Innophos Holdings Inc ....D 609 495-2495
Cranbury (G-1839)
Innophos Investments II Inc ....G 609 495-2495
Cranbury (G-1841)
Innophos Invstmnts Hldings Inc ....G 609 495-2495
Cranbury (G-1842)
◆ Missry Associates Inc ....C 732 752-7500
Edison (G-2574)

2875 Fertilizers, Mixing Only

Growmark Fs LLC ....F 609 267-7054
Eastampton (G-2376)
L & S Contracting Inc ....G 609 397-1281
Hopewell (G-4542)

▼ Reed & Perrine Inc ....E 732 446-6363
Tennent (G-10790)

2879 Pesticides & Agricultural Chemicals, NEC

Agilis Chemicals Inc ....G 973 910-2424
Rockaway (G-9548)
◆ AP&g Co Inc ....D 718 492-3648
Bayonne (G-211)
AP&g Co Inc ....G 718 492-3648
Bayonne (G-212)
◆ Aquatrols Corp of America ....E 856 537-6003
West Deptford (G-11816)
Avantor Performance Mtls LLC ....B 908 859-2151
Phillipsburg (G-8640)
◆ BASF Corporation ....B 973 245-6000
Florham Park (G-3492)
▲ Basfin Corporation ....A 973 245-6000
Florham Park (G-3493)
◆ Bayer Corporation ....A 412 777-2000
Whippany (G-12007)
▲ Big Bucks Enterprises Inc ....G 908 320-7009
Washington (G-11578)
▲ Chem-Is-Try Inc ....G 732 372-7311
Metuchen (G-6100)
Deer Out Animal Repellant LLC ....G 908 769-4242
South Plainfield (G-10353)
◆ Flottec LLC ....G 973 588-4717
Boonton (G-569)
◆ Glysortia LLC ....G 715 426-5358
Plainsboro (G-8884)
Healios Inc ....G 908 731-5061
Flemington (G-3446)
◆ Novartis Corporation ....E 212 307-1122
East Hanover (G-2232)
▲ Pic Corporation ....G 908 862-7977
Linden (G-5429)
Residex LLC ....G 856 232-0880
Blackwood (G-491)
Si Packaging LLC ....F 973 869-9920
Rutherford (G-9744)

2891 Adhesives & Sealants

▲ A D M Tronics Unlimited Inc ....E 201 767-6040
Northvale (G-7566)
Alan Chemical Corporation Inc ....G 973 628-7777
Wayne (G-11602)
▲ Alva-Tech Inc ....F 609 747-1133
Burlington Township (G-997)
Amb Enterprises LLC ....E 973 225-1070
Paterson (G-8206)
Amerasia Intl Tech Inc ....E 609 799-9388
Princeton Junction (G-9147)
▲ American Casein Company ....E 609 387-2988
Burlington (G-954)
American Chemical & Coating Co ....G 908 353-2260
Elizabeth (G-2710)
◆ Andek Corporation ....F 856 866-7600
Moorestown (G-6560)
▲ Annitti Enterprises Inc ....G 973 345-1725
Paterson (G-8213)
Aos Thermal Compounds LLC ....F 732 389-5514
Eatontown (G-2383)
API Americas Inc ....D 732 382-6800
Rahway (G-9174)
▲ Artistic Bias Products Co Inc ....E 732 382-4141
Rahway (G-9175)
▲ Assem - Pak Inc ....E 856 692-3355
Vineland (G-11323)
▼ Baker/Titan Adhesives ....E 973 225-1070
Paterson (G-8219)
Bostik Inc ....D 856 848-8669
Paulsboro (G-8414)
◆ Cardolite Corporation ....E 609 436-0902
Monmouth Junction (G-6335)
Clark Stek-O Corp ....D 201 437-0770
Bayonne (G-218)
◆ Clifton Adhesive Inc ....E 973 694-0845
Wayne (G-11619)
◆ Coim USA Inc ....D 856 224-8560
West Deptford (G-11825)
Compounders Inc ....G 732 938-5007
Farmingdale (G-3381)
Covalnce Spcalty Adhesives LLC ....A 732 356-2870
Middlesex (G-6158)
CR Laurence Co Inc ....F 856 727-1022
Moorestown (G-6570)
Custom Building Products Inc ....D 856 467-9226
Logan Township (G-5612)

Dritac Flooring Products LLC ....F 973 614-9000
Clifton (G-1605)
Elektromek Inc ....F 973 614-9000
Clifton (G-1615)
Flexcraft Industries Inc ....G 973 589-3403
Newark (G-7163)
◆ Frimpeks Inc ....F 201 266-0116
Fairfield (G-3202)
◆ Gabhen Inc ....C 800 631-3572
Totowa (G-10945)
▲ Gluefast Company Inc ....F 732 918-4600
Neptune (G-6915)
HB Fuller Company ....E 732 287-8330
Edison (G-2535)
Henkel US Operations Corp ....E 908 685-7000
Bridgewater (G-843)
Hercules LLC ....G 732 777-4697
Edison (G-2537)
▲ Hudson Industries Corporation ....G 973 402-0100
Fairfield (G-3225)
Kop-Coat Inc ....E 800 221-4466
Rockaway (G-9582)
La Favorite Industries Inc ....F 973 279-1266
Paterson (G-8316)
Mapei Corporation ....F 732 254-4830
Swedesboro (G-10708)
Mapei Corporation ....G 732 254-4830
Swedesboro (G-10707)
▲ Master Bond Inc ....E 201 343-8983
Hackensack (G-3943)
▲ May National Associates NJ Inc ....D 973 473-3330
Lakewood (G-5156)
Mc Ginley Packaging Methods ....G 201 493-9330
Midland Park (G-6232)
Mercury Adhesives Inc ....G 973 472-3307
Passaic (G-8162)
Mon-Eco Industries Inc ....F 732 257-7942
East Brunswick (G-2167)
National Casein New Jersey Inc ....E 856 829-1880
Cinnaminson (G-1480)
▼ National Strch Chem Holdg Corp ....A 908 685-5000
Bridgewater (G-861)
▲ Natl Adhesies Div of Henke ....G 908 685-7000
Bridgewater (G-862)
Norland Products Inc ....E 609 395-1966
Cranbury (G-1863)
Nu Grafix Inc ....E 201 413-1776
Jersey City (G-4794)
Palmetto Adhesives Company ....F 856 451-0400
Bridgeton (G-793)
▲ Permabond LLC ....G 610 323-5003
Somerset (G-10153)
▲ Petronio Shoe Products Corp ....F 973 751-7579
Belleville (G-311)
◆ Plcs Inc ....E 856 722-1333
Mount Laurel (G-6827)
PPG Architectural Finishes Inc ....G 908 353-2477
Elizabeth (G-2767)
▼ Princeton Keynes Group Inc ....F 609 951-2239
Princeton (G-9096)
Princeton Keynes Group Inc ....F 609 208-1777
Newark (G-7274)
Royal Adhesives & Sealants LLC ....E 973 694-0845
Wayne (G-11680)
Rust-Oleum Corporation ....F 732 652-2378
Newark (G-7296)
Saint-Gobain Prfmce Plas Corp ....D 732 652-0910
Somerset (G-10170)
Signature Marketing & Mfg ....G 973 427-3700
Hawthorne (G-4259)
◆ Sika Corporation ....B 201 933-8800
Lyndhurst (G-5708)
Sika Corporation ....G 201 933-8800
Lyndhurst (G-5709)
▼ Solar Compounds Corporation ....E 908 862-2813
Linden (G-5444)
▲ Spiral Binding LLC ....G 973 256-0666
Totowa (G-10973)
Steven Industries Inc ....E 201 437-6500
Bayonne (G-245)
Synthetic Surfaces Inc ....G 908 233-6803
Scotch Plains (G-9858)
▲ Universal Tape Supply Corp ....F 609 653-3191
Somers Point (G-10048)
Zymet Inc ....F 973 428-5245
East Hanover (G-2253)

2892 Explosives

Cartridge Actuated Devices ....E 973 575-8760
Fairfield (G-3157)

Cartridge Actuated Devices ....E 973 347-2281
Byram Township *(G-1021)*

▼ Mjg Technologies Incorporated ....G 856 228-6118
Blackwood *(G-488)*

2893 Printing Ink

AGFA Corporation ....G 908 231-5000
Somerville *(G-10200)*

American Coding and Mkg Ink Co ....G 908 756-0373
Plainfield *(G-8853)*

Athletes Alley ....F 732 842-1127
Shrewsbury *(G-9990)*

Central Ink Corporation ....G 856 467-5562
Swedesboro *(G-10687)*

Champion Ink Co Inc ....G 201 868-4100
North Bergen *(G-7439)*

Chroma Trading Usa Inc ....G 732 956-4431
Morganville *(G-6639)*

CRS Ink Intl Ltd Lblty Co ....G 732 817-0401
Holmdel *(G-4514)*

Custom Chemicals Corp ....A 201 791-5100
Elmwood Park *(G-2814)*

Faust Rudolph Inc ....F 609 298-7334
Cranford *(G-1906)*

Flint Group US LLC ....G 732 329-4627
Dayton *(G-1962)*

Gotham Ink of New England Inc ....G 201 478-5600
Teterboro *(G-10798)*

Ideon LLC ....G 908 431-3126
Hillsborough *(G-4344)*

J M Fry Printing Inks ....G 732 238-1060
East Brunswick *(G-2162)*

Kohl & Madden Prtg Ink Corp ....E 201 935-8666
Carlstadt *(G-1181)*

Lodor Offset Corporation ....F 201 935-7100
Carlstadt *(G-1184)*

Monarch Color Corporation ....F 215 923-2235
Pennsauken *(G-8552)*

▲ Pan Technology Inc ....E 201 438-7878
Carlstadt *(G-1197)*

Prismacolor Corp ....G 973 887-6040
Parsippany *(G-8073)*

▲ Ranger Industries Inc ....E 732 389-3535
Tinton Falls *(G-10844)*

▲ Selective Coatings & Inks ....F 732 938-7677
Wall Township *(G-11508)*

Selective Coatings & Inks ....G 732 493-0707
Ocean *(G-7744)*

Sun Chemical Corporation ....C 201 933-4500
Carlstadt *(G-1223)*

◆ Sun Chemical Corporation ....D 973 404-6000
Parsippany *(G-8094)*

Sun Chemical Corporation ....E 201 438-4831
East Rutherford *(G-2329)*

Sun Chemical Corporation ....F 201 935-8666
Carlstadt *(G-1224)*

▲ Superior Printing Ink Co Inc ....C 201 478-5600
Teterboro *(G-10810)*

Superior Printing Ink Co Inc ....E 856 482-9066
Maple Shade *(G-5911)*

Superior Printing Ink Co Inc ....G 716 685-6763
Teterboro *(G-10811)*

Superior Printing Ink Co Inc ....G 716 685-6763
Teterboro *(G-10812)*

Superior Printing Ink Co Inc ....G 973 242-5868
Newark *(G-7334)*

Supreme Ink Corp ....G 973 344-2922
Newark *(G-7335)*

Total Ink Solutions LLC ....F 201 487-9600
Hackensack *(G-3985)*

Toyo Ink America LLC ....F 201 804-0620
Carlstadt *(G-1231)*

Triangle Ink Co Inc ....F 201 935-2777
Wallington *(G-11530)*

Uvitec Printing Ink Co Inc ....E 973 778-0737
Lodi *(G-5607)*

Vivitone Inc ....F 973 427-8114
Hawthorne *(G-4264)*

2895 Carbon Black

◆ Total American Services Inc ....F 206 626-3500
Jersey City *(G-4838)*

2899 Chemical Preparations, NEC

▲ A D M Tronics Unlimited Inc ....E 201 767-6040
Northvale *(G-7566)*

A J P Scientific Inc ....G 973 472-7200
Clifton *(G-1552)*

Acceledev Chemical LLC ....G 862 239-1524
Wayne *(G-11601)*

Adam Gates & Company LLC ....F 908 829-3386
Hillsborough *(G-4316)*

Advansix Inc ....B 973 526-1800
Parsippany *(G-7941)*

Agilis Chemicals Inc ....G 973 910-2424
Rockaway *(G-9548)*

Airdye Solutions LLC ....E 540 433-9101
Cedar Grove *(G-1269)*

Akzo Nobel Chemicals LLC ....D 732 985-6262
Edison *(G-2454)*

◆ Alden - Leeds Inc ....D 973 589-3544
Kearny *(G-4859)*

Alpha Assembly Solutions Inc ....E 908 561-5170
South Plainfield *(G-10325)*

▲ Alpha Assembly Solutions Inc ....E 908 791-3000
Somerset *(G-10054)*

▲ American Flux & Metal LLC ....E 609 561-7500
Hammonton *(G-4127)*

▲ American Water - Pridesa LLC ....G 856 435-7711
Voorhees *(G-11421)*

◆ Amfine Chemical Corporation ....F 201 818-0159
Hasbrouck Heights *(G-4191)*

Aphelion Orbitals Inc ....G 321 289-0872
Union City *(G-11242)*

◆ Arol Chemical Products Co ....G 973 344-1510
Newark *(G-7094)*

◆ Arro-Mark Company LLC ....F 201 567-4112
Englewood *(G-2871)*

Ashland LLC ....G 908 243-3500
Bridgewater *(G-815)*

Ashland Spcalty Ingredients GP ....E 732 353-7708
Parlin *(G-7929)*

◆ Atlas Refinery Inc ....E 973 589-2002
Newark *(G-7096)*

Avantor Performance Mtls LLC ....B 908 859-2151
Phillipsburg *(G-8640)*

▼ Axim Concrete Technologies ....D 330 966-0444
Lyndhurst *(G-5670)*

◆ BASF Corporation ....B 973 245-6000
Florham Park *(G-3492)*

▲ Basfin Corporation ....A 973 245-6000
Florham Park *(G-3493)*

Beacon C M P Corp ....G 908 851-9393
Kenilworth *(G-4942)*

Bergen International LLC ....G 201 299-4499
East Rutherford *(G-2285)*

Bostik Inc ....D 856 848-8669
Paulsboro *(G-8414)*

BP Corporation North Amer Inc ....E 908 474-5000
Linden *(G-5353)*

◆ Brenntag Specialties Inc ....D 800 732-0562
South Plainfield *(G-10339)*

▲ C & S Specialty Inc ....G 201 750-7740
Norwood *(G-7617)*

C S L Water Treatment Inc ....F 908 647-1400
Warren *(G-11540)*

Caloric Color Co Inc ....F 973 471-4748
Garfield *(G-3725)*

Cantol Inc ....E 609 846-7912
Wildwood *(G-12070)*

Cargille Tab-Pro Corporation ....F 973 267-8883
Carlstadt *(G-1137)*

◆ CC Packaging LLC ....G 732 213-9008
Bayville *(G-252)*

▲ Chem-Is-Try Inc ....G 732 372-7311
Metuchen *(G-6100)*

◆ Chemetall US Inc ....D 908 464-6900
New Providence *(G-7033)*

Chemtreat Inc ....G 609 654-9522
Medford *(G-6066)*

Cleaners Choice Inc ....F 800 652-2533
Totowa *(G-10939)*

Conversion Technology Co Inc ....F 732 752-5660
South Plainfield *(G-10350)*

▲ Croda Inc ....D 732 417-0800
Edison *(G-2495)*

Croda Investments Inc ....G 732 417-0800
Edison *(G-2496)*

Cytec Industries Inc ....G 877 463-7645
Princeton *(G-9026)*

▼ Cytec Industries Inc ....C 973 357-3100
Saddle Brook *(G-9761)*

▼ Delta Procurement Inc ....G 201 623-9353
Carlstadt *(G-1153)*

▲ Elan Inc ....D 973 344-8014
Newark *(G-7150)*

◆ Elementis Global LLC ....C 609 443-2000
East Windsor *(G-2373)*

◆ Elementis Specialties Inc ....C 609 443-2000
East Windsor *(G-2374)*

▲ Elixens America Inc ....G 732 388-3555
Rahway *(G-9187)*

EMD Performance Materials Corp ....B 908 429-3500
Branchburg *(G-657)*

▲ Evans Chemetics LP ....D 201 992-3100
Teaneck *(G-10753)*

▲ Faust Thermographic Supply ....F 908 474-0555
Linden *(G-5374)*

Ferro Corporation ....C 856 467-3000
Bridgeport *(G-765)*

Firefighter One Ltd Lblty Co ....G 973 940-3061
Sparta *(G-10499)*

Fisher Scientific Company LLC ....B 201 796-7100
Fair Lawn *(G-3093)*

◆ Flavors of Origin Inc ....E 732 499-9700
Avenel *(G-131)*

▲ Fluorotherm Polymers Inc ....G 973 575-0760
Parsippany *(G-8014)*

Fragrance Resources Inc ....D 973 458-5231
Keyport *(G-5018)*

Frinton Laboratories Inc ....G 856 722-7037
Moorestown *(G-6578)*

Fuel Management Services Inc ....G 732 929-1964
Toms River *(G-10879)*

Full Circle Mfg Group ....G 908 353-8933
Elizabeth *(G-2736)*

Gamka Sales Co Inc ....E 732 248-1400
Edison *(G-2525)*

Garratt-Callahan Company ....G 732 287-2200
Edison *(G-2527)*

Global Seven Inc ....E 973 209-7474
Rockaway *(G-9571)*

Grayden Industries Inc ....E 201 761-0788
Jersey City *(G-4762)*

▲ Grignard Company LLC ....E 732 340-1111
Rahway *(G-9194)*

▼ Gulbrandsen Technologies Inc ....E 908 735-5458
Clinton *(G-1751)*

◆ Gulco Inc ....G 908 238-2030
Phillipsburg *(G-8651)*

◆ Honeyware Inc ....D 201 997-5900
Kearny *(G-4880)*

Houghton Chemical Corporation ....F 201 460-8071
Carlstadt *(G-1170)*

▲ Hudson Industries Corporation ....G 973 402-0100
Fairfield *(G-3225)*

▲ Hychem Corporation ....G 732 280-8803
Belmar *(G-359)*

▲ Industrial Summit Tech Corp ....E 732 238-2211
Parlin *(G-7932)*

Industrial Water Tech Inc ....G 732 888-1233
Hazlet *(G-4275)*

◆ Infineum USA LP ....A 908 474-0100
Linden *(G-5387)*

Insul-Stop Inc ....E 732 706-1978
Marlboro *(G-5944)*

Intenze Products Inc ....E 201 342-4446
Hackensack *(G-3929)*

Interbahm International Inc ....E 732 499-9700
Avenel *(G-135)*

International Vitamin Corp ....G 973 416-2000
Irvington *(G-4593)*

◆ Interntonal Specialty Pdts Inc ....A 859 815-3333
Wayne *(G-11653)*

Jch Partners & Co LLC ....F 732 664-6440
Howell *(G-4557)*

Jenisse Leisure Products Inc ....F 973 331-1177
Towaco *(G-10997)*

Krohn Technical Products Inc ....F 201 933-9696
Carlstadt *(G-1182)*

Kronos Worldwide Inc ....E 609 860-6200
Cranbury *(G-1849)*

Lanxess Solutions US Inc ....C 973 235-1800
Nutley *(G-7650)*

◆ Lanxess Sybron Chemicals Inc ....C 609 893-1100
Birmingham *(G-468)*

Lodor Offset Corporation ....F 201 935-7100
Carlstadt *(G-1184)*

◆ Lonza Inc ....D 201 316-9200
Allendale *(G-13)*

Lubrizol Advanced Mtls Inc ....E 856 299-3764
Pedricktown *(G-8438)*

Lubrizol Corporation ....G 732 981-0149
Piscataway *(G-8787)*

Mapei Corporation ....E 732 254-4830
Swedesboro *(G-10707)*

▲ Mel Chemicals Inc ....C 908 782-5800
Flemington *(G-3456)*

Morgan Advanced Ceramics Inc ....E 973 808-1621
Fairfield *(G-3264)*

▲ Mri International ....G...... 973 383-3645
Newton *(G-7397)*

◆ No Fire Technologies Inc ....G...... 201 818-1616
South Hackensack *(G-10284)*

Norland Products Inc.........................E...... 609 395-1966
Cranbury *(G-1863)*

Nutech Corp ....G...... 908 707-2097
Franklin Lakes *(G-3622)*

Olon USA Inc ....F...... 973 577-6038
Florham Park *(G-3513)*

▼ Omg Electronic Chemicals Inc ....C...... 908 222-5800
South Plainfield *(G-10418)*

◆ Pariser Industries Inc ....E...... 973 569-9090
Paterson *(G-8360)*

▼ Plant Food Company Inc ....E...... 609 448-0935
Cranbury *(G-1870)*

Polymer Additives Inc ....D...... 856 467-8220
Swedesboro *(G-10719)*

Polymer Additives Inc ....F...... 856 467-8247
Bridgeport *(G-770)*

Por-15 Inc ....E...... 973 887-1999
Whippany *(G-12035)*

Prestone Products Corporation ....E...... 732 577-7800
Freehold *(G-3682)*

Procedyne Corp ....E...... 732 249-8347
New Brunswick *(G-6996)*

Rclc Inc ....E...... 732 877-1788
Woodbridge *(G-12152)*

Robert Nichols Contracting ....F...... 973 902-2632
Ringwood *(G-9455)*

◆ Rockwood Specialties Group Inc .....F...... 609 514-0300
Princeton *(G-9114)*

▲ Royce Associates A Ltd Partnr ....D...... 201 438-5200
East Rutherford *(G-2322)*

Sage Chemical Inc ....E...... 201 489-5172
Hackensack *(G-3970)*

Saltopia Artisan Infused Sea S ....G...... 917 628-8433
Hackettstown *(G-4035)*

Seaboard Industries ....E...... 732 901-5700
Lakewood *(G-5187)*

Sentry Water Management ....E...... 973 616-9000
Riverdale *(G-9486)*

▲ Shamrock Technologies Inc ....C...... 973 242-2999
Newark *(G-7309)*

Sika Corporation ....C...... 201 933-8800
Lyndhurst *(G-5709)*

◆ Sika Corporation ....B...... 201 933-8800
Lyndhurst *(G-5708)*

Sirchie Acquisition Co LLC ....E...... 609 654-0777
Medford *(G-6081)*

◆ SKW Quab Chemicals Inc ....F...... 201 556-0300
Saddle Brook *(G-9794)*

Solenis LLC ....E...... 201 767-7400
Norwood *(G-7635)*

◆ Solvay USA Inc ....B...... 609 860-4000
Princeton *(G-9122)*

◆ Spectrum Laboratory Pdts Inc ....C...... 732 214-1300
New Brunswick *(G-7004)*

Spectrum Laboratory Pdts Inc ....E...... 732 214-1300
New Brunswick *(G-7005)*

▲ Spex Certiprep Inc ....D...... 732 549-7144
Metuchen *(G-6121)*

Stepan Company ....D...... 201 845-3030
Maywood *(G-6061)*

◆ Stonhard Manufacturing Co Inc ....E...... 856 779-7500
Maple Shade *(G-5910)*

◆ Stuart Steel Protection Corp ....E...... 732 469-5544
Somerset *(G-10174)*

Sun Chemical Corporation..................E...... 201 438-4831
East Rutherford *(G-2329)*

Superior Printing Ink Co Inc ....G...... 973 242-5868
Newark *(G-7334)*

Suven Life Sciences Ltd.....................F...... 732 274-0037
Monmouth Junction *(G-6364)*

Sylvan Chemical Corporation.............E...... 201 934-4224
Fair Lawn *(G-3117)*

▲ Torpac Inc ....E...... 973 244-1125
Fairfield *(G-3328)*

▼ Turning Star Inc ....G...... 201 944-3462
Leonia *(G-5322)*

▼ United Energy Corp ....G...... 732 994-5225
Howell *(G-4569)*

▲ Vantage Spclty Ingredients Inc ....C...... 973 345-8600
Warren *(G-11570)*

W R Grace & Co - Conn ....F...... 201 869-5220
North Bergen *(G-7493)*

W R Grace & Co-Conn ....E...... 732 868-6914
Somerset *(G-10197)*

◆ Wasak Inc ....G...... 973 605-8122
Morristown *(G-6751)*

Water Dynamics Incorporated ....G...... 973 428-8330
Whippany *(G-12042)*

▼ William Kenyon & Sons Inc...............E...... 732 985-8980
Piscataway *(G-8836)*

▲ Wilpak Industries Inc ....G...... 201 997-7600
Kearny *(G-4923)*

▲ Wilshire Technologies Inc ....G...... 609 683-1117
Princeton *(G-9139)*

Worldwide Safety Systems LLC ....G...... 888 613-4501
Teaneck *(G-10778)*

Zoomessence Inc ....G...... 732 416-6638
Sayreville *(G-9843)*

29 PETROLEUM REFINING AND RELATED INDUSTRIES

2911 Petroleum Refining

Ashland LLC..G...... 908 243-3500
Bridgewater *(G-815)*

Ashland LLC..D...... 732 353-7718
Parlin *(G-7928)*

Bertone Aromatics ....G...... 201 444-9821
Waldwick *(G-11441)*

BP Corporation North Amer Inc ....G...... 973 633-2200
Wayne *(G-11613)*

BP Corporation North Amer Inc ....G...... 908 474-5000
Linden *(G-5353)*

▼ Bwi Chemicals ....G...... 732 689-0913
Monmouth Junction *(G-6334)*

Columbia Fuel Services Inc ....E...... 732 751-0044
Wall Township *(G-11474)*

CPI Operations LLC ....E...... 856 423-5400
Paulsboro *(G-8416)*

Intertek USA Inc ....E...... 732 969-5200
Carteret *(G-1260)*

Magnalube Inc ....G...... 718 729-1000
Linden *(G-5405)*

McAllister Service Company................G...... 856 665-4545
Pennsauken *(G-8546)*

◆ Mobil Research and Dev Corp ....A...... 856 224-2134
Paulsboro *(G-8421)*

▲ Paulsboro Refining Company LLC ......G...... 973 455-7500
Paulsboro *(G-8424)*

Pbf Energy Company...........................G...... 973 455-7500
Parsippany *(G-8055)*

◆ Pbf Energy Company LLC ....G...... 973 455-7500
Parsippany *(G-8056)*

◆ Pbf Energy Inc ....G...... 973 455-7500
Parsippany *(G-8057)*

◆ Pbf Holding Company LLC ....B...... 888 661-8949
Parsippany *(G-8058)*

◆ Pbf Services Company LLC ....G...... 973 455-7500
Parsippany *(G-8059)*

Pennzoil-Quaker State Company ....E...... 856 423-1388
Paulsboro *(G-8425)*

Purely Organic SA LLC ....G...... 201 942-0400
Jersey City *(G-4810)*

Speedway LLC ....B...... 732 750-7800
Port Reading *(G-8990)*

Starfuels Inc ....G...... 201 685-0400
Englewood *(G-2934)*

Tilcon New York Inc ....G...... 800 789-7625
Parsippany *(G-8102)*

◆ Total American Services Inc ....F...... 206 626-3500
Jersey City *(G-4838)*

▼ United Energy Corp ....G...... 732 994-5225
Howell *(G-4569)*

Valero Ref Company-New Jersey ....A...... 856 224-6000
Paulsboro *(G-8428)*

Wrench Brothers LLC ....G...... 201 222-0301
Jersey City *(G-4851)*

▼ Ziegler Chem & Mineral Corp.............F...... 732 752-4111
Piscataway *(G-8838)*

2951 Paving Mixtures & Blocks

A E Stone Inc......................................E...... 609 641-2781
Egg Harbor Township *(G-2675)*

All Surface Asphalt Paving ....G...... 732 295-3800
Point Pleasant Boro *(G-8930)*

Arawak Paving Co Inc ....E...... 609 561-4100
Hammonton *(G-4130)*

Asphalt Paving Systems Inc ....E...... 609 561-4161
Hammonton *(G-4131)*

Barrett Asphalt Inc.............................E...... 609 561-4100
Hammonton *(G-4132)*

Barrett Industries Corporation ....E...... 973 533-1001
Morristown *(G-6692)*

◆ Barrett Paving Materials Inc ....E...... 973 533-1001
Roseland *(G-9647)*

Beaver Run Farms ....G...... 973 427-1000
Hawthorne *(G-4221)*

Beaver Run Farms ....F...... 973 875-5555
Lafayette *(G-5044)*

Brick-Wall Corp ....E...... 732 787-0226
Atlantic Highlands *(G-109)*

Brick-Wall Corp ....E...... 609 693-6223
Forked River *(G-3534)*

Brunswick Hot Mix Corp ....D...... 908 233-4444
Westfield *(G-11922)*

Central Jersey Hot Mix Asp LLC ....G...... 732 323-0226
Jackson *(G-4656)*

Chevron USA Inc.................................D...... 732 738-2000
Perth Amboy *(G-8610)*

▲ Colas Inc ....G...... 973 290-9082
Morristown *(G-6700)*

Crowfoot Associates Inc ....G...... 609 561-0107
West Berlin *(G-11713)*

D Depasquale Paving LLC ....G...... 301 674-9775
Jackson *(G-4661)*

Dosch-King Company Inc ....F...... 973 887-0145
Whippany *(G-12018)*

▲ Earle The Walter R Corp ....G...... 732 308-1113
Wall Township *(G-11478)*

Earle The Walter R Corp ....G...... 732 657-8551
Jackson *(G-4665)*

Earle Asphalt Company ....G...... 732 657-8551
Jackson *(G-4666)*

Earle Asphalt Company ....C...... 732 308-1113
Wall Township *(G-11479)*

Eastern Concrete Materials Inc ....E...... 973 827-7625
Hamburg *(G-4091)*

Flemington Bituminous Corp ....F...... 908 782-2722
Flemington *(G-3441)*

Hanson Aggregates Wrp Inc ....G...... 972 653-5500
Wall Township *(G-11487)*

Joseph and William Stavola ....E...... 609 924-0300
Kingston *(G-5028)*

Louis N Rothberg & Son Inc ....E...... 732 356-9505
Middlesex *(G-6176)*

National Paving Co Inc ....F...... 856 767-1950
Berlin *(G-439)*

Newark Asphalt Corp ....G...... 973 482-3503
Newark *(G-7253)*

Richard E Pierson Mtls Corp ....G...... 856 740-2400
Williamstown *(G-12103)*

Richard E Pierson Mtls Corp ....E...... 856 691-0083
Vineland *(G-11399)*

Richard E Pierson Mtls Corp ....E...... 856 467-4199
Pilesgrove *(G-8676)*

Riverdale Quarry LLC ....E...... 973 835-0028
Riverdale *(G-9485)*

Rosano Asphalt LLC ....G...... 732 620-8400
Farmingdale *(G-3393)*

Schifano Construction Corp ....F...... 732 752-3450
Middlesex *(G-6194)*

South State Inc ....E...... 856 881-6030
Williamstown *(G-12107)*

Stavola Asphalt Company Inc ....E...... 732 542-2328
Tinton Falls *(G-10848)*

Stavola Construction Mtls Inc ....E...... 732 356-5700
Bound Brook *(G-625)*

Stavola Contracting Co Inc ....G...... 732 935-0156
Englishtown *(G-2998)*

Stavola Holding Corporation ....C...... 732 542-2328
Tinton Falls *(G-10850)*

Stone Industries Inc ....D...... 973 595-6250
Haledon *(G-4085)*

Tilcon New York Inc ....D...... 973 835-0028
Riverdale *(G-9490)*

Tilcon New York Inc ....D...... 800 789-7625
North Bergen *(G-7489)*

Weldon Asphalt Corp ....F...... 973 627-7500
Rockaway *(G-9624)*

Weldon Asphalt Corp ....E...... 908 322-7840
Watchung *(G-11597)*

Weldon Materials Inc ....E...... 201 991-3200
Kearny *(G-4919)*

Ziegler Chem & Mineral Corp..............E...... 732 752-4111
Piscataway *(G-8839)*

2952 Asphalt Felts & Coatings

▼ Actega North America Inc ....C...... 856 829-6300
Delran *(G-2009)*

◆ Fti Inc ....G...... 973 443-0004
Florham Park *(G-3503)*

Icote USA Inc ....G...... 908 359-7575
Hillsborough *(G-4343)*

▲ Karnak Corporation ....D...... 732 388-0300
Clark *(G-1502)*

Karnak Midwest LLC.................G.... 732 388-0300
 Clark (G-1503)
Koadings Inc...........................G.... 732 517-0784
 Allenhurst (G-26)
Lodor Offset Corporation...........F.... 201 935-7100
 Carlstadt (G-1184)
Newark Asphalt Corp................G.... 973 482-3503
 Newark (G-7253)
▲ United Asphalt Co Inc............E.... 856 753-9811
 Berlin (G-444)
▲ Vector Foiltec LLC...............G.... 862 702-8909
 Fairfield (G-3339)

2992 Lubricating Oils & Greases

American Oil & Supply Co............F.... 732 389-5514
 Eatontown (G-2382)
Arol Chemical Products Co..........G.... 973 344-1510
 Newark (G-7094)
◆ Bel-Ray Company Inc.............D.... 732 378-4000
 Wall Township (G-11465)
◆ BP Lubricants USA Inc..........B.... 973 633-2200
 Wayne (G-11614)
Chemours Company..................G.... 856 540-3398
 Deepwater (G-1998)
▼ Cumberland Vacuum Products Inc .G.... 856 691-9155
 Vineland (G-11346)
Federal Lorco Petroleum LLC........D.... 908 352-0542
 Elizabeth (G-2731)
◆ Fti Inc...........................G.... 973 443-0004
 Florham Park (G-3503)
Gordon Terminal Service Co PA.....D.... 201 437-8300
 Bayonne (G-229)
◆ Hangsterfers Laboratories........E.... 856 468-0216
 West Deptford (G-11827)
International Products Corp.........F.... 609 386-8770
 Burlington (G-979)
Lanxess Solutions US Inc...........C.... 973 887-7411
 East Hanover (G-2227)
Lanxess Solutions US Inc...........C.... 732 738-1000
 Fords (G-3530)
Marine Oil Service Inc.............G.... 908 282-6440
 Elizabeth (G-2754)
Mil-Comm Products Company Inc ......F.... 201 935-8561
 East Rutherford (G-2311)
◆ Pbf Holding Company LLC.........B.... 888 661-8949
 Parsippany (G-8058)
Penetone Corporation...............E.... 201 567-3000
 Carlstadt (G-1199)
▲ Pflaumer Brothers Inc...........G.... 609 883-4610
 Ewing (G-3042)
▼ Smb International LLC............F.... 732 222-4888
 West Long Branch (G-11847)
Total Specialties Usa Inc..........D.... 908 862-9300
 Linden (G-5454)

2999 Products Of Petroleum & Coal, NEC

Honeywell International Inc.........C.... 973 455-2000
 Morris Plains (G-6668)
▼ Honeywell Specity Wax & Additv......F.... 973 455-2000
 Morristown (G-6717)

30 RUBBER AND MISCELLANEOUS PLASTICS PRODUCTS

3011 Tires & Inner Tubes

American Tire Distributors..........G.... 973 646-5600
 Totowa (G-10929)
Bkt Exim Us Inc....................G.... 732 817-1400
 Holmdel (G-4509)
Bkt Tires Inc......................G.... 844 258-8473
 Holmdel (G-4510)
Coilhose Pneumatics Inc............E.... 732 432-7177
 East Brunswick (G-2142)
J G Carpenter Contractor...........G.... 732 271-8991
 Middlesex (G-6171)
◆ Leopard Inc.......................F.... 908 964-3600
 Hillside (G-4425)

3021 Rubber & Plastic Footwear

▲ Bear USa Inc.....................F.... 201 943-4748
 Palisades Park (G-7835)
Crocs Inc..........................F.... 609 344-6300
 Atlantic City (G-94)
▲ Lust For Life Footwear LLC......F.... 631 327-2811
 Teaneck (G-10761)
Nike Inc...........................E.... 732 695-0108
 Tinton Falls (G-10842)

▲ Tingley Rubber Corporation.......E.... 800 631-5498
 Piscataway (G-8825)
Vans Inc...........................F.... 732 493-1516
 Tinton Falls (G-10853)

3052 Rubber & Plastic Hose & Belting

Aarubco Rubber Co Inc..............E.... 973 772-8177
 Saddle Brook (G-9749)
▲ Atlantic Rubber Enterprises......G.... 973 697-5900
 Newfoundland (G-7373)
▲ Belting Industries Group LLC......E.... 908 272-8591
 Union (G-11158)
▲ Brecoflex Co LLC.................D.... 732 460-9500
 Eatontown (G-2386)
◆ Colorite Polymers................F.... 800 631-1577
 Ridgefield (G-9356)
Couse & Bolten Co..................G.... 973 344-6330
 Newark (G-7129)
Daniel C Herring Co Inc............F.... 732 530-6557
 Eatontown (G-2389)
Dyna Veyor Inc.....................G.... 908 276-5384
 Newark (G-7146)
Firefighter One Ltd Lblty Co.......G.... 973 940-3061
 Sparta (G-10499)
Forbo Siegling LLC.................F.... 201 567-6100
 Englewood (G-2897)
Harrison Hose and Tubing Inc.......E.... 609 631-8804
 Robbinsville (G-9517)
Hosepharm Ltd Liability Co.........G.... 732 376-0044
 Perth Amboy (G-8617)
Lewis-Goetz and Company Inc.......F.... 856 579-1421
 Swedesboro (G-10706)
◆ Megadyne America LLC............E.... 973 227-4904
 Fairfield (G-3257)
Minor Rubber Co Inc................E.... 973 338-6800
 Bloomfield (G-522)
Novaflex Industries Inc............F.... 856 768-2275
 West Berlin (G-11739)
▲ Passaic Rubber Co................D.... 973 696-9500
 Wayne (G-11671)
◆ Plastic Specialties & Tech Inc....C.... 201 941-2900
 Ridgefield (G-9380)
▲ Polytech Designs Inc.............F.... 973 340-1390
 Clifton (G-1701)
Ptc Electronics Inc................G.... 201 847-0500
 Mahwah (G-5804)
Pure Tech International Inc.........F.... 908 722-4968
 Branchburg (G-695)
▲ Pure Tech International Inc......F.... 908 722-4800
 Branchburg (G-696)
Rubber Fab & Molding Inc...........G.... 908 852-7725
 Johnsonburg (G-4855)
▲ Stiles Enterprises Inc...........F.... 973 625-9660
 Rockaway (G-9610)
T & B Specialties Inc..............G.... 732 928-4500
 Jackson (G-4679)
Targa Industries Inc...............F.... 973 584-3733
 Flanders (G-3418)
▲ Thirty-Three Queen Realty Inc....F.... 973 824-5527
 Newark (G-7341)
◆ US Wire & Cable Corporation......B.... 973 824-5530
 Newark (G-7355)

3053 Gaskets, Packing & Sealing Devices

Alltite Gasket Co..................F.... 732 254-2154
 South River (G-10458)
▲ American Braiding & Mfg Corp.....F.... 732 938-6333
 Howell (G-4545)
▼ Arcy Manufacturing Co Inc........F.... 201 635-1910
 Carlstadt (G-1126)
Aspe Inc...........................E.... 973 808-1155
 Fairfield (G-3141)
▲ Atlantic Rubber Enterprises......G.... 973 697-5900
 Newfoundland (G-7373)
Banks Bros Corporation.............D.... 973 680-4488
 Bloomfield (G-502)
Capital Gasket and Rubber Inc......E.... 856 939-3670
 Runnemede (G-9717)
▲ Cinchseal Associates Inc.........F.... 856 662-5162
 Mount Laurel (G-6788)
Coast Rubber and Gasket Inc........G.... 609 747-0110
 Burlington (G-965)
Cryopak Verification Tech Inc......F.... 732 346-9200
 Edison (G-2497)
Custom Gasket Mfg LLC..............F.... 201 331-6363
 Englewood Cliffs (G-2956)
Datwyler Pharma Packaging..........E.... 856 663-2202
 Pennsauken (G-8500)
Eagleburgmann Industries LP........F.... 856 241-7300
 Swedesboro (G-10695)

East Coast Rubber Products.........G.... 856 384-2747
 Westville (G-11938)
Eastern Molding Co Inc.............G.... 973 759-0220
 Belleville (G-301)
Electro-Ceramic Industries.........E.... 201 342-2630
 Hackensack (G-3909)
Fleet Packaging Inc................G.... 866 302-0340
 South Orange (G-10306)
Frc Electrical Industries Inc......E.... 908 464-3200
 New Providence (G-7036)
Frontline Industries Inc...........F.... 973 373-7211
 Irvington (G-4587)
▲ H K Metal Craft Mfg Corp.........E.... 973 471-7770
 Lodi (G-5585)
J P Rotella Co Inc.................F.... 973 942-2559
 Haledon (G-4083)
Ja-Bar Silicone Corp...............D.... 973 786-5000
 Andover (G-51)
▼ Lamatek Inc......................E.... 856 599-6000
 Paulsboro (G-8418)
Ls Rubber Industries Inc...........F.... 973 680-4488
 Bloomfield (G-519)
▲ Mercer Rubber Company............E.... 856 931-5000
 Bellmawr (G-347)
Metallo Gasket Company Inc.........F.... 732 545-7223
 New Brunswick (G-6981)
▲ Monmouth Rubber Corp.............E.... 732 229-3444
 Long Branch (G-5630)
Mueller Die Cut Solutions Inc......E.... 201 791-5000
 Saddle Brook (G-9777)
▲ Newton Tool & Mfg Inc............D.... 856 241-1500
 Pennsauken (G-8554)
Omega Shielding Products Inc.......F.... 973 366-0080
 Randolph (G-9293)
▼ Paradigm Packaging East LLC......C.... 201 909-3400
 Saddle Brook (G-9780)
Phoenix Packing & Gasket Co........F.... 732 938-7377
 Howell (G-4564)
R S Rubber Corp....................F.... 973 777-2200
 Wallington (G-11529)
▲ Rempac LLC.......................C.... 201 843-4585
 Rochelle Park (G-9536)
Romaco North America Inc...........G.... 609 584-2500
 Hamilton (G-4124)
▲ Seals-Eastern Incorporated.......C.... 732 747-9200
 Red Bank (G-9343)
Specialty Rubber Inc...............G.... 609 704-2555
 Elwood (G-2854)
▲ Sprialseal Inc...................G.... 732 738-6113
 Cliffwood (G-1548)
▲ Stiles Enterprises Inc...........F.... 973 625-9660
 Rockaway (G-9610)
Thomas A Caserta Inc...............F.... 609 586-2807
 Robbinsville (G-9522)
Tricomp Inc........................C.... 973 835-1110
 Pompton Plains (G-8966)
Viziflex Seels Inc.................F.... 201 488-3446
 Saddle Brook (G-9799)

3061 Molded, Extruded & Lathe-Cut Rubber Mechanical Goods

Aarubco Rubber Co Inc..............E.... 973 772-8177
 Saddle Brook (G-9749)
AMP Custom Rubber Inc..............F.... 732 888-2714
 Keyport (G-5015)
Denaka Partners LP.................E.... 609 394-1176
 Trenton (G-11053)
Eastern Molding Co Inc.............G.... 973 759-0220
 Belleville (G-301)
Fermatex Vascular Tech LLC.........F.... 732 681-7070
 Wall Township (G-11481)
Hawthorne Rubber Mfg Corp..........E.... 973 427-3337
 Hawthorne (G-4240)
Kinnarney Rubber Co Inc............F.... 856 468-1320
 Mantua (G-5892)
▲ Manville Rubber Products Inc.....E.... 908 526-9111
 Manville (G-5896)
Mid-State Enterprises Inc..........E.... 973 427-6040
 Hawthorne (G-4247)
Minor Rubber Co Inc................E.... 973 338-6800
 Bloomfield (G-522)
▲ Monmouth Rubber Corp.............E.... 732 229-3444
 Long Branch (G-5630)
Nbs Group Sup Med Pdts Div LLC......G.... 732 745-9292
 New Brunswick (G-6983)
▲ Panova Inc.......................E.... 973 263-1700
 Towaco (G-11000)
▲ Passaic Rubber Co................D.... 973 696-9500
 Wayne (G-11671)

S
I
C

Pierce-Roberts Rubber Company ....F 609 394-5245
Ewing *(G-3043)*

▲ Reiss Corporation ....C 732 446-6100
Rumson *(G-9714)*

▲ Rempac LLC ....D 201 843-4585
Rochelle Park *(G-9536)*

▲ Research & Mfg Corp Amer ....F 908 862-6744
Linden *(G-5433)*

▲ Rubber & Silicone Products Co ....E 973 227-2300
Fairfield *(G-3298)*

Shock Tech Inc ....E 845 368-8600
Mahwah *(G-5812)*

▲ Stiles Enterprises Inc ....F 973 625-9660
Rockaway *(G-9610)*

T & B Specialties Inc ....G 732 928-4500
Jackson *(G-4679)*

▲ Tbmc Inc ....E 864 288-9916
Fairfield *(G-3321)*

Tire Place LLC ....G 732 970-6667
Keyport *(G-5025)*

Tricomp Inc ....C 973 835-1110
Pompton Plains *(G-8966)*

▲ Troy Hills Manufacturing Inc ......G 973 263-1885
Towaco *(G-11005)*

3069 Fabricated Rubber Prdts, NEC

Accu Seal Rubber Inc ....G 732 246-4333
New Brunswick *(G-6942)*

▼ Aero TEC Laboratories Inc ....E 201 825-1400
Ramsey *(G-9231)*

Aerogroup Retail Holdings Inc ......D 732 819-9843
Edison *(G-2451)*

◆ Air Cruisers Company LLC ....C 732 681-3527
Wall Township *(G-11460)*

▲ American Braiding & Mfg Corp ....F 732 938-6333
Howell *(G-4545)*

◆ American Harlequin Corporation ..E 856 234-5505
Moorestown *(G-6558)*

▲ Ames Rubber Corporation ....D 973 827-9101
Hamburg *(G-4088)*

◆ Ansell Healthcare Products LLC ..C 732 345-5400
Iselin *(G-4611)*

Ansell Inc ....D 732 345-5400
Red Bank *(G-9320)*

▲ Ansell Protective Products LLC ...A 732 345-5400
Iselin *(G-4613)*

◆ Asbury Carbons Inc ....G 908 537-2155
Asbury *(G-66)*

Atlantic Flooring LLC ....F 609 296-7700
Ltl Egg Hbr *(G-5641)*

▲ Baby Time International Inc ....G 973 481-7400
Newark *(G-7103)*

Banks Bros Corporation ....D 973 680-4488
Bloomfield *(G-502)*

Bsrm Inc ....G 888 509-0668
Mount Laurel *(G-6784)*

Bumper Specialties Inc ....C 856 345-7650
West Deptford *(G-11819)*

C M H Hele-Shaw Inc ....F 201 974-0570
Hoboken *(G-4462)*

Datwyler Pharma Packaging ....E 856 663-2202
Pennsauken *(G-8500)*

Derv2000 ....G 503 470-9158
Kearny *(G-4871)*

◆ Diversified Foam Products Inc .....D 856 662-1981
Swedesboro *(G-10693)*

Dream Makers Inc ....G 201 248-5502
Park Ridge *(G-7918)*

▲ Dso Fluid Handling Co Inc ....E 732 225-9100
Edison *(G-2505)*

Eastern Molding Co Inc ....G 973 759-0220
Belleville *(G-301)*

Elastograf Inc ....D 973 209-3161
Hamburg *(G-4094)*

◆ Fidelity Industries Inc ....E 973 696-9120
Wayne *(G-11632)*

Fidelity Industries Inc ....E 973 777-2592
Clifton *(G-1619)*

Flooring Concepts NJ LLC ....F 732 409-7600
Manalapan *(G-5848)*

Glopak Corp ....E 908 753-8735
South Plainfield *(G-10373)*

Hawthorne Rubber Mfg Corp ....E 973 427-3337
Hawthorne *(G-4240)*

◆ Henderson Aquatic Inc ....C 856 825-4771
Millville *(G-6307)*

Hutchinson Industries Inc ....F 609 394-1010
Trenton *(G-11064)*

◆ Hutchinson Industries Inc ....C 609 394-1010
Trenton *(G-11065)*

Hutchinson Industries Inc ....F 609 394-1010
Trenton *(G-11066)*

◆ Innocor Inc ....C 732 945-6222
Red Bank *(G-9331)*

Innocor Foam Tech - Acp Inc ....D 732 945-6222
Red Bank *(G-9332)*

Inoac Usa Inc ....D 201 807-0809
Moonachie *(G-6522)*

Kappus Plastic Company Inc ....D 908 537-2288
Hampton *(G-4163)*

Kinnarney Rubber Co Inc ....F 856 468-1320
Mantua *(G-5892)*

La Favorite Industries Inc ....F 973 279-1266
Paterson *(G-8316)*

▼ Lamatek Inc ....E 856 599-6000
Paulsboro *(G-8418)*

◆ Leland Limited Inc ....E 908 561-2000
South Plainfield *(G-10398)*

Linoleum Sales Company Inc ....C 201 438-1844
East Rutherford *(G-2304)*

Ls Rubber Industries Inc ....E 973 680-4488
Bloomfield *(G-519)*

▲ Manville Rubber Products Inc .....E 908 526-9111
Manville *(G-5896)*

Mat Logo Central LLC ....G 973 433-0311
Cedar Grove *(G-1290)*

▲ Mfv International Corporation ......G 973 993-1687
Morristown *(G-6727)*

Miroad Rubber USA LLC ....G 480 280-2543
Edison *(G-2573)*

Ness Plastics Inc ....G 201 854-4072
West New York *(G-11875)*

Norco Manufacturing Inc ....F 201 854-3461
North Bergen *(G-7471)*

Pacific Dnlop Holdings USA LLC ....G 732 345-5400
Red Bank *(G-9339)*

◆ Pacific Dunlop Investments USA ..F 732 345-5400
Red Bank *(G-9340)*

▲ Panova Inc ....E 973 263-1700
Towaco *(G-11000)*

▲ Passaic Rubber Co ....D 973 696-9500
Wayne *(G-11671)*

Pierce-Roberts Rubber Company ....F 609 394-5245
Ewing *(G-3043)*

Pure Rubber Products Co ....G 973 784-3690
Rockaway *(G-9602)*

Rak Foam Sales Inc ....G 908 668-1122
Plainfield *(G-8872)*

▲ Rema Tip Top/North America Inc ..E 201 768-8100
Northvale *(G-7605)*

Rossendale Reddaway Company ....G 973 690-6097
Newark *(G-7292)*

▲ Rp Products LLC ....G 732 254-4222
East Brunswick *(G-2181)*

Schon J Tool & Machine Co ....G 732 928-6665
Jackson *(G-4677)*

Seajay Manufacturing Corp ....F 732 774-0900
Neptune *(G-6931)*

▲ Star-Glo Industries LLC ....C 201 939-6162
East Rutherford *(G-2326)*

Strongwall Industries Inc ....G 201 445-4633
Allendale *(G-19)*

▲ Supply Plus NJ Inc ....F 973 782-5930
Paterson *(G-8390)*

Switlik Parachute Company Inc ......F 609 587-3300
Trenton *(G-11119)*

Sxwell USA LLC ....B 732 345-5400
Iselin *(G-4647)*

Thomas A Caserta Inc ....F 609 586-2807
Robbinsville *(G-9522)*

▲ Tingley Rubber Corporation ....E 800 631-5498
Piscataway *(G-8825)*

Transport Products Inc ....G 973 857-6090
Cedar Grove *(G-1302)*

Tricomp Inc ....C 973 835-1110
Pompton Plains *(G-8966)*

▲ Vibration Muntings Contrls Inc ...D 800 569-8423
Bloomingdale *(G-545)*

▼ Water Master Co ....G 732 247-1900
Highland Park *(G-4305)*

West Phrm Svcs Lakewood Inc ......G 732 730-3295
Lakewood *(G-5205)*

◆ Woodbridge Inoac Technical ....D 201 807-0809
Moonachie *(G-6553)*

Woodbridge Inoac Technical Pro ....D 201 807-0809
Moonachie *(G-6554)*

3081 Plastic Unsupported Sheet & Film

▲ Acrilex Inc ....E 201 333-1500
Jersey City *(G-4698)*

▲ ADM Corporation ....D 732 469-0900
Middlesex *(G-6143)*

Air Protection Packaging Corp ....F 973 577-4343
Linden *(G-5344)*

▼ All American Poly Corp ....C 732 752-3200
Piscataway *(G-8730)*

▼ Allied Plastics Holdings LLC ....D 718 729-5500
Newark *(G-7078)*

Amcor Flexibles Inc ....E 609 267-5900
Mount Holly *(G-6766)*

Amcor Flexibles LLC ....C 856 825-1400
Millville *(G-6275)*

American Renolit Corp La ....E 856 241-4901
Swedesboro *(G-10681)*

American Renolit Corporation ....G 973 706-6912
Wayne *(G-11604)*

American Transparent Plastic ....E 732 287-3000
Edison *(G-2459)*

◆ Arch Crown Inc ....E 973 731-6300
Hillside *(G-4390)*

Ber Plastics Inc ....E 973 839-2100
Riverdale *(G-9475)*

Berry Global Inc ....C 908 353-3850
Elizabeth *(G-2714)*

Berry Global Inc ....G 908 454-0900
Phillipsburg *(G-8643)*

Berry Global Inc ....E 609 395-4199
Cranbury *(G-1814)*

▼ Berry Global Films LLC ....C 201 641-6600
Montvale *(G-6446)*

▲ Broadway Kleer-Guard Corp ....E 609 662-3970
Monroe Township *(G-6380)*

Caloric Color Co Inc ....F 973 471-4748
Garfield *(G-3725)*

Central Plastics Incorporated ....G 973 808-0990
Parsippany *(G-7966)*

◆ Congoleum Corporation ....E 609 584-3000
Trenton *(G-11044)*

Congoleum Corporation ....B 609 584-3000
Trenton *(G-11046)*

Congoleum Corporation ....G 609 584-3601
Trenton *(G-11045)*

Corbco Inc ....G 609 549-6299
Forked River *(G-3536)*

Creative Film Corp ....F 732 367-2166
Lakewood *(G-5097)*

◆ Dicar Inc ....E 973 575-1377
Pine Brook *(G-8697)*

Dow Chemical Company ....D 800 258-2436
Somerset *(G-10090)*

Fordion Packaging Ltd ....F 201 692-1344
Hackensack *(G-3916)*

Gemini Plastic Films Corp ....E 973 340-0700
Garfield *(G-3736)*

◆ Glitterex Corp ....D 908 272-9121
Cranford *(G-1908)*

Glopak Corp ....E 908 753-8735
South Plainfield *(G-10373)*

Heritage Bag Company ....D 856 467-2247
Swedesboro *(G-10702)*

Hillside Plastics Corporation ....G 973 923-2700
Hillside *(G-4414)*

JA Heilferty LLC ....E 201 836-5060
Teaneck *(G-10757)*

Kappus Plastic Company Inc ....D 908 537-2288
Hampton *(G-4163)*

▲ Kayline Processing Inc ....E 609 695-1449
Trenton *(G-11073)*

▲ Kolon USA Incorporated ....F 201 641-5800
Ridgefield Park *(G-9409)*

▲ Lally-Pak Inc ....G 908 351-4141
Hillside *(G-4424)*

◆ Lps Industries Inc ....C 201 438-3515
Moonachie *(G-6529)*

▲ Mark Ronald Associates Inc ....D 908 558-0011
Hillside *(G-4429)*

Montrose Molders Corporation ......C 908 754-3030
South Plainfield *(G-10410)*

▲ Nan Ya Plastics Corp USA ....G 973 992-1775
Livingston *(G-5550)*

▼ Nexus Plastics Incorporated ....D 973 427-3311
Hawthorne *(G-4249)*

Niaflex Corporation ....F 407 851-6620
Livingston *(G-5552)*

Nobelus LLC ....G 800 895-2747
North Brunswick *(G-7531)*

▼ Package Development Co Inc ....E 973 983-8500
Rockaway *(G-9593)*

Pegasus Products Inc ....E 908 707-1122
Branchburg *(G-688)*

▲ Perlin Converting LLC ....F 973 887-0257
　Whippany *(G-12033)*

Petro Packaging Co Inc ....E 908 272-4054
　Cranford *(G-1922)*

▲ Plastic Plus Group LLC ....E 201 561-0405
　Secaucus *(G-9911)*

Prestige Associates Inc ....E 609 393-1509
　Trenton *(G-11105)*

Primex Plastics Corporation ....C 973 470-8000
　Garfield *(G-3751)*

Productive Plastics Inc ....D 856 778-4300
　Mount Laurel *(G-6832)*

Silverton Packaging Corp ....G 732 341-0986
　Monroe Township *(G-6393)*

▲ Ssi North America Inc ....G 973 598-0152
　Randolph *(G-9299)*

Tekni-Plex Inc ....C 908 575-7661
　Branchburg *(G-710)*

▲ Tri-Cor Flexible Packaging Inc ....E 973 940-1500
　Sparta *(G-10526)*

▲ Trinity Plastics Inc ....C 973 994-8018
　Livingston *(G-5566)*

Up United LLC ....E 718 383-5700
　Bridgewater *(G-906)*

▲ US Plastic Sales LLC ....G 908 754-9404
　South Plainfield *(G-10446)*

◆ Vish LLC ....E 201 529-2900
　North Brunswick *(G-7546)*

Zack Painting Co Inc ....E 732 738-7900
　Fords *(G-3531)*

3082 Plastic Unsupported Profile Shapes

▲ Accessrec LLC ....G 973 955-0514
　Clifton *(G-1554)*

▲ All State Plastics Inc ....E 732 654-5054
　South Amboy *(G-10234)*

Alpha Wire Corporation ....C 908 925-8000
　Elizabeth *(G-2708)*

Belle Printing Group LLC ....G 856 235-5151
　Mount Laurel *(G-6782)*

Ber Plastics Inc ....E 973 839-2100
　Riverdale *(G-9475)*

Cobon Plastics Corp ....F 973 344-6330
　Newark *(G-7123)*

▲ Fluorotherm Polymers Inc ....G 973 575-0760
　Parsippany *(G-8014)*

Illinois Tool Works Inc ....G 732 968-5300
　Parsippany *(G-8028)*

▲ K Jabat Inc ....F 732 469-8177
　Green Brook *(G-3860)*

◆ Keystone Plastics Inc ....G 908 561-1300
　South Plainfield *(G-10392)*

◆ Plastic Specialties & Tech Inc ......C 201 941-2900
　Ridgefield *(G-9380)*

▲ Pure Tech International Inc ....G 908 722-4800
　Branchburg *(G-696)*

Resdel Corporation ....E 609 886-1111
　Rio Grande *(G-9461)*

Saint-Gobain Prfmce Plas Corp ....D 856 423-6630
　Mickleton *(G-6138)*

Tpi Partners Inc ....G 908 561-3000
　Stirling *(G-10608)*

Tricomp Inc ....C 973 835-1110
　Pompton Plains *(G-8966)*

▲ X-L Plastics Inc ....C 973 777-9400
　Clifton *(G-1745)*

Zeus Industrial Products Inc ....C 908 292-6500
　Branchburg *(G-721)*

3083 Plastic Laminated Plate & Sheet

Barnegat Light Fibrgls Sup LLC ....G 609 294-8870
　West Creek *(G-11809)*

C & K Plastics Inc ....D 732 549-0011
　Metuchen *(G-6098)*

▲ Dikeman Laminating Corporation ...E 973 473-5696
　Clifton *(G-1599)*

▲ Ensinger Grenloch Inc ....D 856 227-0500
　Grenloch *(G-3866)*

▲ Federal Plastics Corporation ....E 908 272-5800
　Cranford *(G-1907)*

Fedplast Inc ....F 732 901-1153
　Lakewood *(G-5122)*

Flex Products Inc ....D 201 440-1570
　Carlstadt *(G-1162)*

▲ Fluorotherm Polymers Inc ....G 973 575-0760
　Parsippany *(G-8014)*

◆ Gabhen Inc ....C 800 631-3572
　Totowa *(G-10945)*

Graphic Express Menu Co Inc ....E 973 685-0022
　Clifton *(G-1630)*

JMJ Profile Inc ....G 856 767-3930
　West Berlin *(G-11726)*

▲ K Jabat Inc ....F 732 469-8177
　Green Brook *(G-3860)*

▲ La Mart Manufacturing Corp ....G 718 384-6917
　Teaneck *(G-10759)*

▲ McGrory Glass Inc ....D 856 579-3200
　Paulsboro *(G-8420)*

▲ Monmouth Rubber Corp ....E 732 229-3444
　Long Branch *(G-5630)*

◆ Nan Ya Plastics Corp America ....G 973 992-1775
　Livingston *(G-5549)*

▲ O Plast Matic Valves Inc ....G 973 256-3000
　Cedar Grove *(G-1293)*

Owens Plastic Products Inc ....G 856 447-3500
　Cedarville *(G-1324)*

Plastinetics Inc ....G 973 618-9090
　West Caldwell *(G-11797)*

Productive Plastics Inc ....D 856 778-4300
　Mount Laurel *(G-6832)*

▲ Research & Mfg Corp Amer ....F 908 862-6744
　Linden *(G-5433)*

◆ Royal Sovereign Intl Inc ....E 800 397-1025
　Rockleigh *(G-9633)*

◆ Roysons Corporation ....G 973 625-5570
　Rockaway *(G-9606)*

Saint-Gobain Prfmce Plas Corp ....D 856 423-6630
　Mickleton *(G-6138)*

▲ Spiral Binding LLC ....C 973 256-0666
　Totowa *(G-10973)*

Washington Stamp Exchange Inc ....F 973 966-0001
　Florham Park *(G-3523)*

▲ Wood & Laminates Inc ....G 973 773-7475
　Lodi *(G-5609)*

3084 Plastic Pipe

Advanced Drainage Systems Inc ....D 856 467-4779
　Logan Township *(G-5610)*

Endot Industries Inc ....D 973 625-8500
　Rockaway *(G-9564)*

3085 Plastic Bottles

▲ Amcor Phrm Packg USA LLC ....C 856 327-1540
　Millville *(G-6277)*

Amcor Rigid Plastics Usa LLC ....D 856 327-1540
　Millville *(G-6282)*

Brent River Corp ....E 908 722-6021
　Hillsborough *(G-4323)*

Consolidated Container Co LP ....D 908 289-5862
　Elizabeth *(G-2720)*

Flexbiosys Inc ....F 908 300-3244
　Lebanon *(G-5286)*

◆ Imagine Gold LLC ....E 201 488-5988
　South Hackensack *(G-10270)*

Q-Pak Corporation ....E 973 483-4404
　Newark *(G-7281)*

▲ Qualipac America Corp ....E 973 754-9920
　Woodland Park *(G-12230)*

Setco LLC ....G 610 321-9760
　Monroe Township *(G-6391)*

▲ Unette Corporation ....D 973 328-6800
　Randolph *(G-9304)*

3086 Plastic Foam Prdts

A & S Packaging & Display ....E 201 531-1900
　Carlstadt *(G-1120)*

Alliance Corrugated Box Inc ....E 877 525-5269
　Saddle River *(G-9802)*

Arrow Information Packagig LLC ....G 856 317-9000
　Pennsauken *(G-8480)*

Atlantic Can Company ....G 609 518-9950
　Westampton *(G-11911)*

Capitol Foam Products Inc ....E 201 933-5277
　East Rutherford *(G-2291)*

▲ Century Service Affiliates Inc ....E 973 742-3516
　Paterson *(G-8231)*

Craig Robertson ....G 973 293-8666
　Montague *(G-6402)*

Dv8 Enterprises LLC ....F 201 507-6288
　West Berlin *(G-11715)*

▼ Evonik Foams Inc ....E 973 929-8000
　Parsippany *(G-8005)*

Futurex Properties Inc ....E 732 414-6211
　Marlboro *(G-5941)*

Fxi Inc ....D 201 933-8540
　East Rutherford *(G-2298)*

Glopak Corp ....E 908 753-8735
　South Plainfield *(G-10373)*

Granite Packaging Supply Co ....D 856 727-1010
　Moorestown *(G-6579)*

Innocor Foam Technologies LLC ....C 844 824-9348
　Red Bank *(G-9333)*

Instapak Corp Sealed Air ....D 201 791-7600
　Rochelle Park *(G-9529)*

Integrated Packaging Inds Inc ....E 973 839-0500
　Butler *(G-1009)*

Johns Manville Corporation ....G 732 225-9190
　Edison *(G-2548)*

Kohler Industries Inc ....G 336 545-3289
　Paterson *(G-8311)*

▲ New Dimensions Industries LLC .....G 201 531-1010
　West Berlin *(G-11736)*

New Industrial Foam Corp ....G 908 561-4010
　Plainfield *(G-8868)*

▲ Pacor Inc ....E 609 324-1100
　Bordentown *(G-607)*

Plasti Foam ....D 908 722-5254
　Branchburg *(G-690)*

▲ Plastic Plus Inc ....G 973 614-0271
　Passaic *(G-8170)*

Plastico Products LLC ....G 973 923-1944
　Irvington *(G-4600)*

Plastpac Inc ....F 908 272-7200
　Kenilworth *(G-4989)*

Pmc Inc ....B 201 933-8540
　East Rutherford *(G-2317)*

Pmc Inc ....C 732 370-1163
　Lakewood *(G-5173)*

◆ Poly Molding LLC ....F 973 835-7161
　Haskell *(G-4213)*

◆ Rempac Foam Corp ....F 973 881-8880
　Rochelle Park *(G-9535)*

▲ Rempac LLC ....C 201 843-4585
　Rochelle Park *(G-9536)*

▲ Rep Trading Associates Inc ....F 732 591-1140
　Old Bridge *(G-7792)*

Sealed Air Corporation ....C 201 712-7000
　Saddle Brook *(G-9792)*

Sealed Air Corporation ....D 973 890-4735
　Saddle Brook *(G-9793)*

◆ Sekisui America Corporation ....F 201 423-7960
　Secaucus *(G-9927)*

▲ Shell Packaging Corporation ....E 908 871-7000
　Berkeley Heights *(G-422)*

Sierra Packaging Inc ....F 732 571-2900
　Ocean *(G-7745)*

Sonoco Display & Packaging LLC ....G 201 612-4008
　Ridgefield Park *(G-9415)*

▲ T C P Reliable Manufacturing ....E 732 346-9200
　Somerset *(G-10178)*

▲ Tcp Reliable Inc ....G 848 229-2466
　Edison *(G-2638)*

Tech-Pak Inc ....F 201 935-3800
　Wood Ridge *(G-12140)*

Univeg Logistics America Inc ....G 856 241-0097
　Swedesboro *(G-10735)*

▲ US Propack Inc ....E 732 294-4500
　Freehold *(G-3690)*

Utility Development Corp ....G 973 994-4334
　Livingston *(G-5567)*

3087 Custom Compounding Of Purchased Plastic Resins

Bayshore Recycling Corp ....E 732 738-6000
　Keasbey *(G-4924)*

◆ Borealis Compounds Inc ....C 908 850-6200
　Port Murray *(G-8976)*

Diamond Sg Intl Ltd Lblty Co ....G 732 861-9850
　Eatontown *(G-2390)*

▲ Federal Plastics Corporation ....E 908 272-5800
　Cranford *(G-1907)*

◆ Joyce Leslie Inc ....D 201 804-7800
　Hillsborough *(G-4352)*

▼ Lion Extruding Corp ....F 973 344-4648
　Newark *(G-7220)*

Lubrizol Advanced Mtls Inc ....E 856 299-3764
　Pedricktown *(G-8438)*

▲ Nobel Biocare Procera LLC ....E 201 529-7100
　Mahwah *(G-5797)*

▲ Polymeric Resources Corp ....E 973 694-4141
　Wayne *(G-11674)*

▲ Recycle Inc ....D 908 756-2200
　South Plainfield *(G-10433)*

▼ Waste Management NJ Inc ....C 609 434-5200
　Ewing *(G-3069)*

3088 Plastic Plumbing Fixtures

Ace Restoration ....G 267 897-2384
　Sewell *(G-9944)*

S
I
C

Sell All Properties LLC ....F 856 963-8800
Camden *(G-1086)*

▲ Town & Country Plastics Inc .....F 732 780-5300
Marlboro *(G-5961)*

3089 Plastic Prdts

A & D Indus & Mar Repr Inc ....E 732 541-1481
Port Reading *(G-8984)*

A R C Plasmet Corp ....F 201 867-8533
North Bergen *(G-7425)*

A S 4 Plastic Inc ....G 973 925-5223
Paterson *(G-8192)*

▲ A-One Merchandising Corp ....F 718 773-7500
North Arlington *(G-7413)*

Accurate Mold Inc ....E 856 784-8484
Somerdale *(G-10038)*

Acrylics Unlimited ....G 973 862-6014
Lafayette *(G-5043)*

◆ Advantage Molding Products ....F 732 303-8667
Sea Girt *(G-9861)*

▲ Aflex Extrusion Technologies .....E 732 752-0048
Piscataway *(G-8727)*

▲ AJ Siris Products Corp ....F 973 823-0050
Ogdensburg *(G-7769)*

Allgrind Plastics Inc ....F 908 479-4400
Asbury *(G-63)*

Allstar Disposal ....G 973 398-8808
Hopatcong *(G-4533)*

▲ Alva-Tech Inc ....F 609 747-1133
Burlington Township *(G-997)*

▲ Ansmann USA Corp ....E 856 481-3504
Blackwood *(G-470)*

Arbee Company Inc ....F 908 241-7717
Kenilworth *(G-4937)*

Arpac Technology ....G 973 252-0012
Randolph *(G-9270)*

Artus Corp ....E 201 568-1000
Englewood *(G-2873)*

Asi Plastic Inc ....G 973 332-4720
Paterson *(G-8216)*

Associated Plastics Inc ....F 732 574-2800
Rahway *(G-9176)*

▲ B & G Plastics Inc ....G 973 824-9220
Union *(G-11155)*

B & W Plastics Inc ....G 973 383-0020
Sparta *(G-10490)*

◆ Bel-Art Products Inc ....G 973 694-0500
Wayne *(G-11608)*

Berry Global Inc ....C 732 356-2870
Middlesex *(G-6151)*

Berry Global Inc ....C 908 353-3850
Elizabeth *(G-2714)*

Berry Global Inc ....C 980 689-1660
Phillipsburg *(G-8642)*

Berry Global Inc ....E 908 454-0900
Phillipsburg *(G-8643)*

Berry Global Inc ....C 609 395-4199
Cranbury *(G-1814)*

Berry Global Inc ....C 718 205-3115
Elizabeth *(G-2715)*

Big 3 Precision Products Inc ....C 856 293-1400
Millville *(G-6287)*

Birds Beware Corporation ....G 732 671-6377
Middletown *(G-6212)*

▲ Brent River Corp ....E 908 722-6021
Hillsborough *(G-4322)*

Brentrick Inc ....G 973 357-3579
Paterson *(G-8225)*

Brisar Industries Inc ....C 973 278-2500
Paterson *(G-8226)*

Brook Meadow Inventions ....E 973 300-0419
Newton *(G-7382)*

◆ Buckets Plus Inc ....G 732 545-0420
New Brunswick *(G-6949)*

◆ Butler Prtg & Laminating Inc ....C 973 838-8550
Butler *(G-999)*

C & K Plastics Inc ....D 732 549-0011
Metuchen *(G-6098)*

▲ C & N Packaging Inc ....D 631 491-1400
Wayne *(G-11617)*

C G I Cstm Fiberglas & Decking ...F 609 646-5302
Pleasantville *(G-8904)*

Camtec Industries Inc ....F 732 332-9800
Colts Neck *(G-1780)*

Captive Plastics Inc ....C 812 424-2904
Phillipsburg *(G-8645)*

Captive Plastics Inc ....C 732 469-7900
Piscataway *(G-8743)*

Cardinal Fibreglass Industries ......G 718 625-4350
Perth Amboy *(G-8608)*

Carecam International Inc ....E 973 227-0720
Fairfield *(G-3156)*

▲ Case It Inc ....E 800 441-4710
Lyndhurst *(G-5675)*

◆ Case Princeton Co Inc ....E 908 687-1750
Union *(G-11163)*

Celotex ....G 856 663-2626
Pennsauken *(G-8490)*

Chefler Foods LLC ....F 201 596-3710
Saddle Brook *(G-9757)*

Christopher F Maier ....G 908 459-5100
Hope *(G-4539)*

◆ Colorite Plastics Company ......E 201 941-2900
Ridgefield *(G-9355)*

◆ Comar Inc ....E 856 692-6100
Voorhees *(G-11425)*

◆ Comar LLC ....B 856 692-6100
Voorhees *(G-11427)*

Comet Tool Company Inc ....D 856 256-1070
Pitman *(G-8840)*

Competech Smrtcard Sltions Inc ....G 201 256-4184
Englewood Cliffs *(G-2953)*

Componding Engrg Solutions Inc ....F 973 340-4000
Clifton *(G-1587)*

Consolidated Cont Holdings LLC ....D 609 655-0855
Cranbury *(G-1826)*

Container Mfg Inc ....E 732 563-0100
Middlesex *(G-6155)*

▲ Continental Precision Corp ....C 908 754-3030
Piscataway *(G-8752)*

Crossfield Products Corp ....D 908 245-2801
Roselle Park *(G-9691)*

Custom Molders Corp ....D 908 218-7997
Branchburg *(G-653)*

De Leon Plastics Corp ....F 973 653-3480
Paterson *(G-8247)*

▲ Delvco Pharma Packg Svcs Inc ....D 973 278-2500
Paterson *(G-8249)*

Design & Molding Services Inc .....C 732 752-0300
Piscataway *(G-8756)*

▲ Design Display Group Inc ....C 201 438-6000
Carlstadt *(G-1154)*

Dolco Packaging Corp ....E 201 941-2900
Ridgefield *(G-9358)*

Don Shrts Pcture Frmes Molding ....G 732 363-1323
Howell *(G-4552)*

Dor-Win Manufacturing Co ....E 201 796-4300
Elmwood Park *(G-2815)*

◆ Dr Reddys Laboratories Inc .....E 609 375-9900
Princeton *(G-9032)*

▲ Du Technologies Inc ....F 201 729-0070
Moonachie *(G-6515)*

▲ Duerr Tool & Die Co Inc ....F 908 810-9035
Union *(G-11173)*

◆ Dwk Life Sciences Inc ....C 856 825-1100
Millville *(G-6301)*

E & T Plastic Mfg Co Inc ....E 201 596-5017
Teterboro *(G-10792)*

E & T Sales Co Inc ....G 856 787-0900
Mount Laurel *(G-6793)*

East Coast Plastics Inc ....G 856 768-8700
West Berlin *(G-11718)*

▲ Echo Molding Inc ....E 908 688-0099
Union *(G-11178)*

Edwards Creative Products Inc .....E 856 665-3200
Cherry Hill *(G-1361)*

Emdeon Corporation ....A 201 703-3400
Elmwood Park *(G-2819)*

Endot Industries Inc ....D 973 625-8500
Rockaway *(G-9564)*

▲ Engineered Plastic Pdts Inc .....E 908 647-3500
Stirling *(G-10599)*

▲ Engineering Laboratories Inc ....E 201 337-8116
Oakland *(G-7687)*

▲ Enor Corporation ....C 201 750-1680
Englewood *(G-2892)*

▲ Esco Industrial Corporation ......G 973 478-5888
Woodcliff Lake *(G-12190)*

Exothermic Molding Inc ....E 908 272-2299
Kenilworth *(G-4953)*

◆ Farmplast LLC ....E 973 287-6070
Parsippany *(G-8008)*

Fencemax ....G 609 646-2265
Newfield *(G-7366)*

Fibrenetics Inc ....F 732 636-5670
Woodbridge *(G-12148)*

Flex Moulding Inc ....G 201 487-8080
Hackensack *(G-3914)*

Flex Products LLC ....D 201 440-1570
Carlstadt *(G-1162)*

Foster Engraving Corporation ....G 201 489-5979
Hackensack *(G-3918)*

▲ Fram Trak Industries Inc ....E 732 424-8400
Middlesex *(G-6167)*

Fredon Development Inds LLC ....F 973 383-7576
Newton *(G-7389)*

Freedom Vinyl Systems Inc ....G 973 692-0332
Pequannock *(G-8600)*

Garden State Fabricators ....G 732 928-5006
Cream Ridge *(G-1935)*

Garfield Molding Co Inc ....G 973 777-5700
Wallington *(G-11526)*

Gifford Group Inc ....G 212 569-8500
Kearny *(G-4878)*

Gill Associates LLC ....G 973 835-5456
Wayne *(G-11641)*

Glasplex LLC ....G 973 940-8940
Sussex *(G-10671)*

▲ Globe Packaging Co Inc ....G 201 896-1144
Carlstadt *(G-1163)*

Graham Packaging Company LP ....E 717 849-8500
Bordentown *(G-597)*

Greco Industries LLC ....G 732 919-6200
Colts Neck *(G-1787)*

Greenway Products & Svcs LLC ....G 732 442-0200
New Brunswick *(G-6965)*

Grewe Plastics Inc ....G 973 485-7602
Newark *(G-7179)*

Griffen LLC ....G 973 723-5344
Morristown *(G-6711)*

Hall Manufacturing Corp ....E 973 962-6022
Ringwood *(G-9448)*

Hartmann Tool Co Inc ....G 201 343-8700
Hackensack *(G-3925)*

Hathaway Plastic ....G 908 688-9494
Union *(G-11192)*

◆ Hayward Industrial Products ....C 908 351-5400
Elizabeth *(G-2741)*

◆ Hayward Industries Inc ....B 908 351-5400
Elizabeth *(G-2742)*

◆ Heyco Molded Products Inc ......F 732 286-4336
Toms River *(G-10884)*

Highland Products Inc ....G 973 366-0156
Dover *(G-2089)*

▼ Holocraft Corporation ....D 732 502-9500
Neptune *(G-6919)*

Home Organization LLC ....F 201 351-2121
Closter *(G-1760)*

◆ Honeyware Inc ....D 201 997-5900
Kearny *(G-4880)*

Hot Runner Technology ....G 908 431-5711
Hillsborough *(G-4342)*

Icup Inc ....E 856 751-2045
Cherry Hill *(G-1376)*

▲ Injection Works Inc ....E 856 802-6444
Mount Laurel *(G-6804)*

▲ Injectron Corporation ....B 908 753-1990
Plainfield *(G-8865)*

Inman Mold Manufacturing Inc .....G 732 381-3033
Rahway *(G-9198)*

Inman Mold Manufacturing Inc .....G 732 381-3033
Rahway *(G-9199)*

Innova Group Inc ....G 856 696-1053
Vineland *(G-11373)*

Intek Plastics Inc ....E 973 427-7331
Hawthorne *(G-4241)*

Iron Mountain Plastics Inc ....F 201 445-0063
Midland Park *(G-6230)*

▲ J OBrien Co Inc ....E 973 379-8844
Springfield *(G-10558)*

J-Mac Plastics Inc ....E 908 709-1111
Kenilworth *(G-4965)*

▲ Janico Inc ....F 732 370-2223
Freehold *(G-3662)*

◆ Jarden Corporation ....E 201 610-6600
Hoboken *(G-4477)*

◆ Jerhel Plastics Inc ....G 201 436-6662
Bayonne *(G-234)*

▲ Jersey Plastic Molders Inc ....C 973 926-1800
Irvington *(G-4595)*

Kinect Auto Parts Corporation ......G 862 702-8252
Fairfield *(G-3242)*

Koba Corp ....D 732 469-0110
Middlesex *(G-6173)*

L-E-M Plastics and Supplies ....G 201 933-9150
Rutherford *(G-9738)*

Lamart Corp ....F 973 772-6262
Clifton *(G-1656)*

Lamart Corporation ....G 973 772-6262
Clifton *(G-1658)*

◆ Leco Plastics Inc ....F 201 343-3330
   Hackensack (G-3938)
▲ Life of Party LLC ....E 732 828-0886
   North Brunswick (G-7524)
▲ Linden Mold and Tool Corp ....E 732 381-1411
   Rahway (G-9209)
Liquid-Solids Separation Corp ....E 201 236-4833
   Ramsey (G-9245)
LL Building Products Inc ....F 973 628-3000
   Parsippany (G-8039)
LNS Inc ....F 609 927-6656
   Egg Harbor Township (G-2688)
Lumber Super Mart ....G 732 739-1428
   Hazlet (G-4278)
Madan Plastics Inc ....D 908 276-8484
   Cranford (G-1913)
▲ Mainetti Americas Inc ....G 201 215-2900
   Secaucus (G-9903)
◆ Mainetti USA Inc ....F 201 215-2900
   Keasbey (G-4928)
Mamrout Paper Group Corp ....G 718 510-5484
   Edison (G-2564)
▲ Marlo Plastic Products Inc ....E 732 792-1988
   Neptune (G-6923)
McBride Awning Co ....G 732 892-6256
   Point Pleasant Beach (G-8923)
▲ McLean Packaging Corporation ......B 856 359-2600
   Moorestown (G-6600)
▲ Medplast West Berlin Inc ....E 856 753-7600
   West Berlin (G-11733)
▼ Meese Inc ....E 201 796-4490
   Saddle Brook (G-9774)
Metrie Inc ....F 973 584-0040
   Randolph (G-9289)
▲ Mfv International Corporation ....G 973 993-1687
   Morristown (G-6727)
▲ Microcast Technologies Corp ....D 908 523-9503
   Linden (G-5409)
▲ Mighty Mug Incorporated ....G 732 382-3911
   Rahway (G-9215)
Molders Fishing Preserve ....G 732 446-2850
   Jamesburg (G-4687)
Montrose Molders Corporation ....E 908 754-3030
   Piscataway (G-8793)
Multi-Plastics Inc ....E 856 241-9014
   Swedesboro (G-10713)
National Casein New Jersey Inc ....E 856 829-1880
   Cinnaminson (G-1480)
National Diversified Sales Inc ....G 559 562-9888
   Bordentown (G-605)
National Plastic Printing ....G 973 785-1460
   Totowa (G-10957)
Newark Liner & Washer Inc ....F 973 482-5400
   Newark (G-7256)
▲ Newell Brands Inc ....B 201 610-6600
   Hoboken (G-4486)
Nini Disposal ....G 609 587-2411
   Trenton (G-11090)
Nordson Efd LLC ....C 609 259-9222
   Robbinsville (G-9519)
Norlo of New Jersey LLC ....G 646 492-3293
   Montclair (G-6425)
Northland Tooling Technologies ....G 908 850-0023
   Hackettstown (G-4030)
▲ Novembal USA Inc ....E 732 947-3030
   Edison (G-2585)
OK Tool & Die Company Inc ....E 856 629-5757
   Williamstown (G-12094)
▲ Onguard Fence Systems Ltd ....E 908 429-5522
   Branchburg (G-684)
Onguard Fence Systems Ltd ....E 908 429-5522
   Branchburg (G-685)
Onyx Graphics LLC ....G 908 281-0038
   Hillsborough (G-4361)
Oppenheim Plastics Co Inc ....E 201 995-9595
   Woodcliff Lake (G-12197)
Optics Plastics ....G 201 939-3344
   Lyndhurst (G-5699)
◆ Ovadia Corporation ....E 973 256-9200
   Little Falls (G-5483)
Owens Plastic Products Inc ....G 856 447-3500
   Cedarville (G-1324)
P D Q Plastics Inc ....E 201 823-0270
   Bayonne (G-240)
◆ Parkway Plastics Inc ....E 732 752-3636
   Piscataway (G-8798)
▲ Patwin Plastics Inc ....E 908 486-6600
   Linden (G-5426)
Pcr Technologies Inc ....G 973 882-0017
   Pine Brook (G-8713)

Pedibrush LLC ....G 856 796-2963
   Haddon Heights (G-4049)
▲ Pelco Packaging Corporation ....F 973 675-4994
   East Orange (G-2265)
▲ Permalith Plastics LLC ....D 215 925-5659
   Pennsauken (G-8560)
Petro Extrusion Tech Inc ....E 908 789-3338
   Middlesex (G-6187)
Petro Plastics Company Inc ....E 908 789-1200
   Kenilworth (G-4987)
Pfk Coach Phyllis Flood Knerr ....G 856 429-5425
   Haddonfield (G-4061)
▲ Philcorr LLC ....D 856 205-0557
   Vineland (G-11391)
▲ Pierson Industries Inc ....C 973 627-7945
   Rockaway (G-9596)
▲ Plastic Reel Corp of America ....E 201 933-5100
   Carlstadt (G-1203)
Plastics For Chemicals Inc ....G 609 242-9100
   Forked River (G-3540)
Plastics Galore LLC ....G 732 363-8447
   Lakewood (G-5172)
Plastiform Packaging Inc ....E 973 983-8900
   Rockaway (G-9597)
Plastinetics Inc ....G 818 364-1611
   Towaco (G-11001)
Plastpro 2000 Inc ....G 973 992-2090
   Livingston (G-5556)
◆ PMC Group Inc ....F 856 533-1866
   Mount Laurel (G-6828)
Pmp Composites Corporation ....E 609 587-1188
   Trenton (G-10720)
Poly Source Enterprises LLC ....G 732 580-5409
   Freehold (G-3678)
▲ Poly-Version Inc ....E 201 451-7600
   Jersey City (G-4804)
Polycel Structural Foam Inc ....D 908 722-5254
   Branchburg (G-691)
▲ Polycel Structural Foam Inc ....E 908 722-5254
   Branchburg (G-692)
▲ Polymer Dynamix LLC ....F 732 381-1600
   South Plainfield (G-10421)
Polymer Molded Products ....G 732 907-1990
   Bound Brook (G-621)
Precise Technology Inc ....E 856 241-1760
   Swedesboro (G-10720)
Preferred Plastics Inc ....G 856 662-6250
   Pennsauken (G-8562)
Premiere Raceway Sys LLC ....G 732 629-7715
   Piscataway (G-8802)
▲ Princeton Tectonics ....C 609 298-9331
   Pennsauken (G-8565)
Pro Plastics Inc ....G 908 925-5555
   Linden (G-5431)
Productive Plastics Inc ....D 856 778-4300
   Mount Laurel (G-6832)
▲ Protec Secure Card Ltd Lblty ....E 732 542-0700
   Eatontown (G-2419)
Pure TEC Corporation ....G 201 941-2900
   Ridgefield (G-9381)
▲ Pure Tech International Inc ....G 908 722-4800
   Branchburg (G-696)
▲ Qualipac America Corp ....F 973 754-9920
   Woodland Park (G-12230)
◆ Qualteq Inc ....C 908 668-0999
   South Plainfield (G-10429)
R & K Industries Inc ....G 732 531-1123
   Oakhurst (G-7672)
▲ R Squared Sls & Logistics LLC ....G 201 329-9745
   Moonachie (G-6537)
▲ Randy Hangers LLC ....G 201 215-2900
   Secaucus (G-9916)
Rapid Manufacturing Co Inc ....E 732 279-1252
   Toms River (G-10906)
▲ Reachman International Corp ....F 718 388-6565
   Moonachie (G-6539)
Reedy International Corp ....F 732 264-1777
   Keyport (G-5023)
◆ Revere Industries LLC ....C 856 881-3600
   Clayton (G-1527)
Revere Plastics Inc ....G 201 641-0777
   Little Ferry (G-5514)
Ring Container Tech LLC ....F 973 258-0707
   Springfield (G-10577)
▲ Royal Aluminum Co Inc ....D 973 589-8880
   Newark (G-7293)
▲ Royce Associates A Ltd Partnr ....D 201 438-5200
   East Rutherford (G-2322)
Russo Seamless Gutter LLC ....G 732 836-0151
   Brick (G-757)

S&A Molders Inc ....G 732 851-7770
   Manalapan (G-5862)
◆ Sabert Corporation ....C 800 722-3781
   Sayreville (G-9837)
Sabert Corporation ....E 732 721-5544
   Sayreville (G-9838)
▼ Sama Plastics Corp ....E 973 239-7200
   Cedar Grove (G-1300)
Sancon Services Inc ....G 973 344-2500
   Newark (G-7302)
Scott W Springman ....G 856 751-2411
   Cherry Hill (G-1419)
Seajay Manufacturing Corp ....F 732 774-0900
   Neptune (G-6931)
Seal-Spout Corp ....F 908 647-0648
   Liberty Corner (G-5324)
Sealed Air Holdings ....E 201 791-7600
   Elmwood Park (G-2849)
Silver Line Building Pdts LLC ....C 732 752-8704
   Middlesex (G-6198)
Sinclair and Rush Inc ....G 862 262-8189
   Carlstadt (G-1218)
▲ Sonetronics Inc ....D 732 681-5016
   Belmar (G-364)
▲ Stephco Sales Inc ....E 973 278-5454
   Paterson (G-8384)
◆ Stephen Douglas Plastics Inc ....C 973 523-3030
   Paterson (G-8385)
◆ Storemaxx Inc ....F 201 440-8800
   Hackensack (G-3981)
▲ Stull Technologies LLC ....D 732 873-5000
   Somerset (G-10175)
Superseal Manufacturing Co Inc ....E 908 561-5910
   South Plainfield (G-10437)
Survivor II Inc ....E 908 353-1155
   Hillside (G-4442)
T & B Specialties Inc ....G 732 928-4500
   Jackson (G-4679)
T & M Newton Corporation ....G 973 383-1232
   Newton (G-7407)
Tarma Sales ....G 732 969-3318
   Carteret (G-1268)
Team Nisca ....G 732 271-7367
   Somerset (G-10182)
Tech Products Co Inc ....F 201 444-7777
   Midland Park (G-6239)
Techflex Inc ....E 973 300-9242
   Sparta (G-10522)
Technimold Inc ....F 908 232-8331
   Flemington (G-3470)
Technitool Inc ....E 856 768-2707
   West Berlin (G-11754)
Tek Molding ....G 973 702-0450
   Sussex (G-10678)
Tekni-Plex Inc ....C 908 575-7661
   Branchburg (G-710)
Tekni-Plex Inc ....G 908 782-4000
   Flemington (G-3471)
▲ Tektite Industries Inc ....G 609 656-0600
   Trenton (G-11120)
Thermal Chek Inc ....E 856 742-1200
   Westville (G-11950)
▲ Thermo Plastic Tech Inc ....E 908 687-4833
   Union (G-11229)
Thermoplastics Bio-Logics LLC ....F 973 383-2834
   Sparta (G-10524)
▲ Town & Country Plastics Inc ....F 732 780-5300
   Marlboro (G-5961)
Tri Tech Tool & Design Co Inc ....G 732 469-5433
   South Bound Brook (G-10249)
Tripack Industrial USA LLC ....G 973 627-8350
   Rockaway (G-9619)
Triumph Plastics LLC ....G 973 584-5500
   Flanders (G-3421)
Tyz-All Plastics LLC ....G 201 343-1200
   Hackensack (G-3988)
Ua Pipefitters Local 274 ....G 201 943-4700
   Parsippany (G-8105)
▲ Unette Corporation ....D 973 328-6800
   Randolph (G-9304)
▲ Uniplast Industries Inc ....E 201 288-4672
   Hasbrouck Heights (G-4202)
Unit Pack Company Inc ....E 973 239-4112
   Cedar Grove (G-1304)
United Eqp Fabricators LLC ....G 973 242-2737
   Newark (G-7353)
▼ United States Box Corp ....E 973 481-2000
   Fairfield (G-3335)
United Window & Door Mfg Inc ....E 973 912-0600
   Springfield (G-10581)

Vacumet Corp ....G...... 973 628-0405
   Wayne (G-11690)

Valley Plastic Molding Co ....F...... 973 334-2100
   Boonton (G-587)

◆ Van Ness Plastic Molding Co ....C...... 973 778-9500
   Clifton (G-1738)

Vanguard Container Corp ....E...... 732 651-9717
   East Brunswick (G-2195)

▲ Veloso Industries Inc ....G...... 908 925-0999
   Linden (G-5457)

Versatile Distributors Inc ....D...... 973 773-0550
   Livingston (G-5570)

▲ Vinylast Inc ....E...... 732 367-7200
   Lakewood (G-5200)

Viz Mold & Die Ltd ....F...... 201 784-8383
   Northvale (G-7611)

◆ Waldwick Plastics Corp ....G...... 201 445-7436
   Waldwick (G-11455)

▲ Weiss-Aug Co Inc ....C...... 973 887-7600
   East Hanover (G-2249)

Westar Tool LLC ....G...... 856 507-8852
   West Berlin (G-11760)

Whe Research Inc ....G...... 732 240-3871
   Toms River (G-10921)

▲ Whole Year Trading Co Inc ....G...... 732 238-1196
   Dayton (G-1995)

▲ Wilpak Industries Inc ....G...... 201 997-7600
   Kearny (G-4923)

World Plastic Extruders Inc ....D...... 201 933-2915
   Rutherford (G-9746)

◆ WY Industries Inc ....D...... 201 617-8000
   North Bergen (G-7496)

Yuhl Products Inc ....G...... 908 276-5180
   Kenilworth (G-5009)

Zirti LLC ....G...... 201 316-4791
   Allendale (G-24)

31 LEATHER AND LEATHER PRODUCTS

3111 Leather Tanning & Finishing

Buonaventura Bag and Cases LLC ....G...... 212 960-3442
   Clifton (G-1579)

▲ Cejon Inc ....E...... 201 437-8780
   Bayonne (G-217)

▲ Coast To Coast Lea & Vinyl Inc ....G...... 732 525-8877
   Sayreville (G-9818)

▲ Dani Leather USA Inc ....G...... 973 598-0890
   Flanders (G-3403)

Disys Commerce Inc ....G...... 201 567-0457
   Englewood (G-2888)

Jaclyn Holdings Parent LLC ....G...... 201 909-6000
   Maywood (G-6053)

▲ Jaclyn LLC ....D...... 201 909-6000
   Maywood (G-6054)

Maxsyl Leather Co LLC ....D...... 201 864-0579
   Union City (G-11256)

Myers Group LLC ....G...... 973 761-6414
   South Orange (G-10310)

3131 Boot & Shoe Cut Stock & Findings

Cross Counter Inc ....G...... 973 677-0600
   East Orange (G-2255)

Hair Quarters ....G...... 856 624-4072
   Woodstown (G-12238)

Ingersoll-Rand Company ....G...... 973 882-0924
   Pine Brook (G-8706)

Major Bs General Quarters LLC ....G...... 732 710-6088
   Matawan (G-6024)

3142 House Slippers

◆ S Goldberg & Co Inc ....C...... 201 342-1200
   Hackensack (G-3969)

3143 Men's Footwear, Exc Athletic

▲ Bm USA Incorporated ....E...... 800 624-5499
   Carlstadt (G-1132)

Carlascio Custom & Orthopedic ....G...... 201 333-8716
   Jersey City (G-4723)

CB Marathon Opco LLC ....D...... 201 843-5416
   Paramus (G-7860)

Steven Madden Ltd ....D...... 973 533-0121
   Livingston (G-5564)

Vf Outdoor LLC ....G...... 908 352-5390
   Elizabeth (G-2781)

3144 Women's Footwear, Exc Athletic

Carlascio Custom & Orthopedic ....G...... 201 333-8716
   Jersey City (G-4723)

Je TAime Shoes ....G...... 201 845-7463
   Paramus (G-7878)

Schusters Shoes Inc ....G...... 856 885-4551
   Williamstown (G-12105)

3149 Footwear, NEC

◆ Ballet Makers Inc ....B...... 973 595-9000
   Totowa (G-10934)

Carlascio Custom & Orthopedic ....G...... 201 333-8716
   Jersey City (G-4723)

Komar Inc ....B...... 212 725-1500
   Jersey City (G-4772)

◆ S Goldberg & Co Inc ....C...... 201 342-1200
   Hackensack (G-3969)

3151 Leather Gloves & Mittens

Ansell Hawkeye Inc ....E...... 662 258-3200
   Iselin (G-4610)

3161 Luggage

▲ Atco Products Inc ....E...... 973 379-3171
   Springfield (G-10538)

◆ Case Princeton Co Inc ....E...... 908 687-1750
   Union (G-11163)

▲ Gibbons Company Ltd ....E...... 441 294-5047
   Elizabeth (G-2739)

Iacobucci USA Inc ....G...... 732 935-6633
   Eatontown (G-2404)

▲ Jack Georges Inc ....G...... 973 777-6999
   Passaic (G-8150)

▲ Lbu Inc ....E...... 973 773-4800
   Paterson (G-8318)

Ledonne Leather Co Inc ....F...... 201 531-2100
   Lyndhurst (G-5686)

Motion Systems LLC ....F...... 212 686-4666
   Newark (G-7245)

Naluco Inc ....D...... 800 601-8198
   Clifton (G-1678)

Quiet Tone Inc ....G...... 732 431-2826
   Freehold (G-3684)

Samsonite LLC ....A...... 732 493-5146
   Tinton Falls (G-10845)

Selfmade LLC ....G...... 201 792-8968
   Jersey City (G-4826)

▲ Transglobe Usa Inc ....G...... 973 465-1998
   Carlstadt (G-1232)

Tumi Holdings Inc ....D...... 908 756-4400
   South Plainfield (G-10442)

3171 Handbags & Purses

Annette & Jim Dizenzo Sls LLC ....G...... 973 875-0895
   Sussex (G-10666)

Antique Buying Center ....G...... 201 888-0303
   Edgewater (G-2433)

▼ Basu Group ....G...... 908 517-9138
   North Brunswick (G-7507)

▲ Carol S Miller Corporation ....G...... 201 406-4578
   Hillsdale (G-4381)

Gio Vali Handbag Corp ....G...... 973 279-3032
   Paterson (G-8276)

Ledonne Leather Co Inc ....F...... 201 531-2100
   Lyndhurst (G-5686)

▲ M London Inc ....E...... 201 459-6460
   Jersey City (G-4780)

Medici International Inc ....G...... 973 684-6084
   Paterson (G-8334)

Mitzi Intl Handbag & ACC Ltd ....C...... 973 483-5015
   Newark (G-7243)

Tapestry Inc ....F...... 856 488-2220
   Cherry Hill (G-1426)

3172 Personal Leather Goods

Always Be Secure LLC ....G...... 917 887-2286
   Manalapan (G-5838)

▲ Billykirk ....F...... 201 222-9092
   Jersey City (G-4718)

▲ Colemax Group LLC ....G...... 201 489-1080
   River Edge (G-9463)

G-III Leather Fashions Inc ....D...... 212 403-0500
   Dayton (G-1966)

Jaclyn Holdings Parent LLC ....G...... 201 909-6000
   Maywood (G-6053)

▲ Jaclyn LLC ....G...... 201 909-6000
   Maywood (G-6054)

▲ M London Inc ....E...... 201 459-6460
   Jersey City (G-4780)

Maxsyl Leather Co LLC ....D...... 201 864-0579
   Union City (G-11256)

▲ R Neumann & Co ....E...... 201 659-3400
   Hoboken (G-4493)

Tumi Holdings Inc ....D...... 908 756-4400
   South Plainfield (G-10442)

3199 Leather Goods, NEC

Adventure Industries LLC ....G...... 609 426-1777
   East Windsor (G-2341)

▲ Billykirk ....F...... 201 222-9092
   Jersey City (G-4718)

Brook Saddle Ridge Equest ....F...... 609 953-1600
   Shamong (G-9968)

▲ Bucati Leather Inc ....G...... 732 254-0480
   South River (G-10459)

Cunningham Classics Ltd Lblty ....G...... 201 857-4647
   Glen Rock (G-3825)

Dibello USA Inc ....E...... 212 279-9099
   Randolph (G-9273)

◆ Emporium Leather Company Inc ....E...... 201 330-7720
   Secaucus (G-9878)

G S Babu & Co ....F...... 732 939-5190
   Plainsboro (G-8882)

Jaclyn Holdings Parent LLC ....G...... 201 909-6000
   Maywood (G-6053)

▲ Jaclyn LLC ....D...... 201 909-6000
   Maywood (G-6054)

North American Frontier Corp ....E...... 201 222-1931
   Jersey City (G-4792)

▲ R Neumann & Co ....F...... 201 659-3400
   Hoboken (G-4493)

▲ Safe-Strap Company Inc ....E...... 973 442-4623
   Wharton (G-11999)

32 STONE, CLAY, GLASS, AND CONCRETE PRODUCTS

3211 Flat Glass

Artique Glass Studio Inc ....G...... 201 444-3500
   Glen Rock (G-3820)

◆ Edmund Optics Inc ....C...... 856 547-3488
   Barrington (G-177)

Elco Glass Industries Co Inc ....E...... 732 363-6550
   Freehold (G-3652)

▲ Europrojects Intl Inc ....G...... 917 262-0795
   Englewood (G-2894)

Floral Glass Industries Inc ....E...... 201 939-4600
   East Rutherford (G-2297)

Frost Tech Inc ....F...... 732 396-0071
   Rahway (G-9191)

◆ General Glass Intl Corp ....C...... 201 553-1850
   Secaucus (G-9887)

▲ JE Berkowitz LP ....C...... 856 456-7800
   Pedricktown (G-8436)

Jersey Tempered Glass Inc ....E...... 856 273-8700
   Mount Laurel (G-6810)

Just Glass & Mirror Inc ....F...... 856 728-8383
   Williamstown (G-12091)

▲ McGrory Glass Inc ....D...... 856 579-3200
   Paulsboro (G-8420)

Oldcastle Buildingenvelope Inc ....D...... 856 234-9222
   Moorestown (G-6605)

Pierangeli Group Inc ....G...... 856 582-4060
   Gloucester City (G-3842)

Pilkington North America Inc ....C...... 973 470-5703
   Clifton (G-1697)

PPG Ind Inc ....G...... 856 662-9323
   Pennsauken (G-8561)

Spectrum Glass LLC ....G...... 201 750-1251
   Closter (G-1766)

Tri-State Glass & Mirror Inc ....G...... 732 591-5545
   Old Bridge (G-7794)

3221 Glass Containers

Amcor Phrm Packg USA Inc ....C...... 856 825-3050
   Millville (G-6276)

Amcor Phrm Packg USA Inc ....C...... 856 728-9300
   Williamstown (G-12078)

▲ Amcor Phrm Packg USA LLC ....C...... 856 327-1540
   Millville (G-6277)

Amcor Phrm Packg USA LLC ....C...... 856 825-1400
   Millville (G-6278)

Amcor Phrm Packg USA LLC ....C...... 856 825-1400
   Millville (G-6279)

Amcor Phrm Packg USA LLC ....C...... 856 825-1100
   Millville (G-6280)

Ardagh Glass Inc ....B 732 969-0827
Carteret (G-1251)
▲ Assem - Pak Inc ....C 856 692-3355
Vineland (G-11323)
Avant Industries Ltd Inc ....G 973 242-1700
Newark (G-7100)
Cameo Metal Forms Inc ....F 718 788-1106
Woodland Park (G-12213)
▲ Friedrich and Dimmock Inc ....E 856 825-0305
Millville (G-6302)
▲ Gerresheimer Glass Inc ....B 856 692-3600
Vineland (G-11360)
▲ Heinz Glas USA Inc ....F 908 474-0300
Linden (G-5383)
▲ Le Papillon Ltd ....F 908 753-7300
South Plainfield (G-10396)
◆ Leone Industries Inc ....B 856 455-2000
Bridgeton (G-789)
Nipro Glass Americas Corp ....F 856 825-1400
Millville (G-6314)
◆ Nipro Phrmpckging Amricas Corp ....C 856 825-1400
Millville (G-6315)
▲ Piramal Glass - Usa Inc ....E 856 293-6400
Dayton (G-1983)
Piramal Glass - Usa Inc ....C 856 728-9300
Williamstown (G-12097)
Piramal Glass - Usa Inc ....B 856 293-6400
Williamstown (G-12098)
▲ Pochet of America Inc ....C 973 942-4923
Woodland Park (G-12228)
Vivreau Advanced Water Systems ....F 212 502-3749
Fairfield (G-3345)
▲ Worldwide Glass Resources Inc ....E 856 205-1508
Vineland (G-11418)

3229 Pressed & Blown Glassware, NEC

AGC Acquisition LLC ....E 856 692-4435
Vineland (G-11320)
Amcor Phrm Packg USA LLC ....C 856 825-1100
Millville (G-6280)
Betco Glass Inc ....G 856 327-4301
Millville (G-6286)
◆ Buckets Plus Inc ....G 732 545-0420
New Brunswick (G-6949)
◆ Bulbrite Industries Inc ....E 201 531-5900
Moonachie (G-6509)
C Technologies Inc ....E 908 707-1009
Bridgewater (G-826)
Cardinal International Inc ....F 973 628-0900
Wayne (G-11618)
Corning Pharmaceutical GL LLC ....G 856 794-7100
Vineland (G-11342)
Creamer Glass LLC ....G 856 327-2023
Millville (G-6294)
Creamer Glass LLC ....G 856 327-2023
Millville (G-6295)
▲ Crystal World Inc ....E 201 488-0909
Carlstadt (G-1151)
▲ Daum Inc ....G 862 210-8522
Fairfield (G-3172)
▲ Durand Glass Mfg Co Inc ....A 856 327-1850
Millville (G-6300)
◆ E G L Company Inc ....C 908 508-1111
Berkeley Heights (G-409)
Eldon Glass & Mirror Co Inc ....F 973 589-2099
Newark (G-7151)
▼ Fiberguide Industries Inc ....E 908 647-6601
Stirling (G-10600)
Folio Art Glass Inc ....G 732 431-0044
Colts Neck (G-1786)
▲ Friedrich and Dimmock Inc ....E 856 825-0305
Millville (G-6302)
Gbw Manufacturing Inc ....E 973 279-0077
Totowa (G-10947)
▼ Glass Warehouse ....G 856 825-1400
Millville (G-6305)
Glassblowerscom LLC ....G 856 232-7898
Blackwood (G-479)
Glassroots Inc ....E 973 353-9555
Newark (G-7170)
Glassworks Studio Inc ....G 973 656-0800
Morristown (G-6710)
Glocal Expertise Llc ....G 718 928-3839
Jersey City (G-4761)
▲ Go Foton Corporation ....F 732 412-7375
Somerset (G-10106)
▲ Goodlite Products Inc ....F 718 697-7502
Perth Amboy (G-8615)
▲ Hospitality GL Brands USA Inc ....F 800 869-5258
Ridgefield Park (G-9407)
House of Kalon New York ....F 786 259-0786
Secaucus (G-9895)
▲ Icup Inc ....E 856 751-2045
Cherry Hill (G-1376)
▲ Illuminating Experiences LLC ....G 800 734-5858
New Brunswick (G-6967)
Interior Specialties LLC ....F 856 663-1700
Pennsauken (G-8529)
▲ Kraftware Corporation ....E 732 345-7091
Roselle (G-9674)
Kramme Consolidated Inc ....G 856 358-8151
Monroeville (G-6400)
▲ Lumiko USA Inc ....G 609 409-6900
Cranbury (G-1857)
M D Laboratory Supplies Inc ....G 732 322-0773
Franklin Park (G-3628)
▲ Materials Research Group Inc ....G 908 245-3301
Roselle (G-9675)
▲ McGrory Glass Inc ....D 856 579-3200
Paulsboro (G-8420)
Metro Optics LLC ....F 908 413-0004
Flemington (G-3457)
▲ Mg Decor LLC ....F 201 923-5493
Secaucus (G-9904)
Mirrotek International LLC ....E 973 472-1400
Passaic (G-8165)
Nds Technologies Inc ....E 856 691-0330
Vineland (G-11385)
Partners In Vision Inc ....G 888 748-1112
Edison (G-2592)
Princeton Hosted Solutions LLC ....F 856 470-2350
Haddonfield (G-4062)
Princeton Optronics Inc ....E 609 584-9696
Trenton (G-11108)
Q Glass Company Inc ....G 973 335-5191
Towaco (G-11002)
▲ Qis Inc ....F 856 455-3736
Rosenhayn (G-9708)
Quark Enterprises Inc ....E 856 455-0376
Rosenhayn (G-9709)
▲ Radiant Communications Corp ....E 908 757-7444
South Plainfield (G-10432)
▲ Sensors Unlimited Inc ....D 609 333-8000
Princeton (G-9116)
Sterling Products Inc ....F 973 471-2858
Passaic (G-8182)
Technical Glass Products Inc ....G 973 989-5500
Dover (G-2111)
Thomas Clark Fiberglass LLC ....G 609 492-9257
Barnegat (G-167)
Triton Associated Industries ....E 856 697-3050
Buena (G-951)
▲ United Silica Products Inc ....F 973 209-8854
Franklin (G-3606)
▲ Vandermark Merritt GL Studios ....G 908 231-8189
Branchburg (G-715)

3231 Glass Prdts Made Of Purchased Glass

A M K Glass Inc ....G 856 692-1488
Vineland (G-11318)
Above Rest Glass ....G 732 370-1616
Toms River (G-10859)
▲ Ace Fine Art Inc ....G 201 960-4447
Garfield (G-3714)
Ace Glass Incorporated ....D 856 692-3333
Vineland (G-11319)
Amcor Phrm Packg USA LLC ....C 856 825-1100
Millville (G-6280)
Artistic Glass & Doors Inc ....G 856 768-1414
West Berlin (G-11704)
Ascalon Studios Inc ....F 856 768-3779
West Berlin (G-11705)
Atlantic International Tech ....F 973 625-0053
Rockaway (G-9552)
Avant Industries Ltd Inc ....G 973 242-1700
Newark (G-7100)
Bellco Glass Inc ....D 800 257-7043
Vineland (G-11328)
▲ Century Bathworks Inc ....D 973 785-4290
Woodland Park (G-12214)
Century Bathworks Inc ....E 201 785-1414
Woodland Park (G-12215)
▲ Chemglass Inc ....C 856 696-0014
Vineland (G-11336)
◆ Comar Inc ....E 856 692-6100
Voorhees (G-11425)
Comar LLC ....C 856 507-5483
Vineland (G-11337)
◆ Comar LLC ....B 856 692-6100
Voorhees (G-11427)
Comfort Zone ....G 732 869-9990
Ocean Grove (G-7760)
County of Somerset ....C 732 469-3363
Bridgewater (G-830)
CR Laurence Co Inc ....F 201 770-1077
Secaucus (G-9874)
Crown Glass Co Inc ....G 908 642-1764
Branchburg (G-652)
Cumberland Rcycl Corp S Jersey ....E 856 825-4153
Millville (G-6296)
Demco Scientific Glassware Inc ....G 856 327-7898
Millville (G-6299)
◆ Dwk Life Sciences Inc ....C 856 825-1100
Millville (G-6301)
▲ Eastern Glass Resources Inc ....E 973 483-8411
Harrison (G-4180)
Edward W Hiemer & Co ....F 973 772-5081
Clifton (G-1611)
▲ Fbn New Jersey Mfg Inc ....E 973 402-1443
Mountain Lakes (G-6859)
Femenella & Associates Inc ....G 908 722-6526
Branchburg (G-659)
Folio Art Glass Inc ....G 732 431-0044
Colts Neck (G-1786)
▲ Friedrich and Dimmock Inc ....E 856 825-0305
Millville (G-6302)
Gbw Manufacturing Inc ....E 973 279-0077
Totowa (G-10947)
◆ General Glass Intl Corp ....C 201 553-1850
Secaucus (G-9887)
Gerresheimer Glass Inc ....B 856 507-5852
Vineland (G-11361)
▲ Glass Dynamics LLC ....G 856 205-1503
Vineland (G-11362)
Glastron Inc ....E 856 692-0500
Vineland (G-11363)
H S Martin Company Inc ....F 856 692-8700
Vineland (G-11368)
▲ Hanson & Zollinger Inc ....F 856 626-3440
Berlin (G-434)
▲ Icup Inc ....E 856 751-2045
Cherry Hill (G-1376)
Insulite Inc ....F 732 255-1700
Toms River (G-10888)
Interior Specialties LLC ....F 856 663-1700
Pennsauken (G-8529)
▲ JE Berkowitz LP ....C 856 456-7800
Pedricktown (G-8436)
Jersey Tempered Glass Inc ....E 856 273-8700
Mount Laurel (G-6810)
▲ Klein Usa Inc ....F 973 246-8181
East Rutherford (G-2302)
◆ Kubik Maltbie Inc ....E 856 234-0052
Mount Laurel (G-6811)
Linda Spolitino ....G 609 345-3126
Atlantic City (G-102)
▲ McGrory Glass Inc ....D 856 579-3200
Paulsboro (G-8420)
Miric Industries Inc ....F 201 864-0233
North Bergen (G-7468)
Newman Glass Works Inc ....F 215 925-3565
Camden (G-1078)
Oldcastle Buildingenvelope Inc ....D 856 234-9222
Moorestown (G-6605)
Penta Glass Industries Inc ....G 973 478-2110
Garfield (G-3747)
▲ Personlzed Exprssons By Audrey ....F 973 478-5115
Garfield (G-3748)
Pike Machine Products Inc ....D 973 379-9128
Short Hills (G-9983)
Potters Industries LLC ....E 201 507-4169
Carlstadt (G-1206)
▲ Precision Electronic Glass Inc ....D 856 691-2234
Vineland (G-11393)
Proco Inc ....G 609 265-8777
Lumberton (G-5662)
Quality Glass Inc ....F 908 754-2652
South Plainfield (G-10428)
Quark Enterprises Inc ....E 856 455-0376
Rosenhayn (G-9709)
R A O Contract Sales NY Inc ....G 201 652-1500
Paterson (G-8367)
▲ Rambusch Decorating Company ....E 201 333-2525
Jersey City (G-4815)
S P Industries Inc ....D 856 691-3200
Vineland (G-11401)
▲ St Thomas Creations ....E 800 536-2284
Monroe Township (G-6394)
◆ Thermoseal Industries LLC ....D 856 456-3109
Gloucester City (G-3847)

SIC

Triton Associated Industries.................E 856 697-3050
Buena *(G-951)*
Union City Mirror & Table Co.................E 201 867-0050
Union City *(G-11270)*
V M Glass Co.................G 856 794-9333
Vineland *(G-11414)*
William Duling.................G 856 365-6323
Camden *(G-1089)*

3241 Cement, Hydraulic

▼ Anti Hydro International Inc.................F 908 284-9000
Flemington *(G-3427)*
Essroc Corp.................G 856 650-9046
Camden *(G-1063)*
Lafarge North America Inc.................G 201 437-2575
Bayonne *(G-236)*
Lehigh Cement Company.................G 973 579-2111
Sparta *(G-10509)*
Local Concrete Sup & Eqp Corp.................G 201 797-7979
Elmwood Park *(G-2832)*
Tanis Concrete.................E 201 796-1556
Fair Lawn *(G-3119)*

3251 Brick & Structural Clay Tile

Glen-Gery Corporation.................E 908 359-5111
Hillsborough *(G-4336)*
▲ Magpie Marketing Inc.................G 201 507-9155
Rutherford *(G-9739)*
Morgan Advanced Ceramics Inc.................E 973 808-1621
Fairfield *(G-3264)*

3253 Ceramic Tile

Andrevin Inc.................G 732 270-2794
Toms River *(G-10863)*
Best Tile of New Jersey.................G 732 390-7700
East Brunswick *(G-2137)*
Congoleum Corporation.................D 609 584-3601
Trenton *(G-11045)*
▲ Industrie Bitossi Inc.................E 201 796-0722
Elmwood Park *(G-2825)*
▲ L S P Industrial Ceramics Inc.................G 609 397-8330
Lambertville *(G-5217)*
◆ Mannington Mills Inc.................A 856 935-3000
Salem *(G-9806)*
Maya Trading Corporation.................G 201 533-1400
Jersey City *(G-4782)*
▲ Nasco Stone and Tile LLC.................E 732 634-0589
Port Reading *(G-8988)*
▲ RS Marble and Granite Inc.................G 732 802-9220
Port Reading *(G-8989)*
▲ Standard Tile Watchung Corp.................G 908 754-4200
Watchung *(G-11594)*
Stonework Dsign Consulting Inc.................E 973 575-0835
Fairfield *(G-3315)*
▼ Terra Designs Inc.................F 973 328-1135
Dover *(G-2112)*

3255 Clay Refractories

Harbisonwalker Intl Inc.................G 732 388-4011
Rahway *(G-9195)*

3259 Structural Clay Prdts, NEC

R & R Irrigation Co Inc.................F 732 271-7070
Middlesex *(G-6192)*

3261 China Plumbing Fixtures & Fittings

◆ As America Inc.................C 732 980-3000
Piscataway *(G-8738)*
Benco Inc.................F 973 575-4440
Fairfield *(G-3146)*
▲ Ecom 2000 Inc.................F 718 504-7355
Edison *(G-2507)*
▲ Ginsey Industries Inc.................D 856 933-1300
Swedesboro *(G-10699)*
Hitrons Solutions Inc.................E 201 244-0300
Bergenfield *(G-387)*
▲ Hitrons Solutions Inc.................E 201 244-0300
Bergenfield *(G-388)*
◆ Lenape Products Inc.................E 609 394-5376
Trenton *(G-11075)*
◆ New Jersey Porcelain Co Inc.................F 609 394-5376
Trenton *(G-11086)*
▲ Toilettree Products Inc.................G 845 358-5316
Ramsey *(G-9253)*

3262 China, Table & Kitchen Articles

▲ Nikko Ceramics Inc.................F 201 840-5200
Fairview *(G-3366)*

3263 Earthenware, Whiteware, Table & Kitchen Articles

Art Plaque Creations Inc.................F 973 482-2536
Kearny *(G-4862)*

3264 Porcelain Electrical Splys

Curran-Pfeiff Corp.................F 732 225-0555
Edison *(G-2499)*
Electro-Ceramic Industries.................E 201 342-2630
Hackensack *(G-3909)*
Escadaus Inc.................G 973 335-8888
Boonton *(G-567)*
▲ Fermag Technologies Inc.................G 732 985-7300
Toms River *(G-10875)*
House of Prill Inc.................E 732 442-2400
Lincroft *(G-5337)*
Isolantite Manufacturing Co.................E 908 647-3333
Stirling *(G-10602)*
▲ Merrimac Industries Inc.................D 973 575-1300
West Caldwell *(G-11790)*
Mitronics Products Inc.................G 908 647-5006
Gillette *(G-3795)*
Morgan Advanced Ceramics Inc.................E 973 808-1621
Fairfield *(G-3264)*
◆ New Jersey Porcelain Co Inc.................F 609 394-5376
Trenton *(G-11086)*
◆ Oxford Instrs Holdings Inc.................E 732 541-1300
Carteret *(G-1265)*
Pekay Industries Inc.................F 732 938-2722
Farmingdale *(G-3392)*
▲ Top Knobs Usa Inc.................F 908 359-6174
Somerville *(G-10229)*

3269 Pottery Prdts, NEC

Cameo China Inc.................G 201 865-7650
Secaucus *(G-9871)*
▲ Durand Glass Mfg Co Inc.................A 856 327-1850
Millville *(G-6300)*
◆ Franklin Mint LLC.................E 800 843-6468
Fort Lee *(G-3555)*
◆ Larose Industries LLC.................D 973 543-2037
Randolph *(G-9287)*

3271 Concrete Block & Brick

▲ Anchor Concrete Products Inc.................E 732 842-5010
Red Bank *(G-9319)*
Anchor Concrete Products Inc.................D 732 458-9440
Brick *(G-734)*
B&F and Son Masonry Company.................E 201 791-7630
Elmwood Park *(G-2805)*
Bell Supply Co.................E 856 663-3900
Pennsauken *(G-8486)*
Blades Landscaping Inc.................F 856 779-7665
Mount Laurel *(G-6783)*
Clayton Block Co.................D 201 955-6292
North Arlington *(G-7418)*
◆ Clayton Block Company Inc.................E 732 363-1995
Wall Township *(G-11470)*
Clayton Block Company Inc.................G 732 462-1860
Freehold *(G-3647)*
Clayton Block Company Inc.................E 732 681-0186
Wall Township *(G-11471)*
Clayton Block Company Inc.................F 609 693-9600
Forked River *(G-3535)*
Clayton Block Company Inc.................E 732 905-3234
Tinton Falls *(G-10826)*
Clayton Block Company Inc.................G 732 549-1234
Edison *(G-2484)*
Clayton Block Company Inc.................E 732 349-3700
Toms River *(G-10872)*
Clayton Block Company LLC.................E 201 339-8585
Bayonne *(G-219)*
Creative Pavers.................G 201 782-1661
Montvale *(G-6451)*
Crh Americas Inc.................E 732 292-2500
Red Bank *(G-9323)*
Dunbar Concrete Products Inc.................F 973 697-2525
Oak Ridge *(G-7660)*
▲ EP Henry Corporation.................D 856 845-6200
Woodbury *(G-12160)*
▲ GAF Elk Materials Corporation.................C 973 628-4083
Wayne *(G-11639)*
Greenrock Recycling LLC.................G 908 713-0008
Clinton *(G-1750)*
▼ Hycrete Inc.................E 201 386-8110
Little Falls *(G-5477)*
Josantos Cnstr & Dev LLC.................G 732 202-7389
Brick *(G-749)*

Paverart LLC.................G 856 783-7000
Lindenwold *(G-5463)*
▼ Phillips Companies Inc.................D 973 483-4124
Clinton *(G-1753)*
Procrete LLC.................G 609 365-2922
Linwood *(G-5467)*
R P Smith & Son Inc.................F 973 584-4063
Succasunna *(G-10627)*
Reuther Contracting Co Inc.................E 201 863-3550
North Bergen *(G-7480)*
Vogel Precast Inc.................G 732 552-8837
Lakewood *(G-5202)*

3272 Concrete Prdts

A & A Concrete Products Inc.................G 973 835-2239
Riverdale *(G-9473)*
Advanced Pavement Technologies.................F 973 366-8044
Rockaway *(G-9545)*
Associate Fireplace Builders.................G 908 273-5900
Summit *(G-10636)*
▲ Boccella Precast LLC.................F 856 767-3861
Berlin *(G-427)*
▲ Bradbury Burial Vault Co Inc.................E 856 227-2555
Blackwood *(G-473)*
Brent Material Company.................G 908 686-3832
Kenilworth *(G-4946)*
Brewster Vaults & Monuments.................F 856 785-1412
Millville *(G-6290)*
◆ Ceresist Inc.................F 973 345-3231
Paterson *(G-8232)*
Clayton Block Co.................D 201 955-6292
North Arlington *(G-7418)*
Clayton Block Company Inc.................E 732 681-0186
Wall Township *(G-11471)*
Clayton Block Company LLC.................E 201 339-8585
Bayonne *(G-219)*
▲ Concrete Stone & Tile Corp.................E 973 948-7193
Branchville *(G-728)*
▲ Construction Specialties Inc.................E 908 236-0800
Lebanon *(G-5282)*
Cooper Burial Vaults Co.................G 856 547-8405
Barrington *(G-174)*
Cooper-Wilbert Vault Co Inc.................E 856 547-8405
Barrington *(G-175)*
Creter Vault Corp.................E 908 782-7771
Flemington *(G-3432)*
Crossfield Products Corp.................D 908 245-2801
Roselle Park *(G-9691)*
CST Pavers.................F 856 299-5339
Pedricktown *(G-8434)*
▲ CST Products LLC.................E 856 299-5339
Penns Grove *(G-8464)*
Cumberland Marble & Monument.................G 856 691-3334
Vineland *(G-11344)*
Delaware Valley Vault Co Inc.................E 856 227-2555
Blackwood *(G-475)*
Di-Ferraro Inc.................E 973 694-7200
Wayne *(G-11623)*
Diamond Chip Realty LLC.................E 973 383-4651
Sparta *(G-10497)*
Donald Mason Baker Contractor.................G 908 782-2115
Flemington *(G-3437)*
Double Twenties Inc.................F 973 827-7563
Franklin *(G-3598)*
Dunbar Concrete Products Inc.................F 973 697-2525
Oak Ridge *(G-7660)*
Duraamen Engineered Pdts Inc.................G 973 230-1301
Newark *(G-7144)*
▼ Empire Blended Products Inc.................E 732 269-4949
Bayville *(G-254)*
European Stone Art LLC.................F 201 441-9116
South Hackensack *(G-10266)*
Flemington Precast & Sup LLC.................F 908 782-3246
Flemington *(G-3442)*
Flexco Bldg Pdts Ltd Lblty Co.................F 732 780-1700
Marlboro *(G-5940)*
▲ GAF Elk Materials Corporation.................C 973 628-4083
Wayne *(G-11639)*
Garden State Precast Inc.................D 732 938-4436
Wall Township *(G-11485)*
Granville Concrete Products.................G 973 584-6653
Randolph *(G-9280)*
Gravity Vault.................G 732 856-9599
Middletown *(G-6215)*
▼ Grinnell Con Pavingstones Inc.................D 973 383-9300
Sparta *(G-10501)*
H T Hall Inc.................F 732 449-3441
Spring Lake *(G-10533)*
Hanson Aggregates Wrp Inc.................E 972 653-5500
Wall Township *(G-11487)*

Interntnal Dmnsional Stone LLC ....G...... 973 729-0359
  Haskell (G-4208)

◆ J B & Sons Concrete Products ....F...... 856 767-4140
  Berlin (G-435)

J F Gillespie Inc ....E...... 856 692-2233
  Vineland (G-11375)

J L Erectors Inc ....E...... 856 232-9400
  Blackwood (G-482)

▲ Jarco U S Casting Corp ....E...... 201 271-0003
  Union City (G-11250)

Jersey Cast Stone Ltd Lblty Co ....F...... 856 333-6900
  Pennsauken (G-8536)

▲ Jersey Precast Corporation Inc ....C...... 609 689-3700
  Trenton (G-11070)

JM Ahle Co Inc ....G...... 732 388-5507
  Rahway (G-9204)

Jpc Merger Sub LLC ....C...... 609 890-4343
  Trenton (G-11072)

Kelken-Gold Inc ....G...... 732 416-6730
  Sayreville (G-9826)

Kuiken Brothers Company....................E...... 201 796-2082
  Fair Lawn (G-3100)

Liedl ....G...... 908 359-8335
  Hillsborough (G-4355)

▲ Massarellis Lawn Ornaments Inc .....E...... 609 567-9700
  Hammonton (G-4143)

Maund Enterprises Inc ....E...... 609 628-2475
  Tuckahoe (G-11136)

Mershon Concrete LLC ....E...... 609 298-2150
  Bordentown (G-603)

▲ Midstate Filigree Systems Inc..........D...... 609 448-8700
  Cranbury (G-1862)

Northeast Con Pdts & Sup Inc ....G...... 973 728-1667
  Hewitt (G-4291)

P J Gillespie Inc ....E...... 856 327-2993
  Vineland (G-11387)

Paul Bros Inc ....E...... 856 697-5895
  Newfield (G-7370)

Peerless Concrete Products Co ....G...... 973 838-3060
  Butler (G-1015)

Precast Manufacturing Co LLC ....E...... 908 454-2122
  Phillipsburg (G-8665)

Precast Systems Inc ....E...... 609 208-0569
  Allentown (G-33)

Russell Cast Stone Inc ....D...... 856 753-4000
  West Berlin (G-11748)

◆ Sika Corporation ....B...... 201 933-8800
  Lyndhurst (G-5708)

Solid Cast Stone ....G...... 856 694-5245
  Newfield (G-7372)

Strongwall Industries Inc ....G...... 201 445-4633
  Allendale (G-19)

Suburban Monument & Vault................E...... 973 242-7007
  Newark (G-7332)

Trap Rock Industries Inc ....B...... 609 924-0300
  Kingston (G-5030)

Trap-Zap Environmental Systems ....E...... 201 251-9970
  Wyckoff (G-12266)

Tri-State Quikrete ....E...... 973 347-4569
  Flanders (G-3420)

▲ Ulma Form-Works Inc ....D...... 201 882-1122
  Hawthorne (G-4261)

Van Brill Pool & Spa Center ....G...... 856 424-4333
  Marlton (G-6002)

3273 Ready-Mixed Concrete

Abi Inc ....E...... 609 588-8225
  Lawrenceville (G-5249)

Ace-Crete Products Inc ....F...... 732 269-1400
  Bayville (G-247)

Action Supply Inc ....F...... 609 390-0663
  Ocean View (G-7762)

Allied Concrete Co Inc ....G...... 973 627-6150
  Rockaway (G-9549)

Allied Concrete Co Inc ....G...... 973 627-6150
  Rockaway (G-9550)

Atlantic Masonry Supply Inc ....F...... 609 909-9292
  Egg Harbor Township (G-2680)

Clayton Block Company Inc ....F...... 732 349-3700
  Toms River (G-10872)

Clayton Block Company Inc ....F...... 732 364-2404
  Jackson (G-4657)

Clayton Block Company Inc ....E...... 732 549-1234
  Edison (G-2484)

Colonial Concrete Company ....E...... 973 482-1920
  Newark (G-7124)

Colonial Concrete Company ....F...... 201 869-0055
  North Bergen (G-7442)

Concrete On Demand Inc ....F...... 201 337-0005
  Oakland (G-7680)

Construction Dynamics Inc ....F...... 732 840-7766
  Brick (G-738)

County Concrete Corporation ....F...... 973 538-3113
  Morristown (G-6702)

County Concrete Corporation ....D...... 973 744-2188
  Kenvil (G-5010)

Crh Americas Inc ....G...... 908 475-1225
  Brick (G-741)

Diamond Chip Realty LLC....................G...... 973 383-4651
  Sparta (G-10497)

Eastern Concrete Materials Inc ....C...... 201 797-7979
  Saddle Brook (G-9763)

Eastern Concrete Materials Inc ....G...... 908 537-2135
  Glen Gardner (G-3814)

Erial Concrete Inc ....F...... 856 784-8884
  Erial (G-3000)

Ernest R Miles Construction Co ....F...... 856 697-2311
  Newfield (G-7365)

Herbert J Hinchman & Son Inc ....E...... 973 942-2063
  Wayne (G-11647)

Holtec Government Services LLC ....G...... 856 291-0600
  Marlton (G-5978)

Joseph and William Stavola ....G...... 609 924-0300
  Kingston (G-5028)

Kennedy Concrete Inc ....E...... 856 692-8650
  Vineland (G-11378)

L & L Redi-Mix Inc ....G...... 609 859-2271
  Southampton (G-10477)

Le-Ed Construction Inc ....E...... 732 341-4546
  Toms River (G-10893)

Mershon Concrete LLC ....E...... 609 298-2150
  Bordentown (G-603)

Miles Concrete Company Inc ....F...... 856 697-2311
  Newfield (G-7367)

New Jersey Pulverizing Co Inc ....F...... 732 269-1400
  Bayville (G-259)

Penn-Jersey Bldg Mtls Co Inc ....D...... 609 641-6994
  Egg Harbor Township (G-2691)

▼ Phillips Companies Inc....................D...... 973 483-4124
  Clinton (G-1753)

Ralph Clayton & Sons LLC ....E...... 800 662-3044
  Cookstown (G-1808)

Ralph Clayton & Sons LLC ....E...... 609 383-1818
  Egg Harbor Township (G-2693)

Ralph Clayton & Sons LLC ....E...... 609 695-0767
  Trenton (G-11111)

Reuther Material Co Inc ....E...... 201 863-3550
  North Bergen (G-7481)

Salomone Rd-Mix Ltd Liabitlity ....F...... 973 305-0022
  Wayne (G-11682)

SCC Concrete Inc ....F...... 908 859-2172
  Phillipsburg (G-8670)

Short Load Concrete LLC ....G...... 732 469-4420
  Bridgewater (G-895)

Suffolk County Contractors ....E...... 732 349-7726
  Toms River (G-10915)

Tanis Concrete ....E...... 201 796-1556
  Fair Lawn (G-3119)

Trap Rock Industries Inc ....B...... 609 924-0300
  Kingston (G-5030)

VI Concrete Co ....E...... 856 767-0415
  Atco (G-92)

Weldon Materials Inc ....G...... 908 233-4444
  Westfield (G-11934)

Wjv Materials LLC ....E...... 856 299-8244
  Pedricktown (G-8441)

Yogo Mix ....G...... 609 897-1379
  Princeton Junction (G-9167)

3274 Lime

Lime Energy Co...................................G...... 732 791-5380
  Newark (G-7219)

Smith Lime Flour Co Inc ....F...... 973 344-1700
  Kearny (G-4914)

3275 Gypsum Prdts

Art Plaque Creations Inc ....F...... 973 482-2536
  Kearny (G-4862)

Baruffi Bros Inc ....F...... 856 692-6400
  Vineland (G-11327)

Bestwall LLC ....D...... 856 966-7600
  Camden (G-1044)

▲ Durabond Division US Gypsum........F...... 732 636-7900
  Port Reading (G-8987)

New Ngc Inc ....D...... 609 499-1323
  Burlington (G-986)

Proform Acoustic Surfaces LLC ....G...... 201 553-9614
  Secaucus (G-9914)

United States Gypsum Company ....D...... 732 636-7900
  Port Reading (G-8991)

3281 Cut Stone Prdts

A C D Custom Granite Inc ....F...... 732 695-2400
  Ocean (G-7711)

Albert H Hopper Inc ....G...... 201 991-2266
  North Arlington (G-7414)

American Stone Inc ....E...... 973 318-7707
  Hillside (G-4388)

American Stone Inc ....E...... 973 318-7707
  Hillside (G-4389)

Atlas Marble & Granite LLC ....F...... 973 491-5454
  Springfield (G-10539)

▲ Bcg Marble & Granite South LLC .....G...... 732 367-3788
  Jackson (G-4655)

◆ Bcg Marble Gran Fabricators Co .....F...... 201 343-8487
  Hackensack (G-3879)

Bedrock Granite Inc ....E...... 732 741-0010
  Shrewsbury (G-9991)

◆ Cambridge Pavers Inc ....C...... 201 933-5000
  Lyndhurst (G-5673)

▲ Caputo International Inc ....E...... 732 225-5777
  Edison (G-2479)

Charles Deluca ....G...... 973 778-5621
  Lodi (G-5579)

Cole Brothers Marble & Granite ....G...... 856 455-7989
  Elmer (G-2790)

▲ Counter-Fit Inc ....C...... 609 871-8888
  Willingboro (G-12118)

▲ Elana Tile Contractors Inc ....G...... 973 386-0991
  East Hanover (G-2215)

▲ Elite Stone Importers LLC ....G...... 732 542-7900
  Tinton Falls (G-10836)

▲ EP Henry Corporation ....D...... 856 845-6200
  Woodbury (G-12160)

EZ General Construction Corp ....G...... 201 223-1101
  Wayne (G-11631)

◆ Formia Marble & Stone Inc ....F...... 908 259-0606
  Roselle (G-9670)

Gr Stone LLC ....G...... 908 925-7290
  Kenilworth (G-4959)

▲ Gran All Mrble Tile Imprts Inc ....G...... 856 354-4747
  Cherry Hill (G-1372)

▲ Granite and Marble Assoc Inc ....G...... 908 416-1100
  North Plainfield (G-7559)

H T Hall Inc ....F...... 732 449-3441
  Spring Lake (G-10533)

Hanson Aggregates Wrp Inc ....E...... 972 653-5500
  Wall Township (G-11487)

Ilkem Marble and Granite Inc ....G...... 856 433-8714
  Cherry Hill (G-1377)

▲ Industrial Consulting Mktg Inc ....E...... 973 427-2474
  Fair Lawn (G-3096)

Innovative Cutng Concepts LLC ....G...... 609 484-9960
  Egg Harbor Township (G-2685)

Interntnal Dmnsional Stone LLC ....G...... 973 729-0359
  Haskell (G-4208)

▲ Marble Online Corporation ....G...... 201 998-9100
  Kearny (G-4897)

Marmo Enterprises Inc ....G...... 732 649-3011
  Somerset (G-10130)

Marvic Corp ....E...... 908 686-4340
  Union (G-11206)

Murray Paving & Concrete LLC ....E...... 201 670-0030
  Hackensack (G-3950)

Natures Beauty Marble & Gran ....F...... 908 233-5300
  Scotch Plains (G-9852)

▲ Phillipsburg Marble Co Inc...............E...... 908 859-3435
  Phillipsburg (G-8664)

Premier Marble and Gran 2 Inc ....G...... 732 294-7891
  Freehold (G-3681)

◆ Robert Young & Sons Inc ....G...... 973 483-0451
  Newark (G-7291)

Sanford & Birdsall Inc ....G...... 732 223-6966
  Manasquan (G-5880)

Sculptured Stone Inc ....F...... 973 557-1482
  Boonton (G-583)

Solidsurface Designs Inc ....E...... 856 910-7720
  Pennsauken (G-8580)

▲ Sr International Rock Inc...................E...... 908 864-4700
  Bound Brook (G-623)

Statewide Granite and Marble...............F...... 201 653-1700
  Jersey City (G-4833)

Stavola Construction Mtls Inc ....E...... 732 542-2328
  Tinton Falls (G-10849)

Stavola Construction Mtls Inc ....E...... 732 356-5700
  Bound Brook (G-625)

▲ Stone Mar Natural Stone Co LLC .....G...... 856 988-1802
  Marlton (G-6000)

Stone Systems New Jersey LLC ....F...... 973 778-5525
  Fairfield (G-3313)

▲ Stone Truss Systems Inc ....E 973 882-7377
Fairfield (G-3314)

Stoneworld At Redbank Inc ....G 732 383-5110
Red Bank (G-9345)

▲ Thin Stone Systems LLC ....G 973 882-7377
Fairfield (G-3325)

Whole Stones LLC ....G 856 266-0091
Willingboro (G-12123)

3291 Abrasive Prdts

3M Company ....B 973 884-2500
Whippany (G-12004)

▲ Advanced Abrasives Corporation ....F 856 665-9300
Pennsauken (G-8471)

Agsco Corporation ....E 973 244-0005
Pine Brook (G-8681)

▲ Alpex Wheel Co Inc ....F 201 871-1700
Tenafly (G-10781)

▲ Beacut Abrasives Corp ....F 973 249-1420
East Rutherford (G-2283)

Chessco Industries Inc ....F 609 882-0400
Ewing (G-3008)

◆ EMR (usa Holdings) Inc ....F 856 365-7500
Bellmawr (G-339)

▲ Garfield Industries Inc ....E 973 575-3322
Fairfield (G-3206)

Lunzer Inc ....G 201 794-2800
Englewood (G-2911)

▲ Mercury Floor Machines Inc ....E 201 568-4606
Englewood (G-2915)

New Jersey Diamond Products Co .....F 973 684-0949
Paterson (G-8349)

▲ Robinson Tech Intl Corp ....G 973 287-6458
Fairfield (G-3296)

Steel Riser Corp ....G 732 341-7031
Toms River (G-10914)

▲ Supply Plus NY Inc ....G 973 481-4800
Paterson (G-8391)

William R Hall Co ....E 856 784-6700
Lindenwold (G-5464)

3292 Asbestos products

▲ Allied Tile Mfg Corp ....G 718 647-2200
South Plainfield (G-10324)

Blavor Inc ....G 973 265-4165
Montville (G-6483)

Hup & Sons ....G 908 832-7878
Glen Gardner (G-3815)

▲ Hydro-Mechanical Systems Inc ....F 856 848-8888
Westville (G-11943)

◆ Stuart Steel Protection Corp ....E 732 469-5544
Somerset (G-10174)

Wick It LLC ....G 973 249-2970
Passaic (G-8190)

3295 Minerals & Earths: Ground Or Treated

▼ Anthracite Industries Inc ....G 908 537-2155
Asbury (G-65)

◆ Asbury Carbons Inc ....G 908 537-2155
Asbury (G-66)

◆ Asbury Graphite Mills Inc ....E 908 537-2155
Asbury (G-67)

Asbury Graphite Mills Inc ....D 908 537-2157
Asbury (G-68)

Corp American Mica ....G 908 587-5237
Linden (G-5361)

Dicaperl Minerals Corp ....G 856 320-2919
Pennsauken (G-8503)

▲ Fine Minerals Intl Inc ....G 732 318-6760
Edison (G-2520)

◆ G Holdings Inc ....G 973 628-3000
Parsippany (G-8019)

▲ G-I Holdings Inc ....G 973 628-3000
Wayne (G-11638)

Isp Global Technologies Inc ....F 973 628-4000
Wayne (G-11655)

Isp Global Technologies LLC ....G 973 628-4000
Wayne (G-11656)

▲ Mel Chemicals Inc ....C 908 782-5800
Flemington (G-3456)

◆ Minmetals Inc ....F 201 809-1898
Leonia (G-5318)

3296 Mineral Wool

Advantage Fiberglass Inc ....G 609 926-4606
Egg Harbor Township (G-2677)

Fbm Galaxy Inc ....E 856 966-1105
Camden (G-1066)

Insulation Materials Distrs ....G 908 925-2323
Linden (G-5388)

Johns Manville Corporation ....C 856 768-7000
Berlin (G-436)

Owens Corning Sales LLC ....C 201 998-5666
Kearny (G-4904)

▲ Pacor Inc ....E 609 324-1100
Bordentown (G-607)

Passaic Metal & Bldg Sups Co ....D 973 546-9000
Clifton (G-1691)

Pekay Industries Inc ....F 732 938-2722
Farmingdale (G-3392)

◆ United States Mineral Pdts Co ....D 973 347-1200
Stanhope (G-10591)

3297 Nonclay Refractories

▲ Bartley Crucible Refractories ....F 609 393-0066
Trenton (G-11025)

Curran-Pfeiff Corp ....F 732 225-0555
Edison (G-2499)

Morgan Advanced Ceramics Inc ....E 973 808-1621
Fairfield (G-3264)

▲ P & R Castings LLC ....E 732 302-3600
Somerset (G-10150)

Strongwall Industries Inc ....G 201 445-4633
Allendale (G-19)

3299 Nonmetallic Mineral Prdts, NEC

Advanced Cerametrics Inc ....G 609 397-2900
Lambertville (G-5209)

Art Plaque Creations Inc ....F 973 482-2536
Kearny (G-4862)

Bestwall LLC ....D 856 966-7600
Camden (G-1044)

Brambila Jorge Stucco & Stone ....G 856 451-2039
Bridgeton (G-779)

California Stucco Products ....G 201 457-1900
Hackensack (G-3890)

▲ Ceramic Products Inc ....G 201 342-8200
Hackensack (G-3895)

▲ Ceramsource Inc ....F 732 257-5002
East Brunswick (G-2140)

Crystex Composites LLC ....G 973 779-8866
Clifton (G-1594)

Digital Atelier LLC ....G 609 890-6666
Trenton (G-11055)

▲ Environmolds LLC ....F 908 273-5401
Summit (G-10641)

▲ Intersource USA Inc ....G 732 257-5002
East Brunswick (G-2161)

Kingston Nurseries LLC ....F 609 430-0366
Kingston (G-5029)

Mediterranean Stucco Corp ....F 973 491-0160
Newark (G-7239)

Perfect Shapes Inc ....G 856 783-3844
Elmer (G-2795)

Whibco Inc ....E 856 825-5200
Port Elizabeth (G-8971)

33 PRIMARY METAL INDUSTRIES

3312 Blast Furnaces, Coke Ovens, Steel & Rolling Mills

A & A Ironwork Co Inc ....F 973 728-4300
Hewitt (G-4287)

Aibens Imort ....G 609 902-9953
Princeton Junction (G-9146)

◆ Albea Americas Inc ....C 908 689-3000
Washington (G-11573)

Alloy Stainless Products Co ....D 973 256-1616
Totowa (G-10928)

Amrod Corp ....D 973 344-3806
Newark (G-7085)

▲ Anello Fence LLC ....G 973 692-9200
Pequannock (G-8598)

Archer Day Inc ....E 732 396-0600
Avenel (G-124)

▲ Atco Products Inc ....E 973 379-3171
Springfield (G-10538)

Atiair Technology Inc ....G 973 334-4980
Boonton (G-556)

Atlas Copco North America LLC ....G 973 397-3400
Parsippany (G-7955)

Benedict-Miller Inc ....E 908 497-1477
Kenilworth (G-4944)

Bilt Rite Tool & Die Co Inc ....G 973 227-2882
Fairfield (G-3150)

Bloomfield Iron Co Inc ....G 973 748-7040
Belleville (G-296)

Bushwick Metals LLC ....E 908 754-8700
South Plainfield (G-10341)

Camden Iron & Metal Inc ....F 856 365-7500
Camden (G-1047)

◆ Camden Iron & Metal LLC ....D 856 969-7065
Bellmawr (G-334)

CB&i LLC ....C 856 482-3000
Trenton (G-11036)

▲ Century Tube Corp ....E 908 534-2001
Somerville (G-10204)

CMI-Promex Inc ....F 856 351-1000
Pedricktown (G-8433)

DAngelo Metal Products Inc ....F 908 862-8220
Linden (G-5367)

▲ Dso Fluid Handling Co Inc ....E 732 225-9100
Edison (G-2505)

▲ Dynamic Defense Materials LLC ......E 856 552-4150
Marlton (G-5974)

E C Electroplating Inc ....E 973 340-0227
Garfield (G-3731)

▲ Easyflex East Inc ....G 201 853-9005
Little Ferry (G-5503)

Electro Parts Inc ....E 856 767-5923
West Berlin (G-11719)

Equipment Distributing Corp ....E 201 641-8414
Ridgefield Park (G-9405)

Faber Precision Inc ....G 973 983-1844
Rockaway (G-9566)

▲ Ford Fasteners Inc ....G 201 487-3151
Hackensack (G-3915)

Fox Steel Products LLC ....G 856 778-4661
Mount Laurel (G-6799)

G M Stainless Inc ....F 908 575-1834
Branchburg (G-662)

▲ Gerdau Amrsteel Sayreville Inc ....A 732 721-6600
Sayreville (G-9821)

Haas Environmental Inc ....F 609 859-3100
Roseland (G-9652)

Hands On Wheels ....G 609 892-4693
Atlantic City (G-99)

◆ Hoeganaes Corporation ....B 856 303-0366
Cinnaminson (G-1468)

◆ Intra Pac Swedesboro ....D 856 467-0485
Swedesboro (G-10703)

McAlister Welding & Fabg ....F 856 740-3890
Glassboro (G-3809)

New World Stainless LLC ....E 732 412-7137
Somerset (G-10144)

▲ Robinson Tech Intl Corp ....G 973 287-6458
Fairfield (G-3296)

▲ Stainless Metal Source Intl ....G 973 977-2200
Clifton (G-1730)

Tms International LLC ....G 732 721-7477
Sayreville (G-9841)

Unity Steel Rule Die Co ....E 201 569-6400
Englewood (G-2941)

US Pipe Fabrication LLC ....F 856 461-3000
Riverside (G-9507)

Welded Products Co Inc ....G 973 589-0180
Newark (G-7358)

Yarde Metals Inc ....E 973 463-1166
East Hanover (G-2251)

3313 Electrometallurgical Prdts

Alpha Assembly Solutions Inc ....E 908 561-5170
South Plainfield (G-10325)

▲ Alpha Assembly Solutions Inc ....E 908 791-3000
Somerset (G-10054)

3315 Steel Wire Drawing & Nails & Spikes

Amark Industries Inc ....G 973 992-8900
Livingston (G-5524)

Amark Wire LLC ....G 973 882-7818
Fairfield (G-3134)

◆ Arca Industrial (nj) Inc ....G 732 339-0450
Edison (G-2463)

▲ Arrow Fastener Co LLC ....B 201 843-6900
Saddle Brook (G-9752)

Barrette Outdoor Living Inc ....F 609 965-5450
Egg Harbor City (G-2657)

Belmont Whl Fence Mfg Inc ....E 973 472-5121
Garfield (G-3723)

▲ Bergen Cable Technology LLC ....E 973 276-9596
Fairfield (G-3147)

▲ Blue Gauntlet Fencing Gear Inc ....F 201 797-3332
Saddle Brook (G-9755)

Boyle Tool & Die Co Inc ....F 856 853-1819
West Deptford (G-11818)

Bushwick Metals LLC ....G 908 604-1450
South Plainfield (G-10340)

▲ C D E Inc ....D 732 297-2540
North Brunswick *(G-7509)*

▲ Dearborn A Belden Cdt Company ..D 908 925-8000
Elizabeth *(G-2723)*

Evergard Steel Corp ....F 908 925-6800
South Plainfield *(G-10358)*

Fence America New Jersey Inc ....G 973 472-5121
Hackensack *(G-3910)*

Fisk Alloy Inc ....E 973 427-7550
Hawthorne *(G-4234)*

◆ Fisk Alloy Wire Incorporated ....C 973 949-4491
Hawthorne *(G-4235)*

Global Wire & Cable Inc ....E 973 471-1000
Passaic *(G-8145)*

▲ Iwc ....F 732 968-8122
Green Brook *(G-3858)*

▲ Jersey Specialty Co Inc ....E 413 525-2292
Pennsauken *(G-8537)*

▲ Kabel N Elettrotek Amer Inc ....G 973 265-0850
Parsippany *(G-8035)*

▲ Metallia USA LLC ....E 201 585-5000
Fort Lee *(G-3567)*

Ninsa LLC ....G 609 561-7103
Hammonton *(G-4145)*

◆ Okonite Company ....C 201 825-0300
Ramsey *(G-9250)*

Phillips Enterprises Inc ....G 732 493-3191
Ocean *(G-7736)*

◆ Plasma Powders & Systems Inc ....F 732 431-0992
Marlboro *(G-5952)*

▲ Plasti-Clad Metal Products Inc ....G 732 449-2665
Wall Township *(G-11503)*

◆ Railing Dynamics Inc ....F 609 601-1300
Ocean City *(G-7754)*

Roll Tech Industries ....F 609 730-9500
Pennington *(G-8459)*

◆ Sandvik Inc ....C 201 794-5000
Fair Lawn *(G-3112)*

▲ Screentek Manufacturing Co LLC ....F 973 328-2121
Randolph *(G-9296)*

Security Fabricators Inc ....F 908 272-9171
Kenilworth *(G-4996)*

▲ United Wire Hanger Corp ....C 201 288-3212
Hasbrouck Heights *(G-4203)*

◆ US Wire & Cable Corporation ....B 973 824-5530
Newark *(G-7355)*

Wire Fabricators & Insulators ....E 973 768-2839
Livingston *(G-5572)*

Wytech Industries Inc ....D 732 396-3900
Rahway *(G-9228)*

3316 Cold Rolled Steel Sheet, Strip & Bars

American Strip Steel Inc ....F 800 526-1216
South Plainfield *(G-10327)*

American Strip Steel Inc ....G 856 461-8300
Delanco *(G-2002)*

Bigelow Components Corp ....E 973 467-1200
Springfield *(G-10543)*

Fox Steel Products LLC ....G 856 778-4661
Mount Laurel *(G-6799)*

◆ General Sullivan Group Inc ....E 609 745-5004
Pennington *(G-8451)*

Leibrock Metal Products Inc ....G 732 695-0326
Ocean *(G-7731)*

◆ Sandvik Inc ....C 201 794-5000
Fair Lawn *(G-3112)*

3317 Steel Pipe & Tubes

Amer-RAC LLC ....F 856 488-6210
Pennsauken *(G-8476)*

▲ Century Tube Corp ....E 908 534-2001
Somerville *(G-10204)*

Delsea Pipe Inc ....E 856 589-9374
Sewell *(G-9950)*

▲ Dodson Global Inc ....G 732 238-7001
East Brunswick *(G-2144)*

▲ Fluorotherm Polymers Inc ....G 973 575-0760
Parsippany *(G-8014)*

Fox Steel Products LLC ....G 856 778-4661
Mount Laurel *(G-6799)*

Long Island Pipe of NJ ....E 201 939-1100
Lyndhurst *(G-5687)*

◆ M & M International ....F 908 412-8300
South Plainfield *(G-10399)*

▲ Morris Industries Inc ....E 973 835-6600
Pompton Plains *(G-8963)*

Nippon Benkan Kagyo ....E 732 435-0777
New Brunswick *(G-6988)*

▲ Rathgibson North Branch LLC ....C 908 253-3260
Branchburg *(G-697)*

◆ Sandvik Inc ....C 201 794-5000
Fair Lawn *(G-3112)*

▲ Silbo Industries Inc ....C 201 307-0900
Montvale *(G-6479)*

▲ Standard Pipe Products Inc ....G 908 264-8284
Garwood *(G-3787)*

Zekelman Industries Inc ....D 724 342-6851
Westwood *(G-11977)*

3321 Gray Iron Foundries

Bierman-Everett Foundry Co ....G 973 373-8800
South Orange *(G-10301)*

Bridgestate Foundry Corp ....G 856 767-0400
Berlin *(G-428)*

▲ Campbell Foundry Company ....E 973 483-5480
Harrison *(G-4175)*

Campbell Foundry Company ....E 201 998-3765
Kearny *(G-4867)*

Emporia Foundry Inc ....E 973 483-5480
Harrison *(G-4181)*

En Tech Corp ....F 201 784-1034
Closter *(G-1757)*

En Tech Corp ....F 718 389-2058
Closter *(G-1758)*

▲ General Foundries Inc ....E 732 951-9001
North Brunswick *(G-7517)*

McWane Inc ....B 908 454-1161
Phillipsburg *(G-8658)*

United States Pipe Fndry LLC ....C 609 387-6000
Burlington *(G-994)*

▲ Universal Valve Company Inc ....F 908 351-0606
Elizabeth *(G-2780)*

Water Works Supply Company ....F 973 835-2153
Pompton Plains *(G-8968)*

3322 Malleable Iron Foundries

▲ Hafco Foundry & Machine Co ....F 201 447-0433
Midland Park *(G-6228)*

3324 Steel Investment Foundries

Advance Process Systems Lim ....G 201 400-9190
Branchville *(G-724)*

Atlantic Eqp Engineers Inc ....F 201 828-9400
Upper Saddle River *(G-11273)*

Engineered Precision Cast Co ....D 732 671-2424
Middletown *(G-6214)*

▼ Fortune Rvrside Auto Parts Inc ....E 732 381-3355
Rahway *(G-9189)*

Howmet Castings & Services Inc ....A 973 442-2261
Dover *(G-2090)*

Howmet Castings & Services Inc ....B 973 361-0300
Dover *(G-2091)*

Howmet Castings & Services Inc ....B 973 361-2310
Dover *(G-2092)*

Mark I Industries Inc ....F 609 884-0051
Cape May *(G-1103)*

R W Wheaton Co ....G 908 241-4955
Roselle Park *(G-9702)*

Rbc Dain Rauscher ....F 973 778-7300
Woodland Park *(G-12231)*

3325 Steel Foundries, NEC

▲ Accurate Bushing Company Inc ....E 908 789-1121
Garwood *(G-3774)*

D S Jh LLC ....E 973 782-4086
Lincoln Park *(G-5326)*

Double O Manufacturing Inc ....G 732 752-9423
Middlesex *(G-6163)*

H & R Welding LLC ....G 732 920-4881
Brick *(G-745)*

Polmar Iron Work Inc ....F 732 882-0900
Rahway *(G-9217)*

▲ Sas Stressteel Inc ....F 973 244-5995
Fairfield *(G-3301)*

T Wiker Enterprises Inc ....E 609 261-9494
Hainesport *(G-4079)*

3331 Primary Smelting & Refining Of Copper

Amrod Corp ....D 973 344-3806
Newark *(G-7085)*

3334 Primary Production Of Aluminum

▼ Helidex LLC ....G 201 636-2546
East Rutherford *(G-2299)*

Ivey Katrina Owner ....G 973 951-8328
Newark *(G-7202)*

Quick Fab Aluminum Mfg Co ....E 732 367-7200
Lakewood *(G-5175)*

3339 Primary Nonferrous Metals, NEC

Abington Reldan Metals LLC ....G 732 238-8550
South River *(G-10457)*

Alpha Assembly Solutions Inc ....E 908 561-5170
South Plainfield *(G-10325)*

▲ Alpha Assembly Solutions Inc ....E 908 791-3000
Somerset *(G-10054)*

◆ BASF Catalysts LLC ....D 732 205-5000
Iselin *(G-4616)*

◆ Dallas Group of America Inc ....C 908 534-7800
Whitehouse *(G-12045)*

◆ Electrum Inc ....F 732 396-1616
Rahway *(G-9186)*

Ewing Recovery Corp ....G 609 883-0318
Ewing *(G-3017)*

Fisk Alloy Inc ....E 973 427-7550
Hawthorne *(G-4234)*

◆ Fisk Alloy Wire Incorporated ....C 973 949-4491
Hawthorne *(G-4235)*

L D L Technology Inc ....G 973 345-9111
Paterson *(G-8315)*

Matthey Johnson Inc ....C 856 384-7132
West Deptford *(G-11835)*

▲ Mel Chemicals Inc ....C 908 782-5800
Flemington *(G-3456)*

Metallix Direct Gold LLC ....G 732 544-0891
Shrewsbury *(G-10003)*

▲ Metallix Refining Inc ....F 732 936-0050
Shrewsbury *(G-10004)*

▲ National Electronic Alloys Inc ....E 201 337-9400
Oakland *(G-7698)*

▼ Omg Electronic Chemicals Inc ....C 908 222-5800
South Plainfield *(G-10418)*

▲ Path Silicones Inc ....F 201 796-0833
Elmwood Park *(G-2841)*

Perl Pigments LLC ....G 201 836-1212
East Brunswick *(G-2172)*

Premesco Inc ....B 908 686-0513
Union *(G-11216)*

Starfuels Inc ....G 201 685-0400
Englewood *(G-2934)*

▼ Tower Systems Inc ....G 732 237-8800
Bayville *(G-260)*

▲ Umicore Precious Metals NJ LLC ....C 908 222-5006
South Plainfield *(G-10444)*

Umicore USA Inc ....G 908 226-2053
South Plainfield *(G-10445)*

Victors Three-D Inc ....D 201 845-4433
Maywood *(G-6062)*

3341 Secondary Smelting & Refining Of Nonferrous Metals

Aleris Rolled Products Inc ....C 856 881-3600
Clayton *(G-1522)*

Alpha Assembly Solutions Inc ....E 908 561-5170
South Plainfield *(G-10325)*

▲ Alpha Assembly Solutions Inc ....E 908 791-3000
Somerset *(G-10054)*

American Aluminum Alloys LLC ....E 717 417-5966
Pennsauken *(G-8477)*

County of Somerset ....C 732 469-3363
Bridgewater *(G-830)*

Cumberland Rcycl Corp S Jersey ....E 856 825-4153
Millville *(G-6296)*

Emil A Schroth Inc ....E 732 938-5015
Howell *(G-4553)*

Federal Metals & Alloys Co ....G 908 756-0900
South Plainfield *(G-10363)*

Globe Metals Inc ....E 973 589-2563
Newark *(G-7174)*

Johnson Matthey Inc ....C 856 384-7000
West Deptford *(G-11832)*

Kearny Smelting & Ref Corp ....E 201 991-7276
Kearny *(G-4891)*

Matthey Johnson Inc ....C 856 384-7022
Paulsboro *(G-8419)*

Matthey Johnson Inc ....C 856 384-7132
West Deptford *(G-11835)*

▼ Metal MGT Pittsburgh Inc ....E 201 333-2902
Jersey City *(G-4783)*

◆ Minmetals Inc ....F 201 809-1898
Leonia *(G-5318)*

▲ National Electronic Alloys Inc ....E 201 337-9400
Oakland *(G-7698)*

Nedohon Inc ....G 302 533-5512
Wildwood Crest *(G-12076)*

Park Steel & Iron Co ....F 732 775-7500
Neptune *(G-6927)*

◆ Recycling N Hensel Amer Inc ....E 856 753-7614
West Berlin *(G-11746)*

Reldan Metals Inc ....E 732 238-8550
South River *(G-10464)*
Reldan Metals Inc ....C 732 238-8550
South River *(G-10465)*
Semi Conductor Manufacturing ......E 973 478-2880
Clifton *(G-1720)*
◆ Stainless Surplus LLC ....G 914 661-3800
Green Brook *(G-3864)*
▲ State Metal Industries Inc ....D 856 964-1510
Camden *(G-1087)*

3351 Rolling, Drawing & Extruding Of Copper

250 Lackland Holding Inc ....D 732 469-7420
Middlesex *(G-6140)*
▲ Amrod Corp ....G 973 344-2978
Newark *(G-7084)*
Amrod Corp ....D 973 344-3806
Newark *(G-7085)*
▼ AT&T Technologies Inc ....A 201 771-2000
Berkeley Heights *(G-400)*
Belden Inc ....F 908 925-8000
Elizabeth *(G-2712)*
Fisk Alloy Inc ....E 973 427-7550
Hawthorne *(G-4234)*
◆ Fisk Alloy Wire Incorporated ......C 973 949-4491
Hawthorne *(G-4235)*
Freeport Minerals Corporation ......G 908 351-3200
Elizabeth *(G-2734)*
▲ Gulf Cable LLC ....C 201 242-9906
Hasbrouck Heights *(G-4193)*
H Cross Company ....E 201 964-9380
Moonachie *(G-6519)*
Handytube Corporation ....E 732 469-7420
Middlesex *(G-6169)*
Heyco Products Corp ....G 732 286-1800
Toms River *(G-10885)*
▲ Industrial Tube Corporation ....E 908 369-3737
Hillsborough *(G-4345)*
Kearny Smelting & Ref Corp ....E 201 991-7276
Kearny *(G-4891)*
▲ Little Falls Alloys Inc ....E 973 278-1666
Paterson *(G-8323)*
▲ National Electric Wire Co Inc ......E 609 758-3600
Cream Ridge *(G-1938)*

3353 Aluminum Sheet, Plate & Foil

▲ A S Mill Products Inc ....G 212 695-2244
Red Bank *(G-9317)*
Amcor Flexibles Inc ....E 609 267-5900
Mount Holly *(G-6766)*
CMC Composites LLC ....E 732 505-9400
Whiting *(G-12066)*
Eagle Systems Inc ....G 732 226-2111
Ocean *(G-7723)*
▲ Elkom North America Inc ....G 732 786-0490
Manalapan *(G-5844)*
◆ Global Prtners In Shelding Inc ....E 973 574-9077
Fairfield *(G-3210)*
H Cross Company ....E 201 964-9380
Moonachie *(G-6519)*
Myles F Kelly Inc ....F 908 245-2033
Roselle Park *(G-9700)*
Spectrum Glass LLC ....G 201 750-1251
Closter *(G-1766)*
Yarde Metals Inc ....E 973 463-1166
East Hanover *(G-2251)*

3354 Aluminum Extruded Prdts

Alcon Products Inc ....F 609 267-3898
Westampton *(G-11910)*
▲ Aluminum Shapes Inc ....E 856 662-5500
Pennsauken *(G-8475)*
Aluminum Shapes LLC ....B 888 488-7427
Delair *(G-1999)*
▲ Aluseal LLC ....G 856 692-3355
Vineland *(G-11322)*
▲ Ango Electronics Corporation ......F 201 955-0800
North Arlington *(G-7415)*
▲ Coltwell Industries Inc ....F 908 276-7600
Cranford *(G-1901)*
▲ Construction Specialties Inc ....E 908 236-0800
Lebanon *(G-5282)*
Construction Specialties Inc ....E 908 272-2771
Cranford *(G-1902)*
E-TEC Marine Products Inc ....G 732 269-0442
Bayville *(G-253)*
◆ Frameware Inc ....F 800 582-5608
Fairfield *(G-3201)*
Goetz & Ruschmann Inc ....E 973 383-9270
Newton *(G-7391)*

Kwg Industries LLC ....E 908 218-8900
Hillsborough *(G-4354)*
Medicraft Inc ....E 201 797-8820
Elmwood Park *(G-2835)*
Minalex Corporation ....E 908 534-4044
Whitehouse Station *(G-12058)*
Nicks Inc ....G 908 272-3739
Kenilworth *(G-4981)*
Security Fabricators Inc ....F 908 272-9171
Kenilworth *(G-4996)*
▲ Shapes/Arch Holdings LLC ....C 856 662-5500
Delair *(G-2001)*
Unique Aluminum Extrusion LLC ......F 732 271-0006
Middlesex *(G-6207)*

3355 Aluminum Rolling & Drawing, NEC

American Custom Fabricators ....G 732 237-0037
Bayville *(G-248)*
Domel Inc ....E 973 614-1800
Clifton *(G-1603)*
Gentek Building Products Inc ....G 732 381-0900
Avenel *(G-134)*
H Cross Company ....E 201 964-9380
Moonachie *(G-6519)*
▲ Lapp Holding NA Inc ....E 973 660-9700
Florham Park *(G-3509)*
◆ Okonite Company ....G 201 825-0300
Ramsey *(G-9250)*

3356 Rolling, Drawing-Extruding Of Nonferrous Metals

Advance Process Systems Lim ....G 201 400-9190
Branchville *(G-724)*
Alpha Assembly Solutions Inc ....E 908 561-5170
South Plainfield *(G-10325)*
▲ Alpha Assembly Solutions Inc ......E 908 791-3000
Somerset *(G-10054)*
American Aluminum Company ....D 908 233-3500
Mountainside *(G-6868)*
Construction Specialties Inc ....E 908 272-2771
Cranford *(G-1902)*
Fisk Alloy Inc ....E 973 427-7550
Hawthorne *(G-4234)*
◆ Fisk Alloy Wire Incorporated ......C 973 949-4491
Hawthorne *(G-4235)*
H Cross Company ....E 201 964-9380
Moonachie *(G-6519)*
Holistic Solar Usa Inc ....G 732 757-5500
Newark *(G-7191)*
▲ Industrial Tube Corporation ....E 908 369-3737
Hillsborough *(G-4345)*
International Rollforms Inc ....E 856 228-7100
Deptford *(G-2065)*
Kearny Smelting & Ref Corp ....E 201 991-7276
Kearny *(G-4891)*
Komline-Sanderson Engrg Corp ......G 973 579-0090
Sparta *(G-10507)*
Matthey Johnson Inc ....N 856 384-7132
West Deptford *(G-11835)*
New Jersey Gold Buyers Corp ....G 732 765-4653
Marlboro *(G-5949)*
Nickel Savers ....N 201 405-1153
Oakland *(G-7699)*
Nickels Carpet Cleaning ....G 609 892-5783
Mays Landing *(G-6040)*
Nickels N Dimes LLC ....G 732 886-5528
Lakewood *(G-5163)*
▲ Precision Roll Products Inc ....F 973 822-9100
Florham Park *(G-3515)*
◆ Sandvik Inc ....C 201 794-5000
Fair Lawn *(G-3112)*
Swepco Tube LLC ....G 973 778-3000
Clifton *(G-1733)*
Times Tin Cup ....G 973 983-1095
Mountain Lakes *(G-6862)*
Tin Panda Inc ....G 973 916-0707
Clifton *(G-1737)*
Tin Sigh Stop ....G 973 691-2712
Byram Township *(G-1023)*
Titanium Industries Inc ....G 973 428-1900
East Hanover *(G-2246)*
Titanium Smoking Kings LLC ....G 908 339-8876
Phillipsburg *(G-8673)*
Titanium Technical Services ....G 908 323-9899
Flemington *(G-3472)*
Union City Filament Corp ....E 201 945-3366
Ridgefield *(G-9390)*

3357 Nonferrous Wire Drawing

AFL Telecommunications LLC ....D 864 486-7303
Jersey City *(G-4700)*
Alpha Wire Corporation ....C 908 925-8000
Elizabeth *(G-2708)*
▲ Ambro Inc ....E 201 818-9717
Pequannock *(G-8597)*
Arose Inc ....E 856 481-4351
Blackwood *(G-471)*
Ascentta Inc ....F 732 868-1766
Somerset *(G-10064)*
Associated Plastics Inc ....F 732 574-2800
Rahway *(G-9176)*
▼ AT&T Technologies Inc ....A 201 771-2000
Berkeley Heights *(G-400)*
▼ Aw Machinery LLC ....F 973 882-3223
Fairfield *(G-3142)*
Brim Electronics Inc ....F 201 796-2886
Lodi *(G-5578)*
Bruker Ost LLC ....C 732 541-1300
Carteret *(G-1254)*
CDM Electronics Inc ....C 856 740-1200
Turnersville *(G-11141)*
Colonial Wire & Cable Co Inc ....G 732 287-1557
Edison *(G-2486)*
Communications Supply Corp ....E 732 346-1864
Edison *(G-2487)*
▲ Computer Crafts Inc ....C 973 423-3500
Hawthorne *(G-4228)*
▲ Daburn Wire & Cable Corp ....G 973 328-3200
Dover *(G-2084)*
▲ Dearborn A Belden Cdt Company ...D 908 925-8000
Elizabeth *(G-2723)*
Esi ....E 856 629-2492
Sicklerville *(G-10018)*
▲ Flexco Microwave Inc ....E 908 835-1720
Port Murray *(G-8977)*
Francis Metals Company Inc ....F 732 761-0500
Lakewood *(G-5125)*
Global Wire & Cable Inc ....E 973 471-1000
Passaic *(G-8145)*
Harris Driver Co ....G 973 267-8100
Morristown *(G-6712)*
Harrison Electro Mechanical ....F 732 382-6008
Rahway *(G-9196)*
▲ Iboco Corp ....G 732 417-0066
Lakewood *(G-5136)*
▲ Lapp Cable Works Inc ....E 973 660-9632
Florham Park *(G-3508)*
M Parker Autoworks Inc ....E 856 933-0801
Bellmawr *(G-345)*
▲ Micro-Tek Corporation ....G 856 829-3855
Cinnaminson *(G-1477)*
Molecu-Wire Corporation ....F 908 429-0300
Manville *(G-5897)*
National Communications Inc ....E 973 325-3151
West Orange *(G-11901)*
Newtech Group Corp ....G 732 355-0392
Kendall Park *(G-4935)*
Nistica Inc ....E 908 707-9500
Bridgewater *(G-865)*
◆ Okonite Company ....C 201 825-0300
Ramsey *(G-9250)*
Okonite Company ....D 201 825-0300
Paterson *(G-8355)*
Okonite Company ....G 212 239-0660
Woodland Park *(G-12227)*
▲ Paramount Wire Co Inc ....E 973 672-0500
East Orange *(G-2264)*
Prysmian Cbles Systems USA LLC ....F 732 469-5902
Bridgewater *(G-878)*
Seminole Wire & Cable Co Inc ....F 856 324-2929
Pennsauken *(G-8577)*
▲ Sensors Unlimited Inc ....D 609 333-8000
Princeton *(G-9116)*
Service Tech ....E 908 788-0072
Flemington *(G-3465)*
▲ Te Wire & Cable LLC ....C 201 845-9400
Saddle Brook *(G-9796)*
Vytran LLC ....G 732 972-2880
Morganville *(G-6656)*
Wire Fabricators & Insulators ....E 973 768-2839
Livingston *(G-5572)*
Wireworks Corporation ....E 908 686-7400
Hillside *(G-4451)*

3363 Aluminum Die Castings

Bierman-Everett Foundry Co ....G 973 373-8800
South Orange *(G-10301)*

▲ Premier Die Casting Company ....D....... 732 634-3000
Avenel (G-147)

3364 Nonferrous Die Castings, Exc Aluminum

▲ Abco Die Casters Inc ....D....... 973 624-7030
Newark (G-7070)

▲ Carteret Die-Casting Corp ....E....... 732 246-0070
Somerset (G-10074)

▲ Certech Inc ....C....... 201 842-6800
Wood Ridge (G-12135)

Flemington Alumininum & Brass ....G....... 908 782-6333
Flemington (G-3440)

Medalco Metals Inc ....G....... 732 591-0913
Morganville (G-6648)

Medalco Metals Inc ....G....... 908 238-0513
Lebanon (G-5297)

▲ Microcast Technologies Corp ....D....... 908 523-9503
Linden (G-5409)

Union Casting Industries Inc ....F....... 908 686-8888
Union (G-11231)

W & E Baum Bronze Tablet Corp.........E....... 732 866-1881
Freehold (G-3692)

Worldcast Network Inc ....G....... 201 767-2040
Old Tappan (G-7802)

3365 Aluminum Foundries

Aluminum Shapes LLC.......................B....... 888 488-7427
Delair (G-1999)

American Aluminum Casting Co ....E....... 973 372-3200
Irvington (G-4573)

▲ Atlantic Casting & Engineering ....C....... 973 779-2450
Clifton (G-1567)

Bierman-Everett Foundry Co ....G....... 973 373-8800
South Orange (G-10301)

◆ Bon Chef Inc ....D....... 973 383-8848
Lafayette (G-5045)

Pgw Auto Glass LLC ....E....... 856 234-1600
Mount Laurel (G-6825)

Richmond Industries Inc ....E....... 732 355-1616
Dayton (G-1986)

Rosco Inc ....G....... 908 789-1020
Garwood (G-3786)

▲ Shapes/Arch Holdings LLC ....C....... 856 662-5500
Delair (G-2001)

TEC Cast Inc ....E....... 201 935-3885
Carlstadt (G-1227)

TEC Cast Inc ....G....... 201 935-3885
Moonachie (G-6549)

◆ U S Aluminum Inc ....G....... 908 782-5454
Flemington (G-3473)

Union Casting Industries Inc ....F....... 908 686-8888
Union (G-11231)

3366 Copper Foundries

▲ Accurate Bushing Company Inc......E....... 908 789-1121
Garwood (G-3774)

Amrod Corp ....D....... 973 344-3806
Newark (G-7085)

Bierman-Everett Foundry Co ....G....... 973 373-8800
South Orange (G-10301)

▲ Federal Bronze Cast Inds Inc ....E....... 973 589-7575
Newark (G-7161)

▲ Industrial Tube Corporation ....E....... 908 369-3737
Hillsborough (G-4345)

Ivey Katrina Owner ....G....... 973 951-8328
Newark (G-7202)

Oavco Ltd Liability Company ....F....... 609 454-5340
Hamilton (G-4120)

Union Casting Industries Inc ....F....... 908 686-8888
Union (G-11231)

3369 Nonferrous Foundries: Castings, NEC

Alloy Cast Products Inc ....F....... 908 245-2255
Kenilworth (G-4936)

Arde Inc ....D....... 201 784-9880
Carlstadt (G-1128)

Engineered Precision Cast Co ....D....... 732 671-2424
Middletown (G-6214)

Howmet Castings & Services Inc ....A....... 973 442-2261
Dover (G-2090)

▲ Jarco U S Casting Corp ....E....... 201 271-0003
Union City (G-11250)

M D Carbide Tool Corp ....E....... 973 263-0104
Towaco (G-10998)

Microcast Technologies Corp ....G....... 732 943-7356
Avenel (G-140)

▲ Microcast Technologies Corp ....D....... 908 523-9503
Linden (G-5409)

▲ S Jarco-U Castings Corporation ......G....... 201 271-0003
Union City (G-11265)

Tusa Products Inc ....G....... 609 448-8333
Ewing (G-3063)

Ultimate Trading Corp ....D....... 973 228-7700
Fairfield (G-3332)

3398 Metal Heat Treating

Analytic Stress Relieving Inc.............D....... 732 629-7232
Middlesex (G-6146)

Bennett Heat Trting Brzing Inc ....E....... 973 589-0590
Newark (G-7106)

▲ Blue Blade Corp ....E....... 908 272-2620
Kenilworth (G-4945)

Bodycote Thermal Proc Inc ....E....... 908 245-0717
Roselle (G-9663)

Bodycote Thermal Processing ....E....... 908 245-0717
Roselle (G-9664)

Braddock Heat Treating Company ....E....... 732 356-2906
Bridgewater (G-823)

Curtiss-Wright Surfc Tech LLC.............F....... 201 843-7800
Paramus (G-7865)

▲ E F Britten & Co Inc ....F....... 908 276-4800
Cranford (G-1904)

Energy Beams Inc ....F....... 973 291-6555
Bloomingdale (G-543)

Heinzelman Heat Treating LLC ....E....... 201 933-4800
Carlstadt (G-1169)

Kenney Steel Treating Corp ....E....... 201 998-4420
Kearny (G-4892)

Metal Improvement Co Inc ....G....... 253 677-8604
Paramus (G-7887)

▲ Metal Improvement Company LLC..E....... 201 843-7800
Paramus (G-7888)

3399 Primary Metal Prdts, NEC

Acupowder International LLC...............G....... 908 851-4500
Union (G-11146)

Atlantic Eqp Engineers Inc ....F....... 201 828-9400
Upper Saddle River (G-11273)

Bozak Inc ....G....... 732 282-1556
Spring Lake (G-10532)

Bway Corporation ....F....... 609 883-4300
Trenton (G-11031)

Czar Industries Inc ....G....... 609 392-1515
Trenton (G-11051)

▲ FW Winter Inc ....E....... 856 963-7490
Camden (G-1067)

◆ Hoeganaes Corporation ....B....... 856 303-0366
Cinnaminson (G-1468)

Hugo Neu Recycling LLC ....E....... 914 530-2350
Kearny (G-4883)

Matthey Johnson Inc ....C....... 856 384-7132
West Deptford (G-11835)

McW Precision ....F....... 609 859-4400
Southampton (G-10478)

Mv Laboratories Inc ....G....... 908 788-6906
Frenchtown (G-3704)

Performance Alloys & Materials ....G....... 201 865-5268
Secaucus (G-9910)

Scientific Alloys Corp ....F....... 973 478-8323
Clifton (G-1717)

Sentry Mfg LLC ....G....... 856 642-0480
Moorestown (G-6622)

▲ United Sttes Metal Powders Inc.......F....... 908 782-5454
Flemington (G-3474)

34 FABRICATED METAL PRODUCTS, EXCEPT MACHINERY AND TRANSPORTATION EQUIPMENT

3411 Metal Cans

▲ Allstate Can Corporation ....D....... 973 560-9030
Parsippany (G-7944)

Bway Corporation ....C....... 732 997-4100
Dayton (G-1957)

▲ Elemental Container Inc ....G....... 908 687-7720
Union (G-11181)

Foulkrod Associates ....A....... 856 662-6767
Pennsauken (G-8511)

▲ Innovation Foods LLC ....F....... 856 455-2209
Bridgeton (G-786)

▲ JI Packaging Group Corp ....G....... 609 610-0286
Pennington (G-8454)

▲ Medin Technologies Inc ....C....... 973 779-2400
Totowa (G-10955)

▲ Penny Plate LLC ....G....... 856 429-7583
Mount Laurel (G-6824)

▲ Phoenix Container Inc ....C....... 732 247-3931
Trenton (G-11097)

Silgan Containers Mfg Corp ....D....... 732 287-0300
Edison (G-2617)

Sonoco Products Company ....D....... 609 655-0300
Dayton (G-1988)

Tin Can Lids LLC ....G....... 201 503-0677
Tenafly (G-10787)

3412 Metal Barrels, Drums, Kegs & Pails

Andrew B Duffy Inc..........................F....... 856 845-4900
West Deptford (G-11815)

Cutler Bros Box & Lumber Co ....E....... 201 943-2535
Fairview (G-3360)

◆ Granco Group LLC ....G....... 973 515-4721
Roseland (G-9651)

▲ Kraftware Corporation ....E....... 732 345-7091
Roselle (G-1169)

Mauser Usa LLC ....C....... 732 634-6000
Woodbridge (G-12151)

◆ Mauser Usa LLC ....E....... 732 353-7100
East Brunswick (G-2165)

Patrick J Kelly Drums Inc ....E....... 856 963-1795
Camden (G-1081)

▲ Pmm Inc ....E....... 908 692-1465
Colts Neck (G-1790)

Rahway Steel Drum Co Inc ....E....... 732 382-0113
Cranbury (G-1875)

Recycle Inc East ....D....... 908 756-2200
South Plainfield (G-10434)

Romaco North America Inc ....G....... 609 584-2500
Hamilton (G-4124)

Williams Scotsman Inc ....G....... 856 429-0315
Kearny (G-4922)

3421 Cutlery

Art of Shaving - Fl LLC ....G....... 732 410-2520
Freehold (G-3639)

Ben Venuti ....G....... 908 389-9999
Garwood (G-3776)

▲ Du-Mor Blade Co Inc ....E....... 856 829-9384
Cinnaminson (G-1458)

Hobby Blade Specialty Inc ....G....... 908 317-9306
Scotch Plains (G-9851)

▲ IDL Techni-Edge LLC ....C....... 908 497-9818
Kenilworth (G-4962)

Kikuichi New York Inc ....G....... 201 567-8388
Englewood Cliffs (G-2970)

Port A ....F....... 732 776-6511
Asbury Park (G-82)

Revlon Inc ....E....... 732 287-1400
Edison (G-2605)

▲ US Blade Mfg Co Inc ....E....... 908 272-2898
Cranford (G-1930)

3423 Hand & Edge Tools

▲ Acon Watch Crown Company ....F....... 973 546-8585
Garfield (G-3715)

American Logistics Network LLC...........G....... 201 391-1054
Woodcliff Lake (G-12180)

Apex Saw & Tool Co Inc ....G....... 201 438-8777
Lyndhurst (G-5668)

▲ Baumer of America Inc ....F....... 973 263-1569
Towaco (G-10988)

Brasscraft Manufacturing Co ....G....... 856 241-7700
Swedesboro (G-10685)

▲ C T A Manufacturing Corp ....E....... 201 896-1000
Carlstadt (G-1136)

◆ Cementex Products Inc ....E....... 609 387-1040
Burlington (G-962)

▲ Chicago Pneumatic Tool ....F....... 973 928-5222
Clifton (G-1583)

▲ CS Osborne & Co ....D....... 973 483-3232
Harrison (G-4177)

DAKA Manufacturing LLC ....G....... 908 782-0360
Flemington (G-3433)

▲ Danielle Die Cut Products Inc ....E....... 973 278-3000
Paterson (G-8244)

Dicar Diamond Tool Corp ....G....... 973 684-0949
Paterson (G-8250)

▼ Dreyco Inc ....F....... 201 896-9000
Carlstadt (G-1158)

Du-Matt Corporation ....G....... 201 861-4271
West New York (G-11864)

▲ Excel Hobby Blades Corp ....E....... 973 278-4000
Paterson (G-8267)

▲ General Tools & Instrs Co LLC ....E....... 212 431-6100
Secaucus (G-9888)

Grobet File Company Amer LLC ....D....... 201 939-6700
Carlstadt (G-1165)

Grommet Mart Inc ....F ... 973 278-4100
Paterson *(G-8284)*

◆ Hayward Industries Inc ....B ... 908 351-5400
Elizabeth *(G-2742)*

Hexacon Electric Company Inc ....E ... 908 245-6200
Roselle Park *(G-9697)*

▲ IDL Techni-Edge LLC ....C ... 908 497-9818
Kenilworth *(G-4962)*

Indo-US Mim TEC Private Ltd ....G ... 734 327-9842
Princeton *(G-9057)*

J R S Tool & Metal Finishing ....G ... 908 753-2050
South Plainfield *(G-10387)*

▲ Jdv Products Inc ....F ... 201 794-6467
Fair Lawn *(G-3098)*

Jesco Iron Crafts Inc ....F ... 201 488-4545
Bogota *(G-548)*

Jetyd Corporation ....F ... 201 512-9500
Mahwah *(G-5786)*

▲ Legend Stone Products ....G ... 973 473-7088
Clifton *(G-1660)*

◆ Mastercool USA Inc ....E ... 973 252-9119
Randolph *(G-9288)*

▲ National Steel Rule Company ....D ... 908 862-3366
Linden *(G-5415)*

National Steel Rule Company ....F ... 800 922-0885
Linden *(G-5416)*

National Steel Rule Company ....D ... 908 862-3366
Linden *(G-5417)*

▲ Ohaus Corporation ....D ... 973 377-9000
Parsippany *(G-8051)*

▲ Ox Group Usa LLC ....F ... 888 850-6710
Cranford *(G-1920)*

Phoenix Industrial LLC ....G ... 908 955-0114
Whitehouse Station *(G-12061)*

▲ Power Hawk Technologies Inc ....F ... 973 627-4646
Rockaway *(G-9599)*

▲ S & G Tool Aid Corporation ....D ... 973 824-7730
Newark *(G-7297)*

Sine Tru Tool Company Inc ....G ... 732 591-1100
Marlboro *(G-5959)*

Stanley Black & Decker Inc ....F ... 860 225-5111
Jersey City *(G-4831)*

▲ Thirty-Three Queen Realty Inc ....F ... 973 824-5527
Newark *(G-7341)*

3425 Hand Saws & Saw Blades

Forrest Mfg Co Inc ....E ... 973 473-5236
Clifton *(G-1622)*

▲ IDL Techni-Edge LLC ....C ... 908 497-9818
Kenilworth *(G-4962)*

▲ National Steel Rule Company ....D ... 908 862-3366
Linden *(G-5415)*

▲ Tooling Etc LLC ....G ... 732 752-8080
Middlesex *(G-6206)*

3429 Hardware, NEC

4 Way Lock LLC ....G ... 908 359-2002
Hillsborough *(G-4315)*

Airborne Systems N Amer Inc ....G ... 856 663-1275
Pennsauken *(G-8473)*

Allfasteners Usa LLC ....E ... 201 783-8836
Carlstadt *(G-1123)*

◆ American Van Equipment Inc ....C ... 732 905-5900
Lakewood *(G-5071)*

Andrex Inc ....F ... 908 852-2400
Hackettstown *(G-3997)*

▲ Art Materials Service Inc ....D ... 732 545-8888
New Brunswick *(G-6947)*

Artistic Hardware ....G ... 609 383-1909
Northfield *(G-7563)*

◆ Ashley Norton Inc ....F ... 973 835-4027
Pompton Plains *(G-8954)*

▲ Atco Products Inc ....E ... 973 379-3171
Springfield *(G-10538)*

Bildisco Mfg Inc ....F ... 973 673-2400
West Orange *(G-11889)*

Brim Electronics Inc ....F ... 201 796-2886
Lodi *(G-5578)*

Carpenter & Paterson Inc ....E ... 973 772-1800
Bordentown *(G-592)*

▲ Celus Fasteners Mfg Inc ....E ... 800 289-7483
Northvale *(G-7576)*

▲ Charles E Green & Son Inc ....G ... 973 485-3630
Newark *(G-7120)*

CMF Ltd Inc ....E ... 609 695-3600
Ewing *(G-3010)*

Commeatus LLC ....F ... 847 772-5314
Plainsboro *(G-8878)*

▲ Component Hardware Group Inc ....D ... 800 526-3694
Lakewood *(G-5095)*

Confires Fire Prtction Svc LLC ....F ... 908 822-2700
South Plainfield *(G-10349)*

▼ Delta Procurement Inc ....G ... 201 623-9353
Carlstadt *(G-1153)*

Firefighter One Ltd Ltd Lblty Co ....G ... 973 940-3061
Sparta *(G-10499)*

G & S Precision Prototype ....G ... 732 370-3010
Lakewood *(G-5126)*

General Sullivan Group Inc ....E ... 609 745-5000
Pennington *(G-8452)*

Ho-Ho-Kus Inc ....E ... 973 278-2274
Paterson *(G-8290)*

▲ Imperial Weld Ring Corp Inc ....E ... 908 354-0011
Elizabeth *(G-2746)*

Ingersoll-Rand Company ....E ... 856 793-7000
Mount Laurel *(G-6803)*

J Blanco Associates Inc ....F ... 973 427-0619
Hawthorne *(G-4243)*

◆ JC Macelroy Co Inc ....D ... 732 572-7100
Piscataway *(G-8784)*

Jet Test Global LLC ....G ... 702 785-0011
Cherry Hill *(G-1384)*

Ka-Lor Cubicle and Sup Co Inc ....G ... 201 891-8077
Fair Lawn *(G-3099)*

▲ La Milagrosa ....G ... 973 928-1799
Passaic *(G-8156)*

Mariner Sales and Power Inc ....G ... 732 477-7484
Brick *(G-751)*

▲ Modern Sportswear Corporation ....F ... 201 804-2700
Moonachie *(G-6533)*

▲ Mul-T-Lock Usa Inc ....G ... 973 778-3320
Hackensack *(G-3948)*

Oceanview Marine Welding LLC ....G ... 609 624-9669
Ocean View *(G-7765)*

Owens Fasteners Inc ....G ... 856 768-6580
West Berlin *(G-11740)*

Pekay Industries Inc ....E ... 732 938-2722
Farmingdale *(G-3392)*

Penn Elcom Inc ....E ... 973 839-7777
Pompton Plains *(G-8964)*

▲ Polytech Designs Inc ....F ... 973 340-1390
Clifton *(G-1701)*

Ramsay David Cabinetmakers ....F ... 856 234-7776
Moorestown *(G-6618)*

▲ Reich USA Corporation ....F ... 201 684-9400
Mahwah *(G-5808)*

◆ Revere Survival Products Inc ....F ... 973 575-8811
West Caldwell *(G-11803)*

▲ Rotor Clip Company Inc ....B ... 732 469-7707
Somerset *(G-10168)*

RSI Woodworking Products Co ....E ... 609 645-9777
Egg Harbor Township *(G-2695)*

Saint-Gobain Prfmce Plas Corp ....D ... 732 652-0910
Somerset *(G-10170)*

Shade Powers Co Inc ....F ... 201 767-3727
Northvale *(G-7607)*

Steelstran Industries Inc ....G ... 732 566-5040
Matawan *(G-6033)*

Taurus Precision Inc ....F ... 973 785-9254
Little Falls *(G-5491)*

Tiburon Lockers Inc ....G ... 201 750-4960
Rockleigh *(G-9635)*

Truckform Inc ....F ... 908 526-5443
Somerville *(G-10231)*

▲ Unicorp ....C ... 973 674-1700
Orange *(G-7832)*

▲ Versabar Corporation ....F ... 973 279-8400
Totowa *(G-10979)*

▼ Viking Marine Products Inc ....G ... 732 826-4552
Edison *(G-2647)*

World and Main LLC ....E ... 609 860-9990
Cranbury *(G-1892)*

3431 Enameled Iron & Metal Sanitary Ware

▲ Aero Manufacturing Co ....G ... 973 473-5300
Clifton *(G-1558)*

Asd Holding Corp ....G ... 800 442-1902
Piscataway *(G-8739)*

▲ Empire Industries Inc ....G ... 973 279-2050
Paterson *(G-8263)*

▲ Houzer Inc ....F ... 609 584-1900
Hamilton *(G-4108)*

▲ Interlink Products Intl Inc ....E ... 908 862-8090
Linden *(G-5389)*

Mat Manufacturing Corporation ....E ... 800 378-7965
Clifton *(G-1670)*

Sapphire Bath Inc ....G ... 718 215-1262
Paterson *(G-8379)*

Trano Bruce Plumbing & Heating ....G ... 908 654-3685
Mountainside *(G-6889)*

◆ Vigo Industries LLC ....E ... 866 591-7792
Edison *(G-2646)*

3432 Plumbing Fixture Fittings & Trim, Brass

◆ As America Inc ....C ... 732 980-3000
Piscataway *(G-8738)*

Bruce Supply Corp ....F ... 732 661-0500
Keasbey *(G-4925)*

Carpenter & Paterson Inc ....E ... 609 227-2750
Bordentown *(G-593)*

▲ Chatham Brass Co Inc ....G ... 908 668-0500
South Plainfield *(G-10345)*

▲ Danfoss Hago Inc ....C ... 908 232-8687
Mountainside *(G-6873)*

DAngelo Metal Products Inc ....F ... 908 862-8220
Linden *(G-5367)*

▲ Durst Corporation ....G ... 800 852-3906
Cranford *(G-1903)*

▲ El Batal Corporation ....F ... 908 964-3427
Union *(G-11180)*

Grove Supply Inc ....E ... 856 205-0687
Vineland *(G-11365)*

Kessler Industries ....G ... 973 279-1417
Paterson *(G-8309)*

◆ Kissler & Co Inc ....E ... 201 896-9600
Carlstadt *(G-1179)*

Knickerbocker Machine Shop Inc ....D ... 973 256-1616
Totowa *(G-10953)*

Majewski Plumbing & Htg LLC ....G ... 609 374-6001
Villas *(G-11314)*

Msg Fire & Safety Inc ....E ... 732 833-8500
Jackson *(G-4673)*

Plumbing Supply Now LLC ....F ... 732 228-8852
New Brunswick *(G-6991)*

Specialty Products Plus ....G ... 732 380-1188
West Long Branch *(G-11848)*

W C Davis Inc ....F ... 856 547-4750
Haddon Heights *(G-4052)*

Wm Steinen Mfg Co ....D ... 973 887-6400
Parsippany *(G-8116)*

3433 Heating Eqpt

◆ Amec Fster Wheeler N Amer Corp ....D ... 936 448-6323
Hampton *(G-4153)*

Americon Inc ....F ... 609 945-2591
Monmouth Junction *(G-6331)*

Applied Thermal Solutions Inc ....G ... 856 818-8194
Williamstown *(G-12079)*

C & F Burner Co ....E ... 201 998-8080
North Arlington *(G-7417)*

Carlisle Machine Works Inc ....E ... 856 825-0627
Millville *(G-6293)*

Energy Company Inc ....E ... 856 742-1916
Westville *(G-11940)*

▲ Ewc Controls Inc ....E ... 732 446-3110
Manalapan *(G-5846)*

▲ Heat-Timer Corporation ....E ... 973 575-4004
Fairfield *(G-3218)*

Holistic Solar Usa Inc ....G ... 732 757-5500
Newark *(G-7191)*

Inenergy Inc ....E ... 609 466-2512
Ringoes *(G-9438)*

▲ NM Knight Co Inc ....E ... 856 327-4855
Millville *(G-6316)*

▲ Panatech Corporation ....G ... 732 331-5692
Manalapan *(G-5860)*

Stafford Park Solar 1 LLC ....G ... 609 607-9500
Barnegat *(G-166)*

Stamm International Corp ....G ... 201 947-1700
Fort Lee *(G-3583)*

▲ Sun Pacific Power Corp ....F ... 888 845-0242
Manalapan *(G-5864)*

Thermal Transfer Corp ....G ... 412 460-4004
Somerville *(G-10228)*

◆ Triangle Tube/Phase III Co Inc ....D ... 856 228-9940
Paulsboro *(G-8427)*

▲ Trinity Heating & Air Inc ....D ... 732 780-3779
Wall Township *(G-11516)*

Waage Electric Inc ....G ... 908 245-9363
Kenilworth *(G-5004)*

3441 Fabricated Structural Steel

Able Fab Co ....E ... 732 396-0600
Avenel *(G-122)*

◆ Acrow Corporation of America ....E ... 973 244-0080
Parsippany *(G-7938)*

Air & Specialties Sheet Metal ....F ... 908 233-8306
Mountainside *(G-6866)*

Airmet Inc ....G ... 973 481-5550
Newark *(G-7074)*

Ajay Metal Fabricators Inc G 908 523-0557
Linden *(G-5345)*
All American Metal Fabricators G 201 567-2898
Tenafly *(G-10780)*
Allied Metal Industries Inc E 973 824-7347
Newark *(G-7077)*
Alloy Welding Co F 908 218-1551
Branchburg *(G-630)*
American Strip Steel Inc F 800 526-1216
South Plainfield *(G-10327)*
American Strip Steel Inc G 856 461-8300
Delanco *(G-2002)*
Andrew B Duffy Inc F 856 845-4900
West Deptford *(G-11815)*
◆ **Arca Industrial (nj) Inc** G 732 339-0450
Edison *(G-2463)*
Archer Day Inc E 732 396-0600
Avenel *(G-124)*
Architectural Metals Inc G 718 765-0722
Carteret *(G-1250)*
Arnold Steel Co Inc D 732 363-1079
Howell *(G-4546)*
Atlantic Precision Tech LLC G 732 658-3060
North Brunswick *(G-7506)*
Atlas Enterprise F 908 561-1144
South Plainfield *(G-10333)*
B & B Iron Works E 862 238-7203
Clifton *(G-1571)*
B L White Welding & Steel Co G 973 684-4111
Paterson *(G-8218)*
Badger Blades LLC G 908 325-6587
Cranford *(G-1898)*
Banker Steel Nj LLC D 732 968-6061
South Plainfield *(G-10334)*
Bouras Industries Inc A 908 918-9400
Summit *(G-10637)*
Brayco Inc F 609 758-5235
Creamridge *(G-1942)*
Brunnquell Iron Works Inc E 609 409-6101
Cranbury *(G-1817)*
Brunswick Waste System G 908 369-2223
Somerville *(G-10203)*
Burgess Steel Holding LLC G 201 871-3500
Englewood *(G-2879)*
C M C Steel Fabricators Inc C 908 561-3484
South Plainfield *(G-10342)*
C W Grimmer & Sons Inc F 732 741-2189
Tinton Falls *(G-10825)*
▲ **Capital Steel Service LLC** E 609 882-6983
Ewing *(G-3005)*
Capitol Steel Inc F 609 538-9313
Trenton *(G-11032)*
Central Metals Inc D 215 462-7464
Camden *(G-1052)*
Com-Fab Inc G 973 296-0433
Hewitt *(G-4288)*
▲ **Coordinated Metals Inc** D 201 460-7280
Carlstadt *(G-1149)*
▼ **Coronis Building Systems Inc** E 609 261-2200
Columbus *(G-1801)*
Cs Industrial Services LLC G 609 381-4380
Newfield *(G-7364)*
D S Jh LLC E 973 782-4086
Lincoln Park *(G-5326)*
Ddm Steel Cnstr Ltd Lblty Co F 856 794-9400
Vineland *(G-11349)*
Ddm Steel Services Inc F 856 794-1931
Vineland *(G-11350)*
De Jong Iron Works Inc G 973 684-1633
Paterson *(G-8246)*
DMJ Industrial Services LLC G 973 692-8406
Wayne *(G-11624)*
Eagle Steel & Iron LLC G 908 587-1025
Stewartsville *(G-10595)*
Equipment Distributing Corp G 201 641-8414
Ridgefield Park *(G-9405)*
Falstrom Company D 973 777-0013
Passaic *(G-8140)*
Flame Cut Steel Inc F 973 373-9300
Irvington *(G-4586)*
▲ **FMB Systems Inc** D 973 485-5544
Harrison *(G-4184)*
Francis Metals Company Inc F 732 761-0500
Lakewood *(G-5125)*
▼ **Frazier Industrial Company** C 908 876-3001
Long Valley *(G-5637)*
▲ **G J Oliver Inc** D 908 454-9743
Phillipsburg *(G-8649)*
Gavan Graham Elec Pdts Corp E 908 729-9000
Union *(G-11188)*
Geneva Metal Products Co Inc F 973 472-3073
Passaic *(G-8144)*
Giant Stl Fabricators Erectors G 908 241-6766
Roselle *(G-9671)*
Glentech Inc F 908 685-2205
Somerville *(G-10212)*
Grimbilas Enterprises Corp E 973 686-5999
Wayne *(G-11644)*
H Barron Iron Works Inc F 856 456-9092
Gloucester City *(G-3838)*
Hackensack Steel Corp E 201 935-0090
Carlstadt *(G-1167)*
▲ **Harold R Henrich Inc** D 732 370-4455
Lakewood *(G-5132)*
Harris Structural Steel Co Inc E 732 752-6070
South Plainfield *(G-10378)*
Harris Structural Steel Co Inc G 732 752-6070
South Plainfield *(G-10379)*
▼ **Helidex LLC** G 201 636-2546
East Rutherford *(G-2299)*
I K Construction Inc E 908 925-5200
East Orange *(G-2256)*
Ideal Tile Fabrications LLC F 732 751-0074
Farmingdale *(G-3387)*
Imperial Metal Products Inc G 908 647-8181
Bound Brook *(G-618)*
▲ **Industrial Metal Inc** G 908 362-0084
Blairstown *(G-497)*
Industrial Services Entps Inc E 973 361-6780
Rockaway *(G-9574)*
▼ **Infinite Mfg Group Inc** E 973 649-9950
Kearny *(G-4885)*
Innovative Metal Solutions LLC G 609 784-8406
Mount Holly *(G-6774)*
Iron Asylum Incorporated F 856 228-2700
Sewell *(G-9958)*
J & M Cstm Shtmtl Ltd Lblty Co G 856 627-6252
Sicklerville *(G-10020)*
J G Schmidt Steel F 973 473-4822
Passaic *(G-8149)*
◆ **JC Macelroy Co Inc** D 732 572-7100
Piscataway *(G-8784)*
Jemco Inc G 732 446-1112
Manalapan *(G-5852)*
Jersey Metal Works LLC G 732 565-1313
Somerset *(G-10117)*
John Cooper Company Inc F 201 487-4018
Hackensack *(G-3933)*
John F Pearce G 201 440-8765
Moonachie *(G-6525)*
John Maltese Iron Works Inc E 732 249-4350
North Brunswick *(G-7521)*
Leets Steel Inc G 917 416-7977
Sayreville *(G-9828)*
Lehigh Utility Associates Inc F 908 561-5252
South Plainfield *(G-10397)*
Lesli Katchen Steel Cnstr Inc G 732 521-2600
Jamesburg *(G-4686)*
Lingo Inc F 856 273-6594
Mount Laurel *(G-6812)*
Lummus Technology Ventures LLC G 973 893-1515
Bloomfield *(G-521)*
M K Enterprises Inc G 201 891-4199
Wyckoff *(G-12257)*
Main Robert A & Sons Holdg Co E 201 447-3700
Wyckoff *(G-12258)*
Marino International Corp G 732 752-5100
South Plainfield *(G-10404)*
Max Gurtman & Sons Inc G 973 478-7000
Clifton *(G-1671)*
Metal USA Plates and Shapes E 973 242-1000
Newark *(G-7241)*
Metals Plus E 908 862-7677
Linden *(G-5408)*
Metfab Steel Works LLC F 973 675-7676
Orange *(G-7822)*
Morgan Towers Inc G 856 786-7200
Moorestown *(G-6602)*
Napco Separation Equipment Inc G 908 862-7677
Linden *(G-5414)*
Newark Ironworks Inc F 973 424-9790
Newark *(G-7255)*
Nicks Inc G 908 272-3739
Kenilworth *(G-4981)*
Oeg Building Materials Inc E 732 667-3636
Sayreville *(G-9834)*
ONeal Flat Rolled Metals LLC E 609 395-7007
Monroe Township *(G-6388)*
Pabst Enterprises Equipment Co E 908 353-2880
Elizabeth *(G-2764)*
Paone Fabrication Inc G 856 589-3821
Sewell *(G-9964)*
Park Steel & Iron Co F 732 775-7500
Neptune *(G-6927)*
Passaic County Welders Inc E 973 696-1200
Wayne *(G-11670)*
Peter Garafano & Son Inc E 973 278-0350
Paterson *(G-8364)*
Precision Metalcrafters Inc E 856 629-1020
Williamstown *(G-12100)*
Prime Rebar LLC E 908 707-1234
Bridgewater *(G-877)*
Priore Construction Svcs LLC F 973 785-2262
Little Falls *(G-5486)*
R Way Tooling & Met Works LLC F 856 692-2218
Vineland *(G-11394)*
▲ **Ramsey Charles Company** F 845 338-1464
Swedesboro *(G-10723)*
Rcc Fabricators Inc E 609 859-9350
Southampton *(G-10480)*
Riverside Marina Yacht Sls LLC F 856 461-1077
Riverside *(G-9506)*
RS Phillips Steel LLC E 973 827-6464
Sussex *(G-10676)*
Runding LLC G 973 277-8775
Oak Ridge *(G-7666)*
Samna Cnstrctn & Steel Fabrctn F 973 977-8400
Paterson *(G-8375)*
Sea Habor Marine Inc G 732 477-8577
Brick *(G-759)*
Senco Metals LLC G 973 342-1742
Edison *(G-2614)*
Skripak Metal Fabricators Inc G 732 364-9662
Howell *(G-4566)*
Southern New Jersey Stl Co Inc E 856 696-1612
Vineland *(G-11407)*
Springfield Metal Pdts Co Inc F 973 379-4600
Springfield *(G-10578)*
Squillace Stl Fabricators LLC G 908 241-6424
Roselle Park *(G-9703)*
Stainless Steel Fabricators G 856 464-1999
Bellmawr *(G-352)*
Stateline Fabricators LLC E 908 387-8800
Phillipsburg *(G-8672)*
▲ **Stirrup Metal Products Corp** F 973 824-7086
Newark *(G-7330)*
Susan R Bauer Inc G 973 657-1590
Ringwood *(G-9456)*
▲ **T G Manufacturing Inc** F 609 561-0022
Hammonton *(G-4150)*
Theodore E Mozer Inc E 856 829-1432
Palmyra *(G-7851)*
Thomas Russo & Sons Inc G 201 332-4159
Jersey City *(G-4837)*
Tri-Steel Fabricators Inc E 609 392-8660
Trenton *(G-11127)*
Truckform Inc F 908 526-5443
Somerville *(G-10231)*
United Steel Products Co Inc G 609 518-9230
Lumberton *(G-5665)*
Victory Iron Works Inc G 201 485-7181
Wyckoff *(G-12269)*
Vision Railings Ltd Lblty Co F 908 310-8926
Glen Gardner *(G-3817)*
W W Manufacturing Co Inc F 856 451-5700
Bridgeton *(G-802)*
Weir Welding Company Inc E 201 939-2284
Carlstadt *(G-1243)*
Westfield Shtmtl Works Inc E 908 276-5500
Kenilworth *(G-5007)*

3442 Metal Doors, Sash, Frames, Molding & Trim

4 Way Lock LLC G 908 359-2002
Hillsborough *(G-4315)*
Acme & Dorf Door Corp G 973 772-6774
Clifton *(G-1556)*
Alliance Vinyl Windows Co Inc E 856 456-4954
Oaklyn *(G-7710)*
▲ **Allmark Door Company LLC** F 610 358-9800
Springfield *(G-10536)*
Architectural Window Mfg Corp C 201 933-5094
Rutherford *(G-9726)*
Assa Abloy Entrance Systems US E 609 443-5800
Windsor *(G-12124)*
Assa Abloy Entrance Systems US E 609 528-2580
Hamilton *(G-4104)*
Belleville Corp F 201 991-6222
Kearny *(G-4863)*

Beta Industries Corp.................G...201 939-2400
Carlstadt *(G-1130)*

Bildisco Mfg Inc.................F...973 673-2400
West Orange *(G-11889)*

Century Bathworks Inc.................E...201 785-1414
Woodland Park *(G-12215)*

▲ Century Bathworks Inc.................D...973 785-4290
Woodland Park *(G-12214)*

Champion Opco LLC.................F...856 662-3400
West Berlin *(G-11707)*

Dor-Win Manufacturing Co.................G...201 796-4300
Elmwood Park *(G-2815)*

Dorwin Manufacturing Co.................E...201 796-4300
Elmwood Park *(G-2816)*

Elevator Entrance Inc.................E...973 790-9100
Paterson *(G-8259)*

Fast Doors LLC.................G...856 966-3278
Camden *(G-1065)*

Five Star Aluminum Products.................F...201 869-4181
North Bergen *(G-7452)*

Galaxy Metal Products LLC.................E...908 668-5200
Edison *(G-2524)*

Glen G Coats.................G...908 236-2620
Lebanon *(G-5287)*

Gray Overhead Door Co.................F...908 355-3889
Elizabeth *(G-2740)*

▲ Guardrite Steel Door Corp.................G...973 481-4424
Newark *(G-7181)*

Handi-Hut Inc.................E...973 614-1800
Clifton *(G-1633)*

Jersey Steel Door Inc.................G...973 482-4020
Newark *(G-7207)*

LMC-HB Corp.................E...862 239-9814
Paterson *(G-8324)*

Miric Industries Inc.................F...201 864-0233
North Bergen *(G-7468)*

▲ Northern Architectural Systems.......D...201 943-6400
Teterboro *(G-10807)*

Northern Architectural Systems.............E...201 943-6400
Carlstadt *(G-1195)*

Portaseal LLC.................G...973 539-0100
Morristown *(G-6737)*

Quick Fab Aluminum Mfg Co.................E...732 367-7200
Lakewood *(G-5175)*

▲ Randall Mfg Co Inc.................E...973 482-8603
Newark *(G-7284)*

▲ Royal Aluminum Co Inc.................D...973 589-8880
Newark *(G-7293)*

◆ Royal Prime Inc.................D...908 354-7600
Elizabeth *(G-2773)*

▲ RSI Woodworking Products Co.........D...609 484-1600
Egg Harbor Township *(G-2694)*

Security Holdings LLC.................D...201 457-0286
Carlstadt *(G-1216)*

Silver Line Building Pdts LLC.................C...732 752-8704
Middlesex *(G-6198)*

Skyline Windows LLC.................E...201 531-9600
Wood Ridge *(G-12138)*

Surburban Building Pdts Inc.................E...732 901-8900
Howell *(G-4568)*

Taylor Windows Inc.................F...973 672-3000
East Orange *(G-2270)*

◆ Thermwell Products Co Inc.................B...201 684-4400
Mahwah *(G-5820)*

Thomas Erectors Inc.................G...908 810-0030
Hillside *(G-4444)*

Thomas Manufacturing Inc.................E...908 810-0030
Hillside *(G-4445)*

Total Installations.................G...908 943-3211
Elizabeth *(G-2779)*

Tricomp Inc.................C...973 835-1110
Pompton Plains *(G-8966)*

Tuckahoe Manufacturing Inc.................E...856 696-4100
Vineland *(G-11410)*

Verona Aluminum Products Inc.................G...973 857-4809
Verona *(G-11312)*

Warren Capital Inc.................G...732 910-8134
Warren *(G-11572)*

Weathercraft Manufacturing Co.............F...201 262-0055
Emerson *(G-2864)*

Window Factory Inc.................E...856 546-5050
Mount Ephraim *(G-6765)*

▲ Window Shapes Inc.................D...732 549-0708
Metuchen *(G-6131)*

Winstar Windows LLC.................G...973 403-0574
Essex Fells *(G-3001)*

Zulu Fire Doors Ltd Lblty Co.................G...973 569-9858
Paterson *(G-8410)*

3443 Fabricated Plate Work

Able Fab Co.................E...732 396-0600
Avenel *(G-122)*

◆ Acrison Inc.................C...201 440-8300
Moonachie *(G-6499)*

Airmet Inc.................G...973 481-5550
Newark *(G-7074)*

Airzone Systems.................G...201 207-6593
Montville *(G-6482)*

Akw Inc.................G...732 493-1883
Ocean *(G-7714)*

▲ Akw Inc.................G...732 530-9186
Shrewsbury *(G-9988)*

◆ Amec Fster Wheeler N Amer Corp.......D...936 448-6323
Hampton *(G-4153)*

American Auto Carriers Inc.................G...201 573-0371
Woodcliff Lake *(G-12179)*

Andrew B Duffy Inc.................F...856 845-4900
West Deptford *(G-11815)*

Arde.................G...201 440-1453
Norwood *(G-7615)*

Arde Inc.................D...201 784-9880
Carlstadt *(G-1127)*

Arrow Shed LLC.................F...973 835-3200
Haskell *(G-4206)*

▲ Asa Hydraulik of America Inc.................G...908 541-1500
Branchburg *(G-640)*

▲ Asco Valve LLC.................D...973 966-2437
Florham Park *(G-3488)*

Asco Valve LLC.................G...973 386-9000
Parsippany *(G-7953)*

▲ Atlas Industrial Mfg Co.................E...973 779-3970
Clifton *(G-1568)*

▲ Bartell Morrison (usa) LLC.................F...732 566-5400
Freehold *(G-3641)*

Billy D Dumpster Service LLC.................G...609 465-5990
Cape May Court House *(G-1110)*

Brennan Penrod Contractors LLC.................F...856 933-1100
Bellmawr *(G-333)*

Bulkhaul (usa) Limited.................E...908 272-3100
Iselin *(G-4618)*

CB&i LLC.................C...856 482-3000
Trenton *(G-11036)*

Central Metal Fabricators Inc.................F...732 938-6900
Farmingdale *(G-3379)*

▲ Construction Specialties Inc.................E...908 236-0800
Lebanon *(G-5282)*

▲ Corban Energy Group Corp.................E...201 509-8555
Elmwood Park *(G-2812)*

▲ Cospack America Corp.................E...732 548-5858
Edison *(G-2493)*

▲ Crown Engineering Corp.................E...800 631-2153
Farmingdale *(G-3382)*

DC Fabricators Inc.................C...609 499-3000
Florence *(G-3477)*

De Ditrich Process Systems Inc.................E...908 317-2585
Mountainside *(G-6875)*

Deb Maintenance Inc.................E...856 786-0440
Cinnaminson *(G-1453)*

▼ Delta Cooling Towers Inc.................G...973 586-2201
Flanders *(G-3404)*

DI Myers Corp.................F...609 698-8800
Barnegat *(G-161)*

DR Technology Inc.................G...732 780-4664
Freehold *(G-3651)*

Dusenbery Engineering Co Inc.................G...973 539-2200
Morristown *(G-6706)*

▲ E F Britten & Co Inc.................F...908 276-4800
Cranford *(G-1904)*

▲ Edwards Coils Corp.................F...973 835-2800
Pompton Plains *(G-8958)*

Eks Parts Inc.................G...856 227-8811
Sewell *(G-9953)*

Enviro Pak Inc.................F...732 248-1600
Edison *(G-2513)*

Fidelio Limited Partnership.................G...201 307-1626
Woodcliff Lake *(G-12192)*

Force Systems.................F...856 848-8026
Westville *(G-11941)*

Foster Wheeler Arabia Ltd.................G...908 730-4000
Hampton *(G-4156)*

Foster Wheeler Intl Corp.................F...908 730-4000
Hampton *(G-4157)*

Foster Whler Intl Holdings Inc.................G...908 730-4000
Hampton *(G-4159)*

▲ G J Oliver Inc.................D...908 454-9743
Phillipsburg *(G-8649)*

▲ Gate Technologies Inc.................G...973 300-0090
Sparta *(G-10500)*

Harsco Corporation.................E...856 779-7795
Cherry Hill *(G-1374)*

Holler Metal Fabricators Inc.................G...732 635-9050
Metuchen *(G-6109)*

Huber International Corp.................G...732 549-8600
Edison *(G-2539)*

▼ I S Parts International Inc.................E...856 691-2203
Vineland *(G-11372)*

Jaeger Thomas & Melissa DDS.................F...908 735-2722
Lebanon *(G-5292)*

▲ Jersey Tank Fabricators Inc.................E...609 758-7670
South Plainfield *(G-10388)*

◆ Joseph Oat Holdings Inc.................D...856 541-2900
Camden *(G-1072)*

JW Parr Leadburing Co.................G...973 256-8093
Little Falls *(G-5479)*

▲ Kooltronic Inc.................C...609 466-3400
Pennington *(G-8455)*

L & L Welding Contractors.................F...609 395-1600
Dayton *(G-1976)*

◆ Leland Limited Inc.................F...908 561-2000
South Plainfield *(G-10398)*

Linden Well Drilling.................E...908 862-6633
Linden *(G-5403)*

Lobster Life Systems Inc.................F...201 398-0303
Lodi *(G-5592)*

Maarky Thermal Systems Inc.................G...856 470-1504
Cherry Hill *(G-1392)*

Main Robert A & Sons Holdg Co.................E...201 447-3700
Wyckoff *(G-12258)*

▲ Manning & Lewis Engrg Co Inc.................D...908 687-2400
Union *(G-11205)*

▼ Meese Inc.................E...201 796-4490
Saddle Brook *(G-9774)*

Modine Manufacturing Company.........G...856 467-9710
Bridgeport *(G-768)*

Mystic Timber LLC.................G...908 223-7878
Washington *(G-11585)*

Nova Flex Group.................F...856 768-2275
West Berlin *(G-11737)*

▲ Nova Flex Group.................F...856 768-2275
West Berlin *(G-11738)*

▲ Perry Products Corporation.................E...609 267-1600
Hainesport *(G-4076)*

Plate Concepts Inc.................E...908 236-9570
Lebanon *(G-5299)*

▼ Polaris Plate Heat Exchngers L.........G...732 345-7188
Shrewsbury *(G-10008)*

Power Products and Engrg LLC.................E...855 769-3751
Trenton *(G-11102)*

Prospect Transportation Inc.................D...201 933-9999
Carlstadt *(G-1210)*

Pulsonics Inc.................E...800 999-6785
Belleville *(G-313)*

Ras Process Equipment.................E...609 371-1000
Robbinsville *(G-9521)*

Roben Manufacturing Co Inc.................E...732 364-6000
Lakewood *(G-5184)*

Rosenwach Tank Co LLC.................E...732 563-4900
Somerset *(G-10167)*

Rudco Products Inc.................D...856 691-0800
Vineland *(G-11400)*

Russell W Anderson Inc.................G...201 825-2092
Mahwah *(G-5810)*

Scientific Alloys Corp.................F...973 478-8323
Clifton *(G-1717)*

▲ Sheet Metal Products Inc.................D...973 482-0450
Newark *(G-7310)*

▲ Shell Packaging Corporation.................E...908 871-7000
Berkeley Heights *(G-422)*

Springfield Metal Pdts Co Inc.................F...973 379-4600
Springfield *(G-10578)*

SPX Cooling Technologies Inc.................E...908 450-8027
Bridgewater *(G-898)*

Stacks Envmtl Ltd Lblty Co.................G...973 885-2036
Lake Hopatcong *(G-5057)*

▲ Stirrup Metal Products Corp.................G...973 824-7086
Newark *(G-7330)*

Temptrol Corp.................E...856 461-7977
Voorhees *(G-11439)*

Theodore E Mozer Inc.................E...856 829-1432
Palmyra *(G-7851)*

▲ Titanium Fabrication Corp.................D...973 227-5300
Fairfield *(G-3327)*

Tolan Machinery Company Inc.................E...973 983-7212
Rockaway *(G-9615)*

Tolan Machinery Polishing Co.................E...973 983-7212
Rockaway *(G-9616)*

◆ Triangle Tube/Phase III Co Inc.................C...856 228-9940
Paulsboro *(G-8427)*

▲ Ulma Form-Works Inc ....D 201 882-1122
  Hawthorne *(G-4261)*

Waage Electric Inc ....G 908 245-9363
  Kenilworth *(G-5004)*

Wastequip Manufacturing Co ....D 856 784-5500
  Sicklerville *(G-10028)*

Wastequip Manufacturing Co LLC ....E 856 629-9222
  Williamstown *(G-12114)*

Welded Products Co Inc ....E 973 589-0180
  Newark *(G-7358)*

Wind Tunnel Inc ....G 201 485-7793
  Mahwah *(G-5824)*

3444 Sheet Metal Work

67 Pollock Ave Corp ....G 201 432-1156
  Jersey City *(G-4692)*

A B Scantlebury Co Inc ....F 973 770-3000
  Newton *(G-7378)*

A R J Custom Fabrication Inc ....F 609 695-6227
  Trenton *(G-11011)*

A&B Heating & Cooling ....G 908 289-2231
  Elizabeth *(G-2703)*

Abco Metal LLC ....F 973 772-8160
  Paterson *(G-8196)*

Able Fab Co ....E 732 396-0600
  Avenel *(G-122)*

Aerosmith ....G 973 614-9392
  South Hackensack *(G-10252)*

Air & Specialties Sheet Metal ....F 908 233-8306
  Mountainside *(G-6866)*

Air Distribution Systems Inc ....D 856 874-1100
  Cherry Hill *(G-1341)*

Air Power Inc ....E 973 882-5418
  Fairfield *(G-3128)*

Airfiltronix Corp ....G 973 779-5577
  Clifton *(G-1560)*

Airmet Inc ....G 973 481-5550
  Newark *(G-7074)*

Airtec Inc ....G 732 382-3700
  Rahway *(G-9172)*

Ajay Metal Fabricators Inc ....G 908 523-0557
  Linden *(G-5345)*

▲ Allentown Inc ....B 609 259-7951
  Allentown *(G-28)*

Allied Metal Industries Inc ....E 973 824-7347
  Newark *(G-7077)*

Allmike Metal Technology Inc ....F 201 935-2306
  Moonachie *(G-6502)*

Altona Blower & Shtmtl Work ....G 201 641-3520
  Little Ferry *(G-5494)*

Aluma Systems Con Cnstr LLC ......G 908 418-5073
  Linden *(G-5347)*

Amerifab Corp ....G 973 777-2120
  Lodi *(G-5576)*

Andrew B Duffy Inc ....F 856 845-4900
  West Deptford *(G-11815)*

▲ Ango Electronics Corporation ......F 201 955-0800
  North Arlington *(G-7415)*

Architctural Metal Designs Inc ....E 856 765-3000
  Millville *(G-6285)*

▲ Argyle Industries Inc ....F 908 725-8800
  Branchburg *(G-637)*

Artus Corp ....E 201 568-1000
  Englewood *(G-2873)*

Atco Rubber Products Inc ....E 856 794-3393
  Vineland *(G-11324)*

Atlantic Air Enterprises Inc ....F 732 381-4000
  Rahway *(G-9178)*

Atlantic Coastal Welding Inc ....F 732 269-1088
  Bayville *(G-250)*

B & S Sheet Metal Co Inc ....F 973 427-3739
  Hawthorne *(G-4218)*

Babbitt Mfg Co Inc ....F 856 692-3245
  Vineland *(G-11326)*

Banicki Sheet Metal Inc ....G 201 385-5938
  Bergenfield *(G-382)*

BCsmachine & Mfg Corp ....G 908 561-1656
  South Plainfield *(G-10335)*

Belden Inc ....F 908 925-8000
  Elizabeth *(G-2712)*

Benco Inc ....F 973 575-4440
  Fairfield *(G-3146)*

Bergen Homestate Corp ....G 201 372-9740
  Moonachie *(G-6507)*

Bill Chambers Sheet Metal ....G 856 848-4774
  Woodbury Heights *(G-12174)*

Blackhawk Cre Corporation ....F 856 887-0162
  Salem *(G-9803)*

Bloomfield Manufacturing Co ....F 973 575-8900
  Oakland *(G-7676)*

Bonland Industries Inc ....D 973 694-3211
  Wayne *(G-11611)*

Bouras Industries Inc ....A 908 918-9400
  Summit *(G-10637)*

BR Welding Inc ....F 732 363-8253
  Howell *(G-4547)*

Breure Sheet Metal Co Inc ....F 973 772-6423
  Clifton *(G-1578)*

Broadhurst Sheet Metal Works ....G 973 304-4001
  Hawthorne *(G-4223)*

▲ Brook Metal Products Inc ....F 908 355-1601
  Lawrence Township *(G-5241)*

Brothers Sheet Metal ....F 973 579-1788
  Newton *(G-7383)*

Brothers Sheet Metal Inc ....F 973 228-3221
  Roseland *(G-9648)*

Burns Link Manufacturing Co ....F 856 429-6844
  Voorhees *(G-11424)*

C M C Steel Fabricators Inc ....C 908 561-3484
  South Plainfield *(G-10342)*

Cain Machine Inc ....F 856 825-7225
  Millville *(G-6291)*

Cambridge Sheet Metal Inc ....E 973 386-0788
  Blairstown *(G-495)*

Central Metal Fabricators Inc ....F 732 938-6900
  Farmingdale *(G-3379)*

Cheney Flashing Company LLC ....F 609 394-8175
  Trenton *(G-11039)*

Classic Industries Inc ....G 973 227-1366
  Parsippany *(G-7972)*

Clifton Metal Products Co Inc ....F 973 777-6100
  Clifton *(G-1584)*

Coronation Sheet Metal Co ....G 908 686-0930
  Union *(G-11167)*

CPS Metals Inc ....G 856 779-0846
  Maple Shade *(G-5901)*

Crett Construction Inc ....F 973 663-1184
  Lake Hopatcong *(G-5055)*

Custom Fabricators Inc ....G 908 862-4244
  Linden *(G-5365)*

Cutmark Inc ....G 856 234-3428
  Mount Laurel *(G-6791)*

D&N Machine Manufacturing Inc .....E 856 456-1366
  Gloucester City *(G-3835)*

Danson Sheet Metal Inc ....E 201 343-4876
  Hackensack *(G-3903)*

◆ Delair LLC ....D 856 663-2900
  Pennsauken *(G-8502)*

Delaware Valley Sign Corp ....D 609 386-0100
  Burlington *(G-967)*

Demand LLC ....F 908 526-2020
  Somerville *(G-10206)*

Diversified Fab Pdts Ltd Lblty ....G 973 773-3189
  Clifton *(G-1602)*

Dos Industrial Sales LLC ....G 973 887-7800
  East Hanover *(G-2212)*

Duct Mate Inc ....G 201 488-8002
  Hackensack *(G-3907)*

Ducts Inc ....G 973 267-8482
  Morris Plains *(G-6660)*

Ductworks Inc ....F 908 754-8190
  Plainfield *(G-8858)*

▲ Durex Inc ....C 908 688-0800
  Union *(G-11174)*

Dutra Sheet Metal Co ....G 856 692-8058
  Vineland *(G-11354)*

E P Homiek Shtmtl Sups Inc ....E 732 364-7644
  Lakewood *(G-5111)*

Edker Industries Inc ....E 856 786-1971
  Cinnaminson *(G-1460)*

Efco Corp ....F 732 308-1010
  Marlboro *(G-5938)*

Elgee Manufacturing Company ....G 908 647-4100
  Warren *(G-11545)*

Elmco Two Inc ....G 856 365-2244
  Camden *(G-1061)*

◆ Englert Inc ....C 800 364-5378
  Perth Amboy *(G-8612)*

Evs Interactive Inc ....F 718 784-3690
  Riverdale *(G-9480)*

▲ Ewc Controls Inc ....E 732 446-3110
  Manalapan *(G-5846)*

Excel Die Sharpening Corp ....G 908 587-2606
  Linden *(G-5371)*

▼ Fabulous Fabricators LLC ....E 973 779-2400
  Totowa *(G-10944)*

Fairfield Metal Ltd Lblty Co ....F 973 276-8440
  Fairfield *(G-3194)*

Falcon Industries Inc ....D 732 563-9889
  Somerset *(G-10100)*

Fiore Skylights Inc ....F 856 346-0118
  Somerdale *(G-10040)*

Franklen Sheet Metal Co Inc ....F 732 988-0808
  Ocean Grove *(G-7761)*

Frc Electrical Industries Inc ....E 908 464-3200
  New Providence *(G-7036)*

▲ G T M Signs Inc ....G 856 227-2333
  Deptford *(G-2064)*

▲ GAF Elk Materials Corporation .....C 973 628-4083
  Wayne *(G-11639)*

◆ Garvey Corporation ....D 609 561-2450
  Hammonton *(G-4137)*

Gauer Metal Products Co Inc ....E 908 241-4080
  Kenilworth *(G-4958)*

Gaw Associates Inc ....F 856 608-1428
  Cherry Hill *(G-1370)*

General Aviation & Elec Mfg Co ......E 201 487-1700
  Hackensack *(G-3920)*

Geneva Metal Products Co Inc ....F 973 472-3073
  Passaic *(G-8144)*

Giant Stl Fabricators Erectors ....E 908 241-6766
  Roselle *(G-9671)*

Globe Engineering Corp ....G 609 898-0349
  Cape May *(G-1101)*

Golden Metal Products Corp ....E 973 399-1157
  Hillside *(G-4409)*

Great Railing Inc ....F 856 875-0050
  Williamstown *(G-12089)*

H & H Industries Inc ....E 856 663-4444
  Pennsauken *(G-8520)*

Haenssler Shtmtl Works Inc ....F 973 373-6360
  Newark *(G-7182)*

Handi-Hut Inc ....G 973 614-1800
  Clifton *(G-1633)*

Hansen Awning Co ....G 609 886-1685
  Rio Grande *(G-9459)*

▲ Harold R Henrich Inc ....D 732 370-4455
  Lakewood *(G-5132)*

Hays Sheet Metal Inc ....G 856 662-7722
  Pennsauken *(G-8521)*

Hudson Awning Co Inc ....E 201 339-7171
  Bayonne *(G-232)*

Hutchinson Industries Inc ....F 609 394-1010
  Trenton *(G-11064)*

In-Line Shtmtl Fabricators ....G 201 339-8121
  Bayonne *(G-233)*

Independent Metal Sales Inc ....F 609 261-8090
  Hainesport *(G-4074)*

Independent Sheet Metal Co Inc .....D 973 423-1150
  Riverdale *(G-9482)*

Industrial Process & Eqp Inc ....F 973 702-0330
  Sussex *(G-10673)*

Inox Components ....F 856 256-0800
  Pitman *(G-8842)*

Intercoastal Fabricators Inc ....G 856 629-4105
  Williamstown *(G-12090)*

International Shtmtl Plate Mfg ....E 908 722-6614
  Somerville *(G-10216)*

▲ International Swimming Pools ....E 732 565-9229
  New Brunswick *(G-6968)*

Internet-Sales USA Corporation ......G 775 468-8379
  Rockaway *(G-9575)*

J & E Metal Fabricators Inc ....E 732 548-9650
  Metuchen *(G-6112)*

J & M Air Inc ....E 908 707-4040
  Somerville *(G-10217)*

James A Stanlick Jr ....G 973 366-7316
  Wharton *(G-11990)*

Jersey Sheet Metal & Machine ....E 973 366-8628
  Dover *(G-2097)*

Jesco Iron Crafts Inc ....G 201 488-4545
  Bogota *(G-548)*

▲ Jet Precision Metal Inc ....E 973 423-4350
  Hawthorne *(G-4244)*

John E Herbst Heating & Coolg ....G 732 721-0088
  Parlin *(G-7933)*

Joseph Bbinec Shtmtl Works Inc .....E 732 388-0155
  Rahway *(G-9205)*

Kinetron Inc ....F 732 918-7777
  Ocean *(G-7729)*

Klm Mechanical Contractors ....F 201 385-6965
  Dumont *(G-2120)*

Lectro Products Inc ....G 732 462-2463
  Freehold *(G-3666)*

Leibrock Metal Products Inc ....G 732 695-0326
  Ocean *(G-7731)*

Lentine Sheet Metal Inc ....F 908 486-8974
  Linden *(G-5402)*

Lynn Mechanical Contractors ....F 856 829-1717
  Cinnaminson *(G-1474)*

S
I
C

M C Custom Shtmtl Fabrication ....G..... 856 767-9509
West Berlin (G-11732)

Madhu B Goyal MD ....G..... 908 769-0307
South Plainfield (G-10400)

Marino International Corp ....G..... 732 752-5100
South Plainfield (G-10404)

Marlyn Sheet Metal Inc ....F..... 856 863-6900
Clayton (G-1526)

Marx NJ Group LLC ....G..... 732 901-3880
Bound Brook (G-620)

Max Gurtman & Sons Inc ....G..... 973 478-7000
Clifton (G-1671)

▲ Medlaurel Inc ....E..... 856 461-6600
Delanco (G-2007)

Metal Dynamix LLC ....G..... 856 235-4559
Cherry Hill (G-1400)

Metal Specialties New Jersey ....G..... 609 261-9277
Mount Holly (G-6775)

▼ Metalfab Inc ....E..... 973 764-2000
Vernon (G-11299)

Metalix Inc ....G..... 973 546-2500
Little Falls (G-5482)

Michael Anthony Sign Dsign Inc ....E..... 732 453-6120
Piscataway (G-8791)

◆ Middle Atlantic Products Inc ....B..... 973 839-1011
Fairfield (G-3261)

Millar Sheet Metal ....G..... 201 997-1990
Kearny (G-4899)

Millco Custom Fabricators Inc ....G..... 908 756-3640
South Plainfield (G-10407)

Moreng Metal Products Inc ....D..... 973 256-2001
Totowa (G-10956)

Neumann Sheet Metal Inc ....G..... 908 756-0415
Plainfield (G-8867)

New Age Metal Fabg Co Inc ....D..... 973 227-9107
Fairfield (G-3268)

Nordic Metal LLC ....G..... 908 245-8900
Kenilworth (G-4982)

Oeg Building Materials Inc ....E..... 732 667-3636
Sayreville (G-9834)

P L M Manufacturing Company ....G..... 201 342-3636
Hackensack (G-3960)

Pabst Enterprises Equipment Co ....E..... 908 353-2880
Elizabeth (G-2764)

Par Sheet Metal Inc ....F..... 908 241-2477
Roselle (G-9681)

Par Troy Sheet Metal & AC LLC ....G..... 973 227-1150
Fairfield (G-3280)

Park Steel & Iron Co ....F..... 732 775-7500
Neptune (G-6927)

Passaic Metal & Bldg Sups Co ....D..... 973 546-9000
Clifton (G-1691)

Pcr Technologies Inc ....G..... 973 882-0017
Pine Brook (G-8713)

◆ Pemberton Fabricators Inc ....A..... 609 267-0922
Rancocas (G-9260)

Pepco Manufacturing Co ....D..... 856 783-3700
Somerdale (G-10042)

PI Metal Products Inc ....G..... 201 955-0800
Linden (G-5428)

Pioneer Machine & Tool Co Inc ....E..... 856 779-8800
Maple Shade (G-5907)

Postage Bin ....G..... 732 333-0915
Freehold (G-3679)

Precision Metalcrafters Inc ....E..... 856 629-1020
Williamstown (G-12100)

Prism Sheet Metal Inc ....G..... 973 673-0213
Orange (G-7824)

Pro-Deck Supply ....G..... 609 771-1100
Trenton (G-11109)

Professional Envmtl Systems ....E..... 201 991-3000
Kearny (G-4911)

PTL Sheet Metal Inc ....G..... 201 501-8700
Dumont (G-2122)

Quality Sheet Metal & Wldg Inc ....F..... 732 469-7111
Piscataway (G-8804)

R M F Associates Inc ....C..... 908 687-9355
Union (G-11218)

Radiation Systems Inc ....G..... 201 891-7515
Wyckoff (G-12261)

▼ Rails Company Inc ....E..... 973 763-4320
Maplewood (G-5926)

Rainbow Metal Units Corp ....E..... 718 784-3690
Riverdale (G-9484)

Ranco Precision Sheet Metal ....G..... 973 472-8808
Clifton (G-1710)

Rangecraft Manufacturing Inc ....F..... 201 791-0440
Fair Lawn (G-3108)

Rays Seamless Rain Gutters ....G..... 856 629-8407
Sicklerville (G-10024)

Rhoads Metal Works Inc ....E..... 856 486-1551
Pennsauken (G-8573)

Ricklyn Co Inc ....G..... 908 689-6770
Columbia (G-1800)

Roof Deck Inc ....E..... 609 448-6666
East Windsor (G-2365)

S P Sheet Metal Co Inc ....F..... 609 698-8800
Barnegat (G-164)

Schrader & Company Inc ....G..... 973 579-1160
Newton (G-7403)

Seal-Spout Corp ....F..... 908 647-0648
Liberty Corner (G-5324)

◆ Service Metal Fabricating Inc ....D..... 973 625-8882
Rockaway (G-9608)

Service Metal Fabricating Inc ....G..... 973 989-7199
Dover (G-2110)

Shamong Manufacturing Company ......E..... 609 654-2549
Shamong (G-9971)

▲ Sheet Metal Products Inc ....D..... 973 482-0450
Newark (G-7310)

Sonrise Metal Inc ....F..... 973 423-4717
Hopatcong (G-4538)

South Jersey Metal Inc ....E..... 856 228-0642
Deptford (G-2067)

Sperro Metal Products LLC ....E..... 973 335-2000
Montville (G-6494)

Springfield Heating & AC Co ....F..... 908 233-8400
Mountainside (G-6888)

Springfield Metal Pdts Co Inc ....F..... 973 379-4600
Springfield (G-10578)

Star Metal Products ....G..... 908 474-9860
Linden (G-5448)

▲ Stirrup Metal Products Corp ....F..... 973 824-7086
Newark (G-7330)

▲ Super Stud Building Pdts Inc ....D..... 732 662-6200
Edison (G-2633)

T J Eckardt Associates Inc ....E..... 856 767-4111
Berlin (G-442)

Tam Metal Products Inc ....E..... 201 848-7800
Mahwah (G-5818)

Theodore E Mozer Inc ....F..... 856 829-1432
Palmyra (G-7851)

Totowa Metal Fabricators Inc ....F..... 973 423-1943
North Haledon (G-7555)

Trenton Sheet Metal Inc ....E..... 609 695-6328
Trenton (G-11126)

▲ Ulma Form-Works Inc ....D..... 201 882-1122
Hawthorne (G-4261)

Unique Metal Products ....F..... 732 388-1888
Rahway (G-9226)

United Gutter Supply Inc ....E..... 201 933-6316
East Rutherford (G-2335)

USA Industries Inc ....E..... 201 438-6606
Carlstadt (G-1237)

Vfi Fabricators Inc ....E..... 856 629-8786
Williamstown (G-12113)

◆ Ware Industries Inc ....D..... 908 757-9000
South Plainfield (G-10454)

Weathercraft Manufacturing Co ....F..... 201 262-0055
Emerson (G-2864)

Wecom Inc ....E..... 856 863-8400
Glassboro (G-3813)

Welded Products Co Inc ....E..... 973 589-0180
Newark (G-7358)

Westfield Shtmtl Works Inc ....E..... 908 276-5500
Kenilworth (G-5007)

3446 Architectural & Ornamental Metal Work

67 Pollock Ave Corp ....G..... 201 432-1156
Jersey City (G-4692)

A & A Ironwork Co Inc ....F..... 973 728-4300
Hewitt (G-4287)

Abba Metal Works Inc ....G..... 973 684-0808
Paterson (G-8195)

Advanced Products LLC ....E..... 800 724-5464
Lakewood (G-5066)

Airmet Inc ....G..... 973 481-5550
Newark (G-7074)

Alessandra Miscellaneous Metal ....F..... 973 786-6805
Newton (G-7379)

All American Metal Fabricators ....G..... 201 567-2898
Tenafly (G-10780)

Anvil Iron Works Inc ....G..... 856 783-5959
Sicklerville (G-10016)

Architctural Metal Fabricators ....G..... 718 765-0722
Carteret (G-1249)

▲ Architectural Iron Designs ....G..... 908 757-2323
Plainfield (G-8854)

Armetec Corp ....G..... 973 485-2525
Newark (G-7093)

Artistic Railings Inc ....G..... 973 772-8540
Garfield (G-3719)

B L White Welding & Steel Co ....G..... 973 684-4111
Paterson (G-8218)

▲ Bamco Inc ....D..... 732 302-0889
Middlesex (G-6150)

Bedlam Corp ....F..... 973 774-8770
Montclair (G-6408)

Bolt Welding & Iron Works ....G..... 609 393-3993
Trenton (G-11029)

C & S Fencing Inc ....E..... 201 797-5440
Elmwood Park (G-2807)

C W Grimmer & Sons Inc ....F..... 732 741-2189
Tinton Falls (G-10825)

▲ Cacciola Iron Works Inc ....G..... 973 595-0854
Paterson (G-8229)

Carfaro Inc ....E..... 609 890-6600
Trenton (G-11033)

Ciccone Inc ....G..... 732 349-7071
Toms River (G-10871)

▼ Clems Ornemental Iron Works ....D..... 732 968-7200
Piscataway (G-8750)

Columbian Orna Ir Works Inc ....G..... 973 697-0927
Paterson (G-8236)

Consolidated Stl Alum Fence Inc ....E..... 908 272-0494
Kenilworth (G-4948)

▲ Construction Specialties Inc ....G..... 908 236-0800
Lebanon (G-5282)

Creative Metal Works Inc ....F..... 973 579-3717
Sparta (G-10495)

Cusumano Perma-Rail Co ....G..... 908 245-9281
Roselle Park (G-9692)

◆ Delair LLC ....D..... 856 663-2900
Pennsauken (G-8502)

Doortec Archtctural Met GL LLC ....G..... 201 497-5056
River Vale (G-9469)

Empire Lumber & Millwork Co ....E..... 973 242-2700
Newark (G-7153)

F & C Prof Alum Railings Corp ....G..... 908 753-8886
Plainfield (G-8861)

Fairway Building Products LLC ....E..... 609 890-6600
Trenton (G-11059)

▲ FMB Systems Inc ....D..... 973 485-5544
Harrison (G-4184)

G-Tech Elevator Associates LLC ....E..... 866 658-9296
Linden (G-5378)

Garden State Iron Inc ....F..... 732 918-0760
Ocean (G-7726)

George Ciocher Inc ....G..... 732 818-3495
Toms River (G-10880)

Gervens Enterprises Inc ....F..... 973 838-1600
Bloomingdale (G-544)

Harsco Corporation ....E..... 908 454-7169
Plainfield (G-8864)

Integrity Ironworks Corp ....G..... 732 254-2200
Sayreville (G-9824)

International Design & Mfg LLC ....G..... 908 587-2884
Linden (G-5391)

▲ Interntnal Archtctral Irnworks ....E..... 973 741-0749
Irvington (G-4594)

Interstate Architectural & Ir ....G..... 201 941-0393
Cliffside Park (G-1541)

Interstate Panel LLC ....F..... 609 586-4411
Trenton (G-11069)

J G Schmidt Steel ....F..... 973 473-4822
Passaic (G-8149)

J Kaufman Iron Works Inc ....F..... 973 925-9972
Paterson (G-8296)

James A Stanlick Jr ....G..... 973 366-7316
Wharton (G-11990)

James Zylstra Enterprises Inc ....E..... 973 383-6768
Lafayette (G-5047)

Joseph Monga Jr ....G..... 973 595-8517
Paterson (G-8306)

K & A Architectural Met GL LLC ....F..... 908 687-0247
Hillside (G-4423)

Kaufman Stairs Inc ....E..... 908 862-3579
Rahway (G-9206)

La Forge De Style LLC ....G..... 201 488-1955
South Hackensack (G-10275)

Leets Steel Inc ....E..... 917 416-7977
Sayreville (G-9828)

Lingo Inc ....F..... 856 273-6594
Mount Laurel (G-6812)

LMC-HB Corp ....G..... 862 239-9814
Paterson (G-8324)

◆ Lmt Mercer Group Inc ....E..... 888 570-5252
Lawrence Township (G-5243)

Majka Railing Inc ....G..... 973 247-7603
Paterson (G-8329)

Marchione Industries Inc .... F 718 317-4900
Lyndhurst (G-5690)

McNichols Company .... F 877 884-4653
New Brunswick (G-6979)

◆ Merchant & Evans Inc .... E 609 387-3033
Burlington (G-984)

Mershon Concrete LLC .... E 609 298-2150
Bordentown (G-603)

Morsemere Iron Works Inc .... F 201 941-1133
Ridgefield (G-9376)

New Jersey Stair and Rail Inc .... G 732 583-8400
Matawan (G-6025)

Newman Ornamental Iron Works .... F 732 223-9042
Brielle (G-914)

Nicks Inc .... G 908 272-3739
Kenilworth (G-4981)

North Jersey Metal Fabricators .... G 973 305-9830
Wayne (G-11667)

▲ Omnia Industries Inc .... E 973 239-7272
Cedar Grove (G-1295)

Papp Iron Works Inc .... D 908 731-1000
Plainfield (G-8871)

Par Troy Sheet Metal & AC LLC .... G 973 227-1150
Fairfield (G-3280)

Permanore Archtctural Finishes .... G 908 797-4177
Milford (G-6247)

Pioneer Railing Inc .... G 609 387-0981
Beverly (G-464)

Post To Post LLC .... G 609 646-9300
Egg Harbor Township (G-2692)

▲ Rambusch Decorating Company .... E 201 333-2525
Jersey City (G-4815)

Robert J Donaldson Inc .... F 856 629-2737
Williamstown (G-12104)

S & S Socius Inc .... E 732 698-2400
Edison (G-2609)

Security Fabricators Inc .... F 908 272-9171
Kenilworth (G-4996)

Studio Dellarte .... G 718 599-3715
Jersey City (G-4835)

Wayside Fence Company Inc .... E 201 791-7979
Fair Lawn (G-3124)

Zone Defense Inc .... F 973 328-0436
Hackettstown (G-4044)

3448 Prefabricated Metal Buildings & Cmp-nts

Arrow Shed LLC .... E 973 835-3200
Haskell (G-4206)

Diamond Scooters Inc .... G 609 646-0003
Absecon (G-2)

Edward T Brady .... G 732 928-0257
Allentown (G-29)

Everlast Associates Inc .... G 609 261-1888
Southampton (G-10472)

Handi-Hut Inc .... E 973 614-1800
Clifton (G-1633)

Marino Building Systems Corp .... C 732 968-0555
South Plainfield (G-10403)

Mobile Mini Inc .... E 908 561-5033
South Plainfield (G-10408)

Mtn Government Services Inc .... F 703 443-6738
Holmdel (G-4525)

P M C Diners Inc .... F 201 337-6146
Oakland (G-7700)

Pre-Fab Structures Inc .... G 856 768-4257
Atco (G-90)

Walpole Woodworkers Inc .... E 973 539-3555
Morris Plains (G-6681)

3449 Misc Structural Metal Work

Architectural Metal and Glass .... G 732 994-7575
Lakewood (G-5075)

Bolt Welding & Iron Works .... G 609 393-3993
Trenton (G-11029)

Camtec Industries Inc .... F 732 332-9800
Colts Neck (G-1780)

Eagle Steel & Iron LLC .... G 908 587-1025
Stewartsville (G-10595)

Handi-Hut Inc .... E 973 614-1800
Clifton (G-1633)

▲ Haydon Corporation .... D 973 904-0800
Wayne (G-11646)

▼ Helidex LLC .... G 201 636-2546
East Rutherford (G-2299)

Inductotherm Technologies Inc .... G 609 267-9000
Rancocas (G-9259)

Jersey Shore Steel Inc .... G 732 833-8855
Jackson (G-4670)

Kenric Inc .... G 856 294-9161
Swedesboro (G-10704)

Luso Machine Inc .... F 973 242-1717
Newark (G-7228)

Lusotech LLC .... G 973 332-3861
Newark (G-7230)

Mainland Plate Glass Company .... F 609 277-2938
Pleasantville (G-8912)

◆ Metalico Inc .... G 908 497-9610
Cranford (G-1915)

Morsemere Iron Works Inc .... F 201 941-1133
Ridgefield (G-9376)

N E R Associates Inc .... G 908 454-5955
Phillipsburg (G-8661)

New Jersey Steel Corporation .... F 856 337-0054
Haddon Township (G-4053)

Paragon Iron Inc .... G 201 528-7307
Carlstadt (G-1198)

Pipeline Eqp Resources Co LLC .... G 888 232-7372
Boonton (G-579)

RS Phillips Steel LLC .... E 973 827-6464
Sussex (G-10676)

Specialty Measures .... G 609 882-6071
Ewing (G-3055)

Stelfast Inc .... F 440 879-0077
Edison (G-2627)

United Eqp Fabricators LLC .... G 973 242-2737
Newark (G-7353)

W2f Inc .... G 609 735-0135
New Egypt (G-7019)

Wired Products LLC .... F 551 231-5800
Paramus (G-7913)

3451 Screw Machine Prdts

Accurate Screw Machine Corp .... D 973 276-0379
Fairfield (G-3126)

Amark Industries Inc .... G 973 992-8900
Livingston (G-5524)

Automatic Machine Product .... G 973 383-9929
Newton (G-7380)

Bmb Machining LLC .... G 973 256-4010
Woodland Park (G-12211)

C & K Punch & Screw Mch Pdts .... G 201 343-6750
Hackensack (G-3886)

Champion Fasteners Inc .... E 609 267-5222
Lumberton (G-5655)

Chicago Pneumatic Tool .... G 973 276-1377
Fairfield (G-3158)

Congruent Machine Co Inc .... G 973 764-6767
Vernon (G-11297)

▲ Duro Manufacturing Company .... E 908 810-9588
Union (G-11175)

Eastern Machining Corporation .... G 856 694-3303
Franklinville (G-3630)

Edston Manufacturing Company .... E 908 647-0116
Fairfield (G-3182)

▲ Esco Precision Inc .... E 908 722-0800
Hillsborough (G-4331)

F P Schmidt Manufacturing Co .... F 201 343-4241
South Hackensack (G-10267)

Ferrum Industries Inc .... F 201 935-1220
Carlstadt (G-1160)

Form Cut Industries Inc .... E 973 483-5154
Newark (G-7165)

▲ Gadren Machine Co Inc .... F 856 456-4329
Mount Ephraim (G-6763)

H & H Swiss Screw Machine PR .... E 908 688-6390
Hillside (G-4410)

Hi-Grade Products Mfg Co .... G 908 245-4133
Kenilworth (G-4961)

Industrial Machine & Engrg Co .... F 908 862-8874
Linden (G-5386)

▲ International Tool & Mch LLC .... E 908 687-5580
Hillside (G-4419)

◆ J & S Precision Products Co .... E 609 654-0900
Medford (G-6072)

Karl Neuweiler Inc .... G 908 464-6532
Berkeley Heights (G-415)

Labern Machine Products LLC .... G 908 722-1970
Branchburg (G-673)

Main Robert A & Sons Holdg Co .... E 201 447-3700
Wyckoff (G-12258)

Meltom Manufacturing Inc .... G 973 546-0058
Clifton (G-1672)

Metal Components Inc .... E 973 247-1204
North Haledon (G-7551)

Mw Industries Inc .... G 973 244-9200
Fairfield (G-3265)

Nova Precision Products Inc .... C 973 625-1586
Rockaway (G-9590)

O E M Manufacturers Ltd Inc .... G 201 475-8585
Elmwood Park (G-2839)

Orion Precision Industries .... G 732 247-9704
Somerset (G-10147)

Oroszlany Laszlo .... G 201 666-2101
Hillsdale (G-4386)

Peter Yaged .... G 973 427-4219
Hawthorne (G-4253)

S J Screw Company Inc .... E 908 475-2155
Belvidere (G-376)

Salem Manufacturing Corp .... F 973 751-6331
Belleville (G-317)

Sumatic Co Inc .... G 973 772-1288
Garfield (G-3766)

Supermatic Corp .... F 973 627-4433
Rockaway (G-9611)

Telemark Cnc LLC .... G 973 794-4857
Boonton (G-586)

Tool Shop Inc .... G 856 767-8077
West Berlin (G-11758)

Ultimate Spinning Turning Corp .... F 201 372-9740
Moonachie (G-6550)

Welton V Johnson Engineering .... F 908 241-3100
Kenilworth (G-5006)

Zago Manufacturing Company .... E 973 643-6700
Newark (G-7362)

3452 Bolts, Nuts, Screws, Rivets & Washers

▲ Amerifast Corp .... F 908 668-1959
South Plainfield (G-10328)

▲ Arrow Fastener Co LLC .... B 201 843-6900
Saddle Brook (G-9752)

Bigelow Components Corp .... E 973 467-1200
Springfield (G-10543)

▲ Celus Fasteners Mfg Inc .... E 800 289-7483
Northvale (G-7576)

▲ Chicago Pneumatic Tool .... F 973 928-5222
Clifton (G-1583)

Cold Headed Fasteners Inc .... F 856 461-3244
Delanco (G-2004)

Edwin Leonel Ramirez .... G 732 648-5587
Plainfield (G-8860)

F & R Grinding Inc .... F 908 996-0440
Frenchtown (G-3700)

▲ Ford Atlantic Fastener Corp .... E 973 882-1191
Pine Brook (G-8702)

General Sullivan Group Inc .... F 609 745-5000
Pennington (G-8452)

▲ H K Metal Craft Mfg Corp .... E 973 471-7770
Lodi (G-5585)

▲ Industrial Rivet & Fastener Co .... D 201 750-1040
Northvale (G-7584)

◆ JC Macelroy Co Inc .... D 732 572-7100
Piscataway (G-8784)

Kt Mt Corp .... F 877 791-4426
Cinnaminson (G-1473)

Mechanitron Corporation Inc .... G 908 620-1001
Roselle (G-9676)

Mrl Manufacturing Corp .... F 973 790-1744
Haledon (G-4084)

▼ New Jersey Rivet Co LLC .... F 856 963-2237
Camden (G-1077)

Nylok Corporation .... F 201 427-8555
Hawthorne (G-4250)

Oroszlany Laszlo .... G 201 666-2101
Hillsdale (G-4386)

▲ P & R Fasteners Inc .... D 732 302-3600
Somerset (G-10151)

Pin Cancer Campaign .... G 973 600-4170
Newton (G-7400)

▲ Scheinert & Sons Inc .... E 201 791-4600
Saddle Brook (G-9790)

Shallcross Bolt & Specialties .... E 908 925-4700
Linden (G-5441)

▲ Universal Metalcraft Inc .... E 973 345-3284
Wayne (G-11688)

Wm Hbrewster Jr Incorporated .... G 973 227-1050
Fairfield (G-3353)

Zago Manufacturing Company .... G 973 643-6700
Newark (G-7362)

3462 Iron & Steel Forgings

Able Gear & Machine Co .... G 973 983-8055
Rockaway (G-9541)

▲ All Mtals Frge Group Ltd Lblty .... F 973 276-5000
Fairfield (G-3131)

Atlantic Steel Solutions LLC .... F 973 978-0026
Paterson (G-8217)

Bloomfield Iron Co Inc .... G 973 748-7040
Belleville (G-296)

▲ Hafco Foundry & Machine Co ....F 201 447-0433
Midland Park (G-6228)

JDM Engineering Inc ....G 732 780-0770
Freehold (G-3663)

▲ Kumar & Kumar Inc ....G 732 322-0435
Edison (G-2553)

▲ McWilliams Forge Company ....D 973 627-0200
Rockaway (G-9586)

Mpt Industries ....G 973 989-9220
Dover (G-2102)

Pennsylvania Machine Works Inc ....E 856 467-0500
Swedesboro (G-10717)

▲ Piping Supplies Inc ....G 609 561-9323
Williamstown (G-12096)

▲ PSEG Nuclear LLC ....A 856 339-1002
Hancocks Bridge (G-4167)

▲ Razer Scandinavia Inc ....G 732 441-1250
Matawan (G-6030)

S G Manufacturing Co Inc ....D 732 494-6520
Metuchen (G-6119)

Sigma Engineering & Consulting ....F 732 356-3046
Middlesex (G-6197)

State Tool Gear Co Inc ....F 973 642-6181
Newark (G-7329)

Supply Technologies LLC ....G 201 641-7600
Moonachie (G-6547)

▲ Taurus International Corp ....E 201 825-2420
Ramsey (G-9252)

▲ Titanium Industries Inc ....E 973 983-1185
Rockaway (G-9613)

Wyman-Gordon Forgings Inc ....E 973 627-0200
Rockaway (G-9626)

3463 Nonferrous Forgings

▲ McWilliams Forge Company ....D 973 627-0200
Rockaway (G-9586)

▲ Piping Supplies Inc ....G 609 561-9323
Williamstown (G-12096)

Ramco Manufacturing Co Inc ....E 908 245-4500
Kenilworth (G-4991)

3465 Automotive Stampings

▼ Engine Combo LLC ....F 201 290-4399
Irvington (G-4584)

Robert Freeman ....G 973 751-0082
Belleville (G-315)

▲ Taurus International Corp ....E 201 825-2420
Ramsey (G-9252)

Tonys Auto Entp Ltd Lblty Co ....G 203 223-5776
Edison (G-2639)

3466 Crowns & Closures

Amcor Flexibles LLC ....C 856 825-1400
Millville (G-6275)

3469 Metal Stampings, NEC

▲ A K Stamping Co Inc ....D 908 232-7300
Mountainside (G-6865)

◆ A Plus Products Incorporated ....E 732 866-9111
Marlboro (G-5935)

◆ Accurate Forming LLC ....E 973 827-7155
Hamburg (G-4087)

▲ Accurate Tool & Die Co Inc ....G 201 476-9348
Montvale (G-6440)

▲ Acme Cosmetic Components LLC ..E 718 335-3000
Secaucus (G-9865)

Artistic Hardware ....G 609 383-1909
Northfield (G-7563)

Aspe Inc ....E 973 808-1155
Fairfield (G-3141)

▲ Aspen Manufacturing Co Inc ....G 609 871-6400
Beverly (G-459)

B E C Mfg Corp ....E 201 414-0000
Glen Rock (G-3822)

Be CU Manufacturing Co Inc ....E 908 233-3342
Scotch Plains (G-9847)

Bel-Tech Stamping Inc ....F 973 728-8229
West Milford (G-11851)

Bernardaud Na Inc ....G 973 274-3555
Kearny (G-4864)

Bigelow Components Corp ....E 973 467-1200
Springfield (G-10543)

Bilt Rite Tool & Die Co Inc ....G 973 227-2882
Fairfield (G-3150)

Boyle Tool & Die Co Inc ....F 856 853-1819
West Deptford (G-11818)

Camptown Tool & Die Co Inc ....G 908 688-8406
Kenilworth (G-4947)

▲ Carter Manufacturing Co Inc ....E 201 935-0770
Moonachie (G-6512)

▲ Case Medical Inc ....E 201 313-1999
South Hackensack (G-10257)

▲ Charles E Green & Son Inc ....E 973 485-3630
Newark (G-7120)

Cincinnati Thermal Spray Inc ....E 973 379-0003
Springfield (G-10547)

Clover Stamping Inc ....G 973 278-4888
Paterson (G-8234)

▲ Co-Planar Inc ....F 973 625-3500
Denville (G-2032)

▲ Coining Inc ....G 201 791-4020
Montvale (G-6449)

▲ Coining Holding Company ....F 201 791-4020
Montvale (G-6450)

Coining Manufacturing LLC ....G 973 253-0500
Colts Neck (G-1781)

Coining Mfg ....G 973 253-0500
Clifton (G-1585)

▲ Coining Technologies Inc ....D 866 897-2304
Demarest (G-2027)

Contact Untd TI & Stamping Co ....D 973 256-7171
Woodland Park (G-12216)

Deborah Sales & Mfg Co ....G 973 344-8466
Newark (G-7138)

▲ Durex Inc ....C 908 688-0800
Union (G-11174)

Duron Co Inc ....G 973 242-5704
Newark (G-7145)

Eagle Systems Inc ....G 732 226-2111
Ocean (G-7723)

Eclipse Manufacturing LLC ....G 973 340-9939
Garfield (G-3732)

Electronic Parts Specialty Co ....G 609 267-0055
Mount Holly (G-6769)

Elray Manufacturing Company ....E 856 881-1935
Glassboro (G-3804)

Epi Group Ltd Liability Co ....G 917 710-6607
Lakewood (G-5117)

Extruders International Inc ....G 908 241-7750
Roselle Park (G-9695)

F & G Tool & Die Inc ....G 908 241-5880
Kenilworth (G-4954)

F & M Machine Co Inc ....G 908 245-8830
Kenilworth (G-4955)

F G Clover Company Inc ....G 973 627-1160
Rockaway (G-9565)

Fine Manufacturing Inc ....F 201 880-9136
South Hackensack (G-10268)

◆ Frameware Inc ....F 800 582-5608
Fairfield (G-3201)

G Big Corp ....G 973 242-6521
Newark (G-7167)

General Stamping Co Inc ....F 973 627-9500
Columbia (G-1797)

General Wire & Stamping Co ....F 973 366-8080
Randolph (G-9278)

Geneva Metal Products Co Inc ....F 973 472-3073
Passaic (G-8144)

Golden Metal Products Corp ....E 973 399-1157
Hillside (G-4409)

H & T Tool Co Inc ....F 973 227-4858
Fairfield (G-3214)

▲ H K Metal Craft Mfg Corp ....E 973 471-7770
Lodi (G-5585)

▲ Hafco Foundry & Machine Co ....F 201 447-0433
Midland Park (G-6228)

◆ Heyco Molded Products Inc ....F 732 286-4336
Toms River (G-10884)

Heyco Stamped Products ....D 732 286-4336
Toms River (G-10886)

Hnt Industries Inc ....G 908 322-0414
Scotch Plains (G-9850)

House of Gold Inc ....E 856 665-0020
Pennsauken (G-8524)

Ht Stamping Co LLC ....G 973 227-4858
Fairfield (G-3224)

▼ Infor Metal & Tooling Mfg ....F 973 571-9520
Cedar Grove (G-1285)

International Rollforms Inc ....E 856 228-7100
Deptford (G-2065)

▲ J G Schmidt Co Inc ....G 732 563-9500
Green Brook (G-3859)

J J Orly Inc ....F 908 276-9212
Clark (G-1501)

J R M Products Inc ....G 732 203-0200
Union Beach (G-11238)

Jason Metal Products Corp ....G 732 396-1132
Rahway (G-9203)

Jmk Tool Die and Mfg Co Inc ....G 201 845-4710
Rochelle Park (G-9530)

Jordan Manufacturing LLC ....G 973 383-8363
Lafayette (G-5048)

Joy-Rei Enterprises Inc ....G 732 727-0742
Parlin (G-7934)

K H Machine Works ....G 201 867-2338
North Bergen (G-7459)

Laeger Metal Spinning Co Inc ....G 908 925-5530
Linden (G-5399)

Leibrock Metal Products Inc ....G 732 695-0326
Ocean (G-7731)

LMC Precision Inc ....F 973 522-0005
Newark (G-7222)

Luso Machine Inc ....F 973 242-1717
Newark (G-7228)

Magic Metal Works Inc ....G 201 384-8457
Bergenfield (G-389)

Main Robert A & Sons Holdg Co ....E 201 447-3700
Wyckoff (G-12258)

Manttra Inc ....G 877 962-6887
New Brunswick (G-6978)

Manutech Inc ....G 856 358-6136
Elmer (G-2794)

Mechanical Components Corp ....G 732 938-3737
Toms River (G-10896)

▲ Medlaurel Inc ....G 856 461-6600
Delanco (G-2007)

▲ Metal Cutting Corporation ....D 973 239-1100
Cedar Grove (G-1291)

▲ Micro Stamping Corporation ....C 732 302-0800
Somerset (G-10138)

Minitec Corporation ....G 973 989-1426
Dover (G-2100)

Mjse LLC ....F 201 791-9888
Saddle Brook (G-9776)

Molnar Tools Inc ....F 908 580-0671
Warren (G-11560)

Monroe Tool & Die Inc ....G 856 629-5164
Williamstown (G-12092)

▲ National Manufacturing Co Inc ....C 973 635-8846
Chatham (G-1336)

▲ Newell Brands Inc ....B 201 610-6600
Hoboken (G-4486)

Par Metal Products Inc ....F 201 955-0800
North Arlington (G-7422)

Paramount Products Co Inc ....E 732 458-9200
Brick (G-754)

Pcr Technologies Inc ....G 973 882-0017
Pine Brook (G-8713)

Pepco Manufacturing Co ....D 856 783-3700
Somerdale (G-10042)

Peterson Brothers Mfg Co ....E 732 271-8240
Middlesex (G-6186)

Peterson Stamping & Mfg Co ....F 908 241-0900
Kenilworth (G-4986)

Philip Creter Inc ....G 908 686-2910
Union (G-11215)

Phillips Enterprises Inc ....G 732 493-3191
Ocean (G-7736)

Quality Swiss Screw Machine Co ....G 908 289-4334
Elizabeth (G-2770)

R M F Associates Inc ....C 908 687-9355
Union (G-11218)

▼ Rails Company Inc ....E 973 763-4320
Maplewood (G-5926)

Rapid Manufacturing Co Inc ....G 732 279-1252
Toms River (G-10906)

Rebuth Metal Services ....F 908 889-6400
Fanwood (G-3373)

Roseville Tool & Manufacturing ....E 973 992-5405
Livingston (G-5558)

Rostek Innovations LLC ....G 908 996-6007
Frenchtown (G-3705)

S & W Precision Tool Corp ....F 908 526-6097
Bridgewater (G-885)

▲ S H P C Inc ....G 973 589-5242
Newark (G-7298)

Safeguard Coinbox Inc ....G 973 575-0040
Fairfield (G-3299)

Sandik Manufacturing Inc ....G 973 779-0707
Passaic (G-8179)

Short Run Stamping Company Inc ....E 908 862-1070
Linden (G-5442)

Small Quantities NJ Inc ....D 732 248-9009
Edison (G-2622)

Sofield Manufacturing Co Inc ....G 201 931-1530
Ridgefield Park (G-9414)

Sowa Corp ....G 973 297-0008
Newark (G-7321)

Stampex Corp ....F 973 839-4040
Haskell *(G-4214)*

Stamping Com Inc ....G 732 493-4697
Ocean *(G-7747)*

Stamplus Manufacturing Inc ....F 908 241-8844
Roselle *(G-9683)*

▲ Stirrup Metal Products Corp ....F 973 824-7086
Newark *(G-7330)*

TMU Inc ....F 609 884-7656
Cape May *(G-1106)*

Triform Products Inc ....F 973 278-2042
Pompton Plains *(G-8967)*

Tryco Tool & Mfg Co Inc ....F 973 674-6867
Orange *(G-7831)*

Turul Bookbindery Inc ....F 973 361-2810
Wharton *(G-12003)*

Unilite Incorporated ....F 973 667-1674
Nutley *(G-7656)*

United Industries Inc ....D 973 256-7171
Woodland Park *(G-12236)*

United Spport Slutions-Lmt Inc ....E 973 857-9222
Cedar Grove *(G-1305)*

▲ Universal Tools & Mfg Co ....E 973 379-4193
Springfield *(G-10582)*

V H Exacta Corp 856 235-7379
Moorestown *(G-6629)*

◆ Vigo Industries LLC 866 591-7792
Edison *(G-2646)*

Vulcan Tool Company Inc 908 686-0550
Union *(G-11233)*

▲ Weiss-Aug Co Inc ....C 973 887-7600
East Hanover *(G-2249)*

Well Bilt Industries Inc 908 486-6002
Linden *(G-5458)*

Wgjf Manufacturing Corp ....E 908 862-1730
Linden *(G-5459)*

3471 Electroplating, Plating, Polishing, Anodizing & Coloring

A & F Electroplating Inc ....G 973 983-2459
West Orange *(G-11884)*

A & L Industries Inc ....E 973 589-8070
Newark *(G-7064)*

A&A Company Inc ....E 908 561-2378
South Plainfield *(G-10319)*

Accu-Cote Inc 856 845-7323
Thorofare *(G-10818)*

Acme Engraving Co Inc ....E 973 778-0885
Passaic *(G-8124)*

▲ Advanced Metal Processing ....G 856 327-0048
Millville *(G-6274)*

Aerotech Proc Solutions LLC ....G 973 782-4485
Paterson *(G-8199)*

Alcaro & Alcaro Plating Co ....E 973 746-1200
Montclair *(G-6405)*

All Metal Polishing Co Inc ....E 973 589-8070
Newark *(G-7076)*

Ampal Inc ....G 908 782-5454
Flemington *(G-3426)*

Andarn Electro Service Inc ....E 973 523-2220
Paterson *(G-8212)*

Anodizing Corporation ....G 973 694-6449
Wayne *(G-11605)*

Art Metalcraft Plating Co Inc 215 923-6625
Camden *(G-1042)*

Art Mold & Polishing Co Inc ....F 908 518-9191
Roselle *(G-9661)*

▲ B & M Finishers Inc ....E 908 241-5640
Kenilworth *(G-4940)*

Boyko Metal Finishing Co Inc ....G 973 623-4254
Newark *(G-7111)*

Boyko Metal Finishing Co Inc ....D 973 623-4254
Newark *(G-7110)*

Cameo Metal Products Inc 732 388-4000
Rahway *(G-9180)*

Cemp Inc ....F 732 933-1000
Shrewsbury *(G-9992)*

Cramer Plating Inc 908 453-2887
Buttzville *(G-1020)*

DAngelo Metal Products Inc ....F 908 862-8220
Linden *(G-5367)*

Deptford Plating Co Inc 856 227-1144
Deptford *(G-2063)*

▲ Durex Inc.....................................C 908 688-0800
Union *(G-11174)*

Dynasty Metals Inc 800 225-3962
Kearny *(G-4872)*

E C Electroplating Inc ....E 973 340-0227
Garfield *(G-3731)*

Elkem Inc ....G 732 566-1700
Cliffwood *(G-1546)*

FER Plating Inc ....E 201 438-1010
Lyndhurst *(G-5683)*

▲ Foremost Manufacturing Co Inc ......D 908 687-4646
Union *(G-11185)*

G & H Metal Finishers Inc ....G 201 909-9808
Paterson *(G-8274)*

General Magnaplate California ....F 805 642-6262
Linden *(G-5379)*

General Magnaplate Corporation ......D 908 862-6200
Linden *(G-5380)*

Glasseal Products Inc ....C 732 370-9100
Lakewood *(G-5129)*

▲ Hard Crome Solutions 732 500-2568
Metuchen *(G-6108)*

Hill Cross Co Inc ....G 201 864-3393
West New York *(G-11866)*

Ideal Plating & Polishing Co ....F 973 759-5559
Paterson *(G-8292)*

Independence Plating Corp ....F 973 523-1776
Paterson *(G-8293)*

Industrial Hard Chromium Co ....F 973 344-2265
Newark *(G-7196)*

Intrepid Industries Inc 908 534-5300
Lebanon *(G-5291)*

J R S Tool & Metal Finishing 908 753-2050
South Plainfield *(G-10387)*

Kenilworth Anodizing Co 908 241-5640
Kenilworth *(G-4968)*

Madan Plastics Inc 908 276-8484
Cranford *(G-1913)*

Manco Plating Incorporated 973 485-6800
Newark *(G-7234)*

Mara Polishing & Plating Corp ....G 973 242-0800
Newark *(G-7236)*

Master Metal Polishing Corp ....E 973 684-0119
Paterson *(G-8333)*

Mastercraft Metal Finishing ....G 908 354-4404
Elizabeth *(G-2756)*

Metal Finishing Co LLC ....E 973 778-9550
Passaic *(G-8164)*

Miller & Son 973 759-6445
Belleville *(G-307)*

Mold Polishing Company Inc ....G 908 518-9191
Garwood *(G-3779)*

▲ National Mtal Fnshngs Corp Inc ......F 732 752-7770
Middlesex *(G-6183)*

New Brunswick Plating Inc ....D 732 545-6522
New Brunswick *(G-6987)*

Paramount Metal Finishing Co ....C 908 862-0772
Linden *(G-5424)*

▲ Paramount Plating Co Inc 908 862-0772
Linden *(G-5425)*

Patel Metal Plating Inc 732 574-1770
Edison *(G-2593)*

Platinum Plating Specialists 732 221-2575
Clark *(G-1513)*

Polaris Plating Inc ....G 973 278-0033
Parsippany *(G-8069)*

Prem-Khichi Enterprises Inc ....F 973 242-0300
East Brunswick *(G-2174)*

Productive Industrial Finshg ....G 856 427-9646
Voorhees *(G-11436)*

Programatic Platers Inc ....F 718 721-4330
Tenafly *(G-10786)*

Sar Industrial Finishing Inc ....F 609 567-2772
Berlin *(G-441)*

Stainless Stock 732 564-1164
Middlesex *(G-6202)*

▲ Stirrup Metal Products Corp ....F 973 824-7086
Newark *(G-7330)*

Suffern Plating Corp ....E 973 473-4404
Lodi *(G-5604)*

Sun Metal Finishing Inc ....E 973 684-0119
North Haledon *(G-7554)*

Super Chrome Inc ....G 732 774-2210
Asbury Park *(G-85)*

Tolan Polishing Corp ....G 973 983-7212
Rockaway *(G-9617)*

Tomken Plating 856 829-0607
Cinnaminson *(G-1493)*

Trb Electro Corp ....E 973 278-9014
Paterson *(G-8401)*

Vanguard Research Industries ....E 908 753-2770
South Plainfield *(G-10450)*

Vigilant Design 201 432-3900
Jersey City *(G-4843)*

▼ Water Master Co ....G 732 247-1900
Highland Park *(G-4305)*

▲ Zsombor Antal Designs Inc...........F 201 225-1750
River Edge *(G-9468)*

3479 Coating & Engraving, NEC

A S A P Nameplate & Labeling ....F 973 773-3934
Passaic *(G-8122)*

A Smith & Son Inc ....G 609 747-0800
Burlington *(G-952)*

▲ Abco Die Casters Inc ....D 973 624-7030
Newark *(G-7070)*

Acme Engraving Co Inc ....E 973 778-0885
Passaic *(G-8124)*

All American Powdercoating LLC .....G 732 349-7001
Toms River *(G-10861)*

▲ Alpha Processing Co Inc ....E 973 777-1737
Clifton *(G-1562)*

American Galvanizing Co Inc ....D 609 567-2090
Hammonton *(G-4128)*

◆ Andek Corporation ....F 856 866-7600
Moorestown *(G-6560)*

American Metalworks Inc.................E 973 777-2105
Passaic *(G-8125)*

Atlantic Eqp Engineers Inc ....F 201 828-9400
Upper Saddle River *(G-11273)*

▲ Awards Trophy Company ....G 908 687-5775
Hillside *(G-4394)*

Bannister Company Inc 732 828-1353
Milltown *(G-6267)*

◆ Bel-Art Products Inc ....E 973 694-0500
Wayne *(G-11608)*

Boyko Metal Finishing Co Inc ....D 973 623-4254
Newark *(G-7110)*

▲ Brodie System Inc ....F 908 862-8620
Linden *(G-5354)*

◆ Cardolite Corporation ....E 609 436-0902
Monmouth Junction *(G-6335)*

Ceronics Inc ....G 732 566-5600
Matawan *(G-6015)*

Chapter Enterprises Inc ....G 732 560-8500
Bridgewater *(G-827)*

Cincinnati Thermal Spray Inc 973 379-0003
Springfield *(G-10547)*

CRS Ink Intl Ltd Lblty Co 732 817-0401
Holmdel *(G-4514)*

Diamond Hut Jewelry Exchange ......G 201 332-5372
Jersey City *(G-4743)*

Dynamic Coatings LLC 732 998-6625
Matawan *(G-6019)*

Ferro Corporation 908 226-2148
South Plainfield *(G-10364)*

Flexcraft Industries Inc...................G 973 589-3403
Newark *(G-7163)*

Foster Engraving Corporation ....G 201 489-5979
Hackensack *(G-3918)*

Gary R Banks Industrial Group ....F 856 687-2227
West Berlin *(G-11723)*

General Magnaplate California ....F 805 642-6262
Linden *(G-5379)*

General Magnaplate Corporation ......D 908 862-6200
Linden *(G-5380)*

General Magnaplate Wisconsin ....F 800 441-6173
Linden *(G-5381)*

General Plastics Group ....E 973 748-5500
Bloomfield *(G-512)*

Heros Salute Awards Co ....G 973 696-5085
Wayne *(G-11648)*

Hot Dip Galvanizing ....G 732 442-7555
Perth Amboy *(G-8618)*

▲ I V Miller & Sons Inc ....F 732 493-4040
Ocean *(G-7728)*

▲ Innovative Powder Coatings LLC .....G 856 661-0086
Pennsauken *(G-8527)*

Isometric Micro Finish Coating ....G 732 306-6339
Edison *(G-2542)*

Jema-American Inc ....G 732 968-5333
Middlesex *(G-6172)*

Koehler Industries Inc ....E 732 364-2700
Howell *(G-4559)*

Lantier Construction Company ....E 856 780-6366
Moorestown *(G-6592)*

Lordon Inc 908 813-1143
Hackettstown *(G-4018)*

Microsurfaces Inc ....G 201 408-5596
Englewood *(G-2916)*

New Jrsy Glvnzng & Tnnng Wks ....D 973 242-3200
Newark *(G-7251)*

Newark Industrial Spraying ....F 973 344-6855
Newark *(G-7254)*

Nicholas Galvanizing Co Inc ....E 201 795-1010
Jersey City *(G-4789)*

S
I
C

Paramount Metal Finishing Co ....C 908 862-0772
Linden *(G-5424)*
Peerless Coatings LLC ....E 973 427-8771
Hawthorne *(G-4252)*
Penn Metal Finishing Co Inc ....G 609 387-3400
Burlington *(G-987)*
Phoenix Powder Coating LLC ....E 973 907-7500
Haskell *(G-4212)*
▲ Plastics Consulting & Mfg Co ....E 800 222-0317
Camden *(G-1082)*
Powtek Powder Coating Inc ....G 609 394-1144
Ewing *(G-3044)*
Productive Industrial Finshg ....G 856 427-9646
Voorhees *(G-11436)*
S D L Powder Coating Inc ....E 732 473-0800
Toms River *(G-10907)*
Shore Bet Painting and Cnstr ....G 732 996-3455
Bay Head *(G-209)*
▲ Superior Powder Coating Inc ....C 908 351-8707
Elizabeth *(G-2777)*
Technical Nameplate Corp ....E 973 773-4256
Passaic *(G-8184)*
Tresky Corp ....E 732 536-8600
Morganville *(G-6653)*
United Label Corp ....E 973 589-6500
Newark *(G-7354)*
Voigt & Schweitzer LLC ....D 732 442-7555
Perth Amboy *(G-8636)*
W & E Baum Bronze Tablet Corp ....E 732 866-1881
Freehold *(G-3692)*
Weiler & Sons LLC ....G 856 767-8842
Berlin *(G-445)*
▲ Winters Stamp Mfg Co Inc ....F 908 352-3725
Martinsville *(G-6011)*

3482 Small Arms Ammunition

▲ Lightfield Ammunition Corp ....G 732 462-9200
Freehold *(G-3667)*

3483 Ammunition, Large

▲ Lightfield Ammunition Corp ....G 732 462-9200
Freehold *(G-3667)*

3484 Small Arms

2a Holdings Inc ....F 973 378-8011
Maplewood *(G-5913)*
▲ Henry RAC Holding Corp ....D 201 858-4400
Bayonne *(G-231)*
Way It Was Sporting Svc Inc ....G 856 231-0111
Moorestown *(G-6631)*

3489 Ordnance & Access, NEC

American Aluminum Company ....D 908 233-3500
Mountainside *(G-6868)*
Cartridge Actuated Devices ....E 973 347-2281
Byram Township *(G-1021)*
Eastern Regional Waterway ....F 732 684-0409
Brick *(G-743)*
Kongsberg Protech ....G 973 770-0574
Mount Arlington *(G-6756)*

3491 Industrial Valves

Admiral Technology LLC ....E 973 698-5920
Rockaway *(G-9544)*
American Products Company Inc ....D 908 687-4100
Union *(G-11152)*
▲ Armadillo Automation Inc ....E 856 829-2888
Cinnaminson *(G-1447)*
◆ Asco LP ....B 800 972-2726
Florham Park *(G-3483)*
▲ Asco Valve LLC ....D 973 966-2437
Florham Park *(G-3488)*
▲ Automatic Switch Company ....A 973 966-2000
Florham Park *(G-3489)*
Automatic Switch Company ....A 209 941-4111
Florham Park *(G-3490)*
Automatic Switch Company ....F 732 596-1731
Woodbridge *(G-12146)*
Barworth Inc ....G 973 376-4883
Springfield *(G-10541)*
▲ Bio-Chem Fluidics Inc ....D 973 263-3001
Boonton *(G-557)*
▲ Carpathian Industries LLC ....F 201 386-5356
Hoboken *(G-4463)*
▲ Cavagna North America Inc ....E 732 469-2100
Somerset *(G-10080)*
Chase Machine Co ....F 201 438-2214
Lyndhurst *(G-5677)*

Chemiquip Products Co Inc ....G 201 868-4445
Linden *(G-5359)*
Emerson Automation Solutions ....F 856 542-5252
Bridgeport *(G-763)*
▲ Farrell Eqp & Contrls Inc ....F 732 770-4142
Roselle *(G-9669)*
Firefighter One Ltd Lblty Co ....G 973 940-3061
Sparta *(G-10499)*
Fisher Service Co ....G 609 386-5000
Burlington *(G-973)*
Flodyne Controls Inc ....G 908 464-6200
New Providence *(G-7035)*
▲ Gadren Machine Co Inc ....F 856 456-4329
Mount Ephraim *(G-6763)*
Gasflo Products Inc ....E 973 276-9011
Fairfield *(G-3207)*
Gemco Valve Co LLC ....E 732 752-7900
Middlesex *(G-6168)*
◆ Generant Company Inc ....C 814 337-0380
Butler *(G-1004)*
▲ Haier Appliance Products LP ....G 973 617-1800
Wayne *(G-11645)*
◆ Hayward Industrial Products ....C 908 351-5400
Elizabeth *(G-2741)*
▲ Heat-Timer Corporation ....E 973 575-4004
Fairfield *(G-3218)*
▲ Industrial Habonim Valves & AC ....F 201 820-3184
Wayne *(G-11650)*
Instrment Vlve Svcs Burlington ....G 609 386-5000
Burlington *(G-978)*
Magnatrol Valve Corporation ....E 973 427-4341
Hawthorne *(G-4246)*
Magnatrol Valve Corporation ....F 856 829-4580
Roebling *(G-9638)*
Micromat Co ....E 201 529-3738
Ringwood *(G-9452)*
Neptune Research & Development ....E 973 808-8811
West Caldwell *(G-11792)*
▲ O Plast Matic Valves Inc ....D 973 256-3000
Cedar Grove *(G-1293)*
Parker-Hannifin Corporation ....E 973 575-4844
Pine Brook *(G-8712)*
Picut Industries Inc ....D 908 754-1333
Warren *(G-11562)*
Purity Labs ....G 201 372-0236
East Rutherford *(G-2320)*
◆ Simple Home Automation Inc ....C 877 405-2397
Edison *(G-2618)*
◆ Tyco International MGT Co LLC ....E 609 720-4200
Princeton *(G-9133)*
Wm Steinen Mfg Co ....D 973 887-6400
Parsippany *(G-8116)*

3492 Fluid Power Valves & Hose Fittings

A V Hydraulics Ltd Lblty Co ....G 973 621-6800
Newark *(G-7066)*
Air & Hydraulic Power Inc ....G 201 447-1589
Wyckoff *(G-12244)*
▲ American Hose Hydraulic Co Inc ....E 973 684-3225
Paterson *(G-8208)*
▲ Asco Valve LLC ....D 973 966-2437
Florham Park *(G-3488)*
▲ Automatic Switch Company ....A 973 966-2000
Florham Park *(G-3489)*
▲ Gadren Machine Co Inc ....F 856 456-4329
Mount Ephraim *(G-6763)*
◆ Hayward Industrial Products ....C 908 351-5400
Elizabeth *(G-2741)*
Industrial Hydraulics & Rubber ....C 856 966-2600
Camden *(G-1070)*
Novaflex Industries Inc ....F 856 768-2275
West Berlin *(G-11739)*
Parker-Hannifin Corporation ....E 973 575-4844
Pine Brook *(G-8712)*
Robert H Hoover & Sons Inc ....G 973 347-4210
Flanders *(G-3414)*
▲ Universal Valve Company Inc ....F 908 351-0606
Elizabeth *(G-2780)*
▲ Valcor Engineering Corporation ....C 973 467-8400
Springfield *(G-10583)*
▲ Versa Products Company Inc ....C 201 291-0379
Paramus *(G-7912)*
▲ Westlock Controls Corporation ....C 201 794-7650
Saddle Brook *(G-9800)*

3493 Steel Springs, Except Wire

Matthew Warren Inc ....F 908 788-5800
Ringoes *(G-9440)*
◆ Sealy Mattress Co N J Inc ....C 973 345-8800
Paterson *(G-8381)*

Spring Eureka Co Inc ....E 973 589-4960
Newark *(G-7326)*

3494 Valves & Pipe Fittings, NEC

▲ Ammark Corporation ....G 973 616-2555
Pompton Plains *(G-8952)*
▲ Ceodeux Incorporated ....E 724 696-4340
Hackettstown *(G-4000)*
▲ CP Test & Valve Products Inc ....G 201 998-1500
Kearny *(G-4868)*
DAngelo Metal Products Inc ....F 908 862-8220
Linden *(G-5367)*
Dason Stainless Products Co ....F 732 382-7272
Rahway *(G-9183)*
▲ Durst Corporation Inc ....E 800 852-3906
Cranford *(G-1903)*
▲ Everflow Supplies Inc ....E 908 436-1100
Carteret *(G-1256)*
▼ Everlasting Valve Company Inc ....E 908 769-0700
South Plainfield *(G-10359)*
▲ Exclusive Materials LLC ....G 732 886-9956
Lakewood *(G-5119)*
Fluidyne Corp ....E 856 663-1818
Pennsauken *(G-8510)*
▲ Gadren Machine Co Inc ....F 856 456-4329
Mount Ephraim *(G-6763)*
Gasflo Products Inc ....E 973 276-9011
Fairfield *(G-3207)*
Gorton Heating Corp ....E 908 276-1323
Cranford *(G-1909)*
◆ Hayward Industrial Products ....C 908 351-5400
Elizabeth *(G-2741)*
◆ Hayward Industries Inc ....C 908 351-5400
Elizabeth *(G-2742)*
Holby Valve Co Inc ....F 973 465-7400
Newark *(G-7190)*
Imperial Weld Ring Corp Inc ....E 908 354-0011
Elizabeth *(G-2746)*
Knickerbocker Machine Shop Inc ....D 973 256-1616
Totowa *(G-10953)*
Kraissl Company Inc ....E 201 342-0008
Hackensack *(G-3937)*
Lindstrom & King Co Inc ....G 973 279-2511
Paterson *(G-8321)*
▲ Marotta Controls Inc ....C 973 334-7800
Montville *(G-6490)*
Newco Valves LLC ....E 732 257-0300
East Brunswick *(G-2169)*
Nippon Benkan Kagyo ....E 732 435-0777
New Brunswick *(G-6988)*
Pennsylvania Machine Works Inc ....E 856 467-0500
Swedesboro *(G-10717)*
▲ Piping Supplies Inc ....E 609 561-9323
Williamstown *(G-12096)*
Primak Plumbing & Heating Inc ....G 732 270-6282
Toms River *(G-10904)*
Ramco Manufacturing Co Inc ....E 908 245-4500
Kenilworth *(G-4991)*
RGI Inc ....F 973 697-2624
Newfoundland *(G-7376)*
Scientific Machine and Sup Co ....E 732 356-1553
Middlesex *(G-6195)*
◆ Sigma International Group Inc ....F 609 758-0800
Cream Ridge *(G-1941)*
Sims Pump Valve Company Inc ....E 201 792-0600
Hoboken *(G-4496)*
Symcon Inc ....G 973 728-8661
West Milford *(G-11857)*
Syntiro Dynamics LLC ....G 732 377-3307
Wall Township *(G-11513)*
Taylor Forge Stainless Inc ....D 908 722-1313
Branchburg *(G-708)*
Tkl Specialty Piping Inc ....G 908 454-0030
Phillipsburg *(G-8674)*
◆ Vac-U-Max ....E 973 759-4600
Belleville *(G-322)*
▲ Wire Cloth Manufacturers Inc ....E 973 328-1000
Mine Hill *(G-6329)*
Wm Steinen Mfg Co ....D 973 887-6400
Parsippany *(G-8116)*
▲ World Wide Metric Inc ....F 732 247-2300
Branchburg *(G-719)*

3495 Wire Springs

Matthew Warren Inc ....F 908 788-5800
Ringoes *(G-9440)*
Spring Eureka Co Inc ....E 973 589-4960
Newark *(G-7326)*

3496 Misc Fabricated Wire Prdts

Accent Fence Inc ....E...... 609 965-6400
Egg Harbor City (G-2655)
Ace Electronics Inc........................D...... 732 603-9800
Metuchen (G-6093)
Acme Wire Forming LLC...............F...... 201 218-2912
Kinnelon (G-5032)
▲ Allentown Inc............................B...... 609 259-7951
Allentown (G-28)
Alpine Group Inc...........................F...... 201 549-4400
East Rutherford (G-2275)
▼ Aw Machinery LLC.....................F...... 973 882-3223
Fairfield (G-3142)
▲ Bamboo & Rattan Works Inc............G...... 732 255-4239
Toms River (G-10866)
Belden Inc......................................F...... 908 925-8000
Elizabeth (G-2712)
◆ Belleville Wire Cloth Co Inc ....E...... 973 239-0074
Cedar Grove (G-1272)
Belmont Whl Fence Mfg Inc............E...... 973 472-5121
Garfield (G-3723)
▲ Better Sleep Inc ....F...... 908 464-2200
Branchburg (G-643)
Blue Claw Mfg & Supply Company....G...... 856 696-4366
Richland (G-9349)
Boyle Tool & Die Co Inc ....E...... 856 853-1819
West Deptford (G-11818)
▲ Brown and Perkins Inc...............F...... 609 655-1150
Cranbury (G-1816)
▲ Carl Stahl Sava Industries Inc....D...... 973 835-0882
Riverdale (G-9477)
Cerbaco Ltd ....E...... 908 996-1333
Frenchtown (G-3699)
◆ Clements Industries Inc.............E...... 201 440-5500
South Hackensack (G-10258)
Compass Wire Cloth & ....E...... 856 853-7616
Vineland (G-11339)
▲ Compass Wire Cloth Corp ....E...... 856 853-7616
Vineland (G-11340)
Consolidated Stl Alum Fence Inc..........E...... 908 272-0494
Kenilworth (G-4948)
▲ Dearborn A Belden Cdt Company..D...... 908 925-8000
Elizabeth (G-2723)
Deborah Sales & Mfg Co ....G...... 973 344-8466
Newark (G-7138)
◆ Delair LLC.................................D...... 856 663-2900
Pennsauken (G-8502)
Doran Sling and Assembly Corp ....G...... 908 355-1101
Hillside (G-4406)
▲ Ecocom Inc...............................G...... 201 393-0786
Montvale (G-6454)
Edwin R Burger & Son Inc ....E...... 856 468-2300
Sewell (G-9952)
Evergard Steel Corp ....F...... 908 925-6800
South Plainfield (G-10358)
▲ Fisk Alloy Conductors Inc..........C...... 973 825-8500
Hawthorne (G-4233)
Fisk Alloy Inc................................E...... 973 427-7550
Hawthorne (G-4234)
◆ Fisk Alloy Wire Incorporated .....C...... 973 949-4491
Hawthorne (G-4235)
Form Cut Industries Inc..................E...... 973 483-5154
Newark (G-7165)
Gabhen Inc ....G...... 973 256-0666
Totowa (G-10946)
▲ General Metal Manufacturing Co......E...... 973 386-1818
East Hanover (G-2218)
General Wire & Stamping Co ....F...... 973 366-8080
Randolph (G-9278)
◆ Gentek Inc.................................C...... 973 515-0900
Parsippany (G-8024)
▲ High Energy Group Ltd Lblty Co....G...... 732 741-9099
Eatontown (G-2400)
▲ Jcc Military Supply LLC...............G...... 973 341-1314
Paterson (G-8301)
▲ Jersey Strand & Cable Inc..........D...... 908 213-9350
Phillipsburg (G-8654)
M P M Display Inc...........................F...... 973 374-3477
Irvington (G-4597)
Main Robert A & Sons Holdg Co ....E...... 201 447-3700
Wyckoff (G-12258)
Master Wire Manufacturing Co ....F...... 609 561-2900
Hammonton (G-4144)
▲ Metal Textiles Corporation ....D...... 732 287-0800
Edison (G-2569)
New Jersey Wire Cloth Co Inc ....G...... 973 340-0101
Clifton (G-1681)
▲ Newark Wire Cloth Company ......E...... 973 778-4478
Clifton (G-1683)

Newark Wire Works Inc ....E...... 732 661-2001
Edison (G-2580)
Phillips Enterprises Inc ....G...... 732 493-3191
Ocean (G-7736)
▲ Plasti-Clad Metal Products Inc ....F...... 732 449-2665
Wall Township (G-11503)
Precision Ball Specialties ....F...... 856 881-5646
Williamstown (G-12099)
Robert J Donaldson Inc..................F...... 856 629-2737
Williamstown (G-12104)
Robert Main Sons Inc ....E...... 201 447-3700
Fair Lawn (G-3110)
Security Fabricators Inc.................F...... 908 272-9171
Kenilworth (G-4996)
Seminole Wire & Cable Co Inc ....F...... 856 324-2929
Pennsauken (G-8577)
▲ Skorr Products LLC....................F...... 973 523-2606
Paterson (G-8383)
▲ Unique Wire Weaving Co Inc ....E...... 908 688-4600
Hillside (G-4447)
▲ Vibration Muntings Contrls Inc........D...... 800 569-8423
Bloomingdale (G-545)
▲ Vis USA LLC ....E...... 908 575-0606
Branchburg (G-716)
▼ William Kenyon & Sons Inc ....E...... 732 985-8980
Piscataway (G-8836)
▲ Wire Cloth Manufacturers Inc ....E...... 973 328-1000
Mine Hill (G-6329)
Wire Displays Inc ....F...... 973 537-0090
Dover (G-2114)
Wire Fabricators & Insulators........G...... 973 768-2839
Livingston (G-5572)
Wytech Industries Inc....................D...... 732 396-3900
Rahway (G-9228)

3497 Metal Foil & Leaf

Amcor Flexibles Inc.......................E...... 609 267-5900
Mount Holly (G-6766)
API Americas Inc...........................D...... 732 382-6800
Rahway (G-9174)
Constantia Blythewood LLC............D...... 732 974-4100
Belmar (G-356)
▲ Crown Roll Leaf Inc ....C...... 973 742-4000
Paterson (G-8241)
◆ Glitterex Corp............................D...... 908 272-9121
Cranford (G-1908)
▲ Hueck Foils Holding Co..............D...... 732 974-4100
Wall Township (G-11489)
▲ Materials Technology Inc ....D...... 732 246-1000
Somerset (G-10131)
◆ Revere Industries LLC................C...... 856 881-3600
Clayton (G-1527)
Spectrum Foils Inc.........................G...... 973 481-0808
Newark (G-7324)

3498 Fabricated Pipe & Pipe Fittings

A&M Industrial Inc ....F...... 908 862-1800
Avenel (G-121)
Belden Inc......................................F...... 908 925-8000
Elizabeth (G-2712)
Bemis Company Inc........................B...... 908 689-3000
Washington (G-11577)
▲ Century Tube Corp.....................E...... 908 534-2001
Somerville (G-10204)
Coolenheat Inc...............................E...... 908 925-4473
Kendall Park (G-4934)
▲ Custom Alloy Corporation ....C...... 908 638-0257
High Bridge (G-4294)
▲ Esco Industries Corp.................F...... 973 478-5888
Woodcliff Lake (G-12191)
Euro Mechanical Inc ....F...... 201 313-8050
Fairview (G-3361)
▲ Fluorotherm Polymers Inc ....G...... 973 575-0760
Parsippany (G-8014)
▼ Foodline Piping Products Co.........G...... 856 767-1177
West Berlin (G-11720)
Fox Steel Products LLC ....G...... 856 778-4661
Mount Laurel (G-6799)
▲ G & J Steel & Tubing Inc.............D...... 908 526-4445
Hillsborough (G-4334)
Handytube Corporation...................E...... 732 469-7420
Middlesex (G-6169)
Imperial Weld Ring Corp Inc............E...... 908 354-0011
Elizabeth (G-2746)
Jettron Products Inc ....E...... 973 887-0571
East Hanover (G-2226)
M P Tube Works Inc ....G...... 908 317-2500
Mountainside (G-6883)
Piping Solutions Inc.......................F...... 732 537-1009
Bridgewater (G-875)

Precision Mfg Group LLC................D...... 973 785-4630
Cedar Grove (G-1296)
Royal Seamless Corporation..........F...... 732 901-9595
Lakewood (G-5186)
S&W Fabricators Inc.......................G...... 856 881-7418
Glassboro (G-3811)
Samstubend Inc ....F...... 973 278-2555
Paterson (G-8376)
Selling Precision Inc......................E...... 973 728-1214
West Milford (G-11856)
Symcon Inc....................................G...... 973 728-8661
West Milford (G-11857)
Tube Craft of America Inc...............G...... 856 629-5626
Williamstown (G-12110)
▲ U V International LLC..................F...... 973 993-9454
Morristown (G-6747)

3499 Fabricated Metal Prdts, NEC

A Kessler Kreation Inc....................G...... 732 431-2468
Colts Neck (G-1779)
Advanced Precision Systems LLC........G...... 908 730-8892
High Bridge (G-4293)
All State Medal Co Inc ....G...... 973 458-1458
Lodi (G-5575)
Apogee Technologies LLC...............F...... 973 575-8448
Towaco (G-10987)
▲ Awards Trophy Company ....G...... 908 687-5775
Hillside (G-4394)
◆ Cardolite Corporation ....E...... 609 436-0902
Monmouth Junction (G-6335)
Cargille-Sacher Labs Inc ....F...... 973 267-8888
Cedar Knolls (G-1308)
Cold Headed Fasteners Inc.............G...... 856 461-3244
Delanco (G-2004)
◆ Crestron Electronics Inc............C...... 201 767-3400
Rockleigh (G-9628)
▲ D K Trading Inc..........................G...... 856 225-1130
Camden (G-1058)
Escadaus Inc ....G...... 973 335-8888
Boonton (G-567)
Fan of Word ....G...... 201 341-5474
South Orange (G-10305)
▲ Faps Inc.....................................C...... 973 589-5656
Newark (G-7160)
Garden State Highway Pdts Inc........E...... 856 692-7572
Millville (G-6303)
Gbw Manufacturing Inc...................E...... 973 279-0077
Totowa (G-10947)
Go R Design LLC............................E...... 609 286-2146
New Egypt (G-7015)
▲ Hamon Corporation ....D...... 908 333-2000
Somerville (G-10213)
Hookway Enterprises Inc ....F...... 973 691-0382
Netcong (G-6941)
Hurricane Hutch ....G...... 908 256-5912
Chester (G-1437)
▲ Icup Inc.....................................G...... 856 751-2045
Cherry Hill (G-1376)
▲ III Eagle Enterprises Ltd.............E...... 973 237-1111
Ringwood (G-9449)
Intermark Inc ....G...... 908 474-1311
Linden (G-5390)
Ironbound Metal ....G...... 973 242-5704
Newark (G-7200)
▲ Julius E Holland-Moritz Co Inc........G...... 609 397-1231
Lambertville (G-5215)
▲ Kraftware Corporation................E...... 732 345-7091
Roselle (G-9674)
Lighthouse Express Inc ....G...... 732 776-9555
Asbury Park (G-80)
NJ Logo Wear LLC...........................G...... 609 597-9400
Manahawkin (G-5832)
▲ Norco Inc...................................E...... 908 789-1550
Garwood (G-3781)
▲ Permadur Industries Inc.............D...... 908 359-9767
Hillsborough (G-4362)
Pipe Dreams Marine LLC.................G...... 609 628-9353
Tuckahoe (G-11137)
R A O Contract Sales NY Inc............D...... 201 652-1500
Paterson (G-8367)
Raceweld Co Inc ....G...... 908 236-6533
Lebanon (G-5300)
Research and Pvd Materials ....G...... 973 575-4245
Fairfield (G-3293)
RISE Corporation ....E...... 973 575-7480
West Caldwell (G-11804)
Safe Man LLC ....G...... 800 320-2589
Alpha (G-45)
Tricomp Inc....................................C...... 973 835-1110
Pompton Plains (G-8966)

◆ Tropar Manufacturing Co Inc ....E 973 765-0380
Florham Park *(G-3519)*

▲ Tropar Trophy Manufacturing Co .....D ... 973 822-2400
Florham Park *(G-3520)*

Uac Packaging LLC ....G 908 595-6890
Hillsborough *(G-4378)*

▼ United Hospital Supply Corp ....C 609 387-7580
Burlington *(G-993)*

▲ Versabar Corporation ....F 973 279-8400
Totowa *(G-10979)*

Whimsy Diddles LLC ....G 609 560-1323
Chesilhurst *(G-1431)*

Williams Scotsman Inc ....G 856 429-0315
Kearny *(G-4922)*

Wm Hbrewster Jr Incorporated ....G 973 227-1050
Fairfield *(G-3353)*

Zodiac Paintball Inc ....G 973 616-7230
Pompton Plains *(G-8970)*

35 INDUSTRIAL AND COMMERCIAL MACHINERY AND COMPUTER EQUIPMENT

3511 Steam, Gas & Hydraulic Turbines & Engines

Babcock & Wilcox Company ....G 609 261-2424
Cinnaminson *(G-1448)*

Babcock & Wilcox Powr Generatn ....F 973 227-7008
Fairfield *(G-3143)*

▲ Boc Group Inc ....A 908 665-2400
New Providence *(G-7030)*

▲ Hydro-Mechanical Systems Inc ....F 856 848-8888
Westville *(G-11943)*

I4 Sustainability LLC ....G 732 618-3310
Springfield *(G-10557)*

Linde LLC ....G 973 579-2065
Sparta *(G-10510)*

Linde North America Inc ....D 908 464-8100
New Providence *(G-7045)*

▼ Linde North America Inc ....B 908 464-8100
Bridgewater *(G-857)*

Lummus Overseas Corporation ....E 973 893-3000
Bloomfield *(G-520)*

Micheller & Son Hydraulics Inc ....F 908 687-1545
Roselle *(G-9677)*

Ocean Energy Industries Inc ....F 954 828-2177
Oakhurst *(G-7671)*

Polaris America Ltd Lblty Co ....E 614 540-1710
Lakewood *(G-5174)*

Solar Turbines Incorporated ....F 201 825-8200
Upper Saddle River *(G-11285)*

3519 Internal Combustion Engines, NEC

Arrow Machine Company Inc...............G 973 642-2430
Newark *(G-7095)*

Barbs Harley-Davidson ....E 856 456-4141
Mount Ephraim *(G-6762)*

Cast Technology Inc ....G 908 753-5155
South Plainfield *(G-10344)*

Coates International Ltd ....G 732 449-7717
Wall Township *(G-11472)*

Cummins - Allison Corp ....G 201 791-2394
Elmwood Park *(G-2813)*

Cummins Inc ....D 973 491-0100
Kearny *(G-4870)*

Davis Hyundai ....F 609 883-3500
Ewing *(G-3013)*

Grobet File Company Amer LLC ....D 201 939-6700
Carlstadt *(G-1165)*

Henry Jackson Racing Engines ....G 609 758-7476
Cream Ridge *(G-1936)*

Melton Sales & Service ....E 609 699-4800
Bordentown *(G-602)*

Melton Sales & Service ....E 609 699-4800
Columbus *(G-1805)*

◆ Ocean Power & Equipment Co..........G 973 575-5775
West Caldwell *(G-11793)*

Penn Power Group LLC ....F 732 441-1489
Matawan *(G-6028)*

Penske Truck Leasing Co LP ....E 973 575-0169
Parsippany *(G-8060)*

Roy Anania ....G 201 498-1555
Hackensack *(G-3967)*

3523 Farm Machinery & Eqpt

3 IS Technologies Inc ....G 609 238-8213
Hainesport *(G-4067)*

Case Davenport Inc ....G 973 812-7180
Little Falls *(G-5473)*

Edward Brown ....G 973 887-5255
East Hanover *(G-2214)*

Ferratex Services Inc ....E 973 609-5449
Livingston *(G-5529)*

Kinnery Precision LLC ....G 973 473-4664
Passaic *(G-8155)*

▼ Plant Food Company Inc ....F 609 448-0935
Cranbury *(G-1870)*

South Jersey Farmers Exchange ....G 856 769-0062
Woodstown *(G-12240)*

Steve Green Enterprises ....F 732 938-5572
Farmingdale *(G-3394)*

Tifa International LLC ....F 908 647-4570
Hillsborough *(G-4377)*

3524 Garden, Lawn Tractors & Eqpt

Creative Products Inc ....D 732 614-9035
Long Branch *(G-5622)*

Lawn Medic Inc ....G 856 742-1111
Westville *(G-11945)*

McQuade Enterprises LLC ....G 609 501-2437
Millville *(G-6313)*

Robert Colaneri ....G 201 939-4405
East Rutherford *(G-2321)*

W W Manufacturing Co Inc ....F 856 451-5700
Bridgeton *(G-802)*

3531 Construction Machinery & Eqpt

Bestwall LLC ....D 856 966-7600
Camden *(G-1044)*

▲ Breeze-Eastern LLC ....G 973 602-1001
Whippany *(G-12014)*

Breeze-Eastern LLC ....G 973 602-1001
Whippany *(G-12015)*

Busted Knuckle ....G 609 432-7383
Marmora *(G-6005)*

Clark Equipment Company ....A 973 618-2500
Pine Brook *(G-8694)*

Cornell Crane Mfg Ltd ....F 609 742-1900
Westville *(G-11937)*

Corrview International LLC ....G 973 770-0571
Hopatcong *(G-4535)*

County of Warren ....D 908 475-7975
Belvidere *(G-368)*

▲ Custom Converters Inc ....G 201 994-9000
Livingston *(G-5527)*

Dougherty Foundation Products..........G 201 337-5748
Franklin Lakes *(G-3615)*

Dragon Asphalt Equipment LLC ....F 732 922-9290
Lakewood *(G-5110)*

Elite Landscaping & Pavers ....G 732 252-6152
Freehold *(G-3653)*

F and M Equipment Ltd ....D 215 822-0145
South Plainfield *(G-10362)*

Fred McDowell Inc ....G 732 681-5000
Wall Township *(G-11484)*

G & A Pavers Llc ....G 201 562-5947
Englewood *(G-2899)*

Hackettstown Public Works ....G 908 852-2320
Hackettstown *(G-4010)*

Hart Construction Service ....G 908 537-2060
Asbury *(G-70)*

Infrastructure LLC ....G 609 748-1229
Galloway *(G-3712)*

Ingersoll-Rand Company ....E 856 793-7000
Mount Laurel *(G-6803)*

Ingersoll-Rand Intl Inc ....G 559 271-4625
Piscataway *(G-8778)*

Karla Landscaping Pavers ....G 732 333-5852
Howell *(G-4558)*

L Arden Corp ....G 973 523-6400
Paterson *(G-8314)*

Mapei Corporation ....E 732 254-4830
Swedesboro *(G-10707)*

Maritime Solutions Inc ....G 732 752-3831
Middlesex *(G-6178)*

Multi-Pak Corporation ....G 201 342-7474
Hackensack *(G-3949)*

▲ Neu Inc ....G 281 648-9751
Hamilton *(G-4119)*

NJ Paver Restorations LLC ....G 732 558-6011
Hillsborough *(G-4359)*

R & H Spring & Truck Repair ....F 732 681-9000
Wall Township *(G-11504)*

◆ Ransome Equipment Sales LLC ....G 856 797-8100
Lumberton *(G-5663)*

▼ Reinco Inc ....F 908 755-0921
Plainfield *(G-8873)*

Robert Young and Son Inc ....G 973 728-8133
Hewitt *(G-4292)*

▲ Solidia Technologies Inc ....E 908 315-5901
Piscataway *(G-8813)*

Terco Construction LLC ....F 973 551-7759
Newton *(G-7409)*

Trilenium Salvage Co ....G 732 462-2909
Morganville *(G-6654)*

Triple D Enterprises Inc ....E 609 859-3000
Southampton *(G-10483)*

Tuff Mfg Co Inc ....G 201 796-5319
Elmwood Park *(G-2852)*

▲ US Outworkers LLC ....G 973 362-1458
Sussex *(G-10680)*

▼ Wave Dispersion Tech Inc ....G 908 233-7503
Berkeley Heights *(G-424)*

Weldon Concrete Corp ....G 973 228-7473
Roseland *(G-9657)*

3532 Mining Machinery & Eqpt

◆ Amec Fster Wheeler N Amer Corp .....D 936 448-6323
Hampton *(G-4153)*

▲ Enviro-Clear Company Inc ....F 908 638-5507
High Bridge *(G-4295)*

◆ Foremost Machine Builders Inc ....D 973 227-0700
Fairfield *(G-3200)*

Hosokawa Micron International ....C 908 273-6360
Summit *(G-10644)*

International Process Eqp Co ....G 856 665-4007
Pennsauken *(G-8530)*

◆ K-Tron International Inc ....G 856 589-0500
Sewell *(G-9962)*

Pallmann Pulverizers Co Inc ....G 973 471-1450
Clifton *(G-1688)*

3533 Oil Field Machinery & Eqpt

Capuano Plumbing Inc ....G 201 327-0676
Upper Saddle River *(G-11276)*

Grayden Industries Inc ....E 201 761-0788
Jersey City *(G-4762)*

◆ Sandvik Inc ....C 201 794-5000
Fair Lawn *(G-3112)*

3534 Elevators & Moving Stairways

▲ Ahe Manufacturing Inc ....F 609 660-8000
Barnegat *(G-159)*

▲ Amerivator Systems Corporation ......G 973 471-1200
Clifton *(G-1565)*

Archi-Tread Inc ....E 973 725-5738
Kinnelon *(G-5033)*

Diamond Scooters Inc ....G 609 646-0003
Absecon *(G-2)*

Edi/Eci ....E 973 790-9100
Paterson *(G-8253)*

Elevator Cabs of NY Inc ....D 973 790-9100
Paterson *(G-8256)*

▲ Elevator Doors Inc ....C 973 790-9100
Paterson *(G-8257)*

Elevator Enterances NY Inc ....E 973 790-9100
Paterson *(G-8258)*

Elevator Entrance Inc ....E 973 790-9100
Paterson *(G-8259)*

▲ Elevator Technology Corp ....G 973 523-7760
Paterson *(G-8260)*

Flor Lift of N J Inc ....E 973 429-2200
Fairfield *(G-3197)*

G-Tech Elevator Associates LLC ....F 866 658-9296
Linden *(G-5378)*

▲ Krieck Enterprises LLC ....G 908 789-8600
Madison *(G-5727)*

Lj Elevator Service LLC ....G 856 488-5533
Cherry Hill *(G-1389)*

Otis Elevator Company ....E 856 235-5200
Moorestown *(G-6607)*

Otis Elevator Intl Inc ....G 973 575-7030
Fairfield *(G-3277)*

◆ Schindler Elevator Corporation ....B 973 397-6500
Morristown *(G-6740)*

Schindler Elevator Corporation ....E 856 234-2220
Moorestown *(G-6621)*

◆ Schindler Enterprises Inc ....F 973 397-6500
Morristown *(G-6741)*

TEC Elevator Inc ....F 609 938-0647
Marmora *(G-6007)*

3535 Conveyors & Eqpt

Aerocon Inc ....D 800 405-2376
Belleville *(G-295)*

Allstate Conveyor Service....................E...... 856 768-6566
Voorhees *(G-11420)*

Alpha Associates Inc ....E...... 732 730-1800
Lakewood *(G-5067)*

Automated Flexible Conveyors ....F...... 973 340-1695
Clifton *(G-1569)*

Boomerang Systems Inc ....E...... 973 538-1194
Florham Park *(G-3494)*

Buhler Inc ....E...... 201 847-0600
Mahwah *(G-5755)*

Carlisle Machine Works Inc ....E...... 856 825-0627
Millville *(G-6293)*

Century Conveyor Service Inc ....E...... 732 248-4900
Edison *(G-2480)*

▲ Coesia Health & Beauty Inc ....F...... 908 707-8008
Branchburg *(G-648)*

Conveyer Installers America ....G...... 908 453-4729
Belvidere *(G-367)*

Conveyors By North American ....G...... 973 777-6600
Clifton *(G-1590)*

◆ Coperion Corporation ....C...... 201 327-6300
Sewell *(G-9946)*

▲ Coperion K-Tron Pitman Inc ....F...... 856 589-0500
Sewell *(G-9947)*

Das Installations Inc ....F...... 973 473-6858
Garfield *(G-3728)*

Dematic Corp......................................A...... 908 991-9900
Basking Ridge *(G-184)*

Dyna Veyor Inc ....G...... 908 276-5384
Newark *(G-7146)*

Equipment Erectors Inc ....E...... 732 846-1212
Somerset *(G-10097)*

Essex Rise Conveyor Corp ....G...... 973 575-7483
West Caldwell *(G-11775)*

Flexlink Systems Inc...........................E...... 973 983-2700
Branchburg *(G-660)*

Flexlink Systems Inc...........................G...... 908 947-2140
Branchburg *(G-661)*

Flor Lift of N J Inc ....E...... 973 429-2200
Fairfield *(G-3197)*

Flow-Turn Inc ....E...... 908 687-3225
Union *(G-11184)*

▲ Foremost Machine Builders Inc........D...... 973 227-0700
Fairfield *(G-3200)*

▲ Form Lectro Inc ....E...... 973 777-0621
Hackensack *(G-3917)*

◆ Garvey Corporation ....D...... 609 561-2450
Hammonton *(G-4137)*

Gauer Metal Products Co Inc..............E...... 908 241-4080
Kenilworth *(G-4958)*

Hy-Tek Material Handling Inc ....E...... 732 490-6282
Morganville *(G-6642)*

J G Machine Works Inc........................G...... 732 203-2077
Edison *(G-2543)*

◆ K-Tron International Inc ....D...... 856 589-0500
Sewell *(G-9962)*

Keneco Inc...G...... 908 241-3700
Kenilworth *(G-4967)*

Key Handling Systems Inc ....E...... 201 933-9333
Moonachie *(G-6528)*

Knotts Company Inc ....E...... 908 464-4800
Berkeley Heights *(G-416)*

Lamson Airtubes LLC ....F...... 973 300-4267
Lafayette *(G-5049)*

Lynn Mechanical Contractors.............F...... 856 829-1717
Cinnaminson *(G-1474)*

Main Robert A & Sons Holdg Co ....E...... 201 447-3700
Wyckoff *(G-12258)*

▼ Metalfab Inc ....E...... 973 764-2000
Vernon *(G-11299)*

Metalfab Mtl Hdlg Systems LLC ....E...... 973 764-2000
Vernon *(G-11300)*

Pulsonics Inc.......................................F...... 800 999-6785
Belleville *(G-313)*

Reliabotics LLC....................................G...... 732 791-5500
New Brunswick *(G-7000)*

▲ Robotunits Inc ....G...... 732 438-0500
Cranbury *(G-1877)*

Royal Aquarius Empire ....D...... 646 847-3322
Hamilton *(G-4125)*

◆ Sandvik Process Systems Inc..........E...... 973 720-7000
Totowa *(G-10970)*

Sparks Belting Company Inc ....G...... 973 227-4100
Fairfield *(G-3309)*

T O Najarian Associates......................D...... 732 389-0220
Eatontown *(G-2424)*

Tarlton C & T Co Inc............................E...... 908 964-9400
Union *(G-11227)*

TEC Installations Inc...........................F...... 973 684-0503
Paterson *(G-8397)*

Track Systems Inc...............................F...... 201 462-0095
Hasbrouck Heights *(G-4201)*

Traycon Manufacturing Co Inc............E...... 201 939-5555
Carlstadt *(G-1233)*

◆ Unex Manufacturing Inc...................D...... 732 928-2800
Lakewood *(G-5199)*

◆ Vac-U-Max ....E...... 973 759-4600
Belleville *(G-322)*

Vibra Screw Inc ....E...... 973 256-7410
Totowa *(G-10980)*

▲ Volta Belting USA Inc ....F...... 973 276-7905
Pine Brook *(G-8719)*

▲ W & H Systems Inc ....C...... 201 933-7840
Fairfield *(G-3347)*

3536 Hoists, Cranes & Monorails

Bombardier Transportation ....B...... 973 624-9300
Newark *(G-7109)*

Breeze-Eastern LLC ....D...... 973 602-1001
Whippany *(G-12015)*

Courtney Boatlifts Inc ....G...... 732 892-8900
Point Pleasant Boro *(G-8936)*

Electro Lift Inc ....E...... 973 471-0204
Clifton *(G-1612)*

Holtec Government Services LLC ....E...... 856 291-0600
Marlton *(G-5978)*

Konecranes Inc ....F...... 908 259-9696
Kenilworth *(G-4970)*

Maximum Material Handling LLC ....G...... 973 227-1227
Parsippany *(G-8042)*

◆ Palfinger North America ....D...... 609 588-5400
Trenton *(G-11095)*

Pcs Crane Services Inc ....F...... 201 366-4250
Fairview *(G-3368)*

Rudco Products Inc ....D...... 856 691-0800
Vineland *(G-11400)*

▲ Saturn Overhead Equipment LLC ....F...... 732 560-7210
Somerset *(G-10171)*

▼ Teledynamics LLC ....E...... 973 248-3360
Towaco *(G-11004)*

3537 Indl Trucks, Tractors, Trailers & Stackers

▲ Caravan Inc......................................F...... 732 590-0210
Avenel *(G-128)*

Christensen Manufacturing ....F...... 609 466-9700
Pennington *(G-8446)*

Copper Boss Ltd Liability Co...............E...... 888 629-2190
Edison *(G-2492)*

Crown Equipment Corporation.............D...... 201 337-1211
Oakland *(G-7681)*

Dazzledog LLC ....G...... 302 540-6804
Bellmawr *(G-336)*

▲ Excalibur Miretti Group LLC ....F...... 973 808-8399
Fairfield *(G-3188)*

F and M Equipment Ltd ....D...... 215 822-0145
South Plainfield *(G-10362)*

Global Express Freight Inc ....G...... 201 376-6613
Bergenfield *(G-385)*

▲ Hanson & Zollinger Inc ....F...... 856 626-3440
Berlin *(G-434)*

◆ Hilman Incorporated ....D...... 732 462-6277
Marlboro *(G-5943)*

Intech Powercore Corporation ....G...... 201 767-8066
Closter *(G-1761)*

▲ Meto Corp ....F...... 201 405-0311
Parsippany *(G-8046)*

Meto Lift Inc ....F...... 201 405-0311
Parsippany *(G-8047)*

Morse Metal Products Co Inc..............G...... 732 422-3676
Princeton *(G-9078)*

Nardelli Bros Inc ....G...... 856 692-0723
Vineland *(G-11383)*

◆ Palfinger North America ....D...... 609 588-5400
Trenton *(G-11095)*

▲ Permadur Industries Inc ....D...... 908 359-9767
Hillsborough *(G-4362)*

Prestige Forklift Maint Svc ....G...... 732 297-1001
New Brunswick *(G-6993)*

Rentalift Inc ....F...... 973 684-6111
Paterson *(G-8368)*

RISE Corporation ....E...... 973 575-7480
West Caldwell *(G-11804)*

▲ Saturn Overhead Equipment LLC ....F...... 732 560-7210
Somerset *(G-10171)*

◆ Seko Worldwide ....G...... 973 465-6868
Newark *(G-7306)*

Showtime Express ....G...... 732 238-2701
East Brunswick *(G-2183)*

Trucktech Parts & Services.................G...... 973 799-0500
Newark *(G-7348)*

Vanco USA LLC (de) ....C...... 609 499-4141
Bordentown *(G-615)*

Vehicle Technologies Inc ....G...... 609 406-9626
Ewing *(G-3067)*

3541 Machine Tools: Cutting

Alben Metal Products Inc ....G...... 973 279-8891
Paterson *(G-8202)*

Alfa Machine & Tool Co Inc ....F...... 973 227-1962
Fairfield *(G-3129)*

American Mch Tool RPR Rbldg Co ....G...... 973 927-0820
Randolph *(G-9269)*

Armstrong and Sons Inc ....G...... 732 223-1555
Manasquan *(G-5867)*

Array Solders Ltd Liability Co.............G...... 201 432-0095
Jersey City *(G-4710)*

▲ Autodrill LLC ....G...... 908 542-0244
Lebanon *(G-5276)*

Automated Tapping Systems Inc ....F...... 732 899-2282
Brick *(G-735)*

Camden Tool Inc ....E...... 856 966-6800
Camden *(G-1048)*

Charles F Kilian ....G...... 732 458-3554
Brick *(G-736)*

Chase Machine Co ....F...... 201 438-2214
Lyndhurst *(G-5677)*

Coretech International Inc...................F...... 908 454-7999
Alpha *(G-40)*

Cutter Drill & Machine Inc ....G...... 732 206-1112
Howell *(G-4550)*

Eastern Machining Corporation ....G...... 856 694-3303
Franklinville *(G-3630)*

▲ Everite Machine Products Co ....E...... 856 330-6700
Pennsauken *(G-8509)*

▲ Fecken-Kirfel America Inc ....F...... 201 891-5530
Mahwah *(G-5771)*

Gary R Marzili ....G...... 856 782-1546
Sicklerville *(G-10019)*

Gauer Metal Products Co Inc..............E...... 908 241-4080
Kenilworth *(G-4958)*

General Electric Company ....B...... 973 887-6635
Parsippany *(G-8023)*

▼ Glebar Operating LLC ....D...... 201 337-1500
Ramsey *(G-9242)*

High Point Precision Products ....F...... 973 875-6229
Sussex *(G-10672)*

Hone-A-Matic Tool & Cutter Co ....G...... 732 382-6000
Rahway *(G-9197)*

Innovative Manufacturing Inc ....F...... 908 904-1884
Hillsborough *(G-4346)*

J & S Tool ....G...... 973 383-5059
Newton *(G-7393)*

J and M Precision Inc ....G...... 856 661-9595
Pennsauken *(G-8533)*

▲ Jet Pulverizer Co Inc.......................E...... 856 235-5554
Moorestown *(G-6588)*

Joe Mike Precision Fabrication ....F...... 609 953-1144
Medford *(G-6073)*

▲ Komo Machine Inc ....D...... 732 719-6222
Lakewood *(G-5141)*

L & M Machine & Tool Co Inc ....G...... 973 523-5288
Paterson *(G-8313)*

▲ Lever Manufacturing Corp ....E...... 201 684-4400
Mahwah *(G-5789)*

McGonegal Manufacturing Co ....G...... 201 438-2313
East Rutherford *(G-2309)*

Metaport Manufacturing LLC ....G...... 973 383-8363
Lafayette *(G-5051)*

▲ NASA Machine Tools Inc ....E...... 973 633-5200
Lincoln Park *(G-5330)*

New Brunswick Saw Service Inc ....F...... 732 287-4466
Middlesex *(G-6184)*

Nova Precision Products Inc ....G...... 973 625-1586
Rockaway *(G-9590)*

Oroszlany Laszlo ....G...... 201 666-2101
Hillsdale *(G-4386)*

▲ Picut Mfg Co Inc ....G...... 908 754-1333
Warren *(G-11563)*

◆ Rowan Technologies Inc..................D...... 609 267-9000
Rancocas *(G-9262)*

▲ Royal Master Grinders Inc ....D...... 201 337-8500
Oakland *(G-7705)*

Shor International ....E...... 973 520-8777
Madison *(G-5735)*

▼ T A C Technical Instr Corp ....F...... 609 882-2894
Ewing *(G-3059)*

Tool Shop Inc ....G...... 856 767-8077
West Berlin *(G-11758)*

SIC

▲ Tooling Etc LLC..............G....... 732 752-8080
Middlesex *(G-6206)*

Triple-T Cutting Tools Inc............F....... 856 768-0800
West Berlin *(G-11759)*

▲ Uhlmann Packaging Systems LP....D..... 973 402-8855
Towaco *(G-11006)*

Unique Precision Co Inc..........G....... 732 382-8699
Rahway *(G-9227)*

Web Industries Inc..........G....... 973 335-1200
Montville *(G-6497)*

3542 Machine Tools: Forming

▲ Action Packaging Automation..........G....... 609 448-9210
Roosevelt *(G-9639)*

▲ Arrow Fastener Co LLC..........B....... 201 843-6900
Saddle Brook *(G-9752)*

Benton Graphics Inc..........E....... 609 587-4000
Trenton *(G-11026)*

▲ Bergen Cable Technology LLC..........E....... 973 276-9596
Fairfield *(G-3147)*

▲ Bruderer Machinery Inc..........E....... 201 941-2121
Ridgefield *(G-9353)*

Buhler Inc..........E....... 201 847-0600
Mahwah *(G-5755)*

C & S Machinery Rebuilding..........G....... 973 742-7302
Paterson *(G-8228)*

▲ Cozzoli Machine Company..........D....... 732 564-0400
Somerset *(G-10086)*

Doran LLC..........G....... 908 289-9200
Union *(G-11172)*

Edston Manufacturing Company..........G....... 908 647-0116
Fairfield *(G-3182)*

H & W Tool Co Inc..........F....... 973 366-0131
Dover *(G-2088)*

High-Technology Corporation..........F....... 201 488-0010
Hackensack *(G-3926)*

Hone-A-Matic Tool & Cutter Co..........G....... 732 382-6000
Rahway *(G-9197)*

Joy-Rei Enterprises Inc..........G....... 732 727-0742
Parlin *(G-7934)*

▲ Magnetic Metals Corporation..........C....... 856 964-7842
Camden *(G-1076)*

Mastercraft Iron Inc..........F....... 732 988-3113
Neptune *(G-6924)*

▲ Promet Inc..........E....... 303 371-2300
Riverdale *(G-9483)*

Rotech Tool & Mold Co Inc..........G....... 908 241-9669
Kenilworth *(G-4993)*

◆ Royle Systems Group LLC..........E....... 201 644-0345
Teterboro *(G-10809)*

▲ Titanium Industries Inc..........E....... 973 983-1185
Rockaway *(G-9613)*

Trumpf Inc..........E....... 609 925-8200
Cranbury *(G-1886)*

▲ Trumpf Photonics Inc..........C....... 609 925-8200
Cranbury *(G-1887)*

Ultimate Spinning Turning Corp..........G....... 201 372-9740
Moonachie *(G-6550)*

Vantage Tool & Mfg Inc..........G....... 908 647-1010
Warren *(G-11571)*

Williams Scotsman Inc..........G....... 856 429-0315
Kearny *(G-4922)*

3543 Industrial Patterns

Creative Patterns & Mfg..........G....... 973 589-1391
Rockaway *(G-9558)*

▲ Method Assoc Inc..........F....... 732 888-0444
Keyport *(G-5020)*

▲ Motif Industries Inc..........F....... 973 575-1800
East Hanover *(G-2229)*

West Pattern Works Inc..........F....... 609 443-6241
Cranbury *(G-1891)*

3544 Dies, Tools, Jigs, Fixtures & Indl Molds

21st Century Finishing Inc..........E....... 201 797-0212
Clifton *(G-1551)*

A Frieri Machine Tool Inc..........G....... 908 753-7555
South Plainfield *(G-10318)*

▲ A K Stamping Co Inc..........D....... 908 232-7300
Mountainside *(G-6865)*

Accurate Machine & Tool Co..........G....... 908 245-5545
Roselle Park *(G-9687)*

Accurate Mold Inc..........E....... 856 784-8484
Somerdale *(G-10038)*

▲ Accurate Tool & Die Co Inc..........G....... 201 476-9348
Montvale *(G-6440)*

Alfa Machine & Tool Co Inc..........F....... 973 227-1962
Fairfield *(G-3129)*

Algene Marking Equipment Co..........G....... 973 478-9041
Garfield *(G-3716)*

Alloy Cast Products Inc..........F....... 908 245-2255
Kenilworth *(G-4936)*

Almark Tool & Manufacturing Co..........F....... 908 789-2440
Garwood *(G-3775)*

Amerimold Tech Inc..........E....... 732 462-7577
Jackson *(G-4653)*

Art Mold & Polishing Co Inc..........F....... 908 518-9191
Roselle *(G-9661)*

Art Mold & Tool Corporation..........G....... 201 935-3377
East Rutherford *(G-2278)*

B E C Mfg Corp..........E....... 201 414-0000
Glen Rock *(G-3822)*

Bach Tool Precision Inc..........G....... 973 962-6224
Ringwood *(G-9444)*

Barlics Manufacturing Co Inc..........G....... 732 381-6229
Rahway *(G-9179)*

▲ Bihler of America Inc..........E....... 908 213-9001
Phillipsburg *(G-8644)*

Bodine Tool and Machine Co Inc..........E....... 856 234-7800
Moorestown *(G-6564)*

Bonney-Vehslage Tool Co..........F....... 973 589-6975
Springfield *(G-10544)*

Boyle Tool & Die Co Inc..........F....... 856 853-1819
West Deptford *(G-11818)*

Brisar Industries Inc..........C....... 973 278-2500
Paterson *(G-8226)*

▲ C & C Metal Products Corp..........D....... 201 569-7300
Englewood *(G-2880)*

C & K Punch & Screw Mch Pdts..........G....... 201 343-6750
Hackensack *(G-3886)*

C & S Tool Co..........F....... 973 887-6865
East Hanover *(G-2202)*

C and C Tool Co LLC..........G....... 908 431-0330
Hillsborough *(G-4324)*

Camptown Tool & Die Co Inc..........G....... 908 688-8406
Kenilworth *(G-4947)*

▲ Cavalla Inc..........E....... 201 343-3338
Hackensack *(G-3894)*

▲ Charles E Green & Son Inc..........E....... 973 485-3630
Newark *(G-7120)*

City Diecutting Inc..........F....... 973 270-0370
Morristown *(G-6699)*

▲ CK Manufacturing Inc..........E....... 973 808-3500
Fairfield *(G-3159)*

Clover Stamping Inc..........G....... 973 278-4888
Paterson *(G-8234)*

▲ Colwood Electronics Inc..........G....... 732 938-5556
Farmingdale *(G-3380)*

Container Graphics Corp..........E....... 732 922-1180
Neptune *(G-6904)*

▲ Continental Precision Corp..........C....... 908 754-3030
Piscataway *(G-8752)*

Custom Extrusion Tech Inc..........F....... 732 367-5511
Lakewood *(G-5102)*

D & D Technology Inc..........G....... 908 688-5154
Union *(G-11169)*

DEB Manufacturing Inc..........G....... 732 364-7007
Lakewood *(G-5107)*

Dependable Precision Products..........G....... 973 887-3304
Parsippany *(G-7980)*

Die Tech LLC..........G....... 201 343-8324
Hackensack *(G-3905)*

▲ Duerr Tool & Die Co Inc..........G....... 908 810-9035
Hillsborough *(G-11173)*

Dura-Carb Inc..........G....... 973 697-6665
Oak Ridge *(G-7661)*

Dynamic Die Cutting & Finshg..........F....... 973 589-8338
Newark *(G-7147)*

Eb Machine Corp..........G....... 973 442-7729
Wharton *(G-11986)*

Edgar C Barcus Co Inc..........F....... 856 456-0204
Westville *(G-11939)*

Electro Magnetic Products Inc..........E....... 856 235-3011
Moorestown *(G-6575)*

Elray Manufacturing Company..........F....... 856 881-1935
Glassboro *(G-3804)*

F & G Tool & Die Inc..........G....... 908 241-5880
Kenilworth *(G-4954)*

▲ Fancort Industries Inc..........F....... 973 575-0610
West Caldwell *(G-11776)*

G L Tool & Manufacturing Co..........G....... 973 740-0001
Livingston *(G-5532)*

Garden State Precision Inc..........G....... 201 945-6410
Ridgefield *(G-9361)*

Garden State Tool & Mold Corp..........G....... 908 245-2041
South Amboy *(G-10238)*

Gaum Inc..........E....... 609 586-0132
Robbinsville *(G-9516)*

General Tool Specialties Inc..........F....... 908 874-3040
Hillsborough *(G-4335)*

▲ Globe Die-Cutting Products Inc..........C....... 732 494-7744
Metuchen *(G-6105)*

▲ Globe Industries Corp..........G....... 973 992-8990
Clifton *(G-1627)*

Golden Rule Inc..........G....... 856 663-3074
Pennsauken *(G-8516)*

H & W Tool Co Inc..........F....... 973 366-0131
Dover *(G-2088)*

H-E Tool & Mfg Co Inc..........G....... 856 303-8787
Cinnaminson *(G-1466)*

Hanrahan Tool Co Inc..........G....... 732 919-7300
Farmingdale *(G-3386)*

Harris & Tippograph Inc..........G....... 973 523-5204
Paterson *(G-8288)*

Hartmann Tool Co Inc..........G....... 201 343-8700
Hackensack *(G-3925)*

▲ Heinz Glas USA Inc..........F....... 908 474-0300
Linden *(G-5383)*

HNST Mold Inspections LLC..........E....... 201 733-0091
Mahwah *(G-5781)*

Hofmann Tool & Die Corporation..........G....... 201 327-0226
Upper Saddle River *(G-11279)*

Hudson Manufacturing Corp..........F....... 973 376-7070
Millburn *(G-6252)*

Indo-US Mim TEC Private Ltd..........G....... 734 327-9842
Princeton *(G-9057)*

▼ Infor Metal & Tooling Mfg..........F....... 973 571-9520
Cedar Grove *(G-1285)*

Inventors Shop LLC..........E....... 856 303-8787
Cinnaminson *(G-1470)*

Ipsco Apollo Punch & Die Corp..........G....... 973 884-0900
East Hanover *(G-2224)*

J & J Marine Inc..........F....... 856 228-4744
Sewell *(G-9959)*

J P Rotella Co Inc..........F....... 973 942-2559
Haledon *(G-4083)*

J V Q Inc..........F....... 973 523-8806
Paterson *(G-8297)*

J-Mac Plastics Inc..........E....... 908 709-1111
Kenilworth *(G-4965)*

Jmk Tool Die and Mfg Co Inc..........G....... 201 845-4710
Rochelle Park *(G-9530)*

Jordan Manufacturing LLC..........G....... 973 383-8363
Lafayette *(G-5048)*

Kessler Steel Rule Die Inc..........G....... 856 767-0231
West Berlin *(G-11728)*

Koba Corp..........D....... 732 469-0110
Middlesex *(G-6173)*

L & Z Tool and Engineering Inc..........E....... 908 322-2220
Watchung *(G-11592)*

▲ Lasercam LLc..........E....... 201 941-1262
Ridgefield *(G-9370)*

◆ Lawrence Mold and Tool Corp..........E....... 609 392-5422
Lawrenceville *(G-5260)*

Lincoln Mold & Die Corp..........D....... 908 241-3344
Warren *(G-11558)*

▲ Linden Mold and Tool Corp..........E....... 732 381-1411
Rahway *(G-9209)*

Mold Polishing Company Inc..........G....... 908 518-9191
Garwood *(G-3779)*

Monroe Tool & Die Inc..........G....... 856 629-5164
Williamstown *(G-12092)*

▲ Newton Tool & Mfg Inc..........B....... 856 241-1500
Pennsauken *(G-8554)*

Olympic EDM Services Inc..........G....... 973 492-0664
Kinnelon *(G-5039)*

Omega Tool Die..........G....... 856 228-7100
Sewell *(G-9963)*

Orycon Control Technology Inc..........E....... 732 922-2400
Ocean *(G-7732)*

Pahco Machine Inc..........G....... 609 587-1188
Trenton *(G-11094)*

Peterson Steel Rule Die Corp..........F....... 201 935-6180
Carlstadt *(G-1201)*

Philip Creter Inc..........G....... 908 686-2910
Union *(G-11215)*

Pin Point Container Corp..........F....... 856 848-2115
Deptford *(G-2066)*

Precision Ball Specialties..........F....... 856 881-5646
Williamstown *(G-12099)*

Printco..........G....... 908 687-9518
Flemington *(G-3463)*

Progressive Tool & Mfg Corp..........G....... 908 245-7010
Kenilworth *(G-4990)*

Quality Die Shop Inc..........G....... 732 787-0041
North Middletown *(G-7558)*

R G Smith Tool & Mfg Co..........F....... 973 344-1395
Newark *(G-7282)*

Rebuth Metal Services..........G....... 908 889-6400
Fanwood *(G-3373)*

Redkeys Dies Inc .... G 856 456-7890
Gloucester City *(G-3845)*
▲ **Resolv Corporation** .... F 973 220-5141
Orange *(G-7825)*
Rex Tool & Manufacturing Inc .... G 908 925-2727
Linden *(G-5434)*
Richmond Steel Rule Dies Inc .... G 856 661-0900
Pennsauken *(G-8574)*
Romar Machine & Tool Company .... E 201 337-7111
Franklin Lakes *(G-3624)*
Roseville Tool & Manufacturing .... E 973 992-5405
Livingston *(G-5558)*
Rotech Tool & Mold Co Inc .... G 908 241-9669
Kenilworth *(G-4993)*
Schneider & Marquard Inc .... E 973 383-2200
Newton *(G-7402)*
Seajay Manufacturing Corp .... F 732 774-0900
Neptune *(G-6931)*
Sigco Tool & Mfg Co Inc .... E 856 753-6565
West Berlin *(G-11749)*
South Jersey Precision Tl Mold .... F 856 327-0500
Vineland *(G-11405)*
▲ **Spec Steel Rule Dies Inc** .... E 609 443-4435
Windsor *(G-12130)*
Stampex Corp .... F 973 839-4040
Haskell *(G-4214)*
STS Technologies LLC .... F 973 277-5416
Mahwah *(G-5817)*
TEC Cast Inc .... E 201 935-3885
Carlstadt *(G-1227)*
Thal Precision Industries Inc .... G 732 381-6106
Clark *(G-1517)*
▲ **Thomson Lamination Co Inc** .... D 856 779-8521
Maple Shade *(G-5912)*
Totowa Precision Tooling Inc .... F 973 256-2283
Totowa *(G-10976)*
Tryco Tool & Mfg Co Inc .... E 973 674-6867
Orange *(G-7831)*
Turul Bookbindery Inc .... G 973 361-2810
Wharton *(G-12003)*
▲ **Union Tool & Mold Co Inc** .... E 973 763-6611
Maplewood *(G-5931)*
United Die Company Inc .... E 201 997-0250
Kearny *(G-4918)*
Unity Steel Rule Die Co .... E 201 569-6400
Englewood *(G-2941)*
Universal Mold & Tool Inc .... F 856 563-0488
Vineland *(G-11412)*
▲ **Universal Tools & Mfg Co** .... E 973 379-4193
Springfield *(G-10582)*
Valley Die Cutting Inc .... G 973 731-8884
Randolph *(G-9305)*
Vantage Tool & Mfg Inc .... G 908 647-1010
Warren *(G-11571)*
Victory Tool & Mfg Co .... G 973 759-8733
Belleville *(G-325)*
Viking Mold & Tool Corp .... G 609 476-9333
Dorothy *(G-2074)*
Viz Mold & Die Ltd .... F 201 784-8383
Northvale *(G-7611)*
Vmc Die Cutting Corp .... F 973 450-4655
Belleville *(G-326)*
Well Bilt Industries Inc .... F 908 486-6002
Linden *(G-5458)*
West Machine Works Inc .... G 732 549-2183
Metuchen *(G-6130)*
West Pattern Works Inc .... F 609 443-6241
Cranbury *(G-1891)*
Zin-Tech Inc .... E 856 661-0900
Pennsauken *(G-8591)*

3545 Machine Tool Access

Accurate Diamond Tool Corp .... E 201 265-8868
Emerson *(G-2855)*
▼ **Accuratus Ceramic Corp** .... E 908 213-7070
Phillipsburg *(G-8638)*
◆ **Acrison Inc** .... C 201 440-8300
Moonachie *(G-6499)*
Advanced Cutting Services LLC .... G 908 241-5332
Roselle *(G-9659)*
Airbrasive Jet Tech LLC .... G 201 725-7340
Piscataway *(G-8729)*
Alloy Cast Products Inc .... F 908 245-2255
Kenilworth *(G-4936)*
Almark Tool & Manufacturing Co .... F 908 789-2440
Garwood *(G-3775)*
Aloris Tool Technology Co Inc .... E 973 772-1201
Clifton *(G-1561)*
▲ **Alpex Wheel Co Inc** .... F 201 871-1700
Tenafly *(G-10781)*
American Aeronautic Mfg Co .... G 973 442-8138
Pine Brook *(G-8686)*
Astro Tool & Machine Co Inc .... E 732 382-2454
Rahway *(G-9177)*
Automated Tapping Systems Inc .... F 732 899-2282
Brick *(G-735)*
B & S Tool and Cutter Service .... G 201 488-3545
Hackensack *(G-3877)*
B B Supply Corp .... F 201 313-9021
Cliffside Park *(G-1536)*
Bach Tool Precision Inc .... G 973 962-6224
Ringwood *(G-9444)*
▲ **Bar-Lo Carbon Products Inc** .... E 973 227-2717
Fairfield *(G-3144)*
▲ **Belleville Scale & Balance LLC** .... G 973 759-4487
Orange *(G-7817)*
Camden Tool Inc .... E 856 966-6800
Camden *(G-1048)*
Congruent Machine Co Inc .... G 973 764-6767
Vernon *(G-11297)*
Cutter Drill & Machine Inc .... G 732 206-1112
Howell *(G-4550)*
Daven Industries Inc .... E 973 808-8848
Fairfield *(G-3173)*
Defined Pro Machining LLC .... G 973 891-1038
Wharton *(G-11984)*
▲ **Dewitt Bros Tool Co Inc** .... G 908 298-3700
Kenilworth *(G-4951)*
Digivac Company .... F 732 765-0900
Matawan *(G-6017)*
Dmg Mori Usa Inc .... G 973 257-9620
Rockaway *(G-9561)*
◆ **Doosan Machine Tools Amer Corp** .... D 973 618-2500
Pine Brook *(G-8700)*
E P Heller Company .... E 973 377-2878
Madison *(G-5721)*
Energy Beams Inc .... F 973 291-6555
Bloomingdale *(G-543)*
▲ **Engineered Components Inc** .... F 908 788-8393
Three Bridges *(G-10822)*
F & R Grinding Inc .... F 908 996-0440
Frenchtown *(G-3700)*
▲ **Fulcrum Inc** .... G 973 473-6900
Oradell *(G-7809)*
Grobet File Company Amer LLC .... D 201 939-6700
Carlstadt *(G-1165)*
H & W Tool Co Inc .... F 973 366-0131
Dover *(G-2088)*
Hainesport Tool & Machine Co .... F 609 261-0016
Mount Holly *(G-6772)*
▲ **Handler Manufacturing Company** .... E 908 233-7796
Westfield *(G-11926)*
Indo-US Mim TEC Private Ltd .... G 734 327-9842
Princeton *(G-9057)*
▲ **Industrial Brush Co Inc** .... E 800 241-9860
Fairfield *(G-3228)*
International Tool and Mfg Inc .... G 973 227-6767
Fairfield *(G-3233)*
J A Machine & Tool Co Inc .... F 201 767-1308
Closter *(G-1762)*
J and J Contractors .... F 856 765-7521
Millville *(G-6309)*
▲ **Jdv Products Inc** .... F 201 794-6467
Fair Lawn *(G-3098)*
Jnt Technical Services Inc .... E 201 641-2130
Little Ferry *(G-5511)*
K & R Precision Machining LLC .... F 201 385-8855
New Milford *(G-7022)*
Kennametal Inc .... C 412 248-8200
Jersey City *(G-4771)*
KG Systems Inc .... G 973 515-4664
Springfield *(G-10562)*
M D Carbide Tool Corp .... E 973 263-0104
Towaco *(G-10998)*
Martin Tool Company Inc .... F 973 361-9212
Wharton *(G-11992)*
◆ **Maurice S Dessau Co Inc** .... E 201 791-2005
Fair Lawn *(G-3102)*
New Jersey Diamond Products Co .... F 973 684-0949
Paterson *(G-8349)*
Niko Trade Ltd-USA Inc .... G 973 575-4353
Fairfield *(G-3271)*
Precision Ball Specialties .... F 856 881-5646
Williamstown *(G-12099)*
R & H Co Inc .... G 610 258-3177
Phillipsburg *(G-8667)*
R D Associates .... G 973 729-7944
Sparta *(G-10520)*
▲ **Ram Products Inc** .... G 732 651-5500
Dayton *(G-1984)*
Ramco Manufacturing Co Inc .... E 908 245-4500
Kenilworth *(G-4991)*
▲ **Ringfeder Pwr Transm USA Corp** .... E 201 666-3320
Westwood *(G-11970)*
Sandvik Inc .... C 281 275-4800
Fair Lawn *(G-3113)*
◆ **Sandvik Inc** .... C 201 794-5000
Fair Lawn *(G-3112)*
Sine Tru Tool Company Inc .... G 732 591-1100
Marlboro *(G-5959)*
Sk & P Industries Inc .... G 973 482-1864
Newark *(G-7316)*
Ss Tool & Manufacturing Co .... G 908 486-5497
Linden *(G-5447)*
Technodiamant USA Inc .... G 908 850-8505
Tranquility *(G-11008)*
▲ **Teknics Industries Inc** .... D 973 633-7575
Lincoln Park *(G-5333)*
Tool Shop Inc .... G 856 767-8077
West Berlin *(G-11758)*
Totowa Precision Tooling Inc .... F 973 256-2283
Totowa *(G-10976)*
Troy-Onic Inc .... E 973 584-6830
Kenvil *(G-5014)*
▲ **United Instrument Company LLC** .... G 201 767-6000
Northvale *(G-7610)*
▲ **Universal Metalcraft Inc** .... E 973 345-3284
Wayne *(G-11688)*
William T Hutchinson Company .... F 908 688-0533
Union *(G-11235)*
Wrightworks Engineering LLC .... G 609 882-8840
Lawrenceville *(G-5272)*
Zenith Precision Inc .... F 201 933-8640
East Rutherford *(G-2338)*

3546 Power Hand Tools

Black & Decker (us) Inc .... G 201 475-3524
Elmwood Park *(G-2806)*
Chatham Lawn Mowler .... G 973 635-8855
Chatham *(G-1327)*
▲ **Colwood Electronics Inc** .... G 732 938-5556
Farmingdale *(G-3380)*
Congruent Machine Co Inc .... G 973 764-6767
Vernon *(G-11297)*
Dcm Clean Air Products Inc .... G 732 363-2100
Lakewood *(G-5106)*
▲ **Epcos Inc** .... D 732 906-4300
Iselin *(G-4626)*
Epcos Inc .... F 732 603-5941
Lumberton *(G-5657)*
Ingersoll-Rand Company .... C 908 238-7000
Annandale *(G-58)*
Ingersoll-Rand Company .... E 856 793-7000
Mount Laurel *(G-6803)*
J Paul Allen Inc .... G 973 702-1174
Sussex *(G-10674)*
▲ **Jdv Products Inc** .... F 201 794-6467
Fair Lawn *(G-3098)*
Mendham Garden Center .... G 973 543-4178
Mendham *(G-6089)*
▲ **National Steel Rule Company** .... D 908 862-3366
Linden *(G-5415)*
▲ **Newell Brands Inc** .... B 201 610-6600
Hoboken *(G-4486)*
Precision Saw & Tool Corp .... F 973 773-7302
Clifton *(G-1703)*
▲ **Rennsteig Tools Inc** .... G 330 315-3044
Hackensack *(G-3966)*
▲ **S & G Tool Aid Corporation** .... D 973 824-7730
Newark *(G-7297)*
▲ **Singe Corporation** .... G 908 289-7900
Hillside *(G-4440)*
Toydriver LLC .... G 678 637-8500
Garfield *(G-3769)*
William T Hutchinson Company .... F 908 688-0533
Union *(G-11235)*
Winslow Rental & Supply Inc .... G 856 767-5554
Berlin *(G-446)*

3547 Rolling Mill Machinery & Eqpt

Indemax Inc .... G 973 209-2424
Vernon *(G-11298)*

3548 Welding Apparatus

Cerbaco Ltd .... E 908 996-1333
Frenchtown *(G-3699)*
Cni Ceramic Nozzles Inc .... G 973 276-1535
Fairfield *(G-3162)*
Cotterman Inc .... F 856 415-0800
Wenonah *(G-11703)*

SIC

Emabond Solutions LLC ....E...... 201 767-7400
Norwood (G-7621)

Hexacon Electric Company Inc ......E...... 908 245-6200
Roselle Park (G-9697)

▲ Orgo-Thermit Inc ....E...... 732 657-5781
Manchester (G-5887)

◆ Rowan Technologies Inc ....D...... 609 267-9000
Rancocas (G-9262)

◆ Stulz-Sickles Steel Company ......E...... 609 531-2172
Burlington (G-990)

Waage Electric Inc ....G...... 908 245-9363
Kenilworth (G-5004)

Wikstrom Machines Inc ....F...... 732 826-4800
Perth Amboy (G-8637)

3549 Metalworking Machinery, NEC

A D J Group LLC ....G...... 609 743-2099
Bordentown (G-588)

Air & Specialties Sheet Metal ....F...... 908 233-8306
Mountainside (G-6866)

▼ Applied Resources Corp ....E...... 973 328-3882
Wharton (G-11980)

Boomerang Systems Inc ....G...... 973 538-1194
Florham Park (G-3494)

G L Tool & Manufacturing Co ....G...... 973 740-0001
Livingston (G-5532)

▲ K & S Industries Inc ....F...... 908 862-3030
Linden (G-5395)

▲ Lever Manufacturing Corp ....E...... 201 684-4400
Mahwah (G-5789)

◆ Mac Products Inc ....D...... 973 344-5149
Kearny (G-4896)

Precious Metal Processing Cons .....G...... 201 944-8053
Palisades Park (G-7842)

▲ Progressive Ruesch Inc ....E...... 973 962-7700
Ringwood (G-9454)

Seal-Spout Corp ....F...... 908 647-0648
Liberty Corner (G-5324)

TMU Inc ....F...... 609 884-7656
Cape May (G-1106)

Tri-Power Consulting Svcs LLC ......G...... 973 227-7100
Denville (G-2060)

▲ Weber and Scher Mfg Co Inc ......E...... 908 236-8484
Lebanon (G-5303)

Werko Machine Co ....F...... 856 662-0669
Pennsauken (G-8588)

3552 Textile Machinery

A B C Machinery Corp ....G...... 609 971-0990
Forked River (G-3532)

Alfred Heitzman Machine Works .....G...... 201 489-8888
Moonachie (G-6500)

Baxter Corporation ....F...... 201 337-1212
Franklin Lakes (G-3607)

▲ Benjamin Booth Company ....F...... 609 859-1995
Southampton (G-10470)

Burlington Textile Machinery ....F...... 973 279-5900
Paterson (G-8227)

C & S Machine Inc ....F...... 973 882-1097
Fairfield (G-3153)

▲ Catbridge Machinery LLC ....E...... 973 808-0029
Montville (G-6485)

Cire Technologies Inc ....G...... 973 402-8301
Mountain Lakes (G-6855)

◆ Clements Industries Inc ....E...... 201 440-5500
South Hackensack (G-10258)

D R Kenyon & Son Inc ....F...... 908 722-0001
Bridgewater (G-832)

▲ Daf Products Inc ....F...... 201 251-1222
Wyckoff (G-12249)

Excel Industrial Co Inc ....G...... 609 275-1748
Princeton Junction (G-9154)

I F Associates Inc ....E...... 732 223-2900
Allenwood (G-36)

▲ Lever Manufacturing Corp ....E...... 201 684-4400
Mahwah (G-5789)

M & S Machine & Tool Corp ....F...... 973 345-5847
Paterson (G-8327)

◆ Pecata Enterprises Inc ....E...... 973 523-9498
Paterson (G-8362)

▲ Snapco Manufacturing Corp ....E...... 973 282-0300
Hillside (G-4441)

▼ Wizard Technology Inc ....F...... 732 730-0800
Toms River (G-10923)

3553 Woodworking Machinery

Andys Custom Cabinets ....G...... 732 752-6443
Green Brook (G-3854)

Atlas Woodworking Inc ....G...... 201 784-1949
Closter (G-1756)

▲ Design of Tomorrow Inc ....F...... 973 227-1000
Fairfield (G-3177)

Fix It Guy ....G...... 732 278-9000
Toms River (G-10878)

Kitchen and More Inc ....F...... 908 272-3388
Cranford (G-1911)

Logpowercom LLC ....G...... 732 350-9663
Whiting (G-12068)

▲ Samuelson Furniture Inc ....F...... 973 278-4372
Paterson (G-8377)

Stapling Machines Inc ....E...... 973 627-4400
Rockaway (G-9609)

3554 Paper Inds Machinery

175 Derousse LLC ....G...... 856 662-0100
Pennsauken (G-8467)

▼ Alpine Corrugated McHy Inc ....G...... 201 440-3030
Ridgefield Park (G-9397)

◆ Colter & Peterson Inc ....E...... 973 684-0901
West Caldwell (G-11771)

◆ Dietech Services LLC ....G...... 973 667-0798
Nutley (G-7646)

Enser Corporation ....E...... 856 829-5522
Cinnaminson (G-1461)

Holographic Finishing Inc ....G...... 201 941-4651
Ridgefield (G-9365)

▼ Khanna Paper Inc ....G...... 201 706-8050
Hoboken (G-4482)

Microfold Inc ....E...... 201 641-5052
Teterboro (G-10806)

Retrievex ....G...... 732 247-3200
New Brunswick (G-7001)

Rotary Die Systems Inc ....G...... 856 234-3994
Moorestown (G-6619)

Tri-State Knife Grinding Corp ....F...... 609 890-4989
Robbinsville (G-9523)

▲ Woodward Jogger Aerators Inc .....F...... 201 933-6800
East Rutherford (G-2337)

3555 Printing Trades Machinery & Eqpt

▼ Ackley Machine Corporation ....E...... 856 234-3626
Moorestown (G-6555)

Acme Engraving Co Inc ....F...... 973 778-0885
Passaic (G-8124)

Algene Marking Equipment Co ....G...... 973 478-9041
Garfield (G-3716)

▲ Allison Systems Corporation ....F...... 856 461-9111
Riverside (G-9492)

▲ Ancraft Press Corp ....E...... 201 792-9200
Jersey City (G-4705)

▲ Anderson & Vreeland Inc ....E...... 973 227-2270
Fairfield (G-3136)

AT Information Products Inc ....E...... 201 529-0202
Mahwah (G-5750)

▲ Atlantic Zeiser Inc ....E...... 973 228-0800
West Caldwell (G-11766)

▲ Bell-Mark Sales Co Inc ....E...... 973 882-0202
Pine Brook (G-8688)

Benton Graphics Inc ....E...... 609 587-4000
Trenton (G-11026)

▲ Blankets Inc ....E...... 973 589-7800
Newark (G-7108)

BNH Enterprise LLC ....E...... 201 815-0546
Dumont (G-2116)

Charles M Jessup Inc ....E...... 732 324-0430
Keasbey (G-4926)

City Envelope Inc ....E...... 201 792-9292
Jersey City (G-4727)

Clarity Imaging Tech Inc ....E...... 877 272-4362
Saddle Brook (G-9759)

Clarity Imaging Tech Inc ....E...... 413 693-1234
Pennsauken (G-8493)

▲ Clarity Imaging Tech Inc ....G...... 877 272-4362
Pennsauken (G-8494)

▲ Convertech Inc ....E...... 973 328-1850
Wharton (G-11982)

▲ Cronite Co Inc ....E...... 973 887-7900
Parsippany (G-7977)

Custom Roller Inc ....E...... 908 298-7797
Roselle (G-9668)

Deneka Printing Systems Inc ....F...... 609 752-0964
Cream Ridge (G-1934)

Digital Design Inc ....E...... 973 857-9500
Cedar Grove (G-1278)

Domino Printing ....D...... 973 857-0900
Cedar Grove (G-1280)

Ernest Schaefer Inc ....G...... 908 964-1280
Union (G-11182)

Galvanic Prtg & Plate Co Inc ....E...... 201 939-3600
Moonachie (G-6518)

Graham Graphic Group Inc ....G...... 973 827-6177
Ogdensburg (G-7771)

Graphic Equipment Corporation ......E...... 732 494-5350
Metuchen (G-6106)

▲ Interchange Equipment Inc ....E...... 973 473-5005
Passaic (G-8148)

J Nelson Press Inc ....G...... 732 747-0330
Rumson (G-9713)

Karis Graphic Corp ....G...... 201 935-8774
Moonachie (G-6527)

Kirkwood NJ Globe Acqstion LLC ...G...... 201 440-0800
Ridgefield Park (G-9408)

Kohl & Madden Prtg Ink Corp ....E...... 201 935-8666
Carlstadt (G-1181)

Mark/Trece Inc ....E...... 973 884-1005
Whippany (G-12026)

Marko Engraving & Art Corp ....E...... 201 864-6500
Weehawken (G-11698)

Marko Engraving & Art Corp ....F...... 201 945-6555
Fairview (G-3365)

Mgl Printing Solution LLC ....G...... 908 665-1999
New Providence (G-7048)

Mosstype Corporation ....G...... 201 444-8000
Waldwick (G-11450)

Mosstype Holding Corp ....E...... 201 444-8000
Waldwick (G-11451)

N B C Engraving Co Inc ....G...... 201 387-8011
Bergenfield (G-390)

On Demand Machinery ....F...... 908 351-7137
Elizabeth (G-2763)

Packaging Graphics Inc ....G...... 856 767-9000
West Berlin (G-11741)

◆ Pamarco Global Graphics Inc ......E...... 908 241-1200
Roselle (G-9679)

Pamarco Global Graphics Inc ....F...... 856 829-4585
Palmyra (G-7850)

▲ Pamarco Technologies LLC ....E...... 908 241-1200
Roselle (G-9680)

▲ Panpac LLC ....F...... 856 376-3576
Cherry Hill (G-1410)

▲ Polytype America Corp ....E...... 201 995-1000
Mahwah (G-5801)

▼ Printers Service Florida Inc ....G...... 973 589-7800
Newark (G-7276)

Verico Technology LLC ....C...... 201 842-0222
East Rutherford (G-2336)

W R Chesnut Engineering Inc ....F...... 973 227-6995
Fairfield (G-3348)

Wilenta Carting Inc ....F...... 201 325-0044
Secaucus (G-9939)

3556 Food Prdts Machinery

Absecon Island Beverage Co ....G...... 609 653-8123
Egg Harbor Township (G-2676)

◆ AGA Foodservice Inc ....C...... 856 428-4200
Cherry Hill (G-1340)

Allen Steel Co ....G...... 856 785-1171
Leesburg (G-5314)

▲ Am-Mac Incorporated ....F...... 973 575-7567
Fairfield (G-3133)

Arm & Hammer Animal Ntrtn LLC ...G...... 800 526-3563
Princeton (G-9009)

Basha USA LLC ....G...... 201 339-9770
Bayonne (G-213)

Buhler Inc ....E...... 201 847-0600
Mahwah (G-5755)

Buona Vita Inc ....D...... 856 453-7972
Bridgeton (G-780)

Caddy Corporation of America ....D...... 856 467-4222
Swedesboro (G-10686)

Corbion Group ....G...... 973 256-0198
Totowa (G-10940)

Cornell Machine Co Inc ....G...... 973 379-6860
Springfield (G-10549)

D&N Machine Manufacturing Inc ....G...... 856 456-1366
Gloucester City (G-3835)

▲ Dantco Corp ....F...... 973 278-8776
Paterson (G-8245)

▲ Excalibur Bagel Bky Equip Inc .....E...... 201 797-2788
Fair Lawn (G-3091)

▲ Excellent Bakery Equipment Co ....F...... 973 244-1664
Fairfield (G-3091)

Expert Process Systems LLC ....G...... 570 424-0581
Hackettstown (G-4006)

▲ FBM Baking Machines Inc ....F...... 609 860-0577
Cranbury (G-1833)

◆ Gericke USA Inc ....G...... 855 888-0088
Somerset (G-10105)

▲ Gram Equipment ....E...... 201 750-6500
Hamilton (G-4107)

HCH Incorporated ....G 973 300-4551
Sparta (G-10504)
Hill Machine Inc ....G 973 684-2808
Paterson (G-8289)
Industl Envrnmntl Pollutn ....E 908 241-3830
Roselle Park (G-9698)
J Hebrank Inc ....F 973 983-0001
Rockaway (G-9578)
Joe Mike Precision Fabrication ....G 609 953-1144
Medford (G-6073)
◆ Kuhl Corp ....D 908 782-5696
Flemington (G-3454)
M B C Food Machinery Corp ......G 201 489-7000
Hackensack (G-3941)
Machine Control Systems Inc .....G 732 529-6888
Jackson (G-4671)
▲ Magna Industries Inc ....E 732 905-0957
Lakewood (G-5151)
Marlo Manufacturing Co Inc ....E 973 423-0226
Boonton (G-575)
◆ Megas Yeeros LLC ....E 212 777-6342
Lyndhurst (G-5692)
Nowak Inc ....F 973 366-7208
Wharton (G-11994)
Patty-O-Matic Inc ....F 732 938-2757
Farmingdale (G-3391)
Rajbhog Foods Inc ....G 551 222-4700
Jersey City (G-4812)
▲ Rajbhog Foods Inc ....G 201 395-9400
Jersey City (G-4813)
◆ Revent Incorporated ....E 732 777-5187
Somerset (G-10166)
Solbern LLC ....E 973 227-3030
Fairfield (G-3308)
Surfside Foods LLC ....G 856 785-2115
Port Norris (G-8983)
Techno Design Inc ....G 973 478-0930
Garfield (G-3767)
▼ Terriss Consolidated Inds ....F 732 988-0909
Asbury Park (G-86)
TMU Inc ....F 609 884-7656
Cape May (G-1106)
◆ Wilenta Feed Inc ....F 201 325-0044
Secaucus (G-9940)
Willow Technology Inc ....G 732 671-1554
Holmdel (G-4531)
▲ Wyssmont Company Inc ....E 201 947-4600
Fort Lee (G-3592)
Zvonko Stulic & Son Inc ....G 973 589-3773
Newark (G-7363)

3559 Special Ind Machinery, NEC

A S M Technical ....G 973 225-0111
Paterson (G-8193)
Advance Machine Planning Inc ....F 732 356-4438
Middlesex (G-6144)
Advance Process Systems Lim ....G 201 400-9190
Branchville (G-724)
Allied Waste Products Inc ....G 973 473-7638
Wallington (G-11522)
Alvogen Pharma Us Inc ....A 973 796-3400
Pine Brook (G-8685)
AM Cruz International LLC ....G 732 340-0066
Colonia (G-1776)
◆ Amano Cincinnati Incorporated ......D 973 403-1900
Roseland (G-9642)
◆ Amano USA Holdings Inc ....G 973 403-1900
Roseland (G-9643)
Amcor Phrm Packg USA LLC .....E 856 825-1400
Millville (G-6281)
◆ American International Cont ......F 973 917-3331
Boonton (G-554)
American Leistritz Extruder ....F 908 685-2333
Branchburg (G-633)
Autoplast Systems Inc ....G 973 785-8333
Woodland Park (G-12210)
Azego Technology Svcs US Inc ....G 201 327-7500
Oakland (G-7675)
▲ Boc Group Inc ....A 908 665-2400
New Providence (G-7030)
◆ Brother International Corp ....B 908 704-1700
Bridgewater (G-825)
Cain Machine Inc ....F 856 825-7225
Millville (G-6291)
▼ Carl Buck Corporation ....G 973 300-5575
Sparta (G-10491)
Clean Air Group ....G 908 232-4200
Parsippany (G-7973)
▲ Clinton Industries Inc ....E 201 440-0400
Little Ferry (G-5498)

▲ Clordisys Solutions Inc ....E 908 236-4100
Branchburg (G-647)
Colorcraft Sign Co ....F 609 386-1115
Beverly (G-461)
Comfortfit Labs Inc ....E 908 259-9100
Roselle (G-9666)
Concrete Cutting Partners Inc ....G 201 440-2233
Hackensack (G-3898)
◆ Coperion Corporation ....C 201 327-6300
Sewell (G-9946)
County Conservation Co Inc ......F 856 227-6900
Sewell (G-9948)
◆ Cryovation LLC ....G 609 914-4792
Hainesport (G-4071)
▲ Dantco Corp ....G 973 278-8776
Paterson (G-8245)
Dayton Grey Corp ....F 732 869-0060
Asbury Park (G-76)
Deitz Co Inc ....E 732 295-8212
Belmar (G-357)
Eagle Racing Inc ....E 732 367-8487
Lakewood (G-5112)
▼ Eco-Plug-System LLC ....G 855 326-7584
Hewitt (G-4289)
Energy Recycling Co LLC ....G 732 545-6619
Highland Park (G-4303)
Expert Process Systems LLC ....G 570 424-0581
Hackettstown (G-4006)
F P Developments Inc ....E 856 875-7100
Williamstown (G-12086)
▲ Fette Compacting America Inc ....E 973 586-8722
Rockaway (G-9567)
▲ Foremost Machine Builders Inc ....D 973 227-0700
Fairfield (G-3200)
◆ Franklin Miller Inc ....G 973 535-9200
Livingston (G-5531)
G & S Design & Manufacturing ....F 908 862-2444
Linden (G-5377)
Glass Cycle Systems Inc ....G 973 838-0034
Riverdale (G-9481)
◆ Globepharma Inc ....F 732 296-9700
New Brunswick (G-6964)
▲ Gluefast Company Inc ....F 732 918-4600
Neptune (G-6915)
Graham Graphic Group Inc ....G 973 827-6177
Ogdensburg (G-7771)
Grease N Go ....G 856 784-6555
Magnolia (G-5740)
Green Power Chemical LLC ....F 973 770-5600
Hopatcong (G-4536)
Henry Dudley ....G 732 240-6895
Toms River (G-10883)
▼ Hockmeyer Equipment Corp ....G 973 482-0225
Harrison (G-4185)
Hosokawa Micron International ....D 908 273-6360
Summit (G-10645)
Hosokawa Micron International ....D 908 273-6360
Summit (G-10646)
◆ Hosokawa Micron International ....D 908 273-6360
Summit (G-10647)
Hosokawa Micron International ....F 866 507-4974
Pennsauken (G-8523)
▲ Htp Connectivity LLC ....G 973 586-2286
Rockaway (G-9572)
▲ Ileos of America Inc ....E 908 753-7300
South Plainfield (G-10383)
Imperial Sewing Machine Co ....G 973 374-3405
Irvington (G-4591)
Indoor Entertainment of NJ ....E 609 522-6700
Wildwood (G-12073)
Inter Rep Associates Inc ....G 609 465-0077
Cape May Court House (G-1114)
Jason Equipment Corp ....E 973 983-7212
Rockaway (G-9579)
▲ Jaygo Incorporated ....G 908 688-3600
Randolph (G-9285)
▲ Jet Pulverizer Co Inc ....E 856 235-5554
Moorestown (G-6588)
John N Fehlinger Co Inc ....G 973 633-0699
Fairfield (G-3237)
John W Kennedy Company ....G 973 256-5525
Little Falls (G-5478)
▲ Jomar Corp ....E 609 646-8000
Egg Harbor Township (G-2687)
Kahle Automation ....G 973 993-1850
Morristown (G-6719)
▲ Kansai Special Amercn Mch Corp ....G 973 470-8321
East Rutherford (G-2301)
Koch Mdlar Process Systems LLC ....D 201 368-2929
Paramus (G-7882)

▲ Kooltronic Inc ....C 609 466-3400
Pennington (G-8455)
Kyosis LLC ....G 908 202-8894
South River (G-10462)
Linde North America Inc ....D 908 464-8100
New Providence (G-7045)
▼ Linde North America Inc ....B 908 464-8100
Bridgewater (G-857)
Lmt Usa Inc ....G 973 586-8722
Rockaway (G-9585)
◆ Logan Instruments Corporation ....F 732 302-9888
Somerset (G-10125)
M C Technologies Inc ....G 973 839-2779
Pompton Plains (G-8961)
▲ Manning & Lewis Engrg Co Inc ....D 908 687-2400
Union (G-11205)
Mastercraft Electroplating ....G 908 354-4404
Elizabeth (G-2755)
Metal Finishing Co LLC ....G 973 778-9550
Passaic (G-8164)
Miracle Mile Automotive Inc ....G 732 886-6315
Lakewood (G-5160)
◆ N C Carpet Binding & Equipment ....F 973 481-3500
Newark (G-7247)
▲ Nicos Group Inc ....G 201 768-9501
Norwood (G-7631)
P & P Equipment Corporation ....F 201 489-0050
River Edge (G-9467)
▲ Park Plus Inc ....G 201 651-8590
Oakland (G-7701)
Pharma Systems Inc ....G 973 636-9007
Hawthorne (G-4254)
R T Kuntz Co ....F 732 751-1770
Wall Township (G-11505)
▲ Ramco Equipment Corp ....E 908 687-6700
Hillside (G-4436)
▲ Recycle-Tech Corp ....F 201 475-5000
Elmwood Park (G-2847)
▲ Reliable Welding & Mch Work ....E 201 865-1073
North Bergen (G-7478)
Rf360 Technologies Inc ....E 848 999-3582
Iselin (G-4642)
Ridge Manufacturing Corp ....D 973 586-2717
Rockaway (G-9604)
Royal Aquarius Empire ....D 646 847-3322
Hamilton (G-4125)
Safegaurd Document Destruction ....G 609 448-6695
Millstone Township (G-6265)
Safety-Kleen Systems Inc ....F 609 859-2049
Southampton (G-10481)
Science Pump Corporation ....E 856 963-7700
Camden (G-1085)
Seajay Manufacturing Corp ....F 732 774-0900
Neptune (G-6931)
Sony Corporation of America ....F 201 930-1000
Woodcliff Lake (G-12202)
▲ Spadix Technologies Inc ....E 732 356-6906
Middlesex (G-6200)
Specialty Measurements Inc ....F 908 534-1500
Lebanon (G-5302)
Starlight Electro-Optics Inc ....E 908 859-1362
Phillipsburg (G-8671)
Suez Treatment Solutions Inc ....D 201 676-2525
Leonia (G-5320)
Thanks For Being Green LLC ....E 856 333-0991
Pennsauken (G-8584)
Thompson Stone ....G 973 293-7237
Montague (G-6403)
Tilton Rack & Basket Co ....E 973 226-6010
Fairfield (G-3326)
Tosca ....G 973 337-5724
Montclair (G-6438)
Veeco ....E 732 560-5300
Somerset (G-10192)
Veeco Instruments Inc ....E 732 560-5300
Somerset (G-10193)
Vibra Screw Inc ....E 973 256-7410
Totowa (G-10980)
Victor International Marketing ....G 973 267-8900
Morristown (G-6749)
▲ Witte Co Inc ....E 908 689-6500
Washington (G-11590)
▲ Wyssmont Company Inc ....E 201 947-4600
Fort Lee (G-3592)

3561 Pumps & Pumping Eqpt

▲ Apple Air Compressor Corp ....F 888 222-9940
Rutherford (G-9725)
◆ Bio Compression Systems Inc ....E 201 939-0716
Moonachie (G-6508)

Employee Codes: A=Over 500 employees, B=251-500
C=101-250, D=51-100, E=20-50, F=10-19, G=4-9   2018 Harris New Jersey
Manufacturers Directory   573

▲ Boc Group Inc ....A 908 665-2400
New Providence (G-7030)
C & L Machining Company Inc ....G 856 456-1932
Brooklawn (G-920)
Callaghan Pump Controls Inc ....G 201 621-0505
Hackensack (G-3891)
Carter Pump Inc ....G 201 568-9798
Waldwick (G-11442)
Cooper Alloy Corporation ....F 908 688-4120
Hillside (G-4403)
Davis-Standard LLC ....E 908 722-6000
Somerset (G-10089)
Delta Sales Company Inc ....G 973 838-0371
Butler (G-1002)
Dynaflow Engineering Inc ....G 732 356-9790
Middlesex (G-6164)
E Wortmann Machine Works Inc ......F 201 288-1654
Teterboro (G-10793)
Energy Beams Inc ....F 973 291-6555
Bloomingdale (G-543)
Flowserve Corporation ....F 908 859-7000
Phillipsburg (G-8648)
Flowserve Corporation ....D 856 241-7800
Bridgeport (G-766)
Flowserve Corporation ....G 973 334-9444
Parsippany (G-8013)
Flowserve Corporation ....D 973 227-4565
Fairfield (G-3198)
◆ Hayward Industries Inc ....B 908 351-5400
Elizabeth (G-2742)
Hhh Machine Co ....G 908 276-1220
Cranford (G-1910)
Ingersoll-Rand Company ....E 856 793-7000
Mount Laurel (G-6803)
Interntional Cnsld Chemex Corp ....E 732 828-7676
New Brunswick (G-6969)
Kraissl Company Inc ....E 201 342-0008
Hackensack (G-3937)
▲ Leistritz Advanced Tech Corp ....E 201 934-8262
Allendale (G-11)
◆ Linde LLC ....C 908 464-8100
Bridgewater (G-855)
Linde LLC ....G 973 579-2065
Sparta (G-10510)
Linde North America Inc ....D 908 464-8100
New Providence (G-7045)
▼ Linde North America Inc ....B 908 464-8100
Bridgewater (G-857)
Magnatrol Valve Corporation ....F 856 829-4580
Roebling (G-9638)
Melville Industries Inc ....E 856 461-0091
Riverside (G-9503)
▲ Nes Company Inc ....G 973 795-1519
Jersey City (G-4788)
▲ Orion Machinery Co Ltd ....E 201 569-3220
Rutherford (G-9742)
Science Pump Corporation ....E 856 963-7700
Camden (G-1085)
Shoreway Industry ....G 856 307-2020
Clayton (G-1528)
▲ Valcor Engineering Corporation ....C 973 467-8400
Springfield (G-10583)
Valley Tech Inc ....G 908 534-5565
Whitehouse Station (G-12064)
▲ Vanton Pump & Equipment Corp ...E 908 688-4120
Hillside (G-4450)
Xylem Dewatering Solutions Inc ......G 856 467-3636
Bridgeport (G-775)

3562 Ball & Roller Bearings

▲ Accurate Bushing Company Inc .....E 908 789-1121
Garwood (G-3774)
C & L Machining Company Inc ....E 856 456-1932
Brooklawn (G-920)
Emmco Development Corp ....F 732 469-6464
Somerset (G-10093)
Federal Casters Corp ....D 973 483-6700
Harrison (G-4182)
General Dynamics Glbl IMG Tech ....E 973 335-2230
Parsippany (G-8022)
Ingersoll-Rand Company ....E 856 793-7000
Mount Laurel (G-6803)
J C W Inc ....E 732 560-8061
Bridgewater (G-848)
Rbc Bearings Incorporated ....C 609 882-5050
Ewing (G-3048)
▲ Rollon Corporation ....E 973 300-5492
Hackettstown (G-4032)

3563 Air & Gas Compressors

Aavolyn Corp ....E 856 327-8040
Millville (G-6272)
Aer X Dust Corporation ....G 732 946-9462
Holmdel (G-4508)
Argus International Inc ....E 609 466-1677
Ringoes (G-9435)
▲ Armco Compressor Products ....G 201 866-6766
North Bergen (G-7432)
◆ Atlas Copco Hurricane LLC ....D 800 754-7408
Parsippany (G-7954)
▲ Breeze-Eastern LLC ....G 973 602-1001
Whippany (G-12014)
Campbell Hausfeld LLC ....C 856 661-1800
Pennsauken (G-8489)
◆ Croll-Reynolds Co Inc ....E 908 232-4200
Parsippany (G-7976)
Eagletree-Pump Aquisiton Corp ......D 201 569-1173
Rutherford (G-9730)
▼ Emse Corp ....F 973 227-9221
Fairfield (G-3184)
Energy Beams Inc ....F 973 291-6555
Bloomingdale (G-543)
◆ Falcon Safety Products Inc ....D 908 707-4900
Branchburg (G-658)
Fleet Equipment Corporation ....F 201 337-3294
Franklin Lakes (G-3617)
Gas Drying Inc ....F 973 361-2212
Wharton (G-11988)
Ingersoll-Rand Company ....E 856 793-7000
Mount Laurel (G-6803)
Jetstream of Houston LLP ....G 732 448-7830
New Brunswick (G-6972)
Knf Neuberger Inc ....D 609 890-8889
Trenton (G-11074)
Kraissl Company Inc ....E 201 342-0008
Hackensack (G-3937)
▲ Metropolitan Vacuum Clr Co Inc ...D 201 405-2225
Oakland (G-7696)
◆ Orion Machinery Co Ltd ....E 201 569-3220
Rutherford (G-9742)
Polvac Inc ....G 732 828-1662
New Brunswick (G-6992)
▲ Trillium US ....G 973 827-1661
Hamburg (G-4097)
▲ United Vacuum LLC ....F 973 827-1661
Hamburg (G-4098)
◆ Vac-U-Max ....E 973 759-4600
Belleville (G-322)
Vairtec Corporation ....G 201 445-6965
Midland Park (G-6241)

3564 Blowers & Fans

Aer X Dust Corporation ....G 732 946-9462
Holmdel (G-4508)
Air Clean Co Inc ....G 908 355-1515
Elizabeth (G-2706)
Automated Flexible Conveyors ....F 973 340-1695
Clifton (G-1569)
Bioclimatic Air Systems LLC ....E 856 764-4300
Delran (G-2011)
Bioclimatic Inc ....E 856 764-4300
Delran (G-2012)
Bionomic Industries Inc ....F 201 529-1094
Mahwah (G-5753)
Bios International Corp ....E 973 492-8400
Butler (G-998)
Brookaire Company LLC ....F 973 473-7527
Carlstadt (G-1133)
Buhler Inc ....E 201 847-0600
Mahwah (G-5755)
Building Performance Eqp Inc ....F 201 722-1414
Hillsdale (G-4380)
◆ Camfil USA Inc ....C 973 616-7300
Riverdale (G-9476)
Cleanzones LLC ....G 732 534-5590
Jackson (G-4658)
Creative Industrial Kitchens ....G 973 633-0420
Wayne (G-11621)
◆ Croll-Reynolds Co Inc ....E 908 232-4200
Parsippany (G-7976)
Cross Rip Ocean Engrg LLC ....G 973 455-0005
Parsippany (G-7978)
CSM Environmental Systems LLC ....F 908 789-5431
Mountainside (G-6871)
▲ CSM Worldwide Inc ....E 908 233-2882
Bridgewater (G-831)
▲ Csonka Worldwide ....E 609 514-2766
Plainsboro (G-8879)

DR Technology Inc ....G 732 780-4664
Freehold (G-3651)
Encur Inc ....G 732 264-2098
Keyport (G-5016)
Envirnmntal Dynamics Group Inc ....F 609 924-4489
Rocky Hill (G-9637)
Fmdk Technologies Inc ....G 201 828-9822
Mahwah (G-5775)
Gpt Inc ....F 732 446-2400
Manalapan (G-5849)
▲ Hamon Corporation ....D 908 333-2000
Somerville (G-10213)
▲ Handler Manufacturing Company ...E 908 233-7796
Westfield (G-11926)
◆ Hayward Industrial Products ....C 908 351-5400
Elizabeth (G-2741)
Indoor Environmental Tech ....E 973 709-1122
Lincoln Park (G-5327)
◆ JC Macelroy Co Inc ....D 732 572-7100
Piscataway (G-8784)
Klm Mechanical Contractors ....F 201 385-6965
Dumont (G-2120)
▲ Kooltronic Inc ....C 609 466-3400
Pennington (G-8455)
Lm Air Technology Inc ....E 732 381-8200
Rahway (G-9210)
Mer Made Filter ....E 201 236-0217
Ramsey (G-9247)
▲ Metropolitan Vacuum Clr Co Inc ...D 201 405-2225
Oakland (G-7696)
▲ Microelettrica-Usa LLC ....F 973 598-0806
Budd Lake (G-937)
Naava Inc ....G 844 666-2282
Springfield (G-10566)
National Environmental Svcs Co ......G 908 813-1195
Hackettstown (G-4028)
Palude Enterprises Inc ....G 732 241-5478
Howell (G-4562)
Respironics Inc ....C 973 581-6000
Parsippany (G-8079)
Safety Power Inc ....G 908 277-1826
Summit (G-10654)
Science Pump Corporation ....E 856 963-7700
Camden (G-1085)
Stamm International Corp ....E 201 947-1700
Fort Lee (G-3583)
Sternvent Co Inc ....E 908 688-0807
Union (G-11225)
Summit Filter Corp. ....E 908 687-3500
Union (G-11226)
Tri-Dim Filter Corporation ....G 856 786-2447
Cinnaminson (G-1496)
Tri-Dim Filter Corporation ....G 973 709-1122
Lincoln Park (G-5335)
▲ Wire Cloth Manufacturers Inc ....G 973 328-1000
Mine Hill (G-6329)

3565 Packaging Machinery

▲ Action Packaging Automation ....G 609 448-9210
Roosevelt (G-9639)
Ajg Packaging LLC ....G 908 528-6052
Pittstown (G-8848)
Alliance Food Equipment ....F 201 784-1101
Trenton (G-11016)
AT Information Products Inc ....G 201 529-0202
Mahwah (G-5750)
Banarez Enterprises Inc ....G 201 222-7515
Jersey City (G-4713)
▲ Beauty-Fill LLC ....G 908 353-1600
Hillside (G-4397)
▲ Campak Inc ....G 973 994-4888
Livingston (G-5526)
◆ Clements Industries Inc ....E 201 440-5500
South Hackensack (G-10258)
Copack International Inc ....E 973 405-5151
Clifton (G-1591)
▲ Cozzoli Machine Company ....D 732 564-0400
Somerset (G-10086)
Dalemark Industries Inc ....F 732 367-3100
Lakewood (G-5105)
Deitz Co Inc ....E 732 295-8212
Belmar (G-357)
▲ Elite Packaging Corp ....F 732 651-9955
East Brunswick (G-2150)
F P Developments Inc ....E 856 875-7100
Williamstown (G-12086)
Ganz Brothers Inc ....F 201 820-1975
Paramus (G-7870)
Gloucester City Box Works LLC ....F 856 456-9032
Gloucester City (G-3837)

Golden W Ppr Converting Corp ....E 908 412-8889
South Plainfield *(G-10374)*
▲ **Gram Equipment** ....E 201 750-6500
Hamilton *(G-4107)*
Greener Corp ....E 732 341-3880
Bayville *(G-255)*
Groniger USA LLC ....G 704 588-3873
Basking Ridge *(G-189)*
▲ **Hair Systems Inc** ....D 732 446-2202
Englishtown *(G-2994)*
◆ **Heisler Machine & Tool Co** ....E 973 227-6300
Fairfield *(G-3220)*
Hekikat LLC ....G 908 232-1145
Middletown *(G-6217)*
Herma US Inc ....G 973 521-7254
Fairfield *(G-3221)*
▼ **I S Parts International Inc** ....E 856 691-2203
Vineland *(G-11372)*
ID Technology LLC ....E 201 405-0767
Oakland *(G-7692)*
J F C Machine Works LLC ....F 732 203-2077
Holmdel *(G-4518)*
J G Machine Works Inc ....G 732 203-2077
Edison *(G-2543)*
▲ **K & S Industries Inc** ....F 908 862-3030
Linden *(G-5395)*
Kohl & Madden Prtg Ink Corp ....E 201 935-8666
Carlstadt *(G-1181)*
▲ **Kompac Technologies LLC** ....E 908 534-8411
Somerville *(G-10220)*
Labeling Systems LLC ....E 201 405-0767
Oakland *(G-7694)*
Luciano Packaging Technologies ....G 908 722-3222
Branchburg *(G-676)*
Mactec Packaging Tech LLC ....G 732 343-1607
Sayreville *(G-9832)*
▲ **Njrls Enterprises Inc** ....F 732 846-6010
Branchburg *(G-683)*
Pabin Associates Inc ....G 201 288-7216
Hasbrouck Heights *(G-4197)*
▼ **Pace Packaging LLC** ....D 973 227-1040
Fairfield *(G-3279)*
Packaging Machinery & Eqp Co ....G 973 325-2418
West Orange *(G-11903)*
◆ **Per-Fil Industries Inc** ....E 856 461-5700
Riverside *(G-9504)*
PMC Industries Inc ....E 201 342-3684
Hackensack *(G-3963)*
Potdevin Machine Co ....F 973 227-8828
West Caldwell *(G-11798)*
▲ **Pro Pack Inc** ....F 201 485-7587
Wyckoff *(G-12260)*
▲ **Pro-Motion Industries LLC** ....F 856 809-0040
Sicklerville *(G-10023)*
▲ **Pro-Pac Service Inc** ....F 973 962-8080
Ringwood *(G-9453)*
Prodo-Pak Corp ....G 973 772-4500
Garfield *(G-3752)*
▲ **Prodo-Pak Corporation** ....E 973 777-7770
Garfield *(G-3753)*
Quality Carton Inc ....F 201 529-6900
Mahwah *(G-5805)*
Remington Industries Inc ....F 908 233-0153
Mountainside *(G-6887)*
▲ **Romaco Inc** ....E 973 709-0691
Lincoln Park *(G-5332)*
▲ **Scandia Packaging Machinery Co** ....E 973 473-6100
Fairfield *(G-3302)*
Sjd Direct Midwest LLC ....C 732 985-8405
Edison *(G-2620)*
Sjd Direct Midwest LLC ....C 732 287-2525
Edison *(G-2621)*
Specialty Tube Filling LLC ....G 908 262-2219
Hillsborough *(G-4372)*
▲ **Supplyone New York Inc** ....E 718 392-7400
Paterson *(G-8392)*
Techline Extrusion Systems ....G 973 831-0317
Haskell *(G-4215)*
Vacuum Solutions Group Inc ....G 781 762-0414
Teaneck *(G-10776)*
▼ **Wagner Industries Inc** ....F 973 347-0800
Stanhope *(G-10592)*
◆ **Weiler Labeling Systems LLC** ....D 856 273-3377
Moorestown *(G-6632)*
Wrap-Ade Machine Co Inc ....F 973 773-6150
Clifton *(G-1744)*
▲ **Wrapade Packaging Systems LLC** ....F 973 787-1788
Fairfield *(G-3355)*

3566 Speed Changers, Drives & Gears

431 Converters Inc ....G 856 848-8949
Woodbury Heights *(G-12173)*
Able Gear & Machine Co ....G 973 983-8055
Rockaway *(G-9541)*
▲ **Acme Gear Co Inc** ....D 201 568-2245
Englewood *(G-2866)*
Drive Technology Inc ....G 732 422-6500
Monmouth Junction *(G-6342)*
Jetyd Corporation ....F 201 512-9500
Mahwah *(G-5786)*
▲ **Koellmann Gear Corporation** ....C 201 447-0200
Waldwick *(G-11447)*
Martin Sprocket & Gear Inc ....F 973 633-5700
Wayne *(G-11664)*
Numeritool Manufacturing Corp ....G 973 827-7714
Franklin *(G-3603)*
Sew-Eurodrive Inc ....E 856 467-2277
Bridgeport *(G-771)*
Sew-Eurodrive Inc ....D 856 467-2277
Bridgeport *(G-772)*
State Tool Gear Co Inc ....F 973 642-6181
Newark *(G-7329)*
▲ **Walter Machine Co Inc** ....E 201 656-5654
Jersey City *(G-4846)*

3567 Indl Process Furnaces & Ovens

Abp Induction LLC ....F 732 932-6400
North Brunswick *(G-7500)*
Argus International Inc ....E 609 466-1677
Ringoes *(G-9435)*
◆ **C M Furnaces Inc** ....E 973 338-6500
Bloomfield *(G-504)*
Cire Technologies Inc ....G 973 402-8301
Mountain Lakes *(G-6855)*
◆ **Consarc Corporation** ....E 609 267-8000
Rancocas *(G-9256)*
Corbett Industries Inc ....F 201 445-6311
Waldwick *(G-11443)*
Curran-Pfeiff Corp ....F 732 225-0555
Edison *(G-2499)*
▲ **Electroheat Induction Inc** ....G 908 494-0726
Jersey City *(G-4747)*
▲ **Elnik Systems LLC** ....E 973 239-6066
Cedar Grove *(G-1281)*
Energy Beams Inc ....F 973 291-6555
Bloomingdale *(G-543)*
Essex Products International ....E 973 226-2424
Caldwell *(G-1028)*
Gia-Tek LLC ....G 973 228-0875
West Caldwell *(G-11777)*
▲ **Glenro Inc** ....F 973 279-5900
Paterson *(G-8277)*
Hankin Acquisitions Inc ....F 908 722-9595
Hillsborough *(G-4338)*
Hankin Envmtl Systems Inc ....F 908 722-9595
Hillsborough *(G-4339)*
Hary Manufacturing Inc ....F 908 722-7100
Woodbridge *(G-12150)*
▲ **Haydon Corporation** ....D 973 904-0800
Wayne *(G-11646)*
Hed International Inc ....F 609 466-1900
Ringoes *(G-9437)*
◆ **Inductotherm Corporation** ....C 609 267-9000
Rancocas *(G-9258)*
◆ **L & L Kiln Mfg Inc** ....E 856 294-0077
Swedesboro *(G-10705)*
Lydon Bros Corp ....E 201 343-4334
South Hackensack *(G-10276)*
Marsden Inc ....E 856 663-2227
Pennsauken *(G-8544)*
Pennington Furnace Supply Inc ....G 609 737-2500
Pennington *(G-8457)*
Procedyne Corp ....E 732 249-8347
New Brunswick *(G-6996)*
Pv/T Inc ....G 609 267-3933
Rancocas *(G-9261)*
▲ **Radiant Energy Systems Inc** ....E 973 423-5220
Hawthorne *(G-4256)*
Radiation Systems Inc ....G 201 891-7515
Wyckoff *(G-12261)*
◆ **Rowan Technologies Inc** ....D 609 267-9000
Rancocas *(G-9262)*
Saber Associates ....E 973 777-3800
Clifton *(G-1713)*
▲ **Solar Products Inc** ....E 973 248-9370
Pompton Lakes *(G-8948)*
▼ **T-M Vacuum Products Inc** ....E 856 829-2000
Cinnaminson *(G-1490)*

Therma-Tech Corporation ....F 973 345-0076
Paterson *(G-8400)*
Thermal Conduction Engineering ....G 201 865-1084
Secaucus *(G-9934)*
Waage Electric Inc ....G 908 245-9363
Kenilworth *(G-5004)*
▲ **Wyssmont Company Inc** ....E 201 947-4600
Fort Lee *(G-3592)*

3568 Mechanical Power Transmission Eqpt, NEC

A M Gatti Inc ....F 609 396-1577
Trenton *(G-11010)*
Accurate Bronze Bearing Co ....G 973 345-2304
Paterson *(G-8198)*
▲ **Accurate Bushing Company Inc** ....E 908 789-1121
Garwood *(G-3774)*
Amscot Structural Pdts Corp ....E 973 989-8800
Dover *(G-2075)*
▲ **Andantex U S A Inc** ....E 732 493-2812
Ocean *(G-7715)*
▲ **Bcc (USA) Inc** ....G 732 572-5450
Piscataway *(G-8740)*
Brilliant Light Power Inc ....E 609 490-0427
East Windsor *(G-2371)*
Daven Industries Inc ....E 973 808-8848
Fairfield *(G-3173)*
Emmco Development Corp ....F 732 469-6464
Somerset *(G-10093)*
Garlock Bearings Inc ....F 856 848-3200
Thorofare *(G-10819)*
▲ **Gate Technologies Inc** ....G 973 300-0090
Sparta *(G-10500)*
◆ **Ggb North America LLC** ....C 856 848-3200
Thorofare *(G-10821)*
▲ **Hydro-Mechanical Systems Inc** ....F 856 848-8888
Westville *(G-11943)*
Martin Sprocket & Gear Inc ....F 973 633-5700
Wayne *(G-11664)*
Moser Jewel Company ....G 908 454-1155
Phillipsburg *(G-8660)*
▲ **Reich USA Corporation** ....F 201 684-9400
Mahwah *(G-5808)*
S G Manufacturing Co Inc ....D 732 494-6520
Metuchen *(G-6119)*
Valcor Engineering Corporation ....E 973 467-8100
Springfield *(G-10584)*
Woyshner Service Company Inc ....G 856 461-9196
Delran *(G-2024)*

3569 Indl Machinery & Eqpt, NEC

Absolute Protective Systems ....E 732 287-4500
Edison *(G-2448)*
Admiral Filter Company LLC ....F 973 664-0400
Rockaway *(G-9543)*
◆ **Amec Fster Wheeler N Amer Corp** ....D 936 448-6323
Hampton *(G-4153)*
▼ **Amerilubes LLC** ....G 704 399-7701
Waretown *(G-11532)*
▲ **Boc Group Inc** ....A 908 665-2400
New Providence *(G-7030)*
◆ **Camfil USA Inc** ....C 973 616-7300
Riverdale *(G-9476)*
Carol Products Co Inc ....D 732 918-0800
Ocean *(G-7718)*
Celestech Inc ....G 856 986-2221
Haddonfield *(G-4057)*
▲ **Clayton Associates Inc** ....F 732 363-2100
Lakewood *(G-5094)*
Clayton Manufacturing Company ....F 609 409-9400
Cranbury *(G-1823)*
Coilhose Pneumatics Inc ....E 732 432-7177
East Brunswick *(G-2142)*
Complete Filter ....G 732 441-0321
South Amboy *(G-10235)*
Confires Fire Prtction Svc LLC ....F 908 822-2700
South Plainfield *(G-10349)*
Devco Corporation ....G 201 337-1600
Basking Ridge *(G-185)*
▲ **Eaton Filtration LLC** ....B 732 767-4200
Tinton Falls *(G-10833)*
▲ **Enviro-Clear Company Inc** ....F 908 638-5507
High Bridge *(G-4295)*
Eurodia Industrie SA ....G 732 805-4001
Somerset *(G-10098)*
Filtration Solutions Inc ....G 908 684-4000
Hackettstown *(G-4007)*
◆ **Foster Wheeler Zack Inc** ....D 908 730-4000
Hampton *(G-4158)*

S
I
C

◆ Hayward Industries Inc .....B 908 351-5400
Elizabeth *(G-2742)*
◆ Hayward Pool Products Inc .....A 908 351-5400
Elizabeth *(G-2744)*
▲ Heinkel Filtering Systems Inc .....F 856 467-3399
Swedesboro *(G-10701)*
▲ Heller Industries Inc .....D 973 377-6800
Florham Park *(G-3505)*
▲ I & J Fisnar Inc .....F 973 646-5044
Pine Brook *(G-8703)*
Independent Machine Company .....E 973 882-0060
Fairfield *(G-3227)*
Industrial Filters Company .....G 973 575-0533
Fairfield *(G-3229)*
Intech Powercore Corporation .....G 201 767-8066
Closter *(G-1761)*
▲ Integrated Packg Systems Inc .....G 973 664-0020
Denville *(G-2042)*
◆ Kason Corporation .....D 973 467-8140
Millburn *(G-6254)*
▼ Kavon Filter Products Co .....F 732 938-3135
Wall Township *(G-11492)*
Life Liners Inc .....G 973 635-9234
Chatham *(G-1333)*
◆ Linde LLC .....C 908 464-8100
Bridgewater *(G-855)*
Linde LLC .....G 973 579-2065
Sparta *(G-10510)*
Linde North America Inc .....D 908 464-8100
New Providence *(G-7045)*
▼ Linde North America Inc .....B 908 464-8100
Bridgewater *(G-857)*
Liquid-Solids Separation Corp .....E 201 236-4833
Ramsey *(G-9245)*
Madison Park Volunteer Fire Co .....E 732 727-1143
Parlin *(G-7935)*
Mar Cor Purification Inc .....G 973 521-7032
Fairfield *(G-3255)*
Membranes International Inc .....G 973 998-5530
Ringwood *(G-9451)*
Mep Alaska LLC .....G 646 535-9005
Livingston *(G-5543)*
Microdysis Inc .....G 609 642-1184
Bordentown *(G-604)*
▲ Newton Tool & Mfg Inc .....D 856 241-1500
Pennsauken *(G-8554)*
▲ Nichem Co .....G 973 399-9810
Newark *(G-7259)*
NJ Service Testing & Insptn .....G 732 221-6357
Lincroft *(G-5340)*
▲ Palmer Electronics Inc .....F 973 772-5900
Garfield *(G-3744)*
▲ Pem Systems Inc .....E 908 276-0211
Cranford *(G-1921)*
Pulsonics Inc .....F 800 999-6785
Belleville *(G-313)*
Remington Industries Inc .....F 908 233-0153
Mountainside *(G-6887)*
◆ Smartpool LLC .....E 732 730-9880
Lakewood *(G-5189)*
◆ Specified Technologies Inc .....C 908 526-8000
Branchburg *(G-705)*
▲ Stauff Corporation .....E 201 444-7800
Waldwick *(G-11453)*
▲ Steamist Inc .....E 201 933-0700
East Rutherford *(G-2327)*
Summit Filter Corp .....E 908 687-3500
Union *(G-11226)*
T M Industries Inc .....G 908 730-7674
Belvidere *(G-377)*
Teneyck Inc .....D 201 939-1100
Lyndhurst *(G-5711)*
Township of Carneys Point .....F 856 299-4973
Carneys Point *(G-1247)*
Universal Filters Inc .....E 732 774-8555
Asbury Park *(G-87)*
Valeur Corporation .....E 732 329-4666
Monmouth Junction *(G-6369)*

3571 Electronic Computers

Aicumen Technologies Inc .....G 732 668-4204
Princeton *(G-8998)*
Alfred Heitzman Machine Works .....G 201 489-8888
Moonachie *(G-6500)*
Ancol .....G 908 233-8907
Westfield *(G-11920)*
Andlogic Computers .....G 609 610-5752
Hamilton *(G-4103)*
Apple Tree .....G 609 751-5375
Princeton *(G-9005)*
Asi Computer Technologies Inc .....F 732 343-7100
Edison *(G-2467)*
▲ B2x Corporation .....G 201 714-2373
Jersey City *(G-4712)*
▲ Carpenter LLC .....F 609 689-3090
Trenton *(G-11034)*
◆ Crestron Electronics Inc .....C 201 767-3400
Rockleigh *(G-9628)*
▲ Datapro International Inc .....E 732 868-0588
Piscataway *(G-8754)*
▲ DFI-Itox LLC .....E 732 562-0693
Piscataway *(G-8757)*
Dxl Enterprises Inc .....F 201 891-8718
Mahwah *(G-5768)*
Eom Worldwide Sales Corp .....G 732 994-7352
Lakewood *(G-5116)*
Esaw Industries Inc .....G 732 613-1400
East Brunswick *(G-2154)*
Fillimerica Inc .....G 800 435-7257
Montville *(G-6488)*
Five Elements Robotics LLC .....G 800 681-8514
Wall Township *(G-11482)*
▲ Franklin Electronic Publs Inc .....D 609 386-2500
Burlington *(G-974)*
Global Business Dimensions Inc .....E 973 831-5866
Pompton Plains *(G-8960)*
Green Apple Home Imprv LLC .....G 201 300-5554
Garfield *(G-3738)*
▲ Hitechone Inc .....G 201 500-8864
Englewood Cliffs *(G-2964)*
Ideal Data Inc .....F 201 998-9440
North Arlington *(G-7420)*
La Duca Technical Services LLC .....G 570 309-4009
West Milford *(G-11853)*
Lavitsky Computer Laboratories .....G 908 725-6206
Bridgewater *(G-850)*
Maingear Inc .....E 888 624-6432
Kenilworth *(G-4972)*
Mikros Systems Corporation .....G 609 987-1513
Princeton *(G-9074)*
Niksun Inc .....C 609 936-9999
Princeton *(G-9081)*
▼ Novasom Industries Inc .....G 732 994-5652
Lakewood *(G-5167)*
Oracle America Inc .....D 609 750-0640
East Rutherford *(G-2314)*
Oti America Inc .....G 732 429-1900
Iselin *(G-4639)*
Pascack Data Services Inc .....F 973 304-4858
Hawthorne *(G-4251)*
▲ Pcs Revenue Ctrl Systems Inc .....E 201 568-8300
Englewood Cliffs *(G-2978)*
▲ Planitroi Inc .....D 973 664-0700
Denville *(G-2051)*
Princeton Identity Inc .....E 609 256-6994
Hamilton *(G-4123)*
▲ Reliance Electronics Inc .....E 973 237-0400
Totowa *(G-10969)*
Rt Com USA Inc .....G 973 862-4210
Lafayette *(G-5052)*
S G A Business Systems Inc .....G 908 359-4626
Hillsborough *(G-4370)*
Spacetouch Inc .....G 609 712-6572
Princeton *(G-9124)*
Strahan Consulting Group LLC .....G 908 790-0873
Scotch Plains *(G-9857)*
Technical Advantage Inc .....G 973 402-5500
Boonton *(G-585)*
Techno City Inc .....G 862 414-3282
East Rutherford *(G-2330)*
▲ Touch Dynamic Inc .....D 732 382-5701
South Plainfield *(G-10440)*
Xceedium Inc .....D 201 536-1000
Jersey City *(G-4852)*
Zt Systems .....G 201 559-1000
Secaucus *(G-9942)*

3572 Computer Storage Devices

150 Development Group LLC .....G 732 546-3812
Middlesex *(G-6139)*
▲ Altus Pcb LLC .....F 973 928-8777
Cresskill *(G-1943)*
Aurora Research Company Inc .....G 973 827-8055
Franklin *(G-3595)*
B-Hive Ltd Liability Company .....G 302 438-2769
Hightstown *(G-4310)*
Bluecline Networks LLC .....G 609 944-8433
Princeton *(G-9017)*
◆ Computer Printers & Media Sups .....G 732 400-7888
East Brunswick *(G-2143)*
Creative Cmpt Concepts LLC .....G 877 919-7988
Williamstown *(G-12085)*
Dataram Memory .....E 609 799-0071
Princeton *(G-9028)*
Eclearview Technologies Inc .....G 732 695-6999
Ocean *(G-7724)*
EMC Corporation .....D 732 922-6353
Ocean *(G-7725)*
EMC Corporation .....A 732 549-8500
East Brunswick *(G-2152)*
EMC Paving LLC .....G 908 636-1054
Piscataway *(G-8763)*
EMC Squared LLC .....G 973 586-8854
Rockaway *(G-9563)*
Gaw Associates Inc .....F 856 608-1428
Cherry Hill *(G-1370)*
Micronet Enertec Tech Inc .....D 201 225-0190
Montvale *(G-6467)*
▲ Ner Data Products Inc .....E 888 637-3282
Glassboro *(G-3810)*
Pascack Data Services Inc .....F 973 304-4858
Hawthorne *(G-4251)*
▲ Plastic Reel Corp of America .....E 201 933-5100
Carlstadt *(G-1203)*
▲ Pny Technologies Inc .....B 973 515-9700
Parsippany *(G-8068)*
Quantum Integrators Group LLC .....D 609 632-0621
Plainsboro *(G-8897)*
Quantum Renovations .....G 856 278-0176
Pennsville *(G-8593)*
Quantum Vector Corp .....G 201 870-1782
Westwood *(G-11967)*
Ryval Cmpt Svcs Ltd Lblty Co .....G 201 374-1600
Dumont *(G-2123)*
Sony Corporation of America .....B 201 930-1000
Paramus *(G-7902)*
Veeco Instruments Inc .....E 732 560-5300
Somerset *(G-10193)*
Western Digital Corporation .....G 609 734-7479
Princeton *(G-9138)*
Whiptail Technologies LLC .....D 973 585-6375
Whippany *(G-12044)*
▲ Zirex Inc .....G 201 807-6401
Ridgefield Park *(G-9419)*

3575 Computer Terminals

▲ American Gaming & Elec Inc .....D 609 704-3000
Hammonton *(G-4129)*
Computer Company North America .....F 909 265-3390
Bedminster *(G-270)*
Information Technolgy Corp .....G 201 556-1999
Paramus *(G-7876)*
Linden Group Corporation .....F 973 983-8809
Cedar Knolls *(G-1315)*
Maingear Inc .....E 888 624-6432
Kenilworth *(G-4972)*
Metrofuser LLC .....D 908 245-2100
Elizabeth *(G-2757)*
▲ Touch Dynamic Inc .....D 732 382-5701
South Plainfield *(G-10440)*
Zkteco USA LLC .....E 862 505-2101
Fairfield *(G-3356)*

3577 Computer Peripheral Eqpt, NEC

Advancing Opportunities Inc .....G 201 907-0200
Teaneck *(G-10740)*
AEP Networks Inc .....D 732 652-5200
Somerset *(G-10051)*
Alpha Tech Services .....G 973 283-2011
Boonton *(G-553)*
Amedia Networks Inc .....F 732 440-1992
Eatontown *(G-2381)*
American Fibertek Inc .....E 732 302-0660
Somerset *(G-10056)*
Antron Technologies Inc .....G 732 205-0415
Edison *(G-2461)*
Arch Manufacturing & Sales .....G 856 966-3835
Camden *(G-1041)*
Audio Dynamix Inc .....F 201 567-5488
Englewood *(G-2874)*
Automated Control Concepts Inc .....E 732 922-6611
Neptune *(G-6901)*
Behr Technology Inc .....G 908 537-9960
Hampton *(G-4154)*
Berkeley Varitronics Systems .....E 732 548-3737
Metuchen *(G-6096)*
▲ Chiral Photonics Inc .....F 973 732-0030
Pine Brook *(G-8691)*
Cisco Systems Inc .....C 732 635-4200
Iselin *(G-4620)*

Cisco Systems Inc ....G..... 856 642-7000
　Moorestown (G-6567)
Cisco Systems Inc ....E..... 201 782-0842
　Montvale (G-6448)
Conduent State Healthcare LLC ....G..... 973 824-3250
　Newark (G-7126)
Conduent State Healthcare LLC ....G..... 973 754-6134
　Paterson (G-8239)
Corporate Computer Systems ....F..... 732 739-5600
　Newark (G-7127)
Data Base Access Systems Inc ....F..... 973 335-0800
　Mountain Lakes (G-6856)
Dew Associates Inc ....B..... 973 702-0545
　Sparta (G-10496)
Dew Associates Inc ....E..... 973 702-0545
　Sussex (G-10668)
Dialogic Inc ....C..... 973 967-6000
　Parsippany (G-7981)
Diversified Display Pdts LLC ....E..... 908 686-2200
　Hillside (G-4405)
Ems Aviation Inc ....C..... 856 234-5020
　Moorestown (G-6576)
Envirosight LLC ....E..... 973 970-9284
　Randolph (G-9275)
Epiq Systems Inc ....E..... 973 622-6111
　Newark (G-7156)
EVs Broadcast Equipment Inc ....F..... 973 575-7811
　Fairfield (G-3187)
Fotobridge ....G..... 856 809-9400
　West Berlin (G-11721)
Fyth Labs Inc ....G..... 856 313-7362
　Beverly (G-463)
Gulton Incorporated ....A..... 908 791-4622
　South Plainfield (G-10377)
Humanscale Corporation ....C..... 732 537-2944
　Piscataway (G-8777)
I C System Solutions Inc ....F..... 201 666-1122
　Hillsdale (G-4384)
Jetty Life LLC ....G..... 800 900-6435
　Manahawkin (G-5831)
Lexmark International Inc ....F..... 201 307-4601
　Montvale (G-6466)
Lexmark International Inc ....F..... 201 307-4600
　Park Ridge (G-7925)
Link Computer Graphics Inc ....G..... 973 808-8990
　Fairfield (G-3253)
Lucent Technologies World Svcs ....C..... 908 582-3000
　New Providence (G-7046)
Maingear Inc ....E..... 888 624-6432
　Kenilworth (G-4972)
▲ Metrologic Instruments Inc ....C..... 856 228-8100
　Mount Laurel (G-6818)
Micro Innovations Corp ....D..... 732 346-9333
　Edison (G-2571)
MRC Precision Metal Optics Inc ....E..... 941 753-8707
　Northvale (G-7592)
MTS Systems Corporation ....A..... 856 875-4478
　Williamstown (G-12093)
Ncs Pearson Inc ....D..... 201 896-1011
　Lyndhurst (G-5695)
▲ Ner Data Products Inc ....E..... 888 637-3282
　Glassboro (G-3810)
Netscout Systems Inc ....E..... 609 518-4100
　Marlton (G-5990)
Oxberry LLC ....G..... 201 935-3000
　Carlstadt (G-1196)
Paradise Barxon Corp ....E..... 908 707-9141
　Branchburg (G-686)
Parker-Hannifin Corporation ....F..... 856 825-8900
　Millville (G-6319)
▲ Pcs Revenue Ctrl Systems Inc ....E..... 201 568-8300
　Englewood Cliffs (G-2978)
▲ PNC Electronics Inc ....F..... 973 237-0400
　Totowa (G-10964)
R T I Inc ....E..... 201 261-5852
　Oradell (G-7812)
Radcom Equipment Inc ....E..... 201 518-0033
　Paramus (G-7898)
▲ Raritan Inc ....E..... 732 764-8886
　Somerset (G-10162)
▲ Raritan Americas Inc ....C..... 732 764-8886
　Somerset (G-10163)
Ricoh Prtg Systems Amer Inc ....G..... 973 316-6051
　Mountain Lakes (G-6861)
▲ RSR Electronics Inc ....E..... 732 381-8777
　Rahway (G-9222)
▲ S W Electronics & Mfg ....C..... 856 222-9900
　Moorestown (G-6620)
Salescaster Displays Corp ....G..... 908 322-3046
　Scotch Plains (G-9854)

Scantron Corporation ....G..... 201 666-7009
　Westwood (G-11971)
Sony Corporation of America ....B..... 201 930-1000
　Paramus (G-7902)
Source Micro LLC ....F..... 973 328-1749
　Randolph (G-9298)
Sqn Peripherals Inc ....E..... 609 261-5500
　Rancocas (G-9263)
Symbology Enterprises Inc ....F..... 908 725-1699
　Somerville (G-10227)
Technobox Inc ....F..... 856 809-2306
　West Berlin (G-11755)
Telegenix Inc ....F..... 609 265-3910
　Rancocas (G-9264)
Thomas Instrumentation Inc ....F..... 609 624-7777
　Cape May Court House (G-1117)
Total Technology Inc ....E..... 856 617-0502
　Cherry Hill (G-1429)
Umit International Trading LLC ....F..... 973 571-1000
　Cedar Grove (G-1303)
Verint Systems Inc ....D..... 201 438-1429
　Lyndhurst (G-5712)
Western Scientific Computers ....F..... 973 263-9311
　Mountain Lakes (G-6864)
Whale Communications Inc ....E..... 201 947-0054
　Fort Lee (G-3590)
Zaller Studios Inc ....G..... 973 743-5175
　Bloomfield (G-538)
Zebra Technologies Corporation ....B..... 609 383-8743
　Northfield (G-7565)

3578 Calculating & Accounting Eqpt

▲ Atlantic Zeiser Inc ....E..... 973 228-0800
　West Caldwell (G-11766)
Bps Worldwide Inc ....E..... 856 874-0822
　Cherry Hill (G-1352)
Business Control Systems Corp ....F..... 732 283-1301
　Iselin (G-4619)
Comtrex Systems Corporation ....E..... 856 778-0090
　Moorestown (G-6569)
▲ Hpc Pos System Corp ....G..... 973 239-9666
　Cedar Grove (G-1284)
Longport Shields Inc ....G..... 856 727-0227
　Moorestown (G-6598)
◆ Swintec Corp ....F..... 201 935-0115
　Moonachie (G-6548)
United Pos Solutions Inc ....G..... 800 303-2567
　Palisades Park (G-7845)
Worldwide Pt SL Ltd Lblty Co ....F..... 201 928-0222
　Teaneck (G-10777)

3579 Office Machines, NEC

Acedepotcom ....F..... 800 844-0962
　Northvale (G-7568)
◆ Amano Cincinnati Incorporated ....D..... 973 403-1900
　Roseland (G-9642)
◆ Amano USA Holdings Inc ....G..... 973 403-1900
　Roseland (G-9643)
Archive Designs Inc ....G..... 973 242-6400
　Newark (G-7090)
▲ Arrow Fastener Co LLC ....B..... 201 843-6900
　Saddle Brook (G-9752)
Atlantic Business Products ....C..... 201 672-0773
　Lyndhurst (G-5669)
Avante International Tech Inc ....E..... 609 799-9388
　Princeton Junction (G-9149)
◆ Brother International Corp ....B..... 908 704-1700
　Bridgewater (G-825)
Esg LLC ....F..... 973 347-2969
　Budd Lake (G-928)
Hoarders Express LLC ....D..... 856 963-8471
　Camden (G-1068)
J K Office Machine Inc ....G..... 908 273-8811
　Berkeley Heights (G-413)
Opex Corporation ....C..... 856 727-1100
　Moorestown (G-6606)
Pitney Bowes Inc ....F..... 908 903-2870
　Warren (G-11564)
Pitney Bowes Inc ....C..... 800 521-0080
　Newark (G-7271)
Pitney Bowes Inc ....C..... 856 764-2240
　Delran (G-2020)
◆ Swintec Corp ....F..... 201 935-0115
　Moonachie (G-6548)
Time Systems International Co ....E..... 201 871-1200
　Englewood (G-2937)

3581 Automatic Vending Machines

Universal Vending MGT LLC ....F..... 908 233-4373
　Westfield (G-11932)

3582 Commercial Laundry, Dry Clean & Pressing Mchs

▲ Air World Inc ....E..... 201 831-0700
　Mahwah (G-5745)
Airworld Inc ....F..... 973 720-1008
　Paterson (G-8201)
Fairfield Laundry McHy Corp ....E..... 973 575-4330
　Fairfield (G-3193)
Fowler Route Co Inc ....E..... 908 686-3400
　Union (G-11186)
▲ Hoffman/New Yorker Inc ....G..... 201 488-1800
　Hackensack (G-3928)
▲ Multimatic LLC ....G..... 201 767-9660
　Northvale (G-7593)
One Click Cleaners ....C..... 732 804-9802
　Manalapan (G-5858)
Professional Laundry Solutions ....G..... 973 392-0837
　Newark (G-7278)
Sadwith Industries Corp ....G..... 732 531-3856
　Ocean (G-7742)
▲ Utax USA Inc ....G..... 201 433-1200
　Jersey City (G-4842)

3585 Air Conditioning & Heating Eqpt

Ade Inc ....F..... 609 693-6050
　Forked River (G-3533)
▼ Atomizing Systems Inc ....F..... 201 447-1222
　Ho Ho Kus (G-4453)
Ats Mechanical Inc ....G..... 609 298-2323
　Bordentown (G-591)
Banicki Sheet Metal Inc ....E..... 201 385-5938
　Bergenfield (G-382)
Bfhj Holdings Inc ....G..... 908 730-6280
　Montvale (G-6447)
Bgs Inc ....F..... 732 442-5000
　Lakewood (G-5084)
Bolttech Mannings Inc ....D..... 973 537-1576
　Wharton (G-11981)
Calmac Manufacturing Corp ....E..... 201 797-1511
　Fair Lawn (G-3085)
Chiller Solutions LLC ....E..... 973 835-2800
　Pompton Plains (G-8956)
Cold Stat Refregration ....F..... 201 251-2203
　Paramus (G-7861)
Comfortaire Ltd Liability Co ....G..... 856 692-5000
　Vineland (G-11338)
▲ Construction Specialties Inc ....E..... 908 236-0800
　Lebanon (G-5282)
Coolenheat Inc ....E..... 908 925-4473
　Kendall Park (G-4934)
▲ Csonka Worldwide ....E..... 609 514-2766
　Plainsboro (G-8879)
◆ Diversified Heat Transfer Inc ....D..... 800 221-1522
　Towaco (G-10993)
Dolan Assoc Inc ....G..... 973 875-6408
　Sussex (G-10669)
▲ Drytech Inc ....E..... 609 758-1794
　Cookstown (G-1806)
Duct Mate Inc ....G..... 201 488-8002
　Hackensack (G-3907)
Electro Impulse Laboratory Inc ....E..... 732 776-5800
　Neptune (G-6910)
▲ Ener-G Rudox Inc ....E..... 201 438-0111
　East Rutherford (G-2294)
▲ Ewc Controls Inc ....E..... 732 446-3110
　Manalapan (G-5846)
◆ Fujitsu General America Inc ....D..... 973 575-0380
　Fairfield (G-3203)
Harsco Corporation ....E..... 856 779-7795
　Cherry Hill (G-1374)
Heritage Service Solutions LLC ....F..... 856 845-7311
　Westville (G-11942)
▲ Honeywell International Inc ....A..... 973 455-2000
　Morris Plains (G-6666)
Hussmann Corporation ....E..... 800 320-3510
　West Deptford (G-11828)
Iceboxx LLC ....G..... 201 857-0404
　Wyckoff (G-12254)
▲ Icy Cools Inc ....G..... 609 448-0172
　Roosevelt (G-9641)
◆ Ingersoll-Rand US Trane ....D..... 732 652-7100
　Piscataway (G-8779)
Kohlder Manufacturing Inc ....G..... 856 963-1801
　Pennsauken (G-8540)
▲ Kooltronic Inc ....E..... 609 466-3400
　Pennington (G-8455)
▲ Krowne Metal Corp ....G..... 973 305-3300
　Wayne (G-11660)
▲ Lauda-Brinkmann LP ....F..... 856 764-7300
　Delran (G-2017)

Lauda-Brinkmann Management Inc ......F 856 764-7300
Delran (G-2018)

Lennox Industries Inc ....G 908 223-6002
Port Murray (G-8978)

Maco Appliance Parts & Sup Co ....G 609 272-8222
Absecon (G-3)

Mainstream Fluid & Air LLC ....E 908 931-1010
Berkeley Heights (G-419)

Mechanical Technologies LLC ....E 973 616-3800
Pine Brook (G-8709)

ML Mettler Corp ....G 201 869-0170
North Bergen (G-7469)

On Site Manufacturing Inc ....G 812 794-6040
Flemington (G-3458)

Piper Services LLC ....F 844 567-3900
Midland Park (G-6235)

▼ Ryder Technology ....G 215 817-7868
Villas (G-11315)

Sander Mechanical Service Inc ....E 732 560-0600
Branchburg (G-701)

◆ Sealed Unit Parts Co Inc ....C 732 223-1201
Allenwood (G-37)

▲ Sodastream USA Inc ....G 856 755-3400
Mount Laurel (G-6843)

Specialty Fabricators LLC ....E 609 758-6995
Wrightstown (G-12243)

SPX Dry Cooling Usa LLC ....E 908 450-8027
Bridgewater (G-899)

Stamm International Corp ....G 201 947-1700
Fort Lee (G-3583)

▲ Task International (usa) Inc ....F 732 739-0377
Keyport (G-5024)

Tecogen Inc ....E 732 356-5601
Piscataway (G-8821)

▲ Trane Inc ....C 732 652-7100
Piscataway (G-8828)

Trane US Inc ....G 732 652-7100
Piscataway (G-8829)

Trane US Inc ....D 609 587-3400
Trenton (G-11123)

Trane US Inc ....G 973 882-3220
Pine Brook (G-8718)

▲ Walter Machine Co Inc ....E 201 656-5654
Jersey City (G-4846)

York International Corporation ....F 732 346-0606
Edison (G-2653)

Zanotti Transblock USA Corp ....G 917 584-9357
Delran (G-2025)

3586 Measuring & Dispensing Pumps

▲ Newton Tool & Mfg Inc ....D 856 241-1500
Pennsauken (G-8554)

3589 Service Ind Machines, NEC

A Plus Powerwashing ....G 732 245-3816
Neptune (G-6898)

▲ Aero Manufacturing Co ....D 973 473-5300
Clifton (G-1558)

◆ Amano USA Holdings Inc ....G 973 403-1900
Roseland (G-9643)

◆ Aqua Products Inc ....C 973 857-2700
Cedar Grove (G-1271)

Aries Filterworks Inc ....E 856 626-1550
Berlin (G-425)

Arrow Steel Inc ....F 973 523-1122
Paterson (G-8215)

Autoshred LLC ....G 732 244-0950
Toms River (G-10865)

Bellaqua Inc ....G 201 460-8379
East Rutherford (G-2284)

◆ Cantel Medical Corp ....G 973 890-7220
Little Falls (G-5471)

Car Wash Parts Inc ....G 215 633-9250
Ventnor City (G-11290)

Chem-Aqua Inc ....F 972 438-0211
Monmouth Junction (G-6336)

Chen Brothers Machinery Co ....G 973 328-0086
Randolph (G-9272)

▲ Clayton Associates Inc ....F 732 363-2100
Lakewood (G-5094)

Clearwater Well Drilling Co ....G 609 698-1800
Manahawkin (G-5829)

CP Equipment Sales Co ....F 908 687-9621
Union (G-11168)

Dcm Clean Air Products Inc ....G 732 363-2100
Lakewood (G-5106)

▼ Delta Cooling Towers Inc ....G 973 586-2201
Flanders (G-3404)

Detrex Corporation ....G 856 786-8686
Cinnaminson (G-1457)

▲ Dynatec Systems Inc ....F 609 387-0330
Burlington (G-970)

East Brunswick Sewerage Auth ....F 732 257-8313
East Brunswick (G-2148)

Elgee Manufacturing Company ....G 908 647-4100
Warren (G-11545)

Energy Beams Inc ....F 973 291-6555
Bloomingdale (G-543)

Enpro Inc ....E 908 236-2137
Lebanon (G-5285)

Envirnmntal Mgt Chem Wste Svcs ......G 201 848-7676
Mahwah (G-5770)

Es Industrial ....D 732 842-5600
Red Bank (G-9329)

Evoqua Water Technologies LLC ....D 908 851-4250
Union (G-11183)

Favs Corp ....G 856 358-1515
Elmer (G-2792)

Filter Technologies Inc ....G 732 329-2500
Monmouth Junction (G-6344)

Filtrex Inc ....F 973 595-0400
Wayne (G-11633)

Fin-Tek Corporation ....G 973 628-2988
Wayne (G-11634)

◆ Franklin Miller Inc ....F 973 535-9200
Livingston (G-5531)

Glasco Uv LLC ....E 201 934-3348
Mahwah (G-5776)

Global Ecology Corporation ....G 973 655-9001
Roseland (G-9650)

GP Jager Inc ....G 973 750-1180
Kinnelon (G-5035)

▼ Graver Water Systems LLC ....G 908 516-1400
New Providence (G-7039)

Graver Water Systems LLC ....E 973 465-2380
Newark (G-7177)

◆ Hayward Industries Inc ....B 908 351-5400
Elizabeth (G-2742)

Hayward Industries Inc ....G 908 351-0899
Elizabeth (G-2743)

Hickory Industries Inc ....E 201 223-4382
North Bergen (G-7456)

Hobart Sales and Service Inc ....E 973 227-9265
Fairfield (G-3223)

▼ Hungerford & Terry Inc ....E 856 881-3200
Clayton (G-1524)

Innovative Pressure Clg LLC ....G 609 738-3100
Cream Ridge (G-1937)

Interntional Cnsld Chemex Corp ....E 732 828-7676
New Brunswick (G-6969)

J & M Air Inc ....E 908 707-4040
Somerville (G-10217)

▲ Janico Inc ....F 732 370-2223
Freehold (G-3662)

▲ JDV Equipment Corp ....G 973 366-6556
Dover (G-2096)

Karcher North America Inc ....E 856 228-1800
Blackwood (G-486)

◆ Lanxess Sybron Chemicals Inc ....C 609 893-1100
Birmingham (G-468)

Margaritaville Inc ....G 973 728-7562
West Milford (G-11854)

▲ Mercury Floor Machines Inc ....E 201 568-4606
Englewood (G-2915)

Metawater Usa Inc ....G 201 935-3436
Rutherford (G-9740)

Metropolitan Compactors Svc ....G 908 653-0168
Cranford (G-1916)

▲ Metropolitan Vacuum Clr Co Inc ......D 201 405-2225
Oakland (G-7696)

Middlesex Water Company ....F 732 579-0290
Edison (G-2572)

Monitoring Solutions Inc ....G 908 713-0172
Hampton (G-4165)

Multi-Pak Corporation ....E 201 342-7474
Hackensack (G-3949)

Nitto Americas Inc ....F 732 901-7905
Lakewood (G-5165)

Nitto Americas Inc ....E 201 645-4950
Teaneck (G-10763)

NMP Water Systems LLC ....G 201 252-8333
Mahwah (G-5796)

Organica Water Inc ....F 609 651-8885
West Windsor (G-11909)

Pinto of Montville Inc ....G 973 584-2002
Kenvil (G-5012)

▲ Power Container Corp ....E 732 560-3655
Somerset (G-10156)

Powerwash Plus ....G 732 671-6767
Middletown (G-6218)

Premier Compaction Systems ....F 718 328-5990
Woodland Park (G-12229)

Pure H2o Technologies Inc ....G 973 622-0440
Newark (G-7279)

Quality Plus One Catering Inc ....G 732 967-1525
Old Bridge (G-7791)

Randall Manufacturing Co Inc ....E 973 746-2111
Hillside (G-4437)

Rlct Industries LLC ....G 609 712-1318
Pennington (G-8458)

▲ Seaboard Paper and Twine LLC ....E 973 413-8100
Paterson (G-8380)

Site Drainer LLC ....G 862 225-9940
Clifton (G-1726)

South Jersey Water Cond Svc ....E 856 451-0620
Bridgeton (G-798)

▲ Suez Treatment Solutions Inc ....C 201 767-9300
Paramus (G-7907)

T & E Sales of Marlboro Inc ....G 732 549-7551
Metuchen (G-6127)

▲ U V International LLC ....F 973 993-9454
Morristown (G-6747)

Ugsi Chemical Feed Inc ....E 856 896-2160
Vineland (G-11411)

▲ Unique Systems Inc ....F 973 455-0440
Cedar Knolls (G-1322)

Univerclean Ltd ....G 201 674-1563
Fair Lawn (G-3122)

Vac-U-Max ....F 973 759-4600
Belleville (G-323)

Vivreau Advanced Water Systems ....F 212 502-3749
Fairfield (G-3345)

Water Resources New Jersey LLC ....G 609 268-7965
Tabernacle (G-10739)

▲ Waterdoctor Inc ....F 732 972-4510
Ridgefield (G-9393)

3592 Carburetors, Pistons, Rings & Valves

Fujikin of America Inc ....G 201 641-1119
Hasbrouck Heights (G-4192)

▲ Rotarex Inc North America ....D 724 696-3345
Hackettstown (G-4033)

Straval Machine Co Inc ....E 973 340-9955
Elmwood Park (G-2851)

3593 Fluid Power Cylinders & Actuators

GE Aviation Systems LLC ....C 973 428-9898
Whippany (G-12021)

▲ Industrial Habonim Valves & AC ....F 201 820-3184
Wayne (G-11650)

▼ Motion Systems Corp ....D 732 389-1600
Eatontown (G-2414)

Van Hydraulics Inc ....E 732 442-5500
South Plainfield (G-10448)

3594 Fluid Power Pumps & Motors

Industrial Combustion Assn ....F 732 271-0300
Somerset (G-10111)

Mainstream LLC ....G 908 931-1010
Cranford (G-1914)

Neptune Products Inc ....F 973 366-8200
Dover (G-2103)

▲ PMC Liquiflo Equipment Co Inc ....E 908 518-0666
Garwood (G-3785)

Technol Inc ....F 856 848-5480
Westville (G-11949)

3596 Scales & Balances, Exc Laboratory

Advance Scale Company Inc ....E 856 784-4916
Lindenwold (G-5461)

American Garvens Corporation ....G 973 276-1093
Pine Brook (G-8687)

▲ Coperion K-Tron Pitman Inc ....F 856 589-0500
Sewell (G-9947)

Empire Scale & Balance ....G 856 299-1651
Penns Grove (G-8465)

▲ Ohaus Corporation ....D 973 377-9000
Parsippany (G-8051)

Technidyne Corporation ....G 732 363-1055
Toms River (G-10917)

W T Winter Associates Inc ....E 888 808-3611
Fairfield (G-3349)

3599 Machinery & Eqpt, Indl & Commercial, NEC

A B Scantlebury Co Inc ....F 973 770-3000
Newton (G-7378)

A Frieri Machine Tool Inc ....G 908 753-7555
South Plainfield (G-10318)

Abco Tool & Machine Corp ....G...... 973 772-8160
  Garfield (G-3713)

Able Gear & Machine Co ....G...... 973 983-8055
  Rockaway (G-9541)

Accelerated Cnc LLC ....G...... 908 561-8875
  South Plainfield (G-10320)

Ace Metal Kraft Co Inc ....E...... 973 278-6605
  Woodland Park (G-12207)

Advance Machine Inc ....F...... 908 486-7244
  Linden (G-5343)

▲ Aero Products Co Inc ....F...... 973 759-0959
  Belleville (G-294)

Afk Machine Inc ....G...... 973 539-1329
  Randolph (G-9268)

Alben Metal Products Inc ....G...... 973 279-8891
  Paterson (G-8202)

Alex Machine Shop Inc ....G...... 201 768-9110
  Northvale (G-7571)

Alfa Machine & Tool Co Inc ....F...... 973 227-1962
  Fairfield (G-3129)

All Mechanical Services Inc ....F...... 732 442-8292
  Perth Amboy (G-8606)

All Tool Company Inc ....F...... 908 687-3636
  Union (G-11148)

Alpha Lehigh Tool & Mch Co Inc ....E...... 908 454-6481
  Alpha (G-38)

Altech Machine & Tool Inc ....G...... 201 652-4409
  Midland Park (G-6220)

American Machine Spc NJ LLC ....E...... 201 664-0006
  Westwood (G-11954)

American Pipe Benders & Fabric ....G...... 732 287-1122
  Edison (G-2458)

Amex Tool Co ....G...... 908 735-5176
  Asbury (G-64)

Andrex Inc ....F...... 908 852-2400
  Hackettstown (G-3997)

◆ Ansun Protective Metals Inc ....G...... 732 302-0616
  Middlesex (G-6148)

Arch Custom Manufacturing Inc ....G...... 856 966-3835
  Camden (G-1040)

Arch Manufacturing & Sales ....G...... 856 966-3835
  Camden (G-1041)

▲ Argyle Industries Inc ....F...... 908 725-8800
  Branchburg (G-637)

Aries Precision Tool Inc ....G...... 201 252-8550
  Mahwah (G-5749)

▲ Atlantic Casting & Engineering ....C...... 973 779-2450
  Clifton (G-1567)

Atlantic Coastal Welding Inc ....F...... 732 269-1088
  Bayville (G-250)

Atlas Recording Machines Corp ....G...... 732 295-3663
  Point Pleasant Boro (G-8932)

Avony Enterprises Inc ....E...... 212 242-8144
  Trenton (G-11022)

Aztech Mfg Inc ....F...... 609 726-1212
  Pemberton (G-8442)

B & C Machine Co Inc ....G...... 973 823-1120
  Franklin (G-3596)

▲ Barnett Machine Tools Inc ....F...... 973 482-6222
  Harrison (G-4172)

BCsmachine & Mfg Corp ....G...... 908 561-1656
  South Plainfield (G-10335)

Berezin Nilolai ....G...... 856 692-6191
  Vineland (G-11329)

Bertot Industries Inc ....G...... 973 267-0006
  Morristown (G-6695)

Bisaga Inc ....F...... 856 784-7966
  Somerdale (G-10039)

Biwal Manufacturing Co Inc ....G...... 973 778-0105
  Clifton (G-1576)

Bk Machine Shop ....G...... 856 457-7150
  Vineland (G-11332)

Blue Chip Industries Inc ....G...... 908 704-1466
  Somerville (G-10202)

BP Machine Co Inc ....G...... 732 251-0449
  Spotswood (G-10527)

Brenner Metal Products ....E...... 973 778-2466
  Wallington (G-11524)

▲ Brodie System Inc ....F...... 908 862-8620
  Linden (G-5354)

Brusso Hardware LLC ....F...... 212 337-8510
  Belleville (G-297)

C & C Tool and Machine Co LLC ....G...... 856 764-0911
  Riverside (G-9494)

C & N Tooling & Grinding Inc ....F...... 973 598-8411
  Succasunna (G-10619)

C & S Tool Co ....F...... 973 887-6865
  East Hanover (G-2202)

Cadpro Inc ....F...... 856 435-0050
  Williamstown (G-12082)

Cerbaco Ltd ....E...... 908 996-1333
  Frenchtown (G-3699)

Chacko John ....G...... 732 494-1088
  Edison (G-2481)

Chalmers & Kubeck Inc ....G...... 732 993-1251
  New Brunswick (G-6950)

Charles F Kilian ....G...... 732 458-3554
  Brick (G-736)

Charter Machine Company ....F...... 732 494-5350
  Metuchen (G-6099)

◆ Clements Industries Inc ....E...... 201 440-5500
  South Hackensack (G-10258)

Coates Precision Engineering ....G...... 732 449-9382
  Wall Township (G-11473)

▲ Coesia Health & Beauty Inc ....F...... 908 707-8008
  Branchburg (G-648)

Colinear Machine & Design Inc ....G...... 973 300-1681
  Sparta (G-10492)

Components & Controls Inc ....F...... 201 483-9190
  Carlstadt (G-1148)

Computa-Base-Machining Inc ....F...... 856 767-9517
  Berlin (G-432)

Concept Group Inc ....E...... 856 767-5506
  West Berlin (G-11711)

Congruent Machine Co Inc ....G...... 973 764-6767
  Vernon (G-11297)

▲ Connecting Products Inc ....G...... 609 688-1808
  Skillman (G-10030)

Creative Machining Systems ....G...... 609 586-3932
  Trenton (G-11048)

Crown Precision Corp ....G...... 973 470-0097
  Passaic (G-8132)

Cutmark Inc ....G...... 856 234-3428
  Mount Laurel (G-6791)

▲ Cutting Edge Casting Inc ....E...... 908 925-7500
  Linden (G-5366)

Cutting Techniques Inc ....G...... 201 438-2222
  Rockaway (G-9560)

D & H Cutoff Co ....G...... 908 454-4961
  Stewartsville (G-10593)

D N D Corp ....G...... 908 637-4343
  Great Meadows (G-3849)

Daven Industries Inc ....E...... 973 808-8848
  Fairfield (G-3173)

Delva Tool & Machine Corp ....D...... 856 786-8700
  Cinnaminson (G-1455)

Delva Tool & Machine Corp ....D...... 856 829-0109
  Cinnaminson (G-1456)

Dependable Machining Co ....G...... 732 462-0262
  Freehold (G-3650)

Dewalt Manufacturing Co Inc ....G...... 856 423-1207
  Clarksboro (G-1518)

Diamond Machine Co Inc ....G...... 609 490-8940
  Roosevelt (G-9640)

Dihco Inc ....G...... 201 327-0518
  Upper Saddle River (G-11278)

Diversatech Inc ....G...... 609 730-9668
  Pennington (G-8449)

Diversitech Inc ....E...... 973 835-2900
  Riverdale (G-9479)

Drew-Wal Machine & Tool Corp ....G...... 201 641-3887
  Little Ferry (G-5502)

Dynametric Tool Inc ....G...... 973 471-8009
  Clifton (G-1607)

Dynamic Machining Inc ....F...... 856 273-9830
  Cinnaminson (G-1459)

Eastern Machining Corporation ....G...... 856 694-3303
  Franklinville (G-3630)

▲ Edgewater Manufacturing Co Inc ....G...... 201 664-0022
  Fair Lawn (G-3090)

Edhard Corp ....E...... 908 850-8444
  Hackettstown (G-4003)

Edmund Kiss ....G...... 973 810-2312
  Landing (G-5223)

◆ Elaut Usa Inc ....F...... 732 364-9900
  Lakewood (G-5113)

Elmi Machine Tool Corp ....G...... 973 882-1277
  Fairfield (G-3183)

Ethylene Atlantic Corp ....E...... 856 467-0010
  Swedesboro (G-10696)

Eugene Kozak ....G...... 973 442-1001
  Randolph (G-9276)

▲ Evans Machine & Tool Co ....G...... 732 442-1144
  Perth Amboy (G-8613)

▲ Everite Machine Products Co ....E...... 856 330-6700
  Pennsauken (G-8509)

Exactal Tool Ltd Inc ....G...... 908 561-1177
  South Plainfield (G-10360)

F & M Machine Co Inc ....F...... 908 245-8830
  Kenilworth (G-4955)

◆ F & R Machine Corp ....E...... 973 684-8139
  Paterson (G-8268)

F and L Machinery ....G...... 973 218-6216
  Springfield (G-10554)

Fazzio Machine & Steel Inc ....G...... 609 653-1098
  Glassboro (G-3805)

Ferry Machine Corp ....E...... 201 641-9191
  Little Ferry (G-5504)

▲ Fgh Systems Inc ....F...... 973 625-8114
  Denville (G-2039)

Fims Manufacturing Corporation ....E...... 201 845-7088
  Oakland (G-7688)

Fischl Machine & Tool ....G...... 908 829-5621
  Hillsborough (G-4332)

▲ Flexline Inc ....F...... 908 486-3322
  Kenilworth (G-4956)

Fluets Corp ....G...... 908 353-5229
  Hillside (G-4407)

Fluid Filtration Corp ....F...... 973 253-7070
  Garfield (G-3734)

Frank E Ganter Inc ....G...... 856 692-2218
  Vineland (G-11356)

Fredericks Machine Inc ....G...... 609 397-4991
  Rosemont (G-9704)

G & B Machine Inc ....G...... 908 707-1181
  Somerville (G-10209)

G Catalano Inc ....G...... 908 241-6333
  Roselle Park (G-9696)

G L Tool & Manufacturing Co ....G...... 973 740-0001
  Livingston (G-5532)

G P R Company Inc ....G...... 973 227-6160
  Fairfield (G-3204)

Gale Newson Inc ....E...... 732 961-7610
  Jackson (G-4668)

Gamma Machine & Tool Co Inc ....G...... 973 398-8821
  Landing (G-5224)

Gaum Inc ....G...... 609 586-0132
  Robbinsville (G-9516)

Gb Industries II Inc ....G...... 973 728-5900
  Ringwood (G-9447)

Geiger Tool & Mfg Co Inc ....F...... 973 777-2136
  Passaic (G-8142)

Geiger Tool Co Inc ....G...... 973 777-5094
  Passaic (G-8143)

General Electric Company ....B...... 973 887-6635
  Parsippany (G-8023)

General Mch Experimental Works ....G...... 201 843-9035
  Paramus (G-7872)

General Polygon Systems Inc ....F...... 800 825-1655
  Millville (G-6304)

Globe Engineering Corp ....G...... 609 898-0349
  Cape May (G-1101)

▲ Globe Industries Corp ....F...... 973 992-8990
  Clifton (G-1627)

Graphic Equipment Corporation ....E...... 732 494-5350
  Metuchen (G-6106)

Graphic Equipment Corporation ....G...... 732 548-4400
  Metuchen (G-6107)

Great Notch Industries Inc ....G...... 201 343-8110
  Hackensack (G-3923)

Grimaldi Development Corp ....G...... 973 345-0660
  Paterson (G-8282)

▼ Grimco Pneumatic Corp ....G...... 973 345-0660
  Paterson (G-8283)

Grimes Manufacturing Inc ....G...... 732 442-4572
  Perth Amboy (G-8616)

H & H Production Machining ....G...... 973 383-6880
  Sparta (G-10502)

H P Machine Shop Inc ....G...... 856 692-1192
  Vineland (G-11367)

Hanrahan Tool Co Inc ....G...... 732 919-7300
  Farmingdale (G-3386)

Harley Tool & Machine Inc ....G...... 201 244-8899
  Bergenfield (G-386)

Harrison Machine and Tool Inc ....G...... 609 883-0800
  Ewing (G-3020)

Henry Olsen Machine ....G...... 856 662-2121
  Cinnaminson (G-1467)

Hercules Welding & Machine Co ....G...... 856 829-1820
  Palmyra (G-7848)

Hhh Machine Co ....G...... 908 276-1220
  Cranford (G-1910)

Hun Machine Works Inc ....F...... 856 461-6911
  Riverside (G-9500)

Hydracore Inc ....G...... 732 548-5500
  Metuchen (G-6110)

Hydratight Operations Inc ....F...... 732 271-4100
  Somerset (G-10110)

I I Galaxy Inc ....G...... 732 828-2686
  New Brunswick (G-6966)

S
I
C

▼ **Imperial Machine & Tool Co** ....E.... 908 496-8100
Columbia *(G-1798)*

Indoor Entertainment of NJ ....E.... 609 522-6700
Wildwood *(G-12073)*

Industrial Machine Corp ....G.... 973 345-1800
Paterson *(G-8294)*

International Tool and Mfg Inc ....G.... 973 227-6767
Fairfield *(G-3233)*

J & M Manufacturing Inc ....G.... 908 638-4298
High Bridge *(G-4297)*

J A W Products Inc ....F.... 856 829-3210
Cinnaminson *(G-1471)*

J D Machine Parts Inc ....F.... 856 691-8430
Vineland *(G-11374)*

J M C Tool & Mfg Co ....G.... 908 241-8950
Kenilworth *(G-4964)*

J P Rotella Co Inc ....F.... 973 942-2559
Haledon *(G-4083)*

J R Engineering & Machine ....F.... 908 810-6300
Hillside *(G-4420)*

J R S Tool & Metal Finishing ....G.... 908 753-2050
South Plainfield *(G-10387)*

Jaymar Precision Inc ....G.... 856 365-8779
Camden *(G-1071)*

JBAT Inc ....E.... 856 667-7307
Cherry Hill *(G-1383)*

Jordan Tooling & Manufacturing ....G.... 609 261-2636
Hainesport *(G-4075)*

Jsm Co ....G.... 732 695-9577
Tinton Falls *(G-10839)*

K-D Industries Inc ....D.... 973 594-4800
Passaic *(G-8154)*

▼ **Kavon Filter Products Co** ....F.... 732 938-3135
Wall Township *(G-11492)*

▲ **Kelles Incorporated** ....F.... 908 241-9300
Kenilworth *(G-4966)*

Kern & Szalai Co ....F.... 856 802-1500
Moorestown *(G-6590)*

Knudsen Precision Mfg ....F.... 609 538-1100
Ewing *(G-3032)*

Kwg Industries LLC ....E.... 908 218-8900
Hillsborough *(G-4354)*

L & M Machine & Tool Co Inc ....G.... 973 523-5288
Paterson *(G-8313)*

▼ **Lazar Technologies Inc** ....F.... 732 739-9622
Hazlet *(G-4277)*

Legend Machine & Grinding ....F.... 908 685-1100
Bridgewater *(G-851)*

Luso Machine Inc ....F.... 973 242-1717
Newark *(G-7228)*

M & D Prcsion Cntrless Grnding ....G.... 856 764-1616
Riverside *(G-9501)*

M & M Welding & Steel Fabg ....G.... 908 647-6060
Stirling *(G-10603)*

M & RS Miller Auto Gear & Prt ....F.... 201 339-2270
Bayonne *(G-237)*

M & S Holes Corp ....G.... 908 298-6900
Kenilworth *(G-4971)*

M & S Machine & Tool Corp ....F.... 973 345-5847
Paterson *(G-8327)*

M and D Precision Grinding ....G.... 856 764-1616
Riverside *(G-9502)*

M D Carbide Tool Corp ....E.... 973 263-0104
Towaco *(G-10998)*

M4 Machine LLC ....G.... 718 928-9695
Livingston *(G-5541)*

Machine Parts Inc ....F.... 973 491-5444
Newark *(G-7233)*

Machine Plus Inc ....G.... 973 839-8884
Haskell *(G-4210)*

Machine Tech ....F.... 732 738-6810
Edison *(G-2563)*

Manco Industries ....G.... 973 971-3131
Irvington *(G-4598)*

Marlton Pike Precision LLC ....F.... 856 665-1900
Cherry Hill *(G-1395)*

Marshall Maintenance ....C.... 609 394-7153
Trenton *(G-11079)*

Master Tool Corp ....G.... 732 919-1010
Farmingdale *(G-3390)*

Mdi Manufacturing Inc ....F.... 732 994-5599
Lakewood *(G-5157)*

Mechanitron Corporation Inc ....G.... 908 620-1001
Roselle *(G-9676)*

Megawatt Machine Services LLC ....E.... 732 805-4000
Somerset *(G-10134)*

Mercer Machine & Tool Products ....G.... 609 587-1106
Trenton *(G-11080)*

Metal Hose Fabricators Inc ....G.... 908 925-7345
Linden *(G-5407)*

Metronic Engineering Co Inc ....F.... 201 337-1266
Oakland *(G-7695)*

Micheller & Son Hydraulics Inc ....F.... 908 687-1545
Roselle *(G-9677)*

Mid-Lantic Precision Inc ....F.... 856 456-3810
Gloucester City *(G-3840)*

Midway Machine Product Corp ....G.... 609 499-4377
Florence *(G-3479)*

Miemie Design Services Inc ....E.... 609 857-3688
Ltl Egg Hbr *(G-5645)*

Millson Precision Machining ....G.... 732 424-1700
Piscataway *(G-8792)*

Milo Runtak Welding Machinery ....G.... 201 391-0380
Park Ridge *(G-7926)*

Mjs Precision Inc ....G.... 973 209-1300
Franklin *(G-3601)*

Modern Metric Machine Company ....G.... 856 547-4044
Audubon *(G-117)*

Modern Precision Tech Inc ....F.... 856 335-9303
West Berlin *(G-11735)*

Modular Packaging Systems Inc ....F.... 973 970-9393
Rockaway *(G-9587)*

Monmouth Truck Ram Div LLC ....G.... 732 741-5001
Shrewsbury *(G-10007)*

Monroe Machine & Design Inc ....F.... 732 521-3434
Jamesburg *(G-4688)*

N & J Machine Products Corp ....G.... 973 589-0031
Newark *(G-7246)*

N B & Sons LLC ....G.... 856 692-6191
Vineland *(G-11382)*

▲ **National Mtal Fnshngs Corp Inc** ....F.... 732 752-7770
Middlesex *(G-6183)*

National Precision Tool Co ....E.... 973 227-5005
Fairfield *(G-3266)*

▲ **New ERA Converting Machinery** ....E.... 201 670-4848
Paterson *(G-8347)*

New Jersey Balancing Svc Inc ....G.... 973 278-5106
Paterson *(G-8348)*

NJ Precision Tech Inc ....E.... 800 409-3000
Mountainside *(G-6885)*

Norms Auto Parts Inc ....G.... 908 852-5080
Hackettstown *(G-4029)*

Northeast Precast Ltd Lblty Co ....D.... 856 765-9088
Millville *(G-6317)*

Northland Tooling Technologies ....G.... 908 850-0023
Hackettstown *(G-4030)*

▼ **Norwalt Design Inc** ....D.... 973 927-3200
Randolph *(G-9291)*

Nowak Inc ....F.... 973 366-7208
Wharton *(G-11994)*

Numerical Control Program Svc ....G.... 856 665-8737
Cherry Hill *(G-1407)*

Nymar Manufacturing Company ....F.... 973 366-7265
Randolph *(G-9292)*

▲ **O K Tool Corporation** ....G.... 908 561-9920
Plainfield *(G-8870)*

OK Tool & Die Company Inc ....E.... 856 629-5757
Williamstown *(G-12094)*

Olympic EDM Services Inc ....G.... 973 492-0664
Kinnelon *(G-5039)*

Omp Technologies Inc ....F.... 973 808-8500
Fairfield *(G-3276)*

Optimum Precision Inc ....G.... 908 259-9017
Kenilworth *(G-4985)*

P L M Manufacturing Company ....E.... 201 342-3636
Hackensack *(G-3960)*

P M Z Tool Inc ....G.... 908 647-2125
Stirling *(G-10604)*

Pabst Enterprises Equipment Co ....E.... 908 353-2880
Elizabeth *(G-2764)*

Pahco Machine Inc ....G.... 609 587-1188
Trenton *(G-11094)*

Parkway-Kew Corporation ....F.... 732 398-2100
North Brunswick *(G-7533)*

Philip Creter Inc ....G.... 908 686-2910
Union *(G-11215)*

Phoenix Machine Rebuilders Inc ....F.... 973 691-8029
Roxbury Township *(G-9712)*

Phoenix Precision Co ....F.... 973 208-8877
Newfoundland *(G-7375)*

Phoenix Tool & Machine Inc ....G.... 856 753-5565
West Berlin *(G-11742)*

Polo Machine Inc ....G.... 973 340-9984
Garfield *(G-3749)*

Precision Forms Inc ....E.... 973 838-3800
Butler *(G-1016)*

Precision Metal Machining Inc ....E.... 201 843-7427
Carlstadt *(G-1207)*

Precision Metalcrafters Inc ....E.... 856 629-1020
Williamstown *(G-12100)*

Precision Mfg Group LLC ....D.... 973 785-4630
Cedar Grove *(G-1296)*

Precision Specialists Mch LLC ....F.... 856 768-5990
Atco *(G-91)*

Quality Industries Inc ....F.... 973 478-4425
Clifton *(G-1708)*

R G Dunn Acquisitions Co Inc ....E.... 973 762-1300
Maplewood *(G-5925)*

R G Smith Tool & Mfg Co ....F.... 973 344-1395
Newark *(G-7282)*

R J D Machine Products Inc ....F.... 609 392-1515
Trenton *(G-11110)*

R Way Tooling & Met Works LLC ....F.... 856 692-2218
Vineland *(G-11394)*

Raceweld Co Inc ....G.... 908 236-6533
Lebanon *(G-5300)*

Rako Machine Products Inc ....G.... 609 758-1200
Cream Ridge *(G-1940)*

Ramsey Machine & Tool Co Inc ....G.... 973 376-7404
Springfield *(G-10575)*

Raue Screw Machine Products Co ....G.... 973 697-7500
Oak Ridge *(G-7664)*

Rawco LLC ....G.... 908 832-7700
Califon *(G-1036)*

▲ **Reliable Welding & Mch Work** ....E.... 201 865-1073
North Bergen *(G-7478)*

Rendas Tool & Die Inc ....E.... 732 469-4670
Somerset *(G-10165)*

Responsible Machines LLC ....G.... 917 740-2269
Highland Park *(G-4304)*

Reuther Engineering ....F.... 973 485-5800
Edison *(G-2604)*

Ridge Precision Products Inc ....G.... 973 361-3508
Dover *(G-2108)*

Romar Machine & Tool Company ....E.... 201 337-7111
Franklin Lakes *(G-3624)*

Rotary Die Systems Inc ....G.... 856 234-3994
Moorestown *(G-6619)*

Royal Aquarius Empire ....D.... 646 847-3322
Hamilton *(G-4125)*

Ruoff & Sons Inc ....E.... 856 931-2064
Runnemede *(G-9722)*

S & S Precision Company Inc ....G.... 856 662-0006
Pennsauken *(G-8576)*

S&P Machine Company Inc ....F.... 973 365-2101
Passaic *(G-8178)*

Saint-Gobain Prfmce Plas Corp ....D.... 732 652-0910
Somerset *(G-10170)*

Schall Manufacturing Inc ....G.... 732 918-8800
Ocean *(G-7743)*

Select Machine Tool Inc ....G.... 856 933-2100
Mount Ephraim *(G-6764)*

Sensor Products Inc ....E.... 973 884-1755
Madison *(G-5734)*

Sermach Inc ....G.... 732 356-9021
Middlesex *(G-6196)*

Shore Precision Mfg Inc ....F.... 732 914-0949
Toms River *(G-10910)*

Sigma Engineering & Consulting ....F.... 732 356-3046
Middlesex *(G-6197)*

South River Machinery Corp ....G.... 201 487-1736
Hackensack *(G-3978)*

Spectrum Design LLC ....G.... 856 694-1870
Franklinville *(G-3631)*

Spl Holdings LLC ....F.... 856 764-2400
Delran *(G-2023)*

Stanton Precision Products LLC ....G.... 973 838-6951
Butler *(G-1019)*

Star Process Heat Systems LLC ....G.... 732 282-1002
Neptune *(G-6933)*

▲ **Star-Glo Industries LLC** ....C.... 201 939-6162
East Rutherford *(G-2326)*

Steel Mountain Fabricators LLC ....F.... 908 862-2800
Linden *(G-5449)*

Steel Mountain Fabricators LLC ....G.... 201 741-3019
North Bergen *(G-7487)*

Steimling & Son Inc ....F.... 732 613-1550
Sayreville *(G-9840)*

Stollen Machine & Tool Company ....G.... 908 241-0622
Kenilworth *(G-4997)*

Straval Machine Co Inc ....E.... 973 340-9955
Elmwood Park *(G-2851)*

STS Technologies LLC ....F.... 973 277-5416
Mahwah *(G-5817)*

Stuart Mills Inc ....G.... 973 579-5717
Newton *(G-7405)*

Stuart Mills Inc ....G.... 973 579-5717
Newton *(G-7406)*

◆ **Stuart Steel Protection Corp** ....E.... 732 469-5544
Somerset *(G-10174)*

Superior Tool & Mfg Co ....G...... 908 526-9011
Branchburg (G-706)

T & P Machine Shop Inc ....G...... 732 424-9141
Piscataway (G-8820)

T-M Vacuum Products Inc ....F...... 856 829-2000
Cinnaminson (G-1491)

Tam Metal Products Inc ....E...... 201 848-7800
Mahwah (G-5818)

Taurus Precision Inc ....F...... 973 785-9254
Little Falls (G-5491)

Tech Products Co Inc ....E...... 201 444-7777
Midland Park (G-6239)

▲ Testrite Instrument Co Inc ....C...... 201 543-0240
Hackensack (G-3984)

Third River Manufacturing LLC ....G...... 201 935-2795
Carlstadt (G-1229)

Tjk Machine LLC ....G...... 856 691-7811
Vineland (G-11409)

Tomcel Machine Inc ....G...... 973 256-8257
Woodland Park (G-12235)

Totowa Precision Tooling Inc ....F...... 973 256-2283
Totowa (G-10976)

Townsend Machine Inc ....E...... 609 723-2603
Chesterfield (G-1443)

Tracer Tool & Machine Co Inc ....F...... 201 337-6184
Oakland (G-7708)

Triad Tool & Die Co ....G...... 908 534-1784
Branchburg (G-712)

Triangle Automatic Inc ....G...... 973 625-3830
Wharton (G-12002)

Triangle Manufacturing Co Inc ....D...... 201 825-1212
Upper Saddle River (G-11287)

Triple S Industries ....G...... 908 862-0110
Linden (G-5455)

Tru Mfg Corp ....E...... 201 768-4050
Norwood (G-7637)

Unique Precision Co Inc ....G...... 732 382-8699
Rahway (G-9227)

United Machine Inc ....G...... 973 345-4505
Paterson (G-8404)

▲ Universal Metalcraft Inc ....E...... 973 345-3284
Wayne (G-11688)

V & L Machine and Tool Co Inc ....G...... 973 808-5858
Fairfield (G-3336)

Valle Precision Machine Co ....G...... 973 773-3037
Passaic (G-8187)

Vector Precision Machining ....G...... 856 740-5131
Williamstown (G-12112)

Vep Manufacturing ....F...... 732 657-0666
Jackson (G-4681)

▲ Vermes Machine Co Inc ....E...... 856 642-9300
Moorestown (G-6630)

▼ Wagner Industries Inc ....F...... 973 347-0800
Stanhope (G-10592)

Werko Machine Co ....F...... 856 662-0669
Pennsauken (G-8588)

West Machine Works Inc ....G...... 732 549-2183
Metuchen (G-6130)

Whitehouse Machine & Mfg Co ....G...... 908 534-4722
Somerville (G-10232)

▼ William Kenyon & Sons Inc ....E...... 732 985-8980
Piscataway (G-8836)

▲ Win-Tech Precision Products ....G...... 973 887-8727
East Hanover (G-2250)

Woodbridge Machine & Tool Co ....G...... 732 634-0179
Woodbridge (G-12156)

Woods Industrial LLC ....F...... 973 208-0664
West Milford (G-11859)

Zala Machine Co Inc ....E...... 908 431-9106
Hillsborough (G-4379)

Zenex Precision Products Corp ....F...... 973 523-6910
Paterson (G-8409)

36 ELECTRONIC AND OTHER ELECTRICAL EQUIPMENT AND COMPONENTS, EXCEPT COMPUTER

3612 Power, Distribution & Specialty Transformers

A C Transformer Corp ....G...... 973 589-8574
Newark (G-7065)

AFP Transformers Corporation ....D...... 732 248-0305
Edison (G-2453)

Amperite Co Inc ....E...... 201 864-9503
North Bergen (G-7430)

Baltimore Transformer Company ....E...... 973 942-2222
Paterson (G-8220)

Beverly Manufacturing Co Inc ....G...... 856 764-7898
Riverside (G-9493)

Cooper Power Systems LLC ....C...... 732 481-4630
Ocean (G-7719)

Cooper Power Systems LLC ....C...... 856 719-1100
West Berlin (G-11712)

Edko Electronics ....E...... 973 942-2222
Paterson (G-8254)

◆ G & S Motor Equipment Co Inc ....D...... 201 998-9244
Kearny (G-4875)

▲ Galaxy Trans & Magnetics LLC ....F...... 856 753-4546
West Berlin (G-11722)

Glen Magnetics Inc ....G...... 908 454-3717
Alpha (G-41)

▲ Globtek Inc ....B...... 201 784-1000
Northvale (G-7582)

Hbs Electronics Inc ....G...... 973 439-1147
Fairfield (G-3217)

▲ High Energy Group Ltd Lblty Co ....G...... 732 741-9099
Eatontown (G-2400)

High Gate Corp ....F...... 609 267-0680
Mount Holly (G-6773)

▲ Hitran Corporation ....C...... 908 782-5525
Flemington (G-3447)

▲ Hunterdon Transformer Co Inc ....D...... 908 454-2400
Alpha (G-42)

Ivey Katrina Owner ....G...... 973 951-8328
Newark (G-7202)

▲ Jerome Industries Corp ....E...... 908 353-5700
Hackettstown (G-4013)

▼ KG Squared LLC ....G...... 973 627-0643
Rockaway (G-9581)

Magnetika Inc ....E...... 908 454-2600
Phillipsburg (G-8657)

Magnetran Inc ....F...... 856 768-7787
Ocean View (G-7764)

▲ Megatran Industries ....B...... 609 227-4300
Bordentown (G-601)

Mesa Veterans Power LLC ....G...... 856 222-1000
Moorestown (G-6601)

Microsignals Inc ....E...... 800 225-4508
Palisades Park (G-7839)

▲ Model Rectifier Corporation ....E...... 732 225-2100
Edison (G-2575)

Nilsson Electrical Laboratory ....A...... 201 521-4860
Jersey City (G-4790)

◆ Nwl Inc ....B...... 609 298-7300
Bordentown (G-606)

Pioneer Power Solutions Inc ....E...... 212 867-0700
Fort Lee (G-3578)

▲ Power Magne-Tech Corp ....E...... 732 826-4700
Perth Amboy (G-8626)

▲ Power Magnetics Inc ....E...... 609 695-1170
Trenton (G-11101)

▲ Raritan Inc ....E...... 732 764-8886
Somerset (G-10162)

Siemens Corporation ....D...... 732 590-6895
Iselin (G-4645)

Somerset Cpitl Mark Tr MGT Inc ....F...... 848 228-0842
Chesterfield (G-1442)

▲ Transistor Devices Inc ....C...... 908 850-5088
Hackettstown (G-4041)

Transistor Devices Inc ....C...... 908 850-5088
Hackettstown (G-4042)

Voltis LLC ....G...... 607 349-9411
Fairfield (G-3346)

Wolock & Lott Transmission Eqp ....F...... 908 218-9292
Branchburg (G-718)

◆ Zero Surge Inc ....F...... 908 996-7700
Frenchtown (G-3707)

3613 Switchgear & Switchboard Apparatus

Aeropanel Corporation ....D...... 973 335-9636
Boonton (G-552)

Apelio Innovative Inds LLC ....F...... 973 777-8899
Kearny (G-4861)

▲ Astrodyne Corporation ....D...... 908 850-5088
Hackettstown (G-3998)

▲ Automatic Switch Company ....A...... 973 966-2000
Florham Park (G-3489)

Automation & Control Inc ....E...... 856 234-2300
Moorestown (G-6562)

Bel Fuse Inc ....C...... 201 432-0463
Jersey City (G-4715)

Blackhawk Cre Corporation ....F...... 856 887-0162
Salem (G-9803)

BNH Enterprise LLC ....E...... 201 815-0546
Dumont (G-2116)

▲ Circonix Technologies LLC ....F...... 973 962-6160
Ringwood (G-9445)

▲ Comus International Inc ....C...... 973 777-6900
Clifton (G-1588)

Csl Services Inc ....F...... 856 755-9440
Pennsauken (G-8499)

▲ Cutting Board Company ....G...... 908 725-0187
Lebanon (G-5283)

Cutting Board Company ....G...... 908 725-0187
Branchburg (G-655)

Dos Industrial Sales LLC ....G...... 973 887-7800
East Hanover (G-2212)

Eagle Engineering & Automation ....G...... 732 899-2292
Point Pleasant Boro (G-8939)

Electronic Power Designs Inc ....F...... 973 838-7055
Bloomingdale (G-542)

▲ Everite Machine Products Co ....E...... 856 330-6700
Pennsauken (G-8509)

Galaxy Switchgear Inds LLC ....E...... 914 668-8200
Kearny (G-4876)

Ivey Katrina Owner ....G...... 973 951-8328
Newark (G-7202)

Lincoln Electric Pdts Co Inc ....E...... 908 688-2900
Union (G-11201)

Machinery Electrics ....G...... 732 536-0600
Bayville (G-257)

Marine Electric Systems Inc ....E...... 201 531-8600
South Hackensack (G-10278)

Pkm Panel Systems Corp ....F...... 732 238-6760
Old Bridge (G-7789)

▲ Precision Multiple Contrls Inc ....E...... 201 444-0600
Midland Park (G-6236)

Precision Multiple Contrls Inc ....D...... 201 444-0600
Midland Park (G-6237)

Primacy Engineering Inc ....F...... 201 731-3272
Englewood Cliffs (G-2979)

Sensigraphics Inc ....G...... 856 853-9100
Mount Laurel (G-6839)

▲ Sigma-Netics Inc ....E...... 973 227-6372
Riverdale (G-9488)

Symcon Inc ....G...... 973 728-8661
West Milford (G-11857)

Techniques Inc ....E...... 973 256-0947
Woodland Park (G-12234)

▲ Technology Dynamics Inc ....E...... 201 385-0500
Bergenfield (G-396)

Tsi Nomenclature Inc ....G...... 732 340-0646
Avenel (G-157)

3621 Motors & Generators

ABB Motors and Mechanical Inc ....F...... 856 661-1442
Pennsauken (G-8468)

▲ ADI American Distributors LLC ....D...... 973 328-1181
Randolph (G-9267)

Al Tayyar Enrgy- Princeton LLC ....G...... 609 479-8603
Princeton (G-9000)

▲ Allu Group Inc ....F...... 201 288-2236
East Brunswick (G-2132)

Alstrom Energy Group LLC ....G...... 718 824-4901
Old Bridge (G-7773)

American Mdlar Pwr Sltions Inc ....G...... 973 588-4026
Boonton (G-555)

Ametek Inc ....E...... 732 417-0501
Edison (G-2460)

▲ Astrodyne Corporation ....D...... 908 850-5088
Hackettstown (G-3998)

Billows Electric Supply Co Inc ....C...... 856 751-2200
Delran (G-2010)

▲ Blutek Power Inc ....F...... 973 594-1800
Lodi (G-5577)

Boonton Electronics Corp ....E...... 201 261-8797
Parsippany (G-7963)

Cobra Power Systems Inc ....G...... 908 486-1800
Millstone Township (G-6263)

Dewey Electronics Corporation ....E...... 201 337-4700
Oakland (G-7684)

Eagle Engineering & Automation ....E...... 732 899-2292
Point Pleasant Boro (G-8939)

▼ Electro-Miniatures Corp ....D...... 201 460-0510
Moonachie (G-6516)

Electro-Steam Generator Corp ....B...... 609 288-9071
Rancocas (G-9257)

Energy Battery Group Inc ....G...... 404 255-7529
Flemington (G-3439)

▲ Ewc Controls Inc ....E...... 732 446-3110
Manalapan (G-5846)

Fishermens Energy NJ LLC ....F...... 609 286-9650
Cape May (G-1099)

H Power Corp ....G...... 973 249-5444
Clifton (G-1632)

▲ Hansome Energy Systems Inc ....E...... 908 862-9044
Linden (G-5382)

SIC

▲ Hitechone Inc ....G 201 500-8864
  Englewood Cliffs *(G-2964)*
▲ Hydro-Mechanical Systems Inc .....F 856 848-8888
  Westville *(G-11943)*
▲ Innovative Power Solutions LLC .....E 732 544-1075
  Eatontown *(G-2407)*
  Mpower Technologies Inc ....F 973 256-3737
  Clifton *(G-1677)*
▲ Multi-Tech Industries Inc ....E 732 431-0550
  Marlboro *(G-5948)*
◆ Ocean Power Technologies Inc ....E 609 730-0400
  Monroe Township *(G-6387)*
▲ Pht Aerospace LLC ....E 973 831-1230
  Pompton Plains *(G-8965)*
▲ Power Magne-Tech Corp ....E 732 826-4700
  Perth Amboy *(G-8626)*
▲ Power Magnetics Inc ....E 609 695-1170
  Trenton *(G-11101)*
◆ Power Pool Plus Inc ....G 908 454-1124
  Alpha *(G-44)*
  Primacy Engineering Inc ....F 201 731-3272
  Englewood Cliffs *(G-2979)*
  Princeton Tech Group Intl Corp ....G 732 328-9308
  Edison *(G-2596)*
  Rajysan Incorporated ....E 800 433-1382
  Swedesboro *(G-10722)*
  Reliance Electric Company ....E 856 661-1442
  Pennsauken *(G-8572)*
  Servo-Tek Products Company Inc .....E 973 427-4249
  Hawthorne *(G-4258)*
  Technology Dynamics Inc ....D 201 385-0500
  Bergenfield *(G-397)*
  Torque Gun Company LLC ....E 201 512-9800
  South Hackensack *(G-10298)*
◆ Triangle Tube/Phase III Co Inc ....D 856 228-9940
  Paulsboro *(G-8427)*
  Universal Electric Co ....E 201 968-1000
  Hackensack *(G-3989)*
  Valcor Engineering Corporation ....E 973 467-8100
  Springfield *(G-10584)*

3624 Carbon & Graphite Prdts

▲ Asbury Louisiana Inc ....E 908 537-2155
  Asbury *(G-69)*
  Bella Acqua Inc ....F 609 324-9024
  Chesterfield *(G-1441)*
◆ F S R Inc ....D 973 785-4347
  Woodland Park *(G-12218)*
  Hoyt Corporation ....D 201 894-0707
  Englewood *(G-2904)*
▲ Mersen USA Bn Corp ....C 973 334-0700
  Boonton *(G-577)*
▲ Resintech Inc ....C 856 768-9600
  West Berlin *(G-11747)*

3625 Relays & Indl Controls

  Admartec Inc ....G 732 888-8248
  Hazlet *(G-4268)*
  Advanced Industrial Controls ....G 908 725-7575
  Branchburg *(G-628)*
  Alliance Technologies Group ....G 973 664-1151
  East Hanover *(G-2199)*
  American Teletimer Corp ....E 908 654-4200
  Mountainside *(G-6869)*
  Amperite Co Inc ....E 201 864-9503
  North Bergen *(G-7430)*
  Argus International Inc ....E 609 466-1677
  Ringoes *(G-9435)*
  Artisan Controls Corporation ....E 973 598-9400
  Randolph *(G-9271)*
▲ Asco Investment Corp ....C 973 966-2000
  Florham Park *(G-3484)*
▲ Asco Valve LLC ....D 973 966-2437
  Florham Park *(G-3488)*
▲ Astrodyne Corporation ....D 908 850-5088
  Hackettstown *(G-3998)*
  Atc Systems Inc ....G 732 560-0900
  Middlesex *(G-6149)*
▲ Automatic Switch Company ....A 973 966-2000
  Florham Park *(G-3489)*
  Computer Control Corp ....F 973 492-8265
  Butler *(G-1001)*
▲ Comus International Inc ....C 973 777-6900
  Clifton *(G-1588)*
◆ Control & Power Systems Inc ....E 973 439-0500
  Fairfield *(G-3167)*
  Crestron Electronics Inc ....D 201 894-0670
  Cresskill *(G-1944)*
  Deltronics Corporation ....F 856 825-8200
  Millville *(G-6297)*

  Eaton Hydraulics LLC ....E 732 212-4700
  Tinton Falls *(G-10834)*
  Electronic Power Designs Inc ....F 973 838-7055
  Bloomingdale *(G-542)*
▲ Electronic Technology Inc ....C 973 371-5160
  Irvington *(G-4583)*
  Fitness Technologies Inc ....E 201 457-0030
  Hackensack *(G-3913)*
  General Electronic Engineering ....F 732 381-1144
  Rahway *(G-9193)*
▲ Hansome Energy Systems Inc ....E 908 862-9044
  Linden *(G-5382)*
  Harris Corporation ....E 973 284-0123
  Clifton *(G-1635)*
  Harrison Electro Mechanical ....F 732 382-6008
  Rahway *(G-9196)*
  Haz Laboratories ....F 908 453-3300
  Washington *(G-11582)*
▲ Heat-Timer Corporation ....E 973 575-4004
  Fairfield *(G-3218)*
  Howman Associates Inc ....E 732 985-7474
  Edison *(G-2538)*
  Howman Electronics Inc ....F 908 534-2247
  Lebanon *(G-5288)*
▲ Infinova Corporation ....G 732 355-9100
  Monmouth Junction *(G-6347)*
  Innolutions Inc ....G 609 490-9799
  Princeton Junction *(G-9158)*
  Instrumentation Technology Sls ....G 732 388-0866
  Rahway *(G-9200)*
  Intellicon Inc ....G 201 791-9499
  Kearny *(G-4887)*
  ITT Corporation ....D 973 284-0123
  Clifton *(G-1650)*
  Lummus Overseas Corporation ....D 973 893-3000
  Bloomfield *(G-520)*
  M&L Power Systems Maint Inc ....E 732 679-1800
  Old Bridge *(G-7783)*
▲ Megatran Industries ....B 609 227-4300
  Bordentown *(G-601)*
  Mid-State Controls Inc ....E 732 335-0500
  Hazlet *(G-4279)*
  Omega Engineering Inc ....C 856 467-4200
  Bridgeport *(G-769)*
  Panasonic Corp North America ....D 201 348-7000
  Newark *(G-7261)*
▲ Precision Multiple Contrls Inc ....E 201 444-0600
  Midland Park *(G-6236)*
  Precision Multiple Contrls Inc ....E 201 444-0600
  Midland Park *(G-6237)*
  Pressure Controls Inc ....G 973 751-5002
  Belleville *(G-312)*
  Quik-Flex Circuit Inc ....E 856 742-0550
  Gloucester City *(G-3844)*
◆ Rab Lighting Inc ....C 201 784-8600
  Northvale *(G-7602)*
  Redkoh Industries Inc ....G 908 369-1590
  Hillsborough *(G-4368)*
  Relay Specialties Inc ....G 856 547-5000
  Haddon Heights *(G-4050)*
  Reliance Electric Company ....E 856 661-1442
  Pennsauken *(G-8572)*
  Rockwell Automation Inc ....E 973 658-1500
  Parsippany *(G-8080)*
  Rockwell Automation Inc ....G 973 526-3901
  Parsippany *(G-8081)*
◆ Sealed Unit Parts Co Inc ....C 732 223-1201
  Allenwood *(G-37)*
  Servo-Tek Products Company Inc .....E 973 427-4249
  Hawthorne *(G-4258)*
▲ Sigma-Netics Inc ....G 973 227-6372
  Riverdale *(G-9488)*
  Special Technical Services ....G 609 259-2626
  Flanders *(G-3417)*
  Swatch Group Les Btques US Inc ....G 201 271-1400
  Weehawken *(G-11699)*
▲ Textol Systems Inc ....E 800 624-8746
  Carlstadt *(G-1228)*
▲ Transistor Devices Inc ....E 908 850-5088
  Hackettstown *(G-4041)*
  Tsg Inc ....F 973 785-1118
  Little Falls *(G-5492)*
  Tusa Products Inc ....G 609 448-8333
  Ewing *(G-3063)*
  Valcor Engineering Corporation ....E 973 467-8400
  Springfield *(G-10585)*
  Walker Engineering Inc ....F 732 899-2550
  Point Pleasant Boro *(G-8943)*
  Whippany Actuation Systems LLC ....C 973 428-9898
  Whippany *(G-12043)*

  Wireless Telecom Group Inc ....D 973 386-9696
  Parsippany *(G-8114)*
  Xybion Corporation ....C 973 538-2067
  Lawrenceville *(G-5273)*

3629 Electrical Indl Apparatus, NEC

▲ Active Controls LLC ....G 856 669-0940
  Paulsboro *(G-8412)*
▲ Ansmann USA Corp ....G 856 481-3504
  Blackwood *(G-470)*
  Atm Aficionado LLC ....G 973 251-2115
  Livingston *(G-5525)*
  Avionic Instruments LLC ....C 732 388-3500
  Avenel *(G-126)*
  Cellular Empire Inc ....D 800 778-3513
  Linden *(G-5357)*
  Dengen Scientific Corporation ....E 201 687-2983
  Union City *(G-11245)*
▲ Evapco-Blct Dry Cooling Inc ....E 908 379-2665
  Bridgewater *(G-836)*
▲ Fuchs Audio Tech Ltd Lblty Co ....F 973 772-4420
  Clifton *(G-1624)*
  Industronic Inc ....E 908 393-5960
  Bridgewater *(G-845)*
▲ Jsn Holdings LLC ....F 201 857-5900
  Mahwah *(G-5787)*
  Magna-Power Electronics ....D 908 237-2200
  Flemington *(G-3455)*
▲ Mizco International Inc ....D 732 912-2000
  Avenel *(G-141)*
◆ Ocean Power Technologies Inc ....E 609 730-0400
  Monroe Township *(G-6387)*
▲ Power Dynamics Inc ....E 973 560-0019
  Whippany *(G-12036)*
  Powerspec Inc ....E 732 494-9490
  Somerville *(G-10225)*
▲ Princeton Power Systems Inc ....E 609 955-5390
  Lawrenceville *(G-5267)*
  Sparton Aydin LLC ....F 732 935-1320
  Eatontown *(G-2423)*
  Storis Inc ....D 888 478-6747
  Mount Arlington *(G-6760)*
  Timothy P Bryan Elc Co Inc ....G 609 393-8325
  Trenton *(G-11122)*

3631 Household Cooking Eqpt

  Chefman Direct Inc ....E 888 315-8407
  Mahwah *(G-5758)*
  Clean Bbq Inc ....G 732 299-8877
  Edison *(G-2485)*
◆ Jarden Corporation ....E 201 610-6600
  Hoboken *(G-4477)*
◆ Sharp Electronics Corporation ....A 201 529-8200
  Mahwah *(G-5811)*
▲ Signature Marketing Group Ltd ....F 973 575-7785
  Pine Brook *(G-8717)*

3632 Household Refrigerators & Freezers

▲ Bar-Maid Corporation ....C 973 478-7070
  Garfield *(G-3722)*
  Philly Motors and Drives Inc ....E 856 840-8011
  Mount Laurel *(G-6826)*
▲ Troy Hills Manufacturing Inc ....G 973 263-1885
  Towaco *(G-11005)*

3634 Electric Household Appliances

  Aftek Inc ....G 609 588-0900
  Hamilton *(G-4102)*
  Argonautus LLC ....G 908 393-4379
  Bridgewater *(G-813)*
▲ Brabantia USA Inc ....F 201 933-3192
  East Rutherford *(G-2288)*
  Conair Corporation ....D 239 673-2125
  East Windsor *(G-2353)*
  Conair Corporation ....C 609 426-1300
  East Windsor *(G-2354)*
  Edwards Creative Products Inc ....F 856 665-3200
  Cherry Hill *(G-1361)*
  Emerald Electronics Usa Inc ....G 718 872-5544
  Passaic *(G-8137)*
  Expert Appliance Center LLC ....G 732 946-0999
  Marlboro *(G-5939)*
▲ Haydon Corporation ....D 973 904-0800
  Wayne *(G-11646)*
◆ Homeco LLC ....E 732 802-7733
  Piscataway *(G-8774)*
◆ Jarden Corporation ....E 201 610-6600
  Hoboken *(G-4477)*

▲ Maverick Industries Inc ....F 732 417-9666
Edison (G-2565)

▲ Rj Brands LLC ....C 888 315-8407
Mahwah (G-5809)

Rjticeco LLC ....G 973 697-0156
Stockholm (G-10610)

Technology General Corporation ....F ... 973 827-8209
Franklin (G-3605)

Vapor Lounge LLC ....G 973 627-1277
Rockaway (G-9621)

◆ Wanasavealotcom LLC ....F 732 286-6956
Toms River (G-10920)

▲ White Home Products Inc ....G 908 226-2501
Kenilworth (G-5008)

3635 Household Vacuum Cleaners

Hillsborough Vacuum LLC ....G 908 904-6600
Hillsborough (G-4341)

▲ Metropolitan Vacuum Clr Co Inc ......D 201 405-2225
Oakland (G-7696)

Stanley Steemer Intl Inc ....E 973 574-1640
Clifton (G-1731)

3639 Household Appliances, NEC

Arrow Steel Inc...............F 973 523-1122
Paterson (G-8215)

Groupe Seb USA ....F 856 825-6300
Millville (G-6306)

▲ Organize It All Inc ....E 201 488-0808
Bogota (G-549)

▲ PC Marketing Inc ....E 201 943-6100
Ridgefield (G-9379)

◆ Royal Sovereign Intl Inc ....E 800 397-1025
Rockleigh (G-9633)

◆ Triangle Tube/Phase III Co Inc ....D 856 228-9940
Paulsboro (G-8427)

◆ Wanasavealotcom LLC ....F 732 286-6956
Toms River (G-10920)

3641 Electric Lamps

▲ Amati International LLC...............E 201 569-1000
Englewood Cliffs (G-2947)

▲ Bitro Group Inc ....E 201 641-1004
Hackensack (G-3883)

◆ E G L Company Inc...............C 908 508-1111
Berkeley Heights (G-409)

Ethan Allen Retail Inc ....C 973 473-1019
Passaic (G-8139)

Hamamatsu Corporation ....E 908 526-0941
Bridgewater (G-842)

▲ Hamamatsu Corporation ....D 908 231-0960
Bridgewater (G-841)

▲ Hanovia Specialty Lighting LLC ....F 973 651-5510
Fairfield (G-3215)

Hid Ultraviolet LLC ....F 973 383-8535
Sparta (G-10505)

Horiba Instruments Inc ....E 732 623-8335
Piscataway (G-8775)

Lumitron Corp ....F 908 508-9100
Berkeley Heights (G-418)

◆ Maxlite Inc ....C 973 244-7300
West Caldwell (G-11788)

Metal Textiles Corporation ....E 800 843-1215
Edison (G-2570)

Mks Inc ....C 856 451-5545
Bridgeton (G-791)

Natal Lamp & Shade Corp ....E 201 224-7844
Fort Lee (G-3574)

Oxberry LLC ....G 201 935-3000
Carlstadt (G-1196)

Oxford Lamp Inc ....F 732 462-3755
Freehold (G-3676)

Philips Lighting N Amer Corp ....B 732 563-3000
Somerset (G-10154)

Precision Filaments Inc ....G 732 462-3755
Freehold (G-3680)

Rhingo Pro LLC ....G 201 728-9099
Lodi (G-5598)

Standex International Corp ....G 732 469-8452
Middlesex (G-6203)

Superior Lamp Inc ....G 800 257-8353
Cherry Hill (G-1423)

Union City Filament Corp ....E 201 945-3366
Ridgefield (G-9390)

3643 Current-Carrying Wiring Devices

Ametek Inc...............G 732 370-9100
Lakewood (G-5073)

Amperite Co Inc ....E 201 864-9503
North Bergen (G-7430)

▲ Archtech Electronics Corp ....E 732 355-1288
Dayton (G-1952)

Armel Electronics Inc ....E 201 869-4300
North Bergen (G-7433)

Asco Power Services Inc ....F 973 966-2000
Florham Park (G-3485)

Billows Electric Supply Co Inc ....C 856 751-2200
Delran (G-2010)

Bleema Manufacturing Corp ....E 973 371-1771
Irvington (G-4580)

Brim Electronics Inc ....F 201 796-2886
Lodi (G-5578)

Bryan Snook ....F 888 747-3250
Bedminster (G-268)

Cain Machine Inc...............F 856 825-7225
Millville (G-6291)

Calculagraph Co ....D 973 887-9400
East Hanover (G-2204)

Calculagraph Co ....D 973 887-9400
East Hanover (G-2205)

Connector Products Inc ....F 856 829-9190
Pennsauken (G-8498)

Control Products Inc ....D 973 887-5000
East Hanover (G-2210)

▲ Dearborn A Belden Cdt Company ...D 908 925-8000
Elizabeth (G-2723)

East Coast Electronics Inc ....F 908 431-7555
Hillsborough (G-4328)

Esi ....E 856 629-2492
Sicklerville (G-10018)

Frc Electrical Industries Inc ....F 908 464-3200
New Providence (G-7036)

G H Krauss Manufacturing Co ....G 856 662-0815
Cherry Hill (G-1368)

Glasseal Products Inc ....C 732 370-9100
Lakewood (G-5129)

Hofer Connectors Co Inc...............E 973 427-1195
North Haledon (G-7548)

Hofer Machine & Tool Co Inc ....F 973 427-1195
North Haledon (G-7549)

Howman Electronics Inc ....F 908 534-2247
Lebanon (G-5288)

HPH Products Inc ....G 609 883-0052
Ewing (G-3025)

Kraus & Naimer Inc ....E 732 560-1240
Somerset (G-10119)

Lapp Usa Inc...............G 973 660-9700
Florham Park (G-3510)

Lightning Prvntion Systems Inc ....G 856 767-7806
West Berlin (G-11729)

▲ Lumenarc Inc...............F 973 882-5918
West Caldwell (G-11784)

M&L Power Systems Maint Inc ....E 732 679-1800
Old Bridge (G-7783)

◆ Mac Products Inc...............D 973 344-5149
Kearny (G-4896)

Marine Electric Systems Inc ....E 201 531-8600
South Hackensack (G-10278)

▲ Multi-Tech Industries Inc ....F 732 431-0550
Marlboro (G-5948)

Newtech Group Corp...............G 732 355-0392
Kendall Park (G-4935)

Pekay Industries Inc ....F 732 938-2722
Farmingdale (G-3392)

Precision Mfg Group LLC...............D 973 785-4630
Cedar Grove (G-1296)

Pressure Controls Inc...............G 973 751-5002
Belleville (G-312)

◆ Richards Mfg A NJ Ltd Partnr...........C 973 371-1771
Irvington (G-4603)

▲ Richards Mfg Co Sales Inc ....E 973 371-1771
Irvington (G-4604)

▲ Roxboro Holdings Inc ....D 732 919-3119
Wall Township (G-11506)

Signal Systems International ....E 732 793-4668
Lavallette (G-5237)

Simply Amazing LLC ....F 732 249-4151
East Brunswick (G-2184)

Thomas & Betts Corporation ....C 908 852-1122
Hackettstown (G-4040)

Tycom Limited ....G 973 753-3040
Morristown (G-6746)

▲ Unique Wire Weaving Co Inc ....E 908 688-4600
Hillside (G-4447)

Vermont Cableworks Inc ....G 802 674-6555
Edison (G-2643)

Volta Corporation ....E 732 583-3300
Laurence Harbor (G-5236)

3644 Noncurrent-Carrying Wiring Devices

American Fittings Corp ....G 201 664-0027
Fair Lawn (G-3075)

Appleton Grp LLC ....C 973 285-3261
Morristown (G-6687)

Armel Electronics Inc ....E 201 869-4300
North Bergen (G-7433)

Billows Electric Supply Co Inc ....C 856 751-2200
Delran (G-2010)

◆ Heyco Molded Products Inc ....F 732 286-4336
Toms River (G-10884)

Hope Electrical Products Co...............G 973 882-7400
West Caldwell (G-11778)

Liberty Park Raceway LLC ....G 201 333-7223
Jersey City (G-4776)

Moreng Metal Products Inc ....D 973 256-2001
Totowa (G-10956)

Morgan Advanced Ceramics Inc ....E 973 808-1621
Fairfield (G-3264)

Mulberry Metal Products Inc...............D 908 688-8850
Union (G-11210)

▲ Multi-Tech Industries Inc ....F 732 431-0550
Marlboro (G-5948)

Raceway Carwash...............G 215 886-8252
Clementon (G-1533)

Raceway Petroleum Inc ....F 908 222-2999
North Plainfield (G-7561)

Raceway Petroleum Inc ....G 732 729-7350
East Brunswick (G-2178)

Raceway Petroleum Inc ....G 732 613-4404
East Brunswick (G-2179)

▲ Speed Raceway...............G 856 314-8264
Cinnaminson (G-1489)

Thomas & Betts Corporation ....C 908 852-1122
Hackettstown (G-4040)

3645 Residential Lighting Fixtures

▲ Amati International LLC...............E 201 569-1000
Englewood Cliffs (G-2947)

▲ American Brass and Crystal Inc ......E 908 688-8611
Union (G-11150)

Apelio Innovative Inds LLC ....F 973 777-8899
Kearny (G-4861)

Big Eye Lamp Inc...............G 732 557-9400
Whiting (G-12065)

◆ Cast Lighting LLC ....G 973 423-2303
Hawthorne (G-4225)

Cooper Lighting LLC ....D 609 395-4277
Cranbury (G-1827)

▲ Cutting Edge Casting Inc ....E 908 925-7500
Linden (G-5366)

Efficient Lighting Inc ....F 973 846-8568
Parsippany (G-7999)

Encore Led Ltg Ltd Lblty Co ....G 866 694-4533
Wayne (G-11627)

Estrin Calabrese Sales Agency ....G 908 722-9980
Manville (G-5895)

Galaxy Switchgear Inds LLC ....E 914 668-8200
Kearny (G-4876)

▲ Gemini Cut Glass Company Inc ......G 201 568-7722
Englewood (G-2900)

▲ Generation Brands ....G 856 764-0500
Burlington (G-977)

◆ Genie House Corp ....E 609 859-0600
Southampton (G-10473)

Go R Design LLC ....E 609 286-2146
New Egypt (G-7015)

▲ High Energy Group Ltd Lblty Co ......G 732 741-9099
Eatontown (G-2400)

Infinlight Products Inc ....G 888 665-7708
East Windsor (G-2360)

Jay-Bee Lamp & Shade Co Inc ....G 201 265-0762
Paramus (G-7877)

▼ Kurt Versen Inc...............F 201 664-5283
Montvale (G-6464)

◆ Lighting World Inc ....E 732 919-1224
Farmingdale (G-3388)

M + 4 Inc ....G 973 527-3262
Budd Lake (G-934)

Nicholas Longo Sr ....G 856 642-1971
Riverton (G-9508)

▲ Pty Lighting LLC ....G 855 303-4500
Hillside (G-4434)

▲ R B B Corp...............E 973 770-1100
Ledgewood (G-5308)

Robert Wallace ....G 609 649-0596
Stockton (G-10612)

◆ Sea Gull Lighting Products LLC ......B 856 764-0500
Delran (G-2021)

SIC

▲ Starfire Lighting Inc ....E 201 438-9540
Wood Ridge *(G-12139)*

▲ Superior Lighting Inc ....F 908 759-0199
Elizabeth *(G-2776)*

T C S Technologies Inc ....F 908 852-7555
Hackettstown *(G-4039)*

▼ William Spencer ....G 856 235-1830
Mount Laurel *(G-6847)*

3646 Commercial, Indl & Institutional Lighting Fixtures

Absolume LLC ....G 732 523-1231
Lakewood *(G-5063)*

▲ Amati International LLC ....E 201 569-1000
Englewood Cliffs *(G-2947)*

▲ American Brass and Crystal Inc ......E 908 688-8611
Union *(G-11150)*

▲ Amerlux LLC ....C 973 882-5010
Oakland *(G-7674)*

Apelio Innovative Inds LLC ....F 973 777-8899
Kearny *(G-4861)*

Articulight Inc ....G 201 796-2690
Fair Lawn *(G-3077)*

Belfer ....G 732 493-2666
Farmingdale *(G-3378)*

Bellemead Hot Glass ....G 908 281-5516
Hillsborough *(G-4318)*

▲ Compact Fluorescent Systems ....G 908 475-8991
Sparta *(G-10493)*

Cooper Interconnect ....G 856 935-7560
Salem *(G-9804)*

Cooper Lighting LLC ....D 609 395-4277
Cranbury *(G-1827)*

▲ Coronet Inc ....C 973 345-7660
Totowa *(G-10941)*

D and J Industries LLC ....F 201 257-8953
Carlstadt *(G-1152)*

Durabrite Ltg Solutions LLC ....G 201 915-0555
Jersey City *(G-4745)*

Encore Led Ltg Ltd Lblty Co ....G 866 694-4533
Wayne *(G-11627)*

▲ Genesis Lighting Mfg Inc ....G 908 352-6720
Elizabethport *(G-2784)*

◆ Genlyte Thomas Group LLC ....G 800 825-5844
Somerset *(G-10104)*

▲ Hal-O Manufacturing Co Inc ....G 973 824-6122
Newark *(G-7183)*

▲ Illuminating Experiences LLC ....G 800 734-5858
New Brunswick *(G-6967)*

◆ Lighting World Inc ....E 732 919-1224
Farmingdale *(G-3388)*

▲ Luminaire Lighting Corp ....G 732 549-0056
Edison *(G-2560)*

M + 4 Inc ....G 973 527-3262
Budd Lake *(G-934)*

▲ Mercury Lighting Pdts Co Inc ....C 973 244-9444
Fairfield *(G-3259)*

Mks Inc ....G 856 451-5545
Bridgeton *(G-791)*

▲ North American Illumination ....F 973 478-4700
Garfield *(G-3743)*

Picasso Lighting Inds LLC ....G 201 246-8188
Kearny *(G-4909)*

Prg Group Inc ....G 201 758-4000
Secaucus *(G-9913)*

▲ R B B Corp ....E 973 770-1100
Ledgewood *(G-5308)*

◆ Rab Lighting Inc ....C 201 784-8600
Northvale *(G-7602)*

▲ Rambusch Decorating Company .....E 201 333-2525
Jersey City *(G-4815)*

▲ Reggiani Lighting Usa Inc ....F 201 372-1717
Carlstadt *(G-1211)*

Robert Wallace ....G 609 649-0596
Stockton *(G-10612)*

SMS Building Systems Ltd Lblty ......F 856 520-8769
Cherry Hill *(G-1420)*

▲ Specialty Lighting Inds Inc ....E 732 517-0800
Ocean *(G-7746)*

▲ Starfire Lighting Inc ....E 201 438-9540
Wood Ridge *(G-12139)*

▲ Superior Lighting Inc ....F 908 759-0199
Elizabeth *(G-2776)*

▲ Tektite Industries Inc ....E 609 656-0600
Trenton *(G-11120)*

▲ Trinity Manufacturing LLC ....C 732 549-2866
Metuchen *(G-6129)*

Vision Lighting Inc ....G 973 720-1200
Paterson *(G-8408)*

3647 Vehicular Lighting Eqpt

Amperite Co Inc ....E 201 864-9503
North Bergen *(G-7430)*

Elite Emrgncy Lights Ltd Lblty ....F 732 534-2377
Lakewood *(G-5115)*

Spaghetti Engineering Corp ....F 856 719-9989
West Berlin *(G-11751)*

Sun Display Systems LLC ....E 973 226-4334
Fairfield *(G-3317)*

▲ Vehicle Safety Mfg LLC ....E 973 643-3000
Newark *(G-7356)*

3648 Lighting Eqpt, NEC

A P M Hexseal Corporation ....E 201 569-5700
Englewood *(G-2865)*

ABB Lighting Inc ....G 866 222-8866
Toms River *(G-10858)*

Amperite Co Inc ....E 201 864-9503
North Bergen *(G-7430)*

Archlit Inc ....G 973 577-4400
Hopatcong *(G-4534)*

BNH Enterprise LLC ....G 201 815-0546
Dumont *(G-2116)*

▲ Carpenter LLC ....F 609 689-3090
Trenton *(G-11034)*

City of Jersey City ....F 201 547-4470
Jersey City *(G-4728)*

▲ City Theatrical Inc ....E 201 549-1160
Carlstadt *(G-1145)*

Cubalas Emergency Lighting LLC ......G 908 943-1615
Linden *(G-5364)*

▲ Desmar Corporation ....G 908 317-0020
Mountainside *(G-6876)*

◆ Eco Lighting USA Ltd Lblty Co ......G 201 621-5661
South Hackensack *(G-10262)*

Encore Led Ltg Ltd Lblty Co ....G 866 694-4533
Wayne *(G-11627)*

▲ Erco Lighting Inc ....F 732 225-8856
Edison *(G-2515)*

▲ Galaxy Led Inc ....G 201 541-5461
Englewood Cliffs *(G-2961)*

Garden State Irrigation ....F 201 848-1300
Wyckoff *(G-12253)*

◆ Gogreen Power Inc ....F 732 994-5901
Howell *(G-4555)*

▲ High Energy Group Ltd Lblty Co .....G 732 741-9099
Eatontown *(G-2400)*

In The Spotlights ....G 973 361-7768
Rockaway *(G-9573)*

Innovtive Phtnics Slution Corp ....G 732 355-9300
Monmouth Junction *(G-6348)*

▲ John G Papailias Co Inc ....G 201 767-4027
Northvale *(G-7588)*

Lightfox Inc ....E 973 209-9112
Morristown *(G-6723)*

Maxlite Inc ....G 800 555-5629
West Caldwell *(G-11787)*

Michele Maddalena ....G 973 244-0033
Fairfield *(G-3260)*

Musco Sports Lighting LLC ....G 732 751-9114
Wall Township *(G-11498)*

▲ Natale Machine & Tool Co Inc ....F 201 933-5500
Carlstadt *(G-1191)*

Olympia Lighting Inc ....G 201 812-7880
Northvale *(G-7598)*

◆ Pioneer & Co Inc ....E 856 866-9191
Moorestown *(G-6613)*

Princeton Tectonics ....E 609 298-9331
West Berlin *(G-11743)*

▲ Princeton Tectonics ....C 609 298-9331
Pennsauken *(G-8565)*

▼ Proactive Ltg Solutions LLC ....F 800 747-1209
North Arlington *(G-7423)*

◆ Rab Lighting Inc ....G 201 784-8600
Northvale *(G-7602)*

◆ Smartpool LLC ....E 732 730-9880
Lakewood *(G-5189)*

▲ Tektite Industries Inc ....G 609 656-0600
Trenton *(G-11120)*

▲ Trinity Manufacturing LLC ....C 732 549-2866
Metuchen *(G-6129)*

▼ Unilux Inc ....E 201 712-1266
Saddle Brook *(G-9798)*

Wisely Products LLC ....G 929 329-9188
Jersey City *(G-4850)*

Zago Manufacturing Company ....E 973 643-6700
Newark *(G-7362)*

3651 Household Audio & Video Eqpt

360 Media Innovations LLC ....G 201 228-0941
Union *(G-11145)*

▲ Apb-Dynasonics Inc ....G 973 785-1101
Totowa *(G-10931)*

Apogee Sound International LLC ......E 201 934-8500
Ramsey *(G-9234)*

◆ Audio and Video Labs Inc ....B 856 663-9030
Pennsauken *(G-8482)*

Audio Technologies and Codecs ......F 973 624-1116
Newark *(G-7098)*

B and G Music LLC ....G 732 779-4555
Bayville *(G-251)*

▲ Bayview Entertainment LLC ....G 201 880-5331
Pompton Plains *(G-8955)*

▲ Bogen Communications Inc ....D 201 934-8500
Mahwah *(G-5754)*

Bogen Corporation ....E 201 934-8500
Ramsey *(G-9237)*

Broadway Empress Entrmt Inc ....G 973 991-0009
Newark *(G-7117)*

Celco ....F 201 327-1123
Mahwah *(G-5757)*

Concept Professional Systems ....G 732 938-5321
Wall Township *(G-11475)*

◆ Crestron Electronics Inc ....G 201 767-3400
Rockleigh *(G-9628)*

▲ CVE Inc ....D 201 770-0005
Riverdale *(G-9478)*

DMJ Technologies LLC ....G 201 261-5560
New Milford *(G-7021)*

Dtrovision LLC ....E 201 488-3232
Ramsey *(G-9239)*

◆ Emerson Radio Corp ....F 973 428-2000
Parsippany *(G-8001)*

Empirical Labs Inc ....G 973 541-9446
Lake Hiawatha *(G-5054)*

Excite View LLC ....G 201 227-7075
Tenafly *(G-10784)*

Ferro Industries Incorporated ....E 732 246-3200
Colts Neck *(G-1785)*

▲ Funai Corporation Inc ....E 201 806-7635
Rutherford *(G-9732)*

Gabriel Sound Ltd Liability Co ....G 973 831-7800
Pompton Lakes *(G-8947)*

▲ GP Acoustics (us) Inc ....F 732 683-2356
Marlboro *(G-5942)*

Gzgn Inc ....F 201 842-7622
Rutherford *(G-9733)*

Innovative Concepts Design LLC ......F 732 346-0061
Elizabeth *(G-2747)*

Itec Consultants LLC ....G 732 784-8322
Matawan *(G-6022)*

▼ Jvc Industrial America Inc ....E 800 247-3608
Wayne *(G-11657)*

Jvckenwood USA Corporation ....E 973 317-5000
Wayne *(G-11658)*

▲ Kef America Inc ....E 732 414-2074
Marlboro *(G-5946)*

Kultur International Films Ltd ....E 732 229-2343
Red Bank *(G-9334)*

◆ Lg Electronics USA Inc ....B 201 816-2000
Englewood Cliffs *(G-2973)*

▲ Lunar Audio Video LLC ....G 973 233-7700
Sayreville *(G-9831)*

▲ Mardee Company Inc ....G 908 753-4343
South Plainfield *(G-10402)*

▲ Mp Production ....F 973 729-9333
Sparta *(G-10512)*

Murray Electronics Inc ....G 201 405-1158
Oakland *(G-7697)*

◆ Oklahoma Sound Corp ....E 800 261-4112
Clifton *(G-1686)*

Peter-Lisand Machine Corp ....G 201 943-5600
New Milford *(G-7024)*

Philips Elec N Amer Corp ....D 973 804-2100
Ledgewood *(G-5307)*

Phoenix Systems ....G 201 788-5511
North Haledon *(G-7553)*

Premium Distribution Corp ....G 212 533-1100
Secaucus *(G-9912)*

▲ Rcf USA Inc ....G 732 902-6100
Edison *(G-2602)*

Riotsound Inc ....G 917 273-5814
Newton *(G-7401)*

Rock Dreams Electronics LLC ....G 609 890-0808
Trenton *(G-11113)*

Scj Group LLC ....G 201 289-5841
Teaneck *(G-10773)*

◆ Sdi Technologies Inc ....D 732 574-9000
  Rahway *(G-9223)*

Sharkk LLC ....F 302 377-3974
  Livingston *(G-5561)*

◆ Sharp Electronics Corporation ....A 201 529-8200
  Mahwah *(G-5811)*

▲ Sierra Video Systems ....E 530 478-1000
  Clinton *(G-1754)*

Signature Audio Video Systems ....G 732 864-1039
  Toms River *(G-10912)*

▲ Sondpex Corp America LLC ....G 732 940-4430
  Princeton *(G-9123)*

Sony Corporation of America ....B 201 930-1000
  Paramus *(G-7902)*

Sony Corporation of America ....F 201 930-1000
  Woodcliff Lake *(G-12202)*

Sony Electronics Inc ....C 201 930-7030
  Paramus *(G-7903)*

Sony Electronics Inc ....A 201 930-1000
  Paramus *(G-7904)*

Sound Chice Assstive Listening ....G 908 647-2651
  Gillette *(G-3797)*

Sound Professionals Inc ....G 609 267-4400
  Hainesport *(G-4078)*

Sound United LLC ....C 201 762-6500
  Mahwah *(G-5813)*

Stirling Audio Services LLC ....G 732 560-0707
  Middlesex *(G-6204)*

Techflex Inc ....G 973 300-9242
  Sparta *(G-10522)*

Toshiba Amer Consmr Pdts Inc ....G 973 628-8000
  Wayne *(G-11685)*

Tusa Products Inc ....G 609 448-8333
  Ewing *(G-3063)*

V P I Industries Inc ....G 732 583-6895
  Cliffwood *(G-1549)*

Vanderbilt LLC ....E 973 316-3900
  Parsippany *(G-8108)*

▲ Vcom Intl Multi-Media Corp ....D 201 814-0405
  Fairfield *(G-3337)*

Vcom Intl Multi-Media Corp ....D 201 296-0600
  Fairfield *(G-3338)*

Wireworks Corporation ....F 908 686-7400
  Hillside *(G-4451)*

Xbox Exclusive ....G 908 756-3731
  South Plainfield *(G-10455)*

◆ York Telecom Corporation ....D 732 413-6000
  Eatontown *(G-2430)*

Zenith Electronics Corporation ....E 201 816-2071
  Englewood Cliffs *(G-2988)*

3652 Phonograph Records & Magnetic Tape

◆ Audio and Video Labs Inc ....B 856 663-9030
  Pennsauken *(G-8482)*

Audio and Video Labs Inc ....E 856 661-5772
  Delair *(G-2000)*

◆ Disc Makers Inc ....B 800 468-9353
  Pennsauken *(G-8504)*

Masterwork Recording Inc ....G 267 731-7031
  Pennsauken *(G-8545)*

▲ Maxell Corporation of America ....E 973 653-2400
  Woodland Park *(G-12224)*

Metrolpolis Mastering LP ....E 212 604-9433
  Edgewater *(G-2441)*

▲ PM Swapco Inc ....F 201 438-7700
  Lyndhurst *(G-5701)*

Recorded Publications Labs ....E 856 963-3000
  Camden *(G-1084)*

Simtronics Corporation ....G 732 747-0322
  Little Silver *(G-5520)*

Sony Corporation of America ....B 201 930-1000
  Paramus *(G-7902)*

Sony Electronics Inc ....A 201 930-1000
  Woodcliff Lake *(G-12203)*

Sony Music Holdings Inc ....B 201 777-3933
  Rutherford *(G-9745)*

Sun Plastics Co Inc ....F 908 490-0870
  Watchung *(G-11595)*

United Sound Arts Inc ....F 732 229-4949
  Eatontown *(G-2428)*

3661 Telephone & Telegraph Apparatus

Adva Optical Networking Inc ....E 201 258-8300
  Mahwah *(G-5744)*

Alcatel-Lucent USA Inc ....D 908 582-3275
  New Providence *(G-7026)*

▼ AT&T Technologies Inc ....A 201 771-2000
  Berkeley Heights *(G-400)*

Avaya Cala Inc ....G 866 462-8292
  Morristown *(G-6689)*

Avaya Inc ....B 908 953-6000
  Basking Ridge *(G-181)*

Avaya Inc ....C 732 852-2030
  Lincroft *(G-5336)*

◆ Avaya World Services Inc ....E 908 953-6000
  Morristown *(G-6690)*

◆ Bogen Communications Inc ....D 201 934-8500
  Mahwah *(G-5754)*

Bogen Corporation ....G 201 934-8500
  Ramsey *(G-9237)*

Centurum Information Tech Inc ....G 856 751-1111
  Marlton *(G-5967)*

▲ Chromis Fiberoptics Inc ....F 732 764-0900
  Warren *(G-11543)*

Conair Corporation ....C 609 426-1300
  East Windsor *(G-2354)*

Conolog Corporation ....F 908 722-8081
  Branchburg *(G-650)*

D R Tielmann Inc ....G 732 332-1860
  Matawan *(G-6016)*

▲ Dataprobe Inc ....D 201 934-9944
  Allendale *(G-8)*

Dialogic Inc ....C 973 967-6000
  Parsippany *(G-7981)*

Eagle Communications Inc ....G 973 366-6181
  Denville *(G-2038)*

Eastern Instrumentation of ....G 856 231-0668
  Moorestown *(G-6573)*

Fiber-Span Inc ....E 908 253-9080
  Toms River *(G-10876)*

▲ Infinova Corporation ....E 732 355-9100
  Monmouth Junction *(G-6347)*

Iniven LLC ....G 908 722-3770
  Branchburg *(G-669)*

Inlc Technology Corporation ....F 908 834-8390
  Warren *(G-11556)*

Innovance Inc ....G 732 529-2300
  Piscataway *(G-8781)*

▲ Instock Wireless Components ....F 973 335-6550
  Boonton *(G-572)*

▲ IPC Systems Inc ....C 201 253-2000
  Jersey City *(G-4768)*

J C Contracting Inc ....F 973 748-5600
  Rahway *(G-9201)*

LAp Marketing MGT Svcs Inc ....F 609 654-9266
  Cherry Hill *(G-1387)*

Lattice Incorporated ....F 856 910-1166
  Pennsauken *(G-8542)*

Lucent Technologies World Svcs ....C 908 582-3000
  New Providence *(G-7046)*

Lyca Tel LLC ....E 973 286-0771
  Newark *(G-7231)*

▲ Mizco International Inc ....D 732 912-2000
  Avenel *(G-141)*

Nokia Inc ....F 908 582-3149
  Murray Hill *(G-6895)*

Ntt Electronics America Inc ....E 201 556-1770
  Saddle Brook *(G-9778)*

Oe Solutions America Inc ....F 201 568-1188
  Ridgefield Park *(G-9411)*

Optequip Inc ....G 609 758-8609
  Cream Ridge *(G-1939)*

Packetstorm Communications Inc ....F 732 840-3871
  Westwood *(G-11964)*

Parwan Electronics Corporation ....E 732 290-1900
  Matawan *(G-6027)*

▲ Quintum Technologies Inc ....D 732 460-9000
  Eatontown *(G-2421)*

Response Time Incorporated ....E 856 875-0025
  Williamstown *(G-12102)*

Shore Microsystems Inc ....G 732 870-0800
  Long Branch *(G-5633)*

Sierra Communication Intl LLC ....G 866 462-8292
  Morristown *(G-6742)*

▲ Sonetronics Inc ....G 732 681-5016
  Belmar *(G-364)*

Star Dynamic Corp ....D 732 257-7488
  Garfield *(G-3764)*

◆ Swintec Corp ....F 201 935-0115
  Moonachie *(G-6548)*

Technology Corp America Inc ....G 866 462-8292
  Morristown *(G-6744)*

Telcontel Corp ....F 732 441-0800
  Laurence Harbor *(G-5235)*

Telecom Assistance Group Inc ....E 856 753-8585
  West Berlin *(G-11756)*

▲ TMC Corporation ....G 609 860-1830
  Metuchen *(G-6128)*

Tollgrade Communications Inc ....G 732 743-6720
  Piscataway *(G-8827)*

Transcore LP ....F 201 329-9200
  Teterboro *(G-10816)*

Tyco Elec Sbsea Cmmnctions LLC ....B 732 578-7000
  Eatontown *(G-2427)*

Vitex LLC ....G 201 296-0145
  Ridgefield Park *(G-9417)*

Vytran Corporation ....G 732 972-2880
  Morganville *(G-6655)*

Vytran LLC ....E 732 972-2880
  Morganville *(G-6656)*

Zzyzx LLC ....G 908 722-3770
  Branchburg *(G-723)*

3663 Radio & T V Communications, Systs & Eqpt, Broadcast/Studio

Alcatel-Lucent USA Inc ....D 908 582-3275
  New Providence *(G-7026)*

Anatech Microwave Company Inc ....G 973 772-7369
  Garfield *(G-3717)*

▲ Antronix Inc ....A 609 860-0160
  Cranbury *(G-1813)*

Aphelion Orbitals Inc ....G 321 289-0872
  Union City *(G-11242)*

◆ Blitz Safe of America Inc ....E 201 569-5000
  Englewood *(G-2877)*

Blonder Tongue Labs Inc ....C 732 679-4000
  Old Bridge *(G-7775)*

BNS Enterprises Inc ....G 908 285-6556
  Hillsborough *(G-4321)*

▲ Bogen Communications Inc ....D 201 934-8500
  Mahwah *(G-5754)*

Bogen Corporation ....G 201 934-8500
  Ramsey *(G-9237)*

Cabletenna Corp ....G 609 395-9400
  Cranbury *(G-1818)*

Cellebrite Inc ....D 201 848-8552
  Parsippany *(G-7965)*

Centurum Information Tech Inc ....G 856 751-1111
  Marlton *(G-5967)*

◆ Checkpoint Systems Inc ....C 800 257-5540
  West Deptford *(G-11821)*

Checkpoint Systems Inc ....C 856 848-1800
  West Deptford *(G-11822)*

▲ Comm Port Technologies Inc ....G 732 738-8780
  Cranbury *(G-1825)*

◆ Communication Devices Inc ....F 973 334-1980
  Boonton *(G-560)*

Comodo Group Inc ....C 888 266-6361
  Clifton *(G-1586)*

Computeradio ....G 973 220-0087
  Montville *(G-6486)*

Comtron Inc ....F 732 446-7571
  Springfield *(G-10548)*

Conolog Corporation ....F 908 722-8081
  Branchburg *(G-650)*

◆ Crestron Electronics Inc ....C 201 767-3400
  Rockleigh *(G-9628)*

Daysequerra Corporation ....F 856 719-9900
  Pennsauken *(G-8501)*

DMJ and Associates Inc ....E 732 613-7867
  Sayreville *(G-9820)*

Draztic Designs LLC ....E 609 678-4200
  Columbus *(G-1803)*

Eclearview Technologies Inc ....G 732 695-6999
  Ocean *(G-7724)*

Eigent Technologies Inc ....G 732 673-0402
  Holmdel *(G-4515)*

▼ Electromagnetic Tech Inds Inc ....D 973 394-1719
  Boonton *(G-564)*

Engility LLC ....F 703 633-8300
  Princeton Junction *(G-9152)*

Ensync Intrctive Solutions Inc ....G 732 542-4001
  Freehold *(G-3654)*

EVs Broadcast Equipment Inc ....E 973 575-7811
  Fairfield *(G-3186)*

◆ F S R Inc ....D 973 785-4347
  Woodland Park *(G-12218)*

▲ Fei-Elcom Tech Inc ....E 201 767-8030
  Northvale *(G-7580)*

Fiber-Span Inc ....E 908 253-9080
  Toms River *(G-10876)*

Flir Security Inc ....G 201 368-9700
  Ridgefield Park *(G-9406)*

Grass Valley Usa LLC ....E 201 818-4050
  Montvale *(G-6458)*

Hbc Solutions Inc ....G 973 267-5990
  Rockleigh *(G-9630)*

Homan Communications Inc ....G 609 654-9594
  Medford *(G-6070)*

S I C

▲ ID Systems Inc ....C.... 201 996-9000
Woodcliff Lake *(G-12193)*
In-Phase Technologies Inc ....E.... 609 298-9555
Bordentown *(G-599)*
▲ Infinova Corporation ....E.... 732 355-9100
Monmouth Junction *(G-6347)*
Iniven LLC ....G.... 908 722-3770
Branchburg *(G-669)*
Integrated Microwave Tech LLC ....D.... 908 852-3700
Hackettstown *(G-4012)*
International Telematics Corp ....F.... 888 887-0935
Fort Lee *(G-3559)*
Kaleidoscope Sound ....G.... 201 223-2868
Union City *(G-11252)*
▲ Kef America Inc ....E.... 732 414-2074
Marlboro *(G-5946)*
▲ L3 Mobile-Vision Inc ....D.... 973 263-1090
Rockaway *(G-9583)*
L3 Technologies Inc ....A.... 856 338-3000
Camden *(G-1074)*
▲ Lg Elctrnics Mbilecomm USA Inc ....D.... 201 816-2000
Englewood Cliffs *(G-2972)*
Lightning Prvntion Systems Inc ....G.... 856 767-7806
West Berlin *(G-11729)*
Linearizer Technology Inc ....G.... 609 584-8424
Hamilton *(G-4111)*
Lockheed Martin Corporation ....B.... 856 787-3104
Mount Laurel *(G-6814)*
Lucent Technologies World Svcs ....C.... 908 582-3000
New Providence *(G-7046)*
Major Auto Installations Inc ....E.... 973 252-4262
Kenvil *(G-5011)*
Maxentric Technologies LLC ....E.... 201 242-9800
Fort Lee *(G-3566)*
Mediabridge Products LLC ....E.... 856 216-8222
Cherry Hill *(G-1398)*
▲ Merrimac Industries Inc ....D.... 973 575-1300
West Caldwell *(G-11790)*
▲ Microlab/Fxr ....C.... 973 386-9696
Parsippany *(G-8048)*
Microsignals Inc ....E.... 800 225-4508
Palisades Park *(G-7839)*
Miranda MTI Inc ....F.... 973 376-4275
Springfield *(G-10565)*
▲ Mizco International Inc ....D.... 732 912-2000
Avenel *(G-141)*
Modulation Sciences Inc ....F.... 732 302-3090
Somerset *(G-10139)*
Mphase Technologies Inc ....F.... 973 256-3737
Clifton *(G-1676)*
▲ Myat Inc ....E.... 201 529-0145
Mahwah *(G-5794)*
▲ Natural Wireless LLC ....E.... 201 438-2865
East Rutherford *(G-2313)*
Network Communications Cons ....F.... 201 968-0684
Hackensack *(G-3953)*
On Site Communication ....E.... 201 488-4123
South Hackensack *(G-10285)*
Open Terra Inc ....G.... 732 765-9600
Matawan *(G-6026)*
Orbcomm LLC ....E.... 703 433-6300
Rochelle Park *(G-9532)*
OSI Laser Diode Inc ....E.... 732 549-9001
Edison *(G-2590)*
Panasonic Corp North America ....G.... 201 348-7000
Newark *(G-7262)*
Patchamp Inc ....G.... 201 457-1504
Hackensack *(G-3961)*
Peter-Lisand Machine Corp ....G.... 201 943-5600
New Milford *(G-7024)*
Philips Elec N Amer Corp ....D.... 973 471-9450
Clifton *(G-1695)*
Powertrunk Inc ....G.... 201 630-4520
Jersey City *(G-4805)*
Qualcomm Incorporated ....D.... 908 443-8000
Bridgewater *(G-882)*
R F Products Inc ....E.... 856 365-5500
Camden *(G-1083)*
R H A Audio Communications ....G.... 732 257-9180
East Brunswick *(G-2177)*
R P R Graphics Inc ....E.... 908 654-8080
Peapack *(G-8432)*
R&D Microwaves LLC ....E.... 908 212-1696
Boonton *(G-580)*
Radio Systems Design Inc ....E.... 856 467-8000
Swedesboro *(G-10721)*
Radwin Inc ....G.... 201 252-4224
Mahwah *(G-5806)*
Renae Telecom LLC ....D.... 908 362-8112
Elizabeth *(G-2772)*
Rigztools LLC ....G.... 908 361-5433
Fairfield *(G-3294)*
Satellite Pros Inc ....G.... 908 823-9500
Whitehouse Station *(G-12062)*
Selway Partners LLC ....F.... 201 712-7974
Englewood *(G-2929)*
SES Engineering (us) Inc ....D.... 609 987-4000
Princeton *(G-9117)*
Techflex Inc ....E.... 973 300-9242
Sparta *(G-10522)*
Telcontel Corp ....F.... 732 441-0800
Laurence Harbor *(G-5235)*
▲ Telemetrics Inc ....E.... 201 848-9818
Allendale *(G-21)*
Telescript Inc ....G.... 201 767-6733
Norwood *(G-7636)*
Telvue Corporation ....E.... 800 885-8886
Mount Laurel *(G-6844)*
Tone Layout LLC ....G.... 201 438-1746
Ridgefield *(G-9386)*
Turn-Key Technologies Inc ....F.... 732 553-9100
Sayreville *(G-9842)*
Turner Engineering Inc ....F.... 973 263-1000
Mountain Lakes *(G-6863)*
Ussecurenet LLC ....G.... 201 447-0130
Hawthorne *(G-4262)*
Videonet Comm Group LLC ....F.... 732 863-5310
Freehold *(G-3691)*
▲ Vitec Videocom Inc ....E.... 908 852-3700
Secaucus *(G-9938)*
▼ Wide Band Systems Inc ....F.... 973 586-6500
Rockaway *(G-9625)*
Wireless Communications Inc ....F.... 732 926-1000
Metuchen *(G-6132)*
Wireless Electronics Inc ....E.... 856 768-4310
West Berlin *(G-11761)*
Wireworks Corporation ....E.... 908 686-7400
Hillside *(G-4451)*
Zaxcom Inc ....F.... 973 835-5000
Pompton Plains *(G-8969)*
Zzyzx LLC ....G.... 908 722-3770
Branchburg *(G-723)*

3669 Communications Eqpt, NEC

A C L Equipment Corp ....G.... 973 740-9800
Livingston *(G-5521)*
Abris Distribution Inc ....G.... 732 252-9819
Manalapan *(G-5836)*
AT&T Services Inc ....A.... 732 420-3131
Middletown *(G-6210)*
▲ Aurora Multimedia Corporation ....E.... 732 591-5800
Morganville *(G-6637)*
◆ Blitz Safe of America Inc ....F.... 201 569-5000
Englewood *(G-2877)*
▲ Bogen Communications Inc ....D.... 201 934-8500
Mahwah *(G-5754)*
Bogen Corporation ....G.... 201 934-8500
Ramsey *(G-9237)*
Confires Fire Prtction Svc LLC ....F.... 908 822-2700
South Plainfield *(G-10349)*
◆ Crestron Electronics Inc ....C.... 201 767-3400
Rockleigh *(G-9628)*
Cricket Enterprises ....G.... 201 387-7978
Dumont *(G-2117)*
D2cf LLC ....G.... 973 699-4111
West Orange *(G-11892)*
Digitize Inc ....F.... 973 663-1011
Lake Hopatcong *(G-5056)*
Ea Pilot Supply ....G.... 201 934-8449
Bradley Beach *(G-627)*
▲ Electronic Marine Systems Inc ....F.... 732 680-4120
Rahway *(G-9185)*
Elymat Corp ....E.... 201 767-7105
Old Tappan *(G-7798)*
Elymat Industries Inc ....E.... 201 767-7105
Old Tappan *(G-7799)*
▲ Heat-Timer Corporation ....E.... 973 575-4004
Fairfield *(G-3218)*
Hope Center ....F.... 201 798-1234
Jersey City *(G-4766)*
Industronic Inc ....G.... 908 393-5960
Bridgewater *(G-845)*
Institute For Respnsble Online ....G.... 856 722-1048
Mount Laurel *(G-6805)*
Intellgent Trffic Sup Pdts LLC ....G.... 908 791-1200
South Plainfield *(G-10385)*
J C Contracting Inc ....F.... 973 748-5600
Rahway *(G-9201)*
Jen Electric Inc ....F.... 973 467-4901
Springfield *(G-10559)*
Kinly Inc ....E.... 973 585-3000
Cedar Knolls *(G-1314)*
L J Loeffler Systems Inc ....G.... 212 924-7597
Secaucus *(G-9901)*
Merchants Alarm Systems Inc ....E.... 973 779-1296
Wallington *(G-11528)*
▲ Moniteur Devices Inc ....F.... 973 857-1600
Cedar Grove *(G-1292)*
Netquest Corporation ....E.... 856 866-0505
Mount Laurel *(G-6822)*
Octopus Yachts Ltd Lblty Co ....F.... 732 698-8550
Belmar *(G-361)*
Pixell Creative Group LLC ....G.... 609 410-3024
Burlington *(G-988)*
Protection Industries Corp ....F.... 201 333-8050
Jersey City *(G-4808)*
Sightlogix Inc ....E.... 609 951-0008
Princeton *(G-9118)*
Telegenix Inc ....F.... 609 265-3910
Rancocas *(G-9264)*
◆ Tyco International MGT Co LLC ....E.... 609 720-4200
Princeton *(G-9133)*
Work Zone Contractors LLC ....G.... 856 845-8201
Deptford *(G-2069)*
◆ York Telecom Corporation ....D.... 732 413-6000
Eatontown *(G-2430)*

3671 Radio & T V Receiving Electron Tubes

▲ Epcos Inc ....D.... 732 906-4300
Iselin *(G-4626)*
▲ Hamamatsu Corporation ....D.... 908 231-0960
Bridgewater *(G-841)*
Linear Photonics LLC ....G.... 609 584-5747
Hamilton *(G-4109)*
Linearizer Technology Inc ....D.... 609 584-5747
Hamilton *(G-4110)*
Petra Systems Inc ....C.... 908 462-5200
South Plainfield *(G-10419)*
Troy-Onic Inc ....E.... 973 584-6830
Kenvil *(G-5014)*
Union City Filament Corp ....E.... 201 945-3366
Ridgefield *(G-9390)*
World Electronics Inc ....F.... 201 670-1177
Glen Rock *(G-3830)*

3672 Printed Circuit Boards

▲ ADI American Distributors LLC ....D.... 973 328-1181
Randolph *(G-9267)*
▲ Ai-Logix Inc ....E.... 732 469-0880
Somerset *(G-10052)*
▲ Applicad Inc ....E.... 732 751-2555
Wall Township *(G-11463)*
Argus International Inc ....E.... 609 466-1677
Ringoes *(G-9435)*
▼ AT&T Technologies Inc ....A.... 201 771-2000
Berkeley Heights *(G-400)*
▲ Cheringal Associates Inc ....D.... 201 784-8721
Norwood *(G-7618)*
Circuit Reproduction Co ....F.... 201 712-9292
Maywood *(G-6046)*
Computer Control Corp ....F.... 973 492-8265
Butler *(G-1001)*
Data Delay Devices Inc ....E.... 973 202-3268
Clifton *(G-1597)*
▲ Delta Circuits Inc ....E.... 973 575-3000
Fairfield *(G-3175)*
Esi ....E.... 856 629-2492
Sicklerville *(G-10018)*
ESP Associates Inc ....F.... 973 208-9045
Newfoundland *(G-7374)*
GAb Electronic Services LLC ....E.... 856 786-0108
Cinnaminson *(G-1464)*
Garys Kids ....G.... 973 458-1818
Passaic *(G-8141)*
▲ Glenro Inc ....F.... 973 279-5900
Paterson *(G-8277)*
Harrison Electro Mechanical ....F.... 732 382-6008
Rahway *(G-9196)*
J R E Inc ....E.... 973 808-0055
West Caldwell *(G-11780)*
Jnbc Associates LLC ....G.... 973 560-5518
Parsippany *(G-8034)*
Mdj Inc ....E.... 201 457-9260
Hackensack *(G-3945)*
Medco West Electronics Inc ....G.... 201 457-9260
Hackensack *(G-3946)*
Mercury Systems Inc ....E.... 973 244-1040
West Caldwell *(G-11789)*
Modelware Inc ....F.... 732 264-3020
Holmdel *(G-4524)*

Omega Circuit and Engineering ... E ... 732 246-1661
New Brunswick *(G-6990)*

P W B Omni Inc ... G ... 856 384-1300
West Deptford *(G-11838)*

Pcr Technologies Inc ... G ... 973 882-0017
Pine Brook *(G-8713)*

▲ PNC Inc ... C ... 973 284-1600
Nutley *(G-7652)*

Ppi/Time Zero Inc ... C ... 973 278-6500
Fairfield *(G-3285)*

▲ Precision Graphics Inc ... D ... 908 707-8880
Branchburg *(G-693)*

Precision Products Co Inc ... E ... 201 712-5757
Maywood *(G-6060)*

Quik Flex Circuit Inc ... F ... 856 742-0550
Gloucester City *(G-3843)*

▲ R & D Circuits Inc ... C ... 732 549-4554
South Plainfield *(G-10430)*

▲ R R J Co Inc ... E ... 732 544-1514
Colts Neck *(G-1791)*

Redkoh Industries Inc ... G ... 908 369-1590
Hillsborough *(G-4368)*

Scl ... E ... 908 391-9882
Bridgewater *(G-893)*

▲ Shore Printed Circuits Inc ... E ... 732 380-0590
Eatontown *(G-2422)*

Spem Corporation ... E ... 732 356-3366
Piscataway *(G-8816)*

Sure Design ... F ... 732 919-3066
Wall Township *(G-11512)*

Swemco LLC ... C ... 856 222-9900
Moorestown *(G-6625)*

Syscom Technologies Corp ... D ... 856 642-7661
Moorestown *(G-6627)*

T V L Associates Inc ... G ... 973 790-6766
Wayne *(G-11684)*

Techniques Inc ... E ... 973 256-0947
Woodland Park *(G-12234)*

▲ Test Technology Inc ... D ... 856 596-1215
Marlton *(G-6001)*

Thomas Instrumentation Inc ... F ... 609 624-2630
Cape May Court House *(G-1118)*

Toby-Yanni Incorporated ... F ... 973 253-9800
Garfield *(G-3768)*

▲ Transistor Devices Inc ... C ... 908 850-5088
Hackettstown *(G-4041)*

Wireworks Corporation ... E ... 908 686-7400
Hillside *(G-4451)*

3674 Semiconductors

▲ Ace Mountings Co Inc ... F ... 732 721-6200
South Amboy *(G-10233)*

Acolyte Technologies Corp ... G ... 212 629-3239
Perth Amboy *(G-8605)*

Advanced Micro Devices Inc ... C ... 732 787-2892
North Middletown *(G-7556)*

Aeon Corporation ... G ... 609 275-9003
Princeton Junction *(G-9144)*

Akela Laser Corporation ... F ... 732 305-7105
Monroe Township *(G-6377)*

Alcatel-Lucent USA Inc ... D ... 908 582-3275
New Providence *(G-7026)*

Altera Corporation ... G ... 732 649-3477
Somerset *(G-10055)*

American Microsemiconductor ... E ... 973 377-9566
Madison *(G-5719)*

Analog Devices Inc ... E ... 732 868-7100
Somerset *(G-10058)*

Ateksis USA Corp ... G ... 201 340-2655
Garfield *(G-3720)*

Ateksis USA Corp ... G ... 646 508-9074
East Rutherford *(G-2280)*

▲ Atlantic Clean Energy Sup LLC ... G ... 888 900-1581
Branchburg *(G-641)*

▲ Automatic Switch Company ... A ... 973 966-2000
Florham Park *(G-3489)*

Bel Fuse Inc ... C ... 201 432-0463
Jersey City *(G-4715)*

Candela Corporation ... F ... 908 753-6300
South Plainfield *(G-10343)*

Cast Inc ... G ... 201 391-8300
Woodcliff Lake *(G-12185)*

Compufab Sales Inc ... G ... 856 786-0175
Cinnaminson *(G-1452)*

Crystal Deltronic Industries ... E ... 973 328-6898
Dover *(G-2082)*

Crystal Deltronic Industries ... F ... 973 328-7000
Dover *(G-2083)*

Data Delay Devices Inc ... E ... 973 202-3268
Clifton *(G-1597)*

▲ Dialight Corporation ... D ... 732 919-3119
Wall Township *(G-11477)*

Digitron Electronic Corp ... E ... 908 245-2012
Kenilworth *(G-4952)*

Discovery Semiconductors Inc ... E ... 609 434-1311
Ewing *(G-3014)*

Ecs Energy Ltd ... G ... 201 341-5044
Jackson *(G-4667)*

Elena Consultants & Elec ... E ... 908 654-8309
Mountainside *(G-6881)*

Frauscher Sensor Tech USA Inc ... F ... 609 285-5492
Princeton *(G-9047)*

Fuceltech Inc ... G ... 609 275-0070
Princeton Junction *(G-9155)*

G T Associates ... G ... 973 694-6040
Wayne *(G-11637)*

▲ Gce Market Inc ... G ... 856 401-8900
Blackwood *(G-478)*

▲ Hamamatsu Corporation ... D ... 908 231-0960
Bridgewater *(G-841)*

Harrison Electro Mechanical ... F ... 732 382-6008
Rahway *(G-9196)*

Holistic Solar Usa Inc ... G ... 732 757-5500
Newark *(G-7191)*

Hybrid-Tek LLC ... F ... 609 259-3355
Clarksburg *(G-1520)*

Hydraulic Manifolds Usa LLC ... E ... 973 728-1214
West Milford *(G-11852)*

Ii-VI Incorporated ... F ... 973 227-1551
Pine Brook *(G-8704)*

▲ Ii-VI Optoelectronic Dvcs Inc ... B ... 908 668-5000
Warren *(G-11555)*

▲ Imperial Copy Products Inc ... E ... 973 927-5500
Randolph *(G-9284)*

Infineon Tech Americas Corp ... F ... 732 603-5914
Iselin *(G-4629)*

Inphot Inc ... G ... 609 799-7172
Plainsboro *(G-8886)*

Intel Corporation ... G ... 908 894-6035
Hampton *(G-4162)*

Intense Inc ... E ... 732 249-2228
North Brunswick *(G-7520)*

International Diode Corp ... G ... 973 482-6518
Harrison *(G-4186)*

◆ Itech Instruments LLC ... G ... 609 924-7310
Ewing *(G-3026)*

▲ Jerome Industries Corp ... E ... 908 353-5700
Hackettstown *(G-4013)*

▲ Keyence Corporation America ... E ... 201 930-0100
Elmwood Park *(G-2828)*

Kyocera International Inc ... D ... 856 691-7000
Cherry Hill *(G-1386)*

Liberty Cnstr & Inv Group ... G ... 267 784-7931
Cherry Hill *(G-1388)*

Lucent Technologies World Svcs ... C ... 908 582-3000
New Providence *(G-7046)*

M E C Technologies Inc ... E ... 732 505-0308
Toms River *(G-10894)*

Mc Renewable Energy LLC ... F ... 732 369-9933
Manasquan *(G-5873)*

Memory International Corp ... F ... 973 586-2653
Denville *(G-2049)*

Micro-Tek Laboratories Inc ... G ... 973 779-5577
Clifton *(G-1674)*

Microsemi Stor Solutions Inc ... G ... 908 953-9400
Basking Ridge *(G-198)*

Modelware Inc ... F ... 732 264-3020
Holmdel *(G-4524)*

Moser Jewel Company ... G ... 908 454-1155
Phillipsburg *(G-8660)*

▲ Multi-Tech Industries Inc ... F ... 732 431-0550
Marlboro *(G-5948)*

Multilink Technology Corp ... E ... 732 805-9355
Somerset *(G-10142)*

Nanonex Corp ... F ... 732 355-1600
Monmouth Junction *(G-6352)*

▲ Nanopv Corporation ... F ... 609 851-3666
Ewing *(G-3038)*

◆ Nokia of America Corporation ... A ... 908 582-3275
New Providence *(G-7050)*

▲ Nte Electronics Inc ... D ... 973 748-5089
Bloomfield *(G-524)*

Pekay Industries Inc ... F ... 732 938-2722
Farmingdale *(G-3392)*

Princeton Lightwave Inc ... E ... 609 495-2600
Cranbury *(G-1873)*

Renesas Electronics Amer Inc ... E ... 908 685-6000
Bridgewater *(G-883)*

Reuge Management Group Inc ... G ... 888 306-3253
Hoboken *(G-4495)*

Richards Manufacturing Co Inc ... G ... 973 371-1771
Irvington *(G-4602)*

▲ Roxboro Holdings Inc ... D ... 732 919-3119
Wall Township *(G-11506)*

Rudolph Technologies Inc ... G ... 973 448-4307
Ledgewood *(G-5309)*

Semi Conductor Manufacturing ... E ... 973 478-2880
Clifton *(G-1720)*

◆ Sharp Electronics Corporation ... A ... 201 529-8200
Mahwah *(G-5811)*

Solar Rig Technologies LLC ... G ... 973 600-0500
Carlstadt *(G-1221)*

Solid State International Inc ... G ... 201 429-8700
Bloomfield *(G-530)*

Solution and System Inc ... G ... 201 488-7770
Hackensack *(G-3976)*

Sunlight Photonics Inc ... G ... 732 362-7501
Edison *(G-2632)*

Thinfilms Inc ... F ... 908 359-7014
Hillsborough *(G-4376)*

United Silicon Carbide Inc ... F ... 732 355-0550
Monmouth Junction *(G-6368)*

Universal Display Corporation ... C ... 609 671-0980
Ewing *(G-3064)*

Viavi Solutions Inc ... C ... 609 632-0800
Trenton *(G-11131)*

Vicor Industries Inc ... F ... 201 569-1947
Tenafly *(G-10789)*

▼ William Kenyon & Sons Inc ... E ... 732 985-8980
Piscataway *(G-8836)*

Xtreme Powertech LLC ... F ... 201 791-5050
Upper Saddle River *(G-11289)*

Xybion Corporation ... C ... 973 538-2067
Lawrenceville *(G-5273)*

3675 Electronic Capacitors

Electro-Ceramic Industries ... E ... 201 342-2630
Hackensack *(G-3909)*

▲ Electronic Concepts Inc ... C ... 732 542-7880
Eatontown *(G-2392)*

Energy Storage Corp ... D ... 732 542-7880
Eatontown *(G-2394)*

▲ Megatran Industries ... B ... 609 227-4300
Bordentown *(G-601)*

Metuchen Capacitors Inc ... E ... 800 899-6969
Holmdel *(G-4522)*

▲ Nte Electronics Inc ... D ... 973 748-5089
Bloomfield *(G-524)*

Tbt Group Inc ... G ... 856 753-4500
Bellmawr *(G-353)*

3676 Electronic Resistors

▲ Nte Electronics Inc ... D ... 973 748-5089
Bloomfield *(G-524)*

▼ State Electronics Parts Corp ... E ... 973 887-2550
East Hanover *(G-2244)*

3677 Electronic Coils & Transformers

A C Transformer Corp ... G ... 973 589-8574
Newark *(G-7065)*

AFP Transformers Corporation ... D ... 732 248-0305
Edison *(G-2453)*

Alecto Systems LLC ... G ... 973 875-6721
Branchville *(G-725)*

▲ Automatic Switch Company ... A ... 973 966-2000
Florham Park *(G-3489)*

Baltimore Transformer Company ... E ... 973 942-2222
Paterson *(G-8220)*

Behringer Fluid Systems Inc ... G ... 973 948-0226
Branchville *(G-726)*

Bel Fuse Inc ... C ... 201 432-0463
Jersey City *(G-4715)*

Bel Hybrids & Magnetics Inc ... F ... 201 432-0463
Jersey City *(G-4716)*

Celco ... F ... 201 327-1123
Mahwah *(G-5757)*

Edko Electronics ... E ... 973 942-2222
Paterson *(G-8254)*

Electronic Transformer Corp ... E ... 973 942-2222
Paterson *(G-8255)*

Freed Transformer Company ... E ... 973 942-2222
Paterson *(G-8273)*

Fugle-Miller Laboratories Inc ... F ... 732 574-3121
Rahway *(G-9192)*

▲ Jerome Industries Corp ... E ... 908 353-5700
Hackettstown *(G-4013)*

▲ Jinpan International USA Ltd ... G ... 201 460-8778
Carlstadt *(G-1174)*

▲ Jinpan International USA Ltd ... G ... 201 460-8778
Carlstadt *(G-1175)*

SIC

▲ Kef America Inc ....E 732 414-2074
Marlboro *(G-5946)*

▼ KG Squared LLC ....F 973 627-0643
Rockaway *(G-9581)*

▲ Mallika Ashwin Maya Corp ....G 908 393-2571
Hillsborough *(G-4356)*

Microsignals Inc ....E 800 225-4508
Palisades Park *(G-7839)*

NMP Water Systems LLC ....G 201 252-8333
Mahwah *(G-5796)*

SCI-Bore Inc ....G 973 414-9001
East Orange *(G-2268)*

▲ Stonite Coil Corporation ....E 609 585-6600
Trenton *(G-11118)*

Summit Intl Filtration Systems ....G 201 847-2370
Wyckoff *(G-12265)*

Torelco Inc ....F 908 387-0814
Alpha *(G-47)*

▲ Ultra Clean Technologies Corp ....E 856 451-2176
Bridgeton *(G-801)*

3678 Electronic Connectors

Adam Tech Asia Llc ....G 908 687-5000
Union *(G-11147)*

Al Technology Inc ....E 609 799-9388
Princeton Junction *(G-9145)*

Armel Electronics Inc ....E 201 869-4300
North Bergen *(G-7433)*

Barantec Inc ....F 973 779-8774
Clifton *(G-1572)*

Brim Electronics Inc ....F 201 796-2886
Lodi *(G-5578)*

▲ Central Components Mfg LLC ....G 732 469-5720
Middlesex *(G-6154)*

Components Corporation ....F 866 426-6726
Denville *(G-2033)*

Da-Green Electronics Ltd ....E 732 254-2735
South River *(G-10460)*

◆ Fuji Electric Corp America ....D 732 560-9410
Edison *(G-2522)*

▲ Fujipoly America Corporation ....E 732 969-0100
Carteret *(G-1259)*

Glasseal Products Inc ....G 732 370-9100
Lakewood *(G-5129)*

▲ Heilind Electronics Inc ....D 888 881-5420
Lumberton *(G-5658)*

▲ Heilind Mil-Aero LLC ....C 856 722-5535
Lumberton *(G-5659)*

Huber+suhner Astrolab Inc ....E 732 560-3800
Warren *(G-11554)*

▲ I Trade Technology Ltd ....G 615 348-7233
Mahwah *(G-5785)*

Kraus & Naimer Inc ....E 732 560-1240
Somerset *(G-10119)*

◆ Lapp Usa LLC ....C 973 660-9700
Florham Park *(G-3511)*

Napoleon Spring Works Inc ....E 973 278-5588
South Hackensack *(G-10279)*

Newtech Group Corp ....G 732 355-0392
Kendall Park *(G-4935)*

Princetel Inc ....E 609 588-8801
Hamilton *(G-4122)*

▲ Richards Mfg Co Sales Inc ....F 973 371-1771
Irvington *(G-4604)*

Severna Operations Inc ....E 973 503-1600
Parsippany *(G-8085)*

Te Connectivity Corporation ....B 610 893-9800
Eatontown *(G-2425)*

Thomas & Betts Corporation ....C 908 852-1122
Hackettstown *(G-4040)*

▲ Unicorp ....F 973 674-1700
Orange *(G-7832)*

▲ Valconn Electronics Inc ....E 908 687-1600
Union *(G-11232)*

◆ Wire-Pro Inc ....F 856 935-7560
Salem *(G-9810)*

3679 Electronic Components, NEC

A P M Hexseal Corporation ....E 201 569-5700
Englewood *(G-2865)*

Adcomm Inc ....C 201 342-3338
South Hackensack *(G-10251)*

▲ ADI American Distributors LLC ......D 973 328-1181
Randolph *(G-9267)*

Advanced Energy Voorhees Inc ....D 856 627-1287
Voorhees *(G-11419)*

Advanced Technology Group Inc ......E 973 627-6955
Rockaway *(G-9546)*

Aeon Engineering LLC ....G 518 253-7681
Fort Lee *(G-3542)*

▲ Aeroflex Ctrl Components Inc ....D 732 460-0212
Eatontown *(G-2378)*

Algen Design Services Inc ....E 732 389-3630
Eatontown *(G-2379)*

◆ Ameral International Inc ....F 856 456-9000
Brooklawn *(G-919)*

American Fibertek Inc ....E 732 302-0660
Somerset *(G-10056)*

Amperite Co Inc ....G 201 864-9503
North Bergen *(G-7430)*

Andrex Inc ....G 908 852-2400
Hackettstown *(G-3997)*

Andrex Systems Inc ....E 908 835-1720
Port Murray *(G-8975)*

▲ Ango Electronics Corporation ....F 201 955-0800
North Arlington *(G-7415)*

▼ Applied Resources Corp ....E 973 328-3882
Wharton *(G-11980)*

Aspe Inc ....E 973 808-1155
Fairfield *(G-3141)*

▲ Asti Corp ....F 201 501-8900
Bergenfield *(G-381)*

▲ AT&T Technologies Inc ....A 201 771-2000
Berkeley Heights *(G-400)*

Auto Remind Inc ....G 800 277-1299
Fair Lawn *(G-3079)*

◆ Az-Em USA Branchburg NJ ....G 908 429-0020
Branchburg *(G-642)*

Bel Fuse Inc ....C 201 432-0463
Jersey City *(G-4715)*

▲ Bihler of America Inc ....G 908 213-9001
Phillipsburg *(G-8644)*

Billows Electric Supply Co Inc ....C 856 751-2200
Delran *(G-2010)*

Bkh Electronics ....G 210 410-2757
Wanaque *(G-11531)*

Bomar Exo Ltd Liability Co ....F 732 356-7787
Middlesex *(G-6152)*

Bryan Snook ....G 888 747-3250
Bedminster *(G-268)*

Ccard ....G 732 303-8264
Manalapan *(G-5840)*

Circuit Tech Assembly LLC ....F 856 231-0777
Moorestown *(G-6566)*

▲ Clantech Inc ....G 908 281-7667
Hillsborough *(G-4325)*

Coherent Inc ....D 973 240-6851
East Hanover *(G-2207)*

Communication Products Co ....G 973 977-8490
Paterson *(G-8238)*

▲ Compex Corporation ....E 856 719-8657
West Berlin *(G-11710)*

▲ Computer Crafts Inc ....C 973 423-3500
Hawthorne *(G-4228)*

Concept Group Inc ....E 856 767-5506
West Berlin *(G-11711)*

Conolog Corporation ....F 908 722-8081
Branchburg *(G-650)*

Cooper Interconnect ....E 856 935-7560
Salem *(G-9804)*

Creatone Inc ....F 908 789-8700
Mountainside *(G-6870)*

▲ Crestek Inc ....E 609 883-4000
Ewing *(G-3012)*

Crystal Deltronic Industries ....E 973 328-6898
Dover *(G-2082)*

D&N Machine Manufacturing Inc ......E 856 456-1366
Gloucester City *(G-3835)*

Da-Green Electronics Ltd ....E 732 254-2735
South River *(G-10460)*

▲ Dantco Corp ....F 973 278-8776
Paterson *(G-8245)*

Data Delay Devices Inc ....E 973 202-3268
Clifton *(G-1597)*

▲ Dialight Corporation ....D 732 919-3119
Wall Township *(G-11477)*

Doralex Inc ....G 856 764-0694
Delran *(G-2016)*

▲ Douglas Elec Components Inc ....D 973 627-8230
Randolph *(G-9274)*

▼ Electromagnetic Tech Inds Inc ....G 973 394-1719
Boonton *(G-564)*

Electronic Connections Inc ....F 732 367-5588
Lakewood *(G-5114)*

Electronic Mfg Svcs Inc ....E 973 916-1001
Clifton *(G-1614)*

Empire Electronics Inc ....F 973 278-8282
Paterson *(G-8262)*

Empire Telecommunications Inc ....F 201 569-3339
Englewood *(G-2890)*

▲ Epcos Inc ....D 732 906-4300
Iselin *(G-4626)*

Epcos Inc ....F 732 603-5941
Lumberton *(G-5657)*

Esi ....E 856 629-2492
Sicklerville *(G-10018)*

▲ Ewc Controls Inc ....E 732 446-3110
Manalapan *(G-5846)*

Excel Display Corp ....G 732 246-3724
New Brunswick *(G-6959)*

Famcam Inc ....E 973 503-1600
Parsippany *(G-8007)*

Foremost Corp ....G 973 839-3360
Wayne *(G-11635)*

Frc Electrical Industries Inc ....E 908 464-3200
New Providence *(G-7036)*

Fugle-Miller Laboratories Inc ....E 732 574-3121
Rahway *(G-9192)*

▲ G-Way Microwave Inc ....F 201 343-6388
South Hackensack *(G-10269)*

General Reliance Corporation ....E 973 361-1400
Denville *(G-2040)*

Glasseal Products Inc ....G 732 370-9100
Lakewood *(G-5129)*

Glassman High Voltage Inc ....D 908 638-3800
High Bridge *(G-4296)*

GT Microwave Inc ....E 973 361-5700
Randolph *(G-9282)*

Gulton G I D ....G 908 791-4622
South Plainfield *(G-10376)*

Haz Laboratories ....F 908 453-3300
Washington *(G-11582)*

Herley Industries Inc ....D 973 884-2580
Whippany *(G-12024)*

Herley-Cti Inc ....F 973 884-2580
Whippany *(G-12025)*

Heyco Products Corp ....G 732 286-1800
Toms River *(G-10885)*

Idt Energy Inc ....E 877 887-6866
Newark *(G-7194)*

Infiniti Components Inc ....E 908 537-9950
Hampton *(G-4161)*

▲ Interplex Nas Inc ....E 201 367-1300
Northvale *(G-7586)*

◆ Iqe Rf LLC ....D 732 271-5990
Somerset *(G-10113)*

It Surplus Liquidators ....G 732 308-1935
Freehold *(G-3661)*

J A M I Enterprise Inc ....G 732 714-6811
Brick *(G-746)*

J P Rotella Co Inc ....F 973 942-2559
Haledon *(G-4083)*

JB Electronics ....E 609 497-2952
Princeton *(G-9061)*

▲ Jerome Industries Corp ....E 908 353-5700
Hackettstown *(G-4013)*

Jettron Products Inc ....E 973 887-0571
East Hanover *(G-2226)*

JFK Supplies Inc ....F 732 985-7800
Edison *(G-2545)*

Johanson Manufacturing Corp ....C 973 658-1051
Boonton *(G-574)*

K R Electronics Inc ....E 732 636-1900
Avenel *(G-137)*

▼ KG Squared LLC ....F 973 627-0643
Rockaway *(G-9581)*

Kinetics Industries Inc ....E 609 883-9700
Ewing *(G-3030)*

Koamtac Inc ....G 609 734-4335
Princeton *(G-9064)*

Lakeland Transformer Corp ....G 973 835-0818
Haskell *(G-4209)*

▲ Lantek Corporation ....F 973 579-8100
Sparta *(G-10508)*

Lg Electronics USA Inc ....G 732 605-0385
Monroe Township *(G-6383)*

Magnetics & Controls Inc ....F 609 397-8203
Rosemont *(G-9705)*

▲ Maxell Corporation of America ....E 973 653-2400
Woodland Park *(G-12224)*

Meca Electronics Inc ....E 973 625-0661
Denville *(G-2047)*

◆ Mechanical Ingenuity Corp ....E 732 842-8889
Shrewsbury *(G-10002)*

Melstrom Manufacturing Corp ....D 732 938-7400
Wall Township *(G-11497)*

▲ Mennekes Electronics Inc ....E 973 882-8333
Fairfield *(G-3258)*

▲ Merrimac Industries Inc ....D 973 575-1300
West Caldwell *(G-11790)*

▲ Metal Cutting Corporation..............D 973 239-1100
Cedar Grove (G-1291)
Microwave Consulting Corp ....G 973 523-6700
Paterson (G-8339)
Model Electronics Inc........................D 201 961-9200
Ramsey (G-9248)
Model Electronics Inc........................E 201 961-1717
Ramsey (G-9249)
Mwt Materials Inc..............................F 973 928-8300
Passaic (G-8166)
Noah LLC...G 609 637-0039
Lawrenceville (G-5266)
Norsal Distribution Associates............F 908 638-6430
High Bridge (G-4298)
◆ Nwl Inc..B 609 298-7300
Bordentown (G-606)
Patriot American Solutions LLC...........D 862 209-4772
Rockaway (G-9594)
Pcr Technologies Inc..........................G 973 882-0017
Pine Brook (G-8713)
Prima-TEC Electronics Corp ....G 201 947-4052
East Rutherford (G-2319)
Princeton Microwave Technology ....G 609 586-8140
Trenton (G-11107)
Princeton Optronics Inc ....E 609 584-9696
Trenton (G-11108)
▲ Quadrangle Products Inc ....F 732 792-1234
Englishtown (G-2997)
Robert Wynn.......................................G 856 435-6398
Clementon (G-1534)
▲ Roxboro Holdings Inc.....................D 732 919-3119
Wall Township (G-11506)
Rs Microwave Co Inc..........................E 973 492-1207
Butler (G-1018)
Seal Tronics Inc.................................F 864 576-0015
Clifton (G-1718)
Sensigraphics Inc..............................G 856 853-9100
Mount Laurel (G-6839)
Seren Industrial Power Systems..........F 856 205-1131
Vineland (G-11403)
▲ Silverstone Wireless LLC ....G 845 458-5197
Lodi (G-5600)
▲ Solar Products Inc ....E 973 248-9370
Pompton Lakes (G-8948)
Solar Rig Technologies LLC ....G 973 600-0500
Carlstadt (G-1221)
Spem Corporation..............................E 732 356-3366
Piscataway (G-8816)
▲ Spencer Industries Inc ....E 973 751-2200
Belleville (G-318)
Spirent Communications Inc ....G 732 946-4018
Holmdel (G-4530)
▲ Synergy Microwave Corp ....D 973 881-8800
Paterson (G-8394)
▼ T & E Industries Inc ....E 973 672-5454
Orange (G-7830)
Technical Aids To Independence..........F 973 674-1082
East Orange (G-2271)
▲ Technology Dynamics Inc ....E 201 385-0500
Bergenfield (G-396)
Technology Dynamics Inc....................E 201 385-0500
Bergenfield (G-397)
Thomas & Betts Corporation ....C 908 852-1122
Hackettstown (G-4040)
Thomas Instrumentation Inc................F 609 624-2630
Cape May Court House (G-1118)
▲ Thomson Lamination Co Inc............D 856 779-8521
Maple Shade (G-5912)
Tkg Components LLC ....G 609 730-1501
Pennington (G-8460)
Transistor Devices Inc........................C 908 850-5088
Hackettstown (G-4042)
Trek Connect Inc................................E 856 608-0901
Lumberton (G-5664)
Ttss Interactive Products Inc...............E 301 230-1464
Riverdale (G-9491)
Ute Microwave Inc..............................E 732 922-1009
Ocean (G-7748)
Uthe Technology Inc ....G 609 883-4000
Trenton (G-11130)
Utz Technologies Inc..........................E 973 339-1100
Little Falls (G-5493)
▲ Valconn Electronics Inc..................E 908 687-1600
Union (G-11232)
Value Added Vice Solutions LLC..........G 201 400-3247
Brielle (G-916)
▲ VIP Industries Inc ....G 973 472-7500
Clifton (G-1739)
▼ Waveline Incorporated....................E 973 226-9100
Fairfield (G-3350)

West Electronics Inc ....F 609 387-4300
Burlington (G-996)
Western Electronics Dist.....................G 908 475-3303
Belvidere (G-378)
◆ Wire-Pro Inc..................................C 856 935-7560
Salem (G-9810)
Wireworks Corporation ....E 908 686-7400
Hillside (G-4451)
▲ YC Cable (east) Inc........................E 732 868-0800
Piscataway (G-8837)
Zago Manufacturing Company ....E 973 643-6700
Newark (G-7362)

3691 Storage Batteries

E Group Inc..G 856 320-9688
Mount Laurel (G-6795)
▲ Energy Battery ....G 908 751-5918
Flemington (G-3438)
Enersys...D 800 719-7887
Somerset (G-10094)
◆ Gogreen Power Inc.........................F 732 994-5901
Howell (G-4555)
▲ Hoppecke Batteries Inc ....E 856 616-0032
Hainesport (G-4073)
▲ Maxell Corporation of America........G 973 653-2400
Woodland Park (G-12224)
▲ Mizco International Inc ....D 732 912-2000
Avenel (G-141)
Mphase Technologies Inc ....E 973 256-3737
Clifton (G-1676)
Pacific Dnlop Holdings USA LLC ....G 732 345-5400
Red Bank (G-9339)
▲ Skc Powertech Inc ....F 973 347-7000
Budd Lake (G-944)
▲ Tocad America Inc ....E 973 627-9600
Rockaway (G-9614)

3692 Primary Batteries: Dry & Wet

Burlington Atlantic Corp ....G 732 888-7776
Hazlet (G-4271)

3694 Electrical Eqpt For Internal Combustion Engines

Auto Action Group Inc.........................E 908 964-6290
Kenilworth (G-4938)
▲ Dearborn A Belden Cdt Company ...D 908 925-8000
Elizabeth (G-2723)
Dimilo Industries...............................G 973 955-0460
Passaic (G-8134)
Dmf Associated Engines LLC...............D 973 535-9773
Livingston (G-5528)
Doolan Industries Incorporated...........G 856 985-1880
Marlton (G-5973)
Engine Factory Inc.............................G 908 236-9915
Lebanon (G-5284)
▲ Fleetsource LLC.............................F 732 566-4970
Cliffwood (G-1547)
Incom (america) Inc ....G 908 464-3366
Berkeley Heights (G-412)
J & R Rebuilders Inc...........................E 856 627-1414
Laurel Springs (G-5233)
Knite Inc..G 609 258-9550
Ewing (G-3031)
M Parker Autoworks Inc ....E 856 933-0801
Bellmawr (G-345)
Mobile Power Inc...............................G 908 852-3117
Hackettstown (G-4026)

3695 Recording Media

Athlon Group LLC...............................G 201 340-2688
East Rutherford (G-2281)
Cabletime Ltd ....G 973 770-8070
Mount Arlington (G-6752)
▲ Datacolor Inc.................................D 609 924-2189
Lawrenceville (G-5256)
Double Diamond Technologies ....G 609 624-1414
Cape May (G-1097)
▲ Franklin Electronic Publs Inc..........D 609 386-2500
Burlington (G-974)
Fujifilm North America Corp ....B 732 857-3000
Edison (G-2523)
MD International Inc............................G 856 779-7633
Cherry Hill (G-1397)
Network Access Systems Incorpr ....G 732 355-9770
Dayton (G-1981)
Sony Corporation of America ....B 201 930-1000
Paramus (G-7902)
▲ Synergem Inc.................................E 732 692-6308
Avenel (G-154)

3699 Electrical Machinery, Eqpt & Splys, NEC

AAS Technologies Inc ....G 201 342-7300
Hackensack (G-3872)
Abacus Electric & Plumbing................G 908 269-8057
Chester (G-1433)
Almetek Industries Inc........................E 908 850-9700
Hackettstown (G-3996)
Asco Power Technologies LP...............F 732 596-1733
Woodbridge (G-12145)
Asco Power Technologies LP...............F 209 547-8874
Florham Park (G-3486)
◆ Asco Power Technologies LP ....B 973 966-2000
Florham Park (G-3487)
Assa Abloy Entrance Systems US ....E 609 443-5800
Windsor (G-12124)
Assa Abloy Entrance Systems US ....E 609 528-2580
Hamilton (G-4104)
Atlantex Instruments Inc.....................G 201 391-5148
Woodcliff Lake (G-12181)
Avida Incorporated ....G 201 802-0749
Park Ridge (G-7916)
Bio-Key International Inc.....................E 732 359-1100
Wall Township (G-11467)
Blonder Tongue Labs Inc ....C 732 679-4000
Old Bridge (G-7775)
C J Electric ....G 201 891-0739
Wyckoff (G-12247)
Candela Corporation ....F 908 753-6300
South Plainfield (G-10343)
▲ Castle Industries Inc......................E 201 585-8400
Englewood Cliffs (G-2952)
Celco..F 201 327-1123
Mahwah (G-5757)
Chamberlain Group Inc.......................G 201 472-4200
Whippany (G-12016)
◆ Checkpoint Systems Inc ....C 800 257-5540
West Deptford (G-11821)
Checkpoint Systems Inc......................C 856 848-1800
West Deptford (G-11822)
Checkpoint Systems Inc......................C 856 848-1800
West Deptford (G-11824)
▲ Cleary Machinery Co Inc.................G 732 560-3200
South Bound Brook (G-10248)
Commercial Pdts Svcs Group Inc ....G 609 730-4111
Pennington (G-8447)
Connecting Products Inc ....F 609 512-1121
Skillman (G-10029)
Countyline Elec Contrs Corp ....G 732 961-6738
Lakewood (G-5096)
Crest Group Inc.................................F 609 883-4000
Trenton (G-11049)
▲ Crestek Inc....................................E 609 883-4000
Ewing (G-3012)
Cuny & Guerber Inc ....E 201 617-5800
Union City (G-11244)
Daniel Maguire ....E 856 767-8443
West Berlin (G-11714)
▼ Daq Electronics LLC ....E 732 981-0050
Piscataway (G-8753)
▲ Dearborn A Belden Cdt Company ...D 908 925-8000
Elizabeth (G-2723)
▼ Design Assistance Corporation........F 856 241-9500
Swedesboro (G-10691)
Dewey Electronics Corporation............E 201 337-4700
Oakland (G-7684)
Digitize Inc..F 973 663-1011
Lake Hopatcong (G-5056)
▲ Douglas Elec Components Inc..........D 973 627-8230
Randolph (G-9274)
Dranetz Technologies Inc....................D 732 248-4358
Edison (G-2503)
E-Beam Services Inc...........................E 513 933-0031
Cranbury (G-1830)
East Coast Panelboard Inc..................G 732 739-6400
Tinton Falls (G-10832)
East Coast Security Products...............F 973 625-3277
Rockaway (G-9562)
▲ East West Service Co Inc ....G 609 631-9000
Trenton (G-11057)
Eaton Corporation ....E 732 767-9600
Mountainside (G-6880)
Ecsi International Inc..........................E 973 574-8555
Clifton (G-1610)
Edmondmarks Technologies Inc..........E 732 643-0290
Neptune (G-6909)
Electronic Control SEC Inc ....F 973 574-8555
Clifton (G-1613)
▲ Ellenby Technologies Inc................E 856 848-2020
Woodbury Heights (G-12175)

S I C

Engineered Security Systems ... E ... 973 257-0555
Towaco *(G-10995)*

Engineering Dynamics LLC ... G ... 973 794-4500
Boonton *(G-565)*

Enterprisecc Ltd Liability Co ... G ... 201 266-0020
Jersey City *(G-4749)*

Eos Energy Storage LLC ... E ... 732 225-8400
Edison *(G-2514)*

Essex Products International ... E ... 973 226-2424
Caldwell *(G-1028)*

Essexusa LLC ... F ... 201 576-0001
Paramus *(G-7867)*

F Walther Electric Corp ... G ... 732 537-9201
Somerset *(G-10099)*

Fastpulse Technology Inc ... F ... 973 478-5757
Saddle Brook *(G-9765)*

Francis Metals Company Inc ... F ... 732 761-0500
Lakewood *(G-5125)*

Frc Electrical Industries Inc ... E ... 908 464-3200
New Providence *(G-7036)*

◆ **Gogreen Power Inc** ... F ... 732 994-5901
Howell *(G-4555)*

Griffith Electric Supply Co ... G ... 609 632-0253
Windsor *(G-12126)*

Gsi ... G ... 908 608-1325
Summit *(G-10643)*

H G Schaevitz LLC ... G ... 856 727-0250
Moorestown *(G-6582)*

H I D Systems Inc ... G ... 973 383-8535
Sparta *(G-10503)*

◆ **Haas Laser Technologies Inc** ... F ... 973 598-1150
Flanders *(G-3410)*

Henry Bros Electronics Inc ... D ... 201 794-6500
Fair Lawn *(G-3094)*

Hitrons Tech Inc ... G ... 201 941-0024
Ridgefield *(G-9364)*

▲ **I 2 R Corp** ... G ... 732 919-1100
Wall Township *(G-11490)*

Ifortress ... G ... 973 812-6400
Woodland Park *(G-12222)*

▲ **Infinova Corporation** ... E ... 732 355-9100
Monmouth Junction *(G-6347)*

Inrad Optics Inc ... D ... 201 767-1910
Northvale *(G-7585)*

▲ **International Cord Sets Inc** ... F ... 973 227-2118
Fairfield *(G-3232)*

Ironbound Metal ... G ... 973 242-5704
Newark *(G-7200)*

K & A Industries Inc ... G ... 908 226-7000
South Plainfield *(G-10390)*

Ketec ... F ... 856 778-4343
Moorestown *(G-6591)*

▲ **Kft Fire Trainer LLC** ... E ... 201 300-8100
Montvale *(G-6463)*

L & R Manufacturing Co Inc ... C ... 201 991-5330
Kearny *(G-4895)*

◆ **L & R Manufacturing Co Inc** ... D ... 201 991-5330
Kearny *(G-4894)*

Laser Contractors LLC ... G ... 609 517-2407
Medford *(G-6075)*

Lb Electric Co LLC ... G ... 973 366-2188
Denville *(G-2046)*

Ld Electric LLC ... G ... 201 225-1001
Paramus *(G-7883)*

LTS NJ Inc ... G ... 856 780-9888
Mount Laurel *(G-6815)*

M & Z International Inc ... G ... 201 864-3331
West New York *(G-11872)*

Malco Electric LLC ... G ... 856 202-5503
Westville *(G-11946)*

Max Flight Corp ... E ... 732 281-2007
Toms River *(G-10895)*

◆ **Maxlite Inc** ... C ... 973 244-7300
West Caldwell *(G-11788)*

▲ **Metrologic Instruments Inc** ... C ... 856 228-8100
Mount Laurel *(G-6818)*

Mobile Intelligent Alerts Inc ... G ... 201 410-5324
Holmdel *(G-4523)*

Mphase Technologies Inc ... F ... 973 256-3737
Clifton *(G-1676)*

MTS Systems Corporation ... A ... 856 875-4478
Williamstown *(G-12093)*

Multicomm Solutions Inc ... G ... 877 796-8480
Toms River *(G-10898)*

O S I Inc ... F ... 732 754-6271
Metuchen *(G-6116)*

Ocean Energy Industries Inc ... F ... 954 828-2177
Oakhurst *(G-7671)*

OHM Equipment LLC ... G ... 856 765-3011
Millville *(G-6318)*

◆ **Paige Electric Company LP** ... E ... 908 687-7810
Union *(G-11212)*

PCI Inc ... G ... 973 226-8007
West Caldwell *(G-11796)*

Power Brooks Co LLC ... F ... 609 890-0100
Hamilton *(G-4121)*

▲ **PRC Laser Corporation** ... E ... 973 347-0100
Landing *(G-5226)*

Primary Systems Inc ... F ... 732 679-2200
Old Bridge *(G-7790)*

Princeton Lightwave Inc ... E ... 609 495-2600
Cranbury *(G-1873)*

Qsa Global National Corp ... G ... 865 888-6798
Red Bank *(G-9341)*

Quantum Security Systems Inc ... G ... 609 252-0505
Princeton *(G-9108)*

Radnet Inc ... F ... 908 709-1323
Cranford *(G-1924)*

Sant-TEC Electric Inc ... E ... 201 865-4100
North Bergen *(G-7483)*

Secure System Inc ... E ... 732 922-3609
Stirling *(G-10606)*

Security 21 LLC ... G ... 856 384-7474
Woodbury *(G-12169)*

Seminole Wire & Cable Co Inc ... F ... 856 324-2929
Pennsauken *(G-8577)*

Seren Ips Inc ... D ... 856 205-1131
Vineland *(G-11404)*

Signal Crafters Tech Inc ... G ... 973 781-0880
East Hanover *(G-2243)*

Skycam Technologies LLC ... G ... 908 205-5548
Perth Amboy *(G-8631)*

Specialized Fire & SEC Inc ... E ... 212 255-1010
Riverdale *(G-9489)*

Starlight Electro-Optics Inc ... G ... 908 859-1362
Phillipsburg *(G-8671)*

Stud Welding Co The Inc ... G ... 856 866-9300
Moorestown *(G-6624)*

T F S Inc ... E ... 973 890-7651
Totowa *(G-10974)*

Talon7 LLC ... F ... 908 595-2121
Bridgewater *(G-901)*

Techntime Bus Sltons Ltd Lblty ... F ... 973 246-8153
East Rutherford *(G-2331)*

◆ **Tiger Supplies Inc** ... G ... 973 854-8635
Irvington *(G-4606)*

Total Garage Solutions LLC ... F ... 732 749-3993
Wall Township *(G-11515)*

Trec Electric ... G ... 856 374-3433
Sewell *(G-9966)*

Tri Diamond Enterprises LLC ... G ... 609 927-6018
Hammonton *(G-4152)*

U S Laser Corp ... E ... 201 848-9200
Wyckoff *(G-12268)*

Vandermolen Corp ... G ... 973 992-8506
Ledgewood *(G-5313)*

◆ **Vicmarr Audio Inc** ... E ... 732 289-9111
Edison *(G-2645)*

Vision Ten Inc ... F ... 201 935-3000
Carlstadt *(G-1239)*

Wickr Inc ... G ... 516 637-2882
Newark *(G-7360)*

Zenith Mfg & Chemical Corp ... F ... 201 767-1332
Norwood *(G-7638)*

Zinni Electric LLC ... G ... 856 848-8361
Deptford *(G-2070)*

37 TRANSPORTATION EQUIPMENT

3711 Motor Vehicles & Car Bodies

Autoaccess LLC ... F ... 908 240-5919
Sicklerville *(G-10017)*

◆ **BMW of North America LLC** ... A ... 201 307-4000
Woodcliff Lake *(G-12183)*

Bruce Kindberg ... G ... 973 664-0195
Rockaway *(G-9554)*

▲ **Cenntro Automotive Corporation** ... G ... 732 863-0777
Freehold *(G-3644)*

Cliffside Body Corporation ... E ... 201 945-3970
Fairview *(G-3359)*

Daimler Trucks North Amer LLC ... G ... 856 467-6000
Swedesboro *(G-10689)*

Dejana Trck Utility Eqp Co LLC ... E ... 856 303-1315
Cinnaminson *(G-1454)*

Drive-Master Co Inc ... F ... 973 808-9709
Fairfield *(G-3180)*

Elite Emrgncy Lights Ltd Lblty ... F ... 732 534-2377
Lakewood *(G-5115)*

▲ **Faps Inc** ... C ... 973 589-5656
Newark *(G-7160)*

▼ **First Priority Emergency Vhcl** ... E ... 732 657-1104
Manchester *(G-5886)*

First Priority Global Ltd ... F ... 973 347-4321
Flanders *(G-3408)*

Garden St Chasis Remanuf ... E ... 732 283-1910
Woodbridge *(G-12149)*

Jontol Unlimited LLC ... G ... 858 652-1113
Blackwood *(G-485)*

Navistar Inc ... D ... 856 486-2300
Cherry Hill *(G-1403)*

▲ **Odyssey Auto Specialty Inc** ... E ... 973 328-2667
Wharton *(G-11995)*

▼ **Orlando Systems Ltd Lblty Co** ... G ... 908 400-5052
North Plainfield *(G-7560)*

P L Custom Body & Eqp Co Inc ... C ... 732 223-1411
Manasquan *(G-5877)*

Polar Truck Sales ... E ... 201 246-1010
Jersey City *(G-4802)*

R & H Spring & Truck Repair ... F ... 732 681-9000
Wall Township *(G-11504)*

◆ **Rolls-Royce Motor Cars Na LLC** ... A ... 201 307-4117
Woodcliff Lake *(G-12200)*

S L P Engineering Inc ... D ... 732 240-3696
Toms River *(G-10908)*

◆ **Specialty Vhcl Solutions LLC** ... E ... 609 882-1900
Ewing *(G-3056)*

Teo Fabrications Inc ... G ... 973 764-5500
Vernon *(G-11302)*

Tesla Inc ... G ... 201 225-2544
Paramus *(G-7910)*

Toyota Motor Sales ... F ... 973 515-5012
Parsippany *(G-8103)*

Vending Trucks Inc ... E ... 732 969-5400
East Brunswick *(G-2196)*

W2f Inc ... G ... 609 735-0135
New Egypt *(G-7019)*

3713 Truck & Bus Bodies

Alexam Riverdale ... G ... 973 831-0065
Riverdale *(G-9474)*

American Bus & Coach LLC ... E ... 732 283-1982
Iselin *(G-4609)*

Barrier Enterprises Inc ... G ... 973 770-3983
Andover *(G-48)*

Bristol-Donald Company Inc ... E ... 973 589-2640
Newark *(G-7115)*

Christensen Manufacturing ... F ... 609 466-9700
Pennington *(G-8446)*

Cliffside Body Corporation ... E ... 201 945-3970
Fairview *(G-3359)*

▲ **Columbia Industries Inc** ... G ... 201 337-7332
Franklin Lakes *(G-3612)*

▼ **Custom Sales & Service Inc** ... E ... 800 257-7855
Hammonton *(G-4136)*

▼ **Demountable Concepts Inc** ... E ... 856 863-3081
Glassboro *(G-3803)*

Fleet Equipment Corporation ... F ... 201 337-3294
Franklin Lakes *(G-3617)*

Garden St Chasis Remanuf ... E ... 732 283-1910
Woodbridge *(G-12149)*

Jid Transportation LLC ... G ... 201 362-0841
West New York *(G-11870)*

Peter Garafano & Son Inc ... E ... 973 278-0350
Paterson *(G-8364)*

Summit Truck Body Inc ... F ... 908 277-4342
Summit *(G-10661)*

Transtar Truck Body & Wldg Co ... G ... 908 832-2688
Califon *(G-1038)*

▼ **Vacuum Sales Inc** ... E ... 856 627-7790
Laurel Springs *(G-5234)*

Waldwick Vol Amb Corps Inc ... E ... 201 445-8772
Waldwick *(G-11457)*

3714 Motor Vehicle Parts & Access

A-1 Specialized Svcs & Sups ... E ... 732 238-2900
South River *(G-10456)*

▲ **Accurate Tool & Die Co Inc** ... G ... 201 476-9348
Montvale *(G-6440)*

Allied-Signal China Ltd ... E ... 973 455-2000
Morristown *(G-6685)*

▲ **Allison Corp** ... G ... 973 992-3800
Livingston *(G-5523)*

American Refuse Supply Inc ... F ... 973 684-3225
Paterson *(G-8209)*

Banks Bros Corporation ... D ... 973 680-4488
Bloomfield *(G-502)*

Bruce Kindberg ... G ... 973 664-0195
Rockaway *(G-9554)*

▲ **C T A Manufacturing Corp** ... E ... 201 896-1000
Carlstadt *(G-1136)*

▲ **Carolina Fluid Handling Inc** ....A 248 228-8900
West Berlin ***(G-11706)***
▲ **Cervinis Inc** ....F 856 691-1744
Vineland ***(G-11335)***
Chick Capoli Sales ....E 856 768-4500
West Berlin ***(G-11708)***
▲ **Clear Plus Windshield Wipers** ....F 973 546-8800
Garfield ***(G-3726)***
Crestron Electronics Inc ....D 201 894-0670
Cresskill ***(G-1944)***
Custom Auto Radiator Inc ....F 609 242-9700
Forked River ***(G-3537)***
◆ **Elegant USA LLC** ....D 973 812-8820
Totowa ***(G-10943)***
Elite Emrgncy Lights Ltd Lblty ....F 732 534-2377
Lakewood ***(G-5115)***
▲ **Felco Products LLC** ....G 973 890-7979
Paterson ***(G-8271)***
▲ **Fleetsource LLC** ....E 732 566-4970
Cliffwood ***(G-1547)***
Freehold Pntiac Bick GMC Trcks ....D 732 462-7093
Freehold ***(G-3656)***
◆ **Gentek Inc** ....C 973 515-0900
Parsippany ***(G-8024)***
Gorman Industries Inc ....E 973 345-5424
Paterson ***(G-8279)***
Holman Enterprises Inc ....C 856 532-2410
Pennsauken ***(G-8522)***
Holman Enterprises Inc ....E 609 383-6100
Mount Laurel ***(G-6802)***
Honeywell International Inc ....C 973 455-2000
Morristown ***(G-6715)***
◆ **Honeywell International Inc** ....A 973 455-2000
Morris Plains ***(G-6666)***
Ida Automotive Inc ....G 732 591-1245
Morganville ***(G-6643)***
J & R Rebuilders Inc ....G 856 627-1414
Laurel Springs ***(G-5233)***
Jesel Inc ....D 732 901-1800
Lakewood ***(G-5140)***
K & K Automotive Inc ....G 973 777-2235
Passaic ***(G-8153)***
Keystone Automotive Inds Inc ....E 856 829-4700
West Deptford ***(G-11833)***
▲ **Kinedyne LLC** ....F 908 231-1800
Branchburg ***(G-672)***
KRs Automotive Dev Group Inc ....F 732 667-7937
Middlesex ***(G-6174)***
▲ **Kumar Bros USA LLC** ....G 732 266-3091
Englishtown ***(G-2995)***
Level Ten Products Inc ....F 973 827-0900
Hamburg ***(G-4095)***
Ls Rubber Industries Inc ....E 973 680-4488
Bloomfield ***(G-519)***
M P M Building Service ....G 732 946-2600
Holmdel ***(G-4519)***
M P T Racing Inc ....G 973 989-9220
Dover ***(G-2098)***
Machiavelli LLC ....G 862 215-5888
East Orange ***(G-2260)***
▲ **Manley Performance Pdts Inc** ....D 732 905-3366
Lakewood ***(G-5152)***
Matthey Johnson Inc ....C 856 384-7132
West Deptford ***(G-11835)***
Maxzone Vehicle Lighting Corp ....F 732 393-9600
Edison ***(G-2566)***
Momentum Usa Inc ....F 844 300-1553
Edison ***(G-2576)***
▲ **NAPA Concepts Ltd Liability Co** ....G 201 673-2381
North Bergen ***(G-7470)***
Newark Auto Top Co Inc ....F 973 677-9935
East Orange ***(G-2262)***
▲ **Nitto Inc** ....C 732 901-7905
Lakewood ***(G-5164)***
▲ **O T D Inc** ....G 973 890-7979
Totowa ***(G-10958)***
▲ **Ogura Industrial Corp** ....F 586 749-1900
Somerset ***(G-10146)***
▲ **Olde Grandad Industries Inc** ....G 201 997-1899
Passaic ***(G-8168)***
Overdrive Holdings Inc ....F 201 440-1911
South Hackensack ***(G-10286)***
P & A Auto Parts Inc ....E 201 655-7117
Hackensack ***(G-3959)***
Paintmaster Auto Body ....F 732 270-1700
Toms River ***(G-10899)***
▲ **Premier Products Inc** ....D 856 231-1800
Marlton ***(G-5995)***
Quality Remanufacturing Inc ....F 973 523-8800
Paterson ***(G-8366)***
Ram Hydraulics Inc ....G 732 237-0904
Shrewsbury ***(G-10009)***
Rebuilt Parts Co LLC ....F 856 662-3252
Pennsauken ***(G-8570)***
▲ **Research & Mfg Corp Amer** ....F 908 862-6744
Linden ***(G-5433)***
▼ **Rony Inc** ....G 201 891-2551
Wyckoff ***(G-12263)***
▲ **S & G Tool Aid Corporation** ....D 973 824-7730
Newark ***(G-7297)***
S L P Engineering Inc ....D 732 240-3696
Toms River ***(G-10908)***
Shock Tech Inc ....E 845 368-8600
Mahwah ***(G-5812)***
▲ **Tabco Technologies LLC** ....G 201 438-0422
Carlstadt ***(G-1226)***
Tekltd ....G 732 463-2100
Piscataway ***(G-8822)***
Tesla Inc ....G 201 225-2544
Paramus ***(G-7910)***
Top Rated Shopping Bargains ....F 201 630-0770
Hasbrouck Heights ***(G-4200)***
Town Ford Inc ....D 609 298-4990
Bordentown ***(G-613)***
▲ **Transaxle LLC** ....C 856 665-4445
Cinnaminson ***(G-1495)***
Transmission Technology Co ....G 973 305-3600
Lincoln Park ***(G-5334)***
Truckpro LLC ....E 201 229-0599
Teterboro ***(G-10817)***
Turbine Tek Inc ....G 973 872-0903
Wayne ***(G-11687)***
Turbo Solutions LLC ....F 856 209-6900
Pennsauken ***(G-8587)***
Vahlco Racing Wheels LLC ....G 609 758-7013
New Egypt ***(G-7018)***
Valcor Engineering Corporation ....E 973 467-8100
Springfield ***(G-10584)***
◆ **Volvo Car North America LLC** ....B 201 768-7300
Rockleigh ***(G-9636)***
VS Systematics Corp ....G 908 241-5110
Kenilworth ***(G-5003)***
Wayne Motors Inc ....D 973 696-9710
Wayne ***(G-11692)***
Well Manager LLC ....G 609 466-4347
Hopewell ***(G-4544)***
▲ **Wexco Industries Inc** ....E 973 244-5777
Pine Brook ***(G-8720)***

3715 Truck Trailers

ASAP Containers NJ NY Corp ....F 732 659-4402
West Orange ***(G-11886)***
◆ **Automann Inc** ....D 201 529-4996
Somerset ***(G-10068)***
E Loc Total Logistics LLC ....G 609 685-6117
Mount Laurel ***(G-6796)***
◆ **Granco Group LLC** ....G 973 515-4721
Roseland ***(G-9651)***
▲ **Hercules Enterprises LLC** ....D 908 369-0000
Hillsborough ***(G-4340)***
M W Trailer Repair Inc ....F 609 298-1113
Bordentown ***(G-600)***
Richard Shafer ....G 856 358-3483
Elmer ***(G-2796)***
Trac Intermodal LLC ....G 609 452-8900
Princeton ***(G-9130)***
Trac Interstar LLC ....G 609 452-8900
Princeton ***(G-9131)***
Universal Parts New Jersey LLC ....G 732 615-0626
Middletown ***(G-6219)***
Vanco Usa LLC ....D 609 499-4141
Bordentown ***(G-614)***
Vanco USA LLC (de) ....C 609 499-4141
Bordentown ***(G-615)***
Wjm Trucking Inc ....G 856 381-3635
Mullica Hill ***(G-6893)***

3721 Aircraft

Boeing Company ....A 908 464-6959
Berkeley Heights ***(G-401)***
Boeing Company ....A 610 591-1978
Swedesboro ***(G-10684)***
Dassault Aircraft Svcs Corp ....G 201 440-6700
Little Ferry ***(G-5500)***
▼ **Defense Photonics Group Inc** ....F 908 822-1075
South Plainfield ***(G-10354)***
Defense Spport Svcs Intl 2 LLC ....F 856 866-2200
Marlton ***(G-5970)***
Drone Go Home LLC ....G 732 991-3605
Highlands ***(G-4308)***
Easy Aerial Corporation ....G 646 639-4410
Edison ***(G-2506)***
Enroute Computer Solutions Inc ....B 609 569-9255
Egg Harbor Township ***(G-2684)***
Jet Aviation St Louis Inc ....E 201 462-4026
Teterboro ***(G-10800)***
Lockheed Martin Corporation ....C 856 792-9811
Cherry Hill ***(G-1390)***
Lockheed Martin Corporation ....B 856 787-3104
Mount Laurel ***(G-6814)***
Lockheed Martin Corporation ....D 856 722-7782
Moorestown ***(G-6594)***
Pacific Microtronics Inc ....G 973 993-8665
Morris Plains ***(G-6676)***

3724 Aircraft Engines & Engine Parts

Aerospace Industries LLC ....G 973 383-9307
Sparta ***(G-10486)***
Allied-Signal China Ltd ....E 973 455-2000
Morristown ***(G-6685)***
Bright Lights Usa Inc ....E 856 546-5656
Camden ***(G-1046)***
▲ **Bright Lights Usa Inc** ....D 856 546-5656
Barrington ***(G-173)***
Capital Cooling Systems LLC ....G 973 773-8700
Lyndhurst ***(G-5674)***
Dover Tool Connecticut LLC ....F 203 367-6376
Franklin Lakes ***(G-3616)***
Honeywell International Inc ....C 800 601-3099
Morris Plains ***(G-6663)***
Honeywell International Inc ....E 973 455-6633
Morristown ***(G-6714)***
Honeywell International Inc ....E 973 285-5321
Morris Plains ***(G-6664)***
Honeywell International Inc ....A 856 691-5111
Vineland ***(G-11370)***
Honeywell International Inc ....A 856 234-5020
Moorestown ***(G-6585)***
Honeywell International Inc ....D 973 455-2000
Morris Plains ***(G-6665)***
◆ **Honeywell International Inc** ....A 973 455-2000
Morris Plains ***(G-6666)***
Honeywell International Inc ....A 732 919-0010
Wall Township ***(G-11488)***
Honeywell International Inc ....G 908 561-1888
South Plainfield ***(G-10380)***
Honeywell International Inc ....G 800 601-3099
Morris Plains ***(G-6667)***
Honeywell Spain Holdings LLC ....G 973 455-2000
Morristown ***(G-6716)***
Kreisler Industrial Corp ....D 201 773-6829
Elmwood Park ***(G-2829)***
Kreisler Manufacturing Corp ....G 201 791-0700
Elmwood Park ***(G-2830)***
▲ **Parts Life Inc** ....E 856 786-8675
Moorestown ***(G-6609)***

3728 Aircraft Parts & Eqpt, NEC

▲ **Accurate Bushing Company Inc** ....E 908 789-1121
Garwood ***(G-3774)***
Aerospace Manufacturing Inc ....E 973 472-9888
Wallington ***(G-11521)***
◆ **Air Cruisers Company LLC** ....C 732 681-3527
Wall Township ***(G-11460)***
Alpine Machine & Tool Corp ....F 201 666-0959
Westwood ***(G-11953)***
American Aluminum Company ....D 908 233-3500
Mountainside ***(G-6868)***
▲ **Arlington Prcsion Cmpnents LLC** ....E 973 276-1377
Fairfield ***(G-3138)***
Bae Systems Tech Sol Srvc Inc ....E 856 638-1003
Mount Laurel ***(G-6780)***
Bar Fields Inc ....F 347 587-7795
Linden ***(G-5351)***
▲ **Breeze-Eastern LLC** ....G 973 602-1001
Whippany ***(G-12014)***
Breeze-Eastern LLC ....D 973 602-1001
Whippany ***(G-12015)***
▲ **Bright Lights Usa Inc** ....D 856 546-5656
Barrington ***(G-173)***
▼ **Clearway LLC** ....G 973 578-4578
Newark ***(G-7122)***
DEB Manufacturing Inc ....G 732 364-7007
Lakewood ***(G-5107)***
Defense Support Svcs Intl LLC ....F 850 390-4737
Marlton ***(G-5971)***
Doorsills LLC ....G 973 904-0270
Haledon ***(G-4081)***
Drone Go Home LLC ....G 732 991-3605
Highlands ***(G-4308)***

S I C

▲ Drytech Inc ....E 609 758-1794
Cookstown *(G-1806)*

Enginred Arrsting Systems Corp ....E 856 241-8620
Logan Township *(G-5613)*

Exelis Inc/Northrop ....F 973 284-4212
Clifton *(G-1617)*

Export Management Consultants ....E 609 758-1166
Cookstown *(G-1807)*

Goodrich Corporation ....G 973 237-2700
Totowa *(G-10949)*

Ho-Ho-Kus Inc ....E 973 278-2274
Paterson *(G-8290)*

J A Machine & Tool Co Inc ....F 201 767-1308
Closter *(G-1762)*

Keeley Aerospace Ltd ....E 951 582-2113
Cranbury *(G-1846)*

Kreisler Manufacturing Corp ....G 201 791-0700
Elmwood Park *(G-2830)*

Pacific Coast Systems LLC ....G 908 735-9955
Asbury *(G-72)*

Polytechnic Industries Inc ....F 856 235-6550
Mount Laurel *(G-6829)*

Rclc Inc ....E 732 877-1788
Woodbridge *(G-12152)*

▲ Schultz Company ....G 732 922-4334
Neptune *(G-6930)*

Simtek Usa Inc ....G 862 757-8130
Little Falls *(G-5488)*

Terrestrial Imaging LLC ....G 800 359-0530
Brick *(G-760)*

▲ Thales Avionics Inc ....C 732 242-6300
Piscataway *(G-8823)*

Tolin Design Inc ....G 201 261-4455
Emerson *(G-2863)*

Vahl Inc ....E 732 249-4042
East Brunswick *(G-2194)*

Whippany Actuation Systems LLC ....C 973 428-9898
Whippany *(G-12043)*

▲ Zodiac US Corporation ....A 732 681-3527
Wall Township *(G-11520)*

3731 Shipbuilding & Repairing

Allen Steel Co ....G 856 785-1171
Leesburg *(G-5314)*

▼ American Rigging & Repair Inc ......F 866 478-7129
Roselle *(G-9660)*

Bayonne Drydock & Repair Corp ....E 201 823-9295
Bayonne *(G-215)*

Bishop Ascendant Inc ....G 973 210-5298
West Caldwell *(G-11768)*

Conneaut Creek Ship Repr Inc ....G 212 863-9406
Jersey City *(G-4732)*

Island Breeze Intl Inc ....F 856 931-1505
Marlton *(G-5980)*

Kerney Service Group Inc ....E 908 486-2644
Linden *(G-5397)*

Maxwell McKenney Inc ....G 856 310-0700
Haddon Heights *(G-4048)*

Monmouth Marine Engines Inc ....F 732 528-9290
Brielle *(G-913)*

◆ Nvs International Inc ....E 908 523-0266
Linden *(G-5421)*

◆ Ocean Power & Equipment Co ......G 973 575-5775
West Caldwell *(G-11793)*

▲ Simplex Americas LLC ....G 908 237-9099
Flemington *(G-3466)*

Union Dry Dock & Repair Co ....G 201 792-9090
Hoboken *(G-4501)*

Union Dry Dock & Repair Co ....E 201 963-5833
Hoboken *(G-4502)*

White Marine Inc ....F 732 826-4491
Towaco *(G-11007)*

Wittich Bros Marine Inc ....E 732 722-8656
Manasquan *(G-5885)*

3732 Boat Building & Repairing

A & D Indus & Mar Repr Inc ....E 732 541-1481
Port Reading *(G-8984)*

A PS Inlet Marina LLC ....G 732 681-3303
Belmar *(G-355)*

Barnegat Light Fibrgls Sup LLC ....G 609 294-8870
West Creek *(G-11809)*

Camp Marine Services Inc ....G 609 368-1777
Stone Harbor *(G-10613)*

Carver Boat Sales Inc ....G 732 892-0328
Point Pleasant Boro *(G-8934)*

Cherubini Yachts Ltd Lblty Co ....G 856 764-5319
Delran *(G-2015)*

▼ Commercial Water Sports Inc ....G 609 624-3404
Cape May Court House *(G-1113)*

Costa Mar Cnvas Enclosures LLC ......F 609 965-1538
Egg Harbor City *(G-2660)*

D&S Fisheries LLC ....G 914 438-3197
Colts Neck *(G-1783)*

Dorchester Shipyard Inc ....F 856 785-8040
Dorchester *(G-2072)*

Eh Yachts LLC ....D 609 965-2300
Egg Harbor City *(G-2664)*

Henriques Yachts Works ....G 732 269-1180
Bayville *(G-256)*

Jersey Cape Yachts Inc ....D 609 965-8650
Egg Harbor City *(G-2665)*

Lockwood Boat Works Inc ....E 732 721-1605
South Amboy *(G-10241)*

Marine Acquisition Inc ....G 609 965-2300
Egg Harbor City *(G-2667)*

Norma K Corporation ....F 732 477-6441
Point Pleasant Beach *(G-8924)*

Scorpion Charters Spt Fishing ....G 732 477-0985
Brick *(G-758)*

▲ Steelstran Industries Inc ....E 732 574-0700
Avenel *(G-152)*

Sunsplash Marina LLC ....G 609 628-4445
Tuckahoe *(G-11138)*

Supply Technologies LLC ....E 201 641-7600
Moonachie *(G-6547)*

Tf Yachts LLC ....D 609 965-2300
Egg Harbor City *(G-2672)*

Tradewinds Marine Service ....G 848 448-6888
Toms River *(G-10918)*

Union Dry Dock & Repair Co ....E 201 963-5833
Hoboken *(G-4502)*

Van Duyne Bros Inc ....G 609 625-0299
Mays Landing *(G-6043)*

▲ Viking Yacht Company ....B 609 296-6000
New Gretna *(G-7020)*

▲ Yank Marine Inc ....E 609 628-2928
Tuckahoe *(G-11140)*

3743 Railroad Eqpt

American Rail Company Inc ....F 732 785-1110
Brick *(G-733)*

Bombardier Transportation ....G 201 955-5874
Kearny *(G-4866)*

Bombardier Transportation ....G 856 580-5609
Camden *(G-1045)*

Hainesport Industrial Railroad ....F 609 261-8036
Hainesport *(G-4072)*

Marmon Industrial LLC ....F 609 655-4287
Cranbury *(G-1860)*

▲ Multipower International Inc ....G 973 727-0327
Towaco *(G-10999)*

▼ Rails Company Inc ....G 973 763-4320
Maplewood *(G-5926)*

▲ Strato Inc ....D 732 981-1515
Piscataway *(G-8818)*

3751 Motorcycles, Bicycles & Parts

Barbs Harley-Davidson ....E 856 456-4141
Mount Ephraim *(G-6762)*

Bezerra Corporation ....G 973 595-7775
Totowa *(G-10935)*

◆ BMW of North America LLC ....A 201 307-4000
Woodcliff Lake *(G-12183)*

Electric Mobility Corporation ....C 856 468-1000
Sewell *(G-9955)*

◆ Hyper Bicycles Inc ....G 856 694-0352
Malaga *(G-5826)*

Morristown Cycle ....G 973 540-1244
Morristown *(G-6729)*

NJ Grass Choppers ....G 732 414-2850
Manalapan *(G-5856)*

Wheels Motor Sports Inc ....G 732 606-9208
Bayville *(G-262)*

Works Enduro Rider Inc ....G 908 637-6385
Great Meadows *(G-3853)*

3761 Guided Missiles & Space Vehicles

Lockheed Martin Corporation ....B 856 787-3104
Mount Laurel *(G-6814)*

Lockheed Martin Overseas LLC ....G 856 787-3105
Moorestown *(G-6597)*

Savit Corporation ....F 862 209-4516
Rockaway *(G-9607)*

3764 Guided Missile/Space Vehicle Propulsion Units & parts

Aphelion Orbitals Inc ....G 321 289-0872
Union City *(G-11242)*

Lockheed Martin Corporation ....B 856 787-3104
Mount Laurel *(G-6814)*

3769 Guided Missile/Space Vehicle Parts & Eqpt, NEC

Aeropanel Corporation ....D 973 335-9636
Boonton *(G-552)*

Breeze-Eastern LLC ....D 973 602-1001
Whippany *(G-12015)*

▲ Drytech Inc ....E 609 758-1794
Cookstown *(G-1806)*

H & W Tool Co Inc ....F 973 366-0131
Dover *(G-2088)*

▲ McWilliams Forge Company ....D 973 627-0200
Rockaway *(G-9586)*

Zenith Precision Inc ....F 201 933-8640
East Rutherford *(G-2338)*

3792 Travel Trailers & Campers

▼ Orlando Systems Ltd Lblty Co ....G 908 400-5052
North Plainfield *(G-7560)*

3795 Tanks & Tank Components

ALI Envmtl & Tank Svcs LLC ....F 908 755-2962
Scotch Plains *(G-9844)*

AST Construction Inc ....E 609 277-7101
Egg Harbor Township *(G-2679)*

Clogic LLC ....G 973 934-5223
Augusta *(G-119)*

Savit Corporation ....F 862 209-4516
Rockaway *(G-9607)*

3799 Transportation Eqpt, NEC

▲ Parts Life Inc ....E 856 786-8675
Moorestown *(G-6609)*

▼ Savino Del Bene USA Inc ....D 347 960-5568
Avenel *(G-150)*

Sealion Metal Fabricators Inc ....E 856 933-3914
Bellmawr *(G-350)*

Steve Green Enterprises ....F 732 938-5572
Farmingdale *(G-3394)*

38 MEASURING, ANALYZING AND CONTROLLING INSTRUMENTS; PHOTOGRAPHIC, MEDICAL AN

3812 Search, Detection, Navigation & Guidance Systs & Instrs

Aeronautical Instr & Rdo Co ....E 973 473-0034
Lodi *(G-5573)*

Aeropanel Corporation ....D 973 335-9636
Boonton *(G-552)*

Alk Technologies Inc ....C 609 683-0220
Princeton *(G-9002)*

Allied-Signal China Ltd ....E 973 455-2000
Morristown *(G-6685)*

American Gas & Chemical Co Ltd ....E 201 767-7300
Northvale *(G-7572)*

▼ AT&T Technologies Inc ....E 201 771-2000
Berkeley Heights *(G-400)*

Atgi Advanced Tech Group Intl ....E 609 271-8666
Lawrenceville *(G-5250)*

Atlantic Inertial Systems Inc ....D 973 237-2713
Totowa *(G-10932)*

Bae Systems Info & Elec Sys ....B 603 885-4321
Totowa *(G-10933)*

Bae Systems Info & Elec Sys ....A 973 633-6000
Wayne *(G-11607)*

Check-It Electronics Corp ....E 973 520-8435
Elizabeth *(G-2718)*

◆ Checkpoint Systems Inc ....C 800 257-5540
West Deptford *(G-11821)*

Checkpoint Systems Inc ....G 856 848-1800
West Deptford *(G-11822)*

Dassault Procurement Svcs Inc ....D 201 261-4130
Little Ferry *(G-5501)*

Dengen Scientific Corporation ....D 201 687-2983
Union City *(G-11245)*

Dewey Electronics Corporation ....E 201 337-4700
Oakland *(G-7685)*

Drs Infrared Technologies LP ....G 973 898-1500
Parsippany *(G-7986)*

Drs Leonardo Inc ....E 973 775-4440
Newark *(G-7143)*

Drs Leonardo Inc ....E 973 898-1500
Parsippany *(G-7987)*

Drs Leonardo Inc ....E 973 898-1500
Parsippany *(G-7988)*

Drs Leonardo Inc ....E 201 337-3800
Oakland *(G-7686)*

▼ Electromagnetic Tech Inds Inc ....D 973 394-1719
Boonton *(G-564)*

Ferry Machine Corp ....E 201 641-9191
Little Ferry *(G-5504)*

GE Aviation Systems LLC ....C 973 428-9898
Whippany *(G-12021)*

General Plastics Corporation ....E 973 429-5625
Bloomfield *(G-511)*

Glasseal Products Inc ....C 732 370-9100
Lakewood *(G-5129)*

H Galow Co Inc ....E 201 768-0547
Norwood *(G-7624)*

Halberd Match Corp ....E 609 882-7000
Ewing *(G-3019)*

Harris Corporation ....C 973 284-0123
Clifton *(G-1634)*

Harris Corporation ....C 973 284-0123
Clifton *(G-1636)*

Harris Corporation ....C 585 269-6600
Clifton *(G-1637)*

Ho-Ho-Kus Inc ....E 973 278-2274
Paterson *(G-8290)*

◆ Honeywell International Inc ....A 973 455-2000
Morris Plains *(G-6666)*

Honeywell International Inc ....C 973 455-2000
Morristown *(G-6715)*

Innerspace Technology Inc ....E 201 933-1600
Carlstadt *(G-1172)*

Intertek Laboratories Inc ....E 908 903-1800
Stirling *(G-10601)*

Kearfott Corporation ....C 973 785-6000
Woodland Park *(G-12223)*

L3 Technologies Inc ....B 973 446-4000
Budd Lake *(G-932)*

Lockheed Martin ....C 856 762-2222
Marlton *(G-5983)*

Lockheed Martin ....D 856 722-7782
Marlton *(G-5984)*

Lockheed Martin ....C 856 722-2418
Marlton *(G-5985)*

Lockheed Martin Corporation ....A 856 234-1261
Mount Laurel *(G-6813)*

Lockheed Martin Corporation ....D 856 722-7782
Moorestown *(G-6594)*

Lockheed Martin Corporation ....A 856 722-4100
Moorestown *(G-6596)*

Lockheed Martin Corporation ....C 856 722-3336
Moorestown *(G-6595)*

Lockheed Martin Corporation ....B 856 787-3104
Mount Laurel *(G-6814)*

Mantech Systems Engrg Corp ....G 856 566-9155
Voorhees *(G-11435)*

Melton Sales & Service ....E 609 699-4800
Bordentown *(G-602)*

Melton Sales & Service ....E 609 699-4800
Columbus *(G-1805)*

▲ Milspray LLC ....E 732 886-2223
Lakewood *(G-5159)*

▲ Multi-Tech Industries Inc ....F 732 431-0550
Marlboro *(G-5948)*

Mwt Materials Inc ....F 973 928-8300
Passaic *(G-8166)*

National Prtective Systems Inc ....F 732 922-3609
Eatontown *(G-2415)*

Northrop Grumman Systems Corp ....G 908 276-6677
Cranford *(G-1918)*

Oavco Ltd Liability Company ....F 855 535-4227
Princeton *(G-9084)*

Oaviation Corporation ....E 609 619-3060
Princeton *(G-9085)*

Pmc Inc ....F 973 748-5500
Bloomfield *(G-527)*

Premac Inc ....F 732 381-7550
Rahway *(G-9218)*

Primacy Engineering Inc ....F 201 731-3272
Englewood Cliffs *(G-2979)*

Princton Satellite Systems Inc ....G 609 275-9606
Plainsboro *(G-8896)*

Sun Dial & Panel Corporation ....E 973 226-4334
Fairfield *(G-3316)*

▲ Transistor Devices Inc ....C 908 850-5088
Hackettstown *(G-4041)*

3821 Laboratory Apparatus & Furniture

▲ 3d Biotek LLC ....G 908 801-6138
Bridgewater *(G-806)*

Abox Automation Corp ....G 973 659-9611
Pine Brook *(G-8679)*

Accuracy Devices ....G 973 427-8829
Hawthorne *(G-4216)*

Airfiltronix Corp ....G 973 779-5577
Clifton *(G-1560)*

Arrow Engineering Co Inc ....G 908 353-5229
Hillside *(G-4391)*

◆ Arthur H Thomas Company ....B 856 467-2000
Swedesboro *(G-10682)*

Becton Dickinson and Company ....A 201 847-6800
Franklin Lakes *(G-3610)*

Bellco Glass Inc ....D 800 257-7043
Vineland *(G-11328)*

▲ Benchmark Scientific Inc ....E 908 769-5555
Sayreville *(G-9815)*

◆ Bsi Corp ....G 631 589-1118
Nutley *(G-7643)*

▲ C W Brabender Instrs Inc ....E 201 343-8425
South Hackensack *(G-10256)*

Chemspeed Technologies Inc ....G 732 329-1225
North Brunswick *(G-7511)*

Cleanzones LLC ....F 732 534-5590
Jackson *(G-4658)*

Dek Tron International Corp ....E 908 226-1777
Plainfield *(G-8857)*

Delaware Technologies Inc ....F 856 234-7692
Mount Laurel *(G-6792)*

Denton Vacuum LLC ....G 856 439-9100
Moorestown *(G-6572)*

▲ Diagenode Inc ....G 862 209-4680
Denville *(G-2036)*

Difco Laboratories Inc ....G 410 316-4113
Franklin Lakes *(G-3613)*

▼ Emse Corp ....G 973 227-9221
Fairfield *(G-3184)*

Exodon LLC ....F 973 398-2900
Mount Arlington *(G-6754)*

Fluid Dynamics Inc ....G 908 200-5823
Flemington *(G-3443)*

Futurex Inc ....F 201 933-3943
Rochelle Park *(G-9528)*

G & H Sheet Metal Works Inc ....F 973 923-1100
Hillside *(G-4408)*

▲ Handler Manufacturing Company .....E 908 233-7796
Westfield *(G-11926)*

Hel Inc ....G 440 208-7360
Lawrenceville *(G-5258)*

Innovasystems Inc ....F 856 722-0410
Moorestown *(G-6586)*

Knf Neuberger Inc ....D 609 890-8889
Trenton *(G-11074)*

▲ Labnet International Inc ....E 732 417-0700
Iselin *(G-4630)*

Lm Air Technology Inc ....E 732 381-8200
Rahway *(G-9210)*

Micro-Tek Laboratories Inc ....G 973 779-5577
Clifton *(G-1674)*

Microdata Instrument Inc ....F 908 222-1717
South Plainfield *(G-10406)*

MSI Holdings LLC ....G 732 549-7144
Metuchen *(G-6115)*

▲ National Labnet Co ....E 732 417-0700
Iselin *(G-4636)*

▲ Nes Company Inc ....F 973 795-1519
Jersey City *(G-4788)*

▲ Ohaus Corporation ....D 973 377-9000
Parsippany *(G-8051)*

▲ Pacon Manufacturing Corp ....C 732 764-9070
Somerset *(G-10152)*

Randcastle Extrusion Systems ....G 973 239-1150
Cedar Grove *(G-1298)*

S P Industries Inc ....D 215 672-7800
Buena *(G-948)*

Scientific Machine and Sup Co ....E 732 356-1553
Middlesex *(G-6195)*

▲ Scientifix LLC ....G 856 780-5871
Mount Laurel *(G-6838)*

▲ Servolift LLC ....E 973 442-7878
Randolph *(G-9297)*

Spark Holland Inc ....E 609 799-7250
Sicklerville *(G-10026)*

▲ Spex Certiprep Inc ....D 732 549-7144
Metuchen *(G-6121)*

Spex Certiprep Group LLC ....F 208 204-6656
Metuchen *(G-6122)*

Spex Sample Prep LLC ....G 732 549-7144
Metuchen *(G-6124)*

Spex Sample Prep LLC ....E 732 549-7144
Metuchen *(G-6125)*

▲ Thoma Inc ....F 856 608-6887
Moorestown *(G-6628)*

Thomas Scientific ....B 800 345-2100
Swedesboro *(G-10733)*

Thomas Scientific LLC ....G 800 345-2100
Swedesboro *(G-10734)*

Tovatech LLC ....G 973 913-9734
Maplewood *(G-5928)*

Triad Scientific Inc ....G 732 292-1994
Manasquan *(G-5882)*

▼ United Hospital Supply Corp ....C 609 387-7580
Burlington *(G-993)*

Waage Electric Inc ....G 908 245-9363
Kenilworth *(G-5004)*

3822 Automatic Temperature Controls

A T C Companies Inc ....E 732 560-0900
Middlesex *(G-6141)*

Access Northern Security Inc ....F 732 462-2500
Freehold *(G-3634)*

Aginova Inc ....G 732 804-3272
Freehold *(G-3635)*

Amega Scientific Corporation ....F 609 953-7295
Medford *(G-6064)*

▲ Ammark Corporation ....G 973 616-2555
Pompton Plains *(G-8952)*

▲ Armadillo Automation Inc ....E 856 829-2888
Cinnaminson *(G-1447)*

▼ Atomizing Systems Inc ....F 201 447-1222
Ho Ho Kus *(G-4453)*

Brighton Air ....G 973 258-1500
Springfield *(G-10545)*

Building Performance Eqp Inc ....F 201 722-1414
Hillsdale *(G-4380)*

Burling Instruments Inc ....F 973 665-0601
Chatham *(G-1326)*

Calculagraph Co ....D 973 887-9400
East Hanover *(G-2204)*

Chatham Controls Corporation ....G 908 236-6019
Lebanon *(G-5281)*

Check-It Electronics Corp ....E 973 520-8435
Elizabeth *(G-2718)*

Comverge Giants Inc ....G 973 884-5970
Florham Park *(G-3496)*

Comverge Giants Inc ....G 973 884-5970
East Hanover *(G-2209)*

◆ Croll-Reynolds Co Inc ....E 908 232-4200
Parsippany *(G-7976)*

D & A Electronics Mfg ....F 732 938-7400
Wall Township *(G-11476)*

Energy Options Inc ....E 732 512-9100
Edison *(G-2511)*

Fluidsens International Inc ....G 914 338-3932
Twp Washinton *(G-11142)*

▲ Heat-Timer Corporation ....E 973 575-4004
Fairfield *(G-3218)*

Honeywell Asia Pacific Inc ....F 973 455-2000
Morris Plains *(G-6662)*

J & L Controls Inc ....G 732 460-0380
Lincroft *(G-5338)*

Johnson Controls Inc ....G 732 752-2395
Union *(G-11199)*

Johnson Controls Inc ....D 732 225-6700
Edison *(G-2549)*

▲ Megatran Industries ....B 609 227-4300
Bordentown *(G-601)*

Micro-Tek Laboratories Inc ....G 973 779-5577
Clifton *(G-1674)*

Msj Unlimited Services ....G 201 617-0764
Union City *(G-11258)*

National Environmental Svcs Co ....G 973 543-4586
Mendham *(G-6090)*

National Refrigerants Inc ....E 856 455-4555
Bridgeton *(G-792)*

Niagara Conservation Corp ....F 973 829-0800
Cedar Knolls *(G-1319)*

NRG Bluewater Wind LLC ....G 201 748-5000
Hoboken *(G-4487)*

▲ Rees Scientific Corporation ....E 609 530-1055
Ewing *(G-3050)*

◆ Rowan Technologies Inc ....D 609 267-9000
Rancocas *(G-9262)*

Schneder Elc Bldngs Amrcas Inc .....E 201 348-9240
Secaucus *(G-9922)*

Siemens Industry Inc ....E 856 234-7666
Mount Laurel *(G-6841)*

▲ Sigma-Netics Inc ....E 973 227-6372
Riverdale *(G-9488)*

▲ Sisco Manufacturing Co Inc ....F 856 486-7550
Pennsauken *(G-8579)*

Employee Codes: A=Over 500 employees, B=251-500
C=101-250, D=51-100, E=20-50, F=10-19, G=4-9
         2018 Harris New Jersey
Manufacturers Directory
         593

SIC

Sk & P Industries Inc ....G 973 482-1864
Newark (G-7315)
Sulzer Chemtech USA Inc ....C 856 768-2165
West Berlin (G-11752)
Tesa Rentals LLC ....F 973 300-0913
Sparta (G-10523)
Thermo Systems LLC 609 371-3300
East Windsor (G-2368)
▲ Town & Country Plastics Inc ......F 732 780-5300
Marlboro (G-5961)
Trolex Corporation ....E 201 794-8004
Randolph (G-9302)
US Air Power Systems ....G 201 892-5235
Westwood (G-11974)
▲ Vu Sound Incorporated ....F 215 990-2864
Lumberton (G-5666)

3823 Indl Instruments For Meas, Display & Control

Accupac Inc ....C 215 256-7094
Lakewood (G-5064)
Accurate Thermal Systems LLC ......G 609 326-3190
Hainesport (G-4068)
▼ Accuratus Ceramic Corp ....E 908 213-7070
Phillipsburg (G-8638)
◆ Acrison Inc ....C 201 440-8300
Moonachie (G-6499)
ACS Quality Services Inc ....G 856 988-6550
Marlton (G-5964)
Align Sourcing Ltd Lblty Co ....G 609 375-8550
Trenton (G-11014)
American Compressed Gases Inc ......E 201 767-3200
Old Tappan (G-7797)
Amico Technologies Inc ....G 732 901-5900
Lakewood (G-5074)
Anvima Technologies LLC ....G 973 531-7077
Brookside (G-922)
Arcadia Equipment Inc ....E 201 342-3308
Hackensack (G-3874)
▲ Armadillo Automation Inc ....E 856 829-2888
Cinnaminson (G-1447)
Audiocodes Inc ....G 732 469-0880
Somerset (G-10066)
▲ Audiocodes Inc ....G 732 469-0880
Somerset (G-10067)
▲ Boc Group Inc ....A 908 665-2400
New Providence (G-7030)
◆ Btech Inc ....E 973 983-1120
Rockaway (G-9555)
Burling Instruments Inc ....F 973 665-0601
Chatham (G-1326)
▲ Capintec Inc ....E 201 825-9500
Florham Park (G-3495)
Carlisle Machine Works Inc ....E 856 825-0627
Millville (G-6293)
Celco ....F 201 327-1123
Mahwah (G-5757)
▼ Cg Automation Solutions USA ....E 973 379-7400
Springfield (G-10546)
Check-It Electronics Corp ....E 973 520-8435
Elizabeth (G-2718)
▲ Circonix Technologies LLC ....F 973 962-6160
Ringwood (G-9445)
Control Instruments Corp ....E 973 575-9114
Fairfield (G-3168)
◆ Coperion K-Tron Pitman Inc ....F 856 589-0500
Sewell (G-9947)
Corporate Computer Systems ....F 732 739-5600
Newark (G-7127)
▼ Daq Electronics LLC ....E 732 981-0050
Piscataway (G-8753)
Delaware Technologies Inc ....F 856 234-7692
Mount Laurel (G-6792)
Delphian Corporation ....C 201 767-3300
Northvale (G-7577)
Difco Laboratories Inc ....G 410 316-4113
Franklin Lakes (G-3613)
Digital Binscom LLC ....G 908 867-7055
Long Valley (G-5636)
Digivac Company ....F 732 765-0900
Matawan (G-6017)
Dranetz Technologies Inc ....D 732 248-4358
Edison (G-2503)
Elaine Inc ....G 973 345-6200
Woodland Park (G-12217)
▲ Electronic Measuring Devices ....F 973 691-4755
Flanders (G-3406)
Emerson Process Management ....G 908 605-4551
Warren (G-11546)

F S Brainard & Co ....F 609 387-4300
Burlington (G-971)
Fargo Controls Inc ....G 732 389-3376
Eatontown (G-2395)
▲ Gammon Technical Products Inc .....D 732 223-4600
Manasquan (G-5870)
Gerin Corporation Inc ....G 732 774-3256
Neptune (G-6914)
Global Power Technology Inc ....D 732 287-3680
Edison (G-2528)
Intertek Laboratories Inc ....E 908 903-1800
Stirling (G-10601)
▲ Intest Corporation ....G 856 505-8800
Mount Laurel (G-6807)
▲ Istec Corporation ....G 973 383-9888
Sparta (G-10506)
J & W Servo Systems Company ....F 973 335-1007
Rockaway (G-9577)
▲ John G Papailias Co Inc ....G 201 767-4027
Northvale (G-7588)
◆ Kessler-Ellis Products Co ....D 732 935-1320
Eatontown (G-2410)
◆ Linde LLC ....C 908 464-8100
Bridgewater (G-855)
Linde LLC 973 579-2065
Sparta (G-10510)
Linde North America Inc ....G 908 464-8100
New Providence (G-7045)
▼ Linde North America Inc ....B 908 464-8100
Bridgewater (G-857)
Malcam US ....G 973 218-2461
Short Hills (G-9981)
Marine Electric Systems Inc ....E 201 531-8600
South Hackensack (G-10278)
▲ Marotta Controls Inc ....C 973 334-7800
Montville (G-6490)
Matrix Controls Company Inc ....F 732 469-5551
Somerset (G-10132)
Mayfair Tech Ltd Lblty Co ....F 609 802-1262
Princeton (G-9071)
Measurement Control Corp ....G 800 504-9010
West Orange (G-11899)
Mesa Laboratories Inc ....E 973 492-8400
Butler (G-1012)
▲ Meson Group Inc ....E 201 767-7300
Northvale (G-7591)
Micro-Tek Laboratories Inc ....G 973 779-5577
Clifton (G-1674)
▼ Multiforce Systems Corporation .....F 609 683-4242
Princeton (G-9079)
Netquest Corporation ....E 856 866-0505
Mount Laurel (G-6822)
▲ NM Knight Co Inc ....G 856 327-4855
Millville (G-6316)
Omega Engineering Inc ....F 856 467-4200
Swedesboro (G-10716)
Omega Engineering Inc ....C 856 467-4200
Bridgeport (G-769)
Orycon Control Technology Inc ....E 732 922-2400
Ocean (G-7732)
▲ Palmer Electronics Inc ....F 973 772-5900
Garfield (G-3744)
Pavan & Kievit Enterprises ....E 973 546-4615
Garfield (G-3746)
Pressure Controls Inc ....G 973 751-5002
Belleville (G-312)
Process Controls Co ....G 908 269-8465
Chester (G-1438)
Pyrometer Instrument Co Inc ....E 609 443-5522
Windsor (G-12128)
▲ Rees Scientific Corporation ....C 609 530-1055
Ewing (G-3050)
Ribble Company Inc ....F 201 475-1812
Saddle Brook (G-9786)
Rosemount Inc ....F 973 257-2300
Parsippany (G-8082)
▲ Roxboro Holdings Inc ....D 732 919-3119
Wall Township (G-11506)
◆ Sandvik Process Systems Inc ....F 973 720-7000
Totowa (G-10970)
Schneder Elc Bldngs Amrcas Inc .....E 201 348-9240
Secaucus (G-9922)
Siemens Industry Inc ....G 732 302-1686
Warren (G-11567)
Signal Systems International ....F 732 793-4668
Lavallette (G-5237)
Sk & P Industries Inc ....G 973 482-1864
Newark (G-7315)
Sofradir Ec Inc 973 882-0211
Fairfield (G-3307)

▲ Springfeld Prcision Instrs Inc ....E 866 843-3905
Rochelle Park (G-9537)
▼ T A C Technical Instr Corp ....F 609 882-2894
Ewing (G-3059)
Theory Development Corp ....F 201 783-8770
Mahwah (G-5819)
▲ TX Technology Corp ....C 973 442-7500
Denville (G-2061)
V G Controls Inc ....G 973 764-6500
Oakland (G-7709)
Vertiv Services Inc ....E 732 225-3741
Edison (G-2644)

3824 Fluid Meters & Counters

▲ Action Packaging Automation ....G 609 448-9210
Roosevelt (G-9639)
▲ Chem Flowtronic Inc ....G 973 785-0001
Little Falls (G-5474)
Chemiquip Products Co Inc ....G 201 868-4445
Linden (G-5359)
Ellis/Kuhnke Controls Inc ....G 732 291-3334
Eatontown (G-2393)
Heat-Timer Corporation ....E 212 481-2020
Fairfield (G-3219)
Instru-Met Corporation ....G 908 851-0700
Union (G-11195)
▲ Kel Instruments Co Inc ....G 201 847-8353
Wyckoff (G-12255)
◆ Kessler-Ellis Products Co ....D 732 935-1320
Eatontown (G-2410)
▲ Octal Corporation ....E 201 862-1010
Teaneck (G-10764)
◆ Parkeon Inc ....E 856 234-8000
Moorestown (G-6608)
◆ Pemberton Fabricators Inc ....A 609 267-0922
Rancocas (G-9260)
Precision Dealer Services Inc ....E 908 237-1100
Flemington (G-3460)
Rio Supply ....G 856 719-0081
Sicklerville (G-10025)

3825 Instrs For Measuring & Testing Electricity

ABC Digital Electronics Inc ....G 201 666-6888
Old Tappan (G-7796)
Aeronautical Instr & Rdo Co ....E 973 473-0034
Lodi (G-5573)
Agilent Technologies Inc ....E 973 448-7129
Budd Lake (G-923)
◆ Alltest Instruments Inc ....F 732 919-3339
Farmingdale (G-3376)
Alpha Scientific Corporation ....G 908 534-9941
Whitehouse Station (G-12049)
▼ Applied Resources Corp ....E 973 328-3882
Wharton (G-11980)
Ballantine Laboratories Inc ....G 908 713-7742
Annandale (G-56)
Boonton Electronics Corp ....E 201 261-8797
Parsippany (G-7963)
Brookdale Senior Living Inc ....F 856 772-9400
Voorhees (G-11423)
◆ Btech Inc ....E 973 983-1120
Rockaway (G-9555)
▲ Buttonwood Enterprises LLC ....G 201 505-1901
Woodcliff Lake (G-12184)
Byram Laboratories Inc ....E 908 252-0852
Branchburg (G-646)
Celco ....F 201 327-1123
Mahwah (G-5757)
Cisco Systems Inc ....E 201 782-0842
Montvale (G-6448)
◆ Communication Devices Inc ....F 973 334-1980
Boonton (G-560)
Custom Metering Company Inc ....G 973 946-4195
Branchville (G-729)
Datalink Solutions Inc ....F 973 731-9373
West Orange (G-11893)
Dbmcorp Inc ....F 201 677-0008
Oakland (G-7683)
Dranetz Technologies Inc ....D 732 248-4358
Edison (G-2503)
Eastern Instrumentation of ....G 856 231-0668
Moorestown (G-6573)
Electro Impulse Laboratory Inc ....E 732 776-5800
Neptune (G-6910)
EMD Performance Materials Corp .....B 908 429-3500
Branchburg (G-657)
Energy Tracking LLC ....G 973 448-8660
Flanders (G-3407)

Global Power Technology Inc ....D.... 732 287-3680
  Edison *(G-2528)*

Glow Tube Inc ....G.... 609 268-7707
  Shamong *(G-9969)*

Hamamatsu Corporation ....E.... 908 526-0941
  Bridgewater *(G-842)*

▼ Imperial Machine & Tool Co ....E.... 908 496-8100
  Columbia *(G-1798)*

Instru-Met Corporation ....G.... 908 851-0700
  Union *(G-11195)*

Intertek Laboratories Inc ....E.... 908 903-1800
  Stirling *(G-10601)*

▲ Intest Corporation ....G.... 856 505-8800
  Mount Laurel *(G-6807)*

Janke & Company Inc ....G.... 973 334-4477
  Boonton *(G-573)*

▲ Keyence Corporation America ....E.... 201 930-0100
  Elmwood Park *(G-2828)*

Link Computer Graphics Inc ....G.... 973 808-8990
  Fairfield *(G-3253)*

Linseis Inc ....G.... 609 223-2070
  Trenton *(G-11076)*

Marine Electric Systems Inc ....E.... 201 531-8600
  South Hackensack *(G-10278)*

Microdysis Inc ....G.... 609 642-1184
  Bordentown *(G-604)*

Mistras Group Inc ....G.... 609 716-4000
  Princeton Junction *(G-9159)*

Mmtc Inc ....G.... 609 520-9699
  Princeton *(G-9076)*

▲ Multi-Tech Industries Inc ....F.... 732 431-0550
  Marlboro *(G-5948)*

Nanion Technologies Inc ....G.... 973 369-7960
  Livingston *(G-5551)*

Nice Instrumentation ....F.... 732 851-4300
  Manalapan *(G-5855)*

Omnitester Corp ....F.... 856 985-8960
  Marlton *(G-5991)*

Panel Components & Systems ....F.... 973 448-9400
  Stanhope *(G-10589)*

Photonics Management Corp ....G.... 908 231-0960
  Bridgewater *(G-874)*

Powercomm Solutions LLC ....G.... 908 806-7025
  Flemington *(G-3459)*

Pulsar Microwave Corp ....G.... 973 779-6262
  Clifton *(G-1706)*

Quantem Corp ....E.... 609 883-9191
  Ewing *(G-3047)*

Radcom Equipment Inc ....G.... 201 518-0033
  Paramus *(G-7898)*

▲ Rf Vii Inc ....F.... 856 875-2121
  Newfield *(G-7371)*

▲ RSR Electronics Inc ....E.... 732 381-8777
  Rahway *(G-9222)*

▲ Sadelco Inc ....D.... 201 569-3323
  Fort Lee *(G-3581)*

▲ Satec Inc ....E.... 908 258-0924
  Union *(G-11221)*

Seaboard Instrument Co ....G.... 609 641-5300
  Pleasantville *(G-8914)*

Seren Inc ....E.... 856 205-1131
  Vineland *(G-11402)*

▲ Sherry International Inc ....F.... 908 279-7255
  Warren *(G-11566)*

Signal Crafters Tech Inc ....G.... 973 781-0880
  East Hanover *(G-2243)*

Spectrum Instrumentation Corp ....E.... 201 562-1999
  Hackensack *(G-3980)*

▲ Tcp Reliable Inc ....G.... 848 229-2466
  Edison *(G-2638)*

Tel-Instrument Elec Corp ....E.... 201 933-1600
  East Rutherford *(G-2332)*

Thomas Instrumentation Inc ....F.... 609 624-2630
  Cape May Court House *(G-1118)*

▼ Waveline Incorporated ....E.... 973 226-9100
  Fairfield *(G-3350)*

Wireless Telecom Group Inc ....D.... 973 386-9696
  Parsippany *(G-8114)*

▲ Zixel Ltd ....G.... 732 972-3287
  Morganville *(G-6657)*

3826 Analytical Instruments

Acustrip Co Inc ....F.... 973 299-8237
  Denville *(G-2029)*

Acustrip Co Inc ....G.... 973 299-8237
  Mountain Lakes *(G-6853)*

Advanced Imaging Assoc LLC ....G.... 973 823-8999
  Franklin *(G-3593)*

Advanced Technical Support Inc ....D.... 609 298-2522
  Bordentown *(G-589)*

Airscan Inc ....G.... 908 823-9425
  Lebanon *(G-5274)*

◆ Analytical Sales and Svcs Inc ....F.... 973 616-0700
  Flanders *(G-3401)*

Arrow Engineering Co Inc ....G.... 908 353-5229
  Hillside *(G-4391)*

Becton Dickinson and Company ....A.... 201 847-6800
  Franklin Lakes *(G-3610)*

▲ Belair Instrument Company LLC ....E.... 973 912-8900
  Springfield *(G-10542)*

Bergen Open Mri ....G.... 201 652-1213
  Paramus *(G-7858)*

Beta Industries Corp ....E.... 201 939-2400
  Carlstadt *(G-1130)*

Biomedicon ....F.... 856 778-1880
  Moorestown *(G-6563)*

Bios International Corp ....E.... 973 492-8400
  Butler *(G-998)*

▲ C W Brabender Instrs Inc ....E.... 201 343-8425
  South Hackensack *(G-10256)*

▲ Cargille-Sacher Labs Inc ....E.... 973 239-6633
  Cedar Grove *(G-1274)*

Denville Diagnostics Imaging ....E.... 973 586-1212
  Denville *(G-2035)*

Distek Inc ....D.... 732 422-7585
  North Brunswick *(G-7516)*

Dolce Technologies LLC ....G.... 609 497-7319
  Princeton *(G-9031)*

▲ Dynatec Systems Inc ....F.... 609 387-0330
  Burlington *(G-970)*

E S Industries Inc ....G.... 856 753-8400
  West Berlin *(G-11717)*

▲ Eci Technology Inc ....C.... 973 773-8686
  Totowa *(G-10942)*

Edax Inc ....D.... 201 529-4880
  Mahwah *(G-5769)*

Evex Analytical Instruments ....F.... 609 252-9192
  Princeton *(G-9042)*

▲ Ezose Sciences Inc ....G.... 862 926-1950
  Florham Park *(G-3502)*

Fisher Scientific Chemical Div ....E.... 609 633-1422
  Fair Lawn *(G-3092)*

Garden State Mgntc Imaging PC ....F.... 609 581-2727
  Pennsauken *(G-8514)*

▲ Horiba Instruments Inc ....C.... 732 494-8660
  Piscataway *(G-8776)*

Hudson Robotics Inc ....F.... 973 376-7400
  Springfield *(G-10556)*

Isocolor Inc ....G.... 201 935-4494
  Carlstadt *(G-1173)*

JFK Medical Group PC ....F.... 732 632-1650
  Edison *(G-2544)*

M D Laboratory Supplies Inc ....G.... 732 322-0773
  Franklin Park *(G-3628)*

Mesa Laboratories- Bgi Inc ....E.... 973 492-8400
  Butler *(G-1013)*

Microdysis Inc ....G.... 609 642-1184
  Bordentown *(G-604)*

▲ Microsolv Technology Corp ....F.... 732 578-1777
  Eatontown *(G-2413)*

▼ Mnemonics Inc ....G.... 856 234-0970
  Mount Laurel *(G-6820)*

Moa Instrumentation Inc ....G.... 215 547-8308
  Lawrenceville *(G-5264)*

▲ National Labnet Co ....G.... 732 417-0700
  Iselin *(G-4636)*

New ERA Enterprises Inc ....G.... 856 794-2005
  Newfield *(G-7368)*

Novartis Pharmaceuticals Corp ....G.... 862 778-8300
  East Hanover *(G-2236)*

Packaged Gas Systems Inc ....G.... 908 755-2780
  Springfield *(G-10569)*

Perma Pure LLC ....G.... 732 244-0010
  Lakewood *(G-5170)*

▲ Princeton Biomeditech Corp ....D.... 732 274-1000
  Monmouth Junction *(G-6356)*

Princeton Chromatography Inc ....G.... 609 860-1803
  Cranbury *(G-1872)*

Princeton Research Instruments ....G.... 609 924-0570
  Princeton *(G-9101)*

Princeton Separations Inc ....E.... 732 431-3338
  Freehold *(G-3683)*

Pulsetor LLC ....G.... 609 303-0578
  Lambertville *(G-5220)*

Rame-Hart Inc ....G.... 973 335-0560
  Randolph *(G-9295)*

Rame-Hart Instrument Co LLC ....G.... 973 448-0305
  Succasunna *(G-10628)*

Roche Diagnostics Corporation ....F.... 908 253-0707
  Branchburg *(G-700)*

Rudolph Instruments Inc ....G.... 973 227-0139
  Denville *(G-2057)*

Setaram Inc ....G.... 908 262-7060
  Cranbury *(G-1879)*

▲ Siemens Med Sltons Diagnostics .....A.... 973 927-2828
  Flanders *(G-3416)*

Sophion Bioscience Inc ....G.... 732 745-0221
  Paramus *(G-7905)*

Spark Holland Inc ....G.... 609 799-7250
  Sicklerville *(G-10026)*

▲ Temptime Corporation ....D.... 973 984-6000
  Morris Plains *(G-6680)*

Tess-Com Inc ....E.... 412 233-5782
  Middlesex *(G-6205)*

Thermo Fisher Scientific Inc ....F.... 609 239-3185
  Burlington *(G-991)*

Thermo Fisher Scientific Inc ....F.... 732 627-0220
  Somerset *(G-10187)*

▲ Thorlabs Inc ....C.... 973 579-7227
  Newton *(G-7410)*

▲ Topcon Medical Systems Inc ....D.... 201 599-5100
  Oakland *(G-7707)*

Veeco Process Equipment Inc ....C.... 732 560-5300
  Somerset *(G-10194)*

Waters Technologies Corp ....F.... 973 394-5660
  Parsippany *(G-8111)*

3827 Optical Instruments

21st Century Optics Inc ....G.... 808 935-1119
  Warren *(G-11533)*

Anchor Optical Co ....C.... 856 546-1965
  Barrington *(G-170)*

API Nanofabrication & RES Corp ....F.... 732 627-0808
  Somerset *(G-10059)*

Argyle International Inc ....G.... 609 924-9484
  Princeton *(G-9008)*

Artemis Optics and Coatings ....G.... 201 847-0887
  Emerson *(G-2857)*

Avantier Inc ....G.... 732 491-8150
  Metuchen *(G-6095)*

Cercis Inc ....G.... 609 737-5120
  Pennington *(G-8445)*

Cgm Us Inc ....E.... 609 894-4420
  Birmingham *(G-467)*

Chiral Photonics Inc ....F.... 973 732-0030
  Pine Brook *(G-8692)*

Coherent Inc ....D.... 973 240-6851
  East Hanover *(G-2207)*

▲ Datacolor Inc ....D.... 609 924-2189
  Lawrenceville *(G-5256)*

Esco Products Inc ....E.... 973 697-3700
  Oak Ridge *(G-7662)*

▲ High Vision Corporation ....G.... 862 238-7636
  Clifton *(G-1641)*

Ii-VI Wide Band Gap Inc ....G.... 973 227-1551
  Pine Brook *(G-8705)*

Inlc Technology Corporation ....F.... 908 834-8390
  Warren *(G-11556)*

Inrad Optics Inc ....D.... 201 767-1910
  Northvale *(G-7585)*

▼ Integrated Photonics Inc ....D.... 908 281-8000
  Hillsborough *(G-4348)*

Integrated Photonics Inc ....G.... 908 281-8000
  Hillsborough *(G-4349)*

◆ International Crystal Labs ....E.... 973 478-8944
  Garfield *(G-3739)*

Krell Technologies Inc ....G.... 732 617-7091
  Neptune *(G-6921)*

▲ M H Optical Supplies Inc ....E.... 800 445-3090
  South Hackensack *(G-10277)*

MRC Precision Metal Optics Inc ....E.... 941 753-8707
  Northvale *(G-7592)*

Nano-Optic Devices LLC ....F.... 201 594-0226
  Twp Washinton *(G-11143)*

Nanoopto Corporation ....E.... 732 627-0808
  Somerset *(G-10143)*

Norland Products Inc ....E.... 609 395-1966
  Cranbury *(G-1863)*

▲ O & S Research Inc ....E.... 856 829-2800
  Cinnaminson *(G-1481)*

Opt-Sciences Corporation ....F.... 856 829-2800
  Cinnaminson *(G-1482)*

Polarity LLC ....G.... 732 970-3855
  Morganville *(G-6652)*

Princeton Instruments Inc ....G.... 609 587-9797
  Trenton *(G-11106)*

Quantum Coating Inc ....E.... 856 234-5444
  Moorestown *(G-6617)*

Refac Optical Group ....E.... 856 228-1000
  Blackwood *(G-490)*

Roper Scientific Inc ....D...... 520 889-9933
Trenton (G-11114)

Rudolph RES Analytical Corp ....D...... 973 584-1558
Hackettstown (G-4034)

Shanghai Optics Inc ....F...... 732 321-6915
Clark (G-1515)

Sheridan Optical Co Inc ....E...... 856 582-0963
Pitman (G-8846)

Special Optics Inc ....F...... 973 366-7289
Denville (G-2059)

Tag Optics Inc ....G...... 609 356-2142
Princeton (G-9128)

▲ Topcon Medical Systems Inc ....D...... 201 599-5100
Oakland (G-7707)

▲ US Vision Inc ....B...... 856 227-8339
Glendora (G-3833)

Veeco Instruments Inc ....E...... 732 560-5300
Somerset (G-10193)

3829 Measuring & Controlling Devices, NEC

Advanced Shore Imaging Associa ....F...... 732 678-0087
Northfield (G-7562)

AIG Industrial Group Inc ....F...... 201 767-7300
Northvale (G-7569)

Akers Biosciences Inc ....E...... 856 848-8698
West Deptford (G-11814)

Alison Control Inc ....E...... 973 575-7100
Fairfield (G-3130)

Amcor Phrm Packg USA LLC ....C...... 856 825-1100
Millville (G-6280)

American Gas & Chemical Co Ltd.......E...... 201 767-7300
Northvale (G-7572)

◆ American Sensor Tech Inc ....D...... 973 448-1901
Budd Lake (G-924)

Ballantine Laboratories Inc ....E...... 908 713-7742
Annandale (G-56)

Becton Dickinson and Company ....A...... 201 847-6800
Franklin Lakes (G-3610)

Boonton Electronics Corp ....E...... 201 261-8797
Parsippany (G-7963)

▲ C W Brabender Instrs Inc ....E...... 201 343-8425
South Hackensack (G-10256)

▲ Capintec Inc ....E...... 201 825-9500
Florham Park (G-3495)

Checkpoint Security Systems Gr ....C...... 952 933-8858
West Deptford (G-11820)

Checkpoint Systems Inc ....C...... 952 933-8858
West Deptford (G-11823)

▲ Conistics Inc ....G...... 609 584-2600
Hamilton (G-4105)

▲ Coperion K-Tron Pitman Inc ....F...... 856 589-0500
Sewell (G-9947)

▼ Delmhorst Instrument Company ......E...... 973 334-2557
Towaco (G-10992)

Delphian Corporation ....C...... 201 767-7300
Northvale (G-7577)

Digital Binscom LLC ....G...... 908 867-7055
Long Valley (G-5636)

Digivac Company ....F...... 732 765-0900
Matawan (G-6017)

Dranetz Technologies Inc ....D...... 732 248-4358
Edison (G-2503)

▲ DRG International Inc ....E...... 973 564-7555
Springfield (G-10551)

Edax Inc ....D...... 201 529-4880
Mahwah (G-5769)

▲ Euroimmun US Inc ....E...... 973 656-1000
Mountain Lakes (G-6858)

Fluitec International LLC.................G...... 201 946-4584
Bayonne (G-226)

G E Inspection Technologies LP ....D...... 973 448-0077
Flanders (G-3409)

G R Bowler Inc ....G...... 973 525-5172
Andover (G-50)

H S Martin Company Inc ....F...... 856 692-8700
Vineland (G-11368)

Howard A Schaevitz Tech Inc ....E...... 856 662-8000
Budd Lake (G-931)

Innerspace Technology Inc ....G...... 201 933-1600
Carlstadt (G-1172)

Instru-Met Corporation ....G...... 908 851-0700
Union (G-11195)

Instrument Sciences & Tech ....D...... 908 996-9920
Frenchtown (G-3702)

▲ Kanomax Usa Inc ....G...... 973 786-6386
Byram Township (G-1022)

Leak Detection Associates ....G...... 856 401-7718
Vineland (G-11379)

Life Recovery Systems Hd LLC ....G...... 973 283-2800
Kinnelon (G-5038)

▲ Lumiscope Co Inc ....D...... 678 291-3207
East Rutherford (G-2306)

Mab Enterprises Inc ....F...... 973 345-8282
Paterson (G-8328)

Macro Sensors ....F...... 856 662-8000
Budd Lake (G-935)

Magnetic Products and Svcs Inc.......G...... 732 264-6651
Holmdel (G-4520)

Mallinckrodt LLC ....F...... 908 238-6600
Hampton (G-4164)

▲ Maquet Cardiovascular LLC ....D...... 973 709-7000
Wayne (G-11663)

Marine Cont Eqp Crtfction Corp ....G...... 732 938-6622
Farmingdale (G-3389)

Mdr Diagnostics LLC ....G...... 609 396-0021
Mount Laurel (G-6817)

▼ Medical Indicators Inc ....G...... 609 737-1600
Hamilton (G-4114)

▲ Meson Group Inc ....E...... 201 767-7300
Northvale (G-7591)

Micro-Tek Laboratories Inc ....G...... 973 779-5577
Clifton (G-1674)

Mistras Group Inc ....C...... 609 716-4000
Princeton Junction (G-9159)

Netquest Corporation ....E...... 856 866-0505
Mount Laurel (G-6822)

▲ Northwest Instrument Inc.............G...... 973 347-6830
Dover (G-2105)

▼ Orlando Systems Ltd Lblty Co ....G...... 908 400-5052
North Plainfield (G-7560)

▲ Palmer Electronics Inc ....F...... 973 772-5900
Garfield (G-3744)

Physical Acoustics Corporation ....C...... 609 716-4000
Princeton Junction (G-9162)

Ptc Electronics Inc ....G...... 201 847-0500
Mahwah (G-5804)

Radcom Equipment Inc ....G...... 201 518-0033
Paramus (G-7898)

Reliability Maintenance Svcs ....G...... 732 922-8878
Ocean (G-7741)

Roper Scientific Inc ....D...... 520 889-9933
Trenton (G-11114)

Rudolph Technologies Inc ....D...... 973 347-3891
Budd Lake (G-941)

▲ S & G Tool Aid Corporation ....D...... 973 824-7730
Newark (G-7297)

Science Pump Corporation ....E...... 856 963-7700
Camden (G-1085)

Scientific Machine and Sup Co.......G...... 732 356-1553
Middlesex (G-6195)

◆ Scientific Sales Inc ....F...... 609 844-0055
Lawrenceville (G-5268)

▼ Sensor Scientific Inc ....E...... 973 227-7790
Fairfield (G-3305)

SGS UStesting Company ....F...... 973 575-5252
Fairfield (G-3306)

Shock Tech Inc ....E...... 845 368-8600
Mahwah (G-5812)

▲ Sigma-Netics Inc ....E...... 973 227-6372
Riverdale (G-9488)

▲ Springfeld Prcision Instrs Inc ....E...... 866 843-3905
Rochelle Park (G-9537)

Sun Coast Precision Instrument ....G...... 646 852-2331
Cresskill (G-1949)

▲ Superior Signal Company LLC ....F...... 732 251-0800
Old Bridge (G-7793)

Tel-Instrument Elec Corp ....E...... 201 933-1600
East Rutherford (G-2332)

Theory Development Corp ....F...... 201 783-8770
Mahwah (G-5819)

Thwing-Albert Instrument Co ....D...... 856 767-1000
West Berlin (G-11757)

▲ Topcon Medical Systems Inc ....D...... 201 599-5100
Oakland (G-7707)

▲ Transistor Devices Inc ....C...... 908 850-5088
Hackettstown (G-4041)

▲ United Instrument Company LLC.......G...... 201 767-6000
Northvale (G-7610)

Venkateshwara Inc ....F...... 908 964-4777
Somerset (G-10195)

▼ William Kenyon & Sons Inc ....E...... 732 985-8980
Piscataway (G-8836)

3841 Surgical & Medical Instrs & Apparatus

3M Company ....B...... 973 884-2500
Whippany (G-12004)

3M Company ....C...... 908 788-4000
Flemington (G-3422)

▲ A D M Tronics Unlimited Inc ....E...... 201 767-6040
Northvale (G-7566)

A&E Advnced Clsure Systems LLC ......E...... 732 938-2266
Wall Township (G-11459)

Aarisse Health Care Products ....G...... 973 686-1811
Wayne (G-11600)

Abbott Point of Care Inc ....C...... 609 454-9000
Princeton (G-8993)

Abbott Point of Care Inc ....C...... 609 371-8923
East Windsor (G-2339)

▲ Acme International Inc ....G...... 973 594-4866
Clifton (G-1557)

Advanced Precision Inc ....E...... 800 788-9473
Sparta (G-10485)

▲ Alfa Wassermann Inc ....C...... 973 882-8630
West Caldwell (G-11763)

Alfa Wssrmann Dagnstc Tech LLC ......F...... 800 220-4488
West Caldwell (G-11764)

▲ Allergan Inc ....A...... 862 261-7000
Madison (G-5718)

Allergan Holdco Us Inc ....A...... 862 261-7000
Parsippany (G-7943)

Alto Development Corp ....D...... 732 938-2266
Wall Township (G-11461)

▲ America Techma Inc ....G...... 201 894-5887
Englewood Cliffs (G-2948)

American Diagnstc Imaging Inc ....F...... 973 980-1724
Nutley (G-7639)

▲ Anderson Tool & Die Corp ....E...... 908 862-5550
Linden (G-5349)

Antares Pharma Inc ....C...... 609 359-3020
Ewing (G-3003)

Artegraft Inc ....F...... 732 422-8333
North Brunswick (G-7504)

Ascensia Diabetes Care US Inc ....C...... 973 560-6500
Parsippany (G-7952)

Automated Medical Pdts Corp.......G...... 732 602-7717
Sewaren (G-9943)

Baeta Corp ....G...... 201 471-0988
Fort Lee (G-3545)

Bahadir USA LLC ....G...... 856 517-3080
Carneys Point (G-1244)

▲ Bard Healthcare Inc ....F...... 908 277-8000
New Providence (G-7028)

Baxter Healthcare Corporation ....D...... 856 489-2104
Cherry Hill (G-1346)

◆ Bayer Corporation ....A...... 412 777-2000
Whippany (G-12007)

◆ Bayer Healthcare LLC ....A...... 862 404-3000
Whippany (G-12008)

Bayer Hlthcare Phrmcticals Inc ....E...... 973 709-3545
Whippany (G-12010)

▲ Bayer Hlthcare Phrmcticals Inc ....A...... 862 404-3000
Whippany (G-12011)

Bbg Surgical Ltd Liability Co ....G...... 551 404-7920
Lakewood (G-5082)

Bd Ventures LLC ....E...... 201 847-6800
Franklin Lakes (G-3609)

Becton Dickinson and Company ....A...... 201 847-6800
Franklin Lakes (G-3610)

▲ Belair Instrument Company LLC ......E...... 973 912-8900
Springfield (G-10542)

Beltor Manufacturing Corp ....G...... 856 768-5570
Berlin (G-426)

Bernafon LLC ....G...... 888 941-4203
Somerset (G-10069)

◆ Bio Compression Systems Inc.......E...... 201 939-0716
Moonachie (G-6508)

Biodynamics LLC ....G...... 201 227-9255
Englewood (G-2876)

Biomedicon ....F...... 856 778-1880
Moorestown (G-6563)

Biosearch Medical Products Inc.......D...... 908 252-0595
Branchburg (G-644)

Bipore Inc ....F...... 201 767-1993
Northvale (G-7575)

BMA of Colonia ....G...... 732 382-7333
Colonia (G-1777)

Boston Scientific Corporation ....E...... 973 709-7000
Wayne (G-11612)

Burpee Medsystems LLC ....G...... 732 544-8900
Eatontown (G-2387)

▲ C R Bard Inc ....C...... 908 277-8000
New Providence (G-7032)

C R Bard Inc ....G...... 856 461-0946
Delran (G-2013)

▲ Canfield Property Group Inc ....C...... 973 276-0300
Fairfield (G-3155)

◆ Cantel Medical Corp ....G...... 973 890-7220
Little Falls (G-5471)

▲ Capintec Inc ....E...... 201 825-9500
Florham Park (G-3495)

Cardan Medical Products Inc.............G...... 908 964-0800
Union *(G-11162)*

▲ Catalent Pharma Solutions Inc ......B...... 732 537-6200
Somerset *(G-10078)*

Catheter Precision Inc....................F...... 973 691-2000
Ledgewood *(G-5304)*

Cedge Industries Inc.....................F...... 201 641-3222
Ridgefield Park *(G-9400)*

Cenogenics Corporation ....G...... 732 536-6457
Morganville *(G-6638)*

Ch Technologies USA Inc................G...... 201 666-2335
Westwood *(G-11957)*

Clinical Image Retrieval Syste 888 482-2362
Franklin *(G-3597)*

▲ Clordisys Solutions Inc ....E...... 908 236-4100
Branchburg *(G-647)*

Collagen Matrix Inc.......................F...... 201 786-9300
Allendale *(G-7)*

Collagen Matrix Inc.......................D...... 201 405-1477
Oakland *(G-7679)*

▲ Convatec Inc ....B...... 908 904-2500
Bridgewater *(G-829)*

Cordis International Corp...............A...... 732 524-0400
New Brunswick *(G-6953)*

Cranial Technologies Inc...............G...... 201 265-3993
Paramus *(G-7863)*

▲ Crest Ultrasonics Corp ....G...... 609 883-4000
Ewing *(G-3011)*

▲ Crestek Inc ....E...... 609 883-4000
Ewing *(G-3012)*

Cross Medical Specialties Inc........G...... 856 589-3288
Pitman *(G-8841)*

Cura Biomed Inc ....G...... 609 647-1474
Princeton Junction *(G-9151)*

Cytosorbents Corporation ....E...... 732 329-8885
Monmouth Junction *(G-6339)*

Cytosorbents Medical Inc ....E...... 732 329-8885
Monmouth Junction *(G-6340)*

Data Medical Inc ....F...... 800 790-9978
North Bergen *(G-7445)*

Datascope Corp ....E...... 201 995-8000
Mahwah *(G-5762)*

Datascope Corp ....F...... 800 777-4222
Mahwah *(G-5763)*

Dexmed Inc ....G...... 732 831-0507
Elizabeth *(G-2724)*

Dexmed LLC ....G...... 732 831-0507
Elizabeth *(G-2725)*

Diabeto Inc ....G...... 646 397-3175
Piscataway *(G-8758)*

▲ Diagnostix Plus Inc ....G...... 201 530-5505
Teaneck *(G-10748)*

Difco Laboratories Inc ....G...... 410 316-4113
Franklin Lakes *(G-3613)*

▼ Diopsys Inc ....E...... 973 244-0622
Pine Brook *(G-8699)*

▲ Dynasil Corporation America.......G...... 856 767-4600
West Berlin *(G-11716)*

Edda Technology Inc ....F...... 609 919-9889
Princeton *(G-9036)*

Ellis Instruments Inc ....G...... 973 593-9222
Madison *(G-5722)*

▼ Emse Corp ....F...... 973 227-9221
Fairfield *(G-3184)*

Endomedix 848 248-1883
Newark *(G-7154)*

Exalenz Bioscience Inc ....E...... 732 232-4393
Wall Township *(G-11480)*

◆ Excelsior Medical LLC................C...... 732 776-7525
Neptune *(G-6911)*

Ferry Machine Corp ....F...... 201 641-9191
Little Ferry *(G-5504)*

Fresenius Med Care Hldings Inc ....G...... 201 767-7700
Rockleigh *(G-9629)*

Garden State Medical Sup LLC ......G...... 732 348-0312
Lakewood *(G-5127)*

General Graphics Corporation ....G...... 201 664-4083
Hillsdale *(G-4383)*

▲ Genesis Bps LLC ....E...... 201 708-1400
Ramsey *(G-9241)*

Getinge Group Logistics Americ.........E...... 973 709-6000
Wayne *(G-11640)*

Gibraltar Laboratories Inc 973 227-6882
Fairfield *(G-3209)*

Glastron Inc 856 692-0500
Vineland *(G-11363)*

◆ Globe Scientific Inc ....E...... 201 599-1400
Paramus *(G-7873)*

Graydon Products Inc 856 234-9513
Mooréstown *(G-6580)*

H & W Tool Co Inc ....F...... 973 366-0131
Dover *(G-2088)*

H Galow Co Inc 201 768-0547
Norwood *(G-7624)*

Haldor USA Inc ....E...... 856 254-2345
Cherry Hill *(G-1373)*

Haz Laboratories ....G...... 908 453-3300
Washington *(G-11582)*

Health Care Alert LLC ....F...... 732 676-2630
Middletown *(G-6216)*

Healthcare Cart ....G...... 201 406-4797
Blairstown *(G-496)*

Howmedica Osteonics Corp ....G...... 201 541-6569
Englewood *(G-2903)*

Hydromer Inc ....C...... 908 526-2828
Branchburg *(G-665)*

▲ IDL Techni-Edge LLC ....C...... 908 497-9818
Kenilworth *(G-4962)*

Immunostics Inc ....G...... 732 918-0770
Eatontown *(G-2405)*

▲ Immunostics Company Inc ....G...... 732 918-0770
Eatontown *(G-2406)*

▲ Instride Shoes LLC ....E...... 908 874-6670
Hillsborough *(G-4347)*

▼ Integra Lfscnces Holdings Corp.......C...... 609 275-0500
Plainsboro *(G-8887)*

Integra Lifesciences Corp ....C...... 609 275-2700
Plainsboro *(G-8888)*

Integra Lifesciences Corp ....C...... 609 275-2700
Plainsboro *(G-8890)*

Integra Lifesciences Corp ....D...... 609 275-0500
Plainsboro *(G-8889)*

Integra Lifesciences Sales LLC ....B...... 609 275-0500
Plainsboro *(G-8891)*

Intercure Inc ....E...... 973 893-5653
Montclair *(G-6419)*

Ivy Sports Medicine LLC ....G...... 201 573-5423
Montvale *(G-6462)*

Jaktool LLC ....F...... 609 664-2451
Cranbury *(G-1844)*

Jnj International Inv LLC ....G...... 732 524-0400
New Brunswick *(G-6973)*

Johnson & Johnson ....G...... 908 722-9319
Raritan *(G-9311)*

Johnson & Johnson ....C...... 908 874-1000
Morris Plains *(G-6673)*

Johnson & Johnson ....C...... 732 524-0400
New Brunswick *(G-6975)*

◆ Johnson & Johnson ....A...... 732 524-0400
New Brunswick *(G-6974)*

Jrh Service & Sales LLC ....G...... 908 832-9266
Lebanon *(G-5294)*

◆ L & R Manufacturing Co Inc ......D...... 201 991-5330
Kearny *(G-4894)*

Laboratory Diagnostics Co Inc.........F...... 732 536-6300
Morganville *(G-6646)*

Laboratory Diagnostics Co Inc.........G...... 732 972-2145
Morganville *(G-6647)*

▲ Lumiscope Co Inc ....D...... 678 291-3207
East Rutherford *(G-2306)*

▲ Maddak Inc ....G...... 973 628-7600
Wayne *(G-11661)*

Mallinckrodt LLC ....F...... 908 238-6600
Hampton *(G-4164)*

Maxter Corporation ....G...... 609 877-9700
Willingboro *(G-12120)*

Medical Innovation Group LLC ......G...... 832 348-6460
Basking Ridge *(G-197)*

Medicraft Inc ....E...... 201 797-8820
Elmwood Park *(G-2835)*

▲ Medin Technologies Inc ....G...... 973 779-2400
Totowa *(G-10955)*

Medinol Usa Inc ....E...... 201 654-4534
Parsippany *(G-8044)*

Mediscope Manufacturing Inc ....G...... 908 756-2411
Watchung *(G-11593)*

Medpen Inc ....G...... 973 627-8067
Denville *(G-2048)*

◆ Medplast Medical Inc ....G...... 908 561-0717
South Plainfield *(G-10405)*

Medplast Medical Inc ....F...... 732 356-0689
Middlesex *(G-6179)*

Medtronic Usa Inc ....G...... 973 331-7914
Parsippany *(G-8045)*

▲ Micro Stamping Corporation ....C...... 732 302-0800
Somerset *(G-10138)*

Microdose Therapeutx Inc ....E...... 732 355-2100
Ewing *(G-3037)*

◆ Mindray Ds Usa Inc ....A...... 201 995-8000
Mahwah *(G-5791)*

◆ Nephros Inc...............................G...... 201 343-5202
South Orange *(G-10312)*

New American Therapeutics Inc.........G...... 908 282-7444
Haskell *(G-4211)*

Newton Memorial Hospital Inc ....G...... 973 726-0904
Sparta *(G-10514)*

Next Medical Products LLC ....F...... 908 722-4549
Branchburg *(G-682)*

Nextgen Edge Inc ....G...... 610 507-6904
West Milford *(G-11855)*

Northeast Medical Systems Corp.........G...... 856 910-8111
Cherry Hill *(G-1405)*

Nu-Stent Technologies Inc ....G...... 732 729-6270
Hillsborough *(G-4360)*

Oncode-Med Inc ....G...... 908 998-3647
Basking Ridge *(G-201)*

Osteotech Inc ....G...... 732 544-5942
Eatontown *(G-2416)*

Osteotech Inc ....C...... 732 542-2800
Eatontown *(G-2417)*

Osteotech Inc ....F...... 732 542-2800
Eatontown *(G-2418)*

▲ P A K Manufacturing Inc............F...... 973 372-1090
Irvington *(G-4599)*

Pentax of America Inc ....G...... 973 628-6200
Montvale *(G-6468)*

Pharmasource International LLC ....G...... 732 985-6182
Piscataway *(G-8800)*

Phillips Precision Inc....................C...... 201 797-8820
Elmwood Park *(G-2843)*

Precise Cmpnents TI Design Inc ....G...... 973 928-2928
Clifton *(G-1702)*

Precision Spine Inc.......................F...... 601 420-4244
Parsippany *(G-8070)*

RB Health Manufacturing US LLC ....B...... 973 404-2600
Parsippany *(G-8075)*

Redfield Corporation ....G...... 201 845-3990
Rochelle Park *(G-9534)*

Respironics Inc ....C...... 973 581-6000
Parsippany *(G-8079)*

▲ Schering Berlin Inc ....G...... 862 404-3000
Whippany *(G-12038)*

Scimedx Corporation ....E...... 800 221-5598
Dover *(G-2109)*

Sensor Medical Technology LLC.........G...... 425 358-7381
Denville *(G-2058)*

Smartekg LLC ....G...... 201 376-4556
Teaneck *(G-10774)*

Somerset Outpatient Surgery ....G...... 781 635-2807
Somerset *(G-10172)*

Spare Pair Vision Center LLC ....G...... 973 758-1151
Livingston *(G-5563)*

State Technology Inc ....G...... 856 467-8009
Bridgeport *(G-773)*

Steris Instrument MGT Svcs Inc.........G...... 908 904-1317
Hillsborough *(G-4373)*

Stryker ....G...... 856 312-0046
Runnemede *(G-9724)*

Stryker Corporation ....D...... 201 760-8000
Allendale *(G-20)*

Teleflex Incorporated ....D...... 856 349-7234
Gloucester City *(G-3846)*

▲ Terumo Americas Holding Inc ....D...... 732 302-4900
Somerset *(G-10184)*

▲ Terumo Medical Corporation ....C...... 732 302-4900
Somerset *(G-10185)*

▲ Topcon Medical Systems Inc ....D...... 201 599-5100
Oakland *(G-7707)*

Total Tech Medical LLC ....G...... 973 980-6458
Dover *(G-2113)*

Tracer Tool & Machine Co Inc ....F...... 201 337-6184
Oakland *(G-7708)*

▲ Trimline Medical Products Corp.........C...... 908 429-0590
Branchburg *(G-713)*

Unionmed Tech Inc ....G...... 917 714-3418
Bridgewater *(G-905)*

United Medical PC ....F...... 201 339-6111
Bayonne *(G-246)*

▲ US China Allied Products Inc.........G...... 201 461-9886
Fort Lee *(G-3587)*

Vascular Therapies LLC ....G...... 201 266-8310
Cresskill *(G-1950)*

Vela Diagnostics USA Inc ....G...... 973 852-3740
Fairfield *(G-3340)*

Vesag Health Inc ....F...... 732 333-1876
North Brunswick *(G-7545)*

Viatar Ctc Solutions Inc................G...... 617 299-6590
Short Hills *(G-9987)*

◆ Viscot Medical LLC....................E...... 973 887-9273
East Hanover *(G-2248)*

S I C

Vitillo & Sons Inc................F....... 732 886-1393
  Lakewood (G-5201)
Vozeh Equipment Corp.............E....... 201 337-3729
  Franklin Lakes (G-3625)
Westcon Orthopedics Inc.............G....... 908 806-8981
  Neshanic Station (G-6940)
▲ Zeus Scientific Inc.............D....... 908 526-3744
  Branchburg (G-722)
Zimmer Trabecular Met Tech Inc ....C....... 973 576-0032
  Parsippany (G-8118)

3842 Orthopedic, Prosthetic & Surgical Appliances/Splys

3M Company.............B....... 973 884-2500
  Whippany (G-12004)
Ace Box Landau Co Inc.............G....... 201 871-4776
  Englewood Cliffs (G-2946)
Achilles Prosthetcs & Orthotcs ....G....... 201 785-9944
  Ramsey (G-9229)
Acuitive Technologies Inc.............F....... 973 617-7175
  Allendale (G-5)
▲ Aetrex Worldwide Inc.............C....... 201 833-2700
  Teaneck (G-10741)
Ahs Hospital Corp.............E....... 908 522-2000
  Summit (G-10633)
Alexander James Corp.............D....... 908 362-9266
  Blairstown (G-494)
Alkaline Corporation.............G....... 732 531-7830
  Eatontown (G-2380)
Alliance Hand & Physical ....F....... 201 822-0100
  Westwood (G-11952)
◆ Ansell Healthcare Products LLC ....C....... 732 345-5400
  Iselin (G-4611)
Ansell Limited.............E....... 732 345-5400
  Iselin (G-4612)
▲ Ansell Protective Products LLC ....A....... 732 345-5400
  Iselin (G-4613)
Araya Inc.............G....... 201 445-7005
  Ridgewood (G-9420)
Atlantic Prsthtic Orthotic Svc ....G....... 609 927-6330
  Linwood (G-5465)
Banding Centers of America.............G....... 973 805-9977
  Florham Park (G-3491)
▲ Bard Devices Inc.............E....... 908 277-8000
  New Providence (G-7027)
▲ Bard Healthcare Inc.............F....... 908 277-8000
  New Providence (G-7028)
Bard International Inc.............D....... 908 277-8000
  New Providence (G-7029)
Bayside Orthopedics LLC.............G....... 732 691-4898
  Toms River (G-10870)
Becton Dickinson and Company ....A....... 201 847-6800
  Franklin Lakes (G-3610)
▲ Belair Instrument Company LLC ...E....... 973 912-8900
  Springfield (G-10542)
▲ Biomet Fair Lawn LP.............F....... 201 797-7300
  Fair Lawn (G-3084)
Boston Scientific Corporation ....E....... 973 709-7000
  Wayne (G-11612)
Brenner Metal Products ....E....... 973 778-2466
  Wallington (G-11523)
Brick City Wheelchair RPS LLC .....G....... 862 371-4311
  Newark (G-7114)
Burpee Medsystems LLC.............G....... 732 544-8900
  Eatontown (G-2387)
▲ C R Bard Inc.............C....... 908 277-8000
  New Providence (G-7032)
Cape Prosthetics-Orthotics ....G....... 856 810-7900
  Marlton (G-5966)
▲ Capintec Inc.............E....... 201 825-9500
  Florham Park (G-3495)
Carry Easy Inc.............E....... 201 944-0042
  Leonia (G-5315)
Ces Imports LLC.............G....... 610 299-7930
  Stone Harbor (G-10614)
Cocco Enterprises Inc.............F....... 609 393-5939
  Trenton (G-11043)
Cranial Technologies Inc.............G....... 908 754-0572
  Edison (G-2494)
Csus LLC.............G....... 973 298-8599
  Rockaway (G-9559)
▲ Derma Sciences Inc.............C....... 609 514-4744
  Plainsboro (G-8880)
Dexmed Inc.............G....... 732 831-0507
  Elizabeth (G-2724)
Dynamic Safety Usa LLC.............G....... 844 378-7200
  Somerset (G-10091)
Eastern Podiatry Labs Inc.............G....... 609 882-4444
  Ewing (G-3015)

▲ Ebi LLC.............A....... 800 526-2579
  Parsippany (G-7995)
Ebi LP.............E....... 973 299-9022
  Parsippany (G-7996)
Ebi Medical Systems LLC.............F....... 973 299-3330
  Parsippany (G-7997)
Edge Orthotics Inc.............G....... 732 549-3343
  Edison (G-2508)
▲ Electric Mobility Corporation ....C....... 856 468-1000
  Sewell (G-9954)
Endotec Inc.............F....... 973 762-6100
  South Orange (G-10304)
◆ Ethicon Inc.............A....... 732 524-0400
  Somerville (G-10207)
Ethicon Inc.............C....... 908 306-0327
  Bedminster (G-272)
Ethicon Inc.............G....... 908 218-0707
  Bedminster (G-273)
Ethicon Inc.............G....... 908 253-6464
  Bridgewater (G-835)
Extremity Medical LLC.............F....... 973 588-8980
  Parsippany (G-8006)
Garden State Orthopedic Center ....G....... 973 538-4948
  Morristown (G-6709)
Garden State Prosthetics ....G....... 732 922-6650
  Ocean (G-7727)
▲ Gemtor Inc.............E....... 732 583-6200
  Matawan (G-6021)
Genzyme Corporation ....G....... 973 256-2106
  Totowa (G-10948)
Grateful Ped Inc.............F....... 973 478-6511
  Saddle Brook (G-9767)
Hanger Prsthetcs & Ortho Inc.............G....... 973 736-0628
  West Orange (G-11897)
Hanger Prsthetcs & Ortho Inc.............G....... 732 919-7774
  Wall Township (G-11486)
Hanger Prsthetcs & Ortho Inc.............G....... 609 653-8323
  Linwood (G-5466)
Hanger Prsthetcs & Ortho Inc.............G....... 609 889-8447
  Rio Grande (G-9458)
Harry J Lawall & Son Inc ....G....... 856 691-7764
  Vineland (G-11369)
Healqu LLC.............G....... 844 443-2578
  Jersey City (G-4764)
Healthcaredepotonlinecom Inc ....G....... 732 761-9600
  Edison (G-2536)
▲ Howmedica Osteonics Corp ....C....... 201 831-5000
  Mahwah (G-5783)
Icon Orthopedic Concepts LLC ....G....... 973 794-6810
  Boonton (G-571)
Independence Technology LLC ....F....... 908 722-3767
  Somerville (G-10215)
Infront Medical LLC.............G....... 888 515-2532
  Clifton (G-1646)
▼ Integra Lfscnces Holdings Corp ....C....... 609 275-0500
  Plainsboro (G-8887)
Ivy Capital Partners LLC.............G....... 201 573-8400
  Montvale (G-6461)
▲ J C Orthopedic Inc.............G....... 732 458-7900
  Brick (G-747)
J J L & W Inc.............E....... 856 854-3100
  Magnolia (G-5741)
J M M R Inc.............G....... 201 612-5104
  Fair Lawn (G-3097)
▲ Janssen Ortho LLC.............G....... 609 730-2000
  New Brunswick (G-6971)
Jefferson Prosthetic Orthotic ....G....... 973 762-0780
  South Orange (G-10308)
Jentec Inc.............G....... 201 784-1031
  Northvale (G-7587)
▲ Jerome Group Inc.............G....... 856 234-8600
  West Deptford (G-11831)
Jnj International Inv LLC.............G....... 732 524-0400
  New Brunswick (G-6973)
Johnson & Associates Inc ....G....... 856 228-2175
  Blackwood (G-483)
Johnson & Johnson.............G....... 908 722-9319
  Raritan (G-9311)
Johnson & Johnson.............C....... 908 874-1000
  Morris Plains (G-6673)
Johnson & Johnson.............G....... 732 524-0400
  New Brunswick (G-6975)
◆ Johnson & Johnson.............A....... 732 524-0400
  New Brunswick (G-6974)
Johnson & Johnson Medical Inc ....G....... 908 218-0707
  Somerville (G-10219)
K & S Drug & Surgical Inc ....G....... 201 886-9191
  Fort Lee (G-3562)
Kingwood Industrial Pdts Inc ....G....... 908 852-8655
  Hackettstown (G-4015)

Lightfield Llr Corporation.............G....... 732 462-9200
  Freehold (G-3668)
▲ Link Bio Inc.............G....... 973 625-1333
  Rockaway (G-9584)
▲ Lumiscope Co Inc.............G....... 678 291-3207
  East Rutherford (G-2306)
M B R Orthotics Inc.............G....... 201 444-7750
  Wyckoff (G-12256)
▲ Mar Machine Ken Manufacturing ...E....... 973 278-5827
  Paterson (G-8331)
Medical Device Bus Svcs Inc.............G....... 732 524-0400
  New Brunswick (G-6980)
Midlantic Medical Systems Inc ....G....... 908 432-4599
  Skillman (G-10033)
Nahallac LLC.............G....... 908 635-0999
  Whitehouse (G-12047)
North Jrsey Prsthtics Orthtics ....G....... 201 943-4448
  Palisades Park (G-7840)
Nouveau Prosthetics Ltd.............F....... 732 739-0888
  Hazlet (G-4280)
Nouveau Prosthetics Orthotics ....G....... 732 739-0888
  Hazlet (G-4281)
Onkos Surgical Inc.............E....... 973 264-5400
  Parsippany (G-8052)
Ortho-Dynamics Inc.............G....... 973 742-4390
  Paterson (G-8357)
▲ Orthofeet Inc.............E....... 800 524-2845
  Northvale (G-7599)
Ossur Americas Inc.............G....... 856 345-6000
  West Deptford (G-11837)
▲ Oticon Inc.............E....... 732 560-1220
  Somerset (G-10148)
▲ Oticon Medical LLC.............E....... 732 560-0727
  Somerset (G-10149)
◆ Pacific Dunlop Investments USA ....F....... 732 345-5400
  Red Bank (G-9340)
▲ Pacon Manufacturing Corp.............C....... 732 764-9070
  Somerset (G-10152)
▲ Peace Medical Inc.............F....... 800 537-9564
  Wharton (G-11996)
Precise Cmpnents TI Design Inc ....G....... 973 928-2928
  Clifton (G-1702)
Precision Orthotic Lab of Nj ....F....... 856 848-6226
  West Deptford (G-11839)
▲ Preform Laboratories Inc.............G....... 973 523-8610
  Hackensack (G-3964)
Prescription Podiatry Labs ....G....... 609 695-1221
  Trenton (G-11103)
Pro-Fit LLC.............F....... 856 809-9910
  West Berlin (G-11745)
Q-Med Scandinavia Inc.............E....... 609 953-8069
  Edison (G-2600)
▲ Rep Trading Associates Inc.............F....... 732 591-1140
  Old Bridge (G-7792)
Respironics Inc.............C....... 973 581-6000
  Parsippany (G-8079)
Rinko Orthopedic Appliances ....G....... 201 796-3121
  Fair Lawn (G-3109)
▲ Sivantos Inc.............G....... 732 562-6600
  Piscataway (G-8811)
Songbird Hearing Inc.............E....... 732 422-7203
  North Brunswick (G-7539)
Sonic Innovations Inc.............G....... 888 423-7834
  Somerset (G-10173)
Spinal Kinetics LLC.............G....... 908 687-2552
  Union (G-11224)
▲ Superior Intl Srgical Sups LLC ....F....... 609 695-6591
  Ewing (G-3057)
Surgical Lser Sfety Cuncil Inc ....G....... 216 272-0805
  Cherry Hill (G-1424)
Swiss Orthopedic Inc.............G....... 908 874-5522
  Hillsborough (G-4375)
Switlik Parachute Company Inc.............F....... 609 587-3300
  Trenton (G-11119)
Teleflex Incorporated.............D....... 856 349-7234
  Gloucester City (G-3846)
Tgz Acquisition Company LLC ....F....... 856 669-6600
  Cherry Hill (G-1428)
Top Safety Products Company ....F....... 908 707-8680
  Branchburg (G-711)
Total Control Othotics Lab ....G....... 609 499-2200
  Florence (G-3482)
▲ Tronex International Inc.............D....... 973 335-2888
  Budd Lake (G-945)
Tyrx Inc.............E....... 732 246-8676
  Monmouth Junction (G-6367)
▲ Universal Tape Supply Corp.............F....... 609 653-3191
  Somers Point (G-10048)
▲ Water-Jel Holding Company ....D....... 201 507-8300
  Carlstadt (G-1241)

▲ Water-Jel Technologies LLC ....D 201 438-1598
Carlstadt *(G-1242)*

Zimmer Inc ....G 856 778-8300
Mount Laurel *(G-6848)*

Zimmer Trabecular Met Tech Inc ....C 973 576-0032
Parsippany *(G-8118)*

Zounds Inc ....F 856 234-8844
Mount Laurel *(G-6849)*

3843 Dental Eqpt & Splys

American Medical & Dental Sups ....F 877 545-6837
Montvale *(G-6442)*

Anna K Park ....G 856 478-9500
Mullica Hill *(G-6892)*

Dental Models & Designs Inc ....G 973 472-8009
Garfield *(G-3729)*

Dentalworx Lab Ltd Lblty Co ....G 732 981-9096
Edison *(G-2501)*

Dentamach Inc ....F 973 334-2220
Parsippany *(G-7979)*

▲ Dmg America LLC ....E 201 894-5500
Ridgefield Park *(G-9404)*

E P R Industries Inc ....F 856 488-1120
Pennsauken *(G-8507)*

Em Orthodontic Labs Inc ....G 201 652-4411
Waldwick *(G-11446)*

▲ Essential Dental Systems Inc ....E 201 487-9090
South Hackensack *(G-10265)*

Evergreen Dental ....G 856 845-3299
Woodbury Heights *(G-12176)*

▲ Floxite Company Inc ....F 201 529-2019
Mahwah *(G-5774)*

Geistlich Pharma North America ....E 609 779-6560
Princeton *(G-9049)*

▲ Handler Manufacturing Company ....E 908 233-7796
Westfield *(G-11926)*

Integrated Dental Systems LLC ....E 201 676-2457
Englewood Cliffs *(G-2967)*

Integrted Laminate Systems Inc ....D 856 786-6500
Cinnaminson *(G-1469)*

▲ Ivoclar Vivadent Mfg Inc ....D 732 563-4755
Somerset *(G-10114)*

J A W Products Inc ....F 856 829-3210
Cinnaminson *(G-1471)*

Jacquet Jonpaul ....G 856 825-4259
Millville *(G-6310)*

◆ L & R Manufacturing Co Inc ....D 201 991-5330
Kearny *(G-4894)*

Milestone Education LLC ....G 973 535-2717
Livingston *(G-5544)*

▲ Milestone Scientific Inc ....F 973 535-2717
Livingston *(G-5545)*

▲ Mycone Dental Supply Co Inc ....C 856 663-4700
Gibbstown *(G-3792)*

Natural Dental Studios Inc ....G 908 281-0089
Hillsborough *(G-4357)*

Palisades Dental LLc ....G 201 569-0050
Englewood *(G-2920)*

Panthera Dental Inc ....G 201 340-2766
East Rutherford *(G-2316)*

R Yates Consumer Prd LLC ....G 201 569-1030
Englewood *(G-2927)*

Raptor Resources Holdings Inc ....G 732 252-5146
Freehold *(G-3685)*

Samuel H Fields Dental Labs ....E 201 343-4626
Hackensack *(G-3971)*

South East Instruments LLC ....G 201 569-0050
Englewood *(G-2933)*

▲ Spident USA Incorporated ....G 201 944-0511
Little Ferry *(G-5517)*

Ss White Burs Inc ....C 732 905-1100
Lakewood *(G-5190)*

▲ Takara Belmont Usa Inc ....D 732 469-5000
Somerset *(G-10179)*

Takara Belmont Usa Inc ....G 732 469-5000
Somerset *(G-10180)*

◆ Viscot Medical LLC ....E 973 887-9273
East Hanover *(G-2248)*

William R Hall Co ....E 856 784-6700
Lindenwold *(G-5464)*

3844 X-ray Apparatus & Tubes

G E Inspection Technologies LP ....D 973 448-0077
Flanders *(G-3409)*

▼ Glenbrook Technologies Inc ....F 973 361-8866
Randolph *(G-9279)*

Gray Star Inc ....G 973 398-3331
Mount Arlington *(G-6755)*

M T D Inc ....G 908 362-6807
Hardwick *(G-4168)*

Security Defense Systems Corp ....G 973 235-0606
Nutley *(G-7653)*

▲ Swissray America Inc ....E 908 353-0971
Elizabeth *(G-2778)*

Swissray International Inc ....F 800 903-5543
Edison *(G-2636)*

▲ Vatech America Inc ....E 201 210-5028
Fort Lee *(G-3588)*

Vision Ten Inc ....F 201 935-3000
Carlstadt *(G-1239)*

3845 Electromedical & Electrotherapeutic Apparatus

3dimension Dgnstc Slution Corp ....G 201 780-4653
Jersey City *(G-4691)*

3shape Inc ....G 908 219-4641
Warren *(G-11534)*

Affil Endoscopy Services CL ....G 201 842-0020
Clifton *(G-1559)*

Ahs Hospital Corp. ....G 908 522-2000
Summit *(G-10633)*

Andrew Technologies LLC ....G 215 990-0754
Haddonfield *(G-4055)*

▲ Bard Healthcare Inc ....G 908 277-8000
New Providence *(G-7028)*

◆ Bayer Healthcare LLC ....A 862 404-3000
Whippany *(G-12008)*

Burlington Cnty Endoscopy Ctr ....E 609 267-1555
Lumberton *(G-5652)*

▲ C R Bard Inc ....C 908 277-8000
New Providence *(G-7032)*

▲ Capintec Inc ....E 201 825-9500
Florham Park *(G-3495)*

Cgm Us Inc ....G 609 894-4420
Birmingham *(G-467)*

Circulite Inc ....F 201 478-7575
Teaneck *(G-10745)*

Corentec America Inc ....G 949 379-6227
Morristown *(G-6701)*

◆ Datascope Corp ....C 973 244-6100
Fairfield *(G-3171)*

Datascope Corp ....G 201 995-8000
Mahwah *(G-5764)*

Datascope Corp ....E 201 995-8000
Mahwah *(G-5762)*

Davis Center Inc ....G 862 251-4637
Succasunna *(G-10622)*

Diabeto Inc ....G 646 397-3175
Piscataway *(G-8758)*

Dvx LLC ....G 609 924-3590
Princeton *(G-9033)*

Echo Therapeutics Inc ....F 732 201-4189
Edgewater *(G-2437)*

Electrocore Inc ....D 973 290-0097
Basking Ridge *(G-186)*

▲ Enterix Inc ....E 732 429-1899
Edison *(G-2512)*

Ethicon LLC ....D 908 218-3195
Somerville *(G-10208)*

Fluent Diagnostics ....G 201 414-4516
Pequannock *(G-8599)*

Getinge Group Logistics Americ ....E 973 709-6000
Wayne *(G-11640)*

Highlands Acquisition Corp ....G 201 573-8400
Montvale *(G-6459)*

Hilin Life Products Inc ....G 973 648-0265
Newark *(G-7189)*

▲ Impact Instrumentation Inc ....C 973 882-1212
West Caldwell *(G-11779)*

Medtronic Inc ....C 908 289-5969
Swedesboro *(G-10710)*

◆ Mindray Ds Usa Inc ....A 201 995-8000
Mahwah *(G-5791)*

Morris County Imaging ....G 973 532-7900
Morristown *(G-6728)*

Neurotron Medical Inc ....G 609 896-3444
Ewing *(G-3040)*

Newcardio Inc ....F 877 332-4324
Princeton *(G-9080)*

▲ Nextphase Medical Devices LLC .....E 201 968-9400
Waldwick *(G-11452)*

▲ Nextron Medical Tech Inc ....G 973 575-0614
Fairfield *(G-3270)*

Northeast Medical Systems Corp ....G 856 910-8111
Cherry Hill *(G-1405)*

Princeton Trade and Technology ....F 609 683-0215
Princeton *(G-9103)*

Radnet Inc ....G 908 709-1323
Cranford *(G-1925)*

Refine Technology LLC ....F 973 952-0002
Pine Brook *(G-8715)*

Respironics Inc ....C 973 581-6000
Parsippany *(G-8079)*

Rhythmedix LLC ....G 856 282-1080
Mount Laurel *(G-6835)*

Simex Medical Imaging Inc ....G 201 490-0204
Paramus *(G-7901)*

▲ Sonotron Medical Systems Inc ....G 201 767-6040
Northvale *(G-7608)*

St Jude Medical ....F 908 979-3200
Hackettstown *(G-4038)*

St Jude Medical LLC ....G 800 645-5368
Secaucus *(G-9932)*

Surgical Lser Sfety Cuncil Inc ....G 216 272-0805
Cherry Hill *(G-1424)*

Syneron ....G 201 599-9451
Paramus *(G-7909)*

▲ Topcon America Corporation ....B 201 599-5100
Oakland *(G-7706)*

Total Tech Medical LLC ....G 973 980-6458
Dover *(G-2113)*

Universal Medical Inc ....G 800 606-5511
Ewing *(G-3065)*

V L V Associates ....G 973 428-2884
Whippany *(G-12041)*

Vasculogic LLC ....G 908 278-3573
Piscataway *(G-8833)*

Vectracor Inc ....F 973 904-0444
Totowa *(G-10977)*

Vectracor Inc ....F 973 768-0402
Totowa *(G-10978)*

Venetian Care and Rehablitatn ....G 732 721-8200
South Amboy *(G-10246)*

Zounds Inc ....F 856 234-8844
Mount Laurel *(G-6849)*

3851 Ophthalmic Goods

Bausch & Lomb Incorporated ....B 908 927-1400
Bridgewater *(G-820)*

Complete Optical Laboratory ....F 973 338-8886
Bloomfield *(G-508)*

Douglas Liva MD ....G 201 444-7770
Ridgewood *(G-9423)*

Edison Ophthalmology Assoc LLC ....F 908 822-0070
Edison *(G-2510)*

Essilor Laboratories Amer Inc ....F 732 563-9884
Warren *(G-11547)*

Hillcrest Opticians ....G 973 838-6666
Kinnelon *(G-5036)*

I See Optical Laboratories ....F 856 227-9300
Blackwood *(G-481)*

I See Optical Laboratories ....G 856 795-6435
Voorhees *(G-11433)*

Jeffery S Zlotnick Od ....G 732 549-3555
Metuchen *(G-6113)*

▲ Lab Tech Inc ....G 201 767-5613
Northvale *(G-7589)*

▲ Lens Depot Inc ....F 732 993-9766
East Brunswick *(G-2164)*

Lens Lab Express ....G 201 861-0016
West New York *(G-11871)*

Lens Mode Inc ....G 973 467-2000
Millburn *(G-6255)*

▲ Liberty Sport Inc ....E 973 882-0986
Fairfield *(G-3252)*

M & S Optics Inc ....F 856 764-0200
Delran *(G-2019)*

◆ Marcolin USA Eyewear Corp ....D 800 345-8482
Branchburg *(G-678)*

▲ Motif Industries Inc ....F 973 575-1800
East Hanover *(G-2229)*

New Jersey Eye Center Inc ....F 201 384-7333
Bergenfield *(G-391)*

Pam Optical Co ....G 973 744-8882
Montclair *(G-6429)*

Pds Consultants Inc ....E 201 970-2313
Sparta *(G-10517)*

▲ Phillips Safety Products Inc ....F 732 356-1493
Middlesex *(G-6188)*

Richard Danz & Sons Inc ....E 212 697-5722
Glen Rock *(G-3829)*

Sensor Medical Technology LLC ....G 425 358-7381
Denville *(G-2058)*

Smith Optics Inc ....G 208 726-4477
Secaucus *(G-9929)*

Spectacle Shoppe ....G 856 875-5046
Williamstown *(G-12108)*

▲ Topcon Medical Systems Inc ....D 201 599-5100
Oakland *(G-7707)*

S
I
C

Usv Optical Inc ....B 856 228-1000
  Glendora (G-3834)
◆ Viva International Inc ....B 908 595-6200
  Branchburg (G-717)

3861 Photographic Eqpt & Splys

▲ AGFA Corporation ....B 800 540-2432
  Elmwood Park (G-2802)
AGFA Corporation ....E 201 440-0111
  Elmwood Park (G-2803)
AGFA Corporation ....E 201 440-0111
  Carlstadt (G-1121)
▲ AGFA Finance Corp ....C 201 796-0058
  Elmwood Park (G-2804)
▲ Ar2 Products LLC ....G 800 667-1263
  Pompton Plains (G-8953)
▲ Automatic Transfer Inc ....G 908 213-2830
  Alpha (G-39)
B&B Imaging LLC ....G 201 261-3131
  Paramus (G-7856)
Beta Industries Corp ....G 201 939-2400
  Carlstadt (G-1130)
Blue Parachute LLC ....G 732 767-1320
  Metuchen (G-6097)
Central Technology Inc ....F 732 431-3339
  Freehold (G-3645)
Clarity Imaging Tech Inc ....E 413 693-1234
  Pennsauken (G-8493)
Coda Inc ....E 201 825-7400
  Mahwah (G-5760)
Colex Imaging Inc ....G 201 414-5575
  Elmwood Park (G-2810)
Cytotherm LP ....G 609 396-1456
  Trenton (G-11050)
▲ Dyna-Lite Inc ....F 908 687-8800
  Union (G-11176)
▲ E Z Hi-Tech Services Inc ....G 908 317-8203
  Mountainside (G-6879)
Energy Storage Corp ....D 732 542-7880
  Eatontown (G-2394)
Enterprise Solution Products ....G 201 678-9200
  West New York (G-11865)
Fujifilm North America Corp ....B 732 857-3000
  Edison (G-2523)
▼ Fullview Inc ....G 732 275-6500
  Holmdel (G-4516)
▲ Hasselblad Inc ....E 800 456-0203
  Union (G-11191)
▲ Heights Usa Inc ....E 609 530-1300
  Ewing (G-3021)
Howard Packaging Corp ....G 973 904-0022
  Clifton (G-1643)
Hpi International Inc ....F 732 942-9900
  Lakewood (G-5135)
Image Remit Inc ....E 732 940-7900
  North Brunswick (G-7518)
International Laser Group Inc ....E 818 888-0400
  Cherry Hill (G-1382)
Intertest Inc ....E 908 496-8008
  Columbia (G-1799)
Ion360 USA LLC ....G 866 901-0073
  Moorestown (G-6587)
▲ Iris ID Systems Inc ....E 609 819-4747
  Cranbury (G-1843)
James Colucci Enterprises LLC ....E 877 403-4900
  Short Hills (G-9979)
Liveu Inc ....D 201 742-5229
  Hackensack (G-3939)
Mri of West Morris PA ....F 973 927-1010
  Succasunna (G-10625)
▲ Ner Data Products Inc ....E 888 637-3282
  Glassboro (G-3810)
Oxberry LLC ....G 201 935-3000
  Carlstadt (G-1196)
Parker Acquisition Group Inc ....G 908 707-4900
  Branchburg (G-687)
Pentagon Performance Inc ....G 973 975-0400
  Millville (G-6320)
Photographic Analysis Company ....F 973 696-1000
  Wayne (G-11673)
▼ Prestige Camera LLC ....E 718 257-5888
  Somerset (G-10158)
▲ Profoto US Inc ....F 973 822-1300
  Florham Park (G-3516)
▲ Quality Films Corp ....G 718 246-7150
  Hillside (G-4435)
Ricoh Prtg Systems Amer Inc ....G 973 316-6051
  Mountain Lakes (G-6861)
Roper Scientific Inc ....D 520 889-9933
  Trenton (G-11114)

◆ Rpl Supplies Inc ....F 973 767-0880
  Garfield (G-3759)
◆ Samsung Opt-Lctronics Amer Inc ....C 201 325-2612
  Teaneck (G-10772)
◆ Sharp Electronics Corporation ....A 201 529-8200
  Mahwah (G-5811)
▲ Towne Technologies Inc ....F 908 722-9500
  Somerville (G-10230)
Vision Research Inc ....D 973 696-4500
  Wayne (G-11691)
West Essex Graphics Inc ....E 973 227-2400
  Fairfield (G-3351)
Xerox Corporation ....B 609 987-5500
  Princeton (G-9141)
Xybion Corporation ....G 973 538-2067
  Lawrenceville (G-5273)
▲ Zeta Products Inc ....E 908 688-0440
  Annandale (G-62)
Zink Holdings LLC ....C 781 761-5400
  Edison (G-2654)

3873 Watch & Clock Devices & Parts

▲ Acon Watch Crown Company ....F 973 546-8585
  Garfield (G-3715)
▲ Belair Time Corporation ....E 732 905-0100
  Lakewood (G-5083)
◆ Clic Time LLC ....E 201 497-6743
  Woodcliff Lake (G-12187)
Dksh Luxury & Lifestyle N Amer ....E 609 750-8800
  Lawrence Township (G-5242)
Emdur Metal Products Inc ....E 856 541-1100
  Camden (G-1062)
Garrett Moore ....G 908 231-9231
  Bridgewater (G-840)
◆ Movado Group Inc ....B 201 267-8000
  Paramus (G-7890)
Movado Retail Group Inc ....G 201 267-8000
  Paramus (G-7891)
Quantum Vector Corp ....G 201 870-1782
  Westwood (G-11967)
▲ Springfeld Prcision Instrs Inc ....E 866 843-3905
  Rochelle Park (G-7891)
Swatch Group Les Btques US Inc ....G 201 271-1400
  Weehawken (G-11699)
Watchitude LLC ....G 732 745-2626
  New Brunswick (G-7011)
Zeon US Inc ....G 516 532-7167
  North Bergen (G-7498)

39 MISCELLANEOUS MANUFACTURING INDUSTRIES

3911 Jewelry: Precious Metal

Alex and Ani LLC ....G 908 965-1510
  Elizabeth (G-2707)
All State Medal Co Inc ....G 973 458-1458
  Lodi (G-5575)
Anna J Chung Ltd ....F 917 575-8100
  Edgewater (G-2432)
▲ Aubrey David Inc ....E 201 653-2200
  Jersey City (G-4711)
Avanzato Jewelers LLC ....G 609 890-0500
  Trenton (G-11021)
Avigdor Ltd Liability Company ....E 973 898-4770
  Morristown (G-6691)
Aydin Jewelry Menufecturing ....G 201 818-1002
  Ramsey (G-9236)
Barrasso & Blasi Industries ....F 973 761-0595
  Maplewood (G-5914)
Bergio International Inc ....G 973 227-3230
  Fairfield (G-3148)
Bernard D Ascenzo ....G 856 795-0511
  Haddonfield (G-4056)
Bhamra Chain Manufacturing ....G 908 686-4555
  Union (G-11159)
Big Apple Jewelry Mfg ....G 201 531-1600
  East Rutherford (G-2286)
Brad Garman Designs ....G 732 229-6670
  Long Branch (G-5621)
Cherish Designs LLC ....G 856 751-8034
  Mount Laurel (G-6787)
Christian Art ....G 201 867-8096
  West New York (G-11862)
Cinco Star LLC ....G 732 744-1617
  Edison (G-2483)
Creations By Sherry Lynn LLC ....G 800 742-3448
  Florham Park (G-3497)
Creations By Stefano Inc ....G 201 863-8337
  Secaucus (G-9875)

D Paglia & Sons Inc ....F 908 654-5999
  Mountainside (G-6872)
▲ DAmore Jewelers ....E 201 945-0530
  Cliffside Park (G-1537)
Danmola Lara ....G 973 762-7581
  South Orange (G-10302)
David E Connolly Inc ....F 908 654-4600
  Mountainside (G-6874)
DBC Inc ....D 212 819-1177
  Teaneck (G-10747)
▲ Devon Trading Corp ....E 973 812-9190
  Caldwell (G-1026)
Diamond Hut Jewelry Exchange ....G 201 332-5372
  Jersey City (G-4743)
Enamel Art Studio ....G 732 321-0774
  Metuchen (G-6103)
European Imports of LA Inc ....F 973 536-1823
  Paramus (G-7868)
Fehu Jewel LLC ....C 609 297-5491
  Plainsboro (G-8881)
◆ Franklin Mint LLC ....E 800 843-6468
  Fort Lee (G-3555)
Gaurika LLC ....G 201 496-1613
  Cliffside Park (G-1539)
Gem Vault Inc ....G 908 788-1770
  Flemington (G-3444)
▲ George Press Inc ....F 973 992-7797
  Livingston (G-5533)
Gold Buyers At Mall LLC ....G 201 512-5780
  Mahwah (G-5779)
Gold Signature Incorporated ....G 732 777-9170
  Piscataway (G-8769)
Goldstein Setting Co Inc ....F 908 964-1034
  Union (G-11190)
Grassman-Blake Inc ....G 973 379-6170
  Millburn (G-6251)
Great Falls Metalworks Inc ....G 973 523-6811
  Paterson (G-8280)
Greater New Jersey Diamnd Exch ....G 732 752-6446
  Green Brook (G-3856)
▲ H Ritani LLC ....G 888 974-8264
  Closter (G-1759)
Heights Jewelers LLC ....F 201 825-2381
  Allendale (G-10)
▲ Imperium Enterprises LLC ....G 908 206-4970
  Little Ferry (G-5509)
Jct Design Enterprises Inc ....E 212 629-7412
  Union City (G-11251)
Jost Brothers Jewelry Mfg Corp ....F 908 453-2266
  Washington (G-11584)
Jostens Inc ....G 973 584-5843
  Succasunna (G-10624)
Joy Jewelery America Inc ....G 201 689-1150
  River Vale (G-9471)
K B Enterprises of New Jersey ....G 908 451-5282
  Hillsborough (G-4353)
Kole Design LLC ....G 732 409-0211
  Freehold (G-3664)
Krementz & Co ....F 973 621-8300
  Springfield (G-10563)
Labrada Inc ....G 201 461-2641
  Leonia (G-5317)
Lieberfarb Inc ....F 973 676-9090
  Rahway (G-9208)
▲ Littlegifts Inc ....F 212 868-2559
  Secaucus (G-9902)
◆ Lusterline Inc ....G 201 758-5148
  Union City (G-11255)
M S Brown Mfg Jewelers ....G 609 522-7604
  Wildwood (G-12074)
Mdviani Designs Inc ....G 201 840-5410
  Ridgefield (G-9373)
Midas Designs Ltd ....E 201 567-2700
  Maywood (G-6058)
Mj Gross Company - NJ ....G 212 542-3199
  Lakewood (G-5162)
Moonbabies LLC ....G 609 926-0201
  Somers Point (G-10047)
▲ Nadri Inc ....G 201 585-0088
  Fort Lee (G-3572)
NEi Gold Products of NJ ....G 201 488-5858
  Hackensack (G-3951)
Nei Jewelmasters of New Jersey ....D 201 488-5858
  Hackensack (G-3952)
Netfruits Inc ....G 732 249-2588
  New Brunswick (G-6985)
▲ Norco Inc ....E 908 789-1550
  Garwood (G-3781)
▼ Paul Winston Fine Jewelry Grou ......F 800 232-2728
  Englewood Cliffs (G-2977)

Pearl Baumell Company Inc ....G 415 421-2113
  Rutherford *(G-9743)*

Pin People LLC ....F 888 309-7467
  Montvale *(G-6470)*

Premesco Inc ....B 908 686-0513
  Union *(G-11216)*

Pretty Jewelry Co ....G 908 806-3377
  Flemington *(G-3461)*

Provost Square Associates Inc ....F 973 403-8755
  Caldwell *(G-1032)*

Robert Manse Designs LLC ....E 732 428-8305
  Rahway *(G-9220)*

Robertas Jewelers Inc ....G 973 875-5318
  Hamburg *(G-4096)*

Samuel Jewels Inc ....F 201 439-1555
  Bergenfield *(G-394)*

Sara Emporium Inc ....G 201 792-7222
  Jersey City *(G-4823)*

Saud & Son Jewelry Inc ....G 201 866-4445
  West New York *(G-11881)*

Scott Kay Inc ....C 201 287-0100
  Secaucus *(G-9925)*

Scott Kay Sterling LLC ....G 201 287-0100
  Secaucus *(G-9926)*

Shopindia Inc ....G 732 409-0656
  Marlboro *(G-5958)*

Tapia Accessory Group Inc ....E 201 393-0028
  Teterboro *(G-10815)*

Tessler & Weiss/Premesco Inc ....C 800 535-3501
  Union *(G-11228)*

Top Rated Shopping Bargains ....F 201 630-0770
  Hasbrouck Heights *(G-4200)*

Trimarco Inc ....G 973 762-7380
  Maplewood *(G-5929)*

Ultimate Trading Corp ....D 973 228-7700
  Fairfield *(G-3332)*

Unistar Inc ....G 212 840-2100
  Princeton *(G-9134)*

United Diam Inc ....G 732 619-0950
  Matawan *(G-6034)*

W Kodak Jewelers Inc ....G 201 710-5491
  Hoboken *(G-4503)*

W W Jewelers Inc ....D 718 392-4500
  Jersey City *(G-4845)*

Weinman Bros Inc ....E 212 695-8116
  Jersey City *(G-4847)*

Wlxt LLC ....G 732 906-7979
  Metuchen *(G-6133)*

World Class Marketing Corp ....E 201 313-0022
  Fort Lee *(G-3591)*

▲ Zsombor Antal Designs Inc ....F 201 225-1750
  River Edge *(G-9468)*

3914 Silverware, Plated & Stainless Steel Ware

AMG International Inc ....G 404 297-9083
  Parsippany *(G-7945)*

◆ AMG International Inc ....D 201 475-4800
  Parsippany *(G-7946)*

Dynamic Metals Inc ....E 908 769-0522
  Piscataway *(G-8761)*

◆ Freeman Products Inc ....F 201 475-4800
  Parsippany *(G-8017)*

◆ Hampton Forge Ltd ....E 877 935-2892
  Eatontown *(G-2399)*

Hickok Matthews Co Inc ....G 973 335-3400
  Montville *(G-6489)*

▲ III Eagle Enterprises Ltd ....E 973 237-1111
  Ringwood *(G-9449)*

▲ Kraftware Corporation ....E 732 345-7091
  Roselle *(G-9674)*

▲ Medin Technologies Inc ....C 973 779-2400
  Totowa *(G-10955)*

Picture It Inc ....G 732 819-0420
  Edison *(G-2594)*

Trophy King Inc ....G 201 836-1482
  Teaneck *(G-10775)*

3915 Jewelers Findings & Lapidary Work

Corbo Jewelers Inc ....F 973 777-1635
  Clifton *(G-1592)*

▲ Diamond Universe LLC ....F 201 592-9500
  Fort Lee *(G-3551)*

Good As Gold Jewelers Inc ....G 732 286-1111
  Toms River *(G-10881)*

Grassman-Blake Inc ....E 973 379-6170
  Millburn *(G-6251)*

J Michaels Jewelers Inc ....G 908 771-9800
  Berkeley Heights *(G-414)*

Joseph Castings Inc ....F 201 712-0717
  Maywood *(G-6056)*

▲ Master Presentations Inc ....F 732 239-7093
  Lakewood *(G-5155)*

Mdviani Designs Inc ....G 201 840-5410
  Ridgefield *(G-9373)*

Moser Jewel Company ....G 908 454-1155
  Phillipsburg *(G-8660)*

◆ Movado Group Inc ....B 201 267-8000
  Paramus *(G-7890)*

Rcdc Corporation ....G 212 382-0386
  Hoboken *(G-4494)*

Solmor Manufacturing Co Inc ....G 973 824-7203
  Newark *(G-7320)*

Tessler & Weiss/Premesco Inc ....C 800 535-3501
  Union *(G-11228)*

Victors Three-D Inc ....D 201 845-4433
  Maywood *(G-6062)*

Zale Delaware Inc ....G 201 291-0690
  Paramus *(G-7914)*

3931 Musical Instruments

AP Global Enterprises Inc ....G 732 919-6200
  Wall Township *(G-11462)*

▲ Applause Musical Products ....G 856 697-8333
  Landisville *(G-5229)*

▲ D R Handmade Strings Inc ....D 201 599-3113
  Westwood *(G-11958)*

▲ Latin Percussion Inc ....G 973 478-6903
  Garfield *(G-3742)*

▲ Malletech LLC ....F 732 774-0011
  Neptune *(G-6922)*

Master Strap LLC ....G 888 503-7779
  Marlboro *(G-5947)*

Peragallo Organ Company of NJ ....F 973 684-3414
  Paterson *(G-8363)*

Spem Corporation ....E 732 356-3366
  Piscataway *(G-8816)*

Trek II Products Inc ....G 732 214-9200
  New Brunswick *(G-7007)*

▲ Vintage Vibe Ltd Liability Co...........G 973 989-2178
  Rockaway *(G-9622)*

W E Wamsley Restorations Inc ....G 856 795-4001
  Haddonfield *(G-4066)*

3942 Dolls & Stuffed Toys

Chic Btq Doll Design Co LLC ....G 201 784-7727
  Norwood *(G-7619)*

De Zaio Productions Inc ....D 973 423-5000
  Fair Lawn *(G-3089)*

Dream Makers Inc ....G 201 248-5502
  Park Ridge *(G-7918)*

◆ Franklin Mint LLC ....E 800 843-6468
  Fort Lee *(G-3555)*

◆ Homeco LLC ....E 732 802-7733
  Piscataway *(G-8774)*

▲ Kids of America Corp ....E 973 808-8242
  Fairfield *(G-3241)*

▲ New Adventures LLC ....G 973 884-8887
  East Hanover *(G-2231)*

▲ Pretty Ugly LLC ....F 908 620-0931
  Green Brook *(G-3863)*

▲ Reeves International Inc ....G 973 694-5006
  Pequannock *(G-8601)*

▲ Ron Banafato Inc ....G 908 685-9447
  Phillipsburg *(G-8668)*

Tiffanees Toys Inc ....F 732 828-6333
  North Brunswick *(G-7543)*

▲ Treasures LLC ....G 201 723-3506
  Allendale *(G-22)*

3944 Games, Toys & Children's Vehicles

▲ AG&e Holdings Inc ....E 609 704-3000
  Hammonton *(G-4126)*

▲ Ambo Consulting LLC ....G 732 663-0000
  Deal *(G-1997)*

▲ Amloid Corporation ....F 973 328-0654
  Cedar Knolls *(G-1306)*

Answers In Motion LLC ....G 732 267-7792
  Maple Shade *(G-5899)*

▲ Atlas Model Railroad Co Inc ....D 908 687-0880
  Hillside *(G-4392)*

Atlas O LLC ....E 908 687-9590
  Hillside *(G-4393)*

Babysmart LLC ....G 908 766-4900
  Bernardsville *(G-447)*

Bally Technologies Inc ....F 609 641-7711
  Egg Harbor Township *(G-2681)*

Bucci Management Co Inc ....G 609 567-8808
  Hammonton *(G-4134)*

Classic Chess and Games Inc ....G 908 850-6553
  Hackettstown *(G-4001)*

Deluxe Innovations Inc ....G 201 857-5880
  Midland Park *(G-6225)*

Electronics Boutique Amer Inc ....G 856 435-3900
  Clementon *(G-1531)*

◆ Epoch Everlasting Play LLC ....E 973 316-2500
  Parsippany *(G-8002)*

Froyo Skyview LLC ....G 718 607-5656
  Jersey City *(G-4758)*

Hirox - USA Inc ....G 201 342-2600
  Hackensack *(G-3927)*

◆ Horizon Group USA Inc ....C 908 810-1111
  Warren *(G-11553)*

▲ Hygloss Products Inc ....E 973 458-1700
  Wallington *(G-11527)*

▲ Kiddesigns Inc ....E 732 574-9000
  Rahway *(G-9207)*

◆ Larose Industries LLC ....D 973 543-2037
  Randolph *(G-9287)*

Lawrence Katona ....G 609 538-1388
  Ewing *(G-3035)*

▲ Lemniscate Inc ....G 707 824-2272
  Mahwah *(G-5788)*

▲ Majestic Industries Inc ....E 973 473-3434
  Passaic *(G-8158)*

▲ Morgan Cycle LLC ....G 973 218-9233
  Short Hills *(G-9982)*

Poof-Alex Holdings LLC ....G 734 454-9552
  Fairfield *(G-3284)*

Pride Products Mfg LLC ....F 908 353-1900
  Elizabeth *(G-2768)*

▲ Primetime Trading Corp ....E 646 580-8223
  Bayonne *(G-241)*

Proteus Designs LLC ....G 215 519-0135
  Moorestown *(G-6616)*

R & R Distributors Inc ....G 201 804-0077
  Branchville *(G-732)*

Reeves International Inc ....G 973 956-9555
  Wayne *(G-11678)*

Steico USA Inc ....F 732 364-6200
  Lakewood *(G-5191)*

Toysruscom Inc ....G 973 617-3500
  Wayne *(G-11686)*

◆ Wecool Toys Inc ....E 856 296-9766
  Medford *(G-6084)*

Zimpli Kids Inc ....G 732 945-5995
  Neptune *(G-6937)*

3949 Sporting & Athletic Goods, NEC

▲ A & R Sports LLC ....E 201 941-8875
  Randolph *(G-9266)*

AB Coaster LLC ....F 908 879-2713
  Chester *(G-1432)*

◆ Akadema Inc ....E 973 304-1470
  Bloomingdale *(G-540)*

Alden - Leeds Inc ....G 973 344-7986
  Kearny *(G-4858)*

Aquasports Pools LLC ....F 732 247-6298
  New Brunswick *(G-6946)*

◆ Beachcarts USA ....G 201 319-0091
  Secaucus *(G-9867)*

Belleplain Supply Co Inc ....G 609 861-2345
  Woodbine *(G-12141)*

Bergen Manufacturing & Supply ....E 201 854-3461
  North Bergen *(G-7434)*

Big Daddys Sports Haven ....G 856 453-9009
  Millville *(G-6288)*

Captain John Inc ....F 609 494-2094
  Barnegat Light *(G-168)*

CDK Industries LLC ....G 856 488-5456
  Cherry Hill *(G-1356)*

▲ Cover Co Inc ....E 908 707-9797
  Branchburg *(G-651)*

◆ Cressi Sub USA ....G 201 594-1450
  Saddle Brook *(G-9760)*

▲ Crown Products Inc ....E 732 493-0022
  Ocean *(G-7720)*

De Zaio Productions Inc ....G 973 423-5000
  Fair Lawn *(G-3089)*

◆ Delair LLC ....D 856 663-2900
  Pennsauken *(G-8502)*

Elite Surf Snow Skateboard Sp ....G 856 427-7873
  Cherry Hill *(G-1362)*

▲ Endurance Net Inc ....F 609 499-3450
  Florence *(G-3478)*

Fred S Burroughs North Jersey ....D 908 850-8773
  Hackettstown *(G-4008)*

G A D Inc ....G 973 383-3499
  Newton *(G-7390)*

S
I
C

Gamit Force Athc Ltd Lblty Co ....F 908 675-0733
  Long Branch *(G-5624)*
▲ Great Socks LLC ....E 856 964-9700
  Pennsauken *(G-8518)*
Greater ATL Cy Golf Assn LLC ....F 609 652-1800
  Galloway *(G-3711)*
Grill Creations ....G 908 264-8426
  Garwood *(G-3778)*
◆ Hayward Industrial Products ....C 908 351-5400
  Elizabeth *(G-2741)*
Holiday Bowl Inc ....E 201 337-6516
  Oakland *(G-7691)*
Hollywood Tanning Systems Inc ....E 856 302-1368
  Mahwah *(G-5782)*
Impact Protective Eqp LLC ....G 973 377-0903
  Madison *(G-5724)*
Ingui Design LLC ....G 201 264-9126
  Ramsey *(G-9243)*
International Tech Lasers ....G 201 262-4580
  Emerson *(G-2858)*
▲ Interntnal Globl Solutions Inc ......G 201 791-1500
  Elmwood Park *(G-2826)*
▲ Interntonal Riding Helmets Inc ......E 732 772-0165
  Marlboro *(G-5945)*
J & S Enterprises LLC ....F 973 696-9199
  Lincoln Park *(G-5328)*
J and S Sporting Apparel LLC ....G 732 787-5500
  Keansburg *(G-4856)*
JA Cissel Manufacturing Co ....E 732 901-0300
  Lakewood *(G-5137)*
Jersey Cover Corp ....F 732 286-6300
  Toms River *(G-10889)*
Julian Bait Company Inc ....G 732 291-0050
  Atlantic Highlands *(G-114)*
◆ Kayden Manufacturing Inc ....F 201 880-9898
  Hackensack *(G-3935)*
Lacrosse Republic ....G 856 853-8787
  West Deptford *(G-11834)*
◆ Landice Incorporated ....F 973 927-9010
  Randolph *(G-9286)*
Lob-Ster Inc ....G 818 764-6000
  Plainfield *(G-8866)*
Lure Lash ....F 973 783-5274
  Montclair *(G-6421)*
Mulbro Manufacturing & Svc Co ....G 732 805-0290
  Middlesex *(G-6182)*
Newbold Inc ....G 732 469-5654
  Middlesex *(G-6185)*
Offshore Enterprises Inc ....G 609 345-9099
  Atlantic City *(G-105)*
Peloton Interactive Inc ....G 201 784-9510
  Northvale *(G-7601)*
Primal Surf ....G 609 264-1999
  Brigantine *(G-918)*
▲ Prince Sports Inc ....D 609 291-5800
  Bordentown *(G-609)*
◆ Pro Sports Inc ....E 732 294-5561
  Marlboro *(G-5953)*
Pure Soccer Academy Ltd Lblty ....G 877 945-6423
  Pine Brook *(G-8714)*
Rags International Inc ....G 787 632-8447
  Springfield *(G-10574)*
RCM Ltd Inc ....G 201 337-3328
  Oakland *(G-7702)*
Reagent Chemical & RES Inc ....E 908 284-2800
  Ringoes *(G-9442)*
Richard Andrus ....G 856 825-1782
  Millville *(G-6323)*
Rke Atheltic Lettering ....G 732 280-1111
  Belmar *(G-363)*
Ron Jon Surf Shop Fla Inc ....F 609 494-8844
  Ship Bottom *(G-9973)*
Seaville Motorsports ....F 609 624-0040
  Ocean View *(G-7766)*
Silverthorne Furniture Corp ....G 908 689-6969
  Asbury *(G-73)*
▲ Slendertone Distribution Inc ....G 732 660-1177
  Hoboken *(G-4497)*
South County Soccer League Inc ....G 908 310-9052
  Lambertville *(G-5221)*
Ss Equipment Holdings LLC ....E 732 627-0006
  Bridgewater *(G-900)*
Sterling Net & Twine Co Inc ....F 973 783-9800
  Montclair *(G-6436)*
Stingray Sport Pdts Ltd Lblty ....G 201 300-6482
  Fair Lawn *(G-3116)*
◆ Technogym USA Corp ....F 800 804-0952
  Fairfield *(G-3322)*
Tee-Rific Golf Center ....F 908 253-9300
  Branchburg *(G-709)*

Totowa Kickboxing Ltd Lblty Co ....F 973 507-9106
  Totowa *(G-10975)*
Tri State Athc Field Svcs Sups ....G 201 760-9700
  Ramsey *(G-9254)*
◆ Ultimate Trining Munitions Inc ......E 908 725-9000
  Branchburg *(G-714)*
Um Equity Corp ....G 856 354-2200
  Haddonfield *(G-4065)*
USA Industries Inc ....E 201 438-6606
  Carlstadt *(G-1237)*
Willowbrook Golf Center LLC ....F 973 256-6922
  Wayne *(G-11693)*

3951 Pens & Mechanical Pencils

Cameo Metal Forms Inc ....F 718 788-1106
  Woodland Park *(G-12213)*
◆ Cameo Novelty & Pen Corp ....E 973 923-1600
  Hillside *(G-4400)*
▲ Newell Brands Inc ....B 201 610-6600
  Hoboken *(G-4486)*
Pen Company of America LLC ....F 908 374-7949
  Garwood *(G-3784)*
Pen Company of America LLC ....F 908 374-7949
  Linden *(G-5427)*
Touch of Class Promotions LLC ....G 267 994-0860
  Voorhees *(G-11440)*

3952 Lead Pencils, Crayons & Artist's Mtrls

Algene Marking Equipment Co ....G 973 478-9041
  Garfield *(G-3716)*
◆ Asbury Carbons Inc ....G 908 537-2155
  Asbury *(G-66)*
▲ Case It Inc ....G 800 441-4710
  Lyndhurst *(G-5675)*
▲ Chavant Inc ....F 732 751-0003
  Wall Township *(G-11468)*
Congruent Machine Co Inc ....G 973 764-6767
  Vernon *(G-11297)*
Empty Walls Inc ....G 609 452-8488
  Princeton *(G-9038)*
▲ Excel Hobby Blades Corp ....G 973 278-4000
  Paterson *(G-8267)*
Faust Rudolph Inc ....G 609 298-7334
  Cranford *(G-1906)*
▲ General Pencil Company Inc ....G 201 653-5351
  Jersey City *(G-4759)*
▲ Meadowbrook Inventions Inc ....E 908 696-8470
  Bernardsville *(G-451)*
Norwood Industries Inc ....G 856 858-6195
  Haddon Township *(G-4054)*
▲ Pertech Printing Inks Inc ....G 908 354-1700
  Carlstadt *(G-1200)*
Rich Art Color Co Inc ....E 201 767-0009
  Northvale *(G-7606)*
U J Ramelson Co Inc ....G 973 589-5422
  Newark *(G-7349)*
◆ Utrecht Manufacturing Corp ....D 609 409-8001
  Cranbury *(G-1889)*

3953 Marking Devices

A A A Stamp and Seal Mfg Co ....G 201 796-1500
  Saddle Brook *(G-9747)*
A Quick Cut Stamping Embossing ....F 856 321-0050
  Maple Shade *(G-5898)*
Adco Signs of NJ Inc ....E 908 965-2112
  Elizabeth *(G-2705)*
▲ All-State International Inc ....C 908 272-0800
  Cranford *(G-1895)*
American Marking Systems Inc ....D 973 478-5600
  Clifton *(G-1563)*
American Stamp Mfg Co ....F 212 227-1877
  Clifton *(G-1564)*
American Stencyl Inc ....E 201 251-6460
  Glen Rock *(G-3819)*
Blue Ring Stencils LLC ....E 866 763-3873
  Lumberton *(G-5651)*
C Q Corporation ....F 201 935-8488
  East Rutherford *(G-2289)*
Classic Marking Products Inc ....G 973 383-2223
  Roxbury Township *(G-9711)*
Container Graphics Corp ....E 732 922-1180
  Neptune *(G-6904)*
Dalemark Industries Inc ....F 732 367-3100
  Lakewood *(G-5105)*
Digital Design Inc ....E 973 857-9500
  Cedar Grove *(G-1278)*
G & R Graphics Inc ....G 973 731-7438
  South Orange *(G-10307)*
Innovative Art Concepts LLC ....F 201 828-9146
  Ramsey *(G-9244)*

J D Crew Inc ....G 856 665-3676
  Pennsauken *(G-8534)*
L & F Graphics Ltd Lblty Co ....G 973 240-7033
  Paterson *(G-8312)*
Lafarge Road Marking Inc ....G 973 884-0300
  Parsippany *(G-8037)*
Max Pro Services LLC ....G 973 396-2373
  Livingston *(G-5542)*
Newark Stamp & Die Works Inc ....G 973 485-7111
  Newark *(G-7258)*
▲ Pic Graphics ....E 201 420-5040
  Jersey City *(G-4801)*
▲ Private Label Products Inc ....E 201 773-4230
  Fair Lawn *(G-3107)*
▲ Ranger Industries Inc ....E 732 389-3535
  Tinton Falls *(G-10844)*
Shachihata Inc (usa) ....E 732 905-7159
  Lakewood *(G-5188)*
Time Log Industries Inc ....G 609 965-5017
  Egg Harbor City *(G-2673)*
Trodat Usa Inc ....F 732 529-8500
  Somerset *(G-10189)*
▲ Trodat USA LLC ....D 732 562-9500
  Somerset *(G-10190)*
▲ Winters Stamp Mfg Co Inc ....F 908 352-3725
  Martinsville *(G-6011)*

3955 Carbon Paper & Inked Ribbons

Bergen Cnty Crtrdge Xchnge LLC ....G 201 493-8182
  Midland Park *(G-6222)*
▲ Commander Imaging Products Inc ..E 973 742-9298
  Paterson *(G-8237)*
▲ GSC Imaging LLC ....F 856 317-9301
  Pennsauken *(G-8519)*
Hammer Too LLC ....G 908 688-5601
  West Orange *(G-11896)*
International Laser Group Inc ....E 818 888-0400
  Cherry Hill *(G-1382)*
▲ Ner Data Products Inc ....E 888 637-3282
  Glassboro *(G-3810)*
Ricoh Prtg Systems Amer Inc ....G 973 316-6051
  Mountain Lakes *(G-6861)*
◆ Turbon International Inc ....G 800 282-6650
  Cherry Hill *(G-1430)*
Waste Not Computers & Supplies ....G 201 384-4444
  Dumont *(G-2125)*

3961 Costume Jewelry & Novelties

▲ A To Z Bohemian Glass Inc ....E 212 725-2033
  Paterson *(G-8194)*
▲ Alster Import Co Inc ....F 201 332-7245
  Jersey City *(G-4704)*
▲ Ammosa Enterprises Inc ....E 212 779-2890
  Mahwah *(G-5748)*
▲ C & C Metal Products Corp ....D 201 569-7300
  Englewood *(G-2880)*
Golden Treasure Imports Inc ....E 732 723-1830
  Englishtown *(G-2992)*
▲ HMS Monaco Et Cie Ltd ....E 201 533-0007
  Jersey City *(G-4765)*
▲ Infinite Classic Inc ....G 973 227-2790
  Fairfield *(G-3231)*
Jacmel Jewelry Inc ....G 201 223-0435
  Secaucus *(G-9897)*
Lighthouse Express Inc ....G 732 776-9555
  Asbury Park *(G-80)*
▲ Littlegifts Inc ....E 212 868-2559
  Secaucus *(G-9902)*
Meeshaa Inc ....G 908 279-7985
  Edison *(G-2567)*
Nes Jewelry Inc ....D 646 213-4094
  Clifton *(G-1680)*
▲ Norco Inc ....E 908 789-1550
  Garwood *(G-3781)*
▲ Q-Eximtrade Inc ....G 732 366-4667
  Carteret *(G-1267)*
San Marel Designs Inc ....G 973 426-9554
  Budd Lake *(G-942)*
▲ Scaasis Originals Inc ....E 732 775-7474
  Neptune *(G-6928)*
▲ Superior Jewelry Co ....F 215 677-8100
  Northfield *(G-7564)*
Swarovski North America Ltd ....G 732 632-1856
  Edison *(G-2634)*
Swarovski North America Ltd ....G 856 686-1805
  Deptford *(G-2068)*
Swarovski North America Ltd ....G 856 662-5453
  Cherry Hill *(G-1425)*
Swarovski North America Ltd ....G 201 265-4888
  Paramus *(G-7908)*

Swarovski North America Ltd ....G 609 344-1323
Atlantic City *(G-108)*

Tapia Accessory Group Inc ....E 201 393-0028
Teterboro *(G-10815)*

▲ Tsi Accessory Group Inc ....D 847 965-1700
Parsippany *(G-8104)*

Ultimate Trading Corp ....D 973 228-7700
Fairfield *(G-3332)*

Umbrella & Chairs LLC ....G 973 284-1240
Englewood *(G-2939)*

3965 Fasteners, Buttons, Needles & Pins

◆ Allary Corporation ....F 908 851-0077
Union *(G-11149)*

Alpine Machine & Tool Corp ....F 201 666-0959
Westwood *(G-11953)*

Amershoe Corp ....G 201 569-7300
Englewood *(G-2869)*

Arlo Corporation ....G 973 618-0030
Roseland *(G-9645)*

▲ C & C Metal Products Corp ....D 201 569-7300
Englewood *(G-2880)*

▲ Captive Fasteners Corp ....B 201 337-6800
Oakland *(G-7678)*

▲ Case It Inc ....E 800 441-4710
Lyndhurst *(G-5675)*

Communique Inc ....G 973 751-7588
Belleville *(G-298)*

▲ Crown Fastener & Supply Corp ....G 845 268-5150
Ringwood *(G-9446)*

Fastenation Inc ....G 973 591-1277
Clifton *(G-1618)*

▲ Geisler Ganz Corp ....G 201 223-1200
Secaucus *(G-9886)*

Nyltite Corp of America ....E 908 561-1300
South Plainfield *(G-10417)*

Omaha Standard Inc Tr NJ ....G 609 588-5400
Trenton *(G-11093)*

Primesource Building Pdts Inc ....E 732 296-0600
New Brunswick *(G-6994)*

▲ Quality Stays LLC ....G 800 868-8195
Clifton *(G-1709)*

▲ Royal Slide Sales Co Inc ....G 973 777-1177
Garfield *(G-3757)*

Royal Zipper Manufg Company ....F 973 777-1177
Garfield *(G-3758)*

▲ Snapco Manufacturing Corp ....E 973 282-0300
Hillside *(G-4441)*

Straps Manufacturing NJ Inc ....F 201 368-5201
Wyckoff *(G-12264)*

▲ Yale Hook & Eye Co Inc ....F 973 824-1440
Hillside *(G-4452)*

YKK (usa) Inc ....G 201 935-4200
Lyndhurst *(G-5715)*

▲ Zoag LLC ....G 862 591-2969
Clifton *(G-1748)*

3991 Brooms & Brushes

▲ Andon Brush Co Inc ....E 973 256-6611
Little Falls *(G-5469)*

Around Clock Sweeping LLC ....G 973 887-1144
Parsippany *(G-7949)*

▲ Benjamin Booth Company ....F 609 859-1995
Southampton *(G-10470)*

▲ Charles E Green & Son Inc ....E 973 485-3630
Newark *(G-7120)*

▲ Danline Inc ....G 973 376-1000
Springfield *(G-10550)*

◆ Delta Lambskin Products Inc ....E 201 871-9233
Englewood *(G-2887)*

▲ Fifty/Fifty Group Inc ....G 201 343-1243
Hackensack *(G-3911)*

Gordon Brush Mfg Co Inc ....G 973 827-4600
Franklin *(G-3600)*

▲ Industrial Brush Co Inc ....G 800 241-9860
Fairfield *(G-3228)*

◆ Keystone Plastics Inc ....D 908 561-1300
South Plainfield *(G-10392)*

M W Jenkins Sons Inc ....F 973 239-5150
Cedar Grove *(G-1289)*

Manufacturers Brush Corp ....G 973 882-6966
Dover *(G-2099)*

▲ Newark Brush Company LLC ....F 973 376-1000
Springfield *(G-10568)*

Rubigo Cosmetics ....G 973 636-6573
Little Falls *(G-5487)*

▲ Silver Brush Limited ....G 609 443-4900
Windsor *(G-12129)*

▲ Spectrum Paint Applicator ....E 973 732-9180
Newark *(G-7325)*

3993 Signs & Advertising Displays

▲ A Affordable Sign ....F 732 287-0446
Rahway *(G-9171)*

A B S Sign Company Inc ....G 609 522-6833
Wildwood *(G-12069)*

A C Display Studios Inc ....G 609 345-0814
Atlantic City *(G-93)*

A C L Equipment Corp ....G 973 740-9800
Livingston *(G-5521)*

A Sign Company ....G 609 298-3388
Trenton *(G-11012)*

A Sign of Excellence Inc ....G 732 264-0404
Hazlet *(G-4267)*

ABC Sign Systems Inc ....F 856 665-0950
Pennsauken *(G-8469)*

Ace Sign Company Inc ....G 732 826-3858
Perth Amboy *(G-8604)*

Adco Signs of NJ Inc ....E 908 965-2112
Elizabeth *(G-2705)*

Adiant ....F 800 264-8303
Somerville *(G-10199)*

▲ Aesys Inc ....G 201 871-3223
Emerson *(G-2856)*

All Colors Screen Printing LLC ....G 732 777-6033
Highland Park *(G-4300)*

All Nu Trophy & Screen Prtg ....F 201 807-0808
Ridgefield Park *(G-9396)*

Alpha 1 Studio Inc ....G 609 859-2200
Southampton *(G-10469)*

Alu Inc ....E 201 935-2213
Moonachie *(G-6503)*

American Graphic Systems Inc ....G 201 796-0666
Fair Lawn *(G-3076)*

American Sign Instllations LLC ....G 856 506-0610
Millville *(G-6283)*

American Stencyl Inc ....G 201 251-6460
Glen Rock *(G-3819)*

Arnold Furniture Mfrs Inc ....F 973 399-0505
Irvington *(G-4575)*

Art Dmensions ....G 908 322-8488
Scotch Plains *(G-9846)*

Artsign Studio ....G 856 546-4889
Haddon Heights *(G-4045)*

Astro Outdoor Advertising Inc ....G 856 881-4300
Glassboro *(G-3801)*

Atlas Flasher & Supply Co Inc ....E 856 423-3333
Mickleton *(G-6136)*

▲ Aura Badge Co ....D 856 881-9026
Clayton *(G-1523)*

Aura Signs Inc ....G 866 963-7446
Hillsborough *(G-4317)*

▲ Azar International Inc ....E 845 624-8808
Paramus *(G-7855)*

B & A Grafx Inc ....F 646 302-8849
Harrison *(G-4171)*

▲ Bamboo & Rattan Works Inc ....G 732 255-4239
Toms River *(G-10866)*

Bankers Pen Inc ....E 800 499-7367
Garfield *(G-3721)*

Banner Design Inc ....E 908 687-5335
Hillside *(G-4395)*

Bbk Technologies Inc ....G 908 231-0306
Raritan *(G-9307)*

Bergen Digital Graphics LLC ....G 201 825-0011
Upper Saddle River *(G-11274)*

Bergen Sign Company Inc ....E 973 742-7755
Paterson *(G-8222)*

▲ Blanc Industries Inc ....E 973 537-0090
Dover *(G-2078)*

Blazing Visuals ....G 732 781-1401
Point Pleasant Boro *(G-8933)*

Brilliant Brdcstg Concept Inc ....F 732 287-9201
Edison *(G-2475)*

▲ Brinker Industries ....E 973 678-1200
Dover *(G-2080)*

Bruce Kindberg ....G 973 664-0195
Rockaway *(G-9554)*

Brunswick Signs & Exhibit ....G 732 246-2500
North Brunswick *(G-7508)*

Cad Signs LLC ....G 201 267-0457
Hackensack *(G-3887)*

Cad Signs Nyc Corp ....E 201 525-5415
Hackensack *(G-3888)*

▲ Carpenter LLC ....F 609 689-3090
Trenton *(G-11034)*

CDI Group Inc ....F 908 862-1493
Linden *(G-5356)*

▼ Central Art & Enginering Inc ....G 609 758-5922
Cream Ridge *(G-1932)*

Cnr Products Co ....G 201 384-7003
Bergenfield *(G-384)*

Colorcraft Sign Co ....F 609 386-1115
Beverly *(G-461)*

Copyshop ....G 732 721-5700
South Amboy *(G-10236)*

Craft Signs ....G 201 656-1991
Jersey City *(G-4735)*

▲ Creoh Trading Corp ....F 718 821-0570
Lakewood *(G-5098)*

Custom Graphics of Vineland ....E 856 691-7858
Vineland *(G-11347)*

D3 Led LLC ....G 201 583-9486
North Bergen *(G-7444)*

Dale Behre ....G 908 850-4225
Hackettstown *(G-4002)*

Davis Sign Systems Inc ....G 973 394-9909
Boonton *(G-563)*

Daysol Inc ....D 908 272-5900
Kenilworth *(G-4950)*

DCI Signs & Awnings Inc ....E 973 350-0400
Newark *(G-7134)*

Delaware Valley Sign Corp ....D 609 386-0100
Burlington *(G-967)*

▲ Design Display Group Inc ....C 201 438-6000
Carlstadt *(G-1154)*

▲ Design Productions Inc ....G 201 447-5656
Waldwick *(G-11444)*

Designer Sign Systems LLC ....F 212 939-5577
Carlstadt *(G-1155)*

Designs By James ....G 856 692-1316
Vineland *(G-11352)*

Digital Arts Imaging LLC ....F 908 237-4646
Flemington *(G-3435)*

▲ Dimensional Communications Inc ...D 201 767-1500
Mahwah *(G-5766)*

Display Works LLC ....C 201 327-1260
Parsippany *(G-7983)*

Dpj Inc ....F 732 499-8600
Rahway *(G-9184)*

▲ Dublin Management Assoc of NJ ......C 609 387-1600
Burlington *(G-969)*

▲ East Trading West Inv LLC ....G 973 678-0800
Orange *(G-7819)*

Em Signs ....G 973 300-9703
Newton *(G-7386)*

▲ Empro Products Co Inc ....G 973 302-4351
Belleville *(G-302)*

Ervin Advertising Co Inc ....G 732 363-7645
Howell *(G-4554)*

Essex Morris Sign Co ....G 973 386-1755
Whippany *(G-12019)*

▲ Et Manufacturing & Sales Inc ....E 973 777-6662
Passaic *(G-8138)*

▲ Exhibit Co Inc ....E 732 465-1070
Piscataway *(G-8766)*

Exhibit Network Inc ....G 732 751-9600
Oakhurst *(G-7668)*

F & A Signs Inc ....G 732 442-9399
Hopelawn *(G-4540)*

F & S Awning and Blind Co Inc ....G 732 738-4110
Edison *(G-2517)*

Fastsigns ....G 973 887-6700
East Hanover *(G-2216)*

Fedex Office & Print Svcs Inc ....E 856 427-0099
Cherry Hill *(G-1364)*

Fioplex ....G 856 689-7213
Swedesboro *(G-10697)*

Four Way Enterprises Inc ....F 973 633-5757
Wayne *(G-11636)*

Franbeth Inc ....G 856 488-1480
Pennsauken *(G-8512)*

G & R Graphics Inc ....G 973 731-7438
South Orange *(G-10307)*

G-Force River Signs LLC ....G 609 397-4467
Lambertville *(G-5212)*

Garden State Highway Pdts Inc ....E 856 692-7572
Millville *(G-6303)*

General Sign Co Inc ....G 856 753-3535
West Berlin *(G-11724)*

Genesis Marketing Group Inc ....G 201 836-1392
Teaneck *(G-10754)*

GF Supplies LLC ....G 336 539-1666
Elmwood Park *(G-2821)*

Glasscare Inc ....F 201 943-1122
Cliffside Park *(G-1540)*

Graphic Presentations Systems ....F 732 981-1120
Piscataway *(G-8771)*

Graphic Solutions & Signs LLC ....F 201 343-7446
Hackensack *(G-3922)*

Griffin Signs Inc ....E 856 786-8517
Cinnaminson *(G-1465)*

Heros Salute Awards Co ....G 973 696-5085
Wayne *(G-11648)*

Hub Sign Crane Corp ....G 732 252-9090
Manalapan *(G-5850)*

I Associates LLC ....G 215 262-7754
Pennsauken *(G-8525)*

Identity Depot Inc ....G 973 584-9301
Ledgewood *(G-5305)*

◆ Impact Displays Inc ....E 201 804-6262
Carlstadt *(G-1171)*

▼ Infinite Mfg Group Inc ....E 973 649-9950
Kearny *(G-4885)*

Infinite Sign Industries Inc ....E 973 649-9950
Kearny *(G-4886)*

Insign Inc ....E 856 424-1161
Cherry Hill *(G-1381)*

Ionni Sign Inc ....G 973 625-3815
Rockaway *(G-9576)*

J & G Diversified ....G 732 543-2537
New Brunswick *(G-6970)*

J D Crew Inc ....G 856 665-3676
Pennsauken *(G-8534)*

J H M Communications Inc ....F 908 859-6668
Phillipsburg *(G-8653)*

J Vitale Sign Co Inc ....G 732 388-8401
Rahway *(G-9202)*

J&E Business Services LLC ....G 973 984-8444
Morris Plains *(G-6672)*

▲ Jarco U S Casting Corp ....E 201 271-0003
Union City *(G-11250)*

Jencks Signs Corp ....G 908 542-1400
Warren *(G-11557)*

JKA Specialties Mfr Inc ....F 609 859-2090
Southampton *(G-10476)*

Kdf Reprographics Inc ....F 201 784-9991
South Hackensack *(G-10274)*

Kna Graphics Inc ....G 908 272-4232
Kenilworth *(G-4969)*

◆ Kubik Maltbie Inc ....E 856 234-0052
Mount Laurel *(G-6811)*

L & F Graphics Ltd Lblty Co ....G 973 240-7033
Paterson *(G-8312)*

◆ L&M Architectural Graphics Inc ....F 973 575-7665
Fairfield *(G-3245)*

Larue Manufacturing Corp ....F 908 534-2700
Whitehouse *(G-12046)*

Lettering Plus Sign Company ....G 856 299-0404
Pedricktown *(G-8437)*

Lincoln Signs & Awnings Inc ....G 732 442-3151
Perth Amboy *(G-8621)*

M & W Franklin LLC ....G 609 927-0885
Egg Harbor Township *(G-2689)*

M C Signs ....G 609 399-7446
Ocean City *(G-7753)*

▲ Madhouz LLC ....G 609 206-8009
Glassboro *(G-3808)*

Mag Signs ....G 609 747-9600
Burlington *(G-983)*

Manhattan Signs & Designs Ltd ....E 973 278-3603
Paterson *(G-8330)*

Mark-O-Lite Sign Co Inc ....F 732 462-8530
Howell *(G-4561)*

Mashal Signs Co Inc ....G 201 348-8500
West New York *(G-11874)*

Mason Display Innovations Inc ....F 609 860-0675
Cranbury *(G-1861)*

Mc Does Inc ....G 856 985-8730
Marlton *(G-5986)*

McLain Studios Inc ....G 732 775-0271
Asbury Park *(G-81)*

▲ Mechtronics Corporation ....E 845 231-1400
Franklin Lakes *(G-3621)*

▲ Medlaurel Inc ....G 856 461-6600
Delanco *(G-2007)*

▼ Mega Media Concepts Ltd Lblty .....G 973 919-5661
Sparta *(G-10511)*

Mej Signs Inc ....G 609 584-6881
Hamilton *(G-4115)*

Merchandising Display Corp ....G 973 299-8400
Boonton *(G-576)*

▲ Metaline Products Company Inc .....E 732 721-1373
South Amboy *(G-10242)*

Michael Anthony Sign Dsgn Inc ....E 732 453-6120
Piscataway *(G-8791)*

Michele Maddalena ....G 973 244-0033
Fairfield *(G-3260)*

Miller Signs LLC ....G 732 521-0904
Helmetta *(G-4286)*

Montana Electrical Decorating ....G 973 344-1815
Newark *(G-7244)*

Mr Quick Sign ....G 201 670-1690
Midland Park *(G-6233)*

▲ MS Signs Inc ....G 973 569-1111
Paterson *(G-8345)*

Nes Light Inc ....G 201 840-0400
Ridgefield *(G-9377)*

New Dawn Inc ....G 732 774-1377
Neptune *(G-6925)*

Nickel Artistic Services LLC ....G 973 627-0390
Rockaway *(G-9589)*

Nickolaos Kappatos Entps Inc ....F 856 939-1099
Glendora *(G-3832)*

Nomadic North America LLC ....G 703 866-9200
Fairfield *(G-3273)*

North Star Signs Inc ....G 973 244-1144
Highland Lakes *(G-4299)*

NW Sign Industries Inc ....E 856 802-1677
Moorestown *(G-6603)*

NW Sign Industries Inc ....G 856 802-1677
Moorestown *(G-6604)*

Opdyke Awnings Inc ....F 732 449-5940
Wall Township *(G-11501)*

Outfront Media LLC ....D 973 575-6900
Fairfield *(G-3278)*

▲ Ovadia Corporation ....E 973 256-9200
Little Falls *(G-5483)*

Packet Media LLC ....G 856 779-3800
Englishtown *(G-2996)*

Parrish Sign Co Inc ....G 856 696-4040
Vineland *(G-11389)*

Pat Bry Advertising Spc ....G 732 591-0999
Morganville *(G-6650)*

▲ Permalith Plastics LLC ....D 215 925-5659
Pennsauken *(G-8560)*

Premier Disp & Exhibits Inc ....F 856 382-7497
Pennsauken *(G-8563)*

Presentation Solutions Inc ....G 732 961-1960
Jackson *(G-4675)*

Princeton Packet Inc ....C 609 924-3244
Princeton *(G-9097)*

Printing & Signs Express Inc ....G 201 368-1255
Mahwah *(G-5803)*

Printing Lab Ltd Liability Co ....F 201 305-0404
West New York *(G-11877)*

Pro-Pack Corp ....G 908 725-5000
Branchburg *(G-694)*

Progress Displays Inc ....G 908 757-6650
Edison *(G-2597)*

Rand Diversified Companies LLC ....B 732 985-0800
Edison *(G-2601)*

Red Feather Mktg Group LLC ....F 973 377-1988
Madison *(G-5732)*

▲ Resources Inc In Display ....E 908 272-5900
Kenilworth *(G-4992)*

Riccarr Displays Inc ....G 973 983-6701
Rockaway *(G-9603)*

Rich Designs ....G 908 369-5035
Hillsborough *(G-4369)*

Ricztone Inc ....G 609 695-6263
Trenton *(G-11112)*

Riedel Sign Company Inc ....G 201 641-9121
Little Ferry *(G-5515)*

Robden Enterprises Inc ....G 973 273-1200
Newark *(G-7290)*

▲ Roxboro Holdings Inc ....D 732 919-3119
Wall Township *(G-11506)*

S S P Enterprises Inc ....G 732 602-7878
Iselin *(G-4643)*

Salmon Signs ....G 856 589-5600
Pitman *(G-8845)*

▼ Sama Plastics Corp ....E 973 239-7200
Cedar Grove *(G-1300)*

Sign A Rama ....G 609 702-1444
Hainesport *(G-4077)*

Sign A Rama ....G 201 489-6969
Hackensack *(G-3975)*

Sign A Rama ....G 973 471-5558
Clifton *(G-1724)*

Sign Engineers Inc ....G 732 382-4224
Colonia *(G-1778)*

Sign On Inc ....G 201 384-7714
Dumont *(G-2124)*

Sign Shoppe Inc ....G 856 384-2937
Woodbury *(G-12170)*

Sign Spec Inc ....D 856 663-2292
Elmer *(G-2798)*

Sign Up Inc ....G 201 902-8640
Secaucus *(G-9928)*

Signal Sign Company LLC ....F 973 535-9277
Livingston *(G-5562)*

Signs & Custom Metal Inc ....F 201 200-0110
Jersey City *(G-4827)*

Signs of 2000 ....G 973 253-1333
Clifton *(G-1725)*

Signs of Security Inc ....E 973 340-8404
Garfield *(G-3762)*

Sjshore Marketing Ltd Lblty Co ....F 609 390-1400
Marmora *(G-6006)*

Smith Enterprises ....G 215 416-9881
Mount Laurel *(G-6842)*

South Shore Sign Co Inc ....F 718 984-5624
Matawan *(G-6032)*

Spectrum Neon Sign Group LLC ....G 856 317-9223
Pennsauken *(G-8581)*

Speedy Sign-A-Rama ....G 973 605-8313
Morristown *(G-6743)*

Spinningdesigns Inc ....F 732 775-7050
Asbury Park *(G-83)*

Stephen Swinton Studio Inc ....G 908 537-9135
Washington *(G-11588)*

▲ Stone Graphics ....G 732 919-1111
Wall Township *(G-11511)*

Suburban Sign Co Inc ....E 908 862-7222
Linden *(G-5451)*

Sun Neon Sign and Electric Co ....G 856 667-6977
Cherry Hill *(G-1422)*

Sweet Sign Systems Inc ....G 732 521-9300
Jamesburg *(G-4690)*

T L C Specialties Inc ....F 732 244-4225
Toms River *(G-10916)*

Tally Display Corp ....G 973 777-7760
Fairfield *(G-3320)*

Tdk Associates Corp ....G 862 210-8085
Roseland *(G-9656)*

Tech-Pak Inc ....F 201 935-3800
Wood Ridge *(G-12140)*

Technical Nameplate Corp ....E 973 773-4256
Passaic *(G-8184)*

▲ Testrite Instrument Co Inc ....C 201 543-0240
Hackensack *(G-3984)*

Tlg Signs Inc ....G 609 912-0500
Lawrenceville *(G-5270)*

Total Image and Sign ....G 201 941-2307
Ridgefield *(G-9387)*

Touch of Class Promotions LLC ....G 267 994-0860
Voorhees *(G-11440)*

Trademarksign ....F 848 223-4548
Jackson *(G-4680)*

Traffic Safety & Equipment Co ....F 201 327-6050
Mahwah *(G-5822)*

▲ Traffic Safety Service LLC ....E 908 561-4800
South Plainfield *(G-10441)*

▲ Trans World Marketing Corp ....C 201 935-5565
East Rutherford *(G-2334)*

Trukmanns Inc ....E 973 538-7718
Cedar Knolls *(G-1321)*

Two Jays Bingo Supply Inc ....F 609 267-4542
Hainesport *(G-4080)*

Urban Sign & Crane Inc ....G 856 691-8388
Vineland *(G-11413)*

▲ US Propack Inc ....G 732 294-4500
Freehold *(G-3690)*

US Sign and Lighting Svc LLC ....G 973 305-8900
Wayne *(G-11689)*

▲ Visual Graphic Systems Inc ....C 201 528-2700
Carlstadt *(G-1240)*

Vital Signs Medcl Legl Consltn ....F 908 537-7857
Asbury *(G-74)*

Vitillo & Sons Inc ....F 732 886-1393
Lakewood *(G-5201)*

Winemiller Press Inc ....G 732 223-0100
Manasquan *(G-5884)*

Wurz Signsystems LLC ....G 856 461-4397
Pennsauken *(G-8590)*

Yasheel Inc ....G 856 275-6812
Sewell *(G-9967)*

Yates Sign Co Inc ....E 732 578-1818
Farmingdale *(G-3398)*

3995 Burial Caskets

Marchione Industries Inc ....F 718 317-4900
Lyndhurst *(G-5690)*

3996 Linoleum & Hard Surface Floor Coverings, NEC

Congoleum Corporation ....D 609 584-3601
Trenton *(G-11045)*

▲ **Dyerich Flooring Designs Ltd**..........G...... 973 357-0600
Paterson **(G-8252)**

Evertile Flooring Co Inc..........G...... 973 242-7474
Newark **(G-7158)**

Locktile Industries Llc..........F...... 888 562-5845
Newark **(G-7224)**

◆ **Mannington Mills Inc**..........A...... 856 935-3000
Salem **(G-9806)**

S Geno Carpet and Flooring..........G...... 215 669-1400
Mount Royal **(G-6852)**

Takasago Intl Corp USA..........E...... 201 727-4200
Teterboro **(G-10814)**

Tbs Industrial Flooring Pdts..........G...... 732 899-1486
Point Pleasant Beach **(G-8927)**

3999 Manufacturing Industries, NEC

(gt) Global Tech Inc..........F...... 732 447-7083
Dayton **(G-1951)**

A-Wit Technologies Inc..........G...... 800 985-2948
Williamstown **(G-12077)**

Absolute Protective Systems..........E...... 732 287-4500
Edison **(G-2448)**

Acadia Scenic Inc..........E...... 201 653-8889
Jersey City **(G-4697)**

Accurate Screw Machine Corp..........D...... 973 276-0379
Fairfield **(G-3126)**

Adaptive Technology Entps LLC..........G...... 877 847-6272
Medford **(G-6063)**

Afh Industries LLC..........G...... 917 407-6866
Piscataway **(G-8726)**

Almetek Industries Inc..........E...... 908 850-9700
Hackettstown **(G-3996)**

▲ **Amaryllis Inc**..........G...... 973 635-0500
Chatham **(G-1325)**

◆ **American Consolidation Inc**..........D...... 201 438-4351
Carlstadt **(G-1125)**

American National Red Cross..........E...... 973 797-3300
Fairfield **(G-3135)**

American Process Systems..........G...... 908 216-6781
Port Murray **(G-8974)**

Ameritex Industries Corp..........F...... 609 502-0123
Princeton Junction **(G-9148)**

▲ **Amneal Pharmaceuticals LLC**..........E...... 908 947-3120
Bridgewater **(G-809)**

Ana Design Corp..........F...... 609 394-0300
Trenton **(G-11017)**

▲ **Animals Etc Inc**..........G...... 609 386-8442
Burlington **(G-957)**

Anu Industries LLC..........G...... 201 735-7475
Englewood **(G-2870)**

Arafat Lafi..........G...... 201 854-7300
North Bergen **(G-7431)**

Artisan Model Mold..........G...... 908 453-3524
Belvidere **(G-366)**

Artline Heat Transfer Inc..........F...... 973 599-0104
Parsippany **(G-7950)**

▲ **Aura Badge Co**..........D...... 856 881-9026
Clayton **(G-1523)**

Authenticity Brewing LLC..........G...... 862 432-9622
Sparta **(G-10489)**

Berk Gold Stamping Corporation..........E...... 973 786-6052
Andover **(G-49)**

▲ **Bigflysports Inc**..........G...... 201 653-4414
Secaucus **(G-9868)**

Binex Line Corp..........F...... 201 662-7600
Fort Lee **(G-3547)**

Bio-Key International Inc..........E...... 732 359-1100
Wall Township **(G-11467)**

Boruch Trading Ltd Lblty Co..........G...... 718 614-9575
Lakewood **(G-5086)**

BSD Industries Ltd Liability..........G...... 732 534-4341
Lakewood **(G-5091)**

C Bennett Scopes Inc..........G...... 856 464-6889
Mantua **(G-5891)**

Cambrdge Inds For Vslly Impred..........G...... 732 247-6668
Somerset **(G-10072)**

▲ **Candle Artisans Incorporated**..........E...... 908 689-2000
Washington **(G-11579)**

Carbone America Scp Division..........G...... 973 334-0700
Boonton **(G-559)**

◆ **Cellunet Manufacturing Compnay**..........F...... 609 386-3361
Burlington **(G-961)**

Cem Industries Inc..........G...... 908 244-8080
Harrison **(G-4176)**

Central Art & Engineering Inc..........G...... 609 758-5922
Cream Ridge **(G-1931)**

Clover Garden Ctr Ltd Lblty Co..........G...... 856 235-4625
Mount Laurel **(G-6789)**

Competech Smrtcard Sltions Inc..........G...... 201 256-4184
Englewood Cliffs **(G-2953)**

Conair Corporation..........C...... 609 426-1300
East Windsor **(G-2354)**

Connector Mfg Co..........G...... 513 860-4455
Jersey City **(G-4733)**

▲ **Cover Co Inc**..........E...... 908 707-9797
Branchburg **(G-651)**

▲ **Creative Display Inc**..........G...... 732 918-8010
Neptune **(G-6907)**

Custom Docks Inc..........F...... 973 948-3732
Sandyston **(G-9811)**

▲ **Cutting Edge Grower Supply LLC**..........G...... 732 905-9220
Howell **(G-4551)**

Destiny Foundation..........G...... 732 987-9008
Lakewood **(G-5108)**

Digital Outdoor Advg LLC..........G...... 732 616-2232
Tinton Falls **(G-10830)**

Display Works LLC..........G...... 201 327-1260
Parsippany **(G-7983)**

Distek Inc..........D...... 732 422-7585
North Brunswick **(G-7516)**

▲ **Dlite Products Inc**..........G...... 201 444-0822
Wyckoff **(G-12250)**

Dnp Foods America Ltd Lblty Co..........G...... 201 654-5581
Waldwick **(G-11445)**

Doosan Heavy Inds Amer LLC..........G...... 201 944-4554
Englewood Cliffs **(G-2957)**

E-Vents Registration LLC..........F...... 201 722-9221
Westwood **(G-11959)**

Eaton Corporation..........E...... 609 835-4230
Mount Holly **(G-6768)**

Emdur Metal Products Inc..........E...... 856 541-1100
Camden **(G-1062)**

F G Clover Company Inc..........G...... 973 627-1160
Rockaway **(G-9565)**

Fit Fabrication LLC..........G...... 973 685-7344
Clifton **(G-1621)**

Five Kids Group Inc..........G...... 732 774-5331
Neptune **(G-6912)**

Fluid Coating Systems Inc..........G...... 973 767-1028
Garfield **(G-3733)**

▲ **Foldtex II Ltd**..........E...... 908 928-0919
Westfield **(G-11924)**

▲ **Folica Inc**..........E...... 609 860-8430
Dayton **(G-1963)**

Force Industries LLC..........G...... 973 332-1532
Butler **(G-1003)**

◆ **Franklin Mint LLC**..........E...... 800 843-6468
Fort Lee **(G-3555)**

Freeman Technical Sales Inc..........G...... 908 464-4784
New Providence **(G-7037)**

◆ **Fuji Electric Corp America**..........D...... 732 560-9410
Edison **(G-2522)**

G G Tauber Company Inc..........G...... 800 638-6667
Neptune **(G-6913)**

▲ **Galleria Enterprises Inc**..........G...... 646 416-6683
Fairfield **(G-3205)**

▲ **Geisler Ganz Corp**..........G...... 201 223-1200
Secaucus **(G-9886)**

▲ **General Tools Mfg Co LLC**..........G...... 201 770-1380
Secaucus **(G-9889)**

▲ **Gramercy Products Inc**..........E...... 212 868-2559
Secaucus **(G-9892)**

Griffith Electric Sup Co Inc..........B...... 609 695-6121
Trenton **(G-11061)**

Gwenstone LLC..........G...... 732 785-2600
Lakewood **(G-5131)**

Hair Depot Limited..........F...... 973 251-9924
Maplewood **(G-5921)**

Halfway Hounds..........G...... 201 970-6235
Park Ridge **(G-7922)**

▲ **Han Hean U S A Corp**..........G...... 732 494-3256
Edison **(G-2531)**

Harry Shaw Model Maker Inc..........G...... 609 268-0647
Shamong **(G-9970)**

◆ **Hartz Mountain Corporation**..........C...... 800 275-1414
Secaucus **(G-9894)**

Hoyt Corporation..........D...... 201 894-0707
Englewood **(G-2904)**

Hudson Displays Co..........E...... 973 623-8255
Newark **(G-7193)**

Hutchinson Industries Inc..........G...... 609 394-1010
Trenton **(G-11067)**

▲ **Hygloss Products Inc**..........E...... 973 458-1700
Wallington **(G-11527)**

Immunogenetics Inc..........D...... 856 697-1441
Buena **(G-947)**

Industrial Water Institute..........G...... 609 585-4880
Trenton **(G-11068)**

Inman Mold Manufacturing Inc..........G...... 732 381-3033
Rahway **(G-9198)**

▲ **Inopak Ltd**..........F...... 973 962-1121
Ringwood **(G-9450)**

▲ **Jersey Jack Pinball Inc**..........E...... 732 364-9900
Lakewood **(G-5139)**

JKA Specialties Mfr Inc..........F...... 609 859-2090
Southampton **(G-10476)**

Joseph C Hansen Company Inc..........G...... 201 222-1677
Jersey City **(G-4770)**

Kanar Inc..........E...... 201 933-2800
Carlstadt **(G-1176)**

Klein Distributors Inc..........G...... 732 446-7632
Burlington **(G-982)**

Krohn Technical Products Inc..........F...... 201 933-9696
Carlstadt **(G-1182)**

Kudas Industries Inc..........F...... 412 751-0260
Denville **(G-2045)**

▼ **Left-Handed Libra LLC**..........F...... 973 623-1112
Newark **(G-7217)**

Lexi Industries..........G...... 201 297-7900
Northvale **(G-7590)**

Liquid Iron Industries Inc..........G...... 856 336-2639
West Berlin **(G-11730)**

Little House Candles Inc..........G...... 609 758-2996
New Egypt **(G-7017)**

▲ **Littlegifts Inc**..........G...... 212 868-2559
Secaucus **(G-9902)**

▲ **Look of Love Wigs Inc**..........F...... 908 687-9502
Edison **(G-2558)**

▲ **Loving Pets Corporation**..........E...... 609 655-3700
Cranbury **(G-1856)**

Mar-Kal Products Corp..........E...... 973 783-7155
Carlstadt **(G-1187)**

Massage Chair Inc..........G...... 732 201-7777
Brick **(G-753)**

Maxwell & Mollys Closet..........G...... 973 300-0101
Newton **(G-7396)**

◆ **McT Dairies Inc**..........F...... 973 258-9600
Millburn **(G-6256)**

McT Manufacturing Inc..........G...... 877 258-9600
Millburn **(G-6257)**

▲ **Merlin Industries Inc**..........D...... 609 807-1000
Hamilton **(G-4117)**

▲ **Mfv International Corporation**..........G...... 973 993-1687
Morristown **(G-6727)**

▲ **Microelettrica-Usa LLC**..........F...... 973 598-0806
Budd Lake **(G-937)**

▼ **Middle East Marketing Group**..........G...... 201 503-0150
Englewood **(G-2917)**

Minniti J Hair Replacement Inc..........G...... 856 427-9600
Cherry Hill **(G-1401)**

My Magic..........G...... 201 703-1171
Fair Lawn **(G-3105)**

Naomi Pet International Inc..........G...... 201 660-7918
Northvale **(G-7594)**

Natal Lamp & Shade Corp..........E...... 201 224-7844
Fort Lee **(G-3574)**

▲ **National Christmas Pdts Inc**..........E...... 908 709-4141
Cranford **(G-1917)**

▲ **Neilmax Industries Inc**..........G...... 908 756-8800
Edison **(G-2578)**

▲ **New Brunswick Lamp Shade Co**..........E...... 732 545-0377
New Brunswick **(G-6986)**

New Jersey Air Products Inc..........F...... 908 964-9001
Kenilworth **(G-4980)**

▲ **Newell Brands Inc**..........B...... 201 610-6600
Hoboken **(G-4486)**

Novelty Hair Goods Co..........G...... 856 963-5876
Camden **(G-1079)**

Pacent Engineering..........G...... 914 390-9150
Ocean **(G-7733)**

Palumbo Associates Inc..........F...... 908 534-2142
Whitehouse Station **(G-12060)**

Pastel Companies Inc..........G...... 732 508-0635
Howell **(G-4563)**

◆ **Peerless Umbrella Co Inc**..........F...... 973 578-4900
Newark **(G-7267)**

▲ **Pem Systems Inc**..........E...... 908 276-0211
Cranford **(G-1921)**

Pennock Company..........E...... 215 492-7900
Pennsauken **(G-8557)**

Pet Salon Inc..........F...... 609 350-6480
Margate City **(G-5933)**

▲ **Pet Salon Inc**..........G...... 609 350-6480
Margate City **(G-5934)**

Peters Laboratories..........F...... 856 767-4144
Berlin **(G-440)**

Pharmakon Corp..........F...... 856 829-3161
Cinnaminson **(G-1484)**

Polish Nail..........G...... 732 627-9799
Middlesex **(G-6189)**

Power Packaging Services Corp..........G....... 201 261-2566
Paramus *(G-7897)*
Pratt Industries USA Inc..........G....... 973 774-4680
Totowa *(G-10965)*
Prestige Industries LLC..........E....... 866 492-2244
Lyndhurst *(G-5703)*
▲ **Q10 Products LLC**..........F....... 201 567-9299
Clifton *(G-1707)*
Quallis Brands LLC..........G....... 862 252-0664
East Orange *(G-2267)*
▲ **Rainmen USA Incorporated**..........D....... 201 784-3244
Norwood *(G-7634)*
Rapid Models & Prototypes Inc..........G....... 856 933-2929
Runnemede *(G-9720)*
Rapsoco Inc..........G....... 908 977-7321
Elizabeth *(G-2771)*
Razac Products Inc..........G....... 973 622-3700
Newark *(G-7285)*
Rclc Inc..........F....... 732 877-1788
Woodbridge *(G-12152)*
◆ **Rdo Induction Ltd Liability Co**..........G....... 908 835-7222
Washington *(G-11586)*
Red Ray Manufacturing..........G....... 908 722-0040
Branchburg *(G-699)*
▲ **Riverstone Industries Corp**..........G....... 973 586-2564
Rockaway *(G-9605)*
Robel Receptacles Inc..........G....... 609 882-8065
Long Beach Township *(G-5619)*
▲ **RSR Electronics Inc**..........E....... 732 381-8777
Rahway *(G-9222)*
◆ **S Frankford & Sons Inc**..........F....... 856 222-4134
Mount Laurel *(G-6836)*
▲ **Scientific Models Inc**..........E....... 908 464-7070
Berkeley Heights *(G-421)*
Services Equipment Com LLC..........G....... 973 992-4404
Livingston *(G-5560)*
Sherwood Industries Inc..........D....... 609 396-7600
Lawrenceville *(G-5269)*
Shooting Star Inc..........G....... 908 789-2500
Scotch Plains *(G-9856)*
Skaffles Group LLC..........G....... 732 721-0022
Sayreville *(G-9839)*
▲ **Smartlite LLC**..........G....... 973 470-9400
Clifton *(G-1727)*
▲ **Smartplay International Inc**..........E....... 609 880-1860
Beverly *(G-465)*
South Jersey Industries Inc..........D....... 609 561-9000
Hammonton *(G-4149)*
Springworks Group Ltd..........G....... 973 276-7940
Fairfield *(G-3310)*
Standex International Corp..........G....... 732 469-8452
Middlesex *(G-6203)*
▲ **Star Soap/Star Candle/Prayer C**..........C....... 201 690-9090
Ridgefield Park *(G-9416)*
Stephen L Feilinger..........G....... 609 294-1884
Ltl Egg Hbr *(G-5648)*
Steps To Literacy LLC..........E....... 732 560-8363
Bound Brook *(G-626)*
▼ **Strategic Mktg Promotions Inc**..........F....... 845 623-7777
Mahwah *(G-5816)*
◆ **Sun Taiyang Co Ltd**..........D....... 201 549-7100
Moonachie *(G-6546)*
▲ **Sunshine Bouquet Company**..........C....... 732 274-2900
Dayton *(G-1989)*
Suroma Ltd Liability Company..........G....... 908 735-7700
Annandale *(G-61)*
Synthetic Grass Surfaces Inc..........G....... 973 778-9594
Lodi *(G-5605)*
▲ **Takara Belmont Usa Inc**..........D....... 732 469-5000
Somerset *(G-10179)*
Tech Art Inc..........F....... 201 525-0044
Hackensack *(G-3983)*
Technology General Corporation..........F....... 973 827-8209
Franklin *(G-3605)*
▲ **Teluca Inc**..........G....... 973 232-0002
West Orange *(G-11906)*
Ten One Design Ltd Lblty Co..........G....... 201 474-8232
Montclair *(G-6437)*
Tom Ponte Model Makers Inc..........G....... 973 627-5906
Rockaway *(G-9618)*
Tri-Met Industries Inc..........G....... 908 231-0004
Bridgewater *(G-902)*
Triangle Manufacturing Co..........G....... 201 962-7433
Upper Saddle River *(G-11286)*
Tropical Expressions Inc..........G....... 732 899-8680
Point Pleasant Boro *(G-8941)*
Tubari Inc..........E....... 973 779-8693
Passaic *(G-8185)*
◆ **Tyco International MGT Co LLC**..........E....... 609 720-4200
Princeton *(G-9133)*
Ultimate Hair World Ltd Lblty..........F....... 973 622-6900
Bloomfield *(G-535)*
◆ **USA Tealight Inc**..........F....... 732 943-2408
Avenel *(G-158)*
Venture Stationers Inc..........E....... 212 288-7235
Closter *(G-1767)*
Vira Manufacturing Inc..........E....... 732 771-8269
Perth Amboy *(G-8635)*
▲ **Vo-Toys Inc**..........E....... 973 482-8915
Clifton *(G-1740)*
Westrock Converting Company..........G....... 856 438-2200
Marlton *(G-6003)*
▲ **Wg Products Inc**..........G....... 973 256-5999
Totowa *(G-10985)*
Wolf Form Co Inc..........E....... 201 567-6556
Old Tappan *(G-7801)*
Zycal Bioceuticals Mfg LLC..........G....... 888 779-9225
Toms River *(G-10924)*

73 BUSINESS SERVICES

7372 Prepackaged Software

3i Infotech Financial Software..........E....... 732 710-4444
Edison *(G-2444)*
3i Infotech Inc..........G....... 732 710-4444
Edison *(G-2445)*
51maps Inc..........G....... 800 927-5181
Wenonah *(G-11701)*
Able Group Technologies Inc..........G....... 732 591-9299
Morganville *(G-6634)*
Accelerated Technologies Inc..........G....... 609 632-0350
Princeton *(G-8994)*
Accely Inc..........F....... 609 598-1882
Avenel *(G-123)*
Accession Data Systems..........G....... 973 992-7392
Livingston *(G-5522)*
Acclivity LLC..........E....... 973 586-2200
Rockaway *(G-9542)*
Ackk Studios LLC..........G....... 973 876-1327
Bloomfield *(G-500)*
Acqueon Technologies Inc..........G....... 609 945-3139
Princeton *(G-8995)*
Acrelic Interactive LLC..........G....... 908 222-2900
Warren *(G-11535)*
Adherence Solutions LLC..........G....... 800 521-2269
Fairfield *(G-3127)*
Advance Digital Inc..........C....... 201 459-2808
Jersey City *(G-4699)*
Aim Computer Associates Inc..........G....... 201 489-3100
Bergenfield *(G-379)*
Airchartercom LLC..........E....... 212 999-4926
West New York *(G-11860)*
Alaquest International Inc..........F....... 908 713-9399
Lebanon *(G-5275)*
Alcatel-Lucent USA Inc..........D....... 908 582-3275
New Providence *(G-7026)*
Alk Technologies Inc..........C....... 609 683-0220
Princeton *(G-9002)*
Alloy Software Inc..........F....... 973 661-9700
Bloomfield *(G-501)*
Almond Branch Inc..........E....... 973 728-3479
West Milford *(G-11849)*
Alt Shift Creative LLC..........G....... 609 619-0009
Flanders *(G-3400)*
Altibase Incorporated..........G....... 888 837-7333
Mahwah *(G-5747)*
Amber Road Inc..........C....... 201 935-8588
East Rutherford *(G-2276)*
American Soft Solutions Corp..........G....... 732 272-0052
Morganville *(G-6636)*
Amerindia Technologies Inc..........E....... 609 664-2224
Cranbury *(G-1810)*
Angus Systems Group Inc..........E....... 770 521-5553
Middlesex *(G-6147)*
Anju Clinplus LLC..........F....... 732 764-6969
Bound Brook *(G-616)*
Antenna Software Inc..........E....... 201 217-3824
Jersey City *(G-4708)*
Aone Touch Inc..........G....... 732 261-6841
Bordentown *(G-590)*
Aplnow LLC..........G....... 732 223-5575
Manasquan *(G-5866)*
Appex Innovation Solutions LLC..........G....... 215 313-3332
Princeton *(G-9004)*
Applied Voice Speech Tech Inc..........E....... 949 699-2300
Clinton *(G-1749)*
Apprentice Fs Inc..........E....... 201 819-1575
Jersey City *(G-4709)*
Aptimized LLC..........G....... 203 733-2868
Cedar Grove *(G-1270)*
Ariba Inc..........E....... 908 333-3400
Bridgewater *(G-814)*
Artezio LLC..........G....... 609 786-2435
Princeton *(G-9011)*
Astrix Software Technology..........C....... 732 661-0400
Red Bank *(G-9321)*
Athletic Organizational Aids..........E....... 201 652-1485
Midland Park *(G-6221)*
Auraplayer USA Inc..........F....... 617 879-9013
West Orange *(G-11887)*
Aurora Information Systems..........G....... 856 596-4180
Cherry Hill *(G-1344)*
Auto Injury Solutions Inc..........F....... 240 245-3117
Iselin *(G-4614)*
Automated Office Inc..........G....... 888 362-7638
Cherry Hill *(G-1345)*
Automated Resource Group Inc..........D....... 201 391-8357
Montvale *(G-6443)*
Avada Software LLC..........F....... 973 697-1043
Mahwah *(G-5751)*
Avalon Globocare Corp..........G....... 646 762-4517
Freehold *(G-3640)*
Avaya Inc..........C....... 732 852-2030
Lincroft *(G-5336)*
◆ **Avaya World Services Inc**..........E....... 908 953-6000
Morristown *(G-6690)*
Avyakta It Services LLC..........F....... 609 790-7517
East Windsor *(G-2352)*
Aztec Software Associates Inc..........E....... 973 258-0011
Springfield *(G-10540)*
Bandemar Networks LLC..........G....... 732 991-5112
East Brunswick *(G-2136)*
Basic Commerce & Industries..........E....... 609 482-3740
Hammonton *(G-4133)*
Basys Inc..........G....... 732 616-5276
Mount Laurel *(G-6781)*
Bavelle Tech Sltions Ltd Lblty..........F....... 973 992-8086
East Hanover *(G-2201)*
Beseech Ltd Liability Company..........G....... 908 461-7888
Belford *(G-286)*
Bio-Key International Inc..........E....... 732 359-1100
Wall Township *(G-11467)*
Blue Marlin Systems Inc..........D....... 973 722-0816
Long Valley *(G-5635)*
Bluebird Auto Rentl Systems LP..........E....... 973 989-2423
Dover *(G-2079)*
BMC Software Inc..........E....... 973 401-7700
Parsippany *(G-7962)*
BMC Software Inc..........G....... 703 761-0400
Woodcliff Lake *(G-12182)*
Brainstorm Software Corp..........G....... 856 234-4945
Moorestown *(G-6565)*
Brayniac LLC..........F....... 212 993-7222
Hoboken *(G-4460)*
Brittingham Sftwr Design Inc..........G....... 908 832-2691
Califon *(G-1034)*
Burgiss Group LLC..........D....... 201 427-9600
Hoboken *(G-4461)*
Business Dev Solutions Inc..........G....... 856 433-8005
Cherry Hill *(G-1354)*
Business Software Applications..........G....... 908 500-9980
Somerset *(G-10071)*
Buzzboard Inc..........F....... 201 820-0697
Lyndhurst *(G-5672)*
C Systems LLC..........F....... 732 338-9347
Edison *(G-2477)*
Cape Atlantic Software LLC..........G....... 609 442-1331
Egg Harbor Township *(G-2683)*
Cardinal Health Systems Inc..........B....... 732 537-6544
Somerset *(G-10073)*
Catalogic Software Inc..........C....... 201 249-8980
Woodcliff Lake *(G-12186)*
Ce Tech LLC..........G....... 908 229-3803
Whitehouse Station *(G-12050)*
Cegedim Inc..........C....... 908 443-2000
Bedminster *(G-269)*
Channel Logistics LLC..........F....... 856 614-5441
Camden *(G-1053)*
Chisholm Technologies Inc..........G....... 732 859-5578
Shrewsbury *(G-9994)*
Clientsrver Tech Solutions LLC..........G....... 732 710-4495
Iselin *(G-4621)*
Cloudageit Ltd Liability Co..........G....... 888 205-4128
North Brunswick *(G-7513)*
Cognizant Tech Solutions Corp..........D....... 201 801-0233
Teaneck *(G-10746)*
Coles and Blenman Network LLC..........G....... 973 432-7041
Bloomfield *(G-507)*
Com Tek Wrkplace Solutions LLC..........F....... 973 927-6814
Lyndhurst *(G-5678)*

Commvault Americas Inc	G	888 746-3849	
Tinton Falls *(G-10827)*			
Commvault Systems Inc	C	732 870-4000	
Tinton Falls *(G-10828)*			
Compco Analytical Inc	G	201 641-3936	
Little Ferry *(G-5499)*			
Comprehensive Healthcare Systm	D	732 362-2000	
Edison *(G-2488)*			
Computech Applications LLC	G	201 261-5251	
Oradell *(G-7807)*			
Computer Doc Associates Inc	D	908 647-4445	
Martinsville *(G-6009)*			
Computer Sources	G	201 791-9443	
Elmwood Park *(G-2811)*			
Continuity Logic LLC	D	866 321-5079	
Fairfield *(G-3166)*			
Corcentric	F	877 790-7272	
Cherry Hill *(G-1357)*			
Corner Stone Software Inc	G	732 938-5229	
Howell *(G-4549)*			
Criterion Software LLC	F	908 754-1166	
Freehold *(G-3648)*			
Csf Corporation	E	732 302-2222	
Somerset *(G-10087)*			
Custom Business Software LLC	G	732 534-9557	
Freehold *(G-3649)*			
Cybage Software Inc	G	848 219-1221	
Princeton *(G-9025)*			
Cyberextrudercom Inc	G	973 623-7900	
Wayne *(G-11622)*			
Cygate Sftwr & Consulting LLC	G	732 452-1881	
Edison *(G-2500)*			
Cypher Insurance Software	G	856 216-0575	
Stratford *(G-10615)*			
Daddy Donkey Labs LLC	G	646 461-4677	
Fair Haven *(G-3071)*			
Datamotion Inc	E	973 455-1245	
Florham Park *(G-3498)*			
Datayog Inc	F	714 253-6558	
Jersey City *(G-4737)*			
Dcm Group Inc	G	732 516-1173	
Newark *(G-7135)*			
Dell Software Inc	E	201 556-4600	
Rochelle Park *(G-9527)*			
Diacritech LLC	A	732 238-1157	
Jersey City *(G-4742)*			
Dial Connection LLC	F	856 753-6620	
Berlin *(G-433)*			
Direct Computer Resources Inc	E	201 848-0018	
Franklin Lakes *(G-3614)*			
Dma Data Industries Inc	G	201 444-5733	
Wyckoff *(G-12251)*			
Docbox Solutions Ltd Lblty Co	F	201 650-0970	
Montclair *(G-6411)*			
Double Check	G	973 984-2229	
Morris Plains *(G-6659)*			
Dun & Bradstreet Inc	E	973 921-5500	
Short Hills *(G-9977)*			
Dymax Systems Inc	F	732 918-2424	
Neptune *(G-6908)*			
E Pro Inc	F	732 283-0499	
Iselin *(G-4624)*			
Easy Analytic Software Inc	G	856 931-5780	
Bellmawr *(G-338)*			
Ebaotech Inc USA	G	917 977-1145	
Jersey City *(G-4746)*			
Ebic Prparedness Solutions LLC	G	719 244-6209	
Leonia *(G-5316)*			
Eclearview Technologies Inc	G	732 695-6999	
Ocean *(G-7724)*			
Edison Design Group Inc	G	732 993-3341	
Monroe *(G-6373)*			
Edu-Met Interactive Systems Co	F	908 851-9394	
Union *(G-11179)*			
Educhat Inc	G	201 871-8649	
Englewood *(G-2889)*			
Educloud Inc	E	201 944-0445	
Cliffside Park *(G-1538)*			
Effexoft Inc	G	732 221-3642	
Somerset *(G-10092)*			
Elevate Hr Inc	E	973 917-3230	
Parsippany *(G-8000)*			
Enertia LLC	G	856 330-4767	
Pennsauken *(G-8508)*			
Enforsys Inc	E	973 515-8126	
Millburn *(G-6250)*			
Enterprise Services LLC	D	609 259-9400	
Princeton *(G-9039)*			
Eroomsystem Technologies Inc	F	732 730-0116	
Lakewood *(G-5118)*			

Espertech Inc	F	973 577-6406	
Wayne *(G-11629)*			
Ezcom Software Inc	E	201 731-1800	
Englewood *(G-2895)*			
Ezrirx LLC	G	718 502-6610	
Lakewood *(G-5120)*			
Fabricated Software Inc	G	973 857-0524	
Cedar Grove *(G-1282)*			
Factonomy Inc	F	201 848-7812	
Wyckoff *(G-12252)*			
First Internet Systems	F	201 991-1889	
North Arlington *(G-7419)*			
First Mountain Consulting	G	973 325-8480	
West Orange *(G-11894)*			
Fis Avantgard LLC	G	732 530-9303	
Tinton Falls *(G-10837)*			
Fis Data Systems Inc	E	201 945-1774	
Ridgefield *(G-9360)*			
Fis Financial Systems LLC	D	856 784-7230	
Voorhees *(G-11430)*			
Flexicious LLC	G	646 340-5066	
Jersey City *(G-4752)*			
Forge Ahead LLC	G	908 346-4794	
Skillman *(G-10031)*			
Foundation Software Inc	G	908 359-0588	
Belle Mead *(G-291)*			
Four Bros Ventures Inc	G	732 890-9469	
East Brunswick *(G-2155)*			
Foursconsulting Ltd Lblty Co	G	732 599-4324	
South Plainfield *(G-10367)*			
Freyr Inc	C	908 483-7958	
Princeton *(G-9048)*			
Fusar Technologies Inc	G	201 563-0189	
Kearny *(G-4874)*			
Genexosome Technologies Inc	F	646 762-4517	
Freehold *(G-3657)*			
Genomesafe LLC	G	203 676-3752	
West Orange *(G-11895)*			
GL Consulting Inc	E	201 938-0200	
Jersey City *(G-4760)*			
Global IDS Inc	D	609 683-1066	
Princeton *(G-9050)*			
Gray Hair Software Inc	E	856 924-2253	
Mount Laurel *(G-6801)*			
Greycell Labs Inc	E	732 444-0123	
Edison *(G-2529)*			
Gwf Associates LLC	E	732 933-8780	
Eatontown *(G-2398)*			
Harms Software Inc	D	973 402-9500	
Parsippany *(G-8027)*			
Healthper Inc	G	888 257-1804	
Princeton *(G-9054)*			
Healthstar Communications Inc	A	201 560-5370	
Mahwah *(G-5780)*			
Hozric LLC	G	908 420-8821	
Green Brook *(G-3857)*			
Hr Acuity LLC	F	888 598-0161	
Florham Park *(G-3507)*			
I Physician Hub	D	732 274-0155	
Monmouth Junction *(G-6346)*			
I-Exceed Tech Solutions Inc	E	917 693-3207	
Princeton *(G-9056)*			
Idt Global Processing Svcs Inc	G	973 438-3556	
Newark *(G-7195)*			
▼ Image Access Corp	E	201 342-7878	
Rockleigh *(G-9631)*			
Indotronix International Corp	F	609 750-0700	
Plainsboro *(G-8885)*			
Infinix Corp	F	609 936-0101	
Princeton *(G-9058)*			
Inn-Client Server Systems LLC	F	908 782-9500	
Flemington *(G-3449)*			
Innovative Sftwr Solutions Inc	D	856 910-9190	
Maple Shade *(G-5903)*			
Innovi Mobile LLC	F	646 588-0165	
Millburn *(G-6253)*			
Inspire Works Inc	F	908 730-7447	
Annandale *(G-59)*			
Intangible Labs Inc	F	917 375-1301	
Hoboken *(G-4476)*			
Integrate Tech Inc	E	201 693-5625	
Ridgewood *(G-9426)*			
Integration International Inc	E	973 796-2300	
Parsippany *(G-8030)*			
Integration Partners-Ny Corp	B	973 871-2100	
Parsippany *(G-8031)*			
Intellect Design Arena Inc	F	732 769-1037	
Piscataway *(G-8782)*			
Interactive Advisory Software	E	770 951-2929	
Egg Harbor Township *(G-2686)*			

International Bus Mchs Corp	E	201 307-5136	
Park Ridge *(G-7923)*			
Interntnal Digital Systems Inc	F	201 983-7700	
Fort Lee *(G-3560)*			
Intrinsiq Spclty Solutions Inc	E	973 251-2039	
Livingston *(G-5536)*			
Invessence Inc	G	201 977-1955	
Chatham *(G-1329)*			
It Worqs LLC	E	732 494-0009	
Metuchen *(G-6111)*			
J-Tech Creations Inc	E	201 944-2968	
Fort Lee *(G-3561)*			
Junganew LLC	G	201 832-0892	
Rutherford *(G-9737)*			
Juniper Networks Inc	D	908 947-4436	
Bridgewater *(G-849)*			
Justice Laboratory Software	E	973 586-8551	
Denville *(G-2044)*			
Kaizen Technologies Inc	E	732 452-9555	
Edison *(G-2552)*			
Kandasamy Lingeswaran	F	978 631-7662	
Bloomfield *(G-516)*			
Key Software Systems LLC	F	732 409-6068	
Wall Township *(G-11494)*			
Kingster LLC	G	310 951-5127	
Paramus *(G-7881)*			
Kittyhawk Digital LLC	G	269 767-8399	
Emerson *(G-2860)*			
Labvantage Solutions Inc	E	908 707-4100	
Somerset *(G-10121)*			
Lattice Incorporated	F	856 910-1166	
Pennsauken *(G-8542)*			
Limosys LLC	F	212 222-4433	
Englewood Cliffs *(G-2974)*			
Link2consult Inc	G	888 522-0902	
Fort Lee *(G-3564)*			
Liquid Holdings Group Inc	D	212 293-1836	
Hoboken *(G-4484)*			
Lm Matrix Solutions LLC	G	908 756-7952	
Bridgewater *(G-858)*			
Local Wisdom Inc	E	609 269-2320	
Lambertville *(G-5218)*			
Log Storm Security Inc	E	732 393-6000	
Piscataway *(G-8786)*			
Lumeta Corporation	E	732 357-3500	
Somerset *(G-10126)*			
M + P International Inc	E	973 239-3005	
Verona *(G-11307)*			
Machine Atomated Ctrl Tech LLC	G	732 921-8935	
Piscataway *(G-8788)*			
Majesco	G	973 461-5200	
Morristown *(G-6725)*			
Markov Processes International	E	908 608-1558	
Summit *(G-10649)*			
Maxisit Inc	C	732 494-2005	
Metuchen *(G-6114)*			
Medical Transcription Billing	F	732 873-5133	
Somerset *(G-10133)*			
Megaplex Software Inc	G	908 647-3273	
Warren *(G-11559)*			
Melillo Consulting Inc	E	732 563-8400	
Somerset *(G-10135)*			
Mentor Graphics Corporation	C	908 604-0800	
Bedminster *(G-280)*			
Microsoft Corporation	D	732 476-5600	
Iselin *(G-4634)*			
Microsoft Corporation	G	973 785-0982	
Wayne *(G-11665)*			
Microtelecom Ltd Liability Co	G	866 676-5679	
Fort Lee *(G-3569)*			
Microwize Technology Inc	F	800 955-0321	
Paramus *(G-7889)*			
Millennium Info Tech Inc	D	609 750-7120	
Princeton *(G-9075)*			
Mind-Alliance Systems LLC	G	212 920-1911	
Livingston *(G-5546)*			
Mistras Group Inc	C	609 716-4000	
Princeton Junction *(G-9159)*			
Mobilogy Inc	E	201 848-8552	
Parsippany *(G-8049)*			
Moblty Inc	E	973 535-3600	
Livingston *(G-5547)*			
Modelware Inc	F	732 264-3020	
Holmdel *(G-4524)*			
Montgomery Investment Tech	G	610 688-8111	
Cinnaminson *(G-1479)*			
Mosaic Golf LLC	G	201 906-6136	
Hoboken *(G-4485)*			
Mplayer Entertainment LLC	G	302 229-3034	
Cherry Hill *(G-1402)*			

S
I
C

Company	Code	Phone
Ms Health Software Corp, Hackettstown (G-4027)	G	908 850-5564
MSI Technologies LLC, Parsippany (G-8050)	F	973 263-0080
Mtbc Health Inc, Somerset (G-10140)	G	732 873-5133
Mtbc Practice Management Corp, Somerset (G-10141)	C	732 873-5133
Munipol Systems, Marlton (G-5988)	F	856 985-2929
Museami Inc, North Brunswick (G-7528)	F	609 917-3000
Mvn Usa Inc, Holmdel (G-4526)	G	732 817-1400
Nb Ventures Inc, Clark (G-1509)	C	732 382-6565
Nconnex Inc, New Brunswick (G-6984)	G	413 658-5582
Netcom Systems Inc, Edison (G-2579)	E	732 393-6100
Netx Information Systems Inc, Long Beach Township (G-5618)	E	609 298-9118
New Venture Partners LLC, New Providence (G-7049)	A	908 464-8131
Nexagen Networks Inc, Morganville (G-6649)	D	732 598-1277
Nextgen It LLC, Bridgewater (G-864)	E	908 837-9443
Ngenious Solutions Inc, Piscataway (G-8797)	G	732 873-3385
Nicomac Systems Inc, Norwood (G-7630)	G	201 871-0916
Nlyte Software Inc, Edison (G-2583)	E	732 395-6920
Nogpo Inc, Basking Ridge (G-200)	F	908 642-3545
◆ Nokia of America Corporation, New Providence (G-7050)	A	908 582-3275
Northwind Ventures Inc, Vernon (G-11301)	G	917 509-1964
Novega Venture Partners Inc, Holmdel (G-4527)	G	732 528-2600
Nuance Communications Inc, Mahwah (G-5799)	C	201 252-9100
Nxlevel Inc, Lambertville (G-5219)	E	609 483-6900
Objectif Lune LLC, Bloomfield (G-525)	F	973 780-0100
Objectif Lune LLC, Bloomfield (G-526)	G	203 878-7206
Objecutive Inc, Fort Lee (G-3575)	F	201 242-1522
Oli Systems Inc, Cedar Knolls (G-1320)	E	973 539-4996
Onco Inc, Wall Township (G-11500)	F	732 292-7460
One Source Solutions LLC, Freehold (G-3675)	F	732 536-0578
Ontimeworks LLC, New Providence (G-7051)	F	800 689-3568
Onx USA LLC, Edison (G-2588)	E	440 569-2417
Open Solutions Inc, Cherry Hill (G-1408)	E	856 424-0150
Optherium Labs Ou, Holmdel (G-4528)	G	516 253-1777
Oracle America Inc, Edison (G-2589)	D	732 623-4821
Oracle Corporation, Bridgewater (G-869)	C	908 547-6200
Oracle Corporation, East Rutherford (G-2315)	B	201 842-7000
Orangehrm Inc, Secaucus (G-9908)	E	914 458-4254
Orion Cloud Cmpt Solutions Inc, Bridgewater (G-870)	G	732 485-8658
Os33 Services Corp, Iselin (G-4638)	G	866 796-0310
Output Services Group Inc, Ridgefield Park (G-9412)	E	201 871-1100
Oxford Biochronometrics LLC, Montclair (G-6427)	F	201 755-5932
Pace Business Solutions Inc, Manahawkin (G-5833)	E	908 451-0355
Pai Services LLC, Mount Laurel (G-6823)	C	856 231-4667
Parabole LLC, Monmouth Junction (G-6353)	G	609 917-8479
Pario Group LLC, Edison (G-2591)	G	732 906-2302
Patientstar LLC, Moorestown (G-6610)	F	856 722-0808
Paylocity Holding Corporation, Springfield (G-10570)	B	908 917-3027
Pds Prclnical Data Systems Inc, Mount Arlington (G-6759)	E	973 398-2800
Pearson Education Inc, Hoboken (G-4491)	D	914 287-8000
Picture Window Software LLC, Blairstown (G-498)	F	908 362-4000
Pinsonault Associates LLC, Parsippany (G-8066)	E	800 372-9009
Pjm Software Inc, Clifton (G-1698)	G	973 330-0405
Planet Associates Inc, Park Ridge (G-7927)	E	201 693-8700
Plescia & Company Inc, Marlton (G-5994)	F	856 793-0137
Polaris Consulting & Svcs Ltd, Jersey City (G-4803)	F	732 590-8151
Polysystems Inc, Cherry Hill (G-1415)	E	312 332-5670
Predictive Analytcs Dcision, Parsippany (G-8071)	G	973 541-7020
Premier Healthcare Exch Corp, Bedminster (G-283)	D	908 658-3535
Primepoint Inc, Westampton (G-11915)	E	609 298-7373
Priority-Software US LLC, Rockaway (G-9600)	G	973 586-2200
Promia Incorporated, Princeton (G-9106)	E	609 252-1850
Proscape Technologies Inc, Hillsborough (G-4364)	E	215 441-0300
Ptc Inc, Morristown (G-6738)	E	973 631-6195
Qad Inc, Mount Laurel (G-6833)	C	856 273-1717
Qcom Inc, Marlboro (G-5955)	E	732 772-0990
Quadramed Corporation, Eatontown (G-2420)	E	732 751-0400
Quarter Spot, Wayne (G-11676)	F	917 647-9170
Radix M I S, Bloomfield (G-528)	G	973 707-2121
Ramco Systems Corporation, Lawrence Township (G-5246)	E	609 620-4800
Rbs Intrntonal Direct Mktg LLC, Pennsauken (G-8569)	G	856 663-2500
Re Systems Group Inc, Westwood (G-11968)	G	201 883-1572
Real Soft Inc, Monmouth Junction (G-6360)	A	609 409-3636
Red Oak Software Inc, Mountain Lakes (G-6860)	F	973 316-6064
Redi-Data Inc, Fairfield (G-3291)	F	973 227-4380
Redi-Data Inc, Marlton (G-5996)	A	856 988-0551
Redi-Direct Marketing Inc, Fairfield (G-3292)	B	973 808-4500
Redstage Networks LLC, Jersey City (G-4817)	E	888 335-2747
Relational Security Corp, Secaucus (G-9917)	E	201 867-1330
Relatnship Capitl Partners Inc, Short Hills (G-9984)	F	908 962-4881
Relayware Inc, Jersey City (G-4818)	F	201 433-3331
Relpro Inc, Short Hills (G-9985)	G	908 962-4881
Remote Landlord Systems LLC, Lakewood (G-5180)	G	732 534-4445
Revelation Technologies Inc, Westwood (G-11969)	F	201 594-1422
Rey Consulting Inc, Oakland (G-7703)	F	201 337-0051
Rhodium Software Inc, Dayton (G-1985)	G	848 248-2906
Robokiller LLC, South Amboy (G-10244)	E	723 838-1901
RSD America Inc, Teaneck (G-10771)	F	201 996-1000
Rx Trade Zone Inc, Edison (G-2608)	G	833 933-6600
Sage Software Inc, Mount Laurel (G-6837)	D	856 231-4667
Saksoft Inc, Jersey City (G-4821)	C	201 451-4609
Samsung SDS Globl Scl Amer Inc, Ridgefield Park (G-9413)	E	201 229-4456
Saviance Technologies, Metuchen (G-6120)	E	609 448-7095
Scalable Systems Inc, Piscataway (G-8808)	E	732 993-4320
Scimar Technologies LLC, Allentown (G-35)	G	609 208-1796
Scivantage Inc, Jersey City (G-4824)	D	646 452-0001
Screendreamercom Inc, Blackwood (G-492)	G	856 702-6400
Secured MBL Hlth Applctons Inc, Long Branch (G-5632)	G	732 997-9609
Sequel Software Inc, Bridgewater (G-894)	E	908 575-0252
Sfp Software Inc, Mount Laurel (G-6840)	G	856 235-7778
Shiva Software Group Inc, Flanders (G-3415)	E	973 691-5475
Shore Software Inc, Point Pleasant Boro (G-8940)	G	732 899-6878
Sierra Communication Intl LLC, Morristown (G-6742)	G	866 462-8292
Signify Fincl Solutions LLC, Parsippany (G-8086)	E	862 930-4682
Simon & Schuster Inc, Parsippany (G-8087)	D	973 656-6000
Simtronics Corporation, Little Silver (G-5520)	F	732 747-0322
Sirma Group Inc, Jersey City (G-4829)	B	646 357-3067
Sitetracker Inc, Montclair (G-6435)	F	551 486-2087
Smartlinx Solutions LLC, Edison (G-2623)	D	732 385-5507
Software Practices and Tech, Summit (G-10658)	G	908 464-2923
Software Services & Solutions, Lawrence Township (G-5248)	F	203 630-2000
Solbright Group Inc, Newark (G-7319)	F	973 339-3855
Specialneedsware Inc, Newark (G-7323)	F	646 278-9959
Specialty Systems Inc, Toms River (G-10913)	E	732 341-1011
Spectare Systems Inc, Titusville (G-10856)	G	609 303-0957
Sphinx Software Inc, Plainsboro (G-8900)	G	609 275-5085
SRS Software LLC, Montvale (G-6480)	F	201 802-1300
▲ Ssam Sports Inc, Allendale (G-17)	G	917 553-0596
Ssam Sports Inc, Allendale (G-18)	G	917 553-0596
Starbeam Software Solutions, Bergenfield (G-395)	G	201 384-0017
Storis Inc, Mount Arlington (G-6760)	D	888 478-6747
Storm City Entertainment Inc, Sicklerville (G-10027)	F	856 885-6902
Streamserve Inc, Asbury Park (G-84)	E	781 863-1510
Strikeforce Technologies Inc, Edison (G-2628)	G	732 661-9641
Strivr Inc, Livingston (G-5565)	F	973 216-7379
Structured Healthcare MGT Inc, Englewood (G-2935)	E	201 569-3290
Sunbird Software Inc, Somerset (G-10176)	D	732 993-4476
Sunrise Intl Educatn Inc, North Brunswick (G-7541)	D	917 525-0272
Supply Chain Technologies LLC, Shrewsbury (G-10012)	G	856 206-9849
Surround Technologies LLC, Bloomfield (G-534)	G	973 743-1277
Swapshub Company Inc, Piscataway (G-8819)	G	732 529-4813
Swce Inc, Bernardsville (G-455)	E	908 766-5695
Sybase Inc, Parsippany (G-8095)	D	973 537-5700
T N T Information Systems, Plainsboro (G-8901)	G	609 799-9488
Tab Networks, Woodcliff Lake (G-12205)	G	201 746-0067
Tangoe Us Inc, Parsippany (G-8096)	C	973 257-0300

Taptask LLC......G...... 201 294-2371
Clifton *(G-1735)*
Taxstream LLC......D...... 201 610-0390
Hoboken *(G-4500)*
Tech Brains Solutions Inc......E...... 732 952-0552
Somerset *(G-10183)*
Technovision Inc......E...... 732 381-0200
Lyndhurst *(G-5710)*
Thomson Reuters Corporation......F...... 973 662-3070
Nutley *(G-7655)*
Total Cover It LLC......G...... 973 342-4623
South Orange *(G-10316)*
Total Reliance LLC......F...... 732 640-5079
Dayton *(G-1992)*
Transportation Tech Svcs Inc......E...... 732 326-0700
Woodbridge *(G-12155)*
Trendmark LLC......G...... 551 226-7973
Princeton *(G-9132)*
Trisys Inc......F...... 973 360-2300
Florham Park *(G-3518)*
Tropaion Inc......G...... 908 654-3870
Springfield *(G-10580)*
Tunnel Networks Inc......G...... 609 414-9799
East Windsor *(G-2369)*
Turbot Hq Inc......E...... 973 922-0297
Maplewood *(G-5930)*
U S Tech Solutions Inc......D...... 201 524-9600
Jersey City *(G-4840)*
Ubertesters Inc......F...... 201 203-7903
Ridgewood *(G-9434)*
Unicorn Group Inc......D...... 973 360-5904
Fairfield *(G-3333)*
Unicorn Group Inc......E...... 973 360-0688
Florham Park *(G-3522)*
Uniken Inc......G...... 917 324-0399
Chatham *(G-1339)*
Uniphy Health Holdings LLC......E...... 866 874-8616
Newark *(G-7352)*
Universal Business Automation......G...... 973 575-3568
Montville *(G-6496)*
Universal Techncl Resrce Svcs......C...... 973 663-7930
Mount Arlington *(G-6761)*
US Software Group Inc......E...... 732 361-4636
South Plainfield *(G-10447)*
Utah Intermediate Holding Corp......C...... 856 787-2700
Mount Laurel *(G-6845)*
Valuemomentum Inc......D...... 908 755-0025
Piscataway *(G-8832)*
Vantage Business Systems Inc......G...... 609 625-7020
Mays Landing *(G-6044)*
Varsity Software Inc......G...... 609 309-9955
Lawrenceville *(G-5271)*
Venture App LLC......G...... 908 644-3985
Summit *(G-10663)*
Verint Systems Inc......D...... 201 438-1429
Lyndhurst *(G-5712)*
Vertican Technologies Inc......G...... 800 435-7257
Fairfield *(G-3341)*
Vibgyor Solutions Inc......G...... 609 750-9158
Princeton Junction *(G-9165)*
Visionware Systems Inc......F...... 609 924-0800
Skillman *(G-10037)*
Vst Consulting Inc......D...... 732 404-0025
Iselin *(G-4650)*
▲ **Vu Sound Incorporated**......F...... 215 990-2864
Lumberton *(G-5666)*
Vyral Systems Inc......G...... 201 321-2488
Hawthorne *(G-4265)*
Wizcom Corporation......E...... 609 750-0601
Princeton Junction *(G-9166)*
Wizdata Systems Inc......F...... 973 975-4113
Parsippany *(G-8115)*
Workwave LLC......F...... 866 794-1658
Holmdel *(G-4532)*
World Software Corporation......E...... 201 444-3228
Glen Rock *(G-3831)*
X-Factor Cmmnctons Hldings Inc......G...... 877 741-3727
Northvale *(G-7612)*
Xanthus Inc......G...... 973 643-0920
Newark *(G-7361)*
Xchange Software Inc......E...... 732 444-6666
Parlin *(G-7936)*
Yeghen Computer System......F...... 732 996-5500
Ocean *(G-7749)*
Zoluu LLC......G...... 862 686-1774
Fair Lawn *(G-3125)*
Zultner & Company......F...... 609 452-0216
Princeton *(G-9142)*
Zwivel LLC......E...... 844 499-4835
Paramus *(G-7915)*
Zycus Inc......E...... 609 799-5664
Princeton *(G-9143)*

76 MISCELLANEOUS REPAIR SERVICES

7692 Welding Repair

A 1 Fencing Inc......F...... 908 527-1066
Elizabeth *(G-2702)*
Alba Translations CPA......G...... 973 340-1130
Lodi *(G-5574)*
Atlas Enterprise......F...... 908 561-1144
South Plainfield *(G-10333)*
Auto Tig Welding Fabricating......G...... 973 839-8877
Pompton Lakes *(G-8946)*
B L White Welding & Steel Co......G...... 973 684-4111
Paterson *(G-8218)*
Blue Light Welding & Fabg LLC......G...... 856 629-5891
Williamstown *(G-12081)*
Bluewater Industries Inc......F...... 609 427-1012
Dennisville *(G-2028)*
BR Welding Inc......F...... 732 363-8253
Howell *(G-4547)*
Browns Welding Service......G...... 732 988-9530
Neptune *(G-6902)*
Chizzys Service Center......G...... 201 641-7222
Little Ferry *(G-5496)*
CMI-Promex Inc......F...... 856 351-1000
Pedricktown *(G-8433)*
Creative Machining Systems......F...... 609 586-3932
Trenton *(G-11048)*
D J B Welding Inc......G...... 732 657-7478
Jackson *(G-4662)*
D K Tool & Die Welding Group......E...... 908 241-7600
Roselle Park *(G-9693)*
D N D Corp......G...... 908 637-4343
Great Meadows *(G-3849)*
Edward Kurth and Son Inc......E...... 856 227-5252
Sewell *(G-9951)*
Elmco Two Inc......G...... 856 365-2244
Camden *(G-1061)*
Eme Electrical Contractors......G...... 973 228-6608
Caldwell *(G-1027)*
Ferry Machine Corp......E...... 201 641-9191
Little Ferry *(G-5504)*
Folgore Mobil Welding Inc......E...... 732 541-2974
Carteret *(G-1258)*
Frank E Ganter Inc......G...... 856 692-2218
Vineland *(G-11356)*
Ironbound Welding Inc......G...... 973 589-3128
Newark *(G-7201)*
J D Machine Parts Inc......F...... 856 691-8430
Vineland *(G-11374)*
J P Rotella Co Inc......F...... 973 942-2559
Haledon *(G-4083)*
John B Horay Welding......G...... 856 336-2154
West Berlin *(G-11727)*
K H Machine Works......G...... 201 867-2338
North Bergen *(G-7459)*
Kt Welding......G...... 908 862-7370
Linden *(G-5398)*
Laurelton Welding Service Inc......G...... 732 899-6348
Point Pleasant Beach *(G-8922)*
Lodi Welding Co Inc......G...... 908 852-8367
Hackettstown *(G-4017)*
Louis Iron Works Inc......G...... 973 624-2700
Newark *(G-7226)*
Lusotech LLC......G...... 973 332-3861
Newark *(G-7230)*
M & M Welding & Steel Fabg......G...... 908 647-6060
Stirling *(G-10603)*
Machine Plus Inc......G...... 973 839-8884
Haskell *(G-4210)*
McAlister Welding & Fabg......F...... 856 740-3890
Glassboro *(G-3809)*
Micheller & Son Hydraulics Inc......F...... 908 687-1545
Roselle *(G-9677)*
Oceanview Marine Welding LLC......G...... 609 624-9669
Ocean View *(G-7765)*
Off-Road Welding Inc......G...... 908 832-2967
Glen Gardner *(G-3816)*
▲ **Orgo-Thermit Inc**......E...... 732 657-5781
Manchester *(G-5887)*
P K Welding LLC......F...... 908 928-1002
Garwood *(G-3783)*
Pabst Enterprises Equipment Co......E...... 908 353-2880
Elizabeth *(G-2764)*
Pennetta & Sons......E...... 201 420-1693
Jersey City *(G-4798)*
Peter Garafano & Son Inc......E...... 973 278-0350
Paterson *(G-8364)*
Pmje Welding LLC......G...... 973 685-7344
Clifton *(G-1699)*
Precision Welding Machine......G...... 609 625-1465
Mays Landing *(G-6042)*
Reuther Engineering......F...... 973 485-5800
Edison *(G-2604)*
Ricklyn Co Inc......G...... 908 689-6770
Columbia *(G-1800)*
Serious Welding & Mech LLC......F...... 732 698-7478
South River *(G-10466)*
Sine Tru Tool Company Inc......G...... 732 591-1100
Marlboro *(G-5959)*
Specialty Measures......G...... 609 882-6071
Ewing *(G-3055)*
Stecher Dave Welding & Fabg Sp......G...... 856 467-3558
Swedesboro *(G-10729)*
Sulzer Pump Services (us) Inc......F...... 856 542-5046
Bridgeport *(G-774)*
Union City Whirlpool Repair......G...... 908 428-9146
Union City *(G-11271)*
Vep Manufacturing......F...... 732 657-0666
Jackson *(G-4681)*
▲ **Vermes Machine Co Inc**......E...... 856 642-9300
Moorestown *(G-6630)*
W W Manufacturing Co Inc......F...... 856 451-5700
Bridgeton *(G-802)*
Wel-Fab Inc......E...... 609 261-1393
Rancocas *(G-9265)*
Weld Tech Fab......G...... 732 919-2185
Farmingdale *(G-3396)*
Welded Products Co Inc......E...... 973 589-0180
Newark *(G-7358)*
Welding & Radiator Supply Co......G...... 609 965-0433
Egg Harbor City *(G-2674)*
Willow Run Construction Inc......F...... 201 659-7266
Jersey City *(G-4849)*

7694 Armature Rewinding Shops

Absecon Electric Motor Works......G...... 609 641-1523
Absecon *(G-1)*
▲ **Atlantic Kenmark Electric Inc**......F...... 201 991-2117
North Arlington *(G-7416)*
Atlantic Switch Generator LLC......F...... 609 518-1900
Hainesport *(G-4069)*
▲ **Custom Converters Inc**......E...... 201 994-9000
Livingston *(G-5527)*
D Electric Motors Inc......G...... 856 696-5959
Vineland *(G-11348)*
Electrical Motor Repr Co of NJ......F...... 609 392-6149
Trenton *(G-11058)*
General Electric Company......C...... 201 866-2161
North Bergen *(G-7453)*
George J Bender Inc......E...... 908 687-0081
Union *(G-11189)*
Hights Electric Motor Service......G...... 609 448-2298
Hightstown *(G-4312)*
Jarvis Electric Motors Inc......G...... 856 662-7710
Pennsauken *(G-8535)*
Johnnys Service Center......G...... 732 738-0569
Fords *(G-3529)*
Lakewood Elc Mtr Sls & Svc......G...... 732 363-2865
Howell *(G-4560)*
Lockwoods Electric Motor Svc......E...... 609 587-2333
Trenton *(G-11077)*
▲ **Longo Elctrical-Mechanical Inc**......D...... 973 537-0400
Wharton *(G-11991)*
Longo Elctrical-Mechanical Inc......E...... 973 537-0400
Linden *(G-5404)*
Lowder Electric and Cnstr......G...... 732 764-6000
Middlesex *(G-6177)*
▲ **McIntosh Industries Inc**......E...... 908 688-7475
Hillside *(G-4430)*
Motors and Drives Inc......G...... 732 462-7683
Freehold *(G-3672)*
Motors and Drives Inc......G...... 609 344-8058
Atlantic City *(G-103)*
New Jersey Electric Motors......G...... 908 526-5225
Somerville *(G-10221)*
Phil Desiere Electric Mtr Svc......F...... 856 692-8442
Vineland *(G-11390)*
Precision Devices Inc......G...... 609 882-2230
Ewing *(G-3045)*
RSI Company......G...... 973 227-7800
Fairfield *(G-3297)*
◆ **SMS Electric Motor Car LLC**......F...... 215 428-2502
Bridgewater *(G-896)*
Story Electric Mtr Repr Co Inc......G...... 973 256-1636
Little Falls *(G-5490)*

SIC

Employee Codes: A=Over 500 employees, B=251-500
C=101-250, D=51-100, E=20-50, F=10-19, G=4-9
2018 Harris New Jersey
Manufacturers Directory
609

Universal Electric Co ....E 201 968-1000
   Hackensack *(G-3989)*

Universal Electric Mtr Svc Inc ....F 201 968-1000
   Hackensack *(G-3990)*

Willier Elc Mtr Repr Co Inc ....E 856 627-2262
   Gibbsboro *(G-3791)*

Willier Elc Mtr Repr Co Inc ....E 856 627-3535
   Gibbsboro *(G-3790)*

ALPHABETIC SECTION

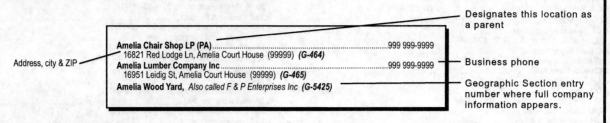

Designates this location as a parent

Amelia Chair Shop LP (PA) 999 999-9999
  16821 Red Lodge Ln, Amelia Court House (99999) *(G-464)*

Address, city & ZIP

Amelia Lumber Company Inc 999 999-9999
  16951 Leidig St, Amelia Court House (99999) *(G-465)*

Amelia Wood Yard, *Also called F & P Enterprises Inc (G-5425)*

Business phone

Geographic Section entry number where full company information appears.

See footnotes for symbols and codes identification.

* Companies listed alphabetically.

* Complete physical or mailing address.

(gt) Global Tech Inc 732 447-7083
  32 Marc Dr Dayton (08810) *(G-1951)*
10-31 Incorporated 908 496-4946
  2 W Crisman Rd Columbia (07832) *(G-1795)*
100 Owned By Ultra Elec Uk, Somerset *Also called AEP Networks Inc (G-10051)*
10x Daily LLC 732 276-6407
  10 Blue Jay Way Lakewood (08701) *(G-5061)*
140 Main Street Corp 732 974-2929
  2175 Highway 35 Ste 13 Sea Girt (08750) *(G-9860)*
150 Development Group LLC 732 546-3812
  400 South Ave Ste 10 Middlesex (08846) *(G-6139)*
175 Derousse LLC 856 662-0100
  175 Derousse Ave Pennsauken (08110) *(G-8467)*
1800iprint, Lumberton *Also called New Jersey Tech Group LLC (G-5661)*
201 Food Packing Inc 973 463-0777
  7 Great Meadow Ln East Hanover (07936) *(G-2198)*
202 Smoothie LLC 973 985-4973
  11 Danielle Dr Wayne (07470) *(G-11599)*
21st Century Finishing Inc 201 797-0212
  40 Webro Rd Clifton (07012) *(G-1551)*
21st Century Media Newsppr LLC (HQ) 215 504-4200
  600 Perry St Trenton (08618) *(G-11009)*
21st Century Optics Inc 808 935-1119
  5 Powderhorn Dr Warren (07059) *(G-11533)*
24 Horas Inc 973 817-7400
  68 Madison St Ste A Newark (07105) *(G-7062)*
250 Lackland Holding LLC 732 469-7420
  250 Lackland Dr Middlesex (08846) *(G-6140)*
26 Flavors LLC 855 662-7299
  29 Riverside Ave Newark (07104) *(G-7063)*
2a Holdings Inc 973 378-8011
  12 Hoffman St Maplewood (07040) *(G-5913)*
3 IS Technologies Inc 609 238-8213
  4 Colfax Ln Hainesport (08036) *(G-4067)*
35 Food Corp 732 442-1640
  545 Us Highway 9 N Woodbridge (07095) *(G-12144)*
360 Media Innovations LLC 201 228-0941
  1511a Stuyvesant Ave Union (07083) *(G-11145)*
3d Biotek LLC 908 801-6138
  1031 Us 206 Ste 202 Bridgewater (08807) *(G-806)*
3dimension Dgnstc Slution Corp 201 780-4653
  394 Union St Fl 1 Jersey City (07304) *(G-4691)*
3forty Group Inc 973 773-1806
  90 Dayton Ave Ste 6a Passaic (07055) *(G-8121)*
3i Infotech Financial Software 732 710-4444
  450 Rritan Ctr Pkwy Ste B Edison (08837) *(G-2444)*
3i Infotech Inc 732 710-4444
  450 Rritan Ctr Pkwy Ste B Edison (08837) *(G-2445)*
3M Company 908 788-4000
  500 Rte 202 Flemington (08822) *(G-3422)*
3M Company 973 884-2500
  140 Algonquin Pkwy Whippany (07981) *(G-12004)*
3r Biopharma LLC 914 486-1898
  324 Perry Dr North Brunswick (08902) *(G-7499)*
3rd Generation Enterprises 201 528-7274
  283 Veterans Blvd Carlstadt (07072) *(G-1119)*
3shape Inc 908 219-4641
  10 Independence Blvd # 150 Warren (07059) *(G-11534)*
4 D Motion, Allendale *Also called Ssam Sports Inc (G-18)*
4 Over Inc 201 440-1656
  4 Empire Blvd Moonachie (07074) *(G-6498)*
4 Way Lock LLC 908 359-2002
  5 Ilene Ct Ste 12 Hillsborough (08844) *(G-4315)*
42 Design Square LLC 888 272-5979
  350 Parsippany Rd Apt 128 Parsippany (07054) *(G-7937)*
431 Converters Inc 856 848-8949
  230 Glassboro Rd Woodbury Heights (08097) *(G-12173)*
5 Elements Robotics, Wall Township *Also called Five Elements Robotics LLC (G-11482)*

5 Kids Group Ltd Liability Co 732 774-5331
  37 State Route 35 N Neptune (07753) *(G-6896)*
50 Plus Monthly Inc 973 584-7911
  5 Clearfield Rd Succasunna (07876) *(G-10618)*
51maps Inc 800 927-5181
  500 E Mantua Ave Wenonah (08090) *(G-11701)*
67 Pollock Ave Corp 201 432-1156
  67 Pollock Ave Jersey City (07305) *(G-4692)*
7th Seventh Day Wellness Ctr 856 308-0991
  6 Sherwick Ct Sicklerville (08081) *(G-10015)*
814 Americas, Elizabeth *Also called Smithfield Packaged Meats Corp (G-2774)*
9001 Corporation 201 963-2233
  507 Summit Ave Ste 7 Jersey City (07306) *(G-4693)*
9002 Corporation 201 792-9595
  318 Central Ave Jersey City (07307) *(G-4694)*
911 Tatical Direct, Toms River *Also called Enailsupply Corporation (G-10874)*
A & A Coating, South Plainfield *Also called A&A Company Inc (G-10319)*
A & A Concrete Products Inc 973 835-2239
  2 S Corporate Dr Riverdale (07457) *(G-9473)*
A & A Ironwork Co Inc 973 728-4300
  955 Burnt Meadow Rd Hewitt (07421) *(G-4287)*
A & A Soft Pretzel Company 856 338-0208
  1100 N 32nd St Camden (08105) *(G-1039)*
A & D Indus & Mar Repr Inc 732 541-1481
  900 Port Reading Ave B2 Port Reading (07064) *(G-8984)*
A & F Electroplating Inc 973 983-2459
  106 Ashland Ave West Orange (07052) *(G-11884)*
A & J Carpets Inc 856 227-1753
  4461 Route 42 Blackwood (08012) *(G-469)*
A & L Industries Inc 973 589-8070
  23 George St Newark (07105) *(G-7064)*
A & R Sewing Company Inc 201 332-0622
  451 Communipaw Ave Jersey City (07304) *(G-4695)*
A & R Sports LLC 201 941-8875
  10 Middlebury Blvd Ste 1 Randolph (07869) *(G-9266)*
A & S Frozen Inc 201 672-0510
  96 E Union Ave East Rutherford (07073) *(G-2274)*
A & S Packaging & Display 201 531-1900
  120 Kero Rd Carlstadt (07072) *(G-1120)*
A 1 Fencing Inc 908 527-1066
  166 7th St Elizabeth (07201) *(G-2702)*
A A A Stamp and Seal Mfg Co 201 796-1500
  361 N Midland Ave Saddle Brook (07663) *(G-9747)*
A A K, Edison *Also called Aak USA Inc (G-2446)*
A A Sayia & Company Inc 201 659-1179
  1 Newark St Ste 29 Hoboken (07030) *(G-4455)*
A A World Class Corp, Fort Lee *Also called World Class Marketing Corp (G-3591)*
A Affordable Sign 732 287-0446
  1053 Madison Ave Rahway (07065) *(G-9171)*
A and P Pharmacy 908 850-7640
  7 Naughright Rd Ste V Hackettstown (07840) *(G-3994)*
A Andersen Shtmtl Fabrication, Linden *Also called Lentine Sheet Metal Inc (G-5402)*
A B C Machinery Corp 609 971-0990
  712 Old Shore Rd Ste 1 Forked River (08731) *(G-3532)*
A B S Sign Company Inc 609 522-6833
  3008 Park Blvd Wildwood (08260) *(G-12069)*
A B Scantlebury Co Inc 973 770-3000
  108 Phil Hardin Rd Newton (07860) *(G-7378)*
A B T, Totowa *Also called Advanced Biotech Overseas LLC (G-10926)*
A B Tees LLC 201 239-0022
  7 Sherman Ave Fl 3 Jersey City (07307) *(G-4696)*
A C Bakery Distributors Inc 973 977-2255
  1 Industrial Plz Paterson (07503) *(G-8191)*
A C C, Neptune *Also called Automated Control Concepts Inc (G-6901)*
A C D, Burlington *Also called American Custom Drying Co (G-955)*
A C D Custom Granite Inc 732 695-2400
  1304 Roller Rd Ocean (07712) *(G-7711)*

A
L
P
H
A
B
E
T
I
C

(PA)=Parent Co (HQ)=Headquarters (DH)=Div Headquarters

A C Display Studios Inc ... 609 345-0814
2715 Arctic Ave Atlantic City (08401) *(G-93)*
A C E, Vineland *Also called Ace Glass Incorporated (G-11319)*
A C F, Bayville *Also called American Custom Fabricators (G-248)*
A C L Equipment Corp (PA) ... 973 740-9800
Northfield Rd Livingston (07039) *(G-5521)*
A C Transformer Corp ... 973 589-8574
89 Madison St Newark (07105) *(G-7065)*
A Cheerful Giver Inc ... 856 358-4438
300 Front St Elmer (08318) *(G-2787)*
A D J Group LLC ... 609 743-2099
12 Trainor Cir Bordentown (08505) *(G-588)*
A D M Tronics Unlimited Inc (PA) ... 201 767-6040
224 Pegasus Ave Ste A Northvale (07647) *(G-7566)*
A Division NJ Bus Forms, Englewood *Also called Infoseal LLC (G-2905)*
A E Stone Inc (PA) ... 609 641-2781
1435 Doughty Rd Egg Harbor Township (08234) *(G-2675)*
A F C, Fair Lawn *Also called Associated Fabrics Corporation (G-3078)*
A Frieri Machine Tool Inc ... 908 753-7555
1112 Belmont Ave South Plainfield (07080) *(G-10318)*
A G S, Cliffwood *Also called Fleetsource LLC (G-1547)*
A Gimenez Trading LLC ... 973 697-2240
5 Wegmann Way Oak Ridge (07438) *(G-7659)*
A H Hoffmann LLC ... 732 988-6000
209 W Sylvania Ave Neptune (07753) *(G-6897)*
A I T, Princeton Junction *Also called Amerasia Intl Tech Inc (G-9147)*
A I T, Princeton Junction *Also called AI Technology Inc (G-9145)*
A J P Scientific Inc ... 973 472-7200
82 Industrial St E Clifton (07012) *(G-1552)*
A K Stamping Co Inc ... 908 232-7300
1159 Us Highway 22 Mountainside (07092) *(G-6865)*
A Kessler Kreation Inc ... 732 431-2468
31 Continental Ct Colts Neck (07722) *(G-1779)*
A L Don Co, Matawan *Also called Steelstran Industries Inc (G-6033)*
A L M, Wayne *Also called Polymeric Resources Corp (G-11674)*
A L Wilson Chemical Co ... 201 997-3300
1050 Harrison Ave Kearny (07032) *(G-4857)*
A M D, Millville *Also called Architctural Metal Designs Inc (G-6285)*
A M Gatti Inc ... 609 396-1577
524 Tindall Ave Trenton (08610) *(G-11010)*
A M Graphics Inc ... 201 767-5320
68 Schraalenburg Rd Ste 6 Harrington Park (07640) *(G-4169)*
A M K Glass Inc ... 856 692-1488
2880 Industrial Way Vineland (08360) *(G-11318)*
A M M, Belvidere *Also called Artisan Model Mold (G-366)*
A N Laggren Awngs Canvas Mfg ... 908 756-1948
1414 South Ave Plainfield (07062) *(G-8852)*
A O S, Eatontown *Also called American Oil & Supply Co (G-2382)*
A P A I, Roosevelt *Also called Action Packaging Automation (G-9639)*
A P M Hexseal Corporation ... 201 569-5700
44 Honeck St Englewood (07631) *(G-2865)*
A Plus Installation, Bloomfield *Also called A Plus Installs LLC (G-499)*
A Plus Installs LLC ... 201 255-4412
29 27 Curtis St Fl 1 Flr 1 Bloomfield (07003) *(G-499)*
A Plus Powerwashing ... 732 245-3816
503 Moore Rd Neptune (07753) *(G-6898)*
A Plus Products Incorporated ... 732 866-9111
8 Timber Ln Marlboro (07746) *(G-5935)*
A PS Inlet Marina LLC ... 732 681-3303
610 5th Ave Belmar (07719) *(G-355)*
A Quick Cut Stamping Embossing ... 856 321-0050
803 N Forklanding Rd Maple Shade (08052) *(G-5898)*
A R Bothers Woodworking Inc ... 908 725-2891
236 Dukes Pkwy E Somerville (08876) *(G-10198)*
A R C Plasmet Corp ... 201 867-8533
4131 Bergen Tpke North Bergen (07047) *(G-7425)*
A R J Custom Fabrication Inc ... 609 695-6227
151 Taylor St Trenton (08638) *(G-11011)*
A S 4 Plastic Inc ... 973 925-5223
116 Getty Ave Paterson (07503) *(G-8192)*
A S A P Nameplate & Labeling ... 973 773-3934
92 1st St Passaic (07055) *(G-8122)*
A S M, Fairfield *Also called Accurate Screw Machine Corp (G-3126)*
A S M Technical ... 973 225-0111
34 Waite St Paterson (07524) *(G-8193)*
A S Mill Products Inc ... 212 695-2244
280 State Route 35 # 104 Red Bank (07701) *(G-9317)*
A Sign Company ... 609 298-3388
258 Old York Rd Trenton (08620) *(G-11012)*
A Sign of Excellence Inc ... 732 264-0404
6 Surrey Dr Hazlet (07730) *(G-4267)*
A Smith & Son Inc ... 609 747-0800
300 W Broad St Burlington (08016) *(G-952)*
A Stitch Ahead ... 609 586-1068
448 Whitehead Rd Ste 3 Trenton (08619) *(G-11013)*
A T C Companies Inc (PA) ... 732 560-0900
207 Blackford Ave Middlesex (08846) *(G-6141)*
A T L, Ramsey *Also called Aero TEC Laboratories Inc (G-9231)*
A T S Rheosystems, Bordentown *Also called Advanced Technical Support Inc (G-589)*
A To Z Bohemian Glass Inc ... 212 725-2033
250 E 17th St Paterson (07524) *(G-8194)*
A To Z Printing & Promotion ... 973 916-9995
1455 Main Ave Ste 2 Clifton (07011) *(G-1553)*
A V Hydraulics Ltd Lblty Co ... 973 621-6800
2 Avenue C Newark (07114) *(G-7066)*
A W Eurostile, Ocean *Also called Akw Inc (G-7714)*
A W Eurostile, Shrewsbury *Also called Akw Inc (G-9988)*
A W Ross Inc ... 973 471-5900
297 Monroe St Ste 1 Passaic (07055) *(G-8123)*
A Zeregas Sons Inc (PA) ... 201 797-1400
20-01 Broadway Fair Lawn (07410) *(G-3072)*
A&A Company Inc ... 908 561-2378
2700 S Clinton Ave South Plainfield (07080) *(G-10319)*
A&B Heating & Cooling ... 908 289-2231
107 Trumbull St Elizabeth (07206) *(G-2703)*
A&C Catalysts Inc ... 908 474-9393
1600 W Blancke St Linden (07036) *(G-5342)*
A&E Advnced Clsure Systems LLC ... 732 938-2266
5206 Asbury Rd Wall Township (07727) *(G-11459)*
A&E Medical, Wall Township *Also called Alto Development Corp (G-11461)*
A&E Promotions LLC ... 732 382-2300
118 Woodlake Ct A Holmdel (07733) *(G-4506)*
A&J Flooring Outlet, Blackwood *Also called A & J Carpets Inc (G-469)*
A&M Industrial Inc ... 908 862-1800
22b Cragwood Rd Avenel (07001) *(G-121)*
A&M Petro Marine Division, Avenel *Also called A&M Industrial Inc (G-121)*
A&P, Hackettstown *Also called A and P Pharmacy (G-3994)*
A&R Printing Corporation ... 732 886-0505
421 W County Line Rd Lakewood (08701) *(G-5062)*
A-1 Fasteners, Camden *Also called Art Metalcraft Plating Co Inc (G-1042)*
A-1 Plastic Bags Inc ... 973 344-4441
136 Tichenor St Newark (07105) *(G-7067)*
A-1 Specialized Svcs & Sups ... 732 238-2900
369 Whitehead Ave South River (08882) *(G-10456)*
A-1 Tablecloth Co Inc ... 201 727-4364
450 Huyler St Ste 102 South Hackensack (07606) *(G-10250)*
A-1 Thrifty Centers, Woodbridge *Also called Stone Mountain Printing Inc (G-12154)*
A-One Merchandising Corp ... 718 773-7500
170 Schuyler Ave North Arlington (07031) *(G-7413)*
A-Wit Technologies Inc ... 800 985-2948
656 Ironwood Dr Williamstown (08094) *(G-12077)*
A. L. Don Co., Avenel *Also called Steelstran Industries Inc (G-152)*
A1 Copying Center, Manasquan *Also called Ahern Blueprinting Inc (G-5865)*
A1 Custom Countertops Inc ... 856 200-3596
20 Old Salem Rd Woodstown (08098) *(G-12237)*
AA Graphics Inc ... 201 398-0710
431 N Midland Ave Saddle Brook (07663) *(G-9748)*
AAA Pharmaceutical (PA) ... 609 288-6060
681 Main St Lumberton (08048) *(G-5649)*
AAA Pharmaceutical Inc ... 856 423-2700
157-160 W Jefferson St Paulsboro (08066) *(G-8411)*
AAA Umbrella Co, Norwood *Also called Rainmen USA Incorporated (G-7634)*
Aak USA Inc (HQ) ... 973 344-1300
499 Thornall St Ste 5 Edison (08837) *(G-2446)*
Aall American Fasteners, Cinnaminson *Also called Kt Mt Corp (G-1473)*
Aarc, Jersey City *Also called All Amrcan Recycl Corp Clifton (G-4701)*
Aarhuskarlshamn USA Inc (PA) ... 973 344-1300
131 Marsh St Newark (07114) *(G-7068)*
Aarisse Health Care Products ... 973 686-1811
11 Robin Hood Way Wayne (07470) *(G-11600)*
Aarubco Rubber Co Inc ... 973 772-8177
259 2nd St Saddle Brook (07663) *(G-9749)*
AAS Technologies Inc ... 201 342-7300
290 Lodi St Hackensack (07601) *(G-3872)*
Aavolyn Corp ... 856 327-8040
207 Bogden Blvd Ste M Millville (08332) *(G-6272)*
AB Aerospace, Linden *Also called Bar Fields Inc (G-5351)*
AB Coaster LLC ... 908 879-2713
360 State Route 24 Ste 4 Chester (07930) *(G-1432)*
AB Science Usa LLC ... 973 218-2437
51 John F Kennedy Pkwy Short Hills (07078) *(G-9974)*
Abacus Electric & Plumbing ... 908 269-8057
95 W Main St Ste 252 Chester (07930) *(G-1433)*
Abatetech Inc ... 609 265-2107
30 Maple Ave Lumberton (08048) *(G-5650)*
ABB Lighting Inc ... 866 222-8866
1501 Industrial Way Toms River (08755) *(G-10858)*
ABB Motors and Mechanical Inc ... 856 661-1442
103 Central Ave 400 B Pennsauken (08110) *(G-8468)*
Abba Metal Works Inc ... 973 684-0808
337 River St Paterson (07524) *(G-8195)*
Abbey Commemoratives, Kenilworth *Also called Arbee Company Inc (G-4937)*
Abbott Artkives LLC ... 201 232-9477
187 Branch Brook Dr Belleville (07109) *(G-293)*
Abbott Laboratories ... 732 346-6649
18 Mayfield Ave Edison (08837) *(G-2447)*

612 2018 Harris New Jersey Manufacturers Directory (G-0000) Company's Geographic Section entry number

Abbott Laboratories 609 443-9300
400 College Rd E Princeton (08540) *(G-8992)*

Abbott Laboratories 856 988-5572
10000 Lincoln Dr E # 201 Marlton (08053) *(G-5963)*

Abbott Laboratories Parsippany 973 428-4000
30 N Jefferson Rd Whippany (07981) *(G-12005)*

Abbott Point of Care Inc (HQ) 609 454-9000
400 College Rd E Princeton (08540) *(G-8993)*

Abbott Point of Care Inc 609 371-8923
104 Windsor Center Dr East Windsor (08520) *(G-2339)*

Abbott Screen Printing, Belleville Also called Abbott Artkives LLC *(G-293)*

Abby Bindery Co Inc 973 690-5509
121 Christie St Newark (07105) *(G-7069)*

ABC Digital Electronics Inc 201 666-6888
44 Country Squire Rd Old Tappan (07675) *(G-7796)*

ABC Printing 973 664-1160
20 Wall St Ste C Rockaway (07866) *(G-9540)*

ABC Sign Systems Inc 856 665-0950
7970 National Hwy Pennsauken (08110) *(G-8469)*

Abco Die Casters Inc 973 624-7030
39 Tompkins Point Rd Newark (07114) *(G-7070)*

Abco Metal LLC 973 772-8160
138 3rd Ave Paterson (07514) *(G-8196)*

Abco Tool & Machine Corp 973 772-8160
2 Elm St Garfield (07026) *(G-3713)*

ABG Accessories, Elizabeth Also called Elegant Headwear Co Inc *(G-2728)*

ABG Lab LLC 973 559-5663
20-21 Wagaraw Rd Bldg 31b Fair Lawn (07410) *(G-3073)*

Abi Inc 609 588-8225
227 Bakers Basin Rd Lawrenceville (08648) *(G-5249)*

Ability2work A NJ Nnprfit Corp 908 782-3458
42 State Route 12 Flemington (08822) *(G-3423)*

Abington Reldan Metals LLC 732 238-8550
395-402 Whitehead South River (08882) *(G-10457)*

Able Fab Co 732 396-0600
18 Mileed Way Avenel (07001) *(G-122)*

Able Gear & Machine Co 973 983-8055
91 Stickle Ave Rockaway (07866) *(G-9541)*

Able Group Technologies Inc 732 591-9299
281 State Route 79 N Morganville (07751) *(G-6634)*

Abon Pharmaceuticals LLC 201 367-1702
140 Legrand Ave Northvale (07647) *(G-7567)*

Aboudi Printing LLC 732 542-2929
132 Lewis St Ste B Eatontown (07724) *(G-2377)*

About Our Town Inc 732 968-1615
2 Lakeview Ave Ste 312 Piscataway (08854) *(G-8723)*

Above Environmental Services 973 702-7021
57 Vernon Crossing Rd Vernon (07462) *(G-11295)*

Above Rest Glass 732 370-1616
2345 Route 9 Ste 31 Toms River (08755) *(G-10859)*

Abox Automation Corp 973 659-9611
45 Us Highway 46 Ste 606 Pine Brook (07058) *(G-8679)*

Abp Induction LLC 732 932-6400
1460 Livingston Ave 200-1 North Brunswick (08902) *(G-7500)*

Abraxis Bioscience Inc (HQ) 908 673-9000
86 Morris Ave Summit (07901) *(G-10630)*

Abraxis Bioscience Inc 908 673-9000
86 Morris Ave Summit (07901) *(G-10631)*

Abrazil LLC 732 658-5191
1 Jacques Ave Kendall Park (08824) *(G-4933)*

Abris Distribution Inc (PA) 732 252-9819
522 Us Highway 9 Ste 377 Manalapan (07726) *(G-5836)*

ABS Company, The, Chester Also called AB Coaster LLC *(G-1432)*

Absecon Electric Motor Works 609 641-1523
500 White Horse Pike Absecon (08201) *(G-1)*

Absecon Island Beverage Co 609 653-8123
6754 Washington Ave B Egg Harbor Township (08234) *(G-2676)*

Absecon Mills Inc 609 965-5373
901 W Aloe St Cologne (08213) *(G-1775)*

Absolume LLC 732 523-1231
1153 Tiffany Ln Lakewood (08701) *(G-5063)*

Absolute Business Services Inc 856 265-9447
325 Maurice St Millville (08332) *(G-6273)*

Absolute Protective Systems 732 287-4500
3 Kellogg Ct Ste 13 Edison (08817) *(G-2448)*

Abuelito Cheese Inc 973 345-3503
607 Main St Paterson (07503) *(G-8197)*

AC Bakery, Paterson Also called A C Bakery Distributors Inc *(G-8191)*

AC Catalyts, Linden Also called A&C Catalysts Inc *(G-5342)*

Academia Furniture LLC 973 472-0100
74 Passaic St Wood Ridge (07075) *(G-12133)*

Academia Furniture Industries, Wood Ridge Also called Academia Furniture LLC *(G-12133)*

Academy of Proplayers, Bloomingdale Also called Akadema Inc *(G-540)*

Acadia Scenic Inc 201 653-8889
130 Bay St Jersey City (07302) *(G-4697)*

ACC Coatings LLC 732 469-8600
201 Pond Ave Middlesex (08846) *(G-6142)*

ACC Foods Ltd Liability Co 856 848-8877
280 Jessup Rd West Deptford (08086) *(G-11813)*

Acceledev Chemical LLC (PA) 862 239-1524
18 Apple Ln Wayne (07470) *(G-11601)*

Acceledev Chemical LLC 732 274-1451
11 Deerpark Dr Ste 119 Monmouth Junction (08852) *(G-6330)*

Accelerated Cnc LLC 908 561-8875
2500 S Clinton Ave South Plainfield (07080) *(G-10320)*

Accelerated Technologies Inc 609 632-0350
2 Research Way Fl 2 # 2 Princeton (08540) *(G-8994)*

Accelis Pharma, Monroe Township Also called Novotec Pharma LLC *(G-6386)*

Accelrx Labs LLC 609 301-6446
55 Lake Dr East Windsor (08520) *(G-2340)*

Accely Inc 609 598-1882
381 Blair Rd Avenel (07001) *(G-123)*

Accent Fence Inc 609 965-6400
1450 Bremen Ave Egg Harbor City (08215) *(G-2655)*

Accent Press Inc 973 785-3127
132 Winifred Dr Totowa (07512) *(G-10925)*

Accent Printing Solutions, New Providence Also called Bowmar Enterprises Inc *(G-7031)*

Access Controls International, Freehold Also called Access Northern Security Inc *(G-3634)*

Access Northern Security Inc (PA) 732 462-2500
303 W Main St Ste 4 Freehold (07728) *(G-3634)*

Access Publishing Co, Ocean Also called Access Response Inc *(G-7712)*

Access Response Inc 732 660-0770
3321 Doris Ave Ocean (07712) *(G-7712)*

Accession Data Systems 973 992-7392
25 Hickory Pl Livingston (07039) *(G-5522)*

Accessories Plus, Ogdensburg Also called AJ Siris Products Corp *(G-7769)*

Accessrec LLC 973 955-0514
55 Park Slope Clifton (07011) *(G-1554)*

Acclivity LLC 973 586-2200
300 Round Hill Dr Ste 2 Rockaway (07866) *(G-9542)*

Accu Seal Rubber Inc 732 246-4333
18f Home News Row New Brunswick (08901) *(G-6942)*

Accu-Cote Inc 856 845-7323
3410 Jessup Rd Thorofare (08086) *(G-10818)*

Accucolor LLC (PA) 732 870-1999
185 Broadway Long Branch (07740) *(G-5620)*

Accumix Pharmaceuticals LLC 609 632-2225
42 Morris Dr Old Bridge (08857) *(G-7772)*

Accupac Inc 215 256-7094
1700 Oak St Lakewood (08701) *(G-5064)*

Accuracy Devices 973 427-8829
321 Central Ave Hawthorne (07506) *(G-4216)*

Accurate Bronze Bearing Co 973 345-2304
64 Illinois Ave Paterson (07503) *(G-8198)*

Accurate Bushing Company Inc 908 789-1121
443 North Ave Ste 1 Garwood (07027) *(G-3774)*

Accurate Diamond Tool Corp 201 265-8868
1 Palisade Ave Emerson (07630) *(G-2855)*

Accurate Forming LLC 973 827-7155
24 Ames Blvd Hamburg (07419) *(G-4087)*

Accurate Machine & Tool Co 908 245-5545
135 W Clay Ave Roselle Park (07204) *(G-9687)*

Accurate Mold Inc 856 784-8484
900 Chestnut Ave Ste G Somerdale (08083) *(G-10038)*

Accurate Plastic Printers LLC 973 591-0180
30 Colfax Ave Clifton (07013) *(G-1555)*

Accurate Screw Machine, Fairfield Also called Mw Industries Inc *(G-3265)*

Accurate Screw Machine Corp 973 276-0379
10 Audrey Pl Fairfield (07004) *(G-3126)*

Accurate Thermal Systems LLC 609 326-3190
4104 Sylon Blvd Hainesport (08036) *(G-4068)*

Accurate Tool & Die Co Inc 201 476-9348
6 Westminster Ct Montvale (07645) *(G-6440)*

Accurate Transmissions, Montvale Also called Accurate Tool & Die Co Inc *(G-6440)*

Accuratus Ceramic Corp 908 213-7070
35 Howard St Phillipsburg (08865) *(G-8638)*

Ace Bag & Burlap Company Inc 973 242-2200
166 Frelinghuysen Ave Newark (07114) *(G-7071)*

Ace Box Co, Englewood Cliffs Also called Ace Box Landau Co Inc *(G-2946)*

Ace Box Landau Co Inc 201 871-4776
600 E Palisade Ave Ste 23 Englewood Cliffs (07632) *(G-2946)*

Ace Crete Product, Bayville Also called New Jersey Pulverizing Co Inc *(G-259)*

Ace Electronics Inc 732 603-9800
235 Liberty St Metuchen (08840) *(G-6093)*

Ace Fine Art Inc 201 960-4447
141 Lanza Ave Bldg 3d Garfield (07026) *(G-3714)*

Ace Glass Incorporated (HQ) 856 692-3333
1430 N West Blvd Vineland (08360) *(G-11319)*

Ace Lthgraphers of Morris Cnty 973 428-4911
22 Russo Pl Berkeley Heights (07922) *(G-398)*

Ace Metal Kraft Co Inc 973 278-6605
815 Mcbride Ave Woodland Park (07424) *(G-12207)*

Ace Mountings Co Inc (PA) 732 721-6200
11 Cross Ave South Amboy (08879) *(G-10233)*

Ace Powder Coating, Newark Also called A & L Industries Inc *(G-7064)*

Ace Restoration 267 897-2384
24 Mariner Dr Sewell (08080) *(G-9944)*

A L P H A B E T I C

Ace Sign Company Inc 732 826-3858
419 Summit Ave Perth Amboy (08861) *(G-8604)*

Ace-Crete Products Inc 732 269-1400
250 Hickory Ln Bayville (08721) *(G-247)*

Aceco Industrial Packaging Co, Newark *Also called Ace Bag & Burlap Company Inc (G-7071)*

Acedepotcom (PA) 800 844-0962
159 Paris Ave Northvale (07647) *(G-7568)*

Aces Led, Branchburg *Also called Atlantic Clean Energy Sup LLC (G-641)*

Acetris Health LLC 201 961-9000
Park 80 West Plz 1 Saddle Brook (07663) *(G-9750)*

Acetylon Pharmaceuticals Inc (HQ) 908 673-9000
86 Morris Ave Summit (07901) *(G-10632)*

Acey Industries Inc 973 595-1222
9 Cranberry Ct North Haledon (07508) *(G-7547)*

Acg North America LLC 908 757-3425
262 Old New Brunswick Rd A Piscataway (08854) *(G-8724)*

Achievement Journal LLC 732 297-1570
5 Larson Ct North Brunswick (08902) *(G-7501)*

Achilles Prosthetcs & Orthotcs 201 785-9944
503 N Franklin Tpke # 12 Ramsey (07446) *(G-9229)*

Aci, Wall Township *Also called Applicad Inc (G-11463)*

Aci, Moorestown *Also called Automation & Control Inc (G-6562)*

Acino Products Ltd Lblty Co 609 695-4300
9b S Gold Dr Hamilton (08691) *(G-4101)*

Ackerson Drapery Decorator Svc 732 797-1967
500 James St Ste 14 Lakewood (08701) *(G-5065)*

Ackk Studios LLC 973 876-1327
411 E Passaic Ave Bloomfield (07003) *(G-500)*

Ackley Machine Corporation 856 234-3626
1273 N Church St Ste 106 Moorestown (08057) *(G-6555)*

Acme & Dorf Door Corp 973 772-6774
490 Getty Ave 500 Clifton (07011) *(G-1556)*

Acme Cosmetic Components LLC 718 335-3000
80 Seaview Dr Ste 1 Secaucus (07094) *(G-9865)*

Acme Drapemaster America Inc 732 512-0613
125 Clearview Rd Edison (08837) *(G-2449)*

Acme Engraving Co Inc (PA) 973 778-0885
19-37 Delaware Ave Passaic (07055) *(G-8124)*

Acme Flagpole Division, Mount Laurel *Also called Lingo Inc (G-6812)*

Acme Gear Co Inc 201 568-2245
130 W Forest Ave Englewood (07631) *(G-2866)*

Acme International Inc 973 594-4866
2a Monhegan St Clifton (07013) *(G-1557)*

Acme Manufacturing Co 732 541-2800
900 Port Reading Ave A2 Port Reading (07064) *(G-8985)*

Acme Markets Inc 609 884-7217
Lafayette & Ocean Sts Cape May (08204) *(G-1090)*

Acme Ring Div, Maplewood *Also called Barrasso & Blasi Industries (G-5914)*

Acme Wire Forming LLC 201 218-2912
18 Pepperidge Tree Ter Kinnelon (07405) *(G-5032)*

Acnd Partners Inc 848 200-7460
1 Honey Ct Metuchen (08840) *(G-6094)*

Acolyte Technologies Corp 212 629-3239
1000 Amboy Ave Perth Amboy (08861) *(G-8605)*

Acon Watch Crown Company 973 546-8585
260 Division Ave Garfield (07026) *(G-3715)*

Acorn Industry Inc 732 536-6256
6 Hoffer Ct Englishtown (07726) *(G-2989)*

Acqua Bella Mfg and Supply, Chesterfield *Also called Bella Acqua Inc (G-1441)*

Acqueon Technologies Inc 609 945-3139
100 Overlook Ctr Fl 2 Princeton (08540) *(G-8995)*

Acrelic Interactive LLC (PA) 908 222-2900
16 Mount Bethel Rd Warren (07059) *(G-11535)*

Acrilex Inc (PA) 201 333-1500
230 Culver Ave Jersey City (07305) *(G-4698)*

Acrison Inc (PA) 201 440-8300
20 Empire Blvd Moonachie (07074) *(G-6499)*

Acrison International, Moonachie *Also called Acrison Inc (G-6499)*

Acro Display Inc (PA) 215 229-1100
2250 Sherman Ave Unit A1 Pennsauken (08110) *(G-8470)*

Acrow Corporation of America (PA) 973 244-0080
181 New Rd Ste 202 Parsippany (07054) *(G-7938)*

Acrylics Unlimited 973 862-6014
11 Millpond Dr Unit 2 Lafayette (07848) *(G-5043)*

ACS Quality Services Inc 856 988-6550
20 Elmgate Rd Marlton (08053) *(G-5964)*

Actavis Elizabeth LLC (HQ) 908 527-9100
200 Elmora Ave Elizabeth (07202) *(G-2704)*

Actavis Elizabeth LLC 908 527-9100
1 Executive Dr Fort Lee (07024) *(G-3541)*

Actavis Elizabeth LLC 973 442-3200
5 Giralda Farms Madison (07940) *(G-5716)*

Actavis Laboratories Fl Inc (HQ) 862 261-7000
400 Interpace Pkwy Ste A1 Parsippany (07054) *(G-7939)*

Actavis LLC 732 947-5300
47 Brunswick Ave Edison (08817) *(G-2450)*

Actavis LLC 800 272-5525
360 Mount Kemble Ave # 3 Morristown (07960) *(G-6683)*

Actavis LLC 732 843-4904
661 Us Highway 1 North Brunswick (08902) *(G-7502)*

Actavis Pharma Inc (HQ) 862 261-7000
400 Interpace Pkwy Ste A1 Parsippany (07054) *(G-7940)*

Actavis US, Elizabeth *Also called Actavis Elizabeth LLC (G-2704)*

Actega North America Inc (HQ) 856 829-6300
950 S Chester Ave Ste B2 Delran (08075) *(G-2009)*

Actega North America Inc 856 829-6300
1450 Taylors Ln Cinnaminson (08077) *(G-1444)*

Action Copy Centers Inc 973 744-5520
590 Valley Rd Ste 2 Montclair (07043) *(G-6404)*

Action Graphics Inc (PA) 973 633-6500
600 Ryerson Rd Ste G Lincoln Park (07035) *(G-5325)*

Action Graphics Inc 856 783-1825
424 E Gibbsboro Rd Lindenwold (08021) *(G-5460)*

Action Instant Printing Center, Brielle *Also called Toms River Printing Corp (G-915)*

Action Packaging Automation 609 448-9210
15 Oscar Dr Roosevelt (08555) *(G-9639)*

Action Press Park Slope 718 624-3457
5 Rustic Ln Holmdel (07733) *(G-4507)*

Action Supply Inc 609 390-0663
1413 Stagecoach Rd Ocean View (08230) *(G-7762)*

Active Controls LLC 856 669-0940
1501 Grandview Ave # 400 Paulsboro (08066) *(G-8412)*

Active Imprints, Monmouth Junction *Also called Wally Enterprises Inc (G-6371)*

Active Learning Associates 908 284-0404
126 Main St Flemington (08822) *(G-3424)*

Acton Mobile Industries Inc 610 485-5100
2013 Route 130 N Burlington (08016) *(G-953)*

Acuitive Technologies Inc 973 617-7175
50 Commerce Dr Allendale (07401) *(G-5)*

Acupac Packaging Inc 201 529-3434
55 Ramapo Valley Rd Mahwah (07430) *(G-5743)*

Acupowder International LLC (HQ) 908 851-4500
901 Lehigh Ave Union (07083) *(G-11146)*

Acustrip Co Inc (PA) 973 299-8237
124 E Main St Apt 109b Denville (07834) *(G-2029)*

Acustrip Co Inc 973 299-8237
10 Craven Rd Mountain Lakes (07046) *(G-6853)*

Ad Lines, Trenton *Also called Central Record Publications (G-11038)*

Adagio Teas Inc (PA) 973 253-7400
170 Kipp Ave Elmwood Park (07407) *(G-2801)*

Adam Gates & Company LLC 908 829-3386
249 Homestead Rd Ste 5 Hillsborough (08844) *(G-4316)*

Adam Metal Products Company, Ledgewood *Also called R B B Corp (G-5308)*

Adam Spence Vascular Tech, Wall Township *Also called Fermatex Vascular Tech LLC (G-11481)*

Adam Tech Asia Llc (HQ) 908 687-5000
909 Rahway Ave Union (07083) *(G-11147)*

Adams Bill Printing & Graphics 856 455-7177
300 Ramah Rd Bridgeton (08302) *(G-776)*

Adams Printing, Bridgeton *Also called Adams Bill Printing & Graphics (G-776)*

Adaptech, Medford *Also called Adaptive Technology Entps LLC (G-6063)*

Adaptive Technology Entps LLC 877 847-6272
141 Taunton Blvd Medford (08055) *(G-6063)*

Adco Chemical Company Inc 973 589-0880
49 Rutherford St Newark (07105) *(G-7072)*

Adco Signs of NJ Inc 908 965-2112
57 Westfield Ave Elizabeth (07208) *(G-2705)*

Adcomm Government Systems, South Hackensack *Also called Adcomm Inc (G-10251)*

Adcomm Inc 201 342-3338
89 Leuning St Ste 9 South Hackensack (07606) *(G-10251)*

Add Rob Litho LLC 201 556-0700
11 W Passaic St Ste 1 Rochelle Park (07662) *(G-9525)*

Addressing Machine & Sup Div, Hillside *Also called Singe Corporation (G-4440)*

Ade Inc 609 693-6050
719 Old Shore Rd Forked River (08731) *(G-3533)*

Adello Biologics LLC (PA) 312 620-1500
20 New England Ave Piscataway (08854) *(G-8725)*

Adherence Solutions LLC 800 521-2269
75 Lane Rd Ste 404 Fairfield (07004) *(G-3127)*

Adhesive Films Inc (PA) 973 882-4944
4 Barnet Rd Pine Brook (07058) *(G-8680)*

Adhesves Sealants Coatings Div, Edison *Also called HB Fuller Company (G-2535)*

Adhisa Molding 862 324-5222
11 Patton Dr West Caldwell (07006) *(G-11762)*

ADI American Distributors LLC (PA) 973 328-1181
2 Emery Ave Ste 1 Randolph (07869) *(G-9267)*

Adiant (PA) 800 264-8303
92 E Main St Ste 405 Somerville (08876) *(G-10199)*

Adidas North America Inc 201 843-4555
1 Garden State Plz Paramus (07652) *(G-7852)*

Adidas North America Inc 732 695-0085
1 Premium Outlet Blvd Tinton Falls (07753) *(G-10823)*

Adidas Outlet Store Tinton FLS, Tinton Falls *Also called Adidas North America Inc (G-10823)*

Adler International Ltd (PA) 201 843-4525
205 Maywood Ave Maywood (07607) *(G-6045)*

2018 Harris New Jersey
Manufacturers Directory

(G-0000) Company's Geographic Section entry number

ADM Corporation..732 469-0900
100 Lincoln Blvd Middlesex (08846) *(G-6143)*

ADM Tronics, Northvale *Also called Sonotron Medical Systems Inc* *(G-7608)*

Adma Biologics Inc (PA)...201 478-5552
465 State Rt 17 Ramsey (07446) *(G-9230)*

Admartec Inc...732 888-8248
12 Crown Plz Ste 204 Hazlet (07730) *(G-4268)*

Admera Health LLC...908 222-0533
126 Corporate Blvd South Plainfield (07080) *(G-10321)*

Admints & Zagabor, Bellmawr *Also called Hit Promo LLC* *(G-342)*

Admiral Filter Company LLC.....................................973 664-0400
18 Green Pond Rd Ste 3 Rockaway (07866) *(G-9543)*

Admiral Technology LLC..973 698-5920
18 Green Pond Rd Ste 3 Rockaway (07866) *(G-9544)*

Adorage Inc...201 886-7000
1055 River Rd Apt Th10 Edgewater (07020) *(G-2431)*

Adotta America, Englewood *Also called Europrojects Intl Inc* *(G-2894)*

Adpro Imprints..732 531-2133
1206 State Route 35 Ocean (07712) *(G-7713)*

Adron Inc..973 334-1600
94 Fanny Rd Boonton (07005) *(G-551)*

ADS, Logan Township *Also called Advanced Drainage Systems Inc* *(G-5610)*

ADS, Cherry Hill *Also called Air Distribution Systems Inc* *(G-1341)*

ADS Sales Co Inc..732 591-0500
1010 Campus Dr Morganville (07751) *(G-6635)*

Adtranz, Kearny *Also called Bombardier Transportation* *(G-4866)*

Adva Optical Networking Inc......................................201 258-8300
1 International Blvd # 705 Mahwah (07495) *(G-5744)*

Advance Digital Inc...201 459-2808
185 Hudson St Ste 3100 Jersey City (07311) *(G-4699)*

Advance Machine Inc..908 486-7244
531 Pennsylvania Ave Linden (07036) *(G-5343)*

Advance Machine Planning Inc..................................732 356-4438
200 Egel Ave Middlesex (08846) *(G-6144)*

Advance Printing Co, Garwood *Also called Ocsidot Inc* *(G-3782)*

Advance Process Systems Lim...................................201 400-9190
130 Gunn Rd Branchville (07826) *(G-724)*

Advance Scale Company Inc (PA).............................856 784-4916
2400 Egg Harbor Rd Lindenwold (08021) *(G-5461)*

Advanced Abrasives Corporation...............................856 665-9300
7980 National Hwy Pennsauken (08110) *(G-8471)*

Advanced Biotech, Totowa *Also called Centrome Inc* *(G-10938)*

Advanced Biotech Overseas LLC (PA)........................973 339-6242
10 Taft Rd Totowa (07512) *(G-10926)*

Advanced Brewing Sys LLC.......................................973 633-1777
91 Savoy Pl Prospect Park (07508) *(G-9168)*

Advanced Cerametrics Inc (PA).................................609 397-2900
245 N Main St Lambertville (08530) *(G-5209)*

Advanced Cutting Services LLC.................................908 241-5332
169 E Highland Pkwy Roselle (07203) *(G-9659)*

Advanced Drainage Systems Inc................................856 467-4779
300 Progress Ct Logan Township (08085) *(G-5610)*

Advanced Energy Voorhees Inc.................................856 627-1287
1007 Laurel Oak Rd Voorhees (08043) *(G-11419)*

Advanced Food Systems Inc.....................................732 873-6776
21 Roosevelt Ave Somerset (08873) *(G-10049)*

Advanced Formulations, Long Valley *Also called Millennium Research LLC* *(G-5639)*

Advanced Imaging Assoc LLC (PA)............................973 823-8999
190 Munsonhurst Rd Ste 1 Franklin (07416) *(G-3593)*

Advanced Industrial Controls....................................908 725-7575
10 County Line Rd Ste 30 Branchburg (08876) *(G-628)*

Advanced Metal Processing.......................................856 327-0048
326 S Wade Blvd Millville (08332) *(G-6274)*

Advanced Micro Devices Inc......................................732 787-2892
16 Snyder Dr North Middletown (07748) *(G-7556)*

Advanced Pavement Technologies.............................973 366-8044
195 Green Pond Rd Rockaway (07866) *(G-9545)*

Advanced Precision Inc...800 788-9473
15 Wilson Dr Ste B Sparta (07871) *(G-10485)*

Advanced Precision Systems LLC...............................908 730-8892
6 Sunset Dr High Bridge (08829) *(G-4293)*

Advanced Products LLC...800 724-5464
1915 Swarthmore Ave Lakewood (08701) *(G-5066)*

Advanced Protective Products...................................201 794-2000
17-10 River Rd Ste 4c Fair Lawn (07410) *(G-3074)*

Advanced Sewer...973 278-1948
10 Memorial Dr Woodland Park (07424) *(G-12208)*

Advanced Shore Imaging Associa..............................732 678-0087
2605 Shore Rd Northfield (08225) *(G-7562)*

Advanced Studies In Medicine, Somerville *Also called Galen Publishing LLC* *(G-10210)*

Advanced Technical Support Inc................................609 298-2522
231 Crosswicks Rd Bordentown (08505) *(G-589)*

Advanced Technology Group Inc................................973 627-6955
101 Round Hill Dr Ste 3 Rockaway (07866) *(G-9546)*

Advancing Opportunities Inc....................................201 907-0200
639 Teaneck Rd Teaneck (07666) *(G-10740)*

Advansix Inc (PA)..973 526-1800
300 Kimball Dr Ste 101 Parsippany (07054) *(G-7941)*

Advanstar Communications Inc..................................973 944-7777
5 Paragon Dr Montvale (07645) *(G-6441)*

Advanstar Communications Inc..................................732 596-0276
485 Us Highway 1 S # 200 Iselin (08830) *(G-4608)*

Advantage Asia, Garfield *Also called Clear Plus Windshield Wipers* *(G-3726)*

Advantage Business Media LLC (PA)..........................973 920-7000
100 Enterprise Dr Ste 600 Rockaway (07866) *(G-9547)*

Advantage Ds LLC..856 307-9600
8 Deptford Rd Glassboro (08028) *(G-3800)*

Advantage Engineering Group, Boonton *Also called Technical Advantage Inc* *(G-585)*

Advantage Fiberglass Inc..609 926-4606
4 Prospect Ave Egg Harbor Township (08234) *(G-2677)*

Advantage Molding Products.....................................732 303-8667
2106 Highway 35 Sea Girt (08750) *(G-9861)*

Advantage Publications, Fort Lee *Also called N J W Magazine* *(G-3571)*

Advaxis Inc (PA)...609 452-9813
305 College Rd E Princeton (08540) *(G-8996)*

Adventure Industries LLC (PA)..................................609 426-1777
59 Lake Dr East Windsor (08520) *(G-2341)*

Advertisers Service Group Inc...................................201 440-5577
65 Railroad Ave Ridgefield Park (07660) *(G-9395)*

Advisory Dumas Group LLC.......................................850 778-1624
7 Van Buren Pl Lawrence Township (08648) *(G-5239)*

Advocate Publishing Corp...973 497-4200
171 Clifton Ave Newark (07104) *(G-7073)*

AE Litho Offset Printers Inc (PA)...............................800 235-8888
450 Broad St Beverly (08010) *(G-456)*

AE Litho Offset Printers Inc......................................609 239-0700
450 Broad St Beverly (08010) *(G-457)*

Aelitho Group, Beverly *Also called AE Litho Offset Printers Inc* *(G-456)*

Aeon Corporation...609 275-9003
186 Princeton Hightstown Princeton Junction (08550) *(G-9144)*

Aeon Engineering LLC...518 253-7681
442 Main St Ste 5 Fort Lee (07024) *(G-3542)*

Aeon Industries Inc...732 246-3224
76 Veronica Ave Somerset (08873) *(G-10050)*

AEP Networks Inc..732 652-5200
347 Elizabeth Ave Ste 100 Somerset (08873) *(G-10051)*

Aer X Dust Corporation...732 946-9462
12 Windingbrook Way Holmdel (07733) *(G-4508)*

Aero Manufacturing Co...973 473-5300
310 Allwood Rd Clifton (07012) *(G-1558)*

Aero Products Co Inc..973 759-0959
21 N 8th St Belleville (07109) *(G-294)*

Aero TEC Laboratories Inc (PA).................................201 825-1400
45 Spear Rd Ramsey (07446) *(G-9231)*

Aerocon, Belleville *Also called Vac-U-Max* *(G-322)*

Aerocon Inc..800 405-2376
69 William St Belleville (07109) *(G-295)*

Aeroflex Ctrl Components Inc....................................732 460-0212
40 Industrial Way E Eatontown (07724) *(G-2378)*

Aerogroup Retail Holdings Inc...................................732 819-9843
207 Meadow Rd Ste A Edison (08817) *(G-2451)*

Aeronautical Instr & Rdo Co (PA)..............................973 473-0034
234 Garibaldi Ave Lodi (07644) *(G-5573)*

Aeropanel Corporation...973 335-9636
661 Myrtle Ave Boonton (07005) *(G-552)*

Aerosmith..973 614-9392
176 Saddle River Ave B South Hackensack (07606) *(G-10252)*

Aerospace Industries LLC...973 383-9307
520 Lafayette Rd Sparta (07871) *(G-10486)*

Aerospace Manufacturing Inc..................................973 472-9888
80 Van Winkle Ave Wallington (07057) *(G-11521)*

Aerospace Nylok, Hawthorne *Also called Nylok Corporation* *(G-4250)*

Aerotech Proc Solutions LLC.....................................973 782-4485
57 Wood St Paterson (07524) *(G-8199)*

Aesys Inc...201 871-3223
27 Bland St Emerson (07630) *(G-2856)*

Aeterna Zentaris Inc..908 626-5428
20 Independence Blvd # 401 Warren (07059) *(G-11536)*

Aetrex Worldwide Inc (PA).......................................201 833-2700
414 Alfred Ave Teaneck (07666) *(G-10741)*

AF Pharma LLC...908 769-7040
1500 Garden St Apt 2i Hoboken (07030) *(G-4456)*

Affil Endoscopy Services CL......................................201 842-0020
925 Clifton Ave Ste 100 Clifton (07013) *(G-1559)*

Affinity Chemical Woodbine LLC................................973 873-4070
82 Crenshaw Dr Flanders (07836) *(G-3399)*

Affordable Lead Solutions LLC..................................856 207-1348
26 Blew Valley Ln Bridgeton (08302) *(G-777)*

Affordable Offset Printing Inc....................................856 661-0722
809 Hylton Rd Ste 11 Pennsauken (08110) *(G-8472)*

Affordable Roofing, Pennsauken *Also called Affordable Offset Printing Inc* *(G-8472)*

Afh Industries LLC...917 407-6866
141 Ethel Rd W Piscataway (08854) *(G-8726)*

Afi, Somerset *Also called American Fibertek Inc* *(G-10056)*

Afk Machine Inc (PA)..973 539-1329
50 High Ridge Rd Randolph (07869) *(G-9268)*

AFL Telecommunications LLC 864 486-7303
123 Town Square Pl Jersey City (07310) *(G-4700)*

Aflag Pharmaceuticals LLC 732 609-4139
163 Jefferson Blvd Edison (08817) *(G-2452)*

Aflex Extrusion Technologies 732 752-0048
240b N Randolphville Rd Piscataway (08854) *(G-8727)*

AFP Transformers Corporation 732 248-0305
206 Talmadge Rd Edison (08817) *(G-2453)*

Africa Imports Inc 201 457-1995
240 S Main St Ste A South Hackensack (07606) *(G-10253)*

Africa World Press 609 695-3200
541 W Ingham Ave Ste B Ewing (08638) *(G-3002)*

Africa World Red Sea Press, Ewing *Also called Red Sea Press Inc (G-3049)*

African Sun Times, East Orange *Also called African Telecom Inc (G-2254)*

African Telecom Inc 973 675-9919
463 N Arlington Ave East Orange (07017) *(G-2254)*

Aftek Inc 609 588-0900
2960 E State Street Ext Hamilton (08619) *(G-4102)*

AG&e Holdings Inc (PA) 609 704-3000
223 Pratt St Hammonton (08037) *(G-4126)*

AGA Foodservice Inc (PA) 856 428-4200
110 Woodcrest Rd Cherry Hill (08003) *(G-1340)*

Agape Child Care Center, West Milford *Also called Almond Branch Inc (G-11849)*

Agape Inc 973 923-7625
487 Chancellor Ave Irvington (07111) *(G-4570)*

Agate Lacquer Tri-Nat LLC 732 968-1080
824 South Ave Middlesex (08846) *(G-6145)*

Agau Inc 732 583-4343
1077 State Route 34 Ste M Matawan (07747) *(G-6012)*

AGC Acquisition LLC 856 692-4435
3740 N West Blvd Vineland (08360) *(G-11320)*

AGFA Corporation (HQ) 800 540-2432
611 River Dr Ste 305 Elmwood Park (07407) *(G-2802)*

AGFA Corporation 201 440-0111
580 Gotham Pkwy Carlstadt (07072) *(G-1121)*

AGFA Corporation 908 231-5000
1318 State Hwy 31 Somerville (08876) *(G-10200)*

AGFA Corporation 201 440-0111
611 River Dr Ste 305 Elmwood Park (07407) *(G-2803)*

AGFA Corporation 201 288-4101
580 Gotham Pkwy Carlstadt (07072) *(G-1122)*

AGFA Corporation, Elmwood Park, Elmwood Park *Also called AGFA Finance Corp (G-2804)*

AGFA Finance Corp 201 796-0058
611 River Dr Elmwood Park (07407) *(G-2804)*

AGFA Graphics, Elmwood Park *Also called AGFA Corporation (G-2802)*

Agile Therapeutics Inc 609 683-1880
101 Poor Farm Rd Princeton (08540) *(G-8997)*

Agilent Technologies Inc 973 448-7129
550 Clark Dr Ste 2 Budd Lake (07828) *(G-923)*

Agilex Flavors & Fragrances, Branchburg *Also called Mid Ocean Partners (G-681)*

Agilex Flavors Fragrances Inc (HQ) 732 885-0702
140 Centennial Ave Piscataway (08854) *(G-8728)*

Agilis Chemicals Inc 973 910-2424
100 Enterprise Dr Ste 301 Rockaway (07866) *(G-9548)*

Aginova Inc (PA) 732 804-3272
3 Chambry Ct Freehold (07728) *(G-3635)*

Agno Pharma 609 223-0638
5 Wingate Ct Allentown (08501) *(G-27)*

Agrilink Foods, Parsippany *Also called Birds Eye Foods Inc (G-7961)*

Agrium Advanced Tech US Inc 732 296-8448
1470 Jersey Ave North Brunswick (08902) *(G-7503)*

Agsco Corporation 973 244-0005
60 Chapin Rd Pine Brook (07058) *(G-8681)*

Agway, Burlington *Also called Klein Distributors Inc (G-982)*

Agway Energy Services LLC 973 887-5300
240 State Route 10 Whippany (07981) *(G-12006)*

Ahb Foods, Mount Laurel *Also called American Harvest Baking Co Inc (G-6778)*

Ahe Manufacturing Inc 609 660-8000
127 S Main St Barnegat (08005) *(G-159)*

Ahern Blueprinting Inc 732 223-1476
231 Parker Ave Manasquan (08736) *(G-5865)*

Ahs Hospital Corp 908 522-2000
99 Beauvoir Ave Summit (07901) *(G-10633)*

Ahzanis Castle LLC 973 874-3191
134 E Main St Paterson (07522) *(G-8200)*

Ai Container, Boonton *Also called American International Cont (G-554)*

AI Technology Inc 609 799-9388
70 Washington Rd Princeton Junction (08550) *(G-9145)*

Ai-Logix Inc 732 469-0880
27 Worlds Fair Dr Ste 2 Somerset (08873) *(G-10052)*

Aibens Imort 609 902-9953
7 York Rd Princeton Junction (08550) *(G-9146)*

Aic, Branchburg *Also called Advanced Industrial Controls (G-628)*

Aicumen Technologies Inc 732 668-4204
11 Nestlewood Way Princeton (08540) *(G-8998)*

AIG Industrial Group Inc (HQ) 201 767-7300
220 Pegasus Ave Northvale (07647) *(G-7569)*

Aim Computer Associates Inc 201 489-3100
19 Dover Ct Bergenfield (07621) *(G-379)*

Ainsworth Media 856 854-1400
732 Haddon Ave Collingswood (08108) *(G-1769)*

Air & Hydraulic Power Inc 201 447-1589
555 Goffle Rd Wyckoff (07481) *(G-12244)*

Air & Specialties Sheet Metal 908 233-8306
276 Sheffield St Mountainside (07092) *(G-6866)*

Air BP, Linden *Also called BP Corporation North Amer Inc (G-5353)*

Air Clean Co Inc 908 355-1515
1135 Chestnut St Elizabeth (07201) *(G-2706)*

Air Cruisers Company LLC (HQ) 732 681-3527
1747 State Route 34 Wall Township (07727) *(G-11460)*

Air Distribution Systems Inc 856 874-1100
1000 Astoria Blvd Cherry Hill (08003) *(G-1341)*

Air Liquide Advanced Materials 908 231-9060
197 Meister Ave Bldg A Branchburg (08876) *(G-629)*

Air Power Inc 973 882-5418
25 Commerce Rd Ste N Fairfield (07004) *(G-3128)*

Air Products, Paulsboro *Also called Coim USA Inc (G-8415)*

Air Products and Chemicals Inc 732 446-5676
405 Route 33 Manalapan (07726) *(G-5837)*

Air Protection Packaging Corp 973 577-4343
1200 Fuller Rd Ste 2 Linden (07036) *(G-5344)*

Air World Inc 201 831-0700
126 Christie Ave Mahwah (07430) *(G-5745)*

Airborne Systems N Amer Inc (HQ) 856 663-1275
5800 Magnolia Ave Pennsauken (08109) *(G-8473)*

Airborne Systems N Amer NJ Inc 856 663-1275
5800 Magnolia Ave Pennsauken (08109) *(G-8474)*

Airborne Systems NA, Pennsauken *Also called Airborne Systems N Amer Inc (G-8473)*

Airbrasive Jet Tech LLC 201 725-7340
151 Old New Brunswick Rd Piscataway (08854) *(G-8729)*

Airbrush Action Inc 732 223-7878
79 S Main St Ste 1 Barnegat (08005) *(G-160)*

Aircharctercom LLC 212 999-4926
6515 Kennedy Blvd E West New York (07093) *(G-11860)*

Airdye Solutions LLC (PA) 540 433-9101
21 Glen Rock Rd Cedar Grove (07009) *(G-1269)*

Airfiltronix Corp (HQ) 973 779-5577
154 Huron Ave Clifton (07013) *(G-1560)*

Airgas Usa LLC 609 685-4241
1910 Old Cuthbert Rd Cherry Hill (08034) *(G-1342)*

Airgas Usa LLC 908 754-7700
2330 Hamilton Blvd South Plainfield (07080) *(G-10322)*

Airgas Usa LLC 856 933-0544
270 Benigno Blvd Bldg 5 Bellmawr (08031) *(G-330)*

Airgas Usa LLC 856 829-7878
600 Union Landing Rd Cinnaminson (08077) *(G-1445)*

Airmet Inc 973 481-5550
794 N 6th St Newark (07107) *(G-7074)*

Airmet Metal Works, Newark *Also called Airmet Inc (G-7074)*

Airoyal Division, Butler *Also called Delta Sales Company Inc (G-1002)*

Airscan Inc 908 823-9425
291 Rt 22 Ste 12 Lebanon (08833) *(G-5274)*

Airtec Inc 732 382-3700
17 W Scott Ave Rahway (07065) *(G-9172)*

Airtec-Unique, Rahway *Also called Airtec Inc (G-9172)*

Airtech Vacuum, Rutherford *Also called Apple Air Compressor Corp (G-9725)*

Airworld Inc 973 720-1008
70 Spruce St Paterson (07501) *(G-8201)*

Airzone Systems 201 207-6593
28 Valhalla Rd Montville (07045) *(G-6482)*

AlSha&anna Nation of Trends 201 951-8197
2 Park Sq Apt 2210 Rahway (07065) *(G-9173)*

Aiva Naturals LLC 201 825-0749
50 Park Pl Ste 1100 Newark (07102) *(G-7075)*

AJ Siris Products Corp 973 823-0050
150 Main St Ogdensburg (07439) *(G-7769)*

Ajay Metal Fabricators Inc 908 523-0557
355 Dalziel Rd Linden (07036) *(G-5345)*

Ajg Packaging LLC 908 528-6052
10 Northwood Dr Pittstown (08867) *(G-8848)*

Ajj Powernutrition LLC 908 452-5164
1930 State Route 57 Hackettstown (07840) *(G-3995)*

AK Associates LLC 732 786-0002
33 Sherwood Ct Jackson (08527) *(G-4652)*

AK Contracting LLC 908 220-8527
32b Seafoam Ave Winfield Park (07036) *(G-12131)*

Akadema Inc 973 304-1470
46 Star Lake Rd Ste B Bloomingdale (07403) *(G-540)*

Akay USA LLC 732 254-7177
500 Hartle St Sayreville (08872) *(G-9812)*

Akcros Chemicals Inc 800 500-7890
500 Jersey Ave New Brunswick (08901) *(G-6943)*

Akela Laser Corporation 732 305-7105
1095 Cranbury S Riv 14 Monroe Township (08831) *(G-6377)*

Akers Biosciences Inc 856 848-8698
201 Grove Rd West Deptford (08086) *(G-11814)*

Akila Holdings Inc 609 454-5034
12 Hampstead Ct Princeton (08540) *(G-8999)*

AKILA HOLDINGS INC LLC, Princeton *Also called Akila Holdings Inc* ***(G-8999)***
Akorn Inc....609 662-9100
5 Cedarbrook Dr Cranbury (08512) ***(G-1809)***
Akorn Inc....732 659-6443
72 Veronica Ave Ste 6 Somerset (08873) ***(G-10053)***
Akrimax Pharmaceuticals LLC....908 372-0506
11 Commerce Dr Ste 103 Cranford (07016) ***(G-1894)***
Aks Pharma Inc....856 521-0710
201 Front St Elmer (08318) ***(G-2788)***
Akw Inc....732 493-1883
1414 Roller Rd Rear Ocean (07712) ***(G-7714)***
Akw Inc (PA)....732 530-9186
41 Newman Springs Rd E Shrewsbury (07702) ***(G-9988)***
Akzo Chemicals, Edison *Also called Akzo Nobel Chemicals LLC* ***(G-2454)***
Akzo Nobel Chemicals LLC....732 985-6262
340 Meadow Rd Edison (08837) ***(G-2454)***
Al and John Inc....973 742-4990
147 Clinton Rd Caldwell (07006) ***(G-1024)***
Al Richrds Homemade Chocolates....201 436-0915
851 Broadway Bayonne (07002) ***(G-210)***
Al Tayyar Enrgy- Princeton LLC....609 479-8603
63 Moran Ave Ste B Princeton (08542) ***(G-9000)***
Aladdin Color Inc....609 518-9858
19 E Main St Ste D Moorestown (08057) ***(G-6556)***
Aladdin Manufacturing Corp....973 616-4600
100 Alexander Ave Pompton Plains (07444) ***(G-8951)***
Aladen Athletic Wear LLC....973 838-2425
465 W Main St Ste 5 Wyckoff (07481) ***(G-12245)***
Alan Chemical Corporation Inc....973 628-7777
573 Valley Rd Ste 1 Wayne (07470) ***(G-11602)***
Alan Duffy Printing....856 768-1046
2389 Atco Ave Atco (08004) ***(G-88)***
Alan Paul Accessories Inc....609 924-4022
66 Witherspoon St # 3300 Princeton (08542) ***(G-9001)***
Alan Paul Neckware, Princeton *Also called Alan Paul Accessories Inc* ***(G-9001)***
Alaquest International Inc....908 713-9399
28 Molasses Hill Rd Lebanon (08833) ***(G-5275)***
Alba Translations CPA....973 340-1130
436 Main St Lodi (07644) ***(G-5574)***
Albea Americas Inc (HQ)....908 689-3000
191 State Route 31 N Washington (07882) ***(G-11573)***
Alben Metal Products Inc....973 279-8891
11 Iowa Ave Paterson (07503) ***(G-8202)***
Albert Forte Neckwear Co Inc....856 423-2342
127 Fellowship Ln Mullica Hill (08062) ***(G-6891)***
Albert H Hopper Inc....201 991-2266
329 Ridge Rd North Arlington (07031) ***(G-7414)***
Albert Paper Products Company....973 373-0330
464 Coit St Irvington (07111) ***(G-4571)***
Alboum W Hat Company Inc....201 399-4110
1439 Springfield Ave Irvington (07111) ***(G-4572)***
Alcami New Jersey Corporation....732 346-5100
165 Fieldcrest Ave Edison (08837) ***(G-2455)***
Alcan Baltek Corporation....201 767-1400
108 Fairway Ct Northvale (07647) ***(G-7570)***
Alcaro & Alcaro Plating Co....973 746-1200
112 Pine St Montclair (07042) ***(G-6405)***
Alcatel-Lucent USA Inc....908 582-3275
600 Mountain Ave 700 New Providence (07974) ***(G-7026)***
Alcatel-Lucent USA Inc., New Providence *Also called Nokia of America Corporation* ***(G-7050)***
Alchemy Billboards LLC....973 977-8828
125 5th Ave Paterson (07524) ***(G-8203)***
Alco Trimming....201 854-8608
8608 Grand Ave Rear North Bergen (07047) ***(G-7426)***
Alcoa Howmet, Dover, Dover *Also called Howmet Castings & Services Inc* ***(G-2091)***
Alcoa Hwmet Dver Alloy Oprtons, Dover *Also called Howmet Castings & Services Inc* ***(G-2092)***
Alcon Products Inc....609 267-3898
161 Burrs Rd Westampton (08060) ***(G-11910)***
Alcop Adhesive Label Co....609 871-4400
826 Perkins Ln Beverly (08010) ***(G-458)***
Alden - Leeds Inc....973 344-7986
100 Hackensack Ave Kearny (07032) ***(G-4858)***
Alden - Leeds Inc (PA)....973 589-3544
55 Jacobus Ave Ste 1 Kearny (07032) ***(G-4859)***
Alden Leeds, Kearny *Also called Alden - Leeds Inc* ***(G-4859)***
Alecto Systems LLC....973 875-6721
130 Gunn Rd Branchville (07826) ***(G-725)***
Alembic Pharmaceuticals Inc (HQ)....908 393-9604
750 Us Highway 202 # 100 Bridgewater (08807) ***(G-807)***
Alere Distribution, Freehold *Also called Alere Inc* ***(G-3637)***
Alere Inc....732 620-4244
500 Halls Mill Rd Freehold (07728) ***(G-3636)***
Alere Inc....732 358-5921
569 Halls Mill Rd Freehold (07728) ***(G-3637)***
Aleris Rolled Products Inc....856 881-3600
838 N Delsea Dr Clayton (08312) ***(G-1522)***
Alessandra Miscellaneous Metal....973 786-6805
75 Mill St Ste B Newton (07860) ***(G-7379)***
Alete Printing LLC....856 468-3536
722 Dartmouth Ct Wenonah (08090) ***(G-11702)***
Alex and Ani LLC....908 965-1510
651 Kapkowski Rd Ste 1274 Elizabeth (07201) ***(G-2707)***
Alex Machine Shop Inc....201 768-9110
267 Livingston St Northvale (07647) ***(G-7571)***
Alex Real LLC....732 730-8770
1876 Lakewood Rd Toms River (08755) ***(G-10860)***
Alex Silk Co Inc....973 427-0499
53 Braen Ave Hawthorne (07506) ***(G-4217)***
Alexam Riverdale....973 831-0065
4000 Riverdale Rd Riverdale (07457) ***(G-9474)***
Alexander Communications Group....973 265-2300
36 Midvale Rd Ste 2e Mountain Lakes (07046) ***(G-6854)***
Alexander James Corp....908 362-9266
845 State Route 94 Blairstown (07825) ***(G-494)***
Alexander Marketing Services, Mountain Lakes *Also called Alexander Communications Group* ***(G-6854)***
Alfa Machine & Tool Co Inc....973 227-1962
19 Just Rd Fairfield (07004) ***(G-3129)***
Alfa Wassermann Inc (PA)....973 882-8630
4 Henderson Dr West Caldwell (07006) ***(G-11763)***
Alfa Wssrmann Dagnstc Tech LLC....800 220-4488
4 Henderson Dr West Caldwell (07006) ***(G-11764)***
Alfred Dunner Inc....212 944-6660
200 Walsh Dr Parsippany (07054) ***(G-7942)***
Alfred Heitzman Machine Works....201 489-8888
303 E Park St Moonachie (07074) ***(G-6500)***
Alfred Sports Inc....973 822-8987
30 Main St Madison (07940) ***(G-5717)***
Algar/Display Connection Corp....201 438-1000
131 W Commercial Ave Moonachie (07074) ***(G-6501)***
Algen Design Services Inc....732 389-3630
40 Industrial Way E Eatontown (07724) ***(G-2379)***
Algene Marking Equipment Co....973 478-9041
232 Palisade Ave Garfield (07026) ***(G-3716)***
Align Pharmaceuticals LLC....908 834-0960
200 Connell Dr Ste 1500 Berkeley Heights (07922) ***(G-399)***
Align Sourcing Ltd Lblty Co....609 375-8550
46 Doe Dr Trenton (08620) ***(G-11014)***
Alisa, Englishtown *Also called Golden Treasure Imports Inc* ***(G-2992)***
Alison Control Inc....973 575-7100
35 Daniel Rd W Fairfield (07004) ***(G-3130)***
Alk Technologies Inc (HQ)....609 683-0220
1 Independence Way # 400 Princeton (08540) ***(G-9002)***
Alkaline Corporation....732 531-7830
38 Industrial Way E Ste 2 Eatontown (07724) ***(G-2380)***
Alkaline Corporation....732 531-7830
714 W Park Ave Oakhurst (07755) ***(G-7667)***
All American Metal Fabricators....201 567-2898
34 Harold St Tenafly (07670) ***(G-10780)***
All American Oil Recovery Co....973 628-9278
1067 State Route 23 Wayne (07470) ***(G-11603)***
All American Poly Corp (PA)....732 752-3200
40 Turner Pl Piscataway (08854) ***(G-8730)***
All American Powdercoating LLC....732 349-7001
2002 Route 9 Toms River (08755) ***(G-10861)***
All American Print & Copy Ctr....732 758-6200
500 State Route 35 Red Bank (07701) ***(G-9318)***
All Amrcan Recycl Corp Clifton....201 656-3363
2 Hope St Jersey City (07307) ***(G-4701)***
All Colors Screen Printing LLC....732 777-6033
176 Woodbridge Ave Highland Park (08904) ***(G-4300)***
All County Recycling Inc....609 393-6445
391 Enterprise Ave Trenton (08638) ***(G-11015)***
ALl Envmtl & Tank Svcs LLC....908 755-2962
2560 Us Highway 22 346 Scotch Plains (07076) ***(G-9844)***
All In Color Inc....973 626-0987
132 Beckwith Ave Paterson (07503) ***(G-8204)***
All In Icing....973 896-5990
24 Woods Edge Rd Stanhope (07874) ***(G-10587)***
All Madina Inc....973 226-7772
592 Passaic Ave West Caldwell (07006) ***(G-11765)***
All Mechanical Services Inc....732 442-8292
430 High St Perth Amboy (08861) ***(G-8606)***
All Metal Polishing Co Inc....973 589-8070
23 George St Newark (07105) ***(G-7076)***
All Mtals Frge Group Ltd Lblty (PA)....973 276-5000
75 Lane Rd Ste 303 Fairfield (07004) ***(G-3131)***
All Natural Products....212 391-2870
4000 Bordentown Ave # 20 Sayreville (08872) ***(G-9813)***
All Nu Trophy & Screen Prtg....201 807-0808
243 Teaneck Rd Ridgefield Park (07660) ***(G-9396)***
All Print Resources Group Inc....201 994-0600
256 Sheffield St Mountainside (07092) ***(G-6867)***
All Racks Industries Inc....212 244-1069
101 Roselle St Linden (07036) ***(G-5346)***
All Seasons Construction Inc....908 852-0955
43 Flocktown Rd Long Valley (07853) ***(G-5634)***

ALPHABETIC

All Seasons Door & Window Inc (PA) 732 238-7100
28 Edgeboro Rd East Brunswick (08816) *(G-2131)*

All Seasons Pool & Spa, Marlton *Also called Van Brill Pool & Spa Center* *(G-6002)*

All Smith Spinning and Turning, Moonachie *Also called Bergen Homestate Corp* *(G-6507)*

All Sports Stadium, Washington *Also called Armin Kososki* *(G-11575)*

All State Medal Co Inc 973 458-1458
16 Adams Pl Lodi (07644) *(G-5575)*

All State Plastics Inc 732 654-5054
237 Raritan St South Amboy (08879) *(G-10234)*

All Structures LLC 732 233-7071
21 Rumson Rd Little Silver (07739) *(G-5519)*

All Surface Asphalt Paving 732 295-3800
528 Hardenberg Ave Point Pleasant Boro (08742) *(G-8930)*

All Tool Company Inc 908 687-3636
899 Rahway Ave Union (07083) *(G-11148)*

All-Lace Processing Corp 201 867-1974
1109 Grand Ave Ste 4 North Bergen (07047) *(G-7427)*

All-State Fence Inc 732 431-4944
347 Mount Pleasant Ave # 300 West Orange (07052) *(G-11885)*

All-State International Inc (PA) 908 272-0800
1 Commerce Dr Cranford (07016) *(G-1895)*

All-State Legal, Cranford *Also called All-State International Inc* *(G-1895)*

Allary Corporation 908 851-0077
2204 Morris Ave Ste 209 Union (07083) *(G-11149)*

Allegra Marketing Print & Mail, Marmora *Also called Sjshore Marketing Ltd Lblty Co* *(G-6006)*

Allegro Nutrition Inc 732 364-3777
1023 Waverly Ave Neptune (07753) *(G-6899)*

Allegro Printing Corporation 609 641-7060
408 S 4th Ave Galloway (08205) *(G-3708)*

Allen Cabinets and Millwork 973 694-0665
60 Newark Pompton Tpke Pequannock (07440) *(G-8596)*

Allen Flavors Inc (PA) 908 561-5995
23 Progress St Edison (08820) *(G-2456)*

Allen Flavors Inc 908 753-0544
220 Saint Nicholas Ave South Plainfield (07080) *(G-10323)*

Allen Steel Co 856 785-1171
202 High St Leesburg (08327) *(G-5314)*

Allentown Inc (PA) 609 259-7951
165 Route 526 Allentown (08501) *(G-28)*

Allergan Inc 908 306-0374
1 Crossroads Dr Bedminster (07921) *(G-265)*

Allergan Inc 862 261-7000
16 Airport Rd Morristown (07960) *(G-6684)*

Allergan Inc (HQ) 862 261-7000
5 Giralda Farms Madison (07940) *(G-5718)*

Allergan Holdco Us Inc (HQ) 862 261-7000
400 Interpace Pkwy Ste D Parsippany (07054) *(G-7943)*

Allergan Pharmacy, Parsippany *Also called Watson Laboratories Inc* *(G-8112)*

Allersearch Labs, Eatontown *Also called Alkaline Corporation* *(G-2380)*

Allfasteners Usa LLC 201 783-8836
480 Meadow Ln Carlstadt (07072) *(G-1123)*

Allgrind Plastics Inc 908 479-4400
6 Vliet Farm Rd Asbury (08802) *(G-63)*

Alliance Contract Mfg, Berlin *Also called Hanson & Zollinger Inc* *(G-434)*

Alliance Corrugated Box Inc 877 525-5269
10 E Saddle River Rd Saddle River (07458) *(G-9802)*

Alliance Design Group, Totowa *Also called Alliance Design Inc* *(G-10927)*

Alliance Design Inc 973 904-9450
434 Union Blvd Totowa (07512) *(G-10927)*

Alliance Display, Totowa *Also called Westrock Rkt Company* *(G-10984)*

Alliance Food Equipment 201 784-1101
1 S Gold Dr Trenton (08691) *(G-11016)*

Alliance Hand & Physical 201 822-0100
24 Booker St Ste 3 Westwood (07675) *(G-11952)*

Alliance Sand Co Inc (PA) 908 534-4116
51 Tannery Rd Somerville (08876) *(G-10201)*

Alliance Sensors Group, Moorestown *Also called H G Schaevitz LLC* *(G-6582)*

Alliance Store Fixture, Moonachie *Also called Amko Displays Corporation* *(G-6505)*

Alliance Technologies Group 973 664-1151
57 Eagle Rock Ave East Hanover (07936) *(G-2199)*

Alliance Vinyl Windows Co Inc 856 456-4954
301 Crescent Blvd Oaklyn (08107) *(G-7710)*

Allied Asphalt Division, Piscataway *Also called Ziegler Chem & Mineral Corp* *(G-8839)*

Allied Bias Products Corp 201 432-6050
430 Communipaw Ave Ste 3 Jersey City (07304) *(G-4702)*

Allied Concrete Co Inc (PA) 973 627-6150
205 Franklin Ave Rockaway (07866) *(G-9549)*

Allied Concrete Co Inc 973 627-6150
205 Franklin Ave Rockaway (07866) *(G-9550)*

Allied Elastic Braid Inc 201 941-8875
280 N Midland Ave Bldg C1 Saddle Brook (07663) *(G-9751)*

Allied Embroidery, Englewood *Also called Sniderman John* *(G-2932)*

Allied Envelope Co Inc (PA) 201 440-2000
33 Commerce Rd Carlstadt (07072) *(G-1124)*

Allied Enviornmental Signage, Farmingdale *Also called Yates Sign Co Inc* *(G-3398)*

Allied Felt Group Div, Bloomingdale *Also called Central Shippee Inc* *(G-541)*

Allied Group Inc 973 543-4994
5 Cold Hill Rd S Ste 19 Mendham (07945) *(G-6086)*

Allied Metal, North Bergen *Also called Allied Specialty Group Inc* *(G-7428)*

Allied Metal Industries Inc 973 824-7347
118 Harper St 144 Newark (07114) *(G-7077)*

Allied Old English Inc 732 636-2060
100 Markley St Port Reading (07064) *(G-8986)*

Allied Pharma Inc 732 738-3295
20 Corrielle St Fords (08863) *(G-3526)*

Allied Plastics Holdings LLC (PA) 718 729-5500
560 Ferry St Newark (07105) *(G-7078)*

Allied Plastics New Jersey LLC 973 956-9200
155 Sherman Ave Paterson (07502) *(G-8205)*

Allied Printing Resources, Carlstadt *Also called Allied Envelope Co Inc* *(G-1124)*

Allied Printing-Graphics Inc 973 227-0520
4 Madison Rd Fairfield (07004) *(G-3132)*

Allied Specialty Foods Inc 856 507-1100
1585 W Forest Grove Rd Vineland (08360) *(G-11321)*

Allied Specialty Group Inc (PA) 201 223-4600
3223 Dell Ave North Bergen (07047) *(G-7428)*

Allied Steaks, Vineland *Also called Allied Specialty Foods Inc* *(G-11321)*

Allied Steel Dist & Svc Ctr, Newark *Also called Allied Metal Industries Inc* *(G-7077)*

Allied Tile Mfg Corp 718 647-2200
631 Montrose Ave South Plainfield (07080) *(G-10324)*

Allied Waste Products Inc 973 473-7638
61 Midland Ave Ste 61-71 Wallington (07057) *(G-11522)*

Allied-Signal China Ltd 973 455-2000
101 Columbia Rd Morristown (07960) *(G-6685)*

Allison Corp (PA) 973 992-3800
15-33 Okner Pkwy Livingston (07039) *(G-5523)*

Allison Systems Corporation 856 461-9111
220 Adams St Riverside (08075) *(G-9492)*

Allmark Door Company LLC (PA) 610 358-9800
15 Stern Ave Springfield (07081) *(G-10536)*

Allmike Metal Technology Inc 201 935-2306
65 Anderson Ave Moonachie (07074) *(G-6502)*

Allos Therapeutics Inc 609 936-3760
302 Carnegie Ctr Ste 200 Princeton (08540) *(G-9003)*

Alloy Cast Products Inc 908 245-2255
700 Swenson Dr Kenilworth (07033) *(G-4936)*

Alloy Software Inc 973 661-9700
400 Broadacres Dr Ste 100 Bloomfield (07003) *(G-501)*

Alloy Stainless Products Co, Totowa *Also called Knickerbocker Machine Shop Inc* *(G-10953)*

Alloy Stainless Products Co 973 256-1616
611 Union Blvd Totowa (07512) *(G-10928)*

Alloy Welding Co 908 218-1551
6 Culnen Dr Ste A Branchburg (08876) *(G-630)*

Allstar Disposal 973 398-8808
118 Hudson Ave Hopatcong (07843) *(G-4533)*

Allstate Can Corporation 973 560-9030
1 Woodhollow Rd Parsippany (07054) *(G-7944)*

Allstate Conveyor Service 856 768-6566
256 Terrace Blvd Voorhees (08043) *(G-11420)*

Allstate Paper Box Co Inc (PA) 973 589-2600
223 Raymond Blvd Newark (07105) *(G-7079)*

Alltec Stores, Fairfield *Also called Vcom Intl Multi-Media Corp* *(G-3338)*

Alltest Instruments Inc 732 919-3339
500 Central Ave Farmingdale (07727) *(G-3376)*

Alltite Gasket Co 732 254-2154
323 William St South River (08882) *(G-10458)*

Allu Group Inc 201 288-2236
25 Kimberly Rd Ste A East Brunswick (08816) *(G-2132)*

Allure Box & Display Co 212 807-7070
216 Charles St Hackensack (07601) *(G-3873)*

Alm Media LLC 973 642-0075
238 Mulberry St Fl 2 Newark (07102) *(G-7080)*

Alma Park Alpacas 732 620-1052
2800 Monmouth Rd Jobstown (08041) *(G-4853)*

Almark Tool & Manufacturing Co 908 789-2440
27 South Ave Garwood (07027) *(G-3775)*

Almatica Pharma Inc 877 447-7979
10 Bloomfield Ave B Pine Brook (07058) *(G-8682)*

Almetek Industries Inc 908 850-9700
2 Joy Dr Hackettstown (07840) *(G-3996)*

Almike Metal Products, Moonachie *Also called Allmike Metal Technology Inc* *(G-6502)*

Almond Branch Inc 973 728-3479
184 Marshall Hill Rd West Milford (07480) *(G-11849)*

Aln, Woodcliff Lake *Also called American Logistics Network LLC* *(G-12180)*

Aloe Creme Laboratories Div, Branchburg *Also called Aloe Science Inc* *(G-631)*

Aloe Science Inc 908 231-8888
160 Meister Ave Ste 20 Branchburg (08876) *(G-631)*

Aloris Tool Technology Co Inc 973 772-1201
407 Getty Ave Clifton (07011) *(G-1561)*

Alpex Wheel Co Inc (PA) 201 871-1700
29 Atwood Ave Tenafly (07670) *(G-10781)*

Alpha 1 Studio Inc 609 859-2200
3 Linda Ln Southampton (08088) *(G-10469)*

Alpha Advanced Materials, Somerset *Also called Alpha Assembly Solutions Inc* *(G-10054)*

Alpha Assembly Solutions Inc 908 561-5170
109 Corporate Blvd South Plainfield (07080) *(G-10325)*

(G-0000) Company's Geographic Section entry number

Alpha Assembly Solutions Inc (HQ) 908 791-3000
  300 Atrium Dr Fl 3 Somerset (08873) *(G-10054)*

Alpha Associates Inc 732 730-1800
  145 Lehigh Ave Lakewood (08701) *(G-5067)*

Alpha Engneered Composites LLC (PA) 732 634-5700
  145 Lehigh Ave Lakewood (08701) *(G-5068)*

Alpha Industries, Lyndhurst *Also called Epsilon Plastics Inc (G-5680)*

Alpha Industries MGT Inc (PA) 201 933-6000
  Page And Schuyler Ave Lyndhurst (07071) *(G-5667)*

Alpha Lehigh Tool & Mch Co Inc 908 454-6481
  41 Industrial Rd Alpha (08865) *(G-38)*

Alpha Plastics, Middlesex *Also called Fram Trak Industries Inc (G-6167)*

Alpha Processing Co Inc 973 777-1737
  210 Delawanna Ave Clifton (07014) *(G-1562)*

Alpha Scientific Corporation 908 534-9941
  442 Rt 202 206n Pmb 435 Whitehouse Station (08889) *(G-12049)*

Alpha Tech Services 973 283-2011
  121 Hawkins Pl Ste 197 Boonton (07005) *(G-553)*

Alpha Wire, Elizabeth *Also called Belden Inc (G-2712)*

Alpha Wire Corporation (PA) 908 925-8000
  711 Lidgerwood Ave Elizabeth (07202) *(G-2708)*

AlphaGraphics, Cherry Hill *Also called C Jackson Associates Inc (G-1355)*

AlphaGraphics, Totowa *Also called Viskal Printing LLC (G-10982)*

AlphaGraphics, Midland Park *Also called Wilker Graphics LLC (G-6242)*

AlphaGraphics, Red Bank *Also called D & S Ventures Inc (G-9324)*

AlphaGraphics, Cranbury *Also called Your Printer V20 Ltd (G-1893)*

AlphaGraphics 201 327-2200
  1 Lethbridge Plz Ste 22 Mahwah (07430) *(G-5746)*

AlphaGraphics 856 761-8000
  5 N Olney Ave Ste 200 Cherry Hill (08003) *(G-1343)*

AlphaGraphics 321, North Brunswick *Also called Carl A Venable Inc (G-7510)*

Alphagraphics Printshops of th, Parsippany *Also called Digital Print Solutions Inc (G-7982)*

AlphaGraphics Printshops of Th 973 984-0066
  60 Speedwell Ave Morristown (07960) *(G-6686)*

Alpharma US Inc 201 228-5090
  400 Crossing Blvd Ste 701 Bridgewater (08807) *(G-808)*

Alphawire, Elizabeth *Also called Alpha Wire Corporation (G-2708)*

Alpine Bakery Inc 201 902-0605
  521-523 30th St Union City (07087) *(G-11239)*

Alpine Corrugated McHy Inc 201 440-3030
  100 Challenger Rd Ste 304 Ridgefield Park (07660) *(G-9397)*

Alpine Creamery 973 726-0777
  14 White Deer Plz Sparta (07871) *(G-10487)*

Alpine Custom Floors 201 533-0100
  173 Sherman Ave Jersey City (07307) *(G-4703)*

Alpine Group Inc (PA) 201 549-4400
  1 Meadowlands Plz Ste 800 East Rutherford (07073) *(G-2275)*

Alpine Machine & Tool Corp 201 666-0959
  42 Bergenline Ave Westwood (07675) *(G-11953)*

Alpine Trading Company Inc 201 871-6111
  400 Overpeck Pl Englewood (07631) *(G-2867)*

Alpro Inc 201 342-4498
  50 Romanelli Ave South Hackensack (07606) *(G-10254)*

Alster Import Co Inc 201 332-7245
  16 Burma Rd Jersey City (07305) *(G-4704)*

Alstrom Energy Group LLC 718 824-4901
  11 Jocama Blvd Ste 11a Old Bridge (08857) *(G-7773)*

Alt Shift Creative LLC 609 619-0009
  15 Mountain Ave Flanders (07836) *(G-3400)*

Altaflo LLC 973 300-3344
  23 Wilson Dr Ste 1 Sparta (07871) *(G-10488)*

Altantic Printing and Design 732 557-9600
  467 Lakehurst Rd Toms River (08755) *(G-10862)*

Altech Machine & Tool Inc 201 652-4409
  230 Bank St Midland Park (07432) *(G-6220)*

Alteon 201 934-1624
  170 Williams Dr Ramsey (07446) *(G-9232)*

Altera Corporation 732 649-3477
  106 Charles St Somerset (08873) *(G-10055)*

Alternate Side Street Suspende 201 291-7878
  16 Arcadian Way Ste C1 Paramus (07652) *(G-7853)*

Alternative Air Fixture, Willingboro *Also called Alternative Air LLC (G-12116)*

Alternative Air LLC (PA) 609 261-5870
  30 Echo Ln Willingboro (08046) *(G-12116)*

Altibase Incorporated 888 837-7333
  1 International Blvd Mahwah (07495) *(G-5747)*

Altima Innovations Inc 732 474-1500
  211 Evans Way Branchburg (08876) *(G-632)*

Altivity Packaging, Wayne *Also called Graphic Packaging Intl LLC (G-11643)*

Alto Development Corp (PA) 732 938-2266
  5206 Asbury Rd Wall Township (07727) *(G-11461)*

Altona Blower & Shtmtl Work 201 641-3520
  23 N Washington Ave Little Ferry (07643) *(G-5494)*

Altona Blower & Shtmtl Works, Little Ferry *Also called Altona Blower & Shtmtl Work (G-5494)*

Altus Pcb LLC 973 928-8777
  45 Legion Dr Cresskill (07626) *(G-1943)*

Alu Inc 201 935-2213
  240 Anderson Ave Moonachie (07074) *(G-6503)*

Aluma Systems Con Cnstr LLC 908 418-5073
  1800 Lower Rd Linden (07036) *(G-5347)*

Aluminum Shapes Inc 856 662-5500
  9000 River Rd Pennsauken (08110) *(G-8475)*

Aluminum Shapes LLC 888 488-7427
  9000 River Rd Delair (08110) *(G-1999)*

Aluseal LLC 856 692-3355
  1649 Castpa Pl Vineland (08360) *(G-11322)*

Alva-Tech Inc 609 747-1133
  1208 Columbus Rd Ste G Burlington Township (08016) *(G-997)*

Alvaro P Escandon Inc 973 274-1040
  528 Ferry St Newark (07105) *(G-7081)*

Alvaro Stairs LLC 201 864-6754
  4201 Tonnelle Ave Ste 12 North Bergen (07047) *(G-7429)*

Alvogen Group Inc (PA) 973 796-3400
  10 Bloomfield Ave Pine Brook (07058) *(G-8683)*

Alvogen Inc 973 796-3400
  10 Bloomfield Ave Ste 3 Pine Brook (07058) *(G-8684)*

Alvogen Pharma Us Inc 973 796-3400
  10 Bloomfield Ave Pine Brook (07058) *(G-8685)*

Always Be Secure LLC 917 887-2286
  195 Route 9 Ste 109 Manalapan (07726) *(G-5838)*

Alzo International Inc 732 254-1901
  650 Jernee Mill Rd Sayreville (08872) *(G-9814)*

AM Best Company Inc (PA) 908 439-2200
  1 Ambest Rd Oldwick (08858) *(G-7803)*

AM Best Company Inc 908 439-2200
  Am Best Rd Oldwick (08858) *(G-7804)*

AM Cruz International LLC 732 340-0066
  13 New York Ave Colonia (07067) *(G-1776)*

AM Wood Inc 732 246-1506
  18 Kennedy Blvd East Brunswick (08816) *(G-2133)*

Am-Mac Incorporated 973 575-7567
  311 Route 46 W Ste C Fairfield (07004) *(G-3133)*

Amalco, Mountainside *Also called American Aluminum Company (G-6868)*

Amalia Carrara Inc 201 348-4500
  2111 Kerrigan Ave Union City (07087) *(G-11240)*

Amano Cincinnati Distributor, Roseland *Also called Amano Cincinnati Incorporated (G-9642)*

Amano Cincinnati Incorporated (HQ) 973 403-1900
  140 Harrison Ave Roseland (07068) *(G-9642)*

Amano USA Holdings Inc (HQ) 973 403-1900
  140 Harrison Ave Roseland (07068) *(G-9643)*

Amante International Ltd 908 518-1688
  510 Codding Rd Westfield (07090) *(G-11919)*

Amarin Corporation PLC 908 719-1315
  1430 Us Highway 206 # 100 Bedminster (07921) *(G-266)*

Amark Industries Inc (PA) 973 992-8900
  293 Eisenhower Pkwy # 100 Livingston (07039) *(G-5524)*

Amark Wire LLC 973 882-7818
  18 Passaic Ave Unit 6 Fairfield (07004) *(G-3134)*

Amaryllis Inc (PA) 973 635-0500
  418 River Rd Chatham (07928) *(G-1325)*

Amati International LLC 201 569-1000
  560 Sylvan Ave Ste 2053 Englewood Cliffs (07632) *(G-2947)*

Amb Enterprises LLC (PA) 973 225-1070
  25 Lake St Paterson (07501) *(G-8206)*

Amber Road Inc (PA) 201 935-8588
  1 Meadowlands Plz # 1500 East Rutherford (07073) *(G-2276)*

Ambix Laboratories, Totowa *Also called Organics Corporation America (G-10960)*

Ambo Consulting LLC 732 663-0000
  82 Norwood Ave Ste 2 Deal (07723) *(G-1997)*

Ambro Inc 201 818-9717
  303 Newark Pompton Tpke Pequannock (07440) *(G-8597)*

Ambro Manufacturing Inc 908 806-8337
  6 Kings Ct Flemington (08822) *(G-3425)*

Amcor Flexibles Inc 609 267-5900
  220 Shreve St Mount Holly (08060) *(G-6766)*

Amcor Flexibles LLC 856 825-1400
  1633 Wheaton Ave Millville (08332) *(G-6275)*

Amcor Flexibles Mil, Millville *Also called Amcor Flexibles LLC (G-6275)*

Amcor Flexibles Mount Holly, Mount Holly *Also called Amcor Flexibles Inc (G-6766)*

Amcor Phrm Packg USA Inc 856 825-3050
  1600 Malone St Millville (08332) *(G-6276)*

Amcor Phrm Packg USA Inc 856 728-9300
  918 E Malaga Rd Williamstown (08094) *(G-12078)*

Amcor Phrm Packg USA LLC (HQ) 856 327-1540
  625 Sharp St N Millville (08332) *(G-6277)*

Amcor Phrm Packg USA LLC 856 825-1400
  1200 N 10th St Millville (08332) *(G-6278)*

Amcor Phrm Packg USA LLC 856 825-1400
  1633 Wheaton Ave Millville (08332) *(G-6279)*

Amcor Phrm Packg USA LLC 856 825-1100
  1501 N 10th St Millville (08332) *(G-6280)*

Amcor Phrm Packg USA LLC 856 825-1400
  1101 Wheaton Ave Millville (08332) *(G-6281)*

Amcor Rigid Plastics Usa LLC 856 327-1540
  625 Sharp St N Millville (08332) *(G-6282)*

A
L
P
H
A
B
E
T
I
C

AMD Fine Linens LLC 201 568-5255
471 S Dean St Englewood (07631) *(G-2868)*

Amec Fster Wheeler N Amer Corp (HQ) 936 448-6323
53 Frontage Rd Hampton (08827) *(G-4153)*

Amedia Networks Inc 732 440-1992
541 Industrial Way W B Eatontown (07724) *(G-2381)*

Amega Scientific Corporation 609 953-7295
617 Stokes Rd Medford (08055) *(G-6064)*

Amer-RAC LLC 856 488-6210
8128 River Rd Pennsauken (08110) *(G-8476)*

Ameral International Inc 856 456-9000
7 Railroad Ln Brooklawn (08030) *(G-919)*

Amerasia Intl Tech Inc 609 799-9388
70 Washington Rd Princeton Junction (08550) *(G-9147)*

America Oggi, Norwood Also called Gruppo Editoriale Oggi Inc *(G-7623)*

America Techma Inc 201 894-5887
385 Sylvan Ave Ste 28 Englewood Cliffs (07632) *(G-2948)*

American & Hispanic Bus Journa, South Orange Also called Diversity Plus
Magazine *(G-10303)*

American Aeronautic Mfg Co 973 442-8138
45 Us Highway 46 Ste 606 Pine Brook (07058) *(G-8686)*

American Aluminum Alloys LLC 717 417-5966
701 N 36th St Pennsauken (08110) *(G-8477)*

American Aluminum Casting Co (PA) 973 372-3200
324 Coit St Irvington (07111) *(G-4573)*

American Aluminum Company 908 233-3500
230 Sheffield St Mountainside (07092) *(G-6868)*

American Architectual Stone, North Plainfield Also called Granite and Marble Assoc
Inc *(G-7559)*

American Auto Carriers Inc 201 573-0371
188 Broadway Ste 1 Woodcliff Lake (07677) *(G-12179)*

American Baby Headwear Co Inc (PA) 908 558-0017
1000 Jefferson Ave Elizabeth (07201) *(G-2709)*

American Bank Note Holographic (HQ) 609 208-0591
2 Applegate Dr Robbinsville (08691) *(G-9510)*

American Banknote Corporation (PA) 203 941-4090
2200 Fletcher Ave Ste 501 Fort Lee (07024) *(G-3543)*

American Beryllia Inc 973 248-8080
16 1st Ave Haskell (07420) *(G-4205)*

American Biltrite Inc 856 778-0700
105 Whittendale Dr Moorestown (08057) *(G-6557)*

American Bindery Depot Inc 732 287-2370
191 Talmadge Rd Edison (08817) *(G-2457)*

American Braiding & Mfg Corp 732 938-6333
247 Old Tavern Rd Howell (07731) *(G-4545)*

American Brass and Crystal Inc 908 688-8611
835 Lehigh Ave Union (07083) *(G-11150)*

American Bus & Coach LLC 732 283-1982
1020 Green St Iselin (08830) *(G-4609)*

American Business Paper Inc 732 363-5788
222 River Ave Lakewood (08701) *(G-5069)*

American Casein Company (PA) 609 387-2988
109 Elbow Ln Burlington (08016) *(G-954)*

American Chemical & Coating Co 908 353-2260
410 Division St Elizabeth (07201) *(G-2710)*

American Coding and Mkg Ink Co 908 756-0373
1220 North Ave Plainfield (07062) *(G-8853)*

American Compressed Gases Inc (PA) 201 767-3200
189 Central Ave Old Tappan (07675) *(G-7797)*

American Consolidation Inc 201 438-4351
500 Washington Ave Carlstadt (07072) *(G-1125)*

American Custom Drying Co 609 387-3933
109 Elbow Ln Burlington (08016) *(G-955)*

American Custom Fabricators 732 237-0037
215 Hickory Ln Ste A Bayville (08721) *(G-248)*

American Dawn Inc 856 467-9211
520 Pdricktown Rd Ste B Bridgeport (08014) *(G-761)*

American Diagnstc Imaging Inc 973 980-1724
410 Centre St 2 Nutley (07110) *(G-7639)*

American Directory Publishing 609 494-4055
1816 Long Beach Blvd Surf City (08008) *(G-10664)*

American Display, Whitehouse Also called Larue Manufacturing Corp *(G-12046)*

American Drawtech Company Inc 973 684-1600
53 E 34th St Paterson (07514) *(G-8207)*

American Envelope 908 241-9900
612 E Elizabeth Ave Linden (07036) *(G-5348)*

American Estates Wines Inc 908 273-5060
19 Hillside Ave Summit (07901) *(G-10634)*

American Fibertek Inc 732 302-0660
120 Belmont Dr Somerset (08873) *(G-10056)*

American Fittings Corp (PA) 201 664-0027
17-10 Willow St Fair Lawn (07410) *(G-3075)*

American Flux & Metal LLC 609 561-7500
352 Fleming Pike Hammonton (08037) *(G-4127)*

American Flyer, Clifton Also called Naluco Inc *(G-1678)*

American Food & Bev Inds LLC 347 241-9827
50 S Center St Ste 20 Orange (07050) *(G-7816)*

American Foreclosures Inc 201 501-0200
15 W Main St Apt 1 Bergenfield (07621) *(G-380)*

American Fur Felt LLC 973 344-3026
53 Rome St Newark (07105) *(G-7082)*

American Galvanizing Co Inc 609 567-2090
1919 S 12th St Hammonton (08037) *(G-4128)*

American Gaming & Elec Inc (HQ) 609 704-3000
233 Pratt St Hammonton (08037) *(G-4129)*

American Garvens Corporation 973 276-1093
19a Chapin Rd Pine Brook (07058) *(G-8687)*

American Gas & Chemical Co Ltd 201 767-7300
220 Pegasus Ave Northvale (07647) *(G-7572)*

American Graphic Solutions, Lakewood Also called American Business Paper Inc *(G-5069)*

American Graphic Systems Inc 201 796-0666
39-26 Broadway Fair Lawn (07410) *(G-3076)*

American Graphix, Elizabeth Also called On Demand Machinery *(G-2763)*

American Harlequin Corporation 856 234-5505
1531 Glen Ave Moorestown (08057) *(G-6558)*

American Harvest Baking Co Inc (PA) 856 642-9955
823 E Gate Dr Ste 3 Mount Laurel (08054) *(G-6778)*

American Home Essentials Inc 908 561-3200
600 Mont Rose Ave South Plainfield (07080) *(G-10326)*

American Home Mfg LLC 732 465-1530
4 Corporate Pl Piscataway (08854) *(G-8731)*

American Hose Hydraulic Co Inc (PA) 973 684-3225
700 21st Ave Paterson (07513) *(G-8208)*

American Ingredients Inc 714 630-6000
265 Harrison Tpke Kearny (07032) *(G-4860)*

American International Cont 973 917-3331
3 Mars Ct Ste 4 Boonton (07005) *(G-554)*

American Intr Resources Inc 908 851-0014
1206 Francyne Way Union (07083) *(G-11151)*

American Jewel Window Systems, Livingston Also called Versatile Distributors Inc *(G-5570)*

American Leistritz Extruder 908 685-2333
169 Meister Ave Branchburg (08876) *(G-633)*

American Lighting, Garfield Also called North American Illumination *(G-3743)*

American Logistics Network LLC 201 391-1054
188 Broadway Ste 1 Woodcliff Lake (07677) *(G-12180)*

American Machine Spc NJ LLC 201 664-0006
51 Bergenline Ave Westwood (07675) *(G-11954)*

American Marking Systems Inc (PA) 973 478-5600
1015 Paulison Ave Clifton (07011) *(G-1563)*

American Mch Tool RPR Rbldg Co 973 927-0820
12 Middlebury Blvd Randolph (07869) *(G-9269)*

American Mdlar Pwr Sltions Inc 973 588-4026
429 Rockaway Valley Rd Boonton (07005) *(G-555)*

American Medical & Dental Sups 877 545-6837
240 W Grand Ave Montvale (07645) *(G-6442)*

American Micro Technologies, Linden Also called American Envelope *(G-5348)*

American Microsemiconductor 973 377-9566
133 Kings Rd Madison (07940) *(G-5719)*

American National Red Cross 973 797-3300
209 Fairfield Rd Fairfield (07004) *(G-3135)*

American Oil & Supply Co 732 389-5514
22 Meridian Rd Ste 6 Eatontown (07724) *(G-2382)*

American Panel TEC, South Plainfield Also called Marino Building Systems Corp *(G-10403)*

American Pharmaceutical LLC 732 645-3030
1 New England Ave Piscataway (08854) *(G-8732)*

American Pipe Benders & Fabric 732 287-1122
191 Vineyard Rd Ste 5 Edison (08817) *(G-2458)*

American Plastic Works Inc 800 494-7326
1270 Glen Ave Moorestown (08057) *(G-6559)*

American Plus Printers Inc 732 528-2170
2604 Atlantic Ave Ste 300 Wall (07719) *(G-11458)*

American Power Cord Corp 973 574-8301
4 Smalley Ave Somerset (08873) *(G-10057)*

American Printing, Colts Neck Also called Laser Dim Graphics & Prtg Inc *(G-1789)*

American Process Systems 908 216-6781
131 Cherry Tree Bend Rd Port Murray (07865) *(G-8974)*

American Products Company Inc 908 687-4100
610 Rahway Ave Ste 1 Union (07083) *(G-11152)*

American Prvate Label Pdts LLC 845 733-8151
24b Munsonhurst Rd Franklin (07416) *(G-3594)*

American Rail Company Inc 732 785-1110
1133 Industrial Pkwy B Brick (08724) *(G-733)*

American Refuse Supply Inc (PA) 973 684-3225
700 21st Ave Paterson (07513) *(G-8209)*

American Renolit Corp La 856 241-4901
301 Berkeley Dr B Swedesboro (08085) *(G-10681)*

American Renolit Corporation 973 706-6912
1310 Hamburg Tpke Ste 5 Wayne (07470) *(G-11604)*

American Rigging & Repair Inc 866 478-7129
356 W 1st Ave Roselle (07203) *(G-9660)*

American Sensor Tech Inc (HQ) 973 448-1901
450 Clark Dr Ste 4 Budd Lake (07828) *(G-924)*

American Shale Oil LLC (HQ) 973 438-3500
520 Broad St Ste 1 Newark (07102) *(G-7083)*

American Sign Instllations LLC 856 506-0610
209 S 15th St Millville (08332) *(G-6283)*

American Soc of Mech Engineers 973 244-2282
150 Clove Rd Ste 6 Little Falls (07424) *(G-5468)*

(G-0000) Company's Geographic Section entry number

American Soft Solutions Corp 732 272-0052
704 Ginesi Dr Ste 26 Morganville (07751) (G-6636)
American Spraytech LLC 908 725-6060
205 Meister Ave Branchburg (08876) (G-634)
American Stairs Inc 732 363-3734
687 Prospect St Ste 420 Lakewood (08701) (G-5070)
American Stamp Mfg Co 212 227-1877
1015 Paulison Ave Clifton (07011) (G-1564)
American Standard, Piscataway Also called Asd Holding Corp (G-8739)
American Standard Brands, Piscataway Also called As America Inc (G-8738)
American Standard Intl Inc 732 652-7100
1 Centennial Ave Ste 101 Piscataway (08854) (G-8733)
American Sten-Cyl, Glen Rock Also called American Stencyl Inc (G-3819)
American Stencyl Inc 201 251-6460
479 S Broad St Glen Rock (07452) (G-3819)
American Stone Inc 973 318-7707
215 Us Highway 22 Hillside (07205) (G-4388)
American Stone Inc (PA) 973 318-7707
215 Us Highway 22 Hillside (07205) (G-4389)
American Strip Steel Inc (HQ) 800 526-1216
400 Metuchen Rd South Plainfield (07080) (G-10327)
American Strip Steel Inc 856 461-8300
901 Coopertown Rd Delanco (08075) (G-2002)
American Teletimer Corp 908 654-4200
1167 Globe Ave Mountainside (07092) (G-6869)
American Tire Distributors 973 646-5600
50 Us Highway 46 Totowa (07512) (G-10929)
American Traffic & St Sign Co, Orange Also called East Trading West Inv LLC (G-7819)
American Transparent Plastic 732 287-3000
180 National Rd Edison (08817) (G-2459)
American Van Equipment Inc (PA) 732 905-5900
149 Lehigh Ave Lakewood (08701) (G-5071)
American Water - Pridesa LLC (PA) 856 435-7711
1025 Laurel Oak Rd Voorhees (08043) (G-11421)
American Youth Enterprises Inc 609 909-1900
120 Marlin Ln Mays Landing (08330) (G-6036)
American/Krengel Stamp Mfg Co, Clifton Also called American Stamp Mfg Co (G-1564)
Americare Laboratories Ltd. 973 279-5100
126 Pennsylvania Ave # 104 Paterson (07503) (G-8210)
Americhem Enterprises Inc 732 363-4840
6 Round Valley Ln Lakewood (08701) (G-5072)
Ameriderm Laboratories, Paterson Also called Americare Laboratories Ltd (G-8210)
Amerifab Corp. 973 777-2120
196 Garibaldi Ave Ste 1 Lodi (07644) (G-5576)
Amerifast Corp. 908 668-1959
104 Sylvania Pl South Plainfield (07080) (G-10328)
Amerigen Pharmaceuticals Ltd (PA) 732 993-9826
197 State Route 18 East Brunswick (08816) (G-2134)
Amerilubes LLC 704 399-7701
5 Mantoloking Ln Waretown (08758) (G-11532)
Amerimold Tech Inc 732 462-7577
150 Park Ave Jackson (08527) (G-4653)
Amerindia Technologies Inc 609 664-2224
101 Interchange Plz # 201 Cranbury (08512) (G-1810)
Ameritex Industries Corp 609 502-0123
39 Everett Dr Ste 2 Princeton Junction (08550) (G-9148)
Amerivator Systems Corporation 973 471-1200
220 Scoles Ave Clifton (07012) (G-1565)
Amerlux Lighting Systems, Oakland Also called Amerlux LLC (G-7674)
Amerlux LLC (PA) 973 882-5010
178 Bauer Dr Oakland (07436) (G-7674)
Amershoe Corp 201 569-7300
456 Nordhoff Pl Englewood (07631) (G-2869)
Amertech Towerservices LLC 732 389-2200
149 Avenue At The Cmn Shrewsbury (07702) (G-9989)
Ames Rubber Corporation (PA) 973 827-9101
19 Ames Blvd Hamburg (07419) (G-4088)
Ametek Inc 732 417-0501
52 Mayfield Ave Edison (08837) (G-2460)
Ametek Inc 732 370-9100
485 Oberlin Ave S Lakewood (08701) (G-5073)
Ametek CTS, Edison Also called Ametek Inc (G-2460)
Amex Tool Co. 908 735-5176
4 Fox Hill Ln Asbury (08802) (G-64)
AMF Graphics Inc 201 994-1500
12 Empire Blvd Moonachie (07074) (G-6504)
Amfico, Fair Lawn Also called American Fittings Corp (G-3075)
Amfine Chemical Corporation (HQ) 201 818-0159
777 Perrace Ave Ste 602b Hasbrouck Heights (07604) (G-4191)
AMG International Inc 404 297-9083
71 Walsh Dr Parsippany (07054) (G-7945)
AMG International Inc (PA) 201 475-4800
71 Walsh Dr Ste 101 Parsippany (07054) (G-7946)
Amici Imports Inc 908 272-8300
335 Centennial Ave Unit 7 Cranford (07016) (G-1896)
Amico Technologies Inc 732 901-5900
1200 River Ave Ste 3a Lakewood (08701) (G-5074)
Amicus Therapeutics Inc (PA) 609 662-2000
1 Cedarbrook Dr Cranbury (08512) (G-1811)

Amiee Lynn Accessories, Ridgefield Also called Lynn Amiee Inc (G-9372)
Amish Dairy Products LLC 973 256-7676
41 Vreeland Ave Ste 208 Totowa (07512) (G-10930)
Amit Fuel Company 973 684-9409
703 Mcbride Ave Woodland Park (07424) (G-12209)
Amko Displays Corporation 201 460-7199
7 Purcell Ct Moonachie (07074) (G-6505)
Amloid Corporation 973 328-0654
7 Ridgedale Ave Ste 1a Cedar Knolls (07927) (G-1306)
Ammark Corporation 973 616-2555
230 W Parkway Ste 12 Pompton Plains (07444) (G-8952)
Ammosa Enterprises Inc (PA) 212 779-2890
1 Lethbridge Plz Ste 12 Mahwah (07430) (G-5748)
Ammosa Jewelry, Mahwah Also called Ammosa Enterprises Inc (G-5748)
Amneal Pharmaceuticals LLC 908 947-3120
1 New England Ave Bldg A Piscataway (08854) (G-8734)
Amneal Pharmaceuticals LLC 908 947-3120
47 Colonial Dr Bldg B Piscataway (08854) (G-8735)
Amneal Pharmaceuticals LLC 908 409-6823
65 Readington Rd Bldg B Branchburg (08876) (G-635)
Amneal Pharmaceuticals LLC (HQ) 908 947-3120
400 Crossing Blvd Fl 3 Bridgewater (08807) (G-809)
Amneal Pharmaceuticals LLC 908 231-1911
131 Chambers Brook Rd Branchburg (08876) (G-636)
Amneal Pharmaceuticals LLC 973 357-0222
209 Mclean Blvd Paterson (07504) (G-8211)
Amneal-Agila LLC 908 947-3120
400 Crossing Blvd Fl 3 Bridgewater (08807) (G-810)
Amoco, Burlington Also called American Casein Company (G-954)
Amorosos Baking Co 215 471-4740
151 Benigno Blvd Bellmawr (08031) (G-331)
AMP Custom Rubber Inc 732 888-2714
3 Cass St Ste 8 Keyport (07735) (G-5015)
Ampal Inc 908 782-5454
408 Us Highway 202 Flemington (08822) (G-3426)
Ampericon Inc 609 945-2591
1 Tamaron Ct Monmouth Junction (08852) (G-6331)
Amperite Co Inc 201 864-9503
4201 Tonnelle Ave Ste 6 North Bergen (07047) (G-7430)
Amps, Boonton Also called American Mdlar Pwr Sltions Inc (G-555)
Amrod Corp (PA) 973 344-2978
305a Craneway St Newark (07114) (G-7084)
Amrod Corp. 973 344-3806
305a Craneway St Newark (07114) (G-7085)
AMS, New Brunswick Also called Art Materials Service Inc (G-6947)
AMS Products LLC 973 442-5790
105 W Dewey Ave Ste 305 Wharton (07885) (G-11978)
AMS Toy Intl Inc 973 442-5790
105 W Dewey Ave Wharton (07885) (G-11979)
Amscan Inc 973 983-0888
25 Green Pond Rd Rockaway (07866) (G-9551)
Amscot Structural Pdts Corp 973 989-8800
241 E Blackwell St Dover (07801) (G-2075)
Amt Stitch Inc 732 376-0009
257 New Brunswick Ave Perth Amboy (08861) (G-8607)
Amy Publications LLC 973 235-1800
11 Robert St Nutley (07110) (G-7640)
Amys Omelette Hse Burlington (PA) 609 386-4800
637 High St Burlington (08016) (G-956)
Ana Design Corp 609 394-0300
1 Ott St Trenton (08638) (G-11017)
Anadys Pharmaceuticals Inc 972 235-4295
340 Kingsland St Nutley (07110) (G-7641)
Analog Devices Inc 732 868-7100
285 Davidson Ave Ste 402 Somerset (08873) (G-10058)
Analytic Stress Relieving Inc 732 629-7232
190 Egel Ave Middlesex (08846) (G-6146)
Analytical Sales and Svcs Inc 973 616-0700
179 Rte 206 Flanders (07836) (G-3401)
Analytical Testing, Edison Also called Alcami New Jersey Corporation (G-2455)
Anatech Microwave Company Inc 973 772-7369
70 Outwater Ln Ste 3 Garfield (07026) (G-3717)
Anatolian Naturals Inc. 201 893-0142
1 Bridge Plz N Ste 275 Fort Lee (07024) (G-3544)
Anchor, Red Bank Also called Crh Americas Inc (G-9323)
Anchor Concrete Products Inc (HQ) 732 842-5010
331 Newman Springs Rd # 236 Red Bank (07701) (G-9319)
Anchor Concrete Products Inc. 732 458-9440
975 Burnt Tavern Rd Brick (08724) (G-734)
Anchor Home Products, West Milford Also called Anchor Sales & Marketing Inc (G-11850)
Anchor Optical Co 856 546-1965
101 E Gloucester Pike Barrington (08007) (G-170)
Anchor Sales & Marketing Inc 973 545-2277
755 Macopin Rd 1 West Milford (07480) (G-11850)
Anco Fine Cheese, Moonachie Also called Schratter Foods Incorporated (G-6541)
Ancol. 908 233-8907
860 Bradford Ave Westfield (07090) (G-11920)
Ancraft Press Corp 201 792-9200
234 16th St Fl 8 Jersey City (07310) (G-4705)

A
L
P
H
A
B
E
T
I
C

Andantex U S A Inc 732 493-2812
1705 Valley Rd Ocean (07712) *(G-7715)*

Andarn Electro Service Inc 973 523-2220
72 Michigan Ave Paterson (07503) *(G-8212)*

Andek Corporation 856 866-7600
850 Glen Ave Moorestown (08057) *(G-6560)*

Anderson & Vreeland Inc (PA) 973 227-2270
8 Evans St Fairfield (07004) *(G-3136)*

Anderson Publishing Ltd 908 301-1995
180 Glenside Ave Scotch Plains (07076) *(G-9845)*

Anderson Tool & Die Corp 908 862-5550
1430 W Blancke St Linden (07036) *(G-5349)*

Andis Inc 973 627-0400
124 E Main St Denville (07834) *(G-2030)*

Andlogic Computers 609 610-5752
866 Nj 33 6 Hamilton (08619) *(G-4103)*

Andon Brush Co Inc 973 256-6611
1 Merrit Ave Little Falls (07424) *(G-5469)*

Andrea Aromatics Inc 609 695-7710
150 Enterprise Ave Trenton (08638) *(G-11018)*

Andrea Company, Orange *Also called Savignano Food Corp (G-7826)*

Andrevin Inc 732 270-2794
792 Fischer Blvd Toms River (08753) *(G-10863)*

Andrew B Duffy Inc 856 845-4900
322 Crown Point Rd West Deptford (08086) *(G-11815)*

Andrew P Mc Hugh Inc 856 547-8953
124 Clements Bridge Rd # 2 Barrington (08007) *(G-171)*

Andrew Technologies LLC 215 990-0754
3 S Haddon Ave Ste 3 # 3 Haddonfield (08033) *(G-4055)*

Andrews Glass Company, Vineland *Also called AGC Acquisition LLC (G-11320)*

Andrex Inc 908 852-2400
101 Bilby Rd Ste E Hackettstown (07840) *(G-3997)*

Andrex Systems Inc 908 835-1720
17 Karrville Rd Port Murray (07865) *(G-8975)*

Andritz Separation Inc 732 269-5305
555 Hickory Ln Bayville (08721) *(G-249)*

Andrus Bait Company, Millville *Also called Richard Andrus (G-6323)*

Andy Graphics Service Bureau 201 866-9407
3711 Park Ave Union City (07087) *(G-11241)*

Andys Custom Cabinets 732 752-6443
143 Jefferson Ave Green Brook (08812) *(G-3854)*

Anello Fence LLC 973 692-9200
50 State Rt 23 Pequannock (07440) *(G-8598)*

Angelo Bakery Corp 973 537-7220
330 S Salem St Ste 10 Dover (07801) *(G-2076)*

Angelos Italian Ices Icecream 201 962-7575
96 E Main St Ramsey (07446) *(G-9233)*

Angelos Panetteria Inc 201 435-4659
14 Wales Ave Jersey City (07306) *(G-4706)*

Angels Bakery USA LLC 718 389-1400
110 Raskulinecz Rd Carteret (07008) *(G-1248)*

Ango Electronics Corporation 201 955-0800
29 Ewing Ave North Arlington (07031) *(G-7415)*

Angus Anywhere, Middlesex *Also called Angus Systems Group Inc (G-6147)*

Angus Systems Group Inc 770 521-5553
1273 Bound Brook Rd # 11 Middlesex (08846) *(G-6147)*

Anheuser-Busch LLC 973 645-7700
30 Montgomery St Ste 700 Jersey City (07302) *(G-4707)*

Anhydrides & Chemicals Inc 973 465-0077
2 Margaretta St Newark (07105) *(G-7086)*

Animals Etc Inc 609 386-8442
210 Mitchell Ave Burlington (08016) *(G-957)*

Anisha Enterprises Inc 908 964-3380
2165 Morris Ave Ste 1 Union (07083) *(G-11153)*

Anju Clinplus LLC 732 764-6969
1661 Route 22 West Bound Brook (08805) *(G-616)*

Ankur International Inc 609 409-6009
1206 Cranbury S River Rd Cranbury (08512) *(G-1812)*

Ann Hemyng Candy Inc 215 536-7004
1195 Crim Rd Bridgewater (08807) *(G-811)*

Anna J Chung Ltd 917 575-8100
5 Park St Edgewater (07020) *(G-2432)*

Anna K Park 856 478-9500
50 N Main St Mullica Hill (08062) *(G-6892)*

Anne Alanna Inc 609 465-3787
41 Pierces Point Rd Cape May Court House (08210) *(G-1109)*

Annette & Jim Dizenzo Sls LLC (PA) 973 875-0895
6 Glenview Ln Sussex (07461) *(G-10666)*

Annin & Co (PA) 973 228-9400
105 Eisenhower Pkwy # 203 Roseland (07068) *(G-9644)*

Annin & Co 973 239-9000
163 Bloomfield Ave Verona (07044) *(G-11303)*

Annin Flag Makers, Roseland *Also called Annin & Co (G-9644)*

Annitti Enterprises Inc 973 345-1725
138 Grand St Paterson (07501) *(G-8213)*

Anodizing Corporation 973 694-6449
10 Legrande Ter Wayne (07470) *(G-11605)*

Ans Nutrition Inc 212 235-5205
700 Central Ave Farmingdale (07727) *(G-3377)*

ANS Plastics Corporation 732 247-2776
625 Jersey Ave Ste 11a New Brunswick (08901) *(G-6944)*

Ansell Hawkeye Inc (HQ) 662 258-3200
111 Wood Ave S Ste 210 Iselin (08830) *(G-4610)*

Ansell Healthcare Products LLC (HQ) 732 345-5400
111 Wood Ave S Ste 210 Iselin (08830) *(G-4611)*

Ansell Inc 732 345-5400
200 Schult Dr Ste 2 Red Bank (07701) *(G-9320)*

Ansell Limited 732 345-5400
111 Wood Ave S Ste 210 Iselin (08830) *(G-4612)*

Ansell Protective Products LLC 732 345-5400
111 Wood Ave S Ste 210 Iselin (08830) *(G-4613)*

Ansell Red Bank,, Red Bank *Also called Ansell Inc (G-9320)*

Ansmann USA Corp 856 481-3504
1001 Lower Landing Rd # 101 Blackwood (08012) *(G-470)*

Ansonia Bridal Veils, North Bergen *Also called Kathy Gibson Designs Inc (G-7461)*

Ansun Protective Metals Inc 732 302-0616
130 Lincoln Blvd Middlesex (08846) *(G-6148)*

Answers In Motion LLC 732 267-7792
204 S Lippincott Ave Maple Shade (08052) *(G-5899)*

Ant Stores, Clifton *Also called Light Inc (G-1662)*

Antares Pharma Inc (PA) 609 359-3020
100 Princeton S Ste 300 Ewing (08628) *(G-3003)*

Antenna Software Inc (HQ) 201 217-3824
111 Town Square Pl # 520 Jersey City (07310) *(G-4708)*

Anthony & Sons Bakery Itln Bky 973 625-2323
20 Luger Rd Denville (07834) *(G-2031)*

Anthony Excavating & Dem 609 926-8804
22 English Ln Egg Harbor Township (08234) *(G-2678)*

Anthracite Industries Inc (HQ) 908 537-2155
405 Old Main St Asbury (08802) *(G-65)*

Anti Hydro International Inc 908 284-9000
45 River Rd Ste 200 Flemington (08822) *(G-3427)*

Antique Bakery & Pizzeria 201 714-9323
122 Willow Ave Ste A Hoboken (07030) *(G-4457)*

Antique Buying Center 201 888-0303
725 River Rd Ste 279 Edgewater (07020) *(G-2433)*

Antonio Mozzarella Factory Inc (PA) 973 353-9411
631 Frelinghuysen Ave Newark (07114) *(G-7087)*

Antonio Mozzarella Factory Inc 973 353-9411
631 Frelinghuysen Ave # 2 Newark (07114) *(G-7088)*

Antonio's Pasta, Woodbridge *Also called 35 Food Corp (G-12144)*

Antron Technologies Inc 732 205-0415
40 Brunswick Ave Ste 104 Edison (08817) *(G-2461)*

Antronics, Cranbury *Also called Cabletenna Corp (G-1818)*

Antronix Inc (PA) 609 860-0160
440 Forsgate Dr Cranbury (08512) *(G-1813)*

Anu Industries LLC 201 735-7475
209 Wilbur St Englewood (07631) *(G-2870)*

Anuco Inc 973 887-9465
911 Charles Dr Unit 3 East Hanover (07936) *(G-2200)*

Anvil Iron Works Inc 856 783-5959
Little Mill Rd Sicklerville (08081) *(G-10016)*

Anvima Technologies LLC 973 531-7077
68 Woodland Rd Brookside (07926) *(G-922)*

Aone Touch Inc 732 261-6841
22 Sagamore Ln Bordentown (08505) *(G-590)*

Aos Thermal Compounds LLC 732 389-5514
22 Meridian Rd Ste 6 Eatontown (07724) *(G-2383)*

AP Deauville LLC 732 545-0200
594 Jersey Ave Ste 1 New Brunswick (08901) *(G-6945)*

AP Global Enterprises Inc 732 919-6200
5044 Industrial Rd Wall Township (07727) *(G-11462)*

AP International, Wall Township *Also called AP Global Enterprises Inc (G-11462)*

AP Packaging, Linden *Also called Air Protection Packaging Corp (G-5344)*

AP&g Co Inc 718 492-3648
75 E 2nd St Bayonne (07002) *(G-211)*

AP&g Co Inc 718 492-3648
75 E 2nd St Bayonne (07002) *(G-212)*

Apb-Dynasonics Inc 973 785-1101
145 Shepherds Ln Totowa (07512) *(G-10931)*

Apco Extruders Inc 732 287-3000
180 National Rd Edison (08817) *(G-2462)*

Apelio Innovative Inds LLC 973 777-8899
46 Sellers St Kearny (07032) *(G-4861)*

Apex Saw & Tool Co Inc 201 438-8777
595 New York Ave Lyndhurst (07071) *(G-5668)*

Aphelion Orbitals Inc 321 289-0872
540 39th St Ste 40 Union City (07087) *(G-11242)*

Aphena Phrma Slutions - NJ LLC 973 947-5441
2 Cranberry Rd Unit A3 Parsippany (07054) *(G-7947)*

API, Sparta *Also called Advanced Precision Inc (G-10485)*

API Americas Inc 732 382-6800
329 New Brunswick Ave Rahway (07065) *(G-9174)*

API Inc 973 227-9335
10 Industrial Rd Fairfield (07004) *(G-3137)*

API Nanofabrication & RES Corp 732 627-0808
1600 Cottontail Ln Ste 1 Somerset (08873) *(G-10059)*

(G-0000) Company's Geographic Section entry number

Apicore LLC (HQ) 732 748-8882
49 Napoleon Ct Ste 1 Somerset (08873) *(G-10060)*

Apicore US LLC 732 748-8882
49 Napoleon Ct Somerset (08873) *(G-10061)*

Apl2000, Manasquan *Also called Aplnow LLC (G-5866)*

Aplnow LLC (PA) 732 223-5575
2640 Highway 70 Ste 4 Manasquan (08736) *(G-5866)*

Apogee Sound International LLC 201 934-8500
50 Spring St Ste 1 Ramsey (07446) *(G-9234)*

Apogee Technologies LLC 973 575-8448
3 Cole Rd Towaco (07082) *(G-10987)*

Apollo East LLC 856 486-1882
7895 Airport Hwy Pennsauken (08109) *(G-8478)*

Apollo Graphics NJ, Cinnaminson *Also called Samuel Elliott Inc (G-1486)*

Apollo Machine Shop, Hillsdale *Also called Oroszlany Laszlo (G-4386)*

Apparel Strgc Alliances LLC 732 833-7771
41 Greenwich Dr Jackson (08527) *(G-4654)*

Appco Pharma LLC (PA) 732 271-8300
120 Belmont Dr Somerset (08873) *(G-10062)*

Appco Pharma LLC 732 271-8300
262 Old New Brunswick Rd Piscataway (08854) *(G-8736)*

Appco Pharma LLC 732 271-8300
120 Belmont Dr Somerset (08873) *(G-10063)*

Appco Pharmaceuticals Corp., Somerset *Also called Appco Pharma LLC (G-10062)*

Appetito Provisions Company 201 864-3410
406 Lafayette Rd Harrington Park (07640) *(G-4170)*

Appetizers Made Easy Inc 201 531-1212
25 Branca Rd Ste B East Rutherford (07073) *(G-2277)*

Appex Innovation Solutions LLC 215 313-3332
103 Carnegie Ctr Princeton (08540) *(G-9004)*

Applause Musical Products 856 697-8333
108 Buena Vista Ave Landisville (08326) *(G-5229)*

Apple Air Compressor Corp (PA) 888 222-9940
301 Veterans Blvd Rutherford (07070) *(G-9725)*

Apple Corrugated Box Ltd 201 635-1269
1 Passaic St Unit 76 Wood Ridge (07075) *(G-12134)*

Apple Tree 609 751-5375
47 Hulfish St Ste 441 Princeton (08542) *(G-9005)*

Applechem Inc 862 210-8344
105 Lock St Ste 205 Newark (07103) *(G-7089)*

Applegate Farm Homemade Ice Cr (PA) 973 744-5900
616 Grove St Montclair (07043) *(G-6406)*

Applegate Farms LLC 908 725-2768
750 Rte 202 Ste 300 Bridgewater (08807) *(G-812)*

Apples & Honey Press LLC 973 379-7200
11 Edison Pl Springfield (07081) *(G-10537)*

Appleton Grp LLC 973 285-3261
55 Madison Ave Morristown (07960) *(G-6687)*

Applicad Inc 732 751-2555
5029 Industrial Rd Wall Township (07727) *(G-11463)*

Applied Color Systems, Lawrenceville *Also called Datacolor Inc (G-5256)*

Applied Image Inc 732 410-2444
800 Business Park Dr Freehold (07728) *(G-3638)*

Applied Microphone Technology, Sparta *Also called Mp Production (G-10512)*

Applied Nutrition Corp 973 734-0023
10 Saddle Rd Cedar Knolls (07927) *(G-1307)*

Applied Optronics, South Plainfield *Also called Candela Corporation (G-10343)*

Applied Psychological Services, Princeton *Also called Princeton Information Center (G-9095)*

Applied Resources Corp (PA) 973 328-3882
105 W Dewey Ave Ste 311 Wharton (07885) *(G-11980)*

Applied Thermal Solutions Inc 856 818-8194
93 Eldridge Ave Williamstown (08094) *(G-12079)*

Applied Voice Speech Tech Inc 949 699-2300
9 Cypress Ct Clinton (08809) *(G-1749)*

Apprentice Fs Inc 201 819-1575
155 Palisade Ave Jersey City (07306) *(G-4709)*

Aprecia Pharmaceuticals Co 215 359-3300
89 Twin Rivers Dr East Windsor (08520) *(G-2342)*

Aptalis Pharma LLC 862 261-7000
400 Interpace Pkwy Ste A1 Parsippany (07054) *(G-7948)*

Aptapharma Corporation 856 665-0025
1533 Union Ave Pennsauken (08110) *(G-8479)*

Aptimized LLC 203 733-2868
579 Pompton Ave Cedar Grove (07009) *(G-1270)*

Apw Company, Rockaway *Also called KG Squared LLC (G-9581)*

Aqua Controls, West Deptford *Also called Aquatrols Corp of America (G-11816)*

Aqua Products Inc 856 829-8444
2703 River Rd Cinnaminson (08077) *(G-1446)*

Aqua Products Inc (HQ) 973 857-2700
25 Rutgers Ave Cedar Grove (07009) *(G-1271)*

Aquarius Biotechnologies Inc 908 443-1860
1545 Rte 206 S Ste 302 Bedminster (07921) *(G-267)*

Aquasports Pools LLC 732 247-6298
999 Jersey Ave New Brunswick (08901) *(G-6946)*

Aquatrols Corp of America 856 537-6003
1273 Imperial Way West Deptford (08066) *(G-11816)*

Aquestive Therapeutics Inc (PA) 908 941-1900
30 Technology Dr Warren (07059) *(G-11537)*

Ar2 Products LLC 800 667-1263
210 W Parkway Ste 9 Pompton Plains (07444) *(G-8953)*

Arab Voice Newspaper 973 523-7815
956 Main St Paterson (07503) *(G-8214)*

Arafat Lafi 201 854-7300
7329 Broadway North Bergen (07047) *(G-7431)*

Aralez Management, Princeton *Also called Aralez Pharmaceuticals MGT Inc (G-9006)*

Aralez Pharmaceuticals MGT Inc 609 917-9330
400 Alexander Park Princeton (08540) *(G-9006)*

Aralez Pharmaceuticals US Inc 609 917-9330
400 Alexander Park Princeton (08540) *(G-9007)*

Aramani Inc 201 945-1160
369 Henry St Fairview (07022) *(G-3357)*

Arawak Paving Co Inc (PA) 609 561-4100
7503 Weymouth Rd Hammonton (08037) *(G-4130)*

Araya Inc 201 445-7005
10 Garber Sq Ste A Ridgewood (07450) *(G-9420)*

Araya Rebirth, Ridgewood *Also called Araya Inc (G-9420)*

Arbee Company Inc 908 241-7717
16 N 26th St Kenilworth (07033) *(G-4937)*

ARC International N Amer LLC (HQ) 856 825-5620
601 S Wade Blvd Millville (08332) *(G-6284)*

Arca Industrial (nj) Inc 732 339-0450
3 Kellogg Ct Ste 2 Edison (08817) *(G-2463)*

Arcadia Equipment Inc 201 342-3308
140 Lawrence St Hackensack (07601) *(G-3874)*

Arch America, Delair *Also called Shapes/Arch Holdings LLC (G-2001)*

Arch Chemicals Inc 908 561-5200
70 Tyler Pl South Plainfield (07080) *(G-10329)*

Arch Crown Inc 973 731-6300
460 Hillside Ave Ste 1 Hillside (07205) *(G-4390)*

Arch Custom Manufacturing Inc 856 966-3835
1215 S 6th St Camden (08104) *(G-1040)*

Arch Manufacturing & Sales 856 966-3835
1213 S 6th St Camden (08104) *(G-1041)*

Arch Personal Care Products LP 908 226-9329
70 Tyler Pl South Plainfield (07080) *(G-10330)*

Archer Day Inc 732 396-0600
18 Mileed Way Avenel (07001) *(G-124)*

Archer Plastics Inc 856 692-0242
1510 Jesse Bridge Rd Elmer (08318) *(G-2789)*

Archer Seating Clearing House, Elmer *Also called Archer Plastics Inc (G-2789)*

Archi-Tread Inc 973 725-5738
191 Brook Valley Rd Kinnelon (07405) *(G-5033)*

Architctral Cbinetry Mllwk LLC 908 213-2001
1425 3rd Ave Phillipsburg (08865) *(G-8639)*

Architctral Metals Fabricaters, Carteret *Also called Architectural Metals Inc (G-1250)*

Architctural Metal Designs Inc 856 765-3000
1505 Pineland Ave Millville (08332) *(G-6285)*

Architctural Metal Fabricators 718 765-0722
66 Grant Ave Carteret (07008) *(G-1249)*

Architectural Acrylics, Cherry Hill *Also called Scott W Springman (G-1419)*

Architectural Iron Designs 908 757-2323
950 S 2nd St Plainfield (07063) *(G-8854)*

Architectural Metal and Glass 732 994-7575
644 Cross St Ste 14 Lakewood (08701) *(G-5075)*

Architectural Metals Inc 718 765-0722
66 Grant Ave Carteret (07008) *(G-1250)*

Architectural Wdwkg Assoc 908 996-7866
4 7th St Frenchtown (08825) *(G-3696)*

Architectural Window Mfg Corp 201 933-5094
359 Veterans Blvd Rutherford (07070) *(G-9726)*

Archive Designs Inc 973 242-6400
238 Emmet St Newark (07114) *(G-7090)*

Archlit Inc 973 577-4400
42 Ithanell Rd Hopatcong (07843) *(G-4534)*

Archon Vitamin LLC (PA) 732 537-1220
3775 Park Ave Unit 1 Edison (08820) *(G-2464)*

Archon Vitamin LLC 973 371-1700
3775 Park Ave Unit 1 Edison (08820) *(G-2465)*

Archtech Electronics Corp 732 355-1288
117 Docks Corner Rd Ste A Dayton (08810) *(G-1952)*

Arctic Foods Inc 908 689-0590
251 E Washington Ave Washington (07882) *(G-11574)*

Arctic Glacier USA Inc 973 771-3391
363 Bloomfield Ave Ste 3b Montclair (07042) *(G-6407)*

Arctic Ice Cream Co, Ewing *Also called Arctic Products Co Inc (G-3004)*

Arctic Products Co Inc 609 393-4264
22 Arctic Pkwy Ewing (08638) *(G-3004)*

Arcy Manufacturing Co Inc 201 635-1910
575 Industrial Rd Carlstadt (07072) *(G-1126)*

Ardagh Glass Inc 732 969-0827
50 Bryla St Carteret (07008) *(G-1251)*

Arde 201 440-1453
500 Walnut St Norwood (07648) *(G-7615)*

Arde Barinco or Arde, Carlstadt *Also called Arde Inc (G-1127)*

Arde Inc (HQ) 201 784-9880
875 Washington Ave Carlstadt (07072) *(G-1127)*

(PA)=Parent Co (HQ)=Headquarters (DH)=Div Headquarters

Arde Inc 201 784-9880
875 Washington Ave Carlstadt (07072) *(G-1128)*

Ardmore Inc 973 481-2406
29 Riverside Ave Bldg 14 Newark (07104) *(G-7091)*

Area Auto Racing News Inc 609 888-3618
2831 S Broad St Trenton (08610) *(G-11019)*

Arglen Industries Inc 732 888-8100
1 Bethany Rd Ste 44 Hazlet (07730) *(G-4269)*

Argo Corp 609 652-4560
Richard Stockton College Pomona (08240) *(G-8944)*

Argonautus LLC 908 393-4379
867 Country Club Rd Bridgewater (08807) *(G-813)*

Argus International Inc (PA) 609 466-1677
424 Route 31 N Ringoes (08551) *(G-9435)*

Argyle Industries Inc 908 725-8800
160 Meister Ave Ste 12 Branchburg (08876) *(G-637)*

Argyle International Inc 609 924-9484
254 Wall St Princeton (08540) *(G-9008)*

Arias Mountain-Coffee LLC (PA) 973 927-9595
22 E Blackwell St Dover (07801) *(G-2077)*

Ariba Inc 908 333-3400
1160 Us Highway 22 # 110 Bridgewater (08807) *(G-814)*

Ariel Laboratories LP 908 755-4080
31 Davis St South Plainfield (07080) *(G-10331)*

Aries Filterworks Inc 856 626-1550
117 Jackson Rd Berlin (08009) *(G-425)*

Aries Precision Tool Inc 201 252-8550
300 State Rt 17 Ste H Mahwah (07430) *(G-5749)*

Arisaph Pharmaceuticals Inc 617 986-4500
1037 Raymond Blvd # 1520 Newark (07102) *(G-7092)*

Arizona Iced Tea, Maplewood *Also called Maplewood Beverage Packers LLC (G-5923)*

Arla Foods Ingredients N Amer 908 604-8551
106 Allen Rd Ste 401 Basking Ridge (07920) *(G-180)*

Arlington Machine & Tool Co, Fairfield *Also called Arlington Prcsion Cmpnents LLC (G-3138)*

Arlington Prcsion Cmpnents LLC 973 276-1377
90 New Dutch Ln Fairfield (07004) *(G-3138)*

Arlo Corporation 973 618-0030
119 Harrison Ave Roseland (07068) *(G-9645)*

Arm & Hammer Animal & Fd Prod, Princeton *Also called Arm & Hammer Animal Ntrtn LLC (G-9009)*

Arm & Hammer Animal Ntrtn LLC (HQ) 800 526-3563
469 N Harrison St Princeton (08540) *(G-9009)*

Arm National Food Inc 609 695-4911
539 Chestnut Ave Trenton (08611) *(G-11020)*

Armadillo Automation Inc 856 829-2888
835 Industrial Hwy Ste 4 Cinnaminson (08077) *(G-1447)*

Armadillo Metalworks Inc 973 777-2105
61 Willet St Ste 1 Passaic (07055) *(G-8125)*

Armco Compressor Products 201 866-6766
2042 46th St North Bergen (07047) *(G-7432)*

Armco Machine, North Bergen *Also called Armco Compressor Products (G-7432)*

Armel Electronics Inc 201 869-4300
1601 75th St North Bergen (07047) *(G-7433)*

Armetec Corp 973 485-2525
166 Abington Ave Newark (07107) *(G-7093)*

Armin Kososki 908 689-0411
297 State Route 31 S Washington (07882) *(G-11575)*

Armkel LLC (HQ) 609 683-5900
469 N Harrison St Princeton (08540) *(G-9010)*

Armorpoxy Inc 908 810-9613
805 Lehigh Ave Union (07083) *(G-11154)*

Armotek Industries Inc 856 829-4585
1 Roto Ave Palmyra (08065) *(G-7846)*

Armstrong and Sons Inc 732 223-1555
2335 Highway 34 Manasquan (08736) *(G-5867)*

Arna Marketing Group Inc 908 625-7395
60 Readington Rd Branchburg (08876) *(G-638)*

Arna Marketing Inc 908 231-1100
60 Readington Rd Branchburg (08876) *(G-639)*

Arnhem Inc 908 709-4045
1 Elm St Ste 1 # 1 Westfield (07090) *(G-11921)*

Arnhem Group, The, Westfield *Also called Arnhem Inc (G-11921)*

Arno Therapeutics Inc 862 703-7170
200 Route 31 Ste 104 Flemington (08822) *(G-3428)*

Arnold Desks Inc 908 686-5656
120 Coit St Irvington (07111) *(G-4574)*

Arnold Furniture Mfrs Inc (PA) 973 399-0505
400 Coit St Irvington (07111) *(G-4575)*

Arnold Gisler Furn Fabricators, Irvington *Also called Arnold Kolax Furniture Inc (G-4576)*

Arnold Kolax Furniture Inc 973 375-3344
146 Coit St Irvington (07111) *(G-4576)*

Arnold Reception Desks Inc 973 375-8101
120 Coit St Irvington (07111) *(G-4577)*

Arnold Steel Co Inc 732 363-1079
79 Randolph Rd Howell (07731) *(G-4546)*

Arnolds Desk, Irvington *Also called Arnold Desks Inc (G-4574)*

Arnolds Yacht Basin Inc (PA) 732 892-3000
1671 Beaver Dam Rd Ste 1 Point Pleasant Boro (08742) *(G-8931)*

Arol Chemical Products Co 973 344-1510
649 Ferry St Newark (07105) *(G-7094)*

Aroma Chemicals, Monmouth Junction *Also called Bwi Chemicals (G-6334)*

Aromac Inc 973 365-1090
6 Chelsea Rd Clifton (07012) *(G-1566)*

Aromatech, Piscataway *Also called Aromatic Technologies Inc (G-8737)*

Aromatic Technologies Inc 732 393-7300
140 Centennial Ave Piscataway (08854) *(G-8737)*

Arome America LLC 908 806-7003
2 Van Fleet Rd Neshanic Station (08853) *(G-6938)*

Aromiens Inc 732 225-8689
98 Mayfield Ave Edison (08837) *(G-2466)*

Arose Inc (PA) 856 481-4351
1001 Lower Landing Rd # 412 Blackwood (08012) *(G-471)*

Around Clock Sweeping LLC 973 887-1144
45 Essex Rd Parsippany (07054) *(G-7949)*

Arpac Technology 973 252-0012
45 Park Ave Randolph (07869) *(G-9270)*

Arquest Inc (PA) 609 395-9500
14 Scotto Farm Ln Millstone Township (08535) *(G-6262)*

Array Solders Ltd Liability Co 201 432-0095
329 Mercer Loop Jersey City (07302) *(G-4710)*

Arro-Mark Company LLC 201 567-4112
158 W Forest Ave Englewood (07631) *(G-2871)*

Arrow Engineering Co Inc 908 353-5229
260 Pennsylvania Ave Hillside (07205) *(G-4391)*

Arrow Fastener Co Inc 201 843-6900
271 Mayhill St Saddle Brook (07663) *(G-9752)*

Arrow Information Packagig LLC 856 317-9000
7100 Westfield Ave Pennsauken (08110) *(G-8480)*

Arrow Machine Company Inc 973 642-2430
117 Norfolk St Newark (07103) *(G-7095)*

Arrow Paper Company Inc (PA) 908 756-1111
633 North Ave Plainfield (07060) *(G-8855)*

Arrow Shed LLC 973 835-3200
1 3rd Ave Haskell (07420) *(G-4206)*

Arrow Steel Inc 973 523-1122
629 E 19th St Paterson (07514) *(G-8215)*

Arrow Thin Films, Emerson *Also called Artemis Optics and Coatings (G-2857)*

Art Craft, Florham Park *Also called Washington Stamp Exchange Inc (G-3523)*

Art Display Essentials, Columbia *Also called 10-31 Incorporated (G-1795)*

Art Dmensions 908 322-8488
1998 Us Highway 22 Scotch Plains (07076) *(G-9846)*

Art Flag Co Inc 212 334-1890
890 River Rd Fair Haven (07704) *(G-3070)*

Art Guild Inc 732 390-5300
12 Connerty Ct Unit B East Brunswick (08816) *(G-2135)*

Art Materials Service Inc 732 545-8888
625 Joyce Kilmer Ave New Brunswick (08901) *(G-6947)*

Art Metalcraft Plating Co Inc 215 923-6625
529 S 2nd St Camden (08103) *(G-1042)*

Art Mold & Polishing Co Inc 908 518-9191
220 Columbus Ave Roselle (07203) *(G-9661)*

Art Mold & Tool Corporation 201 935-3377
742 Paterson Ave East Rutherford (07073) *(G-2278)*

Art of Shaving - Fl LLC 732 410-2520
3710 Us Highway 9 Freehold (07728) *(G-3639)*

Art Plaque Creations Inc 973 482-2536
70 Arlington Ave Kearny (07032) *(G-4862)*

Art Press Printing, Barrington *Also called Andrew P Mc Hugh Inc (G-171)*

Art-Deco Division, Woodland Park *Also called Pochet of America Inc (G-12228)*

Artale Graphics 212 868-0015
2614 Summit Ter Linden (07036) *(G-5350)*

Artegraft Inc 732 422-8333
206 N Center Dr North Brunswick (08902) *(G-7504)*

Artemis Optics and Coatings 201 847-0887
9 Ackerman Ave Emerson (07630) *(G-2857)*

Artex Knitting Mills Inc 856 456-2800
300 Harvard Ave Westville (08093) *(G-11936)*

Artezio LLC 609 786-2435
195 Nassau St Rear 32 Princeton (08542) *(G-9011)*

Artflag, Fair Haven *Also called Art Flag Co Inc (G-3070)*

Arthroglide, Fair Lawn *Also called J M M R Inc (G-3097)*

Arthur A Kaplan Co Inc 201 806-2100
30 Murray Hill Pkwy # 300 East Rutherford (07073) *(G-2279)*

Arthur A Topilow William Lrner 732 528-0760
1707 Atlantic Ave Manasquan (08736) *(G-5868)*

Arthur H Thomas Company (PA) 856 467-2000
1654 High Hill Rd Swedesboro (08085) *(G-10682)*

Arthur Schuman Inc (PA) 973 227-0030
40 New Dutch Ln Fairfield (07004) *(G-3139)*

Artic Ice Manufacturing Co 973 772-7000
158 Semel Ave Garfield (07026) *(G-3718)*

Articulight Inc 201 796-2690
15-06 Morlot Ave Fair Lawn (07410) *(G-3077)*

Artique Glass Studio Inc 201 444-3500
483 S Broad St Glen Rock (07452) *(G-3820)*

Artisan Controls Corporation (PA) 973 598-9400
111 Canfield Ave Ste B-18 Randolph (07869) *(G-9271)*

Artisan Model Mold 908 453-3524
275 Buckhorn Dr Belvidere (07823) *(G-366)*

Artisan Oven Inc 201 488-6261
105 S State St Hackensack (07601) *(G-3875)*

Artistic Bias Products Co Inc 732 382-4141
1905 Elizabeth Ave Rahway (07065) *(G-9175)*

Artistic Creations, Westfield *Also called Foldtex II Ltd (G-11924)*

Artistic Doors and Windows Inc 732 726-9400
10 S Inman Ave Avenel (07001) *(G-125)*

Artistic Glass & Doors Inc 856 768-1414
154 Cooper Rd Ste 201 West Berlin (08091) *(G-11704)*

Artistic Hardware 609 383-1909
430 Tilton Rd Ste 2 Northfield (08225) *(G-7563)*

Artistic Railings Inc (PA) 973 772-8540
500 River Dr Garfield (07026) *(G-3719)*

Artistic Typography Corp 845 783-1990
161 Coolidge Ave Englewood (07631) *(G-2872)*

Artline Heat Transfer Inc 973 599-0104
2 Eastmans Rd Parsippany (07054) *(G-7950)*

Artmolds Journal LLC 908 273-5600
18 Bank St Ste 1 Summit (07901) *(G-10635)*

Arts Embroidery LLC 732 870-2400
175 Monmouth Rd West Long Branch (07764) *(G-11843)*

Arts Weekly Inc 973 812-6766
52 Sindle Ave Little Falls (07424) *(G-5470)*

Arts Windows Inc 732 905-9595
154537 W Unit 1 St 37 Toms River (08755) *(G-10864)*

Artsign Studio 856 546-4889
916 Kings Hwy Ste C Haddon Heights (08035) *(G-4045)*

Artus Corp 201 568-1000
201 S Dean St Englewood (07631) *(G-2873)*

Arysta LLC 856 417-8100
11 Technology Dr Logan Township (08085) *(G-5611)*

Arysta/ Labrea Bakery, Logan Township *Also called Arysta LLC (G-5611)*

As America Inc (HQ) 732 980-3000
1 Centennial Ave Ste 101 Piscataway (08854) *(G-8738)*

Asa Hydraulik of America Inc 908 541-1500
160 Meister Ave Ste 20a Branchburg (08876) *(G-640)*

ASAP Containers NJ NY Corp 732 659-4402
25 Mountain Dr West Orange (07052) *(G-11886)*

ASAP Nameplate and Label Co, Passaic *Also called Technical Nameplate Corp (G-8184)*

ASAP Postal Printing 609 597-7421
775 N Main St Manahawkin (08050) *(G-5828)*

ASAP Printed Products, Passaic *Also called A S A P Nameplate & Labeling (G-8122)*

Asbury Carbons Inc (PA) 908 537-2155
405 Old Main St Asbury (08802) *(G-66)*

Asbury Graphite Mills Inc (HQ) 908 537-2155
405 Old Main St Asbury (08802) *(G-67)*

Asbury Graphite Mills Inc 908 537-2157
156 Asbury West Portal Rd Asbury (08802) *(G-68)*

Asbury Louisiana Inc (HQ) 908 537-2155
405 Old Main St Asbury (08802) *(G-69)*

Asbury Park Press Inc 732 922-6000
3600 Route 66 Neptune (07753) *(G-6900)*

Asbury Syrup Company Inc 732 774-5746
3504 Rose Ave Ste 3 Ocean (07712) *(G-7716)*

Asbury Towel Company Inc 732 370-3908
1295 Towbin Ave Lakewood (08701) *(G-5076)*

Ascalon Art Studios, West Berlin *Also called Ascalon Studios Inc (G-11705)*

Ascalon Studios Inc 856 768-3779
430 Cooper Rd West Berlin (08091) *(G-11705)*

Ascend Laboratories LLC 201 476-1977
339 Jefferson Rd Ste 101 Parsippany (07054) *(G-7951)*

Ascendia Pharmaceuticals LLC 732 638-4028
661 Us Highway 1 2 North Brunswick (08902) *(G-7505)*

Ascensia Diabetes Care US Inc (HQ) 973 560-6500
5 Woodhollow Rd Ste 3 Parsippany (07054) *(G-7952)*

Ascent Aromatics Inc 908 755-0120
120 Case Dr South Plainfield (07080) *(G-10332)*

Ascentta Inc 732 868-1766
370 Campus Dr Ste 105 Somerset (08873) *(G-10064)*

Asco LP (HQ) 800 972-2726
160 Park Ave Florham Park (07932) *(G-3483)*

Asco Investment Corp 973 966-2000
50-60 Hanover Rd Florham Park (07932) *(G-3484)*

Asco Power Services Inc (HQ) 973 966-2000
160 Park Ave Florham Park (07932) *(G-3485)*

Asco Power Technologies LP 732 596-1733
1460 Us Highway 9 N # 209 Woodbridge (07095) *(G-12145)*

Asco Power Technologies LP 209 547-8874
50 Hanover Rd Florham Park (07932) *(G-3486)*

Asco Power Technologies LP (HQ) 973 966-2000
160 Park Ave Florham Park (07932) *(G-3487)*

Asco Power Technology, Florham Park *Also called Automatic Switch Company (G-3490)*

Asco Valve LLC (PA) 973 966-2437
50-60 Hanover Rd Florham Park (07932) *(G-3488)*

Asco Valve LLC 973 386-9000
7 Eastmans Rd Parsippany (07054) *(G-7953)*

Asco Valve Mfg, Florham Park *Also called Asco Valve LLC (G-3488)*

Asd Holding Corp 800 442-1902
1 Centennial Ave Piscataway (08854) *(G-8739)*

Ash Ingredients Inc 201 689-1322
65 Harristown Rd Ste 307 Glen Rock (07452) *(G-3821)*

Asha44 LLC 201 306-3600
175 Us Highway 46 Unit A Fairfield (07004) *(G-3140)*

Ashland, Wayne *Also called Interntonal Specialty Pdts Inc (G-11653)*

Ashland LLC 908 243-3500
1005 Route 202/206 Bridgewater (08807) *(G-815)*

Ashland LLC 732 353-7718
50 S Minnisink Ave Ste 2 Parlin (08859) *(G-7928)*

Ashland Spcalty Ingredients GP 908 243-3500
1005 Route 202/206 Bridgewater (08807) *(G-816)*

Ashland Spcalty Ingredients GP 732 353-7708
50 S Minnisink Ave Ste 1 Parlin (08859) *(G-7929)*

Ashley Norton Inc 973 835-4027
210 W Parkway Ste 1 Pompton Plains (07444) *(G-8954)*

Asi, Woodland Park *Also called Autoplast Systems Inc (G-12210)*

Asi Computer Technologies Inc 732 343-7100
131 Fieldcrest Ave Edison (08837) *(G-2467)*

Asi Plastic Inc 973 332-4720
120 Getty Ave Paterson (07503) *(G-8216)*

Asiamerica Group Inc 201 497-5993
245 Old Hook Rd Westwood (07675) *(G-11955)*

Asme, Little Falls *Also called American Soc of Mech Engineers (G-5468)*

Aspe Inc 973 808-1155
2 Daniel Rd Ste 101 Fairfield (07004) *(G-3141)*

Aspen Appliance Parts, Beverly *Also called Aspen Manufacturing Co Inc (G-459)*

Aspen Manufacturing Co Inc 609 871-6400
703 Van Rossum Ave Unit 5 Beverly (08010) *(G-459)*

Asphalt Paving Systems Inc (PA) 609 561-4161
500 N Egg Harbor Rd Hammonton (08037) *(G-4131)*

Asphalt Plant, Roseland *Also called Weldon Concrete Corp (G-9657)*

Aspire Pharmaceuticals Inc (PA) 732 447-1444
41 Veronica Ave Somerset (08873) *(G-10065)*

Assa Abloy Entrance Systems US 609 443-5800
92 N Main St Unit A Windsor (08561) *(G-12124)*

Assa Abloy Entrance Systems US 609 528-2580
300 Horizon Center Blvd # 309 Hamilton (08691) *(G-4104)*

Assem - Pak Inc 856 692-3355
1649 Castpa Pl Vineland (08360) *(G-11323)*

Asset Backed Alert, Hoboken *Also called Harrison Scott Pblications Inc (G-4472)*

Associate Fireplace Builders 908 273-5900
331 Springfield Ave Summit (07901) *(G-10636)*

Associated Asphalt Mktg LLC 210 249-9988
400 Grove Rd West Deptford (08066) *(G-11817)*

Associated Cleaning Systems 201 530-9197
569 Oritani Pl Teaneck (07666) *(G-10742)*

Associated Fabrics Corporation 201 300-6053
15-01 Pollitt Dr Ste 7 Fair Lawn (07410) *(G-3078)*

Associated Marble Co, Lodi *Also called Charles Deluca (G-5579)*

Associated Plastics Inc 732 574-2800
179 E Inman Ave Rahway (07065) *(G-9176)*

Associated University Presses, Plainsboro *Also called Rosemont Publishing &
Printing (G-8899)*

Assured Automtn Flow Solutions, Roselle *Also called Farrell Eqp & Contrls Inc (G-9669)*

AST Construction Inc 609 277-7101
5 Canale Dr Egg Harbor Township (08234) *(G-2679)*

Asti Corp 201 501-8900
45 W Broad St Bergenfield (07621) *(G-381)*

Asti Magnetics, Bergenfield *Also called Asti Corp (G-381)*

Astor Chocolate Corp (PA) 732 901-1000
651 New Hampshire Ave Lakewood (08701) *(G-5077)*

Astra Cleaners of Hazlet 732 264-4144
35 Hazlet Ave Hazlet (07730) *(G-4270)*

Astral Diagnostics Inc 856 224-0900
1224 Forest Pkwy Ste 200 Paulsboro (08066) *(G-8413)*

Astrazeneca Pharmaceuticals LP 973 975-0324
Fl 2 Flr Morristown (07960) *(G-6688)*

Astrix Software Technology (PA) 732 661-0400
125 Half Mile Rd Ste 200 Red Bank (07701) *(G-9321)*

Astrix Technology Group, Red Bank *Also called Astrix Software Technology (G-9321)*

Astro Outdoor Advertising Inc (PA) 856 881-4300
230 E High St Glassboro (08028) *(G-3801)*

Astro Sign Co, Glassboro *Also called Astro Outdoor Advertising Inc (G-3801)*

Astro Tool & Machine Co Inc 732 382-2454
810 Martin St Rahway (07065) *(G-9177)*

Astrodyne Corporation (PA) 908 850-5088
36 Newburgh Rd Hackettstown (07840) *(G-3998)*

Astrodyne Tdi, Hackettstown *Also called Transistor Devices Inc (G-4041)*

Astrodyne Tdi, Hackettstown *Also called Transistor Devices Inc (G-4042)*

AT Information Products Inc (PA) 201 529-0202
575 Corporate Dr Ste 401 Mahwah (07430) *(G-5750)*

AT&T Services Inc 732 420-3131
200 S Laurel Ave Middletown (07748) *(G-6210)*

AT&T Technologies Inc 201 771-2000
1 Oak Way Berkeley Heights (07922) *(G-400)*

(PA)=Parent Co (HQ)=Headquarters (DH)=Div Headquarters

Atara LLC 916 765-2217
4315 Park Ave Apt 2i Union City (07087) *(G-11243)*

Atc Labs, Newark *Also called Audio Technologies and Codecs* *(G-7098)*

Atc Systems Inc 732 560-0900
207 Blackford Ave Middlesex (08846) *(G-6149)*

Atco Pallet Company 856 461-8141
1000 Creek Rd Delanco (08075) *(G-2003)*

Atco Products Inc 973 379-3171
115 Victory Rd Springfield (07081) *(G-10538)*

Atco Rubber Products Inc 856 794-3393
1480 N West Blvd Vineland (08360) *(G-11324)*

Ateksis USA Corp 201 340-2655
141 Lanza Ave Garfield (07026) *(G-3720)*

Ateksis USA Corp (HQ) 646 508-9074
1 Meadowlands Plz Ste 200 East Rutherford (07073) *(G-2280)*

Atg, Rockaway *Also called Advanced Technology Group Inc* *(G-9546)*

Atgi Advanced Tech Group Intl 609 271-8666
1217 Colts Cir Lawrenceville (08648) *(G-5250)*

Athletes Alley 732 842-1127
483 Broad St Shrewsbury (07702) *(G-9990)*

Athletic Organizational Aids 201 652-1485
54 Fairhaven Dr Midland Park (07432) *(G-6221)*

Athlon Group LLC 201 340-2688
1 Meadowlands Plz Ste 200 East Rutherford (07073) *(G-2281)*

Atiair Technology Inc 973 334-4980
429 Rockaway Valley Rd # 1100 Boonton (07005) *(G-556)*

ATL 201 825-1400
45 Spear Rd Ramsey (07446) *(G-9235)*

Atlantank, Carlstadt *Also called Atlantic Coolg Tech & Svcs LLC (G-1129)*

Atlantex Instruments Inc 201 391-5148
7 Reeds Ln Woodcliff Lake (07677) *(G-12181)*

Atlantic Air Enterprises Inc 732 381-4000
856 Elston St Rahway (07065) *(G-9178)*

Atlantic Associates Intl Inc 856 662-1717
7001 Westfield Ave Pennsauken (08110) *(G-8481)*

Atlantic Boatlifts, Point Pleasant Boro *Also called Courtney Boatlifts Inc (G-8936)*

Atlantic Business Products 201 672-0773
230 Clay Ave Lyndhurst (07071) *(G-5669)*

ATLANTIC C&E, Clifton *Also called Atlantic Casting & Engineering (G-1567)*

Atlantic Can Company 609 518-9950
1200 Highland Dr Westampton (08060) *(G-11911)*

Atlantic Casting & Engineering 973 779-2450
810 Bloomfield Ave Clifton (07012) *(G-1567)*

Atlantic City News, Ventnor City *Also called Phildelphia-Newspapers-Llc (G-11293)*

Atlantic City Week 609 646-4848
8025 Black Horse Pike # 350 Pleasantville (08232) *(G-8902)*

Atlantic Clean Energy Sup LLC 888 900-1581
18 Culnen Dr Branchburg (08876) *(G-641)*

Atlantic Coast Woodwork Inc 609 294-2478
160 Country Club Blvd Ltl Egg Hbr (08087) *(G-5640)*

Atlantic Coastal Welding Inc 732 269-1088
16 Butler Blvd Bayville (08721) *(G-250)*

Atlantic Coolg Tech & Svcs LLC 201 939-0900
80 Kero Rd Carlstadt (07072) *(G-1129)*

Atlantic Eqp Engineers Inc 201 828-9400
24 Industrial Ave Upper Saddle River (07458) *(G-11273)*

Atlantic Exterior Wall Systems 973 646-8200
25 Mansard Ct Wayne (07470) *(G-11606)*

Atlantic Flooring LLC 609 296-7700
121 Middle Holly Ln Ltl Egg Hbr (08087) *(G-5641)*

Atlantic Hemotology & Oncology, Manasquan *Also called Arthur A Topilow William Lrner (G-5868)*

Atlantic Indus WD Pdts LLC 609 965-4555
411 S London Ave Egg Harbor City (08215) *(G-2656)*

Atlantic Inertial Systems Inc 973 237-2713
20f Commerce Way Totowa (07512) *(G-10932)*

Atlantic International Tech 973 625-0053
114 Beach St Ste 3 Rockaway (07866) *(G-9552)*

Atlantic Kenmark Electric Inc 201 991-2117
11 Ewing Ave North Arlington (07031) *(G-7416)*

Atlantic Lining Co Inc 609 723-2400
2206 Saylors Pond Rd 2 Jobstown (08041) *(G-4854)*

Atlantic Masonry Supply Inc 609 909-9292
6422 Black Horse Pike Egg Harbor Township (08234) *(G-2680)*

Atlantic Mills Inc 973 344-2001
1 Market St Ste 9 Passaic (07055) *(G-8126)*

Atlantic Paste & Glue Co Inc, Bayonne *Also called AP&g Co Inc (G-212)*

Atlantic Precision Tech LLC 732 658-3060
432 Quarry Ln North Brunswick (08902) *(G-7506)*

Atlantic Protective Pouches, Toms River *Also called Whe Research Inc (G-10921)*

Atlantic Prsthtic Orthotic Svc 609 927-6330
199 New Rd Ste 56 Linwood (08221) *(G-5465)*

Atlantic Prtg & Graphics LLC 732 493-4222
1301 W Park Ave Ste D Ocean (07712) *(G-7717)*

Atlantic Rubber Enterprises 973 697-5900
35 Union Valley Rd Newfoundland (07435) *(G-7373)*

Atlantic Spring, Ringoes *Also called Matthew Warren Inc (G-9440)*

Atlantic Steel Solutions LLC 973 978-0026
74 Railroad Ave Bldg 102 Paterson (07501) *(G-8217)*

Atlantic Switch Generator LLC 609 518-1900
4108 Sylon Blvd Hainesport (08036) *(G-4069)*

Atlantic Towers, Bayville *Also called Tower Systems Inc (G-260)*

Atlantic U S, Old Bridge *Also called Quality Plus One Catering Inc (G-7791)*

Atlantic Waste Services 201 368-0428
28 North Dr Rochelle Park (07662) *(G-9526)*

Atlantic Wood Industries Inc 609 267-4700
1517 Hwy 38 Hainesport (08036) *(G-4070)*

Atlantic Woodworking Inc 201 773-9277
280 N Midland Ave Ste 230 Saddle Brook (07663) *(G-9753)*

Atlantic Zeiser Inc 973 228-0800
15 Patton Dr West Caldwell (07006) *(G-11766)*

Atlantis Aromatics Inc 732 919-1112
5047 Industrial Rd Ste 4 Wall Township (07727) *(G-11464)*

Atlas Auto Trim Inc 732 985-6800
81 Us Highway 1 Edison (08817) *(G-2468)*

Atlas Copco Hurricane LLC 800 754-7408
7 Campus Dr Ste 200 Parsippany (07054) *(G-7954)*

Atlas Copco North America LLC (HQ) 973 397-3400
7 Campus Dr Ste 200 Parsippany (07054) *(G-7955)*

Atlas Enterprise 908 561-1144
2505 S Clinton Ave South Plainfield (07080) *(G-10333)*

Atlas Flasher & Supply Co Inc 856 423-3333
430 Swedesboro Ave Mickleton (08056) *(G-6136)*

Atlas Industrial Mfg Co (PA) 973 779-3970
81 Somerset Pl Clifton (07012) *(G-1568)*

Atlas Marble & Granite LLC 973 491-5454
44 Fadem Rd Springfield (07081) *(G-10539)*

Atlas Model Railroad Co Inc 908 687-0880
378 Florence Ave Hillside (07205) *(G-4392)*

Atlas O LLC 908 687-9590
378 Florence Ave Hillside (07205) *(G-4393)*

Atlas Recording Machines Corp 732 295-3663
2140 Bridge Ave Point Pleasant Boro (08742) *(G-8932)*

Atlas Refinery Inc 973 589-2002
142 Lockwood St Newark (07105) *(G-7096)*

Atlas Welders & Fabricators, South Plainfield *Also called Atlas Enterprise (G-10333)*

Atlas Woodwork Inc 973 621-9595
212 Wright St Newark (07114) *(G-7097)*

Atlas Woodworking Inc 201 784-1949
15 Naugle St Closter (07624) *(G-1756)*

Atm Aficionado LLC 973 251-2115
184 S Livingston Ave Livingston (07039) *(G-5525)*

Atomizing Systems Inc 201 447-1222
1 Hollywood Ave Ste 1 # 1 Ho Ho Kus (07423) *(G-4453)*

Atrium Publishing, Springfield *Also called Wpi Communications Inc (G-10586)*

Ats Mechanical Inc 609 298-2323
74 Crosswicks St Bordentown (08505) *(G-591)*

Attitudes In Dressing Inc (PA) 908 354-7218
107 Trumbull St Bldg B8 Elizabeth (07206) *(G-2711)*

Aubrey David Inc 201 653-2200
186 Griffith St Jersey City (07307) *(G-4711)*

Audio and Video Labs Inc (HQ) 856 663-9030
7905 N Crescent Blvd Pennsauken (08110) *(G-8482)*

Audio and Video Labs Inc 856 661-5772
7905 N Crescent Blvd Delair (08110) *(G-2000)*

Audio Dynamix Inc 201 567-5488
170 Coolidge Ave Englewood (07631) *(G-2874)*

Audio Technologies and Codecs (PA) 973 624-1116
105 Lock St Ste 411 Newark (07103) *(G-7098)*

Audiocodes Inc 732 469-0880
27 Worlds Fair Dr Ste 2 Somerset (08873) *(G-10066)*

Audiocodes Inc (HQ) 732 469-0880
27 Worlds Fair Dr Ste 2 Somerset (08873) *(G-10067)*

Audrey Hepburn Collection, Boonton *Also called Evh LLC (G-568)*

Augenbrauns Bridal Passaic LLC 845 425-3439
200 Central Ave Lakewood (08701) *(G-5078)*

Augmentus LLC 855 240-1100
306 Wshngton Blvd Ste 303 Hoboken (07030) *(G-4458)*

Aunt Gussies Cookies Crackers, Garfield *Also called Direct Sales and Services Inc (G-3730)*

Aunt Kittys Foods Inc 856 691-2100
270 N Mill Rd Vineland (08360) *(G-11325)*

Auntie Annes Hmde Sft Prtzls 856 772-3737
1337 Voorhees Town Ctr Voorhees (08043) *(G-11422)*

Auntie Annes Soft Pretzels 856 845-3667
1750 Deptford Center Rd # 2086 Woodbury (08096) *(G-12157)*

Auntie Annes Soft Pretzels 856 722-0433
400 W Route 38 Moorestown (08057) *(G-6561)*

Aura Badge Co 856 881-9026
264 W Clayton Ave Clayton (08312) *(G-1523)*

Aura Detergent LLC 718 824-2162
649 Ferry St Newark (07105) *(G-7099)*

Aura Signs Inc 866 963-7446
6 Ilene Ct Ste 9 Hillsborough (08844) *(G-4317)*

Auraplayer USA Inc 617 879-9013
21 Dale Dr West Orange (07052) *(G-11887)*

Aurex Labs Ltd Lblty Co 609 308-2304
10 Lake Dr East Windsor (08520) *(G-2343)*

Auro Health LLC (HQ) 732 839-9400
2572 Brunswick Pike Lawrence Township (08648) *(G-5240)*

(G-0000) Company's Geographic Section entry number

Aurobindo Pharma 732 839-9400
279 Prncton Hightstown Rd East Windsor (08520) *(G-2344)*
Aurobindo Pharma USA 732 839-9402
279 Prncton Hightstown Rd East Windsor (08520) *(G-2345)*
Aurobindo Pharma USA Inc 732 839-9400
2400 Us Highway 130 Dayton (08810) *(G-1953)*
Aurobindo Pharma USA Inc (HQ) 732 839-9400
279 Prnctn Hightstown Rd East Windsor (08520) *(G-2346)*
Aurobindo Pharma USA Inc 609 409-6774
279 Prncton Hightstown Rd East Windsor (08520) *(G-2347)*
Aurobindo Pharma USA LLC 732 839-9400
279 Prnceton Hightstown Rd East Windsor (08520) *(G-2348)*
Aurolife Pharma LLC 732 839-9746
6 Wheeling Rd Dayton (08810) *(G-1954)*
Aurolife Pharma LLC 732 839-9408
203 Windsor Center Dr East Windsor (08520) *(G-2349)*
Aurolife Pharma LLC (HQ) 732 839-4377
2400 Us Highway 130 Dayton (08810) *(G-1955)*
Auromedics Pharma LLC 732 823-4122
279 Prncton Hightstown Rd East Windsor (08520) *(G-2350)*
Auromedics Pharma LLC 732 839-9400
279 Prncton Hightstown Rd East Windsor (08520) *(G-2351)*
Aurora Apparel Inc 201 646-4590
1 Riverside Sq Mall # 146 Hackensack (07601) *(G-3876)*
Aurora Apparels, Hackensack Also called Aurora Apparel Inc *(G-3876)*
Aurora Information Systems 856 596-4180
1873 Marlton Pike E # 220 Cherry Hill (08003) *(G-1344)*
Aurora Multimedia Corporation 732 591-5800
205 Commercial Ct Morganville (07751) *(G-6637)*
Aurora Research Company Inc 973 827-8055
200 Munsonhurst Rd # 201 Franklin (07416) *(G-3595)*
Aurorae, Ramsey Also called Ingui Design LLC *(G-9243)*
Aus Inc (PA) 856 234-9200
155 Gaither Dr Ste A Mount Laurel (08054) *(G-6779)*
Ausome LLC 732 951-8818
80 E State Rt 4 Ste 290 Paramus (07652) *(G-7854)*
Austarpharma LLC 732 225-2930
18 Mayfield Ave Edison (08837) *(G-2469)*
Authenticity Brewing LLC 862 432-9622
23 Kroghs Ln Sparta (07871) *(G-10489)*
Auto Action Group Inc 908 964-6290
121 N Michigan Ave Ste A Kenilworth (07033) *(G-4938)*
Auto Chic, Dover Also called M P T Racing Inc *(G-2098)*
Auto Injury Solutions Inc 240 245-3117
485 Us Highway 1 S Iselin (08830) *(G-4614)*
Auto Remind Inc 800 277-1299
14-25 Plaza Rd Ste N35 Fair Lawn (07410) *(G-3079)*
Auto Shopper, Toms River Also called Showcase Publications Inc *(G-10911)*
Auto Tig Welding Fabricating 973 839-8877
88 Cannonball Rd Ste B Pompton Lakes (07442) *(G-8946)*
Auto-Stak Systems Inc (PA) 201 358-9070
49 Old Hook Rd Westwood (07675) *(G-11956)*
Autoaccess LLC 908 240-5919
451 Church Rd Sicklerville (08081) *(G-10017)*
Autodrill LLC 908 542-0244
1221 Us Highway 22 Ste 6 Lebanon (08833) *(G-5276)*
Automann Inc (PA) 201 529-4996
850 Randolph Rd Somerset (08873) *(G-10068)*
Automann USA, Somerset Also called Automann Inc *(G-10068)*
Automated Control Concepts Inc (PA) 732 922-6611
3535 State Route 66 # 14 Neptune (07753) *(G-6901)*
Automated Flexible Conveyors 973 340-1695
55 Walman Ave Clifton (07011) *(G-1569)*
Automated Medical Pdts Corp 732 602-7717
440 Cliff Rd Sewaren (07077) *(G-9943)*
Automated Office Inc 888 362-7638
9 Executive Campus Cherry Hill (08002) *(G-1345)*
Automated Resource Group Inc 201 391-8357
135 Chestnut Ridge Rd # 2 Montvale (07645) *(G-6443)*
Automated Tapping Systems Inc 732 899-2282
22 Davos Rd Brick (08724) *(G-735)*
Automatic Machine Product 973 383-9929
56 Paterson Ave Newton (07860) *(G-7380)*
Automatic Plating-Accu-Cote, Thorofare Also called Accu-Cote Inc *(G-10818)*
Automatic Roll, Edison Also called Northeast Foods Inc *(G-2584)*
Automatic Switch Company (HQ) 973 966-2000
50-60 Hanover Rd Florham Park (07932) *(G-3489)*
Automatic Switch Company 209 941-4111
50 Hanover Rd Florham Park (07932) *(G-3490)*
Automatic Switch Company 732 596-1731
1460 Us Highway 9 N # 209 Woodbridge (07095) *(G-12146)*
Automatic Transfer Inc 908 213-2830
2 Industrial Rd Alpha (08865) *(G-39)*
Automation & Control Inc 856 234-2300
1491 Lancer Dr Moorestown (08057) *(G-6562)*
Automation Dynamics Systems, Old Tappan Also called ABC Digital Electronics Inc *(G-7796)*
Automotive Database Marketing, Woodcliff Lake Also called Ihs Inc *(G-12194)*
Autopartsource, Edison Also called Momentum Usa Inc *(G-2576)*

Autoplast Systems Inc 973 785-8333
256 Bergen Blvd Woodland Park (07424) *(G-12210)*
Autoshred LLC 732 244-0950
1358 Hooper Ave Toms River (08753) *(G-10865)*
Avacyn Pharmaceuticals Inc 201 836-2599
719 Downing St Teaneck (07666) *(G-10743)*
Avada Software LLC 973 697-1043
1 International Blvd # 400 Mahwah (07495) *(G-5751)*
Avail Inc (PA) 732 560-2222
564a Union Ave Bridgewater (08807) *(G-817)*
Avalon Globocare Corp (PA) 646 762-4517
4400 Route 9 N Freehold (07728) *(G-3640)*
Avalon Pearls, Little Ferry Also called Imperium Enterprises LLC *(G-5509)*
Avant Industries Ltd Inc (PA) 973 242-1700
780 Frelinghuysen Ave Newark (07114) *(G-7100)*
Avante International Tech Inc 609 799-9388
70 Washington Rd Princeton Junction (08550) *(G-9149)*
Avantegarde Image LLC 732 363-8701
535 E County Line Rd Lakewood (08701) *(G-5079)*
Avanti, Cranbury Also called Kt America Corp *(G-1850)*
Avanti Linens Inc (PA) 201 641-7766
234 Moonachie Rd Ste 1 Moonachie (07074) *(G-6506)*
Avantier Inc (PA) 732 491-8150
148 Main St Metuchen (08840) *(G-6095)*
AVANTIK, Springfield Also called Belair Instrument Company LLC *(G-10542)*
Avantor Performance Mtls LLC 908 859-2151
600 N Broad St Phillipsburg (08865) *(G-8640)*
Avanzato Jewelers LLC 609 890-0500
2440 Whthrse Hmlton Sq Rd Trenton (08690) *(G-11021)*
Avaya Cala Inc 866 462-8292
350 Mount Kemble Ave Morristown (07960) *(G-6689)*
Avaya Inc 908 953-6000
211 Mount Airy Rd Basking Ridge (07920) *(G-181)*
Avaya Inc 732 852-2030
307 Mddletown Lincroft Rd Lincroft (07738) *(G-5336)*
Avaya World Services Inc 908 953-6000
350 Mount Kemble Ave Morristown (07960) *(G-6690)*
Avebe North America Inc 609 520-1400
4 Independence Way Princeton (08540) *(G-9012)*
Avenel Pallet Co Inc 732 752-0500
1800 S 2nd St Dunellen (08812) *(G-2126)*
Aventis Inc 800 981-2491
55 Corporate Dr Bridgewater (08807) *(G-818)*
Aventis Phrmcticals Foundation 908 981-5000
55 Corporate Dr Bridgewater (08807) *(G-819)*
Aversas Italian Bakery Inc 856 227-8005
801 Route 168 Blackwood (08012) *(G-472)*
Avery Dennison Corporation 201 956-6100
16-00 Pollitt Dr Ste 3 Fair Lawn (07410) *(G-3080)*
Aviation International News, Midland Park Also called Convention News Company
Inc *(G-6224)*
Avida Incorporated 201 802-0749
174 Kinderkamack Rd Ste A Park Ridge (07656) *(G-7916)*
Avigdor Jewelry, Morristown Also called Avigdor Ltd Liability Company *(G-6691)*
Avigdor Ltd Liability Company 973 898-4770
25 Tikvah Way Morristown (07960) *(G-6691)*
Avionic Instruments LLC 732 388-3500
1414 Randolph Ave Avenel (07001) *(G-126)*
Avitex Co Inc (PA) 973 242-2410
461 Frelinghuysen Ave Newark (07114) *(G-7101)*
Avitex Co Inc 973 242-2410
32 Noble St Newark (07114) *(G-7102)*
Avl Digital Group, Pennsauken Also called Audio and Video Labs Inc *(G-8482)*
Avon Products Inc 973 779-5590
1166 Broad St Clifton (07013) *(G-1570)*
Avony Enterprises Inc 212 242-8144
39 Meade St Ste 122 Trenton (08638) *(G-11022)*
Avstar Publishing Corp. 908 236-6210
3 Burlinghoff Ln Lebanon (08833) *(G-5277)*
Avyakta It Services LLC 609 790-7517
37 Sussex Ln East Windsor (08520) *(G-2352)*
Aw Machinery LLC 973 882-3223
7 Just Rd Fairfield (07004) *(G-3142)*
Awards Trophy Company 908 687-5775
611 Us Highway 22 Hillside (07205) *(G-4394)*
Awnings By Texas Canvas, Fairfield Also called Texas Canvas Co Inc *(G-3324)*
Axg Corporation 212 213-3313
700 Plaza Dr Ste 204 Secaucus (07094) *(G-9866)*
Axiam Printing, Union Also called Anisha Enterprises Inc *(G-11153)*
Axim Concrete Technologies 330 966-0444
201 Polito Ave Lyndhurst (07071) *(G-5670)*
Axiom Ingredients LLC 732 669-2458
33 Wood Ave S Ste 600 Iselin (08830) *(G-4615)*
Aydin Jewelry Menufacturing 201 818-1002
119 E Main St Ramsey (07446) *(G-9236)*
Ayerspace Inc 212 582-8410
25 Fairfield Ave West Caldwell (07006) *(G-11767)*
Ayr Composition Inc 908 241-8118
320 Chestnut St Roselle Park (07204) *(G-9688)*

A
L
P
H
A
B
E
T
I
C

Ayr Graphics & Printing Inc 908 241-8118
320 Chestnut St Roselle Park (07204) *(G-9689)*

Az-Em USA Branchburg NJ 908 429-0020
70 Meister Ave Branchburg (08876) *(G-642)*

Azar Displays, Paramus *Also called Azar International Inc (G-7855)*

Azar International Inc (PA) 845 624-8808
80 W Century Rd Ste 400 Paramus (07652) *(G-7855)*

Azco Steel Company, South Plainfield *Also called Bushwick Metals LLC (G-10341)*

Azego Technology Svcs US Inc (PA) 201 327-7500
103 Bauer Dr Ste A Oakland (07436) *(G-7675)*

Azimuth Renewable Energy, Manasquan *Also called Mc Renewable Energy LLC (G-5873)*

Aztec Graphics Inc 609 587-1000
420 Whitehead Rd Trenton (08619) *(G-11023)*

Aztec Software Associates Inc 973 258-0011
51 Commerce St Springfield (07081) *(G-10540)*

Aztech Mfg Inc 609 726-1212
147 W Hampton St Pemberton (08068) *(G-8442)*

Aztek Sand Grav Cmpny-Division, Hammonton *Also called Arawak Paving Co Inc (G-4130)*

Azuma Foods Intl Inc USA 201 372-1112
20 Murray Hill Pkwy # 130 East Rutherford (07073) *(G-2282)*

B & A Grafx Inc 646 302-8849
1 Cape May St Harrison (07029) *(G-4171)*

B & B Custom Cabinets, Matawan *Also called Kitchen Crafters Plus (G-6023)*

B & B Iron Works 862 238-7203
1 Broad St Clifton (07013) *(G-1571)*

B & B Millwork & Doors Inc 973 249-0300
327 Monroe Ave Kenilworth (07033) *(G-4939)*

B & B Poultry Co Inc 856 692-8893
Almond Rd Norma (08347) *(G-7412)*

B & B Press Inc 908 840-4093
24 Cokesbury Rd Ste 11 Lebanon (08833) *(G-5278)*

B & C Custom WD Handrail Corp 732 530-6640
26 Sunset Ave Red Bank (07701) *(G-9322)*

B & C Machine Co Inc 973 823-1120
22 Lasinski Rd Ste I Franklin (07416) *(G-3596)*

B & F Mason Contractors, Elmwood Park *Also called B&F and Son Masonry Company (G-2805)*

B & G International, Union *Also called B & G Plastics Inc (G-11155)*

B & G Plastics Inc (PA) 973 824-9220
1085 Morris Ave Ste 5d Union (07083) *(G-11155)*

B & H Printers Inc 908 688-6990
470 Schooleys Mountain Rd # 1 Hackettstown (07840) *(G-3999)*

B & L Printing Co, Hillsborough *Also called Premium Service Printing (G-4363)*

B & M Finishers Inc 908 241-5640
201 S 31st St Kenilworth (07033) *(G-4940)*

B & R Bindery Division, Trenton *Also called B & R Printing Inc (G-11024)*

B & R Printing Inc 609 448-3328
84 Hummingbird Dr Trenton (08690) *(G-11024)*

B & S Sheet Metal Co Inc 973 427-3739
60 5th Ave Hawthorne (07506) *(G-4218)*

B & S Tool and Cutter Service 201 488-3545
99 John St Hackensack (07601) *(G-3877)*

B & W Plastics Inc 973 383-0020
20 Wilson Dr Sparta (07871) *(G-10490)*

B and G Music LLC 732 779-4555
2 Teal Pl Bayville (08721) *(G-251)*

B and W Printing Company Inc 908 241-3060
730 Fairfield Ave Kenilworth (07033) *(G-4941)*

B B Supply Corp 201 313-9021
421 Nelson Ave Cliffside Park (07010) *(G-1536)*

B C T, Upper Saddle River *Also called Business Cards Tomorrow (G-11275)*

B D, Franklin Lakes *Also called Becton Dickinson and Company (G-3610)*

B E C Mfg Corp 201 414-0000
649 Lincoln Ave Glen Rock (07452) *(G-3822)*

B F Goodrich Performance Mtls, Pedricktown *Also called Lubrizol Advanced Mtls Inc (G-8438)*

B L White Welding & Steel Co 973 684-4111
527 E 33rd St Paterson (07504) *(G-8218)*

B P, Wayne *Also called BP Lubricants USA Inc (G-11614)*

B P Graphics Inc 732 942-2315
315 4th St Lakewood (08701) *(G-5080)*

B Spinelli Farm Containers 732 566-5619
3992 Highway 516 Matawan (07747) *(G-6013)*

B T O Industries Inc 973 243-0011
11 Lenox Ter West Orange (07052) *(G-11888)*

B T Partners Inc 609 652-6511
3 N New York Rd Ste 23 Galloway (08205) *(G-3709)*

B Tech, Rockaway *Also called Btech Inc (G-9555)*

B V S, Metuchen *Also called Berkeley Varitronics Systems (G-6096)*

B W I, Branchburg *Also called Bridgewater Wholesalers Inc (G-645)*

B Witching Bath Company LLC (PA) 973 423-1820
174 Lincoln Ave Hawthorne (07506) *(G-4219)*

B&B Imaging LLC 201 261-3131
733 Bush Pl Paramus (07652) *(G-7856)*

B&F and Son Masonry Company 201 791-7630
10 North St Elmwood Park (07407) *(G-2805)*

B&G Foods Inc (PA) 973 401-6500
4 Gatehall Dr Ste 110 Parsippany (07054) *(G-7956)*

B&G Foods Inc. 973 403-6795
426 Eagle Rock Ave Roseland (07068) *(G-9646)*

B&G Foods Inc. 973 401-6500
4 Gatehall Dr Ste 110 Parsippany (07054) *(G-7957)*

B&G Foods North America Inc (HQ) 973 401-6500
4 Gatehall Dr Ste 110 Parsippany (07054) *(G-7958)*

B&M Technologies Inc 201 291-8505
109 5th St Ste 1 Saddle Brook (07663) *(G-9754)*

B-Hive Ltd Liability Company 302 438-2769
10 Olivia Rd Hightstown (08520) *(G-4310)*

B-Tea Beverage LLC 201 512-8400
12-17 River Rd Fair Lawn (07410) *(G-3081)*

B.I. Foods, Pennsauken *Also called Beef International Inc (G-8485)*

B2x Corporation 201 714-2373
10 Exchange Pl Fl 25 Jersey City (07302) *(G-4712)*

Bab Printing Jan Service (PA) 908 272-6224
945 Lincoln Ave E Cranford (07016) *(G-1897)*

Babbitt Mfg Co Inc 856 692-3245
719 E Park Ave Vineland (08360) *(G-11326)*

Babcock & Wilcox Company 609 261-2424
1000 Taylors Ln Ste 4 Cinnaminson (08077) *(G-1448)*

Babcock & Wilcox Powr Generatn 973 227-7008
277 Fairfield Rd Ste 331a Fairfield (07004) *(G-3143)*

Baby Time International Inc 973 481-7400
250 Passaic St Newark (07104) *(G-7103)*

Babysmart LLC 908 766-4900
174 Hardscrabble Rd Bernardsville (07924) *(G-447)*

Bach Tool Precision Inc 973 962-6224
51 Executive Pkwy Ringwood (07456) *(G-9444)*

Backroads Inc 973 948-4176
160 County Road 521 Newton (07860) *(G-7381)*

Badge Company of New Jersey, Annandale *Also called Suroma Ltd Liability Company (G-61)*

Badger Blades LLC 908 325-6587
216 North Ave E Ste 2 Cranford (07016) *(G-1898)*

Bae Systems Info & Elec Sys 603 885-4321
100 Campus Rd Ste 1 Totowa (07512) *(G-10933)*

Bae Systems Info & Elec Sys 973 633-6000
164 Totowa Rd Wayne (07470) *(G-11607)*

Bae Systems Tech Sol Srvc Inc 856 638-1003
8000 Midlantic Dr 700n Mount Laurel (08054) *(G-6780)*

Baer Aggregates Inc 908 454-4412
454 River Rd Phillipsburg (08865) *(G-8641)*

Baeta Corp 201 471-0988
1 Bridge Plz N Ste 2 Fort Lee (07024) *(G-3545)*

Bagel Chateau, Westfield *Also called S M Z Enterprises Inc (G-11930)*

Bagel Chateau, Millburn *Also called Millburn Bagel Inc (G-6258)*

Bagel Club 908 806-6022
20 Commerce St Ste 5 Flemington (08822) *(G-3429)*

Bagel Street 609 936-1755
660 Plainsboro Rd Ste 18 Plainsboro (08536) *(G-8875)*

Bahadir USA LLC 856 517-3080
431 S Pnnsville Auburn Rd Carneys Point (08069) *(G-1244)*

Bai Lar Interior Services Inc 732 738-0350
554 New Brunswick Ave Fords (08863) *(G-3527)*

Baker Adhesives, Paterson *Also called Amb Enterprises LLC (G-8206)*

Baker General Contracting, Flemington *Also called Donald Mason Baker Contractor (G-3437)*

Baker/Titan Adhesives 973 225-1070
25 Lake St Paterson (07501) *(G-8219)*

Bakers Perfection Inc 973 983-0700
198 Green Pond Rd Ste 5 Rockaway (07866) *(G-9553)*

Bakers Puff Pastry, Paterson *Also called Mardon Associates Inc (G-8332)*

Bal-Edge Corporation 973 895-8826
151 Industrial Way E Eatontown (07724) *(G-2384)*

Bal-Togs, North Bergen *Also called BT Industries Inc (G-7436)*

Bali Designs, Rahway *Also called Robert Manse Designs LLC (G-9220)*

Ballantine Laboratories Inc 908 713-7742
312 Old Allerton Rd Annandale (08801) *(G-56)*

Ballard Collection Inc 908 604-0082
221 Stirling Rd Warren (07059) *(G-11538)*

Ballet Makers Inc (PA) 973 595-9000
1 Campus Rd Totowa (07512) *(G-10934)*

Bally Gaming, Egg Harbor Township *Also called Bally Technologies Inc (G-2681)*

Bally Technologies Inc 609 641-7711
3133 Fire Rd Egg Harbor Township (08234) *(G-2681)*

Balthazar Bakery, Englewood *Also called Provence LLC (G-2926)*

Baltimore Transformer Company 973 942-2222
460 Totowa Ave Paterson (07522) *(G-8220)*

Bamboo & Rattan Works Inc 732 255-4239
1931 Silverton Rd Toms River (08753) *(G-10866)*

Bamco Inc 732 302-0889
30 Baekeland Ave Middlesex (08846) *(G-6150)*

Banarez Enterprises Inc 201 222-7515
175 Baldwin Ave Jersey City (07306) *(G-4713)*

Bandemar Networks LLC 732 991-5112
3 New Dover Rd East Brunswick (08816) *(G-2136)*

Banding Centers of America 973 805-9977
83 Hanover Rd Ste 160 Florham Park (07932) ***(G-3491)***
Banicki Sheet Metal Inc 201 385-5938
44 Garden St Bergenfield (07621) ***(G-382)***
Banker Steel Nj LLC 732 968-6061
1640 New Market Ave South Plainfield (07080) ***(G-10334)***
Bankers Line, The, Garfield *Also called Bankers Pen Inc* ***(G-3721)***
Bankers Pen Inc 800 499-7367
141 Lanza Ave Bldg 12 Garfield (07026) ***(G-3721)***
Banks Bros Corporation (PA) 973 680-4488
24 Federal Plz Bloomfield (07003) ***(G-502)***
Banner Design Inc 908 687-5335
600 N Union Ave Ste 11 Hillside (07205) ***(G-4395)***
Bannister Company Inc 732 828-1353
216 Brook Dr Milltown (08850) ***(G-6267)***
Bannon Group Ltd 201 451-6500
234 16th St Fl 8 Jersey City (07310) ***(G-4714)***
Banquet Services International 732 270-1188
2214 Route 37 E Ste 1 Toms River (08753) ***(G-10867)***
Bar Fields Inc 347 587-7795
1400 W Elizabeth Ave Linden (07036) ***(G-5351)***
Bar Lan Inc 856 596-2330
327 Gull Cv Brigantine (08203) ***(G-917)***
Bar-Lo Carbon Products Inc 973 227-2717
31 Daniel Rd Fairfield (07004) ***(G-3144)***
Bar-Maid Corporation 973 478-7070
362 Midland Ave Ste 2 Garfield (07026) ***(G-3722)***
Barantec Inc 973 779-8774
777 Passaic Ave Ste 345 Clifton (07012) ***(G-1572)***
Barbeitos Inc 732 726-9543
6 Pocahont Pl Avenel (07001) ***(G-127)***
Barbieri, Anthony J, Carlstadt *Also called Designer Sign Systems LLC* ***(G-1155)***
Barbs Harley-Davidson 856 456-4141
926 Black Horse Pike Mount Ephraim (08059) ***(G-6762)***
Bard Asia Pacific Division, New Providence *Also called Bard International Inc* ***(G-7029)***
Bard Devices Inc (HQ) 908 277-8000
730 Central Ave New Providence (07974) ***(G-7027)***
Bard Healthcare Inc 908 277-8000
730 Central Ave New Providence (07974) ***(G-7028)***
Bard International Inc (HQ) 908 277-8000
111 Spring St New Providence (07974) ***(G-7029)***
Barkercraft, Westville *Also called Intelco* ***(G-11944)***
Barkin Expanding Envelope Co, Manchester *Also called Red Wallet Connection Inc* ***(G-5889)***
Barlics Manufacturing Co Inc 732 381-6229
815 Martin St Rahway (07065) ***(G-9179)***
Barmensen Labs LLC 732 593-3515
2685 Hwy 516 Old Bridge (08857) ***(G-7774)***
Barnegat Light Fibrgls Sup LLC 609 294-8870
304 Forge Rd Unit 12 West Creek (08092) ***(G-11809)***
Barnes & Noble Booksellers Inc 201 272-3635
125 Chubb Ave Fl 3 Lyndhurst (07071) ***(G-5671)***
Barnes & Noble.com, Lyndhurst *Also called Barnes & Noble Booksellers Inc* ***(G-5671)***
Barnet Products Corporation 201 346-4620
920 Sylvan Ave 210 Englewood Cliffs (07632) ***(G-2949)***
Barnett Machine Tools Inc 973 482-6222
401 Supor Blvd Bldg 3n Harrison (07029) ***(G-4172)***
Baron Herzog, Bayonne *Also called Royal Wine Corporation* ***(G-243)***
Barr Laboratories Inc 201 767-1589
265 Livingston St Northvale (07647) ***(G-7573)***
Barr Laboratories Inc 845 362-1100
232 Pegasus Ave Northvale (07647) ***(G-7574)***
Barrasso & Blasi Industries 973 761-0595
1581 Springfield Ave Maplewood (07040) ***(G-5914)***
Barrett Asphalt Inc 609 561-4100
7503 Weymouth Rd Hammonton (08037) ***(G-4132)***
Barrett Industries Corporation (HQ) 973 533-1001
73 Headquarters Plz Morristown (07960) ***(G-6692)***
Barrett Paving Materials Inc (HQ) 973 533-1001
3 Becker Farm Rd Ste 307 Roseland (07068) ***(G-9647)***
Barrette Outdoor Living Inc 609 965-5450
545 Tilton Rd Ste 100 Egg Harbor City (08215) ***(G-2657)***
Barrier Enterprises Inc 973 770-3983
175 Stanhope Sparta Rd Andover (07821) ***(G-48)***
Barrington Press Inc (PA) 201 843-6556
37 Spring Valley Ave Paramus (07652) ***(G-7857)***
Barry Callebaut USA LLC 856 663-2260
1500 Suckle Hwy Pennsauken (08110) ***(G-8483)***
Barry Callebaut USA LLC 856 663-2260
1600 Suckle Hwy Pennsauken (08110) ***(G-8484)***
Barry Urner Publications Inc 732 240-5330
1001 Corporate Cir Toms River (08755) ***(G-10868)***
Bartell Morrison (usa) LLC 732 566-5400
200 Commerce Ave Freehold (07728) ***(G-3641)***
Bartlett Printing & Graphic 609 386-1525
4495 Route 130 S Burlington (08016) ***(G-958)***
Bartley Crucible Refractories 609 393-0066
15 Muirhead Ave Trenton (08638) ***(G-11025)***
Barton & Cooney LLC (PA) 609 747-9300
300 Richards Run Burlington (08016) ***(G-959)***
Baruffi Bros Inc (PA) 856 692-6400
907 N Main Rd Bldg D Vineland (08360) ***(G-11327)***
Barworth Inc 973 376-4883
673 Morris Tpke Springfield (07081) ***(G-10541)***
BASF Catalysts LLC (HQ) 732 205-5000
25 Middlesex Tpke Iselin (08830) ***(G-4616)***
BASF Catalysts LLC 732 205-5000
700 Blair Rd Carteret (07008) ***(G-1252)***
BASF Corporation (HQ) 973 245-6000
100 Park Ave Florham Park (07932) ***(G-3492)***
BASF Corporation 908 689-2500
2 Pleasant View Ave Washington (07882) ***(G-11576)***
BASF Corporation 848 221-2786
227 Oak Ridge Pkwy Toms River (08755) ***(G-10869)***
BASF Corporation 732 205-5086
25 Middlesex Tpke Iselin (08830) ***(G-4617)***
BASF Corporation 732 205-2700
2655 Route 22 W Union (07083) ***(G-11156)***
BASF Corporation 973 426-5429
450 Clark Dr Ste 3 Budd Lake (07828) ***(G-925)***
BASF Engineering Plastics, Budd Lake *Also called BASF Corporation* ***(G-925)***
Basfin Corporation (HQ) 973 245-6000
100 Park Ave Florham Park (07932) ***(G-3493)***
Basha USA LLC 201 339-9770
390 Broadway Bayonne (07002) ***(G-213)***
Bashian Bros Inc (PA) 201 330-1001
65 Railroad Ave Ste 8 Ridgefield (07657) ***(G-9350)***
Bashian Rugs, Ridgefield *Also called Bashian Bros Inc* ***(G-9350)***
Basic Commerce & Industries 609 482-3740
856 S Route 30 Ste 5a Hammonton (08037) ***(G-4133)***
Basic Ltd 718 871-6106
575 Prospect St Ste 241 Lakewood (08701) ***(G-5081)***
Basic Plastics Company Inc (PA) 973 977-8151
318 Mclean Blvd Bldg 5 Paterson (07504) ***(G-8221)***
Basic Solutions Ltd 201 978-7691
330 Adams Ct Manalapan (07726) ***(G-5839)***
Baskin-Robbins, Teaneck *Also called Dunkin Donuts Baskin Robbins* ***(G-10750)***
Bassano Graphics, Hawthorne *Also called Bassano Prtrs & Lithographers* ***(G-4220)***
Bassano Prtrs & Lithographers 973 423-1400
67 Royal Ave Hawthorne (07506) ***(G-4220)***
Bassil Bookbinding Company Inc 201 440-4925
535 S River St Hackensack (07601) ***(G-3878)***
Basu Group 908 517-9138
227 Us Hwy One North Brunswick (08902) ***(G-7507)***
Basys Inc 732 616-5276
1200 S Church St Ste 7 Mount Laurel (08054) ***(G-6781)***
Batallure Beauty LLC (PA) 609 716-1200
104 Carnegie Ctr Ste 202 Princeton (08540) ***(G-9013)***
Bathware House Ltd Lblty Co 732 546-3220
524 W Edgar Rd Linden (07036) ***(G-5352)***
Battistini Foods 609 476-2184
20 Brandywine Ct Egg Harbor Township (08234) ***(G-2682)***
Bau-Lo Wooden Furniture Inc 212 664-9188
63 Chancellor Park Dr Mays Landing (08330) ***(G-6037)***
Bauer Enterprises, Ringwood *Also called Susan R Bauer Inc* ***(G-9456)***
Bauer Publishing Company LP (HQ) 201 569-6699
270 Sylvan Ave Ste 210 Englewood Cliffs (07632) ***(G-2950)***
Bauer Sport Shop 201 384-6522
48 Dumont Ave Dumont (07628) ***(G-2115)***
Baum, W & E, Freehold *Also called W & E Baum Bronze Tablet Corp* ***(G-3692)***
Baumar Industries Inc 973 667-5490
29 E Centre St Nutley (07110) ***(G-7642)***
Baumer of America Inc 973 263-1569
425 Main Rd Towaco (07082) ***(G-10988)***
Baumgartner Associates, Somerset *Also called Pacon Manufacturing Corp* ***(G-10152)***
Bausch & Lomb Incorporated 908 927-1400
400 Somerset Corp Blvd Bridgewater (08807) ***(G-820)***
Bausch Health Companies Inc (HQ) 908 927-1400
400 Somerset Corp Blvd Bridgewater (08807) ***(G-821)***
Bavelle Tech Sltions Ltd Lblty 973 992-8086
100 Eagle Rock Ave # 301 East Hanover (07936) ***(G-2201)***
Baxter Corporation (PA) 201 337-1212
511 Commerce St Franklin Lakes (07417) ***(G-3607)***
Baxter Healthcare Corporation 732 225-4700
100 Raritan Center Pkwy # 120 Edison (08837) ***(G-2470)***
Baxter Healthcare Corporation 856 489-2104
2 Esterbrook Ln Cherry Hill (08003) ***(G-1346)***
Bay Shore Press Inc 732 957-0070
320 Kings Hwy E Middletown (07748) ***(G-6211)***
Bay State Milling Company 973 772-3400
404 Getty Ave Clifton (07011) ***(G-1573)***
Bayer Consumer Care Inc 973 267-6198
36 Columbia Rd Morristown (07960) ***(G-6693)***
Bayer Corporation (HQ) 412 777-2000
100 Bayer Blvd Whippany (07981) ***(G-12007)***
Bayer Hcp Inc For FDA Purposes, Whippany *Also called Bayer Hlthcare Phrmcticals Inc* ***(G-12009)***
Bayer Healthcare LLC 973 254-5000
36 Columbia Rd Morristown (07960) ***(G-6694)***

ALPHABETIC

Bayer Healthcare LLC (HQ) 862 404-3000
100 Bayer Blvd Whippany (07981) *(G-12008)*
Bayer Hlthcare Phrmcticals Inc 862 404-3000
100 Bayer Blvd Whippany (07981) *(G-12009)*
Bayer Hlthcare Phrmcticals Inc 973 709-3545
100 Bayer Blvd Whippany (07981) *(G-12010)*
Bayer Hlthcare Phrmcticals Inc (HQ) 862 404-3000
100 Bayer Blvd Whippany (07981) *(G-12011)*
Bayonne Community News 201 437-2460
447 Broadway Bayonne (07002) *(G-214)*
Bayonne Drydock & Repair Corp 201 823-9295
100 Military Ocean Trml Bayonne (07002) *(G-215)*
Bayshore Recycling Corp 732 738-6000
75 Crows Mill Rd Keasbey (08832) *(G-4924)*
Bayside Orthopedics LLC 732 691-4898
780 Route 37 W Ste 330 Toms River (08755) *(G-10870)*
Bayview Entertainment LLC 201 880-5331
210 W Parkway Ste 7 Pompton Plains (07444) *(G-8955)*
Bbg Surgical Ltd Liability Co 551 404-7920
1995 Rutgers Blvd Lakewood (08701) *(G-5082)*
Bbk Technologies Inc 908 231-0306
13 Rte 206 S Raritan (08869) *(G-9307)*
Bbm Group LLC 201 482-6500
280 Broad Ave Fl 3 Palisades Park (07650) *(G-7834)*
Bcc (USA) Inc 732 572-5450
143 Ethel Rd W Piscataway (08854) *(G-8740)*
Bcg Marble & Granite South LLC 732 367-3788
150 Faraday Ave Jackson (08527) *(G-4655)*
Bcg Marble Gran Fabricators Co 201 343-8487
167 Sussex St Hackensack (07601) *(G-3879)*
BCI, Hammonton *Also called Basic Commerce & Industries (G-4133)*
BCsmachine & Mfg Corp 908 561-1656
3575 Kennedy Rd South Plainfield (07080) *(G-10335)*
BCT, Egg Harbor City *Also called Business Cards Tomorrow Inc (G-2658)*
Bd Biscnces Systems Rgents Inc (PA) 201 847-6800
1 Becton Dr Franklin Lakes (07417) *(G-3608)*
Bd Ventures LLC 201 847-6800
1 Becton Dr Franklin Lakes (07417) *(G-3609)*
Bdd, Bayonne *Also called Bayonne Drydock & Repair Corp (G-215)*
Be CU Manufacturing Co Inc (PA) 908 233-3342
2347 Beryllium Rd Scotch Plains (07076) *(G-9847)*
Bea's Brooklyn's Best, Old Bridge *Also called Deluxe Gourmet Spc Ltd Lblty (G-7776)*
Beach Nutts Media Inc 609 886-4113
2503 Bayshore Rd Villas (08251) *(G-11313)*
Beachcarts USA 201 319-0091
296 Julianne Ter Secaucus (07094) *(G-9867)*
Beachcomber, The, Surf City *Also called Jersey Shore News Mgazines Inc (G-10665)*
Beachwood Canvas Works LLC 732 929-1783
39 Lake Ave Island Heights (08732) *(G-4651)*
Beacon C M P Corp 908 851-9393
295 N Michigan Ave Ste G Kenilworth (07033) *(G-4942)*
Beacon Offset Printing LLC 201 488-4241
204 Russell Pl Hackensack (07601) *(G-3880)*
Beacon, The, Clifton *Also called Diocese of Paterson (G-1600)*
Beacut Abrasives Corp 973 249-1420
788 Paterson Ave East Rutherford (07073) *(G-2283)*
Bear USa Inc (PA) 201 943-4748
460 Bergen Blvd Ste 370 Palisades Park (07650) *(G-7835)*
Bearhands Ltd 201 807-9898
90 Dayton Ave Ste 9 Passaic (07055) *(G-8127)*
Bearing Castings USA, Piscataway *Also called Bcc (USA) Inc (G-8740)*
Beatrice Home Fashions Inc (PA) 908 561-7370
151 Helen St South Plainfield (07080) *(G-10336)*
Beau Label 973 318-7800
385 Hillside Ave Hillside (07205) *(G-4396)*
Beauty Wood Designs 908 687-9697
284 Concord Ave Union (07083) *(G-11157)*
Beauty-Fill LLC 908 353-1600
1319 N Broad St Hillside (07205) *(G-4397)*
Beauty-Pack LLC 732 802-8200
170 Circle Dr N Piscataway (08854) *(G-8741)*
Beaver Run Farms (PA) 973 427-1000
10 Wagaraw Rd Hawthorne (07506) *(G-4221)*
Beaver Run Farms 973 875-5555
300 Beaver Run Rd Lafayette (07848) *(G-5044)*
Bebe Girdle, Harrison *Also called Dolce Vita Intimates LLC (G-4178)*
Bebus Cabinetry LLC 201 729-9300
12 Ames Ave Rutherford (07070) *(G-9727)*
Becton, Dickinson and Company (PA) 201 847-6800
1 Becton Dr Franklin Lakes (07417) *(G-3610)*
Becton Dickinson Re Inc 201 847-6800
1 Becton Dr Franklin Lakes (07417) *(G-3611)*
Bedding Industries of America, North Brunswick *Also called Ther-A-Pedic Sleep Products (G-7542)*
Bedding Shoppe Inc 973 334-9000
811 Route 46 Parsippany (07054) *(G-7959)*
Bedlam Corp 973 774-8770
33 Church St Montclair (07042) *(G-6408)*

Bedrock Granite Inc 732 741-0010
803 Shrewsbury Ave Shrewsbury (07702) *(G-9991)*
Beef International Inc 856 663-6763
7010 Central Hwy Pennsauken (08109) *(G-8485)*
Beers Steel Erecting, Hackensack *Also called John Cooper Company Inc (G-3933)*
Behr Technology Inc 908 537-9960
223 State Route 31 Hampton (08827) *(G-4154)*
Behringer Fluid Systems Inc 973 948-0226
17 Ridge Rd Branchville (07826) *(G-726)*
Behrman House Inc 973 379-7200
241 Millburn Ave B Millburn (07041) *(G-6248)*
Beilis Development LLC 862 203-3650
20-21 Wagaraw Rd Bldg 31b Fair Lawn (07410) *(G-3082)*
Bel Fuse Inc (PA) 201 432-0463
206 Van Vorst St Jersey City (07302) *(G-4715)*
Bel Hybrids & Magnetics Inc (HQ) 201 432-0463
206 Van Vorst St Jersey City (07302) *(G-4716)*
Bel-Art Products Inc (HQ) 973 694-0500
661 Rte 23 Wayne (07470) *(G-11608)*
Bel-Capri, Hackensack *Also called Losurdo Foods Inc (G-3940)*
Bel-Ray Company Inc (HQ) 732 378-4000
1201 Bowman Ave Wall Township (07727) *(G-11465)*
Bel-Tech Stamping Inc 973 728-8229
26 Industrial Rd Ste A West Milford (07480) *(G-11851)*
Belair Instrument Company LLC (PA) 973 912-8900
36 Commerce St Springfield (07081) *(G-10542)*
Belair Time Corporation 732 905-0100
1995 Swarthmore Ave Ste 3 Lakewood (08701) *(G-5083)*
Belden Inc 908 925-8000
711 Lidgerwood Ave Elizabeth (07202) *(G-2712)*
Belfer 732 493-2666
10 Ruckle Ave Farmingdale (07727) *(G-3378)*
Belfer Lighting Manufacturing, Farmingdale *Also called Lighting World Inc (G-3388)*
Bell arte Inc 908 355-1199
10 W Mravlag Pl Elizabeth (07201) *(G-2713)*
Bell Container Corp 973 344-4400
615 Ferry St Newark (07105) *(G-7104)*
Bell Supply Co (PA) 856 663-3900
7221 N Crescent Blvd Pennsauken (08110) *(G-8486)*
Bell'arte, Elizabeth *Also called Bell arte Inc (G-2713)*
Bell-Mark Sales Co Inc (PA) 973 882-0202
331 Changebridge Rd Ste 1 Pine Brook (07058) *(G-8688)*
Bella Acqua Inc 609 324-9024
214 Sykesville Rd Ste 1a Chesterfield (08515) *(G-1441)*
Bella Palermo Pastry Shop 908 931-0298
541 Boulevard Kenilworth (07033) *(G-4943)*
Bellaqua Inc 201 460-8379
251 Paterson Ave East Rutherford (07073) *(G-2284)*
Bellco Glass Inc 800 257-7043
340 Edrudo Rd Vineland (08360) *(G-11328)*
Belle Printing Group LLC (PA) 856 235-5151
3838 Church Rd Mount Laurel (08054) *(G-6782)*
Bellemead Hot Glass 908 281-5516
884 Route 206 Hillsborough (08844) *(G-4318)*
Belleplain Supply Co Inc 609 861-2345
346 Hands Mill Rd Woodbine (08270) *(G-12141)*
Belleplain Supply Gun Center, Woodbine *Also called Belleplain Supply Co Inc (G-12141)*
Bellerophon Therapeutics Inc 908 574-4770
184 Liberty Corner Rd # 302 Warren (07059) *(G-11539)*
Belleville Corp 201 991-6222
328 Belleville Tpke Kearny (07032) *(G-4863)*
Belleville Scale & Balance LLC 973 759-4487
50 S Center St Ste 13 Orange (07050) *(G-7817)*
Belleville Wire Cloth Co Inc (PA) 973 239-0074
18 Rutgers Ave Cedar Grove (07009) *(G-1272)*
Bellevue Parfums USA LLC 908 262-7774
2 Jill Ct Bldg 21 Hillsborough (08844) *(G-4319)*
Bellia & Sons 856 845-2234
1047 N Broad St Woodbury (08096) *(G-12158)*
Bellino, Englewood *Also called AMD Fine Linens LLC (G-2868)*
Bellview Farms Inc 856 697-7172
150 Atlantic St Landisville (08326) *(G-5230)*
Bellview Winery, Landisville *Also called Bellview Farms Inc (G-5230)*
Bellwood Aeromatics Inc 201 670-4617
4 Spielman Rd Fairfield (07004) *(G-3145)*
Belmont Bakery, North Haledon *Also called Mini Frost Foods Corporation (G-7552)*
Belmont Whl Fence Mfg Inc 973 472-5121
112 Monroe St Garfield (07026) *(G-3723)*
Belting Industries Group LLC (HQ) 908 272-8591
1090 Lousons Rd Union (07083) *(G-11158)*
Beltor Manufacturing Corp 856 768-5570
50 Union Ave Ste 12 Berlin (08009) *(G-426)*
Bemis Company Inc 908 689-3000
31 State St Washington (07882) *(G-11577)*
Ben & Jerrys of Hoboken 201 792-1966
405 Washington St Hoboken (07030) *(G-4459)*
Ben Aharon & Son Inc 201 541-2388
15 Smith St Englewood (07631) *(G-2875)*

Ben Venuti 908 389-9999
512 North Ave Garwood (07027) *(G-3776)*

Benchmark Scientific Inc 908 769-5555
2600a Main St Sayreville (08872) *(G-9815)*

Benckiser N Reckitt Amer Inc 973 404-2600
399 Interpace Pkwy # 101 Parsippany (07054) *(G-7960)*

Benco Inc 973 575-4440
10 Madison Rd Ste E Fairfield (07004) *(G-3146)*

Benco Products New York, Fairfield *Also called Benco Inc (G-3146)*

Bender Enterprises, Union *Also called George J Bender Inc (G-11189)*

Benedict-Miller LLC (PA) 908 497-1477
123 N 8th St Kenilworth (07033) *(G-4944)*

Beneduce Vineyard 908 996-3823
1 Jeremiah Ln Pittstown (08867) *(G-8849)*

Benjamin Booth Company 609 859-1995
523 Meadowyck Ln Southampton (08088) *(G-10470)*

Benjamin Moore, Flanders *Also called Technical Coatings Co (G-3419)*

Benjamin Moore & Co (HQ) 201 573-9600
101 Paragon Dr Montvale (07645) *(G-6444)*

Benjamin Moore & Co 973 344-1200
134 Lister Ave Newark (07105) *(G-7105)*

Benjamin Moore & Co 973 569-5000
203 Kuller Rd Clifton (07011) *(G-1574)*

Benjamin Moore & Co 201 573-9600
1 Paragon Dr Ste 255 Montvale (07645) *(G-6445)*

Bennett Cabinets 732 548-1616
1251 Us Highway 1 Edison (08837) *(G-2471)*

Bennett Heat Trting Brzing Inc (PA) 973 589-0590
690 Ferry St Newark (07105) *(G-7106)*

Bentley Laboratories LLC (PA) 732 512-0200
111 Fieldcrest Ave Edison (08837) *(G-2472)*

Benton Bindery Inc 732 431-9064
43 Sycamore Ave Freehold (07728) *(G-3642)*

Benton Graphics Inc 609 587-4000
3 Industrial Dr Trenton (08619) *(G-11026)*

Ber Plastics Inc 973 839-2100
5 Curtis St Riverdale (07457) *(G-9475)*

Berat Corporation 609 953-7700
208 Route 70 Medford (08055) *(G-6065)*

Berennial International 973 675-6266
355 Main St Orange (07050) *(G-7818)*

Berezin Nilolai 856 692-6191
402 E Wheat Rd Vineland (08360) *(G-11329)*

Berg East Imports Inc 908 354-5252
120 E Gloucester Pike Barrington (08007) *(G-172)*

Berg Furniture USA, Barrington *Also called Berg East Imports Inc (G-172)*

Bergen Cable Technology LLC (PA) 973 276-9596
343 Kaplan Dr Fairfield (07004) *(G-3147)*

Bergen Cnty Crtrdge Xchnge LLC 201 493-8182
268 Greenwood Ave Midland Park (07432) *(G-6222)*

Bergen Digital Graphics LLC 201 825-0011
346 State Rt 17 Upper Saddle River (07458) *(G-11274)*

Bergen Homestate Corp 201 372-9740
9 Willow St Moonachie (07074) *(G-6507)*

Bergen Instant Printing Inc 201 945-7303
350 Broad Ave Ridgefield (07657) *(G-9351)*

Bergen International LLC (PA) 201 299-4499
196 Paterson Ave Ste 202 East Rutherford (07073) *(G-2285)*

Bergen Manufacturing & Supply 201 854-3461
2025 85th St North Bergen (07047) *(G-7434)*

Bergen Marzipan & Chocolate 201 385-8343
205 S Washington Ave Bergenfield (07621) *(G-383)*

Bergen Open Mri 201 652-1213
1 W Ridgewood Ave Ste G2 Paramus (07652) *(G-7858)*

Bergen Screen Printing, North Haledon *Also called Acey Industries Inc (G-7547)*

Bergen Sign Company Inc (PA) 973 742-7755
161 E Railway Ave Paterson (07503) *(G-8222)*

Bergenline Gelato LLC 201 861-1100
7903 Bergenline Ave North Bergen (07047) *(G-7435)*

Bergio International Inc (PA) 973 227-3230
12 Daniel Rd Fairfield (07004) *(G-3148)*

Berje Incorporated (PA) 973 748-8980
700 Blair Rd Carteret (07008) *(G-1253)*

Berk Gold Stamping Corporation (PA) 973 786-6052
196 Pequest Rd Andover (07821) *(G-49)*

Berkeley Times, Lakehurst *Also called Micro Media Publications Inc (G-5059)*

Berkeley Varitronics Systems 732 548-3737
255 Liberty St Metuchen (08840) *(G-6096)*

Berlitz Languages US Inc (HQ) 609 759-5371
7 Roszel Rd Fl 3 Princeton (08540) *(G-9014)*

Berlitz Publishing Company Inc 609 514-9650
7 Roszel Rd Princeton (08540) *(G-9015)*

Bernafon LLC 888 941-4203
2501 Cottontail Ln # 102 Somerset (08873) *(G-10069)*

Bernard D Ascenzo 856 795-0511
61 Centre St Haddonfield (08033) *(G-4056)*

Bernard Miller Fabricators 856 541-9499
1135 Mount Ephraim Ave Camden (08103) *(G-1043)*

Bernardaud Na Inc 973 274-3555
1 Jacobus Ave Kearny (07032) *(G-4864)*

Bernardsville News 908 766-3900
17 Morristown Rd Bernardsville (07924) *(G-448)*

Bernardsville Print Center, Bernardsville *Also called R & B Printing Inc (G-454)*

Berry Blast Smoothies LLC 856 692-6174
1194 Sharp Rd Vineland (08360) *(G-11330)*

Berry Business Forms, Cranford *Also called Berry Business Procedure Co (G-1899)*

Berry Business Procedure Co 908 272-6464
6 Park St Cranford (07016) *(G-1899)*

Berry Global Inc 732 356-2870
87 Lincoln Blvd Middlesex (08846) *(G-6151)*

Berry Global Inc 908 353-3850
100 Dowd Ave Elizabeth (07206) *(G-2714)*

Berry Global Inc 980 689-1660
190 Strykers Rd Phillipsburg (08865) *(G-8642)*

Berry Global Inc 908 454-0900
190 Strykers Rd Phillipsburg (08865) *(G-8643)*

Berry Global Inc 609 395-4199
4 Aurora Dr Ste 403 Cranbury (08512) *(G-1814)*

Berry Global Inc 718 205-3115
322 3rd St Elizabeth (07206) *(G-2715)*

Berry Global Films LLC (HQ) 201 641-6600
95 Chestnut Ridge Rd Montvale (07645) *(G-6446)*

Bert's Cake Studio, Lawrence Township *Also called Advisory Dumas Group LLC (G-5239)*

Bertolotti LLC 201 941-3116
54 Industrial Ave Fairview (07022) *(G-3358)*

Bertone Aromatics 201 444-9821
26 Dora Ave Waldwick (07463) *(G-11441)*

Bertot Industries Inc 973 267-0006
23 Malcolm St Ste 1 Morristown (07960) *(G-6695)*

Besam Entrance Solutions, Hamilton *Also called Assa Abloy Entrance Systems US (G-4104)*

Beseech Ltd Liability Company 908 461-7888
259 East Rd Belford (07718) *(G-286)*

Best American Hands 203 247-2028
475 Bloy St Hillside (07205) *(G-4398)*

Best Cast, River Edge *Also called Zsombor Antal Designs Inc (G-9468)*

Best Draperies Inc 856 429-5453
1 Kresson Rd Cherry Hill (08034) *(G-1347)*

Best Drapery & Blind Mfg Co, Cherry Hill *Also called Best Draperies Inc (G-1347)*

Best Drapery and Design, Cherry Hill *Also called Best Drapery Inc (G-1348)*

Best Drapery Inc 856 429-2242
1 Crescent Way Cherry Hill (08002) *(G-1348)*

Best Electric Motor Co, Freehold *Also called Motors and Drives Inc (G-3672)*

Best Linen Factory Inc 973 279-8244
93 Harrison St Ste 6 Paterson (07501) *(G-8223)*

Best of Farms LLC 201 512-8400
12-17 River Rd Fair Lawn (07410) *(G-3083)*

Best Pmbooks.com, Mountainside *Also called Writers & Poets (G-6890)*

Best Provision Co Inc (PA) 973 242-5000
144 Avon Ave Newark (07108) *(G-7107)*

Best Tile of New Jersey 732 390-7700
272 State Route 18 Ste 3 East Brunswick (08816) *(G-2137)*

Best Value Rugs & Carpets Inc 732 752-3528
334 Rt 22 W Dunellen (08812) *(G-2127)*

Bestar, Manalapan *Also called Onwards Inc (G-5859)*

Bestmark National LLC 862 772-4863
171 Coit St Irvington (07111) *(G-4578)*

Bestwall LLC 856 966-7600
1101 S Front St Camden (08103) *(G-1044)*

Bestwork Inds For The Blind 856 424-2510
1940 Olney Ave 200 Cherry Hill (08003) *(G-1349)*

Beta Industries Corp 201 939-2400
707 Commercial Ave Carlstadt (07072) *(G-1130)*

Beta Plastics 201 933-1400
120 Amor Ave Carlstadt (07072) *(G-1131)*

Beta Tech, Carlstadt *Also called Beta Industries Corp (G-1130)*

Betco Glass Inc 856 327-4301
824 Columbia Ave Millville (08332) *(G-6286)*

Beterrific Corp (PA) 201 735-7711
900 Palisade Ave Apt 1d Fort Lee (07024) *(G-3546)*

Bethel Bindery 609 296-5043
1500 Route 539 Ltl Egg Hbr (08087) *(G-5642)*

Bethel Industries Inc 201 656-8222
3423 John F Kennedy Blvd Jersey City (07307) *(G-4717)*

Betsy & Adam Ltd 212 302-3750
90 Dayton Ave Ste 36 Passaic (07055) *(G-8128)*

Better Foods Jeyer LLC 888 717-6412
185 Industrial Ave Ridgefield Park (07660) *(G-9398)*

Better Image Graphics Inc 856 262-0735
1041 Glassboro Rd Ste E6 Williamstown (08094) *(G-12080)*

Better Listen LLC 917 623-9834
492c Cedar Ln Teaneck (07666) *(G-10744)*

Better Sleep Inc 908 464-2200
100 Readington Rd Branchburg (08876) *(G-643)*

Better Team USA Corporation 973 365-0947
95b Industrial St E Clifton (07012) *(G-1575)*

Beverage Works Nj Inc 973 439-5700
10 Dwight Pl Fairfield (07004) *(G-3149)*

Beverage Works Nj Inc (PA) 732 938-7600
1800 State Route 34 # 203 Wall Township (07719) *(G-11466)*

A
L
P
H
A
B
E
T
I
C

Beverly Manufacturing Co Inc.................856 764-7898
63 Webster St Riverside (08075) *(G-9493)*
Beverly Transformers, Riverside *Also called Beverly Manufacturing Co Inc (G-9493)*
Bezerra Corporation.................973 595-7775
232 Union Blvd Totowa (07512) *(G-10935)*
Bezwada Biomedical LLC.................908 281-7529
15 Ilene Ct Ste 1 Hillsborough (08844) *(G-4320)*
Bfhj Holdings Inc (PA).................908 730-6280
26 Chestnut Ridge Rd Montvale (07645) *(G-6447)*
Bga Construction Inc (PA).................973 809-9745
321 Changebridge Rd Pine Brook (07058) *(G-8689)*
Bgs Inc.................732 442-5000
910 E County Line Rd # 101 Lakewood (08701) *(G-5084)*
Bhamra Chain Manufacturing.................908 686-4555
1020 Springfield Rd Union (07083) *(G-11159)*
Bhavika Fuel LLC.................609 926-4500
45 W Laurel Dr Somers Point (08244) *(G-10045)*
Biach, Somerset *Also called Hydratight Operations Inc (G-10110)*
Biazzo Dairy Products Inc.................201 941-8579
1145 Edgewater Ave Ridgefield (07657) *(G-9352)*
Bib and Tucker Inc (PA).................201 489-9600
51 Main St Hackensack (07601) *(G-3881)*
Bie Real Estate Holdings LLC.................856 691-9765
3539 Reilly Ct Vineland (08360) *(G-11331)*
Bierman-Everett Foundry Co.................973 373-8800
7 Speir Dr South Orange (07079) *(G-10301)*
Big 3 Precision Products Inc.................856 293-1400
30 Gorton Rd Millville (08332) *(G-6287)*
Big Apple Jewelry Mfg.................201 531-1600
62 Railroad Ave East Rutherford (07073) *(G-2286)*
Big Bucks Enterprises Inc.................908 320-7009
55 Willow St Washington (07882) *(G-11578)*
Big Daddys Sports Haven.................856 453-9009
595 Sherman Ave Millville (08332) *(G-6288)*
Big Dog Natural, Lakewood *Also called Gwenstone Inc (G-5131)*
Big Eye Lamp Inc.................732 557-9400
870 Route 530 Ste 2 Whiting (08759) *(G-12065)*
Big Red Pin LLC.................732 993-9765
28 May St Apt 1 Edison (08837) *(G-2473)*
Bigelow Components Corp.................973 467-1200
74 Diamond Rd Springfield (07081) *(G-10543)*
Bigflysports Inc.................201 653-4414
60 Metro Way Ste 2 Secaucus (07094) *(G-9868)*
Bigflysports Com, Secaucus *Also called Bigflysports Inc (G-9868)*
Bihler of America Inc.................908 213-9001
85 Industrial Rd Bldg B Phillipsburg (08865) *(G-8644)*
Bildisco Door Mfg, West Orange *Also called Bildisco Mfg Inc (G-11889)*
Bildisco Mfg Inc.................973 673-2400
21 Central Ave West Orange (07052) *(G-11889)*
Bill Chambers Sheet Metal.................856 848-4774
371 Glassboro Rd Ste 5 Woodbury Heights (08097) *(G-12174)*
Bill's Canvas Shop, Woodbine *Also called G & J Solutions Inc (G-12142)*
Billiards and Bars, Asbury *Also called Silverthorne Furniture Corp (G-73)*
Billows Electric Supply Co Inc (PA).................856 751-2200
1813 Underwood Blvd Delran (08075) *(G-2010)*
Bills Printing Service Inc.................609 888-1841
2829 S Broad St Trenton (08610) *(G-11027)*
Billy D Dumpster Service LLC.................609 465-5990
1 Kimbles Beach Rd Cape May Court House (08210) *(G-1110)*
Billykirk.................201 222-9092
150 Bay St Fl 3 Jersey City (07302) *(G-4718)*
Bilt Rite Tool & Die Co Inc.................973 227-2882
29 Montesano Rd Fairfield (07004) *(G-3150)*
Bimbo Bakeries Usa Inc.................732 886-1881
160 Airport Rd Ste 4 Lakewood (08701) *(G-5085)*
Bimbo Bakeries Usa Inc.................732 390-7715
5 Alvin Ct East Brunswick (08816) *(G-2138)*
Bimbo Bakeries Usa Inc.................856 435-0500
1340 Blckwood Clemtons Rd Clementon (08021) *(G-1530)*
Bimbo Bakeries Usa Inc.................973 872-6167
100 Riverview Dr Wayne (07470) *(G-11609)*
Bimbo Bakeries USA Inc.................973 256-8200
930 Riverview Dr Ste 100 Totowa (07512) *(G-10936)*
Bimini Bay Outfitters Ltd.................201 529-3550
43 Mckee Dr Ste 1 Mahwah (07430) *(G-5752)*
Bind-Rite Graphics Inc.................201 863-8100
100 Castle Rd Secaucus (07094) *(G-9869)*
Bind-Rite Robbinsville LLC.................609 208-1917
1 Applegate Dr Robbinsville (08691) *(G-9511)*
Bind-Rite Services Inc.................201 440-5585
16 Horizon Blvd South Hackensack (07606) *(G-10255)*
Bindgraphics Inc.................908 245-1110
490 W 1st Ave Roselle (07203) *(G-9662)*
Bindi Dessert, Kearny *Also called Bindi North America Inc (G-4865)*
Bindi North America Inc (PA).................973 812-8118
630 Belleville Tpke Kearny (07032) *(G-4865)*
Binding Products Inc.................212 947-1192
430 Communipaw Ave Ste 1 Jersey City (07304) *(G-4719)*

Binex Line Corp.................201 662-7600
2 Executive Dr Ste 755 Fort Lee (07024) *(G-3547)*
Bio Compression Systems Inc.................201 939-0716
120 W Commercial Ave Moonachie (07074) *(G-6508)*
Bio-Chem Fluidics Inc.................973 263-3001
85 Fulton St Unit 12 Boonton (07005) *(G-557)*
Bio-Chem Valve, Boonton *Also called Bio-Chem Fluidics Inc (G-557)*
Bio-Key International Inc (PA).................732 359-1100
3349 Hwy 138 Ste E Wall Township (07719) *(G-11467)*
Bio-Nature Labs Ltd Lblty Co.................732 738-5550
195 Campus Dr Edison (08837) *(G-2474)*
Bioactive Resources LLC.................908 561-3114
138 Sylvania Pl South Plainfield (07080) *(G-10337)*
Biochemical Sciences Inc.................856 467-1813
200 Commodore Dr Swedesboro (08085) *(G-10683)*
Bioclimatic Air Systems LLC.................856 764-4300
600 Delran Pkwy Ste D Delran (08075) *(G-2011)*
Bioclimatic Inc (PA).................856 764-4300
600 Delran Pkwy Ste D Delran (08075) *(G-2012)*
Biodynamics LLC (HQ).................201 227-9255
84 Honeck St Englewood (07631) *(G-2876)*
Biogenesis Inc.................201 678-1992
296 Washington Ave Hackensack (07601) *(G-3882)*
Biogenesis-Labs, Hackensack *Also called Biogenesis Inc (G-3882)*
Biomedicon.................856 778-1880
30 E Central Ave Moorestown (08057) *(G-6563)*
Biomedtrix LLC.................973 331-7800
9 Whippany Rd Bldg B2-7 Whippany (07981) *(G-12012)*
Biomedtrix LLC.................973 331-7800
50 Intervale Rd Ste 5 Boonton (07005) *(G-558)*
Biomet Bone Healing Tech, Parsippany *Also called Ebi LLC (G-7995)*
Biomet Fair Lawn LP.................201 797-7300
20-01 Pollitt Dr Fair Lawn (07410) *(G-3084)*
Biomet Spine and Biomet Trauma, Parsippany *Also called Ebi LP (G-7996)*
Bionomic Industries Inc.................201 529-1094
777 Corporate Dr Mahwah (07430) *(G-5753)*
Bionpharma Inc.................609 380-3313
600 Alexander Rd Ste 2-4b Princeton (08540) *(G-9016)*
Biopharm International, Iselin *Also called Advanstar Communications Inc (G-4608)*
Biopharma Research Council.................732 403-3137
1 Sheila Dr Tinton Falls (07724) *(G-10824)*
Biophore LLC.................609 275-3713
4510 Quail Ridge Dr Plainsboro (08536) *(G-8876)*
Bios International Corp.................973 492-8400
10 Park Pl Ste 3 Butler (07405) *(G-998)*
Biosearch Medical Products Inc.................908 252-0595
35 Industrial Pkwy Branchburg (08876) *(G-644)*
Biotech Atlantic Inc.................732 389-4789
6 Industrial Way W Ste E1 Eatontown (07724) *(G-2385)*
Biotech Support Group LLC.................732 613-1967
29 Hershey Rd East Brunswick (08816) *(G-2139)*
Biovail Distribution Company.................908 927-1400
700 Us Highway 202/206 Bridgewater (08807) *(G-822)*
Bioxygen Distribution Corp.................732 212-1799
370 Ocean Ave Sea Bright (07760) *(G-9859)*
Bipore Inc.................201 767-1993
31 Industrial Pkwy Northvale (07647) *(G-7575)*
Birds Beware Corporation.................732 671-6377
50 Townsend Dr Middletown (07748) *(G-6212)*
Birds Eye Foods Inc (HQ).................585 383-1850
121 Woodcrest Rd Cherry Hill (08003) *(G-1350)*
Birds Eye Foods Inc.................920 435-5300
399 Jefferson Rd Parsippany (07054) *(G-7961)*
Birnn Chocolates Inc.................732 214-8680
314 Cleveland Ave Highland Park (08904) *(G-4301)*
Bisaga Inc.................856 784-7966
212 Ashland Ave Somerdale (08083) *(G-10039)*
Bishop Ascendant Inc.................973 210-5298
1083 Bloomfield Ave West Caldwell (07006) *(G-11768)*
Bistis Press Printing Co.................973 373-8033
1310 Clinton Ave Irvington (07111) *(G-4579)*
Bitro Group Inc.................201 641-1004
300 Lodi St Hackensack (07601) *(G-3883)*
Bittner Industries Inc.................856 817-8400
2060 Springdale Rd # 700 Cherry Hill (08003) *(G-1351)*
Bitwine Inc.................888 866-9435
4 Thatcher Rd Tenafly (07670) *(G-10782)*
Bivalve Packing Inc (HQ).................856 785-0270
6957 Miller Ave Port Norris (08349) *(G-8979)*
Biwal Manufacturing Co Inc.................973 778-0105
48 Industrial St W Clifton (07012) *(G-1576)*
Bk Machine Shop.................856 457-7150
586 N West Blvd Vineland (08360) *(G-11332)*
Bkh Electronics.................210 410-2757
9j Brookside Hts Wanaque (07465) *(G-11531)*
Bkt Exim Us Inc (HQ).................732 817-1400
960 Holmdel Rd Ste 2-02 Holmdel (07733) *(G-4509)*
Bkt Tires Inc.................844 258-8473
960 Holmdel Rd Ste 2 Holmdel (07733) *(G-4510)*

Blacher Canvas Products Inc 732 968-3666
604 Bound Brook Rd Dunellen (08812) *(G-2128)*

Black & Decker (us) Inc 201 475-3524
213 Us Highway 46 Elmwood Park (07407) *(G-2806)*

Black Lagoon Inc 609 815-1654
78 Orourke Dr Trenton (08691) *(G-11028)*

Black Prince, Clifton *Also called Prince Black Distillery Inc (G-1704)*

Black Sea Fisheries 973 553-1580
306 Whiteman St Apt 6 Fort Lee (07024) *(G-3548)*

Blackhawk Cre Corporation (PA) 856 887-0162
25 New Market St Salem (08079) *(G-9803)*

Blades Landscaping Inc 856 779-7665
2028 Briggs Rd Mount Laurel (08054) *(G-6783)*

Blades Ldscpg Lawn Maint & Ir, Mount Laurel *Also called Blades Landscaping Inc (G-6783)*

Blanc Industries Inc (PA) 973 537-0090
88 King St Ste 1 Dover (07801) *(G-2078)*

Blankets Inc 973 589-7800
26 Blanchard St Newark (07105) *(G-7108)*

Blaustein M Furs, Short Hills *Also called M Blaustein Inc (G-9980)*

Blavor Inc 973 265-4165
1 Mountain Ave Montville (07045) *(G-6483)*

Blazing Visuals 732 781-1401
2138 Bridge Ave Point Pleasant Boro (08742) *(G-8933)*

Bleema Manufacturing Corp 973 371-1771
517 Lyons Ave Irvington (07111) *(G-4580)*

Blispak Acquisition Corp 973 884-4141
1 Apollo Dr Ste 3 Whippany (07981) *(G-12013)*

Blissful Bites 973 670-6928
36 Butternut Dr Vernon (07462) *(G-11296)*

Blitz Safe of America Inc 201 569-5000
33 Honeck St Englewood (07631) *(G-2877)*

Blizzard Parts & Service, Paterson *Also called P & S Blizzard Corporation (G-8358)*

Blonder Tongue Labs Inc (PA) 732 679-4000
1 Jake Brown Rd Old Bridge (08857) *(G-7775)*

Bloomfield Drapery Co Inc 973 777-3566
948 Paterson Ave Ste A East Rutherford (07073) *(G-2287)*

Bloomfield Iron Co Inc 973 748-7040
21 Florence Ave Belleville (07109) *(G-296)*

Bloomfield Life Inc 973 233-5001
632 Pompton Ave Cedar Grove (07009) *(G-1273)*

Bloomfield Manufacturing Co (PA) 973 575-8900
29 Crosby Ln Oakland (07436) *(G-7676)*

Bloomfield News LLC 973 226-2127
172 Orton Rd West Caldwell (07006) *(G-11769)*

Blu-J2 LLC 201 750-1407
91 Alpine Ct Demarest (07627) *(G-2026)*

Blue Apple Books LLC 973 763-8191
515 Valley St Ste 170 Maplewood (07040) *(G-5915)*

Blue Blade Corp 908 272-2620
123 N 8th St Kenilworth (07033) *(G-4945)*

Blue Blade Steel, Kenilworth *Also called Blue Blade Corp (G-4945)*

Blue Chip Industries Inc 908 704-1466
50 Old Camplain Rd Somerville (08876) *(G-10202)*

Blue Claw Mfg & Supply Company 856 696-4366
118 Clover Ln Richland (08350) *(G-9349)*

Blue Dog Graphics, Hackensack *Also called Typestyle Inc (G-3987)*

Blue Dome Inc 646 415-9331
335 Clifton Ave Clifton (07011) *(G-1577)*

Blue Dome Press, Clifton *Also called Blue Dome Inc (G-1577)*

Blue Fish Clothing Inc 908 996-3720
62 Trenton Ave Frnt Frnt Frenchtown (08825) *(G-3697)*

Blue Gauntlet Fencing Co, Saddle Brook *Also called Blue Gauntlet Fencing Gear Inc (G-9755)*

Blue Gauntlet Fencing Gear Inc 201 797-3332
280 N Midland Ave Bldg W Saddle Brook (07663) *(G-9755)*

Blue Light Welding & Fabg LLC 856 629-5891
2164 Grant Ave Williamstown (08094) *(G-12081)*

Blue Marlin Systems Inc 973 722-0816
2 Ranney Rd Long Valley (07853) *(G-5635)*

Blue Monkey Inc 201 805-0055
456b Sylvan St Saddle Brook (07663) *(G-9756)*

Blue Ocean Pharma LLC 908 428-4668
4 Spring Hill Rd Annandale (08801) *(G-57)*

Blue Parachute LLC 732 767-1320
263 Amboy Ave Ste 1 Metuchen (08840) *(G-6097)*

Blue Ribbon Awards Inc 732 560-0046
12 Worlds Fair Dr Ste J Somerset (08873) *(G-10070)*

Blue Ring Stencils LLC (PA) 866 763-3873
140 Mount Holly By Pass Lumberton (08048) *(G-5651)*

Bluebird Auto Rentl Systems LP (PA) 973 989-2423
200 Mineral Springs Rd Dover (07801) *(G-2079)*

Blueclone Networks LLC 609 944-8433
103 Carnegie Ctr Ste 300 Princeton (08540) *(G-9017)*

Bluewater Inc 973 532-1225
50 Division Ave Ste 42 Millington (07946) *(G-6260)*

Bluewater Industries Inc 609 427-1012
1089 Rt 47 Dennisville (08214) *(G-2028)*

Bluewater Wldg & Fabrication, Dennisville *Also called Bluewater Industries Inc (G-2028)*

Blusa Defense Manufacturing, Barrington *Also called Bright Lights Usa Inc (G-173)*

Blutek Power Inc 973 594-1800
300 1 State Rte 17 Ste B2 Lodi (07644) *(G-5577)*

Bm USA Incorporated (HQ) 800 624-5499
75 Triangle Blvd Carlstadt (07072) *(G-1132)*

BMA of Colonia 732 382-7333
1250 State Rt 27 Colonia (07067) *(G-1777)*

Bmb Machining LLC 973 256-4010
86 Lackawanna Ave 208b Woodland Park (07424) *(G-12211)*

BMC Software Inc 973 401-7700
6 Campus Dr Ste 7 Parsippany (07054) *(G-7962)*

BMC Software Inc 703 761-0400
50 Tice Blvd Woodcliff Lake (07677) *(G-12182)*

Bmca, Parsippany *Also called Standard Industries Inc (G-8092)*

Bmca Holdings Corporation (HQ) 973 628-3000
1361 Alps Rd Wayne (07470) *(G-11610)*

Bmg Entertainment, Rutherford *Also called Sony Music Holdings Inc (G-9745)*

Bmk Enterprises, Rockaway *Also called Bruce Kindberg (G-9554)*

Bmo Bindery, Newark *Also called Abby Bindery Co Inc (G-7069)*

BMW Group, Woodcliff Lake *Also called BMW of North America LLC (G-12183)*

BMW of North America LLC (HQ) 201 307-4000
300 Chestnut Ridge Rd Woodcliff Lake (07677) *(G-12183)*

Bng Industries LLC 862 229-2414
1 Cape May St Ste 2 Harrison (07029) *(G-4173)*

BNH Enterprise LLC 201 815-0546
76 Romano Dr Dumont (07628) *(G-2116)*

BNP Media Inc 201 291-9001
210 E Rte 4 Ste 203 Paramus (07652) *(G-7859)*

BNS Enterprises Inc 908 285-6556
186 Wildflower Ln Hillsborough (08844) *(G-4321)*

BO&nic, Wall Township *Also called Nicholas Oliver LLC (G-11499)*

Boards and Beams Co LLC 973 299-6100
1275 Blmfield Ave Bldg 10 Towaco (07082) *(G-10989)*

Bob's Custom Docks, Sandyston *Also called Custom Docks Inc (G-9811)*

Bobit Business Media Inc 856 596-0999
49 S Maple Ave Marlton (08053) *(G-5965)*

Boc Gases, Sparta *Also called Linde LLC (G-10510)*

Boc Group Inc 908 665-2400
575 Mountain Ave New Providence (07974) *(G-7030)*

Boccella Precast LLC 856 767-3861
324 New Brooklyn Rd Berlin (08009) *(G-427)*

Bodine Tool and Machine Co Inc 856 234-7800
1273 N Church St Ste 104 Moorestown (08057) *(G-6564)*

Body Boost Labs Ltd Lblty Co 609 519-1070
36 W Brookline Dr Laurel Springs (08021) *(G-5232)*

Body Wrappers, Elizabeth *Also called Garylin Togs (G-2737)*

Body Wrappers, Elizabeth *Also called Attitudes In Dressing Inc (G-2711)*

Bodybio Inc (PA) 856 825-8338
45 Reese Rd Millville (08332) *(G-6289)*

Bodycote Thermal Proc Inc 908 245-0717
304 Cox St Roselle (07203) *(G-9663)*

Bodycote Thermal Processing 908 245-0717
304 Cox St Roselle (07203) *(G-9664)*

Boeing 908 464-6959
400 Connell Dr Ste 6200 Berkeley Heights (07922) *(G-401)*

Boeing Company 610 591-1978
800 Arlington Blvd Swedesboro (08085) *(G-10684)*

Bogen Communications Inc 201 934-8500
1200 Macarthur Blvd # 303 Mahwah (07430) *(G-5754)*

Bogen Corporation (PA) 201 934-8500
50 Spring St Ste 1 Ramsey (07446) *(G-9237)*

Bold Hat Makers, Newark *Also called Headwear Creations Inc (G-7188)*

Bolt Welding & Iron Works 609 393-3993
78 Wall St Trenton (08609) *(G-11029)*

Bolttech Mannings Inc 973 537-1576
321 Richard Mine Rd Ste 1 Wharton (07885) *(G-11981)*

Bolttech-Mannings, Wharton *Also called Bolttech Mannings Inc (G-11981)*

Bomar Crystal Company, Middlesex *Also called Bomar Exo Ltd Liability Co (G-6152)*

Bomar Exo Ltd Liability Co 732 356-7787
200b Wood Ave Middlesex (08846) *(G-6152)*

Bombardier Transportation 201 955-5874
1148 Newark Tpke Kearny (07032) *(G-4866)*

Bombardier Transportation 973 624-9300
60 Earhart Dr Newark (07114) *(G-7109)*

Bombardier Transportation 856 580-5609
700 Beideman Ave Camden (08105) *(G-1045)*

Bon Architectual Mill Work LLC 856 320-2872
9120 Pennsauken Hwy Pennsauken (08110) *(G-8487)*

Bon Chef Inc (PA) 973 383-8848
205 State Route 94 Lafayette (07848) *(G-5045)*

Bon Jour, Norwood *Also called Mt Embroidery & Promotions LLC (G-7629)*

Bon Jour Promotions, Norwood *Also called Bon-Jour Group LLC (G-7616)*

Bon Venture Services LLC 973 584-5699
34 Ironia Rd Flanders (07836) *(G-3402)*

Bon-Jour Group LLC 201 646-1070
1100 Blanch Ave Norwood (07648) *(G-7616)*

Bon-Ton Instant Blnds Intriors, Egg Harbor Township *Also called SF Lutz LLC (G-2696)*

Bondi Digital Publishing LLC 212 405-1655
33 Hilliard Ave Edgewater (07020) *(G-2434)*

A
L
P
H
A
B
E
T
I
C

Bonland Industries Inc (PA) 973 694-3211
50 Newark Pompton Tpke Wayne (07470) *(G-11611)*

Bonney-Vehslage Tool Co 973 589-6975
3 Dundar Rd Springfield (07081) *(G-10544)*

Bono USA Inc 973 978-7361
19 Gardner Rd Ste E Fairfield (07004) *(G-3151)*

Bookazine Co Inc (PA) 201 339-7777
75 Hook Rd Bayonne (07002) *(G-216)*

Bookcode Corp 732 742-0481
2312 Plaza Dr Woodbridge (07095) *(G-12147)*

Boomerang Systems Inc (PA) 973 538-1194
30a Vreeland Rd Florham Park (07932) *(G-3494)*

Boonton Electronics Corp 201 261-8797
25 Eastmans Rd Parsippany (07054) *(G-7963)*

Boonton Plastic Molding Co, Boonton Also called Valley Plastic Molding Co *(G-587)*

Boost Company, The, Riverside Also called Drink A Toast Company Inc *(G-9497)*

Bopp Films, Livingston Also called Inteplast Group Corporation *(G-5535)*

Borak Group Inc 718 665-8500
255 Us Highway 1 And 9 Jersey City (07306) *(G-4720)*

Borealis Compounds Inc 908 850-6200
176 Thomas Rd Port Murray (07865) *(G-8976)*

Boro Printing Inc 732 229-1899
813 Broadway West Long Branch (07764) *(G-11844)*

Borton Enterprises 856 453-9221
178 Woodruff Rd Bridgeton (08302) *(G-778)*

Boruch Trading Ltd Lblty Co 718 614-9575
69 Gudz Rd Lakewood (08701) *(G-5086)*

Bosco Products Inc 973 334-7534
441 Main Rd Towaco (07082) *(G-10990)*

Bossen Architectural Millwork 856 786-1100
1818 Bannard St Cinnaminson (08077) *(G-1449)*

Bossett Sailmakers, Manasquan Also called North Sales *(G-5876)*

Bostik Inc 856 848-8669
2000 Nolte Dr Paulsboro (08066) *(G-8414)*

Boston Scientific Corporation 973 709-7000
45 Barbour Pond Dr Wayne (07470) *(G-11612)*

Boston Tea Company LLC 201 440-3004
560 Hudson St Ste 1-5 Hackensack (07601) *(G-3884)*

Bot Beverages, Lawrenceville Also called Bot LLC *(G-5251)*

Bot LLC 609 439-1537
12 Clementon Way Lawrenceville (08648) *(G-5251)*

Bottos Gnine Itln Style Susage, Mount Royal Also called CW Brown Foods Inc *(G-6850)*

Boulevard Lunch Service Inc 732 381-5772
251 Willow Way Clark (07066) *(G-1498)*

Bouras Industries Inc (PA) 908 918-9400
25 Deforest Ave Ste 100 Summit (07901) *(G-10637)*

Bowmar Enterprises Inc 908 277-3000
558 Cent Ave New Providence (07974) *(G-7031)*

Boxworks Inc 856 456-9030
1100 Market St Bellmawr (08031) *(G-332)*

Boyds Pharmacy Inc 609 499-0100
306 Broad St Florence (08518) *(G-3476)*

Boyko Metal Finishing Co Inc (PA) 973 623-4254
100 Poinier St Newark (07114) *(G-7110)*

Boyko Metal Finishing Co Inc 973 623-4254
100 Poinier St Newark (07114) *(G-7111)*

Boyle Tool & Die Co Inc 856 853-1819
135 Crown Point Rd West Deptford (08086) *(G-11818)*

Bozak Inc 732 282-1556
204 State Route 71 Ste B1 Spring Lake (07762) *(G-10532)*

Bozzone Custom Woodwork Inc 973 334-5598
4 Taylortown Rd Montville (07045) *(G-6484)*

BP Corporation North Amer Inc 973 633-2200
1500 Valley Rd Wayne (07470) *(G-11613)*

BP Corporation North Amer Inc 908 474-5000
Park And Brunswick Ave Linden (07036) *(G-5353)*

BP Lubricants USA Inc (HQ) 973 633-2200
1500 Valley Rd Wayne (07470) *(G-11614)*

BP Machine Co Inc 732 251-0449
10 American Way Ste 3 Spotswood (08884) *(G-10527)*

BP Print Group Inc 732 905-9830
315 4th St Lakewood (08701) *(G-5087)*

Bps Worldwide Inc 856 874-0822
1860 Greentree Rd Cherry Hill (08003) *(G-1352)*

BR Welding Inc 732 363-8253
3 Brook Rd Howell (07731) *(G-4547)*

Brabantia USA Inc 201 933-3192
20 Murray Hill Pkwy # 260 East Rutherford (07073) *(G-2288)*

Bracco Diagnostics Inc (HQ) 609 514-2200
259 Prospect Plains Rd Monroe Township (08831) *(G-6378)*

Bracco Research USA Inc 609 514-2517
4c Cedarbrook Dr Cranbury (08512) *(G-1815)*

Bracco USA Inc (HQ) 609 514-2200
259 Prospect Plains Rd Monroe Township (08831) *(G-6379)*

Braco Manufacturing Inc 732 752-7777
4031b New Brunswick Ave South Plainfield (07080) *(G-10338)*

Brad Garman Designs 732 229-6670
30 New Ct Long Branch (07740) *(G-5621)*

Bradbury Burial Vault Co Inc 856 227-2555
761 Lower Landing Rd Blackwood (08012) *(G-473)*

Braddock Heat Treating Company 732 356-2906
123 Chimney Rock Rd Bridgewater (08807) *(G-823)*

Bradley Corrugated Box Co Inc 973 483-0505
900 S 2nd St Harrison (07029) *(G-4174)*

Brady Manufacturing Co, Allentown Also called Edward T Brady *(G-29)*

Braen Stone Company, Haledon Also called Stone Industries Inc *(G-4085)*

Brainstorm Cell Thrpeutics Inc 201 488-0460
3 University Plaza Dr Hackensack (07601) *(G-3885)*

Brainstorm Software Corp 856 234-4945
16 Apple Orchard Rd Moorestown (08057) *(G-6565)*

Brambila Jorge Stucco & Stone 856 451-2039
148 S Giles St Bridgeton (08302) *(G-779)*

Branchville Bagels Inc 973 948-7077
332 Us Highway 206 N Branchville (07826) *(G-727)*

Brand Aromatics Intl Inc 732 363-1204
1600 Oak St Lakewood (08701) *(G-5088)*

Branded Screen Printing 908 879-7411
45 Warren St Ste A Chester (07930) *(G-1434)*

Brasscraft Manufacturing Co 856 241-7700
1 Warner Ct Swedesboro (08085) *(G-10685)*

Bravo Pack Inc 856 872-2937
90 Twinbridge Dr Pennsauken (08110) *(G-8488)*

Brawer Bros Inc (PA) 973 238-0163
375 Diamond Bridge Ave Hawthorne (07506) *(G-4222)*

Brayco Inc 609 758-5235
951 County Hwy 537 Creamridge (08514) *(G-1942)*

Brayniac LLC 212 993-7222
80 River St Ste 5d Hoboken (07030) *(G-4460)*

Brazilian Press & Advertising 973 344-4555
78 Fillmore St Ste 1 Newark (07105) *(G-7112)*

Brazilian Voice 973 491-6200
412 Chestnut St Newark (07105) *(G-7113)*

Bread & Bagels 856 667-2333
1600 Church Rd Cherry Hill (08002) *(G-1353)*

Bread Guy Inc 973 881-9002
840 E 28th St Paterson (07513) *(G-8224)*

Brecoflex Co LLC 732 460-9500
222 Industrial Way W Eatontown (07724) *(G-2386)*

Breen Color Concentrates LLC 609 397-8200
11 Kari Dr Lambertville (08530) *(G-5210)*

Breeze-Eastern LLC (HQ) 973 602-1001
35 Melanie Ln Whippany (07981) *(G-12014)*

Breeze-Eastern LLC 973 602-1001
35 Melanie Ln Whippany (07981) *(G-12015)*

Brennan Penrod Contractors LLC 856 933-1100
420 Benigno Blvd Unit B Bellmawr (08031) *(G-333)*

Brenner Metal Products (PA) 973 778-2466
16 Main Ave Wallington (07057) *(G-11523)*

Brenner Metal Products 973 778-2466
51 Paterson Ave Wallington (07057) *(G-11524)*

Brenntag Specialties Inc (HQ) 800 732-0562
1 Cragwood Rd Ste 302 South Plainfield (07080) *(G-10339)*

Brent Material Company 908 686-3832
308 N 14th St Kenilworth (07033) *(G-4946)*

Brent River Corp (HQ) 908 722-6021
208 Cougar Ct Hillsborough (08844) *(G-4322)*

Brent River Corp 908 722-6021
208 Cougar Ct Hillsborough (08844) *(G-4323)*

Brentrick Inc 973 357-3579
527 E 39th St Paterson (07504) *(G-8225)*

Breure Sheet Metal Co Inc 973 772-6423
46 Walman Ave Clifton (07011) *(G-1578)*

Brewster Vaults & Monuments 856 785-1412
1017 Steep Run Rd Millville (08332) *(G-6290)*

Breyer Manufacturing, Wayne Also called Reeves International Inc *(G-11678)*

Brian Lenhart Interactive LLC 610 737-5314
2 Ridge Dr E Berkeley Heights (07922) *(G-402)*

Brian's Embroidery, Kenvil Also called Pro Image Promotions Inc *(G-5013)*

Briars Usa 732 821-7600
891 Georges Rd Monmouth Junction (08852) *(G-6332)*

Brick City Wheelchair RPS LLC 862 371-4311
92 Hansbury Ave Newark (07112) *(G-7114)*

Brick-Wall Corp (PA) 732 787-0225
25 1st Ave Ste 200 Atlantic Highlands (07716) *(G-109)*

Brick-Wall Corp 609 693-6223
2215 Lacey Rd Forked River (08731) *(G-3534)*

Bridgeport Parts Dist Ctr, Swedesboro Also called Daimler Trucks North Amer LLC *(G-10689)*

Bridgestate Foundry Corp 856 767-0400
175 Jackson Rd Berlin (08009) *(G-428)*

Bridgewater Wholesalers Inc (PA) 908 526-7555
210 Industrial Pkwy Branchburg (08876) *(G-645)*

Bridor USA Inc 856 691-8000
2260 Industrial Way Vineland (08360) *(G-11333)*

Bright Hrzons Fmly Sltions LLC 609 520-7501
890 Ridge Rd Monmouth Junction (08852) *(G-6333)*

Bright Ideas Usa LLC 732 886-8865
890 Morris Ave Lakewood (08701) *(G-5089)*

Bright Lights Usa Inc 856 546-5656
9th & Liberty Camden (08104) *(G-1046)*

(G-0000) Company's Geographic Section entry number

Bright Lights Usa Inc (PA) 856 546-5656
145 Shreve Ave Barrington (08007) *(G-173)*

Brighton Air 973 258-1500
21 Springfield Ave Springfield (07081) *(G-10545)*

Brilliant Brdcstg Concept Inc 732 287-9201
1871 Woodbridge Ave Ste 2 Edison (08817) *(G-2475)*

Brilliant Light Power Inc 609 490-0427
493 Old Trenton Rd East Windsor (08512) *(G-2371)*

Brim Electronics Inc 201 796-2886
120 Home Pl Lodi (07644) *(G-5578)*

Brim Technologies, Eatontown *Also called Bal-Edge Corporation (G-2384)*

Brimar Industries Inc 973 340-7889
64 Outwater Ln Ste 2 Garfield (07026) *(G-3724)*

Bringhurst Bros Inc 856 767-0110
38 W Taunton Rd Berlin (08009) *(G-429)*

Bringhurst Meats, Berlin *Also called Bringhurst Bros Inc (G-429)*

Brinker Displays, Dover *Also called Brinker Industries (G-2080)*

Brinker Industries 973 678-1200
88 King St Ste 1 Dover (07801) *(G-2080)*

Brisar Delvco, Paterson *Also called Delvco Pharma Packg Svcs Inc (G-8249)*

Brisar Delvco Packaging Svcs, Paterson *Also called Brisar Industries Inc (G-8226)*

Brisar Industries Inc 973 278-2500
150 E 7th St Paterson (07524) *(G-8226)*

Brisco Apparel Co Inc 718 715-7110
575 Prospect St Ste 230 Lakewood (08701) *(G-5090)*

Bristol-Donald Company Inc 973 589-2640
50 Roanoke Ave Newark (07105) *(G-7115)*

Bristol-Myers Squibb, Trenton *Also called E R Squibb & Sons Inter-AM (G-11056)*

Bristol-Myers Squibb, Princeton *Also called E R Squibb & Sons Inter-AM (G-9034)*

Bristol-Myers Squibb Company 800 332-2056
104 Georges Rd New Brunswick (08901) *(G-6948)*

Bristol-Myers Squibb Company 609 897-3771
777 Scudders Mill Rd Plainsboro (08536) *(G-8877)*

Bristol-Myers Squibb Company 609 419-5000
100 Nassau Park Blvd # 200 Princeton (08540) *(G-9018)*

Bristol-Myers Squibb Company 212 546-4000
311 Pnnington Rocky Hl Rd Pennington (08534) *(G-8444)*

Bristol-Myers Squibb Company 609 252-4875
Province Line Rd Rr 206 Princeton (08540) *(G-9019)*

Bristol-Myers Squibb Company 908 218-3700
685 Us Highway 202/206 Bridgewater (08807) *(G-824)*

Bristol-Myers Squibb Company 212 546-4000
171 Long Ave Hillside (07205) *(G-4399)*

Bristol-Myers Squibb Company 609 302-3000
3401 Princeton Pike Lawrenceville (08648) *(G-5252)*

Brite Concepts Inc 201 270-8544
90 W Palisade Ave Englewood (07631) *(G-2878)*

Brittingham Sftwr Design Inc 908 832-2691
440 Hwy 513 Califon (07830) *(G-1034)*

Brix City Brewing 201 440-0865
4 Alsan Way Little Ferry (07643) *(G-5495)*

Broadhurst Sheet Metal Works 973 304-4001
230 Warburton Ave Hawthorne (07506) *(G-4223)*

Broadview Technologies Inc 973 465-0077
7 Amsterdam St 33 Newark (07105) *(G-7116)*

Broadway Empress Entrmt Inc 973 991-0009
15-21 Oraton St Newark (07104) *(G-7117)*

Broadway Kleer-Guard Corp 609 662-3970
1 S Middlesex Ave Monroe Township (08831) *(G-6380)*

Brodie System Inc 908 862-8620
1539 W Elizabeth Ave Linden (07036) *(G-5354)*

Brogan Tennyson Group Inc 732 355-0700
2245 Us Highway 130 # 102 Dayton (08810) *(G-1956)*

Bromilows Candy Co (PA) 973 684-1496
350 Rifle Camp Rd Woodland Park (07424) *(G-12212)*

Brook Hollow Winery LLC 908 496-8200
594 State Hwy 94 Columbia (07832) *(G-1796)*

Brook Meadow Inventions 973 300-0419
1 Brooks Plz Newton (07860) *(G-7382)*

Brook Metal Products Inc 908 355-1601
16 Sunset Rd Lawrence Township (08648) *(G-5241)*

Brook Saddle Ridge Equest 609 953-1600
10 Saddle Brook Ct Shamong (08088) *(G-9968)*

Brookaire Company LLC 973 473-7527
329 Veterans Blvd Carlstadt (07072) *(G-1133)*

Brookdale Senior Living Inc 856 772-9400
207 Laurel Rd Voorhees (08043) *(G-11423)*

Brookline Chemical Corp 301 767-1177
26 Hanes Dr Wayne (07470) *(G-11615)*

Brooklyn Bean Roastery, South Plainfield *Also called Two Rivers Coffee LLC (G-10443)*

Brooks Power Systems, Hamilton *Also called Power Brooks Co LLC (G-4121)*

Brother International Corp (HQ) 908 704-1700
200 Crossing Blvd Bridgewater (08807) *(G-825)*

Brothers Sheet Metal (PA) 973 579-1788
15 Grandview Dr Newton (07860) *(G-7383)*

Brothers Sheet Metal Inc 973 228-3221
15 Grand Roseland (07068) *(G-9648)*

Brown and Perkins Inc 609 655-1150
1193 Cranbury S River Rd Cranbury (08512) *(G-1816)*

Brown Chemical Co Inc (PA) 201 337-0900
302 W Oakland Ave Oakland (07436) *(G-7677)*

Browns Awning Co, Ocean City *Also called Robert Brown (G-7756)*

Browns Welding Service 732 988-9530
105 Oxonia Ave Neptune (07753) *(G-6902)*

Bruce Kindberg 973 664-0195
305 Us Highway 46 Rockaway (07866) *(G-9554)*

Bruce McCoy Sr 609 217-6153
5402 Tall Pnes Pine Hill (08021) *(G-8721)*

Bruce Supply Corp 732 661-0500
300 Smith St Keasbey (08832) *(G-4925)*

Bruce Teleky Inc 718 965-9694
430 Communipaw Ave Ste 2 Jersey City (07304) *(G-4721)*

Bruderer Machinery Inc (PA) 201 941-2121
1200 Hendricks Cswy Ridgefield (07657) *(G-9353)*

Bruere Heating & AC, Clifton *Also called Breure Sheet Metal Co Inc (G-1578)*

Bruker Ost LLC 732 541-1300
600 Milik St Carteret (07008) *(G-1254)*

Brummer's Chocolates, Westfield *Also called George Brummer (G-11925)*

Brunnquell Iron Works Inc 609 409-6101
2557 Us Highway 130 Ste 3 Cranbury (08512) *(G-1817)*

Brunswick Hot Mix Corp 908 233-4444
141 Central Ave Westfield (07090) *(G-11922)*

Brunswick Signs & Exhibit 732 246-2500
1510 Jersey Ave North Brunswick (08902) *(G-7508)*

Brunswick Waste System 908 369-2223
Beekman Ln Somerville (08876) *(G-10203)*

Brusso Hardware LLC 212 337-8510
67-69 Greylock Ave Belleville (07109) *(G-297)*

Bryan Snook 888 747-3250
90 Washington Valley Rd Bedminster (07921) *(G-268)*

Bsa Consulting, Somerset *Also called Business Software Applications (G-10071)*

BSC USA LLC 908 487-4437
111 Grand Ave Ste 220 Palisades Park (07650) *(G-7836)*

BSD Industries Ltd Liability 732 534-4341
110 Columbus Ave S Lakewood (08701) *(G-5091)*

Bsdi, Califon *Also called Brittingham Sftwr Design Inc (G-1034)*

Bsi Corp 631 589-1118
52 E Centre St Ste 2 Nutley (07110) *(G-7643)*

Bsrm Inc 888 509-0668
691 Cornwallis Dr Mount Laurel (08054) *(G-6784)*

BT Industries Inc 201 866-0201
6605-09 Smith Ave North Bergen (07047) *(G-7436)*

Btech Inc 973 983-1120
10 Astro Pl Ste A Rockaway (07866) *(G-9555)*

Btm, Paterson *Also called Burlington Textile Machinery (G-8227)*

Bucati Leather Inc 732 254-0480
427 Whitehead Ave Ste 2 South River (08882) *(G-10459)*

Bucci Management Co Inc 609 567-8808
603 N 1st Rd Hammonton (08037) *(G-4134)*

Buckets Plus Inc 732 545-0420
345 Sandford St New Brunswick (08901) *(G-6949)*

Buckhead Beef N E, Edison *Also called Buckhead Meat Company (G-2476)*

Buckhead Meat Company 732 661-4900
220 Raritan Center Pkwy Edison (08837) *(G-2476)*

Bucks County Brewing Co Inc 609 929-0148
80 Lambert Ln Ste 120 Lambertville (08530) *(G-5211)*

Budd Oil, Dover *Also called Region Oil (G-2107)*

Budget Banners, Ocean *Also called Adpro Imprints (G-7713)*

Budget Instant Printing, Clark *Also called Phillip Balderose (G-1512)*

Budget Print Center 973 743-0073
332 Broad St Bloomfield (07003) *(G-503)*

Buhler Inc 201 847-0600
40 Whitney Rd Mahwah (07430) *(G-5755)*

Builders Firstsource Inc 856 767-3153
210 Williamstown Rd Berlin (08009) *(G-430)*

Buildgreen Solutions, Lakewood *Also called Bgs Inc (G-5084)*

Building Materials Corp Amer, Wayne *Also called Bmca Holdings Corporation (G-11610)*

Building Materials Mfg Corp 973 628-3000
1361 Alps Rd Wayne (07470) *(G-11616)*

Building Performance Eqp Inc 201 722-1414
80 Broadway Ste 101 Hillsdale (07642) *(G-4380)*

Bulbrite Industries Inc 201 531-5900
145 W Commercial Ave Moonachie (07074) *(G-6509)*

Bulkhaul (usa) Limited (HQ) 908 272-3100
485 Us Highway 1 S E230b Iselin (08830) *(G-4618)*

Bumble Bee Foods LLC 609 884-0440
994 Ocean Dr Cape May (08204) *(G-1091)*

Bumper Specialties Inc 856 345-7650
1607 Imperial Way West Deptford (08066) *(G-11819)*

Bunn Industries Incorporated (PA) 609 890-2900
2651 E State Street Ext Trenton (08619) *(G-11030)*

Buona Vita Inc 856 453-7972
1 S Industrial Blvd Bridgeton (08302) *(G-780)*

Buonaventura Bag and Cases LLC 212 960-3442
95 Main Ave Ste 1 Clifton (07014) *(G-1579)*

Buono Bagel-To The Max, Ramsey *Also called Frell Corp (G-9240)*

Burdol Inc 856 453-0336
1791 S Burlington Rd Bridgeton (08302) *(G-781)*

Burger Maker Inc 201 939-4747
666 16th St Carlstadt (07072) *(G-1134)*

Burgess Steel Holding LLC 201 871-3500
200 W Forest Ave Englewood (07631) *(G-2879)*

Burgiss Group LLC 201 427-9600
111 River St Fl 10th Hoboken (07030) *(G-4461)*

Burkley Case, Clifton *Also called Buonaventura Bag and Cases LLC (G-1579)*

Burling Instruments Inc 973 665-0601
16 River Rd Chatham (07928) *(G-1326)*

Burlington Atlantic Corp 732 888-7776
1 Crown Plz Hazlet (07730) *(G-4271)*

Burlington Cnty Endoscopy Ctr 609 267-1555
140 Mount Holly By Pass # 5 Lumberton (08048) *(G-5652)*

Burlington Coat Factory 908 994-9562
651 Kapkowski Rd Ste 30 Elizabeth (07201) *(G-2716)*

Burlington County Times, Willingboro *Also called Burlington Times Inc (G-12117)*

Burlington Design Center Inc 856 778-7772
3019 Marne Hwy Mount Laurel (08054) *(G-6785)*

Burlington Press Corporation 609 387-0030
328 High St Burlington (08016) *(G-960)*

Burlington Textile Machinery 973 279-5900
39 Mcbride Ave Paterson (07501) *(G-8227)*

Burlington Times Inc (HQ) 609 871-8000
4284 Route 130 Willingboro (08046) *(G-12117)*

Burns Link Manufacturing Co 856 429-6844
253 American Way Voorhees (08043) *(G-11424)*

Burpee Medsystems LLC 732 544-8900
15 Christopher Way Eatontown (07724) *(G-2387)*

Bush Refrigeration, Pennsauken *Also called Kohlder Manufacturing Inc (G-8540)*

Bushwick Metals LLC 908 604-1450
1641 New Market Ave South Plainfield (07080) *(G-10340)*

Bushwick Metals LLC 908 754-8700
1641 New Market Ave South Plainfield (07080) *(G-10341)*

Business Card Express, Marlton *Also called Five Macs Inc (G-5975)*

Business Cards Tomorrow 201 236-0088
11 Industrial Ave Upper Saddle River (07458) *(G-11275)*

Business Cards Tomorrow Inc 609 965-0808
129 Cincinnati Ave Egg Harbor City (08215) *(G-2658)*

Business Control Systems Corp 732 283-1301
1173 Green St Iselin (08830) *(G-4619)*

Business Dev Solutions Inc 856 433-8005
311 Hadleigh Dr Cherry Hill (08003) *(G-1354)*

Business Software Applications 908 500-9980
6 Sunny Ct Somerset (08873) *(G-10071)*

BUSINESS TODAY, Princeton *Also called Foundation For Student Comm (G-9046)*

Busted Knuckle 609 432-7383
100 Route Us 9 S Unit A Marmora (08223) *(G-6005)*

Butler Prtg & Laminating Inc 973 838-8550
250 Hamburg Tpke Butler (07405) *(G-999)*

Butler Sign Co., Wayne *Also called Four Way Enterprises Inc (G-11636)*

Butterfly Bakery Inc 973 815-1501
615 Bridle Path Wyckoff (07481) *(G-12246)*

Butterfly Bow Ties LLC 973 626-2536
911 Garden St Union (07083) *(G-11160)*

Buttonwood Enterprises LLC 201 505-1901
52 Winding Way Woodcliff Lake (07677) *(G-12184)*

Buy Buy Baby Inc (HQ) 908 688-0888
650 Liberty Ave Union (07083) *(G-11161)*

Buyers Laboratory, LLC, Fairfield *Also called Keypoint Intelligence LLC (G-3240)*

Buzzboard Inc 201 820-0697
1050 Wall St W Ste 630 Lyndhurst (07071) *(G-5672)*

Bway Corporation 732 997-4100
7 Wheeling Rd Dayton (08810) *(G-1957)*

Bway Corporation 609 883-4300
6 Litho Rd Trenton (08648) *(G-11031)*

Bwi Chemicals 732 689-0913
6 Libby Dr Monmouth Junction (08852) *(G-6334)*

Bylada Foods LLC (PA) 201 933-7474
140 W Commercial Ave Moonachie (07074) *(G-6510)*

Byram Laboratories Inc (PA) 908 252-0852
1 Columbia Rd Branchburg (08876) *(G-646)*

Byram Labs, Branchburg *Also called Byram Laboratories Inc (G-646)*

C & C Metal Products Corp (PA) 201 569-7300
456 Nordhoff Pl Englewood (07631) *(G-2880)*

C & C Tool and Machine Co LLC 856 764-0911
38 W Scott St Riverside (08075) *(G-9494)*

C & D Sales 609 383-9292
73 E West Jersey Ave Pleasantville (08232) *(G-8903)*

C & E Canners Inc 609 561-1078
1249 Mays Landing Rd Hammonton (08037) *(G-4135)*

C & F Burner Co 201 998-8080
39 River Rd North Arlington (07031) *(G-7417)*

C & K Plastics Inc 732 549-0011
159 Liberty St Metuchen (08840) *(G-6098)*

C & K Punch & Screw Mch Pdts 201 343-6750
160 Hobart St Hackensack (07601) *(G-3886)*

C & L Machining Company Inc 856 456-1932
110 S New Broadway Brooklawn (08030) *(G-920)*

C & M Shade Corp 201 807-1200
53 Dwight Pl Fairfield (07004) *(G-3152)*

C & N Packaging Inc 631 491-1400
155 Us Highway 46 Ste 200 Wayne (07470) *(G-11617)*

C & N Tooling & Grinding Inc 973 598-8411
19 State Route 10 E # 14 Succasunna (07876) *(G-10619)*

C & S Fencing Inc 201 797-5440
75 Midland Ave 77 Elmwood Park (07407) *(G-2807)*

C & S Machine Inc 973 882-1097
22 Commerce Rd Ste Q Fairfield (07004) *(G-3153)*

C & S Machinery Rebuilding 973 742-7302
636 E 19th St Ste 642 Paterson (07514) *(G-8228)*

C & S Specialty Inc 201 750-7740
121 Piermont Rd Norwood (07648) *(G-7617)*

C & S Tool Co 973 887-6865
304 Ridgedale Ave East Hanover (07936) *(G-2202)*

C A D, Fairfield *Also called Cartridge Actuated Devices (G-3157)*

C A P S, Englewood *Also called Central Admxture Phrm Svcs Inc (G-2883)*

C A R, Forked River *Also called Custom Auto Radiator Inc (G-3537)*

C and C Tool Co LLC 908 431-0330
198 Us Highway 206 Ste 1 Hillsborough (08844) *(G-4324)*

C and R Printing Corporation 201 528-8912
400 Gotham Pkwy Ste 4 Carlstadt (07072) *(G-1135)*

C Bennett Scopes Inc 856 464-6889
550 Bridgeton Pike Mantua (08051) *(G-5891)*

C C S, Newark *Also called Corporate Computer Systems (G-7127)*

C D E Inc 732 297-2540
950 Schweitzer Pl North Brunswick (08902) *(G-7509)*

C E I, Ridgefield *Also called Cosmetic Essence LLC (G-9357)*

C E S, Clifton *Also called Componding Engrg Solutions Inc (G-1587)*

C G Automation Group, Union City *Also called Cuny & Guerber Inc (G-11244)*

C G I Cstm Fiberglas & Decking 609 646-5302
48 S Main St Pleasantville (08232) *(G-8904)*

C Harry Marean Printing 609 965-4708
1717 Philadelphia Ave Egg Harbor City (08215) *(G-2659)*

C J Electric 201 891-0739
327 Franklin Ave Wyckoff (07481) *(G-12247)*

C Jackson Associates Inc 856 761-8000
2050 Springdale Rd # 700 Cherry Hill (08003) *(G-1355)*

C M C Steel Fabricators Inc 908 561-3484
14 Harmich Rd South Plainfield (07080) *(G-10342)*

C M Furnaces Inc 973 338-6500
103 Dewey St Bloomfield (07003) *(G-504)*

C M H Hele-Shaw Inc 201 974-0570
1714 Willow Ave Hoboken (07030) *(G-4462)*

C M M Rentals, Vineland *Also called Cumberland Marble & Monument (G-11344)*

C Q Corporation 201 935-8488
480 Paterson Ave East Rutherford (07073) *(G-2289)*

C R Bard Inc (HQ) 908 277-8000
730 Central Ave New Providence (07974) *(G-7032)*

C R Bard Inc 856 461-0946
1822 Underwood Blvd Delran (08075) *(G-2013)*

C S Hot Stamping 201 840-4004
20 Edgewater Pl Edgewater (07020) *(G-2435)*

C S L Water Quality, Warren *Also called C S L Water Treatment Inc (G-11540)*

C S L Water Treatment Inc 908 647-1400
156 Mount Bethel Rd Warren (07059) *(G-11540)*

C S T Pavers, Branchville *Also called Concrete Stone & Tile Corp (G-728)*

C Systems LLC 732 338-9347
510 Thornall St Ste 310 Edison (08837) *(G-2477)*

C T A Manufacturing Corp 201 896-1000
263 Veterans Blvd Carlstadt (07072) *(G-1136)*

C Technologies Inc 908 707-1009
757 Rte 202/206 Ste 102 Bridgewater (08807) *(G-826)*

C V P, Vineland *Also called Cumberland Vacuum Products Inc (G-11346)*

C W Brabender Instrs Inc 201 343-8425
50 E Wesley St South Hackensack (07606) *(G-10256)*

C W Brown & Company, Mount Royal *Also called CW Brown Foods Inc (G-6851)*

C W Grimmer & Sons Inc 732 741-2189
75 W Gilbert St Tinton Falls (07701) *(G-10825)*

C.B.M. Co., Randolph *Also called Chen Brothers Machinery Co (G-9272)*

C/S Corporate, Lebanon *Also called Construction Specialties Inc (G-5282)*

C2 Imaging LLC (HQ) 646 557-6300
201 Plaza Two Jersey City (07311) *(G-4722)*

C3 Concepts Inc 212 840-1116
1435 51st St Ste 2d North Bergen (07047) *(G-7437)*

Cabinet Tronics Inc 609 267-2625
100 Birmingham Rd Birmingham (08011) *(G-466)*

Cabio Newspaper 201 902-0811
604 56th St West New York (07093) *(G-11861)*

Cabletenna Corp 609 395-9400
440 Forsgate Dr Cranbury (08512) *(G-1818)*

Cabletime Ltd 973 770-8070
100 Valley Rd Ste 203 Mount Arlington (07856) *(G-6752)*

Cabletime USA, Mount Arlington *Also called Cabletime Ltd (G-6752)*

Caboki LLC..609 642-2108
  3 Corporate Dr Cranbury (08512) *(G-1819)*

Cacciola Iron Works Inc....................................973 595-0854
  65 N 9th St Paterson (07522) *(G-8229)*

Cad Signs LLC..201 267-0457
  169 Lodi St Hackensack (07601) *(G-3887)*

Cad Signs Nyc Corp..201 525-5415
  169 Lodi St Hackensack (07601) *(G-3888)*

Cadbury Adams USA LLC (HQ)...........................973 503-2000
  100 Deforest Ave East Hanover (07936) *(G-2203)*

Caddy Corporation of America...........................856 467-4222
  509 Sharptown Rd Swedesboro (08085) *(G-10686)*

Cadence Distributors LLC.................................646 808-3031
  200 S Newman St Unit 8 Hackensack (07601) *(G-3889)*

Cadpro Inc..856 435-0050
  431 S Main St Williamstown (08094) *(G-12082)*

Caesars Pasta LLC...856 227-2585
  1001 Lower Landing Rd Blackwood (08012) *(G-474)*

Cain Machine Inc..856 825-7225
  1501 Oakland Ave Ste R Millville (08332) *(G-6291)*

Cake Specialty Inc...973 238-0500
  255 Goffle Rd Hawthorne (07506) *(G-4224)*

Calandra Italian & French Bky............................973 484-5598
  204 1st Ave W Newark (07107) *(G-7118)*

Calandra's Bakery, Newark *Also called Calandra Italian & French Bky (G-7118)*

Calculagraph Co (PA)..973 887-9400
  280 Ridgedale Ave East Hanover (07936) *(G-2204)*

Calculagraph Co...973 887-9400
  272 Ridgedale Ave 280 East Hanover (07936) *(G-2205)*

Caldwell Progress, Bernardsville *Also called Parker Publications Inc (G-453)*

Calgonate, Branchburg *Also called Top Safety Products Company (G-711)*

California Closet Co, Fairfield *Also called Rainbow Closets Inc (G-3289)*

California Stucco Products.................................201 457-1900
  85 Zabriskie St Ste 1 Hackensack (07601) *(G-3890)*

Caligor Rx Inc..212 988-0590
  801 Penhorn Ave Ste 4 Secaucus (07094) *(G-9870)*

Caliz - Malko LLC...973 207-5200
  66 Clinton Rd Fairfield (07004) *(G-3154)*

Callaghan Pump Controls Inc...........................201 621-0505
  106 Hobart St Hackensack (07601) *(G-3891)*

Calmac Manufacturing Corp...............................201 797-1511
  3-00 Banta Pl Fair Lawn (07410) *(G-3085)*

Caloric Color Co Inc...973 471-4748
  176 Saddle River Rd A Garfield (07026) *(G-3725)*

Calyptus Pharmaceuticals Inc...........................908 720-6049
  174 Nassau St Ste 364 Princeton (08542) *(G-9020)*

Camber Pharmaceuticals Inc.............................732 529-0430
  1031 Centennial Ave Piscataway (08854) *(G-8742)*

Cambrdge Inds For Vslly Impred........................732 247-6668
  1230 Hamilton St Somerset (08873) *(G-10072)*

Cambrex Corporation (PA).................................201 804-3000
  1 Meadowlands Plz # 1510 East Rutherford (07073) *(G-2290)*

Cambridge Bagel Factory, Bloomfield *Also called Cambridge Bagels Inc (G-505)*

Cambridge Bagels Inc.......................................973 743-5683
  648 Bloomfield Ave Bloomfield (07003) *(G-505)*

Cambridge Industries Co Inc.............................973 465-4565
  7 Amsterdam St 33 Newark (07105) *(G-7119)*

Cambridge Pavers Inc......................................201 933-5000
  1 Jerome Ave Lyndhurst (07071) *(G-5673)*

Cambridge Pavingstones, Lyndhurst *Also called Cambridge Pavers Inc (G-5673)*

Cambridge Sheet Metal Inc..............................973 386-0788
  93 Union Brick Rd Blairstown (07825) *(G-495)*

Cambridge Therapeutic Tech LLC.......................914 420-5555
  90 Main St Ste 107 Hackensack (07601) *(G-3892)*

Camden Iron & Metal Inc (HQ)..........................856 365-7500
  1500 S 6th St Camden (08104) *(G-1047)*

Camden Iron & Metal LLC (PA)..........................856 969-7065
  143 Harding Ave Ste 20 Bellmawr (08031) *(G-334)*

Camden Tool Inc...856 966-6800
  129 York St Camden (08102) *(G-1048)*

Cameco Inc...973 239-2845
  100 Pine St Verona (07044) *(G-11304)*

Cameo China Inc...201 865-7650
  501 Penhorn Ave Ste 12 Secaucus (07094) *(G-9871)*

Cameo China East, Secaucus *Also called Cameo China Inc (G-9871)*

Cameo Metal Forms, Rahway *Also called Cameo Metal Products Inc (G-9180)*

Cameo Metal Forms Inc.....................................718 788-1106
  12 Andrews Dr Woodland Park (07424) *(G-12213)*

Cameo Metal Products Inc.................................732 388-4000
  1745 Elizabeth Ave Rahway (07065) *(G-9180)*

Cameo Novelty & Pen Corp................................973 923-1600
  400 Hillside Ave Hillside (07205) *(G-4400)*

Camfil USA Inc (HQ)..973 616-7300
  1 N Corporate Dr Riverdale (07457) *(G-9476)*

Camp Marine Services Inc.................................609 368-1777
  1000 Stone Harbor Blvd Stone Harbor (08247) *(G-10613)*

Campak Inc..973 994-4888
  119 Naylon Ave Livingston (07039) *(G-5526)*

Campbell Converting Corp.................................609 835-2720
  703 Van Rossum Ave Unit 2 Beverly (08010) *(G-460)*

Campbell Foundry Company (PA).......................973 483-5480
  800 Bergen St Harrison (07029) *(G-4175)*

Campbell Foundry Company...............................201 998-3765
  1235 Harrison Tpke Kearny (07032) *(G-4867)*

Campbell Group, Harrison *Also called Campbell Foundry Company (G-4175)*

Campbell Hausfeld LLC....................................856 661-1800
  8550 Remington Ave Pennsauken (08110) *(G-8489)*

Campbell Soup Company (PA)............................856 342-4800
  1 Campbell Pl Camden (08103) *(G-1049)*

Campbell Soup Supply Co LLC (HQ)...................856 342-4800
  1 Campbell Pl Camden (08103) *(G-1050)*

Campbell's Pharmacy, Sea Girt *Also called 140 Main Street Corp (G-9860)*

Campbell-Soup Company, Camden *Also called Campbell Soup Supply Co LLC (G-1050)*

Camptown Tool & Die Co Inc..............................908 688-8406
  25 Sidney Cir Kenilworth (07033) *(G-4947)*

Campus Coordinates LLC...................................732 866-6060
  1711 Ginesi Dr Ste 1 Freehold (07728) *(G-3643)*

Camtec Industries Inc.......................................732 332-9800
  28 Saddle Ridge Rd Colts Neck (07722) *(G-1780)*

Canac Kitchens of NJ Inc...................................201 567-9585
  99 N Dean St Englewood (07631) *(G-2881)*

Canada Dry Bottling Co NY LP............................201 489-6600
  88 Polifly Rd Hackensack (07601) *(G-3893)*

Canada Dry of Delaware Valley, Pennsauken *Also called Foulkrod Associates (G-8511)*

Canary' Closets & Cabinetry, Union *Also called John Canary Custom Wdwkg Inc (G-11198)*

Candela Corporation..908 753-6300
  111 Corporate Blvd Ste I South Plainfield (07080) *(G-10343)*

Candle Artisans Incorporated...........................908 689-2000
  253 E Washington Ave Washington (07882) *(G-11579)*

Candy Treasure LLC...201 830-3600
  66 Welsh Rd Lebanon (08833) *(G-5279)*

Canfield Clinic Systems, Fairfield *Also called Canfield Property Group Inc (G-3155)*

Canfield Property Group Inc...............................973 276-0300
  253 Passaic Ave Ste 1 Fairfield (07004) *(G-3155)*

Cantel Medical Corp (PA)...................................973 890-7220
  150 Clove Rd Ste 36 Little Falls (07424) *(G-5471)*

Cantol Inc (HQ)..609 846-7912
  4701 Mediterranean Ave Wildwood (08260) *(G-12070)*

Cantone Press Inc..201 569-3435
  161 Coolidge Ave Englewood (07631) *(G-2882)*

Canvas 4 Life Inc...973 276-3200
  30 Chapin Rd Ste 1210 Pine Brook (07058) *(G-8690)*

Canvas Creations...609 465-8428
  14 Swainton Goshen Rd Cape May Court House (08210) *(G-1111)*

Caolion BNC Co Ltd..201 641-4709
  65 Challenger Rd Ste 44 Ridgefield Park (07660) *(G-9399)*

Capco Enterprises Inc.......................................973 884-0044
  34 Deforest Ave Ste 4 East Hanover (07936) *(G-2206)*

Cape Atlantic Software LLC...............................609 442-1331
  6523 Mill Rd Egg Harbor Township (08234) *(G-2683)*

Cape May Brewing Company, Cape May *Also called Cape May Brewing Ltd Lblty Co (G-1092)*

Cape May Brewing Company, Cape May *Also called Cape May Brewing Ltd Lblty Co (G-1093)*

Cape May Brewing Ltd Lblty Co..........................609 849-9933
  1288 Hornet Rd Cape May (08204) *(G-1092)*

Cape May Brewing Ltd Lblty Co (PA)...................609 849-9933
  409 Breakwater Rd Cape May (08204) *(G-1093)*

Cape May County Herald, Rio Grande *Also called Seawave Corp (G-9462)*

Cape May Foods, Millville *Also called Lamonica Fine Foods LLC (G-6311)*

Cape May Foods LLC...856 825-8111
  48 Gorton Rd Millville (08332) *(G-6292)*

Cape May Star & Wave, Cape May *Also called Sample Media Inc (G-1104)*

Cape May Winery & Vineyard, Cape May *Also called W J R B Inc (G-1107)*

Cape Prosthetics-Orthotics...............................856 810-7900
  100 Brick Rd Ste 315 Marlton (08053) *(G-5966)*

Cape Publishing Inc..609 898-4500
  513 Washington St Fl 2 Cape May (08204) *(G-1094)*

Capezio, Totowa *Also called Ballet Makers Inc (G-10934)*

Capintec Inc (HQ)...201 825-9500
  7 Vreeland Rd Ste 101 Florham Park (07932) *(G-3495)*

Capital Contracting & Design (PA)......................908 561-8411
  640 North Ave Plainfield (07060) *(G-8856)*

Capital Cooling Systems LLC.............................973 773-8700
  1050 Wall St W Ste 202 Lyndhurst (07071) *(G-5674)*

Capital Foods Inc...908 587-9050
  1701 E Elizabeth Ave Linden (07036) *(G-5355)*

Capital Gasket and Rubber Inc..........................856 939-3670
  325 E Clements Bridge Rd Runnemede (08078) *(G-9717)*

Capital Label and Affixing Co............................856 786-1700
  1100 Taylors Ln Ste 5 Cinnaminson (08077) *(G-1450)*

Capital Printing Corporation..............................732 560-1515
  420 South Ave Middlesex (08846) *(G-6153)*

Capital Soap Products LLC................................973 333-6100
  62 Kearney St Paterson (07522) *(G-8230)*

Capital Steel Service LLC 609 882-6983
82 Stokes Ave Ewing (08638) *(G-3005)*

Capitol Bindery Inc 609 883-5971
312 Stokes Ave Ewing (08638) *(G-3006)*

Capitol Box Corp (PA) 201 867-6018
1300 6th St North Bergen (07047) *(G-7438)*

Capitol Foam Products Inc 201 933-5277
75 E Union Ave East Rutherford (07073) *(G-2291)*

Capitol Steel Inc 609 538-9313
10 Escher St Trenton (08609) *(G-11032)*

Capitol Steel Products, Trenton Also called Capitol Steel Inc *(G-11032)*

Caporale Engraving Co Inc 201 569-8711
30 Roberts Rd Englewood Cliffs (07632) *(G-2951)*

Capra Custom Cabinetry 908 797-9848
259 E Washington Ave Washington (07882) *(G-11580)*

Caps Padel, Cherry Hill Also called Daman International Inc *(G-1359)*

Capsugel Inc (HQ) 862 242-1700
412 Mount Kemble Ave 200c Morristown (07960) *(G-6696)*

Capsugel Holdings Us Inc (HQ) 862 242-1700
412 Mount Kemble Ave 200c Morristown (07960) *(G-6697)*

Capsugel US, Morristown Also called Capsugel Inc *(G-6696)*

Capsugel Us LLC 862 242-1700
412 Mount Kemble Ave Morristown (07960) *(G-6698)*

Captain John Inc 609 494-2094
16 E 12th St Barnegat Light (08006) *(G-168)*

Captivate Internationallc 732 734-0403
28 May St Apt 1 Edison (08837) *(G-2478)*

Captive Fasteners Corp 201 337-6800
19 Thornton Rd Oakland (07436) *(G-7678)*

Captive Plastics Inc 812 424-2904
190 Strykers Rd Phillipsburg (08865) *(G-8645)*

Captive Plastics Inc 732 469-7900
251 Circle Dr N Piscataway (08854) *(G-8743)*

Capuano Plumbing Inc 201 327-0676
327 W Saddle River Rd Upper Saddle River (07458) *(G-11276)*

Caputo International Inc 732 225-5777
112 Northfield Ave Edison (08837) *(G-2479)*

Car Boline, Rahway Also called Carboline Company *(G-9181)*

Car Wash Parts Inc 215 633-9250
6927 Atlantic Ave Ventnor City (08406) *(G-11290)*

Caraco Pharmaceutical Labs 609 819-8200
270 Prospect Plains Rd Cranbury (08512) *(G-1820)*

Caraustar Clifton Primary Pack 973 472-4900
43 Samworth Rd Clifton (07012) *(G-1580)*

Caraustar Industries Inc 908 782-0505
869 State Route 12 Frenchtown (08825) *(G-3698)*

Caravan Inc 732 590-0210
160 Essex Ave E Avenel (07001) *(G-128)*

Caravan Ingredients Inc 973 256-8886
100 Adams Dr Totowa (07512) *(G-10937)*

Caravan Ingredients Inc 201 672-0510
96 E Union Ave East Rutherford (07073) *(G-2292)*

Caravan Products, East Rutherford Also called A & S Frozen Inc *(G-2274)*

Carboline Company 908 233-3150
449 South Ave E Westfield (07090) *(G-11923)*

Carboline Company 732 388-2912
842 Elston St Rahway (07065) *(G-9181)*

Carbone America Scp Division 973 334-0700
400 Myrtle Ave 1 Boonton (07005) *(G-559)*

Cardan Medical Products Inc 908 964-0800
1060 Commerce Ave Union (07083) *(G-11162)*

Cardinal Fibreglass Industries 718 625-4350
1050 State St Perth Amboy (08861) *(G-8608)*

Cardinal Health Systems Inc (HQ) 732 537-6544
14 Schoolhouse Rd Somerset (08873) *(G-10073)*

Cardinal International Inc 973 628-0900
30 Corporate Dr Wayne (07470) *(G-11618)*

Cardinal Millville DC ARC Intl, Millville Also called ARC International N Amer LLC *(G-6284)*

Cardolite Corporation (PA) 609 436-0902
11 Deerpark Dr Ste 124 Monmouth Junction (08852) *(G-6335)*

Carecam International Inc 973 227-0720
10 Plog Rd Fairfield (07004) *(G-3156)*

Caret Corporation (PA) 973 423-5999
101 E Main St Ste 1202 Little Falls (07424) *(G-5472)*

Carfaro, Trenton Also called Fairway Building Products LLC *(G-11059)*

Carfaro Inc 609 890-6600
2075 E State Street Ext Trenton (08619) *(G-11033)*

Cargill Incorporated 908 820-9800
132 Corbin St Elizabeth (07201) *(G-2717)*

Cargille Laboratories, Cedar Grove Also called Cargille-Sacher Labs Inc *(G-1274)*

Cargille Tab-Pro Corporation 973 267-8883
50 Broad St Carlstadt (07072) *(G-1137)*

Cargille-Sacher Labs Inc (PA) 973 239-6633
55 Commerce Rd Cedar Grove (07009) *(G-1274)*

Cargille-Sacher Labs Inc. 973 267-8888
4 E Frederick Pl Cedar Knolls (07927) *(G-1308)*

Carib Chemical Co Inc 201 791-6700
103 Main Ave Elmwood Park (07407) *(G-2808)*

Carib Chemical Co Inc (PA) 201 791-6700
125 Main Ave Elmwood Park (07407) *(G-2809)*

Carib International, Elmwood Park Also called Carib Chemical Co Inc *(G-2808)*

Carib-Display Co (PA) 732 583-1648
18 Northland Ln Matawan (07747) *(G-6014)*

Caribe Express Associates Inc (PA) 201 869-2822
6710 Bergenline Ave Guttenberg (07093) *(G-3867)*

Cariletha Company Inc 609 222-3055
2206 Sedgefield Dr Mount Laurel (08054) *(G-6786)*

Carl A Venable Inc 732 985-6677
65 Hidden Lake Dr North Brunswick (08902) *(G-7510)*

Carl Buck Corporation 973 300-5575
14 Park Lake Rd Ste 3 Sparta (07871) *(G-10491)*

Carl Stahl Sava Industries Inc (HQ) 973 835-0882
4 N Corporate Dr Riverdale (07457) *(G-9477)*

Carl Streit & Son Co 732 775-0803
703 Atkins Ave Neptune (07753) *(G-6903)*

Carlascio Custom & Orthopedic (PA) 201 333-8716
283 Grove St Apt 1 Jersey City (07302) *(G-4723)*

Carlee Corporation 201 768-6800
28 Piermont Rd Rockleigh (07647) *(G-9627)*

Carlisle Machine Works Inc 856 825-0627
412 S Wade Blvd Ste 5 Millville (08332) *(G-6293)*

Carlyle Custom Convertibles (PA) 973 546-4502
6 Empire Blvd Moonachie (07074) *(G-6511)*

Carnegie Deli Inc 201 507-5557
605 Washington Ave Carlstadt (07072) *(G-1138)*

Carnegie Pharmaceuticals Inc 732 783-7010
600 Delran Pkwy Delran (08075) *(G-2014)*

Carner Bros, Roseland Also called Zc Utility Services LLC *(G-9658)*

Carneys Point Fire Company Aux, Carneys Point Also called Township of Carneys Point *(G-1247)*

Carol Healey 973 875-1990
14 Bantry Ter Sussex (07461) *(G-10667)*

Carol Products Co Inc 732 918-0800
1750 Brielle Ave Ste A1 Ocean (07712) *(G-7718)*

Carol S Miller Corporation 201 406-4578
98 Saddlewood Dr Hillsdale (07642) *(G-4381)*

Carolace Embroidery Co Inc (PA) 201 945-2151
65 Railroad Ave Ste 3 Ridgefield (07657) *(G-9354)*

Carole Cosmetics LLC 973 283-2893
10 Park Pl Ste 4 Butler (07405) *(G-1000)*

Carole Hchman Design Group Inc (HQ) 866 267-3945
90 Hudson St Fl 9 Jersey City (07302) *(G-4724)*

Carolina Fluid Handling Inc 248 228-8900
140 Bradford Dr West Berlin (08091) *(G-11706)*

Carpathian Industries LLC 201 386-5356
51 Newark St Ste 508 Hoboken (07030) *(G-4463)*

Carpenter & Paterson Inc 973 772-1800
2 Altran Ct 2 # 2 Bordentown (08505) *(G-592)*

Carpenter & Paterson Inc 609 227-2750
2 Altran Ct Ste 2 # 2 Bordentown (08505) *(G-593)*

Carpenter Emergency Lighting, Trenton Also called Carpenter LLC *(G-11034)*

Carpenter LLC 609 689-3090
2 Marlen Dr Trenton (08691) *(G-11034)*

Carpet Hardware Systems, Montclair Also called Bedlam Corp *(G-6408)*

Carrier Transicold of NJ, Matawan Also called Penn Power Group LLC *(G-6028)*

Carry Cases Plus, Paterson Also called Century Service Affiliates Inc *(G-8231)*

Carry Easy Inc 201 944-0042
131 Fort Lee Rd Fl 2 Leonia (07605) *(G-5315)*

Carson & Gebel Ribbon Co LLC 973 627-4200
17 Green Pond Rd Rockaway (07866) *(G-9556)*

Carstens Publications Inc 973 383-3355
108 Phil Hardin Rd Newton (07860) *(G-7384)*

Carter Manufacturing Co Inc 201 935-0770
55 Anderson Ave Moonachie (07074) *(G-6512)*

Carter Pump Inc 201 568-9798
152d Franklin Tpke Waldwick (07463) *(G-11442)*

Carteret Die-Casting Corp 732 246-0070
74 Veronica Ave Somerset (08873) *(G-10074)*

Cartolith Group 908 624-9833
28 Sager Pl Hillside (07205) *(G-4401)*

Carton Brewing Company LLC 732 654-2337
6 E Washington Ave Atlantic Highlands (07716) *(G-110)*

Cartridge Actuated Devices (HQ) 973 575-8760
51 Dwight Pl Fairfield (07004) *(G-3157)*

Cartridge Actuated Devices 973 347-2281
40 Old Indian Spring Rd Byram Township (07821) *(G-1021)*

Cartridge World of Union, West Orange Also called Hammer Too LLC *(G-11896)*

Cartridge World Paramus, Paramus Also called B&B Imaging LLC *(G-7856)*

Carver Boat Sales Inc 732 892-0328
714 Canal St Point Pleasant Boro (08742) *(G-8934)*

Carwin Phrm Assoc LLC 732 344-6987
1301 Hwy 36 Ste 12 Hazlet (07730) *(G-4272)*

Cary Compounds LLC 732 274-2626
5 Nicholas Ct Dayton (08810) *(G-1958)*

Casa Di Bertacchi Corporation 856 696-5600
1910 Gallagher Dr Vineland (08360) *(G-11334)*

(G-0000) Company's Geographic Section entry number

Casas News Publishing Co.....908 245-6767
325 E Westfield Ave Roselle Park (07204) ***(G-9690)***
Case Davenport Inc.....973 812-7180
280 Main St Apt 211 Little Falls (07424) ***(G-5473)***
Case It Inc.....800 441-4710
1050 Valley Brook Ave B Lyndhurst (07071) ***(G-5675)***
Case Medical Inc.....201 313-1999
19 Empire Blvd South Hackensack (07606) ***(G-10257)***
Case Pork Roll Co Inc.....609 396-8171
644 Washington St Trenton (08611) ***(G-11035)***
Case Princeton Co Inc.....908 687-1750
1119 Morris Ave Union (07083) ***(G-11163)***
Cases By Source Inc.....201 831-0005
215 Island Rd Mahwah (07430) ***(G-5756)***
Casino Player Publishing LLC.....609 404-0600
333 E Jimmie Leeds Rd # 7 Galloway (08205) ***(G-3710)***
Cassies Restaurant, Englewood *Also called Lbd Corp* ***(G-2908)***
Cast Inc.....201 391-8300
11 Stonewall Ct Woodcliff Lake (07677) ***(G-12185)***
Cast Lighting LLC (PA).....973 423-2303
1120 Goffle Rd Hawthorne (07506) ***(G-4225)***
Cast Technology Inc.....908 753-5155
161 West St South Plainfield (07080) ***(G-10344)***
Castellane Manufacturing Co.....609 625-3427
1405 Cantillon Blvd Mays Landing (08330) ***(G-6038)***
Castle Creek Phrmceuticals LLC.....862 286-0400
6 Century Dr Ste 2 Parsippany (07054) ***(G-7964)***
Castle Industries Inc.....201 585-8400
120 Sylvan Ave Ste 3 Englewood Cliffs (07632) ***(G-2952)***
Castle Printing, Ledgewood *Also called Steb Inc* ***(G-5311)***
Castle Printing Center, Ledgewood *Also called Steb Inc* ***(G-5310)***
Castle Woodcraft Assoc LLC.....732 349-1519
161 Atlantic City Blvd Pine Beach (08741) ***(G-8678)***
Catalent Inc (PA).....732 537-6200
14 Schoolhouse Rd Somerset (08873) ***(G-10075)***
Catalent Cts LLC.....201 785-0275
75 Commerce Dr Allendale (07401) ***(G-6)***
Catalent CTS Kansas City LLC.....732 537-6200
14 Schoolhouse Rd Somerset (08873) ***(G-10076)***
Catalent Pharma Solutions LLC (HQ).....732 537-6200
14 Schoolhouse Rd Somerset (08873) ***(G-10077)***
Catalent Pharma Solutions Inc (HQ).....732 537-6200
14 Schoolhouse Rd Somerset (08873) ***(G-10078)***
Catalent US Holding I LLC.....877 587-1835
14 Schoolhouse Rd Somerset (08873) ***(G-10079)***
Catalogic Software Inc.....201 249-8980
50 Tice Blvd Ste 110 Woodcliff Lake (07677) ***(G-12186)***
Catalogue Publishers Inc.....973 423-3600
20-10 Maple Ave 35f-2 Fair Lawn (07410) ***(G-3086)***
Catalyst Chemicals and Ref Div, West Deptford *Also called Johnson Matthey Inc* ***(G-11832)***
Catalyst Chemicals and Ref Div, West Deptford *Also called Matthey Johnson Inc* ***(G-11835)***
Catamaran Media, Pleasantville *Also called Current Newspaper LLC* ***(G-8906)***
Catbridge Machinery LLC.....973 808-0029
115 Main Rd Montville (07045) ***(G-6485)***
Catching Zzz LLC.....888 339-1604
91 New England Ave Piscataway (08854) ***(G-8744)***
Catchmaster, Bayonne *Also called AP&g Co Inc* ***(G-211)***
Catering By Maddalenas Inc.....609 466-7510
415 Route 31 N Ringoes (08551) ***(G-9436)***
Catheter Precision Inc.....973 691-2000
1705 Us Highway 46 Ste 6 Ledgewood (07852) ***(G-5304)***
Catholic Star Herald.....856 583-6142
15 N 7th St Camden (08102) ***(G-1051)***
Caudalie Usa Inc.....201 939-4969
30 Commerce Rd Carlstadt (07072) ***(G-1139)***
Cava Winery and Vineyard Inc.....973 823-9463
3619 State Rt 94 Hamburg (07419) ***(G-4089)***
Cavagna North America Inc.....732 469-2100
50 Napoleon Ct Somerset (08873) ***(G-10080)***
Cavalier Chemical Co Inc.....908 558-0110
42 Colonial Way Short Hills (07078) ***(G-9975)***
Cavalla Inc.....201 343-3338
111 Union St Hackensack (07601) ***(G-3894)***
Cavalli Cabinets Inc.....201 528-7070
1531 S Washington Ave # 1 Piscataway (08854) ***(G-8745)***
Caw LLC.....973 429-7004
248 Montgomery St Bloomfield (07003) ***(G-506)***
CB Marathon Opco LLC.....201 843-5416
1 Garden State Plz Paramus (07652) ***(G-7860)***
CB&i LLC.....856 482-3000
200 Horizon Center Blvd Trenton (08691) ***(G-11036)***
Cbt Supply Inc.....973 586-2783
83 Jacobs Rd Rockaway (07866) ***(G-9557)***
CC Packaging LLC (PA).....732 213-9008
93 Storm Jib Ct Bayville (08721) ***(G-252)***
CCA Industries Inc.....201 935-3232
1099 Wall St W Ste 275 Lyndhurst (07071) ***(G-5676)***
CCA/Custom Change Aprons, Toms River *Also called Philip Papalia* ***(G-10902)***
Ccard.....732 303-8264
17 Belle Terre Dr Manalapan (07726) ***(G-5840)***
Ccbcc Operations LLC.....609 324-7424
948 Farnsworth Ave Bordentown (08505) ***(G-594)***
CCC, Kenvil *Also called County Concrete Corporation* ***(G-5010)***
Ccg Marketing Solutions, West Caldwell *Also called Corporate Mailings Inc* ***(G-11772)***
CCL Label Inc.....609 443-3700
120 Stockton St Hightstown (08520) ***(G-4311)***
CCL Label Inc.....609 586-1332
104 N Gold Dr Robbinsville (08691) ***(G-9512)***
CCL Label Inc.....856 273-0700
92 Ark Rd Lumberton (08048) ***(G-5653)***
CCL Label (delaware) Inc.....609 259-1055
104 N Gold Dr Trenton (08691) ***(G-11037)***
CCL Label Tubedec, Lumberton *Also called CCL Label Inc* ***(G-5653)***
CDI, Boonton *Also called Communication Devices Inc* ***(G-560)***
CDI Group Inc.....908 862-1493
1135 W Elizabeth Ave Linden (07036) ***(G-5356)***
CDK Industries LLC.....856 488-5456
900 Haddonfield Rd Ste 6 Cherry Hill (08002) ***(G-1356)***
CDM Electronics Inc (PA).....856 740-1200
130 American Blvd Turnersville (08012) ***(G-11141)***
Cds., Sparta *Also called Gate Technologies Inc* ***(G-10500)***
Cdss, Princeton *Also called Chryslis Data Sltons Svcs Corp* ***(G-9022)***
Ce De Candy Inc (PA).....908 964-0660
1091 Lousons Rd Union (07083) ***(G-11164)***
Ce Tech LLC.....908 229-3803
8 Fairway Dr Whitehouse Station (08889) ***(G-12050)***
Cedar Hill Landscaping.....732 469-1400
127 Cedar Grove Ln Somerset (08873) ***(G-10081)***
Cedar Hill Topsoil, Somerset *Also called Cedar Hill Landscaping* ***(G-10081)***
Cedge Industries Inc (PA).....201 641-3222
71 Preston St Ridgefield Park (07660) ***(G-9400)***
Cegedim Inc (HQ).....908 443-2000
1425 Us Highway 206 Bedminster (07921) ***(G-269)***
Cei Holdings Inc (PA).....732 888-7788
2182 State Route 35 Holmdel (07733) ***(G-4511)***
Cejon Inc.....201 437-8780
53 Hook Rd Bayonne (07002) ***(G-217)***
Celator Pharmaceuticals Inc (HQ).....609 243-0123
200 Princeton S Ewing (08628) ***(G-3007)***
Celco, Berkeley Heights *Also called Connell Mining Products LLC* ***(G-406)***
Celco.....201 327-1123
14 Industrial Ave Ste 2 Mahwah (07430) ***(G-5757)***
Celebration (us) Inc.....609 261-5200
681 Main St Lumberton (08048) ***(G-5654)***
Celestech Inc.....856 986-2221
221 Kngs Hwy W Hddonfield Haddonfield (08033) ***(G-4057)***
Celgene Cellular.....908 673-9000
45 Horsehill Rd Cedar Knolls (07927) ***(G-1309)***
Celgene Cellular Therapeutics, Warren *Also called Celgene Corporation* ***(G-11541)***
Celgene Corporation.....908 464-8101
300 Connell Dr Ste 6000 Berkeley Heights (07922) ***(G-403)***
Celgene Corporation.....732 271-1001
7 Powderhorn Dr Warren (07059) ***(G-11541)***
Celgene Corporation.....908 967-1432
400 Connell Dr Ste 4000 Berkeley Heights (07922) ***(G-404)***
Celgene Corporation.....908 897-4603
556 Morris Ave Summit (07901) ***(G-10638)***
Celgene Corporation (PA).....908 673-9000
86 Morris Ave Summit (07901) ***(G-10639)***
Celgene Corporation.....908 673-9000
106 Allen Rd Basking Ridge (07920) ***(G-182)***
Celimmune.....908 399-2954
110 Old Driftway Ln Lebanon (08833) ***(G-5280)***
Cell Distributors Inc (PA).....718 473-0162
319 Ridge Rd Dayton (08810) ***(G-1959)***
Celldex Therapeutics Inc (PA).....908 200-7500
53 Frontage Rd Ste 220 Hampton (08827) ***(G-4155)***
Cellebrite Inc.....201 848-8552
7 Campus Dr Ste 210 Parsippany (07054) ***(G-7965)***
Cellular Empire Inc.....800 778-3513
1400 W Elizabeth Ave Linden (07036) ***(G-5357)***
Cellular Innovations, Avenel *Also called Mizco International Inc* ***(G-141)***
Cellular Sciences Inc.....908 237-1561
84 Park Ave Flemington (08822) ***(G-3430)***
Cellunet Manufacturing Compnay.....609 386-3361
460 Veterans Dr Burlington (08016) ***(G-961)***
Celotex.....856 663-2626
1500 John Tipton Blvd Pennsauken (08110) ***(G-8490)***
Celsion Corporation (PA).....609 896-9100
997 Lenox Dr Ste 100 Lawrenceville (08648) ***(G-5253)***
Celtic Passions LLC.....973 865-7046
35 Park Dr Nutley (07110) ***(G-7644)***
Celus Fasteners Mfg Inc (PA).....800 289-7483
200 Paris Ave Northvale (07647) ***(G-7576)***
Cem Industries Inc.....908 244-8080
300 Somerset St Apt 217 Harrison (07029) ***(G-4176)***
Cementex Insulated Tools, Burlington *Also called Cementex Products Inc* ***(G-962)***

ALPHABETIC

Cementex Products Inc.............................609 387-1040
650 Jacksonville Rd Burlington (08016) *(G-962)*

Cemp Inc...732 933-1000
479 Broad St Shrewsbury (07702) *(G-9992)*

Cenntro Automotive Corporation (PA)........732 863-0777
125 Halls Mill Rd Unit 4 Freehold (07728) *(G-3644)*

Cenntro Motors, Freehold *Also called Cenntro Automotive Corporation* *(G-3644)*

Cenogenics Corporation (PA).....................732 536-6457
100 County Road 520 Morganville (07751) *(G-6638)*

Center Stage Productions, Fair Lawn *Also called De Zaio Productions Inc* *(G-3089)*

Central Admxture Phrm Svcs Inc................201 541-0080
160 W Forest Ave Englewood (07631) *(G-2883)*

Central Art & Engineering Inc....................609 758-5922
500 Goldman Dr Cream Ridge (08514) *(G-1931)*

Central Art & Enginering Inc......................609 758-5922
500 Goldman Dr Cream Ridge (08514) *(G-1932)*

Central Bakery, Hackensack *Also called Artisan Oven Inc* *(G-3875)*

Central Components Mfg LLC.....................732 469-5720
440 Lincoln Blvd Middlesex (08846) *(G-6154)*

Central Concrete Aggregates, Forked River *Also called Pioneer Concrete Corp* *(G-3539)*

Central Ink Corporation.............................856 467-5562
2085 Center Square Rd A Swedesboro (08085) *(G-10687)*

Central Jersey Hot Mix Asp LLC................732 323-0226
577 S Hope Chapel Rd Jackson (08527) *(G-4656)*

Central Letter Shop Inc.............................973 808-9595
14 Henderson Dr West Caldwell (07006) *(G-11770)*

Central Metal Fabricators Inc....................732 938-6900
300 Central Ave Farmingdale (07727) *(G-3379)*

Central Metals Inc....................................215 462-7464
1054 S 2nd St Camden (08103) *(G-1052)*

Central Mills Inc.......................................732 329-2009
473 Ridge Rd Dayton (08810) *(G-1960)*

Central Mills Inc (PA)...............................732 329-2009
473 Ridge Rd Dayton (08810) *(G-1961)*

Central Plastics Incorporated....................973 808-0990
333 New Rd Ste 3 Parsippany (07054) *(G-7966)*

Central Poly-Bag Corp..............................908 862-7570
2400 Bedle Pl Linden (07036) *(G-5358)*

Central Record Publications......................609 654-5000
600 Perry St Trenton (08618) *(G-11038)*

Central Safety Equipment Co (PA).............609 386-6448
300 W Broad St Burlington (08016) *(G-963)*

Central Shippee Inc..................................973 838-1100
46 Star Lake Rd Bloomingdale (07403) *(G-541)*

Central Technology Inc..............................732 431-3339
843 State Route 33 Ste 11 Freehold (07728) *(G-3645)*

Centrome Inc..973 339-6242
10 Taft Rd Totowa (07512) *(G-10938)*

Centryco, Burlington *Also called Central Safety Equipment Co* *(G-963)*

Centurum Information Tech Inc (HQ)..........856 751-1111
651 Route 73 N Ste 107 Marlton (08053) *(G-5967)*

Century Bathworks Inc (PA)......................973 785-4290
250 Lackawanna Ave Ste 2 Woodland Park (07424) *(G-12214)*

Century Bathworks Inc..............................201 785-1414
250 Lackawanna Ave Ste 1 Woodland Park (07424) *(G-12215)*

Century Conveyor Service Inc (PA)............732 248-4900
4 Gladys Ct Edison (08817) *(G-2480)*

Century Metals, Ewing *Also called Ewing Recovery Corp* *(G-3017)*

Century Printing Corp...............................732 981-0544
10 New England Ave Piscataway (08854) *(G-8746)*

Century Service Affiliates Inc (PA)............973 742-3516
510 E 31st St Paterson (07504) *(G-8231)*

Century Shower Door, Woodland Park *Also called Century Bathworks Inc* *(G-12214)*

Century Tube Corp....................................908 534-2001
22 Tannery Rd Somerville (08876) *(G-10204)*

Cenveo Inc...201 434-2100
25 Linden Ave E Jersey City (07305) *(G-4725)*

Ceodeux Incorporated...............................724 696-4340
101 Bilby Rd Ste B Hackettstown (07840) *(G-4000)*

Cerami Wood Products Inc.........................732 968-7222
154 12th St Piscataway (08854) *(G-8747)*

Ceramic Products Inc................................201 342-8200
221 Park St Hackensack (07601) *(G-3895)*

Ceramic Tile Outlet, East Brunswick *Also called Best Tile of New Jersey* *(G-2137)*

Ceramsource Inc.......................................732 257-5002
26 Kennedy Blvd Ste B East Brunswick (08816) *(G-2140)*

Cerbaco Ltd...908 996-1333
809 Harrison St Frenchtown (08825) *(G-3699)*

Cercis Inc..609 737-5120
25 Route 31 S Ste C2030 Pennington (08534) *(G-8445)*

Ceresist Inc..973 345-3231
176 E 7th St Ste 2 Paterson (07524) *(G-8232)*

Cerexa Inc..510 285-9200
400 Interpace Pkwy Ste A1 Parsippany (07054) *(G-7967)*

Ceronics Inc...732 566-5600
5 Dock St Matawan (07747) *(G-6015)*

Certech Inc (HQ)......................................201 842-6800
1 Park Pl W Wood Ridge (07075) *(G-12135)*

Certified Cabinet Corp..............................732 741-0755
9 S Main St Marlboro (07746) *(G-5936)*

Certified Clam Corp..................................732 872-6650
190 Bay Ave Ste 1 Highlands (07732) *(G-4307)*

Certified Labeling Solutions, Hillsborough *Also called Distributor Label Products* *(G-4327)*

Certified Processing Corp..........................973 923-5200
184 Us Highway 22 Hillside (07205) *(G-4402)*

Cervini's Auto Design, Vineland *Also called Cervinis Inc* *(G-11335)*

Cervinis Inc..856 691-1744
3656 N Mill Rd Vineland (08360) *(G-11335)*

Ces Fence, East Hanover *Also called Comprelli Equipment and Svc* *(G-2208)*

Ces Imports LLC.......................................610 299-7930
252 93rd St Stone Harbor (08247) *(G-10614)*

CET Films, Lakewood *Also called Custom Extrusion Tech Inc* *(G-5102)*

Cetylite Industries Inc...............................856 665-6111
9051 River Rd Pennsauken (08110) *(G-8491)*

CFS, Sparta *Also called Compact Fluorescent Systems* *(G-10493)*

Cg Automation Solutions USA (PA)............973 379-7400
60 Fadem Rd Springfield (07081) *(G-10546)*

Cgi North America, Jersey City *Also called Dg3 Group America Inc* *(G-4739)*

Cgm Us Inc (PA)......................................609 894-4420
300 Birmingham Rd Birmingham (08011) *(G-467)*

Cgs Sales and Service LLC........................856 665-6154
6950 River Rd Pennsauken (08110) *(G-8492)*

Cgw News LLC...973 473-3972
107 Mount Prospect Ave Clifton (07013) *(G-1581)*

Ch Technologies USA Inc..........................201 666-2335
778 Carver Ave Westwood (07675) *(G-11957)*

Chacko John..732 494-1088
21 Remington Dr Edison (08820) *(G-2481)*

Challenge Printing Co Inc (PA)..................973 471-4700
2 Bridewell Pl Clifton (07014) *(G-1582)*

Challenge Printing Company The, Clifton *Also called Challenge Printing Co Inc* *(G-1582)*

Chalmers & Kubeck Inc.............................732 993-1251
8 Jules Ln New Brunswick (08901) *(G-6950)*

Chamberlain Group Inc..............................201 472-4200
35 Melanie Ln Whippany (07981) *(G-12016)*

Chambord Prints Inc.................................201 795-2007
38 Jackson St Hoboken (07030) *(G-4464)*

Champion Fasteners Inc (PA)....................609 267-5222
707 Smithville Rd Lumberton (08048) *(G-5655)*

Champion Ink Co Inc.................................201 868-4100
2045 88th St North Bergen (07047) *(G-7439)*

Champion Opco LLC..................................856 662-3400
414 Bloomfield Dr Ste 1 West Berlin (08091) *(G-11707)*

Champion Plastics Div, Clifton *Also called X-L Plastics Inc* *(G-1745)*

Champion Sports Products Co, Marlboro *Also called Pro Sports Inc* *(G-5953)*

Champion Window Delaware Vly, West Berlin *Also called Champion Opco LLC* *(G-11707)*

Champions Oncology Inc (PA)....................201 808-8400
1 University Plz Ste 307 Hackensack (07601) *(G-3896)*

Chandler Pharmacy & Surgicals, New Brunswick *Also called Chandler Pharmacy LLC (G-6951)*

Chandler Pharmacy LLC............................732 543-1568
272 George St New Brunswick (08901) *(G-6951)*

Chanel Inc..732 885-5500
876 Centennial Ave Ste 1 Piscataway (08854) *(G-8748)*

Channel Logistics LLC...............................856 614-5441
121 Market St Ste 2 Camden (08102) *(G-1053)*

Chapter Enterprises Inc.............................732 560-8500
1472 Rte 22 Bridgewater (08807) *(G-827)*

Charabot & Co Inc....................................201 812-2762
400 International Dr Budd Lake (07828) *(G-926)*

Charcole Products, Belleville *Also called William R Tatz Industries* *(G-328)*

Chariot Courier & Trans Svcs.....................888 532-9125
7 Parr Dr Sayreville (08872) *(G-9816)*

Charles Deluca...973 778-5621
239 Garibaldi Ave Lodi (07644) *(G-5579)*

Charles E Green & Son Inc........................973 485-3630
625 3rd St Newark (07107) *(G-7120)*

Charles F Kilian..732 458-3554
682 Rolling Hills Ct Brick (08724) *(G-736)*

Charles Kerr Enterprises Inc......................732 738-6500
1090 King Georges Post Rd # 802 Edison (08837) *(G-2482)*

Charles Komar & Sons Inc (PA).................212 725-1500
90 Hudson St Fl 9 Jersey City (07302) *(G-4726)*

Charles M Jessup Inc................................732 324-0430
177 Smith St Keasbey (08832) *(G-4926)*

Charter Fincl Pubg Netwrk Inc...................732 450-8866
499 Broad St Shrewsbury (07702) *(G-9993)*

Charter Machine, Metuchen *Also called Graphic Equipment Corporation* *(G-6107)*

Charter Machine Company.........................732 494-5350
55 Wester Ave Metuchen (08840) *(G-6099)*

Chartwell Promotions Ltd Inc.....................732 780-6900
1 Chartwell Ct Freehold (07728) *(G-3646)*

Chase Machine Co....................................201 438-2214
127 Park Ave Lyndhurst (07071) *(G-5677)*

Chatham Bookseller Inc.............................973 822-1361
8 Green Village Rd Madison (07940) *(G-5720)*

   (G-0000) Company's Geographic Section entry number

Chatham Brass Co Inc 908 668-0500
1253 New Market Ave Ste D South Plainfield (07080) *(G-10345)*
Chatham Controls Corporation 908 236-6019
6 Corral Cir Lebanon (08833) *(G-5281)*
Chatham Lawn Mowler 973 635-8855
14 Commerce St Chatham (07928) *(G-1327)*
Chatham Lawnmower Service, Chatham *Also called Chatham Lawn Mowler (G-1327)*
Chatham Print & Design, Chatham *Also called Thewal Inc (G-1338)*
Chatlos Systems, Denville *Also called TX Technology Corp (G-2061)*
Chavant Inc 732 751-0003
5043 Industrial Rd Wall Township (07727) *(G-11468)*
Check-It Electronics Corp 973 520-8435
560 Trumbull St Elizabeth (07206) *(G-2718)*
Checkpoint Security Systems Gr 952 933-8858
101 Wolf Dr West Deptford (08086) *(G-11820)*
Checkpoint Systems Inc (HQ) 800 257-5540
101 Wolf Dr West Deptford (08086) *(G-11821)*
Checkpoint Systems Inc 856 848-1800
101 Wolf Dr West Deptford (08086) *(G-11822)*
Checkpoint Systems Inc 952 933-8858
101 Wolf Dr West Deptford (08086) *(G-11823)*
Checkpoint Systems Inc 856 848-1800
101 Wolf Dr West Deptford (08086) *(G-11824)*
Cheesecake Factory Inc 973 921-0930
1200 Morris Tpke Ste D103 Short Hills (07078) *(G-9976)*
Cheesecake Factory, The, Short Hills *Also called Cheesecake Factory Inc (G-9976)*
Chefler Foods LLC 201 596-3710
400 Lyster Ave Saddle Brook (07663) *(G-9757)*
Chefman, Mahwah *Also called Rj Brands LLC (G-5809)*
Chefman Direct Inc 888 315-8407
10 Sharp Plz Mahwah (07495) *(G-5758)*
Chelten House Products Inc 856 467-1600
607 Heron Dr Bridgeport (08014) *(G-762)*
Chem Flowtronic Inc 973 785-0001
195 Paterson Ave Ste 4 Little Falls (07424) *(G-5474)*
Chem Power Mfg Div, Cedar Knolls *Also called Foster and Company Inc (G-1312)*
Chem-Aqua Inc 972 438-0211
34 Stouts Ln Monmouth Junction (08852) *(G-6336)*
Chem-Fleur Inc 973 589-4266
150 Firmench Way Newark (07114) *(G-7121)*
Chem-Is-Try Inc 732 372-7311
160 Liberty St Ste 4 Metuchen (08840) *(G-6100)*
Chemaid Laboratories Inc (HQ) 201 843-3300
100 Mayhill St Saddle Brook (07663) *(G-9758)*
Chembiopower Inc 908 209-5595
211 Warren St Ste 503 Warren (07059) *(G-11542)*
Chemetall Americas, New Providence *Also called Chemetall US Inc (G-7033)*
Chemetall US Inc (HQ) 908 464-6900
675 Central Ave New Providence (07974) *(G-7033)*
Chemglass Inc 856 696-0014
3800 N Mill Rd Vineland (08360) *(G-11336)*
Chemical Products Division, Linden *Also called Exxon Mobil Corporation (G-5373)*
Chemical Resources Inc (PA) 609 520-0000
103 Carnegie Ctr Ste 100 Princeton (08540) *(G-9021)*
Chemicals Services, Linden *Also called Just In Time Chemical Sales & (G-5393)*
Chemiquip Products Co Inc 201 868-4445
109 Bradford Ave Linden (07036) *(G-5359)*
Chemmark Development Inc 908 561-0923
70 Tyler Pl South Plainfield (07080) *(G-10346)*
Chemo Dynamics Inc 732 721-4700
3 Crossman Rd S Sayreville (08872) *(G-9817)*
Chemours Company 856 540-3398
Bldg 603 Rr 130 Deepwater (08023) *(G-1998)*
Chemres, Princeton *Also called Chemical Resources Inc (G-9021)*
Chemspeed Technologies Inc 732 329-1225
113 N Center Dr North Brunswick (08902) *(G-7511)*
Chemstaff Inc 201 265-8655
640 Iroquois St Oradell (07649) *(G-7805)*
Chemtract LLC 732 820-0427
2144 Gilbride Rd Martinsville (08836) *(G-6008)*
Chemtrade Chemicals Corp (HQ) 973 515-0900
90 E Halsey Rd Ste 301 Parsippany (07054) *(G-7968)*
Chemtrade Gcc Holding Company (HQ) 973 515-0900
90 E Halsey Rd Ste 301 Parsippany (07054) *(G-7969)*
Chemtrade Solutions LLC (HQ) 973 515-0900
90 E Halsey Rd Ste 301 Parsippany (07054) *(G-7970)*
Chemtrade Solutions LLC 908 464-1500
235 Snyder Ave Berkeley Heights (07922) *(G-405)*
Chemtrade Water Chemical Inc (HQ) 973 515-0900
90 E Halsey Rd Ste 301 Parsippany (07054) *(G-7971)*
Chemtreat Inc 609 654-9522
520 Stokes Rd Ste B11 Medford (08055) *(G-6066)*
Chen Brothers Machinery Co 973 328-0086
503 State Route 10 Randolph (07869) *(G-9272)*
Cheney Flashing Company LLC 609 394-8175
623 Prospect St Trenton (08618) *(G-11039)*
Chenille Products Inc 201 703-1917
30 Henry Ave Palisades Park (07650) *(G-7837)*

Cheringal Associates Inc 201 784-8721
500 Walnut St Norwood (07648) *(G-7618)*
Cherish Designs LLC 856 751-8034
3111 Route 38 Unit 316 Mount Laurel (08054) *(G-6787)*
Cherishmet Inc 201 842-7612
301 State Rt 17 Ste 800 Rutherford (07070) *(G-9728)*
Cherokee Pharma Llc 732 422-7800
1085 Cranbury S Riv 1 Jamesburg (08831) *(G-4684)*
Cherokee Rubber Company, Flanders *Also called Targa Industries Inc (G-3418)*
Cherri Stone Interactive LLC 844 843-7765
182 N Crest Pl Lakewood (08701) *(G-5092)*
Cherry Hill Precision Co, Cherry Hill *Also called JBAT Inc (G-1383)*
Cherubini Yachts Ltd Lblty Co 856 764-5319
51 Norman Ave Delran (08075) *(G-2015)*
Chessco Industries Inc 609 882-0400
1013 Whitehead Road Ext Ewing (08638) *(G-3008)*
Cheveux Cosmetics Corporation 732 446-7516
30 Park Ave Englishtown (07726) *(G-2990)*
Chevron Phillips Chem Co LP 732 738-2000
1200 State St Perth Amboy (08861) *(G-8609)*
Chevron USA Inc 732 738-2000
1200 State St Perth Amboy (08861) *(G-8610)*
Chic Bebe Inc 201 941-5414
53 Howard Park Dr Tenafly (07670) *(G-10783)*
Chic Btq Doll Design Co LLC 201 784-7727
331 Piermont Rd Ste 8 Norwood (07648) *(G-7619)*
Chic LLC 732 354-0035
200 State Route 18 Ste 1 East Brunswick (08816) *(G-2141)*
Chicago Pneumatic Tool 973 276-1377
90 New Dutch Ln Fairfield (07004) *(G-3158)*
Chicago Pneumatic Tool (HQ) 973 928-5222
222 Getty Ave Clifton (07011) *(G-1583)*
Chick Capoli Sales 856 768-4500
420 Commerce Ln Ste 7 West Berlin (08091) *(G-11708)*
Chiha Inc 201 861-2000
5711 Kennedy Blvd North Bergen (07047) *(G-7440)*
Chiha Sales, North Bergen *Also called Chiha Inc (G-7440)*
Children's Tecnology Review, Flemington *Also called Active Learning Associates (G-3424)*
Childrens Research & Dev Co 856 546-8814
216 9th Ave Haddon Heights (08035) *(G-4046)*
Chiller Solutions LLC 973 835-2800
101 Alexander Ave Unit 3 Pompton Plains (07444) *(G-8956)*
China Assured, Howell *Also called Pastel Companies Inc (G-4563)*
Chips Ice Cream LLC 732 840-6332
149 Newtons Corner Rd Howell (07731) *(G-4548)*
Chiral Photonics Inc 973 732-0030
26 Chapin Rd Ste 1104 Pine Brook (07058) *(G-8691)*
Chiral Photonics Inc 973 732-0030
26 Chapin Rd Ste 1104 Pine Brook (07058) *(G-8692)*
Chirgotis, Wm G, Chatham *Also called National Home Planning Service (G-1335)*
Chisholm Technologies Inc 732 859-5578
450 Shrewsbury Plz # 301 Shrewsbury (07702) *(G-9994)*
Chizzy's Truck & Auto Repair, Little Ferry *Also called Chizzys Service Center (G-5496)*
Chizzys Service Center 201 641-7222
44 Bergen Tpke Little Ferry (07643) *(G-5496)*
Chocmod USA Inc 201 585-8730
2200 Fletcher Ave Ste 3 Fort Lee (07024) *(G-3549)*
Chocolate Face Cupcake 609 624-2253
1963 Route 9 N Cape May Court House (08210) *(G-1112)*
Chocolate Factory, Bridgewater *Also called Ann Hemyng Candy Inc (G-811)*
Choice Cabinetry LLC 908 707-8801
61 5th St Somerville (08876) *(G-10205)*
CHR International Inc 201 262-8186
296 Kinderkamack Rd # 220 Oradell (07649) *(G-7806)*
Chris's Cookies, Teterboro *Also called Food & Beverage Inc (G-10795)*
Christensen Manufacturing 609 466-9700
11 Moores Mill Mt Rose Rd Pennington (08534) *(G-8446)*
Christian Art 201 867-8096
567 52nd St Ste 15 West New York (07093) *(G-11862)*
Christian Mssons In Many Lands 732 449-8880
2751 18th Ave Wall Township (07719) *(G-11469)*
Christine Valmy Inc (PA) 973 575-1050
285 Changebridge Rd Ste 1 Pine Brook (07058) *(G-8693)*
Christopher F Maier 908 459-5100
352 Great Meadows Rd Hope (07844) *(G-4539)*
Christopher Fischer, North Bergen *Also called C3 Concepts Inc (G-7437)*
Christopher Szuco 732 684-7643
1061 Windsor Rd Millstone Twp (08535) *(G-6266)*
Chroma Inks USA, Morganville *Also called Chroma Trading Usa Inc (G-6639)*
Chroma Trading Usa Inc 732 956-4431
18 Guest Dr Morganville (07751) *(G-6639)*
Chromak Research Inc 732 560-1366
350 Campus Dr Somerset (08873) *(G-10082)*
Chromis Fiberoptics Inc 732 764-0900
6 Powderhorn Dr Warren (07059) *(G-11543)*
Chromocell Corporation (PA) 732 565-1113
685 Us Highway 1 North Brunswick (08902) *(G-7512)*
Chryslis Data Sltons Svcs Corp (PA) 609 375-2000
100 Overlook Ctr Fl 2 Princeton (08540) *(G-9022)*

ALPHABETIC

Church & Dwight Co Inc (PA) 609 806-1200
500 Charles Ewing Blvd Ewing (08628) ***(G-3009)***
Church & Dwight Co Inc 732 730-3100
800 Airport Rd Lakewood (08701) ***(G-5093)***
Church & Dwight Co Inc 609 655-6101
326 Cranbury Half Acre Rd Cranbury (08512) ***(G-1821)***
Church & Dwight Co Inc 609 683-8021
101 Thanet Cir Ste 1 Princeton (08540) ***(G-9023)***
Church Vestment Mfg Co Inc 973 942-2833
41 Paterson Ave Ste 1 Paterson (07522) ***(G-8233)***
Ciao Cupcake 609 964-6167
7 Wycklow Dr Trenton (08691) ***(G-11040)***
Ciao Milano, Englewood Cliffs *Also called Fyi Marketing Inc* ***(G-2960)***
Cibo Vita Inc 201 773-4873
16-00 Pollitt Dr Ste 3 Fair Lawn (07410) ***(G-3087)***
CIC Letter Service Inc 201 896-1900
111 Commerce Rd Carlstadt (07072) ***(G-1140)***
Ciccone Inc 732 349-7071
2002 Route 9 Toms River (08755) ***(G-10871)***
Ciccone Brothers, Toms River *Also called Ciccone Inc* ***(G-10871)***
Cielito Lindo 580 286-1127
224 French St New Brunswick (08901) ***(G-6952)***
Cimware USA Inc 201 493-0521
226 Brookside Ave Ridgewood (07450) ***(G-9421)***
Cinchseal Associates Inc 856 662-5162
23b Roland Ave Mount Laurel (08054) ***(G-6788)***
Cincinnati Thermal Spray Inc 973 379-0003
80 Fadem Rd Springfield (07081) ***(G-10547)***
Cinco Star LLC 732 744-1617
2 Karnell Ct Edison (08820) ***(G-2483)***
Cinderella Cheese Cake, Riverside *Also called Cinderella Cheesecake Co Inc* ***(G-9495)***
Cinderella Cheesecake Co Inc 856 461-6302
208 N Fairview St Riverside (08075) ***(G-9495)***
Cir Systems, Franklin *Also called Clinical Image Retrieval Syste* ***(G-3597)***
Circa Promotions Inc 732 264-1200
58 Village Ct Hazlet (07730) ***(G-4273)***
Circle D Light, Carlstadt *Also called Natale Machine & Tool Co Inc* ***(G-1191)***
Circle Fabrics, Carlstadt *Also called Circle Visual Inc* ***(G-1141)***
Circle Visual Inc 212 719-5153
340 13th St Carlstadt (07072) ***(G-1141)***
Circonix Technologies LLC (HQ) 973 962-6160
29 Executive Pkwy Ringwood (07456) ***(G-9445)***
Circuit Reproduction Co 201 712-9292
219 Hergesell Ave Maywood (07607) ***(G-6046)***
Circuit Tech Assembly LLC 856 231-0777
341 New Albany Rd Ste 130 Moorestown (08057) ***(G-6566)***
Circulite Inc 201 478-7575
500 F W Burr Blvd Ste 40 Teaneck (07666) ***(G-10745)***
Cire Technologies Inc 973 402-8301
251 Boulevard Mountain Lakes (07046) ***(G-6855)***
Cisco Systems Inc 732 635-4200
111 Wood Ave S Ste 2 Iselin (08830) ***(G-4620)***
Cisco Systems Inc 856 642-7000
308 Harper Dr Ste 100 Moorestown (08057) ***(G-6567)***
Cisco Systems Inc 201 782-0842
1 Paragon Dr Ste 275 Montvale (07645) ***(G-6448)***
Cispharma Inc 609 235-9807
1212 Cranbury S River Rd Cranbury (08512) ***(G-1822)***
Citgo, Clifton *Also called Masouleh Corp* ***(G-1668)***
Citi-Chem Inc 609 231-6655
122 E Kings Hwy Ste 503 Maple Shade (08052) ***(G-5900)***
Citius Pharmaceuticals Inc (PA) 978 938-0338
11 Commerce Dr Ste 100 Cranford (07016) ***(G-1900)***
Citizen of Morris County, The, Denville *Also called Andis Inc* ***(G-2030)***
Citroil Aromatic, Carlstadt *Also called Citroil Enterprises Inc* ***(G-1142)***
Citroil Enterprises Inc 201 933-8405
444 Washington Ave Carlstadt (07072) ***(G-1142)***
Citromax Flavors Inc 201 933-8405
444 Washington Ave Carlstadt (07072) ***(G-1143)***
Citromax Usa Inc 201 933-8405
444 Washington Ave Carlstadt (07072) ***(G-1144)***
City Design Group Inc 201 329-7711
201 Gates Rd Ste C Little Ferry (07643) ***(G-5497)***
City Diecutting Inc 973 270-0370
1 Cory Rd Ste C Morristown (07960) ***(G-6699)***
City Envelope Inc 201 792-9292
235 Orient Ave 1 Jersey City (07305) ***(G-4727)***
City Fresh Market, Union City *Also called Socio Produce Inc* ***(G-11266)***
City Master Barbers Inc 732 536-6400
12 Us Highway 9 Ste 4 Morganville (07751) ***(G-6640)***
City of Jersey City 201 547-4470
575 State Rt 440 Jersey City (07305) ***(G-4728)***
City Theatrical Inc 201 549-1160
475 Barell Ave Carlstadt (07072) ***(G-1145)***
Civic Research Institute Inc (PA) 609 683-4450
4478 Route 27 Ste 202 Kingston (08528) ***(G-5027)***
CJ TMI Manufacturing Amer LLC 609 669-0100
2 Applegate Dr Robbinsville (08691) ***(G-9513)***
CJS Hesse, Forked River *Also called Brick-Wall Corp* ***(G-3534)***
CK, Metuchen *Also called C & K Plastics Inc* ***(G-6098)***
CK Manufacturing Inc 973 808-3500
8 Gardner Rd Fairfield (07004) ***(G-3159)***
Cko Kickboxing, Totowa *Also called Totowa Kickboxing Ltd Lblty Co* ***(G-10975)***
Clantech Inc 908 281-7667
198 Us Highway 206 Ste 10 Hillsborough (08844) ***(G-4325)***
Claremont Distilled Spirits 973 227-7027
25 Commerce Rd Fairfield (07004) ***(G-3160)***
Clarici Graphics Inc 609 587-7204
88 Youngs Rd Trenton (08619) ***(G-11041)***
Clarity Imaging Tech Inc 877 272-4362
250 Pehle Ave Ste 402 Saddle Brook (07663) ***(G-9759)***
Clarity Imaging Tech Inc 413 693-1234
4350 Haddonfield Rd # 300 Pennsauken (08109) ***(G-8493)***
Clarity Imaging Tech Inc (HQ) 877 272-4362
4350 Haddonfield Rd # 300 Pennsauken (08109) ***(G-8494)***
Clark Cooper, Roebling *Also called Magnatrol Valve Corporation* ***(G-9638)***
Clark Equipment Company 973 618-2500
19a Chapin Rd Pine Brook (07058) ***(G-8694)***
Clark Printing Inc 201 845-4888
6 Audrey Pl Fairfield (07004) ***(G-3161)***
Clark Stek-O Corp 201 437-0770
148 E 5th St Bayonne (07002) ***(G-218)***
Classic Chess and Games Inc 908 850-6553
52 Main St Hackettstown (07840) ***(G-4001)***
Classic Cooking LLC 718 439-0200
1600 St Grges Ave Ste 301 Rahway (07065) ***(G-9182)***
Classic Coves, Budd Lake *Also called M + 4 Inc* ***(G-934)***
Classic Designer Woodwork Inc 201 280-3711
60 Hazelhurst Ave Glen Rock (07452) ***(G-3823)***
Classic Graphic Inc 856 753-0055
35 W White Horse Pike Berlin (08009) ***(G-431)***
Classic Impressions 908 689-3137
2 Witte Ln Great Meadows (07838) ***(G-3848)***
Classic Industries Inc 973 227-1366
50 Us Highway 46 Ste 100 Parsippany (07054) ***(G-7972)***
Classic Marking Products Inc 973 383-2223
3 Gold Mine Rd Ste 104 Roxbury Township (07836) ***(G-9711)***
Classic Printers & Converters 732 985-1100
140 Ethel Rd W Ste K Piscataway (08854) ***(G-8749)***
Classic Silks Com I 908 204-0940
131 Roundtop Rd Bernardsville (07924) ***(G-449)***
Clausen Company Inc 732 738-1165
1055 King George Rd Fords (08863) ***(G-3528)***
Clawson Machine Division, Franklin *Also called Technology General Corporation* ***(G-3605)***
Clayton Associates Inc 732 363-2100
1650 Oak St Lakewood (08701) ***(G-5094)***
Clayton Block, Trenton *Also called Ralph Clayton & Sons LLC* ***(G-11111)***
Clayton Block Co 201 955-6292
2 Porete Ave North Arlington (07031) ***(G-7418)***
Clayton Block Company Inc (PA) 732 363-1995
1355 Campus Pkwy Ste 200 Wall Township (07753) ***(G-11470)***
Clayton Block Company Inc 732 462-1860
225 Throckmorton St Freehold (07728) ***(G-3647)***
Clayton Block Company Inc 732 681-0186
1601 18th Ave Wall Township (07719) ***(G-11471)***
Clayton Block Company Inc 732 549-1234
1025 Route 1 Edison (08837) ***(G-2484)***
Clayton Block Company Inc 732 349-3700
194 Chestnut St Toms River (08753) ***(G-10872)***
Clayton Block Company Inc 732 364-2404
1215 E Veterans Hwy Jackson (08527) ***(G-4657)***
Clayton Block Company Inc 609 693-9600
2011 Lacey Rd Forked River (08731) ***(G-3535)***
Clayton Block Company Inc 732 905-3234
100 Commerce Dr Tinton Falls (07753) ***(G-10826)***
Clayton Block Company LLC (HQ) 201 339-8585
440 Hook Rd Bayonne (07002) ***(G-219)***
Clayton Concrete, Cookstown *Also called Ralph Clayton & Sons LLC* ***(G-1808)***
Clayton Concrete, Jackson *Also called Clayton Block Company Inc* ***(G-4657)***
Clayton Industries, Cranbury *Also called Clayton Manufacturing Company* ***(G-1823)***
Clayton Manufacturing Company 609 409-9400
10 S River Rd Ste 6 Cranbury (08512) ***(G-1823)***
Clayton Rolling Mill, Clayton *Also called Aleris Rolled Products Inc* ***(G-1522)***
Clean Air Group 908 232-4200
6 Campus Dr Ste 2 Parsippany (07054) ***(G-7973)***
Clean Bbq Inc 732 299-8877
47 Langstaff Ave Edison (08817) ***(G-2485)***
Clean-Tex Services Inc 908 912-2700
198 Reservoir St Trenton (08618) ***(G-11042)***
Cleaners Choice Inc 800 652-2533
999 Riverview Dr Ste 201 Totowa (07512) ***(G-10939)***
Cleanzones LLC 732 534-5590
640 Herman Rd Ste 2 Jackson (08527) ***(G-4658)***
Clear Control LLC 973 823-8200
93 Main St Ogdensburg (07439) ***(G-7770)***
Clear Cut Window Distrs of NJ 201 512-1804
127 Tam O Shanter Dr Mahwah (07430) ***(G-5759)***

Clear Plus Windshield Wipers..................................973 546-8800
100 Outwater Ln Garfield (07026) *(G-3726)*

Clearcut New Jersey, Pennsauken *Also called Richmond Steel Rule Dies Inc (G-8574)*

Cleardrain, Riverside *Also called Melville Industries Inc (G-9503)*

Clearwater Well Drilling Co..................................609 698-1800
1073 Prospect Ave Manahawkin (08050) *(G-5829)*

Clearway LLC..................................973 578-4578
414 Wilson Ave Newark (07105) *(G-7122)*

Cleary Machinery Co Inc..................................732 560-3200
24 Cedar St South Bound Brook (08880) *(G-10248)*

Clem's, Piscataway *Also called Clems Ornemental Iron Works (G-8750)*

Clements Industries Inc..................................201 440-5500
50 Ruta Ct South Hackensack (07606) *(G-10258)*

Clems Ornemental Iron Works..................................732 968-7200
110 11th St Piscataway (08854) *(G-8750)*

Clench, Lodi *Also called Tony Jones Apparel Inc (G-5606)*

Clenesco Products Corp..................................908 245-5255
298 Cox St Roselle (07203) *(G-9665)*

Cleve Shirtmakers Inc..................................201 825-6122
200 Meadowlands Pkwy # 2 Secaucus (07094) *(G-9872)*

Cli Group, The, Paterson *Also called Custom Laminations Inc (G-8243)*

Clic Time LLC..................................201 497-6743
50 Tice Blvd Ste 340 Woodcliff Lake (07677) *(G-12187)*

Clientsrver Tech Solutions LLC..................................732 710-4495
2 Austin Ave Fl 2 # 2 Iselin (08830) *(G-4621)*

Cliffside Body Corporation..................................201 945-3970
130 Broad Ave Fairview (07022) *(G-3359)*

Clifton Adhesive Inc..................................973 694-0845
48 Burgess Pl Wayne (07470) *(G-11619)*

Clifton Adhesives, Wayne *Also called Royal Adhesives & Sealants LLC (G-11680)*

Clifton Metal Products Co Inc..................................973 777-6100
41 Clifton Blvd Clifton (07011) *(G-1584)*

Clincial Genomics, Edison *Also called Enterix Inc (G-2512)*

Clinical Image Retrieval Syste..................................888 482-2362
12 Cork Hill Rd Ste 2 Franklin (07416) *(G-3597)*

Clinton Envelope, Pennsauken *Also called Tpg Graphics LLC (G-8586)*

Clinton Industries Inc..................................201 440-0400
207 Redneck Ave Little Ferry (07643) *(G-5498)*

Clip Strip Corp..................................201 342-9155
343 S River St Hackensack (07601) *(G-3897)*

Clogic LLC..................................973 934-5223
4 Sunset Ln Augusta (07822) *(G-119)*

Clogic Defense, Augusta *Also called Clogic LLC (G-119)*

Clordisys Solutions Inc..................................908 236-4100
50 Tannery Rd Ste 1 Branchburg (08876) *(G-647)*

Closets By Dsign - Cntl Jersey, Hamilton *Also called Denmatt Industries LLC (G-4106)*

Clothes Horse International..................................856 829-8460
2200 Wallace Blvd Ste A Cinnaminson (08077) *(G-1451)*

Clothing Emporium Inc..................................973 773-3250
682 Main Ave Passaic (07055) *(G-8129)*

Cloudageit Ltd Liability Co..................................888 205-4128
1308 Plymouth Rd North Brunswick (08902) *(G-7513)*

Clover Garden Ctr Ltd Lblty Co..................................856 235-4625
1017 S Church St Mount Laurel (08054) *(G-6789)*

Clover Hill Coffee Co, Colts Neck *Also called Colt Media Inc (G-1782)*

Clover Stamping Inc..................................973 278-4888
60 Spruce St Paterson (07501) *(G-8234)*

Clyde Otis Music Group..................................845 425-8198
494 N Woodland St Englewood (07631) *(G-2884)*

CMC Composites LLC..................................732 505-9400
870 Route 530 Ste 12 Whiting (08759) *(G-12066)*

CMC Joist & Deck, South Plainfield *Also called C M C Steel Fabricators Inc (G-10342)*

CMF Ltd Inc..................................609 695-3600
599 W Ingham Ave Ewing (08638) *(G-3010)*

Cmg, Branchburg *Also called Custom Molders Group LLC (G-654)*

Cmg Plastics, Branchburg *Also called Custom Molders Corp (G-653)*

CMI-Promex Inc..................................856 351-1000
7 Benjamin Green Rd Pedricktown (08067) *(G-8433)*

Cmic Cmo USA Corporation..................................609 395-9700
Cedar Brook Corporate Ctr Cranbury (08512) *(G-1824)*

Cmml, Wall Township *Also called Christian Mssons In Many Lands (G-11469)*

CMS Technology Inc..................................512 913-1898
10 Finderne Ave Ste A Bridgewater (08807) *(G-828)*

Cmyk Printing Inc..................................201 458-1300
651 Garden St Carlstadt (07072) *(G-1146)*

CNG Publishing Company..................................973 768-0978
43 Manchester Way Burlington (08016) *(G-964)*

Cni Ceramic Nozzles Inc..................................973 276-1535
23 Commerce Rd Ste L Fairfield (07004) *(G-3162)*

Cno Corporation..................................732 785-5799
611 Yellowbrick Rd Brick (08724) *(G-737)*

Cnr Products Co..................................201 384-7003
74 Portland Ave Bergenfield (07621) *(G-384)*

Cns Confectionery Products LLC..................................201 823-1400
33 Hook Rd Bayonne (07002) *(G-220)*

Co-Planar Inc..................................973 625-3500
88 Ford Rd Denville (07834) *(G-2032)*

Coast Rubber and Gasket Inc..................................609 747-0110
1208 Columbus Rd Ste G Burlington (08016) *(G-965)*

Coast Star..................................732 223-0076
13 Broad St Manasquan (08736) *(G-5869)*

Coast To Coast Lea & Vinyl Inc (PA)..................................732 525-8877
1 Crossman Rd S Sayreville (08872) *(G-9818)*

Coastal Creations, Lavallette *Also called Signal Systems International (G-5237)*

Coastal Metal Recycling Corp..................................732 738-6000
75 Crows Mill Rd Keasbey (08832) *(G-4927)*

Coaster Inc..................................732 775-3010
1011 Main St Ste B Asbury Park (07712) *(G-75)*

Coaster, The, Asbury Park *Also called Coaster Inc (G-75)*

Coates International Ltd (PA)..................................732 449-7717
2100 Highway 34 Wall Township (07719) *(G-11472)*

Coates Precision Engineering..................................732 449-9382
2100 State Route 34 Wall Township (07719) *(G-11473)*

Cobham McRelectronic Solutions, Eatontown *Also called Aeroflex Ctrl Components Inc (G-2378)*

Cobon Plastics Corp..................................973 344-6330
90 South St Newark (07114) *(G-7123)*

Cobra Power Systems Inc (PA)..................................908 486-1800
304 Monmouth Rd Millstone Township (08510) *(G-6263)*

Cobra Products Inc..................................856 241-7700
1 Warner Ct Swedesboro (08085) *(G-10688)*

Cobyco Inc..................................732 446-4448
65 Wilson Ave Manalapan (07726) *(G-5841)*

Coca Cola Bottling Co Mid Amer..................................732 398-4800
60 Deans Rhode Hall Rd Monmouth Junction (08852) *(G-6337)*

Coca-Cola Refreshments USA Inc..................................732 398-4800
60 Deans Rhode Hall Rd Monmouth Junction (08852) *(G-6338)*

Coca-Cola Refreshments USA Inc..................................201 635-6300
118 Moonachie Ave Carlstadt (07072) *(G-1147)*

Cocco Enterprises Inc (PA)..................................609 393-5939
3575 Quakerbridge Rd # 204 Trenton (08619) *(G-11043)*

Cockpit Usa Inc..................................212 575-1616
725 New Point Rd Elizabeth (07201) *(G-2719)*

Coco International Inc..................................973 694-1200
6 Highpoint Dr Wayne (07470) *(G-11620)*

Cocoa Processing Corp..................................908 688-0415
580 Luis Munoz Marin Blvd Jersey City (07310) *(G-4729)*

Cocoa Services Inc..................................856 234-1700
905 N Lenola Rd Moorestown (08057) *(G-6568)*

Cococare Products Inc..................................973 989-8880
85 Franklin Rd Ste 3a Dover (07801) *(G-2081)*

Coda Inc (PA)..................................201 825-7400
30 Industrial Ave Ste 1 Mahwah (07430) *(G-5760)*

Codenoll, Mountain Lakes *Also called Data Base Access Systems Inc (G-6856)*

Coesia Health & Beauty Inc (PA)..................................908 707-8008
335 Chambers Brook Rd Branchburg (08876) *(G-648)*

Coffee Associates Inc (PA)..................................201 945-1060
178 Old River Rd Edgewater (07020) *(G-2436)*

Coffee Company LLC (PA)..................................609 399-5533
928 Boardwalk Ocean City (08226) *(G-7750)*

Coffee Company LLC..................................609 398-2326
917 Asbury Ave Ocean City (08226) *(G-7751)*

Cognati Cheese Company Inc..................................201 807-9100
205 Moonachie Rd Moonachie (07074) *(G-6513)*

Cognizant Tech Solutions Corp (PA)..................................201 801-0233
500 Frank W Burr Blvd Teaneck (07666) *(G-10746)*

Cohansey Cove..................................609 884-7726
705 Jonathan Hoffman Rd Cape May (08204) *(G-1095)*

Coherent Inc..................................973 240-6851
31 Farinella Dr East Hanover (07936) *(G-2207)*

Coherent Advnced Crystal Group, East Hanover *Also called Coherent Inc (G-2207)*

Coilhose Pneumatics Inc..................................732 432-7177
19 Kimberly Rd East Brunswick (08816) *(G-2142)*

Coim USA Inc..................................856 224-1668
675 Billingsport Rd Paulsboro (08066) *(G-8415)*

Coim USA Inc (HQ)..................................856 224-8560
286 Mantua Grove Rd # 1 West Deptford (08066) *(G-11825)*

Coining Inc..................................201 791-4020
15 Mercedes Dr Montvale (07645) *(G-6449)*

Coining Holding Company (HQ)..................................201 791-4020
15 Mercedes Dr Montvale (07645) *(G-6450)*

Coining Manufactures, Montvale *Also called Coining Holding Company (G-6450)*

Coining Manufacturing LLC..................................973 253-0500
11 Lafayette Ky Colts Neck (07722) *(G-1781)*

Coining Mfg..................................973 253-0500
35 Monhegan St Ste 4 Clifton (07013) *(G-1585)*

Coining Technologies Inc..................................866 897-2304
35 Monhegan St Demarest (07627) *(G-2027)*

Colaneri Brothers, East Rutherford *Also called Robert Colaneri (G-2321)*

Colas Inc (HQ)..................................973 290-9082
73 Headquarters Plz 10t Morristown (07960) *(G-6700)*

Cold Headed Fasteners Inc..................................856 461-3244
401 Creek Rd Ste D Delanco (08075) *(G-2004)*

Cold Spring Ice Inc..................................609 884-3405
906 Schellenger St Cape May (08204) *(G-1096)*

A
L
P
H
A
B
E
T
I
C

Cold Stat Refregiration 201 251-2203
60 Eisenhower Dr Paramus (07652) *(G-7861)*
Cole Brothers Marble & Granite 856 455-7989
892 Parvin Mill Rd Elmer (08318) *(G-2790)*
Colemax Group LLC (PA) 201 489-1080
41 Grand Ave Ste 103 River Edge (07661) *(G-9463)*
Coles and Blenman Network LLC 973 432-7041
117 Orange St Bloomfield (07003) *(G-507)*
Colex Imaging Inc 201 414-5575
55-57 Bushes Ln Elmwood Park (07407) *(G-2810)*
Colfajas Inc 973 727-4813
5 West St Succasunna (07876) *(G-10620)*
Colgate-Palmolive Company 732 878-6062
251 S 8th Ave Highland Park (08904) *(G-4302)*
Colgate-Palmolive Company 732 878-7500
909 River Rd Piscataway (08854) *(G-8751)*
Colgate-Palmolive Company 609 239-6001
400 Elbow Ln Burlington (08016) *(G-966)*
Colibri Scentique Ltd Lblty Co 201 445-5715
68 Chadwick Pl Glen Rock (07452) *(G-3824)*
Colie Sail Makers Inc 732 892-4344
1649 Bay Ave Point Pleasant Boro (08742) *(G-8935)*
Colinear Machine & Design Inc 973 300-1681
7 Wilson Dr Sparta (07871) *(G-10492)*
Collagen Matrix Inc. 201 786-9300
110 Commerce Dr Allendale (07401) *(G-7)*
Collagen Matrix Inc (PA) 201 405-1477
15 Thornton Rd Oakland (07436) *(G-7679)*
Collection Xiix Ltd 201 854-7740
7001 Anpesil Dr Ste 2 North Bergen (07047) *(G-7441)*
College Spun Media Inc 973 945-5040
95 River St Ste 408 Hoboken (07030) *(G-4465)*
Collins and Company LLC 973 427-4068
121 Wagaraw Rd Hawthorne (07506) *(G-4226)*
Colonial - Bende Ribbons Inc 973 777-8700
180 Autumn St Passaic (07055) *(G-8130)*
Colonial Concrete Company (HQ) 973 482-1920
1196 Mccarter Hwy Newark (07104) *(G-7124)*
Colonial Concrete Company 201 869-0055
9301 Railroad Ave Ste 1 North Bergen (07047) *(G-7442)*
Colonial Uphl & Win Treatments 609 641-3124
425 S Main St Pleasantville (08232) *(G-8905)*
Colonial Wire & Cable Co Inc 732 287-1557
85 National Rd Edison (08817) *(G-2486)*
Colonna Brothers Inc (PA) 800 626-8384
4102 Bergen Tpke North Bergen (07047) *(G-7443)*
Color Coded LLC 718 482-1063
249 Thomas Mcgovern Dr # 3 Jersey City (07305) *(G-4730)*
Color Comp Inc 856 262-3040
1041 Glassboro Rd Ste E5 Williamstown (08094) *(G-12083)*
Color Company, Linden *Also called Colorflo Inc (G-5360)*
Color Decor Ltd Liability Co 973 689-2699
518 E 36th St Paterson (07504) *(G-8235)*
Color Logic Inc 973 515-0099
8 Woodhollow Rd Ste Pl-3 Parsippany (07054) *(G-7974)*
Color Screen Pros Inc 973 268-5080
100 Verona Ave Newark (07104) *(G-7125)*
Color Techniques Inc 908 412-9292
260 Ryan St South Plainfield (07080) *(G-10347)*
Colorcraft Sign Co 609 386-1115
400 Magnolia St Beverly (08010) *(G-461)*
Colorflo Inc 908 862-3010
1261 W Elizabeth Ave Linden (07036) *(G-5360)*
Colorful Story Books Inc 908 561-3333
4301 New Brunswick Ave South Plainfield (07080) *(G-10348)*
Colorite Plastics Company (HQ) 201 941-2900
101 Railroad Ave Ridgefield (07657) *(G-9355)*
Colorite Polymers 800 631-1577
101 Railroad Ave Ridgefield (07657) *(G-9356)*
Coloron Plastics Corporation 908 685-1210
169 Meister Ave Branchburg (08876) *(G-649)*
Colorsource Inc 856 488-8100
7025 Central Hwy Pennsauken (08109) *(G-8495)*
Colortec Printing and Mailing 856 767-0108
424 Kelley Dr Ste A West Berlin (08091) *(G-11709)*
Colortec Printing Ink, Parsippany *Also called Prismacolor Corp (G-8073)*
Colt Media Inc 732 946-3276
4 Wedgewood Ave Colts Neck (07722) *(G-1782)*
Colter & Peterson Inc (PA) 973 684-0901
19 Fairfield Pl West Caldwell (07006) *(G-11771)*
Colton Industries Inc 908 277-2040
117 Colt Rd Summit (07901) *(G-10640)*
Coltwell Industries Inc 908 276-7600
55 Winans Ave Cranford (07016) *(G-1901)*
Columbia Fuel Services Inc 732 751-0044
1717 Highway 34 Wall Township (07727) *(G-11474)*
Columbia Industries Inc (PA) 201 337-7332
567 Commerce St Franklin Lakes (07417) *(G-3612)*
Columbia Marketing Corp 973 275-1700
221 Rutgers St Maplewood (07040) *(G-5916)*

Columbia Paint Lab Inc 201 435-4884
452 Communipaw Ave Jersey City (07304) *(G-4731)*
Columbia Press Inc 973 575-6535
12 Industrial Rd Fairfield (07004) *(G-3163)*
Columbian Orna Ir Works Inc 973 697-0927
332 Vreeland Ave Paterson (07513) *(G-8236)*
Colwood Electronics Inc 732 938-5556
44 Main St Farmingdale (07727) *(G-3380)*
Com Tek Wrkplace Solutions LLC 973 927-6814
1099 Wall St W Ste 269 Lyndhurst (07071) *(G-5678)*
Com-Fab Inc 973 296-0433
921 Burnt Meadow Rd B Hewitt (07421) *(G-4288)*
Comar Inc (PA) 856 692-6100
201 Laurel Rd Fl 2 Voorhees (08043) *(G-11425)*
Comar Inc 856 507-5461
201 Laurel Rd Fl 2 Voorhees (08043) *(G-11426)*
Comar LLC (HQ) 856 692-6100
220 Laurel Rd Fl 2 Voorhees (08043) *(G-11427)*
Comar LLC 856 507-5483
3100 N Mill Rd Vineland (08360) *(G-11337)*
Comar Glass, Voorhees *Also called Comar Inc (G-11425)*
Comar Plastics, Voorhees *Also called Comar LLC (G-11427)*
Comarco Products Inc 856 342-7557
501 Jackson St Camden (08104) *(G-1054)*
Comarco Quality Pork Products, Camden *Also called Comarco Products Inc (G-1054)*
Comet Tool Company Inc 856 256-1070
651 Lambs Rd Pitman (08071) *(G-8840)*
Comex Systems Inc. 800 543-6959
101 Pleasant Hill Rd Chester (07930) *(G-1435)*
Comfort Rvolution Holdings LLC 732 272-9111
187 Rte 36 Ste 205 West Long Branch (07764) *(G-11845)*
Comfort Zone 732 869-9990
44 Main Ave Ocean Grove (07756) *(G-7760)*
Comfortaire Htg & A Conditio, Vineland *Also called Comfortaire Ltd Liability Co (G-11338)*
Comfortaire Ltd Liability Co 856 692-5000
1435 E Sherman Ave Vineland (08361) *(G-11338)*
Comfortfit Labs Inc. 908 259-9100
246 Columbus Ave Roselle (07203) *(G-9666)*
Comm Port Technologies Inc 732 738-8780
1 Corporate Dr Ste F Cranbury (08512) *(G-1825)*
Command Nutritionals LLC 973 227-8210
10 Washington Ave Ste 1 Fairfield (07004) *(G-3164)*
Command Web Offset Company Inc (PA) 201 863-8100
100 Castle Rd Secaucus (07094) *(G-9873)*
Commander Imaging Products Inc 973 742-9298
70 Spruce St Ste 8 Paterson (07501) *(G-8237)*
Commeatus LLC 847 772-5314
5216 Fox Run Dr Plainsboro (08536) *(G-8878)*
Commerce Enterprises Inc 201 368-2100
61 S Paramus Rd Ste 135 Paramus (07652) *(G-7862)*
Commerce Financial Prtrs Corp. 908 241-9880
305 Cox St Roselle (07203) *(G-9667)*
Commerce Register Inc 201 445-3000
190 Godwin Ave Midland Park (07432) *(G-6223)*
Commercial Composition & Prtg 856 662-0557
1601 Sherman Ave Ste B Pennsauken (08110) *(G-8496)*
Commercial Pdts Svcs Group Inc (PA) 609 730-4111
1580 Reed Rd Pennington (08534) *(G-8447)*
Commercial Products Co Inc 973 427-6887
117 Ethel Ave Ste 143 Hawthorne (07506) *(G-4227)*
Commercial Water Sports Inc 609 624-3404
28 Clermont Dr Cape May Court House (08210) *(G-1113)*
Communication Devices Inc (PA) 973 334-1980
85 Fulton St Unit 2 Boonton (07005) *(G-560)*
Communication Products Co 973 977-8490
201 Mclean Blvd Paterson (07504) *(G-8238)*
Communications Supply Corp 732 346-1864
104 Sunfield Ave Edison (08837) *(G-2487)*
Communique Inc 973 751-7588
120 Greylock Ave Belleville (07109) *(G-298)*
Community News Network Inc 856 428-3399
6 S Haddon Ave Ste 1 Haddonfield (08033) *(G-4058)*
Community News Service LLC 609 396-1511
15 Princess Rd K Lawrenceville (08648) *(G-5254)*
Community Pride Publications 609 921-8760
55 Prnceton Hightstown Rd Princeton Junction (08550) *(G-9150)*
Commvault Americas Inc 888 746-3849
1 Commvault Way Tinton Falls (07724) *(G-10827)*
Commvault Systems Inc (PA) 732 870-4000
1 Commvault Way Tinton Falls (07724) *(G-10828)*
Comodo Group Inc (PA) 888 266-6361
1255 Broad St Clifton (07013) *(G-1586)*
Compact Fluorescent Systems 908 475-8991
463 Stanhope Rd Sparta (07871) *(G-10493)*
Compass Wire Cloth & 856 853-7616
1942 N Mill Rd Vineland (08360) *(G-11339)*
Compass Wire Cloth Corp 856 853-7616
1942 N Mill Rd Vineland (08360) *(G-11340)*
Compco Analytical Inc 201 641-3936
215 Gates Rd Ste U Little Ferry (07643) *(G-5499)*

Competech Smrtcard Sltions Inc 201 256-4184
440 Sylvan Ave Ste 250 Englewood Cliffs (07632) *(G-2953)*

Compex Corporation 856 719-8657
439 Commerce Ln Ste 1 West Berlin (08091) *(G-11710)*

Complete Filter 732 441-0321
3 Donamar Ln South Amboy (08879) *(G-10235)*

Complete Optical Laboratory 973 338-8886
1255 Broad St Ste 202 Bloomfield (07003) *(G-508)*

Compliance Educational Systems, Marlton *Also called Plescia & Company Inc* *(G-5994)*

Componding Engrg Solutions Inc 973 340-4000
473 Us Highway 46 Clifton (07011) *(G-1587)*

Component Hardware Group Inc (PA) 800 526-3694
1890 Swarthmore Ave Lakewood (08701) *(G-5095)*

Components & Controls Inc 201 483-9190
493 Washington Ave Carlstadt (07072) *(G-1148)*

Components Corporation 866 426-6726
6 Kinsey Pl Denville (07834) *(G-2033)*

Composecure LLC 908 518-0500
309 Pierce St Somerset (08873) *(G-10083)*

Composecure LLC (PA) 908 518-0500
500 Memorial Dr Ste 4 Somerset (08873) *(G-10084)*

Composing Room Inc (PA) 856 662-9111
9100 Pennsauken Hwy Pennsauken (08110) *(G-8497)*

Composition Printing, Jersey City *Also called Logomania Inc* *(G-4778)*

Compounders Inc 732 938-5007
15 Marl Rd Farmingdale (07727) *(G-3381)*

Comprehensive Connectivity Com, Fairfield *Also called Vcom Intl Multi-Media Corp* *(G-3337)*

Comprehensive Healthcare Systm 732 362-2000
2025 Lincoln Hwy Edison (08817) *(G-2488)*

Comprehensive Mktg Systems, Union *Also called Comprehensive Mktg Systems* *(G-11165)*

Comprehensive Mktg Systems 908 810-9778
850 Springfield Rd # 353 Union (07083) *(G-11165)*

Comprelli Equipment and Svc 973 428-8687
9 Brace Dr East Hanover (07936) *(G-2208)*

Comptime Inc 201 760-2400
385 N Franklin Tpke Ste 6 Ramsey (07446) *(G-9238)*

Comptime Print & Copy Center, Ramsey *Also called Comptime Inc* *(G-9238)*

Compufab Sales Inc 856 786-0175
2303 Garry Rd Ste 1 Cinnaminson (08077) *(G-1452)*

Computa-Base-Machining Inc 856 767-9517
411 N Grove St Berlin (08009) *(G-432)*

Computech Applications LLC 201 261-5251
768 Howard Ct E Oradell (07649) *(G-7807)*

Computer Aided Software Tech, Woodcliff Lake *Also called Cast Inc* *(G-12185)*

Computer Company North America 909 265-3390
356 Wren Ln Bedminster (07921) *(G-270)*

Computer Control Corp 973 492-8265
10 Park Pl Ste 1 Butler (07405) *(G-1001)*

Computer Crafts Inc 973 423-3500
57 Thomas Rd N Hawthorne (07506) *(G-4228)*

Computer Doc Associates Inc 908 647-4445
2007 Washington Valley Rd Martinsville (08836) *(G-6009)*

Computer Printers & Media Sups 732 400-7888
6 Alvin Ct East Brunswick (08816) *(G-2143)*

Computer Sources 201 791-9443
37 Leliarts Ln Elmwood Park (07407) *(G-2811)*

Computeradio 973 220-0087
7 Brittany Rd Montville (07045) *(G-6486)*

Comtrex Systems Corporation (PA) 856 778-0090
101 Foster Rd B Moorestown (08057) *(G-6569)*

Comtron Inc 732 446-7571
12 Commerce St Springfield (07081) *(G-10548)*

Comus International Inc (PA) 973 777-6900
454 Allwood Rd Clifton (07012) *(G-1588)*

Comverge Giants Inc 973 884-5970
25a Vreeland Rd Ste 300 Florham Park (07932) *(G-3496)*

Comverge Giants Inc (HQ) 973 884-5970
120 Eagle Rock Ave # 190 East Hanover (07936) *(G-2209)*

Con Cap Sports Wear 973 778-2628
64 Passaic St Wood Ridge (07075) *(G-12136)*

Conagraphics Inc 973 331-1113
1180 Us Highway 46 Ste 2 Parsippany (07054) *(G-7975)*

Conair Corporation 239 673-2125
150 Milford Rd East Windsor (08520) *(G-2353)*

Conair Corporation 609 426-1300
150 Milford Rd East Windsor (08520) *(G-2354)*

Concept Group Inc (PA) 856 767-5506
380 Cooper Rd West Berlin (08091) *(G-11711)*

Concept Professional Systems 732 938-5321
5005 Belmar Blvd Ste B1 Wall Township (07727) *(G-11475)*

Concord Products Company Inc 856 933-3000
360 Columbia Dr Sewell (08080) *(G-9945)*

Concord Truss Co, Woodbury Heights *Also called Woodbury Roof Truss Inc* *(G-12178)*

Concorde Specialty Gases Inc 732 544-9899
36 Eaton Rd Eatontown (07724) *(G-2388)*

Concrete Cutting Partners Inc 201 440-2233
508 Hudson St Hackensack (07601) *(G-3898)*

Concrete On Demand Inc 201 337-0005
45 Edison Ave Ste 1 Oakland (07436) *(G-7680)*

Concrete Stone & Tile Corp (PA) 973 948-7193
17 Ridge Rd Branchville (07826) *(G-728)*

Conduent State Healthcare LLC 973 824-3250
60 Park Pl Ste 605 Newark (07102) *(G-7126)*

Conduent State Healthcare LLC 973 754-6134
100 Hamilton Plz Ste 400 Paterson (07505) *(G-8239)*

Conexion Printing, Hawthorne *Also called Tekno Inc* *(G-4260)*

Confectionately Yours LLC 732 821-6863
3391 State Route 27 # 121 Franklin Park (08823) *(G-3626)*

Confires Fire Prtction Svc LLC 908 822-2700
910 Oak Tree Ave South Plainfield (07080) *(G-10349)*

Congoleum Corporation (PA) 609 584-3000
3500 Quakerbridge Rd Trenton (08619) *(G-11044)*

Congoleum Corporation 609 584-3601
3705 Quakerbridge Rd # 211 Trenton (08619) *(G-11045)*

Congoleum Corporation 609 584-3000
1945 E State Street Ext Trenton (08619) *(G-11046)*

Congruent Machine Co Inc 973 764-6767
107 Maple Grange Rd Vernon (07462) *(G-11297)*

Conistics Inc 609 584-2600
1800 E State St Ste 148 Hamilton (08609) *(G-4105)*

Conneaut Creek Ship Repr Inc 212 863-9406
333 Washington St Ste 201 Jersey City (07302) *(G-4732)*

Connecting Products Inc 609 512-1121
186 Tamarack Cir Skillman (08558) *(G-10029)*

Connecting Products Inc 609 688-1808
194 Tamarack Cir Ste 1 Skillman (08558) *(G-10030)*

Connector Mfg Co 513 860-4455
123 Town Square Pl Jersey City (07310) *(G-4733)*

Connector Products Inc 856 829-9190
1300 John Tipton Blvd Pennsauken (08110) *(G-8498)*

Connell Mining Products LLC 908 673-3700
200 Connell Dr Berkeley Heights (07922) *(G-406)*

Conolog Corporation (PA) 908 722-8081
5 Columbia Rd Branchburg (08876) *(G-650)*

Conopco Inc 201 894-7760
940 Sylvan Ave Englewood Cliffs (07632) *(G-2954)*

Conopco Inc 856 722-1664
305 Fellowship Rd Ste 114 Mount Laurel (08054) *(G-6790)*

Conopco Inc 920 499-2509
800 Sylvan Ave Englewood Cliffs (07632) *(G-2955)*

Consarc Corporation (HQ) 609 267-8000
100 Indel Ave Rancocas (08073) *(G-9256)*

Consoldate Cntiner Holdings NJ, Cranbury *Also called Consolidated Cont Holdings LLC* *(G-1826)*

Consolidated Stl Alum Fence Inc 908 272-0494
316 N 12th St Kenilworth (07033) *(G-4948)*

Consolidated Cont Holdings LLC 609 655-0855
4 Pleasant Hill Rd Cranbury (08512) *(G-1826)*

Consolidated Container Co LP 908 289-5862
28-36 Slater Dr Elizabeth (07206) *(G-2720)*

Consolidated Packg Group Inc 201 440-4240
30 Bergen Tpke Ridgefield Park (07660) *(G-9401)*

Consolidated Stl Alum Fence I, Kenilworth *Also called Consolidated Stl Alum Fence Inc* *(G-4948)*

Constant Services Inc 973 227-2990
17 Commerce Rd Ste 2 Fairfield (07004) *(G-3165)*

Constantia Blythewood LLC 732 974-4100
1111 N Point Blvd Belmar (07719) *(G-356)*

Constantine Engrg Labs Co, Mahwah *Also called Celco* *(G-5757)*

Constitution Arms, Maplewood *Also called 2a Holdings Inc* *(G-5913)*

Constitution Co, Woodbury *Also called Dewechter Inc* *(G-12159)*

Construction Dynamics Inc 732 840-7766
1381 Sally Ike Rd Brick (08724) *(G-738)*

Construction Services, Wayne *Also called Orsillo & Company* *(G-11668)*

Construction Specialties (PA) 908 236-0800
3 Werner Way Ste 100 Lebanon (08833) *(G-5282)*

Construction Specialties Inc 908 272-2771
49 Meeker Ave Cranford (07016) *(G-1902)*

Consumer Graphics Inc 732 469-4699
18 Fordham Rd Somerset (08873) *(G-10085)*

Contact Len Lab, Millburn *Also called Lens Mode Inc* *(G-6255)*

Contact Untd TI & Stamping Co 973 256-7171
6 Andrews Dr Woodland Park (07424) *(G-12216)*

Container Graphics Corp 732 922-1180
3535 Highway 66 Ste 2 Neptune (07753) *(G-6904)*

Container Manufacturing, Middlesex *Also called Container Mfg Inc* *(G-6155)*

Container Mfg Inc 732 563-0100
50 Baekeland Ave Middlesex (08846) *(G-6155)*

Conte Farms 609 268-0513
299 Flyatt Rd Tabernacle (08088) *(G-10737)*

Contech, Elizabeth *Also called Consolidated Container Co LP* *(G-2720)*

Contempocork LLC 201 262-7738
175 Dorchester Rd River Edge (07661) *(G-9464)*

Contemporary Cabling Company 732 382-5064
90 Brookside Ter Clark (07066) *(G-1499)*

A
L
P
H
A
B
E
T
I
C

Contemprary Grphics Bndery Inc 856 663-7277
1200 Ferry Ave Camden (08104) *(G-1055)*

Contes Pasta Company Inc 856 697-3400
310 Wheat Rd Vineland (08360) *(G-11341)*

Conti-Robert and Co JV 732 520-5000
2045 Lincoln Hwy Edison (08817) *(G-2489)*

Continental Aromatics 973 238-9300
1 Thomas Rd S Hawthorne (07506) *(G-4229)*

Continental Cap & Import, Wood Ridge *Also called Con Cap Sports Wear* *(G-12136)*

Continental Cast Stone East, West Berlin *Also called Russell Cast Stone Inc* *(G-11748)*

Continental Cookies Inc 201 498-1966
185 S Newman St Hackensack (07601) *(G-3899)*

Continental Food & Bev Inc 973 815-1600
495 River Rd Clifton (07014) *(G-1589)*

Continental Precision Corp (PA) 908 754-3030
25 Howard St Piscataway (08854) *(G-8752)*

Continental Woodworking Co 609 654-0820
617 Stokes Rd Ste 4305 Medford (08055) *(G-6067)*

Continntal Concession Sups Inc 516 629-4906
1135 Springfield Rd Union (07083) *(G-11166)*

Continuity Logic LLC 866 321-5079
55 Lane Rd Ste 303 Fairfield (07004) *(G-3166)*

Contour Next, Parsippany *Also called Ascensia Diabetes Care US Inc* *(G-7952)*

Contract Coatings Inc 201 343-3131
161 Beech St Hackensack (07601) *(G-3900)*

Contract Filling Inc 973 433-0053
10 Cliffside Dr Cedar Grove (07009) *(G-1275)*

Contravir Pharmaceuticals Inc (PA) 732 902-4000
399 Thornall St Ste 1 Edison (08837) *(G-2490)*

Control & Power Systems Inc 973 439-0500
17 Spielman Rd Fairfield (07004) *(G-3167)*

Control Demolition, Bayonne *Also called Control Industries Inc* *(G-221)*

Control Group, Norwood *Also called Norwood Printing Inc* *(G-7632)*

Control Group, Norwood *Also called Cheringal Associates Inc* *(G-7618)*

Control Industries Inc (PA) 201 437-3826
197 E 22nd St Ste 4 Bayonne (07002) *(G-221)*

Control Instruments Corp 973 575-9114
25 Law Dr Fairfield (07004) *(G-3168)*

Control Products, East Hanover *Also called Calculagraph Co* *(G-2204)*

Control Products Inc 973 887-5000
272 Ridgedale Ave 280 East Hanover (07936) *(G-2210)*

Convatec Healthcare A, S.A.R., Bridgewater *Also called Convatec Inc* *(G-829)*

Convatec Inc (HQ) 908 904-2500
1160 Rte 22 Ste 201 Bridgewater (08807) *(G-829)*

Convenience Works, West Deptford *Also called Hussmann Corporation* *(G-11828)*

Convention News Company Inc (PA) 201 444-5075
214 Franklin Ave Midland Park (07432) *(G-6224)*

Conversion Technology Co Inc 732 752-5660
4301 New Brunswick Ave A South Plainfield (07080) *(G-10350)*

Convertech Inc 973 328-1850
353 Richard Mine Rd Ste 4 Wharton (07885) *(G-11982)*

Converter Company, The, Woodbury Heights *Also called 431 Converters Inc* *(G-12173)*

Converting Resources, Paterson *Also called Stonebridge Paper LLC* *(G-8386)*

Conveyer Installers America 908 453-4729
5 Tamarack Rd Belvidere (07823) *(G-367)*

Conveyors By North American 973 777-6600
156 Huron Ave Clifton (07013) *(G-1590)*

Cookie Cupboard, Cedar Grove *Also called Fairfield Gourmet Food Corp* *(G-1283)*

Cookman Creamery LLC 732 361-5215
1 Mariners Bnd Brielle (08730) *(G-911)*

Coolenheat Inc 908 925-4473
11 Clinton Ct Kendall Park (08824) *(G-4934)*

Cooper Alloy Corporation 908 688-4120
201 Sweetland Ave Ste 1 Hillside (07205) *(G-4403)*

Cooper Burial Vaults Co 856 547-8405
621 Atlantic Ave Barrington (08007) *(G-174)*

Cooper Interconnect 856 935-7560
23 S Front St Salem (08079) *(G-9804)*

Cooper Lighting LLC 609 395-4277
1 Broadway Rd Cranbury (08512) *(G-1827)*

Cooper Power Systems LLC 732 481-4630
42 Cindy Ln Ocean (07712) *(G-7719)*

Cooper Power Systems LLC 856 719-1100
402 Bloomfield Dr Ste 1 West Berlin (08091) *(G-11712)*

Cooper-Wilbert Vault Co Inc (PA) 856 547-8405
621 Atlantic Ave Barrington (08007) *(G-175)*

Coordinated Metals Inc 201 460-7280
626 16th St Carlstadt (07072) *(G-1149)*

Coors Brewing Company 732 767-3300
329 Hana Rd Edison (08817) *(G-2491)*

Copack International Inc 973 405-5151
23 Carol St Clifton (07014) *(G-1591)*

Coperion Corporation (HQ) 201 327-6300
590 Woodbury Glassboro Rd Sewell (08080) *(G-9946)*

Coperion K-Tron Pitman Inc (HQ) 856 589-0500
590 Woodbury Glassboro Rd Sewell (08080) *(G-9947)*

Copper Boss Ltd Liability Co 888 629-2190
40 Mayfield Ave Edison (08837) *(G-2492)*

Copy Depot, The, Randolph *Also called Graphics Depot Inc* *(G-9281)*

Copy-Rite Printing 609 597-9182
378 N Main St Ste A Manahawkin (08050) *(G-5830)*

Copyshop 732 721-5700
921 Us Highway 9 South Amboy (08879) *(G-10236)*

Cor Products Inc 973 731-4952
20 Standish Ave West Orange (07052) *(G-11890)*

Corban Energy Group Corp 201 509-8555
418 Falmouth Ave Elmwood Park (07407) *(G-2812)*

Corbco Inc 609 549-6299
40 Canterbury Dr Forked River (08731) *(G-3536)*

Corbett Industries Inc 201 445-6311
39 Hewson Ave Ste B Waldwick (07463) *(G-11443)*

Corbi Printing Co Inc 856 547-2444
106 W Atlantic Ave Audubon (08106) *(G-116)*

Corbion Group 973 256-0198
100 Adams Dr Totowa (07512) *(G-10940)*

Corbo Jewelers Inc 973 777-1635
1055 Bloomfield Ave Clifton (07012) *(G-1592)*

Corbo Jewelers of Styertowne, Clifton *Also called Corbo Jewelers Inc* *(G-1592)*

Corcentric 877 790-7272
457 Haddonfield Rd # 220 Cherry Hill (08002) *(G-1357)*

Cordes Machine Div, Mountainside *Also called Remington Industries Inc* *(G-6887)*

Cordes Printing Inc 201 652-7272
460 Braen Ave Wyckoff (07481) *(G-12248)*

Cordis International Corp 732 524-0400
1 Johnson And Johnson Plz New Brunswick (08933) *(G-6953)*

Core 3 Brewery Ltd Lblty Co 856 562-0386
3171 Coles Mill Rd Franklinville (08322) *(G-3629)*

Core Acquisition LLC (PA) 732 983-6025
215 Wood Ave Ste 215 # 215 Middlesex (08846) *(G-6156)*

Core Laboratories LP 609 896-2673
11 Princess Rd Ste H Lawrenceville (08648) *(G-5255)*

Core Tech Solutions Inc 609 443-1400
50 Lake Dr East Windsor (08520) *(G-2355)*

Corentec America Inc 949 379-6227
60 Washington St Ste 202 Morristown (07960) *(G-6701)*

Corepharma LLC 732 983-6025
215 Wood Ave Ste 215 # 215 Middlesex (08846) *(G-6157)*

Coretech International Inc 908 454-7999
41 Industrial Rd Alpha (08865) *(G-40)*

Corgi Spirits LLC 862 219-3114
150 Pacific Ave Bldg P Jersey City (07304) *(G-4734)*

Corim Industries, Brick *Also called Corim International Coffee Imp* *(G-739)*

Corim International Coffee Imp (PA) 800 942-4201
1112 Industrial Pkwy Brick (08724) *(G-739)*

Cormedix Inc (PA) 908 517-9500
400 Connell Dr Ste 5000 Berkeley Heights (07922) *(G-407)*

Corn Products International, Bridgewater *Also called Ingredion Incorporated* *(G-846)*

Cornell Crane Mfg Ltd 609 742-1900
224 Llenroc Ln Westville (08093) *(G-11937)*

Cornell Machine Co Inc 973 379-6860
45 Brown Ave Springfield (07081) *(G-10549)*

Corner Stone Software Inc 732 938-5229
1246 Hwy 33 Howell (07731) *(G-4549)*

Cornerstone Imaging, Flemington *Also called Cornerstone Prints Imaging LLC* *(G-3431)*

Cornerstone Prints Imaging LLC 908 782-7966
179 State Route 31 Ste 8 Flemington (08822) *(G-3431)*

Corning Pharmaceutical GL LLC 856 794-7100
563 Crystal Ave Vineland (08360) *(G-11342)*

Coronation Sheet Metal Co 908 686-0930
2198 Stanley Ter Union (07083) *(G-11167)*

Coronet Inc 973 345-7660
55 Shepherds Ln Totowa (07512) *(G-10941)*

Coronet Led, Totowa *Also called Coronet Inc* *(G-10941)*

Coronis Building Systems Inc 609 261-2200
92 Columbus Jobstown Rd Columbus (08022) *(G-1801)*

Corp American Mica 908 587-5237
1015 Pennsylvania Ave Linden (07036) *(G-5361)*

Corporate Computer Systems 732 739-5600
33 Washington St Ste 1002 Newark (07102) *(G-7127)*

Corporate Envelope & Prtg Co 732 752-4333
299r Us Highway 22 Green Brook (08812) *(G-3855)*

Corporate Mailings Inc (PA) 973 439-1168
14 Henderson Dr West Caldwell (07006) *(G-11772)*

Corporate Mailings Inc. 973 808-0009
26 Parsippany Rd Whippany (07981) *(G-12017)*

Corrigan Center For Integrativ 973 239-0700
67 Haller Dr Cedar Grove (07009) *(G-1276)*

Corrview International LLC 973 770-0571
9 Pahaquarry Rd Hopatcong (07843) *(G-4535)*

Corte Provisions, Newark *Also called Seabrite Corp* *(G-7305)*

Cosmetic Coatings Inc 201 438-7150
219 Broad St Carlstadt (07072) *(G-1150)*

Cosmetic Concepts Inc 973 546-1234
20 Chestnut St Garfield (07026) *(G-3727)*

Cosmetic Essence LLC (HQ) 732 888-7788
2182 Hwy 35 Holmdel (07733) *(G-4512)*

(G-0000) Company's Geographic Section entry number

Cosmetic Essence LLC 201 941-9800
1135 Pleasantview Ter Ridgefield (07657) *(G-9357)*

Cosmetic Essence Inc 732 888-7788
2182 State Route 35 Holmdel (07733) *(G-4513)*

Cosmic Custom Screen Printing (PA) 856 629-8337
935 S Black Horse Pike Williamstown (08094) *(G-12084)*

Cosmopolitan Food Group Inc 908 998-1818
50 Harrison St Ste 208 Hoboken (07030) *(G-4466)*

Cospack America Corp 732 548-5858
3856 Park Ave Edison (08820) *(G-2493)*

Cosrich Group Inc (HQ) 866 771-7473
51 La France Ave 55 Bloomfield (07003) *(G-509)*

Costa Custom Cabinets Inc 973 429-7004
248 Montgomery St Bloomfield (07003) *(G-510)*

Costa Mar Cnvas Enclosures LLC 609 965-1538
1324 Moss Mill Rd Egg Harbor City (08215) *(G-2660)*

Costa's Cabinets, Bloomfield Also called Costa Custom Cabinets Inc *(G-510)*

Costume Gallery Inc 609 386-6601
700 Creek Rd Delanco (08075) *(G-2005)*

Cottage Lace and Ribbon Co Inc (PA) 732 776-9353
210 3rd Ave Ste 21 Neptune (07753) *(G-6905)*

Cotterman Inc 856 415-0800
100 Hayes Ave Wenonah (08090) *(G-11703)*

Cottrell Graphics & Advg Spc 732 349-7430
2121 Route 9 Toms River (08755) *(G-10873)*

Coty Research and Development, Morris Plains Also called Coty US LLC *(G-6658)*

Coty US LLC 973 490-8700
410 American Rd Morris Plains (07950) *(G-6658)*

Counter Efx Inc 908 203-0155
301 Roycefield Rd Bldg 5 Hillsborough (08844) *(G-4326)*

Counter-Fit Inc 609 871-8888
1 Ironside Ct Willingboro (08046) *(G-12118)*

Countertops Plus Inc 973 365-2232
61 Willet St Passaic (07055) *(G-8131)*

Counting Sheep Coffee Inc 973 589-4104
41 Malvern St Newark (07105) *(G-7128)*

Country Club Ice Cream 973 729-5570
4 Tyler St Sparta (07871) *(G-10494)*

Country Home Bakers LLC - GA 856 931-7052
361 Benigno Blvd Ste C Bellmawr (08031) *(G-335)*

Country Oven 732 494-4838
1585 Oak Tree Rd Ste 207 Iselin (08830) *(G-4622)*

County Concrete Corporation 973 538-3113
Ridgedale Ave Morristown (07960) *(G-6702)*

County Concrete Corporation (PA) 973 744-2188
50 Railroad Ave Kenvil (07847) *(G-5010)*

County Conservation Co Inc 856 227-6900
212 Blckwood Barnsboro Rd Sewell (08080) *(G-9948)*

County Graphics Forms MGT LLC 908 474-9797
2 Stercho Rd Linden (07036) *(G-5362)*

County Line Phrmaceuticals LLC 262 439-8109
10 Bloomfield Ave Ste 3 Pine Brook (07058) *(G-8695)*

County of Somerset 732 469-3363
40 Polhemus Ln Bridgewater (08807) *(G-830)*

County of Warren 908 475-7975
519 S 185 County Rd Belvidere (07823) *(G-368)*

Countyline Elec Contrs Corp 732 961-6738
2037 Lanes Mill Rd Lakewood (08701) *(G-5096)*

Courier News, Somerville Also called Gannett Co Inc *(G-10211)*

Courier Newspaper, The, Middletown Also called Bay Shore Press Inc *(G-6211)*

Courtney Boatlifts Inc 732 892-8900
1209 Bay Ave Point Pleasant Boro (08742) *(G-8936)*

Couse & Bolten Co 973 344-6330
90 S St Dock 5 Newark (07114) *(G-7129)*

Couture Exchange 732 933-1123
691 Broad St Shrewsbury (07702) *(G-9995)*

Covalnce Spcalty Adhesives LLC 732 356-2870
87 Lincoln Blvd Middlesex (08846) *(G-6158)*

Covalnce Spcialty Coatings LLC 732 356-2870
87 Lincoln Blvd Middlesex (08846) *(G-6159)*

Coventry of New Jersey Inc 856 988-5521
10000 Lincoln Dr E # 201 Marlton (08053) *(G-5968)*

Cover Co Inc 908 707-9797
19 Readington Rd Branchburg (08876) *(G-651)*

Covia Holdings Corporation 856 785-2700
1100 Whitehead Rd Dividing Creek (08315) *(G-2071)*

Covia Holdings Corporation 856 451-6400
1660 S Burlington Rd Bridgeton (08302) *(G-782)*

Cox Stationers and Printers 908 928-1010
1634 E Elizabeth Ave Linden (07036) *(G-5363)*

Cozy Formal Wear Inc (PA) 973 661-9781
695 Passaic Ave Nutley (07110) *(G-7645)*

Cozy Home Fashions, Secaucus Also called Sander Sales Enterprises Ltd *(G-9920)*

Cozzoli Machine Company (PA) 732 564-0400
50 Schoolhouse Rd Somerset (08873) *(G-10086)*

Cozzolino Inc 973 731-9292
20 Standish Ave West Orange (07052) *(G-11891)*

CP Equipment Sales Co 908 687-9621
1504 Oakland Ave Union (07083) *(G-11168)*

CP Test & Valve Products Inc 201 998-1500
234 Sanford Ave Kearny (07032) *(G-4868)*

CPB Inc 856 697-2700
701 S Harding Hwy Buena (08310) *(G-946)*

CPI Operations LLC 856 423-5400
4 Paradise Rd Paulsboro (08066) *(G-8416)*

Cpl Aromas Inc 732 469-0680
1812 Front St Scotch Plains (07076) *(G-9848)*

CPM Supplies, East Brunswick Also called Computer Printers & Media Sups *(G-2143)*

CPS Metals Inc 856 779-0846
450 S Fellowship Rd Maple Shade (08052) *(G-5901)*

CR Laurence Co Inc 856 727-1022
1511 Lancer Dr Moorestown (08057) *(G-6570)*

CR Laurence Co Inc 201 770-1077
70 Seaview Dr Secaucus (07094) *(G-9874)*

Cr Ocean Engineering, LLC, Parsippany Also called Cross Rip Ocean Engrg LLC *(G-7978)*

CRA-Z Works Co Inc 732 390-8238
242 Main St Sayreville (08872) *(G-9819)*

Craft Signs 201 656-1991
136 Franklin St Jersey City (07307) *(G-4735)*

Craft-Pak Inc 718 763-0700
1 Ashley Pl Towaco (07082) *(G-10991)*

Craftmaster Printing Inc (PA) 732 775-0011
2024 State Route 33 Neptune (07753) *(G-6906)*

Craftsmen Photo Lithographers 973 316-5791
38 Beach St East Hanover (07936) *(G-2211)*

Craig Fabrics Inc (PA) 201 869-9126
7014 Jackson St Guttenberg (07093) *(G-3868)*

Craig Robertson 973 293-8666
19 State Route 23 Montague (07827) *(G-6402)*

Cramer Plating Inc 908 453-2887
4 Hoyt Ln Buttzville (07829) *(G-1020)*

Cranford Diagnostic Imaging, Cranford Also called Radnet Inc *(G-1924)*

Cranial Technologies Inc 908 754-0572
2163 Oak Tree Rd Edison (08820) *(G-2494)*

Cranial Technologies Inc 201 265-3993
115 W Century Rd Ste 280 Paramus (07652) *(G-7863)*

Crave Foods LLC 973 233-1220
19 Club Rd Montclair (07043) *(G-6409)*

Cravings 732 531-7122
310 Main St Allenhurst (07711) *(G-25)*

Cravings Gourmet Desserts, Allenhurst Also called Cravings *(G-25)*

Crazy Steve's Pickles & Salsa, Trenton Also called Crazy Steves Concoctions LLC *(G-11047)*

Crazy Steves Concoctions LLC 908 787-2089
38 Herbert Rd Trenton (08691) *(G-11047)*

Cream Ridge Winery 609 259-9797
145 Route 539 Cream Ridge (08514) *(G-1933)*

Creamer Glass LLC 856 327-2023
2201 Quince Ln Millville (08332) *(G-6294)*

Creamer Glass LLC 856 327-2023
411 N 10th St Millville (08332) *(G-6295)*

Creamy Creation LLC (HQ) 585 344-3300
61 S Paramus Rd Ste 535 Paramus (07652) *(G-7864)*

Creating Your Design LLC 973 357-1080
95 Montgomery St Paterson (07501) *(G-8240)*

Creations By Sherry Lynn LLC 800 742-3448
90 Park Ave 414 Florham Park (07932) *(G-3497)*

Creations By Stefano Inc 201 863-8337
1261 Paterson Plank Rd Secaucus (07094) *(G-9875)*

Creationsrewards Net LLC 908 526-3127
116 S 19th Ave Manville (08835) *(G-5893)*

Creative Cabinet Designs Inc 973 402-5886
301 Main St Boonton (07005) *(G-561)*

Creative Cmpt Concepts LLC 877 919-7988
2030 N Black Horse Pike Williamstown (08094) *(G-12085)*

Creative Color Lithographers 908 789-2295
611 South Ave Garwood (07027) *(G-3777)*

Creative Competitions Inc 856 256-2797
406 Ganttown Rd Sewell (08080) *(G-9949)*

Creative Concepts Corporation 201 750-1234
70 Oak St Ste 202 Norwood (07648) *(G-7620)*

Creative Concepts of NJ LLC 732 833-1776
580 N County Line Rd Jackson (08527) *(G-4659)*

Creative Desserts 732 477-0808
42 Capri Dr Brick (08723) *(G-740)*

Creative Display Inc 732 918-8010
349 Essex Rd Neptune (07753) *(G-6907)*

Creative Embroidery Corp 973 497-5700
305 3rd Ave W Ste 3 Newark (07107) *(G-7130)*

Creative Film Corp 732 367-2166
700 Vassar Ave Ste 2 Lakewood (08701) *(G-5097)*

Creative Industrial Kitchens 973 633-0420
8 Leo Pl Wayne (07470) *(G-11621)*

Creative Innovations Inc 973 636-9060
20-21 Wagaraw Rd Bldg 31b Fair Lawn (07410) *(G-3088)*

Creative Machining Systems 609 586-3932
124 Youngs Rd Trenton (08619) *(G-11048)*

Creative Metal Works Inc 973 579-3717
22b Gail Ct Sparta (07871) *(G-10495)*

A L P H A B E T I C

Creative Organization, Clifton *Also called Q10 Products LLC* ***(G-1707)***
Creative Patterns & Mfg..........973 589-1391
114 Beach St Ste 4 Rockaway (07866) ***(G-9558)***
Creative Pavers..........201 782-1661
45 Akers Ave Montvale (07645) ***(G-6451)***
Creative Products Inc..........732 614-9035
92 Shrewsbury Dr Long Branch (07740) ***(G-5622)***
Creative Safety Products, South Hackensack *Also called Encore Enterprises Inc* ***(G-10264)***
Creative Serving, Union *Also called Durex Inc* ***(G-11174)***
Creative Wood Products Inc..........732 370-0051
370 Whitesville Rd Ste 8 Jackson (08527) ***(G-4660)***
Creatone Inc..........908 789-8700
1011 Us Highway 22 Ste 1 Mountainside (07092) ***(G-6870)***
Creoh Packaging, Lakewood *Also called Creoh Trading Corp* ***(G-5098)***
Creoh Trading Corp..........718 821-0570
910 E County Line Rd Lakewood (08701) ***(G-5098)***
Creoh Usa LLC..........718 821-0570
1771 Madison Ave Ste 7 Lakewood (08701) ***(G-5099)***
Crescent Bottling Co Inc..........856 964-2268
1001 N 25th St Camden (08105) ***(G-1056)***
Crescent Uniforms LLC..........732 398-1866
33 Hasbrouck Dr Franklin Park (08823) ***(G-3627)***
Cressi Sub USA..........201 594-1450
3 Rosol Ln Saddle Brook (07663) ***(G-9760)***
Crest Foam Industries, Moonachie *Also called Inoac Usa Inc* ***(G-6522)***
Crest Foam Industries Inc, Moonachie *Also called Woodbridge Inoac Technical* ***(G-6553)***
Crest Group Inc (HQ)..........609 883-4000
Scotch Trenton Mercer Air Trenton (08628) ***(G-11049)***
Crest Ultrasonics Corp (HQ)..........609 883-4000
18 Graphics Dr Ewing (08628) ***(G-3011)***
Crest Wood Fence, Andover *Also called New Jersey Fence & Guardrail* ***(G-53)***
Crestek Inc (PA)..........609 883-4000
18 Graphics Dr Ewing (08628) ***(G-3012)***
Creston Electronics, Cresskill *Also called Crestron Electronics Inc* ***(G-1944)***
Crestron Electronics Inc..........201 894-0670
101 Broadway Cresskill (07626) ***(G-1944)***
Crestron Electronics Inc (PA)..........201 767-3400
15 Volvo Dr Rockleigh (07647) ***(G-9628)***
Cresttek, Trenton *Also called Crest Group Inc* ***(G-11049)***
Creter Vault Corp (PA)..........908 782-7771
417 Us Highway 202 Flemington (08822) ***(G-3432)***
Crett Construction Inc..........973 663-1184
18 Cella St Lake Hopatcong (07849) ***(G-5055)***
Crh Americas Inc..........908 475-1225
975 Burnt Tavern Rd Brick (08724) ***(G-741)***
Crh Americas Inc..........732 292-2500
331 Newman Springs Rd Red Bank (07701) ***(G-9323)***
Cricket Enterprises..........201 387-7978
60 Hillcrest Dr Dumont (07628) ***(G-2117)***
Crijuodama Baking Corp T..........732 451-1250
1900 Highway 70 Ste 209 Lakewood (08701) ***(G-5100)***
Crincoli Woodwork Co Inc..........908 352-9332
160 Spring St Elizabeth (07201) ***(G-2721)***
Crispy Green Inc..........973 679-4515
10 Madison Rd Ste D Fairfield (07004) ***(G-3169)***
Criterion Publishing Co..........732 548-8300
87 Forrest St Metuchen (08840) ***(G-6101)***
Criterion Software LLC..........908 754-1166
205 Us Highway 9 30 Freehold (07728) ***(G-3648)***
Croce & Longo Associates, Cherry Hill *Also called Croces Pasta Poducts* ***(G-1358)***
Croces Pasta Poducts..........856 795-6000
811 Marlton Pike W Cherry Hill (08002) ***(G-1358)***
Crocs Inc..........609 344-6300
113 N Arkansas Ave Atlantic City (08401) ***(G-94)***
Croda Inc (HQ)..........732 417-0800
300 Columbus Cir Ste A Edison (08837) ***(G-2495)***
Croda Investments Inc (HQ)..........732 417-0800
300 Columbus Cir Ste A Edison (08837) ***(G-2496)***
Croll-Reynolds Co Inc (PA)..........908 232-4200
6 Campus Dr Ste 2 Parsippany (07054) ***(G-7976)***
Crompton Corp..........732 826-6600
1000 Convery Blvd Perth Amboy (08861) ***(G-8611)***
Cronite Co Inc (PA)..........973 887-7900
120 E Halsey Rd Parsippany (07054) ***(G-7977)***
Cronos Design, Lodi *Also called Cronos-Prim Colorado LLC* ***(G-5580)***
Cronos-Prim Colorado LLC..........303 369-7477
300-2 State Rt 17 S Lodi (07644) ***(G-5580)***
Cross Counter Inc (PA)..........973 677-0600
200 Freeway Dr E East Orange (07018) ***(G-2255)***
Cross Country Box Co Inc..........973 673-8349
474 Getty Ave Clifton (07011) ***(G-1593)***
Cross H Co, Moonachie *Also called H Cross Company* ***(G-6519)***
Cross Medical Specialties Inc..........856 589-3288
450 Andbro Dr Unit 7 Pitman (08071) ***(G-8841)***
Cross Rip Ocean Engrg LLC..........973 455-0005
6 Campus Dr Parsippany (07054) ***(G-7978)***
Cross-Dock Solutions, Edison *Also called Copper Boss Ltd Liability Co* ***(G-2492)***
Crossfield Products Corp..........908 245-2801
140 Valley Rd Roselle Park (07204) ***(G-9691)***
Crossfire Publications..........516 352-9087
551 Bloomfield Ave C14 Caldwell (07006) ***(G-1025)***
Crowfoot Asphalt, West Berlin *Also called Crowfoot Associates Inc* ***(G-11713)***
Crowfoot Associates Inc..........609 561-0107
Winslow Township West Berlin (08091) ***(G-11713)***
Crown Clothing Co..........856 691-0343
609 Paul St Vineland (08360) ***(G-11343)***
Crown Engineering Corp..........800 631-2153
550 Sqnkum Yellowbrook Rd Farmingdale (07727) ***(G-3382)***
Crown Equipment Corporation..........201 337-1211
104 Bauer Dr Oakland (07436) ***(G-7681)***
Crown Fastener & Supply Corp..........845 268-5150
8 Industrial Pkwy Ste 3 Ringwood (07456) ***(G-9446)***
Crown Glass Co Inc..........908 642-1764
990 Evergreen Dr Branchburg (08876) ***(G-652)***
Crown Lift Trucks, Oakland *Also called Crown Equipment Corporation* ***(G-7681)***
Crown Precision Corp..........973 470-0097
61 Willet St Ste 6 Passaic (07055) ***(G-8132)***
Crown Products Inc..........732 493-0022
1302 Roller Rd Ocean (07712) ***(G-7720)***
Crown Roll Leaf Inc (PA)..........973 742-4000
91 Illinois Ave Paterson (07503) ***(G-8241)***
Crown Roll Leaf Inc..........973 684-2600
12 Columbia Ave Paterson (07503) ***(G-8242)***
Crown Trophy..........973 808-8400
101 Us Highway 46 Ste 136 Pine Brook (07058) ***(G-8696)***
CRS Ink Intl Ltd Lblty Co..........732 817-0401
11 Main St Holmdel (07733) ***(G-4514)***
Crt International Inc..........973 887-7737
260 Wagner St Middlesex (08846) ***(G-6160)***
Crush Rite, Stockholm *Also called Rjticeco LLC* ***(G-10610)***
Crust and Crumb Bakery..........609 492-4966
800 N Bay Ave Ste 9 Beach Haven (08008) ***(G-264)***
Crw Graphics, Pennsauken *Also called Composing Room Inc* ***(G-8497)***
Cryopak Verification Tech Inc (PA)..........732 346-9200
551 Raritan Center Pkwy Edison (08837) ***(G-2497)***
Cryovation LLC (PA)..........609 914-4792
9b Mary Way Hainesport (08036) ***(G-4071)***
Crystal Beverage Corporation (PA)..........201 991-2342
174 Sanford Ave Kearny (07032) ***(G-4869)***
Crystal Deltronic Industries (PA)..........973 328-6898
60 Harding Ave Dover (07801) ***(G-2082)***
Crystal Deltronic Industries..........973 328-7000
60 Harding Ave Dover (07801) ***(G-2083)***
Crystal Ware, Lakewood *Also called Cw International Sales LLC* ***(G-5103)***
Crystal World Inc..........201 488-0909
283 Veterans Blvd Carlstadt (07072) ***(G-1151)***
Crystex Composites LLC..........973 779-8866
125 Clifton Blvd Clifton (07011) ***(G-1594)***
Cs Apparel Inc..........732 906-9666
8 Rio Vista Dr Edison (08820) ***(G-2498)***
Cs Industrial Services LLC..........609 381-4380
303 Catawba Ave Newfield (08344) ***(G-7364)***
CS Osborne & Co (PA)..........973 483-3232
125 Jersey St Harrison (07029) ***(G-4177)***
CSC Brands LP..........800 257-8443
1 Campbell Pl Camden (08103) ***(G-1057)***
Csf Corporation (PA)..........732 302-2222
285 Davidson Ave Ste 103 Somerset (08873) ***(G-10087)***
Csi, Fairfield *Also called Constant Services Inc* ***(G-3165)***
Csl Services Inc..........856 755-9440
7905 Browning Rd Ste 316 Pennsauken (08109) ***(G-8499)***
CSM Environmental Systems LLC..........908 789-5431
269 Sheffield St Ste 1 Mountainside (07092) ***(G-6871)***
CSM Worldwide Inc (PA)..........908 233-2882
36 S Adamsville Rd 7 Bridgewater (08807) ***(G-831)***
Csonka Worldwide..........609 514-2766
501 Plainsboro Rd Ph Plainsboro (08536) ***(G-8879)***
Csr, Paramus *Also called Cold Stat Refregiration* ***(G-7861)***
CSS, Englewood Cliffs *Also called Competech Smrtcard Sltions Inc* ***(G-2953)***
CST Pavers..........856 299-5339
345 Route 130 Pedricktown (08067) ***(G-8434)***
CST Products LLC..........856 299-5339
345 Route 130 Penns Grove (08069) ***(G-8464)***
Csus LLC..........973 298-8599
300 Forge Way Ste 3 Rockaway (07866) ***(G-9559)***
Ctechnologiesinc.com, Bridgewater *Also called C Technologies Inc* ***(G-826)***
Cubalas Emergency Lighting LLC..........908 943-1615
811 Roselle St Linden (07036) ***(G-5364)***
Cubist Pharmaceuticals LLC (HQ)..........908 740-4000
2000 Galloping Hill Rd Kenilworth (07033) ***(G-4949)***
Cuisinarts Division, East Windsor *Also called Conair Corporation* ***(G-2354)***
Cuisine Innvtons Unlimited LLC..........732 730-9310
180 Lehigh Ave Lakewood (08701) ***(G-5101)***
Cultech Inc..........732 225-2722
3500 Hadley Rd South Plainfield (07080) ***(G-10351)***
Cumberland & Salem Guide, Bridgeton *Also called James Kinkade* ***(G-787)***

Cumberland Dairy Inc (PA).....800 257-8484
899 Landis Ave Rosenhayn (08352) ***(G-9706)***
Cumberland Dairy Inc.....856 451-1300
80 Edward Ave Bridgeton (08302) ***(G-783)***
Cumberland Marble & Monument.....856 691-3334
2858 S West Blvd Vineland (08360) ***(G-11344)***
Cumberland News Inc.....856 691-2244
603 E Landis Ave Vineland (08360) ***(G-11345)***
Cumberland Rcycl Corp S Jersey.....856 825-4153
N Delsea Dr Millville (08332) ***(G-6296)***
Cumberland Vacuum Products Inc.....856 691-9155
720 S West Blvd Vineland (08360) ***(G-11346)***
Cummins - Allison Corp.....201 791-2394
495 Boulevard Ste 6 Elmwood Park (07407) ***(G-2813)***
Cummins Inc.....973 491-0100
435 Bergen Ave Kearny (07032) ***(G-4870)***
Cummins-Allison, Elmwood Park *Also called Cummins - Allison Corp* ***(G-2813)***
Cunningham Classics Ltd Lblty.....201 857-4647
536 S Broad St Ste 2 Glen Rock (07452) ***(G-3825)***
Cunningham Marine Hydraulics, Hoboken *Also called C M H Hele-Shaw Inc* ***(G-4462)***
Cuny & Guerber Inc.....201 617-5800
2100 Kerrigan Ave Union City (07087) ***(G-11244)***
Cupcake Celebrations.....973 885-0826
107 Paddock Dr Columbus (08022) ***(G-1802)***
Cupcake Kitschen.....862 221-8872
1042 Ash Dr Mahwah (07430) ***(G-5761)***
Cupcakes By Carousel (PA).....201 389-3090
192 E Ridgewood Ave Ridgewood (07450) ***(G-9422)***
Cura Biomed Inc.....609 647-1474
103 S Longfellow Dr Princeton Junction (08550) ***(G-9151)***
Curran & Connors Inc.....609 514-0104
5 Independence Way # 300 Princeton (08540) ***(G-9024)***
Curran-Pfeiff Corp.....732 225-0555
Liddle Ave Edison (08837) ***(G-2499)***
Current Newspaper LLC.....609 383-8994
1000 W Washington Ave Pleasantville (08232) ***(G-8906)***
Curtain Care Plus Inc.....800 845-6155
17 Industrial St W Clifton (07012) ***(G-1595)***
Curtiss-Wright, Paramus *Also called Metal Improvement Company LLC* ***(G-7888)***
Curtiss-Wright Surfc Tech LLC (HQ).....201 843-7800
80 E Rte 4 Ste 310 Paramus (07652) ***(G-7865)***
Curvon Corporation.....732 747-3832
34 Apple St Tinton Falls (07724) ***(G-10829)***
Custom Alley.....609 294-1875
36 Ship Dr Ltl Egg Hbr (08087) ***(G-5643)***
Custom Alloy Corporation (PA).....908 638-0257
3 Washington Ave Ste 5 High Bridge (08829) ***(G-4294)***
Custom Auto Radiator Inc.....609 242-9700
441 S Main St Forked River (08731) ***(G-3537)***
Custom Bedding Co.....973 761-1100
1677 Springfield Ave Maplewood (07040) ***(G-5917)***
Custom Book Bindery Inc.....973 815-1400
9 Sheridan Ave Clifton (07011) ***(G-1596)***
Custom Building Products Inc.....856 467-9226
2115 High Hill Rd Logan Township (08085) ***(G-5612)***
Custom Business Software LLC.....732 534-9557
87 Broad St Freehold (07728) ***(G-3649)***
Custom Cabinets By Jim Bucko.....609 522-6646
135 W Burk Ave Wildwood (08260) ***(G-12071)***
Custom Chemicals Corp.....201 791-5100
30 Paul Kohner Pl Elmwood Park (07407) ***(G-2814)***
Custom Converters Inc.....201 994-9000
115 Naylon Ave Livingston (07039) ***(G-5527)***
Custom Counters By Precision.....973 773-0111
11-17 Linden St Passaic (07055) ***(G-8133)***
Custom Creations (PA).....201 651-9676
294 W Oakland Ave Oakland (07436) ***(G-7682)***
Custom Decorators Service.....973 625-0516
415 E Main St Ste 3 Denville (07834) ***(G-2034)***
Custom Docks Inc.....973 948-3732
234 Us Highway 206 N Sandyston (07826) ***(G-9811)***
Custom Essence.....732 249-6405
53 Veronica Ave Somerset (08873) ***(G-10088)***
Custom Extrusion Tech Inc.....732 367-5511
1650 Corporate Rd W Lakewood (08701) ***(G-5102)***
Custom Fabricators Inc.....908 862-4244
400 Commerce Rd Linden (07036) ***(G-5365)***
Custom Gasket Mfg LLC.....201 331-6363
640 E Palisade Ave Englewood Cliffs (07632) ***(G-2956)***
Custom Golf, Oakland *Also called RCM Ltd Inc* ***(G-7702)***
Custom Graphics of Vineland.....856 691-7858
71 W Landis Ave Vineland (08360) ***(G-11347)***
Custom Kitchen By Lubrich, Manasquan *Also called Michael Lubrich* ***(G-5874)***
Custom Labels Inc.....973 473-1934
345 Kaplan Dr Fairfield (07004) ***(G-3170)***
Custom Laminations Inc.....973 279-9174
932 Market St Paterson (07513) ***(G-8243)***
Custom Liners Inc.....732 940-0084
345 State Rt 17 Upper Saddle River (07458) ***(G-11277)***
Custom Metering Company Inc.....973 946-4195
36 Mattison Ave Branchville (07826) ***(G-729)***
Custom Mobile Food Equipment, Hammonton *Also called Custom Sales & Service Inc* ***(G-4136)***
Custom Molders Corp.....908 218-7997
160 Meister Ave Ste 1 Branchburg (08876) ***(G-653)***
Custom Molders Group LLC (PA).....908 218-7997
160 Meister Ave Ste 1 Branchburg (08876) ***(G-654)***
Custom Quick Label Inc.....856 596-7555
300 Greentree Rd # 207 Marlton (08053) ***(G-5969)***
Custom Roller Inc (PA).....908 298-7797
240b Columbus Ave Roselle (07203) ***(G-9668)***
Custom Sales & Service Inc.....800 257-7855
275 S 2nd Rd Hammonton (08037) ***(G-4136)***
Custom Wood Furniture Inc.....973 579-4880
37 E Clinton St Ste 1 Newton (07860) ***(G-7385)***
Custom Woodwork, Red Bank *Also called F T Millwork Inc* ***(G-9330)***
Customer Complaint Dept, Monmouth Junction *Also called Tris Pharma Inc* ***(G-6365)***
Cusumano Perma-Rail Co.....908 245-9281
213 W Westfield Ave Roselle Park (07204) ***(G-9692)***
Cutler Bros Box & Lumber Co (PA).....201 943-2535
711 W Prospect Ave Fairview (07022) ***(G-3360)***
Cutmark Inc.....856 234-3428
102 Gaither Dr Ste 2 Mount Laurel (08054) ***(G-6791)***
Cutter Drill & Machine Inc.....732 206-1112
175 Ramtown Greenville Rd # 7 Howell (07731) ***(G-4550)***
Cutting Board Company (PA).....908 725-0187
291 Route 22 E Bldg 6 Lebanon (08833) ***(G-5283)***
Cutting Board Company.....908 725-0187
2 Dreahook Rd Branchburg (08876) ***(G-655)***
Cutting Edge Casting Inc.....908 925-7500
1233 W Saint Georges Ave Linden (07036) ***(G-5366)***
Cutting Edge Grower Supply LLC.....732 905-9220
97 Glen Arden Dr Howell (07731) ***(G-4551)***
Cutting Edge Industries, Linden *Also called Cutting Edge Casting Inc* ***(G-5366)***
Cutting Edge Stencils, Ramsey *Also called Innovative Art Concepts LLC* ***(G-9244)***
Cutting Records Inc.....201 488-8444
190 Main St Ste 403 Hackensack (07601) ***(G-3901)***
Cutting Techniques Inc.....201 438-2222
18 Green Pond Rd Ste 1 Rockaway (07866) ***(G-9560)***
Cvc Specialty Chemicals Inc (HQ).....856 533-3000
844 N Lenola Rd V Moorestown (08057) ***(G-6571)***
Cvc Thermoset Specialties, Moorestown *Also called Cvc Specialty Chemicals Inc* ***(G-6571)***
CVE Inc.....201 770-0005
5 N Corporate Dr Riverdale (07457) ***(G-9478)***
CW Brown Foods Inc (PA).....856 423-3700
161 Kings Hwy Mount Royal (08061) ***(G-6850)***
CW Brown Foods Inc.....856 423-3700
161 Kings Hwy Mount Royal (08061) ***(G-6851)***
Cw International Sales LLC.....732 367-4444
600 James St Lakewood (08701) ***(G-5103)***
Cwi Architectural Millwork LLC.....856 307-7900
8 Deptford Rd Dept D Glassboro (08028) ***(G-3802)***
Cyalume Specialty Products Inc.....732 469-7760
100 W Main St Ste A10 Bound Brook (08805) ***(G-617)***
Cybage Software Inc.....848 219-1221
500 College Rd E Ste 203 Princeton (08540) ***(G-9025)***
Cyberextrudercom Inc.....973 623-7900
1401 Valley Rd Ste 208 Wayne (07470) ***(G-11622)***
Cyclacel Pharmaceuticals Inc (PA).....908 517-7330
200 Connell Dr Ste 1500 Berkeley Heights (07922) ***(G-408)***
Cyclase Dynamics Inc.....973 420-3259
16 E 27th St Barnegat Light (08006) ***(G-169)***
Cygate Sftwr & Consulting LLC.....732 452-1881
22 Meridian Rd Unit 9 Edison (08820) ***(G-2500)***
Cypher Insurance Software.....856 216-0575
32 Sunnybrook Rd Stratford (08084) ***(G-10615)***
Cypra Wallcoverings Inc.....732 525-0340
32 Merritt Ave South Amboy (08879) ***(G-10237)***
Cypress Pharmaceuticals Inc.....601 856-4393
10 N Park Pl Ste 201 Morristown (07960) ***(G-6703)***
Cytec Industries Inc.....877 463-7645
504 Carnegie Ctr Princeton (08540) ***(G-9026)***
Cytec Industries Inc (HQ).....973 357-3100
250 Pehle Ave Ste 306 Saddle Brook (07663) ***(G-9761)***
Cytec Solvay Group, Saddle Brook *Also called Cytec Industries Inc* ***(G-9761)***
Cytosorbents Corporation (PA).....732 329-8885
7 Deerpark Dr Ste K Monmouth Junction (08852) ***(G-6339)***
Cytosorbents Medical Inc (HQ).....732 329-8885
7 Deerpark Dr Ste K Monmouth Junction (08852) ***(G-6340)***
Cytotherm LP.....609 396-1456
110 Sewell Ave Trenton (08610) ***(G-11050)***
Czar Industries Inc.....609 392-1515
1424-1426 Heath Ave Trenton (08638) ***(G-11051)***
D & A Electronics Mfg.....732 938-7400
5303 Asbury Rd Wall Township (07727) ***(G-11476)***
D & A Granulation LLC.....732 994-7480
1970 Rutgers Univ Blvd Lakewood (08701) ***(G-5104)***

ALPHABETIC

D & D Technology Inc..908 688-5154
254 Elmwood Ave Union (07083) *(G-11169)*

D & F Wicker Import Co Inc (PA)....................973 736-5861
295 State Route 10 E Succasunna (07876) *(G-10621)*

D & G LLC..201 289-5750
29 1st St Apt 605 Hackensack (07601) *(G-3902)*

D & H Cutoff Co..908 454-4961
2600 State Route 57 Stewartsville (08886) *(G-10593)*

D & H Pallets LLC...973 481-2981
45 Verona Ave Newark (07104) *(G-7131)*

D & I Printing Co Inc.......................................201 871-3620
23 Chestnut St Englewood (07631) *(G-2885)*

D & N Machine Co, Gloucester City Also called D&N Machine Manufacturing Inc *(G-3835)*

D & S Ventures Inc..732 758-0095
68 White St Ste 4 Red Bank (07701) *(G-9324)*

D A F, Wyckoff Also called Daf Products Inc *(G-12249)*

D A K Office Services Inc................................609 586-8222
3100 Quakerbridge Rd Trenton (08619) *(G-11052)*

D and J Industries LLC...................................201 257-8953
435 Meadow Ln Carlstadt (07072) *(G-1152)*

D and M Discount Fuels.................................856 935-0919
383 E Broadway Salem (08079) *(G-9805)*

D C Herring Co, Eatontown Also called Daniel C Herring Co Inc *(G-2389)*

D C R, Franklin Lakes Also called Direct Computer Resources Inc *(G-3614)*

D D P, Hillside Also called Diversified Display Pdts LLC *(G-4405)*

D Depasquale Paving LLC..............................301 674-9775
1 Reagan Dr Jackson (08527) *(G-4661)*

D Electric Motors Inc.....................................856 696-5959
94 W Sherman Ave Vineland (08360) *(G-11348)*

D J B Welding Inc..732 657-7478
1461 Toms River Rd Jackson (08527) *(G-4662)*

D K Tool & Die Welding Group (PA)................908 241-7600
181 W Clay Ave Roselle Park (07204) *(G-9693)*

D K Trading Inc...856 225-1130
941 S 2nd St Camden (08103) *(G-1058)*

D Kwitman & Son Inc (PA)..............................201 798-5511
1015 Adams St Hoboken (07030) *(G-4467)*

D Kwitman & Son Inc......................................201 798-5511
1015 Adams St Hoboken (07030) *(G-4468)*

D L Imprints..732 493-8555
1701 Valley Rd Ste E Ocean (07712) *(G-7721)*

D L Printing Co Inc...732 750-1917
283 Prospect Ave Avenel (07001) *(G-129)*

D L V Lounge Inc...973 783-6988
300 Bloomfield Ave Montclair (07042) *(G-6410)*

D N D Corp...908 637-4343
13 Cemetery Rd Great Meadows (07838) *(G-3849)*

D P I, West Caldwell Also called Direct Prtg Impressions Inc *(G-11773)*

D P X, Parsippany Also called Dpi Newco LLC *(G-7985)*

D Paglia & Sons Inc.......................................908 654-5999
280 Sheffield St Mountainside (07092) *(G-6872)*

D R Handmade Strings Inc.............................201 599-3113
40 Carver Ave Westwood (07675) *(G-11958)*

D R Kenyon & Son Inc....................................908 722-0001
400 Us Highway 22 Bridgewater (08807) *(G-832)*

D R Music, Westwood Also called D R Handmade Strings Inc *(G-11958)*

D R Printing, Parsippany Also called Printing Industries LLC *(G-8072)*

D R Tielmann Inc...732 332-1860
1208 State Route 34 Ste 1 Matawan (07747) *(G-6016)*

D S F Inc..908 218-5153
401 Us Highway 202 Raritan (08869) *(G-9308)*

D S F Millwork, Raritan Also called D S F Inc *(G-9308)*

D S Jh LLC...973 782-4086
107 Beaverbrook Rd Ste 3 Lincoln Park (07035) *(G-5326)*

D S M, Parsippany Also called DSM Nutritional Products LLC *(G-7989)*

D&B, Short Hills Also called Dun & Bradstreet Inc *(G-9977)*

D&E Nutraceuticals Inc.................................212 235-5200
700 Central Ave Farmingdale (07727) *(G-3383)*

D&N Machine Manufacturing Inc...................856 456-1366
334 Nicholson Rd Gloucester City (08030) *(G-3835)*

D&S Fisheries LLC..914 438-3197
6 Birch Ln Colts Neck (07722) *(G-1783)*

D'Orazio Frozen Foods, Bellmawr Also called DOrazio Foods Inc *(G-337)*

D-K Tool & Die Welding, Roselle Park Also called D K Tool & Die Welding Group *(G-9693)*

D2cf LLC (PA)...973 699-4111
108 Coccio Dr West Orange (07052) *(G-11892)*

D3 Led LLC...201 583-9486
1609 54th St North Bergen (07047) *(G-7444)*

Da-Green Electronics Ltd.............................732 254-2735
37 Main St South River (08882) *(G-10460)*

Dab Design Inc...732 224-8686
331 Newman Springs Rd # 143 Red Bank (07701) *(G-9325)*

Daburn Electronics & Cable, Dover Also called Daburn Wire & Cable Corp *(G-2084)*

Daburn Wire & Cable Corp............................973 328-3200
44 Richboynton Rd Dover (07801) *(G-2084)*

Daco Limited Partnership (PA)......................973 263-1100
100 Fulton St Boonton (07005) *(G-562)*

Daddy Donkey Labs LLC................................646 461-4677
115 Park Rd Fair Haven (07704) *(G-3071)*

Daf Products Inc..201 251-1222
420 Braen Ave Wyckoff (07481) *(G-12249)*

Daiichi Sankyo Inc...908 992-6400
211 Mount Airy Rd Basking Ridge (07920) *(G-183)*

Daily Dish..973 537-9700
915 Berkshire Valley Rd Wharton (07885) *(G-11983)*

Daily Dog Walker LLC.....................................609 755-5364
4 Chestnut Dr Robbinsville (08691) *(G-9514)*

Daily Dollar LLC...732 236-9709
48 E Sedgwick St Monroe Township (08831) *(G-6381)*

Daily News LP...212 210-2100
125 Theodore Conrad Dr Jersey City (07305) *(G-4736)*

Daily Plan It Executive Center.......................609 514-9494
707 Alexander Rd Ste 208 Princeton (08540) *(G-9027)*

Daily Record, The, Parsippany Also called Gannett Co Inc *(G-8020)*

Daily Targum, New Brunswick Also called Targum Publishing Company *(G-7006)*

Daimler Trucks North Amer LLC......................856 467-6000
1140 Commerce Blvd Swedesboro (08085) *(G-10689)*

Dainippon Sumitomo Pharma Amer (HQ).....201 592-2050
1 Bridge Plz N Ste 510 Fort Lee (07024) *(G-3550)*

Dairy Delight LLC..201 939-7878
1 Industrial Dr Rutherford (07070) *(G-9729)*

Dairy Maid Confectionery Co.........................609 399-0100
852 Boardwalk Ocean City (08226) *(G-7752)*

Dairy Queen, Clarksburg Also called Millstone Dq Inc *(G-1521)*

Dairy Queen..732 892-5700
2506 Bridge Ave Point Pleasant Boro (08742) *(G-8937)*

Dairyland, Irvington Also called Agape Inc *(G-4570)*

DAKA Manufacturing LLC.............................908 782-0360
19 Floral Rd Flemington (08822) *(G-3433)*

Dale Behre..908 850-4225
108 East Ave Ste 6 Hackettstown (07840) *(G-4002)*

Dalemark Industries Inc.................................732 367-3100
575 Prospect St Ste 211 Lakewood (08701) *(G-5105)*

Dales's Custom Auto & Sign, Hackettstown Also called Dale Behre *(G-4002)*

Dallas Group of America Inc (PA)..................908 534-7800
374 Rte 22 Whitehouse (08888) *(G-12045)*

Daman International Inc..................................917 945-9708
105 Rye Rd Cherry Hill (08003) *(G-1359)*

Damascus Bakery NJ LLC...............................718 855-1456
60 Mcclellan St Newark (07114) *(G-7132)*

Damask Candies, Swedesboro Also called Damask Kandies *(G-10690)*

Damask Kandies...856 467-1661
2255 Route 322 Swedesboro (08085) *(G-10690)*

Damco, Princeton Also called Accelerated Technologies Inc *(G-8994)*

DAmore Jewelers...201 945-0530
731 Anderson Ave Cliffside Park (07010) *(G-1537)*

Dan Maguire Electrical Contr, West Berlin Also called Daniel Maguire *(G-11714)*

Dan Mar Jewelers, Union Also called Goldstein Setting Co Inc *(G-11190)*

Dana Poly Corp...800 474-1020
85 Harrison St Dover Dover (07801) *(G-2085)*

Danfoss Hago Inc...908 232-8687
1120 Globe Ave Mountainside (07092) *(G-6873)*

DAngelo Metal Products Inc...........................908 862-8220
360 Dalziel Rd Linden (07036) *(G-5367)*

Dani Leather USA Inc......................................973 598-0890
37 Ironia Rd Ste 2 Flanders (07836) *(G-3403)*

Daniel & Ellissa, Carlstadt Also called New Top Inc *(G-1193)*

Daniel C Herring Co Inc...................................732 530-6557
20 Meridian Rd Ste 6 Eatontown (07724) *(G-2389)*

Daniel Fashions Inc...201 869-1008
6108 Hudson Ave West New York (07093) *(G-11863)*

Daniel Maguire...856 767-8443
140 Collings Ave West Berlin (08091) *(G-11714)*

Danielle Die Cut Products Inc.........................973 278-3000
238 Lindbergh Pl Ste 3 Paterson (07503) *(G-8244)*

Danielle Fashion, West New York Also called Daniel Fashions Inc *(G-11863)*

Danline Inc...973 376-1000
1 Silver Ct Springfield (07081) *(G-10550)*

Danline Quality Brushes, Springfield Also called Danline Inc *(G-10550)*

Danmar Press Inc..201 487-4400
24 E Wesley St South Hackensack (07606) *(G-10259)*

Danmark Enterprises Inc (PA)........................732 321-3366
692 Oak Tree Ave South Plainfield (07080) *(G-10352)*

Danmola Lara..973 762-7581
524 N Wyoming Ave South Orange (07079) *(G-10302)*

Dans Woodwork...973 751-4506
37 Branch Brook Dr Belleville (07109) *(G-299)*

Danson Sheet Metal Inc.................................201 343-4876
140 Atlantic St Hackensack (07601) *(G-3903)*

Dantco Corp..973 278-8776
9 Oak St Paterson (07501) *(G-8245)*

Dantco Mixers, Paterson Also called Dantco Corp *(G-8245)*

Daq Electronics LLC.......................................732 981-0050
262 Old New Brunswick Rd B Piscataway (08854) *(G-8753)*

2018 Harris New Jersey
Manufacturers Directory
(G-0000) Company's Geographic Section entry number

Darby Litho Inc 908 231-8883
301 N Main St Manville (08835) *(G-5894)*

Darling Ingredients Inc 973 465-1900
825 Wilson Ave Newark (07105) *(G-7133)*

Daros Group 908 454-7811
200 Arbor Dr Stewartsville (08886) *(G-10594)*

DArtagnan Inc (PA) 973 344-0565
600 Green Ln Union (07083) *(G-11170)*

Darwin Press Inc 609 737-1349
280 N Main St Pennington (08534) *(G-8448)*

Das Installations Inc 973 473-6858
176 Saddle River Rd D Garfield (07026) *(G-3728)*

Dason Stainless Products Co 732 382-7272
1773 Elizabeth Ave Rahway (07065) *(G-9183)*

Dassault Aircraft Svcs Corp (HQ) 201 440-6700
200 Riser Rd Little Ferry (07643) *(G-5500)*

Dassault Procurement Svcs Inc (HQ) 201 261-4130
200 Riser Rd Little Ferry (07643) *(G-5501)*

Data Base Access Systems Inc 973 335-0800
60 Midvale Rd Ste 206 Mountain Lakes (07046) *(G-6856)*

Data Cntrum Communications Inc 201 391-1911
135 Chestnut Ridge Rd # 2 Montvale (07645) *(G-6452)*

Data Communique Inc 201 508-6000
65 Challenger Rd Fl 4 Ridgefield Park (07660) *(G-9402)*

Data Communique Intl Inc 201 508-6000
65 Challenger Rd Ste 400 Ridgefield Park (07660) *(G-9403)*

Data Delay Devices Inc (PA) 973 202-3268
3 Mount Prospect Ave Clifton (07013) *(G-1597)*

Data Medical Inc 800 790-9978
2075 91st St North Bergen (07047) *(G-7445)*

Datacolor Inc (HQ) 609 924-2189
5 Princess Rd Lawrenceville (08648) *(G-5256)*

Datalink Solutions Inc 973 731-9373
27 Fundus Rd West Orange (07052) *(G-11893)*

Datamotion Inc (PA) 973 455-1245
200 Park Ave Ste 302 Florham Park (07932) *(G-3498)*

Datapro International Inc 732 868-0588
201 Circle Dr N Ste 101 Piscataway (08854) *(G-8754)*

Dataprobe Inc (PA) 201 934-9944
1 Pearl Ct B Allendale (07401) *(G-8)*

Dataram Memory 609 799-0071
777 Alexander Rd Ste 100 Princeton (08540) *(G-9028)*

Datascan Graphics Inc 973 543-4803
55 Madison Ave Ste 400 Morristown (07960) *(G-6704)*

Datascope Corp (HQ) 973 244-6100
15 Law Dr Fairfield (07004) *(G-3171)*

Datascope Corp 201 995-8000
800 Macarthur Blvd Mahwah (07430) *(G-5762)*

Datascope Corp 800 777-4222
1300 Macarthur Blvd Mahwah (07430) *(G-5763)*

Datascope Corp 201 995-8000
1300 Macarthur Blvd Mahwah (07430) *(G-5764)*

Datascope Patient Monitoring, Mahwah *Also called Datascope Corp (G-5762)*

Datatel, Fairfield *Also called Middle Atlantic Products Inc (G-3261)*

Datayog Inc 714 253-6558
155 Morgan St Jersey City (07302) *(G-4737)*

Dato Company Inc (PA) 732 225-2272
8 Plainsboro Rd Cranbury (08512) *(G-1828)*

Datwyler Pharma Packaging 856 663-2202
9012 Pennsauken Hwy Pennsauken (08110) *(G-8500)*

Daum Inc (HQ) 862 210-8522
368 Passaic Ave Ste 300 Fairfield (07004) *(G-3172)*

Dauphin North America, Boonton *Also called Daco Limited Partnership (G-562)*

Dauson Corrugated Container 973 827-1494
3627 State Rt 23 Hamburg (07419) *(G-4090)*

Daven Industries Inc 973 808-8848
55 Dwight Pl Fairfield (07004) *(G-3173)*

Daves Salad House Inc 908 965-0773
577 Pennsylvania Ave Elizabeth (07201) *(G-2722)*

David Bradley Chocolatier Inc (PA) 609 443-4747
92 N Main St Bldg 19 Windsor (08561) *(G-12125)*

David Bradley Chocolatier Inc 732 536-7719
520 Us Highway 9 Englishtown (07726) *(G-2991)*

David E Connolly Inc 908 654-4600
1091 Bristol Rd Mountainside (07092) *(G-6874)*

David Gross Group, Lakewood *Also called Mj Gross Company - NJ (G-5162)*

David Leiz Custom Woodwork 908 486-1533
2301 E Edgar Rd Bldg 5a Linden (07036) *(G-5368)*

David Mitchell Inc 856 429-2610
210 Park Dr Voorhees (08043) *(G-11428)*

David Ramsay, Moorestown *Also called Ramsay David Cabinetmakers (G-6618)*

David Sisco Jr 908 454-0880
1223 S Main St Phillipsburg (08865) *(G-8646)*

Davidmark LLC 609 277-7361
711 N Main St Ste 7 Pleasantville (08232) *(G-8907)*

Davion Inc (PA) 973 485-0793
2 Progress Rd North Brunswick (08902) *(G-7514)*

Davis Center Inc 862 251-4637
19 State Route 10 E # 25 Succasunna (07876) *(G-10622)*

Davis Hyundai 609 883-3500
1655 N Olden Avenue Ext Ewing (08638) *(G-3013)*

Davis Hyundai & Mitsubishi, Ewing *Also called Davis Hyundai (G-3013)*

Davis Sign Systems Inc 973 394-9909
65 Harrison St Boonton (07005) *(G-563)*

Davis-Standard LLC 908 722-6000
220 Davidson Ave Ste 401 Somerset (08873) *(G-10089)*

Davlyn Industries Inc 609 655-5974
366 Prncton Hightstown Rd East Windsor (08520) *(G-2356)*

Davy Jnes Swmming Pool Pnt Div, Trenton *Also called Performance Industries Inc (G-11096)*

Dawn Bible Students Assn 201 438-6421
199 Railroad Ave East Rutherford (07073) *(G-2293)*

Dawnex Industries, Riverdale *Also called Rainbow Metal Units Corp (G-9484)*

Dax Haircare, Fairfield *Also called Imperial Dax Co Inc (G-3226)*

Daybrook Holdings Inc (PA) 973 538-6766
161 Madison Ave Ste 200 Morristown (07960) *(G-6705)*

Daysequerra Corporation 856 719-9900
7209 Browning Rd Pennsauken (08109) *(G-8501)*

Daysol Inc 908 272-5900
40 Boright Ave Kenilworth (07033) *(G-4950)*

Dayton Grey Corp 732 869-0060
1008 1st Ave Asbury Park (07712) *(G-76)*

Dazzledog LLC 302 540-6804
143 Harding Ave Ste 7 Bellmawr (08031) *(G-336)*

Db Designs Inc 732 616-5018
10 Damascus Dr Marlboro (07746) *(G-5937)*

DBC Inc 212 819-1177
300 Frank W Burr Blvd # 56 Teaneck (07666) *(G-10747)*

Dbmcorp Inc 201 677-0008
32a Spruce St Oakland (07436) *(G-7683)*

DC Fabricators Inc 609 499-3000
801 W Front St Florence (08518) *(G-3477)*

Dcg Printing Inc 732 530-4441
661 State Rte 35 Shrewsbury (07702) *(G-9996)*

DCI Signs & Awnings Inc 973 350-0400
110 Riverside Ave Newark (07104) *(G-7134)*

Dcm Clean Air Products Inc 732 363-2100
1650 Oak St Lakewood (08701) *(G-5106)*

Dcm Group Inc 732 516-1173
563 Broad St Newark (07102) *(G-7135)*

Dcw Packaging, Sussex *Also called Carol Healey (G-10667)*

Ddm Steel Cnstr Ltd Lblty Co 856 794-9400
3659 N Delsea Dr Vineland (08360) *(G-11349)*

Ddm Steel Services Inc 856 794-1931
3659 N Delsea Dr Vineland (08360) *(G-11350)*

De Ditrich Process Systems Inc (PA) 908 317-2585
244 Sheffield St Mountainside (07092) *(G-6875)*

De Jong Iron Works Inc 973 684-1633
223 Godwin Ave 231 Paterson (07501) *(G-8246)*

De Leon Plastics Corp 973 653-3480
473 Getty Ave Paterson (07503) *(G-8247)*

De Rossi & Son Co Inc 856 691-0061
411 S 6th St Vineland (08360) *(G-11351)*

De Saussure Equipment Co Inc 201 845-6517
23 W Howcroft Rd Maywood (07607) *(G-6047)*

De Zaio Productions Inc 973 423-5000
20-10 Maple Ave Bldg 31c Fair Lawn (07410) *(G-3089)*

Dealaman Enterprises Inc 908 647-5533
214 Mountainview Rd Warren (07059) *(G-11544)*

Deans Graphics 609 261-8817
16 Mill St Ste D Mount Holly (08060) *(G-6767)*

Dearborn A Belden Cdt Company (HQ) 908 925-8000
711 Lidgerwood Ave Elizabeth (07202) *(G-2723)*

Deb El Food Products LLC (PA) 908 282-0120
520 Broad St Fl 6 Newark (07102) *(G-7136)*

Deb El Foods, Newark *Also called Deb El Food Products LLC (G-7136)*

Deb Maintenance Inc 856 786-0440
1000 Union Landing Rd Cinnaminson (08077) *(G-1453)*

DEB Manufacturing Inc 732 364-7007
850 Towbin Ave Lakewood (08701) *(G-5107)*

Deb-El Foods Corporation 908 351-0330
520 Broad St Newark (07102) *(G-7137)*

Deborah Sales & Mfg Co 973 344-8466
109 Meeker Ave Newark (07114) *(G-7138)*

Decorating With Fabric Inc 845 352-5064
1 Broadway Park Ridge (07656) *(G-7917)*

Decoration Operations, Williamstown *Also called Piramal Glass - Usa Inc (G-12098)*

Decorative Iron Works, Paterson *Also called Joseph Monga Jr (G-8306)*

Dee & L LLC 201 858-0138
67 Lefante Dr Bayonne (07002) *(G-222)*

Dee Jay Printing Inc 973 227-7787
16 Passaic Ave Unit 3 Fairfield (07004) *(G-3174)*

Deep Foods Inc (PA) 908 810-7500
1090 Springfield Rd Ste 1 Union (07083) *(G-11171)*

Deer Out Animal Repellant LLC 908 769-4242
3651 S Clinton Ave South Plainfield (07080) *(G-10353)*

Deerbrook Fabrics, Guttenberg *Also called O Stitch Matic Inc (G-3870)*

Deerbrook Fabrics 201 945-4141
427 69th St Guttenberg (07093) *(G-3869)*

A L P H A B E T I C

Defense Photonics Group Inc 908 822-1075
126 Corporate Blvd Ste A South Plainfield (07080) *(G-10354)*
Defense Spport Svcs Intl 2 LLC 856 866-2200
901 Lincoln Dr W Ste 200 Marlton (08053) *(G-5970)*
Defense Support Svcs Intl LLC (HQ) 850 390-4737
901 Lincoln Dr W Ste 200 Marlton (08053) *(G-5971)*
Defined Pro Machining LLC 973 891-1038
105 W Dewey Ave Ste 419 Wharton (07885) *(G-11984)*
Degree Day Systems Inc 973 627-7959
33 Village Park Rd Cedar Grove (07009) *(G-1277)*
Degussa, Parsippany *Also called Evonik Corporation (G-8003)*
Deitz Co Inc 732 295-8212
1750 Hwy 34 Belmar (07719) *(G-357)*
Deitz, Michael & Sons, Hillside *Also called M Deitz & Sons Inc (G-4427)*
Dejana Trck Grter Philadelphia, Cinnaminson *Also called Dejana Trck Utility Eqp Co LLC (G-1454)*
Dejana Trck Utility Eqp Co LLC 856 303-1315
2502 Route 130 N Cinnaminson (08077) *(G-1454)*
Dek Tron International Corp 908 226-1777
244 E 3rd St Plainfield (07060) *(G-8857)*
Del Bakers Inc 856 461-0089
412 Kossuth St Riverside (08075) *(G-9496)*
Del Buono Bakery Inc 856 546-9585
319 Black Horse Pike Haddon Heights (08035) *(G-4047)*
Delair LLC 856 663-2900
9000 River Rd Pennsauken (08110) *(G-8502)*
Delaware Technologies Inc 856 234-7692
641 Mount Laurel Rd Mount Laurel (08054) *(G-6792)*
Delaware Valley Box & Lbr Co, Trenton *Also called Bunn Industries Incorporated (G-11030)*
Delaware Valley Installation 856 546-0097
200 Evergreen Rd Runnemede (08078) *(G-9718)*
Delaware Valley News, Frenchtown *Also called Hunterdon County Democrat Inc (G-3701)*
Delaware Valley Sign Corp (PA) 609 386-0100
112 Connecticut Dr Burlington (08016) *(G-967)*
Delaware Valley Vault, Blackwood *Also called Bradbury Burial Vault Co Inc (G-473)*
Delaware Valley Vault Co Inc 856 227-2555
761 Lower Landing Rd Blackwood (08012) *(G-475)*
Deleet Merchandising Corp (PA) 212 962-6565
26 Blanchard St Newark (07105) *(G-7139)*
Delgard Premier Alum Fencing, Pennsauken *Also called Delair LLC (G-8502)*
Delgen Press Inc 973 472-2266
250 Delawanna Ave Clifton (07014) *(G-1598)*
Delicious Bagels Inc (PA) 732 892-9265
2259 Bridge Ave Point Pleasant Boro (08742) *(G-8938)*
Delicious Fresh Pierogi Inc 908 245-0550
594 Chestnut St Roselle Park (07204) *(G-9694)*
Delight Foods USA LLC 201 369-1199
438 Saint Pauls Ave Jersey City (07306) *(G-4738)*
Delisa Pallet Corp 732 667-7070
116 South Ave Middlesex (08846) *(G-6161)*
Dell Aquila Baking Company 201 886-0613
308 W Hudson Ave Englewood (07631) *(G-2886)*
Dell Software Inc 201 556-4600
80 Parkway Rochelle Park (07662) *(G-9527)*
Delmhorst Instrument Company 973 334-2557
51 Indian Ln E Towaco (07082) *(G-10992)*
Delphian Corporation 201 767-7300
220 Pegasus Ave Northvale (07647) *(G-7577)*
Delsea Pipe Inc 856 589-9374
445 Delsea Dr Sewell (08080) *(G-9950)*
Delta Circuits Inc 973 575-3000
26 Spielman Rd Fairfield (07004) *(G-3175)*
Delta Cooling Towers Inc (PA) 973 586-2201
185 Us Highway 206 Flanders (07836) *(G-3404)*
Delta Corrugated Ppr Pdts Corp 201 941-1910
199 W Ruby Ave Palisades Park (07650) *(G-7838)*
Delta Galil USA Inc (HQ) 201 902-0055
1 Harmon Plz Fl 5 Secaucus (07094) *(G-9876)*
Delta Lambskin Products Inc 201 871-9233
595 Ridge Rd Englewood (07631) *(G-2887)*
Delta Paper Corporation 856 532-0333
122 Kissel Rd Burlington (08016) *(G-968)*
Delta Procurement Inc 201 623-9353
400 Gotham Pkwy Carlstadt (07072) *(G-1153)*
Delta Sales Company Inc 973 838-0371
1355 State Rt 23 Butler (07405) *(G-1002)*
Deltech Resins Co (PA) 973 589-0880
49 Rutherford St Newark (07105) *(G-7140)*
Deltronics Corporation 856 825-8200
224 Bogden Blvd Millville (08332) *(G-6297)*
Delucca's Bakery, Riverside *Also called Del Bakers Inc (G-9496)*
Deluxe Check Printers, Mountain Lakes *Also called Deluxe Corporation (G-6857)*
Deluxe Corporation 973 334-8000
105 Route 46 W Mountain Lakes (07046) *(G-6857)*
Deluxe Foods International 845 825-3442
29 E 25th St Paterson (07514) *(G-8248)*
Deluxe Gourmet Spc Ltd Lblty 732 485-7519
85 Corona Ct Old Bridge (08857) *(G-7776)*
Deluxe Innovations Inc 201 857-5880
140 Greenwood Ave Ste 2a Midland Park (07432) *(G-6225)*
Delva Tool & Machine Corp (PA) 856 786-8700
1603 Industrial Hwy Cinnaminson (08077) *(G-1455)*
Delva Tool & Machine Corp 856 829-0109
1911 Rowland St Cinnaminson (08077) *(G-1456)*
Delvco Pharma Packg Svcs Inc 973 278-2500
150 E 7th St Paterson (07524) *(G-8249)*
Demaio Inc 609 965-4094
543 Columbia Rd Egg Harbor City (08215) *(G-2661)*
Demand LLC 908 526-2020
36 S Adamsville Rd 1 Somerville (08876) *(G-10206)*
Dematic Corp 908 991-9900
150 Allen Rd Ste 102 Basking Ridge (07920) *(G-184)*
Dematte Oil Service Inc 856 692-9125
1780 Hance Bridge Rd Millville (08332) *(G-6298)*
Demco Scientific Glassware Inc 856 327-7898
25 N 6th St Millville (08332) *(G-6299)*
Demountable Concepts Inc 856 863-3081
200 Acorn Rd Glassboro (08028) *(G-3803)*
Denaka Partners LP 609 394-1176
31 Wolverton St 35 Trenton (08611) *(G-11053)*
Denali Company LLC (PA) 732 219-7771
211 Broad St Red Bank (07701) *(G-9326)*
Denby USA Limited 800 374-6479
1065 Rte 22 Ste 3b Bridgewater (08807) *(G-833)*
Deneka Printing Systems Inc (PA) 609 752-0964
100c Goldman Dr Cream Ridge (08514) *(G-1934)*
Dengen Scientific Corporation 201 687-2983
315 4th St Union City (07087) *(G-11245)*
Denmatt Industries LLC 609 689-0099
2080 E State Street Ext Hamilton (08619) *(G-4106)*
Dennis Kessler Steel Rule Die, West Berlin *Also called Kessler Steel Rule Die Inc (G-11728)*
Dental Designs, Garfield *Also called Dental Models & Designs Inc (G-3729)*
Dental Manufacturing, Pennsauken *Also called E P R Industries Inc (G-8507)*
Dental Models & Designs Inc 973 472-8009
20 Passaic St Ste 3 Garfield (07026) *(G-3729)*
Dentalworx Lab Ltd Lblty Co 732 981-9096
1000 New Durham Rd Edison (08817) *(G-2501)*
Dentamach Inc 973 334-2220
14 Walsh Dr Ste 102 Parsippany (07054) *(G-7979)*
Dentistry Today Inc 973 882-4700
100 Passaic Ave Ste 220 Fairfield (07004) *(G-3176)*
Denton Vacuum LLC 856 439-9100
1259 N Church St Moorestown (08057) *(G-6572)*
Denville Dairy, Denville *Also called Rolo Systems (G-2056)*
Denville Diagnostic Imaging, Denville *Also called Denville Diagnostics Imaging (G-2035)*
Denville Diagnostics Imaging 973 586-1212
161 E Main St Ste 101 Denville (07834) *(G-2035)*
Deosen Usa Inc 908 382-6518
1140 Stelton Rd Ste 205 Piscataway (08854) *(G-8755)*
Dependable Machining Co 732 462-0262
53 Weaverville Rd Freehold (07728) *(G-3650)*
Dependable Precision Products 973 887-3304
42 Schindler Ct Parsippany (07054) *(G-7980)*
Deptford Plating Co Inc 856 227-1144
Dein Ave Rr 41 Deptford (08096) *(G-2063)*
Derma Sciences Inc (HQ) 609 514-4744
311 Enterprise Dr Plainsboro (08536) *(G-8880)*
Dermarite Industries LLC 973 247-3491
7777 W Side Ave North Bergen (07047) *(G-7446)*
Dermatological Soc of NJ Inc 856 546-5600
208 White Horse Pike Barrington (08007) *(G-176)*
Dermatology & Laser Center PA 732 222-8323
279 3rd Ave Ste 603 Long Branch (07740) *(G-5623)*
Deroche Canvas, Belvidere *Also called Pv Deroche LLC (G-374)*
Derv2000 ....503 470-9158
420 Belgrove Dr Kearny (07032) *(G-4871)*
Desiere Electric Motor Service, Vineland *Also called Phil Desiere Electric Mtr Svc (G-11390)*
Design & Molding Services Inc 732 752-0300
25 Howard St Piscataway (08854) *(G-8756)*
Design Assistance Corporation 856 241-9500
3 Killdeer Ct Ste 301 Swedesboro (08085) *(G-10691)*
Design Display Group Inc (PA) 201 438-6000
105 Amor Ave Carlstadt (07072) *(G-1154)*
Design Factory Nj Inc 908 964-8833
1210 Liberty Ave Hillside (07205) *(G-4404)*
Design N Stitch Inc 201 488-1314
107 Pink St Hackensack (07601) *(G-3904)*
Design of Tomorrow Inc 973 227-1000
24 Sherwood Ln Fairfield (07004) *(G-3177)*
Design Productions Inc 201 447-5656
9 Industrial Park Waldwick (07463) *(G-11444)*
Designcore Ltd 718 499-0337
585 Windsor Dr Ste 1 Secaucus (07094) *(G-9877)*
Designer, Garfield *Also called US Magic Box Inc (G-3770)*
Designer Bagel, South Plainfield *Also called Danmark Enterprises Inc (G-10352)*
Designer Kitchens 732 370-5500
250 Faraday Ave Jackson (08527) *(G-4663)*

Designer Sign Systems LLC 212 939-5577
  50 Broad St Carlstadt (07072) *(G-1155)*
Designs By James 856 692-1316
  892 N Delsea Dr Vineland (08360) *(G-11352)*
Desisti Lighting, Mountainside *Also called Desmar Corporation (G-6876)*
Desmar Corporation 908 317-0020
  1011 Us Highway 22 Ste 3 Mountainside (07092) *(G-6876)*
Dessau Company, Fair Lawn *Also called Maurice S Dessau Co Inc (G-3102)*
Destiny Foundation 732 987-9008
  564 Marc Dr Lakewood (08701) *(G-5108)*
Detail Doctor, Shrewsbury *Also called Cemp Inc (G-9992)*
Detailed Designs, Plainfield *Also called Injectron Corporation (G-8865)*
Detergent 20 LLC 732 545-0200
  594 Jersey Ave New Brunswick (08901) *(G-6954)*
Detrex Corporation 856 786-8686
  835 Industrial Hwy Ste 1 Cinnaminson (08077) *(G-1457)*
Devatal Inc 609 586-1575
  644 Newkirk Ave Trenton (08610) *(G-11054)*
Devco Corporation 201 337-1600
  131 Morristown Rd Bldg B Basking Ridge (07920) *(G-185)*
Devece & Shaffer Inc 856 829-7282
  400 Legion Ave Palmyra (08065) *(G-7847)*
Devon Products 732 438-3855
  230 W Parkway Ste 3 Pompton Plains (07444) *(G-8957)*
Devon Trading Corp 973 812-9190
  5 Fairfield Rd Caldwell (07006) *(G-1026)*
Devotion Spirits Inc 877 415-3190
  566b Hwy 35 Red Bank (07701) *(G-9327)*
Devotion Vodka, Red Bank *Also called Devotion Spirits Inc (G-9327)*
Dew Associates Inc (PA) 973 702-0545
  48 Woodport Rd Sparta (07871) *(G-10496)*
Dew Associates Inc 973 702-0545
  7 Armstrong Rd Sussex (07461) *(G-10668)*
Dewalt Industrial Tools, Elmwood Park *Also called Black & Decker (us) Inc (G-2806)*
Dewalt Manufacturing Co Inc 856 423-1207
  88 W Cohawkin Rd Clarksboro (08020) *(G-1518)*
Dewechter Inc 856 845-0225
  58 S Broad St Woodbury (08096) *(G-12159)*
Dewey Electronics Corporation (PA) 201 337-4700
  27 Muller Rd Oakland (07436) *(G-7684)*
Dewey Electronics Corporation 201 337-4700
  27 Muller Rd Oakland (07436) *(G-7685)*
Dewitt Bros Tool Co Inc 908 298-3700
  140 Market St Kenilworth (07033) *(G-4951)*
Dewy Meadow Farms Inc (PA) 908 218-5655
  1018 Rector Rd Bridgewater (08807) *(G-834)*
Dewy Meadow Foods, Inc., Bridgewater *Also called Dewy Meadow Farms Inc (G-834)*
Dex Media Inc 908 237-0956
  27 Minneakoning Rd # 204 Flemington (08822) *(G-3434)*
Dex Media Inc 856 988-2700
  401 Route 73 N Bldg 20 Marlton (08053) *(G-5972)*
Dex-O-Tex Floor Coverings, Roselle Park *Also called Crossfield Products Corp (G-9691)*
Dexmed Inc 732 831-0507
  433 N Broad St Fl 1 Elizabeth (07208) *(G-2724)*
Dexmed LLC 732 831-0507
  433 N Broad St Fl 1 Elizabeth (07208) *(G-2725)*
Dezine Line Inc 973 989-1009
  17 Robert St Ste B2 Wharton (07885) *(G-11985)*
DFI-Itox LLC 732 562-0693
  15 Corporate Pl S Ste 201 Piscataway (08854) *(G-8757)*
Dg3 Group America Inc (HQ) 201 793-5000
  100 Burma Rd Jersey City (07305) *(G-4739)*
Dg3 Holdings LLC (HQ) 201 793-5000
  100 Burma Rd Jersey City (07305) *(G-4740)*
Dg3 North America Inc 201 793-5000
  100 Burma Rd Jersey City (07305) *(G-4741)*
Di-Ferraro Inc 973 694-7200
  28 Burgess Pl Wayne (07470) *(G-11623)*
Diabeto Inc 646 397-3175
  200 Centennial Ave # 200 Piscataway (08854) *(G-8758)*
Diacritech LLC 732 238-1157
  201 Marin Blvd Apt 1112 Jersey City (07302) *(G-4742)*
Diagenode Inc 862 209-4680
  400 Morris Ave Ste 101 Denville (07834) *(G-2036)*
Diagnostix Plus Inc 201 530-5505
  811 Queen Anne Rd Teaneck (07666) *(G-10748)*
Dial Connection LLC 856 753-6620
  1040 S Route 73 Berlin (08009) *(G-433)*
Dialight Corporation (HQ) 732 919-3119
  1501 State Route 34 Wall Township (07727) *(G-11477)*
Dialogic Inc (HQ) 973 967-6000
  4 Gatehall Dr Parsippany (07054) *(G-7981)*
Diamex International Corp (PA) 973 838-8844
  23 Birch Rd Kinnelon (07405) *(G-5034)*
Diamond Bright Metal Proc, Middlesex *Also called Stainless Stock (G-6202)*
Diamond Chip Realty LLC 973 383-4651
  33 Demarest Rd Sparta (07871) *(G-10497)*
Diamond Essence, Edison *Also called Meeshaa Inc (G-2567)*

Diamond Foods USA Inc 732 543-2186
  832 Ridgewood Ave North Brunswick (08902) *(G-7515)*
Diamond Hut Jewelry Exchange 201 332-5372
  Hudson Mall Rr 440 Jersey City (07304) *(G-4743)*
Diamond Machine Co Inc 609 490-8940
  30 N Valley Rd Roosevelt (08555) *(G-9640)*
Diamond Sand & Gravel, Sparta *Also called Diamond Chip Realty LLC (G-10497)*
Diamond Scooters Inc 609 646-0003
  645 S Mill Rd Ste 1 Absecon (08201) *(G-2)*
Diamond Sg Intl Ltd Lblty Co 732 861-9850
  20 Meridian Rd Ste 9 Eatontown (07724) *(G-2390)*
Diamond Systems USA Corp 973 777-9075
  176 Saddle River Ave C South Hackensack (07606) *(G-10260)*
Diamond Universe LLC 201 592-9500
  2460 Lemoine Ave Ste 302 Fort Lee (07024) *(G-3551)*
Diamond Wholesale Co 201 727-9595
  30 Congress Dr Moonachie (07074) *(G-6514)*
Diane Matson Inc 609 288-6833
  49 Brighton Rd Westampton (08060) *(G-11912)*
Diaz Foods 404 629-3616
  4 Rosol Ln Saddle Brook (07663) *(G-9762)*
Dibello USA Inc 212 279-9099
  41 Forrest Rd Randolph (07869) *(G-9273)*
Dicaperl Minerals Corp 856 320-2919
  9111 River Rd Pennsauken (08110) *(G-8503)*
Dicar Inc (HQ) 973 575-1377
  30 Chapin Rd Pine Brook (07058) *(G-8697)*
Dicar Inc 973 575-4220
  5 Bader Rd Pine Brook (07058) *(G-8698)*
Dicar Diamond Tool Corp 973 684-0949
  108 Kentucky Ave Paterson (07503) *(G-8250)*
Die Tech LLC 201 343-8324
  58 Mckinley St Hackensack (07601) *(G-3905)*
Dietech Services LLC 973 667-0798
  40 Holmes St Nutley (07110) *(G-7646)*
Difco Laboratories Inc (HQ) 410 316-4113
  1 Becton Dr Franklin Lakes (07417) *(G-3613)*
Digipol Technologies, Denville *Also called Rudolph Instruments Inc (G-2057)*
Digitails, West Berlin *Also called Spaghetti Engineering Corp (G-11751)*
Digital Arts Imaging LLC 908 237-4646
  105 State Route 31 Ste 10 Flemington (08822) *(G-3435)*
Digital Atelier LLC 609 890-6666
  60 Sculptors Way Ste A Trenton (08619) *(G-11055)*
Digital Binscom LLC 908 867-7055
  59 E Mill Rd Ste 1-103 Long Valley (07853) *(G-5636)*
Digital Color Concepts Inc 908 264-0504
  256 Sheffield St Mountainside (07092) *(G-6877)*
Digital Design Inc 973 857-9500
  67 Sand Park Rd Cedar Grove (07009) *(G-1278)*
Digital Dimension Three, Lyndhurst *Also called Popnfold Papers Inc (G-5702)*
Digital Outdoor Advg LLC 732 616-2232
  788 Shrewsbury Ave Ste 22 Tinton Falls (07724) *(G-10830)*
Digital Print Solutions Inc 973 263-1890
  5 Eastmans Rd Parsippany (07054) *(G-7982)*
Digital Printed Communications, Morristown *Also called Pica Printings Inc (G-6735)*
Digital Productions Inc 856 224-1111
  100 Berkeley Dr Swedesboro (08085) *(G-10692)*
Digital Xpress LLC 973 627-2609
  3 Luger Rd Ste 3 # 3 Denville (07834) *(G-2037)*
Digitize Inc 973 663-1011
  158 Edison Rd Lake Hopatcong (07849) *(G-5056)*
Digitron Electronic Corp 908 245-2012
  144 Market St Kenilworth (07033) *(G-4952)*
Digivac Company 732 765-0900
  105 B Church St Ste 4 Matawan (07747) *(G-6017)*
Dihco Inc 201 327-0518
  612 E Crescent Ave Ste A Upper Saddle River (07458) *(G-11278)*
Dijon Enterprises LLC 201 876-9463
  21 Curie Ave Wallington (07057) *(G-11525)*
Dikeman Laminating Corporation 973 473-5696
  181 Sargeant Ave Clifton (07013) *(G-1599)*
Diligaf Enterprises Inc (HQ) 201 684-0900
  500 Corporate Dr Mahwah (07430) *(G-5765)*
Dillon Yarn Corporation (PA) 973 684-1600
  53 E 34th St Paterson (07514) *(G-8251)*
Dim Inc 908 925-2043
  10 Grant St Linden (07036) *(G-5369)*
Dimensional Communications Inc 201 767-1500
  1595 Macarthur Blvd Mahwah (07430) *(G-5766)*
Dimilo Industries 973 955-0460
  90 Dayton Ave Ste 38 Passaic (07055) *(G-8134)*
Dina Hernandez 973 772-8883
  236 Harrison Ave Ste A Lodi (07644) *(G-5581)*
Diocesan Media Center, The, Camden *Also called Diocese of Camden New Jersey (G-1059)*
Diocese of Camden New Jersey (PA) 856 756-7900
  631 Market St Camden (08102) *(G-1059)*
Diocese of Paterson 973 279-8845
  597 Valley Rd Clifton (07013) *(G-1600)*
Diopsys Inc 973 244-0622
  16 Chapin Rd Ste 912 Pine Brook (07058) *(G-8699)*

A
L
P
H
A
B
E
T
I
C

Dipietro Foods Inc 973 762-4077
269 Wyoming Ave Maplewood (07040) *(G-5918)*
Direct Computer Resources Inc (PA) 201 848-0018
120 Birch Rd Franklin Lakes (07417) *(G-3614)*
Direct Development LLC 732 739-8890
97 Apple St 2 Tinton Falls (07724) *(G-10831)*
Direct Prtg Impressions Inc 973 227-6111
33 Fairfield Pl West Caldwell (07006) *(G-11773)*
Direct Sales and Services Inc 973 340-4480
141 Lanza Ave Bldg 8 Garfield (07026) *(G-3730)*
Directory & Almanac, Newark *Also called Advocate Publishing Corp (G-7073)*
Disc Makers Inc 800 468-9353
7905 N Crescent Blvd Pennsauken (08110) *(G-8504)*
Discount Digital Print LLC 201 659-9600
629 Grove St Fl 3 Jersey City (07310) *(G-4744)*
Discount Packaging Corporation 201 836-0521
200 Chadwick Rd Teaneck (07666) *(G-10749)*
Discovery Semiconductors Inc 609 434-1311
119 Silvia St Ewing (08628) *(G-3014)*
Dishman Usa Inc 732 560-4300
476 Union Ave Ste 2 Middlesex (08846) *(G-6162)*
Dispersion Technology Inc 732 364-4488
1885 Swarthmore Ave Lakewood (08701) *(G-5109)*
Display Equation LLC 201 343-4135
135 Spring Valley Ave Hackensack (07601) *(G-3906)*
Display Impressions 856 488-1777
9265 Commerce Hwy Pennsauken (08110) *(G-8505)*
Display Pro Manufacturing, Kenilworth *Also called Daysol Inc (G-4950)*
Display Works LLC (PA) 201 327-1260
1 Gatehall Dr Ste 210 Parsippany (07054) *(G-7983)*
Disposable Hygiene LLC (PA) 973 779-1982
60 Page Rd Clifton (07012) *(G-1601)*
Distek Inc 732 422-7585
121 N Center Dr North Brunswick (08902) *(G-7516)*
Distinctive Wdwrk By Rob Hoffm 609 877-8122
703 Van Rossum Ave Unit 1 Beverly (08010) *(G-462)*
Distinctive Woodwork Inc 609 714-8505
70 Stacy Haines Rd Ste D Lumberton (08048) *(G-5656)*
Distributor Label Products 908 704-9997
51 Old Camplain Rd Hillsborough (08844) *(G-4327)*
Distributors Buying Service, Pleasantville *Also called Shy Kramer & Associates (G-8915)*
Disys Commerce Inc 201 567-0457
100 W Forest Ave Ste H Englewood (07631) *(G-2888)*
Diversatech Inc 609 730-9668
1584 Reed Rd Pennington (08534) *(G-8449)*
Diversfied Globl Grphics Group, Jersey City *Also called Dg3 Holdings LLC (G-4740)*
Diversfied Globl Grphics Group, Jersey City *Also called Dg3 North America Inc (G-4741)*
Diversfield Impressions, Irvington *Also called Diversified Impressions Inc (G-4581)*
Diversified Display Pdts LLC 908 686-2200
777 Ramsey Ave Hillside (07205) *(G-4405)*
Diversified Fab Pdts Ltd Lblty 973 773-3189
158 River Rd Clifton (07014) *(G-1602)*
Diversified Fixtures, Lakewood *Also called Vitillo & Sons Inc (G-5201)*
Diversified Foam Products Inc 856 662-1981
121 High Hill Rd Swedesboro (08085) *(G-10693)*
Diversified Heat Transfer Inc 800 221-1522
439 Main Rd Towaco (07082) *(G-10993)*
Diversified Impressions Inc 973 399-9041
119 Coit St Irvington (07111) *(G-4581)*
Diversified Industries, Swedesboro *Also called Diversified Foam Products Inc (G-10693)*
Diversitech Inc 973 835-2900
18 Hamburg Tpke Riverdale (07457) *(G-9479)*
Diversity Direct, Monmouth Junction *Also called Real Soft Inc (G-6360)*
Diversity In Action, Roseland *Also called Know America Media LLC (G-9653)*
Diversity Plus Magazine 973 275-1405
111 S Orange Ave Ste 28 South Orange (07079) *(G-10303)*
Diversity/Careers In Enginrng, Springfield *Also called Renard Commumnications Inc (G-10576)*
Diversityinc Media LLC 973 494-0539
100 Overlook Ctr Fl 2 Princeton (08540) *(G-9029)*
Divine Printing 732 632-8800
131 Liberty St Metuchen (08840) *(G-6102)*
Division Name Process Systems, Mickleton *Also called Saint-Gobain Prfmce Plas Corp (G-6138)*
DJeet 732 224-8887
637 Broad St Shrewsbury (07702) *(G-9997)*
Dksh Luxury & Lifestyle N Amer 609 750-8800
9 Princess Rd Ste D Lawrence Township (08648) *(G-5242)*
DI Myers Corp 609 698-8800
446 N Main St Barnegat (08005) *(G-161)*
Dlite Products Inc 201 444-0822
540 Ravine Ct Wyckoff (07481) *(G-12250)*
Dm Graphic Center LLC 973 882-8990
26 Commerce Rd Ste L Fairfield (07004) *(G-3178)*
Dma Data Industries Inc 201 444-5733
479 Goffle Rd Wyckoff (07481) *(G-12251)*
DMC, Edison *Also called Dollfus Mieg Company Inc (G-2502)*
DMC Soft, Cherry Hill *Also called Automated Office Inc (G-1345)*

DMD Stairs & Rails LLC 732 901-0102
370 Whitesville Rd Ste 8 Jackson (08527) *(G-4664)*
Dmf Associated Engines LLC 973 535-9773
W Hobart Gap Rd Livingston (07039) *(G-5528)*
Dmg, Edison *Also called Aerogroup Retail Holdings Inc (G-2451)*
Dmg America LLC 201 894-5500
65 Challenger Rd Ste 340 Ridgefield Park (07660) *(G-9404)*
Dmg Mori Seiki, Rockaway *Also called Dmg Mori Usa Inc (G-9561)*
Dmg Mori Usa Inc 973 257-9620
400 Commons Way Ste A Rockaway (07866) *(G-9561)*
DMJ and Associates Inc 732 613-7867
27 William St Sayreville (08872) *(G-9820)*
DMJ Industrial Services LLC 973 692-8406
1 Hilltop Ter Wayne (07470) *(G-11624)*
DMJ Technologies LLC 201 261-5560
775 Maple St New Milford (07646) *(G-7021)*
Dmr Sign Systems, Dover *Also called Envirmmntal Dsign Grphic Entps (G-2086)*
DMS Inc 973 928-3040
218 Little Falls Rd 7-8 Cedar Grove (07009) *(G-1279)*
DMS Laboratories Inc 908 782-3353
2 Darts Mill Rd Flemington (08822) *(G-3436)*
Dmv-Fnterra Excipients USA LLC 609 858-2111
61 S Paramus Rd Paramus (07652) *(G-7866)*
DMW&h, Fairfield *Also called W & H Systems Inc (G-3347)*
Dmz Industries, Fairfield *Also called Control & Power Systems Inc (G-3167)*
Dnp Foods America Ltd Lblty Co 201 654-5581
2 Dipippo Ct Waldwick (07463) *(G-11445)*
DO Productions LLC 856 866-3566
11 Gregg St Lodi (07644) *(G-5582)*
Docbox Solutions Ltd Lblty Co 201 650-0970
140 Upper Mountain Ave Montclair (07042) *(G-6411)*
Dock Resins Corporation 908 862-2351
76 Porcupine Rd Pedricktown (08067) *(G-8435)*
Doctor Tee Shirt, Manasquan *Also called J & G Graphics Inc (G-5872)*
Dodson Global Inc 732 238-7001
27 Cotters Ln East Brunswick (08816) *(G-2144)*
Doerre Fence Co LLC 732 751-9700
392 Adelphia Rd Farmingdale (07727) *(G-3384)*
Dohrman Printing Co Inc 201 933-0346
445 Industrial Rd Carlstadt (07072) *(G-1156)*
Dolan & Traynor Inc 973 696-8700
32 Riverview Dr Wayne (07470) *(G-11625)*
Dolan Assoc Inc 973 875-6408
71 Holland Rd A Sussex (07461) *(G-10669)*
Dolan LLC 800 451-9998
421 Executive Dr Princeton (08540) *(G-9030)*
Dolce Brothers Printing Inc (PA) 201 843-0400
29 Brook Ave Maywood (07607) *(G-6048)*
Dolce Printing 201 843-0400
29 Brook Ave Maywood (07607) *(G-6049)*
Dolce Technologies LLC 609 497-7319
90 Nassau St Fl 4 Princeton (08542) *(G-9031)*
Dolce Vita Intimates LLC (PA) 973 482-8400
1000 1st St Harrison (07029) *(G-4178)*
Dolco Packaging, Branchburg *Also called Tekni-Plex Inc (G-710)*
Dolco Packaging Corp (HQ) 201 941-2900
101 Railroad Ave Ridgefield (07657) *(G-9358)*
Dollfus Mieg Company Inc 732 662-1005
86 Northfield Ave Edison (08837) *(G-2502)*
Domel Inc 973 614-1800
3 Grunwald St Clifton (07013) *(G-1603)*
Dominion Colour Corp USA 973 279-9591
881 Allwood Rd Ste 2 Clifton (07012) *(G-1604)*
Domino Foods Inc (HQ) 732 590-1173
99 Wood Ave S Ste 901 Iselin (08830) *(G-4623)*
Domino Printing 973 857-0900
67 Sand Park Rd Cedar Grove (07009) *(G-1280)*
Domino Sugar, Iselin *Also called Domino Foods Inc (G-4623)*
Doms Bakery Grand Inc 201 653-1948
506 Grand St Hoboken (07030) *(G-4469)*
Don Schreiber Co, Lebanon *Also called Johnthan Leasing Corp (G-5293)*
Don Shrts Pcture Frmes Molding 732 363-1323
294 Lanes Mill Rd Howell (07731) *(G-4552)*
Don Shurts Frames & Molding, Howell *Also called Don Shrts Pcture Frmes Molding (G-4552)*
Donald Mason Baker Contractor (PA) 908 782-2115
188 Thatchers Hill Rd Flemington (08822) *(G-3437)*
Donna Karan International Inc 609 345-3402
1931 Atlantic Ave Atlantic City (08401) *(G-95)*
Donnelley Financial LLC 973 882-7000
5 Henderson Dr West Caldwell (07006) *(G-11774)*
Donnelly Construction, Wayne *Also called Donnelly Industries Inc (G-11626)*
Donnelly Industries Inc 973 672-1800
557 Rte 23 Wayne (07470) *(G-11626)*
Donray Printing Inc 973 515-8100
2 Eastmans Rd Parsippany (07054) *(G-7984)*
Dons Drapery Manufacturing 973 751-1544
145 Heckel St Belleville (07109) *(G-300)*
Doolan Industries Incorporated (PA) 856 985-1880
5 Blue Anchor St Marlton (08053) *(G-5973)*

Door Center Enterprises Inc 609 333-1233
105 Crusher Rd Hopewell (08525) (G-4541)

Door Stop LLC 718 599-5112
109 Kero Rd Carlstadt (07072) (G-1157)

Doorsills LLC 973 904-0270
302 Legion Pl Haledon (07508) (G-4081)

Doorstop, Carlstadt Also called Door Stop LLC (G-1157)

Doortec Archtctural Met GL LLC (PA) 201 497-5056
303 Martin St River Vale (07675) (G-9469)

Doosan Heavy Inds Amer LLC 201 944-4554
140 Sylvan Ave Englewood Cliffs (07632) (G-2957)

Doosan Machine Tools, Pine Brook Also called Clark Equipment Company (G-8694)

Doosan Machine Tools Amer Corp (HQ) 973 618-2500
19a Chapin Rd Pine Brook (07058) (G-8700)

Dor-Win Manufacturing Co 201 796-4300
109 Midland Ave Elmwood Park (07407) (G-2815)

Dorado Systems LLC 856 354-0048
8 Kings Hwy E Haddonfield (08033) (G-4059)

Doralex Inc 856 764-0694
403 Saint Mihiel Dr Delran (08075) (G-2016)

Doran Company, Union Also called Doran LLC (G-11172)

Doran LLC 908 289-9200
599 Green Ln Union (07083) (G-11172)

Doran Sling and Assembly Corp 908 355-1101
1285 Central Ave Ste 2 Hillside (07205) (G-4406)

DOrazio Foods Inc 856 931-1900
960 Creek Rd Bellmawr (08031) (G-337)

Dorchester Shipyard Inc 856 785-8040
13 Front St Dorchester (08316) (G-2072)

Dorf Feature Service Inc 908 518-1802
187 Mill Ln Ste 3 Mountainside (07092) (G-6878)

Dorwin Manufacturing Co 201 796-4300
109 Midland Ave Elmwood Park (07407) (G-2816)

Dorzar Corporation 973 589-6363
50 Avenue L Ste 5 Newark (07105) (G-7141)

Dos Industrial Sales LLC 973 887-7800
7d Great Meadow Ln East Hanover (07936) (G-2212)

Dosch-King Company Inc (PA) 973 887-0145
16 Troy Hills Rd Whippany (07981) (G-12018)

Dosch-King Emulsions, Whippany Also called Dosch-King Company Inc (G-12018)

Dosis Fragrance LLC 718 874-0074
250 Passaic St Newark (07104) (G-7142)

DOT Graphix Inc 609 994-3416
79 S Main St Ste 13 Barnegat (08005) (G-162)

Double Check 973 984-2229
101 Gibraltar Dr Ste 1e Morris Plains (07950) (G-6659)

Double Diamond Technologies 609 624-1414
705 Route 9 Cape May (08204) (G-1097)

Double O Manufacturing Inc 732 752-9423
2b Smalley Ave Middlesex (08846) (G-6163)

Double Twenties Inc 973 827-7563
20 Park Dr Franklin (07416) (G-3598)

Dougherty Foundation Products 201 337-5748
851 Meadow Ln Franklin Lakes (07417) (G-3615)

Douglas Elec Components Inc 973 627-8230
5 Middlebury Blvd Randolph (07869) (G-9274)

Douglas Liva MD 201 444-7770
625 Franklin Tpke Ridgewood (07450) (G-9423)

Douglas Maybury Assoc 908 879-5878
385 State Route 24 Ste 3e Chester (07930) (G-1436)

Douglass Industries Inc 609 804-6040
412 Boston Ave Egg Harbor City (08215) (G-2662)

Douglass Weave Appeal, Egg Harbor City Also called Douglass Industries Inc (G-2662)

Dove Chocolate Discoveries LLC 866 922-3683
400 Valley Rd Ste 200 Mount Arlington (07856) (G-6753)

Dover Tool Connecticut LLC (PA) 203 367-6376
620 Franklin Lake Rd Franklin Lakes (07417) (G-3616)

Dow Chemical Company 800 258-2436
1 Riverview Dr Somerset (08873) (G-10090)

Dow Chemical Company 856 663-2627
1500 John Tipton Blvd Pennsauken (08110) (G-8506)

Dow Chemical Company 732 969-5723
78 Lafayette St Carteret (07008) (G-1255)

Dow Jones & Company Inc 609 520-4000
4300 N Rt 1 & Ridge Rd Cranbury (08512) (G-1829)

Dow Jones & Company Inc 609 520-5238
4300 Us Highway 1 Monmouth Junction (08852) (G-6341)

Dowden Health Media Inc (HQ) 201 740-6100
110 Summit Ave Ste 1 Montvale (07645) (G-6453)

Down Shore Publishing Corp 609 978-1233
638 Teal St West Creek (08092) (G-11810)

Downtown Printing Center Inc 732 246-7990
46 Paterson St Ste 1 New Brunswick (08901) (G-6955)

Dpc Cirrus 973 927-2828
62 Flanders Bartley Rd Flanders (07836) (G-3405)

Dpc Instrument Systems, Flanders Also called Siemens Med Sltons Diagnostics (G-3416)

Dpi Copies Prtg & Graphics Inc 856 874-1355
2070 Marlton Pike E Ste 3 Cherry Hill (08003) (G-1360)

Dpi Newco LLC 973 257-8113
45 Waterview Blvd Parsippany (07054) (G-7985)

Dpj Inc 732 499-8600
245 E Inman Ave Rahway (07065) (G-9184)

Dpk Consulting LLC 732 764-0100
220 Old New Brunswick Rd # 201 Piscataway (08854) (G-8759)

Dpsg, Avenel Also called Snapple Distributors Inc (G-151)

Dr Pregers Sensible Foods Inc 201 703-1300
9 Boumar Pl Elmwood Park (07407) (G-2817)

Dr Reddys Laboratories Inc (HQ) 609 375-9900
107 College Rd E Princeton (08540) (G-9032)

Dr Schar Usa Inc 856 803-5100
305 Heron Dr Swedesboro (08085) (G-10694)

Dr Sofa, Guttenberg Also called Sofa Doctor Inc (G-3871)

DR Technology Inc 732 780-4664
73 South St Freehold (07728) (G-3651)

Dragon Asphalt Equipment LLC 732 922-9290
845 Towbin Ave Lakewood (08701) (G-5110)

Drake Corp 732 254-1530
110 Tices Ln East Brunswick (08816) (G-2145)

Dranetz Technologies Inc (HQ) 732 248-4358
1000 New Durham Rd Edison (08817) (G-2503)

Drapekings, North Bergen Also called Dru Whitacre Media Svcs Ltd (G-7448)

Drapery & More Inc 201 271-9661
2321 Kennedy Blvd Ste 1 North Bergen (07047) (G-7447)

Drawbase Software, Lyndhurst Also called Com Tek Wrkplace Solutions LLC (G-5678)

Draztic Designs LLC 609 678-4200
205 Petticoat Bridge Rd Columbus (08022) (G-1803)

Dream Makers Inc 201 248-5502
53 Glendale Rd Park Ridge (07656) (G-7918)

Dream On ME Industries Inc (PA) 732 752-7220
1532 S Washington Ave # 1 Piscataway (08854) (G-8760)

Dream Well Collection Inc 732 545-5900
633 Nassau St New Brunswick (08902) (G-6956)

Dreamstar Construction LLC 732 393-2572
248 Clubhouse Dr Middletown (07748) (G-6213)

Dreamwell, New Brunswick Also called Dream Well Collection Inc (G-6956)

Drew & Rogers Inc (PA) 973 575-6210
30 Plymouth St Ste 2 Fairfield (07004) (G-3179)

Drew-Wal Machine & Tool Corp 201 641-3887
76 Monroe St Little Ferry (07643) (G-5502)

Dreyco Inc (PA) 201 896-9000
263 Veterans Blvd Carlstadt (07072) (G-1158)

DRG International Inc (PA) 973 564-7555
841 Mountain Ave Springfield (07081) (G-10551)

Drifire LLC 866 266-4035
28 Kennedy Blvd Ste 300 East Brunswick (08816) (G-2146)

Drink A Toast Company Inc 856 461-1000
603 Harrison St Riverside (08075) (G-9497)

Driscoll Foods, Clifton Also called Metropolitan Foods Inc (G-1673)

Driscoll Label Company Inc 973 585-7291
19 West St East Hanover (07936) (G-2213)

Dritac Flooring Products LLC 973 614-9000
60 Webro Rd Clifton (07012) (G-1605)

Drive Technology Inc 732 422-6500
2031 Us Highway 130 1l Monmouth Junction (08852) (G-6342)

Drive-Master Co Inc 973 808-9709
37 Daniel Rd Fairfield (07004) (G-3180)

Drom International Inc 973 316-8400
5 Jacksonville Rd Towaco (07082) (G-10994)

Drone Go Home LLC 732 991-3605
25 Grand Tour Highlands (07732) (G-4308)

Drs Data & Imaging Systems, Oakland Also called Drs Leonardo Inc (G-7686)

Drs Infrared Technologies LP 973 898-1500
5 Sylvan Way Ste 305 Parsippany (07054) (G-7986)

Drs Leonardo Inc 973 775-4440
95 William St Newark (07102) (G-7143)

Drs Leonardo Inc 973 898-1500
5 Sylvan Way Parsippany (07054) (G-7987)

Drs Leonardo Inc 973 898-1500
5 Sylvan Way Parsippany (07054) (G-7988)

Drs Leonardo Inc 201 337-3800
133 Bauer Dr Oakland (07436) (G-7686)

Drs Srvillance Support Systems, Parsippany Also called Drs Leonardo Inc (G-7988)

Dru Whitacre Media Svcs Ltd (PA) 201 770-9950
3200 Liberty Ave Ste 2c North Bergen (07047) (G-7448)

Drug Delivery Technology LLC 973 299-1200
219 Changebridge Rd Montville (07045) (G-6487)

Drytech Inc 609 758-1794
54 Wrghtstown Cokstown Rd Cookstown (08511) (G-1806)

Dse Healthcare Solutions LLC 732 417-1870
164 Northfield Ave Edison (08837) (G-2504)

DSM Nutritional Products LLC 908 475-7093
206 Macks Island Dr Belvidere (07823) (G-369)

DSM Nutritional Products LLC 908 475-0150
253 260 Macks Island Dr Belvidere (07823) (G-370)

DSM Nutritional Products LLC 908 475-5300
200 Roche Dr Belvidere (07823) (G-371)

DSM Nutritional Products LLC 908 475-5300
218 Roche Dr Belvidere (07823) (G-372)

A
L
P
H
A
B
E
T
I
C

DSM Nutritional Products LLC (HQ) 800 526-0189
45 Waterview Blvd Parsippany (07054) *(G-7989)*

DSM Sight & Life Inc 973 257-8208
45 Waterview Blvd Parsippany (07054) *(G-7990)*

Dso Fluid Handling Co Inc 732 225-9100
300 Mcgaw Dr Ste 2 Edison (08837) *(G-2505)*

Dso Sanitary Supply, Edison Also called Dso Fluid Handling Co Inc *(G-2505)*

Dsrv Inc 973 631-1200
330 Waterloo Valley Rd # 200 Budd Lake (07828) *(G-927)*

Dtrovision LLC 201 488-3232
535 E Crescent Ave Ste 1 Ramsey (07446) *(G-9239)*

Du Technologies Inc 201 729-0070
300 W Commercial Ave Moonachie (07074) *(G-6515)*

Du-Matt Corporation 201 861-4271
12 65th St West New York (07093) *(G-11864)*

Du-Mor Blade Co Inc 856 829-9384
1002 Union Landing Rd Cinnaminson (08077) *(G-1458)*

Dubell Lumber Co (PA) 609 654-4143
148 Route 70 Medford (08055) *(G-6068)*

Dublin Management Assoc of NJ 609 387-1600
7 Campus Dr Burlington (08016) *(G-969)*

Dubon Corp 212 812-2171
1356 Stanley Ter Elizabeth (07208) *(G-2726)*

Duct Mate Inc 201 488-8002
190 Lexington Ave Hackensack (07601) *(G-3907)*

Ducts Inc 973 267-8482
8 Moraine Rd Morris Plains (07950) *(G-6660)*

Ductworks Inc 908 754-8190
434 W Front St Plainfield (07060) *(G-8858)*

Dudley Lab, Toms River Also called Henry Dudley *(G-10883)*

Duerr Tool & Die Co Inc (PA) 908 810-9035
1135 Springfield Rd Union (07083) *(G-11173)*

Dulce A Dessert Bar LLC 908 461-2418
609 S Atlantic Ave Matawan (07747) *(G-6018)*

Dun & Bradstreet Inc 973 921-5500
103 John F Kennedy Pkwy Short Hills (07078) *(G-9977)*

Dun-Rite Communications Inc 201 444-0080
31 Industrial Ave Mahwah (07430) *(G-5767)*

Dun-Rite Sand & Gravel Co (PA) 856 692-2520
573 E Grant Ave Vineland (08360) *(G-11353)*

Dunbar Concrete Products Inc 973 697-2525
173 Oak Ridge Rd Oak Ridge (07438) *(G-7660)*

Dunbar Sales Company Inc 201 437-6500
39 Avenue C Ste 1 Bayonne (07002) *(G-223)*

Dune Grass Publishing LLC 609 774-6562
39 Indiana Ave Blackwood (08012) *(G-476)*

Dunkin Donuts Baskin Robbins 201 692-1900
332 Cedar Ln Teaneck (07666) *(G-10750)*

Dunkin' Donuts, Ringoes Also called Jay Jariwala *(G-9439)*

Dunkin' Donuts, Rockaway Also called O O M Inc *(G-9592)*

Dunkin' Donuts, Jersey City Also called 9001 Corporation *(G-4693)*

Dunkin' Donuts, Jersey City Also called 9002 Corporation *(G-4694)*

Dunkin' Donuts, Cinnaminson Also called G N J Inc *(G-1463)*

Dunkin' Donuts, West Caldwell Also called All Madina Inc *(G-11765)*

Dunkin' Donuts, Mount Laurel Also called J K P Donuts Inc *(G-6809)*

Dunn Meadow Pharmacy, Fort Lee Also called LLC Dunn Meadow *(G-3565)*

Dupont, Parlin Also called E I Du Pont De Nemours & Co *(G-7930)*

Dura-Carb Inc 973 697-6665
204 Chamberlain Rd Oak Ridge (07438) *(G-7661)*

Duraamen Engineered Pdts Inc (PA) 973 230-1301
457 Frelinghuysen Ave Newark (07114) *(G-7144)*

Durabak Depot, Teaneck Also called Worldwide Safety Systems LLC *(G-10778)*

Durabond Division US Gypsum 732 636-7900
300 Markley St Port Reading (07064) *(G-8987)*

Durabrite Ltg Solutions LLC 201 915-0555
4 Beacon Way Apt 514 Jersey City (07304) *(G-4745)*

Duragates, Plainfield Also called Architectural Iron Designs *(G-8854)*

Duran Cutting Corp 973 916-0006
90 Dayton Ave Ste 6 Passaic (07055) *(G-8135)*

Durand Glass Mfg Co Inc 856 327-1850
901 S Wade Blvd Millville (08332) *(G-6300)*

Duratape International, Union Also called Wet-N-Stick LLC *(G-11234)*

Durex Inc (PA) 908 688-0800
5 Stahuber Ave Union (07083) *(G-11174)*

Durisan, Passaic Also called Sanit Technologies LLC *(G-8180)*

Duro Bag Manufacturing Company 908 351-2400
750 Dowd Ave Elizabeth (07201) *(G-2727)*

Duro Manufacturing Company 908 810-9588
5 Stahuber Ave Union (07083) *(G-11175)*

Duron Co Inc 973 242-5704
238 Emmet St Newark (07114) *(G-7145)*

Durst Corporation Inc (PA) 800 852-3906
129 Dermody St Cranford (07016) *(G-1903)*

Dusenbery Engineering Co Inc 973 539-2200
309 E Hanover Ave Morristown (07960) *(G-6706)*

Dutra Sheet Metal Co 856 692-8058
1940 S West Blvd Ste E Vineland (08360) *(G-11354)*

Dux Paint LLC 973 473-2376
18 Mill St Lodi (07644) *(G-5583)*

Dv8 Enterprises LLC 201 507-6288
151 Cooper Rd West Berlin (08091) *(G-11715)*

Dvs Industries, Burlington Also called Delaware Valley Sign Corp *(G-967)*

Dvx LLC 609 924-3590
31 Airpark Rd Ste 2 Princeton (08540) *(G-9033)*

Dwk Life Sciences Inc (HQ) 856 825-1100
1501 N 10th St Millville (08332) *(G-6301)*

Dxl Enterprises Inc 201 891-8718
575 Corporate Dr Ste 420 Mahwah (07430) *(G-5768)*

Dye Into Print Inc 973 772-8019
167 Fornelius Ave Clifton (07013) *(G-1606)*

Dyer Communications Inc 732 219-5788
75 W Front St Ste 2 Red Bank (07701) *(G-9328)*

Dyerich Flooring Designs Ltd 973 357-0600
35 Dale Ave Paterson (07505) *(G-8252)*

Dymax Systems Inc 732 918-2424
3455 State Route 66 Ste 6 Neptune (07753) *(G-6908)*

Dyna Veyor Inc 908 276-5384
10 Hudson St Newark (07103) *(G-7146)*

Dyna-Lite Inc 908 687-8800
1050 Commerce Ave Ste 2 Union (07083) *(G-11176)*

Dyna-Sea Group Inc 201 928-0133
765 Carroll Pl Teaneck (07666) *(G-10751)*

Dynaclear Packaging, Wyckoff Also called Pro Pack Inc *(G-12260)*

Dynaflow Engineering Inc 732 356-9790
106 Egel Ave Middlesex (08846) *(G-6164)*

Dynametric Tool Inc 973 471-8009
27 Somerset Pl Clifton (07012) *(G-1607)*

Dynamic Blending Company Inc 856 541-6626
1475 S 6th St Camden (08104) *(G-1060)*

Dynamic Coatings LLC 732 998-6625
253 Main St Ste 120 Matawan (07747) *(G-6019)*

Dynamic Defense Materials LLC 856 552-4150
100 Sharp Rd Marlton (08053) *(G-5974)*

Dynamic Die Cutting & Finshg 973 589-8338
104-110 South St Newark (07114) *(G-7147)*

Dynamic Machining Inc 856 273-9830
1920 Bannard St Cinnaminson (08077) *(G-1459)*

Dynamic Metals Inc 908 769-0522
1713 S 2nd St Piscataway (08854) *(G-8761)*

Dynamic Printing & Graphics 973 473-7177
250 Delawanna Ave Clifton (07014) *(G-1608)*

Dynamic Safety International, Somerset Also called Dynamic Safety Usa LLC *(G-10091)*

Dynamic Safety Usa LLC 844 378-7200
400 Apgar Dr Ste H Somerset (08873) *(G-10091)*

Dynasil Corporation America 856 767-4600
385 Cooper Rd West Berlin (08091) *(G-11716)*

Dynasty Metals Inc 800 225-3962
183 Garfield Ave Kearny (07032) *(G-4872)*

Dynatec Systems Inc (PA) 609 387-0330
360 Connecticut Dr Burlington (08016) *(G-970)*

E & E Group Corp 201 814-0414
7 Maple Ave 2 South Hackensack (07606) *(G-10261)*

E & H Laminating & Slitting Co, Paterson Also called Annitti Enterprises Inc *(G-8213)*

E & J Gallo Winery 973 877-0118
1037 Raymond Blvd Ste 220 Newark (07102) *(G-7148)*

E & M Bindery Inc 973 777-9300
11 Peekay Dr Clifton (07014) *(G-1609)*

E & T Plastic Mfg Co Inc 201 596-5017
200 Green St Teterboro (07608) *(G-10792)*

E & T Sales Co Inc 856 787-0900
824 E Gate Dr Ste E Mount Laurel (08054) *(G-6793)*

E & W Piece Dye Works 973 942-8718
293 Morrissee Ave Haledon (07508) *(G-4082)*

E and E USA, Passaic Also called Emerald Electronics Usa Inc *(G-8137)*

E B R Manufacturing Inc 973 263-8810
10 Woodhaven Rd Parsippany (07054) *(G-7991)*

E Berkowitz & Co Inc 856 608-1118
520 Fellowship Rd B202 Mount Laurel (08054) *(G-6794)*

E C D Ventures Inc 856 875-1100
3501 Route 42 Ste 130 Blackwood (08012) *(G-477)*

E C Electroplating Inc 973 340-0227
125 Clark St Garfield (07026) *(G-3731)*

E C S, Pennington Also called Electrochemical Society Inc *(G-8450)*

E C S, Egg Harbor Township Also called Enroute Computer Solutions Inc *(G-2684)*

E C S I, Clifton Also called Ecsi International Inc *(G-1610)*

E F Britten & Co Inc 908 276-4800
22 South Ave W Cranford (07016) *(G-1904)*

E G L, Berkeley Heights Also called E G L Company Inc *(G-409)*

E G L Company Inc 908 508-1111
100 Industrial Rd Berkeley Heights (07922) *(G-409)*

E Group Inc 856 320-9688
129 Gaither Dr Ste M Mount Laurel (08054) *(G-6795)*

E I Du Pont De Nemours & Co 732 257-1579
250 Cheesequake Rd Parlin (08859) *(G-7930)*

E J M Store Fixtures Inc 973 372-7907
460 Coit St Irvington (07111) *(G-4582)*

2018 Harris New Jersey
Manufacturers Directory

(G-0000) Company's Geographic Section entry number

E L Baxter Co Inc....732 229-8219
1227 Deal Rd Ocean (07712) ***(G-7722)***
E Loc Total Logistics LLC....609 685-6117
144 Canterbury Rd Mount Laurel (08054) ***(G-6796)***
E M D, Flanders *Also called Electronic Measuring Devices* ***(G-3406)***
E M R Photoelectric Div, Princeton Junction *Also called Schlumberger Technology Corp* ***(G-9163)***
E Nevin Miller Inc....201 444-5784
21 Debra Ct Hawthorne (07506) ***(G-4230)***
E P Heller Company....973 377-2878
21 Samson Ave 25 Madison (07940) ***(G-5721)***
E P Homiek Shtmtl Sups Inc....732 364-7644
1352 River Ave Ste 4 Lakewood (08701) ***(G-5111)***
E P R Industries Inc....856 488-1120
4576 S Crescent Blvd Pennsauken (08109) ***(G-8507)***
E Pro Inc (PA)....732 283-0499
555 Us Highway 1 S # 330 Iselin (08830) ***(G-4624)***
E R Squibb & Sons LLC (HQ)....732 246-3195
25 Kennedy Blvd East Brunswick (08816) ***(G-2147)***
E R Squibb & Sons Inter-AM....609 818-3715
3 Hamilton Health Pl Trenton (08690) ***(G-11056)***
E R Squibb & Sons Inter-AM (HQ)....609 252-4111
3551 Lawrenceville Rd Princeton (08540) ***(G-9034)***
E S Industries Inc....856 753-8400
701 S Route 73 A West Berlin (08091) ***(G-11717)***
E S S, Towaco *Also called Engineered Security Systems* ***(G-10995)***
E W Williams Publications (HQ)....201 592-7007
2125 Center Ave Ste 305 Fort Lee (07024) ***(G-3552)***
E Wortmann Machine Works Inc....201 288-1654
50 Hollister Rd Teterboro (07608) ***(G-10793)***
E Z HI Tech International, Mountainside *Also called E Z Hi-Tech Services Inc* ***(G-6879)***
E Z Hi-Tech Services Inc (PA)....908 317-8203
1140 Route 22 Mountainside (07092) ***(G-6879)***
E-Beam Services Inc....513 933-0031
118 Melrich Rd Cranbury (08512) ***(G-1830)***
E-Lo Sportswear LLC....862 902-5220
1 Cape May St Harrison (07029) ***(G-4179)***
E-TEC Marine Products Inc....732 269-0442
245 Hickory Ln Bayville (08721) ***(G-253)***
E-Vents Registration LLC....201 722-9221
40 Tillman St Westwood (07675) ***(G-11959)***
E5 Usa Inc....973 773-0750
61 Willet St Ste 24 Passaic (07055) ***(G-8136)***
Ea Pilot Supply....201 934-8449
603 Fletcher Lake Ave Bradley Beach (07720) ***(G-627)***
Eagle Communications Inc....973 366-6181
2902 Vantage Ct Denville (07834) ***(G-2038)***
Eagle Drives & Controls, Point Pleasant Boro *Also called Eagle Engineering & Automation* ***(G-8939)***
Eagle Engineering & Automation....732 899-2292
2111 Herbertsville Rd Point Pleasant Boro (08742) ***(G-8939)***
Eagle Fabrication Inc....732 739-5300
63 Ohio Dr Ltl Egg Hbr (08087) ***(G-5644)***
Eagle Gutter Supply, East Rutherford *Also called United Gutter Supply Inc* ***(G-2335)***
Eagle Pharmaceuticals Inc (PA)....201 326-5300
50 Tice Blvd Ste 315 Woodcliff Lake (07677) ***(G-12188)***
Eagle Products Div, Paterson *Also called Gorman Industries Inc* ***(G-8279)***
Eagle Racing Inc....732 367-8487
810 Cross St Ste 4 Lakewood (08701) ***(G-5112)***
Eagle Steel & Iron LLC....908 587-1025
102 Willever Way Stewartsville (08886) ***(G-10595)***
Eagle Systems Inc....732 226-2111
1310 Roller Rd Ocean (07712) ***(G-7723)***
Eagle Work Clothes Inc (PA)....908 964-8888
20 Quail Run Florham Park (07932) ***(G-3499)***
Eagleburgmann Industries LP....856 241-7300
614 Heron Dr Ste 8 Swedesboro (08085) ***(G-10695)***
Eagletree-Pump Aquisiton Corp....201 569-1173
301 Veterans Blvd Rutherford (07070) ***(G-9730)***
Eaglevision Usa LLC....908 322-1892
150 North Ave Fanwood (07023) ***(G-3372)***
Earle The Walter R Corp (PA)....732 308-1113
1800 State Route 34 # 205 Wall Township (07719) ***(G-11478)***
Earle The Walter R Corp....732 657-8551
655 S Hope Chapel Rd Jackson (08527) ***(G-4665)***
Earle Asphalt Company....732 657-8551
655 S Hope Chapel Rd Jackson (08527) ***(G-4666)***
Earle Asphalt Company (PA)....732 308-1113
1800 State Route 34 # 205 Wall Township (07719) ***(G-11479)***
Earle Companies, The, Wall Township *Also called Earle Asphalt Company* ***(G-11479)***
Earth Color New York Inc (HQ)....973 884-1300
249 Pomeroy Rd Parsippany (07054) ***(G-7992)***
Earth Digital, Parsippany *Also called Earthcolor Inc* ***(G-7994)***
Earth Thebault Inc (HQ)....973 884-1300
249 Pomeroy Rd Parsippany (07054) ***(G-7993)***
Earthcolor Inc (HQ)....973 884-1300
249 Pomeroy Rd Parsippany (07054) ***(G-7994)***
Earthwork Associates Inc....609 624-9395
477 Corsons Tavern Rd Ocean View (08230) ***(G-7763)***

East Brunswick Sewerage Auth....732 257-8313
25 Harts Ln East Brunswick (08816) ***(G-2148)***
East Coast Custom, Sayreville *Also called CRA-Z Works Co Inc* ***(G-9819)***
East Coast Distributors Inc....732 223-5995
1 Industrial Way W E Eatontown (07724) ***(G-2391)***
East Coast Electronics Inc....908 431-7555
216 Us Highway 206 20a Hillsborough (08844) ***(G-4328)***
East Coast Media LLC....908 575-9700
14 Park Ave Hillsborough (08844) ***(G-4329)***
East Coast Pallets LLC....732 308-3616
17 Sweetmans Ln Manalapan (07726) ***(G-5842)***
East Coast Panelboard Inc....732 739-6400
101 Tornillo Way Tinton Falls (07712) ***(G-10832)***
East Coast Plastics Inc....856 768-8700
427 Commerce Ln Ste 7 West Berlin (08091) ***(G-11718)***
East Coast Power Systems, Tinton Falls *Also called East Coast Panelboard Inc* ***(G-10832)***
East Coast Rubber Products....856 384-2747
1000 Delsea Dr Ste D2 Westville (08093) ***(G-11938)***
East Coast Security Products....973 625-3277
53 Green Pond Rd Ste 1 Rockaway (07866) ***(G-9562)***
East Coast Storage Eqp Co Inc (PA)....732 451-1316
620 Burtis St Brick (08723) ***(G-742)***
East Trading West Inv LLC....973 678-0800
200 S Jefferson St Orange (07050) ***(G-7819)***
East West Service Co Inc....609 631-9000
2 Marlen Dr Trenton (08691) ***(G-11057)***
Eastern Cold Drawn, North Brunswick *Also called C D E Inc* ***(G-7509)***
Eastern Concrete Materials Inc (HQ)....201 797-7979
250 Pehle Ave Ste 503 Saddle Brook (07663) ***(G-9763)***
Eastern Concrete Materials Inc....973 702-7866
80 Estate Dr 23n Sussex (07461) ***(G-10670)***
Eastern Concrete Materials Inc....973 827-7625
3620 State Rt 23 N Hamburg (07419) ***(G-4091)***
Eastern Concrete Materials Inc....908 537-2135
1 Railroad Ave Glen Gardner (08826) ***(G-3814)***
Eastern Glass Resources Inc (PA)....973 483-8411
770 Supor Blvd Harrison (07029) ***(G-4180)***
Eastern Instrumentation of....856 231-0668
710 E Main St Ste 1a Moorestown (08057) ***(G-6573)***
Eastern Machining Corporation....856 694-3303
1197 Fries Mill Rd Franklinville (08322) ***(G-3630)***
Eastern Molding Co Inc....973 759-0220
597 Main St Belleville (07109) ***(G-301)***
Eastern Podiatry Labs Inc....609 882-4444
1702 5th St Ewing (08638) ***(G-3015)***
Eastern Regional Waterway....732 684-0409
2316 2nd Ave Brick (08723) ***(G-743)***
Eastern Sign Company, Egg Harbor Township *Also called M & W Franklin LLC* ***(G-2689)***
Eastside Express Corporation....908 486-3300
2025 E Linden Ave Linden (07036) ***(G-5370)***
Easy Aerial Corporation....646 639-4410
198 Pear Blossom Dr Edison (08837) ***(G-2506)***
Easy Analytic Software Inc....856 931-5780
101 Haag Ave Bellmawr (08031) ***(G-338)***
Easy Stop Food & Fuel Corp....973 517-0478
19 Exeter Ln Hamburg (07419) ***(G-4092)***
Easy Street Publications Inc....917 699-7820
1473 Ridgeway St Union (07083) ***(G-11177)***
Easy Undies LLC....201 715-4909
23 Springfield Ave Springfield (07081) ***(G-10552)***
Easydook Midatlantic, Ocean View *Also called Seaville Motorsports* ***(G-7766)***
Easyflex East Inc....201 853-9005
101 Industrial Ave Little Ferry (07643) ***(G-5503)***
Easylving Brand, The, Springfield *Also called Easy Undies LLC* ***(G-10552)***
Eatem Corporation....856 692-1663
1829 Gallagher Dr Vineland (08360) ***(G-11355)***
Eatem Foods, Vineland *Also called Eatem Corporation* ***(G-11355)***
Eaton Corporation....732 767-9600
1115 Globe Ave A Mountainside (07092) ***(G-6880)***
Eaton Corporation....609 835-4230
96 Stemmers Ln Mount Holly (08060) ***(G-6768)***
Eaton Filtration LLC....732 767-4200
44 Apple St Ste 3 Tinton Falls (07724) ***(G-10833)***
Eaton Hydraulics LLC....732 212-4700
44 Apple St Tinton Falls (07724) ***(G-10834)***
Eb Machine Corp....973 442-7729
320 Richard Mine Rd Wharton (07885) ***(G-11986)***
Ebaotech Inc USA....917 977-1145
2500 Plaza Five Fl 25 Jersey City (07311) ***(G-4746)***
Ebco Tool, East Hanover *Also called Edward Brown* ***(G-2214)***
Ebelle Debelle Phrm Inc....973 823-0665
5 Witherwood Dr Hamburg (07419) ***(G-4093)***
Ebi LLC....800 526-2579
100 Interpace Pkwy Parsippany (07054) ***(G-7995)***
Ebi LP....973 299-9022
399 Jefferson Rd Parsippany (07054) ***(G-7996)***
Ebi Medical Systems LLC....973 299-3330
100 Interpace Pkwy Ste 1 Parsippany (07054) ***(G-7997)***

ALPHABETIC

Ebic Prparedness Solutions LLC..................719 244-6209
236 Overlook Ave Leonia (07605) *(G-5316)*

Ebin New York Inc.................................201 288-8887
506 Us Highway 46 Teterboro (07608) *(G-10794)*

Ebmachine, Wharton *Also called Eb Machine Corp (G-11986)*

Ebocent, Paramus *Also called European Imports of LA Inc (G-7868)*

Ebsco Industries Inc.............................201 933-1800
201 Highway 17 Ste 300 Rutherford (07070) *(G-9731)*

Ebsco Industries Inc.............................732 542-8600
1151 Broad St Ste 212 Shrewsbury (07702) *(G-9998)*

Ebsco Industries Inc.............................201 569-2500
30 Park Rd Ste 2 Tinton Falls (07724) *(G-10835)*

Ebsco Information Services, Shrewsbury *Also called Ebsco Industries Inc (G-9998)*

Ebsco Publishing Inc.............................201 968-9899
2 University Plz Ste 310 Hackensack (07601) *(G-3908)*

ECB USA Inc..973 575-3226
333 Fairfield Rd Fairfield (07004) *(G-3181)*

Ecca, Bloomfield *Also called Complete Optical Laboratory (G-508)*

Ecce Panis Inc.....................................877 706-0510
447 Gotham Pkwy Carlstadt (07072) *(G-1159)*

Echo Molding Inc..................................908 688-0099
911 Springfield Rd Ste 1 Union (07083) *(G-11178)*

Echo Therapeutics Inc (PA)....................732 201-4189
1809 Hudson Park Edgewater (07020) *(G-2437)*

Eci, Hackensack *Also called Electro-Ceramic Industries (G-3909)*

Eci, Lakewood *Also called Electronic Connections Inc (G-5114)*

Eci Technology Inc................................973 773-8686
60 Gordon Dr Totowa (07512) *(G-10942)*

Eclearview Technologies Inc...................732 695-6999
60 Barberry Dr Ocean (07712) *(G-7724)*

Eclecticism Publishing LLC.....................212 714-4714
33 Stanwyck Ct Robbinsville (08691) *(G-9515)*

Eclipse International, North Brunswick *Also called Mattress Dev Co Del LLC (G-7525)*

Eclipse Manufacturing LLC.....................973 340-9939
438 Lanza Ave Garfield (07026) *(G-3732)*

Eclipse Sleep Products LLC.....................732 628-0002
1375 Jersey Ave Ste 1 New Brunswick (08902) *(G-6957)*

Eco Lighting USA Ltd Lblty Co.................201 621-5661
217 Huyler St South Hackensack (07606) *(G-10262)*

Eco LLC...609 683-9030
344 Nassau St Ste F Princeton (08540) *(G-9035)*

Eco-Plug-System LLC............................855 326-7584
1946 Union Valley Rd Hewitt (07421) *(G-4289)*

Ecocom Inc...201 393-0786
221 W Grand Ave Ste 168 Montvale (07645) *(G-6454)*

Ecolab Inc..856 596-4845
110 Marter Ave Ste 411 Moorestown (08057) *(G-6574)*

Ecom 2000 Inc (PA)..............................718 504-7355
3775 Park Ave Unit 3 Edison (08820) *(G-2507)*

Ecomelectronics, Edison *Also called Ecom 2000 Inc (G-2507)*

Econ Forms, Marlboro *Also called Efco Corp (G-5938)*

Ecp, Cherry Hill *Also called Edwards Creative Products Inc (G-1361)*

Ecs Energy Ltd....................................201 341-5044
16 Meadow Run Ct Jackson (08527) *(G-4667)*

Ecseco, Brick *Also called East Coast Storage Eqp Co Inc (G-742)*

Ecsi International Inc (HQ).......................973 574-8555
790 Bloomfield Ave Ste C1 Clifton (07012) *(G-1610)*

Edax Inc (HQ)......................................201 529-4880
91 Mckee Dr Mahwah (07430) *(G-5769)*

Edda Technology Inc.............................609 919-9889
5 Independence Way # 210 Princeton (08540) *(G-9036)*

Eddie Domani......................................908 469-8863
20 Butler St Elizabethport (07206) *(G-2783)*

Ede Pharmaceutical, Hamburg *Also called Ebelle Debelle Phrm Inc (G-4093)*

Edenbridge Pharmaceuticals LLC..............201 292-1292
169 Lackawanna Ave # 110 Parsippany (07054) *(G-7998)*

Edesia Oil LLC.....................................732 851-7979
225 County Road 522 B Manalapan (07726) *(G-5843)*

Edgar C Barcus Co Inc...........................856 456-0204
416 Gateway Blvd Westville (08093) *(G-11939)*

Edge Orthopedics, Boonton *Also called Icon Orthopedic Concepts LLC (G-571)*

Edge Orthotics Inc................................732 549-3343
209 Pierson Ave Edison (08837) *(G-2508)*

Edge Therapeutics Inc..........................800 208-3343
300 Connell Dr Ste 4000 Berkeley Heights (07922) *(G-410)*

Edge Ventures Inc.................................877 841-1402
24 Front Ct Old Bridge (08857) *(G-7777)*

Edgeco, Ridgefield Park *Also called Cedge Industries Inc (G-9400)*

Edgell Communications, Newark *Also called Ensembleiq Inc (G-7155)*

Edgemont Pharmaceuticals LLC...............908 375-8039
92 Roxiticus Rd Far Hills (07931) *(G-3374)*

Edgewater Manufacturing Co Inc (PA).........201 664-0022
17-10 Willow St Fair Lawn (07410) *(G-3090)*

Edgewell Personal Care LLC...................973 753-3000
240 Cedar Knolls Rd Cedar Knolls (07927) *(G-1310)*

Edgewell Personal Care LLC...................201 785-8000
75 Commerce Dr Allendale (07401) *(G-9)*

Edhard Corp..908 850-8444
279 Blau Rd Hackettstown (07840) *(G-4003)*

Edi/Eci..973 790-9100
15 Jane St Paterson (07522) *(G-8253)*

Edison Design Group Inc (PA).................732 993-3341
95 Cobblestone Blvd Monroe (08831) *(G-6373)*

Edison Finishing..................................732 287-6660
191 Vineyard Rd Ste 3 Edison (08817) *(G-2509)*

Edison Lithog & Prtg Corp (PA)................201 902-9191
3725 Tonnelle Ave North Bergen (07047) *(G-7449)*

Edison Ophthalmology Assoc LLC..............908 822-0070
2177 Oak Tree Rd Ste 203t Edison (08820) *(G-2510)*

Edker Industries Inc.............................856 786-1971
1401 Union Landing Rd Cinnaminson (08077) *(G-1460)*

Edko Electronics..................................973 942-2222
460 Totowa Ave Paterson (07522) *(G-8254)*

Edmondmarks Technologies Inc................732 643-0290
3535 State Route 66 Ste 3 Neptune (07753) *(G-6909)*

Edmund Kiss.......................................973 810-2312
12 Orben Dr Unit 1 Landing (07850) *(G-5223)*

Edmund Optics Inc (PA)........................856 547-3488
101 E Gloucester Pike Barrington (08007) *(G-177)*

Edmund Scientific Co, Barrington *Also called Edmund Optics Inc (G-177)*

EDS, South Hackensack *Also called Essential Dental Systems Inc (G-10265)*

Edsall Group USA Inc.............................908 874-6953
115 Stryker Ln Hillsborough (08844) *(G-4330)*

Edston Manufacturing Company................908 647-0116
125 Clinton Rd Unit 2 Fairfield (07004) *(G-3182)*

Edu-Met Interactive Systems Co................908 851-9394
407 Chestnut St Union (07083) *(G-11179)*

Educational & Lab Systems, Fairfield *Also called Design of Tomorrow Inc (G-3177)*

Educhat Inc..201 871-8649
17 Lane Dr Englewood (07631) *(G-2889)*

Educloud Inc.......................................201 944-0445
206 Grant Ave Cliffside Park (07010) *(G-1538)*

Edward Berger Inc...............................609 571-9676
1510 Farrell Ct Old Bridge (08857) *(G-7778)*

Edward Brown.....................................973 887-5255
8 Great Meadow Ln B East Hanover (07936) *(G-2214)*

Edward Kurth and Son Inc.......................856 227-5252
220 Blckwood Barnsboro Rd Sewell (08080) *(G-9951)*

Edward P Paul & Co Inc (PA)....................908 757-4212
525 South Ave Plainfield (07060) *(G-8859)*

Edward T Brady...................................732 928-0257
12 Waldron Rd Allentown (08501) *(G-29)*

Edward W Hiemer & Co..........................973 772-5081
141 Wabash Ave Clifton (07011) *(G-1611)*

Edwards Brothers Inc...........................856 848-6900
1301 Metropolitan Ave # 300 West Deptford (08066) *(G-11826)*

Edwards Coils Corp...............................973 835-2800
101 Alexander Ave Unit 3 Pompton Plains (07444) *(G-8958)*

Edwards Creative Products Inc.................856 665-3200
910 Beechwood Ave Cherry Hill (08002) *(G-1361)*

Edwards Engineering, Pompton Plains *Also called Chiller Solutions LLC (G-8956)*

Edwin Leonel Ramirez...........................732 648-5587
918 Putnam Ave Plainfield (07060) *(G-8860)*

Edwin R Burger & Son Inc.......................856 468-2300
732 Main St Sewell (08080) *(G-9952)*

Efco Corp...732 308-1010
77 Vanderburg Rd Marlboro (07746) *(G-5938)*

Effexoft Inc..732 221-3642
1553 State Route 27 # 1100 Somerset (08873) *(G-10092)*

Efficient Lighting Inc............................973 846-8568
2 Cranberry Rd Ste 5b Parsippany (07054) *(G-7999)*

Egg Harbor Boats, Egg Harbor City *Also called Eh Yachts LLC (G-2664)*

Egg Harbor Rope Products Inc..................609 965-2435
5105 White Horse Pike Egg Harbor City (08215) *(G-2663)*

Egg Harbor Yacht-Div, Egg Harbor City *Also called Marine Acquisition Inc (G-2667)*

Eh Yachts LLC.....................................609 965-2300
801 Philadelphia Ave Egg Harbor City (08215) *(G-2664)*

Eick-Rbert A Qulty Bookbinding, Madison *Also called Robert A Eick Qlty Bookbinding (G-5733)*

Eigent Technologies Inc.........................732 673-0402
10 Cindy Ln Holmdel (07733) *(G-4515)*

Eight OClock Coffee Company (HQ).............201 571-9214
155 Chestnut Ridge Rd # 2 Montvale (07645) *(G-6455)*

Eisai Inc (HQ)......................................201 692-1100
100 Tice Blvd Woodcliff Lake (07677) *(G-12189)*

Ej Machine & Tool Co, Landing *Also called Edmund Kiss (G-5223)*

Ejz Foods LLC.....................................201 229-0500
21 Empire Blvd South Hackensack (07606) *(G-10263)*

Ekr Therapeutics Incorporated.................877 435-2524
1545 Us Highway 206 # 300 Bedminster (07921) *(G-271)*

Eks Parts Inc.......................................856 227-8811
220 Blckwood Barnsboro Rd Sewell (08080) *(G-9953)*

Ektelon, Viking Athletics, Bordentown *Also called Prince Sports Inc (G-609)*

El Batal Corporation..............................908 964-3427
1060 Commerce Ave Union (07083) *(G-11180)*

El Estelcil, Union City *Also called U S A Distributors Inc (G-11269)*

(G-0000) Company's Geographic Section entry number

El Jay Poultry Corp (PA) 856 435-0900
1010 Hddonfield Berlin Rd Voorhees (08043) *(G-11429)*
Elaine Inc 973 345-6200
1 Hazel St Woodland Park (07424) *(G-12217)*
Elaine K Josephson Inc 609 259-2256
7f Jules Ln New Brunswick (08901) *(G-6958)*
Elan Food Laboratories Inc 973 344-8014
268 Doremus Ave Newark (07105) *(G-7149)*
Elan Inc (PA) 973 344-8014
268 Doremus Ave Newark (07105) *(G-7150)*
Elan Vanilla, Newark *Also called Elan Food Laboratories Inc (G-7149)*
Elana Tile Contractors Inc 973 386-0991
8 Merry Ln Ste B East Hanover (07936) *(G-2215)*
Elastograf Inc 973 209-3161
19 Ames Blvd Hamburg (07419) *(G-4094)*
Elaut Usa Inc (PA) 732 364-9900
1000 Towbin Ave Lakewood (08701) *(G-5113)*
Elbee Litho Inc 732 698-7738
292 Dunhams Corner Rd East Brunswick (08816) *(G-2149)*
Elco Glass Industries Co Inc 732 363-6550
16 Tree Line Dr Freehold (07728) *(G-3652)*
Elder & Jenks Co Div, Bayonne *Also called Muralo Company Inc (G-238)*
Eldon Glass & Mirror Co Inc 973 589-2099
58 Stockton St 76 Newark (07105) *(G-7151)*
Electedface LLC 609 924-3636
26 Snowden Ln Princeton (08540) *(G-9037)*
Election Graphics Inc 201 758-9966
15 Rockland Ter Verona (07044) *(G-11305)*
Electric Catalytic Pdts Group, Union *Also called Evoqua Water Technologies LLC (G-11183)*
Electric Mobility Corporation (PA) 856 468-1000
591 Mantua Blvd Sewell (08080) *(G-9954)*
Electric Mobility Corporation 856 468-1000
599 Mantua Blvd Sewell (08080) *(G-9955)*
Electrical Motor Repr Co of NJ 609 392-6149
809 E State St Trenton (08609) *(G-11058)*
Electro Impulse Laboratory Inc 732 776-5800
1805 State Route 33 Neptune (07753) *(G-6910)*
Electro Lift Inc 973 471-0204
204 Sargeant Ave Clifton (07013) *(G-1612)*
Electro Magnetic Products Inc 856 235-3011
355 Crider Ave Moorestown (08057) *(G-6575)*
Electro Mechanical Tech, Hillside *Also called McIntosh Industries Inc (G-4430)*
Electro Parts Inc 856 767-5923
465 E Taunton Ave Ste 201 West Berlin (08091) *(G-11719)*
Electro Plated Wire, Hawthorne *Also called Fisk Alloy Wire Incorporated (G-4235)*
Electro-Ceramic Industries 201 342-2630
75 Kennedy St Hackensack (07601) *(G-3909)*
Electro-Miniatures Corp (PA) 201 460-0510
68 W Commercial Ave Moonachie (07074) *(G-6516)*
Electro-Steam Generator Corp 609 288-9071
50 Indel Ave Rancocas (08073) *(G-9257)*
Electrochemical Society Inc 609 737-1902
65 S Main St Pennington (08534) *(G-8450)*
Electrocore Inc 973 290-0097
150 Allen Rd Ste 201 Basking Ridge (07920) *(G-186)*
Electroheat Induction Inc 908 494-0726
81 Oakland Ave 3 Jersey City (07306) *(G-4747)*
Electroid Co Div, Springfield *Also called Valcor Engineering Corporation (G-10584)*
Electromagnetic Tech Inds Inc 973 394-1719
50 Intervale Rd Ste 11 Boonton (07005) *(G-564)*
Electronic Assemblies, Inc Esi, Sicklerville *Also called Esi (G-10018)*
Electronic Brazing Co Div, Boonton *Also called Janke & Company Inc (G-573)*
Electronic Concepts Inc (HQ) 732 542-7880
526 Industrial Way W Eatontown (07724) *(G-2392)*
Electronic Connections Inc (PA) 732 367-5588
195 Lehigh Ave Ste 3 Lakewood (08701) *(G-5114)*
Electronic Control SEC Inc (PA) 973 574-8555
790 Bloomfield Ave Ste C1 Clifton (07012) *(G-1613)*
Electronic Manufacturing Co, Maplewood *Also called R G Dunn Acquisitions Co Inc (G-5925)*
Electronic Marine Systems Inc (PA) 732 680-4120
800 Ferndale Pl Rahway (07065) *(G-9185)*
Electronic Measuring Devices 973 691-4755
15 Mill Rd Flanders (07836) *(G-3406)*
Electronic Mfg Svcs Inc 973 916-1001
48 Industrial St W Clifton (07012) *(G-1614)*
Electronic Parts Specialty Co 609 267-0055
10 Eagle Ave Ste 1100 Mount Holly (08060) *(G-6769)*
Electronic Power Designs Inc 973 838-7055
132 Union Ave Bloomingdale (07403) *(G-542)*
Electronic Specialty Products, Newfoundland *Also called ESP Associates Inc (G-7374)*
Electronic Systems, Clifton *Also called Harris Corporation (G-1634)*
Electronic Technology Inc 973 371-5160
511 Lyons Ave Irvington (07111) *(G-4583)*
Electronic Transformer Corp 973 942-2222
460 Totowa Ave Paterson (07522) *(G-8255)*
Electronics Boutique Amer Inc 856 435-3900
1468 Blckwood Clmenton Rd Clementon (08021) *(G-1531)*
Electronix Express, Rahway *Also called RSR Electronics Inc (G-9222)*
Electrophysics, Fairfield *Also called Sofradir Ec Inc (G-3307)*
Electrum Inc 732 396-1616
827 Martin St Rahway (07065) *(G-9186)*
Electrum Recovery Works, Rahway *Also called Electrum Inc (G-9186)*
Elegant Desserts Inc 201 933-7309
275 Warren St Lyndhurst (07071) *(G-5679)*
Elegant Headwear Co Inc (PA) 908 558-1200
1000 Jefferson Ave Elizabeth (07201) *(G-2728)*
Elegant USA LLC 973 812-8820
100 Bomont Pl Totowa (07512) *(G-10943)*
Eleison Pharmaceuticals Inc 215 416-7620
311 Farnsworth Ave Ste 1 Bordentown (08505) *(G-595)*
Elektromek Inc 973 614-9000
60 Webro Rd Clifton (07012) *(G-1615)*
Elemental Container Inc 908 687-7720
860 Springfield Rd Union (07083) *(G-11181)*
Elemental Interiors 646 861-3596
204 Bellevue Ave Montclair (07043) *(G-6412)*
Elementis Chromium Inc (PA) 609 443-2000
469 Old Trenton Rd East Windsor (08512) *(G-2372)*
Elementis Global LLC (HQ) 609 443-2000
469 Old Trenton Rd East Windsor (08512) *(G-2373)*
Elementis Specialities, East Windsor *Also called Elementis Global LLC (G-2373)*
Elementis Specialties Inc (HQ) 609 443-2000
469 Old Trenton Rd East Windsor (08512) *(G-2374)*
Elementis Specialties Inc 201 432-0800
469 Old Trenton Rd East Windsor (08512) *(G-2375)*
Elements Accessories Inc 646 801-5187
16 Essex Rd Maplewood (07040) *(G-5919)*
Elements Global Group LLC 908 468-8407
527 Meyersville Rd Gillette (07933) *(G-3794)*
Elements Truffles LLC 908 731-2088
2 2nd St Apt 1002 Jersey City (07302) *(G-4748)*
Elena Consultants & Elec 908 654-8309
1175 Globe Ave Mountainside (07092) *(G-6881)*
Elevate Hr Inc 973 917-3230
1055 Parsippany Blvd # 511 Parsippany (07054) *(G-8000)*
Elevator Cabs of NY Inc 973 790-9100
15 Jane St Paterson (07522) *(G-8256)*
Elevator Doors Inc 973 790-9100
15 Jane St Paterson (07522) *(G-8257)*
Elevator Doors-Elevator Cabs, Paterson *Also called Elevator Cabs of NY Inc (G-8256)*
Elevator Enterances NY Inc 973 790-9100
15 Jane St Paterson (07522) *(G-8258)*
Elevator Entrance Inc 973 790-9100
15 Jane St Paterson (07522) *(G-8259)*
Elevator Technology Corp 973 523-7760
337 Market St Paterson (07501) *(G-8260)*
Elgee Manufacturing Company 908 647-4100
225 Stirling Rd Warren (07059) *(G-11545)*
Elgee Power Vac Sweeper, Warren *Also called Elgee Manufacturing Company (G-11545)*
Eli Lilly and Company 908 704-1807
1181 Us Highway 202 N Branchburg (08876) *(G-656)*
Elie Tahari Ltd (PA) 973 671-6300
16 Bleeker St Millburn (07041) *(G-6249)*
Elis Hot Bagels Inc 732 566-4523
1055c Hwy 34 Matawan (07747) *(G-6020)*
Elite Cabinetry Corp 973 583-0194
97 Main St Newark (07105) *(G-7152)*
Elite Emrgncy Lights Ltd Lblty 732 534-2377
1000 Bennett Blvd Ste 6 Lakewood (08701) *(G-5115)*
Elite Graphix LLC 732 274-2356
45 Stouts Ln Ste 2 Monmouth Junction (08852) *(G-6343)*
Elite Laboratories Inc 201 750-2646
165 Ludlow Ave Northvale (07647) *(G-7578)*
Elite Landscaping & Pavers 732 252-6152
3102 Kapalua Ct Freehold (07728) *(G-3653)*
Elite Packaging Corp 732 651-9955
40 Cotters Ln Ste E East Brunswick (08816) *(G-2150)*
Elite Pharmaceuticals Inc (PA) 201 750-2646
165 Ludlow Ave Northvale (07647) *(G-7579)*
Elite Printing Service 973 729-0366
30 Heritage Dr Sparta (07871) *(G-10498)*
Elite Stone Importers LLC 732 542-7900
45 Park Rd Tinton Falls (07724) *(G-10836)*
Elite Surf Snow Skateboard Sp 856 427-7873
259 Marlton Pike E Cherry Hill (08034) *(G-1362)*
Elixens America Inc 732 388-3555
1443 Pinewood St Bldg 4u Rahway (07065) *(G-9187)*
Elkay Products Co Inc 973 376-7550
35 Brown Ave Springfield (07081) *(G-10553)*
Elkem Inc 732 566-1700
443 County Rd Cliffwood (07721) *(G-1546)*
Elkem Silicones USA Corp (HQ) 732 227-2060
2 Tower Center Blvd # 1601 East Brunswick (08816) *(G-2151)*
Elkom North America Inc 732 786-0490
680 Madison Ave Manalapan (07726) *(G-5844)*
Ellenby Technologies Inc 856 848-2020
412 Grandview Ave Woodbury Heights (08097) *(G-12175)*
Ellis Controls, Eatontown *Also called Ellis/Kuhnke Controls Inc (G-2393)*

ALPHABETIC

Ellis Instruments Inc 973 593-9222
21 Cook Ave Madison (07940) *(G-5722)*

Ellis/Kuhnke Controls Inc 732 291-3334
132 Lewis St Ste A2 Eatontown (07724) *(G-2393)*

Elmco Two Inc 856 365-2244
1045 Cambridge Ave Camden (08105) *(G-1061)*

Elmer Times Co Inc 856 358-6171
21 State St Elmer (08318) *(G-2791)*

Elmi Machine Tool Corp 973 882-1277
15 Spielman Rd 2 Fairfield (07004) *(G-3183)*

Elmwood Press Inc 201 794-6273
85 Main Ave Elmwood Park (07407) *(G-2818)*

Elnik Systems LLC 973 239-6066
107 Commerce Rd Cedar Grove (07009) *(G-1281)*

Eloa - New Jersey, Warren *Also called Essilor Laboratories Amer Inc (G-11547)*

Elray Manufacturing Company 856 881-1935
17 Liberty St Glassboro (08028) *(G-3804)*

Elusys Therapeutics Inc 973 808-0222
25 Riverside Dr Ste 1 Pine Brook (07058) *(G-8701)*

Elvi Pharma LLC 732 640-2707
60 Ethel Rd W Ste 1 Piscataway (08854) *(G-8762)*

Elymat Corp 201 767-7105
180 Old Tappan Rd Ste 11 Old Tappan (07675) *(G-7798)*

Elymat Industries Inc 201 767-7105
180 Old Tappan Rd Ste 3 Old Tappan (07675) *(G-7799)*

Em Orthodontic Labs Inc 201 652-4411
6 Lafayette Pl Waldwick (07463) *(G-11446)*

Em Signs 973 300-9703
80 Merriam Ave Newton (07860) *(G-7386)*

Emabond Solutions LLC 201 767-7400
49 Walnut St Ste 2 Norwood (07648) *(G-7621)*

Embroideries Unlimited Inc 201 692-1560
532 Wyndham Rd Teaneck (07666) *(G-10752)*

Embroidery Concepts 973 942-8555
41 Paterson Ave 43 Paterson (07522) *(G-8261)*

Embroidery In Stitches Inc 732 460-2660
1020 Campus Dr Morganville (07751) *(G-6641)*

EMC Aviation, Cookstown *Also called Export Management Consultants (G-1807)*

EMC Corporation 732 922-6353
8 The Fellsway Ocean (07712) *(G-7725)*

EMC Corporation 732 549-8500
1 Tower Center Blvd Fl 23 East Brunswick (08816) *(G-2152)*

EMC Paving LLC 908 636-1054
57 Justice St Piscataway (08854) *(G-8763)*

EMC Squared LLC 973 586-8854
30 Rolling Ridge Dr Rockaway (07866) *(G-9563)*

EMC Technologists, Wall Township *Also called I 2 R Corp (G-11490)*

EMC Toy, Ocean *Also called EMC Corporation (G-7725)*

Emc3, Marlton *Also called Doolan Industries Incorporated (G-5973)*

EMD Performance Materials Corp 908 429-3500
70 Meister Ave Branchburg (08876) *(G-657)*

Emdeon Corporation 201 703-3400
669 River Dr Ste 240 Elmwood Park (07407) *(G-2819)*

Emdur Art Products, Camden *Also called Emdur Metal Products Inc (G-1062)*

Emdur Metal Products Inc 856 541-1100
1115 Mount Vernon St Camden (08103) *(G-1062)*

Eme Electrical Contractors 973 228-6608
35 Roseland Ave Caldwell (07006) *(G-1027)*

Emerald Electronics Usa Inc 718 872-5544
90 Dayton Ave 50 Passaic (07055) *(G-8137)*

Emerging Technologies, Bridgeton *Also called Mks Inc (G-791)*

Emerson Automation Solutions 856 542-5252
4 Killdeer Ct Ste 200 Bridgeport (08014) *(G-763)*

Emerson Process Management 908 605-4551
20 Independence Blvd Warren (07059) *(G-11546)*

Emerson Radio Corp (PA) 973 428-2000
35 Waterview Blvd Parsippany (07054) *(G-8001)*

Emerson Speed Printing Inc 201 265-7977
379 Kinderkamack Rd Oradell (07649) *(G-7808)*

Emil A Schroth Inc 732 938-5015
Copper Av Yellow Brook Rd Howell (07731) *(G-4553)*

Emil Dipalma Inc 973 477-2766
182 Stephens State Pk Rd Hackettstown (07840) *(G-4004)*

Emisphere Technologies Inc 973 532-8000
4 Becker Farm Rd Ste 103 Roseland (07068) *(G-9649)*

Emmco Development Corp 732 469-6464
243 Belmont Dr Somerset (08873) *(G-10093)*

Empanada King, Clifton *Also called Nijama Corporation (G-1684)*

Empire Architectural Millwork, Newark *Also called Empire Lumber & Millwork Co (G-7153)*

Empire Blended Distributors, Bayville *Also called Empire Blended Products Inc (G-254)*

Empire Blended Products Inc 732 269-4949
250 Hickory Ln Bayville (08721) *(G-254)*

Empire Electronics Inc 973 278-8282
70 Spruce St Ste 2 Paterson (07501) *(G-8262)*

Empire Industries Inc 973 279-2050
40 Warren St Paterson (07524) *(G-8263)*

Empire Lumber & Millwork Co 973 242-2700
377 Frelinghuysen Ave Newark (07114) *(G-7153)*

Empire Scale & Balance 856 299-1651
35 S Broad St Ste D Penns Grove (08069) *(G-8465)*

Empire Specialty Foods Inc 646 773-2630
6 Brookdale Rd East Brunswick (08816) *(G-2153)*

Empire Telecommunications Inc 201 569-3339
15 S Van Brunt St Englewood (07631) *(G-2890)*

Empirical Group LLC 201 571-0300
155 Chestnut Ridge Rd Montvale (07645) *(G-6456)*

Empirical Labs Inc 973 541-9446
41 N Beverwyck Rd Lake Hiawatha (07034) *(G-5054)*

Employment Horizons Inc 973 538-8822
10 Ridgedale Ave Cedar Knolls (07927) *(G-1311)*

Emporia Foundry Inc 973 483-5480
800 Bergen St Harrison (07029) *(G-4181)*

Emporium Leather Company Inc 201 330-7720
501 Penhorn Ave Ste 9 Secaucus (07094) *(G-9878)*

Empro Products Co Inc 973 302-4351
47 Montgomery St Belleville (07109) *(G-302)*

Empty Walls Inc 609 452-8488
3495 Us Highway 1 Ste 21 Princeton (08540) *(G-9038)*

EMR (usa Holdings) Inc (HQ) 856 365-7500
143 Harding Ave Ste 1 Bellmawr (08031) *(G-339)*

Ems Aviation Inc 856 234-5020
121 Whittendale Dr Ste A Moorestown (08057) *(G-6576)*

Emse Corp 973 227-9221
10 Plog Rd Fairfield (07004) *(G-3184)*

Emseco, Fairfield *Also called Emse Corp (G-3184)*

En Tech Corp 201 784-1034
91 Ruckman Rd Ste 1 Closter (07624) *(G-1757)*

En Tech Corp (PA) 718 389-2058
91 Ruckman Rd Closter (07624) *(G-1758)*

Ena Meat Packing Inc (PA) 973 742-4790
240 E 5th St Paterson (07524) *(G-8264)*

Enailsupply Corporation 909 725-1698
2161 Whitesville Rd Ste C Toms River (08755) *(G-10874)*

Enamel Art Studio 732 321-0774
120 Liberty St Metuchen (08840) *(G-6103)*

Enchantmints, Mahwah *Also called Lemniscate Inc (G-5788)*

Encore Enterprises Inc (PA) 201 489-5044
57 Leuning St South Hackensack (07606) *(G-10264)*

Encore International LLC 973 423-3880
270 Lafayette Ave Hawthorne (07506) *(G-4231)*

Encore Led Ltg Ltd Lblty Co 866 694-4533
155 Us Highway 46 Wayne (07470) *(G-11627)*

Encore Pharmaceutical Inc 973 267-9331
49 Moraine Rd Morris Plains (07950) *(G-6661)*

Encore Poly 201 845-4510
240 W Passaic St Ste 7 Maywood (07607) *(G-6050)*

Encur Inc 732 264-2098
200 Division St Keyport (07735) *(G-5016)*

Endo Phrmaceuticals Valera Inc 609 235-3230
8 Clarke Dr Cranbury (08512) *(G-1831)*

Endomedix 848 248-1883
211 Warren St Ste 1 Newark (07103) *(G-7154)*

Endot Industries Inc (PA) 973 625-8500
60 Green Pond Rd Rockaway (07866) *(G-9564)*

Endotec Inc (PA) 973 762-6100
20 Valley St Ste 210 South Orange (07079) *(G-10304)*

Endurance Net Inc 609 499-3450
763 B Railroad Ave Florence (08518) *(G-3478)*

Ener-G Rudox Inc 201 438-0111
180 E Union Ave East Rutherford (07073) *(G-2294)*

Energy Battery 908 751-5918
1200 County Road 523 Flemington (08822) *(G-3438)*

Energy Battery Group Inc 404 255-7529
1200 County Road 523 Flemington (08822) *(G-3439)*

Energy Beams Inc 973 291-6555
185 Hamburg Tpke Bloomingdale (07403) *(G-543)*

Energy Chem America Inc 201 816-2307
920 Sylvan Ave Englewood Cliffs (07632) *(G-2958)*

Energy Combustion Systems, Westville *Also called Energy Company Inc (G-11940)*

Energy Company Inc 856 742-1916
50 Cutler Ave Ste 6 Westville (08093) *(G-11940)*

Energy Options Inc. 732 512-9100
3 Ethel Rd Ste 300 Edison (08817) *(G-2511)*

Energy Recycling Co LLC 732 545-6619
233 Cleveland Ave Highland Park (08904) *(G-4303)*

Energy Storage Corp (PA) 732 542-7880
526 Industrial Way W Eatontown (07724) *(G-2394)*

Energy Tracking LLC 973 448-8660
16 Southwind Dr Flanders (07836) *(G-3407)*

Enersys 800 719-7887
80 Veronica Ave Ste 1 Somerset (08873) *(G-10094)*

Enertia LLC 856 330-4767
10471049 Thomas Busch Pennsauken (08110) *(G-8508)*

Enforsys Inc (PA) 973 515-8126
27 Bleeker St 222 Millburn (07041) *(G-6250)*

Enforsys Systems, Millburn *Also called Enforsys Inc (G-6250)*

ENG SCIENTIFIC, Clifton *Also called A J P Scientific Inc (G-1552)*

Engelhard, Iselin *Also called BASF Catalysts LLC (G-4616)*

Engelhard Corporation 732 205-5000
101 Wood Ave S Iselin (08830) *(G-4625)*

Engility LLC 703 633-8300
15 Roszel Rd Princeton Junction (08550) *(G-9152)*

Engine Combo LLC 201 290-4399
300 Nye Ave Irvington (07111) *(G-4584)*

Engine Efficiency Associates, Rahway Also called Electronic Marine Systems Inc *(G-9185)*

Engine Factory Inc 908 236-9915
24 Cokesbury Rd Ste 15 Lebanon (08833) *(G-5284)*

Engineered Components Inc 908 788-8393
546 Old York Rd Three Bridges (08887) *(G-10822)*

Engineered Mtl Arresting Sys, Logan Township Also called Enginred Arrsting Systems Corp *(G-5613)*

Engineered Plastic Pdts Inc (PA) 908 647-3500
269 Mercer St Stirling (07980) *(G-10599)*

Engineered Precision Cast Co 732 671-2424
952 Palmer Ave Middletown (07748) *(G-6214)*

Engineered Security Systems (PA) 973 257-0555
1 Indian Ln E Towaco (07082) *(G-10995)*

Engineered Silicone Pdts LLC 973 300-5120
75 Mill St Ste 2 Newton (07860) *(G-7387)*

Engineering Dynamics LLC 973 794-4500
429 Rockaway Valley Rd # 1300 Boonton (07005) *(G-565)*

Engineering Laboratories Inc 201 337-8116
360 W Oakland Ave Oakland (07436) *(G-7687)*

Enginred Arrsting Systems Corp 856 241-8620
2239 High Hill Rd Logan Township (08085) *(G-5613)*

Englert Inc (PA) 800 364-5378
1200 Amboy Ave Perth Amboy (08861) *(G-8612)*

Englewood Lab LLC (PA) 201 567-2267
88 W Sheffield Ave Englewood (07631) *(G-2891)*

Engo Co 908 754-6600
128 Case Dr South Plainfield (07080) *(G-10355)*

Engraved Images Ltd 908 234-0323
Demunn Pl Rr 202 Far Hills (07931) *(G-3375)*

Enjou Chocolat Morristown Inc 973 993-9090
8 Dehart St Ste 1 Morristown (07960) *(G-6707)*

Enor Corporation 201 750-1680
246 S Dean St Englewood (07631) *(G-2892)*

Enpro Inc 908 236-2137
1401 Us Highway 22 Lebanon (08833) *(G-5285)*

Enroute Computer Solutions Inc 609 569-9255
2511 Fire Rd Ste A4 Egg Harbor Township (08234) *(G-2684)*

Ensembleiq Inc 973 252-0100
1 Gateway Ctr Fl 1 # 1 Newark (07102) *(G-7155)*

Enser Corporation (PA) 856 829-5522
1902 Taylors Ln Ste B Cinnaminson (08077) *(G-1461)*

Ensign Overseas (usa) Ltd 201 662-7150
8800 Boulevard East 4a North Bergen (07047) *(G-7450)*

Ensign Vidal USA, North Bergen Also called Ensign Overseas (usa) Ltd *(G-7450)*

Ensinger Grenloch Inc (HQ) 856 227-0500
1 Main St Grenloch (08032) *(G-3866)*

Ensinger Hyde, Grenloch Also called Ensinger Grenloch Inc *(G-3866)*

Enspharma, Morris Plains Also called Encore Pharmaceutical Inc *(G-6661)*

Ensync Intrctive Solutions Inc 732 542-4001
83 South St Ste 202 Freehold (07728) *(G-3654)*

Enteris Biopharma Inc 973 453-3518
83 Fulton St Boonton (07005) *(G-566)*

Enterix Inc 732 429-1899
236 Fernwood Ave Edison (08837) *(G-2512)*

Enterprise Container LLC (PA) 201 797-7200
575 N Midland Ave Saddle Brook (07663) *(G-9764)*

Enterprise Press Inc 212 741-2111
1 W Forest Ave Ste 2d Englewood (07631) *(G-2893)*

Enterprise Services LLC 609 259-9400
989 Lenox Dr Princeton (08544) *(G-9039)*

Enterprise Solution Products 201 678-9200
28 Av At Pt Imperial 23 West New York (07093) *(G-11865)*

Enterprisecc Ltd Liability Co 201 266-0020
521 Palisade Ave Jersey City (07307) *(G-4749)*

Entourage Imaging Inc 888 926-6571
39 Everett Dr Ste 1-2 Princeton Junction (08550) *(G-9153)*

Entourage Yearbooks, Princeton Junction Also called Entourage Imaging Inc *(G-9153)*

Envelopes & Printed Pdts Inc 973 942-1232
135 Fairview Ave Prospect Park (07508) *(G-9169)*

Envigo Crs Inc (HQ) 732 873-2550
100 Mettlers Rd Somerset (08873) *(G-10095)*

Envirnmntal Dsign Grphic Entps 973 361-1829
215 State Route 10 Dover (07869) *(G-2086)*

Envirnmntal Dynamics Group Inc (PA) 609 924-4489
5 Crscent Ave Rocky Hill (08553) *(G-9637)*

Envirnmntal Mgt Chem Wste Svcs (PA) 201 848-7676
45 Whitney Rd Bldg B Mahwah (07430) *(G-5770)*

Enviro Pak Inc 732 248-1600
125 National Rd Edison (08817) *(G-2513)*

Enviro Safe Wtr Trtmnt Systems, Elmer Also called Favs Corp *(G-2792)*

Enviro-Clear Company Inc 908 638-5507
152 Cregar Rd High Bridge (08829) *(G-4295)*

Envirochem Inc 732 238-6700
425 Whitehead Ave South River (08882) *(G-10461)*

Environmental Coatings & Cnstr 973 509-9456
36 Eagle Rock Way Montclair (07042) *(G-6413)*

Environmental Technical Drlg, Farmingdale Also called Environmental Technical Drlg *(G-3385)*

Environmental Technical Drlg 732 938-3222
408 Cranberry Rd Farmingdale (07727) *(G-3385)*

Environmolds LLC 908 273-5401
18 Bank St Ste 1 Summit (07901) *(G-10641)*

Envirosight LLC (PA) 973 970-9284
111 Canfield Ave Ste B-3 Randolph (07869) *(G-9275)*

Enzon Pharmaceuticals Inc (PA) 732 980-4500
20 Commerce Dr Ste 135 Cranford (07016) *(G-1905)*

Enzon Pharmaceuticals Inc 732 980-4500
300 Corporate Ct Ste C South Plainfield (07080) *(G-10356)*

Eom Worldwide Sales Corp 732 994-7352
39 Harmony Dr Lakewood (08701) *(G-5116)*

Eon Labs Inc 609 627-8600
506 Carnegie Ctr Ste 400 Princeton (08540) *(G-9040)*

Eos Energy Storage LLC 732 225-8400
214 Fernwood Ave Bldg B Edison (08837) *(G-2514)*

EP Henry Corporation (PA) 856 845-6200
201 Park Ave Woodbury (08096) *(G-12160)*

Ep Systems Inc 570 424-0581
470 Schooleys Mountain Rd Hackettstown (07840) *(G-4005)*

Epco, Middletown Also called Engineered Precision Cast Co *(G-6214)*

Epcos Inc (HQ) 732 906-4300
485b Us Highway 1 S # 200 Iselin (08830) *(G-4626)*

Epcos Inc 732 603-5941
120 Munt Holly Byp Unit 2 Lumberton (08048) *(G-5657)*

Epcos Inc A Tdk Group Company, Iselin Also called Epcos Inc *(G-4626)*

Epd, Bloomingdale Also called Electronic Power Designs Inc *(G-542)*

Epi, Caldwell Also called Essex Products International *(G-1028)*

Epi Group Ltd Liability Co 917 710-6607
410 Monmouth Ave Lakewood (08701) *(G-5117)*

Epic Holding Inc 732 249-6867
15 Footes Ln Morristown (07960) *(G-6708)*

Epic Industries, Morristown Also called Epic Holding Inc *(G-6708)*

Epic Millwork LLC 732 296-0273
1022 Hamilton St Ste J Somerset (08873) *(G-10096)*

Epicore Networks USA Inc 609 267-9118
4 Lina Ln Mount Holly (08060) *(G-6770)*

Epiq Systems Inc 973 622-6111
50 Park Pl Ste 701 Newark (07102) *(G-7156)*

Epoch Everlasting Play LLC 973 316-2500
75d Lackawanna Ave Parsippany (07054) *(G-8002)*

Epoch Press Inc 973 357-0080
7 Highpoint Dr Wayne (07470) *(G-11628)*

Epoch Times 908 548-8026
50 Cragwood Rd Ste 305 South Plainfield (07080) *(G-10357)*

Epolin Chemical LLC (HQ) 973 465-9495
358-364 Adams St Newark (07105) *(G-7157)*

Epolin Inc, Newark Also called Epolin Chemical LLC *(G-7157)*

Eppley Building & Design Inc 973 636-9499
220 Goffle Rd Ste B Hawthorne (07506) *(G-4232)*

Epsilon Plastics Inc (HQ) 201 933-6000
Page & Schuyler Ave 8 Lyndhurst (07071) *(G-5680)*

Equipment Distributing Corp (PA) 201 641-8414
3 Eucker St Ridgefield Park (07660) *(G-9405)*

Equipment Erectors Inc 732 846-1212
15 Veronica Ave Somerset (08873) *(G-10097)*

Equistar Chemicals, Newark Also called Lyondell Chemical Company *(G-7232)*

Erco Ceilings Somers Point Inc 609 517-2531
5 Chestnut St Somers Point (08244) *(G-10046)*

Erco Lighting Inc (PA) 732 225-8856
160 Rrtan Ctr Pkwy Ste 10 Edison (08837) *(G-2515)*

Erial Concrete Inc 856 784-8884
965 Hickstown Rd Erial (08081) *(G-3000)*

Erj Baking LLC 201 906-1300
235 N Pleasant Ave Ridgewood (07450) *(G-9424)*

Ernest R Miles Construction Co 856 697-2311
1445 Catawba Ave Newfield (08344) *(G-7365)*

Ernest Schaefer Inc 908 964-1280
731 Lehigh Ave Union (07083) *(G-11182)*

Eroomsystem Technologies Inc (PA) 732 730-0116
150 Airport Rd Ste 1200 Lakewood (08701) *(G-5118)*

Ervin Advertising Co Inc (PA) 732 363-7645
4880 Us Hwy Rte 9 S Howell (07731) *(G-4554)*

Es Industrial 732 842-5600
10 Mechanic St Ste 200 Red Bank (07701) *(G-9329)*

Esaw Industries Inc 732 613-1400
5 Litchfield Rd East Brunswick (08816) *(G-2154)*

Escada US Subco LLC 201 865-5200
55 Hartz Way Ste 17 Secaucus (07094) *(G-9879)*

Escadaus Inc 973 335-8888
2 Wood Glen Way Boonton (07005) *(G-567)*

Esco Industrial Corporation 973 478-5888
30 Stonewall Ct Woodcliff Lake (07677) *(G-12190)*

A
L
P
H
A
B
E
T
I
C

Esco Industries Corp 973 478-5888
30 Stonewall Ct Woodcliff Lake (07677) *(G-12191)*

Esco Optics, Oak Ridge *Also called Esco Products Inc (G-7662)*

Esco Precision Inc 908 722-0800
71 Old Camplain Rd Hillsborough (08844) *(G-4331)*

Esco Products Inc 973 697-3700
95 Chamberlain Rd Oak Ridge (07438) *(G-7662)*

Esg LLC 973 347-2969
21 Tall Oaks Ln Budd Lake (07828) *(G-928)*

Esi 856 629-2492
1541 New Broklyn Erial Rd Sicklerville (08081) *(G-10018)*

Esjay Pharma LLC 609 469-5920
70 Lake Dr East Windsor (08520) *(G-2357)*

Esjay Pharma LLC (PA) 732 438-1816
27 Ridgeview Way Allentown (08501) *(G-30)*

ESP, Newton *Also called Engineered Silicone Pdts LLC (G-7387)*

ESP Associates Inc 973 208-9045
2713 State Rt 23 Ste 8a Newfoundland (07435) *(G-7374)*

Espertech Inc 973 577-6406
26 Hamilton Ave Wayne (07470) *(G-11629)*

Esquire Business Forms 609 883-1155
1668 N Olden Avenue Ext Ewing (08638) *(G-3016)*

Esquire Graphics & Bus Forms, Ewing *Also called Esquire Business Forms (G-3016)*

Ess, South Hackensack *Also called On Site Communication (G-10285)*

Ess Group Inc 609 755-3139
129 Eayrestown Rd Southampton (08088) *(G-10471)*

Essential Dental Systems Inc 201 487-9090
89 Leuning St Ste 8 South Hackensack (07606) *(G-10265)*

Essential Machining, Brick *Also called Charles F Kilian (G-736)*

Essentra Packaging US Inc 856 439-1700
1224 N Church St Moorestown (08057) *(G-6577)*

Essex Coatings LLC 732 855-9400
135 Essex Ave E Avenel (07001) *(G-130)*

Essex Computers, Paramus *Also called Essexusa LLC (G-7867)*

Essex Morris Sign Co 973 386-1755
30 Troy Rd Ste 2 Whippany (07981) *(G-12019)*

Essex Products International 973 226-2424
494 Mountain Ave Caldwell (07006) *(G-1028)*

Essex Rise Conveyor Corp 973 575-7483
4 Fairfield Cres West Caldwell (07006) *(G-11775)*

Essex West Graphics Inc (PA) 973 227-2400
305 Fairfield Ave Fairfield (07004) *(G-3185)*

Essexusa LLC 201 576-0001
185 N State Rt 17 Paramus (07652) *(G-7867)*

Essilor Laboratories Amer Inc 732 563-9884
5 Powderhorn Dr Warren (07059) *(G-11547)*

Essroc Corp 856 650-9046
2500 S Broadway Camden (08104) *(G-1063)*

Estrin Calabrese Sales Agency 908 722-9980
17 S Main St Ste 3 Manville (08835) *(G-5895)*

ET Browne Drug Co Inc (PA) 201 894-9020
440 Sylvan Ave Englewood Cliffs (07632) *(G-2959)*

Et Manufacturing & Sales Inc 973 777-6662
90 Dayton Ave Ste C5 Passaic (07055) *(G-8138)*

Ethan Allen Retail Inc 973 473-1019
1 Market St Ste 1 # 1 Passaic (07055) *(G-8139)*

Ethel M Chocolates, Mount Arlington *Also called Mars Retail Group Inc (G-6757)*

Ethicon Endo - Surgery, Bridgewater *Also called Ethicon Inc (G-835)*

Ethicon Endo-Surgery, Bedminster *Also called Ethicon Inc (G-273)*

Ethicon Inc (HQ) 732 524-0400
Us Route 22 Somerville (08876) *(G-10207)*

Ethicon Inc 908 306-0327
135 Us Highway 202 206 # 4 Bedminster (07921) *(G-272)*

Ethicon Inc 908 218-0707
135 Us Highway 202 206 # 4 Bedminster (07921) *(G-273)*

Ethicon Inc 908 253-6464
520 Us Highway 22 Ste 1 Bridgewater (08807) *(G-835)*

Ethicon LLC (HQ) 908 218-3195
Rr 22 Box W Somerville (08876) *(G-10208)*

Ethylene Atlantic Corp 856 467-0010
136 Church St Swedesboro (08085) *(G-10696)*

Eti, Irvington *Also called Electronic Technology Inc (G-4583)*

Ets Claude Blandin, Fairfield *Also called ECB USA Inc (G-3181)*

Eugene Kozak 973 442-1001
193 Franklin Rd Randolph (07869) *(G-9276)*

Euro American Foods Group, Bayonne *Also called European Amrcn Foods Group Inc (G-224)*

Euro Kraft Group LLC 856 451-7450
71 Bridgeton Ave Bridgeton (08302) *(G-784)*

Euro Mechanical Inc 201 313-8050
16 Industrial Ave Fairview (07022) *(G-3361)*

Eurodia Industrie SA 732 805-4001
20 Worlds Fair Dr Ste F Somerset (08873) *(G-10098)*

Euroimmun US Inc 973 656-1000
1 Bloomfield Ave 1 # 1 Mountain Lakes (07046) *(G-6858)*

European Amrcn Foods Group Inc (PA) 201 436-6106
698 Kennedy Blvd Bayonne (07002) *(G-224)*

European Amrcn Foods Group Inc 201 583-1101
425 Route 3 Secaucus (07094) *(G-9880)*

European Coffee Classics Inc 856 428-7202
1401 Berlin Rd Ste A Cherry Hill (08034) *(G-1363)*

European Country Kitchens Inc 908 735-6659
272 Pittstown Rd Pittstown (08867) *(G-8850)*

European Imports of LA Inc 973 536-1823
25 Columbine Rd Paramus (07652) *(G-7868)*

European Pretzel One LLC 201 867-6117
1619 54th St North Bergen (07047) *(G-7451)*

European Stone Art LLC 201 441-9116
208 Huyler St South Hackensack (07606) *(G-10266)*

Europrojects Intl Inc (PA) 917 262-0795
500 Nordhoff Pl Ste 5 Englewood (07631) *(G-2894)*

Eva Maria Wolfe 412 777-2000
6 Westbelt Wayne (07470) *(G-11630)*

Evans Chemetics LP (PA) 201 992-3100
Glenpointe Center West 4 Teaneck (07666) *(G-10753)*

Evans Machine & Tool Co 732 442-1144
410 Summit Ave Perth Amboy (08861) *(G-8613)*

Evapco-Blct Dry Cooling Inc 908 379-2665
981 Us Highway 22 Ste 103 Bridgewater (08807) *(G-836)*

Eve of Milady, Union City *Also called Milady Bridals Inc (G-11257)*

Evening Journal Association (HQ) 201 653-1000
1 Harmon Plz Ste 1000 Secaucus (07094) *(G-9881)*

Evening News, The, Salem *Also called Medianews Group Inc (G-9807)*

Evenus Pharmaceutical Labs Inc 609 395-8625
506 Carnegie Ctr Ste 100 Princeton (08540) *(G-9041)*

Everbind Marco, Lodi *Also called Marco Book Co Inc (G-5594)*

Evereast Trading Inc 201 944-6484
2125 Center Ave Ste 215 Fort Lee (07024) *(G-3553)*

Everflow Supplies Inc (PA) 908 436-1100
100 Middlesex Ave Carteret (07008) *(G-1256)*

Evergard Steel Corp 908 925-6800
3313 Revere Rd South Plainfield (07080) *(G-10358)*

Evergreen Dental 856 845-3299
549 S Evergreen Ave Woodbury Heights (08097) *(G-12176)*

Evergreen Information Svcs Inc 973 339-9672
275 Paterson Ave Ste 101 Little Falls (07424) *(G-5475)*

Evergreen Printing Company, Bellmawr *Also called Green Horse Media LLC (G-341)*

Everite Machine Products Co (PA) 856 330-6700
1555 Route 73 Pennsauken (08110) *(G-8509)*

Everlast Associates Inc 609 261-1888
203 Route 530 Southampton (08088) *(G-10472)*

Everlast Sheds, Southampton *Also called Everlast Associates Inc (G-10472)*

Everlasting Valve Company Inc 908 769-0700
108 Somogyi Ct South Plainfield (07080) *(G-10359)*

Evertile Flooring Co Inc 973 242-7474
127 Frelinghuysen Ave Newark (07114) *(G-7158)*

Evertlast Interiors 732 252-9965
52 Main St Ste 6 Manalapan (07726) *(G-5845)*

Everythingbenefits, New Providence *Also called Ontimeworks LLC (G-7051)*

Evex Analytical Instruments 609 252-9192
857 State Rd Princeton (08540) *(G-9042)*

Evex Instruments, Princeton *Also called Evex Analytical Instruments (G-9042)*

Evh LLC 973 257-0076
6 Mars Ct Unit F5 Boonton (07005) *(G-568)*

Evigto Inc 201 951-2187
327 Undercliff Ave Edgewater (07020) *(G-2438)*

Eviva LLC (PA) 973 925-4028
30 Wood St Paterson (07524) *(G-8265)*

Evo9x, Edison *Also called H & A Global Enterprises Inc (G-2530)*

Evolve Furniture Group, Marlton *Also called Global Industries Inc (G-5977)*

Evonik Corporation 732 981-5000
2 Turner Pl Piscataway (08854) *(G-8764)*

Evonik Corporation (HQ) 973 929-8000
299 Jefferson Rd Parsippany (07054) *(G-8003)*

Evonik Corporation 503 907-1210
2 Turner Pl Piscataway (08854) *(G-8765)*

Evonik Cyro LLC (HQ) 973 929-8000
299 Jefferson Rd Parsippany (07054) *(G-8004)*

Evonik Foams Inc (HQ) 973 929-8000
299 Jefferson Rd Parsippany (07054) *(G-8005)*

Evoqua Water Technologies LLC 908 851-4250
2 Milltown Ct Union (07083) *(G-11183)*

Evoqua Water Technologies LLC 908 353-7400
624 Evans St Elizabeth (07201) *(G-2729)*

Evs, Fairfield *Also called EVs Broadcast Equipment Inc (G-3187)*

EVs Broadcast Equipment Inc (HQ) 973 575-7811
9 Law Dr Ste 4 Fairfield (07004) *(G-3186)*

EVs Broadcast Equipment Inc 973 575-7811
700 Route 46 E Ste 300 Fairfield (07004) *(G-3187)*

Evs Interactive Inc 718 784-3690
100 Riverdale Rd Riverdale (07457) *(G-9480)*

Ewc Controls Inc 732 446-3110
385 State Route 33 Manalapan (07726) *(G-5846)*

Ewing Recovery Corp 609 883-0318
1565 6th St Ewing (08638) *(G-3017)*

Ex-Press Printing, Linden *Also called Noble Metals Corp (G-5420)*

2018 Harris New Jersey
Manufacturers Directory

(G-0000) Company's Geographic Section entry number

Exactal Tool & Die, South Plainfield *Also called Exactal Tool Ltd Inc* ***(G-10360)***
Exactal Tool Ltd Inc....908 561-1177
3586 Kennedy Rd Ste 3 South Plainfield (07080) ***(G-10360)***
Exalent Packaging Inc....973 742-9600
55 1st Ave Paterson (07514) ***(G-8266)***
Exalenz Bioscience Inc....732 232-4393
1712 M St Wall Township (07719) ***(G-11480)***
Excalibur Bagel Bky Equip Inc....201 797-2788
4-1 Banta Pl Fair Lawn (07410) ***(G-3091)***
Excalibur Miretti Group LLC....973 808-8399
285 Eldridge Rd Fairfield (07004) ***(G-3188)***
Excavating, Newton *Also called Terco Construction LLC* ***(G-7409)***
Excel Blades, Paterson *Also called Excel Hobby Blades Corp* ***(G-8267)***
Excel Color Graphics Inc....856 848-3345
207 W Jersey Ave Woodbury Heights (08097) ***(G-12177)***
Excel Die Sharpening Corp....908 587-2606
19 Grant St Linden (07036) ***(G-5371)***
Excel Display Corp....732 246-3724
100 Jersey Ave Ste A6 New Brunswick (08901) ***(G-6959)***
Excel Hobby Blades Corp....973 278-4000
481 Getty Ave Paterson (07503) ***(G-8267)***
Excel Industrial Co Inc....609 275-1748
17 Huntington Dr Princeton Junction (08550) ***(G-9154)***
Excelhigh Inc....212 947-8543
910 Oak Tree Ave Ste H South Plainfield (07080) ***(G-10361)***
Excell Brands Ltd Liability Co....908 561-1130
3 Independence Way # 114 Princeton (08540) ***(G-9043)***
Excellence In Baking Inc....732 287-1313
2062 State Route 27 Edison (08817) ***(G-2516)***
Excellent Bakery Equipment Co....973 244-1664
19 Spielman Rd Fairfield (07004) ***(G-3189)***
Excellent Prtg & Graphics LLC....973 773-6661
333 Hazel St Clifton (07011) ***(G-1616)***
Excellentia Flavours LLC (PA)....732 749-9840
30 Stewart Pl Fairfield (07004) ***(G-3190)***
Excellentia International, Fairfield *Also called Excellentia Flavours LLC* ***(G-3190)***
Excelsior Medical LLC (HQ)....732 776-7525
1933 Heck Ave Neptune (07753) ***(G-6911)***
Excerpta Medica Inc (HQ)....908 547-2100
685 Us Highway 202/206 Bridgewater (08807) ***(G-837)***
Excite View LLC....201 227-7075
4 Thatcher Rd Ste 2001 Tenafly (07670) ***(G-10784)***
Exclusive Materials LLC....732 886-9956
1385 Pasadena St Lakewood (08701) ***(G-5119)***
Executive Clothiers, Shrewsbury *Also called Michael Duru Clothiers LLC* ***(G-10005)***
Exelis Geospatial Systems, Clifton *Also called Harris Corporation* ***(G-1637)***
Exelis Inc/Northrop....973 284-4212
77 River Rd Clifton (07014) ***(G-1617)***
Exeltis Usa Inc (HQ)....973 324-0200
180 Park Ave Ste 101 Florham Park (07932) ***(G-3500)***
Exeltis USA Dermatology LLC....973 805-4060
180 Park Ave Ste 101 Florham Park (07932) ***(G-3501)***
Exemplify Biopharma Inc....732 500-3208
3000 Eastpark Blvd Cranbury (08512) ***(G-1832)***
Exhibit Co Inc....732 465-1070
239 Old New Brunswick Rd Piscataway (08854) ***(G-8766)***
Exhibit Network Inc....732 751-9600
434 Brookside Ave Oakhurst (07755) ***(G-7668)***
Exit Zero Cookhouse Inc....609 770-8479
109 Sunset Blvd Ste B Cape May (08204) ***(G-1098)***
Exma Industries, Lakewood *Also called Exclusive Materials LLC* ***(G-5119)***
Exodon LLC....973 398-2900
111 Howard Blvd Ste 204 Mount Arlington (07856) ***(G-6754)***
Exothermic Molding Inc....908 272-2299
50 Lafayette Pl Kenilworth (07033) ***(G-4953)***
Expert Appliance Center LLC....732 946-0999
460 County Road 520 Marlboro (07746) ***(G-5939)***
Expert Process Systems LLC....570 424-0581
470 Schooleys Mountain Rd A Hackettstown (07840) ***(G-4006)***
Export Management Consultants....609 758-1166
54 Wrghtstown Cokstown Rd Cookstown (08511) ***(G-1807)***
Express Press, Galloway *Also called Allegro Printing Corporation* ***(G-3708)***
Express Printing Inc....908 925-6300
209 W Saint Georges Ave Linden (07036) ***(G-5372)***
Express Printing Services Inc....973 585-7355
26 Commerce Rd Ste L Fairfield (07004) ***(G-3191)***
Exquisities, Clifton *Also called International Delights LLC* ***(G-1648)***
Extra Office Inc....732 381-9774
580 Leesville Ave Rahway (07065) ***(G-9188)***
Extracts and Ingredients, Union *Also called Morre-TEC Industries Inc* ***(G-11208)***
Extreme Digital Graphics Inc....973 227-5599
7 Kingsbridge Rd Ste 1 Fairfield (07004) ***(G-3192)***
Extreme Pallet Inc....973 286-1717
315 Astor St Newark (07114) ***(G-7159)***
Extremity Medical LLC....973 588-8980
300 Interpace Pkwy # 410 Parsippany (07054) ***(G-8006)***
Extruders International Inc....908 241-7750
181 W Clay Ave Roselle Park (07204) ***(G-9695)***
Exxon Mobil Corporation....732 321-6100
1900 E Linden Ave Ste A Linden (07036) ***(G-5373)***
Eyelet Embroideries Inc....201 945-2151
65 Railroad Ave Ste 3 Ridgefield (07657) ***(G-9359)***
Eyetech Inc....646 454-1779
700 Us Highway 202/206 Bridgewater (08807) ***(G-838)***
EZ General Construction Corp....201 223-1101
155 Webster Dr Wayne (07470) ***(G-11631)***
Ez-Dumpster LLC....908 752-2787
829 Madison Ave Bridgewater (08807) ***(G-839)***
Ezcom Software Inc....201 731-1800
25 Rockwood Pl Ste 420 Englewood (07631) ***(G-2895)***
Ezose Sciences Inc....862 926-1950
300 Campus Dr Ste 300 Florham Park (07932) ***(G-3502)***
Ezrirx LLC (PA)....718 502-6610
1525 Prospect St Ste 203 Lakewood (08701) ***(G-5120)***
F & A Signs Inc....732 442-9399
49 W Pond Rd Hopelawn (08861) ***(G-4540)***
F & C Prof Alum Railings Corp....908 753-8886
1149 W Front St Plainfield (07063) ***(G-8861)***
F & D, Millville *Also called Friedrich and Dimmock Inc* ***(G-6302)***
F & G Tool & Die Inc....908 241-5880
195 Sumner Ave Kenilworth (07033) ***(G-4954)***
F & M Expressions Unlimited, Mahwah *Also called Flanagan Holdings Inc* ***(G-5772)***
F & M Machine Co Inc....908 245-8830
751 Lexington Ave Kenilworth (07033) ***(G-4955)***
F & R Grinding Inc....908 996-0440
138 County Road 513 Frenchtown (08825) ***(G-3700)***
F & R Machine Corp....973 684-8139
41 Bleeker St Paterson (07524) ***(G-8268)***
F & R Pallets Inc....856 964-8516
201 Erie St Camden (08102) ***(G-1064)***
F & S Awning and Blind Co Inc....732 738-4110
13 Coral St Edison (08837) ***(G-2517)***
F and L Machinery....973 218-6216
48 Commerce St Springfield (07081) ***(G-10554)***
F and M Equipment Ltd....215 822-0145
2820 Hamilton Blvd South Plainfield (07080) ***(G-10362)***
F G Clover Company Inc....973 627-1160
40 Stickle Ave Rockaway (07866) ***(G-9565)***
F I Companies, Old Bridge *Also called Forman Industries Inc* ***(G-7779)***
F L Feldman Associates....732 776-8544
811 Memorial Dr Asbury Park (07712) ***(G-77)***
F M B Systems, Harrison *Also called FMB Systems Inc* ***(G-4184)***
F M C Research and Dev Div, Ewing *Also called FMC Corporation* ***(G-3018)***
F M T, Hillsborough *Also called Fischl Machine & Tool* ***(G-4332)***
F M W Piping Contractors, Carteret *Also called Folgore Mobil Welding Inc* ***(G-1258)***
F P Developments Inc....856 875-7100
402 S Main St Williamstown (08094) ***(G-12086)***
F P Schmidt Manufacturing Co....201 343-4241
143 Leuning St South Hackensack (07606) ***(G-10267)***
F S Brainard & Co....609 387-4300
5 Terri Ln Ste 15 Burlington (08016) ***(G-971)***
F S R Inc....973 785-4347
244 Bergen Blvd Woodland Park (07424) ***(G-12218)***
F S T Printing Inc....732 560-3749
1324 Bound Brook Rd Middlesex (08846) ***(G-6165)***
F T Millwork Inc....732 741-1216
9 Catherine St Red Bank (07701) ***(G-9330)***
F W Bennett & Son Inc....973 383-4050
403 Sparta Rd Lafayette (07848) ***(G-5046)***
F Walther Electric Corp....732 537-9201
12 Worlds Fair Dr Ste F Somerset (08873) ***(G-10099)***
F&S Awning & Sign, Edison *Also called F & S Awning and Blind Co Inc* ***(G-2517)***
F&S Produce Company Inc....856 453-0316
913 Bridgeton Ave Rosenhayn (08352) ***(G-9707)***
Faber Precision Inc....973 983-1844
198 Green Pond Rd Ste 6 Rockaway (07866) ***(G-9566)***
Fabian Couture Group Intl Inc....800 367-6251
205 Chubb Ave Bldg C Lyndhurst (07071) ***(G-5681)***
Fabian Formals Inc....201 460-7776
205 Chubb Ave Ste 2 Lyndhurst (07071) ***(G-5682)***
Fablok Mills Inc....908 464-1950
140 Spring St New Providence (07974) ***(G-7034)***
Fabric Bee, South Hackensack *Also called Pioneer Embroidery Co* ***(G-10289)***
Fabric Chemical Corporation....201 432-0440
61 Cornelison Ave Jersey City (07304) ***(G-4750)***
Fabricated Software Inc....973 857-0524
25 Canfield Rd Cedar Grove (07009) ***(G-1282)***
Fabricolor Holding Intl LLC....973 742-5800
24 1/2 Van Houten St Paterson (07505) ***(G-8269)***
Fabrictex LLC....732 225-3990
278 Raritan Center Pkwy Edison (08837) ***(G-2518)***
Fabulous Fabricators LLC....973 779-2400
11 Jackson Rd Totowa (07512) ***(G-10944)***
Fabuwood Cabinetry Corp....201 432-6555
99 Caven Point Rd Jersey City (07305) ***(G-4751)***
Factonomy Inc....201 848-7812
459 Oldwoods Rd Wyckoff (07481) ***(G-12252)***

ALPHABETIC

Factory Fit, Bellmawr *Also called M Parker Autoworks Inc* *(G-345)*

FAEEC, Basking Ridge *Also called Foundation For Embryonic* *(G-187)*

Fairfield Gourmet Food Corp (PA) 973 575-4365
11 Cliffside Dr Cedar Grove (07009) *(G-1283)*

Fairfield Laundry McHy Corp 973 575-4330
5 Montesano Rd Ste 1 Fairfield (07004) *(G-3193)*

Fairfield Metal Ltd Lblty Co 973 276-8440
9 Audrey Pl Fairfield (07004) *(G-3194)*

Fairfield Stamping, Saddle Brook *Also called Mjse LLC* *(G-9776)*

Fairfield Textiles Corp (PA) 973 227-1656
34 Waite St Paterson (07524) *(G-8270)*

Fairway Building Products LLC 609 890-6600
2075 E State Street Ext Trenton (08619) *(G-11059)*

Falcon Graphics Inc 908 232-1991
70 Westfield Ave Clark (07066) *(G-1500)*

Falcon Industries Inc 732 563-9889
371 Campus Dr Somerset (08873) *(G-10100)*

Falcon Papers & Plastics, Avenel *Also called G R Impex Ltd Liability Co* *(G-133)*

Falcon Printing, Clark *Also called Falcon Graphics Inc* *(G-1500)*

Falcon Printing & Graphics 732 462-6862
339 W Main St Freehold (07728) *(G-3655)*

Falcon Safety Products Inc (HQ) 908 707-4900
25 Imclone Dr Branchburg (08876) *(G-658)*

Falstrom Company 973 777-0013
1 Falstrom Ct Passaic (07055) *(G-8140)*

Famcam Inc 973 503-1600
3 Eastmans Rd Parsippany (07054) *(G-8007)*

Family House of Lamps, Riverton *Also called Nicholas Longo Sr* *(G-9508)*

Family Screen Printing Inc 856 933-2780
124 Harding Ave Ste 124 Bellmawr (08031) *(G-340)*

Fan of Word 201 341-5474
249 Waverly Pl South Orange (07079) *(G-10305)*

Fancort Industries Inc 973 575-0610
31 Fairfield Pl West Caldwell (07006) *(G-11776)*

Fancyheat Corporation 973 589-1450
40 Veronica Ave Somerset (08873) *(G-10101)*

Fantasia Industries Corp 201 261-7070
20 Park Pl Paramus (07652) *(G-7869)*

Fanwood Crushed Stone Company 908 322-7840
1 New Providence Rd Watchung (07069) *(G-11591)*

Faps Inc (PA) 973 589-5656
371 Craneway St Newark (07114) *(G-7160)*

Farbest Brands, Park Ridge *Also called Farbest-Tallman Foods Corp* *(G-7919)*

Farbest-Tallman Foods Corp (PA) 714 897-7199
1 Maynard Dr Ste 3101 Park Ridge (07656) *(G-7919)*

Fargo Controls Inc 732 389-3376
20 Hampton Rd Eatontown (07724) *(G-2395)*

Farmplast LLC 973 287-6070
125 E Halsey Rd Parsippany (07054) *(G-8008)*

Farrell Eqp & Contrls Inc 732 770-4142
263 Cox St Roselle (07203) *(G-9669)*

Fashion Central LLC 732 887-7683
556 Warren Ave Lakewood (08701) *(G-5121)*

Fashion Institute of Ncc, Newark *Also called New Community Corp* *(G-7249)*

Fashion Windows Etc, Paterson *Also called Metro Mills Inc* *(G-8337)*

Fast Copy Printing Center 732 739-4646
81 Broad St Keyport (07735) *(G-5017)*

Fast Doors LLC 856 966-3278
1661 Davis St Camden (08103) *(G-1065)*

Fast T'S, Keyport *Also called Fast Copy Printing Center* *(G-5017)*

Fast-Pak Trading Inc 201 293-4757
375 County Ave Ste 2 Secaucus (07094) *(G-9882)*

Fastenation Inc 973 591-1277
120 Brighton Rd Ste 2 Clifton (07012) *(G-1618)*

Fastpulse Technology Inc 973 478-5757
220 Midland Ave Saddle Brook (07663) *(G-9765)*

Fastsigns, Lawrenceville *Also called Tlg Signs Inc* *(G-5270)*

Fastsigns, Newark *Also called Robden Enterprises Inc* *(G-7290)*

Fastsigns, Upper Saddle River *Also called Bergen Digital Graphics LLC* *(G-11274)*

Fastsigns, Marlton *Also called Mc Does Inc* *(G-5986)*

Fastsigns, Secaucus *Also called Sign Up Inc* *(G-9928)*

Fastsigns, Raritan *Also called Bbk Technologies Inc* *(G-9307)*

Fastsigns 973 887-6700
50 State Route 10 Ste 2 East Hanover (07936) *(G-2216)*

Faubel Pharma Services 908 730-7563
3 3rd St Ste 102 Bordentown (08505) *(G-596)*

Faulding Holdings Inc 908 527-9100
200 Elmora Ave Elizabeth (07202) *(G-2730)*

Faulkner Information Svcs LLC 856 662-2070
143 Old Marlton Pike Medford (08055) *(G-6069)*

Faust Rudolph Inc 609 298-7334
542 South Ave E Cranford (07016) *(G-1906)*

Faust Thermographic Supply 908 474-0555
325 Cantor Ave Linden (07036) *(G-5374)*

Favs Corp 856 358-1515
331 Husted Station Rd Elmer (08318) *(G-2792)*

Fazzio Machine & Steel Inc 609 653-1098
3278 Glassboro Crs Kys Rd Glassboro (08028) *(G-3805)*

FBM Baking Machines Inc 609 860-0577
1 Corporate Dr Ste D Cranbury (08512) *(G-1833)*

Fbm Galaxy Inc 856 966-1105
2201 Mount Ephraim Ave Camden (08104) *(G-1066)*

Fbn New Jersey Mfg Inc 973 402-1443
8 Morris Ave Mountain Lakes (07046) *(G-6859)*

FEC, Franklin Lakes *Also called Fleet Equipment Corporation* *(G-3617)*

Fecken-Kirfel America Inc 201 891-5530
6 Leighton Pl Ste 1 Mahwah (07430) *(G-5771)*

Federal Bronze Cast Inds Inc (PA) 973 589-7575
9 Backus St Newark (07105) *(G-7161)*

Federal Casters Corp (PA) 973 483-6700
785 Harrison Ave Harrison (07029) *(G-4182)*

Federal Equipment & Mfg Co Inc 973 340-7600
194 Westervelt Pl Lodi (07644) *(G-5584)*

Federal Lorco Petroleum LLC 908 352-0542
450 S Front St Elizabeth (07202) *(G-2731)*

Federal Metals & Alloys Co 908 756-0900
4216 S Clinton Ave South Plainfield (07080) *(G-10363)*

Federal Petroleum, Elizabeth *Also called Federal Lorco Petroleum LLC* *(G-2731)*

Federal Plastics Corporation 908 272-5800
570 South Ave E Bldg F1 Cranford (07016) *(G-1907)*

Federal Pretzel Baking Co (PA) 215 467-0505
300 Eagle Ct Bridgeport (08014) *(G-764)*

Federal Reclamation Center, South Plainfield *Also called Federal Metals & Alloys Co* *(G-10363)*

Fedex Corporation 201 525-5070
1071 Main St River Edge (07661) *(G-9465)*

Fedex Offic 5720, River Edge *Also called Fedex Corporation* *(G-9465)*

Fedex Office & Print Svcs Inc 856 427-0099
1160 Route 70 E Cherry Hill (08034) *(G-1364)*

Fedex Office & Print Svcs Inc 732 636-3580
1 Quality Way Iselin (08830) *(G-4627)*

Fedex Office & Print Svcs Inc 732 249-9222
212 Rte 18 New Brunswick (08901) *(G-6960)*

Fedex Office & Print Svcs Inc 856 273-5959
1211 Route 73 Ste E Mount Laurel (08054) *(G-6797)*

Fedex Office & Print Svcs Inc 201 672-0508
120 Route 17 East Rutherford (07073) *(G-2295)*

Fedex Office & Print Svcs Inc 973 376-3966
55 Route 22 Springfield (07081) *(G-10555)*

Fedex Office Commercial Press, Roselle *Also called Howard Press Inc* *(G-9673)*

Fedplast Inc 732 901-1153
1174 Buckwald Ct Lakewood (08701) *(G-5122)*

Feed Your Soul Ltd Lblty Co 201 204-0720
78 John Miller Way # 100 Kearny (07032) *(G-4873)*

Fehlberg Mfg Inc 973 399-1905
10 Renee Pl 16 Irvington (07111) *(G-4585)*

Fehu Jewel LLC 609 297-5491
2912 Quail Ridge Dr Plainsboro (08536) *(G-8881)*

Fei-Elcom Tech Inc 201 767-8030
260 Union St Northvale (07647) *(G-7580)*

Felco Products LLC 973 890-7979
18 Furler St Paterson (07512) *(G-8271)*

Fellowship In Prayer Inc 609 924-6863
291 Witherspoon St Princeton (08542) *(G-9044)*

Femco, Lodi *Also called Federal Equipment & Mfg Co Inc* *(G-5584)*

Femenella & Associates Inc 908 722-6526
10 County Line Rd Ste 24 Branchburg (08876) *(G-659)*

Femto Calibrations, Somerset *Also called Venkateshwara Inc* *(G-10195)*

Fence America New Jersey Inc 973 472-5121
210 S Newman St Ste 1 Hackensack (07601) *(G-3910)*

Fencemax 609 646-2265
1624 Harding Hwy Newfield (08344) *(G-7366)*

FER Plating Inc 201 438-1010
52 Park Ave Lyndhurst (07071) *(G-5683)*

Ferber Plastics, Passaic *Also called Et Manufacturing & Sales Inc* *(G-8138)*

Ferguson Containers Co Inc 908 454-9755
16 Industrial Rd Phillipsburg (08865) *(G-8647)*

Ferland Industries Inc 732 246-3200
14 Evergreen Ln Colts Neck (07722) *(G-1784)*

Fermag Technologies Inc 732 985-7300
146 Village Rd Toms River (08755) *(G-10875)*

Fermatex Vascular Tech LLC 732 681-7070
1746 Rte 34 Wall Township (07727) *(G-11481)*

Fernandes Custom Cabinets 732 446-2829
233 Pease Rd Manalapan (07726) *(G-5847)*

Ferolito Vultaggio & Sons 908 282-4480
535 Dowd Ave Elizabeth (07201) *(G-2732)*

Ferrante Press Inc 609 239-4257
516 Bloomfield Ave Verona (07044) *(G-11306)*

Ferrara Bakery & Cafe Inc 732 826-8700
915 Amboy Ave Perth Amboy (08861) *(G-8614)*

Ferratex Services Inc 973 609-5449
354 Eisenhower Pkwy Livingston (07039) *(G-5529)*

Ferrero U S A Inc (HQ) 732 764-9300
7 Sylvan Way Fl 4 Parsippany (07054) *(G-8009)*

Ferrett Printing Inc 856 686-4896
468 Warwick Rd Woodbury (08096) *(G-12161)*

Ferring Pharmaceuticals Inc (HQ) 973 796-1600
100 Interpace Pkwy Parsippany (07054) *(G-8010)*

Ferring Production Inc 973 796-1600
100 Interpace Pkwy Parsippany (07054) *(G-8011)*

Ferro Corporation 856 467-3000
170 Route 130 S Bridgeport (08014) *(G-765)*

Ferro Corporation 732 287-4925
54 Kellogg Ct Edison (08817) *(G-2519)*

Ferro Corporation 908 226-2148
2501 S Clinton Ave South Plainfield (07080) *(G-10364)*

Ferro Industries Incorporated 732 246-3200
14 Evergreen Ln Colts Neck (07722) *(G-1785)*

Ferrum Industries Inc 201 935-1220
735 Commercial Ave Carlstadt (07072) *(G-1160)*

Ferry Machine Corp 201 641-9191
75 Industrial Ave Little Ferry (07643) *(G-5504)*

Fette Compacting America Inc 973 586-8722
400 Forge Way Rockaway (07866) *(G-9567)*

Fette-America, Rockaway *Also called Lmt Usa Inc (G-9585)*

Ff1 Professional Safety Svcs, Sparta *Also called Firefighter One Ltd Lblty Co (G-10499)*

Fgh Systems Inc 973 625-8114
10 Prospect Pl Denville (07834) *(G-2039)*

Fh Group International Inc 201 210-2426
265 Secaucus Rd Secaucus (07094) *(G-9883)*

Fiabila USA Inc 973 659-9510
114 Iron Mountain Rd Mine Hill (07803) *(G-6326)*

Fiber-Span Inc 908 253-9080
670 Commons Way Toms River (08755) *(G-10876)*

Fibercontrol, Matawan *Also called D R Tielmann Inc (G-6016)*

Fiberguide Industries Inc (HQ) 908 647-6601
1 Bay St Ste 1 # 1 Stirling (07980) *(G-10600)*

Fibertech Group Inc (HQ) 856 697-1600
450 N East Blvd Landisville (08326) *(G-5231)*

Fibrenetics Inc 732 636-5670
2 Cutters Dock Rd Woodbridge (07095) *(G-12148)*

Fidelio Limited Partnership 201 307-1626
188 Broadway Ste 1 Woodcliff Lake (07677) *(G-12192)*

Fidelity Chemical Products Div, South Plainfield *Also called Omg Electronic Chemicals Inc (G-10418)*

Fidelity Industries Inc (PA) 973 696-9120
559 Rte 23 Wayne (07470) *(G-11632)*

Fidelity Industries Inc 973 777-2592
750 Bloomfield Ave Ste 1 Clifton (07012) *(G-1619)*

Fidelity Wallcoverings, Wayne *Also called Fidelity Industries Inc (G-11632)*

Fields Samuel H Dental Labs, Hackensack *Also called Samuel H Fields Dental Labs (G-3971)*

Fieldsboro Plant, Bordentown *Also called Stepan Company (G-611)*

Fifty/Fifty Group Inc 201 343-1243
343 S River St Hackensack (07601) *(G-3911)*

Filipe Custom Woodwork 908 486-0033
1600 E Edgar Rd Linden (07036) *(G-5375)*

Fillimerica Inc 800 435-7257
170 Chngbrdge Rd Bldg A42 Montville (07045) *(G-6488)*

Fillo Factory Inc 201 439-1036
10 Fairway Ct Northvale (07647) *(G-7581)*

Filter Process & Supply, Monmouth Junction *Also called Filter Technologies Inc (G-6344)*

Filter Technologies Inc 732 329-2500
45 Stouts Ln Ste 3 Monmouth Junction (08852) *(G-6344)*

Filtration Solutions Inc. 908 684-4000
432 Sand Shore Rd Ste 8 Hackettstown (07840) *(G-4007)*

Filtrex Inc. 973 595-0400
450 Hamburg Tpke Ste 2 Wayne (07470) *(G-11633)*

Fims Manufacturing Corporation 201 845-7088
8 Allerman Rd Oakland (07436) *(G-7688)*

Fin-Tek Corporation (PA) 973 628-2988
6 Leo Pl Wayne (07470) *(G-11634)*

Fin-Tek Ozone, Wayne *Also called Fin-Tek Corporation (G-11634)*

Financial Advisor Magazine, Shrewsbury *Also called Charter Fincl Pubg Netwrk Inc (G-9993)*

Financial Information Inc 908 222-5300
1 Cragwood Rd Ste 2 South Plainfield (07080) *(G-10365)*

Fine Linen Inc 908 469-3634
107 Trumbull St Elizabeth (07206) *(G-2733)*

Fine Manufacturing Inc 201 880-9136
80 Wesley St South Hackensack (07606) *(G-10268)*

Fine Minerals Intl Inc 732 318-6760
11 Progress St Edison (08820) *(G-2520)*

Fine Organics Corporation (PA) 973 478-7690
420 Kuller Rd Ste 2 Clifton (07011) *(G-1620)*

Fine Wear U S A 201 313-3777
22 E Columbia Ave Fort Lee (07024) *(G-3554)*

Finex Trade 609 921-2747
315 Riverside Dr Princeton (08540) *(G-9045)*

Finlandia Cheese Inc (HQ) 973 316-6699
2001 Us Highway 46 # 303 Parsippany (07054) *(G-8012)*

Finn & Emma LLC 973 227-7770
1275 Bloomfield Ave Ste 5 Fairfield (07004) *(G-3195)*

Finn Emma, Fairfield *Also called Finn & Emma LLC (G-3195)*

Fioplex 856 689-7213
49 Fredrick Blvd Swedesboro (08085) *(G-10697)*

Fiore Skylights Inc 856 346-0118
700 Grace St Somerdale (08083) *(G-10040)*

Firefighter One Ltd Lblty Co 973 940-3061
34 Wilson Dr Sparta (07871) *(G-10499)*

Firefreeze Worldwide Inc 973 627-0722
272 Us Highway 46 Rockaway (07866) *(G-9568)*

Fireplace Place Summit, The, Summit *Also called Associate Fireplace Builders (G-10636)*

Firma Foods USA Corporation 201 794-1181
25 Rockwood Pl Ste 220 Englewood (07631) *(G-2896)*

Firmenich, Newark *Also called Chem-Fleur Inc (G-7121)*

Firmenich 609 580-4498
21 Distribution Way Monmouth Junction (08852) *(G-6345)*

First For Women Magazine, Englewood Cliffs *Also called Bauer Publishing Company LP (G-2950)*

First Friday Global Inc 201 776-6709
130 Mount Pleasant Ave Newark (07104) *(G-7162)*

First Internet Systems 201 991-1889
16 Geraldine Rd North Arlington (07031) *(G-7419)*

First Juice Inc 973 895-3085
19 Tulip Ln Randolph (07869) *(G-9277)*

First Mountain Consulting 973 325-8480
3 Colony Ct West Orange (07052) *(G-11894)*

First National Servicing & Dev 732 341-5409
102 Starc Rd Toms River (08755) *(G-10877)*

First Nighter Formals, Lyndhurst *Also called Fabian Formals Inc (G-5682)*

First Priority Emergency Vhicl (HQ) 732 657-1104
2444 Ridgeway Blvd # 500 Manchester (08759) *(G-5886)*

First Priority Global Ltd (PA) 973 347-4321
160 Gold Mine Rd Flanders (07836) *(G-3408)*

First Priority Specialty Pdts, Manchester *Also called First Priority Emergency Vhicl (G-5886)*

Fis Avantgard LLC 732 530-9303
106 Apple St Ste 110 Tinton Falls (07724) *(G-10837)*

Fis Data Systems Inc 201 945-1774
1008 Virgil Ave Ridgefield (07657) *(G-9360)*

Fis Financial Systems LLC 856 784-7230
600 Laurel Oak Rd Voorhees (08043) *(G-11430)*

Fischl Machine & Tool 908 829-5621
5 Ilene Ct Ste 7 Hillsborough (08844) *(G-4332)*

Fischlers Dawnpoint 856 428-2092
212 Walt Whitman Blvd Cherry Hill (08003) *(G-1365)*

Fisher Canvas Products Inc 609 239-2733
415 Saint Mary St Burlington (08016) *(G-972)*

Fisher Scientific Chemical Div 609 633-1422
1 Reagent Ln Fair Lawn (07410) *(G-3092)*

Fisher Scientific Company LLC 201 796-7100
1 Reagent Ln Fair Lawn (07410) *(G-3093)*

Fisher Service Co 609 386-5000
120 Kissel Rd Burlington (08016) *(G-973)*

Fisher, Harold & Sons, Delanco *Also called Harold F Fisher & Sons Inc (G-2006)*

Fisherman's Pride, Newark *Also called Ruggiero Sea Food Inc (G-7294)*

Fishermens Energy NJ LLC 609 286-9650
985 Ocean Dr Cape May (08204) *(G-1099)*

Fisk Alloy Conductors Inc (HQ) 973 825-8500
10 Thomas Rd N Hawthorne (07506) *(G-4233)*

Fisk Alloy Inc (PA) 973 427-7550
10 Thomas Rd N Hawthorne (07506) *(G-4234)*

Fisk Alloy Wire Incorporated 973 949-4491
10 Thomas Rd N Hawthorne (07506) *(G-4235)*

Fit Fabrication LLC 973 685-7344
310 Colfax Ave Clifton (07013) *(G-1621)*

Fit Graphix (PA) 201 488-4670
390 Maple Hill Dr Hackensack (07601) *(G-3912)*

Fitness Technologies Inc 201 457-0030
10 Banta Pl Ste 202 Hackensack (07601) *(G-3913)*

Five Elements Robotics LLC 800 681-8514
1333 Campus Pkwy Wall Township (07753) *(G-11482)*

Five Kids Group Inc 732 774-5331
37 Highway 35 N Fl 2 Neptune (07753) *(G-6912)*

Five Macs Inc 856 596-3150
8 E Stow Rd Ste 140 Marlton (08053) *(G-5975)*

Five Star Aluminum Products 201 869-4181
2012 86th St North Bergen (07047) *(G-7452)*

Five Star Building Products, North Bergen *Also called Five Star Aluminum Products (G-7452)*

Five Star Supplies NJ Corp 908 862-8801
1301 W Elizabeth Ave A Linden (07036) *(G-5376)*

Fix It Guy 732 278-9000
2562 Balfrey Dr Toms River (08753) *(G-10878)*

Fixturecraft, Ewing *Also called S L Enterprises Inc (G-3054)*

Fizzics Group LLC 917 545-4533
1775 State Route 34 D14 Wall Township (07727) *(G-11483)*

Flame Cut Steel Inc 973 373-9300
300 Coit St Irvington (07111) *(G-4586)*

Flanagan Holdings Inc (PA) 201 512-3338
211 Island Rd Mahwah (07430) *(G-5772)*

Flavor & Fragrance Spc Inc (PA) 201 828-9400
3 Industrial Ave Mahwah (07430) *(G-5773)*

Flavor and Fd Ingredients Inc 201 298-6964
256 Lackland Dr Middlesex (08846) *(G-6166)*

Flavor and Fd Ingredients Inc (PA) 732 805-0335
21 Worlds Fair Dr Somerset (08873) *(G-10102)*

Flavor and Fragrance Division, Teterboro *Also called Mastertaste Inc (G-10805)*

Flavor Associates Inc 973 238-9300
1 Thomas Rd N Hawthorne (07506) *(G-4236)*

Flavor Development Corp 201 784-8188
388 Chestnut St Norwood (07648) *(G-7622)*

Flavor Dynamics Inc 888 271-8424
640 Montrose Ave South Plainfield (07080) *(G-10366)*

Flavor Materials International, Carlstadt *Also called Flavors of Origin Inc (G-1161)*

Flavor Materials International, Avenel *Also called Flavors of Origin Inc (G-131)*

Flavor Solutions Inc 732 354-1931
120 New England Ave Piscataway (08854) *(G-8767)*

Flavors of Origin Inc 201 460-8306
700 Gotham Pkwy Carlstadt (07072) *(G-1161)*

Flavors of Origin Inc (PA) 732 499-9700
10 Engelhard Ave Avenel (07001) *(G-131)*

Flavour Tee International LLC 201 440-3281
66 Industrial Ave Little Ferry (07643) *(G-5505)*

Flech Paper Products Inc 973 357-8111
55 1st Ave Ste 1 Paterson (07514) *(G-8272)*

Fleck Knitwear Co Inc 908 754-8888
400 Leland Ave Plainfield (07062) *(G-8862)*

Fleet Equipment Corporation 201 337-3294
567 Commerce St Franklin Lakes (07417) *(G-3617)*

Fleet Packaging Inc 866 302-0340
75 S Orange Ave Ste 216 South Orange (07079) *(G-10306)*

Fleetsource LLC 732 566-4970
423 County Rd Cliffwood (07721) *(G-1547)*

Flemington Alumininum & Brass 908 782-6333
24 Junction Rd Flemington (08822) *(G-3440)*

Flemington Bituminous Corp 908 782-2722
356 State Route 31 Flemington (08822) *(G-3441)*

Flemington Knitting Mills 908 995-9590
123 Dawn Rd Milford (08848) *(G-6244)*

Flemington Precast & Sup LLC 908 782-3246
18 Allen St Flemington (08822) *(G-3442)*

Flex Moulding Inc 201 487-8080
22 E Lafayette St Hackensack (07601) *(G-3914)*

Flex Products LLC 201 440-1570
640 Dell Rd Ste 1 Carlstadt (07072) *(G-1162)*

Flexabar Corporation (PA) 732 901-6500
1969 Rutgers Blvd Lakewood (08701) *(G-5123)*

Flexbiosys Inc 908 300-3244
291 Us Highway 22 Ste 32 Lebanon (08833) *(G-5286)*

Flexco Bldg Pdts Ltd Lblty Co 732 780-1700
15 Timber Ln Marlboro (07746) *(G-5940)*

Flexco Microwave Inc 908 835-1720
17 Karrville Rd Port Murray (07865) *(G-8977)*

Flexcon Container, Berkeley Heights *Also called Shell Packaging Corporation (G-422)*

Flexcraft Company, Neptune *Also called Holocraft Corporation (G-6919)*

Flexcraft Industries Inc 973 589-3403
390 Adams St Newark (07114) *(G-7163)*

Flexdell Corp 732 901-7771
1969 Rutgers Blvd Lakewood (08701) *(G-5124)*

Flexi Printing Plate Co Inc 201 939-3600
50 Commercial Ave Moonachie (07074) *(G-6517)*

Flexible Components, Somerset *Also called Saint-Gobain Prfmce Plas Corp (G-10170)*

Flexible Foam, Red Bank *Also called Innocor Foam Tech - Acp Inc (G-9332)*

Flexicious LLC 646 340-5066
57 Sip Ave Apt 4b Jersey City (07306) *(G-4752)*

Flexline Inc 908 486-3322
11 Columbus Ave Kenilworth (07033) *(G-4956)*

Flexlink Systems Inc 973 983-2700
335 Chambers Brook Rd Branchburg (08876) *(G-660)*

Flexlink Systems Inc 908 947-2140
335 Chambers Brook Rd Branchburg (08876) *(G-661)*

Flexo-Craft Prints Inc 973 482-7200
1000 1st St Harrison (07029) *(G-4183)*

Flexon Inds Div US Wire Cable, Newark *Also called US Wire & Cable Corporation (G-7355)*

Flexon Industries, Newark *Also called Thirty-Three Queen Realty Inc (G-7341)*

Flexpaq, South Plainfield *Also called Ileos of America Inc (G-10383)*

Flextron Systems, Gloucester City *Also called Quik Flex Circuit Inc (G-3843)*

Flint Group North America, Dayton *Also called Flint Group US LLC (G-1962)*

Flint Group US LLC 732 329-4627
6 Corn Rd Dayton (08810) *(G-1962)*

Flir Security Inc 201 368-9700
65 Challenger Rd Ridgefield Park (07660) *(G-9406)*

FLM Graphics Corporation (PA) 973 575-9450
123 Lehigh Dr Fairfield (07004) *(G-3196)*

Flodyne Controls Inc 908 464-6200
48 Commerce Dr New Providence (07974) *(G-7035)*

Flooring Concepts NJ LLC 732 409-7600
211 Park Ave Manalapan (07726) *(G-5848)*

Floors At Home, Brick *Also called Cno Corporation (G-737)*

Floors For Less Corporation 201 933-9663
94 Carlton Ave East Rutherford (07073) *(G-2296)*

Flor Lift of N J Inc 973 429-2200
19 Gardner Rd Ste M Fairfield (07004) *(G-3197)*

Floral Glass Industries Inc 201 939-4600
99 Murray Hill Pkwy # 10 East Rutherford (07073) *(G-2297)*

Florentine Press Inc 201 386-9200
234 16th St Jersey City (07310) *(G-4753)*

Florlift of NJ, Fairfield *Also called Flor Lift of N J Inc (G-3197)*

Flortek Corporation 201 436-7700
39 W 55th St Bayonne (07002) *(G-225)*

Flottec LLC (PA) 973 588-4717
338 W Main St Boonton (07005) *(G-569)*

Flow-Turn Inc 908 687-3225
1050 Commerce Ave Union (07083) *(G-11184)*

Flowserve Corporation 908 859-7000
222 Cameron Dr Ste 200 Phillipsburg (08865) *(G-8648)*

Flowserve Corporation 856 241-7800
401 Heron Dr Bridgeport (08014) *(G-766)*

Flowserve Corporation 973 334-9444
333 Littleton Rd Ste 303 Parsippany (07054) *(G-8013)*

Flowserve Corporation 973 227-4565
142 Clinton Rd Fairfield (07004) *(G-3198)*

Floxite Company Inc 201 529-2019
31 Industrial Ave Ste 2 Mahwah (07430) *(G-5774)*

Fluent Diagnostics 201 414-4516
22 W Parkway Pequannock (07440) *(G-8599)*

Fluets Corp 908 353-5229
260 Pennsylvania Ave Hillside (07205) *(G-4407)*

Fluid Coating Systems Inc 973 767-1028
13 Barthold St Garfield (07026) *(G-3733)*

Fluid Dynamics Inc 908 200-5823
18 Commerce St Ste 1819 Flemington (08822) *(G-3443)*

Fluid Filtration Corp 973 253-7070
102 Van Winkle Ave Garfield (07026) *(G-3734)*

Fluidsens International Inc 914 338-3932
703 Beechwood Dr Twp Washinton (07676) *(G-11142)*

Fluidyne Corp 856 663-1818
9100 Collins Ave Pennsauken (08110) *(G-8510)*

Fluitec International LLC 201 946-4584
179 W 5th St Bayonne (07002) *(G-226)*

Fluoropharma Medical Inc 973 744-1565
8 Hillside Ave Ste 108 Montclair (07042) *(G-6414)*

Fluorotherm Polymers Inc 973 575-0760
333 New Rd Ste 1 Parsippany (07054) *(G-8014)*

Flying Fish Studio 609 884-2760
130 Park Blvd West Cape May (08204) *(G-11808)*

Flying Models, Newton *Also called Carstens Publications Inc (G-7384)*

FMB Systems Inc 973 485-5544
70 Supor Blvd Harrison (07029) *(G-4184)*

FMC Corporation 973 256-0768
1130 Mcbride Ave Woodland Park (07424) *(G-12219)*

FMC Corporation 732 541-3000
500 Roosevelt Ave Carteret (07008) *(G-1257)*

FMC Corporation 609 963-6200
801-701 Princeton S Ewing (08628) *(G-3018)*

Fmdk Technologies Inc 201 828-9822
63 Ramapo Valley Rd 63w Mahwah (07430) *(G-5775)*

Fmw Drilling, Cinnaminson *Also called Foundation Monitoring (G-1462)*

Foam Rubber Fabricators Inc 973 751-1445
740 Washington Ave Ste 1 Belleville (07109) *(G-303)*

Foamex, East Rutherford *Also called Fxi Inc (G-2298)*

Foil-On, Moonachie *Also called Screen-Trans Development Corp (G-6542)*

Folditure, Hoboken *Also called Gendell Assoicates PA (G-4471)*

Foldtex II Ltd 908 928-0919
705 E Broad St Westfield (07090) *(G-11924)*

Foley-Waite Associates Inc 908 298-0700
746 Colfax Ave Kenilworth (07033) *(G-4957)*

Folgore Mobil Welding Inc 732 541-2974
526 Roosevelt Ave Carteret (07008) *(G-1258)*

Folica Inc (PA) 609 860-8430
11 Corn Rd Ste B Dayton (08810) *(G-1963)*

Folica.com, Dayton *Also called Folica Inc (G-1963)*

Folio Art Glass Inc 732 431-0044
73 State Route 34 S Colts Neck (07722) *(G-1786)*

Food & Beverage Inc 201 288-8881
100 Hollister Rd Unit C-1 Teterboro (07608) *(G-10795)*

Food Circus Super Markets Inc 732 291-4079
9 East Ave 36 Atlantic Highlands (07716) *(G-111)*

Food Ingredient Solutions LLC (PA) 201 440-4377
10 Malcolm Ave Ste 1 Teterboro (07608) *(G-10796)*

Food Mfg 973 920-7000
100 Enterprise Dr Rockaway (07866) *(G-9569)*

Food Sciences Corp (PA) 856 778-4192
821 E Gate Dr Mount Laurel (08054) *(G-6798)*

Foodline Piping Products Co 856 767-1177
225 Edgewood Ave West Berlin (08091) *(G-11720)*

Foodtek Inc (PA) 973 257-4000
9 Whippany Rd Bldg C-2 Whippany (07981) *(G-12020)*

Forbes Magazine, Jersey City *Also called Nsgv Inc* ***(G-4793)***
Forbes Magazine, Jersey City *Also called Forbes Media LLC* ***(G-4754)***
Forbes Media LLC 212 620-2200
499 Washington Blvd Jersey City (07310) ***(G-4754)***
Forbo Siegling LLC 201 567-6100
130 Coolidge Ave Englewood (07631) ***(G-2897)***
Force Industries LLC 973 332-1532
32 Boonton Ave 1 Butler (07405) ***(G-1003)***
Force Systems 856 848-8026
29 Hayes Ave Westville (08093) ***(G-11941)***
Ford Atlanic, Pine Brook *Also called Ford Atlantic Fastener Corp* ***(G-8702)***
Ford Atlantic Fastener Corp 973 882-1191
341 Changebridge Rd Pine Brook (07058) ***(G-8702)***
Ford Fasteners Inc 201 487-3151
110 S Newman St Hackensack (07601) ***(G-3915)***
Fordham Inc 973 575-7840
20 Gloria Ln Fairfield (07004) ***(G-3199)***
Fordion Packaging Ltd 201 692-1344
185 Linden St Ste 3 Hackensack (07601) ***(G-3916)***
Fordoz Pharma Corp 609 469-5949
69 Prnceton Hightstown Rd East Windsor (08520) ***(G-2358)***
Forem Packaging Inc 973 589-0402
2 Joseph St Newark (07105) ***(G-7164)***
Foremost Corp 973 839-3360
2025 Hamburg Tpke Ste A Wayne (07470) ***(G-11635)***
Foremost Machine Builders Inc 973 227-0700
23 Spielman Rd Fairfield (07004) ***(G-3200)***
Foremost Manufacturing Co Inc 908 687-4646
941 Ball Ave Union (07083) ***(G-11185)***
Foresight Enviroprobe Inc 609 259-1244
19 Trenton Lakewood Rd Clarksburg (08510) ***(G-1519)***
Foresight Group LLC 888 992-8880
119 Cherry Hill Rd # 230 Parsippany (07054) ***(G-8015)***
Forest Laboratories LLC 631 436-4534
185 Hudson St Jersey City (07311) ***(G-4755)***
Forest Laboratories LLC 631 501-5399
1900 Plaza Five Jersey City (07311) ***(G-4756)***
Forest Pharmaceuticals Inc (HQ) 862 261-7000
400 Interpace Pkwy Ste A1 Parsippany (07054) ***(G-8016)***
Forge Ahead LLC 908 346-4794
1800 Route 206 Skillman (08558) ***(G-10031)***
Forget ME Not Chocolates By NA 856 753-8916
121 Lakeside Dr Atco (08004) ***(G-89)***
Forino Kitchen Cabinets Inc 201 573-0990
33 S Maple Ave Park Ridge (07656) ***(G-7920)***
Form Cut Industries Inc 973 483-5154
195 Mount Pleasant Ave Newark (07104) ***(G-7165)***
Form Lectro Inc 973 777-0621
1 University Plaza Dr Hackensack (07601) ***(G-3917)***
Form Tops Lminators of Trenton 609 409-4357
37 Merlot Ct Jamesburg (08831) ***(G-4685)***
Forman Industries Inc 732 727-8100
3150 Bordentown Ave Old Bridge (08857) ***(G-7779)***
Formia Marble & Stone Inc 908 259-0606
219 E 11th Ave Roselle (07203) ***(G-9670)***
Formica Bros Bakery 609 348-8934
2310 Arctic Ave Ste 1 Atlantic City (08401) ***(G-96)***
Formica's Bake Shop, Atlantic City *Also called Formica Bros Bakery* ***(G-96)***
Formosa Plastics Corp USA (PA) 973 992-2090
9 Peach Tree Hill Rd Livingston (07039) ***(G-5530)***
Forms & Flyers of New Jersey 856 629-0718
102 Sicklerville Rd Williamstown (08094) ***(G-12087)***
Fornazor International Inc (PA) 201 664-4000
455 Hillsdale Ave Hillsdale (07642) ***(G-4382)***
Forrest Mfg Co Inc 973 473-5236
457 River Rd Clifton (07014) ***(G-1622)***
Forsters Cleaning & Tailoring 201 659-4411
248 Central Ave Jersey City (07307) ***(G-4757)***
Fort Nassau Graphics, West Deptford *Also called Publishers Inc* ***(G-11840)***
Fortune Brands Home & SEC Inc 973 402-6440
603 Cornelia St Boonton (07005) ***(G-570)***
Fortune Metal Recycling, Rahway *Also called Fortune Rvrside Auto Parts Inc* ***(G-9189)***
Fortune Rvrside Auto Parts Inc (PA) 732 381-3355
900 Leesville Ave Rahway (07065) ***(G-9189)***
Fossil Fuel 973 366-9111
105 W Dewey Ave Wharton (07885) ***(G-11987)***
Foster and Company Inc (PA) 973 267-4100
15 Wing Dr Cedar Knolls (07927) ***(G-1312)***
Foster Engraving Corporation 201 489-5979
174 S Main St Ste B Hackensack (07601) ***(G-3918)***
Foster Wheeler, Hampton *Also called Foster Whler Intl Holdings Inc* ***(G-4159)***
Foster Wheeler, Hampton *Also called Foster Wheeler Intl Corp* ***(G-4157)***
Foster Wheeler Arabia Ltd 908 730-4000
53 Frontage Rd Hampton (08827) ***(G-4156)***
Foster Wheeler Intl Corp (HQ) 908 730-4000
Perryville Corporate Pk 5 Hampton (08827) ***(G-4157)***
Foster Wheeler Zack Inc (HQ) 908 730-4000
53 Frontage Rd Hampton (08827) ***(G-4158)***
Foster Whler Intl Holdings Inc (HQ) 908 730-4000
Perryville Corporate Pk 5 Hampton (08827) ***(G-4159)***
Foto Fantasy 732 548-8446
2850 Woodbridge Ave Edison (08837) ***(G-2521)***
Fotobridge 856 809-9400
154 Cooper Rd Ste 203 West Berlin (08091) ***(G-11721)***
Fougera Pharmaceuticals Inc 973 514-4241
1 Health Plz East Hanover (07936) ***(G-2217)***
Foulkrod Associates 856 662-6767
8275 N Crescent Blvd Pennsauken (08110) ***(G-8511)***
Foundation For Embryonic 973 656-2847
140 Allen Rd Basking Ridge (07920) ***(G-187)***
Foundation For Student Comm 609 258-1111
48 University Pl Ste 305 Princeton (08540) ***(G-9046)***
Foundation Monitoring 856 829-0410
515 Wellfleet Rd Cinnaminson (08077) ***(G-1462)***
Foundation Software Inc 908 359-0588
58 Livingston Dr Belle Mead (08502) ***(G-291)***
Four Bros Ventures Inc 732 890-9469
15 Timothy Ln East Brunswick (08816) ***(G-2155)***
Four Star Color, Newton *Also called Four Star Reproductions Inc* ***(G-7388)***
Four Star Reproductions Inc 862 268-8200
52 Paterson Ave Ste 2 Newton (07860) ***(G-7388)***
Four Way Enterprises Inc 973 633-5757
582 Fairfield Rd Wayne (07470) ***(G-11636)***
Foursconsulting Ltd Lblty Co 732 599-4324
295 Durham Ave Ste 206 South Plainfield (07080) ***(G-10367)***
Fowler Route Co Inc (PA) 908 686-3400
565 Rahway Ave Union (07083) ***(G-11186)***
Fox Steel Products LLC 856 778-4661
8 Fox Run Dr Mount Laurel (08054) ***(G-6799)***
Fpc USA, Livingston *Also called Formosa Plastics Corp USA* ***(G-5530)***
Fractal Solutions Corp 201 608-6828
725 River Rd Unit 32135 Edgewater (07020) ***(G-2439)***
Fragales Bakery Inc 973 546-0327
6874 Gaston Ave Garfield (07026) ***(G-3735)***
Fragrance Exchange Inc 732 641-2210
1075 Cranbury Rd Ste 7 Monroe Township (08831) ***(G-6382)***
Fragrance Factory, Northvale *Also called Takasago Intl Corp USA* ***(G-7609)***
Fragrance Factory Inc 973 835-2002
12 Peck Ave Pompton Plains (07444) ***(G-8959)***
Fragrance Resources Inc (HQ) 973 777-2979
600 State Route 36 Hazlet (07730) ***(G-4274)***
Fragrance Resources Inc 973 458-5231
275 Clark St Keyport (07735) ***(G-5018)***
Fragrance Solutions Corp 732 832-7800
3357 S Clinton Ave South Plainfield (07080) ***(G-10368)***
Fralinger's Org Salt Wtr Taffy, Atlantic City *Also called Fralingers Inc* ***(G-97)***
Fralingers Inc (PA) 609 345-2177
1325 Boardwalk Ste 1 Atlantic City (08401) ***(G-97)***
Fralingers Inc 609 345-2177
1519 Boardwalk Atlantic City (08401) ***(G-98)***
Fram Trak Industries Inc 732 424-8400
205 Hallock Ave Middlesex (08846) ***(G-6167)***
Frameco Inc 973 989-1424
158 W Clinton St Ste B Dover (07801) ***(G-2087)***
Framesmith Gallery, The, Princeton *Also called Empty Walls Inc* ***(G-9038)***
Frameware Inc 800 582-5608
8 Audrey Pl Fairfield (07004) ***(G-3201)***
Franbeth Inc 856 488-1480
5505 N Crescent Blvd Pennsauken (08110) ***(G-8512)***
Francis Cable Systems, Lakewood *Also called Francis Metals Company Inc* ***(G-5125)***
Francis Metals Company Inc 732 761-0500
687 Prospect St Ste 430 Lakewood (08701) ***(G-5125)***
Franco Manufacturing Co Inc (PA) 732 494-0500
555 Prospect St Metuchen (08840) ***(G-6104)***
Frank & Jims Inc 609 646-1655
711 N Main St Ste 3 Pleasantville (08232) ***(G-8908)***
Frank B Ross Co Inc (PA) 732 669-0810
970 New Brunswick Ave H Rahway (07065) ***(G-9190)***
Frank Burton & Sons Inc 856 455-1202
333 W Broad St Bridgeton (08302) ***(G-785)***
Frank E Ganter Inc 856 692-2218
224 S Lincoln Ave Vineland (08361) ***(G-11356)***
Frank Ferreira Cab & Mill Work 732 564-1499
74 King George Rd Warren (07059) ***(G-11548)***
Frank J Zechman 732 495-0077
515 Highway 36 Belford (07718) ***(G-287)***
Frank Jims Storm Windows Doors, Pleasantville *Also called Frank & Jims Inc* ***(G-8908)***
Frankford Umbrellas, Mount Laurel *Also called S Frankford & Sons Inc* ***(G-6836)***
Franklen Sheet Metal Co Inc 732 988-0808
122 S Main St Ocean Grove (07756) ***(G-7761)***
Franklin Electronic Publs Inc (PA) 609 386-2500
3 Terri Ln Ste 6 Burlington (08016) ***(G-974)***
Franklin Graphics Inc 201 935-5900
60 Brickell Ave Westwood (07675) ***(G-11960)***
Franklin Miller Inc 973 535-9200
60 Okner Pkwy Livingston (07039) ***(G-5531)***

ALPHABETIC

Franklin Mint LLC 800 843-6468
400 Kelby St Ste 15 Fort Lee (07024) ***(G-3555)***
Franklin Mint Trading, Fort Lee *Also called Franklin Mint LLC* ***(G-3555)***
Franklin Precast Tanks, Franklin *Also called Double Twenties Inc* ***(G-3598)***
Franklin Press, Westwood *Also called Franklin Graphics Inc* ***(G-11960)***
Franks Cabinet Shop Inc 908 658-4396
1992 Burnt Mills Rd Pluckemin (07978) ***(G-8919)***
Franks Upholstery & Draperies 856 779-8585
621 S Forklanding Rd Maple Shade (08052) ***(G-5902)***
Fratelli Beretta Usa Inc 201 438-0723
750 Clark Dr Budd Lake (07828) ***(G-929)***
Frauscher Sensor Tech USA Inc 609 285-5492
300 Carnegie Ctr Ste 320 Princeton (08540) ***(G-9047)***
Frazier Industrial Company (PA) 908 876-3001
91 Fairview Ave Long Valley (07853) ***(G-5637)***
Frc Electrical Industries Inc 908 464-3200
705 Central Ave Ste 3 New Providence (07974) ***(G-7036)***
Fred McDowell Inc 732 681-5000
34 St Hwy Wall Township (07753) ***(G-11484)***
Fred S Burroughs North Jersey 908 850-8773
6 Rushmore Ln Hackettstown (07840) ***(G-4008)***
Fredericks Machine Inc 609 397-4991
99 Kingwood Stockton Rd Rosemont (08556) ***(G-9704)***
Fredon Development Inds LLC 973 383-7576
393 State Route 94 S Newton (07860) ***(G-7389)***
Fredon Welding & Iron Works, Lafayette *Also called James Zylstra Enterprises Inc* ***(G-5047)***
Freed Transformer Company 973 942-2222
460 Totowa Ave Paterson (07522) ***(G-8273)***
Freedom Plastics LLC 201 337-9450
37 Edison Ave Oakland (07436) ***(G-7689)***
Freedom Vinyl Systems Inc 973 692-0332
67 2nd St Pequannock (07440) ***(G-8600)***
Freehold Buick, Freehold *Also called Freehold Pntiac Bick GMC Trcks* ***(G-3656)***
Freehold Pntiac Bick GMC Trcks 732 462-7093
4404 Us Highway 9 Freehold (07728) ***(G-3656)***
Freeman Products, Parsippany *Also called AMG International Inc* ***(G-7945)***
Freeman Products Inc (PA) 201 475-4800
71 Walsh Dr Ste 101 Parsippany (07054) ***(G-8017)***
Freeman Products Worldwide, Parsippany *Also called AMG International Inc* ***(G-7946)***
Freeman Technical Sales Inc 908 464-4784
148 Maple St New Providence (07974) ***(G-7037)***
Freeport Minerals Corporation 908 351-3200
48 94 Bayway Ave Elizabeth (07202) ***(G-2734)***
Freeport-Mcmoran Inc 908 558-4361
48-94 Bayway Ave Elizabeth (07202) ***(G-2735)***
Freeze, Dayton *Also called Central Mills Inc* ***(G-1961)***
Frell Corp 201 825-2500
885 State Rt 17 Ste 5 Ramsey (07446) ***(G-9240)***
French Color Fragrance Co Inc (PA) 201 567-6883
488 Grand Ave Englewood (07631) ***(G-2898)***
French Creek Sheep & Wool Co 610 286-5700
5000 Boardwalk Apt 1717 Ventnor City (08406) ***(G-11291)***
French Textile Co Inc 973 471-5000
835 Bloomfield Ave Ste 1 Clifton (07012) ***(G-1623)***
French Toast, Dayton *Also called Lollytogs Ltd* ***(G-1978)***
French Toast, Dayton *Also called Frenchtoastcom LLC* ***(G-1964)***
French Toast, Dayton *Also called Lollytogs Ltd* ***(G-1979)***
Frenchtoastcom LLC 732 438-5500
321 Herrod Blvd Dayton (08810) ***(G-1964)***
Frenchtown Partition Plant, Frenchtown *Also called Caraustar Industries Inc* ***(G-3698)***
Fresenius Med Care Hldings Inc 201 767-7700
22 Paris Ave Rockleigh (07647) ***(G-9629)***
Freshpet Inc (PA) 201 520-4000
400 Plaza Dr Fl 1 Secaucus (07094) ***(G-9884)***
Frewitt USA Inc 908 829-5245
249 Homestead Rd Hillsborough (08844) ***(G-4333)***
Freyr Inc 908 483-7958
150 College Rd W Ste 102 Princeton (08540) ***(G-9048)***
Friday Morning Quarterback 856 424-6873
1930 Marlton Pike E F36 Cherry Hill (08003) ***(G-1366)***
Friedrich and Dimmock Inc 856 825-0305
2127 Wheaton Ave Millville (08332) ***(G-6302)***
Friends Hardwood Floors Inc 732 859-4019
60 Monmouth Rd Oakhurst (07755) ***(G-7669)***
Frimpeks Inc 201 266-0116
30 Sherwood Ln Ste 6 Fairfield (07004) ***(G-3202)***
Frinton Laboratories Inc 856 722-7037
204 Winding Way Moorestown (08057) ***(G-6578)***
Fritnationalsupply, Newark *Also called Ivey Katrina Owner* ***(G-7202)***
Frontend Graphics Inc 856 547-1600
1951 Old Cuthbert Rd # 414 Cherry Hill (08034) ***(G-1367)***
Frontline Industries Inc 973 373-7211
990 Chancellor Ave Irvington (07111) ***(G-4587)***
Frontline Med Cmmnications Inc (HQ) 973 206-2328
7 Century Dr Ste 302 Parsippany (07054) ***(G-8018)***
Frontline Med Communications, Parsippany *Also called Frontline Med Cmmnications Inc* ***(G-8018)***
Frost King, Mahwah *Also called Thermwell Products Co Inc* ***(G-5820)***
Frost Tech Inc 732 396-0071
830 Elston St Rahway (07065) ***(G-9191)***
Froyo Skyview LLC 718 607-5656
42 Dales Ave Jersey City (07306) ***(G-4758)***
Frozen Falls LLC 908 350-3939
413 King Gorge Rd Ste 202 Basking Ridge (07920) ***(G-188)***
Fs Solutions, New Brunswick *Also called Jetstream of Houston LLP* ***(G-6972)***
Fti Inc 973 443-0004
8 Vreeland Rd Florham Park (07932) ***(G-3503)***
Fu WEI Inc 732 937-8388
40 Cotters Ln Bldg B East Brunswick (08816) ***(G-2156)***
Fu WEI International, East Brunswick *Also called Fu WEI Inc* ***(G-2156)***
Fuceltech Inc 609 275-0070
11 Glengarry Way Princeton Junction (08550) ***(G-9155)***
Fuchs Audio Tech Ltd Lblty Co 973 772-4420
407 Getty Ave Clifton (07011) ***(G-1624)***
Fuel Management Services Inc 732 929-1964
13 Main Bayway Toms River (08753) ***(G-10879)***
Fuel One Inc 732 726-9500
869 Us Highway 1 Avenel (07001) ***(G-132)***
Fugle-Miller Laboratories Inc 732 574-3121
1401 Witherspoon St Ste 1 Rahway (07065) ***(G-9192)***
Fuji Electric Corp America (HQ) 732 560-9410
50 Northfield Ave Edison (08837) ***(G-2522)***
Fujifilm North America Corp 732 857-3000
1100 King Georges Post Rd Edison (08837) ***(G-2523)***
Fujikin of America Inc 201 641-1119
777 Terrace Ave Ste 110 Hasbrouck Heights (07604) ***(G-4192)***
Fujipoly America Corporation 732 969-0100
900 Milik St Carteret (07008) ***(G-1259)***
Fujitsu General America Inc 973 575-0380
353 Route 46 W Fairfield (07004) ***(G-3203)***
Fulcrum Inc 973 473-6900
660 Kinderkamack Rd # 203 Oradell (07649) ***(G-7809)***
Fulfillment Printing and Mail 609 953-9500
77 Oswego Trl Medford Lakes (08055) ***(G-6085)***
Full Circle Mfg Group 908 353-8933
534 S Front St Elizabeth (07202) ***(G-2736)***
Full House Printing Inc 201 798-7073
303 1st St Hoboken (07030) ***(G-4470)***
Full Service Mailers Inc 973 478-8813
123 S Newman St Hackensack (07601) ***(G-3919)***
Fullview Inc 732 275-6500
3 Fieldpoint Dr Holmdel (07733) ***(G-4516)***
Funai Corporation Inc (HQ) 201 806-7635
201 Route 17 Ste 903 Rutherford (07070) ***(G-9732)***
Funnibonz LLC 609 915-3685
3 Lake View Ct Princeton Junction (08550) ***(G-9156)***
Furniture of America NJ 201 605-8200
50 Enterprise Ave N Secaucus (07094) ***(G-9885)***
Furs By Severyn, Linden *Also called S & H R Inc* ***(G-5436)***
Fusar Technologies Inc 201 563-0189
78 John Miller Way # 310 Kearny (07032) ***(G-4874)***
Future Signs, Trenton *Also called Ricztone Inc* ***(G-11112)***
Futurex Inc 201 933-3943
114 Essex St Ste 100 Rochelle Park (07662) ***(G-9528)***
Futurex Properties Inc (PA) 732 414-6211
4 Timber Ln Marlboro (07746) ***(G-5941)***
Futurrex Inc 973 209-1563
24 Munsonhurst Rd Ste F Franklin (07416) ***(G-3599)***
FW Winter Inc 856 963-7490
550 Delaware Ave Camden (08102) ***(G-1067)***
Fxi Inc 201 933-8540
13 Manor Rd East Rutherford (07073) ***(G-2298)***
Fyi Marketing Inc 646 546-5226
22 Laurie Dr Englewood Cliffs (07632) ***(G-2960)***
Fyth Labs Inc 856 313-7362
455 Warren St E Beverly (08010) ***(G-463)***
G & A Coml Seating Pdts Corp 908 233-8000
152 Glen Rd Mountainside (07092) ***(G-6882)***
G & A Pavers Llc 201 562-5947
2123 Sterling Blvd Englewood (07631) ***(G-2899)***
G & B Machine Inc 908 707-1181
35 N Middaugh St Ste B Somerville (08876) ***(G-10209)***
G & F Graphic Services, Pennsauken *Also called Inserts East Incorporated* ***(G-8528)***
G & H Metal Finishers Inc 201 909-9808
282 Dakota St Paterson (07503) ***(G-8274)***
G & H Sheet Metal Works Inc 973 923-1100
1423 Chestnut Ave Hillside (07205) ***(G-4408)***
G & H Soho Inc 201 216-9400
413 Market St Elmwood Park (07407) ***(G-2820)***
G & J Solutions Inc 609 861-9838
419 Madison Ave Woodbine (08270) ***(G-12142)***
G & J Steel & Tubing Inc 908 526-4445
406 Roycefield Rd Hillsborough (08844) ***(G-4334)***
G & M Custom Formica Work 732 888-0360
120 Francis St Ste 5 Keyport (07735) ***(G-5019)***
G & M Printwear 856 742-5551
549 S Broadway Ste 2 Gloucester City (08030) ***(G-3836)***

G & R Fuel Corp 973 732-0530
822 Clinton Ave Newark (07108) *(G-7166)*

G & R Graphics Inc 973 731-7438
303 Irvington Ave South Orange (07079) *(G-10307)*

G & S Design & Manufacturing 908 862-2444
330 Dalziel Rd Linden (07036) *(G-5377)*

G & S Motor Equipment Co Inc 201 998-9244
1800 Harrison Ave Kearny (07032) *(G-4875)*

G & S Precision Prototype 732 370-3010
115 Somerset Ave Lakewood (08701) *(G-5126)*

G & S Technologies, Kearny *Also called G & S Motor Equipment Co Inc* *(G-4875)*

G & W Laboratories Inc (PA) 908 753-2000
111 Coolidge St South Plainfield (07080) *(G-10369)*

G & W Laboratories Inc. 732 474-0729
1551 S Washington Ave Piscataway (08854) *(G-8768)*

G & W Laboratories Inc. 908 753-2000
101 Coolidge St South Plainfield (07080) *(G-10370)*

G & Y Specialty Foods LLC 956 821-9652
2 Andrews Dr Ste 5 Woodland Park (07424) *(G-12220)*

G A D Inc 973 383-3499
914 Cedar Ridge Rd Newton (07860) *(G-7390)*

G A F, Wayne *Also called G-I Holdings Inc* *(G-11638)*

G Big Corp 973 242-6521
189 Frelinghuysen Ave Newark (07114) *(G-7167)*

G Catalano Inc 908 241-6333
222 Valley Rd Roselle Park (07204) *(G-9696)*

G E C, Metuchen *Also called Graphic Equipment Corporation* *(G-6106)*

G E Inspection Technologies LP 973 448-0077
199 Us Highway 206 Flanders (07836) *(G-3409)*

G G Tauber Company Inc 800 638-6667
3535 State Route 66 Ste 1 Neptune (07753) *(G-6913)*

G H Krauss Manufacturing Co 856 662-0815
1209 Route 38 Cherry Hill (08002) *(G-1368)*

G Holdings Inc (PA) 973 628-3000
1 Campus Dr Parsippany (07054) *(G-8019)*

G I Trade Copy, Riverside *Also called Good Impressions Inc* *(G-9498)*

G J Chemical Co (PA) 973 589-1450
40 Veronica Ave Somerset (08873) *(G-10103)*

G J Haerer Co Inc (PA) 973 614-8090
372 Ridgewood Ave Glen Ridge (07028) *(G-3818)*

G J Oliver Inc 908 454-9743
50 Industrial Rd Phillipsburg (08865) *(G-8649)*

G L Tool & Manufacturing Co 973 740-0001
26 Okner Pkwy Livingston (07039) *(G-5532)*

G M Fence Co, East Hanover *Also called General Metal Manufacturing Co* *(G-2218)*

G M Stainless Inc (PA) 908 575-1834
41 Imclone Dr Branchburg (08876) *(G-662)*

G N J Inc (PA) 856 786-1127
N Riderton Rd Rr 130 Cinnaminson (08077) *(G-1463)*

G P R Company Inc 973 227-6160
8 Spielman Rd Fairfield (07004) *(G-3204)*

G R Bowler Inc 973 525-7172
511 Maxim Dr Andover (07821) *(G-50)*

G R Impex Ltd Liability Co (PA) 732 931-7001
2 Terminal Way Bldg A Avenel (07001) *(G-133)*

G R P Signs, Newark *Also called Silver Edmar* *(G-7313)*

G S Babu & Co 732 939-5190
57 Woodland Dr Plainsboro (08536) *(G-8882)*

G T Associates 973 694-6040
440 Indian Rd Wayne (07470) *(G-11637)*

G T M Signs Inc. 856 227-2333
1960 Harris Dr Deptford (08096) *(G-2064)*

G W Laboratories, Piscataway *Also called G & W Laboratories Inc* *(G-8768)*

G&W PA Laboratories LLC 908 753-2000
111 Coolidge St South Plainfield (07080) *(G-10371)*

G-Force River Signs LLC 609 397-4467
9 S Main St Lambertville (08530) *(G-5212)*

G-I Holdings Inc (HQ) 973 628-3000
1361 Alps Rd Wayne (07470) *(G-11638)*

G-III Apparel Group Ltd 732 438-0209
308 Herrod Blvd Dayton (08810) *(G-1965)*

G-III Leather Fashions Inc 212 403-0500
308 Herrod Blvd Dayton (08810) *(G-1966)*

G-Tech Elevator Associates LLC 866 658-9296
12 Sherman St Linden (07036) *(G-5378)*

G-Way Microwave Inc 201 343-6388
38 Leuning St South Hackensack (07606) *(G-10269)*

GAb Electronic Services LLC 856 786-0108
1703 Industrial Hwy Ste 8 Cinnaminson (08077) *(G-1464)*

Gabhen Inc (PA) 800 631-3572
1 Maltese Dr Totowa (07512) *(G-10945)*

Gabhen Inc. 973 256-0666
1 Maltese Dr Totowa (07512) *(G-10946)*

Gabriel Sound Ltd Liability Co 973 831-7800
138 Cannonball Rd Pompton Lakes (07442) *(G-8947)*

Gadde Pharma LLC 609 651-7772
41 Madison Dr Plainsboro (08536) *(G-8883)*

Gade Float Valves, Mount Ephraim *Also called Gadren Machine Co Inc* *(G-6763)*

Gadren Machine Co Inc (PA) 856 456-4329
108 Main St Mount Ephraim (08059) *(G-6763)*

GAF Elk Materials Corporation 973 628-4083
1361 Alps Rd Wayne (07470) *(G-11639)*

Gail Gersons Wine & Dine Resta 732 758-0888
812 Broad St Shrewsbury (07702) *(G-9999)*

Gaisers Erpean Style Provs Inc 908 686-3421
2019 Morris Ave Union (07083) *(G-11187)*

Galaxy Led Inc 201 541-5461
600 Sylvan Ave Ste 106 Englewood Cliffs (07632) *(G-2961)*

Galaxy Metal Products LLC 908 668-5200
2960 Woodbridge Ave Edison (08837) *(G-2524)*

Galaxy of Graphics, East Rutherford *Also called Arthur A Kaplan Co Inc* *(G-2279)*

Galaxy Switchgear Inds LLC 914 668-8200
46 Sellers St Kearny (07032) *(G-4876)*

Galaxy Trans & Magnetics LLC 856 753-4546
386 Cooper Rd West Berlin (08091) *(G-11722)*

Gale Newson Inc (PA) 732 961-7610
460 Faraday Ave Ste 7 Jackson (08527) *(G-4668)*

Galen Publishing LLC 908 253-9001
166 W Main St Somerville (08876) *(G-10210)*

Gallant Laboratories Inc 609 654-4146
2407 Delancey Way Marlton (08053) *(G-5976)*

Galleria Enterprises Inc 646 416-6683
26 Commerce Rd Ste I Fairfield (07004) *(G-3205)*

Gallery of Rugs Inc 908 934-0040
447 Springfield Ave Summit (07901) *(G-10642)*

Galvanic LLC 609 600-2604
514 Washington St Cape May (08204) *(G-1100)*

Galvanic Prtg & Plate Co Inc 201 939-3600
50 Commercial Ave Moonachie (07074) *(G-6518)*

Galvanotech, Linden *Also called G & S Design & Manufacturing* *(G-5377)*

Galves Auto Price List Inc 201 393-0051
430 Industrial Ave Ste 3 Teterboro (07608) *(G-10797)*

Gambay Inc 856 330-4397
1545 Route 73 Pennsauken (08110) *(G-8513)*

Gambert Custom Shirts, Newark *Also called Gambert Shirt Corp* *(G-7168)*

Gambert Shirt Corp 973 424-9105
436 Ferry St Ste 2 Newark (07105) *(G-7168)*

Gamit Force Athc Ltd Lblty Co. 908 675-0733
459 Atlantic Ave Long Branch (07740) *(G-5624)*

Gamka Sales Co Inc 732 248-1400
983 New Durham Rd Edison (08817) *(G-2525)*

Gamma Machine & Tool Co Inc 973 398-8821
32 Oneida Ave Landing (07850) *(G-5224)*

Gammon Technical Products Inc (PA) 732 223-4600
2300 Highway 34 Manasquan (08736) *(G-5870)*

Gangi Graphics Inc 732 840-8680
1669 Route 88 Brick (08724) *(G-744)*

Gann Law Books Inc 973 268-1200
1 Washington Park # 1300 Newark (07102) *(G-7169)*

Gannett Co Inc 908 243-6953
92 E Main St Ste 202 Somerville (08876) *(G-10211)*

Gannett Co Inc. 973 428-6200
800 Jefferson Rd Parsippany (07054) *(G-8020)*

Gannett Stllite Info Ntwrk Inc 973 428-6200
800 Jefferson Rd Parsippany (07054) *(G-8021)*

Gannett Stllite Info Ntwrk Inc 856 691-5000
891 E Oak Rd Vineland (08360) *(G-11357)*

Gannett Stllite Info Ntwrk LLC. 609 561-2300
891 E Oak Rd Unit A Vineland (08360) *(G-11358)*

Gannett Stllite Info Ntwrk LLC. 856 663-6000
301 Cuthbert Blvd Cherry Hill (08002) *(G-1369)*

Ganz Brothers Inc 201 820-1975
12 Mulberry Ct Paramus (07652) *(G-7870)*

Garafano Tank Service, Paterson *Also called Peter Garafano & Son Inc* *(G-8364)*

Gardellas Rvioli Itln Deli LLC 856 697-3509
527 S Brewster Rd Vineland (08360) *(G-11359)*

Garden St Chasis Remanuf 732 283-1910
1 Pennville Rd Woodbridge (07095) *(G-12149)*

Garden State Alnce Orthopaedic, Morristown *Also called Garden State Orthopedic Center* *(G-6709)*

Garden State Btlg Ltd Lblty Co 201 991-2342
174 Sanford Ave Kearny (07032) *(G-4877)*

Garden State Fabricators 732 928-5006
575 Monmouth Rd Cream Ridge (08514) *(G-1935)*

Garden State Fuel 856 442-0061
600 Buck Rd Monroeville (08343) *(G-6399)*

Garden State Highway Pdts Inc (PA) 856 692-7572
301 Riverside Dr D Millville (08332) *(G-6303)*

Garden State Iron Inc 732 918-0760
3418 Sunset Ave Ocean (07712) *(G-7726)*

Garden State Irrigation 201 848-1300
500 W Main St Ste 5 Wyckoff (07481) *(G-12253)*

Garden State Medical Sup LLC 732 348-0312
1995 Rutgers Univ Blvd Lakewood (08701) *(G-5127)*

Garden State Mgntc Imaging PC 609 581-2727
6027 S Crescent Blvd Pennsauken (08110) *(G-8514)*

Garden State Orthopedic Center 973 538-4948
95 Mount Kemble Ave Morristown (07960) *(G-6709)*

A
L
P
H
A
B
E
T
I
C

Garden State Precast Inc 732 938-4436
1630 Wyckoff Rd Wall Township (07727) *(G-11485)*
Garden State Precision Inc 201 945-6410
510 Church St Ridgefield (07657) *(G-9361)*
Garden State Prosthetics 732 922-6650
3500 Sunset Ave Ocean (07712) *(G-7727)*
Garden State Recycl Edison LLC 732 393-0200
355 Meadow Rd Edison (08837) *(G-2526)*
Garden State Sign, Howell *Also called Ervin Advertising Co Inc* *(G-4554)*
Garden State Tool & Mold Corp 908 245-2041
501 Bordentown Ave South Amboy (08879) *(G-10238)*
Garden State Woman Mag LLC 908 879-7143
210 Parker Rd Long Valley (07853) *(G-5638)*
Gardner Resources Inc 732 872-0755
188 Bay Ave Highlands (07732) *(G-4309)*
Garelick Farms LLC 609 499-2600
Cumberland Blvd Rr 130 Burlington (08016) *(G-975)*
Garfield Industries Inc 973 575-3322
62 Clinton Rd Ste 1 Fairfield (07004) *(G-3206)*
Garfield Molding Co Inc 973 777-5700
10 Midland Ave Wallington (07057) *(G-11526)*
Garley Inc 215 788-5756
46 Tall Timber Ln Burlington (08016) *(G-976)*
Garlock Bearings Inc 856 848-3200
700 Mid Atlantic Pkwy Thorofare (08086) *(G-10819)*
Garment Bar, Deptford *Also called International Rollforms Inc* *(G-2065)*
Garratt-Callahan Company 732 287-2200
306 Talmadge Rd Edison (08817) *(G-2527)*
Garrett Moore 908 231-9231
1048 Hoffman Rd Bridgewater (08807) *(G-840)*
Garrison Printing Company Inc 856 488-1900
7155 Airport Hwy Pennsauken (08109) *(G-8515)*
Garvey Corporation (PA) 609 561-2450
208 S Route 73 Hammonton (08037) *(G-4137)*
Gary Ell Photography, Burlington *Also called Pixell Creative Group LLC* *(G-988)*
Gary R Banks Industrial Group 856 687-2227
575 N Route 73 Ste C6 West Berlin (08091) *(G-11723)*
Gary R Marzili 856 782-1546
840 Jarvis Rd Sicklerville (08081) *(G-10019)*
Garylin Togs 908 354-7218
107 Trumbull St Elizabeth (07206) *(G-2737)*
Garys Kids 973 458-1818
314 Monroe St Passaic (07055) *(G-8141)*
Gas Drying Inc 973 361-2212
355 W Dewey Ave Wharton (07885) *(G-11988)*
Gasflo Products Inc 973 276-9011
19 Industrial Rd Fairfield (07004) *(G-3207)*
Gaspari Nutrition, Neptune *Also called Allegro Nutrition Inc* *(G-6899)*
Gass Custom Woodworking 201 493-9282
169 Birchwood Rd Paramus (07652) *(G-7871)*
Gate Technologies Inc 973 300-0090
27 Wilson Dr Unit C Sparta (07871) *(G-10500)*
Gatehuse Media PA Holdings Inc 732 246-7677
104 Church St New Brunswick (08901) *(G-6961)*
Gateway Property Solutions Ltd 732 901-9700
730 Airport Rd Unit 1 Lakewood (08701) *(G-5128)*
Gator Communications Group LLC 973 233-6700
175 Us Highway 46 Fairfield (07004) *(G-3208)*
Gauer Metal Products Co Inc 908 241-4080
175 N Michigan Ave Kenilworth (07033) *(G-4958)*
Gaum Inc (PA) 609 586-0132
1080 Us Highway 130 Robbinsville (08691) *(G-9516)*
Gaurika Jewels, Cliffside Park *Also called Gaurika LLC* *(G-1539)*
Gaurika LLC 201 496-1613
250 Gorge Rd Cliffside Park (07010) *(G-1539)*
Gavan Graham Elec Pdts Corp (PA) 908 729-9000
751 Rahway Ave Union (07083) *(G-11188)*
Gaw Associates Inc 856 608-1428
670 Deer Rd Bldg A Cherry Hill (08034) *(G-1370)*
Gaw Technology, Cherry Hill *Also called Gaw Associates Inc* *(G-1370)*
Gb Industries II Inc 973 728-5900
341 Margaret King Ave Ringwood (07456) *(G-9447)*
Gbd Cabinet Shop, Pluckemin *Also called Franks Cabinet Shop Inc* *(G-8919)*
Gbw Manufacturing Inc 973 279-0077
20 W End Rd Totowa (07512) *(G-10947)*
Gcah, Madison *Also called General Commis Archives & Hstr* *(G-5723)*
Gce Market Inc (PA) 856 401-8900
1001 Lower Landing Rd # 307 Blackwood (08012) *(G-478)*
GCI, Secaucus *Also called General Glass Intl Corp* *(G-9887)*
Gdb International Inc (PA) 732 246-3001
1 Home News Row New Brunswick (08901) *(G-6962)*
GE Appliances, Wayne *Also called Haier Appliance Products LP* *(G-11645)*
GE Aviation Systems LLC 973 428-9898
110 Algonquin Pkwy Whippany (07981) *(G-12021)*
GE Healthcare Inc 908 757-0500
900 Durham Ave South Plainfield (07080) *(G-10372)*
Ge-Ro Desk Company, Newark *Also called R J Hoppe Store Construction* *(G-7283)*
Geiger Tool & Mfg Co Inc 973 777-2136
50 Liberty St Passaic (07055) *(G-8142)*

Geiger Tool Co Inc 973 777-5094
50 Liberty St Passaic (07055) *(G-8143)*
Geisler Ganz Corp 201 223-1200
505 Windsor Dr Secaucus (07094) *(G-9886)*
Geislers Liquor Store 856 845-0482
195 Crown Point Rd Thorofare (08086) *(G-10820)*
Geistlich Pharma North America 609 779-6560
202 Carnegie Ctr Ste 103 Princeton (08540) *(G-9049)*
Gel Concepts LLC 973 884-8995
30 Leslie Ct Whippany (07981) *(G-12022)*
Gel Spice Co Inc (PA) 201 339-0700
48 Hook Rd Bayonne (07002) *(G-227)*
Gel Spice Co LLC 201 339-0700
48 Hook Rd Bayonne (07002) *(G-228)*
Gel United Ltd Liability Co 855 435-8683
635 N Midland Ave 3184 Saddle Brook (07663) *(G-9766)*
Gelbsteins Bakery, Lakewood *Also called Y & J Bakers Inc* *(G-5208)*
Gelotti Confections LLC 973 403-9968
194 Bloomfield Ave Caldwell (07006) *(G-1029)*
Gem Vault Inc 908 788-1770
23 Turntable Jct Flemington (08822) *(G-3444)*
Gemco Valve Co LLC 732 752-7900
301 Smalley Ave Middlesex (08846) *(G-6168)*
Gemcraft Inc 732 449-8944
1921 State Route 71 Belmar (07719) *(G-358)*
Gemini Cut Glass Company Inc 201 568-7722
4 E Forest Ave Englewood (07631) *(G-2900)*
Gemini Plastic Films Corp 973 340-0700
535 Midland Ave Garfield (07026) *(G-3736)*
Gemini Sound, Elizabeth *Also called Innovative Concepts Design LLC* *(G-2747)*
Gemtor Inc 732 583-6200
1 Johnson Ave Matawan (07747) *(G-6021)*
Genavite LLC 973 779-1532
235 Clifton Blvd Clifton (07011) *(G-1625)*
Gendell Assoicates PA 201 656-4498
1031 Bloomfield St Hoboken (07030) *(G-4471)*
Gene Mignola Inc 732 775-9291
704 Cookman Ave Asbury Park (07712) *(G-78)*
General A & E, Hackensack *Also called General Aviation & Elec Mfg Co* *(G-3920)*
General Aviation & Elec Mfg Co 201 487-1700
30 Jersey Pl Hackensack (07601) *(G-3920)*
General Carbon Corporation 973 523-2223
33 Paterson St Paterson (07501) *(G-8275)*
General Chemical, Berkeley Heights *Also called Chemtrade Solutions LLC* *(G-405)*
General Civil Company Inc 866 435-1200
710 Irish Hill Rd Runnemede (08078) *(G-9719)*
General Commis Archives & Hstr 973 408-3189
36 Madison Ave Madison (07940) *(G-5723)*
General Dynamics Glbl IMG Tech 973 335-2230
222 New Rd Ste 1 Parsippany (07054) *(G-8022)*
General Electric Company 973 887-6635
700 Parsippany Rd Parsippany (07054) *(G-8023)*
General Electric Company 201 866-2161
6001 Tonnelle Ave North Bergen (07047) *(G-7453)*
General Electronic Engineering (PA) 732 381-1144
132 W Main St Rahway (07065) *(G-9193)*
General Film Products Inc 908 351-0454
107 Trumbull St Ste 302 Elizabeth (07206) *(G-2738)*
General Foam, East Rutherford *Also called Pmc Inc* *(G-2317)*
General Foundries Inc (PA) 732 951-9001
1 Progress Rd North Brunswick (08902) *(G-7517)*
General Glass Intl Corp 201 553-1850
101 Venture Way Secaucus (07094) *(G-9887)*
General Graphics Corporation (PA) 201 664-4083
63 Briarcliff Rd Hillsdale (07642) *(G-4383)*
General Hydraulics, Springfield *Also called Barworth Inc* *(G-10541)*
General Machine Kraft, Phillipsburg *Also called N E R Associates Inc* *(G-8661)*
General Magnaplate California 805 642-6262
1331 W Edgar Rd Linden (07036) *(G-5379)*
General Magnaplate Corporation (PA) 908 862-6200
1331 W Edgar Rd Linden (07036) *(G-5380)*
General Magnaplate Wisconsin 800 441-6173
1331 W Edgar Rd Linden (07036) *(G-5381)*
General Mch Experimental Works 201 843-9035
117 Gertrude Ave Ste 1 Paramus (07652) *(G-7872)*
General Metal & Glass Co, Camden *Also called William Duling* *(G-1089)*
General Metal Manufacturing Co 973 386-1818
170 State Route 10 East Hanover (07936) *(G-2218)*
General Pallet LLC 732 549-1000
97 River Rd Flemington (08822) *(G-3445)*
General Pencil Company Inc (PA) 201 653-5351
67 Fleet St Jersey City (07306) *(G-4759)*
General Performance Products, Parsippany *Also called Chemtrade Chemicals Corp* *(G-7968)*
General Plastics Corporation 973 429-5625
55 La France Ave Bloomfield (07003) *(G-511)*
General Plastics Group 973 748-5500
55 La France Ave Bloomfield (07003) *(G-512)*

General Polygon Systems Inc 800 825-1655
203 Peterson St Millville (08332) *(G-6304)*

General Reliance Corporation 973 361-1400
88 Ford Rd Ste 20 Denville (07834) *(G-2040)*

General Sign Co Inc 856 753-3535
105 Chestnut Ave West Berlin (08091) *(G-11724)*

General Stamping Co Inc 973 627-9500
309 State Route 94 Columbia (07832) *(G-1797)*

General Sullivan Group Inc (PA) 609 745-5004
85 Route 31 N Pennington (08534) *(G-8451)*

General Sullivan Group Inc 609 745-5000
85 Route 31 N Pennington (08534) *(G-8452)*

General Tool Specialties Inc 908 874-3040
284 Sunnymeade Rd Hillsborough (08844) *(G-4335)*

General Tools & Instrs Co LLC (PA) 212 431-6100
75 Seaview Dr Secaucus (07094) *(G-9888)*

General Tools Mfg Co LLC 201 770-1380
75 Seaview Dr Secaucus (07094) *(G-9889)*

General Wire & Stamping Co 973 366-8080
1 Emery Ave Ste 3 Randolph (07869) *(G-9278)*

Generant Company Inc 814 337-0380
1865 Route 23 S Butler (07405) *(G-1004)*

Generation Brands 856 764-0500
6 Campus Dr Burlington (08016) *(G-977)*

Genesis Bps LLC 201 708-1400
465 Route 17 S Ramsey (07446) *(G-9241)*

Genesis Lighting Mfg Inc 908 352-6720
107 Trumbull St Ste 104 Elizabethport (07206) *(G-2784)*

Genesis Marketing Group Inc 201 836-1392
269 Edgemont Ter Teaneck (07666) *(G-10754)*

Geneva Metal Products Co Inc 973 472-3073
157 10th St Passaic (07055) *(G-8144)*

Genevieves Home Made Candy Sp, Garfield *Also called Genevieves Inc (G-3737)*

Genevieves Inc 973 772-8816
174 Ray St Garfield (07026) *(G-3737)*

Genexosome Technologies Inc 646 762-4517
4400 Route 9 N Freehold (07728) *(G-3657)*

Genie House Corp (PA) 609 859-0600
139 Red Lion Rd Southampton (08088) *(G-10473)*

Genlyte Thomas Group LLC (HQ) 800 825-5844
200 Franklin Square Dr Somerset (08873) *(G-10104)*

Genomesafe LLC 203 676-3752
4 Linden Ave West Orange (07052) *(G-11895)*

Gentek Inc (PA) 973 515-0900
90 E Halsey Rd Ste 301 Parsippany (07054) *(G-8024)*

Gentek Building Products Inc 732 381-0900
11 Cragwood Rd Avenel (07001) *(G-134)*

Genua & Mulligan Printing 973 894-1500
1 Trenton Ave Clifton (07011) *(G-1626)*

Genzyme Biosurgery, Ridgefield *Also called Genzyme Corporation (G-9362)*

Genzyme Corporation 973 256-2106
25 Madison Rd Totowa (07512) *(G-10948)*

Genzyme Corporation 201 313-9660
1125 Pleasantview Ter Ridgefield (07657) *(G-9362)*

Geolytics Inc 908 707-1505
3322 Us Highway 22 # 806 Branchburg (08876) *(G-663)*

George Brummer 908 232-1904
125 E Broad St Westfield (07090) *(G-11925)*

George Ciocher Inc 732 818-3495
1241 Birmingham Ave Toms River (08757) *(G-10880)*

George Glove Company Inc 201 251-1200
301 Greenwood Ave Ste 1 Midland Park (07432) *(G-6226)*

George H Buchanan Company 856 241-3960
2 Mallard Ct Swedesboro (08085) *(G-10698)*

George H Buchanan Printing, Swedesboro *Also called George H Buchanan
Company (G-10698)*

George J Bender Inc 908 687-0081
1 Milltown Ct Union (07083) *(G-11189)*

George Pnterman Kitchens Baths, Manasquan *Also called Sanford & Birdsall Inc (G-5880)*

George Press Inc 973 992-7797
74 S Livingston Ave Livingston (07039) *(G-5533)*

George Scher Engineering, Lebanon *Also called Weber and Scher Mfg Co Inc (G-5303)*

Georges Wine and Spirits Galle 973 948-9950
7 Main St Branchville (07826) *(G-730)*

Georgia-Pacific, Camden *Also called Bestwall LLC (G-1044)*

Georgia-Pacific LLC 908 995-2228
623 Riegelsville Rd Milford (08848) *(G-6245)*

Gep, Clark *Also called Nb Ventures Inc (G-1509)*

Gerardi Press Inc 973 627-2600
3 Luger Rd Ste 3 # 3 Denville (07834) *(G-2041)*

Gerber Products Company (HQ) 973 593-7500
12 Vreeland Rd Fl 2 Florham Park (07932) *(G-3504)*

Gerdau Amrsteel Sayreville Inc 732 721-6600
N Crossman Rd Sayreville (08872) *(G-9821)*

Gericke USA Inc 855 888-0088
14 Worlds Fair Dr Ste C Somerset (08873) *(G-10105)*

Gerin Corporation Inc 732 774-3256
1109 7th Ave Neptune (07753) *(G-6914)*

Gerresheimer Glass Inc (HQ) 856 692-3600
537 Crystal Ave Vineland (08360) *(G-11360)*

Gerresheimer Glass Inc 856 507-5852
91 W Forest Grove Rd Vineland (08360) *(G-11361)*

Gervens Enterprises Inc 973 838-1600
122 Hamburg Tpke Ste D Bloomingdale (07403) *(G-544)*

Getinge Group Logistics Americ 973 709-6000
45 Barbour Pond Dr Wayne (07470) *(G-11640)*

GF Supplies LLC (PA) 336 539-1666
319 E 54th St Elmwood Park (07407) *(G-2821)*

Ggb North America LLC (HQ) 856 848-3200
700 Mid Atlantic Pkwy Thorofare (08086) *(G-10821)*

Gia-Tek LLC 973 228-0875
66 Westover Ave West Caldwell (07006) *(G-11777)*

Giambri's Candy, Clementon *Also called Giambris Quality Sweets Inc (G-1532)*

Giambris Quality Sweets Inc 856 783-1099
26 Brand Ave Clementon (08021) *(G-1532)*

Giannella Deli, Paterson *Also called Lo Presti & Sons LLC (G-8325)*

Giant Stl Fabricators Erectors 908 241-6766
197 E Highland Pkwy Roselle (07203) *(G-9671)*

Gibbons Company Ltd 441 294-5047
614 Progress St Elizabeth (07201) *(G-2739)*

Gibraltar Laboratories Inc (PA) 973 227-6882
122 Fairfield Rd Fairfield (07004) *(G-3209)*

Gifford Group Inc 212 569-8500
35 Obrien St Kearny (07032) *(G-4878)*

Gilbert Storms Jr 973 835-5729
1456 Ringwood Ave Apt 1 Haskell (07420) *(G-4207)*

Gilbys, Haskell *Also called Gilbert Storms Jr (G-4207)*

Gild-N-Son Manufacturing, Kearny *Also called Belleville Corp (G-4863)*

Gill Assoc Idntfcation Systems, Wayne *Also called Gill Associates LLC (G-11641)*

Gill Associates LLC 973 835-5456
2025 Hamburg Tpke Ste M Wayne (07470) *(G-11641)*

Gillespie Industries, Vineland *Also called P J Gillespie Inc (G-11387)*

Ginsey Industries Inc 856 933-1300
2078 Center Square Rd Swedesboro (08085) *(G-10699)*

Gio Vali Handbag Corp 973 279-3032
463 Grand St Paterson (07505) *(G-8276)*

Giovali Handbag, Paterson *Also called Gio Vali Handbag Corp (G-8276)*

Givaudan East, East Hanover *Also called Givaudan Fragrances Corp (G-2221)*

Givaudan Flavors, East Hanover *Also called Givaudan Fragrances Corp (G-2220)*

Givaudan Flavors Corporation 973 463-8192
6 Santa Fe Way Cranbury (08512) *(G-1834)*

Givaudan Flavors Corporation 609 409-6200
6 Santa Fe Way Cranbury (08512) *(G-1835)*

Givaudan Flavors Corporation 973 386-9800
245 Merry Ln East Hanover (07936) *(G-2219)*

Givaudan Fragrances Corp 973 386-9800
245 Merry Ln East Hanover (07936) *(G-2220)*

Givaudan Fragrances Corp 973 576-9500
717 Ridgedale Ave East Hanover (07936) *(G-2221)*

Givaudan Fragrances Corp 973 560-1939
717 Ridgedale Ave East Hanover (07936) *(G-2222)*

Givaudan Fragrances Corp 973 448-6500
300 Waterloo Valley Rd Budd Lake (07828) *(G-930)*

GL Associates, Jersey City *Also called GL Consulting Inc (G-4760)*

GL Consulting Inc (PA) 201 938-0200
210 Hudson St Ste 1000 Jersey City (07311) *(G-4760)*

Glamorous Glo 732 361-3235
42 Carolyn Ct Eatontown (07724) *(G-2396)*

Glasco Uv LLC 201 934-3348
126 Christie Ave Mahwah (07430) *(G-5776)*

Glasplex LLC 973 940-8940
8 Estate Dr Sussex (07461) *(G-10671)*

Glass Cycle Systems Inc 973 838-0034
5 Mathews Ave Riverdale (07457) *(G-9481)*

Glass Dynamics LLC 856 205-1503
2662 Hance Bridge Rd Vineland (08361) *(G-11362)*

Glass House, The, Lumberton *Also called Proco Inc (G-5662)*

Glass Warehouse 856 825-1400
1101 Wheaton Ave Millville (08332) *(G-6305)*

Glassblowerscom LLC (PA) 856 232-7898
234 Bells Lake Rd Blackwood (08012) *(G-479)*

Glassboro News & Food Store 856 881-1181
255 E High St Glassboro (08028) *(G-3806)*

Glasscare Inc 201 943-1122
666 Anderson Ave Cliffside Park (07010) *(G-1540)*

Glasseal Products Inc 732 370-9100
485 Oberlin Ave S Lakewood (08701) *(G-5129)*

Glassman High Voltage Inc (PA) 908 638-3800
124 W Main St High Bridge (08829) *(G-4296)*

Glassroots Inc 973 353-9555
10 Bleeker St Newark (07102) *(G-7170)*

Glassworks Studio Inc 973 656-0800
151 South St Ste B103 Morristown (07960) *(G-6710)*

Glastron Inc 856 692-0500
510 N West Blvd Vineland (08360) *(G-11363)*

Glaxosmithkline Consumer (HQ) 251 591-4188
184 Libery Corner Rd Warren (07059) *(G-11549)*

Glaxosmithkline Consumer Hlth (HQ) 215 751-5046
184 Liberty Corner Rd Warren (07059) *(G-11550)*

Glaxosmithkline LLC 856 952-6023
505 S Vineyard Blvd Collingswood (08108) *(G-1770)*

Glaxosmithkline LLC 609 472-8175
24 Cohasset Ln Cherry Hill (08003) *(G-1371)*

Glebar Company, Ramsey *Also called Glebar Operating LLC* *(G-9242)*

Glebar Operating LLC 201 337-1500
565 E Crescent Ave Ramsey (07446) *(G-9242)*

Gleeson Agency, East Rutherford *Also called Dawn Bible Students Assn* *(G-2293)*

Gleicher Manufacturing Corp 908 233-2211
851 Jerusalem Rd Scotch Plains (07076) *(G-9849)*

Glen G Coats 908 236-2620
119 Main St Lebanon (08833) *(G-5287)*

Glen Magnetics Inc 908 454-3717
1165 3rd Ave Alpha (08865) *(G-41)*

Glen Rock Ham, Caldwell *Also called Al and John Inc* *(G-1024)*

Glen Rock Stair Corp 201 337-9595
551 Commerce St Franklin Lakes (07417) *(G-3618)*

Glen-Gery Brick, Hillsborough *Also called Glen-Gery Corporation* *(G-4336)*

Glen-Gery Corporation 908 359-5111
75 Hamilton Rd Hillsborough (08844) *(G-4336)*

Glenbrook Technologies Inc 973 361-8866
11 Emery Ave Randolph (07869) *(G-9279)*

Glenburnie Feed & Grain 856 986-8128
87 Chapel Hill Rd Mount Laurel (08054) *(G-6800)*

Glenmark Phrmceuticals Inc USA (HQ) 201 684-8000
750 Corporate Dr Mahwah (07430) *(G-5777)*

Glenmark Therapeutics Inc USA 201 684-8000
750 Corporate Dr Mahwah (07430) *(G-5778)*

Glenro Inc (PA) 973 279-5900
39 Mcbride Ave Paterson (07501) *(G-8277)*

Glentech Inc 908 685-2205
46 4th St Somerville (08876) *(G-10212)*

Glenwood LLC 201 569-0050
111 Cedar Ln Englewood (07631) *(G-2901)*

Glenwood-Palisades, Englewood *Also called Glenwood LLC* *(G-2901)*

Glidden Professional Paint Ctr, Elizabeth *Also called PPG Architectural Finishes Inc* *(G-2767)*

Glitterex Corp 908 272-9121
7 Commerce Dr Cranford (07016) *(G-1908)*

Glitterwrap Inc (HQ) 800 745-4883
701 Ford Rd Ste 1 Rockaway (07866) *(G-9570)*

Global Beverage Corporation 201 599-5925
700 Kinderkamack Rd # 314 Oradell (07649) *(G-7810)*

Global Business Dimensions Inc (PA) 973 831-5866
220 W Parkway Ste 8 Pompton Plains (07444) *(G-8960)*

Global Colorants Inc 973 751-2227
5 Macbeth Dr Old Bridge (08857) *(G-7780)*

Global Commodities Exportacao 201 613-1532
126 Jackson St Newark (07105) *(G-7171)*

Global Direct Marketing Group 856 427-6116
229 Kings Hwy E Haddonfield (08033) *(G-4060)*

Global Ecology Corporation (PA) 973 655-9001
101 Eisenhower Pkwy # 300 Roseland (07068) *(G-9650)*

Global Express Freight Inc 201 376-6613
136 W Central Ave Bergenfield (07621) *(G-385)*

Global Force and Artic Bloc, Newark *Also called Global Manufacturing LLC* *(G-7172)*

Global Graphics Intergration 973 334-9653
14 Willard Ln Towaco (07082) *(G-10996)*

Global IDS Inc 609 683-1066
182 Nassau St Ste 202 Princeton (08542) *(G-9050)*

Global Industries Inc (PA) 856 596-3390
17 W Stow Rd Marlton (08053) *(G-5977)*

Global Ingredients Inc 973 278-6677
317 9th Ave Paterson (07514) *(G-8278)*

Global Manufacturing LLC 973 494-5413
35 William St Fl 2 Newark (07102) *(G-7172)*

Global Plastics, Moonachie *Also called Reachman International Corp* *(G-6539)*

Global Power Technology Inc (PA) 732 287-3680
1000 New Durham Rd Edison (08817) *(G-2528)*

Global Prtners In Shelding Inc 973 574-9077
5 Just Rd Fairfield (07004) *(G-3210)*

Global Seven Inc 973 209-7474
198 Green Pond Rd Ste 4 Rockaway (07866) *(G-9571)*

Global Spclty Products-Usa Inc 609 518-7577
10 Eagle Ave Ste 500 Mount Holly (08060) *(G-6771)*

Global Strategy Institute A 973 615-7447
55 Park Ave Unit 35 Bloomfield (07003) *(G-513)*

Global Teak Inc 609 208-2854
530 S Rte 73 Winslow (08095) *(G-12132)*

Global Weavers Corp 973 824-5500
9-13 Dey St Newark (07103) *(G-7173)*

Global Wire & Cable Inc 973 471-1000
61 Willet St Ste 4b Passaic (07055) *(G-8145)*

Globe Casing Co, Carlstadt *Also called Globe Packaging Co Inc* *(G-1163)*

Globe Die-Cutting Products Inc 732 494-7744
76 Liberty St Metuchen (08840) *(G-6105)*

Globe Engineering Corp 609 898-0349
1213 Delaware Ave Cape May (08204) *(G-1101)*

Globe Industries Corp 973 992-8990
48 Industrial St W Clifton (07012) *(G-1627)*

Globe Manufacturing Sales Co, Mountainside *Also called A K Stamping Co Inc* *(G-6865)*

Globe Metals Inc 973 589-2563
7 Avenue L Newark (07105) *(G-7174)*

Globe Packaging Co Inc 201 896-1144
368 Paterson Plank Rd Carlstadt (07072) *(G-1163)*

Globe Pharma Inc 732 296-9700
2b Janine Pl New Brunswick (08901) *(G-6963)*

Globe Photo Engraving Co LLC 201 489-2300
19 N Washington Ave Ste 1 Little Ferry (07643) *(G-5506)*

Globe Photo Engraving Corp 201 489-2300
19 N Washington Ave Little Ferry (07643) *(G-5507)*

Globe Scientific Inc 201 599-1400
610 Winters Ave Ste 1 Paramus (07652) *(G-7873)*

Globepharma Inc 732 296-9700
2b Janine Pl New Brunswick (08901) *(G-6964)*

Globtek Inc (PA) 201 784-1000
186 Veterans Dr Northvale (07647) *(G-7582)*

Glocal Expertise Llc 718 928-3839
185 Zabriskie St Jersey City (07307) *(G-4761)*

Glopak Corp 908 753-8735
132 Case Dr South Plainfield (07080) *(G-10373)*

Gloucester City Box Works LLC 856 456-9032
775 Charles St Gloucester City (08030) *(G-3837)*

Gloucester County Times 856 845-7484
309 S Broad St Woodbury (08096) *(G-12162)*

Glow Tube Inc 609 268-7707
83 Springers Brook Rd Shamong (08088) *(G-9969)*

Glue Fold Inc 973 575-8400
40 Webro Rd Clifton (07012) *(G-1628)*

Gluefast Company Inc 732 918-4600
3535 State Route 66 Ste 1 Neptune (07753) *(G-6915)*

Glyderm, Morristown *Also called Lautus Phrmceuticals Ltd Lblty* *(G-6721)*

Glysortia LLC 715 426-5358
281 Hampshire Dr Plainsboro (08536) *(G-8884)*

GM Construction, Fairfield *Also called Michele Maddalena* *(G-3260)*

GM Precision Machine, Sicklerville *Also called Gary R Marzili* *(G-10019)*

GMC-I New Wrld Btiligungs GMBH, Edison *Also called Global Power Technology Inc* *(G-2528)*

Gmp Publications Inc 609 859-3400
4 Linda Ln Ste B Southampton (08088) *(G-10474)*

Gmpc Printing 973 546-6060
1 Trenton Ave Clifton (07011) *(G-1629)*

Gms Litho Corp 973 575-9400
16 Passaic Ave Unit 3 Fairfield (07004) *(G-3211)*

Go Foton Corporation (PA) 732 412-7375
28 Worlds Fair Dr Somerset (08873) *(G-10106)*

Go R Design LLC 609 286-2146
74 Hemlock Dr New Egypt (08533) *(G-7015)*

Go Waddle Inc 301 452-5084
23 Baldwin Dr Berkeley Heights (07922) *(G-411)*

Goetz & Ruschmann Inc 973 383-9270
1 Brooks Plz Newton (07860) *(G-7391)*

Goffco Industries LLC 973 492-0150
10 Park Pl Ste 300 Butler (07405) *(G-1005)*

Gogreen Power Inc 732 994-5901
4675 Us Highway 9 Howell (07731) *(G-4555)*

Gold Buyers At Mall LLC (PA) 201 512-5780
1 International Blvd # 200 Mahwah (07495) *(G-5779)*

Gold Signature Incorporated 732 777-9170
1260 Stelton Rd Piscataway (08854) *(G-8769)*

Gold Star Distribution LLC 973 882-5300
120 Eagle Rock Ave # 326 East Hanover (07936) *(G-2223)*

Golden Champion North America 732 481-9000
1405 State Route 18 # 205 Old Bridge (08857) *(G-7781)*

Golden Fluff Inc 732 367-5448
118 Monmouth Ave Lakewood (08701) *(G-5130)*

Golden Metal Products Corp 973 399-1157
100 Hoffman Pl Ste 1 Hillside (07205) *(G-4409)*

Golden Platter Foods Inc 973 344-8770
37 Tompkins Point Rd Newark (07114) *(G-7175)*

Golden Rule Creations Inc 201 337-4050
250 Terrace Rd Franklin Lakes (07417) *(G-3619)*

Golden Rule Inc 856 663-3074
7150 N Park Dr Ste 620 Pennsauken (08109) *(G-8516)*

Golden Treasure Imports Inc 732 723-1830
522 Us Highway 9 Englishtown (07726) *(G-2992)*

Golden Tropics Ltd 973 484-0202
1489-1495 Mccarter Hwy Newark (07104) *(G-7176)*

Golden W Ppr Converting Corp 908 412-8889
121 Helen St South Plainfield (07080) *(G-10374)*

Goldsmith & Revere, Ridgefield Park *Also called Dmg America LLC* *(G-9404)*

Goldstar Performance Products, East Hanover *Also called Gold Star Distribution LLC* *(G-2223)*

Goldstein & Burton Inc 201 440-0065
20 Potash Rd Oakland (07436) *(G-7690)*

(G-0000) Company's Geographic Section entry number

Goldstein Setting Co Inc 908 964-1034
2464 Morris Ave Union (07083) *(G-11190)*

Golf Odyssey LLC 973 564-6223
60 Woodcrest Ave Short Hills (07078) *(G-9978)*

Good As Gold Jewelers Inc 732 286-1111
226 Route 37 W Ste 9 Toms River (08755) *(G-10881)*

Good Earth Teas Inc 831 423-7913
155 Chestnut Ridge Rd Montvale (07645) *(G-6457)*

Good Humor/Breyers, Englewood Cliffs *Also called Conopco Inc (G-2955)*

Good Impressions Inc 856 461-3232
28 E Scott St Riverside (08075) *(G-9498)*

Good Impressions Inc (PA) 908 689-3071
325 W Washington Ave Washington (07882) *(G-11581)*

Good Neighbor Pharmacy, Florence *Also called Boyds Pharmacy Inc (G-3476)*

Good To Go Inc 856 627-8241
310 S Burnt Mill Rd Voorhees (08043) *(G-11431)*

Goodlite Products Inc 718 697-7502
500 Division St Perth Amboy (08861) *(G-8615)*

Goodrich Corporation 973 237-2700
20 Commerce Way Totowa (07512) *(G-10949)*

Gopole, Pompton Plains *Also called Ar2 Products LLC (G-8953)*

Goralski Embroidery, Park Ridge *Also called Goralski Inc (G-7921)*

Goralski Inc 201 573-1529
4 Marti Rd Park Ridge (07656) *(G-7921)*

Gordon Brush Mfg Co Inc 973 827-4600
15 Park Dr Franklin (07416) *(G-3600)*

Gordon Fergusson Intr Dctg Ser, Maplewood *Also called Gordon Frgson Intr Dsigns
Svcs (G-5920)*

Gordon Frgson Intr Dsigns Svcs 973 378-2330
205 Rutgers St Maplewood (07040) *(G-5920)*

Gordon International Inc 732 431-3361
6 Paragon Way Ste 110 Freehold (07728) *(G-3658)*

Gordon Terminal Service Co PA 201 437-8300
2 Hook Rd Bayonne (07002) *(G-229)*

Gordon Terminal Service Co. NJ, Bayonne *Also called Gordon Terminal Service Co
PA (G-229)*

Gorgias Press 732 699-0343
46 Orris Ave Piscataway (08854) *(G-8770)*

Gorgo Pallet Company, Vineland *Also called Lt Chini Inc (G-11381)*

Gorman Industries Inc 973 345-5424
700 21st Ave Paterson (07513) *(G-8279)*

Gorton Heating Corp 908 276-1323
546 South Ave E Cranford (07016) *(G-1909)*

Gotham Group, The, Egg Harbor Township *Also called Winsome Digital Inc (G-2700)*

Gotham Ink of New England Inc (HQ) 201 478-5600
100 North St Teterboro (07608) *(G-10798)*

Gotham Project, Bayonne *Also called GP Wine Works LLC (G-230)*

Gottscho Printing Systems, Branchburg *Also called Flexlink Systems Inc (G-661)*

Gourmet Basics, Piscataway *Also called Snack Innovations Inc (G-8812)*

Gourmet Kitchen LLC 732 775-5222
1238 Corlies Ave Neptune (07753) *(G-6916)*

Gowasabi, Palisades Park *Also called Sushi House Inc (G-7844)*

Goya Foods Inc 201 348-4900
100 Seaview Dr Secaucus (07094) *(G-9890)*

Goya Foods Inc 201 865-3470
650 New County Rd Secaucus (07094) *(G-9891)*

GP Acoustics (us) Inc 732 683-2356
10 Timber Ln Marlboro (07746) *(G-5942)*

GP Chemicals Inc 201 869-2200
7225 Bergenline Ave 3b North Bergen (07047) *(G-7454)*

GP Jager Inc 973 750-1180
143 Miller Rd Kinnelon (07405) *(G-5035)*

GP Wine Works LLC 201 997-6055
82 E 3rd St Bayonne (07002) *(G-230)*

Gps Specialty Doors, Fairfield *Also called Global Prtners In Shelding Inc (G-3210)*

Gpschartscom 609 226-8842
5021 Winchester Ave Ventnor City (08406) *(G-11292)*

Gpt Inc 732 446-2400
227 State Route 33 Manalapan (07726) *(G-5849)*

Gr Stone LLC 908 925-7290
91 Market St Kenilworth (07033) *(G-4959)*

Grab Em Snacks Ltd Lblty Co 908 333-3229
216 Us Highway 206 Hillsborough (08844) *(G-4337)*

Graduation Outlet, Fairfield *Also called Trim and Tassels LLC (G-3331)*

Grafwed Internet Media Studios 201 632-1771
37 Millington Dr Midland Park (07432) *(G-6227)*

Graham Graphic Group Inc 973 827-6177
8 Main St Ogdensburg (07439) *(G-7771)*

Graham Packaging Company LP 717 849-8500
201 Elizabeth St Bordentown (08505) *(G-597)*

Gram Equipment, Trenton *Also called Alliance Food Equipment (G-11016)*

Gram Equipment (PA) 201 750-6500
1 S Gold Dr Hamilton (08691) *(G-4107)*

Gramercy Products Inc 212 868-2559
600 Mdwlands Pkwy Ste 131 Secaucus (07094) *(G-9892)*

Gran All Mrble Tile Imprts Inc (PA) 856 354-4747
932 Marlton Pike W Cherry Hill (08002) *(G-1372)*

Granco Group LLC 973 515-4721
101 Eisenhower Pkwy # 300 Roseland (07068) *(G-9651)*

Grand Displays Inc 201 994-1500
3725 Tonnelle Ave North Bergen (07047) *(G-7455)*

Grand Displays Inc (PA) 201 994-1500
1700 Suckle Hwy Pennsauken (08110) *(G-8517)*

Grand Life Inc 201 556-8975
40 Broad St Carlstadt (07072) *(G-1164)*

Grandpa Po's Nutra Nuts, Ridgewood *Also called Nutra Nuts Inc (G-9427)*

Grandview Printing Co Inc 973 890-0006
33 W End Rd Totowa (07512) *(G-10950)*

Granite and Marble Assoc Inc 908 416-1100
310 Tremont Ave North Plainfield (07063) *(G-7559)*

Granite Packaging Supply Co (HQ) 856 727-1010
111 Whittendale Dr Moorestown (08057) *(G-6579)*

Grant Industries, Elmwood Park *Also called Carib Chemical Co Inc (G-2809)*

Grant Industries Inc 201 791-8700
103 Main Ave Elmwood Park (07407) *(G-2822)*

Grant Industries Inc (PA) 201 791-6700
125 Main Ave Elmwood Park (07407) *(G-2823)*

Grant Industries Inc 201 791-6700
125 Main Ave Elmwood Park (07407) *(G-2824)*

Granulation Technology Inc 973 276-0740
12 Industrial Rd Fairfield (07004) *(G-3212)*

Granville Concrete Products 973 584-6653
1076 State Route 10 Randolph (07869) *(G-9280)*

Grape Bginnings Handson Winery 732 380-7356
151 Industrial Way E B Eatontown (07724) *(G-2397)*

Graph Tech Sales & Service 201 218-1749
6 Farmstead Ln Fairfield (07004) *(G-3213)*

Graphcorr LLC 732 355-0088
4 Corn Rd Dayton (08810) *(G-1967)*

Graphic Action Inc 908 213-0055
296 S Main St Phillipsburg (08865) *(G-8650)*

Graphic Arts Printing 201 343-6554
170 Parmelee Ave Hawthorne (07506) *(G-4237)*

Graphic Arts Systems, Ocean *Also called Eagle Systems Inc (G-7723)*

Graphic Concepts, Bound Brook *Also called Star Promotions Inc (G-624)*

Graphic Equipment Corporation (PA) 732 494-5350
55 Wester Ave Metuchen (08840) *(G-6106)*

Graphic Equipment Corporation 732 548-4400
19 Wester Ave Metuchen (08840) *(G-6107)*

Graphic Express Menu Co Inc 973 685-0022
200 Clifton Blvd Ste 6 Clifton (07011) *(G-1630)*

Graphic Image 856 262-8900
1401 N Blck Horse Pike A Williamstown (08094) *(G-12088)*

Graphic Imagery Inc 908 755-2882
556 Central Ave Ste 1 New Providence (07974) *(G-7038)*

Graphic Impressions, Middlesex *Also called Promo Graphic Inc (G-6191)*

Graphic Impressions Inc 201 487-8788
316 Prospect Ave Apt 10f Hackensack (07601) *(G-3921)*

Graphic Impressions Prtg Co 856 728-2266
4391 Route 42 Blackwood (08012) *(G-480)*

Graphic Management 908 654-8400
21 Lafayette Pl Kearny (07032) *(G-4879)*

Graphic Packaging Intl Inc 973 709-9100
5 Haul Rd Wayne (07470) *(G-11642)*

Graphic Packaging Intl LLC 732 424-2100
5 Haul Rd Wayne (07470) *(G-11643)*

Graphic Presentations Systems 732 981-1120
262 Old New Brnswk Rd F Piscataway (08854) *(G-8771)*

Graphic Solutions & Signs LLC 201 343-7446
82 Burlews Ct Hackensack (07601) *(G-3922)*

Graphic Systems, Piscataway *Also called Graphic Presentations Systems (G-8771)*

Graphicolor Corporation 856 691-2507
1370 S Main Rd Vineland (08360) *(G-11364)*

Graphics Depot Inc 973 927-8200
11 Middlebury Blvd Ste 4 Randolph (07869) *(G-9281)*

Grass Valley Usa LLC 201 818-4050
135 Chestnut Ridge Rd # 3 Montvale (07645) *(G-6458)*

Grassman-Blake Inc 973 379-6170
58 E Willow St Millburn (07041) *(G-6251)*

Grateful Ped Inc 973 478-6511
339 10th St Saddle Brook (07663) *(G-9767)*

Graver Chemical Products, Newark *Also called Graver Water Systems LLC (G-7177)*

Graver Water Division, New Providence *Also called Graver Water Systems LLC (G-7039)*

Graver Water Systems LLC (HQ) 908 516-1400
675 Central Ave Ste 3 New Providence (07974) *(G-7039)*

Graver Water Systems LLC 973 465-2380
72 Lockwood St Newark (07105) *(G-7177)*

Gravity Vault 732 856-9599
37 Kanes Ln Middletown (07748) *(G-6215)*

Gray Hair Software Inc 856 924-2253
124 Gaither Dr Ste 160 Mount Laurel (08054) *(G-6801)*

Gray Overhead Door Co 908 355-3889
439 3rd Ave Elizabeth (07206) *(G-2740)*

Gray Star Inc 973 398-3331
200 Valley Rd Ste 103 Mount Arlington (07856) *(G-6755)*

A
L
P
H
A
B
E
T
I
C

Grayden Industries Inc 201 761-0788
  84 Constitution Way Jersey City (07305) *(G-4762)*

Graydon Products Inc 856 234-9513
  800 Glen Ave Moorestown (08057) *(G-6580)*

Graytor Printing Company Inc 201 933-0100
  149 Park Ave Lyndhurst (07071) *(G-5684)*

Grease N Go 856 784-6555
  334 S White Horse Pike Magnolia (08049) *(G-5740)*

Great Eastern Color Lith 201 843-5656
  210 E State Rt 4 Ste 211 Paramus (07652) *(G-7874)*

Great Falls Metalworks Inc 973 523-6811
  301 E 22nd St Paterson (07514) *(G-8280)*

Great Northern Commercial Svcs 908 475-8855
  401 Greenwich St Belvidere (07823) *(G-373)*

Great Northern Corporation 856 241-0080
  500a Pedricktown Rd Swedesboro (08085) *(G-10700)*

Great Notch Industries Inc 201 343-8110
  140 Liberty St Hackensack (07601) *(G-3923)*

Great Railing Inc 856 875-0050
  1086 N Black Horse Pike Williamstown (08094) *(G-12089)*

Great Socks LLC (PA) 856 964-9700
  7001 N Park Dr Pennsauken (08109) *(G-8518)*

Greater ATL Cy Golf Assn LLC 609 652-1800
  401 S New York Rd Galloway (08205) *(G-3711)*

Greater Media Newspapers (HQ) 732 358-5200
  198 Us Highway 9 Ste 100 Englishtown (07726) *(G-2993)*

Greater Media Newspapers 732 254-7004
  201 Hartle St Ste B Sayreville (08872) *(G-9822)*

Greater New Jersey Diamnd Exch 732 752-6446
  299 Us Highway 22 Ste 22 Green Brook (08812) *(G-3856)*

Greater New York Box Co Inc 609 631-7900
  1400 E State St Trenton (08609) *(G-11060)*

Greco Industries LLC 732 919-6200
  7 Colts Gait Ln Colts Neck (07722) *(G-1787)*

Green Apple Home Imprv LLC 201 300-5554
  96 Belmont Ave Apt 2 Garfield (07026) *(G-3738)*

Green Building Solutions, Pennington *Also called Commercial Pdts Svcs Group Inc (G-8447)*

Green Distribution LLC 201 293-4381
  565 Windsor Dr Ste 1 Secaucus (07094) *(G-9893)*

Green Fresh Fruit Salad, Pleasantville *Also called Salad Chef Inc (G-8913)*

Green Horse Media LLC 856 933-0222
  101 Haag Ave Bellmawr (08031) *(G-341)*

Green Labs LLC 862 220-4845
  211 Warren St Ste 206 Newark (07103) *(G-7178)*

Green Land & Logging LLC 908 894-2361
  328 Rosemont Ringoes Rd Stockton (08559) *(G-10611)*

Green Life America, Elmwood Park *Also called Interntnal Globl Solutions Inc (G-2826)*

Green Power Chemical LLC 973 770-5600
  151 Sparta Stanhope Rd Hopatcong (07843) *(G-4536)*

Green Power Chemical Sciences, Hopatcong *Also called Green Power Chemical LLC (G-4536)*

Green Village Packing Co, Green Village *Also called Kleemeyer & Merkel Inc (G-3865)*

Greenbaum Interiors LLC (PA) 973 279-3000
  101 Washington St Paterson (07505) *(G-8281)*

Greenbrook Stairs Inc 908 221-9145
  14 Dayton St Bernardsville (07924) *(G-450)*

Greenbuilt Intl Bldg Co 609 300-9091
  1081 Pndleton Ct Voorhees Voorhees (08043) *(G-11432)*

Greene Bros Spclty Cof Rasters (PA) 908 979-0022
  313 High St Hackettstown (07840) *(G-4009)*

Greene's Beans Cafe, Hackettstown *Also called Greene Bros Spclty Cof Rasters (G-4009)*

Greener Corners Ltd Lblty Co 201 638-2218
  1178 W Laurelton Pkwy Teaneck (07666) *(G-10755)*

Greener Corp (PA) 732 341-3880
  4 Helmly St Bayville (08721) *(G-255)*

Greenproducts.info, Rockaway *Also called Internet-Sales USA Corporation (G-9575)*

Greenrock Recycling LLC 908 713-0008
  3 Frontage Rd Clinton (08809) *(G-1750)*

Greenway Products & Svcs LLC (PA) 732 442-0200
  14 Home News Row New Brunswick (08901) *(G-6965)*

Greetingtap 347 731-4263
  832 Spicer Ave South Plainfield (07080) *(G-10375)*

Gregory Associates, Hasbrouck Heights *Also called Pabin Associates Inc (G-4197)*

Gregory Press Inc 908 686-6473
  7 Mark Rd Ste A Kenilworth (07033) *(G-4960)*

Greif Inc 609 448-5300
  200 Rike Dr Millstone Township (08535) *(G-6264)*

Grenade Supply Co 267 968-3115
  278 N Union St Ste 135 Lambertville (08530) *(G-5213)*

Grewe Plastics Inc 973 485-7602
  123 S 15th St Newark (07107) *(G-7179)*

Grey House Publishing Inc 201 968-0500
  2 University Plz Hackensack (07601) *(G-3924)*

Greycell Labs Inc 732 444-0123
  190 State Route 27 # 102 Edison (08820) *(G-2529)*

Griff Decorative Film, Lakewood *Also called Creative Film Corp (G-5097)*

Griffen LLC 973 723-5344
  44 Prospect St Apt 531 Morristown (07960) *(G-6711)*

Griffin Signs Inc 856 786-8517
  484 N Randolph Ave Cinnaminson (08077) *(G-1465)*

Griffith Electric Sup Co Inc (PA) 609 695-6121
  5 2nd St Trenton (08611) *(G-11061)*

Griffith Electric Supply Co 609 632-0253
  1381 Route 130 N Windsor (08561) *(G-12126)*

Griffith Shade Company Inc 973 667-1474
  308 Washington Ave Ste 1 Nutley (07110) *(G-7647)*

Grignard Company LLC 732 340-1111
  505 Capobianco Plz Rahway (07065) *(G-9194)*

Grill Creations 908 264-8426
  100 North Ave Ste 8 Garwood (07027) *(G-3778)*

Grimaldi Development Corp 973 345-0660
  65 1st Ave Paterson (07514) *(G-8282)*

Grimbilas Enterprises Corp 973 686-5999
  29 Hanes Dr Wayne (07470) *(G-11644)*

Grimco Pneumatic Corp 973 345-0660
  65 1st Ave Paterson (07514) *(G-8283)*

Grimes Manufacturing Inc 732 442-4572
  599 State St Perth Amboy (08861) *(G-8616)*

Grinnell Con Pavingstones Inc 973 383-9300
  482 Houses Corner Rd Sparta (07871) *(G-10501)*

Grip Tight Tools, Union *Also called El Batal Corporation (G-11180)*

Grobet File Company Amer LLC (PA) 201 939-6700
  750 Washington Ave Carlstadt (07072) *(G-1165)*

Grobet USA, Carlstadt *Also called Grobet File Company Amer LLC (G-1165)*

Groezinger Provisions Inc 732 775-3220
  1200 7th Ave Neptune (07753) *(G-6917)*

Grommet Mart Inc 973 278-4100
  85-99 Hazel St Paterson (07503) *(G-8284)*

Groniger USA LLC 704 588-3873
  180 Mount Airy Rd Basking Ridge (07920) *(G-189)*

Groomershelper.com, Margate City *Also called Pet Salon Inc (G-5934)*

Gross Bros Printing Co Inc 201 865-4606
  3125 Summit Ave Union City (07087) *(G-11246)*

Gross Printing Associates Inc 718 832-1110
  180 Brighton Rd Clifton (07012) *(G-1631)*

Group Martin LLC Jj 862 240-1813
  90 South St Newark (07114) *(G-7180)*

Groupe Seb USA 856 825-6300
  2121 Eden Rd Millville (08332) *(G-6306)*

Grove Supply Inc 856 205-0687
  144 W Forest Grove Rd Vineland (08360) *(G-11365)*

Grow Company Inc 201 941-8777
  55 Railroad Ave Ridgefield (07657) *(G-9363)*

Growmark Fs LLC 609 267-7054
  2545 Route 206 Eastampton (08060) *(G-2376)*

Gruppo Editoriale Oggi Inc 201 358-6582
  475 Walnut St Norwood (07648) *(G-7623)*

GS Fresh Beets Incorporated 856 692-1740
  2321 Industrial Way Vineland (08360) *(G-11366)*

GSC, Columbia *Also called General Stamping Co Inc (G-1797)*

GSC Imaging LLC 856 317-9301
  7150 N Park Dr Ste 540 Pennsauken (08109) *(G-8519)*

Gsds, Mahwah *Also called Diligaf Enterprises Inc (G-5765)*

Gsi 908 608-1325
  12 Princeton St Summit (07901) *(G-10643)*

Gsk Consumer Health Inc (HQ) 919 269-5000
  184 Liberty Corner Rd # 78 Warren (07059) *(G-11551)*

Gsk Consumer Healthcare 973 539-0645
  2 Sylvan Way Parsippany (07054) *(G-8025)*

GT Microwave Inc 973 361-5700
  2 Emery Ave Ste 2 # 2 Randolph (07869) *(G-9282)*

GTM Marketing Inc 856 227-2333
  1960 Harris Dr Woodbury (08096) *(G-12163)*

Guardian Drug Company Inc 609 860-2600
  2 Charles Ct Dayton (08810) *(G-1968)*

Guardrite Steel Door Corp 973 481-4424
  81-87 Springdale Ave Newark (07107) *(G-7181)*

Guerbet LLC 812 333-0059
  821 Alexander Rd Ste 204 Princeton (08540) *(G-9051)*

Guernsey Crest Ice Cream Co 973 742-4620
  134 19th Ave Paterson (07513) *(G-8285)*

Guess Inc 201 941-3683
  39 The Promenade Bldg 300 Edgewater (07020) *(G-2440)*

Gulbrandsen Chemicals, Clinton *Also called Gulbrandsen Technologies Inc (G-1751)*

Gulbrandsen Technologies Inc (PA) 908 735-5458
  2 Main St Clinton (08809) *(G-1751)*

Gulco Inc 908 238-2030
  1 Riverside Way Phillipsburg (08865) *(G-8651)*

Gulf Cable LLC (PA) 201 242-9906
  777 Terrace Ave Ste 101 Hasbrouck Heights (07604) *(G-4193)*

Gulton G I D 908 791-4622
  116 Corporate Blvd Ste A South Plainfield (07080) *(G-10376)*

Gulton Incorporated 908 791-4622
  116 Corporate Blvd Ste A South Plainfield (07080) *(G-10377)*

Gum Runners LLC 201 333-0756
  333 Washington St 2 Jersey City (07302) *(G-4763)*

Guttenplans Frozen Dough Inc 732 495-9480
  100 State Route 36 E North Middletown (07748) *(G-7557)*

Gutter Cleaning, Sicklerville *Also called Rays Seamless Rain Gutters* ***(G-10024)***
Guylian USA Inc....201 871-4144
560 Sylvan Ave Ste 2105 Englewood Cliffs (07632) ***(G-2962)***
Gwenstone Inc....732 785-2600
1790 Swarthmore Ave Lakewood (08701) ***(G-5131)***
Gwf Associates LLC....732 933-8780
1 Sheila Dr Ste 8 Eatontown (07724) ***(G-2398)***
Gwynn-E Co....215 423-6400
222 Cedar St Moorestown (08057) ***(G-6581)***
Gzgn Inc....201 842-7622
301 Nj 17 Ste 800 Rutherford (07070) ***(G-9733)***
H & A Global Enterprises Inc....732 318-2587
178 Northfield Ave Edison (08837) ***(G-2530)***
H & H Graphic Printing Inc....201 369-9700
400 Gotham Pkwy Ste 1 Carlstadt (07072) ***(G-1166)***
H & H Industries Inc....856 663-4444
7612 N Crescent Blvd Pennsauken (08110) ***(G-8520)***
H & H Production Machining....973 383-6880
30 White Lake Rd Sparta (07871) ***(G-10502)***
H & H Sheet Metal & Machining, Sparta *Also called H & H Production Machining* ***(G-10502)***
H & H Swiss Screw Machine PR....908 688-6390
1478 Chestnut Ave Hillside (07205) ***(G-4410)***
H & L Printing Co....201 288-0877
309 Boulevard Hasbrouck Heights (07604) ***(G-4194)***
H & R Welding LLC....732 920-4881
307 Drum Point Rd Brick (08723) ***(G-745)***
H & S Fuel Inc....908 769-1362
1100 South Ave Plainfield (07062) ***(G-8863)***
H & S Graphics, Lodi *Also called Santangelo Printing Co Inc* ***(G-5599)***
H & T, Clayton *Also called Hungerford & Terry Inc* ***(G-1524)***
H & T Tool Co Inc....973 227-4858
19 Gardner Rd Ste C Fairfield (07004) ***(G-3214)***
H & W Tool Co Inc (PA)....973 366-0131
22 Lee Ave Dover (07801) ***(G-2088)***
H Barron Iron Works Inc....856 456-9092
316 Water St Gloucester City (08030) ***(G-3838)***
H C Graphics Screenprinting....973 247-0544
238 Lindbergh Pl Ste 3 Paterson (07503) ***(G-8286)***
H Cross Company....201 964-9380
150 W Commercial Ave Moonachie (07074) ***(G-6519)***
H G Schaevitz LLC....856 727-0250
102 Commerce Dr Ste 8 Moorestown (08057) ***(G-6582)***
H Galow Co Inc....201 768-0547
15 Maple St Norwood (07648) ***(G-7624)***
H I D Systems Inc....973 383-8535
520 Lafayette Rd Sparta (07871) ***(G-10503)***
H K Metal Craft Mfg Corp....973 471-7770
35 Industrial Rd Lodi (07644) ***(G-5585)***
H Lauzon Furniture Co Inc....201 837-7598
1098 Decatur Ave Teaneck (07666) ***(G-10756)***
H M Hays Sheet Metal Co, Pennsauken *Also called Hays Sheet Metal Inc* ***(G-8521)***
H P C P O S Systems, Cedar Grove *Also called Hpc Pos System Corp* ***(G-1284)***
H P Machine Shop Inc....856 692-1192
415 Oxford St Vineland (08360) ***(G-11367)***
H Power Corp....973 249-5444
1373 Broad St Clifton (07013) ***(G-1632)***
H Ritani LLC....888 974-8264
101 Carlson Ct Closter (07624) ***(G-1759)***
H S Martin Company Inc....856 692-8700
1149 S East Blvd Vineland (08360) ***(G-11368)***
H T Hall Inc (PA)....732 449-3441
1716 State Route 71 Ste 1 Spring Lake (07762) ***(G-10533)***
H&H Swiss, Hillside *Also called H & H Swiss Screw Machine PR* ***(G-4410)***
H-E Tool & Mfg Co Inc....856 303-8787
800 Industrial Hwy Unit A Cinnaminson (08077) ***(G-1466)***
H.N. Lucas & Son, Delran *Also called Spl Holdings LLC* ***(G-2023)***
Haas Environmental Inc (PA)....609 859-3100
75 Eisenhower Pkwy # 200 Roseland (07068) ***(G-9652)***
Haas Laser Technologies Inc (PA)....973 598-1150
37 Ironia Rd Flanders (07836) ***(G-3410)***
Hackensack Steel Corp....201 935-0090
645 Industrial Rd Carlstadt (07072) ***(G-1167)***
Hackettstown Public Works....908 852-2320
309 E Plane St Hackettstown (07840) ***(G-4010)***
Haenssler Shtmtl Works Inc....973 373-6360
592 Hawthorne Ave Newark (07112) ***(G-7182)***
Hafco Foundry & Machine Co....201 447-0433
301 Greenwood Ave Ste 2 Midland Park (07432) ***(G-6228)***
Hahns Woodworking....908 722-2742
181 Meister Ave Branchburg (08876) ***(G-664)***
Hai Tai Boutique, Hackensack *Also called D & G LLC* ***(G-3902)***
Haier Appliance Products LP (HQ)....973 617-1800
1800 Valley Rd Wayne (07470) ***(G-11645)***
Haights Cross Cmmnications Inc (PA)....212 209-0500
295 Prncton Hightstown Rd Princeton Junction (08550) ***(G-9157)***
Hain Celestial Group Inc....201 935-4500
50 Knickerbocker Rd Moonachie (07074) ***(G-6520)***
Haineport Tools & Maintenance, Mount Holly *Also called Hainesport Tool & Machine Co* ***(G-6772)***
Hainesport Industrial Railroad....609 261-8036
5900 Delaware Ave Hainesport (08036) ***(G-4072)***
Hainesport Tool & Machine Co....609 261-0016
1924 Ark Rd Mount Holly (08060) ***(G-6772)***
Hair Depot Limited....973 251-9924
53 Peachtree Rd Maplewood (07040) ***(G-5921)***
Hair Quarters....856 624-4072
221 Borton Dr Woodstown (08098) ***(G-12238)***
Hair Systems Inc....732 446-2202
30 Park Ave Englishtown (07726) ***(G-2994)***
Hakakian Behzad....973 267-2506
52 Horsehill Rd Cedar Knolls (07927) ***(G-1313)***
Hal Leonard LLC....973 337-5034
33 Plymouth St Ste 302 Montclair (07042) ***(G-6415)***
Hal-O Manufacturing Co Inc....973 824-6122
137 Meeker Ave Ste 143 Newark (07114) ***(G-7183)***
Halberd Match Corp....609 882-7000
1230 Parkway Ave Ste 306 Ewing (08628) ***(G-3019)***
Haldor USA Inc....856 254-2345
100 Springdale Rd 83-206 Cherry Hill (08003) ***(G-1373)***
Halfway Hounds....201 970-6235
108 E Main St Park Ridge (07656) ***(G-7922)***
Hall Manufacturing Corp....973 962-6022
297 Margaret King Ave Ringwood (07456) ***(G-9448)***
Hallco Inc....609 729-0161
5914 New Jersey Ave Wildwood (08260) ***(G-12072)***
Halo Farm Inc....609 695-3311
970 Spruce St Lawrenceville (08648) ***(G-5257)***
Halo Mark, Bound Brook *Also called Marx NJ Group LLC* ***(G-620)***
Halo Pharmaceutical Inc (HQ)....973 428-4000
30 N Jefferson Rd Whippany (07981) ***(G-12023)***
Halo Pub Ice Cream....609 921-1710
9 Hulfish St Princeton (08542) ***(G-9052)***
Halo Pub Inc....609 586-1811
4617 Nottingham Way Trenton (08690) ***(G-11062)***
Halsey News....973 645-0017
2 Prudential Dr Newark (07102) ***(G-7184)***
Halsted Bag, Cranbury *Also called Halsted Corporation* ***(G-1836)***
Halsted Corporation....201 333-0670
51 Commerce Dr Ste 3 Cranbury (08512) ***(G-1836)***
Halton Laboratories LLC....609 917-9330
400 Alexander Park Princeton (08540) ***(G-9053)***
Hamamatsu Corporation (HQ)....908 231-0960
360 Foothill Rd Bridgewater (08807) ***(G-841)***
Hamamatsu Corporation....908 526-0941
360 Foothill Rd Bridgewater (08807) ***(G-842)***
Hamilton Embroidery Co Inc....201 867-4084
907 21st St Union City (07087) ***(G-11247)***
Hammer Manufacturing, Linden *Also called Wgjf Manufacturing Corp* ***(G-5459)***
Hammer Press Printers Inc....973 334-4500
2 Cranberry Rd Ste 2 # 2 Parsippany (07054) ***(G-8026)***
Hammer Too LLC....908 688-5601
623 Eagle Rock Ave West Orange (07052) ***(G-11896)***
Hammonton Gazette Inc....609 704-1939
14 Tilton St Hammonton (08037) ***(G-4138)***
Hammonton News, The, Vineland *Also called Gannett Stllite Info Ntwrk LLC* ***(G-11358)***
Hamon Corporation (HQ)....908 333-2000
58 E Main St Somerville (08876) ***(G-10213)***
Hampton Forge Ltd (PA)....877 935-2892
446 Highway 35 Ste 3 Eatontown (07724) ***(G-2399)***
Hampton Industries Inc....973 574-8900
1 Market St Ste 13 Passaic (07055) ***(G-8146)***
Han Hean U S A Corp....732 494-3256
3856 Park Ave Edison (08820) ***(G-2531)***
Hand Craft Mfg, Newark *Also called Personality Handkerchiefs Inc* ***(G-7269)***
Handcraft Manufacturing Corp....973 565-0077
640 Frelinghuysen Ave # 1 Newark (07114) ***(G-7185)***
Handi-Hut Inc....973 614-1800
3 Grunwald St Clifton (07013) ***(G-1633)***
Handler Manufacturing Company....908 233-7796
612 North Ave E Westfield (07090) ***(G-11926)***
Handmade Furniture, West Creek *Also called Woodward Wood Products Design* ***(G-11812)***
Hands On Wheels....609 892-4693
509 Atlantic Ave Atlantic City (08401) ***(G-99)***
Handy Store Fixtures Inc....973 242-1600
337 Sherman Ave Newark (07114) ***(G-7186)***
Handytube Corporation....732 469-7420
250 Lackland Dr Ste 1 Middlesex (08846) ***(G-6169)***
Hanes Companies - NJ LLC....201 729-9100
104 Sunfield Ave Edison (08837) ***(G-2532)***
Hanger Prsthetcs & Ortho Inc....973 736-0628
59 Main St Ste 111 West Orange (07052) ***(G-11897)***
Hanger Prsthetcs & Ortho Inc....732 919-7774
5100 Belmar Blvd Wall Township (07727) ***(G-11486)***
Hanger Prsthetcs & Ortho Inc....609 653-8323
210 New Rd Ste 7 Linwood (08221) ***(G-5466)***
Hanger Prsthetcs & Ortho Inc....609 889-8447
1 Secluded Ln Rio Grande (08242) ***(G-9458)***
Hangsterfers Laboratories (PA)....856 468-0216
175 Ogden Rd West Deptford (08051) ***(G-11827)***

ALPHABETIC

Hankin Acquisitions Inc...908 722-9595
1 Harvard Way Ste 6 Hillsborough (08844) ***(G-4338)***
Hankin Envmtl Systems Inc...908 722-9595
1 Harvard Way Ste 6 Hillsborough (08844) ***(G-4339)***
Hanover Direct Inc (PA)...201 863-7300
1500 Harbor Blvd Ste 3 Weehawken (07086) ***(G-11695)***
Hanover Direct Operating Group, Weehawken *Also called Hanover Direct Inc* ***(G-11695)***
Hanovia Colight, Fairfield *Also called Hanovia Specialty Lighting LLC* ***(G-3215)***
Hanovia Specialty Lighting LLC...973 651-5510
6 Evans St Fairfield (07004) ***(G-3215)***
Hanrahan Tool Co Inc...732 919-7300
415 Cranberry Rd Farmingdale (07727) ***(G-3386)***
Hansen Awning Co...609 886-1685
18 Church Rd Rio Grande (08242) ***(G-9459)***
Hansen Lithography Ltd...732 270-1188
2214 Route 37 E Ste 1 Toms River (08753) ***(G-10882)***
Hansome Energy Systems Inc (PA)...908 862-9044
365 Dalziel Rd Linden (07036) ***(G-5382)***
Hanson & Zollinger Inc...856 626-3440
117 Jackson Rd Berlin (08009) ***(G-434)***
Hanson Aggregates Wrp Inc (HQ)...972 653-5500
1333 Campus Pkwy Wall Township (07753) ***(G-11487)***
Hanssem...732 425-7695
50 Idlewild Rd Edison (08817) ***(G-2533)***
Hanssem Corporation (HQ)...908 754-4949
20 Kilmer Rd Edison (08817) ***(G-2534)***
HANWHA TECHWIN AMERICA, Teaneck *Also called Samsung Opt-Lctronics Amer Inc* ***(G-10772)***
Hapa, Branchburg *Also called Flexlink Systems Inc* ***(G-660)***
Happle Printing...609 476-0100
81 Cape May Ave Dorothy (08317) ***(G-2073)***
Happy Chef Inc...973 492-2525
22 Park Pl Ste 2 Butler (07405) ***(G-1006)***
Harbisonwalker Intl Inc...732 388-4011
868 Elston St Rahway (07065) ***(G-9195)***
Hard Crome Solutions...732 500-2568
195 Central Ave Metuchen (08840) ***(G-6108)***
Harlequin Floors, Moorestown *Also called American Harlequin Corporation* ***(G-6558)***
Harley Davidson Camden County, Mount Ephraim *Also called Barbs Harley-Davidson* ***(G-6762)***
Harley Tool & Machine Inc...201 244-8899
24 Mcdermott Pl Bergenfield (07621) ***(G-386)***
Harmony Elastomers LLC...973 340-4000
34 Trenton Ave Paterson (07513) ***(G-8287)***
Harmony Sand & Gravel Inc...908 475-4690
County Rd 519 Phillipsburg (08865) ***(G-8652)***
Harms Software Inc...973 402-9500
28 Eastmans Rd Parsippany (07054) ***(G-8027)***
Harold F Fisher & Sons Inc...800 624-2868
200 Ash St Delanco (08075) ***(G-2006)***
Harold R Henrich Inc...732 370-4455
300 Syracuse Ct Lakewood (08701) ***(G-5132)***
Harris & Tippograph Inc...973 523-5204
93 Harrison St Ste 2 Paterson (07501) ***(G-8288)***
Harris Broadcast, Rockleigh *Also called Hbc Solutions Inc* ***(G-9630)***
Harris Corporation...973 284-0123
77 River Rd Clifton (07014) ***(G-1634)***
Harris Corporation...973 284-0123
77 River Rd Clifton (07014) ***(G-1635)***
Harris Corporation...973 284-0123
77 River Rd Clifton (07014) ***(G-1636)***
Harris Corporation...585 269-6600
77 River Rd Clifton (07014) ***(G-1637)***
Harris Driver Co (PA)...973 267-8100
200 Madison Ave Ste 2 Morristown (07960) ***(G-6712)***
Harris Freeman & Co Inc...856 787-9026
344 New Albany Rd Moorestown (08057) ***(G-6583)***
Harris Structural Steel Co Inc (PA)...732 752-6070
1640 New Market Ave South Plainfield (07080) ***(G-10378)***
Harris Structural Steel Co Inc...732 752-6070
1640 New Market Ave South Plainfield (07080) ***(G-10379)***
Harris Tea Company, Moorestown *Also called Harris Freeman & Co Inc* ***(G-6583)***
Harrison Electro Mechanical...732 382-6008
1607 Coach St Rahway (07065) ***(G-9196)***
Harrison Hose and Tubing Inc...609 631-8804
2705 Kuser Rd Robbinsville (08691) ***(G-9517)***
Harrison Machine and Tool Inc...609 883-0800
21 Lexington Ave Ewing (08618) ***(G-3020)***
Harrison Press, Trenton *Also called North Eastern Business Forms* ***(G-11091)***
Harrison Scott Pblications Inc...201 659-1700
5 Marine View Plz Ste 400 Hoboken (07030) ***(G-4472)***
Harry J Lawall & Son Inc...856 691-7764
3071 E Chestnut Ave C9 Vineland (08361) ***(G-11369)***
Harry Shaw Model Maker Inc...609 268-0647
401 Stokes Rd Shamong (08088) ***(G-9970)***
Harsco Corporation...856 779-7795
1960 Old Cuthbert Rd # 100 Cherry Hill (08034) ***(G-1374)***
Harsco Corporation...908 454-7169
709 Loretta Ter Plainfield (07062) ***(G-8864)***
Hart Construction Service...908 537-2060
466 Mine Rd Asbury (08802) ***(G-70)***
Hartin Paint & Filler Corp...201 438-3300
219 Broad St Carlstadt (07072) ***(G-1168)***
Hartmann Tool Co Inc...201 343-8700
147 Lodi St Hackensack (07601) ***(G-3925)***
Hartz Mountain Corporation (HQ)...800 275-1414
400 Plaza Dr Ste 400 # 400 Secaucus (07094) ***(G-9894)***
Harvard Printing Group, Fairfield *Also called Gator Communications Group LLC* ***(G-3208)***
Harvard Printing Group...973 672-0800
175 Us Highway 46 Fairfield (07004) ***(G-3216)***
Harve Benard Ltd (PA)...973 249-1230
125 Delawanna Ave Clifton (07014) ***(G-1638)***
Harvester Inc...201 445-1122
31 Cordier St Irvington (07111) ***(G-4588)***
Harvester Chemical, Irvington *Also called Harvester Inc* ***(G-4588)***
Harwill Corporation...609 895-1955
92 N Main St Windsor (08561) ***(G-12127)***
Harwill Express Press, Windsor *Also called Harwill Corporation* ***(G-12127)***
Hary Manufacturing Inc...908 722-7100
210 Grove Ave Woodbridge (07095) ***(G-12150)***
Hasselblad Bron Incorporated, Union *Also called Hasselblad Inc* ***(G-11191)***
Hasselblad Inc...800 456-0203
1080a Garden State Rd Union (07083) ***(G-11191)***
Hat Box...732 961-2262
605 E County Line Rd # 1 Lakewood (08701) ***(G-5133)***
Hathaway Plastic...908 688-9494
911 Springfield Rd Ste 1 Union (07083) ***(G-11192)***
Hatteras Press Inc...732 935-9800
56 Park Rd Tinton Falls (07724) ***(G-10838)***
Hausmann Enterprises LLC...201 767-0255
130 Union St Northvale (07647) ***(G-7583)***
Hausmann Industries, Northvale *Also called Hausmann Enterprises LLC* ***(G-7583)***
Hawk Dairy Inc...973 466-9030
30 Jabez St Newark (07105) ***(G-7187)***
Hawk Graphics Inc...973 895-5569
1248 Sussex Tpke Randolph (07869) ***(G-9283)***
Hawks and Co, Westville *Also called Heritage Service Solutions LLC* ***(G-11942)***
Hawthorne Kitchens Inc...973 427-9010
120 5th Ave Hawthorne (07506) ***(G-4238)***
Hawthorne Machine Products, Hawthorne *Also called Peter Yaged* ***(G-4253)***
Hawthorne Paint Company Inc...973 423-2335
18 Mill St Lodi (07644) ***(G-5586)***
Hawthorne Press...973 427-3330
463 Lafayette Ave Hawthorne (07506) ***(G-4239)***
Hawthorne Rubber Mfg Corp...973 427-3337
35 4th Ave Hawthorne (07506) ***(G-4240)***
Haydon Corporation (PA)...973 904-0800
415 Hamburg Tpke Ste 1 Wayne (07470) ***(G-11646)***
Hayes Mindish Inc...609 641-9880
1401 N Main St Ste 7 Pleasantville (08232) ***(G-8909)***
Haymarket Media Inc...201 799-4800
140 E Ridgewood Ave 370s Paramus (07652) ***(G-7875)***
Hays Sheet Metal Inc...856 662-7722
7070 Bldg B Kaighns Ave Pennsauken (08109) ***(G-8521)***
Hayward Flow Control, Elizabeth *Also called Hayward Pool Products Inc* ***(G-2744)***
Hayward Industrial Products (HQ)...908 351-5400
620 Division St Elizabeth (07201) ***(G-2741)***
Hayward Industries Inc (PA)...908 351-5400
620 Division St Elizabeth (07201) ***(G-2742)***
Hayward Industries Inc...908 351-0899
628 Henry St Bldg 6 Elizabeth (07201) ***(G-2743)***
Hayward Plastic Products Div, Elizabeth *Also called Hayward Industrial Products* ***(G-2741)***
Hayward Pool Products Inc...908 351-5400
620 Division St Elizabeth (07201) ***(G-2744)***
Haywood Pool Products, Elizabeth *Also called Hayward Industries Inc* ***(G-2742)***
Haz Laboratories...908 453-3300
39 Hartmans Corner Rd Washington (07882) ***(G-11582)***
HB Fuller Company...732 287-8330
59 Brunswick Ave Edison (08817) ***(G-2535)***
HB Technik USA Ltd Lblty Prtnr...973 875-8688
99 George Hill Rd Branchville (07826) ***(G-731)***
Hb-GM Acquistion, Clifton *Also called Harve Benard Ltd* ***(G-1638)***
Hbc Solutions Inc...973 267-5990
22 Paris Ave Ste 110 Rockleigh (07647) ***(G-9630)***
Hbs Electronics Inc...973 439-1147
1275 Bloomfield Ave # 17 Fairfield (07004) ***(G-3217)***
HCH Incorporated...973 300-4551
99 Demarest Rd Ste 4 Sparta (07871) ***(G-10504)***
Hd Microsystems, Parlin *Also called Hitachi Chem Dupont Microsyst* ***(G-7931)***
Head Piece Heaven...201 262-0788
449 2nd St Oradell (07649) ***(G-7811)***
Headquarters Pub LLC...609 347-2579
2 Convention Blvd Atlantic City (08401) ***(G-100)***
Headwear Creations Inc...973 622-1144
200 Wright St Newark (07114) ***(G-7188)***
Healios Inc...908 731-5061
56 Main St Ste 1d Flemington (08822) ***(G-3446)***

Healqu LLC....844 443-2578
210 Fairmount Ave Jersey City (07306) ***(G-4764)***
Health & Natural Beauty, Piscataway *Also called Health and Natural Beauty USA* ***(G-8772)***
Health and Natural Beauty USA....732 640-1830
140 Ethel Rd W Ste W Piscataway (08854) ***(G-8772)***
Health Care Alert LLC....732 676-2630
1715 State Route 35 # 208 Middletown (07748) ***(G-6216)***
Health Monitor Network, Montvale *Also called Data Cntrum Communications Inc* ***(G-6452)***
Health Science Funding LLC....973 984-6159
55 Madison Ave Morristown (07960) ***(G-6713)***
Healthcare Cart....201 406-4797
71 Auble Rd Blairstown (07825) ***(G-496)***
Healthcaredepotonlinecom Inc....732 761-9600
2177 Oak Tree Rd Ste 202 Edison (08820) ***(G-2536)***
Healthper Inc (PA)....888 257-1804
124 Brookstone Dr Princeton (08540) ***(G-9054)***
Healthstar Communications Inc (PA)....201 560-5370
1000 Wyckoff Ave Ste 202 Mahwah (07430) ***(G-5780)***
Heard Woodworking LLC....908 232-3978
31 Normandy Dr Westfield (07090) ***(G-11927)***
Heat-Timer Corporation (PA)....973 575-4004
20 New Dutch Ln Fairfield (07004) ***(G-3218)***
Heat-Timer Corporation....212 481-2020
20 New Dutch Ln Fairfield (07004) ***(G-3219)***
Heat-Timer Service, Fairfield *Also called Heat-Timer Corporation* ***(G-3219)***
Heavenly Havens Creamery LLC....609 259-6600
33 S Main St Allentown (08501) ***(G-31)***
Heavenly Souffle, Millington *Also called Rw Delights Inc* ***(G-6261)***
Hed International Inc....609 466-1900
449 Route 31 N Ringoes (08551) ***(G-9437)***
Hedaya Home Fashions Inc (PA)....908 352-0808
1111 Jefferson Ave Elizabeth (07201) ***(G-2745)***
Heidelberg Press, Westampton *Also called Diane Matson Inc* ***(G-11912)***
Heidi's European Pretzel, North Bergen *Also called European Pretzel One LLC* ***(G-7451)***
Heights Jewelers LLC....201 825-2381
11 Ceely Ct Allendale (07401) ***(G-10)***
Heights Usa Inc....609 530-1300
1445 Lower Ferry Rd Ewing (08618) ***(G-3021)***
Heilind Electronics Inc....888 881-5420
120 Mount Holly Byp Lumberton (08048) ***(G-5658)***
Heilind Electronics Inc, Lumberton *Also called Heilind Electronics Inc* ***(G-5658)***
Heilind Mil-Aero LLC (HQ)....856 722-5535
100c Mount Holly Byp Lumberton (08048) ***(G-5659)***
Heinkel Filtering Systems Inc....856 467-3399
520 Sharptown Rd Swedesboro (08085) ***(G-10701)***
Heinrich Bauer Publishing LP....201 569-6699
270 Sylvan Ave Ste 100 Englewood (07632) ***(G-2902)***
Heinrich Bauer Verlag (HQ)....201 569-0006
270 Sylvan Ave Ste 100 Englewood Cliffs (07632) ***(G-2963)***
Heinz Glas USA Inc....908 474-0300
360 Hurst St Linden (07036) ***(G-5383)***
Heinzelman Heat Treating LLC....201 933-4800
790 Washington Ave Carlstadt (07072) ***(G-1169)***
Heisler Industries, Fairfield *Also called Heisler Machine & Tool Co* ***(G-3220)***
Heisler Machine & Tool Co....973 227-6300
224 Passaic Ave Fairfield (07004) ***(G-3220)***
Hekikat LLC....908 232-1145
24 Doherty Dr Middletown (07748) ***(G-6217)***
Hel Inc....440 208-7360
4 Princess Rd Ste 208 Lawrenceville (08648) ***(G-5258)***
Helen Morley LLC....201 348-6459
35 Buckingham Rd Cresskill (07626) ***(G-1945)***
Helidex LLC....201 636-2546
186 Paterson Ave Ste 303 East Rutherford (07073) ***(G-2299)***
Helidex Offshore, East Rutherford *Also called Helidex LLC* ***(G-2299)***
Heliolite, Cranbury *Also called Lumiko USA Inc* ***(G-1857)***
Heller Industries Inc (PA)....973 377-6800
4 Vreeland Rd Ste 1 Florham Park (07932) ***(G-3505)***
Helsinn Therapeutics US Inc....908 231-1435
170 Wood Ave S Fl 1 Iselin (08830) ***(G-4628)***
Hempel (usa) Inc....201 939-2801
127 Kingsland Ave Clifton (07014) ***(G-1639)***
Henderson Aquatic Inc (PA)....856 825-4771
1 Whitall Ave Millville (08332) ***(G-6307)***
Hengrui Therapeutics Inc....609 423-2155
506 Carnegie Ctr Ste 102 Princeton (08540) ***(G-9055)***
Henkel US Operations Corp....908 685-7000
10 Finderne Ave Ste B Bridgewater (08807) ***(G-843)***
Henriques Yachts Works....732 269-1180
198 Hilton Ave Bayville (08721) ***(G-256)***
Henry Bros Electronics Inc (HQ)....201 794-6500
17-01 Pollitt Dr Ste 5 Fair Lawn (07410) ***(G-3094)***
Henry Dudley....732 240-6895
1508 Wellington Ave Toms River (08757) ***(G-10883)***
Henry Jackson Racing Engines....609 758-7476
787 Monmouth Rd Cream Ridge (08514) ***(G-1936)***
Henry Olsen Machine....856 662-2121
2504 Route 73 Cinnaminson (08077) ***(G-1467)***
Henry RAC Holding Corp....201 858-4400
59 E 1st St Bayonne (07002) ***(G-231)***
Henry Repeating Arms Company, Bayonne *Also called Henry RAC Holding Corp* ***(G-231)***
Herald News, Woodland Park *Also called North Jersey Media Group Inc* ***(G-12226)***
Herald News (PA)....973 569-7000
1 Garret Mountain Plz # 201 Woodland Park (07424) ***(G-12221)***
Herbakraft Incorporated....732 463-1000
121 Ethel Rd W Ste 6 Piscataway (08854) ***(G-8773)***
Herbalist & Alchemist Inc....908 689-9020
51 S Wandling Ave Washington (07882) ***(G-11583)***
Herbert J Hinchman & Son Inc....973 942-2063
26 Pike Dr Wayne (07470) ***(G-11647)***
Herborium Group Inc (PA)....201 849-4431
1 Bridge Plz N Ste 275 Fort Lee (07024) ***(G-3556)***
Herbst John E Heating & Coolg, Parlin *Also called John E Herbst Heating & Coolg* ***(G-7933)***
Hercules Enterprises LLC....908 369-0000
321 Valley Rd Hillsborough (08844) ***(G-4340)***
Hercules LLC....732 777-4697
20 Lee St Edison (08817) ***(G-2537)***
Hercules Welding & Machine Co....856 829-1820
618 W 5th St Palmyra (08065) ***(G-7848)***
Hercules World Industries, Newfoundland *Also called Atlantic Rubber Enterprises* ***(G-7373)***
Heritage Bag Company....856 467-2247
2123 High Hill Rd Swedesboro (08085) ***(G-10702)***
Heritage Inc....201 447-2600
225 Franklin Ave Ste 4 Midland Park (07432) ***(G-6229)***
Heritage Pharma Holdings Inc (HQ)....732 429-1000
1 Tower Center Blvd # 1700 East Brunswick (08816) ***(G-2157)***
Heritage Pharma Labs Inc....732 238-7880
8 Elkins Rd East Brunswick (08816) ***(G-2158)***
Heritage Pharma Labs Inc (HQ)....732 238-7880
21 Cotters Ln Ste B East Brunswick (08816) ***(G-2159)***
Heritage Pharmaceuticals Inc (HQ)....732 429-1000
1 Tower Center Blvd # 1700 East Brunswick (08816) ***(G-2160)***
Heritage Publishing....732 747-7770
440 State Route 34 Ste 2 Colts Neck (07722) ***(G-1788)***
Heritage Service Solutions LLC....856 845-7311
1000 Delsea Dr Ste A1 Westville (08093) ***(G-11942)***
Herley Industries Inc....973 884-2580
9 Whippany Rd Whippany (07981) ***(G-12024)***
Herley-Cti Inc (HQ)....973 884-2580
9 Whippany Rd Whippany (07981) ***(G-12025)***
Herma US Inc....973 521-7254
39 Plymouth St Unit 300 Fairfield (07004) ***(G-3221)***
Herman Eickhoff....609 871-1809
400 John F Kennedy Way Willingboro (08046) ***(G-12119)***
Hermitage Press of New Jersey (PA)....609 882-3600
1595 5th St Ewing (08638) ***(G-3022)***
Heros Salute Awards Co....973 696-5085
1875 State Route 23 Ste 1 Wayne (07470) ***(G-11648)***
Herr Foods Incorporated....732 356-1295
790 New Brunswick Rd Somerset (08873) ***(G-10107)***
Herr Foods Incorporated....732 905-1600
100 Kenyon Dr Lakewood (08701) ***(G-5134)***
Hershey Industries Inc....908 353-3344
1209 Central Ave Hillside (07205) ***(G-4411)***
Hess Corporation....609 882-8477
601 Jack Stephan Way Ewing (08628) ***(G-3023)***
Hexacon Electric Company Inc....908 245-6200
161 W Clay Ave Roselle Park (07204) ***(G-9697)***
Heyco Molded Products Inc (HQ)....732 286-4336
1800 Industrial Way Toms River (08755) ***(G-10884)***
Heyco Products Corp (HQ)....732 286-1800
1800 Industrial Way Toms River (08755) ***(G-10885)***
Heyco Stamped Products....732 286-4336
1800 Industrial Way Toms River (08755) ***(G-10886)***
Hhh Machine Co....908 276-1220
20 Quine St Cranford (07016) ***(G-1910)***
Hi-Grade Products Mfg Co....908 245-4133
752 Jefferson Ave Kenilworth (07033) ***(G-4961)***
Hibrett Puratex, Pennsauken *Also called Atlantic Associates Intl Inc* ***(G-8481)***
Hickok Matthews Co Inc....973 335-3400
337 Main Rd Montville (07045) ***(G-6489)***
Hickory Industries Inc....201 223-4382
4900 W Side Ave North Bergen (07047) ***(G-7456)***
Hicube Coating LLC....973 883-7404
200 Circle Ave Clifton (07011) ***(G-1640)***
Hid Ultraviolet LLC....973 383-8535
520 Lafayette Rd Sparta (07871) ***(G-10505)***
High Energy Group Ltd Lblty Co....732 741-9099
331 Newman Spg Rd Eatontown (07724) ***(G-2400)***
High Gate Corp....609 267-0680
100 Campus Dr Mount Holly (08060) ***(G-6773)***
High Point Brewing Co Inc....973 838-7400
22 Park Pl Butler (07405) ***(G-1007)***
High Point Precision Products....973 875-6229
1 First St Sussex (07461) ***(G-10672)***
High Point Wheat Beer Company, Butler *Also called High Point Brewing Co Inc* ***(G-1007)***
High Tech Manufacturing Inc....973 372-7907
460 Coit St Bldg D Irvington (07111) ***(G-4589)***

ALPHABETIC

High Vision Corporation 862 238-7636
211 River Rd Clifton (07014) *(G-1641)*
High-Technology Corporation (PA) 201 488-0010
144 South St Hackensack (07601) *(G-3926)*
Highland Products Inc 973 366-0156
River St Dover (07801) *(G-2089)*
Highlands Acquisition Corp 201 573-8400
1 Paragon Dr Ste 125 Montvale (07645) *(G-6459)*
Highpont Corporation 201 460-1364
63 E Pierrepont Ave Rutherford (07070) *(G-9734)*
Highroad Press LLC 201 708-6900
220 Anderson Ave Moonachie (07074) *(G-6521)*
Hights Electric Motor Service 609 448-2298
156 Stockton St Hightstown (08520) *(G-4312)*
Hikma Injectables USA Inc 732 542-1191
200 Industrial Way W Eatontown (07724) *(G-2401)*
Hikma Pharmaceuticals USA Inc (HQ) 732 542-1191
246 Industrial Way W Eatontown (07724) *(G-2402)*
Hikma Pharmaceuticals USA Inc 732 542-1191
465 Industrial Way W Eatontown (07724) *(G-2403)*
Hikma Pharmaceuticals USA Inc 856 424-3700
2 Esterbrook Ln Cherry Hill (08003) *(G-1375)*
Hilin Life Products Inc 973 648-0265
211 Warren St Ste 211 # 211 Newark (07103) *(G-7189)*
Hill Cross Co Inc 201 864-3393
543 56th St West New York (07093) *(G-11866)*
Hill Machine Inc (PA) 973 684-2808
295 Governor St Paterson (07501) *(G-8289)*
Hill Mixers Machine, Paterson *Also called Hill Machine Inc (G-8289)*
Hill Pharma Inc 973 521-7400
6 Madison Rd Fairfield (07004) *(G-3222)*
Hill-Rom Holdings Inc 856 486-2117
202 Commerce Dr Ste 2 Moorestown (08057) *(G-6584)*
Hillard Bloom Packing Co Inc 856 785-0120
2601 Ogden Ave Port Norris (08349) *(G-8980)*
Hillary's Fashions, Warren *Also called Hillarys Fashion Boutique LLC (G-11552)*
Hillarys Fashion Boutique LLC 732 667-7733
177 Washington Valley Rd Warren (07059) *(G-11552)*
Hillcrest Opticians 973 838-6666
11 Kiel Ave Ste D-1 Kinnelon (07405) *(G-5036)*
Hillman Rollers, Marlboro *Also called Hilman Incorporated (G-5943)*
Hillsborough Vacuum LLC 908 904-6600
54 Buckland Dr Hillsborough (08844) *(G-4341)*
Hillside Bottling Corp 908 353-6773
1 Evans Terminal Hillside (07205) *(G-4412)*
Hillside Candy LLC (PA) 973 926-2300
35 Hillside Ave Hillside (07205) *(G-4413)*
Hillside Candy LLC 908 241-4747
1112 Walnut St Roselle (07203) *(G-9672)*
Hillside Plastics Corporation 973 923-2700
125 Long Ave Hillside (07205) *(G-4414)*
Hilman Incorporated (PA) 732 462-6277
12 Timber Ln Marlboro (07746) *(G-5943)*
Hinck Turkey Farm Inc 732 681-0508
3930 Belmar Blvd Neptune (07753) *(G-6918)*
Hirox - USA Inc (HQ) 201 342-2600
100 Commerce Way Ste 4 Hackensack (07601) *(G-3927)*
Hisamitsu Phrm Co Inc 973 765-0122
100 Campus Dr Ste 117 Florham Park (07932) *(G-3506)*
Hispanic Outlook In Higher 201 587-8800
299 Market St Ste 140 Saddle Brook (07663) *(G-9768)*
Hispanic Outlook-12 Mag Inc 201 587-8800
42-32 Debruin Dr Fair Lawn (07410) *(G-3095)*
Hit Promo LLC 856 739-4474
440 Benigno Blvd Unit D Bellmawr (08031) *(G-342)*
Hitachi Chem Dupont Microsyst (PA) 732 613-2404
250 Cheesequake Rd Parlin (08859) *(G-7931)*
Hitechone Inc 201 500-8864
440 Sylvan Ave Ste 2508 Englewood Cliffs (07632) *(G-2964)*
Hitran Corporation 908 782-5525
362 Highway 31 Flemington (08822) *(G-3447)*
Hitrons Solutions Inc 201 244-0300
88 Portland Ave Ste M Bergenfield (07621) *(G-387)*
Hitrons Solutions Inc 201 244-0300
88 Portland Ave Ste M Bergenfield (07621) *(G-388)*
Hitrons Tech Inc 201 941-0024
1 Remsen Pl Ste 107 Ridgefield (07657) *(G-9364)*
Hks Marketing, Bayonne *Also called Royal Wine Corporation (G-244)*
HMS Monaco Et Cie Ltd 201 533-0007
629 Grove St Fl 5 Jersey City (07310) *(G-4765)*
HNST Mold Inspections LLC 201 733-0091
143 Church St Mahwah (07430) *(G-5781)*
Hnt Industries Inc 908 322-0414
233 Union Ave Scotch Plains (07076) *(G-9850)*
Ho-Ho-Kus Inc 973 278-2274
189 Lyon St 201 Paterson (07524) *(G-8290)*
Hoarders Express LLC 856 963-8471
529 Market St Camden (08102) *(G-1068)*
Hobart Feg Service Center, Fairfield *Also called Hobart Sales and Service Inc (G-3223)*

Hobart Group Holdings LLC 908 470-1780
240 Main St Gladstone (07934) *(G-3798)*
Hobart Sales and Service Inc 973 227-9265
4 Gloria Ln Fairfield (07004) *(G-3223)*
Hobby Blade Specialty Inc 908 317-9306
725 Jerusalem Rd Scotch Plains (07076) *(G-9851)*
Hobby Publications Inc 732 536-5160
83 South St Ste 307 Freehold (07728) *(G-3659)*
Hoboken Executive Art Inc 201 420-8262
320 Washington St Ste A Hoboken (07030) *(G-4473)*
Hoboken Mary Ltd Liability Co 201 234-9910
1109 Washington St Apt 2 Hoboken (07030) *(G-4474)*
Hoboken Reporter 201 553-0130
4400 Dell Ave North Bergen (07047) *(G-7457)*
Hock & Mandel, Lodi *Also called All State Medal Co Inc (G-5575)*
Hockmeyer Equipment Corp (PA) 973 482-0225
610 Supor Blvd Harrison (07029) *(G-4185)*
Hoda Inc 609 695-3000
532 Mulberry St Trenton (08638) *(G-11063)*
Hoeganaes Corporation (HQ) 856 303-0366
1001 Taylors Ln Cinnaminson (08077) *(G-1468)*
Hofer Connectors Co Inc 973 427-1195
126 Linda Vista Ave North Haledon (07508) *(G-7548)*
Hofer Machine & Tool Co Inc 973 427-1195
126 Linda Vista Ave North Haledon (07508) *(G-7549)*
Hoffman/New Yorker Inc (PA) 201 488-1800
46 Clinton Pl Hackensack (07601) *(G-3928)*
Hoffmann-La Roche Inc (HQ) 973 890-2268
150 Clove Rd Ste 88th Little Falls (07424) *(G-5476)*
Hoffmann-La Roche Inc 973 235-8216
701 Union Blvd Totowa (07512) *(G-10951)*
Hoffmann-La Roche Inc 973 235-3092
340 Kingsland St Nutley (07110) *(G-7648)*
Hoffmann-La Roche Inc 973 235-1016
500 Kingsland St Nutley (07110) *(G-7649)*
Hofmann Tool & Die Corporation 201 327-0226
356 State Rt 17 Upper Saddle River (07458) *(G-11279)*
Hojiblanca USA Inc 201 384-3007
175 Washington Ave Ste 18 Dumont (07628) *(G-2118)*
Holby Valve Co Inc 973 465-7400
24 Ferdon St Newark (07105) *(G-7190)*
Holiday Bowl Inc 201 337-6516
29 Spruce St Oakland (07436) *(G-7691)*
Holistic Solar Usa Inc 732 757-5500
105 Lock St Ste 407 Newark (07103) *(G-7191)*
Holland Manufacturing Co Inc (PA) 973 584-8141
15 Main St Succasunna (07876) *(G-10623)*
Holler Metal Fabricators Inc 732 635-9050
215 Liberty St Metuchen (08840) *(G-6109)*
Holly Packaging Inc 856 327-8281
1101 N 10th St Millville (08332) *(G-6308)*
Hollywood Tanning Systems Inc 856 302-1368
380 Franklin Tpke Mahwah (07430) *(G-5782)*
Hollywood Tans, Mahwah *Also called Hollywood Tanning Systems Inc (G-5782)*
Holman Enterprises Inc 856 532-2410
9040 Burrough Dover Ln Pennsauken (08110) *(G-8522)*
Holman Enterprises Inc 609 383-6100
1311 Route 73 Mount Laurel (08054) *(G-6802)*
Holman Jaguar and Infinite, Mount Laurel *Also called Holman Enterprises Inc (G-6802)*
Holmdel Acpnctr & Ntrl Med Ctr 732 888-4910
721 N Beers St Ste Suite Holmdel (07733) *(G-4517)*
Holocraft Corporation (PA) 732 502-9500
50 Flexcraft Dr Neptune (07753) *(G-6919)*
Holographic Finishing Inc 201 941-4651
501 Hendricks Cswy Ridgefield (07657) *(G-9365)*
Holtec Government Services LLC 856 291-0600
525 Route 73 N Ste 304 Marlton (08053) *(G-5978)*
Holtec International 856 797-0900
1 Holtec Blvd Camden (08104) *(G-1069)*
Homan Communications Inc 609 654-9594
194 Route 70 Ste 9 Medford (08055) *(G-6070)*
Homasote Company 609 883-3300
932 Lower Ferry Rd Ewing (08628) *(G-3024)*
Home and Garden Kraft LLC 908 995-9355
93 Crab Apple Hill Rd Milford (08848) *(G-6246)*
Home Care America, Madison *Also called Krieck Enterprises LLC (G-5727)*
Home News & Tribune, Neptune *Also called Asbury Park Press Inc (G-6900)*
Home News Tribune 908 243-6600
92 E Main St Ste 202 Somerville (08876) *(G-10214)*
Home Organization LLC 201 351-2121
570 Piermont Rd Ste 136 Closter (07624) *(G-1760)*
Home Rubber Company, Trenton *Also called Denaka Partners LP (G-11053)*
Home Warehouse Outlet, Jersey City *Also called Orient Originals Inc (G-4796)*
Homeco LLC 732 802-7733
739 South Ave Piscataway (08854) *(G-8774)*
Homespun Global LLC 917 674-9684
4000 Bordentown Ave # 18 Sayreville (08872) *(G-9823)*
Homestyle Kitchens & Baths LLC 908 979-9000
453 Route 46 E Hackettstown (07840) *(G-4011)*

2018 Harris New Jersey
Manufacturers Directory

(G-0000) Company's Geographic Section entry number

Hometown Office Sups & Prtg Co, Bordentown *Also called Hometown Office Sups & Prtg Co (G-598)*
Hometown Office Sups & Prtg Co 609 298-9020
  192 Us Highway 130 Bordentown (08505) *(G-598)*
Hone-A-Matic Tool & Cutter Co 732 382-6000
  187 Wescott Dr Rahway (07065) *(G-9197)*
Honeyware Inc (PA) 201 997-5900
  244 Dukes St Kearny (07032) *(G-4880)*
Honeywell, Mount Laurel *Also called Metrologic Instruments Inc (G-6818)*
Honeywell Asia Pacific Inc (HQ) 973 455-2000
  115 Tabor Rd Morris Plains (07950) *(G-6662)*
Honeywell Authorized Dealer, Branchburg *Also called Sander Mechanical Service Inc (G-701)*
Honeywell Authorized Dealer, Pennsauken *Also called McAllister Service Company (G-8546)*
Honeywell Authorized Dealer, Berlin *Also called T J Eckardt Associates Inc (G-442)*
Honeywell Authorized Dealer, Bordentown *Also called Ats Mechanical Inc (G-591)*
Honeywell International Inc 800 601-3099
  115 Tabor Rd Morris Plains (07950) *(G-6663)*
Honeywell International Inc 973 455-6633
  20 Airport Rd Morristown (07960) *(G-6714)*
Honeywell International Inc 973 285-5321
  8 Waterloo Dr Morris Plains (07950) *(G-6664)*
Honeywell International Inc 856 691-5111
  2658 N West Blvd Vineland (08360) *(G-11370)*
Honeywell International Inc 856 234-5020
  121 Whittendale Dr Moorestown (08057) *(G-6585)*
Honeywell International Inc 973 455-2000
  115 Tabor Rd Morris Plains (07950) *(G-6665)*
Honeywell International Inc (PA) 973 455-2000
  115 Tabor Rd Morris Plains (07950) *(G-6666)*
Honeywell International Inc 732 919-0010
  5047 Industrial Rd Ste 2 Wall Township (07727) *(G-11488)*
Honeywell International Inc 908 561-1888
  107 Corporate Blvd South Plainfield (07080) *(G-10380)*
Honeywell International Inc 973 455-2000
  Columbia Tpke Morristown (07962) *(G-6715)*
Honeywell International Inc 800 601-3099
  115 Tabor Rd Morris Plains (07950) *(G-6667)*
Honeywell International Inc 973 455-2000
  115 Tabor Rd Morris Plains (07950) *(G-6668)*
Honeywell Spain Holdings LLC (HQ) 973 455-2000
  101 Columbia Rd Morristown (07960) *(G-6716)*
Honeywell Speclty Wax & Additv (HQ) 973 455-2000
  101 Columbia Rd Morristown (07960) *(G-6717)*
Honig Chemical & Proc Corp 973 344-0881
  414 Wilson Ave Newark (07105) *(G-7192)*
Hood Products LLC 201 426-0700
  18 Mill St Lodi (07644) *(G-5587)*
Hoof Fe Dye Works, Paterson *Also called North Jersey Skein Dyeing Co (G-8352)*
Hookway Enterprises Inc 973 691-0382
  130 Allen St Netcong (07857) *(G-6941)*
Hopatcong Fuel On You LLC 973 770-0854
  107 Tulsa Trl Hopatcong (07843) *(G-4537)*
Hope Center 201 798-1234
  43 Charles St Jersey City (07307) *(G-4766)*
Hope Electrical Products Co 973 882-7400
  3 Fairfield Cres West Caldwell (07006) *(G-11778)*
Hopewell Valley Vineyards LLC 609 737-4465
  46 Yard Rd Pennington (08534) *(G-8453)*
Hoppecke Batteries Inc 856 616-0032
  2 Berry Dr Hainesport (08036) *(G-4073)*
Horiba Instruments Inc 732 623-8335
  20 Knightsbridge Rd Piscataway (08854) *(G-8775)*
Horiba Instruments Inc 732 494-8660
  20 Knightsbridge Rd Piscataway (08854) *(G-8776)*
Horiba Scientific, Piscataway *Also called Horiba Instruments Inc (G-8776)*
Horizon Group USA Inc (PA) 908 810-1111
  45 Technology Dr Warren (07059) *(G-11553)*
Horizon Label LLC 856 767-0777
  1049 Industrial Dr West Berlin (08091) *(G-11725)*
Horizon Printing, Clark *Also called Tanter Inc (G-1516)*
Horizon Products NJ LLC 201 773-7015
  40 W Ridgewood Ave Ridgewood (07450) *(G-9425)*
Horowitz, Newark *Also called Manischewitz Company (G-7235)*
Horphag Research (usa) Inc 201 459-0300
  5 Marine View Plz Ste 403 Hoboken (07030) *(G-4475)*
Horsetracs 732 228-7646
  99 Oak Ave West Creek (08092) *(G-11811)*
Hosepharm Ltd Liability Co 732 376-0044
  351 Smith St Perth Amboy (08861) *(G-8617)*
Hosokawa Micron International 908 273-6360
  10 Chatham Rd Summit (07901) *(G-10644)*
Hosokawa Micron International 908 273-6360
  10 Chatham Rd Summit (07901) *(G-10645)*
Hosokawa Micron International 908 273-6360
  10 Chatham Rd Summit (07901) *(G-10646)*
Hosokawa Micron International (HQ) 908 273-6360
  10 Chatham Rd Summit (07901) *(G-10647)*

Hosokawa Micron International 866 507-4974
  751 Hylton Rd Pennsauken (08110) *(G-8523)*
Hosokawa Micron Powder Systems, Summit *Also called Hosokawa Micron International (G-10645)*
Hosokawa Micron Powder Systems, Summit *Also called Hosokawa Micron International (G-10647)*
Hosokawa Tech, Summit *Also called Hosokawa Micron International (G-10644)*
Hospital & Health Care Compen, Oakland *Also called John R Zabka Associates Inc (G-7693)*
Hospitality GL Brands USA Inc 800 869-5258
  185 Industrial Ave Ridgefield Park (07660) *(G-9407)*
Hot Dip Galvanizing 732 442-7555
  1190 Amboy Ave Perth Amboy (08861) *(G-8618)*
Hot Runner Technology 908 431-5711
  216 Us Highway 206 Hillsborough (08844) *(G-4342)*
Hotpack, Buena *Also called S P Industries Inc (G-948)*
Houghton Chemical Corporation 201 460-8071
  30 Amor Ave Carlstadt (07072) *(G-1170)*
House Foods America Corp 732 537-9500
  801 Randolph Rd Somerset (08873) *(G-10108)*
House of Cupcakes 862 225-9536
  259 Allwood Rd Clifton (07012) *(G-1642)*
House of Cupcakes LLC 908 413-3076
  51 Suydam Rd Somerset (08873) *(G-10109)*
House of Gold Inc 856 665-0020
  1505 Suckle Hwy Pennsauken (08110) *(G-8524)*
House of Herbs Inc 973 779-2422
  38 Ann St Passaic (07055) *(G-8147)*
House of Kalon New York 786 259-0786
  2 Radio Ave Apt C24 Secaucus (07094) *(G-9895)*
House of Prill Inc 732 442-2400
  716 Newman Springs Rd # 303 Lincroft (07738) *(G-5337)*
House Pearl Fashions (us) Ltd (HQ) 973 778-7551
  300-2 D&E Rr 17 Lodi (07644) *(G-5588)*
Household and Per Pdts Indust, Montvale *Also called Rodman Media Corp (G-6478)*
Houses Magazine Inc 973 605-1877
  173 Morris St Morris Plains (07950) *(G-6669)*
Houzer Inc (HQ) 609 584-1900
  2605 Kuser Rd Hamilton (08691) *(G-4108)*
Hovione LLC 609 918-2600
  40 Lake Dr East Windsor (08520) *(G-2359)*
Howard A Schaevitz Tech Inc (HQ) 856 662-8000
  450 Clark Dr Ste 4 Budd Lake (07828) *(G-931)*
Howard Lippincott 856 764-8282
  74 Norman Ave Riverside (08075) *(G-9499)*
Howard Packaging Corp 973 904-0022
  86 Cobble St Clifton (07013) *(G-1643)*
Howard Press Inc 908 245-4400
  450 W 1st Ave Roselle (07203) *(G-9673)*
Howell Precision Tool Co, Farmingdale *Also called Hanrahan Tool Co Inc (G-3386)*
HOWELL TOWNSHIP PAL, Howell *Also called Howell Township Police (G-4556)*
Howell Township Police 732 919-2805
  115 Kent Rd Howell (07731) *(G-4556)*
Howes Standard Publishing Co 856 691-2000
  1980 S West Blvd Vineland (08360) *(G-11371)*
Howman Associates Inc 732 985-7474
  12 Garden St Edison (08817) *(G-2538)*
Howman Controls, Edison *Also called Howman Associates Inc (G-2538)*
Howman Electronics Inc 908 534-2247
  291 Us Highway 22 Ste 40 Lebanon (08833) *(G-5288)*
Howman Engineering, Lebanon *Also called Howman Electronics Inc (G-5288)*
Howmedica Osteonics Corp 201 541-6569
  53 Bancker St Englewood (07631) *(G-2903)*
Howmedica Osteonics Corp (HQ) 201 831-5000
  325 Corporate Dr Mahwah (07430) *(G-5783)*
Howmet Castings & Services Inc 973 442-2261
  9 Roy St Dover (07801) *(G-2090)*
Howmet Castings & Services Inc 973 361-0300
  9 Roy St Dover (07801) *(G-2091)*
Howmet Castings & Services Inc 973 361-2310
  10 Roy St Dover (07801) *(G-2092)*
Hoyt Corporation 201 894-0707
  520 S Dean St Englewood (07631) *(G-2904)*
Hozric LLC 908 420-8821
  11 Ridge Rd Green Brook (08812) *(G-3857)*
Hpc Pos System Corp (PA) 973 239-9666
  220 Little Falls Rd # 4 Cedar Grove (07009) *(G-1284)*
HPH Products Inc 609 883-0052
  182 Carlton Ave Ewing (08618) *(G-3025)*
Hpi International Inc 732 942-9900
  301 1st St Lakewood (08701) *(G-5135)*
Hr Acuity LLC 888 598-0161
  25a Vreeland Rd Ste 101 Florham Park (07932) *(G-3507)*
HR Industries Inc 201 941-8000
  605 Broad Ave Ste 102 Ridgefield (07657) *(G-9366)*
HRA International Inc (PA) 609 395-0939
  489 Hillrose Way Monroe (08831) *(G-6374)*
HRP Capital Inc (PA) 201 242-4938
  173 Bridge Plz N Fort Lee (07024) *(G-3557)*

A
L
P
H
A
B
E
T
I
C

Hsh Assoc Financial Publishers 973 838-3330
1200 State Rt 23 Butler (07405) ***(G-1008)***

Ht Stamping Co LLC 973 227-4858
19 Gardner Rd Ste C Fairfield (07004) ***(G-3224)***

Htp Connectivity LLC 973 586-2286
300 Round Hill Dr Ste 4 Rockaway (07866) ***(G-9572)***

Hub Print & Copy Center LLC 201 585-7887
2037 Lemoine Ave Fort Lee (07024) ***(G-3558)***

Hub Sign Crane Corp 732 252-9090
67 Wood Ave Manalapan (07726) ***(G-5850)***

Hub, The, Fort Lee *Also called Hub Print & Copy Center LLC* ***(G-3558)***

Huber International Corp 732 549-8600
499 Thornall St Ste 8 Edison (08837) ***(G-2539)***

Huber+suhner Astrolab Inc 732 560-3800
4 Powderhorn Dr Warren (07059) ***(G-11554)***

Hudson & Bergen Company 201 991-4900
350 Belleville Tpke Kearny (07032) ***(G-4881)***

Hudson Awning & Sign Co, Bayonne *Also called Hudson Awning Co Inc* ***(G-232)***

Hudson Awning Co Inc 201 339-7171
27 Cottage St Bayonne (07002) ***(G-232)***

Hudson Bread, North Bergen *Also called Prestige Bread Jersey Cy Inc* ***(G-7476)***

Hudson Cakery 201 319-0363
1816 Willow Ave Weehawken (07086) ***(G-11696)***

Hudson Cosmetic Mfg Corp 973 472-2323
93 Entin Rd Ste 4 Clifton (07014) ***(G-1644)***

Hudson Displays Co 973 623-8255
687 Frelinghuysen Ave # 1 Newark (07114) ***(G-7193)***

Hudson Drapery Service, Jersey City *Also called Forsters Cleaning & Tailoring* ***(G-4757)***

Hudson Group (hg) Inc (HQ) 201 939-5050
1 Meadowlands Plz East Rutherford (07073) ***(G-2300)***

Hudson Industries Corporation (HQ) 973 402-0100
271 Us Highway 46 F207 Fairfield (07004) ***(G-3225)***

Hudson Manufacturing Corp 973 376-7070
12 E Willow St Millburn (07041) ***(G-6252)***

Hudson Reporter, Bayonne *Also called Newspaper Media Group LLC* ***(G-239)***

Hudson Robotics Inc 973 376-7400
10 Stern Ave Springfield (07081) ***(G-10556)***

Hudson Valley Enviromental Inc 732 967-0060
2063 Basswood Ct Toms River (08755) ***(G-10887)***

Hudson West Publishing Co 201 991-1600
39 Seeley Ave Kearny (07032) ***(G-4882)***

Hueck Foils Holding Co (HQ) 732 974-4100
1955 State Route 34 3c Wall Township (07719) ***(G-11489)***

Hugo Neu Recycling LLC 914 530-2350
78 John Miller Way Ste 1 Kearny (07032) ***(G-4883)***

Humanscale Corporation 732 537-2944
220 Circle Dr N Piscataway (08854) ***(G-8777)***

Hummel Chemical, South Plainfield *Also called Hummel Croton Inc* ***(G-10381)***

Hummel Croton Inc 908 754-1800
10 Harmich Rd South Plainfield (07080) ***(G-10381)***

Hummel Distributing Corp (PA) 908 688-5300
850 Springfield Rd Union (07083) ***(G-11193)***

Hummel Printing Inc 908 688-5300
850 Springfield Rd Union (07083) ***(G-11194)***

Hun Machine Works Inc 856 461-6911
51 Whittaker St Riverside (08075) ***(G-9500)***

Hungerford & Terry Inc (PA) 856 881-3200
226 N Atlantic Ave Clayton (08312) ***(G-1524)***

Hunterdon Brewing Company LLC 908 454-7445
12 Coddington Rd Whitehouse Station (08889) ***(G-12051)***

Hunterdon County Democrat Inc (PA) 908 782-4747
200 State Route 31 # 202 Flemington (08822) ***(G-3448)***

Hunterdon County Democrat Inc 908 996-4047
207 Harrison St Frenchtown (08825) ***(G-3701)***

Hunterdon Observer, Flemington *Also called Hunterdon County Democrat Inc* ***(G-3448)***

Hunterdon Transformer Co Inc (PA) 908 454-2400
75 Industrial Rd Alpha (08865) ***(G-42)***

Hup & Sons 908 832-7878
10 White Tail Ln Glen Gardner (08826) ***(G-3815)***

Hurricane Hutch 908 256-5912
190 Lamerson Rd Chester (07930) ***(G-1437)***

Hussmann Corporation 800 320-3510
875 Kings Hwy Ste 205 West Deptford (08096) ***(G-11828)***

Hutcheon and Simon, Hackensack *Also called Danson Sheet Metal Inc* ***(G-3903)***

Hutchinson Cabinets 856 468-5500
244 Bark Bridge Rd Sewell (08080) ***(G-9956)***

Hutchinson Industries Inc 609 394-1010
251 Southard St Trenton (08609) ***(G-11064)***

Hutchinson Industries Inc (HQ) 609 394-1010
460 Southard St Trenton (08638) ***(G-11065)***

Hutchinson Industries Inc 609 394-1010
84 Parker Ave Ste 86 Trenton (08609) ***(G-11066)***

Hutchinson Industries Inc 609 394-1010
106 108 Mulberry St Trenton (08609) ***(G-11067)***

Hve, Toms River *Also called Hudson Valley Enviromental Inc* ***(G-10887)***

Hy-Tek Material Handling Inc 732 490-6282
704 Ginesi Dr Ste 25 Morganville (07751) ***(G-6642)***

Hy-Test Packaging Corp 973 754-7000
515 E 41st St Paterson (07504) ***(G-8291)***

Hybrid-Tek LLC 609 259-3355
9 Trenton Lakewood Rd # 2 Clarksburg (08510) ***(G-1520)***

Hychem Corporation 732 280-8803
611 Main St Ste B-2 Belmar (07719) ***(G-359)***

Hycrete Inc 201 386-8110
409 Main St Little Falls (07424) ***(G-5477)***

Hydracore Inc 732 548-5500
60 Liberty St Metuchen (08840) ***(G-6110)***

Hydratight Operations Inc 732 271-4100
12 Worlds Fair Dr Ste A Somerset (08873) ***(G-10110)***

Hydraulic Manifolds Usa LLC 973 728-1214
264 Marshall Hill Rd West Milford (07480) ***(G-11852)***

Hydro Milling Group Inc 732 450-2488
20 Thomas Ave Shrewsbury (07702) ***(G-10000)***

Hydro-Mechanical Systems Inc 856 848-8888
1030 Delsea Dr Unit 8 Westville (08093) ***(G-11943)***

Hydromer Inc (PA) 908 526-2828
35 Industrial Pkwy Branchburg (08876) ***(G-665)***

Hygloss Products Inc 973 458-1700
45 Hathaway St Wallington (07057) ***(G-11527)***

Hygrade Business Group Inc (PA) 800 836-7714
30 Seaview Dr Secaucus (07094) ***(G-9896)***

Hyman W Fisher Inc 973 992-9155
121 E Northfield Rd Livingston (07039) ***(G-5534)***

Hyp Hair Inc 201 843-4004
372 Orange Rd Montclair (07042) ***(G-6416)***

Hyper Bicycles Inc 856 694-0352
177 Malaga Park Dr Malaga (08328) ***(G-5826)***

I & J Fisnar Inc 973 646-5044
19 Chapin Rd Bldg C Pine Brook (07058) ***(G-8703)***

I 2 R Corp (PA) 732 919-1100
5033 Industrial Rd Ste 6 Wall Township (07727) ***(G-11490)***

I Associates LLC 215 262-7754
9255 Commerce Hwy Pennsauken (08110) ***(G-8525)***

I C S, Fairfield *Also called International Cord Sets Inc* ***(G-3232)***

I C System Solutions Inc 201 666-1122
270 Broadway Hillsdale (07642) ***(G-4384)***

I F A, Allenwood *Also called I F Associates Inc* ***(G-36)***

I F Associates Inc 732 223-2900
3303 Atlantic Ave Allenwood (08720) ***(G-36)***

I F F, Dayton *Also called Interntnal Flvors Frgrnces Inc* ***(G-1972)***

I F T, Piscataway *Also called Interntonal Fragrance Tech Inc* ***(G-8783)***

I Fcb Holdings Inc (HQ) 201 934-2000
933 Macarthur Blvd Mahwah (07430) ***(G-5784)***

I I Galaxy Inc 732 828-2686
235 Jersey Ave Ste 3 New Brunswick (08901) ***(G-6966)***

I K Construction Inc 908 925-5200
174 Evergreen Pl 805 East Orange (07018) ***(G-2256)***

I M N G, Parsippany *Also called Interntonal Med News Group LLC* ***(G-8032)***

I Physician Hub 732 274-0155
462 New Rd Monmouth Junction (08852) ***(G-6346)***

I Print Nb 201 662-1133
9252 Kennedy Blvd North Bergen (07047) ***(G-7458)***

I S Parts International Inc 856 691-2203
3603 N Mill Rd Vineland (08360) ***(G-11372)***

I See Optical Laboratories (PA) 856 227-9300
44 W Church St Blackwood (08012) ***(G-481)***

I See Optical Laboratories 856 795-6435
312 W Somerdale Rd Voorhees (08043) ***(G-11433)***

I T C Printing Promotion 908 918-1122
24 Beechwood Rd Summit (07901) ***(G-10648)***

I T S Products, South Plainfield *Also called Intellgent Trffic Sup Pdts LLC* ***(G-10385)***

I T W Covid, Cranbury *Also called Illinois Tool Works Inc* ***(G-1837)***

I Trade Technology Ltd (PA) 615 348-7233
115 Franklin Tpke Ste 144 Mahwah (07430) ***(G-5785)***

I V Miller & Sons Inc 732 493-4040
15 Cindy Ln Ocean (07712) ***(G-7728)***

I W Tremont Co, Hawthorne *Also called IW Tremont Co Inc* ***(G-4242)***

I-Exceed Tech Solutions Inc 917 693-3207
103 Carnegie Ctr Ste 300 Princeton (08540) ***(G-9056)***

I-Yell-O Foods Inc 732 525-2201
603 Washington Ave South Amboy (08879) ***(G-10239)***

I.S.t, Parlin *Also called Industrial Summit Tech Corp* ***(G-7932)***

I3 Software, Newark *Also called Dcm Group Inc* ***(G-7135)***

I4 Sustainability LLC 732 618-3310
140 Mountain Ave Ste 303 Springfield (07081) ***(G-10557)***

Iacobucci USA Inc 732 935-6633
151 Industrial Way E A2 Eatontown (07724) ***(G-2404)***

Iacovelli Stairs Incorporated 609 693-3476
707 Challenger Way Forked River (08731) ***(G-3538)***

Iam International Inc 908 713-9651
4 Saddle Ridge Dr Lebanon (08833) ***(G-5289)***

IBC Pharmaceuticals Inc 973 540-9595
300 The American Rd Morris Plains (07950) ***(G-6670)***

IBM, Park Ridge *Also called International Bus Mchs Corp* ***(G-7923)***

Iboco Corp 732 417-0066
1205 Paco Way Ste B Lakewood (08701) ***(G-5136)***

Ice Cold Novelty Products Inc 732 751-0011
5005 Belmar Blvd Ste B2 Wall Township (07727) ***(G-11491)***

Iceberg Coffee LLC..908 675-6972
    865 Rte 33 Ste 4 Freehold (07728) *(G-3660)*

Iceboxx LLC..201 857-0404
    600 Braen Ave Wyckoff (07481) *(G-12254)*

Icelandirect Inc...800 763-4690
    127 Kingsland Ave Ste 101 Clifton (07014) *(G-1645)*

Ichrom Solutions, Sicklerville *Also called Spark Holland Inc (G-10026)*

ICM, Fair Lawn *Also called Industrial Consulting Mktg Inc (G-3096)*

Icon Orthopedic Concepts LLC............................973 794-6810
    6 Mars Ct Ste 3 Boonton (07005) *(G-571)*

Icote USA Inc (PA)..908 359-7575
    465 Amwell Rd Hillsborough (08844) *(G-4343)*

Ics Corporation..215 427-3355
    100 Friars Blvd West Deptford (08086) *(G-11829)*

Icup Inc..856 751-2045
    1152 Marlkress Rd Ste 200 Cherry Hill (08003) *(G-1376)*

Icy Cools Inc...609 448-0172
    15 Oscar Dr Roosevelt (08555) *(G-9641)*

Icykidz...973 342-9665
    539 Union Ave Irvington (07111) *(G-4590)*

ID Systems Inc (PA)...201 996-9000
    123 Tice Blvd Woodcliff Lake (07677) *(G-12193)*

ID Technology LLC..201 405-0767
    48 Spruce St Oakland (07436) *(G-7692)*

Ida Automotive Inc...732 591-1245
    600 Texas Rd Morganville (07751) *(G-6643)*

Ideal Data Inc...201 998-9440
    420 River Rd North Arlington (07031) *(G-7420)*

Ideal Jacobs Corporation....................................973 275-5100
    515 Valley St Bsmt 1 Maplewood (07040) *(G-5922)*

Ideal Plating, Paterson *Also called Independence Plating Corp (G-8293)*

Ideal Plating & Polishing Co...............................973 759-5559
    107 Alabama Ave Paterson (07503) *(G-8292)*

Ideal Tile Company Toms River, Toms River *Also called Andrevin Inc (G-10863)*

Ideal Tile Fabrications LLC.................................732 751-0074
    304a Squankum Rd Farmingdale (07727) *(G-3387)*

Identity Depot Inc..973 584-9301
    244 Main St Ledgewood (07852) *(G-5305)*

Ideon LLC..908 431-3126
    249 Homestead Rd Ste 1 Hillsborough (08844) *(G-4344)*

IDL Techni-Edge LLC..908 497-9818
    30 Boright Ave Kenilworth (07033) *(G-4962)*

IDS, Fort Lee *Also called Interntnal Digital Systems Inc (G-3560)*

IDS, Englewood Cliffs *Also called Integrated Dental Systems LLC (G-2967)*

Idt Energy Inc (HQ)...877 887-6866
    520 Broad St Fl 9 Newark (07102) *(G-7194)*

Idt Global Processing Svcs Inc............................973 438-3556
    520 Broad St Newark (07102) *(G-7195)*

Ifc Products Inc...908 587-1221
    568 E Elizabeth Ave Linden (07036) *(G-5384)*

Ifc Solutions Inc..908 862-8810
    1601 E Linden Ave Linden (07036) *(G-5385)*

Ifortress..973 812-6400
    228 Lackawanna Ave Woodland Park (07424) *(G-12222)*

Igi Corp...908 753-5570
    6 Ingersoll Rd South Plainfield (07080) *(G-10382)*

Ihs Inc..201 391-0084
    50 Tice Blvd Ste 130 Woodcliff Lake (07677) *(G-12194)*

Ii-VI Advanced Materials Sic S, Pine Brook *Also called Ii-VI Incorporated (G-8704)*

Ii-VI Incorporated...973 227-1551
    20 Chapin Rd Ste 1007 Pine Brook (07058) *(G-8704)*

Ii-VI Optoelectronic Dvcs Inc (HQ).......................908 668-5000
    141 Mount Bethel Rd Warren (07059) *(G-11555)*

Ii-VI Wide Band Gap Inc.....................................973 227-1551
    20 Chapin Rd Ste 1005 Pine Brook (07058) *(G-8705)*

Ikaria Therapeutics LLC......................................908 238-6600
    Perryvle 3 Corp Park Fl 3 Hampton (08827) *(G-4160)*

Ileos of America Inc..908 753-7300
    550 Hadley Rd South Plainfield (07080) *(G-10383)*

Ilg, Cherry Hill *Also called International Laser Group Inc (G-1382)*

Ilkem Marble & Granite, Cherry Hill *Also called Ilkem Marble and Granite Inc (G-1377)*

Ilkem Marble and Granite Inc..............................856 433-8714
    2010 Springdale Rd # 300 Cherry Hill (08003) *(G-1377)*

Ill Eagle Enterprises Ltd....................................973 237-1111
    101 Miller Ln Ringwood (07456) *(G-9449)*

Ill-Eagle Enterprises, Ringwood *Also called Ill Eagle Enterprises Ltd (G-9449)*

Illinois Tool Works Inc.......................................609 395-5600
    32 Commerce Dr Ste 1 Cranbury (08512) *(G-1837)*

Illinois Tool Works Inc.......................................732 968-5300
    6 Ringwood Dr Parsippany (07054) *(G-8028)*

Illinois Tools, Passaic *Also called Atlantic Mills Inc (G-8126)*

Illuminating Experiences LLC...............................800 734-5858
    625 Jersey Ave Ste 7 New Brunswick (08901) *(G-6967)*

Ilsi, Fairfield *Also called Industrial Lbeling Systems Inc (G-3230)*

Imaan Trading Inc..201 779-2062
    286 Bergen Ave Jersey City (07305) *(G-4767)*

Image Access Corp (PA)......................................201 342-7878
    22 Paris Ave Ste 210 Rockleigh (07647) *(G-9631)*

Image Builder Appliques, Woodcliff Lake *Also called Uniport Industries Corporation (G-12206)*

Image First Uniforms, Englewood *Also called Alpine Trading Company Inc (G-2867)*

Image Makers Instant Printing.............................973 633-1771
    1581 State Route 23 Wayne (07470) *(G-11649)*

Image Point..908 684-1768
    69 Water St Newton (07860) *(G-7392)*

Image Remit Inc...732 940-7900
    205 N Center Dr North Brunswick (08902) *(G-7518)*

Image Screen Printing Inc...................................732 560-1817
    532 Lincoln Blvd Middlesex (08846) *(G-6170)*

Imagery Embroidary Corporation..........................201 343-9333
    2907 Jeannette St 2911 Union City (07087) *(G-11248)*

Images Costume Productions...............................609 859-7372
    881 Westminster Dr N Southampton (08088) *(G-10475)*

Imagine Audio LLC...856 488-1466
    304 Haddonfield Rd Cherry Hill (08002) *(G-1378)*

Imagine Gold LLC...201 488-5988
    60 Romanelli Ave South Hackensack (07606) *(G-10270)*

Imagine Screen Printing, Dayton *Also called Central Mills Inc (G-1960)*

Imagine Screen Prtg & Prod LLC...........................732 329-2009
    473 Ridge Rd Dayton (08810) *(G-1969)*

Imclone LLC...908 218-9588
    33 Imclone Dr Branchburg (08876) *(G-666)*

Imclone Systems LLC (HQ)...................................908 541-8000
    440 Us Highway 22 Bridgewater (08807) *(G-844)*

Imclone Systems LLC...908 218-0147
    33 Imclone Dr Branchburg (08876) *(G-667)*

Imclone Systems LLC...908 541-8100
    50 Imclone Dr Branchburg (08876) *(G-668)*

Immtech Pharmaceuticals Inc.............................212 791-2911
    93 Prospect Ave Montclair (07042) *(G-6417)*

Immune Pharmaceuticals Inc (PA)........................201 464-2677
    550 Sylvan Ave Ste 101 Englewood Cliffs (07632) *(G-2965)*

Immunogenetics Inc..856 697-1441
    Lincoln Ave & Wheat Rd Buena (08310) *(G-947)*

Immunomedics Inc (PA)......................................973 605-8200
    300 The American Rd Morris Plains (07950) *(G-6671)*

Immunostics Inc...732 918-0770
    38 Industrial Way E Ste 5 Eatontown (07724) *(G-2405)*

Immunostics Company Inc....................................732 918-0770
    38 Industrial Way E Ste 1 Eatontown (07724) *(G-2406)*

Impact Air 45, Englewood *Also called Palisades Dental LLc (G-2920)*

Impact Design Inc..908 289-2900
    248 3rd St Elizabethport (07206) *(G-2785)*

Impact Displays Inc..201 804-6262
    310 13th St Carlstadt (07072) *(G-1171)*

Impact Instrumentation Inc.................................973 882-1212
    27 Fairfield Pl West Caldwell (07006) *(G-11779)*

Impact Medical, West Caldwell *Also called Impact Instrumentation Inc (G-11779)*

Impact Printing...862 225-9167
    15 Vogt Ln 1 Little Ferry (07643) *(G-5508)*

Impact Protective Eqp LLC...................................973 377-0903
    8 Westerly Ave Madison (07940) *(G-5724)*

Impact Unlimited Inc (PA)..................................732 274-2000
    250 Ridge Rd Dayton (08810) *(G-1970)*

Impact Visal Systems, Cream Ridge *Also called Central Art & Enginering Inc (G-1932)*

Impact Xm, Dayton *Also called Impact Unlimited Inc (G-1970)*

Imperial Copy Products Inc..................................973 927-5500
    961 State Route 10 1ee Randolph (07869) *(G-9284)*

Imperial Dax Co Inc..973 227-6105
    120 New Dutch Ln Fairfield (07004) *(G-3226)*

Imperial Design...856 742-8480
    729 Charles St Gloucester City (08030) *(G-3839)*

Imperial Drug & Spice Corp.................................201 348-1551
    5620 Kennedy Blvd W West New York (07093) *(G-11867)*

Imperial Electro-Plating, Lyndhurst *Also called FER Plating Inc (G-5683)*

Imperial Machine & Tool Co (PA)..........................908 496-8100
    8 W Crisman Rd Columbia (07832) *(G-1798)*

Imperial Metal Products Inc................................908 647-8181
    8 W Chimney Rock Rd Bound Brook (08805) *(G-618)*

Imperial Sewing Machine Co................................973 374-3405
    584 S 21st St Irvington (07111) *(G-4591)*

Imperial Weld Ring Corp Inc................................908 354-0011
    80 Front St 88 Elizabeth (07206) *(G-2746)*

Imperium Enterprises LLC...................................908 206-4970
    100 Industrial Ave Ste 1 Little Ferry (07643) *(G-5509)*

Impex, Jersey City *Also called Delight Foods USA LLC (G-4738)*

Important Papers Inc..856 751-4544
    12 Downing St Cherry Hill (08003) *(G-1379)*

Important Papers & Printing, Cherry Hill *Also called Important Papers Inc (G-1379)*

Importers Service Corp.......................................732 248-1946
    65 Brunswick Ave Edison (08817) *(G-2540)*

Impressions Unlimited Prtg LLC............................856 256-0200
    638 Delsea Dr Sewell (08080) *(G-9957)*

Imprint Ink, Shrewsbury *Also called Athletes Alley (G-9990)*

Imprintz Cstm Printed Graphics...........................609 386-5673
    691 Main St Lumberton (08048) *(G-5660)*

A L P H A B E T I C

IMS, Princeton *Also called Intelligent Mtl Solutions Inc* ***(G-9059)***
In Mocean Group LLC 732 960-2415
2400 Rte 1 North Brunswick (08902) ***(G-7519)***
In The Spotlights 973 361-7768
301 Mount Hope Ave # 2091 Rockaway (07866) ***(G-9573)***
In-Line Shtmtl Fabricators 201 339-8121
85 E 21st St Bayonne (07002) ***(G-233)***
In-Phase Technologies Inc 609 298-9555
401 Bordentown Hedding Rd Bordentown (08505) ***(G-599)***
INB Manhattan Drug Company Inc (HQ) 973 926-0816
225 Long Ave Ste 15 Hillside (07205) ***(G-4415)***
INB Manhattan Drug Company Inc 973 926-0816
210 Route 22 Hillside (07205) ***(G-4416)***
INB Manhattan Drug Company Inc 973 926-0816
225 Long Ave Ste 6 Hillside (07205) ***(G-4417)***
Inc Drom International, Towaco *Also called Drom International Inc* ***(G-10994)***
Inca Kola, Clifton *Also called Continental Food & Bev Inc* ***(G-1589)***
Incast, Montvale *Also called Investment Casting Institute* ***(G-6460)***
Incom (america) Inc 908 464-3366
330 Snyder Ave Berkeley Heights (07922) ***(G-412)***
Increase Beverage Intl Inc 609 303-3117
7250 Westfield Ave Ste M Pennsauken (08110) ***(G-8526)***
Indampharm Inc 732 970-0002
281 Route 79 N Ste 219 Morganville (07751) ***(G-6644)***
Indemax Inc 973 209-2424
1 Industrial Dr Vernon (07462) ***(G-11298)***
Independence Plating Corp (PA) 973 523-1776
107 Alabama Ave Paterson (07503) ***(G-8293)***
Independence Technology LLC 908 722-3767
W Ethicon Bldg Rr 22 Somerville (08876) ***(G-10215)***
Independent Enclosures, Wharton *Also called Independent Welding Co* ***(G-11989)***
Independent Machine Company 973 882-0060
2 Stewart Pl Fairfield (07004) ***(G-3227)***
Independent Metal Sales Inc 609 261-8090
1900 Park Ave W Hainesport (08036) ***(G-4074)***
Independent Press, The, Bloomfield *Also called Worrall Community Newspapers* ***(G-537)***
Independent Sheet Metal Co Inc 973 423-1150
2 N Corporate Dr 2 # 2 Riverdale (07457) ***(G-9482)***
Independent Welding Co 973 361-9731
105 W Dewey Ave Ste 307 Wharton (07885) ***(G-11989)***
India Cafe, South Plainfield *Also called Sukhadias Sweets & Snacks* ***(G-10436)***
Indo-US Mim TEC Private Ltd 734 327-9842
214 Carnegie Ctr Ste 104 Princeton (08540) ***(G-9057)***
Indoor Entertainment of NJ 609 522-6700
5301 Ocean Ave Wildwood (08260) ***(G-12073)***
Indoor Environmental Tech 973 709-1122
600 Ryerson Rd Ste F Lincoln Park (07035) ***(G-5327)***
Indotronix International Corp 609 750-0700
101 Morgan Ln Ste 210 Plainsboro (08536) ***(G-8885)***
Inductotherm Corporation (HQ) 609 267-9000
10 Indel Ave Rancocas (08073) ***(G-9258)***
Inductotherm Group, Rancocas *Also called Inductotherm Technologies Inc* ***(G-9259)***
Inductotherm Technologies Inc (HQ) 609 267-9000
10 Indel Ave Rancocas (08073) ***(G-9259)***
Indusco, Fairfield *Also called Industrial Brush Co Inc* ***(G-3228)***
Industl Envrnmntl Pollutn 908 241-3830
176 W Westfield Ave Roselle Park (07204) ***(G-9698)***
Industrial Brush Co Inc 800 241-9860
105 Clinton Rd Ste 1 Fairfield (07004) ***(G-3228)***
Industrial Combustion Assn 732 271-0300
20 Worlds Fair Dr Ste C Somerset (08873) ***(G-10111)***
Industrial Consulting Mktg Inc 973 427-2474
20-21 Wagaraw Rd Bldg 39 Fair Lawn (07410) ***(G-3096)***
Industrial Ferguson Foundry, Union *Also called Union Casting Industries Inc* ***(G-11231)***
Industrial Filters Company 973 575-0533
9 Industrial Rd Fairfield (07004) ***(G-3229)***
Industrial Habonim Valves & AC 201 820-3184
22 Riverview Dr Ste 103 Wayne (07470) ***(G-11650)***
Industrial Hard Chromium Co 973 344-2265
7 Rome St Newark (07105) ***(G-7196)***
Industrial Hydraulics & Rubber 856 966-2600
458 Atlantic Ave Camden (08104) ***(G-1070)***
Industrial Lbeling Systems Inc 973 808-8188
50 Kulick Rd Fairfield (07004) ***(G-3230)***
Industrial Machine & Engrg Co, Linden *Also called Industrial Machine & Engrg Co* ***(G-5386)***
Industrial Machine & Engrg Co 908 862-8874
1807 W Elizabeth Ave Linden (07036) ***(G-5386)***
Industrial Machine Corp 973 345-1800
44 Lehigh Ave Paterson (07503) ***(G-8294)***
Industrial Metal Inc 908 362-0084
169 Cedar Lake Rd Blairstown (07825) ***(G-497)***
Industrial Process & Eqp Inc 973 702-0330
803 State Rt 23 Sussex (07461) ***(G-10673)***
Industrial Rivet & Fastener Co (PA) 201 750-1040
200 Paris Ave Northvale (07647) ***(G-7584)***
Industrial Services Entps Inc 973 361-6780
159 Us Highway 46 Ste 1 Rockaway (07866) ***(G-9574)***
Industrial Stl & Fastener Corp 610 667-2220
167 Old Blmont Ave Fl 2 Flr 2 Cherry Hill (08034) ***(G-1380)***
Industrial Summit Tech Corp (HQ) 732 238-2211
250 Cheesequake Rd Parlin (08859) ***(G-7932)***
Industrial Tube Corporation 908 369-3737
297 Valley Rd Hillsborough (08844) ***(G-4345)***
Industrial Water Institute 609 585-4880
33 Maitland Rd Trenton (08620) ***(G-11068)***
Industrial Water Tech Inc 732 888-1233
6 Village Ct Hazlet (07730) ***(G-4275)***
Industrie Bitossi Inc (HQ) 201 796-0722
410 Market St Elmwood Park (07407) ***(G-2825)***
Industronic Inc 908 393-5960
1011 Us Highway 22 # 301 Bridgewater (08807) ***(G-845)***
Industry Publications Inc 973 331-9545
140 Littleton Rd Ste 320 Parsippany (07054) ***(G-8029)***
Inenergy Inc 609 466-2512
293 Wertsville Rd Ringoes (08551) ***(G-9438)***
Infineon Tech Americas Corp 732 603-5914
186 Wood Ave S Iselin (08830) ***(G-4629)***
Infineum USA LP (HQ) 908 474-0100
1900 E Linden Ave Linden (07036) ***(G-5387)***
Infinite Classic Inc 973 227-2790
30 Sherwood Ln Ste 8 Fairfield (07004) ***(G-3231)***
Infinite Mfg Group Inc 973 649-9950
35 Obrien St Kearny (07032) ***(G-4884)***
Infinite Mfg Group Inc (PA) 973 649-9950
35 Obrien St Kearny (07032) ***(G-4885)***
Infinite Sign, Kearny *Also called Infinite Mfg Group Inc* ***(G-4885)***
Infinite Sign Industries Inc 973 649-9950
35 Obrien St Kearny (07032) ***(G-4886)***
Infiniti Components Inc (PA) 908 537-9950
223 State Route 31 Hampton (08827) ***(G-4161)***
Infinity Compounding LLC 856 467-3030
2079 Center Square Rd Logan Township (08085) ***(G-5614)***
Infinity Ltl Engnred Compounds, Logan Township *Also called Infinity Compounding LLC* ***(G-5614)***
Infinix Corp 609 936-0101
4390 Us Highway 1 Ste 213 Princeton (08540) ***(G-9058)***
Infinlight Products Inc (PA) 888 665-7708
859130 N 126e East Windsor (08520) ***(G-2360)***
Infinova Corporation 732 355-9100
51 Stouts Ln Ste 1 Monmouth Junction (08852) ***(G-6347)***
Infinova Networks, Monmouth Junction *Also called Infinova Corporation* ***(G-6347)***
Infor Metal & Tooling Mfg 973 571-9520
16 Commerce Rd Cedar Grove (07009) ***(G-1285)***
Information Services Intl, Budd Lake *Also called Mars Incorporated* ***(G-936)***
Information Technolgy Corp 201 556-1999
121 Gertrude Ave Paramus (07652) ***(G-7876)***
Information Today Inc 908 219-0279
630 Central Ave Fl 2 New Providence (07974) ***(G-7040)***
Information Today Inc (PA) 609 654-6266
143 Old Marlton Pike Medford (08055) ***(G-6071)***
Infoseal LLC 201 569-4500
55 W Sheffield Ave Englewood (07631) ***(G-2905)***
Infrastructure LLC 609 748-1229
124 Old Port Republic Rd Galloway (08205) ***(G-3712)***
Infront Medical LLC 888 515-2532
1033 Us Highway 46 A202 Clifton (07013) ***(G-1646)***
Ingersoll-Rand Company 908 238-7000
1467 Route 31 S Annandale (08801) ***(G-58)***
Ingersoll-Rand Company 973 882-0924
26 Chapin Rd Ste 1107 Pine Brook (07058) ***(G-8706)***
Ingersoll-Rand Company 856 793-7000
3001 Irwin Rd Mount Laurel (08054) ***(G-6803)***
Ingersoll-Rand Intl Inc 559 271-4625
1 Centennial Ave Ste 101 Piscataway (08854) ***(G-8778)***
Ingersoll-Rand US Trane (HQ) 732 652-7100
1 Centennial Ave Ste 101 Piscataway (08854) ***(G-8779)***
Ingredion Incorporated 908 685-5000
10 Finderne Ave Ste A Bridgewater (08807) ***(G-846)***
Ingui Design LLC 201 264-9126
46 N Central Ave Ramsey (07446) ***(G-9243)***
Iniven, Branchburg *Also called Zzyzx LLC* ***(G-723)***
Iniven LLC 908 722-3770
5 Columbia Rd Branchburg (08876) ***(G-669)***
Injectable Mfg Fcilty, Cherry Hill *Also called Hikma Pharmaceuticals USA Inc* ***(G-1375)***
Injection Works Inc 856 802-6444
104 Gaither Dr Mount Laurel (08054) ***(G-6804)***
Injectron Corporation 908 753-1990
1000 S 2nd St Plainfield (07063) ***(G-8865)***
Ink On Paper Communications (PA) 732 758-6280
450 Shrewsbury Plz # 372 Shrewsbury (07702) ***(G-10001)***
Ink Well Printers LLC 908 272-8090
38 S 21st St Kenilworth (07033) ***(G-4963)***
Inlc Technology Corporation 908 834-8390
30 Technology Dr Ste 1d Warren (07059) ***(G-11556)***
Inman Mold Manufacturing Inc (PA) 732 381-3033
815 Martin St Rahway (07065) ***(G-9198)***
Inman Mold Manufacturing Inc 732 381-3033
273 E Inman Ave Rahway (07065) ***(G-9199)***

Inn-Client Server Systems LLC 908 782-9500
45 River Rd Ste 301 Flemington (08822) ***(G-3449)***
Innan Molding, Rahway *Also called Barlics Manufacturing Co Inc* ***(G-9179)***
Innerspace Technology Inc 201 933-1600
728 Garden St Carlstadt (07072) ***(G-1172)***
Inno Pharma LLC 732 885-2939
860 Centennial Ave Piscataway (08854) ***(G-8780)***
Innocor Inc (HQ) 732 945-6222
200 Schulz Dr Ste 2 Red Bank (07701) ***(G-9331)***
Innocor Foam Tech - Acp Inc (HQ) 732 945-6222
200 Schulz Dr Ste 2 Red Bank (07701) ***(G-9332)***
Innocor Foam Technologies LLC (HQ) 844 824-9348
200 Schulz Dr Ste 2 Red Bank (07701) ***(G-9333)***
Innolutions Inc 609 490-9799
4 Wellesley Ct Princeton Junction (08550) ***(G-9158)***
Innophos Inc 973 587-8735
259 Prospect Plains Rd A Cranbury (08512) ***(G-1838)***
Innophos Holdings Inc (PA) 609 495-2495
259 Prospect Plains Rd A Cranbury (08512) ***(G-1839)***
Innophos Inc (HQ) 609 495-2495
259 Prospect Plains Rd A Cranbury (08512) ***(G-1840)***
Innophos Investments II Inc (HQ) 609 495-2495
259 Prospect Plains Rd Cranbury (08512) ***(G-1841)***
Innophos Invstmnts Hldings Inc (HQ) 609 495-2495
259 Prospect Plains Rd Cranbury (08512) ***(G-1842)***
Innova Group Inc 856 696-1053
327 Tuckahoe Rd Vineland (08360) ***(G-11373)***
Innovance Inc 732 529-2300
15 Corporate Pl S Ste 101 Piscataway (08854) ***(G-8781)***
Innovance Networks, Piscataway *Also called Innovance Inc* ***(G-8781)***
Innovasystems Inc 856 722-0410
1245 N Church St Ste 6 Moorestown (08057) ***(G-6586)***
Innovation Design Center, Voorhees *Also called Comar Inc* ***(G-11426)***
Innovation Foods LLC 856 455-2209
71 Bridgeton Ave Bridgeton (08302) ***(G-786)***
Innovation In Medtech LLC 888 202-5939
5 Rolling Hill Dr Chatham (07928) ***(G-1328)***
Innovative Art Concepts LLC 201 828-9146
630 Swan St Ramsey (07446) ***(G-9244)***
Innovative Concepts Design LLC 732 346-0061
107 Trumbull St Ste 203 Elizabeth (07206) ***(G-2747)***
Innovative Cosmtc Concepts LLC (PA) 212 391-8110
399 Thornall St Ste 26 Edison (08837) ***(G-2541)***
Innovative Cosmtc Concepts LLC 973 225-0264
61 Kuller Rd Clifton (07011) ***(G-1647)***
Innovative Cutng Concepts LLC 609 484-9960
203 Cates Rd Egg Harbor Township (08234) ***(G-2685)***
Innovative Design, Edison *Also called Innovative Cosmtc Concepts LLC* ***(G-2541)***
Innovative Design Inc 201 227-2555
80 Broadway Cresskill (07626) ***(G-1946)***
Innovative Disposables LLC 908 222-7111
3611 Kennedy Rd South Plainfield (07080) ***(G-10384)***
Innovative Manufacturing Inc 908 904-1884
198 Us Highway 206 Ste 4 Hillsborough (08844) ***(G-4346)***
Innovative Metal Solutions LLC 609 784-8406
10 Eagle Ave Ste 400b Mount Holly (08060) ***(G-6774)***
Innovative Photonic Solutions, Monmouth Junction *Also called Innovtive Phtnics Slution Corp* ***(G-6348)***
Innovative Powder Coatings LLC 856 661-0086
9105 Burrough Dover Ln Pennsauken (08110) ***(G-8527)***
Innovative Power Solutions LLC 732 544-1075
373 South St Eatontown (07724) ***(G-2407)***
Innovative Pressure Clg LLC 609 738-3100
10 Arnytown Hrnerstown Rd Cream Ridge (08514) ***(G-1937)***
Innovative Resin Systems Inc 973 465-6887
257 Wilson Ave Newark (07105) ***(G-7197)***
Innovative Resin Systems Inc (PA) 973 465-6887
70 Verkade Dr Wayne (07470) ***(G-11651)***
Innovative Resin Systems Inc 973 633-5342
70 Verkade Dr Wayne (07470) ***(G-11652)***
Innovative Sftwr Solutions Inc 856 910-9190
3000 S Lenola Rd Maple Shade (08052) ***(G-5903)***
Innovi Mobile LLC 646 588-0165
45 Essex St Ste 201 Millburn (07041) ***(G-6253)***
Innovtive Phtnics Slution Corp 732 355-9300
4250 Us Highway 1 Ste 1 Monmouth Junction (08852) ***(G-6348)***
Ino Therapeutics LLC (HQ) 908 238-6600
1425 Us Route 206 Bedminster (07921) ***(G-274)***
Inoac Usa Inc 201 807-0809
100 Carol Pl Moonachie (07074) ***(G-6522)***
Inopak Ltd 973 962-1121
24 Executive Pkwy Ringwood (07456) ***(G-9450)***
Inox Components 856 256-0800
And 553 Rr 55 Pitman (08071) ***(G-8842)***
Inphot Inc 609 799-7172
13 Blossom Hill Dr Plainsboro (08536) ***(G-8886)***
Inrad Optics, Northvale *Also called MRC Precision Metal Optics Inc* ***(G-7592)***
Inrad Optics Inc (PA) 201 767-1910
181 Legrand Ave Northvale (07647) ***(G-7585)***

Inserch By Merc U.S.a, Hackensack *Also called Merc USA Inc* ***(G-3947)***
Inserts East Incorporated 856 663-8181
7045 Central Hwy Pennsauken (08109) ***(G-8528)***
Insign Inc 856 424-1161
1937 Olney Ave Cherry Hill (08003) ***(G-1381)***
Insmed Incorporated (PA) 908 977-9900
10 Finderne Ave Bldg 10 # 10 Bridgewater (08807) ***(G-847)***
Inspire Pharmaceuticals Inc 908 423-1000
1 Merck Dr Whitehouse Station (08889) ***(G-12052)***
Inspire Works Inc 908 730-7447
154 River Rd Annandale (08801) ***(G-59)***
Installations Unlimited, Kenilworth *Also called Auto Action Group Inc* ***(G-4938)***
Instant Business Cards, Belmar *Also called Watonka Printing Inc* ***(G-365)***
Instant Imprints 973 252-9500
286 Us Highway 206 119b Flanders (07836) ***(G-3411)***
Instant Printing, Orange *Also called Berennial International* ***(G-7818)***
Instant Printing of Dover Inc 973 366-6855
241 E Blackwell St Dover (07801) ***(G-2093)***
Instapak Corp Sealed Air 201 791-7600
80 Parker Ave Fl 2 Rochelle Park (07662) ***(G-9529)***
Institutational Edge LLC 201 944-5447
120 Van Nostrand Ave # 201 Englewood Cliffs (07632) ***(G-2966)***
Institute For Respnsble Online 856 722-1048
82 Hillside Ln Mount Laurel (08054) ***(G-6805)***
Instock Wireless Components 973 335-6550
50 Intervale Rd Ste 15 Boonton (07005) ***(G-572)***
Instore Magazine, Montclair *Also called Retail Management Pubg Inc* ***(G-6434)***
Instrctnal Cmpt Based Training, Bridgewater *Also called Excerpta Medica Inc* ***(G-837)***
Instride Shoes LLC 908 874-6670
29 Polhemus Dr Hillsborough (08844) ***(G-4347)***
Instrment Vlve Svcs Burlington 609 386-5000
120 Kissel Rd Burlington (08016) ***(G-978)***
Instru-Met Corporation 908 851-0700
931 Lehigh Ave Union (07083) ***(G-11195)***
Instrument Sciences & Tech 908 996-9920
1131 State Route 12 Frenchtown (08825) ***(G-3702)***
Instrumentation Technology Sls 732 388-0866
205 E Inman Ave Rahway (07065) ***(G-9200)***
Insul-Stop Inc 732 706-1978
240 Boundary Rd Marlboro (07746) ***(G-5944)***
Insulation Material Distrs, Linden *Also called Insulation Materials Distrs* ***(G-5388)***
Insulation Materials Distrs 908 925-2323
501 S Park Ave Linden (07036) ***(G-5388)***
Insulite Inc 732 255-1700
1890 Church Rd Toms River (08753) ***(G-10888)***
Int'l Purchasing Exchange, Somerset *Also called Sysco Guest Supply LLC* ***(G-10177)***
Intangible Labs Inc 917 375-1301
2 Hudson Pl Fl 7 Hoboken (07030) ***(G-4476)***
Intarome Fragrance Corporation (PA) 201 767-8700
370 Chestnut St Norwood (07648) ***(G-7625)***
Intech Powercore Corporation 201 767-8066
250 Herbert Ave Closter (07624) ***(G-1761)***
Integra, Plainsboro *Also called Derma Sciences Inc* ***(G-8880)***
Integra Lfscnces Holdings Corp (PA) 609 275-0500
311 Enterprise Dr Plainsboro (08536) ***(G-8887)***
Integra Lifesciences Corp (HQ) 609 275-2700
311 Enterprise Dr Plainsboro (08536) ***(G-8888)***
Integra Lifesciences Corp 609 275-0500
311 Enterprise Dr Plainsboro (08536) ***(G-8889)***
Integra Lifesciences Corp 609 275-2700
105 Morgan Ln Plainsboro (08536) ***(G-8890)***
Integra Lifesciences Sales LLC 609 275-0500
311 Enterprise Dr Plainsboro (08536) ***(G-8891)***
Integrate Tech Inc 201 693-5625
778 E Ridgewood Ave Ridgewood (07450) ***(G-9426)***
Integrated Biopharma Inc (PA) 888 319-6962
225 Long Ave Ste 13 Hillside (07205) ***(G-4418)***
Integrated Dental Systems LLC 201 676-2457
300 Sylvan Ave Ste 104 Englewood Cliffs (07632) ***(G-2967)***
Integrated Microwave Tech LLC (HQ) 908 852-3700
101 Bilby Rd Ste 15 Hackettstown (07840) ***(G-4012)***
Integrated Packaging Inds Inc (PA) 973 839-0500
45 Carey Ave Ste 210 Butler (07405) ***(G-1009)***
Integrated Packg Systems Inc 973 664-0020
3 Luger Rd Ste 5 Denville (07834) ***(G-2042)***
Integrated Photonics Inc (HQ) 908 281-8000
132 Stryker Ln Ste 1 Hillsborough (08844) ***(G-4348)***
Integrated Photonics Inc 908 281-8000
132 Stryker Ln Ste 1 Hillsborough (08844) ***(G-4349)***
Integration International Inc (PA) 973 796-2300
160 Littleton Rd Ste 106 Parsippany (07054) ***(G-8030)***
Integration Partners-Ny Corp 973 871-2100
1719 State Rt 10 Ste 114 Parsippany (07054) ***(G-8031)***
Integrity Ironworks Corp 732 254-2200
33 Brookside Ave Sayreville (08872) ***(G-9824)***
Integrity Medical Devices Del 609 567-8175
360 Fairview Ave Hammonton (08037) ***(G-4139)***
Integrted Laminate Systems Inc 856 786-6500
1301 Industrial Hwy Cinnaminson (08077) ***(G-1469)***

ALPHABETIC

Intek Plastics Inc 973 427-7331
150 5th Ave Hawthorne (07506) *(G-4241)*
Intel Corporation 908 894-6035
53 Frontage Rd Ste 210 Hampton (08827) *(G-4162)*
Intelco (PA) 856 456-6755
250 Harvard Ave Westville (08093) *(G-11944)*
Intelco 856 384-8562
1927 Nolte Dr Paulsboro (08066) *(G-8417)*
Intellect Design Arena Inc (HQ) 732 769-1037
20 Corporate Pl S Piscataway (08854) *(G-8782)*
Intellect Neurosciences Inc 201 608-5101
550 Sylvan Ave Ste 101 Englewood Cliffs (07632) *(G-2968)*
INTELLECT SEEC, Piscataway *Also called Intellect Design Arena Inc (G-8782)*
Intellgent Trffic Sup Pdts LLC 908 791-1200
3005 Hadley Rd Ste 5 South Plainfield (07080) *(G-10385)*
Intellicon Inc 201 791-9499
46 Sellers St Kearny (07032) *(G-4887)*
Intelligent Mtl Solutions Inc 609 514-4031
201 Washington Rd Princeton (08540) *(G-9059)*
Intelligentproject LLC 732 928-3421
15 Walter Dr Ste 4 Jackson (08527) *(G-4669)*
Intellisphere LLC (HQ) 609 716-7777
666 Plainsboro Rd Ste 300 Plainsboro (08536) *(G-8892)*
Intense Inc 732 249-2228
1200 Airport Rd Ste A North Brunswick (08902) *(G-7520)*
Intenze Products Inc (PA) 201 342-4446
15 Van Orden Pl Hackensack (07601) *(G-3929)*
Inteplast Group Corporation (PA) 973 994-8000
9 Peach Tree Hill Rd Livingston (07039) *(G-5535)*
Inter City Press Inc 908 236-9911
143 Petticoat Ln Lebanon (08833) *(G-5290)*
Inter Parfums Inc 609 860-1967
60 Stults Rd Dayton (08810) *(G-1971)*
Inter Rep Associates Inc (PA) 609 465-0077
131 Kimbles Beach Rd Cape May Court House (08210) *(G-1114)*
Inter Trend, Union *Also called Deep Foods Inc (G-11171)*
Interactive Advisory Software 770 951-2929
3393 Bargaintown Rd # 200 Egg Harbor Township (08234) *(G-2686)*
Interbahm International Inc 732 499-9700
10 Engelhard Ave Avenel (07001) *(G-135)*
Interchange Equipment Inc 973 473-5005
90 Dayton Ave Ste 120 Passaic (07055) *(G-8148)*
Interchange Group Inc 973 783-7032
52 Watchung Ave Montclair (07043) *(G-6418)*
Intercoastal Fabricators Inc 856 629-4105
300 Thomas Ave Ste 301 Williamstown (08094) *(G-12090)*
Intercure Inc 973 893-5653
356 Bloomfield Ave Ste 5 Montclair (07042) *(G-6419)*
Intercure Limited and Resperat, Montclair *Also called Intercure Inc (G-6419)*
Interfashion Cosmetics Corp 201 288-5858
32 Henry St Teterboro (07608) *(G-10799)*
Interfoam, Paterson *Also called Kohler Industries Inc (G-8311)*
Interganic Fzco LLC 224 436-0372
125 Stryker Ln Ste 3 Hillsborough (08844) *(G-4350)*
Intergrated Media Solutions, Manalapan *Also called Lead Conversion Plus (G-5853)*
Intergrated Scales Systems, Fairfield *Also called Lizard Label Co (G-3254)*
Interior Art & Design Inc 201 488-8855
59 Oak St Hackensack (07601) *(G-3930)*
Interior Specialties LLC 856 663-1700
6006 S Crescent Blvd Pennsauken (08109) *(G-8529)*
Interlink Products Intl Inc 908 862-8090
1315 E Elizabeth Ave Linden (07036) *(G-5389)*
Intermark Inc 908 474-1311
601 E Linden Ave Linden (07036) *(G-5390)*
International Aromatics Inc (PA) 201 964-0900
200 Anderson Ave Moonachie (07074) *(G-6523)*
International Beauty Products 973 575-6400
26 Chapin Rd Ste 1108 Pine Brook (07058) *(G-8707)*
International Bus Mchs Corp 201 307-5136
225 Brae Blvd Park Ridge (07656) *(G-7923)*
International Chefs Inc 917 645-2900
33 Bella Vista Ave Saddle Brook (07663) *(G-9769)*
International Coconut Corp 908 289-1555
225 W Grand St Elizabeth (07202) *(G-2748)*
International Container Co 201 440-1600
409 S River St Hackensack (07601) *(G-3931)*
International Cord Sets Inc 973 227-2118
6 Spielman Rd Fairfield (07004) *(G-3232)*
International Crystal Labs (PA) 973 478-8944
11 Erie St Ste 2 Garfield (07026) *(G-3739)*
International Data Group Inc 732 460-9404
6 Windsor Dr Eatontown (07724) *(G-2408)*
International Delights LLC 973 928-5431
230 Brighton Rd Clifton (07012) *(G-1648)*
International Design & Mfg LLC 908 587-2884
1217 Pennsylvania Ave Linden (07036) *(G-5391)*
International Diode Corp 973 482-6518
229 Cleveland Ave Harrison (07029) *(G-4186)*
International Foodsource LLC 973 361-7044
52 Richboynton Rd Dover (07801) *(G-2094)*
International Graphics Inc 908 753-5570
6 Ingersoll Rd South Plainfield (07080) *(G-10386)*
International Laser Group Inc (HQ) 818 888-0400
4 Executive Campus # 104 Cherry Hill (08002) *(G-1382)*
International Molasses Corp 201 368-8036
121 E Hunter Ave Maywood (07607) *(G-6051)*
International Molasses Corp 201 368-8036
88 Market St Fl 2 Saddle Brook (07663) *(G-9770)*
International Olive Oil Inc 732 612-3338
2271 Landmark Pl Ste C Manasquan (08736) *(G-5871)*
International Paper Company 856 853-7000
33 Phoenix Dr West Deptford (08086) *(G-11830)*
International Paper Company 732 828-1700
101 Ford Ave Milltown (08850) *(G-6268)*
International Paper Company 856 931-8000
370 Benigno Blvd Bellmawr (08031) *(G-343)*
International Paper Company 732 251-2000
140 Summerhill Rd Spotswood (08884) *(G-10528)*
International Paper Company 856 546-7000
100 E Gloucester Pike Barrington (08007) *(G-178)*
International Paper Company 973 405-2400
261 River Rd Clifton (07014) *(G-1649)*
International Playthings, Parsippany *Also called Epoch Everlasting Play LLC (G-8002)*
International Point of Sale, Teaneck *Also called Worldwide Pt SL Ltd Lblty Co (G-10777)*
International Process Eqp Co 856 665-4007
9300 N Crescent Blvd Pennsauken (08110) *(G-8530)*
International Processing Corp 732 826-4240
1250 Amboy Ave Perth Amboy (08861) *(G-8619)*
International Products Corp (PA) 609 386-8770
201 Connecticut Dr Burlington (08016) *(G-979)*
International Roll Forms, Sewell *Also called Omega Tool Die (G-9963)*
International Rollforms Inc (PA) 856 228-7100
8 International Ave Deptford (08096) *(G-2065)*
International Shtmtl Plate Mfg 908 722-6614
112 Veterans Mem Dr E Somerville (08876) *(G-10216)*
International Swimming Pools 732 565-9229
14c Van Dyke Ave New Brunswick (08901) *(G-6968)*
International Tech Lasers (PA) 201 262-4580
70 Kinderkamack Rd Ste 7 Emerson (07630) *(G-2858)*
International Telematics Corp 888 887-0935
1 Bridge Plz N Ste 100 Fort Lee (07024) *(G-3559)*
International Tool & Mch LLC 908 687-5580
446 Hillside Ave Hillside (07205) *(G-4419)*
International Tool and Mfg Inc 973 227-6767
30 Sherwood Ln Ste 10 Fairfield (07004) *(G-3233)*
International Vitamin Corp 973 371-4400
209 40th St Irvington (07111) *(G-4592)*
International Vitamin Corp 973 416-2000
191 40th St Irvington (07111) *(G-4593)*
Internet-Sales USA Corporation 775 468-8379
65 Fleetwood Dr Rockaway (07866) *(G-9575)*
Internl Traders Asso Silicon, Hackensack *Also called Solution and System Inc (G-3976)*
Interntional Cnsld Chemex Corp 732 828-7676
235 Jersey Ave New Brunswick (08901) *(G-6969)*
Interntnal Archtctral Irnworks 973 741-0749
181 Coit St Irvington (07111) *(G-4594)*
Interntnal Bscits Cnfctons Inc 856 813-1008
10000 Lincoln Dr E # 102 Marlton (08053) *(G-5979)*
Interntnal Digital Systems Inc 201 983-7700
400 Kelby St Ste 6 Fort Lee (07024) *(G-3560)*
Interntnal Dmnsional Stone LLC 973 729-0359
14 Doty Rd Unit B Haskell (07420) *(G-4208)*
Interntnal Flvors Frgrnces Inc 732 264-4500
800 Rose Ln Union Beach (07735) *(G-11236)*
Interntnal Flvors Frgrnces Inc 732 264-4500
800 Rose Ln Union Beach (07735) *(G-11237)*
Interntnal Flvors Frgrnces Inc 732 329-4600
150 Docks Corner Rd Dayton (08810) *(G-1972)*
Interntnal Flvors Frgrnces Inc 732 264-4500
600 Highway 36 Hazlet (07730) *(G-4276)*
Interntnal Folding Ppr Box Sls 201 941-3100
1039 Hoyt Ave Ridgefield (07657) *(G-9367)*
Interntnal Globl Solutions Inc 201 791-1500
130 Kipp Ave Elmwood Park (07407) *(G-2826)*
Interntnal Ingrdent Sltons Inc 856 778-6623
3001 Irwin Rd Ste A Mount Laurel (08054) *(G-6806)*
Interntnal Pharma Remedies Inc 201 417-3891
244 Dixon Ave Paterson (07501) *(G-8295)*
Interntonal Flavors Fragrances, Hazlet *Also called Interntnal Flvors Frgrnces Inc (G-4276)*
Interntonal Fragrance Tech Inc 770 345-3079
140 Centennial Ave Piscataway (08854) *(G-8783)*
Interntonal Med News Group LLC (HQ) 973 290-8237
7 Century Dr Ste 302 Parsippany (07054) *(G-8032)*
Interntonal Riding Helmets Inc 732 772-0165
15 Timber Ln Marlboro (07746) *(G-5945)*
Interntonal Specialty Pdts Inc (HQ) 859 815-3333
1361 Alps Rd Wayne (07470) *(G-11653)*
Interplast Inc 609 386-4990
100 Connecticut Dr Burlington (08016) *(G-980)*

Interplast Universal Inds 973 471-4100
  199 Garibaldi Ave Lodi (07644) *(G-5589)*

Interplex Nas Inc 201 367-1300
  232 Pegasus Ave Northvale (07647) *(G-7586)*

Intersil Design Center, Bridgewater *Also called Renesas Electronics Amer Inc* *(G-883)*

Intersource USA Inc 732 257-5002
  25 Kimberly Rd Ste A East Brunswick (08816) *(G-2161)*

Interspec, Wall Township *Also called Thortel Fireproof Fabrics Inc* *(G-11514)*

Interstate Architectural & Ir 201 941-0393
  243 Laird Ave Cliffside Park (07010) *(G-1541)*

Interstate Cnncting Components, Lumberton *Also called Heilind Mil-Aero LLC* *(G-5659)*

Interstate Panel LLC (PA) 609 586-4411
  67 Benson Ave Trenton (08610) *(G-11069)*

Intertape Polymer Corp 201 391-3315
  648 Athlone Ter River Vale (07675) *(G-9470)*

Intertek Caleb Brett, Carteret *Also called Intertek USA Inc* *(G-1260)*

Intertek Laboratories Inc 908 903-1800
  340 Union St Stirling (07980) *(G-10601)*

Intertek USA Inc 732 969-5200
  1000 Port Carteret Dr C Carteret (07008) *(G-1260)*

Intertest Inc (PA) 908 496-8008
  303 State Route 94 Ste 1 Columbia (07832) *(G-1799)*

Intervet Inc 908 423-6273
  2 Giralda Farms Madison (07940) *(G-5725)*

Intest Corporation (PA) 856 505-8800
  804 E Gate Dr Ste 200 Mount Laurel (08054) *(G-6807)*

Intex Millwork Solutions LLC 856 293-4100
  45 Mill St Mays Landing (08330) *(G-6039)*

Intra Pac Swedesboro (HQ) 856 467-0485
  20 Ashton Ave Swedesboro (08085) *(G-10703)*

Intrepid Industries Inc 908 534-5300
  291 Us Highway 22 Ste 3 Lebanon (08833) *(G-5291)*

Intrinsiq Spclty Solutions Inc 973 251-2039
  354 Eisenhower Pkwy # 2025 Livingston (07039) *(G-5536)*

Invaderm Corporation 973 572-5676
  25 Worlds Fair Dr Somerset (08873) *(G-10112)*

Inventek Colloidal Clrs LLC 856 206-0058
  106 Gaither Dr Mount Laurel (08054) *(G-6808)*

Inventiv Health Clinical LLC (HQ) 973 348-1000
  131 Morristown Rd Basking Ridge (07920) *(G-190)*

Inventors Shop LLC 856 303-8787
  800 Industrial Hwy Unit A Cinnaminson (08077) *(G-1470)*

Inversand Company Inc (HQ) 856 881-2345
  226 N Atlantic Ave Clayton (08312) *(G-1525)*

Invessence Inc 201 977-1955
  1 Main St Ste 202 Chatham (07928) *(G-1329)*

Investment Casting Institute 201 573-9770
  1 Paragon Dr Ste 110 Montvale (07645) *(G-6460)*

Invitation Studio 732 740-5558
  12 Hemingway Ct Morganville (07751) *(G-6645)*

Ion360 USA LLC 866 901-0073
  513 S Lenola Rd Ste 208 Moorestown (08057) *(G-6587)*

Ionni Sign Inc (PA) 973 625-3815
  14 White Meadow Ave Rockaway (07866) *(G-9576)*

Iop Communications, Shrewsbury *Also called Ink On Paper Communications* *(G-10001)*

Ip Moulding Inc 574 825-6554
  9 Peach Tree Hill Rd Livingston (07039) *(G-5537)*

IPC Information Systems, Jersey City *Also called IPC Systems Inc* *(G-4768)*

IPC Systems Inc (PA) 201 253-2000
  3 2nd St Fl Plz10 Jersey City (07311) *(G-4768)*

Ipe, Sussex *Also called Industrial Process & Eqp Inc* *(G-10673)*

Ipec, Pennsauken *Also called International Process Eqp Co* *(G-8530)*

Iphysicianhub, Monmouth Junction *Also called I Physician Hub* *(G-6346)*

Ipp/Pressworks, Cherry Hill *Also called Pressworks* *(G-1416)*

Ips, Eatontown *Also called Innovative Power Solutions LLC* *(G-2407)*

Ips, Denville *Also called Integrated Packg Systems Inc* *(G-2042)*

Ipsco Apollo Punch & Die Corp 973 884-0900
  10 Great Meadow Ln East Hanover (07936) *(G-2224)*

Ipsen Biopharmaceuticals Inc 908 275-6300
  106 Allen Rd Ste 301 Basking Ridge (07920) *(G-191)*

Iqe Rf LLC 732 271-5990
  394 Elizabeth Ave Ste 1 Somerset (08873) *(G-10113)*

Iris ID Systems Inc 609 819-4747
  8 Clarke Dr Ste 1 Cranbury (08512) *(G-1843)*

Iron Asylum Incorporated 856 228-2700
  233 Delsea Dr Sewell (08080) *(G-9958)*

Iron Chef, Passaic *Also called Mirrotek International LLC* *(G-8165)*

Iron Mountain Plastics Inc 201 445-0063
  112 Greenwood Ave Midland Park (07432) *(G-6230)*

Iron4u Inc 609 514-5163
  5 Independence Way # 300 Princeton (08540) *(G-9060)*

Ironbound Express Inc 973 491-5151
  65 Jabez St Newark (07105) *(G-7198)*

Ironbound Intermodal Inds Inc 973 491-5151
  65 Jabez St Newark (07105) *(G-7199)*

Ironbound Metal 973 242-5704
  238 Emmet St Newark (07114) *(G-7200)*

Ironbound Welding Inc 973 589-3128
  156 Walnut St Newark (07105) *(G-7201)*

ISC, Edison *Also called Importers Service Corp* *(G-2540)*

Isco 856 672-9182
  1 Commerce Dr Bldg 3 Barrington (08007) *(G-179)*

Isdin Corp 862 242-8129
  36 Cattano Ave Morristown (07960) *(G-6718)*

Island Breeze Intl Inc 856 931-1505
  24 S Maple Ave Marlton (08053) *(G-5980)*

Isocolor Inc 201 935-4494
  631 Central Ave Carlstadt (07072) *(G-1173)*

Isolantite Manufacturing Co 908 647-3333
  337 Warren Ave Stirling (07980) *(G-10602)*

Isometric Micro Finish Coating 732 306-6339
  477 Plainfield Rd Edison (08820) *(G-2542)*

Isowave Division, Dover *Also called Crystal Deltronic Industries* *(G-2082)*

Isowave Division, Dover *Also called Crystal Deltronic Industries* *(G-2083)*

Isp Chemco LLC (PA) 973 628-4000
  1361 Alps Rd Wayne (07470) *(G-11654)*

Isp Chemicals LLC 973 635-1551
  116 Summit Ave Chatham (07928) *(G-1330)*

Isp Global Technologies Inc (HQ) 973 628-4000
  1361 Alps Rd Wayne (07470) *(G-11655)*

Isp Global Technologies LLC (HQ) 973 628-4000
  1361 Alps Rd Wayne (07470) *(G-11656)*

Isp Sutton Laboratories, Chatham *Also called Isp Chemicals LLC* *(G-1330)*

Istec Corporation 973 383-9888
  5 Park Lake Rd Ste 6 Sparta (07871) *(G-10506)*

Istec Flow Measurement & Ctrl, Sparta *Also called Istec Corporation* *(G-10506)*

It Cosmetics, Jersey City *Also called LOreal USA Products Inc* *(G-4779)*

It Surplus Liquidators 732 308-1935
  179 South St Ste 1 Freehold (07728) *(G-3661)*

It Talent, Somerset *Also called Tech Brains Solutions Inc* *(G-10183)*

It Worqs LLC 732 494-0009
  16 Pearl St Ste 102 Metuchen (08840) *(G-6111)*

Italian Tile Decor, Elmwood Park *Also called Industrie Bitossi Inc* *(G-2825)*

Italian Treasures 856 770-9188
  1020 Voorhees Town Ctr Voorhees (08043) *(G-11434)*

Itec Consultants LLC 732 784-8322
  38 Hyer Ct Matawan (07747) *(G-6022)*

Itech Instruments LLC 609 924-7310
  816 Silvia St Ewing (08628) *(G-3026)*

Itg Brands LLC 973 386-9087
  50 Williams Pkwy Ste B East Hanover (07936) *(G-2225)*

Itl, Emerson *Also called International Tech Lasers* *(G-2858)*

ITM, Hillside *Also called International Tool & Mch LLC* *(G-4419)*

Its The Pitts Inc 609 645-7319
  619 Church St Pleasantville (08232) *(G-8910)*

ITT Corporation 973 284-0123
  100 Kingsland Rd Clifton (07014) *(G-1650)*

ITT Defense Electronics & Svcs, Clifton *Also called ITT Corporation* *(G-1650)*

Iultrasonic, Maplewood *Also called Tovatech LLC* *(G-5928)*

Ivax Pharmaceuticals LLC 201 767-1700
  400 Chestnut Ridge Rd Woodcliff Lake (07677) *(G-12195)*

Ivey Katrina Owner 973 951-8328
  95 Montrose St Newark (07106) *(G-7202)*

Ivoclar Vivadent Mfg Inc 732 563-4755
  500 Memorial Dr Somerset (08873) *(G-10114)*

Ivy Capital Partners LLC 201 573-8400
  102 Chestnut Ridge Rd # 1 Montvale (07645) *(G-6461)*

Ivy Inn, Princeton *Also called Ldm Inc* *(G-9066)*

Ivy Sports Medicine LLC 201 573-5423
  102 Chestnut Ridge Rd # 1 Montvale (07645) *(G-6462)*

Ivy-Dry Inc 973 575-1992
  299b Fairfield Ave Fairfield (07004) *(G-3234)*

IW Tremont Co Inc 973 427-3800
  18 Utter Ave Hawthorne (07506) *(G-4242)*

Iwc 732 968-8122
  12 Red Bud Ln Green Brook (08812) *(G-3858)*

Iweddingband.com, New Brunswick *Also called Netfruits Inc* *(G-6985)*

Iweiss Inc 201 402-6500
  815 Fairview Ave Ste 10 Fairview (07022) *(G-3362)*

Iws License Corp 732 872-0014
  29 4th Ave Atlantic Highlands (07716) *(G-112)*

Iza and Vanessa Music, Englewood *Also called Clyde Otis Music Group* *(G-2884)*

J & E Metal Fabricators Inc 732 548-9650
  1 Coan Pl Metuchen (08840) *(G-6112)*

J & G Diversified 732 543-2537
  235 Jersey Ave Ste 5 New Brunswick (08901) *(G-6970)*

J & G Graphics Inc 732 223-6660
  221 Parker Ave Manasquan (08736) *(G-5872)*

J & J Marine Inc 856 228-4744
  1596 Hurffville Rd Sewell (08080) *(G-9959)*

J & J Snack Foods Corp (PA) 856 665-9533
  6000 Central Hwy Pennsauken (08109) *(G-8531)*

J & J Snack Foods Corp 856 467-9552
  300 Eagle Ct Bridgeport (08014) *(G-767)*

A
L
P
H
A
B
E
T
I
C

J & J Snack Foods Corp....856 933-3597
361 Benigno Blvd Ste A Bellmawr (08031) *(G-344)*
J & J Snack Foods Corp PA (HQ)....856 665-9533
6000 Central Hwy Pennsauken (08109) *(G-8532)*
J & J Tool & Die, Sewell *Also called J & J Marine Inc (G-9959)*
J & L Controls Inc....732 460-0380
15 Leland Ter Lincroft (07738) *(G-5338)*
J & M Air Inc....908 707-4040
189 S Bridge St Somerville (08876) *(G-10217)*
J & M Cstm Shtmtl Ltd Lblty Co....856 627-6252
1331 New Broklyn Erial Rd Sicklerville (08081) *(G-10020)*
J & M Manufacturing Inc....908 638-4298
54 Main St High Bridge (08829) *(G-4297)*
J & R Custom Woodworking Inc....973 625-4114
449 E Main St Denville (07834) *(G-2043)*
J & R Foods Inc....732 229-4020
309 Morris Ave Ste 5 Long Branch (07740) *(G-5625)*
J & R Pallets, Camden *Also called F & R Pallets Inc (G-1064)*
J & R Rebuilders Inc....856 627-1414
330 Washington Ave Laurel Springs (08021) *(G-5233)*
J & S Enterprises LLC....973 696-9199
175 Beaverbrook Rd Lincoln Park (07035) *(G-5328)*
J & S Finishing Inc....201 854-0338
443 62nd St Fl 1 West New York (07093) *(G-11868)*
J & S Housewares Corp, Newark *Also called Global Weavers Corp (G-7173)*
J & S Precision Products Co....609 654-0900
16 Medford Evesboro Rd Medford (08055) *(G-6072)*
J & S Tool....973 383-5059
56 Paterson Ave Ste 4 Newton (07860) *(G-7393)*
J & T Embroidery Inc....201 867-4897
646 36th St Union City (07087) *(G-11249)*
J & W Servo Systems Company....973 335-1007
53 Green Pond Rd Ste 2 Rockaway (07866) *(G-9577)*
J A M I Enterprise Inc....732 714-6811
1129 Industrial Pkwy A Brick (08724) *(G-746)*
J A Machine & Tool Co Inc....201 767-1308
84 Herbert Ave Closter (07624) *(G-1762)*
J A Visual Group, Hackensack *Also called Njiw Limited Liability Company (G-3954)*
J A W Products Inc....856 829-3210
835 Industrial Hwy # 125 Cinnaminson (08077) *(G-1471)*
J and J Contractors....856 765-7521
604 5th St N Millville (08332) *(G-6309)*
J and M Precision Inc....856 661-9595
8103 River Rd Pennsauken (08110) *(G-8533)*
J and S Sporting Apparel LLC....732 787-5500
224 Main St Keansburg (07734) *(G-4856)*
J B & Sons Concrete Products (PA)....856 767-4140
358 New Brooklyn Rd Berlin (08009) *(G-435)*
J B Offset Printing Corp....201 264-4400
475 Walnut St Norwood (07648) *(G-7626)*
J Blanco Associates Inc....973 427-0619
280 9th Ave 1 Hawthorne (07506) *(G-4243)*
J C Contracting Inc....973 748-5600
681 Mill St Rahway (07065) *(G-9201)*
J C Hansen, Jersey City *Also called Joseph C Hansen Company Inc (G-4770)*
J C Orthopedic Inc....732 458-7900
1680 Route 88 Brick (08724) *(G-747)*
J C Penney Optical, Glendora *Also called US Vision Inc (G-3833)*
J C Penney Optical, Glendora *Also called Usv Optical Inc (G-3834)*
J C W Inc....732 560-8061
795 E Main St Bridgewater (08807) *(G-848)*
J D Crew Inc....856 665-3676
1426 Union Ave Pennsauken (08110) *(G-8534)*
J D M Associates Inc....973 773-8699
127 Kipp Ave Lodi (07644) *(G-5590)*
J D Machine Parts Inc....856 691-8430
158 W Weymouth Rd Vineland (08360) *(G-11374)*
J E B Urban Renewal Associates, Wayne *Also called Anodizing Corporation (G-11605)*
J E I, Brick *Also called J A M I Enterprise Inc (G-746)*
J F C Machine Works LLC....732 203-2077
2182 State Route 35 Holmdel (07733) *(G-4518)*
J F Gillespie Inc....856 692-2233
2547 Brunetta Dr Vineland (08360) *(G-11375)*
J F I Printing....973 759-3444
357 Cortlandt St Belleville (07109) *(G-304)*
J G Carpenter Contractor....732 271-8991
300 Lincoln Blvd Middlesex (08846) *(G-6171)*
J G Machine Works Inc....732 203-2077
2147 State Route 27 Ste D Edison (08817) *(G-2543)*
J G Papailias, Northvale *Also called John G Papailias Co Inc (G-7588)*
J G Schmidt Co Inc....732 563-9500
354 U S Rt 22 Green Brook (08812) *(G-3859)*
J G Schmidt Iron Works, Passaic *Also called J G Schmidt Steel (G-8149)*
J G Schmidt Steel....973 473-4822
211 Central Ave Passaic (07055) *(G-8149)*
J Gennaro Trucking....973 773-0805
13 Garfield Pl Garfield (07026) *(G-3740)*
J H M Communications Inc....908 859-6668
1593 Springtown Rd Phillipsburg (08865) *(G-8653)*
J Harris Company....917 731-5080
57 Barnsdale Rd Madison (07940) *(G-5726)*
J Hebrank Inc....973 983-0001
20 Pine St Rockaway (07866) *(G-9578)*
J J L & W Inc....856 854-3100
424 N White Horse Pike Magnolia (08049) *(G-5741)*
J J Orly Inc....908 276-9212
67 Walnut Ave Ste 307 Clark (07066) *(G-1501)*
J Josephson Inc (HQ)....201 440-7000
35 Horizon Blvd South Hackensack (07606) *(G-10271)*
J Josephson Inc....201 440-7000
35 Empire Blvd South Hackensack (07606) *(G-10272)*
J Josephson Inc....201 426-2646
14 Central Blvd South Hackensack (07606) *(G-10273)*
J K A Specialties, Southampton *Also called JKA Specialties Mfr Inc (G-10476)*
J K Design Inc....908 428-4700
465 Amwell Rd Hillsborough (08844) *(G-4351)*
J K Office Machine Inc....908 273-8811
33 Debbie Pl Berkeley Heights (07922) *(G-413)*
J K P Donuts Inc....856 234-9844
807 Route 73 Mount Laurel (08054) *(G-6809)*
J K Print Management, Hillsborough *Also called J K Design Inc (G-4351)*
J Kaufman Iron Works Inc....973 925-9972
217 Godwin Ave Paterson (07501) *(G-8296)*
J L Erectors Inc....856 232-9400
835 Camden Ave Blackwood (08012) *(G-482)*
J M C Tool & Mfg Co....908 241-8950
845 Fairfield Ave Kenilworth (07033) *(G-4964)*
J M Fry Printing Inks....732 238-1060
124 Tices Ln Ste A East Brunswick (08816) *(G-2162)*
J M M R Inc....201 612-5104
25-9 Broadway Fair Lawn (07410) *(G-3097)*
J Media LLC (PA)....201 600-4573
55 Walnut St Ste 105a Norwood (07648) *(G-7627)*
J Michaels Jewelers Inc....908 771-9800
370 Springfield Ave Berkeley Heights (07922) *(G-414)*
J Nelson Press Inc....732 747-0330
111 E River Rd Rumson (07760) *(G-9713)*
J OBrien Co Inc....973 379-8844
40 Commerce St Springfield (07081) *(G-10558)*
J P Egan Industries Inc....973 642-1500
676 S 14th St Newark (07103) *(G-7203)*
J P Rotella Co Inc....973 942-2559
20 E Barbour St Haledon (07508) *(G-4083)*
J Paul Allen Inc....973 702-1174
127 Sally Harden Rd Sussex (07461) *(G-10674)*
J R E Inc....973 808-0055
22 Fairfield Pl West Caldwell (07006) *(G-11780)*
J R Engineering & Machine....908 810-6300
663 Ramsey Ave Hillside (07205) *(G-4420)*
J R M Products Inc....732 203-0200
701 Locust St Union Beach (07735) *(G-11238)*
J R S Mch & Tl Sls Corp Ameri, South Plainfield *Also called J R S Tool & Metal Finishing (G-10387)*
J R S Tool & Metal Finishing....908 753-2050
107 Borman Rd South Plainfield (07080) *(G-10387)*
J S Manufacturing, Edison *Also called Chacko John (G-2481)*
J S Paluch Co Inc....732 238-2412
6 Alvin Ct Ste 1 East Brunswick (08816) *(G-2163)*
J S R, Hillside *Also called Jomel Seams Reasonable LLC (G-4422)*
J Spinelli & Sons Excavating, Elmer *Also called J Spinelli & Sons Inc (G-2793)*
J Spinelli & Sons Inc....856 691-3133
615 Gershal Ave Elmer (08318) *(G-2793)*
J T Baker Chemical Co, Phillipsburg *Also called Avantor Performance Mtls LLC (G-8640)*
J T Murdoch Shoes....973 748-6484
623 Bloomfield Ave Bloomfield (07003) *(G-514)*
J V Q Inc....973 523-8806
245 E 17th St Paterson (07524) *(G-8297)*
J Vitale Sign Co Inc....732 388-8401
2204 Elizabeth Ave Ste 1 Rahway (07065) *(G-9202)*
J&E Business Services LLC....973 984-8444
39 E Hanover Ave Ste C7 Morris Plains (07950) *(G-6672)*
J&K Ingredients, Paterson *Also called Jk Ingredients Inc (G-8304)*
J&N Pharma LLC....201 391-3139
50 Tice Blvd Ste 340 Woodcliff Lake (07677) *(G-12196)*
J&S Houseware Corp....973 824-5500
9 Dey St Ste 13 Newark (07103) *(G-7204)*
J-M Eagle, Livingston *Also called J-M Manufacturing Company Inc (G-5538)*
J-M Manufacturing Company Inc....800 621-4404
9 Peach Tree Hill Rd Livingston (07039) *(G-5538)*
J-Mac Plastics Inc (PA)....908 709-1111
40 Lafayette Pl Kenilworth (07033) *(G-4965)*
J-Tech Creations Inc....201 944-2968
1 Bridge Plz N Ste 275 Fort Lee (07024) *(G-3561)*
J.E. Holland-Moritz Co., Inc., Lambertville *Also called Julius E Holland-Moritz Co Inc (G-5215)*
JA Cissel Manufacturing Co....732 901-0300
1995 Rutgers Blvd Lakewood (08701) *(G-5137)*

JA Heilferty LLC..201 836-5060
133 Cedar Ln Teaneck (07666) *(G-10757)*
Ja-Bar Silicone Corp..973 786-5000
252 Brighton Rd Andover (07821) *(G-51)*
Jace Systems, Cherry Hill *Also called Tgz Acquisition Company LLC* *(G-1428)*
Jachts - Columbia Can LLC..............................973 925-8020
90 6th Ave Paterson (07524) *(G-8298)*
Jack Georges Inc..973 777-6999
823 Main Ave Passaic (07055) *(G-8150)*
Jackie Evans Fashions, Passaic *Also called Jackie Evans Inc* *(G-8151)*
Jackie Evans Inc...973 471-6991
18 3rd St 26 Passaic (07055) *(G-8151)*
Jaclo Industries, Cranford *Also called Durst Corporation Inc* *(G-1903)*
Jaclyn Inc...201 909-6000
197 W Spring Valley Ave # 101 Maywood (07607) *(G-6052)*
Jaclyn Holdings Parent LLC (PA).....................201 909-6000
197 W Spring Valley Ave Maywood (07607) *(G-6053)*
Jaclyn LLC (HQ)..201 909-6000
197 W Spring Valley Ave # 101 Maywood (07607) *(G-6054)*
Jacmel Jewelry Inc..201 223-0435
401 Penhorn Ave Ste 1 Secaucus (07094) *(G-9897)*
Jacquar Fuel...732 441-0700
107 Hawkins Rd Manalapan (07726) *(G-5851)*
Jacquard Fabrics Inc.......................................732 905-4545
1965 Swarthmore Ave Lakewood (08701) *(G-5138)*
Jacquard Fabrics Co, Lakewood *Also called Jacquard Fabrics Inc* *(G-5138)*
Jacqueline Embroidery Co...............................732 278-8121
445 Thompson St Apt G Hackensack (07601) *(G-3932)*
Jacqueline Mazza LLC.....................................732 718-2944
6 Saw Mill Dr Somerset (08873) *(G-10115)*
Jacquet Jonpaul...856 825-4259
25 E Main St Ste D Millville (08332) *(G-6310)*
Jad Bagels LLC...201 567-4500
52 E Palisade Ave Englewood (07631) *(G-2906)*
Jade Apparel Group, Newark *Also called Sinai Manufacturing Corp* *(G-7314)*
Jade Eastern Trading Inc (PA).........................201 440-8500
13 Division St Ste A Moonachie (07074) *(G-6524)*
Jaeger Thomas & Melissa DDS.........................908 735-2722
1128 State Rd 31 Lebanon (08833) *(G-5292)*
Jai Ganesh Fuel LLC.......................................201 246-8995
815 Kearny Ave Kearny (07032) *(G-4888)*
Jak Diversified II Inc......................................973 439-1182
241 Clinton Rd West Caldwell (07006) *(G-11781)*
Jaktool LLC...609 664-2451
259 Prospect Plains Rd Cranbury (08512) *(G-1844)*
James A Stanlick Jr...973 366-7316
845 Berkshire Valley Rd Wharton (07885) *(G-11990)*
James Candy Company (PA)............................609 344-1519
1519 Boardwalk Atlantic City (08401) *(G-101)*
James Colucci Enterprises LLC........................877 403-4900
150 Jfk Pkwy Short Hills (07078) *(G-9979)*
James D Morrissey Inc.....................................609 859-2860
223 Sooy Place Rd Vincentown (08088) *(G-11317)*
James Howard Inc...973 928-1560
1500 Main Ave Ste 3 Clifton (07011) *(G-1651)*
James Kinkade..856 451-1177
9 Oak Dr Bridgeton (08302) *(G-787)*
James R Macauley Inc......................................856 767-3474
1 Industrial Dr Waterford Works (08089) *(G-11598)*
James Smith (PA)...732 229-8273
375 Broadway Long Branch (07740) *(G-5626)*
James Zylstra Enterprises Inc..........................973 383-6768
52 State Route 15 Lafayette (07848) *(G-5047)*
Jamm Litho, Long Branch *Also called Accucolor LLC* *(G-5620)*
Jamol Laboratories Inc....................................201 262-6363
13 Ackerman Ave Emerson (07630) *(G-2859)*
Jan Packaging Inc...973 361-7200
100 Harrison St Dover (07801) *(G-2095)*
Jane Carter Solution, Newark *Also called Left-Handed Libra LLC* *(G-7217)*
Janet Shops Inc..973 748-4992
550 Bloomfield Ave Bloomfield (07003) *(G-515)*
Janico Inc...732 370-2223
88 Industrial Ct Freehold (07728) *(G-3662)*
Janke & Company Inc.......................................973 334-4477
283 Myrtle Ave Boonton (07005) *(G-573)*
Jannetti Publications.......................................856 256-2300
200 E Holly Ave Sewell (08080) *(G-9960)*
Janssen Global Services LLC...........................908 704-4000
700 Route 202 Raritan (08869) *(G-9309)*
Janssen Ortho LLC (HQ)..................................609 730-2000
1 Johnson And Johnson Plz New Brunswick (08901) *(G-6971)*
Janssen Pharmaceuticals Inc...........................908 218-7701
1 Cottontail Ln Somerset (08873) *(G-10116)*
Janssen Pharmaceuticals Inc (HQ)..................609 730-2000
1125 Trnton Harbourton Rd Titusville (08560) *(G-10855)*
Janssen Research & Dev LLC (HQ)..................908 704-4000
920 Us Highway 202 Raritan (08869) *(G-9310)*
Jarahian Millwork Inc......................................732 240-5151
870 Route 530 Ste 4 Whiting (08759) *(G-12067)*

Jarchem Industries Inc....................................973 344-0600
414 Wilson Ave Newark (07105) *(G-7205)*
Jarco U S Casting Corp...................................201 271-0003
4407 Park Ave Union City (07087) *(G-11250)*
Jarden Corporation (HQ).................................201 610-6600
221 River St Hoboken (07030) *(G-4477)*
Jarit, Plainsboro *Also called Integra Lifesciences Corp* *(G-8888)*
Jarvis Electric Motors Inc...............................856 662-7710
6001 S Crescent Blvd Pennsauken (08110) *(G-8535)*
Jasco Printing, Tabernacle *Also called Jasco Specialties and Forms* *(G-10738)*
Jasco Specialties and Forms...........................856 627-5511
86 Patty Bowker Rd Tabernacle (08088) *(G-10738)*
Jason Equipment Corp.....................................973 983-7212
164 Franklin Ave Rockaway (07866) *(G-9579)*
Jason Industrial Inc., Fairfield *Also called Megadyne America LLC* *(G-3257)*
Jason Metal Products Corp..............................732 396-1132
1072 Randolph Ave Rahway (07065) *(G-9203)*
Jason Mills LLC...732 651-7200
440 S Main St Ste 7 Milltown (08850) *(G-6269)*
Jasper Fashion Ltd Lblty Co............................917 561-4533
336 Murray St Elizabeth (07202) *(G-2749)*
Jassmine Corp..848 565-0515
489 Getty Ave Clifton (07011) *(G-1652)*
Jav Latin America Express...............................201 868-5004
6321 Bergenline Ave West New York (07093) *(G-11869)*
Java Developer's Journal, Woodcliff Lake *Also called Sys-Con Publications Inc* *(G-12204)*
Jay Bee Oil & Gas Company, Union *Also called Jay-Bee Oil & Gas Inc* *(G-11196)*
Jay Franco & Sons Inc.....................................732 721-0022
115 Kennedy Dr Sayreville (08872) *(G-9825)*
Jay Gerish Company..973 403-0655
2 York Ave West Caldwell (07006) *(G-11782)*
Jay Jariwala...908 806-8266
1019 Us Highway 202 Ringoes (08551) *(G-9439)*
Jay-Bee Lamp & Shade Co Inc.........................201 265-0762
540 Salem St Paramus (07652) *(G-7877)*
Jay-Bee Oil & Gas Inc (PA).............................908 686-1493
1720 Us Highway 22 E # 1 Union (07083) *(G-11196)*
Jaygo Incorporated...908 688-3600
7 Emery Ave Randolph (07869) *(G-9285)*
Jaymar Precision Inc.......................................856 365-8779
1169 Cooper St Camden (08102) *(G-1071)*
JB Electronics..609 497-2952
101 Wall St Princeton (08540) *(G-9061)*
JBAT Inc...856 667-7307
28 Coles Ave Cherry Hill (08002) *(G-1383)*
Jbq Printing & Marketing, Hackettstown *Also called B & H Printers Inc* *(G-3999)*
JC Macelroy Co Inc (PA).................................732 572-7100
91 Ethel Rd W Piscataway (08854) *(G-8784)*
JC Pallets Inc...973 345-1102
354 Marshall St Paterson (07503) *(G-8299)*
JC Printing & Advertising Inc...........................973 881-8612
168 8th Ave Paterson (07514) *(G-8300)*
Jcc Military Supply LLC...................................973 341-1314
125 5th Ave Paterson (07524) *(G-8301)*
Jcdecaux Mallscape LLC..................................201 288-2024
440 State Rt 17 Ste 9 Hasbrouck Heights (07604) *(G-4195)*
Jch Partners & Co LLC.....................................732 664-6440
8 Man O War Ln Howell (07731) *(G-4557)*
Jct Design Enterprises Inc...............................212 629-7412
1701 Summit Ave Union City (07087) *(G-11251)*
JDM Engineering Inc..732 780-0770
60 Jerseyville Ave Freehold (07728) *(G-3663)*
JDV Equipment Corp..973 366-6556
1 Princeton Ave Ste 2 Dover (07801) *(G-2096)*
Jdv Products Inc...201 794-6467
22-01 Raphael St Fair Lawn (07410) *(G-3098)*
JE Berkowitz LP..856 456-7800
1 Gateway Blvd Pedricktown (08067) *(G-8436)*
Je TAime Shoes..201 845-7463
Garden State Plz Mall Paramus (07652) *(G-7878)*
Jean's Canvas Products, Belford *Also called Kerry Wilkens Inc* *(G-288)*
Jefferson Printing Serivce...............................973 491-0019
184 Jefferson St Newark (07105) *(G-7206)*
Jefferson Prosthetic Orthotic..........................973 762-0780
120 Prospect St Ste B South Orange (07079) *(G-10308)*
Jeffery S Zlotnick Od......................................732 549-3555
39 Bridge St Ste A Metuchen (08840) *(G-6113)*
Jeffrey Danee Inc...973 872-9388
372 E 23rd St Paterson (07514) *(G-8302)*
Jeffrey Klein Ribbon Designs, Paterson *Also called Klein Ribbon Corp* *(G-8310)*
Jem Printing Inc..908 782-9986
35 Main St Flemington (08822) *(G-3450)*
Jema-American Inc..732 968-5333
824 South Ave Middlesex (08846) *(G-6172)*
Jemco Inc...732 446-1112
85 Tracy Station Rd Manalapan (07726) *(G-5852)*
Jems Pharma LLC...609 386-0141
301 High St Burlington (08016) *(G-981)*

A
L
P
H
A
B
E
T
I
C

Jen Electric Inc 973 467-4901
  631 Morris Ave Springfield (07081) *(G-10559)*
Jen Mar Graphics Inc 973 256-6622
  60 Commerce Way Ste A Totowa (07512) *(G-10952)*
Jencks Signs Corp 908 542-1400
  16 Geiger Ln Warren (07059) *(G-11557)*
Jenisse Leisure Products Inc 973 331-1177
  5 Van Duyne Ct Towaco (07082) *(G-10997)*
Jenkins Brush Co, Cedar Grove *Also called M W Jenkins Sons Inc (G-1289)*
Jenny Jump Farm, Hope *Also called Christopher F Maier (G-4539)*
Jentec Inc 201 784-1031
  20 Charles St Ste C Northvale (07647) *(G-7587)*
Jerhel Plastics Inc 201 436-6662
  63 Hook Rd Bayonne (07002) *(G-234)*
Jerome Group Inc 856 234-8600
  1414 Metropolitan Ave West Deptford (08066) *(G-11831)*
Jerome Industries Corp (HQ) 908 353-5700
  36 Newburgh Rd Hackettstown (07840) *(G-4013)*
Jerome Medical, West Deptford *Also called Jerome Group Inc (G-11831)*
Jersey Beat 201 864-9054
  3726 Park Ave Apt E2 Weehawken (07086) *(G-11697)*
Jersey Boring & Drlg Co Inc 973 242-3800
  36 Pier Ln W Fairfield (07004) *(G-3235)*
Jersey Bound Latino LLC 908 591-2830
  841 Hueston St Union (07083) *(G-11197)*
Jersey Bound Latino Magazine, Union *Also called Jersey Bound Latino LLC (G-11197)*
Jersey Cape Yachts Inc 609 965-8650
  2143 River Rd Egg Harbor City (08215) *(G-2665)*
Jersey Cast Stone Ltd Lblty Co 856 333-6900
  6845 Westfield Ave Pennsauken (08110) *(G-8536)*
Jersey Cider Works LLC (PA) 917 604-0067
  42 Erwin Park Rd Montclair (07042) *(G-6420)*
Jersey Cider Works LLC 908 940-4115
  360 County Road 579 Asbury (08802) *(G-71)*
Jersey Concrete, Toms River *Also called Clayton Block Company Inc (G-10872)*
Jersey Cover Corp 732 286-6300
  1746 Route 9 Toms River (08755) *(G-10889)*
Jersey Girl Brewing Company 908 269-5523
  426 Sand Shore Rd Hackettstown (07840) *(G-4014)*
Jersey Jack Pinball Inc 732 364-9900
  1645 Oak St Lakewood (08701) *(G-5139)*
Jersey Job Guide Inc 732 263-9675
  422 Morris Ave Ste 5 Long Branch (07740) *(G-5627)*
Jersey Journal, Secaucus *Also called Evening Journal Association (G-9881)*
Jersey Lift Truck, Paterson *Also called Rentalift Inc (G-8368)*
Jersey Metal Works LLC 732 565-1313
  1022 Hamilton St Untid Somerset (08873) *(G-10117)*
Jersey Ordnance Inc 609 267-2112
  600 Highland Dr Ste 602 Westampton (08060) *(G-11913)*
Jersey Plastic Molders Inc 973 926-1800
  149 Shaw Ave Irvington (07111) *(G-4595)*
Jersey Precast, Trenton *Also called Jpc Merger Sub LLC (G-11072)*
Jersey Precast Corporation Inc 609 689-3700
  853 Nottingham Way Trenton (08638) *(G-11070)*
Jersey Printing Associates Inc 732 872-9654
  153 1st Ave Ste 1 Atlantic Highlands (07716) *(G-113)*
Jersey Sheet Metal & Machine 973 366-8628
  90 E Dickerson St Dover (07801) *(G-2097)*
Jersey Shore Cosmetics LLC 908 500-9954
  23 Pleasant View Way Flemington (08822) *(G-3451)*
Jersey Shore News Mgazines Inc (PA) 609 494-5900
  1816 Long Beach Blvd Surf City (08008) *(G-10665)*
Jersey Shore Publications 732 892-1276
  749 Bay Ave Brick (08724) *(G-748)*
Jersey Shore Steel Inc 732 833-8855
  636 Herman Rd Jackson (08527) *(G-4670)*
Jersey Shore Vacation Magazine, Brick *Also called Jersey Shore Publications (G-748)*
Jersey Specialty Co Inc 413 525-2292
  7861 Airport Hwy Pennsauken (08109) *(G-8537)*
Jersey Steel Door Inc 973 482-4020
  95 N 11th St Newark (07107) *(G-7207)*
Jersey Strand & Cable Inc 908 213-9350
  259 Center St Ste 3 Phillipsburg (08865) *(G-8654)*
Jersey Tank Fabricators Inc 609 758-7670
  1271 New Market Ave Ste D South Plainfield (07080) *(G-10388)*
Jersey Tempered Glass Inc 856 273-8700
  2035 Briggs Rd Mount Laurel (08054) *(G-6810)*
Jesco Iron Crafts Inc 201 488-4545
  201 W Fort Lee Rd Bogota (07603) *(G-548)*
Jescraft, Bogota *Also called Jesco Iron Crafts Inc (G-548)*
Jese Apparel LLC (PA) 732 969-3200
  8 Nicholas Ct B Dayton (08810) *(G-1973)*
Jesel Inc 732 901-1800
  1985 Cedarbridge Ave # 2 Lakewood (08701) *(G-5140)*
Jet Aviation Aircraft Maint, Teterboro *Also called Jet Aviation St Louis Inc (G-10800)*
Jet Aviation St Louis Inc 201 462-4026
  113 Chrles A Lindbergh Dr Teterboro (07608) *(G-10800)*
Jet Precision Metal Inc 973 423-4350
  7 Schoon Ave Hawthorne (07506) *(G-4244)*

Jet Pulverizer Co Inc 856 235-5554
  1255 N Church St Moorestown (08057) *(G-6588)*
Jet Test Global LLC 702 785-0011
  800 Kings Hwy N Ste 307 Cherry Hill (08034) *(G-1384)*
Jetstream of Houston LLP 732 448-7830
  17 Jules Ln New Brunswick (08901) *(G-6972)*
Jettron Products Inc 973 887-0571
  56 State Route 10 East Hanover (07936) *(G-2226)*
Jetty Life LLC 800 900-6435
  509 N Main St 3 Manahawkin (08050) *(G-5831)*
Jetyd Corporation 201 512-9500
  218 Island Rd Mahwah (07430) *(G-5786)*
Jevek Solutions, Cranbury *Also called Jaktool LLC (G-1844)*
Jewish Media Group, Teaneck *Also called Jewish Standard Inc (G-10758)*
Jewish Standard Inc 201 837-8818
  1086 Teaneck Rd Ste 2f Teaneck (07666) *(G-10758)*
Jewish Times of South Jersey 609 646-2063
  21 W Delilah Rd Pleasantville (08232) *(G-8911)*
JF Braun & Sons Inc 908 393-7400
  2 Slater Dr Elizabeth (07206) *(G-2750)*
Jfc Technologies, Bound Brook *Also called Cyalume Specialty Products Inc (G-617)*
JFK Medical Group PC (PA) 732 632-1650
  60 James St Edison (08820) *(G-2544)*
JFK Supplies Inc 732 985-7800
  85 Lexington Ave Edison (08817) *(G-2545)*
JG Tire, Middlesex *Also called J G Carpenter Contractor (G-6171)*
Jgs, Green Brook *Also called J G Schmidt Co Inc (G-3859)*
JHM Signs, Phillipsburg *Also called J H M Communications Inc (G-8653)*
Jhp Group Holdings Inc 973 658-3569
  1 Upper Pond Rd Ste 4 Parsippany (07054) *(G-8033)*
Jiaherb Inc (HQ) 973 439-6869
  1 Chapin Rd Ste 1 # 1 Pine Brook (07058) *(G-8708)*
Jiangsu Hengrui Medicine Co 609 395-8625
  506 Carnegie Ctr Princeton (08540) *(G-9062)*
Jid Transportation LLC 201 362-0841
  158 61st St Apt 2 West New York (07093) *(G-11870)*
Jig Grinding Specialists, Pennsauken *Also called J and M Precision Inc (G-8533)*
Jigsaw Publishing Inc 973 838-4838
  8 Hemlock Ct Butler (07405) *(G-1010)*
Jimcam Publishing Inc 201 843-5700
  19 W Pleasant Ave Fl 1 Maywood (07607) *(G-6055)*
Jimenez Pallets LLC 862 267-3900
  244 Dukes St Kearny (07032) *(G-4889)*
Jimmys Cookies LLC 973 779-8500
  125 Entin Rd Clifton (07014) *(G-1653)*
Jing, Carlstadt *Also called Jinpan International USA Ltd (G-1175)*
Jinpan International USA Ltd 201 460-8778
  390 Veterans Blvd Carlstadt (07072) *(G-1174)*
Jinpan International USA Ltd 201 460-8778
  390 Veterans Blvd Carlstadt (07072) *(G-1175)*
JIT Manufacturing Inc 973 247-7300
  50 Peel St Paterson (07524) *(G-8303)*
Jjs Own Ltd Liability Company 551 486-8510
  71 Pickens St Little Ferry (07643) *(G-5510)*
Jk Ingredients Inc 973 340-8700
  160 E 5th St Paterson (07524) *(G-8304)*
JKA Specialties Mfr Inc 609 859-2090
  157 Eayrestown Rd Southampton (08088) *(G-10476)*
Jl Packaging Group Corp (PA) 609 610-0286
  2 Birch St Pennington (08534) *(G-8454)*
Jlb Hauling Ltd Liability Co 856 514-2771
  90 Dolbow Ave Pennsville (08070) *(G-8592)*
Jli Marketing & Printing Corp 732 828-8877
  6 Corporate Dr Ste 1 Cranbury (08512) *(G-1845)*
JM Ahle Co Inc 732 388-5507
  625 Leesville Ave Rahway (07065) *(G-9204)*
JM Huber Corporation (PA) 732 603-3630
  499 Thornall St Ste 8 Edison (08837) *(G-2546)*
Jmc Design & Graphics Inc 973 276-9033
  144 Fairfield Rd Fairfield (07004) *(G-3236)*
Jmd Printing, Newton *Also called Skylands Press (G-7404)*
Jmee Financial Division, Washington *Also called Arctic Foods Inc (G-11574)*
JMJ Profile Inc 856 767-3930
  154 Cooper Rd Ste 1303 West Berlin (08091) *(G-11726)*
Jmk Tool Die and Mfg Co Inc (PA) 201 845-4710
  19 W Passaic St Rochelle Park (07662) *(G-9530)*
Jmm Studios 609 861-3094
  1524 Dehirsch Ave Woodbine (08270) *(G-12143)*
Jmp Press Inc 201 444-0236
  19 Sheridan Ave Ho Ho Kus (07423) *(G-4454)*
Jnbc Associates LLC 973 560-5511
  100 Jefferson Rd Parsippany (07054) *(G-8034)*
Jnj International Inv LLC 732 524-0400
  One Johnson/Johnson Plaza New Brunswick (08933) *(G-6973)*
Jnt Technical Services Inc 201 641-2130
  85 Industrial Ave Little Ferry (07643) *(G-5511)*
Jobe Industries Inc 908 862-0400
  1600 W Elizabeth Ave Linden (07036) *(G-5392)*

(G-0000) Company's Geographic Section entry number

Joe Mike Precision Fabrication 609 953-1144
  6 Tidswell Ave Medford (08055) *(G-6073)*

Joey's Fine Foods, Newark *Also called Local Baking Products Inc (G-7223)*

Joffe Lumber & Supply Co Inc 856 825-9550
  18 Burns Ave Vineland (08360) *(G-11376)*

Joffe Millwork & Supply, Vineland *Also called Joffe Lumber & Supply Co Inc (G-11376)*

Johanna Foods Inc (PA) 908 788-2200
  20 Johanna Farms Rd Flemington (08822) *(G-3452)*

Johansen Book Bindery Inc 201 438-4263
  71 E Van Ness Ave Rutherford (07070) *(G-9735)*

Johanson Manufacturing Corp 973 658-1051
  301 Rockaway Valley Rd Boonton (07005) *(G-574)*

John Anthony Bread Distributor 973 523-9258
  298 21st Ave Paterson (07501) *(G-8305)*

John B Horay Welding 856 336-2154
  399 Blaine Ave West Berlin (08091) *(G-11727)*

John B Stetson Company 212 563-1848
  86 Hudson St Hoboken (07030) *(G-4478)*

John Canary Custom Wdwkg Inc 908 851-2894
  697 Rahway Ave Union (07083) *(G-11198)*

John Cooper Company Inc 201 487-4018
  250 Maywood Ave Ste C Hackensack (07601) *(G-3933)*

John E Herbst Heating & Coolg 732 721-0088
  3143 Bordentown Ave 2b Parlin (08859) *(G-7933)*

John F Pearce 201 440-8765
  76 Frederick St Moonachie (07074) *(G-6525)*

John G Papailias Co Inc 201 767-4027
  245 Pegasus Ave Northvale (07647) *(G-7588)*

John H Abbott Inc 609 561-0303
  2101 Woodland Ave Hammonton (08037) *(G-4140)*

John J Chando Jr Inc 732 793-2122
  209 Downer Ave Mantoloking (08738) *(G-5890)*

John M Sniderman Inc (PA) 201 450-4291
  405 Henry St Fairview (07022) *(G-3363)*

John Maltese Iron Works Inc 732 249-4350
  1453 Jersey Ave North Brunswick (08902) *(G-7521)*

John N Fehlinger Co Inc 973 633-0699
  16 Passaic Ave Unit 8 Fairfield (07004) *(G-3237)*

John Patrick Publishing LLC 609 883-2700
  1707 4th St Ewing (08638) *(G-3027)*

John R Zabka Associates Inc (PA) 201 405-0075
  3 Post Rd Ste 3 # 3 Oakland (07436) *(G-7693)*

John S Swift Co, Teterboro *Also called John S Swift Print of NJ Inc (G-10802)*

John S Swift Company Inc 201 935-2002
  375 North St Ste N Teterboro (07608) *(G-10801)*

John S Swift Print of NJ Inc 201 678-3232
  375 North St Ste N Teterboro (07608) *(G-10802)*

John W Kennedy Company 973 256-5525
  60 Sindle Ave Little Falls (07424) *(G-5478)*

John Wiley & Sons Inc (PA) 201 748-6000
  111 River St Ste 2000 Hoboken (07030) *(G-4479)*

John Wiley & Sons Inc 732 302-2265
  41 Saw Mill Pond Rd Edison (08817) *(G-2547)*

John Wiley & Sons Inc 201 748-6000
  111 River St Ste 4 Hoboken (07030) *(G-4480)*

John Wiley and Sons, Hoboken *Also called Wiley Publishing LLC (G-4504)*

John Wm Macy Cheesesticks Inc 201 791-8036
  80 Kipp Ave Elmwood Park (07407) *(G-2827)*

JOHN WM. MACY'S CHEESESTICKS, Elmwood Park *Also called John Wm Macy Cheesesticks Inc (G-2827)*

Johnnys Service Center 732 738-0569
  53 Lawrence St Fords (08863) *(G-3529)*

Johns Manville Corporation 856 768-7000
  437 N Grove St Berlin (08009) *(G-436)*

Johns Manville Corporation 732 225-9190
  Liddle Ave Edison (08837) *(G-2548)*

Johnson & Associates Inc 856 228-2175
  900 Route 168 Ste F4 Blackwood (08012) *(G-483)*

Johnson & Johnson (PA) 732 524-0400
  1 Johnson And Johnson Plz New Brunswick (08933) *(G-6974)*

Johnson & Johnson 732 524-0400
  35 Azalea Pl Piscataway (08854) *(G-8785)*

Johnson & Johnson 732 524-0400
  51 Pettit Pl Princeton (08540) *(G-9063)*

Johnson & Johnson 917 573-8007
  472 Chestnut St Ridgefield (07657) *(G-9368)*

Johnson & Johnson 732 524-0400
  10 Stymiest Rd Lambertville (08530) *(G-5214)*

Johnson & Johnson 732 524-0400
  6 Greenwood Ct Branchburg (08876) *(G-670)*

Johnson & Johnson 732 524-0400
  205 Waverly Ct Trenton (08691) *(G-11071)*

Johnson & Johnson 908 722-9319
  1000 Rte 202 Raritan (08869) *(G-9311)*

Johnson & Johnson 908 704-6809
  1101 Us Highway 202 Raritan (08869) *(G-9312)*

Johnson & Johnson 908 526-5425
  1003 Us Highway 202 P Raritan (08869) *(G-9313)*

Johnson & Johnson 908 874-1000
  201 Tabor Rd Morris Plains (07950) *(G-6673)*

Johnson & Johnson 908 725-7256
  51 Chubb Way Somerville (08876) *(G-10218)*

Johnson & Johnson 732 524-0400
  100 Albany St Ste 100 # 100 New Brunswick (08901) *(G-6975)*

Johnson & Johnson 732 422-5000
  691 Rte 1 North Brunswick (08902) *(G-7522)*

Johnson & Johnson Consumer Inc (HQ) 908 874-1000
  199 Grandview Rd Skillman (08558) *(G-10032)*

Johnson & Johnson Medical Inc (HQ) 908 218-0707
  Us Rt 22 Somerville (08876) *(G-10219)*

Johnson & Mayer Inc 201 646-1717
  58 Hobart St Hackensack (07601) *(G-3934)*

Johnson Associates Systems, Blackwood *Also called Johnson & Associates Inc (G-483)*

Johnson Controls Inc 856 245-9977
  1001 Lower Landing Rd # 409 Blackwood (08012) *(G-484)*

Johnson Controls Inc 732 225-6700
  264 Fernwood Ave Edison (08837) *(G-2549)*

Johnson Controls Inc 732 752-2395
  50 Progress St Union (07083) *(G-11199)*

Johnson Matthey Inc 856 384-7000
  2001 Nolte Dr West Deptford (08066) *(G-11832)*

Johnson Matthey Phrm Mtls, West Deptford *Also called Matthey Johnson Inc (G-11836)*

Johnston Letter Co Inc 973 482-7535
  209 Pleasant Hill Rd Flanders (07836) *(G-3412)*

Johnthan Leasing Corp 908 226-3434
  17 Water St Lebanon (08833) *(G-5293)*

Jolt Company Inc (PA) 201 288-0535
  100 Hollister Rd Unit 1 Teterboro (07608) *(G-10803)*

Jolt Energy Gum, Jersey City *Also called Gum Runners LLC (G-4763)*

Jomar Corp 609 646-8000
  115 E Parkway Dr Egg Harbor Township (08234) *(G-2687)*

Jomel Industries Inc 973 282-0300
  140 Central Ave Ste 1 Hillside (07205) *(G-4421)*

Jomel Seams Reasonable LLC (PA) 973 282-0300
  140 Cent Ave Hillside (07205) *(G-4422)*

Jon-Da Printing Co Inc 201 653-6200
  234 16th St Jersey City (07310) *(G-4769)*

Jonas Media Group Inc 973 438-1900
  520 Broad St Ste 400 Newark (07102) *(G-7208)*

Jones New York, Gillette *Also called Nine West Holdings Inc (G-3796)*

Jontol Unlimited LLC (PA) 858 652-1113
  1134 S Black Horse Pike Blackwood (08012) *(G-485)*

Jordache Ltd 908 226-4930
  200 Helen St South Plainfield (07080) *(G-10389)*

Jordan Manufacturing LLC 973 383-8363
  28 Randazzo Rd Lafayette (07848) *(G-5048)*

Jordan Tooling & Manufacturing 609 261-2636
  1307 Maine Ave Hainesport (08036) *(G-4075)*

Jorgensen Carr Ltd 201 792-2278
  45 Glenwood Pl East Orange (07017) *(G-2257)*

Jory Engravers Inc 201 939-1546
  23 W Erie Ave Rutherford (07070) *(G-9736)*

Josantos Cnstr & Dev LLC 732 202-7389
  13 Riverview Dr Brick (08723) *(G-749)*

Jose Moreira 201 991-9001
  712 Kearny Ave Kearny (07032) *(G-4890)*

Josemi Inc 917 710-2110
  1201 Hudson St Apt 216s Hoboken (07030) *(G-4481)*

Joseph and William Stavola (PA) 609 924-0300
  460 River Rd Kingston (08528) *(G-5028)*

Joseph Bbinec Shtmtl Works Inc 732 388-0155
  774 Martin St Rahway (07065) *(G-9205)*

Joseph Burns Inc 732 356-8355
  241 W Union Ave Bound Brook (08805) *(G-619)*

Joseph C Hansen Company Inc 201 222-1677
  629 Grove St Ste 26 Jersey City (07310) *(G-4770)*

Joseph Castings Inc 201 712-0717
  25 Brook Ave Maywood (07607) *(G-6056)*

Joseph Epstein Food Entps, East Rutherford *Also called Appetizers Made Easy Inc (G-2277)*

Joseph Mnniti Hair Replacement, Cherry Hill *Also called Minniti J Hair Replacement Inc (G-1401)*

Joseph Monga Jr 973 595-8517
  7383 Belmont Ave Paterson (07522) *(G-8306)*

Joseph Naticchia 609 882-7709
  1597 5th St Ewing (08638) *(G-3028)*

Joseph Oat Holdings Inc 856 541-2900
  2500 S Broadway Ste 10 Camden (08104) *(G-1072)*

Joseph Titone & Sons', Burlington *Also called Cellunet Manufacturing Compnay (G-961)*

Jost Brothers Jewelry Mfg Corp 908 453-2266
  295 Jost Dr Washington (07882) *(G-11584)*

Jostens Inc 973 584-5843
  86 Roseville Rd Succasunna (07876) *(G-10624)*

Journal News V Inc 201 986-1458
  424 Acorn Dr Paramus (07652) *(G-7879)*

Journal of Commerce Inc, Newark *Also called Teg New Jersey Inc (G-7338)*

Journal Register Company, Trenton *Also called 21st Century Media Newsppr LLC (G-11009)*

Joy Jewelery America Inc 201 689-1150
  228 Rivervale Rd Ste A River Vale (07675) *(G-9471)*

Joy Snacks LLC 732 272-0707
365 Blair Rd Ste A Avenel (07001) *(G-136)*

Joy-Rei Enterprises Inc 732 727-0742
3143 Bordentown Ave 5b Parlin (08859) *(G-7934)*

Joyce Food LLC (PA) 973 491-9696
80 Avenue K Newark (07105) *(G-7209)*

Joyce Leslie Inc (PA) 201 804-7800
401 Towne Centre Dr Hillsborough (08844) *(G-4352)*

Joyrei Enterprises, Parlin Also called Joy-Rei Enterprises Inc *(G-7934)*

JP Group International LLC 201 820-1444
525 Palmer Ave Maywood (07607) *(G-6057)*

Jpc Merger Sub LLC 609 890-4343
853 Nottingham Way Trenton (08638) *(G-11072)*

Jppc, Ewing Also called John Patrick Publishing LLC *(G-3027)*

JRC Web Accessories 973 625-3888
46 Passaic Ave Fairfield (07004) *(G-3238)*

Jrh Service & Sales LLC 908 832-9266
30 Boulder Hill Rd Lebanon (08833) *(G-5294)*

Jrm Industries Inc (PA) 973 779-9340
1 Mattimore St Passaic (07055) *(G-8152)*

JS Paluch Co Inc 732 516-1900
510 Thornall St Ste 140 Edison (08837) *(G-2550)*

Jsc Wire & Cable, Pennsauken Also called Jersey Specialty Co Inc *(G-8537)*

Jsm Co 732 695-9577
1052 Wayside Rd Tinton Falls (07712) *(G-10839)*

Jsn Holdings LLC 201 857-5900
1 International Blvd Mahwah (07495) *(G-5787)*

Jt Fuels LLC 973 527-4470
1470 Us Highway 46 Ledgewood (07852) *(G-5306)*

Jtp Romark Logistics, Westfield Also called Romark Logistics CES LLC *(G-11929)*

Jtwo Inc 201 410-1616
4 Birch Rd Kinnelon (07405) *(G-5037)*

Jubili Bead & Yarn Shoppe 856 858-7844
713 Haddon Ave Collingswood (08108) *(G-1771)*

Judith Roth Studio Collection 973 543-4455
3 Stone House Rd Mendham (07945) *(G-6087)*

Juliali Woodwork 856 225-0772
1700 Admiral Wilson Blvd Pennsauken (08109) *(G-8538)*

Julian Bait Company Inc 732 291-0050
990 State Route 36 Atlantic Highlands (07716) *(G-114)*

Julian Enterprises, Atlantic Highlands Also called Julian Bait Company Inc *(G-114)*

Julius E Holland-Moritz Co Inc 609 397-1231
599 Brunswick Pike Lambertville (08530) *(G-5215)*

Jump Start Press 732 892-4994
802 Cedar Ave Point Pleasant Beach (08742) *(G-8920)*

Junction Drugs, Fort Lee Also called K & S Drug & Surgical Inc *(G-3562)*

June Jacobs Labs LLC (PA) 201 329-9100
46 Graphic Pl Moonachie (07074) *(G-6526)*

Junganew LLC 201 832-0892
1 Orient Way Ste F104 Rutherford (07070) *(G-9737)*

Juniper Networks Inc 908 947-4436
200 Somerset Corp Blvd Bridgewater (08807) *(G-849)*

Jury Vrdict Rview Publications 973 376-9002
45 Springfield Ave Ste 2 Springfield (07081) *(G-10560)*

Just A Touch of Baking LLC 732 679-5123
3141 Us Highway 9 Old Bridge (08857) *(G-7782)*

Just Glass & Mirror Inc 856 728-8383
1250 N Black Horse Pike Williamstown (08094) *(G-12091)*

Just In Time Chemical Sales Inc 908 862-7726
1711 W Elizabeth Ave Linden (07036) *(G-5393)*

Just Plastics, Kearny Also called Gifford Group Inc *(G-4878)*

Just US Books Inc 973 672-7701
356 Glenwood Ave Ste 7a East Orange (07017) *(G-2258)*

Justice Laboratory Software 973 586-8551
1 Indian Rd Ste 2 Denville (07834) *(G-2044)*

Juvenile Planet, Lakewood Also called Steico USA Inc *(G-5191)*

Juventio LLC 973 908-8097
466 Southern Blvd Ste 2 Chatham (07928) *(G-1331)*

Jvc Industrial America Inc (HQ) 800 247-3608
1700 Valley Rd Ste 1 Wayne (07470) *(G-11657)*

Jvckenwood USA Corporation 973 317-5000
1700 Valley Rd Wayne (07470) *(G-11658)*

Jvm Sales Corp 908 862-4866
3401a Tremley Point Rd Linden (07036) *(G-5394)*

Jvs Copy Services Inc 856 415-9090
460 Main St Sewell (08080) *(G-9961)*

JW Parr Leadburing Co (PA) 973 256-8093
87 Parkway Little Falls (07424) *(G-5479)*

K & A Architectural Met GL LLC 908 687-0247
766b Ramsey Ave Hillside (07205) *(G-4423)*

K & A Industries Inc 908 226-7000
51 Cragwood Rd Ste 204 South Plainfield (07080) *(G-10390)*

K & C Fundraising, Clayton Also called William Cromley *(G-1529)*

K & E Components, Riverdale Also called Diversitech Inc *(G-9479)*

K & K Automotive Inc 973 777-2235
979 Main Ave Passaic (07055) *(G-8153)*

K & R Precision Machining LLC 201 385-8855
336 Birchwood Rd New Milford (07646) *(G-7022)*

K & S Drug & Surgical Inc 201 886-9191
266 Columbia Ave Fort Lee (07024) *(G-3562)*

K & S Industries Inc 908 862-3030
333 Dalziel Rd Linden (07036) *(G-5395)*

K & Z Pickle Co, Camden Also called Kaplan & Zubrin *(G-1073)*

K 2 Mill Work, Columbus Also called K2 Millwork Ltd Liability Co *(G-1804)*

K B Enterprises of New Jersey 908 451-5282
15 Ilene Ct Ste 1211 Hillsborough (08844) *(G-4353)*

K H Machine Works 201 867-2338
4322 Grand Ave North Bergen (07047) *(G-7459)*

K Jabat Inc 732 469-8177
342 Us Highway 22 Green Brook (08812) *(G-3860)*

K K S Criterion Chocolates 732 542-7847
125 Lewis St Eatontown (07724) *(G-2409)*

K M Media Group LLC 973 330-3000
220 Entin Rd Clifton (07014) *(G-1654)*

K R B Printing For Business 856 751-5200
1165 Marlkress Rd Ste G Cherry Hill (08003) *(G-1385)*

K R Electronics Inc 732 636-1900
91 Avenel St Avenel (07001) *(G-137)*

K Ron Art & Mirrors Inc 201 313-7080
395 Broad Ave Ridgefield (07657) *(G-9369)*

K-D Industries Inc 973 594-4800
18 Falstrom Ct Passaic (07055) *(G-8154)*

K-Deer, Westwood Also called Kristine Deer Inc *(G-11961)*

K-Tron International Inc (HQ) 856 589-0500
590 Woodbury Glassboro Rd Sewell (08080) *(G-9962)*

K2 Millwork Ltd Liability Co 609 379-6411
2180 Hedding Rd Columbus (08022) *(G-1804)*

Ka-Lor Cubicle and Sup Co Inc 201 891-8077
14-24 Abbott Rd Fair Lawn (07410) *(G-3099)*

Kabab & Curry Express 732 416-6560
4 Brunswick Ave Edison (08817) *(G-2551)*

Kabel N Elettrotek Amer Inc 973 265-0850
2 Cranberry Rd Ste 5a Parsippany (07054) *(G-8035)*

Kadakia International Group, South Plainfield Also called Kadakia International
Inc *(G-10391)*

Kadakia International Inc 908 754-4445
669 Montrose Ave South Plainfield (07080) *(G-10391)*

Kahle Automation 973 993-1850
89 Headquarters Plz S Morristown (07960) *(G-6719)*

Kairos Enterprises LLC 201 731-3181
210 Sylvan Ave Ste 22 Englewood Cliffs (07632) *(G-2969)*

Kaizen Technologies Inc (PA) 732 452-9555
1 State Route 27 Ste 10 Edison (08820) *(G-2552)*

Kaleidoscope Sound 201 223-2868
514 Monastery Pl Union City (07087) *(G-11252)*

Kalustyan Corporation 908 688-0853
855 Rahway Ave Union (07083) *(G-11200)*

Kamat Pharmatech LLC 732 406-6421
675 Us Highway 1 North Brunswick (08902) *(G-7523)*

Kampack Inc (HQ) 973 589-7400
100 Frontage Rd Newark (07114) *(G-7210)*

Kampack Inc 973 589-7400
100 Frontage Rd Newark (07114) *(G-7211)*

Kanar Inc 201 933-2800
1 Kero Rd Carlstadt (07072) *(G-1176)*

Kandasamy Lingeswaran 978 631-7662
38 Patton Dr Bloomfield (07003) *(G-516)*

Kane Wood Fuel 856 589-3292
512 Cedar Ave Pitman (08071) *(G-8843)*

Kanomax Usa Inc 973 786-6386
219 Us Highway 206 Byram Township (07821) *(G-1022)*

Kansai Special Amercn Mch Corp 973 470-8321
1 Madison St Ste F11 East Rutherford (07073) *(G-2301)*

Kansai Special USA, East Rutherford Also called Kansai Special Amercn Mch Corp *(G-2301)*

Kansas City Design Inc 609 460-4629
201 S Main St Lambertville (08530) *(G-5216)*

Kaplan & Zubrin (PA) 856 964-1083
Second Kaighns Ave Camden (08103) *(G-1073)*

Kappus Plastic Company Inc 908 537-2288
61 State Route 31 65 Hampton (08827) *(G-4163)*

Karcher North America Inc 856 228-1800
500 University Ct Blackwood (08012) *(G-486)*

Karebay Biochem Inc 732 823-1545
11 Deerpark Dr Ste 102a Monmouth Junction (08852) *(G-6349)*

Karen Lee Ballard, Warren Also called Ballard Collection Inc *(G-11538)*

Karis Graphic Corp. 201 935-8774
43 Romeo St Moonachie (07074) *(G-6527)*

Karl Neuweiler Inc 908 464-6532
23 Russo Pl Berkeley Heights (07922) *(G-415)*

Karla Landscaping Pavers 732 333-5852
11 Woodland Dr Howell (07731) *(G-4558)*

Karnak Corporation (PA) 732 388-0300
330 Central Ave Clark (07066) *(G-1502)*

Karnak Midwest LLC (HQ) 732 388-0300
330 Central Ave Clark (07066) *(G-1503)*

Kas Oriental Rugs Inc (PA) 732 545-1900
62 Veronica Ave Ste A Somerset (08873) *(G-10118)*

Kasanova Inc 201 368-8400
175 State Rt 17 Wood Ridge (07075) *(G-12137)*

Kashee & Sons Inc (PA) 201 867-6900
600 Meadowlands Pkwy 21b Secaucus (07094) *(G-9898)*

Kashmir 856 691-8969
3926 N Delsea Dr Vineland (08360) *(G-11377)*

Kashmir Crown Baking LLC (PA) 908 474-1470
710 W Linden Ave Linden (07036) *(G-5396)*

Kason Corporation (PA) 973 467-8140
6771 E Willow St Millburn (07041) *(G-6254)*

Kasper, Elizabeth *Also called Nine West Holdings Inc (G-2758)*

Kasper, Englewood *Also called Nine West Holdings Inc (G-2919)*

Katadin Inc 908 526-0166
53 Dreahook Rd Branchburg (08876) *(G-671)*

Kate Spade & Company 201 295-7569
5901 W Side Ave North Bergen (07047) *(G-7460)*

Kate Spade & Company 609 395-3109
120 Herrod Blvd Ste 8 Dayton (08810) *(G-1974)*

Kathy Gibson Designs Inc (PA) 201 420-0088
1435 51st St Ste 2 North Bergen (07047) *(G-7461)*

Kathy Jeanne Inc 973 575-9898
7 Industrial Rd Fairfield (07004) *(G-3239)*

Katies Closets 973 300-4007
3 Lower Hill Rd Newton (07860) *(G-7394)*

Katis Kupcakes 609 332-2172
233 Hedgeman Rd Moorestown (08057) *(G-6589)*

Katzs Delicatessen Mfg 212 254-2246
100 Industrial Rd Carlstadt (07072) *(G-1177)*

Kaufman Stairs Inc (PA) 908 862-3579
150 E Inman Ave Rahway (07065) *(G-9206)*

Kavon Filter Products Co 732 938-3135
5022 Industrial Rd Wall Township (07727) *(G-11492)*

Kay Printing & Envelope Co Inc 973 330-3000
220 Entin Rd Clifton (07014) *(G-1655)*

Kay Window Fashions Inc 862 591-1554
271 2nd St Saddle Brook (07663) *(G-9771)*

Kayden Manufacturing Inc 201 880-9898
83a Burlews Ct Ste A Hackensack (07601) *(G-3935)*

Kayline Processing Inc (PA) 609 695-1449
31 Coates St Trenton (08611) *(G-11073)*

KB Food Enterprises Inc 973 278-2800
19 E 5th St Paterson (07524) *(G-8307)*

Kdf Reprographics Inc 201 784-9991
65 Worth St South Hackensack (07606) *(G-10274)*

Kearfott Corporation (HQ) 973 785-6000
1150 Mcbride Ave Ste 1 Woodland Park (07424) *(G-12223)*

Kearny Recycle, Kearny *Also called Tilcon New York Inc (G-4917)*

Kearny Smelting & Ref Corp 201 991-7276
936 Harrison Ave Ste 5 Kearny (07032) *(G-4891)*

Keco Engineered Controls, Lakewood *Also called Amico Technologies Inc (G-5074)*

Kedrion Biopharma Inc (HQ) 201 242-8900
400 Kelby St Ste 11 Fort Lee (07024) *(G-3563)*

Keefe Printing Inc 732 295-2099
501 Atlantic Ave Point Pleasant Beach (08742) *(G-8921)*

Keeley Aerospace Ltd 951 582-2113
2559 Us Highway 130 Cranbury (08512) *(G-1846)*

Kef America, Marlboro *Also called GP Acoustics (us) Inc (G-5942)*

Kef America Inc 732 414-2074
10 Timber Ln Marlboro (07746) *(G-5946)*

Kel Instruments Co Inc 201 847-8353
471 Clinton Ave Wyckoff (07481) *(G-12255)*

Kelken Construction Systems, Sayreville *Also called Kelken-Gold Inc (G-9826)*

Kelken-Gold Inc 732 416-6730
550 Hartle St Ste C Sayreville (08872) *(G-9826)*

Kelleigh USA Inc 732 248-1161
1445 Lower Ferry Rd Ste 2 Ewing (08618) *(G-3029)*

Kelles Incorporated 908 241-9300
20 Hoiles Dr Ste D Kenilworth (07033) *(G-4966)*

Kelles Machining Center, Kenilworth *Also called Kelles Incorporated (G-4966)*

Kellogg Company 201 634-9140
164 Monroe Ave River Edge (07661) *(G-9466)*

Kellogg Company 609 567-1688
322 S Egg Harbor Rd Hammonton (08037) *(G-4141)*

Kellogg's Eggo, Hammonton *Also called Kellogg Company (G-4141)*

Kelsey Humus, Great Meadows *Also called Partac Peat Corporation (G-3851)*

Kempak Industries 908 687-4188
33 Fernhill Rd Springfield (07081) *(G-10561)*

Kempton Wood Products 732 449-8673
2800 Ridgewood Rd Wall Township (07719) *(G-11493)*

Ken Bauer & Sons, Hillsdale *Also called Ken Bauer Inc (G-4385)*

Ken Bauer Inc 201 664-6881
277 Broadway Ste A Hillsdale (07642) *(G-4385)*

Keneco Inc 908 241-3700
123 N 8th St Kenilworth (07033) *(G-4967)*

Kenilworth Anodizing Co 908 241-5640
201 S 31st St Ste A Kenilworth (07033) *(G-4968)*

Kenlen Wire Products Division, Livingston *Also called Amark Industries Inc (G-5524)*

Kennametal Inc 412 248-8200
123 Town Square Pl Jersey City (07310) *(G-4771)*

Kennedy Concrete Inc 856 692-8650
1969 S East Ave Vineland (08360) *(G-11378)*

Kennedy Shop N Bag, Willingboro *Also called Herman Eickhoff (G-12119)*

Kennetex Inc 610 444-0600
53 E 34th St Paterson (07514) *(G-8308)*

Kenneth Asmar Custom Interiors 732 544-6137
548 Shrewsbury Ave Tinton Falls (07701) *(G-10840)*

Kenney Steel Treating Corp 201 998-4420
100 Quincy Pl Kearny (07032) *(G-4892)*

Kenric Inc 856 294-9161
110 Richardson Ave Swedesboro (08085) *(G-10704)*

Kenrich Petrochemicals Inc 201 823-9000
570 Broadway Bayonne (07002) *(G-235)*

Kep Marine, Eatontown *Also called Sparton Aydin LLC (G-2423)*

Kerk Cabinetry LLC 856 881-4213
45 Dogwood Ave Glassboro (08028) *(G-3807)*

Kern & Szalai Co 856 802-1500
351 Crider Ave Moorestown (08057) *(G-6590)*

Kern & Szalai Machine Company, Moorestown *Also called Kern & Szalai Co (G-6590)*

Kerney Service Group Inc (PA) 908 486-2644
1700 E Elizabeth Ave Linden (07036) *(G-5397)*

Kerney Ship Repair, Linden *Also called Kerney Service Group Inc (G-5397)*

Kerrigan Lewis Wire/Cdt, Elizabeth *Also called Dearborn A Belden Cdt Company (G-2723)*

Kerry Flavor Systems Us LLC 513 771-4682
160 Terminal Ave Clark (07066) *(G-1504)*

Kerry Inc 201 373-1111
546 Us Highway 46 Teterboro (07608) *(G-10804)*

Kerry Inc 908 237-1595
26 Minneakoning Rd Flemington (08822) *(G-3453)*

Kerry Ingredients, Flemington *Also called Kerry Inc (G-3453)*

Kerry Ingredients & Flavours, Clark *Also called Kerry Flavor Systems Us LLC (G-1504)*

Kerry Ingredients and Flavours, Clark *Also called Mastertaste Inc (G-1508)*

Kerry Ingredients and Flavours, Teterboro *Also called Kerry Inc (G-10804)*

Kerry Wilkens Inc 732 787-0070
780 State Route 36 Belford (07718) *(G-288)*

Keskes Printing LLC 856 767-4733
5 W Taunton Ave Berlin (08009) *(G-437)*

Kessler Industries 973 279-1417
40 Warren St Paterson (07524) *(G-8309)*

Kessler Steel Rule Die Inc 856 767-0231
1004 Industrial Dr Ste 10 West Berlin (08091) *(G-11728)*

Kessler-Ellis Products Co (PA) 732 935-1320
10 Industrial Way E Ste 6 Eatontown (07724) *(G-2410)*

Kestrel Closets LLC 973 586-1144
29 Hillside Rd Rockaway (07866) *(G-9580)*

Ket, Eatontown *Also called Kessler-Ellis Products Co (G-2410)*

Ketec 856 778-4343
1256 N Church St Ste A Moorestown (08057) *(G-6591)*

Keurig Dr Pepper Inc 908 684-4400
562 Ervey Rd Andover (07821) *(G-52)*

Keurig Dr Pepper Inc 732 969-1600
1200 Milik St Carteret (07008) *(G-1261)*

Keurig Dr Pepper Inc 201 933-0070
600 Commercial Ave Carlstadt (07072) *(G-1178)*

Keurig Dr Pepper Inc 201 832-0695
100 Electric Ave Secaucus (07094) *(G-9899)*

Keurig Dr Pepper Inc 732 388-5545
433 Blair Rd Avenel (07001) *(G-138)*

Key Handling Systems Inc 201 933-9333
137 W Commercial Ave Moonachie (07074) *(G-6528)*

Key Software Systems LLC 732 409-6068
5100 Belmar Blvd Ste 8 Wall Township (07727) *(G-11494)*

Keydata International, Piscataway *Also called Datapro International Inc (G-8754)*

Keyence Corporation America (HQ) 201 930-0100
669 River Dr Ste 403 Elmwood Park (07407) *(G-2828)*

Keypoint Intelligence LLC 201 489-6439
108 John St Hackensack (07601) *(G-3936)*

Keypoint Intelligence LLC (HQ) 973 797-2100
80 Little Falls Rd Fairfield (07004) *(G-3240)*

Keysight Technologies, Budd Lake *Also called Agilent Technologies Inc (G-923)*

Keystone Adjustable Cap Co Inc 856 356-2809
1591 Hylton Rd Ste B Pennsauken (08110) *(G-8539)*

Keystone Automotive Inds Inc 856 829-4700
39 Phoenix Dr West Deptford (08086) *(G-11833)*

Keystone Dyeing and Finishing (PA) 718 482-7780
10 Pine Hill Ct Dayton (08810) *(G-1975)*

Keystone Folding Box Company 973 483-1054
367 Verona Ave Newark (07104) *(G-7212)*

Keystone Industries, Gibbstown *Also called Mycone Dental Supply Co Inc (G-3792)*

Keystone Packaging Service 908 454-8567
555 Warren St Phillipsburg (08865) *(G-8655)*

Keystone Plastics Inc 908 561-1300
3451 S Clinton Ave South Plainfield (07080) *(G-10392)*

Keystone Printing Inc 201 387-7252
21c E Madison Ave Dumont (07628) *(G-2119)*

Kft Fire Trainer LLC 201 300-8100
17 Philips Pkwy Montvale (07645) *(G-6463)*

A
L
P
H
A
B
E
T
I
C

KG Squared LLC 973 627-0643
5 Astro Pl Ste B Rockaway (07866) *(G-9581)*

KG Systems Inc 973 515-4664
765 Mountain Ave Ste 120 Springfield (07081) *(G-10562)*

Khanna Paper Inc 201 706-8050
50 Harrison St Ste 118 Hoboken (07030) *(G-4482)*

Kicksonfirecom LLC 718 753-4248
28 Lighthouse Dr South Amboy (08879) *(G-10240)*

Kidcuteture LLC 609 532-0149
5 Rosalind Dr Lawrenceville (08648) *(G-5259)*

Kidde Fire Trainers, Montvale Also called Kft Fire Trainer LLC *(G-6463)*

Kiddesigns Inc 732 574-9000
1299 Main St Rahway (07065) *(G-9207)*

Kids of America Corp 973 808-8242
103 Route 46 W Fairfield (07004) *(G-3241)*

Kiehls Since 1851 Inc 201 843-1125
355 N Highway 17 Paramus (07652) *(G-7880)*

Kik Custom Products, Freehold Also called Prestone Products Corporation *(G-3682)*

Kikuichi New York Inc 201 567-8388
560 Sylvan Ave Ste 3110 Englewood Cliffs (07632) *(G-2970)*

Killian Graphics 973 635-5844
142 Southern Blvd Chatham (07928) *(G-1332)*

Kimbo Educational, Eatontown Also called United Sound Arts Inc *(G-2428)*

Kinect Auto Parts Corporation 862 702-8252
75 Lane Rd Ste 201 Fairfield (07004) *(G-3242)*

Kinedyne LLC (HQ) 908 231-1800
3040 Us Highway 22 # 150 Branchburg (08876) *(G-672)*

Kinetics Control Systems, Ewing Also called Kinetics Industries Inc *(G-3030)*

Kinetics Industries Inc 609 883-9700
140 Stokes Ave Ewing (08638) *(G-3030)*

Kinetron Inc 732 918-7777
1416 Roller Rd Ocean (07712) *(G-7729)*

Kingline, Ringwood Also called Crown Fastener & Supply Corp *(G-9446)*

Kingster LLC 310 951-5127
618 Mazur Ave Paramus (07652) *(G-7881)*

Kingston Nurseries LLC 609 430-0366
140 Mapleton Rd Kingston (08528) *(G-5029)*

Kingwood Industrial Pdts Inc 908 852-8655
261 Main St Unit 12 Hackettstown (07840) *(G-4015)*

Kini Products Inc 732 299-5555
7 Forest Hill Dr New Egypt (08533) *(G-7016)*

Kinly Inc 973 585-3000
2 Ridgedale Ave Ste 100 Cedar Knolls (07927) *(G-1314)*

Kinnarney Rubber Co Inc 856 468-1320
450 Main St Mantua (08051) *(G-5892)*

Kinnery Metal, Passaic Also called Kinnery Precision LLC *(G-8155)*

Kinnery Precision LLC 973 473-4664
11 Exchange Pl Passaic (07055) *(G-8155)*

Kinzee Industries Inc 201 408-4301
80 Brayton St Englewood (07631) *(G-2907)*

Kirkwood NJ Globe Acqstion LLC 201 440-0800
1 Teaneck Rd Ridgefield Park (07660) *(G-9408)*

Kirms Printing Co Inc 732 774-8000
1520 Washington Ave Neptune (07753) *(G-6920)*

Kissler & Co Inc 201 896-9600
770 Central Blvd Carlstadt (07072) *(G-1179)*

Kitchen & Bath Design Center, Linden Also called Filipe Custom Woodwork *(G-5375)*

Kitchen and More Inc 908 272-3388
542 South Ave E Cranford (07016) *(G-1911)*

Kitchen Cabinet 856 228-8989
5100 Route 42 Blackwood (08012) *(G-487)*

Kitchen Crafters Plus 732 566-7995
1 Suydam Pl Matawan (07747) *(G-6023)*

Kitchen King Inc (PA) 732 341-9660
1561 Route 9 Ste 9 Toms River (08755) *(G-10890)*

Kitchen Table Bakers Inc 516 931-5113
100 Passaic Ave Ste 215 Fairfield (07004) *(G-3243)*

Kitchenexpo, Toms River Also called Universal Interlock Corp *(G-10919)*

Kitchens By Frank Inc 732 364-1343
2345 Route 9 Ste 5 Toms River (08755) *(G-10891)*

Kittyhawk Digital LLC 269 767-8399
35 Linwood Ave Emerson (07630) *(G-2860)*

Klabin Fragrances Inc 973 857-3600
71 Village Park Rd Cedar Grove (07009) *(G-1286)*

Kleemeyer & Merkel Inc 973 377-0875
68 Britten Rd Green Village (07935) *(G-3865)*

Klein Distributors Inc 732 446-7632
600 E Route 130 Burlington (08016) *(G-982)*

Klein Ribbon Corp 973 684-4671
176 E 7th St Ste 2 Paterson (07524) *(G-8310)*

Klein Usa Inc 973 246-8181
1 Madison St Ste F East Rutherford (07073) *(G-2302)*

Klm Mechanical Contractors 201 385-6965
109 W Shore Ave Dumont (07628) *(G-2120)*

Klus Pharma Inc 609 651-4466
8 Clarke Dr Ste 4 Cranbury (08512) *(G-1847)*

Kmba Fashions Inc 973 789-1652
272 Elmwood Ave Bldg 3 East Orange (07018) *(G-2259)*

Kmsco Inc 732 238-8666
42 Cindy Ln Ocean (07712) *(G-7730)*

Kna Graphics Inc 908 272-4232
303 N 14th St Kenilworth (07033) *(G-4969)*

Knf Neuberger Inc 609 890-8889
2 Black Forest Rd Trenton (08691) *(G-11074)*

Knickerbocker Bed Company 201 933-3100
770 Commercial Ave Carlstadt (07072) *(G-1180)*

Knickerbocker Machine Shop Inc (PA) 973 256-1616
611 Union Blvd Totowa (07512) *(G-10953)*

Knight Foods LLC 973 385-1230
874 Pompton Ave Ste A2 Cedar Grove (07009) *(G-1287)*

Knight Gas Burner Co, Millville Also called NM Knight Co Inc *(G-6316)*

Knite Inc 609 258-9550
18 W Piper Ave Ste 201 Ewing (08628) *(G-3031)*

Knobware, Englewood Also called C & C Metal Products Corp *(G-2880)*

Knock Out Graphics Inc 732 774-3331
522 Cookman Ave Ste 3n Asbury Park (07712) *(G-79)*

Knotts Company Inc 908 464-4800
350 Snyder Ave Berkeley Heights (07922) *(G-416)*

Know America Media LLC (PA) 770 650-1102
157 Eagle Rock Ave Roseland (07068) *(G-9653)*

Knudsen Precision Mfg 609 538-1100
113 Walters Ave Ewing (08638) *(G-3032)*

Koadings Inc 732 517-0784
540 N Edgemere Dr Allenhurst (07711) *(G-26)*

Koamtac Inc 609 734-4335
116 Village Blvd Ste 305 Princeton (08540) *(G-9064)*

Koba Corp 732 469-0110
60 Baekeland Ave Middlesex (08846) *(G-6173)*

Kobo Products Inc (PA) 908 757-0033
3474 S Clinton Ave South Plainfield (07080) *(G-10393)*

Kobo Products Inc 908 941-3406
690 Montrose Ave South Plainfield (07080) *(G-10394)*

Kobo Products Inc 908 757-0033
234 Saint Nicholas Ave South Plainfield (07080) *(G-10395)*

Kobolak & Son Inc 856 829-6106
1818 Bannard St Cinnaminson (08077) *(G-1472)*

Koch Mdlar Process Systems LLC (PA) 201 368-2929
45 Eisenhower Dr Ste 350 Paramus (07652) *(G-7882)*

Kodak W Jewelers of Bayonne, Hoboken Also called W Kodak Jewelers Inc *(G-4503)*

Koday Press Inc 201 387-0001
69 Armour Pl Dumont (07628) *(G-2121)*

Koehler Industries Inc 732 364-2700
25 Arnold Blvd Howell (07731) *(G-4559)*

Koellmann Gear Corporation 201 447-0200
8 Industrial Park Waldwick (07463) *(G-11447)*

Kohl & Madden Prtg Ink Corp (HQ) 201 935-8666
651 Garden St Carlstadt (07072) *(G-1181)*

Kohlder Manufacturing Inc 856 963-1801
1700 Admiral Wilson Blvd Pennsauken (08109) *(G-8540)*

Kohler Industries Inc 336 545-3289
155 Mcbride Ave Ste 1 Paterson (07501) *(G-8311)*

Kohouts Bakery 973 772-7270
75 Jewell St Fl 1 Garfield (07026) *(G-3741)*

Kole Design LLC 732 409-0211
35 Cedar Ct Freehold (07728) *(G-3664)*

Kolon USA Incorporated 201 641-5800
65 Challenger Rd Ridgefield Park (07660) *(G-9409)*

Komar Company, The, Jersey City Also called Charles Komar & Sons Inc *(G-4726)*

Komar Inc 212 725-1500
90 Hudson St Fl 9 Jersey City (07302) *(G-4772)*

Komar Intimates LLC (HQ) 212 725-1500
90 Hudson St Jersey City (07302) *(G-4773)*

Komar Kids LLC (HQ) 212 725-1500
90 Hudson St Jersey City (07302) *(G-4774)*

Komar Sleepwear, Jersey City Also called Komar Inc *(G-4772)*

Komatsu Northeast, South Plainfield Also called F and M Equipment Ltd *(G-10362)*

Komfort & Kare, Magnolia Also called J J L & W Inc *(G-5741)*

Komline-Sanderson Engrg Corp 973 579-0090
34 White Lake Rd Ste C Sparta (07871) *(G-10507)*

Komo Innovative Cnc Solutions, Lakewood Also called Komo Machine Inc *(G-5141)*

Komo Machine Inc 732 719-6222
1 Komo Dr Lakewood (08701) *(G-5141)*

Kompac Technologies LLC 908 534-8411
7 Commerce St Ste 1 Somerville (08876) *(G-10220)*

Konecranes Inc 908 259-9696
834 Fairfield Ave Kenilworth (07033) *(G-4970)*

Kongsberg Protech 973 770-0574
200 Valley Rd Ste 204 Mount Arlington (07856) *(G-6756)*

Kooltronic Inc (PA) 609 466-3400
30 Pennington Hopewell Rd Pennington (08534) *(G-8455)*

Koomus, Ridgefield Also called Tone Layout LLC *(G-9386)*

Kop Marble Granite Inc 973 283-8000
155 Lions Head Dr W Wayne (07470) *(G-11659)*

Kop-Coat Inc 800 221-4466
36 Pine St Rockaway (07866) *(G-9582)*

Koppers Chocolate LLC 212 243-0220
45 Jackson Dr Cranford (07016) *(G-1912)*

Korean Bergen News Inc 201 894-9061
210 Sylvan Ave Ste 23 Englewood Cliffs (07632) ***(G-2971)***
Korfund Dynamics, Bloomingdale *Also called Vibration Muntings Contrls Inc* ***(G-545)***
Kos Pharmaceuticals Inc (HQ) 609 495-0500
1 Cedarbrook Dr Cranbury (08512) ***(G-1848)***
Kozak Precision Products, Randolph *Also called Eugene Kozak* ***(G-9276)***
Kp Fuel Corporation 973 350-1202
864 Mount Prospect Ave Newark (07104) ***(G-7213)***
Kraemer Koating, Lakewood *Also called Miracle Mile Automotive Inc* ***(G-5160)***
Kraemer Properties Inc (PA) 732 886-6557
1925 Swarthmore Ave Ste 3 Lakewood (08701) ***(G-5142)***
Kraftape Printers Inc 973 824-3005
124 Orchard St Newark (07102) ***(G-7214)***
Kraftware Corporation (PA) 732 345-7091
270 Cox St Roselle (07203) ***(G-9674)***
Kraftwork Custom Design 609 883-8444
182 Homecrest Ave Ewing (08638) ***(G-3033)***
Kraissl Company Inc 201 342-0008
299 Williams Ave Hackensack (07601) ***(G-3937)***
Kramme Consolidated Inc (PA) 856 358-8151
Main St Monroeville (08343) ***(G-6400)***
Kraus & Naimer Inc (PA) 732 560-1240
760 New Brunswick Rd Somerset (08873) ***(G-10119)***
Krauses Homemade Candy Inc 201 943-4790
461 Fairview Ave 465 Fairview (07022) ***(G-3364)***
Kreisler Industrial, Elmwood Park *Also called Kreisler Manufacturing Corp* ***(G-2830)***
Kreisler Industrial Corp (HQ) 201 773-6829
180 Van Riper Ave Elmwood Park (07407) ***(G-2829)***
Kreisler Manufacturing Corp (PA) 201 791-0700
180 Van Riper Ave Elmwood Park (07407) ***(G-2830)***
Krell Technologies Inc 732 617-7091
11 Evergreen Ave Neptune (07753) ***(G-6921)***
Krementz & Co (PA) 973 621-8300
51 Commerce St Springfield (07081) ***(G-10563)***
Krementz Gemstones, Springfield *Also called Krementz & Co* ***(G-10563)***
Krfc Custom Woodworking Inc 732 363-0522
1328 River Ave Ste 25 Lakewood (08701) ***(G-5143)***
Krfc Design Center, Lakewood *Also called Krfc Custom Woodworking Inc* ***(G-5143)***
Krieck Enterprises LLC 908 789-8600
125 Park Ave Madison (07940) ***(G-5727)***
Krimstock Enterprises, Pennsauken *Also called J D Crew Inc* ***(G-8534)***
Kristine Deer Inc 201 497-3333
174 Westwood Ave Westwood (07675) ***(G-11961)***
Kristino Handbags & ACC, Sussex *Also called Annette & Jim Dizenzo Sls LLC* ***(G-10666)***
Krogh's Restaurant, Sparta *Also called Summerlands Inc* ***(G-10521)***
Krohn Industries, Carlstadt *Also called Krohn Technical Products Inc* ***(G-1182)***
Krohn Technical Products Inc 201 933-9696
303 Veterans Blvd Carlstadt (07072) ***(G-1182)***
Kronos Worldwide Inc 609 860-6200
5 Cedarbrook Dr Ste 2 Cranbury (08512) ***(G-1849)***
Krowne Metal Corp 973 305-3300
100 Haul Rd Wayne (07470) ***(G-11660)***
KRs Automotive Dev Group Inc 732 667-7937
278 Lincoln Blvd Ste 2 Middlesex (08846) ***(G-6174)***
Krystal Clear Media Group LLC 302 715-1069
5 Lawrence St Ste Ph34 Bloomfield (07003) ***(G-517)***
Kt America Corp 609 655-5333
2650 Us Highway 130 Ste I Cranbury (08512) ***(G-1850)***
Kt Mt Corp (PA) 877 791-4426
2303 Garry Rd Unit 12 Cinnaminson (08077) ***(G-1473)***
Kt Welding 908 862-7370
328 Spruce St Linden (07036) ***(G-5398)***
Ktb Acquisition Sub Inc (HQ) 973 240-0200
100 Passaic Ave Fairfield (07004) ***(G-3244)***
Kubik Maltbie Inc 856 234-0052
7000 Commerce Pkwy Ste C Mount Laurel (08054) ***(G-6811)***
Kudas Industries Inc 412 751-0260
6 Dorchester Dr Denville (07834) ***(G-2045)***
Kuehne Chemical Company Inc (PA) 973 589-0700
86 N Hackensack Ave Kearny (07032) ***(G-4893)***
Kufall Printing 732 505-9847
4 Oak Ridge Pkwy Toms River (08755) ***(G-10892)***
Kuhl Corp 908 782-5696
39 Kuhl Rd Flemington (08822) ***(G-3454)***
Kuiken Brothers Company (PA) 201 796-2082
6-02 Fair Lawn Ave Fair Lawn (07410) ***(G-3100)***
Kultur International Films Ltd 732 229-2343
2 Bridge Ave Ste 633 Red Bank (07701) ***(G-9334)***
Kultur Video, Red Bank *Also called Kultur International Films Ltd* ***(G-9334)***
Kumar & Kumar Inc 732 322-0435
57 Denise Dr Edison (08820) ***(G-2553)***
Kumar Bros USA LLC (PA) 732 266-3091
74 Oxford Ct Englishtown (07726) ***(G-2995)***
Kupelian Foods Inc 201 440-8055
146 Bergen Tpke Ridgefield Park (07660) ***(G-9410)***
Kurt Versen Inc 201 664-5283
1 Paragon Dr Ste 157 Montvale (07645) ***(G-6464)***
Kushner Draperies Mfg LLC 856 317-9696
5305 Marlton Pike Pennsauken (08109) ***(G-8541)***
Kvk Usa Inc 732 846-2355
19 Home News Row Bldg A New Brunswick (08901) ***(G-6976)***
Kwality Foods Ltd Liability Co 732 906-1941
1734 Oak Tree Rd Edison (08820) ***(G-2554)***
Kwg Industries LLC 908 218-8900
330 Roycefield Rd Unit B Hillsborough (08844) ***(G-4354)***
Kwik Enterprises LLC 732 663-1559
1806 Bellmore St Oakhurst (07755) ***(G-7670)***
Kwik Kopy Printing, Brigantine *Also called Bar Lan Inc* ***(G-917)***
Kync Design LLC 201 293-4677
701 Penhorn Ave Ste 1 Secaucus (07094) ***(G-9900)***
Kyocera International Inc 856 691-7000
1515 Burnt Mill Rd Cherry Hill (08003) ***(G-1386)***
Kyosis LLC 908 202-8894
148 Whitehead Ave Ste 1 South River (08882) ***(G-10462)***
Kyowa Hakko Kirin Cal Inc 609 580-7400
212 Carnegie Ctr Ste 101 Princeton (08540) ***(G-9065)***
Kyowa Kirin Inc 908 234-1096
135 Rte 202 206 Ste 6 Bedminster (07921) ***(G-275)***
L & F Graphics Ltd Lblty Co 973 240-7033
207 E 15th St Paterson (07524) ***(G-8312)***
L & L Kiln Mfg Inc 856 294-0077
505 Sharptown Rd Swedesboro (08085) ***(G-10705)***
L & L Redi-Mix Inc (PA) 609 859-2271
1939 Route 206 Southampton (08088) ***(G-10477)***
L & L Welding Contractors 609 395-1600
3 Wheeling Rd Dayton (08810) ***(G-1976)***
L & M Machine & Tool Co Inc 973 523-5288
105 Lehigh Ave Paterson (07503) ***(G-8313)***
L & R Manufacturing Co Inc (PA) 201 991-5330
577 Elm St Kearny (07032) ***(G-4894)***
L & R Manufacturing Co Inc 201 991-5330
John Hay Ave Kearny (07032) ***(G-4895)***
L & S Contracting Inc 609 397-1281
259 Route 31 N Hopewell (08525) ***(G-4542)***
L & T, Closter *Also called Luxury and Trash Ltd Lblty Co* ***(G-1763)***
L & Z Tool and Engineering Inc 908 322-2220
1691 Us Highway 22 Watchung (07069) ***(G-11592)***
L A Dreyfus Co 732 549-1600
3775 Park Ave Edison (08820) ***(G-2555)***
L A S Printing Co 201 991-5362
3035 John F Kennedy Blvd Jersey City (07306) ***(G-4775)***
L and Ds Sapore Ravioli Cheese 732 563-9190
429b Lincoln Blvd Middlesex (08846) ***(G-6175)***
L Arden Corp 973 523-6400
72 Putnam St Paterson (07524) ***(G-8314)***
L D L Technology Inc 973 345-9111
137 Pennsylvania Ave Paterson (07503) ***(G-8315)***
L E Rosellis Food Specialties 609 654-4816
155 Church Rd Medford (08055) ***(G-6074)***
L Gambert LLC 973 344-3440
61 Freeman St Ste 4 Newark (07105) ***(G-7215)***
L Gambert Shirts, Newark *Also called L Gambert LLC* ***(G-7215)***
L J Loeffler Systems Inc 212 924-7597
95 Centre Ave Secaucus (07094) ***(G-9901)***
L L Teach Inc 732 223-1605
401 Kenli Ln Brielle (08730) ***(G-912)***
L N S Industries, Egg Harbor Township *Also called LNS Inc* ***(G-2688)***
L P Music Group, Garfield *Also called Latin Percussion Inc* ***(G-3742)***
L S P Industrial Ceramics Inc 609 397-8330
34 Mount Airy Village Rd Lambertville (08530) ***(G-5217)***
L&M Architectural Graphics Inc 973 575-7665
20 Montesano Rd Fairfield (07004) ***(G-3245)***
L&M Signs, Fairfield *Also called L&M Architectural Graphics Inc* ***(G-3245)***
L&W Audio/Video Inc 212 980-2862
1034 Clinton St Apt 101 Hoboken (07030) ***(G-4483)***
L-3 Cmmnctons Mbile-Vision Inc, Rockaway *Also called L3 Mobile-Vision Inc* ***(G-9583)***
L-E-M Plastics and Supplies 201 933-9150
255 Highland Cross Ste 4 Rutherford (07070) ***(G-9738)***
L3 Mobile-Vision Inc 973 263-1090
400 Commons Way Ste F Rockaway (07866) ***(G-9583)***
L3 Technologies Inc 856 338-3000
1 Federal St Camden (08103) ***(G-1074)***
L3 Technologies Inc 973 446-4000
450 Clark Dr Ste 1 Budd Lake (07828) ***(G-932)***
La Bonbonniere, Edison *Also called Excellence In Baking Inc* ***(G-2516)***
La Casa De Tortilla 732 398-0660
2017 State Route 27 Somerset (08873) ***(G-10120)***
La Cour Inc (PA) 973 227-3300
36 Kulick Rd Fairfield (07004) ***(G-3246)***
La Duca Technical Services LLC 570 309-4009
51 Shadowy Ln West Milford (07480) ***(G-11853)***
La Favorite Industries Inc 973 279-1266
33 Shady St Paterson (07524) ***(G-8316)***
La Forchetta 973 304-4797
27 Utter Ave Hawthorne (07506) ***(G-4245)***
La Forge De Style LLC 201 488-1955
57 Romanelli Ave South Hackensack (07606) ***(G-10275)***
La Marca Industries, Watchung *Also called L & Z Tool and Engineering Inc* ***(G-11592)***

ALPHABETIC

La Mart Manufacturing Corp.................718 384-6917
1465 Palisade Ave Teaneck (07666) *(G-10759)*
La Milagrosa.................973 928-1799
32 Wall St Passaic (07055) *(G-8156)*
La Pace Imports Inc.................973 895-5420
3 Ascot Ln Morristown (07960) *(G-6720)*
La Sierra Coffee Roasters, Dover *Also called Arias Mountain-Coffee LLC (G-2077)*
La Tribuna Publication Inc.................201 617-1360
300 36th St Apt 1 Union City (07087) *(G-11253)*
Lab Express Inc.................973 227-1700
10 Madison Rd Ste A Fairfield (07004) *(G-3247)*
Lab Express International, Fairfield *Also called Lab Express Inc (G-3247)*
Lab Tech Inc (PA).................201 767-5613
170 Legrand Ave Northvale (07647) *(G-7589)*
Label Graphics II, Fairfield *Also called Label Graphics Mfg Inc (G-3248)*
Label Graphics Mfg Inc (PA).................973 890-5665
175 Paterson Ave Little Falls (07424) *(G-5480)*
Label Graphics Mfg Inc.................973 276-1555
315 Fairfield Rd Fairfield (07004) *(G-3248)*
Label Master Inc.................973 546-3110
89 Dell Glen Ave Lodi (07644) *(G-5591)*
Label Solutions Inc.................201 599-0909
151 W Passaic St 2 Rochelle Park (07662) *(G-9531)*
Labeling Systems LLC.................201 405-0767
48 Spruce St Oakland (07436) *(G-7694)*
Labern Machine Products LLC.................908 722-1970
3388 Us Highway 22 Branchburg (08876) *(G-673)*
Labern Realty, Branchburg *Also called Labern Machine Products LLC (G-673)*
Labnet International Inc.................732 417-0700
33 Wood Ave S Ste 600 Iselin (08830) *(G-4630)*
Laboratory Diagnostics Co Inc (HQ).................732 536-6300
100 County Road 520 Morganville (07751) *(G-6646)*
Laboratory Diagnostics Co Inc.................732 972-2145
712 Ginesi Dr Morganville (07751) *(G-6647)*
Labrada Inc.................201 461-2641
41 Palmer Pl Leonia (07605) *(G-5317)*
Labvantage Solutions Inc (HQ).................908 707-4100
265 Davidson Ave Ste 220 Somerset (08873) *(G-10121)*
Lacoa Inc.................973 754-1000
21 Wallace St Elmwood Park (07407) *(G-2831)*
Lacrosse Republic.................856 853-8787
711 Mantua Pike Ste 2 West Deptford (08096) *(G-11834)*
Laeger Metal Spinning Co Inc.................908 925-5530
1514 E Elizabeth Ave Linden (07036) *(G-5399)*
Laennec Publishing Inc.................973 882-9500
4 Woodhollow Rd Ste 1 Parsippany (07054) *(G-8036)*
Lafarge North America Inc.................201 437-2575
6 Commerce St Bayonne (07002) *(G-236)*
Lafarge Road Marking Inc.................973 884-0300
400 Lanidex Plz Parsippany (07054) *(G-8037)*
Laird & Company (PA).................732 542-0312
1 Laird Rd Eatontown (07724) *(G-2411)*
Lakeland Transformer Corp.................973 835-0818
6 Paul Pl Haskell (07420) *(G-4209)*
Lakewood Elc Mtr Sls & Svc.................732 363-2865
6850 Us Highway 9 Howell (07731) *(G-4560)*
Lally-Pak Inc.................908 351-4141
1209 Central Ave Hillside (07205) *(G-4424)*
Lamart Corp.................973 772-6262
37 Chestnut St Clifton (07011) *(G-1656)*
Lamart Corporation (PA).................973 772-6262
16 Richmond St Clifton (07011) *(G-1657)*
Lamart Corporation.................973 772-6262
162 Circle Ave Clifton (07011) *(G-1658)*
Lamart Manufacturing Co, Teaneck *Also called La Mart Manufacturing Corp (G-10759)*
Lamatek Inc (PA).................856 599-6000
1226 Forest Pkwy Paulsboro (08066) *(G-8418)*
Lamb Printing Inc.................908 852-0837
700 Grand Ave Hackettstown (07840) *(G-4016)*
Laminated Industries Inc.................908 862-5995
2000 Brunswick Ave Linden (07036) *(G-5400)*
Laminated Paperboard Corp.................908 862-5995
2000 Brunswick Ave Linden (07036) *(G-5401)*
Laminetics Inc.................732 367-1116
1151 River Ave Lakewood (08701) *(G-5144)*
Lamitech Inc (HQ).................609 860-8037
322 Half Acre Rd Cranbury (08512) *(G-1851)*
Lamonica Fine Foods LLC.................856 776-2126
48 Gorton Rd Millville (08332) *(G-6311)*
Lamson Airtubes LLC.................973 300-4267
10 Millpond Dr Unit 4 Lafayette (07848) *(G-5049)*
Lanco Container, Paterson *Also called Lanco-York Inc (G-8317)*
Lanco-York Inc (PA).................973 278-7400
864 E 25th St Paterson (07513) *(G-8317)*
Landew Sawdust Co Inc.................973 344-5255
21 Poinier St Newark (07114) *(G-7216)*
Landice Incorporated.................973 927-9010
111 Canfield Ave Ste A-1 Randolph (07869) *(G-9286)*
Landice Treadmills, Randolph *Also called Landice Incorporated (G-9286)*

Landsberg New Jersey Div 1088, Cranbury *Also called Orora Packaging Solutions (G-1865)*
Langan Engineering Environmen (PA).................973 560-4900
300 Kimball Dr Ste 4 Parsippany (07054) *(G-8038)*
Lantek Corporation.................973 579-8100
29 Brookfield Dr Sparta (07871) *(G-10508)*
Lantier Construction Company.................856 780-6366
12 Greenvale Rd Moorestown (08057) *(G-6592)*
Lanxess Solutions US Inc.................732 826-1018
1000 Coventry Blvd Perth Amboy (08861) *(G-8620)*
Lanxess Solutions US Inc.................973 235-1800
10 Kingsland St Nutley (07110) *(G-7650)*
Lanxess Solutions US Inc.................973 887-7411
215 Merry Ln East Hanover (07936) *(G-2227)*
Lanxess Solutions US Inc.................732 738-1000
1020 King George Post Rd Fords (08863) *(G-3530)*
Lanxess Sybron Chemicals Inc (HQ).................609 893-1100
200 Birmingham Rd Birmingham (08011) *(G-468)*
LAp Marketing MGT Svcs Inc.................609 654-9266
104 Old Carriage Rd Cherry Hill (08034) *(G-1387)*
Lapp Cable Works Inc.................973 660-9632
29 Hanover Rd Florham Park (07932) *(G-3508)*
Lapp Holding NA Inc (HQ).................973 660-9700
29 Hanover Rd Florham Park (07932) *(G-3509)*
Lapp Usa Inc.................973 660-9700
29 Hanover Rd Florham Park (07932) *(G-3510)*
Lapp Usa LLC.................973 660-9700
29 Hanover Rd Florham Park (07932) *(G-3511)*
Laraccas Manufacturing Inc.................973 571-1452
395 Little Falls Rd Cedar Grove (07009) *(G-1288)*
Laras Designs, South Orange *Also called Danmola Lara (G-10302)*
Lardieri Custom Woodworking.................732 905-6334
1830 Swarthmore Ave Ste 6 Lakewood (08701) *(G-5145)*
Larose Industries LLC (PA).................973 543-2037
1578 Sussex Tpke Randolph (07869) *(G-9287)*
Larsen Marine Services LLC.................609 408-3564
333 45th Pl Sea Isle City (08243) *(G-9863)*
Larson-Juhl US LLC.................973 439-1801
165 Clinton Rd Caldwell (07006) *(G-1030)*
Larue Manufacturing Corp.................908 534-2700
Salem Indstrl Park 8 Whitehouse (08888) *(G-12046)*
Laser Contractors LLC.................609 517-2407
433 Mckendimen Rd Medford (08055) *(G-6075)*
Laser Dim Graphics & Prtg Inc.................732 821-9000
2 Parkwood Ln Colts Neck (07722) *(G-1789)*
Laser Save, Freehold *Also called Central Technology Inc (G-3645)*
Laser Xpressions Inc.................732 303-9530
3710 Us Highway 9 Fl 2 Freehold (07728) *(G-3665)*
Lasercam LLc (PA).................201 941-1262
1039 Hoyt Ave Ridgefield (07657) *(G-9370)*
Lasermetrics Division, Saddle Brook *Also called Fastpulse Technology Inc (G-9765)*
Laserwave Graphics Inc.................732 745-7764
24a Joyce Kilmer Ave N New Brunswick (08901) *(G-6977)*
Lassonde Pappas and Co Inc (HQ).................856 455-1000
1 Collins Dr Ste 200 Carneys Point (08069) *(G-1245)*
Lassonde Pappas and Co Inc.................856 455-1001
1019 Parsonage Rd Bridgeton (08302) *(G-788)*
Latex Products Division, Hawthorne *Also called Mid-State Enterprises Inc (G-4247)*
Latin Percussion Inc (HQ).................973 478-6903
160 Belmont Ave Ste 1 Garfield (07026) *(G-3742)*
Latino U S A.................732 870-1475
647 Broadway Long Branch (07740) *(G-5628)*
Latino USA Newspaper, Long Branch *Also called Latino U S A (G-5628)*
Latta Graphics Inc.................201 440-4040
651 Garden St Carlstadt (07072) *(G-1183)*
Lattice Incorporated (PA).................856 910-1166
7150 N Park Dr Ste 500 Pennsauken (08109) *(G-8542)*
Lattimer, Vineland *Also called I S Parts International Inc (G-11372)*
Lauda-Brinkmann LP.................856 764-7300
1819 Underwood Blvd Ste 2 Delran (08075) *(G-2017)*
Lauda-Brinkmann Management Inc.................856 764-7300
1819 Underwood Blvd Ste 2 Delran (08075) *(G-2018)*
Lauderdale Millwork Inc.................908 508-9550
77 Industrial Rd Berkeley Heights (07922) *(G-417)*
Laureate Press.................609 646-1545
1336 W Central Ave Egg Harbor City (08215) *(G-2666)*
Laurel Manufacturers, Delanco *Also called Medlaurel Inc (G-2007)*
Laurelton Welding Service Inc.................732 899-6348
117 Channel Dr Point Pleasant Beach (08742) *(G-8922)*
Lautus Phrmceuticals Ltd Lblty.................908 273-2777
7 Kitchell Rd Morristown (07960) *(G-6721)*
Lava Lunch, Maplewood *Also called Elements Accessories Inc (G-5919)*
Lavitsky Computer Laboratories.................908 725-6206
865 Sherwood Rd Bridgewater (08807) *(G-850)*
Lawless Jerky LLC.................310 869-5733
37 N Maple Ave Apt 30 Marlton (08053) *(G-5981)*
Lawn Doctor of Mercer County, New Brunswick *Also called Elaine K Josephson Inc (G-6958)*
Lawn Medic Inc.................856 742-1111
512 River Dr Westville (08093) *(G-11945)*

2018 Harris New Jersey
Manufacturers Directory

(G-0000) Company's Geographic Section entry number

Lawn Medic of Delaware Valley, Westville *Also called Lawn Medic Inc* ***(G-11945)***
Lawrence Custom Drapery Shop 609 882-4007
323 4th St Ewing (08638) ***(G-3034)***
Lawrence Educational Services, Brielle *Also called L L Teach Inc* ***(G-912)***
Lawrence Katona 609 538-1388
63 Carlton Ave Ewing (08618) ***(G-3035)***
Lawrence M Gichan Incorporated 201 330-3222
900 Dell Ave North Bergen (07047) ***(G-7462)***
Lawrence Mold and Tool Corp (PA) 609 392-5422
1412 Ohio Ave Lawrenceville (08648) ***(G-5260)***
Lawrence Packaging, Moonachie *Also called Lps Industries Inc* ***(G-6529)***
Lawyers Diary & Manual, New Providence *Also called Skinder-Strauss LLC* ***(G-7054)***
Lawyers Diary and Manual LLC 973 642-1440
890 Mountain Ave Ste 300 New Providence (07974) ***(G-7041)***
LAZAR CAPPER, Hazlet *Also called Lazar Technologies Inc* ***(G-4277)***
Lazar Technologies Inc 732 739-9622
39 Evergreen St Hazlet (07730) ***(G-4277)***
Lb Book Bindery LLC 973 244-0442
19 Gardner Rd Ste I Fairfield (07004) ***(G-3249)***
Lb Electric Co LLC 973 366-2188
12 Knoll Top Ct Denville (07834) ***(G-2046)***
Lbd Corp 201 541-6760
18 S Dean St Englewood (07631) ***(G-2908)***
Lbu Inc 973 773-4800
7 4th Ave 33 Paterson (07524) ***(G-8318)***
LCI Graphics Inc 973 893-2913
2400 Main St Ste 8 Sayreville (08872) ***(G-9827)***
Ld Electric LLC 201 225-1001
300 N Farview Ave Paramus (07652) ***(G-7883)***
Ldm Inc 609 921-8555
248 Nassau St Princeton (08542) ***(G-9066)***
Le BEC Fin Fine Foods, Linden *Also called Dim Inc* ***(G-5369)***
Le Bon Magot Ltd Liability Co 609 895-0211
69 Lawrncvlle Pnnngton Rd Lawrenceville (08648) ***(G-5261)***
Le Papillon Ltd 908 753-7300
500 Hadley Rd South Plainfield (07080) ***(G-10396)***
Le Papillon of New Jersey, South Plainfield *Also called Le Papillon Ltd* ***(G-10396)***
Le-Ed Concrete & Supply Co, Toms River *Also called Le-Ed Construction Inc* ***(G-10893)***
Le-Ed Construction Inc 732 341-4546
1609 Route 9 Toms River (08755) ***(G-10893)***
Lead Bead Publishing Company 732 246-0410
46 Shelly Dr Somerset (08873) ***(G-10122)***
Lead Conversion Plus 802 497-1557
500 Craig Rd Ste 101 Manalapan (07726) ***(G-5853)***
Leader Newsgroup LLC 201 438-6801
251 Ridge Rd Lyndhurst (07071) ***(G-5685)***
Leader Printers, Wildwood *Also called Hallco Inc* ***(G-12072)***
Leading Pharma LLC (PA) 201 746-9160
3 Oak Rd Fairfield (07004) ***(G-3250)***
Leading Pharma LLC 201 746-9160
155 Chestnut Ridge Rd # 3 Montvale (07645) ***(G-6465)***
Leak Detection Associates 856 401-7718
3003 N Mill Rd 1a Vineland (08360) ***(G-11379)***
Learning Links-Usa Inc 516 437-9071
26 Haypress Rd Cranbury (08512) ***(G-1852)***
Leather Head Sports, Glen Rock *Also called Cunningham Classics Ltd Lblty* ***(G-3825)***
Lebanon Cheese Company Inc 908 236-2611
3 Railroad Ave Lebanon (08833) ***(G-5295)***
Lebanon Door Company, Lebanon *Also called Glen G Coats* ***(G-5287)***
Leco Plastics Inc 201 343-3330
130 Gameville St Hackensack (07601) ***(G-3938)***
Lectro Products Inc 732 462-2463
22 Francis Mills Rd Freehold (07728) ***(G-3666)***
Ledonne Leather Co Inc 201 531-2100
730 5th St Lyndhurst (07071) ***(G-5686)***
Lee Sims Chocolates, Jersey City *Also called Sims Lee Inc* ***(G-4828)***
Lees Woodworking Inc 732 681-1002
726 Walling Ave Wall Township (07719) ***(G-11495)***
Leets Steel Inc 917 416-7977
495 Raritan St Sayreville (08872) ***(G-9828)***
Leeward International Inc 201 836-8830
400 Frank W Burr Blvd # 68 Teaneck (07666) ***(G-10760)***
Left-Handed Libra LLC 973 623-1112
50 Park Pl Ste 1001 Newark (07102) ***(G-7217)***
Legacy Converting Inc (PA) 609 642-7020
3 Security Dr Ste 301 Cranbury (08512) ***(G-1853)***
Legacy Vulcan LLC 973 253-8828
208 Piaget Ave Clifton (07011) ***(G-1659)***
Legend Machine & Grinding 908 685-1100
36 S Adamsville Rd Bridgewater (08807) ***(G-851)***
Legend Stone Products 973 473-7088
185 River Rd Clifton (07014) ***(G-1660)***
Leggett & Platt Incorporated 732 225-2440
521 Sunfield Ave Edison (08837) ***(G-2556)***
Leggett & Platt 2502, Edison *Also called Leggett & Platt Incorporated* ***(G-2556)***
Leggett & Platt Incorporated 904 786-0750
17 Sandy Point Dr Brick (08723) ***(G-750)***
Leggs Hns Bli Plytx Fctry Outl 908 289-7262
651 Kapkowski Rd Ste 1008 Elizabeth (07201) ***(G-2751)***
Lehigh Cement Company 973 579-2111
66 Demarest Rd Sparta (07871) ***(G-10509)***
Lehigh Phoenis, Rockaway *Also called Phoenix Color Corp* ***(G-9595)***
Lehigh Utility Associates Inc 908 561-5252
1300 New Market Ave South Plainfield (07080) ***(G-10397)***
Lehigh Valley Dairy Farms, Burlington *Also called Tuscan/Lehigh Dairies Inc* ***(G-992)***
Leibrock Metal Products Inc 732 695-0326
1800 Brielle Ave Ocean (07712) ***(G-7731)***
Leistritz Advanced Tech Corp (HQ) 201 934-8262
165 Chestnut St Ste 1 Allendale (07401) ***(G-11)***
Leistritz Pump, Allendale *Also called Leistritz Advanced Tech Corp* ***(G-11)***
Leiz Custom Woodworking, Linden *Also called David Leiz Custom Woodwork* ***(G-5368)***
Leland Limited Inc 908 561-2000
2614 S Clinton Ave South Plainfield (07080) ***(G-10398)***
Lemniscate Inc 707 824-2272
1 International Blvd # 400 Mahwah (07495) ***(G-5788)***
Lemon Inc 201 417-5412
72 Mohawk Ave Norwood (07648) ***(G-7628)***
Lenape Products Inc 609 394-5376
610 Plum St Trenton (08638) ***(G-11075)***
Leng-Dor USA Inc (HQ) 732 254-4300
11 Commerce Dr Cranbury (08512) ***(G-1854)***
Lennox Industries Inc 908 223-6002
555 Route 57 Port Murray (07865) ***(G-8978)***
Lens Depot Inc 732 993-9766
40c Cotters Ln Ste D East Brunswick (08816) ***(G-2164)***
Lens Lab Express 201 861-0016
5917 Bergenline Ave West New York (07093) ***(G-11871)***
Lens Mode Inc 973 467-2000
150 Main St Ste 1 Millburn (07041) ***(G-6255)***
Lens Savers Division, Garfield *Also called International Crystal Labs* ***(G-3739)***
Lentine Sheet Metal Inc 908 486-8974
1210 E Elizabeth Ave Linden (07036) ***(G-5402)***
Leo Pharma Inc 973 637-1690
7 Giralda Farms Ste 2 Madison (07940) ***(G-5728)***
Leo Prager Inc 201 266-8888
2322 Sterling Blvd Englewood (07631) ***(G-2909)***
Leo's Famous Yum Yum, Medford *Also called Leos Ice Cream Company* ***(G-6076)***
Leon Levin, East Brunswick *Also called Chic LLC* ***(G-2141)***
Leonard's Novelty Bakery, Moonachie *Also called Royal Baking Co Inc* ***(G-6540)***
Leone Industries Inc 856 455-2000
443 S East Ave Bridgeton (08302) ***(G-789)***
Leopard Inc 908 964-3600
1 Montgomery St Hillside (07205) ***(G-4425)***
Leos Ice Cream Company 856 797-8771
7 Tomlinson Mill Rd Ste 5 Medford (08055) ***(G-6076)***
Les Metalliers Champenois, Paterson *Also called LMC-HB Corp* ***(G-8324)***
Les Tout Petite Inc 201 941-8675
600 Grand Ave Ridgefield (07657) ***(G-9371)***
Lesli Katchen Steel Cnstr Inc 732 521-2600
300 Buckelew Ave Ste 109 Jamesburg (08831) ***(G-4686)***
Lettering Plus Sign Company 856 299-0404
438 Perkintown Rd Pedricktown (08067) ***(G-8437)***
Lettie Press Inc 201 391-6388
1 Evelyn St Park Ridge (07656) ***(G-7924)***
Level Designs Group LLC 973 761-1675
495 W South Orange Ave South Orange (07079) ***(G-10309)***
Level Ten Products Inc 973 827-0900
3670 State Rt 94 Hamburg (07419) ***(G-4095)***
Lever Manufacturing Corp 201 684-4400
420 State Rt 17 Mahwah (07430) ***(G-5789)***
Levi Strauss & Co 732 493-4595
1 Premium Outlet Blvd Tinton Falls (07753) ***(G-10841)***
Levine Industries Inc (PA) 973 742-1000
70 Levine St Paterson (07503) ***(G-8319)***
Levine Packaging Co, Paterson *Also called Levine Industries Inc* ***(G-8319)***
Levine Packaging Supply Corp 973 575-3456
400 Us Highway 46 Fairfield (07004) ***(G-3251)***
Levomed Inc 908 359-4804
2 Rue Matisse Somerset (08873) ***(G-10123)***
Levy & Rappel, Saddle Brook *Also called Grateful Ped Inc* ***(G-9767)***
Levy Innovation 908 303-4492
3 Brigade Hill Rd Morristown (07960) ***(G-6722)***
Lewis Scheller Printing Corp 732 843-5050
1723 Hwy 27 Somerset (08873) ***(G-10124)***
Lewis-Goetz and Company Inc 856 579-1421
1 Killdeer Ct Ste 4 Swedesboro (08085) ***(G-10706)***
Lexi Industries 201 297-7900
252 Livingston St Northvale (07647) ***(G-7590)***
Lexicon Pharmaceuticals Inc 609 466-5500
110 Allen Rd Ste 3 Basking Ridge (07920) ***(G-192)***
Lexington Graphics Corp 973 345-2493
161 Elmwood Dr Clifton (07013) ***(G-1661)***
Lexisnexis Matthew Bender, Newark *Also called Matthew Bender & Company Inc* ***(G-7237)***
Lexmark International Inc 201 307-4601
135 Chestnut Ridge Rd # 2 Montvale (07645) ***(G-6466)***

ALPHABETIC

Lexmark International Inc.....201 307-4600
1 Maynard Dr Ste 3 Park Ridge (07656) *(G-7925)*
Lexora Home, Newark *Also called Lexora Inc (G-7218)*
Lexora Inc.....855 453-9672
80 Wheeler Point Rd Newark (07105) *(G-7218)*
Lf Graphics, Paterson *Also called L & F Graphics Ltd Lblty Co (G-8312)*
Lg Elctrnics Mbilecomm USA Inc (HQ).....201 816-2000
1000 Sylvan Ave Englewood Cliffs (07632) *(G-2972)*
Lg Electronics USA Inc (HQ).....201 816-2000
1000 Sylvan Ave Englewood Cliffs (07632) *(G-2973)*
Lg Electronics USA Inc.....732 605-0385
380 Deans Rhode Hall Rd Monroe Township (08831) *(G-6383)*
Lg Group Aic, Englewood Cliffs *Also called Lg Electronics USA Inc (G-2973)*
Lg Infocomm U.S.A., Englewood Cliffs *Also called Lg Elctrnics Mbilecomm USA Inc (G-2972)*
LG&p Group LLC.....201 634-9099
650 From Rd Fl 5 Paramus (07652) *(G-7884)*
LG&p In-Store Agency, Paramus *Also called LG&p Group LLC (G-7884)*
Liberty Cnstr & Inv Group.....267 784-7931
1878 Marlton Pike E Ste 7 Cherry Hill (08003) *(G-1388)*
Liberty Coca-Cola Bevs LLC.....215 427-4500
1250 Glen Ave Moorestown (08057) *(G-6593)*
Liberty Coca-Cola Bevs LLC.....856 988-3844
5 E Stow Rd Ste G Marlton (08053) *(G-5982)*
Liberty Envelope Inc.....973 546-5600
45 E 5th St Paterson (07524) *(G-8320)*
Liberty Lamp & Shade, Paramus *Also called Jay-Bee Lamp & Shade Co Inc (G-7877)*
Liberty Park Raceway LLC.....201 333-7223
99 Caven Point Rd Jersey City (07305) *(G-4776)*
Liberty Sport Inc.....973 882-0986
107 Fairfield Rd Fairfield (07004) *(G-3252)*
Licensee Services Inc.....609 465-2003
502 S Main St Cape May Court House (08210) *(G-1115)*
Licini Bros Provision, Union City *Also called Licini Brothers Inc (G-11254)*
Licini Brothers Inc.....201 865-1130
907 West St Union City (07087) *(G-11254)*
Lidestri Foods Inc.....856 661-3218
1550 John Tipton Blvd Pennsauken (08110) *(G-8543)*
Lidestri Foods of New Jersey, Pennsauken *Also called Lidestri Foods Inc (G-8543)*
Lieberfarb Inc.....973 676-9090
2100 Felver Ct Rahway (07065) *(G-9208)*
Liedl.....908 359-8335
462 Long Hill Rd Hillsborough (08844) *(G-4355)*
Lieth Holdings LLC (PA).....201 358-8282
30 Westwood Ave Ste A Westwood (07675) *(G-11962)*
Life Liners Inc (PA).....973 635-9234
6 Essex Rd Chatham (07928) *(G-1333)*
Life of Party LLC.....732 828-0886
832 Ridgewood Ave Ste 4 North Brunswick (08902) *(G-7524)*
Life Recovery Systems Hd LLC (PA).....973 283-2800
170 Kinnelon Rd Rm 5 Kinnelon (07405) *(G-5038)*
Life Science Laboratories LLC.....732 367-1900
170 Oberlin Ave N Ste 26 Lakewood (08701) *(G-5146)*
Life Science Labs Mfg LLC.....732 367-9937
170 Oberlin Ave N Ste 26 Lakewood (08701) *(G-5147)*
Life Scnce Labs Spplements LLC.....732 367-1749
216 River Ave Lakewood (08701) *(G-5148)*
Life Skills Education Inc.....507 645-2994
51 Commerce St Springfield (07081) *(G-10564)*
Lifecell Corporation.....908 947-1100
220 Evans Way Ste 3 Branchburg (08876) *(G-674)*
Lifecell Corporation (HQ).....908 947-1100
1 Millennium Way Branchburg (08876) *(G-675)*
Lifegas, Dayton *Also called Linde Gas North America LLC (G-1977)*
Light Inc.....973 777-2704
345 Clifton Ave Clifton (07011) *(G-1662)*
Lightfield Ammunition Corp.....732 462-9200
912 State Route 33 Freehold (07728) *(G-3667)*
Lightfield Llr Corporation.....732 462-9200
912 State Route 33 Freehold (07728) *(G-3668)*
Lightfox Inc.....973 209-9112
67 E Park Pl Ste 750 Morristown (07960) *(G-6723)*
Lighthouse Express Inc.....732 776-9555
809 Memorial Dr Asbury Park (07712) *(G-80)*
Lighting World Inc.....732 919-1224
10 Ruckle Ave Farmingdale (07727) *(G-3388)*
Lightingindustries Picasso, Kearny *Also called Picasso Lighting Inds LLC (G-4909)*
Lightning Press Inc.....973 890-4422
140 Furler St Totowa (07512) *(G-10954)*
Lightning Prvntion Systems Inc.....856 767-7806
154 Cooper Rd Ste 1201 West Berlin (08091) *(G-11729)*
Lightscape Materials Inc.....609 734-2224
201 Washington Rd Princeton (08540) *(G-9067)*
Ligno Tech USA Inc.....908 429-6660
721 Us Highway 202 Bridgewater (08807) *(G-852)*
Lignotech U S A, Bridgewater *Also called Ligno Tech USA Inc (G-852)*
Lilly, Bridgewater *Also called Imclone Systems LLC (G-844)*
Lime Energy Co.....732 791-5380
100 Mulberry St 4 Newark (07102) *(G-7219)*
Limecrest Quarry Developer LLC.....973 383-7100
217 Limecrest Rd Lafayette (07848) *(G-5050)*
Limosys LLC.....212 222-4433
550 Sylvan Ave Ste 100 Englewood Cliffs (07632) *(G-2974)*
Limpert Brothers Inc.....856 691-1353
200 N West Blvd Vineland (08360) *(G-11380)*
Lincoln Electric Pdts Co Inc.....908 688-2900
947 Lehigh Ave Union (07083) *(G-11201)*
Lincoln Mercury of Wayne, Wayne *Also called Wayne Motors Inc (G-11692)*
Lincoln Mold & Die Corp.....908 241-3344
13 Deerwood Trl Warren (07059) *(G-11558)*
Lincoln Signs & Awnings Inc.....732 442-3151
895 State St Perth Amboy (08861) *(G-8621)*
Linda Spolitino.....609 345-3126
1917 Kuehnle Ave Atlantic City (08401) *(G-102)*
Linde Elec & Specialty Gasses, Alpha *Also called Linde North America Inc (G-43)*
Linde Gas North America LLC.....908 329-9300
1 Greenwich St Stewartsville (08886) *(G-10596)*
Linde Gas North America LLC.....908 777-9125
225 Strykers Rd Phillipsburg (08865) *(G-8656)*
Linde Gas North America LLC.....732 438-9977
174 Ridge Rd Ste A Dayton (08810) *(G-1977)*
Linde Gas North America LLC (HQ).....800 932-0803
200 Somerset Corp Blvd # 7000 Bridgewater (08807) *(G-853)*
Linde Gas USA LLC (HQ).....908 464-8100
200 Somset Cor B Ste 7000 Bridgewater (08807) *(G-854)*
Linde Global Helium Inc.....908 464-8100
575 Mountain Ave New Providence (07974) *(G-7042)*
Linde Group, Bridgewater *Also called Linde North America Inc (G-857)*
Linde LLC (HQ).....908 464-8100
200 Somerset Corporate Bl Bridgewater (08807) *(G-855)*
Linde LLC.....908 329-9619
1 Greenwich St Ste 200 Stewartsville (08886) *(G-10597)*
Linde LLC.....512 330-0153
200 Somerset Corp Blvd # 7000 Bridgewater (08807) *(G-856)*
Linde LLC.....908 464-8100
100 Mountain Ave New Providence (07974) *(G-7043)*
Linde LLC.....973 579-2065
20 Demarest Rd Sparta (07871) *(G-10510)*
Linde Merchant Production Inc (HQ).....908 464-8100
575 Mountain Ave New Providence (07974) *(G-7044)*
Linde North America Inc.....908 464-8100
575 Mountain Ave New Providence (07974) *(G-7045)*
Linde North America Inc (HQ).....908 464-8100
200 Somerset Corporate Bl Bridgewater (08807) *(G-857)*
Linde North America Inc.....908 454-7455
80 Industrial Rd Alpha (08865) *(G-43)*
Linden Group Corporation.....973 983-8809
2b Wing Dr Cedar Knolls (07927) *(G-1315)*
Linden Mold and Tool Corp.....732 381-1411
155 Wescott Dr Rahway (07065) *(G-9209)*
Linden Well Drilling.....908 862-6633
2020 Clinton St Linden (07036) *(G-5403)*
Linder & Company Inc.....201 386-8788
1183 W Side Ave Jersey City (07306) *(G-4777)*
Linder Graphics, Jersey City *Also called Linder & Company Inc (G-4777)*
Lindstrom & King Co Inc.....973 279-2511
108 Mclean Blvd Paterson (07514) *(G-8321)*
Linear Photonics LLC.....609 584-5747
3 Nami Ln Ste 7c Hamilton (08619) *(G-4109)*
Linearizer Technology Inc (PA).....609 584-5747
3 Nami Ln Unit C9 Hamilton (08619) *(G-4110)*
Linearizer Technology Inc.....609 584-8424
3 Nami Ln Unit C9 Hamilton (08619) *(G-4111)*
Linen Enterprises, Moorestown *Also called Star Linen Inc (G-6623)*
Linen For Tables.....973 345-8472
407 20th Ave Paterson (07513) *(G-8322)*
Lingo Inc.....856 273-6594
10 Opal Ct Mount Laurel (08054) *(G-6812)*
Link Bio Inc.....973 625-1333
101 Round Hill Dr Ste 7 Rockaway (07866) *(G-9584)*
Link Color NA Inc.....201 438-8222
23c Poplar St East Rutherford (07073) *(G-2303)*
Link Computer Graphics Inc.....973 808-8990
17a Daniel Rd Fairfield (07004) *(G-3253)*
Link Instruments, Fairfield *Also called Link Computer Graphics Inc (G-3253)*
Link News.....732 222-4300
176 Broadway Long Branch (07740) *(G-5629)*
Link2consult Inc.....888 522-0902
1 Bridge Plz N Ste 275 Fort Lee (07024) *(G-3564)*
Linker Machines, Rockaway *Also called J Hebrank Inc (G-9578)*
Linoleum Sales Company Inc.....201 438-1844
135 Park Ave East Rutherford (07073) *(G-2304)*
Linseis Inc.....609 223-2070
109 N Gold Dr Trenton (08691) *(G-11076)*
Linthicum Sails.....856 783-4288
607 Grace St Somerdale (08083) *(G-10041)*
Lion Extruding Corp.....973 344-4648
106 Rutherford St Newark (07105) *(G-7220)*

696 2018 Harris New Jersey Manufacturers Directory (G-0000) Company's Geographic Section entry number

Lion Sales Corp 732 417-9363
125 Jackson Ave Ste 5 Edison (08837) (G-2557)

Lioni Latticini Inc (PA) 908 686-6061
555 Lehigh Ave Union (07083) (G-11202)

Lioni Mozzarella & Specialty 908 624-9450
555 Lehigh Ave Union (07083) (G-11203)

Lioni Specialty Foods, Union Also called Lioni Mozzarella & Specialty (G-11203)

Lipoid LLC 973 735-2692
744 Broad St Ste 1801 Newark (07102) (G-7221)

Lippincott Marine, Riverside Also called Howard Lippincott (G-9499)

Lippman Enterprises LLC 732 316-4946
250 Kennedy Dr Fl 2 Sayreville (08872) (G-9829)

Liquid Elements 856 321-7646
1000 E Park Ave Maple Shade (08052) (G-5904)

Liquid Holdings Group Inc 212 293-1836
111 River St Ste 1204 Hoboken (07030) (G-4484)

Liquid Iron Industries Inc 856 336-2639
150 Cooper Rd Ste B4 West Berlin (08091) (G-11730)

Liquid-Solids Separation Corp (HQ) 201 236-4833
25 Arrow Rd Ramsey (07446) (G-9245)

Lisabelle, Maywood Also called JP Group International LLC (G-6057)

Lithos Estiatorio Ltd Lblty Co 973 758-1111
405 Eisenhower Pkwy Livingston (07039) (G-5539)

Lithuanian Bakery T J Inc 908 354-0970
131 Inslee Pl Elizabeth (07206) (G-2752)

Little Falls Alloys Inc (PA) 973 278-1666
171-191 Caldwell Ave Paterson (07501) (G-8323)

Little Falls Shop Rite Super 973 256-0909
171 Browertown Rd Ste 2 Little Falls (07424) (G-5481)

Little Fox Inc 609 919-9691
720 E Palisade Ave # 104 Englewood Cliffs (07632) (G-2975)

Little House Candles Inc 609 758-2996
20 Province Line Rd New Egypt (08533) (G-7017)

Little Jimmy's, Iselin Also called Magliones Italian Ices LLC (G-4631)

Little Miss Cupcake LLC 732 370-3083
200 Tudor Ct Lakewood (08701) (G-5149)

Littlegifts Inc 212 868-2559
600 Mdwlands Pkwy Ste 131 Secaucus (07094) (G-9902)

Liva Eye Center, Ridgewood Also called Douglas Liva MD (G-9423)

Liveu Inc 201 742-5229
2 University Plz Ste 505 Hackensack (07601) (G-3939)

Living Fashions Llc 732 626-5200
602 Hartle St Sayreville (08872) (G-9830)

Livingston Bagel Warren Inc 973 994-1915
37 E Northfield Rd Livingston (07039) (G-5540)

Liz Claiborne, North Bergen Also called Kate Spade & Company (G-7460)

Liz Claiborne, Dayton Also called Kate Spade & Company (G-1974)

Liz Fields Llc 201 408-5640
41 Smith St Englewood (07631) (G-2910)

Lizard Label Co (PA) 973 808-3322
20 Kulick Rd Ste A Fairfield (07004) (G-3254)

Lj Elevator Service LLC 856 488-5533
515 Hanover Ave Cherry Hill (08002) (G-1389)

LL Building Products Inc (HQ) 973 628-3000
1 Campus Dr Parsippany (07054) (G-8039)

LLC Dunn Meadow 201 297-4603
1555 Center Ave Ste 1 Fort Lee (07024) (G-3565)

Llc, Incoco Products, Clifton Also called Innovative Cosmtc Concepts LLC (G-1647)

Lloyd's Awnings, Millville Also called Lloyds of Millville Inc (G-6312)

Lloyds of Millville Inc 856 825-0345
208 S Wade Blvd Millville (08332) (G-6312)

Lm Air Technology Inc 732 381-8200
1467 Pinewood St Rahway (07065) (G-9210)

Lm Foods LLC 732 855-9500
100 Raskulinecz Rd Carteret (07008) (G-1262)

Lm Matrix Solutions LLC 908 756-7952
991 Us Highway 22 Ste 200 Bridgewater (08807) (G-858)

Lm PC Products, Beverly Also called Fyth Labs Inc (G-463)

LMC Precision Inc 973 522-0005
91 Rome St Newark (07105) (G-7222)

LMC-HB Corp 862 239-9814
23 27 East 23rd St Paterson (07514) (G-8324)

Lmp Printing Corp 973 428-1987
1 Trenton Ave Clifton (07011) (G-1663)

Lmt Mercer Group Inc (PA) 888 570-5252
690 Puritan Ave Lawrence Township (08648) (G-5243)

Lmt Usa Inc 973 586-8722
400 Forge Way Rockaway (07866) (G-9585)

LNS Inc 609 927-6656
24 Buckingham Dr Egg Harbor Township (08234) (G-2688)

Lo Gatto Bookbinding 201 438-4344
390 Paterson Ave East Rutherford (07073) (G-2305)

Lo Presti & Sons LLC 973 523-9258
298 21st Ave Paterson (07501) (G-8325)

Lob-Ster Inc 818 764-6000
1118 North Ave Plainfield (07062) (G-8866)

Lobster House, Cape May Also called Cold Spring Ice Inc (G-1096)

Lobster Life Systems Inc 201 398-0303
10 Dell Glen Ave Ste 5a Lodi (07644) (G-5592)

Lobster Sports, Plainfield Also called Lob-Ster Inc (G-8866)

Local Baking Products Inc 973 482-1400
135 Manchester Pl Newark (07104) (G-7223)

Local Concrete Sup & Eqp Corp 201 797-7979
475 Market St Ste 3fl Elmwood Park (07407) (G-2832)

Local Wisdom Inc 609 269-2320
287 S Main St Ste 2 Lambertville (08530) (G-5218)

Locker Lady, The, Union Also called American Intr Resources Inc (G-11151)

Lockheed Martin 856 762-2222
3000 Lincoln Dr E Ste E Marlton (08053) (G-5983)

Lockheed Martin 856 722-7782
3000 Lincoln Dr E Ste E Marlton (08053) (G-5984)

Lockheed Martin 856 722-2418
3000 Lincoln Dr E Ste E Marlton (08053) (G-5985)

Lockheed Martin Adv, Cherry Hill Also called Lockheed Martin Corporation (G-1390)

Lockheed Martin Corporation 856 234-1261
750 Centerton Rd Mount Laurel (08054) (G-6813)

Lockheed Martin Corporation 856 722-7782
199 Bortons Landing Rd Moorestown (08057) (G-6594)

Lockheed Martin Corporation 856 792-9811
3 Executive Campus # 600 Cherry Hill (08002) (G-1390)

Lockheed Martin Corporation 856 787-3104
532 Fellowship Rd Mount Laurel (08054) (G-6814)

Lockheed Martin Corporation 856 722-3336
199 Bortons Landing Rd Moorestown (08057) (G-6595)

Lockheed Martin Corporation 856 722-4100
199 Bortons Landing Rd Moorestown (08057) (G-6596)

Lockheed Martin Overseas LLC 856 787-3105
199 Bortons Landing Rd Moorestown (08057) (G-6597)

Locktile Industries Llc 888 562-5845
127 Frelinghuysen Ave Newark (07114) (G-7224)

Lockwood Boat Works Inc 732 721-1605
1825 State Route 35 South Amboy (08879) (G-10241)

Lockwoods Electric Motor Svc 609 587-2333
2239 Nottingham Way Trenton (08619) (G-11077)

Lodi Cml Cooperative LLC 201 820-2380
170 Gregg St Ste 5 Lodi (07644) (G-5593)

Lodi Welding Co Inc 908 852-8367
133 Willow Grove St Hackettstown (07840) (G-4017)

Lodor Offset Corporation 201 935-7100
111 Amor Ave Carlstadt (07072) (G-1184)

Log Storm Security Inc 732 393-6000
1551 S Washington Ave # 401 Piscataway (08854) (G-8786)

Logan Instruments Corporation 732 302-9888
19c Schoolhouse Rd Ste C Somerset (08873) (G-10125)

Logomania Inc 201 798-0531
110 1/2 Erie St Jersey City (07302) (G-4778)

Logomatcentral.com, Cedar Grove Also called Mat Logo Central LLC (G-1290)

Logpowercom LLC 732 350-9663
47 Lacey Rd Whiting (08759) (G-12068)

Lola Products, Hackensack Also called Fifty/Fifty Group Inc (G-3911)

Lollytogs Ltd 732 438-5500
321 Herrod Blvd Dayton (08810) (G-1978)

Lollytogs Ltd 732 438-5500
321 Herrod Blvd Dayton (08810) (G-1979)

London Nite, Passaic Also called Betsy & Adam Ltd (G-8128)

Long Island Pipe of NJ 201 939-1100
700 Schuyler Ave Lyndhurst (07071) (G-5687)

Longo Associates Inc 201 825-1500
100 Hilltop Rd Ramsey (07446) (G-9246)

Longo Elctrical-Mechanical Inc 973 537-0400
1625 Pennsylvania Ave Linden (07036) (G-5404)

Longo Elctrical-Mechanical Inc (PA) 973 537-0400
1 Harry Shupe Blvd Wharton (07885) (G-11991)

Longo Industries, Wharton Also called Longo Elctrical-Mechanical Inc (G-11991)

Longport Shields Inc 856 727-0227
5 Twosome Dr Moorestown (08057) (G-6598)

Longrun Press Inc 856 719-9202
1002 Industrial Dr West Berlin (08091) (G-11731)

Longstreet, Avenel Also called Stretch-O-Rama Inc (G-153)

Longview Coffee Co NJ Inc 908 788-4186
843 State Route 12 B10 Frenchtown (08825) (G-3703)

Longview Coffee Company, Frenchtown Also called Longview Coffee Co NJ Inc (G-3703)

Lont & Overkamp Pubg Co Inc 973 942-2243
200 Entin Rd Clifton (07014) (G-1664)

Lonza Biologics Inc 603 610-4809
90 Boroline Rd Allendale (07401) (G-12)

Lonza Inc (HQ) 201 316-9200
90 Boroline Rd Ste 1 Allendale (07401) (G-13)

Look of Love Wigs Inc (PA) 908 687-9502
1795b State Route 27 Edison (08817) (G-2558)

Lopes Sausage Co 973 344-3063
304 Walnut St Newark (07105) (G-7225)

Lordon Inc 908 813-1143
453 Us Highway 46 E Ste 1 Hackettstown (07840) (G-4018)

LOreal Usa Inc 732 499-6617
30 Terminal Ave Clark (07066) (G-1505)

LOreal Usa Inc 212 818-1500
100 Terminal Ave Clark (07066) (G-1506)

A
L
P
H
A
B
E
T
I
C

LOreal Usa Inc 732 499-6690
159 Terminal Ave Clark (07066) **(G-1507)**

LOreal Usa Inc 609 860-7500
35 Broadway Rd Cranbury (08512) **(G-1855)**

LOreal USA Products Inc 732 873-3520
111 Town Square Pl # 317 Jersey City (07310) **(G-4779)**

Loree Jon Pool Tables Plus, Green Brook *Also called Pool Tables Plus Inc* **(G-3862)**

Lornan Litho Inc 609 818-1198
130 Route 31 N Ste E Pennington (08534) **(G-8456)**

Losurdo Foods Inc (PA) 201 343-6680
20 Owens Rd Hackensack (07601) **(G-3940)**

Lotito Foods Inc 973 684-2900
510 E 35th St Paterson (07504) **(G-8326)**

Louis A Nelson Inc 973 743-7404
224 Glenwood Ave Bloomfield (07003) **(G-518)**

Louis Iron Works Inc 973 624-2700
218 Lackawanna Ave Newark (07103) **(G-7226)**

Louis N Rothberg & Son Inc 732 356-9505
550 Cedar Ave Middlesex (08846) **(G-6176)**

Love Beets, Vineland *Also called GS Fresh Beets Incorporated* **(G-11366)**

Love Pallet LLC 908 964-3385
460 Mundet Pl Hillside (07205) **(G-4426)**

Loveline Industries Inc 973 928-3427
90 Dayton Ave Ste 33 Passaic (07055) **(G-8157)**

Loving Care Pharmacy 732 832-2862
1653 State Route 27 # 102 Edison (08817) **(G-2559)**

Loving Pets Corporation 609 655-3700
110 Melrich Rd Ste 1 Cranbury (08512) **(G-1856)**

Lowder Electric and Cnstr 732 764-6000
250 Hallock Ave Ste B Middlesex (08846) **(G-6177)**

Lowell / Edwards, Hoboken *Also called L&W Audio/Video Inc* **(G-4483)**

Lowell Electronics, Glen Rock *Also called World Electronics Inc* **(G-3830)**

LP Thebault Co 973 884-1300
249 Pomeroy Rd Parsippany (07054) **(G-8040)**

LPI, Passaic *Also called Geiger Tool Co Inc* **(G-8143)**

Lps Industries Inc (PA) 201 438-3515
10 Caesar Pl Moonachie (07074) **(G-6529)**

Lrk Inc 609 924-6881
830 State Rd Ste 3 Princeton (08540) **(G-9068)**

Lrp and P Graphics, Cherry Hill *Also called Pad and Publ Assembly Corp* **(G-1409)**

Lrp and P Graphics 856 424-0158
1165 Marlkress Rd Ste M Cherry Hill (08003) **(G-1391)**

Lrp and Profit, Cherry Hill *Also called Lrp and P Graphics* **(G-1391)**

Ls Rubber Industries Inc (HQ) 973 680-4488
24 Federal Plz Bloomfield (07003) **(G-519)**

Lsl Supplements, Lakewood *Also called Life Scnce Labs Spplements LLC* **(G-5148)**

Lt Chini Inc 856 692-0303
646 S Delsea Dr Vineland (08360) **(G-11381)**

LTS Lhmann Thrapy Systems Corp 973 575-5170
21 Henderson Dr West Caldwell (07006) **(G-11783)**

LTS NJ Inc 856 780-9888
109 W Park Dr Unit C Mount Laurel (08054) **(G-6815)**

Lubrizol Advanced Mtls Inc 856 299-3764
76 Porcupine Rd Pedricktown (08067) **(G-8438)**

Lubrizol Advanced Mtls Inc 973 471-1300
1 Industrial St W Clifton (07012) **(G-1665)**

Lubrizol Corporation 732 981-0149
377 Hoes Ln Ste 210 Piscataway (08854) **(G-8787)**

Lucas World Inc 832 293-3770
100 International Dr Budd Lake (07828) **(G-933)**

Luccas Bakery Inc 609 561-5558
631 Egg Harbor Rd Hammonton (08037) **(G-4142)**

Lucent Technologies World Svcs 908 582-3000
600 Mountain Ave New Providence (07974) **(G-7046)**

Luciano Brothers, Millville *Also called Cumberland Rcycl Corp S Jersey* **(G-6296)**

Luciano Packaging Technologies 908 722-3222
29 County Line Rd Branchburg (08876) **(G-676)**

Lucid Lighting, Stockton *Also called Robert Wallace* **(G-10612)**

Lucky Dog Custom Apparel, Pleasantville *Also called Its The Pitts Inc* **(G-8910)**

Lucy's Ravioli Kitchen, Princeton *Also called Lrk Inc* **(G-9068)**

Luis Network, Norwood *Also called J Media LLC* **(G-7627)**

Lukach Interiors Inc 973 777-1499
208 River Rd Clifton (07014) **(G-1666)**

Lukoil N Arlington Ltd Lblty 856 722-6425
302 Harper Dr Ste 303 Moorestown (08057) **(G-6599)**

Lumber Super Mart 732 739-1428
State Hwy No 36 Hazlet (07730) **(G-4278)**

Lumenarc Inc 973 882-5918
37 Fairfield Pl West Caldwell (07006) **(G-11784)**

Lumeta Corporation (PA) 732 357-3500
300 Atrium Dr Ste 300 # 300 Somerset (08873) **(G-10126)**

Lumiko USA Inc 609 409-6900
47 Commerce Dr 3 Cranbury (08512) **(G-1857)**

Luminaire Lighting Corp 732 549-0056
5 Sutton Pl Edison (08817) **(G-2560)**

Luminer Converting Group, Lakewood *Also called Kraemer Properties Inc* **(G-5142)**

Lumiscope Co Inc 678 291-3207
33 Whelan Rd East Rutherford (07073) **(G-2306)**

Lumitron Arospc Ltg Components, Berkeley Heights *Also called Lumitron Corp* **(G-418)**

Lumitron Corp 908 508-9100
35 Russo Pl Berkeley Heights (07922) **(G-418)**

Lummus Overseas Corporation 973 893-3000
1515 Broad St Bloomfield (07003) **(G-520)**

Lummus Technology Ventures LLC 973 893-1515
1515 Broad St Ste A110 Bloomfield (07003) **(G-521)**

Lunar Audio Video LLC 973 233-7700
701 Hartle St Unit 703 Sayreville (08872) **(G-9831)**

Lunds Fisheries Inc 609 884-7600
997 Ocean Dr Cape May (08204) **(G-1102)**

Lunet Inc 201 261-3883
300 N State Rt 17 Ste 3 Paramus (07652) **(G-7885)**

Lunzer Inc 201 794-2800
1 W Forest Ave Ste 1i Englewood (07631) **(G-2911)**

Lupin Pharmaceuticals Inc 908 603-6075
390 Campus Dr Somerset (08873) **(G-10127)**

Lupin Pharmaceuticals Inc 908 603-6000
400 Campus Dr Somerset (08873) **(G-10128)**

Lure Lash 973 783-5274
416 Bloomfield Ave Montclair (07042) **(G-6421)**

Luso Americano 973 344-3200
66 Union St Newark (07105) **(G-7227)**

Luso Glass, Newark *Also called Eldon Glass & Mirror Co Inc* **(G-7151)**

Luso Machine Inc 973 242-1717
29 Avenue C Newark (07114) **(G-7228)**

Luso-Americano Co Inc 973 344-3200
88 Ferry St Ste 1 Newark (07105) **(G-7229)**

Lusotech LLC 973 332-3861
82-84 Vanderpool St Newark (07114) **(G-7230)**

Lust For Life Footwear LLC 631 327-2811
1086 Teaneck Rd Ste 3d Teaneck (07666) **(G-10761)**

Lusterline Inc 201 758-5148
501 30th St Ste 1a Union City (07087) **(G-11255)**

Lux Home Inc 845 623-2821
483 N Rte 17 Paramus (07652) **(G-7886)**

Luxury and Trash Ltd Lblty Co 201 315-4018
1 Closter Cmns 258 Closter (07624) **(G-1763)**

Luye Pharma USA Ltd 609 799-7600
502 Carnegie Ctr Ste 103 Princeton (08540) **(G-9069)**

LV Adhesive Inc 201 507-0080
341 Michele Pl Carlstadt (07072) **(G-1185)**

Lvmh Fragrance Brands US LLC 212 931-2668
208 Fernwood Ave Edison (08837) **(G-2561)**

Lyca Tel LLC (PA) 973 286-0771
24 Commerce St Ste 100 Newark (07102) **(G-7231)**

Lycatel, Newark *Also called Lyca Tel LLC* **(G-7231)**

Lyciret Corp 973 882-0322
377 Crane St Orange (07050) **(G-7820)**

Lycored Corp (HQ) 973 882-0322
377 Crane St Orange (07050) **(G-7821)**

Lycored USA, Orange *Also called Lycored Corp* **(G-7821)**

Lydem LLC 856 566-1419
1 E Broad St Palmyra (08065) **(G-7849)**

Lydon Bros Corp 201 343-4334
254 Green St South Hackensack (07606) **(G-10276)**

Lyle/Carlstrom Associates Inc 908 526-2270
131 Chambers Brook Rd Branchburg (08876) **(G-677)**

Lympha Press USA 732 792-9677
265 Willow Brook Rd # 4 Freehold (07728) **(G-3669)**

Lynch Industries, Burlington *Also called Dublin Management Assoc of NJ* **(G-969)**

Lynn Amiee Inc 201 840-6766
65 Railroad Ave Ste 209 Ridgefield (07657) **(G-9372)**

Lynn Mechanical Contractors 856 829-1717
1810 Rowland St Cinnaminson (08077) **(G-1474)**

Lynx USA, South Hackensack *Also called Napoleon Spring Works Inc* **(G-10279)**

Lyondell Chemical Company 973 578-2200
300 Doremus Ave Newark (07105) **(G-7232)**

Lyondellbasell 732 985-6262
340 Meadow Rd Edison (08837) **(G-2562)**

M & D Prcsion Cntrless Grnding 856 764-1616
120 Kossuth St Riverside (08075) **(G-9501)**

M & E Packaging Corp 201 635-1381
900 Page Ave Fl 2 Lyndhurst (07071) **(G-5688)**

M & M International 908 412-8300
3619 Kennedy Rd Ste A South Plainfield (07080) **(G-10399)**

M & M Mars, Hackettstown *Also called Mars Incorporated* **(G-4020)**

M & M Printing Corp 201 288-7787
216 Boulevard Hasbrouck Heights (07604) **(G-4196)**

M & M Welding & Machine, Stirling *Also called M & M Welding & Steel Fabg* **(G-10603)**

M & M Welding & Steel Fabg 908 647-6060
344 Essex St Stirling (07980) **(G-10603)**

M & RS Miller Auto Gear & Prt 201 339-2270
699 Kennedy Blvd Bayonne (07002) **(G-237)**

M & S Holes Corp 908 298-6900
20 Hoiles Dr Ste A1 Kenilworth (07033) **(G-4971)**

M & S Machine & Tool Corp 973 345-5847
108 Maryland Ave Paterson (07503) **(G-8327)**

(G-0000) Company's Geographic Section entry number

M & S Optics Inc 856 764-0200
2910 Route 130 Delran (08075) *(G-2019)*

M & W Franklin LLC 609 927-0885
3011 Ocean Heights Ave B Egg Harbor Township (08234) *(G-2689)*

M & Z International Inc 201 864-3331
358 Oswego Ct West New York (07093) *(G-11872)*

M + 4 Inc 973 527-3262
98 Crease Rd Budd Lake (07828) *(G-934)*

M + P International Inc 973 239-3005
271 Grove Ave Ste G Verona (07044) *(G-11307)*

M and D Precision Grinding 856 764-1616
120 Kossuth St Riverside (08075) *(G-9502)*

M and R Manufacturing 732 905-1061
575 Prospect St Ste 202 Lakewood (08701) *(G-5150)*

M B C Food Machinery Corp 201 489-7000
78 Mckinley St Hackensack (07601) *(G-3941)*

M B R Orthotics Inc 201 444-7750
579 Goffle Rd Wyckoff (07481) *(G-12256)*

M Blaustein Inc (PA) 973 379-1080
516 Millburn Ave Short Hills (07078) *(G-9980)*

M C Custom Shtmtl Fabrication 856 767-9509
215 Old Egg Harbor Rd C West Berlin (08091) *(G-11732)*

M C Signs 609 399-7446
323 Ocean Ave Ocean City (08226) *(G-7753)*

M C Technologies Inc 973 839-2779
4 Kinney Pl Pompton Plains (07444) *(G-8961)*

M Chasen & Son Inc 973 374-8956
123 S 20th St Irvington (07111) *(G-4596)*

M D Carbide Tool Corp 973 263-0104
19 Old Jacksonville Rd Towaco (07082) *(G-10998)*

M D I, Cranbury Also called Mason Display Innovations Inc *(G-1861)*

M D Laboratory Supplies Inc 732 322-0773
4 Minebrook Ln Franklin Park (08823) *(G-3628)*

M Deitz & Sons Inc 908 686-8800
490 Hillside Ave Hillside (07205) *(G-4427)*

M E C Technologies Inc 732 505-0308
2200 Industrial Way S Toms River (08755) *(G-10894)*

M E I, Flemington Also called Mel Chemicals Inc *(G-3456)*

M G S 609 698-7000
309 Route 72 Barnegat (08005) *(G-163)*

M G X Inc 732 329-0088
45 Stouts Ln Monmouth Junction (08852) *(G-6350)*

M H Optical Supplies Inc 800 445-3090
128 Leuning St South Hackensack (07606) *(G-10277)*

M Hand Pallets 908 887-2100
864 North Ave E Elizabeth (07201) *(G-2753)*

M J Powers & Co Publishers 973 898-1200
65 Madison Ave Ste 220 Morristown (07960) *(G-6724)*

M K Enterprises Inc 201 891-4199
430 W Main St Wyckoff (07481) *(G-12257)*

M K Woodworking Inc 609 771-1350
1476 Prospect St Ewing (08638) *(G-3036)*

M London Inc (PA) 201 459-6460
629 Grove St Fl 8 Jersey City (07310) *(G-4780)*

M P I, Newark Also called Machine Parts Inc *(G-7233)*

M P M Building Service 732 946-2600
6 Brook Ln Holmdel (07733) *(G-4519)*

M P M Display Inc 973 374-3477
74 Woolsey St Irvington (07111) *(G-4597)*

M P S, Holmdel Also called Magnetic Products and Svcs Inc *(G-4520)*

M P T Racing Inc 973 989-9220
85 Franklin Rd Ste 6b Dover (07801) *(G-2098)*

M P Tube Works Inc 908 317-2500
237 Sheffield St Mountainside (07092) *(G-6883)*

M Parker Autoworks Inc 856 933-0801
150 Heller Pl 17w Bellmawr (08031) *(G-345)*

M R, Bloomfield Also called Minor Rubber Co Inc *(G-522)*

M R C Millwork & Trim Inc. 201 954-2176
319 Hobar Ct Franklin Lakes (07417) *(G-3620)*

M Rafi Sons Garment Industries 732 381-7660
1463 Pinewood St Rahway (07065) *(G-9211)*

M S Brown Jewelers, Wildwood Also called M S Brown Mfg Jewelers *(G-12074)*

M S Brown Mfg Jewelers (PA) 609 522-7604
3304 Pacific Ave Wildwood (08260) *(G-12074)*

M S C Paper Products Corp 908 686-2200
777 Ramsey Ave Hillside (07205) *(G-4428)*

M S Plastics and Packg Co 973 492-2400
10 Park Pl Ste 100 Butler (07405) *(G-1011)*

M T D Inc 908 362-6807
24 Slabtown Creek Rd Hardwick (07825) *(G-4168)*

M W Jenkins Sons Inc 973 239-5150
444 Pompton Ave Cedar Grove (07009) *(G-1289)*

M W Trailer Repair Inc 609 298-1113
400 Rising Sun Rd Bordentown (08505) *(G-600)*

M&L Power Systems Maint Inc 732 679-1800
109 White Oak Ln Ste 82 Old Bridge (08857) *(G-7783)*

M/C Communications LLC 908 766-0402
180 Mount Airy Rd Ste 202 Basking Ridge (07920) *(G-193)*

M/C Communications LLC 609 838-7952
5 Commerce Way Ste 202 Hamilton (08691) *(G-4112)*

M2 Communications Inc 201 433-1746
30 Montgomery St Ste 700 Jersey City (07302) *(G-4781)*

M2 Electric LLC 973 770-4596
3 Iron Mountain Rd Mine Hill (07803) *(G-6327)*

M2 Enterprises, Mine Hill Also called M2 Electric LLC *(G-6327)*

M4 Machine LLC 718 928-9695
7 Industrial Pkwy 18 Livingston (07039) *(G-5541)*

Maarky Thermal Systems Inc 856 470-1504
1415 Marlton Pike E # 604 Cherry Hill (08034) *(G-1392)*

Mab Enterprises Inc 973 345-8282
225 Grand St Paterson (07501) *(G-8328)*

MAC Cosmetics Inc 856 661-9024
2000 Route 38 Ste 200 Cherry Hill (08002) *(G-1393)*

Mac Power, Kearny Also called Mac Products Inc *(G-4896)*

Mac Products Inc 973 344-5149
60 Pennsylvania Ave Kearny (07032) *(G-4896)*

Machiavelli LLC 862 215-5888
64 Eaton Pl East Orange (07017) *(G-2260)*

Machine Atomated Ctrl Tech LLC 732 921-8935
1308 Centennial Ave # 109 Piscataway (08854) *(G-8788)*

Machine Control Systems Inc 732 529-6888
47 Portchester Dr Jackson (08527) *(G-4671)*

Machine Parts Inc 973 491-5444
17 Ferdon St Newark (07105) *(G-7233)*

Machine Plus Inc 973 839-8884
97 4th Ave Haskell (07420) *(G-4210)*

Machine Tech 732 738-6810
3125 Woodbridge Ave Ste 4 Edison (08837) *(G-2563)*

Machinery Electrics 732 536-0600
904 Main St Bayville (08721) *(G-257)*

Macie Publishing Company 973 983-8700
13 E Main St Ste 3 Mendham (07945) *(G-6088)*

Mack Trading LLC 973 794-4904
486 Lake Shore Dr Hewitt (07421) *(G-4290)*

Maclearie Printing LLC 732 681-2772
917 18th Ave Wall Township (07719) *(G-11496)*

Macleods Pharma Usa Inc 609 269-5250
666 Plainsboro Rd Ste 230 Plainsboro (08536) *(G-8893)*

Maco Appliance Parts & Sup Co 609 272-8222
1101 N New Rd Absecon (08201) *(G-3)*

Macro Sensors, Budd Lake Also called Howard A Schaevitz Tech Inc *(G-931)*

Macro Sensors 856 662-8000
450 Clark Dr Ste 4 Budd Lake (07828) *(G-935)*

Macromedia Incorporated (PA) 201 646-4000
150 River St Hackensack (07601) *(G-3942)*

Mactec Packaging Tech LLC 732 343-1607
550 Hartle St Ste A Sayreville (08872) *(G-9832)*

Madan Plastics Inc 908 276-8484
370 North Ave E Cranford (07016) *(G-1913)*

Maddak Inc (HQ) 973 628-7600
661 State Route 23 Wayne (07470) *(G-11661)*

Made Solutions LLC 201 254-3693
18-01 River Rd Fair Lawn (07410) *(G-3101)*

Madhouz LLC 609 206-8009
8 Deptford Rd Dept A Glassboro (08028) *(G-3808)*

Madhu B Goyal MD 908 769-0307
908 Oak Tree Ave Ste C South Plainfield (07080) *(G-10400)*

Madison Eagle, Madison Also called Parker Publications *(G-5730)*

Madison Industries Inc 732 727-2225
554 Water Works Rd Old Bridge (08857) *(G-7784)*

Madison Park Volunteer Fire Co 732 727-1143
3011 Cheesequake Rd Parlin (08859) *(G-7935)*

Madison Shoe Company, Carlstadt Also called Bm USA Incorporated *(G-1132)*

Mafco Magnasweet, Camden Also called Mafco Worldwide Corporation *(G-1075)*

Mafco Worldwide Corporation (HQ) 856 964-8840
300 Jefferson St Camden (08104) *(G-1075)*

Mag Signs 609 747-9600
1208 Columbus Rd Ste F Burlington (08016) *(G-983)*

Magazinexperts LLC 973 383-0888
103 Spring St Newton (07860) *(G-7395)*

Maggio Fine, Bellmawr Also called Maggio Printing LLC *(G-346)*

Maggio Printing LLC 856 931-7805
171 Heller Pl Bellmawr (08031) *(G-346)*

Magic Metal Works Inc 201 384-8457
40 W Englewood Ave Bergenfield (07621) *(G-389)*

Magic Printing Corp 732 726-0620
386 Avenel St Avenel (07001) *(G-139)*

Magliones Italian Ices LLC 732 283-0705
111 Madison St Iselin (08830) *(G-4631)*

Magna Industries Inc 732 905-0957
1825 Swarthmore Ave Ste 1 Lakewood (08701) *(G-5151)*

Magna Publishing, Montclair Also called Hyp Hair Inc *(G-6416)*

Magna-Power Electronics 908 237-2200
39 Royal Rd Flemington (08822) *(G-3455)*

Magnalube Inc 718 729-1000
1331 W Edgar Rd Linden (07036) *(G-5405)*

Magnatrol Valve Corporation 973 427-4341
21 Horton Ave Hawthorne (07506) *(G-4246)*

A
L
P
H
A
B
E
T
I
C

Magnatrol Valve Corporation 856 829-4580
  941 Hamilton Ave Roebling (08554) *(G-9638)*

Magnesium Elektron Powders NJ, Manchester *Also called Reade Manufacturing*
Company (G-5888)

Magnetic Metals Corporation (HQ) 856 964-7842
  1900 Hayes Ave Camden (08105) *(G-1076)*

Magnetic Products and Svcs Inc 732 264-6651
  2135 State Route 35 Ste 1 Holmdel (07733) *(G-4520)*

Magnetic Ticket & Label Corp 973 759-6500
  151 Cortlandt St Belleville (07109) *(G-305)*

Magnetics & Controls Inc 609 397-8203
  99 Kingwood Stockton Rd Rosemont (08556) *(G-9705)*

Magnetika Inc 908 454-2600
  300 Red School Ln Phillipsburg (08865) *(G-8657)*

Magnetran Inc 856 768-7787
  24 Elizabeth Ln Ocean View (08230) *(G-7764)*

Magnifica Inc 323 202-0386
  5 Cedarbrook Dr Cranbury (08512) *(G-1858)*

Magnum Computer Recycling, Pennsauken *Also called Thanks For Being Green*
LLC (G-8584)

Magnum Energy Partners, Livingston *Also called Mep Alaska LLC (G-5543)*

Magnuson Products 973 472-9292
  6 Chelsea Rd Clifton (07012) *(G-1667)*

Magpie Marketing Inc 201 507-9155
  194 Woodland Ave Rutherford (07070) *(G-9739)*

Magruder Color Company Inc 817 837-3293
  14 Takolusa Dr Holmdel (07733) *(G-4521)*

Maidenform 732 621-2216
  485 Us Highway 1 S Iselin (08830) *(G-4632)*

Maidenform Brands Inc (HQ) 888 573-0299
  485 Us Highway 1 S Iselin (08830) *(G-4633)*

Maier's Sunbeam Bakery, East Brunswick *Also called Bimbo Bakeries Usa Inc (G-2138)*

Mail Direct Paper Company LLC 201 933-2782
  515 Vly Brook Ave Ste A Lyndhurst (07071) *(G-5689)*

Mail-Well Envelope, Jersey City *Also called Cenveo Inc (G-4725)*

Main Attractions, Edison *Also called Sconda Canvas Products Inc (G-2612)*

Main Fuel LLC 201 941-2707
  73 Palisade Ave Cliffside Park (07010) *(G-1542)*

Main Robert A & Sons Holdg Co (PA) 201 447-3700
  555 Goffle Rd Wyckoff (07481) *(G-12258)*

Main Street Auto & Fuel LLC 732 238-0044
  227 Main St Sayreville (08872) *(G-9833)*

Main Street Graphics Inc 856 755-3523
  30 W Main St Maple Shade (08052) *(G-5905)*

Main Tape Company Inc (PA) 609 395-1704
  1 Capital Dr Ste 101 Cranbury (08512) *(G-1859)*

Mainetti Americas Inc (PA) 201 215-2900
  115 Enterprise Ave S Secaucus (07094) *(G-9903)*

Mainetti USA Inc (HQ) 201 215-2900
  300 Mac Ln Keasbey (08832) *(G-4928)*

Maingear Inc 888 624-6432
  206 Market St Kenilworth (07033) *(G-4972)*

Mainland Plate Glass Company 609 277-2938
  53 E West Jersey Ave Pleasantville (08232) *(G-8912)*

Mainstream LLC 908 931-1010
  230 Cristiani St Cranford (07016) *(G-1914)*

Mainstream Fluid & Air LLC 908 931-1010
  47 Russo Pl Berkeley Heights (07922) *(G-419)*

Maje Systems Inc 856 845-5363
  45 Delaware St Ste 1 Woodbury (08096) *(G-12164)*

Majer Design, Ewing *Also called M K Woodworking Inc (G-3036)*

Majesco (HQ) 973 461-5200
  412 Mount Kemble Ave 110c Morristown (07960) *(G-6725)*

Majestic Industries Inc 973 473-3434
  2 Canal St Passaic (07055) *(G-8158)*

Majewski Plumbing & Htg LLC 609 374-6001
  14 E Miami Ave Villas (08251) *(G-11314)*

Majka Railing Inc 973 247-7603
  125 Mcbride Ave Paterson (07501) *(G-8329)*

Major Auto Installations Inc 973 252-4262
  47 N Dell Ave Ste 10 Kenvil (07847) *(G-5011)*

Major Bs General Quarters LLC 732 710-6088
  46 Oak Knoll Dr Matawan (07747) *(G-6024)*

Major Printing Co Inc 908 686-7296
  934 Savitt Pl Union (07083) *(G-11204)*

Major Products Co Inc (HQ) 201 641-5555
  66 Industrial Ave Little Ferry (07643) *(G-5512)*

Make Wine With US, Wallington *Also called Dijon Enterprises LLC (G-11525)*

Malcam US 973 218-2461
  51 John F Kennedy Pkwy Short Hills (07078) *(G-9981)*

Malco Electric LLC 856 202-5503
  602 Ryan Ave Westville (08093) *(G-11946)*

Malletech LLC 732 774-0011
  1107 11th Ave Neptune (07753) *(G-6922)*

Mallika Ashwin Maya Corp 908 393-2571
  10 Old Camplain Rd Hillsborough (08844) *(G-4356)*

Mallinckrodt Ard Inc 510 400-0700
  1425 Us Highway 206 Bedminster (07921) *(G-276)*

Mallinckrodt Ard Inc (HQ) 908 238-6600
  1425 Us Highway 206 Bedminster (07921) *(G-277)*

Mallinckrodt LLC 908 238-6600
  53 Frontage Rd Hampton (08827) *(G-4164)*

Mallinckrodt Parmaceuticals, Hampton *Also called Mallinckrodt LLC (G-4164)*

Mallinckrodt Pharmaceuticals, Bedminster *Also called Mallinckrodt Ard Inc (G-276)*

Malt Products Corporation (PA) 201 845-4420
  88 Market St Saddle Brook (07663) *(G-9772)*

Malt Products Corporation 201 845-9106
  88 Market St Saddle Brook (07663) *(G-9773)*

Mam, Hillsborough *Also called Mallika Ashwin Maya Corp (G-4356)*

Mamamancinis Holdings Inc (PA) 201 531-1212
  25 Branca Rd East Rutherford (07073) *(G-2307)*

Mamrout Paper Group Corp 718 510-5484
  55 Talmadge Rd Edison (08817) *(G-2564)*

Man-How Inc 609 392-4895
  1150 Southard St Ste 3 Trenton (08638) *(G-11078)*

Manco Industries 973 971-3131
  673 S 21st St Irvington (07111) *(G-4598)*

Manco Plating Incorporated 973 485-6800
  390 Park Ave Newark (07107) *(G-7234)*

Mandip Inc 732 752-4875
  240 Woodrow Ave W Piscataway (08854) *(G-8789)*

Mane USA Inc (HQ) 973 633-5533
  60 Demarest Dr Wayne (07470) *(G-11662)*

Mango Custom Cabinets Inc 908 813-3077
  216 W Stiger St Hackettstown (07840) *(G-4019)*

Manhattan Door Corp 718 963-1111
  109 Kero Rd Carlstadt (07072) *(G-1186)*

Manhattan Gunite, Closter *Also called En Tech Corp (G-1758)*

Manhattan Signs & Designs Ltd 973 278-3603
  130 Beckwith Ave Ste 2b Paterson (07503) *(G-8330)*

Manischewitz Company (HQ) 201 553-1100
  80 Avenue K Newark (07105) *(G-7235)*

Manley Performance Pdts Inc (PA) 732 905-3366
  1960 Swarthmore Ave Lakewood (08701) *(G-5152)*

Manna Group LLC 856 881-7650
  137 Gaither Dr Ste F Mount Laurel (08054) *(G-6816)*

Manner Textile Processing Inc 973 942-8718
  41 Oakdale Ct North Haledon (07508) *(G-7550)*

Manning & Lewis Engrg Co Inc 908 687-2400
  675 Rahway Ave Ste 1 Union (07083) *(G-11205)*

Manning Publication Co 856 375-2597
  1233 Heartwood Dr Cherry Hill (08003) *(G-1394)*

Mannington Mills Inc (PA) 856 935-3000
  75 Mannington Mills Rd Salem (08079) *(G-9806)*

Mannington Rsilient Floors Div, Salem *Also called Mannington Mills Inc (G-9806)*

Mantech Systems Engrg Corp 856 566-9155
  1000 Haddonfield Berlin R Voorhees (08043) *(G-11435)*

Manttra Inc 877 962-6887
  1130 Somerset St New Brunswick (08901) *(G-6978)*

Manufacturers Brush Corp 973 882-6966
  69 King St Ste 6 Dover (07801) *(G-2099)*

Manufacturing / Consultants, Manalapan *Also called Ccard (G-5840)*

Manufacturing Branch, Phillipsburg *Also called Magnetika Inc (G-8657)*

Manufacturing Chem Dyestuff, Cranford *Also called Orient Corporation of America (G-1919)*

Manutech Inc 856 358-6136
  29 State St Elmer (08318) *(G-2794)*

Manva Industries Inc 973 667-2606
  48 Franklin Ave Nutley (07110) *(G-7651)*

Manville Rubber Products Inc 908 526-9111
  1009 Kennedy Blvd Manville (08835) *(G-5896)*

Manzi Printing 732 542-1927
  132 Lewis St Ste B2 Eatontown (07724) *(G-2412)*

Mapei Corporation 732 254-4830
  2155 High Hill Rd Swedesboro (08085) *(G-10707)*

Mapei Corporation 732 254-4830
  2155 High Hill Rd Swedesboro (08085) *(G-10708)*

Mapleton Nurseries, Kingston *Also called Kingston Nurseries LLC (G-5029)*

Maplewood Beverage Packers LLC 973 416-4582
  45 Camptown Rd Maplewood (07040) *(G-5923)*

Maquet, Fairfield *Also called Datascope Corp (G-3171)*

Maquet, Mahwah *Also called Datascope Corp (G-5763)*

Maquet Cardiac Assist, Mahwah *Also called Datascope Corp (G-5764)*

Maquet Cardiovascular LLC 973 709-7000
  45 Barbour Pond Dr Wayne (07470) *(G-11663)*

Mar Cor Purification Inc 973 521-7032
  341 Kaplan Dr Fairfield (07004) *(G-3255)*

Mar Machine Ken Manufacturing 973 278-5827
  477 E 30th St Paterson (07504) *(G-8331)*

Mar-Kal Products Corp 973 783-7155
  145 Commerce Rd Carlstadt (07072) *(G-1187)*

Mara Polishing & Plating Corp 973 242-0800
  105 W Peddie St Newark (07112) *(G-7236)*

Maranatha Ceramic Tile & Marbl 609 758-1168
  253 Cokstown New Egypt Rd Wrightstown (08562) *(G-12242)*

Maranatha Stairs, Wrightstown *Also called Maranatha Ceramic Tile & Marbl (G-12242)*

(G-0000) Company's Geographic Section entry number

Marathon Enterprises Inc (PA) 201 935-3330
  9 Smith St Englewood (07631) *(G-2912)*

Marble and Granite, Wayne *Also called EZ General Construction Corp (G-11631)*

Marble and Granite Design Ctr, Cranbury *Also called Ankur International Inc (G-1812)*

Marble Online Corporation 201 998-9100
  260 Schuyler Ave Fl 1 Kearny (07032) *(G-4897)*

Marbleworld Manufacturing, Hammonton *Also called Bucci Management Co Inc (G-4134)*

Marburn Stores Inc 908 412-1962
  4975 Stelton Rd South Plainfield (07080) *(G-10401)*

Marcal Manufacturing LLC (HQ) 201 703-6225
  1 Market St Elmwood Park (07407) *(G-2833)*

Marcal Paper Mills LLC 800 631-8451
  1 Market St Elmwood Park (07407) *(G-2834)*

Marchione Industries Inc 718 317-4900
  136 Park Ave Lyndhurst (07071) *(G-5690)*

Marco Book Co Inc 973 458-0485
  60 Industrial Rd Lodi (07644) *(G-5594)*

Marcolin USA Eyewear Corp (HQ) 800 345-8482
  3140 Rte 22 Branchburg (08876) *(G-678)*

Marcotex International Inc 201 991-8200
  69 Sellers St Kearny (07032) *(G-4898)*

Mardee Company Inc 908 753-4343
  242 Saint Nicholas Ave South Plainfield (07080) *(G-10402)*

Mardee Video Company, South Plainfield *Also called Mardee Company Inc (G-10402)*

Mardon Associates Inc 973 977-2251
  1 Industrial Plz Paterson (07503) *(G-8332)*

Margaritaville Inc 973 728-7562
  129 Lincoln Ave West Milford (07480) *(G-11854)*

Maria, Paterson *Also called Mar Machine Ken Manufacturing (G-8331)*

Marian, Glen Rock *Also called Melissa Spice Trading Corp (G-3826)*

Mariano Press LLC 732 247-3659
  14 Veronica Ave Somerset (08873) *(G-10129)*

Mariell, Budd Lake *Also called San Marel Designs Inc (G-942)*

Marijon Dyeing & Finishing Co 201 933-9770
  219 Murray Hill Pkwy East Rutherford (07073) *(G-2308)*

Marine Acquisition Inc 609 965-2300
  801 Philadelphia Ave Egg Harbor City (08215) *(G-2667)*

Marine Cont Eqp Crtfction Corp 732 938-6622
  160 Sqnkum Yellowbrook Rd Farmingdale (07727) *(G-3389)*

Marine East, Brick *Also called Mariner Sales and Power Inc (G-751)*

Marine Electric Systems Inc 201 531-8600
  80 Wesley St South Hackensack (07606) *(G-10278)*

Marine Oil Service Inc 908 282-6440
  450 S Front St Elizabeth (07202) *(G-2754)*

Mariner Sales and Power Inc (PA) 732 477-7484
  834 Mantoloking Rd Brick (08723) *(G-751)*

Mariners Annual, Edison *Also called Charles Kerr Enterprises Inc (G-2482)*

Marino Building Systems Corp 732 968-0555
  1640 New Market Ave 1a South Plainfield (07080) *(G-10403)*

Marino International Corp 732 752-5100
  1640 New Market Ave South Plainfield (07080) *(G-10404)*

Marino Ware Division, South Plainfield *Also called Ware Industries Inc (G-10454)*

Maritime Solutions Inc 732 752-3831
  200 Pond Ave Middlesex (08846) *(G-6178)*

Mark Alan Printing & Graphics 732 981-9011
  1032 Stelton Rd Ste 2 Piscataway (08854) *(G-8790)*

Mark I Industries Inc 609 884-0051
  910 Shunpike Rd Cape May (08204) *(G-1103)*

Mark I Interiors, Plainfield *Also called A N Laggren Awngs Canvas Mfg (G-8852)*

Mark Lithographers, Cedar Knolls *Also called Mark Lithography Inc (G-1316)*

Mark Lithography Inc 973 538-5557
  4 Saddle Rd Cedar Knolls (07927) *(G-1316)*

Mark Ronald Associates Inc (PA) 908 558-0011
  1227 Central Ave Hillside (07205) *(G-4429)*

Mark's Hmmade Ice Cream Dlghts, North Bergen *Also called Marks Ice Cream (G-7463)*

Mark-O-Lite Sign Co Inc 732 462-8530
  1420 Us Highway 9 Howell (07731) *(G-4561)*

Mark/Trece Inc 973 884-1005
  160 Algonquin Pkwy Ste 1 Whippany (07981) *(G-12026)*

Markbilt Inc 201 891-7842
  308 Canterbury Ln Wyckoff (07481) *(G-12259)*

Marketing Administration Assoc 732 840-3021
  1101 Industrial Pkwy Brick (08724) *(G-752)*

Marko Engraving & Art Corp (PA) 201 864-6500
  19 Baldwin Ave Weehawken (07086) *(G-11698)*

Marko Engraving & Art Corp 201 945-6555
  439 Fairview Ave Fairview (07022) *(G-3365)*

Markov Processes International 908 608-1558
  475 Sprngfeld Ave Ste 401 Summit (07901) *(G-10649)*

Marks Ice Cream (PA) 201 861-5099
  8205 Bergenline Ave North Bergen (07047) *(G-7463)*

Marks Management Systems Inc 856 866-0588
  590 E Kings Hwy Maple Shade (08052) *(G-5906)*

Markus Wiener Publishers Inc 609 921-1141
  231 Nassau St Princeton (08542) *(G-9070)*

Marlene Embroidery Inc (PA) 201 868-1682
  6805 Madison St West New York (07093) *(G-11873)*

Marlene Lace, North Bergen *Also called Marlene Trimmings LLC (G-7464)*

Marlene Trimmings LLC 201 926-3108
  407 77th St North Bergen (07047) *(G-7464)*

Marlin Candle Co, Ltl Egg Hbr *Also called Stephen L Feilinger (G-5648)*

Marlo Manufacturing Co Inc 973 423-0226
  301 Division St Boonton (07005) *(G-575)*

Marlo Plastic Products Inc 732 792-1988
  3535 State Route 66 Ste 1 Neptune (07753) *(G-6923)*

Marlow Candy & Nut Co Inc 201 569-7606
  65 Honeck St Englewood (07631) *(G-2913)*

Marlton Creative Design Center, Marlton *Also called Packaging Corporation America (G-5992)*

Marlton Pike Precision LLC 856 665-1900
  728 Beechwood Ave Cherry Hill (08002) *(G-1395)*

Marlyn Sheet Metal Inc 856 863-6900
  606 N Delsea Dr Clayton (08312) *(G-1526)*

Marmaxx Operating Corp 973 575-7910
  901 Bloomfield Ave West Caldwell (07006) *(G-11785)*

Marmo Enterprises Inc 732 649-3011
  468 Elizabeth Ave Somerset (08873) *(G-10130)*

Marmon Industrial LLC 609 655-4287
  101 Interchange Plz # 106 Cranbury (08512) *(G-1860)*

Marotta Controls Inc (PA) 973 334-7800
  78 Boonton Ave Montville (07045) *(G-6490)*

Marquis, Moonachie *Also called Jade Eastern Trading Inc (G-6524)*

Marquis - Whos Who Inc 908 673-1006
  430 Mountain Ave Ste 403 New Providence (07974) *(G-7047)*

Mars Incorporated 908 852-1000
  700 High St Hackettstown (07840) *(G-4020)*

Mars Incorporated 908 850-2420
  800 High St Hackettstown (07840) *(G-4021)*

Mars Incorporated 973 691-3500
  100 International Dr Budd Lake (07828) *(G-936)*

Mars Chocolate North Amer LLC (HQ) 908 852-1000
  800 High St Hackettstown (07840) *(G-4022)*

Mars Chocolate North Amer LLC 908 979-5070
  700 High St Hackettstown (07840) *(G-4023)*

Mars Food Us LLC 908 852-1000
  800 High St Hackettstown (07840) *(G-4024)*

Mars Retail Group Inc 973 398-2078
  400 Valley Rd Ste 204 Mount Arlington (07856) *(G-6757)*

Mars Wrigley Conf US LLC 908 852-1000
  800 High St Hackettstown (07840) *(G-4025)*

Marsden Inc 856 663-2227
  6800 Westfield Ave Pennsauken (08110) *(G-8544)*

Marshall Industrial Tech, Trenton *Also called Marshall Maintenance (G-11079)*

Marshall Maintenance (PA) 609 394-7153
  529 S Clinton Ave Trenton (08611) *(G-11079)*

Marshalls, West Caldwell *Also called Marmaxx Operating Corp (G-11785)*

Marte Cabinets Countertops LLC 973 525-9502
  48 Palmer St Apt 1 Passaic (07055) *(G-8159)*

Martin Corporation 856 451-0900
  171 N Pearl St Bridgeton (08302) *(G-790)*

Martin Sprocket & Gear Inc 973 633-5700
  7 Highpoint Dr Wayne (07470) *(G-11664)*

Martin Tool Company Inc 973 361-9212
  60 State Route 15 S Wharton (07885) *(G-11992)*

Martins Specialty Sausage Co (PA) 856 423-4000
  150 Harmony Rd Mickleton (08056) *(G-6137)*

Marty Anderson & Assoc Inc 201 798-0507
  4200 Grand Ave North Bergen (07047) *(G-7465)*

Marvic Corp 908 686-4340
  2450 Iorio Ct Union (07083) *(G-11206)*

Marvic Formica In Design, Union *Also called Marvic Corp (G-11206)*

Marx NJ Group LLC 732 901-3880
  14 Easy St Ste 14e4 Bound Brook (08805) *(G-620)*

Mary Bridget Enterprises 609 267-4830
  2305 Garry Rd Ste B Cinnaminson (08077) *(G-1475)*

Marzullo 973 955-5309
  55 Passaic St Passaic (07055) *(G-8160)*

Mas Epoxies, Cinnaminson *Also called Phoenix Resins Inc (G-1485)*

Masco Cabinetry LLC 732 363-3797
  450 Oberlin Ave S Lakewood (08701) *(G-5153)*

Masco Cabinetry LLC 732 942-5138
  440-450 Oberlin Ave S Lakewood (08701) *(G-5154)*

Mashal Signs Co Inc 201 348-8500
  568 55th St West New York (07093) *(G-11874)*

Mason Candlelight Company, Middlesex *Also called Standex International Corp (G-6203)*

Mason Display Innovations Inc 609 860-0675
  5 Boxal Dr Cranbury (08512) *(G-1861)*

Masouleh Corp (PA) 973 470-8900
  301 River Rd Clifton (07014) *(G-1668)*

Massage Chair Inc 732 201-7777
  1692 Route 88 Ste 1 Brick (08724) *(G-753)*

Massarellis Lawn Ornaments Inc 609 567-9700
  500 S Egg Harbor Rd Hammonton (08037) *(G-4143)*

Massimo Zanetti Beverage USA 201 440-1700
  10 Empire Blvd Moonachie (07074) *(G-6530)*

Massina Wildlife Management, Washington *Also called Big Bucks Enterprises Inc (G-11578)*

Master Bond Inc 201 343-8983
154 Hobart St Hackensack (07601) *(G-3943)*

Master Craft Interiors, Saddle Brook *Also called RFS Commercial (G-9785)*

Master Drapery Workroom Inc 908 272-4404
220 N 14th St Kenilworth (07033) *(G-4973)*

Master Martini USA Inc. 908 455-4434
460 Route 22 W Whitehouse Station (08889) *(G-12053)*

Master Metal Finishers, Paterson *Also called Master Metal Polishing Corp (G-8333)*

Master Metal Polishing Corp 973 684-0119
57 Wood St Paterson (07524) *(G-8333)*

Master Presentations Inc 732 239-7093
182 Hadassah Ln Lakewood (08701) *(G-5155)*

Master Printing Inc 201 842-9100
445 Industrial Rd Carlstadt (07072) *(G-1188)*

Master Repro Inc 201 447-4800
95 Greenwood Ave Midland Park (07432) *(G-6231)*

Master Shoe Products, Belleville *Also called Petronio Shoe Products Corp (G-311)*

Master Strap LLC 888 503-7779
20 Hastings Rd Ste B Marlboro (07746) *(G-5947)*

Master Tool Corp 732 919-1010
342 Sqnkum Yellowbrook Rd Farmingdale (07727) *(G-3390)*

Master Wire Fence, Hammonton *Also called Master Wire Manufacturing Co (G-4144)*

Master Wire Manufacturing Co 609 561-2900
1019 Black Horse Pike Hammonton (08037) *(G-4144)*

Mastercool USA Inc (PA) 973 252-9119
1 Aspen Dr Ste 1 Randolph (07869) *(G-9288)*

Mastercraft Electroplating 908 354-4404
801 Magnolia Ave Ste 4 Elizabeth (07201) *(G-2755)*

Mastercraft Iron Inc 732 988-3113
1111 10th Ave Neptune (07753) *(G-6924)*

Mastercraft Metal Finishing 908 354-4404
801 Magnolia Ave Elizabeth (07201) *(G-2756)*

Mastercrafts, South Hackensack *Also called Robert J Smith (G-10293)*

Mastergraphx, Monmouth Junction *Also called M G X Inc (G-6350)*

Masterpiece Kitchens Inc 609 518-7887
2060 Springdale Rd # 800 Cherry Hill (08003) *(G-1396)*

Masters Interiors Inc 973 253-0784
1500 Main Ave Ste 23 Clifton (07011) *(G-1669)*

Mastertaste Inc (HQ) 732 882-0202
160 Terminal Ave Clark (07066) *(G-1508)*

Mastertaste Inc 201 373-1111
546 Us Highway 46 Teterboro (07608) *(G-10805)*

Masterwork Recording Inc 267 731-7031
7503 Baxter Ave Pennsauken (08109) *(G-8545)*

Mastery Education, Saddle Brook *Also called Peoples Eductl Holdings Inc (G-9781)*

Mat, Branchville *Also called R & R Distributors Inc (G-732)*

Mat Logo Central LLC 973 433-0311
216 Little Falls Rd Cedar Grove (07009) *(G-1290)*

Mat Manufacturing Corporation 800 378-7965
409 River Rd 3 Clifton (07014) *(G-1670)*

Matchless United Companies (HQ) 908 862-7300
801 E Linden Ave Ste 1 Linden (07036) *(G-5406)*

Material Imports 201 229-1180
10 Oxford Dr Moonachie (07074) *(G-6531)*

Materials Research Group Inc 908 245-3301
244 W 1st Ave Roselle (07203) *(G-9675)*

Materials Technology Inc 732 246-1000
220 Churchill Ave Somerset (08873) *(G-10131)*

Mateson Chemical Corporation 215 423-3200
510 Whitmore St Cinnaminson (08077) *(G-1476)*

Math League Press, Tenafly *Also called Mathematics League Inc (G-10785)*

Mathcloud, Cliffside Park *Also called Educloud Inc (G-1538)*

Mathematics League Inc 201 568-6328
17 Lancaster Rd Tenafly (07670) *(G-10785)*

Matheson Gas Products, Basking Ridge *Also called Matheson Tri-Gas Inc (G-196)*

Matheson Gas Products Inc 201 867-4101
959 Us Highway 46 Parsippany (07054) *(G-8041)*

Matheson Tri-Gas Inc 908 991-9200
150 Allen Rd Ste 302 Basking Ridge (07920) *(G-194)*

Matheson Tri-Gas Inc (HQ) 908 991-9200
150 Allen Rd Ste 302 Basking Ridge (07920) *(G-195)*

Matheson Tri-Gas Inc 908 991-9200
150 Allen Rd Ste 301 Basking Ridge (07920) *(G-196)*

Matinas Biopharma Holdings Inc 908 443-1860
1545 Route 206 Ste 302 Bedminster (07921) *(G-278)*

Matinas Biopharma Holdings Inc (PA) 908 443-1860
1545 Route 206 Ste 302 Bedminster (07921) *(G-279)*

Matisse Chocolatier Inc (PA) 201 568-2288
260 Grand Ave Ste 6 Englewood (07631) *(G-2914)*

Matrix Apparel, Spring Lake *Also called Matrix Sales Group LLC (G-10534)*

Matrix Controls Company Inc 732 469-5551
330 Elizabeth Ave Somerset (08873) *(G-10132)*

Matrix Sales Group LLC 908 461-4148
309 Morris Ave Ste E Spring Lake (07762) *(G-10534)*

Matrixx Initiatives Inc (PA) 877 942-2626
1 Grand Blvd Bridgewater (08807) *(G-859)*

Matter Magazine, Maplewood *Also called Visual Impact Advertising Inc (G-5932)*

Matthew Bender & Company Inc (HQ) 518 487-3000
744 Broad St Fl 8 Newark (07102) *(G-7237)*

Matthew Warren Inc 908 788-5800
137 Us Highway 202 Ringoes (08551) *(G-9440)*

Matthey Johnson Inc. 856 384-7022
2003 Nolte Dr Paulsboro (08066) *(G-8419)*

Matthey Johnson Inc. 856 384-7132
2001 Nolte Dr West Deptford (08066) *(G-11835)*

Matthey Johnson Inc. 856 384-7001
2003 Nolte Dr West Deptford (08066) *(G-11836)*

Matthias Paper Corporation (PA) 856 467-6970
301 Arlington Blvd Swedesboro (08085) *(G-10709)*

Mattress Dev Co Del LLC 732 628-0800
1375 Jersey Ave North Brunswick (08902) *(G-7525)*

Mauden International, Pine Brook *Also called International Beauty Products (G-8707)*

Maund Enterprises Inc 609 628-2475
112 Buckhill Rd Tuckahoe (08250) *(G-11136)*

Maurice S Dessau Co Inc 201 791-2005
15-01 Pollitt Dr Ste 10 Fair Lawn (07410) *(G-3102)*

Mauser Usa LLC 732 634-6000
14 Convery Blvd Woodbridge (07095) *(G-12151)*

Mauser Usa LLC (HQ) 732 353-7100
2 Tower Center Blvd 20-1 East Brunswick (08816) *(G-2165)*

Maverick Caterers LLC 718 433-3776
20 Railroad Ave Hackensack (07601) *(G-3944)*

Maverick Housewares, Edison *Also called Maverick Industries Inc (G-2565)*

Maverick Industries Inc 732 417-9666
94 Mayfield Ave Edison (08837) *(G-2565)*

Maverick Oil Co. 732 747-8637
9 Central Ave Red Bank (07701) *(G-9335)*

Max Flight Corp 732 281-2007
7 Executive Dr Toms River (08755) *(G-10895)*

Max Gurtman & Sons Inc 973 478-7000
622 Lexington Ave Clifton (07011) *(G-1671)*

Max Pro Services LLC 973 396-2373
184 S Livingston Ave Livingston (07039) *(G-5542)*

Maxell Corporation of America (HQ) 973 653-2400
3 Garret Mountain Plz # 300 Woodland Park (07424) *(G-12224)*

Maxentric Technologies LLC (PA) 201 242-9800
2071 Lemoine Ave Ste 302 Fort Lee (07024) *(G-3566)*

Maximum Humn Prfmce Hldngs LLC (PA) 973 785-9055
165 Clinton Rd West Caldwell (07006) *(G-11786)*

Maximum Material Handling LLC 973 227-1227
750 Edwards Rd Parsippany (07054) *(G-8042)*

Maxisit Inc 732 494-2005
203 Main St Metuchen (08840) *(G-6114)*

Maxlite Inc 800 555-5629
10 York Ave West Caldwell (07006) *(G-11787)*

Maxlite Inc (PA) 973 244-7300
12 York Ave West Caldwell (07006) *(G-11788)*

Maxsyl Leather Co LLC 201 864-0579
131 35th St Union City (07087) *(G-11256)*

Maxter Corporation 609 877-9700
18 Chalford Ln Willingboro (08046) *(G-12120)*

Maxwell & Mollys Closet 973 300-0101
218 Spring St Newton (07860) *(G-7396)*

Maxwell McKenney Inc. 856 310-0700
116 White Horse Pike # 6 Haddon Heights (08035) *(G-4048)*

Maxzone Vehicle Lighting Corp 732 393-9600
24 Kilmer Rd Edison (08817) *(G-2566)*

May National Associates NJ Inc 973 473-3330
995 Towbin Ave Lakewood (08701) *(G-5156)*

Maya Liquidation, Jersey City *Also called Maya Trading Corporation (G-4782)*

Maya Trading Corporation 201 533-1400
746-748 Tonnelle Ave Jersey City (07307) *(G-4782)*

Mayab Happy Tacos Inc 732 293-0400
450 Florida Grove Rd Perth Amboy (08861) *(G-8622)*

Mayabeque Products Inc 201 869-0531
7424 Bergenline Ave Ste 1 North Bergen (07047) *(G-7466)*

Mayfair Tech Ltd Lblty Co 609 802-1262
66 Witherspoon St Princeton (08542) *(G-9071)*

Mays Landing Sand & Gravel Co (HQ) 856 447-4294
1101 Railroad Ave Newport (08345) *(G-7377)*

Maywood Furniture, Maywood *Also called De Saussure Equipment Co Inc (G-6047)*

Mbox Usa, Inc, Fair Lawn *Also called Auto Remind Inc (G-3079)*

Mbs Installations Inc 888 446-9135
29 Summerhill Ave Jackson (08527) *(G-4672)*

Mc, Cedar Grove *Also called Metal Cutting Corporation (G-1291)*

Mc Does Inc 856 985-8730
906 Route 73 N Marlton (08053) *(G-5986)*

Mc Ginley Packaging Methods 201 493-9330
80 Greenwood Ave Midland Park (07432) *(G-6232)*

Mc Lain Screen Printing, Asbury Park *Also called McLain Studios Inc (G-81)*

Mc Lean Corrugated Containers, Pennsauken *Also called McLean Packaging Corporation (G-8549)*

Mc Renewable Energy LLC 732 369-9933
50 Fletcher Ave Manasquan (08736) *(G-5873)*

McAlister Welding & Fabg 856 740-3890
112 Maple Leaf Ct Glassboro (08028) *(G-3809)*

(G-0000) Company's Geographic Section entry number

McAllister Service Company (PA) 856 665-4545
7116 Park Ave Pennsauken (08109) *(G-8546)*

McBride Awning Co 732 892-6256
304 Richmond Ave Point Pleasant Beach (08742) *(G-8923)*

McC Norsal, Paterson *Also called Microwave Consulting Corp (G-8339)*

McCain Ellios Foods Inc 201 368-0600
11 Gregg St Lodi (07644) *(G-5595)*

McCormicks Bindery Inc 856 663-8035
5815 Magnolia Ave Pennsauken (08109) *(G-8547)*

McGinnis Printing 732 758-0060
20 Monmouth St Red Bank (07701) *(G-9336)*

McGonegal Manufacturing Co 201 438-2313
405 Railroad Ave East Rutherford (07073) *(G-2309)*

McGraw-Hill Glbl Edctn Hldngs 609 371-8301
104 Windsor Center Dr East Windsor (08520) *(G-2361)*

McGrory Glass Inc 856 579-3200
1400 Grandview Ave Paulsboro (08066) *(G-8420)*

MCI Service Parts 732 967-9081
35 Cotters Ln East Brunswick (08816) *(G-2166)*

McIntosh Industries Inc 908 688-7475
676 Ramsey Ave Hillside (07205) *(G-4430)*

McKella 2-8-0 Inc 856 813-1153
7025 Central Hwy Pennsauken (08109) *(G-8548)*

McKella 280, Pennsauken *Also called McKella 2-8-0 Inc (G-8548)*

McLain Studios Inc 732 775-0271
1203 Main St Asbury Park (07712) *(G-81)*

McLean Packaging Corporation (PA) 856 359-2600
1504 Glen Ave Moorestown (08057) *(G-6600)*

McLean Packaging Corporation 856 359-2600
1000 Thomas Busch Mem Hwy Pennsauken (08110) *(G-8549)*

McMunn Associates 856 858-3440
900 Haddon Ave Ste 302 Collingswood (08108) *(G-1772)*

McNichols Company 877 884-4653
2 Home News Row New Brunswick (08901) *(G-6979)*

McQuade Enterprises LLC 609 501-2437
511 N 6th St Millville (08332) *(G-6313)*

McT Dairies Inc (HQ) 973 258-9600
15 Bleeker St Ste 103 Millburn (07041) *(G-6256)*

McT Manufacturing Inc 877 258-9600
15 Bleeker St Ste 101 Millburn (07041) *(G-6257)*

McW Precision 609 859-4400
137 Eayrestown Rd Southampton (08088) *(G-10478)*

McWane Inc 908 454-1161
183 Sitgreaves St Phillipsburg (08865) *(G-8658)*

McWilliams Forge Company (HQ) 973 627-0200
387 Franklin Ave Rockaway (07866) *(G-9586)*

MD International Inc 856 779-7633
383 Kings Hwy N Ste B1 Cherry Hill (08034) *(G-1397)*

Mdb Construction 908 628-8010
236 Cokesbury Rd Lebanon (08833) *(G-5296)*

Mdc, Boonton *Also called Merchandising Display Corp (G-576)*

Mdi Manufacturing Inc 732 994-5599
100 Syracuse Ct Lakewood (08701) *(G-5157)*

Mdj Inc 201 457-9260
25 Dicarolis Ct 21 Hackensack (07601) *(G-3945)*

Mdr Diagnostics LLC 609 396-0021
199 6th Ave Ste C Mount Laurel (08054) *(G-6817)*

Mdr LLC 973 731-7100
401 Pleasant Valley Way # 2 West Orange (07052) *(G-11898)*

Mdviani Designs Inc 201 840-5410
724 Bergen Blvd Ste 2 Ridgefield (07657) *(G-9373)*

Mead Wilbert, Wayne *Also called Di-Ferraro Inc (G-11623)*

Meadowbrook Inventions Inc 908 696-8470
260 Mine Brook Rd Bernardsville (07924) *(G-451)*

Meadowfarmalpacas Aol.com, Lawrenceville *Also called Meadowgate Farm Alpacas (G-5262)*

Meadowgate Farm Alpacas 609 219-0529
3071 Lawrenceville Rd Lawrenceville (08648) *(G-5262)*

Meadowlands Bindery Inc 201 935-6161
146 W Commercial Ave Moonachie (07074) *(G-6532)*

Meadowlands Castle, Lyndhurst *Also called Medieval Times USA Inc (G-5691)*

Meadows Knitting Corp 973 482-6400
1875 Mccarter Hwy Newark (07104) *(G-7238)*

Measurement & Computing Co, West Orange *Also called Measurement Control Corp (G-11899)*

Measurement Control Corp 800 504-9010
9 Cummings Cir West Orange (07052) *(G-11899)*

Meca Electronics Inc 973 625-0661
459 E Main St Denville (07834) *(G-2047)*

Mech-Tronics, Mount Holly *Also called High Gate Corp (G-6773)*

Mechanical Components Corp 732 938-3737
1 Executive Dr Unit B Toms River (08755) *(G-10896)*

Mechanical Ingenuity Corp 732 842-8889
61 Riordan Pl Shrewsbury (07702) *(G-10002)*

Mechanical Technologies LLC 973 616-3800
10 Bloomfield Ave Ste 6 Pine Brook (07058) *(G-8709)*

Mechanictron, Roselle *Also called Mechanitron Corporation Inc (G-9676)*

Mechanitron Corporation Inc 908 620-1001
310 W 1st Ave Roselle (07203) *(G-9676)*

Mechtronics Corporation (PA) 845 231-1400
939 Huron Rd Franklin Lakes (07417) *(G-3621)*

Med Connection LLC 908 213-7012
65 Howard St Phillipsburg (08865) *(G-8659)*

Med-Con Tech Ltd Lblty Co 888 654-0856
24 E Main St Unit 5033 Clinton (08809) *(G-1752)*

Medalco Metals Inc 732 591-0913
281 Highway 79 N Morganville (07751) *(G-6648)*

Medalco Metals Inc 908 238-0513
5 Chrystal Dr Lebanon (08833) *(G-5297)*

Medallion International Inc 973 616-3401
233 W Parkway Pompton Plains (07444) *(G-8962)*

Medavante Inc (HQ) 609 528-9400
100 American Metro Blvd # 106 Hamilton (08619) *(G-4113)*

Medchem Express LLC 732 783-7915
11 Deerpark Dr Monmouth Junction (08852) *(G-6351)*

Medco West Electronics Inc 201 457-9260
25 Dicarolis Ct 21 Hackensack (07601) *(G-3946)*

Medford Cedar Products Inc 609 859-1400
59 Old Red Lion Rd Southampton (08088) *(G-10479)*

Medford Soft Pretzels Inc 856 662-8792
102 Williamsburg Ct Marlton (08053) *(G-5987)*

Medi-Physics, South Plainfield *Also called GE Healthcare Inc (G-10372)*

Media Vista Inc 732 747-8060
60 Broad St Ste 100 Red Bank (07701) *(G-9337)*

Mediabridge Products LLC 856 216-8222
1951 Old Cuthbert Rd Cherry Hill (08034) *(G-1398)*

Medianews Group Inc 856 451-1000
93 5th St Salem (08079) *(G-9807)*

Mediavista News, Red Bank *Also called Media Vista Inc (G-9337)*

Medical Device, Newark *Also called Endomedix (G-7154)*

Medical Device Bus Svcs Inc 732 524-0400
1 Johnson And Johnson Plz New Brunswick (08933) *(G-6980)*

Medical Indicators Inc 609 737-1600
16 Thmas J Rhdes Indus Dr Hamilton (08619) *(G-4114)*

Medical Innovation Group LLC 832 348-6460
416 Mount Airy Rd Basking Ridge (07920) *(G-197)*

Medical Manager, Elmwood Park *Also called Emdeon Corporation (G-2819)*

Medical Scrubs Collectn NJ LLC (HQ) 732 719-8600
1655 Corporate Rd W Lakewood (08701) *(G-5158)*

Medical Strategic Planning Inc 732 219-5090
5 Shelbern Dr Lincroft (07738) *(G-5339)*

Medical Transcription Billing (PA) 732 873-5133
7 Clyde Rd Somerset (08873) *(G-10133)*

Medici International Inc 973 684-6084
85 5th Ave Build18 Paterson (07524) *(G-8334)*

Medicines Company (PA) 973 290-6000
8 Sylvan Way Parsippany (07054) *(G-8043)*

Medicis Pharmaceutical Corp (HQ) 866 246-8245
700 Us Highway 202/206 Bridgewater (08807) *(G-860)*

Medicon Inc 201 669-7456
17 Beechwood Rd Allendale (07401) *(G-14)*

Medicraft Inc 201 797-8820
50 Bushes Ln Elmwood Park (07407) *(G-2835)*

Medieval Times USA Inc 201 933-2220
149 Polito Ave Lyndhurst (07071) *(G-5691)*

Medimtriks Pharmaceuticals Inc 973 882-7512
383 Us Highway 46 Fairfield (07004) *(G-3256)*

Medin Technologies Inc 973 779-2400
11 Jackson Rd Totowa (07512) *(G-10955)*

Medinol Usa Inc 201 654-4534
8 Campus Dr Fl 2 Parsippany (07054) *(G-8044)*

Mediscope Manufacturing Inc (PA) 908 756-2411
744 Mountain Blvd Fl 2w Watchung (07069) *(G-11593)*

Mediterranean Chef Inc 855 628-0903
3 Borinski Dr Lincoln Park (07035) *(G-5329)*

Mediterranean Stucco Corp 973 491-0160
111 Main St Newark (07105) *(G-7239)*

Meditron Devices, Waldwick *Also called Nextphase Medical Devices LLC (G-11452)*

Medlaurel Inc 856 461-6600
620 Cooper St Delanco (08075) *(G-2007)*

Medpen Inc 973 627-8067
52 Memory Ln Denville (07834) *(G-2048)*

Medplast Medical Inc (HQ) 908 561-0717
6 Century Ln South Plainfield (07080) *(G-10405)*

Medplast Medical Inc 732 356-0689
278 Lincoln Blvd Middlesex (08846) *(G-6179)*

Medplast West Berlin Inc (HQ) 856 753-7600
225 Old Egg Harbor Rd West Berlin (08091) *(G-11733)*

Medtech Precision Molds, Middlesex *Also called Medplast Medical Inc (G-6179)*

Medtronic Inc 908 289-5969
1130 Commerce Blvd # 100 Swedesboro (08085) *(G-10710)*

Medtronic Usa Inc 973 331-7914
300 Interpace Pkwy # 340 Parsippany (07054) *(G-8045)*

Meese Inc (HQ) 201 796-4490
535 N Midland Ave Saddle Brook (07663) *(G-9774)*

Meeshaa Inc 908 279-7985
18 Tingley Ln Edison (08820) *(G-2567)*

Mega Industries LLC 973 779-8772
79 South St Passaic (07055) *(G-8161)*

A
L
P
H
A
B
E
T
I
C

Mega Media Concepts Ltd Lblty 973 919-5661
　26 Gail Ct Ste 1 Sparta (07871) *(G-10511)*
Megadyne America LLC (HQ) 973 227-4904
　340 Kaplan Dr Fairfield (07004) *(G-3257)*
Megalith Pharmaceuticals Inc 877 436-7220
　302 Carnegie Ctr Princeton (08540) *(G-9072)*
Megaplex Software Inc 908 647-3273
　21 Broadway Rd Warren (07059) *(G-11559)*
Megas Yeeros LLC 212 777-6342
　165 Chubb Ave Lyndhurst (07071) *(G-5692)*
Megasafe, Netcong *Also called Hookway Enterprises Inc (G-6941)*
Megatran Industries (PA) 609 227-4300
　312 Rising Sun Rd Bordentown (08505) *(G-601)*
Megawatt Machine Services LLC 732 805-4000
　417 Elizabeth Ave Somerset (08873) *(G-10134)*
MEI, East Brunswick *Also called Mon-Eco Industries Inc (G-2167)*
Mej Signs Inc 609 584-6881
　3100 Quakerbridge Rd # 5 Hamilton (08619) *(G-4115)*
Mel Chemicals Inc (HQ) 908 782-5800
　500 Brbrtown Pt Breeze Rd Flemington (08822) *(G-3456)*
Melillo Consulting Inc (PA) 732 563-8400
　285 Davidson Ave Ste 202 Somerset (08873) *(G-10135)*
Melissa Spice Trading Corp 862 262-7773
　123 Glen Ave Glen Rock (07452) *(G-3826)*
Melita USA, Cherry Hill *Also called European Coffee Classics Inc (G-1363)*
Melitta Usa Inc 856 428-7202
　1401 Berlin Rd Ste A Cherry Hill (08034) *(G-1399)*
Mellon D P M L L C (HQ) 732 563-0030
　2 Worlds Fair Dr Ste 310 Somerset (08873) *(G-10136)*
Melstrom Manufacturing Corp 732 938-7400
　5303 Asbury Rd Wall Township (07727) *(G-11497)*
Meltdown 609 207-0527
　13302 Long Beach Blvd Long Beach Township (08008) *(G-5617)*
Meltom Manufacturing Inc 973 546-0058
　22 Franklin Ave Clifton (07011) *(G-1672)*
Melton Industries, Bordentown *Also called Melton Sales & Service (G-602)*
Melton Industries, Columbus *Also called Melton Sales & Service (G-1805)*
Melton Sales & Service 609 699-4800
　1723 Burlington Bordentown (08505) *(G-602)*
Melton Sales & Service (PA) 609 699-4800
　13 Petticoat Bridge Rd Columbus (08022) *(G-1805)*
Melville Industries Inc 856 461-0091
　219 Saint Mihiel Dr Ste 2 Riverside (08075) *(G-9503)*
Mem Group, Englewood *Also called Middle East Marketing Group (G-2917)*
Membranes International Inc 973 998-5530
　219 Margaret King Ave # 2 Ringwood (07456) *(G-9451)*
Memco, Roselle *Also called Pamarco Global Graphics Inc (G-9679)*
Memory International Corp 973 586-2653
　25 Redwood Rd Denville (07834) *(G-2049)*
Menardi-Criswell, Pennsauken *Also called Hosokawa Micron International (G-8523)*
Menasha Packaging Company LLC 973 893-1300
　160 Chubb Ave Ste 101 Lyndhurst (07071) *(G-5693)*
Menasha Packaging Company LLC 732 985-0800
　112 Truman Dr Edison (08817) *(G-2568)*
Mendels Muffins and Stuff Inc 973 881-9900
　53 Jersey St Paterson (07501) *(G-8335)*
Mendez Dairy Co Inc 732 442-6337
　450 Fayette St Perth Amboy (08861) *(G-8623)*
Mendham Garden Center 973 543-4178
　11 W Main St Mendham (07945) *(G-6089)*
Mendles Just Bread Inc 973 881-9900
　53 Jersey St Paterson (07501) *(G-8336)*
Mennekes Electronics Inc 973 882-8333
　277 Fairfield Rd Ste 111 Fairfield (07004) *(G-3258)*
Mennen Company (HQ) 973 630-1500
　191 E Hanover Ave Morristown (07960) *(G-6726)*
Menshen Packaging USA Inc 201 445-7436
　21 Industrial Park Waldwick (07463) *(G-11448)*
Mentor Graphics Corporation 908 604-0800
　550 Hills Dr Ste 100 Bedminster (07921) *(G-280)*
Menu Express 856 216-7777
　1053 Thomas Busch Mem Hwy Pennsauken (08110) *(G-8550)*
Menu Foods Inc, Pennsauken *Also called Simmons Pet Food Nj Inc (G-8578)*
Menu Solutions Inc 718 575-5160
　233 Cortlandt St Belleville (07109) *(G-306)*
Mep Alaska LLC 646 535-9005
　29 Vanderbilt Dr Livingston (07039) *(G-5543)*
Mer Made Filter 201 236-0217
　25 Arrow Rd Ramsey (07446) *(G-9247)*
Merc USA Inc 201 489-3527
　41 Newman St Hackensack (07601) *(G-3947)*
Mercer C AlphaGraphics 609 921-0959
　100 Youngs Rd Hamilton (08619) *(G-4116)*
Mercer Digital Printing LLC 609 919-9190
　650 Whitehead Rd 2 Lawrenceville (08648) *(G-5263)*
Mercer Gasket and Shim, Bellmawr *Also called Mercer Rubber Company (G-347)*
Mercer Machine & Tool Products 609 587-1106
　332 Darcy Ave Trenton (08629) *(G-11080)*

Mercer Rubber Company 856 931-5000
　110 Benigno Blvd Bellmawr (08031) *(G-347)*
Merchandising Display Corp 973 299-8400
　14 Deer Trl Boonton (07005) *(G-576)*
Merchant & Evans Inc (PA) 609 387-3033
　308 Connecticut Dr Burlington (08016) *(G-984)*
Merchants Alarm Systems Inc 973 779-1296
　203 Paterson Ave Ste 5 Wallington (07057) *(G-11528)*
Merck & Co Inc (PA) 908 740-4000
　2000 Galloping Hill Rd Kenilworth (07033) *(G-4974)*
Merck & Co Inc 908 740-4000
　251 S 31st St Kenilworth (07033) *(G-4975)*
Merck & Co Inc 800 224-5318
　2 Giralda Farms Madison (07940) *(G-5729)*
Merck & Co Inc 908 298-4000
　2000 Galloping Hill Rd Kenilworth (07033) *(G-4976)*
Merck & Co Inc 908 298-4000
　566 Morris Ave Summit (07901) *(G-10650)*
Merck & Co Inc 908 740-4000
　126 E Lincoln Ave Rahway (07065) *(G-9212)*
Merck Animal Health, Madison *Also called Intervet Inc (G-5725)*
Merck Holdings LLC (HQ) 908 423-1000
　1 Merck Dr Whitehouse Station (08889) *(G-12054)*
Merck Research Laboratories 732 594-4000
　126 E Lincoln Ave Rahway (07065) *(G-9213)*
Merck Resource Management Inc 908 423-1000
　1 Merck Dr Whitehouse Station (08889) *(G-12055)*
Merck Sharp & Dohme Corp (HQ) 908 740-4000
　2000 Galloping Hill Rd Kenilworth (07033) *(G-4977)*
Merck Sharp & Dohme Corp 908 423-1000
　2000 Galloping Hill Rd Kenilworth (07033) *(G-4978)*
Merck Sharp & Dohme Corp 908 423-3000
　2 Merck Dr Whitehouse Station (08889) *(G-12056)*
Merck Sharp & Dohme Corp 732 594-4000
　126 E Lincoln Ave Rahway (07065) *(G-9214)*
Merck Sharp & Dohme Corp 908 685-3892
　203 River Rd Branchburg (08876) *(G-679)*
Merck Sharp & Dohme Europe Inc (HQ) 908 423-1000
　300 Franklin Square Dr Somerset (08873) *(G-10137)*
Merck Sharpe & Dohme De PR Inc 908 423-1000
　1 Merck Dr Whitehouse Station (08889) *(G-12057)*
Mercury Adhesives Inc 973 472-3307
　140 Dayton Ave Passaic (07055) *(G-8162)*
Mercury Floor Machines Inc 201 568-4606
　110 S Van Brunt St Englewood (07631) *(G-2915)*
Mercury Lighting Pdts Co Inc 973 244-9444
　20 Audrey Pl Fairfield (07004) *(G-3259)*
Mercury Plastic Bag Co Inc (PA) 973 778-7200
　168 7th St Passaic (07055) *(G-8163)*
Mercury Systems Inc 973 244-1040
　2 Henderson Dr Ste B West Caldwell (07006) *(G-11789)*
Merial Inc 732 729-5700
　631 Us Highway 1 North Brunswick (08902) *(G-7526)*
Merlin Controls, Mahwah *Also called Fmdk Technologies Inc (G-5775)*
Merlin Industries Inc (PA) 609 807-1000
　2904 E State Street Ext Hamilton (08619) *(G-4117)*
Merrill Corporation 973 643-4403
　60 Park Pl Ste 400 Newark (07102) *(G-7240)*
Merrill Corporation 908 810-3740
　649 Rahway Ave Union (07083) *(G-11207)*
Merrimac Industries Inc (HQ) 973 575-1300
　41 Fairfield Pl West Caldwell (07006) *(G-11790)*
Mersen USA Bn Corp (HQ) 973 334-0700
　400 Myrtle Ave Boonton (07005) *(G-577)*
Mershon Concrete LLC 609 298-2150
　5251 Us Highway 130 Bordentown (08505) *(G-603)*
Mesa Laboratories Inc 973 492-8400
　10 Park Pl Butler (07405) *(G-1012)*
Mesa Laboratories- Bgi Inc 973 492-8400
　10 Park Pl Butler (07405) *(G-1013)*
Mesa Veterans Power LLC 856 222-1000
　365 New Albany Rd Ste C Moorestown (08057) *(G-6601)*
Meson Group Inc (PA) 201 767-7300
　220 Pegasus Ave Northvale (07647) *(G-7591)*
Mesys, South Hackensack *Also called Marine Electric Systems Inc (G-10278)*
Metal Components Inc 973 247-1204
　92 Marilyn St North Haledon (07508) *(G-7551)*
Metal Cutting Corporation 973 239-1100
　89 Commerce Rd Cedar Grove (07009) *(G-1291)*
Metal Dynamix LLC 856 235-4559
　670 Deer Rd Ste 201 Cherry Hill (08034) *(G-1400)*
Metal Fabrication, Newark *Also called Ironbound Metal (G-7200)*
Metal Fabricators, Phillipsburg *Also called R & H Co Inc (G-8667)*
Metal Finishing Co LLC 973 778-9550
　25 Prospect St Passaic (07055) *(G-8164)*
Metal Hose Fabricators Inc 908 925-7345
　1122 Fedirko Ct Linden (07036) *(G-5407)*
Metal Improvement Co Inc 253 677-8604
　80 E Rte 4 Ste 310 Paramus (07652) *(G-7887)*

(G-0000) Company's Geographic Section entry number

Metal Improvement Company LLC (HQ) 201 843-7800
80 E Rte 4 Ste 310 Paramus (07652) **(G-7888)**
Metal MGT Pittsburgh Inc 201 333-2902
1 Linden Ave E Jersey City (07305) **(G-4783)**
Metal Powder Inds Federation 609 452-7700
105 College Rd E Ste 101 Princeton (08540) **(G-9073)**
Metal Specialties New Jersey 609 261-9277
1 Compass Ln Mount Holly (08060) **(G-6775)**
Metal Textiles Corporation (HQ) 732 287-0800
970 New Durham Rd Edison (08817) **(G-2569)**
Metal Textiles Corporation 800 843-1215
206 Talmadge Rd Edison (08817) **(G-2570)**
Metal USA Plates and Shapes 973 242-1000
178-204 Frelinghuyen Ave Newark (07114) **(G-7241)**
Metalfab Inc 973 764-2000
Prices Switch Rd Vernon (07462) **(G-11299)**
Metalfab Mtl Hdlg Systems LLC 973 764-2000
11 Prices Switch Rd Vernon (07462) **(G-11300)**
Metalgraphics, East Brunswick *Also called Prem-Khichi Enterprises Inc* **(G-2174)**
Metalico Inc (PA) 908 497-9610
135 Dermody St Cranford (07016) **(G-1915)**
Metaline Products Company Inc 732 721-1373
101 N Feltus St South Amboy (08879) **(G-10242)**
Metalix Inc 973 546-2500
9 Villa Rd Little Falls (07424) **(G-5482)**
Metallia USA LLC 201 585-5000
2200 Fletcher Ave Ste 7 Fort Lee (07024) **(G-3567)**
Metallix Direct Gold LLC 732 544-0891
59 Avenue At The Cmn # 201 Shrewsbury (07702) **(G-10003)**
Metallix Refining Inc (PA) 732 936-0050
59 Avenue At The Cmn # 201 Shrewsbury (07702) **(G-10004)**
Metallo Gasket Company Inc 732 545-7223
16 Bethany St New Brunswick (08901) **(G-6981)**
Metals Plus 908 862-7677
200 Marion Ave Linden (07036) **(G-5408)**
Metaport Manufacturing LLC 973 383-8363
28 Randazzo Rd Lafayette (07848) **(G-5051)**
Metawater Usa Inc (PA) 201 935-3436
301 State Rt 17 Ste 504 Rutherford (07070) **(G-9740)**
Metfab Steel Works LLC 973 675-7676
560 Freeman St Orange (07050) **(G-7822)**
Method Assoc Inc 732 888-0444
120 Francis St Ste 2 Keyport (07735) **(G-5020)**
Meto Corp 201 405-0311
29 E Halsey Rd Parsippany (07054) **(G-8046)**
Meto Engineering, Parsippany *Also called Meto Corp* **(G-8046)**
Meto Lift Inc 201 405-0311
29 E Halsey Rd Parsippany (07054) **(G-8047)**
Metrie Inc 973 584-0040
1578 Sussex Tpke Ste 300 Randolph (07869) **(G-9289)**
METRO ELECTRIC DUSTER, Oakland *Also called Metropolitan Vacuum Clr Co Inc* **(G-7696)**
Metro Features, New Milford *Also called Metro Publishing Group Inc* **(G-7023)**
Metro Flag Co, Wharton *Also called National Flag & Display Co Inc* **(G-11993)**
Metro Industrial Supply, Roselle *Also called American Rigging & Repair Inc* **(G-9660)**
Metro Mills Inc 973 942-6034
151 Linwood Ave Paterson (07502) **(G-8337)**
Metro Optics LLC 908 413-0004
38 Winding Way Flemington (08822) **(G-3457)**
Metro Prtg & Promotions LLC 973 316-1600
311 Mechanic St 2 Boonton (07005) **(G-578)**
Metro Publishing Group Inc 201 385-2000
626 Mccarthy Dr New Milford (07646) **(G-7023)**
Metro Seliger Industries Inc 201 438-4530
330 Washington Ave Carlstadt (07072) **(G-1189)**
Metro Tag & Label Inc 201 845-4747
24 Park Ave 2 West Orange (07052) **(G-11900)**
Metro Web Corp 201 553-0700
5901 Tonnelle Ave North Bergen (07047) **(G-7467)**
Metrofuser LLC (PA) 908 245-2100
475 Division St Bldg 1 Elizabeth (07201) **(G-2757)**
Metrolab Div, Newark *Also called Sk & P Industries Inc* **(G-7316)**
Metrolab Division, Newark *Also called Sk & P Industries Inc* **(G-7315)**
Metrologic Instruments Inc (HQ) 856 228-8100
534 Fellowship Rd Mount Laurel (08054) **(G-6818)**
Metrolpolis Mastering LP 212 604-9433
33 Hilliard Ave Edgewater (07020) **(G-2441)**
Metronic Engineering Co Inc 201 337-1266
32 Iron Horse Rd Oakland (07436) **(G-7695)**
Metroplex Products Company Inc 732 249-0653
377 Deans Rhode Hall Rd Monroe Township (08831) **(G-6384)**
Metropolitan Cabinet Works, Fair Lawn *Also called Creative Innovations Inc* **(G-3088)**
Metropolitan Compactors Svc 908 653-0168
21 Quine St Cranford (07016) **(G-1916)**
Metropolitan Foods Inc (PA) 973 672-9400
174 Delawanna Ave Clifton (07014) **(G-1673)**
Metropolitan Manufacturing Inc 201 933-8111
450 Murray Hill Pkwy East Rutherford (07073) **(G-2310)**
Metropolitan Vacuum Clr Co Inc 201 405-2225
5 Raritan Rd Oakland (07436) **(G-7696)**
Metrowest Jewish News, Whippany *Also called New Jersey Jewish News* **(G-12027)**
Mettler Mechanical, North Bergen *Also called ML Mettler Corp* **(G-7469)**
Metuchen Capacitors Inc 800 899-6969
2139 Highway 35 Ste 2 Holmdel (07733) **(G-4522)**
Mfb Soft Pretzels Inc 609 953-6773
617 Stokes Rd Medford (08055) **(G-6077)**
Mfv International Corporation 973 993-1687
89 Headquarters Plz Morristown (07960) **(G-6727)**
Mg Decor LLC 201 923-5493
2 Radio Ave Apt C24 Secaucus (07094) **(G-9904)**
Mgl Forms, New Providence *Also called Mgl Printing Solution LLC* **(G-7048)**
Mgl Printing Solution LLC 908 665-1999
154 South St Ste 1 New Providence (07974) **(G-7048)**
Michael Anthony Sign & Awng Co, Piscataway *Also called Michael Anthony Sign Dsign Inc* **(G-8791)**
Michael Anthony Sign Dsign Inc 732 453-6120
250 Stelton Rd Ste 1 Piscataway (08854) **(G-8791)**
Michael Duru Clothiers LLC 732 741-1999
801 Broad St Shrewsbury (07702) **(G-10005)**
Michael Foods, Elizabethport *Also called Papettis Hygrade Egg Pdts Inc* **(G-2786)**
Michael Graphics Inc 732 846-8680
209 Farmsedge Rd Branchburg (08853) **(G-680)**
Michael Lubrich 732 223-4235
5 Mount Ln Manasquan (08736) **(G-5874)**
Michael's Quick Printing, Hightstown *Also called National Certified Printing* **(G-4313)**
Michaels Cabinet Connection 609 889-6611
1054 Route 47 S Rio Grande (08242) **(G-9460)**
Michele Maddalena 973 244-0033
1275 Bloomfield Ave Fairfield (07004) **(G-3260)**
Michelex Corporation (PA) 201 977-1177
204 Haledon Ave Prospect Park (07508) **(G-9170)**
Michelle Ste Wine Estates Ltd 973 770-8100
200 Valley Rd Ste 200 Mount Arlington (07856) **(G-6758)**
Micheller & Son Hydraulics Inc 908 687-1545
534 W 1st Ave Ste 540 Roselle (07203) **(G-9677)**
Micro Innovations Corp 732 346-9333
1090 King Georges Post Rd Edison (08837) **(G-2571)**
Micro Logic Inc (PA) 201 962-7510
31 Industrial Ave Ste 7 Mahwah (07430) **(G-5790)**
Micro Media Publications Inc 732 657-7344
15 Union Ave Lakehurst (08733) **(G-5059)**
Micro Medical Technologies, Somerset *Also called Micro Stamping Corporation* **(G-10138)**
Micro Stamping Corporation (PA) 732 302-0800
140 Belmont Dr Somerset (08873) **(G-10138)**
Micro-Mark, Berkeley Heights *Also called Scientific Models Inc* **(G-421)**
Micro-Tek Corporation 856 829-3855
1600 Taylors Ln Cinnaminson (08077) **(G-1477)**
Micro-Tek Laboratories Inc (PA) 973 779-5577
154 Huron Ave Clifton (07013) **(G-1674)**
Micro-Tube Fabricators, Middlesex *Also called 250 Lackland Holding Inc* **(G-6140)**
Microcast Technologies Corp 732 943-7356
17 Mileed Way Avenel (07001) **(G-140)**
Microcast Technologies Corp (PA) 908 523-9503
1611 W Elizabeth Ave Linden (07036) **(G-5409)**
Microdata Instrument Inc 908 222-1717
1207 Hogan Dr South Plainfield (07080) **(G-10406)**
Microdose Defense Products, Ewing *Also called Microdose Therapeutx Inc* **(G-3037)**
Microdose Therapeutx Inc 732 355-2100
7 Graphics Dr Ewing (08628) **(G-3037)**
Microdysis Inc 609 642-1184
1200 Florence Columbus Rd Bordentown (08505) **(G-604)**
Microelettrica-Usa LLC 973 598-0806
300 International Dr # 2 Budd Lake (07828) **(G-937)**
Microfeed LLC 201 886-9200
1053 Anderson Ave Fort Lee (07024) **(G-3568)**
Microfold Inc 201 641-5052
375 North St Ste C Teterboro (07608) **(G-10806)**
Microgen Inc 973 575-9025
33 Clinton Rd Ste 102 West Caldwell (07006) **(G-11791)**
Microlab/Fxr 973 386-9696
25 Eastmans Rd Parsippany (07054) **(G-8048)**
Micromat Co 201 529-3738
1165 Greenwood Lake Tpke E Ringwood (07456) **(G-9452)**
Micron Powder Systems, Summit *Also called Hosokawa Micron International* **(G-10646)**
Micronet Enertec Tech Inc 201 225-0190
28 W Grand Ave Ste 3 Montvale (07645) **(G-6467)**
Microseal Industries Inc 973 523-0704
610 E 36th St Paterson (07513) **(G-8338)**
Microsemi Stor Solutions Inc 908 953-9400
180 Mount Airy Rd Basking Ridge (07920) **(G-198)**
Microsignals Inc 800 225-4508
29 Fairview St Ste 1a Palisades Park (07650) **(G-7839)**
Microsoft Corporation 732 476-5600
101 Wood Ave S Ste 900 Iselin (08830) **(G-4634)**
Microsoft Corporation 973 785-0982
1400 Willowbrook Mall Wayne (07470) **(G-11665)**
Microsolv Technology Corp 732 578-1777
1 Industrial Way W Bldg D Eatontown (07724) **(G-2413)**

ALPHABETIC

Microsurfaces Inc 201 408-5596
1 W Forest Ave Ste 2b Englewood (07631) *(G-2916)*

Microtelecom Ltd Liability Co (PA) 866 676-5679
1 Bridge Plz N Ste 275 Fort Lee (07024) *(G-3569)*

Microwave Consulting Corp 973 523-6700
150 Railroad Ave Paterson (07501) *(G-8339)*

Microwize Technology Inc (PA) 800 955-0321
1 Kalisa Way Ste 104 Paramus (07652) *(G-7889)*

Mid Atlantic Graphixinc 609 569-9990
2558 Tilton Rd Egg Harbor Township (08234) *(G-2690)*

Mid Ocean Partners 908 707-0100
130 Industrial Pkwy Branchburg (08876) *(G-681)*

Mid State Bindery 908 755-9388
262 Lackland Dr Middlesex (08846) *(G-6180)*

Mid-Lantic Precision Inc 856 456-3810
940 Market St Gloucester City (08030) *(G-3840)*

Mid-State Controls Inc 732 335-0500
8 Crown Plz Ste 102 Hazlet (07730) *(G-4279)*

Mid-State Enterprises Inc 973 427-6040
155 Van Winkle Ave Hawthorne (07506) *(G-4247)*

Midas Designs Ltd 201 567-2700
124 Lafayette Ave Maywood (07607) *(G-6058)*

Middle Atlantic Products Inc (HQ) 973 839-1011
300 Fairfield Rd Fairfield (07004) *(G-3261)*

Middle East Marketing Group (PA) 201 503-0150
266 S Dean St Englewood (07631) *(G-2917)*

Middleburg Yarn Processing Co (PA) 973 238-1800
375 Diamond Bridge Ave Hawthorne (07506) *(G-4248)*

Middlesex Publications 732 435-0005
850 Us Highway 1 Fl 4 Flr 4 North Brunswick (08902) *(G-7527)*

Middlesex Water Company 732 579-0290
100 Fairview Ave Edison (08817) *(G-2572)*

Midhattan Woodworking Corp 732 727-3020
3130 Bordentown Ave Old Bridge (08857) *(G-7785)*

Midland Farms Inc 800 749-6455
845 E 25th St Paterson (07513) *(G-8340)*

Midland Screen Printing Inc 201 703-0066
280 N Midland Ave Ste 218 Saddle Brook (07663) *(G-9775)*

Midlantic Color Graphics LLC 856 786-3113
2303 Garry Rd Ste 9 Cinnaminson (08077) *(G-1478)*

Midlantic Medical Systems Inc 908 432-4599
61 Fieldstone Rd Skillman (08558) *(G-10033)*

Midstate Filigree Systems Inc 609 448-8700
22 Brick Yard Rd Cranbury (08512) *(G-1862)*

Midway Machine Product Corp 609 499-4377
763a Railroad Ave Florence (08518) *(G-3479)*

Miemie Design Services Inc 609 857-3688
1341 Radio Rd Ltl Egg Hbr (08087) *(G-5645)*

Mighty Mug Incorporated 732 382-3911
665 Martin St Rahway (07065) *(G-9215)*

MII Organics, Hillsborough *Also called Interganic Fzco LLC (G-4350)*

Mike Dolly Screen Printing 732 294-8979
17 Elm St Freehold (07728) *(G-3670)*

Mikros Systems Corporation (PA) 609 987-1513
707 Alexander Rd Princeton (08540) *(G-9074)*

Mil-Comm Products Company Inc 201 935-8561
2 Carlton Ave Ste C East Rutherford (07073) *(G-2311)*

Milady Bridals Inc 201 348-4500
2111 Kerrigan Ave Union City (07087) *(G-11257)*

Miles Concrete Co, Newfield *Also called Ernest R Miles Construction Co (G-7365)*

Miles Concrete Company Inc 856 697-2311
1445 Catawba Ave Newfield (08344) *(G-7367)*

Milestone Education LLC 973 535-2717
220 S Orange Ave Livingston (07039) *(G-5544)*

Milestone Scientific Inc (PA) 973 535-2717
220 S Orange Ave Ste 102 Livingston (07039) *(G-5545)*

Milk Farm, Lawrenceville *Also called Halo Farm Inc (G-5257)*

Millar Sheet Metal 201 997-1990
39 Rizzolo Rd Ste 2 Kearny (07032) *(G-4899)*

Millburn Bagel Inc 973 258-1334
321 Millburn Ave Ste 14 Millburn (07041) *(G-6258)*

Millco Custom Fabricators Inc 908 756-3640
601 Montrose Ave South Plainfield (07080) *(G-10407)*

Millenium Graphics, Marlboro *Also called SAM Graphics Inc (G-5956)*

Millenium Worldwide, Newton *Also called Riotsound Inc (G-7401)*

Millennium Info Tech Inc 609 750-7120
4390 Us Highway 1 Ste 121 Princeton (08540) *(G-9075)*

Millennium Research LLC 908 867-7646
99 W Mill Rd Long Valley (07853) *(G-5639)*

Millennium Systems Intl, Parsippany *Also called Harms Software Inc (G-8027)*

Miller & Son 973 759-6445
24 Belleville Ave Belleville (07109) *(G-307)*

Miller Auto Parts, Bayonne *Also called M & RS Miller Auto Gear & Prt (G-237)*

Miller Berry & Sons Inc 856 785-1420
2615 Robinstown Rd Port Norris (08349) *(G-8981)*

Miller Signs LLC 732 521-0904
14 Main St Helmetta (08828) *(G-4286)*

Milligan & Higgins Div, Fairfield *Also called Hudson Industries Corporation (G-3225)*

Millington Quarry Inc 908 542-0055
135 Stonehouse Rd Basking Ridge (07920) *(G-199)*

Millner Kitchens Inc 609 890-7300
200b Whitehead Rd Ste 108 Hamilton (08619) *(G-4118)*

Millner Kitchens Inc 609 890-7300
200 Whitehead Rd Ste 108 Trenton (08619) *(G-11081)*

Millner Lumber Co, Trenton *Also called Millner Kitchens Inc (G-11081)*

Millson Precision Machining 732 424-1700
145 11th St Piscataway (08854) *(G-8792)*

Millstone Dq Inc 609 259-6733
40 Trenton Lakewood Rd Clarksburg (08510) *(G-1521)*

Milltex Manufacturing, Brick *Also called Marketing Administration Assoc (G-752)*

Millville Vials, Millville *Also called Nipro Phrmpckging Amricas Corp (G-6315)*

Millwood Inc 732 967-8818
7 Brick Plant Rd Ste C South River (08882) *(G-10463)*

Milo Runtak Welding Machinery 201 391-0380
174 Kinderkamack Rd Ste A Park Ridge (07656) *(G-7926)*

Milspray LLC (HQ) 732 886-2223
845 Towbin Ave Lakewood (08701) *(G-5159)*

Milspray Military Technologies, Lakewood *Also called Milspray LLC (G-5159)*

Mimeocom Inc 973 286-2901
158 Mount Olivet Ave Newark (07114) *(G-7242)*

Minalex Corporation 908 534-4044
25 Coddington Rd Whitehouse Station (08889) *(G-12058)*

Minardi Baking Co Inc 973 742-1107
20 Luger Rd Denville (07834) *(G-2050)*

Mincing Overseas Spice Company, Dayton *Also called Mincing Trading Corporation (G-1980)*

Mincing Trading Corporation 732 355-9944
10 Tower Rd Dayton (08810) *(G-1980)*

Mind-Alliance Systems LLC 212 920-1911
21 Herbert Ter Livingston (07039) *(G-5546)*

Mindray Ds Usa Inc 201 995-8000
800 Macarthur Blvd Mahwah (07430) *(G-5791)*

Mindray North America, Mahwah *Also called Mindray Ds Usa Inc (G-5791)*

Mindwise Media LLC 973 701-0685
26 Floral St Chatham (07928) *(G-1334)*

Mine Hill Spartan 973 442-2280
274 Us Highway 46 Mine Hill (07803) *(G-6328)*

Minerva Custom Products LLC 201 447-4731
49 Lockwood Dr Waldwick (07463) *(G-11449)*

Minhura Inc 862 763-4078
24 William St North Arlington (07031) *(G-7421)*

Mini Frost Foods Corporation 973 427-4258
23 Willow Brook Ct North Haledon (07508) *(G-7552)*

Miniature Folding Inc 201 773-6477
14 Wenzel St Elmwood Park (07407) *(G-2836)*

Minitec Corporation 973 989-1426
158 W Clinton St Ste V Dover (07801) *(G-2100)*

Minmetals Inc (PA) 201 809-1898
120 Schor Ave Leonia (07605) *(G-5318)*

Minniti J Hair Replacement Inc 856 427-9600
905 Marlton Pike W Cherry Hill (08002) *(G-1401)*

Minor Rubber Co Inc (PA) 973 338-6800
49 Ackerman St Bloomfield (07003) *(G-522)*

Mint Printing LLC 973 546-2060
475 Westminster Pl Lodi (07644) *(G-5596)*

Minuteman Press, Ho Ho Kus *Also called Jmp Press Inc (G-4454)*

Minuteman Press, Northvale *Also called Palm Press Inc (G-7600)*

Minuteman Press, Clifton *Also called Lmp Printing Corp (G-1663)*

Minuteman Press, Somerville *Also called Roan Printing Inc (G-10226)*

Minuteman Press, Secaucus *Also called Sonata Graphics Inc (G-9930)*

Minuteman Press, Hasbrouck Heights *Also called M & M Printing Corp (G-4196)*

Minuteman Press, Middlesex *Also called Scarlet Printing (G-6193)*

Minuteman Press, Ewing *Also called Tedco Inc (G-3060)*

Minuteman Press, Clifton *Also called Genua & Mulligan Printing (G-1626)*

Minuteman Press, Berlin *Also called Classic Graphic Inc (G-431)*

Minuteman Press, Wall Township *Also called Verni Vito (G-11517)*

Minuteman Press, Cherry Hill *Also called Bittner Industries Inc (G-1351)*

Minuteman Press 973 403-0146
359 Bloomfield Ave Caldwell (07006) *(G-1031)*

Minuteman Press 732 536-8788
349 Us Highway 9 Ste 5 Manalapan (07726) *(G-5854)*

Minwax Group (inc) 201 818-7500
10 Montinview Rd Ste N300 Upper Saddle River (07458) *(G-11280)*

Miracle Mile Automotive Inc 732 886-6315
1925 Swarthmore Ave Ste 1 Lakewood (08701) *(G-5160)*

Miracle Verde Group LLC 201 399-2222
47 Sellers St Kearny (07032) *(G-4900)*

Miranda MTI Inc 973 376-4275
195 Mountain Ave Springfield (07081) *(G-10565)*

Mire Enterprises LLC 732 882-1010
1501 W Blancke St Ste 3 Linden (07036) *(G-5410)*

Miric Industries Inc 201 864-0233
1516 Union Tpke North Bergen (07047) *(G-7468)*

Miric Revolving Swinging Doors, North Bergen *Also called Miric Industries Inc (G-7468)*

Miroad Rubber USA LLC 480 280-2543
182 Whitman Ave Edison (08817) *(G-2573)*

Mironova Labs, Fairfield *Also called Pharmatech International Inc* ***(G-3283)***
Mirrotek International LLC...973 472-1400
90 Dayton Ave Passaic (07055) ***(G-8165)***
Mischief International Inc...201 840-6888
501 Broad Ave Ste 12 Ridgefield (07657) ***(G-9374)***
Misco Enterprises, Edison *Also called Missry Associates Inc* ***(G-2574)***
MISS Sportswear Inc...212 391-2535
745 Joyce Kilmer Ave New Brunswick (08901) ***(G-6982)***
Missa Bay Citrus Company...856 241-0900
101 Arlington Blvd Swedesboro (08085) ***(G-10711)***
Missa Bay LLC (HQ)...856 241-0900
101 Arlington Blvd Swedesboro (08085) ***(G-10712)***
Mission Systems & Training, Marlton *Also called Lockheed Martin* ***(G-5984)***
Missionary Society of St Paul...201 825-7300
997 Macarthur Blvd Mahwah (07430) ***(G-5792)***
Missry Associates Inc...732 752-7500
250 Carter Dr Ste 3 Edison (08817) ***(G-2574)***
Mister Boardwalk, Lakewood *Also called Wardale Corp* ***(G-5204)***
Mister Boardwalk, Lakewood *Also called M and R Manufacturing* ***(G-5150)***
Mister Cookie Face Inc...732 370-5533
1989 Rutgers Blvd Lakewood (08701) ***(G-5161)***
Mister Good Lube Inc...732 842-3266
473 Broad St Shrewsbury (07702) ***(G-10006)***
Mistras Group Inc (PA)...609 716-4000
195 Clarksville Rd Ste 2 Princeton Junction (08550) ***(G-9159)***
Mitronics Products Inc...908 647-5006
239 Morristown Rd Gillette (07933) ***(G-3795)***
Mitsubishi Tanabe Pharma (HQ)...908 607-1950
525 Wshngton Blvd Fl 1400 Flr 1400 Jersey City (07310) ***(G-4784)***
Mitzi Intl Handbag & ACC Ltd...973 483-5015
250 Passaic St Newark (07104) ***(G-7243)***
Mizco International Inc...732 912-2000
80 Essex Ave E Avenel (07001) ***(G-141)***
Mj Corporate Sales Inc...856 778-0055
109 W Park Dr Unit A Mount Laurel (08054) ***(G-6819)***
Mj Family Care, Paterson *Also called Conduent State Healthcare LLC* ***(G-8239)***
Mj Gross Company - NJ...212 542-3199
2 Commonwealth Dr Lakewood (08701) ***(G-5162)***
Mjg Technologies Incorporated...856 228-6118
832 Camden Ave Blackwood (08012) ***(G-488)***
Mjs of Spotswood LLC...732 251-7400
19 Summerhill Rd Spotswood (08884) ***(G-10529)***
Mjs Pizza Bar & Grill, Spotswood *Also called Mjs of Spotswood LLC* ***(G-10529)***
Mjs Precision Inc...973 209-1300
12 Cork Hill Rd Ste 3 Franklin (07416) ***(G-3601)***
Mjse LLC...201 791-9888
374 N Midland Ave Saddle Brook (07663) ***(G-9776)***
Mk Wood Inc...973 450-5110
681 Main St Belleville (07109) ***(G-308)***
Mks Inc...856 451-5545
7 N Industrial Blvd Bridgeton (08302) ***(G-791)***
ML Mettler Corp...201 869-0170
8905 Bergenwood Ave North Bergen (07047) ***(G-7469)***
ML Woodwork Inc...201 953-2175
255 Falmouth Ave Elmwood Park (07407) ***(G-2837)***
Mm Packaging Group LLC...908 759-0101
2401 E Linden Ave Linden (07036) ***(G-5411)***
Mmp Ergonomics Co, Hasbrouck Heights *Also called Track Systems Inc* ***(G-4201)***
Mmtc Inc...609 520-9699
12 Roszel Rd Ste A203 Princeton (08540) ***(G-9076)***
Mnemonics Inc...856 234-0970
102 Gaither Dr Ste 4 Mount Laurel (08054) ***(G-6820)***
Moa Instrumentation Inc...215 547-8308
20 Carla Way Lawrenceville (08648) ***(G-5264)***
Mobil Research and Dev Corp...856 224-2134
600 Billingsport Rd Paulsboro (08066) ***(G-8421)***
Mobile Intelligent Alerts Inc...201 410-5324
72 Middletown Rd Holmdel (07733) ***(G-4523)***
Mobile Mini Inc...908 561-5033
2400 Roosevelt Ave South Plainfield (07080) ***(G-10408)***
Mobile Power Inc...908 852-3117
392 Watters Rd Hackettstown (07840) ***(G-4026)***
Mobile Solutions Intl LLC...609 448-3089
26 Wildflower Trl Robbinsville (08691) ***(G-9518)***
Mobility123, Absecon *Also called Diamond Scooters Inc* ***(G-2)***
Mobilogy Inc (HQ)...201 848-8552
7 Campus Dr Ste 210 Parsippany (07054) ***(G-8049)***
Moblty Inc...973 535-3600
651 W Mount Pleasant Ave # 270 Livingston (07039) ***(G-5547)***
Mococo Partners Corp...862 204-3461
439 E 22nd St Paterson (07514) ***(G-8341)***
Mocvd Systems, Somerset *Also called Veeco* ***(G-10192)***
Mod Media Ltd Liability Co...973 249-6157
15 Oak Rd Ste 2 Fairfield (07004) ***(G-3262)***
Mod-Tek Converting LLC...856 662-6884
2550 Haddonfield Rd Ste E Pennsauken (08110) ***(G-8551)***
Mod-U-Kraf Homes LLC (HQ)...540 482-0273
140 Bradford Dr Ste A West Berlin (08091) ***(G-11734)***
Model Electronics Inc (PA)...201 961-9200
615 E Crescent Ave Ramsey (07446) ***(G-9248)***
Model Electronics Inc...201 961-1717
526 State Rt 17 Ramsey (07446) ***(G-9249)***
Model Rectifier Corporation...732 225-2100
80 Newfield Ave Ste 4 Edison (08837) ***(G-2575)***
Modelware Inc...732 264-3020
28 Red Coach Ln Holmdel (07733) ***(G-4524)***
Modern Drummer Publications...973 239-4140
271 Us Highway 46 H212 Fairfield (07004) ***(G-3263)***
Modern Fuel Inc...973 471-1501
158 Colfax Ave Clifton (07013) ***(G-1675)***
Modern Graphic Arts, Clifton *Also called Sandy Alexander Inc* ***(G-1715)***
Modern Metric Machine Company...856 547-4044
101 W Nicholson Rd Audubon (08106) ***(G-117)***
Modern Precision Tech Inc...856 335-9303
225 Old Egg Harbor Rd West Berlin (08091) ***(G-11735)***
Modern Showcase Inc...201 935-2929
610 Commercial Ave Carlstadt (07072) ***(G-1190)***
Modern Sportswear Corporation...201 804-2700
102 W Commercial Ave Moonachie (07074) ***(G-6533)***
Modern Store Equipment...609 241-7438
2045 Route 130 N Burlington (08016) ***(G-985)***
Modernlinefurniture Inc...908 486-0200
531 N Stiles St Linden (07036) ***(G-5412)***
Modine Manufacturing Company...856 467-9710
244 High Hills Rd Bridgeport (08014) ***(G-768)***
Modroto, Saddle Brook *Also called Meese Inc* ***(G-9774)***
Modular Packaging Systems Inc...973 970-9393
385 Franklin Ave Ste C Rockaway (07866) ***(G-9587)***
Modulation Sciences Inc...732 302-3090
12 Worlds Fair Dr Ste A Somerset (08873) ***(G-10139)***
Mohawk Industries...973 982-6200
150 Western Rd Kearny (07032) ***(G-4901)***
Mojo Organics Inc...201 633-6519
101 Hudson St Fl 21 Jersey City (07302) ***(G-4785)***
Mold Polishing Company Inc...908 518-9191
45 North Ave Ste 3 Garwood (07027) ***(G-3779)***
Molders Fishing Preserve...732 446-2850
318 John Wall Rd Jamesburg (08831) ***(G-4687)***
Moldworks Worldwide LLC...908 474-8082
985 E Linden Ave Linden (07036) ***(G-5413)***
Molecu-Wire Corporation...908 429-0300
1215 Kennedy Blvd Manville (08835) ***(G-5897)***
Molnar Tool and Dye, Ocean *Also called Stamping Com Inc* ***(G-7747)***
Molnar Tools Inc...908 580-0671
3 Stoningham Dr Warren (07059) ***(G-11560)***
Momentum Usa Inc (PA)...844 300-1553
120 Fieldcrest Ave Edison (08837) ***(G-2576)***
Mon-Eco Industries Inc...732 257-7942
5 Joanna Ct Ste G East Brunswick (08816) ***(G-2167)***
Monarch Art Plastics Co LLC...856 235-5151
3838 Church Rd Mount Laurel (08054) ***(G-6821)***
Monarch Color Corporation...215 923-2235
7247 Browning Rd Pennsauken (08109) ***(G-8552)***
Monarch Plastics, Mount Laurel *Also called Monarch Art Plastics Co LLC* ***(G-6821)***
Monarch Robe and Towel Company, South Plainfield *Also called Monarch Towel Company Inc* ***(G-10409)***
Monarch Towel Company Inc (PA)...800 729-7623
301 Hollywood Ave South Plainfield (07080) ***(G-10409)***
Mondelez Global LLC...201 794-4000
22-11 State Rt 208 Fair Lawn (07410) ***(G-3103)***
Mondelez Global LLC...201 794-4080
21-05 Route 208 Fair Lawn (07410) ***(G-3104)***
Mondelez International Inc...973 503-2000
200 Deforest Ave East Hanover (07936) ***(G-2228)***
Moniteur Devices Inc...973 857-1600
36 Commerce Rd Cedar Grove (07009) ***(G-1292)***
Monitor Newspaper, Tinton Falls *Also called Direct Development LLC* ***(G-10831)***
Monitoring Solutions Inc (PA)...908 713-0172
78 State Route 173 Ste 7 Hampton (08827) ***(G-4165)***
Monmouth Bioproducts LLC...732 863-0300
918 State Route 33 Ste 3 Freehold (07728) ***(G-3671)***
Monmouth Hose & Hydraulics, Shrewsbury *Also called Monmouth Truck Ram Div LLC* ***(G-10007)***
Monmouth Journal...732 747-7007
212 Maple Ave Ste 1 Red Bank (07701) ***(G-9338)***
Monmouth Marine Engines Inc...732 528-9290
536 Union Ln Brielle (08730) ***(G-913)***
Monmouth Rubber & Plastics, Long Branch *Also called Monmouth Rubber Corp* ***(G-5630)***
Monmouth Rubber Corp...732 229-3444
75 Long Branch Ave Long Branch (07740) ***(G-5630)***
Monmouth Truck Ram Div LLC...732 741-5001
799 Shrewsbury Ave Shrewsbury (07702) ***(G-10007)***
Monogram Center Inc...732 442-1800
437 Amboy Ave Perth Amboy (08861) ***(G-8624)***
Monroe Machine & Design Inc...732 521-3434
566 Buckelew Ave Jamesburg (08831) ***(G-4688)***

ALPHABETIC

Monroe Tool & Die Inc 856 629-5164
197 Sharp Rd Williamstown (08094) *(G-12092)*

Monroeville Vineyard & Winery 856 521-0523
314 Richwood Rd Monroeville (08343) *(G-6401)*

Monster Coatings Inc 973 983-7662
12 Midway Ct Rockaway (07866) *(G-9588)*

Montage Media Corporation 201 891-3200
1000 Wyckoff Ave Mahwah (07430) *(G-5793)*

Montana Electrical Decorating 973 344-1815
62 Mcwhorter St Newark (07105) *(G-7244)*

Montclair Fuel LLC 973 744-4300
651 Bloomfield Ave Montclair (07042) *(G-6422)*

Montclair Local News LLC 973 744-6243
132 High St Montclair (07042) *(G-6423)*

Montclair Times Editorial, Montclair Also called North Jersey Media Group Inc *(G-6426)*

Monte Printing & Graphics Inc 908 241-6600
225 W Clay Ave Roselle Park (07204) *(G-9699)*

Montego Bay, Ridgefield Also called PC Marketing Inc *(G-9379)*

Montena Taranto Foods Inc 201 943-8484
400 Victoria Ter Ridgefield (07657) *(G-9375)*

Montgomery Investment Tech (PA) 610 688-8111
700 Route 130 N Ste 105 Cinnaminson (08077) *(G-1479)*

Montgomery News 908 874-0020
88 Orchard Rd Ste 10 Skillman (08558) *(G-10034)*

Montrose Molders, Piscataway Also called Continental Precision Corp *(G-8752)*

Montrose Molders Corporation 908 754-3030
25 Howard St Piscataway (08854) *(G-8793)*

Montrose Molders Corporation 908 754-3030
230 Saint Nicholas Ave South Plainfield (07080) *(G-10410)*

Moon, Ridgefield Park Also called Oe Solutions America Inc *(G-9411)*

Moonbabies LLC 609 926-0201
505 New Rd Ste 7 Somers Point (08244) *(G-10047)*

Moosavi Oriental Rugs, Secaucus Also called Moosavi Rugs Inc *(G-9905)*

Moosavi Rugs Inc 201 617-9500
100 Park Plaza Dr 208n Secaucus (07094) *(G-9905)*

More Copy Printing Service 201 327-1106
302 State Rt 17 Upper Saddle River (07458) *(G-11281)*

More Than A Notion Fabrics Ltd 732 821-5580
4437 Route 27 Princeton (08540) *(G-9077)*

Moreira, Jose B, Attorney, Kearny Also called Jose Moreira *(G-4890)*

Morelli Contracting LLC 732 356-8800
201 Egel Ave Ste B Middlesex (08846) *(G-6181)*

Moreng Metal Products Inc 973 256-2001
100 W End Rd Totowa (07512) *(G-10956)*

Morgan Advanced Ceramics Inc 973 808-1621
26 Madison Rd Fairfield (07004) *(G-3264)*

Morgan Cycle LLC 973 218-9233
227 Old Short Hills Rd Short Hills (07078) *(G-9982)*

Morgan Printing Service Inc 732 721-2959
333 S Pine Ave South Amboy (08879) *(G-10243)*

Morgan Technical Ceramics, Wood Ridge Also called Certech Inc *(G-12135)*

Morgan Towers Inc 856 786-7200
212 W Route 38 Ste 300 Moorestown (08057) *(G-6602)*

Morre-TEC Industries Inc 908 688-9009
1 Gary Rd Union (07083) *(G-11208)*

Morris County Duplicating 973 993-8484
8 Farview Ave Cedar Knolls (07927) *(G-1317)*

Morris County Imaging 973 532-7900
310 Madison Ave Ste 110 Morristown (07960) *(G-6728)*

Morris Industries Inc (PA) 973 835-6600
777 State Rt 23 Pompton Plains (07444) *(G-8963)*

Morris Plains Pip Inc 973 533-9330
465 W Mount Pleasant Ave Livingston (07039) *(G-5548)*

Morrison Press Inc 201 488-4848
10 Mckinley St Ste 3 Closter (07624) *(G-1764)*

Morristown Cycle 973 540-1244
103 Washington St Morristown (07960) *(G-6729)*

Morse Metal Products Co Inc (PA) 732 422-3676
1 Hunters Run Princeton (08540) *(G-9078)*

Morsemere Iron Works Inc 201 941-1133
1085 Linden Ave Ste 2 Ridgefield (07657) *(G-9376)*

Morton Salt Inc 732 826-8414
920 State St Perth Amboy (08861) *(G-8625)*

Mosaic Golf LLC 201 906-6136
900 Monroe St Apt 312 Hoboken (07030) *(G-4485)*

Moscova Enterprises Inc 848 628-4873
101 Hudson St Jersey City (07302) *(G-4786)*

Moser Jewel Company 908 454-1155
518 State Route 57 Phillipsburg (08865) *(G-8660)*

Mosse Beverage Industries LLC 732 977-5558
15 Osprey Ln Bayville (08721) *(G-258)*

Mosstype Corporation 201 444-8000
150 Franklin Tpke Waldwick (07463) *(G-11450)*

Mosstype Holding Corp (PA) 201 444-8000
150 Franklin Tpke Waldwick (07463) *(G-11451)*

Mostly Software Development, West Orange Also called First Mountain Consulting *(G-11894)*

Motif Industries Inc 973 575-1800
299 Ridgedale Ave Ste 5 East Hanover (07936) *(G-2229)*

Motion Control Tech Inc 973 361-2226
158 W Clinton St Ste Ff Dover (07801) *(G-2101)*

Motion Systems Corp 732 389-1600
600 Industrial Way W Eatontown (07724) *(G-2414)*

Motion Systems LLC (HQ) 212 686-4666
250 Passaic St Newark (07104) *(G-7245)*

Motomco, Woodland Park Also called Elaine Inc *(G-12217)*

Motor Sport Industry, East Brunswick Also called MCI Service Parts *(G-2166)*

Motors and Drives Inc (PA) 732 462-7683
5 Asbury Ave Freehold (07728) *(G-3672)*

Motors and Drives Inc 609 344-8058
1413 Marmora Ave Atlantic City (08401) *(G-103)*

Mount Hope Quarry, Parsippany Also called Tilcon New York Inc *(G-8102)*

Mountain Millwork 908 647-1100
142 Mountain Ave Warren (07059) *(G-11561)*

Mountain Printing Company Inc 856 767-7600
27 N Atlantic Ave Berlin (08009) *(G-438)*

Mountain Top Logging LLC 908 413-2982
99 Main St Lebanon (08833) *(G-5298)*

Movado Group Inc (PA) 201 267-8000
650 From Rd 375 Paramus (07652) *(G-7890)*

Movado Retail Group Inc 201 267-8000
650 From Rd Ste 375 Paramus (07652) *(G-7891)*

Mp Custom FL LLC 973 417-2288
624 Alps Rd Wayne (07470) *(G-11666)*

Mp Millwork, Wayne Also called Mp Custom FL LLC *(G-11666)*

MP Plastic Llc 973 279-9300
14 Florida Ave Paterson (07503) *(G-8342)*

Mp Production 973 729-9333
104 Hillside Rd Sparta (07871) *(G-10512)*

Mphase Technologies Inc (PA) 973 256-3737
777 Passaic Ave Ste 385 Clifton (07012) *(G-1676)*

Mplayer Entertainment LLC 302 229-3034
329 Greenleigh Ct Cherry Hill (08002) *(G-1402)*

Mpower Technologies Inc 973 256-3737
777 Passaic Ave Ste 385 Clifton (07012) *(G-1677)*

Mpt Delivery Systems Inc 973 278-0283
95 Prince St Paterson (07501) *(G-8343)*

Mpt Delivery Systems Inc 973 279-4132
95 Prince St Paterson (07501) *(G-8344)*

Mpt Industries 973 989-9220
85 Franklin Rd Ste 6b Dover (07801) *(G-2102)*

Mr Good Lube, Shrewsbury Also called Mister Good Lube Inc *(G-10006)*

Mr Green Tea Ice Cream Corp 732 446-9800
25 Church St Unit 104 Keyport (07735) *(G-5021)*

Mr Green Tea Ice Cream Corp 732 446-9800
42 E Front St Keyport (07735) *(G-5022)*

Mr Ice Buckets, New Brunswick Also called Buckets Plus Inc *(G-6949)*

Mr Pauls Custom Cabinets 732 528-9427
2416 Highway 35 Ste E Manasquan (08736) *(G-5875)*

Mr Quick Sign 201 670-1690
30 Dairy St Midland Park (07432) *(G-6233)*

Mr Quickly Inc 908 687-6000
1965 Morris Ave Union (07083) *(G-11209)*

MRC Global (us) Inc 732 225-4005
28 Kennedy Blvd Ste 100 East Brunswick (08816) *(G-2168)*

MRC Precision Metal Optics Inc. 941 753-8707
181 Legrand Ave Northvale (07647) *(G-7592)*

Mri International 973 383-3645
44 Clinton St Newton (07860) *(G-7397)*

Mri of West Morris PA 973 927-1010
66 Sunset Strip Ste 105 Succasunna (07876) *(G-10625)*

Mrl Manufacturing Corp 973 790-1744
59 Lee Ave Haledon (07508) *(G-4084)*

Mrs Fieldbrook Food, Lakewood Also called Mister Cookie Face Inc *(G-5161)*

Mrs Mazzulas Food Products 732 248-0555
240 Carter Dr Edison (08817) *(G-2577)*

Mrs Sullivans Inc (PA) 908 246-8937
1990 Washington Valley Rd Martinsville (08836) *(G-6010)*

Mrs. Sullivan's Pies, Martinsville Also called Mrs Sullivans Inc *(G-6010)*

Ms Health Software Corp 908 850-5564
128 Willow Grove St Hackettstown (07840) *(G-4027)*

MS Signs Inc 973 569-1111
6 Morris St Paterson (07501) *(G-8345)*

MSC Marketing & Technology 201 507-9100
808 Page Ave 8 Lyndhurst (07071) *(G-5694)*

Msg Fire & Safety Inc 732 833-8500
8 Short Hills Blvd Jackson (08527) *(G-4673)*

MSI, Middlesex Also called Maritime Solutions Inc *(G-6178)*

MSI, Palisades Park Also called Microsignals Inc *(G-7839)*

MSI Holdings LLC 732 549-7144
203 Norcross Ave Metuchen (08840) *(G-6115)*

MSI Technologies LLC (PA) 973 263-0080
1055 Parsippany Blvd 205a Parsippany (07054) *(G-8050)*

Msj Unlimited Services 201 617-0764
519 35th St Union City (07087) *(G-11258)*

Msn Pharmaceuticals Inc 908 360-1500
20 Duke Rd Piscataway (08854) *(G-8794)*

Mt Embroidery & Promotions LLC 201 646-1070
  1100 Blanch Ave Norwood (07648) *(G-7629)*

MTBC, Somerset *Also called Medical Transcription Billing (G-10133)*

Mtbc Health Inc (HQ) 732 873-5133
  7 Clyde Rd Somerset (08873) *(G-10140)*

Mtbc Practice Management Corp 732 873-5133
  7 Clyde Rd Somerset (08873) *(G-10141)*

Mteixeira Soapstone VA LLC 201 757-8608
  1100 Palisade Ave Fort Lee (07024) *(G-3570)*

MTI Solar, Somerset *Also called Materials Technology Inc (G-10131)*

Mtn Government Services Inc (HQ) 703 443-6738
  200 Telegraph Rd Holmdel (07733) *(G-4525)*

MTS Systems Corporation 856 875-4478
  745 Debra Dr Williamstown (08094) *(G-12093)*

Mualema LLC 609 820-6098
  2214 Town Ct N Lawrence Township (08648) *(G-5244)*

Mueller Die Cut Solutions Inc 201 791-5000
  150 N Midland Ave Saddle Brook (07663) *(G-9777)*

Muirhead Ringoes NJ Inc 609 695-7803
  1040 Pennsylvania Ave Trenton (08638) *(G-11082)*

Mul-T-Lock Usa Inc 973 778-3320
  100 Commerce Way Ste 2 Hackensack (07601) *(G-3948)*

Mulberry Metal Products Inc (PA) 908 688-8850
  2199 Stanley Ter Union (07083) *(G-11210)*

Mulbro Manufacturing & Svc Co 732 805-0290
  488 Lincoln Blvd Middlesex (08846) *(G-6182)*

Mule Road Pharmacy 732 244-3737
  600 Mule Rd Toms River (08757) *(G-10897)*

Multi Packaging Solutions Inc 908 757-6000
  901 Durham Ave South Plainfield (07080) *(G-10411)*

Multi-Pak Corporation 201 342-7474
  180 Atlantic St Hackensack (07601) *(G-3949)*

Multi-Pak Packaging, West Caldwell *Also called Jak Diversified II Inc (G-11781)*

Multi-Plastics Inc 856 241-9014
  210 Commodore Dr Swedesboro (08085) *(G-10713)*

Multi-Plastics Extrusions Inc 732 388-2300
  30 Production Way Avenel (07001) *(G-142)*

Multi-Tech Industries Inc 732 431-0550
  64 S Main St Marlboro (07746) *(G-5948)*

Multi-Tex Products Corp 201 991-7262
  54 2nd Ave Kearny (07032) *(G-4902)*

Multicomm Solutions Inc 877 796-8480
  1285 Rolls Ct Toms River (08755) *(G-10898)*

Multiforce Systems Corporation 609 683-4242
  101 Wall St Princeton (08540) *(G-9079)*

Multilink Technology Corp 732 805-9355
  300 Atrium Dr Fl 2 Somerset (08873) *(G-10142)*

Multimatic Dry Cleaning Mch, Northvale *Also called Multimatic LLC (G-7593)*

Multimatic LLC (PA) 201 767-9660
  162 Veterans Dr Northvale (07647) *(G-7593)*

Multipower International Inc 973 727-0327
  7 Woodshire Ter Towaco (07082) *(G-10999)*

Municipal Record Service, Audubon *Also called Corbi Printing Co Inc (G-116)*

Munipol Systems 856 985-2929
  1 Eves Dr Ste 111 Marlton (08053) *(G-5988)*

Munzing, Bloomfield *Also called Ultra Additives LLC (G-536)*

Munzing North America LP (HQ) 973 279-1306
  1455 Broad St Ste 3 Bloomfield (07003) *(G-523)*

Muralo Company Inc (PA) 201 437-0770
  148 E 5th St Bayonne (07002) *(G-238)*

Murdoch, J T Shoes, Bloomfield *Also called J T Murdoch Shoes (G-514)*

Murray Electronics Inc 201 405-1158
  12 Fox Ct Oakland (07436) *(G-7697)*

Murray Paving & Concrete LLC 201 670-0030
  210 S Newman St Ste 1 Hackensack (07601) *(G-3950)*

Musco Lighting, Wall Township *Also called Musco Sports Lighting LLC (G-11498)*

Musco Sports Lighting LLC 732 751-9114
  5146 W Hurley Pond Rd # 1 Wall Township (07727) *(G-11498)*

Muse Monthly LLC 609 443-3509
  192 Dorchester Dr East Windsor (08520) *(G-2362)*

Museami Inc 609 917-3000
  2 King Arthur Ct Ste A North Brunswick (08902) *(G-7528)*

Mushroom Wisdom Inc 973 470-0010
  1 Madison St Ste F6 East Rutherford (07073) *(G-2312)*

Music Trades Corp 201 871-1965
  80 West St Ste 200 Englewood (07631) *(G-2918)*

Music Trades Magazine, Englewood *Also called Music Trades Corp (G-2918)*

Musikraft, Landisville *Also called Applause Musical Products (G-5229)*

Musings Press Ltd Liability Co 347 210-8820
  1013 Palisade Ave Apt B1 Union City (07087) *(G-11259)*

Mv Laboratories Inc (PA) 908 788-6906
  843 State Route 12 B17 Frenchtown (08825) *(G-3704)*

Mvn Usa Inc 732 817-1400
  960 Holmdel Rd Holmdel (07733) *(G-4526)*

Mw Industries Inc 973 244-9200
  10 Audrey Pl Fairfield (07004) *(G-3265)*

Mwt Materials Inc 973 928-8300
  90 Dayton Ave Ste 6e Passaic (07055) *(G-8166)*

My House Kitchen Inc 201 262-9000
  492 N Rte 17 Paramus (07652) *(G-7892)*

My Magic 201 703-1171
  0 Plaza Rd Fair Lawn (07410) *(G-3105)*

My Way Prints Inc 973 492-1212
  1376 State Rt 23 Ste E Butler (07405) *(G-1014)*

Myat Inc (PA) 201 529-0145
  360 Franklin Tpke Mahwah (07430) *(G-5794)*

Mycone Dental Supply Co Inc (PA) 856 663-4700
  480 S Democrat Rd Gibbstown (08027) *(G-3792)*

Myers Group LLC 973 761-6414
  74 Blanchard Rd South Orange (07079) *(G-10310)*

Mylan Laboratories Inc 973 761-1600
  76 S Orange Ave Ste 301 South Orange (07079) *(G-10311)*

Myles F Kelly Inc 908 245-2033
  210 W Westfield Ave Roselle Park (07204) *(G-9700)*

Myos Rens Technology Inc 973 509-0444
  45 Horsehill Rd Ste 106 Cedar Knolls (07927) *(G-1318)*

Myriams Dream Book Bindery 609 345-5555
  1102 Atlantic Ave Atlantic City (08401) *(G-104)*

Mystic Timber LLC 908 223-7878
  95 Youmans Ave Washington (07882) *(G-11585)*

Mysuperfoods Ltd Liability Co 646 283-7455
  371 Springfield Ave Ste 2 Summit (07901) *(G-10651)*

Myx Beverage LLC 585 978-3542
  424 W 33rd St Ste 520 Secaucus (07094) *(G-9906)*

Myx Fusions, Secaucus *Also called Myx Beverage LLC (G-9906)*

N & J Machine Products Corp 973 589-0031
  52 Bruen St Newark (07105) *(G-7246)*

N B & Sons LLC 856 692-6191
  402 E Wheat Rd Vineland (08360) *(G-11382)*

N B C Engraving Co Inc 201 387-8011
  160 Woodbine St Bergenfield (07621) *(G-390)*

N C Carpet Binding & Equipment 973 481-3500
  858 Summer Ave Newark (07104) *(G-7247)*

N E A Products Co, Belleville *Also called Robert Freeman (G-315)*

N E R Associates Inc 908 454-5955
  45 Howard St Phillipsburg (08865) *(G-8661)*

N G C, Kendall Park *Also called Newtech Group Corp (G-4935)*

N J S, Flanders *Also called North Jersey Specialists Inc (G-3413)*

N J W Magazine 201 886-2185
  177 Main St Ste 232 Fort Lee (07024) *(G-3571)*

N Research, West Caldwell *Also called Neptune Research & Development (G-11792)*

N V E Pharmaceuticals, Andover *Also called V E N Inc (G-55)*

N W Sign Industries, Moorestown *Also called NW Sign Industries Inc (G-6603)*

N&K Trading Inc 609 616-3110
  1980 Us Highway 1 Bldg 3 North Brunswick (08902) *(G-7529)*

Naava Inc (PA) 844 666-2282
  21 Fadem Rd Ste 7 Springfield (07081) *(G-10566)*

Nabisco, Fair Lawn *Also called Mondelez Global LLC (G-3103)*

Nabisco, Fair Lawn *Also called Mondelez Global LLC (G-3104)*

Nabisco Royal Argentina Inc (HQ) 973 503-2000
  200 Deforest Ave East Hanover (07936) *(G-2230)*

Nablus Pastry & Sweets 973 881-8003
  1050 Main St Fl 1 Paterson (07503) *(G-8346)*

Nadri Inc 201 585-0088
  2 Executive Dr Ste 500 Fort Lee (07024) *(G-3572)*

Nahallac LLC 908 635-0999
  6 Carman Ln Whitehouse (08888) *(G-12047)*

Naluco Inc 800 601-8198
  23 Carol St Clifton (07014) *(G-1678)*

Namf, Fairfield *Also called New Age Metal Fabg Co Inc (G-3268)*

Nan Bread Distribution 201 475-9311
  41 Leliarts Ln Elmwood Park (07407) *(G-2838)*

Nan Ya Plastics Corp America (PA) 973 992-1775
  9 Peach Tree Hill Rd Livingston (07039) *(G-5549)*

Nan Ya Plastics Corp USA (HQ) 973 992-1775
  9 Peach Tree Hill Rd Livingston (07039) *(G-5550)*

Nana Creations Inc 201 263-1112
  329 Lincoln Ave Fort Lee (07024) *(G-3573)*

Nanasi Enterprises, Hackensack *Also called Nei Jewelmasters of New Jersey (G-3952)*

Nanion Technologies Inc 973 369-7960
  1 Naylon Pl Ste 3 Livingston (07039) *(G-5551)*

Nanking Express 732 549-7788
  1538 Oak Tree Rd Iselin (08830) *(G-4635)*

Nano-Optic Devices LLC 201 594-0226
  280 S Chestnut St Twp Washinton (07676) *(G-11143)*

Nanodesal, Pennington *Also called Rlct Industries LLC (G-8458)*

Nanonex Corp 732 355-1600
  1 Deerpark Dr Ste O Monmouth Junction (08852) *(G-6352)*

Nanoopto, Somerset *Also called API Nanofabrication & RES Corp (G-10059)*

Nanoopto Corporation 732 627-0808
  1600 Cottontail Ln Ste 1 Somerset (08873) *(G-10143)*

Nanopv Corporation (PA) 609 851-3666
  122 Mountainview Rd Ewing (08560) *(G-3038)*

Nanopv Technology, Ewing *Also called Nanopv Corporation (G-3038)*

Naomi Pet International Inc 201 660-7918
  20 Charles St Ste D Northvale (07647) *(G-7594)*

**A
L
P
H
A
B
E
T
I
C**

NAPA Auto Parts, Hackettstown *Also called Norms Auto Parts Inc* ***(G-4029)***
NAPA Concepts Ltd Liability Co 201 673-2381
36-3 Bergen Ridge Rd North Bergen (07047) ***(G-7470)***
Napco Separation Equipment Inc 908 862-7677
200 Marion Ave Linden (07036) ***(G-5414)***
Napoleon Spring Works Inc 973 278-5588
25 Empire Blvd South Hackensack (07606) ***(G-10279)***
Nardelli Bros Inc 856 692-0723
1145 N Main Rd Vineland (08360) ***(G-11383)***
Narva Inc 973 218-1200
101 Victory Rd Springfield (07081) ***(G-10567)***
NASA Machine Tools Inc 973 633-5200
1 Frassetto Way Ste B Lincoln Park (07035) ***(G-5330)***
Nasco Stone and Tile LLC 732 634-0589
200 Markley St Port Reading (07064) ***(G-8988)***
Nassau Communications Inc 609 208-9099
650 Whitehead Rd Lawrence Township (08648) ***(G-5245)***
Nassau Printers, Lawrence Township *Also called Nassau Communications Inc* ***(G-5245)***
Nassaus Window Fashions Inc 201 689-6030
799 N State Rt 17 Paramus (07652) ***(G-7893)***
Natal Lamp & Shade Corp 201 224-7844
5 Horizon Rd Apt 2601 Fort Lee (07024) ***(G-3574)***
Natale Machine & Tool Co Inc 201 933-5500
339 13th St Carlstadt (07072) ***(G-1191)***
Natali Vineyards LLC 609 465-0075
221 Route 47 N Cape May Court House (08210) ***(G-1116)***
Natalie Lamp & Shade, Fort Lee *Also called Natal Lamp & Shade Corp* ***(G-3574)***
Nathji Plus Inc 609 877-7600
1 Rose St Willingboro (08046) ***(G-12121)***
Naticchia's Custom Woodworking, Ewing *Also called Joseph Naticchia* ***(G-3028)***
National Auto Detailing Netwrk 856 931-5529
111 Harding Ave Bellmawr (08031) ***(G-348)***
National Casein New Jersey Inc 856 829-1880
401 Marthas Ln Cinnaminson (08077) ***(G-1480)***
National Certified Printing 609 443-6323
387 Mercer St A Hightstown (08520) ***(G-4313)***
National Christmas Pdts Inc 908 709-4141
2 Commerce Dr Cranford (07016) ***(G-1917)***
National Color Graphics 856 435-6800
1755 Wiliamstown Erial Rd Sicklerville (08081) ***(G-10021)***
National Communications Inc 973 325-3151
69 Washington St West Orange (07052) ***(G-11901)***
National Display Group Inc 856 661-1212
6850 River Rd Pennsauken (08110) ***(G-8553)***
National Diversified Sales Inc 559 562-9888
401 Bordentown Hedding Rd Bordentown (08505) ***(G-605)***
National Electric Wire Co Inc 609 758-3600
100 Goldman Dr Cream Ridge (08514) ***(G-1938)***
National Electronic Alloys Inc (PA) 201 337-9400
3 Fir Ct Oakland (07436) ***(G-7698)***
National Environmental Svcs Co (PA) 973 543-4586
7 Hampshire Dr Mendham (07945) ***(G-6090)***
National Environmental Svcs Co 908 813-1195
700 Grand Ave Hackettstown (07840) ***(G-4028)***
National Fence Systems Inc 732 636-5600
1033 Rte One Avenel Avenel (07001) ***(G-143)***
National Flag & Display Co Inc 973 366-1776
353 Richard Mine Rd Ste 5 Wharton (07885) ***(G-11993)***
National Fuel LLC 973 227-4549
287 Changebridge Rd Pine Brook (07058) ***(G-8710)***
National Gypsum Company, Burlington *Also called New Ngc Inc* ***(G-986)***
National Home Planning Service 973 376-3200
79 Thornley Dr Chatham (07928) ***(G-1335)***
National Housing Institute 973 509-1600
60 S Fullerton Ave # 206 Montclair (07042) ***(G-6424)***
National Labnet Co 732 417-0700
33 Wood Ave S Ste 600 Iselin (08830) ***(G-4636)***
National Lecithim Inc (PA) 973 940-8920
93 Spring St Ste 303 Newton (07860) ***(G-7398)***
National Manufacturing Co Inc 973 635-8846
12 River Rd Chatham (07928) ***(G-1336)***
National Metals, Middlesex *Also called National Mtal Fnshngs Corp Inc* ***(G-6183)***
National Mtal Fnshngs Corp Inc (PA) 732 752-7770
897 South Ave Middlesex (08846) ***(G-6183)***
National Paint Supply, North Brunswick *Also called Nautical Marine Paint Corp* ***(G-7530)***
National Paving Co Inc (HQ) 856 767-1950
148 Williamstown Rd Berlin (08009) ***(G-439)***
National Plastic Printing 973 785-1460
130 Furler St Totowa (07512) ***(G-10957)***
National Precision Tool Co 973 227-5005
24 Sherwood Ln Fairfield (07004) ***(G-3266)***
National Prtective Systems Inc 732 922-3609
1 Meridian Rd Eatontown (07724) ***(G-2415)***
National Public Seating, Clifton *Also called NPS Public Furniture Corp* ***(G-1685)***
National Refrigerants Inc 856 455-4555
661 Kenyon Ave Bridgeton (08302) ***(G-792)***
National Register Publishing, New Providence *Also called Marquis - Whos Who Inc* ***(G-7047)***
National Reprographics Inc 609 896-4100
3175 Princeton Pike Lawrenceville (08648) ***(G-5265)***
National Sports Sales, Belleville *Also called Red Diamond Company* ***(G-314)***
National Steel Rule Company (PA) 908 862-3366
750 Commerce Rd Linden (07036) ***(G-5415)***
National Steel Rule Company 800 922-0885
620 Commerce Rd Linden (07036) ***(G-5416)***
National Steel Rule Company 908 862-3366
712 Commerce Rd Linden (07036) ***(G-5417)***
National Strch Chem Holdg Corp (HQ) 908 685-5000
10 Finderne Ave Bridgewater (08807) ***(G-861)***
National Tax Training School, Mahwah *Also called Union Institute Inc* ***(G-5823)***
National Tree Company, Cranford *Also called National Christmas Pdts Inc* ***(G-1917)***
National Woodworking Co 908 851-9316
985 Tinkettle Turn Union (07083) ***(G-11211)***
Natl Adhesies Div of Henke 908 685-7000
10 Finderne Ave Bridgewater (08807) ***(G-862)***
Natural Dental Studios Inc 908 281-0089
216 Us Highway 206 Ste 23 Hillsborough (08844) ***(G-4357)***
Natural Flavors Inc 973 589-1230
268 Doremus Ave Newark (07105) ***(G-7248)***
Natural Green, Bridgewater *Also called J C W Inc* ***(G-848)***
Natural Wireless LLC 201 438-2865
23a Poplar St East Rutherford (07073) ***(G-2313)***
Nature Labs LLC 856 839-0400
46 N West Ave Ste B Vineland (08360) ***(G-11384)***
Naturee Nuts Inc 732 786-4663
636 N Michigan Ave Kenilworth (07033) ***(G-4979)***
Natures Beauty Marble & Gran 908 233-5300
2476 Plainfield Ave Scotch Plains (07076) ***(G-9852)***
Natures Choice Corporation (PA) 973 969-3299
482 Houses Corner Rd Sparta (07871) ***(G-10513)***
Natures Rule LLC 888 819-4220
1319 N Broad St Hillside (07205) ***(G-4431)***
Naturex Holdings Inc (HQ) 201 440-5000
375 Huyler St South Hackensack (07606) ***(G-10280)***
Naturex Inc 201 440-5000
125 Phillips Ave South Hackensack (07606) ***(G-10281)***
Naturex Inc (HQ) 201 440-5000
375 Huyler St South Hackensack (07606) ***(G-10282)***
Nautica Retail USA 212 541-5757
545 Washington Blvd Fl 8 Jersey City (07310) ***(G-4787)***
Nautical Marine Paint Corp (PA) 732 821-3200
1999 Elizabeth St North Brunswick (08902) ***(G-7530)***
Nautilus Neurosciences Inc 908 437-1320
135 Rte 202 Bedminster (07921) ***(G-281)***
Navinta LLC 609 883-1135
1499 Lower Ferry Rd Ewing (08618) ***(G-3039)***
Navistar Inc 856 486-2300
535 Route 38 Ste 300 Cherry Hill (08002) ***(G-1403)***
Naz-Dar/East, South Hackensack *Also called Process Supply Company Inc* ***(G-10291)***
Nb Bookbinding Inc 973 247-1200
356 Getty Ave Bldg 2 Clifton (07011) ***(G-1679)***
Nb Ventures Inc (PA) 732 382-6565
100 Walnut Ave Ste 304 Clark (07066) ***(G-1509)***
Nbs Group Sup Med Pdts Div LLC 732 745-9292
257 Livingston Ave Fl 3 New Brunswick (08901) ***(G-6983)***
Nbs Medical, New Brunswick *Also called Nbs Group Sup Med Pdts Div LLC* ***(G-6983)***
NC Carpet, Newark *Also called N C Carpet Binding & Equipment* ***(G-7247)***
Nconnex Inc 413 658-5582
1 Richmond St Apt 3079 New Brunswick (08901) ***(G-6984)***
Ncs Pearson Inc 201 896-1011
1099 Wall St W Lyndhurst (07071) ***(G-5695)***
Nds, Bordentown *Also called National Diversified Sales Inc* ***(G-605)***
Nds Technologies Inc 856 691-0330
891 E Oak Rd Unit B Vineland (08360) ***(G-11385)***
Nedco Conveyor Technology, Union *Also called Tarlton C & T Co Inc* ***(G-11227)***
Nedohon Inc (PA) 302 533-5512
302 E Newark Ave Wildwood Crest (08260) ***(G-12076)***
NEi Gold Products of NJ 201 488-5858
44 Burlews Ct Hackensack (07601) ***(G-3951)***
Nei House of Chains, Hackensack *Also called NEi Gold Products of NJ* ***(G-3951)***
Nei Jewelmasters of New Jersey (PA) 201 488-5858
44 Burlews Ct Hackensack (07601) ***(G-3952)***
Neighborhood Shoppers (PA) 856 988-7722
10000 Grntree Ctr Ste 201 Marlton (08053) ***(G-5989)***
Neill Supply Co, Lyndhurst *Also called Long Island Pipe of NJ* ***(G-5687)***
Neilmax Industries Inc 908 756-8800
15a Progress St Edison (08820) ***(G-2578)***
Nellsam Group Inc 201 951-9459
36 Washington Ave Fl 1 Cliffside Park (07010) ***(G-1543)***
Nema Associates Inc 973 274-0052
408 E Elizabeth Ave Linden (07036) ***(G-5418)***
Nema Food Distribution Inc 973 256-4415
18 Commerce Rd Ste D Fairfield (07004) ***(G-3267)***
Nephros Inc (PA) 201 343-5202
380 Lackawanna Pl South Orange (07079) ***(G-10312)***
Neptune Products Inc 973 366-8200
353 E Blackwell St Dover (07801) ***(G-2103)***

Neptune Research & Development 973 808-8811
   267 Fairfield Ave West Caldwell (07006) *(G-11792)*

Ner Data Products Inc (HQ) 888 637-3282
   307 Delsea Dr S Glassboro (08028) *(G-3810)*

Nes Company Inc 973 795-1519
   2500 Plz 5 Haborsde Finan Jersey City (07395) *(G-4788)*

Nes Enterprises Inc 201 964-1400
   513 Washington Ave Carlstadt (07072) *(G-1192)*

Nes Jewelry Inc 646 213-4094
   43 Samworth Rd Clifton (07012) *(G-1680)*

Nes Light Inc 201 840-0400
   1179 Edgewater Ave Ridgefield (07657) *(G-9377)*

Nesco, Mendham *Also called National Environmental Svcs Co (G-6090)*

Ness Plastics Inc 201 854-4072
   6040 Kennedy Blvd E 22f West New York (07093) *(G-11875)*

Nestle Beverage Division, Freehold *Also called Nestle Usa Inc (G-3673)*

Nestle Health Science, Bridgewater *Also called Nestle Healthcare Ntrtn Inc (G-863)*

Nestle Healthcare Ntrtn Inc (HQ) 952 848-6000
   1007 Us Hwy 202206 Bridgewater (08807) *(G-863)*

Nestle Infant Nutrition, Florham Park *Also called Gerber Products Company (G-3504)*

Nestle Usa Inc 732 462-1300
   61 Jerseyville Ave Freehold (07728) *(G-3673)*

Nestle Usa Inc 973 390-9555
   326 Smith St Keasbey (08832) *(G-4929)*

Netcom, Hackensack *Also called Network Communications Cons (G-3953)*

Netcom Systems Inc (PA) 732 393-6100
   200 Metroplex Dr Edison (08817) *(G-2579)*

Netfruits Inc 732 249-2588
   100 Jersey Ave New Brunswick (08901) *(G-6985)*

Netquest Corporation 856 866-0505
   523 Fellowship Rd Ste 205 Mount Laurel (08054) *(G-6822)*

Netscout Systems Inc 609 518-4100
   2000 Lincoln Dr E Marlton (08053) *(G-5990)*

Network Access Systems Incorpr 732 355-9770
   19 Issac Dr Dayton (08810) *(G-1981)*

Network Communications Cons 201 968-0684
   20 E Kennedy St Hackensack (07601) *(G-3953)*

Network Typesetting Inc 732 819-0949
   1637 Stelton Rd Ste B4 Piscataway (08854) *(G-8795)*

Netx Information Systems Inc (PA) 609 298-9118
   76 Auburn Rd Long Beach Township (08008) *(G-5618)*

Neu Inc 281 648-9751
   1 N Johnston Ave Ste 2 Hamilton (08609) *(G-4119)*

Neu Haus Inc 201 845-0040
   1 Garden State Plz Paramus (07652) *(G-7894)*

Neumann Sheet Metal Inc 908 756-0415
   759 North Ave Plainfield (07062) *(G-8867)*

Neurotron Medical Inc 609 896-3444
   800 Silvia St Ewing (08628) *(G-3040)*

Neuweiler, K H, Berkeley Heights *Also called Karl Neuweiler Inc (G-415)*

New Adventures LLC 973 884-8887
   6 Deforest Ave Ste 7 East Hanover (07936) *(G-2231)*

New Age Metal Fabg Co Inc 973 227-9107
   26 Daniel Rd W Fairfield (07004) *(G-3268)*

New American Therapeutics Inc 908 282-7444
   1069 Ringwood Ave 311b Haskell (07420) *(G-4211)*

New Art Ring Co, Maplewood *Also called Trimarco Inc (G-5929)*

New Brunswick Lamp Shade Co 732 545-0377
   7 Terminal Rd New Brunswick (08901) *(G-6986)*

New Brunswick Plating Inc (PA) 732 545-6522
   596 Jersey Ave New Brunswick (08901) *(G-6987)*

New Brunswick Saw Service Inc 732 287-4466
   400 Lincoln Blvd Middlesex (08846) *(G-6184)*

New Community Corp 973 643-5300
   200 S Orange Ave Newark (07103) *(G-7249)*

New Dawn Inc 732 774-1377
   60 Steiner Ave Neptune (07753) *(G-6925)*

New Dimensions Industries LLC 201 531-1010
   151 Cooper Rd West Berlin (08091) *(G-11736)*

New England Bedding Trnspt Inc 631 484-0147
   102 3rd Ave Kearny (07032) *(G-4903)*

New England Wood Crafters 856 241-9270
   226 Spruce Trl Swedesboro (08085) *(G-10714)*

New ERA Converting Machinery 201 670-4848
   235 Rt 20 N Paterson (07504) *(G-8347)*

New ERA Enterprises Inc 856 794-2005
   208 N West Blvd Newfield (08344) *(G-7368)*

New Great American Veal, Newark *Also called Dorzar Corporation (G-7141)*

New Heaven Chemicals Iowa LLC 201 506-9109
   18 Jenny Ln Sussex (07461) *(G-10675)*

New Horizon Graphics Inc 609 584-1301
   2 Christine Ave Trenton (08619) *(G-11083)*

New Horizon Press Publishers 908 604-6311
   34 Church St Liberty Corner (07938) *(G-5323)*

New Industrial Foam Corp 908 561-4010
   1355 W Front St Ste 3 Plainfield (07063) *(G-8868)*

New Jersey 50 Plus, Toms River *Also called Pentacle Publishing Corp (G-10901)*

New Jersey Air Products Inc 908 964-9001
   4 Mark Rd S Kenilworth (07033) *(G-4980)*

New Jersey Automotive Mag, Nutley *Also called Thomas Greco Publishing Inc (G-7654)*

New Jersey Balancing Svc Inc 973 278-5106
   138 Michigan Ave Ste 40 Paterson (07503) *(G-8348)*

New Jersey Bindery Svcs LLC 732 200-8024
   4301 New Brunswick Ave South Plainfield (07080) *(G-10412)*

New Jersey Bus & Indust Assn (PA) 609 393-7707
   10 W Lafayette St Trenton (08608) *(G-11084)*

New Jersey Business Magazine 973 882-5004
   310 Passaic Ave Ste 201 Fairfield (07004) *(G-3269)*

New Jersey Department Treasury 609 292-5133
   101 Carroll St Trenton (08609) *(G-11085)*

New Jersey Diamond Products Co 973 684-0949
   108 Kentucky Ave Paterson (07503) *(G-8349)*

New Jersey Drapery Service, Verona *Also called Proclean Services Inc (G-11309)*

New Jersey Electric Motors 908 526-5225
   84 Somerset St Ste A Somerville (08876) *(G-10221)*

New Jersey Eye Center Inc 201 384-7333
   1 N Washington Ave Bergenfield (07621) *(G-391)*

New Jersey Fence & Guardrail 973 786-5400
   32 Main St Andover (07821) *(G-53)*

New Jersey Gold Buyers Corp (PA) 732 765-4653
   460 County Road 520 Marlboro (07746) *(G-5949)*

New Jersey Hardwoods Inc 908 754-0990
   1340 W Front St Plainfield (07063) *(G-8869)*

New Jersey Headwear Corp 973 497-0102
   305 3rd Ave W Ste 5 Newark (07107) *(G-7250)*

New Jersey Herald (HQ) 973 383-1500
   2 Spring St Newton (07860) *(G-7399)*

New Jersey Jewish News (PA) 973 887-3900
   901 State Route 10 Whippany (07981) *(G-12027)*

New Jersey Jury, Springfield *Also called Jury Vrdict Rview Publications (G-10560)*

New Jersey Label LLC 201 880-5102
   30 Wesley St Unit 7 South Hackensack (07606) *(G-10283)*

New Jersey Line X, Bridgewater *Also called Chapter Enterprises Inc (G-827)*

New Jersey Monthly LLC 973 539-8230
   55 S Park Pl Morristown (07960) *(G-6730)*

New Jersey National Guard, Woodbury *Also called NJ Dept Military Vtrans (G-12165)*

New Jersey Polverizing, Bayville *Also called Ace-Crete Products Inc (G-247)*

New Jersey Porcelain Co Inc (PA) 609 394-5376
   600 Plum St Trenton (08638) *(G-11086)*

New Jersey Pulverizing Co Inc 732 269-1400
   250 Hickory Ln Bayville (08721) *(G-259)*

New Jersey Reprographics Inc 908 789-1616
   110 Center St Garwood (07027) *(G-3780)*

New Jersey Rivet Co LLC 856 963-2237
   1785 Haddon Ave Camden (08103) *(G-1077)*

New Jersey Stair and Rail Inc 732 583-8400
   746 Lloyd Rd Matawan (07747) *(G-6025)*

New Jersey Steel Corporation 856 337-0054
   2840 Mount Ephraim Ave Haddon Township (08104) *(G-4053)*

New Jersey Tech Group LLC 609 301-6405
   1632 Route 38 Lumberton (08048) *(G-5661)*

New Jersey Wire Cloth Co Inc 973 340-0101
   55 Park Slope Clifton (07011) *(G-1681)*

New Jrsey Sfood Mktg Group LLC 609 296-7026
   143 Leektown Rd Egg Harbor City (08215) *(G-2668)*

New Jrsey State Leag Mncplties 609 695-3481
   222 W State St Trenton (08608) *(G-11087)*

New Jrsy Glvnzng & Tnnng Wks 973 242-3200
   139 Haynes Ave Newark (07114) *(G-7251)*

New Life Color Reproductions 201 943-7005
   610 Broad Ave Ridgefield (07657) *(G-9378)*

New Life Pharma Ltd Lblty Co 201 784-7812
   265 Livingston St Northvale (07647) *(G-7595)*

New Life Resources Inc 201 750-7880
   153 Walnut St Northvale (07647) *(G-7596)*

New Line Prtg & Tech Solutions 973 405-6133
   790 Bloomfield Ave Ste 3 Clifton (07012) *(G-1682)*

New Manna Inc 973 675-8561
   426 Prospect St East Orange (07017) *(G-2261)*

New Ngc Inc 609 499-1323
   1818 River Rd Burlington (08016) *(G-986)*

New Satellite Network LLC 908 922-0967
   1942 Sunset Pl Scotch Plains (07076) *(G-9853)*

New Standard Printing Corp 973 366-0006
   118 Lincoln Ave Dover (07801) *(G-2104)*

New Top Inc 201 438-3990
   40 Broad St Carlstadt (07072) *(G-1193)*

New Venture Partners LLC 908 464-8131
   430 Mountain Ave Ste 404 New Providence (07974) *(G-7049)*

New View Media 973 691-3002
   1 Old Wolfe Rd Ste 203 Budd Lake (07828) *(G-938)*

New World International Inc 973 881-8100
   46 Lewis St Paterson (07501) *(G-8350)*

New World Leather, South Orange *Also called Myers Group LLC (G-10310)*

New World Stainless LLC 732 412-7137
   100 Randolph Rd Ste 5 Somerset (08873) *(G-10144)*

New York Blackboard of NJ Inc 973 926-1600
   83 Us Highway 22 Hillside (07205) *(G-4432)*

New York Botany Inc 201 564-7444
20 Charles St Ste B Northvale (07647) ***(G-7597)***
New York Daily News, Jersey City *Also called Daily News LP* ***(G-4736)***
New York Folding Box Co Inc 973 347-6932
20 Continental Dr Stanhope (07874) ***(G-10588)***
New York Fur, Fairview *Also called Prime Fur & Leather Inc* ***(G-3369)***
New York Kitchen Specialist, Springfield *Also called Narva Inc* ***(G-10567)***
New York Popular Inc 718 499-2020
400 Federal Blvd Carteret (07008) ***(G-1263)***
New York Poultry Co 908 523-1600
3351 Tremley Point Rd # 2 Linden (07036) ***(G-5419)***
New York-NJ Trail Conference (PA) 201 512-9348
600 Ramapo Valley Rd Mahwah (07430) ***(G-5795)***
Newage Painting Corporation 908 547-4734
78 Fillmore St Ste 7 Newark (07105) ***(G-7252)***
Newark Asphalt Corp 973 482-3503
1500 Mccarter Hwy Newark (07104) ***(G-7253)***
Newark Auto Products, East Orange *Also called Newark Auto Top Co Inc* ***(G-2262)***
Newark Auto Top Co Inc 973 677-9935
23 Centerway East Orange (07017) ***(G-2262)***
Newark Brush Company LLC 973 376-1000
1 Silver Ct Springfield (07081) ***(G-10568)***
Newark Fibers Inc (PA) 201 768-6800
28 Piermont Rd Rockleigh (07647) ***(G-9632)***
Newark Industrial Spraying 973 344-6855
12 Amsterdam St Newark (07105) ***(G-7254)***
Newark Ironworks Inc 973 424-9790
41 Frelinghuysen Ave # 43 Newark (07114) ***(G-7255)***
Newark Liner & Washer Inc 973 482-5400
819 Broadway Newark (07104) ***(G-7256)***
Newark Morning Ledger Co (PA) 973 392-4141
1 Gateway Ctr Ste 1100 Newark (07102) ***(G-7257)***
Newark Morning Ledger Co 732 560-1560
20 Duke Rd Piscataway (08854) ***(G-8796)***
Newark Morning Ledger Co 973 882-6120
26 Riverside Dr Pine Brook (07058) ***(G-8711)***
Newark Stamp & Die Works Inc 973 485-7111
35 Verona Ave Newark (07104) ***(G-7258)***
Newark Steel & Orna Sup Co, Newark *Also called Newark Ironworks Inc* ***(G-7255)***
Newark Trade Digital Graphics, Orange *Also called Newark Trade Typographers* ***(G-7823)***
Newark Trade Typographers 973 674-3727
177 Oakwood Ave Orange (07050) ***(G-7823)***
Newark Wire Cloth Company 973 778-4478
160 Fornelius Ave Clifton (07013) ***(G-1683)***
Newark Wire Works Inc 732 661-2001
1059 King Georges Rd 10 Edison (08837) ***(G-2580)***
Newbold Inc 732 469-5654
200 Egel Ave Middlesex (08846) ***(G-6185)***
Newbold Target, Middlesex *Also called Newbold Inc* ***(G-6185)***
Newcardio Inc 877 332-4324
103 Carnegie Ctr Ste 300 Princeton (08540) ***(G-9080)***
Newco Valves LLC 732 257-0300
19a Cotters Ln East Brunswick (08816) ***(G-2169)***
Newell Brands, Hoboken *Also called Jarden Corporation* ***(G-4477)***
Newell Brands Inc (PA) 201 610-6600
221 River St Ste 13 Hoboken (07030) ***(G-4486)***
Newfuturevest Two LLC (PA) 609 586-8004
17a Marlen Dr Trenton (08691) ***(G-11088)***
Newline Prtg & Tech Solutions 973 405-6133
1011 Us Highway 22 Ste 1 Mountainside (07092) ***(G-6884)***
Newman Glass Works Inc 215 925-3565
1515 Haddon Ave Camden (08103) ***(G-1078)***
Newman Ornamental Iron Works 732 223-9042
207 Union Ave Brielle (08730) ***(G-914)***
Newmans, East Brunswick *Also called Newco Valves LLC* ***(G-2169)***
Newmarket Pharmaceuticals LLC 609 252-9600
4 Pitcairn Ave Trenton (08628) ***(G-11089)***
News Inc Gloucester City 856 456-1199
34 S Broadway Gloucester City (08030) ***(G-3841)***
Newspaper Media Group LLC (PA) 856 779-3800
2 Executive Campus # 400 Cherry Hill (08002) ***(G-1404)***
Newspaper Media Group LLC 201 798-7800
447 Broadway Bayonne (07002) ***(G-239)***
Newtech Group Corp 732 355-0392
54 Inverness Dr Kendall Park (08824) ***(G-4935)***
Newton Biopharma Solutions LLC 908 874-7145
8 Fine Rd Hillsborough (08844) ***(G-4358)***
Newton Memorial Hospital Inc 973 726-0904
89 Sparta Ave Ste 210 Sparta (07871) ***(G-10514)***
Newton Screen Printing Co 973 827-0486
75 Main St Franklin (07416) ***(G-3602)***
Newton Screenprinting, Franklin *Also called Newton Screen Printing Co* ***(G-3602)***
Newton Tool, Newton *Also called T & M Newton Corporation* ***(G-7407)***
Newton Tool & Mfg Inc 856 241-1500
7249b Browning Rd Pennsauken (08109) ***(G-8554)***
Newtype Inc 973 361-6000
447 State Route 10 Ste 14 Randolph (07869) ***(G-9290)***
Nexagen Networks Inc (PA) 732 598-1277
704 Ginesi Dr Ste 21 Morganville (07751) ***(G-6649)***
Nexira Inc 908 704-7480
15 Somerset St Somerville (08876) ***(G-10222)***
Next Medical Products LLC 908 722-4549
45 Columbia Rd Branchburg (08876) ***(G-682)***
Nextgen Edge Inc 610 507-6904
50 Beacon Hill Rd Apt A West Milford (07480) ***(G-11855)***
Nextgen It LLC 908 837-9443
991 Us Highway 22 Ste 200 Bridgewater (08807) ***(G-864)***
Nextphase Medical Devices LLC (PA) 201 968-9400
150 Hopper Ave Waldwick (07463) ***(G-11452)***
Nextron Infusion Services, Fairfield *Also called Nextron Medical Tech Inc* ***(G-3270)***
Nextron Medical Tech Inc 973 575-0614
45 Kulick Rd Fairfield (07004) ***(G-3270)***
Nextwave Web LLC 973 742-4339
229 Marshall St Paterson (07503) ***(G-8351)***
Nexus Plastics Incorporated 973 427-3311
1 Loretto Ave Hawthorne (07506) ***(G-4249)***
Nexxbrands, West Long Branch *Also called Shrem Consulting Ltd Lblty Co* ***(G-11846)***
Nfs, Avenel *Also called National Fence Systems Inc* ***(G-143)***
Ngenious Solutions Inc 732 873-3385
30 Knightsbridge Rd # 525 Piscataway (08854) ***(G-8797)***
Niaflex Corporation 407 851-6620
9 Peach Tree Hill Rd Livingston (07039) ***(G-5552)***
Niagara Conservation Corp 973 829-0800
45 Horsehill Rd Ste 102 Cedar Knolls (07927) ***(G-1319)***
Nice Instrumentation 732 851-4300
205 Park Ave Manalapan (07726) ***(G-5855)***
Nichem Co 973 399-9810
750 Frelinghuysen Ave Newark (07114) ***(G-7259)***
Nicholas Galvanizing Co Inc 201 795-1010
120 Duffield Ave Jersey City (07306) ***(G-4789)***
Nicholas Longo Sr 856 642-1971
205 2nd St Riverton (08077) ***(G-9508)***
Nicholas Oliver LLC 732 690-7144
1933 State Route 35 Wall Township (07719) ***(G-11499)***
Nick's Railings, Kenilworth *Also called Nicks Inc* ***(G-4981)***
Nickel Artistic Services LLC 973 627-0390
39 Us Highway 46 Rockaway (07866) ***(G-9589)***
Nickel Savers 201 405-1153
90 Andrew Ave Oakland (07436) ***(G-7699)***
Nickels Carpet Cleaning 609 892-5783
957 Morningside Dr Mays Landing (08330) ***(G-6040)***
Nickels N Dimes LLC 732 886-5528
80 Gudz Rd Lakewood (08701) ***(G-5163)***
Nickolaos Kappatos Entps Inc 856 939-1099
1215 Black Horse Pike Glendora (08029) ***(G-3832)***
Nickos Construction Inc 267 240-3997
17 Arcadian Dr Sicklerville (08081) ***(G-10022)***
Nicks Inc 908 272-3739
39 N 23rd St Kenilworth (07033) ***(G-4981)***
Nicks Workshop Inc 856 784-6097
171 Clementon Rd W Gibbsboro (08026) ***(G-3788)***
Nicolosi Foods Inc 201 624-1702
2214 Summit Ave Union City (07087) ***(G-11260)***
Nicomac Systems Inc 201 871-0916
54 Summit St Norwood (07648) ***(G-7630)***
Nicos Group Inc 201 768-9501
80 Oak St Ste 201 Norwood (07648) ***(G-7631)***
Nifty Packaging, Old Bridge *Also called Rep Trading Associates Inc* ***(G-7792)***
Nighthawk Interactive LLC 732 243-9922
1090 King Georges Post Rd # 402 Edison (08837) ***(G-2581)***
Nijama Corporation 973 272-3223
132 Getty Ave Clifton (07011) ***(G-1684)***
Nike Inc 732 695-0108
1 Premium Outlet Blvd # 699 Tinton Falls (07753) ***(G-10842)***
Nikko Ceramics Inc (HQ) 201 840-5200
815 Fairview Ave Ste 9 Fairview (07022) ***(G-3366)***
Niko Trade Ltd-USA Inc 973 575-4353
271 Us Highway 46 D107 Fairfield (07004) ***(G-3271)***
Niksun Inc (PA) 609 936-9999
457 N Harrison St Princeton (08540) ***(G-9081)***
Nilsson Electrical Laboratory 201 521-4860
333 W Side Ave Jersey City (07305) ***(G-4790)***
Nine West Holdings Inc 908 647-6168
977 Valley Rd Gillette (07933) ***(G-3796)***
Nine West Holdings Inc 908 354-8895
651 Kapkowski Rd Ste 2032 Elizabeth (07201) ***(G-2758)***
Nine West Holdings Inc 201 541-7004
33 E Palisade Ave Englewood (07631) ***(G-2919)***
Nini Disposal 609 587-2411
410 Whitehead Rd Trenton (08619) ***(G-11090)***
Ninsa LLC 609 561-7103
125 Lincoln St Hammonton (08037) ***(G-4145)***
Nippon Benkan Kagyo 732 435-0777
475 Jersey Ave New Brunswick (08901) ***(G-6988)***
Nippon Paint (usa) Inc (HQ) 201 692-1111
300 Frank W Burr Blvd # 10 Teaneck (07666) ***(G-10762)***
Nippon Paint America, Teaneck *Also called Nippon Paint (usa) Inc* ***(G-10762)***
Nipro Glass Americas Corp 856 825-1400
1633 Wheaton Ave Millville (08332) ***(G-6314)***

Nipro Phrmpckging Amricas Corp (HQ)......856 825-1400
1200 N 10th St Millville (08332) ***(G-6315)***

Nirwana Foods LLC......201 659-2200
778 Newark Ave Jersey City (07306) ***(G-4791)***

Nistica Inc......908 707-9500
745 Us Highway 202/206 # 201 Bridgewater (08807) ***(G-865)***

Nitka Graphics Inc......201 797-3000
13-63 Henrietta Ct Fair Lawn (07410) ***(G-3106)***

Nitta Casings Inc......908 218-4400
141 Southside Ave Bridgewater (08807) ***(G-866)***

Nitto Inc (HQ)......732 901-7905
1990 Rutgers Blvd Lakewood (08701) ***(G-5164)***

Nitto Americas Inc......732 901-7905
1990 Rutgers Blvd Lakewood (08701) ***(G-5165)***

Nitto Americas Inc......201 645-4950
300 Frank W Burr Blvd Teaneck (07666) ***(G-10763)***

Nitto Denko Automotive, Lakewood *Also called Nitto Inc* ***(G-5164)***

Nitto Inc......732 901-0035
1975 Swarthmore Ave Lakewood (08701) ***(G-5166)***

NJ Advance Media LLC......732 902-4300
2015 State Route 27 # 300 Edison (08817) ***(G-2582)***

NJ Copy Center LLC......973 788-1600
10 Madison Rd Ste C Fairfield (07004) ***(G-3272)***

NJ Dept Military Vtrans......856 384-8831
658 N Evergreen Ave Woodbury (08096) ***(G-12165)***

NJ Fuel Haulers Inc......732 740-3681
3617 Us Highway 9 Old Bridge (08857) ***(G-7786)***

NJ Grass Choppers......732 414-2850
254 Monmouth Rd Manalapan (07726) ***(G-5856)***

NJ Logo Wear LLC......609 597-9400
100 Mckinley Ave Ste 6 Manahawkin (08050) ***(G-5832)***

NJ Memorial Art, Verona *Also called Ferrante Press Inc* ***(G-11306)***

NJ Paver Restorations LLC......732 558-6011
857 Amwell Rd Hillsborough (08844) ***(G-4359)***

NJ Precision Tech Inc......800 409-3000
1081 Bristol Rd Mountainside (07092) ***(G-6885)***

NJ Press Media......732 643-3604
3601 State Route 66 Neptune (07753) ***(G-6926)***

NJ Service Testing & Insptn......732 221-6357
26 Oak St Lincroft (07738) ***(G-5340)***

Njbia, Trenton *Also called New Jersey Bus & Indust Assn* ***(G-11084)***

Njiw Limited Liability Company......201 355-2955
87 Burlews Ct Hackensack (07601) ***(G-3954)***

Njr Clean Energy Ventures Corp......732 938-1000
1415 Wyckoff Rd Belmar (07719) ***(G-360)***

Njrls Enterprises Inc......732 846-6010
3380 Us Highway 22 3a Branchburg (08876) ***(G-683)***

Njs Associates Company......973 960-8688
1170 Route 22 Ste 209 Bridgewater (08807) ***(G-867)***

Nlyte Software Inc......732 395-6920
275 Raritan Center Pkwy Edison (08837) ***(G-2583)***

NM Knight Co Inc......856 327-4855
1001 S 2nd St Millville (08332) ***(G-6316)***

Nmn Closet Inc......201 438-2462
40 Veterans Blvd Carlstadt (07072) ***(G-1194)***

NMP Water Systems LLC......201 252-8333
63 Ramapo Valley Rd # 103 Mahwah (07430) ***(G-5796)***

Nmr Manufacturing LLC......908 769-3234
25 Davis St South Plainfield (07080) ***(G-10413)***

No Fire Technologies Inc......201 818-1616
5 James St South Hackensack (07606) ***(G-10284)***

Noah LLC......609 637-0039
610 Lawrenceville Rd Lawrenceville (08648) ***(G-5266)***

Nobel Biocare Procera LLC......201 529-7100
800 Corporate Dr Mahwah (07430) ***(G-5797)***

Nobelus LLC......800 895-2747
1665 Jersey Ave North Brunswick (08902) ***(G-7531)***

Noble Metals, Linden *Also called Express Printing Inc* ***(G-5372)***

Noble Metals Corp......908 925-6300
209 W Saint Georges Ave Linden (07036) ***(G-5420)***

Nobleworks Inc......201 420-0095
500 Paterson Plank Rd Union City (07087) ***(G-11261)***

Nogpo Inc......908 642-3545
4 Patriot Hill Dr Basking Ridge (07920) ***(G-200)***

Nokia Inc......908 582-3149
600-700 Mountain Ave Murray Hill (07974) ***(G-6895)***

Nokia of America Corporation (HQ)......908 582-3275
600 Mountain Ave Ste 700 New Providence (07974) ***(G-7050)***

Nomadic North America LLC......703 866-9200
46 Just Rd Fairfield (07004) ***(G-3273)***

Non Profit Times, Morris Plains *Also called Npt Publishing Group Inc* ***(G-6675)***

Nonzero Foundation Inc......609 688-0793
321 Prospect Ave Princeton (08540) ***(G-9082)***

Noodle Fan......732 446-2820
557 Englishtown Rd Monroe Township (08831) ***(G-6385)***

Noodle Gogo......908 222-8898
4811 Stelton Rd South Plainfield (07080) ***(G-10414)***

Noopys Research Inc......856 358-6001
108 Harding Hwy Newfield (08344) ***(G-7369)***

Norco Inc......908 789-1550
237 South Ave Garwood (07027) ***(G-3781)***

Norco Manufacturing Inc......201 854-3461
2025 85th St North Bergen (07047) ***(G-7471)***

Nordic Metal LLC......908 245-8900
500 S 31st St Kenilworth (07033) ***(G-4982)***

Nordson Efd LLC......609 259-9222
8 Applegate Dr Robbinsville (08691) ***(G-9519)***

Norland Products Inc......609 395-1966
2540 Us Highway 130 # 100 Cranbury (08512) ***(G-1863)***

Norlo of New Jersey LLC......646 492-3293
105 Alexander Ave Montclair (07043) ***(G-6425)***

Norma K Corporation......732 477-6441
30 Broadway Point Pleasant Beach (08742) ***(G-8924)***

Norman Weil Inc......201 940-7345
140 E Ridgewood Ave # 415 Paramus (07652) ***(G-7895)***

Norman Weil Textile, Paramus *Also called Norman Weil Inc* ***(G-7895)***

Norms Auto Parts Inc......908 852-5080
135 Willow Grove St Hackettstown (07840) ***(G-4029)***

Norpak Corporation (PA)......973 589-4200
70 Blanchard St Newark (07105) ***(G-7260)***

Norsal Distribution Associates......908 638-6430
150 Cregar Rd High Bridge (08829) ***(G-4298)***

North America Printing......973 726-7713
156 Woodport Rd Sparta (07871) ***(G-10515)***

North American Composites Co......609 625-8101
5450 Atlantic Ave Mays Landing (08330) ***(G-6041)***

North American Frontier Corp......201 222-1931
195 New York Ave Jersey City (07307) ***(G-4792)***

North American Illumination......973 478-4700
79 Commerce St Ste 2 Garfield (07026) ***(G-3743)***

North Bergen Asphalt, North Bergen *Also called Tilcon New York Inc* ***(G-7489)***

North Bergen Marble & Granite......201 945-9988
217 Palisade Ave Cliffside Park (07010) ***(G-1544)***

North Church Gravel Inc......201 796-1556
173 Oak Ridge Rd Oak Ridge (07438) ***(G-7663)***

North Eastern Business Forms......609 392-1161
1111 Chestnut Ave Trenton (08611) ***(G-11091)***

North Eastern Pallet Exchange......908 289-0018
725 Spring St Ste 2 Elizabeth (07201) ***(G-2759)***

North Jersey Com. Newspaper, Woodland Park *Also called Herald News* ***(G-12221)***

NORTH JERSEY MEDIA GROUP FOUNDATION, Woodland Park *Also called North Jersey Media Group Inc* ***(G-12225)***

North Jersey Media Group Inc (HQ)......201 646-4000
1 Garret Mountain Plz # 201 Woodland Park (07424) ***(G-12225)***

North Jersey Media Group Inc......201 933-1166
9 Lincoln Ave Rutherford (07070) ***(G-9741)***

North Jersey Media Group Inc......973 233-5000
130 Valley Rd Ste D Montclair (07042) ***(G-6426)***

North Jersey Media Group Inc......973 569-7100
1 Garret Mountain Plz # 201 Woodland Park (07424) ***(G-12226)***

North Jersey Media Group Inc......201 485-7800
6 Leighton Pl Mahwah (07430) ***(G-5798)***

North Jersey Metal Fabricators......973 305-9830
130 Ryerson Ave Ste 107 Wayne (07470) ***(G-11667)***

North Jersey Paper Products......973 372-4646
625 18th St Union City (07087) ***(G-11262)***

North Jersey Skein Dyeing Co......201 247-4202
152 Putnam St Paterson (07524) ***(G-8352)***

North Jersey Specialists Inc......973 927-1616
5 Laurel Dr Unit 6 Flanders (07836) ***(G-3413)***

North Jrsey Prsthtics Orthtics......201 943-4448
39 Broad Ave Palisades Park (07650) ***(G-7840)***

North Sales......732 528-8899
2422 Highway 34 Manasquan (08736) ***(G-5876)***

North Star Signs Inc......973 244-1144
3 Callan Ct Highland Lakes (07422) ***(G-4299)***

Northcott Silk USA Inc......201 672-9600
1099 Wall St W Ste 250 Lyndhurst (07071) ***(G-5696)***

Northeast Bindery Inc......908 436-3737
419 Trumbull St Elizabeth (07206) ***(G-2760)***

Northeast Chemicals Inc......732 238-9980
110 Tices Ln Ste 2-3 East Brunswick (08816) ***(G-2170)***

Northeast Con Pdts & Sup Inc......973 728-1667
937 Burnt Meadow Rd Hewitt (07421) ***(G-4291)***

Northeast Foods Inc......732 549-2243
1 Gourmet Ln Ste 1 # 1 Edison (08837) ***(G-2584)***

Northeast Medical Systems Corp......856 910-8111
901 Beechwood Ave Cherry Hill (08002) ***(G-1405)***

Northeast Precast Ltd Lblty Co......856 765-9088
92 Reese Rd Millville (08332) ***(G-6317)***

Northeast Pro-Tech Inc (PA)......973 777-5654
61 Willet St Bldg L Passaic (07055) ***(G-8167)***

Northeast Tomato Company Inc......973 684-4890
4 22 Erie St Paterson (07524) ***(G-8353)***

Northern Architectural Systems (PA)......201 943-6400
111 Central Ave Teterboro (07608) ***(G-10807)***

Northern Architectural Systems......201 943-6400
599 Gotham Pkwy Carlstadt (07072) ***(G-1195)***

ALPHABETIC

Northern State Periodicals LLC 973 782-6100
251 Vreeland Ave Ste B Paterson (07504) ***(G-8354)***
Northland Tooling Technologies 908 850-0023
999 Willow Grove St Ste 2 Hackettstown (07840) ***(G-4030)***
Northrop Grumman Systems Corp 908 276-6677
12 Park St Cranford (07016) ***(G-1918)***
Northstar Travel Media LLC (PA) 201 902-2000
100 Lighting Way Ste 200 Secaucus (07094) ***(G-9907)***
Northwest Instrument Inc 973 347-6830
69 King St Dover (07801) ***(G-2105)***
Northwind Ventures Inc 917 509-1964
39 Woodland Dr Vernon (07462) ***(G-11301)***
Norwalt Design Inc 973 927-3200
961 Route 10 E Ste 2a Randolph (07869) ***(G-9291)***
Norwood Industries Inc 856 858-6195
107 Norwood Ave Haddon Township (08108) ***(G-4054)***
Norwood Printing Inc 201 784-8721
530 Walnut St Norwood (07648) ***(G-7632)***
Noshpeak, Bloomfield *Also called Kandasamy Lingeswaran* ***(G-516)***
Notie Corp 609 259-3477
177 Route 526 Allentown (08501) ***(G-32)***
Nourhan Trading Group Inc 732 381-8110
27 Engelhard Ave Avenel (07001) ***(G-144)***
Nouveau Prosthetics Ltd 732 739-0888
984 State Route 36 Hazlet (07730) ***(G-4280)***
Nouveau Prosthetics Orthotics 732 739-0888
984 State Route 36 Hazlet (07730) ***(G-4281)***
Nouveautes Inc 973 882-8850
70 Clinton Rd Ste 1 Fairfield (07004) ***(G-3274)***
Nova Chemicals Inc 973 726-0056
56 Castlewood Trl Sparta (07871) ***(G-10516)***
Nova Flex Group 856 768-2275
1024 Industrial Dr West Berlin (08091) ***(G-11737)***
Nova Flex Group (HQ) 856 768-2275
1024 Industrial Dr West Berlin (08091) ***(G-11738)***
Nova Polymers Inc 973 227-6695
8 Evans St Fairfield (07004) ***(G-3275)***
Nova Precision Products Inc 973 625-1586
160 Franklin Ave Rockaway (07866) ***(G-9590)***
Novacote Flexpack, West Deptford *Also called Coim USA Inc* ***(G-11825)***
Novacyl Inc 609 259-0444
1 Union St Ste 108 Robbinsville (08691) ***(G-9520)***
Novaera Solutions Inc 732 452-3605
33 Wood Ave S Ste 600 Iselin (08830) ***(G-4637)***
Novaflex Industries Inc 856 768-2275
1024 Industrial Dr West Berlin (08091) ***(G-11739)***
Novapac Laboratories Inc 973 414-8800
510 Ryerson Rd Ste 1 Lincoln Park (07035) ***(G-5331)***
Novartis Corporation (HQ) 212 307-1122
1 S Ridgedale Ave East Hanover (07936) ***(G-2232)***
Novartis Corporation 862 778-8300
1 Health Plz East Hanover (07936) ***(G-2233)***
Novartis Corporation 973 503-7488
59 State Route 10 East Hanover (07936) ***(G-2234)***
Novartis Corporation 973 377-4794
25 Vreeland Rd B Florham Park (07932) ***(G-3512)***
Novartis Pharmaceuticals, East Hanover *Also called Novartis Corporation* ***(G-2233)***
Novartis Pharmaceuticals Corp (HQ) 862 778-8300
1 Health Plz East Hanover (07936) ***(G-2235)***
Novartis Pharmaceuticals Corp 862 778-8300
1 Health Plz East Hanover (07936) ***(G-2236)***
Novartis Pharmaceuticals Corp 973 538-1296
220 E Hanover Ave Morris Plains (07950) ***(G-6674)***
Novartis Pharmaceuticals Corp 862 778-8300
1 S Ridgedale Ave East Hanover (07936) ***(G-2237)***
Novasom Industries Inc 732 994-5652
15 Enclave Blvd Lakewood (08701) ***(G-5167)***
Novega Venture Partners Inc 732 528-2600
23 Main St Holmdel (07733) ***(G-4527)***
Novel Ingredient Services LLC 973 808-5900
43 West St East Hanover (07936) ***(G-2238)***
Novel Laboratories Inc 908 603-6000
400 Campus Dr Somerset (08873) ***(G-10145)***
Novel Technology Labs, Kearny *Also called A L Wilson Chemical Co* ***(G-4857)***
Novelty Cone Co Inc 856 665-9525
807 Sherman Ave Pennsauken (08110) ***(G-8555)***
Novelty Hair Goods Co 856 963-5876
1138 S Broadway 40 Camden (08103) ***(G-1079)***
Novembal USA Inc 732 947-3030
3 Greek Ln Edison (08817) ***(G-2585)***
Novitium Pharma LLC 609 469-5920
70 Lake Dr East Windsor (08520) ***(G-2363)***
Novo Nordisk Inc (HQ) 609 987-5800
800 Scudders Mill Rd Plainsboro (08536) ***(G-8894)***
Novo Nordisk Inc 609 987-5800
1100 Camput Rd Princeton (08540) ***(G-9083)***
Novotec Pharma LLC 609 632-2239
20 Spruce Meadows Dr Monroe Township (08831) ***(G-6386)***
Nowak Inc 973 366-7208
17 Robert St Wharton (07885) ***(G-11994)***

NP Bio Fuels LLC 856 467-2273
18 Reisling Pl Swedesboro (08085) ***(G-10715)***
NPS, East Hanover *Also called Novartis Pharmaceuticals Corp* ***(G-2235)***
NPS Public Furniture Corp 973 594-1100
149 Entin Rd Clifton (07014) ***(G-1685)***
Npt Publishing Group Inc 973 401-0202
201 Littleton Rd Ste 2 Morris Plains (07950) ***(G-6675)***
NRG Bluewater Wind LLC 201 748-5000
22 Hudson Pl Ste 3 Hoboken (07030) ***(G-4487)***
Nsgv Inc 212 620-2200
499 Washington Blvd Fl 9 Jersey City (07310) ***(G-4793)***
Nte Electronics Inc 973 748-5089
44 Farrand St Bloomfield (07003) ***(G-524)***
Ntt Electronics America Inc 201 556-1770
250 Pehle Ave Ste 706 Saddle Brook (07663) ***(G-9778)***
Nu Grafix Inc 201 413-1776
430 Communipaw Ave Jersey City (07304) ***(G-4794)***
Nu Products Seasonings, Oakland *Also called Goldstein & Burton Inc* ***(G-7690)***
Nu Steel, Avenel *Also called Tatara Group Inc* ***(G-155)***
Nu Tech, Franklin Lakes *Also called Nutech Corp* ***(G-3622)***
Nu World, Carteret *Also called Nu-World Corporation* ***(G-1264)***
Nu-EZ Custom Bindery LLC 201 488-4140
111 Essex St Ste 1 Hackensack (07601) ***(G-3955)***
Nu-Meat Technology Inc 908 754-3400
601 Hadley Rd South Plainfield (07080) ***(G-10415)***
Nu-Plan Business Systems Inc 732 231-6944
64 Washington St Clark (07066) ***(G-1510)***
Nu-Stent Technologies Inc 732 729-6270
1 Ilene Ct Hillsborough (08844) ***(G-4360)***
Nu-World Corporation (HQ) 732 541-6300
300 Milik St Carteret (07008) ***(G-1264)***
Nu-World Corporation 732 541-6300
340 Mill Rd Edison (08817) ***(G-2586)***
Nuance Communications Inc 201 252-9100
1111 Macarthur Blvd Mahwah (07430) ***(G-5799)***
Nuchas Tsq LLC 212 913-9682
5905 Kennedy Blvd North Bergen (07047) ***(G-7472)***
Nuclear Diagnostic Pdts Inc 856 489-5733
2 Keystone Ave Ste 200 Cherry Hill (08003) ***(G-1406)***
Nuclear Diagnostic Pdts Inc (PA) 973 664-9696
101 Round Hill Dr Ste 4 Rockaway (07866) ***(G-9591)***
Numerical Control Program Svc 856 665-8737
917 Northwood Ave Cherry Hill (08002) ***(G-1407)***
Numeritool Manufacturing Corp 973 827-7714
58 Woodland Rd Franklin (07416) ***(G-3603)***
Nutech Corp 908 707-2097
322 Freemans Ln Franklin Lakes (07417) ***(G-3622)***
Nutibles, East Hanover *Also called Capco Enterprises Inc* ***(G-2206)***
Nutra Nuts Inc (PA) 323 260-7457
247 Emmett Pl Ridgewood (07450) ***(G-9427)***
Nutra-Med Packaging Inc 973 625-2274
118 Algonquin Pkwy Whippany (07981) ***(G-12028)***
Nutri Sport Pharmacal Inc 973 827-9287
200 N Church Rd Franklin (07416) ***(G-3604)***
Nutri-Force Nutrition, North Bergen *Also called Vs Hercules LLC* ***(G-7492)***
Nutri-Pet Research Inc 732 786-8822
227 State Route 33 Ste 10 Manalapan (07726) ***(G-5857)***
Nutrition Zone, Hackettstown *Also called Ajj Powernutrition LLC* ***(G-3995)***
Nutro Laboratories Inc 908 755-7984
650 Hadley Rd Ste C South Plainfield (07080) ***(G-10416)***
Nutsco Inc 856 966-6400
1115 S 2nd St Camden (08103) ***(G-1080)***
Nvs International Inc 908 523-0266
1600 Lower Rd Linden (07036) ***(G-5421)***
NW Sign Industries Inc 856 802-1677
360 Crider Ave Moorestown (08057) ***(G-6603)***
NW Sign Industries Inc (PA) 856 802-1677
360 Crider Ave Moorestown (08057) ***(G-6604)***
Nwl Inc (HQ) 609 298-7300
312 Rising Sun Rd Bordentown (08505) ***(G-606)***
Nwl Capacitors, Bordentown *Also called Nwl Inc* ***(G-606)***
Nwl Transformers, Bordentown *Also called Megatran Industries* ***(G-601)***
Nxlevel Inc 609 483-6900
201 S Main St Ste 5 Lambertville (08530) ***(G-5219)***
Nxlevel Solutions, Lambertville *Also called Nxlevel Inc* ***(G-5219)***
Nyc Concrete Materials, Saddle Brook *Also called Eastern Concrete Materials Inc* ***(G-9763)***
Nyc Concrete Materials, Elmwood Park *Also called Local Concrete Sup & Eqp Corp* ***(G-2832)***
Nyc Rugs, Englewood *Also called Ben Aharon & Son Inc* ***(G-2875)***
Nyc Woodworking Inc 718 222-1221
39 Kingfisher Ct Marlboro (07746) ***(G-5950)***
Nylok Corporation 201 427-8555
S11 Thomas Rd S Hawthorne (07506) ***(G-4250)***
Nyltite Corp of America 908 561-1300
3451 S Clinton Ave South Plainfield (07080) ***(G-10417)***
Nymar Manufacturing Company 973 366-7265
215 State Route 10 2-4 Randolph (07869) ***(G-9292)***
Nyp Corp (frmr Ny-Pters Corp) (PA) 908 351-6550
805 E Grand St Elizabeth (07201) ***(G-2761)***

ALPHABETIC SECTION Omega Packaging Corp

O & S Research Inc......856 829-2800
1912 Bannard St Cinnaminson (08077) *(G-1481)*
O Berk Company LLC......201 941-1610
215 Bergen Blvd Fairview (07022) *(G-3367)*
O E M Manufacturers Ltd Inc......201 475-8585
65 Leliarts Ln Elmwood Park (07407) *(G-2839)*
O K Tool Corporation......908 561-9920
1233 North Ave Plainfield (07062) *(G-8870)*
O O M Inc......973 328-9408
387 Us Highway 46 Rockaway (07866) *(G-9592)*
O Plast Matic Valves Inc......973 256-3000
1384 Pompton Ave Ste 1 Cedar Grove (07009) *(G-1293)*
O S C, Clifton *Also called Oklahoma Sound Corp (G-1686)*
O S I Inc......732 754-6271
101 Hillside Ave Metuchen (08840) *(G-6116)*
O Stitch Matic Inc......201 861-3045
427 69th St Guttenberg (07093) *(G-3870)*
O T D Inc......973 890-7979
18 Furler St Totowa (07512) *(G-10958)*
O'Neil Color Compounding Corp, Garfield *Also called Primex Color Compounding (G-3750)*
O'Shea's Printing Services, Hackensack *Also called OShea Services Inc (G-3957)*
Oasis CD Manufacturing, Delair *Also called Audio and Video Labs Inc (G-2000)*
Oasis Entertainment Group......973 256-7077
17 Frederick Ct Cedar Grove (07009) *(G-1294)*
Oasis Foods Co, Hillside *Also called Oasis Trading Co Inc (G-4433)*
Oasis Trading Co Inc......908 964-0477
635 Ramsey Ave Hillside (07205) *(G-4433)*
Oav Air Bearing, Princeton *Also called Oavco Ltd Liability Company (G-9084)*
Oav Air Bearings, Hamilton *Also called Oavco Ltd Liability Company (G-4120)*
Oavco Ltd Liability Company (PA)......855 535-4227
103 Carnegie Ctr Princeton (08540) *(G-9084)*
Oavco Ltd Liability Company......609 454-5340
1800 E State St Ste 130 Hamilton (08609) *(G-4120)*
Oaviation Corporation......609 619-3060
103 Carnegie Ctr Ste 212 Princeton (08540) *(G-9085)*
Obare Services Ltd Lblty Co......908 456-1887
593 Meadow St Elizabeth (07201) *(G-2762)*
Oberg & Lindquist Corp (PA)......201 664-1300
671 Broadway Westwood (07675) *(G-11963)*
Object Design, Wharton *Also called AMS Products LLC (G-11978)*
Objectif Lune LLC (HQ)......973 780-0100
300 Broadacres Dr Ste 410 Bloomfield (07003) *(G-525)*
Objectif Lune LLC......203 878-7206
300 Broadacres Dr Ste 410 Bloomfield (07003) *(G-526)*
Objecutive Inc......201 242-1522
2125 Center Ave Ste 411 Fort Lee (07024) *(G-3575)*
Observer Park......201 798-7007
51 Garden St Hoboken (07030) *(G-4488)*
Observer, The, Kearny *Also called Hudson West Publishing Co (G-4882)*
Ocean City Coffee Company, Ocean City *Also called Coffee Company LLC (G-7750)*
Ocean City Coffee Company, Ocean City *Also called Coffee Company LLC (G-7751)*
Ocean City Sentinel The, Ocean City *Also called Sample Media Inc (G-7757)*
Ocean Drive Clothing Co., Kenilworth *Also called Ocean Drive Inc (G-4983)*
Ocean Drive Inc......908 964-2591
530 N Michigan Ave Kenilworth (07033) *(G-4983)*
Ocean Energy Industries Inc......954 828-2177
715 W Park Ave Unit 1073 Oakhurst (07755) *(G-7671)*
Ocean Power & Equipment Co......973 575-5775
1140 Bloomfield Ave # 107 West Caldwell (07006) *(G-11793)*
Ocean Power Technologies Inc (PA)......609 730-0400
28 Engelhard Dr Ste B Monroe Township (08831) *(G-6387)*
Ocean Star......732 899-7606
421 River Ave Point Pleasant Beach (08742) *(G-8925)*
Ocean-Craft International, Northfield *Also called Superior Jewelry Co (G-7564)*
Oceanic Graphic Intl Inc......201 883-1816
105 Main St Ste 1 Hackensack (07601) *(G-3956)*
Oceanic Graphic Printing, Hackensack *Also called Oceanic Graphic Intl Inc (G-3956)*
Oceanic Trading, Neptune *Also called Scaasis Originals Inc (G-6928)*
Oceanview Marine Welding LLC......609 624-9669
414 Wodbine Ocean View Rd Ocean View (08230) *(G-7765)*
Ocsidot Inc......908 789-3300
116 South Ave Garwood (07027) *(G-3782)*
Octal Corporation......201 862-1010
125 Galway Pl Ste B Teaneck (07666) *(G-10764)*
Octopus Yachts Ltd Lblty Co......732 698-8550
2400 Belmar Blvd Ste C-1 Belmar (07719) *(G-361)*
Odyssey Auto Specialty Inc......973 328-2667
317 Richard Mine Rd Wharton (07885) *(G-11995)*
Odyssey of The Mind, Sewell *Also called Creative Competitions Inc (G-9949)*
Oe Solutions America Inc......201 568-1188
65 Challenger Rd Ste 240 Ridgefield Park (07660) *(G-9411)*
Oeg Building Materials Inc......732 667-3636
6001 Bordentown Ave Sayreville (08872) *(G-9834)*
Off-Road Welding Inc......908 832-2967
417 Little Brook Rd Glen Gardner (08826) *(G-3816)*
Office Needs Inc......732 381-7770
1120 Raritan Rd Ste 2 Clark (07066) *(G-1511)*
Officeclocks.com, Bridgewater *Also called Garrett Moore (G-840)*
Officemate International Corp (PA)......732 225-7422
90 Newfeld Ave Rritan Ctr Raritan Ctr Edison (08837) *(G-2587)*
Offshore Enterprises Inc......609 345-9099
433 N Maryland Ave Atlantic City (08401) *(G-105)*
Oggi Media Group LLC......201 358-6582
475 Walnut St Norwood (07648) *(G-7633)*
Ogura Industrial Corp (HQ)......586 749-1900
100 Randolph Rd Somerset (08873) *(G-10146)*
Ohaus Corporation (HQ)......973 377-9000
7 Campus Dr Ste 310 Parsippany (07054) *(G-8051)*
OHM Equipment LLC......856 765-3011
2525 S 2nd St Millville (08332) *(G-6318)*
OHM Laboratories Inc (HQ)......732 418-2235
1385 Livingston Ave North Brunswick (08902) *(G-7532)*
OHM Laboratories Inc......609 720-9200
2 Independence Way Princeton (08540) *(G-9086)*
OHM Laboratories Inc......732 514-1072
14 Terminal Rd New Brunswick (08901) *(G-6989)*
Oia, Bogota *Also called Organize It All Inc (G-549)*
Oil Technologies Services Inc (PA)......856 845-4142
1501 Grandview Ave Ste 1 Paulsboro (08066) *(G-8422)*
Oil Technologies Services Inc......856 845-4142
1501 Grandview Ave Ste 1 Paulsboro (08066) *(G-8423)*
Oil Technologies Services Inc......856 845-4142
1177 W Elizabeth Ave Linden (07036) *(G-5422)*
Oilco Liquid Handling Systems, Monmouth Junction *Also called Valeur Corporation (G-6369)*
Oiltest Inc......908 245-9330
109 Aldene Rd Ste 4 Roselle (07203) *(G-9678)*
OK Tool & Die Company Inc......856 629-5757
603 Blue Bell Rd Williamstown (08094) *(G-12094)*
Oklahoma Sound Corp (PA)......800 261-4112
149 Entin Rd Clifton (07014) *(G-1686)*
Okonite Company (PA)......201 825-0300
102 Hilltop Rd Ramsey (07446) *(G-9250)*
Okonite Company......201 825-0300
959 Market St Paterson (07513) *(G-8355)*
Okonite Company......212 239-0660
3 Garret Mountain Plz # 304 Woodland Park (07424) *(G-12227)*
Old Barracks Association Inc......609 396-1776
101 Barrack St Trenton (08608) *(G-11092)*
OLD BARRACKS MUSEUM, Trenton *Also called Old Barracks Association Inc (G-11092)*
Old Bridge Chemicals Inc......732 727-2225
554 Water Works Rd Old Bridge (08857) *(G-7787)*
Old Fashion Kitchen Inc (PA)......732 364-4100
1045 Towbin Ave Lakewood (08701) *(G-5168)*
Old Fashion Woodworking Inc......973 808-9663
273 E Inman Ave Rahway (07065) *(G-9216)*
Old Fashioned Kitchen, Lakewood *Also called Old Fashion Kitchen Inc (G-5168)*
Old Hights Print Shop Inc......609 443-4700
16 Nancy Ct Jackson (08527) *(G-4674)*
Old Monmouth Candy Co, Freehold *Also called Old Monmouth Peanut Brittle Co (G-3674)*
Old Monmouth Peanut Brittle Co......732 462-1311
627 Park Ave Freehold (07728) *(G-3674)*
Old York Cellars......908 284-9463
80 Old York Rd Ringoes (08551) *(G-9441)*
Oldcastle Apg Northeast, Brick *Also called Crh Americas Inc (G-741)*
Oldcastle Buildingenvelope Inc......856 234-9222
1500 Glen Ave Moorestown (08057) *(G-6605)*
Olde Grandad Industries Inc......201 997-1899
1 Market St Ste 15 Passaic (07055) *(G-8168)*
Oli Systems Inc......973 539-4996
240 Cedar Knolls Rd # 301 Cedar Knolls (07927) *(G-1320)*
Olivos USA Inc (HQ)......201 893-0142
1 Bridge Plz N Ste 275 Fort Lee (07024) *(G-3576)*
Olon USA Inc......973 577-6038
100 Campus Dr Ste 105 Florham Park (07932) *(G-3513)*
Olsen, H Machine, Cinnaminson *Also called Henry Olsen Machine (G-1467)*
Olympia Lighting Inc......201 812-7880
148 Veterans Dr Northvale (07647) *(G-7598)*
Olympic Custom Tools, Kinnelon *Also called Olympic EDM Services Inc (G-5039)*
Olympic EDM Services Inc......973 492-0664
20 Kiel Ave Kinnelon (07405) *(G-5039)*
Omaha Standard Inc Tr NJ......609 588-5400
572 Whitehead Rd Trenton (08619) *(G-11093)*
Omaha Standards, Trenton *Also called Palfinger North America (G-11095)*
Omega Circuit and Engineering......732 246-1661
8 Terminal Rd New Brunswick (08901) *(G-6990)*
Omega Engineering Inc......856 467-4200
1 Killdeer Ct Swedesboro (08085) *(G-10716)*
Omega Engineering Inc......856 467-4200
1 Omega Cir Bridgeport (08014) *(G-769)*
Omega Graphics, Shrewsbury *Also called Dcg Printing Inc (G-9996)*
Omega Heat Transfer Co Inc......732 340-0023
36 Rock Spring Ave West Orange (07052) *(G-11902)*
Omega Packaging Corp......973 890-9505
55 Kings Rd Totowa (07512) *(G-10959)*

ALPHABETIC

Omega Plastics Corp (HQ)..201 507-9100
  Page & Schuyler Ave Ste 5 Lyndhurst (07071) *(G-5697)*
Omega Process Controls, Bridgeport *Also called Omega Engineering Inc (G-769)*
Omega Shielding Products Inc..................................973 366-0080
  9 Emery Ave Randolph (07869) *(G-9293)*
Omega Tool Die...856 228-7100
  8 International Ave Sewell (08080) *(G-9963)*
Omg Electronic Chemicals Inc.................................908 222-5800
  400 Corporate Ct Ste A South Plainfield (07080) *(G-10418)*
Omni Baking Company LLC..856 205-1485
  2621 Freddy Ln Bldg 7 Vineland (08360) *(G-11386)*
Omni Wall Coverings, Edison *Also called W C Omni Incorporated (G-2648)*
Omnia Industries Inc..973 239-7272
  5 Cliffside Dr Cedar Grove (07009) *(G-1295)*
Omniactive Hlth Tchnlogies Inc (HQ).........................866 588-3629
  67 E Park Pl Ste 500 Morristown (07960) *(G-6731)*
Omniflow USA, Springfield *Also called I4 Sustainability LLC (G-10557)*
Omnitester Corp (PA)...856 985-8960
  101 Flintlock Ln Marlton (08053) *(G-5991)*
Omp Technologies Inc..973 808-8500
  24 Commerce Rd Ste H Fairfield (07004) *(G-3276)*
Omthera Pharmaceuticals Inc....................................908 741-4399
  707 State Rd Ste 206 Princeton (08540) *(G-9087)*
On Demand Machinery..908 351-7137
  150 Broadway Elizabeth (07206) *(G-2763)*
On Demand Print Group..201 636-2270
  442 Valley Brook Ave Lyndhurst (07071) *(G-5698)*
On Site Communication..201 488-4123
  15 Worth St South Hackensack (07606) *(G-10285)*
On Site Manufacturing Inc..812 794-6040
  1042 County Road 523 Flemington (08822) *(G-3458)*
Onco Inc...732 292-7460
  1451 State Route 34 # 302 Wall Township (07727) *(G-11500)*
Oncobiologics Inc..609 619-3990
  7 Clarke Dr Cranbury (08512) *(G-1864)*
Oncode-Med Inc...908 998-3647
  11 Georgetown Ct Basking Ridge (07920) *(G-201)*
One Two Three Inc..856 251-1238
  537 Mantua Pike Ste B Woodbury (08096) *(G-12166)*
One Click Cleaners..732 804-9802
  43 Kipling Way Manalapan (07726) *(G-5858)*
One Source Solutions LLC...732 536-0578
  3 Industrial Ct Ste 3 # 3 Freehold (07728) *(G-3675)*
One-Source Communications.......................................973 463-0250
  9 Whippany Rd Bldg C-4 Whippany (07981) *(G-12029)*
ONeal Flat Rolled Metals LLC...................................609 395-7007
  1 Fitzgerald Ave Monroe Township (08831) *(G-6388)*
Oneder, Newark *Also called Specialneedsware Inc (G-7323)*
Onguard Fence Systems Ltd.......................................908 429-5522
  18 Culnen Dr Branchburg (08876) *(G-684)*
Onguard Fence Systems Ltd.......................................908 429-5522
  18 Culnen Dr Branchburg (08876) *(G-685)*
Onkos Surgical Inc...973 264-5400
  77 E Halsey Rd Parsippany (07054) *(G-8052)*
Onpharma Inc...408 335-6850
  400 Somerset Corporate Bl Bridgewater (08807) *(G-868)*
Ont Sutter...201 265-0262
  17c Palisade Ave Emerson (07630) *(G-2861)*
Ontimeworks LLC...800 689-3568
  1253 Springfield Ave New Providence (07974) *(G-7051)*
Onwards Inc...732 309-7348
  10 Connor Dr Manalapan (07726) *(G-5859)*
Onx USA LLC...440 569-2417
  274 Raritan Center Pkwy Edison (08837) *(G-2588)*
Onyx Graphics LLC..908 281-0038
  115 Stryker Ln Ste 4 Hillsborough (08844) *(G-4361)*
Onyx Valve, Cinnaminson *Also called Armadillo Automation Inc (G-1447)*
Opalsoft Consulting, Cherry Hill *Also called MD International Inc (G-1397)*
Opdyke Awnings Inc...732 449-5940
  2036 State Route 35 Wall Township (07719) *(G-11501)*
Open Solutions Inc..856 424-0150
  2091 Springdale Rd Ste 7 Cherry Hill (08003) *(G-1408)*
Open Terra Inc...732 765-9600
  20 Reddington Dr Matawan (07747) *(G-6026)*
Opex Corporation..856 727-1100
  835 Lancer Dr Moorestown (08057) *(G-6606)*
Opici Import Co Inc..201 689-3256
  25 De Boer Dr Glen Rock (07452) *(G-3827)*
Oppenheim Plastics Co Inc...201 995-9595
  90 Broadway Woodcliff Lake (07677) *(G-12197)*
Opt, Monroe Township *Also called Ocean Power Technologies Inc (G-6387)*
Opt-Sciences Corporation (PA)...................................856 829-2800
  1912 Bannard St Cinnaminson (08077) *(G-1482)*
Optequip Inc..609 758-8609
  176 Burlington Path Rd Cream Ridge (08514) *(G-1939)*
Optherium Labs Ou...516 253-1777
  21 Riverside Ln Holmdel (07733) *(G-4528)*
Optics Plastics..201 939-3344
  537 New York Ave Lyndhurst (07071) *(G-5699)*

Optimer Pharmaceuticals LLC....................................858 909-0736
  2000 Galloping Hill Rd Kenilworth (07033) *(G-4984)*
Optimum Precision Inc..908 259-9017
  147 N Michigan Ave Kenilworth (07033) *(G-4985)*
Optimum Precision Machine & TI, Kenilworth *Also called Optimum Precision Inc (G-4985)*
Options Edge LLC...973 701-0051
  53 Division Ave Apt 12 Summit (07901) *(G-10652)*
Oracle America Inc...732 623-4821
  399 Thornall St Ste 39 Edison (08837) *(G-2589)*
Oracle America Inc...609 750-0640
  1 Meadowlands Plz Ste 700 East Rutherford (07073) *(G-2314)*
Oracle Corporation..908 547-6200
  400 Crossing Blvd Fl 6 Bridgewater (08807) *(G-869)*
Oracle Corporation..201 842-7000
  1 Meadowlands Plz # 1400 East Rutherford (07073) *(G-2315)*
Oral Fixation LLC..609 937-9972
  53 Railroad Pl A Hopewell (08525) *(G-4543)*
Oral Manufacturing, Eatontown *Also called Hikma Pharmaceuticals USA Inc (G-2403)*
Orange Mattress, Maplewood *Also called Custom Bedding Co (G-5917)*
Orange Sanitary, Orange *Also called Serranis Bakery (G-7827)*
Orangehrm Inc...914 458-4254
  538 Teal Plz Secaucus (07094) *(G-9908)*
Orbcomm LLC (HQ)..703 433-6300
  395 W Passaic St Ste 3 Rochelle Park (07662) *(G-9532)*
Orcas International Inc..973 448-2801
  9 Lenel Rd Landing (07850) *(G-5225)*
Orcas Naturals, Landing *Also called Orcas International Inc (G-5225)*
Orchid Chemicals, Princeton *Also called Orchid Pharmaceuticals Inc (G-9088)*
Orchid Pharmaceuticals Inc..609 951-2209
  116 Village Blvd Ste 200 Princeton (08540) *(G-9088)*
Orens Daily Roast Inc..201 432-2008
  430 Communipaw Ave Ste 13 Jersey City (07304) *(G-4795)*
Organica Aromatics Corp..609 443-3333
  20 Lake D East Windsor (08520) *(G-2364)*
Organica Water Inc (PA)..609 651-8885
  61 Prnceton Hightstown Rd West Windsor (08550) *(G-11909)*
Organics Corporation America.....................................973 890-9002
  55 W End Rd Totowa (07512) *(G-10960)*
Organize It All Inc (PA)..201 488-0808
  24 River Rd Ste 201 Bogota (07603) *(G-549)*
Organon USA Inc...908 423-1000
  1 Merck Dr Whitehouse Station (08889) *(G-12059)*
Orgo-Thermit Inc (PA)...732 657-5781
  3500 Colonial Dr Manchester (08759) *(G-5887)*
Orient Corporation of America (HQ)............................908 298-0990
  6 Commerce Dr Ste 301 Cranford (07016) *(G-1919)*
Orient Originals Inc...201 332-5005
  55 Edward Hart Dr Jersey City (07305) *(G-4796)*
Original Bagel & Bialy Co Inc......................................973 227-5777
  2 Fairfield Cres West Caldwell (07006) *(G-11794)*
Original Miami Onion Roll Inc......................................973 389-2202
  111 Berkshire Ave Paterson (07502) *(G-8356)*
Orion Cloud Cmpt Solutions Inc..................................732 485-8658
  1200 Rte 22 Ste 2000 Bridgewater (08807) *(G-870)*
Orion Machinery Co Ltd...201 569-3220
  301 Veterans Blvd Rutherford (07070) *(G-9742)*
Orion Precision Industries..732 247-9704
  8 Veronica Ave Somerset (08873) *(G-10147)*
Orlando Systems Ltd Lblty Co.....................................908 400-5052
  375 North Dr Apt A10 North Plainfield (07060) *(G-7560)*
Orlando's Italian Bakery, Lodi *Also called Dina Hernandez (G-5581)*
Ornate Millwork LLC..866 464-5596
  15 Hazelwood Ln Lakewood (08701) *(G-5169)*
Orora Packaging Solutions..609 249-5200
  1 Capital Dr Ste 102 Cranbury (08512) *(G-1865)*
Orora Visual LLC...973 916-2804
  1155 Bloomfield Ave Clifton (07012) *(G-1687)*
Oroszlany Laszlo...201 666-2101
  121 Patterson St Hillsdale (07642) *(G-4386)*
Orsillo & Company...973 248-1833
  189 Berdan Ave Wayne (07470) *(G-11668)*
Ortho Biotech Products LP..908 541-4000
  430 Route 22 Bridgewater (08807) *(G-871)*
Ortho-Clinical Diagnostics Inc (PA)............................908 218-8000
  1001 Us Highway 202 Raritan (08869) *(G-9314)*
Ortho-Dynamics Inc..973 742-4390
  210 E 16th St Paterson (07524) *(G-8357)*
Ortho-Mcneil Phrm Inc, Raritan *Also called Ortho-Mcneil Phrm LLC (G-9315)*
Ortho-Mcneil Phrm LLC (HQ)......................................908 203-4090
  1000 Rte 202 Raritan (08869) *(G-9315)*
Orthodox Baking Co Inc...973 844-9393
  555 Cortlandt St Belleville (07109) *(G-309)*
Orthofeet Inc..800 524-2845
  152 Veterans Dr Ste A Northvale (07647) *(G-7599)*
Orycon Control Technology Inc....................................732 922-2400
  3407 Rose Ave Ocean (07712) *(G-7732)*
Os33 Services Corp (PA)...866 796-0310
  120 Wood Ave S Ste 505 Iselin (08830) *(G-4638)*

(G-0000) Company's Geographic Section entry number

Osem USA Inc 201 871-4433
333 Sylvan Ave Ste 302 Englewood Cliffs (07632) *(G-2976)*

OSG Billing Services, Ridgefield Park *Also called Output Services Group Inc* *(G-9412)*

OShea Services Inc 201 343-8668
483 Main St Hackensack (07601) *(G-3957)*

OSI Laser Diode Inc 732 549-9001
4 Olsen Ave Edison (08820) *(G-2590)*

Ossb and L Pharma LLC 732 940-8701
6 Bel Air Ct Milltown (08850) *(G-6270)*

Ossur Americas Inc 856 345-6000
680 Grove Rd West Deptford (08086) *(G-11837)*

Osteotech Inc 732 544-5942
51 James Way Eatontown (07724) *(G-2416)*

Osteotech Inc (HQ) 732 542-2800
51 James Way Eatontown (07724) *(G-2417)*

Osteotech Inc 732 542-2800
201 Industrial Way W Eatontown (07724) *(G-2418)*

OSullivan Communications Corp (PA) 973 227-5112
1 Fairfield Cres West Caldwell (07006) *(G-11795)*

Otex Specialty Narrow Fabrics (PA) 908 879-3636
4 Essex Ave Ste 403 Bernardsville (07924) *(G-452)*

Oti America Inc 732 429-1900
517 Us Highway 1 S # 2150 Iselin (08830) *(G-4639)*

Oticon Inc (HQ) 732 560-1220
580 Howard Ave Somerset (08873) *(G-10148)*

Oticon Medical LLC 732 560-0727
580 Howard Ave Somerset (08873) *(G-10149)*

Otis Elevator Company 856 235-5200
30 Twosome Dr Ste 4 Moorestown (08057) *(G-6607)*

Otis Elevator Intl Inc 973 575-7030
105 Fairfield Rd Fairfield (07004) *(G-3277)*

Otis Graphics Inc 201 438-7120
290 Grant Ave Lyndhurst (07071) *(G-5700)*

Our Town, Maywood *Also called Jimcam Publishing Inc (G-6055)*

Outfront Media LLC 973 575-6900
185 Us Highway 46 Fairfield (07004) *(G-3278)*

Output Services Group Inc (PA) 201 871-1100
100 Challenger Rd Ste 303 Ridgefield Park (07660) *(G-9412)*

Outsourcing Today LLC 973 439-0060
103 Eisenhower Pkwy # 206 Roseland (07068) *(G-9654)*

Outwater Plastics Industries, Bogota *Also called Outwater Plstcs/Industries Inc (G-550)*

Outwater Plstcs/Industries Inc (PA) 201 498-8750
24 River Rd Ste 108 Bogota (07603) *(G-550)*

Ovadia Corporation 973 256-9200
101 E Main St Ste 501 Little Falls (07424) *(G-5483)*

Oven Art LLC 973 910-2266
200 S Newman St Unit 7 Hackensack (07601) *(G-3958)*

Oven Arts, Hackensack *Also called Oven Art LLC (G-3958)*

Over The Rainbow Bridge Crysta, Sicklerville *Also called 7th Seventh Day Wellness Ctr (G-10015)*

Overdrive Holdings Inc 201 440-1911
540 Huyler St South Hackensack (07606) *(G-10286)*

Overlook Hospital, Summit Mri, Summit *Also called Ahs Hospital Corp (G-10633)*

Owens Corning Sales LLC 201 998-5666
1249 Newark Tpke Kearny (07032) *(G-4904)*

Owens Fasteners Inc 856 768-6580
154 Cooper Rd Ste 101 West Berlin (08091) *(G-11740)*

Owens Plastic Products Inc 856 447-3500
393 Main St Cedarville (08311) *(G-1324)*

Ox Group Usa LLC 888 850-6710
95 Dermody St Cranford (07016) *(G-1920)*

Oxberry LLC 201 935-3000
180 Broad St Carlstadt (07072) *(G-1196)*

Oxford Biochronometrics LLC 201 755-5932
29 S Willow St Montclair (07042) *(G-6427)*

Oxford Instrs Holdings Inc (HQ) 732 541-1300
600 Milik St Carteret (07008) *(G-1265)*

Oxford Lamp Inc 732 462-3755
17 Bannard St Ste 30 Freehold (07728) *(G-3676)*

Oxford Lighting Co, Freehold *Also called Oxford Lamp Inc (G-3676)*

Oxford Quarry, Oxford *Also called Tilcon New York Inc (G-7833)*

Ozone Confectioners Bakers Sup 201 791-4444
27 W Lincoln St Verona (07044) *(G-11308)*

P & A Auto Parts Inc (PA) 201 655-7117
530 River St Hackensack (07601) *(G-3959)*

P & P Equipment Corporation 201 489-0050
286 Kinderkamack Rd River Edge (07661) *(G-9467)*

P & R Castings LLC 732 302-3600
325 Pierce St Somerset (08873) *(G-10150)*

P & R Fasteners Inc (PA) 732 302-3600
325 Pierce St Somerset (08873) *(G-10151)*

P & R PUBLISHING, Phillipsburg *Also called Presbyterian Reformed Pubg Co (G-8666)*

P & S Blizzard Corporation 973 523-1700
722 Madison Ave Paterson (07501) *(G-8358)*

P A K Manufacturing Inc 973 372-1090
704 S 21st St Irvington (07111) *(G-4599)*

P B M, Monmouth Junction *Also called Princeton Biomeditech Corp (G-6356)*

P C C, Totowa *Also called Precision Custom Coatings LLC (G-10966)*

P C G, Fairfield *Also called Print Communications Group Inc (G-3287)*

P C M, Camden *Also called Plastics Consulting & Mfg Co (G-1082)*

P D Q Digital, Englewood *Also called PDQ Print & Copy Inc (G-2921)*

P D Q Plastics Inc 201 823-0270
7 Hook Rd Bayonne (07002) *(G-240)*

P D Salco Inc 973 716-0517
61 Shrewsbury Dr Livingston (07039) *(G-5553)*

P E G, Vineland *Also called Precision Electronic Glass Inc (G-11393)*

P J Gillespie Inc 856 327-2993
2565 Brunetta Dr Vineland (08360) *(G-11387)*

P J Murphy Forest Pdts Corp (PA) 973 316-0800
150 River Rd Ste L1 Montville (07045) *(G-6491)*

P K Welding LLC 908 928-1002
520 South Ave Garwood (07027) *(G-3783)*

P L Custom Body & Eqp Co Inc 732 223-1411
2201 Atlantic Ave Manasquan (08736) *(G-5877)*

P L M Manufacturing Company 201 342-3636
293 Hudson St Hackensack (07601) *(G-3960)*

P M C Diners Inc 201 337-6146
56 Spruce St Oakland (07436) *(G-7700)*

P M Construction Co, Phillipsburg *Also called Philip Mamrak (G-8663)*

P M M I, Carlstadt *Also called Precision Metal Machining Inc (G-1207)*

P M Z Tool Inc 908 647-2125
321 Warren Ave Stirling (07980) *(G-10604)*

P O V Incorporated (PA) 914 258-4361
29 Park St Montclair (07042) *(G-6428)*

P P G Auto Glass, Mount Laurel *Also called Pgw Auto Glass LLC (G-6825)*

P R I, Princeton *Also called Princeton Research Instruments (G-9101)*

P R S, Princeton *Also called Pharmaceutical Regulatory Svcs (G-9091)*

P R X, Clifton *Also called Pharm-Rx Chemical Corporation (G-1694)*

P S I Cement Inc 609 716-1515
12 Robert Dr Princeton Junction (08550) *(G-9160)*

P W B Omni Inc 856 384-1300
1319 Vallee Dr West Deptford (08096) *(G-11838)*

P W Perkins Co Inc 856 769-3525
221 Commissioners Pike Woodstown (08098) *(G-12239)*

P-Americas LLC 973 739-4900
15 Melanie Ln Whippany (07981) *(G-12030)*

Pabin Associates Inc (PA) 201 288-7216
281 Springfield Ave Hasbrouck Heights (07604) *(G-4197)*

Pabst Enterprises Equipment Co 908 353-2880
676 Pennsylvania Ave Elizabeth (07201) *(G-2764)*

Pac Team America Inc (PA) 201 599-5000
205 Robin Rd Ste 200 Paramus (07652) *(G-7896)*

Pace Business Solutions Inc 908 451-0355
297 Route 72 W Manahawkin (08050) *(G-5833)*

Pace Packaging LLC 973 227-1040
3 Sperry Rd Fairfield (07004) *(G-3279)*

Pace Press Incorporated 201 935-7711
1 Caesar Pl Moonachie (07074) *(G-6534)*

Pace Target Brokerage Inc 856 629-2551
716 Clayton Rd Williamstown (08094) *(G-12095)*

Pacent Engineering 914 390-9150
3430 Sunset Ave Ste 18 Ocean (07712) *(G-7733)*

Pacific Coast Systems LLC 908 735-9955
4 Fox Hill Ln Asbury (08802) *(G-72)*

Pacific Dnlop Holdings USA LLC (HQ) 732 345-5400
200 Schulz Dr Red Bank (07701) *(G-9339)*

Pacific Dunlop Investments USA (HQ) 732 345-5400
200 Schulz Dr Red Bank (07701) *(G-9340)*

Pacific Microtronics Inc 973 993-8665
8 Laurel Ln Morris Plains (07950) *(G-6676)*

Pacifichealth Laboratories Inc (PA) 732 739-2900
800 Lanidex Plz Ste 220 Parsippany (07054) *(G-8053)*

Pacira Pharmaceuticals Inc (PA) 973 254-3560
5 Sylvan Way Ste 300 Parsippany (07054) *(G-8054)*

Package Development Co Inc 973 983-8500
100 Round Hill Dr Ste 8 Rockaway (07866) *(G-9593)*

Packaged Gas Systems Inc (PA) 908 755-2780
18 Stern Ave Springfield (07081) *(G-10569)*

Packageman 201 898-1922
331 Main St Belleville (07109) *(G-310)*

Packaging Corporation America 856 596-5020
8 E Stow Rd Ste 100 Marlton (08053) *(G-5992)*

Packaging Corporation America 908 452-9271
101 Bilby Rd Bldg 1 Hackettstown (07840) *(G-4031)*

Packaging Corporation America 856 696-0114
46 N West Ave Ste A Vineland (08360) *(G-11388)*

Packaging Graphics Inc 856 767-9000
435 Commerce Ln West Berlin (08091) *(G-11741)*

Packaging Machinery & Eqp Co 973 325-2418
181 Watson Ave West Orange (07052) *(G-11903)*

Packet Media LLC (PA) 856 779-3800
198 Us Highway 9 Ste 100 Englishtown (07726) *(G-2996)*

Packet Publications, Princeton *Also called Princeton Packet Inc (G-9097)*

Packetstorm Communications Inc 732 840-3871
6 Sullivan St Westwood (07675) *(G-11964)*

Packom LLC (PA) 201 378-8382
385 Main St Little Falls (07424) *(G-5484)*

Pacon Manufacturing Corp................................732 764-9070
400 Pierce St Somerset (08873) *(G-10152)*

Pacor Inc (PA)................................609 324-1100
333 Rising Sun Rd Bordentown (08505) *(G-607)*

Pad and Publ Assembly Corp................................856 424-0158
1165 Marlkress Rd Ste M Cherry Hill (08003) *(G-1409)*

Page 2 LLC................................862 239-9830
508 Hamburg Tpke Ste 108 Wayne (07470) *(G-11669)*

Page Stamp LLC................................732 390-1700
110 Kings Mill Rd Monroe Township (08831) *(G-6389)*

Pahco Machine Inc (PA)................................609 587-1188
572 Whitehead Rd Ste 101 Trenton (08619) *(G-11094)*

Pai Services LLC................................856 231-4667
305 Fellowship Rd Ste 300 Mount Laurel (08054) *(G-6823)*

Paige Company Containers Inc (PA)................................201 461-7800
1 Paul Kohner Pl Elmwood Park (07407) *(G-2840)*

Paige Electric Company LP (PA)................................908 687-7810
1160 Springfield Rd Union (07083) *(G-11212)*

Painting Inc................................201 489-6565
60 Leuning St South Hackensack (07606) *(G-10287)*

Paintmaster Auto Body................................732 270-1700
1920 Route 37 E Ste 1 Toms River (08753) *(G-10899)*

Painton Studios Inc................................732 752-8842
299 Us Highway 22 Ste 21 Green Brook (08812) *(G-3861)*

Palatin Technologies Inc................................609 495-2200
4b Cedarbrook Dr Cranbury (08512) *(G-1866)*

Palfinger North America................................609 588-5400
572 Whitehead Rd Ste 301 Trenton (08619) *(G-11095)*

Palisade Lumber & Supply Inc (PA)................................201 656-4400
432 Palisade Ave Jersey City (07307) *(G-4797)*

Palisades Dental LLc................................201 569-0050
111 Cedar Ln Englewood (07631) *(G-2920)*

Palisades Magnolia Prpts LLC................................201 424-7180
169 Roosevelt Pl Unit B Palisades Park (07650) *(G-7841)*

Pallet Services Inc................................856 514-3908
66 Pennsgrve Pedrcktwn Rd Pedricktown (08067) *(G-8439)*

Pallmann Industries, Clifton *Also called Pallmann Pulverizers Co Inc (G-1688)*

Pallmann Pulverizers Co Inc................................973 471-1450
820 Bloomfield Ave Clifton (07012) *(G-1688)*

Palm Press Inc................................201 767-6504
202 Livingston St Northvale (07647) *(G-7600)*

Palma Inc................................973 429-1490
628 State Route 10 Ste 2 Whippany (07981) *(G-12031)*

Palmarozzo Bindery................................908 688-5300
850 Springfield Rd Union (07083) *(G-11213)*

Palmer Electronics Inc................................973 772-5900
156 Belmont Ave Garfield (07026) *(G-3744)*

Palmer Industries Div, Garfield *Also called Palmer Electronics Inc (G-3744)*

Palmer's Cocoa Butter Formula, Englewood Cliffs *Also called ET Browne Drug Co Inc (G-2959)*

Palmetto Adhesives Company................................856 451-0400
1785 S Burlington Rd Bridgeton (08302) *(G-793)*

Palnet, Williamstown *Also called Premier Asset Logistics Networ (G-12101)*

Palsgaard Incorporated................................973 998-7951
101 Gibraltar Dr Ste 2b Morris Plains (07950) *(G-6677)*

Palude Enterprises Inc................................732 241-5478
1933 Hwy 35 Ste 105-144 Howell (07731) *(G-4562)*

Palumbo Associates Inc................................908 534-2142
27 Ridge Rd Whitehouse Station (08889) *(G-12060)*

Palumbo Millwork Inc................................732 938-3266
5033 Industrial Rd Ste 8 Wall Township (07727) *(G-11502)*

Pam International Co Inc (PA)................................201 291-1200
45 Mayhill St Saddle Brook (07663) *(G-9779)*

Pam Optical Co................................973 744-8882
107 Park St Montclair (07042) *(G-6429)*

Pamarco Global Graphics Inc (HQ)................................908 241-1200
235 E 11th Ave Roselle (07203) *(G-9679)*

Pamarco Global Graphics Inc................................856 829-4585
1 Roto Ave Palmyra (08065) *(G-7850)*

Pamarco Technologies LLC (PA)................................908 241-1200
235 E 11th Ave Roselle (07203) *(G-9680)*

Pan American Coffee Company (PA)................................201 963-2329
500 16th St Hoboken (07030) *(G-4489)*

Pan Graphics Inc................................973 478-2100
45 Hartmann Ave Garfield (07026) *(G-3745)*

Pan Technology Inc................................201 438-7878
117 Moonachie Ave Carlstadt (07072) *(G-1197)*

Panasonic Corp North America................................201 348-7000
2 Riverfront Plz Ste 200 Newark (07102) *(G-7261)*

Panasonic Corp North America................................201 348-7000
2 Riverfront Plz Ste 200 Newark (07102) *(G-7262)*

Panasource Ingredients, Edison *Also called Prosweetz Ingredients Inc (G-2599)*

Panatech Corporation................................732 331-5692
5 Elkridge Way Manalapan (07726) *(G-5860)*

Panel Components & Systems (PA)................................973 448-9400
149 Main St Stanhope (07874) *(G-10589)*

Panos Brands LLC................................800 229-1706
1209 W Saint Georges Ave Linden (07036) *(G-5423)*

Panos Holding Company (HQ)................................201 843-8900
395 W Passaic St Ste 2 Rochelle Park (07662) *(G-9533)*

Panova Inc................................973 263-1700
33 Jacksonville Rd Ste 2 Towaco (07082) *(G-11000)*

Panpac LLC................................856 376-3576
1971 Old Cuthbert Rd Cherry Hill (08034) *(G-1410)*

Panther Printing Inc................................239 542-1050
29 Northfield Ave West Orange (07052) *(G-11904)*

Panthera Dental Inc................................201 340-2766
1 Meadowlands Plz Ste 200 East Rutherford (07073) *(G-2316)*

Pantina Cosmetics Inc................................201 288-7767
30 Henry St Teterboro (07608) *(G-10808)*

Pao Ba Avo LLC................................908 962-9090
545 Edgar Rd Elizabeth (07202) *(G-2765)*

Paone Fabrication Inc................................856 589-3821
345 Chapel Heights Rd Sewell (08080) *(G-9964)*

Papa Johns New Jersey................................609 395-0045
1267 S River Rd Ste 400 Cranbury (08512) *(G-1867)*

Paper Board Products, Hackensack *Also called International Container Co (G-3931)*

Paper Clip Communication Inc................................973 256-1333
125 Paterson Ave Ste 4 Little Falls (07424) *(G-5485)*

Paper Dove Press LLC................................201 641-7938
16 Monnett St Little Ferry (07643) *(G-5513)*

Paper Tube and Core, Paterson *Also called Paper Tubes Cores & Boxes Inc (G-8359)*

Paper Tubes Cores & Boxes Inc................................973 977-8823
239 Lindbergh Pl Paterson (07503) *(G-8359)*

Papertec, Garfield *Also called Wjj and Company LLC (G-3773)*

Papery of Marlton LLC................................856 985-1776
300 Route 73 S Ste B Marlton (08053) *(G-5993)*

Papettis Hygrade Egg Pdts Inc (HQ)................................908 282-7900
1 Papetti Plz Elizabethport (07206) *(G-2786)*

Papillon Ribbon & Bow Inc................................973 928-6128
35 Monhegan St Clifton (07013) *(G-1689)*

Papp Iron Works Inc................................908 731-1000
950 S 2nd St Plainfield (07063) *(G-8871)*

Pappas Lassonde Holdings Inc (HQ)................................856 455-1000
1 Collins Dr Ste 200 Carneys Point (08069) *(G-1246)*

Papyrus, Marlton *Also called Schurman Fine Papers (G-5998)*

Par Code Symbology Inc................................973 918-0550
119 Harrison Ave Roseland (07068) *(G-9655)*

Par Metal Products, North Arlington *Also called Ango Electronics Corporation (G-7415)*

Par Metal Products Inc................................201 955-0800
21 Ewing Ave North Arlington (07031) *(G-7422)*

Par Sheet Metal Inc................................908 241-2477
220 W 1st Ave Roselle (07203) *(G-9681)*

Par Troy Sheet Metal & AC LLC................................973 227-1150
122 Clinton Rd Fairfield (07004) *(G-3280)*

Parabole LLC................................609 917-8479
1100 Cornwall Rd Monmouth Junction (08852) *(G-6353)*

Paradigm Packaging East LLC (HQ)................................201 909-3400
141 5th St Saddle Brook (07663) *(G-9780)*

Paradise................................973 425-0505
1098 Mount Kemble Ave # 2 Morristown (07960) *(G-6732)*

Paradise Barxon Corp................................908 707-9141
185 Industrial Pkwy Ste H Branchburg (08876) *(G-686)*

Paradise Publishing Group LLC................................609 227-7642
25 Middlebury Ln Ste 3b Willingboro (08046) *(G-12122)*

Paragon Iron Inc................................201 528-7307
550 Industrial Rd Unit D Carlstadt (07072) *(G-1198)*

Paramount Bakeries Inc (PA)................................973 482-6638
61 Davenport Ave Newark (07107) *(G-7263)*

Paramount Bakeries Inc................................973 482-6638
18-28 Springdale Ave East Orange (07019) *(G-2263)*

Paramount Bakeries Inc................................973 481-4763
412 428 N 5th St Newark (07107) *(G-7264)*

Paramount Cosmetics, Clifton *Also called Hudson Cosmetic Mfg Corp (G-1644)*

Paramount Cosmetics Inc................................973 472-2323
93 Entin Rd Ste 4 Clifton (07014) *(G-1690)*

Paramount Fixture Corporation................................973 485-1585
175 Mount Pleasant Ave Newark (07104) *(G-7265)*

Paramount Fixture Sales, Newark *Also called Paramount Fixture Corporation (G-7265)*

Paramount Metal Finishing Co................................908 862-0772
1515 W Elizabeth Ave Linden (07036) *(G-5424)*

Paramount Modular Concepts, Oakland *Also called P M C Diners Inc (G-7700)*

Paramount Packaging, Haddonfield *Also called Global Direct Marketing Group (G-4060)*

Paramount Plating, Linden *Also called Paramount Metal Finishing Co (G-5424)*

Paramount Plating Co Inc................................908 862-0772
1515 W Elizabeth Ave Linden (07036) *(G-5425)*

Paramount Products Co Inc................................732 458-9200
1104 Industrial Pkwy Brick (08724) *(G-754)*

Paramount Wire Co Inc................................973 672-0500
2-8 Central Ave East Orange (07018) *(G-2264)*

Paravista Inc................................732 752-1222
123 Lehigh Dr Fairfield (07004) *(G-3281)*

Paravista Imaging and Printing, Fairfield *Also called Paravista Inc (G-3281)*

Pario Group LLC................................732 906-2302
70 Stephenville Pkwy Edison (08820) *(G-2591)*

Paris Corporation New Jersey (PA)................................609 265-9200
800 Highland Dr Westampton (08060) *(G-11914)*

Pariser Industries Inc (PA)................................973 569-9090
91 Michigan Ave Paterson (07503) *(G-8360)*

Park Ave Printing, Trenton *Also called Steven Madola* **(G-11117)**

Park Electric Motor Co, Atlantic City *Also called Motors and Drives Inc* **(G-103)**

Park Plus Inc (PA) 201 651-8590
31 Iron Horse Rd Ste 1 Oakland (07436) **(G-7701)**

Park Printing Services Inc 856 675-1600
7300 N Crescent Blvd # 21 Pennsauken (08110) **(G-8556)**

Park Steel & Iron Co (PA) 732 775-7500
9 Evergreen Ave Neptune (07753) **(G-6927)**

Parkeon Inc 856 234-8000
40 Twosome Dr Ste 7 Moorestown (08057) **(G-6608)**

Parker Acquisition Group Inc (PA) 908 707-4900
25 Imclone Dr Branchburg (08876) **(G-687)**

Parker Labs 973 276-9500
286 Eldridge Rd Fairfield (07004) **(G-3282)**

Parker Publications 908 766-3900
155 Main St Madison (07940) **(G-5730)**

Parker Publications Corporated, Whippany *Also called Recorder Publishing Co Inc* **(G-12037)**

Parker Publications Inc 908 766-3900
17 Morristown Rd 19 Bernardsville (07924) **(G-453)**

Parker-Hannifin Corporation 856 825-8900
525 Orange St Millville (08332) **(G-6319)**

Parker-Hannifin Corporation 973 575-4844
45 Us Highway 46 Ste 602 Pine Brook (07058) **(G-8712)**

Parking Survival Experts, Paramus *Also called Alternate Side Street Suspende* **(G-7853)**

Parkway Plastics Inc 732 752-3636
561 Stelton Rd Piscataway (08854) **(G-8798)**

Parkway Printing Inc 732 308-0300
52 N Main St Ste 11 Marlboro (07746) **(G-5951)**

Parkway-Kew Corporation 732 398-2100
2095 Excelsior Ave North Brunswick (08902) **(G-7533)**

Parmelee Wrench, Harrison *Also called CS Osborne & Co* **(G-4177)**

Parr, J W Leadburing Co, Little Falls *Also called JW Parr Leadburing Co* **(G-5479)**

Parrish Sign Co Inc 856 696-4040
2242 S Delsea Dr Vineland (08360) **(G-11389)**

Parsells Printing Inc 973 473-2700
938 Spring Valley Rd # 1 Maywood (07607) **(G-6059)**

Parsons Cabinets Inc 973 279-4954
79 Beverly Rd Montclair (07043) **(G-6430)**

Partac Peat Corp 908 637-4191
95 Shades Of Death Rd Great Meadows (07838) **(G-3850)**

Partac Peat Corporation 908 637-4631
95 Kelsey Park Great Meadows (07838) **(G-3851)**

Partake Foods, Jersey City *Also called Vivis Life LLC* **(G-4844)**

Parth Enterprises Inc 732 404-0665
665 State Route 27 Iselin (08830) **(G-4640)**

Partners In Vision Inc 888 748-1112
1090 King Georges Post Rd # 103 Edison (08837) **(G-2592)**

Parts Life Inc 856 786-8675
30 Twosome Dr Ste 1 Moorestown (08057) **(G-6609)**

Party City Corporation 973 537-1707
477 State Route 10 # 102 Randolph (07869) **(G-9294)**

Party City of North Bergen 201 865-0040
3111 Kennedy Blvd North Bergen (07047) **(G-7473)**

Parwan Electronics Corporation (PA) 732 290-1900
1230 Hwy 34 Matawan (07747) **(G-6027)**

Pascack Data Services Inc 973 304-4858
200 Central Ave Ste 100 Hawthorne (07506) **(G-4251)**

Pascack Press 201 664-2105
69 Woodland Ave Westwood (07675) **(G-11965)**

Pascack Valley Copy Center 201 664-1917
69 Woodland Ave Westwood (07675) **(G-11966)**

Passaic Color & Chemical, Paterson *Also called Royce Associates A Ltd Partnr* **(G-8372)**

Passaic County Welders Inc 973 696-1200
100 Parish Dr Wayne (07470) **(G-11670)**

Passaic Metal & Bldg Sups Co (PA) 973 546-9000
5 Central Ave Ste 1 Clifton (07011) **(G-1691)**

Passaic Rubber Co (PA) 973 696-9500
45 Demarest Dr Wayne (07470) **(G-11671)**

Pastarama Distributors Inc 609 847-0378
164 Center St Sewell (08080) **(G-9965)**

Pastel Companies Inc (PA) 732 508-0635
4 Hummingbird Ct Howell (07731) **(G-4563)**

Pat Bry Advertising Spc 732 591-0999
Tennant Rd Rr 79 Morganville (07751) **(G-6650)**

Pata Pal, Denville *Also called Qualserv Imports Inc* **(G-2052)**

Patagonia Pharmaceuticals LLC 201 264-7866
50 Tice Blvd Ste A26 Woodcliff Lake (07677) **(G-12198)**

Patchamp Inc 201 457-1504
20 E Kennedy St Hackensack (07601) **(G-3961)**

Patchworks Co Inc 973 627-2002
18 N Salem St Dover (07801) **(G-2106)**

Patel Metal Plating Inc 732 574-1770
6 Emerson St Edison (08820) **(G-2593)**

Patel Printing Plus Corp 908 964-6422
1036 Commerce Ave Union (07083) **(G-11214)**

Patella Construction Corp 973 916-0100
99 South St Passaic (07055) **(G-8169)**

Patella Woodworking, Passaic *Also called Patella Construction Corp* **(G-8169)**

Paterson Bleachery Inc (PA) 973 684-1034
207 E 15th St 219 Paterson (07524) **(G-8361)**

Paterson Laundry & Die Div, Paterson *Also called Fairfield Textiles Corp* **(G-8270)**

Paterson Stamp Works, Clifton *Also called American Marking Systems Inc* **(G-1563)**

Path Silicones Inc (PA) 201 796-0833
21 Wallace St Elmwood Park (07407) **(G-2841)**

Patheon Biologics (nj) LLC 609 919-3300
201 College Rd E Princeton (08540) **(G-9089)**

Patheon Biologics LLC 609 919-3300
201 College Rd E Princeton (08540) **(G-9090)**

Pathmark Stores Inc 973 762-5044
407 Valley St South Orange (07079) **(G-10313)**

Pathmark Stores Inc 856 853-5533
1450 Clements Bridge Rd Woodbury (08096) **(G-12167)**

Pathmark Stores Inc 732 505-6440
1256 Indian Head Rd # 35 Toms River (08755) **(G-10900)**

Patientstar LLC 856 722-0808
308 Harper Dr Ste 105 Moorestown (08057) **(G-6610)**

Patrick J Kelly Drums Inc 856 963-1795
1810 River Ave Camden (08105) **(G-1081)**

Patriot American Solutions LLC 862 209-4772
5 Astro Pl Rockaway (07866) **(G-9594)**

Patriot Pickle Inc 973 709-9487
20 Edison Dr Wayne (07470) **(G-11672)**

Patron America, Carlstadt *Also called Jinpan International USA Ltd* **(G-1174)**

Patterson Smith Publishing 973 744-3291
23 Prospect Ter Montclair (07042) **(G-6431)**

Patty-O-Matic Inc 732 938-2757
Lakewood Farmingdale Rd Farmingdale (07727) **(G-3391)**

Patwin Plastics Inc 908 486-6600
2300 E Linden Ave Linden (07036) **(G-5426)**

Paul Bros Inc 856 697-5895
113 Church St Newfield (08344) **(G-7370)**

Paul Burkhardt & Sons Inc 856 435-2020
648 7th Ave Lindenwold (08021) **(G-5462)**

Paul Dyeing Company 973 484-1121
626 Orange St Newark (07107) **(G-7266)**

Paul Englehardt 908 637-4556
Island Rd Great Meadows (07838) **(G-3852)**

Paul Fago Cabinet Making Inc 856 384-0496
425 S Columbia St Woodbury (08096) **(G-12168)**

Paul Winston Fine Jewelry Grou (PA) 800 232-2728
619 E Palisade Ave Ste 1 Englewood Cliffs (07632) **(G-2977)**

Paulaur Corporation 609 395-8844
105 Melrich Rd Cranbury (08512) **(G-1868)**

Paulist Press Inc 201 825-7300
997 Macarthur Blvd Mahwah (07430) **(G-5800)**

Paulsboro Refining Company LLC 973 455-7500
800 Billingsport Rd Paulsboro (08066) **(G-8424)**

Pavan & Kievit Enterprises 973 546-4615
113 Dewitt St Ste 210 Garfield (07026) **(G-3746)**

Paverart LLC 856 783-7000
2512 Egg Harbor Rd Ste C Lindenwold (08021) **(G-5463)**

Pavexpress 201 330-8300
499 River Rd Clifton (07014) **(G-1692)**

Paylocity Holding Corporation 908 917-3027
21 Fadem Rd Ste 10 Springfield (07081) **(G-10570)**

Pba of West Windsor 609 799-6535
376 N Post Rd Princeton Junction (08550) **(G-9161)**

Pbf Energy, Paulsboro *Also called Paulsboro Refining Company LLC* **(G-8424)**

Pbf Energy Company 973 455-7500
1 Sylvan Way Ste 2 Parsippany (07054) **(G-8055)**

Pbf Energy Company LLC (HQ) 973 455-7500
1 Sylvan Way Ste 2 Parsippany (07054) **(G-8056)**

Pbf Energy Inc (PA) 973 455-7500
1 Sylvan Way Ste 2 Parsippany (07054) **(G-8057)**

Pbf Holding Company LLC (HQ) 888 661-8949
1 Sylvan Way Ste 2 Parsippany (07054) **(G-8058)**

Pbf Services Company LLC 973 455-7500
1 Sylvan Way Ste 2 Parsippany (07054) **(G-8059)**

Pbf Tdo, Parsippany *Also called Pbf Energy Company LLC* **(G-8056)**

PBF TDO, Parsippany *Also called Pbf Holding Company LLC* **(G-8058)**

PC & S, Stanhope *Also called Panel Components & Systems* **(G-10589)**

PC Marketing Inc (PA) 201 943-6100
1040 Wilt Ave Ridgefield (07657) **(G-9379)**

PC Science Training Center, Denville *Also called Justice Laboratory Software* **(G-2044)**

PCA, Hackettstown *Also called Packaging Corporation America* **(G-4031)**

PCA/Supply Services 302a, Vineland *Also called Packaging Corporation America* **(G-11388)**

PCC, Somerset *Also called Power Container Corp* **(G-10156)**

PCC Asia LLC (PA) 973 890-3873
200 Maltese Dr Totowa (07512) **(G-10961)**

PCI, Lebanon *Also called Plate Concepts Inc* **(G-5299)**

PCI Inc 973 226-8007
185 Fairfield Ave Ste 4c West Caldwell (07006) **(G-11796)**

Pcr Technologies Inc 973 882-0017
26 Chapin Rd Ste 1111 Pine Brook (07058) **(G-8713)**

Pcs Crane Services Inc 201 366-4250
83 Broad Ave Fairview (07022) **(G-3368)**

A
L
P
H
A
B
E
T
I
C

Pcs Revenue Ctrl Systems Inc 201 568-8300
  560 Sylvan Ave Ste 2050 Englewood Cliffs (07632) *(G-2978)*

Pdec, Eatontown *Also called East Coast Distributors Inc* *(G-2391)*

PDM Litho Inc 718 301-1740
  220 Entin Rd Clifton (07014) *(G-1693)*

PDM Packaging Inc 201 864-1115
  4102 Bergen Tpke North Bergen (07047) *(G-7474)*

PDQ Print & Copy Inc 201 569-2288
  161 Coolidge Ave Englewood (07631) *(G-2921)*

Pdr Equity LLC (PA) 201 358-7200
  200 Jefferson Park Whippany (07981) *(G-12032)*

Pdr Network, Whippany *Also called Pdr Equity LLC (G-12032)*

Pds Consultants Inc 201 970-2313
  22 Rainbow Trl Sparta (07871) *(G-10517)*

Pds Prclnical Data Systems Inc 973 398-2800
  100 Valley Rd Ste 204 Mount Arlington (07856) *(G-6759)*

Pe Burkhardt & Sons, Lindenwold *Also called Paul Burkhardt & Sons Inc (G-5462)*

Peace Medical Inc 800 537-9564
  105 W Dewey Ave Unit 1-2 Wharton (07885) *(G-11996)*

Peachtree Kay, Clifton *Also called K M Media Group LLC (G-1654)*

Peacock Communications Inc (PA) 973 763-3311
  215 Rutgers St Maplewood (07040) *(G-5924)*

Peacock Products Inc 201 385-5585
  48 Woodbine St Bergenfield (07621) *(G-392)*

Peak Finance Holdings LLC (HQ) 856 969-7100
  121 Woodcrest Rd Cherry Hill (08003) *(G-1411)*

Pearl Baumell Company Inc 415 421-2113
  201 State Rt 17 Ste 302 Rutherford (07070) *(G-9743)*

Pearson Business Services, Old Tappan *Also called Pearson Technology Centre Inc (G-7800)*

Pearson Education Inc (HQ) 201 236-7000
  221 River St Hoboken (07030) *(G-4490)*

Pearson Education Inc 914 287-8000
  221 River St Hoboken (07030) *(G-4491)*

Pearson Education Inc 609 395-6000
  258 Prospect Plains Rd Cranbury (08512) *(G-1869)*

Pearson Education Inc 201 785-2721
  221 River St Ste 200 Hoboken (07030) *(G-4492)*

Pearson Inc 201 236-7000
  1 Lake St Upper Saddle River (07458) *(G-11282)*

Pearson Longman, Hoboken *Also called Pearson Education Inc (G-4491)*

Pearson Technology Centre Inc (HQ) 201 767-5000
  200 Old Tappan Rd Ste 1 Old Tappan (07675) *(G-7800)*

PEC, Matawan *Also called Parwan Electronics Corporation (G-6027)*

Pecata Enterprises Inc 973 523-9498
  18 Market St Paterson (07501) *(G-8362)*

Pechter's, Harrison *Also called R P Baking LLC (G-4189)*

Pechters Southern NJ LLC 856 786-8000
  2 Surrey Ln Cinnaminson (08077) *(G-1483)*

Pedestal Pallet Inc 732 968-7488
  777 N Avenue Ext Dunellen (08812) *(G-2129)*

Pedibrush LLC 856 796-2963
  211 7th Ave Haddon Heights (08035) *(G-4049)*

Peeq Media, Somerset *Also called Toppan Printing Co Amer Inc (G-10188)*

Peer & Picone Woodworking, Pittstown *Also called European Country Kitchens Inc (G-8850)*

Peerless Coating Services, Hawthorne *Also called Peerless Coatings LLC (G-4252)*

Peerless Coatings LLC 973 427-8771
  220a Goffle Rd Hawthorne (07506) *(G-4252)*

Peerless Concrete Products Co 973 838-3060
  246 Main St Butler (07405) *(G-1015)*

Peerless Umbrella Co Inc (PA) 973 578-4900
  427 Ferry St Newark (07105) *(G-7267)*

Pegasus Group Publishing Inc 973 884-9100
  188 State Route 10 Fl 2 East Hanover (07936) *(G-2239)*

Pegasus Home Fashions Inc 908 965-1919
  107 Trumbull St Elizabeth (07206) *(G-2766)*

Pegasus Products Inc 908 707-1122
  19 Readington Rd Branchburg (08876) *(G-688)*

Pekay Industries Inc 732 938-2722
  452 Sqnkum Yellowbrook Rd Farmingdale (07727) *(G-3392)*

Pelco Packaging Corporation 973 675-4994
  545 N Arlington Ave Ste 7 East Orange (07017) *(G-2265)*

Pella Window Store, Paramus *Also called Lux Home Inc (G-7886)*

Peloton Interactive Inc 201 784-9510
  206 Pegasus Ave Northvale (07647) *(G-7601)*

Pem Systems Inc 908 276-0211
  39a Myrtle St Cranford (07016) *(G-1921)*

Pem-All Fire Extinguisher Co, Cranford *Also called Pem Systems Inc (G-1921)*

Pemberton Fabricators Inc 609 267-0922
  30 Indel Ave Rancocas (08073) *(G-9260)*

Pemco Dental Corporation 800 526-4170
  35 Stern Ave Springfield (07081) *(G-10571)*

Pemfab, Rancocas *Also called Pemberton Fabricators Inc (G-9260)*

Pen Company of America LLC 908 374-7949
  502 South Ave Garwood (07027) *(G-3784)*

Pen Company of America LLC (HQ) 908 374-7949
  1401 S Park Ave Linden (07036) *(G-5427)*

Pen Master, Randolph *Also called Larose Industries LLC (G-9287)*

Pendotech, Princeton *Also called Mayfair Tech Ltd Lblty Co (G-9071)*

Penetone Corporation (PA) 201 567-3000
  700 Gotham Pkwy Ste 2 Carlstadt (07072) *(G-1199)*

Penick Corporation 856 678-3601
  33 Industrial Park Rd Newark (07114) *(G-7268)*

Penn Color Inc 201 791-5100
  30 Kohner Dr Elmwood Park (07407) *(G-2842)*

Penn Elcom Inc 973 839-7777
  232 W Parkway Pompton Plains (07444) *(G-8964)*

Penn Jersey Advance Centl Svcs, Secaucus *Also called Penn Jersey Advance Inc (G-9909)*

Penn Jersey Advance Inc 201 775-6610
  1 Harmon Plz Fl 9 Secaucus (07094) *(G-9909)*

Penn Jersey Press Inc 856 627-2200
  10 United States Ave E Gibbsboro (08026) *(G-3789)*

Penn Metal Finishing Co Inc 609 387-3400
  700 Jacksonville Rd Burlington (08016) *(G-987)*

Penn Power Group LLC 732 441-1489
  4118 Hiway 34 Matawan (07747) *(G-6028)*

Penn Rillton Div, The, Bridgeton *Also called Whibco Inc (G-804)*

Penn-Jersey Bldg Mtls Co Inc (PA) 609 641-6994
  6761 Washington Ave Egg Harbor Township (08234) *(G-2691)*

Pennant Ingredients Inc 856 428-4300
  1941 Old Cuthbert Rd Cherry Hill (08034) *(G-1412)*

Pennetta & Sons 201 420-1693
  428 Hoboken Ave Jersey City (07306) *(G-4798)*

Pennington Furnace Supply Inc 609 737-2500
  6 Brookside Ave Pennington (08534) *(G-8457)*

Pennock Company 215 492-7900
  7135 Colonial Ln Pennsauken (08109) *(G-8557)*

Pennock Floral Co, Pennsauken *Also called Pennock Company (G-8557)*

Pennsylvania Crusher, Sewell *Also called K-Tron International Inc (G-9962)*

Pennsylvania Machine Works Inc 856 467-0500
  Rr 551 Swedesboro (08085) *(G-10717)*

Penny Plate LLC (HQ) 856 429-7583
  1400 Horizon Way Ste 300 Mount Laurel (08054) *(G-6824)*

Penny Press 856 547-1991
  908 N White Horse Pike Stratford (08084) *(G-10616)*

Pennzoil-Quaker State Company 856 423-1388
  1224 Forest Pkwy Ste 100 Paulsboro (08066) *(G-8425)*

Penske Truck Leasing Co LP 973 575-0169
  600 Edwards Rd Parsippany (07054) *(G-8060)*

Penta Digital Incorporated 201 839-5392
  234 16th St Fl 8 Jersey City (07310) *(G-4799)*

Penta Glass Industries Inc 973 478-2110
  71 Hepworth Pl Garfield (07026) *(G-3747)*

Penta International Corp 973 740-2300
  50 Okner Pkwy Livingston (07039) *(G-5554)*

Penta Manufacturing Company, Livingston *Also called Penta International Corp (G-5554)*

Pentacle Publishing Corp 732 240-3000
  1830 Route 9 Ste 1 Toms River (08755) *(G-10901)*

Pentagon Performance Inc 973 975-0400
  112 Leddon St Millville (08332) *(G-6320)*

Pentagraphix Offset Prtg Inc 201 526-9300
  629 Grove St Ste 701 Jersey City (07310) *(G-4800)*

Pentax of America Inc 973 628-6200
  3 Paragon Dr Montvale (07645) *(G-6468)*

Peoples Education Inc 201 712-0090
  25 Philips Pkwy 105 Montvale (07645) *(G-6469)*

Peoples Eductl Holdings Inc (PA) 201 712-0090
  299 Market St Ste 240 Saddle Brook (07663) *(G-9781)*

Pepco Manufacturing Co (PA) 856 783-3700
  210 E Evergreen Ave Somerdale (08083) *(G-10042)*

Pepsi 732 238-1598
  5 Lexington Ave East Brunswick (08816) *(G-2171)*

Pepsi-Cola Metro Btlg Co Inc 201 955-2691
  680 Belleville Tpke Kearny (07032) *(G-4905)*

Pepsi-Cola Metro Btlg Co Inc 732 922-9000
  3411 Sunset Ave Ocean (07712) *(G-7734)*

Pepsi-Cola Metro Btlg Co Inc 732 424-3000
  2200 New Brunswick Ave Piscataway (08854) *(G-8799)*

Pepsi-Cola Nat Brnd Bevs Ltd (PA) 856 665-6200
  8275 N Crescent Blvd Pennsauken (08110) *(G-8558)*

Pepsico, East Brunswick *Also called Pepsi (G-2171)*

Pepsico, Piscataway *Also called Pepsi-Cola Metro Btlg Co Inc (G-8799)*

Pepsico, Whippany *Also called P-Americas LLC (G-12030)*

Pepsico Inc 856 661-4604
  8275 N Route 130 Pennsauken (08110) *(G-8559)*

Pequod Communications, Princeton *Also called Wong Robinson & Co Inc (G-9140)*

Per-Fil Industries Inc 856 461-5700
  407 Adams St Riverside (08075) *(G-9504)*

Peragallo Organ Company of NJ 973 684-3414
  306 Buffalo Ave Paterson (07503) *(G-8363)*

Peragallo Pipe Organ, Paterson *Also called Peragallo Organ Company of NJ (G-8363)*

Perc, Boonton *Also called Pipeline Eqp Resources Co LLC (G-579)*

Perceptions Inc 973 344-5333
  280 Central Ave Kearny (07032) *(G-4906)*

Perco Inc 908 464-3000
  620 Springfield Ave Berkeley Heights (07922) *(G-420)*

(G-0000) Company's Geographic Section entry number

Perdue Farms Inc 609 298-4100
120 Route 130 Bordentown (08505) *(G-608)*
Perfect Clicks LLC 845 323-6116
172 Broadway Rear Bldg Woodcliff Lake (07677) *(G-12199)*
Perfect Printing Inc 856 787-1877
1533 Glen Ave Moorestown (08057) *(G-6611)*
Perfect Shapes Inc 856 783-3844
110 Salem St Elmer (08318) *(G-2795)*
Perfecto Foods LLC 201 889-5328
79 Stuyvesant Ave Kearny (07032) *(G-4907)*
Performance Alloys & Materials 201 865-5268
462 Dunlin Plz Secaucus (07094) *(G-9910)*
Performance Industries Inc 609 392-1450
51 Tucker St Trenton (08618) *(G-11096)*
Performance Laboratories Inc, Hackensack Also called Preform Laboratories Inc *(G-3964)*
Perfumania Inc 732 493-4116
1 Premium Outlet Blvd # 269 Tinton Falls (07753) *(G-10843)*
Peribu Collections LLC, Skillman Also called Peribu Global Sourcing *(G-10035)*
Peribu Global Sourcing 704 560-2035
5 Brookside Dr Skillman (08558) *(G-10035)*
Perimeter Solutions LP 732 541-3000
500 Roosevelt Ave Carteret (07008) *(G-1266)*
Perk & Pantry 856 451-4333
97 Trench Rd Ste 4 Bridgeton (08302) *(G-794)*
Perkins Plumbing & Heating 201 327-2736
89 Fawnhill Rd Upper Saddle River (07458) *(G-11283)*
Perl Pigments LLC 201 836-1212
400 Cotters Ln East Brunswick (08816) *(G-2172)*
Perlen Packaging, Whippany Also called Perlin Converting LLC *(G-12033)*
Perlin Converting LLC 973 887-0257
135 Algonquin Pkwy Whippany (07981) *(G-12033)*
Perma Pure LLC (HQ) 732 244-0010
1001 New Hampshire Ave Lakewood (08701) *(G-5170)*
Permabond LLC (PA) 610 323-5003
223 Churchill Ave Somerset (08873) *(G-10153)*
Permadur Industries Inc 908 359-9767
186 Route 206 Hillsborough (08844) *(G-4362)*
Permagraphics Inc 201 814-1200
25 Graphic Pl Moonachie (07074) *(G-6535)*
Permalith Plastics LLC 215 925-5659
6901 N Crescent Blvd Pennsauken (08110) *(G-8560)*
Permanore Archtctural Finishes 908 797-4177
3 Parkland Dr Milford (08848) *(G-6247)*
Pernix Therapeutics LLC 800 793-2145
10 N Park Pl Ste 201 Morristown (07960) *(G-6733)*
Pernix Thrpeutics Holdings Inc (PA) 800 793-2145
10 N Park Pl Ste 201 Morristown (07960) *(G-6734)*
Perry Products Corporation 609 267-1600
25 Mount Laurel Rd Hainesport (08036) *(G-4076)*
Personal Secure, Stirling Also called Secure System Inc *(G-10606)*
Personality Handkerchiefs Inc 973 565-0077
640 Frelinghuysen Ave Newark (07114) *(G-7269)*
Personlzed Exprssons By Audrey 973 478-5115
63 Harrison Ave Garfield (07026) *(G-3748)*
Pertech Corp K & E Printing, Carlstadt Also called Pertech Printing Inks Inc *(G-1200)*
Pertech Printing Inks Inc 908 354-1700
140 Grand St Carlstadt (07072) *(G-1200)*
Pet Devices LLC 929 244-0012
184 S Livingston Ave Livingston (07039) *(G-5555)*
Pet Salon Inc 609 350-6480
8510 Ventnor Ave Margate City (08402) *(G-5933)*
Pet Salon Inc (PA) 609 350-6480
3 S Franklin Ave Margate City (08402) *(G-5934)*
Peter Garafano & Son Inc 973 278-0350
500 Marshall St Paterson (07503) *(G-8364)*
Peter L Demaree 732 531-2133
1206 State Route 35 Ocean (07712) *(G-7735)*
Peter Morley LLC 732 264-0010
21 Village Ct Hazlet (07730) *(G-4282)*
Peter Thomas Roth Labs LLC 201 329-9100
45 Mayhill St Saddle Brook (07663) *(G-9782)*
Peter Yaged 973 427-4219
58 Braen Ave Hawthorne (07506) *(G-4253)*
Peter-Lisand Machine Corp 201 943-5600
262 Voorhis Ave New Milford (07646) *(G-7024)*
Peters Laboratories 856 767-4144
1 Hillside Ln Berlin (08009) *(G-440)*
Peterson Brothers Mfg Co 732 271-8240
10 Baekeland Ave Middlesex (08846) *(G-6186)*
Peterson Stamping & Mfg Co 908 241-0900
75 N Michigan Ave Kenilworth (07033) *(G-4986)*
Peterson Steel Rule Die Corp 201 935-6180
35 Broad St Carlstadt (07072) *(G-1201)*
Petit Pois Corp 856 608-9644
50 Twosome Dr Ste 3 Moorestown (08057) *(G-6612)*
Petnet Solutions Inc 865 218-2000
86-110 Orchard St Ste 2 Hackensack (07601) *(G-3962)*
Petra Solar, South Plainfield Also called Petra Systems Inc *(G-10419)*
Petra Systems Inc 908 462-5200
1 Cragwood Rd Ste 303 South Plainfield (07080) *(G-10419)*

Petro Inc 877 745-7687
40 Cragwood Rd Ste D South Plainfield (07080) *(G-10420)*
Petro Extrusion Tech Inc 908 789-3338
205 Hallock Ave Ste B Middlesex (08846) *(G-6187)*
Petro Extrusion Technology, Middlesex Also called Petro Extrusion Tech Inc *(G-6187)*
Petro Packaging Co Inc 908 272-4054
16 Quine St Cranford (07016) *(G-1922)*
Petro Pallet LLC 732 230-3287
575 Ridge Rd Monmouth Junction (08852) *(G-6354)*
Petro Plastics Company Inc 908 789-1200
500 Hoiles Dr Kenilworth (07033) *(G-4987)*
Petroleum Trends International 732 494-0405
312 Amboy Ave Ste 2 Metuchen (08840) *(G-6117)*
Petronio Shoe Products Corp 973 751-7579
305 Cortlandt St Belleville (07109) *(G-311)*
Pfizer, Peapack Also called Pharmacia & Upjohn Company LLC *(G-8431)*
Pfizer Inc 732 591-2106
11 Erin Ln Old Bridge (08857) *(G-7788)*
Pfizer Inc 973 993-0977
182 Tabor Rd Morris Plains (07950) *(G-6678)*
Pfizer Inc 201 294-8060
8810 Durham Ave North Bergen (07047) *(G-7475)*
Pfizer Inc 908 251-5685
43 Spruce Hollow Rd Dunellen (08812) *(G-2130)*
Pfizer Inc 973 660-5000
1 Giralda Farms Madison (07940) *(G-5731)*
Pfizer Inc 609 434-4920
1001 Jack Stephan Way Ewing (08628) *(G-3041)*
Pfizer Inc 908 901-8000
100 Rte 206 N Peapack (07977) *(G-8429)*
Pfizer Inc 212 733-2323
400 Crossing Blvd Fl 7 Bridgewater (08807) *(G-872)*
Pfizer Inc 973 739-0430
400 Webro Rd Parsippany (07054) *(G-8061)*
Pfk Coach Phyllis Flood Knerr 856 429-5425
119 Walnut St Haddonfield (08033) *(G-4061)*
Pflaumer Brothers Inc (PA) 609 883-4610
1008 Whitehead Road Ext Ewing (08638) *(G-3042)*
Pg Marble, Freehold Also called Premier Marble and Gran 2 Inc *(G-3681)*
Pgi Nonwovens, Landisville Also called Fibertech Group Inc *(G-5231)*
Pgw Auto Glass LLC 856 234-1600
823 E Gate Dr Mount Laurel (08054) *(G-6825)*
Pharm Ops Inc 908 454-7733
101 Broad St Phillipsburg (08865) *(G-8662)*
Pharm-Rx Chemical Corporation 973 917-1400
4 Brighton Rd Ste 308 Clifton (07012) *(G-1694)*
Pharma Synergy LLC 856 241-2316
103 Somerfield Rd Swedesboro (08085) *(G-10718)*
Pharma Systems Inc 973 636-9007
662 Goffle Rd Ste 3 Hawthorne (07506) *(G-4254)*
Pharmaceutic Litho Label Inc (PA) 336 785-4000
450 North Ave E Cranford (07016) *(G-1923)*
Pharmaceutical Innovations 973 242-2900
897 Frelinghuysen Ave Newark (07114) *(G-7270)*
Pharmaceutical Regulatory Svcs (PA) 609 497-9694
58 Fairway Dr Princeton (08540) *(G-9091)*
Pharmachem Laboratories, Paterson Also called Mpt Delivery Systems Inc *(G-8343)*
Pharmachem Laboratories Inc 973 256-1340
15 Adams Dr Totowa (07512) *(G-10962)*
Pharmachem Laboratories Inc 201 343-3611
130 Wesley St South Hackensack (07606) *(G-10288)*
Pharmachem Laboratories LLC (HQ) 201 246-1000
265 Harrison Tpke Kearny (07032) *(G-4908)*
Pharmachem Laboratories, Inc., Kearny Also called Pharmachem Laboratories LLC *(G-4908)*
Pharmacia & Upjohn Inc (HQ) 908 901-8000
100 Route 206 N Peapack (07977) *(G-8430)*
Pharmacia & Upjohn Company LLC (HQ) 908 901-8000
100 Rte 206 N Peapack (07977) *(G-8431)*
Pharmaderm, East Hanover Also called Fougera Pharmaceuticals Inc *(G-2217)*
Pharmakon Corp 856 829-3161
2200 Wallace Blvd Ste C Cinnaminson (08077) *(G-1484)*
Pharmaseq Inc 732 355-0100
11 Deerpark Dr Ste 104 Monmouth Junction (08852) *(G-6355)*
Pharmasource International LLC 732 985-6182
1090 Stelton Rd Piscataway (08854) *(G-8800)*
Pharmatech International Inc 973 244-0393
21 Just Rd Fairfield (07004) *(G-3283)*
Pharmedium Services LLC 847 457-2362
36 Stults Rd Dayton (08810) *(G-1982)*
Pharmetic Mfg Company LLC 732 254-1901
650 Jernee Mill Rd Sayreville (08872) *(G-9835)*
Pharming Healthcare Inc 908 376-3058
685 Us Highway 202/206 Bridgewater (08807) *(G-873)*
Pharmion Corporation (HQ) 908 673-9000
86 Morris Ave Summit (07901) *(G-10653)*
Phelps Dodge, Elizabeth Also called Freeport Minerals Corporation *(G-2734)*
Phibro Animal Health Corp (HQ) 201 329-7300
300 Frank W Burr Blvd Teaneck (07666) *(G-10765)*

Phibro Animal Health Holdings, Teaneck *Also called Phibro-Tech Inc* **(G-10767)**
Phibro Anmal Hlth Holdings Inc (PA) 201 329-7300
300 Frank W Burr Blvd Teaneck (07666) **(G-10766)**
Phibro-Tech Inc (HQ) 201 329-7300
300 Frank W Burr Blvd # 21 Teaneck (07666) **(G-10767)**
Phibrochem Inc 201 329-7300
300 Frank W Burr Blvd # 21 Teaneck (07666) **(G-10768)**
Phil Desiere Electric Mtr Svc 856 692-8442
1338 Almond Rd Vineland (08360) **(G-11390)**
Philadelphia Division, Swedesboro *Also called Lewis-Goetz and Company Inc* **(G-10706)**
Philadelphia Inquirer 856 779-3840
53 Haddonfield Rd Ste 300 Cherry Hill (08002) **(G-1413)**
Philcorr LLC 856 205-0557
2317 Almond Rd Vineland (08360) **(G-11391)**
Phildelphia-Newspapers-Llc 609 823-0453
109 S Dorset Ave Ventnor City (08406) **(G-11293)**
Phildesco Inc 732 937-6560
50 Division St Ste 207 Somerville (08876) **(G-10223)**
Philip Creter Inc 908 686-2910
20 Monroe St Union (07083) **(G-11215)**
Philip Holzer and Assoc LLC 212 691-9500
350 Michele Pl Carlstadt (07072) **(G-1202)**
Philip Lief Group Inc 609 430-1000
371 Sayre Dr Princeton (08540) **(G-9092)**
Philip Mamrak 908 454-6089
531 Victory Ave Phillipsburg (08865) **(G-8663)**
Philip Morris USA Inc 908 781-6400
2 Crossroads Dr Ste 200b Bedminster (07921) **(G-282)**
Philip Papalia 732 349-5530
21 Dugan Ln Toms River (08755) **(G-10902)**
Philips Elec N Amer Corp 973 804-2100
1 Samsung Pl Ledgewood (07852) **(G-5307)**
Philips Elec N Amer Corp 973 471-9450
215 Entin Rd Clifton (07014) **(G-1695)**
Philips Entertainment Lighting, Somerset *Also called Genlyte Thomas Group LLC* **(G-10104)**
Philips Lighting N Amer Corp. 732 563-3000
200 Franklin Square Dr Somerset (08873) **(G-10154)**
Phillip Balderose 732 574-1330
70 Westfield Ave Clark (07066) **(G-1512)**
Phillips Companies Inc (PA) 973 483-4124
7 Frontage Rd Clinton (08809) **(G-1753)**
Phillips Enterprises Inc 732 493-3191
3600 Sunset Ave Ocean (07712) **(G-7736)**
Phillips Precision Inc 201 797-8820
7 Paul Kohner Pl Elmwood Park (07407) **(G-2843)**
Phillips Precision Medicraft, Elmwood Park *Also called Phillips Precision Inc* **(G-2843)**
Phillips Safety Products Inc 732 356-1493
123 Lincoln Blvd Ste 2 Middlesex (08846) **(G-6188)**
Phillips Scientific Co, Mahwah *Also called Theory Development Corp* **(G-5819)**
Phillipsburg Marble Co Inc 908 859-3435
1 Marble Hill Rd Phillipsburg (08865) **(G-8664)**
Philly Motors and Drives Inc 856 840-8011
103 Central Ave Ste 400b Mount Laurel (08054) **(G-6826)**
Phoenician Bakery, The, North Brunswick *Also called Phoenician Inc* **(G-7534)**
Phoenician Inc 732 545-3915
608 Georges Rd North Brunswick (08902) **(G-7534)**
Phoenix Alliance Group LLC 732 495-4800
337 State Route 36 Port Monmouth (07758) **(G-8973)**
Phoenix Business Forms Inc 856 691-2266
2231 N East Blvd Vineland (08360) **(G-11392)**
Phoenix Chemical Inc 908 707-0232
151 Industrial Pkwy Branchburg (08876) **(G-689)**
Phoenix Color Corp 800 632-4111
40 Green Pond Rd Rockaway (07866) **(G-9595)**
Phoenix Container Inc 732 247-3931
6 Litho Rd Trenton (08648) **(G-11097)**
Phoenix Down Corporation 973 812-8100
85 Route 46 Totowa (07512) **(G-10963)**
Phoenix Friction Products, Middlesex *Also called KRs Automotive Dev Group Inc* **(G-6174)**
Phoenix Fuels Life, Cresskill *Also called Phoenix National Petroleum Co* **(G-1947)**
Phoenix Glass LLC 856 692-0100
615 Alvine Rd Pittsgrove (08318) **(G-8847)**
Phoenix Industrial LLC 908 955-0114
531 Route 22 E 194 Whitehouse Station (08889) **(G-12061)**
Phoenix Industries LLC 973 366-4199
105 W Dewey Ave Ste 204 Wharton (07885) **(G-11997)**
Phoenix Machine Rebuilders Inc 973 691-8029
4 Gold Mine Rd Roxbury Township (07836) **(G-9712)**
Phoenix Manufacturing Inc 732 380-1666
1306 Brielle Ave Ocean (07712) **(G-7737)**
Phoenix National Petroleum Co 201 568-5568
157 Hillside Ave Cresskill (07626) **(G-1947)**
Phoenix Packing & Gasket Co 732 938-7377
247 Old Tavern Rd Howell (07731) **(G-4564)**
Phoenix Pkg & Gasket Mfg Co, Howell *Also called Phoenix Packing & Gasket Co* **(G-4564)**
Phoenix Powder Coating LLC 973 907-7500
400 Union Ave Ste 2 Haskell (07420) **(G-4212)**
Phoenix Precision Co. 973 208-8877
2963 State Rt 23 Newfoundland (07435) **(G-7375)**

Phoenix Resins Inc 888 627-3769
602 Union Landing Rd Cinnaminson (08077) **(G-1485)**
Phoenix Systems 201 788-5511
39 Morningside Ave North Haledon (07508) **(G-7553)**
Phoenix Tool & Machine Inc 856 753-5565
1044 Industrial Dr Ste 5 West Berlin (08091) **(G-11742)**
Photo Offset Prtg & Pubg Co 609 587-4900
536 Highway 33 Trenton (08619) **(G-11098)**
Photo Screen of N J, Carlstadt *Also called Screen Reproductions Co Inc* **(G-1215)**
Photographic Analysis Company (PA) 973 696-1000
190 Parish Dr Wayne (07470) **(G-11673)**
Photographic Tech Intl, Newton *Also called Mri International* **(G-7397)**
Photon Technology Intl, Birmingham *Also called Cgm Us Inc* **(G-467)**
Photonics Management Corp (HQ) 908 231-0960
360 Foothill Rd Bridgewater (08807) **(G-874)**
Photoscribe, Teaneck *Also called DBC Inc* **(G-10747)**
Pht Aerospace LLC (PA) 973 831-1230
230 W Parkway Ste 2 Pompton Plains (07444) **(G-8965)**
Physical Acoustics Corporation 609 716-4000
195 Clarksville Rd Princeton Junction (08550) **(G-9162)**
Physicans Educatn Resource LLC 609 378-3701
666 Plainsboro Rd Ste 300 Plainsboro (08536) **(G-8895)**
Physician's Weekly, Basking Ridge *Also called M/C Communications LLC* **(G-193)**
Physicians Weekly LLC 609 981-7354
180 Mount Airy Rd Ste 202 Basking Ridge (07920) **(G-202)**
Physicians Weekly LLC (HQ) 908 766-0421
180 Mount Airy Rd Ste 202 Basking Ridge (07920) **(G-203)**
Physitemp Instruments, Clifton *Also called Micro-Tek Laboratories Inc* **(G-1674)**
Phytoceuticals Inc 201 791-2255
37 Midland Ave Ste 1 Elmwood Park (07407) **(G-2844)**
PI Metal Products Inc 201 955-0800
1717 Pennsylvania Ave Linden (07036) **(G-5428)**
Pic Corporation 908 862-7977
1101 W Elizabeth Ave Linden (07036) **(G-5429)**
Pic Graphics 201 420-5040
926 Newark Ave Ste 400 Jersey City (07306) **(G-4801)**
Pica Printings Inc 973 540-0420
103 Ridgedale Ave Ste 4 Morristown (07960) **(G-6735)**
Picasso Lighting Inds LLC 201 246-8188
46 Sellers St Kearny (07032) **(G-4909)**
Picture Framing Magazine, Freehold *Also called Hobby Publications Inc* **(G-3659)**
Picture It Awards, Edison *Also called Picture It Inc* **(G-2594)**
Picture It Inc 732 819-0420
1703 State Route 27 Ste 2 Edison (08817) **(G-2594)**
Picture Knits Inc 973 340-3131
489 Getty Ave Clifton (07011) **(G-1696)**
Picture Window Software LLC 908 362-4000
47 Cook Rd Blairstown (07825) **(G-498)**
Picut Industries Inc (PA) 908 754-1333
140 Mount Bethel Rd Warren (07059) **(G-11562)**
Picut Mfg Co Inc 908 754-1333
140 Mount Bethel Rd Warren (07059) **(G-11563)**
Piemonte & Liebhauser LLC 973 937-6200
325 Columbia Tpke Ste 108 Florham Park (07932) **(G-3514)**
Pierangeli Group Inc 856 582-4060
221 Jersey Ave Gloucester City (08030) **(G-3842)**
Pierce-Roberts Rubber Company 609 394-5245
1450 Heath Ave Ewing (08638) **(G-3043)**
Pierre Fbre Phrmaceuticals Inc 973 898-1042
8 Campus Dr Ste 2 Parsippany (07054) **(G-8062)**
Pierrepont & Co, Rutherford *Also called Highpont Corporation* **(G-9734)**
Pierson Industries Inc 973 627-7945
7 Astro Pl Rockaway (07866) **(G-9596)**
Pike Machine Products Inc 973 379-9128
17 Clive Hills Rd Short Hills (07078) **(G-9983)**
Pilkington North America Inc 973 470-5703
125 Kingsland Ave Clifton (07014) **(G-1697)**
Pillar of Fire (PA) 732 356-0102
10 Chapel Dr Zarephath (08890) **(G-12270)**
Pilot Chemical Company Ohio 732 634-6613
267 Homestead Ave Avenel (07001) **(G-145)**
Pim Brands LLC 732 560-8300
500 Pierce St Somerset (08873) **(G-10155)**
Pin Cancer Campaign 973 600-4170
34 County Road 519 Newton (07860) **(G-7400)**
Pin Express, Plainfield *Also called Edwin Leonel Ramirez* **(G-8860)**
Pin People LLC 888 309-7467
1 Paragon Dr Ste 150 Montvale (07645) **(G-6470)**
Pin Point Container Corp 856 848-2115
669 Tanyard Rd Deptford (08096) **(G-2066)**
Pine Hill Printing Inc 856 346-2915
200 Erial Rd Pine Hill (08021) **(G-8722)**
Pine Park Kitchens Inc 732 987-6520
225 2nd St Lakewood (08701) **(G-5171)**
Pinelands Brewing Ltd Lblty Co 609 296-6169
140 7th Ave Unit 15 Ltl Egg Hbr (08087) **(G-5646)**
Pinnacle Cosmetic Packg LLC 908 241-7777
80 Market St Kenilworth (07033) **(G-4988)**

2018 Harris New Jersey
Manufacturers Directory

(G-0000) Company's Geographic Section entry number

Pinnacle Cosmetics Packaging, Kenilworth *Also called Pinnacle Cosmetic Packg LLC* ***(G-4988)***
Pinnacle Food Group Inc....856 969-7100
6 Executive Campus # 100 Cherry Hill (08002) ***(G-1414)***
Pinnacle Foods Finance LLC (HQ)....973 541-6620
399 Jefferson Rd Parsippany (07054) ***(G-8063)***
Pinnacle Foods Group LLC (HQ)....856 969-8238
399 Jefferson Rd Parsippany (07054) ***(G-8064)***
Pinnacle Foods Inc (PA)....973 541-6620
399 Jefferson Rd Parsippany (07054) ***(G-8065)***
Pinnacle Grphic Communications, Morris Plains *Also called J&E Business Services LLC* ***(G-6672)***
Pinnacle Materials Inc (PA)....732 254-7676
39 Edgeboro Rd East Brunswick (08816) ***(G-2173)***
Pinnacle Press Inc....201 652-0500
41 Prospect St Midland Park (07432) ***(G-6234)***
Pinsonault Associates LLC....800 372-9009
5 Woodhollow Rd Ste 2 Parsippany (07054) ***(G-8066)***
Pinto of Montville Inc....973 584-2002
25 Pine St Kenvil (07847) ***(G-5012)***
Pinto Printing....856 232-2550
12 Sycamore Dr Blackwood (08012) ***(G-489)***
Pioneer & Co Inc....856 866-9191
97 Foster Rd Ste 5 Moorestown (08057) ***(G-6613)***
Pioneer Associates Inc (PA)....201 592-7007
2125 Center Ave Ste 305 Fort Lee (07024) ***(G-3577)***
Pioneer Concrete Corp....609 693-6151
2011 Lacey Rd Forked River (08731) ***(G-3539)***
Pioneer Embroidery Co....973 777-6418
31 Saddle River Ave South Hackensack (07606) ***(G-10289)***
Pioneer Industries, Carlstadt *Also called Security Holdings LLC* ***(G-1216)***
Pioneer Machine & Tool Co Inc....856 779-8800
425 E Broadway Maple Shade (08052) ***(G-5907)***
Pioneer Power Solutions Inc (PA)....212 867-0700
400 Kelby St Ste 12 Fort Lee (07024) ***(G-3578)***
Pioneer Railing Inc....609 387-0981
401 Railroad Ave Beverly (08010) ***(G-464)***
PIP Printing, Butler *Also called My Way Prints Inc* ***(G-1014)***
PIP Printing, Parsippany *Also called Conagraphics Inc* ***(G-7975)***
PIP Printing, Paramus *Also called Barrington Press Inc* ***(G-7857)***
PIP Printing, Livingston *Also called Morris Plains Pip Inc* ***(G-5548)***
Pipe Dreams Marine LLC....609 628-9353
251 Mill Rd Tuckahoe (08250) ***(G-11137)***
Pipeline Eqp Resources Co LLC....888 232-7372
9 Mars Ct Ste 4 Boonton (07005) ***(G-579)***
Pipeline Renewal Technologies, Randolph *Also called Envirosight LLC* ***(G-9275)***
Piper Heating and Cooling, Midland Park *Also called Piper Services LLC* ***(G-6235)***
Piper Services LLC....844 567-3900
268 Greenwood Ave Midland Park (07432) ***(G-6235)***
Piping Solutions Inc....732 537-1009
81 Chimney Rock Rd Ste 4 Bridgewater (08807) ***(G-875)***
Piping Supplies Inc....609 561-9323
18 E Black Horse Pike Williamstown (08094) ***(G-12096)***
Piramal Glass - Usa Inc (HQ)....856 293-6400
329 Herrod Blvd Dayton (08810) ***(G-1983)***
Piramal Glass - Usa Inc....856 728-9300
918 E Malaga Rd Williamstown (08094) ***(G-12097)***
Piramal Glass - Usa Inc....856 293-6400
918 E Malaga Rd Williamstown (08094) ***(G-12098)***
Pirate Brands LLC....973 401-6500
4 Gatehall Dr Ste 110 Parsippany (07054) ***(G-8067)***
Pirolli Printing Co Inc....856 933-1285
860 W Browning Rd Bellmawr (08031) ***(G-349)***
Pitney Bowes Inc....908 903-2870
15 Mountainview Rd Warren (07059) ***(G-11564)***
Pitney Bowes Inc....800 521-0080
158 Mount Olivet Ave Newark (07114) ***(G-7271)***
Pitney Bowes Inc....856 764-2240
1835 Underwood Blvd Ste 1 Delran (08075) ***(G-2020)***
Pixell Creative Group LLC....609 410-3024
302 Wood St Burlington (08016) ***(G-988)***
Pj Food Service, Cranbury *Also called Papa Johns New Jersey* ***(G-1867)***
Pjm Software Inc....973 330-0405
33 Mayer Dr Clifton (07012) ***(G-1698)***
Pkc Finewoodworking LLC....201 951-8880
31 Springbrook Rd E Montville (07045) ***(G-6492)***
Pkm Panel Systems Corp....732 238-6760
4420 Bordentown Ave Old Bridge (08857) ***(G-7789)***
Pl Custom Emergency Vehicles, Manasquan *Also called P L Custom Body & Eqp Co Inc* ***(G-5877)***
Plagidos Winery LLC....609 567-4633
570 N 1st Rd Hammonton (08037) ***(G-4146)***
Plan It Roi, Denville *Also called Planitroi Inc* ***(G-2051)***
Planet Associates Inc....201 693-8700
24 Wampum Rd Park Ridge (07656) ***(G-7927)***
Planet Popcorn LLC....732 294-8680
Freehold Mall Freehold (07728) ***(G-3677)***
Planitroi Inc (PA)....973 664-0700
100-10 Ford Rd Ste 10 Denville (07834) ***(G-2051)***
Plant Food Company Inc....609 448-0935
38 Hightstwn Crnbry Sta Cranbury (08512) ***(G-1870)***
Plantfusion....732 537-1220
3775 Park Ave Edison (08820) ***(G-2595)***
Plasma Powders & Systems Inc....732 431-0992
228 Boundary Rd Ste 2 Marlboro (07746) ***(G-5952)***
Plasti Foam....908 722-5254
68 County Line Rd Branchburg (08876) ***(G-690)***
Plasti-Clad Metal Products Inc....732 449-2665
2601 Ridgewood Rd Wall Township (07719) ***(G-11503)***
Plastic By All LLC....732 785-5900
1127 Industrial Pkwy B Brick (08724) ***(G-755)***
Plastic Plus Group LLC....201 561-0405
600 Mdwlands Pkwy Ste 134 Secaucus (07094) ***(G-9911)***
Plastic Plus Inc....973 614-0271
184 Willet St Passaic (07055) ***(G-8170)***
Plastic Profiles Co Div, Parsippany *Also called Central Plastics Incorporated* ***(G-7966)***
Plastic Reel Corp of America (PA)....201 933-5100
40 Triangle Blvd Carlstadt (07072) ***(G-1203)***
Plastic Specialties & Tech Inc (HQ)....201 941-2900
101 Railroad Ave Ridgefield (07657) ***(G-9380)***
Plastico Products LLC....973 923-1944
34 Loretto St Irvington (07111) ***(G-4600)***
Plastics Consulting & Mfg Co....800 222-0317
1435 Ferry Ave Camden (08104) ***(G-1082)***
Plastics For Chemicals Inc (PA)....609 242-9100
710 Old Shore Rd Forked River (08731) ***(G-3540)***
Plastics Galore LLC....732 363-8447
1970 Swarthmore Ave Ste 8 Lakewood (08701) ***(G-5172)***
Plastiform Packaging Inc....973 983-8900
114 Beach St Ste 6 Rockaway (07866) ***(G-9597)***
Plastinetics Inc....818 364-1611
439 Main Rd Towaco (07082) ***(G-11001)***
Plastinetics Inc....973 618-9090
195 Fairfield Ave West Caldwell (07006) ***(G-11797)***
Plastpac Inc (PA)....908 272-7200
30 Boright Ave Kenilworth (07033) ***(G-4989)***
Plastpro 2000 Inc....973 992-2090
9 Peach Tree Hill Rd Livingston (07039) ***(G-5556)***
Plastpro Doors, Livingston *Also called Plastpro 2000 Inc* ***(G-5556)***
Plate Concepts Inc....908 236-9570
1221 Us Highway 22 Ste 3 Lebanon (08833) ***(G-5299)***
Platinum Designs LLC....908 782-4010
87 W Main St Somerville (08876) ***(G-10224)***
Platinum Plating Specialists....732 221-2575
11 Blake Dr Clark (07066) ***(G-1513)***
Platon Interiors....201 567-5533
180 S Van Brunt St Englewood (07631) ***(G-2922)***
Platypus Print Productions LLC....732 772-1212
253 State Route 79 N Morganville (07751) ***(G-6651)***
Plcs Inc....856 722-1333
102 Gaither Dr Ste 1 Mount Laurel (08054) ***(G-6827)***
Pleasant, Point Pleasant Beach *Also called Norma K Corporation* ***(G-8924)***
Plescia & Company Inc....856 793-0137
205 Shady Ln Marlton (08053) ***(G-5994)***
Plextone, Kenilworth *Also called Seagrave Coatings Corp* ***(G-4994)***
Plexus Publishing Inc....609 654-6500
143 Old Marlton Pike Medford (08055) ***(G-6078)***
Plumbing Supply Now LLC....732 228-8852
167 Black Horse Ln New Brunswick (08902) ***(G-6991)***
Plus Packaging Inc....973 538-2216
10 Mount Pleasant Rd Morristown (07960) ***(G-6736)***
PM Swapco Inc....201 438-7700
1099 Wall St W Ste 390 Lyndhurst (07071) ***(G-5701)***
PMC, Midland Park *Also called Precision Multiple Contrls Inc* ***(G-6237)***
Pmc Inc....201 933-8540
13 Manor Rd East Rutherford (07073) ***(G-2317)***
Pmc Inc....973 748-5500
55 La France Ave Bloomfield (07003) ***(G-527)***
Pmc Inc....732 370-1163
1 Gusmer Dr Lakewood (08701) ***(G-5173)***
PMC Group Inc (PA)....856 533-1866
1288 Route 73 Ste 401 Mount Laurel (08054) ***(G-6828)***
PMC Industries Inc....201 342-3684
275 Hudson St Hackensack (07601) ***(G-3963)***
PMC Liquiflo Equipment Co Inc....908 518-0666
443 North Ave Garwood (07027) ***(G-3785)***
PMC Thermocouple Division, Saddle Brook *Also called Te Wire & Cable LLC* ***(G-9796)***
Pmje Welding LLC....973 685-7344
310 Colfax Ave Unit A Clifton (07013) ***(G-1699)***
Pmm Inc....908 692-1465
11 Lafayette Ky Colts Neck (07722) ***(G-1790)***
Pmp Composites Corporation....609 587-1188
572 Whitehead Rd Ste 101 Trenton (08619) ***(G-11099)***
Pmv Pharmaceuticals Inc....650 241-2822
8 Clarke Dr Ste 3 Cranbury (08512) ***(G-1871)***
PNC Electronics Inc....973 237-0400
20 W End Rd Totowa (07512) ***(G-10964)***

PNC Inc 973 284-1600
115 E Centre St Nutley (07110) *(G-7652)*

Pneutronics Division, Pine Brook *Also called Parker-Hannifin Corporation* *(G-8712)*

Pny Technologies Inc (PA) 973 515-9700
100 Jefferson Rd Parsippany (07054) *(G-8068)*

Pochet of America Inc 973 942-4923
1 Garret Mountain Plz # 502 Woodland Park (07424) *(G-12228)*

Point Lobster Company Inc 732 892-1718
1 Saint Louis Ave Point Pleasant Beach (08742) *(G-8926)*

Polar Truck Sales 201 246-1010
350 Sip Ave Jersey City (07306) *(G-4802)*

Polaris America Ltd Lblty Co 614 540-1710
1985 Rutgers Blvd Lakewood (08701) *(G-5174)*

Polaris Communications Inc 201 928-0780
1300 Wellington Ave Teaneck (07666) *(G-10769)*

Polaris Consulting & Svcs Ltd 732 590-8151
111 Town Square Pl # 340 Jersey City (07310) *(G-4803)*

Polaris Plate Heat Exchngers L 732 345-7188
1151 Broad St Ste 218 Shrewsbury (07702) *(G-10008)*

Polaris Plating Inc 973 278-0033
36 Teaneck Rd Parsippany (07054) *(G-8069)*

Polaris Thermal, Shrewsbury *Also called Polaris Plate Heat Exchngers L* *(G-10008)*

Polarity LLC 732 970-3855
330 Mockingbird Ln Morganville (07751) *(G-6652)*

Polish Nail 732 627-9799
570 Union Ave Middlesex (08846) *(G-6189)*

Polish Press, Mahwah *Also called Missionary Society of St Paul* *(G-5792)*

Polmar Iron Work Inc 732 882-0900
673 New Brunswick Ave Rahway (07065) *(G-9217)*

Polo Machine Inc 973 340-9984
223 Banta Ave Garfield (07026) *(G-3749)*

Polonica Inc 732 855-0008
147 Ethel Rd W Piscataway (08854) *(G-8801)*

Polvac Inc 732 828-1662
235 Jersey Ave Ste 1 New Brunswick (08901) *(G-6992)*

Poly Bag Division, Hamburg *Also called Dauson Corrugated Container* *(G-4090)*

Poly Molding LLC 973 835-7161
96 4th Ave Haskell (07420) *(G-4213)*

Poly Source Enterprises LLC 732 580-5409
17 Duchess Ct Freehold (07728) *(G-3678)*

Poly-Dyn International, South Plainfield *Also called Polymer Dynamix LLC* *(G-10421)*

Poly-Gel LLC 973 884-3300
30 Leslie Ct Whippany (07981) *(G-12034)*

Poly-Version Inc 201 451-7600
49 Fisk St Jersey City (07305) *(G-4804)*

Polyair Inter Pack Inc 201 804-1725
495 Meadow Ln Carlstadt (07072) *(G-1204)*

Polyair Inter Pack Inc 201 804-1700
495 Meadow Ln Carlstadt (07072) *(G-1205)*

Polyair Packaging Division, Carlstadt *Also called Polyair Inter Pack Inc* *(G-1204)*

Polycast, Hackensack *Also called Spartech LLC* *(G-3979)*

Polycel Structural Foam Inc 908 722-5254
68 County Line Rd Branchburg (08876) *(G-691)*

Polycel Structural Foam Inc 908 722-5254
68 County Line Rd Branchburg (08876) *(G-692)*

Polyfil Corporation 973 627-4070
74 Green Pond Rd Rockaway (07866) *(G-9598)*

Polymathes Holdings I LLC (PA) 609 945-1690
20 Nassau St Ste M Princeton (08542) *(G-9093)*

Polymer Additives Inc 856 467-8247
170 Us Route 130 S Bridgeport (08014) *(G-770)*

Polymer Additives Inc 856 467-8220
170 Us 130 Swedesboro (08085) *(G-10719)*

Polymer Dynamix LLC 732 381-1600
238 Saint Nicholas Ave South Plainfield (07080) *(G-10421)*

Polymer Molded Products 732 907-1990
10 Easy St Bound Brook (08805) *(G-621)*

Polymer Technologies Inc 973 778-9100
10 Clifton Blvd Ste 3 Clifton (07011) *(G-1700)*

Polymeric Resources Corp (PA) 973 694-4141
55 Haul Rd Ste A Wayne (07470) *(G-11674)*

Polymite, Allenhurst *Also called Koadings Inc* *(G-26)*

Polysystems Inc 312 332-5670
2 Executive Campus # 320 Cherry Hill (08002) *(G-1415)*

Polytech Designs Inc 973 340-1390
26 W 1st St Clifton (07011) *(G-1701)*

Polytechnic Industries Inc 856 235-6550
14 Roland Ave Mount Laurel (08054) *(G-6829)*

Polytype America Corp 201 995-1000
10 Industrial Ave Ste 4 Mahwah (07430) *(G-5801)*

Polyvel Inc 609 567-0080
100 9th St Hammonton (08037) *(G-4147)*

Pom Gear, Linden *Also called Cellular Empire Inc* *(G-5357)*

Pomi USA Inc 732 541-4115
253 Main St Ste 380 Matawan (07747) *(G-6029)*

Pompton Lakes Quarry, Pompton Lakes *Also called Tilcon New York Inc* *(G-8950)*

Poof-Alex Holdings LLC 734 454-9552
40 Lane Rd Fairfield (07004) *(G-3284)*

Pool Ladder, Hackensack *Also called Kayden Manufacturing Inc* *(G-3935)*

Pool Tables Plus Inc (PA) 732 968-8228
299 Us Highway 22 Ste 24 Green Brook (08812) *(G-3862)*

Poor Boy Pallet LLC 856 451-3771
45 Finley Rd Bridgeton (08302) *(G-795)*

Poplar Bindery Inc 856 727-8030
300 Mill St Moorestown (08057) *(G-6614)*

Popnfold Papers Inc 201 933-2015
205 Chubb Ave Fl 2 Lyndhurst (07071) *(G-5702)*

Popularity Products, Carteret *Also called New York Popular Inc* *(G-1263)*

Por-15 Inc 973 887-1999
64 S Jefferson Rd Ste 2 Whippany (07981) *(G-12035)*

Porfirio Foods Inc 609 393-4116
320 Anderson St Trenton (08611) *(G-11100)*

Port A (PA) 732 776-6511
911 Kingsley St Asbury Park (07712) *(G-82)*

Portable Container Services, Roseland *Also called Granco Group LLC* *(G-9651)*

Portaseal LLC 973 539-0100
1 John St Morristown (07960) *(G-6737)*

Porton Usa LLC (HQ) 908 791-9100
3001 Hadley Rd Ste 1-4 South Plainfield (07080) *(G-10422)*

Posner, Butler *Also called Carole Cosmetics LLC* *(G-1000)*

Post To Post LLC 609 646-9300
2545 Fire Rd Ste 1 Egg Harbor Township (08234) *(G-2692)*

Postage Bin 732 333-0915
31 E Main St Ste 4 Freehold (07728) *(G-3679)*

Postcard Press Inc 310 747-3878
435 N Midland Ave Saddle Brook (07663) *(G-9783)*

Potdevin Machine Co 973 227-8828
26 Fairfield Pl West Caldwell (07006) *(G-11798)*

Potters Industries LLC 201 507-4169
600 Industrial Rd Carlstadt (07072) *(G-1206)*

Potti-Bags Inc 201 796-5555
120 Ackerman Ave Elmwood Park (07407) *(G-2845)*

Pov Reports, Montclair *Also called P O V Incorporated* *(G-6428)*

Power Bag and Film LLC 908 832-6648
189 W Valley Brook Rd Califon (07830) *(G-1035)*

Power Brooks Co LLC 609 890-0100
2 Marlen Dr Hamilton (08691) *(G-4121)*

Power By Gogreen, Howell *Also called Gogreen Power Inc* *(G-4555)*

Power Container Corp 732 560-3655
33 Schoolhouse Rd Ste 2 Somerset (08873) *(G-10156)*

Power Dynamics Inc 973 560-0019
145 Algonquin Pkwy Ste 2 Whippany (07981) *(G-12036)*

Power Hawk Technologies Inc 973 627-4646
300 Forge Way Ste 2 Rockaway (07866) *(G-9599)*

Power Magne-Tech Corp 732 826-4700
653 Sayre Ave Perth Amboy (08861) *(G-8626)*

Power Magnetic, Perth Amboy *Also called Power Magne-Tech Corp* *(G-8626)*

Power Magnetics Inc (PA) 609 695-1170
377 Reservoir St Trenton (08618) *(G-11101)*

Power Packaging Services Corp 201 261-2566
20 Park Pl Paramus (07652) *(G-7897)*

Power Pool Plus Inc 908 454-1124
7 Edge Rd Alpha (08865) *(G-44)*

Power Products and Engrg LLC 855 769-3751
324 Meadowbrook Rd Trenton (08691) *(G-11102)*

Powercomm Solutions LLC 908 806-7025
15 Minneakoning Rd # 311 Flemington (08822) *(G-3459)*

Powerhuse Frmltons Ltd Labilit 888 666-7715
150 Maple Ave Ste 216 South Plainfield (07080) *(G-10423)*

Powerspec Inc 732 494-9490
25 4th St Somerville (08876) *(G-10225)*

Powertrunk Inc 201 630-4520
66 York St Ste 4 Jersey City (07302) *(G-4805)*

Powerwash Plus 732 671-6767
25 Oriole Rd Middletown (07748) *(G-6218)*

Powtek Powder Coating Inc 609 394-1144
233 Dickinson St Ewing (08638) *(G-3044)*

Ppe, Trenton *Also called Power Products and Engrg LLC* *(G-11102)*

PPG Architectural Finishes Inc 908 353-2477
1001 Newark Ave Elizabeth (07208) *(G-2767)*

PPG Auto Glass, Pennsauken *Also called PPG Ind Inc* *(G-8561)*

PPG Ind Inc 856 662-9323
75 Twinbridge Dr Ste C Pennsauken (08110) *(G-8561)*

PPG Industries Inc 856 273-7870
823 E Gate Dr Ste 4 Mount Laurel (08054) *(G-6830)*

Ppi, Millville *Also called Pentagon Performance Inc* *(G-6320)*

Ppi/Time Zero Inc (PA) 973 278-6500
11 Madison Rd Fairfield (07004) *(G-3285)*

PQ Corporation 732 750-9040
2 Paddock St Avenel (07001) *(G-146)*

PR Products Distributors Inc 973 928-1120
189 Berdan Ave Ste 281 Wayne (07470) *(G-11675)*

Prads, Parsippany *Also called Predictive Analytcs Dcision* *(G-8071)*

Pratt Displays, Totowa *Also called Pratt Industries USA Inc* *(G-10965)*

Pratt Displays, Allendale *Also called Pratt Industries USA Inc* *(G-15)*

Pratt Industries USA Inc 973 774-4680
11 Commerce Way Unit C Totowa (07512) *(G-10965)*

(G-0000) Company's Geographic Section entry number

Pratt Industries USA Inc...201 934-1900
3 Pearl Ct Unit 3f Allendale (07401) *(G-15)*

Praxair Inc...732 738-4150
60 Crows Mill Rd Keasbey (08832) *(G-4930)*

Praxair Cryomag Services Inc..732 738-4000
Industrial Ave Keasbey (08832) *(G-4931)*

Praxair Distribution Inc...908 862-7200
515 E Edgar Rd Linden (07036) *(G-5430)*

Praxair Distribution Inc...973 589-7895
425 Avenue P Newark (07105) *(G-7272)*

PRC Laser Corporation (HQ)..973 347-0100
350 N Frontage Rd Landing (07850) *(G-5226)*

PRC of America, Carlstadt *Also called Plastic Reel Corp of America (G-1203)*

Pre-Fab Structures Inc (PA)...856 768-4257
907 Wedgewood Way Atco (08004) *(G-90)*

Preachers Illustration Service, Ventnor City *Also called Voicings Publication Inc (G-11294)*

Precast Manufacturing Co LLC.......................................908 454-2122
187 Strykers Rd Phillipsburg (08865) *(G-8665)*

Precast Systems Inc...609 208-0569
57 Sharon Station Rd Allentown (08501) *(G-33)*

Precious Cosmetics Packaging.......................................973 478-4633
40 Meta Ln Lodi (07644) *(G-5597)*

Precious Metal Processing Cons.....................................201 944-8053
430 Bergen Blvd Palisades Park (07650) *(G-7842)*

Precise Cmpnents TI Design Inc.....................................973 928-2928
10 Clifton Blvd Unit A4 Clifton (07011) *(G-1702)*

Precise Continental, Harrison *Also called Precise Corporate Printing Inc (G-4187)*

Precise Corporate Printing Inc.......................................973 350-0330
1 Cape May St Ste 250 Harrison (07029) *(G-4187)*

Precise Technology Inc...856 241-1760
406 Heron Dr Ste A Swedesboro (08085) *(G-10720)*

Precision Ball Specialties...856 881-5646
1451 Glassboro Rd Williamstown (08094) *(G-12099)*

Precision Custom Coatings LLC (PA)...............................973 890-3873
200 Maltese Dr Totowa (07512) *(G-10966)*

Precision Cut Kits, Ewing *Also called Lawrence Katona (G-3035)*

Precision Dealer Services Inc...908 237-1100
4 Ryerson Rd Flemington (08822) *(G-3460)*

Precision Devices Inc...609 882-2230
20 Lexington Ave Ste 3 Ewing (08618) *(G-3045)*

Precision Electronic Glass Inc..856 691-2234
1013 Hendee Rd Vineland (08360) *(G-11393)*

Precision Filaments Inc..732 462-3755
17 Bannard St Ste 30 Freehold (07728) *(G-3680)*

Precision Forms Inc...973 838-3800
97 Decker Rd Butler (07405) *(G-1016)*

Precision Graphics Inc..908 707-8880
21 County Line Rd Branchburg (08876) *(G-693)*

Precision Metal Machining Inc..201 843-7427
800 Central Blvd Ste C Carlstadt (07072) *(G-1207)*

Precision Metalcrafters Inc..856 629-1020
17 Filbert St Williamstown (08094) *(G-12100)*

Precision Mfg Group LLC (HQ).......................................973 785-4630
501 Little Falls Rd Cedar Grove (07009) *(G-1296)*

Precision Multiple Contrls Inc (PA)..................................201 444-0600
33 Greenwood Ave Midland Park (07432) *(G-6236)*

Precision Multiple Contrls Inc...201 444-0600
33 Greenwood Ave Midland Park (07432) *(G-6237)*

Precision Optical Lab, Williamstown *Also called Spectacle Shoppe (G-12108)*

Precision Orthotic Lab of Nj..856 848-6226
1595 Imperial Way Ste 103 West Deptford (08066) *(G-11839)*

Precision Press, Garwood *Also called New Jersey Reprographics Inc (G-3780)*

Precision Printing Group Inc..856 753-0900
606 Stamford Dr # 606 Mount Laurel (08054) *(G-6831)*

Precision Products Co Inc...201 712-5757
219 Hergesell Ave Maywood (07607) *(G-6060)*

Precision Roll Products Inc..973 822-9100
306 Columbia Tpke Florham Park (07932) *(G-3515)*

Precision Saw & Tool Corp..973 773-7302
56 Colfax Ave Clifton (07013) *(G-1703)*

Precision Shape Solutions, Dover *Also called Service Metal Fabricating Inc (G-2110)*

Precision Specialists Mch LLC..856 768-5990
1005 Martha Blvd Atco (08004) *(G-91)*

Precision Specialties, Belleville *Also called Communique Inc (G-298)*

Precision Spine Inc (PA)...601 420-4244
5 Sylvan Way Fl 2 Parsippany (07054) *(G-8070)*

Precision Welding, Wharton *Also called James A Stanlick Jr (G-11990)*

Precision Welding Machine..609 625-1465
13th St Mays Landing (08330) *(G-6042)*

Predictive Analytcs Dcision..973 541-7020
2001 Route 46 Ste 310 Parsippany (07054) *(G-8071)*

Preferred Plastics Inc..856 662-6250
6512 Park Ave Pennsauken (08109) *(G-8562)*

Preform Laboratories Inc..973 523-8610
34 George St Hackensack (07601) *(G-3964)*

Prem-Khichi Enterprises Inc..973 242-0300
9 Colburn Rd East Brunswick (08816) *(G-2174)*

Premac Inc..732 381-7550
167 Wescott Dr Rahway (07065) *(G-9218)*

Premesco Inc...908 686-0513
2389 Vauxhall Rd Union (07083) *(G-11216)*

Premesco Seamless Ring Co Div, Union *Also called Premesco Inc (G-11216)*

Premier Asset Logistics Networ (PA)...............................877 725-6381
100 N Black Horse Pike # 100 Williamstown (08094) *(G-12101)*

Premier Compaction Systems..718 328-5990
264 Lackawanna Ave Ste 1 Woodland Park (07424) *(G-12229)*

Premier Consumer Products Inc.....................................201 568-9700
106 Grand Ave Ste 120 Englewood (07631) *(G-2923)*

Premier Die Casting Company.......................................732 634-3000
1177 Rahway Ave Avenel (07001) *(G-147)*

Premier Disp & Exhibits Inc...856 382-7497
7070 Colonial Hwy Pennsauken (08109) *(G-8563)*

Premier Graphics Inc...732 872-9933
165 1st Ave C Atlantic Highlands (07716) *(G-115)*

Premier Healthcare Exch Corp (PA).................................908 658-3535
2 Crossroads Dr Ste 101b Bedminster (07921) *(G-283)*

Premier Marble and Gran 2 Inc......................................732 294-7891
200 Commerce Ave Ste 200 # 200 Freehold (07728) *(G-3681)*

Premier Press Inc...856 665-0722
7120 Airport Hwy Pennsauken (08109) *(G-8564)*

Premier Printing Solutions LLC......................................732 525-0740
508 Raritan St Ste D Sayreville (08872) *(G-9836)*

Premier Products Inc...856 231-1800
1002 Lincoln Dr W Ste B Marlton (08053) *(G-5995)*

Premier Ribbon Company...973 589-2600
223 Raymond Blvd Newark (07105) *(G-7273)*

Premier Specialties Inc..732 469-6615
201 Egel Ave Ste 3a Middlesex (08846) *(G-6190)*

Premiere Raceway Sys LLC...732 629-7715
230 Saint Nicholas Ave Piscataway (08854) *(G-8802)*

Premio Foods Inc (PA)...800 864-7622
50 Utter Ave Hawthorne (07506) *(G-4255)*

Premium Clor Graphics Handpack, Carlstadt *Also called Premium Color Group LLC (G-1208)*

Premium Color Group LLC..973 472-7007
651 Garden St Carlstadt (07072) *(G-1208)*

Premium Distribution Corp..212 533-1100
401 Penhorn Ave Ste 2 Secaucus (07094) *(G-9912)*

Premium Imports Inc...718 486-7125
90 Dayton Ave Ste 98 Passaic (07055) *(G-8171)*

Premium Service Printing..908 707-1311
46 Old Camplain Rd Hillsborough (08844) *(G-4363)*

Prentco, Flemington *Also called Printco (G-3463)*

Presbyterian Reformed Pubg Co.....................................908 454-0505
1102 Marble Hill Rd Phillipsburg (08865) *(G-8666)*

Prescription Dynamics Inc...201 746-6262
310 Ridge Rd Mahwah (07430) *(G-5802)*

Prescription Podiatry Labs...609 695-1221
826 S Broad St Trenton (08611) *(G-11103)*

Presentation Solutions Inc..732 961-1960
432 Clearstream Rd Jackson (08527) *(G-4675)*

President Cont Group II LLC (PA).....................................201 933-7500
200 W Commercial Ave Moonachie (07074) *(G-6536)*

Presperse Corporation (HQ)...732 356-5200
19 Schoolhouse Rd Somerset (08873) *(G-10157)*

Press of Atlantic City, Vineland *Also called South Jersey Publishing Co (G-11406)*

Press of Atlantic City, The, Pleasantville *Also called South Jersey Publishing Co (G-8916)*

Press of Atlantic City, The, Pleasantville *Also called Wilmington Trust Sp Services (G-8918)*

Press Room Inc..609 689-3817
100 Youngs Rd Ste 2 Trenton (08619) *(G-11104)*

Pressto Graphics..732 286-9300
109 Foxwood Ter Toms River (08755) *(G-10903)*

Pressure Controls Inc..973 751-5002
406 Cortlandt St Belleville (07109) *(G-312)*

Pressure Pipe Division, Burlington *Also called United States Pipe Fndry LLC (G-994)*

Pressure Wash, West Milford *Also called Margaritaville Inc (G-11854)*

Pressworks..856 427-9001
1879 Old Cuthbert Rd # 28 Cherry Hill (08034) *(G-1416)*

Prestige Associates Inc..609 393-1509
39 Meade St Trenton (08638) *(G-11105)*

Prestige Bread Jersey Cy Inc...201 422-7900
5601-5711 Tonnelle Ave North Bergen (07047) *(G-7476)*

Prestige Camera LLC..718 257-5888
245 Belmont Dr Somerset (08873) *(G-10158)*

Prestige Forklift Maint Svc..732 297-1001
31 Timber Ridge Rd New Brunswick (08902) *(G-6993)*

Prestige Industries LLC..866 492-2244
1099 Wall St W Ste 353 Lyndhurst (07071) *(G-5703)*

Prestige Laboratories Inc..973 772-8922
100 Oak St East Rutherford (07073) *(G-2318)*

Prestige Millwork LLC..908 526-5100
27e Kearney St Ste B Bridgewater (08807) *(G-876)*

Presto Printing Service Inc..908 756-5337
19 S Plainfield Ave South Plainfield (07080) *(G-10424)*

Prestone Products Corporation......................................732 577-7800
250 Halls Mill Rd Freehold (07728) *(G-3682)*

Pretty Jewelry Co...908 806-3377
80 Main St 82 Flemington (08822) *(G-3461)*

Pretty Lil Cupcakes....201 256-1205
317 Essex St Harrison (07029) ***(G-4188)***
Pretty Ugly LLC....908 620-0931
290 Us Highway 22 Green Brook (08812) ***(G-3863)***
Prg Group Inc....201 758-4000
915 Secaucus Rd Secaucus (07094) ***(G-9913)***
Priamo Designs Ltd....201 861-8808
6614 Broadway West New York (07093) ***(G-11876)***
Pride Products Mfg LLC....908 353-1900
5 Slater Dr Elizabeth (07206) ***(G-2768)***
Prima-TEC Electronics Corp....201 947-4052
316 Main St East Rutherford (07073) ***(G-2319)***
Primacy Engineering Inc (PA)....201 731-3272
560 Sylvan Ave Ste 1212 Englewood Cliffs (07632) ***(G-2979)***
Primak Plumbing & Heating Inc....732 270-6282
904 Dorset Psge Toms River (08753) ***(G-10904)***
Primal Surf....609 264-1999
3106 Revere Blvd Brigantine (08203) ***(G-918)***
Primary Systems Inc....732 679-2200
30 State Route 18 Old Bridge (08857) ***(G-7790)***
Prime Choice Foods, Passaic *Also called House of Herbs Inc* ***(G-8147)***
Prime Coding Services LLC....732 254-3036
58 Frost Ave East Brunswick (08816) ***(G-2175)***
Prime Fur & Leather Inc....201 941-9600
29 Industrial Ave 31 Fairview (07022) ***(G-3369)***
Prime Ingredients Inc....201 791-6655
280 N Midland Ave Ste 340 Saddle Brook (07663) ***(G-9784)***
Prime Rebar LLC....908 707-1234
36 Adamsville Rd Bridgewater (08807) ***(G-877)***
Primepak Company, Teaneck *Also called JA Heilferty LLC* ***(G-10757)***
Primepoint LLC....609 298-7373
2 Springside Rd Westampton (08060) ***(G-11915)***
Primesource Building Pdts Inc....732 296-0600
20 Van Dyke Ave New Brunswick (08901) ***(G-6994)***
Primetime Trading Corp....646 580-8223
148 E 5th St Bayonne (07002) ***(G-241)***
Primex Color Compounding (HQ)....800 282-7933
61 River Dr Garfield (07026) ***(G-3750)***
Primex Plastics Corporation....973 470-8000
65 River Dr Garfield (07026) ***(G-3751)***
Primo Division, Irvington *Also called Jersey Plastic Molders Inc* ***(G-4595)***
Prince Agri Products Inc (HQ)....201 329-7300
300 Frank W Burr Blvd Teaneck (07666) ***(G-10770)***
Prince Black Distillery Inc....212 695-6187
691 Clifton Ave Clifton (07011) ***(G-1704)***
Prince Chikovani Inc....347 622-2789
363 Avenue A Fl 1 Bayonne (07002) ***(G-242)***
Prince Sports Inc....609 291-5800
334 Rising Sun Rd Bordentown (08505) ***(G-609)***
Prince Sterilization Svcs LLC....973 227-6882
122 Fairfield Rd Fairfield (07004) ***(G-3286)***
Prince-Chikovani, Bayonne *Also called Prince Chikovani Inc* ***(G-242)***
Princetel Inc (PA)....609 588-8801
2560 E State Street Ext Hamilton (08619) ***(G-4122)***
Princeton Alumni Weekly, Princeton *Also called Princton Almni Pblications Inc* ***(G-9105)***
Princeton Biomeditech Corp....908 281-0112
75 Orchard Rd Skillman (08558) ***(G-10036)***
Princeton Biomeditech Corp (PA)....732 274-1000
4242 Us Highway 1 Monmouth Junction (08852) ***(G-6356)***
Princeton Biopharma Strategies....609 203-5303
660 Pretty Brook Rd Princeton (08540) ***(G-9094)***
Princeton Chromatography Inc....609 860-1803
1206 S River Rd Ste 1 Cranbury (08512) ***(G-1872)***
Princeton Corp Graphics Inc....732 545-6163
3 Terminal Rd New Brunswick (08901) ***(G-6995)***
Princeton Enduring Biotech Inc....732 406-3041
190 Major Rd Monmouth Junction (08852) ***(G-6357)***
Princeton Enduring Biotech Inc....732 406-3041
190 Major Rd Monmouth Junction (08852) ***(G-6358)***
Princeton Hosted Solutions LLC....856 470-2350
30 Washington Ave Ste D2 Haddonfield (08033) ***(G-4062)***
Princeton Identity Inc....609 256-6994
300 Horizon Center Blvd # 306 Hamilton (08691) ***(G-4123)***
Princeton Information Center....609 924-7019
330 N Harrison St Ste 6 Princeton (08540) ***(G-9095)***
Princeton Instruments, Trenton *Also called Roper Scientific Inc* ***(G-11114)***
Princeton Instruments Inc....609 587-9797
3660 Quakerbridge Rd Trenton (08619) ***(G-11106)***
Princeton Keynes Group Inc (PA)....609 951-2239
116 Village Blvd Ste 200 Princeton (08540) ***(G-9096)***
Princeton Keynes Group Inc....609 208-1777
470 Mulberry St Newark (07114) ***(G-7274)***
Princeton Lightwave Inc....609 495-2600
2555 Route 130 Ste 1 Cranbury (08512) ***(G-1873)***
Princeton Microwave Technology....609 586-8140
5 Nami Ln Ste 1 Trenton (08619) ***(G-11107)***
Princeton Optronics Inc....609 584-9696
1 Electronics Dr Trenton (08619) ***(G-11108)***
Princeton Packet Inc (HQ)....609 924-3244
300 Witherspoon St Princeton (08542) ***(G-9097)***
Princeton Plasma Physics....609 243-2000
100 Stellarator Rd Princeton (08540) ***(G-9098)***
Princeton Power Systems Inc....609 955-5390
3175 Princeton Pike Lawrenceville (08648) ***(G-5267)***
Princeton Publishing Group....609 577-0693
650 Rosedale Rd Princeton (08540) ***(G-9099)***
Princeton Quadrangle Club....609 258-0376
33 Prospect Ave Princeton (08540) ***(G-9100)***
Princeton Research Instruments....609 924-0570
42 Cherry Valley Rd Princeton (08540) ***(G-9101)***
Princeton Separations Inc....732 431-3338
100 Commerce Ave Freehold (07728) ***(G-3683)***
Princeton Supply Corp....609 683-9100
301 N Harrison St Ste 473 Princeton (08540) ***(G-9102)***
Princeton Tech Group Intl Corp....732 328-9308
182 Whitman Ave Edison (08817) ***(G-2596)***
Princeton Tectonics....609 298-9331
110 Collings Ave West Berlin (08091) ***(G-11743)***
Princeton Tectonics (PA)....609 298-9331
1777 Hylton Rd Pennsauken (08110) ***(G-8565)***
Princeton Trade and Technology....609 683-0215
1 Wall St Princeton (08540) ***(G-9103)***
Princeton University Press (PA)....609 258-4900
41 William St Ste 1 Princeton (08540) ***(G-9104)***
Princetonian Graphics Inc....732 329-8282
45 Stouts Ln Ste 4 Monmouth Junction (08852) ***(G-6359)***
Princton Almni Pblications Inc....609 258-4885
194 Nassau St Ste 38 Princeton (08542) ***(G-9105)***
Princton Satellite Systems Inc....609 275-9606
6 Market St Ste 926 Plainsboro (08536) ***(G-8896)***
Print Communications Group Inc....973 882-9444
175 Us Highway 46 Unit A Fairfield (07004) ***(G-3287)***
Print Factory Ltd Liability Co....973 866-5230
730 Clifton Ave Clifton (07013) ***(G-1705)***
Print Factory Nyc, Clifton *Also called Print Factory Ltd Liability Co* ***(G-1705)***
Print Group Inc....201 487-4400
24 E Wesley St South Hackensack (07606) ***(G-10290)***
Print Group The, South Hackensack *Also called Print Group Inc* ***(G-10290)***
Print Mail Communications LLC (PA)....856 488-0345
7025 Colonial Hwy Ste 2 Pennsauken (08109) ***(G-8566)***
Print Media LLC....973 467-0007
232 Morris Ave Springfield (07081) ***(G-10572)***
Print Peel....201 507-0080
341 Michele Pl Carlstadt (07072) ***(G-1209)***
Print Post....973 732-0950
274 Chestnut St Newark (07105) ***(G-7275)***
Print Shop, Trenton *Also called New Jersey Department Treasury* ***(G-11085)***
Print Shop, The, Matawan *Also called Agau Inc* ***(G-6012)***
Print Shoppe Inc....908 782-9213
15 Minneakoning Rd # 305 Flemington (08822) ***(G-3462)***
Print Signs and Designs, Bridgeton *Also called Burdol Inc* ***(G-781)***
Print Solutions LLC....201 567-9622
320 S Dean St Englewood (07631) ***(G-2924)***
Print Tech LLC (PA)....908 232-2287
49 Fadem Rd Springfield (07081) ***(G-10573)***
Print Tech LLC....908 232-0767
349 South Ave E Westfield (07090) ***(G-11928)***
Printco....908 687-9518
12 Minneakoning Rd 103b Flemington (08822) ***(G-3463)***
Printech, Flemington *Also called Jem Printing Inc* ***(G-3450)***
Printers of Salem County LLC....856 935-5032
38 Market St Salem (08079) ***(G-9808)***
Printers Place Inc (PA)....973 744-8889
8 S Fullerton Ave Montclair (07042) ***(G-6432)***
Printers Plus, Lakewood *Also called A&R Printing Corporation* ***(G-5062)***
Printers Service Florida Inc (PA)....973 589-7800
26 Blanchard St Newark (07105) ***(G-7276)***
Printing & Signs Express Inc....201 368-1255
634 Wyckoff Ave Mahwah (07430) ***(G-5803)***
Printing Center Inc....973 383-6362
1 White Lake Rd Sparta (07871) ***(G-10518)***
Printing Craftsman Inc....201 943-0276
130 Bergen Blvd Fairview (07022) ***(G-3370)***
Printing Craftsmen, Fairview *Also called Printing Craftsman Inc* ***(G-3370)***
Printing Delite Inc....973 676-3033
279 To 281 Sanford St East Orange (07018) ***(G-2266)***
Printing Industries LLC....973 334-9775
1543 Us Hwy Rte 46 E Parsippany (07054) ***(G-8072)***
Printing Lab Ltd Liability Co....201 305-0404
609 55th St West New York (07093) ***(G-11877)***
Printing Plus of South Jersey....856 767-3941
406 N Route 73 West Berlin (08091) ***(G-11744)***
Printing Techniques, Nutley *Also called Manva Industries Inc* ***(G-7651)***
Printmaker International Ltd (HQ)....212 629-9260
503 Chancellor Ave Irvington (07111) ***(G-4601)***
Printology....201 345-4632
229 Godwin Ave Midland Park (07432) ***(G-6238)***
Printsmith....908 245-3000
253 W Westfield Ave Roselle Park (07204) ***(G-9701)***

Printwrap Corporation 973 239-1144
　95 Sand Park Rd　Cedar Grove　(07009)　(G-1297)
Priore Construction Svcs LLC 973 785-2262
　5 Peckman Rd　Little Falls　(07424)　(G-5486)
Priority-Software US LLC (HQ) 973 586-2200
　300 Round Hill Dr Ste 2　Rockaway　(07866)　(G-9600)
Prisco Digital Ltd Lblty Co (PA) 973 589-7800
　26 Blanchard St　Newark　(07105)　(G-7277)
Prisco Printers Service, Newark Also called Deleet Merchandising Corp (G-7139)
Prism Color Corporation 856 234-7515
　31 Twosome Dr Ste 1　Moorestown　(08057)　(G-6615)
Prism Dgtal Communications LLC 973 232-5038
　1011 Us Highway 22 Ste A　Mountainside　(07092)　(G-6886)
Prism Sheet Metal Inc 973 673-0213
　50 S Center St Ste 9　Orange　(07050)　(G-7824)
Prismacolor Corp 973 887-6040
　120 E Halsey Rd　Parsippany　(07054)　(G-8073)
Prismatix Decal Inc 201 525-2800
　324 Railroad Ave　Hackensack　(07601)　(G-3965)
Private Label Products Inc 201 773-4230
　20-21 Wagaraw Rd Bldg 34　Fair Lawn　(07410)　(G-3107)
Pro Academy, East Rutherford Also called Techntime Bus Sltons Ltd Lblty (G-2331)
Pro Gad Sales, Newton Also called G A D Inc (G-7390)
Pro Image Promotions Inc 973 252-8000
　480 Us Highway 46　Kenvil　(07847)　(G-5013)
Pro Pack Inc 201 485-7587
　500 W Main St Ste 12　Wyckoff　(07481)　(G-12260)
Pro Plastics Inc 908 925-5555
　1190 Sylvan St　Linden　(07036)　(G-5431)
Pro Screen Printing Inc 201 246-7600
　590 Belleville Tpke # 24　Kearny　(07032)　(G-4910)
Pro Sports　Inc 732 294-5561
　1 Champion Way　Marlboro　(07746)　(G-5953)
Pro Tapes & Specialties　Inc 732 346-0900
　621 Us Highway 1 Unit A　North Brunswick　(08902)　(G-7535)
Pro World 856 406-1020
　961 Bethel Ave　Pennsauken　(08110)　(G-8567)
Pro-Deck Supply 609 771-1100
　3 Pembroke Ct　Trenton　(08648)　(G-11109)
Pro-Fit　LLC 856 809-9910
　215 Edgewood Ave　West Berlin　(08091)　(G-11745)
Pro-Motion Industries LLC 856 809-0040
　102 Allied Pkwy　Sicklerville　(08081)　(G-10023)
Pro-Pac Service Inc 973 962-8080
　15 Van Natta Dr　Ringwood　(07456)　(G-9453)
Pro-Pack Corp 908 725-5000
　160 Meister Ave Ste 18　Branchburg　(08876)　(G-694)
Proactive Ltg Solutions LLC 800 747-1209
　21 Ewing Ave　North Arlington　(07031)　(G-7423)
Procedyne Corp (PA) 732 249-8347
　11 Industrial Dr　New Brunswick　(08901)　(G-6996)
Process Controls Co 908 269-8465
　530 Main St Ste 6a　Chester　(07930)　(G-1438)
Process Supply Company　Inc 201 487-1616
　208 Huyler St　South Hackensack　(07606)　(G-10291)
Proclean Services Inc 973 857-5408
　150 Linden Ave　Verona　(07044)　(G-11309)
Proco Inc 609 265-8777
　15 Queen St　Lumberton　(08048)　(G-5662)
Procrete LLC 609 365-2922
　4 Evergreen Rd　Linwood　(08221)　(G-5467)
Procter & Gamble Mfg Co 732 602-4500
　100 Essex Ave E　Avenel　(07001)　(G-148)
Prodo-Pak Corp 973 772-4500
　130 Monroe St　Garfield　(07026)　(G-3752)
Prodo-Pak Corporation 973 777-7770
　77 Commerce St　Garfield　(07026)　(G-3753)
Product Club Corp 973 664-0565
　41 Pine St Ste 15　Rockaway　(07866)　(G-9601)
Product Identification Co Inc 973 227-7770
　141 Lanza Ave Bldg 19　Garfield　(07026)　(G-3754)
Productive Industrial Finshg 856 427-9646
　103 American Way　Voorhees　(08043)　(G-11436)
Productive Plastics Inc (PA) 856 778-4300
　103 W Park Dr　Mount Laurel　(08054)　(G-6832)
Professional Envmtl Systems 201 991-3000
　1806 Harrison Ave　Kearny　(07032)　(G-4911)
Professional Laundry Solutions 973 392-0837
　443 Orange St　Newark　(07107)　(G-7278)
Professional Printing Services 856 428-6300
　116 N Haddon Ave Ste G　Haddonfield　(08033)　(G-4063)
Professional Reproductions Inc 212 268-1222
　75 Vanderburg Rd　Marlboro　(07746)　(G-5954)
Profiles of Frameware, Fairfield Also called Frameware Inc (G-3201)
Proform Acoustic Surfaces LLC 201 553-9614
　307 Julianne Ter　Secaucus　(07094)　(G-9914)
Proforma, Cedar Grove Also called Repromatic Printing Inc (G-1299)
Proforma Ayr Graphics & Prtg, Roselle Park Also called Ayr Graphics & Printing
Inc (G-9689)

Profoto US Inc 973 822-1300
　220 Park Ave Ste 120　Florham Park　(07932)　(G-3516)
Progard, Englewood Also called Enor Corporation (G-2892)
Programatic Platers Inc 718 721-4330
　32 Laurel Ave　Tenafly　(07670)　(G-10786)
Progress Displays Inc 908 757-6650
　39 Progress St　Edison　(08820)　(G-2597)
Progress Printing Co 201 433-3133
　338 Montgomery St　Jersey City　(07302)　(G-4806)
Progress Woodwork 732 906-8680
　225 Pierson Ave　Edison　(08837)　(G-2598)
Progressive 4 Color Ltd Lblty 973 736-5800
　24 Park Ave　West Orange　(07052)　(G-11905)
Progressive Machine Company, Hackensack Also called P L M Manufacturing
Company (G-3960)
Progressive Offset Inc 201 569-3900
　161 Coolidge Ave　Englewood　(07631)　(G-2925)
Progressive Ruesch Inc 973 962-7700
　21 Van Natta Dr　Ringwood　(07456)　(G-9454)
Progressive Tool & Mfg Corp 908 245-7010
　708 Fairfield Ave　Kenilworth　(07033)　(G-4990)
Prohaska & Co Inc 732 238-3420
　34 Allwood Rd　East Brunswick　(08816)　(G-2176)
Project Feed Usa　Inc 201 443-7143
　127a Dwight St　Jersey City　(07305)　(G-4807)
Promeko Inc 201 861-9446
　543 59th St　West New York　(07093)　(G-11878)
Promet Inc 303 371-2300
　8220 Sanctuary Blvd　Riverdale　(07457)　(G-9483)
Promia Incorporated 609 252-1850
　322 Commons Way　Princeton　(08540)　(G-9106)
Promius Pharma　LLC 609 282-1400
　107 College Rd E Ste 100　Princeton　(08540)　(G-9107)
Promo Graphic Inc 732 629-7300
　112 Wood Ave　Middlesex　(08846)　(G-6191)
Promotion In Motion　Inc (PA) 201 962-8530
　25 Commerce Dr　Allendale　(07401)　(G-16)
Promotion In Motion　Inc 732 560-8300
　500 Pierce St　Somerset　(08873)　(G-10159)
Promotion In Motion Companies, Allendale Also called Promotion In Motion　Inc (G-16)
Promotional Graphics Inc 973 423-3900
　81 E 26th St　Paterson　(07514)　(G-8365)
Pronto Printing & Copying Ctr 201 426-0009
　630 Swan St　Ramsey　(07446)　(G-9251)
Proscape Technologies Inc 215 441-0300
　14 Dogwood Dr　Hillsborough　(08844)　(G-4364)
Prospect Group LLC 718 635-4007
　260 Centennial Ave　Piscataway　(08854)　(G-8803)
Prospect Transportation　Inc (PA) 201 933-9999
　630 Industrial Rd　Carlstadt　(07072)　(G-1210)
Prosthetic Orthotic Solutions, Marlton Also called Cape Prosthetics-Orthotics (G-5966)
Prosweetz Ingredients Inc 732 512-0886
　98a Mayfield Ave　Edison　(08837)　(G-2599)
Protameen Chemicals Inc (PA) 973 256-4374
　375 Minnisink Rd　Totowa　(07512)　(G-10967)
Protec Secure Card Ltd Lblty 732 542-0700
　80 Corbett Way　Eatontown　(07724)　(G-2419)
Protech Oxyplast, Fairfield Also called Protech Powder Coatings　Inc (G-3288)
Protech Powder Coatings　Inc (PA) 973 276-1292
　21 Audrey Pl　Fairfield　(07004)　(G-3288)
Protection Industries Corp 201 333-8050
　107 York St　Jersey City　(07302)　(G-4808)
Proteus Designs LLC 215 519-0135
　900 N Lenola Rd Bldg 9　Moorestown　(08057)　(G-6616)
Protoform Inc 609 261-6920
　112 Burrs Rd　Westampton　(08060)　(G-11916)
Provence LLC 201 503-9717
　214 S Dean St　Englewood　(07631)　(G-2926)
Provost Square Associates Inc 973 403-8755
　6 Provost Sq　Caldwell　(07006)　(G-1032)
Proximo Distillers　LLC 201 204-1718
　333 Washington St Fl 4　Jersey City　(07302)　(G-4809)
Prudent Publishing Co　Inc 973 347-4554
　400 N Frontage Rd　Landing　(07850)　(G-5227)
Prysmian Cbles Systems USA LLC 732 469-5902
　111 Chimney Rock Rd　Bridgewater　(08807)　(G-878)
PSC, Eatontown Also called Protec Secure Card Ltd Lblty (G-2419)
PSEG Nuclear LLC 856 339-1002
　80 Park Plz　Hancocks Bridge　(08038)　(G-4167)
Psnj, Cinnaminson Also called Pechters Southern NJ LLC (G-1483)
Ptc Electronics Inc 201 847-0500
　45 Whitney Rd Ste B9　Mahwah　(07430)　(G-5804)
Ptc Inc 973 631-6195
　89 Headquarters Plz　Morristown　(07960)　(G-6738)
Ptc Therapeutics　Inc 908 222-7000
　100 Corporate Ct　South Plainfield　(07080)　(G-10425)
PTL Sheet Metal Inc 201 501-8700
　70 Davies Ave　Dumont　(07628)　(G-2122)

A
L
P
H
A
B
E
T
I
C

Pts Intermediate Holdings LLC 732 537-6200
  14 Schoolhouse Rd Somerset (08873) *(G-10160)*

Pty Lighting LLC (PA) 855 303-4500
  100 Hoffman Pl Hillside (07205) *(G-4434)*

Publishers Inc 856 853-2800
  1757 Imperial Way West Deptford (08066) *(G-11840)*

Publishers Partnership Co 201 689-1613
  23 N Pleasant Ave Ridgewood (07450) *(G-9428)*

Publishing Technology Inc 732 563-9292
  317 George St Ste 320 New Brunswick (08901) *(G-6997)*

Puebla Foods Inc (PA) 973 246-6311
  26 Jefferson St Passaic (07055) *(G-8172)*

Puebla Foods Inc 973 473-4494
  26 Jefferson St Passaic (07055) *(G-8173)*

Pueblo Latino Laundry LLC 201 864-1666
  1717 Bergenline Ave Union City (07087) *(G-11263)*

Puent-Romer Communications Inc 973 509-7591
  423 Bloomfield Ave Montclair (07042) *(G-6433)*

Pulaski Meat Products Co 908 925-5380
  123 N Wood Ave Linden (07036) *(G-5432)*

Pulasky Meat Products Co, Linden *Also called Pulaski Meat Products Co (G-5432)*

Pulsar Microwave Corp 973 779-6262
  48 Industrial St W Clifton (07012) *(G-1706)*

Pulse Magazine, The, Lyndhurst *Also called Leader Newsgroup LLC (G-5685)*

Pulsetor LLC 609 303-0578
  243 N Union St Ste 207 Lambertville (08530) *(G-5220)*

Pulsonics Inc 800 999-6785
  69 William St Belleville (07109) *(G-313)*

Puratos Corporation 856 266-1736
  8030 National Hwy Pennsauken (08110) *(G-8568)*

Puratos Corporation (HQ) 856 428-4300
  1941 Old Cuthbert Rd Cherry Hill (08034) *(G-1417)*

Purdue Pharma LP 203 588-8000
  100 Prnctn S Corpt Ctr # 250 Ewing (08628) *(G-3046)*

Pure H2o Technologies Inc 973 622-0440
  211 Warren St Ste 19 Newark (07103) *(G-7279)*

Pure Rubber Products Co. 973 784-3690
  300 Round Hill Dr Ste 5 Rockaway (07866) *(G-9602)*

Pure Soccer Academy Ltd Lblty 877 945-6423
  330 Changebridge Rd # 101 Pine Brook (07058) *(G-8714)*

Pure TEC Corporation (HQ) 201 941-2900
  101 Railroad Ave Ridgefield (07657) *(G-9381)*

Pure Tech International Inc 908 722-4968
  3040 Us Highway 22 # 130 Branchburg (08876) *(G-695)*

Pure Tech International Inc (HQ) 908 722-4800
  201 Industrial Pkwy Branchburg (08876) *(G-696)*

Purelink, Ramsey *Also called Dtrovision LLC (G-9239)*

Purely Organic SA LLC 201 942-0400
  142 Liberty Ave Jersey City (07306) *(G-4810)*

Purevolution 973 919-4047
  62 Fayson Lake Rd Kinnelon (07405) *(G-5040)*

Purity Labs 201 372-0236
  1 Maple St East Rutherford (07073) *(G-2320)*

Push Beverages LLC 973 766-2663
  7 Longfellow Dr Succasunna (07876) *(G-10626)*

Putterwheel, Allendale *Also called Ssam Sports Inc (G-17)*

Pv Deroche LLC 908 475-2266
  283 County Route 519 Belvidere (07823) *(G-374)*

Pv/T Inc 609 267-3933
  100 Indel Ave Rancocas (08073) *(G-9261)*

Pvh Corp 908 685-0050
  651 Kapkowski Rd Ste 1416 Elizabeth (07201) *(G-2769)*

Pvh Corp 609 344-6273
  32 N Michigan Ave Atlantic City (08401) *(G-106)*

Pvh Corp 908 685-0050
  1001 Frontier Rd Ste 100 Bridgewater (08807) *(G-879)*

Pvh Corp 732 833-9602
  537 Monmouth Rd Ste 332 Jackson (08527) *(G-4676)*

Pvh Corp 908 685-0050
  1001 Frontier Rd 100 Bridgewater (08807) *(G-880)*

Pvh Corp 908 685-0148
  1001 Frontier Rd 100 Bridgewater (08807) *(G-881)*

Pvh Corp 908 788-5880
  41 Liberty Vlg Flemington (08822) *(G-3464)*

Pwg Lighting, Hillside *Also called Pty Lighting LLC (G-4434)*

Pyramid Food Services Corp 973 900-6513
  93-105 Albert Ave Newark (07105) *(G-7280)*

Pyrometer Instrument Co Inc 609 443-5522
  92 N Main St Bldg 18d Windsor (08561) *(G-12128)*

Q Glass Company Inc 973 335-5191
  624 Rte 202 Towaco (07082) *(G-11002)*

Q P 195 Inc 732 531-8860
  827 W Park Ave Ocean (07712) *(G-7738)*

Q P 500 Inc 732 531-8860
  827 W Park Ave Ocean (07712) *(G-7739)*

Q&Q Pharma Research Company 973 267-0160
  19 Meadow Bluff Rd Morris Plains (07950) *(G-6679)*

Q-Eximtrade Inc (PA) 732 366-4667
  1336 Roosevelt Ave Carteret (07008) *(G-1267)*

Q-Med Scandinavia Inc 609 953-8069
  2035 State Route 27 # 2150 Edison (08817) *(G-2600)*

Q-Pak Corporation 973 483-4404
  2145 Mccarter Hwy Newark (07104) *(G-7281)*

Q10 Products LLC 201 567-9299
  1 Entin Rd Ste 7a Clifton (07014) *(G-1707)*

Qad Inc 856 273-1717
  10000 Midlantic Dr 100w Mount Laurel (08054) *(G-6833)*

Qcom Inc 732 772-0990
  475 County Road 520 # 200 Marlboro (07746) *(G-5955)*

Qis Inc 856 455-3736
  778 Vineland Ave Rosenhayn (08352) *(G-9708)*

Qsa Global National Corp 865 888-6798
  331 Newman Springs Rd Red Bank (07701) *(G-9341)*

Qsa National, Red Bank *Also called Qsa Global National Corp (G-9341)*

Quad/Graphics Inc 609 534-7308
  80 Stemmers Ln Westampton (08060) *(G-11917)*

Quad/Graphics Inc 732 469-0189
  13 Jensen Dr Ste 100 Somerset (08873) *(G-10161)*

Quadelle Textile Corp 201 865-1112
  573 56th St West New York (07093) *(G-11879)*

Quadramed Corporation 732 751-0400
  23 Christopher Way # 303 Eatontown (07724) *(G-2420)*

Quadrangle Products Inc 732 792-1234
  28 Harrison Ave Unit D Englishtown (07726) *(G-2997)*

Quadrant Media Corp Inc (PA) 973 701-8900
  7 Century Dr Ste 302 Parsippany (07054) *(G-8074)*

Quagen Pharmaceuticals LLC (PA) 973 228-9600
  11 Patton Dr West Caldwell (07006) *(G-11799)*

Quagen Pharmaceuticals LLC 973 228-9600
  34 Fairfield Pl West Caldwell (07006) *(G-11800)*

Quaker Soap Div, Newark *Also called Darling Ingredients Inc (G-7133)*

Qualco Inc 973 473-1222
  225 Passaic St Passaic (07055) *(G-8174)*

Qualcomm Incorporated 908 443-8000
  500 Smrst Corp Blvd Fl 4 Bridgewater (08807) *(G-882)*

Qualipac America Corp 973 754-9920
  1 Garret Mountain Plz # 502 Woodland Park (07424) *(G-12230)*

Qualis Packaging Inc (PA) 908 782-0305
  550 Hadley Rd South Plainfield (07080) *(G-10426)*

Quality Bath, Lakewood *Also called Tlw Bath Ltd Liability Company (G-5196)*

Quality Carton Inc (PA) 201 529-6900
  1 International Blvd # 610 Mahwah (07495) *(G-5805)*

Quality Cosmetics Mfg 908 755-9588
  4455 S Clinton Ave South Plainfield (07080) *(G-10427)*

Quality Die Shop Inc 732 787-0041
  17 Argonne Pl North Middletown (07748) *(G-7558)*

Quality Eyework, South Hackensack *Also called M H Optical Supplies Inc (G-10277)*

Quality Films Corp 718 246-7150
  500 Hillside Ave Hillside (07205) *(G-4435)*

Quality Glass Inc 908 754-2652
  2300 S Clinton Ave Ste C South Plainfield (07080) *(G-10428)*

Quality Indexing LLC 908 810-0200
  939 Lehigh Ave Union (07083) *(G-11217)*

Quality Industries Inc 973 478-4425
  204 Getty Ave Clifton (07011) *(G-1708)*

Quality Ingredients Corp 908 879-2227
  385 State Route 24 Ste 3d Chester (07930) *(G-1439)*

Quality Medical Supplies, Leonia *Also called Carry Easy Inc (G-5315)*

Quality Plus One Catering Inc (PA) 732 967-1525
  10 Kerry Ct Old Bridge (08857) *(G-7791)*

Quality Print Solutions 888 679-7237
  589 Franklin Tpke Ridgewood (07450) *(G-9429)*

Quality Remanufacturing Inc 973 523-8800
  565 E 37th St Paterson (07504) *(G-8366)*

Quality Sheet Metal & Wldg Inc 732 469-7111
  23 Clawson St Piscataway (08854) *(G-8804)*

Quality Solid Surface Inc 973 772-8600
  333 Vreeland Ave Garfield (07026) *(G-3755)*

Quality Stays LLC (PA) 800 868-8195
  10 Underwood Pl Ste 2 Clifton (07013) *(G-1709)*

Quality Sweets 732 283-3799
  1396 Oak Tree Rd Iselin (08830) *(G-4641)*

Quality Swiss Screw Machine Co 908 289-4334
  849 4th Ave Elizabeth (07202) *(G-2770)*

Quallis Brands LLC 862 252-0664
  211 Glenwood Ave East Orange (07017) *(G-2267)*

Qualserv Imports Inc 973 620-9234
  3125 State Route 10 Denville (07834) *(G-2052)*

Qualteq Inc 908 668-0999
  800 Montrose Ave Cn1037 South Plainfield (07080) *(G-10429)*

Quantem Corp 609 883-9191
  1457 Lower Ferry Rd Ste 1 Ewing (08618) *(G-3047)*

Quantum Coating Inc 856 234-5444
  1259 N Church St Bldg 1 Moorestown (08057) *(G-6617)*

Quantum Integrators Group LLC 609 632-0621
  8 Madison Dr Plainsboro (08536) *(G-8897)*

Quantum Pharmaceuticals Inc 973 222-6485
  3 Arielle Way Sparta (07871) *(G-10519)*

(G-0000) Company's Geographic Section entry number

Quantum Renovations 856 278-0176
  8 Meghans Way Pennsville (08070) *(G-8593)*

Quantum Security Systems Inc 609 252-0505
  124 Fairfield Rd Princeton (08540) *(G-9108)*

Quantum Vector Corp 201 870-1782
  700 Broadway Westwood (07675) *(G-11967)*

Quark Enterprises Inc 856 455-0376
  320 Morton Ave Rosenhayn (08352) *(G-9709)*

Quarter Spot 917 647-9170
  145 Us Highway 46 Fl 3 Wayne (07470) *(G-11676)*

Quatrx Pharmaceuticals Company (PA) 734 913-9900
  300 Campus Dr Ste 300 Florham Park (07932) *(G-3517)*

Ques Aprv A R Knitwear Inc 201 869-1333
  2201 74th St North Bergen (07047) *(G-7477)*

Quest Diagnostics Incorporated (PA) 973 520-2700
  500 Plaza Dr Ste G Secaucus (07094) *(G-9915)*

Quest Intl Flvors Frgrnces Inc 973 576-9500
  717 Ridgedale Ave East Hanover (07936) *(G-2240)*

Qugen Inc 609 716-6300
  666 Plainsboro Rd Ste 215 Plainsboro (08536) *(G-8898)*

Quick Bias Bnding Trmming Inds 732 422-0123
  9 Creekside Ct North Brunswick (08902) *(G-7536)*

Quick Fab Aluminum Mfg Co 732 367-7200
  1830 Swarthmore Ave Ste 1 Lakewood (08701) *(G-5175)*

Quick Frozen Foods Intl 201 592-7007
  2125 Center Ave Ste 305 Fort Lee (07024) *(G-3579)*

Quickie Print & Copy Shop, Ocean Also called Q P 500 Inc *(G-7739)*

Quickly Printing, Union Also called Mr Quickly Inc *(G-11209)*

Quiet Tone Inc 732 431-2826
  12 Vine St Freehold (07728) *(G-3684)*

Quik Flex Circuit Inc 856 742-0550
  85 Nicholson Rd Gloucester City (08030) *(G-3843)*

Quik-Fab Aluminum Mfg, Lakewood Also called Quick Fab Aluminum Mfg Co *(G-5175)*

Quik-Flex Circuit Inc 856 742-0550
  85 Nicholson Rd Gloucester City (08030) *(G-3844)*

Quik-Sab, Lakewood Also called Vinylast Inc *(G-5200)*

Quikie Print & Copy Shop, Ocean Also called Q P 195 Inc *(G-7738)*

Quinnova Pharmaceuticals Inc 877 660-6263
  1 Main St Ste E Chatham (07928) *(G-1337)*

Quintum Technologies Inc (HQ) 732 460-9000
  71 James Way Eatontown (07724) *(G-2421)*

Qwik Pack & Ship, Blackwood Also called E C D Ventures Inc *(G-477)*

R & B Printing Inc 908 766-4073
  19-21 Mine Brook Rd Fl 1 Bernardsville (07924) *(G-454)*

R & D Circuits Inc (PA) 732 549-4554
  3601 S Clinton Ave South Plainfield (07080) *(G-10430)*

R & H Co Inc 610 258-3177
  1286 Strykers Rd Phillipsburg (08865) *(G-8667)*

R & H Spring & Truck Repair 732 681-9000
  4806 W Hurley Pond Rd Wall Township (07719) *(G-11504)*

R & K Industries Inc 732 531-1123
  259 Overbrook Ave Oakhurst (07755) *(G-7672)*

R & M Chemical Technologies 908 537-9516
  7 Imlaydale Rd Hampton (08827) *(G-4166)*

R & M Manufacturing Inc 609 495-8032
  20 Abeel Rd Monroe Township (08831) *(G-6390)*

R & R Distributors Inc 201 804-0077
  18 Summit Dr Branchville (07826) *(G-732)*

R & R Fuel Inc 201 223-0786
  3205 Hudson Ave Union City (07087) *(G-11264)*

R & R Irrigation Co Inc 732 271-7070
  283 Lincoln Blvd Middlesex (08846) *(G-6192)*

R & R Printing & Copy Center 732 249-9450
  46 Old Camplain Rd Hillsborough (08844) *(G-4365)*

R A O Contract Sales, Paterson Also called R A O Contract Sales NY Inc *(G-8367)*

R A O Contract Sales NY Inc 201 652-1500
  94 Fulton St Ste 4 Paterson (07501) *(G-8367)*

R B B Corp 973 770-1100
  7 Orben Dr Ledgewood (07852) *(G-5308)*

R B Badat Landscaping Inc 609 877-7138
  507 Woodlane Rd Mount Holly (08060) *(G-6776)*

R C Fine Foods Inc 908 359-5500
  139 Stryker Ln Hillsborough (08844) *(G-4366)*

R D Associates 973 729-7944
  97 Warren Rd Sparta (07871) *(G-10520)*

R D I, Ocean City Also called Railing Dynamics Inc *(G-7754)*

R E Pierson Materials, Williamstown Also called Richard E Pierson Mtls Corp *(G-12103)*

R E Pierson Materials, Vineland Also called Richard E Pierson Mtls Corp *(G-11399)*

R E Pierson Materials, Pilesgrove Also called Richard E Pierson Mtls Corp *(G-8676)*

R F Products Inc (PA) 856 365-5500
  1500 Davis St Camden (08103) *(G-1083)*

R G Dunn Acquisitions Co Inc 973 762-1300
  71 Newark Way Maplewood (07040) *(G-5925)*

R G Smith Tool & Mfg Co 973 344-1395
  245 South St Newark (07114) *(G-7282)*

R H A Audio Communications, East Brunswick Also called R H A Audio Communications *(G-2177)*

R H A Audio Communications 732 257-9180
  725 State Route 18 East Brunswick (08816) *(G-2177)*

R H Vassallo Inc 856 358-8841
  Us Rte 40 & State 47 Malaga (08328) *(G-5827)*

R J Blen Grphic Arts Cnverting 732 545-3501
  6 Jules Ln New Brunswick (08901) *(G-6998)*

R J D Machine Products Inc 609 392-1515
  1424-1428 Heath Ave Trenton (08638) *(G-11110)*

R J Hoppe Store Construction 973 485-5665
  340 N 5th St Newark (07107) *(G-7283)*

R L Plastics Inc 732 340-1100
  20 Production Way Avenel (07001) *(G-149)*

R L R Foil Stamping LLC 973 778-9464
  245 4th St Ste 4 Passaic (07055) *(G-8175)*

R L S Enterprises, Branchburg Also called Njrls Enterprises Inc *(G-683)*

R M A, Hillside Also called Mark Ronald Associates Inc *(G-4429)*

R M F Associates Inc 908 687-9355
  202 Carolyn Rd Union (07083) *(G-11218)*

R Neumann & Co 201 659-3400
  300 Observer Hwy Hoboken (07030) *(G-4493)*

R P Baking LLC 973 483-3374
  840 Jersey St Harrison (07029) *(G-4189)*

R P I, Lebanon Also called Reed Presentations Inc *(G-5301)*

R P L, Garfield Also called Rpl Supplies Inc *(G-3759)*

R P R Graphics Inc 908 654-8080
  87 Main St Peapack (07977) *(G-8432)*

R P Smith & Son Inc 973 584-4063
  199 Main St Succasunna (07876) *(G-10627)*

R R Donnelley & Sons Company 973 439-8321
  5 Henderson Dr West Caldwell (07006) *(G-11801)*

R R J Co Inc 732 544-1514
  13 Provincial Pl Colts Neck (07722) *(G-1791)*

R S Rubber Corp 973 777-2200
  55 Paterson Ave Wallington (07057) *(G-11529)*

R Squared Sls & Logistics LLC 201 329-9745
  30 Congress Dr Moonachie (07074) *(G-6537)*

R T I Inc 201 261-5852
  401 Hasbrouck Blvd Oradell (07649) *(G-7812)*

R T Kuntz Co 732 751-1770
  5146 W Hurley Pond Rd # 2 Wall Township (07727) *(G-11505)*

R Tape Corporation (HQ) 908 753-5570
  6 Ingersoll Rd South Plainfield (07080) *(G-10431)*

R V Livolsi Incorporated (PA) 732 286-2200
  20 E Water St Toms River (08753) *(G-10905)*

R W Wheaton Co 908 241-4955
  215 W Clay Ave Roselle Park (07204) *(G-9702)*

R Way Tooling & Met Works LLC 856 692-2218
  224 S Lincoln Ave Vineland (08361) *(G-11394)*

R World Enterprises 201 795-2428
  197 Congress St Jersey City (07307) *(G-4811)*

R Yates Consumer Prd LLC 201 569-1030
  204 Green St Englewood (07631) *(G-2927)*

R&D Consulting, Brookside Also called Anvima Technologies LLC *(G-922)*

R&D Altanova, South Plainfield Also called R & D Circuits Inc *(G-10430)*

R&D Microwaves LLC 908 212-1696
  301 Rockaway Valley Rd # 3 Boonton (07005) *(G-580)*

R&L Sheet Metal, Towaco Also called Apogee Technologies LLC *(G-10987)*

R&R Cosmetics LLC 732 340-1000
  1140 Randolph Ave Rahway (07065) *(G-9219)*

R-Way Machine and Fabrication, Vineland Also called R Way Tooling & Met Works LLC *(G-11394)*

R-Way Tooling Co, Vineland Also called Frank E Ganter Inc *(G-11356)*

Ra Liquidating, Woodbridge Also called Rclc Inc *(G-12152)*

Raason Cabinetry, Englishtown Also called Acorn Industry Inc *(G-2989)*

Rab Lighting Inc (PA) 201 784-8600
  170 Ludlow Ave Northvale (07647) *(G-7602)*

Raceway Carwash 215 886-8252
  1471 Blckwood Clmenton Rd Clementon (08021) *(G-1533)*

Raceway Petroleum Inc 908 222-2999
  643 Us Highway 22 North Plainfield (07060) *(G-7561)*

Raceway Petroleum Inc 732 729-7350
  114 Ryders Ln East Brunswick (08816) *(G-2178)*

Raceway Petroleum Inc 732 613-4404
  523 State Route 18 East Brunswick (08816) *(G-2179)*

Raceweld Co Inc 908 236-6533
  1120 Us Highway 22 Lebanon (08833) *(G-5300)*

Radcom Equipment Inc 201 518-0033
  10 Forest Ave Paramus (07652) *(G-7898)*

Radha Beauty Products LLC 732 993-6242
  100 Stonehurst Ct Northvale (07647) *(G-7603)*

Radiant Communications Corp (PA) 908 757-7444
  5001 Hadley Rd South Plainfield (07080) *(G-10432)*

Radiant Cut Diamond, Hoboken Also called Rcdc Corporation *(G-4494)*

Radiant Energy Systems Inc 973 423-5220
  175 N Ethel Ave Hawthorne (07506) *(G-4256)*

Radiation Systems Inc 201 891-7515
  455 W Main St Wyckoff (07481) *(G-12261)*

A
L
P
H
A
B
E
T
I
C

Radio Systems Design Inc....856 467-8000
601 Heron Dr Swedesboro (08085) *(G-10721)*
Radix Computer Carrers, Bloomfield *Also called Radix M I S (G-528)*
Radix M I S....973 707-2121
50 Hazelwood Rd Bloomfield (07003) *(G-528)*
Radnet Inc....908 709-1323
25 S Union Ave Cranford (07016) *(G-1924)*
Radnet Inc....908 709-1323
25 S Union Ave Cranford (07016) *(G-1925)*
Radwin Inc....201 252-4224
900 Corporate Dr Mahwah (07430) *(G-5806)*
Rafael Pharmaceuticals Inc (PA)....609 409-7050
1 Duncan Dr Cranbury (08512) *(G-1874)*
Raffettos Corp....201 372-1222
62 W Commercial Ave Moonachie (07074) *(G-6538)*
Ragar Co Inc....732 493-1416
2106 Kings Hwy Ocean (07712) *(G-7740)*
Rags International Inc....787 632-8447
15 Tooker Ave Springfield (07081) *(G-10574)*
Rahway Steel Drum Co Inc....732 382-0113
26 Brick Yard Rd Cranbury (08512) *(G-1875)*
Railing Designs Unlimited, Belleville *Also called Bloomfield Iron Co Inc (G-296)*
Railing Dynamics Inc....609 593-5400
1201 N 10th St Millville (08332) *(G-6321)*
Railing Dynamics Inc (HQ)....609 601-1300
3814 Waterview Blvd Ocean City (08226) *(G-7754)*
Railpace Co Inc....732 388-4984
257 Oak Ridge Rd Clark (07066) *(G-1514)*
Rails Company Inc (PA)....973 763-4320
101 Newark Way Maplewood (07040) *(G-5926)*
Rainbow Closets Inc (PA)....973 882-3800
4 Gardner Rd Ste 5 Fairfield (07004) *(G-3289)*
Rainbow Metal Units Corp....718 784-3690
1 Kenner Ct Riverdale (07457) *(G-9484)*
Rainmen USA Incorporated (PA)....201 784-3244
10 Maple St Norwood (07648) *(G-7634)*
Rajbhog Foods Inc....551 222-4700
60 Amity St Jersey City (07304) *(G-4812)*
Rajbhog Foods Inc (PA)....201 395-9400
812 Newark Ave Jersey City (07306) *(G-4813)*
Rajbhog Foods(nj) Inc....551 222-4700
60 Amity St Jersey City (07304) *(G-4814)*
Rajysan Incorporated....800 433-1382
3 Hawk Ct Swedesboro (08085) *(G-10722)*
Rak Foam Sales Inc....908 668-1122
1355 W Front St Ste 2 Plainfield (07063) *(G-8872)*
Rako Machine Products Inc....609 758-1200
845 Monmouth Rd Cream Ridge (08514) *(G-1940)*
Ralph Clayton & Sons LLC....800 662-3044
58 Goldman Dr Cookstown (08511) *(G-1808)*
Ralph Clayton & Sons LLC....609 695-0767
1144 New York Ave Trenton (08638) *(G-11111)*
Ralph Clayton & Sons LLC....609 383-1818
103 Chestnut Ave Egg Harbor Township (08234) *(G-2693)*
Ralph Lauren Corporation....201 531-6000
9 Polito Ave Fl 5 Lyndhurst (07071) *(G-5704)*
Ram Hydraulics Inc....732 237-0904
745 Shrewsbury Ave Shrewsbury (07702) *(G-10009)*
Ram Products Inc....732 651-5500
182 Ridge Rd Ste D Dayton (08810) *(G-1984)*
Ramblewood Cleaners Inc (PA)....856 235-6051
1155 Route 73 Ste B Mount Laurel (08054) *(G-6834)*
Rambusch Decorating Company....201 333-2525
160 Cornelison Ave Jersey City (07304) *(G-4815)*
Rambusch Lighting, Jersey City *Also called Rambusch Decorating Company (G-4815)*
Ramco, Hillside *Also called Randall Manufacturing Co Inc (G-4437)*
Ramco Equipment Corp....908 687-6700
32 Montgomery St Hillside (07205) *(G-4436)*
Ramco Manufacturing Co Inc (PA)....908 245-4500
365 Carnegie Ave Kenilworth (07033) *(G-4991)*
Ramco Systems Corporation (HQ)....609 620-4800
3150 Us Highway 1 Ste 206 Lawrence Township (08648) *(G-5246)*
Rame Hart Instrument, Succasunna *Also called Rame-Hart Instrument Co LLC (G-10628)*
Rame-Hart Inc....973 335-0560
5 Emery Ave Ste 1 Randolph (07869) *(G-9295)*
Rame-Hart Instrument Co LLC....973 448-0305
19 State Route 10 E # 11 Succasunna (07876) *(G-10628)*
Ramsay David Cabinetmakers....856 234-7776
310 Mill St Moorestown (08057) *(G-6618)*
Ramsey Building Supply, Midland Park *Also called Precision Multiple Contrls Inc (G-6236)*
Ramsey Charles Company....845 338-1464
617 Heron Dr Swedesboro (08085) *(G-10723)*
Ramsey Graphics and Printing....201 300-2912
262 Market St Ste 1 Elmwood Park (07407) *(G-2846)*
Ramsey Machine & Tool Co Inc....973 376-7404
60 Tooker Ave Springfield (07081) *(G-10575)*
Ranbaxy Pharmaceuticals, Princeton *Also called OHM Laboratories Inc (G-9086)*
Ranbaxy USA Inc....609 720-9200
2 Independence Way Princeton (08540) *(G-9109)*
Ranco Precision Sheet Metal....973 472-8808
40 Colorado St Clifton (07014) *(G-1710)*
Rand Diversified Companies LLC....732 985-0800
112 Truman Dr Edison (08817) *(G-2601)*
Randall Manufacturing Co, Hillside *Also called Ramco Equipment Corp (G-4436)*
Randall Manufacturing Co Inc....973 746-2111
32 Montgomery St Hillside (07205) *(G-4437)*
Randall Mfg Co Inc....973 482-8603
200 Sylvan Ave Newark (07104) *(G-7284)*
Randcastle Extrusion Systems....973 239-1150
220 Little Falls Rd # 6 Cedar Grove (07009) *(G-1298)*
Randells Cstm Fniture Kitchens....856 216-9400
1864 Marlton Pike E Cherry Hill (08003) *(G-1418)*
Randy Hangers LLC....201 215-2900
115 Enterprise Ave S Secaucus (07094) *(G-9916)*
Rangecraft Manufacturing Inc....201 791-0440
4-40 Banta Pl Fair Lawn (07410) *(G-3108)*
Ranger Industries Inc (PA)....732 389-3535
15 Park Rd Tinton Falls (07724) *(G-10844)*
Ransome Equipment Sales LLC....856 797-8100
106 Ark Rd Lumberton (08048) *(G-5663)*
Ranx Pharmaceuticals Inc....571 214-8989
1085 Cranbury S River Rd Jamesburg (08831) *(G-4689)*
Raphel Marketing Inc....609 348-6646
118 S Newton Pl Atlantic City (08401) *(G-107)*
Rapid Manufacturing Co Inc....732 279-1252
25 Bay Point Dr Toms River (08753) *(G-10906)*
Rapid Models & Prototypes Inc....856 933-2929
101 C Rose Ave Runnemede (08078) *(G-9720)*
Rapid Transfer Co Inc....201 529-0002
1 Lethbridge Plz Ste 16 Mahwah (07430) *(G-5807)*
Rapsoco Inc....908 977-7321
648 Newark Ave Elizabeth (07208) *(G-2771)*
Raptor Resources Holdings Inc (PA)....732 252-5146
41 Howe Ln Freehold (07728) *(G-3685)*
Raritan Inc (HQ)....732 764-8886
400 Cottontail Ln Somerset (08873) *(G-10162)*
Raritan Americas Inc (HQ)....732 764-8886
400 Cottontail Ln Somerset (08873) *(G-10163)*
Raritan Computer, Somerset *Also called Raritan Americas Inc (G-10163)*
Raritan Container, New Brunswick *Also called Raritan Packaging Industries (G-6999)*
Raritan Packaging Industries....732 246-7200
570 Jersey Ave New Brunswick (08901) *(G-6999)*
Raritan Phrmctcals Incoporated....732 238-1685
8 Joanna Ct East Brunswick (08816) *(G-2180)*
Ras Process Equipment....609 371-1000
324 Meadowbrook Rd Robbinsville (08691) *(G-9521)*
Rascal Company, The, Sewell *Also called Electric Mobility Corporation (G-9954)*
Rascal Company, The, Sewell *Also called Electric Mobility Corporation (G-9955)*
Rasi Laboratories Inc....732 873-8500
320 Half Acre Rd Cranbury (08512) *(G-1876)*
Rasi Labs, Cranbury *Also called Rasi Laboratories Inc (G-1876)*
Rasta Imposta, Runnemede *Also called Silvertop Associates Inc (G-9723)*
Rastelli Brothers Inc (PA)....856 803-1100
300 Heron Dr Swedesboro (08085) *(G-10724)*
Rastelli Foods Group Inc....856 803-1100
300 Heron Dr Swedesboro (08085) *(G-10725)*
Rastelli's Foods, Swedesboro *Also called Rastelli Brothers Inc (G-10724)*
Rathgibson North Branch LLC....908 253-3260
100 Aspen Hill Rd Branchburg (08876) *(G-697)*
Raue Screw Machine Products Co....973 697-7500
173 Oak Ridge Rd Oak Ridge (07438) *(G-7664)*
Rauhauser's Own Make Candies, Ocean City *Also called Rauhausers Inc (G-7755)*
Rauhausers Inc....609 399-1465
721 Asbury Ave Ocean City (08226) *(G-7755)*
Rawco LLC....908 832-7700
452 County Road 513 Califon (07830) *(G-1036)*
Rawco Precision Manufacturing, Califon *Also called Rawco LLC (G-1036)*
Raybeam Manufacturing Corp....201 941-4529
700 Grand Ave Ste 5 Ridgefield (07657) *(G-9382)*
Rayge Candy Co....732 458-2179
11 Beverly Beach Rd Brick (08724) *(G-756)*
Rays Reproduction Inc....201 666-5650
39 Bland St Emerson (07630) *(G-2862)*
Rays Seamless Rain Gutters....856 629-8407
33 Hawthorne Rd Sicklerville (08081) *(G-10024)*
Razac Products Inc....973 622-3700
25 Brenner St Newark (07108) *(G-7285)*
Razer Scandinavia Inc....732 441-1250
432 State Route 34 Ste 1a Matawan (07747) *(G-6030)*
RB, Parsippany *Also called Benckiser N Reckitt Amer Inc (G-7960)*
RB Health Manufacturing US LLC....973 404-2600
399 Interpace Pkwy Parsippany (07054) *(G-8075)*
RB Manufacturing LLC....908 533-2000
799 Us Highway 206 Hillsborough (08844) *(G-4367)*
RB Manufacturing LLC (HQ)....973 404-2600
399 Interpace Pkwy Parsippany (07054) *(G-8076)*
Rbc Bearings Incorporated....609 882-5050
400 Sullivan Way Ewing (08628) *(G-3048)*

Rbc Dain Rauscher...973 778-7300
  3 Garret Mountain Plz # 201 Woodland Park (07424) *(G-12231)*

Rbdel Inc..609 324-0040
  272 Dunns Mill Rd Bordentown (08505) *(G-610)*

Rbi Toys, Phillipsburg *Also called Ron Banafato Inc (G-8668)*

Rbs Intrntonal Direct Mktg LLC (PA)..........................856 663-2500
  825 Hylton Rd Pennsauken (08110) *(G-8569)*

Rcc Fabricators Inc...609 859-9350
  2035 Route 206 Southampton (08088) *(G-10480)*

Rcdc Corporation..212 382-0386
  59 Madison St 2 Hoboken (07030) *(G-4494)*

Rcf USA Inc...732 902-6100
  110 Talmadge Rd Edison (08817) *(G-2602)*

Rclc Inc (PA)..732 877-1788
  1480 Us Highway 9 N # 301 Woodbridge (07095) *(G-12152)*

RCM Ltd Inc...201 337-3328
  25 Cardinal Dr Oakland (07436) *(G-7702)*

Rdi, East Windsor *Also called Roof Deck Inc (G-2365)*

Rdl Marketing Group LLC..732 446-0817
  352a Sweetmans Ln Perrineville (08535) *(G-8602)*

Rdo Induction Ltd Liability Co................................908 835-7222
  2170 State Route 57 W Washington (07882) *(G-11586)*

Re Systems Group LLC..201 883-1572
  700 Broadway Ste 204 Westwood (07675) *(G-11968)*

Reachman International Corp...................................718 388-6565
  75 Knickerbocker Rd Moonachie (07074) *(G-6539)*

Reade Manufacturing Company (HQ)...........................732 657-6451
  2590 Ridgeway Blvd Manchester (08759) *(G-5888)*

Readington Farms Inc (HQ)...................................908 534-2121
  12 Mill Rd Whitehouse (08888) *(G-12048)*

Ready Pac Fods - Swedesboro NJ..............................609 360-0953
  101 Arlington Blvd Swedesboro (08085) *(G-10726)*

Ready Pac Produce Inc...609 499-1900
  700 Railroad Ave Florence (08518) *(G-3480)*

Ready-Pac Club Chef, Florence *Also called Ready Pac Produce Inc (G-3480)*

Reagent Chemical & RES Inc....................................908 284-2800
  115 Us Highway 202 Ste E Ringoes (08551) *(G-9442)*

Real Kosher LLC...973 690-5394
  146 Christie St Newark (07105) *(G-7286)*

Real Soft Inc...609 409-3636
  68 Culver Rd Ste 100 Monmouth Junction (08852) *(G-6360)*

Rebtex Inc..908 722-3549
  40 Industrial Pkwy Branchburg (08876) *(G-698)*

Rebuilt Parts Co LLC..856 662-3252
  7929 River Rd Pennsauken (08110) *(G-8570)*

Rebuth Metal Services (PA).....................................908 889-6400
  130 Farley Ave Fanwood (07023) *(G-3373)*

Reckitt Benckiser LLC (HQ)....................................973 404-2600
  399 Interpace Pkwy # 101 Parsippany (07054) *(G-8077)*

Reckitt Benckiser LLC...973 404-2600
  1 Philips Pkwy Montvale (07645) *(G-6471)*

Recombine LLC..646 470-7422
  3 Regent St Ste 301 Livingston (07039) *(G-5557)*

Reconserve Inc..732 826-4240
  1250 Amboy Ave Perth Amboy (08861) *(G-8627)*

Recorded Publications Labs...................................856 963-3000
  1100 E State St Camden (08105) *(G-1084)*

Recorder Newspaper, Stirling *Also called Recorder Publishing Co (G-10605)*

Recorder Newspaper...973 226-4000
  6 Brookside Ave Caldwell (07006) *(G-1033)*

Recorder Publishing Co...908 647-1180
  254 Mercer St Stirling (07980) *(G-10605)*

Recorder Publishing Co Inc (PA)..............................908 766-3900
  100 S Jefferson Rd # 104 Whippany (07981) *(G-12037)*

Recruit Co Ltd...201 216-0600
  111 Pavonia Ave Jersey City (07310) *(G-4816)*

Recruit USA, Jersey City *Also called Recruit Co Ltd (G-4816)*

Rectico Inc..973 575-0009
  12 Gloria Ln Ste 1 Fairfield (07004) *(G-3290)*

Recycle Inc...908 756-2200
  20a Harmich Rd South Plainfield (07080) *(G-10433)*

Recycle Inc East..908 756-2200
  20a Harmich Rd South Plainfield (07080) *(G-10434)*

Recycle-Tech Corp...201 475-5000
  418 Falmouth Ave Elmwood Park (07407) *(G-2847)*

Recycled Pprbd Inc Clifton....................................201 768-7468
  1 Ackerman Ave Clifton (07011) *(G-1711)*

Recycling, Bridgewater *Also called County of Somerset (G-830)*

Recycling N Hensel Amer Inc...................................856 753-7614
  1003 Industrial Dr West Berlin (08091) *(G-11746)*

Red Bank Cabinet, Tinton Falls *Also called Kenneth Asmar Custom Interiors (G-10840)*

Red Bank Gstrntrology Assoc PA..............................732 842-4294
  365 Broad St Ste 2e Red Bank (07701) *(G-9342)*

Red Diamond Company...973 759-2005
  368 Cortlandt St Belleville (07109) *(G-314)*

Red Feather Mktg Group LLC...................................973 377-1988
  332 Main St Madison (07940) *(G-5732)*

Red Letter Press Inc..609 597-5257
  16 Deerhorn Trl Upper Saddle River (07458) *(G-11284)*

Red Oak Software Inc (PA).....................................973 316-6064
  115 Us Highway 46 F1000 Mountain Lakes (07046) *(G-6860)*

Red Ray Manufacturing..908 722-0040
  10 County Line Rd Ste 3 Branchburg (08876) *(G-699)*

Red Sea Press Inc..609 695-3200
  541 W Ingham Ave Ste B Ewing (08638) *(G-3049)*

Red Square Foods Inc..732 846-0190
  62 Berry St Somerset (08873) *(G-10164)*

Red The Tailor, Lakewood *Also called Red The Uniform Tailor Inc (G-5176)*

Red The Uniform Tailor Inc (PA).............................848 299-0100
  475 Oberlin Ave S Ste 2 Lakewood (08701) *(G-5176)*

Red Wallet Connection Inc......................................201 223-2644
  106 Cardigan Ct Manchester (08759) *(G-5889)*

Reda Furniture LLC..732 948-1703
  25 Ocean Ave Manasquan (08736) *(G-5878)*

Reddaway Manufacturing Co Inc..............................973 589-1410
  32 Euclid Ave Newark (07105) *(G-7287)*

Redfield Corporation...201 845-3990
  336 W Passaic St Ste 3 Rochelle Park (07662) *(G-9534)*

Redhawk Distribution Inc......................................516 884-9911
  6835 Westfield Ave Pennsauken (08110) *(G-8571)*

Redhedink LLC...973 890-2320
  135 Minnisink Rd Totowa (07512) *(G-10968)*

Redi-Data Inc (PA)...973 227-4380
  5 Audrey Pl Fairfield (07004) *(G-3291)*

Redi-Data Inc...856 988-0551
  600 Route 73 N Ste 10a Marlton (08053) *(G-5996)*

Redi-Direct Marketing Inc (PA)..............................973 808-4500
  107 Little Falls Rd Fairfield (07004) *(G-3292)*

Redkeys Dies Inc...856 456-7890
  1307 Market St Gloucester City (08030) *(G-3845)*

Redkoh Datatest Industries, Hillsborough *Also called Redkoh Industries Inc (G-4368)*

Redkoh Industries Inc (PA)....................................908 369-1590
  300 Valley Rd Hillsborough (08844) *(G-4368)*

Redmond Bcms Inc...973 664-2000
  103 Pocono Rd Denville (07834) *(G-2053)*

Redpuro Import, Warren *Also called Redpuro LLC (G-11565)*

Redpuro LLC..908 370-4460
  106 Mount Horeb Rd Apt 8b Warren (07059) *(G-11565)*

Redstage Networks LLC..888 335-2747
  111 Town Square Pl Jersey City (07310) *(G-4817)*

Redyref, Riverdale *Also called Evs Interactive Inc (G-9480)*

Reed & Perrine Inc..732 446-6363
  396 Main St Tennent (07763) *(G-10790)*

Reed & Perrine Sales Inc.......................................732 446-6363
  396 Main St Tennent (07763) *(G-10791)*

Reed Presentations Inc (PA)..................................908 832-0007
  17 Water St Lebanon (08833) *(G-5301)*

Reed-Lane Inc..973 709-1090
  359 Newark Pompton Tpke Wayne (07470) *(G-11677)*

Reedy International Corp.......................................732 264-1777
  25 E Front St Ste 200 Keyport (07735) *(G-5023)*

Rees Scientific Corporation....................................609 530-1055
  1007 Whitehead Road Ext # 1 Ewing (08638) *(G-3050)*

Reeves Enterprises Inc..800 883-6752
  562 Central Ave New Providence (07974) *(G-7052)*

Reeves International Inc (PA)..................................973 694-5006
  14 Industrial Rd Pequannock (07440) *(G-8601)*

Reeves International Inc...973 956-9555
  34 Owens Dr Wayne (07470) *(G-11678)*

Refac Optical Group (PA).......................................856 228-1000
  1 Harmon Dr Blackwood (08012) *(G-490)*

Refferals Only Inc...609 921-1033
  3321 Lawrenceville Rd Princeton (08540) *(G-9110)*

Refine Technology LLC...973 952-0002
  26 Chapin Rd Ste 1107 Pine Brook (07058) *(G-8715)*

Refresco Us Inc...973 361-9794
  92 N Main St Wharton (07885) *(G-11998)*

Refrig-It Warehouse...973 344-4545
  77 Hackensack Ave Kearny (07032) *(G-4912)*

Refuel Inc...917 645-2974
  150 Wesley St South Hackensack (07606) *(G-10292)*

Regado Biosciences Inc...908 580-2109
  106 Allen Rd Ste 401 Basking Ridge (07920) *(G-204)*

Regal Crown Fd Svc Specialist................................508 752-2679
  20 Edison Dr Wayne (07470) *(G-11679)*

Regal Litho Prtrs Ltd Lblty Co................................732 901-1500
  1725 Oak St Lakewood (08701) *(G-5177)*

Regency Cabinetry LLC..732 363-5630
  525 Oberlin Ave S Lakewood (08701) *(G-5178)*

Regency Cabinetry LLC (PA)...................................732 363-5630
  525 Oberlin Ave S Lakewood (08701) *(G-5179)*

Regent, Lakewood *Also called Regency Cabinetry LLC (G-5179)*

Regent Cabinets LLC (PA).......................................732 363-5630
  1719 State Rt 10 Ste 220 Parsippany (07054) *(G-8078)*

Regentree LLC...609 734-4328
  116 Village Blvd Ste 200 Princeton (08540) *(G-9111)*

Reggiani Lighting Usa Inc......................................201 372-1717
  372 Starke Rd Carlstadt (07072) *(G-1211)*

Reggie's Roast Coffees, Linden *Also called Mire Enterprises LLC (G-5410)*

A
L
P
H
A
B
E
T
I
C

Regi US Inc 862 702-3901
  8 Fairfield Cres Unit 1 West Caldwell (07006) *(G-11802)*

Regina Wine Co 973 589-6911
  828 Raymond Blvd Newark (07105) *(G-7288)*

Region Oil 973 366-3100
  15 Richboynton Rd Dover (07801) *(G-2107)*

Regional Directory, Surf City *Also called American Directory Publishing (G-10664)*

Register & Transfer, Roselle *Also called Commerce Financial Prtrs Corp (G-9667)*

Register Lithographers Ltd 973 916-2804
  1155 Bloomfield Ave Clifton (07012) *(G-1712)*

Rehtek Machine Co., Passaic *Also called S&P Machine Company Inc (G-8178)*

Reich USA Corporation 201 684-9400
  300 Rte 17 Ste H Mahwah (07430) *(G-5808)*

Reilys Candy Inc 609 953-0040
  719 Stokes Rd 721 Medford (08055) *(G-6079)*

Reinco Inc 908 755-0921
  520 North Ave Plainfield (07060) *(G-8873)*

Reiss Corporation (PA) 732 446-6100
  36 Bingham Ave Rumson (07760) *(G-9714)*

Reiss Manufacturing, Rumson *Also called Reiss Corporation (G-9714)*

Reiss Manufacturing Inc (HQ) 732 446-6100
  36 Bingham Ave Rumson (07760) *(G-9715)*

Relational Security Corp 201 867-1330
  1 Harmon Plz Ste 700 Secaucus (07094) *(G-9917)*

Relatnship Capitl Partners Inc 908 962-4881
  51 Jfk Pkwy Fl 1 Short Hills (07078) *(G-9984)*

Relaxzen Inc 732 936-1500
  621 Shrewsbury Ave Shrewsbury (07702) *(G-10010)*

Relay Specialties Inc 856 547-5000
  1810 Prospect Ridge Blvd Haddon Heights (08035) *(G-4050)*

Relayware Inc 201 433-3331
  30 Montgomery St Ste 1210 Jersey City (07302) *(G-4818)*

Reldan Metals Company, South River *Also called Abington Reldan Metals LLC (G-10457)*

Reldan Metals Inc (PA) 732 238-8550
  396 Whitehead Ave 402 South River (08882) *(G-10464)*

Reldan Metals Inc 732 238-8550
  396 Whitehead Ave 402 South River (08882) *(G-10465)*

Reliability Maintenance Svcs 732 922-8878
  823 W Park Ave Pmb 245 Ocean (07712) *(G-7741)*

Reliable Envelope and Graphics 201 794-7756
  85 Main Ave Elmwood Park (07407) *(G-2848)*

Reliable Hermetic Seals, Bedminster *Also called Bryan Snook (G-268)*

Reliable Pallet Services LLC 973 900-2260
  460 Hillside Ave Ste 1 Hillside (07205) *(G-4438)*

Reliable Pallet Services LLC 732 243-9642
  74 Liberty St Metuchen (08840) *(G-6118)*

Reliable Paper Recycling Inc 201 333-5244
  1 Caven Point Ave Jersey City (07305) *(G-4819)*

Reliable Rbr Plastic McHy Div, North Bergen *Also called Reliable Welding & Mch Work (G-7478)*

Reliable Welding & Mch Work 201 865-1073
  2008 Union Tpke North Bergen (07047) *(G-7478)*

Reliable Wood Products LLC 856 456-6300
  145 Broadway Westville (08093) *(G-11947)*

Reliabotics LLC 732 791-5500
  24 Van Dyke Ave New Brunswick (08901) *(G-7000)*

Reliance Electric Company 856 661-1442
  1035 Thomas Busch Mem Hwy Pennsauken (08110) *(G-8572)*

Reliance Electronics Inc 973 237-0400
  145 Shepherds Ln Totowa (07512) *(G-10969)*

Reliance Graphics Inc (PA) 973 239-5411
  80 Pompton Ave Ste 1 Verona (07044) *(G-11310)*

Reliance Vitamin LLC 732 537-1220
  3775 Park Ave Unit 1 Edison (08820) *(G-2603)*

Reliant Vitamins, Edison *Also called Plantfusion (G-2595)*

Relpro Inc 908 962-4881
  51 Jfk Pkwy Fl 1w Short Hills (07078) *(G-9985)*

Relsec, Secaucus *Also called Relational Security Corp (G-9917)*

Relx Inc 973 812-1900
  1167 Mcbride Ave Ste 3 Woodland Park (07424) *(G-12232)*

Rema Corrosion Control 201 256-8400
  240 Pegasus Ave Northvale (07647) *(G-7604)*

Rema Tip Top/North America Inc (HQ) 201 768-8100
  240 Pegasus Ave Unit 2 Northvale (07647) *(G-7605)*

Remco Press Inc 201 751-5703
  4201 Tonnelle Ave Ste 4 North Bergen (07047) *(G-7479)*

Reminder Newspaper 856 825-8811
  2 W Vine St Millville (08332) *(G-6322)*

Remington Industries Inc 908 233-0153
  269 Sheffield St Ste 2 Mountainside (07092) *(G-6887)*

Remote Landlord Systems LLC 732 534-4445
  525 E County Line Rd Lakewood (08701) *(G-5180)*

Rempac Foam Corp 973 881-8880
  370 W Passaic St Rochelle Park (07662) *(G-9535)*

Rempac LLC (PA) 201 843-4585
  370 W Passaic St Rochelle Park (07662) *(G-9536)*

Renae Telecom LLC 908 362-8112
  745 Thomas St Elizabeth (07202) *(G-2772)*

Renaissance Creations LLC 551 206-1878
  95 8th St Fl 2 Passaic (07055) *(G-8176)*

Renaissance House 201 408-4048
  465 Westview Ave Englewood (07631) *(G-2928)*

Renaissance Lakewood LLC (HQ) 732 901-2052
  1200 Paco Way Lakewood (08701) *(G-5181)*

Renaissance Lakewood LLC 732 367-9000
  1720 Oak St Lakewood (08701) *(G-5182)*

Renaissance Pharmaceuticals, Lakewood *Also called Renaissance Lakewood LLC (G-5181)*

Renaissance Pharmaceuticals, Lakewood *Also called Renaissance Lakewood LLC (G-5182)*

Renard Commumnications Inc 973 912-8550
  197 Mountain Ave Springfield (07081) *(G-10576)*

Renault Winery Inc 609 965-2111
  72 N Bremen Ave Egg Harbor City (08215) *(G-2669)*

Renault Winery Restaurant, Egg Harbor City *Also called Renault Winery Inc (G-2669)*

Rendas Tool & Die Inc 732 469-4670
  417 Elizabeth Ave Somerset (08873) *(G-10165)*

Renell Label Print Inc 201 652-6544
  15 Sunflower Ave Paramus (07652) *(G-7899)*

Renesas Electronics Amer Inc 908 685-6000
  440 Us Highway 22 Ste 100 Bridgewater (08807) *(G-883)*

Rennoc Corporation 856 327-5400
  1450 E Chestnut Ave Ste B Vineland (08361) *(G-11395)*

Rennsteig Tools Inc (HQ) 330 315-3044
  411 Hackensack Ave # 200 Hackensack (07601) *(G-3966)*

Rentalift Inc 973 684-6111
  48 Alabama Ave Paterson (07503) *(G-8368)*

Rep Trading Associates Inc 732 591-1140
  4 Jocama Blvd Old Bridge (08857) *(G-7792)*

Reporte Hispano 609 933-1400
  42 Dorann Ave Princeton (08540) *(G-9112)*

Repro Tronics Inc 201 722-1880
  348 Golf View Dr Ltl Egg Hbr (08087) *(G-5647)*

Repromatic Printing Inc 973 239-7610
  216 Little Falls Rd # 3 Cedar Grove (07009) *(G-1299)*

Resdel Corporation (PA) 609 886-1111
  Industrial Park Rio Grande (08242) *(G-9461)*

Research & Education Assn 732 819-8880
  61 Ethel Rd W Piscataway (08854) *(G-8805)*

Research & Mfg Corp Amer (PA) 908 862-6744
  1130 W Elizabeth Ave Linden (07036) *(G-5433)*

Research and Pvd Materials 973 575-4245
  373 Us Highway 46 Bldg E Fairfield (07004) *(G-3293)*

Research Dev & Manufacture, Dayton *Also called (gt) Global Tech Inc (G-1951)*

Research Institute of America, Newark *Also called Thomson Reuters Corporation (G-7343)*

Research Manufacturing, Linden *Also called Research & Mfg Corp Amer (G-5433)*

Residex LLC 856 232-0880
  1001 Lower Landing Rd # 106 Blackwood (08012) *(G-491)*

Resintech Inc (PA) 856 768-9600
  160 Cooper Rd West Berlin (08091) *(G-11747)*

Resolv Corporation 973 220-5141
  164 Elmwynd Dr Orange (07050) *(G-7825)*

Resources Inc In Display (PA) 908 272-5900
  40 Boright Ave Kenilworth (07033) *(G-4992)*

Respirerx Pharmaceuticals Inc (PA) 201 444-4947
  126 Valley Rd Ste C Glen Rock (07452) *(G-3828)*

Respironics Inc 973 581-6000
  5 Woodhollow Rd Ste 1 Parsippany (07054) *(G-8079)*

Respironics Healthscan, Parsippany *Also called Respironics Inc (G-8079)*

Response Time Incorporated 856 875-0025
  1 Fiber Optic Ln Williamstown (08094) *(G-12102)*

Responsible Machines LLC 917 740-2269
  70 Lawrence Ave Highland Park (08904) *(G-4304)*

Restomotive Laboratories, Whippany *Also called Por-15 Inc (G-12035)*

Restortions By Peter Schichtel 973 605-8818
  10 New St Morristown (07960) *(G-6739)*

Retail Management Pubg Inc 212 981-0217
  28 Valley Rd Montclair (07042) *(G-6434)*

Retawa, Hoboken *Also called Reuge Management Group Inc (G-4495)*

Retrievex 732 247-3200
  5 Home News Row New Brunswick (08901) *(G-7001)*

Retrographics Publishing Inc 201 501-0505
  3 Reuten Dr Closter (07624) *(G-1765)*

Retrospect The For Local News, Collingswood *Also called Ainsworth Media (G-1769)*

Reuge Management Group Inc 888 306-3253
  89 River St Unit 1002 Hoboken (07030) *(G-4495)*

Reuther Contracting Co Inc 201 863-3550
  5303 Tonnelle Ave 5311 North Bergen (07047) *(G-7480)*

Reuther Engineering 973 485-5800
  154 Silver Lake Ave Edison (08817) *(G-2604)*

Reuther Material, North Bergen *Also called Reuther Contracting Co Inc (G-7480)*

Reuther Material Co Inc 201 863-3550
  5303 Tonnelle Ave North Bergen (07047) *(G-7481)*

Revelation Art Gallery, Denville *Also called Revelation Gallery Inc (G-2054)*

Revelation Gallery Inc 973 627-6558
  22 Broadway Denville (07834) *(G-2054)*

Revelation Software, Westwood Also called Revelation Technologies Inc (G-11969)
Revelation Technologies Inc (HQ) 201 594-1422
  99 Kinderkamack Rd # 109 Westwood (07675) (G-11969)
Revent Incorporated 732 777-5187
  22 Roosevelt Ave Somerset (08873) (G-10166)
Revere Industries LLC (PA) 856 881-3600
  838 N Delsea Dr Clayton (08312) (G-1527)
Revere Packaging, Clayton Also called Revere Industries LLC (G-1527)
Revere Plastics Inc 201 641-0777
  16 Industrial Ave Little Ferry (07643) (G-5514)
Revere Survival Products Inc 973 575-8811
  3 Fairfield Cres West Caldwell (07006) (G-11803)
Review and Judge LLC 732 987-3905
  910 E County Line Rd 202c Lakewood (08701) (G-5183)
Review Printing Inc 856 589-7200
  53 E Holly Ave 55 Pitman (08071) (G-8844)
Reviva Labs Inc 856 428-3885
  705 Hopkins Rd Haddonfield (08033) (G-4064)
Revlon Inc 732 287-1400
  2147 State Route 27 Fl 3 Edison (08817) (G-2605)
Revlon Consumer Products Corp 732 287-1400
  2121 State Route 27 Edison (08817) (G-2606)
Rex Lumber Company 732 446-4200
  1 Station St Manalapan (07726) (G-5861)
Rex Sign, Neptune Also called New Dawn Inc (G-6925)
Rex Tool & Manufacturing Inc 908 925-2727
  544 E Elizabeth Ave Linden (07036) (G-5434)
Rex Vinegar Co, Newark Also called Regina Wine Co (G-7288)
Rex Wine Vinegar Company 973 589-6911
  828 Raymond Blvd Ste 830 Newark (07105) (G-7289)
Rey Consulting Inc 201 337-0051
  350 Ramapo Valley Rd Oakland (07436) (G-7703)
Rf Vii Inc 856 875-2121
  104 Church St Newfield (08344) (G-7371)
Rf360 Technologies Inc 848 999-3582
  485b Us Highway 1 S # 210 Iselin (08830) (G-4642)
Rfc Container LLC (PA) 856 692-0404
  2066 S East Ave Vineland (08360) (G-11396)
RFC CONTAINER COMPANY, Vineland Also called Rfc Container LLC (G-11396)
Rff Services LLC 201 564-0040
  40 Edison Ave Ste C Oakland (07436) (G-7704)
Rfm Printing Inc 732 938-4400
  1715 Hwy 34 Belmar (07719) (G-362)
RFS Commercial 201 796-0006
  280 N Midland Ave Bldg M Saddle Brook (07663) (G-9785)
Rga Graphics, Clifton Also called Kay Printing & Envelope Co Inc (G-1655)
RGI Inc 973 697-2624
  27 Union Valley Rd Newfoundland (07435) (G-7376)
Rhingo Pro LLC 201 728-9099
  32 Us Highway 46 E Lodi (07644) (G-5598)
Rhoads Metal Works Inc 856 486-1551
  1551 John Tipton Blvd Pennsauken (08110) (G-8573)
Rhoads OHara Architectural 856 692-4100
  3690 N West Blvd Vineland (08360) (G-11397)
Rhodia, Princeton Also called Solvay Holding Inc (G-9121)
Rhodium Software Inc 848 248-2906
  10 Scotto Pl Dayton (08810) (G-1985)
Rhythmedix LLC 856 282-1080
  5000 Atrium Way Ste 1 Mount Laurel (08054) (G-6835)
Ribble Company Inc 201 475-1812
  280 N Midland Ave Ste 380 Saddle Brook (07663) (G-9786)
Ribbon Bazaar, Neptune Also called Cottage Lace and Ribbon Co Inc (G-6905)
Riccarr Displays Inc 973 983-6701
  52 Green Pond Rd Rockaway (07866) (G-9603)
Ricci Bros Sand Company Inc 856 785-0166
  2099 Dragston Rd Port Norris (08349) (G-8982)
Ricci Brothers Sand, Port Norris Also called Ricci Bros Sand Company Inc (G-8982)
Rich Art Color Co Inc 201 767-0009
  202 Pegasus Ave Northvale (07647) (G-7606)
Rich Designs 908 369-5035
  867 Amwell Rd Hillsborough (08844) (G-4369)
Rich Products Corporation 856 696-5600
  1910 Gallagher Dr Vineland (08360) (G-11398)
Rich Products Corporation 800 356-7094
  100 American Legion Dr Riverside (08075) (G-9505)
Richard Andrus 856 825-1782
  708 E Main St Millville (08332) (G-6323)
Richard Danz & Sons Inc 212 697-5722
  390 Prospect St Glen Rock (07452) (G-3829)
Richard E Pierson Mtls Corp 856 740-2400
  151 Industrial Dr Williamstown (08094) (G-12103)
Richard E Pierson Mtls Corp 856 691-0083
  184 W Sherman Ave Vineland (08360) (G-11399)
Richard E Pierson Mtls Corp (PA) 856 467-4199
  426 Swedesboro Rd Pilesgrove (08098) (G-8676)
Richard J Bell Co Inc 201 847-0887
  465 W Main St Wyckoff (07481) (G-12262)
Richard Rein 609 452-7000
  15 Princess Rd K Lawrence Township (08648) (G-5247)

Richard Shafer 856 358-3483
  38 Martin Ave Elmer (08318) (G-2796)
Richards Industries, West Caldwell Also called RISE Corporation (G-11804)
Richards Manufacturing Co Inc 973 371-1771
  517 Lyons Ave Irvington (07111) (G-4602)
Richards Mfg A NJ Ltd Partnr 973 371-1771
  517 Lyons Ave Irvington (07111) (G-4603)
Richards Mfg Co Sales Inc 973 371-1771
  517 Lyons Ave Irvington (07111) (G-4604)
Richmond Industries Inc 732 355-1616
  1 Chris Ct Dayton (08810) (G-1986)
Richmond Steel Rule Dies Inc 856 661-0900
  1416 Union Ave Pennsauken (08110) (G-8574)
Ricklyn Co Inc 908 689-6770
  43 Centerville Rd Columbia (07832) (G-1800)
Ricks Cleanouts Inc 973 340-7454
  654 River Dr Garfield (07026) (G-3756)
Rico Foods Inc 973 278-0589
  527 E 18th St Paterson (07514) (G-8369)
Rico Products, Paterson Also called Rico Foods Inc (G-8369)
Ricoh Prtg Systems Amer Inc 973 316-6051
  115 Route 46 Bldg F Mountain Lakes (07046) (G-6861)
Ricoh Systems, Mountain Lakes Also called Ricoh Prtg Systems Amer Inc (G-6861)
Riconpharma LLC (HQ) 973 627-4685
  100 Ford Rd Ste 9 Denville (07834) (G-2055)
Ricztone Inc 609 695-6263
  19 Bow Hill Ave Trenton (08610) (G-11112)
Ridge Manufacturing Corp 973 586-2717
  5 Astro Pl Ste A Rockaway (07866) (G-9604)
Ridge Precision Products Inc 973 361-3508
  288 Us Highway 46 Ste D Dover (07801) (G-2108)
Ridgewood Energy O Fund LLC 201 447-9000
  14 Philips Pkwy Montvale (07645) (G-6472)
Ridgewood Energy S Fund LLC 201 307-0470
  14 Philips Pkwy Montvale (07645) (G-6473)
Ridgewood Energy T Fund LLC 800 942-5550
  14 Philips Pkwy Montvale (07645) (G-6474)
Ridgewood Energy U Fund LLC 201 447-9000
  14 Philips Pkwy Montvale (07645) (G-6475)
Ridgewood Energy V Fund LLC 800 942-5550
  14 Philips Pkwy Montvale (07645) (G-6476)
Ridgewood Energy Y Fund LLC 201 447-9000
  14 Philips Pkwy Montvale (07645) (G-6477)
Ridgewood Press Inc 201 670-9797
  609 Franklin Tpke Ridgewood (07450) (G-9430)
Riedel Sign Company Inc 201 641-9121
  15 Warren St Little Ferry (07643) (G-5515)
Riegel Cmmunications Group Inc 609 771-0555
  1 Graphics Dr Ewing (08628) (G-3051)
Riegel Holding Company Inc 609 771-0361
  1 Graphics Dr Ewing (08628) (G-3052)
Riegel Printing Company, Ewing Also called Riegel Holding Company Inc (G-3052)
Riephoff Saw Mill Inc 609 259-7265
  763 Route 524 Allentown (08501) (G-34)
Right Angle, Hoboken Also called Hoboken Executive Art Inc (G-4473)
Rigo Industries Inc 973 881-1780
  50 California Ave Paterson (07503) (G-8370)
Rigztools LLC 908 361-5433
  1275 Bloomfield Ave Fairfield (07004) (G-3294)
Rimtec Corporation, Burlington Also called Rimtec Enterprises Inc (G-989)
Rimtec Enterprises Inc 609 387-0011
  1702 Beverly Rd Burlington (08016) (G-989)
Ring Container Tech LLC 973 258-0707
  50 Fadem Rd Springfield (07081) (G-10577)
Ringfeder Pwr Transm USA Corp 201 666-3320
  165 Carver Ave Westwood (07675) (G-11970)
Rinko Orthopedic Appliances 201 796-3121
  25-09 Broadway Ste 1 Fair Lawn (07410) (G-3109)
Rio Supply 856 719-0081
  100 Allied Pkwy Sicklerville (08081) (G-10025)
Riotsound Inc 917 273-5814
  17 Hampton House Rd # 15 Newton (07860) (G-7401)
Ripe Life Wines LLC 201 560-3233
  253 Indian Trail Dr Franklin Lakes (07417) (G-3623)
RISE Corporation 973 575-7480
  4 Fairfield Cres West Caldwell (07006) (G-11804)
Rising Health LLC 201 961-9000
  Park 80 W Plz Saddle Brook (07663) (G-9787)
Rising Pharmaceuticals Inc (HQ) 201 961-9000
  Park 80 W Plz I 250 Pehle Saddle Brook (07663) (G-9788)
Risse & Risse Graphics Inc 856 751-7671
  901 E Clements Bridge Rd # 3 Runnemede (08078) (G-9721)
Rive Technology Inc 732 329-4441
  1 Deerpark Dr Ste A Monmouth Junction (08852) (G-6361)
River Horse Brewery Co Inc 609 883-0890
  2 Graphics Dr Ewing (08628) (G-3053)
Riverbend Advertiser 908 475-3431
  401 Greenwich St Belvidere (07823) (G-375)
Riverdale Color Mfg Inc (PA) 732 376-9300
  1 Walnut St Perth Amboy (08861) (G-8628)

Riverdale Quarry, Riverdale Also called Tilcon New York Inc *(G-9490)*

Riverdale Quarry LLC 973 835-0028
125 Hamburg Tpke Riverdale (07457) *(G-9485)*

Riverside Marina Yacht Sls LLC 856 461-1077
74 Norman Ave Ste 1 Riverside (08075) *(G-9506)*

Riverstone Industries Corp 973 586-2564
65 Fleetwood Dr Ste 200 Rockaway (07866) *(G-9605)*

Rj Bielan Graphic Arts, New Brunswick Also called R J Blen Grphic Arts Cnverting *(G-6998)*

Rj Brands LLC (PA) 888 315-8407
200 Performance Dr # 207 Mahwah (07495) *(G-5809)*

Rjb Design Group Co., Wyckoff Also called Richard J Bell Co Inc *(G-12262)*

Rjd Machine Products, Trenton Also called Czar Industries Inc *(G-11051)*

Rjticeco LLC 973 697-0156
4 Northwoods Trl Stockholm (07460) *(G-10610)*

Rke Atheltic Lettering 732 280-1111
1901 State Route 71 1c Belmar (07719) *(G-363)*

Rlct Industries LLC 609 712-1318
2 E Acres Dr Pennington (08534) *(G-8458)*

Rmx, Mount Laurel Also called Rhythmedix LLC *(G-6835)*

Road Dept, Belvidere Also called County of Warren *(G-368)*

Roan Printing Inc 908 526-5990
4 E Main St Somerville (08876) *(G-10226)*

Robard, Mount Laurel Also called Food Sciences Corp *(G-6798)*

Robden Enterprises Inc 973 273-1200
210 Market St Newark (07102) *(G-7290)*

Robel Receptacles Inc 609 882-8065
180 Marina Blvd Long Beach Township (08008) *(G-5619)*

Roben Manufacturing Co Inc 732 364-6000
760 Vassar Ave Lakewood (08701) *(G-5184)*

Robert A Eick Qlty Bookbinding 973 822-2100
34 Central Ave Madison (07940) *(G-5733)*

Robert Brown 609 398-6262
1125 West Ave 1 Ocean City (08226) *(G-7756)*

Robert Colaneri 201 939-4405
236 Park Ave 238 East Rutherford (07073) *(G-2321)*

Robert Freeman 973 751-0082
320 Washington Ave Belleville (07109) *(G-315)*

Robert Gaiser Inc 973 838-9254
292 Main St Butler (07405) *(G-1017)*

Robert H Hoover & Sons Inc 973 347-4210
149 Gold Mine Rd Flanders (07836) *(G-3414)*

Robert J Donaldson Inc 856 629-2737
1287 Glassboro Rd Williamstown (08094) *(G-12104)*

Robert J Smith 201 641-6555
152 Louis St South Hackensack (07606) *(G-10293)*

Robert Main Sons Inc 201 447-3700
20-21 Wagaraw Rd Fair Lawn (07410) *(G-3110)*

Robert Manse Designs LLC 732 428-8305
2100 Felver Ct Rahway (07065) *(G-9220)*

Robert Nichols Contracting 973 902-2632
407 Conklintown Rd Ringwood (07456) *(G-9455)*

Robert Stewart Inc (PA) 973 751-5151
120 Little St Belleville (07109) *(G-316)*

Robert Wallace 609 649-0596
811 Rosemont Ringoes Rd Stockton (08559) *(G-10612)*

Robert Weidener 201 703-5700
9 12th St Fair Lawn (07410) *(G-3111)*

Robert Wynn 856 435-6398
36 Windmill Dr Clementon (08021) *(G-1534)*

Robert Young & Sons Inc 973 483-0451
25 Grafton Ave Newark (07104) *(G-7291)*

Robert Young and Son Inc 973 728-8133
830 Burnt Meadow Rd Hewitt (07421) *(G-4292)*

Roberta's Hut, Hamburg Also called Robertas Jewelers Inc *(G-4096)*

Robertas Jewelers Inc 973 875-5318
175 State Rt 23 S Ste D Hamburg (07419) *(G-4096)*

Robertet Inc (HQ) 201 337-7100
400 International Dr Budd Lake (07828) *(G-939)*

Robertet Flavors Inc 732 271-1804
10 Colonial Dr Piscataway (08854) *(G-8806)*

Robertet Flavors & Fragrances, Piscataway Also called Robertet Flavors Inc *(G-8806)*

Robertet Fragrances Inc (HQ) 201 405-1000
400 International Dr Budd Lake (07828) *(G-940)*

Robertet Fragrances Inc 973 575-4550
30 Stewart Pl Fairfield (07004) *(G-3295)*

Robertson Industries, Montague Also called Craig Robertson *(G-6402)*

Robinson Tech Intl Corp 973 287-6458
310 Fairfield Rd Fairfield (07004) *(G-3296)*

Robokiller LLC 723 838-1901
101 S Broadway South Amboy (08879) *(G-10244)*

Robotunits Inc 732 438-0500
8 Corporate Dr Ste 1 Cranbury (08512) *(G-1877)*

Rocco Press Advg Typography 973 790-4000
171 Walnut St Paterson (07522) *(G-8371)*

Roche Diagnostics Corporation 908 253-0707
1080 Us Highway 202 S Branchburg (08876) *(G-700)*

Rock Dreams Electronics LLC 609 890-0808
362 State Highway 33 Trenton (08619) *(G-11113)*

Rock of Ages Monuments, Spring Lake Also called H T Hall Inc *(G-10533)*

Rock Solid Woodworking LLC 732 974-1261
508 Washington Blvd Apt A Sea Girt (08750) *(G-9862)*

Rock Team Alliance, Marlton Also called Westrock Rkt Company *(G-6004)*

Rocket Ship & Print Inc 973 275-1144
71 S Orange Ave South Orange (07079) *(G-10314)*

Rockline Industries Inc 973 257-2884
1 Kramer Way Montville (07045) *(G-6493)*

Rockport, Paramus Also called CB Marathon Opco LLC *(G-7860)*

Rockwell Automation Inc 973 658-1500
299 Cherry Hill Rd # 200 Parsippany (07054) *(G-8080)*

Rockwell Automation Inc 973 526-3901
700 Lanidex Plz Ste 101 Parsippany (07054) *(G-8081)*

Rockwood Corporation 908 355-8600
410 Clermont Ter Ste D Union (07083) *(G-11219)*

Rockwood Holdings Inc (HQ) 609 514-0300
100 Overlook Ctr Ste 101 Princeton (08540) *(G-9113)*

Rockwood Specialties Group Inc (HQ) 609 514-0300
100 Overlook Ctr Ste 101 Princeton (08540) *(G-9114)*

Rodman Media Corp 201 825-2552
25 Philips Pkwy Fl 2 Montvale (07645) *(G-6478)*

Roelynn Litho Inc 732 942-9650
687 Prospect St Ste 410 Lakewood (08701) *(G-5185)*

ROFIN-SINAR TECHNOLOGIES INC., Landing Also called PRC Laser Corporation *(G-5226)*

Roger Software Distribution, Teaneck Also called RSD America Inc *(G-10771)*

Rohm America, Parsippany Also called Evonik Cyro LLC *(G-8004)*

Roi Rnovations, Princeton Also called Refferals Only Inc *(G-9110)*

Rolferrys Specialties Inc 856 456-2999
601 New Broadway Brooklawn (08030) *(G-921)*

Roll Tech Industries 609 730-9500
55 Route 31 S Ste A Pennington (08534) *(G-8459)*

Rollon Corporation 973 300-5492
101 Bilby Rd Ste B Hackettstown (07840) *(G-4032)*

Rolls Offset Group Inc (PA) 201 727-1110
264 Castle Ter Lyndhurst (07071) *(G-5705)*

Rolls-Royce Motor Cars Na LLC 201 307-4117
300 Chestnut Ridge Rd Woodcliff Lake (07677) *(G-12200)*

Rolo Systems 973 627-4214
34a Broadway Denville (07834) *(G-2056)*

Roma Moulding Inc 732 346-0999
115 Northfield Ave Edison (08837) *(G-2607)*

Roma Vinegar, Newark Also called Rex Wine Vinegar Company *(G-7289)*

Romaco Inc 973 709-0691
6 Frassetto Way Ste D Lincoln Park (07035) *(G-5332)*

Romaco North America Inc 609 584-2500
8 Commerce Way Ste 115 Hamilton (08691) *(G-4124)*

Roman & Sunstone, Parsippany Also called Tsi Accessory Group Inc *(G-8104)*

Romar Machine & Tool Company 201 337-7111
521 Commerce St Franklin Lakes (07417) *(G-3624)*

Romark Logistics CES LLC (PA) 908 789-2800
822 South Ave W Westfield (07090) *(G-11929)*

Romax Parking Solutions, Oakland Also called Park Plus Inc *(G-7701)*

Rombiolo LLC 973 680-0405
168 Broughton Ave Bloomfield (07003) *(G-529)*

Romulus Emprises Inc 609 683-4549
60 Woodside Ave Hightstown (08520) *(G-4314)*

Ron Banafato Inc 908 685-9447
1161 3rd Ave Phillipsburg (08865) *(G-8668)*

Ron Jon Surf Shop Fla Inc 609 494-8844
201 W 9th St Ship Bottom (08008) *(G-9973)*

Ronald Perry 201 702-2407
14 Westervelt Pl 1 Jersey City (07304) *(G-4820)*

Roned Printing & Reproduction 973 386-1848
6 Deforest Ave Ste 2 East Hanover (07936) *(G-2241)*

Ronell Industries Inc (PA) 908 245-5255
298 Cox St Roselle (07203) *(G-9682)*

Ronsil Silicone Rubber Div, Rumson Also called Reiss Manufacturing Inc *(G-9715)*

Rony Inc 201 891-2551
393 Crescent Ave Ste 12 Wyckoff (07481) *(G-12263)*

Roof Deck Inc 609 448-6666
80 Twin Rivers Dr East Windsor (08520) *(G-2365)*

Room Service Amenities, Morganville Also called ADS Sales Co Inc *(G-6635)*

Roper Scientific Inc (HQ) 520 889-9933
3660 Quakerbridge Rd Trenton (08619) *(G-11114)*

Rosalindas Discount Furniture 973 928-2838
76 Lexington Ave Passaic (07055) *(G-8177)*

Rosano Asphalt LLC 732 620-8400
Asbury Rd Ste 360 Farmingdale (07727) *(G-3393)*

Rosco Inc 908 789-1020
55 South Ave Garwood (07027) *(G-3786)*

Rose Brand East, Secaucus Also called Rose Brand Wipers Inc *(G-9918)*

Rose Brand Wipers Inc (PA) 201 809-1730
4 Emerson Ln Secaucus (07094) *(G-9918)*

Rose Brand Wipers Inc 201 770-1441
4 Emerson Ln Secaucus (07094) *(G-9919)*

Roseland Manufacturing, Roseland Also called B&G Foods Inc *(G-9646)*

Roselli, L E, Medford Also called L E Rosellis Food Specialties *(G-6074)*

Rosemont Publishing & Printing 609 269-8094
10 Schalks Crossing Rd Plainsboro (08536) *(G-8899)*

(G-0000) Company's Geographic Section entry number

Rosemount Inc 973 257-2300
1160 Parsippany Blvd # 102 Parsippany (07054) *(G-8082)*

Rosenwach Group, Somerset Also called Rosenwach Tank Co LLC *(G-10167)*

Rosenwach Tank Co LLC 732 563-4900
1100 Randolph Rd Somerset (08873) *(G-10167)*

Roseville Tool & Manufacturing 973 992-5405
22 Okner Pkwy Livingston (07039) *(G-5558)*

Rossendale Reddaway Company (PA) 973 690-6097
32 Euclid Ave Newark (07105) *(G-7292)*

Rossow Cosmetics - Usa Inc 732 872-1464
100 Matawan Rd Ste 350 Matawan (07747) *(G-6031)*

Rossow USA, Matawan Also called Rossow Cosmetiques - Usa Inc *(G-6031)*

Rostek Innovations LLC 908 996-6007
2 7th St Frenchtown (08825) *(G-3705)*

Rotarex Inc North America 724 696-3345
101 Bilby Rd Ste B Hackettstown (07840) *(G-4033)*

Rotarex Trade, Hackettstown Also called Rotarex Inc North America *(G-4033)*

Rotary Die Systems Inc 856 234-3994
876 N Lenola Rd Ste 9a Moorestown (08057) *(G-6619)*

Rotech Tool & Mold Co Inc 908 241-9669
824 Fairfield Ave Kenilworth (07033) *(G-4993)*

Rotor Clamp, Somerset Also called Rotor Clip Company Inc *(G-10168)*

Rotor Clip Company Inc (PA) 732 469-7707
187 Davidson Ave Somerset (08873) *(G-10168)*

Rotta Pharmaceuticals Inc 732 751-9020
86 W Main St Freehold (07728) *(G-3686)*

Round Cups LLC 732 734-0244
1301 W Elizabeth Ave D Linden (07036) *(G-5435)*

Rouses Pt Pharmaceuticals LLC 239 390-1495
11 Commerce Dr Ste 101 Cranford (07016) *(G-1926)*

Route 22 Fuel LLC 908 526-5270
1240 Us Highway 22 Bridgewater (08807) *(G-884)*

Rowan Technologies Inc (PA) 609 267-9000
10 Indel Ave Rancocas (08073) *(G-9262)*

Roxboro Holdings Inc (HQ) 732 919-3119
1501 State Route 34 Wall Township (07727) *(G-11506)*

Roy Anania 201 498-1555
149 S State St Hackensack (07601) *(G-3967)*

Roy D Smith Inc 201 384-4163
20 Foster St Bergenfield (07621) *(G-393)*

Roy Press Inc 732 922-9460
57 Bridgewaters Dr Apt 17 Oceanport (07757) *(G-7767)*

Roy Press Printers, Oceanport Also called Roy Press Inc *(G-7767)*

Royal Adhesives & Sealants LLC 973 694-0845
48 Burgess Pl Wayne (07470) *(G-11680)*

Royal Aluminum Co Inc 973 589-8880
620 Market St Ste 1 Newark (07105) *(G-7293)*

Royal Aquarius Empire 646 847-3322
2462 Yardville Hamilton (08690) *(G-4125)*

Royal Aquarius Engrg Inds, Hamilton Also called Royal Aquarius Empire *(G-4125)*

Royal Baking Co Inc 201 296-0888
8 Empire Blvd Moonachie (07074) *(G-6540)*

Royal Cabinet Company Inc 908 203-8000
15 Easy St Bound Brook (08805) *(G-622)*

Royal Cosmetics Corporation 732 246-7275
4 Jules Ln A New Brunswick (08901) *(G-7002)*

Royal Crest Home Fashions Inc 201 461-4600
170 Fair St Palisades Park (07650) *(G-7843)*

Royal Lace Co Inc 718 495-9327
902 E Hazelwood Ave Rahway (07065) *(G-9221)*

Royal Master Grinders Inc 201 337-8500
143 Bauer Dr Oakland (07436) *(G-7705)*

Royal Oak Railings LLC 973 208-8900
3 Field Ct Oak Ridge (07438) *(G-7665)*

Royal Pallet Inc 973 299-0445
771 Knoll Rd Boonton (07005) *(G-581)*

Royal Pharmaceuticals LLC 732 292-2661
2317 Highway 34 Ste 1d Manasquan (08736) *(G-5879)*

Royal Powdered Metals, Flemington Also called United Sttes Metal Powders Inc *(G-3474)*

Royal Prime Inc 908 354-7600
1027 Newark Ave Ste 1 Elizabeth (07208) *(G-2773)*

Royal Printing Service 201 863-3131
441 51st St West New York (07093) *(G-11880)*

Royal Seamless Corporation 732 901-9595
1000 Airport Rd Ste 203 Lakewood (08701) *(G-5186)*

Royal Slide Sales, Garfield Also called Royal Zipper Manufg Company *(G-3758)*

Royal Slide Sales Co Inc (PA) 973 777-1177
42 Hepworth Pl Garfield (07026) *(G-3757)*

Royal Sovereign Intl Inc (PA) 800 397-1025
2 Volvo Dr Rockleigh (07647) *(G-9633)*

Royal Wine Corporation 718 384-2400
63 Lefante Dr Bayonne (07002) *(G-243)*

Royal Wine Corporation 201 535-9006
63 Lefante Dr Bayonne (07002) *(G-244)*

Royal Zipper Manufg Company 973 777-1177
42 Hepworth Pl Garfield (07026) *(G-3758)*

Royale Cosmetics, New Brunswick Also called Royal Cosmetics Corporation *(G-7002)*

Royale Pigments & Chem Inc 201 845-4666
12 N State Rt 17 Ste 203 Paramus (07652) *(G-7900)*

Royalty Press Inc 856 663-2288
165 Broadway Westville (08093) *(G-11948)*

Royalty Press Group, Westville Also called Royalty Press Inc *(G-11948)*

Royce Associates A Ltd Partnr (PA) 201 438-5200
35 Carlton Ave East Rutherford (07073) *(G-2322)*

Royce Associates A Ltd Partnr 973 279-0400
28 Paterson St Paterson (07501) *(G-8372)*

Royce International Corp 201 438-5200
35 Carlton Ave East Rutherford (07073) *(G-2323)*

Royce Leather, Secaucus Also called Emporium Leather Company Inc *(G-9878)*

Royer Graphics Inc 856 344-7935
101 Lincoln Dr Clementon (08021) *(G-1535)*

Royer Group Inc 856 324-0171
7120 Airport Hwy Pennsauken (08109) *(G-8575)*

Royle Systems Group LLC 201 644-0345
375 North St Ste M Teterboro (07608) *(G-10809)*

Roysons Corporation 973 625-5570
40 Vanderhoof Ave Rockaway (07866) *(G-9606)*

Roysons Wall Covering, Rockaway Also called Roysons Corporation *(G-9606)*

Rp Products LLC 732 254-4222
646 State Route 18 East Brunswick (08816) *(G-2181)*

RPC Driveline Service, Pennsauken Also called Rebuilt Parts Co LLC *(G-8570)*

RPI Industries Inc 609 714-2330
220 Route 70 Medford (08055) *(G-6080)*

Rpl, Camden Also called Recorded Publications Labs *(G-1084)*

Rpl Supplies Inc 973 767-0880
141 Lanza Ave Bldg 3a Garfield (07026) *(G-3759)*

RPM Prfrmnce Catings Group Inc (HQ) 888 788-4323
280 West Ave Long Branch (07740) *(G-5631)*

Rq Floors Corp (PA) 201 654-3587
425 Victoria Ter Ridgefield (07657) *(G-9383)*

Rq Floors Corp 201 654-3587
550 Huyler St South Hackensack (07606) *(G-10294)*

RR Bowker LLC (HQ) 908 286-1090
630 Central Ave New Providence (07974) *(G-7053)*

RS Marble and Granite Inc 732 802-9220
900 Port Reading Ave B3 Port Reading (07064) *(G-8989)*

Rs Microwave Co Inc 973 492-1207
22 Park Pl Butler (07405) *(G-1018)*

RS Phillips Steel LLC 973 827-6464
128 Lake Pochung Rd Sussex (07461) *(G-10676)*

RSD America Inc 201 996-1000
300 Frank W Burr Blvd # 54 Teaneck (07666) *(G-10771)*

RSI Company 973 227-7800
333 Us Highway 46 Fairfield (07004) *(G-3297)*

Rsi-Fairfield Division, Fairfield Also called RSI Company *(G-3297)*

Rsi, Egg Harbor Township Also called RSI Woodworking Products Co *(G-2694)*

RSI Woodworking Products Co (PA) 609 484-1600
3092 English Creek Ave Egg Harbor Township (08234) *(G-2694)*

RSI Woodworking Products Co 609 645-9777
3049 Fernwood Ave Egg Harbor Township (08234) *(G-2695)*

RSR Electronics Inc 732 381-8777
900 Hart St Rahway (07065) *(G-9222)*

Rt Com USA Inc 973 862-4210
10 Millpond Dr Unit 2 Lafayette (07848) *(G-5052)*

Rti, Fairfield Also called Robinson Tech Intl Corp *(G-3296)*

Rti Computer Services, Oradell Also called R T I Inc *(G-7812)*

RTS Packaging LLC 908 782-0505
869 State Hwy 12 Frenchtown (08825) *(G-3706)*

Rubber & Silicone Products Co 973 227-2300
17 Montesano Rd Fairfield (07004) *(G-3298)*

Rubber Fab & Molding Inc 908 852-7725
1100 Rte 519 Johnsonburg (07846) *(G-4855)*

Rubigo Cosmetics 973 636-6573
101 E Main St Bldg 12 Little Falls (07424) *(G-5487)*

Rudco Products Inc (PA) 856 691-0800
114 E Oak Rd Vineland (08360) *(G-11400)*

Rudolph Instruments Inc 973 227-0139
400 Morris Ave Ste 120 Denville (07834) *(G-2057)*

Rudolph RES Analytical Corp 973 584-1558
55 Newburgh Rd Hackettstown (07840) *(G-4034)*

Rudolph Technologies Inc 973 448-4307
1705 Us Highway 46 Ste 3 Ledgewood (07852) *(G-5309)*

Rudolph Technologies Inc 973 347-3891
550 Clark Dr Ste 1 Budd Lake (07828) *(G-941)*

Ruffino Packaging Co, Hackensack Also called Ruffino Paper Box Mfg Co *(G-3968)*

Ruffino Paper Box Mfg Co 201 487-1260
63 Green St Hackensack (07601) *(G-3968)*

Ruggiero Sea Food Inc (PA) 973 589-0524
474 Wilson Ave Newark (07105) *(G-7294)*

Ruggiero Sea Food Inc 973 589-0524
117 Avenue L Newark (07105) *(G-7295)*

Rumblewood Cleaners, Mount Laurel Also called Ramblewood Cleaners Inc *(G-6834)*

Rumsons Kitchens Inc 732 842-1810
103 E River Rd Rumson (07760) *(G-9716)*

Runding LLC 973 277-8775
90 Greendale Dr Oak Ridge (07438) *(G-7666)*

Ruoff & Sons Inc 856 931-2064
1030 Rose Ave Runnemede (08078) *(G-9722)*

A
L
P
H
A
B
E
T
I
C

Rush Graphics Inc 973 427-9393
  1122 Goffle Rd 32 Hawthorne (07506) *(G-4257)*

Rush Index Tabs Inc 201 531-1555
  60 Willow St East Rutherford (07073) *(G-2324)*

Rush Manufacturing, Clifton *Also called Mat Manufacturing Corporation* *(G-1670)*

Rush Printing and Binding Svcs, East Rutherford *Also called Rush Index Tabs Inc* *(G-2324)*

Russco Bindery, Clifton *Also called Lont & Overkamp Pubg Co Inc* *(G-1664)*

Russell Cast Stone Inc 856 753-4000
  400 Cooper Rd West Berlin (08091) *(G-11748)*

Russell W Anderson Inc 201 825-2092
  1 Fyke Rd Mahwah (07430) *(G-5810)*

Russo Seamless Gutter LLC 732 836-0151
  45 Cherie Dr Brick (08724) *(G-757)*

Rust-Oleum Corporation 732 652-2378
  480 Frelinghuysen Ave Newark (07114) *(G-7296)*

Rust-Oleum Corporation 732 469-8100
  323 Campus Dr Somerset (08873) *(G-10169)*

Rutler Screen Printing Inc 908 859-3327
  169 Belview Rd Phillipsburg (08865) *(G-8669)*

Rvs Publishing Inc 856 810-7743
  875 Route 73 N Ste H Marlton (08053) *(G-5997)*

Rw Delights Inc 718 683-1038
  50 Division Ave Ste 44 Millington (07946) *(G-6261)*

Rx Trade Zone Inc 833 933-6600
  22 Meridian Rd Unit 15 Edison (08820) *(G-2608)*

Ryder Global, Villas *Also called Ryder Technology* *(G-11315)*

Ryder Technology 215 817-7868
  36 E Drumbed Rd Villas (08251) *(G-11315)*

Ryval Cmpt Svcs Ltd Lblty Co 201 374-1600
  111 Washington Ave Dumont (07628) *(G-2123)*

S & G Optical, Warren *Also called 21st Century Optics Inc* *(G-11533)*

S & G Tool Aid Corporation 973 824-7730
  43 E Alpine St Newark (07114) *(G-7297)*

S & H R Inc 908 925-3797
  401 N Wood Ave Ste 1 Linden (07036) *(G-5436)*

S & M Press Inc 973 546-6111
  169 Semel Ave Ste 2 Garfield (07026) *(G-3760)*

S & M Retaining Rings, Newton *Also called Schneider & Marquard Inc* *(G-7402)*

S & S Manufacturing, Edison *Also called S & S Socius Inc* *(G-2609)*

S & S Precision Company Inc 856 662-0006
  2205 Sherman Ave Pennsauken (08110) *(G-8576)*

S & S Printing, Somerdale *Also called Staines Inc* *(G-10044)*

S & S Socius Inc 732 698-2400
  115 Fieldcrest Ave Edison (08837) *(G-2609)*

S & W Precision Tool Corp 908 526-6097
  3 Holly Ct Bridgewater (08807) *(G-885)*

S and D Fuel LLC 908 248-8188
  1351 Magie Ave Union (07083) *(G-11220)*

S C T, Franklin Lakes *Also called Vozeh Equipment Corp* *(G-3625)*

S D L Powder Coating Inc 732 473-0800
  1591 Route 37 W Ste E4 Toms River (08755) *(G-10907)*

S Frankford & Sons Inc 856 222-4134
  110 Gaither Dr Ste A Mount Laurel (08054) *(G-6836)*

S G A Business Systems Inc 908 359-4626
  83 Haverford Ct Hillsborough (08844) *(G-4370)*

S G A Custom Shirtmakers, Newark *Also called Skip Gambert & Associates Inc* *(G-7317)*

S G Manufacturing Co Inc 732 494-6520
  15 Oliver St Metuchen (08840) *(G-6119)*

S Geno Carpet and Flooring 215 669-1400
  153 Sunset Dr Mount Royal (08061) *(G-6852)*

S Goldberg & Co Inc (PA) 201 342-1200
  3 University Plz Ste 400 Hackensack (07601) *(G-3969)*

S H P C Inc 973 589-5242
  187 Christie St Newark (07105) *(G-7298)*

S J Magazine, Marlton *Also called Rvs Publishing Inc* *(G-5997)*

S J Quarry Materials Inc 856 691-3133
  615 Gershal Ave Elmer (08318) *(G-2797)*

S J Screw Company Inc 908 475-2155
  Front & Hardwick St Belvidere (07823) *(G-376)*

S J T Imaging Inc 201 262-7744
  475 Kinderkamack Rd Ste 2 Oradell (07649) *(G-7813)*

S Jarco-U Castings Corporation 201 271-0003
  109 45th St Union City (07087) *(G-11265)*

S Johnson & Son, Belvidere *Also called S J Screw Company Inc* *(G-376)*

S K, Totowa *Also called Sk Custom Creations Inc* *(G-10972)*

S L Enterprises Inc (PA) 908 272-8145
  1603 N Olden Ave Ewing (08638) *(G-3054)*

S L P Engineering Inc 732 240-3696
  1501 Industrial Way Toms River (08755) *(G-10908)*

S M P, Mawhah *Also called Strategic Mktg Promotions Inc* *(G-5816)*

S M Z Enterprises Inc 908 232-1921
  223 South Ave E Westfield (07090) *(G-11930)*

S P Industries Inc 856 691-3200
  1172 N West Blvd Vineland (08360) *(G-11401)*

S P Industries Inc 215 672-7800
  1002 Harding Hwy Buena (08310) *(G-948)*

S P Sheet Metal Co Inc 609 698-8800
  446 N Main St Barnegat (08005) *(G-164)*

S S P Enterprises Inc 732 602-7878
  825 Us Highway 1 S Iselin (08830) *(G-4643)*

S V O Inc 973 983-8380
  28 State Route 10 W Succasunna (07876) *(G-10629)*

S W Electronics & Mfg (PA) 856 222-9900
  1215 N Church St Moorestown (08057) *(G-6620)*

S W I International Inc 973 334-2525
  487 Division St Boonton (07005) *(G-582)*

S&A Molders Inc 732 851-7770
  75 Mount Vernon Rd Manalapan (07726) *(G-5862)*

S&P Machine Company Inc 973 365-2101
  135 Monroe St Passaic (07055) *(G-8178)*

S&S Precision, Pennsauken *Also called S & S Precision Company Inc* *(G-8576)*

S&W Fabricators Inc 856 881-7418
  100 Delsea Dr S Glassboro (08028) *(G-3811)*

SA Richards Inc 201 947-3850
  1600 Parker Ave Apt 23a Fort Lee (07024) *(G-3580)*

Saad Collection Inc 732 763-4015
  160 Rrtan Ctr Pkwy Unit 5 Edison (08837) *(G-2610)*

Saber Associates 973 777-3800
  1111 Paulison Ave Clifton (07011) *(G-1713)*

Sabert Corporation (PA) 800 722-3781
  2288 Main St Sayreville (08872) *(G-9837)*

Sabert Corporation 732 721-5544
  879 Main St Ste 899 Sayreville (08872) *(G-9838)*

Sabett Hot Dog, Englewood *Also called Marathon Enterprises Inc* *(G-2912)*

Sabre Die Cutting Co Inc 973 357-9800
  68 Mill St Paterson (07501) *(G-8373)*

Saddle Brook Controls, Saddle Brook *Also called Ribble Company Inc* *(G-9786)*

Saddlebrook Ridge Equest Ctr, Shamong *Also called Brook Saddle Ridge Equest* *(G-9968)*

Saddleman Elegant, Totowa *Also called Elegant USA LLC* *(G-10943)*

Sadelco Inc 201 569-3323
  96 Linwood Plz Fort Lee (07024) *(G-3581)*

Sadwith Industries Corp 732 531-3856
  1015 Berkeley Ave Ocean (07712) *(G-7742)*

Safas Corporation (PA) 973 772-5252
  2 Ackerman Ave Clifton (07011) *(G-1714)*

Safe Man LLC 800 320-2589
  801 Vulcanite Ave Alpha (08865) *(G-45)*

Safe-Strap Company Inc 973 442-4623
  105 W Dewey Ave Ste 410 Wharton (07885) *(G-11999)*

Safegaurd Document Destruction 609 448-6695
  800 Rike Dr Millstone Township (08535) *(G-6265)*

Safeguard Business Systems, Hazlet *Also called Peter Morley LLC* *(G-4282)*

Safeguard Coinbox Inc 973 575-0040
  101 Clinton Rd Fairfield (07004) *(G-3299)*

Safer Holding Corp 973 485-1458
  1875 Mccarter Hwy Newark (07104) *(G-7299)*

Safer Textile, Newark *Also called Safer Holding Corp* *(G-7299)*

Safer Textile Processing Corp 973 482-6400
  1875 Mccarter Hwy Newark (07104) *(G-7300)*

Safer Textiles, Newark *Also called Meadows Knitting Corp* *(G-7238)*

Safety Power Inc 908 277-1826
  55 Union Pl Ste 178 Summit (07901) *(G-10654)*

Safety-Kleen Systems Inc 609 859-2049
  123 Red Lion Rd Southampton (08088) *(G-10481)*

Safetysign.com, Garfield *Also called Brimar Industries Inc* *(G-3724)*

Safire Silk Inc 201 636-4061
  135 Grand St Carlstadt (07072) *(G-1212)*

Sage Chemical Inc 201 489-5172
  2 University Plz Ste 204 Hackensack (07601) *(G-3970)*

Sage Payroll Services, Mount Laurel *Also called Pai Services LLC* *(G-6823)*

Sage Software Inc 856 231-4667
  305 Fellowship Rd Ste 300 Mount Laurel (08054) *(G-6837)*

Sahar USA Inc 201 868-4900
  2029 83rd St North Bergen (07047) *(G-7482)*

Sahara Textile Inc 973 247-9900
  52 Courtland St Paterson (07503) *(G-8374)*

Saint La Salle Auxiliary Inc 732 842-4359
  850 Newman Springs Rd Lincroft (07738) *(G-5341)*

Saint-Gobain Prfmce Plas Corp 973 696-4700
  150 Dey Rd Wayne (07470) *(G-11681)*

Saint-Gobain Prfmce Plas Corp 856 423-6630
  210 Harmony Rd Mickleton (08056) *(G-6138)*

Saint-Gobain Prfmce Plas Corp 732 652-0910
  1600 Cottontail Ln Somerset (08873) *(G-10170)*

Saker Shoprites Inc 908 925-1550
  1911 Pennsylvania Ave Linden (07036) *(G-5437)*

Saksoft Inc (HQ) 201 451-4609
  30 Montgomery St Ste 1240 Jersey City (07302) *(G-4821)*

Salad Chef Inc 609 641-5455
  125 Shadeland Ave Pleasantville (08232) *(G-8913)*

Salem Manufacturing Corp 973 751-6331
  115 Roosevelt Ave Belleville (07109) *(G-317)*

Salem Oak Vineyards Ltd Lblty 856 889-2121
  62 N Railroad Ave Pedricktown (08067) *(G-8440)*

Salem Packing Co 856 878-0002
  705 Salem Quinton Rd Salem (08079) *(G-9809)*

Salem Press, Hackensack *Also called Ebsco Publishing Inc* *(G-3908)*

Salem Publishing, Hackensack Also called Grey House Publishing Inc *(G-3924)*
Salerno's Custom Cabinetry, Saddle Brook Also called Salernos Kitchen Cabinets *(G-9789)*
Salernos Kitchen Cabinets 201 794-1990
　599 N Midland Ave Saddle Brook (07663) *(G-9789)*
Salescaster Displays Corp 908 322-3046
　2095 Portland Ave Scotch Plains (07076) *(G-9854)*
Salix Pharmaceuticals Ltd (HQ) 866 246-8245
　400 Somerset Corp Blvd Bridgewater (08807) *(G-886)*
Sally Miller LLC 732 729-4840
　30 N Main St Milltown (08850) *(G-6271)*
Salmon Signs 856 589-5600
　478 W Holly Ave Pitman (08071) *(G-8845)*
Salomone Rd-Mix Ltd Liabitlity 973 305-0022
　17 Demarest Dr Wayne (07470) *(G-11682)*
Salon Interiors Inc 201 488-7888
　62 Leuning St South Hackensack (07606) *(G-10295)*
Saltopia Artisan Infused Sea S 917 628-8433
　9 Reservoir Rd Hackettstown (07840) *(G-4035)*
Salus Pharma LLC 732 329-8089
　11 Deerpark Dr Ste 118 Monmouth Junction (08852) *(G-6362)*
SAM Graphics Inc 732 431-0440
　35 Vanderburg Rd Marlboro (07746) *(G-5956)*
Sam Hak Food Corp 908 688-4993
　10 Montgomery St Ste 20 Hillside (07205) *(G-4439)*
Sama Plastics Corp 973 239-7200
　20 Sand Park Rd Cedar Grove (07009) *(G-1300)*
Samad Brothers Inc 201 372-0909
　419 Murray Hill Pkwy East Rutherford (07073) *(G-2325)*
Samax Enterprise Inc 973 350-9400
　29-75 Riverside Ave Ste 2 Newark (07104) *(G-7301)*
Samna Cnstrctn & Steel Fabrctn 973 977-8400
　75 Dale Ave Paterson (07501) *(G-8375)*
Sample Media Inc (PA) 609 399-5411
　112 E 8th St Ocean City (08226) *(G-7757)*
Sample Media Inc 609 884-2021
　600 Park Blvd Ste 5 Cape May (08204) *(G-1104)*
Samson Sign Company, Waldwick Also called Superior Trademark Inc *(G-11454)*
Samsonite LLC 732 493-5146
　1 Premium Outlet Blvd # 825 Tinton Falls (07753) *(G-10845)*
Samstubend Inc 973 278-2555
　31 Maryland Ave Paterson (07503) *(G-8376)*
Samsung Capacitor, Dumont Also called BNH Enterprise LLC *(G-2116)*
Samsung Opt-Lctronics Amer Inc 201 325-2612
　500 Frank W Burr Blvd # 43 Teaneck (07666) *(G-10772)*
Samsung Pleomax America, Ridgefield Park Also called Zirex Inc *(G-9419)*
Samsung SDS Globl Scl Amer Inc (HQ) 201 229-4456
　100 Challenger Rd Ste 601 Ridgefield Park (07660) *(G-9413)*
Samuel Elliott Inc. 856 773-6000
　1818 Bannard St Cinnaminson (08077) *(G-1486)*
Samuel H Fields Dental Labs 201 343-4626
　197 Union St Hackensack (07601) *(G-3971)*
Samuel Jewels Inc 201 439-1555
　50 Mcdermott Pl Bergenfield (07621) *(G-394)*
Samuelson Furniture Inc 973 278-4372
　11-13 Maryland Ave Paterson (07503) *(G-8377)*
San Marel Designs Inc 973 426-9554
　98 Us Highway 46 Ste 10 Budd Lake (07828) *(G-942)*
Sancon Dumpster Rental Svcs, Newark Also called Sancon Services Inc *(G-7302)*
Sancon Services Inc. 973 344-2500
　50 E Peddie St Newark (07114) *(G-7302)*
Sander Mechanical Service Inc 732 560-0600
　55 Columbia Rd Branchburg (08876) *(G-701)*
Sander Sales Enterprises Ltd 201 808-6705
　200 Seaview Dr Fl 2 Secaucus (07094) *(G-9920)*
Sandik Manufacturing Inc 973 779-0707
　100 8th St Ste 8 Passaic (07055) *(G-8179)*
Sandkamp Woodworks LLC 201 200-0101
　430 Communipaw Ave Ste 1 Jersey City (07304) *(G-4822)*
Sandoval Graphic Co, Somerdale Also called Sandoval Graphics & Printing *(G-10043)*
Sandoval Graphics & Printing 856 435-7320
　9 Minnetonka Rd Somerdale (08083) *(G-10043)*
Sandoz Inc (HQ) 609 627-8500
　100 College Rd W Princeton (08540) *(G-9115)*
Sandoz Inc. 862 778-8300
　1 Health Plz East Hanover (07936) *(G-2242)*
Sandvik Inc (HQ) 201 794-5000
　17-02 Nevins Rd Fair Lawn (07410) *(G-3112)*
Sandvik Inc. 281 275-4800
　17-2 Nevins Rd Fair Lawn (07410) *(G-3113)*
Sandvik & Coromant, Fair Lawn Also called Sandvik Inc *(G-3112)*
Sandvik Coromant, Fair Lawn Also called Sandvik Inc *(G-3113)*
Sandvik Process Systems Inc 973 720-7000
　21 Campus Rd Totowa (07512) *(G-10970)*
Sandy Alexander Inc (PA) 973 470-8100
　200 Entin Rd Clifton (07014) *(G-1715)*
Sanford & Birdsall Inc 732 223-6966
　1704 Atlantic Ave Manasquan (08736) *(G-5880)*
Sanherb Biotech Inc 347 946-5896
　4 Mccullough Close Belle Mead (08502) *(G-292)*

Sanit Technologies LLC 862 238-7555
　90 Dayton Ave Ste 1811 Passaic (07055) *(G-8180)*
Sanitary Soap Company 973 279-8500
　81 Dale Ave Paterson (07501) *(G-8378)*
Sanket Corporation 732 287-0201
　15 Wood Acres Dr Edison (08820) *(G-2611)*
Sankyo U S A, Basking Ridge Also called Daiichi Sankyo Inc *(G-183)*
Sanofi Inc 800 981-2491
　55 Corporate Dr Bridgewater (08807) *(G-887)*
Sanofi Avntis Phrmctcals Group, Bridgewater Also called Sanofi US Services Inc *(G-890)*
Sanofi US Services Inc (HQ) 336 407-4994
　55 Corporate Dr Bridgewater (08807) *(G-888)*
Sanofi US Services Inc. 908 231-4000
　200 Cronjing Blvd Fl 2 Flr 2 Bridgewater (08807) *(G-889)*
Sanofi US Services Inc. 908 231-4000
　1041 Rte 202/206 Bridgewater (08807) *(G-890)*
Sanofi-Synthelabo Inc 908 231-2000
　55 Corporate Dr Bridgewater (08807) *(G-891)*
Sant-TEC Electric Inc (PA) 201 865-4100
　2017 41st St North Bergen (07047) *(G-7483)*
Santangelo Printing Co Inc 973 779-5880
　196 Garibaldi Ave Lodi (07644) *(G-5599)*
Santon Inc 201 444-9080
　128 Grand View Dr Toms River (08753) *(G-10909)*
Sapore Ravioli & Cheese, Middlesex Also called L and Ds Sapore Ravioli Cheese *(G-6175)*
Saporito Inc 201 265-8212
　959 Edgewater Ave Ridgefield (07657) *(G-9384)*
Sapphire Bath Inc 718 215-1262
　93 Harrison St Ste 5 Paterson (07501) *(G-8379)*
Sapphire Envelope & Graphics 856 782-2227
　214 Davis Rd Magnolia (08049) *(G-5742)*
Sapphire Flvors Fragrances LLC 973 200-8849
　6 Commerce Rd Fairfield (07004) *(G-3300)*
Saputo Cheese USA Inc 201 508-6400
　861 Washington Ave Carlstadt (07072) *(G-1213)*
Sar Industrial Finishing Inc 609 567-2772
　104 N Route 73 Berlin (08009) *(G-441)*
Sara Beth Division, Jersey City Also called Carole Hchman Design Group Inc *(G-4724)*
Sara Emporium Inc 201 792-7222
　833 Newark Ave Jersey City (07306) *(G-4823)*
Sarkli-Repechage Ltd 201 549-4200
　300 Castle Rd Secaucus (07094) *(G-9921)*
Sas Stresssteel Inc 973 244-5995
　100 New Dutch Ln Fairfield (07004) *(G-3301)*
Satec Inc 908 258-0924
　10 Milltown Ct Union (07083) *(G-11221)*
Satellite Pros Inc 908 823-9500
　148 Main St Whitehouse Station (08889) *(G-12062)*
Satex Fabrics Ltd 212 221-5555
　704 76th St North Bergen (07047) *(G-7484)*
Sato Lbling Solutions Amer Inc 973 287-3641
　30 Chapin Rd Ste 1201 Pine Brook (07058) *(G-8716)*
Saturn Beauty Group LLC 908 561-5000
　140 Ethel Rd W Ste G Piscataway (08854) *(G-8807)*
Saturn Overhead Equipment LLC 732 560-7210
　100 Apgar Dr Somerset (08873) *(G-10171)*
Sau-Sea Swimming Pool Products 609 859-8500
　1855 Route 206 Southampton (08088) *(G-10482)*
Saud & Son Jewelry Inc 201 866-4445
　441 60th St West New York (07093) *(G-11881)*
Saud Jewelry, West New York Also called Saud & Son Jewelry Inc *(G-11881)*
Sausea Swimming Pool Enamels, Southampton Also called Sau-Sea Swimming Pool Products *(G-10482)*
Saviance Technologies 609 448-7095
　16 Bridge St Metuchen (08840) *(G-6120)*
Savient Pharmaceuticals Inc (HQ) 732 418-9300
　400 Crossing Blvd Fl 3 Bridgewater (08807) *(G-892)*
Savignano Food Corp 973 673-3355
　107 S Jefferson St Orange (07050) *(G-7826)*
Savino Del Bene USA Inc (HQ) 347 960-5568
　34 Engelhard Ave Avenel (07001) *(G-150)*
Savit Corporation 862 209-4516
　400 Commons Way Ste D Rockaway (07866) *(G-9607)*
Savita Naturals Ltd 856 467-4949
　617 Heron Dr Swedesboro (08085) *(G-10727)*
Savoury Systems Intl Inc 908 526-2524
　230 Industrial Pkwy Ste C Branchburg (08876) *(G-702)*
Sawdust Depot LLC 973 344-5255
　704 Hulses Corner Rd Howell (07731) *(G-4565)*
Sawitz Store Fixture, Carlstadt Also called Sawitz Studios Inc *(G-1214)*
Sawitz Studios Inc 201 842-9444
　130 Grand St Carlstadt (07072) *(G-1214)*
Saxa Pharmaceuticals LLC 862 571-7630
　22 Candlelight Dr Holmdel (07733) *(G-4529)*
Saxton Falls Sand & Gravel Co 908 852-0121
　Waterloo Valley Rd Budd Lake (07828) *(G-943)*
Saybolt LP 908 523-2000
　1026 W Elizabeth Ave # 5 Linden (07036) *(G-5438)*

Saybolt North America Inc 973 884-3200
300 Lanidex Plz Parsippany (07054) *(G-8083)*
Scaasis Originals Inc 732 775-7474
1006 11th Ave Neptune (07753) *(G-6928)*
Scafa Modern Art Group, The, Lyndhurst *Also called Scafa-Tornabene Art Pubg Co (G-5706)*
Scafa-Tornabene Art Pubg Co 201 842-8500
165 Chubb Ave Ste 4 Lyndhurst (07071) *(G-5706)*
Scala Pastry 732 398-9808
1896 Us Highway 130 North Brunswick (08902) *(G-7537)*
Scalable Systems Inc 732 993-4320
15 Corporate Pl S Ste 222 Piscataway (08854) *(G-8808)*
Scandia Packaging Machinery Co 973 473-6100
15 Industrial Rd Fairfield (07004) *(G-3302)*
Scantron Corporation 201 666-7009
99 Kinderkamack Rd # 211 Westwood (07675) *(G-11971)*
Scarlet Printing 732 560-1415
253 Beechwood Ave Middlesex (08846) *(G-6193)*
SCC Concrete Inc 908 859-2172
1051 River Rd Phillipsburg (08865) *(G-8670)*
Scen'a Video Tape, Ridgefield Park *Also called Kolon USA Incorporated (G-9409)*
Schairer Brothers 609 965-0996
254 S Bremen Ave Egg Harbor City (08215) *(G-2670)*
Schall Manufacturing Inc 732 918-8800
3501 Rose Ave Ocean (07712) *(G-7743)*
Scheinert & Sons Inc 201 791-4600
404 N Midland Ave 2 Saddle Brook (07663) *(G-9790)*
Scheller, Lewis Printing, Somerset *Also called Lewis Scheller Printing Corp (G-10124)*
Schellmark Inc 732 345-7143
7 Thistledown St Tinton Falls (07753) *(G-10846)*
Schellmark Interactive, Tinton Falls *Also called Schellmark Inc (G-10846)*
Scher Chemicals Inc 973 471-1300
Industrial West Clifton (07012) *(G-1716)*
Scher Fabrics Inc 212 382-2266
18 Duncan Way Freehold (07728) *(G-3687)*
Schering Berlin Inc (HQ) 862 404-3000
100 Bayer Blvd Whippany (07981) *(G-12038)*
Scherng-Plough Pdts Caribe Inc 908 423-1000
1 Merck Dr Whitehouse Station (08889) *(G-12063)*
Schiapparelli Biosystems, West Caldwell *Also called Alfa Wassermann Inc (G-11763)*
Schifano Construction Corp 732 752-3450
1 Smalley Ave Middlesex (08846) *(G-6194)*
Schiff & Co 973 227-1830
1120 Bloomfield Ave # 103 West Caldwell (07006) *(G-11805)*
Schiffenhaus Industries Inc (HQ) 973 484-5000
2013 Mccarter Hwy Newark (07104) *(G-7303)*
Schindler Elevator Corporation (HQ) 973 397-6500
20 Whippany Rd Morristown (07960) *(G-6740)*
Schindler Elevator Corporation 856 234-2220
840 N Lenola Rd Ste 4 Moorestown (08057) *(G-6621)*
Schindler Enterprises Inc (HQ) 973 397-6500
20 Whippany Rd Morristown (07960) *(G-6741)*
Schlumberger Technology Corp 609 275-3815
20 Wallace Rd Princeton Junction (08550) *(G-9163)*
Schmutzerland, Englewood *Also called Umbrella & Chairs LLC (G-2939)*
Schneder Elc Bldngs Amrcas Inc 201 348-9240
210 Meadowlands Pkwy Secaucus (07094) *(G-9922)*
Schneider & Marquard Inc 973 383-2200
112 Phil Hardin Rd Newton (07860) *(G-7402)*
Schneiders Kitchens Inc 908 689-5649
252 State Route 31 N Washington (07882) *(G-11587)*
Scholastic Book Fairs Inc 609 578-4142
2540 Us Highway 130 # 105 Cranbury (08512) *(G-1878)*
Scholastic Inc 201 633-2400
100 Plaza Dr Fl 4 Secaucus (07094) *(G-9923)*
Scholastic National Field Off, Secaucus *Also called Scholastic Uk Group LLC (G-9924)*
Scholastic Uk Group LLC 201 633-2400
100 Plaza Dr Fl 4 Secaucus (07094) *(G-9924)*
Schon J Tool & Machine Co 732 928-6665
150 Park Ave Jackson (08527) *(G-4677)*
Schon Tool, Jackson *Also called Schon J Tool & Machine Co (G-4677)*
School Publications Co Inc 732 988-1100
1520 Washington Ave Neptune (07753) *(G-6929)*
School Spirit Promotions 609 588-6902
3 Ely Ct Trenton (08690) *(G-11115)*
Schott Nyc Corp 800 631-5407
735 Rahway Ave Union (07083) *(G-11222)*
Schrader & Company Inc 973 579-1160
188 Halsey Rd Newton (07860) *(G-7403)*
Schratter Foods Incorporated 973 575-3226
205 Moonachie Rd Moonachie (07074) *(G-6541)*
Schripps European Bread Inc 201 867-0909
5410 Tonnelle Ave North Bergen (07047) *(G-7485)*
Schroth's Gold & Silversmiths, Montville *Also called Hickok Matthews Co Inc (G-6489)*
Schulke Inc 973 521-7163
30 Two Bridges Rd Ste 225 Fairfield (07004) *(G-3303)*
Schultz Company 732 922-4334
2530 Asbury Ave Neptune (07753) *(G-6930)*
Schuman Cheese, Fairfield *Also called Arthur Schuman Inc (G-3139)*
Schurman Fine Papers 856 985-1776
300 State Hwy Rte 73 Marlton (08053) *(G-5998)*
Schusters Shoes Inc 856 885-4551
1122 Rembrandt Way 1 Williamstown (08094) *(G-12105)*
Schutz Container Systems Inc (HQ) 908 429-1637
200 Aspen Hill Rd Branchburg (08876) *(G-703)*
Schutz Corp (HQ) 908 526-6161
200 Aspen Hill Rd Branchburg (08876) *(G-704)*
Schuyler Printing Inc 201 997-8083
71 Kearny Ave Kearny (07032) *(G-4913)*
Schweid & Sons, Carlstadt *Also called Burger Maker Inc (G-1134)*
Schweitzer-Mauduit Intl Inc 732 723-6100
85 Main St Spotswood (08884) *(G-10530)*
SCI, Wall Township *Also called Selective Coatings & Inks (G-11508)*
SCI, Ocean *Also called Selective Coatings & Inks (G-7744)*
SCI-Bore Inc 973 414-9001
364 Glenwood Ave Ste 8c East Orange (07017) *(G-2268)*
Sciecure Pharma Inc 732 329-8089
11 Deerpark Dr Ste 120 Monmouth Junction (08852) *(G-6363)*
Science Pump Corporation 856 963-7700
1431 Ferry Ave Camden (08104) *(G-1085)*
Scientific Alloys Corp 973 478-8323
5 Troast Ct Clifton (07011) *(G-1717)*
Scientific Design Company (PA) 201 641-0500
49 Industrial Ave Little Ferry (07643) *(G-5516)*
Scientific Machine and Sup Co 732 356-1553
700 Cedar Ave Middlesex (08846) *(G-6195)*
Scientific Models Inc 908 464-7070
340 Snyder Ave Berkeley Heights (07922) *(G-421)*
Scientific Sales Inc 609 844-0055
3 Glenbrook Ct Lawrenceville (08648) *(G-5268)*
Scientifix LLC 856 780-5871
520 Fellowship Rd E508 Mount Laurel (08054) *(G-6838)*
Scimar Technologies LLC 609 208-1796
32 Cliffwood Dr Allentown (08501) *(G-35)*
Scimedx Corporation 800 221-5598
53 Richboynton Rd Dover (07801) *(G-2109)*
Scivantage Inc (PA) 646 452-0001
499 Washington Blvd Fl 11 Jersey City (07310) *(G-4824)*
Scj Group LLC 201 289-5841
492 Cedar Ln Ste 102c Teaneck (07666) *(G-10773)*
Scl 908 391-9882
7 Emmons Ct Bridgewater (08807) *(G-893)*
Scodix Inc 855 726-3491
250 Pehle Ave Ste 101 Saddle Brook (07663) *(G-9791)*
Sconda Canvas Products Inc 732 225-3500
85 Newfield Ave Edison (08837) *(G-2612)*
Scories Inc 973 923-1372
28 Vassar Ave Newark (07112) *(G-7304)*
Scorpio Posters Inc 718 499-2001
4 Timber Ln Ste B Marlboro (07746) *(G-5957)*
Scorpion Charters Spt Fishing 732 477-0985
401 Valley Way Brick (08723) *(G-758)*
Scott Graphics Printing Co Inc 201 262-0473
690 River Rd Ste D New Milford (07646) *(G-7025)*
Scott Kay Inc 201 287-0100
55 Hartz Way Ste 1 Secaucus (07094) *(G-9925)*
Scott Kay Sterling LLC 201 287-0100
55 Hartz Way Ste 1 Secaucus (07094) *(G-9926)*
Scott W Springman 856 751-2411
5 Rockhill Rd Ste 3 Cherry Hill (08003) *(G-1419)*
Scotts Company LLC 201 246-0180
125 Baler Blvd North Arlington (07031) *(G-7424)*
Screen Play Inc 973 227-9014
1275 Bloomfield Ave Ste 5 Fairfield (07004) *(G-3304)*
Screen Printing & Embroidery, Pleasantville *Also called C & D Sales (G-8903)*
Screen Printing & Embroidery 732 256-9610
5005 Belmar Blvd Ste B6 Wall Township (07727) *(G-11507)*
Screen Reproductions Co Inc 201 935-0830
850 Washington Ave Carlstadt (07072) *(G-1215)*
Screen Tech Inc of New Jersey 908 862-8000
1800 W Blancke St Linden (07036) *(G-5439)*
Screen-Trans Development Corp 201 933-7800
100 Grand St Moonachie (07074) *(G-6542)*
Screendreamercom Inc 856 702-6400
901 Route 168 Ste 405 Blackwood (08012) *(G-492)*
Screened Images Inc 732 651-8181
7 Joanna Ct Ste H East Brunswick (08816) *(G-2182)*
Screens & Fabricated Metals, Woodland Park *Also called Century Bathworks Inc (G-12215)*
Screens Incorporated 973 633-8558
130 Ryerson Ave Ste 219 Wayne (07470) *(G-11683)*
Screentek Manufacturing Co LLC 973 328-2121
220 Franklin Rd B Randolph (07869) *(G-9296)*
Sct Software, Shrewsbury *Also called Supply Chain Technologies LLC (G-10012)*
Sculptured Stone Inc 973 557-1482
501b Division St Boonton (07005) *(G-583)*
Scunci Division, East Windsor *Also called Conair Corporation (G-2353)*
Scynexis Inc 201 884-5485
1 Evertrust Plz Fl 13 Jersey City (07302) *(G-4825)*

Sdi Technologies Inc (PA)........732 574-9000
1299 Main St Rahway (07065) ***(G-9223)***
SE Tylos USA........973 837-8001
140 Commerce Way Totowa (07512) ***(G-10971)***
Sea Breeze Fruit Flavors Inc........973 334-7777
441 Main Rd Towaco (07082) ***(G-11003)***
Sea Gull Lighting Products LLC (HQ)........856 764-0500
1829 Underwood Blvd Ste 2 Delran (08075) ***(G-2021)***
Sea Habor Marine Inc........732 477-8577
310 Firehouse Rd Brick (08723) ***(G-759)***
Sea Harvest Inc........609 884-3000
985 Ocean Dr Cape May (08204) ***(G-1105)***
Sea Isle Ice Co Inc (PA)........609 263-8748
230 42nd St Sea Isle City (08243) ***(G-9864)***
Seaboard Industries........732 901-5700
1957 Rutgers University B Lakewood (08701) ***(G-5187)***
Seaboard Instrument Co........609 641-5300
4 N 1st St Pleasantville (08232) ***(G-8914)***
Seaboard Paper and Twine LLC........973 413-8100
37 E 6th St Paterson (07524) ***(G-8380)***
Seabrite Corp........973 491-0399
574 Ferry St Newark (07105) ***(G-7305)***
Seabrook Brothers & Sons Inc........856 455-8080
85 Finley Rd Bridgeton (08302) ***(G-796)***
Seagrave Coatings Corp........201 933-1000
209 N Michigan Ave Kenilworth (07033) ***(G-4994)***
Seagull Stain Glass, Atlantic City *Also called Linda Spolitino* ***(G-102)***
Seahawk Services, Paulsboro *Also called Oil Technologies Services Inc* ***(G-8422)***
Seahawk Services, Paulsboro *Also called Oil Technologies Services Inc* ***(G-8423)***
Seahawk Services, Linden *Also called Oil Technologies Services Inc* ***(G-5422)***
Seajay Manufacturing Corp........732 774-0900
9 Memorial Dr Ste 1 Neptune (07753) ***(G-6931)***
Seal Tronics Inc........864 576-0015
320 Colfax Ave Clifton (07013) ***(G-1718)***
Seal-Spout Corp........908 647-0648
50 Allen Rd Liberty Corner (07938) ***(G-5324)***
Sealed Air Corporation........201 712-7000
301 Mayhill St Saddle Brook (07663) ***(G-9792)***
Sealed Air Corporation........973 890-4735
301 Mayhill St Saddle Brook (07663) ***(G-9793)***
Sealed Air Holdings........201 791-7600
200 Riverfront Blvd # 301 Elmwood Park (07407) ***(G-2849)***
Sealed Unit Parts Co Inc........732 223-1201
2230 Landmark Pl Allenwood (08720) ***(G-37)***
Sealion Metal Fabricators Inc........856 933-3914
776 Creek Rd Bellmawr (08031) ***(G-350)***
Seals-Eastern Incorporated........732 747-9200
134 Pearl St Red Bank (07701) ***(G-9343)***
Sealy Mattress Co N J Inc........973 345-8800
697 River St Paterson (07524) ***(G-8381)***
Sealy Paterson, Paterson *Also called Sealy Mattress Co N J Inc* ***(G-8381)***
Seating Expert Inc........201 299-9109
721 Boulevard Kenilworth (07033) ***(G-4995)***
Seaview Golf Resort, Galloway *Also called Greater ATL Cy Golf Assn LLC* ***(G-3711)***
Seaville Motorsports........609 624-0040
3024 N Route 9 Ocean View (08230) ***(G-7766)***
Seawave Corp........609 886-8600
1508 Route 47 Rio Grande (08242) ***(G-9462)***
Sebastian & King Ltd Lblty Co........908 874-6953
816 Robin Rd Hillsborough (08844) ***(G-4371)***
Second Skin LLC........212 931-0621
935 Sedgewick Ct Westfield (07090) ***(G-11931)***
Secord Inc........908 754-2147
1812 Front St Scotch Plains (07076) ***(G-9855)***
Secure System Inc........732 922-3609
320 Essex St Ste 3 Stirling (07980) ***(G-10606)***
Secured MBL Hlth Applctons Inc........732 997-9609
29 Long Branch Ave Long Branch (07740) ***(G-5632)***
Security 21 LLC........856 384-7474
119 Steeplechase Ct Woodbury (08096) ***(G-12169)***
Security Defense Systems Corp........973 235-0606
160 Park Ave Ste 1 Nutley (07110) ***(G-7653)***
Security Fabricators Inc........908 272-9171
321 Lafayette Ave Kenilworth (07033) ***(G-4996)***
Security Holdings LLC (PA)........201 457-0286
111 Kero Rd Carlstadt (07072) ***(G-1216)***
Security Systems Unlimited, Mount Laurel *Also called E Berkowitz & Co Inc* ***(G-6794)***
Sekisui America Corporation (HQ)........201 423-7960
333 Meadowlands Pkwy Secaucus (07094) ***(G-9927)***
Seko Logistics, Newark *Also called Seko Worldwide* ***(G-7306)***
Seko Worldwide........973 465-6868
74 Avenue L Newark (07105) ***(G-7306)***
Seldom Seen Designs LLC........973 535-8805
6215 Town Center Way Livingston (07039) ***(G-5559)***
Select Enterprises Inc........732 287-8622
71 Executive Ave Edison (08817) ***(G-2613)***
Select Machine Tool Inc........856 933-2100
19 Thompson Ave Mount Ephraim (08059) ***(G-6764)***
Select Records, Lyndhurst *Also called PM Swapco Inc* ***(G-5701)***

Selective Coatings & Inks (PA)........732 938-7677
5008 Industrial Rd Wall Township (07727) ***(G-11508)***
Selective Coatings & Inks........732 493-0707
1750 Brielle Ave Ste B4 Ocean (07712) ***(G-7744)***
Selfmade Boutique, Jersey City *Also called Selfmade LLC* ***(G-4826)***
Selfmade LLC........201 792-8968
290 Hoboken Ave Jersey City (07306) ***(G-4826)***
Sell All Properties LLC........856 963-8800
301 Market St Ste 1 Camden (08102) ***(G-1086)***
Selling Precision, West Milford *Also called Hydraulic Manifolds Usa LLC* ***(G-11852)***
Selling Precision Inc........973 728-1214
264 Marshall Hill Rd West Milford (07480) ***(G-11856)***
Selway Partners LLC (PA)........201 712-7974
74 Grand Ave B Englewood (07631) ***(G-2929)***
Semels Embroidery Inc........973 473-6868
1078 Route 46 Clifton (07013) ***(G-1719)***
Semi Conductor Manufacturing........973 478-2880
5 Troast Ct Clifton (07011) ***(G-1720)***
Semi-Hex, Jersey City *Also called General Pencil Company Inc* ***(G-4759)***
Semiconductor Manufacturing, Clifton *Also called Semi Conductor Manufacturing* ***(G-1720)***
Seminole Wire & Cable Co Inc........856 324-2929
7861 Airport Hwy Pennsauken (08109) ***(G-8577)***
Seminole Wire Products, Pennsauken *Also called Seminole Wire & Cable Co Inc* ***(G-8577)***
Senat Poultry LLC........973 742-9316
28 Warren St Paterson (07524) ***(G-8382)***
Senco Metals LLC........973 342-1742
5056 Woodbridge Ave Edison (08837) ***(G-2614)***
Senor Lopez (PA)........732 229-7622
15 Spring Ct Tinton Falls (07724) ***(G-10847)***
Sensible Collection Inc........201 831-1063
2 University Plz Ste 100 Hackensack (07601) ***(G-3972)***
Sensient Cosmetics Technology, South Plainfield *Also called Sensient Technologies Corp* ***(G-10435)***
Sensient Technologies Corp........908 757-4500
107 Wade Ave South Plainfield (07080) ***(G-10435)***
Sensigraphics Inc........856 853-9100
105 W Park Dr Mount Laurel (08054) ***(G-6839)***
Sensonics Inc........856 547-7702
125 White Horse Pike Haddon Heights (08035) ***(G-4051)***
Sensonics International, Haddon Heights *Also called Sensonics Inc* ***(G-4051)***
Sensor Medical Technology LLC........425 358-7381
4 Stewart Ct Denville (07834) ***(G-2058)***
Sensor Products Inc........973 884-1755
300 Madison Ave Ste 200 Madison (07940) ***(G-5734)***
Sensor Scientific Inc (PA)........973 227-7790
6 Kingsbridge Rd Ste 4 Fairfield (07004) ***(G-3305)***
Sensoredge Inc........973 975-4163
140 Littleton Rd Ste 220 Parsippany (07054) ***(G-8084)***
Sensors Unlimited Inc........609 333-8000
330 Carter Rd Ste 100 Princeton (08540) ***(G-9116)***
Sentrex Ingredients LLC........908 862-4440
350 Cantor Ave Linden (07036) ***(G-5440)***
Sentrimed Ltd Liability Co........914 582-8631
49 Holly Oak Dr Voorhees (08043) ***(G-11437)***
Sentry Mfg LLC........856 642-0480
351 Crider Ave Moorestown (08057) ***(G-6622)***
Sentry Water Management........973 616-9000
35 Newark Pompton Tpke Riverdale (07457) ***(G-9486)***
Sepers Countryside Nursery LLC........856 451-0719
282 Harmony Rd Bridgeton (08302) ***(G-797)***
Seqirus USA Inc........908 739-0200
25 Deforest Ave Summit (07901) ***(G-10655)***
Sequel Software Inc........908 575-0252
1065 Us Highway 22 Ste 3 Bridgewater (08807) ***(G-894)***
Sequin City, North Bergen *Also called Sequins of Distinction Inc* ***(G-7486)***
Sequins of Distinction Inc........201 348-8111
1302 13th St North Bergen (07047) ***(G-7486)***
Seren Inc........856 205-1131
1670 Gallagher Dr Vineland (08360) ***(G-11402)***
Seren Industrial Power Systems, Vineland *Also called Seren Inc* ***(G-11402)***
Seren Industrial Power Systems........856 205-1131
1670 Gallagher Dr Vineland (08360) ***(G-11403)***
Seren Ips Inc........856 205-1131
1670 Gallagher Dr Vineland (08360) ***(G-11404)***
Seri-Arts, Carlstadt *Also called Vernon Display Graphics Inc* ***(G-1238)***
Serious Welding & Mech LLC........732 698-7478
427 Whitehead Ave Ste 3 South River (08882) ***(G-10466)***
Sermach Inc........732 356-9021
311 Lincoln Blvd Ste C Middlesex (08846) ***(G-6196)***
Serranis Bakery........973 678-1777
114 S Essex Ave Orange (07050) ***(G-7827)***
Serratelli Hat Company Inc........973 623-4133
418 Central Ave Newark (07107) ***(G-7307)***
Service Apex, Bridgewater *Also called Avail Inc* ***(G-817)***
Service Data Corp Inc........908 522-0020
265 Oak Ridge Ave Summit (07901) ***(G-10656)***
Service Data Forms, Summit *Also called Service Data Corp Inc* ***(G-10656)***
Service Machine Co, Middlesex *Also called Sermach Inc* ***(G-6196)***

ALPHABETIC

Service Metal Fabricating Inc (PA)....973 625-8882
10 Stickle Ave Rockaway (07866) ***(G-9608)***
Service Metal Fabricating Inc....973 989-7199
243 E Blackwell St Dover (07801) ***(G-2110)***
Service Seal Div, Kenilworth *Also called Flexline Inc* ***(G-4956)***
Service Tech....908 788-0072
109 Rake Factory Rd Flemington (08822) ***(G-3465)***
Services Equipment Com LLC....973 992-4404
4 Tamarack Dr Livingston (07039) ***(G-5560)***
Servo-Tek Products Company Inc....973 427-4249
1096 Goffle Rd Hawthorne (07506) ***(G-4258)***
Servolift LLC....973 442-7878
35 Righter Rd Ste A Randolph (07869) ***(G-9297)***
Servometer, Cedar Grove *Also called Precision Mfg Group LLC* ***(G-1296)***
SES Engineering (us) Inc....609 987-4000
4 Research Way Princeton (08540) ***(G-9117)***
Setaram Inc (HQ)....908 262-7060
2555 Us Highway 130 Ste 2 Cranbury (08512) ***(G-1879)***
Setco LLC....610 321-9760
34 Engelhard Dr Monroe Township (08831) ***(G-6391)***
Setcon Industries Inc....973 283-0500
5 Mathews Ave Ste 7 Riverdale (07457) ***(G-9487)***
Seven Mile Pubg & Creative....609 967-7707
355 24th St Avalon (08202) ***(G-120)***
Seven Up Bottling Company, Hackensack *Also called Canada Dry Bottling Co NY LP* ***(G-3893)***
Severino Pasta Mfg Co Inc....856 854-3716
110 Haddon Ave Collingswood (08108) ***(G-1773)***
Severna Operations Inc....973 503-1600
3 Eastmans Rd Parsippany (07054) ***(G-8085)***
Seviroli Foods Inc....856 931-1900
960 Creek Rd Bellmawr (08031) ***(G-351)***
Sew-Eurodrive Inc....856 467-2277
200 High Hill Rd Bridgeport (08014) ***(G-771)***
Sew-Eurodrive Inc....856 467-2277
2107 High Hill Rd Bridgeport (08014) ***(G-772)***
SF Lutz LLC....609 646-9490
3143 Fire Rd Ste F Egg Harbor Township (08234) ***(G-2696)***
Sfp Software Inc....856 235-7778
162 Knotty Oak Dr Mount Laurel (08054) ***(G-6840)***
Sfx Installations, Mount Laurel *Also called Scientifix LLC* ***(G-6838)***
SGB Packaging Group Inc....201 488-3030
401 Hackensack Ave Fl 7 Hackensack (07601) ***(G-3973)***
Sgfootwear Company, Hackensack *Also called S Goldberg & Co Inc* ***(G-3969)***
Sgh Inc....609 698-8868
79 S Main St Ste 2 Barnegat (08005) ***(G-165)***
Sgi Apparel Ltd....201 342-1200
3 University Plz Ste 400 Hackensack (07601) ***(G-3974)***
SGS UStesting Company (HQ)....973 575-5252
291 Fairfield Ave Fairfield (07004) ***(G-3306)***
Sgw Fuel Delivery....609 209-8773
353 Churchill Ave Trenton (08610) ***(G-11116)***
Shabazz Fruit Cola Company LLC....973 230-4641
24 Wyndmoor Ave Newark (07112) ***(G-7308)***
Shachihata Inc (usa)....732 905-7159
525 Oberlin Ave S Lakewood (08701) ***(G-5188)***
Shade Powers Co Inc....201 767-3727
112 Paris Ave Ste C Northvale (07647) ***(G-7607)***
Shafer Brothers Trailers, Elmer *Also called Richard Shafer* ***(G-2796)***
Shaffer Products Inc....908 206-1980
20 Milltown Rd Union (07083) ***(G-11223)***
Shahnawaz Food LLC....908 413-4206
78 Roxy Ave Edison (08820) ***(G-2615)***
Shallcross Bolt & Specialties....908 925-4700
1 Mccandless St Linden (07036) ***(G-5441)***
Shamong Manufacturing Company....609 654-2549
33 Bunker Hill Rd Shamong (08088) ***(G-9971)***
Shamrock Technologies Inc (PA)....973 242-2999
Foot Of Pacific St Newark (07114) ***(G-7309)***
Shanghai Freemen Americas LLC (HQ)....732 981-1288
377 Hoes Ln Ste 240 Piscataway (08854) ***(G-8809)***
Shanghai Optics Inc....732 321-6915
17 Brant Ave Ste 6 Clark (07066) ***(G-1515)***
Shani Auto Fuel Corp....856 241-9767
541 Kings Hwy Woolwich Township (08085) ***(G-12241)***
Shapes/Arch Holdings LLC (PA)....856 662-5500
9000 River Rd Delair (08110) ***(G-2001)***
Sharagano, Harrison *Also called E-Lo Sportswear LLC* ***(G-4179)***
Sharkk LLC....302 377-3974
70 S Orange Ave Ste 105 Livingston (07039) ***(G-5561)***
Sharmatek Inc....908 852-5087
999 Willow Grove St Hackettstown (07840) ***(G-4036)***
Sharp Electronics Corporation (HQ)....201 529-8200
100 Jaguar Land Rover Way Mahwah (07495) ***(G-5811)***
Sharp Impressions Inc....201 573-4943
163 Belmont Ave Ste 1 Garfield (07026) ***(G-3761)***
Sharp Manufacturing Co Amer, Mahwah *Also called Sharp Electronics Corporation* ***(G-5811)***
Sharrott Wine....609 567-9463
370 S Egg Harbor Rd Hammonton (08037) ***(G-4148)***

Shasun USA Inc....732 465-0700
15 Corporate Pl S Ste 222 Piscataway (08854) ***(G-8810)***
Shaw Industries Inc....609 655-8300
1267 S River Rd Ste 100 Cranbury (08512) ***(G-1880)***
Shearman Cabinets....973 677-0071
195 N Munn Ave East Orange (07017) ***(G-2269)***
Sheet Metal Products Inc....973 482-0450
794 N 6th St Newark (07107) ***(G-7310)***
Sheex Inc....856 334-3021
10000 Lincoln Dr E # 303 Marlton (08053) ***(G-5999)***
Sheex Performance Sleep, Marlton *Also called Sheex Inc* ***(G-5999)***
Shekia Group LLC....732 372-7666
1130 King Georges Post Rd Edison (08837) ***(G-2616)***
Shelan Chemical Company Inc....732 796-1003
174 Tournament Dr Monroe Township (08831) ***(G-6392)***
Shelby Mechanical Inc....856 665-4540
1009 Broad St Cinnaminson (08077) ***(G-1487)***
Shell Packaging Corporation (PA)....908 871-7000
200 Connell Dr Ste 1200 Berkeley Heights (07922) ***(G-422)***
SHELTERFORCE MAGAZINE, Montclair *Also called National Housing Institute* ***(G-6424)***
Sheridan Communications, Alpha *Also called Sheridan Printing Company Inc* ***(G-46)***
Sheridan Optical Co Inc....856 582-0963
108 Clinton Ave Pitman (08071) ***(G-8846)***
Sheridan Optical Lab, Pitman *Also called Sheridan Optical Co Inc* ***(G-8846)***
Sheridan Printing Company Inc....908 454-0700
1425 3rd Ave Alpha (08865) ***(G-46)***
Sheris Cookery Inc....973 589-2060
33 Delancey St Newark (07105) ***(G-7311)***
Sherman Group Holdings....201 735-9000
2200 Fletcher Ave Office Fort Lee (07024) ***(G-3582)***
Sherman Nat Inc (HQ)....201 735-9000
10 Sterling Blvd Ste 302 Englewood (07631) ***(G-2930)***
Sherman Printing Co Inc....973 345-2493
161 Elmwood Dr Clifton (07013) ***(G-1721)***
Shermans 1400 Brdway N Y C Ltd....201 735-9000
10 Sterling Blvd Englewood (07631) ***(G-2931)***
Sheroy Printing Inc....973 242-4040
40 Commerce St Newark (07102) ***(G-7312)***
Sherry International Inc....908 279-7255
31 Mountain Blvd Bldg M Warren (07059) ***(G-11566)***
Sherwood Brands Corporation....973 249-8200
120 Jersey Ave New Brunswick (08901) ***(G-7003)***
Sherwood Industries Inc....609 396-7600
1333 Brunswick Ave # 200 Lawrenceville (08648) ***(G-5269)***
Shields Business Solutions, Moorestown *Also called Longport Shields Inc* ***(G-6598)***
Shindo International Inc....973 470-8100
200 Entin Rd Clifton (07014) ***(G-1722)***
Shipmaster, Monroe Township *Also called Broadway Kleer-Guard Corp* ***(G-6380)***
Shiseido America Inc (HQ)....609 371-5800
366 Prncton Hightstown Rd East Windsor (08520) ***(G-2366)***
Shiseido Americas Corporation....609 371-5800
366 Prncton Hightstown Rd East Windsor (08520) ***(G-2367)***
Shiva Fuel Inc....732 826-3228
737 New Brunswick Ave Perth Amboy (08861) ***(G-8629)***
Shiva Software Group Inc....973 691-5475
2 Fennimore Ct Flanders (07836) ***(G-3415)***
Shm, Englewood *Also called Structured Healthcare MGT Inc* ***(G-2935)***
Shock Tech Inc (PA)....845 368-8600
211 Island Rd Mahwah (07430) ***(G-5812)***
Shooting Star Inc....908 789-2500
2500 Plainfield Ave Scotch Plains (07076) ***(G-9856)***
Shop Rite 299, Neptune *Also called Shop Rite Supermarkets Inc* ***(G-6932)***
Shop Rite 633, Absecon *Also called Shop-Rite Supermarkets Inc* ***(G-4)***
Shop Rite of Medford, Medford *Also called Berat Corporation* ***(G-6065)***
Shop Rite Supermarkets Inc....732 775-4250
2200 Highway 66 Neptune (07753) ***(G-6932)***
Shop Rite Supermarkets Inc....732 442-1717
Convery Blvd Fayette Perth Amboy (08861) ***(G-8630)***
Shop-Rite Supermarkets Inc....609 646-2448
616 White Horse Pike Absecon (08201) ***(G-4)***
Shopindia Inc....732 409-0656
3 Topaz Ct Marlboro (07746) ***(G-5958)***
Shoppe, Villas *Also called Beach Nutts Media Inc* ***(G-11313)***
Shoppe CMC Shoppers Guide (PA)....609 886-4112
2503 Bayshore Rd Villas (08251) ***(G-11316)***
Shopper Discount Guide, Marlton *Also called Neighborhood Shoppers* ***(G-5989)***
Shoprite, Perth Amboy *Also called Shop Rite Supermarkets Inc* ***(G-8630)***
Shor International....973 520-8777
77 Fairwood Rd Madison (07940) ***(G-5735)***
Shore Awning Co....732 775-3351
1933 State Route 35 # 126 Wall Township (07719) ***(G-11509)***
Shore Bet Painting and Cnstr....732 996-3455
102 Osborne Ave Bay Head (08742) ***(G-209)***
Shore Drilling Inc....732 935-1776
23 Branch Ave Oceanport (07757) ***(G-7768)***
Shore Microsystems Inc (PA)....732 870-0800
45 Memorial Pkwy Long Branch (07740) ***(G-5633)***

Shore Point Distrg Co Inc 732 308-3334
100 Shore Point Dr Freehold (07728) *(G-3688)*

Shore Precision Mfg Inc 732 914-0949
1000 Industrial Way Ste D Toms River (08755) *(G-10910)*

Shore Printed Circuits Inc 732 380-0590
3 Meridian Rd Eatontown (07724) *(G-2422)*

Shore Software Inc 732 899-6878
1102 Arnold Ave Point Pleasant Boro (08742) *(G-8940)*

Shoreway Industry 856 307-2020
260 W Clayton Ave Clayton (08312) *(G-1528)*

Short Load Concrete LLC 732 469-4420
81 Chimney Rock Rd Ste 1 Bridgewater (08807) *(G-895)*

Short Run Stamping Company Inc (PA) 908 862-1070
925 E Linden Ave Linden (07036) *(G-5442)*

Shotmeyer Bros, Lafayette Also called Beaver Run Farms *(G-5044)*

Showcase Printing of Iselin 732 283-0438
181 E James Pl Iselin (08830) *(G-4644)*

Showcase Publications Inc (PA) 732 349-1134
90 Irons St Toms River (08753) *(G-10911)*

Showtech Inc 973 249-6336
40 Entin Rd Clifton (07014) *(G-1723)*

Showtime Express 732 238-2701
5 Lexington Ave East Brunswick (08816) *(G-2183)*

Shree Ji Printing Corporation 201 842-9500
55 Veterans Blvd Carlstadt (07072) *(G-1217)*

Shrem Consulting Ltd Lblty Co 917 371-0581
457 Monmouth Rd West Long Branch (07764) *(G-11846)*

Shrivers Salt Wtr Taffy Fudge 609 399-0100
852 Boardwalk Ocean City (08226) *(G-7758)*

Shure-Pak Corporation 856 825-0808
1500 N Ten St Millville (08332) *(G-6324)*

Shuren Upholstery, Ewing Also called Lawrence Custom Drapery Shop *(G-3034)*

Shy Kramer & Associates 609 646-2063
21 W Delilah Rd Pleasantville (08232) *(G-8915)*

Si Packaging LLC 973 869-9920
1 Orient Way Ste F191 Rutherford (07070) *(G-9744)*

Sibi Distributors 908 658-4448
1370 Meiners Dr Basking Ridge (07920) *(G-205)*

Sic-Naics LLC 929 344-2633
331 Newman Springs Rd Red Bank (07701) *(G-9344)*

Siccode, Red Bank Also called Sic-Naics LLC *(G-9344)*

Siding Depot, Clifton Also called Passaic Metal & Bldg Sups Co *(G-1691)*

Sidney Scheinert & Son, Saddle Brook Also called Scheinert & Sons Inc *(G-9790)*

Siegfried USA Holding Inc (HQ) 856 678-3601
33 Industrial Park Rd Pennsville (08070) *(G-8594)*

Siegfried USA LLC (HQ) 856 678-3601
33 Industrial Park Rd Pennsville (08070) *(G-8595)*

Siemens Corporation 732 590-6895
170 Wood Ave S Fl 1 Iselin (08830) *(G-4645)*

Siemens Fire Safety, Mount Laurel Also called Siemens Industry Inc *(G-6841)*

Siemens Industry Inc 856 234-7666
2000 Crawford Pl Ste 300 Mount Laurel (08054) *(G-6841)*

Siemens Industry Inc 732 302-1686
163 Washington Valley Rd Warren (07059) *(G-11567)*

Siemens Med Sltons Diagnostics 973 927-2828
62 Flanders Bartley Rd Flanders (07836) *(G-3416)*

Sierra Communication Intl LLC (HQ) 866 462-8292
350 Mount Kemble Ave Morristown (07960) *(G-6742)*

Sierra Packaging Inc 732 571-2900
2106 Kings Hwy Ocean (07712) *(G-7745)*

Sierra Video Systems 530 478-1000
6 State Route 173 Clinton (08809) *(G-1754)*

Sigco Tool & Mfg Co Inc 856 753-6565
110 Collings Ave West Berlin (08091) *(G-11749)*

Sight2site Media LLC 856 637-2479
269 W White Horse Pike Pomona (08240) *(G-8945)*

Sightlogix Inc 609 951-0008
745 Alexander Rd Ste 5 Princeton (08540) *(G-9118)*

Sigma Engineering & Consulting 732 356-3046
220 Lincoln Blvd Ste A Middlesex (08846) *(G-6197)*

Sigma Extruding Corp (HQ) 201 933-5353
Page & Schuyler Ave Lyndhurst (07071) *(G-5707)*

Sigma International Group Inc (PA) 609 758-0800
700 Goldman Dr Cream Ridge (08514) *(G-1941)*

Sigma Plastics Group, Lyndhurst Also called Omega Plastics Corp *(G-5697)*

Sigma Plastics Group, The, Lyndhurst Also called Alpha Industries MGT Inc *(G-5667)*

Sigma Stretch Film, Lyndhurst Also called Sigma Extruding Corp *(G-5707)*

Sigma-Netics Inc 973 227-6372
2 N Corporate Dr Riverdale (07457) *(G-9488)*

Sign A Rama 609 702-1444
1413 Rte 38 Hainesport (08036) *(G-4077)*

Sign A Rama 201 489-6969
379 Main St Hackensack (07601) *(G-3975)*

Sign A Rama 973 471-5558
681 Van Houten Ave Clifton (07013) *(G-1724)*

Sign Engineers Inc 732 382-4224
13 New York Ave Colonia (07067) *(G-1778)*

Sign On Inc 201 384-7714
149 Washington Ave Apt A Dumont (07628) *(G-2124)*

Sign Shoppe Inc 856 384-2937
370 Glassboro Rd Woodbury (08097) *(G-12170)*

Sign Spec Inc 856 663-2292
602 Centerton Rd Elmer (08318) *(G-2798)*

Sign Tech, Westfield Also called Print Tech LLC *(G-11928)*

Sign Up Inc 201 902-8640
255 State Rt 3 Ste 104a Secaucus (07094) *(G-9928)*

Sign-A-Rama, Hainesport Also called Sign A Rama *(G-4077)*

Sign-A-Rama, Hackensack Also called Sign A Rama *(G-3975)*

Sign-A-Rama, Kenilworth Also called Kna Graphics Inc *(G-4969)*

Sign-A-Rama, Ledgewood Also called Identity Depot Inc *(G-5305)*

Sign-A-Rama, Hamilton Also called Mej Signs Inc *(G-4115)*

Sign-A-Rama, Clifton Also called Sign A Rama *(G-1724)*

Signal Crafters Tech Inc 973 781-0880
57 Eagle Rock Ave East Hanover (07936) *(G-2243)*

Signal Graphics, Egg Harbor Township Also called Mid Atlantic Graphixinc *(G-2690)*

Signal Sign Company LLC 973 535-9277
105 Dorsa Ave Livingston (07039) *(G-5562)*

Signal Systems International (PA) 732 793-4668
1700 Grand Central Ave Lavallette (08735) *(G-5237)*

Signarama Roseland, Roseland Also called Tdk Associates Corp *(G-9656)*

Signature Audio Video Systems 732 864-1039
164 Kettle Creek Rd Toms River (08753) *(G-10912)*

Signature Crafts, Hawthorne Also called Signature Marketing & Mfg *(G-4259)*

Signature Marketing & Mfg 973 427-3700
301 Wagaraw Rd Hawthorne (07506) *(G-4259)*

Signature Marketing Group Ltd (PA) 973 575-7785
25 Riverside Dr Ste 4 Pine Brook (07058) *(G-8717)*

Signify Fincl Solutions LLC 862 930-4682
300 Interpace Pkwy Bldg A Parsippany (07054) *(G-8086)*

Signmasters Inc 973 614-8300
217 Brook Ave Ste 2 Passaic (07055) *(G-8181)*

Signpros, Glendora Also called Nickolaos Kappatos Entps Inc *(G-3832)*

Signs & Custom Metal Inc 201 200-0110
62 Monitor St Jersey City (07304) *(G-4827)*

Signs By Tomorrow, Iselin Also called S S P Enterprises Inc *(G-4643)*

Signs of 2000 ....973 253-1333
421 Broad St Clifton (07013) *(G-1725)*

Signs of Security Inc 973 340-8404
64 Outwater Ln Ste 2 Garfield (07026) *(G-3762)*

Sigo Signs, Elmwood Park Also called GF Supplies LLC *(G-2821)*

Sika, Lakewood Also called May National Associates NJ Inc *(G-5156)*

Sika Corporation (HQ) 201 933-8800
201 Polito Ave Lyndhurst (07071) *(G-5708)*

Sika Corporation 201 933-8800
875 Valley Brook Ave Lyndhurst (07071) *(G-5709)*

Sika Corporation 856 298-2313
251 S White Horse Pike Audubon (08106) *(G-118)*

Sika Liquid Plasics Division, Audubon Also called Sika Corporation *(G-118)*

Silab Inc 732 335-1030
1301 State Route 36 Ste 8 Hazlet (07730) *(G-4283)*

Silbo Industries Inc 201 307-0900
50 Chestnut Ridge Rd # 204 Montvale (07645) *(G-6479)*

Silgan Containers Mfg Corp 732 287-0300
135 National Rd Edison (08817) *(G-2617)*

Silicon Press Inc 908 273-8919
25 Beverly Rd Summit (07901) *(G-10657)*

Siloa Inc 908 234-9040
2493c Lamington Rd Bedminster (07921) *(G-284)*

Silver & Gold Connection 1294, Paramus Also called Zale Delaware Inc *(G-7914)*

Silver Brush Limited 609 443-4900
92 N Main St Ste 19-I Windsor (08561) *(G-12129)*

Silver Edmar 973 817-7483
186 Van Buren St Newark (07105) *(G-7313)*

Silver Line Building Pdts LLC 732 752-8704
207 Pond Ave Middlesex (08846) *(G-6198)*

Silver Palate Kitchens Inc 201 568-0110
211 Knickerbocker Rd Cresskill (07626) *(G-1948)*

Silver Silk, Carlstadt Also called Safire Silk Inc *(G-1212)*

Silverstone Wireless LLC (PA) 845 458-5197
6 9 Park Pl Lodi (07644) *(G-5600)*

Silverthorne Furniture Corp 908 689-6969
149 Asbury Broadway Rd Asbury (08802) *(G-73)*

Silverton Packaging Corp 732 341-0986
75 Fairway Blvd Monroe Township (08831) *(G-6393)*

Silvertop Associates Inc (PA) 856 939-9599
600 E Clements Bridge Rd Runnemede (08078) *(G-9723)*

Silverwear, Dayton Also called Jese Apparel LLC *(G-1973)*

Silvi Concrete of Brick, Brick Also called Construction Dynamics Inc *(G-738)*

Sima Enterprises, Wall Township Also called Sima S Enterprises LLC *(G-11510)*

Sima S Enterprises LLC 877 223-7639
1298 Evans Rd Wall Township (07719) *(G-11510)*

Simex Medical Imaging Inc 201 490-0204
68 Alden Rd Paramus (07652) *(G-7901)*

Simi Granola LLC 848 459-5619
10 S New Prospect Rd Jackson (08527) *(G-4678)*

Simmons Pet Food Nj Inc 856 662-7412
9130 Griffith Morgan Ln Pennsauken (08110) *(G-8578)*
Simon & Schuster Inc 856 461-6500
100 Front St Delran (08075) *(G-2022)*
Simon & Schuster Inc 973 656-6000
1639 State Rt 10 Ste 200 Parsippany (07054) *(G-8087)*
Simple Home Automation Inc 877 405-2397
32 Brunswick Ave Edison (08817) *(G-2618)*
Simplex Americas LLC 908 237-9099
20 Bartles Corner Rd Flemington (08822) *(G-3466)*
Simply Amazing LLC 732 249-4151
233 State Route 18 Ste 22 East Brunswick (08816) *(G-2184)*
Sims Lee Inc (PA) 201 433-1308
743 Bergen Ave Jersey City (07306) *(G-4828)*
Sims Metal Management, Jersey City *Also called Metal MGT Pittsburgh Inc (G-4783)*
Sims Pump Valve Company Inc 201 792-0600
1314 Park Ave Hoboken (07030) *(G-4496)*
Simtek Usa Inc 862 757-8130
13 Fairfield Ave Little Falls (07424) *(G-5488)*
Simtronics Corporation 732 747-0322
50 Birch Ave Ste 100 Little Silver (07739) *(G-5520)*
Sinai Manufacturing Corp 973 522-1003
133 Kossuth St Newark (07105) *(G-7314)*
Sinclair and Rush Inc 862 262-8189
640 Dell Rd Carlstadt (07072) *(G-1218)*
Sine Tru Tool Company Inc 732 591-1100
238 Boundary Rd Ste 2 Marlboro (07746) *(G-5959)*
Singe Corporation 908 289-7900
1290 Central Ave Hillside (07205) *(G-4440)*
Single Vender Outsource, Succasunna *Also called S V O Inc (G-10629)*
Sino Monthly Jersey, Edison *Also called Sino Monthly New Jersey Inc (G-2619)*
Sino Monthly New Jersey Inc 732 650-0688
18 Sheppard Pl Edison (08817) *(G-2619)*
Sir Speedy, Montclair *Also called Action Copy Centers Inc (G-6404)*
Sir Speedy, Cranbury *Also called Dato Company Inc (G-1828)*
Sir Speedy, Clifton *Also called Tanzola Printing Inc (G-1734)*
Sir Speedy, Hawthorne *Also called E Nevin Miller Inc (G-4230)*
Sir Speedy, Pennsauken *Also called Franbeth Inc (G-8512)*
Sir Speedy, Newark *Also called Sheroy Printing Inc (G-7312)*
Sir Speedy, Piscataway *Also called Mark Alan Printing & Graphics (G-8790)*
Sir Speedy, Trenton *Also called D A K Office Services Inc (G-11052)*
Sir Speedy, Maple Shade *Also called Marks Management Systems Inc (G-5906)*
Sir Speedy, Paramus *Also called Lunet Inc (G-7885)*
Sir Speedy, Sewell *Also called Yasheel Inc (G-9967)*
Sirchie Acquisition Co LLC 609 654-0777
612 Gravelly Hollow Rd Medford (08055) *(G-6081)*
Sirchie Finger Print Labs, Medford *Also called Sirchie Acquisition Co LLC (G-6081)*
Sirma Group Inc 646 357-3067
1 Evertrust Plz Ste 1103 Jersey City (07302) *(G-4829)*
Sisco Manufacturing Co Inc 856 486-7550
7930 National Hwy Pennsauken (08110) *(G-8579)*
SISSCO DIVISION, Hillsborough *Also called Permadur Industries Inc (G-4362)*
Site Drainer LLC 862 225-9940
18 Sebago St Clifton (07013) *(G-1726)*
Sitetracker Inc (PA) 551 486-2087
491 Bloomfield Ave # 301 Montclair (07042) *(G-6435)*
Sivantos Inc (HQ) 732 562-6600
10 Constitution Ave Piscataway (08854) *(G-8811)*
Sj Magazine 856 722-9300
1000 S Lenola Rd Ste 102 Maple Shade (08052) *(G-5908)*
Sjd Direct Midwest LLC 732 985-8405
112 Truman Dr Edison (08817) *(G-2620)*
Sjd Direct Midwest LLC 732 287-2525
3 Ethel Rd Ste 301 Edison (08817) *(G-2621)*
Sjshore Marketing Ltd Lblty Co 609 390-1400
533 S Shore Rd Ste 1 Marmora (08223) *(G-6006)*
Sk & P Industries Inc (PA) 973 482-1864
73 Norfolk St Newark (07103) *(G-7315)*
Sk & P Industries Inc 973 482-1864
73 Norfolk St Newark (07103) *(G-7316)*
Sk Custom Creations Inc 973 754-9261
50 Furler St Totowa (07512) *(G-10972)*
Sk Life Science Inc 201 421-3800
22-10 State Rt 208 Fair Lawn (07410) *(G-3114)*
Skaffles Group LLC (PA) 732 721-0022
115 Kennedy Dr Sayreville (08872) *(G-9839)*
Skc Powertech Inc 973 347-7000
850 Clark Dr Ste 2 Budd Lake (07828) *(G-944)*
Ski Setting Company, Green Brook *Also called Greater New Jersey Diamnd Exch (G-3856)*
Skinder-Strauss LLC (PA) 973 642-1440
890 Mountain Ave Ste 300 New Providence (07974) *(G-7054)*
Skinwear Temporary Tattoos, Hackensack *Also called Johnson & Mayer Inc (G-3934)*
Skip Gambert & Associates Inc 973 344-3373
436 Ferry St Ste 2 Newark (07105) *(G-7317)*
Sklsi, Fair Lawn *Also called Sk Life Science Inc (G-3114)*
Skorr Products LLC 973 523-2606
90 George St Paterson (07503) *(G-8383)*

Skripak Metal Fabricators Inc 732 364-9662
15 Berkshire Dr Howell (07731) *(G-4566)*
Sks Fuel Inc 973 200-0796
941 Mcbride Ave Woodland Park (07424) *(G-12233)*
SKW Quab Chemicals Inc 201 556-0300
250 Pehle Ave Ste 403 Saddle Brook (07663) *(G-9794)*
Sky Growth Intermediate 201 802-4000
300 Tice Blvd Woodcliff Lake (07677) *(G-12201)*
Skycam Technologies LLC 908 205-5548
235 Kearny Ave Perth Amboy (08861) *(G-8631)*
Skylands Press 973 383-5006
57 Trinity St Newton (07860) *(G-7404)*
Skyline Steel Corporation 973 428-6100
8 Woodhollow Rd Ste 102 Parsippany (07054) *(G-8088)*
Skyline Windows LLC 201 531-9600
210 Park Pl E Wood Ridge (07075) *(G-12138)*
Sleep Innovations, Red Bank *Also called Innocor Inc (G-9331)*
Slendertone Distribution Inc 732 660-1177
221 River St Ste 9 Hoboken (07030) *(G-4497)*
Slp Performance, Toms River *Also called S L P Engineering Inc (G-10908)*
Slt Foods Inc 732 661-1030
303 Ridge Rd Dayton (08810) *(G-1987)*
Slt Imports, Dayton *Also called Slt Foods Inc (G-1987)*
Slys Express LLC 908 787-7516
518 Lindegar St Linden (07036) *(G-5443)*
Small Molecules Inc 201 918-4664
38 Jackson St Hoboken (07030) *(G-4498)*
Small Quantities NJ Inc 732 248-9009
66 Ethel Rd Edison (08817) *(G-2622)*
Smart Candle, Clifton *Also called Smartlite LLC (G-1727)*
Smart Desks, Rockaway *Also called Cbt Supply Inc (G-9557)*
Smart Gear Toys, Deal *Also called Ambo Consulting LLC (G-1997)*
Smartekg LLC 201 376-4556
287 Rutland Ave Teaneck (07666) *(G-10774)*
Smarties, Union *Also called Ce De Candy Inc (G-11164)*
Smartlinx Solutions LLC (PA) 732 385-5507
333 Thornall St Ste 401 Edison (08837) *(G-2623)*
Smartlite LLC 973 470-9400
25 Madison Ave Clifton (07011) *(G-1727)*
Smartplay International Inc 609 880-1860
1550 Bridgeboro Rd Beverly (08010) *(G-465)*
Smartpool LLC 732 730-9880
687 Prospect St Lakewood (08701) *(G-5189)*
Smartwinders, Fairfield *Also called Independent Machine Company (G-3227)*
Smb International LLC 732 222-4888
121 State Route 36 # 180 West Long Branch (07764) *(G-11847)*
Smf, Linden *Also called Steel Mountain Fabricators LLC (G-5449)*
SMI Incorprated, Lebanon *Also called Specialty Measurements Inc (G-5302)*
Smith Bearing, Garwood *Also called Accurate Bushing Company Inc (G-3774)*
Smith Enterprises 215 416-9881
100 Hillside Ln Mount Laurel (08054) *(G-6842)*
Smith Lime Flour Co Inc 973 344-1700
60 Central Ave Kearny (07032) *(G-4914)*
Smith Optics Inc 208 726-4477
300 Lighting Way Ste 400 Secaucus (07094) *(G-9929)*
Smithfield Packaged Meats Corp 908 354-2674
814 2nd Ave Elizabeth (07202) *(G-2774)*
Smitteez Sportswear, Keansburg *Also called J and S Sporting Apparel LLC (G-4856)*
Smitteez Sportswear, Long Branch *Also called James Smith (G-5626)*
Smittys Door Service Inc 908 284-0506
170 Oak Grove Rd Pittstown (08867) *(G-8851)*
Smock, Thomas Woodworking, Eatontown *Also called Thomas Smock Woodworking (G-2426)*
SMR Research Corporation 908 852-7677
300 Valentine St Ste A Hackettstown (07840) *(G-4037)*
SMS Building Systems Ltd Lblty 856 520-8769
5 N Olney Ave Ste 100a Cherry Hill (08003) *(G-1420)*
SMS Electric Motor Car LLC 215 428-2502
18 Totten Dr Bridgewater (08807) *(G-896)*
SMS International, Clifton *Also called Stainless Metal Source Intl (G-1730)*
Snack Innovations Inc (PA) 718 509-9366
41 Ethel Rd W Piscataway (08854) *(G-8812)*
Snap Set Specialists Inc 856 629-9552
300 Thomas Ave Bldg 6 Williamstown (08094) *(G-12106)*
Snapco Manufacturing Corp 973 282-0300
140 Central Ave Ste 1 Hillside (07205) *(G-4441)*
Snapple Beverage Corp (del) 201 933-0070
600 Commercial Ave Carlstadt (07072) *(G-1219)*
Snapple Distributors Inc (HQ) 732 815-2800
433 Blair Rd Ste 1 Avenel (07001) *(G-151)*
Sneaker Swarm LLC 908 693-9262
581 Main St Ste 640 Woodbridge (07095) *(G-12153)*
Sniderman John 201 569-5482
133 E Palisade Ave Apt H Englewood (07631) *(G-2932)*
Sno Skins Inc 973 884-8801
622 State Route 10 Ste 19 Whippany (07981) *(G-12039)*
Snotex USA Inc 973 762-0358
116 Irvington Ave Apt 2f South Orange (07079) *(G-10315)*

Snowdon Inc 732 230-3796
66 Maybury Hill Rd Princeton (08540) **(G-9119)**
SNS Oriental Rugs LLC 201 355-8786
455 Barell Ave Carlstadt (07072) **(G-1220)**
So Many Waves, Newark *Also called Razac Products Inc* **(G-7285)**
Socafe LLC 973 589-4104
41-43 Malvern St Newark (07105) **(G-7318)**
Society Trnsaction Periodicals, Piscataway *Also called Transaction Publishers Inc* **(G-8830)**
Socio Produce Inc 201 348-3660
518 32nd St Union City (07087) **(G-11266)**
Sock Company Inc (PA) 201 307-0675
40 Carver Ave Westwood (07675) **(G-11972)**
Socks 47 Ltd Liability Company 201 866-2222
4620 Bergenline Ave Union City (07087) **(G-11267)**
Sodastream USA Inc 856 755-3400
136 Gaither Dr Ste 200 Mount Laurel (08054) **(G-6843)**
Sofa Doctor Inc 718 292-6300
148 71st St Guttenberg (07093) **(G-3871)**
Sofield Manufacturing Co Inc 201 931-1530
2 Main St Ridgefield Park (07660) **(G-9414)**
Sofradir Ec Inc 973 882-0211
373 Us Highway 46 Fairfield (07004) **(G-3307)**
Software Practices and Tech 908 464-2923
73 Stone Ridge Rd Summit (07901) **(G-10658)**
Software Services & Solutions 203 630-2000
15 Laurel Wood Dr Lawrence Township (08648) **(G-5248)**
Soh LLC 646 943-4066
150 Bay St Apt 715 Jersey City (07302) **(G-4830)**
Sohha Savory Yogurt, Lawrence Township *Also called Mualema LLC* **(G-5244)**
Solar Compounds Corporation 908 862-2813
1201 W Blancke St Linden (07036) **(G-5444)**
Solar Products Inc 973 248-9370
228 Wanaque Ave Pompton Lakes (07442) **(G-8948)**
Solar Rig Technologies LLC 973 600-0500
651 Garden St Carlstadt (07072) **(G-1221)**
Solar Turbines Incorporated 201 825-8200
600 E Crescent Ave # 305 Upper Saddle River (07458) **(G-11285)**
Solaris Pharma Corporation 908 864-0404
1031 Rte 202/206 200 Bridgewater (08807) **(G-897)**
Solbern LLC 973 227-3030
8 Kulick Rd Fairfield (07004) **(G-3308)**
Solbright Group Inc (PA) 973 339-3855
1 Gateway Ctr Ste 26 Newark (07102) **(G-7319)**
Solenis LLC 201 767-7400
49 Walnut St Norwood (07648) **(G-7635)**
Solgar Inc (HQ) 201 944-2311
500 Willow Tree Rd Leonia (07605) **(G-5319)**
Solgar Vitamin & Her, Leonia *Also called Solgar Inc* **(G-5319)**
Solgen Pharmaceuticals Inc 732 983-6025
1514 Edison Glen Ter Edison (08837) **(G-2624)**
Solid Cast Stone 856 694-5245
470 Grubb Rd Newfield (08344) **(G-7372)**
Solid Color Inc 212 239-3930
78 John Miller Way # 420 Kearny (07032) **(G-4915)**
Solid State International Inc 201 429-8700
46 Farrand St Bloomfield (07003) **(G-530)**
Solidia Technologies Inc 908 315-5901
11 Colonial Dr Piscataway (08854) **(G-8813)**
Solidsurface Designs Inc 856 910-7720
1651 Sherman Ave Pennsauken (08110) **(G-8580)**
Soligenix Inc (PA) 609 538-8200
29 Emmons Dr Ste B10 Princeton (08540) **(G-9120)**
Solmor Manufacturing Co Inc 973 824-7203
164 Emmet St Ste 2 Newark (07114) **(G-7320)**
Solutia Inc 908 862-0278
2000 Brunswick Ave Linden (07036) **(G-5445)**
Solution and System Inc 201 488-7770
411 Hackensack Ave Hackensack (07601) **(G-3976)**
Solv-TEC Incorporated 609 261-4242
75 N Main St Medford (08055) **(G-6082)**
Solvay Holding Inc 609 860-4000
504 Carnegie Ctr Princeton (08540) **(G-9121)**
Solvay Spclty Polymers USA LLC 856 853-8119
10 Leonard Ln West Deptford (08086) **(G-11841)**
Solvay USA Inc (HQ) 609 860-4000
504 Carnegie Ctr Princeton (08540) **(G-9122)**
Solvay USA Inc 732 297-0100
219 Black Horse Ln North Brunswick (08902) **(G-7538)**
Solvay USA Inc 609 860-4000
Cn 1120 Cranbury (08512) **(G-1881)**
Solvent & Envmtl Svcs Div, Cinnaminson *Also called Detrex Corporation* **(G-1457)**
Soma Labs Inc 732 271-3444
248 Wagner St 252 Middlesex (08846) **(G-6199)**
Somerset Cpitl Mark Tr MGT Inc 848 228-0842
1 Donlonton Cir Chesterfield (08515) **(G-1442)**
Somerset Outpatient Surgery 781 635-2807
100 Franklin Square Dr # 100 Somerset (08873) **(G-10172)**
Somerset Wood Products Co 908 526-0030
1 Johnson Dr Raritan (08869) **(G-9316)**
Somerville Acquisitions Co Inc (PA) 908 782-9500
45 River Rd Ste 300 Flemington (08822) **(G-3467)**
Somes Uniforms Inc (PA) 201 843-1199
314 Main St Hackensack (07601) **(G-3977)**
Something Different Linen Inc 973 272-0601
167 Fornelius Ave Clifton (07013) **(G-1728)**
Sonata Graphics Inc 201 866-0186
1247 Paterson Plank Rd # 65 Secaucus (07094) **(G-9930)**
Sondpex Corp America LLC 732 940-4430
4185 Route 27 Princeton (08540) **(G-9123)**
Sondpex Electronics, Princeton *Also called Sondpex Corp America LLC* **(G-9123)**
Sondra Roberts Inc 212 684-3344
3 Empire Blvd South Hackensack (07606) **(G-10296)**
Sonetronics Inc (PA) 732 681-5016
1718 State Route 71 Belmar (07719) **(G-364)**
Songbird Hearing Inc 732 422-7203
210 N Center Dr North Brunswick (08902) **(G-7539)**
Sonia Fashion Inc 201 864-3483
422 11th St Union City (07087) **(G-11268)**
Sonic Innovations Inc 888 423-7834
2501 Cottontail Ln Somerset (08873) **(G-10173)**
Sonneborn LLC (HQ) 201 760-2940
600 Parsippany Rd Ste 100 Parsippany (07054) **(G-8089)**
Sonneborn Holding LLC 201 760-2940
600 Parsippany Rd Ste 100 Parsippany (07054) **(G-8090)**
Sonoco Corrflex, Ridgefield Park *Also called Sonoco Display & Packaging LLC* **(G-9415)**
Sonoco Display & Packaging LLC 201 612-4008
55 Challenger Rd Ste 500 Ridgefield Park (07660) **(G-9415)**
Sonoco Products Company 609 655-0300
5 Stults Rd Dayton (08810) **(G-1988)**
Sonoco Products Company 908 713-6900
67 Beaver Ave Ste 11 Annandale (08801) **(G-60)**
Sonotron Medical Systems Inc 201 767-6040
224 Pegasus Ave Northvale (07647) **(G-7608)**
Sonrise Metal Inc 973 423-4717
32 Shore Rd Hopatcong (07843) **(G-4538)**
Sony Corporation of America 201 930-1000
115 W Century Rd Ste 250 Paramus (07652) **(G-7902)**
Sony Corporation of America 201 930-1000
123 Tice Blvd Woodcliff Lake (07677) **(G-12202)**
Sony Electronics Inc 201 930-7030
115 W Century Rd Ste 2 Paramus (07652) **(G-7903)**
Sony Electronics Inc 201 930-1000
123 Tice Blvd Woodcliff Lake (07677) **(G-12203)**
Sony Electronics Inc 201 930-1000
115 W Century Rd Ste 250 Paramus (07652) **(G-7904)**
Sony Music Holdings Inc 201 777-3933
301 State Rte Hwy Rutherford (07070) **(G-9745)**
Sophies Fashions 973 272-8321
352 Lanza Ave Apt 1 Garfield (07026) **(G-3763)**
Sophion Bioscience Inc 732 745-0221
215 College Rd Paramus (07652) **(G-7905)**
Sound Chice Assstive Listening 908 647-2651
498 Long Hill Rd Gillette (07933) **(G-3797)**
Sound Professionals Inc 609 267-4400
3444 Sylon Blvd Hainesport (08036) **(G-4078)**
Sound United LLC 201 762-6500
100 Corporate Dr Mahwah (07430) **(G-5813)**
Soundview Paper Company, Elmwood Park *Also called Marcal Manufacturing LLC* **(G-2833)**
Soundview Paper Holdings LLC (PA) 201 796-4000
1 Market St Elmwood Park (07407) **(G-2850)**
Source Direct Inc 856 768-7445
2200 Garry Rd Ste 3 Cinnaminson (08077) **(G-1488)**
Source Direct Plastics Div, Cinnaminson *Also called Source Direct Inc* **(G-1488)**
Source Micro LLC 973 328-1749
5 Rolling Ridge Rd Randolph (07869) **(G-9298)**
Source One, Totowa *Also called Fabulous Fabricators LLC* **(G-10944)**
Source Packaging, Mahwah *Also called Cases By Source Inc* **(G-5756)**
Sourland Mountain Wdwkg LLC T 908 806-7661
17 Higginsville Rd Neshanic Station (08853) **(G-6939)**
South Amboy Designer T Shirt L 732 456-2594
603 Washington Ave Ste 5b South Amboy (08879) **(G-10245)**
South American Imports Corp 201 941-2020
7 Cecelia Ave Cliffside Park (07010) **(G-1545)**
South Bergenite Editorial, Rutherford *Also called North Jersey Media Group Inc* **(G-9741)**
South Brunswick Furniture Inc 732 658-8850
1015 Edward St Linden (07036) **(G-5446)**
South County Soccer League Inc 908 310-9052
3 Ferry St Lambertville (08530) **(G-5221)**
South East Instruments LLC 201 569-0050
111 Cedar Ln Englewood (07631) **(G-2933)**
South Jersey Countertop Co 856 768-7960
1044 Industrial Dr Ste 12 West Berlin (08091) **(G-11750)**
South Jersey Farmers Exchange 856 769-0062
101 East Ave Woodstown (08098) **(G-12240)**
South Jersey Industries Inc 609 561-9000
1 S Jersey Plz Hammonton (08037) **(G-4149)**
South Jersey Metal Inc 856 228-0642
1651 Hurffville Rd Deptford (08096) **(G-2067)**

ALPHABETIC

South Jersey Precision TI Mold 856 327-0500
　4375 S Lincoln Ave Vineland (08361) *(G-11405)*
South Jersey Pretzel Inc 856 435-5055
　912 N White Horse Pike A Stratford (08084) *(G-10617)*
South Jersey Publishing Co (HQ) 609 272-7000
　1000 W Washington Ave Pleasantville (08232) *(G-8916)*
South Jersey Publishing Co 856 692-0455
　22 W Landis Ave Vineland (08360) *(G-11406)*
South Jersey Water Cond Svc 856 451-0620
　760 Shiloh Pike Bridgeton (08302) *(G-798)*
South River Food Machinery, Hackensack *Also called South River Machinery Corp* *(G-3978)*
South River Machinery Corp 201 487-1736
　115 S River St Hackensack (07601) *(G-3978)*
South Shore Sign Co Inc 718 984-5624
　550 Morristown Rd Matawan (07747) *(G-6032)*
South Shore Signs, Matawan *Also called South Shore Sign Co Inc* *(G-6032)*
South State Inc 856 881-6030
　1340 Glassboro Rd Williamstown (08094) *(G-12107)*
South State Speed Shop, Hackensack *Also called Roy Anania* *(G-3967)*
Southern New Jersey Stl Co Inc (PA) 856 696-1612
　2591 N East Blvd Vineland (08360) *(G-11407)*
Southern NJ Steel, Vineland *Also called Southern New Jersey Stl Co Inc* *(G-11407)*
Southern Ocean Mar Sportswear, Barnegat *Also called Sgh Inc* *(G-165)*
Southwest Stainless LP 732 961-1520
　507 Oak Glen Rd Howell (07731) *(G-4567)*
Southwind Equestrian 856 364-9690
　385 Lebanon Rd Millville (08332) *(G-6325)*
Sowa Corp 973 297-0008
　223 Murray St Newark (07114) *(G-7321)*
Soyka-Smith Design Research, Montclair *Also called Interchange Group Inc* *(G-6418)*
Sozio Inc 732 572-5600
　51 Ethel Rd W Piscataway (08854) *(G-8814)*
Space and Navigation, Budd Lake *Also called L3 Technologies Inc* *(G-932)*
Space-Eyes, Camden *Also called Channel Logistics LLC* *(G-1053)*
Spacetouch Inc 609 712-6572
　34 Chambers St Princeton (08542) *(G-9124)*
Spadix Technologies Inc 732 356-6906
　110 Egel Ave Middlesex (08846) *(G-6200)*
Spaghetti Engineering Corp 856 719-9989
　150 Cooper Rd Ste C7 West Berlin (08091) *(G-11751)*
Spare Pair Vision Center LLC 973 758-1151
　184 S Lvingston Ave Ste 8 Livingston (07039) *(G-5563)*
Spark Holland Inc 609 799-7250
　542 Berlin Cross Keys Rd 3-376 Sicklerville (08081) *(G-10026)*
Spark Wire Products Co Inc 973 773-6945
　158 River Rd Clifton (07014) *(G-1729)*
Sparks Belting Company Inc 973 227-4100
　5 Spielman Rd Fairfield (07004) *(G-3309)*
Spartech LLC 201 489-4000
　215 S Newman St Hackensack (07601) *(G-3979)*
Spartech LLC 973 344-2700
　297 Ferry St Newark (07105) *(G-7322)*
Sparton Aydin LLC 732 935-1320
　10 Industrial Way E Eatontown (07724) *(G-2423)*
Spc Publication, Neptune *Also called School Publications Co Inc* *(G-6929)*
Spct, Elizabeth *Also called Superior Powder Coating Inc* *(G-2777)*
Spec Steel Rule Dies Inc 609 443-4435
　92 N Main St Bldg 1b Windsor (08561) *(G-12130)*
Special Optics Inc 973 366-7289
　3 Stewart Ct Denville (07834) *(G-2059)*
Special T S Screen Prtg & EMB, Flemington *Also called Ambro Manufacturing Inc* *(G-3425)*
Special Technical Services 609 259-2626
　11 Carlton Rd Flanders (07836) *(G-3417)*
Specialized Fire & SEC Inc 212 255-1010
　20 Cotluss Rd Ste 9 Riverdale (07457) *(G-9489)*
Specialized Metal Stamping, Glen Rock *Also called B E C Mfg Corp* *(G-3822)*
Specialneedsware Inc 646 278-9959
　60 Park Pl Ste 504 Newark (07102) *(G-7323)*
Specialty Casting Inc 856 845-3105
　42 Curtis Ave Woodbury (08096) *(G-12171)*
Specialty Fabricators LLC 609 758-6995
　118 Meany Rd Wrightstown (08562) *(G-12243)*
Specialty Lighting Inds Inc 732 517-0800
　1306 Doris Ave Ocean (07712) *(G-7746)*
Specialty Measurements Inc 908 534-1500
　1309 Us Highway 22 Lebanon (08833) *(G-5302)*
Specialty Measures 609 882-6071
　15 Dawes Ave Ewing (08638) *(G-3055)*
Specialty Products & Insul Co, Camden *Also called Fbm Galaxy Inc* *(G-1066)*
Specialty Products Plus 732 380-1188
　215 Locust Ave West Long Branch (07764) *(G-11848)*
Specialty Rubber Inc 609 704-2555
　4500 White Horse Pike Elwood (08217) *(G-2854)*
Specialty Systems Inc (PA) 732 341-1011
　1451 Route 37 W Ste 1 Toms River (08755) *(G-10913)*
Specialty Tube Filling LLC 908 262-2219
　1 Ilene Ct Bldg 8u6 Hillsborough (08844) *(G-4372)*

Specialty Vhcl Solutions LLC 609 882-1900
　804 Silvia St Ewing (08628) *(G-3056)*
Specified Technologies Inc 908 526-8000
　210 Evans Way Branchburg (08876) *(G-705)*
Spectacle Shoppe 856 875-5046
　202 Dickens Ct Williamstown (08094) *(G-12108)*
Spectare Systems Inc 609 303-0957
　17 Independence Way Titusville (08560) *(G-10856)*
Spectra Mattress Inc 732 545-5900
　633 Nassau St North Brunswick (08902) *(G-7540)*
Spectraform, Linden *Also called Thomas H Cox & Son Inc* *(G-5453)*
Spectrum Chemicals & Lab Pdts, New Brunswick *Also called Spectrum Laboratory Pdts Inc* *(G-7004)*
Spectrum Communications, Kenvil *Also called Major Auto Installations Inc* *(G-5011)*
Spectrum Design LLC 856 694-1870
　1106 Grant Ave Franklinville (08322) *(G-3631)*
Spectrum Foils Inc 973 481-0808
　29 Riverside Ave Bldg 1 Newark (07104) *(G-7324)*
Spectrum Glass LLC 201 750-1251
　360 Homans Ave Closter (07624) *(G-1766)*
Spectrum Instrumentation Corp 201 562-1999
　15 Warren St Ste 25 Hackensack (07601) *(G-3980)*
Spectrum Laboratory Pdts Inc (PA) 732 214-1300
　769 Jersey Ave New Brunswick (08901) *(G-7004)*
Spectrum Laboratory Pdts Inc 732 214-1300
　755 769 & 777 Jersey Ave New Brunswick (08901) *(G-7005)*
Spectrum Neon Sign Group LLC 856 317-9223
　9130 Pennsauken Hwy Ste B Pennsauken (08110) *(G-8581)*
Spectrum Paint Applicator 973 732-9180
　425 Ferry St Fl 2 Newark (07105) *(G-7325)*
Spectrum Plastics 732 564-1899
　250 Circle Dr N Piscataway (08854) *(G-8815)*
Spectrum Quality Products, New Brunswick *Also called Spectrum Laboratory Pdts Inc* *(G-7005)*
Speed Center USA, Saddle Brook *Also called Blue Monkey Inc* *(G-9756)*
Speed Raceway 856 314-8264
　1103 Route 130 S Cinnaminson (08077) *(G-1489)*
Speedway, Swedesboro *Also called Cobra Products Inc* *(G-10688)*
Speedway LLC 732 750-7800
　750 Cliff Rd Port Reading (07064) *(G-8990)*
Speedwell Targets, Union *Also called Rockwood Corporation* *(G-11219)*
Speedy Sign-A-Rama 973 605-8313
　166 Ridgedale Ave Ste 4 Morristown (07960) *(G-6743)*
Spem Corporation 732 356-3366
　403 Bell St Piscataway (08854) *(G-8816)*
Spencer Industries Inc (PA) 973 751-2200
　80 Holmes St Belleville (07109) *(G-318)*
Spencer's, Mount Laurel *Also called William Spencer* *(G-6847)*
Sperro Metal Products LLC 973 335-2000
　2 Skyline Dr Montville (07045) *(G-6494)*
Sperry Marine Division, Cranford *Also called Northrop Grumman Systems Corp* *(G-1918)*
Spex Certiprep Inc (PA) 732 549-7144
　203 Norcross Ave Metuchen (08840) *(G-6121)*
Spex Certiprep Group LLC 208 204-6656
　203 Norcross Ave Metuchen (08840) *(G-6122)*
Spex Certprep Group LLC 732 549-7144
　203 Norcross Ave Metuchen (08840) *(G-6123)*
Spex Sample Prep LLC 732 549-7144
　65 Liberty St Metuchen (08840) *(G-6124)*
Spex Sample Prep LLC (PA) 732 549-7144
　203 Norcross Ave Metuchen (08840) *(G-6125)*
Sphinx Software Inc 609 275-5085
　2 Red Oak Dr Plainsboro (08536) *(G-8900)*
SPI, Summit *Also called Safety Power Inc* *(G-10654)*
Spice Chain Corporation 732 518-1100
　9 Elkins Rd East Brunswick (08816) *(G-2185)*
Spice Grill 973 882-4646
　111 Us Highway 46 Parsippany (07054) *(G-8091)*
Spident USA Incorporated 201 944-0511
　205 Redneck Ave Little Ferry (07643) *(G-5517)*
Spinal Kinetics LLC (PA) 908 687-2552
　950 W Chestnut St Union (07083) *(G-11224)*
Spindlers Bake Shop 201 288-1345
　247 Boulevard Hasbrouck Heights (07604) *(G-4198)*
Spinningdesigns Inc 732 775-7050
　910 1st Ave Asbury Park (07712) *(G-83)*
Spiral Binding LLC (PA) 973 256-0666
　1 Maltese Dr Totowa (07512) *(G-10973)*
Spiral James Burn, Totowa *Also called Gabhen Inc* *(G-10945)*
Spiralseal, Cliffwood *Also called Sprialseal Inc* *(G-1548)*
Spirent Communications Inc 732 946-4018
　101 Crawfords Corner Rd Holmdel (07733) *(G-4530)*
Spirit Tex LLC 201 440-1113
　201 Gates Rd Ste E Little Ferry (07643) *(G-5518)*
Spl Holdings LLC 856 764-2400
　211 Carriage Ln Delran (08075) *(G-2023)*
Sports Factory, Lincoln Park *Also called J & S Enterprises LLC* *(G-5328)*

(G-0000) Company's Geographic Section entry number

Sports Impact Inc 732 257-1451
52 Yorktown Rd East Brunswick (08816) *(G-2186)*

Sports Stop Inc 856 881-2763
31 Delsea Dr N Glassboro (08028) *(G-3812)*

Sportstar World Wide Inc 732 254-9214
19 Thomas St South River (08882) *(G-10467)*

Spotless Shade, Edison *Also called Spotless Venetian Blind Servic (G-2625)*

Spotless Venetian Blind Servic 732 548-1711
1217 Us Highway 1 Edison (08837) *(G-2625)*

Spray Tech & Marketing, Parsippany *Also called Industry Publications Inc (G-8029)*

Spray-Tek Inc (PA) 732 469-0050
344 Cedar Ave Middlesex (08846) *(G-6201)*

Sprialseal Inc 732 738-6113
284 Cliffwood Ave Cliffwood (07721) *(G-1548)*

Spring Aire, Mountainside *Also called Springfield Heating & AC Co (G-6888)*

Spring Eureka Co Inc 973 589-4960
9 Manufacturers Pl Newark (07105) *(G-7326)*

Spring Time Mattress Mfg Corp (PA) 973 473-5400
25 Saddle River Ave South Hackensack (07606) *(G-10297)*

Springdale Farm Market Inc 856 424-8674
1638 Springdale Rd Cherry Hill (08003) *(G-1421)*

Springer Scnce + Bus Media LLC 201 348-4033
333 Mdwlands Pkwy Fl 2 Secaucus (07094) *(G-9931)*

Springfeld Prcision Instrs Inc 866 843-3905
114 Essex St Rochelle Park (07662) *(G-9537)*

Springfield Heating & AC Co 908 233-8400
217 Sheffield St Mountainside (07092) *(G-6888)*

Springfield Metal Pdts Co Inc 973 379-4600
8 Commerce St Springfield (07081) *(G-10578)*

Springtime Bedding, South Hackensack *Also called Spring Time Mattress Mfg Corp (G-10297)*

Springworks Group Ltd 973 276-7940
123 Lehigh Dr Fairfield (07004) *(G-3310)*

SPS Alfachem Inc (PA) 973 676-5141
164 Elmwynd Dr Orange (07050) *(G-7828)*

SPX Cooling Technologies Inc 908 450-8027
1200 Us Highway 22 Ste 14 Bridgewater (08807) *(G-898)*

SPX Dry Cooling Usa LLC 908 450-8027
1200 Rte 22 Ste 1 Bridgewater (08807) *(G-899)*

Sqn Banking Systems, Rancocas *Also called Sqn Peripherals Inc (G-9263)*

Sqn Peripherals Inc (HQ) 609 261-5500
65 Indel Ave Rancocas (08073) *(G-9263)*

Squash Beef LLC 917 577-8723
12 Downing Hill Ln Colts Neck (07722) *(G-1792)*

Squillace Stl Fabricators LLC 908 241-6424
240 W Westfield Ave Roselle Park (07204) *(G-9703)*

Squire Corrugated Cont Corp 908 862-9111
110 Allen Rd Ste 3 Basking Ridge (07920) *(G-206)*

Sr International Rock Inc 908 864-4700
7 Easy St Ste E Bound Brook (08805) *(G-623)*

SR Shirts & Stuff LLC 973 335-3086
4 Hickory Dr Montville (07045) *(G-6495)*

Sre Ventures LLC 973 785-0099
163 E Main St Little Falls (07424) *(G-5489)*

SRS Software LLC 201 802-1300
155 Chestnut Ridge Rd Montvale (07645) *(G-6480)*

Ss Equipment Holdings LLC 732 627-0006
1425 Frontier Rd Bridgewater (08807) *(G-900)*

Ss Tool & Manufacturing Co 908 486-5497
1 Garfield St Linden (07036) *(G-5447)*

Ss White Burs Inc 732 905-1100
1145 Towbin Ave Lakewood (08701) *(G-5190)*

Ssam Sports Inc (PA) 917 553-0596
234 Macintyre Ln Allendale (07401) *(G-17)*

Ssam Sports Inc 917 553-0596
2 Myrtle Ave Unit 599 Allendale (07401) *(G-18)*

Ssi North America, Randolph *Also called Surface Source Intl Inc (G-9300)*

Ssi North America Inc 973 598-0152
961 State Route 10 Ste 2i Randolph (07869) *(G-9299)*

St Jude Medical 908 979-3200
999 Willow Grove St Hackettstown (07840) *(G-4038)*

St Jude Medical LLC 800 645-5368
333 Mdwlands Pkwy Ste 502 Secaucus (07094) *(G-9932)*

St Louis Trimming Div, Englewood Cliffs *Also called Trimtex Company Inc (G-2984)*

St Martin Cabinetry Inc 732 902-6020
100 Newfield Ave Ste B Edison (08837) *(G-2626)*

St Thomas Creations (HQ) 800 536-2284
3a S Middlesex Ave Monroe Township (08831) *(G-6394)*

Stacks Envmtl Ltd Lblty Co 973 885-2036
5 Crescent Dr Lake Hopatcong (07849) *(G-5057)*

Stafford Park Solar 1 LLC 609 607-9500
500 Barnegat Blvd N Barnegat (08005) *(G-166)*

Stained Glass Overlay, West Berlin *Also called Artistic Glass & Doors Inc (G-11704)*

Staines Inc 856 784-2718
610 S White Horse Pike Somerdale (08083) *(G-10044)*

Stainless Metal Source Intl 973 977-2200
207 Piaget Ave Clifton (07011) *(G-1730)*

Stainless Steel Fabricators 856 464-1999
900 Creek Rd Bellmawr (08031) *(G-352)*

Stainless Stock 732 564-1164
333 Cedar Ave Ste 1 Middlesex (08846) *(G-6202)*

Stainless Surplus LLC 914 661-3800
6 Pheasant Run Green Brook (08812) *(G-3864)*

Stair Store, The, Lakewood *Also called American Stairs Inc (G-5070)*

Stairshop, Red Bank *Also called B & C Custom WD Handrail Corp (G-9322)*

Stairworks Inc 908 276-2829
335 Centennial Ave Unit 8 Cranford (07016) *(G-1927)*

Stamm International Corp (PA) 201 947-1700
1530 Palisade Ave Ste Phd Fort Lee (07024) *(G-3583)*

Stampex Corp 973 839-4040
75 4th Ave Haskell (07420) *(G-4214)*

Stamping Com Inc 732 493-4697
3600 Sunset Ave Ocean (07712) *(G-7747)*

Stamplus Manufacturing Inc 908 241-8844
654 W 1st Ave Roselle (07203) *(G-9683)*

Stanbee Company Inc (PA) 201 933-9666
70 Broad St Carlstadt (07072) *(G-1222)*

Stand Out Signs, Hopelawn *Also called F & A Signs Inc (G-4540)*

Standard Coating Corporation 201 945-5058
461 Broad Ave Ridgefield (07657) *(G-9385)*

Standard Embossing Plate Mfg 973 344-6670
129 Pulaski St Newark (07105) *(G-7327)*

Standard Industries Inc 856 241-0241
700 2nd St Ste C&D Swedesboro (08085) *(G-10728)*

Standard Industries Inc (HQ) 973 628-3000
1 Campus Dr Parsippany (07054) *(G-8092)*

Standard Merchandising, Pennsauken *Also called Great Socks LLC (G-8518)*

Standard Pipe Products Inc 908 264-8284
15 North Ave Garwood (07027) *(G-3787)*

Standard Prtg & Mail Svcs Inc 973 790-3333
30 Plymouth St Ste A Fairfield (07004) *(G-3311)*

Standard Tile Watchung Corp 908 754-4200
1515 Us Highway 22 Ste 24 Watchung (07069) *(G-11594)*

Standex International Corp 732 469-8452
820 Lincoln Blvd Middlesex (08846) *(G-6203)*

Stanek Netting Co Inc (PA) 973 680-1616
111 Orange St Bloomfield (07003) *(G-531)*

Stanger Robert A & Co LP 732 389-3600
1129 Broad St Fl 2 Shrewsbury (07702) *(G-10011)*

Stanlar Enterprises Inc 973 680-4488
24 Federal Plz Bloomfield (07003) *(G-532)*

Stanley Black & Decker Inc 860 225-5111
123 Town Square Pl Jersey City (07310) *(G-4831)*

Stanley Steemer Carpet Clr 79, Clifton *Also called Stanley Steemer Intl Inc (G-1731)*

Stanley Steemer Intl Inc 973 574-1640
10 Clifton Blvd Ste B2 Clifton (07011) *(G-1731)*

Stanley Tools, Jersey City *Also called Stanley Black & Decker Inc (G-4831)*

Stanson Corporation (PA) 973 344-8666
2 N Hackensack Ave Kearny (07032) *(G-4916)*

Stanton Precision Products LLC 973 838-6951
10 Park Pl Bldg 4 Butler (07405) *(G-1019)*

Stapling Machines Inc (PA) 973 627-4400
41 Pine St Ste 101 Rockaway (07866) *(G-9609)*

Star Bindery Inc 609 519-5732
963 Lincoln Ave Franklinville (08322) *(G-3632)*

Star Binding & Trimming LLC 201 864-2220
80 Industrial Rd Lodi (07644) *(G-5601)*

Star Candle Company, Ridgefield Park *Also called Star Soap/Star Candle/Prayer C (G-9416)*

Star Creations Inc (PA) 212 221-3570
1506 Stelton Rd Piscataway (08854) *(G-8817)*

Star Dynamic Corp 732 257-7488
100 Outwater Ln Garfield (07026) *(G-3764)*

Star Embroidery Corp 973 481-4300
305 3rd Ave W Ste 7 Newark (07107) *(G-7328)*

Star Group, The, Lodi *Also called Star Narrow Fabrics Inc (G-5602)*

Star Ledger, Piscataway *Also called Newark Morning Ledger Co (G-8796)*

Star Ledger, Pine Brook *Also called Newark Morning Ledger Co (G-8711)*

Star Linen Inc (PA) 800 782-7999
1501 Lancer Dr Moorestown (08057) *(G-6623)*

Star Litho Inc 973 641-1603
175 Us Highway 46 Unit C Fairfield (07004) *(G-3312)*

Star Metal Products 908 474-9860
1125 W Elizabeth Ave Linden (07036) *(G-5448)*

Star Narrow Fabrics Inc 973 778-8600
80a Industrial Rd Lodi (07644) *(G-5602)*

Star National, Newark *Also called S H P C Inc (G-7298)*

Star Pharma Inc 718 466-1790
42 Devon Dr East Brunswick (08816) *(G-2187)*

Star Process Heat Systems LLC 732 282-1002
208 Iris Dr Neptune (07753) *(G-6933)*

Star Promotions Inc 732 356-5959
11 Maiden Ln Bound Brook (08805) *(G-624)*

Star Ravioli Manufacturing Co 201 933-6427
2 Anderson Ave Ste 2 # 2 Moonachie (07074) *(G-6543)*

Star Snacks Co LLC 201 200-9820
111 Port Jersey Blvd Jersey City (07305) *(G-4832)*

Star Soap/Star Candle/Prayer C 201 690-9090
300 Industrial Ave Ridgefield Park (07660) *(G-9416)*

A
L
P
H
A
B
E
T
I
C

Star-Glo Industries LLC (PA) 201 939-6162
2 Carlton Ave East Rutherford (07073) *(G-2326)*

Starbeam Software Solutions 201 384-0017
373 Wildrose Ave Bergenfield (07621) *(G-395)*

Starfire Lighting Inc 201 438-9540
7 Donna Dr Wood Ridge (07075) *(G-12139)*

Starfuels Inc 201 685-0400
285 Grand Ave Englewood (07631) *(G-2934)*

Starlight Electro-Optics Inc 908 859-1362
660 Hrmony Brass Cstle Rd Phillipsburg (08865) *(G-8671)*

Starnet Business Solutions 201 252-2863
46 Industrial Ave Ste 2 Mahwah (07430) *(G-5814)*

Starnet Printing Inc 201 760-2600
46 Industrial Ave Ste 2 Mahwah (07430) *(G-5815)*

Starphil Inc 908 353-8943
107 Trumbull St R12 Elizabeth (07206) *(G-2775)*

State Electronics Parts Corp 973 887-2550
36 State Route 10 Ste 6 East Hanover (07936) *(G-2244)*

State Metal Industries Inc (PA) 856 964-1510
941 S 2nd St Camden (08103) *(G-1087)*

State Metal Trading, Camden *Also called D K Trading Inc (G-1058)*

State Technology Inc 856 467-8009
610 Pedricktown Rd Bridgeport (08014) *(G-773)*

State Tool Gear Co Inc 973 642-6181
211 Camden St Newark (07103) *(G-7329)*

Stateline Fabricators LLC 908 387-8800
100 Foul Rift Rd Phillipsburg (08865) *(G-8672)*

Statewide Granite & Marble, Jersey City *Also called Statewide Granite and Marble (G-4833)*

Statewide Granite and Marble 201 653-1700
109 Carlton Ave Jersey City (07306) *(G-4833)*

Stauff Corporation (HQ) 201 444-7800
7 William Demarest Pl Waldwick (07463) *(G-11453)*

Stauts Printing & Graphics 609 654-5382
12 Maine Trl Medford (08055) *(G-6083)*

Stavola Asphalt Company Inc (PA) 732 542-2328
175 Drift Rd Tinton Falls (07724) *(G-10848)*

Stavola Construction Mtls Inc (PA) 732 542-2328
175 Drift Rd Tinton Falls (07724) *(G-10849)*

Stavola Construction Mtls Inc 732 356-5700
810 Thompson Ave Bound Brook (08805) *(G-625)*

Stavola Contracting, Bound Brook *Also called Stavola Construction Mtls Inc (G-625)*

Stavola Contracting Co Inc 732 935-0156
120 Old Bergen Mill Rd Englishtown (07726) *(G-2998)*

Stavola Holding Corporation 732 542-2328
175 Drift Rd Tinton Falls (07724) *(G-10850)*

Stavola Paving Company, Tinton Falls *Also called Stavola Asphalt Company Inc (G-10848)*

Steamist Inc 201 933-0700
25 E Union Ave Ste 1 East Rutherford (07073) *(G-2327)*

Steb Inc (PA) 973 584-0990
1501 Us Highway 46 Ledgewood (07852) *(G-5310)*

Steb Inc 973 584-0990
1501 Us Highway 46 Ledgewood (07852) *(G-5311)*

Stecher Dave Welding & Fabg Sp 856 467-3558
1040 Township Line Rd Swedesboro (08085) *(G-10729)*

Steel Mountain Fabricators LLC (PA) 908 862-2800
1312 W Elizabeth Ave Linden (07036) *(G-5449)*

Steel Mountain Fabricators LLC 201 741-3019
2712 Secaucus Rd North Bergen (07047) *(G-7487)*

Steel Riser Corp 732 341-7031
402 Marc Dr Toms River (08753) *(G-10914)*

Steelstran Industries Inc 732 566-5040
Foot Of Dock St Matawan (07747) *(G-6033)*

Steelstran Industries Inc (PA) 732 574-0700
35 Mileed Way Avenel (07001) *(G-152)*

Stefan Enterprises Inc 973 253-6005
141 Lanza Ave Bldg 16e Garfield (07026) *(G-3765)*

Steico USA Inc 732 364-6200
250 Carey St Lakewood (08701) *(G-5191)*

Steimling & Son Inc 732 613-1550
7 Nickel Ave Sayreville (08872) *(G-9840)*

Steiner Paper Corp 732 651-6009
72 Lone Star Ln Manalapan (07726) *(G-5863)*

Stelfast Inc 440 879-0077
104 Sunfield Ave Edison (08837) *(G-2627)*

Stepan Company 201 845-3030
100 W Hunter Ave Maywood (07607) *(G-6061)*

Stepan Company 609 298-1222
4th St Fieldsboro Bordentown (08505) *(G-611)*

Stephan L Green Trailers, Farmingdale *Also called Steve Green Enterprises (G-3394)*

Stephco Sales Inc 973 278-5454
238 Lindbergh Pl Ste 3 Paterson (07503) *(G-8384)*

Stephen Douglas Plastics Inc 973 523-3030
22 Green St 36 Paterson (07501) *(G-8385)*

Stephen Gould Corporation (PA) 973 428-1500
35 S Jefferson Rd Whippany (07981) *(G-12040)*

Stephen L Feilinger 609 294-1884
655 Route 9 N Ltl Egg Hbr (08087) *(G-5648)*

Stephen Swinton Studio Inc 908 537-9135
49 New Hampton Rd Washington (07882) *(G-11588)*

Steppin Out Magazine 201 703-0911
21-07 Maple Ave Fair Lawn (07410) *(G-3115)*

Steps Clothing Inc 201 420-1496
30 Mall Dr W Unit B59a Jersey City (07310) *(G-4834)*

Steps To Literacy LLC 732 560-8363
4 Easy St Bound Brook (08805) *(G-626)*

Steri-Pharma LLC (PA) 201 857-8210
120 N State Rt 17 Paramus (07652) *(G-7906)*

Sterigenics US LLC 856 241-8880
303 Heron Dr Swedesboro (08085) *(G-10730)*

Steris Instrument MGT Svcs Inc 908 904-1317
10 Ilene Ct Hillsborough (08844) *(G-4373)*

Sterling Marine Products, Montclair *Also called Sterling Net & Twine Co Inc (G-6436)*

Sterling Net & Twine Co Inc (PA) 973 783-9800
18 Label St Montclair (07042) *(G-6436)*

Sterling Products Inc 973 471-2858
90 Dayton Ave Ste 77 Passaic (07055) *(G-8182)*

Sterling Publishing Co Inc 732 248-6563
1 Barnes And Noble Way Monroe Township (08831) *(G-6395)*

Sterling Publishing Warehouse, Monroe Township *Also called Sterling Publishing Co Inc (G-6395)*

Sterling Sound, Edgewater *Also called Metrolpolis Mastering LP (G-2441)*

Sterling System, Edison *Also called Cygate Sftwr & Consulting LLC (G-2500)*

Stern Knit Inc 732 364-8055
3 Fillmore Ave Lakewood (08701) *(G-5192)*

Sternvent Co Inc 908 688-0807
No5 Stahuber Ave Union (07083) *(G-11225)*

Stessl & Neugebauer Inc 908 277-3340
9 Industrial Pl Summit (07901) *(G-10659)*

Stetsers JD Canvas Pdts Inc 856 423-4901
644 Billings Ave Paulsboro (08066) *(G-8426)*

Steve Green Enterprises 732 938-5572
74 Sqankum Yellowbrook Rd Farmingdale (07727) *(G-3394)*

Steven Industries Inc 201 437-6500
39 Avenue C Ste 1 Bayonne (07002) *(G-245)*

Steven Madden Ltd 973 533-0121
112 Eisenhower Pkwy Livingston (07039) *(G-5564)*

Steven Madola 609 989-8022
2001 S Broad St Trenton (08610) *(G-11117)*

Steven Orros 732 972-1104
106 Timber Hill Dr Monroe Township (08831) *(G-6396)*

Steven's Dunbar Companies, Bayonne *Also called Dunbar Sales Company Inc (G-223)*

Stevens Publishing Co 908 284-9326
5 Hageman Dr Flemington (08822) *(G-3468)*

Steward LLC 609 816-8825
345 Witherspoon St Princeton (08542) *(G-9125)*

Steward Mag, Princeton *Also called Steward LLC (G-9125)*

Stewart Business Forms Inc 856 768-2011
138 Frankford Ave Blackwood (08012) *(G-493)*

Stewart-Morris Inc 973 822-2777
71 Kings Rd Ste 1 Madison (07940) *(G-5736)*

STI, Ewing *Also called Surface Technology Inc (G-3058)*

STI, Branchburg *Also called Specified Technologies Inc (G-705)*

Stiles Enterprises Inc 973 625-9660
114 Beach St Rockaway (07866) *(G-9610)*

Stimson Lane Wine & Spirit, Mount Arlington *Also called Michelle Ste Wine Estates Ltd (G-6758)*

Stingray Sport Pdts Ltd Lblty 201 300-6482
20-10 Maple Ave Bldg 35e Fair Lawn (07410) *(G-3116)*

Stirling Audio Services LLC 732 560-0707
201 Wood Ave Middlesex (08846) *(G-6204)*

Stirrup Metal Products Corp 973 824-7086
215 Emmet St Newark (07114) *(G-7330)*

Stobbs Printing Co Inc 973 748-4441
18 Washington St Bloomfield (07003) *(G-533)*

Stollen Machine & Tool Company 908 241-0622
761 Lexington Ave Kenilworth (07033) *(G-4997)*

Stoncor Group Inc (HQ) 800 257-7953
1000 E Park Ave Maple Shade (08052) *(G-5909)*

Stone Graphics 732 919-1111
5020 Industrial Rd Wall Township (07727) *(G-11511)*

Stone Industries Inc (PA) 973 595-6250
400 Central Ave 402 Haledon (07508) *(G-4085)*

Stone Mar Natural Stone Co LLC (PA) 856 988-1802
8 E Stow Rd Ste 200 Marlton (08053) *(G-6000)*

Stone Mountain Printing Inc 732 636-8450
74 Main St Fl 1 Woodbridge (07095) *(G-12154)*

Stone Surfaces Inc 201 935-8803
890 Paterson Plank Rd East Rutherford (07073) *(G-2328)*

Stone Systems New Jersey LLC 973 778-5525
5 Washington Ave Fairfield (07004) *(G-3313)*

Stone Truss Systems Inc (PA) 973 882-7377
23 Commerce Rd Ste O Fairfield (07004) *(G-3314)*

Stone World Magazine, Paramus *Also called BNP Media Inc (G-7859)*

Stonebridge Paper LLC 973 413-8100
37 E 6th St Paterson (07524) *(G-8386)*

Stonework Dsign Consulting Inc (PA) 973 575-0835
25 Pier Ln W Fairfield (07004) *(G-3315)*

(G-0000) Company's Geographic Section entry number

Stoneworld At Redbank Inc 732 383-5110
247 Cooper Rd Red Bank (07701) *(G-9345)*
Stonhard, Maple Shade *Also called Stoncor Group Inc (G-5909)*
Stonhard Manufacturing Co Inc (HQ) 856 779-7500
1000 E Park Ave Maple Shade (08052) *(G-5910)*
Stonite Coil Corporation 609 585-6600
476 Route 156 Trenton (08620) *(G-11118)*
Store 266, Atlantic Highlands *Also called Food Circus Super Markets Inc (G-111)*
Storemaxx Inc 201 440-8800
343 S River St Hackensack (07601) *(G-3981)*
Storis Inc (PA) 888 478-6747
400 Valley Rd Ste 302 Mount Arlington (07856) *(G-6760)*
Storis Management Systems, Mount Arlington *Also called Storis Inc (G-6760)*
Storm City Entertainment Inc 856 885-6902
700 Liberty Pl Sicklerville (08081) *(G-10027)*
Story Electric Mtr Repr Co Inc 973 256-1636
20 Francisco Ave Little Falls (07424) *(G-5490)*
Storybook Knits, Kinnelon *Also called Jtwo Inc (G-5037)*
Str8line Publishing Company 919 717-6740
511 Frelinghuysen Ave Newark (07114) *(G-7331)*
Strahan Consulting Group LLC 908 790-0873
1290 Martine Ave Scotch Plains (07076) *(G-9857)*
Strap-Its, Demarest *Also called Blu-J2 LLC (G-2026)*
Straps Manufacturing NJ Inc 201 368-5201
480 Braen Ave Wyckoff (07481) *(G-12264)*
Strategic Content Imaging 201 863-8100
100 Castle Rd Secaucus (07094) *(G-9933)*
Strategic Mktg Promotions Inc (PA) 845 623-7777
1200 Macarthur Blvd # 251 Mahwah (07430) *(G-5816)*
Strato Inc 732 981-1515
100 New England Ave Ste 1 Piscataway (08854) *(G-8818)*
Straval Machine Co Inc 973 340-9955
20 Bushes Ln Elmwood Park (07407) *(G-2851)*
Streamserve Inc (HQ) 781 863-1510
100 Tormee Dr Asbury Park (07712) *(G-84)*
Street Lights Dept, Jersey City *Also called City of Jersey City (G-4728)*
Stretch-O-Rama Inc 732 855-1400
5 Paddock St Avenel (07001) *(G-153)*
Strides Pharma Inc 609 773-5000
2 Tower Center Blvd # 1102 East Brunswick (08816) *(G-2188)*
Strikeforce Technologies Inc 732 661-9641
1090 King Georges Post Rd Edison (08837) *(G-2628)*
Strive Pharmaceuticals Inc (PA) 609 269-2001
19 Lexington Ave East Brunswick (08816) *(G-2189)*
Strivr Inc 973 216-7379
20 Downing Pl Livingston (07039) *(G-5565)*
Strongwall Industries Inc 201 445-4633
90 Heather Ct Allendale (07401) *(G-19)*
Structural Foam Plastics, Branchburg *Also called Plasti Foam (G-690)*
Structural Steel Fabricators, Lincoln Park *Also called D S Jh LLC (G-5326)*
Structured Healthcare MGT Inc 201 569-3290
456 Nordhoff Pl Englewood (07631) *(G-2935)*
Stryker 856 312-0046
165 E 9th Ave Unit F Runnemede (08078) *(G-9724)*
Stryker Corporation 201 760-8000
2 Pearl Ct Allendale (07401) *(G-20)*
Stryker Orthopaedics, Englewood *Also called Howmedica Osteonics Corp (G-2903)*
Stryker Orthopaedics, Mahwah *Also called Howmedica Osteonics Corp (G-5783)*
STS Technologies LLC 973 277-5416
282 Franklin Tpke Mahwah (07430) *(G-5817)*
Stuart Mills Inc (PA) 973 579-5717
25 Stillwater Rd Newton (07860) *(G-7405)*
Stuart Mills Inc 973 579-5717
25 Stillwater Rd Newton (07860) *(G-7406)*
Stuart Steel Protection Corp 732 469-5544
411 Elizabeth Ave Somerset (08873) *(G-10174)*
Stud Welding Co The Inc 856 866-9300
750 Glen Ave Moorestown (08057) *(G-6624)*
Studio Dellarte 718 599-3715
234 16th St Fl 1 Jersey City (07310) *(G-4835)*
Studio L Contracting LLC 201 837-1650
18 Dicarolis Ct Hackensack (07601) *(G-3982)*
Studio042, Montclair *Also called Puent-Romer Communications Inc (G-6433)*
Stull Technologies LLC 732 873-5000
17 Veronica Ave Somerset (08873) *(G-10175)*
Stulz-Sickles Steel Company (PA) 609 531-2172
2 Campus Dr Burlington (08016) *(G-990)*
Stuyvesant Press Inc 973 399-3880
119 Coit St Irvington (07111) *(G-4605)*
Style Plus, Trenton *Also called Man-How Inc (G-11078)*
Stylex Inc 856 461-5600
740 Coopertown Rd Delanco (08075) *(G-2008)*
Stylus Custom Apparel Inc 908 587-0800
729 E Elizabeth Ave Linden (07036) *(G-5450)*
Subito Music Service Inc 973 857-3440
60 Depot St Verona (07044) *(G-11311)*
Subsidariry of Vac-U-Max, Belleville *Also called Aerocon Inc (G-295)*
Suburban Aluminum Mfg, Howell *Also called Surburban Building Pdts Inc (G-4568)*
Suburban Auto Seat Co Inc (PA) 973 778-9227
35 Industrial Rd Lodi (07644) *(G-5603)*
Suburban Essex Magazine, Fairfield *Also called Vicinity Publications Inc (G-3343)*
Suburban Fence Company, Trenton *Also called Hoda Inc (G-11063)*
Suburban Monument & Vault 973 242-7007
203 Sherman Ave Newark (07114) *(G-7332)*
Suburban Parent Magazine, North Brunswick *Also called Middlesex Publications (G-7527)*
Suburban Sign Co Inc 908 862-7222
210 Marion Ave Linden (07036) *(G-5451)*
Success Publishers LLC 609 443-0792
29 Hampton Hollow Dr Perrineville (08535) *(G-8603)*
Success Sewing Inc 973 622-0328
50 Columbia St Ste 2 Newark (07102) *(G-7333)*
Sudarshan North America Inc 201 652-2046
76 N Walnut St Ridgewood (07450) *(G-9431)*
Sueta Music Ed Publications 888 725-2333
13 E Main St Ste 3 Mendham (07945) *(G-6091)*
Suez Treatment Solutions Inc (HQ) 201 767-9300
461 From Rd Ste 400 Paramus (07652) *(G-7907)*
Suez Treatment Solutions Inc 201 676-2525
600 Willow Tree Rd Leonia (07605) *(G-5320)*
Suffern Plating Corp 973 473-4404
210 Garibaldi Ave Lodi (07644) *(G-5604)*
Suffolk County Contractors 732 349-7726
242 Dover Rd Unit 2 Toms River (08757) *(G-10915)*
Suffolk Molds, Wayne *Also called C & N Packaging Inc (G-11617)*
Suffolk Recycling, Toms River *Also called Suffolk County Contractors (G-10915)*
Sugar & Plumm Upper West LLC 201 334-1600
146 Redneck Ave Moonachie (07074) *(G-6544)*
Sugar and Plumm LLC 201 334-1600
146 Redneck Ave Moonachie (07074) *(G-6545)*
Sugarush 732 414-9044
37 E Front St Red Bank (07701) *(G-9346)*
Suite K Value Added Svcs LLC 732 590-0647
31 Executive Ave Edison (08817) *(G-2629)*
Suite K Value Added Svcs LLC 609 655-6890
31 Executive Ave Edison (08817) *(G-2630)*
Suite K Value Added Svcs LLC (PA) 609 655-6890
31 Executive Ave Edison (08817) *(G-2631)*
Suite-K, Edison *Also called Suite K Value Added Svcs LLC (G-2630)*
Suite-K, Edison *Also called Suite K Value Added Svcs LLC (G-2631)*
Sukhadia's Indian Grill, Parsippany *Also called Sukhadias Sweets & Snacks (G-8093)*
Sukhadias Sweets & Snacks 973 227-6400
61 New Rd Parsippany (07054) *(G-8093)*
Sukhadias Sweets & Snacks (PA) 908 222-0069
124 Case Dr South Plainfield (07080) *(G-10436)*
Sullivan Steel Service, Pennington *Also called General Sullivan Group Inc (G-8451)*
Sullivan-Carson Inc (PA) 856 566-1400
1010 Hddonfield Berlin Rd Voorhees (08043) *(G-11438)*
Sultan Foods Inc 908 874-6953
115 Stryker Ln Ste 13 Hillsborough (08844) *(G-4374)*
Sulzer Bingham Pumps, Bridgeport *Also called Sulzer Pump Services (us) Inc (G-774)*
Sulzer Chemtech USA Inc 856 768-2165
1008 Industrial Dr Ste F West Berlin (08091) *(G-11752)*
Sulzer Pump Services (us) Inc 856 542-5046
621 Heron Dr Bridgeport (08014) *(G-774)*
Suman Realty LLC 908 350-8039
103 Saint Josephs Dr Stirling (07980) *(G-10607)*
Sumangel Jewellers, Piscataway *Also called Star Creations Inc (G-8817)*
Sumatic Co Inc 973 772-1288
102 Dewitt St Garfield (07026) *(G-3766)*
Summerlands Inc 973 729-8428
23 White Deer Plz Sparta (07871) *(G-10521)*
Summit Filter Corp 908 687-3500
20 Milltown Rd Union (07083) *(G-11226)*
Summit Hill Flavors, Somerset *Also called Flavor and Fd Ingredients Inc (G-10102)*
Summit Intl Filtration Systems 201 847-2370
500 W Main St Ste 10 Wyckoff (07481) *(G-12265)*
Summit Millwork & Supply Inc 908 273-1486
235 Morris Ave Summit (07901) *(G-10660)*
Summit Professional Networks 201 526-1230
33 41 Newark St Fl 2 Hoboken (07030) *(G-4499)*
Summit Research Laboratory 908 782-9500
45 River Rd Ste 300 Flemington (08822) *(G-3469)*
Summit Truck Body Inc (PA) 908 277-4342
50 Franklin Pl Summit (07901) *(G-10661)*
Sun Basket Inc 408 669-4418
600 Highland Dr Ste 614 Westampton (08060) *(G-11918)*
Sun Chemical Corporation 201 933-4500
631 Central Ave Carlstadt (07072) *(G-1223)*
Sun Chemical Corporation (HQ) 973 404-6000
35 Waterview Blvd Ste 100 Parsippany (07054) *(G-8094)*
Sun Chemical Corporation 201 438-4831
390 Central Ave East Rutherford (07073) *(G-2329)*
Sun Chemical Corporation 201 935-8666
651 Garden St Carlstadt (07072) *(G-1224)*
Sun Coast Precision Instrument 646 852-2331
80 Broadway Fl 1 Cresskill (07626) *(G-1949)*

A L P H A B E T I C

Sun Dial & Panel Corporation 973 226-4334
2 Daniel Rd Ste 102 Fairfield (07004) *(G-3316)*

Sun Display Systems, Fairfield *Also called Sun Dial & Panel Corporation (G-3316)*

Sun Display Systems LLC 973 226-4334
2 Daniel Rd Fairfield (07004) *(G-3317)*

Sun Metal Finishing Inc 973 684-0119
5 Sicomac Rd 105 North Haledon (07508) *(G-7554)*

Sun Neon Sign and Electric Co 856 667-6977
4 Saddle Ln Cherry Hill (08002) *(G-1422)*

Sun Noodle New Jersey LLC 201 530-1100
40 Kero Rd Carlstadt (07072) *(G-1225)*

Sun Pacific Power Corp 888 845-0242
215 Gordons Corner Rd 1a Manalapan (07726) *(G-5864)*

Sun Pharmaceutical Inds Inc 313 871-8400
2 Independence Way Princeton (08540) *(G-9126)*

Sun Pharmaceutical Inds Inc 609 495-2800
1 Commerce Dr Cranbury (08512) *(G-1882)*

Sun Pharmaceutical Inds Inc (HQ) 609 495-2800
270 Prospect Plains Rd Cranbury (08512) *(G-1883)*

Sun Plastics Co Inc 908 490-0870
35 Blue Wolf Trl Watchung (07069) *(G-11595)*

Sun Taiyang Co Ltd 201 549-7100
85 Oxford Dr 2 Moonachie (07074) *(G-6546)*

Sun Trading, Moonachie *Also called Sun Taiyang Co Ltd (G-6546)*

Sunbird Software Inc 732 993-4476
200 Cottontail Ln B106e Somerset (08873) *(G-10176)*

Sunbrite Dye Co Inc (PA) 973 777-9830
35 8th St Ste 6 Passaic (07055) *(G-8183)*

Sunday Star Ledger, Newark *Also called Newark Morning Ledger Co (G-7257)*

Sunflower Seed 908 735-3822
38 Old Highway 22 Clinton (08809) *(G-1755)*

Sungard, Voorhees *Also called Fis Financial Systems LLC (G-11430)*

Sunglo Fabrics Inc 201 935-0830
50 California Ave Paterson (07503) *(G-8387)*

Sungood, Kenilworth *Also called Naturee Nuts Inc (G-4979)*

Sunham Home Fashions LLC 908 363-1100
700 Central Park Ave New Providence (07974) *(G-7055)*

Sunlight Photonics Inc 732 362-7501
2045 State Route 27 1w Edison (08817) *(G-2632)*

Sunovion Pharmaceuticals Inc 201 592-2050
1 Bridge Plz N Ste 510 Fort Lee (07024) *(G-3584)*

Sunpak Division, Rockaway *Also called Tocad America Inc (G-9614)*

Sunrise Glamour LLC 800 960-2426
33 Wood Ave S Ste 600 Iselin (08830) *(G-4646)*

Sunrise Intl Educatn Inc 917 525-0272
1542 Edly Cove Ct North Brunswick (08902) *(G-7541)*

Sunrise Pharmaceutical Inc 732 382-6085
665 E Lincoln Ave Rahway (07065) *(G-9224)*

Sunrise Snacks Rockland Inc 845 352-2676
787 E 27th St Paterson (07504) *(G-8388)*

Sunset Lettering, Madison *Also called Alfred Sports Inc (G-5717)*

Sunset Printing and Engrv Corp 973 537-9600
10 Kice Ave Wharton (07885) *(G-12000)*

Sunset Stationers, Wharton *Also called Sunset Printing and Engrv Corp (G-12000)*

Sunshine Bouquet Company (PA) 732 274-2900
3 Chris Ct Ste A Dayton (08810) *(G-1989)*

Sunshine Container, Orange *Also called Sunshine Metal & Sign Inc (G-7829)*

Sunshine Lane Mixed Media, Mendham *Also called Surviving Life Corp (G-6092)*

Sunshine Metal & Sign Inc 973 676-4432
461 Maryland St Orange (07050) *(G-7829)*

Sunsplash Marina LLC 609 628-4445
5 Mosquito Landing Rd Tuckahoe (08250) *(G-11138)*

Supco, Allenwood *Also called Sealed Unit Parts Co Inc (G-37)*

Super Chrome Inc 732 774-2210
1004 1st Ave Asbury Park (07712) *(G-85)*

Super Stud Building Pdts Inc 732 662-6200
2960 Woodbridge Ave Edison (08837) *(G-2633)*

Super Wash, Boonton *Also called S W I International Inc (G-582)*

Superfine Online Inc 212 827-0063
205 E 11th Ave Roselle (07203) *(G-9684)*

Superior Custom Kitchens LLC 908 753-6005
126 Mount Bethel Rd Warren (07059) *(G-11568)*

Superior Intl Srgical Sups LLC 609 695-6591
46 Oak Ln Ewing (08618) *(G-3057)*

Superior Jewelry Co 215 677-8100
430 Tilton Rd Ste 1 Northfield (08225) *(G-7564)*

Superior Lamp Inc 800 257-8353
1060 Kings Hwy N Ste 120 Cherry Hill (08034) *(G-1423)*

Superior Lighting Inc 908 759-0199
1245 Virginia St Elizabeth (07208) *(G-2776)*

Superior Marine Canvas 856 241-1724
75 Belfiore Dr Swedesboro (08085) *(G-10731)*

Superior Powder Coating Inc (PA) 908 351-8707
600 Progress St Elizabeth (07201) *(G-2777)*

Superior Printing Ink Co Inc (PA) 201 478-5600
100 North St Teterboro (07608) *(G-10810)*

Superior Printing Ink Co Inc 856 482-9066
540 E Linwood Ave Maple Shade (08052) *(G-5911)*

Superior Printing Ink Co Inc 716 685-6763
100 North St Teterboro (07608) *(G-10811)*

Superior Printing Ink Co Inc 716 685-6763
100 North St Teterboro (07608) *(G-10812)*

Superior Printing Ink Co Inc 973 242-5868
252 Wright St Newark (07114) *(G-7334)*

Superior Promotional Bags, Toms River *Also called Alex Real LLC (G-10860)*

Superior Signal Company LLC 732 251-0800
178 W Greystone Rd Old Bridge (08857) *(G-7793)*

Superior Smoke, Old Bridge *Also called Superior Signal Company LLC (G-7793)*

Superior Tool & Mfg Co 908 526-9011
42 Columbia Rd Ste 2 Branchburg (08876) *(G-706)*

Superior Trademark Inc 201 652-1900
45 Zazzetti St Waldwick (07463) *(G-11454)*

Supermatic Corp 973 627-4433
27 Old Beach Glen Rd Rockaway (07866) *(G-9611)*

Supermedia LLC 973 649-9900
50 Burnett Ave Maplewood (07040) *(G-5927)*

Superseal Manufacturing Co Inc (HQ) 908 561-5910
125 Helen St South Plainfield (07080) *(G-10437)*

Supertex Inc 973 345-1000
860 Market St Paterson (07513) *(G-8389)*

Supplies-Supplies Inc 908 272-5100
85 Maple St Watchung (07069) *(G-11596)*

Supply Chain Technologies LLC 856 206-9849
1161 Broad St Ste 312 Shrewsbury (07702) *(G-10012)*

Supply One Plastics, Moorestown *Also called Granite Packaging Supply Co (G-6579)*

Supply Plus NJ Inc 973 782-5930
3 E 26th St Paterson (07514) *(G-8390)*

Supply Plus NY Inc 973 481-4800
3 E 26th St Paterson (07514) *(G-8391)*

Supply Technologies LLC 201 641-7600
50 Graphic Pl Moonachie (07074) *(G-6547)*

Supplyone New York Inc 718 392-7400
143 Getty Ave Paterson (07503) *(G-8392)*

Supreme Graphics and Prtg Inc 718 989-9817
1027 State St Perth Amboy (08861) *(G-8632)*

Supreme Ink Corp 973 344-2922
65 Mcwhorter St Newark (07105) *(G-7335)*

Supreme Manufacturing Co Inc 732 254-0087
5 Connerty Ct East Brunswick (08816) *(G-2190)*

Surati NJ LLC 732 251-3404
15 American Way Spotswood (08884) *(G-10531)*

Surburban Building Pdts Inc (PA) 732 901-8900
1178 Lkwood Frmingdale Rd Howell (07731) *(G-4568)*

Sure Design 732 919-3066
5027 Industrial Rd Ste 3 Wall Township (07727) *(G-11512)*

Sureway Prtg & Graphics LLC 609 430-4333
338 Wall St Princeton (08540) *(G-9127)*

Surface Source Intl Inc 973 598-0152
961 State Route 10 Ste 2i Randolph (07869) *(G-9300)*

Surface Technology Inc 609 259-0099
1405 Lower Ferry Rd Ewing (08618) *(G-3058)*

Surfside Foods LLC 856 785-2115
1733 Main St Port Norris (08349) *(G-8983)*

Surfside Products, Port Norris *Also called Surfside Foods LLC (G-8983)*

Surgical Lser Sfety Cuncil Inc 216 272-0805
405 Hialeah Dr Cherry Hill (08002) *(G-1424)*

Suroma Ltd Liability Company 908 735-7700
223 Hamden Rd Annandale (08801) *(G-61)*

Surround Technologies LLC (PA) 973 743-1277
650 Bloomfield Ave # 211 Bloomfield (07003) *(G-534)*

Suruchi Foods LLC 201 432-2201
114 Baldwin Ave Ste A Jersey City (07306) *(G-4836)*

Survirvor Windows II, Hillside *Also called Survivor II Inc (G-4442)*

Surviving Life Corp 973 543-3370
3 Muirfield Ln Mendham (07945) *(G-6092)*

Survivor II Inc 908 353-1155
1239 Central Ave Hillside (07205) *(G-4442)*

Susan Mills Inc (PA) 908 355-1400
1285 Central Ave Hillside (07205) *(G-4443)*

Susan R Bauer Inc 973 657-1590
427 Margaret King Ave Ringwood (07456) *(G-9456)*

Sushi House Inc 201 482-0609
225 Commercial Ave Palisades Park (07650) *(G-7844)*

Sussex Humus & Supply Inc 973 779-8812
29 Kenyon St Clifton (07013) *(G-1732)*

Sussex Wine Merchants, Moorestown *Also called Petit Pois Corp (G-6612)*

Sustanble Bldg Innovations Inc 800 560-4143
2435 Highway 34 Ste 204 Manasquan (08736) *(G-5881)*

Sutherland Packaging Inc 973 786-5141
254 Brighton Rd Andover (07821) *(G-54)*

Suuchi Inc 201 284-0789
2321 Kennedy Blvd Ste S4 North Bergen (07047) *(G-7488)*

Suven Life Sciences Ltd 732 274-0037
1100 Cornwall Rd Ste 5 Monmouth Junction (08852) *(G-6364)*

Suzie Mac Specialties Inc 732 238-3500
3 Joanna Ct Ste C East Brunswick (08816) *(G-2191)*

Sv Pharma Inc 732 651-1336
9 Autumn Ln East Brunswick (08816) *(G-2192)*

(G-0000) Company's Geographic Section entry number

Svtc Pharma Inc..201 652-0013
  60 E Ridgewood Ave Ridgewood (07450) *(G-9432)*

Swapshub Company Inc.......................................732 529-4813
  15 Corporate Pl S Ste 130 Piscataway (08854) *(G-8819)*

Swarovski North America Ltd................................732 632-1856
  55 Parsonage Rd Unit 333 Edison (08837) *(G-2634)*

Swarovski North America Ltd................................856 686-1805
  1750 Deptford Center Rd Deptford (08096) *(G-2068)*

Swarovski North America Ltd................................856 662-5453
  2000 Route 38 Cherry Hill (08002) *(G-1425)*

Swarovski North America Ltd................................201 265-4888
  700 Paramus Park Paramus (07652) *(G-7908)*

Swarovski North America Ltd................................609 344-1323
  2801 Pacific Ave Atlantic City (08401) *(G-108)*

Swatch Group Les Btques US Inc.........................201 271-1400
  1200 Harbor Blvd Weehawken (07086) *(G-11699)*

Swce Group, The, Bernardsville Also called Swce Inc *(G-455)*

Swce Inc (PA)...908 766-5695
  360 Mount Harmony Rd Bernardsville (07924) *(G-455)*

Sweet Delight..732 263-9100
  65 Monmouth Rd Oakhurst (07755) *(G-7673)*

Sweet Eats Bakery, Voorhees Also called Good To Go Inc *(G-11431)*

Sweet Orange LLC...908 522-0011
  545 Morris Ave Summit (07901) *(G-10662)*

Sweet Potato Pie Inc...973 279-3405
  140 Auburn St Paterson (07501) *(G-8393)*

Sweet Sign Systems Inc......................................732 521-9300
  9 Davison Ave Ste 5 Jamesburg (08831) *(G-4690)*

Sweet Solutions Inc..732 512-0777
  117 Fieldcrest Ave Edison (08837) *(G-2635)*

Sweetly Spirited Cupcakes Ltd.............................917 846-4238
  10 Newport Dr Princeton Junction (08550) *(G-9164)*

Swemco, Moorestown Also called S W Electronics & Mfg *(G-6620)*

Swemco LLC (HQ)...856 222-9900
  121 Whittendale Dr Ste A Moorestown (08057) *(G-6625)*

Swepco Tube LLC...973 778-3000
  1 Clifton Blvd Clifton (07011) *(G-1733)*

Swintec Corp (PA)...201 935-0115
  320 W Coml Ave Ste 1 Moonachie (07074) *(G-6548)*

Swiss Madison LLC..434 623-4766
  19 Stults Rd Dayton (08810) *(G-1990)*

Swiss Orthopedic Inc...908 874-5522
  188 Us Highway 206 Hillsborough (08844) *(G-4375)*

Swissray America Inc...908 353-0971
  1180 Mclester St Ste 2 Elizabeth (07201) *(G-2778)*

Swissray International Inc (HQ)...........................800 903-5543
  1090 King Georges Rd 1203 Edison (08837) *(G-2636)*

Swissray Medical Systems, Elizabeth Also called Swissray America Inc *(G-2778)*

Swisstex Company...201 861-8000
  220 61st St Ste 2 West New York (07093) *(G-11882)*

Switlik Parachute Company Inc.............................609 587-3300
  Lalor & Hancock Sts Trenton (08609) *(G-11119)*

Sxwell USA LLC...732 345-5400
  111 Wood Ave S Ste 210 Iselin (08830) *(G-4647)*

Sybase Inc...973 537-5700
  400 Interpace Pkwy Ste D1 Parsippany (07054) *(G-8095)*

Sylvan Chemical Corporation..............................201 934-4224
  7 Prescott Pl Fair Lawn (07410) *(G-3117)*

Symbiomix Therapeutics LLC (HQ).....................609 722-7250
  105 Lock St Ste 409 Newark (07103) *(G-7336)*

Symbology Enterprises Inc (PA)..........................908 725-1699
  50 Division St Ste 203 Somerville (08876) *(G-10227)*

Symcon Controls, West Milford Also called Symcon Inc *(G-11857)*

Symcon Inc..973 728-8661
  47 Cedar Ln West Milford (07480) *(G-11857)*

Symphony Inc..856 727-9596
  1263 Glen Ave Ste 220 Moorestown (08057) *(G-6626)*

Symphony Pastries, Moorestown Also called Symphony Inc *(G-6626)*

Symrise Inc (HQ)..201 288-3200
  300 North St Teterboro (07608) *(G-10813)*

Symrise Inc..201 288-3200
  250 Pehle Ave Ste 207 Saddle Brook (07663) *(G-9795)*

Symrise Inc..908 429-6824
  180 Industrial Pkwy Branchburg (08876) *(G-707)*

Symtech Enterprise Intl, Branchburg Also called Paradise Barxon Corp *(G-686)*

Synasia Inc..732 205-9880
  240 Amboy Ave Metuchen (08840) *(G-6126)*

Syncom Pharmaceuticals Inc (PA).......................973 787-2405
  125 Clinton Rd Unit 5 Fairfield (07004) *(G-3318)*

Synergem Inc...732 692-6308
  2323 Randolph Ave Ste 2 Avenel (07001) *(G-154)*

Synergetica International Inc................................732 780-5865
  9 Inverness Dr Marlboro (07746) *(G-5960)*

Synergy Microwave Corp (PA).............................973 881-8800
  201 Mclean Blvd Paterson (07504) *(G-8394)*

Syneron...201 599-9451
  707 Reeder Rd Paramus (07652) *(G-7909)*

Synray Corporation..908 245-2600
  209 N Michigan Ave Kenilworth (07033) *(G-4998)*

Synthetic Grass Surfaces Inc...............................973 778-9594
  6 Robert Ct Lodi (07644) *(G-5605)*

Synthetic Grass Surfaces NJ, Lodi Also called Synthetic Grass Surfaces Inc *(G-5605)*

Synthetic Surfaces Inc (PA)...............................908 233-6803
  2450 Plainfield Ave Scotch Plains (07076) *(G-9858)*

Syntiro Dynamics LLC...732 377-3307
  1606 Cammar Dr Wall Township (07719) *(G-11513)*

Sys-Con Publications Inc.....................................201 802-3000
  577 Chestnut Ridge Rd # 6 Woodcliff Lake (07677) *(G-12204)*

Sysco Guest Supply LLC (HQ)...........................732 537-2297
  300 Davidson Ave Somerset (08873) *(G-10177)*

Syscom Technologies Corp..................................856 642-7661
  1537 Glen Ave Moorestown (08057) *(G-6627)*

Sytheon Ltd..973 988-1075
  315 Wootton St Ste N Boonton (07005) *(G-584)*

T & B Specialties Inc...732 928-4500
  479 Wright Debow Rd Jackson (08527) *(G-4679)*

T & C, Marlboro Also called Town & Country Plastics Inc *(G-5961)*

T & E Industries Inc...973 672-5454
  215 Watchung Ave Orange (07050) *(G-7830)*

T & E Sales of Marlboro Inc...............................732 549-7551
  913 Middlesex Ave Metuchen (08840) *(G-6127)*

T & M Newton Corporation...................................973 383-1232
  119 Fredon Springdale Rd Newton (07860) *(G-7407)*

T & M Pallet Co Inc...908 454-3042
  116 Edison Rd Stewartsville (08886) *(G-10598)*

T & P Machine Shop Inc......................................732 424-9141
  600 Prospect Ave Ste E Piscataway (08854) *(G-8820)*

T & T Cabinet Works Inc......................................973 279-0909
  388 River St Paterson (07524) *(G-8395)*

T A C Technical Instr Corp...................................609 882-2894
  152 Mercer Cty Airport Ewing (08628) *(G-3059)*

T A G, West Berlin Also called Telecom Assistance Group Inc *(G-11756)*

T and C Neuromax LLC..201 447-2020
  106 Prospect St Ridgewood (07450) *(G-9433)*

T C E, Secaucus Also called Thermal Conduction Engineering *(G-9934)*

T C P Reliable Manufacturing...............................732 346-9200
  285 Davidson Ave Ste 303 Somerset (08873) *(G-10178)*

T C S Technologies Inc..908 852-7555
  430 Sand Shore Rd Ste 1 Hackettstown (07840) *(G-4039)*

T F S Inc...973 890-7651
  40 Vreeland Ave Ste 101 Totowa (07512) *(G-10974)*

T G Manufacturing Inc...609 561-0022
  206 Old Forks Rd Hammonton (08037) *(G-4150)*

T G Type-O-Graphics Inc......................................973 253-3333
  19-03 Maple Ave Ste 3 Fair Lawn (07410) *(G-3118)*

T J Eckardt Associates Inc...................................856 767-4111
  230 Williamstown Rd Berlin (08009) *(G-442)*

T J'S Ice Cream Plus, Ocean City Also called Tjs Ice Cream *(G-7759)*

T L C Specialties Inc...732 244-4225
  188 Walnut St Toms River (08753) *(G-10916)*

T M Baxter Services LLC.....................................908 500-9065
  1307 Washington Gdns Washington (07882) *(G-11589)*

T M Industries Inc...908 730-7674
  2013 Brookfield Glen Dr Belvidere (07823) *(G-377)*

T N T Information Systems....................................609 799-9488
  666 Plainsboro Rd Ste 100 Plainsboro (08536) *(G-8901)*

T O Najarian Associates.......................................732 389-0220
  1 Industrial Way W Ste D5 Eatontown (07724) *(G-2424)*

T V L Associates Inc...973 790-6766
  3 Donna Ln Wayne (07470) *(G-11684)*

T Wiker Enterprises Inc.......................................609 261-9494
  5900 Delaware Ave Hainesport (08036) *(G-4079)*

T-M Vacuum Products Inc (PA)..........................856 829-2000
  630 S Warrington Ave Cinnaminson (08077) *(G-1490)*

T-M Vacuum Products Inc...................................856 829-2000
  630 S Warrington Ave Cinnaminson (08077) *(G-1491)*

T-Net Technology, Cedar Grove Also called Umit International Trading LLC *(G-1303)*

T.P. Bryan Electric, Trenton Also called Timothy P Bryan Elc Co Inc *(G-11122)*

Tab Networks..201 746-0067
  50 Tice Blvd Ste 365 Woodcliff Lake (07677) *(G-12205)*

Tabco Technologies LLC (PA)..............................201 438-0422
  400 Gotham Pkwy Carlstadt (07072) *(G-1226)*

Tablecloth Co Inc..973 942-1555
  514 Totowa Ave Paterson (07522) *(G-8396)*

Tabloid Graphic Services Inc..............................856 486-0410
  7101 Westfield Ave Pennsauken (08110) *(G-8582)*

Tach-It, South Hackensack Also called Clements Industries Inc *(G-10258)*

Tactic, Ewing Also called T A C Technical Instr Corp *(G-3059)*

Tadbik NJ Inc..973 882-9595
  17 Madison Rd Fairfield (07004) *(G-3319)*

Tag, Teterboro Also called Tapia Accessory Group Inc *(G-10815)*

Tag Minerals Inc...732 252-5146
  41 Howe Ln Freehold (07728) *(G-3689)*

Tag Optics Inc...609 356-2142
  200 N Harrison St Princeton (08540) *(G-9128)*

Tahari Arthur S Levine, Millburn Also called Tahari ASL LLC *(G-6259)*

Tahari ASL LLC (PA)...888 734-7459
  16 Bleeker St Millburn (07041) *(G-6259)*

A
L
P
H
A
B
E
T
I
C

Takara Belmont Usa Inc (HQ)...732 469-5000
101 Belmont Dr Somerset (08873) **(G-10179)**
Takara Belmont Usa Inc...732 469-5000
101 Belmont Dr Somerset (08873) **(G-10180)**
TAKASAGO INTERNATIONAL CORPORATION (U.S.A.), Teterboro *Also called Takasago Intl Corp USA* **(G-10814)**
Takasago Intl Corp USA (HQ)...201 767-9001
4 Volvo Dr Rockleigh (07647) **(G-9634)**
Takasago Intl Corp USA...201 767-9001
267 Union St Northvale (07647) **(G-7609)**
Takasago Intl Corp USA...201 727-4200
100 Green St Teterboro (07608) **(G-10814)**
Talent Investment LLC...732 931-0088
12 Crown Plz Hazlet (07730) **(G-4284)**
Talent Technology Center, Hazlet *Also called Talent Investment LLC* **(G-4284)**
Talenti Gelato LLC (HQ)...800 298-4020
800 Sylvan Ave Englewood Cliffs (07632) **(G-2980)**
Tally Display Corp...973 777-7760
19 Gardner Rd Ste A Fairfield (07004) **(G-3320)**
Talon7 LLC...908 595-2121
991 Us Highway 22 Ste 200 Bridgewater (08807) **(G-901)**
Tam Metal Products Inc...201 848-7800
55 Whitney Rd Mahwah (07430) **(G-5818)**
Tamaras European American Deli...973 875-5461
13 Essex Rd Sussex (07461) **(G-10677)**
Tanda Sleep, Piscataway *Also called Catching Zzz LLC* **(G-8744)**
Tandem Color Imaging Graphics (PA)...973 513-9779
207 Wanaque Ave Pompton Lakes (07442) **(G-8949)**
Tandem Graphics, Pompton Lakes *Also called Tandem Color Imaging Graphics* **(G-8949)**
Tandem Technologies, Woodbridge *Also called Transportation Tech Svcs Inc* **(G-12155)**
Tangent Graphics Inc...201 488-2840
23 Chestnut St Englewood (07631) **(G-2936)**
Tangoe Us Inc (HQ)...973 257-0300
169 Lackawanna Ave Ste 2b Parsippany (07054) **(G-8096)**
Tanis Concrete...201 796-1556
17-68 River Rd Fair Lawn (07410) **(G-3119)**
Tanter Inc...732 382-3555
151 Westfield Ave Ste 3 Clark (07066) **(G-1516)**
Tanzola Printing Inc...973 779-0858
270 Colfax Ave Clifton (07013) **(G-1734)**
Tap For Message, South Plainfield *Also called Greetingtap* **(G-10375)**
Tap Into LLC...908 370-1158
66 W 4th St New Providence (07974) **(G-7056)**
Tap Pharmaceutical Products...908 470-9700
500 Hills Dr Ste 125 Bedminster (07921) **(G-285)**
Tape Graphics...201 393-9500
208 Boulevard Ste A Hasbrouck Heights (07604) **(G-4199)**
Tapes and Coatings, Middlesex *Also called Covalnce Spcialty Coatings LLC* **(G-6159)**
Tapestry Inc...856 488-2220
2000 Route 38 Ste 1720 Cherry Hill (08002) **(G-1426)**
Tapia Accessory Group Inc...201 393-0028
370 North St Ste 2 Teterboro (07608) **(G-10815)**
Tapintonet...908 279-0303
598 Central Ave Ste 7 New Providence (07974) **(G-7057)**
Taptask LLC...201 294-2371
83 Rolling Hills Rd Clifton (07013) **(G-1735)**
Taree Pharma LLC...609 252-9596
342 Herrontown Rd Princeton (08540) **(G-9129)**
Targa Industries Inc...973 584-3733
5 Laurel Dr Unit 13 Flanders (07836) **(G-3418)**
Targanta Therapeutics Corp (HQ)...973 290-6000
8 Sylvan Way Parsippany (07054) **(G-8097)**
Target Coatings Inc...800 752-9922
17-12 River Rd Fair Lawn (07410) **(G-3120)**
Targeted Healthcare, Plainsboro *Also called Intellisphere LLC* **(G-8892)**
Targum Publishing Company...732 247-1286
126 College Ave Ste 431 New Brunswick (08901) **(G-7006)**
Tarlton C & T Co Inc (PA)...908 964-9400
967 Lehigh Ave Union (07083) **(G-11227)**
Tarma Sales...732 969-3318
641 Roosevelt Ave Carteret (07008) **(G-1268)**
Taro Pharmaceuticals USA Inc...609 655-9002
1 Commerce Dr Cranbury (08512) **(G-1884)**
Taryag Legacy Foundation Inc...732 569-2467
1136 Somerset Ave Lakewood (08701) **(G-5193)**
Task International (usa) Inc...732 739-0377
3 Cass St Keyport (07735) **(G-5024)**
Taste It Presents Inc...908 241-9191
200 Sumner Ave Kenilworth (07033) **(G-4999)**
Taste Italy Manufacturing LLC...856 223-0707
1301 Bremen Ave Egg Harbor City (08215) **(G-2671)**
Tasty Bake Distributing Center, Egg Harbor Township *Also called Tasty Baking Company* **(G-2697)**
Tasty Baking Company...609 641-8588
203 Cates Rd Egg Harbor Township (08234) **(G-2697)**
Tasty Cake South Jersey...856 428-8414
1871 Old Cuthbert Rd B Cherry Hill (08034) **(G-1427)**
Tatara Group Inc...732 231-6031
381 Blair Rd Avenel (07001) **(G-155)**
Taunton Graphics Inc...856 719-8084
1049 Industrial Dr West Berlin (08091) **(G-11753)**
Taurus International Corp...201 825-2420
275 N Franklin Tpke Ste 3 Ramsey (07446) **(G-9252)**
Taurus Precision Inc...973 785-9254
129 Paterson Ave Little Falls (07424) **(G-5491)**
Taxstream LLC...201 610-0390
95 River St Ste 5c Hoboken (07030) **(G-4500)**
Taylor Communications Inc...732 560-3410
625 Pierce St Ste A Somerset (08873) **(G-10181)**
Taylor Communications Inc...732 561-8210
7 Costco Dr Monroe Township (08831) **(G-6397)**
Taylor Communications Inc...973 467-8259
899 Mountain Ave Ste 2f Springfield (07081) **(G-10579)**
Taylor Farms New Jersey Inc...856 241-0097
406 Heron Dr Ste A Swedesboro (08085) **(G-10732)**
Taylor Forge Stainless Inc...908 722-1313
22 Readington Rd Branchburg (08876) **(G-708)**
Taylor Made Cabinets Inc...609 978-6900
516 E Bay Ave Manahawkin (08050) **(G-5834)**
Taylor Made Custom Cabinetry...856 786-5433
7035 Central Hwy 200 Pennsauken (08109) **(G-8583)**
Taylor Products Inc...732 225-4620
255 Raritan Center Pkwy Edison (08837) **(G-2637)**
Taylor Window Factory, East Orange *Also called Taylor Windows Inc* **(G-2270)**
Taylor Windows Inc...973 672-3000
61 Central Ave East Orange (07018) **(G-2270)**
Tbb Inc (PA)...973 589-8875
115-129 Kossuth St Newark (07105) **(G-7337)**
Tbc Color Imaging Inc...973 470-8100
200 Entin Rd Clifton (07014) **(G-1736)**
Tbc Digital, Clifton *Also called Tbc Color Imaging Inc* **(G-1736)**
Tbl Licencing, Elizabeth *Also called Vf Outdoor LLC* **(G-2781)**
Tbl Performance Plastics, Sparta *Also called Thermoplastics Bio-Logics LLC* **(G-10524)**
Tbmc Inc...864 288-9916
340 Kaplan Dr Fairfield (07004) **(G-3321)**
Tbs Industrial Flooring Pdts...732 899-1486
300 New Jersey Ave Point Pleasant Beach (08742) **(G-8927)**
Tbt Group Inc...856 753-4500
191 Heller Pl Bellmawr (08031) **(G-353)**
Tcp Reliable Inc (PA)...848 229-2466
551 Raritan Center Pkwy Edison (08837) **(G-2638)**
Tcp/Reliable, Somerset *Also called T C P Reliable Manufacturing* **(G-10178)**
Tdk Associates Corp...862 210-8085
12 Eisenhower Pkwy Ste 9 Roseland (07068) **(G-9656)**
Te Connectivity Corporation...610 893-9800
250 Industrial Way W Eatontown (07724) **(G-2425)**
Te Subcom, Eatontown *Also called Tyco Elec Sbsea Cmmnctions LLC* **(G-2427)**
Te Wire & Cable LLC...201 845-9400
107 5th St Saddle Brook (07663) **(G-9796)**
Tea Elle Woodworks...732 938-9660
53 Main St Farmingdale (07727) **(G-3395)**
Team Nisca...732 271-7367
100 Randolph Rd Somerset (08873) **(G-10182)**
TEC, Irvington *Also called Engine Combo LLC* **(G-4584)**
TEC Cast Inc (PA)...201 935-3885
440 Meadow Ln Carlstadt (07072) **(G-1227)**
TEC Cast Inc...201 935-3885
2 W Commercial Ave Moonachie (07074) **(G-6549)**
TEC Elevator Inc...609 938-0647
510 Route Us 9 S Marmora (08223) **(G-6007)**
TEC Installations Inc...973 684-0503
375 E 22nd St Paterson (07514) **(G-8397)**
Tech Art Inc...201 525-0044
25 Green St Hackensack (07601) **(G-3983)**
Tech Brains Solutions Inc...732 952-0552
220 Davidson Ave Ste 303 Somerset (08873) **(G-10183)**
Tech Products Co Inc...201 444-7777
300 Greenwood Ave Midland Park (07432) **(G-6239)**
Tech-Ni Fold Usa Inc...973 383-6691
4 Wisteria Rd Lafayette (07848) **(G-5053)**
Tech-Pak Inc...201 935-3800
3 Ethel Blvd Wood Ridge (07075) **(G-12140)**
Techart, Hackensack *Also called Tech Art Inc* **(G-3983)**
Techenzyme Inc...732 632-8600
75 State Route 27 Ste 300 Iselin (08830) **(G-4648)**
Techflex Inc (HQ)...973 300-9242
104 Demarest Rd Ste 1 Sparta (07871) **(G-10522)**
Techline Extrusion Systems...973 831-0317
89 4th Ave Haskell (07420) **(G-4215)**
Technical Advantage Inc (PA)...973 402-5500
34 Farber Hill Rd Boonton (07005) **(G-585)**
Technical Aids To Independence...973 674-1082
219 S 18th St Unit 2 East Orange (07018) **(G-2271)**
Technical Coatings Co (HQ)...973 927-8600
360 Us Highway 206 Flanders (07836) **(G-3419)**
Technical Glass Products Inc...973 989-5500
243 E Blackwell St Dover (07801) **(G-2111)**

Technical Nameplate Corp 973 773-4256
92 1st St Passaic (07055) (G-8184)

Technical Oil Products Co Inc (PA) 973 940-8920
93 Spring St Ste 303 Newton (07860) (G-7408)

Technical Processing Inc 973 278-4950
81 Dale Ave Paterson (07501) (G-8398)

Technical Systems Group, Little Falls Also called Tsg Inc (G-5492)

Technick Products Inc 908 791-0400
238 Saint Nicholas Ave South Plainfield (07080) (G-10438)

Technidyne Corporation 732 363-1055
2190 Route 9 Ste 9 Toms River (08755) (G-10917)

Technimold Inc 908 232-8331
112 Pine Bank Rd Flemington (08822) (G-3470)

Technique Precision, Somerdale Also called Bisaga Inc (G-10039)

Techniques Inc 973 256-0947
14 Alexandria Ct Woodland Park (07424) (G-12234)

Technitool Inc 856 768-2707
1028 Industrial Dr West Berlin (08091) (G-11754)

Techno City Inc 862 414-3282
1 Meadowlands Plz Ste 200 East Rutherford (07073) (G-2330)

Techno Design Inc 973 478-0930
11 Erie St Ste 1 Garfield (07026) (G-3767)

Technobox Inc 856 809-2306
154 Cooper Rd Ste 901 West Berlin (08091) (G-11755)

Technodiamant USA Inc 908 850-8505
35a Kennedy Rd Tranquility (07879) (G-11008)

Technogym USA Corp (HQ) 800 804-0952
700 Us Highway 46 Fairfield (07004) (G-3322)

Technol Inc 856 848-5480
1030 Delsea Dr Unit 8e Westville (08093) (G-11949)

Technology Corp America Inc 866 462-8292
350 Mount Kemble Ave Morristown (07960) (G-6744)

Technology Dynamics Inc (PA) 201 385-0500
100 School St Ste 1 Bergenfield (07621) (G-396)

Technology Dynamics Inc 201 385-0500
100 School St Bergenfield (07621) (G-397)

Technology General Corporation (PA) 973 827-8209
12 Cork Hill Rd Franklin (07416) (G-3605)

Technology Reviews Inc 973 537-9511
14 Red Barn Ln Randolph (07869) (G-9301)

Technology Solutions Sector, Mount Laurel Also called Bae Systems Tech Sol Srvc Inc (G-6780)

Technovations, Randolph Also called Technology Reviews Inc (G-9301)

Technovision Inc 732 381-0200
10 Stuyvesant Ave Bsmt 7 Lyndhurst (07071) (G-5710)

Techtime Bus Sltons Ltd Lblty 973 246-8153
1 Madison St Ste B4 East Rutherford (07073) (G-2331)

Techsetters Inc 856 240-7905
900 Haddon Ave Ste 300 Collingswood (08108) (G-1774)

Teckchek (PA) 919 497-0136
77 Milltown Rd Ste C4 East Brunswick (08816) (G-2193)

Tecnicam, Livingston Also called Campak Inc (G-5526)

Tecogen Inc 732 356-5601
417 Bell St Piscataway (08854) (G-8821)

Tectubes USA Inc 856 589-1250
1299 W Forest Grove Rd Vineland (08360) (G-11408)

Ted-Steel Indstries, Linden Also called Ted-Steel Industries Ltd (G-5452)

Ted-Steel Industries Ltd 212 279-3878
101 Roselle St Linden (07036) (G-5452)

Tedco Inc 609 883-0799
35 Scotch Rd Ewing (08628) (G-3060)

Tee-Rific Golf Center 908 253-9300
3091 Us Highway 22 Branchburg (08876) (G-709)

Teefx Screen Printing LLC 973 942-6800
250 Belmont Ave Haledon (07508) (G-4086)

Teg New Jersey Inc 973 776-8660
2 Penn Plz E 12 Newark (07105) (G-7338)

Teixeira's Bakery, Newark Also called Tbb Inc (G-7337)

Tek Molding 973 702-0450
1440 County Rd 565 Sussex (07461) (G-10678)

Tek-Pak Div, Rochelle Park Also called Rempac LLC (G-9536)

Tekkote Corporation 201 585-1708
580 Willow Tree Rd Leonia (07605) (G-5321)

Tekltd (PA) 732 463-2100
95 Mitchell Ave Piscataway (08854) (G-8822)

Tekni-Plex Inc 908 575-7661
201 Industrial Pkwy Branchburg (08876) (G-710)

Tekni-Plex Inc 908 782-4000
112 Church St Flemington (08822) (G-3471)

Teknics Industries Inc 973 633-7575
170 Beaverbrook Rd Ste 1 Lincoln Park (07035) (G-5333)

Teknics Sales, Lincoln Park Also called Teknics Industries Inc (G-5333)

Tekno Inc 973 423-2004
86 5th Ave Hawthorne (07506) (G-4260)

Tektite Industries Inc 609 656-0600
309 N Clinton Ave Trenton (08638) (G-11120)

Tektite Mfg Division, Trenton Also called Tektite Industries Inc (G-11120)

Tel-Instrument Elec Corp (PA) 201 933-1600
1 Branca Rd East Rutherford (07073) (G-2332)

Telcontel Corp 732 441-0800
11 Industrial Dr Laurence Harbor (08879) (G-5235)

Telecom Assistance Group Inc 856 753-8585
150 Cooper Rd Ste F15 West Berlin (08091) (G-11756)

Teledynamics LLC 973 248-3360
45 Indian Ln E Ste 1 Towaco (07082) (G-11004)

Teleflex Incorporated 856 349-7234
860 Charles St Gloucester City (08030) (G-3846)

Telegenix Inc 609 265-3910
71 Indel Ave Rancocas (08073) (G-9264)

Telemark Cnc LLC 973 794-4857
429 Rockaway Valley Rd Boonton (07005) (G-586)

Telemetrics Inc 201 848-9818
75 Commerce Dr Allendale (07401) (G-21)

Telescript Inc (PA) 201 767-6733
445 Livingston St Norwood (07648) (G-7636)

Teligent Inc (PA) 856 697-1441
105 Lincoln Ave Buena (08310) (G-949)

Teligent Inc 856 697-1441
711 S Harding Hwy Buena (08310) (G-950)

Tellas Ltd 201 399-8888
600 Sylvan Ave Ste 4 Englewood Cliffs (07632) (G-2981)

Teluca Inc 973 232-0002
414 Eagle Rock Ave West Orange (07052) (G-11906)

Telvue Corporation (PA) 800 885-8886
16000 Horizon Way Ste 100 Mount Laurel (08054) (G-6844)

Templar Food Products, New Providence Also called Reeves Enterprises Inc (G-7052)

Temptime Corporation (HQ) 973 984-6000
116 The American Rd Morris Plains (07950) (G-6680)

Temptrol Corp 856 461-7977
242 Terrace Blvd Ste E Voorhees (08043) (G-11439)

Ten One Design Ltd Lblty Co 201 474-8232
149 Chestnut St Montclair (07042) (G-6437)

Tenax Finishing Products Co 973 589-9000
390 Adams St Newark (07114) (G-7339)

Teneyck Inc 201 939-1100
700 Schuyler Ave Lyndhurst (07071) (G-5711)

Teo Fabrications Inc 973 764-5500
95 Maple Grange Rd Vernon (07462) (G-11302)

Terco Construction LLC 973 551-7759
71 Newton Sparta Rd Newton (07860) (G-7409)

Terhune Bros Woodworking 973 962-6686
58 Bearfort Ter Ringwood (07456) (G-9457)

Terminal Printing Co 201 659-5924
85 Washington Ave Belleville (07109) (G-319)

Terra Chips, Moonachie Also called Hain Celestial Group Inc (G-6520)

Terra Designs Inc (PA) 973 328-1135
241 E Blackwell St Rear Dover (07801) (G-2112)

Terrestrial Imaging LLC 800 359-0530
375 Herbertsville Rd Brick (08724) (G-760)

Terrignos Bakery 856 451-6368
632 N Pearl St Bridgeton (08302) (G-799)

Terriss Consolidated Inds 732 988-0909
807 Summerfield Ave Asbury Park (07712) (G-86)

Terumo Americas Holding Inc (HQ) 732 302-4900
2101 Cottontail Ln Somerset (08873) (G-10184)

Terumo Medical Corporation (HQ) 732 302-4900
2101 Cottontail Ln Somerset (08873) (G-10185)

Tesa Rentals LLC 973 300-0913
286 Houses Corner Rd Sparta (07871) (G-10523)

Tesla Inc 201 225-2544
530 N Rte 17 Paramus (07652) (G-7910)

Tesla Motors, Paramus Also called Tesla Inc (G-7910)

Tess-Com Inc (PA) 412 233-5782
400 South Ave Ste 11 Middlesex (08846) (G-6205)

Tessler & Weiss/Premesco Inc 800 535-3501
2389 Vauxhall Rd Union (07083) (G-11228)

Test Technology Inc (HQ) 856 596-1215
5 E Stow Rd Marlton (08053) (G-6001)

Testrite Instrument Co Inc 201 543-0240
216 S Newman St Hackensack (07601) (G-3984)

Testrite Visual Products, Hackensack Also called Testrite Instrument Co Inc (G-3984)

Tetley USA Inc (HQ) 800 728-0084
890 Mountain Ave Ste 105 New Providence (07974) (G-7058)

Tetra Lubricants, Florham Park Also called Fti Inc (G-3503)

Teva Api Inc 201 307-6900
400 Interpace Pkwy Ste A1 Parsippany (07054) (G-8098)

Teva Pharmaceuticals 888 838-2872
400 Interpace Pkwy Ste A1 Parsippany (07054) (G-8099)

Teva Pharmaceuticals Usa Inc 845 362-1100
400 Interpace Pkwy Ste A1 Parsippany (07054) (G-8100)

Teva Pharmaceuticals Usa Inc 973 575-2775
8 Gloria Ln Ste 10 Fairfield (07004) (G-3323)

Teva Womens Health Inc 201 930-3300
400 Campus Dr Somerset (08873) (G-10186)

Tevco Enterprises Inc 908 754-7306
110 Pomponio Ave South Plainfield (07080) (G-10439)

Tex Gul Inc 973 857-3200
874 Pompton Ave Ste A2 Cedar Grove (07009) (G-1301)

Tex Print USA LLC.....201 773-6531
20-21 Wagaraw Rd 31a-1 Fair Lawn (07410) ***(G-3121)***
Tex Spar Co Inc.....732 367-9439
155 Oberlin Ave N Lakewood (08701) ***(G-5194)***
Tex-Net Inc.....609 499-9111
763 Railroad Ave B Florence (08518) ***(G-3481)***
Texas Canvas Co Inc (PA).....973 278-3802
1275 Bloomfield Ave 54b Fairfield (07004) ***(G-3324)***
Textol Systems Inc.....800 624-8746
735 Commercial Ave Carlstadt (07072) ***(G-1228)***
Textron Inc.....201 945-1500
143 River Rd Edgewater (07020) ***(G-2442)***
Texx Team LLC.....201 289-1039
589 Hillsdale Ave Hillsdale (07642) ***(G-4387)***
Tf Yachts LLC.....609 965-2300
801 Philadelphia Ave Egg Harbor City (08215) ***(G-2672)***
TFH Publications Inc.....732 897-6860
85 W Sylvania Ave Neptune (07753) ***(G-6934)***
TFH Publications Inc.....732 988-8400
211 W Sylvania Ave Neptune (07753) ***(G-6935)***
Tfi OEM Commercial Group, Lakewood *Also called Masco Cabinetry LLC* ***(G-5154)***
Tgm, Hammonton *Also called T G Manufacturing Inc* ***(G-4150)***
Tgz Acquisition Company LLC.....856 669-6600
5 Rockhill Rd Ste 2 Cherry Hill (08003) ***(G-1428)***
Thal Precision Industries Inc.....732 381-6106
19a Walnut Ave Clark (07066) ***(G-1517)***
Thales Avionics Inc (HQ).....732 242-6300
140 Centennial Ave Piscataway (08854) ***(G-8823)***
Thanks For Being Green LLC.....856 333-0991
5070b Central Hwy Pennsauken (08109) ***(G-8584)***
That 10 Minute Oil Change Pl.....201 587-0220
257 Rochelle Ave Rochelle Park (07662) ***(G-9538)***
The Aquarian Weekly, Little Falls *Also called Arts Weekly Inc* ***(G-5470)***
The Creative Print Group Inc.....856 486-1700
7905 Browning Rd Ste 112 Pennsauken (08109) ***(G-8585)***
The Door Center Publishing, Hopewell *Also called Door Center Enterprises Inc* ***(G-4541)***
The Vine, Princeton *Also called Venture Info Network* ***(G-9136)***
The Westfield Leader, Westfield *Also called Watthung Communications Inc* ***(G-11933)***
Thebgb Inc (PA).....917 749-5309
840 E 28th St Paterson (07513) ***(G-8399)***
Themac, East Rutherford *Also called McGonegal Manufacturing Co* ***(G-2309)***
Theodore E Mozer Inc.....856 829-1432
14 E 4th St Palmyra (08065) ***(G-7851)***
Theory Development Corp.....201 783-8770
31 Industrial Ave Ste 1 Mahwah (07430) ***(G-5819)***
Thepositive Press.....856 266-8765
2020 Bannard St Cinnaminson (08077) ***(G-1492)***
Ther-A-Pedic Sleep Products (PA).....732 628-0800
1375 Jersey Ave North Brunswick (08902) ***(G-7542)***
Therapeutic Proteins Inc.....312 620-1500
20 New England Ave Piscataway (08854) ***(G-8824)***
Therma-Tech Corporation.....973 345-0076
300 Dakota St Ste 1 Paterson (07503) ***(G-8400)***
Thermal Chek Inc.....856 742-1200
912 Broadway Westville (08093) ***(G-11950)***
Thermal Conduction Engineering.....201 865-1084
865 Roosevelt Ave Secaucus (07094) ***(G-9934)***
Thermal Transfer Corp.....412 460-4004
58 E Main St Somerville (08876) ***(G-10228)***
Thermo Cote Inc.....973 464-3575
198 Green Pond Rd Ste 5 Rockaway (07866) ***(G-9612)***
Thermo Fisher Scientific Inc.....609 239-3185
19 London Rd Burlington (08016) ***(G-991)***
Thermo Fisher Scientific Inc.....732 627-0220
265 Davidson Ave Ste 101 Somerset (08873) ***(G-10187)***
Thermo Plastic Tech Inc.....908 687-4833
1119 Morris Ave Union (07083) ***(G-11229)***
Thermo Systems LLC.....609 371-3300
84 Twin Rivers Dr East Windsor (08520) ***(G-2368)***
Thermo X-Press Printing LLC.....973 585-6505
12d Great Meadow Ln East Hanover (07936) ***(G-2245)***
Thermo-Graphics Inc.....908 486-0100
386 Avenel St Avenel (07001) ***(G-156)***
Thermoplastic Processes, Stirling *Also called Tpi Partners Inc* ***(G-10608)***
Thermoplastics Bio-Logics LLC.....973 383-2834
18 White Lake Rd Sparta (07871) ***(G-10524)***
Thermoseal Industries LLC.....856 456-3109
600 Jersey Ave Gloucester City (08030) ***(G-3847)***
Thermwell Products Co Inc (PA).....201 684-4400
420 State Rt 17 Mahwah (07430) ***(G-5820)***
Thermwell Products Co Inc.....201 684-4400
420 State Rt 17 Mahwah (07430) ***(G-5821)***
Thewal Inc.....973 635-1880
12 Center St Chatham (07928) ***(G-1338)***
Thibaut & Walker Co Inc.....973 589-3331
49 Rutherford St Newark (07105) ***(G-7340)***
Thiladel Phia, Moorestown *Also called CR Laurence Co Inc* ***(G-6570)***
Thin Stone Systems LLC.....973 882-7377
23 Commerce Rd Ste O Fairfield (07004) ***(G-3325)***
Thind Fuel Service LLC.....732 613-1808
178 Hillside Ave South River (08882) ***(G-10468)***
Thinfilms Inc.....908 359-7014
15 Ilene Ct Ste 6 Hillsborough (08844) ***(G-4376)***
Things 2 B, Elmer *Also called Perfect Shapes Inc* ***(G-2795)***
Think Tin, Parsippany *Also called Allstate Can Corporation* ***(G-7944)***
Third Ave Chocolate Shoppe.....732 449-7535
1118 3rd Ave Spring Lake (07762) ***(G-10535)***
Third River Manufacturing LLC.....201 935-2795
503 Washington Ave Carlstadt (07072) ***(G-1229)***
Thirty-Three Queen Realty Inc (PA).....973 824-5527
1 Flexon Plz Newark (07114) ***(G-7341)***
Thoma Inc (PA).....856 608-6887
1640 Nixon Dr 323 Moorestown (08057) ***(G-6628)***
Thomas & Betts Corporation.....908 852-1122
1 Esna Park Hackettstown (07840) ***(G-4040)***
Thomas A Caserta Inc.....609 586-2807
11 S Gold Dr Ste E Robbinsville (08691) ***(G-9522)***
Thomas Clark Fiberglass LLC.....609 492-9257
145 Old Halfway Rd Barnegat (08005) ***(G-167)***
Thomas Cobb & Sons.....856 451-0671
146 Cobbs Mill Rd Bridgeton (08302) ***(G-800)***
Thomas Erectors Inc.....908 810-0030
630 Ramsey Ave Hillside (07205) ***(G-4444)***
Thomas Greco Publishing Inc (PA).....973 667-6965
244 Chestnut St Ste 4 Nutley (07110) ***(G-7654)***
Thomas H Cox & Son Inc.....908 928-1010
1634 E Elizabeth Ave Linden (07036) ***(G-5453)***
Thomas Instrumentation Inc.....609 624-7777
118 Kings Hwy Cape May Court House (08210) ***(G-1117)***
Thomas Instrumentation Inc (PA).....609 624-2630
133 Landing Rd Cape May Court House (08210) ***(G-1118)***
Thomas Manufacturing Inc.....908 810-0030
630 Ramsey Ave Ste 1 Hillside (07205) ***(G-4445)***
Thomas Publishing Company LLC.....973 543-4994
95 W Main St Ste 8 Chester (07930) ***(G-1440)***
Thomas Register, Chester *Also called Thomas Publishing Company LLC* ***(G-1440)***
Thomas Russo & Sons Inc.....201 332-4159
854 Communipaw Ave Jersey City (07304) ***(G-4837)***
Thomas Scientific, Swedesboro *Also called Arthur H Thomas Company* ***(G-10682)***
Thomas Scientific Inc.....800 345-2100
1654 High Hill Rd Swedesboro (08085) ***(G-10733)***
Thomas Scientific LLC (HQ).....800 345-2100
1654 High Hill Rd Swedesboro (08085) ***(G-10734)***
Thomas Smock Woodworking.....732 542-9167
306 Broad St Eatontown (07724) ***(G-2426)***
Thompson Stone.....973 293-7237
3 Myrtle Dr Montague (07827) ***(G-6403)***
Thomsom Health Care Inc.....201 358-7300
5 Paragon Dr Montvale (07645) ***(G-6481)***
Thomson Financial, Newark *Also called Thomson Reuters (markets) LLC* ***(G-7342)***
Thomson Lamination Co Inc.....856 779-8521
504 E Linwood Ave Maple Shade (08052) ***(G-5912)***
Thomson Reuters (markets) LLC.....973 286-7200
2 Gateway Ctr Fl 11 Newark (07102) ***(G-7342)***
Thomson Reuters Corporation.....973 662-3070
492 River Rd Nutley (07110) ***(G-7655)***
Thomson Reuters Corporation.....212 337-4281
2 Gateway Ctr Fl 11 Newark (07102) ***(G-7343)***
Thorlabs Inc (PA).....973 579-7227
56 Sparta Ave Newton (07860) ***(G-7410)***
Thortel Fireproof Fabrics Inc.....732 938-4114
5025 Industrial Rd Wall Township (07727) ***(G-11514)***
Thrombogenics Inc.....732 590-2900
101 Wood Ave S Ste 610 Iselin (08830) ***(G-4649)***
Thumann Incorporated (PA).....201 935-3636
670 Dell Rd Ste 1 Carlstadt (07072) ***(G-1230)***
THUMANNS, Carlstadt *Also called Thumann Incorporated* ***(G-1230)***
Thwing-Albert Instrument Co.....856 767-1000
14 W Collings Ave West Berlin (08091) ***(G-11757)***
Tiburon Lockers Inc.....201 750-4960
22 Paris Ave Ste 106 Rockleigh (07647) ***(G-9635)***
Tic, East Rutherford *Also called Tel-Instrument Elec Corp* ***(G-2332)***
Tifa International LLC.....908 647-4570
109 Stryker Ln Ste 4 Hillsborough (08844) ***(G-4377)***
Tifa Worldwide, Hillsborough *Also called Tifa International LLC* ***(G-4377)***
Tifab, Fairfield *Also called Titanium Fabrication Corp* ***(G-3327)***
Tiffanees Toys Inc.....732 828-6333
601 Nassau St Ste 593 North Brunswick (08902) ***(G-7543)***
Tiffany Packaging.....973 726-8130
270 Sparta Ave Sparta (07871) ***(G-10525)***
Tiger Supplies Inc.....973 854-8635
27 Selvage St Irvington (07111) ***(G-4606)***
Tilcon New York Inc (HQ).....800 789-7625
9 Entin Rd Parsippany (07054) ***(G-8101)***
Tilcon New York Inc.....973 835-0028
125 Hamburg Tpke Riverdale (07457) ***(G-9490)***
Tilcon New York Inc.....800 789-7625
2414 95th St North Bergen (07047) ***(G-7489)***

Tilcon New York Inc....800 789-7625
Foot Of Broad St Pompton Lakes (07442) ***(G-8950)***
Tilcon New York Inc....800 789-7625
411 Bergen Ave Kearny (07032) ***(G-4917)***
Tilcon New York Inc....800 789-7625
9 Entin Rd Ste 12 Parsippany (07054) ***(G-8102)***
Tilcon New York Inc....800 789-7625
Mount Pisgah Ave Oxford (07863) ***(G-7833)***
Tilcon New York Inc....973 347-2405
11 Lackawanna Dr Stanhope (07874) ***(G-10590)***
Tilton Rack & Basket Co....973 226-6010
66 Passaic Ave Fairfield (07004) ***(G-3326)***
Time Log Industries Inc....609 965-5017
312 N Leipzig Ave Egg Harbor City (08215) ***(G-2673)***
Time Systems International Co....201 871-1200
142 S Van Brunt St Englewood (07631) ***(G-2937)***
Timeline Promotions Inc....973 226-1512
19 Aldrin Dr West Caldwell (07006) ***(G-11806)***
Times of Trenton Pubg Corp....609 989-5454
413 River View Plz Trenton (08611) ***(G-11121)***
Times The Villadom Inc....201 652-0744
333 Godwin Ave Midland Park (07432) ***(G-6240)***
Times Tin Cup....973 983-1095
35 Rainbow Trl Mountain Lakes (07046) ***(G-6862)***
Timothy P Bryan Elc Co Inc....609 393-8325
1926 Chestnut Ave Trenton (08611) ***(G-11122)***
Timplex Corp....973 875-5500
1370 State Rt 23 Sussex (07461) ***(G-10679)***
Tin Can Lids LLC....201 503-0677
48 Lylewood Dr Tenafly (07670) ***(G-10787)***
Tin Man Snacks LLC....732 329-9100
351 Herrod Blvd Dayton (08810) ***(G-1991)***
Tin Panda Inc....973 916-0707
875 Bloomfield Ave Clifton (07012) ***(G-1737)***
Tin Sigh Stop....973 691-2712
5 Meteor Trl Byram Township (07821) ***(G-1023)***
Tingley Rubber Corporation (PA)....800 631-5498
1551 S Washington Ave # 403 Piscataway (08854) ***(G-8825)***
Tinton Falls Systems, Tinton Falls *Also called Commvault Americas Inc* ***(G-10827)***
Tipico Products Co Inc....732 942-8820
490 Oberlin Ave S Lakewood (08701) ***(G-5195)***
Tire Place LLC (PA)....732 970-6667
408 State Route 35 Keyport (07735) ***(G-5025)***
Titan, Clifton *Also called Chicago Pneumatic Tool* ***(G-1583)***
Titan America LLC....973 690-5896
178 Marsh St Newark (07114) ***(G-7344)***
Titan Trading Co, Wyckoff *Also called Straps Manufacturing NJ Inc* ***(G-12264)***
Titanium Fabrication Corp (PA)....973 227-5300
110 Lehigh Dr Fairfield (07004) ***(G-3327)***
Titanium Industries Inc (PA)....973 983-1185
18 Green Pond Rd Ste 1 Rockaway (07866) ***(G-9613)***
Titanium Industries Inc....973 428-1900
64 State Route 10 East Hanover (07936) ***(G-2246)***
Titanium Smoking Kings LLC....908 339-8876
509 March Blvd Phillipsburg (08865) ***(G-8673)***
Titanium Technical Services....908 323-9899
21 New York Ave Flemington (08822) ***(G-3472)***
Tjk Machine LLC....856 691-7811
870 E Elmer Rd Vineland (08360) ***(G-11409)***
Tjs Ice Cream....609 398-5055
100 E Atlantic Blvd Ocean City (08226) ***(G-7759)***
Tkg Components LLC....609 730-1501
55 Route 31 S Pennington (08534) ***(G-8460)***
Tkl Specialty Piping Inc....908 454-0030
175 Broad St Phillipsburg (08865) ***(G-8674)***
Tko Visual Communications....610 770-7700
108-136 Martin Luther Newark (07104) ***(G-7345)***
TLC Signs & Banners, Toms River *Also called T L C Specialties Inc* ***(G-10916)***
Tlg Signs Inc....609 912-0500
2901 Us Highway 1 Ste 3 Lawrenceville (08648) ***(G-5270)***
Tlw Bath Ltd Liability Company....732 942-7117
1144 E Cnty Ln Rd Lakewood (08701) ***(G-5196)***
TMC Corporation....609 860-1830
335 High St Bldg B1 Metuchen (08840) ***(G-6128)***
Tmg Enterprises Inc (PA)....732 469-2900
200 Circle Dr N Piscataway (08854) ***(G-8826)***
Tms International LLC....732 721-7477
1 Crossman Rd N Sayreville (08872) ***(G-9841)***
TMU Inc....609 884-7656
910 Shunpike Rd Ste A Cape May (08204) ***(G-1106)***
Tnss Enterprises, Bloomfield *Also called Ultimate Hair World Ltd Lblty* ***(G-535)***
Toadhall Promotions, Manasquan *Also called Winemiller Press Inc* ***(G-5884)***
Toby-Yanni Incorporated....973 253-9800
62 Plauderville Ave Garfield (07026) ***(G-3768)***
Tocad America Inc (HQ)....973 627-9600
53 Green Pond Rd Ste 4 Rockaway (07866) ***(G-9614)***
Todd Shelton LLC....844 626-6355
450 Murray Hill Pkwy C2 East Rutherford (07073) ***(G-2333)***
Tofutti Brands Inc....908 272-2400
50 Jackson Dr Cranford (07016) ***(G-1928)***

Toilettree Products Inc....845 358-5316
41 Orchard St Ste 1 Ramsey (07446) ***(G-9253)***
Token Torch Ltd Liability Co....973 629-1805
3 Hudson Ave East Orange (07018) ***(G-2272)***
Tolan Machinery Company Inc....973 983-7212
164 Franklin Ave Rockaway (07866) ***(G-9615)***
Tolan Machinery Polishing Co....973 983-7212
164 Franklin Ave Rockaway (07866) ***(G-9616)***
Tolan Polishing Corp....973 983-7212
164 Franklin Ave Rockaway (07866) ***(G-9617)***
Tolin Design Inc....201 261-4455
16 Bland St Emerson (07630) ***(G-2863)***
Toll Compaction Group, Neptune *Also called Toll Compaction Service Inc* ***(G-6936)***
Toll Compaction Service Inc (PA)....732 776-8225
14 Memorial Dr Neptune (07753) ***(G-6936)***
Tollgrade Communications Inc....732 743-6720
30 Knightsbridge Rd # 602 Piscataway (08854) ***(G-8827)***
Toltec Products LLC....908 832-2131
68 Beavers Rd Califon (07830) ***(G-1037)***
Tom James Company....732 826-8400
581 Cortlandt St Perth Amboy (08861) ***(G-8633)***
Tom James of Perth Amboy 2, Perth Amboy *Also called Tom James Company* ***(G-8633)***
Tom Ponte Model Makers Inc....973 627-5906
25 Pine St Ste 2 Rockaway (07866) ***(G-9618)***
Tomasello Winery Inc (PA)....609 561-0567
225 N White Horse Pike Hammonton (08037) ***(G-4151)***
Tomcel Machine Inc....973 256-8257
86 Lackawanna Ave Ste 301 Woodland Park (07424) ***(G-12235)***
Tomken Plating....856 829-0607
625 Pear St Cinnaminson (08077) ***(G-1493)***
Tommax Inc....732 224-1046
65 Mechanic St Ste 205 Red Bank (07701) ***(G-9347)***
Tommys Pallet Yard LLC....609 424-3996
2499 Old York Rd Bordentown (08505) ***(G-612)***
Toms River Printing Corp....732 240-2033
11 S Tamarack Dr Brielle (08730) ***(G-915)***
Tomwar Corp....856 740-0111
413 Paradise Rd Williamstown (08094) ***(G-12109)***
Tone Embroidery Corp....201 943-1082
333 Bergen Blvd Fairview (07022) ***(G-3371)***
Tone Kraft Inc....856 283-8043
727 S Randolph Ave Cinnaminson (08077) ***(G-1494)***
Tone Layout LLC....201 438-1746
1015 Hudson Ave Ridgefield (07657) ***(G-9386)***
Toni Embroidery....201 664-6909
475 Broadway Westwood (07675) ***(G-11973)***
Tony Jones Apparel Inc....973 773-6200
300-1 State Rt 17 S 1c Lodi (07644) ***(G-5606)***
Tonymacx86 LLC....973 584-5273
23 Lookout Dr Ledgewood (07852) ***(G-5312)***
Tonys Auto Entp Ltd Lblty Co....203 223-5776
98 Loring Ave Edison (08817) ***(G-2639)***
Too Cool of Ocean City....908 810-6363
530 N Michigan Ave Kenilworth (07033) ***(G-5000)***
Tool Shop Inc....856 767-8077
335 Chestnut Ave West Berlin (08091) ***(G-11758)***
Tooling & Mfg Unlimited, Cape May *Also called TMU Inc* ***(G-1106)***
Tooling Etc LLC....732 752-8080
250 Hallock Ave Middlesex (08846) ***(G-6206)***
Top Knobs Usa Inc (HQ)....908 359-6174
3 Millennium Way Somerville (08876) ***(G-10229)***
Top Line Seating Inc....908 241-9051
540 S 31st St Kenilworth (07033) ***(G-5001)***
Top Rated Shopping Bargains....201 630-0770
92 Railroad Ave Hasbrouck Heights (07604) ***(G-4200)***
Top Safety Products Company....908 707-8680
160 Meister Ave Ste 16 Branchburg (08876) ***(G-711)***
Topaz Skin Care Inc....201 489-0686
1530 Palisade Ave Ste 1 Fort Lee (07024) ***(G-3585)***
Topcon America Corporation (HQ)....201 599-5100
111 Bauer Dr Oakland (07436) ***(G-7706)***
Topcon Medical Systems Inc (HQ)....201 599-5100
111 Bauer Dr Oakland (07436) ***(G-7707)***
Topifram Laboratories Inc....201 894-9020
440 Sylvan Ave Ste 100 Englewood Cliffs (07632) ***(G-2982)***
Toppan Printing Co Amer Inc....732 469-8400
1100 Randolph Rd Somerset (08873) ***(G-10188)***
Toppan Vintage Inc....201 226-9220
109 5th St Saddle Brook (07663) ***(G-9797)***
Torelco Inc....908 387-0814
55 Industrial Rd Alpha (08865) ***(G-47)***
Tornqvist Div, Wayne *Also called Grimbilas Enterprises Corp* ***(G-11644)***
Torpac Capsules, Fairfield *Also called Torpac Inc* ***(G-3328)***
Torpac Inc....973 244-1125
333 Us Highway 46 Fairfield (07004) ***(G-3328)***
Torque Gun Co, The, South Hackensack *Also called Torque Gun Company LLC* ***(G-10298)***
Torque Gun Company LLC....201 512-9800
120 Wesley St South Hackensack (07606) ***(G-10298)***
Torrent Pharma Inc (HQ)....269 544-2299
150 Allen Rd Ste 102 Basking Ridge (07920) ***(G-207)***

ALPHABETIC

(PA)=Parent Co (HQ)=Headquarters (DH)=Div Headquarters

Tosca 973 337-5724
15 Church St Montclair (07042) *(G-6438)*

Toscana Cheese Company Inc 201 617-1500
575 Windsor Dr Secaucus (07094) *(G-9935)*

Toshiba Amer Consmr Pdts Inc 973 628-8000
82 Totowa Rd Wayne (07470) *(G-11685)*

Total American Services Inc (PA) 206 626-3500
100 Town Square Pl # 401 Jersey City (07310) *(G-4838)*

Total Control Othotics Lab 609 499-2200
14 W Front St Florence (08518) *(G-3482)*

Total Cover It LLC 973 342-4623
223 Waverly Pl South Orange (07079) *(G-10316)*

Total Garage Solutions LLC 732 749-3993
1709 State Route 34 Ste 2 Wall Township (07727) *(G-11515)*

Total Image and Sign 201 941-2307
719 Grand Ave Ste 1 Ridgefield (07657) *(G-9387)*

Total Ink Solutions LLC 201 487-9600
200 S Newman St Unit 4 Hackensack (07601) *(G-3985)*

Total Installations 908 943-3211
941 Olive St Elizabeth (07201) *(G-2779)*

Total Logistics, Hainesport *Also called T Wiker Enterprises Inc (G-4079)*

Total Lubricants USA, Linden *Also called Total Specialties Usa Inc (G-5454)*

Total Reliance LLC 732 640-5079
11b Corn Rd Dayton (08810) *(G-1992)*

Total Relief Services, Livingston *Also called Max Pro Services LLC (G-5542)*

Total Remodeling, Elizabeth *Also called Total Installations (G-2779)*

Total Specialties Usa Inc 908 862-9300
5 N Stiles St Linden (07036) *(G-5454)*

Total Tech Medical LLC 973 980-6458
289 Munt Hope Ave Apt J14 Dover (07801) *(G-2113)*

Total Technology Inc 856 617-0502
950 Kings Hwy N Ste 105 Cherry Hill (08034) *(G-1429)*

Totalcat Group Inc (HQ) 908 497-9610
186 North Ave E Cranford (07016) *(G-1929)*

Totally T Shirts & More Inc 609 894-0011
201 W Hampton St Pemberton (08068) *(G-8443)*

Totowa Asphalt, Parsippany *Also called Tilcon New York Inc (G-8101)*

Totowa Kickboxing Ltd Lblty Co 973 507-9106
1 Us Highway 46 Totowa (07512) *(G-10975)*

Totowa Metal Fabricators Inc 973 423-1943
40 Lee Dr North Haledon (07508) *(G-7555)*

Totowa Precision Tooling Inc 973 256-2283
442 Riverview Dr Totowa (07512) *(G-10976)*

Touch Dynamic Inc (PA) 732 382-5701
121 Corporate Blvd South Plainfield (07080) *(G-10440)*

Touch of Class Promotions LLC 267 994-0860
19 Festival Dr Voorhees (08043) *(G-11440)*

Touch of Lace, Fairview *Also called Tone Embroidery Corp (G-3371)*

Toufayan Bakeries, Ridgefield *Also called Toufayan Bakery Inc (G-9388)*

Toufayan Bakery Inc (PA) 201 861-4131
175 Railroad Ave Ridgefield (07657) *(G-9388)*

Tovatech LLC 973 913-9734
205 Rutgers St Maplewood (07040) *(G-5928)*

Tovli Inc 718 417-6677
49 Hunter St Newark (07114) *(G-7346)*

Toweltails, Hackensack *Also called Sensible Collection Inc (G-3972)*

Tower Systems Inc 732 237-8800
235 Hickory Ln Bayville (08721) *(G-260)*

Town & Country Plastics Inc 732 780-5300
10b Timber Ln Marlboro (07746) *(G-5961)*

Town Ford Inc 609 298-4990
860 Us Highway 206 Bordentown (08505) *(G-613)*

Town of Hackettstown, The, Hackettstown *Also called Hackettstown Public Works (G-4010)*

Towne Technologies Inc 908 722-9500
6-10 Bell Ave Somerville (08876) *(G-10230)*

Townsend Machine Inc 609 723-2603
246 Sykesville Rd Chesterfield (08515) *(G-1443)*

Township of Carneys Point 856 299-4973
Walker Ave & D St Carneys Point (08069) *(G-1247)*

Toydriver LLC 678 637-8500
100 Outwater Ln Garfield (07026) *(G-3769)*

Toyo Ink America LLC 201 804-0620
350 Starke Rd Ste 400 Carlstadt (07072) *(G-1231)*

Toyota Motor Sales 973 515-5012
300 Webro Rd Parsippany (07054) *(G-8103)*

Toys "R" Us, Wayne *Also called Toysruscom Inc (G-11686)*

Toysruscom Inc 973 617-3500
1 Geoffrey Way Wayne (07470) *(G-11686)*

Tpg Graphics LLC 856 314-0117
9130 Pennsauken Hwy Ste C Pennsauken (08110) *(G-8586)*

Tpi Partners Inc 908 561-3000
1268 Valley Rd Stirling (07980) *(G-10608)*

Tq3 north America Inc (PA) 973 882-7900
23 Commerce Rd Ste I Fairfield (07004) *(G-3329)*

Trac Intermodal LLC (HQ) 609 452-8900
750 College Rd E Princeton (08540) *(G-9130)*

Trac Interstar LLC (HQ) 609 452-8900
750 College Rd E Princeton (08540) *(G-9131)*

Tracer Tool & Machine Co Inc (PA) 201 337-6184
32 Iron Horse Rd Oakland (07436) *(G-7708)*

Track Systems Inc 201 462-0095
174 Boulevard Ste 6 Hasbrouck Heights (07604) *(G-4201)*

Trade Images, Buena *Also called CPB Inc (G-946)*

Trade Thermographers Inc 201 489-2060
82 Chestnut Ave Rochelle Park (07662) *(G-9539)*

Trademark Plastics Corporation 908 925-5900
494 Broad St Rm 202 Newark (07102) *(G-7347)*

Trademarksign 848 223-4548
631 Herman Rd Jackson (08527) *(G-4680)*

Tradewinds Marine Service 848 448-6888
122 Eton Ct Toms River (08757) *(G-10918)*

Traffic Safety & Equipment Co 201 327-6050
457 State Rt 17 Mahwah (07430) *(G-5822)*

Traffic Safety Service LLC 908 561-4800
601 Hadley Rd South Plainfield (07080) *(G-10441)*

Trane Inc (HQ) 732 652-7100
1 Centennial Ave Ste 101 Piscataway (08854) *(G-8828)*

Trane US Inc 732 652-7100
1 Centennial Ave Ste 101 Piscataway (08854) *(G-8829)*

Trane US Inc 609 587-3400
2231 E State Street Ext Trenton (08619) *(G-11123)*

Trane US Inc 973 882-3220
26 Chapin Rd Ste 1103 Pine Brook (07058) *(G-8718)*

Trano Bruce Plumbing & Heating 908 654-3685
872 Woodland Ave Mountainside (07092) *(G-6889)*

Trans World Marketing Corp (PA) 201 935-5565
360 Murray Hill Pkwy East Rutherford (07073) *(G-2334)*

Transaction Publishers Inc (PA) 732 445-2280
10 Corporate Pl S Ste 102 Piscataway (08854) *(G-8830)*

Transaxle LLC (PA) 856 665-4445
2501 Route 73 Cinnaminson (08077) *(G-1495)*

Transcore LP 201 329-9200
25 Central Ave Teterboro (07608) *(G-10816)*

Transfer Truck & Equipment, Flanders *Also called Robert H Hoover & Sons Inc (G-3414)*

Transglobe Usa Inc 973 465-1998
175 Broad St Carlstadt (07072) *(G-1232)*

Transistor Devices Inc (PA) 908 850-5088
36 Newburgh Rd Hackettstown (07840) *(G-4041)*

Transistor Devices Inc 908 850-5088
36 Newburgh Rd Hackettstown (07840) *(G-4042)*

Transmar Group LLC 973 359-4040
200 South St Ste 4 Morristown (07960) *(G-6745)*

Transmission Technology Co 973 305-3600
1 High Mountain Trl Lincoln Park (07035) *(G-5334)*

Transport Products Inc 973 857-6090
20 Village Park Rd Cedar Grove (07009) *(G-1302)*

Transportation Tech Svcs Inc 732 326-0700
1480 Us Highway 9 N # 204 Woodbridge (07095) *(G-12155)*

Transtar Truck Body & Wldg Co 908 832-2688
514 County Road 513 Califon (07830) *(G-1038)*

Trap Rock Industries Inc (PA) 609 924-0300
460 River Rd Kingston (08528) *(G-5030)*

Trap Rock Industries Inc 609 924-0300
Pennington Hwy Rr 31 Pennington (08534) *(G-8461)*

Trap Rock Industries Inc 609 924-0300
Rr 29 Titusville (08560) *(G-10857)*

Trap Rock Industries LLC 609 924-0300
460 River Rd Kingston (08528) *(G-5031)*

Trap-Zap Environmental Systems 201 251-9970
255 Braen Ave Wyckoff (07481) *(G-12266)*

Travel Weekly 201 902-1931
100 Lighting Way Ste 200 Secaucus (07094) *(G-9936)*

Traycon Manufacturing Co Inc 201 939-5555
555 Barell Ave Carlstadt (07072) *(G-1233)*

Trb Electro Corp 973 278-9014
6 Morris St Paterson (07501) *(G-8401)*

Treasure Chest Corp 973 328-7747
10 N Main St Ste 1 Wharton (07885) *(G-12001)*

Treasure Hunt, Phillipsburg *Also called David Sisco Jr (G-8646)*

Treasures LLC 201 723-3506
32 Ada Pl Allendale (07401) *(G-22)*

Trec Electric 856 374-3433
11 Kensington Ct Sewell (08080) *(G-9966)*

Tree-Ripe Products, East Hanover *Also called 201 Food Packing Inc (G-2198)*

Trek Inc 732 269-6300
43 Cranmer Rd Bayville (08721) *(G-261)*

Trek Connect Inc 856 608-0901
120 Munt Holly Byp Unit 7 Lumberton (08048) *(G-5664)*

Trek II Products Inc 732 214-9200
400 Jersey Ave Ste 1 New Brunswick (08901) *(G-7007)*

Tremont Printing Co 973 227-0742
72 Deer Park Rd Fairfield (07004) *(G-3330)*

Trend Printing/Intl Label 201 941-6611
1183 Edgewater Ave Ridgefield (07657) *(G-9389)*

Trendmark LLC 551 226-7973
465 Meadow Rd Apt 10207 Princeton (08540) *(G-9132)*

Trent Box Manufacturing Co 609 587-7515
1384 Yardville Ham Rd Trenton (08691) *(G-11124)*

Trenton Corrugated Products 609 695-0808
17 Shelton Ave Ewing (08618) *(G-3061)*

Trenton Printing LLC 609 695-6485
1150 Southard St Ste 2 Trenton (08638) *(G-11125)*

Trenton Sheet Metal Inc 609 695-6328
30 Adam Ave Trenton (08618) *(G-11126)*

Trentypo Inc 609 883-5971
304 Stokes Ave Ewing (08638) *(G-3062)*

Tresky Corp 732 536-8600
704 Ginesi Dr Ste 11 Morganville (07751) *(G-6653)*

Tretina Printing Inc 732 264-2324
1301 Cncrd Hwy 36 101 Hazlet (07730) *(G-4285)*

Trf Music Inc 201 335-0005
106 Apple St Ste 302 Tinton Falls (07724) *(G-10851)*

Trf Production Music Libraries, Tinton Falls Also called Trf Music Inc *(G-10851)*

Tri Diamond Electric, Hammonton Also called Tri Diamond Enterprises LLC *(G-4152)*

Tri Diamond Enterprises LLC 609 927-6018
735 Wiltseys Mill Rd Hammonton (08037) *(G-4152)*

Tri Dim Filter, Cinnaminson Also called Tri-Dim Filter Corporation *(G-1496)*

Tri G Manufacturing LLC 732 460-1881
8 Iroquois Ct Colts Neck (07722) *(G-1793)*

Tri State Athc Field Svcs Sups 201 760-9700
145 N Franklin Tpke # 109 Ramsey (07446) *(G-9254)*

Tri Tech Telecom, Columbus Also called Draztic Designs LLC *(G-1803)*

Tri Tech Tool & Design Co Inc 732 469-5433
30 Cherry St South Bound Brook (08880) *(G-10249)*

Tri-Chem Inc 973 751-9200
681 Main St Ste 24 Belleville (07109) *(G-320)*

Tri-Cor Flexible Packaging Inc 973 940-1500
27 Brookfield Dr Sparta (07871) *(G-10526)*

Tri-Delta Plastics, Hillsborough Also called Brent River Corp *(G-4322)*

Tri-Dim Filter, Lincoln Park Also called Indoor Environmental Tech *(G-5327)*

Tri-Dim Filter Corporation 856 786-2447
1306 Sylvania Ave Cinnaminson (08077) *(G-1496)*

Tri-Dim Filter Corporation 973 709-1122
600 Ryerson Rd Ste F Lincoln Park (07035) *(G-5335)*

Tri-G Manufacturing, Colts Neck Also called Tri G Manufacturing LLC *(G-1793)*

Tri-Met Industries Inc 908 231-0004
36 Adamsville Rd Bridgewater (08807) *(G-902)*

Tri-Power Consulting Svcs LLC 973 227-7100
2 Richwood Pl Denville (07834) *(G-2060)*

Tri-State Alum & Stainless Inc 908 693-7337
81 Chimney Rock Rd Ste 6 Bridgewater (08807) *(G-903)*

Tri-State Buns LLC 973 418-8323
808 Warren St 810 Harrison (07029) *(G-4190)*

Tri-State Glass & Mirror Inc (PA) 732 591-5545
11a Jocama Blvd Old Bridge (08857) *(G-7794)*

Tristate Knife Grinding Corp 609 890-4989
3 S Gold Dr Robbinsville (08691) *(G-9523)*

Tri-State Orthopedic, Mount Laurel Also called Zimmer Inc *(G-6848)*

Tri-State Pharmaceutical LLC 732 905-7592
1985 Swarthmore Ave Ste 3 Lakewood (08701) *(G-5197)*

Tri-State Quikrete 973 347-4569
150 Gold Mine Rd Flanders (07836) *(G-3420)*

Tri-Steel Fabricators Inc 609 392-8660
501 Prospect St Trenton (08618) *(G-11127)*

Triad Pharmaceutical, Newark Also called Arisaph Pharmaceuticals Inc *(G-7092)*

Triad Scientific Inc 732 292-1994
6 Stockton Lake Blvd Manasquan (08736) *(G-5882)*

Triad Tool & Die Co 908 534-1784
9 Commerce St Branchburg (08876) *(G-712)*

Triaddisplay, Hillsborough Also called Aura Signs Inc *(G-4317)*

Triangle Automatic Inc 973 625-3830
105 W Dewey Ave 305 Wharton (07885) *(G-12002)*

Triangle Home Fashions LLC 732 355-9800
9 Nicholas Ct Ste A Dayton (08810) *(G-1993)*

Triangle Ink Co Inc (PA) 201 935-2777
53-57 Van Dyke St Wallington (07057) *(G-11530)*

Triangle Manufacturing Co 201 962-7433
116 Pleasant Ave Upper Saddle River (07458) *(G-11286)*

Triangle Manufacturing Co Inc 201 825-1212
120 Pleasant Ave Upper Saddle River (07458) *(G-11287)*

Triangle Reprocenter, Toms River Also called R V Livolsi Incorporated *(G-10905)*

Triangle Tube/Phase III Co Inc 856 228-9940
1240 Forest Pkwy Ste 100 Paulsboro (08066) *(G-8427)*

Triarco Industries LLC 973 942-5100
259 Prospect Plains Rd A Cranbury (08512) *(G-1885)*

Tribuna Hispana 609 646-9167
1614 Dolphin Ave Pleasantville (08232) *(G-8917)*

Trico Web LLC 201 438-3860
75 Broad St Carlstadt (07072) *(G-1234)*

Tricomp Inc 973 835-1110
230 W Parkway Ste 14 Pompton Plains (07444) *(G-8966)*

Triefeldt Studios Inc 609 656-2380
1115 Hamilton Ave Trenton (08629) *(G-11128)*

Triform Products Inc 973 278-2042
164 W Parkway Pompton Plains (07444) *(G-8967)*

Trigen Laboratories LLC 732 721-0070
400 Crossing Blvd Bridgewater (08807) *(G-904)*

Trilenium Salvage Co 732 462-2909
147 Tennent Rd Morganville (07751) *(G-6654)*

Trilex Cleaners, Twp Washinton Also called Trilex Ltd *(G-11144)*

Trilex Ltd 201 664-5576
50 Hemlock Dr Twp Washinton (07676) *(G-11144)*

Trillium US 973 827-1661
3627 State Rt 23 Hamburg (07419) *(G-4097)*

Trilogy Publications LLC 201 816-1211
560 Sylvan Ave Ste 1240 Englewood Cliffs (07632) *(G-2983)*

Trim and Tassels LLC 973 808-1566
204 Passaic Ave Unit 3 Fairfield (07004) *(G-3331)*

Trim Brush Company Inc 973 887-2525
22 Littell Rd Bldg 1 East Hanover (07936) *(G-2247)*

Trim Factory Inc 856 769-8746
1210 Route 40 Pilesgrove (08098) *(G-8677)*

Trimarco Inc 973 762-7380
1847 Springfield Ave # 1849 Maplewood (07040) *(G-5929)*

Trimline Medical Products Corp 908 429-0590
34 Columbia Rd Branchburg (08876) *(G-713)*

Trimtex Company Inc 201 945-2151
325 Sylvan Ave Ste 102 Englewood Cliffs (07632) *(G-2984)*

Trinity Heating & Air Inc (PA) 732 780-3779
2211 Allenwood Rd Wall Township (07719) *(G-11516)*

Trinity LLC, Metuchen Also called Trinity Manufacturing LLC *(G-6129)*

Trinity Manufacturing LLC 732 549-2866
60 Leonard St Metuchen (08840) *(G-6129)*

Trinity Plastics Inc (HQ) 973 994-8018
9 Peach Tree Hill Rd Livingston (07039) *(G-5566)*

Trinity Press Inc 973 881-0690
655 Market St Paterson (07513) *(G-8402)*

Trinity Solar Systems, Wall Township Also called Trinity Heating & Air Inc *(G-11516)*

Tripack Industrial USA LLC 973 627-8350
52 Green Pond Rd Rockaway (07866) *(G-9619)*

Triple D Enterprises Inc 609 859-3000
135 Eayrestown Rd Southampton (08088) *(G-10483)*

Triple S Express 908 686-0557
1991 William St Union (07083) *(G-11230)*

Triple S Industries 908 862-0110
1108 E Linden Ave Linden (07036) *(G-5455)*

Triple-T Cutting Tools Inc 856 768-0800
15 Edgewood Ave Ste A West Berlin (08091) *(G-11759)*

Tripp Nyc Inc 201 520-0420
5200 W Side Ave North Bergen (07047) *(G-7490)*

Tris Pharma Inc 732 940-0358
2031 Us Highway 130 Ste H Monmouth Junction (08852) *(G-6365)*

Tris Pharma Inc (PA) 732 940-2800
2033 Rte 130 Ste D Monmouth Junction (08852) *(G-6366)*

Tristate Crating Pallet Co Inc 973 357-8293
85 Fulton St Paterson (07501) *(G-8403)*

Trisys Inc 973 360-2300
215 Ridgedale Ave Ste 2 Florham Park (07932) *(G-3518)*

Triton Associated Industries 856 697-3050
N Brewster Rd Buena (08310) *(G-951)*

Triumph Brewing of Princeton 609 773-0111
287 S Main St Ste 16 Lambertville (08530) *(G-5222)*

Triumph Knitting Machine Svc (PA) 201 646-0022
238 Main St Ste 102 Hackensack (07601) *(G-3986)*

Triumph Plastics LLC 973 584-5500
99 Bartley Flanders Rd Flanders (07836) *(G-3421)*

Trodat Usa Inc (HQ) 732 529-8500
48 Heller Park Ln Somerset (08873) *(G-10189)*

Trodat USA LLC 732 562-9500
48 Heller Park Ln Somerset (08873) *(G-10190)*

Trolex Corporation 201 794-8004
6 Aspen Dr Randolph (07869) *(G-9302)*

Tronex International Inc (PA) 973 335-2888
300 International Dr Budd Lake (07828) *(G-945)*

Tropaion Inc 908 654-3870
955 S Springfield Ave C302 Springfield (07081) *(G-10580)*

Tropar Manufacturing Co Inc (PA) 973 765-0380
5 Vreeland Rd Florham Park (07932) *(G-3519)*

Tropar Trophy Manufacturing Co (PA) 973 822-2400
5 Vreeland Rd Florham Park (07932) *(G-3520)*

Trophy King Inc 201 836-1482
309 Queen Anne Rd Teaneck (07666) *(G-10775)*

Tropical Bottling Corporation 786 636-6169
700 Kinderkamack Rd Oradell (07649) *(G-7814)*

Tropical Cheese Industries (PA) 732 442-4898
452 Fayette St Perth Amboy (08861) *(G-8634)*

Tropical Expressions Inc 732 899-8680
2127 Bridge Ave Point Pleasant Boro (08742) *(G-8941)*

Troy Corporation (PA) 973 443-4200
8 Vreeland Rd Florham Park (07932) *(G-3521)*

Troy Hills Manufacturing Inc 973 263-1885
2 Como Ct Towaco (07082) *(G-11005)*

Troy-Onic Inc 973 584-6830
90 N Dell Ave Kenvil (07847) *(G-5014)*

Tru Mfg Corp 201 768-4050
40 Oak St Ste 2 Norwood (07648) *(G-7637)*

A
L
P
H
A
B
E
T
I
C

Truckeros News LLC......732 340-1043
1720 Lawrence St Rahway (07065) ***(G-9225)***
Truckform Inc......908 526-5443
50 James St Somerville (08876) ***(G-10231)***
Truckpro LLC......201 229-0599
150 Central Ave Teterboro (07608) ***(G-10817)***
Truckpro 192, Teterboro *Also called Truckpro LLC* ***(G-10817)***
Trucktech Parts & Services......973 799-0500
13 Avenue C Newark (07114) ***(G-7348)***
True Religion Apparel Inc......973 564-9030
1200 Morris Tpke Ste D107 Short Hills (07078) ***(G-9986)***
True Religion Brand Jeans, Short Hills *Also called True Religion Apparel Inc* ***(G-9986)***
True Romance, Englewood Cliffs *Also called Paul Winston Fine Jewelry Grou* ***(G-2977)***
Trugman-Nash, Millburn *Also called McT Dairies Inc* ***(G-6256)***
Truimph Knitting Mills, Hackensack *Also called Triumph Knitting Machine Svc* ***(G-3986)***
Trukmann's Reprographics, Cedar Knolls *Also called Trukmanns Inc* ***(G-1321)***
Trukmanns Inc......973 538-7718
4 Wing Dr Cedar Knolls (07927) ***(G-1321)***
Trumpf Inc......609 925-8200
2601 Route 130 Cranbury (08512) ***(G-1886)***
Trumpf Photonics Inc......609 925-8200
2601 Us Highway 130 Cranbury (08512) ***(G-1887)***
Truss Engineering......201 871-4800
120 Charlotte Pl Ste 206 Englewood (07632) ***(G-2938)***
Tryco Tool & Mfg Co Inc......973 674-6867
363 S Jefferson St Orange (07050) ***(G-7831)***
Trylon, Lyndhurst *Also called Marchione Industries Inc* ***(G-5690)***
Tsb, Harrison *Also called Tri-State Buns LLC* ***(G-4190)***
Tsg Inc......973 785-1118
28 Muller Pl Little Falls (07424) ***(G-5492)***
Tsi Accessory Group Inc (HQ)......847 965-1700
141 New Rd Ste 210 Parsippany (07054) ***(G-8104)***
Tsi Nomenclature Inc......732 340-0646
1400 Rahway Ave Avenel (07001) ***(G-157)***
Ttss Interactive Products Inc......301 230-1464
100 Riverdale Rd Riverdale (07457) ***(G-9491)***
Tubari Inc......973 779-8693
90 Dayton Ave Ste 48 Passaic (07055) ***(G-8185)***
Tube Craft of America Inc......856 629-5626
667 Lebanon Ave Williamstown (08094) ***(G-12110)***
Tube Line, New Brunswick *Also called Nippon Benkan Kagyo* ***(G-6988)***
Tuckahoe Brewing Company LLC......609 645-2739
3092 English Creek Ave Egg Harbor Twp (08234) ***(G-2701)***
Tuckahoe Manufacturing Inc......856 696-4100
327 Tuckahoe Rd Vineland (08360) ***(G-11410)***
Tuckahoe Sand & Gravel Co Inc......609 861-2082
And Sharp Rd Rr 610 Tuckahoe (08250) ***(G-11139)***
Tuerff Sziber Capitol Copy Svc......609 989-8776
116 W State St Trenton (08608) ***(G-11129)***
Tuff Mfg Co Inc......201 796-5319
4 Midland Ave Elmwood Park (07407) ***(G-2852)***
Tuff Mutters LLC......973 291-6679
2 Kiel Ave Unit 155 Kinnelon (07405) ***(G-5041)***
Tulex Pharmaceuticals Inc......609 619-3098
5 Cedarbrook Dr Cranbury (08512) ***(G-1888)***
Tumi Holdings Inc (HQ)......908 756-4400
1001 Durham Ave Ste 1b South Plainfield (07080) ***(G-10442)***
Tun Tavern Brewery & Rest, Atlantic City *Also called Headquarters Pub LLC* ***(G-100)***
Tunnel Barrel & Drum Co Inc......201 933-1444
329 Veterans Blvd Carlstadt (07072) ***(G-1235)***
Tunnel Networks Inc......609 414-9799
53 Winchester Dr East Windsor (08520) ***(G-2369)***
Turbine Tek Inc......973 872-0903
130 Ryerson Ave Ste 303 Wayne (07470) ***(G-11687)***
Turbo Solutions LLC (PA)......856 209-6900
8500 Remington Ave Unit 1 Pennsauken (08110) ***(G-8587)***
Turbon International Inc (HQ)......800 282-6650
4 Executive Campus # 104 Cherry Hill (08002) ***(G-1430)***
Turbon USA, Cherry Hill *Also called Turbon International Inc* ***(G-1430)***
Turbot Hq Inc......973 922-0297
105 Oakview Ave Maplewood (07040) ***(G-5930)***
Turn-Key Technologies Inc......732 553-9100
2400 Main St Ste 11 Sayreville (08872) ***(G-9842)***
Turner Engineering Inc......973 263-1000
14 Morris Ave Mountain Lakes (07046) ***(G-6863)***
Turning Star Inc......201 944-3462
600 Willow Tree Rd Leonia (07605) ***(G-5322)***
Turnkey Solutions, Mahwah *Also called Envirnmntal Mgt Chem Wste Svcs* ***(G-5770)***
Turquoise Chemistry Inc......908 561-0002
537 New Durham Rd Piscataway (08854) ***(G-8831)***
Turul Bookbindery Inc......973 361-2810
60 State Route 15 S Wharton (07885) ***(G-12003)***
Tusa Products Inc......609 448-8333
1515 Parkway Ave Ewing (08628) ***(G-3063)***
Tuscan/Lehigh Dairies Inc (HQ)......570 385-1884
117 Cumberland Blvd Burlington (08016) ***(G-992)***
Tuscany Especially Itln Foods......732 308-1118
13a S Main St Store 5 Marlboro (07746) ***(G-5962)***
TWI Pharmaceuticals Usa Inc......201 762-1410
115 W Century Rd Ste 180 Paramus (07652) ***(G-7911)***
Twill Inc......908 665-1700
22 Russo Pl Berkeley Heights (07922) ***(G-423)***
Twisted Networking, Freehold *Also called Custom Business Software LLC* ***(G-3649)***
Two 12 Fashion LLC......848 222-1562
1525 Prospect St Ste 205 Lakewood (08701) ***(G-5198)***
Two Jays Bingo Supply Inc (PA)......609 267-4542
709 Park Ave E Hainesport (08036) ***(G-4080)***
Two Jays Specialties, Hainesport *Also called Two Jays Bingo Supply Inc* ***(G-4080)***
Two River Times, Red Bank *Also called Dyer Communications Inc* ***(G-9328)***
Two Rivers Coffee LLC......908 205-0018
101 Kentile Rd Unit 13 South Plainfield (07080) ***(G-10443)***
Two Vic's Sports Stop, Glassboro *Also called Sports Stop Inc* ***(G-3812)***
TX Technology Corp......973 442-7500
100 Ford Rd Ste 18 Denville (07834) ***(G-2061)***
Tyco Elec Sbsea Cmmnctions LLC (HQ)......732 578-7000
250 Industrial Way W Eatontown (07724) ***(G-2427)***
Tyco International MGT Co LLC (HQ)......609 720-4200
9 Roszel Rd Ste 2 Princeton (08540) ***(G-9133)***
Tycom Limited (HQ)......973 753-3040
10 Park Ave Morristown (07960) ***(G-6746)***
Typecom LLC (PA)......201 969-1901
1275 15th St Apt 19a Fort Lee (07024) ***(G-3586)***
Typeline......201 251-2201
506 Spencer Dr Wyckoff (07481) ***(G-12267)***
Typen Graphics Inc......973 838-6544
170 Kinnelon Rd Rm 12 Kinnelon (07405) ***(G-5042)***
Typestyle Inc......201 343-3343
222 River St Hackensack (07601) ***(G-3987)***
Tyrx Inc......732 246-8676
1 Deerpark Dr Ste G Monmouth Junction (08852) ***(G-6367)***
Tyz-All Plastics LLC......201 343-1200
130 Gamewell St Hackensack (07601) ***(G-3988)***
U I S Industries Inc (PA)......201 946-2600
15 Exchange Pl Ste 1120 Jersey City (07302) ***(G-4839)***
U J Ramelson Co Inc......973 589-5422
165 Thomas St Newark (07114) ***(G-7349)***
U P N Pallet Co Inc......856 299-1192
305 N Virginia Ave Penns Grove (08069) ***(G-8466)***
U S 1 Publishing Co, Lawrence Township *Also called Richard Rein* ***(G-5247)***
U S A Distributors Inc......201 348-1959
3510 Bergenline Ave Ste 4 Union City (07087) ***(G-11269)***
U S Aluminum Inc......908 782-5454
408 Us Highway 202 Flemington (08822) ***(G-3473)***
U S Box, Fairfield *Also called United States Box Corp* ***(G-3335)***
U S Ink Division, East Rutherford *Also called Sun Chemical Corporation* ***(G-2329)***
U S Laser Corp......201 848-9200
825 Windham Ct N Ste 2 Wyckoff (07481) ***(G-12268)***
U S S, Cedar Grove *Also called United Spport Slutions-Lmt Inc* ***(G-1305)***
U S Screening Corp......973 242-1110
780 Frelinghuysen Ave Newark (07114) ***(G-7350)***
U S Silica Company......856 785-0720
9035 Noble St Mauricetown (08329) ***(G-6035)***
U S Tech Solutions Inc (PA)......201 524-9600
10 Exchange Pl Ste 1710 Jersey City (07302) ***(G-4840)***
U T C, Fairfield *Also called Ultimate Trading Corp* ***(G-3332)***
U V International, Morristown *Also called U V International LLC* ***(G-6747)***
U V International LLC (PA)......973 993-9454
360 Mount Kemble Ave # 2 Morristown (07960) ***(G-6747)***
U-Solution Promo Inc USP, Belle Mead *Also called Sanherb Biotech Inc* ***(G-292)***
Ua Pipefitters Local 274......201 943-4700
205 Jefferson Rd Parsippany (07054) ***(G-8105)***
Uac Packaging LLC......908 595-6890
330 Roycefield Rd Unit C Hillsborough (08844) ***(G-4378)***
Ubertesters Inc......201 203-7903
72 S Maple Ave Ridgewood (07450) ***(G-9434)***
Ubi, Plainfield *Also called United Bedding Industries LLC* ***(G-8874)***
Udico, Kearny *Also called United Die Company Inc* ***(G-4918)***
Uehling Instrument Company, Garfield *Also called Pavan & Kievit Enterprises* ***(G-3746)***
Uff, Hillside *Also called United Forms Finishing Corp* ***(G-4448)***
Ufp Berlin LLC......856 767-0596
159 Jackson Rd Berlin (08009) ***(G-443)***
Ugsi Chemfeed, Inc., Vineland *Also called Ugsi Chemical Feed Inc* ***(G-11411)***
Ugsi Chemical Feed Inc......856 896-2160
1901 W Garden Rd Vineland (08360) ***(G-11411)***
Uhlmann Packaging Systems LP......973 402-8855
44 Indian Ln E Towaco (07082) ***(G-11006)***
Ukrainian National Association (PA)......973 292-9800
2200 State Rt 10 Ste 201 Parsippany (07054) ***(G-8106)***
Ulma Form-Works Inc (HQ)......201 882-1122
58 5th Ave Hawthorne (07506) ***(G-4261)***
Ultimate Hair World Ltd Lblty......973 622-6900
16 Molter Pl Bloomfield (07003) ***(G-535)***
Ultimate Home Products Div, Kearny *Also called Marcotex International Inc* ***(G-4898)***
Ultimate Outdoors, Glen Gardner *Also called Vision Railings Ltd Lblty Co* ***(G-3817)***

Ultimate Spinning Turning Corp 201 372-9740
9 Willow St Moonachie (07074) *(G-6550)*
Ultimate Textile, Paterson *Also called Pecata Enterprises Inc (G-8362)*
Ultimate Trading Corp 973 228-7700
4 Just Rd Fairfield (07004) *(G-3332)*
Ultimate Trining Munitions Inc (PA) 908 725-9000
55 Readington Rd Branchburg (08876) *(G-714)*
Ultra Additives LLC (HQ) 973 279-1306
1455 Broad St Ste 3 Bloomfield (07003) *(G-536)*
Ultra Chemical Inc (PA) 732 224-0200
2 Bridge Ave Ste 631 Red Bank (07701) *(G-9348)*
Ultra Clean Technologies Corp 856 451-2176
1274 Highway 77 Bridgeton (08302) *(G-801)*
Ultra Electronics Herley, Whippany *Also called Herley-Cti Inc (G-12025)*
Ultraflex Systems Florida Inc 973 627-8608
1578 Sussex Tpke Ste 400 Randolph (07869) *(G-9303)*
Um Equity Corp (HQ) 856 354-2200
56 N Haddon Ave Ste 300 Haddonfield (08033) *(G-4065)*
Umbrella & Chairs LLC 973 284-1240
8 Old Quarry Rd Englewood (07631) *(G-2939)*
Umbrella Publishing, Butler *Also called Jigsaw Publishing LLC (G-1010)*
Umbrellas Unlimited 201 476-1011
808 Rivervale Rd River Vale (07675) *(G-9472)*
Umc Inc 973 325-0031
24 Burnett Ter West Orange (07052) *(G-11907)*
Umicore Precious Metals NJ LLC 908 222-5006
3950 S Clinton Ave South Plainfield (07080) *(G-10444)*
Umicore USA Inc 908 226-2053
3900 S Clinton Ave South Plainfield (07080) *(G-10445)*
Umit International Trading LLC 973 571-1000
14 Village Park Rd A-B Cedar Grove (07009) *(G-1303)*
Uncle Eds Creamery 609 818-0100
155 W Delaware Ave Pennington (08534) *(G-8462)*
Under Armour Inc 732 493-2444
1 Premium Outlet Blvd # 101 Tinton Falls (07753) *(G-10852)*
Unette Corporation 973 328-6800
1578 Sussex Tpke Ste 5 Randolph (07869) *(G-9304)*
Unex Manufacturing Inc (PA) 732 928-2800
691 New Hampshire Ave Lakewood (08701) *(G-5199)*
UNI-Tech Drilling Company Inc 856 694-4200
61 Grays Ferry Rd Franklinville (08322) *(G-3633)*
UNI-Vac, Hamburg *Also called United Vacuum LLC (G-4098)*
Unicorn Group Inc (PA) 973 360-0688
25b Hanover Rd Florham Park (07932) *(G-3522)*
Unicorn Group Inc 973 360-5904
23 Daniel Rd Fairfield (07004) *(G-3333)*
Unicorp 973 674-1700
291 Cleveland St Orange (07050) *(G-7832)*
Unified Resources, Kenilworth *Also called Resources Inc In Display (G-4992)*
Unifoil Corporation 973 244-9900
12 Daniel Rd Fairfield (07004) *(G-3334)*
Uniforms By Cozy, Nutley *Also called Cozy Formal Wear Inc (G-7645)*
Uniken Inc 917 324-0399
466 Southern Blvd Ste 2 Chatham (07928) *(G-1339)*
Unilever Bestfoods North Amer (HQ) 201 894-4000
800 Sylvan Ave Englewood Cliffs (07632) *(G-2985)*
Unilever Hpc-USA, Englewood Cliffs *Also called Unilever United States Inc (G-2986)*
Unilever United States Inc (HQ) 201 894-4000
700 Sylvan Ave Englewood Cliffs (07632) *(G-2986)*
Unilever United States Inc 800 298-5018
800 Sylvan Ave Englewood Cliffs (07632) *(G-2987)*
Unilite Incorporated 973 667-1674
151 River Rd Nutley (07110) *(G-7656)*
Unilux Inc (HQ) 201 712-1266
59 5th St Saddle Brook (07663) *(G-9798)*
Unimac Graphics LLC 201 372-1000
350 Michele Pl Carlstadt (07072) *(G-1236)*
Union Beverage Packers LLC 908 206-9111
600 N Union Ave Ste 7 Hillside (07205) *(G-4446)*
Union Casting Industries Inc (PA) 908 686-8888
2365 Us Highway 22 W Union (07083) *(G-11231)*
Union City Filament Corp 201 945-3366
1039 Hoyt Ave A Ridgefield (07657) *(G-9390)*
Union City Mirror & Table Co 201 867-0050
129 34th St Union City (07087) *(G-11270)*
Union City Whirlpool Repair 908 428-9146
507 43rd St Union City (07087) *(G-11271)*
Union Container Corp 973 242-3600
439 Frelinghuysen Ave Newark (07114) *(G-7351)*
Union County Seating & Sup Co 908 241-4949
135 N Michigan Ave Kenilworth (07033) *(G-5002)*
Union Dry Dock & Repair Co (PA) 201 792-9090
51 Newark St Ste 504 Hoboken (07030) *(G-4501)*
Union Dry Dock & Repair Co 201 963-5833
901 Sinatra Dr Hoboken (07030) *(G-4502)*
Union Hill Corp 732 786-9422
29 Park Ave Englishtown (07726) *(G-2999)*
Union Institute Inc 800 914-8138
67 Ramapo Valley Rd # 102 Mahwah (07430) *(G-5823)*

Union Tool & Mold Co Inc 973 763-6611
220 Rutgers St Maplewood (07040) *(G-5931)*
Unionmed Tech Inc 917 714-3418
1031 Us Highway 202/206 # 101 Bridgewater (08807) *(G-905)*
Unionville Vineyards LLC 908 788-0400
9 Rocktown Rd Ringoes (08551) *(G-9443)*
Unionwear, Newark *Also called New Jersey Headwear Corp (G-7250)*
Unipack Inc 973 450-9880
681 Main St Ste 27 Belleville (07109) *(G-321)*
UNIPACK,INC., Belleville *Also called Unipack Inc (G-321)*
Uniphy Health Holdings LLC 866 874-8616
211 Warren St Newark (07103) *(G-7352)*
Uniplast Industries Inc 201 288-4672
1-5 Plant Rd Hasbrouck Heights (07604) *(G-4202)*
Uniport Industries Corporation 201 391-7676
23 Campbell Ave Woodcliff Lake (07677) *(G-12206)*
Unipro, Totowa *Also called O T D Inc (G-10958)*
Unique Aluminum Extrusion LLC 732 271-0006
333 Cedar Ave Ste 6 Middlesex (08846) *(G-6207)*
Unique Embroidery Inc 201 943-9191
64 Bushes Ln Elmwood Park (07407) *(G-2853)*
Unique Encapsulation Tech LLC 973 448-2801
9 Lenel Rd Landing (07850) *(G-5228)*
Unique Encapsulation Tech Orca, Landing *Also called Unique Encapsulation Tech LLC (G-5228)*
Unique Impressions Ltd Lblty 201 751-4088
718 25th St Union City (07087) *(G-11272)*
Unique Metal Products 732 388-1888
17 W Scott Ave Rahway (07065) *(G-9226)*
Unique Precision Co Inc 732 382-8699
2095 Elizabeth Ave Rahway (07065) *(G-9227)*
Unique Screen Printing Corp 908 925-3773
10 Mckinley St 16 Linden (07036) *(G-5456)*
Unique Systems Inc 973 455-0440
4 Saddle Rd Cedar Knolls (07927) *(G-1322)*
Unique Wire Weaving Co Inc 908 688-4600
762 Ramsey Ave Hillside (07205) *(G-4447)*
Unique/Pereny, Ringoes *Also called Hed International Inc (G-9437)*
Uniquiwa's, Jersey City *Also called Ronald Perry (G-4820)*
Unisphere Media LLC 908 795-3701
630 Central Ave New Providence (07974) *(G-7059)*
Unistar Creations, Princeton *Also called Unistar Inc (G-9134)*
Unistar Inc 212 840-2100
61 Castleton Rd Princeton (08540) *(G-9134)*
Unit Pack Company Inc 973 239-4112
7 Lewis Rd Cedar Grove (07009) *(G-1304)*
Unitao Nutraceuticals LLC 973 983-1121
6 Reservoir Pl Rockaway (07866) *(G-9620)*
United Asphalt Co Inc 856 753-9811
237 N Grove St Berlin (08009) *(G-444)*
United Bedding Industries LLC 908 668-0220
300 W 4th St Plainfield (07060) *(G-8874)*
United Cabinet Works LLC 917 686-3395
9 Bonn Pl Apt 2 Weehawken (07086) *(G-11700)*
United City Ice Cube Co Inc 201 945-8387
695 Elm Ave Ridgefield (07657) *(G-9391)*
United Crbral Plsy Bldg Blocks, Teaneck *Also called Advancing Opportunities Inc (G-10740)*
United Diam Inc 732 619-0950
12 Grenoble Ct Matawan (07747) *(G-6034)*
United Die Company Inc 201 997-0250
199 Devon Ter Kearny (07032) *(G-4918)*
United Energy Corp (PA) 732 994-5225
3598 Us Highway 9 Ste 303 Howell (07731) *(G-4569)*
United Envelope LLC (PA) 201 699-5800
65 Railroad Ave Ridgefield (07657) *(G-9392)*
United Eqp Fabricators LLC 973 242-2737
175 Orange St Newark (07103) *(G-7353)*
United Farm Processing Corp 856 451-4612
458 Garrison Rd Rosenhayn (08352) *(G-9710)*
United Federated Systems, Totowa *Also called T F S Inc (G-10974)*
United Forms Finishing Corp 908 687-0494
1413 Chestnut Ave Ste 2 Hillside (07205) *(G-4448)*
United Gutter Supply Inc 201 933-6316
1 Maple St Ste 1 East Rutherford (07073) *(G-2335)*
United Hospital Supply Corp 609 387-7580
4422 Route 130 S Burlington (08016) *(G-993)*
United Industries Inc (PA) 973 256-7171
6 Andrews Dr Woodland Park (07424) *(G-12236)*
United Instrument Company LLC 201 767-6000
207 Washington St Ste A Northvale (07647) *(G-7610)*
United Label Corp 973 589-6500
65 Chambers St Newark (07105) *(G-7354)*
United Machine Inc 973 345-4505
239 Lindbergh Pl Ste 2a Paterson (07503) *(G-8404)*
United Medical PC (PA) 201 339-6111
988 Broadway Bayonne (07002) *(G-246)*
United Mijovi Amer Ltd Lblty 732 718-1001
21 Roseland Pl New Brunswick (08902) *(G-7008)*

United Natural Trading Co 732 650-9905
96 Executive Ave Edison (08817) *(G-2640)*

United Plastics Group Inc 732 873-8777
30 Commerce Dr Somerset (08873) *(G-10191)*

United Pos Solutions Inc 800 303-2567
535 Broad Ave Palisades Park (07650) *(G-7845)*

United Resin Inc 856 358-2574
321 Willow Grove Rd Elmer (08318) *(G-2799)*

United Shippers Associates, Whippany *Also called Corporate Mailings Inc (G-12017)*

United Silica Products Inc 973 209-8854
3 Park Dr Franklin (07416) *(G-3606)*

United Silicon Carbide Inc 732 355-0550
7 Deerpark Dr Ste E Monmouth Junction (08852) *(G-6368)*

United Silicon Carbide Inc 732 565-9500
100 Jersey Ave Bldg A New Brunswick (08901) *(G-7009)*

United Sound Arts Inc 732 229-4949
1 Industrial Way W D-E Eatontown (07724) *(G-2428)*

United Spport Slutions-Lmt Inc 973 857-9222
134 Sand Park Rd Cedar Grove (07009) *(G-1305)*

United State Annuities, Monroe *Also called Webannuitiescom Inc (G-6376)*

United States Box Corp 973 481-2000
14 Madison Rd Ste E Fairfield (07004) *(G-3335)*

United States Cold Storage Inc (HQ) 856 354-8181
2 Aquarium Dr Ste 400 Camden (08103) *(G-1088)*

United States Gypsum Company 732 636-7900
300 Markley St Port Reading (07064) *(G-8991)*

United States Mineral Pdts Co (HQ) 973 347-1200
41 Furnace St Stanhope (07874) *(G-10591)*

United States Pipe Fndry LLC 609 387-6000
1101 E Pearl St Ste 1 Burlington (08016) *(G-994)*

United Steel Products Co Inc 609 518-9230
130 Mount Holly By Pass # 5 Lumberton (08048) *(G-5665)*

United Sttes Metal Powders Inc (PA) 908 782-5454
408 Us Highway 202 Flemington (08822) *(G-3474)*

United Tool & Stamping Co, Woodland Park *Also called United Industries Inc (G-12236)*

United Vacuum LLC 973 827-1661
3627 State Rt 23 Bldg 3 Hamburg (07419) *(G-4098)*

United Window & Door Mfg Inc (PA) 973 912-0600
24 Fadem Rd 36 Springfield (07081) *(G-10581)*

United Wire Hanger Corp 201 288-3212
1-5 Plant Rd Hasbrouck Heights (07604) *(G-4203)*

Unitex International Inc 856 786-5000
2702 Cindel Dr Ste 3 Cinnaminson (08077) *(G-1497)*

Unity Engraving Company, Englewood *Also called Unity Graphics & Engraving Co (G-2940)*

Unity Graphics & Engraving Co 201 541-5462
210 S Van Brunt St Englewood (07631) *(G-2940)*

Unity Steel Rule Die Co 201 569-6400
210 S Van Brunt St Englewood (07631) *(G-2941)*

Univeg Logistics America Inc 856 241-0097
100 Dartmouth Dr Ste 400 Swedesboro (08085) *(G-10735)*

Univerclean Ltd 201 674-1563
8-46 Susan Pl Fair Lawn (07410) *(G-3122)*

Universal Business Automation 973 575-3568
170 Changebridge Rd D3 Montville (07045) *(G-6496)*

Universal Company, Bloomfield *Also called Zwier Corp (G-539)*

Universal Display Corporation (PA) 609 671-0980
375 Phillips Blvd Ste 1 Ewing (08618) *(G-3064)*

Universal Electric Co. 201 968-1000
131 S Newman St Hackensack (07601) *(G-3989)*

Universal Electric Mtr Svc Inc 201 968-1000
131 S Newman St Hackensack (07601) *(G-3990)*

Universal Filters Inc 732 774-8555
1207 Main St Ste A Asbury Park (07712) *(G-87)*

Universal Forest Products, Berlin *Also called Ufp Berlin LLC (G-443)*

Universal Interlock Corp 732 818-8484
910 Hooper Ave Toms River (08753) *(G-10919)*

Universal Labs, New Brunswick *Also called Universal Prtein Spplmnts Corp (G-7010)*

Universal Medical Inc 800 606-5511
275 Phillips Blvd Ewing (08618) *(G-3065)*

Universal Metalcraft Inc 973 345-3284
24 Burgess Pl Wayne (07470) *(G-11688)*

Universal Mold & Tool Inc 856 563-0488
1200 S West Blvd Ste 4e Vineland (08360) *(G-11412)*

Universal Nutrition, New Brunswick *Also called Princeton Corp Graphics Inc (G-6995)*

Universal Pallet Inc 732 356-2624
118 Smoke Rise Dr Warren (07059) *(G-11569)*

Universal Parts New Jersey LLC 732 615-0626
3 Chanowich Ct Middletown (07748) *(G-6219)*

Universal Prtein Spplmnts Corp (PA) 732 545-3130
3 Terminal Rd New Brunswick (08901) *(G-7010)*

Universal Systems Installers 732 656-9002
10 Red Oak Ct Monroe (08831) *(G-6375)*

Universal Tape Supply Corp (PA) 609 653-3191
110 W New Jersey Ave Somers Point (08244) *(G-10048)*

Universal Techncl Resrce Svcs 973 663-7930
200 Valley Rd Ste 102 Mount Arlington (07856) *(G-6761)*

Universal Thd & Scallop Cutng, North Bergen *Also called Walker Eight Corp (G-7494)*

Universal Tools & Mfg Co 973 379-4193
115 Victory Rd Springfield (07081) *(G-10582)*

Universal Valve Company Inc 908 351-0606
478 Schiller St Elizabeth (07206) *(G-2780)*

Universal Vending MGT LLC 908 233-4373
425 North Ave E Ste 2 Westfield (07090) *(G-11932)*

University Fashions By Janet 856 228-1615
1888 Winslow Rd Bldg B Williamstown (08094) *(G-12111)*

University Publications Inc 212 268-4222
562 Morley Ct Belford (07718) *(G-289)*

Unix Cabinetry Inc 201 995-6969
468 Totowa Ave Ste 2 Paterson (07522) *(G-8405)*

Unlimited Silk Screen Products 609 882-0653
41 Lexington Ave Ewing (08618) *(G-3066)*

Up Solution, Palisades Park *Also called United Pos Solutions Inc (G-7845)*

Up United LLC 718 383-5700
495 N Bridge St Bridgewater (08807) *(G-906)*

UPS Store 5952, Bordentown *Also called Rbdel Inc (G-610)*

UPS Store, The, Little Falls *Also called Sre Ventures LLC (G-5489)*

Uptown Bagels, Logan Township *Also called Uptown Bakeries (G-5615)*

Uptown Bakeries, Bridgeport *Also called J & J Snack Foods Corp (G-767)*

Uptown Bakeries 856 467-9552
300 Eagle Ct Logan Township (08085) *(G-5615)*

Urban Millwork & Supply Corp 973 278-7072
90 2nd Ave Paterson (07514) *(G-8406)*

Urban Sign & Crane Inc 856 691-8388
527 E Chestnut Ave Vineland (08360) *(G-11413)*

Urban State 646 836-4311
209 Hollywood Ave Hillside (07205) *(G-4449)*

Urigen Pharmaceuticals Inc 732 640-0160
675 Us Highway 1 Ste 206b North Brunswick (08902) *(G-7544)*

Urso Fuel Corp. 973 325-3324
10 Rollinson St West Orange (07052) *(G-11908)*

US Advanced Materials Division, Parsippany *Also called Sun Chemical Corporation (G-8094)*

US Air Power Systems 201 892-5235
56 Otoole St Westwood (07675) *(G-11974)*

US Blade Mfg Co Inc 908 272-2898
90 Myrtle St Cranford (07016) *(G-1930)*

US China Allied Products Inc 201 461-9886
555 North Ave Apt 12h Fort Lee (07024) *(G-3587)*

US Display Group Inc 931 455-9585
100 Electric Ave Secaucus (07094) *(G-9937)*

US Gov Turamco, Carlstadt *Also called Delta Procurement Inc (G-1153)*

US Led Installation Group, Cherry Hill *Also called Liberty Cnstr & Inv Group (G-1388)*

US Magic Box Inc 973 772-2070
221 Macarthur Ave Garfield (07026) *(G-3770)*

US Minerals, Stanhope *Also called United States Mineral Pdts Co (G-10591)*

US News & World Report Inc 212 716-6800
125 Theodore Conrad Dr Jersey City (07305) *(G-4841)*

US NJ Summit West, Summit *Also called Celgene Corporation (G-10638)*

US Outworkers LLC 973 362-1458
6 Hunter Ridge Rd Sussex (07461) *(G-10680)*

US Pipe Fabrication LLC 856 461-3000
200 Rhawn St Riverside (08075) *(G-9507)*

US Plastic Sales LLC 908 754-9404
651 Metuchen Rd South Plainfield (07080) *(G-10446)*

US Propack Inc 732 294-4500
341 Fairfield Rd Freehold (07728) *(G-3690)*

US Sign and Lighting Svc LLC 973 305-8900
105 Dorsa Ave Wayne (07470) *(G-11689)*

US Software Group Inc 732 361-4636
1550 Park Ave Ste 202 South Plainfield (07080) *(G-10447)*

US Vision, Blackwood *Also called Refac Optical Group (G-490)*

US Vision Inc (HQ) 856 227-8339
1 Harmon Dr Glendora (08029) *(G-3833)*

US Wire & Cable Corporation (PA) 973 824-5530
366 Frelinghuysen Ave Newark (07114) *(G-7355)*

USA Head Office & Warehouse, South Hackensack *Also called Youniversal Labortories (G-10300)*

USA Industries Inc 201 438-6606
111 Kero Rd Carlstadt (07072) *(G-1237)*

USA Tealight Inc 732 943-2408
4 Cragwood Rd Avenel (07001) *(G-158)*

USA Wood Door Inc 856 384-9663
1475 Imperial Way West Deptford (08066) *(G-11842)*

Uscap, Fort Lee *Also called US China Allied Products Inc (G-3587)*

Ussecurenet LLC 201 447-0130
1086 Goffle Rd Ste 101 Hawthorne (07506) *(G-4262)*

Ussg, South Plainfield *Also called US Software Group Inc (G-10447)*

Usv Optical Inc (HQ) 856 228-1000
1 Harmon Dr Glen Oaks Par Glendora (08029) *(G-3834)*

Utah Intermediate Holding Corp 856 787-2700
1020 Briggs Rd Mount Laurel (08054) *(G-6845)*

Utax USA Inc 201 433-1200
30 Montgomery St Ste 1320 Jersey City (07302) *(G-4842)*

Ute Microwave Inc 732 922-1009
3500 Sunset Ave Ste D1 Ocean (07712) *(G-7748)*

Uthe Technology Inc (HQ) 609 883-4000
Scotch Rd Trenton (08628) *(G-11130)*

(G-0000) Company's Geographic Section entry number

Utility Development Corp..................................973 994-4334
  112 Naylon Ave Livingston (07039) *(G-5567)*

Utrecht Art Supply, Cranbury Also called Utrecht Manufacturing Corp *(G-1889)*

Utrecht Manufacturing Corp (HQ)...................609 409-8001
  6 Corp Dr Ste 1 Cranbury (08512) *(G-1889)*

Utrs, Mount Arlington Also called Universal Techncl Resrce Svcs *(G-6761)*

Utz Technologies Inc (PA)...............................973 339-1100
  4 Peckman Rd Little Falls (07424) *(G-5493)*

Uvitec Printing Ink Co Inc..............................973 778-0737
  14 Mill St Lodi (07644) *(G-5607)*

V & L Machine and Tool Co Inc........................973 808-5858
  30 Sherwood Ln Ste 11 Fairfield (07004) *(G-3336)*

V & S Perth Amboy, Perth Amboy Also called Voigt & Schweitzer LLC *(G-8636)*

V A Design, South Plainfield Also called Visual Architectural Designs *(G-10451)*

V A Metal Products, Paterson Also called Alben Metal Products Inc *(G-8202)*

V and S Woodworks Inc...................................201 568-0659
  105 Piermont Rd Tenafly (07670) *(G-10788)*

V Custom Millwork Inc....................................732 469-9600
  1480 Us Highway 22 Bridgewater (08807) *(G-907)*

V E N Inc...973 786-7862
  15 Whitehall Rd Andover (07821) *(G-55)*

V F I Fabricators, Williamstown Also called Vfi Fabricators Inc *(G-12113)*

V G Controls Inc..973 764-6500
  17 Raritan Rd Ste 2 Oakland (07436) *(G-7709)*

V H Exacta Corp..856 235-7379
  107 Whittendale Dr Moorestown (08057) *(G-6629)*

V I P, Clifton Also called Vo-Toys Inc *(G-1740)*

V L V Associates...973 428-2884
  34 Troy Rd Whippany (07981) *(G-12041)*

V M Display...973 365-8027
  90 Dayton Ave Ste 1g Passaic (07055) *(G-8186)*

V M Glass Co...856 794-9333
  3231 N Mill Rd Vineland (08360) *(G-11414)*

V P I Industries Inc..732 583-6895
  77 Cliffwood Ave Ste 3b Cliffwood (07721) *(G-1549)*

V S M, Newark Also called Vehicle Safety Mfg LLC *(G-7356)*

Vac-U-Max (PA)...973 759-4600
  69 William St Belleville (07109) *(G-322)*

Vac-U-Max...973 759-4600
  69 William St Belleville (07109) *(G-323)*

Vacs Bandage Company Inc.............................973 345-3355
  163 Pennsylvania Ave Paterson (07503) *(G-8407)*

Vacumet Corp..973 628-0405
  22 Riverview Dr Ste 101 Wayne (07470) *(G-11690)*

Vacuum Sales Inc..856 627-7790
  51 Stone Rd Laurel Springs (08021) *(G-5234)*

Vacuum Solutions Group Inc...........................781 762-0414
  555 Cedar Ln Ste 1 Teaneck (07666) *(G-10776)*

Vahl Inc..732 249-4042
  34 Kennedy Blvd Ste 2 East Brunswick (08816) *(G-2194)*

Vahlco Racing Wheels LLC.............................609 758-7013
  849 Route 539 New Egypt (08533) *(G-7018)*

Vairtec Corporation...201 445-6965
  265 Greenwood Ave Midland Park (07432) *(G-6241)*

Valconn Electronics Inc...................................908 687-1600
  909 Rahway Ave Union (07083) *(G-11232)*

Valcor Engineering Corporation (PA)...............973 467-8400
  2 Lawrence Rd Springfield (07081) *(G-10583)*

Valcor Engineering Corporation......................973 467-8100
  2 Lawrence Rd Springfield (07081) *(G-10584)*

Valcor Engineering Corporation......................973 467-8400
  2 Lawrence Rd Springfield (07081) *(G-10585)*

Valeant, Bridgewater Also called Bausch Health Companies Inc *(G-821)*

Valeant Phrmcticals N Amer LLC (HQ).............908 927-1400
  400 Somerset Corp Blvd Bridgewater (08807) *(G-908)*

Valenzano Winery..856 701-7871
  1090 Route 206 Shamong (08088) *(G-9972)*

Valeritas Holdings Inc....................................908 927-9920
  750 Route 202 Ste 600 Bridgewater (08807) *(G-909)*

Valero Ref Company-New Jersey......................856 224-6000
  800 Billingsport Rd Paulsboro (08066) *(G-8428)*

Valeur Corporation..732 329-4666
  596 Ridge Rd Monmouth Junction (08852) *(G-6369)*

Validus Pharmaceuticals LLC (PA)..................973 265-2777
  119 Cherry Hill Rd # 310 Parsippany (07054) *(G-8107)*

Valle Precision Machine Co.............................973 773-3037
  58 Myrtle Ave Passaic (07055) *(G-8187)*

Valley Die Cutting Inc......................................973 731-8884
  100 Washington St Randolph (07869) *(G-9305)*

Valley Plastic Molding Co................................973 334-2100
  30 Plane St Ste 4 Boonton (07005) *(G-587)*

Valley Prtg & Graphic Design, Westwood Also called Pascack Valley Copy Center *(G-11966)*

Valley Tech Inc..908 534-5565
  295 Us Highway 22 E 201w Whitehouse Station (08889) *(G-12064)*

Valtris Specialty Chemicals, Bridgeport Also called Polymer Additives Inc *(G-770)*

Valtris Specialty Chemicals, Swedesboro Also called Polymer Additives Inc *(G-10719)*

Valuation Services Group, Mount Laurel Also called Aus Inc *(G-6779)*

Value Added Vice Solutions LLC......................201 400-3247
  1111 Shore Dr Brielle (08730) *(G-916)*

Valued Naturals, Dover Also called International Foodsource LLC *(G-2094)*

Valuemomentum Inc (HQ)..............................908 755-0025
  220 Old New Brunswick Rd # 100 Piscataway (08854) *(G-8832)*

Valuewalk LLC...973 767-2181
  381 Terhune Ave Passaic (07055) *(G-8188)*

Van Brill Pool & Spa Center............................856 424-4333
  850 Route 70 W Marlton (08053) *(G-6002)*

Van Duyne Bros Inc...609 625-0299
  5112 Oakwood Blvd Mays Landing (08330) *(G-6043)*

Van Grouw Welding & Fabg, Wyckoff Also called M K Enterprises Inc *(G-12257)*

Van Heusen, Elizabeth Also called Pvh Corp *(G-2769)*

Van Heusen, Atlantic City Also called Pvh Corp *(G-106)*

Van Heusen, Bridgewater Also called Pvh Corp *(G-879)*

Van Heusen, Jackson Also called Pvh Corp *(G-4676)*

Van Heusen, Bridgewater Also called Pvh Corp *(G-880)*

Van Heusen, Bridgewater Also called Pvh Corp *(G-881)*

Van Heusen, Flemington Also called Pvh Corp *(G-3464)*

Van Hydraulics Inc..732 442-5500
  110 Snyder Rd South Plainfield (07080) *(G-10448)*

Van Ness Plastic Molding Co...........................973 778-9500
  400 Brighton Rd Clifton (07012) *(G-1738)*

Van-Nick Pallet Inc..908 753-1800
  104 Snyder Rd South Plainfield (07080) *(G-10449)*

Vanco Millwork Inc..973 992-3061
  18 Microlab Rd Livingston (07039) *(G-5568)*

Vanco Usa LLC...609 499-4141
  1170 Florence Columbus Rd Bordentown (08505) *(G-614)*

Vanco USA LLC (de)...609 499-4141
  1170 Florence Columbus Rd Bordentown (08505) *(G-615)*

Vanderbilt LLC...973 316-3900
  2 Cranberry Rd Ste 3b Parsippany (07054) *(G-8108)*

Vanderbilt Industries, Parsippany Also called Vanderbilt LLC *(G-8108)*

Vandereems Manufacturing Co........................973 427-2355
  40 Schoon Ave Hawthorne (07506) *(G-4263)*

Vandermark Merritt GL Studios.......................908 231-8189
  1 D Angelo Dr Branchburg (08876) *(G-715)*

Vandermolen Corp...973 992-8506
  106 Hillcrest Ave Ledgewood (07852) *(G-5313)*

Vanguard Container Corp.................................732 651-9717
  35 Cotters Ln Ste 1 East Brunswick (08816) *(G-2195)*

Vanguard Packaging Corp................................973 391-9200
  15 Stratford Dr Livingston (07039) *(G-5569)*

Vanguard Printing..856 358-2665
  531 Garden Rd Elmer (08318) *(G-2800)*

Vanguard Research Industries..........................908 753-2770
  239 Saint Nicholas Ave South Plainfield (07080) *(G-10450)*

Vans Inc..732 493-1516
  1 Premium Outlet Blvd # 815 Tinton Falls (07753) *(G-10853)*

Vantage Business Systems Inc........................609 625-7020
  6019 Main St Mays Landing (08330) *(G-6044)*

Vantage Spclty Ingredients Inc (HQ)...............973 345-8600
  150 Mount Bethel Rd Warren (07059) *(G-11570)*

Vantage Tool & Mfg Inc...................................908 647-1010
  223 Stirling Rd Warren (07059) *(G-11571)*

Vanton Pump & Equipment Corp......................908 688-4120
  201 Sweetland Ave Ste 1 Hillside (07205) *(G-4450)*

Vapor Lounge LLC..973 627-1277
  15 Van Duyne Ave Rockaway (07866) *(G-9621)*

Varsity Software Inc..609 309-9955
  124 Lwrncvlle Pnnngton Rd Lawrenceville (08648) *(G-5271)*

Vascular Therapies LLC...................................201 266-8310
  105 Union Ave Ste 2 Cresskill (07626) *(G-1950)*

Vasculogic LLC..908 278-3573
  37 E Burgess Dr Piscataway (08854) *(G-8833)*

Vascure Natural LLC..732 528-6492
  3828 River Rd Point Pleasant Boro (08742) *(G-8942)*

Vaswani Inc (PA)..877 376-4425
  75 Carter Dr Ste 1 Edison (08817) *(G-2641)*

Vaswani Inc...877 376-4425
  75 Carter Dr Ste 1 Edison (08817) *(G-2642)*

Vaswani Inc...732 377-9794
  201 Circle Dr N Ste 114 Piscataway (08854) *(G-8834)*

Vatech America Inc..201 210-5028
  2200 Fletcher Ave Ste 605 Fort Lee (07024) *(G-3588)*

Vcom Intl Multi-Media Corp (PA)......................201 814-0405
  80 Little Falls Rd Fairfield (07004) *(G-3337)*

Vcom Intl Multi-Media Corp.............................201 296-0600
  80 Little Falls Rd Fairfield (07004) *(G-3338)*

Vct - Qualteq, South Plainfield Also called Qualteq Inc *(G-10429)*

Vector Foiltec LLC...862 702-8909
  55 Lane Rd Ste 110 Fairfield (07004) *(G-3339)*

Vector Precision Machining..............................856 740-5131
  1558 Janvier Rd Williamstown (08094) *(G-12112)*

Vectracor Inc...973 904-0444
  785 Totowa Rd Ste 100 Totowa (07512) *(G-10977)*

Vectracor Inc...973 768-0402
  785 Totowa Rd Ste 100 Totowa (07512) *(G-10978)*

A
L
P
H
A
B
E
T
I
C

Veeco 732 560-5300
394 Elizabeth Ave Somerset (08873) *(G-10192)*

Veeco Instruments Inc 732 560-5300
394 Elizabeth Ave Somerset (08873) *(G-10193)*

Veeco Process Equipment Inc 732 560-5300
394 Elizabeth Ave Somerset (08873) *(G-10194)*

Vehicle Safety Mfg LLC (HQ) 973 643-3000
408 Central Ave Newark (07107) *(G-7356)*

Vehicle Technologies Inc 609 406-9626
17 Decou Ave Ewing (08628) *(G-3067)*

Vela Diagnostics USA Inc 973 852-3740
353c Rte 46 W Ste 250 Fairfield (07004) *(G-3340)*

Veloso Industries Inc 908 925-0999
1020 E Elizabeth Ave Linden (07036) *(G-5457)*

Vending Trucks Inc 732 969-5400
5 Litchfield Rd East Brunswick (08816) *(G-2196)*

Venetian Care and Rehablitatn 732 721-8200
275 John T Oleary Blvd South Amboy (08879) *(G-10246)*

Venetian Caterers, The, Garfield Also called Venetian Corp *(G-3771)*

Venetian Corp 973 546-2250
546 River Dr Garfield (07026) *(G-3771)*

Venkateshwara Inc 908 964-4777
285 Davidson Ave Ste 100 Somerset (08873) *(G-10195)*

Vensun Pharmaceuticals Inc 908 278-8386
103 Carnegie Ctr Ste 300 Princeton (08540) *(G-9135)*

Venture App LLC 908 644-3985
12 Aubrey St Summit (07901) *(G-10663)*

Venture Info Network 609 279-0777
226 Linden Ln Princeton (08540) *(G-9136)*

Venture Shuffelbuard, Lawrence Township Also called Brook Metal Products Inc *(G-5241)*

Venture Stationers Inc 212 288-7235
570 Piermont Rd Closter (07624) *(G-1767)*

Venus Laboratories Inc 973 257-8983
50 Lackawanna Ave Parsippany (07054) *(G-8109)*

Veolia Es 732 469-5100
125 Factory Ln Middlesex (08846) *(G-6208)*

Vep Manufacturing 732 657-0666
575 S Hope Chapel Rd Jackson (08527) *(G-4681)*

Verico Technology LLC 201 842-0222
405 Murray Hill Pkwy East Rutherford (07073) *(G-2336)*

Verint Systems Inc 201 438-1429
9 Polito Ave Fl 9 # 9 Lyndhurst (07071) *(G-5712)*

Verizon, Maplewood Also called Supermedia LLC *(G-5927)*

Verizon Communications Inc 201 666-9934
285 Old Hook Rd Westwood (07675) *(G-11975)*

Verizon Communications Inc 609 646-9939
2546 Fire Rd Egg Harbor Township (08234) *(G-2698)*

Vermeer Pharma LLC 973 270-0073
36 Canfield Rd Morristown (07960) *(G-6748)*

Vermes Machine Co Inc 856 642-9300
351 Crider Ave Moorestown (08057) *(G-6630)*

Vermont Cableworks Inc 802 674-6555
31 National Rd Edison (08817) *(G-2643)*

Verna Printing, Belleville Also called Vernw Printing Company *(G-324)*

Verni Vito 732 449-1760
1818 State Route 35 Ste 8 Wall Township (07719) *(G-11517)*

Vernon Display Graphics Inc 201 935-7117
145 Commerce Rd Carlstadt (07072) *(G-1238)*

Vernw Printing Company 973 751-6462
85 Washington Ave Belleville (07109) *(G-324)*

Verona Aluminum Products Inc 973 857-4809
320 Bloomfield Ave Verona (07044) *(G-11312)*

Veroni Usa Inc 609 970-0320
1110 Commerce Blvd # 200 Logan Township (08085) *(G-5616)*

Versa Products Company Inc 201 291-0379
22 Spring Valley Rd Paramus (07652) *(G-7912)*

Versabar Corporation 973 279-8400
100 Maltese Dr Totowa (07512) *(G-10979)*

Versatile Distributors Inc 973 773-0550
293 Eisenhower Pkwy # 100 Livingston (07039) *(G-5570)*

Versatile Prtg Applications, Bound Brook Also called Joseph Burns Inc *(G-619)*

Verso Paper Management LP 732 938-3167
5100 Belmar Blvd Ste 7 Wall Township (07727) *(G-11518)*

Vertical Group Inc 908 277-3737
106 Allen Rd Ste 207 Basking Ridge (07920) *(G-208)*

Vertical Protective AP LLC 203 904-6099
830 Broad St Ste 3 Shrewsbury (07702) *(G-10013)*

Vertican Technologies Inc 800 435-7257
55 Lane Rd Ste 210 Fairfield (07004) *(G-3341)*

Vertice Pharma LLC (PA) 877 530-1633
630 Central Ave New Providence (07974) *(G-7060)*

Vertis Inc 215 781-1668
80 Stemmers Ln Mount Holly (08060) *(G-6777)*

Vertiv Services Inc 732 225-3741
3a Fernwood Ave Edison (08837) *(G-2644)*

Vesag Health Inc 732 333-1876
675 Us Highway 1 B202c North Brunswick (08902) *(G-7545)*

Vestal Printing, Cliffwood Also called Vestal Publishing Co Inc *(G-1550)*

Vestal Publishing Co Inc 732 583-3232
280 Cliffwood Ave Ste A Cliffwood (07721) *(G-1550)*

Vet Construction Inc 732 987-4922
29 N County Line Rd # 218 Jackson (08527) *(G-4682)*

Vetex, Ewing Also called Vehicle Technologies Inc *(G-3067)*

Vf Outdoor LLC 908 352-5390
651 Kapkowski Rd Ste 2034 Elizabeth (07201) *(G-2781)*

Vfi Fabricators Inc 856 629-8786
300 Thomas Ave Ste 101 Williamstown (08094) *(G-12113)*

Vgyaan Pharmaceuticals LLC 609 452-2770
100 Overlook Ctr Fl 2 Princeton (08540) *(G-9137)*

VI Concrete Co 856 767-0415
2324 Columbia Ave Atco (08004) *(G-92)*

Viatar Ctc Solutions Inc 617 299-6590
29 Clive Hills Rd Short Hills (07078) *(G-9987)*

Viavi Solutions Inc 609 632-0800
2 Applegate Dr Trenton (08691) *(G-11131)*

Vibgyor Solutions Inc 609 750-9158
14 Washington Rd Ste 623 Princeton Junction (08550) *(G-9165)*

Vibra Screw Inc 973 256-7410
755 Union Blvd Totowa (07512) *(G-10980)*

Vibra-Metrics, Princeton Junction Also called Physical Acoustics Corporation *(G-9162)*

Vibration Isolation Co, Paterson Also called Mab Enterprises Inc *(G-8328)*

Vibration Muntings Contrls Inc (PA) .. 800 569-8423
113 Main St Bloomingdale (07403) *(G-545)*

Vicinity Media Group Inc 973 276-1688
165 Passaic Ave Fairfield (07004) *(G-3342)*

Vicinity Publications Inc 973 276-1688
165 Passaic Ave Ste 107 Fairfield (07004) *(G-3343)*

Vicmarr Audio Inc 732 289-9111
9 Kilmer Ct Edison (08817) *(G-2645)*

Vicor Industries Inc 201 569-1947
225 County Rd Tenafly (07670) *(G-10789)*

Victor International Marketing 973 267-8900
35 Airport Rd Ste Ll25 Morristown (07960) *(G-6749)*

Victor Securities Inc 646 481-4835
285 Grand Ave Bldg No3 Englewood (07631) *(G-2942)*

Victoria Offset, Carlstadt Also called Lodor Offset Corporation *(G-1184)*

Victors Settings, Maywood Also called Victors Three-D Inc *(G-6062)*

Victors Three-D Inc 201 845-4433
25 Brook Ave Maywood (07607) *(G-6062)*

Victory Box Corp 908 245-5100
645 W 1st Ave Roselle (07203) *(G-9685)*

Victory International USA LLC 732 417-5900
40 Christopher Way Eatontown (07724) *(G-2429)*

Victory Iron Works Inc 201 485-7181
780 Mountain Ave Wyckoff (07481) *(G-12269)*

Victory Press 201 729-1007
1 Caesar Pl Moonachie (07074) *(G-6551)*

Victory Tool & Mfg Co 973 759-8733
231 Valley St 233 Belleville (07109) *(G-325)*

Videonet Comm Group LLC 732 863-5310
7 Seaman Rd Freehold (07728) *(G-3691)*

Vieiras Bakery, Newark Also called Vieiras Bakery Inc *(G-7357)*

Vieiras Bakery Inc 973 589-7719
34-48 Ave K Newark (07105) *(G-7357)*

Vierheilig Publishing, Midland Park Also called Times The Villadom Inc *(G-6240)*

Vigilant Design 201 432-3900
535 Communipaw Ave Jersey City (07304) *(G-4843)*

Vigo Industries LLC (PA) 866 591-7792
220 Mill Rd Edison (08817) *(G-2646)*

Vigor Inc 973 851-9539
45 Frances St Totowa (07512) *(G-10981)*

Viking Fender Company, Edison Also called Viking Marine Products Inc *(G-2647)*

Viking Marine Products Inc 732 826-4552
977 New Durham Rd Edison (08817) *(G-2647)*

Viking Mold & Tool Corp 609 476-9333
64 Tuckahoe Rd Dorothy (08317) *(G-2074)*

Viking Yacht Company (PA) 609 296-6000
On The Bass Riv Rr 9 New Gretna (08224) *(G-7020)*

Villa Milagro Vineyards LLC 908 995-2072
33 Warren Glen Rd Phillipsburg (08865) *(G-8675)*

Vine Hill Farm 973 383-0100
100 Parsons Rd Newton (07860) *(G-7411)*

Vineland Kosher Poultry Inc (PA) 856 692-1871
1050 S Mill Rd Vineland (08360) *(G-11415)*

Vineland Packaging Corp 856 794-3300
3602 N Mill Rd Vineland (08360) *(G-11416)*

Vineland Specialty Foods L L C 856 742-5001
201 Harvard Ave Westville (08093) *(G-11951)*

Vineland Syrup Inc 856 691-5772
723 S East Blvd Vineland (08360) *(G-11417)*

Vino's Kitchen Renovation, Middlesex Also called Vinos Custom Mllwk & Finshg *(G-6209)*

Vinos Custom Mllwk & Finshg 732 356-1147
562 Lincoln Blvd Middlesex (08846) *(G-6209)*

Vintage Print Gallery 201 501-0505
3 Reuten Dr Closter (07624) *(G-1768)*

Vintage Vibe Ltd Liability Co 973 989-2178
114 Beach St Rockaway (07866) *(G-9622)*

Vinylast Inc 732 367-7200
1830 Swarthmore Ave Ste 1 Lakewood (08701) *(G-5200)*

VIP Industries Inc 973 472-7500
  90 Brighton Rd Clifton (07012) *(G-1739)*

Vira Insight LLC 732 442-6756
  100 Ethel Rd W Piscataway (08854) *(G-8835)*

Vira Manufacturing Inc 732 771-8269
  1 Buckingham Ave Perth Amboy (08861) *(G-8635)*

Virginia Lawyers Weekly, Princeton Also called Dolan LLC *(G-9030)*

Vis USA LLC 908 575-0606
  210 Meister Ave Branchburg (08876) *(G-716)*

Viscot Medical LLC (PA) 973 887-9273
  32 West St East Hanover (07936) *(G-2248)*

Vish Group, North Brunswick Also called Vish LLC *(G-7546)*

Vish LLC 201 529-2900
  1605 Jersey Ave North Brunswick (08902) *(G-7546)*

Vision Lighting Inc 973 720-1200
  48 N 2nd St Paterson (07522) *(G-8408)*

Vision Railings Ltd Lblty Co 908 310-8926
  213 Dee Dee Dr Glen Gardner (08826) *(G-3817)*

Vision Research Inc (HQ) 973 696-4500
  100 Dey Rd Wayne (07470) *(G-11691)*

Vision Ten Inc 201 935-3000
  180 Broad St Carlstadt (07072) *(G-1239)*

Visionware Systems Inc 609 924-0800
  174 Tamarack Cir Skillman (08558) *(G-10037)*

Viskal Printing LLC 973 812-6600
  40e Commerce Way Totowa (07512) *(G-10982)*

Vislink, Hackettstown Also called Integrated Microwave Tech LLC *(G-4012)*

Vistapharm Inc (HQ) 908 376-1622
  630 Central Ave New Providence (07974) *(G-7061)*

Visual Architectural Designs 908 754-3000
  15 Harmich Rd South Plainfield (07080) *(G-10451)*

Visual Engineering Group Inc 908 479-1893
  29 Church St Bloomsbury (08804) *(G-546)*

Visual Graphic Systems Inc 201 528-2700
  330 Washington Ave Carlstadt (07072) *(G-1240)*

Visual Impact Advertising Inc 973 763-4900
  9 Highland Pl Apt 3 Maplewood (07040) *(G-5932)*

Vita-Pure Inc (PA) 908 245-1212
  410 W 1st Ave Roselle (07203) *(G-9686)*

Vitacare Pharma LLC 908 754-1792
  111 Skyline Dr South Plainfield (07080) *(G-10452)*

Vital Signs Medcl Legl Consltn 908 537-7857
  10 Magnolia Ln Asbury (08802) *(G-74)*

Vitamia & Sons, Lodi Also called Vitamia Pasta Boy Inc *(G-5608)*

Vitamia Pasta Boy Inc 973 546-1140
  206 Harrison Ave Ste 214 Lodi (07644) *(G-5608)*

Vitamin Retailer Magazine Inc 732 432-9600
  431 Cranbury Rd Ste C East Brunswick (08816) *(G-2197)*

Vitamin Shoppe Industries Inc (HQ) 201 868-5959
  2101 91st St North Bergen (07047) *(G-7491)*

Vitamin Shoppe, The, North Bergen Also called Vitamin Shoppe Industries Inc *(G-7491)*

Vitamins For Life, Oakhurst Also called Kwik Enterprises LLC *(G-7670)*

Vitaquest International LLC 973 575-9200
  21 Dwight Pl Fairfield (07004) *(G-3344)*

Vitaquest International LLC (PA) 973 575-9200
  8 Henderson Dr West Caldwell (07006) *(G-11807)*

Vitec Videocom Inc 908 852-3700
  700 Penhorn Ave Ste 1 Secaucus (07094) *(G-9938)*

Vitex LLC 201 296-0145
  105 Challenger Rd Ste 401 Ridgefield Park (07660) *(G-9417)*

Vitillo & Sons Inc 732 886-1393
  1930 Swarthmore Ave Lakewood (08701) *(G-5201)*

Viva Chemical Corporation (PA) 201 461-5281
  1512 Palisade Ave Apt 5m Fort Lee (07024) *(G-3589)*

Viva International Group, Branchburg Also called Marcolin USA Eyewear Corp *(G-678)*

Viva International Group, Branchburg Also called Viva International Inc *(G-717)*

Viva International Inc 908 595-6200
  3140 Route 22 Branchburg (08876) *(G-717)*

Vivis Life LLC 201 798-1938
  25 Park Ln S Apt 709 Jersey City (07310) *(G-4844)*

Vivitone Inc (PA) 973 427-8114
  111 Ethel Ave Hawthorne (07506) *(G-4264)*

Vivreau Advanced Water Systems 212 502-3749
  14 Madison Rd Ste 30 Fairfield (07004) *(G-3345)*

Viz Mold & Die Ltd 201 784-8383
  210 Industrial Pkwy Northvale (07647) *(G-7611)*

Viziflex Seels Inc 201 488-3446
  406 N Midland Ave Saddle Brook (07663) *(G-9799)*

Vmc Die Cutting Corp 973 450-4655
  357 Cortlandt St Belleville (07109) *(G-326)*

Vo-Toys Inc (PA) 973 482-8915
  179 Entin Rd Clifton (07014) *(G-1740)*

Vogel Precast Inc 732 552-8837
  1509 Prospect St Lakewood (08701) *(G-5202)*

Voicings Publication Inc 609 822-9401
  3 S Weymouth Ave Ste 2 Ventnor City (08406) *(G-11294)*

Voigt & Schweitzer LLC 732 442-7555
  1190 Amboy Ave Perth Amboy (08861) *(G-8636)*

Vol Employees Beneficiary Assn, Ridgefield Also called Grow Company Inc *(G-9363)*

Volta Belting USA Inc 973 276-7905
  60 Chapin Rd Ste 3 Pine Brook (07058) *(G-8719)*

Volta Corporation (PA) 732 583-3300
  11 Industrial Dr Laurence Harbor (08879) *(G-5236)*

Voltek Division, Secaucus Also called Sekisui America Corporation *(G-9927)*

Voltis LLC 607 349-9411
  55 Dwight Pl Unit A Fairfield (07004) *(G-3346)*

Volvo Car North America LLC (HQ) 201 768-7300
  1 Volvo Dr Rockleigh (07647) *(G-9636)*

Vonage, Holmdel Also called Novega Venture Partners Inc *(G-4527)*

Vozeh Equipment Corp 201 337-3729
  509 Commerce St Ste 1 Franklin Lakes (07417) *(G-3625)*

Vrpark, Rutherford Also called Gzgn Inc *(G-9733)*

Vs Hercules LLC (HQ) 201 868-5959
  2101 91st St North Bergen (07047) *(G-7492)*

VS Systematics Corp 908 241-5110
  300 S Michigan Ave Kenilworth (07033) *(G-5003)*

Vsar Resources LLC 973 233-6000
  30 Engelhard Dr Monroe Township (08831) *(G-6398)*

Vst Consulting Inc 732 404-0025
  200 Middlesex Tpke # 102 Iselin (08830) *(G-4650)*

Vu Sound Incorporated 215 990-2864
  1 Cameron Ln Lumberton (08048) *(G-5666)*

Vu World, Lumberton Also called Vu Sound Incorporated *(G-5666)*

Vulcan Information Packaging, Rutherford Also called Ebsco Industries Inc *(G-9731)*

Vulcan Tool Company Inc 908 686-0550
  1080 Garden State Rd # 1 Union (07083) *(G-11233)*

Vyral Entertainment, Hawthorne Also called Vyral Systems Inc *(G-4265)*

Vyral Systems Inc 201 321-2488
  300 Mountain Ave Hawthorne (07506) *(G-4265)*

Vytran Corporation 732 972-2880
  1400 Campus Dr Morganville (07751) *(G-6655)*

Vytran LLC 732 972-2880
  1400 Campus Dr Morganville (07751) *(G-6656)*

W & E Baum Bronze Tablet Corp 732 866-1881
  89 Bannard St Freehold (07728) *(G-3692)*

W & H Systems Inc 201 933-7840
  253 Passaic Ave Ste 1 Fairfield (07004) *(G-3347)*

W & S Steel Products, Berlin Also called Weiler & Sons LLC *(G-445)*

W A Cleary Products Inc 732 246-2829
  1049 Somerset St Somerset (08873) *(G-10196)*

W B Mason Co Inc 888 926-2766
  151 Heller Pl Bellmawr (08031) *(G-354)*

W B Mason Co Inc 888 926-2766
  350 Commerce Dr Egg Harbor Township (08234) *(G-2699)*

W B Mason Co Inc 888 926-2766
  21 Commerce Dr Cranbury (08512) *(G-1890)*

W C Davis Inc 856 547-4750
  126 W Atlantic Ave Haddon Heights (08035) *(G-4052)*

W C Omni Incorporated 732 248-0999
  166 National Rd Edison (08817) *(G-2648)*

W E Wamsley Restorations Inc 856 795-4001
  26 Tanner St Haddonfield (08033) *(G-4066)*

W F Sherman & Son Inc 732 223-1505
  84 Broad St Manasquan (08736) *(G-5883)*

W G I Corp 732 370-2900
  1875 Swarthmore Ave Lakewood (08701) *(G-5203)*

W Gerriets International Inc 609 771-8111
  130 Winterwood Ave Ewing (08638) *(G-3068)*

W J R B Inc 609 884-1169
  711 Town Bank Rd Cape May (08204) *(G-1107)*

W Kodak Jewelers Inc (PA) 201 710-5491
  60 Newark St Hoboken (07030) *(G-4503)*

W R Chesnut Engineering Inc 973 227-6995
  2 Industrial Rd 101 Fairfield (07004) *(G-3348)*

W R Grace & Co - Conn 201 869-5220
  2133 85th St North Bergen (07047) *(G-7493)*

W R Grace & Co-Conn 732 868-6914
  8 Heller Park Ln Somerset (08873) *(G-10197)*

W R Grace Construction Pdts, North Bergen Also called W R Grace & Co - Conn *(G-7493)*

W T Winter Associates Inc 888 808-3611
  20a Kulick Rd Fairfield (07004) *(G-3349)*

W W Jewelers Inc 718 392-4500
  35 Journal Sq Ste 231 Jersey City (07306) *(G-4845)*

W W Manufacturing Co Inc 856 451-5700
  60 Rosenhayn Ave Bridgeton (08302) *(G-802)*

W W Manufacturing Jewelers, Jersey City Also called W W Jewelers Inc *(G-4845)*

W Y Industries, North Bergen Also called WY Industries Inc *(G-7496)*

W.A. Cleary Products, Somerset Also called W A Cleary Products Inc *(G-10196)*

W2f Inc (PA) 609 735-0135
  167 Archertown Rd New Egypt (08533) *(G-7019)*

Waage Electric Inc 908 245-9363
  720 Colfax Ave Kenilworth (07033) *(G-5004)*

Wacoal America Inc (HQ) 201 933-8400
  1 Wacoal Plz Lyndhurst (07071) *(G-5713)*

Wacoal International Corp (HQ) 201 933-8400
  1 Wacoal Plz Lyndhurst (07071) *(G-5714)*

Waffle Waffle LLC (PA) 201 559-1286
  43 River Rd Nutley (07110) *(G-7657)*

Wagner Carbide Saw Division, Middlesex *Also called Tooling Etc LLC* ***(G-6206)***
Wagner Foto Screen Process............908 624-0800
4 Mark Rd Kenilworth (07033) ***(G-5005)***
Wagner Industries Inc............973 347-0800
51 Sparta Rd Stanhope (07874) ***(G-10592)***
Wagner Provision Co Inc............856 423-1630
54 E Broad St Gibbstown (08027) ***(G-3793)***
Wagner Rack Inc............973 278-6966
2 Broad St Clifton (07013) ***(G-1741)***
Wagonhouse Winery LLC............609 780-8019
1401 State Highway 45 Swedesboro (08085) ***(G-10736)***
Wakefern Food Corp (PA)............908 527-3300
5000 Riverside Dr Keasbey (08832) ***(G-4932)***
Wakefern Food Corp............732 819-0140
Old Post Rd Rr 1 Edison (08837) ***(G-2649)***
Wakefern General Merchandise, Keasbey *Also called Wakefern Food Corp* ***(G-4932)***
Wakefern Personnel, Edison *Also called Wakefern Food Corp* ***(G-2649)***
Walden Farms, Linden *Also called Panos Brands LLC* ***(G-5423)***
Walden Lang In-Pak Service............973 595-5250
474 Getty Ave 2 Clifton (07011) ***(G-1742)***
Walden Mott Corp............201 962-3704
225 N Franklin Tpke Ste 1 Ramsey (07446) ***(G-9255)***
Waldwick Plastics Corp............201 445-7436
21 Industrial Park Waldwick (07463) ***(G-11455)***
Waldwick Printing Co............201 652-5848
1 Harrison Ave Waldwick (07463) ***(G-11456)***
Waldwick Vol Amb Corps Inc............201 445-8772
20 Whites Ln Waldwick (07463) ***(G-11457)***
Walgreen Eastern Co Inc............973 728-3172
1502 Union Valley Rd West Milford (07480) ***(G-11858)***
Walgreen Eastern Co Inc............609 522-1291
5000 Park Blvd Wildwood (08260) ***(G-12075)***
Walgreens, West Milford *Also called Walgreen Eastern Co Inc* ***(G-11858)***
Walgreens, Wildwood *Also called Walgreen Eastern Co Inc* ***(G-12075)***
Walker Eight Corp............201 861-4208
510 73rd St North Bergen (07047) ***(G-7494)***
Walker Engineering Inc............732 899-2550
2111 Herbertsville Rd Point Pleasant Boro (08742) ***(G-8943)***
Wall Street Group Inc............201 333-4784
2 Hollywood Ct B South Plainfield (07080) ***(G-10453)***
Wall Street Journal............609 520-4000
4300 Us Highway 1 Monmouth Junction (08852) ***(G-6370)***
Wallscape, East Brunswick *Also called Rp Products LLC* ***(G-2181)***
Wally Enterprises Inc............732 329-2613
4266 Us Route 1 Monmouth Junction (08852) ***(G-6371)***
Walpole Woodworkers Inc............973 539-3555
540 Tabor Rd Morris Plains (07950) ***(G-6681)***
Walter Machine Co Inc............201 656-5654
84 Cambridge Ave 98 Jersey City (07307) ***(G-4846)***
Wanasavealotcom LLC............732 286-6956
524 Fielders Ln Toms River (08755) ***(G-10920)***
Ward Sand & Material, Vincentown *Also called James D Morrissey Inc* ***(G-11317)***
Wardale Corp............800 813-4050
575 Prospect St Ste 202 Lakewood (08701) ***(G-5204)***
Ware Industries Inc (PA)............908 757-9000
400 Metuchen Rd South Plainfield (07080) ***(G-10454)***
Warehouse, Clifton *Also called Fidelity Industries Inc* ***(G-1619)***
Warehouse Solutions Inc............201 880-1110
3-29 27th St Fl 4 Fair Lawn (07410) ***(G-3123)***
Warner Chilcott (us) LLC............973 442-3200
17 Airport Rd Ste 2 Morristown (07960) ***(G-6750)***
Warner Chilcott (us) LLC (HQ)............862 261-7000
400 Interpace Pkwy Parsippany (07054) ***(G-8110)***
Warner Chilcott Corporation (HQ)............862 261-7000
100 Enterprise Dr Ste 280 Rockaway (07866) ***(G-9623)***
Warner Chilcott Laboratories, Parsippany *Also called Warner Chilcott (us) LLC* ***(G-8110)***
Warp Processing Inc (PA)............973 238-1800
375 Diamond Bridge Ave Hawthorne (07506) ***(G-4266)***
Warren Capital Inc............732 910-8134
6 Westwood Ct Warren (07059) ***(G-11572)***
Warren Pallet Company Inc............908 995-7172
601 County Road 627 Bloomsbury (08804) ***(G-547)***
Wasak Inc............973 605-8122
45 S Park Pl Ste 224 Morristown (07960) ***(G-6751)***
Washington Stamp Exchange Inc............973 966-0001
2 Vreeland Rd Florham Park (07932) ***(G-3523)***
Wasmund Bindery, Toms River *Also called Santon Inc* ***(G-10909)***
Waste Management NJ Inc (HQ)............609 434-5200
107 Silvia St Ewing (08628) ***(G-3069)***
Waste Not Computers & Supplies............201 384-4444
94 Washington Ave Dumont (07628) ***(G-2125)***
Wastequip Manufacturing Co............856 784-5500
1031 Hickstown Rd Sicklerville (08081) ***(G-10028)***
Wastequip Manufacturing Co LLC............856 629-9222
New Brooklyn & Filbert St Williamstown (08094) ***(G-12114)***
Watchitude LLC............732 745-2626
24a Joyce Kilmer Ave N New Brunswick (08901) ***(G-7011)***
Water Dynamics Incorporated............973 428-8330
9 Valley Forge Dr Whippany (07981) ***(G-12042)***
Water Mark Technologies Inc............973 663-3438
762 State Route 15 S 2d Lake Hopatcong (07849) ***(G-5058)***
Water Master Co............732 247-1900
13 S 3rd Ave Highland Park (08904) ***(G-4305)***
Water On Time Bottled............862 252-9798
59 N 14th St East Orange (07017) ***(G-2273)***
Water Resources New Jersey LLC............609 268-7965
1609 Route 206 Tabernacle (08088) ***(G-10739)***
Water Resources of New Jersey, Tabernacle *Also called Water Resources New Jersey LLC* ***(G-10739)***
Water Store, The, East Rutherford *Also called Bellaqua Inc* ***(G-2284)***
Water Works Supply Company (PA)............973 835-2153
660 State Rt 23 Pompton Plains (07444) ***(G-8968)***
Water-Jel Holding Company............201 507-8300
50 Brd St Carlstadt (07072) ***(G-1241)***
Water-Jel Technologies LLC............201 438-1598
50 Broad St Carlstadt (07072) ***(G-1242)***
Waterdoctor Inc............732 972-4510
734 Grand Ave Unit E Ridgefield (07657) ***(G-9393)***
Waterloov, Oakhurst *Also called R & K Industries Inc* ***(G-7672)***
Waters Technologies Corp............973 394-5660
1259 Route 46 Ste 3 Parsippany (07054) ***(G-8111)***
Watonka Printing Inc............732 974-8878
1608 State Route 71 Belmar (07719) ***(G-365)***
Watson Laboratories Inc (HQ)............951 493-5300
400 Interpace Pkwy Parsippany (07054) ***(G-8112)***
Watthung Communications Inc............908 232-4407
251 North Ave W Ste 7 Westfield (07090) ***(G-11933)***
Wave Dispersion Tech Inc (PA)............908 233-7503
45 Industrial Rd Berkeley Heights (07922) ***(G-424)***
Waveline Incorporated............973 226-9100
160 Passaic Ave Fairfield (07004) ***(G-3350)***
Way It Was Sporting Svc Inc............856 231-0111
620 Chestnut St Moorestown (08057) ***(G-6631)***
Wayne County Foods Inc............973 399-0101
360 Coit St Irvington (07111) ***(G-4607)***
Wayne Motors Inc............973 696-9710
1910 State Route 23 Wayne (07470) ***(G-11692)***
Wayside Fence Company Inc............201 791-7979
38-06 Broadway Fair Lawn (07410) ***(G-3124)***
Wcd Enterprises Inc............732 888-4422
1 Main St Keyport (07735) ***(G-5026)***
Wearbest Sil-Tex Mills Ltd (PA)............973 340-8844
325 Midland Ave Garfield (07026) ***(G-3772)***
Weatherbeeta USA Inc............732 287-1182
201 Mill Rd Edison (08837) ***(G-2650)***
Weathercraft Manufacturing Co............201 262-0055
13 Emerson Plz E Emerson (07630) ***(G-2864)***
Weaver Associates Printing, Cranford *Also called Bab Printing Jan Service* ***(G-1897)***
Weavers Fiberglass............609 597-4324
19 Parker St Manahawkin (08050) ***(G-5835)***
Web Industries Inc............973 335-1200
5 Mars Ct Montville (07045) ***(G-6497)***
Web-Cote Ltd............973 827-2299
141 Wheatsworth Rd Hamburg (07419) ***(G-4099)***
Web-Cote Industries, Hamburg *Also called Web-Cote Ltd* ***(G-4099)***
Webannuitiescom Inc (PA)............732 521-5110
8 Talmadge Dr Monroe (08831) ***(G-6376)***
Webb Press............609 386-0100
340 E Broad St Burlington (08016) ***(G-995)***
Webb-Mason Inc............732 747-6585
628 Shrewsbury Ave Ste G Tinton Falls (07701) ***(G-10854)***
Webco Graphics, Lakewood *Also called W G I Corp* ***(G-5203)***
Weber & Doebrich Inc............201 868-6122
119 61st St West New York (07093) ***(G-11883)***
Weber and Scher Mfg Co Inc............908 236-8484
1231 Us Highway 22 Lebanon (08833) ***(G-5303)***
Weber Packaging Inc............201 262-6022
494 Demarest Ave Oradell (07649) ***(G-7815)***
Webers Candy Store............856 455-8277
111 Old Cohansey Rd Bridgeton (08302) ***(G-803)***
Webtech Inc............609 259-2800
108 N Gold Dr Robbinsville (08691) ***(G-9524)***
Wecom Inc............856 863-8400
20 Warrick Ave Glassboro (08028) ***(G-3813)***
Wecool Toys Inc............856 296-9766
19 N Lakeside Dr W Medford (08055) ***(G-6084)***
Wedo, West New York *Also called Weber & Doebrich Inc* ***(G-11883)***
Weekly News, The, Budd Lake *Also called New View Media* ***(G-938)***
Wees Beyond Products Corp............862 238-8800
1 Market St Ste 6 Passaic (07055) ***(G-8189)***
Weidener Construction, Fair Lawn *Also called Robert Weidener* ***(G-3111)***
Weiler & Sons LLC............856 767-8842
170 Jackson Rd Berlin (08009) ***(G-445)***
Weiler Labeling Systems LLC............856 273-3377
1256 N Church St Moorestown (08057) ***(G-6632)***
Weiling Yang............201 440-5329
65 Challenger Rd Ridgefield Park (07660) ***(G-9418)***

Weinman Bros Inc 212 695-8116
111 Town Square Pl # 434 Jersey City (07310) *(G-4847)*

Weir Welding Company Inc (PA) 201 939-2284
316 12th St Carlstadt (07072) *(G-1243)*

Weiss-Aug Co Inc (PA) 973 887-7600
220 Merry Ln East Hanover (07936) *(G-2249)*

Wel-Fab Inc 609 261-1393
50 Indel Ave Rancocas (08073) *(G-9265)*

Weld Tech Fab 732 919-2185
282 Lemon Rd Farmingdale (07727) *(G-3396)*

Welded Products Co Inc 973 589-0180
330 Raymond Blvd Ste 336 Newark (07105) *(G-7358)*

Welding & Radiator Supply Co 609 965-0433
1144 W White Horse Pike Egg Harbor City (08215) *(G-2674)*

Welding Materials, Watchung *Also called Fanwood Crushed Stone Company (G-11591)*

Weldon Asphalt Corp 973 627-7500
311 W Main St Ste 1 Rockaway (07866) *(G-9624)*

Weldon Asphalt Corp 908 322-7840
1 New Providence Rd Watchung (07069) *(G-11597)*

Weldon Asphalt Division, Westfield *Also called Brunswick Hot Mix Corp (G-11922)*

Weldon Concrete Co., Westfield *Also called Weldon Materials Inc (G-11934)*

Weldon Concrete Corp 973 228-7473
1 Eisenhower Pkwy Roseland (07068) *(G-9657)*

Weldon Materials Inc (PA) 908 233-4444
141 Central Ave Westfield (07090) *(G-11934)*

Weldon Materials Inc 201 991-3200
1100 Harrison Ave Kearny (07032) *(G-4919)*

Well Bilt Industries Inc 908 486-6002
2 Maple Ave Linden (07036) *(G-5458)*

Well Manager LLC 609 466-4347
371 Route 31 N Hopewell (08525) *(G-4544)*

Wells-Gardner, Hammonton *Also called American Gaming & Elec Inc (G-4129)*

Wellspring Info Inc 800 268-3682
251 Park St Montclair (07043) *(G-6439)*

Welsch Metal Products Inc 908 782-5996
8 Bartles Corner Rd # 13 Flemington (08822) *(G-3475)*

Welter & Kreutz Printing Co 201 489-9098
51 Worth St South Hackensack (07606) *(G-10299)*

Welton V Johnson Engineering 908 241-3100
22 N 26th St Kenilworth (07033) *(G-5006)*

Wenner Bread Products Inc 631 563-6262
571 Jersey Ave New Brunswick (08901) *(G-7012)*

Werko Machine Co 856 662-0669
9200 Collins Ave Pennsauken (08110) *(G-8588)*

West Dry Industries Inc 908 757-4400
755 W Broad St Westfield (07090) *(G-11935)*

West Electronics, Burlington *Also called F S Brainard & Co (G-971)*

West Electronics Inc 609 387-4300
5 Terri Ln Burlington (08016) *(G-996)*

West Essex Graphics Inc 973 227-2400
305 Fairfield Ave Fairfield (07004) *(G-3351)*

West Essex Tribune Inc 973 992-1771
495 S Livingston Ave Livingston (07039) *(G-5571)*

West Hudson Lumber & Mllwk Co 201 991-7191
60 Arlington Ave Kearny (07032) *(G-4920)*

West Machine Works Inc 732 549-2183
101 Liberty St Metuchen (08840) *(G-6130)*

West Pattern Works Inc 609 443-6241
124 S Main St Cranbury (08512) *(G-1891)*

West Penetone, Carlstadt *Also called Penetone Corporation (G-1199)*

West Phrm Svcs Lakewood Inc 732 730-3295
1200 Paco Way Lakewood (08701) *(G-5205)*

West-Ward Injectables, Inc., Eatontown *Also called Hikma Injectables USA Inc (G-2401)*

Westar Tool LLC 856 507-8852
427 Commerce Ln Ste 7 West Berlin (08091) *(G-11760)*

Westbrook Industries, Scotch Plains *Also called Hnt Industries Inc (G-9850)*

Westbury Press Inc 201 894-0444
1 W Forest Ave Englewood (07631) *(G-2943)*

Westchester Denim Brothers Inc 203 260-1629
736 Slocum Ave Ridgefield (07657) *(G-9394)*

Westchester Lace & Textiles 201 864-2150
3901 Liberty Ave North Bergen (07047) *(G-7495)*

Westcon Orthopedics Inc 908 806-8981
4 Craig Rd Neshanic Station (08853) *(G-6940)*

Western Digital Corporation 609 734-7479
116 Village Blvd Ste 200 Princeton (08540) *(G-9138)*

Western Electronics Dist 908 475-3303
300 5th St Belvidere (07823) *(G-378)*

Western Pacific Foods Inc 908 838-0186
650 Belleville Tpke Ste 2 Kearny (07032) *(G-4921)*

Western Rock Products, Wall Township *Also called Hanson Aggregates Wrp Inc (G-11487)*

Western Scientific Computers 973 263-9311
28 W Shore Rd Mountain Lakes (07046) *(G-6864)*

Westfield Shtmtl Works Inc 908 276-5500
261 Monroe Ave Kenilworth (07033) *(G-5007)*

Westlock Controls Corporation (HQ) 201 794-7650
280 N Midland Ave Ste 232 Saddle Brook (07663) *(G-9800)*

Westrock Converting Company 856 438-2200
5000 Lincoln Dr E Marlton (08053) *(G-6003)*

Westrock CP LLC 732 866-1890
21 Millpond Ln Colts Neck (07722) *(G-1794)*

Westrock CP LLC 973 594-6000
1401 Broad St Ste 1 Clifton (07013) *(G-1743)*

Westrock Rkt Company 973 594-6000
29g Commerce Way Totowa (07512) *(G-10983)*

Westrock Rkt Company 732 274-2500
1 Corn Rd Dayton (08810) *(G-1994)*

Westrock Rkt Company 973 237-9570
1 Center Ct Unit Ab Totowa (07512) *(G-10984)*

Westrock Rkt Company 856 596-8604
5000 Lincoln Dr E Marlton (08053) *(G-6004)*

Westrock Rkt Company 973 484-5000
2013 Mccarter Hwy Newark (07104) *(G-7359)*

Westwood Construction, Millstone Twp *Also called Christopher Szuco (G-6266)*

Westwood Sleep Centers, Westwood *Also called Lieth Holdings LLC (G-11962)*

Wet Planet Beverages, Teterboro *Also called Jolt Company Inc (G-10803)*

Wet-N-Stick LLC 908 687-8273
2816 Morris Ave Ste 21 Union (07083) *(G-11234)*

Wexco Industries Inc 973 244-5777
3 Barnet Rd Pine Brook (07058) *(G-8720)*

Wexford International Inc 908 781-7200
190 Main St Ste 102 Gladstone (07934) *(G-3799)*

Wg Products Inc 973 256-5999
70 Maltese Dr Totowa (07512) *(G-10985)*

Wgjf Manufacturing Corp 908 862-1730
417 Commerce Rd Linden (07036) *(G-5459)*

Whale Communications Inc 201 947-0054
400 Kelby St Ste 8 Fort Lee (07024) *(G-3590)*

What A Tee 2 Inc 201 457-0060
82 Sussex St Hackensack (07601) *(G-3991)*

What's On In Haddonfield, Haddonfield *Also called Community News Network Inc (G-4058)*

Whe Research Inc 732 240-3871
1545 Route 37 W Ste 6 Toms River (08755) *(G-10921)*

Wheal-Grace Corp 973 450-8100
300 Ralph St Belleville (07109) *(G-327)*

Wheatland Tube Co, Westwood *Also called Zekelman Industries Inc (G-11977)*

Wheaton Sands Products, Millville *Also called Glass Warehouse (G-6305)*

Wheaton Science Products, Millville *Also called Amcor Phrm Packg USA LLC (G-6280)*

Wheaton Science Products, Millville *Also called Dwk Life Sciences Inc (G-6301)*

Wheels Motor Sports Inc 732 606-9208
13 Penny Ln Bayville (08721) *(G-262)*

Whibco Inc (PA) 856 455-9200
87 E Commerce St Bridgeton (08302) *(G-804)*

Whibco Inc 856 825-5200
377 Port Commerland Rd Port Elizabeth (08348) *(G-8971)*

Whibco of New Jersey Inc 856 455-9200
377 Port Cumberland Rd Port Elizabeth (08348) *(G-8972)*

Whimsy Diddles LLC 609 560-1323
59 Briarhill Dr Chesilhurst (08089) *(G-1431)*

Whippany Actuation Systems LLC 973 428-9898
110 Algonquin Pkwy Whippany (07981) *(G-12043)*

Whips International, Cherry Hill *Also called CDK Industries LLC (G-1356)*

Whiptail Technologies Inc., Whippany *Also called Whiptail Technologies LLC (G-12044)*

Whiptail Technologies LLC 973 585-6375
9 Whippany Rd Ste 67 Whippany (07981) *(G-12044)*

Whisprwave, Berkeley Heights *Also called Wave Dispersion Tech Inc (G-424)*

White Castle 732 721-3565
987 Us Highway 9 South Amboy (08879) *(G-10247)*

White Eagle Printing Co Inc 609 586-2032
2550 Kuser Rd Trenton (08691) *(G-11132)*

White Home Products Inc 908 226-2501
30 Boright Ave 4 Kenilworth (07033) *(G-5008)*

White Lotus Home Ltd Lblty Co 732 828-2111
745 Joyce Kilmer Ave New Brunswick (08901) *(G-7013)*

White Marine Inc 732 826-4491
7 Old Jacksonville Rd Towaco (07082) *(G-11007)*

Whitehouse Machine & Mfg Co 908 534-4722
3585 Us Highway 22 Somerville (08876) *(G-10232)*

Whitehouse Prtg & Labeling LLC 973 521-7648
50 Kulick Rd Fairfield (07004) *(G-3352)*

Whiteweave Foods, Bridgeton *Also called Wwf Operating Company (G-805)*

Whittle & Mutch Inc 856 235-1165
712 Fellowship Rd Mount Laurel (08054) *(G-6846)*

Whole Stones LLC 856 266-0091
1 Ironside Ct Willingboro (08046) *(G-12123)*

Whole Year Trading Co Inc 732 238-1196
117 Docks Corner Rd Ste B Dayton (08810) *(G-1995)*

Whoot Newspaper, Pleasantville *Also called Atlantic City Week (G-8902)*

Wick It LLC 973 249-2970
1 Gregory Ave Passaic (07055) *(G-8190)*

Wickr Inc 516 637-2882
211 Warren St Ste 34 Newark (07103) *(G-7360)*

Wide Band Systems Inc 973 586-6500
389 Franklin Ave Rockaway (07866) *(G-9625)*

Wikstrom Machines Inc 732 826-4800
412 Summit Ave Perth Amboy (08861) *(G-8637)*

A
L
P
H
A
B
E
T
I
C

Wilcox Press 973 827-7474
6 Main St Hamburg (07419) *(G-4100)*

Wilcoy Press, Pine Hill *Also called Bruce McCoy Sr (G-8721)*

Wild Bills Olde Fashioned Soda, Millington *Also called Bluewater Inc (G-6260)*

Wild Flavors Inc 908 820-9800
132 Corbin St Bldg 1200 Elizabeth (07201) *(G-2782)*

Wild Juice US, Elizabeth *Also called Wild Flavors Inc (G-2782)*

Wilenta Carting Inc 201 325-0044
46 Henry St Secaucus (07094) *(G-9939)*

Wilenta Feed Inc 201 325-0044
46 Henry St Secaucus (07094) *(G-9940)*

Wiley Publishing LLC (HQ) 201 748-6000
111 River St Hoboken (07030) *(G-4504)*

Wiley Subscription Services 201 748-6000
111 River St Hoboken (07030) *(G-4505)*

Wiley-Interscience, Hoboken *Also called Wiley Subscription Services (G-4505)*

Wilker Graphics LLC 201 447-4800
95 Greenwood Ave Midland Park (07432) *(G-6242)*

William Carter Company 201 313-1783
17 The Promenade Edgewater (07020) *(G-2443)*

William Cromley 856 881-6019
101 S Delsea Dr Clayton (08312) *(G-1529)*

William Duling 856 365-6323
613 Kaighn Ave 15 Camden (08103) *(G-1089)*

William Kenyon & Sons Inc (HQ) 732 985-8980
90 Ethel Rd W Piscataway (08854) *(G-8836)*

William Opdyke Awnings Inc (PA) 732 449-5940
2036 State Route 35 Wall Township (07719) *(G-11519)*

William R Hall Co 856 784-6700
901 E Gibbsboro Rd Lindenwold (08021) *(G-5464)*

William R Tatz Industries 973 751-0720
11 Railroad Pl Belleville (07109) *(G-328)*

William Robert Graphics Inc 201 239-7400
234 16th St Fl 7 Jersey City (07310) *(G-4848)*

William Spencer (PA) 856 235-1830
20 Lake Dr Mount Laurel (08054) *(G-6847)*

William T Hutchinson Company 908 688-0533
453 Lehigh Ave Union (07083) *(G-11235)*

Williams Scotsman Inc 856 429-0315
150 Western Rd Kearny (07032) *(G-4922)*

Williams Scotsman - NY Cy, Kearny *Also called Williams Scotsman Inc (G-4922)*

Willier Elc Mtr Repr Co Inc (PA) 856 627-3535
1 Linden Ave Gibbsboro (08026) *(G-3790)*

Willier Elc Mtr Repr Co Inc 856 627-2262
3 Democrat Rd Ste Td Gibbsboro (08026) *(G-3791)*

Willier Technical Services, Gibbsboro *Also called Willier Elc Mtr Repr Co Inc (G-3791)*

Willow Creek Winery Inc 609 770-8782
160 Stevens St 168 Cape May (08204) *(G-1108)*

Willow Iron Works, Jersey City *Also called 67 Pollock Ave Corp (G-4692)*

Willow Run Construction Inc 201 659-7266
67 Pollock Ave Jersey City (07305) *(G-4849)*

Willow Technology Inc 732 671-1554
12 Valley Point Dr Holmdel (07733) *(G-4531)*

Willowbrook Golf Center LLC 973 256-6922
366 Us Highway 46 Wayne (07470) *(G-11693)*

Wilmington Trust Sp Services 609 272-7000
1000 W Washington Ave Pleasantville (08232) *(G-8918)*

Wilpak Industries Inc 201 997-7600
244 Dukes St Kearny (07032) *(G-4923)*

Wilshire Technologies Inc 609 683-1117
318 Wall St Princeton (08540) *(G-9139)*

Wilsonart LLC 800 822-7613
11 Twosome Dr Moorestown (08057) *(G-6633)*

Win-Tech Precision Products 973 887-8727
5a Littell Rd East Hanover (07936) *(G-2250)*

Wind Tunnel Inc 201 485-7793
60 Whitney Rd Ste 13 Mahwah (07430) *(G-5824)*

Windmill Health Products, Fairfield *Also called Vitaquest International LLC (G-3344)*

Windmill Press Inc 856 663-8990
1051 Thomas Busch Mem Hwy Pennsauken (08110) *(G-8589)*

Window Designs By Powers, Northvale *Also called Shade Powers Co Inc (G-7607)*

Window Factory Inc 856 546-5050
603 N Black Horse Pike Mount Ephraim (08059) *(G-6765)*

Window Repairs & Restoration, Gloucester City *Also called Pierangeli Group Inc (G-3842)*

Window Shapes Inc 732 549-0708
225 Liberty St Metuchen (08840) *(G-6131)*

Window Trends 973 887-6676
194 Fieldcrest Rd Parsippany (07054) *(G-8113)*

Windsor Labs LLC 609 301-6446
55 Lake Dr East Windsor (08520) *(G-2370)*

Windtree Therapeutics Inc 973 339-2889
710 Union Blvd Totowa (07512) *(G-10986)*

Winemiller Press Inc 732 223-0100
2411 Atlantic Ave Ste 6 Manasquan (08736) *(G-5884)*

Winery Pak LLC 800 434-4599
3 Wing Dr Ste 101 Cedar Knolls (07927) *(G-1323)*

Winetree Publishing, Monroe Township *Also called Steven Orros (G-6396)*

Wingold Embroidery LLC 732 845-9802
5 Monarch Ln Freehold (07728) *(G-3693)*

Winslow Rental & Supply Inc 856 767-5554
204 Williamstown Rd Berlin (08009) *(G-446)*

Winsome Digital Inc 609 645-2211
202 W Parkway Dr Egg Harbor Township (08234) *(G-2700)*

Winstar Windows LLC 973 403-0574
217 Roseland Ave Essex Fells (07021) *(G-3001)*

Winter Scale & Equipment, Fairfield *Also called W T Winter Associates Inc (G-3349)*

Winters Bank Signs, Martinsville *Also called Winters Stamp Mfg Co Inc (G-6011)*

Winters Stamp Mfg Co Inc 908 352-3725
1024 Mayflower Ct Martinsville (08836) *(G-6011)*

Wire Cloth Manufacturers Inc (PA) 973 328-1000
110 Iron Mountain Rd Mine Hill (07803) *(G-6329)*

Wire Displays Inc 973 537-0090
88 King St Ste 1 Dover (07801) *(G-2114)*

Wire Fabricators & Insulators 973 768-2839
20 Harding Pl Livingston (07039) *(G-5572)*

Wire-Pro Inc (HQ) 856 935-7560
90 W Broadway Salem (08079) *(G-9810)*

Wired Products LLC 551 231-5800
49 E Midland Ave Ste 6 Paramus (07652) *(G-7913)*

Wireless Communications Inc 732 926-1000
55 Liberty St Metuchen (08840) *(G-6132)*

Wireless Communications & Elec, West Berlin *Also called Wireless Electronics Inc (G-11761)*

Wireless Electronics Inc 856 768-4310
153 Cooper Rd West Berlin (08091) *(G-11761)*

Wireless Experience of PA Inc (PA) 732 552-0050
1451 Rte 37 W A Toms River (08755) *(G-10922)*

Wireless Experience, The, Toms River *Also called Wireless Experience of PA Inc (G-10922)*

Wireless Telecom Group Inc (PA) 973 386-9696
25 Eastmans Rd Parsippany (07054) *(G-8114)*

Wireworks Corporation 908 686-7400
380 Hillside Ave Hillside (07205) *(G-4451)*

Wisco Promo & Uniform Inc 973 767-2022
160 Us Highway 46 Saddle Brook (07663) *(G-9801)*

Wise Foods Inc 201 440-2876
150 Carol Pl Moonachie (07074) *(G-6552)*

Wisely Products LLC 929 329-9188
77 Hudson St Apt 2406 Jersey City (07302) *(G-4850)*

Witte Co Inc 908 689-6500
507 Rte 31 S Washington (07882) *(G-11590)*

Wittich Bros Marine Inc 732 722-8656
25a Abe Voorhees Dr Manasquan (08736) *(G-5885)*

Wizard Technology Inc 732 730-0800
2165 Route 9 Toms River (08755) *(G-10923)*

Wizcom Corporation 609 750-0601
19 Washington Rd Ste D Princeton Junction (08550) *(G-9166)*

Wizdata Systems Inc 973 975-4113
140 Littleton Rd Ste 220 Parsippany (07054) *(G-8115)*

Wjj and Company LLC 973 246-7480
141 Lanza Ave Bldg 29 Garfield (07026) *(G-3773)*

Wjm Trucking Inc 856 381-3635
515 Macintosh Dr Mullica Hill (08062) *(G-6893)*

Wjv Materials LLC 856 299-8244
93 Pennsgrve Pedrcktwn Pedricktown (08067) *(G-8441)*

Wl Ring, Metuchen *Also called Wlxt LLC (G-6133)*

Wlxt LLC 732 906-7979
16 Wernik Pl Metuchen (08840) *(G-6133)*

Wm Hbrewster Jr Incorporated 973 227-1050
16 Kulick Rd Fairfield (07004) *(G-3353)*

Wm Leiber Inc 732 938-2080
190 Georgia Tavern Rd Farmingdale (07727) *(G-3397)*

Wm Steinen Mfg Co (PA) 973 887-6400
29 E Halsey Rd Parsippany (07054) *(G-8116)*

Wm.h. Brewster Jr, Fairfield *Also called Wm Hbrewster Jr Incorporated (G-3353)*

Wohners (PA) 201 568-7307
29 Bergen St Englewood (07631) *(G-2944)*

Wolf Form Co Inc 201 567-6556
289 Orangeburgh Rd Old Tappan (07675) *(G-7801)*

Wolock & Lott Transmission Eqp 908 218-9292
25 Chambers Brook Rd Branchburg (08876) *(G-718)*

Woman's World Magazine, Englewood Cliffs *Also called Heinrich Bauer Verlag (G-2963)*

Wong Robinson & Co Inc (PA) 609 951-0300
743 Alexander Rd Ste 15 Princeton (08540) *(G-9140)*

Wood & Laminates Inc 973 773-7475
102 Us Highway 46 E Lodi (07644) *(G-5609)*

Wood Products Inc 609 859-0303
34 Allentown Rd Southampton (08088) *(G-10484)*

Wood Textures 732 230-5005
251 Herrod Blvd Dayton (08810) *(G-1996)*

Wood Works 856 728-4520
1111 N Black Horse Pike Williamstown (08094) *(G-12115)*

Wood's Industrial Services, West Milford *Also called Woods Industrial LLC (G-11859)*

Woodbridge Inoac Technical 201 807-0809
100 Carol Pl Moonachie (07074) *(G-6553)*

Woodbridge Inoac Technical Pro 201 807-0809
100 Carol Pl Moonachie (07074) *(G-6554)*

Woodbridge Machine & Tool Co 732 634-0179
259 Bergen St Woodbridge (07095) *(G-12156)*

Woodbury Roof Truss Inc 856 845-3848
692 S Evergreen Ave Woodbury Heights (08097) *(G-12178)*

Woodhaven Lumber & Millwork (PA) 732 901-0030
200 James St Lakewood (08701) *(G-5206)*

Woodhaven Lumber & Millwork 732 295-8800
1303 Richmond Ave Point Pleasant Beach (08742) *(G-8928)*

Woodhut LLC 732 414-6440
210 Jerseyville Ave Freehold (07728) *(G-3694)*

Woodland Manufacturing Company 609 587-4180
1936 E State Street Ext Trenton (08619) *(G-11133)*

Woodline Works Corporation 732 828-9100
625 Jersey Ave Ste 9 New Brunswick (08901) *(G-7014)*

Woodpeckers Inc 973 751-4744
323 Cortlandt St Belleville (07109) *(G-329)*

Woodriver Industries, Delran *Also called Sea Gull Lighting Products LLC (G-2021)*

Woods Industrial LLC 973 208-0664
81 Hudson Dr West Milford (07480) *(G-11859)*

Woodstock Farms, Edison *Also called United Natural Trading Co (G-2640)*

Woodtec Inc 908 979-0180
300 W Stiger St Hackettstown (07840) *(G-4043)*

Woodward Jogger Aerators Inc (PA) 201 933-6800
45 Carlton Ave East Rutherford (07073) *(G-2337)*

Woodward Wood Products Design 609 597-2708
612 Main St West Creek (08092) *(G-11812)*

Woodworking Inc Corporate 973 227-2211
368 Passaic Ave Ste 300 Fairfield (07004) *(G-3354)*

Word Center Printing 609 586-5825
1905 Highway 33 Ste 10 Trenton (08690) *(G-11134)*

Wordmasters 201 327-4201
213 E Allendale Ave Allendale (07401) *(G-23)*

Work n Gear LLC 856 848-7676
1692 Clements Bridge Rd H Woodbury (08096) *(G-12172)*

Work Zone Contractors LLC 856 845-8201
664 Oak Ave Deptford (08096) *(G-2069)*

Work'n Gear 8047, Woodbury *Also called Work n Gear LLC (G-12172)*

Works Enduro Rider Inc 908 637-6385
1 Jenny Jump Ave Great Meadows (07838) *(G-3853)*

Workwave LLC (HQ) 866 794-1658
101 Crawfords Corner Rd Holmdel (07733) *(G-4532)*

World and Main LLC (PA) 609 860-9990
324a Half Acre Rd Cranbury (08512) *(G-1892)*

World Class Intl Kit 712, Linden *Also called Saker Shoprites Inc (G-5437)*

World Class Marketing Corp (HQ) 201 313-0022
2147 Hudson Ter Fort Lee (07024) *(G-3591)*

World Confections Inc 718 768-8100
14 S Orange Ave Ste A South Orange (07079) *(G-10317)*

World Electronics Inc 201 670-1177
37 Hanover Pl Glen Rock (07452) *(G-3830)*

World Impro, Palisades Park *Also called BSC USA LLC (G-7836)*

World Journal LLC 732 632-8890
41a Bridge St Metuchen (08840) *(G-6134)*

World of Coffee Inc 908 647-1218
328 Essex St Stirling (07980) *(G-10609)*

World of Tea, Stirling *Also called World of Coffee Inc (G-10609)*

World Pac Paper LLC 877 837-2737
600 E Crescent Ave # 301 Upper Saddle River (07458) *(G-11288)*

World Plastic Extruders Inc 201 933-2915
41 Park Ave Rutherford (07070) *(G-9746)*

World Scientific Publishing Co 201 487-9655
27 Warren St Ph 401 Hackensack (07601) *(G-3992)*

World Software Corporation 201 444-3228
266 Harristown Rd Ste 201 Glen Rock (07452) *(G-3831)*

World Wide Metric Inc (PA) 732 247-2300
37 Readington Rd Branchburg (08876) *(G-719)*

World Wide Packaging LLC (PA) 973 805-6500
15 Vreeland Rd Ste 4 Florham Park (07932) *(G-3524)*

Worldcast Network Inc 201 767-2040
20 Foxwood Sq S Old Tappan (07675) *(G-7802)*

Worldox, Glen Rock *Also called World Software Corporation (G-3831)*

Worldwide Glass Resources Inc 856 205-1508
1022 Spruce St Vineland (08360) *(G-11418)*

Worldwide Pt SL Ltd Lblty Co 201 928-0222
555 Cedar Ln Ste 7 Teaneck (07666) *(G-10777)*

Worldwide Safety Systems LLC 888 613-4501
1297 Sussex Rd Teaneck (07666) *(G-10778)*

Worldwide Whl Flr Cvg Inc (PA) 732 906-1400
1055 Us Highway 1 Edison (08837) *(G-2651)*

Worrall Community Newspapers 973 743-4040
266 Liberty St Bloomfield (07003) *(G-537)*

Worthington Biochemical Corp (PA) 732 942-1660
730 Vassar Ave Lakewood (08701) *(G-5207)*

Wostbrock Embroidery Inc 201 445-3074
11 Paterson Ave Ste 1 Midland Park (07432) *(G-6243)*

Woyshner Service Company Inc 856 461-9196
813 Edgewood Ave Delran (08075) *(G-2024)*

Wpi Communications Inc 973 467-8700
55 Morris Ave Ste 312 Springfield (07081) *(G-10586)*

Wpi-Salem Division, Salem *Also called Wire-Pro Inc (G-9810)*

Wrap-Ade Machine Co Inc 973 773-6150
180 Brighton Rd Ste B Clifton (07012) *(G-1744)*

Wrapade, Clifton *Also called Wrap-Ade Machine Co Inc (G-1744)*

Wrapade Packaging Systems LLC 973 787-1788
15 Gardner Rd Ste 200 Fairfield (07004) *(G-3355)*

Wrench Brothers LLC 201 222-0301
327 Newark Ave Jersey City (07302) *(G-4851)*

Wrightworks Engineering LLC 609 882-8840
12 Rosetree Ln Lawrenceville (08648) *(G-5272)*

Write Element LLC 973 584-0373
14 James Rd Randolph (07869) *(G-9306)*

Writers & Poets 908 233-2399
1625 Nottingham Way Mountainside (07092) *(G-6890)*

Wrought Metal Products Div, Riverside *Also called Hun Machine Works Inc (G-9500)*

Wsc International, Delran *Also called Woyshner Service Company Inc (G-2024)*

Wt Media LLC 609 921-3490
4 Applegate Dr Trenton (08691) *(G-11135)*

Wurz Signsystems LLC 856 461-4397
2600 Haddonfield Rd Pennsauken (08110) *(G-8590)*

Wwf Operating Company 856 459-3890
70 Rosenhayn Ave Bridgeton (08302) *(G-805)*

Www.vandlmachinetool.com, Fairfield *Also called V & L Machine and Tool Co Inc (G-3336)*

WY Industries Inc 201 617-8000
2500 Secaucus Rd North Bergen (07047) *(G-7496)*

Wyeth Holdings Corporation, Madison *Also called Wyeth Holdings LLC (G-5737)*

Wyeth Holdings LLC (HQ) 973 660-5000
5 Giralda Farms Madison (07940) *(G-5737)*

Wyeth LLC 973 660-5000
5 Giralda Farms Madison (07940) *(G-5738)*

Wyeth-Ayerst (asia) Ltd (HQ) 973 660-5500
5 Giralda Farms Madison (07940) *(G-5739)*

Wyeth-Ayerst Pharmaceutical 732 274-4221
865 Ridge Rd Monmouth Junction (08852) *(G-6372)*

Wyman-Gordon Forgings Inc 973 627-0200
387 Franklin Ave Rockaway (07866) *(G-9626)*

Wynnpharm Inc 732 409-1005
86 W Main St Freehold (07728) *(G-3695)*

Wyssmont Company Inc 201 947-4600
1470 Bergen Blvd Fort Lee (07024) *(G-3592)*

Wytech Industries Inc (PA) 732 396-3900
960 E Hazelwood Ave Rahway (07065) *(G-9228)*

X Hockey Pro Shops, Bridgewater *Also called Ss Equipment Holdings LLC (G-900)*

X-Factor Cmmnctons Hldings Inc (PA) 877 741-3727
100 Stonehurst Ct Northvale (07647) *(G-7612)*

X-L Plastics Inc 973 777-9400
220 Clifton Blvd Clifton (07011) *(G-1745)*

Xanthus Inc 973 643-0920
105 Lock St Ste 215 Newark (07103) *(G-7361)*

Xbox Exclusive 908 756-3731
111 Eleanor St South Plainfield (07080) *(G-10455)*

Xceedium Inc 201 536-1000
30 Montgomery St Ste 1020 Jersey City (07302) *(G-4852)*

Xcessory LLC 917 647-7523
5901 W Side Ave Fl 7n North Bergen (07047) *(G-7497)*

Xchange Software Inc 732 444-6666
499 Ernston Rd Ste A7 Parlin (08859) *(G-7936)*

Xerox Corporation 609 987-5500
100 Overlook Ctr Ste 310 Princeton (08540) *(G-9141)*

Xtreme Powertech LLC 201 791-5050
123 Pleasant Ave Upper Saddle River (07458) *(G-11289)*

Xybion Corporation (PA) 973 538-2067
2000 Lenox Dr Ste 101 Lawrenceville (08648) *(G-5273)*

Xylem Dewatering Solutions Inc (HQ) 856 467-3636
84 Floodgate Rd Bridgeport (08014) *(G-775)*

Y & J Bakers Inc 732 363-3636
415 Clifton Ave Lakewood (08701) *(G-5208)*

Y C S, Ocean *Also called Yeghen Computer System (G-7749)*

Yale Hook & Eye Co Inc 973 824-1440
33 Race St Hillside (07205) *(G-4452)*

Yamate Chocolatier Inc 732 249-4847
320 Cleveland Ave Highland Park (08904) *(G-4306)*

Yank Marine Inc 609 628-2928
Mosquito Landing Rd Tuckahoe (08250) *(G-11140)*

Yankee Tool Inc. 973 664-0878
17 Edgewater Dr Denville (07834) *(G-2062)*

Yard, Hoboken *Also called Union Dry Dock & Repair Co (G-4502)*

Yarde Metals Inc 973 463-1166
603 Murray Rd East Hanover (07936) *(G-2251)*

Yardworks, Little Silver *Also called All Structures LLC (G-5519)*

Yasheel Inc 856 275-6812
11 Samantha Ct Sewell (08080) *(G-9967)*

Yates Sign Co Inc 732 578-1818
69 Megill Rd Farmingdale (07727) *(G-3398)*

YC Cable (east) Inc 732 868-0800
240 Circle Dr N Piscataway (08854) *(G-8837)*

Yeghen Computer System 732 996-5500
5 Brook Dr Ste 101 Ocean (07712) *(G-7749)*

Yerg Accounting Supplies, Lakehurst *Also called Yerg Inc (G-5060)*

A
L
P
H
A
B
E
T
I
C

Yerg Inc.....973 759-4041
7 Fawnhollow Ln Lakehurst (08759) ***(G-5060)***
Yes Pac, Piscataway *Also called Prospect Group LLC* ***(G-8803)***
Yes Press, Carlstadt *Also called Latta Graphics Inc* ***(G-1183)***
Yi Pin Food Prods, Edison *Also called Yipin Food Products Inc* ***(G-2652)***
Yipin Food Products Inc.....718 788-3059
29 Mack Dr Edison (08817) ***(G-2652)***
YKK (usa) Inc.....201 935-4200
1099 Wall St W Ste 244 Lyndhurst (07071) ***(G-5715)***
Yo Got It.....732 475-7913
606 Arnold Ave Point Pleasant Beach (08742) ***(G-8929)***
Yogo Mix.....609 897-1379
44 Normandy Dr Princeton Junction (08550) ***(G-9167)***
Yogurt Paradise LLC.....732 534-6395
10 S New Prospect Rd Jackson (08527) ***(G-4683)***
Yolo Candy LLC.....201 252-8765
1 International Blvd # 208 Mahwah (07495) ***(G-5825)***
Yonkers Plywood Manufacturing.....732 727-1200
3130 Bordentown Ave Old Bridge (08857) ***(G-7795)***
York International Corporation.....732 346-0606
160 Rritan Ctr Pkwy Ste 6 Edison (08837) ***(G-2653)***
York Street Caterers Inc.....201 868-9088
196 Coolidge Ave Englewood (07631) ***(G-2945)***
York Telecom Corporation (PA).....732 413-6000
81 Corbett Way Eatontown (07724) ***(G-2430)***
Yorktel, Eatontown *Also called York Telecom Corporation* ***(G-2430)***
You Move ME, Bellmawr *Also called Dazzledog LLC* ***(G-336)***
Youniversal Labortories (PA).....201 807-9000
100 Louis St South Hackensack (07606) ***(G-10300)***
Your Printer V20 Ltd.....609 771-4000
6 Corporate Dr Ste 1 Cranbury (08512) ***(G-1893)***
Youre So Invited LLC.....201 664-8600
260 Westwood Ave Westwood (07675) ***(G-11976)***
Yuhl Products Inc.....908 276-5180
15 N 7th St Kenilworth (07033) ***(G-5009)***
Yukon Graphics Inc.....973 575-5700
239 New Rd Ste B110 Parsippany (07054) ***(G-8117)***
Z Fab LLC.....973 248-0686
24 Bodie Rd Wayne (07470) ***(G-11694)***
Z Line Beachwear.....732 793-1234
3263 Route 35 N Lavallette (08735) ***(G-5238)***
Z-Line, Lavallette *Also called Z Line Beachwear* ***(G-5238)***
Z-Tech, Pennsauken *Also called Zin-Tech Inc* ***(G-8591)***
Zack Painting Co Inc.....732 738-7900
900 King George Rd Fords (08863) ***(G-3531)***
Zaffre, Lakewood *Also called Cherri Stone Interactive LLC* ***(G-5092)***
Zago Manufacturing Company.....973 643-6700
21 E Runyon St Newark (07114) ***(G-7362)***
Zahk Sales Inc.....516 633-9179
1405 Boxwood Dr Branchburg (08876) ***(G-720)***
Zaiya Inc.....201 343-3988
185 Kenneth St Hackensack (07601) ***(G-3993)***
Zala Machine Co Inc.....908 431-9106
109 Stryker Ln Ste 11 Hillsborough (08844) ***(G-4379)***
Zala Machine Shop, Hillsborough *Also called Zala Machine Co Inc* ***(G-4379)***
Zale Delaware Inc.....201 291-0690
35 Garden State Plz K33 Paramus (07652) ***(G-7914)***
Zaller Studios Inc.....973 743-5175
265 Watsessing Ave Bloomfield (07003) ***(G-538)***
Zanotti Transblock USA Corp.....917 584-9357
1810 Underwood Blvd 1 Delran (08075) ***(G-2025)***
Zaxcom Inc.....973 835-5000
230 W Parkway Ste 9 Pompton Plains (07444) ***(G-8969)***
Zaxcom Video, Pompton Plains *Also called Zaxcom Inc* ***(G-8969)***
Zc Utility Services LLC.....973 226-1840
10 Steel Ct Roseland (07068) ***(G-9658)***
Zebra Technologies Corporation.....609 383-8743
1501 Tilton Rd Northfield (08225) ***(G-7565)***
Zeeks Tees, Belford *Also called Frank J Zechman* ***(G-287)***
Zeeks Tees.....732 291-2700
515 State Route 36 Belford (07718) ***(G-290)***
Zekelman Industries Inc.....724 342-6851
90 Hurlbut St Westwood (07675) ***(G-11977)***
Zelis Healthcare, Bedminster *Also called Premier Healthcare Exch Corp* ***(G-283)***
Zenas Patisserie.....856 303-8700
308 Broad St Riverton (08077) ***(G-9509)***
Zenex Precision Products Corp.....973 523-6910
69 George St Paterson (07503) ***(G-8409)***
Zenia Pharma LLC.....973 246-9718
575 Grove St Unit F1 Clifton (07013) ***(G-1746)***
Zenith Electronics Corporation.....201 816-2071
1000 Sylvan Ave Fl 1 Englewood Cliffs (07632) ***(G-2988)***
Zenith Energy US LP (PA).....732 515-7410
1 Highland Ave Metuchen (08840) ***(G-6135)***
Zenith Laboratories Inc.....201 767-1700
140 Legrand Ave Northvale (07647) ***(G-7613)***
Zenith Laboratories Inc (HQ).....201 767-1700
140 Legrand Ave Northvale (07647) ***(G-7614)***
Zenith Mfg & Chemical Corp.....201 767-1332
85 Oak St Norwood (07648) ***(G-7638)***
Zenith Precision Inc.....201 933-8640
536 Paterson Ave East Rutherford (07073) ***(G-2338)***
Zenith Ultrasonic, Norwood *Also called Zenith Mfg & Chemical Corp* ***(G-7638)***
Zeon US Inc.....516 532-7167
5903 W Side Ave North Bergen (07047) ***(G-7498)***
Zerega Pasta, Fair Lawn *Also called A Zeregas Sons Inc* ***(G-3072)***
Zero Surge Inc.....908 996-7700
889 State Route 12 Ste 2 Frenchtown (08825) ***(G-3707)***
Zestos Foods LLC.....888 407-5852
1297 Sussex Rd Teaneck (07666) ***(G-10779)***
Zeta Products Inc.....908 688-0440
18 Westgate Dr Annandale (08801) ***(G-62)***
Zeus Industrial Products Inc.....908 292-6500
134 Chubb Way Branchburg (08876) ***(G-721)***
Zeus Scientific Inc.....908 526-3744
200 Evans Way Branchburg (08876) ***(G-722)***
Zicam, Bridgewater *Also called Matrixx Initiatives Inc* ***(G-859)***
Ziegler Chem & Mineral Corp (PA).....732 752-4111
600 Prospect Ave Ste A Piscataway (08854) ***(G-8838)***
Ziegler Chem & Mineral Corp.....732 752-4111
600 Prospect Ave Ste 1 Piscataway (08854) ***(G-8839)***
Ziggy Snack Foods LLC.....917 662-6038
200 Clifton Blvd Ste 1 Clifton (07011) ***(G-1747)***
Zimmer Inc.....856 778-8300
1001 Briggs Rd Ste 275 Mount Laurel (08054) ***(G-6848)***
Zimmer Trabecular Met Tech Inc.....973 576-0032
10 Pomeroy Rd Parsippany (07054) ***(G-8118)***
Zimpli Kids Inc.....732 945-5995
3301 Route 66 Ste 130 Neptune (07753) ***(G-6937)***
Zin-Tech Inc (PA).....856 661-0900
1416 Union Ave Pennsauken (08110) ***(G-8591)***
Zinas Salads Inc.....973 428-0660
11 Great Meadow Ln East Hanover (07936) ***(G-2252)***
Zinicola Baking Co.....973 667-1306
127 King St Nutley (07110) ***(G-7658)***
Zink Holdings LLC.....781 761-5400
114 Tived Ln E Edison (08837) ***(G-2654)***
Zinni Electric LLC.....856 848-8361
66 Grant Ave Deptford (08096) ***(G-2070)***
Zion Industries Inc.....973 998-0162
39 E Hanover Ave Ste G Morris Plains (07950) ***(G-6682)***
Zip Rib, Burlington *Also called Merchant & Evans Inc* ***(G-984)***
Zippityprint LLC.....216 438-0001
182 Harrisonville Rd Mullica Hill (08062) ***(G-6894)***
Zippityprint.com, Mullica Hill *Also called Zippityprint LLC* ***(G-6894)***
Zirex Inc.....201 807-6401
105 Challenger Rd Fl 1 Ridgefield Park (07660) ***(G-9419)***
Zirti LLC.....201 316-4791
8 Cambridge Dr Allendale (07401) ***(G-24)***
Zixel Ltd.....732 972-3287
4 Pegasus Ct Morganville (07751) ***(G-6657)***
Zkteco USA LLC.....862 505-2101
6 Kingsbridge Rd Ste 8 Fairfield (07004) ***(G-3356)***
Zoag LLC.....862 591-2969
4305 Harcourt Rd Clifton (07013) ***(G-1748)***
Zodiac Aerosystems, Wall Township *Also called Zodiac US Corporation* ***(G-11520)***
Zodiac Paintball Inc.....973 616-7230
4 Sage Way Pompton Plains (07444) ***(G-8970)***
Zodiac US Corporation (HQ).....732 681-3527
1747 State Route 34 Wall Township (07727) ***(G-11520)***
Zoetis Inc (PA).....973 822-7000
10 Sylvan Way Ste 105 Parsippany (07054) ***(G-8119)***
Zoetis LLC (HQ).....973 822-7000
10 Sylvan Way Ste 105 Parsippany (07054) ***(G-8120)***
Zoetis Products LLC (HQ).....973 660-5000
100 Campus Dr Ste 3 Florham Park (07932) ***(G-3525)***
Zoetis Products LLC.....973 660-5000
440 Rte 22 Bridgewater (08807) ***(G-910)***
Zollanvari Ltd.....201 330-3344
600 Mdwlands Pkwy Ste 130 Secaucus (07094) ***(G-9941)***
Zoluu LLC.....862 686-1774
0-74 Saddle River Rd Fair Lawn (07410) ***(G-3125)***
Zone Defense Inc.....973 328-0436
428 Sand Shore Rd 7 Hackettstown (07840) ***(G-4044)***
Zone First, Randolph *Also called Trolex Corporation* ***(G-9302)***
Zone Two Inc.....732 237-0766
245 Hickory Ln Unit 2 Bayville (08721) ***(G-263)***
Zoomessence Inc.....732 416-6638
550 Hartle St Ste B Sayreville (08872) ***(G-9843)***
Zoono USA LLC.....732 722-8757
1151 Broad St Ste 115 Shrewsbury (07702) ***(G-10014)***
Zounds Inc.....856 234-8844
3131 Route 38 Ste 19 Mount Laurel (08054) ***(G-6849)***
Zounds Hearing, Mount Laurel *Also called Zounds Inc* ***(G-6849)***
Zsombor Antal Designs Inc.....201 225-1750
822 Kinderkamack Rd River Edge (07661) ***(G-9468)***

Zt Systems 201 559-1000
  333 Meadowlands Pkwy Fl 2 Secaucus (07094) *(G-9942)*

Zultner & Company 609 452-0216
  12 Wallingford Dr Princeton (08540) *(G-9142)*

Zulu Fire Doors Ltd Lblty Co 973 569-9858
  923 Market St Paterson (07513) *(G-8410)*

Zvonko Stulic & Son Inc 973 589-3773
  21 Main St Newark (07105) *(G-7363)*

Zwier Corp 973 748-4009
  497 Bloomfield Ave Bloomfield (07003) *(G-539)*

Zwivel LLC 844 499-4835
  45 Eisenhower Dr Ste 220 Paramus (07652) *(G-7915)*

Zycal Bioceuticals Mfg LLC (PA) 888 779-9225
  5a Executive Dr Toms River (08755) *(G-10924)*

Zycus Inc (HQ) 609 799-5664
  103 Carnegie Ctr Ste 201 Princeton (08540) *(G-9143)*

Zydus Pharmaceuticals USA Inc 609 730-1900
  73 Route 31 N Pennington (08534) *(G-8463)*

Zymes LLC 201 727-1520
  777 Terrace Ave Ste 203 Hasbrouck Heights (07604) *(G-4204)*

Zymet Inc 973 428-5245
  7 Great Meadow Ln East Hanover (07936) *(G-2253)*

Zzyzx LLC 908 722-3770
  5 Columbia Rd Branchburg (08876) *(G-723)*

ALPHABETIC

PRODUCT INDEX

• Product categories are listed in alphabetical order.

A

ABRASIVES
ABRASIVES: Polishing Rouge
ACADEMIC TUTORING SVCS
ACCELERATION INDICATORS & SYSTEM COMPONENTS: Aerospace
ACCELERATORS, RUBBER PROCESSING: Cyclic or Acyclic
ACCOUNTING MACHINES & CASH REGISTERS
ACIDS
ACIDS: Boric
ACRYLIC RESINS
ACTUATORS: Indl, NEC
ACUPUNCTURISTS' OFFICES
ADDITIVE BASED PLASTIC MATERIALS: Plasticizers
ADHESIVES
ADHESIVES & SEALANTS
ADHESIVES: Adhesives, paste
ADHESIVES: Adhesives, plastic
ADHESIVES: Epoxy
ADVERTISING AGENCIES
ADVERTISING AGENCIES: Consultants
ADVERTISING CURTAINS
ADVERTISING DISPLAY PRDTS
ADVERTISING MATERIAL DISTRIBUTION
ADVERTISING REPRESENTATIVES: Electronic Media
ADVERTISING REPRESENTATIVES: Media
ADVERTISING REPRESENTATIVES: Newspaper
ADVERTISING REPRESENTATIVES: Printed Media
ADVERTISING SPECIALTIES, WHOLESALE
ADVERTISING SVCS: Bus Card
ADVERTISING SVCS: Direct Mail
ADVERTISING SVCS: Display
ADVERTISING SVCS: Outdoor
ADVERTISING SVCS: Poster, Outdoor
ADVERTISING SVCS: Sample Distribution
ADVERTISING SVCS: Transit
AEROSOLS
AGENTS, BROKERS & BUREAUS: Personal Service
AGENTS: Loan, Farm Or Business
AGRICULTURAL CHEMICALS: Trace Elements
AGRICULTURAL EQPT: BARN, SILO, POULTRY, DAIRY/LIVESTOCK MACH
AGRICULTURAL EQPT: Fertilizing Machinery
AGRICULTURAL EQPT: Trailers & Wagons, Farm
AGRICULTURAL EQPT: Troughs, Water
AGRICULTURAL EQPT: Turf Eqpt, Commercial
AIR CLEANING SYSTEMS
AIR CONDITIONING & VENTILATION EQPT & SPLYS: Wholesales
AIR CONDITIONING EQPT
AIR CONDITIONING UNITS: Complete, Domestic Or Indl
AIR COOLERS: Metal Plate
AIR MATTRESSES: Plastic
AIR POLLUTION MEASURING SVCS
AIR PURIFICATION EQPT
AIRCRAFT & AEROSPACE FLIGHT INSTRUMENTS & GUIDANCE SYSTEMS
AIRCRAFT & HEAVY EQPT REPAIR SVCS
AIRCRAFT ASSEMBLY PLANTS
AIRCRAFT CONTROL SYSTEMS: Electronic Totalizing Counters
AIRCRAFT ENGINES & ENGINE PARTS: Cooling Systems
AIRCRAFT ENGINES & PARTS
AIRCRAFT EQPT & SPLYS WHOLESALERS
AIRCRAFT FLIGHT INSTRUMENTS
AIRCRAFT MAINTENANCE & REPAIR SVCS
AIRCRAFT PARTS & AUXILIARY EQPT: Aircraft Training Eqpt
AIRCRAFT PARTS & AUXILIARY EQPT: Assys, Subassemblies/Parts
AIRCRAFT PARTS & AUXILIARY EQPT: Body & Wing Assys & Parts
AIRCRAFT PARTS & AUXILIARY EQPT: Body Assemblies & Parts
AIRCRAFT PARTS & AUXILIARY EQPT: Countermeasure Dispensers
AIRCRAFT PARTS & AUXILIARY EQPT: Deicing Eqpt
AIRCRAFT PARTS & AUXILIARY EQPT: Landing Assemblies & Brakes

AIRCRAFT PARTS & AUXILIARY EQPT: Military Eqpt & Armament
AIRCRAFT PARTS & AUXILIARY EQPT: Tanks, Fuel
AIRCRAFT PARTS & EQPT, NEC
AIRCRAFT PARTS WHOLESALERS
AIRCRAFT SEATS
AIRCRAFT SERVICING & REPAIRING
AIRCRAFT TURBINES
AIRCRAFT: Airplanes, Fixed Or Rotary Wing
AIRCRAFT: Autogiros
AIRCRAFT: Research & Development, Manufacturer
AIRPORTS, FLYING FIELDS & SVCS
ALARM SYSTEMS WHOLESALERS
ALARMS: Burglar
ALARMS: Fire
ALCOHOL, ETHYL: For Beverage Purposes
ALKALIES & CHLORINE
ALLOYS: Additive, Exc Copper Or Made In Blast Furnaces
ALTERNATORS: Automotive
ALUMINUM
ALUMINUM PRDTS
ALUMINUM: Coil & Sheet
ALUMINUM: Rolling & Drawing
AMMUNITION
AMMUNITION: Small Arms
AMPLIFIERS
AMPLIFIERS: RF & IF Power
AMUSEMENT & RECREATION SVCS, NEC
AMUSEMENT & RECREATION SVCS: Exhibition Operation
AMUSEMENT & RECREATION SVCS: Game Machines
AMUSEMENT & RECREATION SVCS: Tourist Attraction, Commercial
AMUSEMENT & RECREATION SVCS: Video Game Arcades
AMUSEMENT & RECREATION SVCS: Yoga Instruction
AMUSEMENT ARCADES
AMUSEMENT MACHINES: Coin Operated
AMUSEMENT PARK DEVICES & RIDES
AMUSEMENT PARK DEVICES & RIDES Carousels Or Merry-Go-Rounds
AMUSEMENT PARK DEVICES & RIDES: Carnival Mach & Eqpt, NEC
ANALYZERS: Electrical Testing
ANALYZERS: Network
ANALYZERS: Respiratory
ANESTHESIA EQPT
ANESTHETICS: Bulk Form
ANIMAL FEED & SUPPLEMENTS: Livestock & Poultry
ANIMAL FEED: Wholesalers
ANIMAL FOOD & SUPPLEMENTS: Bird Food, Prepared
ANIMAL FOOD & SUPPLEMENTS: Cat
ANIMAL FOOD & SUPPLEMENTS: Dog
ANIMAL FOOD & SUPPLEMENTS: Dog & Cat
ANIMAL FOOD & SUPPLEMENTS: Feed Supplements
ANIMAL FOOD & SUPPLEMENTS: Livestock
ANIMAL FOOD & SUPPLEMENTS: Poultry
ANIMAL FOOD & SUPPLEMENTS: Slaughtering of nonfood animals
ANODIZING SVC
ANTENNAS: Radar Or Communications
ANTENNAS: Receiving
ANTIBIOTICS
ANTIBIOTICS, PACKAGED
ANTIFREEZE
ANTIHISTAMINE PREPARATIONS
ANTIQUE FURNITURE RESTORATION & REPAIR
APPAREL DESIGNERS: Commercial
APPAREL: Hand Woven
APPLIANCE PARTS: Porcelain Enameled
APPLIANCES, HOUSEHOLD: Kitchen, Major, Exc Refrigs & Stoves
APPLIANCES, HOUSEHOLD: Shampooers, Carpet
APPLIANCES: Household, Refrigerators & Freezers
APPLIANCES: Major, Cooking
APPLIANCES: Small, Electric
APPLICATIONS SOFTWARE PROGRAMMING
AQUARIUM ACCESS, METAL
AQUARIUMS & ACCESS: Plastic
ARCHITECTURAL SVCS

ARCHITECTURAL SVCS: House Designer
ARMATURE REPAIRING & REWINDING SVC
ARMATURES: Ind
ARMOR PLATES
AROMATIC CHEMICAL PRDTS
ART DEALERS & GALLERIES
ART DESIGN SVCS
ART GOODS, WHOLESALE
ART MARBLE: Concrete
ART RESTORATION SVC
ART SPLY STORES
ARTIFICIAL FLOWERS & TREES
ARTIST'S MATERIALS & SPLYS
ARTISTS' MATERIALS, WHOLESALE
ARTISTS' MATERIALS: Clay, Modeling
ARTISTS' MATERIALS: Frames, Artists' Canvases
ARTISTS' MATERIALS: Ink, Drawing, Black & Colored
ARTISTS' MATERIALS: Palettes
ARTISTS' MATERIALS: Pencil Holders
ASBESTOS PRDTS: Clutch Facings
ASBESTOS PRDTS: Pipe Covering, Heat Insulatng Matl, Exc Felt
ASBESTOS PRDTS: Wick
ASBESTOS PRODUCTS
ASH TRAYS: Stamped Metal
ASPHALT & ASPHALT PRDTS
ASPHALT COATINGS & SEALERS
ASPHALT MINING & BITUMINOUS STONE QUARRYING SVCS
ASPHALT MINING SVCS
ASPHALT MIXTURES WHOLESALERS
ASPHALT PLANTS INCLUDING GRAVEL MIX TYPE
ASSEMBLING & PACKAGING SVCS: Cosmetic Kits
ASSEMBLING SVC: Clocks
ASSEMBLING SVC: Plumbing Fixture Fittings, Plastic
ASSOCIATIONS: Business
ASSOCIATIONS: Real Estate Management
ASSOCIATIONS: Scientists'
ASSOCIATIONS: Trade
ATHLETIC ORGANIZATION
ATOMIZERS
AUCTION SVCS: Motor Vehicle
AUDIO & VIDEO EQPT, EXC COMMERCIAL
AUDIO COMPONENTS
AUDIO ELECTRONIC SYSTEMS
AUDIO-VISUAL PROGRAM PRODUCTION SVCS
AUDIOLOGICAL EQPT: Electronic
AUDIOLOGISTS' OFFICES
AUDITING SVCS
AUTO & HOME SUPPLY STORES: Auto & Truck Eqpt & Parts
AUTO & HOME SUPPLY STORES: Automotive Access
AUTO & HOME SUPPLY STORES: Automotive parts
AUTO & HOME SUPPLY STORES: Speed Shops, Incl Race Car Splys
AUTO & HOME SUPPLY STORES: Truck Eqpt & Parts
AUTOCLAVES: Laboratory
AUTOMATED TELLER MACHINE OR ATM REPAIR SVCS
AUTOMATIC REGULATING CONTROL: Building Svcs Monitoring, Auto
AUTOMATIC REGULATING CONTROLS: AC & Refrigeration
AUTOMATIC REGULATING CONTROLS: Appliance, Exc Air-Cond/Refr
AUTOMATIC REGULATING CONTROLS: Elect Air Cleaner, Automatic
AUTOMATIC REGULATING CONTROLS: Electric Heat
AUTOMATIC REGULATING CONTROLS: Energy Cutoff, Residtl/Comm
AUTOMATIC REGULATING CONTROLS: Hardware, Environmental Reg
AUTOMATIC REGULATING CONTROLS: Hydronic Pressure Or Temp
AUTOMATIC REGULATING CONTROLS: Pressure, Air-Cond Sys
AUTOMATIC TELLER MACHINES
AUTOMOBILE FINANCE LEASING
AUTOMOBILE RECOVERY SVCS
AUTOMOBILE STORAGE GARAGE

AUTOMOBILES & OTHER MOTOR VEHICLES WHOLE-SALERS
AUTOMOBILES: Wholesalers
AUTOMOTIVE & TRUCK GENERAL REPAIR SVC
AUTOMOTIVE BODY SHOP
AUTOMOTIVE BODY, PAINT & INTERIOR REPAIR & MAIN-TENANCE SVC
AUTOMOTIVE EMISSIONS TESTING SVCS
AUTOMOTIVE GLASS REPLACEMENT SHOPS
AUTOMOTIVE LETTERING & PAINTING SVCS
AUTOMOTIVE PARTS, ACCESS & SPLYS
AUTOMOTIVE PARTS: Plastic
AUTOMOTIVE PRDTS: Rubber
AUTOMOTIVE REPAIR SHOPS: Engine Repair
AUTOMOTIVE REPAIR SHOPS: Machine Shop
AUTOMOTIVE REPAIR SHOPS: Trailer Repair
AUTOMOTIVE REPAIR SHOPS: Truck Engine Repair, Exc Indl
AUTOMOTIVE REPAIR SHOPS: Wheel Alignment
AUTOMOTIVE REPAIR SVC
AUTOMOTIVE SPLYS & PARTS, NEW, WHOL: Auto Servic-ing Eqpt
AUTOMOTIVE SPLYS & PARTS, NEW, WHOLESALE: Radia-tors
AUTOMOTIVE SPLYS & PARTS, NEW, WHOLESALE: Splys
AUTOMOTIVE SPLYS & PARTS, NEW, WHOLESALE: Trailer Parts
AUTOMOTIVE SPLYS & PARTS, NEW, WHOLESALE: Trim
AUTOMOTIVE SPLYS & PARTS, USED, WHOLESALE
AUTOMOTIVE SPLYS & PARTS, WHOLESALE, NEC
AUTOMOTIVE SPLYS/PART, NEW, WHOL: Spring, Shock Absorb/Strut
AUTOMOTIVE SVCS, EXC REPAIR & CARWASHES: Glass Tinting
AUTOMOTIVE SVCS, EXC REPAIR & CARWASHES: Lubri-cation
AUTOMOTIVE SVCS, EXC REPAIR & CARWASHES: Trailer Maintenance
AUTOMOTIVE SVCS, EXC REPAIR: Washing & Polishing
AUTOMOTIVE TOWING & WRECKING SVC
AUTOMOTIVE WELDING SVCS
AUTOMOTIVE: Seating
AUTOTRANSFORMERS: Electric
AVIATION SCHOOL
AWNINGS & CANOPIES
AWNINGS & CANOPIES: Awnings, Fabric, From Purchased Matls
AWNINGS & CANOPIES: Canopies, Fabric, From Purchased Matls
AWNINGS: Fiberglass
AWNINGS: Metal
AXLES

B

BABY FORMULA
BABY PACIFIERS: Rubber
BADGES, WHOLESALE
BADGES: Identification & Insignia
BAGS & CONTAINERS: Textile, Exc Sleeping
BAGS: Canvas
BAGS: Cement, Made From Purchased Materials
BAGS: Food Storage & Frozen Food, Plastic
BAGS: Food Storage & Trash, Plastic
BAGS: Garment & Wardrobe, Plastic Film
BAGS: Garment, Plastic Film, Made From Purchased Materi-als
BAGS: Laundry, From Purchased Materials
BAGS: Paper
BAGS: Paper, Made From Purchased Materials
BAGS: Plastic
BAGS: Plastic & Pliofilm
BAGS: Plastic, Made From Purchased Materials
BAGS: Rubber Or Rubberized Fabric
BAGS: Shipping
BAGS: Textile
BAGS: Wardrobe, Closet Access, Made From Purchased Ma-terials
BAKERIES, COMMERCIAL: On Premises Baking Only
BAKERIES: On Premises Baking & Consumption
BAKERY MACHINERY
BAKERY PRDTS, FROZEN: Wholesalers
BAKERY PRDTS: Bagels, Fresh Or Frozen
BAKERY PRDTS: Bakery Prdts, Partially Cooked, Exc frozen
BAKERY PRDTS: Biscuits, Baked, Baking Powder & Raised
BAKERY PRDTS: Biscuits, Dry

BAKERY PRDTS: Bread, All Types, Fresh Or Frozen
BAKERY PRDTS: Cakes, Bakery, Exc Frozen
BAKERY PRDTS: Cakes, Bakery, Frozen
BAKERY PRDTS: Cones, Ice Cream
BAKERY PRDTS: Cookies
BAKERY PRDTS: Cookies & crackers
BAKERY PRDTS: Doughnuts, Exc Frozen
BAKERY PRDTS: Dry
BAKERY PRDTS: Frozen
BAKERY PRDTS: Matzoth
BAKERY PRDTS: Pastries, Danish, Frozen
BAKERY PRDTS: Pastries, Exc Frozen
BAKERY PRDTS: Pies, Exc Frozen
BAKERY PRDTS: Pretzels
BAKERY PRDTS: Wholesalers
BAKERY: Wholesale Or Wholesale & Retail Combined
BALLASTS: Lamp
BALLASTS: Lighting
BALLOONS: Toy & Advertising, Rubber
BANQUET HALL FACILITIES
BAR FIXTURES: Wood
BARBECUE EQPT
BARGES BUILDING & REPAIR
BARRELS: Shipping, Metal
BARRETTES
BARRICADES: Metal
BARS: Concrete Reinforcing, Fabricated Steel
BARS: Extruded, Aluminum
BASES, BEVERAGE
BASKETS, GIFT, WHOLESALE
BATH SHOPS
BATHING SUIT STORES
BATHMATS: Rubber
BATHROOM ACCESS & FITTINGS: Vitreous China & Earth-enware
BATTERIES, EXC AUTOMOTIVE: Wholesalers
BATTERIES: Alkaline, Cell Storage
BATTERIES: Rechargeable
BATTERIES: Storage
BATTERIES: Wet
BATTERY CASES: Plastic Or Plastics Combination
BATTERY CHARGERS
BATTERY CHARGERS: Storage, Motor & Engine Generator Type
BEARINGS
BEARINGS & PARTS Ball
BEARINGS: Ball & Roller
BEARINGS: Plastic
BEARINGS: Roller & Parts
BEAUTY & BARBER SHOP EQPT
BEAUTY & BARBER SHOP EQPT & SPLYS WHOLESALERS
BEAUTY SALONS
BEDDING & BEDSPRINGS STORES
BEDDING, BEDSPREADS, BLANKETS & SHEETS
BEDDING, BEDSPREADS, BLANKETS & SHEETS: Com-forters & Quilts
BEDDING, FROM SILK OR MANMADE FIBER
BEDSPREADS & BED SETS, FROM PURCHASED MATERI-ALS
BEDSPREADS, COTTON
BEER, WINE & LIQUOR STORES
BEER, WINE & LIQUOR STORES: Beer, Packaged
BEER, WINE & LIQUOR STORES: Wine
BEESWAX PROCESSING
BELLOWS
BELTING: Fabric
BELTING: Plastic
BELTING: Rubber
BELTING: Transmission, Rubber
BELTS: Conveyor, Made From Purchased Wire
BENCHES: Seating
BEVERAGE BASES & SYRUPS
BEVERAGE STORES
BEVERAGE, NONALCOHOLIC: Iced Tea/Fruit Drink, Bot-tled/Canned
BEVERAGES, ALCOHOLIC: Ale
BEVERAGES, ALCOHOLIC: Beer
BEVERAGES, ALCOHOLIC: Beer & Ale
BEVERAGES, ALCOHOLIC: Brandy
BEVERAGES, ALCOHOLIC: Brandy & Brandy Spirits
BEVERAGES, ALCOHOLIC: Cocktails
BEVERAGES, ALCOHOLIC: Distilled Liquors
BEVERAGES, ALCOHOLIC: Vodka
BEVERAGES, ALCOHOLIC: Wines
BEVERAGES, MILK BASED

BEVERAGES, NONALCOHOLIC: Bottled & canned soft drinks
BEVERAGES, NONALCOHOLIC: Carbonated
BEVERAGES, NONALCOHOLIC: Carbonated, Canned & Bot-tled, Etc
BEVERAGES, NONALCOHOLIC: Flavoring extracts & syrups, nec
BEVERAGES, NONALCOHOLIC: Fruit Drnks, Under 100% Juice, Can
BEVERAGES, NONALCOHOLIC: Fruits, Crushed, For Foun-tain Use
BEVERAGES, NONALCOHOLIC: Soft Drinks, Canned & Bot-tled, Etc
BEVERAGES, NONALCOHOLIC: Tea, Iced, Bottled & Canned, Etc
BEVERAGES, WINE & DISTILLED ALCOHOLIC, WHOLE-SALE: Wine
BEVERAGES, WINE/DISTILLED ALCOH, WHOL: Brandy/Brandy Spirits
BEVERAGES, WINE/DISTILLED ALCOHOLIC, WHOL: Cock-tls, Premixed
BICYCLES, PARTS & ACCESS
BIDETS: Vitreous China
BILLIARD & POOL TABLES & SPLYS
BILLIARD EQPT & SPLYS WHOLESALERS
BILLING & BOOKKEEPING SVCS
BINDING SVC: Books & Manuals
BINDING SVC: Pamphlets
BINDING SVC: Trade
BINDINGS: Bias, Made From Purchased Materials
BIOLOGICAL PRDTS: Bacteriological Media
BIOLOGICAL PRDTS: Exc Diagnostic
BIOLOGICAL PRDTS: Extracts
BIOLOGICAL PRDTS: Vaccines
BIOLOGICAL PRDTS: Vaccines & Immunizing
BLADES: Knife
BLADES: Saw, Hand Or Power
BLANKBOOKS & LOOSELEAF BINDERS
BLANKBOOKS: Albums, Record
BLANKBOOKS: Ledgers & Ledger Sheets
BLANKETS: Horse
BLINDS & SHADES: Vertical
BLINDS : Window
BLOCKS & BRICKS: Concrete
BLOCKS: Acoustical, Concrete
BLOCKS: Landscape Or Retaining Wall, Concrete
BLOCKS: Paving, Asphalt, Not From Refineries
BLOCKS: Paving, Concrete
BLOCKS: Paving, Cut Stone
BLOCKS: Roof Ballast, Concrete
BLOCKS: Sewer & Manhole, Concrete
BLOCKS: Standard, Concrete Or Cinder
BLOOD RELATED HEALTH SVCS
BLOWERS & FANS
BLOWERS & FANS
BLUEPRINTING SVCS
BOAT & BARGE COMPONENTS: Metal, Prefabricated
BOAT BUILDING & REPAIR
BOAT BUILDING & REPAIRING: Fiberglass
BOAT BUILDING & REPAIRING: Lifeboats
BOAT BUILDING & REPAIRING: Yachts
BOAT BUILDING & RPRG: Fishing, Small, Lobster, Crab, Oyster
BOAT DEALERS
BOAT DEALERS: Marine Splys & Eqpt
BOAT DEALERS: Motor
BOAT DEALERS: Sailboats & Eqpt
BOAT DEALERS: Sails & Eqpt
BOAT LIFTS
BOAT REPAIR SVCS
BOAT YARD: Boat yards, storage & incidental repair
BOATS & OTHER MARINE EQPT: Plastic
BODIES: Truck & Bus
BODY PARTS: Automobile, Stamped Metal
BOILER GAGE COCKS
BOILER REPAIR SHOP
BOLTS: Metal
BONDERIZING: Bonderizing, Metal Or Metal Prdts
BOOK STORES
BOOK STORES: Children's
BOOKS, WHOLESALE
BOTTLE CAPS & RESEALERS: Plastic
BOTTLED GAS DEALERS: Liquefied Petro, Dlvrd To Cus-tomers
BOTTLED WATER DELIVERY

BOTTLES: Plastic
BOUTIQUE STORES
BOWLING EQPT & SPLY STORES
BOWLING PIN REFINISH OR REPAIR SVCS
BOXES & CRATES: Rectangular, Wood
BOXES & SHOOK: Nailed Wood
BOXES: Corrugated
BOXES: Fuse, Electric
BOXES: Mail Or Post Office, Collection/Storage, Sheet Metal
BOXES: Paperboard, Folding
BOXES: Paperboard, Set-Up
BOXES: Plastic
BOXES: Solid Fiber
BOXES: Stamped Metal
BOXES: Wirebound, Wood
BOXES: Wooden
BRAKE LININGS
BRASS & BRONZE PRDTS: Die-casted
BRASS FOUNDRY, NEC
BRASS ROLLING & DRAWING
BRASSWORK: Ornamental, Structural
BRAZING: Metal
BRIC-A-BRAC
BRICK, STONE & RELATED PRDTS WHOLESALERS
BRICKS : Ceramic Glazed, Clay
BRIEFCASES
BROADCASTING & COMMS EQPT: Antennas,
   Transmitting/Comms
BROADCASTING & COMMUNICATION EQPT: Transmit-Re-
   ceiver, Radio
BROADCASTING & COMMUNICATIONS EQPT: Cellular
   Radio Telephone
BROADCASTING & COMMUNICATIONS EQPT: Studio Eqpt,
   Radio & TV
BROADCASTING & COMMUNICATIONS EQPT: Transmitting,
   Radio/TV
BROADCASTING STATIONS, RADIO: Religious Music
BROKERS & DEALERS: Securities
BROKERS: Food
BROKERS: Printing
BROOMS & BRUSHES
BROOMS & BRUSHES: Household Or Indl
BROOMS & BRUSHES: Paint Rollers
BROOMS & BRUSHES: Paintbrushes
BROOMS & BRUSHES: Street Sweeping, Hand Or Machine
BRUSHES
BRUSHES & BRUSH STOCK CONTACTS: Electric
BUCKLES & PARTS
BUILDING & OFFICE CLEANING SVCS
BUILDING & STRUCTURAL WOOD MEMBERS
BUILDING COMPONENTS: Structural Steel
BUILDING PRDTS & MATERIALS DEALERS
BUILDING PRDTS: Concrete
BUILDING PRDTS: Stone
BUILDING STONE, ARTIFICIAL: Concrete
BUILDINGS & COMPONENTS: Prefabricated Metal
BUILDINGS, PREFABRICATED: Wholesalers
BUILDINGS: Portable
BUILDINGS: Prefabricated, Metal
BUILDINGS: Prefabricated, Wood
BUILDINGS: Prefabricated, Wood
BULLETIN BOARDS: Cork
BULLION, PRECIOUS METAL, WHOLESALE
BURGLAR ALARM MAINTENANCE & MONITORING SVCS
BURGLARY PROTECTION SVCS
BURIAL VAULTS: Concrete Or Precast Terrazzo
BURLAP & BURLAP PRDTS
BURLAP WHOLESALERS
BURNERS: Gas, Domestic
BURS: Dental
BUS BARS: Electrical
BUSHINGS & BEARINGS
BUSINESS ACTIVITIES: Non-Commercial Site
BUSINESS FORMS WHOLESALERS
BUSINESS FORMS: Printed, Manifold
BUSINESS MACHINE REPAIR, ELECTRIC

C

CABINETS & CASES: Show, Display & Storage, Exc Wood
CABINETS: Bathroom Vanities, Wood
CABINETS: Entertainment
CABINETS: Entertainment Units, Household, Wood
CABINETS: Factory
CABINETS: Kitchen, Metal
CABINETS: Kitchen, Wood

CABINETS: Office, Wood
CABINETS: Show, Display, Etc, Wood, Exc Refrigerated
CABLE & OTHER PAY TELEVISION DISTRIBUTION
CABLE & PAY TELEVISION SVCS: Closed Circuit
CABLE & PAY TELEVISION SVCS: Direct Broadcast Satellite
CABLE TELEVISION PRDTS
CABLE: Coaxial
CABLE: Fiber
CABLE: Fiber Optic
CABLE: Nonferrous, Shipboard
CABLE: Noninsulated
CABLE: Ropes & Fiber
CABLE: Steel, Insulated Or Armored
CACAO BEAN PROCESSING
CAFFEINE & DERIVATIVES
CAGES: Wire
CALCULATING & ACCOUNTING EQPT
CALENDARS, WHOLESALE
CALIBRATING SVCS, NEC
CAMERA & PHOTOGRAPHIC SPLYS STORES: Cameras
CAMERA & PHOTOGRAPHIC SPLYS STORES: Photo-
   graphic Splys
CAMERAS & RELATED EQPT: Photographic
CANDLE SHOPS
CANDLES
CANDLES: Wholesalers
CANDY & CONFECTIONS: Candy Bars, Including Chocolate
   Covered
CANDY & CONFECTIONS: Chocolate Candy, Exc Solid
   Chocolate
CANDY & CONFECTIONS: Fruit & Fruit Peel
CANDY & CONFECTIONS: Licorice
CANDY & CONFECTIONS: Marzipan
CANDY & CONFECTIONS: Nuts, Glace
CANDY & CONFECTIONS: Popcorn Balls/Other Trtd Popcorn
   Prdts
CANDY, NUT & CONFECTIONERY STORES: Candy
CANDY, NUT & CONFECTIONERY STORES: Confectionery
CANDY, NUT & CONFECTIONERY STORES: Produced For
   Direct Sale
CANDY: Chocolate From Cacao Beans
CANDY: Hard
CANNED SPECIALTIES
CANS & TUBES: Ammunition, Board Laminated With Metal
   Foil
CANS: Beverage, Metal, Exc Beer
CANS: Composite Foil-Fiber, Made From Purchased Materials
CANS: Metal
CANS: Tin
CANVAS PRDTS
CANVAS PRDTS, WHOLESALE
CANVAS PRDTS: Boat Seats
CANVAS PRDTS: Convertible Tops, Car/Boat, Fm Purchased
   Mtrl
CAPACITORS: NEC
CAPS: Plastic
CAR WASH EQPT
CAR WASH EQPT & SPLYS WHOLESALERS
CARBIDES
CARBON & GRAPHITE PRDTS, NEC
CARBON BLACK
CARBON PAPER & INKED RIBBONS
CARBON SPECIALTIES Electrical Use
CARBONS: Electric
CARDBOARD PRDTS, EXC DIE-CUT
CARDIOVASCULAR SYSTEM DRUGS, EXC DIAGNOSTIC
CARDS: Color
CARDS: Greeting
CARDS: Identification
CARPET & UPHOLSTERY CLEANING SVCS: Carpet/Furni-
   ture, On Loc
CARPETS & RUGS: Tufted
CARPETS, RUGS & FLOOR COVERING
CARPETS: Hand & Machine Made
CARPETS: Textile Fiber
CARRIER EQPT: Telephone Or Telegraph
CARRYING CASES, WHOLESALE
CARTONS: Egg, Molded Pulp, Made From Purchased Materi-
   als
CASES, WOOD
CASES: Carrying
CASES: Carrying, Clothing & Apparel
CASES: Plastic
CASES: Shipping, Wood, Wirebound
CASH REGISTERS & PARTS

CASINGS: Sheet Metal
CAST STONE: Concrete
CASTERS
CASTINGS GRINDING: For The Trade
CASTINGS: Aerospace Investment, Ferrous
CASTINGS: Aerospace, Aluminum
CASTINGS: Aluminum
CASTINGS: Bronze, NEC, Exc Die
CASTINGS: Commercial Investment, Ferrous
CASTINGS: Copper & Copper-Base Alloy, NEC, Exc Die
CASTINGS: Die, Aluminum
CASTINGS: Die, Nonferrous
CASTINGS: Die, Zinc
CASTINGS: Gray Iron
CASTINGS: Machinery, Nonferrous, Exc Die or Aluminum
   Copper
CASTINGS: Precision
CASTINGS: Zinc
CATALOG & MAIL-ORDER HOUSES
CATALOG SALES
CATALYSTS: Chemical
CATERERS
CAULKING COMPOUNDS
CEILING SYSTEMS: Luminous, Commercial
CELLULOSE DERIVATIVE MATERIALS
CEMENT: Hydraulic
CEMENT: Masonry
CEMENT: Portland
CEMETERY MEMORIAL DEALERS
CERAMIC FIBER
CHAINS: Power Transmission
CHAMBERS & CAISSONS
CHANDELIERS: Commercial
CHANDELIERS: Residential
CHARCOAL: Activated
CHART & GRAPH DESIGN SVCS
CHASING SVC: Metal
CHASSIS: Automobile House Trailer
CHASSIS: Motor Vehicle
CHEESE WHOLESALERS
CHEMICAL ELEMENTS
CHEMICAL PROCESSING MACHINERY & EQPT
CHEMICAL SPLYS FOR FOUNDRIES
CHEMICALS & ALLIED PRDTS WHOLESALERS, NEC
CHEMICALS & ALLIED PRDTS, WHOL: Chemical, Organic,
   Synthetic
CHEMICALS & ALLIED PRDTS, WHOL: Test Kits, Air,
   Water/Soil
CHEMICALS & ALLIED PRDTS, WHOLESALE: Aerosols
CHEMICALS & ALLIED PRDTS, WHOLESALE: Alkalines &
   Chlorine
CHEMICALS & ALLIED PRDTS, WHOLESALE: Aromatic
CHEMICALS & ALLIED PRDTS, WHOLESALE: Chemical Ad-
   ditives
CHEMICALS & ALLIED PRDTS, WHOLESALE: Chemicals,
   Indl
CHEMICALS & ALLIED PRDTS, WHOLESALE: Chemicals,
   Indl & Heavy
CHEMICALS & ALLIED PRDTS, WHOLESALE: Chemicals,
   Rustproofing
CHEMICALS & ALLIED PRDTS, WHOLESALE: Compressed
   Gas
CHEMICALS & ALLIED PRDTS, WHOLESALE: Detergents
CHEMICALS & ALLIED PRDTS, WHOLESALE: Dry Ice
CHEMICALS & ALLIED PRDTS, WHOLESALE: Essential Oils
CHEMICALS & ALLIED PRDTS, WHOLESALE: Indl Gases
CHEMICALS & ALLIED PRDTS, WHOLESALE: Metal Pol-
   ishes
CHEMICALS & ALLIED PRDTS, WHOLESALE: Plastics Film
CHEMICALS & ALLIED PRDTS, WHOLESALE: Plastics Ma-
   terials, NEC
CHEMICALS & ALLIED PRDTS, WHOLESALE: Plastics
   Prdts, NEC
CHEMICALS & ALLIED PRDTS, WHOLESALE: Plastics
   Sheets & Rods
CHEMICALS & ALLIED PRDTS, WHOLESALE: Polyurethane
   Prdts
CHEMICALS & ALLIED PRDTS, WHOLESALE: Resins
CHEMICALS & ALLIED PRDTS, WHOLESALE: Resins, Plas-
   tics
CHEMICALS & ALLIED PRDTS, WHOLESALE: Silicon Lubri-
   cants
CHEMICALS & ALLIED PRDTS, WHOLESALE: Spec
   Clean/Sanitation

INDEX

CHEMICALS & ALLIED PRDTS, WHOLESALE: Waxes, Exc Petroleum
CHEMICALS: Agricultural
CHEMICALS: Aluminum Chloride
CHEMICALS: Aluminum Compounds
CHEMICALS: Aluminum Sulfate
CHEMICALS: Ammonium Compounds, Exc Fertilizers, NEC
CHEMICALS: Barium & Barium Compounds
CHEMICALS: Brine
CHEMICALS: Caustic Soda
CHEMICALS: Fire Retardant
CHEMICALS: High Purity Grade, Organic
CHEMICALS: High Purity, Refined From Technical Grade
CHEMICALS: Inorganic, NEC
CHEMICALS: Medicinal
CHEMICALS: Medicinal, Organic, Uncompounded, Bulk
CHEMICALS: NEC
CHEMICALS: Nickel Compounds Or Salts, Inorganic
CHEMICALS: Nonmetallic Compounds
CHEMICALS: Organic, NEC
CHEMICALS: Phenol
CHEMICALS: Phosphates, Defluorinated/Ammoniated, Exc Fertlr
CHEMICALS: Phosphorus, Elemental
CHEMICALS: Reagent Grade, Refined From Technical Grade
CHEMICALS: Silica Compounds
CHEMICALS: Soda Ash
CHEMICALS: Sodium Bicarbonate
CHEMICALS: Sodium/Potassium Cmpnds,Exc Bleach,Alkalies/Alum
CHEMICALS: Sulfur, Incl Rcvrd/Refined, Fm Sour Natural Gas
CHEMICALS: Water Treatment
CHEMICALS: Zinc Chloride
CHEWING GUM
CHILDREN'S & INFANTS' CLOTHING STORES
CHILDREN'S WEAR STORES
CHINA & GLASS REPAIR SVCS
CHINAWARE WHOLESALERS
CHIROPRACTORS' OFFICES
CHOCOLATE, EXC CANDY FROM BEANS: Chips, Powder, Block, Syrup
CHOCOLATE, EXC CANDY FROM PURCH CHOC: Chips, Powder, Block
CHRISTMAS TREES: Artificial
CHROMATOGRAPHY EQPT
CIGARETTE LIGHTER FLINTS
CIGARETTE LIGHTERS
CIGARETTE STORES
CIRCUIT BOARDS, PRINTED: Television & Radio
CIRCUIT BOARDS: Wiring
CIRCUITS, INTEGRATED: Hybrid
CIRCUITS: Electronic
CLAY MINING, COMMON
CLAYS, EXC KAOLIN & BALL
CLEANING EQPT: Commercial
CLEANING EQPT: Dirt Sweeping Units, Indl
CLEANING EQPT: Floor Washing & Polishing, Commercial
CLEANING EQPT: High Pressure
CLEANING EQPT: Janitors' Carts
CLEANING OR POLISHING PREPARATIONS, NEC
CLEANING PRDTS: Ammonia, Household
CLEANING PRDTS: Bleaches, Household, Dry Or Liquid
CLEANING PRDTS: Degreasing Solvent
CLEANING PRDTS: Deodorants, Nonpersonal
CLEANING PRDTS: Disinfectants, Household Or Indl Plant
CLEANING PRDTS: Drain Pipe Solvents Or Cleaners
CLEANING PRDTS: Drycleaning Preparations
CLEANING PRDTS: Floor Waxes
CLEANING PRDTS: Indl Plant Disinfectants Or Deodorants
CLEANING PRDTS: Metal Polish
CLEANING PRDTS: Polishing Preparations & Related Prdts
CLEANING PRDTS: Sanitation Preps, Disinfectants/Deodorants
CLEANING PRDTS: Specialty
CLEANING PRDTS: Stain Removers
CLEANING SVCS
CLIPPERS: Fingernail & Toenail
CLOCK REPAIR SVCS
CLOSURES: Closures, Stamped Metal
CLOSURES: Plastic
CLOTHING & ACCESS, WOMEN, CHILD & INFANT, WHOL: Blouses
CLOTHING & ACCESS, WOMEN, CHILD & INFANT, WHSLE: Sportswear

CLOTHING & ACCESS, WOMEN, CHILDREN & INFANT, WHOL: Uniforms
CLOTHING & ACCESS, WOMEN, CHILDREN/INFANT, WHOL: Baby Goods
CLOTHING & ACCESS, WOMEN, CHILDREN/INFANT, WHOL: Nightwear
CLOTHING & ACCESS, WOMEN, CHILDREN/INFANT, WHOL: Outerwear
CLOTHING & ACCESS, WOMENS, CHILDREN & INFANTS, WHOL: Hats
CLOTHING & ACCESS: Costumes, Masquerade
CLOTHING & ACCESS: Costumes, Theatrical
CLOTHING & ACCESS: Handicapped
CLOTHING & ACCESS: Handkerchiefs, Exc Paper
CLOTHING & ACCESS: Men's Miscellaneous Access
CLOTHING & APPAREL STORES: Custom
CLOTHING & FURNISHINGS, MEN'S & BOYS', WHOLESALE: Outerwear
CLOTHING & FURNISHINGS, MEN'S & BOYS', WHOLESALE: Scarves
CLOTHING & FURNISHINGS, MEN'S & BOYS', WHOLESALE: Shirts
CLOTHING & FURNISHINGS, MEN'S & BOYS', WHOLESALE: Trousers
CLOTHING & FURNISHINGS, MEN'S & BOYS', WHOLESALE: Umbrellas
CLOTHING & FURNISHINGS, MEN'S & BOYS', WHOLESALE: Uniforms
CLOTHING ACCESS STORES: Belts, Custom
CLOTHING STORES, NEC
CLOTHING STORES: Dancewear
CLOTHING STORES: T-Shirts, Printed, Custom
CLOTHING STORES: Uniforms & Work
CLOTHING STORES: Unisex
CLOTHING: Access
CLOTHING: Access, Women's & Misses'
CLOTHING: Aprons, Exc Rubber/Plastic, Women, Misses, Junior
CLOTHING: Athletic & Sportswear, Men's & Boys'
CLOTHING: Athletic & Sportswear, Women's & Girls'
CLOTHING: Baker, Barber, Lab/Svc Ind Apparel, Washable, Men
CLOTHING: Bathing Suits & Swimwear, Girls, Children & Infant
CLOTHING: Bathrobes, Mens & Womens, From Purchased Materials
CLOTHING: Belts
CLOTHING: Blouses, Women's & Girls'
CLOTHING: Blouses, Womens & Juniors, From Purchased Mtrls
CLOTHING: Brassieres
CLOTHING: Bridal Gowns
CLOTHING: Capes & Jackets, Women's & Misses'
CLOTHING: Caps, Baseball
CLOTHING: Children & Infants'
CLOTHING: Children's, Girls'
CLOTHING: Clergy Vestments
CLOTHING: Coats & Jackets, Leather & Sheep-Lined
CLOTHING: Coats & Suits, Men's & Boys'
CLOTHING: Coats, Leatherette, Oiled Fabric, Etc, Mens & Boys
CLOTHING: Coats, Overcoats & Vests
CLOTHING: Costumes
CLOTHING: Disposable
CLOTHING: Down-Filled, Men's & Boys'
CLOTHING: Dresses
CLOTHING: Dresses & Skirts
CLOTHING: Dressing Gowns, Mens/Womens, From Purchased Matls
CLOTHING: Formal Jackets, Mens & Youth, From Purchased Matls
CLOTHING: Furs
CLOTHING: Garments, Indl, Men's & Boys
CLOTHING: Girdles & Panty Girdles
CLOTHING: Gowns & Dresses, Wedding
CLOTHING: Hats & Caps, NEC
CLOTHING: Hats & Caps, Uniform
CLOTHING: Hats & Headwear, Knit
CLOTHING: Hosiery, Men's & Boys'
CLOTHING: Hosiery, Pantyhose & Knee Length, Sheer
CLOTHING: Hospital, Men's
CLOTHING: Jackets, Field, Military
CLOTHING: Jackets, Overall & Work
CLOTHING: Jeans, Men's & Boys'
CLOTHING: Jerseys, Knit

CLOTHING: Leather
CLOTHING: Leather & sheep-lined clothing
CLOTHING: Lounge, Bed & Leisurewear
CLOTHING: Maternity
CLOTHING: Men's & boy's underwear & nightwear
CLOTHING: Millinery
CLOTHING: Neckwear
CLOTHING: Outerwear, Knit
CLOTHING: Outerwear, Lthr, Wool/Down-Filled, Men, Youth/Boy
CLOTHING: Outerwear, Women's & Misses' NEC
CLOTHING: Raincoats, Exc Vulcanized Rubber, Purchased Matls
CLOTHING: Robes & Dressing Gowns
CLOTHING: Service Apparel, Women's
CLOTHING: Shirts
CLOTHING: Shirts, Dress, Men's & Boys'
CLOTHING: Shirts, Knit
CLOTHING: Shirts, Sports & Polo, Men's & Boys'
CLOTHING: Skirts
CLOTHING: Sleeping Garments, Women's & Children's
CLOTHING: Socks
CLOTHING: Sportswear, Women's
CLOTHING: Suits & Skirts, Women's & Misses'
CLOTHING: Suits, Men's & Boys', From Purchased Materials
CLOTHING: Sweaters & Sweater Coats, Knit
CLOTHING: T-Shirts & Tops, Knit
CLOTHING: T-Shirts & Tops, Women's & Girls'
CLOTHING: Tailored Dress/Sport Coats, Mens & Boys
CLOTHING: Tailored Suits & Formal Jackets
CLOTHING: Ties, Neck, Men's & Boys', From Purchased Material
CLOTHING: Trousers & Slacks, Men's & Boys'
CLOTHING: Underwear, Knit
CLOTHING: Underwear, Men's & Boys'
CLOTHING: Underwear, Women's & Children's
CLOTHING: Uniforms & Vestments
CLOTHING: Uniforms, Ex Athletic, Women's, Misses' & Juniors'
CLOTHING: Uniforms, Firemen's, From Purchased Materials
CLOTHING: Uniforms, Men's & Boys'
CLOTHING: Uniforms, Military, Men/Youth, Purchased Materials
CLOTHING: Uniforms, Policemen's, From Purchased Materials
CLOTHING: Uniforms, Team Athletic
CLOTHING: Uniforms, Work
CLOTHING: WarmUp, Jogging & Sweat Suits, Girls' & Children's
CLOTHING: Waterproof Outerwear
CLOTHING: Womens/Misses Coats, Jackets & Vests, Down-Filled
CLOTHING: Work Apparel, Exc Uniforms
CLOTHING: Work, Men's
CLOTHING: Work, Waterproof, Exc Raincoats
COAL MINING SERVICES
COAL, MINERALS & ORES, WHOLESALE: Coal
COATING COMPOUNDS: Tar
COATING SVC
COATING SVC: Metals & Formed Prdts
COATING SVC: Metals, With Plastic Or Resins
COATING SVC: Rust Preventative
COATING SVC: Silicon
COATINGS: Air Curing
COATINGS: Epoxy
COATINGS: Polyurethane
CODEINE & DERIVATIVES
COFFEE MAKERS: Electric
COFFEE SVCS
COILS & TRANSFORMERS
COILS, WIRE: Aluminum, Made In Rolling Mills
COIN-OPERATED LAUNDRY
COLLECTION AGENCY, EXC REAL ESTATE
COLOR LAKES OR TONERS
COLOR PIGMENTS
COLOR SEPARATION: Photographic & Movie Film
COLORING & FINISHING SVC: Aluminum Or Formed Prdts
COLORS: Pigments, Inorganic
COLORS: Pigments, Organic
COLUMNS, FRACTIONING: Metal Plate
COMFORTERS & QUILTS, FROM MANMADE FIBER OR SILK
COMMERCIAL & INDL SHELVING WHOLESALERS
COMMERCIAL & OFFICE BUILDINGS RENOVATION & REPAIR

COMMERCIAL ART & GRAPHIC DESIGN SVCS
COMMERCIAL ART & ILLUSTRATION SVCS
COMMERCIAL CONTAINERS WHOLESALERS
COMMERCIAL EQPT & SPLYS, WHOLESALE: Hotel
COMMERCIAL EQPT WHOLESALERS, NEC
COMMERCIAL EQPT, WHOLESALE: Bakery Eqpt & Splys
COMMERCIAL EQPT, WHOLESALE: Coffee Brewing Eqpt & Splys
COMMERCIAL EQPT, WHOLESALE: Comm Cooking & Food Svc Eqpt
COMMERCIAL EQPT, WHOLESALE: Display Eqpt, Exc Refrigerated
COMMERCIAL EQPT, WHOLESALE: Restaurant, NEC
COMMERCIAL EQPT, WHOLESALE: Scales, Exc Laboratory
COMMERCIAL EQPT, WHOLESALE: Store Fixtures & Display Eqpt
COMMERCIAL LAUNDRY EQPT
COMMERCIAL PRINTING & NEWSPAPER PUBLISHING COMBINED
COMMERCIAL REFRIGERATORS WHOLESALERS
COMMODITY CONTRACTS BROKERS, DEALERS
COMMON SAND MINING
COMMUNICATION HEADGEAR: Telephone
COMMUNICATIONS EQPT & SYSTEMS, NEC
COMMUNICATIONS EQPT REPAIR & MAINTENANCE
COMMUNICATIONS EQPT WHOLESALERS
COMMUNICATIONS EQPT: Microwave
COMMUNICATIONS SVCS
COMMUNICATIONS SVCS: Cellular
COMMUNICATIONS SVCS: Data
COMMUNICATIONS SVCS: Facsimile Transmission
COMMUNICATIONS SVCS: Internet Connectivity Svcs
COMMUNICATIONS SVCS: Internet Host Svcs
COMMUNICATIONS SVCS: Online Svc Providers
COMMUNICATIONS SVCS: Satellite Earth Stations
COMMUNICATIONS SVCS: Telephone Or Video
COMMUNICATIONS SVCS: Telephone, Data
COMMUNICATIONS SVCS: Telephone, Local
COMMUNICATIONS SVCS: Telephone, Local & Long Distance
COMMUNICATIONS SVCS: Telephone, Voice
COMMUTATORS: Electric Motors
COMMUTATORS: Electronic
COMPACT DISCS OR CD'S, WHOLESALE
COMPACT LASER DISCS: Prerecorded
COMPACTORS: Trash & Garbage, Residential
COMPOST
COMPRESSORS: Air & Gas
COMPRESSORS: Air & Gas, Including Vacuum Pumps
COMPUTER & COMPUTER SOFTWARE STORES
COMPUTER & COMPUTER SOFTWARE STORES: Peripheral Eqpt
COMPUTER & COMPUTER SOFTWARE STORES: Personal Computers
COMPUTER & COMPUTER SOFTWARE STORES: Printers & Plotters
COMPUTER & COMPUTER SOFTWARE STORES: Software & Access
COMPUTER & COMPUTER SOFTWARE STORES: Software, Bus/Non-Game
COMPUTER & COMPUTER SOFTWARE STORES: Software, Computer Game
COMPUTER & DATA PROCESSING EQPT REPAIR & MAINTENANCE
COMPUTER & OFFICE MACHINE MAINTENANCE & REPAIR
COMPUTER & SFTWR STORE: Modem, Monitor, Terminal/Disk Drive
COMPUTER CALCULATING SVCS
COMPUTER DISKETTES WHOLESALERS
COMPUTER FACILITIES MANAGEMENT SVCS
COMPUTER FORMS
COMPUTER GRAPHICS SVCS
COMPUTER INTERFACE EQPT: Indl Process
COMPUTER PAPER WHOLESALERS
COMPUTER PERIPHERAL EQPT REPAIR & MAINTENANCE
COMPUTER PERIPHERAL EQPT, NEC
COMPUTER PERIPHERAL EQPT, WHOLESALE
COMPUTER PERIPHERAL EQPT: Decoders
COMPUTER PERIPHERAL EQPT: Graphic Displays, Exc Terminals
COMPUTER PERIPHERAL EQPT: Input Or Output
COMPUTER PROCESSING SVCS
COMPUTER PROGRAMMING SVCS

COMPUTER PROGRAMMING SVCS: Custom
COMPUTER RELATED MAINTENANCE SVCS
COMPUTER SERVICE BUREAU
COMPUTER SOFTWARE DEVELOPMENT
COMPUTER SOFTWARE DEVELOPMENT & APPLICATIONS
COMPUTER SOFTWARE SYSTEMS ANALYSIS & DESIGN: Custom
COMPUTER SOFTWARE WRITERS
COMPUTER STORAGE DEVICES, NEC
COMPUTER STORAGE UNITS: Auxiliary
COMPUTER SYSTEM SELLING SVCS
COMPUTER SYSTEMS ANALYSIS & DESIGN
COMPUTER TERMINALS
COMPUTER TRAINING SCHOOLS
COMPUTER-AIDED DESIGN SYSTEMS SVCS
COMPUTER-AIDED ENGINEERING SYSTEMS SVCS
COMPUTER-AIDED MANUFACTURING SYSTEMS SVCS
COMPUTERS, NEC
COMPUTERS, NEC, WHOLESALE
COMPUTERS, PERIPH & SOFTWARE, WHLSE: Acctg Machs, Readable
COMPUTERS, PERIPH & SOFTWARE, WHLSE: Personal & Home Entrtn
COMPUTERS, PERIPHERALS & SOFTWARE, WHOLESALE: Printers
COMPUTERS, PERIPHERALS & SOFTWARE, WHOLESALE: Software
COMPUTERS, PERIPHERALS & SOFTWARE, WHOLESALE: Terminals
COMPUTERS: Indl, Process, Gas Flow
COMPUTERS: Mini
COMPUTERS: Personal
CONCENTRATES, DRINK
CONCENTRATES, FLAVORING, EXC DRINK
CONCRETE CURING & HARDENING COMPOUNDS
CONCRETE PRDTS
CONCRETE PRDTS, PRECAST, NEC
CONCRETE: Bituminous
CONCRETE: Dry Mixture
CONCRETE: Ready-Mixed
CONDENSERS: Heat Transfer Eqpt, Evaporative
CONDENSERS: Motors Or Generators
CONDENSERS: Steam
CONDUITS & FITTINGS: Electric
CONFECTIONERY PRDTS WHOLESALERS
CONFECTIONS & CANDY
CONFINEMENT SURVEILLANCE SYS MAINTENANCE & MONITORING SVCS
CONNECTORS & TERMINALS: Electrical Device Uses
CONNECTORS: Cord, Electric
CONNECTORS: Electrical
CONNECTORS: Electronic
CONNECTORS: Power, Electric
CONSTRUCTION & MINING MACHINERY WHOLESALERS
CONSTRUCTION EQPT REPAIR SVCS
CONSTRUCTION EQPT: Blade, Grader, Scraper, Dozer/Snow Plow
CONSTRUCTION EQPT: Cranes
CONSTRUCTION EQPT: Dozers, Tractor Mounted, Material Moving
CONSTRUCTION EQPT: Graders, Road
CONSTRUCTION EQPT: Subgraders
CONSTRUCTION EQPT: Wrecker Hoists, Automobile
CONSTRUCTION MATERIALS, WHOLESALE: Architectural Metalwork
CONSTRUCTION MATERIALS, WHOLESALE: Awnings
CONSTRUCTION MATERIALS, WHOLESALE: Block, Concrete & Cinder
CONSTRUCTION MATERIALS, WHOLESALE: Brick, Exc Refractory
CONSTRUCTION MATERIALS, WHOLESALE: Building Stone
CONSTRUCTION MATERIALS, WHOLESALE: Building Stone, Granite
CONSTRUCTION MATERIALS, WHOLESALE: Building Stone, Marble
CONSTRUCTION MATERIALS, WHOLESALE: Building, Exterior
CONSTRUCTION MATERIALS, WHOLESALE: Cement
CONSTRUCTION MATERIALS, WHOLESALE: Concrete Mixtures
CONSTRUCTION MATERIALS, WHOLESALE: Glass
CONSTRUCTION MATERIALS, WHOLESALE: Gravel

CONSTRUCTION MATERIALS, WHOLESALE: Masons' Materials
CONSTRUCTION MATERIALS, WHOLESALE: Metal Buildings
CONSTRUCTION MATERIALS, WHOLESALE: Millwork
CONSTRUCTION MATERIALS, WHOLESALE: Pallets, Wood
CONSTRUCTION MATERIALS, WHOLESALE: Paving Materials
CONSTRUCTION MATERIALS, WHOLESALE: Prefabricated Structures
CONSTRUCTION MATERIALS, WHOLESALE: Roof, Asphalt/Sheet Metal
CONSTRUCTION MATERIALS, WHOLESALE: Roofing & Siding Material
CONSTRUCTION MATERIALS, WHOLESALE: Sand
CONSTRUCTION MATERIALS, WHOLESALE: Septic Tanks
CONSTRUCTION MATERIALS, WHOLESALE: Siding, Exc Wood
CONSTRUCTION MATERIALS, WHOLESALE: Skylights, All Materials
CONSTRUCTION MATERIALS, WHOLESALE: Stone, Crushed Or Broken
CONSTRUCTION MATERIALS, WHOLESALE: Stucco
CONSTRUCTION MATERIALS, WHOLESALE: Tile & Clay Prdts
CONSTRUCTION MATERIALS, WHOLESALE: Window Frames
CONSTRUCTION MATERIALS, WHOLESALE: Windows
CONSTRUCTION MATLS, WHOL: Lumber, Rough, Dressed/Finished
CONSTRUCTION MTRLS, WHOL: Exterior Flat Glass, Plate/Window
CONSTRUCTION SAND MINING
CONSTRUCTION: Athletic & Recreation Facilities
CONSTRUCTION: Bridge
CONSTRUCTION: Chemical Facility
CONSTRUCTION: Commercial & Institutional Building
CONSTRUCTION: Commercial & Office Building, New
CONSTRUCTION: Dams, Waterways, Docks & Other Marine
CONSTRUCTION: Drainage System
CONSTRUCTION: Electric Power Line
CONSTRUCTION: Foundation & Retaining Wall
CONSTRUCTION: Greenhouse
CONSTRUCTION: Heavy Highway & Street
CONSTRUCTION: Hospital
CONSTRUCTION: Indl Building & Warehouse
CONSTRUCTION: Indl Buildings, New, NEC
CONSTRUCTION: Indl Plant
CONSTRUCTION: Irrigation System
CONSTRUCTION: Marine
CONSTRUCTION: Natural Gas Compressor Station
CONSTRUCTION: Nonresidential Buildings, Custom
CONSTRUCTION: Pharmaceutical Manufacturing Plant
CONSTRUCTION: Power & Communication Transmission Tower
CONSTRUCTION: Refineries
CONSTRUCTION: Religious Building
CONSTRUCTION: Residential, Nec
CONSTRUCTION: Sewer Line
CONSTRUCTION: Single-Family Housing
CONSTRUCTION: Single-family Housing, New
CONSTRUCTION: Steel Buildings
CONSTRUCTION: Street Surfacing & Paving
CONSTRUCTION: Transmitting Tower, Telecommunication
CONSTRUCTION: Warehouse
CONSTRUCTION: Waste Water & Sewage Treatment Plant
CONSTRUCTION: Water & Sewer Line
CONSULTING SVC: Actuarial
CONSULTING SVC: Business, NEC
CONSULTING SVC: Chemical
CONSULTING SVC: Computer
CONSULTING SVC: Data Processing
CONSULTING SVC: Engineering
CONSULTING SVC: Human Resource
CONSULTING SVC: Management
CONSULTING SVC: Marketing Management
CONSULTING SVC: Online Technology
CONSULTING SVC: Sales Management
CONSULTING SVC: Telecommunications
CONSULTING SVCS, BUSINESS: Agricultural
CONSULTING SVCS, BUSINESS: Communications
CONSULTING SVCS, BUSINESS: Energy Conservation
CONSULTING SVCS, BUSINESS: Environmental
CONSULTING SVCS, BUSINESS: Publishing

INDEX

CONSULTING SVCS, BUSINESS: Sys Engnrg, Exc Computer/Prof
CONSULTING SVCS, BUSINESS: Systems Analysis & Engineering
CONSULTING SVCS, BUSINESS: Systems Analysis Or Design
CONSULTING SVCS, BUSINESS: Test Development & Evaluation
CONSULTING SVCS, BUSINESS: Traffic
CONSULTING SVCS: Oil
CONSULTING SVCS: Psychological
CONSULTING SVCS: Scientific
CONTACT LENSES
CONTACTS: Electrical
CONTAINERS, GLASS: Cosmetic Jars
CONTAINERS, GLASS: Medicine Bottles
CONTAINERS: Air Cargo, Metal
CONTAINERS: Cargo, Wood & Wood With Metal
CONTAINERS: Corrugated
CONTAINERS: Foil, Bakery Goods & Frozen Foods
CONTAINERS: Food & Beverage
CONTAINERS: Food, Metal
CONTAINERS: Frozen Food & Ice Cream
CONTAINERS: Glass
CONTAINERS: Metal
CONTAINERS: Plastic
CONTAINERS: Plywood & Veneer, Wood
CONTAINERS: Sanitary, Food
CONTAINERS: Shipping & Mailing, Fiber
CONTAINERS: Shipping, Bombs, Metal Plate
CONTAINERS: Shipping, Metal, Milk, Fluid
CONTAINERS: Shipping, Wood
CONTAINERS: Wood
CONTAINMENT VESSELS: Reactor, Metal Plate
CONTRACTOR: Dredging
CONTRACTORS: Access Control System Eqpt
CONTRACTORS: Antenna Installation
CONTRACTORS: Asbestos Removal & Encapsulation
CONTRACTORS: Asphalt
CONTRACTORS: Awning Installation
CONTRACTORS: Boiler Maintenance Contractor
CONTRACTORS: Boring, Building Construction
CONTRACTORS: Bridge Painting
CONTRACTORS: Building Board-up
CONTRACTORS: Building Eqpt & Machinery Installation
CONTRACTORS: Building Sign Installation & Mntnce
CONTRACTORS: Building Site Preparation
CONTRACTORS: Cable Laying
CONTRACTORS: Carpentry Work
CONTRACTORS: Carpentry, Cabinet & Finish Work
CONTRACTORS: Carpentry, Cabinet Building & Installation
CONTRACTORS: Carpentry, Finish & Trim Work
CONTRACTORS: Carpet Laying
CONTRACTORS: Ceramic Floor Tile Installation
CONTRACTORS: Closet Organizers, Installation & Design
CONTRACTORS: Commercial & Office Building
CONTRACTORS: Communications Svcs
CONTRACTORS: Computer Installation
CONTRACTORS: Concrete
CONTRACTORS: Concrete Block Masonry Laying
CONTRACTORS: Concrete Breaking, Street & Highway
CONTRACTORS: Concrete Repair
CONTRACTORS: Construction Site Cleanup
CONTRACTORS: Core Drilling & Cutting
CONTRACTORS: Countertop Installation
CONTRACTORS: Demolition, Building & Other Structures
CONTRACTORS: Directional Oil & Gas Well Drilling Svc
CONTRACTORS: Drywall
CONTRACTORS: Electric Power Systems
CONTRACTORS: Electrical
CONTRACTORS: Electronic Controls Installation
CONTRACTORS: Energy Management Control
CONTRACTORS: Epoxy Application
CONTRACTORS: Excavating
CONTRACTORS: Excavating Slush Pits & Cellars Svcs
CONTRACTORS: Exterior Painting
CONTRACTORS: Exterior Wall System Installation
CONTRACTORS: Fence Construction
CONTRACTORS: Fiber Optic Cable Installation
CONTRACTORS: Fiberglass Work
CONTRACTORS: Fire Detection & Burglar Alarm Systems
CONTRACTORS: Fire Sprinkler System Installation Svcs
CONTRACTORS: Floor Laying & Other Floor Work
CONTRACTORS: Flooring
CONTRACTORS: Food Svcs Eqpt Installation

CONTRACTORS: Garage Doors
CONTRACTORS: Gas Field Svcs, NEC
CONTRACTORS: General Electric
CONTRACTORS: Glass Tinting, Architectural & Automotive
CONTRACTORS: Glass, Glazing & Tinting
CONTRACTORS: Heating & Air Conditioning
CONTRACTORS: Heating Systems Repair & Maintenance Svc
CONTRACTORS: Highway & Street Construction, General
CONTRACTORS: Highway & Street Paving
CONTRACTORS: Home & Office Intrs Finish, Furnish/Remodel
CONTRACTORS: Hydraulic Eqpt Installation & Svcs
CONTRACTORS: Indl Building Renovation, Remodeling & Repair
CONTRACTORS: Kitchen & Bathroom Remodeling
CONTRACTORS: Lighting Syst
CONTRACTORS: Lightweight Steel Framing Installation
CONTRACTORS: Machine Rigging & Moving
CONTRACTORS: Machinery Installation
CONTRACTORS: Maintenance, Parking Facility Eqpt
CONTRACTORS: Marble Installation, Interior
CONTRACTORS: Masonry & Stonework
CONTRACTORS: Mechanical
CONTRACTORS: Office Furniture Installation
CONTRACTORS: Oil & Gas Building, Repairing & Dismantling Svc
CONTRACTORS: Oil & Gas Field Geological Exploration Svcs
CONTRACTORS: Oil & Gas Well Drilling Svc
CONTRACTORS: Oil & Gas Well On-Site Foundation Building Svcs
CONTRACTORS: Oil Field Lease Tanks: Erectg, Clng/Rprg Svcs
CONTRACTORS: Oil/Gas Field Casing,Tube/Rod Running,Cut/Pull
CONTRACTORS: Oil/Gas Well Construction, Rpr/Dismantling Svcs
CONTRACTORS: On-Site Welding
CONTRACTORS: Ornamental Metal Work
CONTRACTORS: Painting & Wall Covering
CONTRACTORS: Painting, Commercial
CONTRACTORS: Painting, Commercial, Interior
CONTRACTORS: Painting, Indl
CONTRACTORS: Parking Lot Maintenance
CONTRACTORS: Plumbing
CONTRACTORS: Prefabricated Window & Door Installation
CONTRACTORS: Process Piping
CONTRACTORS: Protective Lining Install, Underground Sewage
CONTRACTORS: Resilient Floor Laying
CONTRACTORS: Roofing
CONTRACTORS: Safety & Security Eqpt
CONTRACTORS: Sandblasting Svc, Building Exteriors
CONTRACTORS: Septic System
CONTRACTORS: Sheet Metal Work, NEC
CONTRACTORS: Shoring & Underpinning
CONTRACTORS: Siding
CONTRACTORS: Single-family Home General Remodeling
CONTRACTORS: Solar Energy Eqpt
CONTRACTORS: Sound Eqpt Installation
CONTRACTORS: Spraying, Nonagricultural
CONTRACTORS: Standby Or Emergency Power Specialization
CONTRACTORS: Stone Masonry
CONTRACTORS: Storage Tank Erection, Metal
CONTRACTORS: Store Front Construction
CONTRACTORS: Structural Steel Erection
CONTRACTORS: Svc Well Drilling Svcs
CONTRACTORS: Tile Installation, Ceramic
CONTRACTORS: Timber Removal
CONTRACTORS: Ventilation & Duct Work
CONTRACTORS: Warm Air Heating & Air Conditioning
CONTRACTORS: Water Intake Well Drilling Svc
CONTRACTORS: Water Well Drilling
CONTRACTORS: Water Well Servicing
CONTRACTORS: Waterproofing
CONTRACTORS: Weather Stripping
CONTRACTORS: Well Bailing, Cleaning, Swabbing & Treating Svc
CONTRACTORS: Window Treatment Installation
CONTRACTORS: Windows & Doors
CONTRACTORS: Wood Floor Installation & Refinishing
CONTRACTORS: Wrecking & Demolition
CONTROL CIRCUIT DEVICES

CONTROL EQPT: Buses Or Trucks, Electric
CONTROL EQPT: Electric
CONTROL EQPT: Noise
CONTROL PANELS: Electrical
CONTROLS & ACCESS: Indl, Electric
CONTROLS & ACCESS: Motor
CONTROLS: Air Flow, Refrigeration
CONTROLS: Automatic Temperature
CONTROLS: Environmental
CONTROLS: Relay & Ind
CONTROLS: Thermostats
CONTROLS: Thermostats, Exc Built-in
CONTROLS: Voice
CONTROLS: Water Heater
CONVENIENCE STORES
CONVENTION & TRADE SHOW SVCS
CONVERTERS: Data
CONVERTERS: Frequency
CONVERTERS: Phase Or Rotary, Electrical
CONVERTERS: Power, AC to DC
CONVERTERS: Torque, Exc Auto
CONVEYOR SYSTEMS
CONVEYOR SYSTEMS: Belt, General Indl Use
CONVEYOR SYSTEMS: Bucket Type
CONVEYOR SYSTEMS: Bulk Handling
CONVEYOR SYSTEMS: Pneumatic Tube
CONVEYOR SYSTEMS: Robotic
CONVEYORS & CONVEYING EQPT
COOKING & FOOD WARMING EQPT: Commercial
COOKING & FOODWARMING EQPT: Commercial
COOKING EQPT, HOUSEHOLD: Indoor
COOLING TOWERS: Metal
COOLING TOWERS: Wood
COPPER ORES
COPPER: Rolling & Drawing
CORES: Fiber, Made From Purchased Materials
CORES: Magnetic
CORK & CORK PRDTS
CORK & CORK PRDTS: Tiles
CORRUGATED PRDTS: Boxes, Partition, Display Items, Sheet/Pad
CORRUGATING MACHINES
COSMETIC PREPARATIONS
COSMETICS & TOILETRIES
COSMETICS WHOLESALERS
COSMETOLOGY & PERSONAL HYGIENE SALONS
COSMETOLOGY SCHOOL
COSTUME JEWELRY & NOVELTIES: Apparel, Exc Precious Metals
COSTUME JEWELRY & NOVELTIES: Exc Semi & Precious Metals
COUNTER & SINK TOPS
COUNTERS & COUNTER DISPLAY CASES: Refrigerated
COUNTERS & COUNTING DEVICES
COUNTERS OR COUNTER DISPLAY CASES, EXC WOOD
COUNTERS OR COUNTER DISPLAY CASES, WOOD
COUNTING DEVICES: Controls, Revolution & Timing
COUNTING DEVICES: Gauges, Press Temp Corrections Computing
COUNTING DEVICES: Pedometers
COUPLINGS: Hose & Tube, Hydraulic Or Pneumatic
COUPLINGS: Pipe
COUPON REDEMPTION SVCS
COURIER OR MESSENGER SVCS
COURIER SVCS, AIR: Letter Delivery, Private
COURIER SVCS: Ground
COURIER SVCS: Package By Vehicle
COVERS & PADS Chair, Made From Purchased Materials
COVERS: Automobile Seat
COVERS: Canvas
COVERS: Hot Tub & Spa
CRADLES: Drum
CRANES: Indl Plant
CRANKSHAFTS & CAMSHAFTS: Machining
CREATIVE SVCS: Advertisers, Exc Writers
CREDIT BUREAUS
CRUCIBLES
CRUDE PETROLEUM & NATURAL GAS PRODUCTION
CRUDE PETROLEUM PRODUCTION
CRYSTALS
CUPS & PLATES: Foamed Plastics
CUPS: Paper, Made From Purchased Materials
CURBING: Granite Or Stone
CURTAIN & DRAPERY FIXTURES: Poles, Rods & Rollers
CURTAINS & BEDDING: Knit
CURTAINS: Knit

CURTAINS: Shower
CURTAINS: Window, From Purchased Materials
CUSHIONS & PILLOWS
CUSHIONS & PILLOWS: Bed, From Purchased Materials
CUSHIONS: Textile, Exc Spring & Carpet
CUT STONE & STONE PRODUCTS
CUTLERY, STAINLESS STEEL
CUTOUTS: Distribution
CUTTING SVC: Paper, Exc Die-Cut
CYCLIC CRUDES & INTERMEDIATES
CYLINDER & ACTUATORS: Fluid Power
CYLINDERS: Pressure
CYLINDERS: Pump

D

DAIRY PRDTS STORE: Cheese
DAIRY PRDTS STORE: Ice Cream, Packaged
DAIRY PRDTS STORES
DAIRY PRDTS WHOLESALERS: Fresh
DAIRY PRDTS: Butter
DAIRY PRDTS: Cheese
DAIRY PRDTS: Dairy Based Desserts, Frozen
DAIRY PRDTS: Dietary Supplements, Dairy & Non-Dairy
   Based
DAIRY PRDTS: Dips & Spreads, Cheese Based
DAIRY PRDTS: Dried & Powdered Milk & Milk Prdts
DAIRY PRDTS: Evaporated Milk
DAIRY PRDTS: Farmers' Cheese
DAIRY PRDTS: Frozen Desserts & Novelties
DAIRY PRDTS: Ice Cream & Ice Milk
DAIRY PRDTS: Ice Cream, Bulk
DAIRY PRDTS: Ice Cream, Packaged, Molded, On Sticks,
   Etc.
DAIRY PRDTS: Ice milk, Bulk
DAIRY PRDTS: Imitation Cheese
DAIRY PRDTS: Milk Preparations, Dried
DAIRY PRDTS: Milk, Chocolate
DAIRY PRDTS: Milk, Condensed & Evaporated
DAIRY PRDTS: Milk, Fluid
DAIRY PRDTS: Milk, Processed, Pasteurized, Homoge-
   nized/Btld
DAIRY PRDTS: Natural Cheese
DAIRY PRDTS: Pot Cheese
DAIRY PRDTS: Powdered Cream
DAIRY PRDTS: Processed Cheese
DAIRY PRDTS: Yogurt, Exc Frozen
DATA ENTRY SVCS
DATA PROCESSING & PREPARATION SVCS
DATA PROCESSING SVCS
DATA VERIFICATION SVCS
DATABASE INFORMATION RETRIEVAL SVCS
DECALCOMANIA WORK, EXC CHINA & GLASS
DECORATIVE WOOD & WOODWORK
DEFENSE SYSTEMS & EQPT
DEGREASING MACHINES
DEHYDRATION EQPT
DELAY LINES
DENTAL EQPT
DENTAL EQPT & SPLYS
DENTAL EQPT & SPLYS WHOLESALERS
DENTAL EQPT & SPLYS: Cabinets
DENTAL EQPT & SPLYS: Dental Materials
DENTAL EQPT & SPLYS: Drills, Bone
DENTAL EQPT & SPLYS: Enamels
DENTAL EQPT & SPLYS: Laboratory
DENTAL EQPT & SPLYS: Orthodontic Appliances
DENTAL EQPT & SPLYS: Teeth, Artificial, Exc In Dental Labs
DENTAL INSTRUMENT REPAIR SVCS
DENTISTS' OFFICES & CLINICS
DEODORANTS: Personal
DEPARTMENT STORES
DEPARTMENT STORES: Army-Navy Goods
DEPILATORIES, COSMETIC
DERMATOLOGICALS
DESALTER KITS: Sea Water
DESIGN SVCS, NEC
DESIGN SVCS: Commercial & Indl
DESIGN SVCS: Computer Integrated Systems
DESIGNS SVCS: COSTUME & SCENERY DESIGN SVCS
DESIGNS SVCS: Scenery, Theatrical
DETECTION APPARATUS: Electronic/Magnetic Field,
   Light/Heat
DETECTORS: Water Leak
DETONATORS: Detonators, high explosives
DIAGNOSTIC SUBSTANCES

DIAGNOSTIC SUBSTANCES OR AGENTS: Blood Derivative
DIAGNOSTIC SUBSTANCES OR AGENTS: Electrolyte
DIAGNOSTIC SUBSTANCES OR AGENTS: Enzyme & Isoen-
   zyme
DIAGNOSTIC SUBSTANCES OR AGENTS: Hematology
DIAGNOSTIC SUBSTANCES OR AGENTS: In Vitro
DIAGNOSTIC SUBSTANCES OR AGENTS: In Vivo
DIAGNOSTIC SUBSTANCES OR AGENTS: Radioactive
DIAGNOSTIC SUBSTANCES OR AGENTS: Veterinary
DIAMONDS, GEMS, WHOLESALE
DIAMONDS: Cutting & Polishing
DIAPERS: Disposable
DIATOMACEOUS EARTH: Ground Or Treated
DIE CUTTING SVC: Paper
DIE SETS: Presses, Metal Stamping
DIES & TOOLS: Special
DIES: Cutting, Exc Metal
DIES: Extrusion
DIES: Paper Cutting
DIES: Plastic Forming
DIES: Steel Rule
DIES: Wire Drawing & Straightening
DIFFERENTIAL ASSEMBLIES & PARTS
DIODES & RECTIFIERS
DIODES: Light Emitting
DIORITE: Crushed & Broken
DIRECT SELLING ESTABLISHMENTS, NEC
DIRECT SELLING ESTABLISHMENTS: Beverage Svcs
DIRECT SELLING ESTABLISHMENTS:
   Drapes/Curtains,Door-To-Door
DIRECT SELLING ESTABLISHMENTS: Snacks
DISCOUNT DEPARTMENT STORES
DISCS & TAPE: Optical, Blank
DISHWASHING EQPT: Commercial
DISK & DISKETTE EQPT, EXC DRIVES
DISK DRIVES: Computer
DISKETTE DUPLICATING SVCS
DISPENSERS: Soap
DISPENSING EQPT & PARTS, BEVERAGE: Coolers,
   Milk/Water, Elec
DISPENSING EQPT & PARTS, BEVERAGE: Fountain/Other
   Beverage
DISPLAY FIXTURES: Wood
DISPLAY ITEMS: Corrugated, Made From Purchased Materi-
   als
DISPLAY ITEMS: Solid Fiber, Made From Purchased Materi-
   als
DISPLAY LETTERING SVCS
DISPLAY STANDS: Merchandise, Exc Wood
DOCK EQPT & SPLYS, INDL
DOCUMENT EMBOSSING SVCS
DOLOMITIC MARBLE: Crushed & Broken
DOOR & WINDOW REPAIR SVCS
DOOR FRAMES: Wood
DOOR OPERATING SYSTEMS: Electric
DOORS & WINDOWS WHOLESALERS: All Materials
DOORS & WINDOWS: Storm, Metal
DOORS: Fire, Metal
DOORS: Folding, Plastic Or Plastic Coated Fabric
DOORS: Garage, Overhead, Metal
DOORS: Garage, Overhead, Wood
DOORS: Glass
DOORS: Rolling, Indl Building Or Warehouse, Metal
DOORS: Screen, Metal
DOORS: Wooden
DRAINING OR PUMPING OF METAL MINES
DRAPERIES & CURTAINS
DRAPERIES & DRAPERY FABRICS, COTTON
DRAPERIES: Plastic & Textile, From Purchased Materials
DRAPERY & UPHOLSTERY STORES: Curtains
DRAPERY & UPHOLSTERY STORES: Draperies
DRILL BITS
DRILLING MACHINERY & EQPT: Oil & Gas
DRILLING MACHINERY & EQPT: Water Well
DRINK MIXES, NONALCOHOLIC: Cocktail
DRINKING PLACES: Alcoholic Beverages
DRINKING PLACES: Tavern
DRIVES: High Speed Indl, Exc Hydrostatic
DRUG STORES
DRUGGIST'S SUNDRIES: Rubber
DRUGS & DRUG PROPRIETARIES, WHOL: Biologicals/Al-
   lied Prdts
DRUGS & DRUG PROPRIETARIES, WHOLESALE
DRUGS & DRUG PROPRIETARIES, WHOLESALE: Animal
   Medicines

DRUGS & DRUG PROPRIETARIES, WHOLESALE: Medici-
   nals/Botanicals
DRUGS & DRUG PROPRIETARIES, WHOLESALE: Pharma-
   ceuticals
DRUGS & DRUG PROPRIETARIES, WHOLESALE: Vitamins
   & Minerals
DRUGS ACTING ON THE CENTRAL NERVOUS SYSTEM &
   SENSE ORGANS
DRUGS AFFECTING NEOPLASMS & ENDOCRINE SYS-
   TEMS
DRUGS: Parasitic & Infective Disease Affecting
DRUMS: Brake
DRUMS: Fiber
DRYCLEANING & LAUNDRY SVCS: Commercial & Family
DRYCLEANING EQPT & SPLYS: Commercial
DRYCLEANING PLANTS
DRYCLEANING SVC: Collecting & Distributing Agency
DRYCLEANING SVC: Drapery & Curtain
DRYERS & REDRYERS: Indl
DRYERS: Textile
DUCTING: Metal Plate
DUCTING: Plastic
DUCTS: Sheet Metal
DUMPSTERS: Garbage
DUST OR FUME COLLECTING EQPT: Indl
DYE INTERMEDIATES: Cyclic
DYES & PIGMENTS: Organic
DYES OR COLORS: Food, Synthetic
DYES: Synthetic Organic
DYESTUFFS WHOLESALERS

E

EATING PLACES
EDUCATIONAL SVCS
EDUCATIONAL SVCS, NONDEGREE GRANTING: Continu-
   ing Education
ELASTIC BRAID & NARROW WOVEN FABRICS
ELECTRIC & OTHER SERVICES COMBINED
ELECTRIC MOTOR REPAIR SVCS
ELECTRIC SERVICES
ELECTRIC SVCS, NEC: Power Generation
ELECTRIC TOOL REPAIR SVCS
ELECTRICAL APPARATUS & EQPT WHOLESALERS
ELECTRICAL APPLIANCES, TELEVISIONS & RADIOS
   WHOLESALERS
ELECTRICAL CURRENT CARRYING WIRING DEVICES
ELECTRICAL DEVICE PARTS: Porcelain, Molded
ELECTRICAL DISCHARGE MACHINING, EDM
ELECTRICAL EQPT & SPLYS
ELECTRICAL EQPT FOR ENGINES
ELECTRICAL EQPT REPAIR & MAINTENANCE
ELECTRICAL EQPT REPAIR SVCS
ELECTRICAL EQPT REPAIR SVCS: High Voltage
ELECTRICAL EQPT: Automotive, NEC
ELECTRICAL GOODS, WHOLESALE: Batteries, Storage, Indl
ELECTRICAL GOODS, WHOLESALE: Closed Circuit Televi-
   sion Or TV
ELECTRICAL GOODS, WHOLESALE: Conduits & Raceways
ELECTRICAL GOODS, WHOLESALE: Connectors
ELECTRICAL GOODS, WHOLESALE: Electrical Entertain-
   ment Eqpt
ELECTRICAL GOODS, WHOLESALE: Electronic Parts
ELECTRICAL GOODS, WHOLESALE: Fittings & Construction
   Mat
ELECTRICAL GOODS, WHOLESALE: Flashlights
ELECTRICAL GOODS, WHOLESALE: Generators
ELECTRICAL GOODS, WHOLESALE: High Fidelity Eqpt
ELECTRICAL GOODS, WHOLESALE: Household Appliances,
   NEC
ELECTRICAL GOODS, WHOLESALE: Insulators
ELECTRICAL GOODS, WHOLESALE: Intercommunication
   Eqpt
ELECTRICAL GOODS, WHOLESALE: Irons
ELECTRICAL GOODS, WHOLESALE: Light Bulbs & Related
   Splys
ELECTRICAL GOODS, WHOLESALE: Lighting Fixtures,
   Comm & Indl
ELECTRICAL GOODS, WHOLESALE: Lugs & Connectors
ELECTRICAL GOODS, WHOLESALE: Mobile telephone Eqpt
ELECTRICAL GOODS, WHOLESALE: Modems, Computer
ELECTRICAL GOODS, WHOLESALE: Motor Ctrls, Starters &
   Relays
ELECTRICAL GOODS, WHOLESALE: Motors
ELECTRICAL GOODS, WHOLESALE: Paging & Signaling
   Eqpt

INDEX

ELECTRICAL GOODS, WHOLESALE: Panelboards
ELECTRICAL GOODS, WHOLESALE: Radio & TV Or TV Eqpt & Parts
ELECTRICAL GOODS, WHOLESALE: Radio Parts & Access, NEC
ELECTRICAL GOODS, WHOLESALE: Semiconductor Devices
ELECTRICAL GOODS, WHOLESALE: Signaling, Eqpt
ELECTRICAL GOODS, WHOLESALE: Switches, Exc Electronic, NEC
ELECTRICAL GOODS, WHOLESALE: Switchgear
ELECTRICAL GOODS, WHOLESALE: Telephone & Telegraphic Eqpt
ELECTRICAL GOODS, WHOLESALE: Telephone Eqpt
ELECTRICAL GOODS, WHOLESALE: Transformer & Transmission Eqpt
ELECTRICAL GOODS, WHOLESALE: Tubes, Rcvg & Txmtg Or Indl
ELECTRICAL GOODS, WHOLESALE: Video Eqpt
ELECTRICAL GOODS, WHOLESALE: Wire & Cable
ELECTRICAL GOODS, WHOLESALE: Wire & Cable, Ctrl & Sig
ELECTRICAL GOODS, WHOLESALE: Wire & Cable, Electronic
ELECTRICAL GOODS, WHOLESALE: Wire & Cable, Power
ELECTRICAL INDL APPARATUS, NEC
ELECTRICAL MEASURING INSTRUMENT REPAIR & CALIBRATION SVCS
ELECTRICAL SPLYS
ELECTRICAL SUPPLIES: Porcelain
ELECTROCARS: Golfer Transportation
ELECTRODES: Fluorescent Lamps
ELECTRODES: Indl Process
ELECTROMEDICAL EQPT
ELECTROMEDICAL EQPT WHOLESALERS
ELECTRON TUBES
ELECTRON TUBES: Parts
ELECTRONIC COMPONENTS
ELECTRONIC DEVICES: Solid State, NEC
ELECTRONIC EQPT REPAIR SVCS
ELECTRONIC LOADS & POWER SPLYS
ELECTRONIC PARTS & EQPT WHOLESALERS
ELECTRONIC TRAINING DEVICES
ELECTROPLATING & PLATING SVC
ELEVATORS & EQPT
ELEVATORS WHOLESALERS
ELEVATORS: Installation & Conversion
ELEVATORS: Stair, Motor Powered
EMBLEMS: Embroidered
EMBOSSING SVC: Paper
EMBROIDERING & ART NEEDLEWORK FOR THE TRADE
EMBROIDERING SVC
EMBROIDERING SVC: Schiffli Machine
EMBROIDERY ADVERTISING SVCS
EMBROIDERY KITS
EMERGENCY ALARMS
EMPLOYMENT AGENCY SVCS
EMPLOYMENT SVCS: Labor Contractors
ENAMELS
ENCLOSURES: Electronic
ENCODERS: Digital
ENDOCRINE PRDTS
ENERGY MEASUREMENT EQPT
ENGINE PARTS & ACCESS: Internal Combustion
ENGINE REBUILDING: Diesel
ENGINE REBUILDING: Gas
ENGINEERING SVCS
ENGINEERING SVCS: Aviation Or Aeronautical
ENGINEERING SVCS: Building Construction
ENGINEERING SVCS: Chemical
ENGINEERING SVCS: Construction & Civil
ENGINEERING SVCS: Electrical Or Electronic
ENGINEERING SVCS: Energy conservation
ENGINEERING SVCS: Industrial
ENGINEERING SVCS: Machine Tool Design
ENGINEERING SVCS: Mechanical
ENGINEERING SVCS: Structural
ENGINES & ENGINE PARTS: Guided Missile, Research & Develpt
ENGINES: Diesel & Semi-Diesel Or Duel Fuel
ENGINES: Gasoline, NEC
ENGINES: Internal Combustion, NEC
ENGRAVING SVC, NEC
ENGRAVING SVC: Jewelry & Personal Goods
ENGRAVING SVCS

ENGRAVING: Bank Note
ENGRAVINGS: Plastic
ENTERTAINERS
ENTERTAINERS & ENTERTAINMENT GROUPS
ENTERTAINMENT PROMOTION SVCS
ENTERTAINMENT SVCS
ENVELOPES
ENVELOPES WHOLESALERS
ENZYMES
EPOXY RESINS
EQUIPMENT: Rental & Leasing, NEC
ERASERS: Rubber Or Rubber & Abrasive Combined
ETCHING & ENGRAVING SVC
ETHYLENE-PROPYLENE RUBBERS: EPDM Polymers
EXHAUST SYSTEMS: Eqpt & Parts
EXPANSION JOINTS: Rubber
EXPLOSIVES
EXPLOSIVES, EXC AMMO & FIREWORKS WHOLESALERS
EXTENSION CORDS
EXTERMINATING PRDTS: Household Or Indl Use
EXTRACTS, FLAVORING
EXTRUDED SHAPES, NEC: Copper & Copper Alloy
EYEGLASS CASES
EYEGLASSES
EYES: Artificial
Ethylene Glycols

F

FABRIC STORES
FABRICATED METAL PRODUCTS, NEC
FABRICS & CLOTHING: Rubber Coated
FABRICS: Alpacas, Cotton
FABRICS: Alpacas, Mohair, Woven
FABRICS: Animal Fiber, Narrow Woven
FABRICS: Apparel & Outerwear, Broadwoven
FABRICS: Apparel & Outerwear, Cotton
FABRICS: Automotive, Cotton
FABRICS: Automotive, From Manmade Fiber
FABRICS: Bandage Cloth, Cotton
FABRICS: Basket Weave, Cotton
FABRICS: Broadwoven, Cotton
FABRICS: Broadwoven, Synthetic Manmade Fiber & Silk
FABRICS: Broadwoven, Wool
FABRICS: Canvas
FABRICS: Coated Or Treated
FABRICS: Decorative Trim & Specialty, Including Twist Weave
FABRICS: Denims
FABRICS: Fiberglass, Broadwoven
FABRICS: Hat Band
FABRICS: Jacquard Woven, Cotton
FABRICS: Lace & Decorative Trim, Narrow
FABRICS: Lace & Lace Prdts
FABRICS: Lace, Knit, NEC
FABRICS: Laminated
FABRICS: Laundry, Cotton
FABRICS: Manmade Fiber, Narrow
FABRICS: Nonwoven
FABRICS: Paper, Broadwoven
FABRICS: Pile, Circular Knit
FABRICS: Polypropylene, Broadwoven
FABRICS: Print, Cotton
FABRICS: Resin Or Plastic Coated
FABRICS: Rubberized
FABRICS: Scrub Cloths
FABRICS: Seat Cover, Automobile, Cotton
FABRICS: Shirting, Cotton
FABRICS: Shoe
FABRICS: Spunbonded
FABRICS: Trimmings
FABRICS: Trimmings, Textile
FABRICS: Umbrella Cloth, Cotton
FABRICS: Underwear, Cotton
FABRICS: Upholstery, Cotton
FABRICS: Wall Covering, From Manmade Fiber Or Silk
FABRICS: Warp & Flat Knit Prdts
FABRICS: Warp Knit, Lace & Netting
FABRICS: Weft Or Circular Knit
FABRICS: Woven Wire, Made From Purchased Wire
FABRICS: Woven, Narrow Cotton, Wool, Silk
FACE PLATES
FACILITIES SUPPORT SVCS
FACSIMILE COMMUNICATION EQPT
FAMILY CLOTHING STORES
FANS, VENTILATING: Indl Or Commercial

FARM PRDTS, RAW MATERIALS, WHOLESALE: Nuts & Nut By-Prdts
FARM SPLY STORES
FARM SPLYS WHOLESALERS
FARM SPLYS, WHOLESALE: Feed
FARM SPLYS, WHOLESALE: Fertilizers & Agricultural Chemicals
FARM SPLYS, WHOLESALE: Greenhouse Eqpt & Splys
FARM SPLYS, WHOLESALE: Insecticides
FARM SPLYS, WHOLESALE: Soil, Potting & Planting
FASTENERS WHOLESALERS
FASTENERS: Metal
FASTENERS: Notions, NEC
FASTENERS: Notions, Zippers
FATTY ACID ESTERS & AMINOS
FELT, WHOLESALE
FENCE POSTS: Iron & Steel
FENCES & FENCING MATERIALS
FENCING DEALERS
FENCING MADE IN WIREDRAWING PLANTS
FENCING MATERIALS: Docks & Other Outdoor Prdts, Wood
FENCING MATERIALS: Plastic
FENCING MATERIALS: Snow Fence, Wood
FENCING MATERIALS: Wood
FENCING: Chain Link
FERRITES
FERTILIZER, AGRICULTURAL: Wholesalers
FERTILIZERS: NEC
FERTILIZERS: Nitrogenous
FERTILIZERS: Phosphatic
FIBER & FIBER PRDTS: Acrylic
FIBER & FIBER PRDTS: Organic, Noncellulose
FIBER & FIBER PRDTS: Polyester
FIBER & FIBER PRDTS: Synthetic Cellulosic
FIBER & FIBER PRDTS: Vinyl
FIBER OPTICS
FILE FOLDERS
FILM & SHEET: Unsuppported Plastic
FILM BASE: Cellulose Acetate Or Nitrocellulose Plastics
FILTERS
FILTERS & SOFTENERS: Water, Household
FILTERS & STRAINERS: Pipeline
FILTERS: Air
FILTERS: Air Intake, Internal Combustion Engine, Exc Auto
FILTERS: Gasoline, Internal Combustion Engine, Exc Auto
FILTERS: General Line, Indl
FILTERS: Motor Vehicle
FILTERS: Paper
FILTRATION DEVICES: Electronic
FILTRATION SAND MINING
FINANCIAL SVCS
FINDINGS & TRIMMINGS Fabric, NEC
FINDINGS & TRIMMINGS: Apparel
FINDINGS & TRIMMINGS: Fabric
FINDINGS & TRIMMINGS: Furniture, Fabric
FINGERNAILS, ARTIFICIAL
FINGERPRINT EQPT
FINISHING AGENTS: Textile
FIRE ALARM MAINTENANCE & MONITORING SVCS
FIRE ARMS, SMALL: Guns Or Gun Parts, 30 mm & Below
FIRE ARMS, SMALL: Rifles Or Rifle Parts, 30 mm & below
FIRE DETECTION SYSTEMS
FIRE ESCAPES
FIRE EXTINGUISHER CHARGES
FIRE EXTINGUISHERS: Portable
FIRE OR BURGLARY RESISTIVE PRDTS
FIRE PROTECTION EQPT
FIRE PROTECTION, GOVERNMENT: Local
FIREPLACE & CHIMNEY MATERIAL: Concrete
FIREWOOD, WHOLESALE
FISH & SEAFOOD PROCESSORS: Canned Or Cured
FISH & SEAFOOD PROCESSORS: Fresh Or Frozen
FISH LIVER OILS: For Medicinal Use, Refined Or Concentrated
FISHING EQPT: Lures
FISHING EQPT: Nets & Seines
FITTINGS & ASSEMBLIES: Hose & Tube, Hydraulic Or Pneumatic
FITTINGS: Pipe
FITTINGS: Pipe, Fabricated
FIXTURES & EQPT: Kitchen, Metal, Exc Cast Aluminum
FIXTURES & EQPT: Kitchen, Porcelain Enameled
FIXTURES: Bank, Metal, Ornamental
FIXTURES: Cut Stone
FLAGPOLES

FLAGS: Fabric
FLAT GLASS: Antique
FLAT GLASS: Construction
FLAT GLASS: Laminated
FLAT GLASS: Tempered
FLAT GLASS: Window, Clear & Colored
FLAVORS OR FLAVORING MATERIALS: Synthetic
FLOOR CLEANING & MAINTENANCE EQPT: Household
FLOOR COVERING STORES
FLOOR COVERING STORES: Carpets
FLOOR COVERING STORES: Rugs
FLOOR COVERING: Plastic
FLOOR COVERINGS WHOLESALERS
FLOOR COVERINGS: Aircraft & Automobile
FLOOR COVERINGS: Rubber
FLOOR COVERINGS: Tile, Support Plastic
FLOORING: Hard Surface
FLOORING: Hardwood
FLOORING: Rubber
FLOORING: Tile
FLORIST: Flowers, Fresh
FLORISTS
FLOWER ARRANGEMENTS: Artificial
FLOWERS, ARTIFICIAL, WHOLESALE
FLOWERS, FRESH, WHOLESALE
FLOWERS: Artificial & Preserved
FLUID METERS & COUNTING DEVICES
FLUID POWER PUMPS & MOTORS
FLUID POWER VALVES & HOSE FITTINGS
FLUXES
FLY TRAPS: Electrical
FOAM CHARGE MIXTURES
FOAM RUBBER
FOAM RUBBER, WHOLESALE
FOAMS & RUBBER, WHOLESALE
FOIL & LEAF: Metal
FOIL BOARD: Made From Purchased Materials
FOIL: Aluminum
FOIL: Copper
FOIL: Zinc
FOOD CASINGS: Plastic
FOOD COLORINGS
FOOD COLORINGS: Bakers'
FOOD PRDTS & SEAFOOD: Shellfish, Fresh, Shucked
FOOD PRDTS, BREAKFAST: Cereal, Granola & Muesli
FOOD PRDTS, BREAKFAST: Cereal, Oats, Rolled
FOOD PRDTS, CANNED OR FRESH PACK: Fruit Juices
FOOD PRDTS, CANNED: Baby Food
FOOD PRDTS, CANNED: Barbecue Sauce
FOOD PRDTS, CANNED: Beans & Bean Sprouts
FOOD PRDTS, CANNED: Chili Sauce, Tomato
FOOD PRDTS, CANNED: Ethnic
FOOD PRDTS, CANNED: Fruits
FOOD PRDTS, CANNED: Fruits & Fruit Prdts
FOOD PRDTS, CANNED: Italian
FOOD PRDTS, CANNED: Jams, Including Imitation
FOOD PRDTS, CANNED: Mexican, NEC
FOOD PRDTS, CANNED: Seasonings, Tomato
FOOD PRDTS, CANNED: Soups
FOOD PRDTS, CANNED: Soups, Exc Seafood
FOOD PRDTS, CANNED: Spaghetti & Other Pasta Sauce
FOOD PRDTS, CANNED: Tomato Sauce.
FOOD PRDTS, CANNED: Vegetable Pastes
FOOD PRDTS, CONFECTIONERY, WHOLESALE: Candy
FOOD PRDTS, CONFECTIONERY, WHOLESALE: Nuts, Salted/Roasted
FOOD PRDTS, CONFECTIONERY, WHOLESALE: Pretzels
FOOD PRDTS, CONFECTIONERY, WHOLESALE: Snack Foods
FOOD PRDTS, CONFECTIONERY, WHOLESALE: Syrups, Fountain
FOOD PRDTS, DAIRY, WHOLESALE: Frozen Dairy Desserts
FOOD PRDTS, DAIRY, WHOLESALE: Milk, Canned Or Dried
FOOD PRDTS, FISH & SEAFOOD, WHOLESALE: Seafood
FOOD PRDTS, FISH & SEAFOOD: Clams, Canned, Jarred, Etc
FOOD PRDTS, FISH & SEAFOOD: Clams, Preserved Or Cured
FOOD PRDTS, FISH & SEAFOOD: Fish, Canned, Jarred, Etc
FOOD PRDTS, FISH & SEAFOOD: Fish, Frozen, Prepared
FOOD PRDTS, FISH & SEAFOOD: Fresh, Prepared
FOOD PRDTS, FISH & SEAFOOD: Oysters, Canned, Jarred, Etc
FOOD PRDTS, FISH & SEAFOOD: Prepared Cakes & Sticks

FOOD PRDTS, FISH & SEAFOOD: Seafood, Frozen, Prepared
FOOD PRDTS, FROZEN: Breakfasts, Packaged
FOOD PRDTS, FROZEN: Dinners, Packaged
FOOD PRDTS, FROZEN: Ethnic Foods, NEC
FOOD PRDTS, FROZEN: Fruits, Juices & Vegetables
FOOD PRDTS, FROZEN: NEC
FOOD PRDTS, FROZEN: Pizza
FOOD PRDTS, FROZEN: Snack Items
FOOD PRDTS, FROZEN: Soups
FOOD PRDTS, FROZEN: Vegetables, Exc Potato Prdts
FOOD PRDTS, FROZEN: Whipped Topping
FOOD PRDTS, FRUITS & VEGETABLES, FRESH, WHOLESALE: Vegetable
FOOD PRDTS, MEAT & MEAT PRDTS, WHOLESALE: Fresh
FOOD PRDTS, POULTRY, WHOLESALE: Poultry Prdts, NEC
FOOD PRDTS, WHOL: Canned Goods, Fruit, Veg, Seafood/Meats
FOOD PRDTS, WHOLESALE: Baking Splys
FOOD PRDTS, WHOLESALE: Beans, Dry, Bulk
FOOD PRDTS, WHOLESALE: Breakfast Cereals
FOOD PRDTS, WHOLESALE: Chocolate
FOOD PRDTS, WHOLESALE: Coffee & Tea
FOOD PRDTS, WHOLESALE: Coffee, Green Or Roasted
FOOD PRDTS, WHOLESALE: Cooking Oils
FOOD PRDTS, WHOLESALE: Dried or Canned Foods
FOOD PRDTS, WHOLESALE: Flavorings & Fragrances
FOOD PRDTS, WHOLESALE: Health
FOOD PRDTS, WHOLESALE: Juices
FOOD PRDTS, WHOLESALE: Molasses, Indl
FOOD PRDTS, WHOLESALE: Natural & Organic
FOOD PRDTS, WHOLESALE: Pasta & Rice
FOOD PRDTS, WHOLESALE: Sauces
FOOD PRDTS, WHOLESALE: Sausage Casings
FOOD PRDTS, WHOLESALE: Specialty
FOOD PRDTS, WHOLESALE: Spices & Seasonings
FOOD PRDTS, WHOLESALE: Tea
FOOD PRDTS, WHOLESALE: Water, Mineral Or Spring, Bottled
FOOD PRDTS: Almond Pastes
FOOD PRDTS: Animal & marine fats & oils
FOOD PRDTS: Blackstrap Molasses, Purchd Raw Sugar/Syrup
FOOD PRDTS: Bread Crumbs, Exc Made In Bakeries
FOOD PRDTS: Breakfast Bars
FOOD PRDTS: Cereals
FOOD PRDTS: Chewing Gum Base
FOOD PRDTS: Chocolate, Baking
FOOD PRDTS: Cocoa & Cocoa Prdts
FOOD PRDTS: Cocoa, Butter
FOOD PRDTS: Cocoa, Powdered
FOOD PRDTS: Coconut, Desiccated & Shredded
FOOD PRDTS: Coffee
FOOD PRDTS: Coffee Extracts
FOOD PRDTS: Coffee Roasting, Exc Wholesale Grocers
FOOD PRDTS: Cooking Oils, Refined Vegetable, Exc Corn
FOOD PRDTS: Desserts, Ready-To-Mix
FOOD PRDTS: Doughs & Batters
FOOD PRDTS: Doughs, Frozen Or Refrig From Purchased Flour
FOOD PRDTS: Dressings, Salad, Raw & Cooked Exc Dry Mixes
FOOD PRDTS: Dried & Dehydrated Fruits, Vegetables & Soup Mix
FOOD PRDTS: Edible Oil Prdts, Exc Corn Oil
FOOD PRDTS: Edible fats & oils
FOOD PRDTS: Eggs, Processed
FOOD PRDTS: Eggs, Processed, Dehydrated
FOOD PRDTS: Emulsifiers
FOOD PRDTS: Flavored Ices, Frozen
FOOD PRDTS: Flour
FOOD PRDTS: Flour & Other Grain Mill Products
FOOD PRDTS: Flour Mixes & Doughs
FOOD PRDTS: Flour, Cake From Purchased Flour
FOOD PRDTS: Flours & Flour Mixes, From Purchased Flour
FOOD PRDTS: Fresh Vegetables, Peeled Or Processed
FOOD PRDTS: Fruit Juices
FOOD PRDTS: Fruit Pops, Frozen
FOOD PRDTS: Fruits & Vegetables, Pickled
FOOD PRDTS: Fruits, Dehydrated Or Dried
FOOD PRDTS: Gelatin Dessert Preparations
FOOD PRDTS: Granola & Energy Bars, Nonchocolate
FOOD PRDTS: Granulated Cane Sugar
FOOD PRDTS: Hydrol
FOOD PRDTS: Ice, Blocks

FOOD PRDTS: Ice, Cubes
FOOD PRDTS: Instant Coffee
FOOD PRDTS: Luncheon Meat, Poultry
FOOD PRDTS: Macaroni Prdts, Dry, Alphabet, Rings Or Shells
FOOD PRDTS: Macaroni, Noodles, Spaghetti, Pasta, Etc
FOOD PRDTS: Malt
FOOD PRDTS: Margarine, Including Imitation
FOOD PRDTS: Mayonnaise & Dressings, Exc Tomato Based
FOOD PRDTS: Menhaden Oil
FOOD PRDTS: Mixes, Bread & Roll From Purchased Flour
FOOD PRDTS: Mixes, Cake, From Purchased Flour
FOOD PRDTS: Mixes, Doughnut From Purchased Flour
FOOD PRDTS: Mixes, Pancake From Purchased Flour
FOOD PRDTS: Mixes, Pizza From Purchased Flour
FOOD PRDTS: Mixes, Salad Dressings, Dry
FOOD PRDTS: Mustard, Prepared
FOOD PRDTS: Nuts & Seeds
FOOD PRDTS: Olive Oil
FOOD PRDTS: Oriental Noodles
FOOD PRDTS: Pasta, Uncooked, Packaged With Other Ingredients
FOOD PRDTS: Peanut Butter
FOOD PRDTS: Pickles, Vinegar
FOOD PRDTS: Pizza Doughs From Purchased Flour
FOOD PRDTS: Pizza, Refrigerated
FOOD PRDTS: Popcorn, Popped
FOOD PRDTS: Popcorn, Unpopped
FOOD PRDTS: Potato & Corn Chips & Similar Prdts
FOOD PRDTS: Potato Chips & Other Potato-Based Snacks
FOOD PRDTS: Poultry, Processed, Frozen
FOOD PRDTS: Poultry, Slaughtered & Dressed
FOOD PRDTS: Preparations
FOOD PRDTS: Prepared Sauces, Exc Tomato Based
FOOD PRDTS: Raw cane sugar
FOOD PRDTS: Rice, Milled
FOOD PRDTS: Rice, Packaged & Seasoned
FOOD PRDTS: Salads
FOOD PRDTS: Seasonings & Spices
FOOD PRDTS: Shortening & Solid Edible Fats
FOOD PRDTS: Soup Mixes
FOOD PRDTS: Spices, Including Ground
FOOD PRDTS: Sugar
FOOD PRDTS: Sugar, Cane
FOOD PRDTS: Syrup, Maple
FOOD PRDTS: Syrup, Pancake, Blended & Mixed
FOOD PRDTS: Syrups
FOOD PRDTS: Tea
FOOD PRDTS: Tofu Desserts, Frozen
FOOD PRDTS: Tofu, Exc Frozen Desserts
FOOD PRDTS: Tortillas
FOOD PRDTS: Turkey, Processed, Frozen
FOOD PRDTS: Turkey, Slaughtered & Dressed
FOOD PRDTS: Vegetable Oil Mills, NEC
FOOD PRDTS: Vegetables, Dried or Dehydrated Exc Freeze-Dried
FOOD PRDTS: Vinegar
FOOD PRDTS: Yeast
FOOD PRODUCTS MACHINERY
FOOD STORES: Convenience, Independent
FOOD STORES: Delicatessen
FOOD STORES: Frozen Food &Freezer Plans, Exc Meat
FOOD STORES: Grocery, Independent
FOOD STORES: Supermarkets
FOOD STORES: Supermarkets, Chain
FOOTWEAR, WHOLESALE: Athletic
FOOTWEAR, WHOLESALE: Shoe Access
FOOTWEAR, WHOLESALE: Shoes
FORGINGS
FORGINGS: Automotive & Internal Combustion Engine
FORGINGS: Gear & Chain
FORGINGS: Metal , Ornamental, Ferrous
FORGINGS: Nonferrous
FORGINGS: Nuclear Power Plant, Ferrous
FORMS: Concrete, Sheet Metal
FOUNDRIES: Aluminum
FOUNDRIES: Brass, Bronze & Copper
FOUNDRIES: Gray & Ductile Iron
FOUNDRIES: Iron
FOUNDRIES: Nonferrous
FOUNDRIES: Steel
FOUNDRIES: Steel Investment
FOUNDRY MACHINERY & EQPT
FOUNDRY MATERIALS: Insulsleeves
FOUNDRY SAND MINING

INDEX

FRAMES & FRAMING WHOLESALE
FRANCHISES, SELLING OR LICENSING
FREEZERS: Household
FREIGHT FORWARDING ARRANGEMENTS
FREIGHT HANDLING SVCS: Air
FREIGHT TRANSPORTATION ARRANGEMENTS
FRICTION MATERIAL, MADE FROM POWDERED METAL
FRUIT & VEGETABLE MARKETS
FRUITS & VEGETABLES WHOLESALERS: Fresh
FRUITS: Artificial & Preserved
FUEL CELLS: Solid State
FUEL OIL DEALERS
FUELS: Ethanol
FUELS: Jet
FUELS: Oil
FUND RAISING ORGANIZATION, NON-FEE BASIS
FUNGICIDES OR HERBICIDES
FUR FINISHING & LINING: For The Fur Goods Trade
FUR: Coats
FURNACES & OVENS: Indl
FURNACES & OVENS: Vacuum
FURNACES: Indl, Electric
FURNACES: Indl, Fuel-Fired, Metal Melting
FURNACES: Warm Air, Electric
FURNITURE & CABINET STORES: Cabinets, Custom Work
FURNITURE & CABINET STORES: Custom
FURNITURE & FIXTURES Factory
FURNITURE COMPONENTS: Porcelain Enameled
FURNITURE REPAIR & MAINTENANCE SVCS
FURNITURE STOCK & PARTS: Hardwood
FURNITURE STORES
FURNITURE STORES: Cabinets, Kitchen, Exc Custom Made
FURNITURE STORES: Custom Made, Exc Cabinets
FURNITURE STORES: Office
FURNITURE STORES: Outdoor & Garden
FURNITURE UPHOLSTERY REPAIR SVCS
FURNITURE WHOLESALERS
FURNITURE, HOUSEHOLD: Wholesalers
FURNITURE, OFFICE: Wholesalers
FURNITURE, OUTDOOR & LAWN: Wholesalers
FURNITURE, WHOLESALE: Bar
FURNITURE, WHOLESALE: Chairs
FURNITURE, WHOLESALE: Juvenile
FURNITURE, WHOLESALE: Lockers
FURNITURE, WHOLESALE: Shelving
FURNITURE, WHOLESALE: Sofas & Couches
FURNITURE: Bar furniture
FURNITURE: Benches, Office, Wood
FURNITURE: Cafeteria
FURNITURE: Chair Beds
FURNITURE: Chairs & Couches, Wood, Upholstered
FURNITURE: Chairs, Dental
FURNITURE: Chairs, Folding
FURNITURE: Chairs, Household Upholstered
FURNITURE: Chairs, Household, Metal
FURNITURE: Chairs, Office Exc Wood
FURNITURE: Chairs, Office Wood
FURNITURE: Chests, Cedar
FURNITURE: Church
FURNITURE: Desks & Tables, Office, Wood
FURNITURE: Desks, Wood
FURNITURE: Foundations & Platforms
FURNITURE: Frames, Box Springs Or Bedsprings, Metal
FURNITURE: Hospital
FURNITURE: Hotel
FURNITURE: Household, Metal
FURNITURE: Household, Upholstered, Exc Wood Or Metal
FURNITURE: Household, Wood
FURNITURE: Hydraulic Barber & Beauty Shop Chairs
FURNITURE: Institutional, Exc Wood
FURNITURE: Juvenile, Wood
FURNITURE: Juvenile, Wood
FURNITURE: Kitchen & Dining Room
FURNITURE: Kitchen & Dining Room, Metal
FURNITURE: Laboratory
FURNITURE: Lawn & Garden, Except Wood & Metal
FURNITURE: Lawn, Wood
FURNITURE: Library
FURNITURE: Mattresses & Foundations
FURNITURE: Mattresses, Box & Bedsprings
FURNITURE: Mattresses, Innerspring Or Box Spring
FURNITURE: NEC
FURNITURE: Office Panel Systems, Wood
FURNITURE: Office, Exc Wood
FURNITURE: Office, Wood

FURNITURE: School
FURNITURE: Sleep
FURNITURE: Sofa Beds Or Convertible Sofas)
FURNITURE: Spring Cushions
FURNITURE: Table Tops, Marble
FURNITURE: Tables & Table Tops, Wood
FURNITURE: Tables, Household, Metal
FURNITURE: Upholstered
FURNITURE: Vehicle
FURNITURE: Wall Cases, Office, Exc Wood
FURNITURE: Wardrobes, Household, Wood
FURNITURE: Wicker & Rattan
FURRIERS
FUSES & FUSE EQPT
FUSES: Electric
Furs

G

GAMES & TOYS: Baby Carriages & Restraint Seats
GAMES & TOYS: Blocks
GAMES & TOYS: Board Games, Children's & Adults'
GAMES & TOYS: Craft & Hobby Kits & Sets
GAMES & TOYS: Dolls & Doll Clothing
GAMES & TOYS: Dolls, Exc Stuffed Toy Animals
GAMES & TOYS: Kits, Science, Incl Microscopes/Chemistry Sets
GAMES & TOYS: Marbles
GAMES & TOYS: Models, Airplane, Toy & Hobby
GAMES & TOYS: Models, Railroad, Toy & Hobby
GAMES & TOYS: Trains & Eqpt, Electric & Mechanical
GAMES & TOYS: Wagons, Coaster, Express & Play, Children's
GARBAGE CONTAINERS: Plastic
GARBAGE DISPOSERS & COMPACTORS: Commercial
GAS & OIL FIELD EXPLORATION SVCS
GAS & OIL FIELD SVCS, NEC
GAS & OTHER COMBINED SVCS
GAS STATIONS
GASES: Flourinated Hydrocarbon
GASES: Helium
GASES: Indl
GASES: Nitrogen
GASES: Oxygen
GASKET MATERIALS
GASKETS
GASKETS & SEALING DEVICES
GASOLINE FILLING STATIONS
GASTROINTESTINAL OR GENITOURINARY SYSTEM DRUGS
GATES: Ornamental Metal
GAUGES
GEARS
GEARS: Power Transmission, Exc Auto
GELATIN CAPSULES
GEM STONES MINING, NEC: Natural
GEMSTONE & INDL DIAMOND MINING SVCS
GENERAL COUNSELING SVCS
GENERAL MERCHANDISE, NONDURABLE, WHOLESALE
GENERATING APPARATUS & PARTS: Electrical
GENERATION EQPT: Electronic
GENERATOR REPAIR SVCS
GENERATORS SETS: Motor, Automotive
GENERATORS: Electric
GENERATORS: Storage Battery Chargers
GENERATORS: Ultrasonic
GIFT SHOP
GIFT WRAP: Paper, Made From Purchased Materials
GIFT, NOVELTY & SOUVENIR STORES: Gifts & Novelties
GIFT, NOVELTY & SOUVENIR STORES: Party Favors
GIFTS & NOVELTIES: Wholesalers
GIFTWARE: Brass
GILSONITE MINING SVCS
GLASS & GLASS CERAMIC PRDTS, PRESSED OR BLOWN: Tableware
GLASS FABRICATORS
GLASS PRDTS, FROM PURCHASED GLASS: Art
GLASS PRDTS, FROM PURCHASED GLASS: Glass Beads, Reflecting
GLASS PRDTS, FROM PURCHASED GLASS: Insulating
GLASS PRDTS, FROM PURCHASED GLASS: Mirrored
GLASS PRDTS, FROM PURCHASED GLASS: Novelties, Fruit, Etc
GLASS PRDTS, PRESSED OR BLOWN: Barware
GLASS PRDTS, PRESSED OR BLOWN: Bulbs, Electric Lights

GLASS PRDTS, PRESSED OR BLOWN: Furnishings & Access
GLASS PRDTS, PRESSED OR BLOWN: Glassware, Art Or Decorative
GLASS PRDTS, PRESSED OR BLOWN: Glassware, Novelty
GLASS PRDTS, PRESSED OR BLOWN: Lighting Eqpt Parts
GLASS PRDTS, PRESSED OR BLOWN: Optical
GLASS PRDTS, PRESSED OR BLOWN: Ornaments, Christmas Tree
GLASS PRDTS, PRESSED OR BLOWN: Scientific Glassware
GLASS PRDTS, PRESSED OR BLOWN: Tubing
GLASS PRDTS, PURCHASED GLASS: Glassware, Scientific/Tech
GLASS STORE: Leaded Or Stained
GLASS STORES
GLASS, AUTOMOTIVE: Wholesalers
GLASS: Fiber
GLASS: Flat
GLASS: Indl Prdts
GLASS: Insulating
GLASS: Plate
GLASS: Pressed & Blown, NEC
GLASS: Stained
GLASS: Structural
GLASSWARE STORES
GLASSWARE WHOLESALERS
GLASSWARE: Indl
GLASSWARE: Laboratory
GLASSWARE: Laboratory & Medical
GLOBAL POSITIONING SYSTEMS & EQPT
GLOVES: Fabric
GLOVES: Leather
GLOVES: Plastic
GLOVES: Safety
GLUE
GOLD ORES
GOLD STAMPING, EXC BOOKS
GOLF EQPT
GOLF GOODS & EQPT
GOURMET FOOD STORES
GOVERNMENT, EXECUTIVE OFFICES: County Supervisor/Exec Office
GRAIN & FIELD BEANS WHOLESALERS
GRANITE: Crushed & Broken
GRANITE: Cut & Shaped
GRANITE: Dimension
GRANITE: Dimension
GRAPHIC ARTS & RELATED DESIGN SVCS
GRAPHITE MINING SVCS
GRASSES: Artificial & Preserved
GRAVE VAULTS, METAL
GRAVEL & PEBBLE MINING
GRAVEL MINING
GREASE TRAPS: Concrete
GREASES: Lubricating
GREENSAND MINING SVCS
GREETING CARD SHOPS
GREETING CARDS WHOLESALERS
GRINDING SVC: Precision, Commercial Or Indl
GRINDING SVCS: Ophthalmic Lens, Exc Prescription
GRIT: Steel
GRITS: Crushed & Broken
GROCERIES WHOLESALERS, NEC
GROCERIES, GENERAL LINE WHOLESALERS
GROUP DAY CARE CENTER
GROUTING EQPT: Concrete
GUIDANCE SYSTEMS & EQPT: Space Vehicle
GUIDED MISSILES & SPACE VEHICLES
GUIDED MISSILES & SPACE VEHICLES: Research & Development
GUM & WOOD CHEMICALS
GUTTERS
GUTTERS: Sheet Metal
GYPSUM & CALCITE MINING SVCS
GYPSUM PRDTS
GYROSCOPES

H

HAIR & HAIR BASED PRDTS
HAIR CARE PRDTS
HAIR CARE PRDTS: Bleaches
HAIR CARE PRDTS: Hair Coloring Preparations
HAIR DRESSING, FOR THE TRADE
HAND TOOLS, NEC: Wholesalers
HANDBAGS

HANDBAGS: Women's
HANDLES: Brush Or Tool, Plastic
HANGERS: Garment, Plastic
HANGERS: Garment, Wire
HANGERS: Garment, Wire
HARD RUBBER PRDTS, NEC
HARDWARE
HARDWARE & BUILDING PRDTS: Plastic
HARDWARE STORES
HARDWARE STORES: Builders'
HARDWARE STORES: Door Locks & Lock Sets
HARDWARE STORES: Tools
HARDWARE STORES: Tools, Power
HARDWARE WHOLESALERS
HARDWARE, WHOLESALE: Bolts
HARDWARE, WHOLESALE: Builders', NEC
HARDWARE, WHOLESALE: Power Tools & Access
HARDWARE, WHOLESALE: Screws
HARDWARE, WHOLESALE: Security Devices, Locks
HARDWARE, WHOLESALE: Washers
HARDWARE: Aircraft
HARDWARE: Aircraft & Marine, Incl Pulleys & Similar Items
HARDWARE: Builders'
HARDWARE: Cabinet
HARDWARE: Furniture, Builders' & Other Household
HARDWARE: Luggage
HARDWARE: Parachute
HARNESS ASSEMBLIES: Cable & Wire
HARNESS WIRING SETS: Internal Combustion Engines
HARNESSES, HALTERS, SADDLERY & STRAPS
HEADPHONES: Radio
HEALTH AIDS: Exercise Eqpt
HEALTH FOOD & SUPPLEMENT STORES
HEALTH SCREENING SVCS
HEARING AIDS
HEAT EXCHANGERS
HEAT EXCHANGERS: After Or Inter Coolers Or Condensers, Etc
HEAT TREATING: Metal
HEATERS: Swimming Pool, Electric
HEATING & AIR CONDITIONING UNITS, COMBINATION
HEATING APPARATUS: Steam
HEATING EQPT & SPLYS
HEATING EQPT: Complete
HEATING EQPT: Induction
HEATING PADS: Nonelectric
HEATING UNITS & DEVICES: Indl, Electric
HEAVY DISTILLATES
HELMETS: Athletic
HELP SUPPLY SERVICES
HOBBY GOODS, WHOLESALE
HOBBY SUPPLIES, WHOLESALE
HOBBY, TOY & GAME STORES: Arts & Crafts & Splys
HOISTS
HOLDERS, PAPER TOWEL, GROCERY BAG, ETC: Plastic
HOLDING COMPANIES: Banks
HOLDING COMPANIES: Investment, Exc Banks
HOLDING COMPANIES: Personal, Exc Banks
HOLLOWARE, SILVER
HOME ENTERTAINMENT EQPT: Electronic, NEC
HOME ENTERTAINMENT REPAIR SVCS
HOME FURNISHINGS WHOLESALERS
HOME HEALTH CARE SVCS
HOME IMPROVEMENT & RENOVATION CONTRACTOR AGENCY
HOMEFURNISHING STORE: Bedding, Sheet, Blanket,Spread/Pillow
HOMEFURNISHING STORES: Beddings & Linens
HOMEFURNISHING STORES: Closet organizers & shelving units
HOMEFURNISHING STORES: Fireplaces & Wood Burning Stoves
HOMEFURNISHING STORES: Lighting Fixtures
HOMEFURNISHING STORES: Metalware
HOMEFURNISHING STORES: Mirrors
HOMEFURNISHING STORES: Towels
HOMEFURNISHING STORES: Venetian Blinds
HOMEFURNISHING STORES: Vertical Blinds
HOMEFURNISHING STORES: Window Furnishings
HOMEFURNISHING STORES: Window Shades, NEC
HOMEFURNISHINGS & SPLYS, WHOLESALE: Decorative
HOMEFURNISHINGS, WHOLESALE: Blankets
HOMEFURNISHINGS, WHOLESALE: Blinds, Vertical
HOMEFURNISHINGS, WHOLESALE: Carpets
HOMEFURNISHINGS, WHOLESALE: Curtains

HOMEFURNISHINGS, WHOLESALE: Draperies
HOMEFURNISHINGS, WHOLESALE: Fireplace Eqpt & Access
HOMEFURNISHINGS, WHOLESALE: Kitchenware
HOMEFURNISHINGS, WHOLESALE: Linens, Table
HOMEFURNISHINGS, WHOLESALE: Rugs
HOMEFURNISHINGS, WHOLESALE: Sheets, Textile
HOMEFURNISHINGS, WHOLESALE: Towels
HOMEFURNISHINGS, WHOLESALE: Wood Flooring
HOODS: Range, Sheet Metal
HOPPERS: Metal Plate
HORNS: Marine, Compressed Air Or Steam
HORSE & PET ACCESSORIES: Textile
HORSE ACCESS: Harnesses & Riding Crops, Etc, Exc Leather
HORSESHOES
HOSE: Air Line Or Air Brake, Rubber Or Rubberized Fabric
HOSE: Fire, Rubber
HOSE: Flexible Metal
HOSE: Garden, Plastic
HOSE: Plastic
HOSE: Pneumatic, Rubber Or Rubberized Fabric, NEC
HOSE: Rubber
HOSES & BELTING: Rubber & Plastic
HOSPITAL BEDS WHOLESALERS
HOSPITAL EQPT REPAIR SVCS
HOSPITALS: Medical & Surgical
HOTELS & MOTELS
HOUSEHOLD APPLIANCE REPAIR SVCS
HOUSEHOLD APPLIANCE STORES
HOUSEHOLD ARTICLES: Metal
HOUSEHOLD FURNISHINGS, NEC
HOUSEHOLD SEWING MACHINES WHOLESALERS: Electric
HOUSEWARE STORES
HOUSEWARES, ELECTRIC, EXC COOKING APPLIANCES & UTENSILS
HOUSEWARES, ELECTRIC: Cooking Appliances
HOUSEWARES, ELECTRIC: Dryers, Hand & Face
HOUSEWARES, ELECTRIC: Heaters, Sauna
HOUSEWARES, ELECTRIC: Heating, Bsbrd/Wall, Radiant Heat
HOUSEWARES, ELECTRIC: Ice Crushers
HOUSEWARES, ELECTRIC: Lighters, Cigar
HOUSEWARES: Dishes, China
HOUSEWARES: Dishes, Earthenware
HOUSEWARES: Dishes, Plastic
HUMIDIFIERS & DEHUMIDIFIERS
HYDRAULIC EQPT REPAIR SVC
HYDRAULIC FLUIDS: Synthetic Based
Hard Rubber & Molded Rubber Prdts

I

ICE
ICE CREAM & ICES WHOLESALERS
IGNEOUS ROCK: Crushed & Broken
IGNITION SYSTEMS: Internal Combustion Engine
INCINERATORS
INDL & PERSONAL SVC PAPER WHOLESALERS
INDL & PERSONAL SVC PAPER, WHOL: Bags, Paper/Disp Plastic
INDL & PERSONAL SVC PAPER, WHOL: Boxes, Corrugtd/Solid Fiber
INDL & PERSONAL SVC PAPER, WHOL: Boxes, Setup Paperboard
INDL & PERSONAL SVC PAPER, WHOL: Closures, Paper/Disp Plastc
INDL & PERSONAL SVC PAPER, WHOL: Cups, Disp, Plastic/Paper
INDL & PERSONAL SVC PAPER, WHOL: Paper, Wrap/Coarse/Prdts
INDL & PERSONAL SVC PAPER, WHOLESALE: Boxes & Containers
INDL & PERSONAL SVC PAPER, WHOLESALE: Boxes, Fldng Pprboard
INDL & PERSONAL SVC PAPER, WHOLESALE: Paperboard & Prdts
INDL & PERSONAL SVC PAPER, WHOLESALE: Press Sensitive Tape
INDL & PERSONAL SVC PAPER, WHOLESALE: Shipping Splys
INDL CONTRACTORS: Exhibit Construction
INDL EQPT CLEANING SVCS
INDL EQPT SVCS
INDL GASES WHOLESALERS

INDL MACHINERY & EQPT WHOLESALERS
INDL MACHINERY REPAIR & MAINTENANCE
INDL PATTERNS: Foundry Cores
INDL PROCESS INSTR: Transmit, Process Variables
INDL PROCESS INSTRUMENTS: Analyzers
INDL PROCESS INSTRUMENTS: Boiler Controls, Power & Marine
INDL PROCESS INSTRUMENTS: Control
INDL PROCESS INSTRUMENTS: Controllers, Process Variables
INDL PROCESS INSTRUMENTS: Indl Flow & Measuring
INDL PROCESS INSTRUMENTS: Manometers
INDL PROCESS INSTRUMENTS: Moisture Meters
INDL PROCESS INSTRUMENTS: On-Stream Gas Or Liquid Analysis
INDL PROCESS INSTRUMENTS: PH Instruments
INDL PROCESS INSTRUMENTS: Temperature
INDL PROCESS INSTRUMENTS: Water Quality Monitoring/Cntrl Sys
INDL SPLYS WHOLESALERS
INDL SPLYS, WHOL: Fasteners, Incl Nuts, Bolts, Screws, Etc
INDL SPLYS, WHOLESALE: Abrasives
INDL SPLYS, WHOLESALE: Bearings
INDL SPLYS, WHOLESALE: Bottler Splys
INDL SPLYS, WHOLESALE: Brushes, Indl
INDL SPLYS, WHOLESALE: Clean Room Splys
INDL SPLYS, WHOLESALE: Drums, New Or Reconditioned
INDL SPLYS, WHOLESALE: Fasteners & Fastening Eqpt
INDL SPLYS, WHOLESALE: Filters, Indl
INDL SPLYS, WHOLESALE: Gaskets
INDL SPLYS, WHOLESALE: Gaskets & Seals
INDL SPLYS, WHOLESALE: Gears
INDL SPLYS, WHOLESALE: Plastic Bottles
INDL SPLYS, WHOLESALE: Power Transmission, Eqpt & Apparatus
INDL SPLYS, WHOLESALE: Rubber Goods, Mechanical
INDL SPLYS, WHOLESALE: Staplers & Tackers
INDL SPLYS, WHOLESALE: Tanks, Pressurized
INDL SPLYS, WHOLESALE: Tools
INDL SPLYS, WHOLESALE: Tools, NEC
INDL SPLYS, WHOLESALE: Twine
INDL SPLYS, WHOLESALE: Valves & Fittings
INDUCTORS
INFANTS' WEAR STORES
INFORMATION RETRIEVAL SERVICES
INK OR WRITING FLUIDS
INK: Duplicating
INK: Gravure
INK: Letterpress Or Offset
INK: Lithographic
INK: Printing
INK: Screen process
INSECTICIDES
INSECTICIDES & PESTICIDES
INSPECTION & TESTING SVCS
INSTRUMENT LANDING SYSTEMS OR ILS: Airborne Or Ground
INSTRUMENTS & ACCESSORIES: Surveying
INSTRUMENTS & METERS: Measuring, Electric
INSTRUMENTS, LABORATORY: Amino Acid Analyzers
INSTRUMENTS, LABORATORY: Analyzers, Automatic Chemical
INSTRUMENTS, LABORATORY: Blood Testing
INSTRUMENTS, LABORATORY: Gas Analyzing
INSTRUMENTS, LABORATORY: Liquid Chromatographic
INSTRUMENTS, LABORATORY: Mass Spectroscopy
INSTRUMENTS, LABORATORY: Spectrographs
INSTRUMENTS, LABORATORY: Spectrometers
INSTRUMENTS, MEASURING & CNTRL: Geophysical & Meteorological
INSTRUMENTS, MEASURING & CNTRL: Radiation & Testing, Nuclear
INSTRUMENTS, MEASURING & CNTRL: Testing, Abrasion, Etc
INSTRUMENTS, MEASURING & CNTRL: Whole Body Counters, Nuclear
INSTRUMENTS, MEASURING & CNTRLG: Thermometers/Temp Sensors
INSTRUMENTS, MEASURING & CNTRLNG: Press & Vac Ind, Acft Eng
INSTRUMENTS, MEASURING & CONTROLLING: Dosimetry, Personnel
INSTRUMENTS, MEASURING & CONTROLLING: Gas Detectors

INSTRUMENTS, MEASURING & CONTROLLING: Surveying & Drafting
INSTRUMENTS, MEASURING & CONTROLLING: Ultrasonic Testing
INSTRUMENTS, MEASURING/CNTRLG: Fire Detect Sys, Non-Electric
INSTRUMENTS, MEASURING/CNTRLNG: Med Diagnostic Sys, Nuclear
INSTRUMENTS, OPTICAL: Coating & Grinding, Lens
INSTRUMENTS, OPTICAL: Elements & Assemblies, Exc Ophthalmic
INSTRUMENTS, OPTICAL: Lenses, All Types Exc Ophthalmic
INSTRUMENTS, OPTICAL: Light Sources, Standard
INSTRUMENTS, OPTICAL: Magnifying, NEC
INSTRUMENTS, OPTICAL: Polarizers
INSTRUMENTS, OPTICAL: Test & Inspection
INSTRUMENTS, SURGICAL & MED: Cleaning Eqpt, Ultrasonic Med
INSTRUMENTS, SURGICAL & MED: Needles & Syringes, Hypodermic
INSTRUMENTS, SURGICAL & MEDICAL: Blood & Bone Work
INSTRUMENTS, SURGICAL & MEDICAL: Blood Pressure
INSTRUMENTS, SURGICAL & MEDICAL: Catheters
INSTRUMENTS, SURGICAL & MEDICAL: Hemodialysis
INSTRUMENTS, SURGICAL & MEDICAL: Inhalation Therapy
INSTRUMENTS, SURGICAL & MEDICAL: Lasers, Surgical
INSTRUMENTS, SURGICAL & MEDICAL: Ophthalmic
INSTRUMENTS, SURGICAL/MED: Microsurgical, Exc Electromedical
INSTRUMENTS: Analytical
INSTRUMENTS: Analyzers, Internal Combustion Eng, Electronic
INSTRUMENTS: Combustion Control, Indl
INSTRUMENTS: Electronic, Analog-Digital Converters
INSTRUMENTS: Endoscopic Eqpt, Electromedical
INSTRUMENTS: Eye Examination
INSTRUMENTS: Flow, Indl Process
INSTRUMENTS: Frequency Meters, Electrical, Mech & Electronic
INSTRUMENTS: Indl Process Control
INSTRUMENTS: Laser, Scientific & Engineering
INSTRUMENTS: Liquid Analysis, Indl Process
INSTRUMENTS: Liquid Level, Indl Process
INSTRUMENTS: Measurement, Indl Process
INSTRUMENTS: Measuring & Controlling
INSTRUMENTS: Measuring Electricity
INSTRUMENTS: Measuring, Electrical Energy
INSTRUMENTS: Measuring, Electrical Power
INSTRUMENTS: Medical & Surgical
INSTRUMENTS: Microwave Test
INSTRUMENTS: Nautical
INSTRUMENTS: Optical, Analytical
INSTRUMENTS: Oscillographs & Oscilloscopes
INSTRUMENTS: Photographic, Electronic
INSTRUMENTS: Power Measuring, Electrical
INSTRUMENTS: Pressure Measurement, Indl
INSTRUMENTS: Radio Frequency Measuring
INSTRUMENTS: Telemetering, Indl Process
INSTRUMENTS: Temperature Measurement, Indl
INSTRUMENTS: Test, Digital, Electronic & Electrical Circuits
INSTRUMENTS: Test, Electronic & Electric Measurement
INSTRUMENTS: Test, Electronic & Electrical Circuits
INSTRUMENTS: Testing, Semiconductor
INSTRUMENTS: Thermal Conductive, Indl
INSTRUMENTS: Thermal Property Measurement
INSTRUMENTS: Vibration
INSTRUMENTS: Viscometer, Indl Process
INSULATING BOARD, CELLULAR FIBER
INSULATING COMPOUNDS
INSULATION & CUSHIONING FOAM: Polystyrene
INSULATION & ROOFING MATERIALS: Wood, Reconstituted
INSULATION MATERIALS WHOLESALERS
INSULATION: Fiberglass
INSULATORS, PORCELAIN: Electrical
INSURANCE BROKERS, NEC
INTEGRATED CIRCUITS, SEMICONDUCTOR NETWORKS, ETC
INTERCOMMUNICATIONS SYSTEMS: Electric
INTERIOR DECORATING SVCS
INTERIOR DESIGN SVCS, NEC
INTERIOR DESIGNING SVCS
INTERIOR REPAIR SVCS
INTRAVENOUS SOLUTIONS
INVENTOR

INVERTERS: Nonrotating Electrical
INVERTERS: Rotating Electrical
INVESTMENT FUNDS, NEC
INVESTORS, NEC
IRON & STEEL: Corrugating, Cold-Rolled
IRON OXIDES
IRRADIATION EQPT

J

JANITORIAL & CUSTODIAL SVCS
JANITORIAL EQPT & SPLYS WHOLESALERS
JARS: Plastic
JEWELERS' FINDINGS & MATERIALS
JEWELERS' FINDINGS & MATERIALS: Bearings, Synthetic
JEWELERS' FINDINGS & MATERIALS: Castings
JEWELERS' FINDINGS & MTLS: Jewel Prep, Instr, Tools, Watches
JEWELERS' FINDINGS/MTRLS: Gem Prep, Settings, Real/Imitation
JEWELRY & PRECIOUS STONES WHOLESALERS
JEWELRY APPAREL
JEWELRY FINDINGS & LAPIDARY WORK
JEWELRY REPAIR SVCS
JEWELRY STORES
JEWELRY STORES: Precious Stones & Precious Metals
JEWELRY, PRECIOUS METAL: Bracelets
JEWELRY, PRECIOUS METAL: Medals, Precious Or Semiprecious
JEWELRY, PRECIOUS METAL: Mountings & Trimmings
JEWELRY, PRECIOUS METAL: Necklaces
JEWELRY, PRECIOUS METAL: Pearl, Natural Or Cultured
JEWELRY, PRECIOUS METAL: Pins
JEWELRY, PRECIOUS METAL: Rings, Finger
JEWELRY, PRECIOUS METAL: Rosaries/Other Sm Religious Article
JEWELRY, PRECIOUS METAL: Settings & Mountings
JEWELRY, WHOLESALE
JEWELRY: Decorative, Fashion & Costume
JEWELRY: Precious Metal
JOB PRINTING & NEWSPAPER PUBLISHING COMBINED
JOB TRAINING & VOCATIONAL REHABILITATION SVCS

K

KAOLIN MINING
KITCHEN ARTICLES: Coarse Earthenware
KITCHEN CABINET STORES, EXC CUSTOM
KITCHEN CABINETS WHOLESALERS
KITCHEN TOOLS & UTENSILS WHOLESALERS
KITCHEN UTENSILS: Bakers' Eqpt, Wood
KITCHEN UTENSILS: Wooden
KITCHENWARE STORES
KITS: Plastic
KNIVES: Agricultural Or indl

L

LABELS: Cotton, Printed
LABELS: Paper, Made From Purchased Materials
LABELS: Woven
LABOR RESOURCE SVCS
LABORATORIES, TESTING: Food
LABORATORIES, TESTING: Hazardous Waste
LABORATORIES, TESTING: Product Testing
LABORATORIES, TESTING: Product Testing, Safety/Performance
LABORATORIES: Biological
LABORATORIES: Biological Research
LABORATORIES: Biotechnology
LABORATORIES: Commercial Nonphysical Research
LABORATORIES: Dental Orthodontic Appliance Production
LABORATORIES: Dental, Crown & Bridge Production
LABORATORIES: Electronic Research
LABORATORIES: Environmental Research
LABORATORIES: Medical
LABORATORIES: Medical Pathology
LABORATORIES: Noncommercial Research
LABORATORIES: Physical Research, Commercial
LABORATORIES: Testing
LABORATORIES: Testing
LABORATORY APPARATUS & FURNITURE
LABORATORY APPARATUS, EXC HEATING & MEASURING
LABORATORY APPARATUS: Sample Preparation Apparatus
LABORATORY APPARATUS: Shakers & Stirrers
LABORATORY CHEMICALS: Organic
LABORATORY EQPT, EXC MEDICAL: Wholesalers

LABORATORY EQPT: Chemical
LABORATORY EQPT: Clinical Instruments Exc Medical
LABORATORY EQPT: Incubators
LABORATORY EQPT: Measuring
LACE GOODS & WARP KNIT FABRIC DYEING & FINISHING
LAMINATED PLASTICS: Plate, Sheet, Rod & Tubes
LAMINATING MATERIALS
LAMP & LIGHT BULBS & TUBES
LAMP BULBS & TUBES, ELECTRIC: Filaments
LAMP BULBS & TUBES, ELECTRIC: For Specialized Applications
LAMP BULBS & TUBES, ELECTRIC: Light, Complete
LAMP BULBS & TUBES, ELECTRIC: Parts
LAMP BULBS & TUBES/PARTS, ELECTRIC: Generalized Applications
LAMP STORES
LAMPS: Boudoir, Residential
LAMPS: Incandescent, Filament
LAMPS: Ultraviolet
LAMPS: Wall, Residential
LANDING MATS: Aircraft, Metal
LANGUAGE SCHOOLS
LAPIDARY WORK & DIAMOND CUTTING & POLISHING
LAPIDARY WORK: Jewel Cut, Drill, Polish, Recut/Setting
LARD: From Slaughtering Plants
LASER SYSTEMS & EQPT
LASERS: Welding, Drilling & Cutting Eqpt
LATEX: Foamed
LAUNDRIES, EXC POWER & COIN-OPERATED
LAUNDRY & DRYCLEANING SVCS, EXC COIN-OPERATED: Pickup
LAUNDRY & GARMENT SVCS, NEC: Hand Laundries
LAUNDRY & GARMENT SVCS: Tailor Shop, Exc Custom/Merchant
LAUNDRY EQPT: Commercial
LAUNDRY SVCS: Indl
LAWN & GARDEN EQPT
LAWN MOWER REPAIR SHOP
LEAD
LEAD PENCILS & ART GOODS
LEAD-IN WIRES: Electric Lamp
LEASING & RENTAL SVCS: Earth Moving Eqpt
LEASING & RENTAL: Construction & Mining Eqpt
LEASING & RENTAL: Medical Machinery & Eqpt
LEASING & RENTAL: Other Real Estate Property
LEASING & RENTAL: Trucks, Without Drivers
LEASING: Passenger Car
LEATHER & CANVAS GOODS: Leggings Or Chaps, NEC
LEATHER GOODS: Card Cases
LEATHER GOODS: Cases
LEATHER GOODS: Cosmetic Bags
LEATHER GOODS: Garments
LEATHER GOODS: Personal
LEATHER GOODS: Safety Belts
LEATHER GOODS: Wallets
LEATHER TANNING & FINISHING
LEATHER, LEATHER GOODS & FURS, WHOLESALE
LEATHER: Accessory Prdts
LEATHER: Bag
LEATHER: Handbag
LEATHER: Mechanical
LEATHER: Processed
LEGAL & TAX SVCS
LEGAL OFFICES & SVCS
LEGAL SVCS: General Practice Attorney or Lawyer
LEGAL SVCS: Malpractice & Negligence Law
LENS COATING: Ophthalmic
LETTER WRITING SVCS
LIFE INSURANCE: Fraternal Organizations
LIGHTER FLUID
LIGHTING EQPT: Flashlights
LIGHTING EQPT: Floodlights
LIGHTING EQPT: Motor Vehicle, Flasher Lights
LIGHTING EQPT: Motor Vehicle, NEC
LIGHTING EQPT: Outdoor
LIGHTING EQPT: Spotlights
LIGHTING FIXTURES WHOLESALERS
LIGHTING FIXTURES, NEC
LIGHTING FIXTURES: Airport
LIGHTING FIXTURES: Arc
LIGHTING FIXTURES: Decorative Area
LIGHTING FIXTURES: Fluorescent, Commercial
LIGHTING FIXTURES: Indl & Commercial
LIGHTING FIXTURES: Motor Vehicle
LIGHTING FIXTURES: Public

LIGHTING FIXTURES: Residential
LIGHTING FIXTURES: Street
LIGHTING FIXTURES: Swimming Pool
LIGHTING FIXTURES: Underwater
LIGHTING MAINTENANCE SVC
LIME
LIMESTONE: Crushed & Broken
LINEN SPLY SVC: Non-Clothing
LINENS & TOWELS WHOLESALERS
LINENS: Napkins, Fabric & Nonwoven, From Purchased Materials
LINENS: Tablecloths, From Purchased Materials
LINER STRIPS: Rubber
LINERS & COVERS: Fabric
LINERS & LINING
LIQUEFIED PETROLEUM GAS DEALERS
LIQUID CRYSTAL DISPLAYS
LITHOGRAPHIC PLATES
LOCKS
LOCKS: Safe & Vault, Metal
LOG SPLITTERS
LOGGING
LOOSELEAF BINDERS
LOOSELEAF BINDERS: Library
LOTIONS OR CREAMS: Face
LOUDSPEAKERS
LUBRICATING EQPT: Indl
LUBRICATION SYSTEMS & EQPT
LUGGAGE & BRIEFCASES
LUGGAGE & LEATHER GOODS STORES
LUGGAGE WHOLESALERS
LUGGAGE: Traveling Bags
LUMBER & BLDG MATLS DEALER, RET: Garage Doors, Sell/Install
LUMBER & BLDG MATRLS DEALERS, RET: Bath Fixtures, Eqpt/Sply
LUMBER & BLDG MTRLS DEALERS, RET: Doors, Storm, Wood/Metal
LUMBER & BLDG MTRLS DEALERS, RET: Planing Mill Prdts/Lumber
LUMBER & BLDG MTRLS DEALERS, RET: Windows, Storm, Wood/Metal
LUMBER & BUILDING MATERIALS DEALER, RET: Door & Window Prdts
LUMBER & BUILDING MATERIALS DEALER, RET: Masonry Matls/Splys
LUMBER & BUILDING MATERIALS DEALERS, RET: Solar Heating Eqpt
LUMBER & BUILDING MATERIALS DEALERS, RETAIL: Countertops
LUMBER & BUILDING MATERIALS DEALERS, RETAIL: Tile, Ceramic
LUMBER & BUILDING MATERIALS RET DEALERS: Millwork & Lumber
LUMBER & BUILDING MATLS DEALERS, RET: Concrete/Cinder Block
LUMBER: Hardwood Dimension & Flooring Mills
LUMBER: Plywood, Hardwood
LUMBER: Rails, Fence, Round Or Split
LUMBER: Siding, Dressed
LUMBER: Veneer, Hardwood

M

MACHINE PARTS: Stamped Or Pressed Metal
MACHINE SHOPS
MACHINE TOOL ACCESS: Cutting
MACHINE TOOL ACCESS: Diamond Cutting, For Turning, Etc
MACHINE TOOL ACCESS: Dresser, Abrasive Wheel Or Other
MACHINE TOOL ACCESS: Drill Bushings, Drilling Jig
MACHINE TOOL ACCESS: Drills
MACHINE TOOL ACCESS: Files
MACHINE TOOL ACCESS: Hopper Feed Devices
MACHINE TOOL ACCESS: Machine Attachments & Access, Drilling
MACHINE TOOL ACCESS: Tool Holders
MACHINE TOOL ACCESS: Tools & Access
MACHINE TOOL ATTACHMENTS & ACCESS
MACHINE TOOLS & ACCESS
MACHINE TOOLS, METAL CUTTING: Cutoff
MACHINE TOOLS, METAL CUTTING: Drilling
MACHINE TOOLS, METAL CUTTING: Drilling & Boring
MACHINE TOOLS, METAL CUTTING: Exotic, Including Explosive
MACHINE TOOLS, METAL CUTTING: Grind, Polish, Buff, Lapp

MACHINE TOOLS, METAL CUTTING: Jig, Boring & Grinding
MACHINE TOOLS, METAL CUTTING: Tool Replacement & Rpr Parts
MACHINE TOOLS, METAL FORMING: Bending
MACHINE TOOLS, METAL FORMING: Container, Metal Incl Cans
MACHINE TOOLS, METAL FORMING: Crimping, Metal
MACHINE TOOLS, METAL FORMING: Forming, Metal Deposit
MACHINE TOOLS, METAL FORMING: Magnetic Forming
MACHINE TOOLS, METAL FORMING: Marking
MACHINE TOOLS, METAL FORMING: Mechanical, Pneumatic Or Hyd
MACHINE TOOLS, METAL FORMING: Punching & Shearing
MACHINE TOOLS, METAL FORMING: Rebuilt
MACHINE TOOLS, METAL FORMING: Spinning, Metal
MACHINE TOOLS: Metal Cutting
MACHINE TOOLS: Metal Forming
MACHINERY & EQPT, AGRICULTURAL, WHOL: Farm Eqpt Parts/Splys
MACHINERY & EQPT, AGRICULTURAL, WHOLESALE: Lawn & Garden
MACHINERY & EQPT, INDL, WHOL: Controlling Instruments/Access
MACHINERY & EQPT, INDL, WHOL: Environ Pollution Cntrl, Air
MACHINERY & EQPT, INDL, WHOLESALE: Cement Making
MACHINERY & EQPT, INDL, WHOLESALE: Chemical Process
MACHINERY & EQPT, INDL, WHOLESALE: Compaction
MACHINERY & EQPT, INDL, WHOLESALE: Conveyor Systems
MACHINERY & EQPT, INDL, WHOLESALE: Dairy Prdts Manufacturing
MACHINERY & EQPT, INDL, WHOLESALE: Drilling, Exc Bits
MACHINERY & EQPT, INDL, WHOLESALE: Engines & Parts, Diesel
MACHINERY & EQPT, INDL, WHOLESALE: Engines, Gasoline
MACHINERY & EQPT, INDL, WHOLESALE: Food Manufacturing
MACHINERY & EQPT, INDL, WHOLESALE: Food Product Manufacturng
MACHINERY & EQPT, INDL, WHOLESALE: Hydraulic Systems
MACHINERY & EQPT, INDL, WHOLESALE: Indl Machine Parts
MACHINERY & EQPT, INDL, WHOLESALE: Instruments & Cntrl Eqpt
MACHINERY & EQPT, INDL, WHOLESALE: Machine Tools & Access
MACHINERY & EQPT, INDL, WHOLESALE: Machine Tools & Metalwork
MACHINERY & EQPT, INDL, WHOLESALE: Measure/Test, Electric
MACHINERY & EQPT, INDL, WHOLESALE: Packaging
MACHINERY & EQPT, INDL, WHOLESALE: Plastic Prdts Machinery
MACHINERY & EQPT, INDL, WHOLESALE: Power Plant Machinery
MACHINERY & EQPT, INDL, WHOLESALE: Processing & Packaging
MACHINERY & EQPT, INDL, WHOLESALE: Pulverizing
MACHINERY & EQPT, INDL, WHOLESALE: Recycling
MACHINERY & EQPT, INDL, WHOLESALE: Screening
MACHINERY & EQPT, INDL, WHOLESALE: Sewing
MACHINERY & EQPT, INDL, WHOLESALE: Textile
MACHINERY & EQPT, INDL, WHOLESALE: Textile & Leather
MACHINERY & EQPT, WHOLESALE: Concrete Processing
MACHINERY & EQPT, WHOLESALE: Construction & Mining, Ladders
MACHINERY & EQPT, WHOLESALE: Construction, General
MACHINERY & EQPT: Electroplating
MACHINERY & EQPT: Farm
MACHINERY & EQPT: Gas Producers, Generators/Other Rltd Eqpt
MACHINERY & EQPT: Liquid Automation
MACHINERY & EQPT: Metal Finishing, Plating Etc
MACHINERY & EQPT: Petroleum Refinery
MACHINERY & EQPT: Vibratory Parts Handling Eqpt
MACHINERY BASES
MACHINERY, CALCULATING: Calculators & Adding
MACHINERY, COMMERCIAL LAUNDRY & Drycleaning: Pressing

MACHINERY, COMMERCIAL LAUNDRY: Washing, Incl Coin-Operated
MACHINERY, EQPT & SUPPLIES: Parking Facility
MACHINERY, FOOD PRDTS: Beverage
MACHINERY, FOOD PRDTS: Cutting, Chopping, Grinding, Mixing
MACHINERY, FOOD PRDTS: Dairy & Milk
MACHINERY, FOOD PRDTS: Food Processing, Smokers
MACHINERY, FOOD PRDTS: Homogenizing, Dairy, Fruit/Vegetable
MACHINERY, FOOD PRDTS: Mixers, Commercial
MACHINERY, FOOD PRDTS: Ovens, Bakery
MACHINERY, FOOD PRDTS: Processing, Poultry
MACHINERY, MAILING: Address Labeling
MACHINERY, MAILING: Postage Meters
MACHINERY, METALWORKING: Assembly, Including Robotic
MACHINERY, METALWORKING: Coil Winding, For Springs
MACHINERY, METALWORKING: Rotary Slitters, Metalworking
MACHINERY, OFFICE: Sorters, Filing
MACHINERY, OFFICE: Stapling, Hand Or Power
MACHINERY, OFFICE: Time Clocks &Time Recording Devices
MACHINERY, OFFICE: Typing & Word Processing
MACHINERY, PACKAGING: Carton Packing
MACHINERY, PACKAGING: Packing & Wrapping
MACHINERY, PACKAGING: Vacuum
MACHINERY, PAPER INDUSTRY: Converting, Die Cutting & Stampng
MACHINERY, PAPER INDUSTRY: Cutting
MACHINERY, PAPER INDUSTRY: Fourdrinier
MACHINERY, PRINTING TRADES: Bookbinding Machinery
MACHINERY, PRINTING TRADES: Bronzing Or Dusting
MACHINERY, PRINTING TRADES: Electrotyping
MACHINERY, PRINTING TRADES: Plates
MACHINERY, PRINTING TRADES: Plates, Engravers' Metal
MACHINERY, PRINTING TRADES: Presses, Envelope
MACHINERY, PRINTING TRADES: Presses, Gravure
MACHINERY, PRINTING TRADES: Printing Trade Parts & Attchts
MACHINERY, PRINTING TRADES: Type, Foundry
MACHINERY, SEWING: Sewing & Hat & Zipper Making
MACHINERY, TEXTILE: Card Clothing
MACHINERY, TEXTILE: Fiber & Yarn Preparation
MACHINERY, TEXTILE: Finishing
MACHINERY, TEXTILE: Loom Parts &Attachments, Jacquard
MACHINERY, TEXTILE: Winders
MACHINERY, WOODWORKING: Box Making, For Wooden Boxes
MACHINERY, WOODWORKING: Cabinet Makers'
MACHINERY, WOODWORKING: Furniture Makers
MACHINERY, WOODWORKING: Scarfing
MACHINERY: Assembly, Exc Metalworking
MACHINERY: Automotive Maintenance
MACHINERY: Automotive Related
MACHINERY: Brake Burnishing Or Washing
MACHINERY: Centrifugal
MACHINERY: Concrete Prdts
MACHINERY: Construction
MACHINERY: Cryogenic, Industrial
MACHINERY: Custom
MACHINERY: Die Casting
MACHINERY: Electronic Component Making
MACHINERY: Engraving
MACHINERY: Extruding, Synthetic Filament
MACHINERY: Folding
MACHINERY: Gas Separators
MACHINERY: Gear Cutting & Finishing
MACHINERY: General, Industrial, NEC
MACHINERY: Glass Cutting
MACHINERY: Glassmaking
MACHINERY: Grinding
MACHINERY: Ice Cream
MACHINERY: Ice Making
MACHINERY: Industrial, NEC
MACHINERY: Labeling
MACHINERY: Lapping
MACHINERY: Marking, Metalworking
MACHINERY: Metalworking
MACHINERY: Milling
MACHINERY: Mining
MACHINERY: Ozone
MACHINERY: Packaging
MACHINERY: Paper Industry Miscellaneous
MACHINERY: Pharmaciutical

INDEX

MACHINERY: Plastic Working
MACHINERY: Printing Presses
MACHINERY: Recycling
MACHINERY: Riveting
MACHINERY: Road Construction & Maintenance
MACHINERY: Rubber Working
MACHINERY: Saw & Sawing
MACHINERY: Semiconductor Manufacturing
MACHINERY: Sheet Metal Working
MACHINERY: Sifting & Screening
MACHINERY: Specialty
MACHINERY: Stone Working
MACHINERY: Textile
MACHINERY: Thread Rolling
MACHINERY: Tire Shredding
MACHINERY: Voting
MACHINERY: Woodworking
MACHINES: Forming, Sheet Metal
MACHINISTS' TOOLS & MACHINES: Measuring, Metalworking Type
MACHINISTS' TOOLS: Precision
MACHINISTS' TOOLS: Scales, Measuring, Precision
MAGNETIC INK & OPTICAL SCANNING EQPT
MAGNETIC RESONANCE IMAGING DEVICES: Nonmedical
MAGNETS: Ceramic
MAGNETS: Permanent
MAIL PRESORTING SVCS
MAIL-ORDER BOOK CLUBS
MAIL-ORDER HOUSES: Arts & Crafts Eqpt & Splys
MAIL-ORDER HOUSES: Clothing, Exc Women's
MAIL-ORDER HOUSES: Computer Eqpt & Electronics
MAIL-ORDER HOUSES: Computers & Peripheral Eqpt
MAIL-ORDER HOUSES: Food
MAIL-ORDER HOUSES: Order Taking Office Only
MAILBOX RENTAL & RELATED SVCS
MAILING MACHINES WHOLESALERS
MAILING SVCS, NEC
MANAGEMENT CONSULTING SVCS: Automation & Robotics
MANAGEMENT CONSULTING SVCS: Business
MANAGEMENT CONSULTING SVCS: Construction Project
MANAGEMENT CONSULTING SVCS: Food & Beverage
MANAGEMENT CONSULTING SVCS: General
MANAGEMENT CONSULTING SVCS: Hospital & Health
MANAGEMENT CONSULTING SVCS: Incentive Or Award Program
MANAGEMENT CONSULTING SVCS: Industrial
MANAGEMENT CONSULTING SVCS: Industry Specialist
MANAGEMENT CONSULTING SVCS: Information Systems
MANAGEMENT CONSULTING SVCS: Maintenance
MANAGEMENT CONSULTING SVCS: Manufacturing
MANAGEMENT CONSULTING SVCS: Merchandising
MANAGEMENT CONSULTING SVCS: New Products & Svcs
MANAGEMENT CONSULTING SVCS: Restaurant & Food
MANAGEMENT CONSULTING SVCS: Retail Trade Consultant
MANAGEMENT CONSULTING SVCS: Training & Development
MANAGEMENT CONSULTING SVCS: Transportation
MANAGEMENT SERVICES
MANAGEMENT SVCS, FACILITIES SUPPORT: Environ Remediation
MANAGEMENT SVCS: Administrative
MANAGEMENT SVCS: Business
MANAGEMENT SVCS: Construction
MANAGEMENT SVCS: Hotel Or Motel
MANHOLES & COVERS: Metal
MANICURE PREPARATIONS
MANIFOLDS: Pipe, Fabricated From Purchased Pipe
MANUFACTURED & MOBILE HOME DEALERS
MANUFACTURING INDUSTRIES, NEC
MAPS
MARBLE BOARD
MARBLE, BUILDING: Cut & Shaped
MARBLE: Crushed & Broken
MARINAS
MARINE APPAREL STORES
MARINE CARGO HANDLING SVCS
MARINE CARGO HANDLING SVCS: Marine Terminal
MARINE ENGINE REPAIR SVCS
MARINE HARDWARE
MARINE RELATED EQPT
MARINE SPLY DEALERS
MARINE SPLYS WHOLESALERS
MARINE SVC STATIONS
MARKETS: Meat & fish

MARKING DEVICES
MARKING DEVICES: Embossing Seals & Hand Stamps
MARKING DEVICES: Embossing Seals, Corporate & Official
MARKING DEVICES: Pads, Inking & Stamping
MARKING DEVICES: Screens, Textile Printing
MARKING DEVICES: Seal Presses, Notary & Hand
MARKING DEVICES: Time Stamps, Hand, Rubber Or Metal
MATERIALS HANDLING EQPT WHOLESALERS
MATS OR MATTING, NEC: Rubber
MATS, MATTING & PADS: Auto, Floor, Exc Rubber Or Plastic
MATS: Table, Plastic & Textile
MATTRESS STORES
MEAL DELIVERY PROGRAMS
MEAT & MEAT PRDTS WHOLESALERS
MEAT CUTTING & PACKING
MEAT MARKETS
MEAT PRDTS: Canned
MEAT PRDTS: Canned Exc Baby Food, From Slaughtered Meat
MEAT PRDTS: Cured, From Slaughtered Meat
MEAT PRDTS: Frozen
MEAT PRDTS: Ham, Boiled, From Purchased Meat
MEAT PRDTS: Head Cheese, From Purchased Meat
MEAT PRDTS: Meat By-Prdts, From Slaughtered Meat
MEAT PRDTS: Pork, Cured, From Purchased Meat
MEAT PRDTS: Pork, From Slaughtered Meat
MEAT PRDTS: Sausage Casings, Natural
MEAT PRDTS: Sausages & Related Prdts, From Purchased Meat
MEAT PRDTS: Sausages, From Purchased Meat
MEAT PRDTS: Snack Sticks, Incl Jerky, From Purchased Meat
MEAT PRDTS: Spiced Meats, From Purchased Meat
MEAT PRDTS: Veal, From Slaughtered Meat
MEAT PROCESSED FROM PURCHASED CARCASSES
MEAT PROCESSING MACHINERY
MEATS, PACKAGED FROZEN: Wholesalers
MECHANICAL INSTRUMENT REPAIR SVCS
MED, DENTAL & HOSPITAL EQPT, WHOL: Incontinent Prdts/Splys
MEDIA BUYING AGENCIES
MEDIA: Magnetic & Optical Recording
MEDICAL & HOSPITAL EQPT WHOLESALERS
MEDICAL & SURGICAL SPLYS: Bandages & Dressings
MEDICAL & SURGICAL SPLYS: Clothing, Fire Resistant & Protect
MEDICAL & SURGICAL SPLYS: Cosmetic Restorations
MEDICAL & SURGICAL SPLYS: Cotton, Incl Cotton Balls
MEDICAL & SURGICAL SPLYS: Foot Appliances, Orthopedic
MEDICAL & SURGICAL SPLYS: Ligatures
MEDICAL & SURGICAL SPLYS: Limbs, Artificial
MEDICAL & SURGICAL SPLYS: Orthopedic Appliances
MEDICAL & SURGICAL SPLYS: Personal Safety Eqpt
MEDICAL & SURGICAL SPLYS: Prosthetic Appliances
MEDICAL & SURGICAL SPLYS: Splints, Pneumatic & Wood
MEDICAL & SURGICAL SPLYS: Sponges
MEDICAL & SURGICAL SPLYS: Supports, Abdominal, Ankle, Etc
MEDICAL & SURGICAL SPLYS: Sutures, Non & Absorbable
MEDICAL & SURGICAL SPLYS: Trusses, Orthopedic & Surgical
MEDICAL EQPT REPAIR SVCS, NON-ELECTRIC
MEDICAL EQPT: CAT Scanner Or Computerized Axial Tomography
MEDICAL EQPT: Diagnostic
MEDICAL EQPT: Electromedical Apparatus
MEDICAL EQPT: Electrotherapeutic Apparatus
MEDICAL EQPT: Laser Systems
MEDICAL EQPT: MRI/Magnetic Resonance Imaging Devs, Nuclear
MEDICAL EQPT: Pacemakers
MEDICAL EQPT: Patient Monitoring
MEDICAL EQPT: Sterilizers
MEDICAL EQPT: Ultrasonic Scanning Devices
MEDICAL EQPT: Ultrasonic, Exc Cleaning
MEDICAL EQPT: X-Ray Apparatus & Tubes, Radiographic
MEDICAL EQPT: X-ray Generators
MEDICAL HELP SVCS
MEDICAL SVCS ORGANIZATION
MEDICAL, DENTAL & HOSPITAL EQPT, WHOL: Hosptl Eqpt/Furniture
MEDICAL, DENTAL & HOSPITAL EQPT, WHOL: Surgical Eqpt & Splys
MEDICAL, DENTAL & HOSPITAL EQPT, WHOLESALE: Baths, Whirlpool

MEDICAL, DENTAL & HOSPITAL EQPT, WHOLESALE: Diagnostic, Med
MEDICAL, DENTAL & HOSPITAL EQPT, WHOLESALE: Hearing Aids
MEDICAL, DENTAL & HOSPITAL EQPT, WHOLESALE: Med Eqpt & Splys
MEDICAL, DENTAL & HOSPITAL EQPT, WHOLESALE: Medical Lab
MEDICAL, DENTAL & HOSPITAL EQPT, WHOLESALE: Orthopedic
MEDICAL, DENTAL/HOSPITAL EQPT, WHOL: Veterinarian Eqpt/Sply
MEMBERSHIP ORGANIZATIONS, NEC: Charitable
MEMBERSHIP ORGANIZATIONS, PROF: Education/Teacher Assoc
MEMBERSHIP ORGANIZATIONS, RELIGIOUS: Assembly Of God Church
MEMBERSHIP ORGANIZATIONS, RELIGIOUS: Catholic Church
MEMBERSHIP ORGANIZATIONS, RELIGIOUS: Nonchurch
MEN'S & BOYS' CLOTHING ACCESS STORES
MEN'S & BOYS' CLOTHING STORES
MEN'S & BOYS' CLOTHING WHOLESALERS, NEC
MEN'S & BOYS' SPORTSWEAR CLOTHING STORES
MEN'S & BOYS' SPORTSWEAR WHOLESALERS
MEN'S CLOTHING STORES: Everyday, Exc Suits & Sportswear
METAL & STEEL PRDTS: Abrasive
METAL CUTTING SVCS
METAL FABRICATORS: Architechtural
METAL FABRICATORS: Plate
METAL FABRICATORS: Sheet
METAL FABRICATORS: Structural, Ship
METAL FABRICATORS: Structural, Ship
METAL FINISHING SVCS
METAL MINING SVCS
METAL SERVICE CENTERS & OFFICES
METAL SPINNING FOR THE TRADE
METAL STAMPING, FOR THE TRADE
METAL STAMPINGS: Ornamental
METAL STAMPINGS: Patterned
METAL STAMPINGS: Perforated
METAL TREATING COMPOUNDS
METAL: Battery
METAL SVC CENTERS & WHOL: Structural Shapes, Iron Or Steel
METALS SVC CENTERS & WHOLESALERS: Bars, Metal
METALS SVC CENTERS & WHOLESALERS: Cable, Wire
METALS SVC CENTERS & WHOLESALERS: Ferroalloys
METALS SVC CENTERS & WHOLESALERS: Foundry Prdts
METALS SVC CENTERS & WHOLESALERS: Iron & Steel Prdt, Ferrous
METALS SVC CENTERS & WHOLESALERS: Nonferrous Sheets, Etc
METALS SVC CENTERS & WHOLESALERS: Pipe & Tubing, Steel
METALS SVC CENTERS & WHOLESALERS: Rope, Wire, Exc Insulated
METALS SVC CENTERS & WHOLESALERS: Sheets, Metal
METALS SVC CENTERS & WHOLESALERS: Stampings, Metal
METALS SVC CENTERS & WHOLESALERS: Steel
METALS SVC CENTERS & WHOLESALERS: Steel Decking
METALS SVC CENTERS/WHOL: Forms, Steel Concrete Construction
METALS SVC CNTRS & WHOL: Metal Wires, Ties, Cables/Screening
METALS SVC CTRS & WHOLESALERS: Aluminum Bars, Rods, Etc
METALS: Precious NEC
METALS: Primary Nonferrous, NEC
METALWORK: Miscellaneous
METALWORK: Ornamental
METALWORKING MACHINERY WHOLESALERS
METERS: Power Factor & Phase Angle
METERS: Pyrometers, Indl Process
MGMT CONSULTING SVCS: Matls, Incl Purch, Handle & Invntry
MICA
MICROCIRCUITS, INTEGRATED: Semiconductor
MICROFILM EQPT
MICROFILM EQPT WHOLESALERS
MICROFILM SVCS
MICROPHONES
MICROWAVE COMPONENTS

MICROWAVE OVENS: Household
MILITARY GOODS & REGALIA STORES
MILITARY INSIGNIA
MILL PRDTS: Structural & Rail
MILLINERY SUPPLIES: Veils & Veiling, Bridal, Funeral, Etc
MILLING: Feed, Wheat
MILLING: Grain Cereals, Cracked
MILLWORK
MINE & QUARRY SVCS: Nonmetallic Minerals
MINE EXPLORATION SVCS: Nonmetallic Minerals
MINERAL PIGMENT MINING
MINERAL WOOL
MINERAL WOOL INSULATION PRDTS
MINERALS: Ground Or Otherwise Treated
MINERALS: Ground or Treated
MINING MACHINES & EQPT: Clarifying, Mineral
MINING MACHINES & EQPT: Feeders, Ore & Aggregate
MINING MACHINES & EQPT: Pulverizers, Stone, Stationary
MIXERS: Hot Metal
MIXTURES & BLOCKS: Asphalt Paving
MOBILE COMMUNICATIONS EQPT
MOBILE HOMES
MODELS
MODELS: General, Exc Toy
MODELS: Railroad, Exc Toy
MOLDED RUBBER PRDTS
MOLDING COMPOUNDS
MOLDINGS & TRIM: Metal, Exc Automobile
MOLDINGS & TRIM: Wood
MOLDINGS: Picture Frame
MOLDS: Indl
MOLDS: Plastic Working & Foundry
MONORAIL SYSTEMS
MONUMENTS & GRAVE MARKERS, EXC TERRAZZO
MONUMENTS: Concrete
MONUMENTS: Cut Stone, Exc Finishing Or Lettering Only
MOPS: Floor & Dust
MORTAR: High Temperature, Nonclay
MOTION PICTURE & VIDEO PRODUCTION SVCS
MOTION PICTURE & VIDEO PRODUCTION SVCS: Educational, TV
MOTION PICTURE PRODUCTION & DISTRIBUTION
MOTION PICTURE PRODUCTION & DISTRIBUTION: Television
MOTOR & GENERATOR PARTS: Electric
MOTOR REPAIR SVCS
MOTOR SCOOTERS & PARTS
MOTOR VEHICLE ASSEMBLY, COMPLETE: Ambulances
MOTOR VEHICLE ASSEMBLY, COMPLETE: Autos, Incl Specialty
MOTOR VEHICLE ASSEMBLY, COMPLETE: Bus/Large Spclty Vehicles
MOTOR VEHICLE ASSEMBLY, COMPLETE: Military Motor Vehicle
MOTOR VEHICLE ASSEMBLY, COMPLETE: Snow Plows
MOTOR VEHICLE ASSEMBLY, COMPLETE: Truck & Tractor Trucks
MOTOR VEHICLE ASSEMBLY, COMPLETE: Truck Tractors, Highway
MOTOR VEHICLE DEALERS: Automobiles, New & Used
MOTOR VEHICLE DEALERS: Pickups & Vans, Used
MOTOR VEHICLE DEALERS: Trucks, Tractors/Trailers, New & Used
MOTOR VEHICLE PARTS & ACCESS: Air Conditioner Parts
MOTOR VEHICLE PARTS & ACCESS: Body Components & Frames
MOTOR VEHICLE PARTS & ACCESS: Cleaners, air
MOTOR VEHICLE PARTS & ACCESS: Clutches
MOTOR VEHICLE PARTS & ACCESS: Cylinder Heads
MOTOR VEHICLE PARTS & ACCESS: Engines & Parts
MOTOR VEHICLE PARTS & ACCESS: Fuel Pumps
MOTOR VEHICLE PARTS & ACCESS: Fuel Systems & Parts
MOTOR VEHICLE PARTS & ACCESS: Transmission Housings Or Parts
MOTOR VEHICLE PARTS & ACCESS: Transmissions
MOTOR VEHICLE PARTS & ACCESS: Water Pumps
MOTOR VEHICLE PARTS & ACCESS: Wheel rims
MOTOR VEHICLE PARTS & ACCESS: Windshield Frames
MOTOR VEHICLE PARTS & ACCESS: Wipers, Windshield
MOTOR VEHICLE SPLYS & PARTS WHOLESALERS: New
MOTOR VEHICLE SPLYS & PARTS WHOLESALERS: Used
MOTOR VEHICLE: Hardware
MOTOR VEHICLE: Radiators
MOTOR VEHICLES & CAR BODIES

MOTOR VEHICLES, WHOLESALE: Trailers for passenger vehicles
MOTOR VEHICLES, WHOLESALE: Trailers, Truck, New & Used
MOTOR VEHICLES, WHOLESALE: Truck bodies
MOTORCYCLE ACCESS
MOTORCYCLE DEALERS
MOTORCYCLE PARTS & ACCESS DEALERS
MOTORCYCLE REPAIR SHOPS
MOTORCYCLES & RELATED PARTS
MOTORS: Electric
MOTORS: Generators
MOTORS: Torque
MOUNTING MERCHANDISE ON CARDS
MOUTHWASHES
MOVIE THEATERS, EXC DRIVE-IN
MOVING SVC: Local
MOWERS & ACCESSORIES
MULTIPLEX EQPT: Radio, Television & Broadcast
MUSEUMS
MUSEUMS & ART GALLERIES
MUSIC ARRANGING & COMPOSING SVCS
MUSIC COPYING SVCS
MUSIC DISTRIBUTION APPARATUS
MUSICAL INSTRUMENT LESSONS
MUSICAL INSTRUMENT PARTS & ACCESS, WHOLESALE
MUSICAL INSTRUMENT REPAIR
MUSICAL INSTRUMENTS & ACCESS: NEC
MUSICAL INSTRUMENTS & ACCESS: Pianos
MUSICAL INSTRUMENTS & PARTS: Percussion
MUSICAL INSTRUMENTS & SPLYS STORES
MUSICAL INSTRUMENTS WHOLESALERS
MUSICAL INSTRUMENTS: Guitars & Parts, Electric & Acoustic
MUSICAL INSTRUMENTS: Organs
MUSICAL INSTRUMENTS: Synthesizers, Music
MUSICAL INSTRUMENTS: Violins & Parts

N

NAILS WHOLESALERS
NAME PLATES: Engraved Or Etched
NATIONAL SECURITY, GOVERNMENT: National Guard
NATURAL GAS LIQUIDS PRODUCTION
NATURAL GAS PRODUCTION
NATURAL LIQUEFIED PETROLEUM GAS PRODUCTION
NAVIGATIONAL SYSTEMS & INSTRUMENTS
NET & NETTING PRDTS
NETTING: Rope
NEW & USED CAR DEALERS
NEWS SYNDICATES
NEWSPAPERS & PERIODICALS NEWS REPORTING SVCS
NICKEL ALLOY
NONCURRENT CARRYING WIRING DEVICES
NONDAIRY BASED FROZEN DESSERTS
NONFERROUS: Rolling & Drawing, NEC
NOTIONS: Fasteners, Slide Zippers
NOTIONS: Hooks, Crochet
NOVELTIES
NOVELTIES & SPECIALTIES: Metal
NOVELTIES, DURABLE, WHOLESALE
NOVELTIES: Leather
NOVELTIES: Paper, Made From Purchased Materials
NOVELTIES: Plastic
NOVELTY SHOPS
NOZZLES & SPRINKLERS Lawn Hose
NOZZLES: Fire Fighting
NOZZLES: Spray, Aerosol, Paint Or Insecticide
NUCLEAR FUELS SCRAP REPROCESSING
NURSERIES & LAWN & GARDEN SPLY STORE, RET: Lawn/Garden Splys
NURSERIES & LAWN & GARDEN SPLY STORES, RETAIL: Top Soil
NURSERIES & LAWN/GARDEN SPLY STORE, RET: Lawnmowers/Tractors
NURSERY & GARDEN CENTERS
NUTS: Metal
NYLON FIBERS

O

OFFICE EQPT WHOLESALERS
OFFICE EQPT, WHOLESALE: Calculating Machines
OFFICE EQPT, WHOLESALE: Duplicating Machines
OFFICE FIXTURES: Exc Wood
OFFICE FURNITURE REPAIR & MAINTENANCE SVCS
OFFICE MACHINES, NEC

OFFICE SPLY & STATIONERY STORES
OFFICE SPLY & STATIONERY STORES: Office Forms & Splys
OFFICE SPLYS, NEC, WHOLESALE
OFFICES & CLINICS DOCTORS OF MED: Intrnl Med Practitioners
OFFICES & CLINICS OF DENTISTS: Dental Clinics & Offices
OFFICES & CLINICS OF DENTISTS: Specialist, Practitioners
OFFICES & CLINICS OF DOCTORS OF MEDICINE: Gastronomist
OFFICES & CLINICS OF DOCTORS OF MEDICINE: Group Health Assoc
OFFICES & CLINICS OF DOCTORS OF MEDICINE: Neurosurgeon
OFFICES & CLINICS OF DOCTORS OF MEDICINE: Oculist
OFFICES & CLINICS OF DOCTORS OF MEDICINE: Oncologist
OFFICES & CLINICS OF DOCTORS OF MEDICINE: Ophthalmologist
OFFICES & CLINICS OF DOCTORS OF MEDICINE: Radiologist
OFFICES & CLINICS OF DRS OF MEDICINE: Geriatric
OFFICES & CLINICS OF DRS OF MEDICINE: Physician, Orthopedic
OIL FIELD SVCS, NEC
OIL TREATING COMPOUNDS
OILS & ESSENTIAL OILS
OILS & GREASES: Blended & Compounded
OILS & GREASES: Lubricating
OILS: Essential
OILS: Lubricating
OILS: Lubricating
OILS: Peppermint
OILS: Vegetable Oils, Vulcanized Or Sulfurized
OLEFINS
OMNIBEARING INDICATORS
OPERATOR: Apartment Buildings
OPERATOR: Nonresidential Buildings
OPHTHALMIC GOODS
OPHTHALMIC GOODS WHOLESALERS
OPHTHALMIC GOODS, NEC, WHOLESALE: Frames
OPHTHALMIC GOODS, NEC, WHOLESALE: Lenses
OPHTHALMIC GOODS: Frames & Parts, Eyeglass & Spectacle
OPHTHALMIC GOODS: Lenses, Ophthalmic
OPHTHALMIC GOODS: Protectors, Eye
OPTICAL GOODS STORES
OPTICAL GOODS STORES: Contact Lenses, Prescription
OPTICAL GOODS STORES: Eyeglasses, Prescription
OPTICAL GOODS STORES: Opticians
OPTICAL INSTRUMENTS & APPARATUS
OPTICAL INSTRUMENTS & LENSES
OPTICAL ISOLATORS
OPTOMETRISTS' OFFICES
ORAL PREPARATIONS
ORDNANCE
ORGAN TUNING & REPAIR SVCS
ORGANIZATIONS: Biotechnical Research, Noncommercial
ORGANIZATIONS: Civic & Social
ORGANIZATIONS: Medical Research
ORGANIZATIONS: Noncommercial Social Research
ORGANIZATIONS: Religious
ORGANIZATIONS: Research Institute
ORGANIZATIONS: Scientific Research Agency
ORGANIZERS, CLOSET & DRAWER Plastic
ORIENTED STRANDBOARD
ORNAMENTS: Lawn
ORTHODONTIST
OUTLETS: Electric, Convenience
OVENS: Infrared
OXALIC ACID & METALLIC SALTS

P

PACKAGE DESIGN SVCS
PACKAGED FROZEN FOODS WHOLESALERS, NEC
PACKAGING & LABELING SVCS
PACKAGING MATERIALS, INDL: Wholesalers
PACKAGING MATERIALS, WHOLESALE
PACKAGING MATERIALS: Paper
PACKAGING MATERIALS: Paper, Coated Or Laminated
PACKAGING MATERIALS: Plastic Film, Coated Or Laminated
PACKAGING MATERIALS: Polystyrene Foam
PACKAGING: Blister Or Bubble Formed, Plastic
PACKING & CRATING SVC

I N D E X

PACKING & CRATING SVCS: Containerized Goods For Shipping
PACKING MATERIALS: Mechanical
PACKING SVCS: Shipping
PADS, SCOURING: Soap Impregnated
PADS: Athletic, Protective
PADS: Mattress
PAILS: Meta, Exc Shipping
PAINT & PAINTING SPLYS STORE
PAINTING SVC: Metal Prdts
PAINTS & ADDITIVES
PAINTS & ALLIED PRODUCTS
PAINTS, VARNISHES & SPLYS WHOLESALERS
PAINTS, VARNISHES & SPLYS, WHOLESALE: Paints
PAINTS: Marine
PAINTS: Waterproof
PALLET REPAIR SVCS
PALLETS
PALLETS & SKIDS: Wood
PALLETS: Metal
PALLETS: Plastic
PALLETS: Wooden
PANEL & DISTRIBUTION BOARDS & OTHER RELATED APPARATUS
PANEL & DISTRIBUTION BOARDS: Electric
PANELS, CORRUGATED: Plastic
PANELS: Building, Wood
PANELS: Electric Metering
PANELS: Wood
PAPER & BOARD: Die-cut
PAPER & ENVELOPES: Writing, Made From Purchased Materials
PAPER CONVERTING
PAPER MANUFACTURERS: Exc Newsprint
PAPER PRDTS: Feminine Hygiene Prdts
PAPER PRDTS: Infant & Baby Prdts
PAPER PRDTS: Sanitary
PAPER PRDTS: Towels, Napkins/Tissue Paper, From Purchd Mtrls
PAPER, WHOLESALE: Fine
PAPER, WHOLESALE: Printing
PAPER: Adhesive
PAPER: Bag
PAPER: Card
PAPER: Cardboard
PAPER: Chart & Graph, Ruled
PAPER: Coated & Laminated, NEC
PAPER: Copier
PAPER: Corrugated
PAPER: Envelope
PAPER: Gift Wrap
PAPER: Metallic Covered, Made From Purchased Materials
PAPER: Newsprint
PAPER: Packaging
PAPER: Poster & Art
PAPER: Printer
PAPER: Specialty Or Chemically Treated
PAPER: Wallpaper
PAPER: Wrapping & Packaging
PAPER: Wrapping, Waterproof Or Coated
PAPERBOARD
PAPERBOARD CONVERTING
PAPERBOARD PRDTS: Binders' Board
PAPERBOARD PRDTS: Coated & Treated Board
PAPERBOARD PRDTS: Container Board
PAPERBOARD PRDTS: Folding Boxboard
PAPERBOARD PRDTS: Milk Carton Board
PAPERBOARD PRDTS: Packaging Board
PAPERBOARD PRDTS: Specialty Board
PAPERBOARD PRDTS: Strawboard
PAPERBOARD: Coated
PAPERBOARD: Corrugated
PARACHUTES
PARKING GARAGE
PARKING METERS
PARTITIONS & FIXTURES: Except Wood
PARTITIONS WHOLESALERS
PARTITIONS: Solid Fiber, Made From Purchased Materials
PARTITIONS: Wood & Fixtures
PARTS: Metal
PATENT OWNERS & LESSORS
PATTERNS: Indl
PAVERS
PAVING MATERIALS: Prefabricated, Concrete
PAVING MIXTURES

PAYROLL SVCS
PEARLS, WHOLESALE
PEAT MINING & PROCESSING SVCS
PEAT MINING SVCS
PENS & PARTS: Ball Point
PENS & PENCILS: Mechanical, NEC
PERFUME: Concentrated
PERFUME: Perfumes, Natural Or Synthetic
PERFUMES
PESTICIDES
PESTICIDES WHOLESALERS
PET SPLYS
PET SPLYS WHOLESALERS
PETROLEUM & PETROLEUM PRDTS, WHOLESALE Butane Gas
PETROLEUM PRDTS WHOLESALERS
PETS & PET SPLYS, WHOLESALE
PHARMACEUTICAL PREPARATIONS: Adrenal
PHARMACEUTICAL PREPARATIONS: Digitalis
PHARMACEUTICAL PREPARATIONS: Druggists' Preparations
PHARMACEUTICAL PREPARATIONS: Medicines, Capsule Or Ampule
PHARMACEUTICAL PREPARATIONS: Pills
PHARMACEUTICAL PREPARATIONS: Powders
PHARMACEUTICAL PREPARATIONS: Proprietary Drug PRDTS
PHARMACEUTICAL PREPARATIONS: Solutions
PHARMACEUTICAL PREPARATIONS: Tablets
PHARMACEUTICALS
PHARMACEUTICALS: Mail-Order Svc
PHARMACEUTICALS: Medicinal & Botanical Prdts
PHARMACIES & DRUG STORES
PHOSPHATES
PHOTOCOPY MACHINE REPAIR SVCS
PHOTOCOPY MACHINES
PHOTOCOPY SPLYS WHOLESALERS
PHOTOCOPYING & DUPLICATING SVCS
PHOTOENGRAVING SVC
PHOTOFINISHING LABORATORIES
PHOTOFINISHING LABORATORIES
PHOTOGRAPH DEVELOPING & RETOUCHING SVCS
PHOTOGRAPHIC & OPTICAL GOODS EQPT REPAIR SVCS
PHOTOGRAPHIC CONTROL SYSTEMS: Electronic
PHOTOGRAPHIC EQPT & SPLYS
PHOTOGRAPHIC EQPT & SPLYS WHOLESALERS
PHOTOGRAPHIC EQPT & SPLYS, WHOLESALE: Identity Recorders
PHOTOGRAPHIC EQPT & SPLYS, WHOLESALE: Motion Picture Camera
PHOTOGRAPHIC EQPT & SPLYS, WHOLESALE: Processing
PHOTOGRAPHIC EQPT & SPLYS: Cameras, Still & Motion Pictures
PHOTOGRAPHIC EQPT & SPLYS: Developers, Not Chemical Plants
PHOTOGRAPHIC EQPT & SPLYS: Film, Sensitized
PHOTOGRAPHIC EQPT & SPLYS: Flashlight Apparatus, Exc Bulbs
PHOTOGRAPHIC EQPT & SPLYS: Plates, Sensitized
PHOTOGRAPHIC EQPT & SPLYS: Printing Eqpt
PHOTOGRAPHIC EQPT & SPLYS: Processing Eqpt
PHOTOGRAPHIC EQPT & SPLYS: Toners, Prprd, Not Chem Plnts
PHOTOGRAPHIC EQPT & SPLYS: Trays, Printing & Processing
PHOTOGRAPHIC EQPT & SPLYS: X-Ray Film
PHOTOGRAPHIC EQPT REPAIR SVCS
PHOTOGRAPHIC EQPT/SPLYS, WHOL: Cameras/Projectors/Eqpt/Splys
PHOTOGRAPHIC SVCS
PHOTOGRAPHY SVCS: Commercial
PHOTOGRAPHY: Aerial
PHOTOTYPESETTING SVC
PHYSICAL EXAMINATION SVCS, INSURANCE
PHYSICAL FITNESS CENTERS
PHYSICIANS' OFFICES & CLINICS: Medical doctors
PICTURE FRAMES: Metal
PICTURE FRAMES: Wood
PICTURE PROJECTION EQPT
PIECE GOODS & NOTIONS WHOLESALERS
PIECE GOODS, NOTIONS & DRY GOODS, WHOL: Textile Converters
PIECE GOODS, NOTIONS & DRY GOODS, WHOL: Textiles, Woven

PIECE GOODS, NOTIONS & DRY GOODS, WHOL: Trimmings, Apparel
PIECE GOODS, NOTIONS & DRY GOODS, WHOL: Yard Goods, Woven
PIECE GOODS, NOTIONS & DRY GOODS, WHOLESALE: Fabrics
PIECE GOODS, NOTIONS & DRY GOODS, WHOLESALE: Fabrics, Lace
PIECE GOODS, NOTIONS & DRY GOODS, WHOLESALE: Sewing Access
PIECE GOODS, NOTIONS & OTHER DRY GOODS, WHOL: Flags/Banners
PIECE GOODS, NOTIONS & OTHER DRY GOODS, WHOL: Millinery Sply
PIECE GOODS, NOTIONS & OTHER DRY GOODS, WHOLESALE: Fabrics
PIECE GOODS, NOTIONS & OTHER DRY GOODS, WHOLESALE: Ribbons
PIECE GOODS, NOTIONS & OTHER DRY GOODS, WHOLESALE: Zippers
PIECE GOODS, NOTIONS/DRY GOODS, WHOL: Linen Piece, Woven
PIECE GOODS, NOTIONS/DRY GOODS, WHOL: Silk Piece, Woven
PIGMENTS, INORGANIC: Metallic & Mineral, NEC
PILLOW FILLING MTRLS: Curled Hair, Cotton Waste, Moss
PILLOW TUBING
PILOT SVCS: Aviation
PINS
PIPE & FITTING: Fabrication
PIPE & FITTINGS: Cast Iron
PIPE & FITTINGS: Pressure, Cast Iron
PIPE FITTINGS: Plastic
PIPE JOINT COMPOUNDS
PIPE SECTIONS, FABRICATED FROM PURCHASED PIPE
PIPE, CAST IRON: Wholesalers
PIPE, IRRIGATION: Concrete
PIPE, SEWER: Concrete
PIPE: Concrete
PIPE: Plastic
PIPE: Sewer, Cast Iron
PIPE: Sheet Metal
PIPELINE & POWER LINE INSPECTION SVCS
PIPELINE TERMINAL FACILITIES: Independent
PIPELINES: Crude Petroleum
PIPES & TUBES
PIPES & TUBES: Steel
PIPES: Steel & Iron
PIVOTS: Power Transmission
PLACEMATS: Plastic Or Textile
PLANING MILLS: Millwork
PLANTERS: Plastic
PLANTS: Artificial & Preserved
PLAQUES: Picture, Laminated
PLASMAS
PLASTER WORK: Ornamental & Architectural
PLASTER, ACOUSTICAL: Gypsum
PLASTIC PRDTS
PLASTICIZERS, ORGANIC: Cyclic & Acyclic
PLASTICS FILM & SHEET
PLASTICS FILM & SHEET: Polyethylene
PLASTICS FILM & SHEET: Polypropylene
PLASTICS FILM & SHEET: Polyvinyl
PLASTICS FILM & SHEET: Vinyl
PLASTICS FINISHED PRDTS: Laminated
PLASTICS MATERIAL & RESINS
PLASTICS MATERIALS, BASIC FORMS & SHAPES WHOLESALERS
PLASTICS PROCESSING
PLASTICS SHEET: Packing Materials
PLASTICS: Blow Molded
PLASTICS: Extruded
PLASTICS: Finished Injection Molded
PLASTICS: Injection Molded
PLASTICS: Molded
PLASTICS: Polystyrene Foam
PLASTICS: Thermoformed
PLATE WORK: Metalworking Trade
PLATEMAKING SVC: Color Separations, For The Printing Trade
PLATEMAKING SVC: Embossing, For The Printing Trade
PLATEMAKING SVC: Letterpress
PLATES
PLATES: Plastic Exc Polystyrene Foam
PLATES: Sheet & Strip, Exc Coated Prdts

PLATES: Steel
PLATING & FINISHING SVC: Decorative, Formed Prdts
PLATING & POLISHING SVC
PLATING COMPOUNDS
PLATING SVC: Chromium, Metals Or Formed Prdts
PLATING SVC: Electro
PLATING SVC: NEC
PLAYGROUND EQPT
PLEATING & STITCHING FOR THE TRADE: Decorative &
  Novelty
PLEATING & STITCHING FOR THE TRADE: Lace, Burnt-Out
PLEATING & STITCHING FOR THE TRADE: Scalloping
PLEATING & STITCHING FOR TRADE: Permanent Pleat-
  ing/Pressing
PLEATING & STITCHING SVC
PLUMBING & HEATING EQPT & SPLY, WHOL: Htg
  Eqpt/Panels, Solar
PLUMBING & HEATING EQPT & SPLY, WHOLESALE: Hy-
  dronic Htg Eqpt
PLUMBING & HEATING EQPT & SPLYS WHOLESALERS
PLUMBING & HEATING EQPT & SPLYS, WHOL: Pipe/Fitting,
  Plastic
PLUMBING & HEATING EQPT & SPLYS, WHOL: Plumbing
  Fitting/Sply
PLUMBING & HEATING EQPT & SPLYS, WHOL: Water Purif
  Eqpt
PLUMBING & HEATING EQPT & SPLYS, WHOLESALE: Oil
  Burners
PLUMBING FIXTURES
PLUMBING FIXTURES: Brass, Incl Drain Cocks,
  Faucets/Spigots
PLUMBING FIXTURES: Plastic
PLUMBING FIXTURES: Vitreous
PLUMBING FIXTURES: Vitreous China
POINT OF SALE DEVICES
POLISHING SVC: Metals Or Formed Prdts
POLYAMIDES
POLYESTERS
POLYETHYLENE CHLOROSULFONATED RUBBER
POLYETHYLENE RESINS
POLYPROPYLENE RESINS
POLYTETRAFLUOROETHYLENE RESINS
POLYVINYL CHLORIDE RESINS
POPCORN & SUPPLIES WHOLESALERS
POSTERS, WHOLESALE
POULTRY & POULTRY PRDTS WHOLESALERS
POULTRY & SMALL GAME SLAUGHTERING & PROCESS-
  ING
POULTRY, PACKAGED FROZEN: Wholesalers
POWDER: Metal
POWDERS, FLAVORING, EXC DRINK
POWER SPLY CONVERTERS: Static, Electronic Applications
POWER SUPPLIES: All Types, Static
POWER SUPPLIES: Transformer, Electronic Type
POWER SWITCHING EQPT
POWER TOOLS, HAND: Cartridge-Activated
POWER TOOLS, HAND: Drill Attachments, Portable
POWER TOOLS, HAND: Drills & Drilling Tools
POWER TRANSMISSION EQPT WHOLESALERS
POWER TRANSMISSION EQPT: Aircraft
POWER TRANSMISSION EQPT: Mechanical
PRECAST TERRAZZO OR CONCRETE PRDTS
PRECIOUS METALS
PRECIOUS METALS WHOLESALERS
PRECISION INSTRUMENT REPAIR SVCS
PREFABRICATED BUILDING DEALERS
PREPARATORY SCHOOL
PRERECORDED TAPE, COMPACT DISC & RECORD
  STORES
PRERECORDED TAPE, COMPACT DISC & RECORD
  STORES: Records
PRESCHOOL CENTERS
PRESSURE COOKERS: Stamped Or Drawn Metal
PRIMARY METAL PRODUCTS
PRINT CARTRIDGES: Laser & Other Computer Printers
PRINTED CIRCUIT BOARDS
PRINTERS & PLOTTERS
PRINTERS' SVCS: Folding, Collating, Etc
PRINTERS: Computer
PRINTERS: Magnetic Ink, Bar Code
PRINTING & BINDING: Books
PRINTING & EMBOSSING: Plastic Fabric Articles
PRINTING & ENGRAVING: Financial Notes & Certificates
PRINTING & ENGRAVING: Invitation & Stationery
PRINTING & ENGRAVING: Poster & Decal

PRINTING & STAMPING: Fabric Articles
PRINTING & WRITING PAPER WHOLESALERS
PRINTING INKS WHOLESALERS
PRINTING MACHINERY
PRINTING MACHINERY, EQPT & SPLYS: Wholesalers
PRINTING, COMMERCIAL: Bags, Plastic, NEC
PRINTING, COMMERCIAL: Business Forms, NEC
PRINTING, COMMERCIAL: Calendars, NEC
PRINTING, COMMERCIAL: Cards, Souvenir, NEC
PRINTING, COMMERCIAL: Cards, Visiting, Incl Business,
  NEC
PRINTING, COMMERCIAL: Catalogs, NEC
PRINTING, COMMERCIAL: Decals, NEC
PRINTING, COMMERCIAL: Directories, Exc Telephone, NEC
PRINTING, COMMERCIAL: Envelopes, NEC
PRINTING, COMMERCIAL: Fashion Plates, NEC
PRINTING, COMMERCIAL: Imprinting
PRINTING, COMMERCIAL: Labels & Seals, NEC
PRINTING, COMMERCIAL: Literature, Advertising, NEC
PRINTING, COMMERCIAL: Promotional
PRINTING, COMMERCIAL: Publications
PRINTING, COMMERCIAL: Schedules, Transportation, NEC
PRINTING, COMMERCIAL: Screen
PRINTING, COMMERCIAL: Tags, NEC
PRINTING, COMMERCIAL: Tickets, NEC
PRINTING, LITHOGRAPHIC: Advertising Posters
PRINTING, LITHOGRAPHIC: Atlases
PRINTING, LITHOGRAPHIC: Calendars
PRINTING, LITHOGRAPHIC: Catalogs
PRINTING, LITHOGRAPHIC: Color
PRINTING, LITHOGRAPHIC: Decals
PRINTING, LITHOGRAPHIC: Forms & Cards, Business
PRINTING, LITHOGRAPHIC: Forms, Business
PRINTING, LITHOGRAPHIC: Newspapers
PRINTING, LITHOGRAPHIC: Offset & photolithographic print-
  ing
PRINTING, LITHOGRAPHIC: On Metal
PRINTING, LITHOGRAPHIC: Promotional
PRINTING, LITHOGRAPHIC: Publications
PRINTING, LITHOGRAPHIC: Transfers, Decalcomania Or Dry
PRINTING, LITHOGRAPHIC: Wrappers
PRINTING, LITHOGRAPHIC: Wrappers & Seals
PRINTING: Books
PRINTING: Books
PRINTING: Broadwoven Fabrics. Cotton
PRINTING: Checkbooks
PRINTING: Commercial, NEC
PRINTING: Engraving & Plate
PRINTING: Fabric, Narrow
PRINTING: Flexographic
PRINTING: Gravure, Cards, Exc Greeting
PRINTING: Gravure, Catalogs, No Publishing On-Site
PRINTING: Gravure, Color
PRINTING: Gravure, Forms, Business
PRINTING: Gravure, Labels
PRINTING: Gravure, Magazines, No Publishing On-Site
PRINTING: Gravure, Posters
PRINTING: Gravure, Rotogravure
PRINTING: Gravure, Stationery & Invitation
PRINTING: Laser
PRINTING: Letterpress
PRINTING: Lithographic
PRINTING: Manmade Fiber & Silk, Broadwoven Fabric
PRINTING: Offset
PRINTING: Photo-Offset
PRINTING: Photolithographic
PRINTING: Rotogravure
PRINTING: Screen, Broadwoven Fabrics, Cotton
PRINTING: Screen, Fabric
PRINTING: Screen, Manmade Fiber & Silk, Broadwoven Fab-
  ric
PRINTING: Thermography
PRODUCT STERILIZATION SVCS
PROFESSIONAL EQPT & SPLYS, WHOLESALE: Law En-
  forcement
PROFESSIONAL EQPT & SPLYS, WHOLESALE: Optical
  Goods
PROFESSIONAL EQPT & SPLYS, WHOLESALE: Precision
  Tools
PROFESSIONAL EQPT & SPLYS, WHOLESALE: Scientific &
  Engineerg
PROFESSIONAL EQPT & SPLYS, WHOLESALE: Theatrical
PROFESSIONAL INSTRUMENT REPAIR SVCS
PROFILE SHAPES: Unsupported Plastics
PROMOTION SVCS

PROTECTION EQPT: Lightning
PROTECTIVE FOOTWEAR: Rubber Or Plastic
PUBLIC ADDRESS SYSTEMS
PUBLIC FINANCE, TAXATION & MONETARY POLICY OF-
  FICES
PUBLIC RELATIONS SVCS
PUBLISHERS: Art Copy
PUBLISHERS: Art Copy & Poster
PUBLISHERS: Book
PUBLISHERS: Book Clubs, No Printing
PUBLISHERS: Books, No Printing
PUBLISHERS: Catalogs
PUBLISHERS: Directories, NEC
PUBLISHERS: Directories, Telephone
PUBLISHERS: Guides
PUBLISHERS: Magazines, No Printing
PUBLISHERS: Maps
PUBLISHERS: Miscellaneous
PUBLISHERS: Music Book & Sheet Music
PUBLISHERS: Music, Book
PUBLISHERS: Music, Sheet
PUBLISHERS: Newsletter
PUBLISHERS: Newspaper
PUBLISHERS: Newspapers, No Printing
PUBLISHERS: Pamphlets, No Printing
PUBLISHERS: Periodical Statistical Reports, No Printing
PUBLISHERS: Periodical, With Printing
PUBLISHERS: Periodicals, Magazines
PUBLISHERS: Periodicals, No Printing
PUBLISHERS: Posters
PUBLISHERS: Shopping News
PUBLISHERS: Technical Manuals
PUBLISHERS: Technical Manuals & Papers
PUBLISHERS: Technical Papers
PUBLISHERS: Telephone & Other Directory
PUBLISHERS: Textbooks, No Printing
PUBLISHERS: Trade journals, No Printing
PUBLISHING & BROADCASTING: Internet Only
PUBLISHING & PRINTING: Art Copy
PUBLISHING & PRINTING: Books
PUBLISHING & PRINTING: Catalogs
PUBLISHING & PRINTING: Directories, NEC
PUBLISHING & PRINTING: Guides
PUBLISHING & PRINTING: Magazines: publishing & printing
PUBLISHING & PRINTING: Newsletters, Business Svc
PUBLISHING & PRINTING: Newspapers
PUBLISHING & PRINTING: Pamphlets
PUBLISHING & PRINTING: Periodical Statistical Reports
PUBLISHING & PRINTING: Technical Manuals
PUBLISHING & PRINTING: Technical Papers
PUBLISHING & PRINTING: Textbooks
PUBLISHING & PRINTING: Trade Journals
PULLEYS: Metal
PULP MILLS
PUMP JACKS & OTHER PUMPING EQPT: Indl
PUMP SLEEVES: Rubber
PUMPS
PUMPS & PARTS: Indl
PUMPS & PUMPING EQPT REPAIR SVCS
PUMPS & PUMPING EQPT WHOLESALERS
PUMPS, HEAT: Electric
PUMPS: Domestic, Water Or Sump
PUMPS: Fluid Power
PUMPS: Gasoline, Measuring Or Dispensing
PUMPS: Vacuum, Exc Laboratory
PUNCHES: Forming & Stamping
PURCHASING SVCS
PURIFICATION & DUST COLLECTION EQPT

Q

QUARTZ CRYSTALS: Electronic
QUILTING SVC

R

RACEWAYS
RACKS: Display
RACKS: Garment, Exc Wood
RACKS: Garment, Wood
RACKS: Pallet, Exc Wood
RADAR SYSTEMS & EQPT
RADIO & TELEVISION COMMUNICATIONS EQUIPMENT
RADIO BROADCASTING & COMMUNICATIONS EQPT
RADIO BROADCASTING STATIONS
RADIO COMMUNICATIONS: Airborne Eqpt
RADIO MAGNETIC INSTRUMENTATION

INDEX

RADIO PRODUCERS
RADIO REPAIR SHOP, NEC
RADIO, TELEVISION & CONSUMER ELECTRONICS STORES: Eqpt, NEC
RADIO, TELEVISION/CONSUMER ELEC STORES: Video Cameras/Access
RADIO, TV & CONSUMER ELEC STORES: Automotive Sound Eqpt
RADIO, TV & CONSUMER ELECTRONICS: VCR & Access
RADIOS WHOLESALERS
RAILINGS: Prefabricated, Metal
RAILROAD CARGO LOADING & UNLOADING SVCS
RAILROAD EQPT
RAILROAD EQPT: Cars & Eqpt, Interurban
RAILROAD EQPT: Cars & Eqpt, Train, Freight Or Passenger
RAILROAD EQPT: Cars, Motor
RAILROAD EQPT: Engines, Locomotive, Steam
RAILROAD EQPT: Locomotives & Parts, Electric Or Nonelectric
RAILROAD MAINTENANCE & REPAIR SVCS
RAILROAD RELATED EQPT
RAILROAD SWITCHING & TERMINAL SVCS
RAILS: Elevator, Guide
RAILS: Rails, rolled & drawn, aluminum
RAMPS: Prefabricated Metal
RAZORS, RAZOR BLADES
REAL ESTATE AGENCIES: Rental
REAL ESTATE AGENCIES: Selling
REAL ESTATE AGENTS & MANAGERS
REAL ESTATE INVESTMENT TRUSTS
REAL ESTATE OPERATORS, EXC DEVELOPERS: Apartment Hotel
REAL ESTATE OPERATORS, EXC DEVELOPERS: Commercial/Indl Bldg
RECLAIMED RUBBER: Reworked By Manufacturing Process
RECORD BLANKS: Phonographic
RECORDERS: Sound
RECORDING & PLAYBACK HEADS: Magnetic
RECORDING HEADS: Speech & Musical Eqpt
RECORDING TAPE: Video, Blank
RECORDS & TAPES: Prerecorded
RECORDS OR TAPES: Masters
RECOVERY SVCS: Metal
RECOVERY SVCS: Solvents
RECREATIONAL SPORTING EQPT REPAIR SVCS
RECTIFIERS: Electronic, Exc Semiconductor
RECYCLABLE SCRAP & WASTE MATERIALS WHOLESALERS
RECYCLING: Paper
REELS: Fiber, Textile, Made From Purchased Materials
REFINERS & SMELTERS: Aluminum
REFINERS & SMELTERS: Brass, Secondary
REFINERS & SMELTERS: Copper
REFINERS & SMELTERS: Gold, Secondary
REFINERS & SMELTERS: Lead, Secondary
REFINERS & SMELTERS: Nonferrous Metal
REFINERS & SMELTERS: Platinum Group Metal Refining, Primary
REFINERS & SMELTERS: Platinum Group Metals, Secondary
REFINERS & SMELTERS: Silicon, Primary, Over 99% Pure
REFINERS & SMELTERS: Zinc, Primary, Including Slabs & Dust
REFINERS & SMELTERS: Zinc, Primary, Including Zinc Residue
REFINING LUBRICATING OILS & GREASES, NEC
REFINING: Petroleum
REFLECTIVE ROAD MARKERS, WHOLESALE
REFRACTORIES: Clay
REFRACTORIES: Nonclay
REFRACTORY CASTABLES
REFRIGERATION & HEATING EQUIPMENT
REFRIGERATION EQPT & SPLYS WHOLESALERS
REFRIGERATION EQPT: Complete
REFRIGERATION SVC & REPAIR
REFUSE SYSTEMS
REGULATORS: Transmission & Distribution Voltage
REGULATORS: Transmission & Distribution Voltage
REHABILITATION CENTER, OUTPATIENT TREATMENT
REHABILITATION SVCS
RELAYS & SWITCHES: Indl, Electric
RELAYS: Electric Power
RELAYS: Electronic Usage
RELIGIOUS SPLYS WHOLESALERS
REMOVERS & CLEANERS
REMOVERS: Paint

RENTAL CENTERS: Furniture
RENTAL CENTERS: Party & Banquet Eqpt & Splys
RENTAL SVCS: Business Machine & Electronic Eqpt
RENTAL SVCS: Costume
RENTAL SVCS: Eqpt, Theatrical
RENTAL SVCS: Stores & Yards Eqpt
RENTAL SVCS: Tuxedo
RENTAL: Passenger Car
RENTAL: Trucks, With Drivers
REPRODUCTION SVCS: Video Tape Or Disk
RESEARCH & DEVELOPMENT SVCS, COMMERCIAL: Engineering Lab
RESEARCH, DEV & TESTING SVCS, COMM: Chem Lab, Exc Testing
RESEARCH, DEVELOPMENT & TEST SVCS, COMM: Business Analysis
RESEARCH, DEVELOPMENT & TEST SVCS, COMM: Cmptr Hardware Dev
RESEARCH, DEVELOPMENT & TEST SVCS, COMM: Research, Exc Lab
RESEARCH, DEVELOPMENT & TESTING SVCS, COMM: Research Lab
RESEARCH, DEVELOPMENT & TESTING SVCS, COMMERCIAL: Business
RESEARCH, DEVELOPMENT & TESTING SVCS, COMMERCIAL: Energy
RESEARCH, DEVELOPMENT & TESTING SVCS, COMMERCIAL: Medical
RESEARCH, DEVELOPMENT & TESTING SVCS, COMMERCIAL: Physical
RESEARCH, DVLPMT & TESTING SVCS, COMM: Merger, Acq & Reorg
RESEARCH, DVLPT & TEST SVCS, COMM: Mkt Analysis or Research
RESEARCH, DVLPT & TESTING SVCS, COMM: Survey, Mktg
RESIDENTIAL REMODELERS
RESIDUES
RESINS: Custom Compound Purchased
RESISTORS
RESTAURANT EQPT REPAIR SVCS
RESTAURANT EQPT: Carts
RESTAURANT EQPT: Food Wagons
RESTAURANTS: Delicatessen
RESTAURANTS:Full Svc, American
RESTAURANTS:Full Svc, Diner
RESTAURANTS:Full Svc, Family, Independent
RESTAURANTS:Full Svc, Italian
RESTAURANTS:Limited Svc, Coffee Shop
RESTAURANTS:Limited Svc, Ice Cream Stands Or Dairy Bars
RESTAURANTS:Ltd Svc, Ice Cream, Soft Drink/Fountain Stands
RETAIL BAKERY: Bagels
RETAIL BAKERY: Bread
RETAIL BAKERY: Cakes
RETAIL BAKERY: Cookies
RETAIL BAKERY: Doughnuts
RETAIL BAKERY: Pastries
RETAIL BAKERY: Pretzels
RETAIL LUMBER YARDS
RETAIL STORES, NEC
RETAIL STORES: Artificial Limbs
RETAIL STORES: Awnings
RETAIL STORES: Baby Carriages & Strollers
RETAIL STORES: Batteries, Non-Automotive
RETAIL STORES: Communication Eqpt
RETAIL STORES: Cosmetics
RETAIL STORES: Decals
RETAIL STORES: Electronic Parts & Eqpt
RETAIL STORES: Hair Care Prdts
RETAIL STORES: Hearing Aids
RETAIL STORES: Hospital Eqpt & Splys
RETAIL STORES: Infant Furnishings & Eqpt
RETAIL STORES: Medical Apparatus & Splys
RETAIL STORES: Monuments, Finished To Custom Order
RETAIL STORES: Motors, Electric
RETAIL STORES: Orthopedic & Prosthesis Applications
RETAIL STORES: Perfumes & Colognes
RETAIL STORES: Pet Food
RETAIL STORES: Pet Splys
RETAIL STORES: Pets
RETAIL STORES: Photocopy Machines
RETAIL STORES: Plumbing & Heating Splys
RETAIL STORES: Police Splys

RETAIL STORES: Rock & Stone Specimens
RETAIL STORES: Rubber Stamps
RETAIL STORES: Safety Splys & Eqpt
RETAIL STORES: Spas & Hot Tubs
RETAIL STORES: Telephone Eqpt & Systems
RETAIL STORES: Water Purification Eqpt
RETAIL STORES: Wheelchair Lifts
REUPHOLSTERY & FURNITURE REPAIR
REUPHOLSTERY SVCS
REWINDING SVCS
RHEOSTATS: Electronic
RIBBONS & BOWS
RIBBONS, NEC
RIBBONS: Machine, Inked Or Carbon
RIDING APPAREL STORES
RIVETS: Metal
ROAD CONSTRUCTION EQUIPMENT WHOLESALERS
ROAD MATERIALS: Bituminous, Not From Refineries
ROBOTS, SERVICES OR NOVELTY, WHOLESALE
ROLL FORMED SHAPES: Custom
ROLLERS & FITTINGS: Window Shade
ROLLING MILL EQPT: Finishing
ROLLS & ROLL COVERINGS: Rubber
ROLLS: Rubber, Solid Or Covered
ROOF DECKS
ROOFING GRANULES
ROOFING MATERIALS: Asphalt
ROOFING MATERIALS: Sheet Metal
ROOM COOLERS: Portable
ROPE
RUBBER
RUBBER PRDTS: Appliance, Mechanical
RUBBER PRDTS: Automotive, Mechanical
RUBBER PRDTS: Mechanical
RUBBER PRDTS: Medical & Surgical Tubing, Extrudd & Lathe-Cut
RUBBER PRDTS: Oil & Gas Field Machinery, Mechanical
RUBBER PRDTS: Sheeting
RUBBER PRDTS: Silicone
RUBBER PRDTS: Sponge
RUBBER PRDTS: Wet Suits
RUBBER STAMP, WHOLESALE
RUBBER STRUCTURES: Air-Supported
RUGS : Tufted
RULERS: Metal
RUST RESISTING

S

SAFES & VAULTS: Metal
SAFETY EQPT & SPLYS WHOLESALERS
SAFETY INSPECTION SVCS
SAILS
SALES PROMOTION SVCS
SALT
SALT & SULFUR MINING
SAMPLE BOOKS
SAND & GRAVEL
SAND MINING
SAND: Hygrade
SANITARY SVC, NEC
SANITARY SVCS: Chemical Detoxification
SANITARY SVCS: Environmental Cleanup
SANITARY SVCS: Radioactive Waste Materials, Disposal
SANITARY SVCS: Refuse Collection & Disposal Svcs
SANITARY SVCS: Sewage Treatment Facility
SANITARY SVCS: Waste Materials, Recycling
SANITARY WARE: Metal
SANITATION CHEMICALS & CLEANING AGENTS
SASHES: Door Or Window, Metal
SATELLITE COMMUNICATIONS EQPT
SATELLITES: Communications
SAW BLADES
SAWDUST & SHAVINGS
SAWING & PLANING MILLS
SAWING & PLANING MILLS: Custom
SAWS & SAWING EQPT
SCALES & BALANCES, EXC LABORATORY
SCALES: Indl
SCANNING DEVICES: Optical
SCHOOL BUS SVC
SCHOOLS: Vocational, NEC
SCIENTIFIC INSTRUMENTS WHOLESALERS
SCRAP & WASTE MATERIALS, WHOLESALE: Metal
SCRAP & WASTE MATERIALS, WHOLESALE: Nonferrous Metals Scrap

SCRAP & WASTE MATERIALS, WHOLESALE: Paper
SCRAP & WASTE MATERIALS, WHOLESALE: Plastics
 Scrap
SCREENS: Window, Metal
SCREENS: Window, Wood Framed
SCREW MACHINE PRDTS
SCREW MACHINES
SCREWS: Metal
SEALANTS
SEALING COMPOUNDS: Sealing, synthetic rubber or plastic
SEALS: Hermetic
SEALS: Oil, Rubber
SEARCH & DETECTION SYSTEMS, EXC RADAR
SEARCH & NAVIGATION SYSTEMS
SEARCH & RESCUE SVCS
SEATING: Stadium
SECRETARIAL SVCS
SECURITY CONTROL EQPT & SYSTEMS
SECURITY DEVICES
SECURITY EQPT STORES
SECURITY PROTECTIVE DEVICES MAINTENANCE &
 MONITORING SVCS
SECURITY SYSTEMS SERVICES
SEMICONDUCTOR CIRCUIT NETWORKS
SEMICONDUCTORS & RELATED DEVICES
SENSORS: Radiation
SENSORS: Temperature For Motor Windings
SENSORS: Temperature, Exc Indl Process
SEPTIC TANKS: Concrete
SEWAGE & WATER TREATMENT EQPT
SEWAGE TREATMENT SYSTEMS & EQPT
SEWING CONTRACTORS
SEWING MACHINES & PARTS: Indl
SHADES: Lamp & Light, Residential
SHADES: Lamp Or Candle
SHADES: Window
SHAPES & PILINGS, STRUCTURAL: Steel
SHAPES: Extruded, Aluminum, NEC
SHAVING PREPARATIONS
SHEET METAL SPECIALTIES, EXC STAMPED
SHEETING: Laminated Plastic
SHEETS & SHEETINGS, COTTON
SHEETS: Fabric, From Purchased Materials
SHELLAC
SHELTERED WORKSHOPS
SHELVES & SHELVING: Wood
SHERARDIZING SVC: Metals Or Metal Prdts
SHIELDS OR ENCLOSURES: Radiator, Sheet Metal
SHIMS: Metal
SHIP BLDG/RPRG: Submersible Marine Robots, Manned/Un-
 manned
SHIP BUILDING & REPAIRING: Cargo, Commercial
SHIP BUILDING & REPAIRING: Dredges
SHIP BUILDING & REPAIRING: Fishing Vessels, Large
SHIP BUILDING & REPAIRING: Passenger, Commercial
SHIP BUILDING & REPAIRING: Rigging, Marine
SHIPBUILDING & REPAIR
SHIPPING AGENTS
SHOE MATERIALS: Counters
SHOE MATERIALS: Quarters
SHOE MATERIALS: Rands
SHOE MATERIALS: Rubber
SHOE STORES
SHOE STORES: Athletic
SHOE STORES: Children's
SHOE STORES: Orthopedic
SHOES & BOOTS WHOLESALERS
SHOES: Athletic, Exc Rubber Or Plastic
SHOES: Ballet Slippers
SHOES: Canvas, Rubber Soled
SHOES: Children's, Sandals, Exc Rubber Or Plastic
SHOES: Men's
SHOES: Orthopedic, Children's
SHOES: Orthopedic, Men's
SHOES: Orthopedic, Women's
SHOES: Plastic Or Rubber
SHOES: Plastic Or Rubber Soles With Fabric Uppers
SHOES: Rubber Or Rubber Soled Fabric Uppers
SHOES: Women's, Dress
SHOWCASES & DISPLAY FIXTURES: Office & Store
SHOWER STALLS: Metal
SHREDDERS: Indl & Commercial
SIDING & STRUCTURAL MATERIALS: Wood
SIDING: Sheet Metal
SIGN LETTERING & PAINTING SVCS

SIGN PAINTING & LETTERING SHOP
SIGNALING APPARATUS: Electric
SIGNALS: Traffic Control, Electric
SIGNALS: Transportation
SIGNS & ADVERTISING SPECIALTIES
SIGNS & ADVERTISING SPECIALTIES: Artwork, Advertising
SIGNS & ADVERTISING SPECIALTIES: Displays, Paint
 Process
SIGNS & ADVERTISING SPECIALTIES: Novelties
SIGNS & ADVERTISING SPECIALTIES: Signs
SIGNS & ADVERTSG SPECIALTIES: Displays/Cutouts Win-
 dow/Lobby
SIGNS, ELECTRICAL: Wholesalers
SIGNS, EXC ELECTRIC, WHOLESALE
SIGNS: Electrical
SIGNS: Neon
SILICA MINING
SILICON WAFERS: Chemically Doped
SILICONES
SILK SCREEN DESIGN SVCS
SILVER ORES
SILVERWARE & PLATED WARE
SIMULATORS: Flight
SINK TOPS, PLASTIC LAMINATED
SIRENS: Vehicle, Marine, Indl & Warning
SKIN CARE PRDTS: Suntan Lotions & Oils
SKYLIGHTS
SLAB & TILE, ROOFING: Concrete
SLAB & TILE: Precast Concrete, Floor
SLAB, CROSSING: Concrete
SLAUGHTERING & MEAT PACKING
SLIDES & EXHIBITS: Prepared
SLINGS: Lifting, Made From Purchased Wire
SLIP RINGS
SLIPCOVERS & PADS
SLIPPERS: House
SMOKE DETECTORS
SMOKERS' SPLYS, WHOLESALE
SNOW PLOWING SVCS
SOAPS & DETERGENTS
SOAPS & DETERGENTS: Dishwashing Compounds
SOAPSTONE MINING
SOCIAL SVCS: Individual & Family
SOFT DRINKS WHOLESALERS
SOFTWARE PUBLISHERS: Application
SOFTWARE PUBLISHERS: Business & Professional
SOFTWARE PUBLISHERS: Computer Utilities
SOFTWARE PUBLISHERS: Education
SOFTWARE PUBLISHERS: Home Entertainment
SOFTWARE PUBLISHERS: NEC
SOFTWARE PUBLISHERS: Operating Systems
SOFTWARE PUBLISHERS: Publisher's
SOFTWARE TRAINING, COMPUTER
SOLAR CELLS
SOLAR HEATING EQPT
SOLDERING EQPT: Electrical, Exc Handheld
SOLDERING EQPT: Electrical, Handheld
SOLDERS
SOLVENTS
SOLVENTS: Organic
SONAR SYSTEMS & EQPT
SOUND REPRODUCING EQPT
SOUVENIR SHOPS
SOUVENIRS, WHOLESALE
SPACE VEHICLE EQPT
SPACE VEHICLES
SPEAKER MONITORS
SPEAKER SYSTEMS
SPECIAL EVENTS DECORATION SVCS
SPECIALTY FOOD STORES: Coffee
SPECIALTY FOOD STORES: Health & Dietetic Food
SPECIALTY FOOD STORES: Juices, Fruit Or Vegetable
SPECIALTY FOOD STORES: Tea
SPECIALTY FOOD STORES: Vitamin
SPECIALTY OUTPATIENT CLINICS, NEC
SPICE & HERB STORES
SPONGES: Bleached & Dyed
SPOOLS: Fiber, Made From Purchased Materials
SPORTING & ATHLETIC GOODS: Bowling Alleys & Access
SPORTING & ATHLETIC GOODS: Cases, Gun & Rod
SPORTING & ATHLETIC GOODS: Driving Ranges, Golf,
 Electronic
SPORTING & ATHLETIC GOODS: Fishing Eqpt
SPORTING & ATHLETIC GOODS: Fishing Tackle, General

SPORTING & ATHLETIC GOODS: Guards, Football, Soccer,
 Etc
SPORTING & ATHLETIC GOODS: Gymnasium Eqpt
SPORTING & ATHLETIC GOODS: Hockey Eqpt & Splys, NEC
SPORTING & ATHLETIC GOODS: Hunting Eqpt
SPORTING & ATHLETIC GOODS: Pools, Swimming, Exc
 Plastic
SPORTING & ATHLETIC GOODS: Pools, Swimming, Plastic
SPORTING & ATHLETIC GOODS: Rackets/Frames, Tennis,
 Etc
SPORTING & ATHLETIC GOODS: Rods & Rod Parts, Fishing
SPORTING & ATHLETIC GOODS: Shafts, Golf Club
SPORTING & ATHLETIC GOODS: Shooting Eqpt & Splys,
 General
SPORTING & ATHLETIC GOODS: Skateboards
SPORTING & ATHLETIC GOODS: Target Shooting Eqpt
SPORTING & ATHLETIC GOODS: Targets, Archery & Rifle
 Shooting
SPORTING & ATHLETIC GOODS: Team Sports Eqpt
SPORTING & ATHLETIC GOODS: Tennis Eqpt & Splys
SPORTING & ATHLETIC GOODS: Track & Field Athletic Eqpt
SPORTING & ATHLETIC GOODS: Treadmills
SPORTING & ATHLETIC GOODS: Water Sports Eqpt
SPORTING & ATHLETIC GOODS: Winter Sports
SPORTING & RECREATIONAL GOODS & SPLYS WHOLE-
 SALERS
SPORTING & RECREATIONAL GOODS, WHOLESALE: Ath-
 letic Goods
SPORTING & RECREATIONAL GOODS, WHOLESALE: Boat
 Access & Part
SPORTING & RECREATIONAL GOODS, WHOLESALE: Fish-
 ing
SPORTING & RECREATIONAL GOODS, WHOLESALE: Fish-
 ing Tackle
SPORTING & RECREATIONAL GOODS, WHOLESALE: Golf
SPORTING & RECREATIONAL GOODS, WHOLESALE: Surf-
 ing
SPORTING GOODS
SPORTING GOODS STORES, NEC
SPORTING GOODS STORES: Ammunition
SPORTING GOODS STORES: Baseball Eqpt
SPORTING GOODS STORES: Camping Eqpt
SPORTING GOODS STORES: Firearms
SPORTING GOODS STORES: Hockey Eqpt, Exc Skates
SPORTING GOODS STORES: Pool & Billiard Tables
SPORTING GOODS STORES: Specialty Sport Splys, NEC
SPORTING GOODS STORES: Surfing Eqpt & Splys
SPORTING GOODS STORES: Team sports Eqpt
SPORTING GOODS: Fishing Nets
SPORTING GOODS: Surfboards
SPORTING/ATHLETIC GOODS: Gloves, Boxing, Handball,
 Etc
SPORTS APPAREL STORES
SPORTS CLUBS, MANAGERS & PROMOTERS
SPOUTING: Plastic & Fiberglass Reinforced
SPOUTS: Sheet Metal
SPRAYING & DUSTING EQPT
SPRAYING EQPT: Agricultural
SPRAYS: Artificial & Preserved
SPRINGS: Coiled Flat
SPRINGS: Steel
SPRINGS: Wire
SPRINKLING SYSTEMS: Fire Control
SQUIBS: Electric
STAFFING, EMPLOYMENT PLACEMENT
STAINLESS STEEL
STAINLESS STEEL WARE
STAIRCASES & STAIRS, WOOD
STAMPINGS: Automotive
STAMPINGS: Metal
STAPLES
STAPLES: Steel, Wire Or Cut
STATIONARY & OFFICE SPLYS, WHOL: Computer/Photo-
 copying Splys
STATIONARY & OFFICE SPLYS, WHOLESALE: Blank Books
STATIONARY & OFFICE SPLYS, WHOLESALE: Inked Rib-
 bons
STATIONARY & OFFICE SPLYS, WHOLESALE: Marking De-
 vices
STATIONARY/OFFICE SPLYS, WHOL: Soc Stationery/Greet-
 ing Cards
STATIONARY & OFFICE SPLYS WHOLESALERS
STATIONERY ARTICLES: Pottery
STATIONERY PRDTS
STATIONERY: Made From Purchased Materials

STATUES: Nonmetal
STEEL & ALLOYS: Tool & Die
STEEL FABRICATORS
STEEL MILLS
STEEL, COLD-ROLLED: Strip NEC, From Purchased Hot-Rolled
STEEL, HOT-ROLLED: Sheet Or Strip
STEEL: Cold-Rolled
STEEL: Laminated
STENCILS
STONE: Cast Concrete
STONE: Dimension, NEC
STONE: Quarrying & Processing, Own Stone Prdts
STORE FIXTURES: Exc Wood
STORE FIXTURES: Wood
STORES: Auto & Home Supply
STRAINERS: Line, Piping Systems
STRAPPING
STRAPS: Apparel Webbing
STRAPS: Bindings, Textile
STRAPS: Braids, Textile
STRIPS: Copper & Copper Alloy
STRUCTURAL SUPPORT & BUILDING MATERIAL: Concrete
STUCCO
STUDIOS: Artists & Artists' Studios
STUDS & JOISTS: Sheet Metal
SUBSCRIPTION FULFILLMENT SVCS: Magazine, Newspaper, Etc
SUGAR SUBSTITUTES: Organic
SUGAR SUBSTITUTES: Sorbitol
SUNDRIES & RELATED PRDTS: Medical & Laboratory, Rubber
SUPERMARKETS & OTHER GROCERY STORES
SUPPOSITORIES
SURFACE ACTIVE AGENTS
SURFACE ACTIVE AGENTS: Penetrants
SURFACE ACTIVE AGENTS: Softeners, Textile Assisting
SURFACE ACTIVE AGENTS: Textile Processing Assistants
SURGICAL & MEDICAL INSTRUMENTS WHOLESALERS
SURGICAL APPLIANCES & SPLYS
SURGICAL APPLIANCES & SPLYS
SURGICAL EQPT: See Also Instruments
SURGICAL IMPLANTS
SURVEYING & MAPPING: Land Parcels
SURVEYING SVCS: Photogrammetric Engineering
SVC ESTABLISH EQPT, WHOLESALE: Carpet/Rug Clean Eqpt & Sply
SVC ESTABLISHMENT EQPT & SPLYS WHOLESALERS
SVC ESTABLISHMENT EQPT, WHOL: Cleaning & Maint Eqpt & Splys
SVC ESTABLISHMENT EQPT, WHOL: Concrete Burial Vaults & Boxes
SVC ESTABLISHMENT EQPT, WHOLESALE: Beauty Parlor Eqpt & Sply
SVC ESTABLISHMENT EQPT, WHOLESALE: Floor Machinery, Maint
SVC ESTABLISHMENT EQPT, WHOLESALE: Vacuum Cleaning Systems
SWEEPING COMPOUNDS
SWIMMING POOL & HOT TUB CLEANING & MAINTENANCE SVCS
SWIMMING POOL ACCESS: Leaf Skimmers Or Pool Rakes
SWIMMING POOL EQPT: Filters & Water Conditioning Systems
SWIMMING POOL SPLY STORES
SWIMMING POOLS, EQPT & SPLYS: Wholesalers
SWITCHES
SWITCHES: Electric Power
SWITCHES: Electric Power, Exc Snap, Push Button, Etc
SWITCHES: Electronic
SWITCHES: Electronic Applications
SWITCHES: Time, Electrical Switchgear Apparatus
SWITCHGEAR & SWITCHBOARD APPARATUS
SWITCHING EQPT: Radio & Television Communications
SYRUPS, DRINK
SYRUPS: Pharmaceutical
SYSTEMS ENGINEERING: Computer Related
SYSTEMS INTEGRATION SVCS
SYSTEMS INTEGRATION SVCS: Office Computer Automation
SYSTEMS SOFTWARE DEVELOPMENT SVCS

T

TABLE OR COUNTERTOPS, PLASTIC LAMINATED
TABLE TOPS: Porcelain Enameled

TABLECLOTHS & SETTINGS
TABLES: Lift, Hydraulic
TABLETS: Bronze Or Other Metal
TAGS & LABELS: Paper
TAGS: Paper, Blank, Made From Purchased Paper
TANK COMPONENTS: Military, Specialized
TANK REPAIR SVCS
TANKS & OTHER TRACKED VEHICLE CMPNTS
TANKS: Concrete
TANKS: Cryogenic, Metal
TANKS: Fuel, Including Oil & Gas, Metal Plate
TANKS: Lined, Metal
TANKS: Plastic & Fiberglass
TANKS: Standard Or Custom Fabricated, Metal Plate
TANKS: Water, Metal Plate
TANNERIES: Leather
TANNING AGENTS: Synthetic Organic
TANNING SALON EQPT & SPLYS, WHOLESALE
TANNING SALONS
TAPE DRIVES
TAPE STORAGE UNITS: Computer
TAPES, ADHESIVE: Medical
TAPES: Fabric
TAPES: Gummed, Cloth Or Paper Based, From Purchased Matls
TAPES: Pressure Sensitive
TARGET DRONES
TELECOMMUNICATION EQPT REPAIR SVCS, EXC TELEPHONES
TELECOMMUNICATION SYSTEMS & EQPT
TELECOMMUNICATIONS CARRIERS & SVCS: Wired
TELECOMMUNICATIONS CARRIERS & SVCS: Wireless
TELEGRAPHS & RELATED APPARATUS
TELEMARKETING BUREAUS
TELEMETERING EQPT
TELEPHONE ANSWERING MACHINES
TELEPHONE BOOTHS, EXC WOOD
TELEPHONE CENTRAL OFFICE EQPT: Dial Or Manual
TELEPHONE EQPT INSTALLATION
TELEPHONE EQPT: NEC
TELEPHONE STATION EQPT & PARTS: Wire
TELEPHONE SWITCHING EQPT
TELEPHONE SWITCHING EQPT: Toll Switching
TELEPHONE: Automatic Dialers
TELEPHONE: Fiber Optic Systems
TELEPHONE: Switchboards
TELEVISION BROADCASTING & COMMUNICATIONS EQPT
TELEVISION SETS
TELEVISION SETS WHOLESALERS
TELEVISION: Closed Circuit Eqpt
TEMPORARY HELP SVCS
TEN PIN CENTERS
TERMINAL BOARDS
TEST BORING SVCS: Nonmetallic Minerals
TEST KITS: Pregnancy
TESTERS: Battery
TESTERS: Environmental
TESTERS: Gas, Exc Indl Process
TESTERS: Integrated Circuit
TESTERS: Liquid, Exc Indl Process
TESTERS: Physical Property
TEXTILE & APPAREL SVCS
TEXTILE BAGS WHOLESALERS
TEXTILE CONVERTERS: Knit Goods
TEXTILE FABRICATORS
TEXTILE FINISH: Chem Coat/Treat, Fire Resist, Manmade
TEXTILE FINISHING: Calendering, Cotton
TEXTILE FINISHING: Chem Coating/Treating, Broadwoven, Cotton
TEXTILE FINISHING: Decorative, Cotton, Broadwoven
TEXTILE FINISHING: Dyeing, Broadwoven, Cotton
TEXTILE FINISHING: Dyeing, Manmade Fiber & Silk, Broadwoven
TEXTILE FINISHING: Embossing, Cotton, Broadwoven
TEXTILE MACHINERY ACCESS, HARDWOOD
TEXTILE: Finishing, Cotton Broadwoven
TEXTILE: Finishing, Raw Stock NEC
TEXTILE: Goods, NEC
TEXTILES
TEXTILES: Crash, Linen
TEXTILES: Linen Fabrics
TEXTILES: Mill Waste & Remnant
TEXTILES: Padding & Wadding
THEATRICAL SCENERY
THEOLOGICAL SEMINARIES

THERMOMETERS: Medical, Digital
THERMOPLASTIC MATERIALS
THERMOPLASTICS
THERMOSETTING MATERIALS
THREAD: Embroidery
THYROID PREPARATIONS
TIES, FORM: Metal
TILE: Asphalt, Floor
TILE: Brick & Structural, Clay
TILE: Clay, Drain & Structural
TILE: Mosaic, Ceramic
TILE: Vinyl, Asbestos
TILE: Wall & Floor, Ceramic
TILE: Wall, Ceramic
TIMING DEVICES: Electronic
TIN
TIRE & INNER TUBE MATERIALS & RELATED PRDTS
TIRE & TUBE REPAIR MATERIALS, WHOLESALE
TIRE CORD & FABRIC
TIRE DEALERS
TIRES & INNER TUBES
TIRES & TUBES, WHOLESALE: Automotive
TIRES: Truck
TITANIUM MILL PRDTS
TOBACCO & PRDTS, WHOLESALE: Cigarettes
TOBACCO & PRDTS, WHOLESALE: Cigars
TOBACCO LEAF PROCESSING
TOBACCO: Cigarettes
TOBACCO: Cigars
TOILET PREPARATIONS
TOILET SEATS: Wood
TOILETRIES, COSMETICS & PERFUME STORES
TOILETRIES, WHOLESALE: Perfumes
TOILETRIES, WHOLESALE: Razor Blades
TOILETRIES, WHOLESALE: Toilet Soap
TOILETRIES, WHOLESALE: Toiletries
TOILETS: Portable Chemical, Plastics
TOOL & DIE STEEL
TOOLS: Hand
TOOLS: Hand, Jewelers'
TOOLS: Hand, Power
TOOLS: Hand, Stonecutters'
TOOTHPASTES, GELS & TOOTHPOWDERS
TOWELS: Fabric & Nonwoven, Made From Purchased Materials
TOWELS: Indl
TOWERS, SECTIONS: Transmission, Radio & Television
TOWING & TUGBOAT SVC
TOYS
TOYS & HOBBY GOODS & SPLYS, WHOLESALE: Amusement Goods
TOYS & HOBBY GOODS & SPLYS, WHOLESALE: Arts/Crafts Eqpt/Sply
TOYS & HOBBY GOODS & SPLYS, WHOLESALE: Dolls
TOYS & HOBBY GOODS & SPLYS, WHOLESALE: Toys & Games
TOYS, HOBBY GOODS & SPLYS WHOLESALERS
TOYS: Dolls, Stuffed Animals & Parts
TOYS: Electronic
TOYS: Rubber
TOYS: Video Game Machines
TRADE SHOW ARRANGEMENT SVCS
TRADING STAMP PROMOTION & REDEMPTION
TRAILERS & PARTS: Truck & Semi's
TRAILERS & TRAILER EQPT
TRAILERS: Bodies
TRAILERS: Demountable Cargo Containers
TRAILERS: Semitrailers, Truck Tractors
TRAILERS: Truck, Chassis
TRANSDUCERS: Pressure
TRANSFORMERS: Distribution
TRANSFORMERS: Distribution, Electric
TRANSFORMERS: Electric
TRANSFORMERS: Electronic
TRANSFORMERS: Machine Tool
TRANSFORMERS: Meters, Electronic
TRANSFORMERS: Power Related
TRANSFORMERS: Rectifier
TRANSFORMERS: Specialty
TRANSFORMERS: Tripping
TRANSISTORS
TRANSLATION & INTERPRETATION SVCS
TRANSMISSIONS: Motor Vehicle
TRANSPORTATION EPQT & SPLYS, WHOLESALE: Marine Crafts/Splys

TRANSPORTATION EPQT/SPLYS, WHOL: Guided Missiles/Space Veh
TRANSPORTATION EPQT/SPLYS, WHOL: Marine Propulsn Mach/Eqpt
TRANSPORTATION EQPT & SPLYS WHOLESALERS, NEC
TRANSPORTATION SVCS, WATER: Boat Cleaning
TRANSPORTATION SVCS, WATER: Intracoastal, Freight
TRANSPORTATION SVCS, WATER: Salvaging & Surveying, Marine
TRANSPORTATION SVCS: Railroads, Belt line
TRANSPORTATION: Deep Sea Domestic Freight
TRANSPORTATION: Deep Sea Foreign Freight
TRANSPORTATION: Local Passenger, NEC
TRANSPORTATION: Monorail Transit Systems
TRAP ROCK: Crushed & Broken
TRAPS: Animal & Fish, Wire
TRAVEL AGENCIES
TRAYS: Plastic
TRIM: Window, Wood
TROPHIES, NEC
TROPHIES, PLATED, ALL METALS
TROPHIES: Metal, Exc Silver
TROPHY & PLAQUE STORES
TRUCK & BUS BODIES: Ambulance
TRUCK & BUS BODIES: Automobile Wrecker Truck
TRUCK & BUS BODIES: Bus Bodies
TRUCK & BUS BODIES: Dump Truck
TRUCK & BUS BODIES: Tank Truck
TRUCK & BUS BODIES: Truck Cabs, Motor Vehicles
TRUCK & BUS BODIES: Truck, Motor Vehicle
TRUCK BODIES: Body Parts
TRUCK BODY SHOP
TRUCK DRIVER SVCS
TRUCK GENERAL REPAIR SVC
TRUCK PAINTING & LETTERING SVCS
TRUCK PARTS & ACCESSORIES: Wholesalers
TRUCKING & HAULING SVCS: Building Materials
TRUCKING & HAULING SVCS: Contract Basis
TRUCKING & HAULING SVCS: Haulage & Cartage, Light, Local
TRUCKING & HAULING SVCS: Hazardous Waste
TRUCKING & HAULING SVCS: Machinery, Heavy
TRUCKING & HAULING SVCS: Mail Carriers, Contract
TRUCKING & HAULING SVCS: Petroleum, Local
TRUCKING, AUTOMOBILE CARRIER
TRUCKING, DUMP
TRUCKING, REFRIGERATED: Long-Distance
TRUCKING: Except Local
TRUCKING: Local, With Storage
TRUCKING: Local, Without Storage
TRUCKS & TRACTORS: Industrial
TRUCKS, INDL: Wholesalers
TRUCKS: Forklift
TRUCKS: Indl
TRUSSES & FRAMING: Prefabricated Metal
TRUSSES: Wood, Floor
TRUSSES: Wood, Roof
TUB CONTAINERS: Plastic
TUBE & TUBING FABRICATORS
TUBES: Electron, NEC
TUBES: Light Sensing & Emitting
TUBES: Photomultiplier
TUBES: Steel & Iron
TUBING, COLD-DRAWN: Mech Or Hypodermic Sizes, Stainless
TUBING: Copper
TUBING: Flexible, Metallic
TUBING: Glass
TUBING: Plastic
TUBING: Seamless
TUNGSTEN MILL PRDTS
TURBINES & TURBINE GENERATOR SET UNITS, COMPLETE
TURBINES & TURBINE GENERATOR SET UNITS: Gas, Complete
TURBINES & TURBINE GENERATOR SETS
TURBINES: Hydraulic, Complete
TURBINES: Steam
TURKEY PROCESSING & SLAUGHTERING
TURNKEY VENDORS: Computer Systems
TWINE
TWINE PRDTS
TYPESETTING SVC
TYPESETTING SVC: Computer
TYPESETTING SVC: Hand Composition

TYPEWRITERS & PARTS
TYPOGRAPHY

U

ULTRASONIC EQPT: Cleaning, Exc Med & Dental
ULTRASONIC EQPT: Dental
UMBRELLAS & CANES
UMBRELLAS: Garden Or Wagon
UNIFORM STORES
UNSUPPORTED PLASTICS: Floor Or Wall Covering
UPHOLSTERY WORK SVCS
USED BOOK STORES
USED CAR DEALERS
USED MERCHANDISE STORES
USED MERCHANDISE STORES: Building Materials
USED MERCHANDISE STORES: Musical Instruments
UTENSILS: Household, Cooking & Kitchen, Metal
UTENSILS: Household, Cooking & Kitchen, Porcelain Enameled

V

VACUUM CLEANER STORES
VACUUM CLEANERS: Household
VACUUM CLEANERS: Indl Type
VACUUM PUMPS & EQPT: Laboratory
VACUUM SYSTEMS: Air Extraction, Indl
VALUE-ADDED RESELLERS: Computer Systems
VALVE REPAIR SVCS, INDL
VALVES
VALVES & PARTS: Gas, Indl
VALVES & PIPE FITTINGS
VALVES & REGULATORS: Pressure, Indl
VALVES Solenoid
VALVES: Aerosol, Metal
VALVES: Aircraft, Control, Hydraulic & Pneumatic
VALVES: Aircraft, Hydraulic
VALVES: Control, Automatic
VALVES: Fire Hydrant
VALVES: Fluid Power, Control, Hydraulic & pneumatic
VALVES: Indl
VALVES: Plumbing & Heating
VALVES: Regulating & Control, Automatic
VALVES: Regulating, Process Control
VALVES: Water Works
VANILLIN: Synthetic
VARNISHES, NEC
VARNISHING SVC: Metal Prdts
VAULTS & SAFES WHOLESALERS
VEGETABLE OILS: Medicinal Grade, Refined Or Concentrated
VEGETABLES, FROZEN: Wholesaler
VEHICLES: All Terrain
VENDING MACHINES & PARTS
VENETIAN BLIND REPAIR SHOP
VENETIAN BLINDS & SHADES
VENTILATING EQPT: Metal
VENTILATING EQPT: Sheet Metal
VERIFIERS: Punch Card
VESSELS: Process, Indl, Metal Plate
VETERINARY PHARMACEUTICAL PREPARATIONS
VETERINARY PRDTS: Instruments & Apparatus
VIALS: Glass
VIDEO & AUDIO EQPT, WHOLESALE
VIDEO EQPT
VIDEO REPAIR SVCS
VIDEO TAPE PRODUCTION SVCS
VISUAL COMMUNICATIONS SYSTEMS
VISUAL EFFECTS PRODUCTION SVCS
VITAMINS: Natural Or Synthetic, Uncompounded, Bulk
VITAMINS: Pharmaceutical Preparations
VOCATIONAL REHABILITATION AGENCY
VOCATIONAL TRAINING AGENCY

W

WALL COVERINGS: Rubber
WALLBOARD: Gypsum
WALLPAPER & WALL COVERINGS
WALLPAPER: Embossed Plastic, Textile Backed
WALLS: Curtain, Metal
WAREHOUSING & STORAGE FACILITIES, NEC
WAREHOUSING & STORAGE, REFRIGERATED: Cold Storage Or Refrig
WAREHOUSING & STORAGE: Fur
WAREHOUSING & STORAGE: General

WAREHOUSING & STORAGE: General
WAREHOUSING & STORAGE: Household Goods
WAREHOUSING & STORAGE: Miniwarehouse
WAREHOUSING & STORAGE: Self Storage
WARFARE COUNTER-MEASURE EQPT
WARM AIR HEATING & AC EQPT & SPLYS, WHOLESALE Air Filters
WARM AIR HEATING & AC EQPT & SPLYS, WHOLESALE Furnaces
WARM AIR HEATING/AC EQPT/SPLYS, WHOL Dehumidifiers, Exc Port
WARM AIR HEATING/AC EQPT/SPLYS, WHOL Warm Air Htg Eqpt/Splys
WARP KNIT FABRIC FINISHING
WASHCLOTHS & BATH MITTS, FROM PURCHASED MATERIALS
WASHERS: Metal
WASHERS: Rubber
WATCH & CLOCK STORES
WATCH REPAIR SVCS
WATCHES
WATER HEATERS
WATER PURIFICATION EQPT: Household
WATER PURIFICATION PRDTS: Chlorination Tablets & Kits
WATER SOFTENER SVCS
WATER SPLY: Irrigation
WATER SUPPLY
WATER TREATMENT EQPT: Indl
WATER: Mineral, Carbonated, Canned & Bottled, Etc
WATER: Pasteurized & Mineral, Bottled & Canned
WATER: Pasteurized, Canned & Bottled, Etc
WAXES: Petroleum, Not Produced In Petroleum Refineries
WEATHER STRIP: Sponge Rubber
WEATHER STRIPS: Metal
WEDDING CONSULTING SVCS
WEIGHING MACHINERY & APPARATUS
WEIGHING SVCS: Food & Commodity
WELDING & CUTTING APPARATUS & ACCESS, NEC
WELDING EQPT
WELDING EQPT & SPLYS WHOLESALERS
WELDING EQPT & SPLYS: Electrodes
WELDING EQPT REPAIR SVCS
WELDING EQPT: Electric
WELDING EQPT: Electrical
WELDING REPAIR SVC
WELDING SPLYS, EXC GASES: Wholesalers
WELDING TIPS: Heat Resistant, Metal
WELDMENTS
WET CORN MILLING
WHEELCHAIR LIFTS
WHEELCHAIRS
WHEELS
WHEELS & PARTS
WHEELS: Abrasive
WHEELS: Buffing & Polishing
WHEELS: Water
WHIRLPOOL BATHS: Hydrotherapy
WIG & HAIRPIECE STORES
WIGS & HAIRPIECES
WIGS, DOLL: Hair
WIGS, WHOLESALE
WINCHES
WIND TUNNELS
WINDINGS: Coil, Electronic
WINDMILLS: Electric Power Generation
WINDOW & DOOR FRAMES
WINDOW FRAMES & SASHES: Plastic
WINDOW FRAMES, MOLDING & TRIM: Vinyl
WINDOWS: Frames, Wood
WINE CELLARS, BONDED: Wine, Blended
WIRE
WIRE & CABLE: Aluminum
WIRE & CABLE: Nonferrous, Aircraft
WIRE & CABLE: Nonferrous, Automotive, Exc Ignition Sets
WIRE & CABLE: Nonferrous, Building
WIRE & WIRE PRDTS
WIRE CLOTH & WOVEN WIRE PRDTS, MADE FROM PURCHASED WIRE
WIRE FENCING & ACCESS WHOLESALERS
WIRE MATERIALS: Copper
WIRE MATERIALS: Steel
WIRE PRDTS: Ferrous Or Iron, Made In Wiredrawing Plants
WIRE PRDTS: Steel & Iron
WIRE: Communication
WIRE: Mesh

INDEX

WIRE: Nonferrous
WIRE: Nonferrous, Appliance Fixture
WIRE: Steel, Insulated Or Armored
WIRING DEVICES WHOLESALERS
WOMEN'S & CHILDREN'S CLOTHING WHOLESALERS, NEC
WOMEN'S & GIRLS' SPORTSWEAR WHOLESALERS
WOMEN'S CLOTHING STORES
WOMEN'S CLOTHING STORES: Ready-To-Wear
WOMEN'S SPECIALTY CLOTHING STORES
WOMEN'S SPORTSWEAR STORES
WOOD FENCING WHOLESALERS
WOOD PRDTS: Door Trim
WOOD PRDTS: Moldings, Unfinished & Prefinished
WOOD PRDTS: Mulch Or Sawdust
WOOD PRDTS: Mulch, Wood & Bark

WOOD PRDTS: Poles
WOOD PRDTS: Policemen's Clubs
WOOD PRDTS: Trophy Bases
WOOD PRDTS: Veneer Work, Inlaid
WOOD PRDTS: Yard Sticks
WOOD PRODUCTS: Reconstituted
WOOD TREATING: Creosoting
WOOD TREATING: Flooring, Block
WOOD TREATING: Wood Prdts, Creosoted
WOODWORK & TRIM: Exterior & Ornamental
WOODWORK & TRIM: Interior & Ornamental
WOODWORK: Carved & Turned
WOODWORK: Interior & Ornamental, NEC
WOOL: Glass
WORD PROCESSING SVCS
WOVEN WIRE PRDTS, NEC

WRENCHES
WRITING FOR PUBLICATION SVCS

X-RAY EQPT & TUBES

YACHT BASIN OPERATIONS
YARN & YARN SPINNING
YARN : Crochet, Spun
YARN MILLS: Texturizing
YARN MILLS: Texturizing, Throwing & Twisting
YARN MILLS: Throwing
YARN WHOLESALERS
YARN: Manmade & Synthetic Fiber, Twisting Or Winding
YARN: Specialty & Novelty

PRODUCT SECTION

ABRASIVES

3M Company..B...... 973 884-2500
Whippany *(G-12004)*

Advanced Abrasives Corporation.........F...... 856 665-9300
Pennsauken *(G-8471)*

Beacut Abrasives Corp.........................F...... 973 249-1420
East Rutherford *(G-2283)*

Chessco Industries Inc.........................E...... 609 882-0400
Ewing *(G-3008)*

Lunzer Inc..G...... 201 794-2800
Englewood *(G-2911)*

Mercury Floor Machines Inc..................E...... 201 568-4606
Englewood *(G-2915)*

New Jersey Diamond Products Co........F...... 973 684-0949
Paterson *(G-8349)*

Robinson Tech Intl Corp.......................G...... 973 287-6458
Fairfield *(G-3296)*

William R Hall Co.................................E...... 856 784-6700
Lindenwold *(G-5464)*

ABRASIVES: Polishing Rouge

Agsco Corporation...............................E...... 973 244-0005
Pine Brook *(G-8681)*

ACADEMIC TUTORING SVCS

Davis Center Inc..................................G...... 862 251-4637
Succasunna *(G-10622)*

ACCELERATION INDICATORS & SYSTEM COMPONENTS: Aerospace

Princton Satellite Systems Inc.............G...... 609 275-9606
Plainsboro *(G-8896)*

ACCELERATORS, RUBBER PROCESSING: Cyclic or Acyclic

Brown Chemical Co Inc........................E...... 201 337-0900
Oakland *(G-7677)*

ACCOUNTING MACHINES & CASH REGISTERS

Worldwide Pt SL Ltd Lblty Co...............F...... 201 928-0222
Teaneck *(G-10777)*

ACIDS

Evans Chemetics LP............................D...... 201 992-3100
Teaneck *(G-10753)*

ACIDS: Boric

Solvay Holding Inc...............................A...... 609 860-4000
Princeton *(G-9121)*

Solvay USA Inc....................................C...... 732 297-0100
North Brunswick *(G-7538)*

ACRYLIC RESINS

United Resin Inc..................................F...... 856 358-2574
Elmer *(G-2799)*

ACTUATORS: Indl, NEC

Textol Systems Inc..............................E...... 800 624-8746
Carlstadt *(G-1228)*

Valcor Engineering Corporation............E...... 973 467-8400
Springfield *(G-10585)*

Whippany Actuation Systems LLC........C...... 973 428-9898
Whippany *(G-12043)*

ACUPUNCTURISTS' OFFICES

Holmdel Acpnctr & Ntrl Med Ctr...........G...... 732 888-4910
Holmdel *(G-4517)*

ADDITIVE BASED PLASTIC MATERIALS: Plasticizers

Composecure LLC................................C...... 908 518-0500
Somerset *(G-10083)*

Composecure LLC................................C...... 908 518-0500
Somerset *(G-10084)*

Technology Reviews Inc.......................G...... 973 537-9511
Randolph *(G-9301)*

ADHESIVES

Amb Enterprises LLC...........................E...... 973 225-1070
Paterson *(G-8206)*

Amerasia Intl Tech Inc.........................E...... 609 799-9388
Princeton Junction *(G-9147)*

American Chemical & Coating Co.........G...... 908 353-2260
Elizabeth *(G-2710)*

Annitti Enterprises Inc.........................E...... 973 345-1725
Paterson *(G-8213)*

Baker/Titan Adhesives.........................E...... 973 225-1070
Paterson *(G-8219)*

Bostik Inc...D...... 856 848-8669
Paulsboro *(G-8414)*

Cardolite Corporation...........................E...... 609 436-0902
Monmouth Junction *(G-6335)*

Coim USA Inc.......................................D...... 856 224-8560
West Deptford *(G-11825)*

Dritac Flooring Products LLC................F...... 973 614-9000
Clifton *(G-1605)*

Elektromek Inc.....................................F...... 973 614-9000
Clifton *(G-1615)*

Frimpeks Inc..F...... 201 266-0116
Fairfield *(G-3202)*

HB Fuller Company...............................E...... 732 287-8330
Edison *(G-2535)*

Henkel US Operations Corp..................E...... 908 685-7000
Bridgewater *(G-843)*

Hercules LLC.......................................G...... 732 777-4697
Edison *(G-2537)*

Master Bond Inc...................................E...... 201 343-8983
Hackensack *(G-3943)*

Mercury Adhesives Inc.........................G...... 973 472-3307
Passaic *(G-8162)*

Mon-Eco Industries Inc........................F...... 732 257-7942
East Brunswick *(G-2167)*

National Casein New Jersey Inc............E...... 856 829-1880
Cinnaminson *(G-1480)*

Natl Adhesies Div of Henke..................G...... 908 685-7000
Bridgewater *(G-862)*

Norland Products Inc............................E...... 609 395-1966
Cranbury *(G-1863)*

Palmetto Adhesives Company..............F...... 856 451-0400
Bridgeton *(G-793)*

Petronio Shoe Products Corp...............F...... 973 751-7579
Belleville *(G-311)*

PPG Architectural Finishes Inc.............G...... 908 353-2477
Elizabeth *(G-2767)*

Solar Compounds Corporation..............E...... 908 862-2813
Linden *(G-5444)*

Steven Industries Inc...........................E...... 201 437-6500
Bayonne *(G-245)*

Synthetic Surfaces Inc.........................G...... 908 233-6803
Scotch Plains *(G-9858)*

Zymet Inc...E...... 973 428-5245
East Hanover *(G-2253)*

ADHESIVES & SEALANTS

A D M Tronics Unlimited Inc.................E...... 201 767-6040
Northvale *(G-7566)*

Alan Chemical Corporation Inc.............G...... 973 628-7777
Wayne *(G-11602)*

Alva-Tech Inc.......................................F...... 609 747-1133
Burlington Township *(G-997)*

American Casein Company....................E...... 609 387-2988
Burlington *(G-954)*

Andek Corporation................................F...... 856 866-7600
Moorestown *(G-6560)*

API Americas Inc..................................D...... 732 382-6800
Rahway *(G-9174)*

Artistic Bias Products Co Inc................E...... 732 382-4141
Rahway *(G-9175)*

Clark Stek-O Corp.................................D...... 201 437-0770
Bayonne *(G-218)*

Covalnce Spcalty Adhesives LLC.........A...... 732 356-2870
Middlesex *(G-6158)*

Custom Building Products Inc...............D...... 856 467-9226
Logan Township *(G-5612)*

Flexcraft Industries Inc........................G...... 973 589-3403
Newark *(G-7163)*

Gabhen Inc...C...... 800 631-3572
Totowa *(G-10945)*

Kop-Coat Inc..E...... 800 221-4466
Rockaway *(G-9582)*

Mapei Corporation................................F...... 732 254-4830
Swedesboro *(G-10708)*

Mapei Corporation................................E...... 732 254-4830
Swedesboro *(G-10707)*

Mc Ginley Packaging Methods..............G...... 201 493-9330
Midland Park *(G-6232)*

National Strch Chem Holdg Corp..........A...... 908 685-5000
Bridgewater *(G-861)*

Permabond LLC....................................G...... 610 323-5003
Somerset *(G-10153)*

Princeton Keynes Group Inc..................F...... 609 951-2239
Princeton *(G-9096)*

Princeton Keynes Group Inc..................F...... 609 208-1777
Newark *(G-7274)*

Rust-Oleum Corporation.......................F...... 732 652-2378
Newark *(G-7296)*

Saint-Gobain Prfmce Plas Corp............D...... 732 652-0910
Somerset *(G-10170)*

Spiral Binding LLC................................C...... 973 256-0666
Totowa *(G-10973)*

Universal Tape Supply Corp..................F...... 609 653-3191
Somers Point *(G-10048)*

ADHESIVES: Adhesives, paste

Aos Thermal Compounds LLC..............F...... 732 389-5514
Eatontown *(G-2383)*

ADHESIVES: Adhesives, plastic

Clifton Adhesive Inc.............................E...... 973 694-0845
Wayne *(G-11619)*

ADHESIVES: Epoxy

Sika Corporation..................................B...... 201 933-8800
Lyndhurst *(G-5708)*

ADVERTISING AGENCIES

Access Response Inc............................G...... 732 660-0770
Ocean *(G-7712)*

Advertisers Service Group Inc..............F...... 201 440-5577
Ridgefield Park *(G-9395)*

B T O Industries Inc.............................G...... 973 243-0011
West Orange *(G-11888)*

Employee Codes: A=Over 500 employees, B=251-500
C=101-250, D=51-100, E=20-50, F=10-19, G=4-9

2018 Harris New jersey
Manufacturers Directory

791

PRODUCT

Corporate Mailings Inc ....C 973 439-1168
West Caldwell *(G-11772)*

Corporate Mailings Inc ....D 973 808-0009
Whippany *(G-12017)*

Display Works LLC ....C 201 327-1260
Parsippany *(G-7983)*

Gail Gersons Wine & Dine Resta ....G 732 758-0888
Shrewsbury *(G-9999)*

Global Graphics Intergration ....F 973 334-9653
Towaco *(G-10996)*

Healthstar Communications Inc ....A 201 560-5370
Mahwah *(G-5780)*

Killian Graphics ....G 973 635-5844
Chatham *(G-1332)*

Moscova Enterprises Inc ....F 848 628-4873
Jersey City *(G-4786)*

Neighborhood Shoppers ....G 856 988-7722
Marlton *(G-5989)*

Nema Associates Inc ....F 973 274-0052
Linden *(G-5418)*

Polaris Communications Inc ....F 201 928-0780
Teaneck *(G-10769)*

Pro-Pack Corp ....G 908 725-5000
Branchburg *(G-694)*

Prohaska & Co Inc ....G 732 238-3420
East Brunswick *(G-2176)*

Schellmark Inc ....G 732 345-7143
Tinton Falls *(G-10846)*

Slendertone Distribution Inc ....G 732 660-1177
Hoboken *(G-4497)*

Typecom LLC ....G 201 969-1901
Fort Lee *(G-3586)*

Wt Media LLC ....F 609 921-3490
Trenton *(G-11135)*

ADVERTISING AGENCIES: Consultants

Cherri Stone Interactive LLC ....G 844 843-7765
Lakewood *(G-5092)*

Digital Outdoor Advg LLC ....G 732 616-2232
Tinton Falls *(G-10830)*

Suzie Mac Specialties Inc ....E 732 238-3500
East Brunswick *(G-2191)*

Tap Into LLC ....G 908 370-1158
New Providence *(G-7056)*

ADVERTISING CURTAINS

Prestige Industries LLC ....E 866 492-2244
Lyndhurst *(G-5703)*

ADVERTISING DISPLAY PRDTS

Digital Outdoor Advg LLC ....G 732 616-2232
Tinton Falls *(G-10830)*

Display Works LLC ....C 201 327-1260
Parsippany *(G-7983)*

Hudson Displays Co ....E 973 623-8255
Newark *(G-7193)*

Pharmakon Corp ....F 856 829-3161
Cinnaminson *(G-1484)*

Power Packaging Services Corp ....G 201 261-2566
Paramus *(G-7897)*

Strategic Mktg Promotions Inc ....F 845 623-7777
Mahwah *(G-5816)*

Westrock Converting Company ....G 856 438-2200
Marlton *(G-6003)*

ADVERTISING MATERIAL DISTRIBUTION

Enertia LLC ....G 856 330-4767
Pennsauken *(G-8508)*

ADVERTISING REPRESENTATIVES: Electronic Media

Musings Press Ltd Liability Co ....F 347 210-8820
Union City *(G-11259)*

Retail Management Pubg Inc ....F 212 981-0217
Montclair *(G-6434)*

ADVERTISING REPRESENTATIVES: Media

Data Communique Inc ....E 201 508-6000
Ridgefield Park *(G-9402)*

Diacritech LLC ....A 732 238-1157
Jersey City *(G-4742)*

ADVERTISING REPRESENTATIVES: Newspaper

David Sisco Jr ....G 908 454-0880
Phillipsburg *(G-8646)*

Times of Trenton Pubg Corp ....A 609 989-5454
Trenton *(G-11121)*

ADVERTISING REPRESENTATIVES: Printed Media

J D M Associates Inc ....G 973 773-8699
Lodi *(G-5590)*

Progress Displays Inc ....G 908 757-6650
Edison *(G-2597)*

ADVERTISING SPECIALTIES, WHOLESALE

A&E Promotions LLC ....G 732 382-2300
Holmdel *(G-4506)*

ADS Sales Co Inc ....E 732 591-0500
Morganville *(G-6635)*

All Colors Screen Printing LLC ....G 732 777-6033
Highland Park *(G-4300)*

Circa Promotions Inc ....G 732 264-1200
Hazlet *(G-4273)*

Digital Outdoor Advg LLC ....G 732 616-2232
Tinton Falls *(G-10830)*

Drew & Rogers Inc ....F 973 575-6210
Fairfield *(G-3179)*

G G Tauber Company Inc ....E 800 638-6667
Neptune *(G-6913)*

Genesis Marketing Group Inc ....G 201 836-1392
Teaneck *(G-10754)*

Imprintz Cstm Printed Graphics ....G 609 386-5673
Lumberton *(G-5660)*

J&E Business Services LLC ....G 973 984-8444
Morris Plains *(G-6672)*

Newton Screen Printing Co ....G 973 827-0486
Franklin *(G-3602)*

One Two Three Inc ....F 856 251-1238
Woodbury *(G-12166)*

Penny Press ....G 856 547-1991
Stratford *(G-10616)*

Pro-Pack Corp ....G 908 725-5000
Branchburg *(G-694)*

Wally Enterprises Inc ....F 732 329-2613
Monmouth Junction *(G-6371)*

ADVERTISING SVCS: Bus Card

Silver Edmar ....G 973 817-7483
Newark *(G-7313)*

ADVERTISING SVCS: Direct Mail

About Our Town Inc ....G 732 968-1615
Piscataway *(G-8723)*

Access Response Inc ....G 732 660-0770
Ocean *(G-7712)*

Arna Marketing Group Inc ....D 908 625-7395
Branchburg *(G-638)*

Brisar Industries Inc ....C 973 278-2500
Paterson *(G-8226)*

C and R Printing Corporation ....F 201 528-8912
Carlstadt *(G-1135)*

Central Letter Shop Inc ....E 973 808-9595
West Caldwell *(G-11770)*

Comprehensive Mktg Systems ....G 908 810-9778
Union *(G-11165)*

Ics Corporation ....C 215 427-3355
West Deptford *(G-11829)*

Ideal Data Inc ....F 201 998-9440
North Arlington *(G-7420)*

Johnston Letter Co Inc ....G 973 482-7535
Flanders *(G-3412)*

Madhouz LLC ....G 609 206-8009
Glassboro *(G-3808)*

Metro Seliger Industries Inc ....G 201 438-4530
Carlstadt *(G-1189)*

Redi-Direct Marketing Inc ....B 973 808-4500
Fairfield *(G-3292)*

Total Reliance LLC ....F 732 640-5079
Dayton *(G-1992)*

Verizon Communications Inc ....D 609 646-9939
Egg Harbor Township *(G-2698)*

Zippityprint LLC ....F 216 438-0001
Mullica Hill *(G-6894)*

ADVERTISING SVCS: Display

Dublin Management Assoc of NJ ....C 609 387-1600
Burlington *(G-969)*

Larue Manufacturing Corp ....F 908 534-2700
Whitehouse *(G-12046)*

Madhouz LLC ....G 609 206-8009
Glassboro *(G-3808)*

ADVERTISING SVCS: Outdoor

Fedex Office & Print Svcs Inc ....E 856 427-0099
Cherry Hill *(G-1364)*

Outfront Media LLC ....D 973 575-6900
Fairfield *(G-3278)*

ADVERTISING SVCS: Poster, Outdoor

Stephen Swinton Studio Inc ....G 908 537-9135
Washington *(G-11588)*

ADVERTISING SVCS: Sample Distribution

Redi-Direct Marketing Inc ....B 973 808-4500
Fairfield *(G-3292)*

ADVERTISING SVCS: Transit

David Sisco Jr ....G 908 454-0880
Phillipsburg *(G-8646)*

Grafwed Internet Media Studios ....G 201 632-1771
Midland Park *(G-6227)*

AEROSOLS

American Spraytech LLC ....E 908 725-6060
Branchburg *(G-634)*

AGENTS, BROKERS & BUREAUS: Personal Service

Patty-O-Matic Inc ....F 732 938-2757
Farmingdale *(G-3391)*

AGENTS: Loan, Farm Or Business

Max Pro Services LLC ....G 973 396-2373
Livingston *(G-5542)*

AGRICULTURAL CHEMICALS: Trace Elements

Avantor Performance Mtls LLC ....B 908 859-2151
Phillipsburg *(G-8640)*

Flottec LLC ....G 973 588-4717
Boonton *(G-569)*

AGRICULTURAL EQPT: BARN, SILO, POULTRY, DAIRY/LIVESTOCK MACH

Edward Brown ....G 973 887-5255
East Hanover *(G-2214)*

AGRICULTURAL EQPT: Fertilizing Machinery

Plant Food Company Inc ....E 609 448-0935
Cranbury *(G-1870)*

AGRICULTURAL EQPT: Trailers & Wagons, Farm

Steve Green Enterprises ....F 732 938-5572
Farmingdale *(G-3394)*

AGRICULTURAL EQPT: Troughs, Water

Ferratex Services Inc ....E 973 609-5449
Livingston *(G-5529)*

AGRICULTURAL EQPT: Turf Eqpt, Commercial

South Jersey Farmers Exchange ....G 856 769-0062
Woodstown *(G-12240)*

AIR CLEANING SYSTEMS

Croll-Reynolds Co Inc ....E 908 232-4200
Parsippany *(G-7976)*

Palude Enterprises Inc ....G 732 241-5478
Howell *(G-4562)*

AIR CONDITIONING & VENTILATION EQPT & SPLYS: Wholesales

ML Mettler Corp ....G 201 869-0170
North Bergen **(G-7469)**

Passaic Metal & Bldg Sups Co ....D 973 546-9000
Clifton **(G-1691)**

AIR CONDITIONING EQPT

Ats Mechanical Inc ....G 609 298-2323
Bordentown **(G-591)**

Honeywell International Inc ....A 973 455-2000
Morris Plains **(G-6666)**

Kooltronic Inc ....C 609 466-3400
Pennington **(G-8455)**

Mainstream Fluid & Air LLC ....E 908 931-1010
Berkeley Heights **(G-419)**

Mechanical Technologies LLC ....E 973 616-3800
Pine Brook **(G-8709)**

Task International (usa) Inc ....F 732 739-0377
Keyport **(G-5024)**

AIR CONDITIONING UNITS: Complete, Domestic Or Indl

Construction Specialties Inc ....E 908 236-0800
Lebanon **(G-5282)**

SPX Dry Cooling Usa LLC ....E 908 450-8027
Bridgewater **(G-899)**

Tecogen Inc ....E 732 356-5601
Piscataway **(G-8821)**

AIR COOLERS: Metal Plate

Airzone Systems ....G 201 207-6593
Montville **(G-6482)**

AIR MATTRESSES: Plastic

Glasplex LLC ....G 973 940-8940
Sussex **(G-10671)**

L-E-M Plastics and Supplies ....G 201 933-9150
Rutherford **(G-9738)**

Mamrout Paper Group Corp ....G 718 510-5484
Edison **(G-2564)**

Plastics Galore LLC ....G 732 363-8447
Lakewood **(G-5172)**

AIR POLLUTION MEASURING SVCS

Valley Tech Inc ....G 908 534-5565
Whitehouse Station **(G-12064)**

AIR PURIFICATION EQPT

Air Clean Co Inc ....G 908 355-1515
Elizabeth **(G-2706)**

Bioclimatic Air Systems LLC ....E 856 764-4300
Delran **(G-2011)**

Bionomic Industries Inc ....F 201 529-1094
Mahwah **(G-5753)**

CSM Worldwide Inc ....E 908 233-2882
Bridgewater **(G-831)**

Csonka Worldwide ....E 609 514-2766
Plainsboro **(G-8879)**

DR Technology Inc ....G 732 780-4664
Freehold **(G-3651)**

Encur Inc ....G 732 264-2098
Keyport **(G-5016)**

Lm Air Technology Inc ....E 732 381-8200
Rahway **(G-9210)**

Naava Inc ....G 844 666-2282
Springfield **(G-10566)**

National Environmental Svcs Co ....G 908 813-1195
Hackettstown **(G-4028)**

Safety Power Inc ....G 908 277-1826
Summit **(G-10654)**

AIRCRAFT & AEROSPACE FLIGHT INSTRUMENTS & GUIDANCE SYSTEMS

Bae Systems Info & Elec Sys ....A 973 633-6000
Wayne **(G-11607)**

Honeywell International Inc ....C 973 455-2000
Morristown **(G-6715)**

Lockheed Martin Corporation ....A 856 234-1261
Mount Laurel **(G-6813)**

AIRCRAFT & HEAVY EQPT REPAIR SVCS

Thales Avionics Inc ....C 732 242-6300
Piscataway **(G-8823)**

AIRCRAFT ASSEMBLY PLANTS

Boeing Company ....A 908 464-6959
Berkeley Heights **(G-401)**

Dassault Aircraft Svcs Corp ....G 201 440-6700
Little Ferry **(G-5500)**

Defense Photonics Group Inc ....F 908 822-1075
South Plainfield **(G-10354)**

Easy Aerial Corporation ....G 646 639-4410
Edison **(G-2506)**

Jet Aviation St Louis Inc ....E 201 462-4026
Teterboro **(G-10800)**

Lockheed Martin Corporation ....C 856 792-9811
Cherry Hill **(G-1390)**

Lockheed Martin Corporation ....D 856 722-7782
Moorestown **(G-6594)**

Pacific Microtronics Inc ....G 973 993-8665
Morris Plains **(G-6676)**

AIRCRAFT CONTROL SYSTEMS: Electronic Totalizing Counters

Honeywell International Inc ....A 973 455-2000
Morris Plains **(G-6666)**

AIRCRAFT ENGINES & ENGINE PARTS: Cooling Systems

Capital Cooling Systems LLC ....G 973 773-8700
Lyndhurst **(G-5674)**

AIRCRAFT ENGINES & PARTS

Aerospace Industries LLC ....G 973 383-9307
Sparta **(G-10486)**

Allied-Signal China Ltd ....E 973 455-2000
Morristown **(G-6685)**

Bright Lights Usa Inc ....E 856 546-5656
Camden **(G-1046)**

Bright Lights Usa Inc ....D 856 546-5656
Barrington **(G-173)**

Dover Tool Connecticut LLC ....F 203 367-6376
Franklin Lakes **(G-3616)**

Honeywell International Inc ....C 800 601-3099
Morris Plains **(G-6663)**

Honeywell International Inc ....E 973 455-6633
Morristown **(G-6714)**

Honeywell International Inc ....E 973 285-5321
Morris Plains **(G-6664)**

Honeywell International Inc ....A 856 691-5111
Vineland **(G-11370)**

Honeywell International Inc ....A 856 234-5020
Moorestown **(G-6585)**

Honeywell International Inc ....D 973 455-2000
Morris Plains **(G-6665)**

Honeywell International Inc ....A 973 455-2000
Morris Plains **(G-6666)**

Honeywell International Inc ....A 732 919-0010
Wall Township **(G-11488)**

Honeywell International Inc ....G 908 561-1888
South Plainfield **(G-10380)**

Honeywell International Inc ....A 800 601-3099
Morris Plains **(G-6667)**

Honeywell Spain Holdings LLC ....G 973 455-2000
Morristown **(G-6716)**

Kreisler Industrial Corp ....D 201 773-6829
Elmwood Park **(G-2829)**

Parts Life Inc ....E 856 786-8675
Moorestown **(G-6609)**

AIRCRAFT EQPT & SPLYS WHOLESALERS

Aeropanel Corporation ....D 973 335-9636
Boonton **(G-552)**

Dassault Procurement Svcs Inc ....F 201 261-4130
Little Ferry **(G-5501)**

AIRCRAFT FLIGHT INSTRUMENTS

Dassault Procurement Svcs Inc ....F 201 261-4130
Little Ferry **(G-5501)**

General Plastics Corporation ....E 973 429-5625
Bloomfield **(G-511)**

H Galow Co Inc ....E 201 768-0547
Norwood **(G-7624)**

Pmc Inc ....F 973 748-5500
Bloomfield **(G-527)**

AIRCRAFT MAINTENANCE & REPAIR SVCS

GE Aviation Systems LLC ....C 973 428-9898
Whippany **(G-12021)**

Jet Aviation St Louis Inc ....E 201 462-4026
Teterboro **(G-10800)**

AIRCRAFT PARTS & AUXILIARY EQPT: Aircraft Training Eqpt

Pacific Coast Systems LLC ....G 908 735-9955
Asbury **(G-72)**

AIRCRAFT PARTS & AUXILIARY EQPT: Assys, Subassemblies/Parts

Doorsills LLC ....G 973 904-0270
Haledon **(G-4081)**

Export Management Consultants ....E 609 758-1166
Cookstown **(G-1807)**

AIRCRAFT PARTS & AUXILIARY EQPT: Body & Wing Assys & Parts

Keeley Aerospace Ltd ....E 951 582-2113
Cranbury **(G-1846)**

AIRCRAFT PARTS & AUXILIARY EQPT: Body Assemblies & Parts

Arlington Prcsion Cmpnents LLC ....E 973 276-1377
Fairfield **(G-3138)**

Kreisler Manufacturing Corp ....G 201 791-0700
Elmwood Park **(G-2830)**

Vahl Inc ....E 732 249-4042
East Brunswick **(G-2194)**

AIRCRAFT PARTS & AUXILIARY EQPT: Countermeasure Dispensers

Bae Systems Tech Sol Srvc Inc ....E 856 638-1003
Mount Laurel **(G-6780)**

AIRCRAFT PARTS & AUXILIARY EQPT: Deicing Eqpt

Clearway LLC ....G 973 578-4578
Newark **(G-7122)**

AIRCRAFT PARTS & AUXILIARY EQPT: Landing Assemblies & Brakes

Enginred Arrsting Systems Corp ....E 856 241-8620
Logan Township **(G-5613)**

Zodiac US Corporation ....A 732 681-3527
Wall Township **(G-11520)**

AIRCRAFT PARTS & AUXILIARY EQPT: Military Eqpt & Armament

Polytechnic Industries Inc ....F 856 235-6550
Mount Laurel **(G-6829)**

AIRCRAFT PARTS & AUXILIARY EQPT: Tanks, Fuel

Air Cruisers Company LLC ....C 732 681-3527
Wall Township **(G-11460)**

AIRCRAFT PARTS & EQPT, NEC

Accurate Bushing Company Inc ....E 908 789-1121
Garwood **(G-3774)**

Aerospace Manufacturing Inc ....E 973 472-9888
Wallington **(G-11521)**

Alpine Machine & Tool Corp ....F 201 666-0959
Westwood **(G-11953)**

American Aluminum Company ....D 908 233-3500
Mountainside **(G-6868)**

Bar Fields Inc ....F 347 587-7795
Linden **(G-5351)**

Breeze-Eastern LLC ....G 973 602-1001
Whippany **(G-12014)**

Breeze-Eastern LLC ....D 973 602-1001
Whippany **(G-12015)**

Bright Lights Usa Inc ....D 856 546-5656
Barrington **(G-173)**

DEB Manufacturing Inc ....G 732 364-7007
Lakewood **(G-5107)**

Defense Support Svcs Intl LLC ....F 850 390-4737
Marlton **(G-5971)**

Drytech Inc ....E 609 758-1794
Cookstown **(G-1806)**

PRODUCT

Exelis Inc/Northrop ....F 973 284-4212
Clifton (G-1617)

Goodrich Corporation ....C 973 237-2700
Totowa (G-10949)

Ho-Ho-Kus Inc ....E 973 278-2274
Paterson (G-8290)

J A Machine & Tool Co Inc ....F 201 767-1308
Closter (G-1762)

Rclc Inc ....F 732 877-1788
Woodbridge (G-12152)

Schultz Company ....G 732 922-4334
Neptune (G-6930)

Terrestrial Imaging LLC ....G 800 359-0530
Brick (G-760)

Thales Avionics Inc ....C 732 242-6300
Piscataway (G-8823)

Tolin Design Inc ....G 201 261-4455
Emerson (G-2863)

Whippany Actuation Systems LLC ......C 973 428-9898
Whippany (G-12043)

AIRCRAFT PARTS WHOLESALERS

Aerospace Industries LLC ....G 973 383-9307
Sparta (G-10486)

AIRCRAFT SEATS

Air Cruisers Company LLC ....C 732 681-3527
Wall Township (G-11460)

AIRCRAFT SERVICING & REPAIRING

Defense Spport Svcs Intl 2 LLC ....F 856 866-2200
Marlton (G-5970)

AIRCRAFT TURBINES

Kreisler Manufacturing Corp ....G 201 791-0700
Elmwood Park (G-2830)

AIRCRAFT: Airplanes, Fixed Or Rotary Wing

Boeing Company ....A 610 591-1978
Swedesboro (G-10684)

Defense Spport Svcs Intl 2 LLC ....F 856 866-2200
Marlton (G-5970)

AIRCRAFT: Autogiros

Drone Go Home LLC ....G 732 991-3605
Highlands (G-4308)

AIRCRAFT: Research & Development, Manufacturer

Enroute Computer Solutions Inc ....B 609 569-9255
Egg Harbor Township (G-2684)

Lockheed Martin Corporation ....B 856 787-3104
Mount Laurel (G-6814)

AIRPORTS, FLYING FIELDS & SVCS

Bombardier Transportation..................B 973 624-9300
Newark (G-7109)

Defense Support Svcs Intl LLC ....F 850 390-4737
Marlton (G-5971)

ALARM SYSTEMS WHOLESALERS

Absolute Protective Systems ....E 732 287-4500
Edison (G-2448)

ALARMS: Burglar

Merchants Alarm Systems Inc ....E 973 779-1296
Wallington (G-11528)

ALARMS: Fire

Digitize Inc ....F 973 663-1011
Lake Hopatcong (G-5056)

ALCOHOL, ETHYL: For Beverage Purposes

Creamy Creation LLC ....G 585 344-3300
Paramus (G-7864)

ALKALIES & CHLORINE

Kuehne Chemical Company Inc ....E 973 589-0700
Kearny (G-4893)

PMC Group Inc ....F 856 533-1866
Mount Laurel (G-6828)

Qualco Inc ....E 973 473-1222
Passaic (G-8174)

ALLOYS: Additive, Exc Copper Or Made In Blast Furnaces

Alpha Assembly Solutions Inc ....E 908 561-5170
South Plainfield (G-10325)

Alpha Assembly Solutions Inc ....E 908 791-3000
Somerset (G-10054)

ALTERNATORS: Automotive

Mobile Power Inc ....G 908 852-3117
Hackettstown (G-4026)

ALUMINUM

Helidex LLC ....G 201 636-2546
East Rutherford (G-2299)

Ivey Katrina Owner ....G 973 951-8328
Newark (G-7202)

Quick Fab Aluminum Mfg Co ....E 732 367-7200
Lakewood (G-5175)

ALUMINUM PRDTS

Alcon Products Inc ....F 609 267-3898
Westampton (G-11910)

Aluminum Shapes Inc ....E 856 662-5500
Pennsauken (G-8475)

Aluminum Shapes LLC ....B 888 488-7427
Delair (G-1999)

Ango Electronics Corporation ....F 201 955-0800
North Arlington (G-7415)

Coltwell Industries Inc ....G 908 276-7600
Cranford (G-1901)

Construction Specialties Inc ....B 908 236-0800
Lebanon (G-5282)

Construction Specialties Inc ....E 908 272-2771
Cranford (G-1902)

E-TEC Marine Products Inc ....G 732 269-0442
Bayville (G-253)

Goetz & Ruschmann Inc......................E 973 383-9270
Newton (G-7391)

Kwg Industries LLC ....E 908 218-8900
Hillsborough (G-4354)

Medicraft Inc ....E 201 797-8820
Elmwood Park (G-2835)

Minalex Corporation ....E 908 534-4044
Whitehouse Station (G-12058)

Nicks Inc ....E 908 272-3739
Kenilworth (G-4981)

Security Fabricators Inc ....F 908 272-9171
Kenilworth (G-4996)

Shapes/Arch Holdings LLC ....C 856 662-5500
Delair (G-2001)

Unique Aluminum Extrusion LLC ....F 732 271-0006
Middlesex (G-6207)

ALUMINUM: Coil & Sheet

H Cross Company ....E 201 964-9380
Moonachie (G-6519)

ALUMINUM: Rolling & Drawing

Gentek Building Products Inc..............E 732 381-0900
Avenel (G-134)

AMMUNITION

Lightfield Ammunition Corp ....G 732 462-9200
Freehold (G-3667)

AMMUNITION: Small Arms

Lightfield Ammunition Corp ....G 732 462-9200
Freehold (G-3667)

AMPLIFIERS

Bogen Communications Inc ....D 201 934-8500
Mahwah (G-5754)

Bogen Corporation ....G 201 934-8500
Ramsey (G-9237)

Celco ....E 201 327-1123
Mahwah (G-5757)

Sound Chice Assstive Listening ....G 908 647-2651
Gillette (G-3797)

AMPLIFIERS: RF & IF Power

Fiber-Span Inc ....E 908 253-9080
Toms River (G-10876)

AMUSEMENT & RECREATION SVCS, NEC

Indoor Entertainment of NJ..................E 609 522-6700
Wildwood (G-12073)

AMUSEMENT & RECREATION SVCS: Exhibition Operation

Creating Your Design LLC ....G 973 357-1080
Paterson (G-8240)

AMUSEMENT & RECREATION SVCS: Game Machines

Elaut Usa Inc ....F 732 364-9900
Lakewood (G-5113)

AMUSEMENT & RECREATION SVCS: Tourist Attraction, Commercial

Christopher F Maier ....F 908 459-5100
Hope (G-4539)

AMUSEMENT & RECREATION SVCS: Video Game Arcades

Xbox Exclusive...................................G 908 756-3731
South Plainfield (G-10455)

AMUSEMENT & RECREATION SVCS: Yoga Instruction

Kristine Deer Inc ....G 201 497-3333
Westwood (G-11961)

AMUSEMENT ARCADES

AG&e Holdings Inc ....E 609 704-3000
Hammonton (G-4126)

AMUSEMENT MACHINES: Coin Operated

Jersey Jack Pinball Inc.......................E 732 364-9900
Lakewood (G-5139)

Shooting Star Inc ....G 908 789-2500
Scotch Plains (G-9856)

Smartplay International Inc..................E 609 880-1860
Beverly (G-465)

AMUSEMENT PARK DEVICES & RIDES

Able Gear & Machine Co ....G 973 983-8055
Rockaway (G-9541)

Modular Packaging Systems Inc ....F 973 970-9393
Rockaway (G-9587)

Precision Forms Inc ....G 973 838-3800
Butler (G-1016)

AMUSEMENT PARK DEVICES & RIDES Carousels Or Merry-Go-Rounds

Indoor Entertainment of NJ..................E 609 522-6700
Wildwood (G-12073)

AMUSEMENT PARK DEVICES & RIDES: Carnival Mach & Eqpt, NEC

Elaut Usa Inc ....F 732 364-9900
Lakewood (G-5113)

ANALYZERS: Electrical Testing

Celco ....F 201 327-1123
Mahwah (G-5757)

Linseis Inc ....G 609 223-2070
Trenton (G-11076)

ANALYZERS: Network

Brookdale Senior Living Inc ....F 856 772-9400
Voorhees (G-11423)

Cisco Systems Inc ....E 201 782-0842
Montvale (G-6448)

Datalink Solutions Inc ....F 973 731-9373
West Orange (G-11893)

ANALYZERS: Respiratory

Impact Instrumentation Inc ....C 973 882-1212
West Caldwell (G-11779)

ANESTHESIA EQPT

Medpen Inc ....G 973 627-8067
Denville (G-2048)
Precision Spine Inc ....F 601 420-4244
Parsippany (G-8070)

ANESTHETICS: Bulk Form

Janssen Pharmaceuticals Inc ....A 609 730-2000
Titusville (G-10855)
Linde LLC ....G 973 579-2065
Sparta (G-10510)

ANIMAL FEED & SUPPLEMENTS: Livestock & Poultry

Darling Ingredients Inc ....C 973 465-1900
Newark (G-7133)
Glenburnie Feed & Grain ....G 856 986-8128
Mount Laurel (G-6800)

ANIMAL FEED: Wholesalers

Phibro Anmal Hlth Holdings Inc ....G 201 329-7300
Teaneck (G-10766)
Wilenta Carting Inc ....F 201 325-0044
Secaucus (G-9939)
Wilenta Feed Inc ....F 201 325-0044
Secaucus (G-9940)

ANIMAL FOOD & SUPPLEMENTS: Bird Food, Prepared

R World Enterprises ....G 201 795-2428
Jersey City (G-4811)

ANIMAL FOOD & SUPPLEMENTS: Cat

Mars Incorporated ....F 973 691-3500
Budd Lake (G-936)

ANIMAL FOOD & SUPPLEMENTS: Dog

Gwenstone Inc ....G 732 785-2600
Lakewood (G-5131)
Simmons Pet Food Nj Inc ....B 856 662-7412
Pennsauken (G-8578)

ANIMAL FOOD & SUPPLEMENTS: Dog & Cat

Freshpet Inc ....E 201 520-4000
Secaucus (G-9884)
Mars Food Us LLC ....F 908 852-1000
Hackettstown (G-4024)
Phibro Anmal Hlth Holdings Inc ....G 201 329-7300
Teaneck (G-10766)

ANIMAL FOOD & SUPPLEMENTS: Feed Supplements

Microfeed LLC ....G 201 886-9200
Fort Lee (G-3568)
Pet Devices LLC ....G 929 244-0012
Livingston (G-5555)
Pharmacia & Upjohn Company LLC .....B 908 901-8000
Peapack (G-8431)
Prince Agri Products Inc ....E 201 329-7300
Teaneck (G-10770)

ANIMAL FOOD & SUPPLEMENTS: Livestock

International Processing Corp ....F 732 826-4240
Perth Amboy (G-8619)
Reconserve Inc ....G 732 826-4240
Perth Amboy (G-8627)

ANIMAL FOOD & SUPPLEMENTS: Poultry

New York Poultry Co ....F 908 523-1600
Linden (G-5419)

ANIMAL FOOD & SUPPLEMENTS: Slaughtering of nonfood animals

Buckhead Meat Company ....C 732 661-4900
Edison (G-2476)

ANODIZING SVC

Aerotech Proc Solutions LLC ....G 973 782-4485
Paterson (G-8199)
Andarn Electro Service Inc ....E 973 523-2220
Paterson (G-8212)
Anodizing Corporation ....G 973 694-6449
Wayne (G-11605)
B & M Finishers Inc ....E 908 241-5640
Kenilworth (G-4940)
Independence Plating Corp ....F 973 523-1776
Paterson (G-8293)
Kenilworth Anodizing Co ....E 908 241-5640
Kenilworth (G-4968)
Master Metal Polishing Corp ....E 973 684-0119
Paterson (G-8333)
Super Chrome Inc ....G 732 774-2210
Asbury Park (G-85)
Trb Electro Corp ....E 973 278-9014
Paterson (G-8401)

ANTENNAS: Radar Or Communications

Electromagnetic Tech Inds Inc ....D 973 394-1719
Boonton (G-564)

ANTENNAS: Receiving

Gulton G I D ....G 908 791-4622
South Plainfield (G-10376)
It Surplus Liquidators ....G 732 308-1935
Freehold (G-3661)
Lg Electronics USA Inc ....G 732 605-0385
Monroe Township (G-6383)
Patriot American Solutions LLC ....D 862 209-4772
Rockaway (G-9594)

ANTIBIOTICS

Pfizer Inc ....F 973 660-5000
Madison (G-5731)

ANTIBIOTICS, PACKAGED

Capsugel Inc ....D 862 242-1700
Morristown (G-6696)
Capsugel Us LLC ....B 862 242-1700
Morristown (G-6698)
Pfizer Inc ....C 908 901-8000
Peapack (G-8429)

ANTIFREEZE

Agilis Chemicals Inc ....G 973 910-2424
Rockaway (G-9548)
BASF Corporation ....B 973 245-6000
Florham Park (G-3492)
Basfin Corporation ....A 973 245-6000
Florham Park (G-3493)
Full Circle Mfg Group ....F 908 353-8933
Elizabeth (G-2736)
Prestone Products Corporation ....E 732 577-7800
Freehold (G-3682)

ANTIHISTAMINE PREPARATIONS

Janssen Pharmaceuticals Inc ....A 609 730-2000
Titusville (G-10855)

ANTIQUE FURNITURE RESTORATION & REPAIR

Restortions By Peter Schichtel ....G 973 605-8818
Morristown (G-6739)

APPAREL DESIGNERS: Commercial

Suuchi Inc ....C 201 284-0789
North Bergen (G-7488)
Two 12 Fashion LLC ....G 848 222-1562
Lakewood (G-5198)

APPAREL: Hand Woven

Bearhands Ltd ....G 201 807-9898
Passaic (G-8127)

APPLIANCE PARTS: Porcelain Enameled

Aspen Manufacturing Co Inc ....G 609 871-6400
Beverly (G-459)

APPLIANCES, HOUSEHOLD: Kitchen, Major, Exc Refrigs & Stoves

Organize It All Inc ....E 201 488-0808
Bogota (G-549)
PC Marketing Inc ....E 201 943-6100
Ridgefield (G-9379)
Royal Sovereign Intl Inc ....E 800 397-1025
Rockleigh (G-9633)
Wanasavealotcom LLC ....F 732 286-6956
Toms River (G-10920)

APPLIANCES, HOUSEHOLD: Shampooers, Carpet

Stanley Steemer Intl Inc ....E 973 574-1640
Clifton (G-1731)

APPLIANCES: Household, Refrigerators & Freezers

Bar-Maid Corporation ....C 973 478-7070
Garfield (G-3722)
Philly Motors and Drives Inc ....E 856 840-8011
Mount Laurel (G-6826)

APPLIANCES: Major, Cooking

Signature Marketing Group Ltd ....F 973 575-7785
Pine Brook (G-8717)

APPLIANCES: Small, Electric

Conair Corporation ....D 239 673-2125
East Windsor (G-2353)
Edwards Creative Products Inc ....F 856 665-3200
Cherry Hill (G-1361)
Jarden Corporation ....E 201 610-6600
Hoboken (G-4477)
White Home Products Inc ....G 908 226-2501
Kenilworth (G-5008)

APPLICATIONS SOFTWARE PROGRAMMING

Alloy Software Inc ....F 973 661-9700
Bloomfield (G-501)
Channel Logistics LLC ....F 856 614-5441
Camden (G-1053)
James Colucci Enterprises LLC ....E 877 403-4900
Short Hills (G-9979)
Mobile Intelligent Alerts Inc ....G 201 410-5324
Holmdel (G-4523)
Utah Intermediate Holding Corp ....C 856 787-2700
Mount Laurel (G-6845)

AQUARIUM ACCESS, METAL

Julius E Holland-Moritz Co Inc ....G 609 397-1231
Lambertville (G-5215)

AQUARIUMS & ACCESS: Plastic

Qualteq Inc ....C 908 668-0999
South Plainfield (G-10429)

ARCHITECTURAL SVCS

LMC-HB Corp ....E 862 239-9814
Paterson (G-8324)
National Home Planning Service ....G 973 376-3200
Chatham (G-1335)

ARCHITECTURAL SVCS: House Designer

Marlene Trimmings LLC ....G 201 926-3108
North Bergen (G-7464)

ARMATURE REPAIRING & REWINDING SVC

Longo Elctrical-Mechanical Inc ....D 973 537-0400
Wharton (G-11991)

ARMATURES: Ind

ABB Motors and Mechanical Inc ....F 856 661-1442
Pennsauken (G-8468)

ARMOR PLATES

Dynamic Defense Materials LLC ....G 856 552-4150
Marlton (G-5974)

PRODUCT

AROMATIC CHEMICAL PRDTS

Bertone Aromatics ....G....... 201 444-9821
  Waldwick *(G-11441)*
Bwi Chemicals ....G....... 732 689-0913
  Monmouth Junction *(G-6334)*

ART DEALERS & GALLERIES

Empty Walls Inc ....G....... 609 452-8488
  Princeton *(G-9038)*
Environmolds LLC ....F....... 908 273-5401
  Summit *(G-10641)*
Revelation Gallery Inc ....G....... 973 627-6558
  Denville *(G-2054)*

ART DESIGN SVCS

Digital Atelier LLC ....G....... 609 890-6666
  Trenton *(G-11055)*
J D M Associates Inc ....G....... 973 773-8699
  Lodi *(G-5590)*
Minerva Custom Products LLC ....G....... 201 447-4731
  Waldwick *(G-11449)*

ART GOODS, WHOLESALE

Printers Service Florida Inc ....G....... 973 589-7800
  Newark *(G-7276)*
Scafa-Tornabene Art Pubg Co ....E....... 201 842-8500
  Lyndhurst *(G-5706)*

ART MARBLE: Concrete

Cumberland Marble & Monument ....G....... 856 691-3334
  Vineland *(G-11344)*

ART RESTORATION SVC

Revelation Gallery Inc ....G....... 973 627-6558
  Denville *(G-2054)*

ART SPLY STORES

Utrecht Manufacturing Corp ....D....... 609 409-8001
  Cranbury *(G-1889)*

ARTIFICIAL FLOWERS & TREES

Pennock Company ....E....... 215 492-7900
  Pennsauken *(G-8557)*

ARTIST'S MATERIALS & SPLYS

Meadowbrook Inventions Inc ....E....... 908 696-8470
  Bernardsville *(G-451)*
Rich Art Color Co Inc ....F....... 201 767-0009
  Northvale *(G-7606)*
U J Ramelson Co Inc ....G....... 973 589-5422
  Newark *(G-7349)*
Utrecht Manufacturing Corp ....D....... 609 409-8001
  Cranbury *(G-1889)*

ARTISTS' MATERIALS, WHOLESALE

Silver Brush Limited ....G....... 609 443-4900
  Windsor *(G-12129)*

ARTISTS' MATERIALS: Clay, Modeling

Chavant Inc ....F....... 732 751-0003
  Wall Township *(G-11468)*

ARTISTS' MATERIALS: Frames, Artists' Canvases

Empty Walls Inc ....G....... 609 452-8488
  Princeton *(G-9038)*

ARTISTS' MATERIALS: Ink, Drawing, Black & Colored

Algene Marking Equipment Co ....G....... 973 478-9041
  Garfield *(G-3716)*
Pertech Printing Inks Inc ....E....... 908 354-1700
  Carlstadt *(G-1200)*

ARTISTS' MATERIALS: Palettes

Norwood Industries Inc ....F....... 856 858-6195
  Haddon Township *(G-4054)*

ARTISTS' MATERIALS: Pencil Holders

Case It Inc ....E....... 800 441-4710
  Lyndhurst *(G-5675)*

ASBESTOS PRDTS: Clutch Facings

Hydro-Mechanical Systems Inc ....F....... 856 848-8888
  Westville *(G-11943)*

ASBESTOS PRDTS: Pipe Covering, Heat Insulatng Matl, Exc Felt

Stuart Steel Protection Corp ....E....... 732 469-5544
  Somerset *(G-10174)*

ASBESTOS PRDTS: Wick

Wick It LLC ....G....... 973 249-2970
  Passaic *(G-8190)*

ASBESTOS PRODUCTS

Blavor Inc ....G....... 973 265-4165
  Montville *(G-6483)*

ASH TRAYS: Stamped Metal

House of Gold Inc ....E....... 856 665-0020
  Pennsauken *(G-8524)*

ASPHALT & ASPHALT PRDTS

A E Stone Inc ....E....... 609 641-2781
  Egg Harbor Township *(G-2675)*
Arawak Paving Co Inc ....E....... 609 561-4100
  Hammonton *(G-4130)*
Beaver Run Farms ....G....... 973 427-1000
  Hawthorne *(G-4221)*
Beaver Run Farms ....F....... 973 875-5555
  Lafayette *(G-5044)*
Dosch-King Company Inc ....F....... 973 887-0145
  Whippany *(G-12018)*
Earle Asphalt Company ....D....... 732 657-8551
  Jackson *(G-4666)*
Eastern Concrete Materials Inc ....G....... 973 827-7625
  Hamburg *(G-4091)*
National Paving Co Inc ....F....... 856 767-1950
  Berlin *(G-439)*
Newark Asphalt Corp ....G....... 973 482-3503
  Newark *(G-7253)*
Riverdale Quarry LLC ....G....... 973 835-0028
  Riverdale *(G-9485)*
South State Inc ....E....... 856 881-6030
  Williamstown *(G-12107)*

ASPHALT COATINGS & SEALERS

Lodor Offset Corporation ....F....... 201 935-7100
  Carlstadt *(G-1184)*
Newark Asphalt Corp ....G....... 973 482-3503
  Newark *(G-7253)*

ASPHALT MINING & BITUMINOUS STONE QUARRYING SVCS

Eastern Concrete Materials Inc ....G....... 973 702-7866
  Sussex *(G-10670)*

ASPHALT MINING SVCS

Ziegler Chem & Mineral Corp ....E....... 732 752-4111
  Piscataway *(G-8839)*

ASPHALT MIXTURES WHOLESALERS

Central Jersey Hot Mix Asp LLC ....G....... 732 323-0226
  Jackson *(G-4656)*
Stone Industries Inc ....D....... 973 595-6250
  Haledon *(G-4085)*

ASPHALT PLANTS INCLUDING GRAVEL MIX TYPE

Dragon Asphalt Equipment LLC ....F....... 732 922-9290
  Lakewood *(G-5110)*
Fred McDowell Inc ....G....... 732 681-5000
  Wall Township *(G-11484)*
Robert Young and Son Inc ....G....... 973 728-8133
  Hewitt *(G-4292)*
Weldon Concrete Corp ....G....... 973 228-7473
  Roseland *(G-9657)*

ASSEMBLING & PACKAGING SVCS: Cosmetic Kits

Beauty-Pack LLC ....F....... 732 802-8200
  Piscataway *(G-8741)*
Cei Holdings Inc ....E....... 732 888-7788
  Holmdel *(G-4511)*
Cosmetic Essence LLC ....C....... 732 888-7788
  Holmdel *(G-4512)*
Cosmetic Essence Inc ....E....... 732 888-7788
  Holmdel *(G-4513)*
SGB Packaging Group Inc ....G....... 201 488-3030
  Hackensack *(G-3973)*

ASSEMBLING SVC: Clocks

Emdur Metal Products Inc ....F....... 856 541-1100
  Camden *(G-1062)*
Garrett Moore ....G....... 908 231-9231
  Bridgewater *(G-840)*

ASSEMBLING SVC: Plumbing Fixture Fittings, Plastic

Majewski Plumbing & Htg LLC ....G....... 609 374-6001
  Villas *(G-11314)*
Plumbing Supply Now LLC ....F....... 732 228-8852
  New Brunswick *(G-6991)*
W C Davis Inc ....F....... 856 547-4750
  Haddon Heights *(G-4052)*

ASSOCIATIONS: Business

Seawave Corp ....E....... 609 886-8600
  Rio Grande *(G-9462)*

ASSOCIATIONS: Real Estate Management

McQuade Enterprises LLC ....G....... 609 501-2437
  Millville *(G-6313)*

ASSOCIATIONS: Scientists'

Electrochemical Society Inc ....E....... 609 737-1902
  Pennington *(G-8450)*

ASSOCIATIONS: Trade

Metal Powder Inds Federation ....F....... 609 452-7700
  Princeton *(G-9073)*
New Jersey Bus & Indust Assn ....G....... 609 393-7707
  Trenton *(G-11084)*

ATHLETIC ORGANIZATION

New York-NJ Trail Conference ....F....... 201 512-9348
  Mahwah *(G-5795)*

ATOMIZERS

Accurate Screw Machine Corp ....D....... 973 276-0379
  Fairfield *(G-3126)*
Afh Industries LLC ....G....... 917 407-6866
  Piscataway *(G-8726)*
American Consolidation Inc ....G....... 201 438-4351
  Carlstadt *(G-1125)*
Amneal Pharmaceuticals LLC ....E....... 908 947-3120
  Bridgewater *(G-809)*
Cutting Edge Grower Supply LLC ......G....... 732 905-9220
  Howell *(G-4551)*
Distek Inc ....D....... 732 422-7585
  North Brunswick *(G-7516)*
Griffith Electric Sup Co Inc ....D....... 609 695-6121
  Trenton *(G-11061)*
Hoyt Corporation ....F....... 201 894-0707
  Englewood *(G-2904)*
Industrial Water Institute ....G....... 609 585-4880
  Trenton *(G-11068)*
Mfv International Corporation ....G....... 973 993-1687
  Morristown *(G-6727)*
New Jersey Air Products Inc ....F....... 908 964-9001
  Kenilworth *(G-4980)*
Riverstone Industries Corp ....G....... 973 586-2564
  Rockaway *(G-9605)*
Tri-Met Industries Inc ....G....... 908 231-0004
  Bridgewater *(G-902)*

AUCTION SVCS: Motor Vehicle

Toyota Motor Sales ....F....... 973 515-5012
  Parsippany *(G-8103)*

AUDIO & VIDEO EQPT, EXC COMMERCIAL

360 Media Innovations LLC..............G......201 228-0941
  Union (G-11145)
Bayview Entertainment LLC ....E......201 880-5331
  Pompton Plains (G-8955)
Broadway Empress Entrmt Inc ....G......973 991-0009
  Newark (G-7117)
Crestron Electronics Inc ....C......201 767-3400
  Rockleigh (G-9628)
CVE Inc ....D......201 770-0005
  Riverdale (G-9478)
Emerson Radio Corp ....F......973 428-2000
  Parsippany (G-8001)
Funai Corporation Inc ....E......201 806-7635
  Rutherford (G-9732)
Itec Consultants LLC ....G......732 784-8322
  Matawan (G-6022)
Kef America Inc ....E......732 414-2074
  Marlboro (G-5946)
Lg Electronics USA Inc ....B......201 816-2000
  Englewood Cliffs (G-2973)
Lunar Audio Video LLC ....G......973 233-7700
  Sayreville (G-9831)
Mardee Company Inc ....E......908 753-4343
  South Plainfield (G-10402)
Philips Elec N Amer Corp ....D......973 804-2100
  Ledgewood (G-5307)
Sierra Video Systems ....E......530 478-1000
  Clinton (G-1754)
Signature Audio Video Systems............G......732 864-1039
  Toms River (G-10912)
Sony Corporation of America ....B......201 930-1000
  Paramus (G-7902)
Sony Electronics Inc ....C......201 930-7030
  Paramus (G-7903)
Sony Electronics Inc ....A......201 930-1000
  Paramus (G-7904)
Stirling Audio Services LLC ....G......732 560-0707
  Middlesex (G-6204)
Techflex Inc ....E......973 300-9242
  Sparta (G-10522)
Vcom Intl Multi-Media Corp...................D......201 296-0600
  Fairfield (G-3338)
Wireworks Corporation ....E......908 686-7400
  Hillside (G-4451)
Xbox Exclusive....................................G......908 756-3731
  South Plainfield (G-10455)
Zenith Electronics Corporation ....E......201 816-2071
  Englewood Cliffs (G-2988)

AUDIO COMPONENTS

Sony Corporation of America ....F......201 930-1000
  Woodcliff Lake (G-12202)

AUDIO ELECTRONIC SYSTEMS

Apb-Dynasonics Inc ....G......973 785-1101
  Totowa (G-10931)
Audio Technologies and Codecs ....F......973 624-1116
  Newark (G-7098)
Concept Professional Systems ....G......732 938-5321
  Wall Township (G-11475)
DMJ Technologies LLC ....G......201 261-5560
  New Milford (G-7021)
Dtrovision LLC ....E......201 488-3232
  Ramsey (G-9239)
Empirical Labs Inc ....G......973 541-9446
  Lake Hiawatha (G-5054)
Ferro Industries Incorporated ....E......732 246-3200
  Colts Neck (G-1785)
Innovative Concepts Design LLC.........F......732 346-0061
  Elizabeth (G-2747)
Phoenix Systems ....G......201 788-5511
  North Haledon (G-7553)
Riotsound Inc ....G......917 273-5814
  Newton (G-7401)
Scj Group LLC ....G......201 289-5841
  Teaneck (G-10773)
Sondpex Corp America LLC ....G......732 940-4430
  Princeton (G-9123)
V P I Industries Inc ....P......732 583-6895
  Cliffwood (G-1549)
Vanderbilt LLC....................................E......973 316-3900
  Parsippany (G-8108)

AUDIO-VISUAL PROGRAM PRODUCTION SVCS

Vu Sound Incorporated ....F......215 990-2864
  Lumberton (G-5666)

AUDIOLOGICAL EQPT: Electronic

Davis Center Inc ....G......862 251-4637
  Succasunna (G-10622)

AUDIOLOGISTS' OFFICES

Davis Center Inc ....G......862 251-4637
  Succasunna (G-10622)

AUDITING SVCS

Sony Music Holdings Inc ....B......201 777-3933
  Rutherford (G-9745)

AUTO & HOME SUPPLY STORES: Auto & Truck Eqpt & Parts

Chapter Enterprises Inc ....G......732 560-8500
  Bridgewater (G-827)
Norms Auto Parts Inc ....G......908 852-5080
  Hackettstown (G-4029)

AUTO & HOME SUPPLY STORES: Automotive Access

American Van Equipment Inc ....C......732 905-5900
  Lakewood (G-5071)
M & RS Miller Auto Gear & Prt ....F......201 339-2270
  Bayonne (G-237)

AUTO & HOME SUPPLY STORES: Automotive parts

Custom Auto Radiator Inc....................F......609 242-9700
  Forked River (G-3537)
P & A Auto Parts Inc ....E......201 655-7117
  Hackensack (G-3959)

AUTO & HOME SUPPLY STORES: Speed Shops, Incl Race Car Splys

Bruce Kindberg ....G......973 664-0195
  Rockaway (G-9554)

AUTO & HOME SUPPLY STORES: Truck Eqpt & Parts

Robert H Hoover & Sons Inc.................G......973 347-4210
  Flanders (G-3414)

AUTOCLAVES: Laboratory

Benchmark Scientific Inc ....E......908 769-5555
  Sayreville (G-9815)

AUTOMATED TELLER MACHINE OR ATM REPAIR SVCS

Longport Shields Inc ....G......856 727-0227
  Moorestown (G-6598)

AUTOMATIC REGULATING CONTROL: Building Svcs Monitoring, Auto

J & L Controls Inc ....G......732 460-0380
  Lincroft (G-5338)
Johnson Controls Inc ....E......732 752-2395
  Union (G-11199)

AUTOMATIC REGULATING CONTROLS: AC & Refrigeration

Atomizing Systems Inc ....F......201 447-1222
  Ho Ho Kus (G-4453)
Msj Unlimited Services.........................G......201 617-0764
  Union City (G-11258)
National Refrigerants Inc ....E......856 455-4555
  Bridgeton (G-792)
Siemens Industry Inc ....E......856 234-7666
  Mount Laurel (G-6841)

AUTOMATIC REGULATING CONTROLS: Appliance, Exc Air-Cond/Refr

Vu Sound Incorporated ....F......215 990-2864
  Lumberton (G-5666)

AUTOMATIC REGULATING CONTROLS: Elect Air Cleaner, Automatic

National Environmental Svcs Co..........G......973 543-4586
  Mendham (G-6090)
Sulzer Chemtech USA Inc ....C......856 768-2165
  West Berlin (G-11752)

AUTOMATIC REGULATING CONTROLS: Electric Heat

Heat-Timer Corporation ....E......973 575-4004
  Fairfield (G-3218)

AUTOMATIC REGULATING CONTROLS: Energy Cutoff, Residtl/Comm

Building Performance Eqp Inc...............F......201 722-1414
  Hillsdale (G-4380)

AUTOMATIC REGULATING CONTROLS: Hardware, Environmental Reg

Comverge Giants Inc ....G......973 884-5970
  Florham Park (G-3496)
Comverge Giants Inc ....G......973 884-5970
  East Hanover (G-2209)

AUTOMATIC REGULATING CONTROLS: Hydronic Pressure Or Temp

A T C Companies Inc ....E......732 560-0900
  Middlesex (G-6141)
Sisco Manufacturing Co Inc.................F......856 486-7550
  Pennsauken (G-8579)

AUTOMATIC REGULATING CONTROLS: Pressure, Air-Cond Sys

US Air Power Systems ....G......201 892-5235
  Westwood (G-11974)

AUTOMATIC TELLER MACHINES

Bps Worldwide Inc ....E......856 874-0822
  Cherry Hill (G-1352)
Longport Shields Inc ....G......856 727-0227
  Moorestown (G-6598)

AUTOMOBILE FINANCE LEASING

Volvo Car North America LLC...............B......201 768-7300
  Rockleigh (G-9636)

AUTOMOBILE RECOVERY SVCS

Zc Utility Services LLC ....G......973 226-1840
  Roseland (G-9658)

AUTOMOBILE STORAGE GARAGE

Boomerang Systems Inc ....E......973 538-1194
  Florham Park (G-3494)

AUTOMOBILES & OTHER MOTOR VEHICLES WHOLESALERS

Autoaccess LLC...................................F......908 240-5919
  Sicklerville (G-10017)
P L Custom Body & Eqp Co Inc............C......732 223-1411
  Manasquan (G-5877)

AUTOMOBILES: Wholesalers

BMW of North America LLC..................A......201 307-4000
  Woodcliff Lake (G-12183)
Shock Tech Inc....................................E......845 368-8600
  Mahwah (G-5812)

AUTOMOTIVE & TRUCK GENERAL REPAIR SVC

Bombardier Transportation....................B......973 624-9300
  Newark (G-7109)
Faps Inc ....C......973 589-5656
  Newark (G-7160)
Freehold Pntiac Bick GMC Trcks..........D......732 462-7093
  Freehold (G-3656)
Holman Enterprises Inc ....E......609 383-6100
  Mount Laurel (G-6802)
P & S Blizzard Corporation ....G......973 523-1700
  Paterson (G-8358)

Summit Truck Body Inc ....F 908 277-4342
Summit (G-10661)
Town Ford Inc ....D 609 298-4990
Bordentown (G-613)
Wayne Motors Inc ....D 973 696-9710
Wayne (G-11692)

AUTOMOTIVE BODY SHOP

Dale Behre ....G 908 850-4225
Hackettstown (G-4002)
Freehold Pntiac Bick GMC Trcks ......D 732 462-7093
Freehold (G-3656)
Wayne Motors Inc ....D 973 696-9710
Wayne (G-11692)

AUTOMOTIVE BODY, PAINT & INTERIOR REPAIR & MAINTENANCE SVC

Drive-Master Co Inc ....F 973 808-9709
Fairfield (G-3180)
Holman Enterprises Inc ....E 609 383-6100
Mount Laurel (G-6802)
Summit Truck Body Inc ....F 908 277-4342
Summit (G-10661)
Town Ford Inc ....D 609 298-4990
Bordentown (G-613)

AUTOMOTIVE EMISSIONS TESTING SVCS

Superior Signal Company LLC ....F 732 251-0800
Old Bridge (G-7793)

AUTOMOTIVE GLASS REPLACEMENT SHOPS

Pgw Auto Glass LLC ....E 856 234-1600
Mount Laurel (G-6825)
Quality Glass Inc ....F 908 754-2652
South Plainfield (G-10428)

AUTOMOTIVE LETTERING & PAINTING SVCS

Painting Inc................................F 201 489-6565
South Hackensack (G-10287)

AUTOMOTIVE PARTS, ACCESS & SPLYS

A-1 Specialized Svcs & Sups ....E 732 238-2900
South River (G-10456)
Accurate Tool & Die Co Inc ....G 201 476-9348
Montvale (G-6440)
Allied-Signal China Ltd..................E 973 455-2000
Morristown (G-6685)
Allison Corp................................G 973 992-3800
Livingston (G-5523)
American Refuse Supply Inc ....F 973 684-3225
Paterson (G-8209)
Banks Bros Corporation ....D 973 680-4488
Bloomfield (G-502)
Bruce Kindberg ....G 973 664-0195
Rockaway (G-9554)
C T A Manufacturing Corp...............E 201 896-1000
Carlstadt (G-1136)
Chick Capoli Sales ....E 856 768-4500
West Berlin (G-11708)
Crestron Electronics Inc ....D 201 894-0670
Cresskill (G-1944)
Elegant USA LLC ....D 973 812-8820
Totowa (G-10943)
Elite Emrgncy Lights Ltd Lblty ....F 732 534-2377
Lakewood (G-5115)
Fleetsource LLC ....E 732 566-4970
Cliffwood (G-1547)
Freehold Pntiac Bick GMC Trcks ......D 732 462-7093
Freehold (G-3656)
Gentek Inc.................................C 973 515-0900
Parsippany (G-8024)
Gorman Industries Inc ....E 973 345-5424
Paterson (G-8279)
Holman Enterprises Inc ....E 609 383-6100
Mount Laurel (G-6802)
Honeywell International Inc ....C 973 455-2000
Morristown (G-6715)
Honeywell International Inc ....A 973 455-2000
Morris Plains (G-6666)
Ida Automotive Inc ....G 732 591-1245
Morganville (G-6643)
J & R Rebuilders Inc ....G 856 627-1414
Laurel Springs (G-5233)

Jesel Inc...................................D 732 901-1800
Lakewood (G-5140)
Keystone Automotive Inds Inc ....E 856 829-4700
West Deptford (G-11833)
Kinedyne LLC ....F 908 231-1800
Branchburg (G-672)
Kumar Bros USA LLC ....G 732 266-3091
Englishtown (G-2995)
Ls Rubber Industries Inc ....E 973 680-4488
Bloomfield (G-519)
M P T Racing Inc ....G 973 989-9220
Dover (G-2098)
Machiavelli LLC ....G 862 215-5888
East Orange (G-2260)
Maxzone Vehicle Lighting Corp ....F 732 393-9600
Edison (G-2566)
Newark Auto Top Co Inc ....F 973 677-9935
East Orange (G-2262)
Nitto Inc....................................C 732 901-7905
Lakewood (G-5164)
Ogura Industrial Corp ....F 586 749-1900
Somerset (G-10146)
Olde Grandad Industries Inc ....G 201 997-1899
Passaic (G-8168)
P & A Auto Parts Inc ....E 201 655-7117
Hackensack (G-3959)
Paintmaster Auto Body ....F 732 270-1700
Toms River (G-10899)
Rebuilt Parts Co LLC ....F 856 662-3252
Pennsauken (G-8570)
Research & Mfg Corp Amer ....F 908 862-6744
Linden (G-5433)
Rony Inc....................................G 201 891-2551
Wyckoff (G-12263)
S & G Tool Aid Corporation ....D 973 824-7730
Newark (G-7297)
S L P Engineering Inc ....D 732 240-3696
Toms River (G-10908)
Shock Tech Inc ....E 845 368-8600
Mahwah (G-5812)
Tabco Technologies LLC ....G 201 438-0422
Carlstadt (G-1226)
Tekltd ....F 732 463-2100
Piscataway (G-8822)
Tesla Inc ....E 201 225-2544
Paramus (G-7910)
Town Ford Inc ....D 609 298-4990
Bordentown (G-613)
Turbine Tek Inc ....G 973 872-0903
Wayne (G-11687)
Valcor Engineering Corporation ....E 973 467-8100
Springfield (G-10584)
Volvo Car North America LLC ....B 201 768-7300
Rockleigh (G-9636)
VS Systematics Corp ....G 908 241-5110
Kenilworth (G-5003)
Wayne Motors Inc ....D 973 696-9710
Wayne (G-11692)

AUTOMOTIVE PARTS: Plastic

Kinect Auto Parts Corporation ....G 862 702-8252
Fairfield (G-3242)

AUTOMOTIVE PRDTS: Rubber

Aero TEC Laboratories Inc ....E 201 825-1400
Ramsey (G-9231)
Hutchinson Industries Inc ....F 609 394-1010
Trenton (G-11064)
Hutchinson Industries Inc ....F 609 394-1010
Trenton (G-11065)
Hutchinson Industries Inc ....F 609 394-1010
Trenton (G-11066)

AUTOMOTIVE REPAIR SHOPS: Engine Repair

Gamka Sales Co Inc.....................E 732 248-1400
Edison (G-2525)

AUTOMOTIVE REPAIR SHOPS: Machine Shop

Metal Specialties New Jersey ....G 609 261-9277
Mount Holly (G-6775)

AUTOMOTIVE REPAIR SHOPS: Trailer Repair

Richard Shafer ....G 856 358-3483
Elmer (G-2796)

AUTOMOTIVE REPAIR SHOPS: Truck Engine Repair, Exc Indl

Robert H Hoover & Sons Inc.............G 973 347-4210
Flanders (G-3414)
Trucktech Parts & Services..............G 973 799-0500
Newark (G-7348)

AUTOMOTIVE REPAIR SHOPS: Wheel Alignment

Trucktech Parts & Services..............G 973 799-0500
Newark (G-7348)

AUTOMOTIVE REPAIR SVC

Bruce Kindberg ....G 973 664-0195
Rockaway (G-9554)
J & R Rebuilders Inc ....G 856 627-1414
Laurel Springs (G-5233)
Johnnys Service Center ....G 732 738-0569
Fords (G-3529)

AUTOMOTIVE SPLYS & PARTS, NEW, WHOL: Auto Servicing Eqpt

Blackhawk Cre Corporation.............F 856 887-0162
Salem (G-9803)

AUTOMOTIVE SPLYS & PARTS, NEW, WHOLESALE: Radiators

Bruce Kindberg ....G 973 664-0195
Rockaway (G-9554)
Modine Manufacturing Company ....G 856 467-9710
Bridgeport (G-768)

AUTOMOTIVE SPLYS & PARTS, NEW, WHOLESALE: Splys

Tabco Technologies LLC ....G 201 438-0422
Carlstadt (G-1226)

AUTOMOTIVE SPLYS & PARTS, NEW, WHOLESALE: Trailer Parts

M W Trailer Repair Inc ....F 609 298-1113
Bordentown (G-600)
Overdrive Holdings Inc ....F 201 440-1911
South Hackensack (G-10286)

AUTOMOTIVE SPLYS & PARTS, NEW, WHOLESALE: Trim

Newark Auto Top Co Inc ....F 973 677-9935
East Orange (G-2262)

AUTOMOTIVE SPLYS & PARTS, USED, WHOLESALE

Rebuilt Parts Co LLC ....F 856 662-3252
Pennsauken (G-8570)

AUTOMOTIVE SPLYS & PARTS, WHOLESALE, NEC

BMW of North America LLC.............A 201 307-4000
Woodcliff Lake (G-12183)
Dreyco Inc.................................F 201 896-9000
Carlstadt (G-1158)
M & RS Miller Auto Gear & Prt ....F 201 339-2270
Bayonne (G-237)
P & A Auto Parts Inc ....E 201 655-7117
Hackensack (G-3959)
Volvo Car North America LLC ....B 201 768-7300
Rockleigh (G-9636)
Wexco Industries Inc ....E 973 244-5777
Pine Brook (G-8720)

AUTOMOTIVE SPLYS/PART, NEW, WHOL: Spring, Shock Absorb/Strut

Shock Tech Inc ....E 845 368-8600
Mahwah (G-5812)

AUTOMOTIVE SVCS, EXC REPAIR & CARWASHES: Glass Tinting

Glasscare Inc.............................F 201 943-1122
Cliffside Park (G-1540)

AUTOMOTIVE SVCS, EXC REPAIR & CARWASHES: Lubrication

Grease N Go ....G 856 784-6555
Magnolia (G-5740)

AUTOMOTIVE SVCS, EXC REPAIR & CARWASHES: Trailer Maintenance

Ashland LLC ....G 908 243-3500
Bridgewater (G-815)
Steve Green Enterprises ....F 732 938-5572
Farmingdale (G-3394)

AUTOMOTIVE SVCS, EXC REPAIR: Washing & Polishing

National Auto Detailing Netwrk .....E 856 931-5529
Bellmawr (G-348)
T & E Sales of Marlboro Inc ....G 732 549-7551
Metuchen (G-6127)

AUTOMOTIVE TOWING & WRECKING SVC

J Spinelli & Sons Inc ....E 856 691-3133
Elmer (G-2793)

AUTOMOTIVE WELDING SVCS

Specialty Measures ....G 609 882-6071
Ewing (G-3055)

AUTOMOTIVE: Seating

Johnson Controls Inc ....E 856 245-9977
Blackwood (G-484)
Union County Seating & Sup Co .....E 908 241-4949
Kenilworth (G-5002)

AUTOTRANSFORMERS: Electric

A C Transformer Corp ....G 973 589-8574
Newark (G-7065)

AVIATION SCHOOL

Aus Inc ....G 856 234-9200
Mount Laurel (G-6779)

AWNINGS & CANOPIES

G T M Signs Inc ....G 856 227-2333
Deptford (G-2064)
Hansen Awning Co ....G 609 886-1685
Rio Grande (G-9459)
Michael Anthony Sign Dsign Inc .....E 732 453-6120
Piscataway (G-8791)

AWNINGS & CANOPIES: Awnings, Fabric, From Purchased Matls

Blacher Canvas Products Inc ....G 732 968-3666
Dunellen (G-2128)
G & J Solutions Inc ....F 609 861-9838
Woodbine (G-12142)
Opdyke Awnings Inc ....F 732 449-5940
Wall Township (G-11501)
Sconda Canvas Products Inc ....E 732 225-3500
Edison (G-2612)
Shore Awning Co ....G 732 775-3351
Wall Township (G-11509)
Stetsers JD Canvas Pdts Inc ....G 856 423-4901
Paulsboro (G-8426)
Texas Canvas Co Inc ....G 973 278-3802
Fairfield (G-3324)

AWNINGS & CANOPIES: Canopies, Fabric, From Purchased Matls

Hudson Awning Co Inc ....E 201 339-7171
Bayonne (G-232)

AWNINGS: Fiberglass

McBride Awning Co ....G 732 892-6256
Point Pleasant Beach (G-8923)

AWNINGS: Metal

Hudson Awning Co Inc ....E 201 339-7171
Bayonne (G-232)
Weathercraft Manufacturing Co .....F 201 262-0055
Emerson (G-2864)

AXLES

Turbo Solutions LLC ....F 856 209-6900
Pennsauken (G-8587)

BABY FORMULA

Buy Buy Baby Inc ....F 908 688-0888
Union (G-11161)
Gerber Products Company ....C 973 593-7500
Florham Park (G-3504)

BABY PACIFIERS: Rubber

Baby Time International Inc ....G 973 481-7400
Newark (G-7103)

BADGES, WHOLESALE

Colorcraft Sign Co ....F 609 386-1115
Beverly (G-461)
Touch of Class Promotions LLC .....G 267 994-0860
Voorhees (G-11440)

BADGES: Identification & Insignia

Almetek Industries Inc ....E 908 850-9700
Hackettstown (G-3996)
Aura Badge Co ....D 856 881-9026
Clayton (G-1523)
Competech Smrtcard Sltions Inc .....E 201 256-4184
Englewood Cliffs (G-2953)
E-Vents Registration LLC ....F 201 722-9221
Westwood (G-11959)
G G Tauber Company Inc ....E 800 638-6667
Neptune (G-6913)

BAGS & CONTAINERS: Textile, Exc Sleeping

ADM Corporation ....D 732 469-0900
Middlesex (G-6143)
Elements Accessories Inc ....G 646 801-5187
Maplewood (G-5919)
Philip Papalia ....F 732 349-5530
Toms River (G-10902)
Shaffer Products Inc ....E 908 206-1980
Union (G-11223)

BAGS: Canvas

Halsted Corporation ....E 201 333-0670
Cranbury (G-1836)

BAGS: Cement, Made From Purchased Materials

P S I Cement Inc ....G 609 716-1515
Princeton Junction (G-9160)

BAGS: Food Storage & Frozen Food, Plastic

Refrig-It Warehouse ....E 973 344-4545
Kearny (G-4912)

BAGS: Food Storage & Trash, Plastic

Harris Freeman & Co Inc ....D 856 787-9026
Moorestown (G-6583)

BAGS: Garment & Wardrobe, Plastic Film

Basic Ltd ....E 718 871-6106
Lakewood (G-5081)

BAGS: Garment, Plastic Film, Made From Purchased Materials

Sigma Extruding Corp ....D 201 933-5353
Lyndhurst (G-5707)

BAGS: Laundry, From Purchased Materials

Lbu Inc ....E 973 773-4800
Paterson (G-8318)

BAGS: Paper

Summit Filter Corp ....E 908 687-3500
Union (G-11226)

BAGS: Paper, Made From Purchased Materials

Duro Bag Manufacturing Company .....C 908 351-2400
Elizabeth (G-2727)

BAGS: Plastic

Allied Plastics New Jersey LLC ....D 973 956-9200
Paterson (G-8205)
American Transparent Plastic ....E 732 287-3000
Edison (G-2459)
Apco Extruders Inc ....E 732 287-3000
Edison (G-2462)
CCL Label Inc ....D 609 443-3700
Hightstown (G-4311)
Encore Poly ....G 201 845-4510
Maywood (G-6050)
Ez-Dumpster LLC ....G 908 752-2787
Bridgewater (G-839)
Freedom Plastics LLC ....F 201 337-9450
Oakland (G-7689)
Gemini Plastic Films Corp ....E 973 340-0700
Garfield (G-3736)
Global Direct Marketing Group ....G 856 427-6116
Haddonfield (G-4060)
Goetz & Ruschmann Inc ....E 973 383-9270
Newton (G-7391)
Inteplast Group Corporation ....B 973 994-8000
Livingston (G-5535)
Keystone Packaging Service ....G 908 454-8567
Phillipsburg (G-8655)
M S Plastics and Packg Co ....F 973 492-2400
Butler (G-1011)
Trinity Plastics Inc ....C 973 994-8018
Livingston (G-5566)

BAGS: Plastic & Pliofilm

Ace Box Landau Co Inc ....G 201 871-4776
Englewood Cliffs (G-2946)
Alpha Industries MGT Inc ....C 201 933-6000
Lyndhurst (G-5567)
General Film Products Inc ....E 908 351-0454
Elizabeth (G-2738)
MP Plastic Llc ....E 973 279-9300
Paterson (G-8342)
Tiffany Packaging ....G 973 726-8130
Sparta (G-10525)

BAGS: Plastic, Made From Purchased Materials

A-1 Plastic Bags Inc ....D 973 344-4441
Newark (G-7067)
All American Poly Corp ....C 732 752-3200
Piscataway (G-8730)
ANS Plastics Corporation ....F 732 247-2776
New Brunswick (G-6944)
Basic Plastics Company Inc ....E 973 977-8151
Paterson (G-8221)
Beta Plastics ....C 201 933-1400
Carlstadt (G-1131)
Central Poly-Bag Corp ....F 908 862-7570
Linden (G-5358)
Consolidated Packg Group Inc ....C 201 440-4240
Ridgefield Park (G-9401)
Craft-Pak Inc ....F 718 763-0700
Towaco (G-10991)
Dana Poly Corp ....E 800 474-1020
Dover (G-2085)
Essentra Packaging US Inc ....E 856 439-1700
Moorestown (G-6577)
Flexbiosys Inc ....F 908 300-3244
Lebanon (G-5286)
Halsted Corporation ....E 201 333-0670
Cranbury (G-1836)
Heritage Bag Company ....G 856 467-2247
Swedesboro (G-10702)
Hershey Industries Inc ....F 908 353-3344
Hillside (G-4411)
Lps Industries Inc ....C 201 438-3515
Moonachie (G-6529)
M & E Packaging Corp ....G 201 635-1381
Lyndhurst (G-5688)
Mercury Plastic Bag Co Inc ....E 973 778-7200
Passaic (G-8163)
Nexus Plastics Incorporated ....D 973 427-3311
Hawthorne (G-4249)
Omega Plastics Corp ....D 201 507-9100
Lyndhurst (G-5697)
Plus Packaging Inc ....G 973 538-2216
Morristown (G-6736)
Potti-Bags Inc ....G 201 796-5555
Elmwood Park (G-2845)
Power Bag and Film LLC ....G 908 832-6648
Califon (G-1035)

Employee Codes: A=Over 500 employees, B=251-500
C=101-250, D=51-100, E=20-50, F=10-19, G=4-9

2018 Harris New Jersey
Manufacturers Directory

PRODUCT

799

Source Direct Inc ....F 856 768-7445
Cinnaminson *(G-1488)*

Spectrum Plastics ....G 732 564-1899
Piscataway *(G-8815)*

X-L Plastics Inc 973 777-9400
Clifton *(G-1745)*

BAGS: Rubber Or Rubberized Fabric

Glopak Corp ....E 908 753-8735
South Plainfield *(G-10373)*

Mfv International Corporation ....G 973 993-1687
Morristown *(G-6727)*

BAGS: Shipping

Flexo-Craft Prints Inc ....E 973 482-7200
Harrison *(G-4183)*

BAGS: Textile

Ace Bag & Burlap Company Inc ....F 973 242-2200
Newark *(G-7071)*

AMS Products LLC ....F 973 442-5790
Wharton *(G-11978)*

Kt America Corp ....F 609 655-5333
Cranbury *(G-1850)*

Lbu Inc ....E 973 773-4800
Paterson *(G-8318)*

Mobile Solutions Intl LLC ....G 609 448-3089
Robbinsville *(G-9518)*

Nyp Corp (frmr Ny-Pters Corp) ....D 908 351-6550
Elizabeth *(G-2761)*

BAGS: Wardrobe, Closet Access, Made From Purchased Materials

Katies Closets ....G 973 300-4007
Newton *(G-7394)*

Kestrel Closets LLC ....G 973 586-1144
Rockaway *(G-9580)*

BAKERIES, COMMERCIAL: On Premises Baking Only

A C Bakery Distributors Inc ....F 973 977-2255
Paterson *(G-8191)*

Acme Markets Inc ....E 609 884-7217
Cape May *(G-1090)*

All In Icing ....G 973 896-5990
Stanhope *(G-10587)*

All Natural Products ....F 212 391-2870
Sayreville *(G-9813)*

Alpine Bakery Inc ....G 201 902-0605
Union City *(G-11239)*

Auntie Annes Hmde Sft Prtzls ....F 856 772-3737
Voorhees *(G-11422)*

Auntie Annes Soft Pretzels ....F 856 722-0433
Moorestown *(G-6561)*

Aversas Italian Bakery Inc ....E 856 227-8005
Blackwood *(G-472)*

Bagel Street ....E 609 936-1755
Plainsboro *(G-8875)*

Berat Corporation ....C 609 953-7700
Medford *(G-6065)*

Bimbo Bakeries Usa Inc ....D 856 435-0500
Clementon *(G-1530)*

Blissful Bites ....G 973 670-6928
Vernon *(G-11296)*

Bread Guy Inc ....F 973 881-9002
Paterson *(G-8224)*

Calandra Italian & French Bky ....D 973 484-5598
Newark *(G-7118)*

Campbell Soup Company ....A 856 342-4800
Camden *(G-1049)*

Carnegie Deli Inc ....D 201 507-5557
Carlstadt *(G-1138)*

Chocolate Face Cupcake ....G 609 624-2253
Cape May Court House *(G-1112)*

Ciao Cupcake ....G 609 964-6167
Trenton *(G-11040)*

Cinderella Cheesecake Co Inc ....F 856 461-6302
Riverside *(G-9495)*

Conte Farms ....F 609 268-0513
Tabernacle *(G-10737)*

Crijuodama Baking Corp T ....G 732 451-1250
Lakewood *(G-5100)*

Cupcake Celebrations ....G 973 885-0826
Columbus *(G-1802)*

Cupcake Kitschen ....G 862 221-8872
Mahwah *(G-5761)*

Del Bakers Inc ....E 856 461-0089
Riverside *(G-9496)*

Dell Aquila Baking Company ....G 201 886-0613
Englewood *(G-2886)*

Erj Baking LLC ....G 201 906-1300
Ridgewood *(G-9424)*

Excellence In Baking Inc ....G 732 287-1313
Edison *(G-2516)*

Food Circus Super Markets Inc ....D 732 291-4079
Atlantic Highlands *(G-111)*

Formica Bros Bakery ....F 609 348-8934
Atlantic City *(G-96)*

Herman Eickhoff ....C 609 871-1809
Willingboro *(G-12119)*

House of Cupcakes ....G 862 225-9536
Clifton *(G-1642)*

House of Cupcakes LLC ....G 908 413-3076
Somerset *(G-10109)*

International Delights LLC ....C 973 928-5431
Clifton *(G-1648)*

J & J Snack Foods Corp ....C 856 933-3597
Bellmawr *(G-344)*

J & J Snack Foods Corp ....B 856 665-9533
Pennsauken *(G-8531)*

J & J Snack Foods Corp ....D 856 467-9552
Bridgeport *(G-767)*

Jacqueline Mazza LLC ....G 732 718-2944
Somerset *(G-10115)*

John Anthony Bread Distributor ....G 973 523-9258
Paterson *(G-8305)*

Just A Touch of Baking LLC ....G 732 679-5123
Old Bridge *(G-7782)*

Kashmir Crown Baking LLC ....E 908 474-1470
Linden *(G-5396)*

KB Food Enterprises Inc ....F 973 278-2800
Paterson *(G-8307)*

Little Falls Shop Rite Super ....B 973 256-0909
Little Falls *(G-5481)*

Little Miss Cupcake LLC ....G 732 370-3083
Lakewood *(G-5149)*

Livingston Bagel Warren Inc ....E 973 994-1915
Livingston *(G-5540)*

Lo Presti & Sons LLC ....G 973 523-9258
Paterson *(G-8325)*

Local Baking Products Inc ....G 973 482-1400
Newark *(G-7223)*

Luccas Bakery Inc ....G 609 561-5558
Hammonton *(G-4142)*

Mendels Muffins and Stuff Inc ....G 973 881-9900
Paterson *(G-8335)*

Minardi Baking Co Inc ....E 973 742-1107
Denville *(G-2050)*

Mini Frost Foods Corporation ....E 973 427-4258
North Haledon *(G-7552)*

Nan Bread Distribution ....G 201 475-9311
Elmwood Park *(G-2838)*

Paramount Bakeries Inc ....G 973 482-6638
East Orange *(G-2263)*

Pathmark Stores Inc ....C 856 853-5533
Woodbury *(G-12167)*

Pathmark Stores Inc ....C 732 505-6440
Toms River *(G-10900)*

Pathmark Stores Inc ....C 973 762-5044
South Orange *(G-10313)*

Pechters Southern NJ LLC ....G 856 786-8000
Cinnaminson *(G-1483)*

Pretty Lil Cupcakes ....G 201 256-1205
Harrison *(G-4188)*

R P Baking LLC ....E 973 483-3374
Harrison *(G-4189)*

Rombiolo LLC ....G 973 680-0405
Bloomfield *(G-529)*

Scala Pastry ....G 732 398-9808
North Brunswick *(G-7537)*

Serranis Bakery ....G 973 678-1777
Orange *(G-7827)*

Shop Rite Supermarkets Inc ....C 732 442-1717
Perth Amboy *(G-8630)*

Shop Rite Supermarkets Inc ....C 732 775-4250
Neptune *(G-6932)*

Shop-Rite Supermarkets Inc ....C 609 646-2448
Absecon *(G-4)*

Sibi Distributors ....G 908 658-4448
Basking Ridge *(G-205)*

Springdale Farm Market Inc ....E 856 424-8674
Cherry Hill *(G-1421)*

Sweetly Spirited Cupcakes Ltd ....G 917 846-4238
Princeton Junction *(G-9164)*

Terrignos Bakery ....E 856 451-6368
Bridgeton *(G-799)*

Thebgb Inc ....G 917 749-5309
Paterson *(G-8399)*

Tri-State Buns LLC ....E 973 418-8323
Harrison *(G-4190)*

Y & J Bakers Inc ....E 732 363-3636
Lakewood *(G-5208)*

Zenas Patisserie ....G 856 303-8700
Riverton *(G-9509)*

BAKERIES: On Premises Baking & Consumption

Advisory Dumas Group LLC ....F 850 778-1624
Lawrence Township *(G-5239)*

Aversas Italian Bakery Inc ....E 856 227-8005
Blackwood *(G-472)*

Cake Specialty Inc ....F 973 238-0500
Hawthorne *(G-4224)*

Del Buono Bakery Inc ....E 856 546-9585
Haddon Heights *(G-4047)*

Dina Hernandez ....G 973 772-8883
Lodi *(G-5581)*

Dunkin Donuts Baskin Robbins ....G 201 692-1900
Teaneck *(G-10750)*

Elis Hot Bagels Inc ....E 732 566-4523
Matawan *(G-6020)*

Millburn Bagel Inc ....E 973 258-1334
Millburn *(G-6258)*

Minardi Baking Co Inc ....E 973 742-1107
Denville *(G-2050)*

Mini Frost Foods Corporation ....E 973 427-4258
North Haledon *(G-7552)*

Terrignos Bakery ....E 856 451-6368
Bridgeton *(G-799)*

Wenner Bread Products Inc ....D 631 563-6262
New Brunswick *(G-7012)*

Y & J Bakers Inc ....E 732 363-3636
Lakewood *(G-5208)*

BAKERY MACHINERY

Machine Control Systems Inc ....G 732 529-6888
Jackson *(G-4671)*

Magna Industries Inc ....E 732 905-0957
Lakewood *(G-5151)*

Wilenta Feed Inc ....F 201 325-0044
Secaucus *(G-9940)*

BAKERY PRDTS, FROZEN: Wholesalers

Mini Frost Foods Corporation ....E 973 427-4258
North Haledon *(G-7552)*

BAKERY PRDTS: Bagels, Fresh Or Frozen

Bagel Club ....F 908 806-6022
Flemington *(G-3429)*

Branchville Bagels Inc ....E 973 948-7077
Branchville *(G-727)*

Cambridge Bagels Inc ....F 973 743-5683
Bloomfield *(G-505)*

Danmark Enterprises Inc ....G 732 321-3366
South Plainfield *(G-10352)*

Delicious Bagels Inc ....G 732 892-9265
Point Pleasant Boro *(G-8938)*

Elis Hot Bagels Inc ....E 732 566-4523
Matawan *(G-6020)*

Frell Corp ....F 201 825-2500
Ramsey *(G-9240)*

Jad Bagels LLC ....G 201 567-4500
Englewood *(G-2906)*

Millburn Bagel Inc ....E 973 258-1334
Millburn *(G-6258)*

Original Bagel & Bialy Co Inc ....E 973 227-5777
West Caldwell *(G-11794)*

S M Z Enterprises Inc ....F 908 232-1921
Westfield *(G-11930)*

Uptown Bakeries ....C 856 467-9552
Logan Township *(G-5615)*

BAKERY PRDTS: Bakery Prdts, Partially Cooked, Exc frozen

Ferrara Bakery & Cafe Inc ....F 732 826-8700
Perth Amboy *(G-8614)*

BAKERY PRDTS: Biscuits, Baked, Baking Powder & Raised

Ecce Panis Inc ....G 877 706-0510
Carlstadt *(G-1159)*

Katis Kupcakes ....G...... 609 332-2172
  Moorestown (G-6589)

BAKERY PRDTS: Biscuits, Dry

Interntnal Bscits Cnfctons Inc ....G...... 856 813-1008
  Marlton (G-5979)
Mondelez Global LLC ....A...... 201 794-4000
  Fair Lawn (G-3103)
Nabisco Royal Argentina Inc ....G...... 973 503-2000
  East Hanover (G-2230)

BAKERY PRDTS: Bread, All Types, Fresh Or Frozen

Angelos Panetteria Inc ....G...... 201 435-4659
  Jersey City (G-4706)
Del Buono Bakery Inc ....E...... 856 546-9585
  Haddon Heights (G-4047)
Fragales Bakery Inc ....F...... 973 546-0327
  Garfield (G-3735)
Prestige Bread Jersey Cy Inc ....D...... 201 422-7900
  North Bergen (G-7476)
Schripps European Bread Inc ....E...... 201 867-0909
  North Bergen (G-7485)
Vieiras Bakery Inc ....D...... 973 589-7719
  Newark (G-7357)
Wenner Bread Products Inc ....D...... 631 563-6262
  New Brunswick (G-7012)
Zinicola Baking Co ....G...... 973 667-1306
  Nutley (G-7658)

BAKERY PRDTS: Cakes, Bakery, Exc Frozen

Ability2work A NJ Nnprfit Corp ....F...... 908 782-3458
  Flemington (G-3423)
Advisory Dumas Group LLC ....F...... 850 778-1624
  Lawrence Township (G-5239)
Ahzanis Castle LLC ....G...... 973 874-3191
  Paterson (G-8200)
Cheesecake Factory Inc ....G...... 973 921-0930
  Short Hills (G-9976)
Pao Ba Avo LLC ....G...... 908 962-9090
  Elizabeth (G-2765)
Unilever Bestfoods North Amer ....F...... 201 894-4000
  Englewood Cliffs (G-2985)

BAKERY PRDTS: Cakes, Bakery, Frozen

Aiva Naturals LLC ....G...... 201 825-0749
  Newark (G-7075)
Cinderella Cheesecake Co Inc ....F...... 856 461-6302
  Riverside (G-9495)
Country Oven ....G...... 732 494-4838
  Iselin (G-4622)
Hudson Cakery ....G...... 201 319-0363
  Weehawken (G-11696)
Sugar & Plumm Upper West LLC ....D...... 201 334-1600
  Moonachie (G-6544)
Sugarush ....G...... 732 414-9044
  Red Bank (G-9346)

BAKERY PRDTS: Cones, Ice Cream

Chips Ice Cream LLC ....G...... 732 840-6332
  Howell (G-4548)
Meltdown ....G...... 609 207-0527
  Long Beach Township (G-5617)
Millstone Dq Inc ....G...... 609 259-6733
  Clarksburg (G-1521)
Novelty Cone Co Inc ....E...... 856 665-9525
  Pennsauken (G-8555)

BAKERY PRDTS: Cookies

Caliz - Malko LLC ....G...... 973 207-5200
  Fairfield (G-3154)
Continental Cookies Inc ....F...... 201 498-1966
  Hackensack (G-3899)
Fairfield Gourmet Food Corp ....D...... 973 575-4365
  Cedar Grove (G-1283)
Food & Beverage Inc ....D...... 201 288-8881
  Teterboro (G-10795)
J & J Snack Foods Corp ....B...... 856 665-9533
  Pennsauken (G-8531)
J & J Snack Foods Corp ....D...... 856 467-9552
  Bridgeport (G-767)
Jassmine Corp ....G...... 848 565-0515
  Clifton (G-1652)
Jimmys Cookies LLC ....C...... 973 779-8500
  Clifton (G-1653)
Joyce Food LLC ....C...... 973 491-9696
  Newark (G-7209)

Royal Baking Co Inc ....D...... 201 296-0888
  Moonachie (G-6540)

BAKERY PRDTS: Cookies & crackers

Bakers Perfection Inc ....E...... 973 983-0700
  Rockaway (G-9553)
Birds Eye Foods Inc ....C...... 585 383-1850
  Cherry Hill (G-1350)
Campbell Soup Company ....A...... 856 342-4800
  Camden (G-1049)
Direct Sales and Services Inc ....E...... 973 340-4480
  Garfield (G-3730)
Gerber Products Company ....C...... 973 593-7500
  Florham Park (G-3504)
Grab Em Snacks Ltd Lblty Co ....G...... 908 333-3229
  Hillsborough (G-4337)
John Wm Macy Cheesesticks Inc ....D...... 201 791-8036
  Elmwood Park (G-2827)
Kitchen Table Bakers Inc ....E...... 516 931-5113
  Fairfield (G-3243)
Little Falls Shop Rite Super ....B...... 973 256-0909
  Little Falls (G-5481)
Lo Presti & Sons LLC ....E...... 973 523-9258
  Paterson (G-8325)
Local Baking Products Inc ....E...... 973 482-1400
  Newark (G-7223)
Mini Frost Foods Corporation ....E...... 973 427-4258
  North Haledon (G-7552)
Mondelez Global LLC ....A...... 201 794-4080
  Fair Lawn (G-3104)
Oven Art LLC ....E...... 973 910-2266
  Hackensack (G-3958)

BAKERY PRDTS: Doughnuts, Exc Frozen

9001 Corporation ....E...... 201 963-2233
  Jersey City (G-4693)
9002 Corporation ....E...... 201 792-9595
  Jersey City (G-4694)
G N J Inc ....F...... 856 786-1127
  Cinnaminson (G-1463)
J K P Donuts Inc ....G...... 856 234-9844
  Mount Laurel (G-6809)
Jay Jariwala ....F...... 908 806-8266
  Ringoes (G-9439)
Lodi Cml Cooperative LLC ....G...... 201 820-2380
  Lodi (G-5593)
O O M Inc ....G...... 973 328-9408
  Rockaway (G-9592)

BAKERY PRDTS: Dry

Arysta LLC ....G...... 856 417-8100
  Logan Township (G-5611)
Butterfly Bakery Inc ....E...... 973 815-1501
  Wyckoff (G-12246)
Deep Foods Inc ....C...... 908 810-7500
  Union (G-11171)
Pace Target Brokerage Inc ....E...... 856 629-2551
  Williamstown (G-12095)

BAKERY PRDTS: Frozen

A & S Frozen Inc ....E...... 201 672-0510
  East Rutherford (G-2274)
Country Home Bakers LLC - GA ....C...... 856 931-7052
  Bellmawr (G-335)
I-Yell-O Foods Inc ....G...... 732 525-2201
  South Amboy (G-10239)
J & J Snack Foods Corp ....B...... 856 665-9533
  Pennsauken (G-8531)
J & J Snack Foods Corp ....D...... 856 467-9552
  Bridgeport (G-767)
J & J Snack Foods Corp ....C...... 856 933-3597
  Bellmawr (G-344)
Mardon Associates Inc ....F...... 973 977-2251
  Paterson (G-8332)
Nema Food Distribution Inc ....G...... 973 256-4415
  Fairfield (G-3267)
Rich Products Corporation ....A...... 800 356-7094
  Riverside (G-9505)
Sugar and Plumm LLC ....G...... 201 334-1600
  Moonachie (G-6545)
Wenner Bread Products Inc ....D...... 631 563-6262
  New Brunswick (G-7012)

BAKERY PRDTS: Matzoth

Manischewitz Company ....D...... 201 553-1100
  Newark (G-7235)

BAKERY PRDTS: Pastries, Danish, Frozen

Royal Baking Co Inc ....D...... 201 296-0888
  Moonachie (G-6540)

BAKERY PRDTS: Pastries, Exc Frozen

Nuchas Tsq LLC ....F...... 212 913-9682
  North Bergen (G-7472)
Royal Baking Co Inc ....D...... 201 296-0888
  Moonachie (G-6540)

BAKERY PRDTS: Pies, Exc Frozen

Mendles Just Bread Inc ....G...... 973 881-9900
  Paterson (G-8336)
Sweet Potato Pie Inc ....E...... 973 279-3405
  Paterson (G-8393)

BAKERY PRDTS: Pretzels

A & A Soft Pretzel Company ....G...... 856 338-0208
  Camden (G-1039)
Auntie Annes Hmde Sft Prtzls ....F...... 856 772-3737
  Voorhees (G-11422)
Auntie Annes Soft Pretzels ....E...... 856 845-3667
  Woodbury (G-12157)
European Pretzel One LLC ....F...... 201 867-6117
  North Bergen (G-7451)
Federal Pretzel Baking Co ....E...... 215 467-0505
  Bridgeport (G-764)
J & J Snack Foods Corp ....C...... 856 933-3597
  Bellmawr (G-344)
J & J Snack Foods Corp PA ....G...... 856 665-9533
  Pennsauken (G-8532)
Medford Soft Pretzels Inc ....G...... 856 662-8792
  Marlton (G-5987)
South Jersey Pretzel Inc ....F...... 856 435-5055
  Stratford (G-10617)

BAKERY PRDTS: Wholesalers

Aversas Italian Bakery Inc ....E...... 856 227-8005
  Blackwood (G-472)
Bread Guy Inc ....F...... 973 881-9002
  Paterson (G-8224)
Country Home Bakers LLC - GA ....C...... 856 931-7052
  Bellmawr (G-335)
Del Bakers Inc ....E...... 856 461-0089
  Riverside (G-9496)
Livingston Bagel Warren Inc ....E...... 973 994-1915
  Livingston (G-5540)
Lo Presti & Sons LLC ....E...... 973 523-9258
  Paterson (G-8325)
Luccas Bakery Inc ....E...... 609 561-5558
  Hammonton (G-4142)
Minardi Baking Co Inc ....E...... 973 742-1107
  Denville (G-2050)
Serranis Bakery ....F...... 973 678-1777
  Orange (G-7827)
Uptown Bakeries ....C...... 856 467-9552
  Logan Township (G-5615)
Y & J Bakers Inc ....E...... 732 363-3636
  Lakewood (G-5208)

BAKERY: Wholesale Or Wholesale & Retail Combined

American Harvest Baking Co Inc ....E...... 856 642-9955
  Mount Laurel (G-6778)
Amorosos Baking Co ....B...... 215 471-4740
  Bellmawr (G-331)
Angelo Bakery Corp ....G...... 973 537-7220
  Dover (G-2076)
Angels Bakery USA LLC ....E...... 718 389-1400
  Carteret (G-1248)
Anthony & Sons Bakery Itln Bky ....D...... 973 625-2323
  Denville (G-2031)
Antique Bakery & Pizzeria ....E...... 201 714-9323
  Hoboken (G-4457)
Artisan Oven Inc ....E...... 201 488-6261
  Hackensack (G-3875)
Bimbo Bakeries Usa Inc ....D...... 732 886-1881
  Lakewood (G-5085)
Bimbo Bakeries Usa Inc ....D...... 732 390-7715
  East Brunswick (G-2138)
Bimbo Bakeries Usa Inc ....E...... 973 872-6167
  Wayne (G-11609)
Bridor USA Inc ....D...... 856 691-8000
  Vineland (G-11333)
Cake Specialty Inc ....C...... 973 238-0500
  Hawthorne (G-4224)

Celtic Passions LLC ....F 973 865-7046
Nutley (G-7644)

Cravings ....F 732 531-7122
Allenhurst (G-25)

Creative Desserts ....G 732 477-0808
Brick (G-740)

Crust and Crumb Bakery ....G 609 492-4966
Beach Haven (G-264)

Cupcakes By Carousel ....G 201 389-3090
Ridgewood (G-9422)

Damascus Bakery NJ LLC ....D 718 855-1456
Newark (G-7132)

Doms Bakery Grand Inc ....G 201 653-1948
Hoboken (G-4469)

Dr Schar Usa Inc ....E 856 803-5100
Swedesboro (G-10694)

Feed Your Soul Ltd Lblty Co ....G 201 204-0720
Kearny (G-4873)

Good To Go Inc ....E 856 627-8241
Voorhees (G-11431)

Kohouts Bakery ....G 973 772-7270
Garfield (G-3741)

Mfb Soft Pretzels Inc ....G 609 953-6773
Medford (G-6077)

Mondelez Global LLC ....A 201 794-4000
Fair Lawn (G-3103)

Nablus Pastry & Sweets ....G 973 881-8003
Paterson (G-8346)

Nexira Inc ....F 908 704-7480
Somerville (G-10222)

Northeast Foods Inc ....D 732 549-2243
Edison (G-2584)

Omni Baking Company LLC ......B 856 205-1485
Vineland (G-11386)

Orthodox Baking Co Inc ....E 973 844-9393
Belleville (G-309)

Paramount Bakeries Inc ....G 973 482-6638
Newark (G-7263)

Paramount Bakeries Inc ....E 973 481-4763
Newark (G-7264)

Perk & Pantry ....G 856 451-4333
Bridgeton (G-794)

Provence LLC ....C 201 503-9717
Englewood (G-2926)

Spindlers Bake Shop ....G 201 288-1345
Hasbrouck Heights (G-4198)

Tasty Baking Company ....G 609 641-8588
Egg Harbor Township (G-2697)

Tasty Cake South Jersey ....G 856 428-8414
Cherry Hill (G-1427)

Toufayan Bakery Inc ....C 201 861-4131
Ridgefield (G-9388)

Vitamia Pasta Boy Inc ....F 973 546-1140
Lodi (G-5608)

Zaiya Inc ....E 201 343-3988
Hackensack (G-3993)

BALLASTS: Lamp

Amperite Co Inc ....E 201 864-9503
North Bergen (G-7430)

BALLASTS: Lighting

Magnetika Inc ....E 908 454-2600
Phillipsburg (G-8657)

BALLOONS: Toy & Advertising, Rubber

Ansell Healthcare Products LLC ....C .. 732 345-5400
Iselin (G-4611)

Pacific Dnlop Holdings USA LLC ....G .. 732 345-5400
Red Bank (G-9339)

BANQUET HALL FACILITIES

Renault Winery Inc ....E 609 965-2111
Egg Harbor City (G-2669)

BAR FIXTURES: Wood

Pool Tables Plus Inc ....G 732 968-8228
Green Brook (G-3862)

BARBECUE EQPT

Clean Bbq Inc ....G 732 299-8877
Edison (G-2485)

Jarden Corporation ....E 201 610-6600
Hoboken (G-4477)

BARGES BUILDING & REPAIR

Monmouth Marine Engines Inc ....F 732 528-9290
Brielle (G-913)

Union Dry Dock & Repair Co ....G 201 792-9090
Hoboken (G-4501)

BARRELS: Shipping, Metal

Mauser Usa LLC ....E 732 353-7100
East Brunswick (G-2165)

Williams Scotsman Inc ....G 856 429-0315
Kearny (G-4922)

BARRETTES

Bigflysports Inc ....G 201 653-4414
Secaucus (G-9868)

BARRICADES: Metal

Garden State Highway Pdts Inc ....E 856 692-7572
Millville (G-6303)

BARS: Concrete Reinforcing, Fabricated Steel

Eagle Steel & Iron LLC ....G 908 587-1025
Stewartsville (G-10595)

Jersey Shore Steel Inc ....G 732 833-8855
Jackson (G-4670)

Kenric Inc ....G 856 294-9161
Swedesboro (G-10704)

Lusotech LLC ....G 973 332-3861
Newark (G-7230)

New Jersey Steel Corporation ....F 856 337-0054
Haddon Township (G-4053)

Paragon Iron Inc ....F 201 528-7307
Carlstadt (G-1198)

BARS: Extruded, Aluminum

Aluseal LLC ....G 856 692-3355
Vineland (G-11322)

BASES, BEVERAGE

Bluewater Inc ....G 973 532-1225
Millington (G-6260)

Myx Beverage LLC ....F 585 978-3542
Secaucus (G-9906)

Reeves Enterprises Inc ....G 800 883-6752
New Providence (G-7052)

BASKETS, GIFT, WHOLESALE

Reeves International Inc ....E 973 694-5006
Pequannock (G-8601)

BATH SHOPS

Hawthorne Kitchens Inc ....F 973 427-9010
Hawthorne (G-4238)

BATHING SUIT STORES

Signal Systems International ....G 732 793-4668
Lavallette (G-5237)

BATHMATS: Rubber

Innocor Inc ....C 732 945-6222
Red Bank (G-9331)

Innocor Foam Tech - Acp Inc ....D 732 945-6222
Red Bank (G-9332)

BATHROOM ACCESS & FITTINGS: Vitreous China & Earthenware

Ginsey Industries Inc ....D 856 933-1300
Swedesboro (G-10699)

Hitrons Solutions Inc ....F 201 244-0300
Bergenfield (G-387)

Lenape Products Inc ....E 609 394-5376
Trenton (G-11075)

Toilettree Products Inc ....G 845 358-5316
Ramsey (G-9253)

BATTERIES, EXC AUTOMOTIVE: Wholesalers

Ansmann USA Corp ....G 856 481-3504
Blackwood (G-470)

BNS Enterprises Inc ....G 908 285-6556
Hillsborough (G-4321)

Btech Inc ....E 973 983-1120
Rockaway (G-9555)

Enersys ....D 800 719-7887
Somerset (G-10094)

Paris Corporation New Jersey ....D .. 609 265-9200
Westampton (G-11914)

Tocad America Inc ....E 973 627-9600
Rockaway (G-9614)

BATTERIES: Alkaline, Cell Storage

Gogreen Power Inc ....F 732 994-5901
Howell (G-4555)

BATTERIES: Rechargeable

Mizco International Inc ....D 732 912-2000
Avenel (G-141)

Skc Powertech Inc ....F 973 347-7000
Budd Lake (G-944)

BATTERIES: Storage

E Group Inc ....G 856 320-9688
Mount Laurel (G-6795)

Energy Battery ....G 908 751-5918
Flemington (G-3438)

Enersys ....D 800 719-7887
Somerset (G-10094)

Hoppecke Batteries Inc ....E 856 616-0032
Hainesport (G-4073)

Maxell Corporation of America ....E .. 973 653-2400
Woodland Park (G-12224)

Mphase Technologies Inc ....F 973 256-3737
Clifton (G-1676)

Pacific Dnlop Holdings USA LLC ....G .. 732 345-5400
Red Bank (G-9339)

Tocad America Inc ....E 973 627-9600
Rockaway (G-9614)

BATTERIES: Wet

Burlington Atlantic Corp ....G 732 888-7776
Hazlet (G-4271)

BATTERY CASES: Plastic Or Plastics Combination

Ansmann USA Corp ....G 856 481-3504
Blackwood (G-470)

BATTERY CHARGERS

Ansmann USA Corp ....G 856 481-3504
Blackwood (G-470)

Dengen Scientific Corporation ....E .. 201 687-2983
Union City (G-11245)

Jsn Holdings LLC ....F 201 857-5900
Mahwah (G-5787)

Mizco International Inc ....D 732 912-2000
Avenel (G-141)

Storis Inc ....D 888 478-6747
Mount Arlington (G-6760)

Timothy P Bryan Elc Co Inc ....G .. 609 393-8325
Trenton (G-11122)

BATTERY CHARGERS: Storage, Motor & Engine Generator Type

Energy Battery Group Inc ....G 404 255-7529
Flemington (G-3439)

Mpower Technologies Inc ....F 973 256-3737
Clifton (G-1677)

BEARINGS

Bcc (USA) Inc ....G 732 572-5450
Piscataway (G-8740)

BEARINGS & PARTS Ball

C & L Machining Company Inc ....G .. 856 456-1932
Brooklawn (G-920)

Emmco Development Corp ....F 732 469-6464
Somerset (G-10093)

BEARINGS: Ball & Roller

Accurate Bushing Company Inc ....E .. 908 789-1121
Garwood (G-3774)

General Dynamics Glbl IMG Tech ......E .. 973 335-2230
Parsippany (G-8022)

Ingersoll-Rand Company ....E 856 793-7000
Mount Laurel *(G-6803)*

Rollon Corporation ....E 973 300-5492
Hackettstown *(G-4032)*

BEARINGS: Plastic

Plastics For Chemicals Inc ....G 609 242-9100
Forked River *(G-3540)*

BEARINGS: Roller & Parts

Rbc Bearings Incorporated...................C 609 882-5050
Ewing *(G-3048)*

BEAUTY & BARBER SHOP EQPT

Ameritex Industries Corp ....F 609 502-0123
Princeton Junction *(G-9148)*

Binex Line Corp ....F 201 662-7600
Fort Lee *(G-3547)*

Boruch Trading Ltd Lblty Co ....G 718 614-9575
Lakewood *(G-5086)*

Conair Corporation ....C 609 426-1300
East Windsor *(G-2354)*

Doosan Heavy Inds Amer LLC ....G 201 944-4554
Englewood Cliffs *(G-2957)*

Eaton Corporation ....E 609 835-4230
Mount Holly *(G-6768)*

Freeman Technical Sales Inc ....G 908 464-4784
New Providence *(G-7037)*

Hutchinson Industries Inc ....G 609 394-1010
Trenton *(G-11067)*

Kanar Inc ....F 201 933-2800
Carlstadt *(G-1176)*

Krohn Technical Products Inc ....F 201 933-9696
Carlstadt *(G-1182)*

McT Dairies Inc ....F 973 258-9600
Millburn *(G-6256)*

Neilmax Industries Inc ....G 908 756-8800
Edison *(G-2578)*

Pastel Companies Inc ....G 732 508-0635
Howell *(G-4563)*

Pratt Industries USA Inc ....G 973 774-4680
Totowa *(G-10965)*

Quallis Brands LLC..........................G 862 252-0664
East Orange *(G-2267)*

Sherwood Industries Inc ....D 609 396-7600
Lawrenceville *(G-5269)*

South Jersey Industries Inc ....D 609 561-9000
Hammonton *(G-4149)*

Sun Taiyang Co Ltd ....D 201 549-7100
Moonachie *(G-6546)*

Takara Belmont Usa Inc ....D 732 469-5000
Somerset *(G-10179)*

Zycal Bioceuticals Mfg LLC ....G 888 779-9225
Toms River *(G-10924)*

BEAUTY & BARBER SHOP EQPT & SPLYS WHOLESALERS

Lure Lash ....F 973 783-5274
Montclair *(G-6421)*

BEAUTY SALONS

Protameen Chemicals Inc ....E 973 256-4374
Totowa *(G-10967)*

Scories Inc ....F 973 923-1372
Newark *(G-7304)*

BEDDING & BEDSPRINGS STORES

Bedding Shoppe Inc ....G 973 334-9000
Parsippany *(G-7959)*

Hanover Direct Inc ....B 201 863-7300
Weehawken *(G-11695)*

BEDDING, BEDSPREADS, BLANKETS & SHEETS

Chic Bebe Inc ....G 201 941-5414
Tenafly *(G-10783)*

Colonial Uphl & Win Treatments ....G 609 641-3124
Pleasantville *(G-8905)*

Marketing Administration Assoc ....G 732 840-3021
Brick *(G-752)*

Star Linen Inc ....E 800 782-7999
Moorestown *(G-6623)*

Sunham Home Fashions LLC ....D 908 363-1100
New Providence *(G-7055)*

United Bedding Industries LLC ....E 908 668-0220
Plainfield *(G-8874)*

White Lotus Home Ltd Lblty Co ....F 732 828-2111
New Brunswick *(G-7013)*

BEDDING, BEDSPREADS, BLANKETS & SHEETS: Comforters & Quilts

Global Weavers Corp........................G 973 824-5500
Newark *(G-7173)*

J&S Houseware Corp ....G 973 824-5500
Newark *(G-7204)*

Sahara Textile Inc ....E 973 247-9900
Paterson *(G-8374)*

BEDDING, FROM SILK OR MANMADE FIBER

Chic Bebe Inc ....G 201 941-5414
Tenafly *(G-10783)*

BEDSPREADS & BED SETS, FROM PURCHASED MATERIALS

Ackerson Drapery Decorator Svc.........G 732 797-1967
Lakewood *(G-5065)*

Beatrice Home Fashions Inc ....E 908 561-7370
South Plainfield *(G-10336)*

D Kwitman & Son Inc ....E 201 798-5511
Hoboken *(G-4467)*

BEDSPREADS, COTTON

Metro Mills Inc ....E 973 942-6034
Paterson *(G-8337)*

BEER, WINE & LIQUOR STORES

Crescent Bottling Co Inc ....G 856 964-2268
Camden *(G-1056)*

Geislers Liquor Store ....F 856 845-0482
Thorofare *(G-10820)*

K & S Drug & Surgical Inc ....G 201 886-9191
Fort Lee *(G-3562)*

BEER, WINE & LIQUOR STORES: Beer, Packaged

Carton Brewing Company LLC ....G 732 654-2337
Atlantic Highlands *(G-110)*

Headquarters Pub LLC ....E 609 347-2579
Atlantic City *(G-100)*

BEER, WINE & LIQUOR STORES: Wine

Cream Ridge Winery.........................G 609 259-9797
Cream Ridge *(G-1933)*

Georges Wine and Spirits Galle ....G 973 948-9950
Branchville *(G-730)*

Natali Vineyards LLC ....G 609 465-0075
Cape May Court House *(G-1116)*

W J R B Inc ....G 609 884-1169
Cape May *(G-1107)*

BEESWAX PROCESSING

Frank B Ross Co Inc ....F 732 669-0810
Rahway *(G-9190)*

BELLOWS

Precision Mfg Group LLC ....D 973 785-4630
Cedar Grove *(G-1296)*

BELTING: Fabric

Belting Industries Group LLC...............E 908 272-8591
Union *(G-11158)*

BELTING: Plastic

Brecoflex Co LLC ....D 732 460-9500
Eatontown *(G-2386)*

Dyna Veyor Inc ....G 908 276-5384
Newark *(G-7146)*

BELTING: Rubber

Aarubco Rubber Co Inc ....E 973 772-8177
Saddle Brook *(G-9749)*

Belting Industries Group LLC ....E 908 272-8591
Union *(G-11158)*

Passaic Rubber Co ....D 973 696-9500
Wayne *(G-11671)*

T & B Specialties Inc........................G 732 928-4500
Jackson *(G-4679)*

BELTING: Transmission, Rubber

Polytech Designs Inc ....F 973 340-1390
Clifton *(G-1701)*

BELTS: Conveyor, Made From Purchased Wire

Vis USA LLC ....F 908 575-0606
Branchburg *(G-716)*

BENCHES: Seating

Jcdecaux Mallscape LLC ....G 201 288-2024
Hasbrouck Heights *(G-4195)*

BEVERAGE BASES & SYRUPS

Citromax Flavors Inc ....G 201 933-8405
Carlstadt *(G-1143)*

BEVERAGE STORES

Greene Bros Spclty Cof Rasters ....F 908 979-0022
Hackettstown *(G-4009)*

BEVERAGE, NONALCOHOLIC: Iced Tea/Fruit Drink, Bottled/Canned

Boston Tea Company LLC ....G 201 440-3004
Hackensack *(G-3884)*

Nirwana Foods LLC ....F 201 659-2200
Jersey City *(G-4791)*

BEVERAGES, ALCOHOLIC: Ale

Geislers Liquor Store ....F 856 845-0482
Thorofare *(G-10820)*

Group Martin LLC Jj ....F 862 240-1813
Newark *(G-7180)*

BEVERAGES, ALCOHOLIC: Beer

Anheuser-Busch LLC ....C 973 645-7700
Jersey City *(G-4707)*

Brix City Brewing ....G 201 440-0865
Little Ferry *(G-5495)*

Bucks County Brewing Co Inc ....G 609 929-0148
Lambertville *(G-5211)*

Cape May Brewing Ltd Lblty Co ....F 609 849-9933
Cape May *(G-1092)*

Cape May Brewing Ltd Lblty Co ....E 609 849-9933
Cape May *(G-1093)*

Carton Brewing Company LLC ....G 732 654-2337
Atlantic Highlands *(G-110)*

Fizzics Group LLC ....G 917 545-4533
Wall Township *(G-11483)*

Headquarters Pub LLC ....E 609 347-2579
Atlantic City *(G-100)*

High Point Brewing Co Inc ....G 973 838-7400
Butler *(G-1007)*

Hunterdon Brewing Company LLC ....D 908 454-7445
Whitehouse Station *(G-12051)*

Pinelands Brewing Ltd Lblty Co............F 609 296-6169
Ltl Egg Hbr *(G-5646)*

River Horse Brewery Co Inc ....F 609 883-0890
Ewing *(G-3053)*

Shore Point Distrg Co Inc ....C 732 308-3334
Freehold *(G-3688)*

Tuckahoe Brewing Company LLC ....F 609 645-2739
Egg Harbor Twp *(G-2701)*

BEVERAGES, ALCOHOLIC: Beer & Ale

Advanced Brewing Sys LLC ....G 973 633-1777
Prospect Park *(G-9168)*

Coors Brewing Company ....E 732 767-3300
Edison *(G-2491)*

Core 3 Brewery Ltd Lblty Co................G 856 562-0386
Franklinville *(G-3629)*

Jersey Girl Brewing Company ....G 908 269-5523
Hackettstown *(G-4014)*

Proximo Distillers LLC ....D 201 204-1718
Jersey City *(G-4809)*

Summerlands Inc ....E 973 729-8428
Sparta *(G-10521)*

Triumph Brewing of Princeton..............G 609 773-0111
Lambertville *(G-5222)*

P R O D U C T

BEVERAGES, ALCOHOLIC: Brandy

Laird & Company ....E 732 542-0312
Eatontown *(G-2411)*

BEVERAGES, ALCOHOLIC: Brandy & Brandy Spirits

Monroeville Vineyard & Winery ....F 856 521-0523
Monroeville *(G-6401)*

BEVERAGES, ALCOHOLIC: Cocktails

Hoboken Mary Ltd Liability Co ....G 201 234-9910
Hoboken *(G-4474)*
Shrem Consulting Ltd Lblty Co ....G 917 371-0581
West Long Branch *(G-11846)*

BEVERAGES, ALCOHOLIC: Distilled Liquors

Claremont Distilled Spirits ....F 973 227-7027
Fairfield *(G-3160)*
Corgi Spirits LLC ....G 862 219-3114
Jersey City *(G-4734)*
Prince Black Distillery Inc ....E 212 695-6187
Clifton *(G-1704)*
White Castle ....E 732 721-3565
South Amboy *(G-10247)*

BEVERAGES, ALCOHOLIC: Vodka

Devotion Spirits Inc ....G 877 415-3190
Red Bank *(G-9327)*

BEVERAGES, ALCOHOLIC: Wines

American Estates Wines Inc ....G 908 273-5060
Summit *(G-10634)*
Bellview Farms Inc ....G 856 697-7172
Landisville *(G-5230)*
Beneduce Vineyard ....G 908 996-3823
Pittstown *(G-8849)*
Brook Hollow Winery LLC ....G 908 496-8200
Columbia *(G-1796)*
Cava Winery and Vineyard Inc ....F 973 823-9463
Hamburg *(G-4089)*
Cream Ridge Winery ....G 609 259-9797
Cream Ridge *(G-1933)*
Dijon Enterprises LLC ....G 201 876-9463
Wallington *(G-11525)*
E & J Gallo Winery ....E 973 877-0118
Newark *(G-7148)*
GP Wine Works LLC ....G 201 997-6055
Bayonne *(G-230)*
Grape Bginnings Handson Winery ....G 732 380-7356
Eatontown *(G-2397)*
Hojiblanca USA Inc ....G 201 384-3007
Dumont *(G-2118)*
Hopewell Valley Vineyards LLC ....E 609 737-4465
Pennington *(G-8453)*
Hunterdon Brewing Company LLC ....D 908 454-7445
Whitehouse Station *(G-12051)*
Jersey Cider Works LLC ....G 917 604-0067
Montclair *(G-6420)*
Jersey Cider Works LLC ....G 908 940-4115
Asbury *(G-71)*
Michelle Ste Wine Estates Ltd ....G 973 770-8100
Mount Arlington *(G-6758)*
Natali Vineyards LLC ....G 609 465-0075
Cape May Court House *(G-1116)*
Old York Cellars ....G 908 284-9463
Ringoes *(G-9441)*
Opici Import Co Inc ....E 201 689-3256
Glen Rock *(G-3827)*
Petit Pois Corp ....G 856 608-9644
Moorestown *(G-6612)*
Plagidos Winery LLC ....G 609 567-4633
Hammonton *(G-4146)*
Redpuro LLC ....G 908 370-4460
Warren *(G-11565)*
Ripe Life Wines LLC ....G 201 560-3233
Franklin Lakes *(G-3623)*
Royal Wine Corporation ....C 718 384-2400
Bayonne *(G-243)*
Royal Wine Corporation ....C 201 535-9006
Bayonne *(G-244)*
Salem Oak Vineyards Ltd Lblty ....G 856 889-2121
Pedricktown *(G-8440)*
Sharrott Wine ....G 609 567-9463
Hammonton *(G-4148)*
Southwind Equestrian ....G 856 364-9690
Millville *(G-6325)*

Unionville Vineyards LLC ....G 908 788-0400
Ringoes *(G-9443)*
Valenzano Winery ....G 856 701-7871
Shamong *(G-9972)*
Villa Milagro Vineyards LLC ....G 908 995-2072
Phillipsburg *(G-8675)*
W J R B Inc ....G 609 884-1169
Cape May *(G-1107)*
Wagonhouse Winery LLC ....G 609 780-8019
Swedesboro *(G-10736)*
Willow Creek Winery Inc ....G 609 770-8782
Cape May *(G-1108)*
Winery Pak LLC ....G 800 434-4599
Cedar Knolls *(G-1323)*

BEVERAGES, MILK BASED

Cumberland Dairy Inc ....C 800 257-8484
Rosenhayn *(G-9706)*

BEVERAGES, NONALCOHOLIC: Bottled & canned soft drinks

Beverage Works Nj Inc ....F 973 439-5700
Fairfield *(G-3149)*
Beverage Works Nj Inc ....B 732 938-7600
Wall Township *(G-11466)*
Bot LLC ....G 609 439-1537
Lawrenceville *(G-5251)*
Coca-Cola Refreshments USA Inc ....F 732 398-4800
Monmouth Junction *(G-6338)*
Coca-Cola Refreshments USA Inc ....B 201 635-6300
Carlstadt *(G-1147)*
Crescent Bottling Co Inc ....G 856 964-2268
Camden *(G-1056)*
Evereast Trading Inc ....E 201 944-6484
Fort Lee *(G-3553)*
Global Beverage Corporation ....E 201 599-5925
Oradell *(G-7810)*
Iceberg Coffee LLC ....G 908 675-6972
Freehold *(G-3660)*
Increase Beverage Intl Inc ....F 609 303-3117
Pennsauken *(G-8526)*
Liberty Coca-Cola Bevs LLC ....D 215 427-4500
Moorestown *(G-6593)*
Liberty Coca-Cola Bevs LLC ....E 856 988-3844
Marlton *(G-5982)*
Mococo Partners Corp ....G 862 204-3461
Paterson *(G-8341)*
Push Beverages LLC ....G 973 766-2663
Succasunna *(G-10626)*
Snapple Beverage Corp (del) ....D 201 933-0070
Carlstadt *(G-1219)*
Snapple Distributors Inc ....E 732 815-2800
Avenel *(G-151)*
Tropical Bottling Corporation ....F 786 636-6169
Oradell *(G-7814)*
Unilever United States Inc ....A 201 894-4000
Englewood Cliffs *(G-2986)*

BEVERAGES, NONALCOHOLIC: Carbonated

P-Americas LLC ....G 973 739-4900
Whippany *(G-12030)*
Pepsi ....G 732 238-1598
East Brunswick *(G-2171)*
Pepsi-Cola Metro Btlg Co Inc ....B 732 424-3000
Piscataway *(G-8799)*
Pepsico Inc ....E 856 661-4604
Pennsauken *(G-8559)*
V E N Inc ....G 973 786-7862
Andover *(G-55)*

BEVERAGES, NONALCOHOLIC: Carbonated, Canned & Bottled, Etc

Crystal Beverage Corporation ....G 201 991-2342
Kearny *(G-4869)*
Ferolito Vultaggio & Sons ....E 908 282-4480
Elizabeth *(G-2732)*
Garden State Btlg Ltd Lblty Co ....F 201 991-2342
Kearny *(G-4877)*
Jolt Company Inc ....E 201 288-0535
Teterboro *(G-10803)*
Maplewood Beverage Packers LLC ....C 973 416-4582
Maplewood *(G-5923)*
Relaxzen Inc ....F 732 936-1500
Shrewsbury *(G-10010)*

BEVERAGES, NONALCOHOLIC: Flavoring extracts & syrups, nec

Adron Inc ....E 973 334-1600
Boonton *(G-551)*
Advanced Food Systems Inc ....E 732 873-6776
Somerset *(G-10049)*
Arnhem Inc ....G 908 709-4045
Westfield *(G-11921)*
Asbury Syrup Company Inc ....E 732 774-5746
Ocean *(G-7716)*
Cargill Incorporated ....G 908 820-9800
Elizabeth *(G-2717)*
Centrome Inc ....E 973 339-6242
Totowa *(G-10938)*
Citromax Usa Inc ....E 201 933-8405
Carlstadt *(G-1144)*
Farbest-Tallman Foods Corp ....D 714 897-7199
Park Ridge *(G-7919)*
Flavor and Fd Ingredients Inc ....E 201 298-6964
Middlesex *(G-6166)*
Flavor and Fd Ingredients Inc ....E 732 805-0335
Somerset *(G-10102)*
Flavors of Origin Inc ....E 732 499-9700
Avenel *(G-131)*
Givaudan Flavors Corporation ....E 609 409-6200
Cranbury *(G-1835)*
Givaudan Fragrances Corp ....C 973 386-9800
East Hanover *(G-2220)*
Interbahm International Inc ....E 732 499-9700
Avenel *(G-135)*
Jk Ingredients Inc ....D 973 340-8700
Paterson *(G-8304)*
Kerry Flavor Systems Us LLC ....C 513 771-4682
Clark *(G-1504)*
Kerry Inc ....D 908 237-1595
Flemington *(G-3453)*
Malt Products Corporation ....E 201 845-4420
Saddle Brook *(G-9772)*
Malt Products Corporation ....E 201 845-9106
Saddle Brook *(G-9773)*
Mastertaste Inc ....C 732 882-0202
Clark *(G-1508)*
Novel Ingredient Services LLC ....E 973 808-5900
East Hanover *(G-2238)*
Premier Specialties Inc ....F 732 469-6615
Middlesex *(G-6190)*
R C Fine Foods Inc ....D 908 359-5500
Hillsborough *(G-4366)*
Robertet Inc ....E 201 337-7100
Budd Lake *(G-939)*
Sensient Technologies Corp ....E 908 757-4500
South Plainfield *(G-10435)*
Solvay USA Inc ....B 609 860-4000
Princeton *(G-9122)*
Solvay USA Inc ....C 732 297-0100
North Brunswick *(G-7538)*
Takasago Intl Corp USA ....E 201 727-4200
Teterboro *(G-10814)*
Vineland Syrup Inc ....E 856 691-5772
Vineland *(G-11417)*
Wild Flavors Inc ....F 908 820-9800
Elizabeth *(G-2782)*

BEVERAGES, NONALCOHOLIC: Fruit Drnks, Under 100% Juice, Can

First Juice Inc ....G 973 895-3085
Randolph *(G-9277)*
Mosse Beverage Industries LLC ....G 732 977-5558
Bayville *(G-258)*
Tuscan/Lehigh Dairies Inc ....D 570 385-1884
Burlington *(G-992)*

BEVERAGES, NONALCOHOLIC: Fruits, Crushed, For Fountain Use

Limpert Brothers Inc ....E 856 691-1353
Vineland *(G-11380)*

BEVERAGES, NONALCOHOLIC: Soft Drinks, Canned & Bottled, Etc

3rd Generation Enterprises ....F 201 528-7274
Carlstadt *(G-1119)*
Briars Usa ....G 732 821-7600
Monmouth Junction *(G-6332)*
Canada Dry Bottling Co NY LP ....E 201 489-6600
Hackensack *(G-3893)*

(G-0000) Company's Geographic Section entry number

Ccbcc Operations LLC ....D...... 609 324-7424
Bordentown (G-594)

Coca Cola Bottling Co Mid Amer ....F...... 732 398-4800
Monmouth Junction (G-6337)

Continental Food & Bev Inc ....F...... 973 815-1600
Clifton (G-1589)

Hillside Bottling Corp ....G...... 908 353-6773
Hillside (G-4412)

Keurig Dr Pepper Inc ....D...... 908 684-4400
Andover (G-52)

Keurig Dr Pepper Inc ....F...... 732 969-1600
Carteret (G-1261)

Keurig Dr Pepper Inc ....G...... 201 933-0070
Carlstadt (G-1178)

Keurig Dr Pepper Inc ....D...... 201 832-0695
Secaucus (G-9899)

Keurig Dr Pepper Inc ....D...... 732 388-5545
Avenel (G-138)

Pepsi-Cola Metro Btlg Co Inc ....G...... 201 955-2691
Kearny (G-4905)

Pepsi-Cola Metro Btlg Co Inc ....C...... 732 922-9000
Ocean (G-7734)

Pepsi-Cola Nat Brnd Bevs Ltd ....B...... 856 665-6200
Pennsauken (G-8558)

Shabazz Fruit Cola Company LLC ......G...... 973 230-4641
Newark (G-7308)

Supreme Manufacturing Co Inc ....E...... 732 254-0087
East Brunswick (G-2190)

Union Beverage Packers LLC ....C...... 908 206-9111
Hillside (G-4446)

BEVERAGES, NONALCOHOLIC: Tea, Iced, Bottled & Canned, Etc

B-Tea Beverage LLC ....E...... 201 512-8400
Fair Lawn (G-3081)

Continntal Concession Sups Inc ....E...... 516 629-4906
Union (G-11166)

BEVERAGES, WINE & DISTILLED ALCOHOLIC, WHOLESALE: Wine

Petit Pois Corp ....G...... 856 608-9644
Moorestown (G-6612)

Royal Wine Corporation ....C...... 718 384-2400
Bayonne (G-243)

Royal Wine Corporation ....C...... 201 535-9006
Bayonne (G-244)

BEVERAGES, WINE/DISTILLED ALCOH, WHOL: Brandy/Brandy Spirits

Laird & Company ....E...... 732 542-0312
Eatontown (G-2411)

BEVERAGES, WINE/DISTILLED ALCOHOLIC, WHOL: Cocktls, Premixed

Hoboken Mary Ltd Liability Co ....G...... 201 234-9910
Hoboken (G-4474)

Shrem Consulting Ltd Lblty Co ....G...... 917 371-0581
West Long Branch (G-11846)

BICYCLES, PARTS & ACCESS

Hyper Bicycles Inc ....G...... 856 694-0352
Malaga (G-5826)

BIDETS: Vitreous China

Hitrons Solutions Inc ....F...... 201 244-0300
Bergenfield (G-388)

BILLIARD & POOL TABLES & SPLYS

Silverthorne Furniture Corp ....G...... 908 689-6969
Asbury (G-73)

BILLIARD EQPT & SPLYS WHOLESALERS

Pool Tables Plus Inc ....G...... 732 968-8228
Green Brook (G-3862)

BILLING & BOOKKEEPING SVCS

Verizon Communications Inc ....E...... 201 666-9934
Westwood (G-11975)

BINDING SVC: Books & Manuals

A S A P Nameplate & Labeling ....F...... 973 773-3934
Passaic (G-8122)

Action Copy Centers Inc ....G...... 973 744-5520
Montclair (G-6404)

Allegro Printing Corporation ....G...... 609 641-7060
Galloway (G-3708)

American Graphic Systems Inc ....G...... 201 796-0666
Fair Lawn (G-3076)

Ancraft Press Corp ....F...... 201 792-9200
Jersey City (G-4705)

Bar Lan Inc ....G...... 856 596-2330
Brigantine (G-917)

Bassil Bookbinding Company Inc ....E...... 201 440-4925
Hackensack (G-3878)

Berk Gold Stamping Corporation ....E...... 973 786-6052
Andover (G-49)

Binding Products Inc ....E...... 212 947-1192
Jersey City (G-4719)

Budget Print Center ....G...... 973 743-0073
Bloomfield (G-503)

C Jackson Associates Inc ....E...... 856 761-8000
Cherry Hill (G-1355)

Commerce Financial Prtrs Corp ....E...... 908 241-9880
Roselle (G-9667)

Cornerstone Prints Imaging LLC ....G...... 908 782-7966
Flemington (G-3431)

Craftsmen Photo Lithographers ....E...... 973 316-5791
East Hanover (G-2211)

Creative Color Lithographers ....F...... 908 789-2295
Garwood (G-3777)

Custom Book Bindery Inc ....F...... 973 815-1400
Clifton (G-1596)

D & I Printing Co Inc ....F...... 201 871-3620
Englewood (G-2885)

D A K Office Services Inc ....G...... 609 586-8222
Trenton (G-11052)

Devece & Shaffer Inc ....G...... 856 829-7282
Palmyra (G-7847)

E Nevin Miller Inc ....F...... 201 444-5784
Hawthorne (G-4230)

Fedex Office & Print Svcs Inc ....F...... 732 249-9222
New Brunswick (G-6960)

Fedex Office & Print Svcs Inc ....F...... 856 273-5959
Mount Laurel (G-6797)

Fedex Office & Print Svcs Inc ....E...... 856 427-0099
Cherry Hill (G-1364)

Grandview Printing Co Inc ....F...... 973 890-0006
Totowa (G-10950)

Gross Bros Printing Co Inc ....E...... 201 865-4606
Union City (G-11246)

Holographic Finishing Inc ....F...... 201 941-4651
Ridgefield (G-9365)

Hub Print & Copy Center LLC ....G...... 201 585-7887
Fort Lee (G-3558)

Instant Printing of Dover Inc ....G...... 973 366-6855
Dover (G-2093)

Jersey Printing Associates Inc ....E...... 732 872-9654
Atlantic Highlands (G-113)

Jmp Press Inc ....G...... 201 444-0236
Ho Ho Kus (G-4454)

John S Swift Company Inc ....G...... 201 935-2002
Teterboro (G-10801)

Johnston Letter Co Inc ....G...... 973 482-7535
Flanders (G-3412)

Laser Dim Graphics & Prtg Inc ....F...... 732 821-9000
Colts Neck (G-1789)

Latta Graphics Inc ....E...... 201 440-4040
Carlstadt (G-1183)

Lunet Inc ....G...... 201 261-3883
Paramus (G-7885)

Marco Book Co Inc ....E...... 973 458-0485
Lodi (G-5594)

Mariano Press LLC ....F...... 732 247-3659
Somerset (G-10129)

Marks Management Systems Inc ....G...... 856 866-0588
Maple Shade (G-5906)

Mid State Bindery ....G...... 908 755-9388
Middlesex (G-6180)

Morris Plains Pip Inc ....G...... 973 533-9330
Livingston (G-5548)

Myriams Dream Book Bindery ....G...... 609 345-5555
Atlantic City (G-104)

New Jersey Bindery Svcs LLC ....G...... 732 200-8024
South Plainfield (G-10412)

OShea Services Inc ....G...... 201 343-8668
Hackensack (G-3957)

Pad and Publ Assembly Corp ....E...... 856 424-0158
Cherry Hill (G-1409)

Palm Press Inc ....G...... 201 767-6504
Northvale (G-7600)

Palmarozzo Bindery ....G...... 908 688-5300
Union (G-11213)

Permagraphics Inc ....F...... 201 814-1200
Moonachie (G-6535)

Philip Holzer and Assoc LLC ....E...... 212 691-9500
Carlstadt (G-1202)

Premier Printing Solutions LLC ....G...... 732 525-0740
Sayreville (G-9836)

Printing Craftsman Inc ....F...... 201 943-0276
Fairview (G-3370)

Puent-Romer Communications Inc ......G...... 973 509-7591
Montclair (G-6433)

R & B Printing Inc ....G...... 908 766-4073
Bernardsville (G-454)

Redmond Bcms Inc ....D...... 973 664-2000
Denville (G-2053)

Roan Printing Inc ....F...... 908 526-5990
Somerville (G-10226)

Royer Group Inc ....E...... 856 324-0171
Pennsauken (G-8575)

S & M Press Inc ....F...... 973 546-6111
Garfield (G-3760)

Scarlet Printing ....G...... 732 560-1415
Middlesex (G-6193)

Scott Graphics Printing Co Inc ....G...... 201 262-0473
New Milford (G-7025)

Sheroy Printing Inc ....F...... 973 242-4040
Newark (G-7312)

Sonata Graphics Inc ....G...... 201 866-0186
Secaucus (G-9930)

Standard Prtg & Mail Svcs Inc ....F...... 973 790-3333
Fairfield (G-3311)

Star Promotions Inc ....F...... 732 356-5959
Bound Brook (G-624)

Steb Inc ....G...... 973 584-0990
Ledgewood (G-5310)

Tanter Inc ....G...... 732 382-3555
Clark (G-1516)

Tanzola Printing Inc ....G...... 973 779-0858
Clifton (G-1734)

Tech-Pak Inc ....F...... 201 935-3800
Wood Ridge (G-12140)

Tedco Inc ....G...... 609 883-0799
Ewing (G-3060)

Thewal Inc ....F...... 973 635-1880
Chatham (G-1338)

Toppan Printing Co Amer Inc ....C...... 732 469-8400
Somerset (G-10188)

Verni Vito ....G...... 732 449-1760
Wall Township (G-11517)

Westbury Press Inc ....D...... 201 894-0444
Englewood (G-2943)

Wilker Graphics LLC ....G...... 201 447-4800
Midland Park (G-6242)

Windmill Press Inc ....G...... 856 663-8990
Pennsauken (G-8589)

Yasheel Inc ....G...... 856 275-6812
Sewell (G-9967)

BINDING SVC: Pamphlets

McCormicks Bindery Inc ....E...... 856 663-8035
Pennsauken (G-8547)

BINDING SVC: Trade

Miniature Folding Inc ....F...... 201 773-6477
Elmwood Park (G-2836)

BINDINGS: Bias, Made From Purchased Materials

Quick Bias Bnding Trmming Inds ....F...... 732 422-0123
North Brunswick (G-7536)

BIOLOGICAL PRDTS: Bacteriological Media

Monmouth Bioproducts LLC ....G...... 732 863-0300
Freehold (G-3671)

BIOLOGICAL PRDTS: Exc Diagnostic

A J P Scientific Inc ....G...... 973 472-7200
Clifton (G-1552)

Adma Biologics Inc ....D...... 201 478-5552
Ramsey (G-9230)

Brainstorm Cell Thrpeutics Inc ....E...... 201 488-0460
Hackensack (G-3885)

Devatal Inc ....G...... 609 586-1575
Trenton (G-11054)

Difco Laboratories Inc ....G...... 410 316-4113
Franklin Lakes (G-3613)

DSM Nutritional Products LLC ....C...... 908 475-7093
Belvidere (G-369)

PRODUCT

DSM Nutritional Products LLC ....B 800 526-0189
   Parsippany (G-7989)

Eli Lilly and Company........................E 908 704-1807
   Branchburg (G-656)

Epicore Networks USA Inc ....E 609 267-9118
   Mount Holly (G-6770)

Genzyme Corporation.......................G 973 256-2106
   Totowa (G-10948)

Imclone LLC....................................F 908 218-9588
   Branchburg (G-666)

Imclone Systems LLC........................C 908 541-8000
   Bridgewater (G-844)

Imclone Systems LLC........................D 908 218-0147
   Branchburg (G-667)

Inspire Pharmaceuticals Inc ....C 908 423-1000
   Whitehouse Station (G-12052)

Integra Lfscnces Holdings Corp ....G 609 275-0500
   Plainsboro (G-8887)

Integra Lifesciences Corp ....D 609 275-0500
   Plainsboro (G-8889)

Intervet Inc ....G 908 423-6273
   Madison (G-5725)

Lifecell Corporation ....C 908 947-1100
   Branchburg (G-674)

Lifecell Corporation ....C 908 947-1100
   Branchburg (G-675)

Medchem Express LLC......................G 732 783-7915
   Monmouth Junction (G-6351)

Novaera Solutions Inc ....D 732 452-3605
   Iselin (G-4637)

Princeton Enduring Biotech Inc ....G 732 406-3041
   Monmouth Junction (G-6358)

Princeton Enduring Biotech Inc ....G 732 406-3041
   Monmouth Junction (G-6357)

Seqirus USA Inc ....E 908 739-0200
   Summit (G-10655)

Soligenix Inc ....F 609 538-8200
   Princeton (G-9120)

Teligent Inc ....F 856 697-1441
   Buena (G-950)

Worthington Biochemical Corp ....E 732 942-1660
   Lakewood (G-5207)

Wyeth Holdings LLC.........................G 973 660-5000
   Madison (G-5737)

Zymes LLC......................................F 201 727-1520
   Hasbrouck Heights (G-4204)

BIOLOGICAL PRDTS: Extracts

Weiling Yang...................................G 201 440-5329
   Ridgefield Park (G-9418)

BIOLOGICAL PRDTS: Vaccines

Merck & Co Inc ....B 908 740-4000
   Kenilworth (G-4974)

Merck & Co Inc ....D 908 740-4000
   Rahway (G-9212)

Organon USA Inc ....G 908 423-1000
   Whitehouse Station (G-12059)

BIOLOGICAL PRDTS: Vaccines & Immunizing

Nathji Plus Inc ....G 609 877-7600
   Willingboro (G-12121)

BLADES: Knife

Du-Mor Blade Co Inc........................E 856 829-9384
   Cinnaminson (G-1458)

US Blade Mfg Co Inc ....E 908 272-2898
   Cranford (G-1930)

BLADES: Saw, Hand Or Power

Tooling Etc LLC...............................G 732 752-8080
   Middlesex (G-6206)

BLANKBOOKS & LOOSELEAF BINDERS

Black Lagoon Inc ....G 609 815-1654
   Trenton (G-11028)

Ebsco Industries Inc ....F 201 933-1800
   Rutherford (G-9731)

Walden Lang In-Pak Service ....E 973 595-5250
   Clifton (G-1742)

BLANKBOOKS: Albums, Record

Cutting Records Inc..........................G 201 488-8444
   Hackensack (G-3901)

BLANKBOOKS: Ledgers & Ledger Sheets

Newark Morning Ledger Co ....C 973 882-6120
   Pine Brook (G-8711)

BLANKETS: Horse

Clothes Horse International ....F 856 829-8460
   Cinnaminson (G-1451)

Curvon Corporation...........................E 732 747-3832
   Tinton Falls (G-10829)

BLINDS & SHADES: Vertical

Metro Mills Inc ....E 973 942-6034
   Paterson (G-8337)

Vertical Group Inc ....F 908 277-3737
   Basking Ridge (G-208)

BLINDS : Window

Golden Champion North America ....G 732 481-9000
   Old Bridge (G-7781)

Worldwide Whl Flr Cvg Inc..................D 732 906-1400
   Edison (G-2651)

BLOCKS & BRICKS: Concrete

Clayton Block Co ....D 201 955-6292
   North Arlington (G-7418)

Clayton Block Company Inc ....E 732 549-1234
   Edison (G-2484)

Clayton Block Company Inc ....E 732 349-3700
   Toms River (G-10872)

Clayton Block Company LLC...............E 201 339-8585
   Bayonne (G-219)

Crh Americas Inc ....E 732 292-2500
   Red Bank (G-9323)

Greenrock Recycling LLC ....E 908 713-0008
   Clinton (G-1750)

Hycrete Inc.....................................E 201 386-8110
   Little Falls (G-5477)

Paverart LLC ....E 856 783-7000
   Lindenwold (G-5463)

Phillips Companies Inc......................D 973 483-4124
   Clinton (G-1753)

Procrete LLC ....E 609 365-2922
   Linwood (G-5467)

BLOCKS: Acoustical, Concrete

B&F and Son Masonry Company ....E 201 791-7630
   Elmwood Park (G-2805)

BLOCKS: Landscape Or Retaining Wall, Concrete

Blades Landscaping Inc ....F 856 779-7665
   Mount Laurel (G-6783)

Josantos Cnstr & Dev LLC..................G 732 202-7389
   Brick (G-749)

BLOCKS: Paving, Asphalt, Not From Refineries

D Depasquale Paving LLC ....G 301 674-9775
   Jackson (G-4661)

BLOCKS: Paving, Concrete

Creative Pavers ....G 201 782-1661
   Montvale (G-6451)

BLOCKS: Paving, Cut Stone

Cambridge Pavers Inc ....C 201 933-5000
   Lyndhurst (G-5673)

EP Henry Corporation ....D 856 845-6200
   Woodbury (G-12160)

BLOCKS: Roof Ballast, Concrete

GAF Elk Materials Corporation ....C 973 628-4083
   Wayne (G-11639)

BLOCKS: Sewer & Manhole, Concrete

Dunbar Concrete Products Inc ....F 973 697-2525
   Oak Ridge (G-7660)

Vogel Precast Inc ....G 732 552-8837
   Lakewood (G-5202)

BLOCKS: Standard, Concrete Or Cinder

Anchor Concrete Products Inc ....E 732 842-5010
   Red Bank (G-9319)

Anchor Concrete Products Inc ....D 732 458-9440
   Brick (G-734)

Bell Supply Co.................................E 856 663-3900
   Pennsauken (G-8486)

Clayton Block Company Inc ....E 732 363-1995
   Wall Township (G-11470)

Clayton Block Company Inc ....G 732 462-1860
   Freehold (G-3647)

Clayton Block Company Inc ....E 732 681-0186
   Wall Township (G-11471)

Clayton Block Company Inc ....F 609 693-9600
   Forked River (G-3535)

Clayton Block Company Inc ....E 732 905-3234
   Tinton Falls (G-10826)

EP Henry Corporation ....D 856 845-6200
   Woodbury (G-12160)

R P Smith & Son Inc ....F 973 584-4063
   Succasunna (G-10627)

Reuther Contracting Co Inc ....E 201 863-3550
   North Bergen (G-7480)

BLOOD RELATED HEALTH SVCS

Conduent State Healthcare LLC...........G 973 824-3250
   Newark (G-7126)

BLOWERS & FANS

Aer X Dust Corporation ....G 732 946-9462
   Holmdel (G-4508)

Automated Flexible Conveyors ....F 973 340-1695
   Clifton (G-1569)

Bioclimatic Inc.................................E 856 764-4300
   Delran (G-2012)

Bios International Corp ....G 973 492-8400
   Butler (G-998)

Cleanzones LLC ....F 732 534-5590
   Jackson (G-4658)

CSM Environmental Systems LLC ....F 908 789-5431
   Mountainside (G-6871)

Fmdk Technologies Inc ....G 201 828-9822
   Mahwah (G-5775)

Hamon Corporation...........................D 908 333-2000
   Somerville (G-10213)

Hayward Industrial Products ....C 908 351-5400
   Elizabeth (G-2741)

Indoor Environmental Tech ....E 973 709-1122
   Lincoln Park (G-5327)

JC Macelroy Co Inc ....D 732 572-7100
   Piscataway (G-8784)

Klm Mechanical Contractors ....F 201 385-6965
   Dumont (G-2120)

Kooltronic Inc..................................G 609 466-3400
   Pennington (G-8455)

Mer Made Filter................................G 201 236-0217
   Ramsey (G-9247)

Metropolitan Vacuum Clr Co Inc ....D 201 405-2225
   Oakland (G-7696)

Microelettrica-Usa LLC ....F 973 598-0806
   Budd Lake (G-937)

Respironics Inc ....C 973 581-6000
   Parsippany (G-8079)

Science Pump Corporation ....E 856 963-7700
   Camden (G-1085)

Stamm International Corp ....D 201 947-1700
   Fort Lee (G-3583)

Summit Filter Corp ....E 908 687-3500
   Union (G-11226)

Tri-Dim Filter Corporation ....F 973 709-1122
   Lincoln Park (G-5335)

Wire Cloth Manufacturers Inc ....E 973 328-1000
   Mine Hill (G-6329)

BLOWERS & FANS

Creative Industrial Kitchens ....G 973 633-0420
   Wayne (G-11621)

BLUEPRINTING SVCS

Ahern Blueprinting Inc ....F 732 223-1476
   Manasquan (G-5865)

All American Print & Copy Ctr ....G 732 758-6200
   Red Bank (G-9318)

Bellia & Sons ....E 856 845-2234
   Woodbury (G-12158)

Comptime Inc ....G 201 760-2400
   Ramsey (G-9238)

Professional Reproductions Inc...........F 212 268-1222
Marlboro **(G-5954)**

BOAT & BARGE COMPONENTS: Metal, Prefabricated

Riverside Marina Yacht Sls LLC...........F 856 461-1077
Riverside **(G-9506)**

BOAT BUILDING & REPAIR

A & D Indus & Mar Repr Inc ....E 732 541-1481
Port Reading **(G-8984)**
A PS Inlet Marina LLC...........................G....... 732 681-3303
Belmar **(G-355)**
Barnegat Light Fibrgls Sup LLC...........G....... 609 294-8870
West Creek **(G-11809)**
Carver Boat Sales Inc ....G....... 732 892-0328
Point Pleasant Boro **(G-8934)**
Commercial Water Sports Inc ....G....... 609 624-3404
Cape May Court House **(G-1113)**
Costa Mar Cnvas Enclosures LLC ....F 609 965-1538
Egg Harbor City **(G-2660)**
Dorchester Shipyard Inc ....F 856 785-8040
Dorchester **(G-2072)**
Jersey Cape Yachts Inc ....D....... 609 965-8650
Egg Harbor City **(G-2665)**
Lockwood Boat Works Inc ....E 732 721-1605
South Amboy **(G-10241)**
Marine Acquisition Inc...........................D....... 609 965-2300
Egg Harbor City **(G-2667)**
Steelstran Industries Inc ....E 732 574-0700
Avenel **(G-152)**
Sunsplash Marina LLC ....G....... 609 628-4445
Tuckahoe **(G-11138)**
Supply Technologies LLC ....E 201 641-7600
Moonachie **(G-6547)**
Tradewinds Marine Service ....G....... 848 448-6888
Toms River **(G-10918)**
Union Dry Dock & Repair Co ....E 201 963-5833
Hoboken **(G-4502)**
Yank Marine Inc ....E 609 628-2928
Tuckahoe **(G-11140)**

BOAT BUILDING & REPAIRING: Fiberglass

Henriques Yachts Works ....G....... 732 269-1180
Bayville **(G-256)**

BOAT BUILDING & REPAIRING: Lifeboats

Van Duyne Bros Inc ....G....... 609 625-0299
Mays Landing **(G-6043)**

BOAT BUILDING & REPAIRING: Yachts

Camp Marine Services Inc ....G....... 609 368-1777
Stone Harbor **(G-10613)**
Cherubini Yachts Ltd Lblty Co................G....... 856 764-5319
Delran **(G-2015)**
Eh Yachts LLC ....D....... 609 965-2300
Egg Harbor City **(G-2664)**
Tf Yachts LLC ....E 609 965-2300
Egg Harbor City **(G-2672)**
Viking Yacht Company ....B....... 609 296-6000
New Gretna **(G-7020)**

BOAT BUILDING & RPRG: Fishing, Small, Lobster, Crab, Oyster

D&S Fisheries LLC..................................G....... 914 438-3197
Colts Neck **(G-1783)**
Norma K Corporation ....G....... 732 477-6441
Point Pleasant Beach **(G-8924)**
Scorpion Charters Spt Fishing...............G....... 732 477-0985
Brick **(G-758)**

BOAT DEALERS

Carver Boat Sales Inc ....G....... 732 892-0328
Point Pleasant Boro **(G-8934)**
Custom Docks Inc...................................F 973 948-3732
Sandyston **(G-9811)**
Marine Acquisition Inc............................D....... 609 965-2300
Egg Harbor City **(G-2667)**

BOAT DEALERS: Marine Splys & Eqpt

Fisher Canvas Products Inc....................G....... 609 239-2733
Burlington **(G-972)**
Oil Technologies Services Inc ....G....... 856 845-4142
Paulsboro **(G-8422)**

Oil Technologies Services Inc ....G....... 856 845-4142
Paulsboro **(G-8423)**
Oil Technologies Services Inc ....G....... 856 845-4142
Linden **(G-5422)**

BOAT DEALERS: Motor

Arnolds Yacht Basin Inc.........................G....... 732 892-3000
Point Pleasant Boro **(G-8931)**

BOAT DEALERS: Sailboats & Eqpt

Colie Sail Makers Inc ....G....... 732 892-4344
Point Pleasant Boro **(G-8935)**

BOAT DEALERS: Sails & Eqpt

A PS Inlet Marina LLC...........................G....... 732 681-3303
Belmar **(G-355)**

BOAT LIFTS

Courtney Boatlifts Inc............................G....... 732 892-8900
Point Pleasant Boro **(G-8936)**

BOAT REPAIR SVCS

Riverside Marina Yacht Sls LLC ....F 856 461-1077
Riverside **(G-9506)**

BOAT YARD: Boat yards, storage & incidental repair

A PS Inlet Marina LLC...........................G....... 732 681-3303
Belmar **(G-355)**
Riverside Marina Yacht Sls LLC ....F 856 461-1077
Riverside **(G-9506)**

BOATS & OTHER MARINE EQPT: Plastic

A & D Indus & Mar Repr Inc ....E 732 541-1481
Port Reading **(G-8984)**

BODIES: Truck & Bus

Bristol-Donald Company Inc...................E 973 589-2640
Newark **(G-6277)**
Christensen Manufacturing ....F 609 466-9700
Pennington **(G-8446)**
Cliffside Body Corporation ....E 201 945-3970
Fairview **(G-3359)**
Fleet Equipment Corporation ....F 201 337-3294
Franklin Lakes **(G-3617)**

BODY PARTS: Automobile, Stamped Metal

Engine Combo LLC.................................F 201 290-4399
Irvington **(G-4584)**
Tonys Auto Entp Ltd Lblty Co................G....... 203 223-5776
Edison **(G-2639)**

BOILER GAGE COCKS

Haier Appliance Products LP.................G....... 973 617-1800
Wayne **(G-11645)**

BOILER REPAIR SHOP

Edward Kurth and Son Inc ....E 856 227-5252
Sewell **(G-9951)**

BOLTS: Metal

General Sullivan Group Inc.....................F 609 745-5000
Pennington **(G-8452)**
JC Macelroy Co Inc................................D....... 732 572-7100
Piscataway **(G-8784)**

BONDERIZING: Bonderizing, Metal Or Metal Prdts

Tresky Corp ....G....... 732 536-8600
Morganville **(G-6653)**

BOOK STORES

Barnes & Noble Booksellers Inc............E 201 272-3635
Lyndhurst **(G-5671)**
Light Inc ....G....... 973 777-2704
Clifton **(G-1662)**
New Horizon Press Publishers ....G....... 908 604-6311
Liberty Corner **(G-5323)**
Publishers Partnership Co ....D....... 201 689-1613
Ridgewood **(G-9428)**

BOOK STORES: Children's

Apples & Honey Press LLC....................F 973 379-7200
Springfield **(G-10537)**

BOOKS, WHOLESALE

Behrman House Inc ....F 973 379-7200
Millburn **(G-6248)**
Bookazine Co Inc ....D....... 201 339-7777
Bayonne **(G-216)**
Marco Book Co Inc ....G....... 973 458-0485
Lodi **(G-5594)**
Sterling Publishing Co Inc......................E 732 248-6563
Monroe Township **(G-6395)**

BOTTLE CAPS & RESEALERS: Plastic

Berry Global Inc ....C....... 732 356-2870
Middlesex **(G-6151)**
Berry Global Inc ....C....... 908 353-3850
Elizabeth **(G-2714)**
Berry Global Inc ....E 908 454-0900
Phillipsburg **(G-8643)**
Berry Global Inc ....C....... 718 205-3115
Elizabeth **(G-2715)**
Captive Plastics Inc ....C....... 812 424-2904
Phillipsburg **(G-8645)**
Newark Liner & Washer Inc ....F 973 482-5400
Newark **(G-7256)**

BOTTLED GAS DEALERS: Liquefied Petro, Dlvrd To Customers

Welding & Radiator Supply Co ....G....... 609 965-0433
Egg Harbor City **(G-2674)**

BOTTLED WATER DELIVERY

Vivreau Advanced Water Systems ....F 212 502-3749
Fairfield **(G-3345)**

BOTTLES: Plastic

Amcor Phrm Packg USA LLC ....C....... 856 327-1540
Millville **(G-6277)**
Amcor Rigid Plastics Usa LLC ....D....... 856 327-1540
Millville **(G-6282)**
Brent River Corp ....G....... 908 722-6021
Hillsborough **(G-4323)**
Consolidated Container Co LP ....D....... 908 289-5862
Elizabeth **(G-2720)**
Flexbiosys Inc ....F 908 300-3244
Lebanon **(G-5286)**
Imagine Gold LLC ....E 201 488-5988
South Hackensack **(G-10270)**
Q-Pak Corporation ....E 973 483-4404
Newark **(G-7281)**
Qualipac America Corp ....F 973 754-9920
Woodland Park **(G-12230)**
Setco LLC ....G....... 610 321-9760
Monroe Township **(G-6391)**
Unette Corporation ....D....... 973 328-6800
Randolph **(G-9304)**

BOUTIQUE STORES

Hillarys Fashion Boutique LLC................F 732 667-7733
Warren **(G-11552)**
Selfmade LLC ....G....... 201 792-8968
Jersey City **(G-4826)**

BOWLING EQPT & SPLY STORES

Mulbro Manufacturing & Svc Co ....G....... 732 805-0290
Middlesex **(G-6182)**

BOWLING PIN REFINISH OR REPAIR SVCS

Mulbro Manufacturing & Svc Co ....G....... 732 805-0290
Middlesex **(G-6182)**

BOXES & CRATES: Rectangular, Wood

Arrow Information Packagig LLC ....G....... 856 317-9000
Pennsauken **(G-8480)**
Boxworks Inc ....G....... 856 456-9030
Bellmawr **(G-332)**

BOXES & SHOOK: Nailed Wood

Boxworks Inc...G....... 856 456-9030
Bellmawr **(G-332)**

PRODUCT

T & M Pallet Co Inc..........E...... 908 454-3042
Stewartsville *(G-10598)*

BOXES: Corrugated

Ace Box Landau Co Inc..........G...... 201 871-4776
Englewood Cliffs *(G-2946)*
Albert Paper Products Company......E...... 973 373-0330
Irvington *(G-4571)*
Alliance Corrugated Box Inc........E...... 877 525-5269
Saddle River *(G-9802)*
Allstate Paper Box Co Inc..........D...... 973 589-2600
Newark *(G-7079)*
B Spinelli Farm Containers..........732 566-5619
Matawan *(G-6013)*
Bell Container Corp..........973 344-4400
Newark *(G-7104)*
Bradley Corrugated Box Co Inc......973 483-0505
Harrison *(G-4174)*
Bunn Industries Incorporated......F...... 609 890-2900
Trenton *(G-11030)*
Dauson Corrugated Container......F...... 973 827-1494
Hamburg *(G-4090)*
Delta Corrugated Ppr Pdts Corp....C...... 201 941-1910
Palisades Park *(G-7838)*
Delvco Pharma Packg Svcs Inc......D...... 973 278-2500
Paterson *(G-8249)*
E L Baxter Co Inc..........F...... 732 229-8219
Ocean *(G-7722)*
Enterprise Container LLC..........F...... 201 797-7200
Saddle Brook *(G-9764)*
Ferguson Containers Co Inc..........E...... 908 454-9755
Phillipsburg *(G-8647)*
Georgia-Pacific LLC..........C...... 908 995-2228
Milford *(G-6245)*
Great Northern Corporation..........856 241-0080
Swedesboro *(G-10700)*
HR Industries Inc..........F...... 201 941-8000
Ridgefield *(G-9366)*
International Container Co..........E...... 201 440-1600
Hackensack *(G-3931)*
Kampack Inc..........C...... 973 589-7400
Newark *(G-7211)*
Lanco-York Inc..........E...... 973 278-7400
Paterson *(G-8317)*
Levine Industries Inc..........E...... 973 742-1000
Paterson *(G-8319)*
Levine Packaging Supply Corp......E...... 973 575-3456
Fairfield *(G-3251)*
McLean Packaging Corporation......B...... 856 359-2600
Moorestown *(G-6600)*
McLean Packaging Corporation......D...... 856 359-2600
Pennsauken *(G-8549)*
Menasha Packaging Company LLC...C...... 732 985-0800
Edison *(G-2568)*
Orora Packaging Solutions..........E...... 609 249-5200
Cranbury *(G-1865)*
Packaging Corporation America......856 596-5020
Marlton *(G-5992)*
Packaging Corporation America......G...... 908 452-9271
Hackettstown *(G-4031)*
Paige Company Containers Inc......E...... 201 461-7800
Elmwood Park *(G-2840)*
Pin Point Container Corp..........G...... 856 848-2115
Deptford *(G-2066)*
President Cont Group II LLC..........B...... 201 933-7500
Moonachie *(G-6536)*
Raritan Packaging Industries......E...... 732 246-7200
New Brunswick *(G-6999)*
Rfc Container LLC..........D...... 856 692-0404
Vineland *(G-11396)*
Schiffenhaus Industries Inc..........C...... 973 484-5000
Newark *(G-7303)*
Sutherland Packaging Inc..........D...... 973 786-5141
Andover *(G-54)*
Trent Box Manufacturing Co..........E...... 609 587-7515
Trenton *(G-11124)*
Trenton Corrugated Products..........E...... 609 695-0808
Ewing *(G-3061)*
US Display Group Inc..........F...... 931 455-9585
Secaucus *(G-9937)*
Victory Box Corp..........G...... 908 245-5100
Roselle *(G-9685)*
Vineland Packaging Corp..........E...... 856 794-3300
Vineland *(G-11416)*
Weber Packaging Inc..........G...... 201 262-6022
Oradell *(G-7815)*
Westrock Rkt Company..........D...... 732 274-2500
Dayton *(G-1994)*

BOXES: Fuse, Electric

Hope Electrical Products Co..........G...... 973 882-7400
West Caldwell *(G-11778)*

BOXES: Mail Or Post Office, Collection/Storage, Sheet Metal

Postage Bin..........G...... 732 333-0915
Freehold *(G-3679)*

BOXES: Paperboard, Folding

Albert Paper Products Company......E...... 973 373-0330
Irvington *(G-4571)*
Contemprary Grphics Bndery Inc...C...... 856 663-7277
Camden *(G-1055)*
Cultech Inc..........C...... 732 225-2722
South Plainfield *(G-10351)*
Global Direct Marketing Group......856 427-6116
Haddonfield *(G-4060)*
International Container Co..........E...... 201 440-1600
Hackensack *(G-3931)*
Interntnal Folding Ppr Box Sls......E...... 201 941-3100
Ridgefield *(G-9367)*
Keystone Folding Box Company......D...... 973 483-1054
Newark *(G-7212)*
McLean Packaging Corporation......B...... 856 359-2600
Moorestown *(G-6600)*
Multi Packaging Solutions Inc......G...... 908 757-6000
South Plainfield *(G-10411)*
New York Folding Box Co Inc..........E...... 973 347-6932
Stanhope *(G-10588)*
R J Blen Grphic Arts Cnverting......E...... 732 545-3501
New Brunswick *(G-6998)*
Westrock Rkt Company..........C...... 973 594-6000
Totowa *(G-10983)*

BOXES: Paperboard, Set-Up

Capitol Box Corp..........E...... 201 867-6018
North Bergen *(G-7438)*
Exalent Packaging Inc..........E...... 973 742-9600
Paterson *(G-8266)*
Global Direct Marketing Group......G...... 856 427-6116
Haddonfield *(G-4060)*
Granite Packaging Supply Co......D...... 856 727-1010
Moorestown *(G-6579)*
McLean Packaging Corporation......B...... 856 359-2600
Moorestown *(G-6600)*
McLean Packaging Corporation......D...... 856 359-2600
Pennsauken *(G-8549)*
North Jersey Paper Products......F...... 973 372-4646
Union City *(G-11262)*
Ruffino Paper Box Mfg Co..........F...... 201 487-1260
Hackensack *(G-3968)*
Shure-Pak Corporation..........856 825-0808
Millville *(G-6324)*
United States Box Corp..........E...... 973 481-2000
Fairfield *(G-3335)*

BOXES: Plastic

McLean Packaging Corporation......B...... 856 359-2600
Moorestown *(G-6600)*
United States Box Corp..........E...... 973 481-2000
Fairfield *(G-3335)*

BOXES: Solid Fiber

SA Richards Inc..........G...... 201 947-3850
Fort Lee *(G-3580)*
Woodland Manufacturing Company...F...... 609 587-4180
Trenton *(G-11133)*

BOXES: Stamped Metal

Case Medical Inc..........E...... 201 313-1999
South Hackensack *(G-10257)*

BOXES: Wirebound, Wood

B Spinelli Farm Containers..........732 566-5619
Matawan *(G-6013)*

BOXES: Wooden

Bunn Industries Incorporated......F...... 609 890-2900
Trenton *(G-11030)*
Cutler Bros Box & Lumber Co......E...... 201 943-2535
Fairview *(G-3360)*
E L Baxter Co Inc..........F...... 732 229-8219
Ocean *(G-7722)*

BRAKE LININGS

Rossendale Reddaway Company......G...... 973 690-6097
Newark *(G-7292)*

BRASS & BRONZE PRDTS: Die-casted

Flemington Aluminium & Brass......G...... 908 782-6333
Flemington *(G-3440)*
Union Casting Industries Inc..........F...... 908 686-8888
Union *(G-11231)*
W & E Baum Bronze Tablet Corp...E...... 732 866-1881
Freehold *(G-3692)*

BRASS FOUNDRY, NEC

Industrial Tube Corporation..........E...... 908 369-3737
Hillsborough *(G-4345)*

BRASS ROLLING & DRAWING

Kearny Smelting & Ref Corp..........E...... 201 991-7276
Kearny *(G-4891)*

BRASSWORK: Ornamental, Structural

Bedlam Corp..........F...... 973 774-8770
Montclair *(G-6408)*

BRAZING: Metal

Bennett Heat Trting Brzing Inc......E...... 973 589-0590
Newark *(G-7106)*
E F Britten & Co Inc..........F...... 908 276-4800
Cranford *(G-1904)*

BRIC-A-BRAC

Middle East Marketing Group......G...... 201 503-0150
Englewood *(G-2917)*

BRICK, STONE & RELATED PRDTS WHOLESALERS

Aladdin Manufacturing Corp..........B...... 973 616-4600
Pompton Plains *(G-8951)*

BRICKS : Ceramic Glazed, Clay

Magpie Marketing Inc..........G...... 201 507-9155
Rutherford *(G-9739)*

BRIEFCASES

Jack Georges Inc..........E...... 973 777-6999
Passaic *(G-8150)*

BROADCASTING & COMMS EQPT: Antennas, Transmitting/Comms

Electromagnetic Tech Inds Inc......D...... 973 394-1719
Boonton *(G-564)*
Lightning Prvntion Systems Inc......G...... 856 767-7806
West Berlin *(G-11729)*
Philips Elec N Amer Corp..........D...... 973 471-9450
Clifton *(G-1695)*

BROADCASTING & COMMUNICATION EQPT: Transmit-Receiver, Radio

Conolog Corporation..........F...... 908 722-8081
Branchburg *(G-650)*

BROADCASTING & COMMUNICATIONS EQPT: Cellular Radio Telephone

Cellebrite Inc..........D...... 201 848-8552
Parsippany *(G-7965)*

BROADCASTING & COMMUNICATIONS EQPT: Studio Eqpt, Radio & TV

EVs Broadcast Equipment Inc......E...... 973 575-7811
Fairfield *(G-3186)*
Kaleidoscope Sound..........G...... 201 223-2868
Union City *(G-11252)*

BROADCASTING & COMMUNICATIONS EQPT: Transmitting, Radio/TV

Myat Inc..........E...... 201 529-0145
Mahwah *(G-5794)*

BROADCASTING STATIONS, RADIO: Religious Music

Pillar of Fire ....D....... 732 356-0102
Zarephath *(G-12270)*

BROKERS & DEALERS: Securities

Stanger Robert A & Co LP ....E....... 732 389-3600
Shrewsbury *(G-10011)*

BROKERS: Food

BSC USA LLC ....F....... 908 487-4437
Palisades Park *(G-7836)*
Losurdo Foods Inc ....E....... 201 343-6680
Hackensack *(G-3940)*
Metropolitan Foods Inc ....C....... 973 672-9400
Clifton *(G-1673)*

BROKERS: Printing

Budget Print Center ....G....... 973 743-0073
Bloomfield *(G-503)*
Elbee Litho Inc ....G....... 732 698-7738
East Brunswick *(G-2149)*
Longrun Press Inc ....F....... 856 719-9202
West Berlin *(G-11731)*

BROOMS & BRUSHES

Andon Brush Co Inc ....E....... 973 256-6611
Little Falls *(G-5469)*
Fifty/Fifty Group Inc ....E....... 201 343-1243
Hackensack *(G-3911)*
Gordon Brush Mfg Co Inc ....G....... 973 827-4600
Franklin *(G-3600)*
Industrial Brush Co Inc ....E....... 800 241-9860
Fairfield *(G-3228)*
Keystone Plastics Inc ....D....... 908 561-1300
South Plainfield *(G-10392)*
Newark Brush Company LLC ....F....... 973 376-1000
Springfield *(G-10568)*
Rubigo Cosmetics ....G....... 973 636-6573
Little Falls *(G-5487)*

BROOMS & BRUSHES: Household Or Indl

Benjamin Booth Company ....F....... 609 859-1995
Southampton *(G-10470)*
Danline Inc ....E....... 973 376-1000
Springfield *(G-10550)*
M W Jenkins Sons Inc ....F....... 973 239-5150
Cedar Grove *(G-1289)*

BROOMS & BRUSHES: Paint Rollers

Charles E Green & Son Inc ....G....... 973 485-3630
Newark *(G-7120)*
Delta Lambskin Products Inc ....E....... 201 871-9233
Englewood *(G-2887)*

BROOMS & BRUSHES: Paintbrushes

Silver Brush Limited ....G....... 609 443-4900
Windsor *(G-12129)*
Spectrum Paint Applicator ....E....... 973 732-9180
Newark *(G-7325)*

BROOMS & BRUSHES: Street Sweeping, Hand Or Machine

Around Clock Sweeping LLC ....G....... 973 887-1144
Parsippany *(G-7949)*

BRUSHES

Manufacturers Brush Corp ....G....... 973 882-6966
Dover *(G-2099)*

BRUSHES & BRUSH STOCK CONTACTS: Electric

Hoyt Corporation ....D....... 201 894-0707
Englewood *(G-2904)*
Mersen USA Bn Corp ....C....... 973 334-0700
Boonton *(G-577)*

BUCKLES & PARTS

Allary Corporation ....F....... 908 851-0077
Union *(G-11149)*
Geisler Ganz Corp ....G....... 201 223-1200
Secaucus *(G-9886)*

BUILDING & OFFICE CLEANING SVCS

Professional Laundry Solutions ....G....... 973 392-0837
Newark *(G-7278)*

BUILDING & STRUCTURAL WOOD MEMBERS

Arnold Steel Co Inc ....D....... 732 363-1079
Howell *(G-4546)*
Marino International Corp ....G....... 732 752-5100
South Plainfield *(G-10404)*
Thomas Smock Woodworking ....G....... 732 542-9167
Eatontown *(G-2426)*
Timplex Corp ....F....... 973 875-5500
Sussex *(G-10679)*

BUILDING COMPONENTS: Structural Steel

Arnold Steel Co Inc ....D....... 732 363-1079
Howell *(G-4546)*
Badger Blades LLC ....G....... 908 325-6587
Cranford *(G-1898)*
Burgess Steel Holding LLC ....G....... 201 871-3500
Englewood *(G-2879)*
Capitol Steel Inc ....F....... 609 538-9313
Trenton *(G-11032)*
Central Metals Inc ....D....... 215 462-7464
Camden *(G-1052)*
Com-Fab Inc ....G....... 973 296-0433
Hewitt *(G-4288)*
Coordinated Metals Inc ....D....... 201 460-7280
Carlstadt *(G-1149)*
Coronis Building Systems Inc ....E....... 609 261-2200
Columbus *(G-1801)*
Ddm Steel Cnstr Ltd Lblty Co ....F....... 856 794-9400
Vineland *(G-11349)*
Ddm Steel Services Inc ....F....... 856 794-1931
Vineland *(G-11350)*
H Barron Iron Works Inc ....F....... 856 456-9092
Gloucester City *(G-3838)*
J G Schmidt Steel ....F....... 973 473-4822
Passaic *(G-8149)*
John Maltese Iron Works Inc ....E....... 732 249-4350
North Brunswick *(G-7521)*
Passaic County Welders Inc ....E....... 973 696-1200
Wayne *(G-11670)*
Rcc Fabricators Inc ....E....... 609 859-9350
Southampton *(G-10480)*
Stateline Fabricators LLC ....E....... 908 387-8800
Phillipsburg *(G-8672)*

BUILDING PRDTS & MATERIALS DEALERS

Cusumano Perma-Rail Co ....G....... 908 245-9281
Roselle Park *(G-9692)*
Dubell Lumber Co ....E....... 609 654-4143
Medford *(G-6068)*
Ironbound Welding Inc ....G....... 973 589-3128
Newark *(G-7201)*
Newark Ironworks Inc ....F....... 973 424-9790
Newark *(G-7255)*
Portaseal LLC ....G....... 973 539-0100
Morristown *(G-6737)*
Precision Multiple Contrls Inc ....E....... 201 444-0600
Midland Park *(G-6236)*
Precision Multiple Contrls Inc ....D....... 201 444-0600
Midland Park *(G-6237)*
Superior Custom Kitchens LLC ....E....... 908 753-6005
Warren *(G-11568)*
Timplex Corp ....F....... 973 875-5500
Sussex *(G-10679)*

BUILDING PRDTS: Concrete

Flexco Bldg Pdts Ltd Lblty Co ....F....... 732 780-1700
Marlboro *(G-5940)*
JM Ahle Co Inc ....G....... 732 388-5507
Rahway *(G-9204)*

BUILDING PRDTS: Stone

Interntnal Dmnsional Stone LLC ....G....... 973 729-0359
Haskell *(G-4208)*

BUILDING STONE, ARTIFICIAL: Concrete

Diamond Chip Realty LLC ....E....... 973 383-4651
Sparta *(G-10497)*
Interntnal Dmnsional Stone LLC ....G....... 973 729-0359
Haskell *(G-4208)*

BUILDINGS & COMPONENTS: Prefabricated Metal

Mtn Government Services Inc ....F....... 703 443-6738
Holmdel *(G-4525)*
Pre-Fab Structures Inc ....G....... 856 768-4257
Atco *(G-90)*
Walpole Woodworkers Inc ....E....... 973 539-3555
Morris Plains *(G-6681)*

BUILDINGS, PREFABRICATED: Wholesalers

Benco Inc ....F....... 973 575-4440
Fairfield *(G-3146)*

BUILDINGS: Portable

Arrow Shed LLC ....E....... 973 835-3200
Haskell *(G-4206)*
Edward T Brady ....G....... 732 928-0257
Allentown *(G-29)*
Everlast Associates Inc ....G....... 609 261-1888
Southampton *(G-10472)*
Handi-Hut Inc ....E....... 973 614-1800
Clifton *(G-1633)*
Mobile Mini Inc ....E....... 908 561-5033
South Plainfield *(G-10408)*

BUILDINGS: Prefabricated, Metal

P M C Diners Inc ....F....... 201 337-6146
Oakland *(G-7700)*

BUILDINGS: Prefabricated, Wood

Laraccas Manufacturing Inc ....E....... 973 571-1452
Cedar Grove *(G-1288)*
Marino International Corp ....G....... 732 752-5100
South Plainfield *(G-10404)*
Mod-U-Kraf Homes LLC ....E....... 540 482-0273
West Berlin *(G-11734)*
Sustanble Bldg Innovations Inc ....G....... 800 560-4143
Manasquan *(G-5881)*
Walpole Woodworkers Inc ....E....... 973 539-3555
Morris Plains *(G-6681)*

BUILDINGS: Prefabricated, Wood

R H Vassallo Inc ....G....... 856 358-8841
Malaga *(G-5827)*

BULLETIN BOARDS: Cork

New York Blackboard of NJ Inc ....G....... 973 926-1600
Hillside *(G-4432)*
R A O Contract Sales NY Inc ....E....... 201 652-1500
Paterson *(G-8367)*

BULLION, PRECIOUS METAL, WHOLESALE

BASF Catalysts LLC ....D....... 732 205-5000
Iselin *(G-4616)*

BURGLAR ALARM MAINTENANCE & MONITORING SVCS

Engineered Security Systems ....E....... 973 257-0555
Towaco *(G-10995)*

BURGLARY PROTECTION SVCS

Merchants Alarm Systems Inc ....E....... 973 779-1296
Wallington *(G-11528)*

BURIAL VAULTS: Concrete Or Precast Terrazzo

Bradbury Burial Vault Co Inc ....E....... 856 227-2555
Blackwood *(G-473)*
Brewster Vaults & Monuments ....F....... 856 785-1412
Millville *(G-6290)*
Cooper Burial Vaults Co ....G....... 856 547-8405
Barrington *(G-174)*
Cooper-Wilbert Vault Co Inc ....E....... 856 547-8405
Barrington *(G-175)*
Creter Vault Corp ....E....... 908 782-7771
Flemington *(G-3432)*
Delaware Valley Vault Co Inc ....G....... 856 227-2555
Blackwood *(G-475)*
Di-Ferraro Inc ....E....... 973 694-7200
Wayne *(G-11623)*
Gravity Vault ....G....... 732 856-9599
Middletown *(G-6215)*

PRODUCT

Maund Enterprises Inc ....G...... 609 628-2475
Tuckahoe **(G-11136)**

BURLAP & BURLAP PRDTS

Halsted Corporation ....E...... 201 333-0670
Cranbury **(G-1836)**

BURLAP WHOLESALERS

Nyp Corp (frmr Ny-Pters Corp) ....D...... 908 351-6550
Elizabeth **(G-2761)**

BURNERS: Gas, Domestic

Carlisle Machine Works Inc ....E...... 856 825-0627
Millville **(G-6293)**

BURS: Dental

Ss White Burs Inc ....C...... 732 905-1100
Lakewood **(G-5190)**

BUS BARS: Electrical

Bryan Snook ....G...... 888 747-3250
Bedminster **(G-268)**
M&L Power Systems Maint Inc ....E...... 732 679-1800
Old Bridge **(G-7783)**

BUSHINGS & BEARINGS

Ivey Katrina Owner ....G...... 973 951-8328
Newark **(G-7202)**
Oavco Ltd Liability Company ....F...... 609 454-5340
Hamilton **(G-4120)**

BUSINESS ACTIVITIES: Non-Commercial Site

Adaptive Technology Entps LLC ....G...... 877 847-6272
Medford **(G-6063)**
Ajg Packaging LLC ....G...... 908 528-6052
Pittstown **(G-8848)**
Align Sourcing Ltd Lblty Co ....G...... 609 375-8550
Trenton **(G-11014)**
Atara LLC ....G...... 916 765-2217
Union City **(G-11243)**
Avyakta It Services LLC ....F...... 609 790-7517
East Windsor **(G-2352)**
Beseech Ltd Liability Company........G...... 908 461-7888
Belford **(G-286)**
Better Listen LLC ....G...... 917 623-9834
Teaneck **(G-10744)**
Buttonwood Enterprises LLC ....G...... 201 505-1901
Woodcliff Lake **(G-12184)**
Chariot Courier & Trans Svcs ....F...... 888 532-9125
Sayreville **(G-9816)**
Cherri Stone Interactive LLC ....G...... 844 843-7765
Lakewood **(G-5092)**
Cloudageit Ltd Liability Co ....G...... 888 205-4128
North Brunswick **(G-7513)**
Commeatus LLC ....F...... 847 772-5314
Plainsboro **(G-8878)**
Creative Products Inc ....D...... 732 614-9035
Long Branch **(G-5622)**
Decorating With Fabric Inc ....G...... 845 352-5064
Park Ridge **(G-7917)**
Defined Pro Machining LLC ....G...... 973 891-1038
Wharton **(G-11984)**
Dengen Scientific Corporation ....E...... 201 687-2983
Union City **(G-11245)**
Dibello USA Inc ....G...... 212 279-9099
Randolph **(G-9273)**
Docbox Solutions Ltd Lblty Co ....G...... 201 650-0970
Montclair **(G-6411)**
Durabrite Ltg Solutions LLC ....G...... 201 915-0555
Jersey City **(G-4745)**
Eagle Steel & Iron LLC ....G...... 908 587-1025
Stewartsville **(G-10595)**
Effexoft Inc ....G...... 732 221-3642
Somerset **(G-10092)**
Energy Tracking LLC ....G...... 973 448-8660
Flanders **(G-3407)**
Fan of Word ....G...... 201 341-5474
South Orange **(G-10305)**
Fioplex ....G...... 856 689-7213
Swedesboro **(G-10697)**
Frameware Inc ....F...... 800 582-5608
Fairfield **(G-3201)**
Fred S Burroughs North Jersey ....D...... 908 850-8773
Hackettstown **(G-4008)**

Froyo Skyview LLC ....G...... 718 607-5656
Jersey City **(G-4758)**
Gpschartscom ....G...... 609 226-8842
Ventnor City **(G-11292)**
Hangsterfers Laboratories ....E...... 856 468-0216
West Deptford **(G-11827)**
Inter Rep Associates Inc ....G...... 609 465-0077
Cape May Court House **(G-1114)**
Internet-Sales USA Corporation ....G...... 775 468-8379
Rockaway **(G-9575)**
JI Packaging Group Corp ....G...... 609 610-0286
Pennington **(G-8454)**
Kandasamy Lingeswaran ....F...... 978 631-7662
Bloomfield **(G-516)**
Levomed Inc ....G...... 908 359-4804
Somerset **(G-10123)**
M D Laboratory Supplies Inc ....G...... 732 322-0773
Franklin Park **(G-3628)**
M2 Electric LLC ....F...... 973 770-4596
Mine Hill **(G-6327)**
Master Strap LLC ....G...... 888 503-7779
Marlboro **(G-5947)**
Mobile Intelligent Alerts Inc ....G...... 201 410-5324
Holmdel **(G-4523)**
Mplayer Entertainment LLC ....G...... 302 229-3034
Cherry Hill **(G-1402)**
Nickos Construction Inc ....G...... 267 240-3997
Sicklerville **(G-10022)**
Njiw Limited Liability Company ....F...... 201 355-2955
Hackensack **(G-3954)**
Oncode-Med Inc ....G...... 908 998-3647
Basking Ridge **(G-201)**
Oxford Biochronometrics LLC ....G...... 201 755-5932
Montclair **(G-6427)**
Procrete LLC ....G...... 609 365-2922
Linwood **(G-5467)**
Quallis Brands LLC ....G...... 862 252-0664
East Orange **(G-2267)**
Quantum Pharmaceuticals Inc ....G...... 973 222-6485
Sparta **(G-10519)**
Scimar Technologies LLC ....G...... 609 208-1796
Allentown **(G-35)**
Shrem Consulting Ltd Lblty Co ....G...... 917 371-0581
West Long Branch **(G-11846)**
Sight2site Media LLC ....G...... 856 637-2479
Pomona **(G-8945)**
Sima S Enterprises LLC ....G...... 877 223-7639
Wall Township **(G-11510)**
Ssam Sports Inc ....G...... 917 553-0596
Allendale **(G-17)**
Strivr Inc ....G...... 973 216-7379
Livingston **(G-5565)**
Tap Into LLC ....G...... 908 370-1158
New Providence **(G-7056)**
Tonymacx86 LLC ....G...... 973 584-5273
Ledgewood **(G-5312)**
Trim and Tassels LLC ....G...... 973 808-1566
Fairfield **(G-3331)**
Ultimate Spinning Turning Corp ....G...... 201 372-9740
Moonachie **(G-6550)**
Umbrella & Chairs LLC ....G...... 973 284-1240
Englewood **(G-2939)**
United Cabinet Works LLC ....G...... 917 686-3395
Weehawken **(G-11700)**
Urban State ....G...... 646 836-4311
Hillside **(G-4449)**
Venture App LLC ....G...... 908 644-3985
Summit **(G-10663)**
Vivis Life LLC ....G...... 201 798-1938
Jersey City **(G-4844)**
Vu Sound Incorporated ....F...... 215 990-2864
Lumberton **(G-5666)**
Wittich Bros Marine Inc ....G...... 732 722-8656
Manasquan **(G-5885)**
Zestos Foods LLC ....G...... 888 407-5852
Teaneck **(G-10779)**
Zoluu LLC ....G...... 862 686-1774
Fair Lawn **(G-3125)**

BUSINESS FORMS WHOLESALERS

Berry Business Procedure Co ....G...... 908 272-6464
Cranford **(G-1899)**
Drew & Rogers Inc ....E...... 973 575-6210
Fairfield **(G-3179)**
Important Papers Inc ....G...... 856 751-4544
Cherry Hill **(G-1379)**
Peter Morley LLC ....G...... 732 264-0010
Hazlet **(G-4282)**
Service Data Corp Inc ....G...... 908 522-0020
Summit **(G-10656)**

Stewart Business Forms Inc...........F...... 856 768-2011
Blackwood **(G-493)**

BUSINESS FORMS: Printed, Manifold

Degree Day Systems Inc ....G...... 973 627-7959
Cedar Grove **(G-1277)**
Drew & Rogers Inc ....E...... 973 575-6210
Fairfield **(G-3179)**
Hygrade Business Group Inc ....E...... 800 836-7714
Secaucus **(G-9896)**
Infoseal LLC ....D...... 201 569-4500
Englewood **(G-2905)**
North Eastern Business Forms ....G...... 609 392-1161
Trenton **(G-11091)**
Snap Set Specialists Inc ....G...... 856 629-9552
Williamstown **(G-12106)**
Stewart Business Forms Inc ....F...... 856 768-2011
Blackwood **(G-493)**
Taylor Communications Inc ....D...... 732 560-3410
Somerset **(G-10181)**
Watonka Printing Inc ....G...... 732 974-8878
Belmar **(G-365)**

BUSINESS MACHINE REPAIR, ELECTRIC

Cummins - Allison Corp ....G...... 201 791-2394
Elmwood Park **(G-2813)**
J K Office Machine Inc ....G...... 908 273-8811
Berkeley Heights **(G-413)**

CABINETS & CASES: Show, Display & Storage, Exc Wood

Atlantic Coast Woodwork Inc ....G...... 609 294-2478
Ltl Egg Hbr **(G-5640)**
Custom Creations ....G...... 201 651-9676
Oakland **(G-7682)**

CABINETS: Bathroom Vanities, Wood

Frank Burton & Sons Inc ....G...... 856 455-1202
Bridgeton **(G-785)**
Intelco ....E...... 856 384-8562
Paulsboro **(G-8417)**
Lexora Inc ....G...... 855 453-9672
Newark **(G-7218)**

CABINETS: Entertainment

Bernard Miller Fabricators ....G...... 856 541-9499
Camden **(G-1043)**
L&W Audio/Video Inc ....G...... 212 980-2862
Hoboken **(G-4483)**
Parsons Cabinets Inc ....G...... 973 279-4954
Montclair **(G-6430)**

CABINETS: Entertainment Units, Household, Wood

Imagine Audio LLC ....G...... 856 488-1466
Cherry Hill **(G-1378)**
Silverthorne Furniture Corp ....G...... 908 689-6969
Asbury **(G-73)**

CABINETS: Factory

Acorn Industry Inc ....F...... 732 536-6256
Englishtown **(G-2989)**
Modernlinefurniture Inc ....E...... 908 486-0200
Linden **(G-5412)**
Universal Interlock Corp ....G...... 732 818-8484
Toms River **(G-10919)**
West Hudson Lumber & Mllwk Co.......G...... 201 991-7191
Kearny **(G-4920)**

CABINETS: Kitchen, Metal

Rumsons Kitchens Inc ....G...... 732 842-1810
Rumson **(G-9716)**

CABINETS: Kitchen, Wood

10-31 Incorporated ....E...... 908 496-4946
Columbia **(G-1795)**
A & J Carpets Inc ....G...... 856 227-1753
Blackwood **(G-469)**
A R Bothers Woodworking Inc ....E...... 908 725-2891
Somerville **(G-10198)**
A W Ross Inc ....F...... 973 471-5900
Passaic **(G-8123)**
Allen Cabinets and Millwork ....G...... 973 694-0665
Pequannock **(G-8596)**

Bcg Marble Gran Fabricators Co...........F 201 343-8487
  Hackensack (G-3879)
Bebus Cabinetry LLC ....G 201 729-9300
  Rutherford (G-9727)
Bennett Cabinets ....G 732 548-1616
  Edison (G-2471)
Bernard Miller Fabricators ....G 856 541-9499
  Camden (G-1043)
Capra Custom Cabinetry ....G 908 797-9848
  Washington (G-11580)
Castle Woodcraft Assoc LLC ....F 732 349-1519
  Pine Beach (G-8678)
Cavalli Cabinets Inc ....G 201 528-7070
  Piscataway (G-8745)
Certified Cabinet Corp ....G 732 741-0755
  Marlboro (G-5936)
Choice Cabinetry LLC ....E 908 707-8801
  Somerville (G-10205)
CPB Inc ....E 856 697-2700
  Buena (G-946)
Custom Cabinets By Jim Bucko............G 609 522-6646
  Wildwood (G-12071)
David Leiz Custom Woodwork ....G 908 486-1533
  Linden (G-5368)
Designer Kitchens ....F 732 370-5500
  Jackson (G-4663)
Elite Cabinetry Corp ....G 973 583-0194
  Newark (G-7152)
Euro Kraft Group LLC.............................E 856 451-7450
  Bridgeton (G-784)
European Country Kitchens Inc ....D 908 735-6659
  Pittstown (G-8850)
F L Feldman Associates ....F 732 776-8544
  Asbury Park (G-77)
Fabuwood Cabinetry Corp ....B 201 432-6555
  Jersey City (G-4751)
Fernandes Custom Cabinets ....G 732 446-2829
  Manalapan (G-5847)
Foley-Waite Associates Inc ....F 908 298-0700
  Kenilworth (G-4957)
Forman Industries Inc ....D 732 727-8100
  Old Bridge (G-7779)
Frank Ferreira Cab & Mill Work ....G 732 564-1499
  Warren (G-11548)
Franks Cabinet Shop Inc ....G 908 658-4396
  Pluckemin (G-8919)
G & M Custom Formica Work ....G 732 888-0360
  Keyport (G-5019)
Gambay Inc..G 856 330-4397
  Pennsauken (G-8513)
Gemcraft Inc ....G 732 449-8944
  Belmar (G-358)
Hanssem ....G 732 425-7695
  Edison (G-2533)
Hanssem Corporation ....D 908 754-4994
  Edison (G-2534)
Heard Woodworking LLC ....G 908 232-3978
  Westfield (G-11927)
Hutchinson Cabinets ....E 856 468-5500
  Sewell (G-9956)
J & R Custom Woodworking Inc ....G 973 625-4114
  Denville (G-2043)
John Canary Custom Wdwkg Inc ....F 908 851-2894
  Union (G-11198)
Kasanova Inc ....G 201 368-8400
  Wood Ridge (G-12137)
Ken Bauer Inc ....E 201 664-6881
  Hillsdale (G-4385)
Kerk Cabinetry LLC ....G 856 881-4213
  Glassboro (G-3807)
Kinzee Industries Inc ....F 201 408-4301
  Englewood (G-2907)
Kitchen Cabinet..G 856 228-8989
  Blackwood (G-487)
Kitchen Crafters Plus ....G 732 566-7995
  Matawan (G-6023)
Kitchen King Inc ....F 732 341-9660
  Toms River (G-10890)
Kobolak & Son Inc ....G 856 829-6106
  Cinnaminson (G-1472)
L&W Audio/Video Inc ....G 212 980-2862
  Hoboken (G-4483)
M K Woodworking Inc ....G 609 771-1350
  Ewing (G-3036)
Marte Cabinets Countertops LLC ....G 973 525-9502
  Passaic (G-8159)
Masterpiece Kitchens Inc ....G 609 518-7887
  Cherry Hill (G-1396)
Michael Lubrich...G 732 223-4235
  Manasquan (G-5874)

Michaels Cabinet Connection ....G 609 889-6611
  Rio Grande (G-9460)
Millner Kitchens Inc ....G 609 890-7300
  Hamilton (G-4118)
Mk Wood Inc ....G 973 450-5110
  Belleville (G-308)
Mp Custom FL LLC ....F 973 417-2288
  Wayne (G-11666)
Mr Pauls Custom Cabinets ....G 732 528-9427
  Manasquan (G-5875)
Nmn Closet Inc ....E 201 438-2462
  Carlstadt (G-1194)
Oberg & Lindquist Corp ....E 201 664-1300
  Westwood (G-11963)
Palumbo Millwork Inc ....G 732 938-3266
  Wall Township (G-11502)
Parsons Cabinets Inc ....G 973 279-4954
  Montclair (G-6430)
Paul Burkhardt & Sons Inc....................G 856 435-2020
  Lindenwold (G-5462)
Paul Fago Cabinet Making Inc ....G 856 384-0496
  Woodbury (G-12168)
Pine Park Kitchens Inc ....G 732 987-6520
  Lakewood (G-5171)
Platinum Designs LLC ....G 908 782-4010
  Somerville (G-10224)
Platon Interiors ....G 201 567-5533
  Englewood (G-2922)
R & M Manufacturing Inc ....E 609 495-8032
  Monroe Township (G-6390)
Regency Cabinetry LLC ....G 732 363-5630
  Lakewood (G-5178)
Regency Cabinetry LLC ....F 732 363-5630
  Lakewood (G-5179)
Regent Cabinets LLC ....F 732 363-5630
  Parsippany (G-8078)
Royal Cabinet Company Inc ....E 908 203-8000
  Bound Brook (G-622)
Salernos Kitchen Cabinets ....E 201 794-1990
  Saddle Brook (G-9789)
Shearman Cabinets ....G 973 677-0071
  East Orange (G-2269)
Shekia Group LLC....................................E 732 372-7666
  Edison (G-2616)
St Martin Cabinetry Inc ....G 732 902-6020
  Edison (G-2626)
Studio L Contracting LLC ....G 201 837-1650
  Hackensack (G-3982)
Superior Custom Kitchens LLC...............E 908 753-6005
  Warren (G-11568)
T & T Cabinet Works Inc ....G 973 279-0909
  Paterson (G-8395)
United Cabinet Works LLC ....G 917 686-3395
  Weehawken (G-11700)
Visual Architectural Designs ....F 908 754-3000
  South Plainfield (G-10451)
Vitillo & Sons Inc.....................................F 732 886-1393
  Lakewood (G-5201)

CABINETS: Office, Wood

Arnold Desks Inc.....................................E 908 686-5656
  Irvington (G-4574)
Atlantic Coast Woodwork Inc ....G.......609 294-2478
  Ltl Egg Hbr (G-5640)
Kitchens By Frank Inc ....G.......732 364-1343
  Toms River (G-10891)
Pemco Dental Corporation ....E 800 526-4170
  Springfield (G-10571)
Vinos Custom Mllwk & Finshg.................F........732 356-1147
  Middlesex (G-6209)

CABINETS: Show, Display, Etc, Wood, Exc Refrigerated

10-31 Incorporated ....E 908 496-4946
  Columbia (G-1795)
Costa Custom Cabinets Inc ....F 973 429-7004
  Bloomfield (G-510)
CPB Inc ....E 856 697-2700
  Buena (G-946)

CABLE & OTHER PAY TELEVISION DISTRIBUTION

T V L Associates Inc ....G 973 790-6766
  Wayne (G-11684)

CABLE & PAY TELEVISION SVCS: Closed Circuit

Absolute Protective Systems ....E 732 287-4500
  Edison (G-2448)

CABLE & PAY TELEVISION SVCS: Direct Broadcast Satellite

DMJ and Associates Inc..........................E 732 613-7867
  Sayreville (G-9820)

CABLE TELEVISION PRDTS

Antronix Inc ....A 609 860-0160
  Cranbury (G-1813)
Cabletenna Corp ....G 609 395-9400
  Cranbury (G-1818)
Mediabridge Products LLC ....E 856 216-8222
  Cherry Hill (G-1398)

CABLE: Coaxial

Flexco Microwave Inc ....E 908 835-1720
  Port Murray (G-8977)
Wire Fabricators & Insulators ....E 973 768-2839
  Livingston (G-5572)

CABLE: Fiber

Contemporary Cabling Company ....G 732 382-5064
  Clark (G-1499)
Dun-Rite Communications Inc.................G 201 444-0080
  Mahwah (G-5767)
Huber+suhner Astrolab Inc ....E 732 560-3800
  Warren (G-11554)
Motion Control Tech Inc ....F 973 361-2226
  Dover (G-2101)
Newtech Group Corp ....G 732 355-0392
  Kendall Park (G-4935)

CABLE: Fiber Optic

Ascentta Inc..F 732 868-1766
  Somerset (G-10064)
AT&T Technologies Inc ....A 201 771-2000
  Berkeley Heights (G-400)
Aw Machinery LLC ....F 973 882-3223
  Fairfield (G-3142)
Computer Crafts Inc ....E 973 423-3500
  Hawthorne (G-4228)
Nistica Inc ....E 908 707-9500
  Bridgewater (G-865)
Sensors Unlimited Inc ....D 609 333-8000
  Princeton (G-9116)
Vytran LLC ....E 732 972-2880
  Morganville (G-6656)

CABLE: Nonferrous, Shipboard

Alpha Wire Corporation...........................C 908 925-8000
  Elizabeth (G-2708)

CABLE: Noninsulated

Alpine Group Inc ....F 201 549-4400
  East Rutherford (G-2275)
Gentek Inc...C 973 515-0900
  Parsippany (G-8024)
Jersey Strand & Cable Inc.....................D 908 213-9350
  Phillipsburg (G-8654)

CABLE: Ropes & Fiber

Steelstran Industries Inc ....E 732 574-0700
  Avenel (G-152)

CABLE: Steel, Insulated Or Armored

Arca Industrial (nj) Inc ....G 732 339-0450
  Edison (G-2463)
Bergen Cable Technology LLC ....E 973 276-9596
  Fairfield (G-3147)
Kabel N Elettrotek Amer Inc ....G 973 265-0850
  Parsippany (G-8035)
Okonite Company ....C 201 825-0300
  Ramsey (G-9250)
US Wire & Cable Corporation ....B 973 824-5530
  Newark (G-7355)
Wire Fabricators & Insulators ....E 973 768-2839
  Livingston (G-5572)

PRODUCT

CACAO BEAN PROCESSING

Cocoa Processing Corp ....G 908 688-0415
Jersey City **(G-4729)**

CAFFEINE & DERIVATIVES

Certified Processing Corp ....G 973 923-5200
Hillside **(G-4402)**

CAGES: Wire

Allentown Inc ....B 609 259-7951
Allentown **(G-28)**

CALCULATING & ACCOUNTING EQPT

Atlantic Zeiser Inc ....E 973 228-0800
West Caldwell **(G-11766)**

CALENDARS, WHOLESALE

Judith Roth Studio Collection ....G 973 543-4455
Mendham **(G-6087)**

CALIBRATING SVCS, NEC

State Technology Inc ....G 856 467-8009
Bridgeport **(G-773)**

CAMERA & PHOTOGRAPHIC SPLYS STORES: Cameras

AAS Technologies Inc ....G 201 342-7300
Hackensack **(G-3872)**
Eom Worldwide Sales Corp ....G 732 994-7352
Lakewood **(G-5116)**

CAMERA & PHOTOGRAPHIC SPLYS STORES: Photographic Splys

Gill Associates LLC ....G 973 835-5456
Wayne **(G-11641)**

CAMERAS & RELATED EQPT: Photographic

Ar2 Products LLC ....G 800 667-1263
Pompton Plains **(G-8953)**
Fullview Inc ....G 732 275-6500
Holmdel **(G-4516)**
Intertest Inc ....E 908 496-8008
Columbia **(G-1799)**
Ion360 USA LLC ....G 866 901-0073
Moorestown **(G-6587)**
Liveu Inc ....D 201 742-5229
Hackensack **(G-3939)**
Photographic Analysis Company ....G 973 696-1000
Wayne **(G-11673)**
Prestige Camera LLC ....E 718 257-5888
Somerset **(G-10158)**
Quality Films Corp ....G 718 246-7150
Hillside **(G-4435)**
Roper Scientific Inc ....D 520 889-9933
Trenton **(G-11114)**

CANDLE SHOPS

A Cheerful Giver Inc ....F 856 358-4438
Elmer **(G-2787)**

CANDLES

Ana Design Corp ....F 609 394-0300
Trenton **(G-11017)**
Candle Artisans Incorporated ....E 908 689-2000
Washington **(G-11579)**
Little House Candles Inc ....G 609 758-2996
New Egypt **(G-7017)**
Smartlite LLC ....G 973 470-9400
Clifton **(G-1727)**
Standex International Corp ....G 732 469-8452
Middlesex **(G-6203)**
Star Soap/Star Candle/Prayer C ....G 201 690-9090
Ridgefield Park **(G-9416)**
Stephen L Feilinger ....G 609 294-1884
Ltl Egg Hbr **(G-5648)**
USA Tealight Inc ....F 732 943-2408
Avenel **(G-158)**

CANDLES: Wholesalers

A Cheerful Giver Inc ....F 856 358-4438
Elmer **(G-2787)**

CANDY & CONFECTIONS: Candy Bars, Including Chocolate Covered

Mars Wrigley Conf US LLC ....G 908 852-1000
Hackettstown **(G-4025)**
Minhura Inc ....G 862 763-4078
North Arlington **(G-7421)**
Sherwood Brands Corporation ....F 973 249-8200
New Brunswick **(G-7003)**

CANDY & CONFECTIONS: Chocolate Candy, Exc Solid Chocolate

Al Richrds Homemade Chocolates ....F 201 436-0915
Bayonne **(G-210)**
Bromilows Candy Co ....G 973 684-1496
Woodland Park **(G-12212)**
Enjou Chocolat Morristown Inc ....G 973 993-9090
Morristown **(G-6707)**
Genevieves Inc ....F 973 772-8816
Garfield **(G-3737)**

CANDY & CONFECTIONS: Fruit & Fruit Peel

Cns Confectionery Products LLC ....F 201 823-1400
Bayonne **(G-220)**

CANDY & CONFECTIONS: Licorice

Mafco Worldwide Corporation ....C 856 964-8840
Camden **(G-1075)**

CANDY & CONFECTIONS: Marzipan

Bergen Marzipan & Chocolate ....G 201 385-8343
Bergenfield **(G-383)**

CANDY & CONFECTIONS: Nuts, Glace

Naturee Nuts Inc ....F 732 786-4663
Kenilworth **(G-4979)**

CANDY & CONFECTIONS: Popcorn Balls/Other Trtd Popcorn Prdts

Nutra Nuts Inc ....G 323 260-7457
Ridgewood **(G-9427)**

CANDY, NUT & CONFECTIONERY STORES: Candy

Birnn Chocolates Inc ....G 732 214-8680
Highland Park **(G-4301)**
Bromilows Candy Co ....G 973 684-1496
Woodland Park **(G-12212)**
Damask Kandies ....G 856 467-1661
Swedesboro **(G-10690)**
Enjou Chocolat Morristown Inc ....G 973 993-9090
Morristown **(G-6707)**
Genevieves Inc ....F 973 772-8816
Garfield **(G-3737)**
Giambris Quality Sweets Inc ....G 856 783-1099
Clementon **(G-1532)**
Hillside Candy LLC ....E 908 241-4747
Roselle **(G-9672)**
K K S Criterion Chocolates ....E 732 542-7847
Eatontown **(G-2409)**
Krauses Homemade Candy Inc ....F 201 943-4790
Fairview **(G-3364)**
Matisse Chocolatier Inc ....G 201 568-2288
Englewood **(G-2914)**
Rauhausers Inc ....F 609 399-1465
Ocean City **(G-7755)**
Reilys Candy Inc ....F 609 953-0040
Medford **(G-6079)**
Shrivers Salt Wtr Taffy Fudge ....G 609 399-0100
Ocean City **(G-7758)**
Sims Lee Inc ....G 201 433-1308
Jersey City **(G-4828)**
Webers Candy Store ....G 856 455-8277
Bridgeton **(G-803)**

CANDY, NUT & CONFECTIONERY STORES: Confectionery

Fralingers Inc ....E 609 345-2177
Atlantic City **(G-97)**
James Candy Company ....D 609 344-1519
Atlantic City **(G-101)**
Old Monmouth Peanut Brittle Co ....G 732 462-1311
Freehold **(G-3674)**

CANDY, NUT & CONFECTIONERY STORES: Produced For Direct Sale

George Brummer ....G 908 232-1904
Westfield **(G-11925)**

CANDY: Chocolate From Cacao Beans

Genevieves Inc ....F 973 772-8816
Garfield **(G-3737)**
George Brummer ....G 908 232-1904
Westfield **(G-11925)**
Mars Incorporated ....F 973 691-3500
Budd Lake **(G-936)**

CANDY: Hard

Lucas World Inc ....G 832 293-3770
Budd Lake **(G-933)**

CANNED SPECIALTIES

Bakers Perfection Inc ....E 973 983-0700
Rockaway **(G-9553)**
Campbell Soup Company ....A 856 342-4800
Camden **(G-1049)**
CSC Brands LP ....F 800 257-8443
Camden **(G-1057)**
F&S Produce Company Inc ....E 856 453-0316
Rosenhayn **(G-9707)**
Goya Foods Inc ....B 201 348-4900
Secaucus **(G-9890)**
Mushroom Wisdom Inc ....F 973 470-0010
East Rutherford **(G-2312)**
Nestle Healthcare Ntrtn Inc ....C 952 848-6000
Bridgewater **(G-863)**
Novartis Corporation ....E 212 307-1122
East Hanover **(G-2232)**
Project Feed Usa Inc ....F 201 443-7143
Jersey City **(G-4807)**
Universal Prtein Spplmnts Corp ....D 732 545-3130
New Brunswick **(G-7010)**

CANS & TUBES: Ammunition, Board Laminated With Metal Foil

Hicube Coating LLC ....G 973 883-7404
Clifton **(G-1640)**

CANS: Beverage, Metal, Exc Beer

Foulkrod Associates ....A 856 662-6767
Pennsauken **(G-8511)**

CANS: Composite Foil-Fiber, Made From Purchased Materials

Sonoco Products Company ....D 609 655-0300
Dayton **(G-1988)**

CANS: Metal

Bway Corporation ....C 732 997-4100
Dayton **(G-1957)**
Elemental Container Inc ....G 908 687-7720
Union **(G-11181)**
Medin Technologies Inc ....G 973 779-2400
Totowa **(G-10955)**
Silgan Containers Mfg Corp ....D 732 287-0300
Edison **(G-2617)**
Sonoco Products Company ....D 609 655-0300
Dayton **(G-1988)**

CANS: Tin

JI Packaging Group Corp ....G 609 610-0286
Pennington **(G-8454)**
Tin Can Lids LLC ....G 201 503-0677
Tenafly **(G-10787)**

CANVAS PRDTS

Beachwood Canvas Works LLC ....F 732 929-1783
Island Heights **(G-4651)**
Colie Sail Makers Inc ....G 732 892-4344
Point Pleasant Boro **(G-8935)**
Costa Mar Cnvas Enclosures LLC ....F 609 965-1538
Egg Harbor City **(G-2660)**
Fisher Canvas Products Inc ....G 609 239-2733
Burlington **(G-972)**
Howard Lippincott ....G 856 764-8282
Riverside **(G-9499)**

Lloyds of Millville Inc..................G...... 856 825-0345
   Millville (G-6312)
Meese Inc..............................E...... 201 796-4490
   Saddle Brook (G-9774)
Revere Plastics Inc...................G...... 201 641-0777
   Little Ferry (G-5514)
Robert Brown..........................G...... 609 398-6262
   Ocean City (G-7756)
Superior Marine Canvas................G...... 856 241-1724
   Swedesboro (G-10731)
William Opdyke Awnings Inc............G...... 732 449-5940
   Wall Township (G-11519)

CANVAS PRDTS, WHOLESALE

Howard Lippincott.....................G...... 856 764-8282
   Riverside (G-9499)

CANVAS PRDTS: Boat Seats

Canvas Creations......................G...... 609 465-8428
   Cape May Court House (G-1111)

CANVAS PRDTS: Convertible Tops, Car/Boat, Fm Purchased Mtrl

Pv Deroche LLC........................E...... 908 475-2266
   Belvidere (G-374)

CAPACITORS: NEC

Electro-Ceramic Industries............E...... 201 342-2630
   Hackensack (G-3909)
Electronic Concepts Inc...............C...... 732 542-7880
   Eatontown (G-2392)
Energy Storage Corp...................D...... 732 542-7880
   Eatontown (G-2394)
Megatran Industries...................B...... 609 227-4300
   Bordentown (G-601)
Metuchen Capacitors Inc...............E...... 800 899-6969
   Holmdel (G-4522)
Nte Electronics Inc...................D...... 973 748-5089
   Bloomfield (G-524)
Tbt Group Inc.........................G...... 856 753-4500
   Bellmawr (G-353)

CAPS: Plastic

AJ Siris Products Corp................E...... 973 823-0050
   Ogdensburg (G-7769)

CAR WASH EQPT

Car Wash Parts Inc....................G...... 215 633-9250
   Ventnor City (G-11290)
Chen Brothers Machinery Co............G...... 973 328-0086
   Randolph (G-9272)
Interntional Cnsld Chemex Corp........E...... 732 828-7676
   New Brunswick (G-6969)
T & E Sales of Marlboro Inc...........G...... 732 549-7551
   Metuchen (G-6127)

CAR WASH EQPT & SPLYS WHOLESALERS

Car Wash Parts Inc....................G...... 215 633-9250
   Ventnor City (G-11290)
Chen Brothers Machinery Co............G...... 973 328-0086
   Randolph (G-9272)
Interntional Cnsld Chemex Corp........E...... 732 828-7676
   New Brunswick (G-6969)

CARBIDES

Caribe Express Associates Inc.........G...... 201 869-2822
   Guttenberg (G-3867)
United Silicon Carbide Inc............G...... 732 565-9500
   New Brunswick (G-7009)

CARBON & GRAPHITE PRDTS, NEC

Asbury Louisiana Inc..................E...... 908 537-2155
   Asbury (G-69)
Resintech Inc.........................C...... 856 768-9600
   West Berlin (G-11747)

CARBON BLACK

Total American Services Inc...........F...... 206 626-3500
   Jersey City (G-4838)

CARBON PAPER & INKED RIBBONS

Ner Data Products Inc.................E...... 888 637-3282
   Glassboro (G-3810)

CARBON SPECIALTIES Electrical Use

Bella Acqua Inc.......................F...... 609 324-9024
   Chesterfield (G-1441)

CARBONS: Electric

F S R Inc.............................D...... 973 785-4347
   Woodland Park (G-12218)

CARDBOARD PRDTS, EXC DIE-CUT

Laminated Paperboard Corp.............G...... 908 862-5995
   Linden (G-5401)

CARDIOVASCULAR SYSTEM DRUGS, EXC DIAGNOSTIC

Ebelle Debelle Phrm Inc...............F...... 973 823-0665
   Hamburg (G-4093)

CARDS: Color

American Banknote Corporation.........G...... 203 941-4090
   Fort Lee (G-3543)
Flortek Corporation...................E...... 201 436-7700
   Bayonne (G-225)

CARDS: Greeting

Amaryllis Inc.........................G...... 973 635-0500
   Chatham (G-1325)
Easy Street Publications Inc..........G...... 917 699-7820
   Union (G-11177)
Greetingtap...........................G...... 347 731-4263
   South Plainfield (G-10375)
Magnetic Ticket & Label Corp..........E...... 973 759-6500
   Belleville (G-305)
Nobleworks Inc........................F...... 201 420-0095
   Union City (G-11261)
Prudent Publishing Co Inc.............E...... 973 347-4554
   Landing (G-5227)
Saint La Salle Auxiliary Inc..........G...... 732 842-4359
   Lincroft (G-5341)
Schurman Fine Papers..................E...... 856 985-1776
   Marlton (G-5998)

CARDS: Identification

Competech Smrtcard Sltions Inc........G...... 201 256-4184
   Englewood Cliffs (G-2953)
Protec Secure Card Ltd Lblty..........E...... 732 542-0700
   Eatontown (G-2419)
Team Nisca............................G...... 732 271-7367
   Somerset (G-10182)

CARPET & UPHOLSTERY CLEANING SVCS: Carpet/Furniture, On Loc

Stanley Steemer Intl Inc..............E...... 973 574-1640
   Clifton (G-1731)

CARPETS & RUGS: Tufted

Mohawk Industries.....................G...... 973 982-6200
   Kearny (G-4901)

CARPETS, RUGS & FLOOR COVERING

A & J Carpets Inc.....................G...... 856 227-1753
   Blackwood (G-469)
Amici Imports Inc.....................F...... 908 272-8300
   Cranford (G-1896)
Bamboo & Rattan Works Inc.............G...... 732 255-4239
   Toms River (G-10866)
Bashian Bros Inc......................E...... 201 330-1001
   Ridgefield (G-9350)
Ben Aharon & Son Inc..................G...... 201 541-2388
   Englewood (G-2875)
Cno Corporation.......................G...... 732 785-5799
   Brick (G-737)
Gallery of Rugs Inc...................G...... 908 934-0040
   Summit (G-10642)
Hakakian Behzad.......................E...... 973 267-2506
   Cedar Knolls (G-1313)
Kas Oriental Rugs Inc.................E...... 732 545-1900
   Somerset (G-10118)
Kashee & Sons Inc.....................F...... 201 867-6900
   Secaucus (G-9898)
La Forchetta.........................G...... 973 304-4797
   Hawthorne (G-4245)
Moosavi Rugs Inc......................G...... 201 617-9500
   Secaucus (G-9905)

Samad Brothers Inc....................F...... 201 372-0909
   East Rutherford (G-2325)
Seldom Seen Designs LLC...............G...... 973 535-8805
   Livingston (G-5559)
Shaw Industries Inc...................B...... 609 655-8300
   Cranbury (G-1880)
SNS Oriental Rugs LLC.................G...... 201 355-8786
   Carlstadt (G-1220)
Stiles Enterprises Inc................F...... 973 625-9660
   Rockaway (G-9610)
Worldwide Whl Flr Cvg Inc.............D...... 732 906-1400
   Edison (G-2651)
Zollanvari Ltd........................F...... 201 330-3344
   Secaucus (G-9941)

CARPETS: Hand & Machine Made

Kync Design LLC.......................G...... 201 293-4677
   Secaucus (G-9900)

CARPETS: Textile Fiber

Aladdin Manufacturing Corp............B...... 973 616-4600
   Pompton Plains (G-8951)

CARRIER EQPT: Telephone Or Telegraph

Instock Wireless Components...........F...... 973 335-6550
   Boonton (G-572)
Parwan Electronics Corporation........E...... 732 290-1900
   Matawan (G-6027)

CARRYING CASES, WHOLESALE

Kini Products Inc.....................G...... 732 299-5555
   New Egypt (G-7016)

CARTONS: Egg, Molded Pulp, Made From Purchased Materials

Tekni-Plex Inc........................C...... 908 575-7661
   Branchburg (G-710)

CASES, WOOD

Minerva Custom Products LLC...........G...... 201 447-4731
   Waldwick (G-11449)

CASES: Carrying

Motion Systems LLC....................F...... 212 686-4666
   Newark (G-7245)

CASES: Carrying, Clothing & Apparel

Gibbons Company Ltd...................E...... 441 294-5047
   Elizabeth (G-2739)
Selfmade LLC..........................E...... 201 792-8968
   Jersey City (G-4826)

CASES: Plastic

Case It Inc...........................E...... 800 441-4710
   Lyndhurst (G-5675)
Case Princeton Co Inc.................E...... 908 687-1750
   Union (G-11163)
Dr Reddys Laboratories Inc............E...... 609 375-9900
   Princeton (G-9032)
Garden State Fabricators..............G...... 732 928-5006
   Cream Ridge (G-1935)
Qualipac America Corp.................F...... 973 754-9920
   Woodland Park (G-12230)
Sealed Air Holdings...................G...... 201 791-7600
   Elmwood Park (G-2849)

CASES: Shipping, Wood, Wirebound

Caudalie Usa Inc......................G...... 201 939-4969
   Carlstadt (G-1139)
Minerva Custom Products LLC...........G...... 201 447-4731
   Waldwick (G-11449)

CASH REGISTERS & PARTS

United Pos Solutions Inc..............G...... 800 303-2567
   Palisades Park (G-7845)

CASINGS: Sheet Metal

Middle Atlantic Products Inc..........B...... 973 839-1011
   Fairfield (G-3261)

PRODUCT

CAST STONE: Concrete

Jarco U S Casting Corp..................E...... 201 271-0003
Union City *(G-11250)*

CASTERS

Federal Casters Corp.....................D...... 973 483-6700
Harrison *(G-4182)*
J C W Inc..E...... 732 560-8061
Bridgewater *(G-848)*

CASTINGS GRINDING: For The Trade

Legend Machine & Grinding.................F...... 908 685-1100
Bridgewater *(G-851)*
M and D Precision Grinding...............G...... 856 764-1616
Riverside *(G-9502)*
Unique Precision Co Inc....................G...... 732 382-8699
Rahway *(G-9227)*

CASTINGS: Aerospace Investment, Ferrous

Advance Process Systems Lim...........G...... 201 400-9190
Branchville *(G-724)*
Atlantic Eqp Engineers Inc..............F...... 201 828-9400
Upper Saddle River *(G-11273)*

CASTINGS: Aerospace, Aluminum

Pgw Auto Glass LLC........................E...... 856 234-1600
Mount Laurel *(G-6825)*
TEC Cast Inc...................................E...... 201 935-3885
Carlstadt *(G-1227)*

CASTINGS: Aluminum

Rosco Inc.......................................G...... 908 789-1020
Garwood *(G-3786)*
Union Casting Industries Inc ....F...... 908 686-8888
Union *(G-11231)*

CASTINGS: Bronze, NEC, Exc Die

Federal Bronze Cast Inds Inc.............E...... 973 589-7575
Newark *(G-7161)*

CASTINGS: Commercial Investment, Ferrous

Engineered Precision Cast Co.............D...... 732 671-2424
Middletown *(G-6214)*
Howmet Castings & Services Inc ....A...... 973 442-2261
Dover *(G-2090)*
Howmet Castings & Services Inc ....B...... 973 361-0300
Dover *(G-2091)*
Howmet Castings & Services Inc ....B...... 973 361-2310
Dover *(G-2092)*
R W Wheaton Co...............................G...... 908 241-4955
Roselle Park *(G-9702)*

CASTINGS: Copper & Copper-Base Alloy, NEC, Exc Die

Union Casting Industries Inc ....F...... 908 686-8888
Union *(G-11231)*

CASTINGS: Die, Aluminum

Bierman-Everett Foundry Co ....G...... 973 373-8800
South Orange *(G-10301)*
Premier Die Casting Company ....D...... 732 634-3000
Avenel *(G-147)*

CASTINGS: Die, Nonferrous

Certech Inc ....C...... 201 842-6800
Wood Ridge *(G-12135)*
Medalco Metals Inc ....G...... 732 591-0913
Morganville *(G-6648)*
Medalco Metals Inc ....G...... 908 238-0513
Lebanon *(G-5297)*
Worldcast Network Inc ....G...... 201 767-2040
Old Tappan *(G-7802)*

CASTINGS: Die, Zinc

Abco Die Casters Inc ....D...... 973 624-7030
Newark *(G-7070)*
Carteret Die-Casting Corp.................E...... 732 246-0070
Somerset *(G-10074)*
Microcast Technologies Corp ....D...... 908 523-9503
Linden *(G-5409)*

CASTINGS: Gray Iron

Bierman-Everett Foundry Co ....G...... 973 373-8800
South Orange *(G-10301)*
Bridgestate Foundry Corp ....G...... 856 767-0400
Berlin *(G-428)*
General Foundries Inc ....E...... 732 951-9001
North Brunswick *(G-7517)*

CASTINGS: Machinery, Nonferrous, Exc Die or Aluminum Copper

Arde Inc...D...... 201 784-9880
Carlstadt *(G-1128)*
Tusa Products Inc ....G...... 609 448-8333
Ewing *(G-3063)*

CASTINGS: Precision

Alloy Cast Products Inc.....................F...... 908 245-2255
Kenilworth *(G-4936)*
Jarco U S Casting Corp.....................E...... 201 271-0003
Union City *(G-11250)*

CASTINGS: Zinc

Microcast Technologies Corp ....D...... 908 523-9503
Linden *(G-5409)*

CATALOG & MAIL-ORDER HOUSES

10-31 Incorporated ....E...... 908 496-4946
Columbia *(G-1795)*
Barnes & Noble Booksellers Inc..........E...... 201 272-3635
Lyndhurst *(G-5671)*
Hanover Direct Inc............................B...... 201 863-7300
Weehawken *(G-11695)*
Work n Gear LLC...............................G...... 856 848-7676
Woodbury *(G-12172)*

CATALOG SALES

Edmund Optics Inc ....C...... 856 547-3488
Barrington *(G-177)*

CATALYSTS: Chemical

BASF Catalysts LLC ....D...... 732 205-5000
Iselin *(G-4616)*
Rive Technology Inc ....E...... 732 329-4441
Monmouth Junction *(G-6361)*
Scientific Design Company ....C...... 201 641-0500
Little Ferry *(G-5516)*
Totalcat Group Inc ....G...... 908 497-9610
Cranford *(G-1929)*
West Dry Industries Inc ....G...... 908 757-4400
Westfield *(G-11935)*

CATERERS

Ben & Jerrys of Hoboken ....F...... 201 792-1966
Hoboken *(G-4459)*
Bringhurst Bros Inc ....E...... 856 767-0110
Berlin *(G-429)*
Catering By Maddalenas Inc ....G...... 609 466-7510
Ringoes *(G-9436)*
Georges Wine and Spirits Galle ....G...... 973 948-9950
Branchville *(G-730)*
Sushi House Inc ....E...... 201 482-0609
Palisades Park *(G-7844)*
York Street Caterers Inc ....C...... 201 868-9088
Englewood *(G-2945)*

CAULKING COMPOUNDS

May National Associates NJ Inc ....D...... 973 473-3330
Lakewood *(G-5156)*

CEILING SYSTEMS: Luminous, Commercial

Illuminating Experiences LLC...............G...... 800 734-5858
New Brunswick *(G-6967)*

CELLULOSE DERIVATIVE MATERIALS

Dicaperl Minerals Corp......................G...... 856 320-2919
Pennsauken *(G-8503)*

CEMENT: Hydraulic

Anti Hydro International Inc................F...... 908 284-9000
Flemington *(G-3427)*
Lafarge North America Inc ....G...... 201 437-2575
Bayonne *(G-236)*

Lehigh Cement Company....................G...... 973 579-2111
Sparta *(G-10509)*
Tanis Concrete ....E...... 201 796-1556
Fair Lawn *(G-3119)*

CEMENT: Masonry

Local Concrete Sup & Eqp Corp ....G...... 201 797-7979
Elmwood Park *(G-2832)*

CEMENT: Portland

Essroc Corp.....................................G...... 856 650-9046
Camden *(G-1063)*

CEMETERY MEMORIAL DEALERS

Albert H Hopper Inc ....G...... 201 991-2266
North Arlington *(G-7414)*
Bcg Marble & Granite South LLC ....G...... 732 367-3788
Jackson *(G-4655)*

CERAMIC FIBER

Advanced Cerametrics Inc.................G...... 609 397-2900
Lambertville *(G-5209)*
Ceramic Products Inc.........................G...... 201 342-8200
Hackensack *(G-3895)*
Ceramsource Inc...............................F...... 732 257-5002
East Brunswick *(G-2140)*
Crystex Composites LLC ....E...... 973 779-8866
Clifton *(G-1594)*
Intersource USA Inc..........................F...... 732 257-5002
East Brunswick *(G-2161)*

CHAINS: Power Transmission

Brilliant Light Power Inc....................E...... 609 490-0427
East Windsor *(G-2371)*

CHAMBERS & CAISSONS

Force Systems ....F...... 856 848-8026
Westville *(G-11941)*

CHANDELIERS: Commercial

Bellemead Hot Glass ....G...... 908 281-5516
Hillsborough *(G-4318)*

CHANDELIERS: Residential

Gemini Cut Glass Company Inc ....G...... 201 568-7722
Englewood *(G-2900)*
Pty Lighting LLC ....G...... 855 303-4500
Hillside *(G-4434)*

CHARCOAL: Activated

Evoqua Water Technologies LLC ....F...... 908 353-7400
Elizabeth *(G-2729)*
General Carbon Corporation ....F...... 973 523-2223
Paterson *(G-8275)*

CHART & GRAPH DESIGN SVCS

Graphicolor Corporation ....E...... 856 691-2507
Vineland *(G-11364)*

CHASING SVC: Metal

Weiler & Sons LLC.............................G...... 856 767-8842
Berlin *(G-445)*

CHASSIS: Automobile House Trailer

Orlando Systems Ltd Lblty Co ....G...... 908 400-5052
North Plainfield *(G-7560)*

CHASSIS: Motor Vehicle

Garden St Chasis Remanuf..................E...... 732 283-1910
Woodbridge *(G-12149)*

CHEESE WHOLESALERS

35 Food Corp...................................G...... 732 442-1640
Woodbridge *(G-12144)*
Colonna Brothers Inc.........................D...... 800 626-8384
North Bergen *(G-7443)*
Lioni Mozzarella & Specialty...............E...... 908 624-9450
Union *(G-11203)*
Tipico Products Co Inc.......................D...... 732 942-8820
Lakewood *(G-5195)*
Tropical Cheese Industries ....B...... 732 442-4898
Perth Amboy *(G-8634)*

CHEMICAL ELEMENTS

Acnd Partners Inc ....G....... 848 200-7460
Metuchen *(G-6094)*

Alkaline Corporation.......................E....... 732 531-7830
Oakhurst *(G-7667)*

Elemental Interiors ....G....... 646 861-3596
Montclair *(G-6412)*

Elements Truffles LLC ....G....... 908 731-2088
Jersey City *(G-4748)*

Rlct Industries LLC ....G....... 609 712-1318
Pennington *(G-8458)*

Southwest Stainless LP ....G....... 732 961-1520
Howell *(G-4567)*

Write Element LLC ....G....... 973 584-0373
Randolph *(G-9306)*

CHEMICAL PROCESSING MACHINERY & EQPT

Gluefast Company Inc ....F....... 732 918-4600
Neptune *(G-6915)*

Hosokawa Micron International..........D....... 908 273-6360
Summit *(G-10645)*

Hosokawa Micron International..........D....... 908 273-6360
Summit *(G-10646)*

Hosokawa Micron International..........D....... 908 273-6360
Summit *(G-10647)*

Hosokawa Micron International..........F....... 866 507-4974
Pennsauken *(G-8523)*

Jaygo Incorporated...........................G....... 908 688-3600
Randolph *(G-9285)*

Jet Pulverizer Co Inc........................E....... 856 235-5554
Moorestown *(G-6588)*

Koch Mdlar Process Systems LLC.......D....... 201 368-2929
Paramus *(G-7882)*

Manning & Lewis Engrg Co Inc ....D....... 908 687-2400
Union *(G-11205)*

Miracle Mile Automotive Inc..............G....... 732 886-6315
Lakewood *(G-5160)*

Witte Co Inc ....E....... 908 689-6500
Washington *(G-11590)*

Wyssmont Company Inc ....E....... 201 947-4600
Fort Lee *(G-3592)*

CHEMICAL SPLYS FOR FOUNDRIES

Adam Gates & Company LLC ....F....... 908 829-3386
Hillsborough *(G-4316)*

Sage Chemical Inc ....G....... 201 489-5172
Hackensack *(G-3970)*

CHEMICALS & ALLIED PRDTS WHOLESALERS, NEC

Ambro Inc ....E....... 201 818-9717
Pequannock *(G-8597)*

Arol Chemical Products Co ....G....... 973 344-1510
Newark *(G-7094)*

Barnegat Light Fibrgls Sup LLC..........G....... 609 294-8870
West Creek *(G-11809)*

Chemical Resources Inc ....E....... 609 520-0000
Princeton *(G-9021)*

Chemtrade Solutions LLC ....G....... 973 515-0900
Parsippany *(G-7970)*

Cronite Co Inc ....E....... 973 887-7900
Parsippany *(G-7977)*

Cvc Specialty Chemicals Inc ....F....... 856 533-3000
Moorestown *(G-6571)*

Fuel Management Services Inc............G....... 732 929-1964
Toms River *(G-10879)*

Hychem Corporation ....G....... 732 280-8803
Belmar *(G-359)*

Lab Express Inc ....F....... 973 227-1700
Fairfield *(G-3247)*

Lyciret Corp ....E....... 973 882-0322
Orange *(G-7820)*

Mel Chemicals Inc............................C....... 908 782-5800
Flemington *(G-3456)*

National Auto Detailing Netwrk..........E....... 856 931-5529
Bellmawr *(G-348)*

Pharm-Rx Chemical Corporation ....G....... 973 917-1400
Clifton *(G-1694)*

Polymer Additives Inc ....F....... 856 467-8247
Bridgeport *(G-770)*

Reade Manufacturing Company ....E....... 732 657-6451
Manchester *(G-5888)*

Sage Chemical Inc ....G....... 201 489-5172
Hackensack *(G-3970)*

Sau-Sea Swimming Pool Products ......F....... 609 859-8500
Southampton *(G-10482)*

Si Packaging LLC..............................F....... 973 869-9920
Rutherford *(G-9744)*

Sylvan Chemical Corporation..............E....... 201 934-4224
Fair Lawn *(G-3117)*

Synasia Inc ....G....... 732 205-9880
Metuchen *(G-6126)*

T & B Specialties Inc ....E....... 732 928-4500
Jackson *(G-4679)*

Vantage Spclty Ingredients Inc..........C....... 973 345-8600
Warren *(G-11570)*

Veolia Es ....E....... 732 469-5100
Middlesex *(G-6208)*

CHEMICALS & ALLIED PRDTS, WHOL: Chemical, Organic, Synthetic

Houghton Chemical Corporation ....F....... 201 460-8071
Carlstadt *(G-1170)*

Spectrum Laboratory Pdts Inc ....E....... 732 214-1300
New Brunswick *(G-7005)*

Ultra Chemical Inc............................E....... 732 224-0200
Red Bank *(G-9348)*

CHEMICALS & ALLIED PRDTS, WHOL: Test Kits, Air, Water/Soil

Kel Instruments Co Inc......................G....... 201 847-8353
Wyckoff *(G-12255)*

CHEMICALS & ALLIED PRDTS, WHOLESALE: Aerosols

Milspray LLC.....................................E....... 732 886-2223
Lakewood *(G-5159)*

CHEMICALS & ALLIED PRDTS, WHOLESALE: Alkalines & Chlorine

Ashland LLC.....................................D....... 732 353-7718
Parlin *(G-7928)*

CHEMICALS & ALLIED PRDTS, WHOLESALE: Aromatic

Berje Incorporated ....C....... 973 748-8980
Carteret *(G-1253)*

CHEMICALS & ALLIED PRDTS, WHOLESALE: Chemical Additives

Global Spclty Products-Usa Inc ....F....... 609 518-7577
Mount Holly *(G-6771)*

CHEMICALS & ALLIED PRDTS, WHOLESALE: Chemicals, Indl

Amano USA Holdings Inc....................G....... 973 403-1900
Roseland *(G-9643)*

Amfine Chemical Corporation ....F....... 201 818-0159
Hasbrouck Heights *(G-4191)*

Brenntag Specialties Inc ....D....... 800 732-0562
South Plainfield *(G-10339)*

Brown Chemical Co Inc......................E....... 201 337-0900
Oakland *(G-7677)*

G J Chemical Co ....E....... 973 589-1450
Somerset *(G-10103)*

Gpt Inc ....F....... 732 446-2400
Manalapan *(G-5849)*

Hummel Croton Inc............................F....... 908 754-1800
South Plainfield *(G-10381)*

Inversand Company Inc ....F....... 856 881-2345
Clayton *(G-1525)*

Morre-TEC Industries Inc ....E....... 908 688-9009
Union *(G-11208)*

Northeast Chemicals Inc.....................E....... 732 238-9980
East Brunswick *(G-2170)*

Prestige Laboratories Inc....................E....... 973 772-8922
East Rutherford *(G-2318)*

Raybeam Manufacturing Corp ....G....... 201 941-4529
Ridgefield *(G-9382)*

Rockwood Specialties Group Inc..........F....... 609 514-0300
Princeton *(G-9114)*

CHEMICALS & ALLIED PRDTS, WHOLESALE: Chemicals, Indl & Heavy

Just In Time Chemical Sales & ....G....... 908 862-7726
Linden *(G-5393)*

Royale Pigments & Chem Inc ....G....... 201 845-4666
Paramus *(G-7900)*

CHEMICALS & ALLIED PRDTS, WHOLESALE: Chemicals, Rustproofing

Por-15 Inc...E....... 973 887-1999
Whippany *(G-12035)*

CHEMICALS & ALLIED PRDTS, WHOLESALE: Compressed Gas

Praxair Distribution Inc ....E....... 973 589-7895
Newark *(G-7272)*

CHEMICALS & ALLIED PRDTS, WHOLESALE: Detergents

Detergent 20 LLC ....F....... 732 545-0200
New Brunswick *(G-6954)*

CHEMICALS & ALLIED PRDTS, WHOLESALE: Dry Ice

Artic Ice Manufacturing Co ....G....... 973 772-7000
Garfield *(G-3718)*

CHEMICALS & ALLIED PRDTS, WHOLESALE: Essential Oils

International Olive Oil Inc....................G....... 732 612-3338
Manasquan *(G-5871)*

CHEMICALS & ALLIED PRDTS, WHOLESALE: Indl Gases

Air Liquide Advanced Materials ....F....... 908 231-9060
Branchburg *(G-629)*

E G L Company Inc............................C....... 908 508-1111
Berkeley Heights *(G-409)*

CHEMICALS & ALLIED PRDTS, WHOLESALE: Metal Polishes

Plasma Powders & Systems Inc............G....... 732 431-0992
Marlboro *(G-5952)*

CHEMICALS & ALLIED PRDTS, WHOLESALE: Plastics Film

American Renolit Corporation..............G....... 973 706-6912
Wayne *(G-11604)*

ANS Plastics Corporation ....F....... 732 247-2776
New Brunswick *(G-6944)*

Kadakia International Inc ....G....... 908 754-4445
South Plainfield *(G-10391)*

CHEMICALS & ALLIED PRDTS, WHOLESALE: Plastics Materials, NEC

Acrilex Inc..E....... 201 333-1500
Jersey City *(G-4698)*

Mark Ronald Associates Inc ....D....... 908 558-0011
Hillside *(G-4429)*

Multi-Plastics Inc..............................E....... 856 241-9014
Swedesboro *(G-10713)*

Pro Plastics Inc ....E....... 908 925-5555
Linden *(G-5431)*

CHEMICALS & ALLIED PRDTS, WHOLESALE: Plastics Prdts, NEC

Allentown Inc....................................B....... 609 259-7951
Allentown *(G-28)*

Barlics Manufacturing Co Inc ....G....... 732 381-6229
Rahway *(G-9179)*

Central Plastics Incorporated ....G....... 973 808-0990
Parsippany *(G-7966)*

JA Heilferty LLC ....E....... 201 836-5060
Teaneck *(G-10757)*

Nitto Americas Inc ....F....... 732 901-7905
Lakewood *(G-5165)*

Nitto Americas Inc ....F....... 201 645-4950
Teaneck *(G-10763)*

Sealed Air Holdings ....G....... 201 791-7600
Elmwood Park *(G-2849)*

CHEMICALS & ALLIED PRDTS, WHOLESALE: Plastics Sheets & Rods

E & T Sales Co Inc ....G....... 856 787-0900
Mount Laurel *(G-6793)*

PRODUCT

Grewe Plastics Inc ....G..... 973 485-7602
  Newark (G-7179)
L-E-M Plastics and Supplies ....G..... 201 933-9150
  Rutherford (G-9738)

CHEMICALS & ALLIED PRDTS, WHOLESALE: Polyurethane Prdts

Worldwide Safety Systems LLC ....G..... 888 613-4501
  Teaneck (G-10778)

CHEMICALS & ALLIED PRDTS, WHOLESALE: Resins

Advansix Inc ....B..... 973 526-1800
  Parsippany (G-7941)
Resintech Inc ....C..... 856 768-9600
  West Berlin (G-11747)
Shelan Chemical Company Inc ....G..... 732 796-1003
  Monroe Township (G-6392)
Thibaut & Walker Co Inc ....G..... 973 589-3331
  Newark (G-7340)

CHEMICALS & ALLIED PRDTS, WHOLESALE: Resins, Plastics

Federal Plastics Corporation ....E..... 908 272-5800
  Cranford (G-1907)

CHEMICALS & ALLIED PRDTS, WHOLESALE: Silicon Lubricants

Path Silicones Inc ....F..... 201 796-0833
  Elmwood Park (G-2841)

CHEMICALS & ALLIED PRDTS, WHOLESALE: Spec Clean/Sanitation

Microgen Inc ....G..... 973 575-9025
  West Caldwell (G-11791)

CHEMICALS & ALLIED PRDTS, WHOLESALE: Waxes, Exc Petroleum

Honeywell International Inc ....C..... 973 455-2000
  Morris Plains (G-6668)
Honeywell Speclty Wax & Additv ....F..... 973 455-2000
  Morristown (G-6717)

CHEMICALS: Agricultural

Agilis Chemicals Inc ....G..... 973 910-2424
  Rockaway (G-9548)
Aquatrols Corp of America ....E..... 856 537-6003
  West Deptford (G-11816)
BASF Corporation ....B..... 973 245-6000
  Florham Park (G-3492)
Basfin Corporation ....A..... 973 245-6000
  Florham Park (G-3493)
Chem-Is-Try Inc ....G..... 732 372-7311
  Metuchen (G-6100)
Healios Inc ....G..... 908 731-5061
  Flemington (G-3446)
Novartis Corporation ....E..... 212 307-1122
  East Hanover (G-2232)

CHEMICALS: Aluminum Chloride

Gulco Inc ....E..... 908 238-2030
  Phillipsburg (G-8651)

CHEMICALS: Aluminum Compounds

Allied Specialty Group Inc ....F..... 201 223-4600
  North Bergen (G-7428)
Chemtrade Solutions LLC ....F..... 908 464-1500
  Berkeley Heights (G-405)
Somerville Acquisitions Co Inc ....F..... 908 782-9500
  Flemington (G-3467)
Tri-State Alum & Stainless Inc ....G..... 908 693-7337
  Bridgewater (G-903)

CHEMICALS: Aluminum Sulfate

Chemtrade Solutions LLC ....G..... 973 515-0900
  Parsippany (G-7970)

CHEMICALS: Ammonium Compounds, Exc Fertilizers, NEC

Church & Dwight Co Inc ....B..... 609 806-1200
  Ewing (G-3009)

CHEMICALS: Barium & Barium Compounds

Hummel Croton Inc ....F..... 908 754-1800
  South Plainfield (G-10381)

CHEMICALS: Brine

Water Mark Technologies Inc ....G..... 973 663-3438
  Lake Hopatcong (G-5058)

CHEMICALS: Caustic Soda

Formosa Plastics Corp USA ....B..... 973 992-2090
  Livingston (G-5530)

CHEMICALS: Fire Retardant

No Fire Technologies Inc ....G..... 201 818-1616
  South Hackensack (G-10284)
Turning Star Inc ....G..... 201 944-3462
  Leonia (G-5322)

CHEMICALS: High Purity Grade, Organic

Ultra Chemical Inc ....F..... 732 224-0200
  Red Bank (G-9348)

CHEMICALS: High Purity, Refined From Technical Grade

Avebe North America Inc ....F..... 609 520-1400
  Princeton (G-9012)
Foster and Company Inc ....F..... 973 267-4100
  Cedar Knolls (G-1312)

CHEMICALS: Inorganic, NEC

Affinity Chemical Woodbine LLC ....F..... 973 873-4070
  Flanders (G-3399)
Agilis Chemicals Inc ....G..... 973 910-2424
  Rockaway (G-9548)
AIG Industrial Group Inc ....F..... 201 767-7300
  Northvale (G-7569)
Airgas Usa LLC ....F..... 609 685-4241
  Cherry Hill (G-1342)
Airgas Usa LLC ....E..... 856 829-7878
  Cinnaminson (G-1445)
Akzo Nobel Chemicals LLC ....D..... 732 985-6262
  Edison (G-2454)
American Gas & Chemical Co Ltd ....E..... 201 767-7300
  Northvale (G-7572)
Arch Chemicals Inc ....D..... 908 561-5200
  South Plainfield (G-10329)
Atlantic Associates Intl Inc ....F..... 856 662-1717
  Pennsauken (G-8481)
Avantor Performance Mtls LLC ....B..... 908 859-2151
  Phillipsburg (G-8640)
BASF Corporation ....B..... 973 245-6000
  Florham Park (G-3492)
Basfin Corporation ....A..... 973 245-6000
  Florham Park (G-3493)
Baumar Industries Inc ....G..... 973 667-5490
  Nutley (G-7642)
Bayer Corporation ....A..... 412 777-2000
  Whippany (G-12007)
Biochemical Sciences Inc ....G..... 856 467-1813
  Swedesboro (G-10683)
Chem-Is-Try Inc ....G..... 732 372-7311
  Metuchen (G-6100)
Chemstaff Inc ....E..... 201 265-8655
  Oradell (G-7805)
Chemtrade Chemicals Corp ....D..... 973 515-0900
  Parsippany (G-7968)
Chemtrade Gcc Holding Company ....G..... 973 515-0900
  Parsippany (G-7969)
Chemtrade Water Chemical Inc ....G..... 973 515-0900
  Parsippany (G-7971)
Chessco Industries Inc ....E..... 609 882-0400
  Ewing (G-3008)
Citi-Chem Inc ....E..... 609 231-6655
  Maple Shade (G-5900)
CMS Technology Inc ....E..... 512 913-1898
  Bridgewater (G-828)
Coim USA Inc ....E..... 856 224-1668
  Paulsboro (G-8415)
Cytec Industries Inc ....C..... 973 357-3100
  Saddle Brook (G-9761)
Dallas Group of America Inc ....C..... 908 534-7800
  Whitehouse (G-12045)
E I Du Pont De Nemours & Co ....E..... 732 257-1579
  Parlin (G-7930)
Elementis Chromium Inc ....C..... 609 443-2000
  East Windsor (G-2372)

Elements Global Group LLC ....G..... 908 468-8407
  Gillette (G-3794)
Elkem Silicones USA Corp ....E..... 732 227-2060
  East Brunswick (G-2151)
Engelhard Corporation ....F..... 732 205-5000
  Iselin (G-4625)
Evonik Corporation ....B..... 973 929-8000
  Parsippany (G-8003)
Futurrex Inc ....F..... 973 209-1563
  Franklin (G-3599)
G J Chemical Co ....E..... 973 589-1450
  Somerset (G-10103)
Gentek Inc ....C..... 973 515-0900
  Parsippany (G-8024)
Honeywell International Inc ....G..... 973 455-2000
  Morris Plains (G-6668)
Innophos Inc ....G..... 973 587-8735
  Cranbury (G-1838)
Innophos Holdings Inc ....D..... 609 495-2495
  Cranbury (G-1839)
Innophos Inc ....A..... 609 495-2495
  Cranbury (G-1840)
Innophos Investments II Inc ....G..... 609 495-2495
  Cranbury (G-1841)
Innophos Invstmnts Hldings Inc ....G..... 609 495-2495
  Cranbury (G-1842)
Intelligent Mtl Solutions Inc ....F..... 609 514-4031
  Princeton (G-9059)
JM Huber Corporation ....D..... 732 603-3630
  Edison (G-2546)
Ligno Tech USA Inc ....G..... 908 429-6660
  Bridgewater (G-852)
Liquid Elements ....G..... 856 321-7646
  Maple Shade (G-5904)
Lonza Inc ....D..... 201 316-9200
  Allendale (G-13)
Mateson Chemical Corporation ....G..... 215 423-3200
  Cinnaminson (G-1476)
Mel Chemicals Inc ....C..... 908 782-5800
  Flemington (G-3456)
Meson Group Inc ....E..... 201 767-7300
  Northvale (G-7591)
Morre-TEC Industries Inc ....E..... 908 688-9009
  Union (G-11208)
Morton Salt Inc ....F..... 732 826-8414
  Perth Amboy (G-8625)
Munzing North America LP ....E..... 973 279-1306
  Bloomfield (G-523)
New Heaven Chemicals Iowa LLC ....G..... 201 506-9109
  Sussex (G-10675)
Newfuturevest Two LLC ....G..... 609 586-8004
  Trenton (G-11088)
Northeast Chemicals Inc ....E..... 732 238-9980
  East Brunswick (G-2170)
Nova Chemicals Inc ....G..... 973 726-0056
  Sparta (G-10516)
Old Bridge Chemicals Inc ....E..... 732 727-2225
  Old Bridge (G-7787)
P W Perkins Co Inc ....E..... 856 769-3525
  Woodstown (G-12239)
Phibro-Tech Inc ....E..... 201 329-7300
  Teaneck (G-10767)
Phibrochem Inc ....E..... 201 329-7300
  Teaneck (G-10768)
PQ Corporation ....E..... 732 750-9040
  Avenel (G-146)
Protameen Chemicals Inc ....E..... 973 256-4374
  Totowa (G-10967)
Reade Manufacturing Company ....E..... 732 657-6451
  Manchester (G-5888)
Resintech Inc ....C..... 856 768-9600
  West Berlin (G-11747)
Rockwood Holdings Inc ....E..... 609 514-0300
  Princeton (G-9113)
Sanit Technologies LLC ....F..... 862 238-7555
  Passaic (G-8180)
Setcon Industries Inc ....F..... 973 283-0500
  Riverdale (G-8487)
Solvay Spclty Polymers USA LLC ....C..... 856 853-8119
  West Deptford (G-11841)
Solvay USA Inc ....D..... 609 860-4000
  Cranbury (G-1881)
Spectrum Laboratory Pdts Inc ....E..... 732 214-1300
  New Brunswick (G-7005)
Spex Certprep Group LLC ....G..... 732 549-7144
  Metuchen (G-6123)
Summit Research Laboratory ....E..... 908 782-9500
  Flemington (G-3469)
Synasia Inc ....E..... 732 205-9880
  Metuchen (G-6126)

Youniversal Labortories ....G...... 201 807-9000
South Hackensack (G-10300)

CHEMICALS: Medicinal

Avebe North America Inc ....F.... 609 520-1400
Princeton (G-9012)
Bodybio Inc ....E.... 856 825-8338
Millville (G-6289)
Chromak Research Inc ....G.... 732 560-1366
Somerset (G-10082)
Pharmacia & Upjohn Inc ....B.... 908 901-8000
Peapack (G-8430)
Pharmacia & Upjohn Company LLC ....B.... 908 901-8000
Peapack (G-8431)

CHEMICALS: Medicinal, Organic, Uncompounded, Bulk

Sytheon Ltd ....G.... 973 988-1075
Boonton (G-584)

CHEMICALS: NEC

A D M Tronics Unlimited Inc ....E.... 201 767-6040
Northvale (G-7566)
A J P Scientific Inc ....G.... 973 472-7200
Clifton (G-1552)
Acceledev Chemical LLC ....G.... 862 239-1524
Wayne (G-11601)
Advansix Inc ....B.... 973 526-1800
Parsippany (G-7941)
Akzo Nobel Chemicals LLC ....D.... 732 985-6262
Edison (G-2454)
American Flux & Metal LLC ....E.... 609 561-7500
Hammonton (G-4127)
Amfine Chemical Corporation ....F.... 201 818-0159
Hasbrouck Heights (G-4191)
Ashland LLC ....G.... 908 243-3500
Bridgewater (G-815)
Ashland Spcalty Ingredients GP ....E.... 732 353-7708
Parlin (G-7929)
Atlas Refinery Inc ....E.... 973 589-2002
Newark (G-7096)
Avantor Performance Mtls LLC ....B.... 908 859-2151
Phillipsburg (G-8640)
Beacon C M P Corp ....G.... 908 851-9393
Kenilworth (G-4942)
Bostik Inc ....D.... 856 848-8669
Paulsboro (G-8414)
BP Corporation North Amer Inc ......E.... 908 474-5000
Linden (G-5353)
Brenntag Specialties Inc ....D.... 800 732-0562
South Plainfield (G-10339)
C & S Specialty Inc ....G.... 201 750-7740
Norwood (G-7617)
Cantol Inc ....E.... 609 846-7912
Wildwood (G-12070)
Cargille Tab-Pro Corporation ....F.... 973 267-8883
Carlstadt (G-1137)
CC Packaging LLC ....G.... 732 213-9008
Bayville (G-252)
Chem-Is-Try Inc ....G.... 732 372-7311
Metuchen (G-6100)
Cleaners Choice Inc ....F.... 800 652-2533
Totowa (G-10939)
Croda Inc ....D.... 732 417-0800
Edison (G-2495)
Croda Investments Inc ....G.... 732 417-0800
Edison (G-2496)
Cytec Industries Inc ....G.... 877 463-7645
Princeton (G-9026)
Cytec Industries Inc ....C.... 973 357-3100
Saddle Brook (G-9761)
Delta Procurement Inc ....G.... 201 623-9353
Carlstadt (G-1153)
Elan Inc ....D.... 973 344-8014
Newark (G-7150)
Elementis Specialties Inc ....C.... 609 443-2000
East Windsor (G-2374)
Ferro Corporation ....C.... 856 467-3000
Bridgeport (G-765)
Fisher Scientific Company LLC ....B.... 201 796-7100
Fair Lawn (G-3093)
Fluorotherm Polymers Inc ....G.... 973 575-0760
Parsippany (G-8014)
Frinton Laboratories Inc ....G.... 856 722-7037
Moorestown (G-6578)
Fuel Management Services Inc ....G.... 732 929-1964
Toms River (G-10879)
Global Seven Inc ....E.... 973 209-7474
Rockaway (G-9571)

Grignard Company LLC ....E.... 732 340-1111
Rahway (G-9194)
Gulbrandsen Technologies Inc ....E.... 908 735-5458
Clinton (G-1751)
Gulco Inc ....E.... 908 238-2030
Phillipsburg (G-8651)
Houghton Chemical Corporation ......F.... 201 460-8071
Carlstadt (G-1170)
Hychem Corporation ....G.... 732 280-8803
Belmar (G-359)
Industrial Summit Tech Corp ....G.... 732 238-2211
Parlin (G-7932)
Infineum USA LP ....A.... 908 474-0100
Linden (G-5387)
Interntonal Specialty Pdts Inc ....A.... 859 815-3333
Wayne (G-11653)
Jenisse Leisure Products Inc ....F.... 973 331-1177
Towaco (G-10997)
Kronos Worldwide Inc ....E.... 609 860-6200
Cranbury (G-1849)
Lanxess Solutions US Inc ....C.... 973 235-1800
Nutley (G-7650)
Lodor Offset Corporation ....F.... 201 935-7100
Carlstadt (G-1184)
Lonza Inc ....D.... 201 316-9200
Allendale (G-13)
Lubrizol Advanced Mtls Inc ....E.... 856 299-3764
Pedricktown (G-8438)
Lubrizol Corporation ....G.... 732 981-0149
Piscataway (G-8787)
Mapei Corporation ....E.... 732 254-4830
Swedesboro (G-10707)
Mel Chemicals Inc ....C.... 908 782-5800
Flemington (G-3456)
Mri International ....G.... 973 383-3645
Newton (G-7397)
Nutech Corp ....G.... 908 707-2097
Franklin Lakes (G-3622)
Plant Food Company Inc ....E.... 609 448-0935
Cranbury (G-1870)
Polymer Additives Inc ....D.... 856 467-8220
Swedesboro (G-10719)
Polymer Additives Inc ....F.... 856 467-8247
Bridgeport (G-770)
Procedyne Corp ....E.... 732 249-8347
New Brunswick (G-6996)
Rockwood Specialties Group Inc ......F.... 609 514-0300
Princeton (G-9114)
Royce Associates A Ltd Partnr ....D.... 201 438-5200
East Rutherford (G-2322)
Shamrock Technologies Inc ....C.... 973 242-2999
Newark (G-7309)
Sika Corporation ....B.... 201 933-8800
Lyndhurst (G-5708)
Sirchie Acquisition Co LLC ....E.... 609 654-0777
Medford (G-6081)
SKW Quab Chemicals Inc ....F.... 201 556-0300
Saddle Brook (G-9794)
Solvay USA Inc ....B.... 609 860-4000
Princeton (G-9122)
Spectrum Laboratory Pdts Inc ....C.... 732 214-1300
New Brunswick (G-7004)
Spectrum Laboratory Pdts Inc ....E.... 732 214-1300
New Brunswick (G-7005)
Spex Certiprep Inc ....D.... 732 549-7144
Metuchen (G-6121)
Stepan Company ....D.... 201 845-3030
Maywood (G-6061)
Stonhard Manufacturing Co Inc ....E.... 856 779-7500
Maple Shade (G-5910)
Stuart Steel Protection Corp ....E.... 732 469-5544
Somerset (G-10174)
Sun Chemical Corporation ....E.... 201 438-4831
East Rutherford (G-2329)
Superior Printing Ink Co Inc ....G.... 973 242-5868
Newark (G-7334)
Suven Life Sciences Ltd ....F.... 732 274-0037
Monmouth Junction (G-6364)
Sylvan Chemical Corporation ....E.... 201 934-4224
Fair Lawn (G-3117)
United Energy Corp ....G.... 732 994-5225
Howell (G-4569)
Vantage Spclty Ingredients Inc ....C.... 973 345-8600
Warren (G-11570)
William Kenyon & Sons Inc ....E.... 732 985-8980
Piscataway (G-8836)
Wilshire Technologies Inc ....G.... 609 683-1117
Princeton (G-9139)
Worldwide Safety Systems LLC ....G.... 888 613-4501
Teaneck (G-10778)

Zoomessence Inc ....G.... 732 416-6638
Sayreville (G-9843)

CHEMICALS: Nickel Compounds Or Salts, Inorganic

Omg Electronic Chemicals Inc ....C.... 908 222-5800
South Plainfield (G-10418)

CHEMICALS: Nonmetallic Compounds

R & M Chemical Technologies.........F.... 908 537-9516
Hampton (G-4166)

CHEMICALS: Organic, NEC

Adron Inc ....E.... 973 334-1600
Boonton (G-551)
Agilis Chemicals Inc ....G.... 973 910-2424
Rockaway (G-9548)
Akcros Chemicals Inc ....D.... 800 500-7890
New Brunswick (G-6943)
Aromiens Inc ....G.... 732 225-8689
Edison (G-2466)
Ashland Spcalty Ingredients GP ....C.... 908 243-3500
Bridgewater (G-816)
Ashland Spcalty Ingredients GP ....E.... 732 353-7708
Parlin (G-7929)
ATL ....E.... 201 825-1400
Ramsey (G-9235)
Avantor Performance Mtls LLC ....B.... 908 859-2151
Phillipsburg (G-8640)
BASF Catalysts LLC ....C.... 732 205-5000
Carteret (G-1252)
BASF Corporation ....B.... 973 245-6000
Florham Park (G-3492)
BASF Corporation ....D.... 908 689-2500
Washington (G-11576)
BASF Corporation ....E.... 848 221-2786
Toms River (G-10869)
BASF Corporation ....C.... 732 205-5086
Iselin (G-4617)
BASF Corporation ....C.... 732 205-2700
Union (G-11156)
BASF Corporation ....E.... 973 426-5429
Budd Lake (G-925)
Basfin Corporation ....A.... 973 245-6000
Florham Park (G-3493)
Chem-Fleur Inc ....D.... 973 589-4266
Newark (G-7121)
Chem-Is-Try Inc ....G.... 732 372-7311
Metuchen (G-6100)
Chembiopower Inc ....G.... 908 209-5595
Warren (G-11542)
Chemmark Development Inc...........G.... 908 561-0923
South Plainfield (G-10346)
Coim USA Inc ....E.... 856 224-1668
Paulsboro (G-8415)
Colibri Scentique Ltd Lblty Co ....G.... 201 445-5715
Glen Rock (G-3824)
Crompton Corp ....G.... 732 826-6600
Perth Amboy (G-8611)
Cvc Specialty Chemicals Inc ....F.... 856 533-3000
Moorestown (G-6571)
Deleet Merchandising Corp ....E.... 212 962-6565
Newark (G-7139)
Dow Chemical Company ....E.... 856 663-2627
Pennsauken (G-8506)
Dow Chemical Company ....D.... 732 969-5723
Carteret (G-1255)
Elan Inc ....D.... 973 344-8014
Newark (G-7150)
Energy Chem America Inc ....D.... 201 816-2307
Englewood Cliffs (G-2958)
Epic Holding Inc ....E.... 732 249-6867
Morristown (G-6708)
Evonik Corporation ....D.... 732 981-5000
Piscataway (G-8764)
Evonik Corporation ....B.... 973 929-8000
Parsippany (G-8003)
FMC Corporation ....C.... 609 963-6200
Ewing (G-3018)
Gentek Inc ....C.... 973 515-0900
Parsippany (G-8024)
Givaudan Fragrances Corp ....E.... 973 576-9500
East Hanover (G-2221)
GP Chemicals Inc...................G.... 201 869-2200
North Bergen (G-7454)
Honig Chemical & Proc Corp ....E.... 973 344-0881
Newark (G-7192)
Isp Chemco LLC ....G.... 973 628-4000
Wayne (G-11654)

Isp Global Technologies Inc ....F 973 628-4000
Wayne (G-11655)
Isp Global Technologies LLC ....G 973 628-4000
Wayne (G-11656)
Lanxess Solutions US Inc ....C 732 826-1018
Perth Amboy (G-8620)
Ligno Tech USA Inc ....G 908 429-6660
Bridgewater (G-852)
Lonza Inc ....D 201 316-9200
Allendale (G-13)
Lubrizol Advanced Mtls Inc ....F 973 471-1300
Clifton (G-1665)
Lyondellbasell ....F 732 985-6262
Edison (G-2562)
National Strch Chem Holdg Corp ....A 908 685-5000
Bridgewater (G-861)
Northeast Chemicals Inc ....E 732 238-9980
East Brunswick (G-2170)
Pilot Chemical Company Ohio ....F 732 634-6613
Avenel (G-145)
Protameen Chemicals Inc ....E 973 256-4374
Totowa (G-10967)
Royale Pigments & Chem Inc ....E 201 845-4666
Paramus (G-7900)
Royce Associates A Ltd Partnr ....D 201 438-5200
East Rutherford (G-2322)
Royce International Corp ....G 201 438-5200
East Rutherford (G-2323)
Sanit Technologies LLC ....F 862 238-7555
Passaic (G-8180)
Scher Chemicals Inc ....A 973 471-1300
Clifton (G-1716)
SE Tylos USA ....G 973 837-8001
Totowa (G-10971)
Small Molecules Inc ....G 201 918-4664
Hoboken (G-4498)
Sonneborn LLC ....F 201 760-2940
Parsippany (G-8089)
Stepan Company ....D 609 298-1222
Bordentown (G-611)
Surface Technology Inc ....F 609 259-0099
Ewing (G-3058)
Technical Processing Inc ....F 973 278-4950
Paterson (G-8398)
Troy Corporation ....D 973 443-4200
Florham Park (G-3521)
Umicore Precious Metals NJ LLC ....E 908 222-5006
South Plainfield (G-10444)
Veolia Es ....E 732 469-5100
Middlesex (G-6208)
Viva Chemical Corporation ....G 201 461-5281
Fort Lee (G-3589)

CHEMICALS: Phenol

Solvay Holding Inc ....A 609 860-4000
Princeton (G-9121)
Solvay USA Inc ....C 732 297-0100
North Brunswick (G-7538)
Solvay USA Inc ....B 609 860-4000
Princeton (G-9122)

CHEMICALS: Phosphates, Defluorinated/Ammoniated, Exc Fertlr

Perimeter Solutions LP ....C 732 541-3000
Carteret (G-1266)

CHEMICALS: Phosphorus, Elemental

Augmentus LLC ....G 855 240-1100
Hoboken (G-4458)

CHEMICALS: Reagent Grade, Refined From Technical Grade

Bd Biscnces Systems Rgents Inc ....G 201 847-6800
Franklin Lakes (G-3608)

CHEMICALS: Silica Compounds

Evonik Corporation ....E 503 907-1210
Piscataway (G-8765)

CHEMICALS: Soda Ash

FMC Corporation ....D 973 256-0768
Woodland Park (G-12219)
FMC Corporation ....D 732 541-3000
Carteret (G-1257)
Solvay Holding Inc ....A 609 860-4000
Princeton (G-9121)

Solvay USA Inc ....C 732 297-0100
North Brunswick (G-7538)

CHEMICALS: Sodium Bicarbonate

Church & Dwight Co Inc ....F 732 730-3100
Lakewood (G-5093)
Church & Dwight Co Inc ....F 609 655-6101
Cranbury (G-1821)
Church & Dwight Co Inc ....E 609 683-8021
Princeton (G-9023)
Church & Dwight Co Inc ....B 609 806-1200
Ewing (G-3009)

CHEMICALS: Sodium/Potassium Cmpnds,Exc Bleach,Alkalies/Alum

Kuehne Chemical Company Inc ....E 973 589-0700
Kearny (G-4893)

CHEMICALS: Sulfur, Incl Rcvrd/Refined, Fm Sour Natural Gas

Reagent Chemical & RES Inc ....E 908 284-2800
Ringoes (G-9442)

CHEMICALS: Water Treatment

Alden - Leeds Inc ....D 973 589-3544
Kearny (G-4859)
C S L Water Treatment Inc ....F 908 647-1400
Warren (G-11540)
Chemtreat Inc ....G 609 654-9522
Medford (G-6066)
Garratt-Callahan Company ....G 732 287-2200
Edison (G-2527)
Industrial Water Tech Inc ....G 732 888-1233
Hazlet (G-4275)
Lanxess Sybron Chemicals Inc ....C 609 893-1100
Birmingham (G-468)
Pariser Industries Inc ....F 973 569-9090
Paterson (G-8360)
Robert Nichols Contracting ....F 973 902-2632
Ringwood (G-9455)
Seaboard Industries ....F 732 901-5700
Lakewood (G-5187)
Sentry Water Management ....E 973 616-9000
Riverdale (G-9486)
Solenis LLC ....E 201 767-7400
Norwood (G-7635)
Wasak Inc ....G 973 605-8122
Morristown (G-6751)
Water Dynamics Incorporated ....G 973 428-8330
Whippany (G-12042)

CHEMICALS: Zinc Chloride

Madison Industries Inc ....E 732 727-2225
Old Bridge (G-7784)

CHEWING GUM

Gum Runners LLC ....F 201 333-0756
Jersey City (G-4763)

CHILDREN'S & INFANTS' CLOTHING STORES

Komar Inc ....B 212 725-1500
Jersey City (G-4772)
Marmaxx Operating Corp ....D 973 575-7910
West Caldwell (G-11785)
Sock Company Inc ....E 201 307-0675
Westwood (G-11972)

CHILDREN'S WEAR STORES

Buy Buy Baby Inc ....F 908 688-0888
Union (G-11161)

CHINA & GLASS REPAIR SVCS

Quality Glass Inc ....F 908 754-2652
South Plainfield (G-10428)

CHINAWARE WHOLESALERS

Nikko Ceramics Inc ....F 201 840-5200
Fairview (G-3366)

CHIROPRACTORS' OFFICES

Spinal Kinetics LLC ....G 908 687-2552
Union (G-11224)

CHOCOLATE, EXC CANDY FROM BEANS: Chips, Powder, Block, Syrup

Bergen Marzipan & Chocolate ....G 201 385-8343
Bergenfield (G-383)
Birnn Chocolates Inc ....G 732 214-8680
Highland Park (G-4301)
Bromilows Candy Co ....G 973 684-1496
Woodland Park (G-12212)
Candy Treasure LLC ....G 201 830-3600
Lebanon (G-5279)
Chocmod USA Inc ....E 201 585-8730
Fort Lee (G-3549)
David Bradley Chocolatier Inc ....F 609 443-4747
Windsor (G-12125)
David Bradley Chocolatier Inc ....E 732 536-7719
Englishtown (G-2991)
Dove Chocolate Discoveries LLC ....E 866 922-3683
Mount Arlington (G-6753)
Fralingers Inc ....E 609 345-2177
Atlantic City (G-97)
K K S Criterion Chocolates ....E 732 542-7847
Eatontown (G-2409)
Koppers Chocolate LLC ....D 212 243-0220
Cranford (G-1912)
Mars Incorporated ....D 908 850-2420
Hackettstown (G-4021)
Mars Incorporated ....G 908 852-1000
Hackettstown (G-4020)
Mars Chocolate North Amer LLC ....A 908 852-1000
Hackettstown (G-4022)
Mars Retail Group Inc ....F 973 398-2078
Mount Arlington (G-6757)
Nouveautes Inc ....F 973 882-8850
Fairfield (G-3274)
Promotion In Motion Inc ....D 201 962-8530
Allendale (G-16)
Savita Naturals Ltd ....E 856 467-4949
Swedesboro (G-10727)

CHOCOLATE, EXC CANDY FROM PURCH CHOC: Chips, Powder, Block

Barry Callebaut USA LLC ....E 856 663-2260
Pennsauken (G-8483)
Barry Callebaut USA LLC ....D 856 663-2260
Pennsauken (G-8484)
Bosco Products Inc ....G 973 334-7534
Towaco (G-10990)
Forget ME Not Chocolates By NA ....G 856 753-8916
Atco (G-89)
Matisse Chocolatier Inc ....G 201 568-2288
Englewood (G-2914)
Neu Haus Inc ....G 201 845-0040
Paramus (G-7894)
Third Ave Chocolate Shoppe ....G 732 449-7535
Spring Lake (G-10535)

CHRISTMAS TREES: Artificial

Foldtex II Ltd ....E 908 928-0919
Westfield (G-11924)
National Christmas Pdts Inc ....E 908 709-4141
Cranford (G-1917)

CHROMATOGRAPHY EQPT

Analytical Sales and Svcs Inc ....F 973 616-0700
Flanders (G-3401)
E S Industries Inc ....G 856 753-8400
West Berlin (G-11717)
Waters Technologies Corp ....F 973 394-5660
Parsippany (G-8111)

CIGARETTE LIGHTER FLINTS

Triangle Manufacturing Co ....G 201 962-7433
Upper Saddle River (G-11286)

CIGARETTE LIGHTERS

Rclc Inc ....F 732 877-1788
Woodbridge (G-12152)

CIGARETTE STORES

Sherman Nat Inc ....E 201 735-9000
Englewood (G-2930)

CIRCUIT BOARDS, PRINTED: Television & Radio

Ai-Logix Inc ....E 732 469-0880
  Somerset *(G-10052)*
Applicad Inc ....E 732 751-2555
  Wall Township *(G-11463)*
Harrison Electro Mechanical ....F 732 382-6008
  Rahway *(G-9196)*
Omega Circuit and Engineering ....E 732 246-1661
  New Brunswick *(G-6990)*
Pcr Technologies Inc ....G 973 882-0017
  Pine Brook *(G-8713)*
PNC Inc ....C 973 284-1600
  Nutley *(G-7652)*
Precision Graphics Inc ....D 908 707-8880
  Branchburg *(G-693)*
Shore Printed Circuits Inc ....E 732 380-0590
  Eatontown *(G-2422)*

CIRCUIT BOARDS: Wiring

AT&T Technologies Inc ....A 201 771-2000
  Berkeley Heights *(G-400)*
P W B Omni Inc ....G 856 384-1300
  West Deptford *(G-11838)*

CIRCUITS, INTEGRATED: Hybrid

Hybrid-Tek LLC ....F 609 259-3355
  Clarksburg *(G-1520)*

CIRCUITS: Electronic

Adcomm Inc ....C 201 342-3338
  South Hackensack *(G-10251)*
Advanced Technology Group Inc ....E 973 627-6955
  Rockaway *(G-9546)*
Aeon Engineering LLC ....G 518 253-7681
  Fort Lee *(G-3542)*
American Fibertek Inc ....E 732 302-0660
  Somerset *(G-10056)*
Ango Electronics Corporation ....F 201 955-0800
  North Arlington *(G-7415)*
Applied Resources Corp ....E 973 328-3882
  Wharton *(G-11980)*
Az-Em USA Branchburg NJ ....G 908 429-0020
  Branchburg *(G-642)*
Bihler of America Inc ....C 908 213-9001
  Phillipsburg *(G-8644)*
Billows Electric Supply Co Inc ....C 856 751-2200
  Delran *(G-2010)*
Bkh Electronics ....G 210 410-2757
  Wanaque *(G-11531)*
Ccard ....G 732 303-8264
  Manalapan *(G-5840)*
Circuit Tech Assembly LLC ....F 856 231-0777
  Moorestown *(G-6566)*
Creatone Inc ....F 908 789-8700
  Mountainside *(G-6870)*
D&N Machine Manufacturing Inc ....E 856 456-1366
  Gloucester City *(G-3835)*
Dantco Corp ....F 973 278-8776
  Paterson *(G-8245)*
Data Delay Devices Inc ....E 973 202-3268
  Clifton *(G-1597)*
Doralex Inc ....G 856 764-0694
  Delran *(G-2016)*
Douglas Elec Components Inc ....D 973 627-8230
  Randolph *(G-9274)*
Empire Telecommunications Inc ....F 201 569-3339
  Englewood *(G-2890)*
Ewc Controls Inc ....E 732 446-3110
  Manalapan *(G-5846)*
Famcam Inc ....E 973 503-1600
  Parsippany *(G-8007)*
Foremost Corp ....G 973 839-3360
  Wayne *(G-11635)*
Fugle-Miller Laboratories Inc ....E 732 574-3121
  Rahway *(G-9192)*
Haz Laboratories ....F 908 453-3300
  Washington *(G-11582)*
Iqe Rf LLC ....D 732 271-5990
  Somerset *(G-10113)*
J A M I Enterprise Inc ....G 732 714-6811
  Brick *(G-746)*
J P Rotella Co Inc ....F 973 942-2559
  Haledon *(G-4083)*
JB Electronics ....F 609 497-2952
  Princeton *(G-9061)*
Jettron Products Inc ....E 973 887-0571
  East Hanover *(G-2226)*

Johanson Manufacturing Corp ....C 973 658-1051
  Boonton *(G-574)*
Koamtac Inc ....G 609 734-4335
  Princeton *(G-9064)*
Lantek Corporation ....F 973 579-8100
  Sparta *(G-10508)*
Mechanical Ingenuity Corp ....E 732 842-8889
  Shrewsbury *(G-10002)*
Metal Cutting Corporation ....D 973 239-1100
  Cedar Grove *(G-1291)*
Noah LLC ....G 609 637-0039
  Lawrenceville *(G-5266)*
Norsal Distribution Associates ....F 908 638-6430
  High Bridge *(G-4298)*
Pcr Technologies Inc ....G 973 882-0017
  Pine Brook *(G-8713)*
Prima-TEC Electronics Corp ....G 201 947-4052
  East Rutherford *(G-2319)*
Roxboro Holdings Inc ....D 732 919-3119
  Wall Township *(G-11506)*
Seren Industrial Power Systems ....F 856 205-1131
  Vineland *(G-11403)*
Silverstone Wireless LLC ....G 845 458-5197
  Lodi *(G-5600)*
Spencer Industries Inc ....E 973 751-2200
  Belleville *(G-318)*
Spirent Communications Inc ....G 732 946-4018
  Holmdel *(G-4530)*
Thomas & Betts Corporation ....C 908 852-1122
  Hackettstown *(G-4040)*
Thomas Instrumentation Inc ....F 609 624-2630
  Cape May Court House *(G-1118)*
Ttss Interactive Products Inc ....E 301 230-1464
  Riverdale *(G-9491)*
Utz Technologies Inc ....E 973 339-1100
  Little Falls *(G-5493)*
Western Electronics Dist ....G 908 475-3303
  Belvidere *(G-378)*
Wireworks Corporation ....E 908 686-7400
  Hillside *(G-4451)*

CLAY MINING, COMMON

Partac Peat Corp ....F 908 637-4191
  Great Meadows *(G-3850)*

CLAYS, EXC KAOLIN & BALL

Eaglevision Usa LLC ....G 908 322-1892
  Fanwood *(G-3372)*

CLEANING EQPT: Commercial

Detrex Corporation ....G 856 786-8686
  Cinnaminson *(G-1457)*
Energy Beams Inc ....F 973 291-6555
  Bloomingdale *(G-543)*
Es Industrial ....D 732 842-5600
  Red Bank *(G-9329)*
Karcher North America Inc ....F 856 228-1800
  Blackwood *(G-486)*
Randall Manufacturing Co Inc ....E 973 746-2111
  Hillside *(G-4437)*
Seaboard Paper and Twine LLC ....E 973 413-8100
  Paterson *(G-8380)*
Unique Systems Inc ....G 973 455-0440
  Cedar Knolls *(G-1322)*

CLEANING EQPT: Dirt Sweeping Units, Indl

Elgee Manufacturing Company ....G 908 647-4100
  Warren *(G-11545)*

CLEANING EQPT: Floor Washing & Polishing, Commercial

Amano USA Holdings Inc ....G 973 403-1900
  Roseland *(G-9643)*
Mercury Floor Machines Inc ....E 201 568-4606
  Englewood *(G-2915)*

CLEANING EQPT: High Pressure

A Plus Powerwashing ....G 732 245-3816
  Neptune *(G-6898)*
Innovative Pressure Clg LLC ....G 609 738-3100
  Cream Ridge *(G-1937)*
Margaritaville Inc ....G 973 728-7562
  West Milford *(G-11854)*
Powerwash Plus ....G 732 671-6767
  Middletown *(G-6218)*

CLEANING EQPT: Janitors' Carts

Janico Inc ....F 732 370-2223
  Freehold *(G-3662)*

CLEANING OR POLISHING PREPARATIONS, NEC

Amano USA Holdings Inc ....G 973 403-1900
  Roseland *(G-9643)*
Americhem Enterprises Inc ....G 732 363-4840
  Lakewood *(G-5072)*
Aqua Products Inc ....E 856 829-8444
  Cinnaminson *(G-1446)*
Atlantic Associates Intl Inc ....F 856 662-1717
  Pennsauken *(G-8481)*
Cantol Inc ....E 609 846-7912
  Wildwood *(G-12070)*
Cavalier Chemical Co Inc ....E 908 558-0110
  Short Hills *(G-9975)*
Envirochem Inc ....E 732 238-6700
  South River *(G-10461)*
Fabric Chemical Corporation ....G 201 432-0440
  Jersey City *(G-4750)*
Interntional Cnsld Chemex Corp ....E 732 828-7676
  New Brunswick *(G-6969)*
L & R Manufacturing Co Inc ....D 201 991-5330
  Kearny *(G-4894)*
Magnuson Products ....F 973 472-9292
  Clifton *(G-1667)*
Penetone Corporation ....E 201 567-3000
  Carlstadt *(G-1199)*
Raybeam Manufacturing Corp ....G 201 941-4529
  Ridgefield *(G-9382)*
Trim Brush Company Inc ....G 973 887-2525
  East Hanover *(G-2247)*

CLEANING PRDTS: Ammonia, Household

Q-Pak Corporation ....E 973 483-4404
  Newark *(G-7281)*

CLEANING PRDTS: Bleaches, Household, Dry Or Liquid

Church & Dwight Co Inc ....B 609 806-1200
  Ewing *(G-3009)*

CLEANING PRDTS: Degreasing Solvent

Arol Chemical Products Co ....G 973 344-1510
  Newark *(G-7094)*
Green Power Chemical LLC ....F 973 770-5600
  Hopatcong *(G-4536)*
Horizon Products NJ LLC ....G 201 773-7015
  Ridgewood *(G-9425)*

CLEANING PRDTS: Deodorants, Nonpersonal

Allison Corp ....G 973 992-3800
  Livingston *(G-5523)*
Mennen Company ....B 973 630-1500
  Morristown *(G-6726)*
RB Manufacturing LLC ....C 908 533-2000
  Hillsborough *(G-4367)*
RB Manufacturing LLC ....C 973 404-2600
  Parsippany *(G-8076)*
Reckitt Benckiser LLC ....B 973 404-2600
  Parsippany *(G-8077)*

CLEANING PRDTS: Disinfectants, Household Or Indl Plant

Schulke Inc ....G 973 521-7163
  Fairfield *(G-3303)*
Sterigenics US LLC ....G 856 241-8880
  Swedesboro *(G-10730)*

CLEANING PRDTS: Drain Pipe Solvents Or Cleaners

Advanced Sewer ....F 973 278-1948
  Woodland Park *(G-12208)*
Brasscraft Manufacturing Co ....G 856 241-7700
  Swedesboro *(G-10685)*
Cobra Products Inc ....D 856 241-7700
  Swedesboro *(G-10688)*

PRODUCT

CLEANING PRDTS: Drycleaning Preparations

A L Wilson Chemical Co.............F.......201 997-3300
Kearny **(G-4857)**

Ramblewood Cleaners Inc.........G.......856 235-6051
Mount Laurel **(G-6834)**

CLEANING PRDTS: Floor Waxes

Epic Holding Inc......................E.......732 249-6867
Morristown **(G-6708)**

CLEANING PRDTS: Indl Plant Disinfectants Or Deodorants

Menshen Packaging USA Inc.........D.......201 445-7436
Waldwick **(G-11448)**

CLEANING PRDTS: Metal Polish

Agate Lacquer Tri-Nat LLC............G.......732 968-1080
Middlesex **(G-6145)**

CLEANING PRDTS: Polishing Preparations & Related Prdts

National Auto Detailing Netwrk.......E.......856 931-5529
Bellmawr **(G-348)**

Royce Associates A Ltd Partnr........D.......201 438-5200
East Rutherford **(G-2322)**

Stepan Company........................D.......201 845-3030
Maywood **(G-6061)**

CLEANING PRDTS: Sanitation Preps, Disinfectants/Deodorants

Microgen Inc...........................G.......973 575-9025
West Caldwell **(G-11791)**

Zoono USA LLC........................G.......732 722-8757
Shrewsbury **(G-10014)**

CLEANING PRDTS: Specialty

Associated Cleaning Systems.........G.......201 530-9197
Teaneck **(G-10742)**

Clenesco Products Corp...............F.......908 245-5255
Roselle **(G-9665)**

Fine Organics Corporation............F.......973 478-7690
Clifton **(G-1620)**

Jobe Industries Inc...................G.......908 862-0400
Linden **(G-5392)**

Ronell Industries Inc.................B.......908 245-5255
Roselle **(G-9682)**

CLEANING PRDTS: Stain Removers

Edwards Creative Products Inc.........F.......856 665-3200
Cherry Hill **(G-1361)**

CLEANING SVCS

Associated Cleaning Systems.........G.......201 530-9197
Teaneck **(G-10742)**

CLIPPERS: Fingernail & Toenail

Revlon Inc.............................E.......732 287-1400
Edison **(G-2605)**

CLOCK REPAIR SVCS

Garrett Moore.........................G.......908 231-9231
Bridgewater **(G-840)**

CLOSURES: Closures, Stamped Metal

Amcor Flexibles LLC...................C.......856 825-1400
Millville **(G-6275)**

CLOSURES: Plastic

Associated Plastics Inc...............F.......732 574-2800
Rahway **(G-9176)**

C & N Packaging Inc..................D.......631 491-1400
Wayne **(G-11617)**

Revere Plastics Inc...................G.......201 641-0777
Little Ferry **(G-5514)**

Stull Technologies LLC................D.......732 873-5000
Somerset **(G-10175)**

CLOTHING & ACCESS, WOMEN, CHILD & INFANT, WHOL: Blouses

Chic LLC..............................G.......732 354-0035
East Brunswick **(G-2141)**

CLOTHING & ACCESS, WOMEN, CHILD & INFANT, WHSLE: Sportswear

Ballet Makers Inc.....................B.......973 595-9000
Totowa **(G-10934)**

Jese Apparel LLC......................F.......732 969-3200
Dayton **(G-1973)**

CLOTHING & ACCESS, WOMEN, CHILDREN & INFANT, WHOL: Uniforms

Happy Chef Inc........................E.......973 492-2525
Butler **(G-1006)**

CLOTHING & ACCESS, WOMEN, CHILDREN/INFANT, WHOL: Baby Goods

Baby Time International Inc...........G.......973 481-7400
Newark **(G-7103)**

CLOTHING & ACCESS, WOMEN, CHILDREN/INFANT, WHOL: Nightwear

Charles Komar & Sons Inc.............B.......212 725-1500
Jersey City **(G-4726)**

CLOTHING & ACCESS, WOMEN, CHILDREN/INFANT, WHOL: Outerwear

Paradise..............................G.......973 425-0505
Morristown **(G-6732)**

CLOTHING & ACCESS, WOMENS, CHILDREN & INFANTS, WHOL: Hats

Kathy Jeanne Inc......................F.......973 575-9898
Fairfield **(G-3239)**

CLOTHING & ACCESS: Costumes, Masquerade

Images Costume Productions...........G.......609 859-7372
Southampton **(G-10475)**

Xcessory LLC..........................G.......917 647-7523
North Bergen **(G-7497)**

CLOTHING & ACCESS: Costumes, Theatrical

Ballet Makers Inc.....................B.......973 595-9000
Totowa **(G-10934)**

CLOTHING & ACCESS: Handicapped

Apparel Strgc Alliances LLC...........F.......732 833-7771
Jackson **(G-4654)**

Blu-J2 LLC............................G.......201 750-1407
Demarest **(G-2026)**

E5 Usa Inc............................G.......973 773-0750
Passaic **(G-8136)**

Jese Apparel LLC......................F.......732 969-3200
Dayton **(G-1973)**

Steps Clothing Inc....................E.......201 420-1496
Jersey City **(G-4834)**

CLOTHING & ACCESS: Handkerchiefs, Exc Paper

Lynn Amiee Inc........................E.......201 840-6766
Ridgefield **(G-9372)**

Personality Handkerchiefs Inc.........E.......973 565-0077
Newark **(G-7269)**

CLOTHING & ACCESS: Men's Miscellaneous Access

Better Team USA Corporation..........G.......973 365-0947
Clifton **(G-1575)**

Butterfly Bow Ties LLC................G.......973 626-2536
Union **(G-11160)**

Evigto Inc............................G.......201 951-2187
Edgewater **(G-2438)**

Handcraft Manufacturing Corp.........E.......973 565-0077
Newark **(G-7185)**

Hat Box...............................E.......732 961-2262
Lakewood **(G-5133)**

Kristine Deer Inc......................G.......201 497-3333
Westwood **(G-11961)**

Lion Sales Corp.......................G.......732 417-9363
Edison **(G-2557)**

New York Popular Inc..................D.......718 499-2020
Carteret **(G-1263)**

Paradise..............................G.......973 425-0505
Morristown **(G-6732)**

Philip Papalia.........................F.......732 349-5530
Toms River **(G-10902)**

Premium Imports Inc...................G.......718 486-7125
Passaic **(G-8171)**

Stylus Custom Apparel Inc.............G.......908 587-0800
Linden **(G-5450)**

CLOTHING & APPAREL STORES: Custom

Dezine Line Inc.......................F.......973 989-1009
Wharton **(G-11985)**

Flying Fish Studio.....................G.......609 884-2760
West Cape May **(G-11808)**

Rpl Supplies Inc.......................F.......973 767-0880
Garfield **(G-3759)**

CLOTHING & FURNISHINGS, MEN'S & BOYS', WHOLESALE: Outerwear

Tony Jones Apparel Inc................G.......973 773-6200
Lodi **(G-5606)**

CLOTHING & FURNISHINGS, MEN'S & BOYS', WHOLESALE: Scarves

HRA International Inc..................G.......609 395-0939
Monroe **(G-6374)**

CLOTHING & FURNISHINGS, MEN'S & BOYS', WHOLESALE: Shirts

Fabian Couture Group Intl Inc.........F.......800 367-6251
Lyndhurst **(G-5681)**

Skip Gambert & Associates Inc.........C.......973 344-3373
Newark **(G-7317)**

Spirit Tex LLC........................G.......201 440-1113
Little Ferry **(G-5518)**

CLOTHING & FURNISHINGS, MEN'S & BOYS', WHOLESALE: Trousers

Jade Eastern Trading Inc..............F.......201 440-8500
Moonachie **(G-6524)**

CLOTHING & FURNISHINGS, MEN'S & BOYS', WHOLESALE: Umbrellas

Peerless Umbrella Co Inc..............C.......973 578-4900
Newark **(G-7267)**

S Frankford & Sons Inc................F.......856 222-4134
Mount Laurel **(G-6836)**

CLOTHING & FURNISHINGS, MEN'S & BOYS', WHOLESALE: Uniforms

Eagle Work Clothes Inc................E.......908 964-8888
Florham Park **(G-3499)**

Happy Chef Inc........................E.......973 492-2525
Butler **(G-1006)**

CLOTHING ACCESS STORES: Belts, Custom

G G Tauber Company Inc...............E.......800 638-6667
Neptune **(G-6913)**

CLOTHING STORES, NEC

G-III Apparel Group Ltd...............D.......732 438-0209
Dayton **(G-1965)**

Hillarys Fashion Boutique LLC.........F.......732 667-7733
Warren **(G-11552)**

CLOTHING STORES: Dancewear

Ballet Makers Inc.....................B.......973 595-9000
Totowa **(G-10934)**

Sock Company Inc......................E.......201 307-0675
Westwood **(G-11972)**

CLOTHING STORES: T-Shirts, Printed, Custom

Its The Pitts Inc......................G.......609 645-7319
Pleasantville **(G-8910)**

(G-0000) Company's Geographic Section entry number

James Smith ....G 732 229-8273
Long Branch **(G-5626)**

Tarma Sales ....G 732 969-3318
Carteret **(G-1268)**

Wally Enterprises Inc ....F 732 329-2613
Monmouth Junction **(G-6371)**

CLOTHING STORES: Uniforms & Work

Cozy Formal Wear Inc ....G 973 661-9781
Nutley **(G-7645)**

Five Kids Group Inc ....G 732 774-5331
Neptune **(G-6912)**

Premium Imports Inc ....G 718 486-7125
Passaic **(G-8171)**

CLOTHING STORES: Unisex

Finn & Emma LLC ....G 973 227-7770
Fairfield **(G-3195)**

Komar Inc ....B 212 725-1500
Jersey City **(G-4772)**

CLOTHING: Access

Couture Exchange ....G 732 933-1123
Shrewsbury **(G-9995)**

School Spirit Promotions ....G 609 588-6902
Trenton **(G-11115)**

Too Cool of Ocean City ....G 908 810-6363
Kenilworth **(G-5000)**

CLOTHING: Access, Women's & Misses'

City Design Group Inc ....G 201 329-7711
Little Ferry **(G-5497)**

Collection Xiix Ltd ....C 201 854-7740
North Bergen **(G-7441)**

Davidmark LLC ....G 609 277-7361
Pleasantville **(G-8907)**

Evigto Inc ....G 201 951-2187
Edgewater **(G-2438)**

Sondra Roberts Inc ....E 212 684-3344
South Hackensack **(G-10296)**

CLOTHING: Aprons, Exc Rubber/Plastic, Women, Misses, Junior

Hedaya Home Fashions Inc ....C 908 352-0808
Elizabeth **(G-2745)**

Helen Morley LLC ....E 201 348-6459
Cresskill **(G-1945)**

Philip Papalia ....F 732 349-5530
Toms River **(G-10902)**

CLOTHING: Athletic & Sportswear, Men's & Boys'

Aladen Athletic Wear LLC ....E 973 838-2425
Wyckoff **(G-12245)**

Amante International Ltd ....F 908 518-1688
Westfield **(G-11919)**

Bimini Bay Outfitters Ltd ....E 201 529-3550
Mahwah **(G-5752)**

Central Mills Inc ....G 732 329-2009
Dayton **(G-1960)**

Evh LLC ....F 973 257-0076
Boonton **(G-568)**

Kmba Fashions Inc ....G 973 789-1652
East Orange **(G-2259)**

Leeward International Inc ....F 201 836-8830
Teaneck **(G-10760)**

Merc USA Inc ....F 201 489-3527
Hackensack **(G-3947)**

MISS Sportswear Inc ....G 212 391-2535
New Brunswick **(G-6982)**

Moldworks Worldwide LLC ....G 908 474-8082
Linden **(G-5413)**

Nautica Retail USA ....G 212 541-5757
Jersey City **(G-4787)**

Onwards Inc ....G 732 309-7348
Manalapan **(G-5859)**

Safire Silk Inc ....G 201 636-4061
Carlstadt **(G-1212)**

Selfmade LLC ....G 201 792-8968
Jersey City **(G-4826)**

Senor Lopez ....G 732 229-7622
Tinton Falls **(G-10847)**

Tony Jones Apparel Inc ....G 973 773-6200
Lodi **(G-5606)**

What A Tee 2 Inc ....F 201 457-0060
Hackensack **(G-3991)**

CLOTHING: Athletic & Sportswear, Women's & Girls'

Amante International Ltd ....F 908 518-1688
Westfield **(G-11919)**

Garylin Togs ....D 908 354-7218
Elizabeth **(G-2737)**

Matrix Sales Group LLC ....D 908 461-4148
Spring Lake **(G-10534)**

Sno Skins Inc ....G 973 884-8801
Whippany **(G-12039)**

Tellas Ltd ....E 201 399-8888
Englewood Cliffs **(G-2981)**

What A Tee 2 Inc ....F 201 457-0060
Hackensack **(G-3991)**

CLOTHING: Baker, Barber, Lab/Svc Ind Apparel, Washable, Men

Db Designs Inc ....G 732 616-5018
Marlboro **(G-5937)**

Happy Chef Inc ....E 973 492-2525
Butler **(G-1006)**

Ronald Perry ....F 201 702-2407
Jersey City **(G-4820)**

CLOTHING: Bathing Suits & Swimwear, Girls, Children & Infant

In Mocean Group LLC ....G 732 960-2415
North Brunswick **(G-7519)**

Leeward International Inc ....F 201 836-8830
Teaneck **(G-10760)**

CLOTHING: Bathrobes, Mens & Womens, From Purchased Materials

Carole Hchman Design Group Inc ....C 866 267-3945
Jersey City **(G-4724)**

Monarch Towel Company Inc ......E 800 729-7623
South Plainfield **(G-10409)**

CLOTHING: Belts

Josemi Inc ....G 917 710-2110
Hoboken **(G-4481)**

Straps Manufacturing NJ Inc ......F 201 368-5201
Wyckoff **(G-12264)**

Two 12 Fashion LLC ....G 848 222-1562
Lakewood **(G-5198)**

CLOTHING: Blouses, Women's & Girls'

Cleve Shirtmakers Inc ....G 201 825-6122
Secaucus **(G-9872)**

Gambert Shirt Corp ....E 973 424-9105
Newark **(G-7168)**

Luxury and Trash Ltd Lblty Co ....G 201 315-4018
Closter **(G-1763)**

Metropolitan Manufacturing Inc ....D 201 933-8111
East Rutherford **(G-2310)**

New Jersey Headwear Corp ....C 973 497-0102
Newark **(G-7250)**

Saad Collection Inc ....G 732 763-4015
Edison **(G-2610)**

Second Skin LLC ....F 212 931-0621
Westfield **(G-11931)**

Spirit Tex LLC ....G 201 440-1113
Little Ferry **(G-5518)**

Suuchi Inc ....C 201 284-0789
North Bergen **(G-7488)**

True Religion Apparel Inc ....G 973 564-9030
Short Hills **(G-9986)**

CLOTHING: Blouses, Womens & Juniors, From Purchased Mtrls

Daniel Fashions Inc ....G 201 869-1008
West New York **(G-11863)**

Elie Tahari Ltd ....C 973 671-6300
Millburn **(G-6249)**

Harve Benard Ltd ....C 973 249-1230
Clifton **(G-1638)**

Nicholas Oliver LLC ....G 732 690-7144
Wall Township **(G-11499)**

Tahari ASL LLC ....E 888 734-7459
Millburn **(G-6259)**

CLOTHING: Brassieres

Wacoal America Inc ....C 201 933-8400
Lyndhurst **(G-5713)**

CLOTHING: Bridal Gowns

Amalia Carrara Inc ....E 201 348-4500
Union City **(G-11240)**

Augenbrauns Bridal Passaic LLC ....G 845 425-3439
Lakewood **(G-5078)**

Duran Cutting Corp ....F 973 916-0006
Passaic **(G-8135)**

CLOTHING: Capes & Jackets, Women's & Misses'

Fyi Marketing Inc ....G 646 546-5226
Englewood Cliffs **(G-2960)**

CLOTHING: Caps, Baseball

Con Cap Sports Wear ....F 973 778-2628
Wood Ridge **(G-12136)**

New Jersey Headwear Corp ....C 973 497-0102
Newark **(G-7250)**

CLOTHING: Children & Infants'

Lollytogs Ltd ....F 732 438-5500
Dayton **(G-1978)**

Sally Miller LLC ....G 732 729-4840
Milltown **(G-6271)**

CLOTHING: Children's, Girls'

Attitudes In Dressing Inc ....B 908 354-7218
Elizabeth **(G-2711)**

Bib and Tucker Inc ....G 201 489-9600
Hackensack **(G-3881)**

Blue Fish Clothing Inc ....C 908 996-3720
Frenchtown **(G-3697)**

Central Mills Inc ....C 732 329-2009
Dayton **(G-1961)**

Frenchtoastcom LLC ....F 732 438-5500
Dayton **(G-1964)**

Garylin Togs ....D 908 354-7218
Elizabeth **(G-2737)**

JP Group International LLC ....G 201 820-1444
Maywood **(G-6057)**

Les Tout Petite Inc ....G 201 941-8675
Ridgefield **(G-9371)**

Lollytogs Ltd ....D 732 438-5500
Dayton **(G-1979)**

Lollytogs Ltd ....F 732 438-5500
Dayton **(G-1978)**

CLOTHING: Clergy Vestments

Church Vestment Mfg Co Inc ......G 973 942-2833
Paterson **(G-8233)**

Robert Gaiser Inc ....F 973 838-9254
Butler **(G-1017)**

CLOTHING: Coats & Jackets, Leather & Sheep-Lined

Cockpit Usa Inc ....F 212 575-1616
Elizabeth **(G-2719)**

Schott Nyc Corp ....D 800 631-5407
Union **(G-11222)**

CLOTHING: Coats & Suits, Men's & Boys'

Fordham Inc ....E 973 575-7840
Fairfield **(G-3199)**

New Community Corp ....E 973 643-5300
Newark **(G-7249)**

CLOTHING: Coats, Leatherette, Oiled Fabric, Etc, Mens & Boys

House Pearl Fashions (us) Ltd ....F 973 778-7551
Lodi **(G-5588)**

CLOTHING: Coats, Overcoats & Vests

Burlington Coat Factory ....D 908 994-9562
Elizabeth **(G-2716)**

CLOTHING: Costumes

Jaclyn Inc ....C 201 909-6000
Maywood **(G-6052)**

Employee Codes: A=Over 500 employees, B=251-500
C=101-250, D=51-100, E=20-50, F=10-19, G=4-9

2018 Harris New jersey
Manufacturers Directory

PRODUCT

821

Silvertop Associates Inc ....E 856 939-9599
  Runnemede *(G-9723)*

CLOTHING: Disposable

Keystone Adjustable Cap Co Inc..........E 856 356-2809
  Pennsauken *(G-8539)*

CLOTHING: Down-Filled, Men's & Boys'

Schott Nyc Corp ....D 800 631-5407
  Union *(G-11222)*

CLOTHING: Dresses

Betsy & Adam Ltd ....F 212 302-3750
  Passaic *(G-8128)*
Cs Apparel Inc ....G 732 906-9666
  Edison *(G-2498)*
Donna Karan International Inc ....G 609 345-3402
  Atlantic City *(G-95)*
Elie Tahari Ltd ....C 973 671-6300
  Millburn *(G-6249)*
Hillarys Fashion Boutique LLC ....F 732 667-7733
  Warren *(G-11552)*
Kate Spade & Company ....F 201 295-7569
  North Bergen *(G-7460)*
Kate Spade & Company ....G 609 395-3109
  Dayton *(G-1974)*
Kidcuteture LLC ....G 609 532-0149
  Lawrenceville *(G-5259)*
Metropolitan Manufacturing Inc ....D 201 933-8111
  East Rutherford *(G-2310)*
Milady Bridals Inc ....E 201 348-4500
  Union City *(G-11257)*
Nicholas Oliver LLC ....G 732 690-7144
  Wall Township *(G-11499)*
Printmaker International Ltd ....G 212 629-9260
  Irvington *(G-4601)*
Second Skin LLC ....F 212 931-0621
  Westfield *(G-11931)*
Sophies Fashions ....G 973 272-8321
  Garfield *(G-3763)*
Tahari ASL LLC ....E 888 734-7459
  Millburn *(G-6259)*

CLOTHING: Dresses & Skirts

Sophies Fashions ....G 973 272-8321
  Garfield *(G-3763)*

CLOTHING: Dressing Gowns, Mens/Womens, From Purchased Matls

Chiha Inc ....F 201 861-2000
  North Bergen *(G-7440)*

CLOTHING: Formal Jackets, Mens & Youth, From Purchased Matls

Fabian Formals Inc ....E 201 460-7776
  Lyndhurst *(G-5682)*

CLOTHING: Furs

American Fur Felt LLC ....F 973 344-3026
  Newark *(G-7082)*
M Blaustein Inc ....G 973 379-1080
  Short Hills *(G-9980)*

CLOTHING: Garments, Indl, Men's & Boys

Pro World ....G 856 406-1020
  Pennsauken *(G-8567)*

CLOTHING: Girdles & Panty Girdles

Dolce Vita Intimates LLC ....D 973 482-8400
  Harrison *(G-4178)*

CLOTHING: Gowns & Dresses, Wedding

Head Piece Heaven ....G 201 262-0788
  Oradell *(G-7811)*
Liz Fields Llc ....G 201 408-5640
  Englewood *(G-2910)*
More Than A Notion Fabrics Ltd..........G 732 821-5580
  Princeton *(G-9077)*

CLOTHING: Hats & Caps, NEC

Headwear Creations Inc ....E 973 622-1144
  Newark *(G-7188)*

Jay Gerish Company ....G 973 403-0655
  West Caldwell *(G-11782)*
Kathy Jeanne Inc ....F 973 575-9898
  Fairfield *(G-3239)*
Serratelli Hat Company Inc ....G 973 623-4133
  Newark *(G-7307)*

CLOTHING: Hats & Caps, Uniform

Alboum W Hat Company Inc...............E 201 399-4110
  Irvington *(G-4572)*
Castellane Manufacturing Co ....F 609 625-3427
  Mays Landing *(G-6038)*

CLOTHING: Hats & Headwear, Knit

Artex Knitting Mills Inc ....D 856 456-2800
  Westville *(G-11936)*
Elegant Headwear Co Inc ....C 908 558-1200
  Elizabeth *(G-2728)*

CLOTHING: Hosiery, Men's & Boys'

Great Socks LLC ....E 856 964-9700
  Pennsauken *(G-8518)*
Sock Company Inc ....E 201 307-0675
  Westwood *(G-11972)*

CLOTHING: Hosiery, Pantyhose & Knee Length, Sheer

Great Socks LLC ....E 856 964-9700
  Pennsauken *(G-8518)*
Swisstex Company ....E 201 861-8000
  West New York *(G-11882)*

CLOTHING: Hospital, Men's

Janet Shops Inc ....F 973 748-4992
  Bloomfield *(G-515)*

CLOTHING: Jackets, Field, Military

Sinai Manufacturing Corp ....D 973 522-1003
  Newark *(G-7314)*

CLOTHING: Jackets, Overall & Work

Bethel Industries Inc ....C 201 656-8222
  Jersey City *(G-4717)*

CLOTHING: Jeans, Men's & Boys'

Guess Inc ....E 201 941-3683
  Edgewater *(G-2440)*

CLOTHING: Jerseys, Knit

Fairfield Textiles Corp ....D 973 227-1656
  Paterson *(G-8270)*

CLOTHING: Leather

French Creek Sheep & Wool Co ....E 610 286-5700
  Ventnor City *(G-11291)*
G-III Apparel Group Ltd ....D 732 438-0209
  Dayton *(G-1965)*
Prime Fur & Leather Inc ....F 201 941-9600
  Fairview *(G-3369)*

CLOTHING: Leather & sheep-lined clothing

G-III Leather Fashions Inc ....E 212 403-0500
  Dayton *(G-1966)*

CLOTHING: Lounge, Bed & Leisurewear

Chiha Inc ....F 201 861-2000
  North Bergen *(G-7440)*
D L V Lounge Inc ....G 973 783-6988
  Montclair *(G-6410)*

CLOTHING: Maternity

Second Skin LLC ....F 212 931-0621
  Westfield *(G-11931)*

CLOTHING: Men's & boy's underwear & nightwear

Basic Solutions Ltd ....G 201 978-7691
  Manalapan *(G-5839)*
Central Mills Inc ....C 732 329-2009
  Dayton *(G-1961)*

Sgi Apparel Ltd ....G 201 342-1200
  Hackensack *(G-3974)*

CLOTHING: Millinery

Kathy Gibson Designs Inc ....F 201 420-0088
  North Bergen *(G-7461)*

CLOTHING: Neckwear

Albert Forte Neckwear Co Inc............G 856 423-2342
  Mullica Hill *(G-6891)*
Robert Stewart Inc ....G 973 751-5151
  Belleville *(G-316)*

CLOTHING: Outerwear, Knit

Alan Paul Accessories Inc ....G 609 924-4022
  Princeton *(G-9001)*
D & G LLC ....G 201 289-5750
  Hackensack *(G-3902)*
Flemington Knitting Mills ....F 908 995-9590
  Milford *(G-6244)*
Ralph Lauren Corporation ....G 201 531-6000
  Lyndhurst *(G-5704)*
Triumph Knitting Machine Svc ....E 201 646-0022
  Hackensack *(G-3986)*

CLOTHING: Outerwear, Lthr, Wool/Down-Filled, Men, Youth/Boy

Bear USa Inc ....F 201 943-4748
  Palisades Park *(G-7835)*

CLOTHING: Outerwear, Women's & Misses' NEC

Alfred Dunner Inc ....D 212 944-6660
  Parsippany *(G-7942)*
Bear USa Inc ....F 201 943-4748
  Palisades Park *(G-7835)*
Bestwork Inds For The Blind ....D 856 424-2510
  Cherry Hill *(G-1349)*
Blue Fish Clothing Inc ....C 908 996-3720
  Frenchtown *(G-3697)*
BT Industries Inc ....D 201 866-0201
  North Bergen *(G-7436)*
Fordham Inc ....E 973 575-7840
  Fairfield *(G-3199)*
Great Socks LLC ....E 856 964-9700
  Pennsauken *(G-8518)*
Happy Chef Inc ....E 973 492-2525
  Butler *(G-1006)*
House Pearl Fashions (us) Ltd ....F 973 778-7551
  Lodi *(G-5588)*
Marmaxx Operating Corp ....D 973 575-7910
  West Caldwell *(G-11785)*
Metropolitan Manufacturing Inc ....D 201 933-8111
  East Rutherford *(G-2310)*
New Community Corp ....E 973 643-5300
  Newark *(G-7249)*
Red The Uniform Tailor Inc ....E 848 299-0100
  Lakewood *(G-5176)*
Snotex USA Inc ....G 973 762-0358
  South Orange *(G-10315)*

CLOTHING: Raincoats, Exc Vulcanized Rubber, Purchased Matls

Man-How Inc ....G 609 392-4895
  Trenton *(G-11078)*

CLOTHING: Robes & Dressing Gowns

Charles Komar & Sons Inc ....B 212 725-1500
  Jersey City *(G-4726)*

CLOTHING: Service Apparel, Women's

Escada US Subco LLC ....B 201 865-5200
  Secaucus *(G-9879)*

CLOTHING: Shirts

Central Mills Inc ....C 732 329-2009
  Dayton *(G-1961)*
Cleve Shirtmakers Inc ....E 201 825-6122
  Secaucus *(G-9872)*
Drifire LLC ....E 866 266-4035
  East Brunswick *(G-2146)*
Gambert Shirt Corp ....E 973 424-9105
  Newark *(G-7168)*

(G-0000) Company's Geographic Section entry number

Jade Eastern Trading Inc ....F 201 440-8500
  Moonachie (G-6524)
New Community Corp ....E 973 643-5300
  Newark (G-7249)
New Jersey Headwear Corp..............C 973 497-0102
  Newark (G-7250)
New Top Inc ....E 201 438-3990
  Carlstadt (G-1193)
Pvh Corp ....G 908 685-0050
  Elizabeth (G-2769)
Pvh Corp ....G 908 685-0050
  Bridgewater (G-879)
Ralph Lauren Corporation ....D 201 531-6000
  Lyndhurst (G-5704)
Saad Collection Inc ....G 732 763-4015
  Edison (G-2610)

CLOTHING: Shirts, Dress, Men's & Boys'

L Gambert LLC ....D 973 344-3440
  Newark (G-7215)
Pvh Corp ....G 609 344-6273
  Atlantic City (G-106)
Pvh Corp ....G 732 833-9602
  Jackson (G-4676)
Pvh Corp ....G 908 685-0050
  Bridgewater (G-880)
Pvh Corp ....G 908 685-0148
  Bridgewater (G-881)
Pvh Corp ....F 908 788-5880
  Flemington (G-3464)
Skip Gambert & Associates Inc..........C 973 344-3373
  Newark (G-7317)

CLOTHING: Shirts, Knit

3forty Group Inc ....F 973 773-1806
  Passaic (G-8121)

CLOTHING: Shirts, Sports & Polo, Men's & Boys'

Bimini Bay Outfitters Ltd..................F 201 529-3550
  Mahwah (G-5752)

CLOTHING: Skirts

Chic LLC ....G 732 354-0035
  East Brunswick (G-2141)
Success Sewing Inc..........................G 973 622-0328
  Newark (G-7333)

CLOTHING: Sleeping Garments, Women's & Children's

Central Mills Inc ....C 732 329-2009
  Dayton (G-1961)
Charles Komar & Sons Inc..................B 212 725-1500
  Jersey City (G-4726)
Sgi Apparel Ltd ....G 201 342-1200
  Hackensack (G-3974)
Swisstex Company ....E 201 861-8000
  West New York (G-11882)

CLOTHING: Socks

J T Murdoch Shoes............................F 973 748-6484
  Bloomfield (G-514)
Socks 47 Ltd Liability Company..........G 201 866-2222
  Union City (G-11267)

CLOTHING: Sportswear, Women's

Central Mills Inc ....C 732 329-2009
  Dayton (G-1961)
Counter-Fit Inc ....C 609 871-8888
  Willingboro (G-12118)
Leeward International Inc..................F 201 836-8830
  Teaneck (G-10760)
Les Tout Petite Inc ....G 201 941-8675
  Ridgefield (G-9371)
Nine West Holdings Inc ....E 908 647-6168
  Gillette (G-3796)
Ocean Drive Inc ....G 908 964-2591
  Kenilworth (G-4983)
Printmaker International Ltd ....G 212 629-9260
  Irvington (G-4601)
Swisstex Company ....E 201 861-8000
  West New York (G-11882)
Tripp Nyc Inc ....E 201 520-0420
  North Bergen (G-7490)

CLOTHING: Suits & Skirts, Women's & Misses'

E-Lo Sportswear LLC ....F 862 902-5220
  Harrison (G-4179)

CLOTHING: Suits, Men's & Boys', From Purchased Materials

Harve Benard Ltd ....C 973 249-1230
  Clifton (G-1638)
Tom James Company ....E 732 826-8400
  Perth Amboy (G-8633)

CLOTHING: Sweaters & Sweater Coats, Knit

Fleck Knitwear Co Inc ....E 908 754-8888
  Plainfield (G-8862)
French Creek Sheep & Wool Co..........E 610 286-5700
  Ventnor City (G-11291)
Jtwo Inc ....G 201 410-1616
  Kinnelon (G-5037)

CLOTHING: T-Shirts & Tops, Knit

Supertex Inc ....E 973 345-1000
  Paterson (G-8389)

CLOTHING: T-Shirts & Tops, Women's & Girls'

Chic LLC ....G 732 354-0035
  East Brunswick (G-2141)

CLOTHING: Tailored Dress/Sport Coats, Mens & Boys

Bimini Bay Outfitters Ltd..................F 201 529-3550
  Mahwah (G-5752)

CLOTHING: Tailored Suits & Formal Jackets

Fabian Couture Group Intl Inc ....F 800 367-6251
  Lyndhurst (G-5681)
Michael Duru Clothiers LLC................G 732 741-1999
  Shrewsbury (G-10005)

CLOTHING: Ties, Neck, Men's & Boys', From Purchased Material

HRA International Inc ....G 609 395-0939
  Monroe (G-6374)

CLOTHING: Trousers & Slacks, Men's & Boys'

Ralph Lauren Corporation ....D 201 531-6000
  Lyndhurst (G-5704)

CLOTHING: Underwear, Knit

William Carter Company ....G 201 313-1783
  Edgewater (G-2443)

CLOTHING: Underwear, Men's & Boys'

D & G LLC..G 201 289-5750
  Hackensack (G-3902)
Umc Inc ....G 973 325-0031
  West Orange (G-11907)

CLOTHING: Underwear, Women's & Children's

Carole Hchman Design Group Inc........C 866 267-3945
  Jersey City (G-4724)
D & G LLC..G 201 289-5750
  Hackensack (G-3902)
Fashion Central LLC ....G 732 887-7683
  Lakewood (G-5121)
Maidenform ....A 732 621-2216
  Iselin (G-4632)
Maidenform Brands Inc ....E 888 573-0299
  Iselin (G-4633)

CLOTHING: Uniforms & Vestments

Costume Gallery Inc ....E 609 386-6601
  Delanco (G-2005)
Fine Wear U S A ....G 201 313-3777
  Fort Lee (G-3554)

Global Manufacturing LLC..................G 973 494-5413
  Newark (G-7172)

CLOTHING: Uniforms, Ex Athletic, Women's, Misses' & Juniors'

Eagle Work Clothes Inc ....E 908 964-8888
  Florham Park (G-3499)
Happy Chef Inc................................E 973 492-2525
  Butler (G-1006)

CLOTHING: Uniforms, Firemen's, From Purchased Materials

Firefighter One Ltd Lblty Co ....G 973 940-3061
  Sparta (G-10499)
Trilex Ltd ....E 201 664-5576
  Twp Washinton (G-11144)

CLOTHING: Uniforms, Men's & Boys'

Stretch-O-Rama Inc ....E 732 855-1400
  Avenel (G-153)

CLOTHING: Uniforms, Military, Men/Youth, Purchased Materials

Crown Clothing Co ....C 856 691-0343
  Vineland (G-11343)
De Rossi & Son Co Inc ....C 856 691-0061
  Vineland (G-11351)

CLOTHING: Uniforms, Policemen's, From Purchased Materials

Alpine Trading Company Inc ....E 201 871-6111
  Englewood (G-2867)

CLOTHING: Uniforms, Team Athletic

Rennoc Corporation ....D 856 327-5400
  Vineland (G-11395)

CLOTHING: Uniforms, Work

Enailsupply Corporation ....G 909 725-1698
  Toms River (G-10874)
New Community Corp ....E 973 643-5300
  Newark (G-7249)

CLOTHING: WarmUp, Jogging & Sweat Suits, Girls' & Children's

Lemon Inc ....G 201 417-5412
  Norwood (G-7628)

CLOTHING: Waterproof Outerwear

A J P Scientific Inc............................G 973 472-7200
  Clifton (G-1552)

CLOTHING: Womens/Misses Coats, Jackets & Vests, Down-Filled

Fyi Marketing Inc.............................G 646 546-5226
  Englewood Cliffs (G-2960)

CLOTHING: Work Apparel, Exc Uniforms

Flying Fish Studio............................G 609 884-2760
  West Cape May (G-11808)

CLOTHING: Work, Men's

Ansell Healthcare Products LLC ....C 732 345-5400
  Iselin (G-4611)
B2x Corporation ....G 201 714-2373
  Jersey City (G-4712)
Bestwork Inds For The Blind ....D 856 424-2510
  Cherry Hill (G-1349)
Galvanic LLC ....G 609 600-2604
  Cape May (G-1100)
Luxury and Trash Ltd Lblty Co ....G 201 315-4018
  Closter (G-1763)
Matrix Sales Group LLC ....D 908 461-4148
  Spring Lake (G-10534)
Mischief International Inc ....G 201 840-6888
  Ridgefield (G-9374)
Red The Uniform Tailor Inc ....E 848 299-0100
  Lakewood (G-5176)
Somes Uniforms Inc ....F 201 843-1199
  Hackensack (G-3977)

P R O D U C T

Switlik Parachute Company Inc............F...... 609 587-3300
Trenton (G-11119)

Tellas Ltd ....E...... 201 399-8888
Englewood Cliffs (G-2981)

Todd Shelton LLC ....G...... 844 626-6355
East Rutherford (G-2333)

Trilex Ltd ....E...... 201 664-5576
Twp Washinton (G-11144)

Vertical Protective AP LLC ....G...... 203 904-6099
Shrewsbury (G-10013)

CLOTHING: Work, Waterproof, Exc Raincoats

Eagle Work Clothes Inc ....E...... 908 964-8888
Florham Park (G-3499)

Loveline Industries Inc ....G...... 973 928-3427
Passaic (G-8157)

M Rafi Sons Garment Industries ....G...... 732 381-7660
Rahway (G-9211)

COAL MINING SERVICES

Asbury Carbons Inc ....G...... 908 537-2155
Asbury (G-66)

Starfuels Inc ....E...... 201 685-0400
Englewood (G-2934)

COAL, MINERALS & ORES, WHOLESALE: Coal

Minmetals Inc ....F...... 201 809-1898
Leonia (G-5318)

COATING COMPOUNDS: Tar

Actega North America Inc ....C...... 856 829-6300
Delran (G-2009)

Fti Inc ....G...... 973 443-0004
Florham Park (G-3503)

COATING SVC

All American Powdercoating LLC ....G...... 732 349-7001
Toms River (G-10861)

Dynamic Coatings LLC ....G...... 732 998-6625
Matawan (G-6019)

COATING SVC: Metals & Formed Prdts

Abco Die Casters Inc ....D...... 973 624-7030
Newark (G-7070)

Alpha Processing Co Inc ....E...... 973 777-1737
Clifton (G-1562)

Andek Corporation ....F...... 856 866-7600
Moorestown (G-6560)

Atlantic Eqp Engineers Inc ....F...... 201 828-9400
Upper Saddle River (G-11273)

Boyko Metal Finishing Co Inc ....D...... 973 623-4254
Newark (G-7110)

Cardolite Corporation ....E...... 609 436-0902
Monmouth Junction (G-6335)

Ceronics Inc ....G...... 732 566-5600
Matawan (G-6015)

Chapter Enterprises Inc ....G...... 732 560-8500
Bridgewater (G-827)

Cincinnati Thermal Spray Inc ....G...... 973 379-0003
Springfield (G-10547)

Ferro Corporation ....G...... 908 226-2148
South Plainfield (G-10364)

General Magnaplate California ....F...... 805 642-6262
Linden (G-5379)

General Magnaplate Corporation ....D...... 908 862-6200
Linden (G-5380)

General Magnaplate Wisconsin ....F...... 800 441-6173
Linden (G-5381)

General Plastics Group ....E...... 973 748-5500
Bloomfield (G-512)

Innovative Powder Coatings LLC ....G...... 856 661-0086
Pennsauken (G-8527)

Jema-American Inc ....G...... 732 968-5333
Middlesex (G-6172)

Lordon Inc ....G...... 908 813-1143
Hackettstown (G-4018)

Paramount Metal Finishing Co ....C...... 908 862-0772
Linden (G-5424)

Peerless Coatings LLC ....E...... 973 427-8771
Hawthorne (G-4252)

Penn Metal Finishing Co Inc ....G...... 609 387-3400
Burlington (G-987)

Phoenix Powder Coating LLC ....G...... 973 907-7500
Haskell (G-4212)

S D L Powder Coating Inc ....G...... 732 473-0800
Toms River (G-10907)

COATING SVC: Metals, With Plastic Or Resins

Bel-Art Products Inc ....E...... 973 694-0500
Wayne (G-11608)

Flexcraft Industries Inc ....G...... 973 589-3403
Newark (G-7163)

Plastics Consulting & Mfg Co ....E...... 800 222-0317
Camden (G-1082)

COATING SVC: Rust Preventative

Gary R Banks Industrial Group ....F...... 856 687-2227
West Berlin (G-11723)

COATING SVC: Silicon

Microsurfaces Inc ....G...... 201 408-5596
Englewood (G-2916)

COATINGS: Air Curing

ACC Coatings LLC ....F...... 732 469-8600
Middlesex (G-6142)

RPM Prfrmnce Catings Group Inc ....F...... 888 788-4323
Long Branch (G-5631)

Stoncor Group Inc ....C...... 800 257-7953
Maple Shade (G-5909)

Uvitec Printing Ink Co Inc ....E...... 973 778-0737
Lodi (G-5607)

COATINGS: Epoxy

Armorpoxy Inc ....F...... 908 810-9613
Union (G-11154)

Broadview Technologies Inc ....E...... 973 465-0077
Newark (G-7116)

Duraamen Engineered Pdts Inc ....G...... 973 230-1301
Newark (G-7144)

Master Bond Inc ....E...... 201 343-8983
Hackensack (G-3943)

North Jersey Specialists Inc ....G...... 973 927-1616
Flanders (G-3413)

Palma Inc ....F...... 973 429-1490
Whippany (G-12031)

Philip Mamrak ....G...... 908 454-6089
Phillipsburg (G-8663)

Rema Corrosion Control ....F...... 201 256-8400
Northvale (G-7604)

Sika Corporation ....B...... 201 933-8800
Lyndhurst (G-5708)

Sika Corporation ....C...... 201 933-8800
Lyndhurst (G-5709)

COATINGS: Polyurethane

Worldwide Safety Systems LLC ....G...... 888 613-4501
Teaneck (G-10778)

CODEINE & DERIVATIVES

Mallinckrodt LLC ....F...... 908 238-6600
Hampton (G-4164)

Prime Coding Services LLC ....G...... 732 254-3036
East Brunswick (G-2175)

COFFEE MAKERS: Electric

Argonautus LLC ....G...... 908 393-4379
Bridgewater (G-813)

COFFEE SVCS

Coffee Associates Inc ....E...... 201 945-1060
Edgewater (G-2436)

Quality Plus One Catering Inc ....G...... 732 967-1525
Old Bridge (G-7791)

COILS & TRANSFORMERS

A C Transformer Corp ....G...... 973 589-8574
Newark (G-7065)

AFP Transformers Corporation ....D...... 732 248-0305
Edison (G-2453)

Automatic Switch Company ....A...... 973 966-2000
Florham Park (G-3489)

Behringer Fluid Systems Inc ....G...... 973 948-0226
Branchville (G-726)

Bel Hybrids & Magnetics Inc ....F...... 201 432-0463
Jersey City (G-4716)

Celco ....F...... 201 327-1123
Mahwah (G-5757)

Freed Transformer Company ....E...... 973 942-2222
Paterson (G-8273)

Fugle-Miller Laboratories Inc ....E...... 732 574-3121
Rahway (G-9192)

Jerome Industries Corp ....E...... 908 353-5700
Hackettstown (G-4013)

Kef America Inc ....E...... 732 414-2074
Marlboro (G-5946)

Mallika Ashwin Maya Corp ....G...... 908 393-2571
Hillsborough (G-4356)

Microsignals Inc ....G...... 800 225-4508
Palisades Park (G-7839)

Stonite Coil Corporation ....E...... 609 585-6600
Trenton (G-11118)

Torelco Inc ....F...... 908 387-0814
Alpha (G-47)

COILS, WIRE: Aluminum, Made In Rolling Mills

H Cross Company ....E...... 201 964-9380
Moonachie (G-6519)

COIN-OPERATED LAUNDRY

Pueblo Latino Laundry LLC ....G...... 201 864-1666
Union City (G-11263)

COLLECTION AGENCY, EXC REAL ESTATE

Quadramed Corporation ....E...... 732 751-0400
Eatontown (G-2420)

COLOR LAKES OR TONERS

Ferro Corporation ....E...... 732 287-4925
Edison (G-2519)

COLOR PIGMENTS

Brenntag Specialties Inc ....D...... 800 732-0562
South Plainfield (G-10339)

Riverdale Color Mfg Inc ....E...... 732 376-9300
Perth Amboy (G-8628)

Sudarshan North America Inc ....G...... 201 652-2046
Ridgewood (G-9431)

COLOR SEPARATION: Photographic & Movie Film

Prism Color Corporation ....D...... 856 234-7515
Moorestown (G-6615)

COLORING & FINISHING SVC: Aluminum Or Formed Prdts

Ampal Inc ....G...... 908 782-5454
Flemington (G-3426)

COLORS: Pigments, Inorganic

BASF Catalysts LLC ....D...... 732 205-5000
Iselin (G-4616)

Breen Color Concentrates LLC ....F...... 609 397-8200
Lambertville (G-5210)

Color Techniques Inc ....F...... 908 412-9292
South Plainfield (G-10347)

Custom Chemicals Corp ....A...... 201 791-5100
Elmwood Park (G-2814)

Dispersion Technology Inc ....F...... 732 364-4488
Lakewood (G-5109)

Elementis Specialties Inc ....E...... 201 432-0800
East Windsor (G-2375)

Elementis Specialties Inc ....C...... 609 443-2000
East Windsor (G-2374)

Evonik Corporation ....B...... 973 929-8000
Parsippany (G-8003)

Ferro Corporation ....E...... 732 287-4925
Edison (G-2519)

French Color Fragrance Co Inc ....E...... 201 567-6883
Englewood (G-2898)

Global Colorants Inc ....G...... 973 751-2227
Old Bridge (G-7780)

Kvk Usa Inc ....F...... 732 846-2355
New Brunswick (G-6976)

Lightscape Materials Inc ....G...... 609 734-2224
Princeton (G-9067)

Sensient Technologies Corp ....F...... 908 757-4500
South Plainfield (G-10435)

Vivitone Inc..........................F...... 973 427-8114
Hawthorne (G-4264)

COLORS: Pigments, Organic

Color Techniques Inc..................F...... 908 412-9292
South Plainfield (G-10347)
Dominion Colour Corp USA.................F...... 973 279-9591
Clifton (G-1604)
Penn Color Inc.........................C...... 201 791-5100
Elmwood Park (G-2842)
Sun Chemical Corporation...................D...... 973 404-6000
Parsippany (G-8094)

COLUMNS, FRACTIONING: Metal Plate

Construction Specialties Inc..............E...... 908 236-0800
Lebanon (G-5282)

COMFORTERS & QUILTS, FROM MANMADE FIBER OR SILK

Hanover Direct Inc ....B...... 201 863-7300
Weehawken (G-11695)

COMMERCIAL & INDL SHELVING WHOLESALERS

Warehouse Solutions Inc ....F...... 201 880-1110
Fair Lawn (G-3123)

COMMERCIAL & OFFICE BUILDINGS RENOVATION & REPAIR

Crincoli Woodwork Co Inc ....F...... 908 352-9332
Elizabeth (G-2721)
Donnelly Industries Inc ....D...... 973 672-1800
Wayne (G-11626)

COMMERCIAL ART & GRAPHIC DESIGN SVCS

4 Over Inc..........................F...... 201 440-1656
Moonachie (G-6498)
42 Design Square LLC..................F...... 888 272-5979
Parsippany (G-7937)
Alpha 1 Studio Inc..................G...... 609 859-2200
Southampton (G-10469)
Applied Image Inc ....E...... 732 410-2444
Freehold (G-3638)
C2 Imaging LLC..................E...... 646 557-6300
Jersey City (G-4722)
Drew & Rogers Inc ....E...... 973 575-6210
Fairfield (G-3179)
Eagle Systems Inc ....G...... 732 226-2111
Ocean (G-7723)
Go R Design LLC..................E...... 609 286-2146
New Egypt (G-7015)
Graphic Action Inc ....G...... 908 213-0055
Phillipsburg (G-8650)
Harwill Corporation..................G...... 609 895-1955
Windsor (G-12127)
Jasco Specialties and Forms..................G...... 856 627-5511
Tabernacle (G-10738)
L & F Graphics Ltd Lblty Co ....G...... 973 240-7033
Paterson (G-8312)
L&M Architectural Graphics Inc ....F...... 973 575-7665
Fairfield (G-3245)
Larue Manufacturing Corp ....F...... 908 534-2700
Whitehouse (G-12046)
McKella 2-8-0 Inc..................D...... 856 813-1153
Pennsauken (G-8548)
Monte Printing & Graphics Inc ....G...... 908 241-6600
Roselle Park (G-9699)
Nema Associates Inc ....F...... 973 274-0052
Linden (G-5418)
Onyx Graphics LLC..................G...... 908 281-0038
Hillsborough (G-4361)
Print Factory Ltd Liability Co..................G...... 973 866-5230
Clifton (G-1705)
Promo Graphic Inc..................G...... 732 629-7300
Middlesex (G-6191)
Rays Reproduction Inc ....G...... 201 666-5650
Emerson (G-2862)
Remco Press Inc..................G...... 201 751-5703
North Bergen (G-7479)
Ridgewood Press Inc..................F...... 201 670-9797
Ridgewood (G-9430)
Shindo International Inc..................E...... 973 470-8100
Clifton (G-1722)

Springworks Group Ltd ....G...... 973 276-7940
Fairfield (G-3310)
Star Narrow Fabrics Inc..................G...... 973 778-8600
Lodi (G-5602)
Techsetters Inc..................E...... 856 240-7905
Collingswood (G-1774)
Toppan Printing Co Amer Inc..................C...... 732 469-8400
Somerset (G-10188)

COMMERCIAL ART & ILLUSTRATION SVCS

Blue Parachute LLC..................G...... 732 767-1320
Metuchen (G-6097)
Royer Graphics Inc..................G...... 856 344-7935
Clementon (G-1535)

COMMERCIAL CONTAINERS WHOLESALERS

Granco Group LLC..................G...... 973 515-4721
Roseland (G-9651)
James R Macauley Inc..................G...... 856 767-3474
Waterford Works (G-11598)

COMMERCIAL EQPT & SPLYS, WHOLESALE: Hotel

ADS Sales Co Inc..................E...... 732 591-0500
Morganville (G-6635)

COMMERCIAL EQPT WHOLESALERS, NEC

Atlantic Zeiser Inc..................E...... 973 228-0800
West Caldwell (G-11766)
Edsall Group USA Inc..................D...... 908 874-6953
Hillsborough (G-4330)
Envirosight LLC..................E...... 973 970-9284
Randolph (G-9275)
Ice Cold Novelty Products Inc ....G...... 732 751-0011
Wall Township (G-11491)
Intertest Inc..................E...... 908 496-8008
Columbia (G-1799)
Par Code Symbology Inc..................F...... 973 918-0550
Roseland (G-9655)
Sea Breeze Fruit Flavors Inc..................D...... 973 334-7777
Towaco (G-11003)
Track Systems Inc..................F...... 201 462-0095
Hasbrouck Heights (G-4201)
W T Winter Associates Inc ....E...... 888 808-3611
Fairfield (G-3349)

COMMERCIAL EQPT, WHOLESALE: Bakery Eqpt & Splys

Cns Confectionery Products LLC ....F...... 201 823-1400
Bayonne (G-220)

COMMERCIAL EQPT, WHOLESALE: Coffee Brewing Eqpt & Splys

Rockline Industries Inc..................C...... 973 257-2884
Montville (G-6493)

COMMERCIAL EQPT, WHOLESALE: Comm Cooking & Food Svc Eqpt

Am-Mac Incorporated ....F...... 973 575-7567
Fairfield (G-3133)
Bon Chef Inc..................D...... 973 383-8848
Lafayette (G-5045)
J & M Air Inc..................E...... 908 707-4040
Somerville (G-10217)

COMMERCIAL EQPT, WHOLESALE: Display Eqpt, Exc Refrigerated

CDI Group Inc..................F...... 908 862-1493
Linden (G-5356)
Salescaster Displays Corp..................G...... 908 322-3046
Scotch Plains (G-9854)

COMMERCIAL EQPT, WHOLESALE: Restaurant, NEC

HCH Incorporated ....G...... 973 300-4551
Sparta (G-10504)
Taylor Products Inc ....E...... 732 225-4620
Edison (G-2637)

COMMERCIAL EQPT, WHOLESALE: Scales, Exc Laboratory

Advance Scale Company Inc..................E...... 856 784-4916
Lindenwold (G-5461)
Empire Scale & Balance..................G...... 856 299-1651
Penns Grove (G-8465)
Lps Industries Inc..................C...... 201 438-3515
Moonachie (G-6529)
Ptc Electronics Inc..................G...... 201 847-0500
Mahwah (G-5804)

COMMERCIAL EQPT, WHOLESALE: Store Fixtures & Display Eqpt

Testrite Instrument Co Inc..................C...... 201 543-0240
Hackensack (G-3984)

COMMERCIAL LAUNDRY EQPT

Air World Inc..................E...... 201 831-0700
Mahwah (G-5745)
Airworld Inc ....F...... 973 720-1008
Paterson (G-8201)
Fairfield Laundry McHy Corp..................E...... 973 575-4330
Fairfield (G-3193)
Fowler Route Co Inc ....E...... 908 686-3400
Union (G-11186)
Sadwith Industries Corp..................G...... 732 531-3856
Ocean (G-7742)

COMMERCIAL PRINTING & NEWSPAPER PUBLISHING COMBINED

Asbury Park Press Inc..................A...... 732 922-6000
Neptune (G-6900)
Burlington Times Inc ....B...... 609 871-8000
Willingboro (G-12117)
Central Record Publications..................E...... 609 654-5000
Trenton (G-11038)
Community News Service LLC..................F...... 609 396-1511
Lawrenceville (G-5254)
Hunterdon County Democrat Inc..........D...... 908 782-4747
Flemington (G-3448)
New Jersey Herald ....C...... 973 383-1500
Newton (G-7399)
Newark Morning Ledger Co ....B...... 973 392-4141
Newark (G-7257)
Newspaper Media Group LLC ....E...... 201 798-7800
Bayonne (G-239)
Princeton Packet Inc..................C...... 609 924-3244
Princeton (G-9097)
Recorder Publishing Co Inc..................D...... 908 766-3900
Whippany (G-12037)
South Jersey Publishing Co ....F...... 856 692-0455
Vineland (G-11406)

COMMERCIAL REFRIGERATORS WHOLESALERS

Modern Store Equipment ....F...... 609 241-7438
Burlington (G-985)

COMMODITY CONTRACTS BROKERS, DEALERS

Powerspec Inc..................E...... 732 494-9490
Somerville (G-10225)

COMMON SAND MINING

Alliance Sand Co Inc..................G...... 908 534-4116
Somerville (G-10201)
F W Bennett & Son Inc ....G...... 973 383-4050
Lafayette (G-5046)
New Jersey Pulverizing Co Inc..........F...... 732 269-1400
Bayville (G-259)

COMMUNICATION HEADGEAR: Telephone

Sonetronics Inc..................D...... 732 681-5016
Belmar (G-364)

COMMUNICATIONS EQPT & SYSTEMS, NEC

Institute For Respnsble Online..............G...... 856 722-1048
Mount Laurel (G-6805)

COMMUNICATIONS EQPT REPAIR & MAINTENANCE

Lucent Technologies World Svcs........C 908 582-3000
New Providence (G-7046)
Transcore LP ....F 201 329-9200
Teterboro (G-10816)
Wireless Electronics Inc................E 856 768-4310
West Berlin (G-11761)

COMMUNICATIONS EQPT WHOLESALERS

360 Media Innovations LLC..............G 201 228-0941
Union (G-11145)
Ambro Inc ....E 201 818-9717
Pequannock (G-8597)
Arose Inc...................................E 856 481-4351
Blackwood (G-471)
Bogen Communications Inc..............D 201 934-8500
Mahwah (G-5754)
Enterprisecc Ltd Liability Co.............G 201 266-0020
Jersey City (G-4749)
Industronic Inc..............................G 908 393-5960
Bridgewater (G-845)
Transcore LP ....F 201 329-9200
Teterboro (G-10816)
Vcom Intl Multi-Media Corp..............D 201 814-0405
Fairfield (G-3337)
Vitex LLC ....G 201 296-0145
Ridgefield Park (G-9417)

COMMUNICATIONS EQPT: Microwave

Fei-Elcom Tech Inc ....E 201 767-8030
Northvale (G-7580)
In-Phase Technologies Inc ....E 609 298-9555
Bordentown (G-599)
Merrimac Industries Inc...................D 973 575-1300
West Caldwell (G-11790)
Vitec Videocom Inc ....E 908 852-3700
Secaucus (G-9938)
Wide Band Systems Inc ....F 973 586-6500
Rockaway (G-9625)

COMMUNICATIONS SVCS

Tyco Elec Sbsea Cmmnctions LLC ....B 732 578-7000
Eatontown (G-2427)

COMMUNICATIONS SVCS: Cellular

Instock Wireless Components..............F 973 335-6550
Boonton (G-572)
Princeton Hosted Solutions LLC..........F 856 470-2350
Haddonfield (G-4062)
Verizon Communications Inc..............E 201 666-9934
Westwood (G-11975)
Verizon Communications Inc..............D 609 646-9939
Egg Harbor Township (G-2698)
Wireless Experience of PA Inc.............G 732 552-0050
Toms River (G-10922)

COMMUNICATIONS SVCS: Data

Communications Supply Corp ....E 732 346-1864
Edison (G-2487)
Grafwed Internet Media Studios...........G 201 632-1771
Midland Park (G-6227)
Pentagon Performance Inc ....G 973 975-0400
Millville (G-6320)
Spirent Communications Inc ....G 732 946-4018
Holmdel (G-4530)

COMMUNICATIONS SVCS: Facsimile Transmission

All American Print & Copy Ctr ....G 732 758-6200
Red Bank (G-9318)
E C D Ventures Inc ....G 856 875-1100
Blackwood (G-477)

COMMUNICATIONS SVCS: Internet Connectivity Svcs

Comodo Group Inc ....C 888 266-6361
Clifton (G-1586)
Telvue Corporation ....E 800 885-8886
Mount Laurel (G-6844)
Wcd Enterprises Inc ....G 732 888-4422
Keyport (G-5026)

COMMUNICATIONS SVCS: Internet Host Svcs

North Jersey Media Group Inc............A 201 646-4000
Woodland Park (G-12225)
Strahan Consulting Group LLC ....G 908 790-0873
Scotch Plains (G-9857)
US Software Group Inc....................E 732 361-4636
South Plainfield (G-10447)

COMMUNICATIONS SVCS: Online Svc Providers

Home Organization LLC ....F 201 351-2121
Closter (G-1760)
Mindwise Media LLC.......................G 973 701-0685
Chatham (G-1334)
Solbright Group Inc ....G 973 339-3855
Newark (G-7319)

COMMUNICATIONS SVCS: Satellite Earth Stations

Ussecurenet LLC ....G 201 447-0130
Hawthorne (G-4262)

COMMUNICATIONS SVCS: Telephone Or Video

Bandemar Networks LLC ....G 732 991-5112
East Brunswick (G-2136)
Enterprisecc Ltd Liability Co ....G 201 266-0020
Jersey City (G-4749)

COMMUNICATIONS SVCS: Telephone, Data

Verizon Communications Inc.............E 201 666-9934
Westwood (G-11975)

COMMUNICATIONS SVCS: Telephone, Local

Verizon Communications Inc.............D 609 646-9939
Egg Harbor Township (G-2698)

COMMUNICATIONS SVCS: Telephone, Local & Long Distance

Novega Venture Partners Inc ....G 732 528-2600
Holmdel (G-4527)
Spirent Communications Inc ....G 732 946-4018
Holmdel (G-4530)

COMMUNICATIONS SVCS: Telephone, Voice

Blueclone Networks LLC..................G 609 944-8433
Princeton (G-9017)
Value Added Vice Solutions LLC..........G 201 400-3247
Brielle (G-916)

COMMUTATORS: Electric Motors

Allu Group Inc ....F 201 288-2236
East Brunswick (G-2132)

COMMUTATORS: Electronic

Heyco Products Corp ....G 732 286-1800
Toms River (G-10885)

COMPACT DISCS OR CD'S, WHOLESALE

Audio and Video Labs Inc ....B 856 663-9030
Pennsauken (G-8482)

COMPACT LASER DISCS: Prerecorded

Audio and Video Labs Inc ....B 856 663-9030
Pennsauken (G-8482)
Audio and Video Labs Inc ....E 856 661-5772
Delair (G-2000)
Disc Makers Inc...........................B 800 468-9353
Pennsauken (G-8504)
Simtronics Corporation ....F 732 747-0322
Little Silver (G-5520)
Sony Corporation of America ....B 201 930-1000
Paramus (G-7902)

COMPACTORS: Trash & Garbage, Residential

Arrow Steel Inc ....F 973 523-1122
Paterson (G-8215)

COMPOST

L & S Contracting Inc ....G 609 397-1281
Hopewell (G-4542)

COMPRESSORS: Air & Gas

Aavolyn Corp................................E 856 327-8040
Millville (G-6272)
Aer X Dust Corporation ....G 732 946-9462
Holmdel (G-4508)
Argus International Inc ....E 609 466-1677
Ringoes (G-9435)
Armco Compressor Products.............G 201 866-6766
North Bergen (G-7432)
Atlas Copco Hurricane LLC ....D 800 754-7408
Parsippany (G-7954)
Emse Corp ....G 973 227-9221
Fairfield (G-3184)
Energy Beams Inc ....F 973 291-6555
Bloomingdale (G-543)
Fleet Equipment Corporation ....F 201 337-3294
Franklin Lakes (G-3617)
Metropolitan Vacuum Clr Co Inc..........D 201 405-2225
Oakland (G-7696)
Trillium US ....G 973 827-1661
Hamburg (G-4097)
Vac-U-Max ....E 973 759-4600
Belleville (G-322)

COMPRESSORS: Air & Gas, Including Vacuum Pumps

Breeze-Eastern LLC.......................G 973 602-1001
Whippany (G-12014)
Campbell Hausfeld LLC ....E 856 661-1800
Pennsauken (G-8489)
Gas Drying Inc.............................F 973 361-2212
Wharton (G-11988)
Ingersoll-Rand Company ....E 856 793-7000
Mount Laurel (G-6803)
Knf Neuberger Inc ....D 609 890-8889
Trenton (G-11074)
Kraissl Company Inc ....E 201 342-0008
Hackensack (G-3937)

COMPUTER & COMPUTER SOFTWARE STORES

Andlogic Computers........................G 609 610-5752
Hamilton (G-4103)
Asi Computer Technologies Inc ....F 732 343-7100
Edison (G-2467)
Computer Doc Associates Inc............D 908 647-4445
Martinsville (G-6009)
Maingear Inc ....E 888 624-6432
Kenilworth (G-4972)
R T I Inc ....E 201 261-5852
Oradell (G-7812)

COMPUTER & COMPUTER SOFTWARE STORES: Peripheral Eqpt

Fillimerica Inc ....G 800 435-7257
Montville (G-6488)

COMPUTER & COMPUTER SOFTWARE STORES: Personal Computers

Adaptive Technology Entps LLC..........G 877 847-6272
Medford (G-6063)

COMPUTER & COMPUTER SOFTWARE STORES: Printers & Plotters

Imperial Copy Products Inc ....E 973 927-5500
Randolph (G-9284)

COMPUTER & COMPUTER SOFTWARE STORES: Software & Access

Promia Incorporated......................G 609 252-1850
Princeton (G-9106)

COMPUTER & COMPUTER SOFTWARE STORES: Software, Bus/Non-Game

Automated Office Inc......................G 888 362-7638
Cherry Hill (G-1345)
Bluebird Auto Rentl Systems LP ....E 973 989-2423
Dover (G-2079)

COMPUTER & COMPUTER SOFTWARE STORES: Software, Computer Game

Sony Corporation of America ....F 201 930-1000
  Woodcliff Lake *(G-12202)*

COMPUTER & DATA PROCESSING EQPT REPAIR & MAINTENANCE

Innovative Sftwr Solutions Inc..............D....... 856 910-9190
  Maple Shade *(G-5903)*

COMPUTER & OFFICE MACHINE MAINTENANCE & REPAIR

Able Group Technologies Inc ....G....... 732 591-9299
  Morganville *(G-6634)*
Blueclone Networks LLC...................G....... 609 944-8433
  Princeton *(G-9017)*
Creative Cmpt Concepts LLC ....G....... 877 919-7988
  Williamstown *(G-12085)*
Fis Avantgard LLC ....G....... 732 530-9303
  Tinton Falls *(G-10837)*
Integration International Inc..................E 973 796-2300
  Parsippany *(G-8030)*
Lavitsky Computer Laboratories...........G....... 908 725-6206
  Bridgewater *(G-850)*
Lm Matrix Solutions LLC....................G....... 908 756-7952
  Bridgewater *(G-858)*
Vertiv Services Inc ....E 732 225-3741
  Edison *(G-2644)*

COMPUTER & SFTWR STORE: Modem, Monitor, Terminal/Disk Drive

Techntime Bus Sltons Ltd Lblty ....F 973 246-8153
  East Rutherford *(G-2331)*

COMPUTER CALCULATING SVCS

Metro Seliger Industries Inc.................C 201 438-4530
  Carlstadt *(G-1189)*

COMPUTER DISKETTES WHOLESALERS

Epcos Inc ....F 732 603-5941
  Lumberton *(G-5657)*

COMPUTER FACILITIES MANAGEMENT SVCS

Blueclone Networks LLC....................G....... 609 944-8433
  Princeton *(G-9017)*
Commvault Systems Inc ....C 732 870-4000
  Tinton Falls *(G-10828)*
Criterion Software LLC......................F....... 908 754-1166
  Freehold *(G-3648)*
Ensync Intrctive Solutions Inc.............G....... 732 542-4001
  Freehold *(G-3654)*
Medical Strategic Planning Inc ....G....... 732 219-5090
  Lincroft *(G-5339)*

COMPUTER FORMS

All-State International Inc...................C 908 272-0800
  Cranford *(G-1895)*
Stuyvesant Press Inc........................F 973 399-3880
  Irvington *(G-4605)*

COMPUTER GRAPHICS SVCS

FLM Graphics Corporation ....D....... 973 575-9450
  Fairfield *(G-3196)*
Strahan Consulting Group LLC ....G....... 908 790-0873
  Scotch Plains *(G-9857)*

COMPUTER INTERFACE EQPT: Indl Process

Corporate Computer Systems ....F....... 732 739-5600
  Newark *(G-7127)*
Ribble Company Inc ....F....... 201 475-1812
  Saddle Brook *(G-9786)*

COMPUTER PAPER WHOLESALERS

Paris Corporation New Jersey..............D....... 609 265-9200
  Westampton *(G-11914)*

COMPUTER PERIPHERAL EQPT REPAIR & MAINTENANCE

Central Technology Inc ....F....... 732 431-3339
  Freehold *(G-3645)*
Image Access Corp.........................E 201 342-7878
  Rockleigh *(G-9631)*
R T I Inc ....E 201 261-5852
  Oradell *(G-7812)*
Ryval Cmpt Svcs Ltd Lblty Co...........G....... 201 374-1600
  Dumont *(G-2123)*

COMPUTER PERIPHERAL EQPT, NEC

Advancing Opportunities Inc...............G....... 201 907-0200
  Teaneck *(G-10740)*
AEP Networks Inc..........................D....... 732 652-5200
  Somerset *(G-10051)*
Amedia Networks Inc.......................F....... 732 440-1992
  Eatontown *(G-2381)*
Antron Technologies Inc ....G....... 732 205-0415
  Edison *(G-2461)*
Arch Manufacturing & Sales ....G....... 856 966-3835
  Camden *(G-1041)*
Automated Control Concepts Inc.........E 732 922-6611
  Neptune *(G-6901)*
Behr Technology Inc........................G....... 908 537-9960
  Hampton *(G-4154)*
Berkeley Varitronics Systems ....G....... 732 548-3737
  Metuchen *(G-6096)*
Cisco Systems Inc ....G....... 856 642-7000
  Moorestown *(G-6567)*
Cisco Systems Inc ....E 201 782-0842
  Montvale *(G-6448)*
Conduent State Healthcare LLC ....G....... 973 824-3250
  Newark *(G-7126)*
Conduent State Healthcare LLC ....G....... 973 754-6134
  Paterson *(G-8239)*
Corporate Computer Systems ....F....... 732 739-5600
  Newark *(G-7127)*
Data Base Access Systems Inc ....F....... 973 335-0800
  Mountain Lakes *(G-6856)*
Dew Associates Inc ....B 973 702-0545
  Sparta *(G-10496)*
Dew Associates Inc ....E 973 702-0545
  Sussex *(G-10668)*
Ems Aviation Inc ....B 856 234-5020
  Moorestown *(G-6576)*
Envirosight LLC ....E 973 970-9284
  Randolph *(G-9275)*
Epiq Systems Inc ....G....... 973 622-6111
  Newark *(G-7156)*
Fyth Labs Inc................................G....... 856 313-7362
  Beverly *(G-463)*
Humanscale Corporation ....C 732 537-2944
  Piscataway *(G-8777)*
I C System Solutions Inc ....F....... 201 666-1122
  Hillsdale *(G-4384)*
Link Computer Graphics Inc ....G....... 973 808-8990
  Fairfield *(G-3253)*
Lucent Technologies World Svcs.........C 908 582-3000
  New Providence *(G-7046)*
Maingear Inc ....E 888 624-6432
  Kenilworth *(G-4972)*
Micro Innovations Corp ....D....... 732 346-9333
  Edison *(G-2571)*
MTS Systems Corporation ....A....... 856 875-4478
  Williamstown *(G-12093)*
Ner Data Products Inc ....F....... 888 637-3282
  Glassboro *(G-3810)*
Netscout Systems Inc......................G....... 609 518-4100
  Marlton *(G-5990)*
Oxberry LLC ....G....... 201 935-3000
  Carlstadt *(G-1196)*
Parker-Hannifin Corporation ....F....... 856 825-8900
  Millville *(G-6319)*
Pcs Revenue Ctrl Systems Inc ....E 201 568-8300
  Englewood Cliffs *(G-2978)*
PNC Electronics Inc........................F....... 973 237-0400
  Totowa *(G-10964)*
R T I Inc ....E 201 261-5852
  Oradell *(G-7812)*
Radcom Equipment Inc ....G....... 201 518-0033
  Paramus *(G-7898)*
Raritan Inc ....E 732 764-8886
  Somerset *(G-10162)*
Raritan Americas Inc ....C 732 764-8886
  Somerset *(G-10163)*
RSR Electronics Inc........................E 732 381-8777
  Rahway *(G-9222)*

S W Electronics & Mfg.....................C 856 222-9900
  Moorestown *(G-6620)*
Salescaster Displays Corp.................G....... 908 322-3046
  Scotch Plains *(G-9854)*
Sony Corporation of America ....B 201 930-1000
  Paramus *(G-7902)*
Source Micro LLC ....F....... 973 328-1749
  Randolph *(G-9298)*
Technobox Inc ....G....... 856 809-2306
  West Berlin *(G-11755)*
Telegenix Inc ....F....... 609 265-3910
  Rancocas *(G-9264)*
Thomas Instrumentation Inc...............F....... 609 624-7777
  Cape May Court House *(G-1117)*
Umit International Trading LLC ....F....... 973 571-1000
  Cedar Grove *(G-1303)*
Verint Systems Inc..........................D....... 201 438-1429
  Lyndhurst *(G-5712)*
Western Scientific Computers ....F....... 973 263-9311
  Mountain Lakes *(G-6864)*
Whale Communications Inc ....G....... 201 947-0054
  Fort Lee *(G-3590)*

COMPUTER PERIPHERAL EQPT, WHOLESALE

Abris Distribution Inc ....G....... 732 252-9819
  Manalapan *(G-5836)*
Antron Technologies Inc ....G....... 732 205-0415
  Edison *(G-2461)*
Archtech Electronics Corp..................E 732 355-1288
  Dayton *(G-1952)*
Bcc (USA) Inc ....G....... 732 572-5450
  Piscataway *(G-8740)*
Capintec Inc ....E 201 825-9500
  Florham Park *(G-3495)*
Computer Company North America......F....... 909 265-3390
  Bedminster *(G-270)*
DFI-Itox LLC ....E 732 562-0693
  Piscataway *(G-8757)*
Fusar Technologies Inc ....G....... 201 563-0189
  Kearny *(G-4874)*
Pascack Data Services Inc ....F....... 973 304-4858
  Hawthorne *(G-4251)*
Quadrangle Products Inc ....F....... 732 792-1234
  Englishtown *(G-2997)*

COMPUTER PERIPHERAL EQPT: Decoders

Paradise Barxon Corp ....G....... 908 707-9141
  Branchburg *(G-686)*

COMPUTER PERIPHERAL EQPT: Graphic Displays, Exc Terminals

Zaller Studios Inc ....G....... 973 743-5175
  Bloomfield *(G-538)*

COMPUTER PERIPHERAL EQPT: Input Or Output

American Fibertek Inc ....E 732 302-0660
  Somerset *(G-10056)*

COMPUTER PROCESSING SVCS

Aone Touch Inc ....G....... 732 261-6841
  Bordentown *(G-590)*

COMPUTER PROGRAMMING SVCS

Bavelle Tech Sltions Ltd Lblty ....F....... 973 992-8086
  East Hanover *(G-2201)*
Cloudageit Ltd Liability Co ....G....... 888 205-4128
  North Brunswick *(G-7513)*
Com Tek Wrkplace Solutions LLC ....F....... 973 927-6814
  Lyndhurst *(G-5678)*
Corporate Computer Systems ....F....... 732 739-5600
  Newark *(G-7127)*
Cyberextrudercom Inc ....G....... 973 623-7900
  Wayne *(G-11622)*
Dew Associates Inc ....B 973 702-0545
  Sparta *(G-10496)*
Eclearview Technologies Inc ....G....... 732 695-6999
  Ocean *(G-7724)*
Ensync Intrctive Solutions Inc.............G....... 732 542-4001
  Freehold *(G-3654)*
Fusar Technologies Inc ....G....... 201 563-0189
  Kearny *(G-4874)*
Global Power Technology Inc ....D....... 732 287-3680
  Edison *(G-2528)*

Interntnal Digital Systems Inc...........F....201 983-7700
  Fort Lee *(G-3560)*
JS Paluch Co Inc...........F....732 516-1900
  Edison *(G-2550)*
Medical Strategic Planning Inc...........G....732 219-5090
  Lincroft *(G-5339)*
Microtelecom Ltd Liability Co...........G....866 676-5679
  Fort Lee *(G-3569)*
Netquest Corporation...........856 866-0505
  Mount Laurel *(G-6822)*
Onco Inc...........F....732 292-7460
  Wall Township *(G-11500)*
Real Soft Inc...........A....609 409-3636
  Monmouth Junction *(G-6360)*
Redstage Networks LLC...........F....888 335-2747
  Jersey City *(G-4817)*
Stephen Swinton Studio Inc...........G....908 537-9135
  Washington *(G-11588)*
Structured Healthcare MGT Inc...........E....201 569-3290
  Englewood *(G-2935)*

COMPUTER PROGRAMMING SVCS: Custom

Greycell Labs Inc...........E....732 444-0123
  Edison *(G-2529)*
Indotronix International Corp...........G....609 750-0700
  Plainsboro *(G-8885)*
Thomas Instrumentation Inc...........F....609 624-7777
  Cape May Court House *(G-1117)*
Thomas Instrumentation Inc...........E....609 624-2630
  Cape May Court House *(G-1118)*
Um Equity Corp...........G....856 354-2200
  Haddonfield *(G-4065)*

COMPUTER RELATED MAINTENANCE SVCS

Ensync Intrctive Solutions Inc...........G....732 542-4001
  Freehold *(G-3654)*
Kyosis LLC...........G....908 202-8894
  South River *(G-10462)*
Lm Matrix Solutions LLC...........G....908 756-7952
  Bridgewater *(G-858)*
Pds Prclnical Data Systems Inc...........E....973 398-2800
  Mount Arlington *(G-6759)*
Ryval Cmpt Svcs Ltd Lblty Co...........G....201 374-1600
  Dumont *(G-2123)*

COMPUTER SERVICE BUREAU

Alaquest International Inc...........F....908 713-9399
  Lebanon *(G-5275)*
Commerce Register Inc...........E....201 445-3000
  Midland Park *(G-6223)*
Stephen Swinton Studio Inc...........G....908 537-9135
  Washington *(G-11588)*

COMPUTER SOFTWARE DEVELOPMENT

Audiocodes Inc...........G....732 469-0880
  Somerset *(G-10066)*
Audiocodes Inc...........F....732 469-0880
  Somerset *(G-10067)*
Aztec Software Associates Inc...........E....973 258-0011
  Springfield *(G-10540)*
Burgiss Group LLC...........D....201 427-9600
  Hoboken *(G-4461)*
Comprehensive Healthcare Systm...........D....732 362-2000
  Edison *(G-2488)*
Data Communique Inc...........E....201 508-6000
  Ridgefield Park *(G-9402)*
Energy Tracking LLC...........G....973 448-8660
  Flanders *(G-3407)*
Innerspace Technology Inc...........G....201 933-1600
  Carlstadt *(G-1172)*
Kittyhawk Digital LLC...........G....269 767-8399
  Emerson *(G-2860)*
Lavitsky Computer Laboratories...........G....908 725-6206
  Bridgewater *(G-850)*
Majesco...........G....973 461-5200
  Morristown *(G-6725)*
Maxisit Inc...........C....732 494-2005
  Metuchen *(G-6114)*
Micro Logic Inc...........F....201 962-7510
  Mahwah *(G-5790)*
Mikros Systems Corporation...........G....609 987-1513
  Princeton *(G-9074)*
Netcom Systems Inc...........E....732 393-6100
  Edison *(G-2579)*
Netx Information Systems Inc...........E....609 298-9118
  Long Beach Township *(G-5618)*
Os33 Services Corp...........G....866 796-0310
  Iselin *(G-4638)*

Planet Associates Inc...........E....201 693-8700
  Park Ridge *(G-7927)*
Promia Incorporated...........G....609 252-1850
  Princeton *(G-9106)*
Samsung SDS Globl Scl Amer Inc...........E....201 229-4456
  Ridgefield Park *(G-9413)*
Smartlinx Solutions LLC...........D....732 385-5507
  Edison *(G-2623)*
Software Practices and Tech...........E....908 464-2923
  Summit *(G-10658)*
Specialty Systems Inc...........E....732 341-1011
  Toms River *(G-10913)*
Sunbird Software Inc...........D....732 993-4476
  Somerset *(G-10176)*
Wizcom Corporation...........E....609 750-0601
  Princeton Junction *(G-9166)*
World Software Corporation...........E....201 444-3228
  Glen Rock *(G-3831)*
Xybion Corporation...........C....973 538-2067
  Lawrenceville *(G-5273)*

COMPUTER SOFTWARE DEVELOPMENT & APPLICATIONS

Aginova Inc...........G....732 804-3272
  Freehold *(G-3635)*
Aplnow LLC...........G....732 223-5575
  Manasquan *(G-5866)*
Artezio LLC...........G....609 786-2435
  Princeton *(G-9011)*
Audio Technologies and Codecs...........E....973 624-1116
  Newark *(G-7098)*
Avyakta It Services LLC...........F....609 790-7517
  East Windsor *(G-2352)*
Cegedim Inc...........C....908 443-2000
  Bedminster *(G-269)*
Chryslis Data Sltons Svcs Corp...........G....609 375-2000
  Princeton *(G-9022)*
Clientsrver Tech Solutions LLC...........G....732 710-4495
  Iselin *(G-4621)*
Cognizant Tech Solutions Corp...........D....201 801-0233
  Teaneck *(G-10746)*
Coles and Blenman Network LLC...........G....973 432-7041
  Bloomfield *(G-507)*
Diabeto Inc...........G....646 397-3175
  Piscataway *(G-8758)*
Dialogic Inc...........C....973 967-6000
  Parsippany *(G-7981)*
Ebic Prparedness Solutions LLC...........G....719 244-6209
  Leonia *(G-5316)*
Enertia LLC...........G....856 330-4767
  Pennsauken *(G-8508)*
Enroute Computer Solutions Inc...........B....609 569-9255
  Egg Harbor Township *(G-2684)*
Factonomy Inc...........F....201 848-7812
  Wyckoff *(G-12252)*
Image Access Corp...........E....201 342-7878
  Rockleigh *(G-9631)*
Innovi Mobile LLC...........F....646 588-0165
  Millburn *(G-6253)*
Kicksonfirecom LLC...........G....718 753-4248
  South Amboy *(G-10240)*
Limosys LLC...........F....212 222-4433
  Englewood Cliffs *(G-2974)*
Local Wisdom Inc...........E....609 269-2320
  Lambertville *(G-5218)*
Melillo Consulting Inc...........E....732 563-8400
  Somerset *(G-10135)*
Nb Ventures Inc...........C....732 382-6565
  Clark *(G-1509)*
Ngenious Solutions Inc...........G....732 873-3385
  Piscataway *(G-8797)*
Pai Services LLC...........C....856 231-4667
  Mount Laurel *(G-6823)*
Pds Prclnical Data Systems Inc...........E....973 398-2800
  Mount Arlington *(G-6759)*
Pentax of America Inc...........E....973 628-6200
  Montvale *(G-6468)*
Princton Satellite Systems Inc...........E....609 275-9606
  Plainsboro *(G-8896)*
Robokiller LLC...........E....723 838-1901
  South Amboy *(G-10244)*
Rx Trade Zone Inc...........G....833 933-6600
  Edison *(G-2608)*
Saksoft Inc...........E....201 451-4609
  Jersey City *(G-4821)*
Saviance Technologies...........F....609 448-7095
  Metuchen *(G-6120)*
Secured MBL Hlth Applctons Inc...........G....732 997-9609
  Long Branch *(G-5632)*

Steward LLC...........G....609 816-8825
  Princeton *(G-9125)*
Valuemomentum Inc...........D....908 755-0025
  Piscataway *(G-8832)*
Worldwide Pt SL Ltd Lblty Co...........F....201 928-0222
  Teaneck *(G-10777)*

COMPUTER SOFTWARE SYSTEMS ANALYSIS & DESIGN: Custom

Amerindia Technologies Inc...........E....609 664-2224
  Cranbury *(G-1810)*
Anvima Technologies LLC...........G....973 531-7077
  Brookside *(G-922)*
Appex Innovation Solutions LLC...........G....215 313-3332
  Princeton *(G-9004)*
Bandemar Networks LLC...........G....732 991-5112
  East Brunswick *(G-2136)*
Bluebird Auto Rentl Systems LP...........E....973 989-2423
  Dover *(G-2079)*
Creative Cmpt Concepts LLC...........G....877 919-7988
  Williamstown *(G-12085)*
Genomesafe LLC...........G....203 676-3752
  West Orange *(G-11895)*
Hozric LLC...........G....908 420-8821
  Green Brook *(G-3857)*
I-Exceed Tech Solutions Inc...........G....917 693-3207
  Princeton *(G-9056)*
Ms Health Software Corp...........G....908 850-5564
  Hackettstown *(G-4027)*
Pace Business Solutions Inc...........E....908 451-0355
  Manahawkin *(G-5833)*
Scimar Technologies LLC...........G....609 208-1796
  Allentown *(G-35)*
Sirma Group Inc...........B....646 357-3067
  Jersey City *(G-4829)*

COMPUTER SOFTWARE WRITERS

Antenna Software Inc...........E....201 217-3824
  Jersey City *(G-4708)*
Simtronics Corporation...........F....732 747-0322
  Little Silver *(G-5520)*

COMPUTER STORAGE DEVICES, NEC

150 Development Group LLC...........G....732 546-3812
  Middlesex *(G-6139)*
Altus Pcb LLC...........F....973 928-8777
  Cresskill *(G-1943)*
B-Hive Ltd Liability Company...........G....302 438-2769
  Hightstown *(G-4310)*
Blueclone Networks LLC...........G....609 944-8433
  Princeton *(G-9017)*
Computer Printers & Media Sups...........G....732 400-7888
  East Brunswick *(G-2143)*
Dataram Memory...........E....609 799-0071
  Princeton *(G-9028)*
Eclearview Technologies Inc...........G....732 695-6999
  Ocean *(G-7724)*
EMC Corporation...........D....732 922-6353
  Ocean *(G-7725)*
EMC Corporation...........A....732 549-8500
  East Brunswick *(G-2152)*
EMC Paving LLC...........G....908 636-1054
  Piscataway *(G-8763)*
EMC Squared LLC...........G....973 586-8854
  Rockaway *(G-9563)*
Gaw Associates Inc...........F....856 608-1428
  Cherry Hill *(G-1370)*
Micronet Enertec Tech Inc...........D....201 225-0190
  Montvale *(G-6467)*
Ner Data Products Inc...........E....888 637-3282
  Glassboro *(G-3810)*
Plastic Reel Corp of America...........E....201 933-5100
  Carlstadt *(G-1203)*
Pny Technologies Inc...........B....973 515-9700
  Parsippany *(G-8068)*
Quantum Integrators Group LLC...........E....609 632-0621
  Plainsboro *(G-8897)*
Quantum Renovations...........G....856 278-0176
  Pennsville *(G-8593)*
Quantum Vector Corp...........G....201 870-1782
  Westwood *(G-11967)*
Sony Corporation of America...........B....201 930-1000
  Paramus *(G-7902)*
Veeco Instruments Inc...........E....732 560-5300
  Somerset *(G-10193)*
Whiptail Technologies LLC...........D....973 585-6375
  Whippany *(G-12044)*

COMPUTER STORAGE UNITS: Auxiliary

Creative Cmpt Concepts LLC ....G 877 919-7988
  Williamstown (G-12085)
Ryval Cmpt Svcs Ltd Lblty Co ....G 201 374-1600
  Dumont (G-2123)

COMPUTER SYSTEM SELLING SVCS

Planitroi Inc ....D 973 664-0700
  Denville (G-2051)

COMPUTER SYSTEMS ANALYSIS & DESIGN

Baxter Corporation ....F 201 337-1212
  Franklin Lakes (G-3607)
Microtelecom Ltd Liability Co ....G 866 676-5679
  Fort Lee (G-3569)
Multiforce Systems Corporation ....F 609 683-4242
  Princeton (G-9079)
Pascack Data Services Inc ....F 973 304-4858
  Hawthorne (G-4251)
Planet Associates Inc ....E 201 693-8700
  Park Ridge (G-7927)
Primary Systems Inc ....F 732 679-2200
  Old Bridge (G-7790)
Redkoh Industries Inc ....G 908 369-1590
  Hillsborough (G-4368)
Secured MBL Hlth Applctons Inc ....G 732 997-9609
  Long Branch (G-5632)
Tyco Elec Sbsea Cmmnctions LLC ....B 732 578-7000
  Eatontown (G-2427)

COMPUTER TERMINALS

Information Technolgy Corp ....G 201 556-1999
  Paramus (G-7876)
Maingear Inc ....E 888 624-6432
  Kenilworth (G-4972)
Metrofuser LLC ....D 908 245-2100
  Elizabeth (G-2757)
Zkteco USA LLC ....E 862 505-2101
  Fairfield (G-3356)

COMPUTER TRAINING SCHOOLS

Swce Inc ....E 908 766-5695
  Bernardsville (G-455)

COMPUTER-AIDED DESIGN SYSTEMS SVCS

Enser Corporation ....E 856 829-5522
  Cinnaminson (G-1461)
Senco Metals LLC ....G 973 342-1742
  Edison (G-2614)
Warehouse Solutions Inc ....F 201 880-1110
  Fair Lawn (G-3123)

COMPUTER-AIDED ENGINEERING SYSTEMS SVCS

Circonix Technologies LLC ....F 973 962-6160
  Ringwood (G-9445)
Machine Atomated Ctrl Tech LLC ....G 732 921-8935
  Piscataway (G-8788)

COMPUTER-AIDED MANUFACTURING SYSTEMS SVCS

Sightlogix Inc ....E 609 951-0008
  Princeton (G-9118)

COMPUTERS, NEC

Alfred Heitzman Machine Works ....G 201 489-8888
  Moonachie (G-6500)
Asi Computer Technologies Inc ....F 732 343-7100
  Edison (G-2467)
B2x Corporation ....G 201 714-2373
  Jersey City (G-4712)
Datapro International Inc ....E 732 868-0588
  Piscataway (G-8754)
DFI-Itox LLC ....E 732 562-0693
  Piscataway (G-8757)
Dxl Enterprises Inc ....F 201 891-8718
  Mahwah (G-5768)
Esaw Industries Inc ....G 732 613-1400
  East Brunswick (G-2154)
Fillimerica Inc ....G 800 435-7257
  Montville (G-6488)
Franklin Electronic Publs Inc ....D 609 386-2500
  Burlington (G-974)

Global Business Dimensions Inc ....E 973 831-5866
  Pompton Plains (G-8960)
Hitechone Inc ....G 201 500-8864
  Englewood Cliffs (G-2964)
Ideal Data Inc ....F 201 998-9440
  North Arlington (G-7420)
La Duca Technical Services LLC ....G 570 309-4009
  West Milford (G-11853)
Lavitsky Computer Laboratories ....G 908 725-6206
  Bridgewater (G-850)
Niksun Inc ....C 609 936-9999
  Princeton (G-9081)
Novasom Industries Inc ....G 732 994-5652
  Lakewood (G-5167)
Oracle America Inc ....D 609 750-0640
  East Rutherford (G-2314)
Oti America Inc ....G 732 429-1900
  Iselin (G-4639)
Pcs Revenue Ctrl Systems Inc ....E 201 568-8300
  Englewood Cliffs (G-2978)
Planitroi Inc ....D 973 664-0700
  Denville (G-2051)
Reliance Electronics Inc ....E 973 237-0400
  Totowa (G-10969)
Rt Com USA Inc ....G 973 862-4210
  Lafayette (G-5052)
Spacetouch Inc ....G 609 712-6572
  Princeton (G-9124)
Strahan Consulting Group LLC ....G 908 790-0873
  Scotch Plains (G-9857)
Technical Advantage Inc ....G 973 402-5500
  Boonton (G-585)
Techno City Inc ....G 862 414-3282
  East Rutherford (G-2330)
Xceedium Inc ....D 201 536-1000
  Jersey City (G-4852)
Zt Systems ....G 201 559-1000
  Secaucus (G-9942)

COMPUTERS, NEC, WHOLESALE

AT Information Products Inc ....G 201 529-0202
  Mahwah (G-5750)
Central Technology Inc ....F 732 431-3339
  Freehold (G-3645)
Dymax Systems Inc ....F 732 918-2424
  Neptune (G-6908)

COMPUTERS, PERIPH & SOFTWARE, WHLSE: Acctg Machs, Readable

Aone Touch Inc ....G 732 261-6841
  Bordentown (G-590)

COMPUTERS, PERIPH & SOFTWARE, WHLSE: Personal & Home Entrtn

Maingear Inc ....E 888 624-6432
  Kenilworth (G-4972)

COMPUTERS, PERIPHERALS & SOFTWARE, WHOLESALE: Printers

B&B Imaging LLC ....G 201 261-3131
  Paramus (G-7856)

COMPUTERS, PERIPHERALS & SOFTWARE, WHOLESALE: Software

3shape Inc ....G 908 219-4641
  Warren (G-11534)
Aztec Software Associates Inc ....E 973 258-0011
  Springfield (G-10540)
Five Elements Robotics LLC ....G 800 681-8514
  Wall Township (G-11482)
Freyr Inc ....C 908 483-7958
  Princeton (G-9048)
Nb Ventures Inc ....C 732 382-6565
  Clark (G-1509)
New Line Prtg & Tech Solutions ....G 973 405-6133
  Clifton (G-1682)
RSD America Inc ....F 201 996-1000
  Teaneck (G-10771)

COMPUTERS, PERIPHERALS & SOFTWARE, WHOLESALE: Terminals

National Communications Inc ....E 973 325-3151
  West Orange (G-11901)

COMPUTERS: Indl, Process, Gas Flow

Multiforce Systems Corporation ....F 609 683-4242
  Princeton (G-9079)

COMPUTERS: Mini

Crestron Electronics Inc ....C 201 767-3400
  Rockleigh (G-9628)
Five Elements Robotics LLC ....G 800 681-8514
  Wall Township (G-11482)

COMPUTERS: Personal

Ancol ....G 908 233-8907
  Westfield (G-11920)
Andlogic Computers ....G 609 610-5752
  Hamilton (G-4103)
Apple Tree ....G 609 751-5375
  Princeton (G-9005)
Eom Worldwide Sales Corp ....G 732 994-7352
  Lakewood (G-5116)
Green Apple Home Imprv LLC ....G 201 300-5554
  Garfield (G-3738)
Maingear Inc ....E 888 624-6432
  Kenilworth (G-4972)
Mikros Systems Corporation ....G 609 987-1513
  Princeton (G-9074)
Pascack Data Services Inc ....F 973 304-4858
  Hawthorne (G-4251)
Princeton Identity Inc ....E 609 256-6994
  Hamilton (G-4123)
S G A Business Systems Inc ....G 908 359-4626
  Hillsborough (G-4370)
Touch Dynamic Inc ....D 732 382-5701
  South Plainfield (G-10440)

CONCENTRATES, DRINK

Citroil Enterprises Inc ....F 201 933-8405
  Carlstadt (G-1142)

CONCENTRATES, FLAVORING, EXC DRINK

Sapphire Flvors Fragrances LLC ....F 973 200-8849
  Fairfield (G-3300)
Savoury Systems Intl Inc ....F 908 526-2524
  Branchburg (G-702)

CONCRETE CURING & HARDENING COMPOUNDS

Axim Concrete Technologies ....D 330 966-0444
  Lyndhurst (G-5670)
Gamka Sales Co Inc ....E 732 248-1400
  Edison (G-2525)
Sika Corporation ....C 201 933-8800
  Lyndhurst (G-5709)
W R Grace & Co - Conn ....F 201 869-5220
  North Bergen (G-7493)
W R Grace & Co-Conn ....E 732 868-6914
  Somerset (G-10197)

CONCRETE PRDTS

A & A Concrete Products Inc ....G 973 835-2239
  Riverdale (G-9473)
Clayton Block Company Inc ....E 732 681-0186
  Wall Township (G-11471)
Crossfield Products Corp ....D 908 245-2801
  Roselle Park (G-9691)
CST Pavers ....F 856 299-5339
  Pedricktown (G-8434)
European Stone Art LLC ....F 201 441-9116
  South Hackensack (G-10266)
Garden State Precast Inc ....D 732 938-4436
  Wall Township (G-11485)
Hanson Aggregates Wrp Inc ....E 972 653-5500
  Wall Township (G-11487)
J F Gillespie Inc ....E 856 692-2233
  Vineland (G-11375)
Kelken-Gold Inc ....E 732 416-6730
  Sayreville (G-9826)
P J Gillespie Inc ....E 856 327-2993
  Vineland (G-11387)
Paul Bros Inc ....E 856 697-5895
  Newfield (G-7370)
Russell Cast Stone Inc ....D 856 753-4000
  West Berlin (G-11748)
Sika Corporation ....B 201 933-8800
  Lyndhurst (G-5708)
Solid Cast Stone ....G 856 694-5245
  Newfield (G-7372)

Employee Codes: A=Over 500 employees, B=251-500
C=101-250, D=51-100, E=20-50, F=10-19, G=4-9

2018 Harris New Jersey
Manufacturers Directory

829

PRODUCT

Strongwall Industries Inc ....G...... 201 445-4633
Allendale *(G-19)*
Trap Rock Industries Inc ....B...... 609 924-0300
Kingston *(G-5030)*

CONCRETE PRDTS, PRECAST, NEC

Boccella Precast LLC ....F...... 856 767-3861
Berlin *(G-427)*
Clayton Block Co ....D...... 201 955-6292
North Arlington *(G-7418)*
Clayton Block Company LLC ....E...... 201 339-8585
Bayonne *(G-219)*
Dunbar Concrete Products Inc ....F...... 973 697-2525
Oak Ridge *(G-7660)*
Empire Blended Products Inc ....E...... 732 269-4949
Bayville *(G-254)*
J B & Sons Concrete Products ....F...... 856 767-4140
Berlin *(G-435)*
Jersey Precast Corporation Inc ....C...... 609 689-3700
Trenton *(G-11070)*
Jpc Merger Sub LLC ....C...... 609 890-4343
Trenton *(G-11072)*
Precast Manufacturing Co LLC ....E...... 908 454-2122
Phillipsburg *(G-8665)*
Precast Systems Inc ....E...... 609 208-0569
Allentown *(G-33)*

CONCRETE: Bituminous

Earle The Walter R Corp ....G...... 732 308-1113
Wall Township *(G-11478)*
Earle The Walter R Corp ....G...... 732 657-8551
Jackson *(G-4665)*
Joseph and William Stavola...................E...... 609 924-0300
Kingston *(G-5028)*
Stavola Contracting Co Inc ....G...... 732 935-0156
Englishtown *(G-2998)*

CONCRETE: Dry Mixture

Duraamen Engineered Pdts Inc ....G...... 973 230-1301
Newark *(G-7144)*
Tri-State Quikrete ....E...... 973 347-4569
Flanders *(G-3420)*

CONCRETE: Ready-Mixed

Abi Inc ....E...... 609 588-8225
Lawrenceville *(G-5249)*
Ace-Crete Products Inc ....F...... 732 269-1400
Bayville *(G-247)*
Action Supply Inc ....F...... 609 390-0663
Ocean View *(G-7762)*
Allied Concrete Co Inc ....G...... 973 627-6150
Rockaway *(G-9549)*
Allied Concrete Co Inc ....G...... 973 627-6150
Rockaway *(G-9550)*
Atlantic Masonry Supply Inc ....F...... 609 909-9292
Egg Harbor Township *(G-2680)*
Clayton Block Company Inc ....F...... 732 349-3700
Toms River *(G-10872)*
Clayton Block Company Inc ....F...... 732 364-2404
Jackson *(G-4657)*
Clayton Block Company Inc ....E...... 732 549-1234
Edison *(G-2484)*
Colonial Concrete Company ....E...... 973 482-1920
Newark *(G-7124)*
Colonial Concrete Company ....E...... 201 869-0055
North Bergen *(G-7442)*
Concrete On Demand Inc ....F...... 201 337-0005
Oakland *(G-7680)*
Construction Dynamics Inc ....F...... 732 840-7766
Brick *(G-738)*
County Concrete Corporation ....F...... 973 538-3113
Morristown *(G-6702)*
County Concrete Corporation ....D...... 973 744-2188
Kenvil *(G-5010)*
Crh Americas Inc ....G...... 908 475-1225
Brick *(G-741)*
Diamond Chip Realty LLC ....E...... 973 383-4651
Sparta *(G-10497)*
Eastern Concrete Materials Inc ....C...... 201 797-7979
Saddle Brook *(G-9763)*
Eastern Concrete Materials Inc ....G...... 908 537-2135
Glen Gardner *(G-3814)*
Erial Concrete Inc ....F...... 856 784-8884
Erial *(G-3000)*
Ernest R Miles Construction Co ....F...... 856 697-2311
Newfield *(G-7365)*
Herbert J Hinchman & Son Inc ....E...... 973 942-2063
Wayne *(G-11647)*

Holtec Government Services LLC ....G...... 856 291-0600
Marlton *(G-5978)*
Joseph and William Stavola...................E...... 609 924-0300
Kingston *(G-5028)*
Kennedy Concrete Inc ....E...... 856 692-8650
Vineland *(G-11378)*
L & L Redi-Mix Inc ....E...... 609 859-2271
Southampton *(G-10477)*
Le-Ed Construction Inc ....E...... 732 341-4546
Toms River *(G-10893)*
Mershon Concrete LLC ....E...... 609 298-2150
Bordentown *(G-603)*
Miles Concrete Company Inc ....F...... 856 697-2311
Newfield *(G-7367)*
New Jersey Pulverizing Co Inc ....F...... 732 269-1400
Bayville *(G-259)*
Penn-Jersey Bldg Mtls Co Inc ....D...... 609 641-6994
Egg Harbor Township *(G-2691)*
Phillips Companies Inc ....D...... 973 483-4124
Clinton *(G-1753)*
Ralph Clayton & Sons LLC ....E...... 800 662-3044
Cookstown *(G-1808)*
Ralph Clayton & Sons LLC ....G...... 609 383-1818
Egg Harbor Township *(G-2693)*
Ralph Clayton & Sons LLC ....E...... 609 695-0767
Trenton *(G-11111)*
Reuther Material Co Inc ....E...... 201 863-3550
North Bergen *(G-7481)*
Salomone Rd-Mix Ltd Liabitlity ....F...... 973 305-0022
Wayne *(G-11682)*
SCC Concrete Inc ....F...... 908 859-2172
Phillipsburg *(G-8670)*
Short Load Concrete LLC ....G...... 732 469-4420
Bridgewater *(G-895)*
Suffolk County Contractors ....E...... 732 349-7726
Toms River *(G-10915)*
Tanis Concrete ....E...... 201 796-1556
Fair Lawn *(G-3119)*
Trap Rock Industries Inc ....B...... 609 924-0300
Kingston *(G-5030)*
VI Concrete Co ....F...... 856 767-0415
Atco *(G-92)*
Weldon Materials Inc ....E...... 908 233-4444
Westfield *(G-11934)*
Wjv Materials LLC ....E...... 856 299-8244
Pedricktown *(G-8441)*
Yogo Mix ....G...... 609 897-1379
Princeton Junction *(G-9167)*

CONDENSERS: Heat Transfer Eqpt, Evaporative

Coolenheat Inc ....E...... 908 925-4473
Kendall Park *(G-4934)*
Diversified Heat Transfer Inc ....D...... 800 221-1522
Towaco *(G-10993)*
Harsco Corporation ....E...... 856 779-7795
Cherry Hill *(G-1374)*

CONDENSERS: Motors Or Generators

Evapco-Blct Dry Cooling Inc ....E...... 908 379-2665
Bridgewater *(G-836)*

CONDENSERS: Steam

Amec Fster Wheeler N Amer Corp ....D...... 936 448-6323
Hampton *(G-4153)*
DC Fabricators Inc ....C...... 609 499-3000
Florence *(G-3477)*
Maarky Thermal Systems Inc................G...... 856 470-1504
Cherry Hill *(G-1392)*
Power Products and Engrg LLC............E...... 855 769-3751
Trenton *(G-11102)*

CONDUITS & FITTINGS: Electric

Appleton Grp LLC ....C...... 973 285-3261
Morristown *(G-6687)*
Thomas & Betts Corporation ....C...... 908 852-1122
Hackettstown *(G-4040)*

CONFECTIONERY PRDTS WHOLESALERS

Fralingers Inc ....E...... 609 345-2177
Atlantic City *(G-97)*
James Candy Company ....D...... 609 344-1519
Atlantic City *(G-101)*
Nexira Inc ....F...... 908 704-7480
Somerville *(G-10222)*
PR Products Distributors Inc ....G...... 973 928-1120
Wayne *(G-11675)*

Promotion In Motion Inc ....D...... 201 962-8530
Allendale *(G-16)*
Webers Candy Store ....G...... 856 455-8277
Bridgeton *(G-803)*

CONFECTIONS & CANDY

Ann Hemyng Candy Inc ....G...... 215 536-7004
Bridgewater *(G-811)*
Astor Chocolate Corp ....C...... 732 901-1000
Lakewood *(G-5077)*
Ausome LLC ....G...... 732 951-8818
Paramus *(G-7854)*
Cadbury Adams USA LLC ....E...... 973 503-2000
East Hanover *(G-2203)*
Candy Treasure LLC ....G...... 201 830-3600
Lebanon *(G-5279)*
Capco Enterprises Inc ....F...... 973 884-0044
East Hanover *(G-2206)*
Ce De Candy Inc ....C...... 908 964-0660
Union *(G-11164)*
Dairy Maid Confectionery Co ....G...... 609 399-0100
Ocean City *(G-7752)*
Damask Kandies ....G...... 856 467-1661
Swedesboro *(G-10690)*
David Bradley Chocolatier Inc ....F...... 609 443-4747
Windsor *(G-12125)*
David Bradley Chocolatier Inc ....E...... 732 536-7719
Englishtown *(G-2991)*
Ensign Overseas (usa) Ltd ....G...... 201 662-7150
North Bergen *(G-7450)*
Ferrero U S A Inc ....C...... 732 764-9300
Parsippany *(G-8009)*
Fralingers Inc ....G...... 609 345-2177
Atlantic City *(G-98)*
Fralingers Inc ....E...... 609 345-2177
Atlantic City *(G-97)*
Giambris Quality Sweets Inc ....G...... 856 783-1099
Clementon *(G-1532)*
Guylian USA Inc ....G...... 201 871-4144
Englewood Cliffs *(G-2962)*
Hillside Candy LLC ....F...... 973 926-2300
Hillside *(G-4413)*
Hillside Candy LLC ....E...... 908 241-4747
Roselle *(G-9672)*
James Candy Company ....D...... 609 344-1519
Atlantic City *(G-101)*
Koppers Chocolate LLC ....D...... 212 243-0220
Cranford *(G-1912)*
Krauses Homemade Candy Inc ....E...... 201 943-4790
Fairview *(G-3364)*
Life of Party LLC ....E...... 732 828-0886
North Brunswick *(G-7524)*
Marlow Candy & Nut Co Inc ....E...... 201 569-7606
Englewood *(G-2913)*
Mars Incorporated ....A...... 908 852-1000
Hackettstown *(G-4020)*
Mars Incorporated ....D...... 908 850-2420
Hackettstown *(G-4021)*
Mars Chocolate North Amer LLC ....A...... 908 852-1000
Hackettstown *(G-4022)*
Mars Chocolate North Amer LLC ....A...... 908 979-5070
Hackettstown *(G-4023)*
Old Monmouth Peanut Brittle Co ....G...... 732 462-1311
Freehold *(G-3674)*
Oral Fixation LLC ....G...... 609 937-9972
Hopewell *(G-4543)*
Ozone Confectioners Bakers Sup ....F...... 201 791-4444
Verona *(G-11308)*
Packom LLC ....F...... 201 378-8382
Little Falls *(G-5484)*
Pim Brands LLC ....D...... 732 560-8300
Somerset *(G-10155)*
PR Products Distributors Inc ....G...... 973 928-1120
Wayne *(G-11675)*
Promotion In Motion Inc ....D...... 201 962-8530
Allendale *(G-16)*
Promotion In Motion Inc ....E...... 732 560-8300
Somerset *(G-10159)*
Rauhausers Inc ....F...... 609 399-1465
Ocean City *(G-7755)*
Rayge Candy Co ....F...... 732 458-2179
Brick *(G-756)*
Reilys Candy Inc ....F...... 609 953-0040
Medford *(G-6079)*
Shrivers Salt Wtr Taffy Fudge ....G...... 609 399-0100
Ocean City *(G-7758)*
Sims Lee Inc ....G...... 201 433-1308
Jersey City *(G-4828)*
U I S Industries Inc ....A...... 201 946-2600
Jersey City *(G-4839)*

Webers Candy Store ....G 856 455-8277
  Bridgeton (G-803)
William R Tatz Industries ....G 973 751-0720
  Belleville (G-328)
World Confections Inc ....D 718 768-8100
  South Orange (G-10317)
Yolo Candy LLC ....G 201 252-8765
  Mahwah (G-5825)

CONFINEMENT SURVEILLANCE SYS MAINTENANCE & MONITORING SVCS

SMS Building Systems Ltd Lblty ....F 856 520-8769
  Cherry Hill (G-1420)

CONNECTORS & TERMINALS: Electrical Device Uses

Armel Electronics Inc ....E 201 869-4300
  North Bergen (G-7433)
Glasseal Products Inc ....C 732 370-9100
  Lakewood (G-5129)
Hofer Machine & Tool Co Inc ....F 973 427-1195
  North Haledon (G-7549)
Mac Products Inc ....D 973 344-5149
  Kearny (G-4896)
Thomas & Betts Corporation ....C 908 852-1122
  Hackettstown (G-4040)

CONNECTORS: Cord, Electric

Connector Products Inc ....F 856 829-9190
  Pennsauken (G-8498)
Volta Corporation ....E 732 583-3300
  Laurence Harbor (G-5236)

CONNECTORS: Electrical

Bleema Manufacturing Corp ....E 973 371-1771
  Irvington (G-4580)
Richards Mfg A NJ Ltd Partnr ....C 973 371-1771
  Irvington (G-4603)

CONNECTORS: Electronic

Adam Tech Asia Llc ....G 908 687-5000
  Union (G-11147)
Al Technology Inc ....E 609 799-9388
  Princeton Junction (G-9145)
Armel Electronics Inc ....E 201 869-4300
  North Bergen (G-7433)
Barantec Inc ....F 973 779-8774
  Clifton (G-1572)
Brim Electronics Inc ....E 201 796-2886
  Lodi (G-5578)
Central Components Mfg LLC ....G 732 469-5720
  Middlesex (G-6154)
Components Corporation ....F 866 426-6726
  Denville (G-2033)
Da-Green Electronics Ltd ....E 732 254-2735
  South River (G-10460)
Fuji Electric Corp America ....D 732 560-9410
  Edison (G-2522)
Fujipoly America Corporation ....E 732 969-0100
  Carteret (G-1259)
Glasseal Products Inc ....C 732 370-9100
  Lakewood (G-5129)
Heilind Electronics Inc ....D 888 881-5420
  Lumberton (G-5658)
Heilind Mil-Aero LLC ....E 856 722-5535
  Lumberton (G-5659)
Huber+suhner Astrolab Inc ....E 732 560-3800
  Warren (G-11554)
I Trade Technology Ltd ....G 615 348-7233
  Mahwah (G-5785)
Kraus & Naimer Inc ....E 732 560-1240
  Somerset (G-10119)
Lapp Usa LLC ....C 973 660-9700
  Florham Park (G-3511)
Napoleon Spring Works Inc ....E 973 278-5588
  South Hackensack (G-10279)
Newtech Group Corp ....G 732 355-0392
  Kendall Park (G-4935)
Princetel Inc ....E 609 588-8801
  Hamilton (G-4122)
Richards Mfg Co Sales Inc ....E 973 371-1771
  Irvington (G-4604)
Severna Operations Inc ....E 973 503-1600
  Parsippany (G-8085)
Te Connectivity Corporation ....B 610 893-9800
  Eatontown (G-2425)

Thomas & Betts Corporation ....C 908 852-1122
  Hackettstown (G-4040)
Unicorp ....C 973 674-1700
  Orange (G-7832)
Valconn Electronics Inc ....E 908 687-1600
  Union (G-11232)
Wire-Pro Inc ....C 856 935-7560
  Salem (G-9810)

CONNECTORS: Power, Electric

Dos Industrial Sales LLC ....G 973 887-7800
  East Hanover (G-2212)

CONSTRUCTION & MINING MACHINERY WHOLESALERS

Doosan Machine Tools Amer Corp ......D 973 618-2500
  Pine Brook (G-8700)
Harsco Corporation ....E 856 779-7795
  Cherry Hill (G-1374)
Msg Fire & Safety Inc ....G 732 833-8500
  Jackson (G-4673)
Rajysan Incorporated ....E 800 433-1382
  Swedesboro (G-10722)
Taurus International Corp ....E 201 825-2420
  Ramsey (G-9252)

CONSTRUCTION EQPT REPAIR SVCS

Cleary Machinery Co Inc ....G 732 560-3200
  South Bound Brook (G-10248)
Permadur Industries Inc ....D 908 359-9767
  Hillsborough (G-4362)

CONSTRUCTION EQPT: Blade, Grader, Scraper, Dozer/Snow Plow

R & H Spring & Truck Repair ....F 732 681-9000
  Wall Township (G-11504)

CONSTRUCTION EQPT: Cranes

Cornell Crane Mfg Ltd ....F 609 742-1900
  Westville (G-11937)

CONSTRUCTION EQPT: Dozers, Tractor Mounted, Material Moving

L Arden Corp ....G 973 523-6400
  Paterson (G-8314)

CONSTRUCTION EQPT: Graders, Road

Infrastructure LLC ....G 609 748-1229
  Galloway (G-3712)

CONSTRUCTION EQPT: Subgraders

Ransome Equipment Sales LLC ....G 856 797-8100
  Lumberton (G-5663)

CONSTRUCTION EQPT: Wrecker Hoists, Automobile

Busted Knuckle ....G 609 432-7383
  Marmora (G-6005)
Trilenium Salvage Co ....G 732 462-2909
  Morganville (G-6654)

CONSTRUCTION MATERIALS, WHOLESALE: Architectural Metalwork

Omnia Industries Inc ....E 973 239-7272
  Cedar Grove (G-1295)

CONSTRUCTION MATERIALS, WHOLESALE: Awnings

Babbitt Mfg Co Inc ....F 856 692-3245
  Vineland (G-11326)

CONSTRUCTION MATERIALS, WHOLESALE: Block, Concrete & Cinder

Clayton Block Company Inc ....E 732 681-0186
  Wall Township (G-11471)

CONSTRUCTION MATERIALS, WHOLESALE: Brick, Exc Refractory

Glen-Gery Corporation ....E 908 359-5111
  Hillsborough (G-4336)

CONSTRUCTION MATERIALS, WHOLESALE: Building Stone

El Batal Corporation ....F 908 964-3427
  Union (G-11180)

CONSTRUCTION MATERIALS, WHOLESALE: Building Stone, Granite

Ankur International Inc ....F 609 409-6009
  Cranbury (G-1812)
Ilkem Marble and Granite Inc ....G 856 433-8714
  Cherry Hill (G-1377)
Natures Beauty Marble & Gran ....E 908 233-5300
  Scotch Plains (G-9852)
Sr International Rock Inc ....G 908 864-4700
  Bound Brook (G-623)
Statewide Granite and Marble ....F 201 653-1700
  Jersey City (G-4833)
Whole Stones LLC ....G 856 266-0091
  Willingboro (G-12123)

CONSTRUCTION MATERIALS, WHOLESALE: Building Stone, Marble

Bcg Marble & Granite South LLC ....G 732 367-3788
  Jackson (G-4655)
Bcg Marble Gran Fabricators Co ....F 201 343-8487
  Hackensack (G-3879)
Dolan & Traynor Inc ....E 973 696-8700
  Wayne (G-11625)
North Bergen Marble & Granite ....E 201 945-9988
  Cliffside Park (G-1544)
Phillipsburg Marble Co Inc ....E 908 859-3435
  Phillipsburg (G-8664)

CONSTRUCTION MATERIALS, WHOLESALE: Building, Exterior

Form Tops Lminators of Trenton ....G 609 409-4357
  Jamesburg (G-4685)
Greenbuilt Intl Bldg Co ....C 609 300-9091
  Voorhees (G-11432)
Kuiken Brothers Company ....E 201 796-2082
  Fair Lawn (G-3100)
Ufp Berlin LLC ....C 856 767-0596
  Berlin (G-443)

CONSTRUCTION MATERIALS, WHOLESALE: Cement

Lehigh Cement Company ....G 973 579-2111
  Sparta (G-10509)

CONSTRUCTION MATERIALS, WHOLESALE: Concrete Mixtures

Ernest R Miles Construction Co ....F 856 697-2311
  Newfield (G-7365)
Ralph Clayton & Sons LLC ....E 609 695-0767
  Trenton (G-11111)

CONSTRUCTION MATERIALS, WHOLESALE: Glass

Floral Glass Industries Inc ....E 201 939-4600
  East Rutherford (G-2297)
General Glass Intl Corp ....C 201 553-1850
  Secaucus (G-9887)
McGrory Glass Inc ....D 856 579-3200
  Paulsboro (G-8420)

CONSTRUCTION MATERIALS, WHOLESALE: Gravel

Brick-Wall Corp ....E 732 787-0226
  Atlantic Highlands (G-109)
Herbert J Hinchman & Son Inc ....E 973 942-2063
  Wayne (G-11647)

Employee Codes: A=Over 500 employees, B=251-500
C=101-250, D=51-100, E=20-50, F=10-19, G=4-9

2018 Harris New Jersey
Manufacturers Directory

PRODUCT

831

CONSTRUCTION MATERIALS, WHOLESALE: Masons' Materials

Action Supply Inc ....F 609 390-0663
Ocean View *(G-7762)*
Anchor Concrete Products Inc ....E 732 842-5010
Red Bank *(G-9319)*
Anchor Concrete Products Inc ....D 732 458-9440
Brick *(G-734)*
Precision Multiple Contrls Inc ....E 201 444-0600
Midland Park *(G-6236)*
Precision Multiple Contrls Inc ....D 201 444-0600
Midland Park *(G-6237)*
Reuther Material Co Inc ....E 201 863-3550
North Bergen *(G-7481)*

CONSTRUCTION MATERIALS, WHOLESALE: Metal Buildings

Tilcon New York Inc ....B 800 789-7625
Parsippany *(G-8101)*

CONSTRUCTION MATERIALS, WHOLESALE: Millwork

B & B Millwork & Doors Inc ....G 973 249-0300
Kenilworth *(G-4939)*
V Custom Millwork Inc ....F 732 469-9600
Bridgewater *(G-907)*
Wood Works ....G 856 728-4520
Williamstown *(G-12115)*

CONSTRUCTION MATERIALS, WHOLESALE: Pallets, Wood

Avenel Pallet Co Inc ....F 732 752-0500
Dunellen *(G-2126)*
Delisa Pallet Corp ....F 732 667-7070
Middlesex *(G-6161)*

CONSTRUCTION MATERIALS, WHOLESALE: Paving Materials

South State Inc ....E 856 881-6030
Williamstown *(G-12107)*

CONSTRUCTION MATERIALS, WHOLESALE: Prefabricated Structures

Everlast Associates Inc ....G 609 261-1888
Southampton *(G-10472)*
R H Vassallo Inc ....G 856 358-8841
Malaga *(G-5827)*

CONSTRUCTION MATERIALS, WHOLESALE: Roof, Asphalt/Sheet Metal

US Outworkers LLC ....G 973 362-1458
Sussex *(G-10680)*

CONSTRUCTION MATERIALS, WHOLESALE: Roofing & Siding Material

Armorpoxy Inc ....F 908 810-9613
Union *(G-11154)*
Myles F Kelly Inc ....F 908 245-2033
Roselle Park *(G-9700)*
Passaic Metal & Bldg Sups Co ....D 973 546-9000
Clifton *(G-1691)*
Stavola Asphalt Company Inc ....E 732 542-2328
Tinton Falls *(G-10848)*

CONSTRUCTION MATERIALS, WHOLESALE: Sand

County Concrete Corporation ....D 973 744-2188
Kenvil *(G-5010)*

CONSTRUCTION MATERIALS, WHOLESALE: Septic Tanks

A & A Concrete Products Inc ....G 973 835-2239
Riverdale *(G-9473)*
County Concrete Corporation ....F 973 538-3113
Morristown *(G-6702)*

CONSTRUCTION MATERIALS, WHOLESALE: Siding, Exc Wood

Babbitt Mfg Co Inc ....F 856 692-3245
Vineland *(G-11326)*

CONSTRUCTION MATERIALS, WHOLESALE: Skylights, All Materials

Construction Specialties Inc ....E 908 272-2771
Cranford *(G-1902)*

CONSTRUCTION MATERIALS, WHOLESALE: Stone, Crushed Or Broken

County Concrete Corporation ....F 973 538-3113
Morristown *(G-6702)*
Fanwood Crushed Stone Company ......D 908 322-7840
Watchung *(G-11591)*
R B Badat Landscaping Inc ....G 609 877-7138
Mount Holly *(G-6776)*
Stavola Construction Mtls Inc ....E 732 356-5700
Bound Brook *(G-625)*

CONSTRUCTION MATERIALS, WHOLESALE: Stucco

Mediterranean Stucco Corp ....F 973 491-0160
Newark *(G-7239)*
Perfect Shapes Inc ....G 856 783-3844
Elmer *(G-2795)*

CONSTRUCTION MATERIALS, WHOLESALE: Tile & Clay Prdts

Akw Inc ....G 732 493-1883
Ocean *(G-7714)*
Akw Inc ....F 732 530-9186
Shrewsbury *(G-9988)*

CONSTRUCTION MATERIALS, WHOLESALE: Window Frames

Surburban Building Pdts Inc ....E 732 901-8900
Howell *(G-4568)*

CONSTRUCTION MATERIALS, WHOLESALE: Windows

Alliance Vinyl Windows Co Inc ....E 856 456-4954
Oaklyn *(G-7710)*

CONSTRUCTION MATLS, WHOL: Lumber, Rough, Dressed/Finished

Dubell Lumber Co ....E 609 654-4143
Medford *(G-6068)*
Norwood Industries Inc ....F 856 858-6195
Haddon Township *(G-4054)*

CONSTRUCTION MTRLS, WHOL: Exterior Flat Glass, Plate/Window

Oldcastle Buildingenvelope Inc ....D 856 234-9222
Moorestown *(G-6605)*

CONSTRUCTION SAND MINING

Action Supply Inc ....F 609 390-0663
Ocean View *(G-7762)*
Eastern Concrete Materials Inc ....C 201 797-7979
Saddle Brook *(G-9763)*
Pioneer Concrete Corp ....F 609 693-6151
Forked River *(G-3539)*
Ricci Bros Sand Company Inc ....E 856 785-0166
Port Norris *(G-8982)*
Saxton Falls Sand & Gravel Co ....E 908 852-0121
Budd Lake *(G-943)*
Whibco Inc ....F 856 455-9200
Bridgeton *(G-804)*

CONSTRUCTION: Athletic & Recreation Facilities

Finex Trade ....G 609 921-2747
Princeton *(G-9045)*

CONSTRUCTION: Bridge

Ashland LLC ....D 732 353-7718
Parlin *(G-7928)*

Colas Inc ....G 973 290-9082
Morristown *(G-6700)*

CONSTRUCTION: Chemical Facility

Foster Wheeler Arabia Ltd ....G 908 730-4000
Hampton *(G-4156)*
Foster Wheeler Intl Corp ....F 908 730-4000
Hampton *(G-4157)*
Foster Whler Intl Holdings Inc ....G 908 730-4000
Hampton *(G-4159)*

CONSTRUCTION: Commercial & Institutional Building

Dubell Lumber Co ....E 609 654-4143
Medford *(G-6068)*
John J Chando Jr Inc ....F 732 793-2122
Mantoloking *(G-5890)*

CONSTRUCTION: Commercial & Office Building, New

All Seasons Construction Inc ....G 908 852-0955
Long Valley *(G-5634)*
Jontol Unlimited LLC ....G 858 652-1113
Blackwood *(G-485)*
Terco Construction LLC ....F 973 551-7759
Newton *(G-7409)*

CONSTRUCTION: Dams, Waterways, Docks & Other Marine

Bishop Ascendant Inc ....G 973 210-5298
West Caldwell *(G-11768)*
Courtney Boatlifts Inc ....G 732 892-8900
Point Pleasant Boro *(G-8936)*
Ocean Energy Industries Inc ....F 954 828-2177
Oakhurst *(G-7671)*

CONSTRUCTION: Drainage System

Infrastructure LLC ....G 609 748-1229
Galloway *(G-3712)*

CONSTRUCTION: Electric Power Line

Pioneer Associates Inc ....E 201 592-7007
Fort Lee *(G-3577)*

CONSTRUCTION: Foundation & Retaining Wall

Ernest R Miles Construction Co ....F 856 697-2311
Newfield *(G-7365)*

CONSTRUCTION: Greenhouse

Internet-Sales USA Corporation ....G 775 468-8379
Rockaway *(G-9575)*

CONSTRUCTION: Heavy Highway & Street

Ashland LLC ....D 732 353-7718
Parlin *(G-7928)*
Hackettstown Public Works ....G 908 852-2320
Hackettstown *(G-4010)*
Richard E Pierson Mtls Corp ....F 856 740-2400
Williamstown *(G-12103)*
Richard E Pierson Mtls Corp ....F 856 691-0083
Vineland *(G-11399)*
Richard E Pierson Mtls Corp ....F 856 467-4199
Pilesgrove *(G-8676)*
Stavola Asphalt Company Inc ....E 732 542-2328
Tinton Falls *(G-10848)*
Terco Construction LLC ....F 973 551-7759
Newton *(G-7409)*

CONSTRUCTION: Hospital

Gateway Property Solutions Ltd ....E 732 901-9700
Lakewood *(G-5128)*

CONSTRUCTION: Indl Building & Warehouse

Dreamstar Construction LLC ....F 732 393-2572
Middletown *(G-6213)*
General Civil Company Inc ....F 866 435-1200
Runnemede *(G-9719)*
Lollytogs Ltd ....F 732 438-5500
Dayton *(G-1978)*
Orient Originals Inc ....E 201 332-5005
Jersey City *(G-4796)*

CONSTRUCTION: Indl Buildings, New, NEC

Terco Construction LLC ....F 973 551-7759
  Newton (G-7409)

CONSTRUCTION: Indl Plant

Foster Wheeler Zack Inc ....D 908 730-4000
  Hampton (G-4158)
Hamon Corporation ....D 908 333-2000
  Somerville (G-10213)

CONSTRUCTION: Irrigation System

Terco Construction LLC ....F 973 551-7759
  Newton (G-7409)

CONSTRUCTION: Marine

J & J Marine Inc.............................F 856 228-4744
  Sewell (G-9959)

CONSTRUCTION: Natural Gas Compressor Station

Corban Energy Group Corp ....E 201 509-8555
  Elmwood Park (G-2812)

CONSTRUCTION: Nonresidential Buildings, Custom

Forman Industries Inc ....D 732 727-8100
  Old Bridge (G-7779)

CONSTRUCTION: Pharmaceutical Manufacturing Plant

Leading Pharma LLC ....E 201 746-9160
  Fairfield (G-3250)

CONSTRUCTION: Power & Communication Transmission Tower

Dun-Rite Communications Inc...........G 201 444-0080
  Mahwah (G-5767)

CONSTRUCTION: Refineries

Shelby Mechanical Inc......................E 856 665-4540
  Cinnaminson (G-1487)

CONSTRUCTION: Religious Building

George Ciocher Inc.........................G 732 818-3495
  Toms River (G-10880)

CONSTRUCTION: Residential, Nec

Dreamstar Construction LLC.............F 732 393-2572
  Middletown (G-6213)
EZ General Construction Corp ....G 201 223-1101
  Wayne (G-11631)
Greenbuilt Intl Bldg Co ....C 609 300-9091
  Voorhees (G-11432)
Mdb Construction ....G 908 628-8010
  Lebanon (G-5296)

CONSTRUCTION: Sewer Line

Suffolk County Contractors ....E 732 349-7726
  Toms River (G-10915)

CONSTRUCTION: Single-Family Housing

BNH Enterprise LLC ....G 201 815-0546
  Dumont (G-2116)
Dubell Lumber Co ....E 609 654-4143
  Medford (G-6068)
Greenbuilt Intl Bldg Co ....C 609 300-9091
  Voorhees (G-11432)
Hart Construction Service.................G 908 537-2060
  Asbury (G-70)
Josantos Cnstr & Dev LLC...............G 732 202-7389
  Brick (G-749)
Mod-U-Kraf Homes LLC ....E 540 482-0273
  West Berlin (G-11734)
Vinylast Inc ....E 732 367-7200
  Lakewood (G-5200)

CONSTRUCTION: Single-family Housing, New

All Seasons Construction Inc............G 908 852-0955
  Long Valley (G-5634)
John J Chando Jr Inc ....F 732 793-2122
  Mantoloking (G-5890)
Van Duyne Bros Inc ....G 609 625-0299
  Mays Landing (G-6043)

CONSTRUCTION: Steel Buildings

East Coast Storage Eqp Co Inc ....E 732 451-1316
  Brick (G-742)

CONSTRUCTION: Street Surfacing & Paving

Brunswick Hot Mix Corp ....D 908 233-4444
  Westfield (G-11922)
South State Inc ....E 856 881-6030
  Williamstown (G-12107)

CONSTRUCTION: Transmitting Tower, Telecommunication

Maxentric Technologies LLC ....E 201 242-9800
  Fort Lee (G-3566)

CONSTRUCTION: Warehouse

New Jersey Steel Corporation ....F 856 337-0054
  Haddon Township (G-4053)

CONSTRUCTION: Waste Water & Sewage Treatment Plant

Chem-Aqua Inc ....F 972 438-0211
  Monmouth Junction (G-6336)
Dynatec Systems Inc ....F 609 387-0330
  Burlington (G-970)

CONSTRUCTION: Water & Sewer Line

DMJ and Associates Inc ....E 732 613-7867
  Sayreville (G-9820)
Philip Mamrak................................G 908 454-6089
  Phillipsburg (G-8663)

CONSULTING SVC: Actuarial

Inventors Shop LLC ....E 856 303-8787
  Cinnaminson (G-1470)

CONSULTING SVC: Business, NEC

2a Holdings Inc ....F 973 378-8011
  Maplewood (G-5913)
Adherence Solutions LLC ....G 800 521-2269
  Fairfield (G-3127)
Athlon Group LLC...........................G 201 340-2688
  East Rutherford (G-2281)
BNH Enterprise LLC ....G 201 815-0546
  Dumont (G-2116)
Ch Technologies USA Inc ....G 201 666-2335
  Westwood (G-11957)
Chemstaff Inc ....G 201 265-8655
  Oradell (G-7805)
Electronic Measuring Devices ....F 973 691-4755
  Flanders (G-3406)
Fisher Scientific Company LLC...........B 201 796-7100
  Fair Lawn (G-3093)
Gary R Banks Industrial Group ....F 856 687-2227
  West Berlin (G-11723)
Glocal Expertise Llc........................G 718 928-3839
  Jersey City (G-4761)
Hitrons Solutions Inc ....F 201 244-0300
  Bergenfield (G-388)
Hoboken Executive Art Inc ....G 201 420-8262
  Hoboken (G-4473)
Iam International Inc ....G 908 713-9651
  Lebanon (G-5289)
Industrial Water Tech Inc.................G 732 888-1233
  Hazlet (G-4275)
L L Teach Inc ....E 732 223-1605
  Brielle (G-912)
Light Inc......................................G 973 777-2704
  Clifton (G-1662)
M2 Communications Inc...................E 201 433-1746
  Jersey City (G-4781)
Multiforce Systems Corporation ....F 609 683-4242
  Princeton (G-9079)
Novaera Solutions Inc ....D 732 452-3605
  Iselin (G-4637)

Steps To Literacy LLC ....E 732 560-8363
  Bound Brook (G-626)
Trek II Products Inc.........................G 732 214-9200
  New Brunswick (G-7007)
Wilshire Technologies Inc ....G 609 683-1117
  Princeton (G-9139)

CONSULTING SVC: Chemical

Acceledev Chemical LLC ....G 862 239-1524
  Wayne (G-11601)

CONSULTING SVC: Computer

Aplnow LLC...................................G 732 223-5575
  Manasquan (G-5866)
Auraplayer USA Inc ....F 617 879-9013
  West Orange (G-11887)
Automated Office Inc.......................G 888 362-7638
  Cherry Hill (G-1345)
Burgiss Group LLC ....D 201 427-9600
  Hoboken (G-4461)
Ce Tech LLC ....G 908 229-3803
  Whitehouse Station (G-12050)
Cognizant Tech Solutions Corp..........D 201 801-0233
  Teaneck (G-10746)
Cygate Sftwr & Consulting LLC..........G 732 452-1881
  Edison (G-2500)
Datapro International Inc..................E 732 868-0588
  Piscataway (G-8754)
Dymax Systems Inc ....F 732 918-2424
  Neptune (G-6908)
E Pro Inc ....F 732 283-0499
  Iselin (G-4624)
Fillimerica Inc ....G 800 435-7257
  Montville (G-6488)
Fis Avantgard LLC ....G 732 530-9303
  Tinton Falls (G-10837)
Indotronix International Corp ....G 609 750-0700
  Plainsboro (G-8885)
Innovative Sftwr Solutions Inc..........D 856 910-9190
  Maple Shade (G-5903)
Innovi Mobile LLC ....F 646 588-0165
  Millburn (G-6253)
Integration International Inc..............E 973 796-2300
  Parsippany (G-8030)
Interntnal Digital Systems Inc...........F 201 983-7700
  Fort Lee (G-3560)
Linden Group Corporation ....F 973 983-8809
  Cedar Knolls (G-1315)
MD International Inc........................G 856 779-7633
  Cherry Hill (G-1397)
Mind-Alliance Systems LLC ....G 212 920-1911
  Livingston (G-5546)
Novaera Solutions Inc ....D 732 452-3605
  Iselin (G-4637)
Onx USA LLC ....E 440 569-2417
  Edison (G-2588)
Pace Business Solutions Inc ....E 908 451-0355
  Manahawkin (G-5833)
Pascack Data Services Inc ....F 973 304-4858
  Hawthorne (G-4251)
Princton Satellite Systems Inc...........G 609 275-9606
  Plainsboro (G-8896)
Promia Incorporated.......................G 609 252-1850
  Princeton (G-9106)
R T I Inc......................................E 201 261-5852
  Oradell (G-7812)
Radix M I S ....G 973 707-2121
  Bloomfield (G-528)
Re Systems Group Inc.....................G 201 883-1572
  Westwood (G-11968)
Real Soft Inc ....A 609 409-3636
  Monmouth Junction (G-6360)
RSD America Inc ....F 201 996-1000
  Teaneck (G-10771)
Saviance Technologies ....F 609 448-7095
  Metuchen (G-6120)
Secured MBL Hlth Applctons Inc ....G 732 997-9609
  Long Branch (G-5632)
Software Services & Solutions............F 203 630-2000
  Lawrence Township (G-5248)
Specialty Systems Inc ....E 732 341-1011
  Toms River (G-10913)
Strahan Consulting Group LLC...........G 908 790-0873
  Scotch Plains (G-9857)
Tropaion Inc..................................G 908 654-3870
  Springfield (G-10580)
U S Tech Solutions Inc....................D 201 524-9600
  Jersey City (G-4840)
Unicorn Group Inc ....E 973 360-0688
  Florham Park (G-3522)

Employee Codes: A=Over 500 employees, B=251-500
C=101-250, D=51-100, E=20-50, F=10-19, G=4-9

2018 Harris New Jersey
Manufacturers Directory

833

PRODUCT

Unicorn Group Inc ....D 973 360-5904
Fairfield (G-3333)

CONSULTING SVC: Data Processing

Megaplex Software Inc ....G 908 647-3273
Warren (G-11559)

CONSULTING SVC: Engineering

Cire Technologies Inc ....G 973 402-8301
Mountain Lakes (G-6855)
Componding Engrg Solutions Inc ....F 973 340-4000
Clifton (G-1587)
De Ditrich Process Systems Inc ....E 908 317-2585
Mountainside (G-6875)
Drive Technology Inc ....G 732 422-6500
Monmouth Junction (G-6342)
Ellenby Technologies Inc ....E 856 848-2020
Woodbury Heights (G-12175)
Ensync Intrctive Solutions Inc...............G 732 542-4001
Freehold (G-3654)
Expert Process Systems LLC ....G 570 424-0581
Hackettstown (G-4006)
Forman Industries Inc ....D 732 727-8100
Old Bridge (G-7779)
Foster Whler Intl Holdings Inc ....G 908 730-4000
Hampton (G-4159)
Fyth Labs Inc ....G 856 313-7362
Beverly (G-463)
Hansome Energy Systems Inc ....E 908 862-9044
Linden (G-5382)
John J Chando Jr Inc ....F 732 793-2122
Mantoloking (G-5890)
Koch Mdlar Process Systems LLC.........D 201 368-2929
Paramus (G-7882)
Langan Engineering Environmen...........G 973 560-4900
Parsippany (G-8038)
M C Technologies Inc ....E 973 839-2779
Pompton Plains (G-8961)
Micro-Tek Corporation...........................G 856 829-3855
Cinnaminson (G-1477)
Network Communications Cons..............F 201 968-0684
Hackensack (G-3953)
T O Najarian Associates ....D 732 389-0220
Eatontown (G-2424)
Tsg Inc ....F 973 785-1118
Little Falls (G-5492)

CONSULTING SVC: Human Resource

Elevate Hr Inc ....E 973 917-3230
Parsippany (G-8000)
Hr Acuity LLC ....F 888 598-0161
Florham Park (G-3507)
Real Soft Inc ....A 609 409-3636
Monmouth Junction (G-6360)

CONSULTING SVC: Management

2a Holdings Inc ....F 973 378-8011
Maplewood (G-5913)
Ansell Inc ....D 732 345-5400
Red Bank (G-9320)
Central Components Mfg LLC ....G 732 469-5720
Middlesex (G-6154)
Centurum Information Tech Inc ....G 856 751-1111
Marlton (G-5967)
Defense Spport Svcs Intl 2 LLC.............F 856 866-2200
Marlton (G-5970)
Ecs Energy Ltd...E 201 341-5044
Jackson (G-4667)
Ingersoll-Rand Company ....C 908 238-7000
Annandale (G-58)
Inserts East Incorporated......................C 856 663-8181
Pennsauken (G-8528)
JW Parr Leadburing Co ....G 973 256-8093
Little Falls (G-5479)
Lattice Incorporated ....F 856 910-1166
Pennsauken (G-8542)
Medical Strategic Planning Inc ....G 732 219-5090
Lincroft (G-5339)
Moscova Enterprises Inc ....F 848 628-4873
Jersey City (G-4786)
Nextgen It LLC ....G 908 837-9443
Bridgewater (G-864)
Npt Publishing Group Inc ....F 973 401-0202
Morris Plains (G-6675)
Pds Consultants Inc ....E 201 970-2313
Sparta (G-10517)
Planitroi Inc ....D 973 664-0700
Denville (G-2051)

Schiff & Co ....F 973 227-1830
West Caldwell (G-11805)
Trek Inc ....G 732 269-6300
Bayville (G-261)

CONSULTING SVC: Marketing Management

AB Coaster LLC ....F 908 879-2713
Chester (G-1432)
All In Color Inc ....G 973 626-0987
Paterson (G-8204)
Cherri Stone Interactive LLC ....G 844 843-7765
Lakewood (G-5092)
Global Graphics Intergration ....F 973 334-9653
Towaco (G-10996)
I T C Printing Promotion ....G 908 918-1122
Summit (G-10648)
Jersey Bound Latino LLC ....G 908 591-2830
Union (G-11197)
Kairos Enterprises LLC ....F 201 731-3181
Englewood Cliffs (G-2969)
Oceanic Graphic Intl Inc ....F 201 883-1816
Hackensack (G-3956)
Prism Dgtal Communications LLC.........F 973 232-5038
Mountainside (G-6886)
Raphel Marketing Inc ....G 609 348-6646
Atlantic City (G-107)
Sjshore Marketing Ltd Lblty Co ....F 609 390-1400
Marmora (G-6006)
The Creative Print Group Inc ....F 856 486-1700
Pennsauken (G-8585)
Vending Trucks Inc ....E 732 969-5400
East Brunswick (G-2196)
Victor International Marketing ....G 973 267-8900
Morristown (G-6749)
Vitaquest International LLC ....G 973 575-9200
Fairfield (G-3344)
Vitaquest International LLC ....B 973 575-9200
West Caldwell (G-11807)
Webb-Mason Inc ....G 732 747-6585
Tinton Falls (G-10854)

CONSULTING SVC: Online Technology

Appex Innovation Solutions LLC ....G 215 313-3332
Princeton (G-9004)
Artezio LLC...G 609 786-2435
Princeton (G-9011)
Brayniac LLC..F 212 993-7222
Hoboken (G-4460)
Datamotion Inc ....E 973 455-1245
Florham Park (G-3498)
I Physician Hub ....D 732 274-0155
Monmouth Junction (G-6346)
Local Wisdom Inc ....E 609 269-2320
Lambertville (G-5218)
Manna Group LLC....................................F 856 881-7650
Mount Laurel (G-6816)
Maxentric Technologies LLC ....E 201 242-9800
Fort Lee (G-3566)
Solar Rig Technologies LLC ....G 973 600-0500
Carlstadt (G-1221)

CONSULTING SVC: Sales Management

Advanstar Communications Inc ....E 973 944-7777
Montvale (G-6441)
Shy Kramer & Associates ....F 609 646-2063
Pleasantville (G-8915)

CONSULTING SVC: Telecommunications

Enterprisecc Ltd Liability Co ....G 201 266-0020
Jersey City (G-4749)
Princeton Hosted Solutions LLC...........F 856 470-2350
Haddonfield (G-4062)

CONSULTING SVCS, BUSINESS: Agricultural

SGB Packaging Group Inc ....G 201 488-3030
Hackensack (G-3973)

CONSULTING SVCS, BUSINESS: Communications

Telecom Assistance Group Inc..............E 856 753-8585
West Berlin (G-11756)

CONSULTING SVCS, BUSINESS: Energy Conservation

Pennetta & Sons ....E 201 420-1693
Jersey City (G-4798)

CONSULTING SVCS, BUSINESS: Environmental

Foundation Monitoring...........................G 856 829-0410
Cinnaminson (G-1462)
I 2 R Corp ....G 732 919-1100
Wall Township (G-11490)
Langan Engineering Environmen........G 973 560-4900
Parsippany (G-8038)
Linden Well Drilling ....E 908 862-6633
Linden (G-5403)
National Environmental Svcs Co...........G 908 813-1195
Hackettstown (G-4028)

CONSULTING SVCS, BUSINESS: Publishing

B T O Industries Inc ....G 973 243-0011
West Orange (G-11888)

CONSULTING SVCS, BUSINESS: Sys Engnrg, Exc Computer/Prof

Bavelle Tech Sltions Ltd Lblty ....F 973 992-8086
East Hanover (G-2201)
Clientsrver Tech Solutions LLC...........G 732 710-4495
Iselin (G-4621)
Cloudageit Ltd Liability Co ....G 888 205-4128
North Brunswick (G-7513)
Computer Doc Associates Inc ....D 908 647-4445
Martinsville (G-6009)
Genomesafe LLC ....G 203 676-3752
West Orange (G-11895)
Interntnl Digital Systems Inc................F 201 983-7700
Fort Lee (G-3560)

CONSULTING SVCS, BUSINESS: Systems Analysis & Engineering

Advance Process Systems Lim ....G 201 400-9190
Branchville (G-724)
Defense Spport Svcs Intl 2 LLC.............F 856 866-2200
Marlton (G-5970)
Demaio Inc ....E 609 965-4094
Egg Harbor City (G-2661)
G L Tool & Manufacturing Co ....G 973 740-0001
Livingston (G-5532)
Scalable Systems Inc ....E 732 993-4320
Piscataway (G-8808)

CONSULTING SVCS, BUSINESS: Systems Analysis Or Design

Roper Scientific Inc ....D 520 889-9933
Trenton (G-11114)

CONSULTING SVCS, BUSINESS: Test Development & Evaluation

Biophore LLC ....G 609 275-3713
Plainsboro (G-8876)

CONSULTING SVCS, BUSINESS: Traffic

Griffin Signs Inc ....E 856 786-8517
Cinnaminson (G-1465)

CONSULTING SVCS: Oil

A H Hoffmann LLC ....G 732 988-6000
Neptune (G-6897)
Petroleum Trends International ....G 732 494-0405
Metuchen (G-6117)

CONSULTING SVCS: Psychological

Princeton Information Center ....G 609 924-7019
Princeton (G-9095)

CONSULTING SVCS: Scientific

Sensonics Inc ....F 856 547-7702
Haddon Heights (G-4051)

CONTACT LENSES

Lens Mode Inc ....G... 973 467-2000
Millburn *(G-6255)*

CONTACTS: Electrical

Precision Mfg Group LLC ....D... 973 785-4630
Cedar Grove *(G-1296)*

CONTAINERS, GLASS: Cosmetic Jars

Amcor Phrm Packg USA Inc ....C... 856 728-9300
Williamstown *(G-12078)*
Amcor Phrm Packg USA LLC ....C... 856 327-1540
Millville *(G-6277)*
Amcor Phrm Packg USA LLC ....C... 856 825-1400
Millville *(G-6278)*
Amcor Phrm Packg USA LLC ....C... 856 825-1400
Millville *(G-6279)*
Cameo Metal Forms Inc ....F... 718 788-1106
Woodland Park *(G-12213)*
Heinz Glas USA Inc ....F... 908 474-0300
Linden *(G-5383)*

CONTAINERS, GLASS: Medicine Bottles

Gerresheimer Glass Inc ....B... 856 692-3600
Vineland *(G-11360)*

CONTAINERS: Air Cargo, Metal

Seko Worldwide ....G... 973 465-6868
Newark *(G-7306)*

CONTAINERS: Cargo, Wood & Wood With Metal

Granco Group LLC ....G... 973 515-4721
Roseland *(G-9651)*

CONTAINERS: Corrugated

Apple Corrugated Box Ltd ....F... 201 635-1269
Wood Ridge *(G-12134)*
Boxworks Inc ....G... 856 456-9030
Bellmawr *(G-332)*
Diamex International Corp ....G... 973 838-8844
Kinnelon *(G-5034)*
Global Direct Marketing Group ....G... 856 427-6116
Haddonfield *(G-4060)*
Greater New York Box Co Inc ....G... 609 631-7900
Trenton *(G-11060)*
International Paper Company ....D... 732 828-1700
Milltown *(G-6268)*
New York Folding Box Co Inc ....E... 973 347-6932
Stanhope *(G-10588)*
North Jersey Paper Products ....F... 973 372-4646
Union City *(G-11262)*
Packaging Corporation America ....G... 856 696-0114
Vineland *(G-11388)*
RTS Packaging LLC ....D... 908 782-0505
Frenchtown *(G-3706)*
Squire Corrugated Cont Corp ....D... 908 862-9111
Basking Ridge *(G-206)*
Sunshine Metal & Sign Inc ....G... 973 676-4432
Orange *(G-7829)*
Westrock Rkt Company ....C... 973 484-5000
Newark *(G-7359)*

CONTAINERS: Foil, Bakery Goods & Frozen Foods

Revere Industries LLC ....C... 856 881-3600
Clayton *(G-1527)*

CONTAINERS: Food & Beverage

Innovation Foods LLC ....F... 856 455-2209
Bridgeton *(G-786)*

CONTAINERS: Food, Metal

Allstate Can Corporation ....D... 973 560-9030
Parsippany *(G-7944)*
Penny Plate LLC ....D... 856 429-7583
Mount Laurel *(G-6824)*

CONTAINERS: Frozen Food & Ice Cream

American International Cont ....F... 973 917-3331
Boonton *(G-554)*
Heavenly Havens Creamery LLC ....G... 609 259-6600
Allentown *(G-31)*

CONTAINERS: Glass

Amcor Phrm Packg USA Inc ....C... 856 825-3050
Millville *(G-6276)*
Amcor Phrm Packg USA LLC ....C... 856 825-1100
Millville *(G-6280)*
Ardagh Glass Inc ....B... 732 969-0827
Carteret *(G-1251)*
Avant Industries Ltd Inc ....G... 973 242-1700
Newark *(G-7100)*
Friedrich and Dimmock Inc ....E... 856 825-0305
Millville *(G-6302)*
Leone Industries Inc ....B... 856 455-2000
Bridgeton *(G-789)*
Piramal Glass - Usa Inc ....E... 856 293-6400
Dayton *(G-1983)*
Piramal Glass - Usa Inc ....C... 856 728-9300
Williamstown *(G-12097)*
Piramal Glass - Usa Inc ....B... 856 293-6400
Williamstown *(G-12098)*
Pochet of America Inc ....C... 973 942-4923
Woodland Park *(G-12228)*

CONTAINERS: Metal

Andrew B Duffy Inc ....F... 856 845-4900
West Deptford *(G-11815)*
Cutler Bros Box & Lumber Co ....E... 201 943-2535
Fairview *(G-3360)*
Kraftware Corporation ....E... 732 345-7091
Roselle *(G-9674)*
Mauser Usa LLC ....C... 732 634-6000
Woodbridge *(G-12151)*
Patrick J Kelly Drums Inc ....G... 856 963-1795
Camden *(G-1081)*
Pmm Inc ....F... 908 692-1465
Colts Neck *(G-1790)*
Rahway Steel Drum Co Inc ....E... 732 382-0113
Cranbury *(G-1875)*
Recycle Inc East ....D... 908 756-2200
South Plainfield *(G-10434)*
Romaco North America Inc ....G... 609 584-2500
Hamilton *(G-4124)*

CONTAINERS: Plastic

Berry Global Inc ....B... 980 689-1660
Phillipsburg *(G-8642)*
Berry Global Inc ....C... 609 395-4199
Cranbury *(G-1814)*
C & K Plastics Inc ....D... 732 549-0011
Metuchen *(G-6098)*
Captive Plastics Inc ....C... 732 469-7900
Piscataway *(G-8743)*
Comar Inc ....E... 856 692-6100
Voorhees *(G-11425)*
Comar LLC ....B... 856 692-6100
Voorhees *(G-11427)*
Consolidated Cont Holdings LLC ....D... 609 655-0855
Cranbury *(G-1826)*
Container Mfg Inc ....E... 732 563-0100
Middlesex *(G-6155)*
De Leon Plastics Corp ....F... 973 653-3480
Paterson *(G-8247)*
Dwk Life Sciences Inc ....C... 856 825-1100
Millville *(G-6301)*
E & T Sales Co Inc ....G... 856 787-0900
Mount Laurel *(G-6793)*
Fibrenetics Inc ....F... 732 636-5670
Woodbridge *(G-12148)*
Flex Products LLC ....D... 201 440-1570
Carlstadt *(G-1162)*
Graham Packaging Company LP ....E... 717 849-8500
Bordentown *(G-597)*
Griffen LLC ....G... 973 723-5344
Morristown *(G-6711)*
J OBrien Co Inc ....E... 973 379-8844
Springfield *(G-10558)*
Jarden Corporation ....E... 201 610-6600
Hoboken *(G-4477)*
Jerhel Plastics Inc ....G... 201 436-6662
Bayonne *(G-234)*
Liquid-Solids Separation Corp ....E... 201 236-4833
Ramsey *(G-9245)*
Meese Inc ....E... 201 796-4490
Saddle Brook *(G-9774)*
Mfv International Corporation ....G... 973 993-1687
Morristown *(G-6727)*
National Diversified Sales Inc ....G... 559 562-9888
Bordentown *(G-605)*
Oppenheim Plastics Co Inc ....E... 201 995-9595
Woodcliff Lake *(G-12197)*

Ovadia Corporation ....E... 973 256-9200
Little Falls *(G-5483)*
Plastic Reel Corp of America ....E... 201 933-5100
Carlstadt *(G-1203)*
Plastinetics Inc ....G... 818 364-1611
Towaco *(G-11001)*
Polymer Dynamix LLC ....F... 732 381-1600
South Plainfield *(G-10421)*
Ring Container Tech LLC ....F... 973 258-0707
Springfield *(G-10577)*
Stephco Sales Inc ....E... 973 278-5454
Paterson *(G-8384)*
Stephen Douglas Plastics Inc ....C... 973 523-3030
Paterson *(G-8385)*
Storemaxx Inc ....F... 201 440-8800
Hackensack *(G-3981)*
Techflex Inc ....E... 973 300-9242
Sparta *(G-10522)*
Unette Corporation ....D... 973 328-6800
Randolph *(G-9304)*
Unit Pack Company Inc ....E... 973 239-4112
Cedar Grove *(G-1304)*
Vanguard Container Corp ....E... 732 651-9717
East Brunswick *(G-2195)*
WY Industries Inc ....D... 201 617-8000
North Bergen *(G-7496)*

CONTAINERS: Plywood & Veneer, Wood

Builders Firstsource Inc ....E... 856 767-3153
Berlin *(G-430)*

CONTAINERS: Sanitary, Food

Amscan Inc ....D... 973 983-0888
Rockaway *(G-9551)*
Soundview Paper Holdings LLC ....A... 201 796-4000
Elmwood Park *(G-2850)*
United Plastics Group Inc ....E... 732 873-8777
Somerset *(G-10191)*

CONTAINERS: Shipping & Mailing, Fiber

Slys Express LLC ....G... 908 787-7516
Linden *(G-5443)*

CONTAINERS: Shipping, Bombs, Metal Plate

Enviro Pak Inc ....E... 732 248-1600
Edison *(G-2513)*
Meese Inc ....E... 201 796-4490
Saddle Brook *(G-9774)*

CONTAINERS: Shipping, Metal, Milk, Fluid

Granco Group LLC ....G... 973 515-4721
Roseland *(G-9651)*

CONTAINERS: Shipping, Wood

Vandereems Manufacturing Co ....F... 973 427-2355
Hawthorne *(G-4263)*

CONTAINERS: Wood

Cutler Bros Box & Lumber Co ....E... 201 943-2535
Fairview *(G-3360)*
Jan Packaging Inc ....D... 973 361-7200
Dover *(G-2095)*

CONTAINMENT VESSELS: Reactor, Metal Plate

Ras Process Equipment ....E... 609 371-1000
Robbinsville *(G-9521)*

CONTRACTOR: Dredging

Anthony Excavating & Dem ....G... 609 926-8804
Egg Harbor Township *(G-2678)*

CONTRACTORS: Access Control System Eqpt

Absolute Protective Systems ....E... 732 287-4500
Edison *(G-2448)*
Access Northern Security Inc ....F... 732 462-2500
Freehold *(G-3634)*

CONTRACTORS: Antenna Installation

Dun-Rite Communications Inc ....G... 201 444-0080
Mahwah *(G-5767)*

Jersey Steel Door Inc ....G....... 973 482-4020
Newark (G-7207)

CONTRACTORS: Asbestos Removal & Encapsulation

Abatetech Inc ....E....... 609 265-2107
Lumberton (G-5650)

CONTRACTORS: Asphalt

Murray Paving & Concrete LLC ....E....... 201 670-0030
Hackensack (G-3950)

CONTRACTORS: Awning Installation

F & S Awning and Blind Co Inc.............G....... 732 738-4110
Edison (G-2517)
McBride Awning Co ....G....... 732 892-6256
Point Pleasant Beach (G-8923)

CONTRACTORS: Boiler Maintenance Contractor

Energy Company Inc ....E....... 856 742-1916
Westville (G-11940)
Shelby Mechanical Inc ....E....... 856 665-4540
Cinnaminson (G-1487)

CONTRACTORS: Boring, Building Construction

UNI-Tech Drilling Company Inc ....E....... 856 694-4200
Franklinville (G-3633)

CONTRACTORS: Bridge Painting

Newage Painting Corporation.................G....... 908 547-4734
Newark (G-7252)

CONTRACTORS: Building Board-up

Cargille Tab-Pro Corporation ....F....... 973 267-8883
Carlstadt (G-1137)

CONTRACTORS: Building Eqpt & Machinery Installation

Assa Abloy Entrance Systems US ....E....... 609 443-5800
Windsor (G-12124)
Assa Abloy Entrance Systems US ....E....... 609 528-2580
Hamilton (G-4104)
Benco Inc ....F....... 973 575-4440
Fairfield (G-3146)
DMJ and Associates Inc ....E....... 732 613-7867
Sayreville (G-9820)
Expert Process Systems LLC ....G....... 570 424-0581
Hackettstown (G-4006)
Gervens Enterprises Inc.........................F....... 973 838-1600
Bloomingdale (G-544)
Otis Elevator Company ....E....... 856 235-5200
Moorestown (G-6607)
Verona Aluminum Products Inc..............G....... 973 857-4809
Verona (G-11312)

CONTRACTORS: Building Sign Installation & Mntnce

Banner Design Inc ....G....... 908 687-5335
Hillside (G-4395)
Bergen Sign Company Inc ....E....... 973 742-7755
Paterson (G-8222)
DCI Signs & Awnings Inc ....G....... 973 350-0400
Newark (G-7134)
Delaware Valley Sign Corp ....D....... 609 386-0100
Burlington (G-967)
General Sign Co Inc...............................G....... 856 753-3535
West Berlin (G-11724)
Griffin Signs Inc ....G....... 856 786-8517
Cinnaminson (G-1465)
Ionni Sign Inc ....G....... 973 625-3815
Rockaway (G-9576)
Kdf Reprographics Inc ....F....... 201 784-9991
South Hackensack (G-10274)
Michele Maddalena ....G....... 973 244-0033
Fairfield (G-3260)
Sign Shoppe Inc ....G....... 856 384-2937
Woodbury (G-12170)
Speedy Sign-A-Rama...............................G....... 973 605-8313
Morristown (G-6743)
Sun Neon Sign and Electric Co ....G....... 856 667-6977
Cherry Hill (G-1422)

Tdk Associates Corp ....G....... 862 210-8085
Roseland (G-9656)

CONTRACTORS: Building Site Preparation

All Seasons Construction Inc ....G....... 908 852-0955
Long Valley (G-5634)
Barrett Industries Corporation ....E....... 973 533-1001
Morristown (G-6692)
Barrett Paving Materials Inc...................E....... 973 533-1001
Roseland (G-9647)
General Civil Company Inc ....F....... 866 435-1200
Runnemede (G-9719)

CONTRACTORS: Cable Laying

Tycom Limited ....C....... 973 753-3040
Morristown (G-6746)

CONTRACTORS: Carpentry Work

24 Horas Inc ....F....... 973 817-7400
Newark (G-7062)
Royal Aluminum Co Inc..........................D....... 973 589-8880
Newark (G-7293)

CONTRACTORS: Carpentry, Cabinet & Finish Work

Creative Cabinet Designs Inc ....F....... 973 402-5886
Boonton (G-561)
Cwi Architectural Millwork LLC ....G....... 856 307-7900
Glassboro (G-3802)
Distinctive Woodwork Inc ....E....... 609 714-8505
Lumberton (G-5656)
European Country Kitchens Inc ....D....... 908 735-6659
Pittstown (G-8850)
Mango Custom Cabinets Inc..................F....... 908 813-3077
Hackettstown (G-4019)
Metroplex Products Company Inc..........G....... 732 249-0653
Monroe Township (G-6384)
Narva Inc ....G....... 973 218-1200
Springfield (G-10567)
Parsons Cabinets Inc ....G....... 973 279-4954
Montclair (G-6430)
Restortions By Peter Schichtel ....G....... 973 605-8818
Morristown (G-6739)
Universal Systems Installers ....E....... 732 656-9002
Monroe (G-6375)

CONTRACTORS: Carpentry, Cabinet Building & Installation

Costa Custom Cabinets Inc ....F....... 973 429-7004
Bloomfield (G-510)
Creative Innovations Inc ....F....... 973 636-9060
Fair Lawn (G-3088)
Epic Millwork LLC ....E....... 732 296-0273
Somerset (G-10096)
Hawthorne Kitchens Inc ....F....... 973 427-9010
Hawthorne (G-4238)
Jorgensen Carr Ltd................................G....... 201 792-2278
East Orange (G-2257)
Kitchen Crafters Plus ....G....... 732 566-7995
Matawan (G-6023)
Taylor Made Custom Cabinetry ....F....... 856 786-5433
Pennsauken (G-8583)
Wood & Laminates Inc ....G....... 973 773-7475
Lodi (G-5609)

CONTRACTORS: Carpentry, Finish & Trim Work

Glen Rock Stair Corp ....E....... 201 337-9595
Franklin Lakes (G-3618)
Marty Anderson & Assoc Inc ....G....... 201 798-0507
North Bergen (G-7465)

CONTRACTORS: Carpet Laying

Cole Brothers Marble & Granite ....G....... 856 455-7989
Elmer (G-2790)
Franks Upholstery & Draperies ....G....... 856 779-8585
Maple Shade (G-5902)

CONTRACTORS: Ceramic Floor Tile Installation

Locktile Industries Llc ....F....... 888 562-5845
Newark (G-7224)

CONTRACTORS: Closet Organizers, Installation & Design

Rainbow Closets Inc ....D....... 973 882-3800
Fairfield (G-3289)

CONTRACTORS: Commercial & Office Building

Salon Interiors Inc.................................E....... 201 488-7888
South Hackensack (G-10295)

CONTRACTORS: Communications Svcs

Tyco Elec Sbsea Cmmnctions LLC ....B....... 732 578-7000
Eatontown (G-2427)

CONTRACTORS: Computer Installation

Creative Cmpt Concepts LLC ....G....... 877 919-7988
Williamstown (G-12085)
Pascack Data Services Inc ....F....... 973 304-4858
Hawthorne (G-4251)

CONTRACTORS: Concrete

B&F and Son Masonry Company ....E....... 201 791-7630
Elmwood Park (G-2805)
Concrete Cutting Partners Inc................G....... 201 440-2233
Hackensack (G-3898)
Construction Dynamics Inc ....F....... 732 840-7766
Brick (G-738)
Miles Concrete Company Inc ....G....... 856 697-2311
Newfield (G-7367)
Richard E Pierson Mtls Corp ....G....... 856 740-2400
Williamstown (G-12103)
Richard E Pierson Mtls Corp ....G....... 856 691-0083
Vineland (G-11399)
Richard E Pierson Mtls Corp ....C....... 856 467-4199
Pilesgrove (G-8676)
Tanis Concrete ....E....... 201 796-1556
Fair Lawn (G-3119)

CONTRACTORS: Concrete Block Masonry Laying

General Civil Company Inc ....F....... 866 435-1200
Runnemede (G-9719)

CONTRACTORS: Concrete Breaking, Street & Highway

Control Industries Inc.............................F....... 201 437-3826
Bayonne (G-221)

CONTRACTORS: Concrete Repair

RFS Commercial ....E....... 201 796-0006
Saddle Brook (G-9785)

CONTRACTORS: Construction Site Cleanup

Vet Construction Inc ....F....... 732 987-4922
Jackson (G-4682)

CONTRACTORS: Core Drilling & Cutting

Environmental Technical Drlg ....G....... 732 938-3222
Farmingdale (G-3385)

CONTRACTORS: Countertop Installation

Creative Innovations Inc ....F....... 973 636-9060
Fair Lawn (G-3088)
Intelco ....E....... 856 384-8562
Paulsboro (G-8417)
Narva Inc ....G....... 973 218-1200
Springfield (G-10567)
South Jersey Countertop Co ....G....... 856 768-7960
West Berlin (G-11750)

CONTRACTORS: Demolition, Building & Other Structures

Mdb Construction ....G....... 908 628-8010
Lebanon (G-5296)

CONTRACTORS: Directional Oil & Gas Well Drilling Svc

Jay-Bee Oil & Gas Inc............................D....... 908 686-1493
Union (G-11196)

CONTRACTORS: Drywall

Bell Supply Co...............................E....... 856 663-3900
Pennsauken (G-8486)

Christopher Szuco........................G....... 732 684-7643
Millstone Twp (G-6266)

CONTRACTORS: Electric Power Systems

Norsal Distribution Associates...........F....... 908 638-6430
High Bridge (G-4298)

CONTRACTORS: Electrical

Apelio Innovative Inds LLC...............F....... 973 777-8899
Kearny (G-4861)

Archer Day Inc...........................E....... 732 396-0600
Avenel (G-124)

Automation & Control Inc................E....... 856 234-2300
Moorestown (G-6562)

C J Electric.............................G....... 201 891-0739
Wyckoff (G-12247)

Crestron Electronics Inc................C....... 201 767-3400
Rockleigh (G-9628)

George J Bender Inc.....................E....... 908 687-0081
Union (G-11189)

L&W Audio/Video Inc.....................E....... 212 980-2862
Hoboken (G-4483)

Lb Electric Co LLC......................G....... 973 366-2188
Denville (G-2046)

M&L Power Systems Maint Inc.............E....... 732 679-1800
Old Bridge (G-7783)

Marshall Maintenance....................C....... 609 394-7153
Trenton (G-11079)

R & R Irrigation Co Inc.................E....... 732 271-7070
Middlesex (G-6192)

Trinity Heating & Air Inc...............D....... 732 780-3779
Wall Township (G-11516)

Verizon Communications Inc.............D....... 609 646-9939
Egg Harbor Township (G-2698)

CONTRACTORS: Electronic Controls Installation

Johnson Controls Inc....................D....... 732 225-6700
Edison (G-2549)

CONTRACTORS: Energy Management Control

Bfhj Holdings Inc.......................G....... 908 730-6280
Montvale (G-6447)

CONTRACTORS: Epoxy Application

Newage Painting Corporation.............G....... 908 547-4734
Newark (G-7252)

CONTRACTORS: Excavating

Barrett Industries Corporation..........E....... 973 533-1001
Morristown (G-6692)

Barrett Paving Materials Inc............E....... 973 533-1001
Roseland (G-9647)

Cedar Hill Landscaping..................E....... 732 469-1400
Somerset (G-10081)

Control Industries Inc..................F....... 201 437-3826
Bayonne (G-221)

Earthwork Associates Inc................F....... 609 624-9395
Ocean View (G-7763)

Hudson Valley Enviromental Inc..........G....... 732 967-0060
Toms River (G-10887)

Hup & Sons..............................G....... 908 832-7878
Glen Gardner (G-3815)

Philip Mamrak...........................G....... 908 454-6089
Phillipsburg (G-8663)

CONTRACTORS: Excavating Slush Pits & Cellars Svcs

Zc Utility Services LLC.................G....... 973 226-1840
Roseland (G-9658)

CONTRACTORS: Exterior Painting

Dux Paint LLC...........................F....... 973 473-2376
Lodi (G-5583)

CONTRACTORS: Exterior Wall System Installation

Atlantic Exterior Wall Systems..........D....... 973 646-8200
Wayne (G-11606)

CONTRACTORS: Fence Construction

A 1 Fencing Inc.........................F....... 908 527-1066
Elizabeth (G-2702)

Accent Fence Inc........................E....... 609 965-6400
Egg Harbor City (G-2655)

All-State Fence Inc.....................E....... 732 431-4944
West Orange (G-11885)

C & S Fencing Inc.......................E....... 201 797-5440
Elmwood Park (G-2807)

Consoldated Stl Alum Fence Inc..........E....... 908 272-0494
Kenilworth (G-4948)

Doerre Fence Co LLC.....................F....... 732 751-9700
Farmingdale (G-3384)

Edwin R Burger & Son Inc................E....... 856 468-2300
Sewell (G-9952)

H Barron Iron Works Inc.................F....... 856 456-9092
Gloucester City (G-3838)

Mendham Garden Center...................G....... 973 543-4178
Mendham (G-6089)

National Fence Systems Inc..............D....... 732 636-5600
Avenel (G-143)

Northeast Precast Ltd Lblty Co..........D....... 856 765-9088
Millville (G-6317)

CONTRACTORS: Fiber Optic Cable Installation

Comm Port Technologies Inc..............G....... 732 738-8780
Cranbury (G-1825)

Contemporary Cabling Company............G....... 732 382-5064
Clark (G-1499)

CONTRACTORS: Fiberglass Work

United Eqp Fabricators LLC..............G....... 973 242-2737
Newark (G-7353)

CONTRACTORS: Fire Detection & Burglar Alarm Systems

Checkpoint Security Systems Gr..........C....... 952 933-8858
West Deptford (G-11820)

Checkpoint Systems Inc..................C....... 952 933-8858
West Deptford (G-11823)

Merchants Alarm Systems Inc.............E....... 973 779-1296
Wallington (G-11528)

CONTRACTORS: Fire Sprinkler System Installation Svcs

Absolute Protective Systems.............E....... 732 287-4500
Edison (G-2448)

Tyco International MGT Co LLC............E....... 609 720-4200
Princeton (G-9133)

CONTRACTORS: Floor Laying & Other Floor Work

Armorpoxy Inc...........................F....... 908 810-9613
Union (G-11154)

Flooring Concepts NJ LLC................F....... 732 409-7600
Manalapan (G-5848)

Friends Hardwood Floors Inc.............G....... 732 859-4019
Oakhurst (G-7669)

Tbs Industrial Flooring Pdts............G....... 732 899-1486
Point Pleasant Beach (G-8927)

CONTRACTORS: Flooring

Atlantic Flooring LLC...................F....... 609 296-7700
Ltl Egg Hbr (G-5641)

Flooring Concepts NJ LLC................F....... 732 409-7600
Manalapan (G-5848)

Friends Hardwood Floors Inc.............G....... 732 859-4019
Oakhurst (G-7669)

CONTRACTORS: Food Svcs Eqpt Installation

Marlo Manufacturing Co Inc..............E....... 973 423-0226
Boonton (G-575)

CONTRACTORS: Garage Doors

Gray Overhead Door Co...................F....... 908 355-3889
Elizabeth (G-2740)

CONTRACTORS: Gas Field Svcs, NEC

Ridgewood Energy O Fund LLC.............G....... 201 447-9000
Montvale (G-6472)

CONTRACTORS: General Electric

Eme Electrical Contractors..............G....... 973 228-6608
Caldwell (G-1027)

Lowder Electric and Cnstr...............G....... 732 764-6000
Middlesex (G-6177)

M2 Electric LLC.........................F....... 973 770-4596
Mine Hill (G-6327)

Story Electric Mtr Repr Co Inc..........G....... 973 256-1636
Little Falls (G-5490)

Sun Neon Sign and Electric Co...........G....... 856 667-6977
Cherry Hill (G-1422)

Timothy P Bryan Elc Co Inc..............G....... 609 393-8325
Trenton (G-11122)

CONTRACTORS: Glass Tinting, Architectural & Automotive

Glasscare Inc...........................F....... 201 943-1122
Cliffside Park (G-1540)

CONTRACTORS: Glass, Glazing & Tinting

Above Rest Glass........................G....... 732 370-1616
Toms River (G-10859)

Eldon Glass & Mirror Co Inc.............F....... 973 589-2099
Newark (G-7151)

Frost Tech Inc..........................F....... 732 396-0071
Rahway (G-9191)

Glasscare Inc...........................F....... 201 943-1122
Cliffside Park (G-1540)

Mainland Plate Glass Company............F....... 609 277-2938
Pleasantville (G-8912)

Newman Glass Works Inc..................F....... 215 925-3565
Camden (G-1078)

Penta Glass Industries Inc..............G....... 973 478-2110
Garfield (G-3747)

Semi Conductor Manufacturing............G....... 973 478-2880
Clifton (G-1720)

William Duling..........................G....... 856 365-6323
Camden (G-1089)

CONTRACTORS: Heating & Air Conditioning

Breure Sheet Metal Co Inc...............G....... 973 772-6423
Clifton (G-1578)

Duct Mate Inc...........................G....... 201 488-8002
Hackensack (G-3907)

Heat-Timer Corporation..................E....... 212 481-2020
Fairfield (G-3219)

Marshall Maintenance....................C....... 609 394-7153
Trenton (G-11079)

McAllister Service Company..............E....... 856 665-4545
Pennsauken (G-8546)

Rosenwach Tank Co LLC...................E....... 732 563-4900
Somerset (G-10167)

Springfield Heating & AC Co.............F....... 908 233-8400
Mountainside (G-6888)

CONTRACTORS: Heating Systems Repair & Maintenance Svc

Pennington Furnace Supply Inc...........G....... 609 737-2500
Pennington (G-8457)

CONTRACTORS: Highway & Street Construction, General

Stavola Holding Corporation.............C....... 732 542-2328
Tinton Falls (G-10850)

CONTRACTORS: Highway & Street Paving

A E Stone Inc...........................E....... 609 641-2781
Egg Harbor Township (G-2675)

Arawak Paving Co Inc....................E....... 609 561-4100
Hammonton (G-4130)

Barrett Industries Corporation..........E....... 973 533-1001
Morristown (G-6692)

Barrett Paving Materials Inc............E....... 973 533-1001
Roseland (G-9647)

Brick-Wall Corp.........................E....... 609 693-6223
Forked River (G-3534)

Colas Inc...............................G....... 973 290-9082
Morristown (G-6700)

Dosch-King Company Inc..................F....... 973 887-0145
Whippany (G-12018)

Joseph and William Stavola.................E....... 609 924-0300
Kingston (G-5028)

Murray Paving & Concrete LLC.........E....... 201 670-0030
Hackensack (G-3950)

Philip Mamrak.....................................G....... 908 454-6089
Phillipsburg (G-8663)

Schifano Construction Corp...............F....... 732 752-3450
Middlesex (G-6194)

Suffolk County Contractors.................E....... 732 349-7726
Toms River (G-10915)

Trap Rock Industries Inc....................B....... 609 924-0300
Kingston (G-5030)

CONTRACTORS: Home & Office Intrs Finish, Furnish/Remodel

Majka Railing Inc.................................G....... 973 247-7603
Paterson (G-8329)

Maranatha Ceramic Tile & Marbl........E....... 609 758-1168
Wrightstown (G-12242)

CONTRACTORS: Hydraulic Eqpt Installation & Svcs

Industrial Hydraulics & Rubber...........G....... 856 966-2600
Camden (G-1070)

CONTRACTORS: Indl Building Renovation, Remodeling & Repair

Diamond Scooters Inc..........................G....... 609 646-0003
Absecon (G-2)

Mdb Construction.................................G....... 908 628-8010
Lebanon (G-5296)

CONTRACTORS: Kitchen & Bathroom Remodeling

Artistic Hardware.................................G....... 609 383-1909
Northfield (G-7563)

Eviva LLC...G....... 973 925-4028
Paterson (G-8265)

Ken Bauer Inc......................................E....... 201 664-6881
Hillsdale (G-4385)

Royal Cabinet Company Inc.................E....... 908 203-8000
Bound Brook (G-622)

Sanford & Birdsall Inc.........................G....... 732 223-6966
Manasquan (G-5880)

CONTRACTORS: Lighting Syst

Prg Group Inc.......................................G....... 201 758-4000
Secaucus (G-9913)

Pty Lighting LLC...................................G....... 855 303-4500
Hillside (G-4434)

CONTRACTORS: Lightweight Steel Framing Installation

Jersey Shore Steel Inc........................G....... 732 833-8855
Jackson (G-4670)

CONTRACTORS: Machine Rigging & Moving

Industrial Process & Eqp Inc..............F....... 973 702-0330
Sussex (G-10673)

Woods Industrial LLC..........................F....... 973 208-0664
West Milford (G-11859)

CONTRACTORS: Machinery Installation

Equipment Erectors Inc.......................E....... 732 846-1212
Somerset (G-10097)

Luciano Packaging Technologies.........G....... 908 722-3222
Branchburg (G-676)

Marshall Maintenance..........................C....... 609 394-7153
Trenton (G-11079)

Paramount Metal Finishing Co.............C....... 908 862-0772
Linden (G-5424)

Sigma Engineering & Consulting.........F....... 732 356-3046
Middlesex (G-6197)

CONTRACTORS: Maintenance, Parking Facility Eqpt

Kyosis LLC...G....... 908 202-8894
South River (G-10462)

CONTRACTORS: Marble Installation, Interior

Elana Tile Contractors Inc...................G....... 973 386-0991
East Hanover (G-2215)

Solidsurface Designs Inc.....................E....... 856 910-7720
Pennsauken (G-8580)

Whole Stones LLC................................G....... 856 266-0091
Willingboro (G-12123)

CONTRACTORS: Masonry & Stonework

B&F and Son Masonry Company.........E....... 201 791-7630
Elmwood Park (G-2805)

Donald Mason Baker Contractor.........G....... 908 782-2115
Flemington (G-3437)

Murray Paving & Concrete LLC.........E....... 201 670-0030
Hackensack (G-3950)

Procrete LLC..G....... 609 365-2922
Linwood (G-5467)

T M Baxter Services LLC.....................E....... 908 500-9065
Washington (G-11589)

Thin Stone Systems LLC......................G....... 973 882-7377
Fairfield (G-3325)

CONTRACTORS: Mechanical

Airmet Inc...G....... 973 481-5550
Newark (G-7074)

Klm Mechanical Contractors...............F....... 201 385-6965
Dumont (G-2120)

Lusotech LLC..G....... 973 332-3861
Newark (G-7230)

Pennetta & Sons..................................E....... 201 420-1693
Jersey City (G-4798)

Sander Mechanical Service Inc...........E....... 732 560-0600
Branchburg (G-701)

CONTRACTORS: Office Furniture Installation

Extra Office Inc....................................F....... 732 381-9774
Rahway (G-9188)

CONTRACTORS: Oil & Gas Building, Repairing & Dismantling Svc

General Civil Company Inc...................F....... 866 435-1200
Runnemede (G-9719)

Kabel N Elettrotek Amer Inc................G....... 973 265-0850
Parsippany (G-8035)

CONTRACTORS: Oil & Gas Field Geological Exploration Svcs

Foresight Enviroprobe Inc....................G....... 609 259-1244
Clarksburg (G-1519)

CONTRACTORS: Oil & Gas Well Drilling Svc

Maverick Oil Co....................................E....... 732 747-8637
Red Bank (G-9335)

Shore Drilling Inc.................................G....... 732 935-1776
Oceanport (G-7768)

CONTRACTORS: Oil & Gas Well On-Site Foundation Building Svcs

Region Oil..C....... 973 366-3100
Dover (G-2107)

CONTRACTORS: Oil Field Lease Tanks: Erectg, Clng/Rprg Svcs

Conti-Robert and Co JV........................D....... 732 520-5000
Edison (G-2489)

CONTRACTORS: Oil/Gas Field Casing, Tube/Rod Running, Cut/Pull

Creamer Glass LLC...............................G....... 856 327-2023
Millville (G-6295)

CONTRACTORS: Oil/Gas Well Construction, Rpr/Dismantling Svcs

AK Contracting LLC.............................G....... 908 220-8527
Winfield Park (G-12131)

All Seasons Construction Inc...............G....... 908 852-0955
Long Valley (G-5634)

Gateway Property Solutions Ltd...........E....... 732 901-9700
Lakewood (G-5128)

Mep Alaska LLC...................................G....... 646 535-9005
Livingston (G-5543)

Mister Good Lube Inc..........................G....... 732 842-3266
Shrewsbury (G-10006)

Nickos Construction Inc.......................F....... 267 240-3997
Sicklerville (G-10022)

Refferals Only Inc................................G....... 609 921-1033
Princeton (G-9110)

Robert Weidener...................................G....... 201 703-5700
Fair Lawn (G-3111)

Shelby Mechanical Inc.........................E....... 856 665-4540
Cinnaminson (G-1487)

That 10 Minute Oil Change Pl..............G....... 201 587-0220
Rochelle Park (G-9538)

Vet Construction Inc............................E....... 732 987-4922
Jackson (G-4682)

Zion Industries Inc..............................E....... 973 998-0162
Morris Plains (G-6682)

CONTRACTORS: On-Site Welding

All American Metal Fabricators............G....... 201 567-2898
Tenafly (G-10780)

BR Welding Inc....................................F....... 732 363-8253
Howell (G-4547)

Energy Company Inc............................E....... 856 742-1916
Westville (G-11940)

Independent Welding Co.......................F....... 973 361-9731
Wharton (G-11989)

James A Stanlick Jr..............................G....... 973 366-7316
Wharton (G-11990)

Orgo-Thermit Inc..................................E....... 732 657-5781
Manchester (G-5887)

Wel-Fab Inc..E....... 609 261-1393
Rancocas (G-9265)

Woods Industrial LLC..........................F....... 973 208-0664
West Milford (G-11859)

CONTRACTORS: Ornamental Metal Work

67 Pollock Ave Corp............................G....... 201 432-1156
Jersey City (G-4692)

Abba Metal Works Inc.........................G....... 973 684-0808
Paterson (G-8195)

Coordinated Metals Inc........................D....... 201 460-7280
Carlstadt (G-1149)

CONTRACTORS: Painting & Wall Covering

Brennan Penrod Contractors LLC.........F....... 856 933-1100
Bellmawr (G-333)

CONTRACTORS: Painting, Commercial

Zack Painting Co Inc............................E....... 732 738-7900
Fords (G-3531)

CONTRACTORS: Painting, Commercial, Interior

Forman Industries Inc..........................D....... 732 727-8100
Old Bridge (G-7779)

CONTRACTORS: Painting, Indl

United Spport Slutions-Lmt Inc............E....... 973 857-9222
Cedar Grove (G-1305)

CONTRACTORS: Parking Lot Maintenance

Advanced Pavement Technologies........F....... 973 366-8044
Rockaway (G-9545)

CONTRACTORS: Plumbing

Advanced Sewer...................................F....... 973 278-1948
Woodland Park (G-12208)

Capuano Plumbing Inc.........................G....... 201 327-0676
Upper Saddle River (G-11276)

Cobra Products Inc..............................D....... 856 241-7700
Swedesboro (G-10688)

Eme Electrical Contractors...................G....... 973 228-6608
Caldwell (G-1027)

Frank Burton & Sons Inc......................G....... 856 455-1202
Bridgeton (G-785)

Perkins Plumbing & Heating................G....... 201 327-2736
Upper Saddle River (G-11283)

World and Main LLC............................G....... 609 860-9990
Cranbury (G-1892)

CONTRACTORS: Prefabricated Window & Door Installation

Architectural Window Mfg Corp............C....... 201 933-5094
Rutherford (G-9726)

Europrojects Intl Inc.............................G....... 917 262-0795
Englewood (G-2894)

Verona Aluminum Products Inc.............G....... 973 857-4809
Verona (G-11312)

CONTRACTORS: Process Piping

Industrial Process & Eqp Inc ....F 973 702-0330
Sussex (G-10673)

CONTRACTORS: Protective Lining Install, Underground Sewage

Atlantic Lining Co Inc ....E 609 723-2400
Jobstown (G-4854)

CONTRACTORS: Resilient Floor Laying

Palma Inc ....F 973 429-1490
Whippany (G-12031)

CONTRACTORS: Roofing

Vector Foiltec LLC ....G 862 702-8909
Fairfield (G-3339)

CONTRACTORS: Safety & Security Eqpt

Amerindia Technologies Inc ....E 609 664-2224
Cranbury (G-1810)
Tyco International MGT Co LLC ....E 609 720-4200
Princeton (G-9133)

CONTRACTORS: Sandblasting Svc, Building Exteriors

Jaeger Thomas & Melissa DDS ....F 908 735-2722
Lebanon (G-5292)

CONTRACTORS: Septic System

Vogel Precast Inc ....G 732 552-8837
Lakewood (G-5202)

CONTRACTORS: Sheet Metal Work, NEC

Atlantic Air Enterprises Inc ....F 732 381-4000
Rahway (G-9178)
Crett Construction Inc ....F 973 663-1184
Lake Hopatcong (G-5055)
Danson Sheet Metal Inc ....E 201 343-4876
Hackensack (G-3903)
In-Line Shtmtl Fabricators ....G 201 339-8121
Bayonne (G-233)
Independent Sheet Metal Co Inc............D 973 423-1150
Riverdale (G-9482)
Joseph Bbinec Shtmtl Works Inc ....E 732 388-0155
Rahway (G-9205)
Klm Mechanical Contractors ....F 201 385-6965
Dumont (G-2120)
Mastercraft Iron Inc...............................F 732 988-3113
Neptune (G-6924)

CONTRACTORS: Shoring & Underpinning

Aluma Systems Con Cnstr LLC............G 908 418-5073
Linden (G-5347)

CONTRACTORS: Siding

John Cooper Company Inc ....F 201 487-4018
Hackensack (G-3933)
Window Factory Inc ....E 856 546-5050
Mount Ephraim (G-6765)

CONTRACTORS: Single-family Home General Remodeling

Crincoli Woodwork Co Inc ....F 908 352-9332
Elizabeth (G-2721)
Diamond Scooters Inc...........................G 609 646-0003
Absecon (G-2)
Ken Bauer Inc......................................E 201 664-6881
Hillsdale (G-4385)
Rumsons Kitchens Inc ....G 732 842-1810
Rumson (G-9716)

CONTRACTORS: Solar Energy Eqpt

Holistic Solar Usa Inc ....G 732 757-5500
Newark (G-7191)
Mc Renewable Energy LLC ....F 732 369-9933
Manasquan (G-5873)
Panatech Corporation...........................G 732 331-5692
Manalapan (G-5860)
Trinity Heating & Air Inc ....D 732 780-3779
Wall Township (G-11516)

CONTRACTORS: Sound Eqpt Installation

E Berkowitz & Co Inc ....G 856 608-1118
Mount Laurel (G-6794)

CONTRACTORS: Spraying, Nonagricultural

Zack Painting Co Inc.............................E 732 738-7900
Fords (G-3531)

CONTRACTORS: Standby Or Emergency Power Specialization

Elite Emrgncy Lights Ltd Lblty ....F 732 534-2377
Lakewood (G-5115)

CONTRACTORS: Stone Masonry

Stone Truss Systems Inc ....E 973 882-7377
Fairfield (G-3314)

CONTRACTORS: Storage Tank Erection, Metal

Jersey Tank Fabricators Inc..................E 609 758-7670
South Plainfield (G-10388)

CONTRACTORS: Store Front Construction

Architectural Metal and Glass ....G 732 994-7575
Lakewood (G-5075)

CONTRACTORS: Structural Steel Erection

Arnold Steel Co Inc..............................D 732 363-1079
Howell (G-4546)
Banker Steel Nj LLC..............................D 732 968-6061
South Plainfield (G-10334)
Burgess Steel Holding LLC....................G 201 871-3500
Englewood (G-2879)
CB&i LLC...C 856 482-3000
Trenton (G-11036)
East Coast Storage Eqp Co Inc ....E 732 451-1316
Brick (G-742)
Garden State Iron Inc............................F 732 918-0760
Ocean (G-7726)
Harris Structural Steel Co Inc ....G 732 752-6070
South Plainfield (G-10379)
John Cooper Company Inc ....F 201 487-4018
Hackensack (G-3933)
John Maltese Iron Works Inc ....E 732 249-4350
North Brunswick (G-7521)
Leets Steel Inc.....................................G 917 416-7977
Sayreville (G-9828)
RS Phillips Steel LLC............................E 973 827-6464
Sussex (G-10676)
Tri-Steel Fabricators Inc ....E 609 392-8660
Trenton (G-11127)

CONTRACTORS: Svc Well Drilling Svcs

Foundation Monitoring..........................G 856 829-0410
Cinnaminson (G-1462)

CONTRACTORS: Tile Installation, Ceramic

Maranatha Ceramic Tile & Marbl ....E 609 758-1168
Wrightstown (G-12242)
Terra Designs Inc ....F 973 328-1135
Dover (G-2112)

CONTRACTORS: Timber Removal

Hudson Valley Enviromental Inc ....E 732 967-0060
Toms River (G-10887)

CONTRACTORS: Ventilation & Duct Work

Altona Blower & Shtmtl Work ....G 201 641-3520
Little Ferry (G-5494)
Bonland Industries Inc ....D 973 694-3211
Wayne (G-11611)
Creative Industrial Kitchens ....G 973 633-0420
Wayne (G-11621)
Madhu B Goyal MD ....G 908 769-0307
South Plainfield (G-10400)
Millar Sheet Metal................................G 201 997-1990
Kearny (G-4899)
Professional Envmtl Systems ....E 201 991-3000
Kearny (G-4911)
PTL Sheet Metal Inc..............................G 201 501-8700
Dumont (G-2122)

CONTRACTORS: Warm Air Heating & Air Conditioning

Banicki Sheet Metal Inc........................G 201 385-5938
Bergenfield (G-382)
In-Line Shtmtl Fabricators ....G 201 339-8121
Bayonne (G-233)
John E Herbst Heating & Coolg............G 732 721-0088
Parlin (G-7933)
T J Eckardt Associates Inc ....F 856 767-4111
Berlin (G-442)
Temptrol Corp ....E 856 461-7977
Voorhees (G-11439)

CONTRACTORS: Water Intake Well Drilling Svc

UNI-Tech Drilling Company Inc ....E 856 694-4200
Franklinville (G-3633)

CONTRACTORS: Water Well Drilling

Clearwater Well Drilling Co ....G 609 698-1800
Manahawkin (G-5829)

CONTRACTORS: Water Well Servicing

UNI-Tech Drilling Company Inc ....E 856 694-4200
Franklinville (G-3633)

CONTRACTORS: Waterproofing

Anti Hydro International Inc...................F 908 284-9000
Flemington (G-3427)

CONTRACTORS: Weather Stripping

Portaseal LLC..G 973 539-0100
Morristown (G-6737)

CONTRACTORS: Well Bailing, Cleaning, Swabbing & Treating Svc

Environmental Technical Drlg ....G 732 938-3222
Farmingdale (G-3385)
Perkins Plumbing & Heating..................G 201 327-2736
Upper Saddle River (G-11283)

CONTRACTORS: Window Treatment Installation

Proclean Services Inc...........................F 973 857-5408
Verona (G-11309)

CONTRACTORS: Windows & Doors

Frank & Jims Inc ....G 609 646-1655
Pleasantville (G-8908)
Guardrite Steel Door Corp ....G 973 481-4424
Newark (G-7181)

CONTRACTORS: Wood Floor Installation & Refinishing

AM Wood Inc ....F 732 246-1506
East Brunswick (G-2133)
Contempocork LLC................................G 201 262-7738
River Edge (G-9464)

CONTRACTORS: Wrecking & Demolition

Anthony Excavating & Dem ....G 609 926-8804
Egg Harbor Township (G-2678)
Hudson Valley Enviromental Inc ....E 732 967-0060
Toms River (G-10887)

CONTROL CIRCUIT DEVICES

Admartec Inc ....G 732 888-8248
Hazlet (G-4268)
Quik-Flex Circuit Inc ....E 856 742-0550
Gloucester City (G-3844)

CONTROL EQPT: Buses Or Trucks, Electric

Valcor Engineering Corporation............E 973 467-8100
Springfield (G-10584)

CONTROL EQPT: Electric

Asco Valve LLC.....................................D 973 966-2437
Florham Park (G-3488)

PRODUCT

Atc Systems Inc ....G 732 560-0900
Middlesex (G-6149)
Automatic Switch Company ....A 973 966-2000
Florham Park (G-3489)
Computer Control Corp ....F 973 492-8265
Butler (G-1001)
Electronic Power Designs Inc ......F 973 838-7055
Bloomingdale (G-542)
Harris Corporation ....E 973 284-0123
Clifton (G-1635)
Innolutions Inc ....G 609 490-9799
Princeton Junction (G-9158)
ITT Corporation ....G 973 284-0123
Clifton (G-1650)
Mid-State Controls Inc ....F 732 335-0500
Hazlet (G-4279)
Rockwell Automation Inc ....E 973 658-1500
Parsippany (G-8080)
Walker Engineering Inc ....F 732 899-2550
Point Pleasant Boro (G-8943)

CONTROL EQPT: Noise

Hansome Energy Systems Inc ....E 908 862-9044
Linden (G-5382)
Wireless Telecom Group Inc ....D 973 386-9696
Parsippany (G-8114)

CONTROL PANELS: Electrical

Eagle Engineering & Automation .....G 732 899-2292
Point Pleasant Boro (G-8939)
Everite Machine Products Co ....E 856 330-6700
Pennsauken (G-8509)
Ivey Katrina Owner ....G 973 951-8328
Newark (G-7202)
Machinery Electrics ....G 732 536-0600
Bayville (G-257)
Pkm Panel Systems Corp ....F 732 238-6760
Old Bridge (G-7789)
Sensigraphics Inc ....E 856 853-9100
Mount Laurel (G-6839)

CONTROLS & ACCESS: Indl, Electric

Control & Power Systems Inc ....E 973 439-0500
Fairfield (G-3167)
Electronic Technology Inc ....C 973 371-5160
Irvington (G-4583)
General Electronic Engineering .....F 732 381-1144
Rahway (G-9193)
Infinova Corporation ....E 732 355-9100
Monmouth Junction (G-6347)
Precision Multiple Contrls Inc ....E 201 444-0600
Midland Park (G-6236)
Precision Multiple Contrls Inc ....D 201 444-0600
Midland Park (G-6237)
Rab Lighting Inc ....C 201 784-8600
Northvale (G-7602)

CONTROLS & ACCESS: Motor

Eaton Hydraulics LLC ....E 732 212-4700
Tinton Falls (G-10834)
Servo-Tek Products Company Inc ....E 973 427-4249
Hawthorne (G-4258)

CONTROLS: Air Flow, Refrigeration

Ammark Corporation ....G 973 616-2555
Pompton Plains (G-8952)
Croll-Reynolds Co Inc ....E 908 232-4200
Parsippany (G-7976)
Energy Options Inc ....E 732 512-9100
Edison (G-2511)

CONTROLS: Automatic Temperature

D & A Electronics Mfg ....F 732 938-7400
Wall Township (G-11476)
Rowan Technologies Inc ....D 609 267-9000
Rancocas (G-9262)

CONTROLS: Environmental

Access Northern Security Inc ....F 732 462-2500
Freehold (G-3634)
Amega Scientific Corporation ....F 609 953-7295
Medford (G-6064)
Armadillo Automation Inc ....E 856 829-2888
Cinnaminson (G-1447)
Burling Instruments Inc ....F 973 665-0601
Chatham (G-1326)

Calculagraph Co ....D 973 887-9400
East Hanover (G-2204)
Check-It Electronics Corp ....E 973 520-8435
Elizabeth (G-2718)
Fluidsens International Inc ....G 914 338-3932
Twp Washinton (G-11142)
Honeywell Asia Pacific Inc ....F 973 455-2000
Morris Plains (G-6662)
Johnson Controls Inc ....D 732 225-6700
Edison (G-2549)
Megatran Industries ....B 609 227-4300
Bordentown (G-601)
Micro-Tek Laboratories Inc ....G 973 779-5577
Clifton (G-1674)
Niagara Conservation Corp ....F 973 829-0800
Cedar Knolls (G-1319)
Rees Scientific Corporation ....C 609 530-1055
Ewing (G-3050)
Schneder Elc Bldngs Amrcas Inc ....E 201 348-9240
Secaucus (G-9922)
Sigma-Netics Inc ....E 973 227-6372
Riverdale (G-9488)
Sk & P Industries Inc ....G 973 482-1864
Newark (G-7315)
Tesa Rentals LLC ....F 973 300-0913
Sparta (G-10523)
Thermo Systems LLC ....G 609 371-3300
East Windsor (G-2368)
Town & Country Plastics Inc ....F 732 780-5300
Marlboro (G-5961)
Trolex Corporation ....E 201 794-8004
Randolph (G-9302)

CONTROLS: Relay & Ind

Advanced Industrial Controls ....G 908 725-7575
Branchville (G-628)
Alliance Technologies Group ....G 973 664-1151
East Hanover (G-2199)
Argus International Inc ....E 609 466-1677
Ringoes (G-9435)
Crestron Electronics Inc ....D 201 894-0670
Cresskill (G-1944)
Harrison Electro Mechanical ....F 732 382-6008
Rahway (G-9196)
Heat-Timer Corporation ....E 973 575-4004
Fairfield (G-3218)
Instrumentation Technology Sls .....G 732 388-0866
Rahway (G-9200)
Lummus Overseas Corporation ......G 973 893-3000
Bloomfield (G-520)
Megatran Industries ....B 609 227-4300
Bordentown (G-601)
Omega Engineering Inc ....C 856 467-4200
Bridgeport (G-769)
Pressure Controls Inc ....G 973 751-5002
Belleville (G-312)
Relay Specialties Inc ....E 856 547-5000
Haddon Heights (G-4050)
Reliance Electric Company ....E 856 661-1442
Pennsauken (G-8572)
Rockwell Automation Inc ....G 973 526-3901
Parsippany (G-8081)
Special Technical Services ....G 609 259-2626
Flanders (G-3417)
Xybion Corporation ....C 973 538-2067
Lawrenceville (G-5273)

CONTROLS: Thermostats

Aginova Inc ....G 732 804-3272
Freehold (G-3635)

CONTROLS: Thermostats, Exc Built-in

Chatham Controls Corporation ....G 908 236-6019
Lebanon (G-5281)

CONTROLS: Voice

Value Added Vice Solutions LLC .....G 201 400-3247
Brielle (G-916)

CONTROLS: Water Heater

Brighton Air ....G 973 258-1500
Springfield (G-10545)

CONVENIENCE STORES

Glassboro News & Food Store ....G 856 881-1181
Glassboro (G-3806)

CONVENTION & TRADE SHOW SVCS

Atlas O LLC ....E 908 687-9590
Hillside (G-4393)
Excerpta Medica Inc ....D 908 547-2100
Bridgewater (G-837)
Foundation For Student Comm ....E 609 258-1111
Princeton (G-9046)
Hyman W Fisher Inc ....G 973 992-9155
Livingston (G-5534)
Information Today Inc ....E 609 654-6266
Medford (G-6071)

CONVERTERS: Data

Cisco Systems Inc ....C 732 635-4200
Iselin (G-4620)
Dialogic Inc ....C 973 967-6000
Parsippany (G-7981)
Total Technology Inc ....E 856 617-0502
Cherry Hill (G-1429)

CONVERTERS: Frequency

ADI American Distributors LLC ......D 973 328-1181
Randolph (G-9267)
Technology Dynamics Inc ....D 201 385-0500
Bergenfield (G-397)

CONVERTERS: Phase Or Rotary, Electrical

Power Magnetics Inc ....E 609 695-1170
Trenton (G-11101)

CONVERTERS: Power, AC to DC

Powerspec Inc ....E 732 494-9490
Somerville (G-10225)
Princeton Power Systems Inc ....D 609 955-5390
Lawrenceville (G-5267)

CONVERTERS: Torque, Exc Auto

431 Converters Inc ....G 856 848-8949
Woodbury Heights (G-12173)
Jetyd Corporation ....F 201 512-9500
Mahwah (G-5786)

CONVEYOR SYSTEMS

Knotts Company Inc ....E 908 464-4800
Berkeley Heights (G-416)

CONVEYOR SYSTEMS: Belt, General Indl Use

Conveyer Installers America ....G 908 453-4729
Belvidere (G-367)
Flow-Turn Inc ....E 908 687-3225
Union (G-11184)
Hy-Tek Material Handling Inc ....E 732 490-6282
Morganville (G-6642)
Volta Belting USA Inc ....F 973 276-7905
Pine Brook (G-8719)

CONVEYOR SYSTEMS: Bucket Type

Coesia Health & Beauty Inc ....F 908 707-8008
Branchburg (G-648)

CONVEYOR SYSTEMS: Bulk Handling

Coperion Corporation ....C 201 327-6300
Sewell (G-9946)

CONVEYOR SYSTEMS: Pneumatic Tube

Lamson Airtubes LLC ....F 973 300-4267
Lafayette (G-5049)
Vac-U-Max ....G 973 759-4600
Belleville (G-322)

CONVEYOR SYSTEMS: Robotic

Boomerang Systems Inc ....E 973 538-1194
Florham Park (G-3494)
Reliabotics LLC ....G 732 791-5500
New Brunswick (G-7000)
Royal Aquarius Empire ....D 646 847-3322
Hamilton (G-4125)
T O Najarian Associates ....D 732 389-0220
Eatontown (G-2424)

CONVEYORS & CONVEYING EQPT

Aerocon Inc ....D 800 405-2376
Belleville *(G-295)*
Allstate Conveyor Service..........E 856 768-6566
Voorhees *(G-11420)*
Alpha Associates Inc ....E 732 730-1800
Lakewood *(G-5067)*
Automated Flexible Conveyors ....F ... 973 340-1695
Clifton *(G-1569)*
Buhler Inc ....E 201 847-0600
Mahwah *(G-5755)*
Carlisle Machine Works Inc ....E 856 825-0627
Millville *(G-6293)*
Century Conveyor Service Inc ...E 732 248-4900
Edison *(G-2480)*
Conveyors By North American.............G ... 973 777-6600
Clifton *(G-1590)*
Coperion K-Tron Pitman Inc ......F 856 589-0500
Sewell *(G-9947)*
Das Installations Inc ....F 973 473-6858
Garfield *(G-3728)*
Dematic Corp...............................A 908 991-9900
Basking Ridge *(G-184)*
Dyna Veyor Inc ....G 908 276-5384
Newark *(G-7146)*
Equipment Erectors Inc ....E 732 846-1212
Somerset *(G-10097)*
Essex Rise Conveyor Corp ....G 973 575-7483
West Caldwell *(G-11775)*
Flexlink Systems Inc.....................E 973 983-2700
Branchburg *(G-660)*
Flexlink Systems Inc.....................G 908 947-2140
Branchburg *(G-661)*
Flor Lift Of N J Inc ....E 973 429-2200
Fairfield *(G-3197)*
Foremost Machine Builders Inc...........D ... 973 227-0700
Fairfield *(G-3200)*
Form Lectro Inc ....E 973 777-0621
Hackensack *(G-3917)*
Garvey Corporation ....D 609 561-2450
Hammonton *(G-4137)*
Gauer Metal Products Co Inc .....E 908 241-4080
Kenilworth *(G-4958)*
J G Machine Works Inc.................E 732 203-2077
Edison *(G-2543)*
K-Tron International Inc ....E 856 589-0500
Sewell *(G-9962)*
Keneco Inc ....E 908 241-3700
Kenilworth *(G-4967)*
Key Handling Systems Inc ....E 201 933-9333
Moonachie *(G-6528)*
Lynn Mechanical Contractors................F ... 856 829-1717
Cinnaminson *(G-1474)*
Main Robert A & Sons Holdg Co ....E ... 201 447-3700
Wyckoff *(G-12258)*
Metalfab Inc ....E 973 764-2000
Vernon *(G-11299)*
Metalfab Mtl Hdlg Systems LLC ....E ... 973 764-2000
Vernon *(G-11300)*
Pulsonics Inc ....F 800 999-6785
Belleville *(G-313)*
Robotunits Inc ....G 732 438-0500
Cranbury *(G-1877)*
Sandvik Process Systems Inc ....E 973 720-7000
Totowa *(G-10970)*
Sparks Belting Company Inc .....E 973 227-4100
Fairfield *(G-3309)*
Tarlton C & T Co Inc.....................E 908 964-9400
Union *(G-11227)*
TEC Installations Inc...................E 973 684-0503
Paterson *(G-8397)*
Track Systems Inc ....F 201 462-0095
Hasbrouck Heights *(G-4201)*
Traycon Manufacturing Co Inc ...G 201 939-5555
Carlstadt *(G-1233)*
Unex Manufacturing Inc ....D 732 928-2800
Lakewood *(G-5199)*
Vibra Screw Inc ....E 973 256-7410
Totowa *(G-10980)*
W & H Systems Inc ....C 201 933-7840
Fairfield *(G-3347)*

COOKING & FOOD WARMING EQPT: Commercial

Aero Manufacturing Co ....D 973 473-5300
Clifton *(G-1558)*
J & M Air Inc ....E 908 707-4040
Somerville *(G-10217)*

Pinto of Montville Inc ....G 973 584-2002
Kenvil *(G-5012)*
Power Container Corp ....E 732 560-3655
Somerset *(G-10156)*
Rlct Industries LLC ....G 609 712-1318
Pennington *(G-8458)*

COOKING & FOODWARMING EQPT: Commercial

Hickory Industries Inc ....E 201 223-4382
North Bergen *(G-7456)*

COOKING EQPT, HOUSEHOLD: Indoor

Chefman Direct Inc ....E 888 315-8407
Mahwah *(G-5758)*

COOLING TOWERS: Metal

Delta Cooling Towers Inc ....G 973 586-2201
Flanders *(G-3404)*
SPX Cooling Technologies Inc ....G ... 908 450-8027
Bridgewater *(G-898)*

COOLING TOWERS: Wood

Amertech Towerservices LLC..............E ... 732 389-2200
Shrewsbury *(G-9989)*
Atlantic Coolg Tech & Svcs LLC ....E ... 201 939-0900
Carlstadt *(G-1129)*

COPPER ORES

Freeport-Mcmoran Inc ....G 908 558-4361
Elizabeth *(G-2735)*

COPPER: Rolling & Drawing

Belden Inc ....F 908 925-8000
Elizabeth *(G-2712)*
Fisk Alloy Inc ....G 973 427-7550
Hawthorne *(G-4234)*
Fisk Alloy Wire Incorporated ......C 973 949-4491
Hawthorne *(G-4235)*
Freeport Minerals Corporation ....D ... 908 351-3200
Elizabeth *(G-2734)*
Gulf Cable LLC ....C 201 242-9906
Hasbrouck Heights *(G-4193)*
Heyco Products Corp ....G 732 286-1800
Toms River *(G-10885)*
National Electric Wire Co Inc .....E 609 758-3600
Cream Ridge *(G-1938)*

CORES: Fiber, Made From Purchased Materials

JRC Web Accessories ....F 973 625-3888
Fairfield *(G-3238)*

CORES: Magnetic

Bel Fuse Inc ....C 201 432-0463
Jersey City *(G-4715)*
KG Squared LLC ....F 973 627-0643
Rockaway *(G-9581)*
Lakeland Transformer Corp ....G 973 835-0818
Haskell *(G-4209)*
Magnetics & Controls Inc ....F 609 397-8203
Rosemont *(G-9705)*
Thomson Lamination Co Inc........D 856 779-8521
Maple Shade *(G-5912)*

CORK & CORK PRDTS

AMP Custom Rubber Inc ....F 732 888-2714
Keyport *(G-5015)*

CORK & CORK PRDTS: Tiles

Best Value Rugs & Carpets Inc............G ... 732 752-3528
Dunellen *(G-2127)*
Contempocork LLC.......................G 201 262-7738
River Edge *(G-9464)*
Denby USA Limited ....G 800 374-6479
Bridgewater *(G-833)*

CORRUGATED PRDTS: Boxes, Partition, Display Items, Sheet/Pad

Graphcorr LLC ....F 732 355-0088
Dayton *(G-1967)*

Rectico Inc ....F 973 575-0009
Fairfield *(G-3290)*

CORRUGATING MACHINES

Alpine Corrugated McHy Inc ......G 201 440-3030
Ridgefield Park *(G-9397)*

COSMETIC PREPARATIONS

A D M Tronics Unlimited Inc ....E ... 201 767-6040
Northvale *(G-7566)*
Acupac Packaging Inc..................C 201 529-3434
Mahwah *(G-5743)*
Anatolian Naturals Inc ....G 201 893-0142
Fort Lee *(G-3544)*
AP Deauville LLC ....E 732 545-0200
New Brunswick *(G-6945)*
Ariel Laboratories LP ....G 908 755-4080
South Plainfield *(G-10331)*
Avon Products Inc ....G 973 779-5590
Clifton *(G-1570)*
Barmensen Labs LLC ....G 732 593-3515
Old Bridge *(G-7774)*
Beilis Development LLC ....F 862 203-3650
Fair Lawn *(G-3082)*
Bentley Laboratories LLC ....C 732 512-0200
Edison *(G-2472)*
Biogenesis Inc ....F 201 678-1992
Hackensack *(G-3882)*
Caolion BNC Co Ltd ....C 201 641-4709
Ridgefield Park *(G-9399)*
Carole Cosmetics LLC ....E 973 283-2893
Butler *(G-1000)*
CCA Industries Inc ....E 201 935-3232
Lyndhurst *(G-5676)*
Chanel Inc ....A 732 885-5500
Piscataway *(G-8748)*
Chemaid Laboratories Inc ....C 201 843-3300
Saddle Brook *(G-9758)*
Christine Valmy Inc ....E 973 575-1050
Pine Brook *(G-8693)*
Cococare Products Inc ....E 973 989-8880
Dover *(G-2081)*
Cosmetic Coatings Inc ....E 201 438-7150
Carlstadt *(G-1150)*
Cosmetic Concepts Inc ....C 973 546-1234
Garfield *(G-3727)*
Cosmetic Essence LLC ....C 732 888-7788
Holmdel *(G-4512)*
Cosmetic Essence LLC ....D 201 941-9800
Ridgefield *(G-9357)*
Cosrich Group Inc ....E 866 771-7473
Bloomfield *(G-509)*
Davion Inc ....E 973 485-0793
North Brunswick *(G-7514)*
Davlyn Industries Inc ....G 609 655-5974
East Windsor *(G-2356)*
Encore International LLC ....F 973 423-3880
Hawthorne *(G-4231)*
ET Browne Drug Co Inc ....D 201 894-9020
Englewood Cliffs *(G-2959)*
Fragrance Resources Inc ....F 973 777-2979
Hazlet *(G-4274)*
Gallant Laboratories Inc ....G 609 654-4146
Marlton *(G-5976)*
Gel Concepts LLC ....E 973 884-8995
Whippany *(G-12022)*
Givaudan Fragrances Corp ....C 973 448-6500
Budd Lake *(G-930)*
Grow Company Inc ....E 201 941-8777
Ridgefield *(G-9363)*
Hudson Cosmetic Mfg Corp.........D 973 472-2323
Clifton *(G-1644)*
Imperial Dax Co Inc.....................E 973 227-6105
Fairfield *(G-3226)*
Innovative Cosmtc Concepts LLC........F ... 212 391-8110
Edison *(G-2541)*
Innovative Cosmtc Concepts LLC........D ... 973 225-0264
Clifton *(G-1647)*
Intarome Fragrance Corporation.........D ... 201 767-8700
Norwood *(G-7625)*
Interfashion Cosmetics Corp ......E 201 288-5858
Teterboro *(G-10799)*
June Jacobs Labs LLC ....G 201 329-9100
Moonachie *(G-6526)*
Kobo Products Inc ....E 908 941-3406
South Plainfield *(G-10394)*
Kobo Products Inc ....E 908 757-0033
South Plainfield *(G-10395)*
Kobo Products Inc ....E 908 757-0033
South Plainfield *(G-10393)*

Employee Codes: A=Over 500 employees, B=251-500
C=101-250, D=51-100, E=20-50, F=10-19, G=4-9

2018 Harris New jersey
Manufacturers Directory

841

PRODUCT

Lippman Enterprises LLC ....E 732 316-4946
Sayreville *(G-9829)*

New York Botany Inc ....E 201 564-7444
Northvale *(G-7597)*

Nu-World Corporation ....C 732 541-6300
Carteret *(G-1264)*

Nu-World Corporation ....G 732 541-6300
Edison *(G-2586)*

Omega Packaging Corp ....D 973 890-9505
Totowa *(G-10959)*

Organics Corporation America ....E 973 890-9002
Totowa *(G-10960)*

Pantina Cosmetics Inc ....E 201 288-7767
Teterboro *(G-10808)*

Paramount Cosmetics Inc ....D 973 472-2323
Clifton *(G-1690)*

Peter Thomas Roth Labs LLC ....E 201 329-9100
Saddle Brook *(G-9782)*

Pfizer Inc ....E 973 739-0430
Parsippany *(G-8061)*

Precious Cosmetics Packaging..............F 973 478-4633
Lodi *(G-5597)*

Premier Specialties Inc ....F 732 469-6615
Middlesex *(G-6190)*

Presperse Corporation ....E 732 356-5200
Somerset *(G-10157)*

Promeko Inc ....G 201 861-9446
West New York *(G-11878)*

Quality Cosmetics Mfg ....E 908 755-9588
South Plainfield *(G-10427)*

Revlon Consumer Products Corp ....D 732 287-1400
Edison *(G-2606)*

Rossow Cosmetiques - Usa Inc.............G 732 872-1464
Matawan *(G-6031)*

Royal Cosmetics Corporation ....F 732 246-7275
New Brunswick *(G-7002)*

Rubigo Cosmetics ....G 973 636-6573
Little Falls *(G-5487)*

Sarkli-Repechage Ltd ....D 201 549-4200
Secaucus *(G-9921)*

SGB Packaging Group Inc ....E 201 488-3030
Hackensack *(G-3973)*

Shiseido America Inc ....D 609 371-5800
East Windsor *(G-2366)*

Shiseido Americas Corporation ....D 609 371-5800
East Windsor *(G-2367)*

Sozio Inc ....D 732 572-5600
Piscataway *(G-8814)*

Suite K Value Added Svcs LLC ....F 732 590-0647
Edison *(G-2629)*

Suite K Value Added Svcs LLC ....F 609 655-6890
Edison *(G-2630)*

Suite K Value Added Svcs LLC ....D 609 655-6890
Edison *(G-2631)*

World Wide Packaging LLC ....D 973 805-6500
Florham Park *(G-3524)*

COSMETICS & TOILETRIES

ABG Lab LLC ....G 973 559-5663
Fair Lawn *(G-3073)*

Adorage Inc ....G 201 886-7000
Edgewater *(G-2431)*

Adron Inc ....E 973 334-1600
Boonton *(G-551)*

AlSha&anna Nation of Trends ....G 201 951-8197
Rahway *(G-9173)*

American Spraytech LLC ....E 908 725-6060
Branchburg *(G-634)*

Andrea Aromatics Inc ....E 609 695-7710
Trenton *(G-11018)*

Armkel LLC ....A 609 683-5900
Princeton *(G-9010)*

Art of Shaving - Fl LLC ....G 732 410-2520
Freehold *(G-3639)*

Bellwood Aeromatics Inc ....G 201 670-4617
Fairfield *(G-3145)*

Bio-Nature Labs Ltd Lblty Co ....E 732 738-5550
Edison *(G-2474)*

Bristol-Myers Squibb Company ....E 212 546-4000
Hillside *(G-4399)*

Caret Corporation ....G 973 423-5999
Little Falls *(G-5472)*

Cei Holdings Inc ....E 732 888-7788
Holmdel *(G-4511)*

Conair Corporation ....C 609 426-1300
East Windsor *(G-2354)*

Conopco Inc ....E 856 722-1664
Mount Laurel *(G-6790)*

Contract Filling Inc ....C 973 433-0053
Cedar Grove *(G-1275)*

Cosmetic Essence Inc ....E 732 888-7788
Holmdel *(G-4513)*

Custom Liners Inc ....G 732 940-0084
Upper Saddle River *(G-11277)*

Devon Products ....G 732 438-3855
Pompton Plains *(G-8957)*

Disposable Hygiene LLC ....G 973 779-1982
Clifton *(G-1601)*

Drom International Inc ....E 973 316-8400
Towaco *(G-10994)*

Ebin New York Inc ....E 201 288-8887
Teterboro *(G-10794)*

Edgewell Personal Care LLC ....E 201 785-8000
Allendale *(G-9)*

Englewood Lab LLC ....C 201 567-2267
Englewood *(G-2891)*

Flavor & Fragrance Spc Inc ....D 201 828-9400
Mahwah *(G-5773)*

Fragrance Resources Inc ....D 973 458-5231
Keyport *(G-5018)*

Gentek Inc ....C 973 515-0900
Parsippany *(G-8024)*

Hy-Test Packaging Corp ....C 973 754-7000
Paterson *(G-8291)*

Imaan Trading Inc ....E 201 779-2062
Jersey City *(G-4767)*

Inter Parfums Inc ....E 609 860-1967
Dayton *(G-1971)*

International Beauty Products ....F 973 575-6400
Pine Brook *(G-8707)*

Interntnal Flvors Frgrnces Inc ....C 732 264-4500
Union Beach *(G-11236)*

Interntnal Flvors Frgrnces Inc ....C 732 264-4500
Hazlet *(G-4276)*

Interntonal Fragrance Tech Inc ....E 770 345-3079
Piscataway *(G-8783)*

Isp Chemicals LLC ....E 973 635-1551
Chatham *(G-1330)*

Jersey Shore Cosmetics LLC ....F 908 500-9954
Flemington *(G-3451)*

Jnj International Inv LLC ....G 732 524-0400
New Brunswick *(G-6973)*

Johnson & Johnson ....D 732 422-5000
North Brunswick *(G-7522)*

Johnson & Johnson ....A 732 524-0400
New Brunswick *(G-6974)*

Johnson & Johnson ....C 908 722-9319
Raritan *(G-9311)*

Johnson & Johnson ....C 908 874-1000
Morris Plains *(G-6673)*

Johnson & Johnson ....C 732 524-0400
New Brunswick *(G-6975)*

Lvmh Fragrance Brands US LLC............G 212 931-2668
Edison *(G-2561)*

Medallion International Inc......................F 973 616-3401
Pompton Plains *(G-8962)*

Mid Ocean Partners ....D 908 707-0100
Branchburg *(G-681)*

Mycone Dental Supply Co Inc ....C 856 663-4700
Gibbstown *(G-3792)*

Nellsam Group Inc ....G 201 951-9459
Cliffside Park *(G-1543)*

New Manna Inc ....G 973 675-8561
East Orange *(G-2261)*

New World International Inc....................F 973 881-8100
Paterson *(G-8350)*

Nmr Manufacturing LLC ....G 908 769-3234
South Plainfield *(G-10413)*

Premier Consumer Products Inc ....G 201 568-9700
Englewood *(G-2923)*

Quest Intl Flvors Frgrnces Inc ....B 973 576-9500
East Hanover *(G-2240)*

Regi US Inc ....G 862 702-3901
West Caldwell *(G-11802)*

Revlon Inc ....E 732 287-1400
Edison *(G-2605)*

Robertet Inc ....E 201 337-7100
Budd Lake *(G-939)*

Saturn Beauty Group LLC ....G 908 561-5000
Piscataway *(G-8807)*

Siloa Inc ....G 908 234-9040
Bedminster *(G-284)*

Sunrise Glamour LLC ....G 800 960-2426
Iselin *(G-4646)*

Topaz Skin Care Inc ....G 201 489-0686
Fort Lee *(G-3585)*

Topifram Laboratories Inc......................E 201 894-9020
Englewood Cliffs *(G-2982)*

Unilever United States Inc.....................A 201 894-4000
Englewood Cliffs *(G-2986)*

COSMETICS WHOLESALERS

AJ Siris Products Corp...........................E 973 823-0050
Ogdensburg *(G-7769)*

Kobo Products Inc ....E 908 757-0033
South Plainfield *(G-10393)*

New York Botany Inc ....E 201 564-7444
Northvale *(G-7597)*

Precious Cosmetics Packaging...............F 973 478-4633
Lodi *(G-5597)*

Reviva Labs Inc ....E 856 428-3885
Haddonfield *(G-4064)*

Rubigo Cosmetics ....G 973 636-6573
Little Falls *(G-5487)*

Shiseido America Inc ....D 609 371-5800
East Windsor *(G-2366)*

COSMETOLOGY & PERSONAL HYGIENE SALONS

Clean-Tex Services Inc ....B 908 912-2700
Trenton *(G-11042)*

COSMETOLOGY SCHOOL

Christine Valmy Inc ....E 973 575-1050
Pine Brook *(G-8693)*

COSTUME JEWELRY & NOVELTIES: Apparel, Exc Precious Metals

C & C Metal Products Corp ....D 201 569-7300
Englewood *(G-2880)*

Meeshaa Inc ....G 908 279-7985
Edison *(G-2567)*

Scaasis Originals Inc ....E 732 775-7474
Neptune *(G-6928)*

COSTUME JEWELRY & NOVELTIES: Exc Semi & Precious

A To Z Bohemian Glass Inc ....E 212 725-2033
Paterson *(G-8194)*

Alster Import Co Inc...............................F 201 332-7245
Jersey City *(G-4704)*

Ammosa Enterprises Inc........................E 212 779-2890
Mahwah *(G-5748)*

San Marel Designs Inc..........................G 973 426-9554
Budd Lake *(G-942)*

Superior Jewelry Co ....F 215 677-8100
Northfield *(G-7564)*

COUNTER & SINK TOPS

A1 Custom Countertops Inc ....F 856 200-3596
Woodstown *(G-12237)*

Bernard Miller Fabricators ....G 856 541-9499
Camden *(G-1043)*

Countertops Plus Inc ....F 973 365-2232
Passaic *(G-8131)*

Custom Counters By Precision ....E 973 773-0111
Passaic *(G-8133)*

Marvic Corp ....E 908 686-4340
Union *(G-11206)*

Masco Cabinetry LLC ....C 732 363-3797
Lakewood *(G-5153)*

Masco Cabinetry LLC ....C 732 942-5138
Lakewood *(G-5154)*

Quality Solid Surface Inc.......................G 973 772-8600
Garfield *(G-3755)*

South Jersey Countertop Co ....G 856 768-7960
West Berlin *(G-11750)*

COUNTERS & COUNTER DISPLAY CASES: Refrigerated

Specialty Fabricators LLC......................E 609 758-6995
Wrightstown *(G-12243)*

COUNTERS & COUNTING DEVICES

Chem Flowtronic Inc..............................G 973 785-0001
Little Falls *(G-5474)*

Instru-Met Corporation ....G 908 851-0700
Union *(G-11195)*

Octal Corporation ....E 201 862-1010
Teaneck *(G-10764)*

(G-0000) Company's Geographic Section entry number

COUNTERS OR COUNTER DISPLAY CASES, EXC WOOD

Minerva Custom Products LLC ....G....... 201 447-4731
  Waldwick (G-11449)
Richard J Bell Co Inc ....F 201 847-0887
  Wyckoff (G-12262)

COUNTERS OR COUNTER DISPLAY CASES, WOOD

A W Ross Inc ....F 973 471-5900
  Passaic (G-8123)
Counter Efx Inc ....G....... 908 203-0155
  Hillsborough (G-4326)
Garley Inc..G....... 215 788-5756
  Burlington (G-976)
Millner Kitchens Inc ....G....... 609 890-7300
  Trenton (G-11081)
Wagner Rack Inc ....E 973 278-6966
  Clifton (G-1741)

COUNTING DEVICES: Controls, Revolution & Timing

Ellis/Kuhnke Controls Inc ....G....... 732 291-3334
  Eatontown (G-2393)
Heat-Timer Corporation.......................E 212 481-2020
  Fairfield (G-3219)
Kessler-Ellis Products Co ....D....... 732 935-1320
  Eatontown (G-2410)

COUNTING DEVICES: Gauges, Press Temp Corrections Computing

Chemiquip Products Co Inc..................G....... 201 868-4445
  Linden (G-5359)

COUNTING DEVICES: Pedometers

Kel Instruments Co Inc.........................G....... 201 847-8353
  Wyckoff (G-12255)

COUPLINGS: Hose & Tube, Hydraulic Or Pneumatic

Industrial Hydraulics & Rubber ....G....... 856 966-2600
  Camden (G-1070)
Novaflex Industries Inc........................F 856 768-2275
  West Berlin (G-11739)

COUPLINGS: Pipe

Precision Mfg Group LLC......................D....... 973 785-4630
  Cedar Grove (G-1296)

COUPON REDEMPTION SVCS

S L Enterprises Inc ....G....... 908 272-8145
  Ewing (G-3054)

COURIER OR MESSENGER SVCS

Skinder-Strauss LLC ....E 973 642-1440
  New Providence (G-7054)

COURIER SVCS, AIR: Letter Delivery, Private

Sre Ventures LLC.................................G....... 973 785-0099
  Little Falls (G-5489)

COURIER SVCS: Ground

Parker Publications ....F 908 766-3900
  Madison (G-5730)

COURIER SVCS: Package By Vehicle

Sre Ventures LLC.................................G....... 973 785-0099
  Little Falls (G-5489)

COVERS & PADS Chair, Made From Purchased Materials

Drake Corp..G....... 732 254-1530
  East Brunswick (G-2145)

COVERS: Automobile Seat

Atlas Auto Trim Inc ....G....... 732 985-6800
  Edison (G-2468)
Elegant USA LLC ....D....... 973 812-8820
  Totowa (G-10943)

COVERS: Canvas

Harold F Fisher & Sons Inc ....G....... 800 624-2868
  Delanco (G-2006)

COVERS: Hot Tub & Spa

Cover Co Inc ....E 908 707-9797
  Branchburg (G-651)
Merlin Industries Inc ....D....... 609 807-1000
  Hamilton (G-4117)

CRADLES: Drum

Meto Corp ....F 201 405-0311
  Parsippany (G-8046)
Meto Lift Inc ....F 201 405-0311
  Parsippany (G-8047)

CRANES: Indl Plant

Holtec Government Services LLC ....G....... 856 291-0600
  Marlton (G-5978)
Pcs Crane Services Inc ....F 201 366-4250
  Fairview (G-3368)

CRANKSHAFTS & CAMSHAFTS: Machining

STS Technologies LLC ....F 973 277-5416
  Mahwah (G-5817)

CREATIVE SVCS: Advertisers, Exc Writers

Red Feather Mktg Group LLC ....F 973 377-1988
  Madison (G-5732)

CREDIT BUREAUS

AM Best Company Inc ....A 908 439-2200
  Oldwick (G-7803)
G-III Leather Fashions Inc ....D....... 212 403-0500
  Dayton (G-1966)

CRUCIBLES

Bartley Crucible Refractories ....F 609 393-0066
  Trenton (G-11025)

CRUDE PETROLEUM & NATURAL GAS PRODUCTION

Associated Asphalt Mktg LLC ....E 210 249-9988
  West Deptford (G-11817)
MRC Global (us) Inc ....F 732 225-4005
  East Brunswick (G-2168)
Petro Inc...G....... 877 745-7687
  South Plainfield (G-10420)
Phoenix National Petroleum Co ....G....... 201 568-5568
  Cresskill (G-1947)
Zenith Energy US LP ....G....... 732 515-7410
  Metuchen (G-6135)

CRUDE PETROLEUM PRODUCTION

JM Huber Corporation ....D....... 732 603-3630
  Edison (G-2546)
Speedway LLC ....B....... 732 750-7800
  Port Reading (G-8990)

CRYSTALS

Coherent Inc ....D....... 973 240-6851
  East Hanover (G-2207)
Crystal Deltronic Industries ....E 973 328-6898
  Dover (G-2082)
Epcos Inc ....D....... 732 906-4300
  Iselin (G-4626)
Epcos Inc ....F 732 603-5941
  Lumberton (G-5657)

CUPS & PLATES: Foamed Plastics

Plastico Products LLC..........................G....... 973 923-1944
  Irvington (G-4600)

CUPS: Paper, Made From Purchased Materials

Prospect Group LLC.............................F 718 635-4007
  Piscataway (G-8803)
Round Cups LLC...................................G....... 732 734-0244
  Linden (G-5435)

CURBING: Granite Or Stone

A C D Custom Granite Inc ....F 732 695-2400
  Ocean (G-7711)

CURTAIN & DRAPERY FIXTURES: Poles, Rods & Rollers

A N Laggren Awngs Canvas Mfg...........F 908 756-1948
  Plainfield (G-8852)
Acme Drapemaster America Inc............G....... 732 512-0613
  Edison (G-2449)
Erco Ceilings Somers Point Inc............E 609 517-2531
  Somers Point (G-10046)
Glasscare Inc.......................................F 201 943-1122
  Cliffside Park (G-1540)
Nassaus Window Fashions Inc ....E 201 689-6030
  Paramus (G-7893)
Newell Brands Inc ....B....... 201 610-6600
  Hoboken (G-4486)
SF Lutz LLC ....G....... 609 646-9490
  Egg Harbor Township (G-2696)
Shade Powers Co Inc ....F 201 767-3727
  Northvale (G-7607)

CURTAINS & BEDDING: Knit

D Kwitman & Son Inc ....G....... 201 798-5511
  Hoboken (G-4468)
Hampton Industries Inc ....E 973 574-8900
  Passaic (G-8146)

CURTAINS: Knit

Curtain Care Plus Inc ....G....... 800 845-6155
  Clifton (G-1595)

CURTAINS: Shower

Royal Crest Home Fashions Inc ....D....... 201 461-4600
  Palisades Park (G-7843)

CURTAINS: Window, From Purchased Materials

Beltor Manufacturing Corp ....G....... 856 768-5570
  Berlin (G-426)
Best Linen Factory Inc ....F 973 279-8244
  Paterson (G-8223)
Bloomfield Drapery Co Inc....................F 973 777-3566
  East Rutherford (G-2287)
D Kwitman & Son Inc ....F 201 798-5511
  Hoboken (G-4467)
Drapery & More Inc ....G....... 201 271-9661
  North Bergen (G-7447)
Franks Upholstery & Draperies ....G....... 856 779-8585
  Maple Shade (G-5902)
Iweiss Inc ....E 201 402-6500
  Fairview (G-3362)

CUSHIONS & PILLOWS

AMS Toy Intl Inc ....E 973 442-5790
  Wharton (G-11979)
Innocor Inc..C....... 732 945-6222
  Red Bank (G-9331)
Innocor Foam Tech - Acp Inc................D....... 732 945-6222
  Red Bank (G-9332)
Kas Oriental Rugs Inc..........................E 732 545-1900
  Somerset (G-10118)
Orient Originals Inc.............................E 201 332-5005
  Jersey City (G-4796)
Pegasus Home Fashions Inc ....D....... 908 965-1919
  Elizabeth (G-2766)
Redhawk Distribution Inc ....F 516 884-9911
  Pennsauken (G-8571)

CUSHIONS & PILLOWS: Bed, From Purchased Materials

American Dawn Inc ....G....... 856 467-9211
  Bridgeport (G-761)
AMS Products LLC ....F 973 442-5790
  Wharton (G-11978)
Phoenix Down Corporation....................C....... 973 812-8100
  Totowa (G-10963)

CUSHIONS: Textile, Exc Spring & Carpet

American Dawn Inc ....G....... 856 467-9211
  Bridgeport (G-761)

PRODUCT

CUT STONE & STONE PRODUCTS

Atlas Marble & Granite LLC ....F...... 973 491-5454
Springfield (G-10539)
Charles Deluca ....G...... 973 778-5621
Lodi (G-5579)
Counter-Fit Inc ....C...... 609 871-8888
Willingboro (G-12118)
Elana Tile Contractors Inc ....G...... 973 386-0991
East Hanover (G-2215)
Elite Stone Importers LLC ....G...... 732 542-7900
Tinton Falls (G-10836)
EZ General Construction Corp ....G...... 201 223-1101
Wayne (G-11631)
Granite and Marble Assoc Inc ....G...... 908 416-1100
North Plainfield (G-7559)
H T Hall Inc ....F...... 732 449-3441
Spring Lake (G-10533)
Hanson Aggregates Wrp Inc ....E...... 972 653-5500
Wall Township (G-11487)
Industrial Consulting Mktg Inc ....E...... 973 427-2474
Fair Lawn (G-3096)
Innovative Cutng Concepts LLC ....G...... 609 484-9960
Egg Harbor Township (G-2685)
Marvic Corp ....E...... 908 686-4340
Union (G-11206)
Robert Young & Sons Inc ....G...... 973 483-0451
Newark (G-7291)
Sculptured Stone Inc ....F...... 973 557-1482
Boonton (G-583)
Stone Mar Natural Stone Co LLC ....G...... 856 988-1802
Marlton (G-6000)
Thin Stone Systems LLC ....G...... 973 882-7377
Fairfield (G-3325)

CUTLERY, STAINLESS STEEL

Hampton Forge Ltd ....E...... 877 935-2892
Eatontown (G-2399)

CUTOUTS: Distribution

Cutting Board Company ....G...... 908 725-0187
Lebanon (G-5283)
Cutting Board Company ....G...... 908 725-0187
Branchburg (G-655)

CUTTING SVC: Paper, Exc Die-Cut

American Bindery Depot Inc ....C...... 732 287-2370
Edison (G-2457)

CYCLIC CRUDES & INTERMEDIATES

Chem-Is-Try Inc ....G...... 732 372-7311
Metuchen (G-6100)
Chemical Resources Inc ....E...... 609 520-0000
Princeton (G-9021)
Elementis Specialties Inc ....C...... 609 443-2000
East Windsor (G-2374)
Ferro Corporation ....C...... 856 467-3000
Bridgeport (G-765)
Manner Textile Processing Inc ....D...... 973 942-8718
North Haledon (G-7550)
Novartis Corporation ....E...... 212 307-1122
East Hanover (G-2232)
Royce Associates A Ltd Partnr ....E...... 973 279-0400
Paterson (G-8372)

CYLINDER & ACTUATORS: Fluid Power

GE Aviation Systems LLC ....C...... 973 428-9898
Whippany (G-12021)
Industrial Habonim Valves & AC ....F...... 201 820-3184
Wayne (G-11650)
Motion Systems Corp ....D...... 732 389-1600
Eatontown (G-2414)
Van Hydraulics Inc ....E...... 732 442-5500
South Plainfield (G-10448)

CYLINDERS: Pressure

E F Britten & Co Inc ....F...... 908 276-4800
Cranford (G-1904)
Main Robert A & Sons Holdg Co ....E...... 201 447-3700
Wyckoff (G-12258)

CYLINDERS: Pump

Delta Sales Company Inc ....F...... 973 838-0371
Butler (G-1002)

DAIRY PRDTS STORE: Cheese

Vitamia Pasta Boy Inc ....F...... 973 546-1140
Lodi (G-5608)

DAIRY PRDTS STORE: Ice Cream, Packaged

Magliones Italian Ices LLC ....F...... 732 283-0705
Iselin (G-4631)

DAIRY PRDTS STORES

Halo Farm Inc ....G...... 609 695-3311
Lawrenceville (G-5257)

DAIRY PRDTS WHOLESALERS: Fresh

Finlandia Cheese Inc ....E...... 973 316-6699
Parsippany (G-8012)
Schratter Foods Incorporated ....G...... 973 575-3226
Moonachie (G-6541)

DAIRY PRDTS: Butter

Cookman Creamery LLC ....G...... 732 361-5215
Brielle (G-911)

DAIRY PRDTS: Cheese

Arthur Schuman Inc ....D...... 973 227-0030
Fairfield (G-3139)
Capital Foods Inc ....E...... 908 587-9050
Linden (G-5355)
Lioni Latticini Inc ....D...... 908 686-6061
Union (G-11202)
Lotito Foods Inc ....F...... 973 684-2900
Paterson (G-8326)
Mendez Dairy Co Inc ....D...... 732 442-6337
Perth Amboy (G-8623)
Saporito Inc ....G...... 201 265-8212
Ridgefield (G-9384)
Schratter Foods Incorporated ....G...... 973 575-3226
Moonachie (G-6541)
South American Imports Corp ....G...... 201 941-2020
Cliffside Park (G-1545)
Tipico Products Co Inc ....D...... 732 942-8820
Lakewood (G-5195)

DAIRY PRDTS: Dairy Based Desserts, Frozen

Angelos Italian Ices Icecream ....G...... 201 962-7575
Ramsey (G-9233)
Best of Farms LLC ....G...... 201 512-8400
Fair Lawn (G-3083)
Bindi North America Inc ....E...... 973 812-8118
Kearny (G-4865)
Elegant Desserts Inc ....F...... 201 933-7309
Lyndhurst (G-5679)
Rw Delights Inc ....G...... 718 683-1038
Millington (G-6261)

DAIRY PRDTS: Dietary Supplements, Dairy & Non-Dairy Based

Allegro Nutrition Inc ....E...... 732 364-3777
Neptune (G-6899)
Amish Dairy Products LLC ....G...... 973 256-7676
Totowa (G-10930)
Body Boost Labs Ltd Lblty Co ....F...... 609 519-1070
Laurel Springs (G-5232)
Farbest-Tallman Foods Corp ....D...... 714 897-7199
Park Ridge (G-7919)
Food Sciences Corp ....C...... 856 778-4192
Mount Laurel (G-6798)
Gold Star Distribution LLC ....F...... 973 882-5300
East Hanover (G-2223)
Grow Company Inc ....E...... 201 941-8777
Ridgefield (G-9363)
Horphag Research (usa) Inc ....G...... 201 459-0300
Hoboken (G-4475)
Icelandirect Inc ....F...... 800 763-4690
Clifton (G-1645)
Jersey Ordnance Inc ....G...... 609 267-2112
Westampton (G-11913)
Lycored Corp ....G...... 973 882-0322
Orange (G-7821)
Nutri Sport Pharmacal Inc ....G...... 973 827-9287
Franklin (G-3604)
Orcas International Inc ....F...... 973 448-2801
Landing (G-5225)
Syncom Pharmaceuticals Inc ....E...... 973 787-2405
Fairfield (G-3318)

Unique Encapsulation Tech LLC ....E...... 973 448-2801
Landing (G-5228)
V E N Inc ....C...... 973 786-7862
Andover (G-55)

DAIRY PRDTS: Dips & Spreads, Cheese Based

Cognati Cheese Company Inc ....E...... 201 807-9100
Moonachie (G-6513)
Lioni Mozzarella & Specialty ....E...... 908 624-9450
Union (G-11203)
Saputo Cheese USA Inc ....E...... 201 508-6400
Carlstadt (G-1213)

DAIRY PRDTS: Dried & Powdered Milk & Milk Prdts

Arla Foods Ingredients N Amer ....F...... 908 604-8551
Basking Ridge (G-180)

DAIRY PRDTS: Evaporated Milk

Nestle Usa Inc ....C...... 973 390-9555
Keasbey (G-4929)

DAIRY PRDTS: Farmers' Cheese

Georges Wine and Spirits Galle ....G...... 973 948-9950
Branchville (G-730)

DAIRY PRDTS: Frozen Desserts & Novelties

Applegate Farm Homemade Ice Cr ....F...... 973 744-5900
Montclair (G-6406)
Country Club Ice Cream ....G...... 973 729-5570
Sparta (G-10494)
Cumberland Dairy Inc ....E...... 856 451-1300
Bridgeton (G-783)
Dairy Queen ....F...... 732 892-5700
Point Pleasant Boro (G-8937)
Evereast Trading Inc ....G...... 201 944-6484
Fort Lee (G-3553)
Gelotti Confections LLC ....G...... 973 403-9968
Caldwell (G-1029)
Guernsey Crest Ice Cream Co ....G...... 973 742-4620
Paterson (G-8285)
Heavenly Havens Creamery LLC ....G...... 609 259-6600
Allentown (G-31)
Kwality Foods Ltd Liability Co ....G...... 732 906-1941
Edison (G-2554)
Leos Ice Cream Company ....G...... 856 797-8771
Medford (G-6076)
Magliones Italian Ices LLC ....F...... 732 283-0705
Iselin (G-4631)
Marks Ice Cream ....G...... 201 861-5099
North Bergen (G-7463)
Mr Green Tea Ice Cream Corp ....E...... 732 446-9800
Keyport (G-5021)
Mr Green Tea Ice Cream Corp ....F...... 732 446-9800
Keyport (G-5022)
Piemonte & Liebhauser LLC ....F...... 973 937-6200
Florham Park (G-3514)
Rajbhog Foods(nj) Inc ....C...... 551 222-4700
Jersey City (G-4814)
Rolo Systems ....E...... 973 627-4214
Denville (G-2056)
Sweet Delight ....F...... 732 263-9100
Oakhurst (G-7673)
Tjs Ice Cream ....G...... 609 398-5055
Ocean City (G-7759)
Unilever United States Inc ....A...... 201 894-4000
Englewood Cliffs (G-2986)

DAIRY PRDTS: Ice Cream & Ice Milk

Agape Inc ....F...... 973 923-7625
Irvington (G-4570)

DAIRY PRDTS: Ice Cream, Bulk

Alpine Creamery ....G...... 973 726-0777
Sparta (G-10487)
Arctic Products Co Inc ....F...... 609 393-4264
Ewing (G-3004)
Bergenline Gelato LLC ....G...... 201 861-1100
North Bergen (G-7435)
Bertolotti LLC ....F...... 201 941-3116
Fairview (G-3358)
Cielito Lindo ....G...... 580 286-1127
New Brunswick (G-6952)

Confectionately Yours LLC ....E 732 821-6863
Franklin Park *(G-3626)*
Dunkin Donuts Baskin Robbins ....G 201 692-1900
Teaneck *(G-10750)*
Halo Pub Ice Cream ....F 609 921-1710
Princeton *(G-9052)*
Halo Pub Inc ....F 609 586-1811
Trenton *(G-11062)*
Mister Cookie Face Inc ....C 732 370-5533
Lakewood *(G-5161)*
Sweet Orange LLC ....G 908 522-0011
Summit *(G-10662)*
Talenti Gelato LLC ....E 800 298-4020
Englewood Cliffs *(G-2980)*
Uncle Eds Creamery ....G 609 818-0100
Pennington *(G-8462)*

DAIRY PRDTS: Ice Cream, Packaged, Molded, On Sticks, Etc.

Conopco Inc ....C 920 499-2509
Englewood Cliffs *(G-2955)*
Mars Incorporated ....F 973 691-3500
Budd Lake *(G-936)*

DAIRY PRDTS: Ice milk, Bulk

Deep Foods Inc ....C 908 810-7500
Union *(G-11171)*

DAIRY PRDTS: Imitation Cheese

Mondelez International Inc ....E 973 503-2000
East Hanover *(G-2228)*

DAIRY PRDTS: Milk Preparations, Dried

American Casein Company ....E 609 387-2988
Burlington *(G-954)*

DAIRY PRDTS: Milk, Chocolate

Yamate Chocolatier Inc ....G 732 249-4847
Highland Park *(G-4306)*

DAIRY PRDTS: Milk, Condensed & Evaporated

American Custom Drying Co ....E 609 387-3933
Burlington *(G-955)*
Dairy Delight LLC ....F 201 939-7878
Rutherford *(G-9729)*
Kerry Inc ....D 201 373-1111
Teterboro *(G-10804)*
Robertet Flavors Inc ....F 732 271-1804
Piscataway *(G-8806)*

DAIRY PRDTS: Milk, Fluid

Wwf Operating Company ....F 856 459-3890
Bridgeton *(G-805)*

DAIRY PRDTS: Milk, Processed, Pasteurized, Homogenized/Btld

Cumberland Dairy Inc ....E 856 451-1300
Bridgeton *(G-783)*
Garelick Farms LLC ....C 609 499-2600
Burlington *(G-975)*
Halo Farm Inc ....G 609 695-3311
Lawrenceville *(G-5257)*
Midland Farms Inc ....E 800 749-6455
Paterson *(G-8340)*
Readington Farms Inc ....D 908 534-2121
Whitehouse *(G-12048)*
Tuscan/Lehigh Dairies Inc ....D 570 385-1884
Burlington *(G-992)*
Wakefern Food Corp ....B 732 819-0140
Edison *(G-2649)*
Wakefern Food Corp ....B 908 527-3300
Keasbey *(G-4932)*

DAIRY PRDTS: Natural Cheese

Abuelito Cheese Inc ....G 973 345-3503
Paterson *(G-8197)*
Biazzo Dairy Products Inc ....E 201 941-8579
Ridgefield *(G-9352)*
Colonna Brothers Inc ....D 800 626-8384
North Bergen *(G-7443)*
Finlandia Cheese Inc ....E 973 316-6699
Parsippany *(G-8012)*

Hawk Dairy Inc ....G 973 466-9030
Newark *(G-7187)*
Jvm Sales Corp ....D 908 862-4866
Linden *(G-5394)*
Lebanon Cheese Company Inc ....G 908 236-2611
Lebanon *(G-5295)*
Losurdo Foods Inc ....E 201 343-6680
Hackensack *(G-3940)*
Montena Taranto Foods Inc ....E 201 943-8484
Ridgefield *(G-9375)*
Toscana Cheese Company Inc ....E 201 617-1500
Secaucus *(G-9935)*
Tropical Cheese Industries ....B 732 442-4898
Perth Amboy *(G-8634)*

DAIRY PRDTS: Pot Cheese

Vitamia Pasta Boy Inc ....F 973 546-1140
Lodi *(G-5608)*

DAIRY PRDTS: Powdered Cream

Panos Brands LLC ....E 800 229-1706
Linden *(G-5423)*

DAIRY PRDTS: Processed Cheese

ECB USA Inc ....G 973 575-3226
Fairfield *(G-3181)*
Home and Garden Kraft LLC ....G 908 995-9355
Milford *(G-6246)*
Tone Kraft Inc ....G 856 283-8043
Cinnaminson *(G-1494)*

DAIRY PRDTS: Yogurt, Exc Frozen

Frozen Falls LLC ....G 908 350-3939
Basking Ridge *(G-188)*
Johanna Foods Inc ....B 908 788-2200
Flemington *(G-3452)*
Mualema LLC ....G 609 820-6098
Lawrence Township *(G-5244)*
Yo Got It ....G 732 475-7913
Point Pleasant Beach *(G-8929)*
Yogurt Paradise LLC ....G 732 534-6395
Jackson *(G-4683)*

DATA ENTRY SVCS

Aim Computer Associates Inc ....G 201 489-3100
Bergenfield *(G-379)*
Ideal Data Inc ....F 201 998-9440
North Arlington *(G-7420)*

DATA PROCESSING & PREPARATION SVCS

Chryslis Data Sltons Svcs Corp ....G 609 375-2000
Princeton *(G-9022)*
Ics Corporation ....C 215 427-3355
West Deptford *(G-11829)*
Image Remit Inc ....E 732 940-7900
North Brunswick *(G-7518)*
Maxisit Inc ....C 732 494-2005
Metuchen *(G-6114)*
Pds Prclnical Data Systems Inc ....E 973 398-2800
Mount Arlington *(G-6759)*
The Creative Print Group Inc ....F 856 486-1700
Pennsauken *(G-8585)*

DATA PROCESSING SVCS

Automated Resource Group Inc ....D 201 391-8357
Montvale *(G-6443)*
Corporate Mailings Inc ....D 973 808-0009
Whippany *(G-12017)*
Corporate Mailings Inc ....C 973 439-1168
West Caldwell *(G-11772)*
Fis Data Systems Inc ....E 201 945-1774
Ridgefield *(G-9360)*
Fis Financial Systems LLC ....D 856 784-7230
Voorhees *(G-11430)*
Johnson & Associates Inc ....F 856 228-2175
Blackwood *(G-483)*
S G A Business Systems Inc ....G 908 359-4626
Hillsborough *(G-4370)*
Thomas Publishing Company LLC ....E 973 543-4994
Chester *(G-1440)*

DATA VERIFICATION SVCS

Datamotion Inc ....E 973 455-1245
Florham Park *(G-3498)*

DATABASE INFORMATION RETRIEVAL SVCS

Redi-Data Inc ....F 973 227-4380
Fairfield *(G-3291)*
Redi-Data Inc ....A 856 988-0551
Marlton *(G-5996)*
Redi-Direct Marketing Inc ....B 973 808-4500
Fairfield *(G-3292)*
Teg New Jersey Inc ....A 973 776-8660
Newark *(G-7338)*

DECALCOMANIA WORK, EXC CHINA & GLASS

Mar-Kal Products Corp ....E 973 783-7155
Carlstadt *(G-1187)*

DECORATIVE WOOD & WOODWORK

Architectural Wdwkg Assoc ....G 908 996-7866
Frenchtown *(G-3696)*
Atlas Woodwork Inc ....E 973 621-9595
Newark *(G-7097)*
Distinctive Wdwrk By Rob Hoffm ....G 609 877-8122
Beverly *(G-462)*
Distinctive Woodwork Inc ....G 609 714-8505
Lumberton *(G-5656)*
Edison Finishing ....G 732 287-6660
Edison *(G-2509)*
Jorgensen Carr Ltd ....G 201 792-2278
East Orange *(G-2257)*
Krfc Custom Woodworking Inc ....G 732 363-0522
Lakewood *(G-5143)*
Lardieri Custom Woodworking ....F 732 905-6334
Lakewood *(G-5145)*
M and R Manufacturing ....G 732 905-1061
Lakewood *(G-5150)*
Metroplex Products Company Inc ....G 732 249-0653
Monroe Township *(G-6384)*
Narva Inc ....G 973 218-1200
Springfield *(G-10567)*
Perk & Pantry ....G 856 451-4333
Bridgeton *(G-794)*
Ragar Co Inc ....G 732 493-1416
Ocean *(G-7740)*
Randells Cstm Fniture Kitchens ....F 856 216-9400
Cherry Hill *(G-1418)*
Restortions By Peter Schichtel ....G 973 605-8818
Morristown *(G-6739)*
Studio L Contracting LLC ....G 201 837-1650
Hackensack *(G-3982)*
Taylor Made Custom Cabinetry ....F 856 786-5433
Pennsauken *(G-8583)*

DEFENSE SYSTEMS & EQPT

Dengen Scientific Corporation ....E 201 687-2983
Union City *(G-11245)*
L3 Technologies Inc ....B 973 446-4000
Budd Lake *(G-932)*
Lockheed Martin Corporation ....A 856 722-4100
Moorestown *(G-6596)*
Mantech Systems Engrg Corp ....G 856 566-9155
Voorhees *(G-11435)*
Melton Sales & Service ....E 609 699-4800
Bordentown *(G-602)*
Melton Sales & Service ....E 609 699-4800
Columbus *(G-1805)*
Milspray LLC ....G 732 886-2223
Lakewood *(G-5159)*

DEGREASING MACHINES

Grease N Go ....G 856 784-6555
Magnolia *(G-5740)*
Green Power Chemical LLC ....F 973 770-5600
Hopatcong *(G-4536)*
Safety-Kleen Systems Inc ....F 609 859-2049
Southampton *(G-10481)*

DEHYDRATION EQPT

Gericke USA Inc ....G 855 888-0088
Somerset *(G-10105)*

DELAY LINES

Amperite Co Inc ....E 201 864-9503
North Bergen *(G-7430)*

PRODUCT

DENTAL EQPT

Floxite Company Inc.................................F...... 201 529-2019
  Mahwah *(G-5774)*
Takara Belmont Usa Inc ....E...... 732 469-5000
  Somerset *(G-10180)*

DENTAL EQPT & SPLYS

American Medical & Dental Sups ....F...... 877 545-6837
  Montvale *(G-6442)*
Dentalworx Lab Ltd Lblty Co ....G...... 732 981-9096
  Edison *(G-2501)*
Dentamach Inc ....F...... 973 334-2220
  Parsippany *(G-7979)*
Dmg America LLC ....E...... 201 894-5500
  Ridgefield Park *(G-9404)*
Geistlich Pharma North America ....G...... 609 779-6560
  Princeton *(G-9049)*
Integrated Dental Systems LLC...........E...... 201 676-2457
  Englewood Cliffs *(G-2967)*
J A W Products Inc ....F...... 856 829-3210
  Cinnaminson *(G-1471)*
Milestone Education LLC ....G...... 973 535-2717
  Livingston *(G-5544)*
Milestone Scientific Inc ....F...... 973 535-2717
  Livingston *(G-5545)*
Mycone Dental Supply Co Inc ....C...... 856 663-4700
  Gibbstown *(G-3792)*
Panthera Dental Inc ....G...... 201 340-2766
  East Rutherford *(G-2316)*
R Yates Consumer Prd LLC ....G...... 201 569-1030
  Englewood *(G-2927)*
Raptor Resources Holdings Inc ....G...... 732 252-5146
  Freehold *(G-3685)*
Samuel H Fields Dental Labs ....E...... 201 343-4626
  Hackensack *(G-3971)*
Spident USA Incorporated ....G...... 201 944-0511
  Little Ferry *(G-5517)*
Viscot Medical LLC ....E...... 973 887-9273
  East Hanover *(G-2248)*
William R Hall Co ....E...... 856 784-6700
  Lindenwold *(G-5464)*

DENTAL EQPT & SPLYS WHOLESALERS

J A W Products Inc ....F...... 856 829-3210
  Cinnaminson *(G-1471)*
Mycone Dental Supply Co Inc ....C...... 856 663-4700
  Gibbstown *(G-3792)*
Pemco Dental Corporation ....E...... 800 526-4170
  Springfield *(G-10571)*
Ss White Burs Inc ....C...... 732 905-1100
  Lakewood *(G-5190)*

DENTAL EQPT & SPLYS: Cabinets

Integrted Laminate Systems Inc...........D...... 856 786-6500
  Cinnaminson *(G-1469)*

DENTAL EQPT & SPLYS: Dental Materials

E P R Industries Inc ....F...... 856 488-1120
  Pennsauken *(G-8507)*
Essential Dental Systems Inc ....E...... 201 487-9090
  South Hackensack *(G-10265)*
Ivoclar Vivadent Mfg Inc ....D...... 732 563-4755
  Somerset *(G-10114)*

DENTAL EQPT & SPLYS: Drills, Bone

Palisades Dental LLc ....F...... 201 569-0050
  Englewood *(G-2920)*

DENTAL EQPT & SPLYS: Enamels

Anna K Park ....G...... 856 478-9500
  Mullica Hill *(G-6892)*
Evergreen Dental ....G...... 856 845-3299
  Woodbury Heights *(G-12176)*
Jacquet Jonpaul...................................G...... 856 825-4259
  Millville *(G-6310)*

DENTAL EQPT & SPLYS: Laboratory

Handler Manufacturing Company ....E...... 908 233-7796
  Westfield *(G-11926)*

DENTAL EQPT & SPLYS: Orthodontic Appliances

Em Orthodontic Labs Inc ....G...... 201 652-4411
  Waldwick *(G-11446)*

DENTAL EQPT & SPLYS: Teeth, Artificial, Exc In Dental Labs

Dental Models & Designs Inc ....G...... 973 472-8009
  Garfield *(G-3729)*
Natural Dental Studios Inc ....G...... 908 281-0089
  Hillsborough *(G-4357)*

DENTAL INSTRUMENT REPAIR SVCS

Ss White Burs Inc ....C...... 732 905-1100
  Lakewood *(G-5190)*

DENTISTS' OFFICES & CLINICS

Samuel H Fields Dental Labs ....E...... 201 343-4626
  Hackensack *(G-3971)*

DEODORANTS: Personal

B Witching Bath Company LLC ....G...... 973 423-1820
  Hawthorne *(G-4219)*
Cherri Stone Interactive LLC ....G...... 844 843-7765
  Lakewood *(G-5092)*
Grenade Supply Co..............................G...... 267 968-3115
  Lambertville *(G-5213)*

DEPARTMENT STORES

Gibbons Company Ltd ....E...... 441 294-5047
  Elizabeth *(G-2739)*
Scala Pastry...G...... 732 398-9808
  North Brunswick *(G-7537)*

DEPARTMENT STORES: Army-Navy Goods

Escada US Subco LLC ....B...... 201 865-5200
  Secaucus *(G-9879)*

DEPILATORIES, COSMETIC

American Prvate Label Pdts LLC ....G...... 845 733-8151
  Franklin *(G-3594)*
Arch Personal Care Products LP ....E...... 908 226-9329
  South Plainfield *(G-10330)*

DERMATOLOGICALS

Dermarite Industries LLC ....C...... 973 247-3491
  North Bergen *(G-7446)*
Dermatological Soc of NJ Inc ....G...... 856 546-5600
  Barrington *(G-176)*
Dermatology & Laser Center PA............G...... 732 222-8323
  Long Branch *(G-5623)*
Medimtriks Pharmaceuticals Inc ....E...... 973 882-7512
  Fairfield *(G-3256)*
Phytoceuticals Inc ....G...... 201 791-2255
  Elmwood Park *(G-2844)*
Quinnova Pharmaceuticals Inc ....E...... 877 660-6263
  Chatham *(G-1337)*
Rouses Pt Pharmaceuticals LLC............G...... 239 390-1495
  Cranford *(G-1926)*
Topifram Laboratories Inc ....E...... 201 894-9020
  Englewood Cliffs *(G-2982)*

DESALTER KITS: Sea Water

American Water - Pridesa LLC ....G...... 856 435-7711
  Voorhees *(G-11421)*

DESIGN SVCS, NEC

Fleet Packaging Inc ....G...... 866 302-0340
  South Orange *(G-10306)*
Grafwed Internet Media Studios ....G...... 201 632-1771
  Midland Park *(G-6227)*
Interchange Group Inc..........................F...... 973 783-7032
  Montclair *(G-6418)*
Keeley Aerospace Ltd ....E...... 951 582-2113
  Cranbury *(G-1846)*
Level Designs Group LLC ....G...... 973 761-1675
  South Orange *(G-10309)*
My Way Prints Inc ....G...... 973 492-1212
  Butler *(G-1014)*
Pastel Companies Inc ....G...... 732 508-0635
  Howell *(G-4563)*
Springworks Group Ltd ....G...... 973 276-7940
  Fairfield *(G-3310)*
TMC Corporation ....G...... 609 860-1830
  Metuchen *(G-6128)*

DESIGN SVCS: Commercial & Indl

Eurodia Industrie SA ....G...... 732 805-4001
  Somerset *(G-10098)*
I F Associates Inc ....F...... 732 223-2900
  Allenwood *(G-36)*
Method Assoc Inc ....F...... 732 888-0444
  Keyport *(G-5020)*
Precision Graphics Inc ....D...... 908 707-8880
  Branchburg *(G-693)*
Spectrum Design LLC ....G...... 856 694-1870
  Franklinville *(G-3631)*
Technical Advantage Inc ....G...... 973 402-5500
  Boonton *(G-585)*
Transmission Technology Co ....G...... 973 305-3600
  Lincoln Park *(G-5334)*

DESIGN SVCS: Computer Integrated Systems

Alaquest International Inc ....F...... 908 713-9399
  Lebanon *(G-5275)*
Business Control Systems Corp ....F...... 732 283-1301
  Iselin *(G-4619)*
Com Tek Wrkplace Solutions LLC.........F...... 973 927-6814
  Lyndhurst *(G-5678)*
Commvault Systems Inc ....C...... 732 870-4000
  Tinton Falls *(G-10828)*
Comtrex Systems Corporation ....E...... 856 778-0090
  Moorestown *(G-6569)*
Cyberextrudercom Inc ....G...... 973 623-7900
  Wayne *(G-11622)*
Datapro International Inc ....E...... 732 868-0588
  Piscataway *(G-8754)*
Eclearview Technologies Inc ....G...... 732 695-6999
  Ocean *(G-7724)*
Ensync Intrctive Solutions Inc..............G...... 732 542-4001
  Freehold *(G-3654)*
Henry Bros Electronics Inc ....D...... 201 794-6500
  Fair Lawn *(G-3094)*
Juniper Networks Inc ....D...... 908 947-4436
  Bridgewater *(G-849)*
M + P International Inc ....E...... 973 239-3005
  Verona *(G-11307)*
Maxisit Inc ....C...... 732 494-2005
  Metuchen *(G-6114)*
Medical Strategic Planning Inc ....G...... 732 219-5090
  Lincroft *(G-5339)*
Melillo Consulting Inc ....E...... 732 563-8400
  Somerset *(G-10135)*
MSI Technologies LLC..........................F...... 973 263-0080
  Parsippany *(G-8050)*
Netscout Systems Inc ....G...... 609 518-4100
  Marlton *(G-5990)*
Niksun Inc ....C...... 609 936-9999
  Princeton *(G-9081)*
R T I Inc ....E...... 201 261-5852
  Oradell *(G-7812)*
Real Soft Inc ....A...... 609 409-3636
  Monmouth Junction *(G-6360)*
Ryval Cmpt Svcs Ltd Lblty Co ....G...... 201 374-1600
  Dumont *(G-2123)*
Specialty Systems Inc ....E...... 732 341-1011
  Toms River *(G-10913)*
Techntime Bus Sltons Ltd Lblty ....F...... 973 246-8153
  East Rutherford *(G-2331)*
Transcore LP ....F...... 201 329-9200
  Teterboro *(G-10816)*
Verizon Communications Inc.................D...... 609 646-9939
  Egg Harbor Township *(G-2698)*
Verizon Communications Inc.................E...... 201 666-9934
  Westwood *(G-11975)*

DESIGNS SVCS: COSTUME & SCENERY DESIGN SVCS

Images Costume Productions ....G...... 609 859-7372
  Southampton *(G-10475)*

DESIGNS SVCS: Scenery, Theatrical

Kdf Reprographics Inc ....F...... 201 784-9991
  South Hackensack *(G-10274)*

DETECTION APPARATUS: Electronic/Magnetic Field, Light/Heat

Checkpoint Systems Inc ....C...... 800 257-5540
  West Deptford *(G-11821)*
Checkpoint Systems Inc ....C...... 856 848-1800
  West Deptford *(G-11822)*

(G-0000) Company's Geographic Section entry number

Multi-Tech Industries Inc ....F 732 431-0550
  Marlboro (G-5948)

DETECTORS: Water Leak

United Machine Inc ....G 973 345-4505
  Paterson (G-8404)

DETONATORS: Detonators, high explosives

Cartridge Actuated Devices ....E 973 347-2281
  Byram Township (G-1021)

DIAGNOSTIC SUBSTANCES

Admera Health LLC ....G 908 222-0533
  South Plainfield (G-10321)
Alere Inc ....B 732 358-5921
  Freehold (G-3637)
Astral Diagnostics Inc ....G 856 224-0900
  Paulsboro (G-8413)
Biotech Atlantic Inc ....F 732 389-4789
  Eatontown (G-2385)
Bracco Diagnostics Inc ....C 609 514-2200
  Monroe Township (G-6378)
Bracco USA Inc ....G 609 514-2200
  Monroe Township (G-6379)
Cenogenics Corporation ....E 732 536-6457
  Morganville (G-6638)
Dpc Cirrus ....G 973 927-2828
  Flanders (G-3405)
Fluoropharma Medical Inc ....G 973 744-1565
  Montclair (G-6414)
Immunomedics Inc ....C 973 605-8200
  Morris Plains (G-6671)
Laboratory Diagnostics Co Inc ....F 732 536-6300
  Morganville (G-6646)
Pharmaseq Inc ....G 732 355-0100
  Monmouth Junction (G-6355)
Quest Diagnostics Incorporated ....A 973 520-2700
  Secaucus (G-9915)

DIAGNOSTIC SUBSTANCES OR AGENTS: Blood Derivative

Baxter Healthcare Corporation ....C 732 225-4700
  Edison (G-2470)
Ortho-Clinical Diagnostics Inc ....A 908 218-8000
  Raritan (G-9314)

DIAGNOSTIC SUBSTANCES OR AGENTS: Electrolyte

Ess Group Inc ....G 609 755-3139
  Southampton (G-10471)

DIAGNOSTIC SUBSTANCES OR AGENTS: Enzyme & Isoenzyme

Genzyme Corporation ....G 973 256-2106
  Totowa (G-10948)
Worthington Biochemical Corp ....E 732 942-1660
  Lakewood (G-5207)

DIAGNOSTIC SUBSTANCES OR AGENTS: Hematology

Arthur A Topilow William Lrner ....E 732 528-0760
  Manasquan (G-5868)

DIAGNOSTIC SUBSTANCES OR AGENTS: In Vitro

Akers Biosciences Inc ....E 856 848-8698
  West Deptford (G-11814)
Ascensia Diabetes Care US Inc ....C 973 560-6500
  Parsippany (G-7952)
Dsrv Inc ....F 973 631-1200
  Budd Lake (G-927)
Foundation For Embryonic ....G 973 656-2847
  Basking Ridge (G-187)
Mindray Ds Usa Inc ....A 201 995-8000
  Mahwah (G-5791)
Princeton Biomeditech Corp ....E 908 281-0112
  Skillman (G-10036)
Princeton Biomeditech Corp ....D 732 274-1000
  Monmouth Junction (G-6356)
Recombine LLC ....G 646 470-7422
  Livingston (G-5557)
Sensonics Inc ....F 856 547-7702
  Haddon Heights (G-4051)

DIAGNOSTIC SUBSTANCES OR AGENTS: In Vivo

Alere Inc ....B 732 620-4244
  Freehold (G-3636)

DIAGNOSTIC SUBSTANCES OR AGENTS: Radioactive

Petnet Solutions Inc ....G 865 218-2000
  Hackensack (G-3962)

DIAGNOSTIC SUBSTANCES OR AGENTS: Veterinary

Biomedtrix LLC ....G 973 331-7800
  Boonton (G-558)
Biomedtrix LLC ....F 973 331-7800
  Whippany (G-12012)
DMS Laboratories Inc ....G 908 782-3353
  Flemington (G-3436)

DIAMONDS, GEMS, WHOLESALE

Diamond Wholesale Co ....E 201 727-9595
  Moonachie (G-6514)
Golden Treasure Imports Inc ....G 732 723-1830
  Englishtown (G-2992)
Rcdc Corporation ....G 212 382-0386
  Hoboken (G-4494)

DIAMONDS: Cutting & Polishing

Rcdc Corporation ....G 212 382-0386
  Hoboken (G-4494)

DIAPERS: Disposable

Arquest Inc ....B 609 395-9500
  Millstone Township (G-6262)
Braco Manufacturing Inc ....E 732 752-7777
  South Plainfield (G-10338)
Innovative Disposables LLC ....E 908 222-7111
  South Plainfield (G-10384)

DIATOMACEOUS EARTH: Ground Or Treated

Dicaperl Minerals Corp ....G 856 320-2919
  Pennsauken (G-8503)

DIE CUTTING SVC: Paper

Goetz & Ruschmann Inc ....G 973 383-9270
  Newton (G-7391)
R J Blen Grphic Arts Cnverting ....E 732 545-3501
  New Brunswick (G-6998)
Sabre Die Cutting Co Inc ....E 973 357-9800
  Paterson (G-8373)

DIE SETS: Presses, Metal Stamping

C & C Metal Products Corp ....D 201 569-7300
  Englewood (G-2880)
Electro Magnetic Products Inc ....E 856 235-3011
  Moorestown (G-6575)
Elray Manufacturing Company ....E 856 881-1935
  Glassboro (G-3804)
Stampex Corp ....F 973 839-4040
  Haskell (G-4214)
STS Technologies LLC ....F 973 277-5416
  Mahwah (G-5817)
Tryco Tool & Mfg Co Inc ....E 973 674-6867
  Orange (G-7831)

DIES & TOOLS: Special

A K Stamping Co Inc ....D 908 232-7300
  Mountainside (G-6865)
Accurate Machine & Tool Co ....G 908 245-5545
  Roselle Park (G-9687)
Accurate Tool & Die Co Inc ....G 201 476-9348
  Montvale (G-6440)
Algene Marking Equipment Co ....G 973 478-9041
  Garfield (G-3716)
B E C Mfg Corp ....G 201 414-0000
  Glen Rock (G-3822)
Bach Tool Precision Inc ....G 973 962-6224
  Ringwood (G-9444)
Bihler of America Inc ....C 908 213-9001
  Phillipsburg (G-8644)
Bodine Tool and Machine Co Inc ....E 856 234-7800
  Moorestown (G-6564)

Boyle Tool & Die Co Inc ....F 856 853-1819
  West Deptford (G-11818)
Brisar Industries Inc ....C 973 278-2500
  Paterson (G-8226)
C & K Punch & Screw Mch Pdts ....G 201 343-6750
  Hackensack (G-3886)
Cavalla Inc ....E 201 343-3338
  Hackensack (G-3894)
Charles E Green & Son Inc ....E 973 485-3630
  Newark (G-7120)
City Diecutting Inc ....F 973 270-0370
  Morristown (G-6699)
Die Tech LLC ....G 201 343-8324
  Hackensack (G-3905)
Duerr Tool & Die Co Inc ....F 908 810-9035
  Union (G-11173)
Dura-Carb Inc ....G 973 697-6665
  Oak Ridge (G-7661)
Dynamic Die Cutting & Finshg ....F 973 589-8338
  Newark (G-7147)
F & G Tool & Die Inc ....G 908 241-5880
  Kenilworth (G-4954)
Garden State Precision Inc ....G 201 945-6410
  Ridgefield (G-9361)
Globe Die-Cutting Products Inc ....C 732 494-7744
  Metuchen (G-6105)
Golden Rule Inc ....G 856 663-3074
  Pennsauken (G-8516)
H-E Tool & Mfg Co Inc ....E 856 303-8787
  Cinnaminson (G-1466)
Harris & Tippograph Inc ....G 973 523-5204
  Paterson (G-8288)
Hofmann Tool & Die Corporation ....G 201 327-0226
  Upper Saddle River (G-11279)
Infor Metal & Tooling Mfg ....F 973 571-9520
  Cedar Grove (G-1285)
Jmk Tool Die and Mfg Co Inc ....G 201 845-4710
  Rochelle Park (G-9530)
Jordan Manufacturing LLC ....G 973 383-8363
  Lafayette (G-5048)
L & Z Tool and Engineering Inc ....E 908 322-2220
  Watchung (G-11592)
Olympic EDM Services Inc ....G 973 492-0664
  Kinnelon (G-5039)
Omega Tool Die ....G 856 228-7100
  Sewell (G-9963)
Peterson Steel Rule Die Corp ....E 201 935-6180
  Carlstadt (G-1201)
Philip Creter Inc ....G 908 686-2910
  Union (G-11215)
Printco ....G 908 687-9518
  Flemington (G-3463)
Progressive Tool & Mfg Corp ....G 908 245-7010
  Kenilworth (G-4990)
Rebuth Metal Services ....F 908 889-6400
  Fanwood (G-3373)
Rex Tool & Manufacturing Inc ....G 908 925-2727
  Linden (G-5434)
Thomson Lamination Co Inc ....D 856 779-8521
  Maple Shade (G-5912)
Vantage Tool & Mfg Inc ....G 908 647-1010
  Warren (G-11571)
Victory Tool & Mfg Co ....G 973 759-8733
  Belleville (G-325)
Vmc Die Cutting Corp ....F 973 450-4655
  Belleville (G-326)

DIES: Cutting, Exc Metal

Danielle Die Cut Products Inc ....E 973 278-3000
  Paterson (G-8244)
Grobet File Company Amer LLC ....D 201 939-6700
  Carlstadt (G-1165)

DIES: Extrusion

Alloy Cast Products Inc ....F 908 245-2255
  Kenilworth (G-4936)
Custom Extrusion Tech Inc ....F 732 367-5511
  Lakewood (G-5102)

DIES: Paper Cutting

21st Century Finishing Inc ....E 201 797-0212
  Clifton (G-1551)
Turul Bookbindery Inc ....G 973 361-2810
  Wharton (G-12003)

DIES: Plastic Forming

Hartmann Tool Co Inc ....G 201 343-8700
  Hackensack (G-3925)

PRODUCT

Orycon Control Technology Inc ....E ... 732 922-2400
Ocean *(G-7732)*

DIES: *Steel Rule*

Edgar C Barcus Co Inc ....F ... 856 456-0204
Westville *(G-11939)*

Kessler Steel Rule Die Inc ....G ... 856 767-0231
West Berlin *(G-11728)*

Lasercam LLc ....E ... 201 941-1262
Ridgefield *(G-9370)*

Pin Point Container Corp ....G ... 856 848-2115
Deptford *(G-2066)*

Quality Die Shop Inc ....G ... 732 787-0041
North Middletown *(G-7558)*

Redkeys Dies Inc ....G ... 856 456-7890
Gloucester City *(G-3845)*

Richmond Steel Rule Dies Inc ....G ... 856 661-0900
Pennsauken *(G-8574)*

Spec Steel Rule Dies Inc ....E ... 609 443-4435
Windsor *(G-12130)*

Zin-Tech Inc ....E ... 856 661-0900
Pennsauken *(G-8591)*

DIES: *Wire Drawing & Straightening*

United Die Company Inc ....E ... 201 997-0250
Kearny *(G-4918)*

DIFFERENTIAL ASSEMBLIES & PARTS

NAPA Concepts Ltd Liability Co ....G ... 201 673-2381
North Bergen *(G-7470)*

Transaxle LLC ....C ... 856 665-4445
Cinnaminson *(G-1495)*

DIODES & RECTIFIERS

Harrison Electro Mechanical ....F ... 732 382-6008
Rahway *(G-9196)*

Intense Inc ....E ... 732 249-2228
North Brunswick *(G-7520)*

DIODES: *Light Emitting*

Acolyte Technologies Corp ....G ... 212 629-3239
Perth Amboy *(G-8605)*

Atlantic Clean Energy Sup LLC ....G ... 888 900-1581
Branchburg *(G-641)*

Imperial Copy Products Inc ....E ... 973 927-5500
Randolph *(G-9284)*

Liberty Cnstr & Inv Group ....G ... 267 784-7931
Cherry Hill *(G-1388)*

DIORITE: *Crushed & Broken*

Kop Marble Granite Inc ....G ... 973 283-8000
Wayne *(G-11659)*

DIRECT SELLING ESTABLISHMENTS, NEC

Compco Analytical Inc ....G ... 201 641-3936
Little Ferry *(G-5499)*

DIRECT SELLING ESTABLISHMENTS: *Beverage Svcs*

McT Dairies Inc ....F ... 973 258-9600
Millburn *(G-6256)*

DIRECT SELLING ESTABLISHMENTS: *Drapes/Curtains,Door-To-Door*

A Plus Installs LLC ....G ... 201 255-4412
Bloomfield *(G-499)*

DIRECT SELLING ESTABLISHMENTS: *Snacks*

Ziggy Snack Foods LLC ....E ... 917 662-6038
Clifton *(G-1747)*

DISCOUNT DEPARTMENT STORES

Marmaxx Operating Corp ....D ... 973 575-7910
West Caldwell *(G-11785)*

DISCS & TAPE: *Optical, Blank*

Sony Corporation of America ....B ... 201 930-1000
Paramus *(G-7902)*

DISHWASHING EQPT: *Commercial*

Hobart Sales and Service Inc ....E ... 973 227-9265
Fairfield *(G-3223)*

Univerclean Ltd ....G ... 201 674-1563
Fair Lawn *(G-3122)*

DISK & DISKETTE EQPT, EXC DRIVES

Audio Dynamix Inc ....F ... 201 567-5488
Englewood *(G-2874)*

EVs Broadcast Equipment Inc ....F ... 973 575-7811
Fairfield *(G-3187)*

DISK DRIVES: *Computer*

Western Digital Corporation ....G ... 609 734-7479
Princeton *(G-9138)*

DISKETTE DUPLICATING SVCS

Strategic Content Imaging ....C ... 201 863-8100
Secaucus *(G-9933)*

US Software Group Inc ....E ... 732 361-4636
South Plainfield *(G-10447)*

DISPENSERS: *Soap*

Inopak Ltd ....F ... 973 962-1121
Ringwood *(G-9450)*

DISPENSING EQPT & PARTS, BEVERAGE: *Coolers, Milk/Water, Elec*

Walter Machine Co Inc ....E ... 201 656-5654
Jersey City *(G-4846)*

DISPENSING EQPT & PARTS, BEVERAGE: *Fountain/Other Beverage*

Krowne Metal Corp ....E ... 973 305-3300
Wayne *(G-11660)*

Sodastream USA Inc ....D ... 856 755-3400
Mount Laurel *(G-6843)*

DISPLAY FIXTURES: *Wood*

Acro Display Inc ....E ... 215 229-1100
Pennsauken *(G-8470)*

Banner Design Inc ....E ... 908 687-5335
Hillside *(G-4395)*

Bossen Architectural Millwork ....F ... 856 786-1100
Cinnaminson *(G-1449)*

Capital Contracting & Design ....E ... 908 561-8411
Plainfield *(G-8856)*

Design Display Group Inc ....C ... 201 438-6000
Carlstadt *(G-1154)*

Level Designs Group LLC ....G ... 973 761-1675
South Orange *(G-10309)*

R J Hoppe Store Construction ....G ... 973 485-5665
Newark *(G-7283)*

DISPLAY ITEMS: *Corrugated, Made From Purchased Materials*

Menasha Packaging Company LLC .....C ... 973 893-1300
Lyndhurst *(G-5693)*

Package Development Co Inc ....E ... 973 983-8500
Rockaway *(G-9593)*

Pratt Industries USA Inc ....D ... 201 934-1900
Allendale *(G-15)*

DISPLAY ITEMS: *Solid Fiber, Made From Purchased Materials*

Algar/Display Connection Corp ....D ... 201 438-1000
Moonachie *(G-6501)*

Cases By Source Inc ....E ... 201 831-0005
Mahwah *(G-5756)*

Level Designs Group LLC ....G ... 973 761-1675
South Orange *(G-10309)*

DISPLAY LETTERING SVCS

Monogram Center Inc ....E ... 732 442-1800
Perth Amboy *(G-8624)*

DISPLAY STANDS: *Merchandise, Exc Wood*

M P M Display Inc ....F ... 973 374-3477
Irvington *(G-4597)*

Metaline Products Company Inc ....E ... 732 721-1373
South Amboy *(G-10242)*

V M Display ....F ... 973 365-8027
Passaic *(G-8186)*

DOCK EQPT & SPLYS, INDL

American Process Systems ....G ... 908 216-6781
Port Murray *(G-8974)*

Custom Docks Inc ....F ... 973 948-3732
Sandyston *(G-9811)*

Technology General Corporation ....F ... 973 827-8209
Franklin *(G-3605)*

DOCUMENT EMBOSSING SVCS

Windmill Press Inc ....G ... 856 663-8990
Pennsauken *(G-8589)*

DOLOMITIC MARBLE: *Crushed & Broken*

Tilcon New York Inc ....D ... 800 789-7625
Kearny *(G-4917)*

DOOR & WINDOW REPAIR SVCS

Frank & Jims Inc ....G ... 609 646-1655
Pleasantville *(G-8908)*

Miric Industries Inc ....F ... 201 864-0233
North Bergen *(G-7468)*

Pierangeli Group Inc ....G ... 856 582-4060
Gloucester City *(G-3842)*

DOOR FRAMES: *Wood*

RSI Woodworking Products Co ....D ... 609 484-1600
Egg Harbor Township *(G-2694)*

RSI Woodworking Products Co ....E ... 609 645-9777
Egg Harbor Township *(G-2695)*

USA Wood Door Inc ....E ... 856 384-9663
West Deptford *(G-11842)*

DOOR OPERATING SYSTEMS: *Electric*

Assa Abloy Entrance Systems US ....E ... 609 443-5800
Windsor *(G-12124)*

Assa Abloy Entrance Systems US ....E ... 609 528-2580
Hamilton *(G-4104)*

Chamberlain Group Inc ....G ... 201 472-4200
Whippany *(G-12016)*

Total Garage Solutions LLC ....F ... 732 749-3993
Wall Township *(G-11515)*

DOORS & WINDOWS WHOLESALERS: *All Materials*

Babbitt Mfg Co Inc ....F ... 856 692-3245
Vineland *(G-11326)*

Bridgewater Wholesalers Inc ....C ... 908 526-7555
Branchburg *(G-645)*

Door Center Enterprises Inc ....G ... 609 333-1233
Hopewell *(G-4541)*

Dreamstar Construction LLC ....F ... 732 393-2572
Middletown *(G-6213)*

Passaic Metal & Bldg Sups Co ....D ... 973 546-9000
Clifton *(G-1691)*

DOORS & WINDOWS: *Storm, Metal*

Dor-Win Manufacturing Co ....E ... 201 796-4300
Elmwood Park *(G-2815)*

Royal Aluminum Co Inc ....D ... 973 589-8880
Newark *(G-7293)*

Surburban Building Pdts Inc ....E ... 732 901-8900
Howell *(G-4568)*

Taylor Windows Inc ....F ... 973 672-3000
East Orange *(G-2270)*

Window Shapes Inc ....D ... 732 549-0708
Metuchen *(G-6131)*

DOORS: *Fire, Metal*

Allmark Door Company LLC ....F ... 610 358-9800
Springfield *(G-10536)*

DOORS: *Folding, Plastic Or Plastic Coated Fabric*

Dor-Win Manufacturing Co ....E ... 201 796-4300
Elmwood Park *(G-2815)*

Innova Group Inc ....G ... 856 696-1053
Vineland *(G-11373)*

(G-0000) Company's Geographic Section entry number

DOORS: Garage, Overhead, Metal

Glen G Coats ....G 908 236-2620
Lebanon (G-5287)
Gray Overhead Door Co ....F 908 355-3889
Elizabeth (G-2740)
Portaseal LLC ....G 973 539-0100
Morristown (G-6737)

DOORS: Garage, Overhead, Wood

Total Garage Solutions LLC ......F 732 749-3993
Wall Township (G-11515)

DOORS: Glass

Century Bathworks Inc ....D 973 785-4290
Woodland Park (G-12214)
Klein Usa Inc ....F 973 246-8181
East Rutherford (G-2302)
Pike Machine Products Inc ......D 973 379-9128
Short Hills (G-9983)

DOORS: Rolling, Indl Building Or Warehouse, Metal

Guardrite Steel Door Corp ......G 973 481-4424
Newark (G-7181)

DOORS: Screen, Metal

Century Bathworks Inc ....D 973 785-4290
Woodland Park (G-12214)

DOORS: Wooden

Bildisco Mfg Inc ....F 973 673-2400
West Orange (G-11889)
Door Stop LLC ....F 718 599-5112
Carlstadt (G-1157)
Hahns Woodworking ....F 908 722-2742
Branchburg (G-664)
Manhattan Door Corp ....D 718 963-1111
Carlstadt (G-1186)
RPI Industries Inc ....D 609 714-2330
Medford (G-6080)
Smittys Door Service Inc ....G 908 284-0506
Pittstown (G-8851)
W F Sherman & Son Inc ....F 732 223-1505
Manasquan (G-5883)

DRAINING OR PUMPING OF METAL MINES

Demaio Inc ....E 609 965-4094
Egg Harbor City (G-2661)

DRAPERIES & CURTAINS

Ackerson Drapery Decorator Svc ......G 732 797-1967
Lakewood (G-5065)
Colonial Uphl & Win Treatments ......G 609 641-3124
Pleasantville (G-8905)
D Kwitman & Son Inc ....F 201 798-5511
Hoboken (G-4468)
Gordon Frgson Intr Dsigns Svcs ......G 973 378-2330
Maplewood (G-5920)
Interior Art & Design Inc ....E 201 488-8855
Hackensack (G-3930)
Lawrence Custom Drapery Shop ......F 609 882-4007
Ewing (G-3034)
Marburn Stores Inc ....G 908 412-1962
South Plainfield (G-10401)
Master Drapery Workroom Inc ..F 908 272-4404
Kenilworth (G-4973)
Nassaus Window Fashions Inc ..E 201 689-6030
Paramus (G-7893)
Thortel Fireproof Fabrics Inc ..F 732 938-4114
Wall Township (G-11514)
W Gerriets International Inc ....E 609 771-8111
Ewing (G-3068)

DRAPERIES & DRAPERY FABRICS, COTTON

Bai Lar Interior Services Inc ....G 732 738-0350
Fords (G-3527)
Proclean Services Inc ....F 973 857-5408
Verona (G-11309)

DRAPERIES: Plastic & Textile, From Purchased Materials

Beatrice Home Fashions Inc ....E 908 561-7370
South Plainfield (G-10336)

Dons Drapery Manufacturing ....F 973 751-1544
Belleville (G-300)
Dru Whitacre Media Svcs Ltd ..D 201 770-9950
North Bergen (G-7448)
Forsters Cleaning & Tailoring ..G 201 659-4411
Jersey City (G-4757)
Kushner Draperies Mfg LLC ....E 856 317-9696
Pennsauken (G-8541)
Metro Mills Inc ....E 973 942-6034
Paterson (G-8337)
Stessl & Neugebauer Inc ....F 908 277-3340
Summit (G-10659)

DRAPERY & UPHOLSTERY STORES: Curtains

Curtain Care Plus Inc ....G 800 845-6155
Clifton (G-1595)
Nassaus Window Fashions Inc ..E 201 689-6030
Paramus (G-7893)

DRAPERY & UPHOLSTERY STORES: Draperies

Decorating With Fabric Inc ......G 845 352-5064
Park Ridge (G-7917)
Lawrence Custom Drapery Shop ......F 609 882-4007
Ewing (G-3034)

DRILL BITS

Ram Products Inc ....G 732 651-5500
Dayton (G-1984)

DRILLING MACHINERY & EQPT: Oil & Gas

Grayden Industries Inc ....E 201 761-0788
Jersey City (G-4762)

DRILLING MACHINERY & EQPT: Water Well

Capuano Plumbing Inc ....G 201 327-0676
Upper Saddle River (G-11276)

DRINK MIXES, NONALCOHOLIC: Cocktail

201 Food Packing Inc ....F 973 463-0777
East Hanover (G-2198)

DRINKING PLACES: Alcoholic Beverages

Medieval Times USA Inc ....C 201 933-2220
Lyndhurst (G-5691)

DRINKING PLACES: Tavern

Ldm Inc ....F 609 921-8555
Princeton (G-9066)
Summerlands Inc ....E 973 729-8428
Sparta (G-10521)

DRIVES: High Speed Indl, Exc Hydrostatic

Numeritool Manufacturing Corp ......G 973 827-7714
Franklin (G-3603)
Sew-Eurodrive Inc ....E 856 467-2277
Bridgeport (G-771)

DRUG STORES

140 Main Street Corp ....F 732 974-2929
Sea Girt (G-9860)
Boyds Pharmacy Inc ....F 609 499-0100
Florence (G-3476)
K & S Drug & Surgical Inc ......G 201 886-9191
Fort Lee (G-3562)
Little Falls Shop Rite Super ....B 973 256-0909
Little Falls (G-5481)
Njs Associates Company ....G 973 960-8688
Bridgewater (G-867)
Pathmark Stores Inc ....C 973 762-5044
South Orange (G-10313)
Pathmark Stores Inc ....C 856 853-5533
Woodbury (G-12167)
Pathmark Stores Inc ....C 732 505-6440
Toms River (G-10900)
Pdr Equity LLC ....D 201 358-7200
Whippany (G-12032)
Walgreen Eastern Co Inc ....E 973 728-3172
West Milford (G-11858)
Walgreen Eastern Co Inc ....E 609 522-1291
Wildwood (G-12075)

DRUGGIST'S SUNDRIES: Rubber

Datwyler Pharma Packaging ......E 856 663-2202
Pennsauken (G-8500)

DRUGS & DRUG PROPRIETARIES, WHOL: Biologicals/Allied Prdts

Difco Laboratories Inc ....G 410 316-4113
Franklin Lakes (G-3613)

DRUGS & DRUG PROPRIETARIES, WHOLESALE

Acetris Health LLC ....G 201 961-9000
Saddle Brook (G-9750)
Exeltis Usa Inc ....D 973 324-0200
Florham Park (G-3500)
Genzyme Corporation ....G 973 256-2106
Totowa (G-10948)
Rising Health LLC ....E 201 961-9000
Saddle Brook (G-9787)
Rising Pharmaceuticals Inc ......E 201 961-9000
Saddle Brook (G-9788)

DRUGS & DRUG PROPRIETARIES, WHOLESALE: Animal Medicines

Merck & Co Inc ....B 908 740-4000
Kenilworth (G-4974)
Merck & Co Inc ....D 908 740-4000
Rahway (G-9212)

DRUGS & DRUG PROPRIETARIES, WHOLESALE: Medicinals/Botanicals

Herborium Group Inc ....G 201 849-4431
Fort Lee (G-3556)
Ivy-Dry Inc ....G 973 575-1992
Fairfield (G-3234)

DRUGS & DRUG PROPRIETARIES, WHOLESALE: Pharmaceuticals

Actavis LLC ....D 732 947-5300
Edison (G-2450)
Aeterna Zentaris Inc ....E 908 626-5428
Warren (G-11536)
Amneal Pharmaceuticals LLC ....F 908 947-3120
Piscataway (G-8734)
Amneal Pharmaceuticals LLC ....E 908 231-1911
Branchburg (G-636)
Camber Pharmaceuticals Inc ....E 732 529-0430
Piscataway (G-8742)
Central Admxture Phrm Svcs Inc ......E 201 541-0080
Englewood (G-2883)
Dr Reddys Laboratories Inc ......E 609 375-9900
Princeton (G-9032)
Ezrirx LLC ....G 718 502-6610
Lakewood (G-5120)
Ferring Pharmaceuticals Inc ....C 973 796-1600
Parsippany (G-8010)
Ino Therapeutics LLC ....D 908 238-6600
Bedminster (G-274)
Klus Pharma Inc ....F 609 651-4466
Cranbury (G-1847)
Leading Pharma LLC ....E 201 746-9160
Montvale (G-6465)
Leo Pharma Inc ....B 973 637-1690
Madison (G-5728)
Magnifica Inc ....F 323 202-0386
Cranbury (G-1858)
Medimtriks Pharmaceuticals Inc ......E 973 882-7512
Fairfield (G-3256)
Parker Labs ....G 973 276-9500
Fairfield (G-3282)
Patheon Biologics (nj) LLC ......D 609 919-3300
Princeton (G-9089)
Patheon Biologics LLC ....G 609 919-3300
Princeton (G-9090)
Pernix Therapeutics LLC ....E 800 793-2145
Morristown (G-6733)
Pharmatech International Inc ....F 973 244-0393
Fairfield (G-3283)
Phytoceuticals Inc ....G 201 791-2255
Elmwood Park (G-2844)
Sandoz Inc ....C 609 627-8500
Princeton (G-9115)
Strive Pharmaceuticals Inc ......G 609 269-2001
East Brunswick (G-2189)

Employee Codes: A=Over 500 employees, B=251-500
C=101-250, D=51-100, E=20-50, F=10-19, G=4-9

2018 Harris New jersey
Manufacturers Directory

849

PRODUCT

Taro Pharmaceuticals USA Inc ....E 609 655-9002
Cranbury (G-1884)
Vertice Pharma LLC ....C 877 530-1633
New Providence (G-7060)
Vgyaan Pharmaceuticals LLC..............G 609 452-2770
Princeton (G-9137)
Windtree Therapeutics Inc ....F 973 339-2889
Totowa (G-10986)

DRUGS & DRUG PROPRIETARIES, WHOLESALE: Vitamins & Minerals

Icelandirect Inc ....F 800 763-4690
Clifton (G-1645)
Reliance Vitamin LLC ....C 732 537-1220
Edison (G-2603)
Vitaquest International LLC ....F 973 575-9200
Fairfield (G-3344)
Vitaquest International LLC ....B 973 575-9200
West Caldwell (G-11807)

DRUGS ACTING ON THE CENTRAL NERVOUS SYSTEM & SENSE ORGANS

Allergan Inc ....D 908 306-0374
Bedminster (G-265)
Allergan Inc 862 261-7000
Morristown (G-6684)

DRUGS AFFECTING NEOPLASMS & ENDOCRINE SYSTEMS

Bayer Hlthcare Phrmcticals Inc ....A 862 404-3000
Whippany (G-12009)
Bayer Hlthcare Phrmcticals Inc ....E 973 709-3545
Whippany (G-12010)
Bayer Hlthcare Phrmcticals Inc ....A 862 404-3000
Whippany (G-12011)
Pharmion Corporation 908 673-9000
Summit (G-10653)
Schering Berlin Inc ....G 862 404-3000
Whippany (G-12038)

DRUGS: Parasitic & Infective Disease Affecting

Immtech Pharmaceuticals Inc ....E 212 791-2911
Montclair (G-6417)
Leo Pharma Inc ....B 973 637-1690
Madison (G-5728)

DRUMS: Brake

Momentum Usa Inc ....F 844 300-1553
Edison (G-2576)

DRUMS: Fiber

Tunnel Barrel & Drum Co Inc ....E 201 933-1444
Carlstadt (G-1235)

DRYCLEANING & LAUNDRY SVCS: Commercial & Family

Trilex Ltd ....E 201 664-5576
Twp Washinton (G-11144)

DRYCLEANING EQPT & SPLYS: Commercial

Multimatic LLC ....G 201 767-9660
Northvale (G-7593)

DRYCLEANING PLANTS

Proclean Services Inc ....F 973 857-5408
Verona (G-11309)

DRYCLEANING SVC: Collecting & Distributing Agency

Forsters Cleaning & Tailoring...............G 201 659-4411
Jersey City (G-4757)

DRYCLEANING SVC: Drapery & Curtain

Astra Cleaners of Hazlet......................G 732 264-4144
Hazlet (G-4270)

DRYERS & REDRYERS: Indl

Hary Manufacturing Inc ....F 908 722-7100
Woodbridge (G-12150)

Lydon Bros Corp ....E 201 343-4334
South Hackensack (G-10276)
Marsden Inc ....E 856 663-2227
Pennsauken (G-8544)
Wyssmont Company Inc ....E 201 947-4600
Fort Lee (G-3592)

DRYERS: Textile

Cire Technologies Inc ....G 973 402-8301
Mountain Lakes (G-6855)

DUCTING: Metal Plate

Nova Flex Group ....F 856 768-2275
West Berlin (G-11737)

DUCTING: Plastic

Du Technologies Inc ....F 201 729-0070
Moonachie (G-6515)
Endot Industries Inc ....D 973 625-8500
Rockaway (G-9564)

DUCTS: Sheet Metal

Air Distribution Systems Inc ....D 856 874-1100
Cherry Hill (G-1341)
Air Power Inc ....E 973 882-5418
Fairfield (G-3128)
Ducts Inc ....G 973 267-8482
Morris Plains (G-6660)
M C Custom Shtmtl Fabrication ....G 856 767-9509
West Berlin (G-11732)
Par Troy Sheet Metal & AC LLC ....G 973 227-1150
Fairfield (G-3280)
PTL Sheet Metal Inc ....D 201 501-8700
Dumont (G-2122)
T J Eckardt Associates Inc ....F 856 767-4111
Berlin (G-442)

DUMPSTERS: Garbage

Billy D Dumpster Service LLC ....G 609 465-5990
Cape May Court House (G-1110)
Rudco Products Inc ....D 856 691-0800
Vineland (G-11400)
Wastequip Manufacturing Co ....D 856 784-5500
Sicklerville (G-10028)
Wastequip Manufacturing Co LLC ....E 856 629-9222
Williamstown (G-12114)

DUST OR FUME COLLECTING EQPT: Indl

Buhler Inc ....E 201 847-0600
Mahwah (G-5755)
Sternvent Co Inc ....E 908 688-0807
Union (G-11225)

DYE INTERMEDIATES: Cyclic

French Color Fragrance Co Inc ....E 201 567-6883
Englewood (G-2898)

DYES & PIGMENTS: Organic

Carib Chemical Co Inc ....F 201 791-6700
Elmwood Park (G-2808)
Carib Chemical Co Inc ....F 201 791-6700
Elmwood Park (G-2809)
Coloron Plastics Corporation ....G 908 685-1210
Branchburg (G-649)
Epolin Chemical LLC ....G 973 465-9495
Newark (G-7157)
Magruder Color Company Inc...............C 817 837-3293
Holmdel (G-4521)
Orient Corporation of America ....G 908 298-0990
Cranford (G-1919)
Polymathes Holdings I LLC ....G 609 945-1690
Princeton (G-9093)
Primex Color Compounding ....E 800 282-7933
Garfield (G-3750)
Riverdale Color Mfg Inc ....G 732 376-9300
Perth Amboy (G-8628)
Shelan Chemical Company Inc.............G 732 796-1003
Monroe Township (G-6392)
Totowa Precision Tooling Inc ....F 973 256-2283
Totowa (G-10976)

DYES OR COLORS: Food, Synthetic

SPS Alfachem Inc ....G 973 676-5141
Orange (G-7828)

William R Tatz Industries.....................G 973 751-0720
Belleville (G-328)

DYES: Synthetic Organic

American Chemical & Coating Co.........G 908 353-2260
Elizabeth (G-2710)
Fabricolor Holding Intl LLC..................G 973 742-5800
Paterson (G-8269)
Honeyware Inc ....D 201 997-5900
Kearny (G-4880)

DYESTUFFS WHOLESALERS

Carib Chemical Co Inc ....F 201 791-6700
Elmwood Park (G-2809)

EATING PLACES

Anthony & Sons Bakery Itln Bky ....D 973 625-2323
Denville (G-2031)
Atlantic City Week ....F 609 646-4848
Pleasantville (G-8902)
Auntie Annes Hmde Sft Prtzls ....F 856 772-3737
Voorhees (G-11422)
Bagel Street ....E 609 936-1755
Plainsboro (G-8875)
Berat Corporation ....C 609 953-7700
Medford (G-6065)
Comarco Products Inc ....D 856 342-7557
Camden (G-1054)
Cravings ....F 732 531-7122
Allenhurst (G-25)
Elis Hot Bagels Inc ....E 732 566-4523
Matawan (G-6020)
Food Circus Super Markets Inc ....D 732 291-4079
Atlantic Highlands (G-111)
Hsh Assoc Financial Publishers ....G 973 838-3330
Butler (G-1008)
Limpert Brothers Inc ....E 856 691-1353
Vineland (G-11380)
Lrk Inc ....F 609 924-6881
Princeton (G-9068)
Medieval Times USA Inc ....C 201 933-2220
Lyndhurst (G-5691)
Muirhead Ringoes NJ Inc ....F 609 695-7803
Trenton (G-11082)
Nuchas Tsq LLC ....E 212 913-9682
North Bergen (G-7472)
Ruggiero Sea Food Inc ....D 973 589-0524
Newark (G-7294)
Ruggiero Sea Food Inc ....G 973 589-0524
Newark (G-7295)
Springdale Farm Market Inc.................E 856 424-8674
Cherry Hill (G-1421)
Tomasello Winery Inc ....F 609 561-0567
Hammonton (G-4151)
Universal Interlock Corp ....G 732 818-8484
Toms River (G-10919)

EDUCATIONAL SVCS

Sunrise Intl Educatn Inc ....D 917 525-0272
North Brunswick (G-7541)

EDUCATIONAL SVCS, NONDEGREE GRANTING: Continuing Education

Encore Enterprises Inc ....G 201 489-5044
South Hackensack (G-10264)
Jannetti Publications ....D 856 256-2300
Sewell (G-9960)

ELASTIC BRAID & NARROW WOVEN FABRICS

Sullivan-Carson Inc ....G 856 566-1400
Voorhees (G-11438)

ELECTRIC & OTHER SERVICES COMBINED

Foster Wheeler Zack Inc ....D 908 730-4000
Hampton (G-4158)

ELECTRIC MOTOR REPAIR SVCS

Absecon Electric Motor Works..............G 609 641-1523
Absecon (G-1)
Atlantic Kenmark Electric Inc ....F 201 991-2117
North Arlington (G-7416)
Atlantic Switch Generator LLC ....F 609 518-1900
Hainesport (G-4069)

D Electric Motors Inc ....G..... 856 696-5959
  Vineland *(G-11348)*

Electrical Motor Repr Co of NJ ....F..... 609 392-6149
  Trenton *(G-11058)*

General Electric Company ....C..... 201 866-2161
  North Bergen *(G-7453)*

Jarvis Electric Motors Inc ....G..... 856 662-7710
  Pennsauken *(G-8535)*

Lakewood Elc Mtr Sls & Svc ....G..... 732 363-2865
  Howell *(G-4560)*

Lockwoods Electric Motor Svc ....E..... 609 587-2333
  Trenton *(G-11077)*

Longo Elctrical-Mechanical Inc ....E..... 973 537-0400
  Linden *(G-5404)*

Lowder Electric and Cnstr ....G..... 732 764-6000
  Middlesex *(G-6177)*

McIntosh Industries Inc ....G..... 908 688-7475
  Hillside *(G-4430)*

Motors and Drives Inc ....G..... 732 462-7683
  Freehold *(G-3672)*

Motors and Drives Inc ....G..... 609 344-8058
  Atlantic City *(G-103)*

New Jersey Electric Motors ....G..... 908 526-5225
  Somerville *(G-10221)*

Phil Desiere Electric Mtr Svc ....F..... 856 692-8442
  Vineland *(G-11390)*

Precision Devices Inc ....G..... 609 882-2230
  Ewing *(G-3045)*

RSI Company ....G..... 973 227-7800
  Fairfield *(G-3297)*

SMS Electric Motor Car LLC ....F..... 215 428-2502
  Bridgewater *(G-896)*

Story Electric Mtr Repr Co Inc ....E..... 973 256-1636
  Little Falls *(G-5490)*

Universal Electric Co ....E..... 201 968-1000
  Hackensack *(G-3989)*

Universal Electric Mtr Svc Inc ....E..... 201 968-1000
  Hackensack *(G-3990)*

Willier Elc Mtr Repr Co Inc ....E..... 856 627-2262
  Gibbsboro *(G-3791)*

Willier Elc Mtr Repr Co Inc ....E..... 856 627-3535
  Gibbsboro *(G-3790)*

ELECTRIC SERVICES

C J Electric ....G..... 201 891-0739
  Wyckoff *(G-12247)*

General Electric Company ....C..... 201 866-2161
  North Bergen *(G-7453)*

Lb Electric Co LLC ....G..... 973 366-2188
  Denville *(G-2046)*

ELECTRIC SVCS, NEC: Power Generation

Ocean Power Technologies Inc ....E..... 609 730-0400
  Monroe Township *(G-6387)*

ELECTRIC TOOL REPAIR SVCS

Kissler & Co Inc ....E..... 201 896-9600
  Carlstadt *(G-1179)*

ELECTRICAL APPARATUS & EQPT WHOLESALERS

America Techma Inc ....G..... 201 894-5887
  Englewood Cliffs *(G-2948)*

Antronix Inc ....A..... 609 860-0160
  Cranbury *(G-1813)*

Archtech Electronics Corp ....E..... 732 355-1288
  Dayton *(G-1952)*

Asco Power Technologies LP ....F..... 732 596-1733
  Woodbridge *(G-12145)*

Belden Inc ....F..... 908 925-8000
  Elizabeth *(G-2712)*

Cabletenna Corp ....G..... 609 395-9400
  Cranbury *(G-1818)*

Cisco Systems Inc ....E..... 201 782-0842
  Montvale *(G-6448)*

D Electric Motors Inc ....G..... 856 696-5959
  Vineland *(G-11348)*

DMJ and Associates Inc ....E..... 732 613-7867
  Sayreville *(G-9820)*

Ellenby Technologies Inc ....E..... 856 848-2020
  Woodbury Heights *(G-12175)*

H I D Systems Inc ....G..... 973 383-8535
  Sparta *(G-10503)*

Kinetics Industries Inc ....E..... 609 883-9700
  Ewing *(G-3030)*

Lumiko USA Inc ....G..... 609 409-6900
  Cranbury *(G-1857)*

Luminaire Lighting Corp ....G..... 732 549-0056
  Edison *(G-2560)*

Mac Products Inc ....D..... 973 344-5149
  Kearny *(G-4896)*

Maxlite Inc ....C..... 973 244-7300
  West Caldwell *(G-11788)*

Technology Dynamics Inc ....E..... 201 385-0500
  Bergenfield *(G-396)*

YC Cable (east) Inc ....E..... 732 868-0800
  Piscataway *(G-8837)*

ELECTRICAL APPLIANCES, TELEVISIONS & RADIOS WHOLESALERS

Expert Appliance Center LLC ....G..... 732 946-0999
  Marlboro *(G-5939)*

L&W Audio/Video Inc ....E..... 212 980-2862
  Hoboken *(G-4483)*

Lg Electronics USA Inc ....B..... 201 816-2000
  Englewood Cliffs *(G-2973)*

Sharp Electronics Corporation ....A..... 201 529-8200
  Mahwah *(G-5811)*

W T Winter Associates Inc ....E..... 888 808-3611
  Fairfield *(G-3349)*

Wanasavealotcom LLC ....F..... 732 286-6956
  Toms River *(G-10920)*

ELECTRICAL CURRENT CARRYING WIRING DEVICES

Ametek Inc ....G..... 732 370-9100
  Lakewood *(G-5073)*

Amperite Co Inc ....E..... 201 864-9503
  North Bergen *(G-7430)*

Archtech Electronics Corp ....E..... 732 355-1288
  Dayton *(G-1952)*

Billows Electric Supply Co Inc ....C..... 856 751-2200
  Delran *(G-2010)*

Brim Electronics Inc ....F..... 201 796-2886
  Lodi *(G-5578)*

Cain Machine Inc ....F..... 856 825-7225
  Millville *(G-6291)*

Calculagraph Co ....D..... 973 887-9400
  East Hanover *(G-2204)*

Control Products Inc ....D..... 973 887-5000
  East Hanover *(G-2210)*

Dearborn A Belden Cdt Company ....D..... 908 925-8000
  Elizabeth *(G-2723)*

Frc Electrical Industries Inc ....E..... 908 464-3200
  New Providence *(G-7036)*

G H Krauss Manufacturing Co ....G..... 856 662-0815
  Cherry Hill *(G-1368)*

Hofer Connectors Co Inc ....E..... 973 427-1195
  North Haledon *(G-7548)*

Howell Electronics Inc ....F..... 908 534-2247
  Lebanon *(G-5288)*

HPH Products Inc ....G..... 609 883-0052
  Ewing *(G-3025)*

Kraus & Naimer Inc ....G..... 732 560-1240
  Somerset *(G-10119)*

Lumenarc Inc ....F..... 973 882-5918
  West Caldwell *(G-11784)*

Marine Electric Systems Inc ....E..... 201 531-8600
  South Hackensack *(G-10278)*

Multi-Tech Industries Inc ....F..... 732 431-0550
  Marlboro *(G-5948)*

Newtech Group Corp ....G..... 732 355-0392
  Kendall Park *(G-4935)*

Pekay Industries Inc ....F..... 732 938-2722
  Farmingdale *(G-3392)*

Pressure Controls Inc ....G..... 973 751-5002
  Belleville *(G-312)*

Richards Mfg Co Sales Inc ....E..... 973 371-1771
  Irvington *(G-4604)*

Roxboro Holdings Inc ....D..... 732 919-3119
  Wall Township *(G-11506)*

Signal Systems International ....G..... 732 793-4668
  Lavallette *(G-5237)*

Tycom Limited ....C..... 973 753-3040
  Morristown *(G-6746)*

Unique Wire Weaving Co Inc ....E..... 908 688-4600
  Hillside *(G-4447)*

Vermont Cableworks Inc ....E..... 802 674-6555
  Edison *(G-2643)*

ELECTRICAL DEVICE PARTS: Porcelain, Molded

Electro-Ceramic Industries ....E..... 201 342-2630
  Hackensack *(G-3909)*

ELECTRICAL DISCHARGE MACHINING, EDM

Gale Newson Inc ....E..... 732 961-7610
  Jackson *(G-4668)*

Olympic EDM Services Inc ....G..... 973 492-0664
  Kinnelon *(G-5039)*

ELECTRICAL EQPT & SPLYS

Abacus Electric & Plumbing ....G..... 908 269-8057
  Chester *(G-1433)*

Asco Power Technologies LP ....F..... 732 596-1733
  Woodbridge *(G-12145)*

Asco Power Technologies LP ....F..... 209 547-8874
  Florham Park *(G-3486)*

Asco Power Technologies LP ....B..... 973 966-2000
  Florham Park *(G-3487)*

Avida Incorporated ....G..... 201 802-0749
  Park Ridge *(G-7916)*

Bio-Key International Inc ....E..... 732 359-1100
  Wall Township *(G-11467)*

C J Electric ....G..... 201 891-0739
  Wyckoff *(G-12247)*

Celco ....F..... 201 327-1123
  Mahwah *(G-5757)*

Commercial Pdts Svcs Group Inc ....G..... 609 730-4111
  Pennington *(G-8447)*

Connecting Products Inc ....F..... 609 512-1121
  Skillman *(G-10029)*

Countyline Elec Contrs Corp ....G..... 732 961-6738
  Lakewood *(G-5096)*

Cuny & Guerber Inc ....E..... 201 617-5800
  Union City *(G-11244)*

Daniel Maguire ....E..... 856 767-8443
  West Berlin *(G-11714)*

Dearborn A Belden Cdt Company ....D..... 908 925-8000
  Elizabeth *(G-2723)*

Dewey Electronics Corporation ....E..... 201 337-4700
  Oakland *(G-7684)*

Douglas Elec Components Inc ....D..... 973 627-8230
  Randolph *(G-9274)*

Dranetz Technologies Inc ....D..... 732 248-4358
  Edison *(G-2503)*

E-Beam Services Inc ....E..... 513 933-0031
  Cranbury *(G-1830)*

East Coast Panelboard Inc ....E..... 732 739-6400
  Tinton Falls *(G-10832)*

East West Service Co Inc ....G..... 609 631-9000
  Trenton *(G-11057)*

Eaton Corporation ....E..... 732 767-9600
  Mountainside *(G-6880)*

Edmondmarks Technologies Inc ....E..... 732 643-0290
  Neptune *(G-6909)*

Ellenby Technologies Inc ....E..... 856 848-2020
  Woodbury Heights *(G-12175)*

Engineering Dynamics LLC ....G..... 973 794-4500
  Boonton *(G-565)*

Eos Energy Storage LLC ....E..... 732 225-8400
  Edison *(G-2514)*

Essex Products International ....E..... 973 226-2424
  Caldwell *(G-1028)*

F Walther Electric Corp ....G..... 732 537-9201
  Somerset *(G-10099)*

Francis Metals Company Inc ....F..... 732 761-0500
  Lakewood *(G-5125)*

Frc Electrical Industries Inc ....E..... 908 464-3200
  New Providence *(G-7036)*

Griffith Electric Supply Co ....G..... 609 632-0253
  Windsor *(G-12126)*

H G Schaevitz LLC ....G..... 856 727-0250
  Moorestown *(G-6582)*

H I D Systems Inc ....G..... 973 383-8535
  Sparta *(G-10503)*

Henry Bros Electronics Inc ....D..... 201 794-6500
  Fair Lawn *(G-3094)*

Hitrons Tech Inc ....G..... 201 941-0024
  Ridgefield *(G-9364)*

I 2 R Corp ....G..... 732 919-1100
  Wall Township *(G-11490)*

International Cord Sets Inc ....F..... 973 227-2118
  Fairfield *(G-3232)*

Lb Electric Co LLC ....G..... 973 366-2188
  Denville *(G-2046)*

Ld Electric LLC ....E..... 201 225-1001
  Paramus *(G-7883)*

Malco Electric LLC ....G..... 856 202-5503
  Westville *(G-11946)*

Maxlite Inc ....C..... 973 244-7300
  West Caldwell *(G-11788)*

Mphase Technologies Inc ....F..... 973 256-3737
  Clifton *(G-1676)*

MTS Systems Corporation ....A 856 875-4478
  Williamstown *(G-12093)*

Ocean Energy Industries Inc ....F 954 828-2177
  Oakhurst *(G-7671)*

OHM Equipment LLC ....G 856 765-3011
  Millville *(G-6318)*

Paige Electric Company LP ....E 908 687-7810
  Union *(G-11212)*

PCI Inc ....G 973 226-8007
  West Caldwell *(G-11796)*

Power Brooks Co LLC ....F 609 890-0100
  Hamilton *(G-4121)*

Primary Systems Inc ....F 732 679-2200
  Old Bridge *(G-7790)*

Radnet Inc ....F 908 709-1323
  Cranford *(G-1924)*

Sant-TEC Electric Inc ....E 201 865-4100
  North Bergen *(G-7483)*

Trec Electric ....G 856 374-3433
  Sewell *(G-9966)*

Tri Diamond Enterprises LLC ....G 609 927-6018
  Hammonton *(G-4152)*

Vicmarr Audio Inc ....E 732 289-9111
  Edison *(G-2645)*

Vision Ten Inc ....F 201 935-3000
  Carlstadt *(G-1239)*

Zinni Electric LLC ....G 856 848-8361
  Deptford *(G-2070)*

ELECTRICAL EQPT FOR ENGINES

Dearborn A Belden Cdt Company ....D 908 925-8000
  Elizabeth *(G-2723)*

Dimilo Industries ....G 973 955-0460
  Passaic *(G-8134)*

Dmf Associated Engines LLC ....D 973 535-9773
  Livingston *(G-5528)*

Engine Factory Inc ....E 908 236-9915
  Lebanon *(G-5284)*

Fleetsource LLC ....E 732 566-4970
  Cliffwood *(G-1547)*

J & R Rebuilders Inc ....G 856 627-1414
  Laurel Springs *(G-5233)*

M Parker Autoworks Inc ....E 856 933-0801
  Bellmawr *(G-345)*

ELECTRICAL EQPT REPAIR & MAINTENANCE

ABC Digital Electronics Inc ....G 201 666-6888
  Old Tappan *(G-7796)*

Asco Power Technologies LP ....F 209 547-8874
  Florham Park *(G-3486)*

Binding Products Inc ....E 212 947-1192
  Jersey City *(G-4719)*

Hansome Energy Systems Inc ....E 908 862-9044
  Linden *(G-5382)*

McAllister Service Company ....E 856 665-4545
  Pennsauken *(G-8546)*

Nilsson Electrical Laboratory ....G 201 521-4860
  Jersey City *(G-4790)*

W T Winter Associates Inc ....E 888 808-3611
  Fairfield *(G-3349)*

ELECTRICAL EQPT REPAIR SVCS

Waage Electric Inc ....G 908 245-9363
  Kenilworth *(G-5004)*

ELECTRICAL EQPT REPAIR SVCS: High Voltage

A T C Companies Inc ....E 732 560-0900
  Middlesex *(G-6141)*

Longo Elctrical-Mechanical Inc ....E 973 537-0400
  Linden *(G-5404)*

M&L Power Systems Maint Inc ....E 732 679-1800
  Old Bridge *(G-7783)*

ELECTRICAL EQPT: Automotive, NEC

Auto Action Group Inc ....E 908 964-6290
  Kenilworth *(G-4938)*

ELECTRICAL GOODS, WHOLESALE: Batteries, Storage, Indl

Energy Battery Group Inc ....G 404 255-7529
  Flemington *(G-3439)*

ELECTRICAL GOODS, WHOLESALE: Closed Circuit Television Or TV

L3 Mobile-Vision Inc ....D 973 263-1090
  Rockaway *(G-9583)*

ELECTRICAL GOODS, WHOLESALE: Conduits & Raceways

American Fittings Corp ....G 201 664-0027
  Fair Lawn *(G-3075)*

ELECTRICAL GOODS, WHOLESALE: Connectors

CDM Electronics Inc ....C 856 740-1200
  Turnersville *(G-11141)*

Da-Green Electronics Ltd ....E 732 254-2735
  South River *(G-10460)*

Heilind Electronics Inc ....D 888 881-5420
  Lumberton *(G-5658)*

I Trade Technology Ltd ....G 615 348-7233
  Mahwah *(G-5785)*

ELECTRICAL GOODS, WHOLESALE: Electrical Entertainment Eqpt

Philips Elec N Amer Corp ....D 973 471-9450
  Clifton *(G-1695)*

ELECTRICAL GOODS, WHOLESALE: Electronic Parts

East Coast Electronics Inc ....E 908 431-7555
  Hillsborough *(G-4328)*

Electronic Connections Inc ....F 732 367-5588
  Lakewood *(G-5114)*

Foremost Corp ....G 973 839-3360
  Wayne *(G-11635)*

Infiniti Components Inc ....G 908 537-9950
  Hampton *(G-4161)*

Nitto Americas Inc ....F 732 901-7905
  Lakewood *(G-5165)*

Nitto Americas Inc ....F 201 645-4950
  Teaneck *(G-10763)*

Power Dynamics Inc ....E 973 560-0019
  Whippany *(G-12036)*

State Electronics Parts Corp ....E 973 887-2550
  East Hanover *(G-2244)*

ELECTRICAL GOODS, WHOLESALE: Fittings & Construction Mat

Hofer Connectors Co Inc ....E 973 427-1195
  North Haledon *(G-7548)*

ELECTRICAL GOODS, WHOLESALE: Flashlights

Fuji Electric Corp America ....D 732 560-9410
  Edison *(G-2522)*

ELECTRICAL GOODS, WHOLESALE: Generators

Chatham Lawn Mowler ....G 973 635-8855
  Chatham *(G-1327)*

Power Pool Plus Inc ....G 908 454-1124
  Alpha *(G-44)*

ELECTRICAL GOODS, WHOLESALE: High Fidelity Eqpt

Riotsound Inc ....G 917 273-5814
  Newton *(G-7401)*

ELECTRICAL GOODS, WHOLESALE: Household Appliances, NEC

Boruch Trading Ltd Lblty Co ....G 718 614-9575
  Lakewood *(G-5086)*

ELECTRICAL GOODS, WHOLESALE: Insulators

Tyco Elec Sbsea Cmmnctions LLC ....B 732 578-7000
  Eatontown *(G-2427)*

ELECTRICAL GOODS, WHOLESALE: Intercommunication Eqpt

L J Loeffler Systems Inc ....G 212 924-7597
  Secaucus *(G-9901)*

ELECTRICAL GOODS, WHOLESALE: Irons

Bushwick Metals LLC ....E 908 754-8700
  South Plainfield *(G-10341)*

ELECTRICAL GOODS, WHOLESALE: Light Bulbs & Related Splys

Bulbrite Industries Inc ....E 201 531-5900
  Moonachie *(G-6509)*

ELECTRICAL GOODS, WHOLESALE: Lighting Fixtures, Comm & Indl

Eco Lighting USA Ltd Lblty Co ....G 201 621-5661
  South Hackensack *(G-10262)*

I4 Sustainability LLC ....G 732 618-3310
  Springfield *(G-10557)*

Leland Limited Inc ....F 908 561-2000
  South Plainfield *(G-10398)*

Reggiani Lighting Usa Inc ....F 201 372-1717
  Carlstadt *(G-1211)*

ELECTRICAL GOODS, WHOLESALE: Lugs & Connectors

Richards Mfg Co Sales Inc ....E 973 371-1771
  Irvington *(G-4604)*

ELECTRICAL GOODS, WHOLESALE: Mobile telephone Eqpt

Lg Elctrnics Mbilecomm USA Inc ....D 201 816-2000
  Englewood Cliffs *(G-2972)*

ELECTRICAL GOODS, WHOLESALE: Modems, Computer

Micro Innovations Corp ....D 732 346-9333
  Edison *(G-2571)*

ELECTRICAL GOODS, WHOLESALE: Motor Ctrls, Starters & Relays

Drive Technology Inc ....G 732 422-6500
  Monmouth Junction *(G-6342)*

ELECTRICAL GOODS, WHOLESALE: Motors

Electrical Motor Repr Co of NJ ....F 609 392-6149
  Trenton *(G-11058)*

George J Bender Inc ....E 908 687-0081
  Union *(G-11189)*

Hights Electric Motor Service ....G 609 448-2298
  Hightstown *(G-4312)*

Lakewood Elc Mtr Sls & Svc ....G 732 363-2865
  Howell *(G-4560)*

Phil Desiere Electric Mtr Svc ....F 856 692-8442
  Vineland *(G-11390)*

Universal Electric Co ....E 201 968-1000
  Hackensack *(G-3989)*

Universal Electric Mtr Svc Inc ....F 201 968-1000
  Hackensack *(G-3990)*

Walker Engineering Inc ....F 732 899-2550
  Point Pleasant Boro *(G-8943)*

Willier Elc Mtr Repr Co Inc ....E 856 627-3535
  Gibbsboro *(G-3790)*

ELECTRICAL GOODS, WHOLESALE: Paging & Signaling Eqpt

Turn-Key Technologies Inc ....F 732 553-9100
  Sayreville *(G-9842)*

ELECTRICAL GOODS, WHOLESALE: Panelboards

East Coast Panelboard Inc ....E 732 739-6400
  Tinton Falls *(G-10832)*

ELECTRICAL GOODS, WHOLESALE: Radio & TV Or TV Eqpt & Parts

Philips Elec N Amer Corp ....D 973 471-9450
  Clifton *(G-1695)*

ELECTRICAL GOODS, WHOLESALE: Radio Parts & Access, NEC

Pulsar Microwave Corp ....E...... 973 779-6262
  Clifton *(G-1706)*

ELECTRICAL GOODS, WHOLESALE: Semiconductor Devices

American Microsemiconductor ....E...... 973 377-9566
  Madison *(G-5719)*
Digitron Electronic Corp ....E...... 908 245-2012
  Kenilworth *(G-4952)*
Mulberry Metal Products Inc.................D...... 908 688-8850
  Union *(G-11210)*

ELECTRICAL GOODS, WHOLESALE: Signaling, Eqpt

Intellgent Trffic Sup Pdts LLC..............G...... 908 791-1200
  South Plainfield *(G-10385)*
Salescaster Displays Corp....................G...... 908 322-3046
  Scotch Plains *(G-9854)*

ELECTRICAL GOODS, WHOLESALE: Switches, Exc Electronic, NEC

Asco Valve LLC....................................D...... 973 966-2437
  Florham Park *(G-3488)*

ELECTRICAL GOODS, WHOLESALE: Switchgear

Hoyt Corporation ....D...... 201 894-0707
  Englewood *(G-2904)*

ELECTRICAL GOODS, WHOLESALE: Telephone & Telegraphic Eqpt

Spirent Communications Inc ....G...... 732 946-4018
  Holmdel *(G-4530)*

ELECTRICAL GOODS, WHOLESALE: Telephone Eqpt

National Communications Inc ....E...... 973 325-3151
  West Orange *(G-11901)*

ELECTRICAL GOODS, WHOLESALE: Transformer & Transmission Eqpt

Wolock & Lott Transmission Eqp ....F...... 908 218-9292
  Branchburg *(G-718)*

ELECTRICAL GOODS, WHOLESALE: Tubes, Rcvg & Txmtg Or Indl

Hamamatsu Corporation ....D...... 908 231-0960
  Bridgewater *(G-841)*
Photonics Management Corp ....G...... 908 231-0960
  Bridgewater *(G-874)*

ELECTRICAL GOODS, WHOLESALE: Video Eqpt

Murray Electronics Inc ....G...... 201 405-1158
  Oakland *(G-7697)*

ELECTRICAL GOODS, WHOLESALE: Wire & Cable

Alpha Wire Corporation........................C...... 908 925-8000
  Elizabeth *(G-2708)*
Arose Inc...E...... 856 481-4351
  Blackwood *(G-471)*
Kabel N Elettrotek Amer Inc ....G...... 973 265-0850
  Parsippany *(G-8035)*
Screentek Manufacturing Co LLC ....F...... 973 328-2121
  Randolph *(G-9296)*

ELECTRICAL GOODS, WHOLESALE: Wire & Cable, Ctrl & Sig

Lapp Usa LLC.......................................C...... 973 660-9700
  Florham Park *(G-3511)*
Protection Industries Corp...................F...... 201 333-8050
  Jersey City *(G-4808)*

ELECTRICAL GOODS, WHOLESALE: Wire & Cable, Electronic

Daburn Wire & Cable Corp....................G...... 973 328-3200
  Dover *(G-2084)*
Paige Electric Company LP ....E...... 908 687-7810
  Union *(G-11212)*

ELECTRICAL GOODS, WHOLESALE: Wire & Cable, Power

High Energy Group Ltd Lblty Co ....G...... 732 741-9099
  Eatontown *(G-2400)*

ELECTRICAL INDL APPARATUS, NEC

Active Controls LLC.............................G...... 856 669-0940
  Paulsboro *(G-8412)*
Atm Aficionado LLC ....G...... 973 251-2115
  Livingston *(G-5525)*

ELECTRICAL MEASURING INSTRUMENT REPAIR & CALIBRATION SVCS

Byram Laboratories Inc.......................E...... 908 252-0852
  Branchburg *(G-646)*

ELECTRICAL SPLYS

Billows Electric Supply Co Inc ....C...... 856 751-2200
  Delran *(G-2010)*
Global Business Dimensions Inc ....E...... 973 831-5866
  Pompton Plains *(G-8960)*
Kraus & Naimer Inc.............................E...... 732 560-1240
  Somerset *(G-10119)*
Longo Elctrical-Mechanical Inc ....D...... 973 537-0400
  Wharton *(G-11991)*
Maco Appliance Parts & Sup Co ....G...... 609 272-8222
  Absecon *(G-3)*
Panel Components & Systems ....F...... 973 448-9400
  Stanhope *(G-10589)*
Precision Devices Inc ....G...... 609 882-2230
  Ewing *(G-3045)*

ELECTRICAL SUPPLIES: Porcelain

House of Prill Inc.................................E...... 732 442-2400
  Lincroft *(G-5337)*
Isolantite Manufacturing Co ....E...... 908 647-3333
  Stirling *(G-10602)*
Morgan Advanced Ceramics Inc ....E...... 973 808-1621
  Fairfield *(G-3264)*
Pekay Industries Inc ....F...... 732 938-2722
  Farmingdale *(G-3392)*
Top Knobs Usa Inc ....E...... 908 359-6174
  Somerville *(G-10229)*

ELECTROCARS: Golfer Transportation

Parts Life Inc ....E...... 856 786-8675
  Moorestown *(G-6609)*

ELECTRODES: Fluorescent Lamps

E G L Company Inc ....C...... 908 508-1111
  Berkeley Heights *(G-409)*

ELECTRODES: Indl Process

Siemens Industry Inc ....G...... 732 302-1686
  Warren *(G-11567)*

ELECTROMEDICAL EQPT

Andrew Technologies LLC.....................G...... 215 990-0754
  Haddonfield *(G-4055)*
Bard Healthcare Inc ....F...... 908 277-8000
  New Providence *(G-7028)*
Bayer Healthcare LLC...........................A...... 862 404-3000
  Whippany *(G-12008)*
C R Bard Inc ....C...... 908 277-8000
  New Providence *(G-7032)*
Circulite Inc ....F...... 201 478-7575
  Teaneck *(G-10745)*
Datascope Corp ....G...... 201 995-8000
  Mahwah *(G-5764)*
Datascope Corp ....E...... 201 995-8000
  Mahwah *(G-5762)*
Diabeto Inc ....G...... 646 397-3175
  Piscataway *(G-8758)*
Echo Therapeutics Inc ....F...... 732 201-4189
  Edgewater *(G-2437)*

Electrocore Inc....................................D...... 973 290-0097
  Basking Ridge *(G-186)*
Highlands Acquisition Corp.................G...... 201 573-8400
  Montvale *(G-6459)*
Hilin Life Products Inc ....G...... 973 648-0265
  Newark *(G-7189)*
Medtronic Inc.......................................C...... 908 289-5969
  Swedesboro *(G-10710)*
Mindray Ds Usa Inc ....A...... 201 995-8000
  Mahwah *(G-5791)*
Newcardio Inc......................................F...... 877 332-4324
  Princeton *(G-9080)*
Northeast Medical Systems Corp.........G...... 856 910-8111
  Cherry Hill *(G-1405)*
Radnet Inc...E...... 908 709-1323
  Cranford *(G-1925)*
Rhythmedix LLC...................................G...... 856 282-1080
  Mount Laurel *(G-6835)*
Simex Medical Imaging Inc ....G...... 201 490-0204
  Paramus *(G-7901)*
Sonotron Medical Systems Inc ....G...... 201 767-6040
  Northvale *(G-7608)*
St Jude Medical...................................F...... 908 979-3200
  Hackettstown *(G-4038)*
Syneron ....G...... 201 599-9451
  Paramus *(G-7909)*
Vasculogic LLC....................................G...... 908 278-3573
  Piscataway *(G-8833)*
Vectracor Inc ....F...... 973 904-0444
  Totowa *(G-10977)*
Vectracor Inc ....G...... 973 768-0402
  Totowa *(G-10978)*
Zounds Inc...F...... 856 234-8844
  Mount Laurel *(G-6849)*

ELECTROMEDICAL EQPT WHOLESALERS

Ascensia Diabetes Care US Inc ....C...... 973 560-6500
  Parsippany *(G-7952)*
Orlando Systems Ltd Lblty Co ....G...... 908 400-5052
  North Plainfield *(G-7560)*
State Technology Inc ....G...... 856 467-8009
  Bridgeport *(G-773)*

ELECTRON TUBES

Epcos Inc...D...... 732 906-4300
  Iselin *(G-4626)*
Union City Filament Corp......................E...... 201 945-3366
  Ridgefield *(G-9390)*
World Electronics Inc ....F...... 201 670-1177
  Glen Rock *(G-3830)*

ELECTRON TUBES: Parts

Linear Photonics LLC............................G...... 609 584-5747
  Hamilton *(G-4109)*
Linearizer Technology Inc....................D...... 609 584-5747
  Hamilton *(G-4110)*

ELECTRONIC COMPONENTS

Communication Products Co ....G...... 973 977-8490
  Paterson *(G-8238)*
Tkg Components LLC.............................G...... 609 730-1501
  Pennington *(G-8460)*

ELECTRONIC DEVICES: Solid State, NEC

Elena Consultants & Elec ....E...... 908 654-8309
  Mountainside *(G-6881)*
Pekay Industries Inc ....F...... 732 938-2722
  Farmingdale *(G-3392)*

ELECTRONIC EQPT REPAIR SVCS

Delaware Technologies Inc ....F...... 856 234-7692
  Mount Laurel *(G-6792)*
Instru-Met Corporation ....G...... 908 851-0700
  Union *(G-11195)*
Johnson Controls Inc ....D...... 732 225-6700
  Edison *(G-2549)*
Singe Corporation................................G...... 908 289-7900
  Hillside *(G-4440)*
Test Technology Inc ....D...... 856 596-1215
  Marlton *(G-6001)*

ELECTRONIC LOADS & POWER SPLYS

Algen Design Services Inc ....E...... 732 389-3630
  Eatontown *(G-2379)*
Cooper Interconnect ....G...... 856 935-7560
  Salem *(G-9804)*

P R O D U C T

JFK Supplies Inc ....F 732 985-7800
Edison (G-2545)
Princeton Optronics Inc ....E 609 584-9696
Trenton (G-11108)
Solar Rig Technologies LLC ....G 973 600-0500
Carlstadt (G-1221)

ELECTRONIC PARTS & EQPT WHOLESALERS

ADI American Distributors LLC ....D 973 328-1181
Randolph (G-9267)
Aeroflex Ctrl Components Inc ....D 732 460-0212
Eatontown (G-2378)
Barantec Inc ....F 973 779-8774
Clifton (G-1572)
Brother International Corp ....B 908 704-1700
Bridgewater (G-825)
East West Service Co Inc ....E 609 631-9000
Trenton (G-11057)
Eastern Instrumentation of ....G 856 231-0668
Moorestown (G-6573)
Eaton Corporation ....E 732 767-9600
Mountainside (G-6880)
Epcos Inc ....D 732 906-4300
Iselin (G-4626)
Franklin Electronic Publs Inc ....D 609 386-2500
Burlington (G-974)
Glen Magnetics Inc ....E 908 454-3717
Alpha (G-41)
Gulton G I D ....G 908 791-4622
South Plainfield (G-10376)
J & W Servo Systems Company ....F 973 335-1007
Rockaway (G-9577)
Jerome Industries Corp ....E 908 353-5700
Hackettstown (G-4013)
Kef America Inc ....E 732 414-2074
Marlboro (G-5946)
Link Computer Graphics Inc ....G 973 808-8990
Fairfield (G-3253)
Lucent Technologies World Svcs ....C 908 582-3000
New Providence (G-7046)
Major Auto Installations Inc ....E 973 252-4262
Kenvil (G-5011)
Musings Press Ltd Liability Co ....F 347 210-8820
Union City (G-11259)
Nilsson Electrical Laboratory ....G 201 521-4860
Jersey City (G-4790)
Orlando Systems Ltd Lblty Co ....G 908 400-5052
North Plainfield (G-7560)
P W B Omni Inc ....G 856 384-1300
West Deptford (G-11838)
Panasonic Corp North America ....D 201 348-7000
Newark (G-7261)
Procedyne Corp ....E 732 249-8347
New Brunswick (G-6996)
Ribble Company Inc ....F 201 475-1812
Saddle Brook (G-9786)
RSR Electronics Inc ....E 732 381-8777
Rahway (G-9222)
Sound United LLC ....C 201 762-6500
Mahwah (G-5813)
Vcom Intl Multi-Media Corp ....D 201 296-0600
Fairfield (G-3338)
World Electronics Inc ....F 201 670-1177
Glen Rock (G-3830)
YC Cable (east) Inc ....E 732 868-0800
Piscataway (G-8837)

ELECTRONIC TRAINING DEVICES

Castle Industries Inc ....E 201 585-8400
Englewood Cliffs (G-2952)
Design Assistance Corporation ....F 856 241-9500
Swedesboro (G-10691)
Kft Fire Trainer LLC ....E 201 300-8100
Montvale (G-6463)
Signal Crafters Tech Inc ....G 973 781-0880
East Hanover (G-2243)

ELECTROPLATING & PLATING SVC

G & H Metal Finishers Inc ....G 201 909-9808
Paterson (G-8274)

ELEVATORS & EQPT

Amerivator Systems Corporation ....G 973 471-1200
Clifton (G-1565)
Edi/Eci ....G 973 790-9100
Paterson (G-8253)

Elevator Cabs of NY Inc ....D 973 790-9100
Paterson (G-8256)
Elevator Doors Inc ....C 973 790-9100
Paterson (G-8257)
Elevator Enterances NY Inc ....E 973 790-9100
Paterson (G-8258)
Elevator Entrance Inc ....E 973 790-9100
Paterson (G-8259)
Elevator Technology Corp ....E 973 523-7760
Paterson (G-8260)
Flor Lift of N J Inc ....E 973 429-2200
Fairfield (G-3197)
Otis Elevator Intl Inc ....E 973 575-7030
Fairfield (G-3277)
Schindler Elevator Corporation ....B 973 397-6500
Morristown (G-6740)
Schindler Elevator Corporation ....E 856 234-2220
Moorestown (G-6621)
TEC Elevator Inc ....F 609 938-0647
Marmora (G-6007)

ELEVATORS WHOLESALERS

Otis Elevator Company ....E 856 235-5200
Moorestown (G-6607)
Otis Elevator Intl Inc ....C 973 575-7030
Fairfield (G-3277)

ELEVATORS: Installation & Conversion

G-Tech Elevator Associates LLC ....F 866 658-9296
Linden (G-5378)
Otis Elevator Intl Inc ....C 973 575-7030
Fairfield (G-3277)
Schindler Elevator Corporation ....B 973 397-6500
Morristown (G-6740)
Schindler Elevator Corporation ....E 856 234-2220
Moorestown (G-6621)
Schindler Enterprises Inc ....F 973 397-6500
Morristown (G-6741)

ELEVATORS: Stair, Motor Powered

Archi-Tread Inc ....G 973 725-5738
Kinnelon (G-5033)

EMBLEMS: Embroidered

Chenille Products Inc ....F 201 703-1917
Palisades Park (G-7837)
Golden Rule Creations Inc ....G 201 337-4050
Franklin Lakes (G-3619)
Its The Pitts Inc ....G 609 645-7319
Pleasantville (G-8910)
Patchworks Co Inc ....G 973 627-2002
Dover (G-2106)
Uniport Industries Corporation ....G 201 391-7676
Woodcliff Lake (G-12206)
Wally Enterprises Inc ....F 732 329-2613
Monmouth Junction (G-6371)
World Class Marketing Corp ....G 201 313-0022
Fort Lee (G-3591)

EMBOSSING SVC: Paper

Turul Bookbindery Inc ....G 973 361-2810
Wharton (G-12003)

EMBROIDERING & ART NEEDLEWORK FOR THE TRADE

Ambro Manufacturing Inc ....F 908 806-8337
Flemington (G-3425)
Arts Embroidery LLC ....G 732 870-2400
West Long Branch (G-11843)
C & D Sales ....G 609 383-9292
Pleasantville (G-8903)
CDK Industries LLC ....G 856 488-5456
Cherry Hill (G-1356)
Embroidery In Stitches Inc ....F 732 460-2660
Morganville (G-6641)
Gilbert Storms Jr ....G 973 835-5729
Haskell (G-4207)
Imagery Embroidary Corporation ....F 201 343-9333
Union City (G-11248)
Innovative Design Inc ....G 201 227-2555
Cresskill (G-1946)
J and S Sporting Apparel LLC ....G 732 787-5500
Keansburg (G-4856)
Mary Bridget Enterprises ....E 609 267-4830
Cinnaminson (G-1475)
Mt Embroidery & Promotions LLC ....G 201 646-1070
Norwood (G-7629)

NJ Logo Wear LLC ....G 609 597-9400
Manahawkin (G-5832)
Pro Image Promotions Inc ....G 973 252-8000
Kenvil (G-5013)
Risse & Risse Graphics Inc ....E 856 751-7671
Runnemede (G-9721)
Sgh Inc ....G 609 698-8868
Barnegat (G-165)
Star Embroidery Corp ....E 973 481-4300
Newark (G-7328)
Unique Embroidery Inc ....F 201 943-9191
Elmwood Park (G-2853)
University Fashions By Janet ....G 856 228-1615
Williamstown (G-12111)

EMBROIDERING SVC

A Stitch Ahead ....F 609 586-1068
Trenton (G-11013)
Advantage Ds LLC ....F 856 307-9600
Glassboro (G-3800)
Apollo East LLC ....E 856 486-1882
Pennsauken (G-8478)
Bauer Sport Shop ....G 201 384-6522
Dumont (G-2115)
Bon-Jour Group LLC ....F 201 646-1070
Norwood (G-7616)
Cozy Formal Wear Inc ....G 973 661-9781
Nutley (G-7645)
Creative Embroidery Corp ....E 973 497-5700
Newark (G-7130)
Design N Stitch Inc ....G 201 488-1314
Hackensack (G-3904)
Dezine Line Inc ....G 973 989-1009
Wharton (G-11985)
Embroideries Unlimited Inc ....G 201 692-1560
Teaneck (G-10752)
J & S Finishing Inc ....G 201 854-0338
West New York (G-11868)
J & T Embroidery Inc ....F 201 867-4897
Union City (G-11249)
Midland Screen Printing Inc ....F 201 703-0066
Saddle Brook (G-9775)
Pioneer Embroidery Co ....G 973 777-6418
South Hackensack (G-10289)
Semels Embroidery Inc ....F 973 473-6868
Clifton (G-1719)
Sequins of Distinction Inc ....G 201 348-8111
North Bergen (G-7486)
Sniderman John ....F 201 569-5482
Englewood (G-2932)
South Amboy Designer T Shirt L ....G 732 456-2594
South Amboy (G-10245)
Toni Embroidery ....F 201 664-6909
Westwood (G-11973)
William Cromley ....G 856 881-6019
Clayton (G-1529)
Wostbrock Embroidery Inc ....G 201 445-3074
Midland Park (G-6243)

EMBROIDERING SVC: Schiffli Machine

Carolace Embroidery Co Inc ....D 201 945-2151
Ridgefield (G-9354)
Chenille Products Inc ....F 201 703-1917
Palisades Park (G-7837)
Embroidery Concepts ....G 973 942-8555
Paterson (G-8261)
Eyelet Embroideries Inc ....D 201 945-2151
Ridgefield (G-9359)
Goralski Inc ....E 201 573-1529
Park Ridge (G-7921)
Hamilton Embroidery Co Inc ....F 201 867-4084
Union City (G-11247)
Jacqueline Embroidery Co ....G 732 278-8121
Hackensack (G-3932)
John M Sniderman Inc ....G 201 450-4291
Fairview (G-3363)
Marlene Embroidery Inc ....G 201 868-1682
West New York (G-11873)
O Stitch Matic Inc ....G 201 861-3045
Guttenberg (G-3870)
Quadelle Textile Corp ....F 201 865-1112
West New York (G-11879)
Tone Embroidery Corp ....E 201 943-1082
Fairview (G-3371)
Tri-Chem Inc ....F 973 751-9200
Belleville (G-320)
Weber & Doebrich Inc ....G 201 868-6122
West New York (G-11883)

EMBROIDERY ADVERTISING SVCS

All Colors Screen Printing LLC ....G....... 732 777-6033
  Highland Park *(G-4300)*
L & F Graphics Ltd Lblty Co ....G....... 973 240-7033
  Paterson *(G-8312)*
Madhouz LLC ....G....... 609 206-8009
  Glassboro *(G-3808)*
Red Diamond Company ....G....... 973 759-2005
  Belleville *(G-314)*
Wally Enterprises Inc ....F....... 732 329-2613
  Monmouth Junction *(G-6371)*

EMBROIDERY KITS

Five Kids Group Inc ....G....... 732 774-5331
  Neptune *(G-6912)*

EMERGENCY ALARMS

Blitz Safe of America Inc ....F....... 201 569-5000
  Englewood *(G-2877)*
Confires Fire Prtction Svc LLC ....F....... 908 822-2700
  South Plainfield *(G-10349)*
Cricket Enterprises ....G....... 201 387-7978
  Dumont *(G-2117)*
D2cf LLC ....G....... 973 699-4111
  West Orange *(G-11892)*

EMPLOYMENT AGENCY SVCS

Crystal Deltronic Industries ....F....... 973 328-7000
  Dover *(G-2083)*

EMPLOYMENT SVCS: Labor Contractors

Enser Corporation ....E....... 856 829-5522
  Cinnaminson *(G-1461)*

ENAMELS

Kadakia International Inc ....G....... 908 754-4445
  South Plainfield *(G-10391)*
Tevco Enterprises Inc ....D....... 908 754-7306
  South Plainfield *(G-10439)*

ENCLOSURES: Electronic

Leibrock Metal Products Inc ....G....... 732 695-0326
  Ocean *(G-7731)*
Magic Metal Works Inc ....G....... 201 384-8457
  Bergenfield *(G-389)*
Par Metal Products Inc ....F....... 201 955-0800
  North Arlington *(G-7422)*
Pepco Manufacturing Co ....G....... 856 783-3700
  Somerdale *(G-10042)*
Stamplus Manufacturing Inc ....F....... 908 241-8844
  Roselle *(G-9683)*

ENCODERS: Digital

Flir Security Inc ....G....... 201 368-9700
  Ridgefield Park *(G-9406)*
R P R Graphics Inc ....E....... 908 654-8080
  Peapack *(G-8432)*
Videonet Comm Group LLC ....F....... 732 863-5310
  Freehold *(G-3691)*

ENDOCRINE PRDTS

Ipsen Biopharmaceuticals Inc ....C....... 908 275-6300
  Basking Ridge *(G-191)*

ENERGY MEASUREMENT EQPT

Glow Tube Inc ....G....... 609 268-7707
  Shamong *(G-9969)*
Nice Instrumentation ....F....... 732 851-4300
  Manalapan *(G-5855)*

ENGINE PARTS & ACCESS: Internal Combustion

Coates International Ltd ....G....... 732 449-7717
  Wall Township *(G-11472)*
Davis Hyundai ....F....... 609 883-3500
  Ewing *(G-3013)*
Grobet File Company Amer LLC ....D....... 201 939-6700
  Carlstadt *(G-1165)*

ENGINE REBUILDING: Diesel

Cast Technology Inc ....G....... 908 753-5155
  South Plainfield *(G-10344)*

Melton Sales & Service ....E....... 609 699-4800
  Bordentown *(G-602)*
Melton Sales & Service ....E....... 609 699-4800
  Columbus *(G-1805)*
Penske Truck Leasing Co LP ....E....... 973 575-0169
  Parsippany *(G-8060)*

ENGINE REBUILDING: Gas

Arrow Machine Company Inc ....G....... 973 642-2430
  Newark *(G-7095)*

ENGINEERING SVCS

Adam Gates & Company LLC ....F....... 908 829-3386
  Hillsborough *(G-4316)*
Advance Machine Planning Inc ....F....... 732 356-4438
  Middlesex *(G-6144)*
Aeon Engineering LLC ....G....... 518 253-7681
  Fort Lee *(G-3542)*
Alecto Systems LLC ....G....... 973 875-6721
  Branchville *(G-725)*
American Soc of Mech Engineers ....D....... 973 244-2282
  Little Falls *(G-5468)*
Anvima Technologies LLC ....G....... 973 531-7077
  Brookside *(G-922)*
Applicad Inc ....E....... 732 751-2555
  Wall Township *(G-11463)*
Bel Hybrids & Magnetics Inc ....F....... 201 432-0463
  Jersey City *(G-4716)*
Bishop Ascendant Inc ....G....... 973 210-5298
  West Caldwell *(G-11768)*
Carpenter & Paterson Inc ....E....... 973 772-1800
  Bordentown *(G-592)*
Centurum Information Tech Inc ....G....... 856 751-1111
  Marlton *(G-5967)*
Defense Spport Svcs Intl 2 LLC ....F....... 856 866-2200
  Marlton *(G-5970)*
Dengen Scientific Corporation ....E....... 201 687-2983
  Union City *(G-11245)*
Essex Products International ....E....... 973 226-2424
  Caldwell *(G-1028)*
Fin-Tek Corporation ....G....... 973 628-2988
  Wayne *(G-11634)*
Foster Wheeler Arabia Ltd ....G....... 908 730-4000
  Hampton *(G-4156)*
Foster Wheeler Intl Corp ....F....... 908 730-4000
  Hampton *(G-4157)*
Global Power Technology Inc ....D....... 732 287-3680
  Edison *(G-2528)*
Helidex LLC ....G....... 201 636-2546
  East Rutherford *(G-2299)*
Holtec International ....B....... 856 797-0900
  Camden *(G-1069)*
Hosokawa Micron International ....C....... 908 273-6360
  Summit *(G-10644)*
Jaktool LLC ....F....... 609 664-2451
  Cranbury *(G-1844)*
Jdv Products Inc ....F....... 201 794-6467
  Fair Lawn *(G-3098)*
Jentec Inc ....G....... 201 784-1031
  Northvale *(G-7587)*
Joseph Oat Holdings Inc ....B....... 856 541-2900
  Camden *(G-1072)*
Krell Technologies Inc ....G....... 732 617-7091
  Neptune *(G-6921)*
Lattice Incorporated ....F....... 856 910-1166
  Pennsauken *(G-8542)*
Lockheed Martin Corporation ....D....... 856 722-7782
  Moorestown *(G-6594)*
Lummus Technology Ventures LLC ....G....... 973 893-1515
  Bloomfield *(G-521)*
Magnetic Products and Svcs Inc ....G....... 732 264-6651
  Holmdel *(G-4520)*
Microcast Technologies Corp ....D....... 908 523-9503
  Linden *(G-5409)*
Mistras Group Inc ....C....... 609 716-4000
  Princeton Junction *(G-9159)*
MTS Systems Corporation ....A....... 856 875-4478
  Williamstown *(G-12093)*
Parkway-Kew Corporation ....F....... 732 398-2100
  North Brunswick *(G-7533)*
Performance Alloys & Materials ....G....... 201 865-5268
  Secaucus *(G-9910)*
Primacy Engineering Inc ....F....... 201 731-3272
  Englewood Cliffs *(G-2979)*
Primary Systems Inc ....F....... 732 679-2200
  Old Bridge *(G-7790)*
Princeton Keynes Group Inc ....F....... 609 951-2239
  Princeton *(G-9096)*
Procedyne Corp ....E....... 732 249-8347
  New Brunswick *(G-6996)*

S L P Engineering Inc ....D....... 732 240-3696
  Toms River *(G-10908)*
Shock Tech Inc ....E....... 845 368-8600
  Mahwah *(G-5812)*
Specialty Systems Inc ....E....... 732 341-1011
  Toms River *(G-10913)*
Tbt Group Inc ....E....... 856 753-4500
  Bellmawr *(G-353)*
Tech Products Co Inc ....E....... 201 444-7777
  Midland Park *(G-6239)*
Total Technology Inc ....E....... 856 617-0502
  Cherry Hill *(G-1429)*
Turner Engineering Inc ....F....... 973 263-1000
  Mountain Lakes *(G-6863)*
V G Controls Inc ....G....... 973 764-6500
  Oakland *(G-7709)*

ENGINEERING SVCS: Aviation Or Aeronautical

Thales Avionics Inc ....C....... 732 242-6300
  Piscataway *(G-8823)*

ENGINEERING SVCS: Building Construction

All Seasons Construction Inc ....G....... 908 852-0955
  Long Valley *(G-5634)*

ENGINEERING SVCS: Chemical

Innovasystems Inc ....F....... 856 722-0410
  Moorestown *(G-6586)*
Scientific Design Company ....C....... 201 641-0500
  Little Ferry *(G-5516)*

ENGINEERING SVCS: Construction & Civil

Acrow Corporation of America ....E....... 973 244-0080
  Parsippany *(G-7938)*
Enterprisecc Ltd Liability Co ....G....... 201 266-0020
  Jersey City *(G-4749)*
Tanis Concrete ....E....... 201 796-1556
  Fair Lawn *(G-3119)*

ENGINEERING SVCS: Electrical Or Electronic

Advanced Industrial Controls ....G....... 908 725-7575
  Branchburg *(G-628)*
Automation & Control Inc ....E....... 856 234-2300
  Moorestown *(G-6562)*
Creatone Inc ....F....... 908 789-8700
  Mountainside *(G-6870)*
Edmondmarks Technologies Inc ....E....... 732 643-0290
  Neptune *(G-6909)*
Griffith Electric Sup Co Inc ....D....... 609 695-6121
  Trenton *(G-11061)*
Intertek Laboratories Inc ....E....... 908 903-1800
  Stirling *(G-10601)*
Johnson Controls Inc ....D....... 732 225-6700
  Edison *(G-2549)*
Patriot American Solutions LLC ....D....... 862 209-4772
  Rockaway *(G-9594)*
Thomas Instrumentation Inc ....F....... 609 624-2630
  Cape May Court House *(G-1118)*

ENGINEERING SVCS: Energy conservation

Atlantic Clean Energy Sup LLC ....G....... 888 900-1581
  Branchburg *(G-641)*

ENGINEERING SVCS: Industrial

Foster Wheeler Zack Inc ....D....... 908 730-4000
  Hampton *(G-4158)*
Rapid Models & Prototypes Inc ....G....... 856 933-2929
  Runnemede *(G-9720)*

ENGINEERING SVCS: Machine Tool Design

Edmund Kiss ....G....... 973 810-2312
  Landing *(G-5223)*

ENGINEERING SVCS: Mechanical

Connecting Products Inc ....F....... 609 512-1121
  Skillman *(G-10029)*
Enser Corporation ....E....... 856 829-5522
  Cinnaminson *(G-1461)*
J Blanco Associates Inc ....F....... 973 427-0619
  Hawthorne *(G-4243)*
S J T Imaging Inc ....D....... 201 262-7744
  Oradell *(G-7813)*

Employee Codes: A=Over 500 employees, B=251-500
C=101-250, D=51-100, E=20-50, F=10-19, G=4-9

2018 Harris New jersey
Manufacturers Directory

PRODUCT

855

Sigma Engineering & Consulting ....F 732 356-3046
   Middlesex *(G-6197)*

STS Technologies LLC ....F 973 277-5416
   Mahwah *(G-5817)*

ENGINEERING SVCS: Structural

Coperion Corporation ....C 201 327-6300
   Sewell *(G-9946)*

East Coast Storage Eqp Co Inc ....E 732 451-1316
   Brick *(G-742)*

ENGINES & ENGINE PARTS: Guided Missile, Research & Develpt

Aphelion Orbitals Inc ....G 321 289-0872
   Union City *(G-11242)*

Lockheed Martin Corporation ....B 856 787-3104
   Mount Laurel *(G-6814)*

ENGINES: Diesel & Semi-Diesel Or Duel Fuel

Penn Power Group LLC ....F 732 441-1489
   Matawan *(G-6028)*

ENGINES: Gasoline, NEC

Roy Anania ....G 201 498-1555
   Hackensack *(G-3967)*

ENGINES: Internal Combustion, NEC

Cummins - Allison Corp ....G 201 791-2394
   Elmwood Park *(G-2813)*

Cummins Inc ....D 973 491-0100
   Kearny *(G-4870)*

Henry Jackson Racing Engines ....G 609 758-7476
   Cream Ridge *(G-1936)*

ENGRAVING SVC, NEC

Armotek Industries Inc ....E 856 829-4585
   Palmyra *(G-7846)*

Beauty Wood Designs ....G 908 687-9697
   Union *(G-11157)*

Blue Ribbon Awards Inc ....G 732 560-0046
   Somerset *(G-10070)*

Crown Trophy ....G 973 808-8400
   Pine Brook *(G-8696)*

Pochet of America Inc ....C 973 942-4923
   Woodland Park *(G-12228)*

Precise Corporate Printing Inc ....E 973 350-0330
   Harrison *(G-4187)*

Sunset Printing and Engrv Corp ....E 973 537-9600
   Wharton *(G-12000)*

Winemiller Press Inc ....G 732 223-0100
   Manasquan *(G-5884)*

ENGRAVING SVC: Jewelry & Personal Goods

Awards Trophy Company ....G 908 687-5775
   Hillside *(G-4394)*

Diamond Hut Jewelry Exchange ....G 201 332-5372
   Jersey City *(G-4743)*

Heros Salute Awards Co ....G 973 696-5085
   Wayne *(G-11648)*

Koehler Industries Inc ....G 732 364-2700
   Howell *(G-4559)*

ENGRAVING SVCS

Bannister Company Inc ....F 732 828-1353
   Milltown *(G-6267)*

Jory Engravers Inc ....G 201 939-1546
   Rutherford *(G-9736)*

NJ Logo Wear LLC ....G 609 597-9400
   Manahawkin *(G-5832)*

ENGRAVING: Bank Note

Starnet Business Solutions ....E 201 252-2863
   Mahwah *(G-5814)*

ENGRAVINGS: Plastic

Foster Engraving Corporation ....G 201 489-5979
   Hackensack *(G-3918)*

ENTERTAINERS

Foto Fantasy ....G 732 548-8446
   Edison *(G-2521)*

ENTERTAINERS & ENTERTAINMENT GROUPS

Sony Music Holdings Inc ....B 201 777-3933
   Rutherford *(G-9745)*

ENTERTAINMENT PROMOTION SVCS

Bng Industries LLC ....F 862 229-2414
   Harrison *(G-4173)*

ENTERTAINMENT SVCS

J Media LLC ....G 201 600-4573
   Norwood *(G-7627)*

Pentacle Publishing Corp ....E 732 240-3000
   Toms River *(G-10901)*

ENVELOPES

Bravo Pack Inc ....E 856 872-2937
   Pennsauken *(G-8488)*

Cenveo Inc ....D 201 434-2100
   Jersey City *(G-4725)*

Corporate Envelope & Prtg Co ....G 732 752-4333
   Green Brook *(G-3855)*

Red Wallet Connection Inc ....D 201 223-2644
   Manchester *(G-5889)*

Tpg Graphics LLC ....G 856 314-0117
   Pennsauken *(G-8586)*

United Envelope LLC ....C 201 699-5800
   Ridgefield *(G-9392)*

Washington Stamp Exchange Inc ....F 973 966-0001
   Florham Park *(G-3523)*

Watonka Printing Inc ....E 732 974-8878
   Belmar *(G-365)*

ENVELOPES WHOLESALERS

Allied Envelope Co Inc ....E 201 440-2000
   Carlstadt *(G-1124)*

Arna Marketing Inc ....E 908 231-1100
   Branchburg *(G-639)*

Bravo Pack Inc ....G 856 872-2937
   Pennsauken *(G-8488)*

Cenveo Inc ....D 201 434-2100
   Jersey City *(G-4725)*

Five Macs Inc ....E 856 596-3150
   Marlton *(G-5975)*

ENZYMES

Techenzyme Inc ....G 732 632-8600
   Iselin *(G-4648)*

EPOXY RESINS

Anti Hydro International Inc ....F 908 284-9000
   Flemington *(G-3427)*

Cvc Specialty Chemicals Inc ....F 856 533-3000
   Moorestown *(G-6571)*

Innovative Resin Systems Inc ....G 973 465-6887
   Newark *(G-7197)*

Innovative Resin Systems Inc ....E 973 465-6887
   Wayne *(G-11651)*

Innovative Resin Systems Inc ....G 973 633-5342
   Wayne *(G-11652)*

Phoenix Resins Inc ....F 888 627-3769
   Cinnaminson *(G-1485)*

Sika Corporation ....C 201 933-8800
   Lyndhurst *(G-5709)*

Sika Corporation ....B 201 933-8800
   Lyndhurst *(G-5708)*

EQUIPMENT: Rental & Leasing, NEC

Armstrong and Sons Inc ....G 732 223-1555
   Manasquan *(G-5867)*

Atlas Flasher & Supply Co Inc ....E 856 423-3333
   Mickleton *(G-6136)*

Fleetsource LLC ....E 732 566-4970
   Cliffwood *(G-1547)*

Gamka Sales Co Inc ....G 732 248-1400
   Edison *(G-2525)*

Harsco Corporation ....E 856 779-7795
   Cherry Hill *(G-1374)*

Power Pool Plus Inc ....G 908 454-1124
   Alpha *(G-44)*

Safety-Kleen Systems Inc ....F 609 859-2049
   Southampton *(G-10481)*

Trac Intermodal LLC ....G 609 452-8900
   Princeton *(G-9130)*

Trac Interstar LLC ....G 609 452-8900
   Princeton *(G-9131)*

Traffic Safety Service LLC ....E 908 561-4800
   South Plainfield *(G-10441)*

Vineland Syrup Inc ....E 856 691-5772
   Vineland *(G-11417)*

ERASERS: Rubber Or Rubber & Abrasive Combined

Asbury Carbons Inc ....G 908 537-2155
   Asbury *(G-66)*

ETCHING & ENGRAVING SVC

A Smith & Son Inc ....G 609 747-0800
   Burlington *(G-952)*

Acme Engraving Co Inc ....E 973 778-0885
   Passaic *(G-8124)*

Bannister Company Inc ....F 732 828-1353
   Milltown *(G-6267)*

Foster Engraving Corporation ....G 201 489-5979
   Hackensack *(G-3918)*

W & E Baum Bronze Tablet Corp ....E 732 866-1881
   Freehold *(G-3692)*

ETHYLENE-PROPYLENE RUBBERS: EPDM Polymers

Bezwada Biomedical LLC ....G 908 281-7529
   Hillsborough *(G-4320)*

Kelleigh USA Inc ....G 732 248-1161
   Ewing *(G-3029)*

Nova Polymers Inc ....F 973 227-6695
   Fairfield *(G-3275)*

EXHAUST SYSTEMS: Eqpt & Parts

Matthey Johnson Inc ....C 856 384-7132
   West Deptford *(G-11835)*

EXPANSION JOINTS: Rubber

La Favorite Industries Inc ....F 973 279-1266
   Paterson *(G-8316)*

EXPLOSIVES

Cartridge Actuated Devices ....E 973 575-8760
   Fairfield *(G-3157)*

EXPLOSIVES, EXC AMMO & FIREWORKS WHOLESALERS

Cartridge Actuated Devices ....E 973 347-2281
   Byram Township *(G-1021)*

EXTENSION CORDS

Gogreen Power Inc ....F 732 994-5901
   Howell *(G-4555)*

EXTERMINATING PRDTS: Household Or Indl Use

Si Packaging LLC ....F 973 869-9920
   Rutherford *(G-9744)*

EXTRACTS, FLAVORING

A A Sayia & Company Inc ....G 201 659-1179
   Hoboken *(G-4455)*

Allen Flavors Inc ....C 908 561-5995
   Edison *(G-2456)*

Allen Flavors Inc ....F 908 753-0544
   South Plainfield *(G-10323)*

Brand Aromatics Intl Inc ....G 732 363-1204
   Lakewood *(G-5088)*

Elan Inc ....D 973 344-8014
   Newark *(G-7150)*

Flavor & Fragrance Spc Inc ....D 201 828-9400
   Mahwah *(G-5773)*

Flavor Associates Inc ....F 973 238-9300
   Hawthorne *(G-4236)*

Flavor Dynamics Inc ....E 888 271-8424
   South Plainfield *(G-10366)*

Flavor Solutions Inc ....G 732 354-1931
   Piscataway *(G-8767)*

Flavors of Origin Inc ....G 201 460-8306
   Carlstadt *(G-1161)*

Givaudan Flavors Corporation ....C 973 386-9800
   East Hanover *(G-2219)*

(G-0000) Company's Geographic Section entry number

Ifc Products Inc ....F 908 587-1221
　Linden **(G-5384)**

Interntnal Flvors Frgrnces Inc ....D ... 732 329-4600
　Dayton **(G-1972)**

Mastertaste Inc ....F 201 373-1111
　Teterboro **(G-10805)**

Medallion International Inc ....F 973 616-3401
　Pompton Plains **(G-8962)**

Natural Flavors Inc ....E 973 589-1230
　Newark **(G-7248)**

Penta International Corp ....D ... 973 740-2300
　Livingston **(G-5554)**

Sentrex Ingredients LLC ....G 908 862-4440
　Linden **(G-5440)**

Whittle & Mutch Inc ....F 856 235-1165
　Mount Laurel **(G-6846)**

EXTRUDED SHAPES, NEC: Copper & Copper Alloy

Amrod Corp ....G 973 344-2978
　Newark **(G-7084)**

Amrod Corp ....D ... 973 344-3806
　Newark **(G-7085)**

EYEGLASS CASES

Colemax Group LLC ....G 201 489-1080
　River Edge **(G-9463)**

EYEGLASSES

Essilor Laboratories Amer Inc ....F 732 563-9884
　Warren **(G-11547)**

I See Optical Laboratories ....G 856 795-6435
　Voorhees **(G-11433)**

Marcolin USA Eyewear Corp ....D ... 800 345-8482
　Branchburg **(G-678)**

Motif Industries Inc ....F 973 575-1800
　East Hanover **(G-2229)**

Viva International Inc ....B 908 595-6200
　Branchburg **(G-717)**

EYES: Artificial

Jeffery S Zlotnick Od ....G 732 549-3555
　Metuchen **(G-6113)**

New Jersey Eye Center Inc ....F 201 384-7333
　Bergenfield **(G-391)**

Richard Danz & Sons Inc ....E 212 697-5722
　Glen Rock **(G-3829)**

Ethylene Glycols

Nan Ya Plastics Corp America ....E 973 992-1775
　Livingston **(G-5549)**

FABRIC STORES

Pioneer Embroidery Co ....G 973 777-6418
　South Hackensack **(G-10289)**

FABRICATED METAL PRODUCTS, NEC

Apogee Technologies LLC ....F 973 575-8448
　Towaco **(G-10987)**

Hurricane Hutch ....G 908 256-5912
　Chester **(G-1437)**

Ironbound Metal ....G 973 242-5704
　Newark **(G-7200)**

Safe Man LLC ....G 800 320-2589
　Alpha **(G-45)**

FABRICS & CLOTHING: Rubber Coated

Ansell Protective Products LLC ....A 732 345-5400
　Iselin **(G-4613)**

Pacific Dunlop Investments USA ....F 732 345-5400
　Red Bank **(G-9340)**

Tingley Rubber Corporation ....E 800 631-5498
　Piscataway **(G-8825)**

FABRICS: Alpacas, Cotton

Meadowgate Farm Alpacas ....G 609 219-0529
　Lawrenceville **(G-5262)**

FABRICS: Alpacas, Mohair, Woven

Alma Park Alpacas ....G 732 620-1052
　Jobstown **(G-4853)**

FABRICS: Animal Fiber, Narrow Woven

Paterson Bleachery Inc ....F 973 684-1034
　Paterson **(G-8361)**

FABRICS: Apparel & Outerwear, Broadwoven

Dollfus Mieg Company Inc ....C 732 662-1005
　Edison **(G-2502)**

Soh LLC ....E 646 943-4066
　Jersey City **(G-4830)**

FABRICS: Apparel & Outerwear, Cotton

Aurora Apparel Inc ....G 201 646-4590
　Hackensack **(G-3876)**

Green Distribution LLC ....D ... 201 293-4381
　Secaucus **(G-9893)**

Quantum Vector Corp ....G 201 870-1782
　Westwood **(G-11967)**

Refuel Inc ....G 917 645-2974
　South Hackensack **(G-10292)**

FABRICS: Automotive, Cotton

Allison Corp ....G 973 992-3800
　Livingston **(G-5523)**

FABRICS: Automotive, From Manmade Fiber

Allison Corp ....G 973 992-3800
　Livingston **(G-5523)**

FABRICS: Bandage Cloth, Cotton

Vacs Bandage Company Inc ....F 973 345-3355
　Paterson **(G-8407)**

FABRICS: Basket Weave, Cotton

Gene Mignola Inc ....G 732 775-9291
　Asbury Park **(G-78)**

FABRICS: Broadwoven, Cotton

Picture Knits Inc ....E 973 340-3131
　Clifton **(G-1696)**

Stanek Netting Co Inc ....G 973 680-1616
　Bloomfield **(G-531)**

Tex Gul Inc ....G 973 857-3200
　Cedar Grove **(G-1301)**

Trimtex Company Inc ....D ... 201 945-2151
　Englewood Cliffs **(G-2984)**

FABRICS: Broadwoven, Synthetic Manmade Fiber & Silk

Absecon Mills Inc ....C 609 965-5373
　Cologne **(G-1775)**

Alex Silk Co Inc ....G 973 427-0499
　Hawthorne **(G-4217)**

Fablok Mills Inc ....E 908 464-1950
　New Providence **(G-7034)**

New Community Corp ....E 973 643-5300
　Newark **(G-7249)**

Nyltite Corp of America ....F 908 561-1300
　South Plainfield **(G-10417)**

Nyp Corp (frmr Ny-Pters Corp) ....D ... 908 351-6550
　Elizabeth **(G-2761)**

Paterson Bleachery Inc ....F 973 684-1034
　Paterson **(G-8361)**

Picture Knits Inc ....E 973 340-3131
　Clifton **(G-1696)**

Star Binding & Trimming LLC ....E 201 864-2220
　Lodi **(G-5601)**

Wearbest Sil-Tex Mills Ltd ....D ... 973 340-8844
　Garfield **(G-3772)**

FABRICS: Broadwoven, Wool

C3 Concepts Inc ....E 212 840-1116
　North Bergen **(G-7437)**

French Creek Sheep & Wool Co ....E 610 286-5700
　Ventnor City **(G-11291)**

Paterson Bleachery Inc ....F 973 684-1034
　Paterson **(G-8361)**

FABRICS: Canvas

Canvas 4 Life Inc ....G 973 276-3200
　Pine Brook **(G-8690)**

FABRICS: Coated Or Treated

AK Associates LLC ....G 732 786-0002
　Jackson **(G-4652)**

Alpha Associates Inc ....E 732 730-1800
　Lakewood **(G-5067)**

Ferland Industries Inc ....G 732 246-3200
　Colts Neck **(G-1784)**

Gleicher Manufacturing Corp ....E 908 233-2211
　Scotch Plains **(G-9849)**

Laboratory Diagnostics Co Inc ....F 732 536-6300
　Morganville **(G-6646)**

PCC Asia LLC ....G 973 890-3873
　Totowa **(G-10961)**

Precision Custom Coatings LLC ....B 973 890-3873
　Totowa **(G-10966)**

Safer Textile Processing Corp ....B 973 482-6400
　Newark **(G-7300)**

FABRICS: Decorative Trim & Specialty, Including Twist Weave

Amt Stitch Inc ....G 732 376-0009
　Perth Amboy **(G-8607)**

FABRICS: Denims

Blue Monkey Inc ....G 201 805-0055
　Saddle Brook **(G-9756)**

Westchester Denim Brothers Inc ....G 203 260-1629
　Ridgefield **(G-9394)**

FABRICS: Fiberglass, Broadwoven

Thomas Clark Fiberglass LLC ....G 609 492-9257
　Barnegat **(G-167)**

United Eqp Fabricators LLC ....G 973 242-2737
　Newark **(G-7353)**

FABRICS: Hat Band

Cranial Technologies Inc ....E 201 265-3993
　Paramus **(G-7863)**

FABRICS: Jacquard Woven, Cotton

Jacquard Fabrics Inc ....E 732 905-4545
　Lakewood **(G-5138)**

FABRICS: Lace & Decorative Trim, Narrow

Wingold Embroidery LLC ....G 732 845-9802
　Freehold **(G-3693)**

FABRICS: Lace & Lace Prdts

Westchester Lace & Textiles ....C 201 864-2150
　North Bergen **(G-7495)**

World Class Marketing Corp ....E 201 313-0022
　Fort Lee **(G-3591)**

FABRICS: Lace, Knit, NEC

Royal Lace Co Inc ....E 718 495-9327
　Rahway **(G-9221)**

FABRICS: Laminated

Butler Prtg & Laminating Inc ....C 973 838-8550
　Butler **(G-999)**

Custom Laminations Inc ....E 973 279-9174
　Paterson **(G-8243)**

Daf Products Inc ....F 201 251-1222
　Wyckoff **(G-12249)**

W C Omni Incorporated ....E 732 248-0999
　Edison **(G-2648)**

FABRICS: Laundry, Cotton

Pueblo Latino Laundry LLC ....G 201 864-1666
　Union City **(G-11263)**

FABRICS: Manmade Fiber, Narrow

Reddaway Manufacturing Co Inc ....F 973 589-1410
　Newark **(G-7287)**

FABRICS: Nonwoven

Fabrictex LLC ....G 732 225-3990
　Edison **(G-2518)**

JKA Specialties Mfr Inc ....F 609 859-2090
　Southampton **(G-10476)**

Klein Ribbon Corp ....E 973 684-4671
　Paterson **(G-8310)**

P R O D U C T

FABRICS: Paper, Broadwoven

Invitation Studio .... G 732 740-5558
Morganville **(G-6645)**

FABRICS: Pile, Circular Knit

Susan Mills Inc .... F 908 355-1400
Hillside **(G-4443)**

FABRICS: Polypropylene, Broadwoven

Kt America Corp .... F 609 655-5333
Cranbury **(G-1850)**

FABRICS: Print, Cotton

Designs By James .... G 856 692-1316
Vineland **(G-11352)**
Musings Press Ltd Liability Co .... F 347 210-8820
Union City **(G-11259)**
Teefx Screen Printing LLC .... G 973 942-6800
Haledon **(G-4086)**

FABRICS: Resin Or Plastic Coated

Alpha Engneered Composites LLC ...... C 732 634-5700
Lakewood **(G-5068)**
Commercial Products Co Inc .... F 973 427-6887
Hawthorne **(G-4227)**
DMS Inc .... G 973 928-3040
Cedar Grove **(G-1279)**
Interplast Universal Inds .... E 973 471-4100
Lodi **(G-5589)**
Plastic By All LLC .... G 732 785-5900
Brick **(G-755)**

FABRICS: Rubberized

American Braiding & Mfg Corp .... F 732 938-6333
Howell **(G-4545)**

FABRICS: Scrub Cloths

Medical Scrubs Collectn NJ LLC ..... G 732 719-8600
Lakewood **(G-5158)**

FABRICS: Seat Cover, Automobile, Cotton

Fh Group International Inc .... E 201 210-2426
Secaucus **(G-9883)**

FABRICS: Shirting, Cotton

Avail Inc .... G 732 560-2222
Bridgewater **(G-817)**

FABRICS: Shoe

Stanbee Company Inc .... E 201 933-9666
Carlstadt **(G-1222)**

FABRICS: Spunbonded

Fibertech Group Inc .... C 856 697-1600
Landisville **(G-5231)**

FABRICS: Trimmings

A S A P Nameplate & Labeling ...... F 973 773-3934
Passaic **(G-8122)**
All Nu Trophy & Screen Prtg .... F 201 807-0808
Ridgefield Park **(G-9396)**
Allied Elastic Braid Inc .... E 201 941-8875
Saddle Brook **(G-9751)**
Amcor Phrm Packg USA Inc .... C 856 728-9300
Williamstown **(G-12078)**
Art Guild Inc .... F 732 390-5300
East Brunswick **(G-2135)**
Aztec Graphics Inc .... F 609 587-1000
Trenton **(G-11023)**
Budget Print Center .... G 973 743-0073
Bloomfield **(G-503)**
C Q Corporation .... F 201 935-8488
East Rutherford **(G-2289)**
Clarici Graphics Inc .... E 609 587-7204
Trenton **(G-11041)**
Color Comp Inc .... G 856 262-3040
Williamstown **(G-12083)**
Cox Stationers and Printers .... E 908 928-1010
Linden **(G-5363)**
Creative Embroidery Corp .... E 973 497-5700
Newark **(G-7130)**
Custom Graphics of Vineland .... E 856 691-7858
Vineland **(G-11347)**

Donray Printing Inc .... E 973 515-8100
Parsippany **(G-7984)**
Elegant USA LLC .... D 973 812-8820
Totowa **(G-10943)**
Family Screen Printing Inc .... F 856 933-2780
Bellmawr **(G-340)**
Jrm Industries Inc .... D 973 779-9340
Passaic **(G-8152)**
Klein Ribbon Corp .... E 973 684-4671
Paterson **(G-8310)**
Lukoil N Arlington Ltd Lblty .... E 856 722-6425
Moorestown **(G-6599)**
Mar-Kal Products Corp .... E 973 783-7155
Carlstadt **(G-1187)**
Monogram Center Inc .... E 732 442-1800
Perth Amboy **(G-8624)**
Painting Inc .... F 201 489-6565
South Hackensack **(G-10287)**
Phoenix Glass LLC .... E 856 692-0100
Pittsgrove **(G-8847)**
Prismatix Decal Inc .... E 201 525-2800
Hackensack **(G-3965)**
R & B Printing Inc .... E 908 766-4073
Bernardsville **(G-454)**
Red Diamond Company .... G 973 759-2005
Belleville **(G-314)**
Rutler Screen Printing Inc .... F 908 859-3327
Phillipsburg **(G-8669)**
Safer Textile Processing Corp ...... B 973 482-6400
Newark **(G-7300)**
Scher Fabrics Inc .... E 212 382-2266
Freehold **(G-3687)**
Screened Images Inc .... E 732 651-8181
East Brunswick **(G-2182)**
Semels Embroidery Inc .... F 973 473-6868
Clifton **(G-1719)**
Sniderman John .... E 201 569-5482
Englewood **(G-2932)**
Stefan Enterprises Inc .... E 973 253-6005
Garfield **(G-3765)**
Stone Graphics .... F 732 919-1111
Wall Township **(G-11511)**
Suzie Mac Specialties Inc .... E 732 238-3500
East Brunswick **(G-2191)**
Toppan Printing Co Amer Inc ...... C 732 469-8400
Somerset **(G-10188)**
U S Screening Corp .... E 973 242-1110
Newark **(G-7350)**
Unique Screen Printing Corp ...... E 908 925-3773
Linden **(G-5456)**
Z Line Beachwear .... G 732 793-1234
Lavallette **(G-5238)**
Zone Two Inc .... F 732 237-0766
Bayville **(G-263)**

FABRICS: Trimmings, Textile

Allied Bias Products Corp .... F 201 432-6050
Jersey City **(G-4702)**
Marlene Trimmings LLC .... E 201 926-3108
North Bergen **(G-7464)**
Textol Systems Inc .... E 800 624-8746
Carlstadt **(G-1228)**
Trimtex Company Inc .... D 201 945-2151
Englewood Cliffs **(G-2984)**

FABRICS: Umbrella Cloth, Cotton

Umbrellas Unlimited .... G 201 476-1011
River Vale **(G-9472)**

FABRICS: Underwear, Cotton

Easy Undies LLC .... G 201 715-4909
Springfield **(G-10552)**
Leggs Hns Bli Plytx Fctry Outl ..... G 908 289-7262
Elizabeth **(G-2751)**

FABRICS: Upholstery, Cotton

Absecon Mills Inc .... C 609 965-5373
Cologne **(G-1775)**

FABRICS: Wall Covering, From Manmade Fiber Or Silk

L&M Architectural Graphics Inc ..... F 973 575-7665
Fairfield **(G-3245)**

FABRICS: Warp & Flat Knit Prdts

Stern Knit Inc .... G 732 364-8055
Lakewood **(G-5192)**

FABRICS: Warp Knit, Lace & Netting

All-Lace Processing Corp .... F 201 867-1974
North Bergen **(G-7427)**
Fablok Mills Inc .... E 908 464-1950
New Providence **(G-7034)**
Jason Mills LLC .... G 732 651-7200
Milltown **(G-6269)**

FABRICS: Weft Or Circular Knit

Meadows Knitting Corp .... E 973 482-6400
Newark **(G-7238)**
Trimtex Company Inc .... D 201 945-2151
Englewood Cliffs **(G-2984)**

FABRICS: Woven Wire, Made From Purchased Wire

Newark Wire Cloth Company .... E 973 778-4478
Clifton **(G-1683)**

FABRICS: Woven, Narrow Cotton, Wool, Silk

Allied Elastic Braid Inc .... E 201 941-8875
Saddle Brook **(G-9751)**
Avitex Co Inc .... E 973 242-2410
Newark **(G-7101)**
Avitex Co Inc .... G 973 242-2410
Newark **(G-7102)**
Hamilton Embroidery Co Inc .... F 201 867-4084
Union City **(G-11247)**
Otex Specialty Narrow Fabrics ..... G 908 879-3636
Bernardsville **(G-452)**

FACE PLATES

Mulberry Metal Products Inc .... D 908 688-8850
Union **(G-11210)**

FACILITIES SUPPORT SVCS

Tmg Enterprises Inc .... E 732 469-2900
Piscataway **(G-8826)**

FACSIMILE COMMUNICATION EQPT

Swintec Corp .... F 201 935-0115
Moonachie **(G-6548)**

FAMILY CLOTHING STORES

Marmaxx Operating Corp .... D 973 575-7910
West Caldwell **(G-11785)**
Stretch-O-Rama Inc .... E 732 855-1400
Avenel **(G-153)**

FANS, VENTILATING: Indl Or Commercial

Building Performance Eqp Inc ...... F 201 722-1414
Hillsdale **(G-4380)**

FARM PRDTS, RAW MATERIALS, WHOLESALE: Nuts & Nut By-Prdts

Kalustyan Corporation .... D 908 688-0853
Union **(G-11200)**

FARM SPLY STORES

Mendham Garden Center .... G 973 543-4178
Mendham **(G-6089)**

FARM SPLYS WHOLESALERS

Le-Ed Construction Inc .... E 732 341-4546
Toms River **(G-10893)**

FARM SPLYS, WHOLESALE: Feed

Glenburnie Feed & Grain .... G 856 986-8128
Mount Laurel **(G-6800)**

FARM SPLYS, WHOLESALE: Fertilizers & Agricultural Chemicals

Purely Organic SA LLC .... G 201 942-0400
Jersey City **(G-4810)**

FARM SPLYS, WHOLESALE: Greenhouse Eqpt & Splys

Cutting Edge Grower Supply LLC .... G 732 905-9220
Howell **(G-4551)**

FARM SPLYS, WHOLESALE: Insecticides

Pic Corporation.................................E 908 862-7977
Linden (G-5429)

FARM SPLYS, WHOLESALE: Soil, Potting & Planting

Saxton Falls Sand & Gravel Co ....E 908 852-0121
Budd Lake (G-943)

FASTENERS WHOLESALERS

Industrial Rivet & Fastener Co.............D 201 750-1040
Northvale (G-7584)

FASTENERS: Metal

Celus Fasteners Mfg Inc...................E 800 289-7483
Northvale (G-7576)
CMF Ltd Inc ....E 609 695-3600
Ewing (G-3010)
General Sullivan Group Inc...............F 609 745-5000
Pennington (G-8452)
Imperial Weld Ring Corp Inc ....E 908 354-0011
Elizabeth (G-2746)
Rotor Clip Company Inc ....B 732 469-7707
Somerset (G-10168)
Taurus Precision Inc.......................E 973 785-9254
Little Falls (G-5491)

FASTENERS: Notions, NEC

Alpine Machine & Tool Corp ....F 201 666-0959
Westwood (G-11953)
Amershoe Corp ....G 201 569-7300
Englewood (G-2869)
Arlo Corporation ....G 973 618-0030
Roseland (G-9645)
C & C Metal Products Corp ....D 201 569-7300
Englewood (G-2880)
Captive Fasteners Corp ....B 201 337-6800
Oakland (G-7678)
Communique Inc............................G 973 751-7588
Belleville (G-298)
Crown Fastener & Supply Corp...........G 845 268-5150
Ringwood (G-9446)
Fastenation Inc............................E 973 591-1277
Clifton (G-1618)
Nyltite Corp of America ....F 908 561-1300
South Plainfield (G-10417)
Straps Manufacturing NJ Inc ....F 201 368-5201
Wyckoff (G-12264)

FASTENERS: Notions, Zippers

Case It Inc ....E 800 441-4710
Lyndhurst (G-5675)
Royal Slide Sales Co Inc ....G 973 777-1177
Garfield (G-3757)
Royal Zipper Manufg Company ....F 973 777-1177
Garfield (G-3758)
Snapco Manufacturing Corp ....E 973 282-0300
Hillside (G-4441)

FATTY ACID ESTERS & AMINOS

Barnet Products Corporation ....F 201 346-4620
Englewood Cliffs (G-2949)

FELT, WHOLESALE

Central Shippee Inc ....E 973 838-1100
Bloomingdale (G-541)

FENCE POSTS: Iron & Steel

Anello Fence LLC..........................E 973 692-9200
Pequannock (G-8598)
Robinson Tech Intl Corp ....G 973 287-6458
Fairfield (G-3296)

FENCES & FENCING MATERIALS

General Metal Manufacturing Co...........E 973 386-1818
East Hanover (G-2218)
Master Wire Manufacturing Co ....E 609 561-2900
Hammonton (G-4144)

FENCING DEALERS

All-State Fence Inc.........................E 732 431-4944
West Orange (G-11885)

Blue Gauntlet Fencing Gear Inc ....F 201 797-3332
Saddle Brook (G-9755)
Doerre Fence Co LLC ....F 732 751-9700
Farmingdale (G-3384)
Great Railing Inc ....F 856 875-0050
Williamstown (G-12089)
Hoda Inc ....F 609 695-3000
Trenton (G-11063)
National Fence Systems Inc ....D 732 636-5600
Avenel (G-143)
Walpole Woodworkers Inc ....E 973 539-3555
Morris Plains (G-6681)
Wayside Fence Company Inc ....E 201 791-7979
Fair Lawn (G-3124)

FENCING MADE IN WIREDRAWING PLANTS

Blue Gauntlet Fencing Gear Inc ....F 201 797-3332
Saddle Brook (G-9755)
Fence America New Jersey Inc ....G 973 472-5121
Hackensack (G-3910)

FENCING MATERIALS: Docks & Other Outdoor Prdts, Wood

Comprelli Equipment and Svc ....G 973 428-8687
East Hanover (G-2208)
Larsen Marine Services LLC ....G 609 408-3564
Sea Isle City (G-9863)
Medford Cedar Products Inc ....G 609 859-1400
Southampton (G-10479)
Wardale Corp ....E 800 813-4050
Lakewood (G-5204)

FENCING MATERIALS: Plastic

Fencemax ....G 609 646-2265
Newfield (G-7366)
Freedom Vinyl Systems Inc ....G 973 692-0332
Pequannock (G-8600)
Onguard Fence Systems Ltd ....E 908 429-5522
Branchburg (G-684)
Onguard Fence Systems Ltd ....E 908 429-5522
Branchburg (G-685)

FENCING MATERIALS: Snow Fence, Wood

P & S Blizzard Corporation ....G 973 523-1700
Paterson (G-8358)

FENCING MATERIALS: Wood

All-State Fence Inc.........................E 732 431-4944
West Orange (G-11885)
Doerre Fence Co LLC ....F 732 751-9700
Farmingdale (G-3384)
General Metal Manufacturing Co...........E 973 386-1818
East Hanover (G-2218)
Hoda Inc ....F 609 695-3000
Trenton (G-11063)
National Fence Systems Inc ....D 732 636-5600
Avenel (G-143)
Walpole Woodworkers Inc ....E 973 539-3555
Morris Plains (G-6681)

FENCING: Chain Link

Belmont Whl Fence Mfg Inc ....E 973 472-5121
Garfield (G-3723)
Security Fabricators Inc ....F 908 272-9171
Kenilworth (G-4996)

FERRITES

Fermag Technologies Inc..................G 732 985-7300
Toms River (G-10875)
Merrimac Industries Inc....................D 973 575-1300
West Caldwell (G-11790)

FERTILIZER, AGRICULTURAL: Wholesalers

Big Bucks Enterprises Inc ....E 908 320-7009
Washington (G-11578)

FERTILIZERS: NEC

Growmark Fs LLC..........................F 609 267-7054
Eastampton (G-2376)
Reed & Perrine Inc ....E 732 446-6363
Tennent (G-10790)

FERTILIZERS: Nitrogenous

Agrium Advanced Tech US Inc ....F 732 296-8448
North Brunswick (G-7503)
Growmark Fs LLC..........................F 609 267-7054
Eastampton (G-2376)

FERTILIZERS: Phosphatic

Growmark Fs LLC..........................F 609 267-7054
Eastampton (G-2376)
Innophos Holdings Inc ....D 609 495-2495
Cranbury (G-1839)
Innophos Invstmnts Hldings Inc ....G 609 495-2495
Cranbury (G-1842)
Missry Associates Inc ....C 732 752-7500
Edison (G-2574)

FIBER & FIBER PRDTS: Acrylic

Natures Choice Corporation ....F 973 969-3299
Sparta (G-10513)

FIBER & FIBER PRDTS: Organic, Noncellulose

Allied-Signal China Ltd.....................E 973 455-2000
Morristown (G-6685)
Northeast Pro-Tech Inc.....................F 973 777-5654
Passaic (G-8167)
Solutia Inc...................................G 908 862-0278
Linden (G-5445)

FIBER & FIBER PRDTS: Polyester

Carlee Corporation ....E 201 768-6800
Rockleigh (G-9627)
Nan Ya Plastics Corp America ....E 973 992-1775
Livingston (G-5549)

FIBER & FIBER PRDTS: Synthetic Cellulosic

Cytec Industries Inc........................C 973 357-3100
Saddle Brook (G-9761)
Endot Industries Inc ....D 973 625-8500
Rockaway (G-9564)
Newark Fibers Inc ....G 201 768-6800
Rockleigh (G-9632)
Steiner Paper Corp ....G 732 651-6009
Manalapan (G-5863)

FIBER & FIBER PRDTS: Vinyl

Jaclyn Holdings Parent LLC ....G 201 909-6000
Maywood (G-6053)
Jaclyn LLC ....D 201 909-6000
Maywood (G-6054)

FIBER OPTICS

C Technologies Inc ....E 908 707-1009
Bridgewater (G-826)
Fiberguide Industries Inc ....E 908 647-6601
Stirling (G-10600)
Go Foton Corporation ....F 732 412-7375
Somerset (G-10106)
Metro Optics LLC ....F 908 413-0004
Flemington (G-3457)
Princeton Hosted Solutions LLC..........F 856 470-2350
Haddonfield (G-4062)
Princeton Optronics Inc ....E 609 584-9696
Trenton (G-11108)
Radiant Communications Corp ....E 908 757-7444
South Plainfield (G-10432)

FILE FOLDERS

Red Wallet Connection Inc.................D 201 223-2644
Manchester (G-5889)

FILM & SHEET: Unsuppported Plastic

All American Poly Corp ....C 732 752-3200
Piscataway (G-8730)
Arch Crown Inc ....E 973 731-6300
Hillside (G-4390)
Berry Global Inc ....C 908 353-3850
Elizabeth (G-2714)
Berry Global Inc ....E 908 454-0900
Phillipsburg (G-8643)
Berry Global Inc ....C 609 395-4199
Cranbury (G-1814)
Berry Global Films LLC ....C 201 641-6600
Montvale (G-6446)

Corbco Inc ....G........ 609 549-6299
Forked River *(G-3536)*

Fordion Packaging Ltd ....F........ 201 692-1344
Hackensack *(G-3916)*

Heritage Bag Company ....D........ 856 467-2247
Swedesboro *(G-10702)*

JA Heilferty LLC ....E........ 201 836-5060
Teaneck *(G-10757)*

Kolon USA Incorporated ....F........ 201 641-5800
Ridgefield Park *(G-9409)*

Montrose Molders Corporation ....C........ 908 754-3030
South Plainfield *(G-10410)*

Niaflex Corporation ....F........ 407 851-6620
Livingston *(G-5552)*

Pegasus Products Inc ....E........ 908 707-1122
Branchburg *(G-688)*

Plastic Plus Group LLC ....E........ 201 561-0405
Secaucus *(G-9911)*

Productive Plastics Inc ....D........ 856 778-4300
Mount Laurel *(G-6832)*

Trinity Plastics Inc ....C........ 973 994-8018
Livingston *(G-5566)*

US Plastic Sales LLC ....G........ 908 754-9404
South Plainfield *(G-10446)*

Vish LLC ....E........ 201 529-2900
North Brunswick *(G-7546)*

FILM BASE: Cellulose Acetate Or Nitrocellulose Plastics

Nobelus LLC ....G........ 800 895-2747
North Brunswick *(G-7531)*

FILTERS

Camfil USA Inc ....C........ 973 616-7300
Riverdale *(G-9476)*

Carol Products Co Inc ....D........ 732 918-0800
Ocean *(G-7718)*

Coilhose Pneumatics Inc ....E........ 732 432-7177
East Brunswick *(G-2142)*

Complete Filter ....G........ 732 441-0321
South Amboy *(G-10235)*

Enviro-Clear Company Inc ....F........ 908 638-5507
High Bridge *(G-4295)*

Filtration Solutions Inc ....G........ 908 684-4000
Hackettstown *(G-4007)*

Mar Cor Purification Inc ....G........ 973 521-7032
Fairfield *(G-3255)*

Membranes International Inc ....G........ 973 998-5530
Ringwood *(G-9451)*

Nichem Co ....G........ 973 399-9810
Newark *(G-7259)*

FILTERS & SOFTENERS: Water, Household

Aries Filterworks Inc ....E........ 856 626-1550
Berlin *(G-425)*

Clearwater Well Drilling Co ....G........ 609 698-1800
Manahawkin *(G-5829)*

Filter Technologies Inc ....E........ 732 329-2500
Monmouth Junction *(G-6344)*

Graver Water Systems LLC ....F........ 973 465-2380
Newark *(G-7177)*

Lanxess Sybron Chemicals Inc ....C........ 609 893-1100
Birmingham *(G-468)*

Quality Plus One Catering Inc ....G........ 732 967-1525
Old Bridge *(G-7791)*

FILTERS & STRAINERS: Pipeline

Eaton Filtration LLC ....B........ 732 767-4200
Tinton Falls *(G-10833)*

Hayward Industries Inc ....B........ 908 351-5400
Elizabeth *(G-2742)*

FILTERS: Air

Brookaire Company LLC ....F........ 973 473-7527
Carlstadt *(G-1133)*

Envirnmntal Dynamics Group Inc ....F........ 609 924-4489
Rocky Hill *(G-9637)*

Tri-Dim Filter Corporation ....G........ 856 786-2447
Cinnaminson *(G-1496)*

FILTERS: Air Intake, Internal Combustion Engine, Exc Auto

Star Process Heat Systems LLC ......G........ 732 282-1002
Neptune *(G-6933)*

FILTERS: Gasoline, Internal Combustion Engine, Exc Auto

Fluid Filtration Corp ....F........ 973 253-7070
Garfield *(G-3734)*

FILTERS: General Line, Indl

Admiral Filter Company LLC ....F........ 973 664-0400
Rockaway *(G-9543)*

Industrial Filters Company ....G........ 973 575-0533
Fairfield *(G-3229)*

Kavon Filter Products Co ....F........ 732 938-3135
Wall Township *(G-11492)*

Liquid-Solids Separation Corp ....E........ 201 236-4833
Ramsey *(G-9245)*

Newton Tool & Mfg Inc ....G........ 856 241-1500
Pennsauken *(G-8554)*

Summit Filter Corp ....E........ 908 687-3500
Union *(G-11226)*

Universal Filters Inc ....E........ 732 774-8555
Asbury Park *(G-87)*

FILTERS: Motor Vehicle

Felco Products LLC ....G........ 973 890-7979
Paterson *(G-8271)*

FILTERS: Paper

Allied Group Inc ....E........ 973 543-4994
Mendham *(G-6086)*

Rockline Industries Inc ....C........ 973 257-2884
Montville *(G-6493)*

Seaboard Paper and Twine LLC ......E........ 973 413-8100
Paterson *(G-8380)*

Tekkote Corporation ....D........ 201 585-1708
Leonia *(G-5321)*

FILTRATION DEVICES: Electronic

NMP Water Systems LLC ....G........ 201 252-8333
Mahwah *(G-5796)*

Summit Intl Filtration Systems ....G........ 201 847-2370
Wyckoff *(G-12265)*

Ultra Clean Technologies Corp ....E........ 856 451-2176
Bridgeton *(G-801)*

FILTRATION SAND MINING

Cherishmet Inc ....F........ 201 842-7612
Rutherford *(G-9728)*

Inversand Company Inc ....G........ 856 881-2345
Clayton *(G-1525)*

FINANCIAL SVCS

Invessence Inc ....E........ 201 977-1955
Chatham *(G-1329)*

Michelex Corporation ....E........ 201 977-1177
Prospect Park *(G-9170)*

Optherium Labs Ou ....E........ 516 253-1777
Holmdel *(G-4528)*

SMR Research Corporation ....G........ 908 852-7677
Hackettstown *(G-4037)*

Sueta Music Ed Publications ....F........ 888 725-2333
Mendham *(G-6091)*

FINDINGS & TRIMMINGS Fabric, NEC

Alco Trimming ....G........ 201 854-8608
North Bergen *(G-7426)*

Artistic Bias Products Co Inc ....E........ 732 382-4141
Rahway *(G-9175)*

Star Binding & Trimming LLC ....E........ 201 864-2220
Lodi *(G-5601)*

FINDINGS & TRIMMINGS: Apparel

Green Distribution LLC ....D........ 201 293-4381
Secaucus *(G-9893)*

FINDINGS & TRIMMINGS: Fabric

Newark Auto Top Co Inc ....F........ 973 677-9935
East Orange *(G-2262)*

FINDINGS & TRIMMINGS: Furniture, Fabric

Associated Fabrics Corporation ....G........ 201 300-6053
Fair Lawn *(G-3078)*

FINGERNAILS, ARTIFICIAL

Polish Nail ....G........ 732 627-9799
Middlesex *(G-6189)*

FINGERPRINT EQPT

Bio-Key International Inc ....E........ 732 359-1100
Wall Township *(G-11467)*

FINISHING AGENTS: Textile

Arol Chemical Products Co ....G........ 973 344-1510
Newark *(G-7094)*

Pariser Industries Inc ....E........ 973 569-9090
Paterson *(G-8360)*

FIRE ALARM MAINTENANCE & MONITORING SVCS

Checkpoint Security Systems Gr ....C........ 952 933-8858
West Deptford *(G-11820)*

Checkpoint Systems Inc ....C........ 952 933-8858
West Deptford *(G-11823)*

FIRE ARMS, SMALL: Guns Or Gun Parts, 30 mm & Below

2a Holdings Inc ....F........ 973 378-8011
Maplewood *(G-5913)*

FIRE ARMS, SMALL: Rifles Or Rifle Parts, 30 mm & below

Henry RAC Holding Corp ....D........ 201 858-4400
Bayonne *(G-231)*

Way It Was Sporting Svc Inc ....G........ 856 231-0111
Moorestown *(G-6631)*

FIRE DETECTION SYSTEMS

Protection Industries Corp ....F........ 201 333-8050
Jersey City *(G-4808)*

Tyco International MGT Co LLC ....E........ 609 720-4200
Princeton *(G-9133)*

FIRE ESCAPES

C W Grimmer & Sons Inc ....F........ 732 741-2189
Tinton Falls *(G-10825)*

FIRE EXTINGUISHER CHARGES

Firefighter One Ltd Lblty Co ....G........ 973 940-3061
Sparta *(G-10499)*

FIRE EXTINGUISHERS: Portable

Absolute Protective Systems ....E........ 732 287-4500
Edison *(G-2448)*

C Bennett Scopes Inc ....G........ 856 464-6889
Mantua *(G-5891)*

Pem Systems Inc ....E........ 908 276-0211
Cranford *(G-1921)*

Tyco International MGT Co LLC ....E........ 609 720-4200
Princeton *(G-9133)*

FIRE OR BURGLARY RESISTIVE PRDTS

Crestron Electronics Inc ....C........ 201 767-3400
Rockleigh *(G-9628)*

RISE Corporation ....E........ 973 575-7480
West Caldwell *(G-11804)*

Williams Scotsman Inc ....G........ 856 429-0315
Kearny *(G-4922)*

FIRE PROTECTION EQPT

Life Liners Inc ....G........ 973 635-9234
Chatham *(G-1333)*

Madison Park Volunteer Fire Co ....E........ 732 727-1143
Parlin *(G-7935)*

Pem Systems Inc ....E........ 908 276-0211
Cranford *(G-1921)*

Specified Technologies Inc ....C........ 908 526-8000
Branchburg *(G-705)*

Township of Carneys Point ....F........ 856 299-4973
Carneys Point *(G-1247)*

FIRE PROTECTION, GOVERNMENT: Local

Township of Carneys Point ....F........ 856 299-4973
Carneys Point *(G-1247)*

FIREPLACE & CHIMNEY MATERIAL: Concrete

Associate Fireplace Builders...............G.... 908 273-5900
Summit (G-10636)

Van Brill Pool & Spa Center ....G.... 856 424-4333
Marlton (G-6002)

FIREWOOD, WHOLESALE

Kane Wood Fuel ....G.... 856 589-3292
Pitman (G-8843)

Vine Hill Farm ....G.... 973 383-0100
Newton (G-7411)

FISH & SEAFOOD PROCESSORS: Canned Or Cured

Cape May Foods LLC ....E.... 856 825-8111
Millville (G-6292)

Gerber Products Company ....C.... 973 593-7500
Florham Park (G-3504)

Point Lobster Company Inc ....F.... 732 892-1718
Point Pleasant Beach (G-8926)

Sea Harvest Inc ....E.... 609 884-3000
Cape May (G-1105)

Sushi House Inc ....E.... 201 482-0609
Palisades Park (G-7844)

FISH & SEAFOOD PROCESSORS: Fresh Or Frozen

Azuma Foods Intl Inc USA ....F.... 201 372-1112
East Rutherford (G-2282)

Black Sea Fisheries ....G.... 973 553-1580
Fort Lee (G-3548)

Certified Clam Corp ....F.... 732 872-6650
Highlands (G-4307)

Golden Tropics Ltd ....E.... 973 484-0202
Newark (G-7176)

Hillard Bloom Packing Co Inc ....G.... 856 785-0120
Port Norris (G-8980)

Lm Foods LLC ....D.... 732 855-9500
Carteret (G-1262)

New Jrsey Sfood Mktg Group LLC ....G.... 609 296-7026
Egg Harbor City (G-2668)

Ruggiero Sea Food Inc ....D.... 973 589-0524
Newark (G-7294)

Ruggiero Sea Food Inc ....G.... 973 589-0524
Newark (G-7295)

Sushi House Inc ....E.... 201 482-0609
Palisades Park (G-7844)

FISH LIVER OILS: For Medicinal Use, Refined Or Concentrated

Matinas Biopharma Holdings Inc ....F.... 908 443-1860
Bedminster (G-278)

FISHING EQPT: Lures

Lure Lash...............................F.... 973 783-5274
Montclair (G-6421)

Richard Andrus ....G.... 856 825-1782
Millville (G-6323)

FISHING EQPT: Nets & Seines

Richard Andrus ....G.... 856 825-1782
Millville (G-6323)

FITTINGS & ASSEMBLIES: Hose & Tube, Hydraulic Or Pneumatic

American Hose Hydraulic Co Inc ....E.... 973 684-3225
Paterson (G-8208)

Robert H Hoover & Sons Inc...............G.... 973 347-4210
Flanders (G-3414)

FITTINGS: Pipe

Dason Stainless Products Co ....F.... 732 382-7272
Rahway (G-9183)

Exclusive Materials LLC ....G.... 732 886-9956
Lakewood (G-5119)

Pennsylvania Machine Works Inc ....E.... 856 467-0500
Swedesboro (G-10717)

Piping Supplies Inc ....G.... 609 561-9323
Williamstown (G-12096)

Ramco Manufacturing Co Inc ....E.... 908 245-4500
Kenilworth (G-4991)

Syntiro Dynamics LLC.......................G.... 732 377-3307
Wall Township (G-11513)

Taylor Forge Stainless Inc ....D.... 908 722-1313
Branchburg (G-708)

Tkl Specialty Piping Inc ....G.... 908 454-0030
Phillipsburg (G-8674)

FITTINGS: Pipe, Fabricated

A&M Industrial Inc ....F.... 908 862-1800
Avenel (G-121)

Euro Mechanical Inc ....F.... 201 313-8050
Fairview (G-3361)

FIXTURES & EQPT: Kitchen, Metal, Exc Cast Aluminum

Epi Group Ltd Liability Co...............G.... 917 710-6607
Lakewood (G-5117)

Vigo Industries LLC ....E.... 866 591-7792
Edison (G-2646)

FIXTURES & EQPT: Kitchen, Porcelain Enameled

Artistic Hardware ....G.... 609 383-1909
Northfield (G-7563)

FIXTURES: Bank, Metal, Ornamental

Zone Defense Inc ....F.... 973 328-0436
Hackettstown (G-4044)

FIXTURES: Cut Stone

Sanford & Birdsall Inc ....G.... 732 223-6966
Manasquan (G-5880)

FLAGPOLES

Lingo Inc ....F.... 856 273-6594
Mount Laurel (G-6812)

FLAGS: Fabric

Annin & Co ....E.... 973 228-9400
Roseland (G-9644)

Annin & Co ....C.... 973 239-9000
Verona (G-11303)

Art Flag Co Inc ....F.... 212 334-1890
Fair Haven (G-3070)

National Flag & Display Co Inc ....E.... 973 366-1776
Wharton (G-11993)

Stewart-Morris Inc...............................G.... 973 822-2777
Madison (G-5736)

FLAT GLASS: Antique

Artique Glass Studio Inc ....G.... 201 444-3500
Glen Rock (G-3820)

FLAT GLASS: Construction

McGrory Glass Inc ....D.... 856 579-3200
Paulsboro (G-8420)

FLAT GLASS: Laminated

JE Berkowitz LP ....C.... 856 456-7800
Pedricktown (G-8436)

FLAT GLASS: Tempered

Jersey Tempered Glass Inc ....E.... 856 273-8700
Mount Laurel (G-6810)

FLAT GLASS: Window, Clear & Colored

Elco Glass Industries Co Inc ....E.... 732 363-6550
Freehold (G-3652)

FLAVORS OR FLAVORING MATERIALS: Synthetic

Firmenich ....G.... 609 580-4498
Monmouth Junction (G-6345)

Givaudan Flavors Corporation...............G.... 973 463-8192
Cranbury (G-1834)

Interntnal Flvors Frgrnces Inc ....C.... 732 264-4500
Union Beach (G-11237)

Interntnal Flvors Frgrnces Inc ....G.... 732 264-4500
Hazlet (G-4276)

Zoomessence Inc ....G.... 732 416-6638
Sayreville (G-9843)

FLOOR CLEANING & MAINTENANCE EQPT: Household

Groupe Seb USA ....F.... 856 825-6300
Millville (G-6306)

FLOOR COVERING STORES

Armorpoxy Inc...............................F.... 908 810-9613
Union (G-11154)

Floors For Less Corporation ....G.... 201 933-9663
East Rutherford (G-2296)

FLOOR COVERING STORES: Carpets

A & J Carpets Inc ....G.... 856 227-1753
Blackwood (G-469)

Best Value Rugs & Carpets Inc...............G.... 732 752-3528
Dunellen (G-2127)

Worldwide Whl Flr Cvg Inc...............D.... 732 906-1400
Edison (G-2651)

FLOOR COVERING STORES: Rugs

Amici Imports Inc ....F.... 908 272-8300
Cranford (G-1896)

FLOOR COVERING: Plastic

Crossfield Products Corp ....D.... 908 245-2801
Roselle Park (G-9691)

FLOOR COVERINGS WHOLESALERS

Armorpoxy Inc...............................F.... 908 810-9613
Union (G-11154)

FLOOR COVERINGS: Aircraft & Automobile

Fh Group International Inc ....E.... 201 210-2426
Secaucus (G-9883)

FLOOR COVERINGS: Rubber

Strongwall Industries Inc ....G.... 201 445-4633
Allendale (G-19)

FLOOR COVERINGS: Tile, Support Plastic

Locktile Industries Llc ....F.... 888 562-5845
Newark (G-7224)

FLOORING: Hard Surface

Congoleum Corporation...................D.... 609 584-3601
Trenton (G-11045)

Dyerich Flooring Designs Ltd ....G.... 973 357-0600
Paterson (G-8252)

Evertile Flooring Co Inc.......................G.... 973 242-7474
Newark (G-7158)

Mannington Mills Inc ....A.... 856 935-3000
Salem (G-9806)

S Geno Carpet and Flooring ....G.... 215 669-1400
Mount Royal (G-6852)

Takasago Intl Corp USA ....E.... 201 727-4200
Teterboro (G-10814)

Tbs Industrial Flooring Pdts...............G.... 732 899-1486
Point Pleasant Beach (G-8927)

FLOORING: Hardwood

Alpine Custom Floors...........................F.... 201 533-0100
Jersey City (G-4703)

Atlantic Flooring LLC ....F.... 609 296-7700
Ltl Egg Hbr (G-5641)

Continental Woodworking Co...............G.... 609 654-0820
Medford (G-6067)

Flooring Concepts NJ LLC...................F.... 732 409-7600
Manalapan (G-5848)

Floors For Less Corporation ....G.... 201 933-9663
East Rutherford (G-2296)

Friends Hardwood Floors Inc...............G.... 732 859-4019
Oakhurst (G-7669)

FLOORING: Rubber

Atlantic Flooring LLC ....F.... 609 296-7700
Ltl Egg Hbr (G-5641)

Flooring Concepts NJ LLC...................F.... 732 409-7600
Manalapan (G-5848)

Linoleum Sales Company Inc...............G.... 201 438-1844
East Rutherford (G-2304)

P R O D U C T

FLOORING: Tile

L S P Industrial Ceramics Inc .... G 609 397-8330
Lambertville *(G-5217)*

Maya Trading Corporation .... G 201 533-1400
Jersey City *(G-4782)*

FLORIST: Flowers, Fresh

Clover Garden Ctr Ltd Lblty Co .... G 856 235-4625
Mount Laurel *(G-6789)*

Pennock Company .... E 215 492-7900
Pennsauken *(G-8557)*

FLORISTS

Berat Corporation .... C 609 953-7700
Medford *(G-6065)*

Food Circus Super Markets Inc .... D 732 291-4079
Atlantic Highlands *(G-111)*

Little Falls Shop Rite Super .... B 973 256-0909
Little Falls *(G-5481)*

Pathmark Stores Inc .... C 973 762-5044
South Orange *(G-10313)*

Shop Rite Supermarkets Inc .... C 732 775-4250
Neptune *(G-6932)*

Springdale Farm Market Inc .... E 856 424-8674
Cherry Hill *(G-1421)*

FLOWER ARRANGEMENTS: Artificial

Arafat Lafi .... G 201 854-7300
North Bergen *(G-7431)*

FLOWERS, ARTIFICIAL, WHOLESALE

Missry Associates Inc .... C 732 752-7500
Edison *(G-2574)*

FLOWERS, FRESH, WHOLESALE

Sunshine Bouquet Company .... C 732 274-2900
Dayton *(G-1989)*

FLOWERS: Artificial & Preserved

Dnp Foods America Ltd Lblty Co .... G 201 654-5581
Waldwick *(G-11445)*

Sunshine Bouquet Company .... C 732 274-2900
Dayton *(G-1989)*

FLUID METERS & COUNTING DEVICES

Action Packaging Automation .... G 609 448-9210
Roosevelt *(G-9639)*

Pemberton Fabricators Inc .... A 609 267-0922
Rancocas *(G-9260)*

Precision Dealer Services Inc .... E 908 237-1100
Flemington *(G-3460)*

Rio Supply .... G 856 719-0081
Sicklerville *(G-10025)*

FLUID POWER PUMPS & MOTORS

Industrial Combustion Assn .... F 732 271-0300
Somerset *(G-10111)*

PMC Liquiflo Equipment Co Inc .... E 908 518-0666
Garwood *(G-3785)*

Technol Inc .... F 856 848-5480
Westville *(G-11949)*

FLUID POWER VALVES & HOSE FITTINGS

Asco Valve LLC .... D 973 966-2437
Florham Park *(G-3488)*

Automatic Switch Company .... A 973 966-2000
Florham Park *(G-3489)*

Gadren Machine Co Inc .... F 856 456-4329
Mount Ephraim *(G-6763)*

Parker-Hannifin Corporation .... E 973 575-4844
Pine Brook *(G-8712)*

Universal Valve Company Inc .... F 908 351-0606
Elizabeth *(G-2780)*

Valcor Engineering Corporation .... C 973 467-8400
Springfield *(G-10583)*

FLUXES

Alpha Assembly Solutions Inc .... E 908 561-5170
South Plainfield *(G-10325)*

Alpha Assembly Solutions Inc .... E 908 791-3000
Somerset *(G-10054)*

Morgan Advanced Ceramics Inc .... E 973 808-1621
Fairfield *(G-3264)*

FLY TRAPS: Electrical

Vandermolen Corp .... G 973 992-8506
Ledgewood *(G-5313)*

FOAM CHARGE MIXTURES

Bergen International LLC .... G 201 299-4499
East Rutherford *(G-2285)*

FOAM RUBBER

Diversified Foam Products Inc .... D 856 662-1981
Swedesboro *(G-10693)*

Inoac Usa Inc .... G 201 807-0809
Moonachie *(G-6522)*

Ls Rubber Industries Inc .... E 973 680-4488
Bloomfield *(G-519)*

Woodbridge Inoac Technical .... G 201 807-0809
Moonachie *(G-6553)*

Woodbridge Inoac Technical Pro .... D 201 807-0809
Moonachie *(G-6554)*

FOAM RUBBER, WHOLESALE

Foam Rubber Fabricators Inc .... E 973 751-1445
Belleville *(G-303)*

Supply Plus NY Inc .... G 973 481-4800
Paterson *(G-8391)*

FOAMS & RUBBER, WHOLESALE

Diversified Display Pdts LLC .... E 908 686-2200
Hillside *(G-4405)*

FOIL & LEAF: Metal

Amcor Flexibles Inc .... E 609 267-5900
Mount Holly *(G-6766)*

API Americas Inc .... D 732 382-6800
Rahway *(G-9174)*

Constantia Blythewood LLC .... E 732 974-4100
Belmar *(G-356)*

Crown Roll Leaf Inc .... C 973 742-4000
Paterson *(G-8241)*

Glitterex Corp .... B 908 272-9121
Cranford *(G-1908)*

Spectrum Foils Inc .... G 973 481-0808
Newark *(G-7324)*

FOIL BOARD: Made From Purchased Materials

Eagle Systems Inc .... G 732 226-2111
Ocean *(G-7723)*

Goetz & Ruschmann Inc .... E 973 383-9270
Newton *(G-7391)*

FOIL: Aluminum

Elkom North America Inc .... G 732 786-0490
Manalapan *(G-5844)*

Yarde Metals Inc .... E 973 463-1166
East Hanover *(G-2251)*

FOIL: Copper

Materials Technology Inc .... G 732 246-1000
Somerset *(G-10131)*

FOIL: Zinc

Hueck Foils Holding Co .... G 732 974-4100
Wall Township *(G-11489)*

FOOD CASINGS: Plastic

Globe Packaging Co Inc .... G 201 896-1144
Carlstadt *(G-1163)*

Revere Industries LLC .... C 856 881-3600
Clayton *(G-1527)*

Tyz-All Plastics LLC .... G 201 343-1200
Hackensack *(G-3988)*

FOOD COLORINGS

Grow Company Inc .... E 201 941-8777
Ridgefield *(G-9363)*

Ifc Solutions Inc .... E 908 862-8810
Linden *(G-5385)*

Prime Ingredients Inc .... G 201 791-6655
Saddle Brook *(G-9784)*

FOOD COLORINGS: Bakers'

Global Colorants Inc .... G 973 751-2227
Old Bridge *(G-7780)*

FOOD PRDTS & SEAFOOD: Shellfish, Fresh, Shucked

Bivalve Packing Inc .... G 856 785-0270
Port Norris *(G-8979)*

FOOD PRDTS, BREAKFAST: Cereal, Granola & Muesli

Simi Granola LLC .... F 848 459-5619
Jackson *(G-4678)*

FOOD PRDTS, BREAKFAST: Cereal, Oats, Rolled

Silver Palate Kitchens Inc .... E 201 568-0110
Cresskill *(G-1948)*

FOOD PRDTS, CANNED OR FRESH PACK: Fruit Juices

BSC USA LLC .... F 908 487-4437
Palisades Park *(G-7836)*

Halo Farm Inc .... G 609 695-3311
Lawrenceville *(G-5257)*

Johanna Foods Inc .... B 908 788-2200
Flemington *(G-3452)*

Lassonde Pappas and Co Inc .... D 856 455-1000
Carneys Point *(G-1245)*

Lassonde Pappas and Co Inc .... E 856 455-1001
Bridgeton *(G-788)*

Pappas Lassonde Holdings Inc .... G 856 455-1000
Carneys Point *(G-1246)*

Polonica Inc .... G 732 855-0008
Piscataway *(G-8801)*

Refresco Us Inc .... D 973 361-9794
Wharton *(G-11998)*

FOOD PRDTS, CANNED: Baby Food

Mysuperfoods Ltd Liability Co .... F 646 283-7455
Summit *(G-10651)*

FOOD PRDTS, CANNED: Barbecue Sauce

Funnibonz LLC .... G 609 915-3685
Princeton Junction *(G-9156)*

FOOD PRDTS, CANNED: Beans & Bean Sprouts

B&G Foods Inc .... B 973 401-6500
Parsippany *(G-7956)*

B&G Foods Inc .... B 973 401-6500
Parsippany *(G-7957)*

Goya Foods Inc .... E 201 865-3470
Secaucus *(G-9891)*

FOOD PRDTS, CANNED: Chili Sauce, Tomato

Gardner Resources Inc .... G 732 872-0755
Highlands *(G-4309)*

FOOD PRDTS, CANNED: Ethnic

Crave Foods LLC .... F 973 233-1220
Montclair *(G-6409)*

Fast-Pak Trading Inc .... G 201 293-4757
Secaucus *(G-9882)*

Nema Food Distribution Inc .... G 973 256-4415
Fairfield *(G-3267)*

Sanket Corporation .... F 732 287-0201
Edison *(G-2611)*

FOOD PRDTS, CANNED: Fruits

B&G Foods Inc .... B 973 401-6500
Parsippany *(G-7956)*

B&G Foods Inc .... B 973 401-6500
Parsippany *(G-7957)*

Campbell Soup Company .... A 856 342-4800
Camden *(G-1049)*

Garelick Farms LLC .... C 609 499-2600
Burlington *(G-975)*

Pomi USA Inc .... G 732 541-4115
Matawan *(G-6029)*

Wayne County Foods Inc ....E 973 399-0101
Irvington (G-4607)

FOOD PRDTS, CANNED: Fruits & Fruit Prdts

C & E Canners Inc..............................F 609 561-1078
Hammonton (G-4135)
Cameco Inc...D 973 239-2845
Verona (G-11304)

FOOD PRDTS, CANNED: Italian

Antonio Mozzarella Factory Inc ....F 973 353-9411
Newark (G-7087)
Antonio Mozzarella Factory Inc ....E 973 353-9411
Newark (G-7088)
Bono USA Inc......................................G 973 978-7361
Fairfield (G-3151)
Mrs Mazzulas Food Products ....G 732 248-0555
Edison (G-2577)
Tuscany Especially Itln Foods..............F 732 308-1118
Marlboro (G-5962)

FOOD PRDTS, CANNED: Jams, Including Imitation

B&G Foods Inc....................................C 973 403-6795
Roseland (G-9646)

FOOD PRDTS, CANNED: Mexican, NEC

Mayab Happy Tacos Inc ....E 732 293-0400
Perth Amboy (G-8622)

FOOD PRDTS, CANNED: Seasonings, Tomato

European Amrcn Foods Group Inc ....E 201 436-6106
Bayonne (G-224)

FOOD PRDTS, CANNED: Soups

Aunt Kittys Foods Inc...........................D 856 691-2100
Vineland (G-11325)
Campbell Soup Supply Co LLC ....G 856 342-4800
Camden (G-1050)

FOOD PRDTS, CANNED: Soups, Exc Seafood

Manischewitz Company ....D 201 553-1100
Newark (G-7235)

FOOD PRDTS, CANNED: Spaghetti & Other Pasta Sauce

Lidestri Foods Inc ....D 856 661-3218
Pennsauken (G-8543)

FOOD PRDTS, CANNED: Tomato Sauce.

Losurdo Foods Inc...............................E 201 343-6680
Hackensack (G-3940)

FOOD PRDTS, CANNED: Vegetable Pastes

Northeast Tomato Company Inc.............F 973 684-4890
Paterson (G-8353)

FOOD PRDTS, CONFECTIONERY, WHOLESALE: Candy

Birnn Chocolates Inc ....G 732 214-8680
Highland Park (G-4301)
Damask Kandies ....G 856 467-1661
Swedesboro (G-10690)
Ferrero U S A Inc.................................C 732 764-9300
Parsippany (G-8009)
Marlow Candy & Nut Co Inc ....E 201 569-7606
Englewood (G-2913)
Shrivers Salt Wtr Taffy Fudge...............G 609 399-0100
Ocean City (G-7758)
World Confections Inc..........................D 718 768-8100
South Orange (G-10317)

FOOD PRDTS, CONFECTIONERY, WHOLESALE: Nuts, Salted/Roasted

Cibo Vita Inc ....C 201 773-4873
Fair Lawn (G-3087)
Cns Confectionery Products LLC ....F 201 823-1400
Bayonne (G-220)

FOOD PRDTS, CONFECTIONERY, WHOLESALE: Pretzels

A & A Soft Pretzel Company ....G 856 338-0208
Camden (G-1039)
J & J Snack Foods Corp PA ....G 856 665-9533
Pennsauken (G-8532)

FOOD PRDTS, CONFECTIONERY, WHOLESALE: Snack Foods

Fast-Pak Trading Inc ....G 201 293-4757
Secaucus (G-9882)
Pace Target Brokerage Inc ....E 856 629-2551
Williamstown (G-12095)
Palsgaard Incorporated ....F 973 998-7951
Morris Plains (G-6677)
Zestos Foods LLC ....G 888 407-5852
Teaneck (G-10779)

FOOD PRDTS, CONFECTIONERY, WHOLESALE: Syrups, Fountain

Asbury Syrup Company Inc...................F 732 774-5746
Ocean (G-7716)

FOOD PRDTS, DAIRY, WHOLESALE: Frozen Dairy Desserts

Dairy Queen.. ...... 732 892-5700
Point Pleasant Boro (G-8937)
Rajbhog Foods(nj) Inc..........................C 551 222-4700
Jersey City (G-4814)

FOOD PRDTS, DAIRY, WHOLESALE: Milk, Canned Or Dried

Arla Foods Ingredients N Amer ....F 908 604-8551
Basking Ridge (G-180)
Cns Confectionery Products LLC ....F 201 823-1400
Bayonne (G-220)
Dairy Delight LLC ....F 201 939-7878
Rutherford (G-9729)

FOOD PRDTS, FISH & SEAFOOD, WHOLESALE: Seafood

Certified Clam Corp ....F 732 872-6650
Highlands (G-4307)
Ruggiero Sea Food Inc ....D 973 589-0524
Newark (G-7294)
Ruggiero Sea Food Inc ....G 973 589-0524
Newark (G-7295)

FOOD PRDTS, FISH & SEAFOOD: Clams, Canned, Jarred, Etc

Lamonica Fine Foods LLC ....C 856 776-2126
Millville (G-6311)

FOOD PRDTS, FISH & SEAFOOD: Clams, Preserved Or Cured

Bumble Bee Foods LLC ....C 609 884-0440
Cape May (G-1091)

FOOD PRDTS, FISH & SEAFOOD: Fish, Canned, Jarred, Etc

Manischewitz Company ....D 201 553-1100
Newark (G-7235)

FOOD PRDTS, FISH & SEAFOOD: Fish, Frozen, Prepared

Delight Foods USA LLC ....F 201 369-1199
Jersey City (G-4738)

FOOD PRDTS, FISH & SEAFOOD: Fresh, Prepared

J & R Foods Inc...................................F 732 229-4020
Long Branch (G-5625)
Lamonica Fine Foods LLC ....C 856 776-2126
Millville (G-6311)

FOOD PRDTS, FISH & SEAFOOD: Oysters, Canned, Jarred, Etc

Hillard Bloom Packing Co Inc................G 856 785-0120
Port Norris (G-8980)

FOOD PRDTS, FISH & SEAFOOD: Prepared Cakes & Sticks

Peak Finance Holdings LLC...................G 856 969-7100
Cherry Hill (G-1411)
Pinnacle Foods Finance LLC ....C 973 541-6620
Parsippany (G-8063)
Pinnacle Foods Group LLC ....D 856 969-8238
Parsippany (G-8064)

FOOD PRDTS, FISH & SEAFOOD: Seafood, Frozen, Prepared

CHR International Inc ....G 201 262-8186
Oradell (G-7806)
Lunds Fisheries Inc ....D 609 884-7600
Cape May (G-1102)

FOOD PRDTS, FROZEN: Breakfasts, Packaged

Amys Omelette Hse Burlington ....F 609 386-4800
Burlington (G-956)
Pinnacle Food Group Inc ....E 856 969-7100
Cherry Hill (G-1414)
Rajbhog Foods(nj) Inc..........................C 551 222-4700
Jersey City (G-4814)
Waffle Waffle LLC ....F 201 559-1286
Nutley (G-7657)

FOOD PRDTS, FROZEN: Dinners, Packaged

Deep Foods Inc ....C 908 810-7500
Union (G-11171)

FOOD PRDTS, FROZEN: Ethnic Foods, NEC

Battistini Foods...................................G 609 476-2184
Egg Harbor Township (G-2682)
Delicious Fresh Pierogi Inc ....F 908 245-0550
Roselle Park (G-9694)
Fast-Pak Trading Inc............................G 201 293-4757
Secaucus (G-9882)
L E Rosellis Food Specialties ....F 609 654-4816
Medford (G-6074)
Old Fashion Kitchen Inc.......................D 732 364-4100
Lakewood (G-5168)
Savignano Food Corp...........................E 973 673-3355
Orange (G-7826)
Socio Produce Inc................................G 201 348-3660
Union City (G-11266)
Vineland Specialty Foods L L C.............G 856 742-5001
Westville (G-11951)

FOOD PRDTS, FROZEN: Fruits, Juices & Vegetables

202 Smoothie LLC...............................G 973 985-4973
Wayne (G-11599)
Berry Blast Smoothies LLC ....G 856 692-6174
Vineland (G-11330)
Birds Eye Foods Inc ....C 585 383-1850
Cherry Hill (G-1350)

FOOD PRDTS, FROZEN: NEC

Appetizers Made Easy Inc....................E 201 531-1212
East Rutherford (G-2277)
Arctic Foods Inc..................................E 908 689-0590
Washington (G-11574)
Caesars Pasta LLC ....E 856 227-2585
Blackwood (G-474)
Campbell Soup Company ....A 856 342-4800
Camden (G-1049)
Cuisine Innvtons Unlimited LLC............C 732 730-9310
Lakewood (G-5101)
Dewy Meadow Farms Inc ....F 908 218-5655
Bridgewater (G-834)
Diaz Foods...D 404 629-3616
Saddle Brook (G-9762)
DO Productions LLC............................D 856 866-3566
Lodi (G-5582)
Dr Pregers Sensible Foods Inc..............D 201 703-1300
Elmwood Park (G-2817)

PRODUCT

Peak Finance Holdings LLC....................G....... 856 969-7100
Cherry Hill *(G-1411)*

Pinnacle Foods Finance LLC..................C....... 973 541-6620
Parsippany *(G-8063)*

Pinnacle Foods Group LLC....................D....... 856 969-8238
Parsippany *(G-8064)*

Pinnacle Foods Inc..................................C....... 973 541-6620
Parsippany *(G-8065)*

Rich Products Corporation....................G....... 856 696-5600
Vineland *(G-11398)*

Rico Foods Inc...E....... 973 278-0589
Paterson *(G-8369)*

Severino Pasta Mfg Co Inc.....................E....... 856 854-3716
Collingswood *(G-1773)*

Seviroli Foods Inc...................................E....... 856 931-1900
Bellmawr *(G-351)*

Tovli Inc...E....... 718 417-6677
Newark *(G-7346)*

Unilever United States Inc....................A....... 201 894-4000
Englewood Cliffs *(G-2986)*

FOOD PRDTS, FROZEN: Pizza

McCain Ellios Foods Inc.........................C....... 201 368-0600
Lodi *(G-5595)*

Mjs of Spotswood LLC.............................G....... 732 251-7400
Spotswood *(G-10529)*

FOOD PRDTS, FROZEN: Snack Items

Group Martin LLC Jj..............................F....... 862 240-1813
Newark *(G-7180)*

FOOD PRDTS, FROZEN: Soups

Classic Cooking LLC..............................D....... 718 439-0200
Rahway *(G-9182)*

FOOD PRDTS, FROZEN: Vegetables, Exc Potato Prdts

Birds Eye Foods Inc...............................C....... 920 435-5300
Parsippany *(G-7961)*

Classic Cooking LLC..............................D....... 718 439-0200
Rahway *(G-9182)*

Seabrook Brothers & Sons Inc............C....... 856 455-8080
Bridgeton *(G-796)*

FOOD PRDTS, FROZEN: Whipped Topping

Birds Eye Foods Inc...............................C....... 585 383-1850
Cherry Hill *(G-1350)*

FOOD PRDTS, FRUITS & VEGETABLES, FRESH, WHOLESALE: Vegetable

DArtagnan Inc..D....... 973 344-0565
Union *(G-11170)*

FOOD PRDTS, MEAT & MEAT PRDTS, WHOLESALE: Fresh

Cameco Inc...D....... 973 239-2845
Verona *(G-11304)*

Carl Streit & Son Co..............................G....... 732 775-0803
Neptune *(G-6903)*

DArtagnan Inc..D....... 973 344-0565
Union *(G-11170)*

Kleemeyer & Merkel Inc........................F....... 973 377-0875
Green Village *(G-3865)*

Licini Brothers Inc................................G....... 201 865-1130
Union City *(G-11254)*

Rastelli Brothers Inc.............................D....... 856 803-1100
Swedesboro *(G-10724)*

Rastelli Foods Group Inc......................F....... 856 803-1100
Swedesboro *(G-10725)*

FOOD PRDTS, POULTRY, WHOLESALE: Poultry Prdts, NEC

David Mitchell Inc..................................E....... 856 429-2610
Voorhees *(G-11428)*

FOOD PRDTS, WHOL: Canned Goods, Fruit, Veg, Seafood/Meats

Cameco Inc...D....... 973 239-2845
Verona *(G-11304)*

FOOD PRDTS, WHOLESALE: Baking Splys

Formica Bros Bakery..............................F....... 609 348-8934
Atlantic City *(G-96)*

FOOD PRDTS, WHOLESALE: Beans, Dry, Bulk

Kalustyan Corporation..........................D....... 908 688-0853
Union *(G-11200)*

FOOD PRDTS, WHOLESALE: Breakfast Cereals

Coco International Inc............................E....... 973 694-1200
Wayne *(G-11620)*

FOOD PRDTS, WHOLESALE: Chocolate

Third Ave Chocolate Shoppe..................G....... 732 449-7535
Spring Lake *(G-10535)*

FOOD PRDTS, WHOLESALE: Coffee & Tea

Eight OClock Coffee Company...............D....... 201 571-9214
Montvale *(G-6455)*

Orens Daily Roast Inc.............................F....... 201 432-2008
Jersey City *(G-4795)*

United Mijovi Amer Ltd Lblty................F....... 732 718-1001
New Brunswick *(G-7008)*

FOOD PRDTS, WHOLESALE: Coffee, Green Or Roasted

Coffee Associates Inc............................E....... 201 945-1060
Edgewater *(G-2436)*

Pan American Coffee Company.............E....... 201 963-2329
Hoboken *(G-4489)*

FOOD PRDTS, WHOLESALE: Cooking Oils

Cosmopolitan Food Group Inc..............G....... 908 998-1818
Hoboken *(G-4466)*

FOOD PRDTS, WHOLESALE: Dried or Canned Foods

Metropolitan Foods Inc.........................C....... 973 672-9400
Clifton *(G-1673)*

United Natural Trading Co....................D....... 732 650-9905
Edison *(G-2640)*

FOOD PRDTS, WHOLESALE: Flavorings & Fragrances

Advanced Biotech Overseas LLC..........G....... 973 339-6242
Totowa *(G-10926)*

Beauty-Fill LLC.......................................E....... 908 353-1600
Hillside *(G-4397)*

Charabot & Co Inc.................................F....... 201 812-2762
Budd Lake *(G-926)*

Excell Brands Ltd Liability Co..............G....... 908 561-1130
Princeton *(G-9043)*

Flavors of Origin Inc.............................E....... 732 499-9700
Avenel *(G-131)*

Interbahm International Inc...................E....... 732 499-9700
Avenel *(G-135)*

Natural Flavors Inc................................E....... 973 589-1230
Newark *(G-7248)*

Robertet Inc...E....... 201 337-7100
Budd Lake *(G-939)*

Savoury Systems Intl Inc......................F....... 908 526-2524
Branchburg *(G-702)*

FOOD PRDTS, WHOLESALE: Health

Fast-Pak Trading Inc.............................E....... 201 293-4757
Secaucus *(G-9882)*

Novel Ingredient Services LLC..............G....... 973 808-5900
East Hanover *(G-2238)*

Vitaquest International LLC..................B....... 973 575-9200
West Caldwell *(G-11807)*

Vitaquest International LLC..................F....... 973 575-9200
Fairfield *(G-3344)*

Zestos Foods LLC...................................G....... 888 407-5852
Teaneck *(G-10779)*

FOOD PRDTS, WHOLESALE: Juices

American Food & Bev Inds LLC............D....... 347 241-9827
Orange *(G-7816)*

FOOD PRDTS, WHOLESALE: Molasses, Indl

International Molasses Corp...................E....... 201 368-8036
Saddle Brook *(G-9770)*

FOOD PRDTS, WHOLESALE: Natural & Organic

DArtagnan Inc..D....... 973 344-0565
Union *(G-11170)*

Maverick Caterers LLC...........................E....... 718 433-3776
Hackensack *(G-3944)*

FOOD PRDTS, WHOLESALE: Pasta & Rice

35 Food Corp..G....... 732 442-1640
Woodbridge *(G-12144)*

La Pace Imports Inc...............................F....... 973 895-5420
Morristown *(G-6720)*

Severino Pasta Mfg Co Inc.....................E....... 856 854-3716
Collingswood *(G-1773)*

Slt Foods Inc..F....... 732 661-1030
Dayton *(G-1987)*

FOOD PRDTS, WHOLESALE: Sauces

Gardner Resources Inc...........................G....... 732 872-0755
Highlands *(G-4309)*

FOOD PRDTS, WHOLESALE: Sausage Casings

Nitta Casings Inc....................................C....... 908 218-4400
Bridgewater *(G-866)*

FOOD PRDTS, WHOLESALE: Specialty

Delicious Fresh Pierogi Inc....................F....... 908 245-0550
Roselle Park *(G-9694)*

Farbest-Tallman Foods Corp.................D....... 714 897-7199
Park Ridge *(G-7919)*

Golden Fluff Inc......................................F....... 732 367-5448
Lakewood *(G-5130)*

FOOD PRDTS, WHOLESALE: Spices & Seasonings

A A Sayia & Company Inc.......................G....... 201 659-1179
Hoboken *(G-4455)*

Gel Spice Co Inc.....................................B....... 201 339-0700
Bayonne *(G-227)*

Green Labs LLC.......................................G....... 862 220-4845
Newark *(G-7178)*

Interntnal Ingrdent Sltons Inc.............E....... 856 778-6623
Mount Laurel *(G-6806)*

Kalustyan Corporation..........................D....... 908 688-0853
Union *(G-11200)*

Melissa Spice Trading Corp...................E....... 862 262-7773
Glen Rock *(G-3826)*

Mincing Trading Corporation...............E....... 732 355-9944
Dayton *(G-1980)*

PDM Packaging Inc................................F....... 201 864-1115
North Bergen *(G-7474)*

FOOD PRDTS, WHOLESALE: Tea

Adagio Teas Inc......................................G....... 973 253-7400
Elmwood Park *(G-2801)*

B-Tea Beverage LLC...............................E....... 201 512-8400
Fair Lawn *(G-3081)*

Boston Tea Company LLC.......................G....... 201 440-3004
Hackensack *(G-3884)*

Harris Freeman & Co Inc........................D....... 856 787-9026
Moorestown *(G-6583)*

FOOD PRDTS, WHOLESALE: Water, Mineral Or Spring, Bottled

Shrem Consulting Ltd Lblty Co.............G....... 917 371-0581
West Long Branch *(G-11846)*

FOOD PRDTS: Almond Pastes

Sun Basket Inc.......................................C....... 408 669-4418
Westampton *(G-11918)*

FOOD PRDTS: Animal & marine fats & oils

Bringhurst Bros Inc...............................E....... 856 767-0110
Berlin *(G-429)*

Darling Ingredients Inc.........................C....... 973 465-1900
Newark *(G-7133)*

Epicore Networks USA Inc ....E 609 267-9118
  Mount Holly **(G-6770)**

FOOD PRDTS: Blackstrap Molasses, Purchd Raw Sugar/Syrup

International Molasses Corp ....E 201 368-8036
  Maywood **(G-6051)**

FOOD PRDTS: Bread Crumbs, Exc Made In Bakeries

Colonna Brothers Inc ....D 800 626-8384
  North Bergen **(G-7443)**

FOOD PRDTS: Breakfast Bars

Amys Omelette Hse Burlington ....F 609 386-4800
  Burlington **(G-956)**

FOOD PRDTS: Cereals

Dim Inc ....F 908 925-2043
  Linden **(G-5369)**
Gerber Products Company ....C 973 593-7500
  Florham Park **(G-3504)**
Kellogg Company ....E 201 634-9140
  River Edge **(G-9466)**
Kellogg Company ....D 609 567-1688
  Hammonton **(G-4141)**
Mm Packaging Group LLC ....G 908 759-0101
  Linden **(G-5411)**
Vivis Life LLC ....G 201 798-1938
  Jersey City **(G-4844)**

FOOD PRDTS: Chewing Gum Base

L A Dreyfus Co ....C 732 549-1600
  Edison **(G-2555)**

FOOD PRDTS: Chocolate, Baking

Master Martini USA Inc ....G 908 455-4434
  Whitehouse Station **(G-12053)**

FOOD PRDTS: Cocoa & Cocoa Prdts

Transmar Group LLC ....G 973 359-4040
  Morristown **(G-6745)**

FOOD PRDTS: Cocoa, Butter

Cocoa Services Inc ....F 856 234-1700
  Moorestown **(G-6568)**

FOOD PRDTS: Cocoa, Powdered

Mack Trading LLC ....G 973 794-4904
  Hewitt **(G-4290)**

FOOD PRDTS: Coconut, Desiccated & Shredded

International Coconut Corp ....F 908 289-1555
  Elizabeth **(G-2748)**
Phildesco Inc ....G 732 937-6560
  Somerville **(G-10223)**

FOOD PRDTS: Coffee

26 Flavors LLC ....G 855 662-7299
  Newark **(G-7063)**
Coffee Associates Inc ....E 201 945-1060
  Edgewater **(G-2436)**
Corim International Coffee Imp ....D 800 942-4201
  Brick **(G-739)**
Counting Sheep Coffee Inc ....G 973 589-4104
  Newark **(G-7128)**
Eight OClock Coffee Company ....D 201 571-9214
  Montvale **(G-6455)**
European Coffee Classics Inc ....E 856 428-7202
  Cherry Hill **(G-1363)**
Greene Bros Spclty Cof Rasters ....F 908 979-0022
  Hackettstown **(G-4009)**
Longview Coffee Co NJ Inc ....E 908 788-4186
  Frenchtown **(G-3703)**
Massimo Zanetti Beverage USA ....F 201 440-1700
  Moonachie **(G-6530)**
Nestle Usa Inc ....C 732 462-1300
  Freehold **(G-3673)**
Orens Daily Roast Inc ....F 201 432-2008
  Jersey City **(G-4795)**

Pan American Coffee Company ....E 201 963-2329
  Hoboken **(G-4489)**
Socafe LLC ....F 973 589-4104
  Newark **(G-7318)**

FOOD PRDTS: Coffee Extracts

Adagio Teas Inc ....G 973 253-7400
  Elmwood Park **(G-2801)**

FOOD PRDTS: Coffee Roasting, Exc Wholesale Grocers

Arias Mountain-Coffee LLC ....G 973 927-9595
  Dover **(G-2077)**
Coffee Company LLC ....G 609 399-5533
  Ocean City **(G-7750)**
Coffee Company LLC ....G 609 398-2326
  Ocean City **(G-7751)**
Melitta Usa Inc ....E 856 428-7202
  Cherry Hill **(G-1399)**
Mire Enterprises LLC ....G 732 882-1010
  Linden **(G-5410)**
Two Rivers Coffee LLC ....G 908 205-0018
  South Plainfield **(G-10443)**
World of Coffee Inc ....G 908 647-1218
  Stirling **(G-10609)**

FOOD PRDTS: Cooking Oils, Refined Vegetable, Exc Corn

Oasis Trading Co Inc ....C 908 964-0477
  Hillside **(G-4433)**

FOOD PRDTS: Desserts, Ready-To-Mix

Dulce A Dessert Bar LLC ....G 908 461-2418
  Matawan **(G-6018)**

FOOD PRDTS: Doughs & Batters

Fillo Factory Inc ....E 201 439-1036
  Northvale **(G-7581)**

FOOD PRDTS: Doughs, Frozen Or Refrig From Purchased Flour

Jimmys Cookies LLC ....C 973 779-8500
  Clifton **(G-1653)**
Nijama Corporation ....G 973 272-3223
  Clifton **(G-1684)**

FOOD PRDTS: Dressings, Salad, Raw & Cooked Exc Dry Mixes

Chelten House Products Inc ....C 856 467-1600
  Bridgeport **(G-762)**
Oasis Trading Co Inc ....C 908 964-0477
  Hillside **(G-4433)**
Panos Brands LLC ....E 800 229-1706
  Linden **(G-5423)**

FOOD PRDTS: Dried & Dehydrated Fruits, Vegetables & Soup Mix

International Foodsource LLC ....D 973 361-7044
  Dover **(G-2094)**
JF Braun & Sons Inc ....E 908 393-7400
  Elizabeth **(G-2750)**
Mrs Mazzulas Food Products ....G 732 248-0555
  Edison **(G-2577)**

FOOD PRDTS: Edible Oil Prdts, Exc Corn Oil

Aak USA Inc ....D 973 344-1300
  Edison **(G-2446)**
European Amrcn Foods Group Inc ......E 201 436-6106
  Bayonne **(G-224)**
European Amrcn Foods Group Inc ......B 201 583-1101
  Secaucus **(G-9880)**

FOOD PRDTS: Edible fats & oils

Aarhuskarlshamn USA Inc ....E 973 344-1300
  Newark **(G-7068)**
Technical Oil Products Co Inc ....G 973 940-8920
  Newton **(G-7408)**
Western Pacific Foods Inc ....F 908 838-0186
  Kearny **(G-4921)**

FOOD PRDTS: Eggs, Processed

Deb El Food Products LLC ....G 908 282-0120
  Newark **(G-7136)**
Papettis Hygrade Egg Pdts Inc ....A 908 282-7900
  Elizabethport **(G-2786)**

FOOD PRDTS: Eggs, Processed, Dehydrated

Deb-El Foods Corporation ....C 908 351-0330
  Newark **(G-7137)**

FOOD PRDTS: Emulsifiers

National Lecithim Inc ....G 973 940-8920
  Newton **(G-7398)**
Nexira Inc ....F 908 704-7480
  Somerville **(G-10222)**

FOOD PRDTS: Flavored Ices, Frozen

J & J Snack Foods Corp ....B 856 665-9533
  Pennsauken **(G-8531)**
J & J Snack Foods Corp ....D 856 467-9552
  Bridgeport **(G-767)**
South Jersey Pretzel Inc ....F 856 435-5055
  Stratford **(G-10617)**
Taylor Products Inc ....E 732 225-4620
  Edison **(G-2637)**

FOOD PRDTS: Flour

Better Foods Jeyer LLC ....G 888 717-6412
  Ridgefield Park **(G-9398)**

FOOD PRDTS: Flour & Other Grain Mill Products

Frewitt USA Inc ....E 908 829-5245
  Hillsborough **(G-4333)**
Mayab Happy Tacos Inc ....E 732 293-0400
  Perth Amboy **(G-8622)**

FOOD PRDTS: Flour Mixes & Doughs

Foodtek Inc ....F 973 257-4000
  Whippany **(G-12020)**
R C Fine Foods Inc ....D 908 359-5500
  Hillsborough **(G-4366)**
Slt Foods Inc ....F 732 661-1030
  Dayton **(G-1987)**

FOOD PRDTS: Flour, Cake From Purchased Flour

Peak Finance Holdings LLC ....G 856 969-7100
  Cherry Hill **(G-1411)**
Pinnacle Foods Finance LLC ....C 973 541-6620
  Parsippany **(G-8063)**
Pinnacle Foods Group LLC ....D 856 969-8238
  Parsippany **(G-8064)**

FOOD PRDTS: Flours & Flour Mixes, From Purchased Flour

Fornazor International Inc ....E 201 664-4000
  Hillsdale **(G-4382)**

FOOD PRDTS: Fresh Vegetables, Peeled Or Processed

F&S Produce Company Inc ....E 856 453-0316
  Rosenhayn **(G-9707)**

FOOD PRDTS: Fruit Juices

American Food & Bev Inds LLC ....D 347 241-9827
  Orange **(G-7816)**
Ejz Foods LLC ....G 201 229-0500
  South Hackensack **(G-10263)**
G & Y Specialty Foods LLC ....G 956 821-9652
  Woodland Park **(G-12220)**
Gerber Products Company ....C 973 593-7500
  Florham Park **(G-3504)**
Mojo Organics Inc ....G 201 633-6519
  Jersey City **(G-4785)**

FOOD PRDTS: Fruit Pops, Frozen

Icykidz ....G 973 342-9665
  Irvington **(G-4590)**

P
R
O
D
U
C
T

FOOD PRDTS: Fruits & Vegetables, Pickled

Crazy Steves Concoctions LLC .... G 908 787-2089
   Trenton (G-11047)
United Farm Processing Corp .... F 856 451-4612
   Rosenhayn (G-9710)

FOOD PRDTS: Fruits, Dehydrated Or Dried

Cibo Vita Inc .... C 201 773-4873
   Fair Lawn (G-3087)

FOOD PRDTS: Gelatin Dessert Preparations

Joyce Food LLC .... C 973 491-9696
   Newark (G-7209)
Poly-Gel LLC .... E 973 884-3300
   Whippany (G-12034)

FOOD PRDTS: Granola & Energy Bars, Nonchocolate

Joy Snacks LLC .... F 732 272-0707
   Avenel (G-136)

FOOD PRDTS: Granulated Cane Sugar

Global Commodities Exportacao .... G 201 613-1532
   Newark (G-7171)

FOOD PRDTS: Hydrol

Hydro Milling Group Inc .... G 732 450-2488
   Shrewsbury (G-10000)

FOOD PRDTS: Ice, Blocks

Artic Ice Manufacturing Co .... G 973 772-7000
   Garfield (G-3718)
United States Cold Storage Inc .... B 856 354-8181
   Camden (G-1088)

FOOD PRDTS: Ice, Cubes

United City Ice Cube Co Inc .... G 201 945-8387
   Ridgefield (G-9391)

FOOD PRDTS: Instant Coffee

United Mijovi Amer Ltd Lblty .... F 732 718-1001
   New Brunswick (G-7008)

FOOD PRDTS: Luncheon Meat, Poultry

Nema Food Distribution Inc .... G 973 256-4415
   Fairfield (G-3267)

FOOD PRDTS: Macaroni Prdts, Dry, Alphabet, Rings Or Shells

A Zeregas Sons Inc .... C 201 797-1400
   Fair Lawn (G-3072)
Porfirio Foods Inc .... G 609 393-4116
   Trenton (G-11100)
Silver Palate Kitchens Inc .... E 201 568-0110
   Cresskill (G-1948)
Unilever Bestfoods North Amer .... F 201 894-4000
   Englewood Cliffs (G-2985)

FOOD PRDTS: Macaroni, Noodles, Spaghetti, Pasta, Etc

Casa Di Bertacchi Corporation .... C 856 696-5600
   Vineland (G-11334)
Gardellas Rvioli Itln Deli LLC .... F 856 697-3509
   Vineland (G-11359)
L E Rosellis Food Specialties .... F 609 654-4816
   Medford (G-6074)
Raffettos Corp .... F 201 372-1222
   Moonachie (G-6538)
Severino Pasta Mfg Co Inc .... E 856 854-3716
   Collingswood (G-1773)
Vitamia Pasta Boy Inc .... F 973 546-1140
   Lodi (G-5608)

FOOD PRDTS: Malt

International Molasses Corp .... E 201 368-8036
   Saddle Brook (G-9770)
Malt Products Corporation .... E 201 845-4420
   Saddle Brook (G-9772)
Malt Products Corporation .... E 201 845-9106
   Saddle Brook (G-9773)

FOOD PRDTS: Margarine, Including Imitation

Bimbo Bakeries USA Inc .... C 973 256-8200
   Totowa (G-10936)

FOOD PRDTS: Mayonnaise & Dressings, Exc Tomato Based

Unilever Bestfoods North Amer .... F 201 894-4000
   Englewood Cliffs (G-2985)

FOOD PRDTS: Menhaden Oil

Daybrook Holdings Inc .... G 973 538-6766
   Morristown (G-6705)

FOOD PRDTS: Mixes, Bread & Roll From Purchased Flour

Caravan Ingredients Inc .... C 973 256-8886
   Totowa (G-10937)

FOOD PRDTS: Mixes, Cake, From Purchased Flour

Manischewitz Company .... D 201 553-1100
   Newark (G-7235)
Procter & Gamble Mfg Co .... D 732 602-4500
   Avenel (G-148)
William R Tatz Industries .... G 973 751-0720
   Belleville (G-328)

FOOD PRDTS: Mixes, Doughnut From Purchased Flour

All Madina Inc .... F 973 226-7772
   West Caldwell (G-11765)

FOOD PRDTS: Mixes, Pancake From Purchased Flour

Joyce Food LLC .... C 973 491-9696
   Newark (G-7209)

FOOD PRDTS: Mixes, Pizza From Purchased Flour

Mjs of Spotswood LLC .... G 732 251-7400
   Spotswood (G-10529)

FOOD PRDTS: Mixes, Salad Dressings, Dry

Muirhead Ringoes NJ Inc .... G 609 695-7803
   Trenton (G-11082)

FOOD PRDTS: Mustard, Prepared

RB Manufacturing LLC .... G 908 533-2000
   Hillsborough (G-4367)
RB Manufacturing LLC .... G 973 404-2600
   Parsippany (G-8076)
Reckitt Benckiser LLC .... B 973 404-2600
   Parsippany (G-8077)

FOOD PRDTS: Nuts & Seeds

Cibo Vita Inc .... C 201 773-4873
   Fair Lawn (G-3087)
Cns Confectionery Products LLC .... F 201 823-1400
   Bayonne (G-220)

FOOD PRDTS: Olive Oil

Cosmopolitan Food Group Inc .... G 908 998-1818
   Hoboken (G-4466)
Edesia Oil LLC .... F 732 851-7979
   Manalapan (G-5843)
Finex Trade .... G 609 921-2747
   Princeton (G-9045)
Hojiblanca USA Inc .... G 201 384-3007
   Dumont (G-2118)
International Olive Oil Inc .... G 732 612-3338
   Manasquan (G-5871)
Olivos USA Inc .... G 201 893-0142
   Fort Lee (G-3576)

FOOD PRDTS: Oriental Noodles

CJ TMI Manufacturing Amer LLC .... C 609 669-0100
   Robbinsville (G-9513)

FOOD PRDTS: Pasta, Uncooked, Packaged With Other Ingredients

35 Food Corp .... G 732 442-1640
   Woodbridge (G-12144)
Contes Pasta Company Inc .... E 856 697-3400
   Vineland (G-11341)
Croces Pasta Poducts .... G 856 795-6000
   Cherry Hill (G-1358)
Dipietro Foods Inc .... G 973 762-4077
   Maplewood (G-5918)
European Amrcn Foods Group Inc ...... E 201 436-6106
   Bayonne (G-224)
European Amrcn Foods Group Inc ...... B 201 583-1101
   Secaucus (G-9880)
Firma Foods USA Corporation .... G 201 794-1181
   Englewood (G-2896)
L and Ds Sapore Ravioli Cheese .... F 732 563-9190
   Middlesex (G-6175)
La Pace Imports Inc .... F 973 895-5420
   Morristown (G-6720)
Lrk Inc .... G 609 924-6881
   Princeton (G-9068)
Pastarama Distributors Inc .... G 609 847-0378
   Sewell (G-9965)
Vitamia Pasta Boy Inc .... F 973 546-1140
   Lodi (G-5608)

FOOD PRDTS: Peanut Butter

Procter & Gamble Mfg Co .... D 732 602-4500
   Avenel (G-148)
Unilever Bestfoods North Amer .... F 201 894-4000
   Englewood Cliffs (G-2985)

FOOD PRDTS: Pickles, Vinegar

Regal Crown Fd Svc Specialist .... G 508 752-2679
   Wayne (G-11679)

FOOD PRDTS: Pizza Doughs From Purchased Flour

Losurdo Foods Inc .... E 201 343-6680
   Hackensack (G-3940)

FOOD PRDTS: Pizza, Refrigerated

Papa Johns New Jersey .... D 609 395-0045
   Cranbury (G-1867)
Taste Italy Manufacturing LLC .... G 856 223-0707
   Egg Harbor City (G-2671)

FOOD PRDTS: Popcorn, Popped

Continntal Concession Sups Inc .... E 516 629-4906
   Union (G-11166)
Planet Popcorn LLC .... G 732 294-8680
   Freehold (G-3677)
Ziggy Snack Foods LLC .... E 917 662-6038
   Clifton (G-1747)

FOOD PRDTS: Popcorn, Unpopped

MCI Service Parts .... G 732 967-9081
   East Brunswick (G-2166)

FOOD PRDTS: Potato & Corn Chips & Similar Prdts

Auntie Annes Hmde Sft Prtzls .... F 856 772-3737
   Voorhees (G-11422)
Auntie Annes Soft Pretzels .... E 856 722-0433
   Moorestown (G-6561)
Campbell Soup Company .... A 856 342-4800
   Camden (G-1049)
Golden Fluff Inc .... F 732 367-5448
   Lakewood (G-5130)
Grab Em Snacks Ltd Lblty Co .... G 908 333-3229
   Hillsborough (G-4337)
Hain Celestial Group Inc .... E 201 935-4500
   Moonachie (G-6520)
Herr Foods Incorporated .... E 732 356-1295
   Somerset (G-10107)
Herr Foods Incorporated .... E 732 905-1600
   Lakewood (G-5134)
Ktb Acquisition Sub Inc .... G 973 240-0200
   Fairfield (G-3244)
Mayab Happy Tacos Inc .... E 732 293-0400
   Perth Amboy (G-8622)
Pirate Brands LLC .... F 973 401-6500
   Parsippany (G-8067)

Rajbhog Foods(nj) Inc ....C...... 551 222-4700
Jersey City *(G-4814)*

Snack Innovations Inc ....E...... 718 509-9366
Piscataway *(G-8812)*

Wise Foods Inc ....G...... 201 440-2876
Moonachie *(G-6552)*

Zestos Foods LLC ....G...... 888 407-5852
Teaneck *(G-10779)*

FOOD PRDTS: Potato Chips & Other Potato-Based Snacks

Birds Eye Foods Inc ....C...... 585 383-1850
Cherry Hill *(G-1350)*

FOOD PRDTS: Poultry, Processed, Frozen

Golden Platter Foods Inc ....E...... 973 344-8770
Newark *(G-7175)*

FOOD PRDTS: Poultry, Slaughtered & Dressed

B & B Poultry Co Inc ....C...... 856 692-8893
Norma *(G-7412)*

FOOD PRDTS: Preparations

ACC Foods Ltd Liability Co ....C...... 856 848-8877
West Deptford *(G-11813)*

Allied Old English Inc ....E...... 732 636-2060
Port Reading *(G-8986)*

American Custom Drying Co ....E...... 609 387-3933
Burlington *(G-955)*

Applied Nutrition Corp ....E...... 973 734-0023
Cedar Knolls *(G-1307)*

Arome America LLC ....G...... 908 806-7003
Neshanic Station *(G-6938)*

Barry Callebaut USA LLC ....E...... 856 663-2260
Pennsauken *(G-8483)*

Bylada Foods LLC ....G...... 201 933-7474
Moonachie *(G-6510)*

Caravan Ingredients Inc ....E...... 201 672-0510
East Rutherford *(G-2292)*

Crispy Green Inc ....F...... 973 679-4515
Fairfield *(G-3169)*

Deluxe Foods International ....G...... 845 825-3442
Paterson *(G-8248)*

Deosen Usa Inc ....G...... 908 382-6518
Piscataway *(G-8755)*

DJeet ....G...... 732 224-8887
Shrewsbury *(G-9997)*

DOrazio Foods Inc ....D...... 856 931-1900
Bellmawr *(G-337)*

Dyna-Sea Group Inc ....G...... 201 928-0133
Teaneck *(G-10751)*

Eatem Corporation ....D...... 856 692-1663
Vineland *(G-11355)*

Edsall Group USA Inc ....D...... 908 874-6953
Hillsborough *(G-4330)*

Empire Specialty Foods Inc ....G...... 646 773-2630
East Brunswick *(G-2153)*

Farbest-Tallman Foods Corp ....D...... 714 897-7199
Park Ridge *(G-7919)*

Flavour Tee International LLC ....G...... 201 440-3281
Little Ferry *(G-5505)*

Food Ingredient Solutions LLC ....G...... 201 440-4377
Teterboro *(G-10796)*

Foodtek Inc ....F...... 973 257-4000
Whippany *(G-12020)*

Global Ingredients Inc ....G...... 973 278-6677
Paterson *(G-8278)*

Golden Tropics Ltd ....E...... 973 484-0202
Newark *(G-7176)*

Gourmet Kitchen LLC ....C...... 732 775-5222
Neptune *(G-6916)*

Green Labs LLC ....G...... 862 220-4845
Newark *(G-7178)*

GS Fresh Beets Incorporated ....F...... 856 692-1740
Vineland *(G-11366)*

Iam International Inc ....G...... 908 713-9651
Lebanon *(G-5289)*

J & J Snack Foods Corp ....C...... 856 933-3597
Bellmawr *(G-344)*

Jk Ingredients Inc ....D...... 973 340-8700
Paterson *(G-8304)*

Knight Foods LLC ....G...... 973 385-1230
Cedar Grove *(G-1287)*

L E Rosellis Food Specialties ....F...... 609 654-4816
Medford *(G-6074)*

Le Bon Magot Ltd Liability Co ....G...... 609 895-0211
Lawrenceville *(G-5261)*

Leng-Dor USA Inc ....F...... 732 254-4300
Cranbury *(G-1854)*

Maverick Caterers LLC ....E...... 718 433-3776
Hackensack *(G-3944)*

Mediterranean Chef Inc ....F...... 855 628-0903
Lincoln Park *(G-5329)*

Megas Yeeros LLC ....E...... 212 777-6342
Lyndhurst *(G-5692)*

Metropolitan Foods Inc ....C...... 973 672-9400
Clifton *(G-1673)*

Missa Bay Citrus Company ....F...... 856 241-0900
Swedesboro *(G-10711)*

Missa Bay LLC ....D...... 856 241-0900
Swedesboro *(G-10712)*

Mushroom Wisdom Inc ....F...... 973 470-0010
East Rutherford *(G-2312)*

Nestle Usa Inc ....C...... 732 462-1300
Freehold *(G-3673)*

Omega Packaging Corp ....D...... 973 890-9505
Totowa *(G-10959)*

Palsgaard Incorporated ....F...... 973 998-7951
Morris Plains *(G-6677)*

Panos Holding Company ....G...... 201 843-8900
Rochelle Park *(G-9533)*

Paulaur Corporation ....D...... 609 395-8844
Cranbury *(G-1868)*

Pennant Ingredients Inc ....G...... 856 428-4300
Cherry Hill *(G-1412)*

Perfecto Foods LLC ....G...... 201 889-5328
Kearny *(G-4907)*

Pharmachem Laboratories Inc ....E...... 973 256-1340
Totowa *(G-10962)*

Pharmachem Laboratories Inc ....E...... 201 343-3611
South Hackensack *(G-10288)*

Pharmachem Laboratories LLC ....D...... 201 246-1000
Kearny *(G-4908)*

Prince Chikovani Inc ....G...... 347 622-2789
Bayonne *(G-242)*

Princeton Quadrangle Club ....G...... 609 258-0376
Princeton *(G-9100)*

Puratos Corporation ....E...... 856 266-1736
Pennsauken *(G-8568)*

Puratos Corporation ....C...... 856 428-4300
Cherry Hill *(G-1417)*

Pyramid Food Services Corp ....F...... 973 900-6513
Newark *(G-7280)*

Quality Ingredients Corp ....F...... 908 879-2227
Chester *(G-1439)*

R C Fine Foods Inc ....D...... 908 359-5500
Hillsborough *(G-4366)*

Ready Pac Fods - Swedesboro NJ ....F...... 609 360-0953
Swedesboro *(G-10726)*

Ready Pac Produce Inc ....D...... 609 499-1900
Florence *(G-3480)*

Saker Shoprites Inc ....F...... 908 925-1550
Linden *(G-5437)*

Sunrise Snacks Rockland Inc ....F...... 845 352-2676
Paterson *(G-8388)*

Surfside Foods LLC ....G...... 856 785-2115
Port Norris *(G-8983)*

Suruchi Foods LLC ....G...... 201 432-2201
Jersey City *(G-4836)*

Tamaras European American Deli ....G...... 973 875-5461
Sussex *(G-10677)*

Taste It Presents Inc ....G...... 908 241-9191
Kenilworth *(G-4999)*

Taylor Farms New Jersey Inc ....E...... 856 241-0097
Swedesboro *(G-10732)*

Tin Man Snacks LLC ....E...... 732 329-9100
Dayton *(G-1991)*

United Natural Trading Co ....D...... 732 650-9905
Edison *(G-2640)*

Venetian Corp ....F...... 973 546-2250
Garfield *(G-3771)*

Zinas Salads Inc ....E...... 973 428-0660
East Hanover *(G-2252)*

FOOD PRDTS: Prepared Sauces, Exc Tomato Based

Edsall Group USA Inc ....D...... 908 874-6953
Hillsborough *(G-4330)*

Mamamancinis Holdings Inc ....G...... 201 531-1212
East Rutherford *(G-2307)*

Mirrotek International LLC ....E...... 973 472-1400
Passaic *(G-8165)*

Silver Palate Kitchens Inc ....E...... 201 568-0110
Cresskill *(G-1948)*

Yipin Food Products Inc ....F...... 718 788-3059
Edison *(G-2652)*

FOOD PRDTS: Raw cane sugar

International Molasses Corp ....E...... 201 368-8036
Saddle Brook *(G-9770)*

FOOD PRDTS: Rice, Milled

Diamond Foods USA Inc ....G...... 732 543-2186
North Brunswick *(G-7515)*

Fornazor International Inc ....E...... 201 664-4000
Hillsdale *(G-4382)*

FOOD PRDTS: Rice, Packaged & Seasoned

Sam Hak Food Corp ....E...... 908 688-4993
Hillside *(G-4439)*

FOOD PRDTS: Salads

Daves Salad House Inc ....G...... 908 965-0773
Elizabeth *(G-2722)*

Salad Chef Inc ....F...... 609 641-5455
Pleasantville *(G-8913)*

Sheris Cookery Inc ....F...... 973 589-2060
Newark *(G-7311)*

FOOD PRDTS: Seasonings & Spices

Excellentia Flavours LLC ....F...... 732 749-9840
Fairfield *(G-3190)*

Gel Spice Co LLC ....C...... 201 339-0700
Bayonne *(G-228)*

Interntnal Ingrdent Sltons Inc ....E...... 856 778-6623
Mount Laurel *(G-6806)*

Kalustyan Corporation ....D...... 908 688-0853
Union *(G-11200)*

Mincing Trading Corporation ....E...... 732 355-9944
Dayton *(G-1980)*

Organica Aromatics Corp ....G...... 609 443-3333
East Windsor *(G-2364)*

Spice Chain Corporation ....C...... 732 518-1100
East Brunswick *(G-2185)*

Sultan Foods Inc ....E...... 908 874-6953
Hillsborough *(G-4374)*

FOOD PRDTS: Shortening & Solid Edible Fats

Procter & Gamble Mfg Co ....D...... 732 602-4500
Avenel *(G-148)*

FOOD PRDTS: Soup Mixes

Joyce Food LLC ....C...... 973 491-9696
Newark *(G-7209)*

Major Products Co Inc ....E...... 201 641-5555
Little Ferry *(G-5512)*

Osem USA Inc ....G...... 201 871-4433
Englewood Cliffs *(G-2976)*

Unilever Bestfoods North Amer ....F...... 201 894-4000
Englewood Cliffs *(G-2985)*

FOOD PRDTS: Spices, Including Ground

Gel Spice Co Inc ....B...... 201 339-0700
Bayonne *(G-227)*

Goldstein & Burton Inc ....D...... 201 440-0065
Oakland *(G-7690)*

Melissa Spice Trading Corp ....F...... 862 262-7773
Glen Rock *(G-3826)*

PDM Packaging Inc ....F...... 201 864-1115
North Bergen *(G-7474)*

FOOD PRDTS: Sugar

Akila Holdings Inc ....G...... 609 454-5034
Princeton *(G-8999)*

FOOD PRDTS: Sugar, Cane

Domino Foods Inc ....E...... 732 590-1173
Iselin *(G-4623)*

FOOD PRDTS: Syrup, Maple

Vine Hill Farm ....G...... 973 383-0100
Newton *(G-7411)*

PRODUCT

FOOD PRDTS: Syrup, Pancake, Blended & Mixed

Peak Finance Holdings LLC...................G....... 856 969-7100
  Cherry Hill *(G-1411)*
Pinnacle Foods Finance LLC................C....... 973 541-6620
  Parsippany *(G-8063)*
Pinnacle Foods Group LLC.....................D....... 856 969-8238
  Parsippany *(G-8064)*

FOOD PRDTS: Syrups

B&G Foods Inc ....B....... 973 401-6500
  Parsippany *(G-7956)*
B&G Foods Inc ....B....... 973 401-6500
  Parsippany *(G-7957)*

FOOD PRDTS: Tea

Empirical Group LLC ....E....... 201 571-0300
  Montvale *(G-6456)*
Good Earth Teas Inc ....D....... 831 423-7913
  Montvale *(G-6457)*
Harris Freeman & Co Inc ....D....... 856 787-9026
  Moorestown *(G-6583)*
Longview Coffee Co NJ Inc ....E....... 908 788-4186
  Frenchtown *(G-3703)*
Tetley USA Inc ....E....... 800 728-0084
  New Providence *(G-7058)*

FOOD PRDTS: Tofu Desserts, Frozen

Tofutti Brands Inc ....G....... 908 272-2400
  Cranford *(G-1928)*

FOOD PRDTS: Tofu, Exc Frozen Desserts

Tofutti Brands Inc ....G....... 908 272-2400
  Cranford *(G-1928)*

FOOD PRDTS: Tortillas

La Casa De Tortilla ....G....... 732 398-0660
  Somerset *(G-10120)*
Puebla Foods Inc ....E....... 973 246-6311
  Passaic *(G-8172)*
Puebla Foods Inc ....F....... 973 473-4494
  Passaic *(G-8173)*

FOOD PRDTS: Turkey, Processed, Frozen

Mamamancinis Holdings Inc................G....... 201 531-1212
  East Rutherford *(G-2307)*

FOOD PRDTS: Turkey, Slaughtered & Dressed

El Jay Poultry Corp..............................F....... 856 435-0900
  Voorhees *(G-11429)*

FOOD PRDTS: Vegetable Oil Mills, NEC

Romulus Emprises Inc ....G....... 609 683-4549
  Hightstown *(G-4314)*
Textron Inc ....E....... 201 945-1500
  Edgewater *(G-2442)*
W A Cleary Products Inc ....F....... 732 246-2829
  Somerset *(G-10196)*

FOOD PRDTS: Vegetables, Dried or Dehydrated Exc Freeze-Dried

Elaine K Josephson Inc.........................G....... 609 259-2256
  New Brunswick *(G-6958)*

FOOD PRDTS: Vinegar

American Food & Bev Inds LLC ....D....... 347 241-9827
  Orange *(G-7816)*
Cosmopolitan Food Group Inc ....G....... 908 998-1818
  Hoboken *(G-4466)*
Hojiblanca USA Inc ....G....... 201 384-3007
  Dumont *(G-2118)*
International Olive Oil Inc......................G....... 732 612-3338
  Manasquan *(G-5871)*
Regina Wine Co....................................G....... 973 589-6911
  Newark *(G-7288)*
Rex Wine Vinegar Company ....G....... 973 589-6911
  Newark *(G-7289)*
Silver Palate Kitchens Inc....................E....... 201 568-0110
  Cresskill *(G-1948)*

FOOD PRDTS: Yeast

Sensient Technologies Corp.................E....... 908 757-4500
  South Plainfield *(G-10435)*

FOOD PRODUCTS MACHINERY

AGA Foodservice Inc ....C....... 856 428-4200
  Cherry Hill *(G-1340)*
Allen Steel Co ....G....... 856 785-1171
  Leesburg *(G-5314)*
Am-Mac Incorporated ....F....... 973 575-7567
  Fairfield *(G-3133)*
Buhler Inc ....E....... 201 847-0600
  Mahwah *(G-5755)*
Buona Vita Inc ....D....... 856 453-7972
  Bridgeton *(G-780)*
Caddy Corporation of America ....D....... 856 467-4222
  Swedesboro *(G-10686)*
Corbion Group ....G....... 973 256-0198
  Totowa *(G-10940)*
D&N Machine Manufacturing Inc..........E....... 856 456-1366
  Gloucester City *(G-3835)*
Dantco Corp ....F....... 973 278-8776
  Paterson *(G-8245)*
Excalibur Bagel Bky Equip Inc ....E....... 201 797-2788
  Fair Lawn *(G-3091)*
Excellent Bakery Equipment Co............E....... 973 244-1664
  Fairfield *(G-3189)*
Expert Process Systems LLC ....G....... 570 424-0581
  Hackettstown *(G-4006)*
FBM Baking Machines Inc.....................E....... 609 860-0577
  Cranbury *(G-1833)*
HCH Incorporated ....G....... 973 300-4551
  Sparta *(G-10504)*
Industl Envrnmntl Pollutn ....E....... 908 241-3830
  Roselle Park *(G-9698)*
J Hebrank Inc ....E....... 973 983-0001
  Rockaway *(G-9578)*
Joe Mike Precision Fabrication ....F....... 609 953-1144
  Medford *(G-6073)*
M B C Food Machinery Corp.................G....... 201 489-7000
  Hackensack *(G-3941)*
Marlo Manufacturing Co Inc ....G....... 973 423-0226
  Boonton *(G-575)*
Megas Yeeros LLC ....E....... 212 777-6342
  Lyndhurst *(G-5692)*
Nowak Inc ....G....... 973 366-7208
  Wharton *(G-11994)*
Rajbhog Foods Inc...............................G....... 551 222-4700
  Jersey City *(G-4812)*
Rajbhog Foods Inc...............................G....... 201 395-9400
  Jersey City *(G-4813)*
Solbern LLC...E....... 973 227-3030
  Fairfield *(G-3308)*
Surfside Foods LLC..............................G....... 856 785-2115
  Port Norris *(G-8983)*
Techno Design Inc ....G....... 973 478-0930
  Garfield *(G-3767)*
TMU Inc ....F....... 609 884-7656
  Cape May *(G-1106)*

FOOD STORES: Convenience, Independent

Raceway Petroleum Inc........................E....... 732 613-4404
  East Brunswick *(G-2179)*

FOOD STORES: Delicatessen

Bagel Club ....F....... 908 806-6022
  Flemington *(G-3429)*
Branchville Bagels Inc..........................G....... 973 948-7077
  Branchville *(G-727)*

FOOD STORES: Frozen Food &Freezer Plans, Exc Meat

L E Rosellis Food Specialties ....F....... 609 654-4816
  Medford *(G-6074)*

FOOD STORES: Grocery, Independent

Berat Corporation ....C....... 609 953-7700
  Medford *(G-6065)*
CW Brown Foods Inc ....E....... 856 423-3700
  Mount Royal *(G-6851)*
Dipietro Foods Inc ....G....... 973 762-4077
  Maplewood *(G-5918)*
Georges Wine and Spirits Galle ....G....... 973 948-9950
  Branchville *(G-730)*
Kohouts Bakery ....G....... 973 772-7270
  Garfield *(G-3741)*

Savignano Food Corp...........................E....... 973 673-3355
  Orange *(G-7826)*

FOOD STORES: Supermarkets

Food Circus Super Markets Inc ....D....... 732 291-4079
  Atlantic Highlands *(G-111)*
Lo Presti & Sons LLC ....E....... 973 523-9258
  Paterson *(G-8325)*
Perk & Pantry ....G....... 856 451-4333
  Bridgeton *(G-794)*
Shop Rite Supermarkets Inc ....C....... 732 775-4250
  Neptune *(G-6932)*

FOOD STORES: Supermarkets, Chain

Acme Markets Inc ....E....... 609 884-7217
  Cape May *(G-1090)*
Herman Eickhoff ....C....... 609 871-1809
  Willingboro *(G-12119)*
Little Falls Shop Rite Super ....B....... 973 256-0909
  Little Falls *(G-5481)*
Pathmark Stores Inc ....C....... 973 762-5044
  South Orange *(G-10313)*
Pathmark Stores Inc ....C....... 856 853-5533
  Woodbury *(G-12167)*
Pathmark Stores Inc ....C....... 732 505-6440
  Toms River *(G-10900)*
Saker Shoprites Inc ....F....... 908 925-1550
  Linden *(G-5437)*
Shop Rite Supermarkets Inc ....C....... 732 442-1717
  Perth Amboy *(G-8630)*
Shop-Rite Supermarkets Inc.................C....... 609 646-2448
  Absecon *(G-4)*
Wakefern Food Corp............................B....... 908 527-3300
  Keasbey *(G-4932)*

FOOTWEAR, WHOLESALE: Athletic

Ballet Makers Inc.................................E....... 973 595-9000
  Totowa *(G-10934)*

FOOTWEAR, WHOLESALE: Shoe Access

Sysco Guest Supply LLC ....C....... 732 537-2297
  Somerset *(G-10177)*

FOOTWEAR, WHOLESALE: Shoes

Komar Inc ....B....... 212 725-1500
  Jersey City *(G-4772)*

FORGINGS

All Mtals Frge Group Ltd Lblty ....F....... 973 276-5000
  Fairfield *(G-3131)*
Atlantic Steel Solutions LLC.................F....... 973 978-0026
  Paterson *(G-8217)*
Hafco Foundry & Machine Co ....F....... 201 447-0433
  Midland Park *(G-6228)*
Kumar & Kumar Inc ....G....... 732 322-0435
  Edison *(G-2553)*
Pennsylvania Machine Works Inc ....E....... 856 467-0500
  Swedesboro *(G-10717)*
S G Manufacturing Co Inc ....D....... 732 494-6520
  Metuchen *(G-6119)*
Sigma Engineering & Consulting ....F....... 732 356-3046
  Middlesex *(G-6197)*
Supply Technologies LLC ....E....... 201 641-7600
  Moonachie *(G-6547)*
Wyman-Gordon Forgings Inc ....E....... 973 627-0200
  Rockaway *(G-9626)*

FORGINGS: Automotive & Internal Combustion Engine

JDM Engineering Inc ....G....... 732 780-0770
  Freehold *(G-3663)*
Mpt Industries ....G....... 973 989-9220
  Dover *(G-2102)*
Taurus International Corp ....E....... 201 825-2420
  Ramsey *(G-9252)*

FORGINGS: Gear & Chain

Able Gear & Machine Co ....G....... 973 983-8055
  Rockaway *(G-9541)*

FORGINGS: Metal , Ornamental, Ferrous

Bloomfield Iron Co Inc..........................G....... 973 748-7040
  Belleville *(G-296)*

FORGINGS: Nonferrous

McWilliams Forge Company ....D.....973 627-0200
Rockaway (G-9586)

Ramco Manufacturing Co Inc ....E.....908 245-4500
Kenilworth (G-4991)

FORGINGS: Nuclear Power Plant, Ferrous

McWilliams Forge Company ....D.....973 627-0200
Rockaway (G-9586)

PSEG Nuclear LLC ....A.....856 339-1002
Hancocks Bridge (G-4167)

FORMS: Concrete, Sheet Metal

Efco Corp ....F.....732 308-1010
Marlboro (G-5938)

Ulma Form-Works Inc ....D.....201 882-1122
Hawthorne (G-4261)

FOUNDRIES: Aluminum

Aluminum Shapes LLC ....B.....888 488-7427
Delair (G-1999)

American Aluminum Casting Co ....E.....973 372-3200
Irvington (G-4573)

Atlantic Casting & Engineering ....C.....973 779-2450
Clifton (G-1567)

Bierman-Everett Foundry Co ....G.....973 373-8800
South Orange (G-10301)

Bon Chef Inc ....D.....973 383-8848
Lafayette (G-5045)

Richmond Industries Inc ....E.....732 355-1616
Dayton (G-1986)

Shapes/Arch Holdings LLC ....C.....856 662-5500
Delair (G-2001)

TEC Cast Inc ....D.....201 935-3885
Moonachie (G-6549)

U S Aluminum Inc ....G.....908 782-5454
Flemington (G-3473)

FOUNDRIES: Brass, Bronze & Copper

Accurate Bushing Company Inc ....E.....908 789-1121
Garwood (G-3774)

Amrod Corp ....D.....973 344-3806
Newark (G-7085)

Bierman-Everett Foundry Co ....G.....973 373-8800
South Orange (G-10301)

FOUNDRIES: Gray & Ductile Iron

United States Pipe Fndry LLC ....C.....609 387-6000
Burlington (G-994)

FOUNDRIES: Iron

Hafco Foundry & Machine Co ....F.....201 447-0433
Midland Park (G-6228)

FOUNDRIES: Nonferrous

Engineered Precision Cast Co ....D.....732 671-2424
Middletown (G-6214)

Howmet Castings & Services Inc ....A.....973 442-2261
Dover (G-2090)

M D Carbide Tool Corp ....E.....973 263-0104
Towaco (G-10998)

S Jarco-U Castings Corporation ....G.....201 271-0003
Union City (G-11265)

Ultimate Trading Corp ....D.....973 228-7700
Fairfield (G-3332)

FOUNDRIES: Steel

Accurate Bushing Company Inc ....E.....908 789-1121
Garwood (G-3774)

D S Jh LLC ....E.....973 782-4086
Lincoln Park (G-5326)

Double O Manufacturing Inc ....G.....732 752-9423
Middlesex (G-6163)

H & R Welding LLC ....G.....732 920-4881
Brick (G-745)

Polmar Iron Work Inc ....F.....732 882-0900
Rahway (G-9217)

Sas Stressteel Inc ....F.....973 244-5995
Fairfield (G-3301)

T Wiker Enterprises Inc ....G.....609 261-9494
Hainesport (G-4079)

FOUNDRIES: Steel Investment

Fortune Rvrside Auto Parts Inc ....E.....732 381-3355
Rahway (G-9189)

Mark I Industries Inc ....F.....609 884-0051
Cape May (G-1103)

Rbc Dain Rauscher ....F.....973 778-7300
Woodland Park (G-12231)

FOUNDRY MACHINERY & EQPT

Tosca ....G.....973 337-5724
Montclair (G-6438)

FOUNDRY MATERIALS: Insulsleeves

Whibco Inc ....E.....856 825-5200
Port Elizabeth (G-8971)

FOUNDRY SAND MINING

U S Silica Company ....E.....856 785-0720
Mauricetown (G-6035)

FRAMES & FRAMING WHOLESALE

K Ron Art & Mirrors Inc ....G.....201 313-7080
Ridgefield (G-9369)

Roma Moulding Inc ....F.....732 346-0999
Edison (G-2607)

FRANCHISES, SELLING OR LICENSING

Enzon Pharmaceuticals Inc ....G.....732 980-4500
Cranford (G-1905)

Stanley Steemer Intl Inc ....E.....973 574-1640
Clifton (G-1731)

FREEZERS: Household

Troy Hills Manufacturing Inc ....G.....973 263-1885
Towaco (G-11005)

FREIGHT FORWARDING ARRANGEMENTS

R & M Chemical Technologies ....F.....908 537-9516
Hampton (G-4166)

Savino Del Bene USA Inc ....D.....347 960-5568
Avenel (G-150)

FREIGHT HANDLING SVCS: Air

Copper Boss Ltd Liability Co ....E.....888 629-2190
Edison (G-2492)

FREIGHT TRANSPORTATION ARRANGEMENTS

Colortec Printing and Mailing ....G.....856 767-0108
West Berlin (G-11709)

Fedex Office & Print Svcs Inc ....E.....732 636-3580
Iselin (G-4627)

Lummus Technology Ventures LLC ....G.....973 893-1515
Bloomfield (G-521)

Precision Dealer Services Inc ....E.....908 237-1100
Flemington (G-3460)

Total Reliance LLC ....F.....732 640-5079
Dayton (G-1992)

FRICTION MATERIAL, MADE FROM POWDERED METAL

Cardolite Corporation ....E.....609 436-0902
Monmouth Junction (G-6335)

Hamon Corporation ....D.....908 333-2000
Somerville (G-10213)

FRUIT & VEGETABLE MARKETS

Springdale Farm Market Inc ....E.....856 424-8674
Cherry Hill (G-1421)

FRUITS & VEGETABLES WHOLESALERS: Fresh

Georges Wine and Spirits Galle ....G.....973 948-9950
Branchville (G-730)

Ready Pac Produce Inc ....D.....609 499-1900
Florence (G-3480)

FRUITS: Artificial & Preserved

Venture Stationers Inc ....E.....212 288-7235
Closter (G-1767)

FUEL CELLS: Solid State

Fuceltech Inc ....G.....609 275-0070
Princeton Junction (G-9155)

FUEL OIL DEALERS

McAllister Service Company ....E.....856 665-4545
Pennsauken (G-8546)

FUELS: Ethanol

Amit Fuel Company ....G.....973 684-9409
Woodland Park (G-12209)

Bhavika Fuel LLC ....G.....609 926-4500
Somers Point (G-10045)

D and M Discount Fuels ....G.....856 935-0919
Salem (G-9805)

Daros Group ....G.....908 454-7811
Stewartsville (G-10594)

Easy Stop Food & Fuel Corp ....G.....973 517-0478
Hamburg (G-4092)

Fancyheat Corporation ....F.....973 589-1450
Somerset (G-10101)

Fossil Fuel ....G.....973 366-9111
Wharton (G-11987)

Fuel One Inc ....G.....732 726-9500
Avenel (G-132)

G & R Fuel Corp ....G.....973 732-0530
Newark (G-7166)

H & S Fuel Inc ....G.....908 769-1362
Plainfield (G-8863)

Hopatcong Fuel On You LLC ....G.....973 770-0854
Hopatcong (G-4537)

Jacquar Fuel ....G.....732 441-0700
Manalapan (G-5851)

Jai Ganesh Fuel LLC ....G.....201 246-8995
Kearny (G-4888)

Jt Fuels LLC ....G.....973 527-4470
Ledgewood (G-5306)

Kp Fuel Corporation ....G.....973 350-1202
Newark (G-7213)

Main Fuel LLC ....G.....201 941-2707
Cliffside Park (G-1542)

Main Street Auto & Fuel LLC ....G.....732 238-0044
Sayreville (G-9833)

Modern Fuel Inc ....G.....973 471-1501
Clifton (G-1675)

Montclair Fuel LLC ....G.....973 744-4300
Montclair (G-6422)

National Fuel LLC ....G.....973 227-4549
Pine Brook (G-8710)

NJ Fuel Haulers Inc ....G.....732 740-3681
Old Bridge (G-7786)

NP Bio Fuels LLC ....G.....856 467-2273
Swedesboro (G-10715)

Prospect Transportation Inc ....D.....201 933-9999
Carlstadt (G-1210)

R & R Fuel Inc ....G.....201 223-0786
Union City (G-11264)

Route 22 Fuel LLC ....G.....908 526-5270
Bridgewater (G-884)

S and D Fuel LLC ....G.....908 248-8188
Union (G-11220)

Sgw Fuel Delivery ....G.....609 209-8773
Trenton (G-11116)

Shani Auto Fuel Corp ....G.....856 241-9767
Woolwich Township (G-12241)

Shiva Fuel Inc ....G.....732 826-3228
Perth Amboy (G-8629)

Sks Fuel Inc ....G.....973 200-0796
Woodland Park (G-12233)

Suman Realty LLC ....G.....908 350-8039
Stirling (G-10607)

Thind Fuel Service LLC ....G.....732 613-1808
South River (G-10468)

Unitex International Inc ....G.....856 786-5000
Cinnaminson (G-1497)

Urso Fuel Corp ....G.....973 325-3324
West Orange (G-11908)

FUELS: Jet

Columbia Fuel Services Inc ....F.....732 751-0044
Wall Township (G-11474)

FUELS: Oil

CPI Operations LLC ....E.....856 423-5400
Paulsboro (G-8416)

Starfuels Inc ....G.....201 685-0400
Englewood (G-2934)

FUND RAISING ORGANIZATION, NON-FEE BASIS

New Jersey Jewish News ....E 973 887-3900
Whippany *(G-12027)*

FUNGICIDES OR HERBICIDES

Big Bucks Enterprises Inc ....E 908 320-7009
Washington *(G-11578)*

Glysortia LLC ....G 715 426-5358
Plainsboro *(G-8884)*

FUR FINISHING & LINING: For The Fur Goods Trade

N&K Trading Inc ....E 609 616-3110
North Brunswick *(G-7529)*

FUR: Coats

S & H R Inc ....G 908 925-3797
Linden *(G-5436)*

FURNACES & OVENS: Indl

Abp Induction LLC ....F 732 932-6400
North Brunswick *(G-7500)*

Curran-Pfeiff Corp ....F 732 225-0555
Edison *(G-2499)*

Electroheat Induction Inc ....G 908 494-0726
Jersey City *(G-4747)*

Energy Beams Inc ....F 973 291-6555
Bloomingdale *(G-543)*

Essex Products International ....E 973 226-2424
Caldwell *(G-1028)*

Haydon Corporation ....D 973 904-0800
Wayne *(G-11646)*

L & L Kiln Mfg Inc ....E 856 294-0077
Swedesboro *(G-10705)*

Procedyne Corp ....E 732 249-8347
New Brunswick *(G-6996)*

Saber Associates ....E 973 777-3800
Clifton *(G-1713)*

FURNACES & OVENS: Vacuum

Elnik Systems LLC ....E 973 239-6066
Cedar Grove *(G-1281)*

T-M Vacuum Products Inc ....E 856 829-2000
Cinnaminson *(G-1490)*

FURNACES: Indl, Electric

Consarc Corporation ....E 609 267-8000
Rancocas *(G-9256)*

FURNACES: Indl, Fuel-Fired, Metal Melting

Rowan Technologies Inc ....D 609 267-9000
Rancocas *(G-9262)*

FURNACES: Warm Air, Electric

Lennox Industries Inc ....G 908 223-6002
Port Murray *(G-8978)*

FURNITURE & CABINET STORES: Cabinets, Custom Work

Castle Woodcraft Assoc LLC ....F 732 349-1519
Pine Beach *(G-8678)*

Cozzolino Inc ....E 973 731-9292
West Orange *(G-11891)*

Creative Cabinet Designs Inc ....F 973 402-5886
Boonton *(G-561)*

Hawthorne Kitchens Inc ....F 973 427-9010
Hawthorne *(G-4238)*

Paul Burkhardt & Sons Inc ....G 856 435-2020
Lindenwold *(G-5462)*

Ramsay David Cabinetmakers ....F 856 234-7776
Moorestown *(G-6618)*

Schneiders Kitchens Inc ....G 908 689-5649
Washington *(G-11587)*

Superior Custom Kitchens LLC ....E 908 753-6005
Warren *(G-11568)*

FURNITURE & CABINET STORES: Custom

Lukach Interiors Inc ....F 973 777-1499
Clifton *(G-1666)*

Royal Cabinet Company Inc ....E 908 203-8000
Bound Brook *(G-622)*

Woodtec Inc ....G 908 979-0180
Hackettstown *(G-4043)*

FURNITURE & FIXTURES Factory

G & H Sheet Metal Works Inc ....F 973 923-1100
Hillside *(G-4408)*

Infinite Mfg Group Inc ....E 973 649-9950
Kearny *(G-4885)*

Organize It All Inc ....E 201 488-0808
Bogota *(G-549)*

Rosalindas Discount Furniture ....F 973 928-2838
Passaic *(G-8177)*

FURNITURE COMPONENTS: Porcelain Enameled

Rostek Innovations LLC ....G 908 996-6007
Frenchtown *(G-3705)*

FURNITURE REPAIR & MAINTENANCE SVCS

Rff Services LLC ....F 201 564-0040
Oakland *(G-7704)*

FURNITURE STOCK & PARTS: Hardwood

Eppley Building & Design Inc ....E 973 636-9499
Hawthorne *(G-4232)*

FURNITURE STORES

Bau-Lo Wooden Furniture Inc ....G 212 664-9188
Mays Landing *(G-6037)*

Best Value Rugs & Carpets Inc ....G 732 752-3528
Dunellen *(G-2127)*

Carlyle Custom Convertibles ....D 973 546-4502
Moonachie *(G-6511)*

Ethan Allen Retail Inc ....C 973 473-1019
Passaic *(G-8139)*

Furniture of America NJ ....E 201 605-8200
Secaucus *(G-9885)*

Greenbaum Interiors LLC ....D 973 279-3000
Paterson *(G-8281)*

H Lauzon Furniture Co Inc ....F 201 837-7598
Teaneck *(G-10756)*

South Brunswick Furniture Inc ....C 732 658-8850
Linden *(G-5446)*

White Lotus Home Ltd Lblty Co ....G 732 828-2111
New Brunswick *(G-7013)*

William Opdyke Awnings Inc ....G 732 449-5940
Wall Township *(G-11519)*

William Spencer ....G 856 235-1830
Mount Laurel *(G-6847)*

FURNITURE STORES: Cabinets, Kitchen, Exc Custom Made

Bozzone Custom Woodwork Inc ....G 973 334-5598
Montville *(G-6484)*

FURNITURE STORES: Custom Made, Exc Cabinets

Arnold Reception Desks Inc ....E 973 375-8101
Irvington *(G-4577)*

Crincoli Woodwork Co Inc ....F 908 352-9332
Elizabeth *(G-2721)*

FURNITURE STORES: Office

Bellia & Sons ....E 856 845-2234
Woodbury *(G-12158)*

La Cour Inc ....E 973 227-3300
Fairfield *(G-3246)*

Modernlinefurniture Inc ....E 908 486-0200
Linden *(G-5412)*

W B Mason Co Inc ....D 888 926-2766
Bellmawr *(G-354)*

W B Mason Co Inc ....E 888 926-2766
Egg Harbor Township *(G-2699)*

W B Mason Co Inc ....E 888 926-2766
Cranbury *(G-1890)*

FURNITURE STORES: Outdoor & Garden

Medford Cedar Products Inc ....G 609 859-1400
Southampton *(G-10479)*

Walpole Woodworkers Inc ....E 973 539-3555
Morris Plains *(G-6681)*

FURNITURE UPHOLSTERY REPAIR SVCS

Sofa Doctor Inc ....G 718 292-6300
Guttenberg *(G-3871)*

FURNITURE WHOLESALERS

Best Value Rugs & Carpets Inc ....G 732 752-3528
Dunellen *(G-2127)*

Global Industries Inc ....C 856 596-3390
Marlton *(G-5977)*

Greenbaum Interiors LLC ....D 973 279-3000
Paterson *(G-8281)*

RFS Commercial ....E 201 796-0006
Saddle Brook *(G-9785)*

FURNITURE, HOUSEHOLD: Wholesalers

D & F Wicker Import Co Inc ....E 973 736-5861
Succasunna *(G-10621)*

FURNITURE, OFFICE: Wholesalers

La Cour Inc ....E 973 227-3300
Fairfield *(G-3246)*

Office Needs Inc ....G 732 381-7770
Clark *(G-1511)*

Supplies-Supplies Inc ....E 908 272-5100
Watchung *(G-11596)*

Techntime Bus Sltons Ltd Lblty ....F 973 246-8153
East Rutherford *(G-2331)*

Two Jays Bingo Supply Inc ....F 609 267-4542
Hainesport *(G-4080)*

FURNITURE, OUTDOOR & LAWN: Wholesalers

Wisely Products LLC ....G 929 329-9188
Jersey City *(G-4850)*

FURNITURE, WHOLESALE: Bar

Pool Tables Plus Inc ....G 732 968-8228
Green Brook *(G-3862)*

FURNITURE, WHOLESALE: Chairs

Daco Limited Partnership ....D 973 263-1100
Boonton *(G-562)*

NPS Public Furniture Corp ....D 973 594-1100
Clifton *(G-1685)*

FURNITURE, WHOLESALE: Juvenile

Berg East Imports Inc ....D 908 354-5252
Barrington *(G-172)*

FURNITURE, WHOLESALE: Lockers

American Intr Resources Inc ....G 908 851-0014
Union *(G-11151)*

FURNITURE, WHOLESALE: Shelving

Modern Store Equipment ....F 609 241-7438
Burlington *(G-985)*

FURNITURE, WHOLESALE: Sofas & Couches

Carlyle Custom Convertibles ....D 973 546-4502
Moonachie *(G-6511)*

FURNITURE: Bar furniture

Outwater Plstcs/Industries Inc ....D 201 498-8750
Bogota *(G-550)*

Renaissance Creations LLC ....G 551 206-1878
Passaic *(G-8176)*

FURNITURE: Benches, Office, Wood

Fu WEI Inc ....G 732 937-8388
East Brunswick *(G-2156)*

FURNITURE: Cafeteria

Atlantic Coast Woodwork Inc ....G 609 294-2478
Ltl Egg Hbr *(G-5640)*

FURNITURE: Chair Beds

Bedding Shoppe Inc ....G 973 334-9000
Parsippany *(G-7959)*

FURNITURE: Chairs & Couches, Wood, Upholstered

Carlyle Custom Convertibles ....D 973 546-4502
Moonachie (G-6511)

Woodward Wood Products Design ......F 609 597-2708
West Creek (G-11812)

FURNITURE: Chairs, Dental

Takara Belmont Usa Inc ....D 732 469-5000
Somerset (G-10179)

FURNITURE: Chairs, Folding

Drake Corp..................................G....... 732 254-1530
East Brunswick (G-2145)

FURNITURE: Chairs, Household Upholstered

H Lauzon Furniture Co Inc ....F 201 837-7598
Teaneck (G-10756)

FURNITURE: Chairs, Household, Metal

NPS Public Furniture Corp..................D 973 594-1100
Clifton (G-1685)

FURNITURE: Chairs, Office Exc Wood

Daco Limited Partnership ....D 973 263-1100
Boonton (G-562)

Stylex Inc ....C 856 461-5600
Delanco (G-2008)

FURNITURE: Chairs, Office Wood

Gordon International Inc ....F 732 431-3361
Freehold (G-3658)

Seating Expert Inc..................E 201 299-9109
Kenilworth (G-4995)

Vaswani Inc..................................F 877 376-4425
Edison (G-2642)

Vaswani Inc..................................F 732 377-9794
Piscataway (G-8834)

FURNITURE: Chests, Cedar

Vine Hill Farm..................................G 973 383-0100
Newton (G-7411)

FURNITURE: Church

Christian Art ....G...... 201 867-8096
West New York (G-11862)

FURNITURE: Desks & Tables, Office, Wood

Arnold Reception Desks Inc ....E 973 375-8101
Irvington (G-4577)

FURNITURE: Desks, Wood

R J Hoppe Store Construction..................G...... 973 485-5665
Newark (G-7283)

FURNITURE: Foundations & Platforms

Leggett & Platt Incorporated..................D...... 904 786-0750
Brick (G-750)

FURNITURE: Frames, Box Springs Or Bedsprings, Metal

Christopher Szuco..................................G...... 732 684-7643
Millstone Twp (G-6266)

Knickerbocker Bed Company..................E 201 933-3100
Carlstadt (G-1180)

FURNITURE: Hospital

Hausmann Enterprises LLC..................D...... 201 767-0255
Northvale (G-7583)

Hill-Rom Holdings Inc..................................G...... 856 486-2117
Moorestown (G-6584)

FURNITURE: Hotel

Mp Custom FL LLC..................................F 973 417-2288
Wayne (G-11666)

FURNITURE: Household, Metal

Avantegarde Image LLC..................F 732 363-8701
Lakewood (G-5079)

FURNITURE: Household, Upholstered, Exc Wood Or Metal

South Brunswick Furniture Inc..................C 732 658-8850
Linden (G-5446)

FURNITURE: Household, Wood

10-31 Incorporated..................................E 908 496-4946
Columbia (G-1795)

Atlantic Woodworking Inc..................G...... 201 773-9277
Saddle Brook (G-9753)

Bau-Lo Wooden Furniture Inc..................G...... 212 664-9188
Mays Landing (G-6037)

Bcg Marble Gran Fabricators Co..................F 201 343-8487
Hackensack (G-3879)

Bernard Miller Fabricators ....G...... 856 541-9499
Camden (G-1043)

Bng Industries LLC..................................F 862 229-2414
Harrison (G-4173)

Bozzone Custom Woodwork Inc ....G...... 973 334-5598
Montville (G-6484)

Central Shippee Inc ....E 973 838-1100
Bloomingdale (G-541)

Cerami Wood Products Inc ....F 732 968-7222
Piscataway (G-8747)

Cozzolino Inc..................................G...... 973 731-9292
West Orange (G-11891)

Dab Design Inc ....G...... 732 224-8686
Red Bank (G-9325)

Foley-Waite Associates Inc ....F 908 298-0700
Kenilworth (G-4957)

Greenbaum Interiors LLC..................D...... 973 279-3000
Paterson (G-8281)

Interchange Group Inc..................................F 973 783-7032
Montclair (G-6418)

L&W Audio/Video Inc ....G...... 212 980-2862
Hoboken (G-4483)

My House Kitchen Inc..................................G...... 201 262-9000
Paramus (G-7892)

National Woodworking Co ....G...... 908 851-9316
Union (G-11211)

Robert J Smith ....G...... 201 641-6555
South Hackensack (G-10293)

Salernos Kitchen Cabinets ....E 201 794-1990
Saddle Brook (G-9789)

Sawitz Studios Inc ....E 201 842-9444
Carlstadt (G-1214)

Schneiders Kitchens Inc ....G...... 908 689-5649
Washington (G-11587)

Starphil Inc ....G...... 908 353-8943
Elizabeth (G-2775)

V and S Woodworks Inc ....G...... 201 568-0659
Tenafly (G-10788)

Walpole Woodworkers Inc ....E 973 539-3555
Morris Plains (G-6681)

Woodline Works Corporation ....E 732 828-9100
New Brunswick (G-7014)

Woodpeckers Inc ....F 973 751-4744
Belleville (G-329)

FURNITURE: Hydraulic Barber & Beauty Shop Chairs

Wg Products Inc..................................G...... 973 256-5999
Totowa (G-10985)

FURNITURE: Institutional, Exc Wood

Fortune Brands Home & SEC Inc..................A...... 973 402-6440
Boonton (G-570)

Hausmann Enterprises LLC..................D...... 201 767-0255
Northvale (G-7583)

Jmm Studios ....G...... 609 861-3094
Woodbine (G-12143)

Longo Associates Inc ....F 201 825-1500
Ramsey (G-9246)

FURNITURE: Juvenile, Wood

Berg East Imports Inc..................................D...... 908 354-5252
Barrington (G-172)

FURNITURE: Juvenile, Wood

Dream On ME Industries Inc..................D...... 732 752-7220
Piscataway (G-8760)

FURNITURE: Kitchen & Dining Room

Creative Cabinet Designs Inc ....F 973 402-5886
Boonton (G-561)

FURNITURE: Kitchen & Dining Room (cont.)

Designer Kitchens ....F 732 370-5500
Jackson (G-4663)

Forino Kitchen Cabinets Inc ....G...... 201 573-0990
Park Ridge (G-7920)

Mango Custom Cabinets Inc..................F 908 813-3077
Hackettstown (G-4019)

Renaissance Creations LLC ....G...... 551 206-1878
Passaic (G-8176)

FURNITURE: Kitchen & Dining Room, Metal

South Jersey Metal Inc..................................E 856 228-0642
Deptford (G-2067)

Taylor Made Cabinets Inc..................E 609 978-6900
Manahawkin (G-5834)

FURNITURE: Laboratory

Thoma Inc..................................F 856 608-6887
Moorestown (G-6628)

United Hospital Supply Corp ....C 609 387-7580
Burlington (G-993)

FURNITURE: Lawn & Garden, Except Wood & Metal

Scott W Springman..................................G...... 856 751-2411
Cherry Hill (G-1419)

FURNITURE: Lawn, Wood

R H Vassallo Inc ....G...... 856 358-8841
Malaga (G-5827)

FURNITURE: Library

Renaissance Creations LLC ....G...... 551 206-1878
Passaic (G-8176)

FURNITURE: Mattresses & Foundations

Innocor Inc..................................C 732 945-6222
Red Bank (G-9331)

Innocor Foam Tech - Acp Inc ....D...... 732 945-6222
Red Bank (G-9332)

J P Egan Industries Inc ....G...... 973 642-1500
Newark (G-7203)

Sealy Mattress Co N J Inc ....C 973 345-8800
Paterson (G-8381)

FURNITURE: Mattresses, Box & Bedsprings

Catching Zzz LLC ....G...... 888 339-1604
Piscataway (G-8744)

Comfort Rvolution Holdings LLC..................F 732 272-9111
West Long Branch (G-11845)

Dream Well Collection Inc..................F 732 545-5900
New Brunswick (G-6956)

Eclipse Sleep Products LLC..................D...... 732 628-0002
New Brunswick (G-6957)

Grand Life Inc ....G...... 201 556-8975
Carlstadt (G-1164)

Jomel Industries Inc ....F 973 282-0300
Hillside (G-4421)

Jomel Seams Reasonable LLC..................G...... 973 282-0300
Hillside (G-4422)

Mattress Dev Co Del LLC ....E 732 628-0800
North Brunswick (G-7525)

New England Bedding Trnspt Inc..................G...... 631 484-0147
Kearny (G-4903)

Spectra Mattress Inc..................................G...... 732 545-5900
North Brunswick (G-7540)

Spring Time Mattress Mfg Corp..................D...... 973 473-5400
South Hackensack (G-10297)

White Lotus Home Ltd Lblty Co ....F 732 828-2111
New Brunswick (G-7013)

FURNITURE: Mattresses, Innerspring Or Box Spring

Custom Bedding Co ....G...... 973 761-1100
Maplewood (G-5917)

Leggett & Platt Incorporated..................D...... 732 225-2440
Edison (G-2556)

Ther-A-Pedic Sleep Products ....D...... 732 628-0800
North Brunswick (G-7542)

FURNITURE: NEC

Best American Hands..................................E 203 247-2028
Hillside (G-4398)

Wood Textures ....F 732 230-5005
Dayton (G-1996)

FURNITURE: Office Panel Systems, Wood

M2 Electric LLC ....F 973 770-4596
Mine Hill *(G-6327)*

Mbs Installations Inc ....F 888 446-9135
Jackson *(G-4672)*

FURNITURE: Office, Exc Wood

Concord Products Company Inc ....E 856 933-3000
Sewell *(G-9945)*

Creative Innovations Inc ....F 973 636-9060
Fair Lawn *(G-3088)*

Fehlberg Mfg Inc ....F 973 399-1905
Irvington *(G-4585)*

Gaw Associates Inc ....E 856 608-1428
Cherry Hill *(G-1370)*

Global Industries Inc ....C 856 596-3390
Marlton *(G-5977)*

La Cour Inc ....E 973 227-3300
Fairfield *(G-3246)*

FURNITURE: Office, Wood

Arnold Furniture Mfrs Inc ....F 973 399-0505
Irvington *(G-4575)*

Arnold Kolax Furniture Inc ....E 973 375-3344
Irvington *(G-4576)*

Cbt Supply Inc ....G 973 586-2783
Rockaway *(G-9557)*

Cozzolino Inc ....E 973 731-9292
West Orange *(G-11891)*

Designcore Ltd ....D 718 499-0337
Secaucus *(G-9877)*

G & A Coml Seating Pdts Corp ....G 908 233-8000
Mountainside *(G-6882)*

La Cour Inc ....E 973 227-3300
Fairfield *(G-3246)*

Mp Custom FL LLC ....F 973 417-2288
Wayne *(G-11666)*

Reda Furniture LLC ....F 732 948-1703
Manasquan *(G-5878)*

Renaissance Creations LLC 551 206-1878
Passaic *(G-8176)*

Robert J Smith ....G 201 641-6555
South Hackensack *(G-10293)*

FURNITURE: School

Academia Furniture LLC ....E 973 472-0100
Wood Ridge *(G-12133)*

RFS Commercial ....E 201 796-0006
Saddle Brook *(G-9785)*

Visual Architectural Designs ....F 908 754-3000
South Plainfield *(G-10451)*

FURNITURE: Sleep

Lieth Holdings LLC ....G 201 358-8282
Westwood *(G-11962)*

Sheex Inc ....E 856 334-3021
Marlton *(G-5999)*

FURNITURE: Sofa Beds Or Convertible Sofas)

Carlyle Custom Convertibles ....D 973 546-4502
Moonachie *(G-6511)*

FURNITURE: Spring Cushions

Ayerspace Inc ....G 212 582-8410
West Caldwell *(G-11767)*

FURNITURE: Table Tops, Marble

Formia Marble & Stone Inc ....F 908 259-0606
Roselle *(G-9670)*

Natures Beauty Marble & Gran ....F 908 233-5300
Scotch Plains *(G-9852)*

FURNITURE: Tables & Table Tops, Wood

Union City Mirror & Table Co ....E 201 867-0050
Union City *(G-11270)*

FURNITURE: Tables, Household, Metal

De Saussure Equipment Co Inc ....E 201 845-6517
Maywood *(G-6047)*

FURNITURE: Upholstered

Custom Decorators Service ....G 973 625-0516
Denville *(G-2034)*

Edward P Paul & Co Inc ....G 908 757-4212
Plainfield *(G-8859)*

Furniture of America NJ ....E 201 605-8200
Secaucus *(G-9885)*

Masters Interiors Inc ....E 973 253-0784
Clifton *(G-1669)*

Rff Services LLC ....F 201 564-0040
Oakland *(G-7704)*

Sofa Doctor Inc ....G 718 292-6300
Guttenberg *(G-3871)*

FURNITURE: Vehicle

Suburban Auto Seat Co Inc ....F 973 778-9227
Lodi *(G-5603)*

FURNITURE: Wall Cases, Office, Exc Wood

Denmatt Industries LLC ....F 609 689-0099
Hamilton *(G-4106)*

FURNITURE: Wardrobes, Household, Wood

Rainbow Closets Inc ....D 973 882-3800
Fairfield *(G-3289)*

FURNITURE: Wicker & Rattan

D & F Wicker Import Co Inc ....E 973 736-5861
Succasunna *(G-10621)*

FURRIERS

M Blaustein Inc ....G 973 379-1080
Short Hills *(G-9980)*

S & H R Inc ....G 908 925-3797
Linden *(G-5436)*

FUSES & FUSE EQPT

BNH Enterprise LLC ....G 201 815-0546
Dumont *(G-2116)*

FUSES: Electric

Bel Fuse Inc ....C 201 432-0463
Jersey City *(G-4715)*

Furs

Tubari Inc ....E 973 779-8693
Passaic *(G-8185)*

GAMES & TOYS: Baby Carriages & Restraint Seats

Majestic Industries Inc ....E 973 473-3434
Passaic *(G-8158)*

GAMES & TOYS: Blocks

Poof-Alex Holdings LLC ....G 734 454-9552
Fairfield *(G-3284)*

GAMES & TOYS: Board Games, Children's & Adults'

Classic Chess and Games Inc ....G 908 850-6553
Hackettstown *(G-4001)*

GAMES & TOYS: Craft & Hobby Kits & Sets

Hygloss Products Inc ....E 973 458-1700
Wallington *(G-11527)*

Larose Industries LLC ....D 973 543-2037
Randolph *(G-9287)*

GAMES & TOYS: Dolls & Doll Clothing

Chic Btq Doll Design Co LLC ....G 201 784-7727
Norwood *(G-7619)*

GAMES & TOYS: Dolls, Exc Stuffed Toy Animals

Franklin Mint LLC ....E 800 843-6468
Fort Lee *(G-3555)*

GAMES & TOYS: Kits, Science, Incl Microscopes/Chemistry Sets

Hirox - USA Inc ....G 201 342-2600
Hackensack *(G-3927)*

GAMES & TOYS: Marbles

Bucci Management Co Inc ....G 609 567-8808
Hammonton *(G-4134)*

GAMES & TOYS: Models, Airplane, Toy & Hobby

Lawrence Katona ....G 609 538-1388
Ewing *(G-3035)*

GAMES & TOYS: Models, Railroad, Toy & Hobby

Deluxe Innovations Inc ....G 201 857-5880
Midland Park *(G-6225)*

GAMES & TOYS: Trains & Eqpt, Electric & Mechanical

Atlas Model Railroad Co Inc ....D 908 687-0880
Hillside *(G-4392)*

GAMES & TOYS: Wagons, Coaster, Express & Play, Children's

Morgan Cycle LLC ....G 973 218-9233
Short Hills *(G-9982)*

GARBAGE CONTAINERS: Plastic

Allstar Disposal ....G 973 398-8808
Hopatcong *(G-4533)*

Birds Beware Corporation ....G 732 671-6377
Middletown *(G-6212)*

Greco Industries LLC ....G 732 919-6200
Colts Neck *(G-1787)*

Janico Inc ....F 732 370-2223
Freehold *(G-3662)*

Nini Disposal ....G 609 587-2411
Trenton *(G-11090)*

Sancon Services Inc ....G 973 344-2500
Newark *(G-7302)*

GARBAGE DISPOSERS & COMPACTORS: Commercial

Arrow Steel Inc ....F 973 523-1122
Paterson *(G-8215)*

Metropolitan Compactors Svc ....G 908 653-0168
Cranford *(G-1916)*

Multi-Pak Corporation ....E 201 342-7474
Hackensack *(G-3949)*

Premier Compaction Systems ....F 718 328-5990
Woodland Park *(G-12229)*

GAS & OIL FIELD EXPLORATION SVCS

All American Oil Recovery Co ....E 973 628-9278
Wayne *(G-11603)*

American Shale Oil LLC ....G 973 438-3500
Newark *(G-7083)*

Core Laboratories LP ....F 609 896-2673
Lawrenceville *(G-5255)*

Hess Corporation ....G 609 882-8477
Ewing *(G-3023)*

Masouleh Corp ....E 973 470-8900
Clifton *(G-1668)*

Mep Alaska LLC ....G 646 535-9005
Livingston *(G-5543)*

Ridgewood Energy S Fund LLC ....G 201 307-0470
Montvale *(G-6473)*

Ridgewood Energy T Fund LLC ....G 800 942-5550
Montvale *(G-6474)*

Ridgewood Energy U Fund LLC ....G 201 447-9000
Montvale *(G-6475)*

Ridgewood Energy V Fund LLC ....G 800 942-5550
Montvale *(G-6476)*

Ridgewood Energy Y Fund LLC ....G 201 447-9000
Montvale *(G-6477)*

GAS & OIL FIELD SVCS, NEC

Garden State Fuel ....G 856 442-0061
Monroeville *(G-6399)*

GAS & OTHER COMBINED SVCS

Lantier Construction Company ....E 856 780-6366
Moorestown (G-6592)

GAS STATIONS

Phoenix National Petroleum Co ....G 201 568-5568
Cresskill (G-1947)

Total American Services Inc ....F 206 626-3500
Jersey City (G-4838)

GASES: Flourinated Hydrocarbon

Solvay Holding Inc ....A 609 860-4000
Princeton (G-9121)

Solvay USA Inc ....B 609 860-4000
Princeton (G-9122)

Solvay USA Inc ....C 732 297-0100
North Brunswick (G-7538)

Sonneborn Holding LLC ....B 201 760-2940
Parsippany (G-8090)

GASES: Helium

Linde Global Helium Inc ....E 908 464-8100
New Providence (G-7042)

GASES: Indl

Air Liquide Advanced Materials ....F 908 231-9060
Branchburg (G-629)

Air Products and Chemicals Inc ....E 732 446-5676
Manalapan (G-5837)

Airgas Usa LLC ....F 908 754-7700
South Plainfield (G-10322)

Airgas Usa LLC ....F 856 933-0544
Bellmawr (G-330)

Airgas Usa LLC ....F 609 685-4241
Cherry Hill (G-1342)

Airgas Usa LLC ....E 856 829-7878
Cinnaminson (G-1445)

Boc Group Inc ....A 908 665-2400
New Providence (G-7030)

Coim USA Inc ....E 856 224-1668
Paulsboro (G-8415)

Concorde Specialty Gases Inc ....E 732 544-9899
Eatontown (G-2388)

Linde Gas North America LLC ....G 908 777-9125
Phillipsburg (G-8656)

Linde North America Inc ....D 908 464-8100
New Providence (G-7045)

Linde North America Inc ....B 908 464-8100
Bridgewater (G-857)

Linde North America Inc ....D 908 454-7455
Alpha (G-43)

Matheson Gas Products Inc ....F 201 867-4101
Parsippany (G-8041)

Matheson Tri-Gas Inc ....F 908 991-9200
Basking Ridge (G-194)

Matheson Tri-Gas Inc ....D 908 991-9200
Basking Ridge (G-195)

Matheson Tri-Gas Inc ....E 908 991-9200
Basking Ridge (G-196)

Praxair Inc ....F 732 738-4150
Keasbey (G-4930)

Praxair Cryomag Services Inc ....F 732 738-4000
Keasbey (G-4931)

Praxair Distribution Inc ....F 908 862-7200
Linden (G-5430)

Praxair Distribution Inc ....E 973 589-7895
Newark (G-7272)

GASES: Nitrogen

Linde Gas North America LLC ....F 732 438-9977
Dayton (G-1977)

Linde LLC ....E 908 329-9619
Stewartsville (G-10597)

GASES: Oxygen

Bioxygen Distribution Corp ....G 732 212-1799
Sea Bright (G-9859)

Linde Gas North America LLC ....E 908 329-9300
Stewartsville (G-10596)

Linde Gas North America LLC ....A 800 932-0803
Bridgewater (G-853)

Linde Gas USA LLC ....C 908 464-8100
Bridgewater (G-854)

Linde LLC ....C 908 464-8100
Bridgewater (G-855)

Linde LLC ....B 512 330-0153
Bridgewater (G-856)

Linde LLC ....E 908 464-8100
New Providence (G-7043)

Linde LLC ....G 973 579-2065
Sparta (G-10510)

Linde Merchant Production Inc ....F 908 464-8100
New Providence (G-7044)

GASKET MATERIALS

Banks Bros Corporation ....D 973 680-4488
Bloomfield (G-502)

Capital Gasket and Rubber Inc ....E 856 939-3670
Runnemede (G-9717)

Monmouth Rubber Corp ....E 732 229-3444
Long Branch (G-5630)

GASKETS

Alltite Gasket Co ....F 732 254-2154
South River (G-10458)

Arcy Manufacturing Co Inc ....F 201 635-1910
Carlstadt (G-1126)

Coast Rubber and Gasket Inc ....G 609 747-0110
Burlington (G-965)

Metallo Gasket Company Inc ....F 732 545-7223
New Brunswick (G-6981)

Omega Shielding Products Inc ....F 973 366-0080
Randolph (G-9293)

Phoenix Packing & Gasket Co ....F 732 938-7377
Howell (G-4564)

R S Rubber Corp ....F 973 777-2200
Wallington (G-11529)

Seals-Eastern Incorporated ....C 732 747-9200
Red Bank (G-9343)

Specialty Rubber Inc ....G 609 704-2555
Elwood (G-2854)

Tricomp Inc ....C 973 835-1110
Pompton Plains (G-8966)

GASKETS & SEALING DEVICES

Cinchseal Associates Inc ....E 856 662-5162
Mount Laurel (G-6788)

Custom Gasket Mfg LLC ....F 201 331-6363
Englewood Cliffs (G-2956)

Frontline Industries Inc ....F 973 373-7211
Irvington (G-4587)

H K Metal Craft Mfg Corp ....E 973 471-7770
Lodi (G-5585)

GASOLINE FILLING STATIONS

Chevron USA Inc ....D 732 738-2000
Perth Amboy (G-8610)

Masouleh Corp ....E 973 470-8900
Clifton (G-1668)

GASTROINTESTINAL OR GENITOURINARY SYSTEM DRUGS

Guardian Drug Company Inc ....D 609 860-2600
Dayton (G-1968)

Salix Pharmaceuticals Ltd ....C 866 246-8245
Bridgewater (G-886)

GATES: Ornamental Metal

J Kaufman Iron Works Inc ....F 973 925-9972
Paterson (G-8296)

Robert J Donaldson Inc ....F 856 629-2737
Williamstown (G-12104)

GAUGES

Digivac Company ....F 732 765-0900
Matawan (G-6017)

GEARS

State Tool Gear Co Inc ....F 973 642-6181
Newark (G-7329)

GEARS: Power Transmission, Exc Auto

Koellmann Gear Corporation ....C 201 447-0200
Waldwick (G-11447)

Martin Sprocket & Gear Inc ....F 973 633-5700
Wayne (G-11664)

Walter Machine Co Inc ....E 201 656-5654
Jersey City (G-4846)

GELATIN CAPSULES

International Vitamin Corp ....G 973 416-2000
Irvington (G-4593)

Torpac Inc ....E 973 244-1125
Fairfield (G-3328)

GEM STONES MINING, NEC: Natural

Innovative Cutng Concepts LLC ....G 609 484-9960
Egg Harbor Township (G-2685)

GEMSTONE & INDL DIAMOND MINING SVCS

Diamond Wholesale Co ....E 201 727-9595
Moonachie (G-6514)

Star Creations Inc ....G 212 221-3570
Piscataway (G-8817)

GENERAL COUNSELING SVCS

Corrigan Center For Integrativ ....G 973 239-0700
Cedar Grove (G-1276)

GENERAL MERCHANDISE, NONDURABLE, WHOLESALE

Shy Kramer & Associates ....F 609 646-2063
Pleasantville (G-8915)

GENERATING APPARATUS & PARTS: Electrical

American Mdlar Pwr Sltions Inc ....G 973 588-4026
Boonton (G-555)

Ocean Power Technologies Inc ....E 609 730-0400
Monroe Township (G-6387)

GENERATION EQPT: Electronic

Cellular Empire Inc ....D 800 778-3513
Linden (G-5357)

Fuchs Audio Tech Ltd Lblty Co ....F 973 772-4420
Clifton (G-1624)

Industronic ....G 908 393-5960
Bridgewater (G-845)

Magna-Power Electronics ....D 908 237-2200
Flemington (G-3455)

Ocean Power Technologies Inc ....E 609 730-0400
Monroe Township (G-6387)

Power Dynamics Inc ....E 973 560-0019
Whippany (G-12036)

Sparton Aydin LLC ....F 732 935-1320
Eatontown (G-2423)

GENERATOR REPAIR SVCS

Gamka Sales Co Inc ....E 732 248-1400
Edison (G-2525)

Hights Electric Motor Service ....G 609 448-2298
Hightstown (G-4312)

Power Pool Plus Inc ....G 908 454-1124
Alpha (G-44)

RSI Company ....G 973 227-7800
Fairfield (G-3297)

GENERATORS SETS: Motor, Automotive

Doolan Industries Incorporated ....G 856 985-1880
Marlton (G-5973)

GENERATORS: Electric

Electro-Steam Generator Corp ....B 609 288-9071
Rancocas (G-9257)

GENERATORS: Storage Battery Chargers

Hitechone Inc ....G 201 500-8864
Englewood Cliffs (G-2964)

GENERATORS: Ultrasonic

Seren Ips Inc ....D 856 205-1131
Vineland (G-11404)

GIFT SHOP

A Cheerful Giver Inc ....F 856 358-4438
Elmer (G-2787)

Candy Treasure LLC ....G 201 830-3600
Lebanon (G-5279)

Cream Ridge Winery ....G 609 259-9797
Cream Ridge (G-1933)

PRODUCT

Engraved Images Ltd ....G.... 908 234-0323
  Far Hills (G-3375)
Genevieves Inc ....F 973 772-8816
  Garfield (G-3737)
Jubili Bead & Yarn Shoppe ....G.... 856 858-7844
  Collingswood (G-1771)
Trophy King Inc ....G.... 201 836-1482
  Teaneck (G-10775)

GIFT WRAP: Paper, Made From Purchased Materials

Flexo-Craft Prints Inc ....E 973 482-7200
  Harrison (G-4183)

GIFT, NOVELTY & SOUVENIR STORES: Gifts & Novelties

Matisse Chocolatier Inc ....G.... 201 568-2288
  Englewood (G-2914)
Mj Corporate Sales Inc ....E 856 778-0055
  Mount Laurel (G-6819)
Rolferrys Specialties Inc ....G.... 856 456-2999
  Brooklawn (G-921)

GIFT, NOVELTY & SOUVENIR STORES: Party Favors

Party City Corporation ....F 973 537-1707
  Randolph (G-9294)
Party City of North Bergen ....F 201 865-0040
  North Bergen (G-7473)

GIFTS & NOVELTIES: Wholesalers

A Kessler Kreation Inc ....G.... 732 431-2468
  Colts Neck (G-1779)
C Bennett Scopes Inc ....G.... 856 464-6889
  Mantua (G-5891)
HMS Monaco Et Cie Ltd ....E 201 533-0007
  Jersey City (G-4765)
House of Prill Inc ....E 732 442-2400
  Lincroft (G-5337)
Madhouz LLC ....G.... 609 206-8009
  Glassboro (G-3808)
Nikko Ceramics Inc ....F 201 840-5200
  Fairview (G-3366)
Nouveautes Inc ....F 973 882-8850
  Fairfield (G-3274)
Prismatix Decal Inc ....G.... 201 525-2800
  Hackensack (G-3965)
Qualserv Imports Inc ....G.... 973 620-9234
  Denville (G-2052)
Retrographics Publishing Inc ....G.... 201 501-0505
  Closter (G-1765)
Scaasis Originals Inc ....E 732 775-7474
  Neptune (G-6928)

GIFTWARE: Brass

Lighthouse Express Inc ....G.... 732 776-9555
  Asbury Park (G-80)

GILSONITE MINING SVCS

Ziegler Chem & Mineral Corp ....F 732 752-4111
  Piscataway (G-8838)

GLASS & GLASS CERAMIC PRDTS, PRESSED OR BLOWN: Tableware

Durand Glass Mfg Co Inc ....A 856 327-1850
  Millville (G-6300)

GLASS FABRICATORS

Above Rest Glass ....G.... 732 370-1616
  Toms River (G-10859)
Amcor Phrm Packg USA LLC ....C 856 825-1100
  Millville (G-6280)
Atlantic International Tech ....F 973 625-0053
  Rockaway (G-9552)
Avant Industries Ltd Inc ....G.... 973 242-1700
  Newark (G-7100)
Century Bathworks Inc ....E 201 785-1414
  Woodland Park (G-12215)
Chemglass Inc ....C 856 696-0014
  Vineland (G-11336)
Comar Inc ....E 856 692-6100
  Voorhees (G-11425)
Comar LLC ....C 856 507-5483
  Vineland (G-11337)

Comar LLC ....B 856 692-6100
  Voorhees (G-11427)
County of Somerset ....C 732 469-3363
  Bridgewater (G-830)
CR Laurence Co Inc ....F 201 770-1077
  Secaucus (G-9874)
Crown Glass Co Inc ....G.... 908 642-1764
  Branchburg (G-652)
Cumberland Rcycl Corp S Jersey .....E 856 825-4153
  Millville (G-6296)
Dwk Life Sciences Inc ....C 856 825-1100
  Millville (G-6301)
Eastern Glass Resources Inc ....E 973 483-8411
  Harrison (G-4180)
Fbn New Jersey Mfg Inc ....E 973 402-1443
  Mountain Lakes (G-6859)
Friedrich and Dimmock Inc ....E 856 825-0305
  Millville (G-6302)
Gbw Manufacturing Inc ....E 973 279-0077
  Totowa (G-10947)
Gerresheimer Glass Inc ....B 856 507-5852
  Vineland (G-11361)
Glastron Inc ....E 856 692-0500
  Vineland (G-11363)
Icup Inc ....E 856 751-2045
  Cherry Hill (G-1376)
Jersey Tempered Glass Inc ....E 856 273-8700
  Mount Laurel (G-6810)
Kubik Maltbie Inc ....E 856 234-0052
  Mount Laurel (G-6811)
McGrory Glass Inc ....D 856 579-3200
  Paulsboro (G-8420)
Miric Industries Inc ....F 201 864-0233
  North Bergen (G-7468)
Newman Glass Works Inc ....F 215 925-3565
  Camden (G-1078)
Oldcastle Buildingenvelope Inc ....D 856 234-9222
  Moorestown (G-6605)
Penta Glass Industries Inc ....G.... 973 478-2110
  Garfield (G-3747)
Precision Electronic Glass Inc ....D 856 691-2234
  Vineland (G-11393)
Quality Glass Inc ....F 908 754-2652
  South Plainfield (G-10428)
Quark Enterprises Inc ....E 856 455-0376
  Rosenhayn (G-9709)
S P Industries Inc ....D 856 691-3200
  Vineland (G-11401)
St Thomas Creations ....E 800 536-2284
  Monroe Township (G-6394)
Triton Associated Industries ....E 856 697-3050
  Buena (G-951)
William Duling ....G.... 856 365-6323
  Camden (G-1089)

GLASS PRDTS, FROM PURCHASED GLASS: Art

Personlzed Exprssons By Audrey ......F 973 478-5115
  Garfield (G-3748)

GLASS PRDTS, FROM PURCHASED GLASS: Glass Beads, Reflecting

Potters Industries LLC ....E 201 507-4169
  Carlstadt (G-1206)

GLASS PRDTS, FROM PURCHASED GLASS: Insulating

Insulite Inc ....F 732 255-1700
  Toms River (G-10888)
JE Berkowitz LP ....C 856 456-7800
  Pedricktown (G-8436)
Thermoseal Industries LLC ....D 856 456-3109
  Gloucester City (G-3847)

GLASS PRDTS, FROM PURCHASED GLASS: Mirrored

General Glass Intl Corp ....C 201 553-1850
  Secaucus (G-9887)
Interior Specialties LLC ....F 856 663-1700
  Pennsauken (G-8529)
R A O Contract Sales NY Inc ....G.... 201 652-1500
  Paterson (G-8367)
Union City Mirror & Table Co ....E 201 867-0050
  Union City (G-11270)

GLASS PRDTS, FROM PURCHASED GLASS: Novelties, Fruit, Etc

Proco Inc ....G.... 609 265-8777
  Lumberton (G-5662)

GLASS PRDTS, PRESSED OR BLOWN: Barware

Buckets Plus Inc ....G.... 732 545-0420
  New Brunswick (G-6949)

GLASS PRDTS, PRESSED OR BLOWN: Bulbs, Electric Lights

Bulbrite Industries Inc ....E 201 531-5900
  Moonachie (G-6509)
Goodlite Products Inc ....F 718 697-7502
  Perth Amboy (G-8615)
Lumiko USA Inc ....G.... 609 409-6900
  Cranbury (G-1857)

GLASS PRDTS, PRESSED OR BLOWN: Furnishings & Access

Crystal World Inc ....E 201 488-0909
  Carlstadt (G-1151)
Folio Art Glass Inc ....G.... 732 431-0044
  Colts Neck (G-1786)
Gbw Manufacturing Inc ....E 973 279-0077
  Totowa (G-10947)
Glocal Expertise Llc ....G.... 718 928-3839
  Jersey City (G-4761)
Interior Specialties LLC ....F 856 663-1700
  Pennsauken (G-8529)
Mirrotek International LLC ....F 973 472-1400
  Passaic (G-8165)

GLASS PRDTS, PRESSED OR BLOWN: Glassware, Art Or Decorative

Eldon Glass & Mirror Co Inc ....F 973 589-2099
  Newark (G-7151)
Glassworks Studio Inc ....G.... 973 656-0800
  Morristown (G-6710)
House of Kalon New York ....F 786 259-0786
  Secaucus (G-9895)
Kraftware Corporation ....E 732 345-7091
  Roselle (G-9674)
Vandermark Merritt GL Studios ....G.... 908 231-8189
  Branchburg (G-715)

GLASS PRDTS, PRESSED OR BLOWN: Glassware, Novelty

Hospitality GL Brands USA Inc ....F 800 869-5258
  Ridgefield Park (G-9407)

GLASS PRDTS, PRESSED OR BLOWN: Lighting Eqpt Parts

Illuminating Experiences LLC ....G.... 800 734-5858
  New Brunswick (G-6967)
Sterling Products Inc ....F 973 471-2858
  Passaic (G-8182)

GLASS PRDTS, PRESSED OR BLOWN: Optical

Partners In Vision Inc ....G.... 888 748-1112
  Edison (G-2592)

GLASS PRDTS, PRESSED OR BLOWN: Ornaments, Christmas Tree

Mg Decor LLC ....F 201 923-5493
  Secaucus (G-9904)

GLASS PRDTS, PRESSED OR BLOWN: Scientific Glassware

AGC Acquisition LLC ....E 856 692-4435
  Vineland (G-11320)
Friedrich and Dimmock Inc ....E 856 825-0305
  Millville (G-6302)
Glass Warehouse ....G.... 856 825-1400
  Millville (G-6305)
Kramme Consolidated Inc ....E 856 358-8151
  Monroeville (G-6400)

(G-0000) Company's Geographic Section entry number

Nds Technologies Inc.................E......856 691-0330
Vineland *(G-11385)*

Quark Enterprises Inc................E......856 455-0376
Rosenhayn *(G-9709)*

Technical Glass Products Inc.........G......973 989-5500
Dover *(G-2111)*

GLASS PRDTS, PRESSED OR BLOWN: Tubing

Corning Pharmaceutical GL LLC.........G......856 794-7100
Vineland *(G-11342)*

Creamer Glass LLC.....................G......856 327-2023
Millville *(G-6294)*

Creamer Glass LLC.....................G......856 327-2023
Millville *(G-6295)*

E G L Company Inc......................C......908 508-1111
Berkeley Heights *(G-409)*

GLASS PRDTS, PURCHASED GLASS: Glassware, Scientific/Tech

H S Martin Company Inc................F......856 692-8700
Vineland *(G-11368)*

V M Glass Co...........................G......856 794-9333
Vineland *(G-11414)*

GLASS STORE: Leaded Or Stained

Artique Glass Studio Inc..............G......201 444-3500
Glen Rock *(G-3820)*

Artistic Glass & Doors Inc............G......856 768-1414
West Berlin *(G-11704)*

GLASS STORES

Architectural Metal and Glass.........G......732 994-7575
Lakewood *(G-5075)*

Newman Glass Works Inc................F......215 925-3565
Camden *(G-1078)*

Phoenix Glass LLC....................E......856 692-0100
Pittsgrove *(G-8847)*

GLASS, AUTOMOTIVE: Wholesalers

Pgw Auto Glass LLC...................E......856 234-1600
Mount Laurel *(G-6825)*

PPG Ind Inc............................G......856 662-9323
Pennsauken *(G-8561)*

GLASS: Fiber

Thomas Clark Fiberglass LLC...........G......609 492-9257
Barnegat *(G-167)*

GLASS: Flat

Edmund Optics Inc....................C......856 547-3488
Barrington *(G-177)*

Floral Glass Industries Inc...........E......201 939-4600
East Rutherford *(G-2297)*

Frost Tech Inc.........................F......732 396-0071
Rahway *(G-9191)*

General Glass Intl Corp...............C......201 553-1850
Secaucus *(G-9887)*

Oldcastle Buildingenvelope Inc........D......856 234-9222
Moorestown *(G-6605)*

Pierangeli Group Inc.................G......856 582-4060
Gloucester City *(G-3842)*

Pilkington North America Inc.........C......973 470-5703
Clifton *(G-1697)*

Spectrum Glass LLC....................G......201 750-1251
Closter *(G-1766)*

Tri-State Glass & Mirror Inc..........G......732 591-5545
Old Bridge *(G-7794)*

GLASS: Indl Prdts

M D Laboratory Supplies Inc...........G......732 322-0773
Franklin Park *(G-3628)*

Q Glass Company Inc...................G......973 335-5191
Towaco *(G-11002)*

GLASS: Insulating

Just Glass & Mirror Inc...............F......856 728-8383
Williamstown *(G-12091)*

GLASS: Plate

PPG Ind Inc............................G......856 662-9323
Pennsauken *(G-8561)*

GLASS: Pressed & Blown, NEC

Amcor Phrm Packg USA LLC..............C......856 825-1100
Millville *(G-6280)*

Cardinal International Inc...........F......973 628-0900
Wayne *(G-11618)*

Daum Inc...............................G......862 210-8522
Fairfield *(G-3172)*

Glassblowerscom LLC...................G......856 232-7898
Blackwood *(G-479)*

Glassroots Inc.........................E......973 353-9555
Newark *(G-7170)*

Icup Inc...............................E......856 751-2045
Cherry Hill *(G-1376)*

Materials Research Group Inc..........G......908 245-3301
Roselle *(G-9675)*

McGrory Glass Inc.....................D......856 579-3200
Paulsboro *(G-8420)*

Qis Inc................................F......856 455-3736
Rosenhayn *(G-9708)*

Sensors Unlimited Inc.................D......609 333-8000
Princeton *(G-9116)*

Triton Associated Industries.........E......856 697-3050
Buena *(G-951)*

GLASS: Stained

Ace Fine Art Inc......................G......201 960-4447
Garfield *(G-3714)*

Artistic Glass & Doors Inc............G......856 768-1414
West Berlin *(G-11704)*

Ascalon Studios Inc...................F......856 768-3779
West Berlin *(G-11705)*

Comfort Zone..........................G......732 869-9990
Ocean Grove *(G-7760)*

Edward W Hiemer & Co..................F......973 772-5081
Clifton *(G-1611)*

Femenella & Associates Inc............G......908 722-6526
Branchburg *(G-659)*

Folio Art Glass Inc...................G......732 431-0044
Colts Neck *(G-1786)*

Glass Dynamics LLC....................G......856 205-1503
Vineland *(G-11362)*

Linda Spolitino.......................G......609 345-3126
Atlantic City *(G-102)*

Rambusch Decorating Company...........E......201 333-2525
Jersey City *(G-4815)*

GLASS: Structural

Europrojects Intl Inc.................G......917 262-0795
Englewood *(G-2894)*

GLASSWARE STORES

Folio Art Glass Inc...................G......732 431-0044
Colts Neck *(G-1786)*

GLASSWARE WHOLESALERS

ARC International N Amer LLC...........C......856 825-5620
Millville *(G-6284)*

Durand Glass Mfg Co Inc...............A......856 327-1850
Millville *(G-6300)*

Eastern Glass Resources Inc...........E......973 483-8411
Harrison *(G-4180)*

GLASSWARE: Indl

United Silica Products Inc............F......973 209-8854
Franklin *(G-3606)*

GLASSWARE: Laboratory

Ace Glass Incorporated................D......856 692-3333
Vineland *(G-11319)*

GLASSWARE: Laboratory & Medical

A M K Glass Inc.......................G......856 692-1488
Vineland *(G-11318)*

Bellco Glass Inc.....................D......800 257-7043
Vineland *(G-11328)*

Demco Scientific Glassware Inc........G......856 327-7898
Millville *(G-6299)*

Hanson & Zollinger Inc...............F......856 626-3440
Berlin *(G-434)*

GLOBAL POSITIONING SYSTEMS & EQPT

Comodo Group Inc......................C......888 266-6361
Clifton *(G-1586)*

ID Systems Inc.......................C......201 996-9000
Woodcliff Lake *(G-12193)*

GLOVES: Fabric

American Baby Headwear Co Inc..........D......908 558-0017
Elizabeth *(G-2709)*

George Glove Company Inc.............G......201 251-1200
Midland Park *(G-6226)*

GLOVES: Leather

Ansell Hawkeye Inc...................E......662 258-3200
Iselin *(G-4610)*

GLOVES: Plastic

Poly-Version Inc......................E......201 451-7600
Jersey City *(G-4804)*

GLOVES: Safety

Ansell Protective Products LLC........A......732 345-5400
Iselin *(G-4613)*

Becton Dickinson and Company.........A......201 847-6800
Franklin Lakes *(G-3610)*

Pacific Dunlop Investments USA........F......732 345-5400
Red Bank *(G-9340)*

GLUE

Gluefast Company Inc..................F......732 918-4600
Neptune *(G-6915)*

Hudson Industries Corporation.........G......973 402-0100
Fairfield *(G-3225)*

Signature Marketing & Mfg.............G......973 427-3700
Hawthorne *(G-4259)*

GOLD ORES

Freeport-Mcmoran Inc..................G......908 558-4361
Elizabeth *(G-2735)*

GOLD STAMPING, EXC BOOKS

Berk Gold Stamping Corporation........E......973 786-6052
Andover *(G-49)*

GOLF EQPT

Greater ATL Cy Golf Assn LLC..........F......609 652-1800
Galloway *(G-3711)*

JA Cissel Manufacturing Co............E......732 901-0300
Lakewood *(G-5137)*

GOLF GOODS & EQPT

RCM Ltd Inc...........................G......201 337-3328
Oakland *(G-7702)*

Tex-Net Inc...........................E......609 499-9111
Florence *(G-3481)*

GOURMET FOOD STORES

Delicious Fresh Pierogi Inc...........F......908 245-0550
Roselle Park *(G-9694)*

Gardner Resources Inc.................G......732 872-0755
Highlands *(G-4309)*

Silver Palate Kitchens Inc...........E......201 568-0110
Cresskill *(G-1948)*

GOVERNMENT, EXECUTIVE OFFICES: County Supervisor/Exec Office

County of Somerset....................C......732 469-3363
Bridgewater *(G-830)*

GRAIN & FIELD BEANS WHOLESALERS

Akila Holdings Inc....................G......609 454-5034
Princeton *(G-8999)*

GRANITE: Crushed & Broken

Stone Industries Inc..................D......973 595-6250
Haledon *(G-4085)*

GRANITE: Cut & Shaped

Bcg Marble Gran Fabricators Co........F......201 343-8487
Hackensack *(G-3879)*

Bedrock Granite Inc..................E......732 741-0010
Shrewsbury *(G-9991)*

Caputo International Inc.............G......732 225-5777
Edison *(G-2479)*

Gran All Mrble Tile Imprts Inc........G......856 354-4747
Cherry Hill *(G-1372)*

Marmo Enterprises Inc ....G....... 732 649-3011
Somerset *(G-10130)*
Stone Systems New Jersey LLC ....F....... 973 778-5525
Fairfield *(G-3313)*
Stone Truss Systems Inc ....E....... 973 882-7377
Fairfield *(G-3314)*
Stoneworld At Redbank Inc ....G....... 732 383-5110
Red Bank *(G-9345)*
Whole Stones LLC ....G....... 856 266-0091
Willingboro *(G-12123)*

GRANITE: Dimension

Fanwood Crushed Stone Company ......D....... 908 322-7840
Watchung *(G-11591)*

GRANITE: Dimension

Eastern Concrete Materials Inc ....G....... 908 537-2135
Glen Gardner *(G-3814)*
Stone Surfaces Inc ....D....... 201 935-8803
East Rutherford *(G-2328)*

GRAPHIC ARTS & RELATED DESIGN SVCS

A M Graphics Inc ....G....... 201 767-5320
Harrington Park *(G-4169)*
Advertisers Service Group Inc ....F....... 201 440-5577
Ridgefield Park *(G-9395)*
Alliance Design Inc ....F....... 973 904-9450
Totowa *(G-10927)*
AlphaGraphics ....F....... 856 761-8000
Cherry Hill *(G-1343)*
Banner Design Inc ....E....... 908 687-5335
Hillside *(G-4395)*
Color Comp Inc ....G....... 856 262-3040
Williamstown *(G-12083)*
Design Factory Nj Inc ....G....... 908 964-8833
Hillside *(G-4404)*
Digital Arts Imaging LLC ....F....... 908 237-4646
Flemington *(G-3435)*
Dm Graphic Center LLC ....F....... 973 882-8990
Fairfield *(G-3178)*
Dynamic Printing & Graphics ....F....... 973 473-7177
Clifton *(G-1608)*
Earth Color New York Inc ....E....... 973 884-1300
Parsippany *(G-7992)*
Encore Enterprises Inc ....G....... 201 489-5044
South Hackensack *(G-10264)*
Envirnmntal Dsign Grphic Entps ....G....... 973 361-1829
Dover *(G-2086)*
Falcon Graphics Inc ....G....... 908 232-1991
Clark *(G-1500)*
Franbeth Inc ....G....... 856 488-1480
Pennsauken *(G-8512)*
Frontend Graphics Inc ....G....... 856 547-1600
Cherry Hill *(G-1367)*
Gangi Graphics Inc ....G....... 732 840-8680
Brick *(G-744)*
Graphic Imagery Inc ....F....... 908 755-2882
New Providence *(G-7038)*
J K Design Inc ....E....... 908 428-4700
Hillsborough *(G-4351)*
James Howard Inc ....F....... 973 928-1560
Clifton *(G-1651)*
Laserwave Graphics Inc ....F....... 732 745-7764
New Brunswick *(G-6977)*
Lexington Graphics Corp ....G....... 973 345-2493
Clifton *(G-1661)*
National Color Graphics ....F....... 856 435-6800
Sicklerville *(G-10021)*
Polaris Communications Inc ....F....... 201 928-0780
Teaneck *(G-10769)*
Ramsey Graphics and Printing ....G....... 201 300-2912
Elmwood Park *(G-2846)*
Sandoval Graphics & Printing ....G....... 856 435-7320
Somerdale *(G-10043)*
Stephen Swinton Studio Inc ....G....... 908 537-9135
Washington *(G-11588)*
Typeline ....F....... 201 251-2201
Wyckoff *(G-12267)*
Zippityprint LLC ....F....... 216 438-0001
Mullica Hill *(G-6894)*

GRAPHITE MINING SVCS

Asbury Carbons Inc ....G....... 908 537-2155
Asbury *(G-66)*

GRASSES: Artificial & Preserved

Synthetic Grass Surfaces Inc ....G....... 973 778-9594
Lodi *(G-5605)*

GRAVE VAULTS, METAL

Marchione Industries Inc ....F....... 718 317-4900
Lyndhurst *(G-5690)*

GRAVEL & PEBBLE MINING

Tuckahoe Sand & Gravel Co Inc ....E...... 609 861-2082
Tuckahoe *(G-11139)*

GRAVEL MINING

Trap Rock Industries Inc ....E...... 609 924-0300
Titusville *(G-10857)*

GREASE TRAPS: Concrete

Trap-Zap Environmental Systems ....E...... 201 251-9970
Wyckoff *(G-12266)*

GREASES: Lubricating

Magnalube Inc ....G...... 718 729-1000
Linden *(G-5405)*

GREENSAND MINING SVCS

Hungerford & Terry Inc ....E...... 856 881-3200
Clayton *(G-1524)*

GREETING CARD SHOPS

Papery of Marlton LLC ....G...... 856 985-1776
Marlton *(G-5993)*

GREETING CARDS WHOLESALERS

Nobleworks Inc ....F...... 201 420-0095
Union City *(G-11261)*

GRINDING SVC: Precision, Commercial Or Indl

M & D Prcsion Cntrless Grnding ....G...... 856 764-1616
Riverside *(G-9501)*
Tri-State Knife Grinding Corp ....E...... 609 890-4989
Robbinsville *(G-9523)*

GRINDING SVCS: Ophthalmic Lens, Exc Prescription

I See Optical Laboratories ....F...... 856 227-9300
Blackwood *(G-481)*
Lab Tech Inc ....G...... 201 767-5613
Northvale *(G-7589)*

GRIT: Steel

Steel Riser Corp ....G...... 732 341-7031
Toms River *(G-10914)*

GRITS: Crushed & Broken

Trap Rock Industries Inc ....E...... 609 924-0300
Titusville *(G-10857)*

GROCERIES WHOLESALERS, NEC

Anthony & Sons Bakery Itln Bky ....D...... 973 625-2323
Denville *(G-2031)*
Bimbo Bakeries USA Inc ....C...... 973 256-8200
Totowa *(G-10936)*
Colonna Brothers Inc ....D...... 800 626-8384
North Bergen *(G-7443)*
Del Buono Bakery Inc ....E...... 856 546-9585
Haddon Heights *(G-4047)*
Diamond Foods USA Inc ....G...... 732 543-2186
North Brunswick *(G-7515)*
Elis Hot Bagels Inc ....E...... 732 566-4523
Matawan *(G-6020)*
Foulkrod Associates ....A...... 856 662-6767
Pennsauken *(G-8511)*
G & Y Specialty Foods LLC ....G...... 956 821-9652
Woodland Park *(G-12220)*
R C Fine Foods Inc ....D...... 908 359-5500
Hillsborough *(G-4366)*
Salad Chef Inc ....F...... 609 641-5455
Pleasantville *(G-8913)*
Wakefern Food Corp ....B...... 908 527-3300
Keasbey *(G-4932)*
Wakefern Food Corp ....B...... 732 819-0140
Edison *(G-2649)*

GROCERIES, GENERAL LINE WHOLESALERS

Arm National Food Inc ....G....... 609 695-4911
Trenton *(G-11020)*
Deep Foods Inc ....C....... 908 810-7500
Union *(G-11171)*
Dove Chocolate Discoveries LLC ....E....... 866 922-3683
Mount Arlington *(G-6753)*
Panos Holding Company ....G....... 201 843-8900
Rochelle Park *(G-9533)*
Wakefern Food Corp ....B....... 908 527-3300
Keasbey *(G-4932)*
Zestos Foods LLC ....G....... 888 407-5852
Teaneck *(G-10779)*

GROUP DAY CARE CENTER

Pillar of Fire ....D....... 732 356-0102
Zarephath *(G-12270)*

GROUTING EQPT: Concrete

Corrview International LLC ....G....... 973 770-0571
Hopatcong *(G-4535)*
Mapei Corporation ....E....... 732 254-4830
Swedesboro *(G-10707)*

GUIDANCE SYSTEMS & EQPT: Space Vehicle

Lockheed Martin Corporation ....B....... 856 787-3104
Mount Laurel *(G-6814)*

GUIDED MISSILES & SPACE VEHICLES

Savit Corporation ....F....... 862 209-4516
Rockaway *(G-9607)*

GUIDED MISSILES & SPACE VEHICLES: Research & Development

Lockheed Martin Corporation ....B....... 856 787-3104
Mount Laurel *(G-6814)*

GUM & WOOD CHEMICALS

Importers Service Corp ....E....... 732 248-1946
Edison *(G-2540)*
Sanit Technologies LLC ....F....... 862 238-7555
Passaic *(G-8180)*

GUTTERS

R & K Industries Inc ....G....... 732 531-1123
Oakhurst *(G-7672)*
Russo Seamless Gutter LLC ....G....... 732 836-0151
Brick *(G-757)*

GUTTERS: Sheet Metal

Englert Inc ....C....... 800 364-5378
Perth Amboy *(G-8612)*
Rays Seamless Rain Gutters ....G....... 856 629-8407
Sicklerville *(G-10024)*
United Gutter Supply Inc ....E....... 201 933-6316
East Rutherford *(G-2335)*

GYPSUM & CALCITE MINING SVCS

Titan America LLC ....G....... 973 690-5896
Newark *(G-7344)*

GYPSUM PRDTS

Art Plaque Creations Inc ....F....... 973 482-2536
Kearny *(G-4862)*
Bestwall LLC ....D....... 856 966-7600
Camden *(G-1044)*
Durabond Division US Gypsum ....F....... 732 636-7900
Port Reading *(G-8987)*
United States Gypsum Company ....D....... 732 636-7900
Port Reading *(G-8991)*

GYROSCOPES

Atlantic Inertial Systems Inc ....B....... 973 237-2713
Totowa *(G-10932)*

HAIR & HAIR BASED PRDTS

Cellunet Manufacturing Compnay ....F....... 609 386-3361
Burlington *(G-961)*
Geisler Ganz Corp ....G....... 201 223-1200
Secaucus *(G-9886)*

Left-Handed Libra LLC ....F..... 973 623-1112
Newark (G-7217)

Minniti J Hair Replacement Inc ....G.... 856 427-9600
Cherry Hill (G-1401)

Newell Brands Inc ....B..... 201 610-6600
Hoboken (G-4486)

Novelty Hair Goods Co ....G.... 856 963-5876
Camden (G-1079)

Teluca Inc ....G.... 973 232-0002
West Orange (G-11906)

HAIR CARE PRDTS

Caboki LLC ....G.... 609 642-2108
Cranbury (G-1819)

Cheveux Cosmetics Corporation ....D.... 732 446-7516
Englishtown (G-2990)

Imperial Drug & Spice Corp ....G.... 201 348-1551
West New York (G-11867)

LOreal Usa Inc ....C.... 732 499-6617
Clark (G-1505)

LOreal Usa Inc ....D.... 212 818-1500
Clark (G-1506)

LOreal Usa Inc ....D.... 732 499-6690
Clark (G-1507)

LOreal Usa Inc ....A.... 609 860-7500
Cranbury (G-1855)

Scories Inc ....F.... 973 923-1372
Newark (G-7304)

HAIR CARE PRDTS: Bleaches

Hair Systems Inc ....D.... 732 446-2202
Englishtown (G-2994)

HAIR CARE PRDTS: Hair Coloring Preparations

Fantasia Industries Corp ....E.... 201 261-7070
Paramus (G-7869)

LOreal USA Products Inc ....G.... 732 873-3520
Jersey City (G-4779)

Maje Systems Inc ....G.... 856 845-5363
Woodbury (G-12164)

Product Club Corp ....F.... 973 664-0565
Rockaway (G-9601)

HAIR DRESSING, FOR THE TRADE

Folica Inc ....E.... 609 860-8430
Dayton (G-1963)

Razac Products Inc ....G.... 973 622-3700
Newark (G-7285)

HAND TOOLS, NEC: Wholesalers

Dreyco Inc ....F.... 201 896-9000
Carlstadt (G-1158)

El Batal Corporation ....F.... 908 964-3427
Union (G-11180)

Jdv Products Inc ....F.... 201 794-6467
Fair Lawn (G-3098)

Ox Group Usa LLC ....F.... 888 850-6710
Cranford (G-1920)

Vozeh Equipment Corp ....E.... 201 337-3729
Franklin Lakes (G-3625)

HANDBAGS

Antique Buying Center ....G.... 201 888-0303
Edgewater (G-2433)

Carol S Miller Corporation ....G.... 201 406-4578
Hillsdale (G-4381)

Ledonne Leather Co Inc ....F.... 201 531-2100
Lyndhurst (G-5686)

M London Inc ....E.... 201 459-6460
Jersey City (G-4780)

Medici International Inc ....G.... 973 684-6084
Paterson (G-8334)

Mitzi Intl Handbag & ACC Ltd ....C.... 973 483-5015
Newark (G-7243)

HANDBAGS: Women's

Annette & Jim Dizenzo Sls LLC ....G.... 973 875-0895
Sussex (G-10666)

Basu Group ....G.... 908 517-9138
North Brunswick (G-7507)

Gio Vali Handbag Corp ....G.... 973 279-3032
Paterson (G-8276)

Tapestry Inc ....F.... 856 488-2220
Cherry Hill (G-1426)

HANDLES: Brush Or Tool, Plastic

Pedibrush LLC ....G.... 856 796-2963
Haddon Heights (G-4049)

HANGERS: Garment, Plastic

B & G Plastics Inc ....E.... 973 824-9220
Union (G-11155)

Mainetti Americas Inc ....G.... 201 215-2900
Secaucus (G-9903)

Mainetti USA Inc ....F.... 201 215-2900
Keasbey (G-4928)

Randy Hangers LLC ....G.... 201 215-2900
Secaucus (G-9916)

Uniplast Industries Inc ....E.... 201 288-4672
Hasbrouck Heights (G-4202)

HANGERS: Garment, Wire

United Wire Hanger Corp ....C.... 201 288-3212
Hasbrouck Heights (G-4203)

HANGERS: Garment, Wire

Ecocom Inc ....G.... 201 393-0786
Montvale (G-6454)

HARD RUBBER PRDTS, NEC

Bumper Specialties Inc ....C.... 856 345-7650
West Deptford (G-11819)

Miroad Rubber USA LLC ....G.... 480 280-2543
Edison (G-2573)

HARDWARE

Andrex Inc ....F.... 908 852-2400
Hackettstown (G-3997)

Art Materials Service Inc ....D.... 732 545-8888
New Brunswick (G-6947)

Ashley Norton Inc ....F.... 973 835-4027
Pompton Plains (G-8954)

Brim Electronics Inc ....F.... 201 796-2886
Lodi (G-5578)

Carpenter & Paterson Inc ....G.... 973 772-1800
Bordentown (G-592)

Charles E Green & Son Inc ....E.... 973 485-3630
Newark (G-7120)

Commeatus LLC ....F.... 847 772-5314
Plainsboro (G-8878)

Component Hardware Group Inc ....D.... 800 526-3694
Lakewood (G-5095)

G & S Precision Prototype ....G.... 732 370-3010
Lakewood (G-5126)

Ho-Ho-Kus Inc ....E.... 973 278-2274
Paterson (G-8290)

J Blanco Associates Inc ....F.... 973 427-0619
Hawthorne (G-4243)

JC Macelroy Co Inc ....D.... 732 572-7100
Piscataway (G-8784)

Ka-Lor Cubicle and Sup Co Inc ....G.... 201 891-8077
Fair Lawn (G-3099)

Owens Fasteners Inc ....G.... 856 768-6580
West Berlin (G-11740)

Pekay Industries Inc ....F.... 732 938-2722
Farmingdale (G-3392)

Penn Elcom Inc ....F.... 973 839-7777
Pompton Plains (G-8964)

Revere Survival Products Inc ....F.... 973 575-8811
West Caldwell (G-11803)

RSI Woodworking Products Co ....E.... 609 645-9777
Egg Harbor Township (G-2695)

Saint-Gobain Prfmce Plas Corp ....D.... 732 652-0910
Somerset (G-10170)

Shade Powers Co Inc ....F.... 201 767-3727
Northvale (G-7607)

Steelstran Industries Inc ....G.... 732 566-5040
Matawan (G-6033)

Truckform Inc ....F.... 908 526-5443
Somerville (G-10231)

Unicorp ....C.... 973 674-1700
Orange (G-7832)

Versabar Corporation ....F.... 973 279-8400
Totowa (G-10979)

HARDWARE & BUILDING PRDTS: Plastic

Artus Corp ....E.... 201 568-1000
Englewood (G-2873)

Camtec Industries Inc ....F.... 732 332-9800
Colts Neck (G-1780)

Hayward Industrial Products ....C.... 908 351-5400
Elizabeth (G-2741)

Hayward Industries Inc ....B.... 908 351-5400
Elizabeth (G-2742)

LL Building Products Inc ....F.... 973 628-3000
Parsippany (G-8039)

Lumber Super Mart ....G.... 732 739-1428
Hazlet (G-4278)

Plastpro 2000 Inc ....G.... 973 992-2090
Livingston (G-5556)

Premiere Raceway Sys LLC ....G.... 732 629-7715
Piscataway (G-8802)

HARDWARE STORES

Component Hardware Group Inc ....D.... 800 526-3694
Lakewood (G-5095)

Woodhaven Lumber & Millwork ....E.... 732 295-8800
Point Pleasant Beach (G-8928)

HARDWARE STORES: Builders'

Artistic Hardware ....G.... 609 383-1909
Northfield (G-7563)

HARDWARE STORES: Door Locks & Lock Sets

Door Center Enterprises Inc ....G.... 609 333-1233
Hopewell (G-4541)

HARDWARE STORES: Tools

Molnar Tools Inc ....F.... 908 580-0671
Warren (G-11560)

Precision Saw & Tool Corp ....F.... 973 773-7302
Clifton (G-1703)

Sandvik Inc ....C.... 281 275-4800
Fair Lawn (G-3113)

Shor International ....F.... 973 520-8777
Madison (G-5735)

HARDWARE STORES: Tools, Power

Jarvis Electric Motors Inc ....G.... 856 662-7710
Pennsauken (G-8535)

Rennsteig Tools Inc ....G.... 330 315-3044
Hackensack (G-3966)

HARDWARE WHOLESALERS

Brusso Hardware LLC ....F.... 212 337-8510
Belleville (G-297)

Electro Parts Inc ....G.... 856 767-5923
West Berlin (G-11719)

Industrial Stl & Fastener Corp ....G.... 610 667-2220
Cherry Hill (G-1380)

Ingersoll-Rand Company ....C.... 908 238-7000
Annandale (G-58)

Outwater Plstcs/Industries Inc ....D.... 201 498-8750
Bogota (G-550)

Penn Elcom Inc ....F.... 973 839-7777
Pompton Plains (G-8964)

Permadur Industries Inc ....D.... 908 359-9767
Hillsborough (G-4362)

S H P C Inc ....E.... 973 589-5242
Newark (G-7298)

Shallcross Bolt & Specialties ....E.... 908 925-4700
Linden (G-5441)

HARDWARE, WHOLESALE: Bolts

Stud Welding Co The Inc ....G.... 856 866-9300
Moorestown (G-6624)

HARDWARE, WHOLESALE: Builders', NEC

EP Henry Corporation ....D.... 856 845-6200
Woodbury (G-12160)

HARDWARE, WHOLESALE: Power Tools & Access

E P Heller Company ....E.... 973 377-2878
Madison (G-5721)

HARDWARE, WHOLESALE: Screws

Ford Fasteners Inc ....G.... 201 487-3151
Hackensack (G-3915)

Employee Codes: A=Over 500 employees, B=251-500
C=101-250, D=51-100, E=20-50, F=10-19, G=4-9

2018 Harris New Jersey
Manufacturers Directory

PRODUCT

877

HARDWARE, WHOLESALE: Security Devices, Locks

Mul-T-Lock Usa Inc ....E...... 973 778-3320
Hackensack (G-3948)

HARDWARE, WHOLESALE: Washers

Randall Manufacturing Co Inc ....E... 973 746-2111
Hillside (G-4437)

HARDWARE: Aircraft

Jet Test Global LLC ....G...... 702 785-0011
Cherry Hill (G-1384)

HARDWARE: Aircraft & Marine, Incl Pulleys & Similar Items

Modern Sportswear Corporation ......F... 201 804-2700
Moonachie (G-6533)

HARDWARE: Builders'

Allfasteners Usa LLC ....E...... 201 783-8836
Carlstadt (G-1123)
World and Main LLC ....C...... 609 860-9990
Cranbury (G-1892)

HARDWARE: Cabinet

Artistic Hardware ....G...... 609 383-1909
Northfield (G-7563)

HARDWARE: Furniture, Builders' & Other Household

Ingersoll-Rand Company ....E... 856 793-7000
Mount Laurel (G-6803)
Ramsay David Cabinetmakers..............F... 856 234-7776
Moorestown (G-6618)

HARDWARE: Luggage

Atco Products Inc ....E...... 973 379-3171
Springfield (G-10538)

HARDWARE: Parachute

Airborne Systems N Amer Inc ....G.... 856 663-1275
Pennsauken (G-8473)

HARNESS ASSEMBLIES: Cable & Wire

Ameral International Inc.................F... 856 456-9000
Brooklawn (G-919)
Andrex Inc ....F... 908 852-2400
Hackettstown (G-3997)
Andrex Systems Inc.........................G... 908 835-1720
Port Murray (G-8975)
Computer Crafts Inc ....C... 973 423-3500
Hawthorne (G-4228)
Da-Green Electronics Ltd ....E... 732 254-2735
South River (G-10460)
Electronic Connections Inc.................F... 732 367-5588
Lakewood (G-5114)
Empire Electronics Inc ....F... 973 278-8282
Paterson (G-8262)
Esi ....E... 856 629-2492
Sicklerville (G-10018)
General Reliance Corporation ....E... 973 361-1400
Denville (G-2040)
Melstrom Manufacturing Corp.............D... 732 938-7400
Wall Township (G-11497)
Quadrangle Products Inc ....F... 732 792-1234
Englishtown (G-2997)
Spem Corporation ....E... 732 356-3366
Piscataway (G-8816)
Technical Aids To Independence..........F... 973 674-1082
East Orange (G-2271)
Trek Connect Inc ....E... 856 608-0901
Lumberton (G-5664)
Valconn Electronics Inc...................E... 908 687-1600
Union (G-11232)
VIP Industries Inc ....E... 973 472-7500
Clifton (G-1739)
Wire-Pro Inc ....C... 856 935-7560
Salem (G-9810)
YC Cable (east) Inc ....E... 732 868-0800
Piscataway (G-8837)

HARNESS WIRING SETS: Internal Combustion Engines

Incom (america) Inc ....G...... 908 464-3366
Berkeley Heights (G-412)

HARNESSES, HALTERS, SADDLERY & STRAPS

Brook Saddle Ridge Equest................F... 609 953-1600
Shamong (G-9968)
Emporium Leather Company Inc..........E... 201 330-7720
Secaucus (G-9878)
Jaclyn Holdings Parent LLC ....E... 201 909-6000
Maywood (G-6053)
Jaclyn LLC.................................D... 201 909-6000
Maywood (G-6054)

HEADPHONES: Radio

Maxell Corporation of America.............E... 973 653-2400
Woodland Park (G-12224)

HEALTH AIDS: Exercise Eqpt

Ingui Design LLC ....G... 201 264-9126
Ramsey (G-9243)
Slendertone Distribution Inc...............G... 732 660-1177
Hoboken (G-4497)
Technogym USA Corp ....F... 800 804-0952
Fairfield (G-3322)

HEALTH FOOD & SUPPLEMENT STORES

Applied Nutrition Corp ....E... 973 734-0023
Cedar Knolls (G-1307)

HEALTH SCREENING SVCS

Vesag Health Inc ....F... 732 333-1876
North Brunswick (G-7545)

HEARING AIDS

Kingwood Industrial Pdts Inc ....G... 908 852-8655
Hackettstown (G-4015)
Oticon Inc ....C... 732 560-1220
Somerset (G-10148)
Songbird Hearing Inc.......................E... 732 422-7203
North Brunswick (G-7539)
Sonic Innovations Inc ....G... 888 423-7834
Somerset (G-10173)

HEAT EXCHANGERS

Atlas Industrial Mfg Co ....E... 973 779-3970
Clifton (G-1568)
Joseph Oat Holdings Inc....................D... 856 541-2900
Camden (G-1072)

HEAT EXCHANGERS: After Or Inter Coolers Or Condensers, Etc

Asa Hydraulik of America Inc ....G... 908 541-1500
Branchburg (G-640)
Kooltronic Inc.............................C... 609 466-3400
Pennington (G-8455)
Manning & Lewis Engrg Co Inc ....D... 908 687-2400
Union (G-11205)
Perry Products Corporation ....E... 609 267-1600
Hainesport (G-4076)

HEAT TREATING: Metal

Analytic Stress Relieving Inc...............D... 732 629-7232
Middlesex (G-6146)
Blue Blade Corp ....G... 908 272-2620
Kenilworth (G-4945)
Bodycote Thermal Proc Inc ....E... 908 245-0717
Roselle (G-9663)
Bodycote Thermal Processing ....E... 908 245-0717
Roselle (G-9664)
Braddock Heat Treating Company ....F... 732 356-2906
Bridgewater (G-823)
Curtiss-Wright Surfc Tech LLC ....F... 201 843-7800
Paramus (G-7865)
Energy Beams Inc ....F... 973 291-6555
Bloomingdale (G-543)
Heinzelman Heat Treating LLC ....E... 201 933-4800
Carlstadt (G-1169)
Kenney Steel Treating Corp ....E... 201 998-4420
Kearny (G-4892)

Metal Improvement Co Inc ....G...... 253 677-8604
Paramus (G-7887)
Metal Improvement Company LLC....E....... 201 843-7800
Paramus (G-7888)

HEATERS: Swimming Pool, Electric

Hayward Pool Products Inc ....A... 908 351-5400
Elizabeth (G-2744)
Smartpool LLC ....E... 732 730-9880
Lakewood (G-5189)

HEATING & AIR CONDITIONING UNITS, COMBINATION

Ade Inc ....F... 609 693-6050
Forked River (G-3533)
Dolan Assoc Inc ....G... 973 875-6408
Sussex (G-10669)
Duct Mate Inc..............................G... 201 488-8002
Hackensack (G-3907)
Ener-G Rudox Inc ....E... 201 438-0111
East Rutherford (G-2294)
Fujitsu General America Inc ....D... 973 575-0380
Fairfield (G-3203)
Maco Appliance Parts & Sup Co ....G... 609 272-8222
Absecon (G-3)
Sander Mechanical Service Inc ....E... 732 560-0600
Branchburg (G-701)

HEATING APPARATUS: Steam

Amec Fster Wheeler N Amer Corp ....D... 936 448-6323
Hampton (G-4153)

HEATING EQPT & SPLYS

Ampericon Inc ....F... 609 945-2591
Monmouth Junction (G-6331)
Applied Thermal Solutions Inc ....G... 856 818-8194
Williamstown (G-12079)
C & F Burner Co ....E... 201 998-8080
North Arlington (G-7417)
Ewc Controls Inc...........................E... 732 446-3110
Manalapan (G-5846)
Heat-Timer Corporation....................E... 973 575-4004
Fairfield (G-3218)
NM Knight Co Inc ....E... 856 327-4855
Millville (G-6316)
Stafford Park Solar 1 LLC ....G... 609 607-9500
Barnegat (G-166)
Stamm International Corp ....G... 201 947-1700
Fort Lee (G-3583)
Thermal Transfer Corp ....G... 412 460-4004
Somerville (G-10228)
Triangle Tube/Phase III Co Inc ....D... 856 228-9940
Paulsboro (G-8427)
Waage Electric Inc ....G... 908 245-9363
Kenilworth (G-5004)

HEATING EQPT: Complete

Bolttech Mannings Inc......................D... 973 537-1576
Wharton (G-11981)
Chiller Solutions LLC ....E... 973 835-2800
Pompton Plains (G-8956)

HEATING EQPT: Induction

Inductotherm Corporation ....C... 609 267-9000
Rancocas (G-9258)
Pennington Furnace Supply Inc ....G... 609 737-2500
Pennington (G-8457)
Thermal Conduction Engineering ....G... 201 865-1084
Secaucus (G-9934)

HEATING PADS: Nonelectric

Artline Heat Transfer Inc ....F... 973 599-0104
Parsippany (G-7950)
Rdo Induction Ltd Liability Co..............G... 908 835-7222
Washington (G-11586)

HEATING UNITS & DEVICES: Indl, Electric

Argus International Inc ....E... 609 466-1677
Ringoes (G-9435)
C M Furnaces Inc ....E... 973 338-6500
Bloomfield (G-504)
Corbett Industries Inc.....................F... 201 445-6311
Waldwick (G-11443)
Gia-Tek LLC................................G... 973 228-0875
West Caldwell (G-11777)

Glenro Inc ....F 973 279-5900
  Paterson (G-8277)
Hed International Inc ....F 609 466-1900
  Ringoes (G-9437)
Pv/T Inc ....G 609 267-3933
  Rancocas (G-9261)
Solar Products Inc ....E 973 248-9370
  Pompton Lakes (G-8948)
Waage Electric Inc ....G 908 245-9363
  Kenilworth (G-5004)

HEAVY DISTILLATES

Ashland LLC ....G 908 243-3500
  Bridgewater (G-815)
Ashland LLC ....D 732 353-7718
  Parlin (G-7928)

HELMETS: Athletic

Interntonal Riding Helmets Inc ....E 732 772-0165
  Marlboro (G-5945)

HELP SUPPLY SERVICES

Dxl Enterprises Inc ....F 201 891-8718
  Mahwah (G-5768)

HOBBY GOODS, WHOLESALE

Model Rectifier Corporation ....E 732 225-2100
  Edison (G-2575)
Tri-Chem Inc ....F 973 751-9200
  Belleville (G-320)

HOBBY SUPPLIES, WHOLESALE

Scientific Models Inc ....E 908 464-7070
  Berkeley Heights (G-421)

HOBBY, TOY & GAME STORES: Arts & Crafts & Splys

A Cheerful Giver Inc ....F 856 358-4438
  Elmer (G-2787)

HOISTS

Electro Lift Inc ....E 973 471-0204
  Clifton (G-1612)
Rudco Products Inc ....D 856 691-0800
  Vineland (G-11400)
Saturn Overhead Equipment LLC ....F 732 560-7210
  Somerset (G-10171)

HOLDERS, PAPER TOWEL, GROCERY BAG, ETC: Plastic

A-One Merchandising Corp ....F 718 773-7500
  North Arlington (G-7413)

HOLDING COMPANIES: Banks

Merck Holdings LLC ....F 908 423-1000
  Whitehouse Station (G-12054)

HOLDING COMPANIES: Investment, Exc Banks

Allergan Holdco Us Inc ....G 862 261-7000
  Parsippany (G-7943)
Chemtrade Gcc Holding Company ....G 973 515-0900
  Parsippany (G-7969)
Chemtrade Water Chemical Inc ....G 973 515-0900
  Parsippany (G-7971)
Jaclyn Holdings Parent LLC ....G 201 909-6000
  Maywood (G-6053)
Naturex Holdings Inc ....G 201 440-5000
  South Hackensack (G-10280)
Pappas Lassonde Holdings Inc ....G 856 455-1000
  Carneys Point (G-1246)
Stamm International Corp ....G 201 947-1700
  Fort Lee (G-3583)

HOLDING COMPANIES: Personal, Exc Banks

Healthstar Communications Inc ....A 201 560-5370
  Mahwah (G-5780)
Warner Chilcott Corporation ....E 862 261-7000
  Rockaway (G-9623)

HOLLOWARE, SILVER

Hickok Matthews Co Inc ....G 973 335-3400
  Montville (G-6489)

HOME ENTERTAINMENT EQPT: Electronic, NEC

Excite View LLC ....E 201 227-7075
  Tenafly (G-10784)
Gzgn Inc ....F 201 842-7622
  Rutherford (G-9733)
Jvckenwood USA Corporation ....E 973 317-5000
  Wayne (G-11658)
Rock Dreams Electronics LLC ....G 609 890-0808
  Trenton (G-11113)
Tusa Products Inc ....G 609 448-8333
  Ewing (G-3063)

HOME ENTERTAINMENT REPAIR SVCS

Homan Communications Inc ....G 609 654-9594
  Medford (G-6070)

HOME FURNISHINGS WHOLESALERS

Aladdin Manufacturing Corp ....B 973 616-4600
  Pompton Plains (G-8951)
Floral Glass Industries Inc ....E 201 939-4600
  East Rutherford (G-2297)
House of Prill Inc ....E 732 442-2400
  Lincroft (G-5337)
Q10 Products LLC ....F 201 567-9299
  Clifton (G-1707)
R L Plastics Inc ....G 732 340-1100
  Avenel (G-149)
St Thomas Creations ....G 800 536-2284
  Monroe Township (G-6394)
Wanasavealotcom LLC ....F 732 286-6956
  Toms River (G-10920)

HOME HEALTH CARE SVCS

Aarisse Health Care Products ....G 973 686-1811
  Wayne (G-11600)
Fluent Diagnostics ....G 201 414-4516
  Pequannock (G-8599)

HOME IMPROVEMENT & RENOVATION CONTRACTOR AGENCY

AK Contracting LLC ....G 908 220-8527
  Winfield Park (G-12131)
R & K Industries Inc ....G 732 531-1123
  Oakhurst (G-7672)

HOMEFURNISHING STORE: Bedding, Sheet, Blanket,Spread/Pillow

Homespun Global LLC ....G 917 674-9684
  Sayreville (G-9823)
Nassaus Window Fashions Inc ....E 201 689-6030
  Paramus (G-7893)
Storis Inc ....D 888 478-6747
  Mount Arlington (G-6760)

HOMEFURNISHING STORES: Beddings & Linens

JFK Supplies Inc ....F 732 985-7800
  Edison (G-2545)
Professional Laundry Solutions ....G 973 392-0837
  Newark (G-7278)

HOMEFURNISHING STORES: Closet organizers & shelving units

Interior Specialties LLC ....F 856 663-1700
  Pennsauken (G-8529)

HOMEFURNISHING STORES: Fireplaces & Wood Burning Stoves

Mdb Construction ....G 908 628-8010
  Lebanon (G-5296)

HOMEFURNISHING STORES: Lighting Fixtures

City Theatrical Inc ....E 201 549-1160
  Carlstadt (G-1145)

Efficient Lighting Inc ....F 973 846-8568
  Parsippany (G-7999)
Genie House Corp ....E 609 859-0600
  Southampton (G-10473)
Robert Wallace ....G 609 649-0596
  Stockton (G-10612)
Sun Pacific Power Corp ....F 888 845-0242
  Manalapan (G-5864)

HOMEFURNISHING STORES: Metalware

Abba Metal Works Inc ....G 973 684-0808
  Paterson (G-8195)

HOMEFURNISHING STORES: Mirrors

Just Glass & Mirror Inc ....F 856 728-8383
  Williamstown (G-12091)

HOMEFURNISHING STORES: Towels

Sensible Collection Inc ....G 201 831-1063
  Hackensack (G-3972)

HOMEFURNISHING STORES: Venetian Blinds

A Plus Installs LLC ....G 201 255-4412
  Bloomfield (G-499)

HOMEFURNISHING STORES: Vertical Blinds

Arts Windows Inc ....G 732 905-9595
  Toms River (G-10864)

HOMEFURNISHING STORES: Window Furnishings

Proclean Services Inc ....F 973 857-5408
  Verona (G-11309)
Shade Powers Co Inc ....F 201 767-3727
  Northvale (G-7607)

HOMEFURNISHING STORES: Window Shades, NEC

Griffith Shade Company Inc ....G 973 667-1474
  Nutley (G-7647)
Hudson & Bergen Company ....G 201 991-4900
  Kearny (G-4881)

HOMEFURNISHINGS & SPLYS, WHOLESALE: Decorative

Glocal Expertise Llc ....G 718 928-3839
  Jersey City (G-4761)
House of Kalon New York ....F 786 259-0786
  Secaucus (G-9895)
Marketing Administration Assoc ....G 732 840-3021
  Brick (G-752)
Shopindia Inc ....G 732 409-0656
  Marlboro (G-5958)
Trim and Tassels LLC ....G 973 808-1566
  Fairfield (G-3331)

HOMEFURNISHINGS, WHOLESALE: Blankets

Weatherbeeta USA Inc ....E 732 287-1182
  Edison (G-2650)

HOMEFURNISHINGS, WHOLESALE: Blinds, Vertical

Arts Windows Inc ....G 732 905-9595
  Toms River (G-10864)

HOMEFURNISHINGS, WHOLESALE: Carpets

Kync Design LLC ....G 201 293-4677
  Secaucus (G-9900)

HOMEFURNISHINGS, WHOLESALE: Curtains

D Kwitman & Son Inc ....F 201 798-5511
  Hoboken (G-4467)
Kushner Draperies Mfg LLC ....E 856 317-9696
  Pennsauken (G-8541)

PRODUCT

HOMEFURNISHINGS, WHOLESALE: Draperies

Custom Decorators Service ....G...... 973 625-0516
  Denville (G-2034)
Lawrence Custom Drapery Shop ....F...... 609 882-4007
  Ewing (G-3034)

HOMEFURNISHINGS, WHOLESALE: Fireplace Eqpt & Access

Associate Fireplace Builders ....G...... 908 273-5900
  Summit (G-10636)

HOMEFURNISHINGS, WHOLESALE: Kitchenware

Primetime Trading Corp ....E...... 646 580-8223
  Bayonne (G-241)

HOMEFURNISHINGS, WHOLESALE: Linens, Table

Central Shippee Inc ....E...... 973 838-1100
  Bloomingdale (G-541)
Circle Visual Inc ....E...... 212 719-5153
  Carlstadt (G-1141)
Happy Chef Inc ....E...... 973 492-2525
  Butler (G-1006)

HOMEFURNISHINGS, WHOLESALE: Rugs

Samad Brothers Inc ....F...... 201 372-0909
  East Rutherford (G-2325)
Seldom Seen Designs LLC ....G...... 973 535-8805
  Livingston (G-5559)
SNS Oriental Rugs LLC ....G...... 201 355-8786
  Carlstadt (G-1220)

HOMEFURNISHINGS, WHOLESALE: Sheets, Textile

Homespun Global LLC ....G...... 917 674-9684
  Sayreville (G-9823)
Triangle Home Fashions LLC ....G...... 732 355-9800
  Dayton (G-1993)

HOMEFURNISHINGS, WHOLESALE: Towels

Franco Manufacturing Co Inc ....C...... 732 494-0500
  Metuchen (G-6104)
Jay Franco & Sons Inc ....D...... 732 721-0022
  Sayreville (G-9825)
Sensible Collection Inc.........................G...... 201 831-1063
  Hackensack (G-3972)

HOMEFURNISHINGS, WHOLESALE: Wood Flooring

Worldwide Whl Flr Cvg Inc ....D...... 732 906-1400
  Edison (G-2651)

HOODS: Range, Sheet Metal

Rangecraft Manufacturing Inc ....F...... 201 791-0440
  Fair Lawn (G-3108)

HOPPERS: Metal Plate

Acrison Inc ....C...... 201 440-8300
  Moonachie (G-6499)

HORNS: Marine, Compressed Air Or Steam

Pipe Dreams Marine LLC......................G...... 609 628-9353
  Tuckahoe (G-11137)

HORSE & PET ACCESSORIES: Textile

Tri G Manufacturing LLC ....F...... 732 460-1881
  Colts Neck (G-1793)
Tuff Mutters LLC ....G...... 973 291-6679
  Kinnelon (G-5041)
Union Hill Corp ....G...... 732 786-9422
  Englishtown (G-2999)
Weatherbeeta USA Inc ....E...... 732 287-1182
  Edison (G-2650)

HORSE ACCESS: Harnesses & Riding Crops, Etc, Exc Leather

Horsetracs ....G...... 732 228-7646
  West Creek (G-11811)

HORSESHOES

Razer Scandinavia Inc ....G...... 732 441-1250
  Matawan (G-6030)

HOSE: Air Line Or Air Brake, Rubber Or Rubberized Fabric

Lewis-Goetz and Company Inc ....F...... 856 579-1421
  Swedesboro (G-10706)

HOSE: Fire, Rubber

Firefighter One Ltd Lblty Co ....G...... 973 940-3061
  Sparta (G-10499)

HOSE: Flexible Metal

Andrex Inc ....F...... 908 852-2400
  Hackettstown (G-3997)
Metal Hose Fabricators Inc ....G...... 908 925-7345
  Linden (G-5407)

HOSE: Garden, Plastic

Plastic Specialties & Tech Inc...............C...... 201 941-2900
  Ridgefield (G-9380)
Pure Tech International Inc ....G...... 908 722-4968
  Branchburg (G-695)
Pure Tech International Inc ....G...... 908 722-4800
  Branchburg (G-696)
US Wire & Cable Corporation ....B...... 973 824-5530
  Newark (G-7355)

HOSE: Plastic

Couse & Bolten Co ....G...... 973 344-6330
  Newark (G-7129)
Harrison Hose and Tubing Inc ....E...... 609 631-8804
  Robbinsville (G-9517)
Hosepharm Ltd Liability Co ....G...... 732 376-0044
  Perth Amboy (G-8617)

HOSE: Pneumatic, Rubber Or Rubberized Fabric, NEC

Ptc Electronics Inc ....G...... 201 847-0500
  Mahwah (G-5804)

HOSE: Rubber

Rubber Fab & Molding Inc ....G...... 908 852-7725
  Johnsonburg (G-4855)

HOSES & BELTING: Rubber & Plastic

Atlantic Rubber Enterprises ....G...... 973 697-5900
  Newfoundland (G-7373)
Colorite Polymers ....F...... 800 631-1577
  Ridgefield (G-9356)
Daniel C Herring Co Inc ....F...... 732 530-6557
  Eatontown (G-2389)
Forbo Siegling LLC..............................F...... 201 567-6100
  Englewood (G-2897)
Megadyne America LLC ....E...... 973 227-4904
  Fairfield (G-3257)
Minor Rubber Co Inc ....E...... 973 338-6800
  Bloomfield (G-522)
Novaflex Industries Inc.........................F...... 856 768-2275
  West Berlin (G-11739)
Stiles Enterprises Inc ....G...... 973 625-9660
  Rockaway (G-9610)
Targa Industries Inc ....F...... 973 584-3733
  Flanders (G-3418)
Thirty-Three Queen Realty Inc...............F...... 973 824-5527
  Newark (G-7341)

HOSPITAL BEDS WHOLESALERS

Garden State Medical Sup LLC..............G...... 732 348-0312
  Lakewood (G-5127)

HOSPITAL EQPT REPAIR SVCS

Compco Analytical Inc ....G...... 201 641-3936
  Little Ferry (G-5499)

HOSPITALS: Medical & Surgical

Ahs Hospital Corp................................E...... 908 522-2000
  Summit (G-10633)
Newton Memorial Hospital Inc...............G...... 973 726-0904
  Sparta (G-10514)

HOTELS & MOTELS

Sysco Guest Supply LLC ....C...... 732 537-2297
  Somerset (G-10177)

HOUSEHOLD APPLIANCE REPAIR SVCS

Organize It All Inc ....E...... 201 488-0808
  Bogota (G-549)

HOUSEHOLD APPLIANCE STORES

Arctic Foods Inc ....E...... 908 689-0590
  Washington (G-11574)
JFK Supplies Inc ....F...... 732 985-7800
  Edison (G-2545)
Oberg & Lindquist Corp ....E...... 201 664-1300
  Westwood (G-11963)

HOUSEHOLD ARTICLES: Metal

Advanced Precision Systems LLC.........G...... 908 730-8892
  High Bridge (G-4293)
Faps Inc ....C...... 973 589-5656
  Newark (G-7160)
Gbw Manufacturing Inc ....E...... 973 279-0077
  Totowa (G-10947)
Kraftware Corporation ....E...... 732 345-7091
  Roselle (G-9674)

HOUSEHOLD FURNISHINGS, NEC

Better Sleep Inc ....F...... 908 464-2200
  Branchburg (G-643)
Carlyle Custom Convertibles ....D...... 973 546-4502
  Moonachie (G-6511)
Fine Linen Inc ....F...... 908 469-3634
  Elizabeth (G-2733)
Howard Lippincott ....F...... 856 764-8282
  Riverside (G-9499)
Interior Art & Design Inc ....E...... 201 488-8855
  Hackensack (G-3930)
Leggett & Platt Incorporated ....D...... 904 786-0750
  Brick (G-750)
Sheex Inc ....E...... 856 334-3021
  Marlton (G-5999)
Tex Spar Co Inc ....C...... 732 367-9439
  Lakewood (G-5194)

HOUSEHOLD SEWING MACHINES WHOLESALERS: Electric

Brother International Corp ....B...... 908 704-1700
  Bridgewater (G-825)

HOUSEWARE STORES

Maverick Industries Inc ....F...... 732 417-9666
  Edison (G-2565)

HOUSEWARES, ELECTRIC, EXC COOKING APPLIANCES & UTENSILS

Brabantia USA Inc ....F...... 201 933-3192
  East Rutherford (G-2288)
Expert Appliance Center LLC ....G...... 732 946-0999
  Marlboro (G-5939)
Homeco LLC ....E...... 732 802-7733
  Piscataway (G-8774)

HOUSEWARES, ELECTRIC: Cooking Appliances

Emerald Electronics Usa Inc.................G...... 718 872-5544
  Passaic (G-8137)
Maverick Industries Inc ....F...... 732 417-9666
  Edison (G-2565)
Rj Brands LLC ....C...... 888 315-8407
  Mahwah (G-5809)
Wanasavealotcom LLC ....F...... 732 286-6956
  Toms River (G-10920)

HOUSEWARES, ELECTRIC: Dryers, Hand & Face

Conair Corporation ....C 609 426-1300
East Windsor **(G-2354)**

HOUSEWARES, ELECTRIC: Heaters, Sauna

Aftek Inc ....G 609 588-0900
Hamilton **(G-4102)**

HOUSEWARES, ELECTRIC: Heating, Bsbrd/Wall, Radiant Heat

Haydon Corporation ....D 973 904-0800
Wayne **(G-11646)**

HOUSEWARES, ELECTRIC: Ice Crushers

Rjticeco LLC ....G 973 697-0156
Stockholm **(G-10610)**
Technology General Corporation ....F 973 827-8209
Franklin **(G-3605)**

HOUSEWARES, ELECTRIC: Lighters, Cigar

Vapor Lounge LLC ....G 973 627-1277
Rockaway **(G-9621)**

HOUSEWARES: Dishes, China

Nikko Ceramics Inc ....F 201 840-5200
Fairview **(G-3366)**

HOUSEWARES: Dishes, Earthenware

Art Plaque Creations Inc ....F 973 482-2536
Kearny **(G-4862)**

HOUSEWARES: Dishes, Plastic

Asi Plastic Inc ....G 973 332-4720
Paterson **(G-8216)**
Buckets Plus Inc ....G 732 545-0420
New Brunswick **(G-6949)**
Mighty Mug Incorporated ....G 732 382-3911
Rahway **(G-9215)**
Newell Brands Inc ....B 201 610-6600
Hoboken **(G-4486)**
R Squared Sls & Logistics LLC ....G 201 329-9745
Moonachie **(G-6537)**

HUMIDIFIERS & DEHUMIDIFIERS

Csonka Worldwide ....E 609 514-2766
Plainsboro **(G-8879)**

HYDRAULIC EQPT REPAIR SVC

American Hose Hydraulic Co Inc ....E 973 684-3225
Paterson **(G-8208)**
Micheller & Son Hydraulics Inc ....F 908 687-1545
Roselle **(G-9677)**
MTS Systems Corporation ....A 856 875-4478
Williamstown **(G-12093)**
Van Hydraulics Inc ....E 732 442-5500
South Plainfield **(G-10448)**

HYDRAULIC FLUIDS: Synthetic Based

Firefreeze Worldwide Inc ....E 973 627-0722
Rockaway **(G-9568)**
Lanxess Solutions US Inc ....C 973 887-7411
East Hanover **(G-2227)**

Hard Rubber & Molded Rubber Prdts

Dso Fluid Handling Co Inc ....E 732 225-9100
Edison **(G-2505)**
Kinnarney Rubber Co Inc ....F 856 468-1320
Mantua **(G-5892)**
Ness Plastics Inc ....F 201 854-4072
West New York **(G-11875)**
Norco Manufacturing Inc ....F 201 854-3461
North Bergen **(G-7471)**
Schon J Tool & Machine Co ....G 732 928-6665
Jackson **(G-4677)**
Vibration Muntings Contrls Inc ....D 800 569-8423
Bloomingdale **(G-545)**

ICE

Arctic Glacier USA Inc ....F 973 771-3391
Montclair **(G-6407)**

Cold Spring Ice Inc ....G 609 884-3405
Cape May **(G-1096)**
Sea Isle Ice Co Inc ....E 609 263-8748
Sea Isle City **(G-9864)**

ICE CREAM & ICES WHOLESALERS

Magliones Italian Ices LLC ....F 732 283-0705
Iselin **(G-4631)**
South Jersey Pretzel Inc ....F 856 435-5055
Stratford **(G-10617)**

IGNEOUS ROCK: Crushed & Broken

A E Stone Inc ....E 609 641-2781
Egg Harbor Township **(G-2675)**
R B Badat Landscaping Inc ....E 609 877-7138
Mount Holly **(G-6776)**
Riverdale Quarry LLC ....E 973 835-0028
Riverdale **(G-9485)**
Trap Rock Industries Inc ....E 609 924-0300
Pennington **(G-8461)**

IGNITION SYSTEMS: Internal Combustion Engine

Knite Inc ....G 609 258-9550
Ewing **(G-3031)**

INCINERATORS

Cire Technologies Inc ....G 973 402-8301
Mountain Lakes **(G-6855)**
Hankin Acquisitions Inc ....F 908 722-9595
Hillsborough **(G-4338)**
Hankin Envmtl Systems Inc ....F 908 722-9595
Hillsborough **(G-4339)**

INDL & PERSONAL SVC PAPER WHOLESALERS

A-One Merchandising Corp ....F 718 773-7500
North Arlington **(G-7413)**
American Business Paper Inc ....F 732 363-5788
Lakewood **(G-5069)**
Asbury Syrup Company Inc ....F 732 774-5746
Ocean **(G-7716)**
Borak Group Inc ....D 718 665-8500
Jersey City **(G-4720)**
Granite Packaging Supply Co ....D 856 727-1010
Moorestown **(G-6579)**
Great Eastern Color Lith ....G 201 843-5656
Paramus **(G-7874)**
Mamrout Paper Group Corp ....G 718 510-5484
Edison **(G-2564)**
North Jersey Paper Products ....F 973 372-4646
Union City **(G-11262)**
Schurman Fine Papers ....E 856 985-1776
Marlton **(G-5998)**
Steiner Paper Corp ....G 732 651-6009
Manalapan **(G-5863)**
United States Box Corp ....E 973 481-2000
Fairfield **(G-3335)**

INDL & PERSONAL SVC PAPER, WHOL: Bags, Paper/Disp Plastic

ANS Plastics Corporation ....F 732 247-2776
New Brunswick **(G-6944)**
Broadway Kleer-Guard Corp ....E 609 662-3970
Monroe Township **(G-6380)**
Central Poly-Bag Corp ....F 908 862-7570
Linden **(G-5358)**
Potti-Bags Inc ....G 201 796-5555
Elmwood Park **(G-2845)**

INDL & PERSONAL SVC PAPER, WHOL: Boxes, Corrugtd/Solid Fiber

Ace Box Landau Co Inc ....G 201 871-4776
Englewood Cliffs **(G-2946)**
Alliance Corrugated Box Inc ....E 877 525-5269
Saddle River **(G-9802)**
E C D Ventures Inc ....G 856 875-1100
Blackwood **(G-477)**
Weber Packaging Inc ....G 201 262-6022
Oradell **(G-7815)**

INDL & PERSONAL SVC PAPER, WHOL: Boxes, Setup Paperboard

Capitol Box Corp ....E 201 867-6018
North Bergen **(G-7438)**

INDL & PERSONAL SVC PAPER, WHOL: Closures, Paper/Disp Plastc

Andon Brush Co Inc ....E 973 256-6611
Little Falls **(G-5469)**

INDL & PERSONAL SVC PAPER, WHOL: Cups, Disp, Plastic/Paper

Continntal Concession Sups Inc ....E 516 629-4906
Union **(G-11166)**

INDL & PERSONAL SVC PAPER, WHOL: Paper, Wrap/Coarse/Prdts

Matthias Paper Corporation ....E 856 467-6970
Swedesboro **(G-10709)**
Orora Packaging Solutions ....E 609 249-5200
Cranbury **(G-1865)**

INDL & PERSONAL SVC PAPER, WHOLESALE: Boxes & Containers

Dauson Corrugated Container ....F 973 827-1494
Hamburg **(G-4090)**
Westrock Rkt Company ....C 973 484-5000
Newark **(G-7359)**

INDL & PERSONAL SVC PAPER, WHOLESALE: Boxes, Fldng Pprboard

Interntnl Folding Ppr Box Sls ....E 201 941-3100
Ridgefield **(G-9367)**

INDL & PERSONAL SVC PAPER, WHOLESALE: Paperboard & Prdts

Lamitech Inc ....E 609 860-8037
Cranbury **(G-1851)**

INDL & PERSONAL SVC PAPER, WHOLESALE: Press Sensitive Tape

Pro Tapes & Specialties Inc ....C 732 346-0900
North Brunswick **(G-7535)**
Universal Tape Supply Corp ....F 609 653-3191
Somers Point **(G-10048)**

INDL & PERSONAL SVC PAPER, WHOLESALE: Shipping Splys

Clements Industries Inc ....E 201 440-5500
South Hackensack **(G-10258)**
JFK Supplies Inc ....F 732 985-7800
Edison **(G-2545)**
Levine Industries Inc ....E 973 742-1000
Paterson **(G-8319)**

INDL CONTRACTORS: Exhibit Construction

Dublin Management Assoc of NJ ....C 609 387-1600
Burlington **(G-969)**
Palumbo Associates Inc ....F 908 534-2142
Whitehouse Station **(G-12060)**
Taylor Made Custom Cabinetry ....F 856 786-5433
Pennsauken **(G-8583)**

INDL EQPT CLEANING SVCS

Chen Brothers Machinery Co ....G 973 328-0086
Randolph **(G-9272)**

INDL EQPT SVCS

C & S Machine Inc ....F 973 882-1097
Fairfield **(G-3153)**

INDL GASES WHOLESALERS

Airgas Usa LLC ....F 609 685-4241
Cherry Hill **(G-1342)**
Airgas Usa LLC ....E 856 829-7878
Cinnaminson **(G-1445)**
Frank E Ganter Inc ....G 856 692-2218
Vineland **(G-11356)**

PRODUCT

Praxair Distribution Inc ....F 908 862-7200
Linden *(G-5430)*

INDL MACHINERY & EQPT WHOLESALERS

Brunswick Waste System ....G 908 369-2223
Somerville *(G-10203)*
Carter Pump Inc ....G 201 568-9798
Waldwick *(G-11442)*
Columbia Fuel Services Inc ....F 732 751-0044
Wall Township *(G-11474)*
Components & Controls Inc ....F 201 483-9190
Carlstadt *(G-1148)*
Envirnmntal Mgt Chem Wste Svcs ......G 201 848-7676
Mahwah *(G-5770)*
Envirosight LLC ....E 973 970-9284
Randolph *(G-9275)*
F and L Machinery ....G 973 218-6216
Springfield *(G-10554)*
Fette Compacting America Inc ....E 973 586-8722
Rockaway *(G-9567)*
Fluitec International LLC ....G 201 946-4584
Bayonne *(G-226)*
Ganz Brothers Inc ....F 201 820-1975
Paramus *(G-7870)*
Gas Drying Inc ....F 973 361-2212
Wharton *(G-11988)*
Hamon Corporation ....D 908 333-2000
Somerville *(G-10213)*
Houzer Inc ....F 609 584-1900
Hamilton *(G-4108)*
Intertest Inc ....E 908 496-8008
Columbia *(G-1799)*
J & S Tool ....G 973 383-5059
Newton *(G-7393)*
J OBrien Co Inc ....E 973 379-8844
Springfield *(G-10558)*
JDV Equipment Corp ....G 973 366-6556
Dover *(G-2096)*
Kissler & Co Inc ....E 201 896-9600
Carlstadt *(G-1179)*
Machinery Electrics ....G 732 536-0600
Bayville *(G-257)*
NM Knight Co Inc ....E 856 327-4855
Millville *(G-6316)*
Orion Machinery Co Ltd ....E 201 569-3220
Rutherford *(G-9742)*
Pavan & Kievit Enterprises ....E 973 546-4615
Garfield *(G-3746)*
Plcs Inc ....E 856 722-1333
Mount Laurel *(G-6827)*
Powerspec Inc ....E 732 494-9490
Somerville *(G-10225)*
Progressive Ruesch Inc ....E 973 962-7700
Ringwood *(G-9454)*
Ringfeder Pwr Transm USA Corp ......E 201 666-3320
Westwood *(G-11970)*
Sandvik Inc ....C 281 275-4800
Fair Lawn *(G-3113)*
Specialty Measurements Inc ....E 908 534-1500
Lebanon *(G-5302)*
Traffic Safety & Equipment Co ....F 201 327-6050
Mahwah *(G-5822)*
W T Winter Associates Inc ....E 888 808-3611
Fairfield *(G-3349)*
Wagner Industries Inc ....F 973 347-0800
Stanhope *(G-10592)*
Wrap-Ade Machine Co Inc ....F 973 773-6150
Clifton *(G-1744)*

INDL MACHINERY REPAIR & MAINTENANCE

American Mch Tool RPR Rbldg Co ......G 973 927-0820
Randolph *(G-9269)*
Atlantic Switch Generator LLC ....F 609 518-1900
Hainesport *(G-4069)*
Brunswick Waste System ....G 908 369-2223
Somerville *(G-10203)*
Corbett Industries Inc ....F 201 445-6311
Waldwick *(G-11443)*
Gamka Sales Co Inc ....E 732 248-1400
Edison *(G-2525)*
Hockmeyer Equipment Corp ....D 973 482-0225
Harrison *(G-4185)*
Machine Plus Inc ....G 973 839-8884
Haskell *(G-4210)*
Royal Aquarius Empire ....D 646 847-3322
Hamilton *(G-4125)*
White Marine Inc ....F 732 826-4491
Towaco *(G-11007)*

INDL PATTERNS: Foundry Cores

West Pattern Works Inc ....F 609 443-6241
Cranbury *(G-1891)*

INDL PROCESS INSTR: Transmit, Process Variables

Audiocodes Inc ....G 732 469-0880
Somerset *(G-10066)*
Audiocodes Inc ....F 732 469-0880
Somerset *(G-10067)*

INDL PROCESS INSTRUMENTS: Analyzers

Celco ....F 201 327-1123
Mahwah *(G-5757)*

INDL PROCESS INSTRUMENTS: Boiler Controls, Power & Marine

Process Controls Co ....G 908 269-8465
Chester *(G-1438)*

INDL PROCESS INSTRUMENTS: Control

Acrison Inc ....C 201 440-8300
Moonachie *(G-6499)*
Armadillo Automation Inc ....E 856 829-2888
Cinnaminson *(G-1447)*
Coperion K-Tron Pitman Inc ....F 856 589-0500
Sewell *(G-9947)*

INDL PROCESS INSTRUMENTS: Controllers, Process Variables

Matrix Controls Company Inc ....F 732 469-5551
Somerset *(G-10132)*

INDL PROCESS INSTRUMENTS: Indl Flow & Measuring

Linde LLC ....C 908 464-8100
Bridgewater *(G-855)*
Linde LLC ....E 973 579-2065
Sparta *(G-10510)*

INDL PROCESS INSTRUMENTS: Manometers

Rosemount Inc ....F 973 257-2300
Parsippany *(G-8082)*

INDL PROCESS INSTRUMENTS: Moisture Meters

Elaine Inc ....G 973 345-6200
Woodland Park *(G-12217)*

INDL PROCESS INSTRUMENTS: On-Stream Gas Or Liquid Analysis

Control Instruments Corp ....E 973 575-9114
Fairfield *(G-3168)*
Delphian Corporation ....C 201 767-7300
Northvale *(G-7577)*
Meson Group Inc ....E 201 767-7300
Northvale *(G-7591)*

INDL PROCESS INSTRUMENTS: PH Instruments

Omega Engineering Inc ....C 856 467-4200
Bridgeport *(G-769)*

INDL PROCESS INSTRUMENTS: Temperature

Accurate Thermal Systems LLC ....G 609 326-3190
Hainesport *(G-4068)*
Burling Instruments Inc ....F 973 665-0601
Chatham *(G-1326)*
Capintec Inc ....E 201 825-9500
Florham Park *(G-3495)*
Micro-Tek Laboratories Inc ....G 973 779-5577
Clifton *(G-1674)*
Orycon Control Technology Inc ....E 732 922-2400
Ocean *(G-7732)*

INDL PROCESS INSTRUMENTS: Water Quality Monitoring/Cntrl Sys

ACS Quality Services Inc ....G 856 988-6550
Marlton *(G-5964)*
Delaware Technologies Inc ....F 856 234-7692
Mount Laurel *(G-6792)*

INDL SPLYS WHOLESALERS

Bright Lights Usa Inc ....D 856 546-5656
Barrington *(G-173)*
Captive Fasteners Corp ....B 201 337-6800
Oakland *(G-7678)*
Communique Inc ....G 973 751-7588
Belleville *(G-298)*
Deltronics Corporation ....F 856 825-8200
Millville *(G-6297)*
Dreyco Inc ....F 201 896-9000
Carlstadt *(G-1158)*
Federal Equipment & Mfg Co Inc ......G 973 340-7600
Lodi *(G-5584)*
Foster and Company Inc ....E 973 267-4100
Cedar Knolls *(G-1312)*
Granite Packaging Supply Co ....G 856 727-1010
Moorestown *(G-6579)*
Illinois Tool Works Inc ....G 732 968-5300
Parsippany *(G-8028)*
Industrial Rivet & Fastener Co ....D 201 750-1040
Northvale *(G-7584)*
Ingersoll-Rand Company ....C 908 238-7000
Annandale *(G-58)*
Intellgent Trffic Sup Pdts LLC ....G 908 791-1200
South Plainfield *(G-10385)*
Intersource USA Inc ....F 732 257-5002
East Brunswick *(G-2161)*
Jontol Unlimited LLC ....G 858 652-1113
Blackwood *(G-485)*
Knotts Company Inc ....E 908 464-4800
Berkeley Heights *(G-416)*
Matchless United Companies ....G 908 862-7300
Linden *(G-5406)*
Metallo Gasket Company Inc ....F 732 545-7223
New Brunswick *(G-6981)*
Newco Valves LLC ....E 732 257-0300
East Brunswick *(G-2169)*
O Plast Matic Valves Inc ....D 973 256-3000
Cedar Grove *(G-1293)*
Permadur Industries Inc ....D 908 359-9767
Hillsborough *(G-4362)*
Siemens Industry Inc ....E 856 234-7666
Mount Laurel *(G-6841)*
Steelstran Industries Inc ....E 732 574-0700
Avenel *(G-152)*
Technodiamant USA Inc ....G 908 850-8505
Tranquility *(G-11008)*
Tommax Inc ....F 732 224-1046
Red Bank *(G-9347)*
Tri-Power Consulting Svcs LLC ....E 973 227-7100
Denville *(G-2060)*

INDL SPLYS, WHOL: Fasteners, Incl Nuts, Bolts, Screws, Etc

Champion Fasteners Inc ....E 609 267-5222
Lumberton *(G-5655)*
Cold Headed Fasteners Inc ....G 856 461-3244
Delanco *(G-2004)*
Kt Mt Corp ....F 877 791-4426
Cinnaminson *(G-1473)*
P & R Fasteners Inc ....D 732 302-3600
Somerset *(G-10151)*
Scheinert & Sons Inc ....E 201 791-4600
Saddle Brook *(G-9790)*
Stud Welding Co The Inc ....G 856 866-9300
Moorestown *(G-6624)*

INDL SPLYS, WHOLESALE: Abrasives

Beacut Abrasives Corp ....F 973 249-1420
East Rutherford *(G-2283)*

INDL SPLYS, WHOLESALE: Bearings

Accurate Bronze Bearing Co ....G 973 345-2304
Paterson *(G-8198)*
Bcc (USA) Inc ....G 732 572-5450
Piscataway *(G-8740)*

INDL SPLYS, WHOLESALE: Bottler Splys

Agsco Corporation ....E 973 244-0005
Pine Brook *(G-8681)*

INDL SPLYS, WHOLESALE: Brushes, Indl

Andon Brush Co Inc ....E 973 256-6611
Little Falls *(G-5469)*

INDL SPLYS, WHOLESALE: Clean Room Splys

Borak Group Inc ....D 718 665-8500
Jersey City *(G-4720)*

INDL SPLYS, WHOLESALE: Drums, New Or Reconditioned

Rahway Steel Drum Co Inc ....E 732 382-0113
Cranbury *(G-1875)*
Tunnel Barrel & Drum Co Inc ....E 201 933-1444
Carlstadt *(G-1235)*

INDL SPLYS, WHOLESALE: Fasteners & Fastening Eqpt

Arlo Corporation ....G 973 618-0030
Roseland *(G-9645)*

INDL SPLYS, WHOLESALE: Filters, Indl

Filter Technologies Inc ....G 732 329-2500
Monmouth Junction *(G-6344)*
Mer Made Filter....................................G 201 236-0217
Ramsey *(G-9247)*

INDL SPLYS, WHOLESALE: Gaskets

Capital Gasket and Rubber Inc.............G 856 939-3670
Runnemede *(G-9717)*
R S Rubber Corp ....F 973 777-2200
Wallington *(G-11529)*
Transport Products Inc.........................G 973 857-6090
Cedar Grove *(G-1302)*

INDL SPLYS, WHOLESALE: Gaskets & Seals

Custom Gasket Mfg LLC ....F 201 331-6363
Englewood Cliffs *(G-2956)*
Mercer Rubber Company ....E 856 931-5000
Bellmawr *(G-347)*

INDL SPLYS, WHOLESALE: Gears

State Tool Gear Co Inc.........................F 973 642-6181
Newark *(G-7329)*

INDL SPLYS, WHOLESALE: Plastic Bottles

Mighty Mug Incorporated ....G 732 382-3911
Rahway *(G-9215)*

INDL SPLYS, WHOLESALE: Power Transmission, Eqpt & Apparatus

Brilliant Light Power Inc ....E 609 490-0427
East Windsor *(G-2371)*

INDL SPLYS, WHOLESALE: Rubber Goods, Mechanical

Amerimold Tech Inc..............................E 732 462-7577
Jackson *(G-4653)*
Coast Rubber and Gasket Inc ....G 609 747-0110
Burlington *(G-965)*
Rema Tip Top/North America Inc...........E 201 768-8100
Northvale *(G-7605)*
Specialty Rubber Inc ....G 609 704-2555
Elwood *(G-2854)*
Stiles Enterprises Inc ....F 973 625-9660
Rockaway *(G-9610)*
T & B Specialties Inc...........................G 732 928-4500
Jackson *(G-4679)*

INDL SPLYS, WHOLESALE: Staplers & Tackers

Crown Fastener & Supply Corp.............G 845 268-5150
Ringwood *(G-9446)*

INDL SPLYS, WHOLESALE: Tanks, Pressurized

Corban Energy Group Corp ....E 201 509-8555
Elmwood Park *(G-2812)*

INDL SPLYS, WHOLESALE: Tools

Dicar Diamond Tool Corp......................F 973 684-0949
Paterson *(G-8250)*
Jnt Technical Services Inc ....E 201 641-2130
Little Ferry *(G-5511)*

INDL SPLYS, WHOLESALE: Tools, NEC

Ox Group Usa LLC...............................F 888 850-6710
Cranford *(G-1920)*

INDL SPLYS, WHOLESALE: Twine

Baxter Corporation ....F 201 337-1212
Franklin Lakes *(G-3607)*

INDL SPLYS, WHOLESALE: Valves & Fittings

Amico Technologies Inc........................G 732 901-5900
Lakewood *(G-5074)*
Carpenter & Paterson Inc ....E 973 772-1800
Bordentown *(G-592)*
Ceodeux Incorporated ....E 724 696-4340
Hackettstown *(G-4000)*
Chalmers & Kubeck Inc ....G 732 993-1251
New Brunswick *(G-6950)*
Farrell Eqp & Contrls Inc ....F 732 770-4142
Roselle *(G-9669)*
Nedohon Inc ....G 302 533-5512
Wildwood Crest *(G-12076)*
Rotarex Inc North America ....D 724 696-3345
Hackettstown *(G-4033)*
Silbo Industries Inc ....E 201 307-0900
Montvale *(G-6479)*
Sims Pump Valve Company Inc.............E 201 792-0600
Hoboken *(G-4496)*
Taylor Forge Stainless Inc ....D 908 722-1313
Branchburg *(G-708)*
Teneyck Inc...D 201 939-1100
Lyndhurst *(G-5711)*

INDUCTORS

Alecto Systems LLC ....G 973 875-6721
Branchville *(G-725)*
Bel Fuse Inc..C 201 432-0463
Jersey City *(G-4715)*

INFANTS' WEAR STORES

Bib and Tucker Inc ....G 201 489-9600
Hackensack *(G-3881)*

INFORMATION RETRIEVAL SERVICES

Bio-Key International Inc ....E 732 359-1100
Wall Township *(G-11467)*
J R S Tool & Metal Finishing ....G 908 753-2050
South Plainfield *(G-10387)*
Maxisit Inc..C 732 494-2005
Metuchen *(G-6114)*

INK OR WRITING FLUIDS

Airdye Solutions LLC ....E 540 433-9101
Cedar Grove *(G-1269)*
Arro-Mark Company LLC ....F 201 567-4112
Englewood *(G-2871)*
Caloric Color Co Inc ....F 973 471-4748
Garfield *(G-3725)*
Conversion Technology Co Inc ....F 732 752-5660
South Plainfield *(G-10350)*
Faust Thermographic Supply ....F 908 474-0555
Linden *(G-5374)*
Honeyware Inc ....D 201 997-5900
Kearny *(G-4880)*
Intenze Products Inc............................G 201 342-4446
Hackensack *(G-3929)*
Wilpak Industries Inc ....G 201 997-7600
Kearny *(G-4923)*

INK: Duplicating

Chroma Trading Usa Inc.......................G 732 956-4431
Morganville *(G-6639)*

INK: Gravure

Selective Coatings & Inks ....F 732 938-7677
Wall Township *(G-11508)*
Selective Coatings & Inks ....G 732 493-0707
Ocean *(G-7744)*

INK: Letterpress Or Offset

Central Ink Corporation........................G 856 467-5562
Swedesboro *(G-10687)*

INK: Lithographic

J M Fry Printing Inks............................G 732 238-1060
East Brunswick *(G-2162)*
Supreme Ink Corp ....F 973 344-2922
Newark *(G-7335)*

INK: Printing

AGFA Corporation ....G 908 231-5000
Somerville *(G-10200)*
American Coding and Mkg Ink Co.........G 908 756-0373
Plainfield *(G-8853)*
Athletes Alley ....F 732 842-1127
Shrewsbury *(G-9990)*
Custom Chemicals Corp ....A 201 791-5100
Elmwood Park *(G-2814)*
Faust Rudolph Inc................................F 609 298-7334
Cranford *(G-1906)*
Flint Group US LLC..............................G 732 329-4627
Dayton *(G-1962)*
Gotham Ink of New England Inc............G 201 478-5600
Teterboro *(G-10798)*
Ideon LLC ....G 908 431-3126
Hillsborough *(G-4344)*
Kohl & Madden Prtg Ink Corp ....E 201 935-8666
Carlstadt *(G-1181)*
Lodor Offset Corporation ....E 201 935-7100
Carlstadt *(G-1184)*
Monarch Color Corporation ....F 215 923-2235
Pennsauken *(G-8552)*
Pan Technology Inc ....E 201 438-7878
Carlstadt *(G-1197)*
Prismacolor Corp ....F 973 887-6040
Parsippany *(G-8073)*
Ranger Industries Inc ....E 732 389-3535
Tinton Falls *(G-10844)*
Sun Chemical Corporation ....C 201 933-4500
Carlstadt *(G-1223)*
Sun Chemical Corporation ....D 973 404-6000
Parsippany *(G-8094)*
Sun Chemical Corporation ....E 201 438-4831
East Rutherford *(G-2329)*
Sun Chemical Corporation ....F 201 935-8666
Carlstadt *(G-1224)*
Superior Printing Ink Co Inc ....C 201 478-5600
Teterboro *(G-10810)*
Superior Printing Ink Co Inc ....E 856 482-9066
Maple Shade *(G-5911)*
Superior Printing Ink Co Inc ....G 716 685-6763
Teterboro *(G-10811)*
Superior Printing Ink Co Inc ....G 716 685-6763
Teterboro *(G-10812)*
Superior Printing Ink Co Inc ....G 973 242-5868
Newark *(G-7334)*
Total Ink Solutions LLC........................F 201 487-9600
Hackensack *(G-3985)*
Toyo Ink America LLC ....F 201 804-0620
Carlstadt *(G-1231)*
Uvitec Printing Ink Co Inc ....E 973 778-0737
Lodi *(G-5607)*
Vivitone Inc...F 973 427-8114
Hawthorne *(G-4264)*

INK: Screen process

Champion Ink Co Inc ....G 201 868-4100
North Bergen *(G-7439)*
CRS Ink Intl Ltd Lblty Co......................G 732 817-0401
Holmdel *(G-4514)*
Triangle Ink Co Inc ....F 201 935-2777
Wallington *(G-11530)*

INSECTICIDES

Pic Corporation ....E 908 862-7977
Linden *(G-5429)*

PRODUCT

INSECTICIDES & PESTICIDES

Deer Out Animal Repellant LLC............G 908 769-4242
South Plainfield *(G-10353)*

Residex LLC.................................G 856 232-0880
Blackwood *(G-491)*

INSPECTION & TESTING SVCS

T A C Technical Instr Corp ....F 609 882-2894
Ewing *(G-3059)*

TEC Cast Inc ....D 201 935-3885
Moonachie *(G-6549)*

INSTRUMENT LANDING SYSTEMS OR ILS: Airborne Or Ground

Premac Inc ....F 732 381-7550
Rahway *(G-9218)*

INSTRUMENTS & ACCESSORIES: Surveying

Topcon Medical Systems Inc ....D 201 599-5100
Oakland *(G-7707)*

INSTRUMENTS & METERS: Measuring, Electric

Byram Laboratories Inc ....E 908 252-0852
Branchburg *(G-646)*

Photonics Management Corp ....G 908 231-0960
Bridgewater *(G-874)*

Quantem Corp ....E 609 883-9191
Ewing *(G-3047)*

Seaboard Instrument Co ....G 609 641-5300
Pleasantville *(G-8914)*

INSTRUMENTS, LABORATORY: Amino Acid Analyzers

Ezose Sciences Inc.........................F 862 926-1950
Florham Park *(G-3502)*

INSTRUMENTS, LABORATORY: Analyzers, Automatic Chemical

Eci Technology Inc ....C 973 773-8686
Totowa *(G-10942)*

Microsolv Technology Corp...............F 732 578-1777
Eatontown *(G-2413)*

INSTRUMENTS, LABORATORY: Blood Testing

Princeton Separations Inc.................E 732 431-3338
Freehold *(G-3683)*

INSTRUMENTS, LABORATORY: Gas Analyzing

Packaged Gas Systems Inc ....G 908 755-2780
Springfield *(G-10569)*

Perma Pure LLC ....G 732 244-0010
Lakewood *(G-5170)*

INSTRUMENTS, LABORATORY: Liquid Chromatographic

Princeton Chromatography Inc ....G 609 860-1803
Cranbury *(G-1872)*

INSTRUMENTS, LABORATORY: Mass Spectroscopy

Dolce Technologies LLC ....G 609 497-7319
Princeton *(G-9031)*

Sophion Bioscience Inc ....G 732 745-0221
Paramus *(G-7905)*

INSTRUMENTS, LABORATORY: Spectrographs

Horiba Instruments Inc.....................C 732 494-8660
Piscataway *(G-8776)*

INSTRUMENTS, LABORATORY: Spectrometers

Moa Instrumentation Inc ....G 215 547-8308
Lawrenceville *(G-5264)*

INSTRUMENTS, MEASURING & CNTRL: Geophysical & Meteorological

Instrument Sciences & Tech ....D 908 996-9920
Frenchtown *(G-3702)*

Kanomax Usa Inc ....G 973 786-6386
Byram Township *(G-1022)*

INSTRUMENTS, MEASURING & CNTRL: Radiation & Testing, Nuclear

Capintec Inc..................................E 201 825-9500
Florham Park *(G-3495)*

Theory Development Corp ....F 201 783-8770
Mahwah *(G-5819)*

INSTRUMENTS, MEASURING & CNTRL: Testing, Abrasion, Etc

Instru-Met Corporation ....G 908 851-0700
Union *(G-11195)*

S & G Tool Aid Corporation ....G 973 824-7730
Newark *(G-7297)*

INSTRUMENTS, MEASURING & CNTRL: Whole Body Counters, Nuclear

Orlando Systems Ltd Lblty Co ....G 908 400-5052
North Plainfield *(G-7560)*

INSTRUMENTS, MEASURING & CNTRLG: Thermometers/Temp Sensors

Becton Dickinson and Company.........A 201 847-6800
Franklin Lakes *(G-3610)*

Conistics Inc..................................G 609 584-2600
Hamilton *(G-4105)*

Sensor Scientific Inc ....E 973 227-7790
Fairfield *(G-3305)*

INSTRUMENTS, MEASURING & CNTRLNG: Press & Vac Ind, Acft Eng

Ptc Electronics Inc..........................G 201 847-0500
Mahwah *(G-5804)*

INSTRUMENTS, MEASURING & CONTROLLING: Dosimetry, Personnel

Life Recovery Systems Hd LLC............G 973 283-2800
Kinnelon *(G-5038)*

INSTRUMENTS, MEASURING & CONTROLLING: Gas Detectors

AIG Industrial Group Inc ....F 201 767-7300
Northvale *(G-7569)*

Delphian Corporation ....C 201 767-7300
Northvale *(G-7577)*

Meson Group Inc ....E 201 767-7300
Northvale *(G-7591)*

INSTRUMENTS, MEASURING & CONTROLLING: Surveying & Drafting

Northwest Instrument Inc...................G 973 347-6830
Dover *(G-2105)*

INSTRUMENTS, MEASURING & CONTROLLING: Ultrasonic Testing

G E Inspection Technologies LP ....D 973 448-0077
Flanders *(G-3409)*

INSTRUMENTS, MEASURING/CNTRLG: Fire Detect Sys, Non-Electric

Alison Control Inc............................E 973 575-7100
Fairfield *(G-3130)*

INSTRUMENTS, MEASURING/CNTRLNG: Med Diagnostic Sys, Nuclear

Advanced Shore Imaging Associa........F 732 678-0087
Northfield *(G-7562)*

Euroimmun US Inc ....E 973 656-1000
Mountain Lakes *(G-6858)*

Mallinckrodt LLC ....F 908 238-6600
Hampton *(G-4164)*

INSTRUMENTS, MEASURING & CNTRL: (cont.)

Maquet Cardiovascular LLC ....D 973 709-7000
Wayne *(G-11663)*

Mdr Diagnostics LLC ....E 609 396-0021
Mount Laurel *(G-6817)*

INSTRUMENTS, OPTICAL: Coating & Grinding, Lens

Krell Technologies Inc......................G 732 617-7091
Neptune *(G-6921)*

INSTRUMENTS, OPTICAL: Elements & Assemblies, Exc Ophthalmic

Integrated Photonics Inc ....D 908 281-8000
Hillsborough *(G-4348)*

Integrated Photonics Inc ....G 908 281-8000
Hillsborough *(G-4349)*

International Crystal Labs ....E 973 478-8944
Garfield *(G-3739)*

INSTRUMENTS, OPTICAL: Lenses, All Types Exc Ophthalmic

21st Century Optics Inc.....................G 808 935-1119
Warren *(G-11533)*

Esco Products Inc............................E 973 697-3700
Oak Ridge *(G-7662)*

Inrad Optics Inc...............................G 201 767-1910
Northvale *(G-7585)*

O & S Research Inc..........................E 856 829-2800
Cinnaminson *(G-1481)*

INSTRUMENTS, OPTICAL: Light Sources, Standard

Cercis Inc......................................G 609 737-5120
Pennington *(G-8445)*

INSTRUMENTS, OPTICAL: Magnifying, NEC

Anchor Optical Co ....C 856 546-1965
Barrington *(G-170)*

INSTRUMENTS, OPTICAL: Polarizers

Inlc Technology Corporation ....F 908 834-8390
Warren *(G-11556)*

Polarity LLC...................................G 732 970-3855
Morganville *(G-6652)*

INSTRUMENTS, OPTICAL: Test & Inspection

Datacolor Inc..................................D 609 924-2189
Lawrenceville *(G-5256)*

INSTRUMENTS, SURGICAL & MED: Cleaning Eqpt, Ultrasonic Med

Crest Ultrasonics Corp ....G 609 883-4000
Ewing *(G-3011)*

Crestek Inc.....................................E 609 883-4000
Ewing *(G-3012)*

L & R Manufacturing Co Inc.................D 201 991-5330
Kearny *(G-4894)*

INSTRUMENTS, SURGICAL & MED: Needles & Syringes, Hypodermic

Becton Dickinson and Company.........A 201 847-6800
Franklin Lakes *(G-3610)*

Oncode-Med Inc ....G 908 998-3647
Basking Ridge *(G-201)*

INSTRUMENTS, SURGICAL & MEDICAL: Blood & Bone Work

Catalent Pharma Solutions Inc ....B 732 537-6200
Somerset *(G-10078)*

Datascope Corp ....D 201 995-8000
Mahwah *(G-5762)*

Genesis Bps LLC ....E 201 708-1400
Ramsey *(G-9241)*

H Galow Co Inc................................E 201 768-0547
Norwood *(G-7624)*

New American Therapeutics Inc...........G 908 282-7444
Haskell *(G-4211)*

Phillips Precision Inc........................C 201 797-8820
Elmwood Park *(G-2843)*

INSTRUMENTS, SURGICAL & MEDICAL: Blood Pressure

General Graphics Corporation ....G..... 201 664-4083
Hillsdale (G-4383)
Intercure Inc ....E 973 893-5653
Montclair (G-6419)
Trimline Medical Products Corp ....C 908 429-0590
Branchburg (G-713)

INSTRUMENTS, SURGICAL & MEDICAL: Catheters

Bipore Inc ....F 201 767-1993
Northvale (G-7575)
Catheter Precision Inc ....F 973 691-2000
Ledgewood (G-5304)

INSTRUMENTS, SURGICAL & MEDICAL: Hemodialysis

BMA of Colonia ....E 732 382-7333
Colonia (G-1777)

INSTRUMENTS, SURGICAL & MEDICAL: Inhalation Therapy

Biodynamics LLC...............................G..... 201 227-9255
Englewood (G-2876)
Microdose Therapeutx Inc ....E 732 355-2100
Ewing (G-3037)

INSTRUMENTS, SURGICAL & MEDICAL: Lasers, Surgical

Unionmed Tech Inc ....G..... 917 714-3418
Bridgewater (G-905)

INSTRUMENTS, SURGICAL & MEDICAL: Ophthalmic

Sensor Medical Technology LLC.........G..... 425 358-7381
Denville (G-2058)
Westcon Orthopedics Inc ....G..... 908 806-8981
Neshanic Station (G-6940)

INSTRUMENTS, SURGICAL/MED: Microsurgical, Exc Electromedical

Jrh Service & Sales LLC.....................G..... 908 832-9266
Lebanon (G-5294)

INSTRUMENTS: Analytical

Advanced Technical Support Inc ....D...... 609 298-2522
Bordentown (G-589)
Arrow Engineering Co Inc ....G..... 908 353-5229
Hillside (G-4391)
Becton Dickinson and Company.........A 201 847-6800
Franklin Lakes (G-3610)
Belair Instrument Company LLC.........E 973 912-8900
Springfield (G-10542)
Beta Industries Corp..........................G..... 201 939-2400
Carlstadt (G-1130)
Biomedicon ....F 856 778-1880
Moorestown (G-6563)
C W Brabender Instrs Inc ....E 201 343-8425
South Hackensack (G-10256)
Cargille-Sacher Labs Inc ....E 973 239-6633
Cedar Grove (G-1274)
Distek Inc ....D 732 422-7585
North Brunswick (G-7516)
Edax Inc ....D 201 529-4880
Mahwah (G-5769)
Evex Analytical Instruments ....F 609 252-9192
Princeton (G-9042)
Fisher Scientific Chemical Div............E 609 633-1422
Fair Lawn (G-3092)
Hudson Robotics Inc ....F 973 376-7400
Springfield (G-10556)
Isocolor Inc ....G..... 201 935-4494
Carlstadt (G-1173)
M D Laboratory Supplies Inc ....G..... 732 322-0773
Franklin Park (G-3628)
Mesa Laboratories- Bgi Inc.................E 973 492-8400
Butler (G-1013)
Microdysis Inc ....G..... 609 642-1184
Bordentown (G-604)
National Labnet Co ....E 732 417-0700
Iselin (G-4636)

New ERA Enterprises Inc ....G..... 856 794-2005
Newfield (G-7368)
Novartis Pharmaceuticals Corp..........G..... 862 778-8300
East Hanover (G-2236)
Princeton Research Instruments..........G..... 609 924-0570
Princeton (G-9101)
Pulsetor LLC ....G..... 609 303-0578
Lambertville (G-5220)
Rame-Hart Inc ....E 973 335-0560
Randolph (G-9295)
Rame-Hart Instrument Co LLC ....G..... 973 448-0305
Succasunna (G-10628)
Roche Diagnostics Corporation ....F 908 253-0707
Branchburg (G-700)
Rudolph Instruments Inc ....G..... 973 227-0139
Denville (G-2057)
Siemens Med Sltons Diagnostics........A 973 927-2828
Flanders (G-3416)
Spark Holland Inc..............................G..... 609 799-7250
Sicklerville (G-10026)
Thermo Fisher Scientific Inc...............F 609 239-3185
Burlington (G-991)
Thermo Fisher Scientific Inc...............F 732 627-0220
Somerset (G-10187)
Topcon Medical Systems Inc ....D 201 599-5100
Oakland (G-7707)
Veeco Process Equipment Inc ....C 732 560-5300
Somerset (G-10194)

INSTRUMENTS: Analyzers, Internal Combustion Eng, Electronic

Buttonwood Enterprises LLC ....G..... 201 505-1901
Woodcliff Lake (G-12184)

INSTRUMENTS: Combustion Control, Indl

Carlisle Machine Works Inc ....E 856 825-0627
Millville (G-6293)
NM Knight Co Inc ....E 856 327-4855
Millville (G-6316)

INSTRUMENTS: Electronic, Analog-Digital Converters

Microdysis Inc ....G..... 609 642-1184
Bordentown (G-604)
Thomas Instrumentation Inc ....F 609 624-2630
Cape May Court House (G-1118)

INSTRUMENTS: Endoscopic Eqpt, Electromedical

Affil Endoscopy Services CL ....G..... 201 842-0020
Clifton (G-1559)
Burlington Cnty Endoscopy Ctr ....E 609 267-1555
Lumberton (G-5652)
Ethicon LLC ....D 908 218-3195
Somerville (G-10208)

INSTRUMENTS: Eye Examination

Spare Pair Vision Center LLC ....G..... 973 758-1151
Livingston (G-5563)

INSTRUMENTS: Flow, Indl Process

Boc Group Inc ....A 908 665-2400
New Providence (G-7030)
Kessler-Ellis Products Co ....D 732 935-1320
Eatontown (G-2410)
Linde North America Inc ....D 908 464-8100
New Providence (G-7045)
Linde North America Inc ....B 908 464-8100
Bridgewater (G-857)

INSTRUMENTS: Frequency Meters, Electrical, Mech & Electronic

Sherry International Inc......................F 908 279-7255
Warren (G-11566)

INSTRUMENTS: Indl Process Control

Accuratus Ceramic Corp.....................E 908 213-7070
Phillipsburg (G-8638)
American Compressed Gases Inc........E 201 767-3200
Old Tappan (G-7797)
Amico Technologies Inc ....G..... 732 901-5900
Lakewood (G-5074)
Anvima Technologies LLC ....G..... 973 531-7077
Brookside (G-922)

Arcadia Equipment Inc ....F 201 342-3308
Hackensack (G-3874)
Btech Inc ....E 973 983-1120
Rockaway (G-9555)
Check-It Electronics Corp ....E 973 520-8435
Elizabeth (G-2718)
Circonix Technologies LLC ....F 973 962-6160
Ringwood (G-9445)
Difco Laboratories Inc ....G..... 410 316-4113
Franklin Lakes (G-3613)
Digivac Company ....F 732 765-0900
Matawan (G-6017)
Dranetz Technologies Inc ....D 732 248-4358
Edison (G-2503)
Emerson Process Management ....G..... 908 605-4551
Warren (G-11546)
F S Brainard & Co ....F 609 387-4300
Burlington (G-971)
Fargo Controls Inc ....G..... 732 389-3376
Eatontown (G-2395)
Global Power Technology Inc ....D 732 287-3680
Edison (G-2528)
Intertek Laboratories Inc ....E 908 903-1800
Stirling (G-10601)
Istec Corporation ....F 973 383-9888
Sparta (G-10506)
J & W Servo Systems Company ....F 973 335-1007
Rockaway (G-9577)
Marine Electric Systems Inc ....E 201 531-8600
South Hackensack (G-10278)
Marotta Controls Inc ....C 973 334-7800
Montville (G-6490)
Mayfair Tech Ltd Lblty Co ....F 609 802-1262
Princeton (G-9071)
Mesa Laboratories Inc ....E 973 492-8400
Butler (G-1012)
Netquest Corporation ....E 856 866-0505
Mount Laurel (G-6822)
Omega Engineering Inc ....F 856 467-4200
Swedesboro (G-10716)
Palmer Electronics Inc ....F 973 772-5900
Garfield (G-3744)
Pavan & Kievit Enterprises ....E 973 546-4615
Garfield (G-3746)
Rees Scientific Corporation ....C 609 530-1055
Ewing (G-3050)
Roxboro Holdings Inc ....D 732 919-3119
Wall Township (G-11506)
Schneder Elc Bldngs Amrcas Inc........E 201 348-9240
Secaucus (G-9922)
Sk & P Industries Inc ....G..... 973 482-1864
Newark (G-7315)
Sofradir Ec Inc....................................E 973 882-0211
Fairfield (G-3307)
Springfeld Prcision Instrs Inc ....E 866 843-3905
Rochelle Park (G-9537)
T A C Technical Instr Corp ....F 609 882-2894
Ewing (G-3059)
Theory Development Corp ....F 201 783-8770
Mahwah (G-5819)
V G Controls Inc ....G..... 973 764-6500
Oakland (G-7709)
Vertiv Services Inc ....E 732 225-3741
Edison (G-2644)

INSTRUMENTS: Laser, Scientific & Engineering

Mnemonics Inc ....G..... 856 234-0970
Mount Laurel (G-6820)

INSTRUMENTS: Liquid Analysis, Indl Process

Accupac Inc ....C 215 256-7094
Lakewood (G-5064)
Gammon Technical Products Inc ....D 732 223-4600
Manasquan (G-5870)

INSTRUMENTS: Liquid Level, Indl Process

John G Papailias Co Inc ....G..... 201 767-4027
Northvale (G-7588)
Signal Systems International................G..... 732 793-4668
Lavallette (G-5237)

INSTRUMENTS: Measurement, Indl Process

Digital Binscom LLC...........................G..... 908 867-7055
Long Valley (G-5636)

Employee Codes: A=Over 500 employees, B=251-500
C=101-250, D=51-100, E=20-50, F=10-19, G=4-9

2018 Harris New jersey
Manufacturers Directory

885

PRODUCT

Electronic Measuring Devices ....F 973 691-4755
  Flanders (G-3406)
Malcam US ....G 973 218-2461
  Short Hills (G-9981)
Measurement Control Corp ....G 800 504-9010
  West Orange (G-11899)
Sandvik Process Systems Inc ....E 973 720-7000
  Totowa (G-10970)

INSTRUMENTS: Measuring & Controlling

Akers Biosciences Inc.....................E 856 848-8698
  West Deptford (G-11814)
Amcor Phrm Packg USA LLC ....C 856 825-1100
  Millville (G-6280)
American Gas & Chemical Co Ltd .....E 201 767-7300
  Northvale (G-7572)
Ballantine Laboratories Inc ....G 908 713-7742
  Annandale (G-56)
Boonton Electronics Corp ....E 201 261-8797
  Parsippany (G-7963)
C W Brabender Instrs Inc ....E 201 343-8425
  South Hackensack (G-10256)
Checkpoint Security Systems Gr ....C 952 933-8858
  West Deptford (G-11820)
Checkpoint Systems Inc ....C 952 933-8858
  West Deptford (G-11823)
Coperion K-Tron Pitman Inc ....F 856 589-0500
  Sewell (G-9947)
Delmhorst Instrument Company ....E 973 334-2557
  Towaco (G-10992)
Digital Binscom LLC.......................G 908 867-7055
  Long Valley (G-5636)
Digivac Company ....E 732 765-0900
  Matawan (G-6017)
Dranetz Technologies Inc ....D 732 248-4358
  Edison (G-2503)
DRG International Inc ....E 973 564-7555
  Springfield (G-10551)
Edax Inc ....E 201 529-4880
  Mahwah (G-5769)
G R Bowler Inc ....G 973 525-7172
  Andover (G-50)
H S Martin Company Inc ....F 856 692-8700
  Vineland (G-11368)
Howard A Schaevitz Tech Inc ....E 856 662-8000
  Budd Lake (G-931)
Innerspace Technology Inc ....G 201 933-1600
  Carlstadt (G-1172)
Leak Detection Associates ....G 856 401-7718
  Vineland (G-11379)
Lumiscope Co Inc ....D 678 291-3207
  East Rutherford (G-2306)
Mab Enterprises Inc.......................F 973 345-8282
  Paterson (G-8328)
Macro Sensors ....F 856 662-8000
  Budd Lake (G-935)
Magnetic Products and Svcs Inc ....G 732 264-6651
  Holmdel (G-4520)
Micro-Tek Laboratories Inc ....G 973 779-5577
  Clifton (G-1674)
Mistras Group Inc ....C 609 716-4000
  Princeton Junction (G-9159)
Netquest Corporation ....E 856 866-0505
  Mount Laurel (G-6822)
Physical Acoustics Corporation ....C 609 716-4000
  Princeton Junction (G-9162)
Radcom Equipment Inc ....E 201 518-0033
  Paramus (G-7898)
Roper Scientific Inc ....D 520 889-9933
  Trenton (G-11114)
Rudolph Technologies Inc ....D 973 347-3891
  Budd Lake (G-941)
Science Pump Corporation ....E 856 963-7700
  Camden (G-1085)
Scientific Machine and Sup Co ....E 732 356-1553
  Middlesex (G-6195)
Scientific Sales Inc ....F 609 844-0055
  Lawrenceville (G-5268)
Shock Tech Inc ....E 845 368-8600
  Mahwah (G-5812)
Sigma-Netics Inc ....E 973 227-6372
  Riverdale (G-9488)
Springfeld Prcision Instrs Inc ....E 866 843-3905
  Rochelle Park (G-9537)
Sun Coast Precision Instrument ....G 646 852-2331
  Cresskill (G-1949)
Superior Signal Company LLC ....F 732 251-0800
  Old Bridge (G-7793)
Tel-Instrument Elec Corp ....E 201 933-1600
  East Rutherford (G-2332)

Transistor Devices Inc....................C 908 850-5088
  Hackettstown (G-4041)
United Instrument Company LLC ....G 201 767-6000
  Northvale (G-7610)
Venkateshwara Inc ....F 908 964-4777
  Somerset (G-10195)
William Kenyon & Sons Inc ....E 732 985-8980
  Piscataway (G-8836)

INSTRUMENTS: Measuring Electricity

Agilent Technologies Inc.................E 973 448-7129
  Budd Lake (G-923)
Alltest Instruments Inc ....F 732 919-3339
  Farmingdale (G-3376)
Eastern Instrumentation of ....G 856 231-0668
  Moorestown (G-6573)
Hamamatsu Corporation ....E 908 526-0941
  Bridgewater (G-842)
Imperial Machine & Tool Co ....G 908 496-8100
  Columbia (G-1798)
Instru-Met Corporation ....G 908 851-0700
  Union (G-11195)
Intertek Laboratories Inc.................E 908 903-1800
  Stirling (G-10601)
Keyence Corporation America ....G 201 930-0100
  Elmwood Park (G-2828)
Link Computer Graphics Inc ....G 973 808-8990
  Fairfield (G-3253)
Mistras Group Inc ....C 609 716-4000
  Princeton Junction (G-9159)
Multi-Tech Industries Inc ....F 732 431-0550
  Marlboro (G-5948)
Nanion Technologies Inc ....G 973 369-7960
  Livingston (G-5551)
Panel Components & Systems ....F 973 448-9400
  Stanhope (G-10589)
Powercomm Solutions LLC ....G 908 806-7025
  Flemington (G-3459)
RSR Electronics Inc.......................E 732 381-8777
  Rahway (G-9222)
Tcp Reliable Inc ....G 848 229-2466
  Edison (G-2638)
Tel-Instrument Elec Corp ....E 201 933-1600
  East Rutherford (G-2332)

INSTRUMENTS: Measuring, Electrical Energy

Energy Tracking LLC ....G 973 448-8660
  Flanders (G-3407)

INSTRUMENTS: Measuring, Electrical Power

Janke & Company Inc......................G 973 334-4477
  Boonton (G-573)

INSTRUMENTS: Medical & Surgical

3M Company..................................C 908 788-4000
  Flemington (G-3422)
A D M Tronics Unlimited Inc ....E 201 767-6040
  Northvale (G-7566)
A&E Advnced Clsure Systems LLC .....E 732 938-2266
  Wall Township (G-11459)
Aarisse Health Care Products ....G 973 686-1811
  Wayne (G-11600)
Advanced Precision Inc ....E 800 788-9473
  Sparta (G-10485)
Allergan Inc ....A 862 261-7000
  Madison (G-5718)
Allergan Holdco Us Inc ....A 862 261-7000
  Parsippany (G-7943)
Alto Development Corp ....D 732 938-2266
  Wall Township (G-11461)
America Techma Inc ....G 201 894-5887
  Englewood Cliffs (G-2948)
Antares Pharma Inc ....C 609 359-3020
  Ewing (G-3003)
Artegraft Inc ....F 732 422-8333
  North Brunswick (G-7504)
Baeta Corp ....G 201 471-0988
  Fort Lee (G-3545)
Bard Healthcare Inc ....C 908 277-8000
  New Providence (G-7028)
Baxter Healthcare Corporation ....D 856 489-2104
  Cherry Hill (G-1346)
Bayer Corporation ....A 412 777-2000
  Whippany (G-12007)
Bayer Healthcare LLC.....................A 862 404-3000
  Whippany (G-12008)
Bayer Hlthcare Phrmcticals Inc ....E 973 709-3545
  Whippany (G-12010)

Bayer Hlthcare Phrmcticals Inc ....A 862 404-3000
  Whippany (G-12011)
Bd Ventures LLC ....E 201 847-6800
  Franklin Lakes (G-3609)
Belair Instrument Company LLC ....E 973 912-8900
  Springfield (G-10542)
Beltor Manufacturing Corp ....G 856 768-5570
  Berlin (G-426)
Bernafon LLC ....G 888 941-4203
  Somerset (G-10069)
Bio Compression Systems Inc ....E 201 939-0716
  Moonachie (G-6508)
Biomedicon ....F 856 778-1880
  Moorestown (G-6563)
Biosearch Medical Products Inc ....D 908 252-0595
  Branchburg (G-644)
Boston Scientific Corporation ....E 973 709-7000
  Wayne (G-11612)
Burpee Medsystems LLC ....G 732 544-8900
  Eatontown (G-2387)
C R Bard Inc ....C 908 277-8000
  New Providence (G-7032)
C R Bard Inc ....G 856 461-0946
  Delran (G-2013)
Canfield Property Group Inc ....F 973 276-0300
  Fairfield (G-3155)
Cantel Medical Corp ....G 973 890-7220
  Little Falls (G-5471)
Capintec Inc.................................E 201 825-9500
  Florham Park (G-3495)
Cardan Medical Products Inc ....G 908 964-0800
  Union (G-11162)
Cedge Industries Inc......................F 201 641-3222
  Ridgefield Park (G-9400)
Cenogenics Corporation ....E 732 536-6457
  Morganville (G-6638)
Ch Technologies USA Inc ....G 201 666-2335
  Westwood (G-11957)
Clordisys Solutions Inc ....E 908 236-4100
  Branchburg (G-647)
Collagen Matrix Inc ....E 201 786-9300
  Allendale (G-7)
Collagen Matrix Inc ....D 201 405-1477
  Oakland (G-7679)
Convatec Inc ....B 908 904-2500
  Bridgewater (G-829)
Cordis International Corp.................A 732 524-0400
  New Brunswick (G-6953)
Cranial Technologies Inc.................E 201 265-3993
  Paramus (G-7863)
Cura Biomed Inc ....G 609 647-1474
  Princeton Junction (G-9151)
Cytosorbents Corporation ....E 732 329-8885
  Monmouth Junction (G-6339)
Cytosorbents Medical Inc ....E 732 329-8885
  Monmouth Junction (G-6340)
Data Medical Inc ....F 800 790-9978
  North Bergen (G-7445)
Datascope Corp ....F 800 777-4222
  Mahwah (G-5763)
Dexmed Inc ....G 732 831-0507
  Elizabeth (G-2724)
Dexmed LLC ....G 732 831-0507
  Elizabeth (G-2725)
Difco Laboratories Inc ....G 410 316-4113
  Franklin Lakes (G-3613)
Diopsys Inc ....E 973 244-0622
  Pine Brook (G-8699)
Dynasil Corporation America ....G 856 767-4600
  West Berlin (G-11716)
Emse Corp ....F 973 227-9221
  Fairfield (G-3184)
Endomedix ....G 848 248-1883
  Newark (G-7154)
Excelsior Medical LLC....................C 732 776-7525
  Neptune (G-6911)
Ferry Machine Corp ....E 201 641-9191
  Little Ferry (G-5504)
Fresenius Med Care Hldings Inc ....E 201 767-7700
  Rockleigh (G-9629)
Garden State Medical Sup LLC ....G 732 348-0312
  Lakewood (G-5127)
Getinge Group Logistics Americ ....E 973 709-6000
  Wayne (G-11640)
Glastron Inc ....E 856 692-0500
  Vineland (G-11363)
Globe Scientific Inc ....E 201 599-1400
  Paramus (G-7873)
Graydon Products Inc ....E 856 234-9513
  Moorestown (G-6580)

(G-0000) Company's Geographic Section entry number

H & W Tool Co Inc ....F 973 366-0131
Dover (G-2088)

Haz Laboratories ....F 908 453-3300
Washington (G-11582)

Healthcare Cart ....G 201 406-4797
Blairstown (G-496)

Howmedica Osteonics Corp ....E 201 541-6569
Englewood (G-2903)

Hydromer Inc ....C 908 526-2828
Branchburg (G-665)

IDL Techni-Edge LLC ....C 908 497-9818
Kenilworth (G-4962)

Instride Shoes LLC ....E 908 874-6670
Hillsborough (G-4347)

Integra Lfscnces Holdings Corp ...C 609 275-0500
Plainsboro (G-8887)

Integra Lifesciences Corp ....C 609 275-2700
Plainsboro (G-8888)

Integra Lifesciences Corp ....E 609 275-2700
Plainsboro (G-8890)

Integra Lifesciences Corp ....C 609 275-0500
Plainsboro (G-8889)

Integra Lifesciences Sales LLC ...B 609 275-0500
Plainsboro (G-8891)

Ivy Sports Medicine LLC ....G 201 573-5423
Montvale (G-6462)

Jaktool LLC ....F 609 664-2451
Cranbury (G-1844)

Jnj International Inv LLC ....G 732 524-0400
New Brunswick (G-6973)

Johnson & Johnson ....G 908 722-9319
Raritan (G-9311)

Johnson & Johnson ....C 908 874-1000
Morris Plains (G-6673)

Johnson & Johnson ....C 732 524-0400
New Brunswick (G-6975)

Johnson & Johnson ....A 732 524-0400
New Brunswick (G-6974)

Laboratory Diagnostics Co Inc .....F 732 536-6300
Morganville (G-6646)

Laboratory Diagnostics Co Inc .....G 732 972-2145
Morganville (G-6647)

Lumiscope Co Inc ....D 678 291-3207
East Rutherford (G-2306)

Maddak Inc ....G 973 628-7600
Wayne (G-11661)

Mallinckrodt LLC ....F 908 238-6600
Hampton (G-4164)

Maxter Corporation ....G 609 877-9700
Willingboro (G-12120)

Medicraft Inc ....E 201 797-8820
Elmwood Park (G-2835)

Medin Technologies Inc ....C 973 779-2400
Totowa (G-10955)

Medinol Usa Inc ....E 201 654-4534
Parsippany (G-8044)

Mediscope Manufacturing Inc ......G 908 756-2411
Watchung (G-11593)

Medplast Medical Inc ....C 908 561-0717
South Plainfield (G-10405)

Medplast Medical Inc ....F 732 356-0689
Middlesex (G-6179)

Medtronic Usa Inc ....F 973 331-7914
Parsippany (G-8045)

Micro Stamping Corporation ....C 732 302-0800
Somerset (G-10138)

Mindray Ds Usa Inc ....A 201 995-8000
Mahwah (G-5791)

Nephros Inc ....G 201 343-5202
South Orange (G-10312)

Next Medical Products LLC ....F 908 722-4549
Branchburg (G-682)

Nextgen Edge Inc ....G 610 507-6904
West Milford (G-11855)

Nu-Stent Technologies Inc ....G 732 729-6270
Hillsborough (G-4360)

Osteotech Inc ....E 732 544-5942
Eatontown (G-2416)

Osteotech Inc ....C 732 542-2800
Eatontown (G-2417)

Osteotech Inc ....F 732 542-2800
Eatontown (G-2418)

Precise Cmpnents TI Design Inc ...G 973 928-2928
Clifton (G-1702)

RB Health Manufacturing US LLC ...B 973 404-2600
Parsippany (G-8075)

Redfield Corporation ....G 201 845-3990
Rochelle Park (G-9534)

Respironics Inc ....C 973 581-6000
Parsippany (G-8079)

Schering Berlin Inc ....G 862 404-3000
Whippany (G-12038)

Somerset Outpatient Surgery ....G 781 635-2807
Somerset (G-10172)

Steris Instrument MGT Svcs Inc ...G 908 904-1317
Hillsborough (G-4373)

Stryker ....G 856 312-0046
Runnemede (G-9724)

Stryker Corporation ....D 201 760-8000
Allendale (G-20)

Teleflex Incorporated ....D 856 349-7234
Gloucester City (G-3846)

Terumo Americas Holding Inc ....D 732 302-4900
Somerset (G-10184)

Terumo Medical Corporation ....C 732 302-4900
Somerset (G-10185)

Topcon Medical Systems Inc ....D 201 599-5100
Oakland (G-7707)

Total Tech Medical LLC ....G 973 980-6458
Dover (G-2113)

Tracer Tool & Machine Co Inc ....F 201 337-6184
Oakland (G-7708)

US China Allied Products Inc ....G 201 461-9886
Fort Lee (G-3587)

Vascular Therapies LLC ....G 201 266-8310
Cresskill (G-1950)

Viatar Ctc Solutions Inc ....G 617 299-6590
Short Hills (G-9987)

Viscot Medical LLC ....E 973 887-9273
East Hanover (G-2248)

Vitillo & Sons Inc ....F 732 886-1393
Lakewood (G-5201)

Vozeh Equipment Corp ....E 201 337-3729
Franklin Lakes (G-3625)

INSTRUMENTS: Microwave Test

Boonton Electronics Corp ....E 201 261-8797
Parsippany (G-7963)

Mmtc Inc ....G 609 520-9699
Princeton (G-9076)

Waveline Incorporated ....E 973 226-9100
Fairfield (G-3350)

Wireless Telecom Group Inc ....D 973 386-9696
Parsippany (G-8114)

INSTRUMENTS: Nautical

AT&T Technologies Inc ....A 201 771-2000
Berkeley Heights (G-400)

INSTRUMENTS: Optical, Analytical

Thorlabs Inc ....C 973 579-7227
Newton (G-7410)

INSTRUMENTS: Oscillographs & Oscilloscopes

Spectrum Instrumentation Corp .....E 201 562-1999
Hackensack (G-3980)

INSTRUMENTS: Photographic, Electronic

Samsung Opt-Lctronics Amer Inc ...C 201 325-2612
Teaneck (G-10772)

INSTRUMENTS: Power Measuring, Electrical

Electro Impulse Laboratory Inc ......E 732 776-5800
Neptune (G-6910)

INSTRUMENTS: Pressure Measurement, Indl

Pressure Controls Inc ....G 973 751-5002
Belleville (G-312)

TX Technology Corp ....C 973 442-7500
Denville (G-2061)

INSTRUMENTS: Radio Frequency Measuring

Pulsar Microwave Corp ....E 973 779-6262
Clifton (G-1706)

Rf Vii Inc ....F 856 875-2121
Newfield (G-7371)

Seren Inc ....E 856 205-1131
Vineland (G-11402)

INSTRUMENTS: Telemetering, Indl Process

Cg Automation Solutions USA ....E 973 379-7400
Springfield (G-10546)

Daq Electronics LLC ....E 732 981-0050
Piscataway (G-8753)

INSTRUMENTS: Temperature Measurement, Indl

Intest Corporation ....G 856 505-8800
Mount Laurel (G-6807)

INSTRUMENTS: Test, Digital, Electronic & Electrical Circuits

Intest Corporation ....G 856 505-8800
Mount Laurel (G-6807)

INSTRUMENTS: Test, Electronic & Electric Measurement

Alpha Scientific Corporation ....G 908 534-9941
Whitehouse Station (G-12049)

Communication Devices Inc ....F 973 334-1980
Boonton (G-560)

Dbmcorp Inc ....F 201 677-0008
Oakland (G-7683)

Dranetz Technologies Inc ....D 732 248-4358
Edison (G-2503)

Global Power Technology Inc ....D 732 287-3680
Edison (G-2528)

Marine Electric Systems Inc ....E 201 531-8600
South Hackensack (G-10278)

Zixel Ltd ....G 732 972-3287
Morganville (G-6657)

INSTRUMENTS: Test, Electronic & Electrical Circuits

ABC Digital Electronics Inc ....G 201 666-6888
Old Tappan (G-7796)

Aeronautical Instr & Rdo Co ....E 973 473-0034
Lodi (G-5573)

Applied Resources Corp ....G 973 328-3882
Wharton (G-11980)

Ballantine Laboratories Inc ....G 908 713-7742
Annandale (G-56)

Omnitester Corp ....F 856 985-8960
Marlton (G-5991)

Sadelco Inc ....D 201 569-3323
Fort Lee (G-3581)

Signal Crafters Tech Inc ....G 973 781-0880
East Hanover (G-2243)

INSTRUMENTS: Testing, Semiconductor

Radcom Equipment Inc ....G 201 518-0033
Paramus (G-7898)

INSTRUMENTS: Thermal Conductive, Indl

Align Sourcing Ltd Lblty Co ....G 609 375-8550
Trenton (G-11014)

INSTRUMENTS: Thermal Property Measurement

Setaram Inc ....G 908 262-7060
Cranbury (G-1879)

Temptime Corporation ....D 973 984-6000
Morris Plains (G-6680)

INSTRUMENTS: Vibration

Reliability Maintenance Svcs ....G 732 922-8878
Ocean (G-7741)

INSTRUMENTS: Viscometer, Indl Process

Gerin Corporation Inc ....G 732 774-3256
Neptune (G-6914)

INSULATING BOARD, CELLULAR FIBER

Homasote Company ....C 609 883-3300
Ewing (G-3024)

INSULATING COMPOUNDS

Insul-Stop Inc ....G 732 706-1978
Marlboro (G-5944)

INSULATION & CUSHIONING FOAM: Polystyrene

Evonik Foams Inc ....E 973 929-8000
Parsippany (G-8005)

PRODUCT

Johns Manville Corporation..................E 732 225-9190
Edison *(G-2548)*

Kohler Industries Inc..................G....336 545-3289
Paterson *(G-8311)*

Pacor Inc..................E 609 324-1100
Bordentown *(G-607)*

Poly Molding LLC..................F 973 835-7161
Haskell *(G-4213)*

INSULATION & ROOFING MATERIALS:
Wood, Reconstituted

Bmca Holdings Corporation..................E 973 628-3000
Wayne *(G-11610)*

Johns Manville Corporation..................E 732 225-9190
Edison *(G-2548)*

Standard Industries Inc..................C 856 241-0241
Swedesboro *(G-10728)*

Standard Industries Inc..................A 973 628-3000
Parsippany *(G-8092)*

INSULATION MATERIALS WHOLESALERS

Fbm Galaxy Inc..................E 856 966-1105
Camden *(G-1066)*

Fluid Coating Systems Inc..................G 973 767-1028
Garfield *(G-3733)*

Pacor Inc..................E 609 324-1100
Bordentown *(G-607)*

INSULATION: Fiberglass

Insulation Materials Distrs..................G 908 925-2323
Linden *(G-5388)*

INSULATORS, PORCELAIN: Electrical

Curran-Pfeiff Corp..................F 732 225-0555
Edison *(G-2499)*

Mitronics Products Inc..................G 908 647-5006
Gillette *(G-3795)*

New Jersey Porcelain Co Inc..................F 609 394-5376
Trenton *(G-11086)*

INSURANCE BROKERS, NEC

Webannuitiescom Inc..................G 732 521-5110
Monroe *(G-6376)*

INTEGRATED CIRCUITS, SEMICONDUCTOR NETWORKS, ETC

Advanced Micro Devices Inc..................C 732 787-2892
North Middletown *(G-7556)*

Alcatel-Lucent USA Inc..................D 908 582-3275
New Providence *(G-7026)*

Analog Devices Inc..................E 732 868-7100
Somerset *(G-10058)*

Ateksis USA Corp..................G 201 340-2655
Garfield *(G-3720)*

Ateksis USA Corp..................G 646 508-9074
East Rutherford *(G-2280)*

Candela Corporation..................F 908 753-6300
South Plainfield *(G-10343)*

Digitron Electronic Corp..................E 908 245-2012
Kenilworth *(G-4952)*

Hydraulic Manifolds Usa LLC..................E 973 728-1214
West Milford *(G-11852)*

Nokia of America Corporation..................A 908 582-3275
New Providence *(G-7050)*

Solid State International Inc..................G 201 429-8700
Bloomfield *(G-530)*

Xybion Corporation..................C 973 538-2067
Lawrenceville *(G-5273)*

INTERCOMMUNICATIONS SYSTEMS:
Electric

Abris Distribution Inc..................G 732 252-9819
Manalapan *(G-5836)*

AT&T Services Inc..................A 732 420-3131
Middletown *(G-6210)*

Bogen Communications Inc..................D 201 934-8500
Mahwah *(G-5754)*

Bogen Corporation..................G 201 934-8500
Ramsey *(G-9237)*

Crestron Electronics Inc..................C 201 767-3400
Rockleigh *(G-9628)*

Electronic Marine Systems Inc..................F 732 680-4120
Rahway *(G-9185)*

Elymat Corp..................E 201 767-7105
Old Tappan *(G-7798)*

Elymat Industries Inc..................E 201 767-7105
Old Tappan *(G-7799)*

Industronic Inc..................G 908 393-5960
Bridgewater *(G-845)*

L J Loeffler Systems Inc..................G 212 924-7597
Secaucus *(G-9901)*

Moniteur Devices Inc..................F 973 857-1600
Cedar Grove *(G-1292)*

Netquest Corporation..................E 856 866-0505
Mount Laurel *(G-6822)*

INTERIOR DECORATING SVCS

Greenbaum Interiors LLC..................D 973 279-3000
Paterson *(G-8281)*

INTERIOR DESIGN SVCS, NEC

American Intr Resources Inc..................G 908 851-0014
Union *(G-11151)*

Cronos-Prim Colorado LLC..................G 303 369-7477
Lodi *(G-5580)*

Masters Interiors Inc..................E 973 253-0784
Clifton *(G-1669)*

Ramsay David Cabinetmakers..................F 856 234-7776
Moorestown *(G-6618)*

INTERIOR DESIGNING SVCS

Bai Lar Interior Services Inc..................G 732 738-0350
Fords *(G-3527)*

Carole Hchman Design Group Inc..................C 866 267-3945
Jersey City *(G-4724)*

Good Impressions Inc..................G 856 461-3232
Riverside *(G-9498)*

Gordon Frgson Intr Dsigns Svcs..................G 973 378-2330
Maplewood *(G-5920)*

Insign Inc..................E 856 424-1161
Cherry Hill *(G-1381)*

INTERIOR REPAIR SVCS

Atlas Auto Trim Inc..................G 732 985-6800
Edison *(G-2468)*

Suburban Auto Seat Co Inc..................F 973 778-9227
Lodi *(G-5603)*

INTRAVENOUS SOLUTIONS

Fractal Solutions Corp..................G 201 608-6828
Edgewater *(G-2439)*

Nextron Medical Tech Inc..................D 973 575-0614
Fairfield *(G-3270)*

INVENTOR

Bishop Ascendant Inc..................G 973 210-5298
West Caldwell *(G-11768)*

INVERTERS: Nonrotating Electrical

Avionic Instruments LLC..................C 732 388-3500
Avenel *(G-126)*

INVERTERS: Rotating Electrical

Power Magne-Tech Corp..................E 732 826-4700
Perth Amboy *(G-8626)*

INVESTMENT FUNDS, NEC

Stanger Robert A & Co LP..................E 732 389-3600
Shrewsbury *(G-10011)*

INVESTORS, NEC

Al Tayyar Enrgy- Princeton LLC..................G 609 479-8603
Princeton *(G-9000)*

Capsugel Holdings Us Inc..................G 862 242-1700
Morristown *(G-6697)*

IRON & STEEL: Corrugating, Cold-Rolled

General Sullivan Group Inc..................E 609 745-5004
Pennington *(G-8451)*

IRON OXIDES

Rockwood Holdings Inc..................E 609 514-0300
Princeton *(G-9113)*

IRRADIATION EQPT

Gray Star Inc..................G 973 398-3331
Mount Arlington *(G-6755)*

JANITORIAL & CUSTODIAL SVCS

Aus Inc..................G 856 234-9200
Mount Laurel *(G-6779)*

G T M Signs Inc..................G 856 227-2333
Deptford *(G-2064)*

Ronell Industries Inc..................B 908 245-5255
Roselle *(G-9682)*

JANITORIAL EQPT & SPLYS WHOLESALERS

Americhem Enterprises Inc..................G 732 363-4840
Lakewood *(G-5072)*

T & B Specialties Inc..................G 732 928-4500
Jackson *(G-4679)*

JARS: Plastic

Parkway Plastics Inc..................E 732 752-3636
Piscataway *(G-8798)*

JEWELERS' FINDINGS & MATERIALS

Solmor Manufacturing Co Inc..................G 973 824-7203
Newark *(G-7320)*

Victors Three-D Inc..................D 201 845-4433
Maywood *(G-6062)*

JEWELERS' FINDINGS & MATERIALS:
Bearings, Synthetic

Moser Jewel Company..................G 908 454-1155
Phillipsburg *(G-8660)*

JEWELERS' FINDINGS & MATERIALS:
Castings

Diamond Universe LLC..................F 201 592-9500
Fort Lee *(G-3551)*

Joseph Castings Inc..................F 201 712-0717
Maywood *(G-6056)*

JEWELERS' FINDINGS & MTLS: Jewel Prep, Instr, Tools, Watches

Master Presentations Inc..................F 732 239-7093
Lakewood *(G-5155)*

Movado Group Inc..................B 201 267-8000
Paramus *(G-7890)*

JEWELERS' FINDINGS/MTRLS: Gem Prep, Settings, Real/Imitation

Mdviani Designs Inc..................G 201 840-5410
Ridgefield *(G-9373)*

JEWELRY & PRECIOUS STONES WHOLESALERS

Diamond Hut Jewelry Exchange..................G 201 332-5372
Jersey City *(G-4743)*

Enamel Art Studio..................G 732 321-0774
Metuchen *(G-6103)*

Imperium Enterprises LLC..................G 908 206-4970
Little Ferry *(G-5509)*

Ultimate Trading Corp..................D 973 228-7700
Fairfield *(G-3332)*

Unistar Inc..................G 212 840-2100
Princeton *(G-9134)*

United Diam Inc..................G 732 619-0950
Matawan *(G-6034)*

JEWELRY APPAREL

Creations By Sherry Lynn LLC..................G 800 742-3448
Florham Park *(G-3497)*

Moonbabies LLC..................G 609 926-0201
Somers Point *(G-10047)*

Shopindia Inc..................G 732 409-0656
Marlboro *(G-5958)*

JEWELRY FINDINGS & LAPIDARY WORK

Grassman-Blake Inc..................E 973 379-6170
Millburn *(G-6251)*

Tessler & Weiss/Premesco Inc..................C 800 535-3501
Union *(G-11228)*

JEWELRY REPAIR SVCS

DAmore Jewelers..................F 201 945-0530
Cliffside Park *(G-1537)*

Diamond Hut Jewelry Exchange ....G...... 201 332-5372
　Jersey City (G-4743)
Good As Gold Jewelers Inc ....G...... 732 286-1111
　Toms River (G-10881)
Pretty Jewelry Co ....G...... 908 806-3377
　Flemington (G-3461)
Saud & Son Jewelry Inc ....G...... 201 866-4445
　West New York (G-11881)

JEWELRY STORES

Aubrey David Inc ....E...... 201 653-2200
　Jersey City (G-4711)
DBC Inc ....D...... 212 819-1177
　Teaneck (G-10747)
Diamond Hut Jewelry Exchange ....G...... 201 332-5372
　Jersey City (G-4743)
Scott Kay Inc ....C...... 201 287-0100
　Secaucus (G-9925)
Tsi Accessory Group Inc ....D...... 847 965-1700
　Parsippany (G-8104)

JEWELRY STORES: Precious Stones & Precious Metals

Anna J Chung Ltd ....F...... 917 575-8100
　Edgewater (G-2432)
Avanzato Jewelers LLC ....G...... 609 890-0500
　Trenton (G-11021)
Corbo Jewelers Inc ....F...... 973 777-1635
　Clifton (G-1592)
DAmore Jewelers ....F...... 201 945-0530
　Cliffside Park (G-1537)
Gem Vault Inc ....G...... 908 788-1770
　Flemington (G-3444)
George Press Inc ....F...... 973 992-7797
　Livingston (G-5533)
Goldstein Setting Co Inc ....F...... 908 964-1034
　Union (G-11190)
Good As Gold Jewelers Inc ....G...... 732 286-1111
　Toms River (G-10881)
Hickok Matthews Co Inc ....G...... 973 335-3400
　Montville (G-6489)
J Michaels Jewelers Inc ....G...... 908 771-9800
　Berkeley Heights (G-414)
M S Brown Mfg Jewelers ....G...... 609 522-7604
　Wildwood (G-12074)
Robertas Jewelers Inc ....G...... 973 875-5318
　Hamburg (G-4096)
Saud & Son Jewelry Inc ....G...... 201 866-4445
　West New York (G-11881)
W Kodak Jewelers Inc ....G...... 201 710-5491
　Hoboken (G-4503)

JEWELRY, PRECIOUS METAL: Bracelets

Franklin Mint LLC ....E...... 800 843-6468
　Fort Lee (G-3555)

JEWELRY, PRECIOUS METAL: Medals, Precious Or Semiprecious

Norco Inc ....E...... 908 789-1550
　Garwood (G-3781)

JEWELRY, PRECIOUS METAL: Mountings & Trimmings

Brad Garman Designs ....G...... 732 229-6670
　Long Branch (G-5621)

JEWELRY, PRECIOUS METAL: Necklaces

Bhamra Chain Manufacturing ....G...... 908 686-4555
　Union (G-11159)

JEWELRY, PRECIOUS METAL: Pearl, Natural Or Cultured

Grassman-Blake Inc ....E...... 973 379-6170
　Millburn (G-6251)

JEWELRY, PRECIOUS METAL: Pins

Barrasso & Blasi Industries ....F...... 973 761-0595
　Maplewood (G-5914)
Pin People LLC ....F...... 888 309-7467
　Montvale (G-6470)

JEWELRY, PRECIOUS METAL: Rings, Finger

Jostens Inc ....G...... 973 584-5843
　Succasunna (G-10624)
Lieberfarb Inc ....F...... 973 676-9090
　Rahway (G-9208)
Premesco Inc ....B...... 908 686-0513
　Union (G-11216)
Provost Square Associates Inc ....F...... 973 403-8755
　Caldwell (G-1032)
Tessler & Weiss/Premesco Inc ....C...... 800 535-3501
　Union (G-11228)
Trimarco Inc ....G...... 973 762-7380
　Maplewood (G-5929)

JEWELRY, PRECIOUS METAL: Rosaries/Other Sm Religious Article

Christian Art ....G...... 201 867-8096
　West New York (G-11862)
Devon Trading Corp ....E...... 973 812-9190
　Caldwell (G-1026)
Top Rated Shopping Bargains ....F...... 201 630-0770
　Hasbrouck Heights (G-4200)

JEWELRY, PRECIOUS METAL: Settings & Mountings

Creations By Stefano Inc ....G...... 201 863-8337
　Secaucus (G-9875)
Goldstein Setting Co Inc ....F...... 908 964-1034
　Union (G-11190)
Greater New Jersey Diamnd Exch ....G...... 732 752-6446
　Green Brook (G-3856)

JEWELRY, WHOLESALE

Alster Import Co Inc ....F...... 201 332-7245
　Jersey City (G-4704)
Diamond Universe LLC ....F...... 201 592-9500
　Fort Lee (G-3551)
Gold Signature Incorporated ....G...... 732 777-9170
　Piscataway (G-8769)
Heights Jewelers LLC ....F...... 201 825-2381
　Allendale (G-10)
J Michaels Jewelers Inc ....G...... 908 771-9800
　Berkeley Heights (G-414)
Mj Gross Company - NJ ....G...... 212 542-3199
　Lakewood (G-5162)
Saud & Son Jewelry Inc ....G...... 201 866-4445
　West New York (G-11881)
Scaasis Originals Inc ....E...... 732 775-7474
　Neptune (G-6928)
Scott Kay Sterling LLC ....G...... 201 287-0100
　Secaucus (G-9926)
Superior Jewelry Co ....F...... 215 677-8100
　Northfield (G-7564)
Trimarco Inc ....G...... 973 762-7380
　Maplewood (G-5929)

JEWELRY: Decorative, Fashion & Costume

Golden Treasure Imports Inc ....G...... 732 723-1830
　Englishtown (G-2992)
HMS Monaco Et Cie Ltd ....E...... 201 533-0007
　Jersey City (G-4765)
Infinite Classic Inc ....G...... 973 227-2790
　Fairfield (G-3231)
Jacmel Jewelry Inc ....G...... 201 223-0435
　Secaucus (G-9897)
Lighthouse Express Inc ....G...... 732 776-9555
　Asbury Park (G-80)
Littlegifts Inc ....F...... 212 868-2559
　Secaucus (G-9902)
Nes Jewelry Inc ....D...... 646 213-4094
　Clifton (G-1680)
Norco Inc ....G...... 908 789-1550
　Garwood (G-3781)
Q-Eximtrade Inc ....G...... 732 366-4667
　Carteret (G-1267)
Swarovski North America Ltd ....G...... 732 632-1856
　Edison (G-2634)
Swarovski North America Ltd ....G...... 856 686-1805
　Deptford (G-2068)
Swarovski North America Ltd ....G...... 856 662-5453
　Cherry Hill (G-1425)
Swarovski North America Ltd ....G...... 201 265-4888
　Paramus (G-7908)
Swarovski North America Ltd ....G...... 609 344-1323
　Atlantic City (G-108)
Tapia Accessory Group Inc ....G...... 201 393-0028
　Teterboro (G-10815)

Tsi Accessory Group Inc ....D...... 847 965-1700
　Parsippany (G-8104)
Ultimate Trading Corp ....D...... 973 228-7700
　Fairfield (G-3332)
Umbrella & Chairs LLC ....G...... 973 284-1240
　Englewood (G-2939)

JEWELRY: Precious Metal

Alex and Ani LLC ....G...... 908 965-1510
　Elizabeth (G-2707)
All State Medal Co Inc ....G...... 973 458-1458
　Lodi (G-5575)
Anna J Chung Ltd ....F...... 917 575-8100
　Edgewater (G-2432)
Aubrey David Inc ....E...... 201 653-2200
　Jersey City (G-4711)
Avanzato Jewelers LLC ....G...... 609 890-0500
　Trenton (G-11021)
Avigdor Ltd Liability Company ....E...... 973 898-4770
　Morristown (G-6691)
Aydin Jewelry Menufacturing ....G...... 201 818-1002
　Ramsey (G-9236)
Bergio International Inc ....G...... 973 227-3230
　Fairfield (G-3148)
Bernard D Ascenzo ....G...... 856 795-0511
　Haddonfield (G-4056)
Big Apple Jewelry Mfg ....G...... 201 531-1600
　East Rutherford (G-2286)
Cherish Designs LLC ....G...... 856 751-8034
　Mount Laurel (G-6787)
Cinco Star LLC ....G...... 732 744-1617
　Edison (G-2483)
D Paglia & Sons Inc ....F...... 908 654-5999
　Mountainside (G-6872)
DAmore Jewelers ....F...... 201 945-0530
　Cliffside Park (G-1537)
Danmola Lara ....G...... 973 762-7581
　South Orange (G-10302)
David E Connolly Inc ....F...... 908 654-4600
　Mountainside (G-6874)
DBC Inc ....D...... 212 819-1177
　Teaneck (G-10747)
Diamond Hut Jewelry Exchange ....G...... 201 332-5372
　Jersey City (G-4743)
Enamel Art Studio ....G...... 732 321-0774
　Metuchen (G-6103)
European Imports of LA Inc ....F...... 973 536-1823
　Paramus (G-7868)
Fehu Jewel LLC ....C...... 609 297-5491
　Plainsboro (G-8881)
Gaurika LLC ....G...... 201 496-1613
　Cliffside Park (G-1539)
Gem Vault Inc ....G...... 908 788-1770
　Flemington (G-3444)
George Press Inc ....F...... 973 992-7797
　Livingston (G-5533)
Gold Buyers At Mall LLC ....G...... 201 512-5780
　Mahwah (G-5779)
Gold Signature Incorporated ....G...... 732 777-9170
　Piscataway (G-8769)
Great Falls Metalworks Inc ....G...... 973 523-6811
　Paterson (G-8280)
H Ritani LLC ....E...... 888 974-8264
　Closter (G-1759)
Heights Jewelers LLC ....F...... 201 825-2381
　Allendale (G-10)
Imperium Enterprises LLC ....G...... 908 206-4970
　Little Ferry (G-5509)
Jct Design Enterprises Inc ....E...... 212 629-7412
　Union City (G-11251)
Jost Brothers Jewelry Mfg Corp ....F...... 908 453-2266
　Washington (G-11584)
Joy Jewelery America Inc ....G...... 201 689-1150
　River Vale (G-9471)
K B Enterprises of New Jersey ....G...... 908 451-5282
　Hillsborough (G-4353)
Kole Design LLC ....G...... 732 409-0211
　Freehold (G-3664)
Krementz & Co ....G...... 973 621-8300
　Springfield (G-10563)
Labrada Inc ....G...... 201 461-2641
　Leonia (G-5317)
Littlegifts Inc ....F...... 212 868-2559
　Secaucus (G-9902)
Lusterline Inc ....G...... 201 758-5148
　Union City (G-11255)
M S Brown Mfg Jewelers ....G...... 609 522-7604
　Wildwood (G-12074)
Mdviani Designs Inc ....G...... 201 840-5410
　Ridgefield (G-9373)

Midas Designs Ltd ....G 201 567-2700
   Maywood (G-6058)

Mj Gross Company - NJ ....G 212 542-3199
   Lakewood (G-5162)

Nadri Inc. ....G 201 585-0088
   Fort Lee (G-3572)

NEi Gold Products of NJ ....E 201 488-5858
   Hackensack (G-3951)

Nei Jewelmasters of New Jersey ....D 201 488-5858
   Hackensack (G-3952)

Netfruits Inc ....G 732 249-2588
   New Brunswick (G-6985)

Paul Winston Fine Jewelry Grou ....F 800 232-2728
   Englewood Cliffs (G-2977)

Pearl Baumell Company Inc ....G 415 421-2113
   Rutherford (G-9743)

Pretty Jewelry Co ....G 908 806-3377
   Flemington (G-3461)

Robert Manse Designs LLC ....E 732 428-8305
   Rahway (G-9220)

Robertas Jewelers Inc ....G 973 875-5318
   Hamburg (G-4096)

Samuel Jewels Inc ....F 201 439-1555
   Bergenfield (G-394)

Sara Emporium Inc ....G 201 792-7222
   Jersey City (G-4823)

Saud & Son Jewelry Inc ....G 201 866-4445
   West New York (G-11881)

Scott Kay Inc ....C 201 287-0100
   Secaucus (G-9925)

Scott Kay Sterling LLC ....C 201 287-0100
   Secaucus (G-9926)

Tapia Accessory Group Inc ....E 201 393-0028
   Teterboro (G-10815)

Ultimate Trading Corp ....D 973 228-7700
   Fairfield (G-3332)

Unistar Inc ....G 212 840-2100
   Princeton (G-9134)

United Diam Inc ....G 732 619-0950
   Matawan (G-6034)

W Kodak Jewelers Inc ....G 201 710-5491
   Hoboken (G-4503)

W W Jewelers Inc ....D 718 392-4500
   Jersey City (G-4845)

Weinman Bros Inc ....E 212 695-8116
   Jersey City (G-4847)

Wlxt LLC ....D 732 906-7979
   Metuchen (G-6133)

World Class Marketing Corp ....E 201 313-0022
   Fort Lee (G-3591)

Zsombor Antal Designs Inc ....F 201 225-1750
   River Edge (G-9468)

JOB PRINTING & NEWSPAPER PUBLISHING COMBINED

Evening Journal Association ....F 201 653-1000
   Secaucus (G-9881)

JOB TRAINING & VOCATIONAL REHABILITATION SVCS

Avyakta It Services LLC ....F 609 790-7517
   East Windsor (G-2352)

Reuge Management Group Inc ....G 888 306-3253
   Hoboken (G-4495)

KAOLIN MINING

JM Huber Corporation ....D 732 603-3630
   Edison (G-2546)

KITCHEN ARTICLES: Coarse Earthenware

Durand Glass Mfg Co Inc ....A 856 327-1850
   Millville (G-6300)

KITCHEN CABINET STORES, EXC CUSTOM

European Country Kitchens Inc ....D 908 735-6659
   Pittstown (G-8850)

Millner Kitchens Inc ....G 609 890-7300
   Trenton (G-11081)

Taylor Made Cabinets Inc ....E 609 978-6900
   Manahawkin (G-5834)

KITCHEN CABINETS WHOLESALERS

Bossen Architectural Millwork ....F 856 786-1100
   Cinnaminson (G-1449)

Creative Cabinet Designs Inc ....F 973 402-5886
   Boonton (G-561)

Kinzee Industries Inc ....F 201 408-4301
   Englewood (G-2907)

Mango Custom Cabinets Inc ....F 908 813-3077
   Hackettstown (G-4019)

Metroplex Products Company Inc ....G 732 249-0653
   Monroe Township (G-6384)

Mk Wood Inc ....G 973 450-5110
   Belleville (G-308)

Shekia Group LLC ....E 732 372-7666
   Edison (G-2616)

Vinos Custom Mllwk & Finshg ....G 732 356-1147
   Middlesex (G-6209)

KITCHEN TOOLS & UTENSILS WHOLESALERS

Kraftware Corporation ....E 732 345-7091
   Roselle (G-9674)

KITCHEN UTENSILS: Bakers' Eqpt, Wood

Corbion Group ....G 973 256-0198
   Totowa (G-10940)

HB Technik USA Ltd Lblty Prtnr ....G 973 875-8688
   Branchville (G-731)

KITCHEN UTENSILS: Wooden

Forino Kitchen Cabinets Inc ....G 201 573-0990
   Park Ridge (G-7920)

Wees Beyond Products Corp ....F 862 238-8800
   Passaic (G-8189)

KITCHENWARE STORES

Adagio Teas Inc ....G 973 253-7400
   Elmwood Park (G-2801)

Tatara Group Inc ....G 732 231-6031
   Avenel (G-155)

KITS: Plastic

Triumph Plastics LLC ....G 973 584-5500
   Flanders (G-3421)

KNIVES: Agricultural Or indl

Baumer of America Inc ....F 973 263-1569
   Towaco (G-10988)

LABELS: Cotton, Printed

Star Narrow Fabrics Inc ....G 973 778-8600
   Lodi (G-5602)

LABELS: Paper, Made From Purchased Materials

Aeon Industries Inc ....G 732 246-3224
   Somerset (G-10050)

CCL Label Inc ....C 609 586-1332
   Robbinsville (G-9512)

Custom Quick Label Inc ....G 856 596-7555
   Marlton (G-5969)

Magnetic Ticket & Label Corp ....E 973 759-6500
   Belleville (G-305)

Renell Label Print Inc ....G 201 652-6544
   Paramus (G-7899)

United Label Corp ....F 973 589-6500
   Newark (G-7354)

LABELS: Woven

Beau Label ....D 973 318-7800
   Hillside (G-4396)

LABOR RESOURCE SVCS

Doolan Industries Incorporated ....G 856 985-1880
   Marlton (G-5973)

LABORATORIES, TESTING: Food

Chemo Dynamics Inc ....F 732 721-4700
   Sayreville (G-9817)

LABORATORIES, TESTING: Hazardous Waste

SGS UStesting Company ....F 973 575-5252
   Fairfield (G-3306)

LABORATORIES, TESTING: Product Testing

Chromak Research Inc ....G 732 560-1366
   Somerset (G-10082)

Dengen Scientific Corporation ....E 201 687-2983
   Union City (G-11245)

Randcastle Extrusion Systems ....G 973 239-1150
   Cedar Grove (G-1298)

LABORATORIES, TESTING: Product Testing, Safety/Performance

Lockheed Martin Corporation ....C 856 722-3336
   Moorestown (G-6595)

LABORATORIES: Biological

Genzyme Corporation ....G 973 256-2106
   Totowa (G-10948)

LABORATORIES: Biological Research

Edge Therapeutics Inc ....E 800 208-3343
   Berkeley Heights (G-410)

Emisphere Technologies Inc ....F 973 532-8000
   Roseland (G-9649)

Sanofi US Services Inc ....F 908 231-4000
   Bridgewater (G-890)

Soligenix Inc ....G 609 538-8200
   Princeton (G-9120)

LABORATORIES: Biotechnology

Advanced Biotech Overseas LLC ....G 973 339-6242
   Totowa (G-10926)

Bezwada Biomedical LLC ....G 908 281-7529
   Hillsborough (G-4320)

Biophore LLC ....G 609 275-3713
   Plainsboro (G-8876)

Celldex Therapeutics Inc ....C 908 200-7500
   Hampton (G-4155)

Cmic Cmo USA Corporation ....E 609 395-9700
   Cranbury (G-1824)

Epicore Networks USA Inc ....E 609 267-9118
   Mount Holly (G-6770)

Hydromer Inc ....C 908 526-2828
   Branchburg (G-665)

Imclone Systems LLC ....D 908 218-0147
   Branchburg (G-667)

Leo Pharma Inc ....G 973 637-1690
   Madison (G-5728)

Oli Systems Inc ....E 973 539-4996
   Cedar Knolls (G-1320)

Ptc Therapeutics Inc ....B 908 222-7000
   South Plainfield (G-10425)

SGS UStesting Company ....F 973 575-5252
   Fairfield (G-3306)

SPS Alfachem Inc ....G 973 676-5141
   Orange (G-7828)

LABORATORIES: Commercial Nonphysical Research

Ihs Inc ....G 201 391-0084
   Woodcliff Lake (G-12194)

SGS UStesting Company ....F 973 575-5252
   Fairfield (G-3306)

LABORATORIES: Dental Orthodontic Appliance Production

Em Orthodontic Labs Inc ....G 201 652-4411
   Waldwick (G-11446)

LABORATORIES: Dental, Crown & Bridge Production

Samuel H Fields Dental Labs ....E 201 343-4626
   Hackensack (G-3971)

LABORATORIES: Electronic Research

Bel Hybrids & Magnetics Inc ....F 201 432-0463
   Jersey City (G-4716)

Doralex Inc ....G 856 764-0694
   Delran (G-2016)

Intertek Laboratories Inc ....E 908 903-1800
   Stirling (G-10601)

Sensors Unlimited Inc ....D 609 333-8000
   Princeton (G-9116)

Xybion Corporation ....C 973 538-2067
   Lawrenceville (G-5273)

LABORATORIES: Environmental Research

Indoor Environmental Tech.................E 973 709-1122
Lincoln Park *(G-5327)*

LABORATORIES: Medical

DRG International Inc ....E 973 564-7555
Springfield *(G-10551)*
First National Servicing & Dev.............E 732 341-5409
Toms River *(G-10877)*
Fresenius Med Care Hldings Inc ....G 201 767-7700
Rockleigh *(G-9629)*
Radnet Inc..F 908 709-1323
Cranford *(G-1924)*

LABORATORIES: Medical Pathology

Oncode-Med Inc ....G 908 998-3647
Basking Ridge *(G-201)*

LABORATORIES: Noncommercial Research

Air Liquide Advanced Materials ....F 908 231-9060
Branchburg *(G-629)*
Engility LLC ....F 703 633-8300
Princeton Junction *(G-9152)*
National Housing Institute ....G 973 509-1600
Montclair *(G-6424)*

LABORATORIES: Physical Research, Commercial

Admera Health LLC...............................G 908 222-0533
South Plainfield *(G-10321)*
Alteon ....G 201 934-1624
Ramsey *(G-9232)*
Bayer Healthcare LLC ....A 862 404-3000
Whippany *(G-12008)*
Bristol-Myers Squibb Company ....G 609 252-4875
Princeton *(G-9019)*
Bristol-Myers Squibb Company ....E 212 546-4000
Hillside *(G-4399)*
Centurum Information Tech Inc.............G 856 751-1111
Marlton *(G-5967)*
Collagen Matrix Inc ....D 201 405-1477
Oakland *(G-7679)*
Cyalume Specialty Products Inc ....E 732 469-7760
Bound Brook *(G-617)*
Datwyler Pharma Packaging ....E 856 663-2202
Pennsauken *(G-8500)*
Dengen Scientific Corporation ....E 201 687-2983
Union City *(G-11245)*
Elementis Specialties Inc ....C 609 443-2000
East Windsor *(G-2374)*
Heritage Pharma Labs Inc.....................C 732 238-7880
East Brunswick *(G-2159)*
High-Technology Corporation ....F 201 488-0010
Hackensack *(G-3926)*
J M M R Inc ....G 201 612-5104
Fair Lawn *(G-3097)*
Janssen Global Services LLC................F 908 704-4000
Raritan *(G-9309)*
Janssen Research & Dev LLC ....A 908 704-4000
Raritan *(G-9310)*
LOreal Usa Inc ....D 732 499-6690
Clark *(G-1507)*
Pharmaseq Inc ....G 732 355-0100
Monmouth Junction *(G-6355)*
Scynexis Inc ....F 201 884-5485
Jersey City *(G-4825)*
Topifram Laboratories Inc ....E 201 894-9020
Englewood Cliffs *(G-2982)*

LABORATORIES: Testing

Alcami New Jersey Corporation............D 732 346-5100
Edison *(G-2455)*
Quest Diagnostics Incorporated ....A 973 520-2700
Secaucus *(G-9915)*
SGS UStesting Company ....F 973 575-5252
Fairfield *(G-3306)*

LABORATORIES: Testing

A M K Glass Inc ....G 856 692-1488
Vineland *(G-11318)*
Ballantine Laboratories Inc ....G 908 713-7742
Annandale *(G-56)*
C W Brabender Instrs Inc ....E 201 343-8425
South Hackensack *(G-10256)*
Coperion Corporation ....C 201 327-6300
Sewell *(G-9946)*

Design of Tomorrow Inc ....F 973 227-1000
Fairfield *(G-3177)*
Enroute Computer Solutions Inc...........B 609 569-9255
Egg Harbor Township *(G-2684)*
Gibraltar Laboratories Inc ....E 973 227-6882
Fairfield *(G-3209)*
Reliability Maintenance Svcs................G 732 922-8878
Ocean *(G-7741)*
Sk & P Industries Inc ....G 973 482-1864
Newark *(G-7315)*
Sk & P Industries Inc ....G 973 482-1864
Newark *(G-7316)*
Spex Certiprep Inc ....D 732 549-7144
Metuchen *(G-6121)*
Surface Technology Inc..........................F 609 259-0099
Ewing *(G-3058)*

LABORATORY APPARATUS & FURNITURE

3d Biotek LLC..G 908 801-6138
Bridgewater *(G-806)*
Abox Automation Corp...........................G 973 659-9611
Pine Brook *(G-8679)*
Becton Dickinson and Company...........A 201 847-6800
Franklin Lakes *(G-3610)*
Bsi Corp ....E 631 589-1118
Nutley *(G-7643)*
C W Brabender Instrs Inc ....E 201 343-8425
South Hackensack *(G-10256)*
Diagenode Inc ....G 862 209-4680
Denville *(G-2036)*
Difco Laboratories Inc ....G 410 316-4113
Franklin Lakes *(G-3613)*
Fluid Dynamics Inc ....G 908 200-5823
Flemington *(G-3443)*
G & H Sheet Metal Works Inc................F 973 923-1100
Hillside *(G-4408)*
Handler Manufacturing Company ....E 908 233-7796
Westfield *(G-11926)*
Hel Inc ....G 440 208-7360
Lawrenceville *(G-5258)*
Lm Air Technology Inc...........................E 732 381-8200
Rahway *(G-9210)*
MSI Holdings LLC ....G 732 549-7144
Metuchen *(G-6115)*
S P Industries Inc ....D 215 672-7800
Buena *(G-948)*
Triad Scientific Inc ....G 732 292-1994
Manasquan *(G-5882)*
Waage Electric Inc ....G 908 245-9363
Kenilworth *(G-5004)*

LABORATORY APPARATUS, EXC HEATING & MEASURING

Microdata Instrument Inc ....F 908 222-1717
South Plainfield *(G-10406)*
Randcastle Extrusion Systems ....G 973 239-1150
Cedar Grove *(G-1298)*

LABORATORY APPARATUS: Sample Preparation Apparatus

Delaware Technologies Inc ....F 856 234-7692
Mount Laurel *(G-6792)*

LABORATORY APPARATUS: Shakers & Stirrers

Arrow Engineering Co Inc ....G 908 353-5229
Hillside *(G-4391)*

LABORATORY CHEMICALS: Organic

Acceledev Chemical LLC ....G 732 274-1451
Monmouth Junction *(G-6330)*
Bal-Edge Corporation............................G 973 895-8826
Eatontown *(G-2384)*
Biotech Support Group LLC ....G 732 613-1967
East Brunswick *(G-2139)*
Karebay Biochem Inc ....G 732 823-1545
Monmouth Junction *(G-6349)*
Spectrum Laboratory Pdts Inc...............C 732 214-1300
New Brunswick *(G-7004)*
Spectrum Laboratory Pdts Inc...............E 732 214-1300
New Brunswick *(G-7005)*

LABORATORY EQPT, EXC MEDICAL: Wholesalers

Microsolv Technology Corp....................F 732 578-1777
Eatontown *(G-2413)*
National Labnet Co ....E 732 417-0700
Iselin *(G-4636)*
Orlando Systems Ltd Lblty Co ....G 908 400-5052
North Plainfield *(G-7560)*
Scimedx Corporation ....E 800 221-5598
Dover *(G-2109)*
Tovatech LLC ....G 973 913-9734
Maplewood *(G-5928)*
Triad Scientific Inc ....G 732 292-1994
Manasquan *(G-5882)*

LABORATORY EQPT: Chemical

Scientifix LLC ....G 856 780-5871
Mount Laurel *(G-6838)*
Servolift LLC ....E 973 442-7878
Randolph *(G-9297)*
Spex Certiprep Inc ....D 732 549-7144
Metuchen *(G-6121)*
Spex Certiprep Group LLC ....F 208 204-6656
Metuchen *(G-6122)*
Spex Sample Prep LLC ....F 732 549-7144
Metuchen *(G-6124)*
Spex Sample Prep LLC ....F 732 549-7144
Metuchen *(G-6125)*

LABORATORY EQPT: Clinical Instruments Exc Medical

Exodon LLC...F 973 398-2900
Mount Arlington *(G-6754)*

LABORATORY EQPT: Incubators

Pacon Manufacturing Corp ....C 732 764-9070
Somerset *(G-10152)*

LABORATORY EQPT: Measuring

Dek Tron International Corp....................E 908 226-1777
Plainfield *(G-8857)*
Ohaus Corporation ....D 973 377-9000
Parsippany *(G-8051)*

LACE GOODS & WARP KNIT FABRIC DYEING & FINISHING

Keystone Dyeing and Finishing ....G 718 482-7780
Dayton *(G-1975)*
Rebtex Inc...C 908 722-3549
Branchburg *(G-698)*

LAMINATED PLASTICS: Plate, Sheet, Rod & Tubes

Barnegat Light Fibrgls Sup LLC ....G 609 294-8870
West Creek *(G-11809)*
C & K Plastics Inc ....D 732 549-0011
Metuchen *(G-6098)*
Federal Plastics Corporation ....E 908 272-5800
Cranford *(G-1907)*
Fedplast Inc...F 732 901-1153
Lakewood *(G-5122)*
Flex Products LLC ....D 201 440-1570
Carlstadt *(G-1162)*
Fluorotherm Polymers Inc ....G 973 575-0760
Parsippany *(G-8014)*
Gabhen Inc ....C 800 631-3572
Totowa *(G-10945)*
K Jabat Inc ....F 732 469-8177
Green Brook *(G-3860)*
McGrory Glass Inc ....D 856 579-3200
Paulsboro *(G-8420)*
Nan Ya Plastics Corp America ....E 973 992-1775
Livingston *(G-5549)*
O Plast Matic Valves Inc ....D 973 256-3000
Cedar Grove *(G-1293)*
Owens Plastic Products Inc ....G 856 447-3500
Cedarville *(G-1324)*
Productive Plastics Inc ....D 856 778-4300
Mount Laurel *(G-6832)*
Research & Mfg Corp Amer ....F 908 862-6744
Linden *(G-5433)*
Royal Sovereign Intl Inc ....E 800 397-1025
Rockleigh *(G-9633)*

P
R
O
D
U
C
T

Spiral Binding LLC.................C...... 973 256-0666
Totowa (*G-10973*)

Wood & Laminates Inc..............G...... 973 773-7475
Lodi (*G-5609*)

LAMINATING MATERIALS

Nu Grafix Inc...........................E...... 201 413-1776
Jersey City (*G-4794*)

LAMP & LIGHT BULBS & TUBES

Amati International LLC ....E...... 201 569-1000
Englewood Cliffs (*G-2947*)

Ethan Allen Retail Inc ....C...... 973 473-1019
Passaic (*G-8139*)

Hamamatsu Corporation.............E...... 908 526-0941
Bridgewater (*G-842*)

Hamamatsu Corporation.............D...... 908 231-0960
Bridgewater (*G-841*)

Maxlite Inc...............................C...... 973 244-7300
West Caldwell (*G-11788*)

Mks Inc....................................E...... 856 451-5545
Bridgeton (*G-791*)

Oxberry LLC............................G...... 201 935-3000
Carlstadt (*G-1196*)

Standex International Corp ....G...... 732 469-8452
Middlesex (*G-6203*)

Superior Lamp Inc....................G...... 800 257-8353
Cherry Hill (*G-1423*)

LAMP BULBS & TUBES, ELECTRIC: Filaments

Union City Filament Corp...........E...... 201 945-3366
Ridgefield (*G-9390*)

LAMP BULBS & TUBES, ELECTRIC: For Specialized Applications

Bitro Group Inc........................E...... 201 641-1004
Hackensack (*G-3883*)

Metal Textiles Corporation.........E...... 800 843-1215
Edison (*G-2570*)

LAMP BULBS & TUBES, ELECTRIC: Light, Complete

Philips Lighting N Amer Corp.......B...... 732 563-3000
Somerset (*G-10154*)

LAMP BULBS & TUBES, ELECTRIC: Parts

Oxford Lamp Inc.......................F...... 732 462-3755
Freehold (*G-3676*)

LAMP BULBS & TUBES/PARTS, ELECTRIC: Generalized Applications

Precision Filaments Inc.............G...... 732 462-3755
Freehold (*G-3680*)

Rhingo Pro LLC.........................G...... 201 728-9099
Lodi (*G-5598*)

LAMP STORES

Jay-Bee Lamp & Shade Co Inc ....G...... 201 265-0762
Paramus (*G-7877*)

Nicholas Longo Sr....................G...... 856 642-1971
Riverton (*G-9508*)

LAMPS: Boudoir, Residential

Efficient Lighting Inc ....F...... 973 846-8568
Parsippany (*G-7999*)

LAMPS: Incandescent, Filament

Lumitron Corp ....F...... 908 508-9100
Berkeley Heights (*G-418*)

Natal Lamp & Shade Corp...........E...... 201 224-7844
Fort Lee (*G-3574*)

LAMPS: Ultraviolet

Hanovia Specialty Lighting LLC ......F...... 973 651-5510
Fairfield (*G-3215*)

Hid Ultraviolet LLC...................F...... 973 383-8535
Sparta (*G-10505*)

Horiba Instruments Inc ....E...... 732 623-8335
Piscataway (*G-8775*)

LAMPS: Wall, Residential

Genie House Corp.....................E...... 609 859-0600
Southampton (*G-10473*)

LANDING MATS: Aircraft, Metal

Helidex LLC ....G...... 201 636-2546
East Rutherford (*G-2299*)

LANGUAGE SCHOOLS

Berlitz Languages US Inc...........D...... 609 759-5371
Princeton (*G-9014*)

LAPIDARY WORK & DIAMOND CUTTING & POLISHING

J Michaels Jewelers Inc.............G...... 908 771-9800
Berkeley Heights (*G-414*)

LAPIDARY WORK: Jewel Cut, Drill, Polish, Recut/Setting

Corbo Jewelers Inc...................F...... 973 777-1635
Clifton (*G-1592*)

Good As Gold Jewelers Inc ....G...... 732 286-1111
Toms River (*G-10881*)

Zale Delaware Inc.....................G...... 201 291-0690
Paramus (*G-7914*)

LARD: From Slaughtering Plants

Buckhead Meat Company ....C...... 732 661-4900
Edison (*G-2476*)

LASER SYSTEMS & EQPT

Candela Corporation ....F...... 908 753-6300
South Plainfield (*G-10343*)

Cleary Machinery Co Inc............G...... 732 560-3200
South Bound Brook (*G-10248*)

Fastpulse Technology Inc...........F...... 973 478-5757
Saddle Brook (*G-9765*)

Gsi...G...... 908 608-1325
Summit (*G-10643*)

Haas Laser Technologies Inc.......G...... 973 598-1150
Flanders (*G-3410*)

Inrad Optics Inc.......................D...... 201 767-1910
Northvale (*G-7585*)

Laser Contractors LLC ....G...... 609 517-2407
Medford (*G-6075*)

Metrologic Instruments Inc.........C...... 856 228-8100
Mount Laurel (*G-6818*)

O S I Inc...................................F...... 732 754-6271
Metuchen (*G-6116*)

PRC Laser Corporation..............E...... 973 347-0100
Landing (*G-5226*)

Princeton Lightwave Inc............E...... 609 495-2600
Cranbury (*G-1873*)

Starlight Electro-Optics Inc........G...... 908 859-1362
Phillipsburg (*G-8671*)

Tiger Supplies Inc....................G...... 973 854-8635
Irvington (*G-4606*)

U S Laser Corp ....E...... 201 848-9200
Wyckoff (*G-12268*)

LASERS: Welding, Drilling & Cutting Eqpt

Ironbound Metal ....G...... 973 242-5704
Newark (*G-7200*)

LATEX: Foamed

Ansell Inc................................D...... 732 345-5400
Red Bank (*G-9320*)

LAUNDRIES, EXC POWER & COIN-OPERATED

Fine Wear U S A ....G...... 201 313-3777
Fort Lee (*G-3554*)

LAUNDRY & DRYCLEANING SVCS, EXC COIN-OPERATED: Pickup

Clean-Tex Services Inc ....B...... 908 912-2700
Trenton (*G-11042*)

LAUNDRY & GARMENT SVCS, NEC: Hand Laundries

One Click Cleaners ....G...... 732 804-9802
Manalapan (*G-5858*)

LAUNDRY & GARMENT SVCS: Tailor Shop, Exc Custom/Merchant

Forsters Cleaning & Tailoring.......G...... 201 659-4411
Jersey City (*G-4757*)

LAUNDRY EQPT: Commercial

One Click Cleaners ....G...... 732 804-9802
Manalapan (*G-5858*)

Utax USA Inc............................G...... 201 433-1200
Jersey City (*G-4842*)

LAUNDRY SVCS: Indl

A-1 Tablecloth Co Inc ....C...... 201 727-4364
South Hackensack (*G-10250*)

LAWN & GARDEN EQPT

Creative Products Inc................D...... 732 614-9035
Long Branch (*G-5622*)

Lawn Medic Inc ....G...... 856 742-1111
Westville (*G-11945*)

McQuade Enterprises LLC...........G...... 609 501-2437
Millville (*G-6313*)

W W Manufacturing Co Inc ....F...... 856 451-5700
Bridgeton (*G-802*)

LAWN MOWER REPAIR SHOP

Chatham Lawn Mowler...............G...... 973 635-8855
Chatham (*G-1327*)

Robert Colaneri ....G...... 201 939-4405
East Rutherford (*G-2321*)

LEAD

Alpha Assembly Solutions Inc.......E...... 908 561-5170
South Plainfield (*G-10325*)

Alpha Assembly Solutions Inc.......E...... 908 791-3000
Somerset (*G-10054*)

LEAD PENCILS & ART GOODS

Congruent Machine Co Inc...........G...... 973 764-6767
Vernon (*G-11297*)

Excel Hobby Blades Corp ....E...... 973 278-4000
Paterson (*G-8267*)

Faust Rudolph Inc.....................F...... 609 298-7334
Cranford (*G-1906*)

LEAD-IN WIRES: Electric Lamp

Seminole Wire & Cable Co Inc.......F...... 856 324-2929
Pennsauken (*G-8577*)

LEASING & RENTAL SVCS: Earth Moving Eqpt

Gamka Sales Co Inc..................E...... 732 248-1400
Edison (*G-2525*)

LEASING & RENTAL: Construction & Mining Eqpt

Harsco Corporation ....E...... 856 779-7795
Cherry Hill (*G-1374*)

Winslow Rental & Supply Inc.......G...... 856 767-5554
Berlin (*G-446*)

Xylem Dewatering Solutions Inc ......C...... 856 467-3636
Bridgeport (*G-775*)

LEASING & RENTAL: Medical Machinery & Eqpt

Enertia LLC ....G...... 856 330-4767
Pennsauken (*G-8508*)

Technidyne Corporation..............G...... 732 363-1055
Toms River (*G-10917*)

Tgz Acquisition Company LLC.......F...... 856 669-6600
Cherry Hill (*G-1428*)

LEASING & RENTAL: Other Real Estate Property

Grignard Company LLC ....E..... 732 340-1111
  Rahway *(G-9194)*

LEASING & RENTAL: Trucks, Without Drivers

Brunswick Hot Mix Corp ....D...... 908 233-4444
  Westfield *(G-11922)*
Fleetsource LLC ....E...... 732 566-4970
  Cliffwood *(G-1547)*
Stanley Steemer Intl Inc ....E...... 973 574-1640
  Clifton *(G-1731)*

LEASING: Passenger Car

Freehold Pntiac Bick GMC Trcks..........D..... 732 462-7093
  Freehold *(G-3656)*
Holman Enterprises Inc ....E...... 609 383-6100
  Mount Laurel *(G-6802)*
Town Ford Inc ....D...... 609 298-4990
  Bordentown *(G-613)*
Volvo Car North America LLC..............B...... 201 768-7300
  Rockleigh *(G-9636)*

LEATHER & CANVAS GOODS: Leggings Or Chaps, NEC

G S Babu & Co ....F...... 732 939-5190
  Plainsboro *(G-8882)*

LEATHER GOODS: Card Cases

Tumi Holdings Inc ....D...... 908 756-4400
  South Plainfield *(G-10442)*

LEATHER GOODS: Cases

Billykirk ....F...... 201 222-9092
  Jersey City *(G-4718)*

LEATHER GOODS: Cosmetic Bags

Jaclyn Holdings Parent LLC ....G...... 201 909-6000
  Maywood *(G-6053)*
Jaclyn LLC ....D...... 201 909-6000
  Maywood *(G-6054)*

LEATHER GOODS: Garments

Billykirk ....F...... 201 222-9092
  Jersey City *(G-4718)*
Bucati Leather Inc ....G...... 732 254-0480
  South River *(G-10459)*
Dibello USA Inc ....G...... 212 279-9099
  Randolph *(G-9273)*
North American Frontier Corp ....E...... 201 222-1931
  Jersey City *(G-4792)*

LEATHER GOODS: Personal

G-III Leather Fashions Inc ....D...... 212 403-0500
  Dayton *(G-1966)*
Maxsyl Leather Co LLC ....D...... 201 864-0579
  Union City *(G-11256)*
R Neumann & Co ....F...... 201 659-3400
  Hoboken *(G-4493)*

LEATHER GOODS: Safety Belts

Safe-Strap Company Inc ....E...... 973 442-4623
  Wharton *(G-11999)*

LEATHER GOODS: Wallets

Always Be Secure LLC ....G...... 917 887-2286
  Manalapan *(G-5838)*
M London Inc ....E...... 201 459-6460
  Jersey City *(G-4780)*

LEATHER TANNING & FINISHING

Dani Leather USA Inc ....G...... 973 598-0890
  Flanders *(G-3403)*

LEATHER, LEATHER GOODS & FURS, WHOLESALE

Bucati Leather Inc ....G...... 732 254-0480
  South River *(G-10459)*
Ledonne Leather Co Inc ....F...... 201 531-2100
  Lyndhurst *(G-5686)*

LEATHER: Accessory Prdts

Cejon Inc ....E.... 201 437-8780
  Bayonne *(G-217)*
Disys Commerce Inc ....G.... 201 567-0457
  Englewood *(G-2888)*

LEATHER: Bag

Jaclyn Holdings Parent LLC ....G.... 201 909-6000
  Maywood *(G-6053)*
Jaclyn LLC ....D.... 201 909-6000
  Maywood *(G-6054)*

LEATHER: Handbag

Buonaventura Bag and Cases LLC ......G..... 212 960-3442
  Clifton *(G-1579)*

LEATHER: Mechanical

Coast To Coast Lea & Vinyl Inc ....G.... 732 525-8877
  Sayreville *(G-9818)*

LEATHER: Processed

Maxsyl Leather Co LLC ....D.... 201 864-0579
  Union City *(G-11256)*

LEGAL & TAX SVCS

Max Pro Services LLC ....G.... 973 396-2373
  Livingston *(G-5542)*

LEGAL OFFICES & SVCS

Gann Law Books Inc ....F.... 973 268-1200
  Newark *(G-7169)*
Thomson Reuters Corporation ....F.... 973 662-3070
  Nutley *(G-7655)*

LEGAL SVCS: General Practice Attorney or Lawyer

Jose Moreira ....G.... 201 991-9001
  Kearny *(G-4890)*

LEGAL SVCS: Malpractice & Negligence Law

Madhu B Goyal MD ....G.... 908 769-0307
  South Plainfield *(G-10400)*

LENS COATING: Ophthalmic

Sensor Medical Technology LLC..........G.... 425 358-7381
  Denville *(G-2058)*

LETTER WRITING SVCS

Johnston Letter Co Inc ....G.... 973 482-7535
  Flanders *(G-3412)*

LIFE INSURANCE: Fraternal Organizations

Ukrainian National Association ....E.... 973 292-9800
  Parsippany *(G-8106)*

LIGHTER FLUID

Rclc Inc ....F.... 732 877-1788
  Woodbridge *(G-12152)*

LIGHTING EQPT: Flashlights

Gogreen Power Inc ....F.... 732 994-5901
  Howell *(G-4555)*
Princeton Tectonics ....C.... 609 298-9331
  Pennsauken *(G-8565)*

LIGHTING EQPT: Floodlights

Natale Machine & Tool Co Inc ....F.... 201 933-5500
  Carlstadt *(G-1191)*

LIGHTING EQPT: Motor Vehicle, Flasher Lights

Amperite Co Inc ....E.... 201 864-9503
  North Bergen *(G-7430)*
Elite Emrgncy Lights Ltd Lblty ....F.... 732 534-2377
  Lakewood *(G-5115)*

LIGHTING EQPT: Motor Vehicle, NEC

Spaghetti Engineering Corp ....F.... 856 719-9989
  West Berlin *(G-11751)*

LIGHTING EQPT: Outdoor

Archlit Inc ....G.... 973 577-4400
  Hopatcong *(G-4534)*
Garden State Irrigation ....F.... 201 848-1300
  Wyckoff *(G-12253)*
Princeton Tectonics ....E.... 609 298-9331
  West Berlin *(G-11743)*
Rab Lighting Inc ....C.... 201 784-8600
  Northvale *(G-7602)*
Wisely Products LLC ....G.... 929 329-9188
  Jersey City *(G-4850)*

LIGHTING EQPT: Spotlights

In The Spotlights ....G.... 973 361-7768
  Rockaway *(G-9573)*

LIGHTING FIXTURES WHOLESALERS

Articulight Inc ....G.... 201 796-2690
  Fair Lawn *(G-3077)*
Cuny & Guerber Inc ....E.... 201 617-5800
  Union City *(G-11244)*
Desmar Corporation ....G.... 908 317-0020
  Mountainside *(G-6876)*
Efficient Lighting Inc ....F.... 973 846-8568
  Parsippany *(G-7999)*
Gemini Cut Glass Company Inc ....G.... 201 568-7722
  Englewood *(G-2900)*
Robert Wallace ....G.... 609 649-0596
  Stockton *(G-10612)*

LIGHTING FIXTURES, NEC

A P M Hexseal Corporation ....E.... 201 569-5700
  Englewood *(G-2865)*
Amperite Co Inc ....E.... 201 864-9503
  North Bergen *(G-7430)*
Carpenter LLC ....F.... 609 689-3090
  Trenton *(G-11034)*
City Theatrical Inc ....E.... 201 549-1160
  Carlstadt *(G-1145)*
Cubalas Emergency Lighting LLC ....G.... 908 943-1615
  Linden *(G-5364)*
Desmar Corporation ....G.... 908 317-0020
  Mountainside *(G-6876)*
Eco Lighting USA Ltd Lblty Co.............G.... 201 621-5661
  South Hackensack *(G-10262)*
Erco Lighting Inc ....F.... 732 225-8856
  Edison *(G-2515)*
Galaxy Led Inc ....G.... 201 541-5461
  Englewood Cliffs *(G-2961)*
High Energy Group Ltd Lblty Co ....G.... 732 741-9099
  Eatontown *(G-2400)*
Innovtive Phtnics Slution Corp ....G.... 732 355-9300
  Monmouth Junction *(G-6348)*
John G Papailias Co Inc ....G.... 201 767-4027
  Northvale *(G-7588)*
Lightfox Inc ....E.... 973 209-9112
  Morristown *(G-6723)*
Michele Maddalena ....G.... 973 244-0033
  Fairfield *(G-3260)*
Musco Sports Lighting LLC ....G.... 732 751-9114
  Wall Township *(G-11498)*
Olympia Lighting Inc ....G.... 201 812-7880
  Northvale *(G-7598)*
Proactive Ltg Solutions LLC ....F.... 800 747-1209
  North Arlington *(G-7423)*
Tektite Industries Inc ....G.... 609 656-0600
  Trenton *(G-11120)*
Unilux Inc ....E.... 201 712-1266
  Saddle Brook *(G-9798)*
Zago Manufacturing Company ....E.... 973 643-6700
  Newark *(G-7362)*

LIGHTING FIXTURES: Airport

BNH Enterprise LLC ....G.... 201 815-0546
  Dumont *(G-2116)*

LIGHTING FIXTURES: Arc

Maxlite Inc ....G.... 800 555-5629
  West Caldwell *(G-11787)*

LIGHTING FIXTURES: Decorative Area

Encore Led Ltg Ltd Lblty Co..................G.... 866 694-4533
  Wayne *(G-11627)*
Trinity Manufacturing LLC ....G.... 732 549-2866
  Metuchen *(G-6129)*

Employee Codes: A=Over 500 employees, B=251-500
C=101-250, D=51-100, E=20-50, F=10-19, G=4-9
2018 Harris New Jersey
Manufacturers Directory
893
PRODUCT

LIGHTING FIXTURES: Fluorescent, Commercial

Coronet Inc ....C....... 973 345-7660
Totowa (G-10941)

R B B Corp ....E....... 973 770-1100
Ledgewood (G-5308)

LIGHTING FIXTURES: Indl & Commercial

Absolume LLC ....G....... 732 523-1231
Lakewood (G-5063)

Amati International LLC ....E....... 201 569-1000
Englewood Cliffs (G-2947)

American Brass and Crystal Inc ....E....... 908 688-8611
Union (G-11150)

Amerlux LLC ....C....... 973 882-5010
Oakland (G-7674)

Apelio Innovative Inds LLC ....F....... 973 777-8899
Kearny (G-4861)

Articulight Inc ....G....... 201 796-2690
Fair Lawn (G-3077)

Belfer ....G....... 732 493-2666
Farmingdale (G-3378)

Compact Fluorescent Systems ....G....... 908 475-8991
Sparta (G-10493)

Cooper Interconnect ....G....... 856 935-7560
Salem (G-9804)

Cooper Lighting LLC ....D....... 609 395-4277
Cranbury (G-1827)

D and J Industries LLC ....F....... 201 257-8953
Carlstadt (G-1152)

Durabrite Ltg Solutions LLC ....G....... 201 915-0555
Jersey City (G-4745)

Encore Led Ltg Ltd Lblty Co ....G....... 866 694-4533
Wayne (G-11627)

Genesis Lighting Mfg Inc ....G....... 908 352-6720
Elizabethport (G-2784)

Genlyte Thomas Group LLC ....E....... 800 825-5844
Somerset (G-10104)

Hal-O Manufacturing Co Inc ....G....... 973 824-6122
Newark (G-7183)

Lighting World Inc ....G....... 732 919-1224
Farmingdale (G-3388)

Luminaire Lighting Corp ....G....... 732 549-0056
Edison (G-2560)

M + 4 Inc ....G....... 973 527-3262
Budd Lake (G-934)

Mercury Lighting Pdts Co Inc ....C....... 973 244-9444
Fairfield (G-3259)

Mks Inc ....E....... 856 451-5545
Bridgeton (G-791)

North American Illumination ....F....... 973 478-4700
Garfield (G-3743)

Picasso Lighting Inds LLC ....E....... 201 246-8188
Kearny (G-4909)

Prg Group Inc ....G....... 201 758-4000
Secaucus (G-9913)

Rab Lighting Inc ....C....... 201 784-8600
Northvale (G-7602)

Rambusch Decorating Company ....G....... 201 333-2525
Jersey City (G-4815)

Reggiani Lighting Usa Inc ....F....... 201 372-1717
Carlstadt (G-1211)

Robert Wallace ....G....... 609 649-0596
Stockton (G-10612)

SMS Building Systems Ltd Lblty ......F....... 856 520-8769
Cherry Hill (G-1420)

Specialty Lighting Inds Inc ....E....... 732 517-0800
Ocean (G-7746)

Starfire Lighting Inc ....E....... 201 438-9540
Wood Ridge (G-12139)

Superior Lighting Inc ....F....... 908 759-0199
Elizabeth (G-2776)

Tektite Industries Inc ....G....... 609 656-0600
Trenton (G-11120)

Trinity Manufacturing LLC ....C....... 732 549-2866
Metuchen (G-6129)

Vision Lighting Inc ....G....... 973 720-1200
Paterson (G-8408)

LIGHTING FIXTURES: Motor Vehicle

Sun Display Systems LLC ....E....... 973 226-4334
Fairfield (G-3317)

Vehicle Safety Mfg LLC ....E....... 973 643-3000
Newark (G-7356)

LIGHTING FIXTURES: Public

ABB Lighting Inc ....G....... 866 222-8866
Toms River (G-10858)

LIGHTING FIXTURES: Residential

Amati International LLC ....E....... 201 569-1000
Englewood Cliffs (G-2947)

American Brass and Crystal Inc ....E....... 908 688-8611
Union (G-11150)

Apelio Innovative Inds LLC ....F....... 973 777-8899
Kearny (G-4861)

Big Eye Lamp Inc ....G....... 732 557-9400
Whiting (G-12065)

Cooper Lighting LLC ....D....... 609 395-4277
Cranbury (G-1827)

Cutting Edge Casting Inc ....G....... 908 925-7500
Linden (G-5366)

Estrin Calabrese Sales Agency ....G....... 908 722-9980
Manville (G-5895)

Galaxy Switchgear Inds LLC ....E....... 914 668-8200
Kearny (G-4876)

Generation Brands ....G....... 856 764-0500
Burlington (G-977)

Go R Design LLC ....E....... 609 286-2146
New Egypt (G-7015)

High Energy Group Ltd Lblty Co ....G....... 732 741-9099
Eatontown (G-2400)

Infinlight Products Inc ....G....... 888 665-7708
East Windsor (G-2360)

Kurt Versen Inc ....F....... 201 664-5283
Montvale (G-6464)

Lighting World Inc ....E....... 732 919-1224
Farmingdale (G-3388)

M + 4 Inc ....G....... 973 527-3262
Budd Lake (G-934)

R B B Corp ....E....... 973 770-1100
Ledgewood (G-5308)

Robert Wallace ....G....... 609 649-0596
Stockton (G-10612)

Sea Gull Lighting Products LLC ....B....... 856 764-0500
Delran (G-2021)

Starfire Lighting Inc ....E....... 201 438-9540
Wood Ridge (G-12139)

Superior Lighting Inc ....G....... 908 759-0199
Elizabeth (G-2776)

T C S Technologies Inc ....G....... 908 852-7555
Hackettstown (G-4039)

William Spencer ....G....... 856 235-1830
Mount Laurel (G-6847)

LIGHTING FIXTURES: Street

City of Jersey City ....F....... 201 547-4470
Jersey City (G-4728)

LIGHTING FIXTURES: Swimming Pool

Smartpool LLC ....E....... 732 730-9880
Lakewood (G-5189)

LIGHTING FIXTURES: Underwater

Pioneer & Co Inc ....E....... 856 866-9191
Moorestown (G-6613)

LIGHTING MAINTENANCE SVC

Forman Industries Inc ....D....... 732 727-8100
Old Bridge (G-7779)

LIME

Lime Energy Co ....G....... 732 791-5380
Newark (G-7219)

Smith Lime Flour Co Inc ....F....... 973 344-1700
Kearny (G-4914)

LIMESTONE: Crushed & Broken

Legacy Vulcan LLC ....E....... 973 253-8828
Clifton (G-1659)

Limecrest Quarry Developer LLC ......F....... 973 383-7100
Lafayette (G-5050)

LINEN SPLY SVC: Non-Clothing

Hozric LLC ....G....... 908 420-8821
Green Brook (G-3857)

LINENS & TOWELS WHOLESALERS

American Dawn Inc ....G....... 856 467-9211
Bridgeport (G-761)

Anchor Sales & Marketing Inc ....F....... 973 545-2277
West Milford (G-11850)

Living Fashions Llc ....F....... 732 626-5200
Sayreville (G-9830)

Professional Laundry Solutions ....G....... 973 392-0837
Newark (G-7278)

LINENS: Napkins, Fabric & Nonwoven, From Purchased Materials

Linen For Tables ....G....... 973 345-8472
Paterson (G-8322)

LINENS: Tablecloths, From Purchased Materials

R L Plastics Inc ....G....... 732 340-1100
Avenel (G-149)

Tablecloth Co Inc ....E....... 973 942-1555
Paterson (G-8396)

LINER STRIPS: Rubber

Rema Tip Top/North America Inc ......E....... 201 768-8100
Northvale (G-7605)

LINERS & COVERS: Fabric

Kerry Wilkens Inc ....G....... 732 787-0070
Belford (G-288)

Polyair Inter Pack Inc ....D....... 201 804-1700
Carlstadt (G-1205)

LINERS & LINING

Brennan Penrod Contractors LLC ......F....... 856 933-1100
Bellmawr (G-333)

Jaeger Thomas & Melissa DDS ....F....... 908 735-2722
Lebanon (G-5292)

Linden Well Drilling ....E....... 908 862-6633
Linden (G-5403)

LIQUEFIED PETROLEUM GAS DEALERS

American Compressed Gases Inc ....E....... 201 767-3200
Old Tappan (G-7797)

LIQUID CRYSTAL DISPLAYS

Dialight Corporation ....D....... 732 919-3119
Wall Township (G-11477)

Excel Display Corp ....G....... 732 246-3724
New Brunswick (G-6959)

LITHOGRAPHIC PLATES

AGFA Corporation ....G....... 908 231-5000
Somerville (G-10200)

LOCKS

Tiburon Lockers Inc ....G....... 201 750-4960
Rockleigh (G-9635)

LOCKS: Safe & Vault, Metal

Hookway Enterprises Inc ....F....... 973 691-0382
Netcong (G-6941)

LOG SPLITTERS

Custom Converters Inc ....E....... 201 994-9000
Livingston (G-5527)

LOGGING

Bamboo & Rattan Works Inc ....G....... 732 255-4239
Toms River (G-10866)

Green Land & Logging LLC ....G....... 908 894-2361
Stockton (G-10611)

Kane Wood Fuel ....G....... 856 589-3292
Pitman (G-8843)

Marzullo ....F....... 973 955-5309
Passaic (G-8160)

Mountain Top Logging LLC ....G....... 908 413-2982
Lebanon (G-5298)

LOOSELEAF BINDERS

Flortek Corporation ....E....... 201 436-7700
Bayonne (G-225)

Johnthan Leasing Corp ....E....... 908 226-3434
Lebanon (G-5293)

LOOSELEAF BINDERS: Library

Reed Presentations Inc ....G....... 908 832-0007
Lebanon (G-5301)

2018 Harris New Jersey
Manufacturers Directory

(G-0000) Company's Geographic Section entry number

LOTIONS OR CREAMS: Face

Alkaline Corporation................................G..... 732 531-7830
Eatontown (G-2380)

Americare Laboratories Ltd ....E..... 973 279-5100
Paterson (G-8210)

Millennium Research LLC ....G..... 908 867-7646
Long Valley (G-5639)

Novapac Laboratories Inc ....F..... 973 414-8800
Lincoln Park (G-5331)

R&R Cosmetics LLC................................G..... 732 340-1000
Rahway (G-9219)

Vsar Resources LLC ....F..... 973 233-6000
Monroe Township (G-6398)

LOUDSPEAKERS

GP Acoustics (us) Inc ....F..... 732 683-2356
Marlboro (G-5942)

LUBRICATING EQPT: Indl

Devco Corporation..................................G..... 201 337-1600
Basking Ridge (G-185)

T M Industries Inc ....G..... 908 730-7674
Belvidere (G-377)

LUBRICATION SYSTEMS & EQPT

Amerilubes LLC ....G..... 704 399-7701
Waretown (G-11532)

Intech Powercore Corporation ....G..... 201 767-8066
Closter (G-1761)

LUGGAGE & BRIEFCASES

Atco Products Inc ....E..... 973 379-3171
Springfield (G-10538)

Case Princeton Co Inc............................E..... 908 687-1750
Union (G-11163)

Iacobucci USA Inc ....G..... 732 935-6633
Eatontown (G-2404)

Lbu Inc ....E..... 973 773-4800
Paterson (G-8318)

Ledonne Leather Co Inc ....F..... 201 531-2100
Lyndhurst (G-5686)

Naluco Inc...D..... 800 601-8198
Clifton (G-1678)

Quiet Tone Inc ....G..... 732 431-2826
Freehold (G-3684)

Samsonite LLC..A..... 732 493-5146
Tinton Falls (G-10845)

Transglobe Usa Inc ....G..... 973 465-1998
Carlstadt (G-1232)

LUGGAGE & LEATHER GOODS STORES

Tumi Holdings Inc ....D..... 908 756-4400
South Plainfield (G-10442)

Venture Stationers Inc ....E..... 212 288-7235
Closter (G-1767)

LUGGAGE WHOLESALERS

Naluco Inc...D..... 800 601-8198
Clifton (G-1678)

LUGGAGE: Traveling Bags

Tumi Holdings Inc ....D..... 908 756-4400
South Plainfield (G-10442)

LUMBER & BLDG MATLS DEALER, RET: Garage Doors, Sell/Install

Door Center Enterprises Inc ....G..... 609 333-1233
Hopewell (G-4541)

Glen G Coats ....G..... 908 236-2620
Lebanon (G-5287)

LUMBER & BLDG MATRLS DEALERS, RET: Bath Fixtures, Eqpt/Sply

Tatara Group Inc ....G..... 732 231-6031
Avenel (G-155)

Toilettree Products Inc ....G..... 845 358-5316
Ramsey (G-9253)

LUMBER & BLDG MTRLS DEALERS, RET: Doors, Storm, Wood/Metal

Urban Millwork & Supply Corp ....G..... 973 278-7072
Paterson (G-8406)

LUMBER & BLDG MTRLS DEALERS, RET: Planing Mill Prdts/Lumber

Medford Cedar Products Inc...................G..... 609 859-1400
Southampton (G-10479)

LUMBER & BLDG MTRLS DEALERS, RET: Windows, Storm, Wood/Metal

Hudson & Bergen Company ....G..... 201 991-4900
Kearny (G-4881)

LUMBER & BUILDING MATERIALS DEALER, RET: Door & Window Prdts

Artistic Glass & Doors Inc.......................G..... 856 768-1414
West Berlin (G-11704)

Frank & Jims Inc ....G..... 609 646-1655
Pleasantville (G-8908)

Jersey Steel Door Inc ....G..... 973 482-4020
Newark (G-7207)

Lux Home Inc ....G..... 845 623-2821
Paramus (G-7886)

USA Wood Door Inc ....E..... 856 384-9663
West Deptford (G-11842)

Window Factory Inc ....E..... 856 546-5050
Mount Ephraim (G-6765)

LUMBER & BUILDING MATERIALS DEALER, RET: Masonry Matls/Splys

Efco Corp ....F..... 732 308-1010
Marlboro (G-5938)

J B & Sons Concrete Products ....F..... 856 767-4140
Berlin (G-435)

LUMBER & BUILDING MATERIALS DEALERS, RET: Solar Heating Eqpt

Mc Renewable Energy LLC ....F..... 732 369-9933
Manasquan (G-5873)

Sun Pacific Power Corp ....F..... 888 845-0242
Manalapan (G-5864)

LUMBER & BUILDING MATERIALS DEALERS, RETAIL: Countertops

Solidsurface Designs Inc ....E..... 856 910-7720
Pennsauken (G-8580)

LUMBER & BUILDING MATERIALS DEALERS, RETAIL: Tile, Ceramic

Akw Inc ....G..... 732 530-9186
Shrewsbury (G-9988)

Best Value Rugs & Carpets Inc..............G..... 732 752-3528
Dunellen (G-2127)

Gran All Mrble Tile Imprts Inc ....G..... 856 354-4747
Cherry Hill (G-1372)

Maranatha Ceramic Tile & Marbl ....E..... 609 758-1168
Wrightstown (G-12242)

LUMBER & BUILDING MATERIALS RET DEALERS: Millwork & Lumber

Bossen Architectural Millwork ....F..... 856 786-1100
Cinnaminson (G-1449)

Cwi Architectural Millwork LLC ....G..... 856 307-7900
Glassboro (G-3802)

Kempton Wood Products ....G..... 732 449-8673
Wall Township (G-11493)

Kuiken Brothers Company........................E..... 201 796-2082
Fair Lawn (G-3100)

New Jersey Hardwoods Inc ....E..... 908 754-0990
Plainfield (G-8869)

Vanco Millwork Inc..................................F..... 973 992-3061
Livingston (G-5568)

Wohners ....G..... 201 568-7307
Englewood (G-2944)

Wood Works ....G..... 856 728-4520
Williamstown (G-12115)

Woodhaven Lumber & Millwork ....C..... 732 901-0030
Lakewood (G-5206)

Woodtec Inc...G..... 908 979-0180
Hackettstown (G-4043)

LUMBER & BUILDING MATLS DEALERS, RET: Concrete/Cinder Block

Clayton Block Company Inc ....E..... 732 549-1234
Edison (G-2484)

Clayton Block Company Inc ....E..... 732 681-0186
Wall Township (G-11471)

LUMBER: Hardwood Dimension & Flooring Mills

Gwynn-E Co...G..... 215 423-6400
Moorestown (G-6581)

LUMBER: Plywood, Hardwood

Essex Coatings LLC ....F..... 732 855-9400
Avenel (G-130)

Rhoads OHara Architectural ....G..... 856 692-4100
Vineland (G-11397)

Woodhut LLC ....F..... 732 414-6440
Freehold (G-3694)

LUMBER: Rails, Fence, Round Or Split

New Jersey Fence & Guardrail ....F..... 973 786-5400
Andover (G-53)

Railing Dynamics Inc ....F..... 609 593-5400
Millville (G-6321)

LUMBER: Siding, Dressed

John H Abbott Inc ....G..... 609 561-0303
Hammonton (G-4140)

LUMBER: Veneer, Hardwood

Mannington Mills Inc ....A..... 856 935-3000
Salem (G-9806)

MACHINE PARTS: Stamped Or Pressed Metal

Cincinnati Thermal Spray Inc ....E..... 973 379-0003
Springfield (G-10547)

Eclipse Manufacturing LLC.....................G..... 973 340-9939
Garfield (G-3732)

Elray Manufacturing Company ....E..... 856 881-1935
Glassboro (G-3804)

Extruders International Inc ....G..... 908 241-7750
Roselle Park (G-9695)

Fine Manufacturing Inc ....F..... 201 880-9136
South Hackensack (G-10268)

Hafco Foundry & Machine Co ....G..... 201 447-0433
Midland Park (G-6228)

Infor Metal & Tooling Mfg ....F..... 973 571-9520
Cedar Grove (G-1285)

Joy-Rei Enterprises Inc ....G..... 732 727-0742
Parlin (G-7934)

K H Machine Works ....G..... 201 867-2338
North Bergen (G-7459)

LMC Precision Inc...................................F..... 973 522-0005
Newark (G-7222)

Mechanical Components Corp ....G..... 732 938-3737
Toms River (G-10896)

Medlaurel Inc ....E..... 856 461-6600
Delanco (G-2007)

Metal Cutting Corporation.......................D..... 973 239-1100
Cedar Grove (G-1291)

Philip Creter Inc ....G..... 908 686-2910
Union (G-11215)

Quality Swiss Screw Machine Co...........G..... 908 289-4334
Elizabeth (G-2770)

Sandik Manufacturing Inc ....G..... 973 779-0707
Passaic (G-8179)

TMU Inc ....F..... 609 884-7656
Cape May (G-1106)

V H Exacta Corp ....G..... 856 235-7379
Moorestown (G-6629)

Vulcan Tool Company Inc ....F..... 908 686-0550
Union (G-11233)

MACHINE SHOPS

Atlantic Casting & Engineering ....C..... 973 779-2450
Clifton (G-1567)

Atlas Recording Machines Corp..............G..... 732 295-3663
Point Pleasant Boro (G-8932)

Brenner Metal Products ....E..... 973 778-2466
Wallington (G-11524)

Brusso Hardware LLC ....F..... 212 337-8510
Belleville (G-297)

Cadpro Inc ....F..... 856 435-0050
Williamstown (G-12082)

PRODUCT

Components & Controls Inc ....F 201 483-9190
Carlstadt (G-1148)
Crown Precision Corp ....G 973 470-0097
Passaic (G-8132)
Henry Olsen Machine ....G 856 662-2121
Cinnaminson (G-1467)
Hercules Welding & Machine Co ....G 856 829-1820
Palmyra (G-7848)
Hydratight Operations Inc ....F 732 271-4100
Somerset (G-10110)
Jsm Co ....G 732 695-9577
Tinton Falls (G-10839)
Kavon Filter Products Co ....F 732 938-3135
Wall Township (G-11492)
M4 Machine LLC 718 928-9695
Livingston (G-5541)
Mjs Precision Inc 973 209-1300
Franklin (G-3601)
Philip Creter Inc ....G 908 686-2910
Union (G-11215)
Phoenix Machine Rebuilders Inc ....F 973 691-8029
Roxbury Township (G-9712)
Steel Mountain Fabricators LLC ....F 908 862-2800
Linden (G-5449)
Steel Mountain Fabricators LLC ....G 201 741-3019
North Bergen (G-7487)
Tomcel Machine Inc ....G 973 256-8257
Woodland Park (G-12235)
Triangle Manufacturing Co Inc ....D 201 825-1212
Upper Saddle River (G-11287)
Woods Industrial LLC ....F 973 208-0664
West Milford (G-11859)

MACHINE TOOL ACCESS: Cutting

Advanced Cutting Services LLC ....G 908 241-5332
Roselle (G-9659)
Alloy Cast Products Inc....................F 908 245-2255
Kenilworth (G-4936)
B & S Tool and Cutter Service 201 488-3545
Hackensack (G-3877)
B B Supply Corp 201 313-9021
Cliffside Park (G-1536)
E P Heller Company ....F 973 377-2878
Madison (G-5721)
Grobet File Company Amer LLC ....D 201 939-6700
Carlstadt (G-1165)
Kennametal Inc 412 248-8200
Jersey City (G-4771)
Maurice S Dessau Co Inc ....E 201 791-2005
Fair Lawn (G-3102)
Niko Trade Ltd-USA Inc ....G 973 575-4353
Fairfield (G-3271)
Sine Tru Tool Company Inc ....G 732 591-1100
Marlboro (G-5959)
Tool Shop Inc ....G 856 767-8077
West Berlin (G-11758)

MACHINE TOOL ACCESS: Diamond Cutting, For Turning, Etc

Accurate Diamond Tool Corp ....E 201 265-8868
Emerson (G-2855)
Accuratus Ceramic Corp ....E 908 213-7070
Phillipsburg (G-8638)
Dewitt Bros Tool Co Inc....................G 908 298-3700
Kenilworth (G-4951)
New Jersey Diamond Products Co ....F 973 684-0949
Paterson (G-8349)
Technodiamant USA Inc ....G 908 850-8505
Tranquility (G-11008)

MACHINE TOOL ACCESS: Dresser, Abrasive Wheel Or Other

Airbrasive Jet Tech LLC ....G 201 725-7340
Piscataway (G-8729)

MACHINE TOOL ACCESS: Drill Bushings, Drilling Jig

J and J Contractors ....F 856 765-7521
Millville (G-6309)

MACHINE TOOL ACCESS: Drills

Cutter Drill & Machine Inc ....G 732 206-1112
Howell (G-4550)

MACHINE TOOL ACCESS: Files

Ramco Manufacturing Co Inc ....E 908 245-4500
Kenilworth (G-4991)

MACHINE TOOL ACCESS: Hopper Feed Devices

Acrison Inc ....C 201 440-8300
Moonachie (G-6499)

MACHINE TOOL ACCESS: Machine Attachments & Access, Drilling

William T Hutchinson Company ....F 908 688-0533
Union (G-11235)

MACHINE TOOL ACCESS: Tool Holders

Aloris Tool Technology Co Inc ....E 973 772-1201
Clifton (G-1561)

MACHINE TOOL ACCESS: Tools & Access

Camden Tool Inc ....E 856 966-6800
Camden (G-1048)

MACHINE TOOL ATTACHMENTS & ACCESS

American Aeronautic Mfg Co ....G 973 442-8138
Pine Brook (G-8686)
Automated Tapping Systems Inc ....F 732 899-2282
Brick (G-735)
Engineered Components Inc ....F 908 788-8393
Three Bridges (G-10822)
Hainesport Tool & Machine Co ....F 609 261-0016
Mount Holly (G-6772)
R & H Co Inc 610 258-3177
Phillipsburg (G-8667)
Ringfeder Pwr Transm USA Corp.........E 201 666-3320
Westwood (G-11970)
Ss Tool & Manufacturing Co ....G 908 486-5497
Linden (G-5447)
Teknics Industries Inc ....D 973 633-7575
Lincoln Park (G-5333)
Totowa Precision Tooling Inc ....F 973 256-2283
Totowa (G-10976)

MACHINE TOOLS & ACCESS

Alpex Wheel Co Inc..........................F 201 871-1700
Tenafly (G-10781)
Astro Tool & Machine Co Inc ....E 732 382-2454
Rahway (G-9177)
Daven Industries Inc ....E 973 808-8848
Fairfield (G-3173)
Doosan Machine Tools Amer Corp......D 973 618-2500
Pine Brook (G-8700)
Energy Beams Inc ....F 973 291-6555
Bloomingdale (G-543)
F & R Grinding Inc ....F 908 996-0440
Frenchtown (G-3700)
H & W Tool Co Inc ....F 973 366-0131
Dover (G-2088)
Handler Manufacturing Company ....E 908 233-7796
Westfield (G-11926)
Indo-US Mim TEC Private Ltd ....G 734 327-9842
Princeton (G-9057)
Jdv Products Inc 201 794-6467
Fair Lawn (G-3098)
Jnt Technical Services Inc ....E 201 641-2130
Little Ferry (G-5511)
M D Carbide Tool Corp ....G 973 263-0104
Towaco (G-10998)
Sandvik Inc ....C 281 275-4800
Fair Lawn (G-3113)
Sandvik Inc 201 794-5000
Fair Lawn (G-3112)
Sk & P Industries Inc ....G 973 482-1864
Newark (G-7316)
Troy-Onic Inc ....E 973 584-6830
Kenvil (G-5014)
United Instrument Company LLC.........G 201 767-6000
Northvale (G-7610)

MACHINE TOOLS, METAL CUTTING: Cutoff

Armstrong and Sons Inc ....G 732 223-1555
Manasquan (G-5867)

MACHINE TOOLS, METAL CUTTING: Drilling

Autodrill LLC ....G 908 542-0244
Lebanon (G-5276)

MACHINE TOOLS, METAL CUTTING: Drilling & Boring

Picut Mfg Co Inc ....D 908 754-1333
Warren (G-11563)

MACHINE TOOLS, METAL CUTTING: Exotic, Including Explosive

Gauer Metal Products Co Inc..............E 908 241-4080
Kenilworth (G-4958)

MACHINE TOOLS, METAL CUTTING: Grind, Polish, Buff, Lapp

Web Industries Inc ....F 973 335-1200
Montville (G-6497)

MACHINE TOOLS, METAL CUTTING: Jig, Boring & Grinding

J and M Precision Inc ....G 856 661-9595
Pennsauken (G-8533)

MACHINE TOOLS, METAL CUTTING: Tool Replacement & Rpr Parts

American Mch Tool RPR Rbldg Co ....G 973 927-0820
Randolph (G-9269)
Uhlmann Packaging Systems LP ....D 973 402-8855
Towaco (G-11006)

MACHINE TOOLS, METAL FORMING: Bending

Promet Inc ....G 303 371-2300
Riverdale (G-9483)

MACHINE TOOLS, METAL FORMING: Container, Metal Incl Cans

Williams Scotsman Inc ....G 856 429-0315
Kearny (G-4922)

MACHINE TOOLS, METAL FORMING: Crimping, Metal

Bergen Cable Technology LLC ....E 973 276-9596
Fairfield (G-3147)

MACHINE TOOLS, METAL FORMING: Forming, Metal Deposit

Titanium Industries Inc......................E 973 983-1185
Rockaway (G-9613)

MACHINE TOOLS, METAL FORMING: Magnetic Forming

Magnetic Metals Corporation...............C 856 964-7842
Camden (G-1076)

MACHINE TOOLS, METAL FORMING: Marking

Cozzoli Machine Company ....D 732 564-0400
Somerset (G-10086)

MACHINE TOOLS, METAL FORMING: Mechanical, Pneumatic Or Hyd

Joy-Rei Enterprises Inc ....G 732 727-0742
Parlin (G-7934)

MACHINE TOOLS, METAL FORMING: Punching & Shearing

Bruderer Machinery Inc.....................E 201 941-2121
Ridgefield (G-9353)

MACHINE TOOLS, METAL FORMING: Rebuilt

C & S Machinery Rebuilding ....G 973 742-7302
Paterson (G-8228)

MACHINE TOOLS, METAL FORMING: Spinning, Metal

Ultimate Spinning Turning Corp............G...... 201 372-9740
Moonachie (G-6550)

MACHINE TOOLS: Metal Cutting

Alben Metal Products Inc ....G...... 973 279-8891
Paterson (G-8202)
Alfa Machine & Tool Co Inc..................F...... 973 227-1962
Fairfield (G-3129)
Array Solders Ltd Liability Co ....G...... 201 432-0095
Jersey City (G-4710)
Automated Tapping Systems Inc ....F...... 732 899-2282
Brick (G-735)
Camden Tool Inc ....E...... 856 966-6800
Camden (G-1048)
Charles F Kilian ....G...... 732 458-3554
Brick (G-736)
Chase Machine Co ....F...... 201 438-2214
Lyndhurst (G-5677)
Coretech International Inc ....F...... 908 454-7999
Alpha (G-40)
Cutter Drill & Machine Inc ....G...... 732 206-1112
Howell (G-4550)
Eastern Machining Corporation ....G...... 856 694-3303
Franklinville (G-3630)
Fecken-Kirfel America Inc ....F...... 201 891-5530
Mahwah (G-5771)
Gary R Marzili ....G...... 856 782-1546
Sicklerville (G-10019)
Hone-A-Matic Tool & Cutter Co ....G...... 732 382-6000
Rahway (G-9197)
Innovative Manufacturing Inc ....F...... 908 904-1884
Hillsborough (G-4346)
J & S Tool ....G...... 973 383-5059
Newton (G-7393)
Komo Machine Inc ....D...... 732 719-6222
Lakewood (G-5141)
L & M Machine & Tool Co Inc ....G...... 973 523-5288
Paterson (G-8313)
Lever Manufacturing Corp ....E...... 201 684-4400
Mahwah (G-5789)
Metaport Manufacturing LLC ....G...... 973 383-8363
Lafayette (G-5051)
NASA Machine Tools Inc ....E...... 973 633-5200
Lincoln Park (G-5330)
Nova Precision Products Inc ....C...... 973 625-1586
Rockaway (G-9590)
Oroszlany Laszlo ....G...... 201 666-2101
Hillsdale (G-4386)
Shor International ....E...... 973 520-8777
Madison (G-5735)
T A C Technical Instr Corp ....F...... 609 882-2894
Ewing (G-3059)
Tool Shop Inc ....G...... 856 767-8077
West Berlin (G-11758)
Tooling Etc LLC ....G...... 732 752-8080
Middlesex (G-6206)
Triple-T Cutting Tools Inc ....F...... 856 768-0800
West Berlin (G-11759)

MACHINE TOOLS: Metal Forming

Action Packaging Automation ....G...... 609 448-9210
Roosevelt (G-9639)
Benton Graphics Inc ....E...... 609 587-4000
Trenton (G-11026)
Doran LLC ....G...... 908 289-9200
Union (G-11172)
H & W Tool Co Inc ....F...... 973 366-0131
Dover (G-2088)
High-Technology Corporation ....F...... 201 488-0010
Hackensack (G-3926)
Hone-A-Matic Tool & Cutter Co ....G...... 732 382-6000
Rahway (G-9197)
Rotech Tool & Mold Co Inc ....G...... 908 241-9669
Kenilworth (G-4993)
Royle Systems Group LLC....................E...... 201 644-0345
Teterboro (G-10809)
Vantage Tool & Mfg Inc ....G...... 908 647-1010
Warren (G-11571)

MACHINERY & EQPT, AGRICULTURAL, WHOL: Farm Eqpt Parts/Splys

National Diversified Sales Inc.............G...... 559 562-9888
Bordentown (G-605)

MACHINERY & EQPT, AGRICULTURAL, WHOLESALE: Lawn & Garden

Creative Products Inc ....D...... 732 614-9035
Long Branch (G-5622)
Vandermolen Corp ....G...... 973 992-8506
Ledgewood (G-5313)

MACHINERY & EQPT, INDL, WHOL: Controlling Instruments/Access

American Process Systems...................G...... 908 216-6781
Port Murray (G-8974)
Johnson Controls Inc ....D...... 732 225-6700
Edison (G-2549)

MACHINERY & EQPT, INDL, WHOL: Environ Pollution Cntrl, Air

Tess-Com Inc..E...... 412 233-5782
Middlesex (G-6205)

MACHINERY & EQPT, INDL, WHOLESALE: Cement Making

Nobelus LLC ....G...... 800 895-2747
North Brunswick (G-7531)
P S I Cement Inc..................................G...... 609 716-1515
Princeton Junction (G-9160)

MACHINERY & EQPT, INDL, WHOLESALE: Chemical Process

Servolift LLC ....E...... 973 442-7878
Randolph (G-9297)

MACHINERY & EQPT, INDL, WHOLESALE: Compaction

Premier Compaction Systems ....F...... 718 328-5990
Woodland Park (G-12229)

MACHINERY & EQPT, INDL, WHOLESALE: Conveyor Systems

Das Installations Inc ....F...... 973 473-6858
Garfield (G-3728)
East Coast Storage Eqp Co Inc ....E...... 732 451-1316
Brick (G-742)
Robotunits Inc ....G...... 732 438-0500
Cranbury (G-1877)

MACHINERY & EQPT, INDL, WHOLESALE: Dairy Prdts Manufacturing

Dairy Delight LLC.................................F...... 201 939-7878
Rutherford (G-9729)

MACHINERY & EQPT, INDL, WHOLESALE: Drilling, Exc Bits

Morris Industries Inc ....E...... 973 835-6600
Pompton Plains (G-8963)

MACHINERY & EQPT, INDL, WHOLESALE: Engines & Parts, Diesel

Cummins Inc ....D...... 973 491-0100
Kearny (G-4870)
Rajysan Incorporated ....E...... 800 433-1382
Swedesboro (G-10722)

MACHINERY & EQPT, INDL, WHOLESALE: Engines, Gasoline

Monmouth Marine Engines Inc............F...... 732 528-9290
Brielle (G-913)

MACHINERY & EQPT, INDL, WHOLESALE: Food Manufacturing

Am-Mac Incorporated ....F...... 973 575-7567
Fairfield (G-3133)
Drytech Inc ....E...... 609 758-1794
Cookstown (G-1806)
McT Dairies Inc....................................F...... 973 258-9600
Millburn (G-6256)

MACHINERY & EQPT, INDL, WHOLESALE: Food Product Manufacturng

Solbern LLC..E...... 973 227-3030
Fairfield (G-3308)
Traycon Manufacturing Co Inc ....E...... 201 939-5555
Carlstadt (G-1233)

MACHINERY & EQPT, INDL, WHOLESALE: Hydraulic Systems

American Hose Hydraulic Co Inc ....E...... 973 684-3225
Paterson (G-8208)
Asa Hydraulik of America Inc ....G...... 908 541-1500
Branchburg (G-640)
Bristol-Donald Company Inc.................E...... 973 589-2640
Newark (G-7115)
Micheller & Son Hydraulics Inc ....F...... 908 687-1545
Roselle (G-9677)
Technol Inc ....F...... 856 848-5480
Westville (G-11949)
Van Hydraulics Inc ....E...... 732 442-5500
South Plainfield (G-10448)

MACHINERY & EQPT, INDL, WHOLESALE: Indl Machine Parts

Engineered Components Inc ....F...... 908 788-8393
Three Bridges (G-10822)
Inter Rep Associates Inc ....G...... 609 465-0077
Cape May Court House (G-1114)

MACHINERY & EQPT, INDL, WHOLESALE: Instruments & Cntrl Eqpt

Amega Scientific Corporation ....F...... 609 953-7295
Medford (G-6064)
Panel Components & Systems ....F...... 973 448-9400
Stanhope (G-10589)
Schneder Elc Bldngs Amrcas Inc..........E...... 201 348-9240
Secaucus (G-9922)
Sensor Products Inc ....E...... 973 884-1755
Madison (G-5734)

MACHINERY & EQPT, INDL, WHOLESALE: Machine Tools & Access

Autodrill LLC ....G...... 908 542-0244
Lebanon (G-5276)
Doosan Machine Tools Amer Corp........D...... 973 618-2500
Pine Brook (G-8700)
J R S Tool & Metal Finishing ....G...... 908 753-2050
South Plainfield (G-10387)
Rennsteig Tools Inc ....G...... 330 315-3044
Hackensack (G-3966)
Shor International ....E...... 973 520-8777
Madison (G-5735)

MACHINERY & EQPT, INDL, WHOLESALE: Machine Tools & Metalwork

Lmt Usa Inc..G...... 973 586-8722
Rockaway (G-9585)
Metaport Manufacturing LLC ....G...... 973 383-8363
Lafayette (G-5051)
P M Z Tool Inc ....G...... 908 647-2125
Stirling (G-10604)
Royal Master Grinders Inc ....D...... 201 337-8500
Oakland (G-7705)
Uhlmann Packaging Systems LP ....D...... 973 402-8855
Towaco (G-11006)

MACHINERY & EQPT, INDL, WHOLESALE: Measure/Test, Electric

Keyence Corporation America ....E...... 201 930-0100
Elmwood Park (G-2828)

MACHINERY & EQPT, INDL, WHOLESALE: Packaging

Abox Automation Corp..........................G...... 973 659-9611
Pine Brook (G-8679)
Ajg Packaging LLC ....G...... 908 528-6052
Pittstown (G-8848)
Campak Inc ....G...... 973 994-4888
Livingston (G-5526)
Cavalla Inc ....E...... 201 343-3338
Hackensack (G-3894)

PRODUCT

Integrated Packg Systems Inc ....G...... 973 664-0020
Denville *(G-2042)*
Modular Packaging Systems Inc ....F 973 970-9393
Rockaway *(G-9587)*
Pro Pack Inc ....F 201 485-7587
Wyckoff *(G-12260)*

MACHINERY & EQPT, INDL, WHOLESALE: Plastic Prdts Machinery

Yuhl Products Inc ....G...... 908 276-5180
Kenilworth *(G-5009)*

MACHINERY & EQPT, INDL, WHOLESALE: Power Plant Machinery

Process Controls Co ....G...... 908 269-8465
Chester *(G-1438)*

MACHINERY & EQPT, INDL, WHOLESALE: Processing & Packaging

Beauty-Pack LLC ....F 732 802-8200
Piscataway *(G-8741)*
Blispak Acquisition Corp ....D...... 973 884-4141
Whippany *(G-12013)*

MACHINERY & EQPT, INDL, WHOLESALE: Pulverizing

Pallmann Pulverizers Co Inc ....E 973 471-1450
Clifton *(G-1688)*

MACHINERY & EQPT, INDL, WHOLESALE: Recycling

Energy Recycling Co LLC ....G...... 732 545-6619
Highland Park *(G-4303)*

MACHINERY & EQPT, INDL, WHOLESALE: Screening

Charles M Jessup Inc ....G...... 732 324-0430
Keasbey *(G-4926)*

MACHINERY & EQPT, INDL, WHOLESALE: Sewing

Brother International Corp ....B 908 704-1700
Bridgewater *(G-825)*

MACHINERY & EQPT, INDL, WHOLESALE: Textile

Baxter Corporation ....F 201 337-1212
Franklin Lakes *(G-3607)*
Burlington Textile Machinery ....F 973 279-5900
Paterson *(G-8227)*
Megadyne America LLC ....E 973 227-4904
Fairfield *(G-3257)*

MACHINERY & EQPT, INDL, WHOLESALE: Textile & Leather

Satex Fabrics Ltd ....G...... 212 221-5555
North Bergen *(G-7484)*

MACHINERY & EQPT, WHOLESALE: Concrete Processing

A & A Concrete Products Inc ....G...... 973 835-2239
Riverdale *(G-9473)*

MACHINERY & EQPT, WHOLESALE: Construction & Mining, Ladders

Steelstran Industries Inc ....E 732 574-0700
Avenel *(G-152)*

MACHINERY & EQPT, WHOLESALE: Construction, General

Cleary Machinery Co Inc ....G...... 732 560-3200
South Bound Brook *(G-10248)*
Winslow Rental & Supply Inc ....G...... 856 767-5554
Berlin *(G-446)*

MACHINERY & EQPT: Electroplating

G & S Design & Manufacturing ....F 908 862-2444
Linden *(G-5377)*
Tilton Rack & Basket Co ....E 973 226-6010
Fairfield *(G-3326)*

MACHINERY & EQPT: Farm

3 IS Technologies Inc ....G...... 609 238-8213
Hainesport *(G-4067)*
Case Davenport Inc ....G...... 973 812-7180
Little Falls *(G-5473)*
Kinnery Precision LLC ....G...... 973 473-4664
Passaic *(G-8155)*

MACHINERY & EQPT: Gas Producers, Generators/Other Rltd Eqpt

Boc Group Inc ....A...... 908 665-2400
New Providence *(G-7030)*
Linde North America Inc ....D...... 908 464-8100
New Providence *(G-7045)*
Linde North America Inc ....B 908 464-8100
Bridgewater *(G-857)*
Mep Alaska LLC ....G...... 646 535-9005
Livingston *(G-5543)*

MACHINERY & EQPT: Liquid Automation

I & J Fisnar Inc ....F 973 646-5044
Pine Brook *(G-8703)*
Integrated Packg Systems Inc ....G...... 973 664-0020
Denville *(G-2042)*
Microdysis Inc ....G...... 609 642-1184
Bordentown *(G-604)*
Stauff Corporation ....E 201 444-7800
Waldwick *(G-11453)*
Valeur Corporation ....E 732 329-4666
Monmouth Junction *(G-6369)*

MACHINERY & EQPT: Metal Finishing, Plating Etc

Carl Buck Corporation ....G...... 973 300-5575
Sparta *(G-10491)*
Dayton Grey Corp ....F 732 869-0060
Asbury Park *(G-76)*
Metal Finishing Co LLC ....G...... 973 778-9550
Passaic *(G-8164)*
P & P Equipment Corporation ....F 201 489-0050
River Edge *(G-9467)*
Ramco Equipment Corp ....E 908 687-6700
Hillside *(G-4436)*
Sony Corporation of America ....F 201 930-1000
Woodcliff Lake *(G-12202)*

MACHINERY & EQPT: Petroleum Refinery

John W Kennedy Company ....G...... 973 256-5525
Little Falls *(G-5478)*

MACHINERY & EQPT: Vibratory Parts Handling Eqpt

Vibra Screw Inc ....E 973 256-7410
Totowa *(G-10980)*

MACHINERY BASES

Intermark Inc ....G...... 908 474-1311
Linden *(G-5390)*
Raceweld Co Inc ....G...... 908 236-6533
Lebanon *(G-5300)*
Uac Packaging LLC ....G...... 908 595-6890
Hillsborough *(G-4378)*

MACHINERY, CALCULATING: Calculators & Adding

Swintec Corp ....F 201 935-0115
Moonachie *(G-6548)*

MACHINERY, COMMERCIAL LAUNDRY & Drycleaning: Pressing

Hoffman/New Yorker Inc ....G...... 201 488-1800
Hackensack *(G-3928)*

MACHINERY, COMMERCIAL LAUNDRY: Washing, Incl Coin-Operated

Professional Laundry Solutions ....G...... 973 392-0837
Newark *(G-7278)*

MACHINERY, EQPT & SUPPLIES: Parking Facility

Amano Cincinnati Incorporated ....D...... 973 403-1900
Roseland *(G-9642)*
Amano USA Holdings Inc ....G...... 973 403-1900
Roseland *(G-9643)*
Kyosis LLC ....G...... 908 202-8894
South River *(G-10462)*
Park Plus Inc ....G...... 201 651-8590
Oakland *(G-7701)*

MACHINERY, FOOD PRDTS: Beverage

Absecon Island Beverage Co ....G...... 609 653-8123
Egg Harbor Township *(G-2676)*
Terriss Consolidated Inds ....F 732 988-0909
Asbury Park *(G-86)*

MACHINERY, FOOD PRDTS: Cutting, Chopping, Grinding, Mixing

Wyssmont Company Inc ....E 201 947-4600
Fort Lee *(G-3592)*
Zvonko Stulic & Son Inc ....G...... 973 589-3773
Newark *(G-7363)*

MACHINERY, FOOD PRDTS: Dairy & Milk

Arm & Hammer Animal Ntrtn LLC ....G...... 800 526-3563
Princeton *(G-9009)*

MACHINERY, FOOD PRDTS: Food Processing, Smokers

Basha USA LLC ....G...... 201 339-9770
Bayonne *(G-213)*

MACHINERY, FOOD PRDTS: Homogenizing, Dairy, Fruit/Vegetable

Hill Machine Inc ....G...... 973 684-2808
Paterson *(G-8289)*

MACHINERY, FOOD PRDTS: Mixers, Commercial

Cornell Machine Co Inc ....G...... 973 379-6860
Springfield *(G-10549)*
Willow Technology Inc ....G...... 732 671-1554
Holmdel *(G-4531)*

MACHINERY, FOOD PRDTS: Ovens, Bakery

Revent Incorporated ....E 732 777-5187
Somerset *(G-10166)*

MACHINERY, FOOD PRDTS: Processing, Poultry

Kuhl Corp ....D...... 908 782-5696
Flemington *(G-3454)*

MACHINERY, MAILING: Address Labeling

Acedepotcom ....F 800 844-0962
Northvale *(G-7568)*

MACHINERY, MAILING: Postage Meters

Pitney Bowes Inc ....F 908 903-2870
Warren *(G-11564)*
Pitney Bowes Inc ....C...... 800 521-0080
Newark *(G-7271)*
Pitney Bowes Inc ....C...... 856 764-2240
Delran *(G-2020)*

MACHINERY, METALWORKING: Assembly, Including Robotic

Boomerang Systems Inc ....E 973 538-1194
Florham Park *(G-3494)*

MACHINERY, METALWORKING: Coil Winding, For Springs

K & S Industries Inc.................................F 908 862-3030
Linden (G-5395)

MACHINERY, METALWORKING: Rotary Slitters, Metalworking

Progressive Ruesch Inc ....E 973 962-7700
Ringwood (G-9454)

MACHINERY, OFFICE: Sorters, Filing

Archive Designs Inc.................................G 973 242-6400
Newark (G-7090)
Hoarders Express LLC ....D 856 963-8471
Camden (G-1068)

MACHINERY, OFFICE: Stapling, Hand Or Power

Arrow Fastener Co LLC ....B 201 843-6900
Saddle Brook (G-9752)

MACHINERY, OFFICE: Time Clocks &Time Recording Devices

Amano Cincinnati Incorporated ....D 973 403-1900
Roseland (G-9642)
Amano USA Holdings Inc ....G 973 403-1900
Roseland (G-9643)
Time Systems International Co ....E 201 871-1200
Englewood (G-2937)

MACHINERY, OFFICE: Typing & Word Processing

Brother International Corp ....B 908 704-1700
Bridgewater (G-825)

MACHINERY, PACKAGING: Carton Packing

Golden W Ppr Converting Corp.............E 908 412-8889
South Plainfield (G-10374)
Quality Carton Inc ....F 201 529-6900
Mahwah (G-5805)
Supplyone New York Inc ....E 718 392-7400
Paterson (G-8392)

MACHINERY, PACKAGING: Packing & Wrapping

Gram Equipment.....................................E 201 750-6500
Hamilton (G-4107)
Hair Systems Inc ....D 732 446-2202
Englishtown (G-2994)
Pro Pack Inc ....F 201 485-7587
Wyckoff (G-12260)
Sjd Direct Midwest LLC ....C 732 985-8405
Edison (G-2620)
Sjd Direct Midwest LLC ....C 732 287-2525
Edison (G-2621)

MACHINERY, PACKAGING: Vacuum

Vacuum Solutions Group Inc................G 781 762-0414
Teaneck (G-10776)

MACHINERY, PAPER INDUSTRY: Converting, Die Cutting & Stampng

Holographic Finishing Inc ....F 201 941-4651
Ridgefield (G-9365)
Rotary Die Systems Inc ....G 856 234-3994
Moorestown (G-6619)

MACHINERY, PAPER INDUSTRY: Cutting

Retrievex..G 732 247-3200
New Brunswick (G-7001)

MACHINERY, PAPER INDUSTRY: Fourdrinier

Enser Corporation ....E 856 829-5522
Cinnaminson (G-1461)

MACHINERY, PRINTING TRADES: Bookbinding Machinery

On Demand Machinery ....F 908 351-7137
Elizabeth (G-2763)

MACHINERY, PRINTING TRADES: Bronzing Or Dusting

Wilenta Carting Inc ....F 201 325-0044
Secaucus (G-9939)

MACHINERY, PRINTING TRADES: Electrotyping

BNH Enterprise LLC ....G 201 815-0546
Dumont (G-2116)

MACHINERY, PRINTING TRADES: Plates

Galvanic Prtg & Plate Co Inc................E 201 939-3600
Moonachie (G-6518)
Mark/Trece Inc ....E 973 884-1005
Whippany (G-12026)
Marko Engraving & Art Corp ....F 201 864-6500
Weehawken (G-11698)
Marko Engraving & Art Corp ....F 201 945-6555
Fairview (G-3365)
Mosstype Corporation ....G 201 444-8000
Waldwick (G-11450)
Mosstype Holding Corp ....G 201 444-8000
Waldwick (G-11451)
Packaging Graphics Inc ....E 856 767-9000
West Berlin (G-11741)
Verico Technology LLC ....C 201 842-0222
East Rutherford (G-2336)

MACHINERY, PRINTING TRADES: Plates, Engravers' Metal

N B C Engraving Co Inc.........................G 201 387-8011
Bergenfield (G-390)

MACHINERY, PRINTING TRADES: Presses, Envelope

City Envelope Inc ....G 201 792-9292
Jersey City (G-4727)

MACHINERY, PRINTING TRADES: Presses, Gravure

Allison Systems Corporation.................F 856 461-9111
Riverside (G-9492)

MACHINERY, PRINTING TRADES: Printing Trade Parts & Attchts

Clarity Imaging Tech Inc........................E 877 272-4362
Saddle Brook (G-9759)
Clarity Imaging Tech Inc........................E 413 693-1234
Pennsauken (G-8493)
Clarity Imaging Tech Inc........................G 877 272-4362
Pennsauken (G-8494)

MACHINERY, PRINTING TRADES: Type, Foundry

Ernest Schaefer Inc ....G 908 964-1280
Union (G-11182)

MACHINERY, SEWING: Sewing & Hat & Zipper Making

Brother International Corp ....B 908 704-1700
Bridgewater (G-825)
Comfortfit Labs Inc ....E 908 259-9100
Roselle (G-9666)
N C Carpet Binding & Equipment.........F 973 481-3500
Newark (G-7247)

MACHINERY, TEXTILE: Card Clothing

Benjamin Booth Company ....F 609 859-1995
Southampton (G-10470)

MACHINERY, TEXTILE: Fiber & Yarn Preparation

I F Associates Inc..................................F 732 223-2900
Allenwood (G-36)

MACHINERY, TEXTILE: Finishing

D R Kenyon & Son Inc ....F 908 722-0001
Bridgewater (G-832)

Snapco Manufacturing Corp.................E 973 282-0300
Hillside (G-4441)

MACHINERY, TEXTILE: Loom Parts &Attachments, Jacquard

Baxter Corporation ....F 201 337-1212
Franklin Lakes (G-3607)

MACHINERY, TEXTILE: Winders

Lever Manufacturing Corp ....E 201 684-4400
Mahwah (G-5789)

MACHINERY, WOODWORKING: Box Making, For Wooden Boxes

Stapling Machines Inc ....E 973 627-4400
Rockaway (G-9609)

MACHINERY, WOODWORKING: Cabinet Makers'

Andys Custom Cabinets ....G 732 752-6443
Green Brook (G-3854)
Atlas Woodworking Inc ....G 201 784-1949
Closter (G-1756)
Fix It Guy...G 732 278-9000
Toms River (G-10878)
Kitchen and More Inc.............................F 908 272-3388
Cranford (G-1911)

MACHINERY, WOODWORKING: Furniture Makers

Samuelson Furniture Inc ....F 973 278-4372
Paterson (G-8377)

MACHINERY, WOODWORKING: Scarfing

Design of Tomorrow Inc ....F 973 227-1000
Fairfield (G-3177)

MACHINERY: Assembly, Exc Metalworking

Heller Industries Inc..............................D 973 377-6800
Florham Park (G-3505)
Independent Machine Company ....E 973 882-0060
Fairfield (G-3227)
Palmer Electronics Inc ....F 973 772-5900
Garfield (G-3744)
Pulsonics Inc ....F 800 999-6785
Belleville (G-313)
Remington Industries Inc ....F 908 233-0153
Mountainside (G-6887)

MACHINERY: Automotive Maintenance

Royal Aquarius Empire ....D 646 847-3322
Hamilton (G-4125)

MACHINERY: Automotive Related

Eagle Racing Inc ....G 732 367-8487
Lakewood (G-5112)
Eco-Plug-System LLC ....G 855 326-7584
Hewitt (G-4289)
M C Technologies Inc ....E 973 839-2779
Pompton Plains (G-8961)
Mastercraft Electroplating.....................G 908 354-4404
Elizabeth (G-2755)

MACHINERY: Brake Burnishing Or Washing

Clayton Associates Inc ....F 732 363-2100
Lakewood (G-5094)

MACHINERY: Centrifugal

Celestech Inc 856 986-2221
Haddonfield (G-4057)
Heinkel Filtering Systems Inc................F 856 467-3399
Swedesboro (G-10701)

MACHINERY: Concrete Prdts

Concrete Cutting Partners Inc..............G 201 440-2233
Hackensack (G-3898)

MACHINERY: Construction

Bestwall LLC ....D 856 966-7600
Camden (G-1044)

PRODUCT

Breeze-Eastern LLC ....D.... 973 602-1001
Whippany (G-12015)
Clark Equipment Company ....A.... 973 618-2500
Pine Brook (G-8694)
County of Warren ....D.... 908 475-7975
Belvidere (G-368)
Dougherty Foundation Products ....G.... 201 337-5748
Franklin Lakes (G-3615)
F and M Equipment Ltd ....D.... 215 822-0145
South Plainfield (G-10362)
Ingersoll-Rand Intl Inc ....D.... 559 271-4625
Piscataway (G-8778)
Multi-Pak Corporation ....E.... 201 342-7474
Hackensack (G-3949)
Reinco Inc ....F.... 908 755-0921
Plainfield (G-8873)
Solidia Technologies Inc ....E.... 908 315-5901
Piscataway (G-8813)
Terco Construction LLC ....F.... 973 551-7759
Newton (G-7409)
Tuff Mfg Co Inc ....G.... 201 796-5319
Elmwood Park (G-2852)

MACHINERY: Cryogenic, Industrial

Boc Group Inc ....A.... 908 665-2400
New Providence (G-7030)
Cryovation LLC ....G.... 609 914-4792
Hainesport (G-4071)
Linde North America Inc ....D.... 908 464-8100
New Providence (G-7045)
Linde North America Inc ....B.... 908 464-8100
Bridgewater (G-857)

MACHINERY: Custom

Chacko John ....G.... 732 494-1088
Edison (G-2481)
Coesia Health & Beauty Inc ....F.... 908 707-8008
Branchburg (G-648)
Connecting Products Inc ....G.... 609 688-1808
Skillman (G-10030)
Daven Industries Inc ....E.... 973 808-8848
Fairfield (G-3173)
Globe Industries Corp ....F.... 973 992-8990
Clifton (G-1627)
I I Galaxy Inc ....G.... 732 828-2686
New Brunswick (G-6966)
Imperial Machine & Tool Co ....E.... 908 496-8100
Columbia (G-1798)
Jordan Tooling & Manufacturing ....G.... 609 261-2636
Hainesport (G-4075)
Lazar Technologies Inc ....F.... 732 739-9622
Hazlet (G-4277)
Luso Machine Inc ....F.... 973 242-1717
Newark (G-7228)
National Mtal Fnshngs Corp Inc ....F.... 732 752-7770
Middlesex (G-6183)
New ERA Converting Machinery ....E.... 201 670-4848
Paterson (G-8347)
Northeast Precast Ltd Lblty Co ....D.... 856 765-9088
Millville (G-6317)
Norwalt Design Inc ....D.... 973 927-3200
Randolph (G-9291)
R G Smith Tool & Mfg Co ....F.... 973 344-1395
Newark (G-7282)
Royal Aquarius Empire ....D.... 646 847-3322
Hamilton (G-4125)
Sensor Products Inc ....E.... 973 884-1755
Madison (G-5734)
Spectrum Design LLC ....G.... 856 694-1870
Franklinville (G-3631)
Stuart Steel Protection Corp ....E.... 732 469-5544
Somerset (G-10174)
William Kenyon & Sons Inc ....E.... 732 985-8980
Piscataway (G-8836)

MACHINERY: Die Casting

Buhler Inc ....E.... 201 847-0600
Mahwah (G-5755)

MACHINERY: Electronic Component Making

Azego Technology Svcs US Inc ....G.... 201 327-7500
Oakland (G-7675)
Henry Dudley ....G.... 732 240-6895
Toms River (G-10883)
Htp Connectivity LLC ....G.... 973 586-2286
Rockaway (G-9572)
Rf360 Technologies Inc ....E.... 848 999-3582
Iselin (G-4642)

Ridge Manufacturing Corp ....D.... 973 586-2717
Rockaway (G-9604)

MACHINERY: Engraving

Cronite Co Inc ....E.... 973 887-7900
Parsippany (G-7977)

MACHINERY: Extruding, Synthetic Filament

American Leistritz Extruder ....F.... 908 685-2333
Branchburg (G-633)

MACHINERY: Folding

Microfold Inc ....G.... 201 641-5052
Teterboro (G-10806)

MACHINERY: Gas Separators

Linde LLC ....C.... 908 464-8100
Bridgewater (G-855)
Linde LLC ....G.... 973 579-2065
Sparta (G-10510)

MACHINERY: Gear Cutting & Finishing

Joe Mike Precision Fabrication ....F.... 609 953-1144
Medford (G-6073)

MACHINERY: General, Industrial, NEC

NJ Service Testing & Insptn ....G.... 732 221-6357
Lincroft (G-5340)

MACHINERY: Glass Cutting

Spadix Technologies Inc ....G.... 732 356-6906
Middlesex (G-6200)

MACHINERY: Glassmaking

Cain Machine Inc ....F.... 856 825-7225
Millville (G-6291)
Inter Rep Associates Inc ....G.... 609 465-0077
Cape May Court House (G-1114)

MACHINERY: Grinding

Everite Machine Products Co ....E.... 856 330-6700
Pennsauken (G-8509)
Glebar Operating LLC ....D.... 201 337-1500
Ramsey (G-9242)
Jet Pulverizer Co Inc ....E.... 856 235-5554
Moorestown (G-6588)
McGonegal Manufacturing Co ....E.... 201 438-2313
East Rutherford (G-2309)
Royal Master Grinders Inc ....D.... 201 337-8500
Oakland (G-7705)

MACHINERY: Ice Cream

Gram Equipment ....E.... 201 750-6500
Hamilton (G-4107)

MACHINERY: Ice Making

Iceboxx LLC ....G.... 201 857-0404
Wyckoff (G-12254)

MACHINERY: Industrial, NEC

Arch Custom Manufacturing Inc ....G.... 856 966-3835
Camden (G-1040)
Miemie Design Services Inc ....G.... 609 857-3688
Ltl Egg Hbr (G-5645)
Responsible Machines LLC ....G.... 917 740-2269
Highland Park (G-4304)

MACHINERY: Labeling

AT Information Products Inc ....G.... 201 529-0202
Mahwah (G-5750)
Clements Industries Inc ....E.... 201 440-5500
South Hackensack (G-10258)
Dalemark Industries Inc ....F.... 732 367-3100
Lakewood (G-5105)
Herma US Inc ....G.... 973 521-7254
Fairfield (G-3221)
ID Technology LLC ....E.... 201 405-0767
Oakland (G-7692)
Kompac Technologies LLC ....E.... 908 534-8411
Somerville (G-10220)
Labeling Systems LLC ....E.... 201 405-0767
Oakland (G-7694)

Weiler Labeling Systems LLC ....D.... 856 273-3377
Moorestown (G-6632)

MACHINERY: Lapping

Unique Precision Co Inc ....G.... 732 382-8699
Rahway (G-9227)

MACHINERY: Marking, Metalworking

A D J Group LLC ....G.... 609 743-2099
Bordentown (G-588)
Tri-Power Consulting Svcs LLC ....E.... 973 227-7100
Denville (G-2060)

MACHINERY: Metalworking

Air & Specialties Sheet Metal ....F.... 908 233-8306
Mountainside (G-6866)
Applied Resources Corp ....E.... 973 328-3882
Wharton (G-11980)
G L Tool & Manufacturing Co ....G.... 973 740-0001
Livingston (G-5532)
Lever Manufacturing Corp ....E.... 201 684-4400
Mahwah (G-5789)
Mac Products Inc ....D.... 973 344-5149
Kearny (G-4896)
Precious Metal Processing Cons ....G.... 201 944-8053
Palisades Park (G-7842)
Seal-Spout Corp ....F.... 908 647-0648
Liberty Corner (G-5324)
TMU Inc ....F.... 609 884-7656
Cape May (G-1106)
Weber and Scher Mfg Co Inc ....E.... 908 236-8484
Lebanon (G-5303)
Werko Machine Co ....F.... 856 662-0669
Pennsauken (G-8588)

MACHINERY: Milling

General Electric Company ....B.... 973 887-6635
Parsippany (G-8023)

MACHINERY: Mining

Hosokawa Micron International ....C.... 908 273-6360
Summit (G-10644)
International Process Eqp Co ....G.... 856 665-4007
Pennsauken (G-8530)

MACHINERY: Ozone

Science Pump Corporation ....E.... 856 963-7700
Camden (G-1085)
Suez Treatment Solutions Inc ....D.... 201 676-2525
Leonia (G-5320)

MACHINERY: Packaging

Action Packaging Automation ....G.... 609 448-9210
Roosevelt (G-9639)
Alliance Food Equipment ....F.... 201 784-1101
Trenton (G-11016)
Banarez Enterprises Inc ....G.... 201 222-7515
Jersey City (G-4713)
Campak Inc ....G.... 973 994-4888
Livingston (G-5526)
Copack International Inc ....E.... 973 405-5151
Clifton (G-1591)
Cozzoli Machine Company ....D.... 732 564-0400
Somerset (G-10086)
Deitz Co Inc ....F.... 732 295-8212
Belmar (G-357)
Elite Packaging Corp ....F.... 732 651-9955
East Brunswick (G-2150)
F P Developments Inc ....E.... 856 875-7100
Williamstown (G-12086)
Ganz Brothers Inc ....E.... 201 820-1975
Paramus (G-7870)
Gloucester City Box Works LLC ....F.... 856 456-9032
Gloucester City (G-3837)
Greener Corp ....E.... 732 341-3880
Bayville (G-255)
Groniger USA LLC ....G.... 704 588-3873
Basking Ridge (G-189)
Heisler Machine & Tool Co ....E.... 973 227-6300
Fairfield (G-3220)
Hekikat LLC ....G.... 908 232-1145
Middletown (G-6217)
I S Parts International Inc ....E.... 856 691-2203
Vineland (G-11372)
J G Machine Works Inc ....G.... 732 203-2077
Edison (G-2543)

K & S Industries Inc..............................F 908 862-3030
Linden *(G-5395)*

Kohl & Madden Prtg Ink Corp..........E 201 935-8666
Carlstadt *(G-1181)*

Luciano Packaging Technologies........G 908 722-3222
Branchburg *(G-676)*

Mactec Packaging Tech LLC.............G 732 343-1607
Sayreville *(G-9832)*

Njrls Enterprises Inc.........................F 732 846-6010
Branchburg *(G-683)*

Pabin Associates Inc.........................G 201 288-7216
Hasbrouck Heights *(G-4197)*

Pace Packaging LLC..........................D 973 227-1040
Fairfield *(G-3279)*

Packaging Machinery & Eqp Co........G 973 325-2418
West Orange *(G-11903)*

Per-Fil Industries Inc........................E 856 461-5700
Riverside *(G-9504)*

PMC Industries Inc...........................E 201 342-3684
Hackensack *(G-3963)*

Potdevin Machine Co.........................F 973 227-8828
West Caldwell *(G-11798)*

Pro-Motion Industries LLC................F 856 809-0040
Sicklerville *(G-10023)*

Pro-Pac Service Inc...........................F 973 962-8080
Ringwood *(G-9453)*

Prodo-Pak Corp................................F 973 772-4500
Garfield *(G-3752)*

Prodo-Pak Corporation......................E 973 777-7770
Garfield *(G-3753)*

Remington Industries Inc...................F 908 233-0153
Mountainside *(G-6887)*

Romaco Inc......................................E 973 709-0691
Lincoln Park *(G-5332)*

Scandia Packaging Machinery Co........E 973 473-6100
Fairfield *(G-3302)*

Techline Extrusion Systems..............G 973 831-0317
Haskell *(G-4215)*

Wagner Industries Inc.......................F 973 347-0800
Stanhope *(G-10592)*

Wrap-Ade Machine Co Inc.................G 973 773-6150
Clifton *(G-1744)*

Wrapade Packaging Systems LLC.......F 973 787-1788
Fairfield *(G-3355)*

MACHINERY: Paper Industry Miscellaneous

175 Derousse LLC.............................G 856 662-0100
Pennsauken *(G-8467)*

Colter & Peterson Inc........................E 973 684-0901
West Caldwell *(G-11771)*

Dietech Services LLC.........................G 973 667-0798
Nutley *(G-7646)*

Khanna Paper Inc.............................G 201 706-8050
Hoboken *(G-4482)*

Tri-State Knife Grinding Corp............E 609 890-4989
Robbinsville *(G-9523)*

Woodward Jogger Aerators Inc...........F 201 933-6800
East Rutherford *(G-2337)*

MACHINERY: Pharmaciutical

Alvogen Pharma Us Inc......................A 973 796-3400
Pine Brook *(G-8685)*

Amcor Phrm Packg USA LLC..............E 856 825-1400
Millville *(G-6281)*

American International Cont...............F 973 917-3331
Boonton *(G-554)*

Clordisys Solutions Inc......................E 908 236-4100
Branchburg *(G-647)*

Dantco Corp....................................F 973 278-8776
Paterson *(G-8245)*

Deitz Co Inc.....................................F 732 295-8212
Belmar *(G-357)*

Expert Process Systems LLC.............G 570 424-0581
Hackettstown *(G-4006)*

F P Developments Inc........................E 856 875-7100
Williamstown *(G-12086)*

Fette Compacting America Inc............E 973 586-8722
Rockaway *(G-9567)*

Globepharma Inc..............................F 732 296-9700
New Brunswick *(G-6964)*

Jason Equipment Corp.......................E 973 983-7212
Rockaway *(G-9579)*

Kahle Automation.............................G 973 993-1850
Morristown *(G-6719)*

Lmt Usa Inc.....................................G 973 586-8722
Rockaway *(G-9585)*

Logan Instruments Corporation..........F 732 302-9888
Somerset *(G-10125)*

Nicos Group Inc...............................G 201 768-9501
Norwood *(G-7631)*

Pharma Systems Inc..........................G 973 636-9007
Hawthorne *(G-4254)*

Specialty Measurements Inc...............F 908 534-1500
Lebanon *(G-5302)*

Victor International Marketing............G 973 267-8900
Morristown *(G-6749)*

MACHINERY: Plastic Working

Autoplast Systems Inc......................G 973 785-8333
Woodland Park *(G-12210)*

Coperion Corporation........................C 201 327-6300
Sewell *(G-9946)*

Foremost Machine Builders Inc...........D 973 227-0700
Fairfield *(G-3200)*

Jomar Corp......................................E 609 646-8000
Egg Harbor Township *(G-2687)*

R T Kuntz Co....................................F 732 751-1770
Wall Township *(G-11505)*

Seajay Manufacturing Corp................G 732 774-0900
Neptune *(G-6931)*

MACHINERY: Printing Presses

J Nelson Press Inc............................G 732 747-0330
Rumson *(G-9713)*

Karis Graphic Corp...........................G 201 935-8774
Moonachie *(G-6527)*

Kirkwood NJ Globe Acqstion LLC.......G 201 440-0800
Ridgefield Park *(G-9408)*

Mgl Printing Solution LLC.................G 908 665-1999
New Providence *(G-7048)*

MACHINERY: Recycling

Allied Waste Products Inc...................G 973 473-7638
Wallington *(G-11522)*

Clean Air Group...............................G 908 232-4200
Parsippany *(G-7973)*

County Conservation Co Inc...............F 856 227-6900
Sewell *(G-9948)*

Energy Recycling Co LLC...................G 732 545-6619
Highland Park *(G-4303)*

Glass Cycle Systems Inc....................G 973 838-0034
Riverdale *(G-9481)*

Graham Graphic Group Inc.................G 973 827-6177
Ogdensburg *(G-7771)*

Kooltronic Inc..................................C 609 466-3400
Pennington *(G-8455)*

Recycle-Tech Corp............................F 201 475-5000
Elmwood Park *(G-2847)*

Thanks For Being Green LLC..............E 856 333-0991
Pennsauken *(G-8584)*

MACHINERY: Riveting

Arrow Fastener Co LLC......................B 201 843-6900
Saddle Brook *(G-9752)*

MACHINERY: Road Construction & Maintenance

Hackettstown Public Works................G 908 852-2320
Hackettstown *(G-4010)*

MACHINERY: Rubber Working

Advance Machine Planning Inc...........F 732 356-4438
Middlesex *(G-6144)*

Colorcraft Sign Co............................F 609 386-1115
Beverly *(G-461)*

Reliable Welding & Mch Work.............E 201 865-1073
North Bergen *(G-7478)*

MACHINERY: Saw & Sawing

New Brunswick Saw Service Inc..........F 732 287-4466
Middlesex *(G-6184)*

Rowan Technologies Inc.....................D 609 267-9000
Rancocas *(G-9262)*

MACHINERY: Semiconductor Manufacturing

Advance Process Systems Lim............G 201 400-9190
Branchville *(G-724)*

Ileos of America Inc..........................C 908 753-7300
South Plainfield *(G-10383)*

Starlight Electro-Optics Inc...............G 908 859-1362
Phillipsburg *(G-8671)*

Veeco..E 732 560-5300
Somerset *(G-10192)*

Veeco Instruments Inc.......................E 732 560-5300
Somerset *(G-10193)*

MACHINERY: Sheet Metal Working

Trumpf Inc.......................................E 609 925-8200
Cranbury *(G-1886)*

Trumpf Photonics Inc........................C 609 925-8200
Cranbury *(G-1887)*

MACHINERY: Sifting & Screening

Eurodia Industrie SA.........................G 732 805-4001
Somerset *(G-10098)*

Kason Corporation............................D 973 467-8140
Millburn *(G-6254)*

MACHINERY: Specialty

A S M Technical................................G 973 225-0111
Paterson *(G-8193)*

Indoor Entertainment of NJ................E 609 522-6700
Wildwood *(G-12073)*

MACHINERY: Stone Working

Thompson Stone...............................G 973 293-7237
Montague *(G-6403)*

MACHINERY: Textile

A B C Machinery Corp........................G 609 971-0990
Forked River *(G-3532)*

Alfred Heitzman Machine Works..........G 201 489-8888
Moonachie *(G-6500)*

Burlington Textile Machinery..............F 973 279-5900
Paterson *(G-8227)*

C & S Machine Inc............................F 973 882-1097
Fairfield *(G-3153)*

Catbridge Machinery LLC...................E 973 808-0029
Montville *(G-6485)*

Clements Industries Inc.....................E 201 440-5500
South Hackensack *(G-10258)*

Daf Products Inc...............................F 201 251-1222
Wyckoff *(G-12249)*

Excel Industrial Co Inc.......................G 609 275-1748
Princeton Junction *(G-9154)*

M & S Machine & Tool Corp................F 973 345-5847
Paterson *(G-8327)*

Pecata Enterprises Inc.......................G 973 523-9498
Paterson *(G-8362)*

MACHINERY: Thread Rolling

Edston Manufacturing Company..........G 908 647-0116
Fairfield *(G-3182)*

MACHINERY: Tire Shredding

Safegaurd Document Destruction........G 609 448-6695
Millstone Township *(G-6265)*

MACHINERY: Voting

Avante International Tech Inc..............E 609 799-9388
Princeton Junction *(G-9149)*

MACHINERY: Woodworking

Logpowercom LLC............................G 732 350-9663
Whiting *(G-12068)*

MACHINES: Forming, Sheet Metal

Aluma Systems Con Cnstr LLC............G 908 418-5073
Linden *(G-5347)*

Bergen Homestate Corp.....................G 201 372-9740
Moonachie *(G-6507)*

Dos Industrial Sales LLC...................G 973 887-7800
East Hanover *(G-2212)*

MACHINISTS' TOOLS & MACHINES: Measuring, Metalworking Type

Dmg Mori Usa Inc.............................G 973 257-9620
Rockaway *(G-9561)*

MACHINISTS' TOOLS: Precision

Almark Tool & Manufacturing Co........F 908 789-2440
Garwood *(G-3775)*

Bach Tool Precision Inc......................G 973 962-6224
Ringwood *(G-9444)*

Bar-Lo Carbon Products Inc................E 973 227-2717
Fairfield *(G-3144)*

Congruent Machine Co Inc..................G 973 764-6767
Vernon *(G-11297)*

PRODUCT

Defined Pro Machining LLC ....G 973 891-1038
  Wharton *(G-11984)*
Industrial Brush Co Inc ....E 800 241-9860
  Fairfield *(G-3228)*
International Tool and Mfg Inc ....G 973 227-6767
  Fairfield *(G-3233)*
J A Machine & Tool Co Inc ....F 201 767-1308
  Closter *(G-1762)*
K & R Precision Machining LLC ....F 201 385-8855
  New Milford *(G-7022)*
Martin Tool Company Inc ....F 973 361-9212
  Wharton *(G-11992)*
Precision Ball Specialties ....G 856 881-5646
  Williamstown *(G-12099)*
R D Associates ....G 973 729-7944
  Sparta *(G-10520)*
Universal Metalcraft Inc ....E 973 345-3284
  Wayne *(G-11688)*
Wrightworks Engineering LLC ....G 609 882-8840
  Lawrenceville *(G-5272)*
Zenith Precision Inc ....F 201 933-8640
  East Rutherford *(G-2338)*

MACHINISTS' TOOLS: Scales, Measuring, Precision

Belleville Scale & Balance LLC............G 973 759-4487
  Orange *(G-7817)*
Fulcrum Inc ....G 973 473-6900
  Oradell *(G-7809)*
KG Systems Inc ....G 973 515-4664
  Springfield *(G-10562)*

MAGNETIC INK & OPTICAL SCANNING EQPT

Fotobridge ....G 856 809-9400
  West Berlin *(G-11721)*
Metrologic Instruments Inc ....C 856 228-8100
  Mount Laurel *(G-6818)*

MAGNETIC RESONANCE IMAGING DEVICES: Nonmedical

Advanced Imaging Assoc LLC ....G 973 823-8999
  Franklin *(G-3593)*
Bergen Open Mri ....G 201 652-1213
  Paramus *(G-7858)*
Denville Diagnostics Imaging.............E 973 586-1212
  Denville *(G-2035)*
Garden State Mgntic Imaging PC ....F 609 581-2727
  Pennsauken *(G-8514)*
JFK Medical Group PC ....E 732 632-1650
  Edison *(G-2544)*

MAGNETS: Ceramic

Escadaus Inc ....G 973 335-8888
  Boonton *(G-567)*
Oxford Instrs Holdings Inc ....E 732 541-1300
  Carteret *(G-1265)*

MAGNETS: Permanent

Escadaus Inc ....G 973 335-8888
  Boonton *(G-567)*
Permadur Industries Inc ....D 908 359-9767
  Hillsborough *(G-4362)*
Tricomp Inc ....C 973 835-1110
  Pompton Plains *(G-8966)*

MAIL PRESORTING SVCS

Arna Marketing Group Inc ....D 908 625-7395
  Branchburg *(G-638)*

MAIL-ORDER BOOK CLUBS

Chatham Bookseller Inc ....G 973 822-1361
  Madison *(G-5720)*

MAIL-ORDER HOUSES: Arts & Crafts Eqpt & Splys

Utrecht Manufacturing Corp ....D 609 409-8001
  Cranbury *(G-1889)*

MAIL-ORDER HOUSES: Clothing, Exc Women's

Cockpit Usa Inc ....F 212 575-1616
  Elizabeth *(G-2719)*

Somes Uniforms Inc ....F 201 843-1199
  Hackensack *(G-3977)*

MAIL-ORDER HOUSES: Computer Eqpt & Electronics

Creative Cmpt Concepts LLC ....G 877 919-7988
  Williamstown *(G-12085)*

MAIL-ORDER HOUSES: Computers & Peripheral Eqpt

Datapro International Inc.................E 732 868-0588
  Piscataway *(G-8754)*

MAIL-ORDER HOUSES: Food

Genevieves Inc........................F 973 772-8816
  Garfield *(G-3737)*
Giambris Quality Sweets Inc ....G 856 783-1099
  Clementon *(G-1532)*

MAIL-ORDER HOUSES: Order Taking Office Only

Arna Marketing Inc.....................E 908 231-1100
  Branchburg *(G-639)*

MAILBOX RENTAL & RELATED SVCS

E C D Ventures Inc.....................G 856 875-1100
  Blackwood *(G-477)*
Sre Ventures LLC ....G 973 785-0099
  Little Falls *(G-5489)*

MAILING MACHINES WHOLESALERS

Singe Corporation......................G 908 289-7900
  Hillside *(G-4440)*

MAILING SVCS, NEC

Barton & Cooney LLC...................D 609 747-9300
  Burlington *(G-959)*
C Jackson Associates Inc ....E 856 761-8000
  Cherry Hill *(G-1355)*
CIC Letter Service Inc ....D 201 896-1900
  Carlstadt *(G-1140)*
Corporate Mailings Inc ....D 973 808-0009
  Whippany *(G-12017)*
Corporate Mailings Inc ....C 973 439-1168
  West Caldwell *(G-11772)*
Full Service Mailers Inc ....F 973 478-8813
  Hackensack *(G-3919)*
Hermitage Press of New Jersey ....D 609 882-3600
  Ewing *(G-3022)*
Hummel Distributing Corp ....E 908 688-5300
  Union *(G-11193)*
Hummel Printing Inc ....E 908 688-5300
  Union *(G-11194)*
Ihs Inc ....G 201 391-0084
  Woodcliff Lake *(G-12194)*
Liberty Envelope Inc ....F 973 546-5600
  Paterson *(G-8320)*
Sjshore Marketing Ltd Lblty Co ....F 609 390-1400
  Marmora *(G-6006)*
Standard Prtg & Mail Svcs Inc ....F 973 790-3333
  Fairfield *(G-3311)*
Tmg Enterprises Inc ....E 732 469-2900
  Piscataway *(G-8826)*
Trenton Printing LLC ....F 609 695-6485
  Trenton *(G-11125)*
United Forms Finishing Corp ....F 908 687-0494
  Hillside *(G-4448)*
Your Printer V20 Ltd ....E 609 771-4000
  Cranbury *(G-1893)*

MANAGEMENT CONSULTING SVCS: Automation & Robotics

Robotunits Inc ....G 732 438-0500
  Cranbury *(G-1877)*

MANAGEMENT CONSULTING SVCS: Business

Aus Inc ....G 856 234-9200
  Mount Laurel *(G-6779)*
Nb Ventures Inc ....C 732 382-6565
  Clark *(G-1509)*
Recycling N Hensel Amer Inc ....E 856 753-7614
  West Berlin *(G-11746)*

SMR Research Corporation ....G 908 852-7677
  Hackettstown *(G-4037)*
Utility Development Corp ....G 973 994-4334
  Livingston *(G-5567)*

MANAGEMENT CONSULTING SVCS: Construction Project

Infinite Mfg Group Inc ....E 973 649-9950
  Kearny *(G-4885)*

MANAGEMENT CONSULTING SVCS: Food & Beverage

Advanced Food Systems Inc ....E 732 873-6776
  Somerset *(G-10049)*

MANAGEMENT CONSULTING SVCS: General

Lummus Technology Ventures LLC......G 973 893-1515
  Bloomfield *(G-521)*

MANAGEMENT CONSULTING SVCS: Hospital & Health

Quadramed Corporation ....E 732 751-0400
  Eatontown *(G-2420)*

MANAGEMENT CONSULTING SVCS: Incentive Or Award Program

Genesis Marketing Group Inc ....G 201 836-1392
  Teaneck *(G-10754)*
Hyman W Fisher Inc....................G 973 992-9155
  Livingston *(G-5534)*

MANAGEMENT CONSULTING SVCS: Industrial

Elena Consultants & Elec ....E 908 654-8309
  Mountainside *(G-6881)*
Synthetic Surfaces Inc ....G 908 233-6803
  Scotch Plains *(G-9858)*

MANAGEMENT CONSULTING SVCS: Industry Specialist

Luciano Packaging Technologies ....G 908 722-3222
  Branchburg *(G-676)*
Pflaumer Brothers Inc ....G 609 883-4610
  Ewing *(G-3042)*
Rambusch Decorating Company ....E 201 333-2525
  Jersey City *(G-4815)*
Technology Reviews Inc ....G 973 537-9511
  Randolph *(G-9301)*

MANAGEMENT CONSULTING SVCS: Information Systems

Business Dev Solutions Inc...............G 856 433-8005
  Cherry Hill *(G-1354)*
Comprehensive Healthcare Systm ....D 732 362-2000
  Edison *(G-2488)*
Netcom Systems Inc....................E 732 393-6100
  Edison *(G-2579)*

MANAGEMENT CONSULTING SVCS: Maintenance

Zion Industries Inc ....E 973 998-0162
  Morris Plains *(G-6682)*

MANAGEMENT CONSULTING SVCS: Manufacturing

Schall Manufacturing Inc ....G 732 918-8800
  Ocean *(G-7743)*

MANAGEMENT CONSULTING SVCS: Merchandising

LG&p Group LLC ....E 201 634-9099
  Paramus *(G-7884)*
Njiw Limited Liability Company ....F 201 355-2955
  Hackensack *(G-3954)*

MANAGEMENT CONSULTING SVCS: New Products & Svcs

Convention News Company Inc ....F 201 444-5075
Midland Park *(G-6224)*
Naava Inc ....G 844 666-2282
Springfield *(G-10566)*

MANAGEMENT CONSULTING SVCS: Restaurant & Food

Advisory Dumas Group LLC ....F 850 778-1624
Lawrence Township *(G-5239)*

MANAGEMENT CONSULTING SVCS: Retail Trade Consultant

Neighborhood Shoppers ....G 856 988-7722
Marlton *(G-5989)*

MANAGEMENT CONSULTING SVCS: Training & Development

42 Design Square LLC ....F 888 272-5979
Parsippany *(G-7937)*

MANAGEMENT CONSULTING SVCS: Transportation

Carpenter & Paterson Inc ....E 609 227-2750
Bordentown *(G-593)*

MANAGEMENT SERVICES

Belle Printing Group LLC ....G 856 235-5151
Mount Laurel *(G-6782)*
Data Communique Inc ....E 201 508-6000
Ridgefield Park *(G-9402)*
Deerbrook Fabrics ....F 201 945-4141
Guttenberg *(G-3869)*
Gannett Stllite Info Ntwrk Inc ....C 856 691-5000
Vineland *(G-11357)*
Integration Partners-Ny Corp ....B 973 871-2100
Parsippany *(G-8031)*
Jvc Industrial America Inc ....E 800 247-3608
Wayne *(G-11657)*
Merck Sharp & Dohme Corp ....A 908 740-4000
Kenilworth *(G-4977)*
Pfizer Inc ....D 973 739-0430
Parsippany *(G-8061)*
Qsa Global National Corp ....G 865 888-6798
Red Bank *(G-9341)*
Retail Management Pubg Inc ....F 212 981-0217
Montclair *(G-6434)*
Universal Vending MGT LLC ....F 908 233-4373
Westfield *(G-11932)*

MANAGEMENT SVCS, FACILITIES SUPPORT: Environ Remediation

Abatetech Inc ....E 609 265-2107
Lumberton *(G-5650)*
General Civil Company Inc ....F 866 435-1200
Runnemede *(G-9719)*

MANAGEMENT SVCS: Administrative

Eclearview Technologies Inc ....G 732 695-6999
Ocean *(G-7724)*
El Jay Poultry Corp ....F 856 435-0900
Voorhees *(G-11429)*

MANAGEMENT SVCS: Business

Mind-Alliance Systems LLC ....G 212 920-1911
Livingston *(G-5546)*

MANAGEMENT SVCS: Construction

Dreamstar Construction LLC ....F 732 393-2572
Middletown *(G-6213)*
Vet Construction Inc ....F 732 987-4922
Jackson *(G-4682)*

MANAGEMENT SVCS: Hotel Or Motel

Sysco Guest Supply LLC ....C 732 537-2297
Somerset *(G-10177)*

MANHOLES & COVERS: Metal

Campbell Foundry Company ....E 973 483-5480
Harrison *(G-4175)*
Campbell Foundry Company ....E 201 998-3765
Kearny *(G-4867)*
Emporia Foundry Inc ....E 973 483-5480
Harrison *(G-4181)*
Universal Valve Company Inc ....F 908 351-0606
Elizabeth *(G-2780)*

MANICURE PREPARATIONS

Yankee Tool Inc ....F 973 664-0878
Denville *(G-2062)*

MANIFOLDS: Pipe, Fabricated From Purchased Pipe

Selling Precision Inc ....E 973 728-1214
West Milford *(G-11856)*

MANUFACTURED & MOBILE HOME DEALERS

Silverstone Wireless LLC ....G 845 458-5197
Lodi *(G-5600)*

MANUFACTURING INDUSTRIES, NEC

(gt) Global Tech Inc ....F 732 447-7083
Dayton *(G-1951)*
Anu Industries LLC ....G 201 735-7475
Englewood *(G-2870)*
Authenticity Brewing LLC ....G 862 432-9622
Sparta *(G-10489)*
BSD Industries Ltd Liability ....G 732 534-4341
Lakewood *(G-5091)*
Cambrdge Inds For Vslly Impred ....G 732 247-6668
Somerset *(G-10072)*
Carbone America Scp Division ....G 973 334-0700
Boonton *(G-559)*
Cem Industries Inc ....G 908 244-8080
Harrison *(G-4176)*
Connector Mfg Co ....G 513 860-4455
Jersey City *(G-4733)*
Fit Fabrication LLC ....G 973 685-7344
Clifton *(G-1621)*
Force Industries LLC ....G 973 332-1532
Butler *(G-1003)*
General Tools Mfg Co LLC ....G 201 770-1380
Secaucus *(G-9889)*
Han Hean U S A Corp ....G 732 494-3256
Edison *(G-2531)*
Kudas Industries Inc ....F 412 751-0260
Denville *(G-2045)*
Lexi Industries ....G 201 297-7900
Northvale *(G-7590)*
Liquid Iron Industries Inc ....G 856 336-2639
West Berlin *(G-11730)*
Massage Chair Inc ....G 732 201-7777
Brick *(G-753)*
McT Manufacturing Inc ....G 877 258-9600
Millburn *(G-6257)*
Pacent Engineering ....G 914 390-9150
Ocean *(G-7733)*
Peters Laboratories ....F 856 767-4144
Berlin *(G-440)*
Rapsoco Inc ....G 908 977-7321
Elizabeth *(G-2771)*
Red Ray Manufacturing ....G 908 722-0040
Branchburg *(G-699)*
Robel Receptacles Inc ....G 609 882-8065
Long Beach Township *(G-5619)*
Ten One Design Ltd Lblty Co ....G 201 474-8232
Montclair *(G-6437)*
Vira Manufacturing Inc ....E 732 771-8269
Perth Amboy *(G-8635)*

MAPS

Geolytics Inc ....G 908 707-1505
Branchburg *(G-663)*

MARBLE BOARD

Eagle Fabrication Inc ....E 732 739-5300
Ltl Egg Hbr *(G-5644)*

MARBLE, BUILDING: Cut & Shaped

American Stone Inc ....E 973 318-7707
Hillside *(G-4388)*
American Stone Inc ....F 973 318-7707
Hillside *(G-4389)*
Bcg Marble & Granite South LLC ....G 732 367-3788
Jackson *(G-4655)*
Cole Brothers Marble & Granite ....G 856 455-7989
Elmer *(G-2790)*
Gr Stone LLC ....G 908 925-7290
Kenilworth *(G-4959)*
Ilkem Marble and Granite Inc ....G 856 433-8714
Cherry Hill *(G-1377)*
Marble Online Corporation ....G 201 998-9100
Kearny *(G-4897)*
Phillipsburg Marble Co Inc ....E 908 859-3435
Phillipsburg *(G-8664)*
Premier Marble and Gran 2 Inc ....G 732 294-7891
Freehold *(G-3681)*
Solidsurface Designs Inc ....E 856 910-7720
Pennsauken *(G-8580)*
Sr International Rock Inc ....G 908 864-4700
Bound Brook *(G-623)*
Statewide Granite and Marble ....F 201 653-1700
Jersey City *(G-4833)*

MARBLE: Crushed & Broken

Stone Surfaces Inc ....D 201 935-8803
East Rutherford *(G-2328)*

MARINAS

Camp Marine Services Inc ....G 609 368-1777
Stone Harbor *(G-10613)*
Lockwood Boat Works Inc ....E 732 721-1605
South Amboy *(G-10241)*
Norma K Corporation ....G 732 477-6441
Point Pleasant Beach *(G-8924)*

MARINE APPAREL STORES

Denali Company LLC ....E 732 219-7771
Red Bank *(G-9326)*

MARINE CARGO HANDLING SVCS

Bayonne Drydock & Repair Corp ....E 201 823-9295
Bayonne *(G-215)*

MARINE CARGO HANDLING SVCS: Marine Terminal

Federal Lorco Petroleum LLC ....D 908 352-0542
Elizabeth *(G-2731)*

MARINE ENGINE REPAIR SVCS

Monmouth Marine Engines Inc ....F 732 528-9290
Brielle *(G-913)*

MARINE HARDWARE

Delta Procurement Inc ....G 201 623-9353
Carlstadt *(G-1153)*
Mariner Sales and Power Inc ....G 732 477-7484
Brick *(G-751)*
Oceanview Marine Welding LLC ....G 609 624-9669
Ocean View *(G-7765)*
Viking Marine Products Inc ....G 732 826-4552
Edison *(G-2647)*

MARINE RELATED EQPT

Maritime Solutions Inc ....G 732 752-3831
Middlesex *(G-6178)*
Wave Dispersion Tech Inc ....G 908 233-7503
Berkeley Heights *(G-424)*

MARINE SPLY DEALERS

Camp Marine Services Inc ....G 609 368-1777
Stone Harbor *(G-10613)*
Lockwood Boat Works Inc ....E 732 721-1605
South Amboy *(G-10241)*
Monmouth Marine Engines Inc ....F 732 528-9290
Brielle *(G-913)*
Riverside Marina Yacht Sls LLC ....F 856 461-1077
Riverside *(G-9506)*

MARINE SPLYS WHOLESALERS

World Wide Metric Inc ....F 732 247-2300
Branchburg *(G-719)*

PRODUCT

MARINE SVC STATIONS

A PS Inlet Marina LLC .... G 732 681-3303
Belmar *(G-355)*

MARKETS: Meat & fish

Arm National Food Inc .... G 609 695-4911
Trenton *(G-11020)*

Licini Brothers Inc .... G 201 865-1130
Union City *(G-11254)*

MARKING DEVICES

Adco Signs of NJ Inc .... E 908 965-2112
Elizabeth *(G-2705)*

Blue Ring Stencils LLC .... E 866 763-3873
Lumberton *(G-5651)*

Classic Marking Products Inc ...... G 973 383-2223
Roxbury Township *(G-9711)*

Container Graphics Corp .... E 732 922-1180
Neptune *(G-6904)*

Dalemark Industries Inc .... F 732 367-3100
Lakewood *(G-5105)*

Digital Design Inc .... E 973 857-9500
Cedar Grove *(G-1278)*

G & R Graphics Inc .... E 973 731-7438
South Orange *(G-10307)*

J D Crew Inc .... G 856 665-3676
Pennsauken *(G-8534)*

Lafarge Road Marking Inc .... C 973 884-0300
Parsippany *(G-8037)*

Pic Graphics Inc .... E 201 420-5040
Jersey City *(G-4801)*

Private Label Products Inc .... E 201 773-4230
Fair Lawn *(G-3107)*

Trodat Usa Inc .... F 732 529-8500
Somerset *(G-10189)*

Winters Stamp Mfg Co Inc .... F 908 352-3725
Martinsville *(G-6011)*

MARKING DEVICES: Embossing Seals & Hand Stamps

A A A Stamp and Seal Mfg Co ...... G 201 796-1500
Saddle Brook *(G-9747)*

A Quick Cut Stamping Embossing ...... F 856 321-0050
Maple Shade *(G-5898)*

American Marking Systems Inc ...... D 973 478-5600
Clifton *(G-1563)*

American Stamp Mfg Co .... F 212 227-1877
Clifton *(G-1564)*

Newark Stamp & Die Works Inc ...... G 973 485-7111
Newark *(G-7258)*

Shachihata Inc (usa) .... F 732 905-7159
Lakewood *(G-5188)*

Trodat USA LLC .... D 732 562-9500
Somerset *(G-10190)*

MARKING DEVICES: Embossing Seals, Corporate & Official

All-State International Inc .... C 908 272-0800
Cranford *(G-1895)*

MARKING DEVICES: Pads, Inking & Stamping

Ranger Industries Inc .... E 732 389-3535
Tinton Falls *(G-10844)*

MARKING DEVICES: Screens, Textile Printing

C Q Corporation .... F 201 935-8488
East Rutherford *(G-2289)*

L & F Graphics Ltd Lblty Co .... G 973 240-7033
Paterson *(G-8312)*

MARKING DEVICES: Seal Presses, Notary & Hand

Max Pro Services LLC .... G 973 396-2373
Livingston *(G-5542)*

MARKING DEVICES: Time Stamps, Hand, Rubber Or Metal

Time Log Industries Inc .... G 609 965-5017
Egg Harbor City *(G-2673)*

MATERIALS HANDLING EQPT WHOLESALERS

Elkay Products Co Inc .... F 973 376-7550
Springfield *(G-10553)*

Hy-Tek Material Handling Inc .... E 732 490-6282
Morganville *(G-6642)*

Permadur Industries Inc .... D 908 359-9767
Hillsborough *(G-4362)*

MATS OR MATTING, NEC: Rubber

American Harlequin Corporation ...... E 856 234-5505
Moorestown *(G-6558)*

MATS, MATTING & PADS: Auto, Floor, Exc Rubber Or Plastic

Newark Auto Top Co Inc .... F 973 677-9935
East Orange *(G-2262)*

MATS: Table, Plastic & Textile

Living Fashions Llc .... F 732 626-5200
Sayreville *(G-9830)*

MATTRESS STORES

Custom Bedding Co .... G 973 761-1100
Maplewood *(G-5917)*

Jomel Industries Inc .... G 973 282-0300
Hillside *(G-4421)*

Jomel Seams Reasonable LLC ...... G 973 282-0300
Hillside *(G-4422)*

Lieth Holdings LLC .... G 201 358-8282
Westwood *(G-11962)*

MEAL DELIVERY PROGRAMS

Princeton Quadrangle Club .... G 609 258-0376
Princeton *(G-9100)*

MEAT & MEAT PRDTS WHOLESALERS

Arctic Foods Inc .... E 908 689-0590
Washington *(G-11574)*

Arm National Food Inc .... G 609 695-4911
Trenton *(G-11020)*

Bringhurst Bros Inc .... E 856 767-0110
Berlin *(G-429)*

Megas Yeeros LLC .... E 212 777-6342
Lyndhurst *(G-5692)*

Nu-Meat Technology Inc .... E 908 754-3400
South Plainfield *(G-10415)*

MEAT CUTTING & PACKING

Arm National Food Inc .... G 609 695-4911
Trenton *(G-11020)*

B & B Poultry Co Inc .... C 856 692-8893
Norma *(G-7412)*

Bie Real Estate Holdings LLC ...... G 856 691-9765
Vineland *(G-11331)*

Cameco Inc .... D 973 239-2845
Verona *(G-11304)*

Carl Streit & Son Co .... G 732 775-0803
Neptune *(G-6903)*

Carnegie Deli Inc .... D 201 507-5557
Carlstadt *(G-1138)*

Comarco Products Inc .... D 856 342-7557
Camden *(G-1054)*

Katzs Delicatessen Mfg .... E 212 254-2246
Carlstadt *(G-1177)*

Kleemeyer & Merkel Inc .... F 973 377-0875
Green Village *(G-3865)*

Mamamancinis Holdings Inc .... G 201 531-1212
East Rutherford *(G-2307)*

Nu-Meat Technology Inc .... E 908 754-3400
South Plainfield *(G-10415)*

Premio Foods Inc .... C 800 864-7622
Hawthorne *(G-4255)*

Pulaski Meat Products Co .... E 908 925-5380
Linden *(G-5432)*

Salem Packing Co .... E 856 878-0002
Salem *(G-9809)*

Seabrite Corp .... E 973 491-0399
Newark *(G-7305)*

Tubari Inc .... E 973 779-8693
Passaic *(G-8185)*

MEAT MARKETS

Arctic Foods Inc .... E 908 689-0590
Washington *(G-11574)*

Bringhurst Bros Inc .... E 856 767-0110
Berlin *(G-429)*

Kleemeyer & Merkel Inc .... F 973 377-0875
Green Village *(G-3865)*

Mayabeque Products Inc .... G 201 869-0531
North Bergen *(G-7466)*

Rastelli Brothers Inc .... D 856 803-1100
Swedesboro *(G-10724)*

Rastelli Foods Group Inc .... F 856 803-1100
Swedesboro *(G-10725)*

MEAT PRDTS: Canned

B&G Foods Inc .... B 973 401-6500
Parsippany *(G-7956)*

B&G Foods Inc .... B 973 401-6500
Parsippany *(G-7957)*

B&G Foods North America Inc ...... F 973 401-6500
Parsippany *(G-7958)*

MEAT PRDTS: Canned Exc Baby Food, From Slaughtered Meat

DArtagnan Inc .... D 973 344-0565
Union *(G-11170)*

Nourhan Trading Group Inc .... G 732 381-8110
Avenel *(G-144)*

Rastelli Brothers Inc .... D 856 803-1100
Swedesboro *(G-10724)*

Rastelli Foods Group Inc .... F 856 803-1100
Swedesboro *(G-10725)*

MEAT PRDTS: Cured, From Slaughtered Meat

Veroni Usa Inc .... E 609 970-0320
Logan Township *(G-5616)*

York Street Caterers Inc .... C 201 868-9088
Englewood *(G-2945)*

MEAT PRDTS: Frozen

Rajbhog Foods(nj) Inc .... C 551 222-4700
Jersey City *(G-4814)*

MEAT PRDTS: Ham, Boiled, From Purchased Meat

Al and John Inc .... B 973 742-4990
Caldwell *(G-1024)*

MEAT PRDTS: Head Cheese, From Purchased Meat

Red Square Foods Inc .... F 732 846-0190
Somerset *(G-10164)*

MEAT PRDTS: Meat By-Prdts, From Slaughtered Meat

Applegate Farms LLC .... C 908 725-2768
Bridgewater *(G-812)*

MEAT PRDTS: Pork, Cured, From Purchased Meat

Case Pork Roll Co Inc .... E 609 396-8171
Trenton *(G-11035)*

MEAT PRDTS: Pork, From Slaughtered Meat

Bringhurst Bros Inc .... E 856 767-0110
Berlin *(G-429)*

Dealaman Enterprises Inc .... E 908 647-5533
Warren *(G-11544)*

MEAT PRDTS: Sausage Casings, Natural

Nitta Casings Inc .... C 908 218-4400
Bridgewater *(G-866)*

MEAT PRDTS: Sausages & Related Prdts, From Purchased Meat

Fratelli Beretta Usa Inc .... D 201 438-0723
Budd Lake *(G-929)*

MEAT PRDTS: Sausages, From Purchased Meat

Appetito Provisions Company ....E 201 864-3410
Harrington Park (G-4170)

Casa Di Bertacchi Corporation ....C 856 696-5600
Vineland (G-11334)

CW Brown Foods Inc ....E 856 423-3700
Mount Royal (G-6850)

Highpont Corporation ....G 201 460-1364
Rutherford (G-9734)

Lopes Sausage Co ....G 973 344-3063
Newark (G-7225)

Mayabeque Products Inc ....G 201 869-0531
North Bergen (G-7466)

Premio Foods Inc ....C 800 864-7622
Hawthorne (G-4255)

Pulaski Meat Products Co ....E 908 925-5380
Linden (G-5432)

Smithfield Packaged Meats Corp ....E 908 354-2674
Elizabeth (G-2774)

Thumann Incorporated ....C 201 935-3636
Carlstadt (G-1230)

MEAT PRDTS: Snack Sticks, Incl Jerky, From Purchased Meat

Lawless Jerky LLC ....G 310 869-5733
Marlton (G-5981)

MEAT PRDTS: Spiced Meats, From Purchased Meat

Martins Specialty Sausage Co ....F 856 423-4000
Mickleton (G-6137)

MEAT PRDTS: Veal, From Slaughtered Meat

Dorzar Corporation ....E 973 589-6363
Newark (G-7141)

MEAT PROCESSED FROM PURCHASED CARCASSES

A Gimenez Trading LLC ....G 973 697-2240
Oak Ridge (G-7659)

Allied Specialty Foods Inc ....D 856 507-1100
Vineland (G-11321)

Applegate Farms LLC ....C 908 725-2768
Bridgewater (G-812)

Arm National Food Inc ....G 609 695-4911
Trenton (G-11020)

Best Provision Co Inc ....D 973 242-5000
Newark (G-7107)

Bringhurst Bros Inc ....E 856 767-0110
Berlin (G-429)

Buckhead Meat Company ....C 732 661-4900
Edison (G-2476)

Campbell Soup Supply Co LLC ....G 856 342-4800
Camden (G-1050)

CW Brown Foods Inc ....G 856 423-3700
Mount Royal (G-6851)

Dubon Corp ....G 212 812-2171
Elizabeth (G-2726)

Ena Meat Packing Inc ....E 973 742-4790
Paterson (G-8264)

Gaisers Erpean Style Provs Inc ....F 908 686-3421
Union (G-11187)

Groezinger Provisions Inc ....F 732 775-3220
Neptune (G-6917)

Kupelian Foods Inc ....G 201 440-8055
Ridgefield Park (G-9410)

Licini Brothers Inc ....G 201 865-1130
Union City (G-11254)

Mamamancinis Holdings Inc ....G 201 531-1212
East Rutherford (G-2307)

Marathon Enterprises Inc ....F 201 935-3330
Englewood (G-2912)

Nicolosi Foods Inc ....G 201 624-1702
Union City (G-11260)

Real Kosher LLC ....G 973 690-5394
Newark (G-7286)

Shahnawaz Food LLC ....F 908 413-4206
Edison (G-2615)

Wagner Provision Co Inc ....F 856 423-1630
Gibbstown (G-3793)

MEAT PROCESSING MACHINERY

Patty-O-Matic Inc ....F 732 938-2757
Farmingdale (G-3391)

MEATS, PACKAGED FROZEN: Wholesalers

Delight Foods USA LLC ....F 201 369-1199
Jersey City (G-4738)

Nema Food Distribution Inc ....G 973 256-4415
Fairfield (G-3267)

MECHANICAL INSTRUMENT REPAIR SVCS

Deltronics Corporation ....F 856 825-8200
Millville (G-6297)

Serious Welding & Mech LLC ....F 732 698-7478
South River (G-10466)

MED, DENTAL & HOSPITAL EQPT, WHOL: Incontinent Prdts/Splys

Easy Undies LLC ....G 201 715-4909
Springfield (G-10552)

MEDIA BUYING AGENCIES

Outsourcing Today LLC ....F 973 439-0060
Roseland (G-9654)

MEDIA: Magnetic & Optical Recording

Fujifilm North America Corp ....B 732 857-3000
Edison (G-2523)

Synergem Inc ....E 732 692-6308
Avenel (G-154)

MEDICAL & HOSPITAL EQPT WHOLESALERS

America Techma Inc ....G 201 894-5887
Englewood Cliffs (G-2948)

Belair Instrument Company LLC ....E 973 912-8900
Springfield (G-10542)

Brenner Metal Products ....E 973 778-2466
Wallington (G-11523)

Dmg America LLC ....E 201 894-5500
Ridgefield Park (G-9404)

First National Servicing & Dev ....E 732 341-5409
Toms River (G-10877)

Hydromer Inc ....C 908 526-2828
Branchburg (G-665)

Krieck Enterprises LLC ....G 908 789-8600
Madison (G-5727)

Nbs Group Sup Med Pdts Div LLC ....G 732 745-9292
New Brunswick (G-6983)

Tronex International Inc ....D 973 335-2888
Budd Lake (G-945)

MEDICAL & SURGICAL SPLYS: Bandages & Dressings

3M Company ....B 973 884-2500
Whippany (G-12004)

Banding Centers of America ....G 973 805-9977
Florham Park (G-3491)

MEDICAL & SURGICAL SPLYS: Clothing, Fire Resistant & Protect

Ces Imports LLC ....G 610 299-7930
Stone Harbor (G-10614)

MEDICAL & SURGICAL SPLYS: Cosmetic Restorations

Araya Inc ....G 201 445-7005
Ridgewood (G-9420)

MEDICAL & SURGICAL SPLYS: Cotton, Incl Cotton Balls

Dexmed Inc ....G 732 831-0507
Elizabeth (G-2724)

MEDICAL & SURGICAL SPLYS: Foot Appliances, Orthopedic

Aetrex Worldwide Inc ....C 201 833-2700
Teaneck (G-10741)

Ortho-Dynamics Inc ....G 973 742-4390
Paterson (G-8357)

Orthofeet Inc ....E 800 524-2845
Northvale (G-7599)

MEDICAL & SURGICAL SPLYS: Ligatures

Ethicon Inc ....C 908 306-0327
Bedminster (G-272)

Ethicon Inc ....C 908 218-0707
Bedminster (G-273)

Healqu LLC ....G 844 443-2578
Jersey City (G-4764)

MEDICAL & SURGICAL SPLYS: Limbs, Artificial

Cape Prosthetics-Orthotics ....G 856 810-7900
Marlton (G-5966)

Edge Orthotics Inc ....G 732 549-3343
Edison (G-2508)

Garden State Orthopedic Center ....G 973 538-4948
Morristown (G-6709)

Hanger Prsthetcs & Ortho Inc ....G 973 736-0628
West Orange (G-11897)

Hanger Prsthetcs & Ortho Inc ....G 609 653-8323
Linwood (G-5466)

Harry J Lawall & Son Inc ....G 856 691-7764
Vineland (G-11369)

Jefferson Prosthetic Orthotic ....G 973 762-0780
South Orange (G-10308)

Nouveau Prosthetics Ltd ....F 732 739-0888
Hazlet (G-4280)

Nouveau Prosthetics Orthotics ....F 732 739-0888
Hazlet (G-4281)

Pro-Fit LLC ....F 856 809-9910
West Berlin (G-11745)

MEDICAL & SURGICAL SPLYS: Orthopedic Appliances

Achilles Prosthetcs & Orthotcs ....G 201 785-9944
Ramsey (G-9229)

Bayside Orthopedics LLC ....G 732 691-4898
Toms River (G-10870)

Cocco Enterprises Inc ....F 609 393-5939
Trenton (G-11043)

Cranial Technologies Inc ....G 908 754-0572
Edison (G-2494)

Eastern Podiatry Labs Inc ....G 609 882-4444
Ewing (G-3015)

Extremity Medical LLC ....E 973 588-8980
Parsippany (G-8006)

Grateful Ped Inc ....F 973 478-6511
Saddle Brook (G-9767)

Icon Orthopedic Concepts LLC ....G 973 794-6810
Boonton (G-571)

Ivy Capital Partners LLC ....G 201 573-8400
Montvale (G-6461)

J C Orthopedic Inc ....G 732 458-7900
Brick (G-747)

M B R Orthotics Inc. ....G 201 444-7750
Wyckoff (G-12256)

Precision Orthotic Lab of Nj ....F 856 848-6226
West Deptford (G-11839)

Rinko Orthopedic Appliances ....G 201 796-3121
Fair Lawn (G-3109)

Sivantos Inc ....B 732 562-6600
Piscataway (G-8811)

Tgz Acquisition Company LLC ....F 856 669-6600
Cherry Hill (G-1428)

Total Control Othotics Lab ....G 609 499-2200
Florence (G-3482)

MEDICAL & SURGICAL SPLYS: Personal Safety Eqpt

Ansell Limited ....E 732 345-5400
Iselin (G-4612)

Dynamic Safety Usa LLC ....G 844 378-7200
Somerset (G-10091)

Gemtor Inc ....E 732 583-6200
Matawan (G-6021)

Surgical Lser Sfety Cuncil Inc ....G 216 272-0805
Cherry Hill (G-1424)

MEDICAL & SURGICAL SPLYS: Prosthetic Appliances

Atlantic Prsthtic Orthotic Svc ....G 609 927-6330
Linwood (G-5465)

Garden State Prosthetics ....G 732 922-6650
Ocean (G-7727)

J J L & W Inc ....E 856 854-3100
Magnolia (G-5741)

J M M R Inc ....G...... 201 612-5104
Fair Lawn **(G-3097)**

Johnson & Associates Inc ......F 856 228-2175
Blackwood **(G-483)**

Mar Machine Ken Manufacturing ....E 973 278-5827
Paterson **(G-8331)**

North Jrsey Prsthtics Orthtics ....G...... 201 943-4448
Palisades Park **(G-7840)**

Ossur Americas Inc ....G...... 856 345-6000
West Deptford **(G-11837)**

Swiss Orthopedic Inc ....G...... 908 874-5522
Hillsborough **(G-4375)**

MEDICAL & SURGICAL SPLYS: Splints, Pneumatic & Wood

Jerome Group Inc ....D...... 856 234-8600
West Deptford **(G-11831)**

MEDICAL & SURGICAL SPLYS: Sponges

Nahallac LLC ....G...... 908 635-0999
Whitehouse **(G-12047)**

MEDICAL & SURGICAL SPLYS: Supports, Abdominal, Ankle, Etc

Preform Laboratories Inc ....E 973 523-8610
Hackensack **(G-3964)**

MEDICAL & SURGICAL SPLYS: Sutures, Non & Absorbable

Ethicon Inc ....A...... 732 524-0400
Somerville **(G-10207)**

MEDICAL & SURGICAL SPLYS: Trusses, Orthopedic & Surgical

Spinal Kinetics LLC ....G...... 908 687-2552
Union **(G-11224)**

MEDICAL EQPT REPAIR SVCS, NON-ELECTRIC

Cross Medical Specialties Inc ....F 856 589-3288
Pitman **(G-8841)**

MEDICAL EQPT: CAT Scanner Or Computerized Axial Tomography

3shape Inc ....G...... 908 219-4641
Warren **(G-11534)**

Morris County Imaging ....G...... 973 532-7900
Morristown **(G-6728)**

MEDICAL EQPT: Diagnostic

Abbott Point of Care Inc ....C...... 609 454-9000
Princeton **(G-8993)**

Abbott Point of Care Inc ....C...... 609 371-8923
East Windsor **(G-2339)**

Alfa Wassermann Inc ....C...... 973 882-8630
West Caldwell **(G-11763)**

Alfa Wssrmann Dagnstc Tech LLC ......F 800 220-4488
West Caldwell **(G-11764)**

American Diagnstc Imaging Inc ......F 973 980-1724
Nutley **(G-7639)**

Ascensia Diabetes Care US Inc ....C...... 973 560-6500
Parsippany **(G-7952)**

Bahadir USA LLC ....G...... 856 517-3080
Carneys Point **(G-1244)**

Clinical Image Retrieval Syste ....G...... 888 482-2362
Franklin **(G-3597)**

Diabeto Inc ....G...... 646 397-3175
Piscataway **(G-8758)**

Diagnostix Plus Inc ....G...... 201 530-5505
Teaneck **(G-10748)**

Edda Technology Inc ....F 609 919-9889
Princeton **(G-9036)**

Exalenz Bioscience Inc ....E 732 232-4393
Wall Township **(G-11480)**

Gibraltar Laboratories Inc ....E 973 227-6882
Fairfield **(G-3209)**

Health Care Alert LLC ....F 732 676-2630
Middletown **(G-6216)**

Immunostics Inc ....G...... 732 918-0770
Eatontown **(G-2405)**

Immunostics Company Inc ....E 732 918-0770
Eatontown **(G-2406)**

Medical Innovation Group LLC ....G...... 832 348-6460
Basking Ridge **(G-197)**

Newton Memorial Hospital Inc ....G...... 973 726-0904
Sparta **(G-10514)**

Northeast Medical Systems Corp ....G...... 856 910-8111
Cherry Hill **(G-1405)**

Pharmasource International LLC ....G...... 732 985-6182
Piscataway **(G-8800)**

Scimedx Corporation ....E 800 221-5598
Dover **(G-2109)**

Smartekg LLC ....G...... 201 376-4556
Teaneck **(G-10774)**

State Technology Inc ....G...... 856 467-8009
Bridgeport **(G-773)**

United Medical PC ....F 201 339-6111
Bayonne **(G-246)**

Vela Diagnostics USA Inc ....G...... 973 852-3740
Fairfield **(G-3340)**

Vesag Health Inc ....F 732 333-1876
North Brunswick **(G-7545)**

Zeus Scientific Inc ....D...... 908 526-3744
Branchburg **(G-722)**

MEDICAL EQPT: Electromedical Apparatus

Fluent Diagnostics ....G...... 201 414-4516
Pequannock **(G-8599)**

Neurotron Medical Inc ....G...... 609 896-3444
Ewing **(G-3040)**

Nextphase Medical Devices LLC ....E 201 968-9400
Waldwick **(G-11452)**

MEDICAL EQPT: Electrotherapeutic Apparatus

Datascope Corp ....C...... 973 244-6100
Fairfield **(G-3171)**

MEDICAL EQPT: Laser Systems

Cgm Us Inc ....E 609 894-4420
Birmingham **(G-467)**

Refine Technology LLC ....F 973 952-0002
Pine Brook **(G-8715)**

Surgical Lser Sfety Cuncil Inc ....G...... 216 272-0805
Cherry Hill **(G-1424)**

Topcon America Corporation ....B...... 201 599-5100
Oakland **(G-7706)**

MEDICAL EQPT: MRI/Magnetic Resonance Imaging Devs, Nuclear

Ahs Hospital Corp ....E 908 522-2000
Summit **(G-10633)**

MEDICAL EQPT: Pacemakers

Nextron Medical Tech Inc ....D...... 973 575-0614
Fairfield **(G-3270)**

St Jude Medical LLC ....E 800 645-5368
Secaucus **(G-9932)**

Venetian Care and Rehablitatn ....G...... 732 721-8200
South Amboy **(G-10246)**

MEDICAL EQPT: Patient Monitoring

Capintec Inc ....E 201 825-9500
Florham Park **(G-3495)**

Respironics Inc ....C...... 973 581-6000
Parsippany **(G-8079)**

Universal Medical Inc ....F 800 606-5511
Ewing **(G-3065)**

MEDICAL EQPT: Sterilizers

Alkaline Corporation ....G...... 732 531-7830
Eatontown **(G-2380)**

MEDICAL EQPT: Ultrasonic Scanning Devices

3dimension Dgnstc Slution Corp ....G...... 201 780-4653
Jersey City **(G-4691)**

Corentec America Inc ....G...... 949 379-6227
Morristown **(G-6701)**

Enterix Inc ....G...... 732 429-1899
Edison **(G-2512)**

Total Tech Medical LLC ....G...... 973 980-6458
Dover **(G-2113)**

V L V Associates ....F 973 428-2884
Whippany **(G-12041)**

MEDICAL EQPT: Ultrasonic, Exc Cleaning

Dvx LLC ....G...... 609 924-3590
Princeton **(G-9033)**

MEDICAL EQPT: X-Ray Apparatus & Tubes, Radiographic

G E Inspection Technologies LP ....D...... 973 448-0077
Flanders **(G-3409)**

Vatech America Inc ....E 201 210-5028
Fort Lee **(G-3588)**

MEDICAL EQPT: X-ray Generators

Swissray International Inc ....F 800 903-5543
Edison **(G-2636)**

MEDICAL HELP SVCS

Chromak Research Inc ....G...... 732 560-1366
Somerset **(G-10082)**

MEDICAL SVCS ORGANIZATION

I Physician Hub ....D...... 732 274-0155
Monmouth Junction **(G-6346)**

Midlantic Medical Systems Inc ....G...... 908 432-4599
Skillman **(G-10033)**

MEDICAL, DENTAL & HOSPITAL EQPT, WHOL: Hosptl Eqpt/Furniture

Biomedicon ....F 856 778-1880
Moorestown **(G-6563)**

MEDICAL, DENTAL & HOSPITAL EQPT, WHOL: Surgical Eqpt & Splys

Akorn Inc ....D...... 732 659-6443
Somerset **(G-10053)**

Lumiscope Co Inc ....D...... 678 291-3207
East Rutherford **(G-2306)**

MEDICAL, DENTAL & HOSPITAL EQPT, WHOLESALE: Baths, Whirlpool

Asd Holding Corp ....G...... 800 442-1902
Piscataway **(G-8739)**

MEDICAL, DENTAL & HOSPITAL EQPT, WHOLESALE: Diagnostic, Med

Spectrum Laboratory Pdts Inc ....C...... 732 214-1300
New Brunswick **(G-7004)**

SPS Alfachem Inc ....G...... 973 676-5141
Orange **(G-7828)**

MEDICAL, DENTAL & HOSPITAL EQPT, WHOLESALE: Hearing Aids

Oticon Inc ....C...... 732 560-1220
Somerset **(G-10148)**

MEDICAL, DENTAL & HOSPITAL EQPT, WHOLESALE: Med Eqpt & Splys

3M Company ....C...... 908 788-4000
Flemington **(G-3422)**

Bard International Inc ....D...... 908 277-8000
New Providence **(G-7029)**

Bellco Glass Inc ....D...... 800 257-7043
Vineland **(G-11328)**

Bergen Manufacturing & Supply ....E 201 854-3461
North Bergen **(G-7434)**

Bsi Corp ....E 631 589-1118
Nutley **(G-7643)**

Carry Easy Inc ....E 201 944-0042
Leonia **(G-5315)**

Case Medical Inc ....E 201 313-1999
South Hackensack **(G-10257)**

Cryopak Verification Tech Inc ....G...... 732 346-9200
Edison **(G-2497)**

Cura Biomed Inc ....G...... 609 647-1474
Princeton Junction **(G-9151)**

Dexmed Inc ....G...... 732 831-0507
Elizabeth **(G-2724)**

Diagnostix Plus Inc ....G...... 201 530-5505
Teaneck **(G-10748)**

Distek Inc ....G...... 732 422-7585
North Brunswick **(G-7516)**

DRG International Inc ....E 973 564-7555
Springfield (G-10551)
Electric Mobility Corporation.................C 856 468-1000
Sewell (G-9954)
Ellis Instruments Inc ....G 973 593-9222
Madison (G-5722)
Fresenius Med Care Hldings Inc ....G 201 767-7700
Rockleigh (G-9629)
Maddak Inc ....G 973 628-7600
Wayne (G-11661)
Medical Indicators Inc ....F 609 737-1600
Hamilton (G-4114)
Oxford Instrs Holdings Inc ....E 732 541-1300
Carteret (G-1265)
Photonics Management Corp ....G 908 231-0960
Bridgewater (G-874)
Redfield Corporation ....G 201 845-3990
Rochelle Park (G-9534)

MEDICAL, DENTAL & HOSPITAL EQPT, WHOLESALE: Medical Lab

Friedrich and Dimmock Inc ....E 856 825-0305
Millville (G-6302)
Globe Scientific Inc ....E 201 599-1400
Paramus (G-7873)
Tovatech LLC ....G 973 913-9734
Maplewood (G-5928)

MEDICAL, DENTAL & HOSPITAL EQPT, WHOLESALE: Orthopedic

Howmedica Osteonics Corp ....C 201 831-5000
Mahwah (G-5783)

MEDICAL, DENTAL/HOSPITAL EQPT, WHOL: Veterinarian Eqpt/Sply

Biomedtrix LLC ....F 973 331-7800
Whippany (G-12012)
Biomedtrix LLC ....G 973 331-7800
Boonton (G-558)
DMS Laboratories Inc ....G 908 782-3353
Flemington (G-3436)

MEMBERSHIP ORGANIZATIONS, NEC: Charitable

DSM Sight & Life Inc ....G 973 257-8208
Parsippany (G-7990)

MEMBERSHIP ORGANIZATIONS, PROF: Education/Teacher Assoc

Investment Casting Institute ....G 201 573-9770
Montvale (G-6460)

MEMBERSHIP ORGANIZATIONS, RELIGIOUS: Assembly Of God Church

Almond Branch Inc ....E 973 728-3479
West Milford (G-11849)
Hope Center..F 201 798-1234
Jersey City (G-4766)

MEMBERSHIP ORGANIZATIONS, RELIGIOUS: Catholic Church

Diocese of Camden New Jersey...........A 856 756-7900
Camden (G-1059)

MEMBERSHIP ORGANIZATIONS, RELIGIOUS: Nonchurch

Christian Mssons In Many Lands ....G 732 449-8880
Wall Township (G-11469)

MEN'S & BOYS' CLOTHING ACCESS STORES

Gilbert Storms Jr.................................G 973 835-5729
Haskell (G-4207)
Stretch-O-Rama Inc ....E 732 855-1400
Avenel (G-153)

MEN'S & BOYS' CLOTHING STORES

Elie Tahari Ltd ....C 973 671-6300
Millburn (G-6249)

Hat Box ....E 732 961-2262
Lakewood (G-5133)
Pvh Corp ....G 908 685-0050
Bridgewater (G-879)
Sock Company Inc...............................E 201 307-0675
Westwood (G-11972)
Todd Shelton LLC ....G 844 626-6355
East Rutherford (G-2333)

MEN'S & BOYS' CLOTHING WHOLESALERS, NEC

Burlington Coat Factory ....D 908 994-9562
Elizabeth (G-2716)
Handcraft Manufacturing Corp ....E 973 565-0077
Newark (G-7185)
Merc USA Inc ....F 201 489-3527
Hackensack (G-3947)
New Top Inc ....E 201 438-3990
Carlstadt (G-1193)
New York Popular Inc ....D 718 499-2020
Carteret (G-1263)
Personality Handkerchiefs Inc...............E 973 565-0077
Newark (G-7269)
Selfmade LLC ....E 201 792-8968
Jersey City (G-4826)
Trilex Ltd ....E 201 664-5576
Twp Washinton (G-11144)

MEN'S & BOYS' SPORTSWEAR CLOTHING STORES

Cockpit Usa Inc ....F 212 575-1616
Elizabeth (G-2719)

MEN'S & BOYS' SPORTSWEAR WHOLESALERS

Bimini Bay Outfitters Ltd......................F 201 529-3550
Mahwah (G-5752)
Chartwell Promotions Ltd Inc ....G 732 780-6900
Freehold (G-3646)
Cockpit Usa Inc ....F 212 575-1616
Elizabeth (G-2719)
Monogram Center Inc ....E 732 442-1800
Perth Amboy (G-8624)

MEN'S CLOTHING STORES: Everyday, Exc Suits & Sportswear

John B Stetson Company ....G 212 563-1848
Hoboken (G-4478)

METAL & STEEL PRDTS: Abrasive

EMR (usa Holdings) Inc........................F 856 365-7500
Bellmawr (G-339)

METAL CUTTING SVCS

Kwg Industries LLC ....E 908 218-8900
Hillsborough (G-4354)

METAL FABRICATORS: Architechtural

67 Pollock Ave Corp ....G 201 432-1156
Jersey City (G-4692)
A & A Ironwork Co Inc ....F 973 728-4300
Hewitt (G-4287)
Advanced Products LLC ....E 800 724-5464
Lakewood (G-5066)
Airmet Inc ....G 973 481-5550
Newark (G-7074)
Anvil Iron Works Inc ....G 856 783-5959
Sicklerville (G-10016)
Architctural Metal Fabricators ....G 718 765-0722
Carteret (G-1249)
Architectural Iron Designs ....G 908 757-2323
Plainfield (G-8854)
Armetec Corp ....G 973 485-2525
Newark (G-7093)
B L White Welding & Steel Co ....G 973 684-4111
Paterson (G-8218)
Bamco Inc ....D 732 302-0889
Middlesex (G-6150)
Bolt Welding & Iron Works ....G 609 393-3993
Trenton (G-11029)
Carfaro Inc ....E 609 890-6600
Trenton (G-11033)
Ciccone Inc...G 732 349-7071
Toms River (G-10871)

Clems Ornamental Iron Works ....D 732 968-7200
Piscataway (G-8750)
Columbian Orna Ir Works Inc ....G 973 697-0927
Paterson (G-8236)
Consolidated Stl Alum Fence Inc ....E 908 272-0494
Kenilworth (G-4948)
Creative Metal Works Inc ....F 973 579-3717
Sparta (G-10495)
Cusumano Perma-Rail Co.....................G 908 245-9281
Roselle Park (G-9692)
Doortec Archtctural Met GL LLC ....G 201 497-5056
River Vale (G-9469)
Empire Lumber & Millwork Co ....E 973 242-2700
Newark (G-7153)
F & C Prof Alum Railings Corp ....E 908 753-8886
Plainfield (G-8861)
Fairway Building Products LLC..............E 609 890-6600
Trenton (G-11059)
FMB Systems Inc ....D 973 485-5544
Harrison (G-4184)
George Ciocher Inc..............................G 732 818-3495
Toms River (G-10880)
Harsco Corporation ....E 908 454-7169
Plainfield (G-8864)
Integrity Ironworks Corp ....G 732 254-2200
Sayreville (G-9824)
International Design & Mfg LLC ....G 908 587-2884
Linden (G-5391)
Interntnal Archtctral Irnworks................E 973 741-0749
Irvington (G-4594)
Interstate Architectural & Ir..................G 201 941-0393
Cliffside Park (G-1541)
Interstate Panel LLC ....F 609 586-4411
Trenton (G-11069)
J G Schmidt Steel ....F 973 473-4822
Passaic (G-8149)
James Zylstra Enterprises Inc ....E 973 383-6768
Lafayette (G-5047)
K & A Architectural Met GL LLC ....G 908 687-0247
Hillside (G-4423)
Kaufman Stairs Inc ....E 908 862-3579
Rahway (G-9206)
LMC-HB Corp ....E 862 239-9814
Paterson (G-8324)
Marchione Industries Inc ....F 718 317-4900
Lyndhurst (G-5690)
McNichols Company.............................F 877 884-4653
New Brunswick (G-6979)
Merchant & Evans Inc..........................E 609 387-3033
Burlington (G-984)
Mershon Concrete LLC ....E 609 298-2150
Bordentown (G-603)
Morsemere Iron Works Inc ....F 201 941-1133
Ridgefield (G-9376)
Newman Ornamental Iron Works ....F 732 223-9042
Brielle (G-914)
Omnia Industries Inc ....E 973 239-7272
Cedar Grove (G-1295)
Papp Iron Works Inc ....D 908 731-1000
Plainfield (G-8871)
Par Troy Sheet Metal & AC LLC ....G 973 227-1150
Fairfield (G-3280)
Permanore Archtctural Finishes ....G 908 797-4177
Milford (G-6247)
Pioneer Railing Inc..............................G 609 387-0981
Beverly (G-464)
Rambusch Decorating Company ....E 201 333-2525
Jersey City (G-4815)
S & S Socius Inc.................................E 732 698-2400
Edison (G-2609)
Security Fabricators Inc ....F 908 272-9171
Kenilworth (G-4996)
Studio Dellarte....................................G 718 599-3715
Jersey City (G-4835)

METAL FABRICATORS: Plate

Airmet Inc ....G 973 481-5550
Newark (G-7074)
Akw Inc ....G 732 493-1883
Ocean (G-7714)
Akw Inc ....G 732 530-9186
Shrewsbury (G-9988)
Arrow Shed LLC ....E 973 835-3200
Haskell (G-4206)
Asco Valve LLC ....D 973 966-2437
Florham Park (G-3488)
Asco Valve LLC....................................E 973 386-9000
Parsippany (G-7953)
CB&i LLC ....C 856 482-3000
Trenton (G-11036)

P
R
O
D
U
C
T

Crown Engineering Corp ....E 800 631-2153
Farmingdale (G-3382)
Jersey Tank Fabricators Inc ....E 609 758-7670
South Plainfield (G-10388)
Nova Flex Group ....F 856 768-2275
West Berlin (G-11738)
Pulsonics Inc ....F 800 999-6785
Belleville (G-313)
Scientific Alloys Corp ....F 973 478-8323
Clifton (G-1717)
Shell Packaging Corporation ......E 908 871-7000
Berkeley Heights (G-422)
Springfield Metal Pdts Co Inc .....F 973 379-4600
Springfield (G-10578)
Stirrup Metal Products Corp ....F 973 824-7086
Newark (G-7330)
Theodore E Mozer Inc ....E 856 829-1432
Palmyra (G-7851)
Titanium Fabrication Corp ....D 973 227-5300
Fairfield (G-3327)
Triangle Tube/Phase III Co Inc ....B 856 228-9940
Paulsboro (G-8427)
Ulma Form-Works Inc ....D 201 882-1122
Hawthorne (G-4261)
Waage Electric Inc ....G 908 245-9363
Kenilworth (G-5004)

METAL FABRICATORS: Sheet

67 Pollock Ave Corp ....G 201 432-1156
Jersey City (G-4692)
A R J Custom Fabrication Inc ....F 609 695-6227
Trenton (G-11011)
A&B Heating & Cooling ....G 908 289-2231
Elizabeth (G-2703)
Abco Metal LLC ....F 973 772-8160
Paterson (G-8196)
Aerosmith ....G 973 614-9392
South Hackensack (G-10252)
Air & Specialties Sheet Metal ......E 908 233-8306
Mountainside (G-6866)
Airfiltronix Corp ....G 973 779-5577
Clifton (G-1560)
Airmet Inc ....G 973 481-5550
Newark (G-7074)
Airtec Inc ....G 732 382-3700
Rahway (G-9172)
Ajay Metal Fabricators Inc ....G 908 523-0557
Linden (G-5345)
Allentown Inc ....B 609 259-7951
Allentown (G-28)
Allied Metal Industries Inc ....E 973 824-7347
Newark (G-7077)
Amerifab Corp ....F 973 777-2120
Lodi (G-5576)
Andrew B Duffy Inc ....F 856 845-4900
West Deptford (G-11815)
Ango Electronics Corporation ....F 201 955-0800
North Arlington (G-7415)
Architctural Metal Designs Inc .....E 856 765-3000
Millville (G-6285)
Argyle Industries Inc ....F 908 725-8800
Branchburg (G-637)
Artus Corp ....E 201 568-1000
Englewood (G-2873)
Atlantic Air Enterprises Inc ....F 732 381-4000
Rahway (G-9178)
Atlantic Coastal Welding Inc ....F 732 269-1088
Bayville (G-250)
B & S Sheet Metal Co Inc ....F 973 427-3739
Hawthorne (G-4218)
Babbitt Mfg Co Inc ....F 856 692-3245
Vineland (G-11326)
Banicki Sheet Metal Inc ....F 201 385-5938
Bergenfield (G-382)
BCsmachine & Mfg Corp ....G 908 561-1656
South Plainfield (G-10335)
Belden Inc ....F 908 925-8000
Elizabeth (G-2712)
Benco Inc ....F 973 575-4440
Fairfield (G-3146)
Bill Chambers Sheet Metal ....G 856 848-4774
Woodbury Heights (G-12174)
Blackhawk Cre Corporation ....F 856 887-0162
Salem (G-9803)
Bloomfield Manufacturing Co ....F 973 575-8900
Oakland (G-7676)
BR Welding Inc ....F 732 363-8253
Howell (G-4547)
Breure Sheet Metal Co Inc ....G 973 772-6423
Clifton (G-1578)

Brook Metal Products Inc ....F 908 355-1601
Lawrence Township (G-5241)
Brothers Sheet Metal ....F 973 579-1788
Newton (G-7383)
Brothers Sheet Metal Inc ....F 973 228-3221
Roseland (G-9648)
Cain Machine Inc ....F 856 825-7225
Millville (G-6291)
Cambridge Sheet Metal Inc ....F 973 386-0788
Blairstown (G-495)
Central Metal Fabricators Inc ....F 732 938-6900
Farmingdale (G-3379)
Classic Industries Inc ....G 973 227-1366
Parsippany (G-7972)
CPS Metals Inc ....F 856 779-0846
Maple Shade (G-5901)
Crett Construction Inc ....G 973 663-1184
Lake Hopatcong (G-5055)
Cutmark Inc ....G 856 234-3428
Mount Laurel (G-6791)
Danson Sheet Metal Inc ....E 201 343-4876
Hackensack (G-3903)
Delair LLC ....D 856 663-2900
Pennsauken (G-8502)
Delaware Valley Sign Corp ....D 609 386-0100
Burlington (G-967)
Demand LLC ....F 908 526-2020
Somerville (G-10206)
Duct Mate Inc ....G 201 488-8002
Hackensack (G-3907)
Durex Inc ....C 908 688-0800
Union (G-11174)
Dutra Sheet Metal Co ....G 856 692-8058
Vineland (G-11354)
E P Homiek Shtmtl Sups Inc ....E 732 364-7644
Lakewood (G-5111)
Evs Interactive Inc ....F 718 784-3690
Riverdale (G-9480)
Ewc Controls Inc ....E 732 446-3110
Manalapan (G-5846)
Excel Die Sharpening Corp ....E 908 587-2606
Linden (G-5371)
Fabulous Fabricators LLC ....E 973 779-2400
Totowa (G-10944)
Falcon Industries Inc ....G 732 563-9889
Somerset (G-10100)
Frc Electrical Industries Inc ....E 908 464-3200
New Providence (G-7036)
Garvey Corporation ....D 609 561-2450
Hammonton (G-4137)
Gauer Metal Products Co Inc ....E 908 241-4080
Kenilworth (G-4958)
Geneva Metal Products Co Inc ......F 973 472-3073
Passaic (G-8144)
Giant Stl Fabricators Erectors ......G 908 241-6766
Roselle (G-9671)
Golden Metal Products Corp ....F 973 399-1157
Hillside (G-4409)
H & H Industries Inc ....F 856 663-4444
Pennsauken (G-8520)
Haenssler Shtmtl Works Inc ....F 973 373-6360
Newark (G-7182)
Handi-Hut Inc ....F 973 614-1800
Clifton (G-1633)
Harold R Henrich Inc ....D 732 370-4455
Lakewood (G-5132)
Hutchinson Industries Inc ....F 609 394-1010
Trenton (G-11064)
In-Line Shtmtl Fabricators ....G 201 339-8121
Bayonne (G-233)
Independent Metal Sales Inc ....F 609 261-8090
Hainesport (G-4074)
Independent Sheet Metal Co Inc ...F 973 423-1150
Riverdale (G-9482)
Inox Components ....F 856 256-0800
Pitman (G-8842)
Intercoastal Fabricators Inc ....G 856 629-4105
Williamstown (G-12090)
International Swimming Pools ....E 732 565-9229
New Brunswick (G-6968)
Internet-Sales USA Corporation ....F 775 468-8379
Rockaway (G-9575)
J & M Air Inc ....E 908 707-4040
Somerville (G-10217)
James A Stanlick Jr ....G 973 366-7316
Wharton (G-11990)
Jesco Iron Crafts Inc ....F 201 488-4545
Bogota (G-548)
Jet Precision Metal Inc ....G 973 423-4350
Hawthorne (G-4244)

John E Herbst Heating & Coolg .....G 732 721-0088
Parlin (G-7933)
Joseph Bbinec Shtmtl Works Inc ...E 732 388-0155
Rahway (G-9205)
Klm Mechanical Contractors ....E 201 385-6965
Dumont (G-2120)
Lectro Products Inc ....G 732 462-2463
Freehold (G-3666)
Leibrock Metal Products Inc ....G 732 695-0326
Ocean (G-7731)
Madhu B Goyal MD ....G 908 769-0307
South Plainfield (G-10400)
Marino International Corp ....G 732 752-5100
South Plainfield (G-10404)
Marlyn Sheet Metal Inc ....F 856 863-6900
Clayton (G-1526)
Marx NJ Group LLC ....E 732 901-3880
Bound Brook (G-620)
Max Gurtman & Sons Inc ....G 973 478-7000
Clifton (G-1671)
Medlaurel Inc ....E 856 461-6600
Delanco (G-2007)
Metal Dynamix LLC ....G 856 235-4559
Cherry Hill (G-1400)
Millar Sheet Metal ....G 201 997-1990
Kearny (G-4899)
Millco Custom Fabricators Inc ....G 908 756-3640
South Plainfield (G-10407)
Nordic Metal LLC ....G 908 245-8900
Kenilworth (G-4982)
Oeg Building Materials Inc ....E 732 667-3636
Sayreville (G-9834)
P L M Manufacturing Company ......E 201 342-3636
Hackensack (G-3960)
Pabst Enterprises Equipment Co ...E 908 353-2880
Elizabeth (G-2764)
Par Sheet Metal Inc ....F 908 241-2477
Roselle (G-9681)
Park Steel & Iron Co ....F 732 775-7500
Neptune (G-6927)
Passaic Metal & Bldg Sups Co ......D 973 546-9000
Clifton (G-1691)
Pcr Technologies Inc ....G 973 882-0017
Pine Brook (G-8713)
Pepco Manufacturing Co ....D 856 783-3700
Somerdale (G-10042)
Pl Metal Products Inc ....G 201 955-0800
Linden (G-5428)
Precision Metalcrafters Inc ....E 856 629-1020
Williamstown (G-12100)
Prism Sheet Metal Inc ....G 973 673-0213
Orange (G-7824)
R M F Associates Inc ....C 908 687-9355
Union (G-11218)
Rails Company Inc ....E 973 763-4320
Maplewood (G-5926)
Rainbow Metal Units Corp ....E 718 784-3690
Riverdale (G-9484)
Ranco Precision Sheet Metal ....G 973 472-8808
Clifton (G-1710)
Ricklyn Co Inc ....G 908 689-6770
Columbia (G-1800)
Schrader & Company Inc ....F 973 579-1160
Newton (G-7403)
Service Metal Fabricating Inc ....G 973 989-7199
Dover (G-2110)
Sheet Metal Products Inc ....D 973 482-0450
Newark (G-7310)
Sonrise Metal Inc ....F 973 423-4717
Hopatcong (G-4538)
South Jersey Metal Inc ....E 856 228-0642
Deptford (G-2067)
Sperro Metal Products LLC ....F 973 335-2000
Montville (G-6494)
Springfield Heating & AC Co ....F 908 233-8400
Mountainside (G-6888)
Star Metal Products ....E 908 474-9860
Linden (G-5448)
Stirrup Metal Products Corp ....F 973 824-7086
Newark (G-7330)
Tam Metal Products Inc ....E 201 848-7800
Mahwah (G-5818)
Ware Industries Inc ....D 908 757-9000
South Plainfield (G-10454)
Welded Products Co Inc ....E 973 589-0180
Newark (G-7358)

METAL FABRICATORS: Structural, Ship

Allied Metal Industries Inc ....E 973 824-7347
Newark (G-7077)

(G-0000) Company's Geographic Section entry number

Sea Habor Marine Inc ....G...... 732 477-8577
Brick (G-759)

METAL FABRICATORS: Structural, Ship

Flame Cut Steel Inc ....F...... 973 373-9300
Irvington (G-4586)
Susan R Bauer Inc ....G...... 973 657-1590
Ringwood (G-9456)

METAL FINISHING SVCS

A & L Industries Inc ....E...... 973 589-8070
Newark (G-7064)
Advanced Metal Processing ....G...... 856 327-0048
Millville (G-6274)
Cameo Metal Products Inc ....F...... 732 388-4000
Rahway (G-9180)
Durex Inc ....C...... 908 688-0800
Union (G-11174)
Foremost Manufacturing Co Inc ....D...... 908 687-4646
Union (G-11185)
Paramount Metal Finishing Co ....C...... 908 862-0772
Linden (G-5424)
Prem-Khichi Enterprises Inc ....F...... 973 242-0300
East Brunswick (G-2174)
Sar Industrial Finishing Inc ....F...... 609 567-2772
Berlin (G-441)
Sun Metal Finishing Inc ....E...... 973 684-0119
North Haledon (G-7554)
Vigilant Design ....G...... 201 432-3900
Jersey City (G-4843)

METAL MINING SVCS

Coastal Metal Recycling Corp ....G...... 732 738-6000
Keasbey (G-4927)
Connell Mining Products LLC ....D...... 908 673-3700
Berkeley Heights (G-406)
Industrial Stl & Fastener Corp ....G...... 610 667-2220
Cherry Hill (G-1380)

METAL SERVICE CENTERS & OFFICES

Alloy Stainless Products Co ....D...... 973 256-1616
Totowa (G-10928)
Ansun Protective Metals Inc ....G...... 732 302-0616
Middlesex (G-6148)
Asbury Carbons Inc ....G...... 908 537-2155
Asbury (G-66)
Bedlam Corp ....F...... 973 774-8770
Montclair (G-6408)
Benedict-Miller LLC ....F...... 908 497-1477
Kenilworth (G-4944)
Doolan Industries Incorporated ....G...... 856 985-1880
Marlton (G-5973)
Dynamic Metals Inc ....E...... 908 769-0522
Piscataway (G-8761)
FW Winter Inc ....E...... 856 963-7490
Camden (G-1067)
Independent Metal Sales Inc ....F...... 609 261-8090
Hainesport (G-4074)
Lentine Sheet Metal Inc ....F...... 908 486-8974
Linden (G-5402)
Merchant & Evans Inc ....E...... 609 387-3033
Burlington (G-984)
Metal Cutting Corporation ....D...... 973 239-1100
Cedar Grove (G-1291)
Procedyne Corp ....E...... 732 249-8347
New Brunswick (G-6996)
RS Phillips Steel LLC ....E...... 973 827-6464
Sussex (G-10676)
Steelstran Industries Inc ....E...... 732 574-0700
Avenel (G-152)

METAL SPINNING FOR THE TRADE

F G Clover Company Inc ....G...... 973 627-1160
Rockaway (G-9565)
Laeger Metal Spinning Co Inc ....G...... 908 925-5530
Linden (G-5399)

METAL STAMPING, FOR THE TRADE

A K Stamping Co Inc ....D...... 908 232-7300
Mountainside (G-6865)
Accurate Forming LLC ....E...... 973 827-7155
Hamburg (G-4087)
Acme Cosmetic Components LLC ....E...... 718 335-3000
Secaucus (G-9865)
Camptown Tool & Die Co Inc ....G...... 908 688-8406
Kenilworth (G-4947)

Carter Manufacturing Co Inc ....E...... 201 935-0770
Moonachie (G-6512)
Clover Stamping Inc ....G...... 973 278-4888
Paterson (G-8234)
Co-Planar Inc ....F...... 973 625-3500
Denville (G-2032)
Coining Inc ....C...... 201 791-4020
Montvale (G-6449)
Coining Holding Company ....F...... 201 791-4020
Montvale (G-6450)
Coining Manufacturing LLC ....E...... 973 253-0500
Colts Neck (G-1781)
Coining Mfg ....G...... 973 253-0500
Clifton (G-1585)
Coining Technologies Inc ....D...... 866 897-2304
Demarest (G-2027)
Deborah Sales & Mfg Co ....G...... 973 344-8466
Newark (G-7138)
Durex Inc ....C...... 908 688-0800
Union (G-11174)
Duron Co Inc ....F...... 973 242-5704
Newark (G-7145)
F & G Tool & Die Inc ....E...... 908 241-5880
Kenilworth (G-4954)
F & M Machine Co Inc ....F...... 908 245-8830
Kenilworth (G-4955)
General Stamping Co Inc ....F...... 973 627-9500
Columbia (G-1797)
H & T Tool Co Inc ....F...... 973 227-4858
Fairfield (G-3214)
H K Metal Craft Mfg Corp ....E...... 973 471-7770
Lodi (G-5585)
Heyco Stamped Products ....D...... 732 286-4336
Toms River (G-10886)
International Rollforms Inc ....E...... 856 228-7100
Deptford (G-2065)
J G Schmidt Co Inc ....D...... 732 563-9500
Green Brook (G-3859)
J J Orly Inc ....F...... 908 276-9212
Clark (G-1501)
J R M Products Inc ....G...... 732 203-0200
Union Beach (G-11238)
Jason Metal Products Corp ....G...... 732 396-1132
Rahway (G-9203)
Jmk Tool Die and Mfg Co Inc ....G...... 201 845-4710
Rochelle Park (G-9530)
Jordan Manufacturing LLC ....G...... 973 383-8363
Lafayette (G-5048)
National Manufacturing Co Inc ....C...... 973 635-8846
Chatham (G-1336)
Paramount Products Co Inc ....F...... 732 458-9200
Brick (G-754)
Peterson Brothers Mfg Co ....E...... 732 271-8240
Middlesex (G-6186)
Peterson Stamping & Mfg Co ....F...... 908 241-0900
Kenilworth (G-4986)
Rails Company Inc ....E...... 973 763-4320
Maplewood (G-5926)
Rapid Manufacturing Co Inc ....E...... 732 279-1252
Toms River (G-10906)
Rebuth Metal Services ....F...... 908 889-6400
Fanwood (G-3373)
Roseville Tool & Manufacturing ....E...... 973 992-5405
Livingston (G-5558)
Small Quantities NJ Inc ....D...... 732 248-9009
Edison (G-2622)
Stirrup Metal Products Corp ....F...... 973 824-7086
Newark (G-7330)
Universal Tools & Mfg Co ....E...... 973 379-4193
Springfield (G-10582)
Weiss-Aug Co Inc ....C...... 973 887-7600
East Hanover (G-2249)
Well Bilt Industries Inc ....F...... 908 486-6002
Linden (G-5458)
Wgjf Manufacturing Corp ....F...... 908 862-1730
Linden (G-5459)

METAL STAMPINGS: Ornamental

Hnt Industries Inc ....G...... 908 322-0414
Scotch Plains (G-9850)

METAL STAMPINGS: Patterned

Short Run Stamping Company Inc ....E...... 908 862-1070
Linden (G-5442)
United Spport Slutions-Lmt Inc ....E...... 973 857-9222
Cedar Grove (G-1305)

METAL STAMPINGS: Perforated

Electronic Parts Specialty Co ....G...... 609 267-0055
Mount Holly (G-6769)

METAL TREATING COMPOUNDS

Chemetall US Inc ....D...... 908 464-6900
New Providence (G-7033)

METAL: Battery

American Aluminum Company ....D...... 908 233-3500
Mountainside (G-6868)
Holistic Solar Usa Inc ....G...... 732 757-5500
Newark (G-7191)
Komline-Sanderson Engrg Corp ....G...... 973 579-0090
Sparta (G-10507)

METALS SVC CENTERS & WHOL: Structural Shapes, Iron Or Steel

Stateline Fabricators LLC ....E...... 908 387-8800
Phillipsburg (G-8672)

METALS SVC CENTERS & WHOLESALERS: Bars, Metal

G M Stainless Inc ....F...... 908 575-1834
Branchburg (G-662)
Gauer Metal Products Co Inc ....E...... 908 241-4080
Kenilworth (G-4958)

METALS SVC CENTERS & WHOLESALERS: Cable, Wire

Ace Electronics Inc ....D...... 732 603-9800
Metuchen (G-6093)
T V L Associates Inc ....G...... 973 790-6766
Wayne (G-11684)

METALS SVC CENTERS & WHOLESALERS: Ferroalloys

Cherishmet Inc ....F...... 201 842-7612
Rutherford (G-9728)

METALS SVC CENTERS & WHOLESALERS: Foundry Prdts

Whibco Inc ....F...... 856 455-9200
Bridgeton (G-804)

METALS SVC CENTERS & WHOLESALERS: Iron & Steel Prdt, Ferrous

Stulz-Sickles Steel Company ....E...... 609 531-2172
Burlington (G-990)
Titanium Industries Inc ....E...... 973 983-1185
Rockaway (G-9613)

METALS SVC CENTERS & WHOLESALERS: Nonferrous Sheets, Etc

Dynasty Metals Inc ....E...... 800 225-3962
Kearny (G-4872)
Nedohon Inc ....G...... 302 533-5512
Wildwood Crest (G-12076)

METALS SVC CENTERS & WHOLESALERS: Pipe & Tubing, Steel

Morris Industries Inc ....E...... 973 835-6600
Pompton Plains (G-8963)

METALS SVC CENTERS & WHOLESALERS: Rope, Wire, Exc Insulated

Doran Sling and Assembly Corp ....G...... 908 355-1101
Hillside (G-4406)

METALS SVC CENTERS & WHOLESALERS: Sheets, Metal

Federal Casters Corp ....D...... 973 483-6700
Harrison (G-4182)
Passaic Metal & Bldg Sups Co ....D...... 973 546-9000
Clifton (G-1691)

Employee Codes: A=Over 500 employees, B=251-500
C=101-250, D=51-100, E=20-50, F=10-19, G=4-9

2018 Harris New Jersey
Manufacturers Directory

PRODUCT

909

METALS SVC CENTERS & WHOLESALERS: Stampings, Metal

Microcast Technologies Corp................D...... 908 523-9503
  Linden (G-5409)

METALS SVC CENTERS & WHOLESALERS: Steel

Allied Metal Industries Inc.............E...... 973 824-7347
  Newark (G-7077)
American Strip Steel Inc................F...... 800 526-1216
  South Plainfield (G-10327)
American Strip Steel Inc................G...... 856 461-8300
  Delanco (G-2002)
Bouras Industries Inc................A...... 908 918-9400
  Summit (G-10637)
Bushwick Metals LLC................E...... 908 754-8700
  South Plainfield (G-10341)
Capital Steel Service LLC................E...... 609 882-6983
  Ewing (G-3005)
Efco Corp................F...... 732 308-1010
  Marlboro (G-5938)
EMR (usa Holdings) Inc................F...... 856 365-7500
  Bellmawr (G-339)
Evans Machine & Tool Co................G...... 732 442-1144
  Perth Amboy (G-8613)
Fazzio Machine & Steel Inc................G...... 609 653-1098
  Glassboro (G-3805)
General Sullivan Group Inc................G...... 609 745-5004
  Pennington (G-8451)
General Sullivan Group Inc................G...... 609 745-5000
  Pennington (G-8452)
Harsco Corporation................E...... 908 454-7169
  Plainfield (G-8864)
Industrial Stl & Fastener Corp................G...... 610 667-2220
  Cherry Hill (G-1380)
Ironbound Welding Inc................G...... 973 589-3128
  Newark (G-7201)
McNichols Company................F...... 877 884-4653
  New Brunswick (G-6979)
Minmetals Inc................F...... 201 809-1898
  Leonia (G-5318)
National Electronic Alloys Inc................E...... 201 337-9400
  Oakland (G-7698)
ONeal Flat Rolled Metals LLC................E...... 609 395-7007
  Monroe Township (G-6388)
Rebuth Metal Services................F...... 908 889-6400
  Fanwood (G-3373)
Stainless Metal Source Intl................G...... 973 977-2200
  Clifton (G-1730)

METALS SVC CENTERS & WHOLESALERS: Steel Decking

Great Railing Inc................F...... 856 875-0050
  Williamstown (G-12089)

METALS SVC CENTERS/WHOL: Forms, Steel Concrete Construction

Sas Stressteel Inc................F...... 973 244-5995
  Fairfield (G-3301)

METALS SVC CNTRS & WHOL: Metal Wires, Ties, Cables/Screening

Plasma Powders & Systems Inc................G...... 732 431-0992
  Marlboro (G-5952)
Skorr Products LLC................F...... 973 523-2606
  Paterson (G-8383)

METALS SVC CTRS & WHOLESALERS: Aluminum Bars, Rods, Etc

Argyle Industries Inc................F...... 908 725-8800
  Branchburg (G-637)
Harley Tool & Machine Inc................G...... 201 244-8899
  Bergenfield (G-386)
Kwg Industries LLC................E...... 908 218-8900
  Hillsborough (G-4354)
Tabco Technologies LLC................G...... 201 438-0422
  Carlstadt (G-1226)

METALS: Precious NEC

Abington Reldan Metals LLC................G...... 732 238-8550
  South River (G-10457)
BASF Catalysts LLC................D...... 732 205-5000
  Iselin (G-4616)

Electrum Inc................F...... 732 396-1616
  Rahway (G-9186)
Ewing Recovery Corp................G...... 609 883-0318
  Ewing (G-3017)
Metallix Direct Gold LLC................G...... 732 544-0891
  Shrewsbury (G-10003)
Metallix Refining Inc................F...... 732 936-0050
  Shrewsbury (G-10004)
Premesco Inc................B...... 908 686-0513
  Union (G-11216)
Starfuels Inc................G...... 201 685-0400
  Englewood (G-2934)
Umicore Precious Metals NJ LLC................E...... 908 222-5006
  South Plainfield (G-10444)
Umicore USA Inc................F...... 908 226-2053
  South Plainfield (G-10445)

METALS: Primary Nonferrous, NEC

Dallas Group of America Inc................C...... 908 534-7800
  Whitehouse (G-12045)
Fisk Alloy Inc................C...... 973 427-7550
  Hawthorne (G-4234)
Fisk Alloy Wire Incorporated................C...... 973 949-4491
  Hawthorne (G-4235)
Mel Chemicals Inc................C...... 908 782-5800
  Flemington (G-3456)
National Electronic Alloys Inc................E...... 201 337-9400
  Oakland (G-7698)
Omg Electronic Chemicals Inc................C...... 908 222-5800
  South Plainfield (G-10418)
Tower Systems Inc................G...... 732 237-8800
  Bayville (G-260)
Victors Three-D Inc................D...... 201 845-4433
  Maywood (G-6062)

METALWORK: Miscellaneous

Bolt Welding & Iron Works................G...... 609 393-3993
  Trenton (G-11029)
Camtec Industries Inc................F...... 732 332-9800
  Colts Neck (G-1780)
Handi-Hut Inc................E...... 973 614-1800
  Clifton (G-1633)
Haydon Corporation................D...... 973 904-0800
  Wayne (G-11646)
Inductotherm Technologies Inc................G...... 609 267-9000
  Rancocas (G-9259)
Luso Machine Inc................F...... 973 242-1717
  Newark (G-7228)
Mainland Plate Glass Company................F...... 609 277-2938
  Pleasantville (G-8912)
Metalico Inc................G...... 908 497-9610
  Cranford (G-1915)
Morsemere Iron Works Inc................F...... 201 941-1133
  Ridgefield (G-9376)
N E R Associates Inc................G...... 908 454-5955
  Phillipsburg (G-8661)
Pipeline Eqp Resources Co LLC................ 888 232-7372
  Boonton (G-579)
RS Phillips Steel LLC................E...... 973 827-6464
  Sussex (G-10676)
Stelfast Inc................E...... 440 879-0077
  Edison (G-2627)
United Eqp Fabricators LLC................G...... 973 242-2737
  Newark (G-7353)
W2f Inc................G...... 609 735-0135
  New Egypt (G-7019)
Wired Products LLC................F...... 551 231-5800
  Paramus (G-7913)

METALWORK: Ornamental

Garden State Iron Inc................F...... 732 918-0760
  Ocean (G-7726)
La Forge De Style LLC................G...... 201 488-1955
  South Hackensack (G-10275)
Leets Steel Inc................G...... 917 416-7977
  Sayreville (G-9828)

METALWORKING MACHINERY WHOLESALERS

Bihler of America Inc................C...... 908 213-9001
  Phillipsburg (G-8644)
P & P Equipment Corporation................F...... 201 489-0050
  River Edge (G-9467)

METERS: Power Factor & Phase Angle

Satec Inc................E...... 908 258-0924
  Union (G-11221)

METERS: Pyrometers, Indl Process

Pyrometer Instrument Co Inc................E...... 609 443-5522
  Windsor (G-12128)

MGMT CONSULTING SVCS: Matls, Incl Purch, Handle & Invntry

Defense Support Svcs Intl LLC................F...... 850 390-4737
  Marlton (G-5971)
Pabin Associates Inc................G...... 201 288-7216
  Hasbrouck Heights (G-4197)
Precision Dealer Services Inc................E...... 908 237-1100
  Flemington (G-3460)
T Wiker Enterprises Inc................G...... 609 261-9494
  Hainesport (G-4079)

MICA

Corp American Mica................G...... 908 587-5237
  Linden (G-5361)

MICROCIRCUITS, INTEGRATED: Semiconductor

Modelware Inc................F...... 732 264-3020
  Holmdel (G-4524)
Semi Conductor Manufacturing................E...... 973 478-2880
  Clifton (G-1720)

MICROFILM EQPT

Zeta Products Inc................E...... 908 688-0440
  Annandale (G-62)

MICROFILM EQPT WHOLESALERS

Image Access Corp................E...... 201 342-7878
  Rockleigh (G-9631)
Zeta Products Inc................E...... 908 688-0440
  Annandale (G-62)

MICROFILM SVCS

Image Access Corp................E...... 201 342-7878
  Rockleigh (G-9631)

MICROPHONES

Mp Production................F...... 973 729-9333
  Sparta (G-10512)
Sound Professionals Inc................G...... 609 267-4400
  Hainesport (G-4078)

MICROWAVE COMPONENTS

Aeroflex Ctrl Components Inc................D...... 732 460-0212
  Eatontown (G-2378)
Compex Corporation................E...... 856 719-8657
  West Berlin (G-11710)
Conolog Corporation................F...... 908 722-8081
  Branchburg (G-650)
Electromagnetic Tech Inds Inc................D...... 973 394-1719
  Boonton (G-564)
Electronic Mfg Svcs Inc................F...... 973 916-1001
  Clifton (G-1614)
G-Way Microwave Inc................F...... 201 343-6388
  South Hackensack (G-10269)
GT Microwave Inc................E...... 973 361-5700
  Randolph (G-9282)
Herley Industries Inc................D...... 973 884-2580
  Whippany (G-12024)
Herley-Cti Inc................F...... 973 884-2580
  Whippany (G-12025)
K R Electronics Inc................F...... 732 636-1900
  Avenel (G-137)
Meca Electronics Inc................D...... 973 625-0661
  Denville (G-2047)
Merrimac Industries Inc................D...... 973 575-1300
  West Caldwell (G-11790)
Microwave Consulting Corp................G...... 973 523-6700
  Paterson (G-8339)
Mwt Materials Inc................F...... 973 928-8300
  Passaic (G-8166)
Princeton Microwave Technology................G...... 609 586-8140
  Trenton (G-11107)
Rs Microwave Co Inc................E...... 973 492-1207
  Butler (G-1018)
Synergy Microwave Corp................D...... 973 881-8800
  Paterson (G-8394)
Ute Microwave Inc................E...... 732 922-1009
  Ocean (G-7748)

(G-0000) Company's Geographic Section entry number

Waveline Incorporated ....E 973 226-9100
Fairfield (G-3350)

MICROWAVE OVENS: Household

Sharp Electronics Corporation...........A 201 529-8200
Mahwah (G-5811)

MILITARY GOODS & REGALIA STORES

Red The Uniform Tailor Inc ....E 848 299-0100
Lakewood (G-5176)

MILITARY INSIGNIA

Services Equipment Com LLC..............G 973 992-4404
Livingston (G-5560)

MILL PRDTS: Structural & Rail

A & A Ironwork Co Inc ....F 973 728-4300
Hewitt (G-4287)

MILLINERY SUPPLIES: Veils & Veiling, Bridal, Funeral, Etc

Edward Berger Inc ....E 609 571-9676
Old Bridge (G-7778)
French Textile Co Inc ....F 973 471-5000
Clifton (G-1623)

MILLING: Feed, Wheat

Bay State Milling Company ....D ... 973 772-3400
Clifton (G-1573)

MILLING: Grain Cereals, Cracked

Cibo Vita Inc ....C 201 773-4873
Fair Lawn (G-3087)
Coco International Inc ....E 973 694-1200
Wayne (G-11620)

MILLWORK

Architctral Cbinetry Mllwk LLC..............G 908 213-2001
Phillipsburg (G-8639)
B & B Millwork & Doors Inc ....G 973 249-0300
Kenilworth (G-4939)
Bestmark National LLC ....E 862 772-4863
Irvington (G-4578)
Bon Architectual Mill Work LLC ....G 856 320-2872
Pennsauken (G-8487)
Cabinet Tronics Inc ....F 609 267-2625
Birmingham (G-466)
Castle Woodcraft Assoc LLC ....F 732 349-1519
Pine Beach (G-8678)
Caw LLC ....F 973 429-7004
Bloomfield (G-506)
Cerami Wood Products Inc ....F 732 968-7222
Piscataway (G-8747)
Classic Designer Woodwork Inc ....G 201 280-3711
Glen Rock (G-3823)
Cozzolino Inc ....E 973 731-9292
West Orange (G-11891)
Creating Your Design LLC ....G 973 357-1080
Paterson (G-8240)
Custom Counters By Precision ....E 973 773-0111
Passaic (G-8133)
Custom Wood Furniture Inc ....F 973 579-4880
Newton (G-7385)
Dans Woodwork ....G 973 751-4506
Belleville (G-299)
Design of Tomorrow Inc ....F 973 227-1000
Fairfield (G-3177)
Donnelly Industries Inc ....D 973 672-1800
Wayne (G-11626)
Dor-Win Manufacturing Co ....E 201 796-4300
Elmwood Park (G-2815)
Dreamstar Construction LLC ....F 732 393-2572
Middletown (G-6213)
Empire Lumber & Millwork Co ....E 973 242-2700
Newark (G-7153)
Epic Millwork LLC ....E 732 296-0273
Somerset (G-10096)
Everlast Interiors ....G 732 252-9965
Manalapan (G-5845)
F T Millwork Inc ....G 732 741-1216
Red Bank (G-9330)
Filipe Custom Woodwork ....E 908 486-0033
Linden (G-5375)
Gass Custom Woodworking ....G 201 493-9282
Paramus (G-7871)

Glen Rock Stair Corp ....E 201 337-9595
Franklin Lakes (G-3618)
Hutchinson Cabinets ....E 856 468-5500
Sewell (G-9956)
Ideal Jacobs Corporation ....E 973 275-5100
Maplewood (G-5922)
Intex Millwork Solutions LLC...............E 856 293-4100
Mays Landing (G-6039)
Joseph Naticchia ....F 609 882-7709
Ewing (G-3028)
K2 Millwork Ltd Liability Co ....G 609 379-6411
Columbus (G-1804)
Kempton Wood Products......................G 732 449-8673
Wall Township (G-11493)
Lauderdale Millwork Inc ....G 908 508-9550
Berkeley Heights (G-417)
Lees Woodworking Inc ....G 732 681-1002
Wall Township (G-11495)
Lux Home Inc ....G 845 623-2821
Paramus (G-7886)
M K Woodworking Inc ....G 609 771-1350
Ewing (G-3036)
M R C Millwork & Trim Inc ....G 201 954-2176
Franklin Lakes (G-3620)
ML Woodwork Inc ....G 201 953-2175
Elmwood Park (G-2837)
Mountain Millwork ....G 908 647-1100
Warren (G-11561)
New Jersey Hardwoods Inc ....E 908 754-0990
Plainfield (G-8869)
Nyc Woodworking Inc ....G 718 222-1221
Marlboro (G-5950)
Old Fashion Woodworking Inc ....F 973 808-9663
Rahway (G-9216)
Ornate Millwork LLC ....G 866 464-5596
Lakewood (G-5169)
Palisade Lumber & Supply Inc ....G 201 656-4400
Jersey City (G-4797)
Palumbo Millwork Inc ....G 732 938-3266
Wall Township (G-11502)
Pkc Finewoodworking LLC ....G 201 951-8880
Montville (G-6492)
Precision Dealer Services Inc ....E 908 237-1100
Flemington (G-3460)
Prestige Millwork LLC ....G 908 526-5100
Bridgewater (G-876)
Progress Woodwork ....G 732 906-8680
Edison (G-2598)
R & M Manufacturing Inc ....E 609 495-8032
Monroe Township (G-6390)
R J Hoppe Store Construction ....G 973 485-5665
Newark (G-7283)
Rex Lumber Company ....G 732 446-4200
Manalapan (G-5861)
Rock Solid Woodworking LLC ....G 732 974-1261
Sea Girt (G-9862)
Salernos Kitchen Cabinets ....E 201 794-1990
Saddle Brook (G-9789)
Somerset Wood Products Co ....E 908 526-0030
Raritan (G-9316)
Sourland Mountain Wdwkg LLC T........G 908 806-7661
Neshanic Station (G-6939)
Summit Millwork & Supply Inc............G 908 273-1486
Summit (G-10660)
Tea Elle Woodworks ....G 732 938-9660
Farmingdale (G-3395)
Terhune Bros Woodworking ....G 973 962-6686
Ringwood (G-9457)
Unix Cabinetry Inc ....G 201 995-6969
Paterson (G-8405)
V Custom Millwork Inc ....F 732 469-9600
Bridgewater (G-907)
Vanco Millwork Inc ....F 973 992-3061
Livingston (G-5568)
Visual Architectural Designs ....F 908 754-3000
South Plainfield (G-10451)
West Hudson Lumber & Mllwk Co ....G 201 991-7191
Kearny (G-4920)
Wohners ....G 201 568-7307
Englewood (G-2944)
Wood Works ....G 856 728-4520
Williamstown (G-12115)
Woodhaven Lumber & Millwork ....E 732 295-8800
Point Pleasant Beach (G-8928)
Woodtec Inc ....G 908 979-0180
Hackettstown (G-4043)
Woodworking Inc Corporate ....E 973 227-2211
Fairfield (G-3354)

MINE & QUARRY SVCS: Nonmetallic Minerals

Jlb Hauling Ltd Liability Co..................G 856 514-2771
Pennsville (G-8592)

MINE EXPLORATION SVCS: Nonmetallic Minerals

Tag Minerals Inc ....G 732 252-5146
Freehold (G-3689)

MINERAL PIGMENT MINING

Axiom Ingredients LLC ....F 732 669-2458
Iselin (G-4615)

MINERAL WOOL

Advantage Fiberglass Inc ....G 609 926-4606
Egg Harbor Township (G-2677)
Johns Manville Corporation ....C 856 768-7000
Berlin (G-436)
Owens Corning Sales LLC ....G 201 998-5666
Kearny (G-4904)
Pacor Inc ....E 609 324-1100
Bordentown (G-607)
Passaic Metal & Bldg Sups Co ....D 973 546-9000
Clifton (G-1691)
Pekay Industries Inc ....F 732 938-2722
Farmingdale (G-3392)

MINERAL WOOL INSULATION PRDTS

United States Mineral Pdts Co..............D 973 347-1200
Stanhope (G-10591)

MINERALS: Ground Or Otherwise Treated

Anthracite Industries Inc.....................G 908 537-2155
Asbury (G-65)
Mel Chemicals Inc.............................C 908 782-5800
Flemington (G-3456)

MINERALS: Ground or Treated

Asbury Graphite Mills Inc ....E 908 537-2155
Asbury (G-67)
Asbury Graphite Mills Inc ....D 908 537-2157
Asbury (G-68)
Fine Minerals Intl Inc ....G 732 318-6760
Edison (G-2520)
Isp Global Technologies Inc ....G 973 628-4000
Wayne (G-11655)
Isp Global Technologies LLC ....G 973 628-4000
Wayne (G-11656)
Minmetals Inc ....F 201 809-1898
Leonia (G-5318)

MINING MACHINES & EQPT: Clarifying, Mineral

Enviro-Clear Company Inc ....F 908 638-5507
High Bridge (G-4295)

MINING MACHINES & EQPT: Feeders, Ore & Aggregate

K-Tron International Inc.......................D 856 589-0500
Sewell (G-9962)

MINING MACHINES & EQPT: Pulverizers, Stone, Stationary

Pallmann Pulverizers Co Inc.................E 973 471-1450
Clifton (G-1688)

MIXERS: Hot Metal

Bartell Morrison (usa) LLC...................F 732 566-5400
Freehold (G-3641)

MIXTURES & BLOCKS: Asphalt Paving

All Surface Asphalt Paving ....G 732 295-3800
Point Pleasant Boro (G-8930)
Asphalt Paving Systems Inc ....C 609 561-4161
Hammonton (G-4131)
Brick-Wall Corp ....E 732 787-0226
Atlantic Highlands (G-109)
Brick-Wall Corp ....G 609 693-6223
Forked River (G-3534)

P
R
O
D
U
C
T

Brunswick Hot Mix Corp ....D 908 233-4444
Westfield (G-11922)
Central Jersey Hot Mix Asp LLC ....G 732 323-0226
Jackson (G-4656)
Chevron USA Inc ....D 732 738-2000
Perth Amboy (G-8610)
Crowfoot Associates Inc ....G 609 561-0107
West Berlin (G-11713)
Earle Asphalt Company ....C 732 308-1113
Wall Township (G-11479)
Hanson Aggregates Wrp Inc ....E 972 653-5500
Wall Township (G-11487)
Louis N Rothberg & Son Inc ....E 732 356-9505
Middlesex (G-6176)
Richard E Pierson Mtls Corp ....G 856 740-2400
Williamstown (G-12103)
Richard E Pierson Mtls Corp ....G 856 691-0083
Vineland (G-11399)
Richard E Pierson Mtls Corp ....C 856 467-4199
Pilesgrove (G-8676)
Schifano Construction Corp ....F 732 752-3450
Middlesex (G-6194)
Stavola Asphalt Company Inc ....E 732 542-2328
Tinton Falls (G-10848)
Stavola Construction Mtls Inc ....E 732 356-5700
Bound Brook (G-625)
Stone Industries Inc ....D 973 595-6250
Haledon (G-4085)
Tilcon New York Inc ....G 973 835-0028
Riverdale (G-9490)
Tilcon New York Inc ....D 800 789-7625
North Bergen (G-7489)
Weldon Asphalt Corp ....F 973 627-7500
Rockaway (G-9624)
Weldon Asphalt Corp ....E 908 322-7840
Watchung (G-11597)
Ziegler Chem & Mineral Corp.........E 732 752-4111
Piscataway (G-8839)

MOBILE COMMUNICATIONS EQPT

Mizco International Inc ....D 732 912-2000
Avenel (G-141)
Open Terra Inc ....G 732 765-9600
Matawan (G-6026)
Tone Layout LLC ....G 201 438-1746
Ridgefield (G-9386)

MOBILE HOMES

Acton Mobile Industries Inc ....G 610 485-5100
Burlington (G-953)
Wireless Experience of PA Inc ....G 732 552-0050
Toms River (G-10922)

MODELS

Scientific Models Inc ....E 908 464-7070
Berkeley Heights (G-421)

MODELS: General, Exc Toy

Artisan Model Mold...................G 908 453-3524
Belvidere (G-366)
Central Art & Engineering Inc ....G 609 758-5922
Cream Ridge (G-1931)
Franklin Mint LLC ....E 800 843-6468
Fort Lee (G-3555)
Harry Shaw Model Maker Inc ....G 609 268-0647
Shamong (G-9970)
Rapid Models & Prototypes Inc ....G 856 933-2929
Runnemede (G-9720)

MODELS: Railroad, Exc Toy

Microelettrica-Usa LLC...............F 973 598-0806
Budd Lake (G-937)

MOLDED RUBBER PRDTS

Accu Seal Rubber Inc ....G 732 246-4333
New Brunswick (G-6942)
Eastern Molding Co Inc ....G 973 759-0220
Belleville (G-301)
Elastograf Inc ....D 973 209-3161
Hamburg (G-4094)
Hawthorne Rubber Mfg Corp ....E 973 427-3337
Hawthorne (G-4240)
Manville Rubber Products Inc ....E 908 526-9111
Manville (G-5896)
Panova Inc ....E 973 263-1700
Towaco (G-11000)

Pierce-Roberts Rubber Company ....F 609 394-5245
Ewing (G-3043)
Pure Rubber Products Co ....G 973 784-3690
Rockaway (G-9602)
Seajay Manufacturing Corp ....F 732 774-0900
Neptune (G-6931)
Star-Glo Industries LLC..............C 201 939-6162
East Rutherford (G-2326)
Transport Products Inc ....G 973 857-6090
Cedar Grove (G-1302)
Water Master Co ....G 732 247-1900
Highland Park (G-4305)

MOLDING COMPOUNDS

Custom Molders Group LLC ....G 908 218-7997
Branchburg (G-654)
Infinity Compounding LLC ....E 856 467-3030
Logan Township (G-5614)
Louis A Nelson Inc ....F 973 743-7404
Bloomfield (G-518)
Med Connection LLC ....G 908 213-7012
Phillipsburg (G-8659)
Wexford International Inc ....G 908 781-7200
Gladstone (G-3799)

MOLDINGS & TRIM: Metal, Exc Automobile

Randall Mfg Co Inc ....E 973 482-8603
Newark (G-7284)
Thermwell Products Co Inc ....B 201 684-4400
Mahwah (G-5820)

MOLDINGS & TRIM: Wood

Abatetech Inc ....E 609 265-2107
Lumberton (G-5650)

MOLDINGS: Picture Frame

Don Shrts Pcture Frmes Molding.......G 732 363-1323
Howell (G-4552)
Frameware Inc ....F 800 582-5608
Fairfield (G-3201)
III Eagle Enterprises Ltd ....E 973 237-1111
Ringwood (G-9449)
Roma Moulding Inc ....F 732 346-0999
Edison (G-2607)

MOLDS: Indl

Art Mold & Polishing Co Inc..........F 908 518-9191
Roselle (G-9661)
Art Mold & Tool Corporation ....G 201 935-3377
East Rutherford (G-2278)
C and C Tool Co LLC ....G 908 431-0330
Hillsborough (G-4324)
CK Manufacturing Inc ....E 973 808-3500
Fairfield (G-3159)
DEB Manufacturing Inc ....G 732 364-7007
Lakewood (G-5107)
Dependable Precision Products ....G 973 887-3304
Parsippany (G-7980)
Eb Machine Corp ....G 973 442-7729
Wharton (G-11986)
Garden State Tool & Mold Corp ....G 908 245-2041
South Amboy (G-10238)
H & W Tool Co Inc ....F 973 366-0131
Dover (G-2088)
Hanrahan Tool Co Inc ....G 732 919-7300
Farmingdale (G-3386)
Heinz Glas USA Inc ....F 908 474-0300
Linden (G-5383)
HNST Mold Inspections LLC ....F 201 733-0091
Mahwah (G-5781)
J-Mac Plastics Inc ....E 908 709-1111
Kenilworth (G-4965)
Lawrence Mold and Tool Corp ....G 609 392-5422
Lawrenceville (G-5260)
Linden Mold and Tool Corp ....E 732 381-1411
Rahway (G-9209)
Mold Polishing Company Inc ....G 908 518-9191
Garwood (G-3779)
Pahco Machine Inc ....G 609 587-1188
Trenton (G-11094)
TEC Cast Inc ....E 201 935-3885
Carlstadt (G-1227)
Union Tool & Mold Co Inc ....E 973 763-6611
Maplewood (G-5931)
Universal Mold & Tool Inc ....F 856 563-0488
Vineland (G-11412)
West Pattern Works Inc ....F 609 443-6241
Cranbury (G-1891)

MOLDS: Plastic Working & Foundry

Continental Precision Corp...........C 908 754-3030
Piscataway (G-8752)
Lincoln Mold & Die Corp ....D 908 241-3344
Warren (G-11558)
Rotech Tool & Mold Co Inc ....G 908 241-9669
Kenilworth (G-4993)
Sigco Tool & Mfg Co Inc ....E 856 753-6565
West Berlin (G-11749)
Thal Precision Industries Inc ....G 732 381-6106
Clark (G-1517)
Viking Mold & Tool Corp ....G 609 476-9333
Dorothy (G-2074)

MONORAIL SYSTEMS

Bombardier Transportation...........B 973 624-9300
Newark (G-7109)
Teledynamics LLC ....E 973 248-3360
Towaco (G-11004)

MONUMENTS & GRAVE MARKERS, EXC TERRAZZO

H T Hall Inc ....F 732 449-3441
Spring Lake (G-10533)

MONUMENTS: Concrete

Suburban Monument & Vault ....G 973 242-7007
Newark (G-7332)

MONUMENTS: Cut Stone, Exc Finishing Or Lettering Only

Albert H Hopper Inc ....G 201 991-2266
North Arlington (G-7414)

MOPS: Floor & Dust

Janico Inc ....F 732 370-2223
Freehold (G-3662)

MORTAR: High Temperature, Nonclay

Strongwall Industries Inc ....G 201 445-4633
Allendale (G-19)

MOTION PICTURE & VIDEO PRODUCTION SVCS

Bandemar Networks LLC ....G 732 991-5112
East Brunswick (G-2136)
Recorded Publications Labs...........E 856 963-3000
Camden (G-1084)

MOTION PICTURE & VIDEO PRODUCTION SVCS: Educational, TV

Global Strategy Institute A ....G 973 615-7447
Bloomfield (G-513)

MOTION PICTURE PRODUCTION & DISTRIBUTION

Sony Corporation of America ....F 201 930-1000
Woodcliff Lake (G-12202)

MOTION PICTURE PRODUCTION & DISTRIBUTION: Television

Acadia Scenic Inc ....E 201 653-8889
Jersey City (G-4697)

MOTOR & GENERATOR PARTS: Electric

Al Tayyar Enrgy- Princeton LLC ......G 609 479-8603
Princeton (G-9000)
Reliance Electric Company ....E 856 661-1442
Pennsauken (G-8572)

MOTOR REPAIR SVCS

George J Bender Inc ....E 908 687-0081
Union (G-11189)
Hights Electric Motor Service ....G 609 448-2298
Hightstown (G-4312)
Johnnys Service Center ....G 732 738-0569
Fords (G-3529)

MOTOR SCOOTERS & PARTS

Electric Mobility Corporation.............C 856 468-1000
  Sewell (G-9955)

MOTOR VEHICLE ASSEMBLY, COMPLETE: Ambulances

First Priority Emergency Vhicl.............E 732 657-1104
  Manchester (G-5886)
First Priority Global Ltd ....F 973 347-4321
  Flanders (G-3408)
P L Custom Body & Eqp Co Inc............C 732 223-1411
  Manasquan (G-5877)

MOTOR VEHICLE ASSEMBLY, COMPLETE: Autos, Incl Specialty

Bruce Kindberg ....G 973 664-0195
  Rockaway (G-9554)
Cenntro Automotive Corporation.........G 732 863-0777
  Freehold (G-3644)
Elite Emrgncy Lights Ltd Lblty ....F 732 534-2377
  Lakewood (G-5115)
Odyssey Auto Specialty Inc ....E 973 328-2667
  Wharton (G-11995)
Orlando Systems Ltd Lblty Co ....G 908 400-5052
  North Plainfield (G-7560)
S L P Engineering Inc ....D 732 240-3696
  Toms River (G-10908)
Teo Fabrications Inc ....G 973 764-5500
  Vernon (G-11302)
W2f Inc ....G 609 735-0135
  New Egypt (G-7019)

MOTOR VEHICLE ASSEMBLY, COMPLETE: Bus/Large Spclty Vehicles

Specialty Vhcl Solutions LLC ....E 609 882-1900
  Ewing (G-3056)

MOTOR VEHICLE ASSEMBLY, COMPLETE: Military Motor Vehicle

Jontol Unlimited LLC ....G 858 652-1113
  Blackwood (G-485)

MOTOR VEHICLE ASSEMBLY, COMPLETE: Snow Plows

R & H Spring & Truck Repair ....F 732 681-9000
  Wall Township (G-11504)

MOTOR VEHICLE ASSEMBLY, COMPLETE: Truck & Tractor Trucks

Cliffside Body Corporation ....E 201 945-3970
  Fairview (G-3359)
Dejana Trck Utility Eqp Co LLC ....E 856 303-1315
  Cinnaminson (G-1454)
Polar Truck Sales ....E 201 246-1010
  Jersey City (G-4802)

MOTOR VEHICLE ASSEMBLY, COMPLETE: Truck Tractors, Highway

Daimler Trucks North Amer LLC ....G 856 467-6000
  Swedesboro (G-10689)

MOTOR VEHICLE DEALERS: Automobiles, New & Used

Davis Hyundai ....F 609 883-3500
  Ewing (G-3013)
Drive-Master Co Inc ....F 973 808-9709
  Fairfield (G-3180)
Freehold Pntiac Bick GMC Trcks..........D 732 462-7093
  Freehold (G-3656)
Holman Enterprises Inc ....E 609 383-6100
  Mount Laurel (G-6802)
Town Ford Inc ....D 609 298-4990
  Bordentown (G-613)
Toyota Motor Sales ....F 973 515-5012
  Parsippany (G-8103)
Volvo Car North America LLC ....B 201 768-7300
  Rockleigh (G-9636)
Wayne Motors Inc ....D 973 696-9710
  Wayne (G-11692)

MOTOR VEHICLE DEALERS: Pickups & Vans, Used

Polar Truck Sales ....E 201 246-1010
  Jersey City (G-4802)

MOTOR VEHICLE DEALERS: Trucks, Tractors/Trailers, New & Used

Granco Group LLC ....G 973 515-4721
  Roseland (G-9651)
M W Trailer Repair Inc ....F 609 298-1113
  Bordentown (G-600)
Robert H Hoover & Sons Inc..............G 973 347-4210
  Flanders (G-3414)

MOTOR VEHICLE PARTS & ACCESS: Air Conditioner Parts

Premier Products Inc....................D 856 231-1800
  Marlton (G-5995)

MOTOR VEHICLE PARTS & ACCESS: Body Components & Frames

Cervinis Inc..............................F 856 691-1744
  Vineland (G-11335)

MOTOR VEHICLE PARTS & ACCESS: Cleaners, air

M P M Building Service ....G 732 946-2600
  Holmdel (G-4519)

MOTOR VEHICLE PARTS & ACCESS: Clutches

KRs Automotive Dev Group Inc ....F 732 667-7937
  Middlesex (G-6174)

MOTOR VEHICLE PARTS & ACCESS: Cylinder Heads

Ram Hydraulics Inc......................G 732 237-0904
  Shrewsbury (G-10009)

MOTOR VEHICLE PARTS & ACCESS: Engines & Parts

Holman Enterprises Inc..................C 856 532-2410
  Pennsauken (G-8522)
K & K Automotive Inc ....G 973 777-2235
  Passaic (G-8153)
Manley Performance Pdts Inc.............D 732 905-3366
  Lakewood (G-5152)

MOTOR VEHICLE PARTS & ACCESS: Fuel Pumps

O T D Inc ....G 973 890-7979
  Totowa (G-10958)

MOTOR VEHICLE PARTS & ACCESS: Fuel Systems & Parts

Carolina Fluid Handling Inc ....A 248 228-8900
  West Berlin (G-11706)

MOTOR VEHICLE PARTS & ACCESS: Transmission Housings Or Parts

Quality Remanufacturing Inc ....F 973 523-8800
  Paterson (G-8366)

MOTOR VEHICLE PARTS & ACCESS: Transmissions

Level Ten Products Inc....................F 973 827-0900
  Hamburg (G-4095)
Overdrive Holdings Inc...................F 201 440-1911
  South Hackensack (G-10286)
Truckpro LLC ....E 201 229-0599
  Teterboro (G-10817)

MOTOR VEHICLE PARTS & ACCESS: Water Pumps

Well Manager LLC ....G 609 466-4347
  Hopewell (G-4544)

MOTOR VEHICLE PARTS & ACCESS: Wheel rims

Top Rated Shopping Bargains.............F 201 630-0770
  Hasbrouck Heights (G-4200)

MOTOR VEHICLE PARTS & ACCESS: Windshield Frames

Clear Plus Windshield Wipers ....F 973 546-8800
  Garfield (G-3726)

MOTOR VEHICLE PARTS & ACCESS: Wipers, Windshield

Wexco Industries Inc ....E 973 244-5777
  Pine Brook (G-8720)

MOTOR VEHICLE SPLYS & PARTS WHOLESALERS: New

Allison Corp..............................G 973 992-3800
  Livingston (G-5523)
Gorman Industries Inc....................E 973 345-5424
  Paterson (G-8279)
Holman Enterprises Inc...................C 856 532-2410
  Pennsauken (G-8522)
Lumiko USA Inc ....G 609 409-6900
  Cranbury (G-1857)
Rony Inc.................................G 201 891-2551
  Wyckoff (G-12263)
Taurus International Corp ....E 201 825-2420
  Ramsey (G-9252)

MOTOR VEHICLE SPLYS & PARTS WHOLESALERS: Used

A-1 Specialized Svcs & Sups...............E 732 238-2900
  South River (G-10456)
P & A Auto Parts Inc ....E 201 655-7117
  Hackensack (G-3959)

MOTOR VEHICLE: Hardware

American Van Equipment Inc ....C 732 905-5900
  Lakewood (G-5071)

MOTOR VEHICLE: Radiators

Custom Auto Radiator Inc................F 609 242-9700
  Forked River (G-3537)

MOTOR VEHICLES & CAR BODIES

Autoaccess LLC ....F 908 240-5919
  Sicklerville (G-10017)
BMW of North America LLC ....A 201 307-4000
  Woodcliff Lake (G-12183)
Drive-Master Co Inc ....F 973 808-9709
  Fairfield (G-3180)
Faps Inc ....C 973 589-5656
  Newark (G-7160)
Navistar Inc.............................D 856 486-2300
  Cherry Hill (G-1403)
Rolls-Royce Motor Cars Na LLC..........A 201 307-4117
  Woodcliff Lake (G-12200)
Tesla Inc................................G 201 225-2544
  Paramus (G-7910)
Toyota Motor Sales ....F 973 515-5012
  Parsippany (G-8103)
Vending Trucks Inc ....E 732 969-5400
  East Brunswick (G-2196)

MOTOR VEHICLES, WHOLESALE: Trailers for passenger vehicles

Trac Intermodal LLC ....G 609 452-8900
  Princeton (G-9130)
Trac Interstar LLC ....G 609 452-8900
  Princeton (G-9131)

MOTOR VEHICLES, WHOLESALE: Trailers, Truck, New & Used

M W Trailer Repair Inc ....F 609 298-1113
  Bordentown (G-600)
Peter Garafano & Son Inc.................E 973 278-0350
  Paterson (G-8364)

P
R
O
D
U
C
T

MOTOR VEHICLES, WHOLESALE: Truck bodies

Bristol-Donald Company Inc............E 973 589-2640
Newark *(G-7115)*

Cliffside Body Corporation ....E 201 945-3970
Fairview *(G-3359)*

Fleet Equipment Corporation ....F 201 337-3294
Franklin Lakes *(G-3617)*

MOTORCYCLE ACCESS

Barbs Harley-Davidson ....E 856 456-4141
Mount Ephraim *(G-6762)*

MOTORCYCLE DEALERS

Barbs Harley-Davidson ....E 856 456-4141
Mount Ephraim *(G-6762)*

MOTORCYCLE PARTS & ACCESS DEALERS

Morristown Cycle ....G 973 540-1244
Morristown *(G-6729)*

MOTORCYCLE REPAIR SHOPS

Barbs Harley-Davidson ....E 856 456-4141
Mount Ephraim *(G-6762)*

Morristown Cycle ....G 973 540-1244
Morristown *(G-6729)*

MOTORCYCLES & RELATED PARTS

Morristown Cycle ....G 973 540-1244
Morristown *(G-6729)*

NJ Grass Choppers ....G 732 414-2850
Manalapan *(G-5856)*

Works Enduro Rider Inc ....G 908 637-6385
Great Meadows *(G-3853)*

MOTORS: Electric

Eagle Engineering & Automation ....G 732 899-2292
Point Pleasant Boro *(G-8939)*

Universal Electric Co ....E 201 968-1000
Hackensack *(G-3989)*

MOTORS: Generators

Alstrom Energy Group LLC ....G 718 824-4901
Old Bridge *(G-7773)*

Ametek Inc ....G 732 417-0501
Edison *(G-2460)*

Astrodyne Corporation ....D 908 850-5088
Hackettstown *(G-3998)*

Billows Electric Supply Co Inc ....C 856 751-2200
Delran *(G-2010)*

Blutek Power Inc ....F 973 594-1800
Lodi *(G-5577)*

Boonton Electronics Corp ....E 201 261-8797
Parsippany *(G-7963)*

Cobra Power Systems Inc ....G 908 486-1800
Millstone Township *(G-6263)*

Dewey Electronics Corporation ....E 201 337-4700
Oakland *(G-7684)*

Ewc Controls Inc ....E 732 446-3110
Manalapan *(G-5846)*

H Power Corp ....G 973 249-5444
Clifton *(G-1632)*

Hansome Energy Systems Inc ....E 908 862-9044
Linden *(G-5382)*

Hydro-Mechanical Systems Inc ....F 856 848-8888
Westville *(G-11943)*

Innovative Power Solutions LLC ....E 732 544-1075
Eatontown *(G-2407)*

Multi-Tech Industries Inc ....F 732 431-0550
Marlboro *(G-5948)*

Pht Aerospace LLC ....F 973 831-1230
Pompton Plains *(G-8965)*

Power Pool Plus Inc ....G 908 454-1124
Alpha *(G-44)*

Primacy Engineering Inc ....F 201 731-3272
Englewood Cliffs *(G-2979)*

Princeton Tech Group Intl Corp ....G 732 328-9308
Edison *(G-2596)*

Rajysan Incorporated ....G 800 433-1382
Swedesboro *(G-10722)*

Servo-Tek Products Company Inc ....E 973 427-4249
Hawthorne *(G-4258)*

Triangle Tube/Phase III Co Inc ....D 856 228-9940
Paulsboro *(G-8427)*

MOTORS: Torque

Torque Gun Company LLC ....E 201 512-9800
South Hackensack *(G-10298)*

MOUNTING MERCHANDISE ON CARDS

Comfort Zone ....G 732 869-9990
Ocean Grove *(G-7760)*

MOUTHWASHES

Cadbury Adams USA LLC ....E 973 503-2000
East Hanover *(G-2203)*

MOVIE THEATERS, EXC DRIVE-IN

Sony Corporation of America ....F 201 930-1000
Woodcliff Lake *(G-12202)*

MOVING SVC: Local

E C D Ventures Inc ....G 856 875-1100
Blackwood *(G-477)*

MOWERS & ACCESSORIES

Robert Colaneri ....G 201 939-4405
East Rutherford *(G-2321)*

MULTIPLEX EQPT: Radio, Television & Broadcast

Communication Devices Inc ....F 973 334-1980
Boonton *(G-560)*

MUSEUMS

General Commis Archives & Hstr ....G 973 408-3189
Madison *(G-5723)*

Old Barracks Association Inc ....F 609 396-1776
Trenton *(G-11092)*

MUSEUMS & ART GALLERIES

Mega Media Concepts Ltd Lblty ....G 973 919-5661
Sparta *(G-10511)*

MUSIC ARRANGING & COMPOSING SVCS

Metrolpolis Mastering LP ....E 212 604-9433
Edgewater *(G-2441)*

MUSIC COPYING SVCS

Audio and Video Labs Inc ....B 856 663-9030
Pennsauken *(G-8482)*

MUSIC DISTRIBUTION APPARATUS

Audio and Video Labs Inc ....B 856 663-9030
Pennsauken *(G-8482)*

B and G Music LLC ....G 732 779-4555
Bayville *(G-251)*

MUSICAL INSTRUMENT LESSONS

Hope Center ....F 201 798-1234
Jersey City *(G-4766)*

MUSICAL INSTRUMENT PARTS & ACCESS, WHOLESALE

AP Global Enterprises Inc ....G 732 919-6200
Wall Township *(G-11462)*

MUSICAL INSTRUMENT REPAIR

W E Wamsley Restorations Inc ....G 856 795-4001
Haddonfield *(G-4066)*

MUSICAL INSTRUMENTS & ACCESS: NEC

AP Global Enterprises Inc ....G 732 919-6200
Wall Township *(G-11462)*

Malletech LLC ....F 732 774-0011
Neptune *(G-6922)*

Trek II Products Inc ....G 732 214-9200
New Brunswick *(G-7007)*

MUSICAL INSTRUMENTS & ACCESS: Pianos

Vintage Vibe Ltd Liability Co ....G 973 989-2178
Rockaway *(G-9622)*

MUSICAL INSTRUMENTS & PARTS: Percussion

Latin Percussion Inc ....E 973 478-6903
Garfield *(G-3742)*

MUSICAL INSTRUMENTS & SPLYS STORES

Music Trades Corp ....G 201 871-1965
Englewood *(G-2918)*

Trf Music Inc ....F 201 335-0005
Tinton Falls *(G-10851)*

MUSICAL INSTRUMENTS WHOLESALERS

Latin Percussion Inc ....E 973 478-6903
Garfield *(G-3742)*

MUSICAL INSTRUMENTS: Guitars & Parts, Electric & Acoustic

Applause Musical Products ....G 856 697-8333
Landisville *(G-5229)*

D R Handmade Strings Inc ....D 201 599-3113
Westwood *(G-11958)*

MUSICAL INSTRUMENTS: Organs

Peragallo Organ Company of NJ ....F 973 684-3414
Paterson *(G-8363)*

MUSICAL INSTRUMENTS: Synthesizers, Music

Spem Corporation ....E 732 356-3366
Piscataway *(G-8816)*

MUSICAL INSTRUMENTS: Violins & Parts

W E Wamsley Restorations Inc 856 795-4001
Haddonfield *(G-4066)*

NAILS WHOLESALERS

Crown Fastener & Supply Corp ....G 845 268-5150
Ringwood *(G-9446)*

NAME PLATES: Engraved Or Etched

A S A P Nameplate & Labeling ....F 973 773-3934
Passaic *(G-8122)*

Lantier Construction Company ....E 856 780-6366
Moorestown *(G-6592)*

Technical Nameplate Corp ....E 973 773-4256
Passaic *(G-8184)*

United Label Corp ....F 973 589-6500
Newark *(G-7354)*

Winters Stamp Mfg Co Inc ....F 908 352-3725
Martinsville *(G-6011)*

NATIONAL SECURITY, GOVERNMENT: National Guard

NJ Dept Military Vtrans ....G 856 384-8831
Woodbury *(G-12165)*

NATURAL GAS LIQUIDS PRODUCTION

Pipeline Eqp Resources Co LLC ....G 888 232-7372
Boonton *(G-579)*

NATURAL GAS PRODUCTION

Agway Energy Services LLC ....E 973 887-5300
Whippany *(G-12006)*

Njr Clean Energy Ventures Corp ....B 732 938-1000
Belmar *(G-360)*

NATURAL LIQUEFIED PETROLEUM GAS PRODUCTION

M G S ....G 609 698-7000
Barnegat *(G-163)*

NAVIGATIONAL SYSTEMS & INSTRUMENTS

Drs Leonardo Inc ....E 973 775-4440
Newark *(G-7143)*

Drs Leonardo Inc ....E 973 898-1500
Parsippany *(G-7987)*

Drs Leonardo Inc ....E 201 337-3800
Oakland *(G-7686)*

Harris Corporation ....C 973 284-0123
  Clifton (G-1636)

NET & NETTING PRDTS

Endurance Net Inc ....F 609 499-3450
  Florence (G-3478)

NETTING: Rope

French Textile Co Inc ....F 973 471-5000
  Clifton (G-1623)
Sterling Net & Twine Co Inc ....F 973 783-9800
  Montclair (G-6436)

NEW & USED CAR DEALERS

Cemp Inc..F 732 933-1000
  Shrewsbury (G-9992)

NEWS SYNDICATES

Thomson Reuters Corporation.............F 973 662-3070
  Nutley (G-7655)

NEWSPAPERS & PERIODICALS NEWS REPORTING SVCS

Dorf Feature Service Inc.....................E 908 518-1802
  Mountainside (G-6878)

NICKEL ALLOY

Industrial Tube Corporation ....E 908 369-3737
  Hillsborough (G-4345)
Nickel Savers......................................G 201 405-1153
  Oakland (G-7699)
Nickels Carpet Cleaning......................G 609 892-5783
  Mays Landing (G-6040)
Nickels N Dimes LLC..........................G 732 886-5528
  Lakewood (G-5163)

NONCURRENT CARRYING WIRING DEVICES

American Fittings Corp ....G 201 664-0027
  Fair Lawn (G-3075)
Billows Electric Supply Co Inc ....C 856 751-2200
  Delran (G-2010)
Heyco Molded Products Inc.................F 732 286-4336
  Toms River (G-10884)
Moreng Metal Products Inc ....D 973 256-2001
  Totowa (G-10956)
Morgan Advanced Ceramics Inc ....E 973 808-1621
  Fairfield (G-3264)
Multi-Tech Industries Inc ....F 732 431-0550
  Marlboro (G-5948)

NONDAIRY BASED FROZEN DESSERTS

Ice Cold Novelty Products Inc ....G 732 751-0011
  Wall Township (G-11491)
Mega Industries LLC............................G 973 779-8772
  Passaic (G-8161)

NONFERROUS: Rolling & Drawing, NEC

Construction Specialties Inc................E 908 272-2771
  Cranford (G-1902)
Fisk Alloy Inc.....................................E 973 427-7550
  Hawthorne (G-4234)
Fisk Alloy Wire Incorporated ....C 973 949-4491
  Hawthorne (G-4235)
International Rollforms Inc ....E 856 228-7100
  Deptford (G-2065)
Kearny Smelting & Ref Corp...............E 201 991-7276
  Kearny (G-4891)
Precision Roll Products Inc ....F 973 822-9100
  Florham Park (G-3515)
Swepco Tube LLC...............................C 973 778-3000
  Clifton (G-1733)

NOTIONS: Fasteners, Slide Zippers

YKK (usa) Inc.....................................G 201 935-4200
  Lyndhurst (G-5715)

NOTIONS: Hooks, Crochet

Omaha Standard Inc Tr NJ...................G 609 588-5400
  Trenton (G-11093)

NOVELTIES

Amaryllis Inc......................................G 973 635-0500
  Chatham (G-1325)

Inman Mold Manufacturing Inc ....G 732 381-3033
  Rahway (G-9198)
Tom Ponte Model Makers Inc...............G 973 627-5906
  Rockaway (G-9618)

NOVELTIES & SPECIALTIES: Metal

Icup Inc ....E 856 751-2045
  Cherry Hill (G-1376)

NOVELTIES, DURABLE, WHOLESALE

Adventure Industries LLC....................G 609 426-1777
  East Windsor (G-2341)

NOVELTIES: Leather

Adventure Industries LLC....................G 609 426-1777
  East Windsor (G-2341)
Cunningham Classics Ltd Lblty ....G 201 857-4647
  Glen Rock (G-3825)
R Neumann & Co.................................F 201 659-3400
  Hoboken (G-4493)

NOVELTIES: Paper, Made From Purchased Materials

Johnson & Mayer Inc...........................F 201 646-1717
  Hackensack (G-3934)
Red Letter Press Inc ....G 609 597-5257
  Upper Saddle River (G-11284)

NOVELTIES: Plastic

Christopher F Maier ....F 908 459-5100
  Hope (G-4539)
Edwards Creative Products Inc ....F 856 665-3200
  Cherry Hill (G-1361)
Icup Inc ....E 856 751-2045
  Cherry Hill (G-1376)
Marlo Plastic Products Inc ....E 732 792-1988
  Neptune (G-6923)

NOVELTY SHOPS

Rpl Supplies Inc ....F 973 767-0880
  Garfield (G-3759)
Sherman Nat Inc.................................E 201 735-9000
  Englewood (G-2930)

NOZZLES & SPRINKLERS Lawn Hose

Durst Corporation Inc.........................E 800 852-3906
  Cranford (G-1903)
Msg Fire & Safety Inc ....G 732 833-8500
  Jackson (G-4673)

NOZZLES: Fire Fighting

Confires Fire Prtction Svc LLC.............F 908 822-2700
  South Plainfield (G-10349)
Firefighter One Ltd Lblty Co ....G 973 940-3061
  Sparta (G-10499)

NOZZLES: Spray, Aerosol, Paint Or Insecticide

Zodiac Paintball Inc............................G 973 616-7230
  Pompton Plains (G-8970)

NUCLEAR FUELS SCRAP REPROCESSING

Holtec International ....B 856 797-0900
  Camden (G-1069)

NURSERIES & LAWN & GARDEN SPLY STORE, RET: Lawn/Garden Splys

Lumber Super Mart..............................G 732 739-1428
  Hazlet (G-4278)
Mendham Garden Center ....G 973 543-4178
  Mendham (G-6089)

NURSERIES & LAWN & GARDEN SPLY STORES, RETAIL: Top Soil

Cedar Hill Landscaping ....E 732 469-1400
  Somerset (G-10081)
L & S Contracting Inc ....G 609 397-1281
  Hopewell (G-4542)

NURSERIES & LAWN/GARDEN SPLY STORE, RET: Lawnmowers/Tractors

Chatham Lawn Mowler ....G 973 635-8855
  Chatham (G-1327)

NURSERY & GARDEN CENTERS

Agway Energy Services LLC ....E 973 887-5300
  Whippany (G-12006)

NUTS: Metal

Amerifast Corp....................................F 908 668-1959
  South Plainfield (G-10328)
Nylok Corporation...............................F 201 427-8555
  Hawthorne (G-4250)

NYLON FIBERS

Honeywell International Inc ....A 973 455-2000
  Morris Plains (G-6666)

OFFICE EQPT WHOLESALERS

Binding Products Inc...........................E 212 947-1192
  Jersey City (G-4719)
Brother International Corp ....B 908 704-1700
  Bridgewater (G-825)
Cummins - Allison Corp ....G 201 791-2394
  Elmwood Park (G-2813)
Maxlite Inc..C 973 244-7300
  West Caldwell (G-11788)
Royal Sovereign Intl Inc ....E 800 397-1025
  Rockleigh (G-9633)
Sharp Electronics Corporation.............A 201 529-8200
  Mahwah (G-5811)
Time Systems International Co ....E 201 871-1200
  Englewood (G-2937)

OFFICE EQPT, WHOLESALE: Calculating Machines

Aone Touch Inc ....G 732 261-6841
  Bordentown (G-590)

OFFICE EQPT, WHOLESALE: Duplicating Machines

Imperial Copy Products Inc ....E 973 927-5500
  Randolph (G-9284)

OFFICE FIXTURES: Exc Wood

Cor Products Inc ....G 973 731-4952
  West Orange (G-11890)
High Tech Manufacturing Inc................G 973 372-7907
  Irvington (G-4589)

OFFICE FURNITURE REPAIR & MAINTENANCE SVCS

Extra Office Inc..................................F 732 381-9774
  Rahway (G-9188)
Mbs Installations Inc ....F 888 446-9135
  Jackson (G-4672)

OFFICE MACHINES, NEC

Atlantic Business Products ....G 201 672-0773
  Lyndhurst (G-5669)

OFFICE SPLY & STATIONERY STORES

Important Papers Inc ....G 856 751-4544
  Cherry Hill (G-1379)
Logomania Inc.....................................G 201 798-0531
  Jersey City (G-4778)
Papery of Marlton LLC.........................G 856 985-1776
  Marlton (G-5993)

OFFICE SPLY & STATIONERY STORES: Office Forms & Splys

Bellia & Sons ....E 856 845-2234
  Woodbury (G-12158)
Forms & Flyers of New Jersey.............G 856 629-0718
  Williamstown (G-12087)
Hometown Office Sups & Prtg Co ....G 609 298-9020
  Bordentown (G-598)
Imperial Copy Products Inc ....E 973 927-5500
  Randolph (G-9284)

JFK Supplies Inc ....F 732 985-7800
  Edison (G-2545)
Lamb Printing Inc ....G 908 852-0837
  Hackettstown (G-4016)
Printers Place Inc ....G 973 744-8889
  Montclair (G-6432)
Supplies-Supplies Inc ....F 908 272-5100
  Watchung (G-11596)
Venture Stationers Inc ....E 212 288-7235
  Closter (G-1767)
W B Mason Co Inc ....D 888 926-2766
  Bellmawr (G-354)
W B Mason Co Inc ....E 888 926-2766
  Egg Harbor Township (G-2699)
W B Mason Co Inc ....F 888 926-2766
  Cranbury (G-1890)

OFFICE SPLYS, NEC, WHOLESALE

Office Needs Inc ....G 732 381-7770
  Clark (G-1511)
Thomas H Cox & Son Inc ....E 908 928-1010
  Linden (G-5453)
Wilcox Press ....G 973 827-7474
  Hamburg (G-4100)

OFFICES & CLINICS DOCTORS OF MED: Intrnl Med Practitioners

United Medical PC ....F 201 339-6111
  Bayonne (G-246)

OFFICES & CLINICS OF DENTISTS: Dental Clinics & Offices

Vatech America Inc ....E 201 210-5028
  Fort Lee (G-3588)

OFFICES & CLINICS OF DENTISTS: Specialist, Practitioners

Nobel Biocare Procera LLC ....E 201 529-7100
  Mahwah (G-5797)

OFFICES & CLINICS OF DOCTORS OF MEDICINE: Gastronomist

Red Bank Gstrntrology Assoc PA ....E 732 842-4294
  Red Bank (G-9342)

OFFICES & CLINICS OF DOCTORS OF MEDICINE: Group Health Assoc

I Physician Hub ....D 732 274-0155
  Monmouth Junction (G-6346)

OFFICES & CLINICS OF DOCTORS OF MEDICINE: Neurosurgeon

Spinal Kinetics LLC ....G 908 687-2552
  Union (G-11224)

OFFICES & CLINICS OF DOCTORS OF MEDICINE: Oculist

Richard Danz & Sons Inc ....E 212 697-5722
  Glen Rock (G-3829)

OFFICES & CLINICS OF DOCTORS OF MEDICINE: Oncologist

Arthur A Topilow William Lrner ....E 732 528-0760
  Manasquan (G-5868)

OFFICES & CLINICS OF DOCTORS OF MEDICINE: Ophthalmologist

Douglas Liva MD ....G 201 444-7770
  Ridgewood (G-9423)

OFFICES & CLINICS OF DOCTORS OF MEDICINE: Radiologist

Mri of West Morris PA ....F 973 927-1010
  Succasunna (G-10625)

OFFICES & CLINICS OF DRS OF MEDICINE: Geriatric

Madhu B Goyal MD ....G 908 769-0307
  South Plainfield (G-10400)

OFFICES & CLINICS OF DRS OF MEDICINE: Physician, Orthopedic

Biodynamics LLC ....G 201 227-9255
  Englewood (G-2876)

OIL FIELD SVCS, NEC

Above Environmental Services ....G 973 702-7021
  Vernon (G-11295)
Dematte Oil Service Inc ....G 856 692-9125
  Millville (G-6298)
Mine Hill Spartan ....G 973 442-2280
  Mine Hill (G-6328)
Schlumberger Technology Corp ....C 609 275-3815
  Princeton Junction (G-9163)

OIL TREATING COMPOUNDS

Arol Chemical Products Co ....G 973 344-1510
  Newark (G-7094)

OILS & ESSENTIAL OILS

Elixens America Inc ....G 732 388-3555
  Rahway (G-9187)
EMD Performance Materials Corp ....B 908 429-3500
  Branchburg (G-657)
Fragrance Resources Inc ....D 973 458-5231
  Keyport (G-5018)

OILS & GREASES: Blended & Compounded

Arol Chemical Products Co ....G 973 344-1510
  Newark (G-7094)
Cumberland Vacuum Products Inc ....G 856 691-9155
  Vineland (G-11346)
Hangsterfers Laboratories ....E 856 468-0216
  West Deptford (G-11827)
Total Specialties Usa Inc ....D 908 862-9300
  Linden (G-5454)

OILS & GREASES: Lubricating

American Oil & Supply Co ....F 732 389-5514
  Eatontown (G-2382)
BP Lubricants USA Inc ....B 973 633-2200
  Wayne (G-11614)
Chemours Company ....G 856 540-3398
  Deepwater (G-1998)
Federal Lorco Petroleum LLC ....D 908 352-0542
  Elizabeth (G-2731)
Fti Inc ....G 973 443-0004
  Florham Park (G-3503)
Gordon Terminal Service Co PA ....D 201 437-8300
  Bayonne (G-229)
International Products Corp ....F 609 386-8770
  Burlington (G-979)
Lanxess Solutions US Inc ....C 973 887-7411
  East Hanover (G-2227)
Lanxess Solutions US Inc ....C 732 738-1000
  Fords (G-3530)
Penetone Corporation ....E 201 567-3000
  Carlstadt (G-1199)
Pflaumer Brothers Inc ....G 609 883-4610
  Ewing (G-3042)

OILS: Essential

Flavors of Origin Inc ....E 732 499-9700
  Avenel (G-131)
Grayden Industries Inc ....E 201 761-0788
  Jersey City (G-4762)
Interbahm International Inc ....E 732 499-9700
  Avenel (G-135)

OILS: Lubricating

Wrench Brothers LLC ....G 201 222-0301
  Jersey City (G-4851)

OILS: Lubricating

Marine Oil Service Inc ....G 908 282-6440
  Elizabeth (G-2754)
Mil-Comm Products Company Inc ....F 201 935-8561
  East Rutherford (G-2311)

Pbf Holding Company LLC ....B 888 661-8949
  Parsippany (G-8058)
Smb International LLC ....F 732 222-4888
  West Long Branch (G-11847)

OILS: Peppermint

Jch Partners & Co LLC ....F 732 664-6440
  Howell (G-4557)

OILS: Vegetable Oils, Vulcanized Or Sulfurized

Elementis Global LLC ....C 609 443-2000
  East Windsor (G-2373)

OLEFINS

Lyondell Chemical Company ....G 973 578-2200
  Newark (G-7232)

OMNIBEARING INDICATORS

Atgi Advanced Tech Group Intl ....E 609 271-8666
  Lawrenceville (G-5250)
Oavco Ltd Liability Company ....F 855 535-4227
  Princeton (G-9084)

OPERATOR: Apartment Buildings

Ayerspace Inc ....G 212 582-8410
  West Caldwell (G-11767)
Ukrainian National Association ....E 973 292-9800
  Parsippany (G-8106)

OPERATOR: Nonresidential Buildings

Avant Industries Ltd Inc ....G 973 242-1700
  Newark (G-7100)
Epolin Chemical LLC ....G 973 465-9495
  Newark (G-7157)
Polymathes Holdings I LLC ....G 609 945-1690
  Princeton (G-9093)
Rossendale Reddaway Company ....G 973 690-6097
  Newark (G-7292)

OPHTHALMIC GOODS

Bausch & Lomb Incorporated ....B 908 927-1400
  Bridgewater (G-820)
Complete Optical Laboratory ....F 973 338-8886
  Bloomfield (G-508)
Hillcrest Opticians ....G 973 838-6666
  Kinnelon (G-5036)
Lens Lab Express ....G 201 861-0016
  West New York (G-11871)
Pds Consultants Inc ....E 201 970-2313
  Sparta (G-10517)
Phillips Safety Products Inc ....E 732 356-1493
  Middlesex (G-6188)
Smith Optics Inc ....G 208 726-4477
  Secaucus (G-9929)
Spectacle Shoppe ....G 856 875-5046
  Williamstown (G-12108)
Topcon Medical Systems Inc ....D 201 599-5100
  Oakland (G-7707)
Usv Optical Inc ....B 856 228-1000
  Glendora (G-3834)

OPHTHALMIC GOODS WHOLESALERS

Sensor Medical Technology LLC ....G 425 358-7381
  Denville (G-2058)

OPHTHALMIC GOODS, NEC, WHOLESALE: Frames

Liberty Sport Inc ....E 973 882-0986
  Fairfield (G-3252)

OPHTHALMIC GOODS, NEC, WHOLESALE: Lenses

Lens Depot Inc ....F 732 993-9766
  East Brunswick (G-2164)

OPHTHALMIC GOODS: Frames & Parts, Eyeglass & Spectacle

Liberty Sport Inc ....E 973 882-0986
  Fairfield (G-3252)

OPHTHALMIC GOODS: Lenses, Ophthalmic

Edison Ophthalmology Assoc LLC ......F 908 822-0070
  Edison (G-2510)
Lens Depot Inc ....F 732 993-9766
  East Brunswick (G-2164)
M & S Optics Inc....................................F 856 764-0200
  Delran (G-2019)
Pam Optical Co ....G 973 744-8882
  Montclair (G-6429)

OPHTHALMIC GOODS: Protectors, Eye

Douglas Liva MD ....G 201 444-7770
  Ridgewood (G-9423)

OPTICAL GOODS STORES

Complete Optical Laboratory.................F 973 338-8886
  Bloomfield (G-508)
Pam Optical Co ....G 973 744-8882
  Montclair (G-6429)
US Vision Inc ....B 856 227-8339
  Glendora (G-3833)

OPTICAL GOODS STORES: Contact Lenses, Prescription

Intense Inc ....E 732 249-2228
  North Brunswick (G-7520)

OPTICAL GOODS STORES: Eyeglasses, Prescription

Usv Optical Inc.....................................B 856 228-1000
  Glendora (G-3834)

OPTICAL GOODS STORES: Opticians

Hillcrest Opticians ....G 973 838-6666
  Kinnelon (G-5036)
Lens Lab Express ....G 201 861-0016
  West New York (G-11871)
Partners In Vision Inc ....G 888 748-1112
  Edison (G-2592)
Spectacle Shoppe ....G 856 875-5046
  Williamstown (G-12108)

OPTICAL INSTRUMENTS & APPARATUS

Opt-Sciences Corporation ....F 856 829-2800
  Cinnaminson (G-1482)
Rudolph RES Analytical Corp................D 973 584-1558
  Hackettstown (G-4034)
Shanghai Optics Inc ....F 732 321-6915
  Clark (G-1515)
Topcon Medical Systems Inc ....D 201 599-5100
  Oakland (G-7707)

OPTICAL INSTRUMENTS & LENSES

API Nanofabrication & RES Corp ....F 732 627-0808
  Somerset (G-10059)
Argyle International Inc ....G 609 924-9484
  Princeton (G-9008)
Artemis Optics and Coatings................G 201 847-0887
  Emerson (G-2857)
Avantier Inc ....G 732 491-8150
  Metuchen (G-6095)
Cgm Us Inc ....E 609 894-4420
  Birmingham (G-467)
Chiral Photonics Inc ....F 973 732-0030
  Pine Brook (G-8692)
Coherent Inc ....D 973 240-6851
  East Hanover (G-2207)
High Vision Corporation ....G 862 238-7636
  Clifton (G-1641)
Ii-VI Wide Band Gap Inc ....G 973 227-1551
  Pine Brook (G-8705)
M H Optical Supplies Inc ....E 800 445-3090
  South Hackensack (G-10277)
MRC Precision Metal Optics Inc ....E 941 753-8707
  Northvale (G-7592)
Nano-Optic Devices LLC......................F 201 594-0226
  Twp Washinton (G-11143)
Nanoopto Corporation...........................E 732 627-0808
  Somerset (G-10143)
Norland Products Inc............................E 609 395-1966
  Cranbury (G-1863)
Princeton Instruments Inc.....................G 609 587-9797
  Trenton (G-11106)
Quantum Coating Inc............................E 856 234-5444
  Moorestown (G-6617)

Refac Optical Group ....E 856 228-1000
  Blackwood (G-490)
Roper Scientific Inc ....D 520 889-9933
  Trenton (G-11114)
Sheridan Optical Co Inc ....E 856 582-0963
  Pitman (G-8846)
Special Optics Inc ....F 973 366-7289
  Denville (G-2059)
Tag Optics Inc ....G 609 356-2142
  Princeton (G-9128)
US Vision Inc ....B 856 227-8339
  Glendora (G-3833)
Veeco Instruments Inc..........................E 732 560-5300
  Somerset (G-10193)

OPTICAL ISOLATORS

Ace Mountings Co Inc ....F 732 721-6200
  South Amboy (G-10233)
Crystal Deltronic Industries ....E 973 328-6898
  Dover (G-2082)
Crystal Deltronic Industries ....F 973 328-7000
  Dover (G-2083)

OPTOMETRISTS' OFFICES

Complete Optical Laboratory.................F 973 338-8886
  Bloomfield (G-508)
Jeffery S Zlotnick Od...........................G 732 549-3555
  Metuchen (G-6113)

ORAL PREPARATIONS

Health and Natural Beauty USA.............F 732 640-1830
  Piscataway (G-8772)

ORDNANCE

American Aluminum Company................D 908 233-3500
  Mountainside (G-6868)
Cartridge Actuated Devices ....E 973 347-2281
  Byram Township (G-1021)
Eastern Regional Waterway ....F 732 684-0409
  Brick (G-743)
Kongsberg Protech ....G 973 770-0574
  Mount Arlington (G-6756)

ORGAN TUNING & REPAIR SVCS

Peragallo Organ Company of NJ...........F 973 684-3414
  Paterson (G-8363)

ORGANIZATIONS: Biotechnical Research, Noncommercial

SPS Alfachem Inc ....G 973 676-5141
  Orange (G-7828)

ORGANIZATIONS: Civic & Social

New Jrsey State Leag Mncplties ....F 609 695-3481
  Trenton (G-11087)

ORGANIZATIONS: Medical Research

Agile Therapeutics Inc ....F 609 683-1880
  Princeton (G-8997)
Anadys Pharmaceuticals Inc ....E 972 235-4295
  Nutley (G-7641)
Enterix Inc ....E 732 429-1899
  Edison (G-2512)
Hoffmann-La Roche Inc........................A 973 890-2268
  Little Falls (G-5476)
Thomsom Health Care Inc.....................C 201 358-7300
  Montvale (G-6481)

ORGANIZATIONS: Noncommercial Social Research

Global Strategy Institute A....................G 973 615-7447
  Bloomfield (G-513)

ORGANIZATIONS: Religious

La Tribuna Publication Inc ....E 201 617-1360
  Union City (G-11253)

ORGANIZATIONS: Research Institute

Lockheed Martin Corporation................C 856 722-3336
  Moorestown (G-6595)

ORGANIZATIONS: Scientific Research Agency

Anvima Technologies LLC ....G 973 531-7077
  Brookside (G-922)

ORGANIZERS, CLOSET & DRAWER Plastic

Home Organization LLC ....F 201 351-2121
  Closter (G-1760)
Pfk Coach Phyllis Flood Knerr ....G 856 429-5425
  Haddonfield (G-4061)

ORIENTED STRANDBOARD

JM Huber Corporation ....D 732 603-3630
  Edison (G-2546)

ORNAMENTS: Lawn

Tropical Expressions Inc.......................G 732 899-8680
  Point Pleasant Boro (G-8941)

ORTHODONTIST

Jaeger Thomas & Melissa DDS ....F 908 735-2722
  Lebanon (G-5292)

OUTLETS: Electric, Convenience

Simply Amazing LLC ....F 732 249-4151
  East Brunswick (G-2184)

OVENS: Infrared

Radiant Energy Systems Inc..................E 973 423-5220
  Hawthorne (G-4256)
Radiation Systems Inc...........................G 201 891-7515
  Wyckoff (G-12261)
Therma-Tech Corporation ....F 973 345-0076
  Paterson (G-8400)

OXALIC ACID & METALLIC SALTS

American Beryllia Inc ....E 973 248-8080
  Haskell (G-4205)

PACKAGE DESIGN SVCS

Audio Dynamix Inc................................F 201 567-5488
  Englewood (G-2874)
Integrated Packaging Inds Inc ....E 973 839-0500
  Butler (G-1009)
Pac Team America Inc ....E 201 599-5000
  Paramus (G-7896)
Tekni-Plex Inc ....D 908 782-4000
  Flemington (G-3471)
Weber Packaging Inc ....G 201 262-6022
  Oradell (G-7815)

PACKAGED FROZEN FOODS WHOLESALERS, NEC

Arctic Foods Inc ....E 908 689-0590
  Washington (G-11574)
Arm National Food Inc ....G 609 695-4911
  Trenton (G-11020)
Metropolitan Foods Inc ....C 973 672-9400
  Clifton (G-1673)
Missa Bay LLC ....D 856 241-0900
  Swedesboro (G-10712)

PACKAGING & LABELING SVCS

Alexander James Corp ....D 908 362-9266
  Blairstown (G-494)
American Spraytech LLC ....E 908 725-6060
  Branchburg (G-634)
Assem - Pak Inc ....C 856 692-3355
  Vineland (G-11323)
Brisar Industries Inc ....C 973 278-2500
  Paterson (G-8226)
Copack International Inc ....E 973 405-5151
  Clifton (G-1591)
Envirochem Inc ....E 732 238-6700
  South River (G-10461)
G H Krauss Manufacturing Co...............G 856 662-0815
  Cherry Hill (G-1368)
Gordon Terminal Service Co PA.............D 201 437-8300
  Bayonne (G-229)
Holly Packaging Inc ....E 856 327-8281
  Millville (G-6308)
Hy-Test Packaging Corp........................G 973 754-7000
  Paterson (G-8291)

P
R
O
D
U
C
T

J&E Business Services LLC .... G 973 984-8444
Morris Plains *(G-6672)*

Major Products Co Inc .... E 201 641-5555
Little Ferry *(G-5512)*

Nutra-Med Packaging Inc .... D 973 625-2274
Whippany *(G-12028)*

Rectico Inc .... F 973 575-0009
Fairfield *(G-3290)*

Reed-Lane Inc .... C 973 709-1090
Wayne *(G-11677)*

Refresco Us Inc .... D 973 361-9794
Wharton *(G-11998)*

Robert Freeman .... G 973 751-0082
Belleville *(G-315)*

Sabre Die Cutting Co Inc .... E 973 357-9800
Paterson *(G-8373)*

PACKAGING MATERIALS, INDL: Wholesalers

Raritan Packaging Industries .... E 732 246-7200
New Brunswick *(G-6999)*

PACKAGING MATERIALS, WHOLESALE

Ace Bag & Burlap Company Inc .... F 973 242-2200
Newark *(G-7071)*

Albert Paper Products Company .... E 973 373-0330
Irvington *(G-4571)*

Alliance Corrugated Box Inc .... E 877 525-5269
Saddle River *(G-9802)*

Amcor Flexibles Inc .... E 609 267-5900
Mount Holly *(G-6766)*

Capital Gasket and Rubber Inc .... G 856 939-3670
Runnemede *(G-9717)*

Fleet Packaging Inc .... G 866 302-0340
South Orange *(G-10306)*

Granite Packaging Supply Co .... D 856 727-1010
Moorestown *(G-6579)*

GT Microwave Inc .... G 973 361-5700
Randolph *(G-9282)*

Kolon USA Incorporated .... F 201 641-5800
Ridgefield Park *(G-9409)*

M & E Packaging Corp .... G 201 635-1381
Lyndhurst *(G-5688)*

M S Plastics and Packg Co .... F 973 492-2400
Butler *(G-1011)*

Mm Packaging Group LLC .... G 908 759-0101
Linden *(G-5411)*

Plus Packaging Inc .... G 973 538-2216
Morristown *(G-6736)*

Polyair Inter Pack Inc .... D 201 804-1725
Carlstadt *(G-1204)*

Pro Pack Inc .... F 201 485-7587
Wyckoff *(G-12260)*

US Propack Inc .... G 732 294-4500
Freehold *(G-3690)*

PACKAGING MATERIALS: Paper

Aeon Industries Inc .... G 732 246-3224
Somerset *(G-10050)*

Amcor Flexibles Inc .... E 609 267-5900
Mount Holly *(G-6766)*

Arch Crown Inc .... E 973 731-6300
Hillside *(G-4390)*

Carol Healey .... G 973 875-1990
Sussex *(G-10667)*

Employment Horizons Inc .... B 973 538-8822
Cedar Knolls *(G-1311)*

Gleicher Manufacturing Corp .... E 908 233-2211
Scotch Plains *(G-9849)*

Holland Manufacturing Co Inc .... C 973 584-8141
Succasunna *(G-10623)*

Ileos of America Inc .... F 908 753-7300
South Plainfield *(G-10383)*

Jrm Industries Inc .... D 973 779-9340
Passaic *(G-8152)*

Lps Industries Inc .... C 201 438-3515
Moonachie *(G-6529)*

Multi Packaging Solutions Inc .... G 908 757-6000
South Plainfield *(G-10411)*

Polyair Inter Pack Inc .... D 201 804-1725
Carlstadt *(G-1204)*

Princeton Corp Graphics Inc .... D 732 545-6163
New Brunswick *(G-6995)*

Tekni-Plex Inc .... D 908 782-4000
Flemington *(G-3471)*

US Magic Box Inc .... G 973 772-2070
Garfield *(G-3770)*

PACKAGING MATERIALS: Paper, Coated Or Laminated

Allure Box & Display Co .... F 212 807-7070
Hackensack *(G-3873)*

Delta Paper Corporation .... E 856 532-0333
Burlington *(G-968)*

E & E Group Corp .... G 201 814-0414
South Hackensack *(G-10261)*

Homasote Company .... C 609 883-3300
Ewing *(G-3024)*

PACKAGING MATERIALS: Plastic Film, Coated Or Laminated

Amcor Flexibles LLC .... C 856 825-1400
Millville *(G-6275)*

ANS Plastics Corporation .... F 732 247-2776
New Brunswick *(G-6944)*

Basic Plastics Company Inc .... E 973 977-8151
Paterson *(G-8221)*

Blispak Acquisition Corp .... D 973 884-4141
Whippany *(G-12013)*

Comar Inc .... F 856 507-5461
Voorhees *(G-11426)*

Consolidated Packg Group Inc .... G 201 440-4240
Ridgefield Park *(G-9401)*

Forem Packaging Inc .... F 973 589-0402
Newark *(G-7164)*

Kansas City Design Inc .... G 609 460-4629
Lambertville *(G-5216)*

Lally-Pak Inc .... D 908 351-4141
Hillside *(G-4424)*

LV Adhesive Inc .... E 201 507-0080
Carlstadt *(G-1185)*

MSC Marketing & Technology .... E 201 507-9100
Lyndhurst *(G-5694)*

R Tape Corporation .... C 908 753-5570
South Plainfield *(G-10431)*

PACKAGING MATERIALS: Polystyrene Foam

A & S Packaging & Display .... F 201 531-1900
Carlstadt *(G-1120)*

Alliance Corrugated Box Inc .... E 877 525-5269
Saddle River *(G-9802)*

Arrow Information Packagig LLC .... G 856 317-9000
Pennsauken *(G-8480)*

Atlantic Can Company .... G 609 518-9950
Westampton *(G-11911)*

Century Service Affiliates Inc .... E 973 742-3516
Paterson *(G-8231)*

Craig Robertson .... G 973 293-8666
Montague *(G-6402)*

Futurex Properties Inc .... E 732 414-6211
Marlboro *(G-5941)*

Fxi Inc .... D 201 933-8540
East Rutherford *(G-2298)*

Granite Packaging Supply Co .... D 856 727-1010
Moorestown *(G-6579)*

Integrated Packaging Inds Inc .... E 973 839-0500
Butler *(G-1009)*

New Industrial Foam Corp .... G 908 561-4010
Plainfield *(G-8868)*

Plastpac Inc .... F 908 272-7200
Kenilworth *(G-4989)*

Rep Trading Associates Inc .... E 732 591-1140
Old Bridge *(G-7792)*

Sealed Air Corporation .... C 201 712-7000
Saddle Brook *(G-9792)*

Sealed Air Corporation .... D 973 890-4735
Saddle Brook *(G-9793)*

Shell Packaging Corporation .... E 908 871-7000
Berkeley Heights *(G-422)*

Sierra Packaging Inc .... F 732 571-2900
Ocean *(G-7745)*

Sonoco Display & Packaging LLC .... G 201 612-4008
Ridgefield Park *(G-9415)*

Tcp Reliable Inc .... G 848 229-2466
Edison *(G-2638)*

Tech-Pak Inc .... F 201 935-3800
Wood Ridge *(G-12140)*

Univeg Logistics America Inc .... G 856 241-0097
Swedesboro *(G-10735)*

US Propack Inc .... G 732 294-4500
Freehold *(G-3690)*

Utility Development Corp .... G 973 994-4334
Livingston *(G-5567)*

PACKAGING: Blister Or Bubble Formed, Plastic

Carecam International Inc .... E 973 227-0720
Fairfield *(G-3156)*

Colorite Plastics Company .... E 201 941-2900
Ridgefield *(G-9355)*

Dolco Packaging Corp .... E 201 941-2900
Ridgefield *(G-9358)*

Plastiform Packaging Inc .... E 973 983-8900
Rockaway *(G-9597)*

Pure TEC Corporation .... G 201 941-2900
Ridgefield *(G-9381)*

Tekni-Plex Inc .... C 908 575-7661
Branchburg *(G-710)*

Tekni-Plex Inc .... D 908 782-4000
Flemington *(G-3471)*

PACKING & CRATING SVC

Integrated Packaging Inds Inc .... E 973 839-0500
Butler *(G-1009)*

PACKING & CRATING SVCS: Containerized Goods For Shipping

Bigflysports Inc .... G 201 653-4414
Secaucus *(G-9868)*

Cuny & Guerber Inc .... E 201 617-5800
Union City *(G-11244)*

PACKING MATERIALS: Mechanical

American Braiding & Mfg Corp .... F 732 938-6333
Howell *(G-4545)*

Cryopak Verification Tech Inc .... E 732 346-9200
Edison *(G-2497)*

Fleet Packaging Inc .... G 866 302-0340
South Orange *(G-10306)*

Paradigm Packaging East LLC .... C 201 909-3400
Saddle Brook *(G-9780)*

Romaco North America Inc .... G 609 584-2500
Hamilton *(G-4124)*

PACKING SVCS: Shipping

Hub Print & Copy Center LLC .... G 201 585-7887
Fort Lee *(G-3558)*

Jan Packaging Inc .... D 973 361-7200
Dover *(G-2095)*

Norwood Industries Inc .... F 856 858-6195
Haddon Township *(G-4054)*

Oasis Trading Co Inc .... C 908 964-0477
Hillside *(G-4433)*

Package Development Co Inc .... E 973 983-8500
Rockaway *(G-9593)*

Vaswani Inc .... F 877 376-4425
Edison *(G-2642)*

PADS, SCOURING: Soap Impregnated

Supply Plus NY Inc .... E 973 481-4800
Paterson *(G-8391)*

PADS: Athletic, Protective

Impact Protective Eqp LLC .... G 973 377-0903
Madison *(G-5724)*

PADS: Mattress

Stanlar Enterprises Inc .... E 973 680-4488
Bloomfield *(G-532)*

PAILS: Meta, Exc Shipping

Phoenix Container Inc .... C 732 247-3931
Trenton *(G-11097)*

PAINT & PAINTING SPLYS STORE

Hawthorne Paint Company Inc .... G 973 423-2335
Lodi *(G-5586)*

PAINTING SVC: Metal Prdts

Newark Industrial Spraying .... F 973 344-6855
Newark *(G-7254)*

Productive Industrial Finshg .... G 856 427-9646
Voorhees *(G-11436)*

PAINTS & ADDITIVES

Columbia Paint Lab Inc ....E 201 435-4884
  Jersey City *(G-4731)*
Dux Paint LLC ....F 973 473-2376
  Lodi *(G-5583)*
Elementis Specialties Inc ....C 609 443-2000
  East Windsor *(G-2374)*
Fti Inc ....G 973 443-0004
  Florham Park *(G-3503)*
Hawthorne Paint Company Inc ....G 973 423-2335
  Lodi *(G-5586)*
Kop-Coat Inc ....E 800 221-4466
  Rockaway *(G-9582)*
Milspray LLC ....E 732 886-2223
  Lakewood *(G-5159)*
Ultra Additives LLC ....E 973 279-1306
  Bloomfield *(G-536)*

PAINTS & ALLIED PRODUCTS

Actega North America Inc ....C 856 829-6300
  Delran *(G-2009)*
Actega North America Inc ....F 856 829-6300
  Cinnaminson *(G-1444)*
Advanced Protective Products ....F 201 794-2000
  Fair Lawn *(G-3074)*
Ashland LLC ....G 908 243-3500
  Bridgewater *(G-815)*
Ashland Spcalty Ingredients GP ....E 732 353-7708
  Parlin *(G-7929)*
Benjamin Moore & Co ....C 201 573-9600
  Montvale *(G-6444)*
Benjamin Moore & Co ....C 973 344-1200
  Newark *(G-7105)*
Benjamin Moore & Co ....D 973 569-5000
  Clifton *(G-1574)*
Benjamin Moore & Co ....D 201 573-9600
  Montvale *(G-6445)*
Breen Color Concentrates LLC ....F 609 397-8200
  Lambertville *(G-5210)*
Carboline Company ....F 908 233-3150
  Westfield *(G-11923)*
Chemetall US Inc ....D 908 464-6900
  New Providence *(G-7033)*
Clausen Company Inc ....F 732 738-1165
  Fords *(G-3528)*
Colorflo Inc ....G 908 862-3010
  Linden *(G-5360)*
Covalnce Spcialty Coatings LLC ....D 732 356-2870
  Middlesex *(G-6159)*
Cytec Industries Inc ....C 973 357-3100
  Saddle Brook *(G-9761)*
Dunbar Sales Company Inc ....G 201 437-6500
  Bayonne *(G-223)*
E I Du Pont De Nemours & Co ....E 732 257-1579
  Parlin *(G-7930)*
Elementis Specialties Inc ....E 201 432-0800
  East Windsor *(G-2375)*
Environmental Coatings & Cnstr ....F 973 509-9456
  Montclair *(G-6413)*
Evonik Corporation ....B 973 929-8000
  Parsippany *(G-8003)*
Fluorotherm Polymers Inc ....G 973 575-0760
  Parsippany *(G-8014)*
Gdb International Inc ....D 732 246-3001
  New Brunswick *(G-6962)*
General Plastics Group ....E 973 748-5500
  Bloomfield *(G-512)*
Industrial Summit Tech Corp ....E 732 238-2211
  Parlin *(G-7932)*
J R S Tool & Metal Finishing ....G 908 753-2050
  South Plainfield *(G-10387)*
Lafarge Road Marking Inc ....C 973 884-0300
  Parsippany *(G-8037)*
Muralo Company Inc ....C 201 437-0770
  Bayonne *(G-238)*
Nautical Marine Paint Corp ....E 732 821-3200
  North Brunswick *(G-7530)*
Nippon Paint (usa) Inc ....F 201 692-1111
  Teaneck *(G-10762)*
Penn Metal Finishing Co Inc ....G 609 387-3400
  Burlington *(G-987)*
Plastic Specialties & Tech Inc ....C 201 941-2900
  Ridgefield *(G-9380)*
Prem-Khichi Enterprises Inc ....F 973 242-0300
  East Brunswick *(G-2174)*
Rich Art Color Co Inc ....F 201 767-0009
  Northvale *(G-7606)*
Saint-Gobain Prfmce Plas Corp ....D 732 652-0910
  Somerset *(G-10170)*

Seagrave Coatings Corp ....E 201 933-1000
  Kenilworth *(G-4994)*
Steven Industries Inc ....E 201 437-6500
  Bayonne *(G-245)*
Target Coatings Inc ....G 800 752-9922
  Fair Lawn *(G-3120)*
Tenax Finishing Products Co ....F 973 589-9000
  Newark *(G-7339)*

PAINTS, VARNISHES & SPLYS WHOLESALERS

Worldwide Safety Systems LLC ....G 888 613-4501
  Teaneck *(G-10778)*

PAINTS, VARNISHES & SPLYS, WHOLESALE: Paints

Kop-Coat Inc ....E 800 221-4466
  Rockaway *(G-9582)*
Nautical Marine Paint Corp ....E 732 821-3200
  North Brunswick *(G-7530)*
Steven Industries Inc ....E 201 437-6500
  Bayonne *(G-245)*
Target Coatings Inc ....G 800 752-9922
  Fair Lawn *(G-3120)*

PAINTS: Marine

Flexdell Corp ....G 732 901-7771
  Lakewood *(G-5124)*
Hempel (usa) Inc ....G 201 939-2801
  Clifton *(G-1639)*

PAINTS: Waterproof

Newage Painting Corporation ....G 908 547-4734
  Newark *(G-7252)*
Performance Industries Inc ....E 609 392-1450
  Trenton *(G-11096)*
Sau-Sea Swimming Pool Products ....F 609 859-8500
  Southampton *(G-10482)*
Tq3 north America Inc ....G 973 882-7900
  Fairfield *(G-3329)*

PALLET REPAIR SVCS

F & R Pallets Inc ....E 856 964-8516
  Camden *(G-1064)*
Lt Chini Inc ....G 856 692-0303
  Vineland *(G-11381)*
T & M Pallet Co Inc ....E 908 454-3042
  Stewartsville *(G-10598)*
Warren Pallet Company Inc ....F 908 995-7172
  Bloomsbury *(G-547)*

PALLETS

D & H Pallets LLC ....E 973 481-2981
  Newark *(G-7131)*
F & R Pallets Inc ....E 856 964-8516
  Camden *(G-1064)*
Greenway Products & Svcs LLC ....C 732 442-0200
  New Brunswick *(G-6965)*
JC Pallets Inc ....F 973 345-1102
  Paterson *(G-8299)*
M Hand Pallets ....G 908 887-2100
  Elizabeth *(G-2753)*
Reliable Pallet Services LLC ....G 973 900-2260
  Hillside *(G-4438)*
Reliable Pallet Services LLC ....G 732 243-9642
  Metuchen *(G-6118)*
Royal Pallet Inc ....G 973 299-0445
  Boonton *(G-581)*
Universal Pallet Inc ....G 732 356-2624
  Warren *(G-11569)*
Van-Nick Pallet Inc ....G 908 753-1800
  South Plainfield *(G-10449)*

PALLETS & SKIDS: Wood

Avenel Pallet Co Inc ....F 732 752-0500
  Dunellen *(G-2126)*
Bunn Industries Incorporated ....F 609 890-2900
  Trenton *(G-11030)*
Delisa Pallet Corp ....F 732 667-7070
  Middlesex *(G-6161)*
East Coast Pallets LLC ....G 732 308-3616
  Manalapan *(G-5842)*
Global Direct Marketing Group ....G 856 427-6116
  Haddonfield *(G-4060)*

Isco ....G 856 672-9182
  Barrington *(G-179)*
Riephoff Saw Mill Inc ....F 609 259-7265
  Allentown *(G-34)*
Wm Leiber Inc ....G 732 938-2080
  Farmingdale *(G-3397)*

PALLETS: Metal

RISE Corporation ....E 973 575-7480
  West Caldwell *(G-11804)*

PALLETS: Plastic

Componding Engrg Solutions Inc ....F 973 340-4000
  Clifton *(G-1587)*
P D Q Plastics Inc ....E 201 823-0270
  Bayonne *(G-240)*
Pelco Packaging Corporation ....F 973 675-4994
  East Orange *(G-2265)*

PALLETS: Wooden

Atco Pallet Company ....E 856 461-8141
  Delanco *(G-2003)*
Atlantic Indus WD Pdts LLC ....G 609 965-4555
  Egg Harbor City *(G-2656)*
Cutler Bros Box & Lumber Co ....E 201 943-2535
  Fairview *(G-3360)*
Extreme Pallet Inc ....G 973 286-1717
  Newark *(G-7159)*
General Pallet LLC ....G 732 549-1000
  Flemington *(G-3445)*
Jimenez Pallets LLC ....G 862 267-3900
  Kearny *(G-4889)*
Lawrence M Gichan Incorporated ....F 201 330-3222
  North Bergen *(G-7462)*
Love Pallet LLC ....G 908 964-3385
  Hillside *(G-4426)*
Lt Chini Inc ....G 856 692-0303
  Vineland *(G-11381)*
Millwood Inc ....D 732 967-8818
  South River *(G-10463)*
North Eastern Pallet Exchange ....E 908 289-0018
  Elizabeth *(G-2759)*
Notie Corp ....G 609 259-3477
  Allentown *(G-32)*
Pallet Services Inc ....G 856 514-3908
  Pedricktown *(G-8439)*
Pedestal Pallet Inc ....G 732 968-7488
  Dunellen *(G-2129)*
Petro Pallet LLC ....E 732 230-3287
  Monmouth Junction *(G-6354)*
Poor Boy Pallet LLC ....E 856 451-3771
  Bridgeton *(G-795)*
Premier Asset Logistics Networ ....F 877 725-6381
  Williamstown *(G-12101)*
Select Enterprises Inc ....G 732 287-8622
  Edison *(G-2613)*
T & M Pallet Co Inc ....E 908 454-3042
  Stewartsville *(G-10598)*
Tommys Pallet Yard LLC ....G 609 424-3996
  Bordentown *(G-612)*
Tristate Crating Pallet Co Inc ....E 973 357-8293
  Paterson *(G-8403)*
U P N Pallet Co Inc ....E 856 299-1192
  Penns Grove *(G-8466)*
Warren Pallet Company Inc ....F 908 995-7172
  Bloomsbury *(G-547)*

PANEL & DISTRIBUTION BOARDS & OTHER RELATED APPARATUS

Aeropanel Corporation ....D 973 335-9636
  Boonton *(G-552)*
Automation & Control Inc ....E 856 234-2300
  Moorestown *(G-6562)*

PANEL & DISTRIBUTION BOARDS: Electric

Electronic Power Designs Inc ....F 973 838-7055
  Bloomingdale *(G-542)*
Lincoln Electric Pdts Co Inc ....E 908 688-2900
  Union *(G-11201)*
Symcon Inc ....G 973 728-8661
  West Milford *(G-11857)*
Tsi Nomenclature Inc ....G 732 340-0646
  Avenel *(G-157)*

PANELS, CORRUGATED: Plastic

Onyx Graphics LLC ....G 908 281-0038
  Hillsborough *(G-4361)*

Employee Codes: A=Over 500 employees, B=251-500
C=101-250, D=51-100, E=20-50, F=10-19, G=4-9

2018 Harris New jersey
Manufacturers Directory

919

PRODUCT

Philcorr LLC ....D...... 856 205-0557
Vineland (G-11391)

PANELS: Building, Wood

All Structures LLC ....G...... 732 233-7071
Little Silver (G-5519)

PANELS: Electric Metering

Csl Services Inc ....F...... 856 755-9440
Pennsauken (G-8499)

PANELS: Wood

Yonkers Plywood Manufacturing ....E...... 732 727-1200
Old Bridge (G-7795)

PAPER & BOARD: Die-cut

American Bindery Depot Inc..............C...... 732 287-2370
Edison (G-2457)
Custom Converters Inc ....E...... 201 994-9000
Livingston (G-5527)
Danielle Die Cut Products Inc ....E...... 973 278-3000
Paterson (G-8244)
Dynamic Die Cutting & Finshg ....F...... 973 589-8338
Newark (G-7147)
Gleicher Manufacturing Corp ....E...... 908 233-2211
Scotch Plains (G-9849)
Grand Displays Inc ....F...... 201 994-1500
North Bergen (G-7455)
Grand Displays Inc ....E...... 201 994-1500
Pennsauken (G-8517)
JIT Manufacturing Inc ....F...... 973 247-7300
Paterson (G-8303)
Prestige Associates Inc ....E...... 609 393-1509
Trenton (G-11105)
Pro Tapes & Specialties Inc ....C...... 732 346-0900
North Brunswick (G-7535)
Stephco Sales Inc ....E...... 973 278-5454
Paterson (G-8384)
Vmc Die Cutting Corp ....F...... 973 450-4655
Belleville (G-326)

PAPER & ENVELOPES: Writing, Made From Purchased Materials

ADM Corporation ....D...... 732 469-0900
Middlesex (G-6143)
Arna Marketing Group Inc.................D...... 908 625-7395
Branchburg (G-638)

PAPER CONVERTING

Arrow Paper Company Inc ....G...... 908 756-1111
Plainfield (G-8855)
B & G Plastics Inc ....E...... 973 824-9220
Union (G-11155)
Cartolith Group ....G...... 908 624-9833
Hillside (G-4401)
CCL Label Inc ....C...... 609 443-3700
Hightstown (G-4311)
Georgia-Pacific LLC.........................C...... 908 995-2228
Milford (G-6245)
Laminated Industries Inc ....E...... 908 862-5995
Linden (G-5400)
Legacy Converting Inc ....E...... 609 642-7020
Cranbury (G-1853)
Matthias Paper Corporation ....E...... 856 467-6970
Swedesboro (G-10709)
Princeton Supply Corp......................G...... 609 683-9100
Princeton (G-9102)
R L R Foil Stamping LLC ....F...... 973 778-9464
Passaic (G-8175)
Steiner Paper Corp ....G...... 732 651-6009
Manalapan (G-5863)
Stonebridge Paper LLC ....F...... 973 413-8100
Paterson (G-8386)

PAPER MANUFACTURERS: Exc Newsprint

International Paper Company ....E...... 856 853-7000
West Deptford (G-11830)
International Paper Company ....C...... 856 931-8000
Bellmawr (G-343)
International Paper Company ....C...... 856 546-7000
Barrington (G-178)
International Paper Company ....G...... 973 405-2400
Clifton (G-1649)
Printwrap Corporation ....F...... 973 239-1144
Cedar Grove (G-1297)

Schweitzer-Mauduit Intl Inc...............B...... 732 723-6100
Spotswood (G-10530)
Sealed Air Holdings ....G...... 201 791-7600
Elmwood Park (G-2849)
Steiner Paper Corp ....G...... 732 651-6009
Manalapan (G-5863)
Verso Paper Management LP ....A...... 732 938-3167
Wall Township (G-11518)

PAPER PRDTS: Feminine Hygiene Prdts

Jnj International Inv LLC ....G...... 732 524-0400
New Brunswick (G-6973)
Johnson & Johnson ....D...... 732 524-0400
Piscataway (G-8785)
Johnson & Johnson ....D...... 732 524-0400
Princeton (G-9063)
Johnson & Johnson ....D...... 917 573-8007
Ridgefield (G-9368)
Johnson & Johnson ....D...... 732 524-0400
Lambertville (G-5214)
Johnson & Johnson ....D...... 732 524-0400
Branchburg (G-670)
Johnson & Johnson ....D...... 732 524-0400
Trenton (G-11071)
Johnson & Johnson ....A...... 732 524-0400
New Brunswick (G-6974)
Johnson & Johnson ....C...... 908 722-9319
Raritan (G-9311)
Johnson & Johnson ....C...... 908 874-1000
Morris Plains (G-6673)
Johnson & Johnson ....C...... 732 524-0400
New Brunswick (G-6975)

PAPER PRDTS: Infant & Baby Prdts

Interganic Fzco LLC.........................G...... 224 436-0372
Hillsborough (G-4350)

PAPER PRDTS: Sanitary

Johnson & Johnson ....D...... 732 422-5000
North Brunswick (G-7522)
Keystone Adjustable Cap Co Inc........E...... 856 356-2809
Pennsauken (G-8539)
Marcal Manufacturing LLC.................G...... 201 703-6225
Elmwood Park (G-2833)
Marcal Paper Mills LLC ....A...... 800 631-8451
Elmwood Park (G-2834)
Pacon Manufacturing Corp.................C...... 732 764-9070
Somerset (G-10152)
Soundview Paper Holdings LLC ....A...... 201 796-4000
Elmwood Park (G-2850)

PAPER PRDTS: Towels, Napkins/Tissue Paper, From Purchd Mtrls

Federal Equipment & Mfg Co Inc.........G...... 973 340-7600
Lodi (G-5584)

PAPER, WHOLESALE: Fine

Acedepotcom ....F...... 800 844-0962
Northvale (G-7568)

PAPER, WHOLESALE: Printing

Printwrap Corporation ....F...... 973 239-1144
Cedar Grove (G-1297)

PAPER: Adhesive

LV Adhesive Inc ....E...... 201 507-0080
Carlstadt (G-1185)
Omega Heat Transfer Co Inc..............F...... 732 340-0023
West Orange (G-11902)
Plus Packaging Inc ....G...... 973 538-2216
Morristown (G-6736)
Thermwell Products Co Inc................G...... 201 684-4400
Mahwah (G-5821)
Wet-N-Stick LLC ....G...... 908 687-8273
Union (G-11234)

PAPER: Bag

Case It Inc ....E...... 800 441-4710
Lyndhurst (G-5675)

PAPER: Card

American Banknote Corporation.........G...... 203 941-4090
Fort Lee (G-3543)

PAPER: Cardboard

All County Recycling Inc...................F...... 609 393-6445
Trenton (G-11015)

PAPER: Chart & Graph, Ruled

Gpschartscom ....G...... 609 226-8842
Ventnor City (G-11292)

PAPER: Coated & Laminated, NEC

Avery Dennison Corporation ....G...... 201 956-6100
Fair Lawn (G-3080)
CCL Label Inc ....D...... 609 443-3700
Hightstown (G-4311)
CCL Label (delaware) Inc ....C...... 609 259-1055
Trenton (G-11037)
Custom Laminations Inc ....E...... 973 279-9174
Paterson (G-8243)
Dikeman Laminating Corporation ....E...... 973 473-5696
Clifton (G-1599)
Fedex Office & Print Svcs Inc ....E...... 856 427-0099
Cherry Hill (G-1364)
Gleicher Manufacturing Corp ....E...... 908 233-2211
Scotch Plains (G-9849)
Graphic Express Menu Co Inc ....E...... 973 685-0022
Clifton (G-1630)
Horizon Label LLC ....F...... 856 767-0777
West Berlin (G-11725)
Igi Corp ....G...... 908 753-5570
South Plainfield (G-10382)
International Graphics Inc..................C...... 908 753-5570
South Plainfield (G-10386)
Lacoa Inc ....G...... 973 754-1000
Elmwood Park (G-2831)
Par Code Symbology Inc...................F...... 973 918-0550
Roseland (G-9655)
Renell Label Print Inc ....G...... 201 652-6544
Paramus (G-7899)
Tech-Pak Inc ....F...... 201 935-3800
Wood Ridge (G-12140)
United Label Corp ....F...... 973 589-6500
Newark (G-7354)

PAPER: Copier

Popnfold Papers Inc ....G...... 201 933-2015
Lyndhurst (G-5702)

PAPER: Corrugated

Schiffenhaus Industries Inc ....C...... 973 484-5000
Newark (G-7303)

PAPER: Envelope

Glue Fold Inc ....D...... 973 575-8400
Clifton (G-1628)

PAPER: Gift Wrap

Glitterwrap Inc ....D...... 800 745-4883
Rockaway (G-9570)
Icup Inc ....E...... 856 751-2045
Cherry Hill (G-1376)
M S C Paper Products Corp ....E...... 908 686-2200
Hillside (G-4428)
Schurman Fine Papers ....E...... 856 985-1776
Marlton (G-5998)

PAPER: Metallic Covered, Made From Purchased Materials

Unifoil Corporation ....D...... 973 244-9900
Fairfield (G-3334)

PAPER: Newsprint

Beach Nutts Media Inc......................G...... 609 886-4113
Villas (G-11313)
Delta Paper Corporation...................E...... 856 532-0333
Burlington (G-968)

PAPER: Packaging

Amcor Flexibles LLC ....C...... 856 825-1400
Millville (G-6275)
Borak Group Inc ....D...... 718 665-8500
Jersey City (G-4720)
G R Impex Ltd Liability Co ....F...... 732 931-7001
Avenel (G-133)
Lps Industries Inc ....C...... 201 438-3515
Moonachie (G-6529)

PAPER: Poster & Art

Arthur A Kaplan Co Inc..................E........201 806-2100
East Rutherford *(G-2279)*

PAPER: Printer

Boro Printing Inc.........................G........732 229-1899
West Long Branch *(G-11844)*
Lodor Offset Corporation..............F........201 935-7100
Carlstadt *(G-1184)*
Sre Ventures LLC........................G........973 785-0099
Little Falls *(G-5489)*

PAPER: Specialty Or Chemically Treated

Holland Manufacturing Co Inc..............C........973 584-8141
Succasunna *(G-10623)*
IW Tremont Co Inc........................E........973 427-3800
Hawthorne *(G-4242)*

PAPER: Wallpaper

Rigo Industries Inc......................E........973 881-1780
Paterson *(G-8370)*
Screen Reproductions Co Inc............E........201 935-0830
Carlstadt *(G-1215)*

PAPER: Wrapping & Packaging

Allure Box & Display Co.................F........212 807-7070
Hackensack *(G-3873)*
Flexo-Craft Prints Inc...................E........973 482-7200
Harrison *(G-4183)*

PAPER: Wrapping, Waterproof Or Coated

Norpak Corporation......................E........973 589-4200
Newark *(G-7260)*

PAPERBOARD

Caraustar Industries Inc................E........908 782-0505
Frenchtown *(G-3698)*
International Paper Company..............C........732 251-2000
Spotswood *(G-10528)*
M S C Paper Products Corp..............E........908 686-2200
Hillside *(G-4428)*
Sonoco Products Company................D........908 713-6900
Annandale *(G-60)*
Union Container Corp....................E........973 242-3600
Newark *(G-7351)*
Westrock CP LLC.........................D........732 866-1890
Colts Neck *(G-1794)*
Westrock Rkt Company....................E........973 237-9570
Totowa *(G-10984)*
Wjj and Company LLC....................F........973 246-7480
Garfield *(G-3773)*

PAPERBOARD CONVERTING

Caraustar Clifton Primary Pack..........C........973 472-4900
Clifton *(G-1580)*

PAPERBOARD PRDTS: Binders' Board

Nu-EZ Custom Bindery LLC..............E........201 488-4140
Hackensack *(G-3955)*

PAPERBOARD PRDTS: Coated & Treated Board

Monster Coatings Inc....................G........973 983-7662
Rockaway *(G-9588)*

PAPERBOARD PRDTS: Container Board

Westrock CP LLC.........................E........973 594-6000
Clifton *(G-1743)*

PAPERBOARD PRDTS: Folding Boxboard

Graphic Packaging Intl LLC..............C........732 424-2100
Wayne *(G-11643)*
Multi Packaging Solutions Inc............C........908 757-6000
South Plainfield *(G-10411)*
Shure-Pak Corporation...................G........856 825-0808
Millville *(G-6324)*
United States Box Corp..................E........973 481-2000
Fairfield *(G-3335)*

PAPERBOARD PRDTS: Milk Carton Board

Four Star Reproductions Inc.............E........862 268-8200
Newton *(G-7388)*

PAPERBOARD PRDTS: Packaging Board

JIT Manufacturing Inc...................F........973 247-7300
Paterson *(G-8303)*
Shell Packaging Corporation............E........908 871-7000
Berkeley Heights *(G-422)*
Vanguard Packaging Corp................G........973 391-9200
Livingston *(G-5569)*

PAPERBOARD PRDTS: Specialty Board

Flech Paper Products Inc................F........973 357-8111
Paterson *(G-8272)*

PAPERBOARD PRDTS: Strawboard

Greenbuilt Intl Bldg Co..................C........609 300-9091
Voorhees *(G-11432)*

PAPERBOARD: Coated

Lamitech Inc.............................E........609 860-8037
Cranbury *(G-1851)*
Tekni-Plex Inc...........................D........908 782-4000
Flemington *(G-3471)*

PAPERBOARD: Corrugated

Sunshine Metal & Sign Inc...............G........973 676-4432
Orange *(G-7829)*

PARACHUTES

Air Cruisers Company LLC...............C........732 681-3527
Wall Township *(G-11460)*
Airborne Systems N Amer NJ Inc........C........856 663-1275
Pennsauken *(G-8474)*
Switlik Parachute Company Inc...........G........609 587-3300
Trenton *(G-11119)*

PARKING GARAGE

Kyosis LLC..............................G........908 202-8894
South River *(G-10462)*

PARKING METERS

Parkeon Inc.............................E........856 234-8000
Moorestown *(G-6608)*

PARTITIONS & FIXTURES: Except Wood

Acro Display Inc.........................E........215 229-1100
Pennsauken *(G-8470)*
Benco Inc...............................F........973 575-4440
Fairfield *(G-3146)*
Carib-Display Co.........................G........732 583-1648
Matawan *(G-6014)*
Display Works LLC.......................C........201 327-1260
Parsippany *(G-7983)*
Engo Co................................E........908 754-6600
South Plainfield *(G-10355)*
Imperial Design..........................G........856 742-8480
Gloucester City *(G-3839)*
Insign Inc..............................E........856 424-1161
Cherry Hill *(G-1381)*
Ner Data Products Inc...................E........888 637-3282
Glassboro *(G-3810)*
S L Enterprises Inc......................G........908 272-8145
Ewing *(G-3054)*

PARTITIONS WHOLESALERS

Door Stop LLC...........................F........718 599-5112
Carlstadt *(G-1157)*
Extra Office Inc.........................F........732 381-9774
Rahway *(G-9188)*

PARTITIONS: Solid Fiber, Made From Purchased Materials

Westrock Rkt Company...................C........856 596-8604
Marlton *(G-6004)*

PARTITIONS: Wood & Fixtures

Arrow Information Packagig LLC..........G........856 317-9000
Pennsauken *(G-8480)*
Bamboo & Rattan Works Inc.............G........732 255-4239
Toms River *(G-10866)*
D S F Inc...............................E........908 218-5153
Raritan *(G-9308)*
Designcore Ltd..........................D........718 499-0337
Secaucus *(G-9877)*

Eagle Fabrication Inc

Eagle Fabrication Inc...................E........732 739-5300
Ltl Egg Hbr *(G-5644)*
Intelco.................................D........856 456-6755
Westville *(G-11944)*
Ken Bauer Inc...........................E........201 664-6881
Hillsdale *(G-4385)*
Kubik Maltbie Inc........................E........856 234-0052
Mount Laurel *(G-6811)*
Medlaurel Inc...........................E........856 461-6600
Delanco *(G-2007)*
Parsons Cabinets Inc....................G........973 279-4954
Montclair *(G-6430)*

PARTS: Metal

Cospack America Corp....................E........732 548-5858
Edison *(G-2493)*
I S Parts International Inc................E........856 691-2203
Vineland *(G-11372)*

PATENT OWNERS & LESSORS

Scorpio Posters Inc......................E........718 499-2001
Marlboro *(G-5957)*

PATTERNS: Indl

Creative Patterns & Mfg.................G........973 589-1391
Rockaway *(G-9558)*
Method Assoc Inc........................F........732 888-0444
Keyport *(G-5020)*
Motif Industries Inc......................F........973 575-1800
East Hanover *(G-2229)*

PAVERS

Elite Landscaping & Pavers..............G........732 252-6152
Freehold *(G-3653)*
G & A Pavers Llc........................G........201 562-5947
Englewood *(G-2899)*
Karla Landscaping Pavers...............G........732 333-5852
Howell *(G-4558)*
NJ Paver Restorations LLC..............G........732 558-6011
Hillsborough *(G-4359)*
US Outworkers LLC.......................G........973 362-1458
Sussex *(G-10680)*

PAVING MATERIALS: Prefabricated, Concrete

Advanced Pavement Technologies........F........973 366-8044
Rockaway *(G-9545)*
Concrete Stone & Tile Corp..............E........973 948-7193
Branchville *(G-728)*
CST Products LLC........................E........856 299-5339
Penns Grove *(G-8464)*

PAVING MIXTURES

Barrett Asphalt Inc......................E........609 561-4100
Hammonton *(G-4132)*
Stavola Holding Corporation..............C........732 542-2328
Tinton Falls *(G-10850)*

PAYROLL SVCS

Sage Software Inc........................D........856 231-4667
Mount Laurel *(G-6837)*

PEARLS, WHOLESALE

Pearl Baumell Company Inc..............G........415 421-2113
Rutherford *(G-9743)*

PEAT MINING & PROCESSING SVCS

Sussex Humus & Supply Inc.............G........973 779-8812
Clifton *(G-1732)*

PEAT MINING SVCS

Partac Peat Corp........................F........908 637-4191
Great Meadows *(G-3850)*
Partac Peat Corporation.................F........908 637-4631
Great Meadows *(G-3851)*

PENS & PARTS: Ball Point

Cameo Metal Forms Inc..................F........718 788-1106
Woodland Park *(G-12213)*
Touch of Class Promotions LLC..........G........267 994-0860
Voorhees *(G-11440)*

Employee Codes: A=Over 500 employees, B=251-500
C=101-250, D=51-100, E=20-50, F=10-19, G=4-9

2018 Harris New Jersey
Manufacturers Directory

921

PRODUCT

PENS & PENCILS: Mechanical, NEC

Cameo Novelty & Pen Corp ....E 973 923-1600
Hillside *(G-4400)*
Newell Brands Inc.................................B 201 610-6600
Hoboken *(G-4486)*
Pen Company of America LLC ....E 908 374-7949
Garwood *(G-3784)*
Pen Company of America LLC ....E 908 374-7949
Linden *(G-5427)*

PERFUME: Concentrated

Charabot & Co Inc...............................F 201 812-2762
Budd Lake *(G-926)*
Takasago Intl Corp USA ....C 201 767-9001
Rockleigh *(G-9634)*
Takasago Intl Corp USA ....D 201 767-9001
Northvale *(G-7609)*

PERFUME: Perfumes, Natural Or Synthetic

Custom Essence...................................F 732 249-6405
Somerset *(G-10088)*
Mastertaste Inc...................................F 201 373-1111
Teterboro *(G-10805)*
Radha Beauty Products LLC ....G 732 993-6242
Northvale *(G-7603)*

PERFUMES

Agilex Flavors Fragrances Inc...............G 732 885-0702
Piscataway *(G-8728)*
Ascent Aromatics Inc ....G 908 755-0120
South Plainfield *(G-10332)*
Atlantis Aromatics Inc ....G 732 919-1112
Wall Township *(G-11464)*
Batallure Beauty LLC............................E 609 716-1200
Princeton *(G-9013)*
Bellevue Parfums USA LLC ....F 908 262-7774
Hillsborough *(G-4319)*
Cadence Distributors LLC ....G 646 808-3031
Hackensack *(G-3889)*
Continental Aromatics ....G 973 238-9300
Hawthorne *(G-4229)*
Coty US LLC ....D 973 490-8700
Morris Plains *(G-6658)*
Cpl Aromas Inc....................................F 732 469-0680
Scotch Plains *(G-9848)*
Creative Concepts Corporation...............G 201 750-1234
Norwood *(G-7620)*
Dosis Fragrance LLC............................G 718 874-0074
Newark *(G-7142)*
Excell Brands Ltd Liability Co ....G 908 561-1130
Princeton *(G-9043)*
Fragrance Exchange Inc ....G 732 641-2210
Monroe Township *(G-6382)*
Fragrance Factory Inc ....G 973 835-2002
Pompton Plains *(G-8959)*
Fragrance Solutions Corp ....G 732 832-7800
South Plainfield *(G-10368)*
French Color Fragrance Co Inc ....E 201 567-6883
Englewood *(G-2898)*
International Aromatics Inc.....................F 201 964-0900
Moonachie *(G-6523)*
Klabin Fragrances Inc ....F 973 857-3600
Cedar Grove *(G-1286)*
Perfumania Inc ....G 732 493-4116
Tinton Falls *(G-10843)*
Qualis Packaging Inc ....F 908 782-0305
South Plainfield *(G-10426)*
Robertet Fragrances Inc ....E 201 405-1000
Budd Lake *(G-940)*
Robertet Fragrances Inc ....E 973 575-4550
Fairfield *(G-3295)*
Sahar USA Inc ....E 201 868-4900
North Bergen *(G-7482)*
Victory International USA LLC ....F 732 417-5900
Eatontown *(G-2429)*

PESTICIDES

AP&g Co Inc ....D 718 492-3648
Bayonne *(G-211)*
AP&g Co Inc ....D 718 492-3648
Bayonne *(G-212)*
Bayer Corporation ....A 412 777-2000
Whippany *(G-12007)*

PESTICIDES WHOLESALERS

Growmark Fs LLC ....F 609 267-7054
Eastampton *(G-2376)*

PET SPLYS

Animals Etc Inc ....G 609 386-8442
Burlington *(G-957)*
Gramercy Products Inc ....E 212 868-2559
Secaucus *(G-9892)*
Gwenstone Inc ....G 732 785-2600
Lakewood *(G-5131)*
Halfway Hounds ....G 201 970-6235
Park Ridge *(G-7922)*
Hartz Mountain Corporation ....C 800 275-1414
Secaucus *(G-9894)*
Immunogenetics Inc ....D 856 697-1441
Buena *(G-947)*
Klein Distributors Inc............................G 732 446-7632
Burlington *(G-982)*
Littlegifts Inc.......................................F 212 868-2559
Secaucus *(G-9902)*
Loving Pets Corporation ....E 609 655-3700
Cranbury *(G-1856)*
Maxwell & Mollys Closet ....G 973 300-0101
Newton *(G-7396)*
Naomi Pet International Inc....................E 201 660-7918
Northvale *(G-7594)*
Pet Salon Inc ....F 609 350-6480
Margate City *(G-5933)*
Pet Salon Inc ....E 609 350-6480
Margate City *(G-5934)*
Q10 Products LLC ....F 201 567-9299
Clifton *(G-1707)*
Skaffles Group LLC ....E 732 721-0022
Sayreville *(G-9839)*
Vo-Toys Inc ....E 973 482-8915
Clifton *(G-1740)*

PET SPLYS WHOLESALERS

Hartz Mountain Corporation ....C 800 275-1414
Secaucus *(G-9894)*
Imagine Gold LLC ....E 201 488-5988
South Hackensack *(G-10270)*
Loving Pets Corporation ....E 609 655-3700
Cranbury *(G-1856)*
R World Enterprises ....G 201 795-2428
Jersey City *(G-4811)*
Tuff Mutters LLC ....G 973 291-6679
Kinnelon *(G-5041)*

PETROLEUM & PETROLEUM PRDTS, WHOLESALE Butane Gas

Welding & Radiator Supply Co ....G 609 965-0433
Egg Harbor City *(G-2674)*

PETROLEUM PRDTS WHOLESALERS

Jet Aviation St Louis Inc ....E 201 462-4026
Teterboro *(G-10800)*
Speedway LLC ....B 732 750-7800
Port Reading *(G-8990)*

PETS & PET SPLYS, WHOLESALE

Vo-Toys Inc ....E 973 482-8915
Clifton *(G-1740)*

PHARMACEUTICAL PREPARATIONS: Adrenal

Austarpharma LLC................................D 732 225-2930
Edison *(G-2469)*

PHARMACEUTICAL PREPARATIONS: Digitalis

Diamond Systems USA Corp ....G 973 777-9075
South Hackensack *(G-10260)*

PHARMACEUTICAL PREPARATIONS: Druggists' Preparations

Actavis Elizabeth LLC ....E 973 442-3200
Madison *(G-5716)*
Amneal Pharmaceuticals LLC ....E 908 947-3120
Bridgewater *(G-809)*
Aptapharma Corporation ....E 856 665-0025
Pennsauken *(G-8479)*
Arno Therapeutics Inc ....G 862 703-7170
Flemington *(G-3428)*
Ascendia Pharmaceuticals LLC ....E 732 638-4028
North Brunswick *(G-7505)*

Astrazeneca Pharmaceuticals LP...........F 973 975-0324
Morristown *(G-6688)*
Cyalume Specialty Products Inc ....E 732 469-7760
Bound Brook *(G-617)*
Eagle Pharmaceuticals Inc.....................E 201 326-5300
Woodcliff Lake *(G-12188)*
Ekr Therapeutics Incorporated...............C 877 435-2524
Bedminster *(G-271)*
Faulding Holdings Inc ....C 908 527-9100
Elizabeth *(G-2730)*
Fougera Pharmaceuticals Inc ....E 973 514-4241
East Hanover *(G-2217)*
Glaxosmithkline Consumer Hlth ....G 215 751-5046
Warren *(G-11550)*
Health Science Funding LLC ....F 973 984-6159
Morristown *(G-6713)*
Hill Pharma Inc ....F 973 521-7400
Fairfield *(G-3222)*
Hovione LLC ....D 609 918-2600
East Windsor *(G-2359)*
Intellect Neurosciences Inc....................G 201 608-5101
Englewood Cliffs *(G-2968)*
Klus Pharma Inc...................................F 609 651-4466
Cranbury *(G-1847)*
Luye Pharma USA Ltd ....E 609 799-7600
Princeton *(G-9069)*
Michelex Corporation ....G 201 977-1177
Prospect Park *(G-9170)*
Msn Pharmaceuticals Inc.......................G 908 360-1500
Piscataway *(G-8794)*
Novartis Corporation ....B 973 503-7488
East Hanover *(G-2234)*
OHM Laboratories Inc...........................D 732 418-2235
North Brunswick *(G-7532)*
Quagen Pharmaceuticals LLC ....F 973 228-9600
West Caldwell *(G-11799)*
Raritan Phrmctcals Incoporated.............C 732 238-1685
East Brunswick *(G-2180)*
Renaissance Lakewood LLC ....F 732 901-2052
Lakewood *(G-5181)*
Renaissance Lakewood LLC ....B 732 367-9000
Lakewood *(G-5182)*
Royal Pharmaceuticals LLC ....G 732 292-2661
Manasquan *(G-5879)*
Salus Pharma LLC ....F 732 329-8089
Monmouth Junction *(G-6362)*
Siegfried USA Holding Inc ....E 856 678-3601
Pennsville *(G-8594)*
Symbiomix Therapeutics LLC ....F 609 722-7250
Newark *(G-7336)*
T and C Neuromax LLC ....G 201 447-2020
Ridgewood *(G-9433)*
Tris Pharma Inc ....C 732 940-2800
Monmouth Junction *(G-6366)*
TWI Pharmaceuticals Usa Inc ....G 201 762-1410
Paramus *(G-7911)*
Vascure Natural LLC.............................G 732 528-6492
Point Pleasant Boro *(G-8942)*

PHARMACEUTICAL PREPARATIONS: Medicines, Capsule Or Ampule

Acino Products Ltd Lblty Co ....F 609 695-4300
Hamilton *(G-4101)*
Boyds Pharmacy Inc.............................F 609 499-0100
Florence *(G-3476)*
Camber Pharmaceuticals Inc..................E 732 529-0430
Piscataway *(G-8742)*
Holmdel Acpnctr & Ntrl Med Ctr ....G 732 888-4910
Holmdel *(G-4517)*
Inno Pharma LLC ....F 732 885-2939
Piscataway *(G-8780)*
Prescription Dynamics Inc ....F 201 746-6262
Mahwah *(G-5802)*
Sensoredge Inc ....G 973 975-4163
Parsippany *(G-8084)*

PHARMACEUTICAL PREPARATIONS: Pills

Bristol-Myers Squibb Company ....E 212 546-4000
Pennington *(G-8444)*
Core Acquisition LLC.............................G 732 983-6025
Middlesex *(G-6156)*
Corepharma LLC ....G 732 983-6025
Middlesex *(G-6157)*
Levomed Inc ....G 908 359-4804
Somerset *(G-10123)*
Zydus Pharmaceuticals USA Inc ....E 609 730-1900
Pennington *(G-8463)*

PHARMACEUTICAL PREPARATIONS: Powders

Matthey Johnson Inc ....C 856 384-7132
West Deptford *(G-11835)*

PHARMACEUTICAL PREPARATIONS: Proprietary Drug PRDTS

Applechem Inc ....G..... 862 210-8344
Newark *(G-7089)*
Merck Holdings LLC ....F 908 423-1000
Whitehouse Station *(G-12054)*
Novitium Pharma LLC ....G..... 609 469-5920
East Windsor *(G-2363)*
Pharming Healthcare Inc ....G..... 908 376-3058
Bridgewater *(G-873)*
Quantum Pharmaceuticals Inc ....G..... 973 222-6485
Sparta *(G-10519)*
Vistapharm Inc ....C 908 376-1622
New Providence *(G-7061)*

PHARMACEUTICAL PREPARATIONS: Solutions

Allergan Inc ....A 862 261-7000
Madison *(G-5718)*
Fordoz Pharma Corp ....F 609 469-5949
East Windsor *(G-2358)*
Lydem LLC ....G..... 856 566-1419
Palmyra *(G-7849)*
Medavante Inc ....G..... 609 528-9400
Hamilton *(G-4113)*
Pmv Pharmaceuticals Inc ....G..... 650 241-2822
Cranbury *(G-1871)*
Rafael Pharmaceuticals Inc ....F 609 409-7050
Cranbury *(G-1874)*

PHARMACEUTICAL PREPARATIONS: Tablets

Alembic Pharmaceuticals Inc ....F 908 393-9604
Bridgewater *(G-807)*
Ranbaxy USA Inc ....E 609 720-9200
Princeton *(G-9109)*
Sandoz Inc ....C 609 627-8500
Princeton *(G-9115)*

PHARMACEUTICALS

140 Main Street Corp ....F 732 974-2929
Sea Girt *(G-9860)*
3r Biopharma LLC ....G..... 914 486-1898
North Brunswick *(G-7499)*
A and P Pharmacy ....G..... 908 850-7640
Hackettstown *(G-3994)*
AAA Pharmaceutical ....D..... 609 288-6060
Lumberton *(G-5649)*
AAA Pharmaceutical Inc ....F 856 423-2700
Paulsboro *(G-8411)*
AB Science Usa LLC ....G..... 973 218-2437
Short Hills *(G-9974)*
Abbott Laboratories ....G..... 732 346-6649
Edison *(G-2447)*
Abbott Laboratories ....E 609 443-9300
Princeton *(G-8992)*
Abbott Laboratories ....F 856 988-5572
Marlton *(G-5963)*
Abbott Laboratories Parsippany ....G..... 973 428-4000
Whippany *(G-12005)*
ABG Lab LLC ....G..... 973 559-5663
Fair Lawn *(G-3073)*
Abon Pharmaceuticals LLC ....E 201 367-1702
Northvale *(G-7567)*
Abraxis Bioscience Inc ....D..... 908 673-9000
Summit *(G-10630)*
Abraxis Bioscience Inc ....D..... 908 673-9000
Summit *(G-10631)*
Accelrx Labs LLC ....G..... 609 301-6446
East Windsor *(G-2340)*
Accumix Pharmaceuticals LLC ....G..... 609 632-2225
Old Bridge *(G-7772)*
Acetris Health LLC ....G..... 201 961-9000
Saddle Brook *(G-9750)*
Acetylon Pharmaceuticals Inc ....F 908 673-9000
Summit *(G-10632)*
Acg North America LLC ....E 908 757-3425
Piscataway *(G-8724)*
Actavis Elizabeth LLC ....B 908 527-9100
Elizabeth *(G-2704)*
Actavis Elizabeth LLC ....C 908 527-9100
Fort Lee *(G-3541)*

Actavis Laboratories FI Inc ....G..... 862 261-7000
Parsippany *(G-7939)*
Actavis LLC ....C 800 272-5525
Morristown *(G-6683)*
Actavis LLC ....C 732 843-4904
North Brunswick *(G-7502)*
Actavis LLC ....D..... 732 947-5300
Edison *(G-2450)*
Actavis Pharma Inc ....C 862 261-7000
Parsippany *(G-7940)*
Adello Biologics LLC ....E 312 620-1500
Piscataway *(G-8725)*
Advaxis Inc ....C 609 452-9813
Princeton *(G-8996)*
Aeterna Zentaris Inc ....G..... 908 626-5428
Warren *(G-11536)*
AF Pharma LLC ....G..... 908 769-7040
Hoboken *(G-4456)*
Aflag Pharmaceuticals LLC ....G..... 732 609-4139
Edison *(G-2452)*
Agile Therapeutics Inc ....F 609 683-1880
Princeton *(G-8997)*
Agno Pharma ....G..... 609 223-0638
Allentown *(G-27)*
Akorn Inc ....E 609 662-9100
Cranbury *(G-1809)*
Akorn Inc ....D..... 732 659-6443
Somerset *(G-10053)*
Akrimax Pharmaceuticals LLC ....G..... 908 372-0506
Cranford *(G-1894)*
Aks Pharma Inc ....G..... 856 521-0710
Elmer *(G-2788)*
Alcami New Jersey Corporation ....D..... 732 346-5100
Edison *(G-2455)*
Align Pharmaceuticals LLC ....G..... 908 834-0960
Berkeley Heights *(G-399)*
Allied Pharma Inc ....G..... 732 738-3295
Fords *(G-3526)*
Allos Therapeutics Inc ....G..... 609 936-3760
Princeton *(G-9003)*
Almatica Pharma Inc ....E 877 447-7979
Pine Brook *(G-8682)*
Alpharma US Inc ....E 201 228-5090
Bridgewater *(G-808)*
Altima Innovations Inc ....G..... 732 474-1500
Branchburg *(G-632)*
Alvogen Group Inc ....E 973 796-3400
Pine Brook *(G-8683)*
Alvogen Inc ....C 973 796-3400
Pine Brook *(G-8684)*
Amarin Corporation PLC ....E 908 719-1315
Bedminster *(G-266)*
American Pharmaceutical LLC ....G..... 732 645-3030
Piscataway *(G-8732)*
Amerigen Pharmaceuticals Ltd ....F 732 993-9826
East Brunswick *(G-2134)*
Amicus Therapeutics Inc ....C 609 662-2000
Cranbury *(G-1811)*
Amneal Pharmaceuticals LLC ....F 908 947-3120
Piscataway *(G-8735)*
Amneal Pharmaceuticals LLC ....G..... 908 409-6823
Branchburg *(G-635)*
Amneal Pharmaceuticals LLC ....E 908 231-1911
Branchburg *(G-636)*
Amneal Pharmaceuticals LLC ....E 973 357-0222
Paterson *(G-8211)*
Amneal Pharmaceuticals LLC ....F 908 947-3120
Piscataway *(G-8734)*
Amneal-Agila LLC ....F 908 947-3120
Bridgewater *(G-810)*
Anadys Pharmaceuticals Inc ....E 972 235-4295
Nutley *(G-7641)*
Antares Pharma Inc ....C 609 359-3020
Ewing *(G-3003)*
Aphena Phrma Slutions - NJ LLC ....D..... 973 947-5441
Parsippany *(G-7947)*
API Inc ....F 973 227-9335
Fairfield *(G-3137)*
Apicore LLC ....E 732 748-8882
Somerset *(G-10060)*
Apicore US LLC ....E 732 748-8882
Somerset *(G-10061)*
Appco Pharma LLC ....E 732 271-8300
Somerset *(G-10062)*
Appco Pharma LLC ....E 732 271-8300
Piscataway *(G-8736)*
Appco Pharma LLC ....E 732 271-8300
Somerset *(G-10063)*
Aprecia Pharmaceuticals Co ....E 215 359-3300
East Windsor *(G-2342)*

Aptalis Pharma LLC ....B 862 261-7000
Parsippany *(G-7948)*
Aquarius Biotechnologies Inc ....G..... 908 443-1860
Bedminster *(G-267)*
Aquestive Therapeutics Inc ....F 908 941-1900
Warren *(G-11537)*
Aralez Pharmaceuticals MGT Inc ....G..... 609 917-9330
Princeton *(G-9006)*
Aralez Pharmaceuticals US Inc ....F 609 917-9330
Princeton *(G-9007)*
Arisaph Pharmaceuticals Inc ....G..... 617 986-4500
Newark *(G-7092)*
Aromac Inc ....G..... 973 365-1090
Clifton *(G-1566)*
Ascend Laboratories LLC ....E 201 476-1977
Parsippany *(G-7951)*
Aspire Pharmaceuticals Inc ....D..... 732 447-1444
Somerset *(G-10065)*
Aurex Labs Ltd Lblty Co ....F 609 308-2304
East Windsor *(G-2343)*
Auro Health LLC ....G..... 732 839-9400
Lawrence Township *(G-5240)*
Aurobindo Pharma ....G..... 732 839-9400
East Windsor *(G-2344)*
Aurobindo Pharma USA Inc ....G..... 732 839-9402
East Windsor *(G-2345)*
Aurobindo Pharma USA Inc ....G..... 732 839-9400
Dayton *(G-1953)*
Aurobindo Pharma USA Inc ....E 732 839-9400
East Windsor *(G-2346)*
Aurobindo Pharma USA Inc ....G..... 609 409-6774
East Windsor *(G-2347)*
Aurobindo Pharma USA LLC ....G..... 732 839-9400
East Windsor *(G-2348)*
Aurolife Pharma LLC ....G..... 732 839-9746
Dayton *(G-1954)*
Aurolife Pharma LLC ....G..... 732 839-9408
East Windsor *(G-2349)*
Aurolife Pharma LLC ....C 732 839-4377
Dayton *(G-1955)*
Auromedics Pharma LLC ....F 732 823-4122
East Windsor *(G-2350)*
Auromedics Pharma LLC ....E 732 839-9400
East Windsor *(G-2351)*
Avacyn Pharmaceuticals Inc ....G..... 201 836-2599
Teaneck *(G-10743)*
Aventis Phrmcticals Foundation ....E 908 981-5000
Bridgewater *(G-819)*
Barr Laboratories Inc ....C 201 767-1589
Northvale *(G-7573)*
Barr Laboratories Inc ....E 845 362-1100
Northvale *(G-7574)*
BASF Corporation ....B 973 245-6000
Florham Park *(G-3492)*
Basfin Corporation ....A 973 245-6000
Florham Park *(G-3493)*
Bausch Health Companies Inc ....B 908 927-1400
Bridgewater *(G-821)*
Bayer Consumer Care Inc ....A 973 267-6198
Morristown *(G-6693)*
Bayer Corporation ....A 412 777-2000
Whippany *(G-12007)*
Bayer Healthcare LLC ....F 973 254-5000
Morristown *(G-6694)*
Bayer Healthcare LLC ....A 862 404-3000
Whippany *(G-12008)*
Becton Dickinson Re Inc ....F 201 847-6800
Franklin Lakes *(G-3611)*
Bellerophon Therapeutics Inc ....E 908 574-4770
Warren *(G-11539)*
Bionpharma Inc ....G..... 609 380-3313
Princeton *(G-9016)*
Biopharma Research Council ....G..... 732 403-3137
Tinton Falls *(G-10824)*
Biophore LLC ....G..... 609 275-3713
Plainsboro *(G-8876)*
Biovail Distribution Company ....G..... 908 927-1400
Bridgewater *(G-822)*
Blue Ocean Pharma LLC ....E 908 428-4668
Annandale *(G-57)*
Bracco Research USA Inc ....E 609 514-2517
Cranbury *(G-1815)*
Bristol-Myers Squibb Company ....G..... 800 332-2056
New Brunswick *(G-6948)*
Bristol-Myers Squibb Company ....E 609 897-3771
Plainsboro *(G-8877)*
Bristol-Myers Squibb Company ....G..... 609 419-5000
Princeton *(G-9018)*
Bristol-Myers Squibb Company ....B 908 218-3700
Bridgewater *(G-824)*

PRODUCT

Bristol-Myers Squibb Company	E	212 546-4000
Hillside (G-4399)		
Bristol-Myers Squibb Company	A	609 302-3000
Lawrenceville (G-5252)		
Bristol-Myers Squibb Company	G	609 252-4875
Princeton (G-9019)		
Caligor Rx Inc	E	212 988-0590
Secaucus (G-9870)		
Calyptus Pharmaceuticals Inc	F	908 720-6049
Princeton (G-9020)		
Cambrex Corporation	D	201 804-3000
East Rutherford (G-2290)		
Cambridge Therapeutic Tech LLC	G	914 420-5555
Hackensack (G-3892)		
Capsugel Holdings Us Inc	G	862 242-1700
Morristown (G-6697)		
Caraco Pharmaceutical Labs	G	609 819-8200
Cranbury (G-1820)		
Cardinal Health Systems Inc	B	732 537-6544
Somerset (G-10073)		
Carnegie Pharmaceuticals LLC	G	732 783-7010
Delran (G-2014)		
Carwin Phrm Assoc LLC	G	732 344-6987
Hazlet (G-4272)		
Castle Creek Phrmceuticals LLC	F	862 286-0400
Parsippany (G-7964)		
Catalent Inc	D	732 537-6200
Somerset (G-10075)		
Catalent Cts LLC	C	201 785-0275
Allendale (G-6)		
Catalent CTS Kansas City LLC	G	732 537-6200
Somerset (G-10076)		
Catalent Pharma Solutions LLC	D	732 537-6200
Somerset (G-10077)		
Catalent Pharma Solutions Inc	B	732 537-6200
Somerset (G-10078)		
Catalent US Holding I LLC	G	877 587-1835
Somerset (G-10079)		
Celator Pharmaceuticals Inc	E	609 243-0123
Ewing (G-3007)		
Celgene Cellular	A	908 673-9000
Cedar Knolls (G-1309)		
Celgene Corporation	F	908 464-8101
Berkeley Heights (G-403)		
Celgene Corporation	E	732 271-1001
Warren (G-11541)		
Celgene Corporation	F	908 967-1432
Berkeley Heights (G-404)		
Celgene Corporation	E	908 897-4603
Summit (G-10638)		
Celgene Corporation	C	908 673-9000
Summit (G-10639)		
Celgene Corporation	G	908 673-9000
Basking Ridge (G-182)		
Celimmune	G	908 399-2954
Lebanon (G-5280)		
Celldex Therapeutics Inc	C	908 200-7500
Hampton (G-4155)		
Cellular Sciences Inc	G	908 237-1561
Flemington (G-3430)		
Celsion Corporation	F	609 896-9100
Lawrenceville (G-5253)		
Central Admxture Phrm Svcs Inc	E	201 541-0080
Englewood (G-2883)		
Cerexa Inc	E	510 285-9200
Parsippany (G-7967)		
Cetylite Industries Inc	E	856 665-6111
Pennsauken (G-8491)		
Champions Oncology Inc	D	201 808-8400
Hackensack (G-3896)		
Chandler Pharmacy LLC	G	732 543-1568
New Brunswick (G-6951)		
Chemtract LLC	G	732 820-0427
Martinsville (G-6008)		
Cherokee Pharma Llc	G	732 422-7800
Jamesburg (G-4684)		
Chromocell Corporation	D	732 565-1113
North Brunswick (G-7512)		
Cispharma Inc	F	609 235-9807
Cranbury (G-1822)		
Citius Pharmaceuticals Inc	G	978 938-0338
Cranford (G-1900)		
Cmic Cmo USA Corporation	E	609 395-9700
Cranbury (G-1824)		
Contract Coatings Inc	F	201 343-3131
Hackensack (G-3900)		
Contravir Pharmaceuticals Inc	E	732 902-4000
Edison (G-2490)		
Core Tech Solutions Inc	F	609 443-1400
East Windsor (G-2355)		
Cormedix Inc	G	908 517-9500
Berkeley Heights (G-407)		
County Line Phrmaceuticals LLC	G	262 439-8109
Pine Brook (G-8695)		
Cubist Pharmaceuticals LLC	C	908 740-4000
Kenilworth (G-4949)		
Cyclacel Pharmaceuticals Inc	F	908 517-7330
Berkeley Heights (G-408)		
Cyclase Dynamics Inc	G	973 420-3259
Barnegat Light (G-169)		
Cypress Pharmaceuticals Inc	C	601 856-4393
Morristown (G-6703)		
D&E Nutraceuticals Inc	E	212 235-5200
Farmingdale (G-3383)		
Daiichi Sankyo Inc	F	908 992-6400
Basking Ridge (G-183)		
Dainippon Sumitomo Pharma Amer	E	201 592-2050
Fort Lee (G-3550)		
Derma Sciences Inc	C	609 514-4744
Plainsboro (G-8880)		
Difco Laboratories Inc	G	410 316-4113
Franklin Lakes (G-3613)		
Dishman Usa Inc	F	732 560-4300
Middlesex (G-6162)		
Dmv-Fnterra Excipients USA LLC	G	609 858-2111
Paramus (G-7866)		
Dpi Newco LLC	E	973 257-8113
Parsippany (G-7985)		
DSM Nutritional Products LLC	C	908 475-7093
Belvidere (G-369)		
DSM Nutritional Products LLC	B	908 475-0150
Belvidere (G-370)		
DSM Nutritional Products LLC	C	908 475-5300
Belvidere (G-371)		
DSM Nutritional Products LLC	C	908 475-5300
Belvidere (G-372)		
DSM Nutritional Products LLC	B	800 526-0189
Parsippany (G-7989)		
E R Squibb & Sons LLC	G	732 246-3195
East Brunswick (G-2147)		
E R Squibb & Sons Inter-AM	G	609 818-3715
Trenton (G-11056)		
E R Squibb & Sons Inter-AM	G	609 252-4111
Princeton (G-9034)		
Edenbridge Pharmaceuticals LLC	E	201 292-1292
Parsippany (G-7998)		
Edge Therapeutics Inc	E	800 208-3343
Berkeley Heights (G-410)		
Eisai Inc	C	201 692-1100
Woodcliff Lake (G-12189)		
Eli Lilly and Company	E	908 704-1807
Branchburg (G-656)		
Elite Laboratories Inc	E	201 750-2646
Northvale (G-7578)		
Elite Pharmaceuticals Inc	E	201 750-2646
Northvale (G-7579)		
Elusys Therapeutics Inc	E	973 808-0222
Pine Brook (G-8701)		
Elvi Pharma LLC	F	732 640-2707
Piscataway (G-8762)		
Emisphere Technologies Inc	F	973 532-8000
Roseland (G-9649)		
Encore Pharmaceutical Inc	G	973 267-9331
Morris Plains (G-6661)		
Endo Phrmaceuticals Valera Inc	F	609 235-3230
Cranbury (G-1831)		
Enteris Biopharma Inc	E	973 453-3518
Boonton (G-566)		
Envigo Crs Inc	B	732 873-2550
Somerset (G-10095)		
Enzon Pharmaceuticals Inc	G	732 980-4500
Cranford (G-1905)		
Enzon Pharmaceuticals Inc	D	732 980-4500
South Plainfield (G-10356)		
Eon Labs Inc	A	609 627-8600
Princeton (G-9040)		
Esjay Pharma LLC	G	609 469-5920
East Windsor (G-2357)		
Esjay Pharma LLC	G	732 438-1816
Allentown (G-30)		
Eva Maria Wolfe	G	412 777-2000
Wayne (G-11630)		
Evenus Pharmaceutical Labs Inc	G	609 395-8625
Princeton (G-9041)		
Exeltis Usa Inc	D	973 324-0200
Florham Park (G-3500)		
Exeltis USA Dermatology LLC	E	973 805-4060
Florham Park (G-3501)		
Exemplify Biopharma Inc	G	732 500-3208
Cranbury (G-1832)		
Eyetech Inc	F	646 454-1779
Bridgewater (G-838)		
Faubel Pharma Services	G	908 730-7563
Bordentown (G-596)		
Ferring Pharmaceuticals Inc	C	973 796-1600
Parsippany (G-8010)		
Ferring Production Inc	E	973 796-1600
Parsippany (G-8011)		
First National Servicing & Dev	E	732 341-5409
Toms River (G-10877)		
Five Star Supplies NJ Corp	E	908 862-8801
Linden (G-5376)		
Forest Laboratories LLC	B	631 436-4534
Jersey City (G-4755)		
Forest Laboratories LLC	B	631 501-5399
Jersey City (G-4756)		
Forest Pharmaceuticals Inc	A	862 261-7000
Parsippany (G-8016)		
G & W Laboratories Inc	D	732 474-0729
Piscataway (G-8768)		
G&W PA Laboratories LLC	G	908 753-2000
South Plainfield (G-10371)		
Gadde Pharma LLC	G	609 651-7772
Plainsboro (G-8883)		
GE Healthcare Inc	G	908 757-0500
South Plainfield (G-10372)		
Genzyme Corporation	C	201 313-9660
Ridgefield (G-9362)		
Genzyme Corporation	G	973 256-2106
Totowa (G-10948)		
Glaxosmithkline Consumer	B	251 591-4188
Warren (G-11549)		
Glaxosmithkline LLC	E	856 952-6023
Collingswood (G-1770)		
Glaxosmithkline LLC	E	609 472-8175
Cherry Hill (G-1371)		
Glenmark Phrmceuticals Inc USA	D	201 684-8000
Mahwah (G-5777)		
Glenmark Therapeutics Inc USA	B	201 684-8000
Mahwah (G-5778)		
Glenwood LLC	C	201 569-0050
Englewood (G-2901)		
Globe Pharma Inc	G	732 296-9700
New Brunswick (G-6963)		
Grant Industries Inc	D	201 791-8700
Elmwood Park (G-2822)		
Grant Industries Inc	D	201 791-6700
Elmwood Park (G-2823)		
Grant Industries Inc	F	201 791-6700
Elmwood Park (G-2824)		
Granulation Technology Inc	F	973 276-0740
Fairfield (G-3212)		
Grow Company Inc	E	201 941-8777
Ridgefield (G-9363)		
Gsk Consumer Health Inc	B	919 269-5000
Warren (G-11551)		
Gsk Consumer Healthcare	D	973 539-0645
Parsippany (G-8025)		
Halo Pharmaceutical Inc	D	973 428-4000
Whippany (G-12023)		
Halton Laboratories LLC	G	609 917-9330
Princeton (G-9053)		
Helsinn Therapeutics US Inc	E	908 231-1435
Iselin (G-4628)		
Hengrui Therapeutics Inc	G	609 423-2155
Princeton (G-9055)		
Heritage Pharma Holdings Inc	C	732 429-1000
East Brunswick (G-2157)		
Heritage Pharma Labs Inc	F	732 238-7880
East Brunswick (G-2158)		
Heritage Pharma Labs Inc	C	732 238-7880
East Brunswick (G-2159)		
Heritage Pharmaceuticals Inc	E	732 429-1000
East Brunswick (G-2160)		
Hikma Injectables USA Inc	G	732 542-1191
Eatontown (G-2401)		
Hikma Pharmaceuticals USA Inc	B	732 542-1191
Eatontown (G-2402)		
Hikma Pharmaceuticals USA Inc	G	732 542-1191
Eatontown (G-2403)		
Hikma Pharmaceuticals USA Inc	C	856 424-3700
Cherry Hill (G-1375)		
Hisamitsu Phrm Co Inc	F	973 765-0122
Florham Park (G-3506)		
Hobart Group Holdings LLC	G	908 470-1780
Gladstone (G-3798)		
Hoffmann-La Roche Inc	A	973 890-2268
Little Falls (G-5476)		
Hoffmann-La Roche Inc	F	973 235-8216
Totowa (G-10951)		

Hoffmann-La Roche Inc....D....973 235-3092
Nutley (G-7648)
Hoffmann-La Roche Inc....E....973 235-1016
Nutley (G-7649)
HRP Capital Inc....G....201 242-4938
Fort Lee (G-3557)
I Fcb Holdings Inc....G....201 934-2000
Mahwah (G-5784)
IBC Pharmaceuticals Inc....F....973 540-9595
Morris Plains (G-6670)
Ikaria Therapeutics LLC....G....908 238-6600
Hampton (G-4160)
Imclone Systems LLC....G....908 541-8100
Branchburg (G-668)
Imclone Systems LLC....C....908 541-8000
Bridgewater (G-844)
Imclone Systems LLC....D....908 218-0147
Branchburg (G-667)
Immune Pharmaceuticals Inc....F....201 464-2677
Englewood Cliffs (G-2965)
Immunomedics Inc....C....973 605-8200
Morris Plains (G-6671)
INB Manhattan Drug Company Inc....D....973 926-0816
Hillside (G-4416)
Indampharm Inc....F....732 970-0002
Morganville (G-6644)
Ino Therapeutics LLC....D....908 238-6600
Bedminster (G-274)
Insmed Incorporated....C....908 977-9900
Bridgewater (G-847)
Integra Lifesciences Corp....D....609 275-0500
Plainsboro (G-8889)
Interntnal Pharma Remedies Inc....G....201 417-3891
Paterson (G-8295)
Invaderm Corporation....G....973 572-5676
Somerset (G-10112)
Inventiv Health Clinical LLC....G....973 348-1000
Basking Ridge (G-190)
Ipsen Biopharmaceuticals Inc....C....908 275-6300
Basking Ridge (G-191)
Ivax Pharmaceuticals LLC....G....201 767-1700
Woodcliff Lake (G-12195)
J&N Pharma LLC....G....201 391-3139
Woodcliff Lake (G-12196)
Jak Diversified II Inc....D....973 439-1182
West Caldwell (G-11781)
Janssen Global Services LLC....F....908 704-4000
Raritan (G-9309)
Janssen Research & Dev LLC....A....908 704-4000
Raritan (G-9310)
Jems Pharma LLC....G....609 386-0141
Burlington (G-981)
Jhp Group Holdings Inc....A....973 658-3569
Parsippany (G-8033)
Jiangsu Hengrui Medicine Co....G....609 395-8625
Princeton (G-9062)
Jnj International Inv LLC....G....732 524-0400
New Brunswick (G-6973)
Johnson & Johnson....A....732 524-0400
New Brunswick (G-6974)
Johnson & Johnson....D....908 704-6809
Raritan (G-9312)
Johnson & Johnson....E....908 526-5425
Raritan (G-9313)
Johnson & Johnson....D....908 725-7256
Somerville (G-10218)
Johnson & Johnson....D....732 422-5000
North Brunswick (G-7522)
Johnson & Johnson....G....908 722-9319
Raritan (G-9311)
Johnson & Johnson....C....908 874-1000
Morris Plains (G-6673)
Johnson & Johnson....C....732 524-0400
New Brunswick (G-6975)
Johnson & Johnson Consumer Inc....A....908 874-1000
Skillman (G-10032)
Juventio LLC....G....973 908-8097
Chatham (G-1331)
Kamat Pharmatech LLC....G....732 406-6421
North Brunswick (G-7523)
Kiehls Since 1851 Inc....G....201 843-1125
Paramus (G-7880)
Kos Pharmaceuticals Inc....F....609 495-0500
Cranbury (G-1848)
Kyowa Hakko Kirin Cal Inc....G....609 580-7400
Princeton (G-9065)
Kyowa Kirin Inc....D....908 234-1096
Bedminster (G-275)
Lab Express Inc....F....973 227-1700
Fairfield (G-3247)

Lautus Phrmceuticals Ltd Lblty....G....908 273-2777
Morristown (G-6721)
Leading Pharma LLC....E....201 746-9160
Fairfield (G-3250)
Leading Pharma LLC....E....201 746-9160
Montvale (G-6465)
Lexicon Pharmaceuticals Inc....F....609 466-5500
Basking Ridge (G-192)
Lipoid LLC....G....973 735-2692
Newark (G-7221)
LLC Dunn Meadow....G....201 297-4603
Fort Lee (G-3565)
Lonza Biologics Inc....D....603 610-4809
Allendale (G-12)
Loving Care Pharmacy....G....732 832-2862
Edison (G-2559)
LTS Lhmann Thrapy Systems Corp....A....973 575-5170
West Caldwell (G-11783)
Lupin Pharmaceuticals Inc....G....908 603-6075
Somerset (G-10127)
Lupin Pharmaceuticals Inc....G....908 603-6000
Somerset (G-10128)
Lyciret Corp....E....973 882-0322
Orange (G-7820)
Macleods Pharma Usa Inc....F....609 269-5250
Plainsboro (G-8893)
Magnifica Inc....G....323 202-0386
Cranbury (G-1858)
Mallinckrodt Ard Inc....G....510 400-0700
Bedminster (G-276)
Mallinckrodt Ard Inc....G....908 238-6600
Bedminster (G-277)
Mallinckrodt LLC....F....908 238-6600
Hampton (G-4164)
Matinas Biopharma Holdings Inc....F....908 443-1860
Bedminster (G-279)
Matrixx Initiatives Inc....E....877 942-2626
Bridgewater (G-859)
Matthey Johnson Inc....E....856 384-7001
West Deptford (G-11836)
Medicines Company....C....973 290-6000
Parsippany (G-8043)
Medicis Pharmaceutical Corp....F....866 246-8245
Bridgewater (G-860)
Medicon Inc....G....201 669-7456
Allendale (G-14)
Megalith Pharmaceuticals Inc....G....877 436-7220
Princeton (G-9072)
Merck & Co Inc....B....908 740-4000
Kenilworth (G-4974)
Merck & Co Inc....E....908 740-4000
Kenilworth (G-4975)
Merck & Co Inc....E....800 224-5318
Madison (G-5729)
Merck & Co Inc....D....908 298-4000
Kenilworth (G-4976)
Merck & Co Inc....E....908 298-4000
Summit (G-10650)
Merck & Co Inc....D....908 740-4000
Rahway (G-9212)
Merck Research Laboratories....D....732 594-4000
Rahway (G-9213)
Merck Resource Management Inc....G....908 423-1000
Whitehouse Station (G-12055)
Merck Sharp & Dohme Corp....A....908 740-4000
Kenilworth (G-4977)
Merck Sharp & Dohme Corp....B....908 423-1000
Kenilworth (G-4978)
Merck Sharp & Dohme Corp....E....908 423-3000
Whitehouse Station (G-12056)
Merck Sharp & Dohme Corp....D....732 594-4000
Rahway (G-9214)
Merck Sharp & Dohme Corp....G....908 685-3892
Branchburg (G-679)
Merck Sharp & Dohme Europe Inc....F....908 423-1000
Somerset (G-10137)
Merck Sharpe & Dohme De PR Inc....G....908 423-1000
Whitehouse Station (G-12057)
Merial Inc....E....732 729-5700
North Brunswick (G-7526)
Mitsubishi Tanabe Pharma....E....908 607-1950
Jersey City (G-4784)
Mpt Delivery Systems Inc....G....973 278-0283
Paterson (G-8343)
Mule Road Pharmacy....G....732 244-3737
Toms River (G-10897)
Mylan Laboratories Inc....G....973 761-1600
South Orange (G-10311)
Myos Rens Technology Inc....G....973 509-0444
Cedar Knolls (G-1318)

Nautilus Neurosciences Inc....G....908 437-1320
Bedminster (G-281)
New Life Pharma Ltd Lblty Co....G....201 784-7812
Northvale (G-7595)
New Life Resources Inc....F....201 750-7880
Northvale (G-7596)
Newton Biopharma Solutions LLC....G....908 874-7145
Hillsborough (G-4358)
Njs Associates Company....G....973 960-8688
Bridgewater (G-867)
Novacyl Inc....G....609 259-0444
Robbinsville (G-9520)
Novartis Corporation....E....212 307-1122
East Hanover (G-2232)
Novartis Corporation....D....862 778-8300
East Hanover (G-2233)
Novartis Corporation....C....973 377-4794
Florham Park (G-3512)
Novartis Pharmaceuticals Corp....A....862 778-8300
East Hanover (G-2235)
Novartis Pharmaceuticals Corp....F....973 538-1296
Morris Plains (G-6674)
Novartis Pharmaceuticals Corp....G....862 778-8300
East Hanover (G-2237)
Novartis Pharmaceuticals Corp....G....862 778-8300
East Hanover (G-2236)
Novel Laboratories Inc....C....908 603-6000
Somerset (G-10145)
Novo Nordisk Inc....B....609 987-5800
Plainsboro (G-8894)
Novo Nordisk Inc....G....609 987-5800
Princeton (G-9083)
Novotec Pharma LLC....G....609 632-2239
Monroe Township (G-6386)
Nuclear Diagnostic Pdts Inc....F....856 489-5733
Cherry Hill (G-1406)
Nuclear Diagnostic Pdts Inc....G....973 664-9696
Rockaway (G-9591)
Nutra-Med Packaging Inc....D....973 625-2274
Whippany (G-12028)
OHM Laboratories Inc....D....609 720-9200
Princeton (G-9086)
OHM Laboratories Inc....D....732 514-1072
New Brunswick (G-6989)
Omthera Pharmaceuticals Inc....F....908 741-4399
Princeton (G-9087)
Oncobiologics Inc....D....609 619-3990
Cranbury (G-1864)
Onpharma Inc....G....408 335-6850
Bridgewater (G-868)
Optimer Pharmaceuticals LLC....B....858 909-0736
Kenilworth (G-4984)
Orchid Pharmaceuticals Inc....G....609 951-2209
Princeton (G-9088)
Organon USA Inc....G....908 423-1000
Whitehouse Station (G-12059)
Ortho Biotech Products LP....D....908 541-4000
Bridgewater (G-871)
Ortho-Clinical Diagnostics Inc....A....908 218-8000
Raritan (G-9314)
Ortho-Mcneil Phrm LLC....E....908 203-4090
Raritan (G-9315)
Ossb and L Pharma LLC....G....732 940-8701
Milltown (G-6270)
Pacira Pharmaceuticals Inc....B....973 254-3560
Parsippany (G-8054)
Palatin Technologies Inc....E....609 495-2200
Cranbury (G-1866)
Parker Labs....G....973 276-9500
Fairfield (G-3282)
Patagonia Pharmaceuticals LLC....G....201 264-7866
Woodcliff Lake (G-12198)
Patheon Biologics (nj) LLC....D....609 919-3300
Princeton (G-9089)
Patheon Biologics LLC....D....609 919-3300
Princeton (G-9090)
Pdr Equity LLC....D....201 358-7200
Whippany (G-12032)
Penick Corporation....G....856 678-3601
Newark (G-7268)
Pernix Therapeutics LLC....E....800 793-2145
Morristown (G-6733)
Pernix Thrpeutics Holdings Inc....D....800 793-2145
Morristown (G-6734)
Pfizer Inc....D....732 591-2106
Old Bridge (G-7788)
Pfizer Inc....C....973 993-0977
Morris Plains (G-6678)
Pfizer Inc....C....201 294-8060
North Bergen (G-7475)

Pfizer Inc ....C 908 251-5685
Dunellen (G-2130)

Pfizer Inc ....F 973 660-5000
Madison (G-5731)

Pfizer Inc ....E 609 434-4920
Ewing (G-3041)

Pfizer Inc ....C 212 733-2323
Bridgewater (G-872)

Pharm Ops Inc ....G 908 454-7733
Phillipsburg (G-8662)

Pharm-Rx Chemical Corporation ....G 973 917-1400
Clifton (G-1694)

Pharma Synergy LLC ....G 856 241-2316
Swedesboro (G-10718)

Pharmaceutical Innovations ....E 973 242-2900
Newark (G-7270)

Pharmaceutical Regulatory Svcs ....G 609 497-9694
Princeton (G-9091)

Pharmachem Laboratories Inc ....E 973 256-1340
Totowa (G-10962)

Pharmachem Laboratories Inc 201 343-3611
South Hackensack (G-10288)

Pharmachem Laboratories LLC ....D 201 246-1000
Kearny (G-4908)

Pharmacia & Upjohn Inc ....B 908 901-8000
Peapack (G-8430)

Pharmacia & Upjohn Company LLC ....B 908 901-8000
Peapack (G-8431)

Pharmasource International LLC ....G 732 985-6182
Piscataway (G-8800)

Pharmatech International Inc ....F 973 244-0393
Fairfield (G-3283)

Pharmedium Services LLC ....E 847 457-2362
Dayton (G-1982)

Pierre Fbre Phrmaceuticals Inc ....G 973 898-1042
Parsippany (G-8062)

Porton Usa LLC ....E 908 791-9100
South Plainfield (G-10422)

Prince Sterilization Svcs LLC ....E 973 227-6882
Fairfield (G-3286)

Princeton Biopharma Strategies ....G 609 203-5303
Princeton (G-9094)

Princeton Enduring Biotech Inc ....G 732 406-3041
Monmouth Junction (G-6357)

Princeton Enduring Biotech Inc ....G 732 406-3041
Monmouth Junction (G-6358)

Promius Pharma LLC ....D 609 282-1400
Princeton (G-9107)

Prosweetz Ingredients Inc ....E 732 512-0886
Edison (G-2599)

Protoform Inc ....G 609 261-6920
Westampton (G-11916)

Ptc Therapeutics Inc ....B 908 222-7000
South Plainfield (G-10425)

Pts Intermediate Holdings LLC ....A 732 537-6200
Somerset (G-10160)

Purdue Pharma LP ....C 203 588-8000
Ewing (G-3046)

Q&Q Pharma Research Company ....G 973 267-0160
Morris Plains (G-6679)

Quagen Pharmaceuticals LLC ....F 973 228-9600
West Caldwell (G-11800)

Quatrx Pharmaceuticals Company ......D 734 913-9900
Florham Park (G-3517)

Qugen Inc ....G 609 716-6300
Plainsboro (G-8898)

Ranx Pharmaceuticals Inc ....G 571 214-8989
Jamesburg (G-4689)

Reed-Lane Inc ....C 973 709-1090
Wayne (G-11677)

Regado Biosciences Inc ....G 908 580-2109
Basking Ridge (G-204)

Regentree LLC ....G 609 734-4328
Princeton (G-9111)

Respirerx Pharmaceuticals Inc ....G 201 444-4947
Glen Rock (G-3828)

Riconpharma LLC ....E 973 627-4685
Denville (G-2055)

Rising Health LLC ....G 201 961-9000
Saddle Brook (G-9787)

Rising Pharmaceuticals Inc ....E 201 961-9000
Saddle Brook (G-9788)

Rotta Pharmaceuticals Inc ....G 732 751-9020
Freehold (G-3686)

Sandoz Inc ....A 862 778-8300
East Hanover (G-2242)

Sanofi Inc ....B 800 981-2491
Bridgewater (G-887)

Sanofi US Services Inc ....A 336 407-4994
Bridgewater (G-888)

Sanofi US Services Inc ....E 908 231-4000
Bridgewater (G-889)

Sanofi US Services Inc ....F 908 231-4000
Bridgewater (G-890)

Sanofi-Synthelabo Inc ....A 908 231-2000
Bridgewater (G-891)

Saxa Pharmaceuticals LLC ....G 862 571-7630
Holmdel (G-4529)

Scherng-Plough Pdts Caribe Inc ....G 908 423-1000
Whitehouse Station (G-12063)

Sciecure Pharma Inc ....E 732 329-8089
Monmouth Junction (G-6363)

Scynexis Inc ....F 201 884-5485
Jersey City (G-4825)

Secord Inc ....F 908 754-2147
Scotch Plains (G-9855)

Sentrimed Ltd Liability Co ....G 914 582-8631
Voorhees (G-11437)

Sharmatek Inc ....G 908 852-5087
Hackettstown (G-4036)

Shasun USA Inc ....F 732 465-0700
Piscataway (G-8810)

Siegfried USA LLC ....C 856 678-3601
Pennsville (G-8595)

Sky Growth Intermediate ....B 201 802-4000
Woodcliff Lake (G-12201)

Snowdon Inc ....G 732 230-3796
Princeton (G-9119)

Solaris Pharma Corporation ....G 908 864-0404
Bridgewater (G-897)

Solgen Pharmaceuticals Inc ....E 732 983-6025
Edison (G-2624)

Soligenix Inc ....F 609 538-8200
Princeton (G-9120)

Spray-Tek Inc ....E 732 469-0050
Middlesex (G-6201)

Star Pharma Inc ....G 718 466-1790
East Brunswick (G-2187)

Steri-Pharma LLC ....D 201 857-8210
Paramus (G-7906)

Strides Pharma Inc ....G 609 773-5000
East Brunswick (G-2188)

Strive Pharmaceuticals Inc ....G 609 269-2001
East Brunswick (G-2189)

Sun Pharmaceutical Inds Inc ....E 313 871-8400
Princeton (G-9126)

Sun Pharmaceutical Inds Inc ....F 609 495-2800
Cranbury (G-1882)

Sun Pharmaceutical Inds Inc ....F 609 495-2800
Cranbury (G-1883)

Sunovion Pharmaceuticals Inc ....D 201 592-2050
Fort Lee (G-3584)

Sunrise Pharmaceutical Inc ....E 732 382-6085
Rahway (G-9224)

Sv Pharma Inc ....G 732 651-1336
East Brunswick (G-2192)

Svtc Pharma Inc ....G 201 652-0013
Ridgewood (G-9432)

Synergetica International Inc ....G 732 780-5865
Marlboro (G-5960)

Tap Pharmaceutical Products ....G 908 470-9700
Bedminster (G-285)

Taree Pharma LLC ....G 609 252-9596
Princeton (G-9129)

Targanta Therapeutics Corp ....D 973 290-6000
Parsippany (G-8097)

Taro Pharmaceuticals USA Inc ....E 609 655-9002
Cranbury (G-1884)

Teligent Inc ....C 856 697-1441
Buena (G-949)

Teligent Inc ....F 856 697-1441
Buena (G-950)

Teva Api Inc ....E 201 307-6900
Parsippany (G-8098)

Teva Pharmaceuticals ....F 888 838-2872
Parsippany (G-8099)

Teva Pharmaceuticals Usa Inc ....G 845 362-1100
Parsippany (G-8100)

Teva Pharmaceuticals Usa Inc ....G 973 575-2775
Fairfield (G-3323)

Teva Womens Health Inc ....G 201 930-3300
Somerset (G-10186)

Therapeutic Proteins Inc ....F 312 620-1500
Piscataway (G-8824)

Thrombogenics Inc ....E 732 590-2900
Iselin (G-4649)

Torrent Pharma Inc ....F 269 544-2299
Basking Ridge (G-207)

Tri-State Pharmaceutical LLC ....G 732 905-7592
Lakewood (G-5197)

Trigen Laboratories LLC ....A 732 721-0070
Bridgewater (G-904)

Tulex Pharmaceuticals Inc ....F 609 619-3098
Cranbury (G-1888)

Unipack Inc ....F 973 450-9880
Belleville (G-321)

Urigen Pharmaceuticals Inc ....G 732 640-0160
North Brunswick (G-7544)

Valeant Phrmcticals N Amer LLC ......E 908 927-1400
Bridgewater (G-908)

Valeritas Holdings Inc ....D 908 927-9920
Bridgewater (G-909)

Validus Pharmaceuticals LLC ....G 973 265-2777
Parsippany (G-8107)

Vensun Pharmaceuticals Inc ....F 908 278-8386
Princeton (G-9135)

Vermeer Pharma LLC ....G 973 270-0073
Morristown (G-6748)

Vertice Pharma LLC ....C 877 530-1633
New Providence (G-7060)

Vgyaan Pharmaceuticals LLC ....G 609 452-2770
Princeton (G-9137)

Vita-Pure Inc ....E 908 245-1212
Roselle (G-9686)

Vitacare Pharma LLC ....G 908 754-1792
South Plainfield (G-10452)

Walgreen Eastern Co Inc ....E 973 728-3172
West Milford (G-11858)

Walgreen Eastern Co Inc ....E 609 522-1291
Wildwood (G-12075)

Warner Chilcott (us) LLC ....G 973 442-3200
Morristown (G-6750)

Warner Chilcott (us) LLC ....D 862 261-7000
Parsippany (G-8110)

Warner Chilcott Corporation ....E 862 261-7000
Rockaway (G-9623)

Watson Laboratories Inc ....C 951 493-5300
Parsippany (G-8112)

Windsor Labs LLC ....G 609 301-6446
East Windsor (G-2370)

Windtree Therapeutics Inc ....F 973 339-2889
Totowa (G-10986)

Wyeth Holdings LLC ....E 973 660-5000
Madison (G-5737)

Wyeth LLC ....B 973 660-5000
Madison (G-5738)

Wyeth-Ayerst (asia) Ltd ....G 973 660-5500
Madison (G-5739)

Wyeth-Ayerst Pharmaceutical ....F 732 274-4221
Monmouth Junction (G-6372)

Wynnpharm Inc ....G 732 409-1005
Freehold (G-3695)

Zenia Pharma LLC ....G 973 246-9718
Clifton (G-1746)

Zenith Laboratories Inc ....C 201 767-1700
Northvale (G-7613)

Zenith Laboratories Inc ....C 201 767-1700
Northvale (G-7614)

Zoetis Inc ....B 973 822-7000
Parsippany (G-8119)

Zoetis LLC ....B 973 822-7000
Parsippany (G-8120)

Zoetis Products LLC ....C 973 660-5000
Florham Park (G-3525)

Zoetis Products LLC ....F 973 660-5000
Bridgewater (G-910)

PHARMACEUTICALS: Mail-Order Svc

Vitamin Shoppe Industries Inc ....A 201 868-5959
North Bergen (G-7491)

PHARMACEUTICALS: Medicinal & Botanical Prdts

7th Seventh Day Wellness Ctr ....G 856 308-0991
Sicklerville (G-10015)

Abrazil LLC ....G 732 658-5191
Kendall Park (G-4933)

Akzo Nobel Chemicals LLC ....D 732 985-6262
Edison (G-2454)

American Ingredients Inc ....F 714 630-6000
Kearny (G-4860)

Chem-Is-Try Inc ....G 732 372-7311
Metuchen (G-6100)

Cyalume Specialty Products Inc ....E 732 469-7760
Bound Brook (G-617)

D & A Granulation LLC ....G 732 994-7480
Lakewood (G-5104)

Eleison Pharmaceuticals Inc ....G 215 416-7620
Bordentown (G-595)

Fisher Scientific Company LLC............B 201 796-7100
    Fair Lawn **(G-3093)**

Guerbet LLC.....................................E 812 333-0059
    Princeton **(G-9051)**

Herbalist & Alchemist Inc....................F 908 689-9020
    Washington **(G-11583)**

Herborium Group Inc ....G 201 849-4431
    Fort Lee **(G-3556)**

Ivy-Dry Inc...G 973 575-1992
    Fairfield **(G-3234)**

Janssen Pharmaceuticals Inc..............D 908 218-7701
    Somerset **(G-10116)**

Jiaherb Inc..E 973 439-6869
    Pine Brook **(G-8708)**

Ortho-Mcneil Phrm LLC........................E 908 203-4090
    Raritan **(G-9315)**

Pfizer Inc ....C 212 733-2323
    Bridgewater **(G-872)**

Purevolution ....F 973 919-4047
    Kinnelon **(G-5040)**

Savient Pharmaceuticals Inc ....F 732 418-9300
    Bridgewater **(G-892)**

Sk Life Science Inc ....E 201 421-3800
    Fair Lawn **(G-3114)**

Specialty Measurements Inc................F 908 534-1500
    Lebanon **(G-5302)**

Toll Compaction Service Inc ....E 732 776-8225
    Neptune **(G-6936)**

Zoetis Products LLC.............................C 973 660-5000
    Florham Park **(G-3525)**

PHARMACIES & DRUG STORES

Berat Corporation ....C 609 953-7700
    Medford **(G-6065)**

Mule Road Pharmacy...........................G 732 244-3737
    Toms River **(G-10897)**

Shop Rite Supermarkets Inc ....C 732 775-4250
    Neptune **(G-6932)**

Shop Rite Supermarkets Inc ....C 732 442-1717
    Perth Amboy **(G-8630)**

Shop-Rite Supermarkets Inc................C 609 646-2448
    Absecon **(G-4)**

Teva Pharmaceuticals ....F 888 838-2872
    Parsippany **(G-8099)**

PHOSPHATES

Innophos Inc..G 973 587-8735
    Cranbury **(G-1838)**

Innophos Investments II Inc.................G 609 495-2495
    Cranbury **(G-1841)**

PHOTOCOPY MACHINE REPAIR SVCS

Imperial Copy Products Inc ....E 973 927-5500
    Randolph **(G-9284)**

PHOTOCOPY MACHINES

Enterprise Solution Products ....G 201 678-9200
    West New York **(G-11865)**

PHOTOCOPY SPLYS WHOLESALERS

Enterprise Solution Products ....G 201 678-9200
    West New York **(G-11865)**

PHOTOCOPYING & DUPLICATING SVCS

Berennial International ....G 973 675-6266
    Orange **(G-7818)**

Binding Products Inc ....E 212 947-1192
    Jersey City **(G-4719)**

Budget Print Center ....G 973 743-0073
    Bloomfield **(G-503)**

C2 Imaging LLC....................................E 646 557-6300
    Jersey City **(G-4722)**

E Nevin Miller Inc ....F 201 444-5784
    Hawthorne **(G-4230)**

Fedex Office & Print Svcs Inc..............E 856 427-0099
    Cherry Hill **(G-1364)**

Fedex Office & Print Svcs Inc..............E 732 636-3580
    Iselin **(G-4627)**

Fedex Office & Print Svcs Inc..............F 732 249-9222
    New Brunswick **(G-6960)**

Fedex Office & Print Svcs Inc..............F 856 273-5959
    Mount Laurel **(G-6797)**

Fedex Office & Print Svcs Inc..............G 973 376-3966
    Springfield **(G-10555)**

Fedex Office & Print Svcs Inc..............G 201 672-0508
    East Rutherford **(G-2295)**

Franbeth Inc ....G 856 488-1480
    Pennsauken **(G-8512)**

Good Impressions Inc ....F 908 689-3071
    Washington **(G-11581)**

Good Impressions Inc ....G 856 461-3232
    Riverside **(G-9498)**

Graphic Action Inc ....G 908 213-0055
    Phillipsburg **(G-8650)**

Graphics Depot Inc ....F 973 927-8200
    Randolph **(G-9281)**

Hub Print & Copy Center LLC ....G 201 585-7887
    Fort Lee **(G-3558)**

Instant Printing of Dover Inc ....G 973 366-6855
    Dover **(G-2093)**

J&E Business Services LLC ....G 973 984-8444
    Morris Plains **(G-6672)**

Jvs Copy Services Inc ....F 856 415-9090
    Sewell **(G-9961)**

Laser Dim Graphics & Prtg Inc ....F 732 821-9000
    Colts Neck **(G-1789)**

Lewis Scheller Printing Corp ....G 732 843-5050
    Somerset **(G-10124)**

Lont & Overkamp Pubg Co Inc ....F 973 942-2243
    Clifton **(G-1664)**

Marks Management Systems Inc...........G 856 866-0588
    Maple Shade **(G-5906)**

Mr Quickly Inc ....G 908 687-6000
    Union **(G-11209)**

Penn Jersey Press Inc ....G 856 627-2200
    Gibbsboro **(G-3789)**

Penny Press ....G 856 547-1991
    Stratford **(G-10616)**

Press Room Inc ....F 609 689-3817
    Trenton **(G-11104)**

R & B Printing Inc ....G 908 766-4073
    Bernardsville **(G-454)**

R V Livolsi Incorporated ....G 732 286-2200
    Toms River **(G-10905)**

Ridgewood Press Inc ....F 201 670-9797
    Ridgewood **(G-9430)**

Roan Printing Inc ....F 908 526-5990
    Somerville **(G-10226)**

Santon Inc ....E 201 444-9080
    Toms River **(G-10909)**

Strategic Content Imaging ....C 201 863-8100
    Secaucus **(G-9933)**

Tanzola Printing Inc ....G 973 779-0858
    Clifton **(G-1734)**

Toms River Printing Corp......................G 732 240-2033
    Brielle **(G-915)**

Word Center Printing ....G 609 586-5825
    Trenton **(G-11134)**

PHOTOENGRAVING SVC

Globe Photo Engraving Corp ....F 201 489-2300
    Little Ferry **(G-5507)**

PHOTOFINISHING LABORATORIES

Tko Visual Communications ....F 610 770-7700
    Newark **(G-7345)**

PHOTOFINISHING LABORATORIES

American Teletimer Corp ....E 908 654-4200
    Mountainside **(G-6869)**

Fujifilm North America Corp ....B 732 857-3000
    Edison **(G-2523)**

Little Falls Shop Rite Super ....B 973 256-0909
    Little Falls **(G-5481)**

PHOTOGRAPH DEVELOPING & RETOUCHING SVCS

Old Hights Print Shop Inc ....G 609 443-4700
    Jackson **(G-4674)**

PHOTOGRAPHIC & OPTICAL GOODS EQPT REPAIR SVCS

Samsung Opt-Lctronics Amer Inc ....C 201 325-2612
    Teaneck **(G-10772)**

PHOTOGRAPHIC CONTROL SYSTEMS: Electronic

Atlantex Instruments Inc ....G 201 391-5148
    Woodcliff Lake **(G-12181)**

PHOTOGRAPHIC EQPT & SPLYS

AGFA Corporation ....B 800 540-2432
    Elmwood Park **(G-2802)**

AGFA Corporation ....E 201 440-0111
    Elmwood Park **(G-2803)**

AGFA Corporation ....E 201 440-0111
    Carlstadt **(G-1121)**

AGFA Finance Corp ....C 201 796-0058
    Elmwood Park **(G-2804)**

Beta Industries Corp ....E 201 939-2400
    Carlstadt **(G-1130)**

Central Technology Inc ....F 732 431-3339
    Freehold **(G-3645)**

Clarity Imaging Tech Inc ....E 413 693-1234
    Pennsauken **(G-8493)**

Coda Inc ....E 201 825-7400
    Mahwah **(G-5760)**

Fujifilm North America Corp ....B 732 857-3000
    Edison **(G-2523)**

Hasselblad Inc ....E 800 456-0203
    Union **(G-11191)**

Heights Usa Inc ....E 609 530-1300
    Ewing **(G-3021)**

Howard Packaging Corp ....G 973 904-0022
    Clifton **(G-1643)**

Hpi International Inc ....F 732 942-9900
    Lakewood **(G-5135)**

International Laser Group Inc ....E 818 888-0400
    Cherry Hill **(G-1382)**

Iris ID Systems Inc ....E 609 819-4747
    Cranbury **(G-1843)**

Ner Data Products Inc ....E 888 637-3282
    Glassboro **(G-3810)**

Oxberry LLC ....G 201 935-3000
    Carlstadt **(G-1196)**

Parker Acquisition Group Inc ....G 908 707-4900
    Branchburg **(G-687)**

Pentagon Performance Inc ....G 973 975-0400
    Millville **(G-6320)**

Profoto US Inc ....F 973 822-1300
    Florham Park **(G-3516)**

Rpl Supplies Inc ....F 973 767-0880
    Garfield **(G-3759)**

Towne Technologies Inc ....F 908 722-9500
    Somerville **(G-10230)**

Xerox Corporation ....B 609 987-5500
    Princeton **(G-9141)**

PHOTOGRAPHIC EQPT & SPLYS WHOLESALERS

Gill Associates LLC ....G 973 835-5456
    Wayne **(G-11641)**

Inserts East Incorporated.....................C 856 663-8181
    Pennsauken **(G-8528)**

Kinly Inc ....E 973 585-3000
    Cedar Knolls **(G-1314)**

Tocad America Inc ....E 973 627-9600
    Rockaway **(G-9614)**

PHOTOGRAPHIC EQPT & SPLYS, WHOLESALE: Identity Recorders

Qsa Global National Corp ....G 865 888-6798
    Red Bank **(G-9341)**

PHOTOGRAPHIC EQPT & SPLYS, WHOLESALE: Motion Picture Camera

Plastic Reel Corp of America ....E 201 933-5100
    Carlstadt **(G-1203)**

PHOTOGRAPHIC EQPT & SPLYS, WHOLESALE: Processing

Mri International ....G 973 383-3645
    Newton **(G-7397)**

PHOTOGRAPHIC EQPT & SPLYS: Cameras, Still & Motion Pictures

Vision Research Inc ....D 973 696-4500
    Wayne **(G-11691)**

Xybion Corporation ....C 973 538-2067
    Lawrenceville **(G-5273)**

PRODUCT

PHOTOGRAPHIC EQPT & SPLYS: Developers, Not Chemical Plants

James Colucci Enterprises LLC ....E 877 403-4900
Short Hills (G-9979)

PHOTOGRAPHIC EQPT & SPLYS: Film, Sensitized

Energy Storage Corp ....D 732 542-7880
Eatontown (G-2394)

PHOTOGRAPHIC EQPT & SPLYS: Flashlight Apparatus, Exc Bulbs

Dyna-Lite Inc ....F 908 687-8800
Union (G-11176)

PHOTOGRAPHIC EQPT & SPLYS: Plates, Sensitized

West Essex Graphics Inc ....E 973 227-2400
Fairfield (G-3351)

PHOTOGRAPHIC EQPT & SPLYS: Printing Eqpt

Blue Parachute LLC ....G 732 767-1320
Metuchen (G-6097)
Colex Imaging Inc ....G 201 414-5575
Elmwood Park (G-2810)
E Z Hi-Tech Services Inc ....G 908 317-8203
Mountainside (G-6879)

PHOTOGRAPHIC EQPT & SPLYS: Processing Eqpt

Cytotherm LP ....G 609 396-1456
Trenton (G-11050)

PHOTOGRAPHIC EQPT & SPLYS: Toners, Prprd, Not Chem Plnts

Automatic Transfer Inc ....G 908 213-2830
Alpha (G-39)
B&B Imaging LLC ....G 201 261-3131
Paramus (G-7856)
Ricoh Prtg Systems Amer Inc ....G 973 316-6051
Mountain Lakes (G-6861)

PHOTOGRAPHIC EQPT & SPLYS: Trays, Printing & Processing

Image Remit Inc ....E 732 940-7900
North Brunswick (G-7518)

PHOTOGRAPHIC EQPT & SPLYS: X-Ray Film

Mri of West Morris PA ....F 973 927-1010
Succasunna (G-10625)

PHOTOGRAPHIC EQPT REPAIR SVCS

Photographic Analysis Company ....G 973 696-1000
Wayne (G-11673)

PHOTOGRAPHIC EQPT/SPLYS, WHOL: Cameras/Projectors/Eqpt/Splys

Mizco International Inc ....D 732 912-2000
Avenel (G-141)
Samsung Opt-Lctronics Amer Inc ....C 201 325-2612
Teaneck (G-10772)

PHOTOGRAPHIC SVCS

Globe Photo Engraving Corp ....F 201 489-2300
Little Ferry (G-5507)
New Life Color Reproductions ....G 201 943-7005
Ridgefield (G-9378)

PHOTOGRAPHY SVCS: Commercial

Pixell Creative Group LLC ....G 609 410-3024
Burlington (G-988)
S J T Imaging Inc ....D 201 262-7744
Oradell (G-7813)
Stephen Swinton Studio Inc ....G 908 537-9135
Washington (G-11588)
Visionware Systems Inc ....F 609 924-0800
Skillman (G-10037)

PHOTOGRAPHY: Aerial

Pentagon Performance Inc ....G 973 975-0400
Millville (G-6320)

PHOTOTYPESETTING SVC

L A S Printing Co ....G 201 991-5362
Jersey City (G-4775)
Trentypo Inc ....F 609 883-5971
Ewing (G-3062)

PHYSICAL EXAMINATION SVCS, INSURANCE

Um Equity Corp ....G 856 354-2200
Haddonfield (G-4065)

PHYSICAL FITNESS CENTERS

Totowa Kickboxing Ltd Lblty Co ....F 973 507-9106
Totowa (G-10975)

PHYSICIANS' OFFICES & CLINICS: Medical doctors

Bio Compression Systems Inc ....E 201 939-0716
Moonachie (G-6508)
Endotec Inc ....F 973 762-6100
South Orange (G-10304)
Galen Publishing LLC ....E 908 253-9001
Somerville (G-10210)
Grateful Ped Inc ....F 973 478-6511
Saddle Brook (G-9767)
Medici International Inc ....G 973 684-6084
Paterson (G-8334)

PICTURE FRAMES: Metal

R A O Contract Sales NY Inc ....G 201 652-1500
Paterson (G-8367)

PICTURE FRAMES: Wood

Frameco Inc ....E 973 989-1424
Dover (G-2087)
Hoboken Executive Art Inc ....G 201 420-8262
Hoboken (G-4473)
K Ron Art & Mirrors Inc ....G 201 313-7080
Ridgefield (G-9369)
Larson-Juhl US LLC ....E 973 439-1801
Caldwell (G-1030)
R A O Contract Sales NY Inc ....G 201 652-1500
Paterson (G-8367)
Revelation Gallery Inc ....G 973 627-6558
Denville (G-2054)
Vaswani Inc ....D 877 376-4425
Edison (G-2641)

PICTURE PROJECTION EQPT

Sharp Electronics Corporation ....A 201 529-8200
Mahwah (G-5811)

PIECE GOODS & NOTIONS WHOLESALERS

Artistic Bias Products Co Inc ....E 732 382-4141
Rahway (G-9175)
Foldtex II Ltd ....E 908 928-0919
Westfield (G-11924)
Hedaya Home Fashions Inc ....C 908 352-0808
Elizabeth (G-2745)
John M Sniderman Inc ....G 201 450-4291
Fairview (G-3363)
Uniport Industries Corporation ....G 201 391-7676
Woodcliff Lake (G-12206)

PIECE GOODS, NOTIONS & DRY GOODS, WHOL: Textile Converters

Alpha Associates Inc ....E 732 730-1800
Lakewood (G-5067)
Printmaker International Ltd ....G 212 629-9260
Irvington (G-4601)
Scher Fabrics Inc ....F 212 382-2266
Freehold (G-3687)

PIECE GOODS, NOTIONS & DRY GOODS, WHOL: Textiles, Woven

American Dawn Inc ....G 856 467-9211
Bridgeport (G-761)

Franco Manufacturing Co Inc ....C 732 494-0500
Metuchen (G-6104)

PIECE GOODS, NOTIONS & DRY GOODS, WHOL: Trimmings, Apparel

Alco Trimming ....G 201 854-8608
North Bergen (G-7426)
Green Distribution LLC ....D 201 293-4381
Secaucus (G-9893)

PIECE GOODS, NOTIONS & DRY GOODS, WHOL: Yard Goods, Woven

R L Plastics Inc ....E 732 340-1100
Avenel (G-149)

PIECE GOODS, NOTIONS & DRY GOODS, WHOLESALE: Fabrics

Douglass Industries Inc ....E 609 804-6040
Egg Harbor City (G-2662)

PIECE GOODS, NOTIONS & DRY GOODS, WHOLESALE: Fabrics, Lace

Deerbrook Fabrics ....F 201 945-4141
Guttenberg (G-3869)
Royal Lace Co Inc ....E 718 495-9327
Rahway (G-9221)
Tone Embroidery Corp ....E 201 943-1082
Fairview (G-3371)

PIECE GOODS, NOTIONS & DRY GOODS, WHOLESALE: Sewing Access

Sysco Guest Supply LLC ....C 732 537-2297
Somerset (G-10177)

PIECE GOODS, NOTIONS & OTHER DRY GOODS, WHOL: Flags/Banners

F & S Awning and Blind Co Inc ....G 732 738-4110
Edison (G-2517)
Services Equipment Com LLC ....G 973 992-4404
Livingston (G-5560)

PIECE GOODS, NOTIONS & OTHER DRY GOODS, WHOL: Millinery Sply

Bai Lar Interior Services Inc ....G 732 738-0350
Fords (G-3527)

PIECE GOODS, NOTIONS & OTHER DRY GOODS, WHOLESALE: Fabrics

Associated Fabrics Corporation ....G 201 300-6053
Fair Lawn (G-3078)
Circle Visual Inc ....E 212 719-5153
Carlstadt (G-1141)
Marcotex International Inc ....E 201 991-8200
Kearny (G-4898)

PIECE GOODS, NOTIONS & OTHER DRY GOODS, WHOLESALE: Ribbons

Carson & Gebel Ribbon Co LLC ....E 973 627-4200
Rockaway (G-9556)
Cottage Lace and Ribbon Co Inc ....G 732 776-9353
Neptune (G-6905)
Papillon Ribbon & Bow Inc ....E 973 928-6128
Clifton (G-1689)

PIECE GOODS, NOTIONS & OTHER DRY GOODS, WHOLESALE: Zippers

Royal Slide Sales Co Inc ....G 973 777-1177
Garfield (G-3757)
YKK (usa) Inc ....G 201 935-4200
Lyndhurst (G-5715)

PIECE GOODS, NOTIONS/DRY GOODS, WHOL: Linen Piece, Woven

Linen For Tables ....G 973 345-8472
Paterson (G-8322)

PIECE GOODS, NOTIONS/DRY GOODS, WHOL: Silk Piece, Woven

Craig Fabrics Inc..............................F 201 869-9126
Guttenberg (G-3868)

PIGMENTS, INORGANIC: Metallic & Mineral, NEC

Welsch Metal Products Inc ....G.... 908 782-5996
Flemington (G-3475)

PILLOW FILLING MTRLS: Curled Hair, Cotton Waste, Moss

American Home Mfg LLC ....F 732 465-1530
Piscataway (G-8731)

PILLOW TUBING

Hanover Direct Inc ....B 201 863-7300
Weehawken (G-11695)

PILOT SVCS: Aviation

Rclc Inc ....F 732 877-1788
Woodbridge (G-12152)

PINS

Bigelow Components Corp.................E 973 467-1200
Springfield (G-10543)
Edwin Leonel Ramirez.......................G 732 648-5587
Plainfield (G-8860)
Pin Cancer Campaign ....G 973 600-4170
Newton (G-7400)

PIPE & FITTING: Fabrication

Belden Inc......................................F 908 925-8000
Elizabeth (G-2712)
Bemis Company Inc ....B 908 689-3000
Washington (G-11577)
Coolenheat Inc ....E 908 925-4473
Kendall Park (G-4934)
Custom Alloy Corporation ....C 908 638-0257
High Bridge (G-4294)
Esco Industries Corp ....E 973 478-5888
Woodcliff Lake (G-12191)
Fluorotherm Polymers Inc ....G 973 575-0760
Parsippany (G-8014)
Fox Steel Products LLC ....G 856 778-4661
Mount Laurel (G-6799)
Handytube Corporation ....E 732 469-7420
Middlesex (G-6169)
Imperial Weld Ring Corp Inc ....E 908 354-0011
Elizabeth (G-2746)
Piping Solutions Inc ....G 732 537-1009
Bridgewater (G-875)
Royal Seamless Corporation ....F 732 901-9595
Lakewood (G-5186)
S&W Fabricators Inc ....G 856 881-7418
Glassboro (G-3811)
Symcon Inc.....................................G 973 728-8661
West Milford (G-11857)
Tube Craft of America Inc.................G 856 629-5626
Williamstown (G-12110)
U V International LLC ....F 973 993-9454
Morristown (G-6747)

PIPE & FITTINGS: Cast Iron

Water Works Supply Company............F 973 835-2153
Pompton Plains (G-8968)

PIPE & FITTINGS: Pressure, Cast Iron

McWane Inc ....B 908 454-1161
Phillipsburg (G-8658)

PIPE FITTINGS: Plastic

Esco Industrial Corporation................G 973 478-5888
Woodcliff Lake (G-12190)
Ua Pipefitters Local 274 ....G 201 943-4700
Parsippany (G-8105)

PIPE JOINT COMPOUNDS

Plcs Inc ....E 856 722-1333
Mount Laurel (G-6827)

PIPE SECTIONS, FABRICATED FROM PURCHASED PIPE

Foodline Piping Products Co................G...... 856 767-1177
West Berlin (G-11720)

PIPE, CAST IRON: Wholesalers

M P Tube Works Inc ....G 908 317-2500
Mountainside (G-6883)
Water Works Supply Company............F 973 835-2153
Pompton Plains (G-8968)

PIPE, IRRIGATION: Concrete

Liedl..G 908 359-8335
Hillsborough (G-4355)

PIPE, SEWER: Concrete

Brent Material Company....................G 908 686-3832
Kenilworth (G-4946)

PIPE: Concrete

Ceresist Inc ....F 973 345-3231
Paterson (G-8232)

PIPE: Plastic

Advanced Drainage Systems Inc ....D...... 856 467-4779
Logan Township (G-5610)
Endot Industries Inc ....D...... 973 625-8500
Rockaway (G-9564)

PIPE: Sewer, Cast Iron

En Tech Corp ....F 201 784-1034
Closter (G-1757)
En Tech Corp ....F 718 389-2058
Closter (G-1758)

PIPE: Sheet Metal

Able Fab Co ....E 732 396-0600
Avenel (G-122)
Altona Blower & Shtmtl Work ....G.... 201 641-3520
Little Ferry (G-5494)
Industrial Process & Eqp Inc ....F 973 702-0330
Sussex (G-10673)

PIPELINE & POWER LINE INSPECTION SVCS

Corrview International LLC ....G....... 973 770-0571
Hopatcong (G-4535)

PIPELINE TERMINAL FACILITIES: Independent

Fence America New Jersey Inc ....G....... 973 472-5121
Hackensack (G-3910)

PIPELINES: Crude Petroleum

Total American Services Inc ....F 206 626-3500
Jersey City (G-4838)

PIPES & TUBES

Albea Americas Inc ....C...... 908 689-3000
Washington (G-11573)
Intra Pac Swedesboro ....D...... 856 467-0485
Swedesboro (G-10703)

PIPES & TUBES: Steel

Amer-RAC LLC ....F 856 488-6210
Pennsauken (G-8476)
Century Tube Corp...........................E 908 534-2001
Somerville (G-10204)
Delsea Pipe Inc...............................E 856 589-9374
Sewell (G-9950)
Dodson Global Inc ....G...... 732 238-7001
East Brunswick (G-2144)
Fluorotherm Polymers Inc ....G 973 575-0760
Parsippany (G-8014)
Fox Steel Products LLC ....G 856 778-4661
Mount Laurel (G-6799)
Long Island Pipe of NJ ....E 201 939-1100
Lyndhurst (G-5687)
M & M International ....F 908 412-8300
South Plainfield (G-10399)

Morris Industries Inc..........................E 973 835-6600
Pompton Plains (G-8963)
Nippon Benkan Kagyo........................E 732 435-0777
New Brunswick (G-6988)
Silbo Industries Inc ....F 201 307-0900
Montvale (G-6479)
Standard Pipe Products Inc ....G...... 908 264-8284
Garwood (G-3787)
Zekelman Industries Inc ....D...... 724 342-6851
Westwood (G-11977)

PIPES: Steel & Iron

Bushwick Metals LLC ....E 908 754-8700
South Plainfield (G-10341)
US Pipe Fabrication LLC ....F 856 461-3000
Riverside (G-9507)

PIVOTS: Power Transmission

Emmco Development Corp ....F 732 469-6464
Somerset (G-10093)

PLACEMATS: Plastic Or Textile

B T Partners Inc ....G...... 609 652-6511
Galloway (G-3709)
Hedaya Home Fashions Inc ....C...... 908 352-0808
Elizabeth (G-2745)

PLANING MILLS: Millwork

Mp Custom FL LLC ....F 973 417-2288
Wayne (G-11666)

PLANTERS: Plastic

Whole Year Trading Co Inc ....G.... 732 238-1196
Dayton (G-1995)

PLANTS: Artificial & Preserved

Clover Garden Ctr Ltd Lblty Co ....G...... 856 235-4625
Mount Laurel (G-6789)
Creative Display Inc ....G...... 732 918-8010
Neptune (G-6907)

PLAQUES: Picture, Laminated

Emdur Metal Products Inc..................F 856 541-1100
Camden (G-1062)

PLASMAS

Kedrion Biopharma Inc ....D...... 201 242-8900
Fort Lee (G-3563)
Princeton Plasma Physics ....F 609 243-2000
Princeton (G-9098)

PLASTER WORK: Ornamental & Architectural

Kingston Nurseries LLC......................F 609 430-0366
Kingston (G-5029)

PLASTER, ACOUSTICAL: Gypsum

Proform Acoustic Surfaces LLC...........G...... 201 553-9614
Secaucus (G-9914)

PLASTIC PRDTS

Brook Meadow Inventions ....E 973 300-0419
Newton (G-7382)
C G I Cstm Fiberglas & Decking...........F 609 646-5302
Pleasantville (G-8904)
Celotex ....G...... 856 663-2626
Pennsauken (G-8490)
Lamart Corp....................................F 973 772-6262
Clifton (G-1656)
Optics Plastics ....G...... 201 939-3344
Lyndhurst (G-5699)
Vacumet Corp..................................G...... 973 628-0405
Wayne (G-11690)

PLASTICIZERS, ORGANIC: Cyclic & Acyclic

Cambridge Industries Co Inc ....G.... 973 465-4565
Newark (G-7119)
Just In Time Chemical Sales & ....G.... 908 862-7726
Linden (G-5393)
Kenrich Petrochemicals Inc................E 201 823-9000
Bayonne (G-235)
Lanxess Solutions US Inc ....C...... 732 738-1000
Fords (G-3530)

P
R
O
D
U
C
T

PLASTICS FILM & SHEET

Acrilex Inc ....E 201 333-1500
Jersey City **(G-4698)**

ADM Corporation ....D 732 469-0900
Middlesex **(G-6143)**

Allied Plastics Holdings LLC ....D 718 729-5500
Newark **(G-7078)**

American Renolit Corporation ....G 973 706-6912
Wayne **(G-11604)**

Ber Plastics Inc ....E 973 839-2100
Riverdale **(G-9475)**

Caloric Color Co Inc ....F 973 471-4748
Garfield **(G-3725)**

Creative Film Corp ....F 732 367-2166
Lakewood **(G-5097)**

Dicar Inc ....E 973 575-1377
Pine Brook **(G-8697)**

Dow Chemical Company ....D 800 258-2436
Somerset **(G-10090)**

Glitterex Corp ....D 908 272-9121
Cranford **(G-1908)**

Hillside Plastics Corporation ....D 973 923-2700
Hillside **(G-4414)**

Nexus Plastics Incorporated ....D 973 427-3311
Hawthorne **(G-4249)**

Perlin Converting LLC ....F 973 887-0257
Whippany **(G-12033)**

Primex Plastics Corporation ....C 973 470-8000
Garfield **(G-3751)**

Ssi North America Inc ....G 973 598-0152
Randolph **(G-9299)**

Up United LLC ....E 718 383-5700
Bridgewater **(G-906)**

PLASTICS FILM & SHEET: Polyethylene

American Transparent Plastic ....E 732 287-3000
Edison **(G-2459)**

Gemini Plastic Films Corp ....E 973 340-0700
Garfield **(G-3736)**

Glopak Corp ....E 908 753-8735
South Plainfield **(G-10373)**

Silverton Packaging Corp ....G 732 341-0986
Monroe Township **(G-6393)**

Tri-Cor Flexible Packaging Inc ....E 973 940-1500
Sparta **(G-10526)**

PLASTICS FILM & SHEET: Polypropylene

Central Plastics Incorporated ....G 973 808-0990
Parsippany **(G-7966)**

PLASTICS FILM & SHEET: Polyvinyl

Kappus Plastic Company Inc ....D 908 537-2288
Hampton **(G-4163)**

Kayline Processing Inc ....E 609 695-1449
Trenton **(G-11073)**

Mark Ronald Associates Inc ....D 908 558-0011
Hillside **(G-4429)**

PLASTICS FILM & SHEET: Vinyl

American Renolit Corp La ....G 856 241-4901
Swedesboro **(G-10681)**

Congoleum Corporation ....D 609 584-3601
Trenton **(G-11045)**

Nan Ya Plastics Corp USA ....E 973 992-1775
Livingston **(G-5550)**

PLASTICS FINISHED PRDTS: Laminated

Dikeman Laminating Corporation ....E 973 473-5696
Clifton **(G-1599)**

La Mart Manufacturing Corp ....G 718 384-6917
Teaneck **(G-10759)**

Plastinetics Inc ....G 973 618-9090
West Caldwell **(G-11797)**

Roysons Corporation ....D 973 625-5570
Rockaway **(G-9606)**

PLASTICS MATERIAL & RESINS

Adco Chemical Company Inc ....E 973 589-0880
Newark **(G-7072)**

Advansix Inc ....B 973 526-1800
Parsippany **(G-7941)**

Akzo Nobel Chemicals LLC ....D 732 985-6262
Edison **(G-2454)**

Allied-Signal China Ltd ....E 973 455-2000
Morristown **(G-6685)**

Alpine Group Inc ....F 201 549-4400
East Rutherford **(G-2275)**

Altaflo LLC ....F 973 300-3344
Sparta **(G-10488)**

Amcor Flexibles LLC ....C 856 825-1400
Millville **(G-6275)**

American Plastic Works Inc ....E 800 494-7326
Moorestown **(G-6559)**

ARC International N Amer LLC ....C 856 825-5620
Millville **(G-6284)**

Ashland LLC ....G 908 243-3500
Bridgewater **(G-815)**

Ashland LLC ....G 732 353-7718
Parlin **(G-7928)**

Bergen Manufacturing & Supply ....E 201 854-3461
North Bergen **(G-7434)**

Cary Compounds LLC ....E 732 274-2626
Dayton **(G-1958)**

Chevron Phillips Chem Co LP ....E 732 738-2000
Perth Amboy **(G-8609)**

Clausen Company Inc ....E 732 738-1165
Fords **(G-3528)**

Covalnce Specialty Coatings LLC ....D 732 356-2870
Middlesex **(G-6159)**

Crossfield Products Corp ....D 908 245-2801
Roselle Park **(G-9691)**

Custom Counters By Precision ....E 973 773-0111
Passaic **(G-8133)**

Cytec Industries Inc ....C 973 357-3100
Saddle Brook **(G-9761)**

Deltech Resins Co ....E 973 589-0880
Newark **(G-7140)**

Dock Resins Corporation ....E 908 862-2351
Pedricktown **(G-8435)**

E-Beam Services Inc ....E 513 933-0031
Cranbury **(G-1830)**

Eagle Fabrication Inc ....E 732 739-5300
Ltl Egg Hbr **(G-5644)**

Evonik Cyro LLC ....D 973 929-8000
Parsippany **(G-8004)**

Exxon Mobil Corporation ....E 732 321-6100
Linden **(G-5373)**

Federal Plastics Corporation ....E 908 272-5800
Cranford **(G-1907)**

Flex Moulding Inc ....E 201 487-8080
Hackensack **(G-3914)**

Foam Rubber Fabricators Inc ....E 973 751-1445
Belleville **(G-303)**

Glopak Corp ....E 908 753-8735
South Plainfield **(G-10373)**

Illinois Tool Works Inc ....E 609 395-5600
Cranbury **(G-1837)**

Intelco ....D 856 456-6755
Westville **(G-11944)**

Interntonal Specialty Pdts Inc ....A 859 815-3333
Wayne **(G-11653)**

Interplast Inc ....F 609 386-4990
Burlington **(G-980)**

Intra Pac Swedesboro ....D 856 467-0485
Swedesboro **(G-10703)**

Ip Moulding Inc ....G 574 825-6554
Livingston **(G-5537)**

Kairos Enterprises LLC ....E 201 731-3181
Englewood Cliffs **(G-2969)**

Lanxess Solutions US Inc ....C 732 826-1018
Perth Amboy **(G-8620)**

Multi-Plastics Extrusions Inc ....F 732 388-2300
Avenel **(G-142)**

North American Composites Co ....F 609 625-8101
Mays Landing **(G-6041)**

Palma Inc ....F 973 429-1490
Whippany **(G-12031)**

Petro Packaging Co Inc ....E 908 272-4054
Cranford **(G-1922)**

Phoenix Industries LLC ....E 973 366-4199
Wharton **(G-11997)**

Polymer Technologies Inc ....D 973 778-9100
Clifton **(G-1700)**

Polymeric Resources Corp ....E 973 694-4141
Wayne **(G-11674)**

Polyvel Inc ....E 609 567-0080
Hammonton **(G-4147)**

Rust-Oleum Corporation ....E 732 469-8100
Somerset **(G-10169)**

Safas Corporation ....E 973 772-5252
Clifton **(G-1714)**

Saint-Gobain Prfmce Plas Corp ....C 973 696-4700
Wayne **(G-11681)**

Sika Corporation ....E 856 298-2313
Audubon **(G-118)**

Solidsurface Designs Inc ....E 856 910-7720
Pennsauken **(G-8580)**

Solvay USA Inc ....B 609 860-4000
Princeton **(G-9122)**

Solvay USA Inc ....C 732 297-0100
North Brunswick **(G-7538)**

Spartech LLC ....E 201 489-4000
Hackensack **(G-3979)**

Spartech LLC ....G 973 344-2700
Newark **(G-7322)**

Specialty Casting Inc ....G 856 845-3105
Woodbury **(G-12171)**

Synray Corporation ....E 908 245-2600
Kenilworth **(G-4998)**

Technick Products Inc ....F 908 791-0400
South Plainfield **(G-10438)**

Thibaut & Walker Co Inc ....G 973 589-3331
Newark **(G-7340)**

Trademark Plastics Corporation ....E 908 925-5900
Newark **(G-7347)**

Uvitec Printing Ink Co Inc ....E 973 778-0737
Lodi **(G-5607)**

Weavers Fiberglass ....E 609 597-4324
Manahawkin **(G-5835)**

Wilsonart LLC ....F 800 822-7613
Moorestown **(G-6633)**

Zahk Sales Inc ....G 516 633-9179
Branchburg **(G-720)**

PLASTICS MATERIALS, BASIC FORMS & SHAPES WHOLESALERS

Brook Meadow Inventions ....E 973 300-0419
Newton **(G-7382)**

Chemical Resources Inc ....E 609 520-0000
Princeton **(G-9021)**

D & D Technology Inc ....E 908 688-5154
Union **(G-11169)**

Gdb International Inc ....D 732 246-3001
New Brunswick **(G-6962)**

Reachman International Corp ....F 718 388-6565
Moonachie **(G-6539)**

PLASTICS PROCESSING

A S 4 Plastic Inc ....G 973 925-5223
Paterson **(G-8192)**

Acrylics Unlimited ....G 973 862-6014
Lafayette **(G-5043)**

Arpac Technology ....G 973 252-0012
Randolph **(G-9270)**

Enor Corporation ....C 201 750-1680
Englewood **(G-2892)**

Greenway Products & Svcs LLC ....C 732 442-0200
New Brunswick **(G-6965)**

Grewe Plastics Inc ....G 973 485-7602
Newark **(G-7179)**

Highland Products Inc ....G 973 366-0156
Dover **(G-2089)**

Intek Plastics Inc ....E 973 427-7331
Hawthorne **(G-4241)**

Lamart Corporation ....G 973 772-6262
Clifton **(G-1658)**

Multi-Plastics Inc ....E 856 241-9014
Swedesboro **(G-10713)**

Reachman International Corp ....F 718 388-6565
Moonachie **(G-6539)**

Reedy International Corp ....F 732 264-1777
Keyport **(G-5023)**

Royce Associates A Ltd Partnr ....D 201 438-5200
East Rutherford **(G-2322)**

Sama Plastics Corp ....E 973 239-7200
Cedar Grove **(G-1300)**

Scott W Springman ....E 856 751-2411
Cherry Hill **(G-1419)**

Town & Country Plastics Inc ....F 732 780-5300
Marlboro **(G-5961)**

United Eqp Fabricators LLC ....G 973 242-2737
Newark **(G-7353)**

Whe Research Inc ....G 732 240-3871
Toms River **(G-10921)**

PLASTICS SHEET: Packing Materials

Air Protection Packaging Corp ....F 973 577-4343
Linden **(G-5344)**

Amcor Flexibles Inc ....E 609 267-5900
Mount Holly **(G-6766)**

Amcor Flexibles LLC ....C 856 825-1400
Millville **(G-6275)**

Broadway Kleer-Guard Corp ....E 609 662-3970
Monroe Township **(G-6380)**

2018 Harris New jersey
Manufacturers Directory

(G-0000) Company's Geographic Section entry number

Lally-Pak Inc ....D 908 351-4141
  Hillside (G-4424)
Lps Industries Inc ....C 201 438-3515
  Moonachie (G-6529)
Package Development Co Inc ....E 973 983-8500
  Rockaway (G-9593)
Petro Packaging Co Inc ....E 908 272-4054
  Cranford (G-1922)
Tekni-Plex Inc ....C 908 575-7661
  Branchburg (G-710)

PLASTICS: Blow Molded

Big 3 Precision Products Inc ....G 856 293-1400
  Millville (G-6287)
Holocraft Corporation ....D 732 502-9500
  Neptune (G-6919)
Seajay Manufacturing Corp ....F 732 774-0900
  Neptune (G-6931)

PLASTICS: Extruded

Aflex Extrusion Technologies ....E 732 752-0048
  Piscataway (G-8727)
Brentrick Inc ....G 973 357-3579
  Paterson (G-8225)
E & T Plastic Mfg Co Inc ....C 201 596-5017
  Teterboro (G-10792)
Hall Manufacturing Corp ....E 973 962-6022
  Ringwood (G-9448)
Leco Plastics Inc ....F 201 343-3330
  Hackensack (G-3938)
Patwin Plastics Inc ....E 908 486-6600
  Linden (G-5426)
Petro Extrusion Tech Inc ....E 908 789-3338
  Middlesex (G-6187)
Petro Plastics Company Inc ....E 908 789-1200
  Kenilworth (G-4987)
Poly Source Enterprises LLC ....G 732 580-5409
  Freehold (G-3678)
T & B Specialties Inc ....G 732 928-4500
  Jackson (G-4679)
Thermoplastics Bio-Logics LLC ....F 973 383-2834
  Sparta (G-10524)
World Plastic Extruders Inc ....D 201 933-2915
  Rutherford (G-9746)

PLASTICS: Finished Injection Molded

Design Display Group Inc ....C 201 438-6000
  Carlstadt (G-1154)
Emdeon Corporation ....A 201 703-3400
  Elmwood Park (G-2819)
Engineering Laboratories Inc ....E 201 337-8116
  Oakland (G-7687)
Farmplast LLC ....E 973 287-6070
  Parsippany (G-8008)
Flex Moulding Inc ....G 201 487-8080
  Hackensack (G-3914)
Iron Mountain Plastics Inc ....F 201 445-0063
  Midland Park (G-6230)
LNS Inc ....F 609 927-6656
  Egg Harbor Township (G-2688)
Nordson Efd LLC ....C 609 259-9222
  Robbinsville (G-9519)
Owens Plastic Products Inc ....G 856 447-3500
  Cedarville (G-1324)
Pmp Composites Corporation ....E 609 587-1188
  Trenton (G-11099)
Polymer Molded Products ....G 732 907-1990
  Bound Brook (G-621)
Pro Plastics Inc ....E 908 925-5555
  Linden (G-5431)
S&A Molders Inc ....G 732 851-7770
  Manalapan (G-5862)
Wilpak Industries Inc ....G 201 997-7600
  Kearny (G-4923)
Yuhl Products Inc ....G 908 276-5180
  Kenilworth (G-5009)

PLASTICS: Injection Molded

A R C Plasmet Corp ....F 201 867-8533
  North Bergen (G-7425)
Accurate Mold Inc ....E 856 784-8484
  Somerdale (G-10038)
Allgrind Plastics Inc ....F 908 479-4400
  Asbury (G-63)
Alva-Tech Inc ....F 609 747-1133
  Burlington Township (G-997)
B & W Plastics Inc ....G 973 383-0020
  Sparta (G-10490)

Brent River Corp ....E 908 722-6021
  Hillsborough (G-4322)
Comet Tool Company Inc ....D 856 256-1070
  Pitman (G-8840)
Continental Precision Corp ....C 908 754-3030
  Piscataway (G-8752)
Custom Molders Corp ....D 908 218-7997
  Branchburg (G-653)
Design & Molding Services Inc ....C 732 752-0300
  Piscataway (G-8756)
Duerr Tool & Die Co Inc ....F 908 810-9035
  Union (G-11173)
Echo Molding Inc ....E 908 688-0099
  Union (G-11178)
Engineered Plastic Pdts Inc ....E 908 647-3500
  Stirling (G-10599)
Exothermic Molding Inc ....E 908 272-2299
  Kenilworth (G-4953)
Fram Trak Industries Inc ....E 732 424-8400
  Middlesex (G-6167)
Fredon Development Inds LLC ....F 973 383-7576
  Newton (G-7389)
Gifford Group Inc ....F 212 569-8500
  Kearny (G-4878)
Hathaway Plastic ....G 908 688-9494
  Union (G-11192)
Heyco Molded Products Inc ....F 732 286-4336
  Toms River (G-10884)
Honeyware Inc ....D 201 997-5900
  Kearny (G-4880)
Hot Runner Technology ....G 908 431-5711
  Hillsborough (G-4342)
Injection Works Inc ....E 856 802-6444
  Mount Laurel (G-6804)
Injectron Corporation ....B 908 753-1990
  Plainfield (G-8865)
Inman Mold Manufacturing Inc ....G 732 381-3033
  Rahway (G-9198)
Inman Mold Manufacturing Inc ....G 732 381-3033
  Rahway (G-9199)
J-Mac Plastics Inc ....E 908 709-1111
  Kenilworth (G-4965)
Koba Corp ....G 732 469-0110
  Middlesex (G-6173)
Linden Mold and Tool Corp ....E 732 381-1411
  Rahway (G-9209)
Medplast West Berlin Inc ....E 856 753-7600
  West Berlin (G-11733)
Microcast Technologies Corp ....D 908 523-9503
  Linden (G-5409)
Northland Tooling Technologies ....G 908 850-0023
  Hackettstown (G-4030)
Novembal USA Inc ....E 732 947-3030
  Edison (G-2585)
OK Tool & Die Company Inc ....E 856 629-5757
  Williamstown (G-12094)
Pierson Industries Inc ....C 973 627-7945
  Rockaway (G-9596)
PMC Group Inc ....F 856 533-1866
  Mount Laurel (G-6828)
Polycel Structural Foam Inc ....D 908 722-5254
  Branchburg (G-691)
Polycel Structural Foam Inc ....E 908 722-5254
  Branchburg (G-692)
Precise Technology Inc ....E 856 241-1760
  Swedesboro (G-10720)
Preferred Plastics Inc ....G 856 662-6250
  Pennsauken (G-8562)
Princeton Tectonics ....C 609 298-9331
  Pennsauken (G-8565)
Pure Tech International Inc ....G 908 722-4800
  Branchburg (G-696)
Rapid Manufacturing Co Inc ....E 732 279-1252
  Toms River (G-10906)
Sonetronics Inc ....D 732 681-5016
  Belmar (G-364)
T & M Newton Corporation ....G 973 383-1232
  Newton (G-7407)
Tech Products Co Inc ....F 201 444-7777
  Midland Park (G-6239)
Technimold Inc ....F 908 232-8331
  Flemington (G-3470)
Technitool Inc ....E 856 768-2707
  West Berlin (G-11754)
Tektite Industries Inc ....G 609 656-0600
  Trenton (G-11120)
Tri Tech Tool & Design Co Inc ....E 732 469-5433
  South Bound Brook (G-10249)
Tripack Industrial USA LLC ....G 973 627-8350
  Rockaway (G-9619)

Van Ness Plastic Molding Co ....C 973 778-9500
  Clifton (G-1738)
Waldwick Plastics Corp ....C 201 445-7436
  Waldwick (G-11455)
Weiss-Aug Co Inc ....C 973 887-7600
  East Hanover (G-2249)
Westar Tool LLC ....G 856 507-8852
  West Berlin (G-11760)

PLASTICS: Molded

Advantage Molding Products ....F 732 303-8667
  Sea Girt (G-9861)
Don Shrts Pcture Frmes Molding ......G 732 363-1323
  Howell (G-4552)
East Coast Plastics Inc ....G 856 768-8700
  West Berlin (G-11718)
Garfield Molding Co Inc ....G 973 777-5700
  Wallington (G-11526)
Hartmann Tool Co Inc ....G 201 343-8700
  Hackensack (G-3925)
Jersey Plastic Molders Inc ....C 973 926-1800
  Irvington (G-4595)
Life of Party LLC ....E 732 828-0886
  North Brunswick (G-7524)
Metrie Inc ....F 973 584-0040
  Randolph (G-9289)
Molders Fishing Preserve ....G 732 446-2850
  Jamesburg (G-4687)
Montrose Molders Corporation ....E 908 754-3030
  Piscataway (G-8793)
National Casein New Jersey Inc ....E 856 829-1880
  Cinnaminson (G-1480)
Norlo of New Jersey LLC ....G 646 492-3293
  Montclair (G-6425)
Sinclair and Rush Inc ....G 862 262-8189
  Carlstadt (G-1218)
Tek Molding ....G 973 702-0450
  Sussex (G-10678)
Thermo Plastic Tech Inc ....E 908 687-4833
  Union (G-11229)
Valley Plastic Molding Co ....F 973 334-2100
  Boonton (G-587)
Viz Mold & Die Ltd ....F 201 784-8383
  Northvale (G-7611)

PLASTICS: Polystyrene Foam

Capitol Foam Products Inc ....E 201 933-5277
  East Rutherford (G-2291)
Dv8 Enterprises LLC ....F 201 507-6288
  West Berlin (G-11715)
Glopak Corp ....E 908 753-8735
  South Plainfield (G-10373)
Innocor Foam Technologies LLC ......G 844 824-9348
  Red Bank (G-9333)
Instapak Corp Sealed Air ....D 201 791-7600
  Rochelle Park (G-9529)
New Dimensions Industries LLC ......G 201 531-1010
  West Berlin (G-11736)
Plasti Foam ....D 908 722-5254
  Branchburg (G-690)
Plastic Plus Inc ....G 973 614-0271
  Passaic (G-8170)
Pmc Inc ....B 201 933-8540
  East Rutherford (G-2317)
Pmc Inc ....G 732 370-1163
  Lakewood (G-5173)
Rempac Foam Corp ....F 973 881-8880
  Rochelle Park (G-9535)
Rempac LLC ....C 201 843-4585
  Rochelle Park (G-9536)
Sekisui America Corporation ....F 201 423-7960
  Secaucus (G-9927)
T C P Reliable Manufacturing ....E 732 346-9200
  Somerset (G-10178)

PLASTICS: Thermoformed

Brisar Industries Inc ....C 973 278-2500
  Paterson (G-8226)
Delvco Pharma Packg Svcs Inc ....D 973 278-2500
  Paterson (G-8249)
Madan Plastics Inc ....D 908 276-8484
  Cranford (G-1913)
Productive Plastics Inc ....D 856 778-4300
  Mount Laurel (G-6832)
Veloso Industries Inc ....G 908 925-0999
  Linden (G-5457)

Employee Codes: A=Over 500 employees, B=251-500
C=101-250, D=51-100, E=20-50, F=10-19, G=4-9

2018 Harris New Jersey
Manufacturers Directory

931

PRODUCT

PLATE WORK: Metalworking Trade

Able Fab Co ....E 732 396-0600
  Avenel (G-122)

Sheet Metal Products Inc ....D 973 482-0450
  Newark (G-7310)

Tolan Machinery Polishing Co ......E 973 983-7212
  Rockaway (G-9616)

PLATEMAKING SVC: Color Separations, For The Printing Trade

R P R Graphics Inc ....E 908 654-8080
  Peapack (G-8432)

PLATEMAKING SVC: Embossing, For The Printing Trade

Standard Embossing Plate Mfg .....G 973 344-6670
  Newark (G-7327)

PLATEMAKING SVC: Letterpress

Downtown Printing Center Inc ....F 732 246-7990
  New Brunswick (G-6955)

PLATES

Acme Engraving Co Inc ....E 973 778-0885
  Passaic (G-8124)

Advertisers Service Group Inc ....F 201 440-5577
  Ridgefield Park (G-9395)

Celebration (us) Inc ....C 609 261-5200
  Lumberton (G-5654)

Container Graphics Corp ....E 732 922-1180
  Neptune (G-6904)

E I Du Pont De Nemours & Co ......E 732 257-1579
  Parlin (G-7930)

Essex West Graphics Inc ....E 973 227-2400
  Fairfield (G-3185)

G & R Graphics Inc ....G 973 731-7438
  South Orange (G-10307)

Garrison Printing Company Inc ......E 856 488-1900
  Pennsauken (G-8515)

Globe Photo Engraving Co LLC .....E 201 489-2300
  Little Ferry (G-5506)

Grandview Printing Co Inc ....F 973 890-0006
  Totowa (G-10950)

Hatteras Press Inc ....B 732 935-9800
  Tinton Falls (G-10838)

Howard Press Inc ....D 908 245-4400
  Roselle (G-9673)

Lacoa Inc ....G 973 754-1000
  Elmwood Park (G-2831)

Mariano Press LLC ....F 732 247-3659
  Somerset (G-10129)

Mark/Trece Inc ....E 973 884-1005
  Whippany (G-12026)

Marko Engraving & Art Corp ....F 201 864-6500
  Weehawken (G-11698)

Marko Engraving & Art Corp ....F 201 945-6555
  Fairview (G-3365)

Mosstype Holding Corp ....E 201 444-8000
  Waldwick (G-11451)

Nassau Communications Inc ....F 609 208-9099
  Lawrence Township (G-5245)

Staines Inc ....F 856 784-2718
  Somerdale (G-10044)

Tangent Graphics Inc ....G 201 488-2840
  Englewood (G-2936)

Tech-Ni Fold Usa Inc ....G 973 383-6691
  Lafayette (G-5053)

Toppan Printing Co Amer Inc ....C 732 469-8400
  Somerset (G-10188)

Unity Graphics & Engraving Co ......G 201 541-5462
  Englewood (G-2940)

PLATES: Plastic Exc Polystyrene Foam

Tarma Sales ....G 732 969-3318
  Carteret (G-1268)

PLATES: Sheet & Strip, Exc Coated Prdts

Benedict-Miller LLC ....F 908 497-1477
  Kenilworth (G-4944)

PLATES: Steel

Archer Day Inc ....E 732 396-0600
  Avenel (G-124)

PLATING & FINISHING SVC: Decorative, Formed Prdts

Zsombor Antal Designs Inc ....F 201 225-1750
  River Edge (G-9468)

PLATING & POLISHING SVC

A&A Company Inc ....E 908 561-2378
  South Plainfield (G-10319)

Acme Engraving Co Inc ....E 973 778-0885
  Passaic (G-8124)

Boyko Metal Finishing Co Inc ....G 973 623-4254
  Newark (G-7111)

Boyko Metal Finishing Co Inc ....D 973 623-4254
  Newark (G-7110)

Hard Crome Solutions ....G 732 500-2568
  Metuchen (G-6108)

Intrepid Industries Inc ....G 908 534-5300
  Lebanon (G-5291)

J R S Tool & Metal Finishing ....G 908 753-2050
  South Plainfield (G-10387)

Mold Polishing Company Inc ....G 908 518-9191
  Garwood (G-3779)

Productive Industrial Finshg ....G 856 427-9646
  Voorhees (G-11436)

Stainless Stock ....G 732 564-1164
  Middlesex (G-6202)

Stirrup Metal Products Corp ....F 973 824-7086
  Newark (G-7330)

PLATING COMPOUNDS

Krohn Technical Products Inc ....F 201 933-9696
  Carlstadt (G-1182)

Omg Electronic Chemicals Inc ....C 908 222-5800
  South Plainfield (G-10418)

PLATING SVC: Chromium, Metals Or Formed Prdts

Industrial Hard Chromium Co ....F 973 344-2265
  Newark (G-7196)

Tomken Plating ....G 856 829-0607
  Cinnaminson (G-1493)

PLATING SVC: Electro

A & F Electroplating Inc ....G 973 983-2459
  West Orange (G-11884)

Accu-Cote Inc ....G 856 845-7323
  Thorofare (G-10818)

Alcaro & Alcaro Plating Co ....E 973 746-1200
  Montclair (G-6405)

Cramer Plating Inc ....G 908 453-2887
  Buttzville (G-1020)

Deptford Plating Co Inc ....G 856 227-1144
  Deptford (G-2063)

E C Electroplating Inc ....F 973 340-0227
  Garfield (G-3731)

Elkem Inc ....G 732 566-1700
  Cliffwood (G-1546)

FER Plating Inc ....G 201 438-1010
  Lyndhurst (G-5683)

General Magnaplate Corporation ....D 908 862-6200
  Linden (G-5380)

Hill Cross Co Inc ....G 201 864-3393
  West New York (G-11866)

Ideal Plating & Polishing Co ....F 973 759-5559
  Paterson (G-8292)

Madan Plastics Inc ....D 908 276-8484
  Cranford (G-1913)

Manco Plating Incorporated ....G 973 485-6800
  Newark (G-7234)

Metal Finishing Co LLC ....G 973 778-9550
  Passaic (G-8164)

Miller & Son ....G 973 759-6445
  Belleville (G-307)

National Mtal Fnshngs Corp Inc .....F 732 752-7770
  Middlesex (G-6183)

New Brunswick Plating Inc ....D 732 545-6522
  New Brunswick (G-6987)

Paramount Plating Co Inc ....E 908 862-0772
  Linden (G-5425)

Polaris Plating Inc ....G 973 278-0033
  Parsippany (G-8069)

Suffern Plating Corp ....E 973 473-4404
  Lodi (G-5604)

Vanguard Research Industries ....E 908 753-2770
  South Plainfield (G-10450)

PLATING SVC: NEC

Art Metalcraft Plating Co Inc ....F 215 923-6625
  Camden (G-1042)

DAngelo Metal Products Inc ....F 908 862-8220
  Linden (G-5367)

General Magnaplate California ....F 805 642-6262
  Linden (G-5379)

Glasseal Products Inc ....C 732 370-9100
  Lakewood (G-5129)

Mara Polishing & Plating Corp ......G 973 242-0800
  Newark (G-7236)

Patel Metal Plating Inc ....G 732 574-1770
  Edison (G-2593)

Platinum Plating Specialists ....G 732 221-2575
  Clark (G-1513)

Programatic Platers Inc ....F 718 721-4330
  Tenafly (G-10786)

PLAYGROUND EQPT

De Zaio Productions Inc ....G 973 423-5000
  Fair Lawn (G-3089)

PLEATING & STITCHING FOR THE TRADE: Decorative & Novelty

Avanti Linens Inc ....C 201 641-7766
  Moonachie (G-6506)

PLEATING & STITCHING FOR THE TRADE: Lace, Burnt-Out

Carolace Embroidery Co Inc ....D 201 945-2151
  Ridgefield (G-9354)

PLEATING & STITCHING FOR THE TRADE: Scalloping

Walker Eight Corp ....G 201 861-4208
  North Bergen (G-7494)

PLEATING & STITCHING FOR TRADE: Permanent Pleating/Pressing

Central Safety Equipment Co ....E 609 386-6448
  Burlington (G-963)

PLEATING & STITCHING SVC

Aztec Graphics Inc ....F 609 587-1000
  Trenton (G-11023)

Craig Fabrics Inc ....F 201 869-9126
  Guttenberg (G-3868)

Deerbrook Fabrics ....F 201 945-4141
  Guttenberg (G-3869)

Family Screen Printing Inc ....F 856 933-2780
  Bellmawr (G-340)

Goralski Inc ....E 201 573-1529
  Park Ridge (G-7921)

Monogram Center Inc ....E 732 442-1800
  Perth Amboy (G-8624)

O Stitch Matic Inc ....G 201 861-3045
  Guttenberg (G-3870)

Quadelle Textile Corp ....F 201 865-1112
  West New York (G-11879)

Red Diamond Company ....G 973 759-2005
  Belleville (G-314)

Tone Embroidery Corp ....E 201 943-1082
  Fairview (G-3371)

PLUMBING & HEATING EQPT & SPLY, WHOL: Htg Eqpt/Panels, Solar

Atlantic Clean Energy Sup LLC ....G 888 900-1581
  Branchburg (G-641)

I4 Sustainability LLC ....G 732 618-3310
  Springfield (G-10557)

Mc Renewable Energy LLC ....F 732 369-9933
  Manasquan (G-5873)

Petra Systems Inc ....C 908 462-5200
  South Plainfield (G-10419)

Solar Rig Technologies LLC ....G 973 600-0500
  Carlstadt (G-1221)

Sun Pacific Power Corp ....F 888 845-0242
  Manalapan (G-5864)

PLUMBING & HEATING EQPT & SPLY, WHOLESALE: Hydronic Htg Eqpt

Encur Inc ....G 732 264-2098
Keyport (G-5016)

PLUMBING & HEATING EQPT & SPLYS WHOLESALERS

Frank Burton & Sons Inc ....G 856 455-1202
Bridgeton (G-785)
Samstubend Inc ....F 973 278-2555
Paterson (G-8376)

PLUMBING & HEATING EQPT & SPLYS, WHOL: Pipe/Fitting, Plastic

Morris Industries Inc ....E 973 835-6600
Pompton Plains (G-8963)

PLUMBING & HEATING EQPT & SPLYS, WHOL: Plumbing Fitting/Sply

Durst Corporation Inc ....E 800 852-3906
Cranford (G-1903)
Everflow Supplies Inc ....E 908 436-1100
Carteret (G-1256)
Grove Supply Inc ....E 856 205-0687
Vineland (G-11365)
Kessler Industries ....G 973 279-1417
Paterson (G-8309)
Mat Manufacturing Corporation ......E 800 378-7965
Clifton (G-1670)
U V International LLC ....F 973 993-9454
Morristown (G-6747)

PLUMBING & HEATING EQPT & SPLYS, WHOL: Water Purif Eqpt

Bellaqua Inc ....G 201 460-8379
East Rutherford (G-2284)
Dynatec Systems Inc ....F 609 387-0330
Burlington (G-970)
Favs Corp ....G 856 358-1515
Elmer (G-2792)
Liquid-Solids Separation Corp ....E 201 236-4833
Ramsey (G-9245)

PLUMBING & HEATING EQPT & SPLYS, WHOLESALE: Oil Burners

Industrial Combustion Assn ....F 732 271-0300
Somerset (G-10111)

PLUMBING FIXTURES

As America Inc ....C 732 980-3000
Piscataway (G-8738)
Bruce Supply Corp ....F 732 661-0500
Keasbey (G-4925)
Carpenter & Paterson Inc ....E 609 227-2750
Bordentown (G-593)
Chatham Brass Co Inc ....G 908 668-0500
South Plainfield (G-10345)
Danfoss Hago Inc ....C 908 232-8687
Mountainside (G-6873)
DAngelo Metal Products Inc ....F 908 862-8220
Linden (G-5367)
Grove Supply Inc ....E 856 205-0687
Vineland (G-11365)
Kessler Industries ....G 973 279-1417
Paterson (G-8309)
Kissler & Co Inc ....E 201 896-9600
Carlstadt (G-1179)
Knickerbocker Machine Shop Inc ....D 973 256-1616
Totowa (G-10953)
Specialty Products Plus ....G 732 380-1188
West Long Branch (G-11848)
Wm Steinen Mfg Co ....D 973 887-6400
Parsippany (G-8116)

PLUMBING FIXTURES: Brass, Incl Drain Cocks, Faucets/Spigots

El Batal Corporation ....F 908 964-3427
Union (G-11180)

PLUMBING FIXTURES: Plastic

Ace Restoration ....G 267 897-2384
Sewell (G-9944)

Sell All Properties LLC ....F 856 963-8800
Camden (G-1086)
Town & Country Plastics Inc ....F 732 780-5300
Marlboro (G-5961)

PLUMBING FIXTURES: Vitreous

As America Inc ....C 732 980-3000
Piscataway (G-8738)
Benco Inc ....F 973 575-4440
Fairfield (G-3146)
Ecom 2000 Inc ....F 718 504-7355
Edison (G-2507)

PLUMBING FIXTURES: Vitreous China

New Jersey Porcelain Co Inc ....F 609 394-5376
Trenton (G-11086)

POINT OF SALE DEVICES

Business Control Systems Corp ......F 732 283-1301
Iselin (G-4619)
Comtrex Systems Corporation ....E 856 778-0090
Moorestown (G-6569)
Hpc Pos System Corp ....G 973 239-9666
Cedar Grove (G-1284)

POLISHING SVC: Metals Or Formed Prdts

All Metal Polishing Co Inc ....E 973 589-8070
Newark (G-7076)
Art Mold & Polishing Co Inc ....F 908 518-9191
Roselle (G-9661)
Dynasty Metals Inc ....E 800 225-3962
Kearny (G-4872)
Tolan Polishing Corp ....F 973 983-7212
Rockaway (G-9617)
Water Master Co ....G 732 247-1900
Highland Park (G-4305)

POLYAMIDES

Hitachi Chem Dupont Microsyst ......E 732 613-2404
Parlin (G-7931)

POLYESTERS

Coim USA Inc ....D 856 224-8560
West Deptford (G-11825)

POLYETHYLENE CHLOROSULFONATED RUBBER

Lyondell Chemical Company ....G 973 578-2200
Newark (G-7232)

POLYETHYLENE RESINS

Epsilon Plastics Inc ....D 201 933-6000
Lyndhurst (G-5680)
Honeywell International Inc ....A 973 455-2000
Morris Plains (G-6666)
Polyfil Corporation ....E 973 627-4070
Rockaway (G-9598)
Recycle Inc East ....D 908 756-2200
South Plainfield (G-10434)

POLYPROPYLENE RESINS

Atlantic Lining Co Inc ....E 609 723-2400
Jobstown (G-4854)
Bayer Corporation ....A 412 777-2000
Whippany (G-12007)

POLYTETRAFLUOROETHYLENE RESINS

Cain Machine Inc ....F 856 825-7225
Millville (G-6291)

POLYVINYL CHLORIDE RESINS

Berry Global Films LLC ....C 201 641-6600
Montvale (G-6446)
Breen Color Concentrates LLC ....F 609 397-8200
Lambertville (G-5210)
Formosa Plastics Corp USA ....B 973 992-2090
Livingston (G-5530)
J-M Manufacturing Company Inc ......D 800 621-4404
Livingston (G-5538)
Phoenix Manufactoring Inc ....G 732 380-1666
Ocean (G-7737)
Rimtec Enterprises Inc ....C 609 387-0011
Burlington (G-989)

Surface Source Intl Inc ....F 973 598-0152
Randolph (G-9300)

POPCORN & SUPPLIES WHOLESALERS

Continntal Concession Sups Inc ......E 516 629-4906
Union (G-11166)

POSTERS, WHOLESALE

Scorpio Posters Inc ....E 718 499-2001
Marlboro (G-5957)

POULTRY & POULTRY PRDTS WHOLESALERS

Farbest-Tallman Foods Corp ....D 714 897-7199
Park Ridge (G-7919)

POULTRY & SMALL GAME SLAUGHTERING & PROCESSING

Carl Streit & Son Co ....G 732 775-0803
Neptune (G-6903)
David Mitchell Inc ....E 856 429-2610
Voorhees (G-11428)
Ena Meat Packing Inc ....E 973 742-4790
Paterson (G-8264)
Perdue Farms Inc ....G 609 298-4100
Bordentown (G-608)
Senat Poultry LLC ....E 973 742-9316
Paterson (G-8382)
Vineland Kosher Poultry Inc ....C 856 692-1871
Vineland (G-11415)

POULTRY, PACKAGED FROZEN: Wholesalers

South Jersey Pretzel Inc ....F 856 435-5055
Stratford (G-10617)

POWDER: Metal

Acupowder International LLC ....G 908 851-4500
Union (G-11146)
Atlantic Eqp Engineers Inc ....F 201 828-9400
Upper Saddle River (G-11273)
FW Winter Inc ....E 856 963-7490
Camden (G-1067)
United Sttes Metal Powders Inc ......F 908 782-5454
Flemington (G-3474)

POWDERS, FLAVORING, EXC DRINK

Akay USA LLC ....G 732 254-7177
Sayreville (G-9812)
Robertet Flavors Inc ....F 732 271-1804
Piscataway (G-8806)

POWER SPLY CONVERTERS: Static, Electronic Applications

Infiniti Components Inc ....G 908 537-9950
Hampton (G-4161)
Technology Dynamics Inc ....E 201 385-0500
Bergenfield (G-396)

POWER SUPPLIES: All Types, Static

ADI American Distributors LLC ....D 973 328-1181
Randolph (G-9267)
Advanced Energy Voorhees Inc ....D 856 627-1287
Voorhees (G-11419)
AT&T Technologies Inc ....A 201 771-2000
Berkeley Heights (G-400)
Clantech Inc ....G 908 281-7667
Hillsborough (G-4325)
Crestek Inc ....E 609 883-4000
Ewing (G-3012)
Glassman High Voltage Inc ....D 908 638-3800
High Bridge (G-4296)
Idt Energy Inc ....E 877 887-6866
Newark (G-7194)
Jerome Industries Corp ....E 908 353-5700
Hackettstown (G-4013)
Nwl Inc ....B 609 298-7300
Bordentown (G-606)
Technology Dynamics Inc ....D 201 385-0500
Bergenfield (G-397)
Transistor Devices Inc ....C 908 850-5088
Hackettstown (G-4042)

Employee Codes: A=Over 500 employees, B=251-500
C=101-250, D=51-100, E=20-50, F=10-19, G=4-9

2018 Harris New jersey
Manufacturers Directory

933

PRODUCT

Uthe Technology Inc..................G......609 883-4000
  Trenton (G-11130)
West Electronics Inc......................F......609 387-4300
  Burlington (G-996)

POWER SUPPLIES: Transformer, Electronic Type

Electronic Transformer Corp..............E......973 942-2222
  Paterson (G-8255)
Jinpan International USA Ltd..............G......201 460-8778
  Carlstadt (G-1175)

POWER SWITCHING EQPT

Sigma-Netics Inc..........................E......973 227-6372
  Riverdale (G-9488)
Technology Dynamics Inc...................E......201 385-0500
  Bergenfield (G-396)

POWER TOOLS, HAND: Cartridge-Activated

Dcm Clean Air Products Inc................G......732 363-2100
  Lakewood (G-5106)
Rennsteig Tools Inc.......................G......330 315-3044
  Hackensack (G-3966)

POWER TOOLS, HAND: Drill Attachments, Portable

Toydriver LLC.............................G......678 637-8500
  Garfield (G-3769)

POWER TOOLS, HAND: Drills & Drilling Tools

J Paul Allen Inc..........................G......973 702-1174
  Sussex (G-10674)

POWER TRANSMISSION EQPT WHOLESALERS

Sew-Eurodrive Inc.........................E......856 467-2277
  Bridgeport (G-771)

POWER TRANSMISSION EQPT: Aircraft

Simtek Usa Inc............................G......862 757-8130
  Little Falls (G-5488)

POWER TRANSMISSION EQPT: Mechanical

A M Gatti Inc.............................F......609 396-1577
  Trenton (G-11010)
Accurate Bronze Bearing Co................G......973 345-2304
  Paterson (G-8198)
Accurate Bushing Company Inc..............E......908 789-1121
  Garwood (G-3774)
Andantex U S A Inc........................E......732 493-2812
  Ocean (G-7715)
Daven Industries Inc......................E......973 808-8848
  Fairfield (G-3173)
Garlock Bearings Inc......................F......856 848-3200
  Thorofare (G-10819)
Gate Technologies Inc.....................G......973 300-0090
  Sparta (G-10500)
Hydro-Mechanical Systems Inc..............F......856 848-8888
  Westville (G-11943)
Martin Sprocket & Gear Inc................G......973 633-5700
  Wayne (G-11664)
Moser Jewel Company.......................G......908 454-1155
  Phillipsburg (G-8660)
Reich USA Corporation.....................F......201 684-9400
  Mahwah (G-5808)
S G Manufacturing Co Inc..................D......732 494-6520
  Metuchen (G-6119)
Valcor Engineering Corporation............E......973 467-8100
  Springfield (G-10584)
Woyshner Service Company Inc..............G......856 461-9196
  Delran (G-2024)

PRECAST TERRAZZO OR CONCRETE PRDTS

J L Erectors Inc..........................E......856 232-9400
  Blackwood (G-482)
Massarellis Lawn Ornaments Inc............E......609 567-9700
  Hammonton (G-4143)

PRECIOUS METALS

Matthey Johnson Inc.......................C......856 384-7132
  West Deptford (G-11835)

PRECIOUS METALS WHOLESALERS

Dxl Enterprises Inc.......................F......201 891-8718
  Mahwah (G-5768)
Hickok Matthews Co Inc....................G......973 335-3400
  Montville (G-6489)

PRECISION INSTRUMENT REPAIR SVCS

Sprialseal Inc............................G......732 738-6113
  Cliffwood (G-1548)

PREFABRICATED BUILDING DEALERS

Benco Inc.................................F......973 575-4440
  Fairfield (G-3146)

PREPARATORY SCHOOL

Pillar of Fire............................D......732 356-0102
  Zarephath (G-12270)

PRERECORDED TAPE, COMPACT DISC & RECORD STORES

Sony Music Holdings Inc...................B......201 777-3933
  Rutherford (G-9745)

PRERECORDED TAPE, COMPACT DISC & RECORD STORES: Records

Riotsound Inc.............................G......917 273-5814
  Newton (G-7401)

PRESCHOOL CENTERS

Almond Branch Inc.........................E......973 728-3479
  West Milford (G-11849)

PRESSURE COOKERS: Stamped Or Drawn Metal

Manttra Inc...............................G......877 962-6887
  New Brunswick (G-6978)

PRIMARY METAL PRODUCTS

Czar Industries Inc.......................G......609 392-1515
  Trenton (G-11051)
McW Precision.............................F......609 859-4400
  Southampton (G-10478)
Sentry Mfg LLC............................G......856 642-0480
  Moorestown (G-6622)

PRINT CARTRIDGES: Laser & Other Computer Printers

Bergen Cnty Crtrdge Xchnge LLC............G......201 493-8182
  Midland Park (G-6222)
GSC Imaging LLC...........................F......856 317-9301
  Pennsauken (G-8519)
Hammer Too LLC............................G......908 688-5601
  West Orange (G-11896)
International Laser Group Inc.............E......818 888-0400
  Cherry Hill (G-1382)
Turbon International Inc..................G......800 282-6650
  Cherry Hill (G-1430)

PRINTED CIRCUIT BOARDS

ADI American Distributors LLC.............D......973 328-1181
  Randolph (G-9267)
Argus International Inc...................E......609 466-1677
  Ringoes (G-9435)
Cheringal Associates Inc..................D......201 784-8721
  Norwood (G-7618)
Circuit Reproduction Co...................F......201 712-9292
  Maywood (G-6046)
Computer Control Corp.....................F......973 492-8265
  Butler (G-1001)
Data Delay Devices Inc....................E......973 202-3268
  Clifton (G-1597)
Delta Circuits Inc........................E......973 575-3000
  Fairfield (G-3175)
Esi.......................................E......856 629-2492
  Sicklerville (G-10018)
ESP Associates Inc........................F......973 208-9045
  Newfoundland (G-7374)

GAb Electronic Services LLC...............E......856 786-0108
  Cinnaminson (G-1464)
Garys Kids................................G......973 458-1818
  Passaic (G-8141)
Glenro Inc................................F......973 279-5900
  Paterson (G-8277)
J R E Inc.................................E......973 808-0055
  West Caldwell (G-11780)
Jnbc Associates LLC.......................G......973 560-5518
  Parsippany (G-8034)
Mdj Inc...................................E......201 457-9260
  Hackensack (G-3945)
Medco West Electronics Inc................G......201 457-9260
  Hackensack (G-3946)
Mercury Systems Inc.......................E......973 244-1040
  West Caldwell (G-11789)
Modelware Inc.............................F......732 264-3020
  Holmdel (G-4524)
Ppi/Time Zero Inc.........................C......973 278-6500
  Fairfield (G-3285)
Precision Products Co Inc.................E......201 712-5757
  Maywood (G-6060)
Quik Flex Circuit Inc.....................F......856 742-0550
  Gloucester City (G-3843)
R & D Circuits Inc........................C......732 549-4554
  South Plainfield (G-10430)
R R J Co Inc..............................G......732 544-1514
  Colts Neck (G-1791)
Redkoh Industries Inc.....................G......908 369-1590
  Hillsborough (G-4368)
Scl.......................................E......908 391-9882
  Bridgewater (G-893)
Spem Corporation..........................E......732 356-3366
  Piscataway (G-8816)
Sure Design...............................F......732 919-3066
  Wall Township (G-11512)
Swemco LLC................................G......856 222-9900
  Moorestown (G-6625)
Syscom Technologies Corp..................D......856 642-7661
  Moorestown (G-6627)
T V L Associates Inc......................G......973 790-6766
  Wayne (G-11684)
Techniques Inc............................E......973 256-0947
  Woodland Park (G-12234)
Test Technology Inc.......................D......856 596-1215
  Marlton (G-6001)
Thomas Instrumentation Inc................F......609 624-2630
  Cape May Court House (G-1118)
Toby-Yanni Incorporated...................F......973 253-9800
  Garfield (G-3768)
Transistor Devices Inc....................C......908 850-5088
  Hackettstown (G-4041)
Wireworks Corporation.....................G......908 686-7400
  Hillside (G-4451)

PRINTERS & PLOTTERS

Diversified Display Pdts LLC..............E......908 686-2200
  Hillside (G-4405)
Gulton Incorporated.......................E......908 791-4622
  South Plainfield (G-10377)
Jetty Life LLC............................G......800 900-6435
  Manahawkin (G-5831)

PRINTERS' SVCS: Folding, Collating, Etc

B&B Imaging LLC...........................G......201 261-3131
  Paramus (G-7856)
Campbell Converting Corp..................G......609 835-2720
  Beverly (G-460)
Cox Stationers and Printers...............E......908 928-1010
  Linden (G-5363)
Dm Graphic Center LLC.....................F......973 882-8990
  Fairfield (G-3178)
Semels Embroidery Inc.....................F......973 473-6868
  Clifton (G-1719)
Strategic Content Imaging.................C......201 863-8100
  Secaucus (G-9933)

PRINTERS: Computer

Lexmark International Inc.................F......201 307-4601
  Montvale (G-6466)
Lexmark International Inc.................F......201 307-4600
  Park Ridge (G-7925)
Ricoh Prtg Systems Amer Inc...............G......973 316-6051
  Mountain Lakes (G-6861)

PRINTERS: Magnetic Ink, Bar Code

Alpha Tech Services.......................G......973 283-2011
  Boonton (G-553)

Zebra Technologies Corporation..........B......609 383-8743
Northfield *(G-7565)*

PRINTING & BINDING: Books

Aramani Inc...G......201 945-1160
Fairview *(G-3357)*

PRINTING & EMBOSSING: Plastic Fabric Articles

C S Hot Stamping..................................G......201 840-4004
Edgewater *(G-2435)*

PRINTING & ENGRAVING: Financial Notes & Certificates

All-State International Inc..................C......908 272-0800
Cranford *(G-1895)*
Data Communique Inc.........................E......201 508-6000
Ridgefield Park *(G-9402)*

PRINTING & ENGRAVING: Invitation & Stationery

Bellia & Sons..E......856 845-2234
Woodbury *(G-12158)*
E C D Ventures Inc..............................G......856 875-1100
Blackwood *(G-477)*
Engraved Images Ltd...........................G......908 234-0323
Far Hills *(G-3375)*
Envelopes & Printed Pdts Inc.............G......973 942-1232
Prospect Park *(G-9169)*
Papery of Marlton LLC.........................G......856 985-1776
Marlton *(G-5993)*
Party City Corporation.........................F......973 537-1707
Randolph *(G-9294)*
Party City of North Bergen..................F......201 865-0040
North Bergen *(G-7473)*
Remco Press Inc...................................G......201 751-5703
North Bergen *(G-7479)*
Sharp Impressions Inc ....G......201 573-4943
Garfield *(G-3761)*

PRINTING & ENGRAVING: Poster & Decal

Scorpio Posters Inc............................E......718 499-2001
Marlboro *(G-5957)*

PRINTING & STAMPING: Fabric Articles

Alchemy Billboards LLC.......................G......973 977-8828
Paterson *(G-8203)*
Custom Laminations Inc.......................E......973 279-9174
Paterson *(G-8243)*
Image Point...G......908 684-1768
Newton *(G-7392)*
Mail Direct Paper Company LLC ....F......201 933-2782
Lyndhurst *(G-5689)*

PRINTING & WRITING PAPER WHOLESALERS

G R Impex Ltd Liability Co ....F......732 931-7001
Avenel *(G-133)*
Gdb International Inc............................D......732 246-3001
New Brunswick *(G-6962)*
Thermo X-Press Printing LLC...............G......973 585-6505
East Hanover *(G-2245)*

PRINTING INKS WHOLESALERS

B&B Imaging LLC..................................G......201 261-3131
Paramus *(G-7856)*
Prismacolor Corp..................................G......973 887-6040
Parsippany *(G-8073)*
Superior Printing Ink Co Inc ....E......856 482-9066
Maple Shade *(G-5911)*

PRINTING MACHINERY

Ackley Machine Corporation ....E......856 234-3626
Moorestown *(G-6555)*
Acme Engraving Co Inc........................E......973 778-0885
Passaic *(G-8124)*
Algene Marking Equipment Co............G......973 478-9041
Garfield *(G-3716)*
Ancraft Press Corp ....F......201 792-9200
Jersey City *(G-4705)*
Anderson & Vreeland Inc ....E......973 227-2270
Fairfield *(G-3136)*

AT Information Products Inc ....G......201 529-0202
Mahwah *(G-5750)*
Atlantic Zeiser Inc ....E......973 228-0800
West Caldwell *(G-11766)*
Bell-Mark Sales Co Inc ....E......973 882-0202
Pine Brook *(G-8688)*
Benton Graphics Inc ....E......609 587-4000
Trenton *(G-11026)*
Blankets Inc..E......973 589-7800
Newark *(G-7108)*
Charles M Jessup Inc ....G......732 324-0430
Keasbey *(G-4926)*
Convertech Inc......................................E......973 328-1850
Wharton *(G-11982)*
Custom Roller Inc ....G......908 298-7797
Roselle *(G-9668)*
Deneka Printing Systems Inc.............G......609 752-0964
Cream Ridge *(G-1934)*
Digital Design Inc.................................E......973 857-9500
Cedar Grove *(G-1278)*
Domino Printing.....................................D......973 857-0900
Cedar Grove *(G-1280)*
Graham Graphic Group Inc...................E......973 827-6177
Ogdensburg *(G-7771)*
Graphic Equipment Corporation..........E......732 494-5350
Metuchen *(G-6106)*
Interchange Equipment Inc..................E......973 473-5005
Passaic *(G-8148)*
Kohl & Madden Prtg Ink Corp..............E......201 935-8666
Carlstadt *(G-1181)*
Pamarco Global Graphics Inc.............E......908 241-1200
Roselle *(G-9679)*
Pamarco Global Graphics Inc.............F......856 829-4585
Palmyra *(G-7850)*
Pamarco Technologies LLC.................E......908 241-1200
Roselle *(G-9680)*
Panpac LLC..F......856 376-3576
Cherry Hill *(G-1410)*
Polytype America Corp ....E......201 995-1000
Mahwah *(G-5801)*
Printers Service Florida Inc...............G......973 589-7800
Newark *(G-7276)*
W R Chesnut Engineering Inc..............F......973 227-6995
Fairfield *(G-3348)*

PRINTING MACHINERY, EQPT & SPLYS: Wholesalers

Anderson & Vreeland Inc ....E......973 227-2270
Fairfield *(G-3136)*
AT Information Products Inc ....G......201 529-0202
Mahwah *(G-5750)*
Colter & Peterson Inc ....E......973 684-0901
West Caldwell *(G-11771)*
Deleet Merchandising Corp ....E......212 962-6565
Newark *(G-7139)*
Ernest Schaefer Inc ....E......908 964-1280
Union *(G-11182)*
Interchange Equipment Inc..................E......973 473-5005
Passaic *(G-8148)*
Superior Trademark Inc........................G......201 652-1900
Waldwick *(G-11454)*

PRINTING, COMMERCIAL: Bags, Plastic, NEC

Lally-Pak Inc..D......908 351-4141
Hillside *(G-4424)*

PRINTING, COMMERCIAL: Business Forms, NEC

Campbell Converting Corp ....G......609 835-2720
Beverly *(G-460)*
Earthcolor Inc......................................C......973 884-1300
Parsippany *(G-7994)*
Maggio Printing LLC.............................E......856 931-7805
Bellmawr *(G-346)*
New Line Prtg & Tech Solutions...........G......973 405-6133
Clifton *(G-1682)*
Stewart Business Forms Inc................F......856 768-2011
Blackwood *(G-493)*

PRINTING, COMMERCIAL: Calendars, NEC

Judith Roth Studio Collection ....G......973 543-4455
Mendham *(G-6087)*

PRINTING, COMMERCIAL: Cards, Souvenir, NEC

Italian Treasures.................................G......856 770-9188
Voorhees *(G-11434)*

PRINTING, COMMERCIAL: Cards, Visiting, Incl Business, NEC

Postcard Press Inc.............................E......310 747-3878
Saddle Brook *(G-9783)*

PRINTING, COMMERCIAL: Catalogs, NEC

Platypus Print Productions LLC...........G......732 772-1212
Morganville *(G-6651)*
Polaris Communications Inc.................F......201 928-0780
Teaneck *(G-10769)*

PRINTING, COMMERCIAL: Decals, NEC

Kraftwork Custom Design.....................F......609 883-8444
Ewing *(G-3033)*

PRINTING, COMMERCIAL: Directories, Exc Telephone, NEC

Lamb Printing Inc.................................G......908 852-0837
Hackettstown *(G-4016)*

PRINTING, COMMERCIAL: Envelopes, NEC

American Envelope...............................G......908 241-9900
Linden *(G-5348)*
John Patrick Publishing LLC...............D......609 883-2700
Ewing *(G-3027)*
Liberty Envelope Inc...........................F......973 546-5600
Paterson *(G-8320)*
Reliable Envelope and Graphics ....E......201 794-7756
Elmwood Park *(G-2848)*
Sapphire Envelope & Graphics............F......856 782-2227
Magnolia *(G-5742)*
United Envelope LLC...........................C......201 699-5800
Ridgefield *(G-9392)*

PRINTING, COMMERCIAL: Fashion Plates, NEC

Flanagan Holdings Inc..........................D......201 512-3338
Mahwah *(G-5772)*

PRINTING, COMMERCIAL: Imprinting

Butler Prtg & Laminating Inc ....C......973 838-8550
Butler *(G-999)*

PRINTING, COMMERCIAL: Labels & Seals, NEC

Alcop Adhesive Label Co.....................G......609 871-4400
Beverly *(G-458)*
Brimar Industries Inc...........................E......973 340-7889
Garfield *(G-3724)*
CCL Label Inc.......................................C......609 586-1332
Robbinsville *(G-9512)*
CCL Label Inc......................................E......856 273-0700
Lumberton *(G-5653)*
Classic Printers & Converters ....G......732 985-1100
Piscataway *(G-8749)*
Custom Labels Inc ....G......973 473-1934
Fairfield *(G-3170)*
Distributor Label Products ....E......908 704-9997
Hillsborough *(G-4327)*
Driscoll Label Company Inc................F......973 585-7291
East Hanover *(G-2213)*
Industrial Lbeling Systems Inc............E......973 808-8188
Fairfield *(G-3230)*
Label Solutions Inc..............................G......201 599-0909
Rochelle Park *(G-9531)*
Lizard Label Co....................................F......973 808-3322
Fairfield *(G-3254)*
Product Identification Co Inc................F......973 227-7770
Garfield *(G-3754)*
Promotional Graphics Inc.....................F......973 423-3900
Paterson *(G-8365)*
Sato Lbling Solutions Amer Inc............D......973 287-3641
Pine Brook *(G-8716)*
Star Narrow Fabrics Inc.......................G......973 778-8600
Lodi *(G-5602)*
Stephen Gould Corporation..................D......973 428-1500
Whippany *(G-12040)*

Employee Codes: A=Over 500 employees, B=251-500
C=101-250, D=51-100, E=20-50, F=10-19, G=4-9   2018 Harris New jersey
Manufacturers Directory   935

PRODUCT

Taunton Graphics Inc ....F 856 719-8084
West Berlin (G-11753)

PRINTING, COMMERCIAL: Literature, Advertising, NEC

Avail Inc ....G 732 560-2222
Bridgewater (G-817)
Brite Concepts Inc ....G 201 270-8544
Englewood (G-2878)
Page 2 LLC ....G 862 239-9830
Wayne (G-11669)

PRINTING, COMMERCIAL: Promotional

American Youth Enterprises Inc ....G 609 909-1900
Mays Landing (G-6036)
Graphic Imagery Inc ....F 908 755-2882
New Providence (G-7038)
Harwill Corporation ....G 609 895-1955
Windsor (G-12127)
Hit Promo LLC ....C 856 739-4474
Bellmawr (G-342)
Hygrade Business Group Inc ....E 800 836-7714
Secaucus (G-9896)
J H M Communications Inc ....F 908 859-6668
Phillipsburg (G-8653)
Koday Press Inc ....F 201 387-0001
Dumont (G-2121)
Marlo Plastic Products Inc ....E 732 792-1988
Neptune (G-6923)
Njiw Limited Liability Company ....F 201 355-2955
Hackensack (G-3954)
Patchworks Co Inc ....G 973 627-2002
Dover (G-2106)
Pressworks ....G 856 427-9001
Cherry Hill (G-1416)
Signmasters Inc ....D 973 614-8300
Passaic (G-8181)
Silver Edmar ....G 973 817-7483
Newark (G-7313)
Smith Enterprises ....G 215 416-9881
Mount Laurel (G-6842)

PRINTING, COMMERCIAL: Publications

Active Learning Associates ....G 908 284-0404
Flemington (G-3424)
Digital Color Concepts Inc ....D 908 264-0504
Mountainside (G-6877)
Paper Clip Communication Inc ....F 973 256-1333
Little Falls (G-5485)
University Publications Inc ....G 212 268-4222
Belford (G-289)

PRINTING, COMMERCIAL: Schedules, Transportation, NEC

Chariot Courier & Trans Svcs ....F 888 532-9125
Sayreville (G-9816)

PRINTING, COMMERCIAL: Screen

A B Tees LLC ....G 201 239-0022
Jersey City (G-4696)
Abbott Artkives LLC ....G 201 232-9477
Belleville (G-293)
Adpro Imprints ....G 732 531-2133
Ocean (G-7713)
Advantage Ds LLC ....F 856 307-9600
Glassboro (G-3800)
Alex Real LLC ....F 732 730-8770
Toms River (G-10860)
Alfred Sports Inc ....F 973 822-8987
Madison (G-5717)
All Colors Screen Printing LLC ....G 732 777-6033
Highland Park (G-4300)
All Nu Trophy & Screen Prtg ....F 201 807-0808
Ridgefield Park (G-9396)
Armin Kososki ....G 908 689-0411
Washington (G-11575)
Arnolds Yacht Basin Inc ....G 732 892-3000
Point Pleasant Boro (G-8931)
Art Guild Inc ....F 732 390-5300
East Brunswick (G-2135)
Arts Embroidery LLC ....G 732 870-2400
West Long Branch (G-11843)
Bankers Pen Inc ....E 800 499-7367
Garfield (G-3721)
Branded Screen Printing ....G 908 879-7411
Chester (G-1434)

C & D Sales ....G 609 383-9292
Pleasantville (G-8903)
Campus Coordinates LLC ....G 732 866-6060
Freehold (G-3643)
Central Mills Inc ....G 732 329-2009
Dayton (G-1960)
Cgs Sales and Service LLC ....G 856 665-6154
Pennsauken (G-8492)
Chambord Prints Inc ....E 201 795-2007
Hoboken (G-4464)
Clear Control LLC ....G 973 823-8200
Ogdensburg (G-7770)
Color Screen Pros Inc ....F 973 268-5080
Newark (G-7125)
Colorcraft Sign Co ....F 609 386-1115
Beverly (G-461)
Composing Room Inc ....C 856 662-9111
Pennsauken (G-8497)
Cosmic Custom Screen Printing ....G 856 629-8337
Williamstown (G-12084)
Custom Graphics of Vineland ....E 856 691-7858
Vineland (G-11347)
D L Imprints ....G 732 493-8555
Ocean (G-7721)
Deans Graphics ....G 609 261-8817
Mount Holly (G-6767)
Dezine Line Inc ....F 973 989-1009
Wharton (G-11985)
DOT Graphix Inc ....F 609 994-3416
Barnegat (G-162)
Envirnmntal Dsign Grphic Entps ....G 973 361-1829
Dover (G-2086)
F S T Printing Inc ....G 732 560-3749
Middlesex (G-6165)
Frontend Graphics Inc ....G 856 547-1600
Cherry Hill (G-1367)
G & M Printwear ....F 856 742-5551
Gloucester City (G-3836)
Graphic Image ....G 856 262-8900
Williamstown (G-12088)
GTM Marketing Inc ....G 856 227-2333
Woodbury (G-12163)
H C Graphics Screenprinting ....G 973 247-0544
Paterson (G-8286)
Hary Manufacturing Inc ....F 908 722-7100
Woodbridge (G-12150)
Heritage Inc ....G 201 447-2600
Midland Park (G-6229)
Image Screen Printing Inc ....G 732 560-1817
Middlesex (G-6170)
Imagery Embroidary Corporation ....F 201 343-9333
Union City (G-11248)
Imprintz Cstm Printed Graphics ....G 609 386-5673
Lumberton (G-5660)
J & G Graphics Inc ....G 732 223-6660
Manasquan (G-5872)
J and S Sporting Apparel LLC ....G 732 787-5500
Keansburg (G-4856)
Licensee Services Inc ....F 609 465-2003
Cape May Court House (G-1115)
Maclearie Printing LLC ....G 732 681-2772
Wall Township (G-11496)
Mary Bridget Enterprises ....E 609 267-4830
Cinnaminson (G-1475)
Menu Solutions Inc ....D 718 575-5160
Belleville (G-306)
Midland Screen Printing Inc ....G 201 703-0066
Saddle Brook (G-9775)
Midlantic Color Graphics LLC ....G 856 786-3113
Cinnaminson (G-1478)
Mj Corporate Sales Inc ....G 856 778-0055
Mount Laurel (G-6819)
Monarch Art Plastics Co LLC ....E 856 235-5151
Mount Laurel (G-6821)
Newton Screen Printing Co ....G 973 827-0486
Franklin (G-3602)
NJ Logo Wear LLC ....G 609 597-9400
Manahawkin (G-5832)
O Berk Company LLC ....E 201 941-1610
Fairview (G-3367)
Pecata Enterprises Inc ....G 973 523-9498
Paterson (G-8362)
Printsmith ....G 908 245-3000
Roselle Park (G-9701)
Process Supply Company Inc ....F 201 487-1616
South Hackensack (G-10291)
Promo Graphic Inc ....G 732 629-7300
Middlesex (G-6191)
R & R Printing & Copy Center ....G 732 249-9450
Hillsborough (G-4365)

Red Diamond Company ....G 973 759-2005
Belleville (G-314)
Rolferrys Specialties Inc ....G 856 456-2999
Brooklawn (G-921)
Rutler Screen Printing Inc ....F 908 859-3327
Phillipsburg (G-8669)
Screen Play Inc ....G 973 227-9014
Fairfield (G-3304)
Screen Tech Inc of New Jersey ....D 908 862-8000
Linden (G-5439)
Sports Stop Inc ....F 856 881-2763
Glassboro (G-3812)
Sunglo Fabrics Inc ....F 201 935-0830
Paterson (G-8387)
Tectubes USA Inc ....E 856 589-1250
Vineland (G-11408)
Totally T Shirts & More Inc ....G 609 894-0011
Pemberton (G-8443)
Trukmanns Inc ....E 973 538-7718
Cedar Knolls (G-1321)
U S Screening Corp ....C 973 242-1110
Newark (G-7350)
Unlimited Silk Screen Products ....G 609 882-0653
Ewing (G-3066)
Vernon Display Graphics Inc ....E 201 935-7117
Carlstadt (G-1238)
Wagner Foto Screen Process ....F 908 624-0800
Kenilworth (G-5005)
Wisco Promo & Uniform Inc ....G 973 767-2022
Saddle Brook (G-9801)
Work n Gear LLC ....G 856 848-7676
Woodbury (G-12172)
Zeeks Tees ....F 732 291-2700
Belford (G-290)
Zone Two Inc ....G 732 237-0766
Bayville (G-263)
Zwier Corp ....G 973 748-4009
Bloomfield (G-539)

PRINTING, COMMERCIAL: Tags, NEC

Ideal Jacobs Corporation ....E 973 275-5100
Maplewood (G-5922)

PRINTING, COMMERCIAL: Tickets, NEC

Clothing Emporium Inc ....F 973 773-3250
Passaic (G-8129)

PRINTING, LITHOGRAPHIC: Advertising Posters

Forbes Media LLC ....D 212 620-2200
Jersey City (G-4754)
Orora Visual LLC ....G 973 916-2804
Clifton (G-1687)
Solid Color Inc ....G 212 239-3930
Kearny (G-4915)

PRINTING, LITHOGRAPHIC: Atlases

Allied Envelope Co Inc ....E 201 440-2000
Carlstadt (G-1124)

PRINTING, LITHOGRAPHIC: Calendars

Schellmark Inc ....G 732 345-7143
Tinton Falls (G-10846)

PRINTING, LITHOGRAPHIC: Catalogs

Action Graphics Inc ....E 973 633-6500
Lincoln Park (G-5325)

PRINTING, LITHOGRAPHIC: Color

Colorsource Inc ....E 856 488-8100
Pennsauken (G-8495)
Donray Printing Inc ....E 973 515-8100
Parsippany (G-7984)
Shindo International Inc ....E 973 470-8100
Clifton (G-1722)

PRINTING, LITHOGRAPHIC: Decals

Product Identification Co Inc ....F 973 227-7770
Garfield (G-3754)
Suzie Mac Specialties Inc ....E 732 238-3500
East Brunswick (G-2191)

PRINTING, LITHOGRAPHIC: Forms & Cards, Business

Elite Graphix LLC ....F 732 274-2356
  Monmouth Junction (G-6343)
Print Factory Ltd Liability Co ....G 973 866-5230
  Clifton (G-1705)
Remco Press Inc ....G 201 751-5703
  North Bergen (G-7479)
Supplies-Supplies Inc ....F 908 272-5100
  Watchung (G-11596)
Webb-Mason Inc ....G 732 747-6585
  Tinton Falls (G-10854)

PRINTING, LITHOGRAPHIC: Forms, Business

Absolute Business Services Inc ....G 856 265-9447
  Millville (G-6273)
Crt International Inc ....F 973 887-7737
  Middlesex (G-6160)
Douglas Maybury Assoc ....G 908 879-5878
  Chester (G-1436)
Paris Corporation New Jersey ....D 609 265-9200
  Westampton (G-11914)

PRINTING, LITHOGRAPHIC: Newspapers

Redmond Bcms Inc ....D 973 664-2000
  Denville (G-2053)

PRINTING, LITHOGRAPHIC: Offset & photolithographic printing

Atlantic Prtg & Graphics LLC ....G 732 493-4222
  Ocean (G-7717)
Hometown Office Sups & Prtg Co ....G 609 298-9020
  Bordentown (G-598)
Lamb Printing Inc ....G 908 852-0837
  Hackettstown (G-4016)
Mercer C AlphaGraphics ....G 609 921-0959
  Hamilton (G-4116)

PRINTING, LITHOGRAPHIC: On Metal

AE Litho Offset Printers Inc ....D 800 235-8888
  Beverly (G-456)
AE Litho Offset Printers Inc ....G 609 239-0700
  Beverly (G-457)
Aus Inc ....G 856 234-9200
  Mount Laurel (G-6779)
C Harry Marean Printing ....G 609 965-4708
  Egg Harbor City (G-2659)
Command Web Offset Company Inc .....C 201 863-8100
  Secaucus (G-9873)
Nassau Communications Inc ....F 609 208-9099
  Lawrence Township (G-5245)

PRINTING, LITHOGRAPHIC: Promotional

Corporate Mailings Inc ....C 973 439-1168
  West Caldwell (G-11772)
Corporate Mailings Inc ....D 973 808-0009
  Whippany (G-12017)
Datascan Graphics Inc ....E 973 543-4803
  Morristown (G-6704)
J D M Associates Inc ....G 973 773-8699
  Lodi (G-5590)
Killian Graphics ....G 973 635-5844
  Chatham (G-1332)

PRINTING, LITHOGRAPHIC: Publications

Hansen Lithography Ltd ....G 732 270-1188
  Toms River (G-10882)
Recorder Publishing Co ....E 908 647-1180
  Stirling (G-10605)

PRINTING, LITHOGRAPHIC: Transfers, Decalcomania Or Dry

Superior Trademark Inc ....G 201 652-1900
  Waldwick (G-11454)

PRINTING, LITHOGRAPHIC: Wrappers

Printwrap Corporation ....F 973 239-1144
  Cedar Grove (G-1297)

PRINTING, LITHOGRAPHIC: Wrappers & Seals

Tape Graphics ....G 201 393-9500
  Hasbrouck Heights (G-4199)

PRINTING: Books

Command Web Offset Company Inc .....C 201 863-8100
  Secaucus (G-9873)
Phoenix Color Corp ....E 800 632-4111
  Rockaway (G-9595)

PRINTING: Books

All In Color Inc ....G 973 626-0987
  Paterson (G-8204)
AM Best Company Inc ....A 908 439-2200
  Oldwick (G-7803)
Athletic Organizational Aids ....E 201 652-1485
  Midland Park (G-6221)
Binding Products Inc ....E 212 947-1192
  Jersey City (G-4719)
Extreme Digital Graphics Inc ....F 973 227-5599
  Fairfield (G-3192)
Forbes Media LLC ....D 212 620-2200
  Jersey City (G-4754)
G & H Soho Inc ....F 201 216-9400
  Elmwood Park (G-2820)
Howard Press Inc ....D 908 245-4400
  Roselle (G-9673)
Musings Press Ltd Liability Co ....F 347 210-8820
  Union City (G-11259)
NJ Copy Center LLC ....G 973 788-1600
  Fairfield (G-3272)
Oceanic Graphic Intl Inc ....F 201 883-1816
  Hackensack (G-3956)
Rush Index Tabs Inc ....E 201 531-1555
  East Rutherford (G-2324)
School Publications Co Inc ....E 732 988-1100
  Neptune (G-6929)
Service Data Corp Inc ....G 908 522-0020
  Summit (G-10656)
Starnet Printing Inc ....G 201 760-2600
  Mahwah (G-5815)
Surviving Life Corp ....G 973 543-3370
  Mendham (G-6092)
Wellspring Info Inc ....G 800 268-3682
  Montclair (G-6439)
Wheal-Grace Corp ....E 973 450-8100
  Belleville (G-327)

PRINTING: Broadwoven Fabrics. Cotton

Peter L Demaree ....G 732 531-2133
  Ocean (G-7735)
Premier Printing Solutions LLC ....G 732 525-0740
  Sayreville (G-9836)

PRINTING: Checkbooks

Deluxe Corporation ....C 973 334-8000
  Mountain Lakes (G-6857)

PRINTING: Commercial, NEC

4 Over Inc ....F 201 440-1656
  Moonachie (G-6498)
Action Graphics Inc ....G 856 783-1825
  Lindenwold (G-5460)
Ahern Blueprinting Inc ....F 732 223-1476
  Manasquan (G-5865)
Alliance Design Inc ....F 973 904-9450
  Totowa (G-10927)
AlphaGraphics Printshops of Th ....G 973 984-0066
  Morristown (G-6686)
Altantic Printing and Design ....F 732 557-9600
  Toms River (G-10862)
American Banknote Corporation ....G 203 941-4090
  Fort Lee (G-3543)
American Graphic Systems Inc ....G 201 796-0666
  Fair Lawn (G-3076)
Andy Graphics Service Bureau ....G 201 866-9407
  Union City (G-11241)
Applied Image Inc ....E 732 410-2444
  Freehold (G-3638)
Artistic Typography Corp ....G 845 783-1990
  Englewood (G-2872)
ASAP Postal Printing ....G 609 597-7421
  Manahawkin (G-5828)
Ayr Composition Inc ....G 908 241-8118
  Roselle Park (G-9688)

B & H Printers Inc ....G 908 688-6990
  Hackettstown (G-3999)
B P Graphics Inc ....E 732 942-2315
  Lakewood (G-5080)
Belle Printing Group LLC ....G 856 235-5151
  Mount Laurel (G-6782)
Bistis Press Printing Co ....G 973 373-8033
  Irvington (G-4579)
C and R Printing Corporation ....F 201 528-8912
  Carlstadt (G-1135)
C2 Imaging LLC ....E 646 557-6300
  Jersey City (G-4722)
Circa Promotions Inc ....G 732 264-1200
  Hazlet (G-4273)
Color Logic Inc ....E 973 515-0099
  Parsippany (G-7974)
Colortec Printing and Mailing ....G 856 767-0108
  West Berlin (G-11709)
Commerce Financial Prtrs Corp ....E 908 241-9880
  Roselle (G-9667)
Coventry of New Jersey Inc ....E 856 988-5521
  Marlton (G-5968)
Creative Color Lithographers ....F 908 789-2295
  Garwood (G-3777)
Crown Roll Leaf Inc ....E 973 684-2600
  Paterson (G-8242)
Daily News LP ....F 212 210-2100
  Jersey City (G-4736)
Data Communique Intl Inc ....E 201 508-6000
  Ridgefield Park (G-9403)
Delgen Press Inc ....G 973 472-2266
  Clifton (G-1598)
Digital Xpress LLC ....G 973 627-2609
  Denville (G-2037)
Diligaf Enterprises Inc ....E 201 684-0900
  Mahwah (G-5765)
Display Impressions ....F 856 488-1777
  Pennsauken (G-8505)
Dye Into Print Inc ....D 973 772-8019
  Clifton (G-1606)
Elite Printing Service ....G 973 729-0366
  Sparta (G-10498)
Enterprise Press Inc ....E 212 741-2111
  Englewood (G-2893)
Fedex Office & Print Svcs Inc ....G 201 672-0508
  East Rutherford (G-2295)
Fedex Office & Print Svcs Inc ....E 732 636-3580
  Iselin (G-4627)
Fischlers Dawnpoint ....G 856 428-2092
  Cherry Hill (G-1365)
Fit Graphix ....G 201 488-4670
  Hackensack (G-3912)
Five Macs Inc ....E 856 596-3150
  Marlton (G-5975)
Flexi Printing Plate Co Inc ....F 201 939-3600
  Moonachie (G-6517)
Fordham Inc ....E 973 575-7840
  Fairfield (G-3199)
Forms & Flyers of New Jersey ....G 856 629-0718
  Williamstown (G-12087)
Foto Fantasy ....G 732 548-8446
  Edison (G-2521)
Frank J Zechman ....G 732 495-0077
  Belford (G-287)
Fu WEI Inc ....G 732 937-8388
  East Brunswick (G-2156)
Gator Communications Group LLC ......E 973 233-6700
  Fairfield (G-3208)
Global Graphics Intergration ....F 973 334-9653
  Towaco (G-10996)
Graphic Arts Printing ....G 201 343-6554
  Hawthorne (G-4237)
H & H Graphic Printing Inc ....G 201 369-9700
  Carlstadt (G-1166)
H & L Printing Co ....G 201 288-0877
  Hasbrouck Heights (G-4194)
Hayes Mindish Inc ....G 609 641-9880
  Pleasantville (G-8909)
Howard Press Inc ....D 908 245-4400
  Roselle (G-9673)
Hummel Distributing Corp ....E 908 688-5300
  Union (G-11193)
Hummel Printing Inc ....E 908 688-5300
  Union (G-11194)
Ics Corporation ....C 215 427-3355
  West Deptford (G-11829)
Illinois Tool Works Inc ....E 609 395-5600
  Cranbury (G-1837)
Important Papers Inc ....G 856 751-4544
  Cherry Hill (G-1379)

PRODUCT

Ink On Paper Communications..........G...... 732 758-6280
Shrewsbury (G-10001)
Instant Printing of Dover Inc ....G...... 973 366-6855
Dover (G-2093)
Inter City Press Inc ....E...... 908 236-9911
Lebanon (G-5290)
J F I Printing ....G...... 973 759-3444
Belleville (G-304)
J&E Business Services LLC ....G...... 973 984-8444
Morris Plains (G-6672)
James Howard Inc ....F...... 973 928-1560
Clifton (G-1651)
Jefferson Printing Serivce ....F...... 973 491-0019
Newark (G-7206)
Jimcam Publishing Inc ....G...... 201 843-5700
Maywood (G-6055)
Jrm Industries Inc ....D...... 973 779-9340
Passaic (G-8152)
K M Media Group LLC ....D...... 973 330-3000
Clifton (G-1654)
Kdf Reprographics Inc ....E...... 201 784-9991
South Hackensack (G-10274)
Keefe Printing Inc ....G...... 732 295-2099
Point Pleasant Beach (G-8921)
Kraftape Printers Inc ....G...... 973 824-3005
Newark (G-7214)
Lacoa Inc ....G...... 973 754-1000
Elmwood Park (G-2831)
Laserwave Graphics Inc ....F...... 732 745-7764
New Brunswick (G-6977)
Latta Graphics Inc ....G...... 201 440-4040
Carlstadt (G-1183)
Logomania Inc ....G...... 201 798-0531
Jersey City (G-4778)
Lont & Overkamp Pubg Co Inc ....E...... 973 942-2243
Clifton (G-1664)
Lornan Litho Inc ....F...... 609 818-1198
Pennington (G-8456)
M & M Printing Corp ....G...... 201 288-7787
Hasbrouck Heights (G-4196)
Main Street Graphics Inc ....G...... 856 755-3523
Maple Shade (G-5905)
Mariano Press LLC ....F...... 732 247-3659
Somerset (G-10129)
Mega Media Concepts Ltd Lblty ....G...... 973 919-5661
Sparta (G-10511)
Menu Express......................................F...... 856 216-7777
Pennsauken (G-8550)
Mercer C AlphaGraphics ....G...... 609 921-0959
Hamilton (G-4116)
Merrill Corporation............................D...... 973 643-4403
Newark (G-7240)
Merrill Corporation............................D...... 908 810-3740
Union (G-11207)
Michael Graphics Inc ....E...... 732 846-8680
Branchburg (G-680)
Mike Dolly Screen Printing ....F...... 732 294-8979
Freehold (G-3670)
Mimeocom Inc ....F...... 973 286-2901
Newark (G-7242)
National Color Graphics ....F...... 856 435-6800
Sicklerville (G-10021)
National Plastic Printing....................E...... 973 785-1460
Totowa (G-10957)
National Reprographics Inc ....E...... 609 896-4100
Lawrenceville (G-5265)
New Jersey Label LLC ....F...... 201 880-5102
South Hackensack (G-10283)
New Jersey Tech Group LLC ....G...... 609 301-6405
Lumberton (G-5661)
North America Printing........................G...... 973 726-7713
Sparta (G-10515)
North Eastern Business Forms ....G...... 609 392-1161
Trenton (G-11091)
Ocsidot Inc ....F...... 908 789-3300
Garwood (G-3782)
OShea Services Inc ....G...... 201 343-8668
Hackensack (G-3957)
Outfront Media LLC ....D...... 973 575-6900
Fairfield (G-3278)
Page Stamp LLC ....G...... 732 390-1700
Monroe Township (G-6389)
Palm Press Inc ....G...... 201 767-6504
Northvale (G-7600)
Peacock Products Inc ....F...... 201 385-5585
Bergenfield (G-392)
Penn Jersey Press Inc ....G...... 856 627-2200
Gibbsboro (G-3789)
Penta Digital Incorporated ....G...... 201 839-5392
Jersey City (G-4799)

Perco Inc ....F...... 908 464-3000
Berkeley Heights (G-420)
Phoenix Alliance Group LLC ....F...... 732 495-4800
Port Monmouth (G-8973)
Premier Press Inc ....F...... 856 665-0722
Pennsauken (G-8564)
Premium Color Group LLC ....G...... 973 472-7007
Carlstadt (G-1208)
Press Room Inc....................................F...... 609 689-3817
Trenton (G-11104)
Pressto Graphics ....F...... 732 286-9300
Toms River (G-10903)
Princeton Corp Graphics Inc ....D...... 732 545-6163
New Brunswick (G-6995)
Print Mail Communications LLC.........E...... 856 488-0345
Pennsauken (G-8566)
Print Media LLC ....G...... 973 467-0007
Springfield (G-10572)
Print Solutions LLC ....F...... 201 567-9622
Englewood (G-2924)
Printing & Signs Express Inc ....G...... 201 368-1255
Mahwah (G-5803)
Printing Craftsman Inc ....F...... 201 943-0276
Fairview (G-3370)
Ramsey Graphics and Printing............G...... 201 300-2912
Elmwood Park (G-2846)
Redmond Bcms Inc ....D...... 973 664-2000
Denville (G-2053)
Roan Printing Inc ....F...... 908 526-5990
Somerville (G-10226)
Royalty Press Inc ....G...... 856 663-2288
Westville (G-11948)
Royer Group Inc ....E...... 856 324-0171
Pennsauken (G-8575)
S & M Press Inc ....G...... 973 546-6111
Garfield (G-3760)
S J T Imaging Inc ....D...... 201 262-7744
Oradell (G-7813)
S V O Inc ....G...... 973 983-8380
Succasunna (G-10629)
Samuel Elliott Inc ....E...... 856 773-6000
Cinnaminson (G-1486)
Screen-Trans Development Corp ....G...... 201 933-7800
Moonachie (G-6542)
Semels Embroidery Inc ....G...... 973 473-6868
Clifton (G-1719)
Sjshore Marketing Ltd Lblty Co ....F...... 609 390-1400
Marmora (G-6006)
Skylands Press ....G...... 973 383-5006
Newton (G-7404)
T G Type-O-Graphics Inc ....G...... 973 253-3333
Fair Lawn (G-3118)
Tbc Color Imaging Inc ....G...... 973 470-8100
Clifton (G-1736)
Tekno Inc ....G...... 973 423-2004
Hawthorne (G-4260)
Terminal Printing Co ....G...... 201 659-5924
Belleville (G-319)
Timeline Promotions Inc ....G...... 973 226-1512
West Caldwell (G-11806)
Tko Visual Communications ....F...... 610 770-7700
Newark (G-7345)
Toppan Printing Co Amer Inc..............C...... 732 469-8400
Somerset (G-10188)
Toppan Vintage Inc ....E...... 201 226-9220
Saddle Brook (G-9797)
Travel Weekly ....G...... 201 902-1931
Secaucus (G-9936)
Tremont Printing Co ....G...... 973 227-0742
Fairfield (G-3330)
Trentypo Inc. ....F...... 609 883-5971
Ewing (G-3062)
Trico Web LLC ....G...... 201 438-3860
Carlstadt (G-1234)
Typecom LLC ....G...... 201 969-1901
Fort Lee (G-3586)
Typeline...F...... 201 251-2201
Wyckoff (G-12267)
Unimac Graphics LLC ....C...... 201 372-1000
Carlstadt (G-1236)
United Label Corp ....F...... 973 589-6500
Newark (G-7354)
Vertis Inc ....D...... 215 781-1668
Mount Holly (G-6777)
Wall Street Group Inc ....D...... 201 333-4784
South Plainfield (G-10453)
Whitehouse Prtg & Labeling LLC ....G...... 973 521-7648
Fairfield (G-3352)
Wilmington Trust Sp Services ....G...... 609 272-7000
Pleasantville (G-8918)

Winsome Digital Inc............................F...... 609 645-2211
Egg Harbor Township (G-2700)
Z Fab LLC ....G...... 973 248-0686
Wayne (G-11694)

PRINTING: Engraving & Plate

Caporale Engraving Co Inc ....E...... 201 569-8711
Englewood Cliffs (G-2951)
Pan Graphics Inc.................................D...... 973 478-2100
Garfield (G-3745)

PRINTING: Fabric, Narrow

Asha44 LLC ....E...... 201 306-3600
Fairfield (G-3140)

PRINTING: Flexographic

CCL Label (delaware) Inc ....C...... 609 259-1055
Trenton (G-11037)
Cheringal Associates Inc ....D...... 201 784-8721
Norwood (G-7618)
Flexo-Craft Prints Inc ....E...... 973 482-7200
Harrison (G-4183)
Horizon Label LLC ....F...... 856 767-0777
West Berlin (G-11725)
Trend Printing/Intl Label ....E...... 201 941-6611
Ridgefield (G-9389)

PRINTING: Gravure, Cards, Exc Greeting

Five Macs Inc......................................E...... 856 596-3150
Marlton (G-5975)

PRINTING: Gravure, Catalogs, No Publishing On-Site

R R Donnelley & Sons Company ....C...... 973 439-8321
West Caldwell (G-11801)

PRINTING: Gravure, Color

Link Color NA Inc ....G...... 201 438-8222
East Rutherford (G-2303)

PRINTING: Gravure, Forms, Business

All-State International Inc...................C...... 908 272-0800
Cranford (G-1895)
East Coast Distributors Inc ....F...... 732 223-5995
Eatontown (G-2391)

PRINTING: Gravure, Labels

Challenge Printing Co Inc ....C...... 973 471-4700
Clifton (G-1582)
Label Master Inc ....G...... 973 546-3110
Lodi (G-5591)
Lps Industries Inc ....C...... 201 438-3515
Moonachie (G-6529)
Metro Tag & Label Inc ....G...... 201 845-4747
West Orange (G-11900)
Tadbik NJ Inc ....E...... 973 882-9595
Fairfield (G-3319)

PRINTING: Gravure, Magazines, No Publishing On-Site

Food Mfg ....C...... 973 920-7000
Rockaway (G-9569)

PRINTING: Gravure, Posters

Winemiller Press Inc ....G...... 732 223-0100
Manasquan (G-5884)

PRINTING: Gravure, Rotogravure

American Business Paper Inc ....F...... 732 363-5788
Lakewood (G-5069)
Arna Marketing Inc ....E...... 908 231-1100
Branchburg (G-639)
Constant Services Inc ....E...... 973 227-2990
Fairfield (G-3165)
Lrp and P Graphics ....F...... 856 424-0158
Cherry Hill (G-1391)
New Jersey Department Treasury ....G...... 609 292-5133
Trenton (G-11085)
Pad and Publ Assembly Corp ....E...... 856 424-0158
Cherry Hill (G-1409)
Taylor Communications Inc ....E...... 732 561-8210
Monroe Township (G-6397)

Taylor Communications Inc ....F 973 467-8259
 Springfield *(G-10579)*

Wheal-Grace Corp. ....E 973 450-8100
 Belleville *(G-327)*

PRINTING: Gravure, Stationery & Invitation

Youre So Invited LLC ....G 201 664-8600
 Westwood *(G-11976)*

PRINTING: Laser

American Bank Note Holographic ....D 609 208-0591
 Robbinsville *(G-9510)*

B&M Technologies Inc ....F 201 291-8505
 Saddle Brook *(G-9754)*

Laser Xpressions Inc ....F 732 303-9530
 Freehold *(G-3665)*

Printology ....G 201 345-4632
 Midland Park *(G-6238)*

United Forms Finishing Corp ....F 908 687-0494
 Hillside *(G-4448)*

PRINTING: Letterpress

Allegro Printing Corporation ....G 609 641-7060
 Galloway *(G-3708)*

B and W Printing Company Inc ....G 908 241-3060
 Kenilworth *(G-4941)*

Bassano Prtrs & Lithographers ....E 973 423-1400
 Hawthorne *(G-4220)*

Burdol Inc ....G 856 453-0336
 Bridgeton *(G-781)*

C Harry Marean Printing ....G 609 965-4708
 Egg Harbor City *(G-2659)*

Dewechter Inc ....G 856 845-0225
 Woodbury *(G-12159)*

Downtown Printing Center Inc ....F 732 246-7990
 New Brunswick *(G-6955)*

Ferrante Press Inc ....G 609 239-4257
 Verona *(G-11306)*

Good Impressions Inc ....G 856 461-3232
 Riverside *(G-9498)*

Howes Standard Publishing Co ....E 856 691-2000
 Vineland *(G-11371)*

Keskes Printing LLC ....G 856 767-4733
 Berlin *(G-437)*

Office Needs Inc ....G 732 381-7770
 Clark *(G-1511)*

Pharmaceutic Litho Label Inc ....C 336 785-4000
 Cranford *(G-1923)*

Red Letter Press Inc ....G 609 597-5257
 Upper Saddle River *(G-11284)*

Riegel Cmmunications Group Inc ....F 609 771-0555
 Ewing *(G-3051)*

Rocco Press Advg Typography ....F 973 790-4000
 Paterson *(G-8371)*

Santangelo Printing Co Inc ....F 973 779-5880
 Lodi *(G-5599)*

Sherman Printing Co Inc ....G 973 345-2493
 Clifton *(G-1721)*

Stuyvesant Press Inc ....F 973 399-3880
 Irvington *(G-4605)*

Vernw Printing Company ....G 973 751-6462
 Belleville *(G-324)*

Wilcox Press ....G 973 827-7474
 Hamburg *(G-4100)*

PRINTING: Lithographic

A&E Promotions LLC ....G 732 382-2300
 Holmdel *(G-4506)*

AA Graphics Inc ....G 201 398-0710
 Saddle Brook *(G-9748)*

ABC Printing ....G 973 664-1160
 Rockaway *(G-9540)*

Aboudi Printing LLC ....G 732 542-2929
 Eatontown *(G-2377)*

Accent Press Inc ....G 973 785-3127
 Totowa *(G-10925)*

Accurate Plastic Printers LLC ....E 973 591-0180
 Clifton *(G-1555)*

Action Copy Centers Inc ....G 973 744-5520
 Montclair *(G-6404)*

Advertisers Service Group Inc ....F 201 440-5577
 Ridgefield Park *(G-9395)*

AGFA Corporation ....E 201 288-4101
 Carlstadt *(G-1122)*

Alan Duffy Printing ....G 856 768-1046
 Atco *(G-88)*

Allegro Printing Corporation ....G 609 641-7060
 Galloway *(G-3708)*

Ancraft Press Corp ....F 201 792-9200
 Jersey City *(G-4705)*

Arde ....G 201 440-1453
 Norwood *(G-7615)*

Arglen Industries Inc ....F 732 888-8100
 Hazlet *(G-4269)*

Arna Marketing Group Inc ....D 908 625-7395
 Branchburg *(G-638)*

Asbury Park Press Inc ....A 732 922-6000
 Neptune *(G-6900)*

Asha44 LLC ....E 201 306-3600
 Fairfield *(G-3140)*

Ayr Graphics & Printing Inc ....G 908 241-8118
 Roselle Park *(G-9689)*

Bannon Group Ltd ....G 201 451-6500
 Jersey City *(G-4714)*

Bar Lan Inc ....G 856 596-2330
 Brigantine *(G-917)*

Better Image Graphics Inc ....G 856 262-0735
 Williamstown *(G-12080)*

Big Red Pin LLC ....G 732 993-9765
 Edison *(G-2473)*

Bittner Industries Inc ....G 856 817-8400
 Cherry Hill *(G-1351)*

Bruce McCoy Sr ....G 609 217-6153
 Pine Hill *(G-8721)*

Business Cards Tomorrow ....E 201 236-0088
 Upper Saddle River *(G-11275)*

Business Cards Tomorrow Inc ....F 609 965-0808
 Egg Harbor City *(G-2658)*

Catholic Star Herald ....G 856 583-6142
 Camden *(G-1051)*

Century Printing Corp ....G 732 981-0544
 Piscataway *(G-8746)*

CIC Letter Service Inc ....D 201 896-1900
 Carlstadt *(G-1140)*

Clark Printing Inc ....E 201 845-4888
 Fairfield *(G-3161)*

Classic Graphic Inc ....G 856 753-0055
 Berlin *(G-431)*

Classic Impressions ....G 908 689-3137
 Great Meadows *(G-3848)*

Coast Star ....E 732 223-0076
 Manasquan *(G-5869)*

Corbi Printing Co Inc ....G 856 547-2444
 Audubon *(G-116)*

Cornerstone Prints Imaging LLC ....G 908 782-7966
 Flemington *(G-3431)*

Coventry of New Jersey Inc ....E 856 988-5521
 Marlton *(G-5968)*

D & S Ventures Inc ....G 732 758-0095
 Red Bank *(G-9324)*

Data Communique Intl Inc ....E 201 508-6000
 Ridgefield Park *(G-9403)*

Dato Company Inc ....G 732 225-2272
 Cranbury *(G-1828)*

Delgen Press Inc ....G 973 472-2266
 Clifton *(G-1598)*

Digital Print Solutions Inc ....F 973 263-1890
 Parsippany *(G-7982)*

Digital Productions Inc ....G 856 224-1111
 Swedesboro *(G-10692)*

Digital Xpress LLC ....G 973 627-2609
 Denville *(G-2037)*

Earth Color New York Inc ....E 973 884-1300
 Parsippany *(G-7992)*

Earthcolor Inc ....C 973 884-1300
 Parsippany *(G-7994)*

East Coast Media LLC ....E 908 575-9700
 Hillsborough *(G-4329)*

Edwards Brothers Inc ....G 856 848-6900
 West Deptford *(G-11826)*

Encore Enterprises Inc ....G 201 489-5044
 South Hackensack *(G-10264)*

Express Printing Services Inc ....G 973 585-7355
 Fairfield *(G-3191)*

Fedex Corporation ....G 201 525-5070
 River Edge *(G-9465)*

Franbeth Inc ....G 856 488-1480
 Pennsauken *(G-8512)*

Fulfillment Printing and Mail ....G 609 953-9500
 Medford Lakes *(G-6085)*

Full Service Mailers Inc ....F 973 478-8813
 Hackensack *(G-3919)*

Garrison Printing Company Inc ....E 856 488-1900
 Pennsauken *(G-8515)*

Genua & Mulligan Printing ....G 973 894-1500
 Clifton *(G-1626)*

Gerardi Press Inc ....G 973 627-2600
 Denville *(G-2041)*

Gms Litho Corp ....G 973 575-9400
 Fairfield *(G-3211)*

Graph Tech Sales & Service ....F 201 218-1749
 Fairfield *(G-3213)*

Graphic Management ....E 908 654-8400
 Kearny *(G-4879)*

Graytor Printing Company Inc ....E 201 933-0100
 Lyndhurst *(G-5684)*

Great Eastern Color Lith ....G 201 843-5656
 Paramus *(G-7874)*

Great Northern Commercial Svcs ....G 908 475-8855
 Belvidere *(G-373)*

Gross Printing Associates Inc ....F 718 832-1110
 Clifton *(G-1631)*

Hammer Press Printers Inc ....D 973 334-4500
 Parsippany *(G-8026)*

Harvard Printing Group ....G 973 672-0800
 Fairfield *(G-3216)*

Herald News ....G 973 569-7000
 Woodland Park *(G-12221)*

Highroad Press LLC ....E 201 708-6900
 Moonachie *(G-6521)*

Holographic Finishing Inc ....F 201 941-4651
 Ridgefield *(G-9365)*

I Print Nb ....G 201 662-1133
 North Bergen *(G-7458)*

I T C Printing Promotion ....G 908 918-1122
 Summit *(G-10648)*

Imagine Screen Prtg & Prod LLC ....C 732 329-2009
 Dayton *(G-1969)*

Inserts East Incorporated ....C 856 663-8181
 Pennsauken *(G-8528)*

Instant Imprints ....G 973 252-9500
 Flanders *(G-3411)*

J B Offset Printing Corp ....G 201 264-4400
 Norwood *(G-7626)*

Jasco Specialties and Forms ....G 856 627-5511
 Tabernacle *(G-10738)*

Jem Printing Inc ....G 908 782-9986
 Flemington *(G-3450)*

Johnston Letter Co Inc ....G 973 482-7535
 Flanders *(G-3412)*

Jory Engravers Inc ....G 201 939-1546
 Rutherford *(G-9736)*

Jvs Copy Services Inc ....F 856 415-9090
 Sewell *(G-9961)*

Knock Out Graphics Inc ....F 732 774-3331
 Asbury Park *(G-79)*

L A S Printing Co ....G 201 991-5362
 Jersey City *(G-4775)*

L L Teach Inc ....G 732 223-1605
 Brielle *(G-912)*

Label Solutions Inc ....G 201 599-0909
 Rochelle Park *(G-9531)*

Laser Dim Graphics & Prtg Inc ....F 732 821-9000
 Colts Neck *(G-1789)*

Latta Graphics Inc ....E 201 440-4040
 Carlstadt *(G-1183)*

Laureate Press ....G 609 646-1545
 Egg Harbor City *(G-2666)*

Lexington Graphics Corp ....G 973 345-2493
 Clifton *(G-1661)*

Lithos Estiatorio Ltd Lblty Co ....G 973 758-1111
 Livingston *(G-5539)*

Lmp Printing Corp ....G 973 428-1987
 Clifton *(G-1663)*

Longrun Press Inc ....F 856 719-9202
 West Berlin *(G-11731)*

Mark Alan Printing & Graphics ....G 732 981-9011
 Piscataway *(G-8790)*

Marks Management Systems Inc ....G 856 866-0588
 Maple Shade *(G-5906)*

Merrill Corporation ....D 908 810-3740
 Union *(G-11207)*

Metro Prtg & Promotions LLC ....F 973 316-1600
 Boonton *(G-578)*

Metro Seliger Industries Inc ....C 201 438-4530
 Carlstadt *(G-1189)*

Mint Printing LLC ....G 973 546-2060
 Lodi *(G-5596)*

Minuteman Press ....G 973 403-0146
 Caldwell *(G-1031)*

Minuteman Press ....G 732 536-8788
 Manalapan *(G-5854)*

More Copy Printing Service ....G 201 327-1106
 Upper Saddle River *(G-11281)*

Multi Packaging Solutions Inc ....G 908 757-6000
 South Plainfield *(G-10411)*

Nema Associates Inc ....F 973 274-0052
 Linden *(G-5418)*

New Horizon Graphics Inc.....G.......609 584-1301
Trenton *(G-11083)*

New Jersey Label LLC.....F.......201 880-5102
South Hackensack *(G-10283)*

Nextwave Web LLC.....F.......973 742-4339
Paterson *(G-8351)*

Nu-Plan Business Systems Inc.....G.......732 231-6944
Clark *(G-1510)*

Old Hights Print Shop Inc.....G.......609 443-4700
Jackson *(G-4674)*

On Demand Print Group.....G.......201 636-2270
Lyndhurst *(G-5698)*

One Two Three Inc.....F.......856 251-1238
Woodbury *(G-12166)*

OSullivan Communications Corp.....E.......973 227-5112
West Caldwell *(G-11795)*

Pace Press Incorporated.....D.......201 935-7711
Moonachie *(G-6534)*

Pad and Publ Assembly Corp.....E.......856 424-0158
Cherry Hill *(G-1409)*

Parth Enterprises Inc.....G.......732 404-0665
Iselin *(G-4640)*

PDM Litho Inc.....E.......718 301-1740
Clifton *(G-1693)*

Peacock Communications Inc.....G.......973 763-3311
Maplewood *(G-5924)*

Perfect Printing Inc.....E.......856 787-1877
Moorestown *(G-6611)*

Pharmaceutic Litho Label Inc.....C.......336 785-4000
Cranford *(G-1923)*

Philip Holzer and Assoc LLC.....E.......212 691-9500
Carlstadt *(G-1202)*

Pica Printings Inc.....G.......973 540-0420
Morristown *(G-6735)*

Pinto Printing.....G.......856 232-2550
Blackwood *(G-489)*

Precision Printing Group Inc.....E.......856 753-0900
Mount Laurel *(G-6831)*

Pressto Graphics.....F.......732 286-9300
Toms River *(G-10903)*

Print Mail Communications LLC.....E.......856 488-0345
Pennsauken *(G-8566)*

Print Peel.....E.......201 507-0080
Carlstadt *(G-1209)*

Prisco Digital Ltd Lblty Co.....F.......973 589-7800
Newark *(G-7277)*

Pro Screen Printing Inc.....G.......201 246-7600
Kearny *(G-4910)*

Prohaska & Co Inc.....G.......732 238-3420
East Brunswick *(G-2176)*

Pronto Printing & Copying Ctr.....G.......201 426-0009
Ramsey *(G-9251)*

Q P 195 Inc.....F.......732 531-8860
Ocean *(G-7738)*

Quality Print Solutions.....G.......888 679-7237
Ridgewood *(G-9429)*

Regal Litho Prtrs Ltd Lblty Co.....G.......732 901-1500
Lakewood *(G-5177)*

Reliable Envelope and Graphics.....E.......201 794-7756
Elmwood Park *(G-2848)*

Rocco Press Advg Typography.....F.......973 790-4000
Paterson *(G-8371)*

Rocket Ship & Print Inc.....G.......973 275-1144
South Orange *(G-10314)*

Roy D Smith Inc.....G.......201 384-4163
Bergenfield *(G-393)*

Roy Press Inc.....G.......732 922-9460
Oceanport *(G-7767)*

Royer Group Inc.....E.......856 324-0171
Pennsauken *(G-8575)*

Rush Index Tabs Inc.....E.......201 531-1555
East Rutherford *(G-2324)*

S & M Press Inc.....F.......973 546-6111
Garfield *(G-3760)*

SAM Graphics Inc.....E.......732 431-0440
Marlboro *(G-5956)*

Sample Media Inc.....E.......609 399-5411
Ocean City *(G-7757)*

Sandoval Graphics & Printing.....G.......856 435-7320
Somerdale *(G-10043)*

Sapphire Envelope & Graphics.....E.......856 782-2227
Magnolia *(G-5742)*

School Publications Co Inc.....E.......732 988-1100
Neptune *(G-6929)*

Screen Printing & Embroidery.....G.......732 256-9610
Wall Township *(G-11507)*

Service Data Corp Inc.....G.......908 522-0020
Summit *(G-10656)*

Sheroy Printing Inc.....F.......973 242-4040
Newark *(G-7312)*

Shree Ji Printing Corporation.....E.......201 842-9500
Carlstadt *(G-1217)*

Signs of Security Inc.....E.......973 340-8404
Garfield *(G-3762)*

South Amboy Designer T Shirt L.....G.......732 456-2594
South Amboy *(G-10245)*

Staines Inc.....F.......856 784-2718
Somerdale *(G-10044)*

Steven Madola.....G.......609 989-8022
Trenton *(G-11117)*

Strategic Content Imaging.....C.......201 863-8100
Secaucus *(G-9933)*

Sunset Printing and Engrv Corp.....E.......973 537-9600
Wharton *(G-12000)*

Superfine Online Inc.....G.......212 827-0063
Roselle *(G-9684)*

Supreme Graphics and Prtg Inc.....G.......718 989-9817
Perth Amboy *(G-8632)*

Supreme Ink Corp.....F.......973 344-2922
Newark *(G-7335)*

Tandem Color Imaging Graphics.....G.......973 513-9779
Pompton Lakes *(G-8949)*

Technical Nameplate Corp.....E.......973 773-4256
Passaic *(G-8184)*

Tectubes USA Inc.....E.......856 589-1250
Vineland *(G-11408)*

Tex Print USA LLC.....E.......201 773-6531
Fair Lawn *(G-3121)*

Thermo X-Press Printing LLC.....G.......973 585-6505
East Hanover *(G-2245)*

Toppan Printing Co Amer Inc.....C.......732 469-8400
Somerset *(G-10188)*

Trade Thermographers Inc.....F.......201 489-2060
Rochelle Park *(G-9539)*

Tremont Printing Co.....G.......973 227-0742
Fairfield *(G-3330)*

Trentypo Inc.....F.......609 883-5971
Ewing *(G-3062)*

Trukmanns Inc.....E.......973 538-7718
Cedar Knolls *(G-1321)*

Typeline.....F.......201 251-2201
Wyckoff *(G-12267)*

Unity Graphics & Engraving Co.....E.......201 541-5462
Englewood *(G-2940)*

Vestal Publishing Co Inc.....G.......732 583-3232
Cliffwood *(G-1550)*

Visual Engineering Group Inc.....G.......908 479-1893
Bloomsbury *(G-546)*

W B Mason Co Inc.....D.......888 926-2766
Bellmawr *(G-354)*

W B Mason Co Inc.....E.......888 926-2766
Egg Harbor Township *(G-2699)*

W B Mason Co Inc.....E.......888 926-2766
Cranbury *(G-1890)*

W G I Corp.....F.......732 370-2900
Lakewood *(G-5203)*

Washington Stamp Exchange Inc.....F.......973 966-0001
Florham Park *(G-3523)*

Watonka Printing Inc.....G.......732 974-8878
Belmar *(G-365)*

Webb Press.....G.......609 386-0100
Burlington *(G-995)*

Wilmington Trust Sp Services.....C.......609 272-7000
Pleasantville *(G-8918)*

Zwier Corp.....G.......973 748-4009
Bloomfield *(G-539)*

PRINTING: Manmade Fiber & Silk, Broadwoven Fabric

Stefan Enterprises Inc.....E.......973 253-6005
Garfield *(G-3765)*

PRINTING: Offset

A M Graphics Inc.....G.......201 767-5320
Harrington Park *(G-4169)*

A To Z Printing & Promotion.....G.......973 916-9995
Clifton *(G-1553)*

A&R Printing Corporation.....G.......732 886-0505
Lakewood *(G-5062)*

Accucolor LLC.....G.......732 870-1999
Long Branch *(G-5620)*

Ace Lthgraphers of Morris Cnty.....F.......973 428-4911
Berkeley Heights *(G-398)*

Adams Bill Printing & Graphics.....G.......856 455-7177
Bridgeton *(G-776)*

Add Rob Litho LLC.....G.......201 556-0700
Rochelle Park *(G-9525)*

Affordable Offset Printing Inc.....G.......856 661-0722
Pennsauken *(G-8472)*

Agau Inc.....G.......732 583-4343
Matawan *(G-6012)*

Aladdin Color Inc.....G.......609 518-9858
Moorestown *(G-6556)*

Alete Printing LLC.....G.......856 468-3536
Wenonah *(G-11702)*

All American Print & Copy Ctr.....G.......732 758-6200
Red Bank *(G-9318)*

All Print Resources Group Inc.....G.......201 994-0600
Mountainside *(G-6867)*

Allied Printing-Graphics Inc.....G.......973 227-0520
Fairfield *(G-3132)*

AlphaGraphics.....G.......201 327-2200
Mahwah *(G-5746)*

AlphaGraphics.....F.......856 761-8000
Cherry Hill *(G-1343)*

AlphaGraphics Printshops of Th.....G.......973 984-0066
Morristown *(G-6686)*

American Graphic Systems Inc.....G.......201 796-0666
Fair Lawn *(G-3076)*

American Plus Printers Inc.....E.......732 528-2170
Wall *(G-11458)*

AMF Graphics Inc.....F.......201 994-1500
Moonachie *(G-6504)*

Andrew P Mc Hugh Inc.....G.......856 547-8953
Barrington *(G-171)*

Anisha Enterprises Inc.....G.......908 964-3380
Union *(G-11153)*

Anuco Inc.....F.......973 887-9465
East Hanover *(G-2200)*

B & B Press Inc.....G.......908 840-4093
Lebanon *(G-5278)*

B & R Printing Inc.....G.......609 448-3328
Trenton *(G-11024)*

B and W Printing Company Inc.....G.......908 241-3060
Kenilworth *(G-4941)*

Bab Printing Jan Service.....G.......908 272-6224
Cranford *(G-1897)*

Barrington Press Inc.....F.......201 843-6556
Paramus *(G-7857)*

Bartlett Printing & Graphic.....G.......609 386-1525
Burlington *(G-958)*

Barton & Cooney LLC.....D.......609 747-9300
Burlington *(G-959)*

Bassano Prtrs & Lithographers.....E.......973 423-1400
Hawthorne *(G-4220)*

Beacon Offset Printing LLC.....G.......201 488-4241
Hackensack *(G-3880)*

Berennial International.....G.......973 675-6266
Orange *(G-7818)*

Bergen Instant Printing Inc.....G.......201 945-7303
Ridgefield *(G-9351)*

Berry Business Procedure Co.....G.......908 272-6464
Cranford *(G-1899)*

Bills Printing Service Inc.....G.......609 888-1841
Trenton *(G-11027)*

Bind-Rite Robbinsville LLC.....D.......609 208-1917
Robbinsville *(G-9511)*

Boro Printing Inc.....G.......732 229-1899
West Long Branch *(G-11844)*

Bowmar Enterprises Inc.....G.......908 277-3000
New Providence *(G-7031)*

BP Print Group Inc.....D.......732 905-9830
Lakewood *(G-5087)*

Budget Print Center.....G.......973 743-0073
Bloomfield *(G-503)*

Burdol Inc.....G.......856 453-0336
Bridgeton *(G-781)*

Burlington Press Corporation.....F.......609 387-0030
Burlington *(G-960)*

C Jackson Associates Inc.....E.......856 761-8000
Cherry Hill *(G-1355)*

Cantone Press Inc.....E.......201 569-3435
Englewood *(G-2882)*

Capital Printing Corporation.....D.......732 560-1515
Middlesex *(G-6153)*

Carl A Venable Inc.....G.......732 985-6677
North Brunswick *(G-7510)*

Central Letter Shop Inc.....E.......973 808-9595
West Caldwell *(G-11770)*

Challenge Printing Co Inc.....C.......973 471-4700
Clifton *(G-1582)*

Cmyk Printing Inc.....F.......201 458-1300
Carlstadt *(G-1146)*

Color Coded LLC.....G.......718 482-1063
Jersey City *(G-4730)*

Columbia Press Inc.....E.......973 575-6535
Fairfield *(G-3163)*

Commerce Financial Prtrs Corp.....E.......908 241-9880
Roselle *(G-9667)*

Company	Code	Phone
Comprehensive Mktg Systems Union (G-11165)	G	908 810-9778
Conagraphics Inc Parsippany (G-7975)	G	973 331-1113
Contemprary Grphics Bndery Inc Camden (G-1055)	C	856 663-7277
Copy-Rite Printing Manahawkin (G-5830)	G	609 597-9182
Cordes Printing Inc Wyckoff (G-12248)	G	201 652-7272
Cottrell Graphics & Advg Spc Toms River (G-10873)	G	732 349-7430
County Graphics Forms MGT LLC Linden (G-5362)	E	908 474-9797
Craftmaster Printing Inc Neptune (G-6906)	G	732 775-0011
Craftsmen Photo Lithographers East Hanover (G-2211)	E	973 316-5791
Creative Color Lithographers Garwood (G-3777)	F	908 789-2295
Custom Book Bindery Inc Clifton (G-1596)	F	973 815-1400
D & I Printing Co Inc Englewood (G-2885)	F	201 871-3620
D A K Office Services Inc Trenton (G-11052)	G	609 586-8222
D L Printing Co Inc Avenel (G-129)	G	732 750-1917
Danmar Press Inc South Hackensack (G-10259)	F	201 487-4400
Darby Litho Inc Manville (G-5894)	F	908 231-8883
Dcg Printing Inc Shrewsbury (G-9996)	G	732 530-4441
Dee Jay Printing Inc Fairfield (G-3174)	G	973 227-7787
Design Factory Nj Inc Hillside (G-4404)	G	908 964-8833
Devece & Shaffer Inc Palmyra (G-7847)	G	856 829-7282
Dg3 Group America Inc Jersey City (G-4739)	G	201 793-5000
Dg3 Holdings LLC Jersey City (G-4740)	G	201 793-5000
Dg3 North America Inc Jersey City (G-4741)	B	201 793-5000
Diane Matson Inc Westampton (G-11912)	F	609 288-6833
Diligaf Enterprises Inc Mahwah (G-5765)	E	201 684-0900
Direct Prtg Impressions Inc West Caldwell (G-11773)	F	973 227-6111
Discount Digital Print LLC Jersey City (G-4744)	F	201 659-9600
Diversified Impressions Inc Irvington (G-4581)	G	973 399-9041
Divine Printing Metuchen (G-6102)	G	732 632-8800
Dohrman Printing Co Inc Carlstadt (G-1156)	G	201 933-0346
Dolce Brothers Printing Inc Maywood (G-6048)	E	201 843-0400
Dolce Printing Maywood (G-6049)	F	201 843-0400
Donnelley Financial LLC West Caldwell (G-11774)	F	973 882-7000
Dpi Copies Prtg & Graphics Inc Cherry Hill (G-1360)	F	856 874-1355
Dynamic Printing & Graphics Clifton (G-1608)	F	973 473-7177
E Nevin Miller Inc Hawthorne (G-4230)	F	201 444-5784
Earth Thebault Inc Parsippany (G-7993)	C	973 884-1300
Edison Lithog & Prtg Corp North Bergen (G-7449)	D	201 902-9191
Elbee Litho Inc East Brunswick (G-2149)	G	732 698-7738
Election Graphics Inc Verona (G-11305)	F	201 758-9966
Elmwood Press Inc Elmwood Park (G-2818)	F	201 794-6273
Esquire Business Forms Ewing (G-3016)	G	609 883-1155
Excel Color Graphics Inc Woodbury Heights (G-12177)	G	856 848-3345
Excellent Prtg & Graphics LLC Clifton (G-1616)	F	973 773-6661
Express Printing Inc Linden (G-5372)	G	908 925-6300
Falcon Graphics Inc Clark (G-1500)	G	908 232-1991
Falcon Printing & Graphics Freehold (G-3655)	G	732 462-6862
Fast Copy Printing Center Keyport (G-5017)	F	732 739-4646
Ferrett Printing Inc Woodbury (G-12161)	G	856 686-4896
FLM Graphics Corporation Fairfield (G-3196)	D	973 575-9450
Four Star Reproductions Inc Newton (G-7388)	E	862 268-8200
Franklin Graphics Inc Westwood (G-11960)	G	201 935-5900
Full House Printing Inc Hoboken (G-4470)	G	201 798-7073
G J Haerer Co Inc Glen Ridge (G-3818)	D	973 614-8090
Galvanic Prtg & Plate Co Inc Moonachie (G-6518)	E	201 939-3600
Gangi Graphics Inc Brick (G-744)	G	732 840-8680
Gannett Stllite Info Ntwrk Inc Vineland (G-11357)	C	856 691-5000
George H Buchanan Company Swedesboro (G-10698)	E	856 241-3960
Gmpc Printing Clifton (G-1629)	G	973 546-6060
Goffco Industries LLC Butler (G-1005)	G	973 492-0150
Good Impressions Inc Riverside (G-9498)	G	856 461-3232
Good Impressions Inc Washington (G-11581)	F	908 689-3071
Grandview Printing Co Inc Totowa (G-10950)	F	973 890-0006
Graphic Action Inc Phillipsburg (G-8650)	G	908 213-0055
Graphic Impressions Inc Hackensack (G-3921)	F	201 487-8788
Graphic Impressions Prtg Co Blackwood (G-480)	G	856 728-2266
Graphicolor Corporation Vineland (G-11364)	E	856 691-2507
Graphics Depot Inc Randolph (G-9281)	F	973 927-8200
Green Horse Media LLC Bellmawr (G-341)	C	856 933-0222
Gregory Press Inc Kenilworth (G-4960)	F	908 686-6473
Gross Bros Printing Co Inc Union City (G-11246)	E	201 865-4606
H C Graphics Screenprinting Paterson (G-8286)	G	973 247-0544
Hallco Inc Wildwood (G-12072)	G	609 729-0161
Happle Printing Dorothy (G-2073)	G	609 476-0100
Hatteras Press Inc Tinton Falls (G-10838)	B	732 935-9800
Hawk Graphics Inc Randolph (G-9283)	E	973 895-5569
Hermitage Press of New Jersey Ewing (G-3022)	D	609 882-3600
Howard Press Inc Roselle (G-9673)	G	908 245-4400
Howes Standard Publishing Co Vineland (G-11371)	E	856 691-2000
Hub Print & Copy Center LLC Fort Lee (G-3558)	G	201 585-7887
Image Makers Instant Printing Wayne (G-11649)	G	973 633-1771
Impact Printing Little Ferry (G-5508)	G	862 225-9167
Impressions Unlimited Prtg LLC Sewell (G-9957)	G	856 256-0200
Ink Well Printers LLC Kenilworth (G-4963)	G	908 272-8090
Instant Printing of Dover Inc Dover (G-2093)	G	973 366-6855
JC Printing & Advertising Inc Paterson (G-8300)	G	973 881-8612
Jersey Printing Associates Inc Atlantic Highlands (G-113)	E	732 872-9654
Jli Marketing & Printing Corp Cranbury (G-1845)	F	732 828-8877
Jmc Design & Graphics Inc Fairfield (G-3236)	G	973 276-9033
Jmp Press Inc Ho Ho Kus (G-4454)	G	201 444-0236
John S Swift Company Inc Teterboro (G-10801)	G	201 935-2002
John S Swift Print of NJ Inc Teterboro (G-10802)	G	201 678-3232
Jon-Da Printing Co Inc Jersey City (G-4769)	F	201 653-6200
Joseph Burns Inc Bound Brook (G-619)	G	732 356-8355
K R B Printing For Business Cherry Hill (G-1385)	F	856 751-5200
Kay Printing & Envelope Co Inc Clifton (G-1655)	G	973 330-3000
Keskes Printing LLC Berlin (G-437)	G	856 767-4733
Keystone Printing Inc Dumont (G-2119)	G	201 387-7252
Kirms Printing Co Inc Neptune (G-6920)	E	732 774-8000
Kufall Printing Toms River (G-10892)	G	732 505-9847
Lawn Medic Inc Westville (G-11945)	G	856 742-1111
LCI Graphics Inc Sayreville (G-9827)	F	973 893-2913
Lettie Press Inc Park Ridge (G-7924)	G	201 391-6388
Lewis Scheller Printing Corp Somerset (G-10124)	G	732 843-5050
Liberty Envelope Inc Paterson (G-8320)	F	973 546-5600
Lightning Press Inc Totowa (G-10954)	F	973 890-4422
Lont & Overkamp Pubg Co Inc Clifton (G-1664)	E	973 942-2243
LP Thebault Co Parsippany (G-8040)	F	973 884-1300
Lunet Inc Paramus (G-7885)	G	201 261-3883
M & M Printing Corp Hasbrouck Heights (G-4196)	G	201 288-7787
M G X Inc Monmouth Junction (G-6350)	F	732 329-0088
Major Printing Co Inc Union (G-11204)	G	908 686-7296
Manva Industries Inc Nutley (G-7651)	F	973 667-2606
Manzi Printing Eatontown (G-2412)	G	732 542-1927
Mariano Press LLC Somerset (G-10129)	F	732 247-3659
Mark Lithography Inc Cedar Knolls (G-1316)	E	973 538-5557
Master Printing Inc Carlstadt (G-1188)	E	201 842-9100
Master Repro Inc Midland Park (G-6231)	G	201 447-4800
McGinnis Printing Red Bank (G-9336)	G	732 758-0060
McKella 2-8-0 Inc Pennsauken (G-8548)	D	856 813-1153
Mercer Digital Printing LLC Lawrenceville (G-5263)	G	609 919-9190
Metro Web Corp North Bergen (G-7467)	E	201 553-0700
Michael Graphics Inc Branchburg (G-680)	E	732 846-8680
Mid Atlantic Graphixinc Egg Harbor Township (G-2690)	G	609 569-9990
Monte Printing & Graphics Inc Roselle Park (G-9699)	G	908 241-6600
Morgan Printing Service Inc South Amboy (G-10243)	F	732 721-2959
Morris County Duplicating Cedar Knolls (G-1317)	D	973 993-8484
Morris Plains Pip Inc Livingston (G-5548)	G	973 533-9330
Morrison Press Inc Closter (G-1764)	F	201 488-4848
Mountain Printing Company Inc Berlin (G-438)	E	856 767-7600
Mr Quickly Inc Union (G-11209)	G	908 687-6000
My Way Prints Inc Butler (G-1014)	G	973 492-1212
National Certified Printing Hightstown (G-4313)	G	609 443-6323
New Jersey Reprographics Inc Garwood (G-3780)	G	908 789-1616
New Life Color Reproductions Ridgefield (G-9378)	G	201 943-7005

PRODUCT

New Standard Printing Corp G 973 366-0006
Dover *(G-2104)*

Newline Prtg & Tech Solutions F 973 405-6133
Mountainside *(G-6884)*

Nitka Graphics Inc F 201 797-3000
Fair Lawn *(G-3106)*

Noble Metals Corp G 908 925-6300
Linden *(G-5420)*

Norwood Printing Inc F 201 784-8721
Norwood *(G-7632)*

Ocsidot Inc F 908 789-3300
Garwood *(G-3782)*

One-Source Communications E 973 463-0250
Whippany *(G-12029)*

OShea Services Inc G 201 343-8668
Hackensack *(G-3957)*

Otis Graphics Inc F 201 438-7120
Lyndhurst *(G-5700)*

Palm Press Inc G 201 767-6504
Northvale *(G-7600)*

Panther Printing Inc G 239 542-1050
West Orange *(G-11904)*

Paravista Inc E 732 752-1222
Fairfield *(G-3281)*

Park Printing Services Inc F 856 675-1600
Pennsauken *(G-8556)*

Parkway Printing Inc G 732 308-0300
Marlboro *(G-5951)*

Parsells Printing Inc G 973 473-2700
Maywood *(G-6059)*

Pascack Valley Copy Center G 201 664-1917
Westwood *(G-11966)*

Patel Printing Plus Corp F 908 964-6422
Union *(G-11214)*

PDQ Print & Copy Inc F 201 569-2288
Englewood *(G-2921)*

Penn Jersey Press Inc G 856 627-2200
Gibbsboro *(G-3789)*

Penny Press G 856 547-1991
Stratford *(G-10616)*

Pentagraphix Offset Prtg Inc F 201 526-9300
Jersey City *(G-4800)*

Permagraphics Inc F 201 814-1200
Moonachie *(G-6535)*

Phoenix Business Forms Inc G 856 691-2266
Vineland *(G-11392)*

Pine Hill Printing Inc G 856 346-2915
Pine Hill *(G-8722)*

Pinnacle Press Inc G 201 652-0500
Midland Park *(G-6234)*

Pirolli Printing Co Inc F 856 933-1285
Bellmawr *(G-349)*

Premier Graphics Inc E 732 872-9933
Atlantic Highlands *(G-115)*

Premier Printing Solutions LLC G 732 525-0740
Sayreville *(G-9836)*

Premium Service Printing G 908 707-1311
Hillsborough *(G-4363)*

Presto Printing Service Inc G 908 756-5337
South Plainfield *(G-10424)*

Princetonian Graphics Inc F 732 329-8282
Monmouth Junction *(G-6359)*

Print Post G 973 732-0950
Newark *(G-7275)*

Print Shoppe Inc G 908 782-9213
Flemington *(G-3462)*

Print Tech LLC D 908 232-2287
Springfield *(G-10573)*

Print Tech LLC G 908 232-0767
Westfield *(G-11928)*

Printers of Salem County LLC G 856 935-5032
Salem *(G-9808)*

Printers Place Inc G 973 744-8889
Montclair *(G-6432)*

Printing Center Inc E 973 383-6362
Sparta *(G-10518)*

Printing Craftsman Inc F 201 943-0276
Fairview *(G-3370)*

Printing Delite Inc G 973 676-3033
East Orange *(G-2266)*

Printing Industries LLC G 973 334-9775
Parsippany *(G-8072)*

Printing Plus of South Jersey G 856 767-3941
West Berlin *(G-11744)*

Prism Color Corporation D 856 234-7515
Moorestown *(G-6615)*

Prism Dgtal Communications LLC F 973 232-5038
Mountainside *(G-6886)*

Professional Printing Services G 856 428-6300
Haddonfield *(G-4063)*

Professional Reproductions Inc F 212 268-1222
Marlboro *(G-5954)*

Progress Printing Co F 201 433-3133
Jersey City *(G-4806)*

Progressive 4 Color Ltd Lblty G 973 736-5800
West Orange *(G-11905)*

Progressive Offset Inc E 201 569-3900
Englewood *(G-2925)*

Publishers Inc E 856 853-2800
West Deptford *(G-11840)*

Puent-Romer Communications Inc G 973 509-7591
Montclair *(G-6433)*

Q P 500 Inc G 732 531-8860
Ocean *(G-7739)*

Quad/Graphics Inc E 609 534-7308
Westampton *(G-11917)*

Quad/Graphics Inc E 732 469-0189
Somerset *(G-10161)*

R & B Printing Inc G 908 766-4073
Bernardsville *(G-454)*

R L R Foil Stamping LLC F 973 778-9464
Passaic *(G-8175)*

R V Livolsi Incorporated G 732 286-2200
Toms River *(G-10905)*

Rays Reproduction Inc G 201 666-5650
Emerson *(G-2862)*

Register Lithographers Ltd D 973 916-2804
Clifton *(G-1712)*

Reliance Graphics Inc G 973 239-5411
Verona *(G-11310)*

Repro Tronics Inc G 201 722-1880
Ltl Egg Hbr *(G-5647)*

Repromatic Printing Inc G 973 239-7610
Cedar Grove *(G-1299)*

Review Printing Inc G 856 589-7200
Pitman *(G-8844)*

Rfm Printing Inc F 732 938-4400
Belmar *(G-362)*

Ridgewood Press Inc F 201 670-9797
Ridgewood *(G-9430)*

Riegel Holding Company Inc D 609 771-0361
Ewing *(G-3052)*

Roan Printing Inc F 908 526-5990
Somerville *(G-10226)*

Roelynn Litho Inc F 732 942-9650
Lakewood *(G-5185)*

Rolls Offset Group Inc E 201 727-1110
Lyndhurst *(G-5705)*

Roned Printing & Reproduction G 973 386-1848
East Hanover *(G-2241)*

Royal Printing Service E 201 863-3131
West New York *(G-11880)*

Royer Graphics Inc G 856 344-7935
Clementon *(G-1535)*

Rush Graphics Inc E 973 427-9393
Hawthorne *(G-4257)*

Sandy Alexander Inc C 973 470-8100
Clifton *(G-1715)*

Santangelo Printing Co Inc F 973 779-5880
Lodi *(G-5599)*

Scarlet Printing G 732 560-1415
Middlesex *(G-6193)*

Schuyler Printing Inc G 201 997-8083
Kearny *(G-4913)*

Scodix Inc F 855 726-3491
Saddle Brook *(G-9791)*

Scott Graphics Printing Co Inc G 201 262-0473
New Milford *(G-7025)*

Sherman Printing Co Inc G 973 345-2493
Clifton *(G-1721)*

Showcase Printing of Iselin G 732 283-0438
Iselin *(G-4644)*

Sonata Graphics Inc G 201 866-0186
Secaucus *(G-9930)*

Star Litho Inc G 973 641-1603
Fairfield *(G-3312)*

Stauts Printing & Graphics G 609 654-5382
Medford *(G-6083)*

Steb Inc G 973 584-0990
Ledgewood *(G-5310)*

Steb Inc F 973 584-0990
Ledgewood *(G-5311)*

Stobbs Printing Co Inc G 973 748-4441
Bloomfield *(G-533)*

Stone Mountain Printing Inc G 732 636-8450
Woodbridge *(G-12154)*

Stuyvesant Press Inc F 973 399-3880
Irvington *(G-4605)*

Sureway Prtg & Graphics LLC G 609 430-4333
Princeton *(G-9127)*

Tabloid Graphic Services Inc D 856 486-0410
Pennsauken *(G-8582)*

Tangent Graphics Inc G 201 488-2840
Englewood *(G-2936)*

Tanter Inc G 732 382-3555
Clark *(G-1516)*

Tanzola Printing Inc G 973 779-0858
Clifton *(G-1734)*

Tedco Inc G 609 883-0799
Ewing *(G-3060)*

The Creative Print Group Inc F 856 486-1700
Pennsauken *(G-8585)*

Thermo-Graphics Inc G 908 486-0100
Avenel *(G-156)*

Thewal Inc F 973 635-1880
Chatham *(G-1338)*

Thomas H Cox & Son Inc E 908 928-1010
Linden *(G-5453)*

Tmg Enterprises Inc E 732 469-2900
Piscataway *(G-8826)*

Toms River Printing Corp G 732 240-2033
Brielle *(G-915)*

Trenton Printing LLC F 609 695-6485
Trenton *(G-11125)*

Trinity Press Inc E 973 881-0690
Paterson *(G-8402)*

Tuerff Sziber Capitol Copy Svc G 609 989-8776
Trenton *(G-11129)*

Twill Inc F 908 665-1700
Berkeley Heights *(G-423)*

Typestyle Inc G 201 343-3343
Hackensack *(G-3987)*

Vanguard Printing G 856 358-2665
Elmer *(G-2800)*

Verni Vito G 732 449-1760
Wall Township *(G-11517)*

Vernw Printing Company G 973 751-6462
Belleville *(G-324)*

Vintage Print Gallery G 201 501-0505
Closter *(G-1768)*

Viskal Printing LLC G 973 812-6600
Totowa *(G-10982)*

Waldwick Printing Co G 201 652-5848
Waldwick *(G-11456)*

Welter & Kreutz Printing Co G 201 489-9098
South Hackensack *(G-10299)*

Westbury Press Inc D 201 894-0444
Englewood *(G-2943)*

White Eagle Printing Co Inc E 609 586-2032
Trenton *(G-11132)*

Wilcox Press G 973 827-7474
Hamburg *(G-4100)*

Wilker Graphics LLC G 201 447-4800
Midland Park *(G-6242)*

William Robert Graphics Inc G 201 239-7400
Jersey City *(G-4848)*

Wong Robinson & Co Inc E 609 951-0300
Princeton *(G-9140)*

Yasheel Inc G 856 275-6812
Sewell *(G-9967)*

Your Printer V20 Ltd E 609 771-4000
Cranbury *(G-1893)*

Yukon Graphics Inc G 973 575-5700
Parsippany *(G-8117)*

Zippityprint LLC F 216 438-0001
Mullica Hill *(G-6894)*

PRINTING: Photo-Offset

AGFA Corporation E 201 440-0111
Carlstadt *(G-1121)*

Downtown Printing Center Inc F 732 246-7990
New Brunswick *(G-6955)*

Emerson Speed Printing Inc G 201 265-7977
Oradell *(G-7808)*

Phillip Balderose G 732 574-1330
Clark *(G-1512)*

Photo Offset Prtg & Pubg Co G 609 587-4900
Trenton *(G-11098)*

Print Group Inc F 201 487-4400
South Hackensack *(G-10290)*

Standard Prtg & Mail Svcs Inc F 973 790-3333
Fairfield *(G-3311)*

Star Promotions Inc F 732 356-5959
Bound Brook *(G-624)*

Tretina Printing Inc F 732 264-2324
Hazlet *(G-4285)*

PRINTING: Photolithographic

Artale Graphics F 212 868-0015
Linden *(G-5350)*

942 2018 Harris New jersey Manufacturers Directory (G-0000) Company's Geographic Section entry number

Linder & Company Inc.................F 201 386-8788
Jersey City (G-4777)

PRINTING: Rotogravure

Acme Engraving Co Inc.....................E 973 778-0885
Passaic (G-8124)

PRINTING: Screen, Broadwoven Fabrics, Cotton

Anne Alanna Inc.................G 609 465-3787
Cape May Court House (G-1109)
Aztec Graphics Inc.................F 609 587-1000
Trenton (G-11023)
Chartwell Promotions Ltd Inc ....G 732 780-6900
Freehold (G-3646)
Mt Embroidery & Promotions LLC ....G 201 646-1070
Norwood (G-7629)
Rolferrys Specialties Inc ....G 856 456-2999
Brooklawn (G-921)
Screened Images Inc ....E 732 651-8181
East Brunswick (G-2182)
Unique Screen Printing Corp.................E 908 925-3773
Linden (G-5456)

PRINTING: Screen, Fabric

Acey Industries Inc.................G 973 595-1222
North Haledon (G-7547)
Ambro Manufacturing Inc ....F 908 806-8337
Flemington (G-3425)
Art Flag Co Inc ....F 212 334-1890
Fair Haven (G-3070)
Designs By James ....G 856 692-1316
Vineland (G-11352)
James Smith ....G 732 229-8273
Long Branch (G-5626)
McLain Studios Inc ....G 732 775-0271
Asbury Park (G-81)
Nes Enterprises Inc ....G 201 964-1400
Carlstadt (G-1192)
Tarma Sales ....G 732 969-3318
Carteret (G-1268)
Total Ink Solutions LLC ....F 201 487-9600
Hackensack (G-3985)
Wally Enterprises Inc ....F 732 329-2613
Monmouth Junction (G-6371)

PRINTING: Screen, Manmade Fiber & Silk, Broadwoven Fabric

Chartwell Promotions Ltd Inc ....G 732 780-6900
Freehold (G-3646)
Design N Stitch Inc ....G 201 488-1314
Hackensack (G-3904)
Gilbert Storms Jr ....G 973 835-5729
Haskell (G-4207)
Screened Images Inc ....E 732 651-8181
East Brunswick (G-2182)
Unique Screen Printing Corp.................E 908 925-3773
Linden (G-5456)

PRINTING: Thermography

Magic Printing Corp.................F 732 726-0620
Avenel (G-139)
Print Communications Group Inc.........D 973 882-9444
Fairfield (G-3287)
Trade Thermographers Inc.................F 201 489-2060
Rochelle Park (G-9539)
Watonka Printing Inc ....G 732 974-8878
Belmar (G-365)

PRODUCT STERILIZATION SVCS

E-Beam Services Inc.................E 513 933-0031
Cranbury (G-1830)

PROFESSIONAL EQPT & SPLYS, WHOLESALE: Law Enforcement

Jontol Unlimited LLC.................G 858 652-1113
Blackwood (G-485)

PROFESSIONAL EQPT & SPLYS, WHOLESALE: Optical Goods

Complete Optical Laboratory.................F 973 338-8886
Bloomfield (G-508)
Lens Lab Express ....G 201 861-0016
West New York (G-11871)

PROFESSIONAL EQPT & SPLYS, WHOLESALE: Precision Tools

Oroszlany Laszlo ....G 201 666-2101
Hillsdale (G-4386)

PROFESSIONAL EQPT & SPLYS, WHOLESALE: Scientific & Engineerg

Arthur H Thomas Company ....B 856 467-2000
Swedesboro (G-10682)
Magnetic Products and Svcs Inc.................G 732 264-6651
Holmdel (G-4520)
Thomas Scientific Inc.................B 800 345-2100
Swedesboro (G-10733)
Thomas Scientific LLC.................G 800 345-2100
Swedesboro (G-10734)

PROFESSIONAL EQPT & SPLYS, WHOLESALE: Theatrical

American Harlequin Corporation ....E 856 234-5505
Moorestown (G-6558)
Rose Brand Wipers Inc.................C 201 809-1730
Secaucus (G-9918)
W Gerriets International Inc.................G 609 771-8111
Ewing (G-3068)

PROFESSIONAL INSTRUMENT REPAIR SVCS

Rf Vii Inc.................F 856 875-2121
Newfield (G-7371)
Sk & P Industries Inc ....G 973 482-1864
Newark (G-7316)
State Technology Inc.................G 856 467-8009
Bridgeport (G-773)

PROFILE SHAPES: Unsupported Plastics

Accessrec LLC.................G 973 955-0514
Clifton (G-1554)
All State Plastics Inc.................E 732 654-5054
South Amboy (G-10234)
Belle Printing Group LLC.................G 856 235-5151
Mount Laurel (G-6782)
Fluorotherm Polymers Inc.................G 973 575-0760
Parsippany (G-8014)
Keystone Plastics Inc.................D 908 561-1300
South Plainfield (G-10392)
Saint-Gobain Prfmce Plas Corp.................D 856 423-6630
Mickleton (G-6138)
Tricomp Inc.................C 973 835-1110
Pompton Plains (G-8966)
Zeus Industrial Products Inc.................C 908 292-6500
Branchburg (G-721)

PROMOTION SVCS

AlphaGraphics ....G 201 327-2200
Mahwah (G-5746)
Apollo East LLC.................E 856 486-1882
Pennsauken (G-8478)
Fu WEI Inc.................G 732 937-8388
East Brunswick (G-2156)
Hit Promo LLC.................C 856 739-4474
Bellmawr (G-342)
Timeline Promotions Inc.................G 973 226-1512
West Caldwell (G-11806)

PROTECTION EQPT: Lightning

Lightning Prvntion Systems Inc.................G 856 767-7806
West Berlin (G-11729)

PROTECTIVE FOOTWEAR: Rubber Or Plastic

Lust For Life Footwear LLC ....F 631 327-2811
Teaneck (G-10761)
Tingley Rubber Corporation ....E 800 631-5498
Piscataway (G-8825)

PUBLIC ADDRESS SYSTEMS

Oklahoma Sound Corp.................E 800 261-4112
Clifton (G-1686)

PUBLIC FINANCE, TAXATION & MONETARY POLICY OFFICES

New Jersey Department Treasury ....E 609 292-5133
Trenton (G-11085)

PUBLIC RELATIONS SVCS

Rbs Intrntonal Direct Mktg LLC ....G 856 663-2500
Pennsauken (G-8569)
The Creative Print Group Inc ....F 856 486-1700
Pennsauken (G-8585)

PUBLISHERS: Art Copy

Arthur A Kaplan Co Inc.................E 201 806-2100
East Rutherford (G-2279)

PUBLISHERS: Art Copy & Poster

Bruce Teleky Inc.................G 718 965-9694
Jersey City (G-4721)
M/C Communications LLC.................F 908 766-0402
Basking Ridge (G-193)
M/C Communications LLC.................E 609 838-7952
Hamilton (G-4112)
Physicians Weekly LLC.................G 609 981-7354
Basking Ridge (G-202)
Physicians Weekly LLC.................E 908 766-0421
Basking Ridge (G-203)
Sonata Graphics Inc ....G 201 866-0186
Secaucus (G-9930)

PUBLISHERS: Book

Alexander Communications Group.......F 973 265-2300
Mountain Lakes (G-6854)
AM Best Company Inc ....B 908 439-2200
Oldwick (G-7804)
Apples & Honey Press LLC.................F 973 379-7200
Springfield (G-10537)
Barnes & Noble Booksellers Inc.................E 201 272-3635
Lyndhurst (G-5671)
Bookcode Corp ....G 732 742-0481
Woodbridge (G-12147)
CNG Publishing Company ....G 973 768-0978
Burlington (G-964)
Evergreen Information Svcs Inc.................F 973 339-9672
Little Falls (G-5475)
Franklin Electronic Publs Inc.................D 609 386-2500
Burlington (G-974)
Hispanic Outlook In Higher ....G 201 587-8800
Saddle Brook (G-9768)
Hispanic Outlook-12 Mag Inc ....G 201 587-8800
Fair Lawn (G-3095)
Howard Press Inc.................D 908 245-4400
Roselle (G-9673)
Hudson Group (hg) Inc ....B 201 939-5050
East Rutherford (G-2300)
JS Paluch Co Inc.................F 732 516-1900
Edison (G-2550)
Mathematics League Inc ....G 201 568-6328
Tenafly (G-10785)
Metal Powder Inds Federation ....F 609 452-7700
Princeton (G-9073)
Missionary Society of St Paul ....E 201 825-7300
Mahwah (G-5792)
New York-NJ Trail Conference ....F 201 512-9348
Mahwah (G-5795)
NJ Dept Military Vtrans ....G 856 384-8831
Woodbury (G-12165)
Pearson Education Inc ....A 201 236-7000
Hoboken (G-4490)
Pearson Education Inc ....E 609 395-6000
Cranbury (G-1869)
Philip Lief Group Inc.................G 609 430-1000
Princeton (G-9092)
Princeton Publishing Group ....G 609 577-0693
Princeton (G-9099)
Princeton University Press ....D 609 258-4900
Princeton (G-9104)
Railpace Co Inc ....G 732 388-4984
Clark (G-1514)
Renaissance House ....G 201 408-4048
Englewood (G-2928)
Research & Education Assn ....E 732 819-8880
Piscataway (G-8805)
School Publications Co Inc.................E 732 988-1100
Neptune (G-6929)
Silicon Press Inc ....G 908 273-8919
Summit (G-10657)

Employee Codes: A=Over 500 employees, B=251-500
C=101-250, D=51-100, E=20-50, F=10-19, G=4-9

2018 Harris New jersey
Manufacturers Directory

943

PRODUCT

Taryag Legacy Foundation Inc ....F 732 569-2467
Lakewood *(G-5193)*
Transaction Publishers Inc ....F 732 445-2280
Piscataway *(G-8830)*
Trilogy Publications LLC ....G 201 816-1211
Englewood Cliffs *(G-2983)*

PUBLISHERS: Book Clubs, No Printing

Plexus Publishing Inc ....E 609 654-6500
Medford *(G-6078)*

PUBLISHERS: Books, No Printing

Africa World Press ....G 609 695-3200
Ewing *(G-3002)*
AM Best Company Inc ....A 908 439-2200
Oldwick *(G-7803)*
Behrman House Inc ....F 973 379-7200
Millburn *(G-6248)*
Berlitz Languages US Inc ....D 609 759-5371
Princeton *(G-9014)*
Berlitz Publishing Company Inc ....E 609 514-9650
Princeton *(G-9015)*
Blue Apple Books LLC ....G 973 763-8191
Maplewood *(G-5915)*
Blue Dome Inc ....G 646 415-9331
Clifton *(G-1577)*
Carstens Publications Inc ....E 973 383-3355
Newton *(G-7384)*
Chatham Bookseller Inc ....G 973 822-1361
Madison *(G-5720)*
Colt Media Inc ....G 732 946-3276
Colts Neck *(G-1782)*
Comex Systems Inc ....G 800 543-6959
Chester *(G-1435)*
Creative Competitions Inc ....F 856 256-2797
Sewell *(G-9949)*
Darwin Press Inc ....G 609 737-1349
Pennington *(G-8448)*
Galves Auto Price List Inc ....F 201 393-0051
Teterboro *(G-10797)*
Haights Cross Cmmnications Inc.........E 212 209-0500
Princeton Junction *(G-9157)*
Jump Start Press ....G 732 892-4994
Point Pleasant Beach *(G-8920)*
Just US Books Inc ....G 973 672-7701
East Orange *(G-2258)*
Learning Links-Usa Inc ....G 516 437-9071
Cranbury *(G-1852)*
Manning Publication Co ....G 856 375-2597
Cherry Hill *(G-1394)*
Markus Wiener Publishers Inc..............G 609 921-1141
Princeton *(G-9070)*
Matthew Bender & Company Inc ....E 518 487-3000
Newark *(G-7237)*
Modern Drummer Publications ....F 973 239-4140
Fairfield *(G-3263)*
New Horizon Press Publishers ....G 908 604-6311
Liberty Corner *(G-5323)*
Patterson Smith Publishing ....G 973 744-3291
Montclair *(G-6431)*
Paulist Press Inc ....G 201 825-7300
Mahwah *(G-5800)*
Pearson Education Inc ....F 201 785-2721
Hoboken *(G-4492)*
Presbyterian Reformed Pubg Co ....F 908 454-0505
Phillipsburg *(G-8666)*
Red Sea Press Inc ....G 609 695-3200
Ewing *(G-3049)*
Rosemont Publishing & Printing ....F 609 269-8094
Plainsboro *(G-8899)*
RR Bowker LLC ....C 908 286-1090
New Providence *(G-7053)*
Scholastic Inc ....G 201 633-2400
Secaucus *(G-9923)*
Simon & Schuster Inc ....E 973 656-6000
Parsippany *(G-8087)*
Springer Scnce + Bus Media LLC ....D 201 348-4033
Secaucus *(G-9931)*
Sterling Publishing Co Inc ....E 732 248-6563
Monroe Township *(G-6395)*
Stevens Publishing Co ....E 908 284-9326
Flemington *(G-3468)*
Thomson Reuters Corporation ....B 212 337-4281
Newark *(G-7343)*
Wordmasters ....G 201 327-4201
Allendale *(G-23)*
Writers & Poets ....G 908 233-2399
Mountainside *(G-6890)*

PUBLISHERS: Catalogs

Bookazine Co Inc ....D 201 339-7777
Bayonne *(G-216)*
Brogan Tennyson Group Inc ....F 732 355-0700
Dayton *(G-1956)*
Catalogue Publishers Inc ....F 973 423-3600
Fair Lawn *(G-3086)*

PUBLISHERS: Directories, NEC

Dex Media Inc ....F 908 237-0956
Flemington *(G-3434)*
Information Today Inc ....F 908 219-0279
New Providence *(G-7040)*
Jonas Media Group Inc ....F 973 438-1900
Newark *(G-7208)*
Thomas Publishing Company LLC ....E 973 543-4994
Chester *(G-1440)*
Walden Mott Corp ....G 201 962-3704
Ramsey *(G-9255)*

PUBLISHERS: Directories, Telephone

Supermedia LLC ....B 973 649-9900
Maplewood *(G-5927)*
Verizon Communications Inc ....E 201 666-9934
Westwood *(G-11975)*
Verizon Communications Inc ....D 609 646-9939
Egg Harbor Township *(G-2698)*

PUBLISHERS: Guides

Community Pride Publications ....F 609 921-8760
Princeton Junction *(G-9150)*
Jersey Job Guide Inc ....G 732 263-9675
Long Branch *(G-5627)*

PUBLISHERS: Magazines, No Printing

Advanstar Communications Inc ....E 973 944-7777
Montvale *(G-6441)*
Advanstar Communications Inc ....E 732 596-0276
Iselin *(G-4608)*
AM Best Company Inc ....A 908 439-2200
Oldwick *(G-7803)*
B T O Industries Inc ....G 973 243-0011
West Orange *(G-11888)*
Backroads Inc ....G 973 948-4176
Newton *(G-7381)*
Bauer Publishing Company LP ....G 201 569-6699
Englewood Cliffs *(G-2950)*
Bobit Business Media Inc ....G 856 596-0999
Marlton *(G-5965)*
Carstens Publications Inc ....E 973 383-3355
Newton *(G-7384)*
Casino Player Publishing LLC ....E 609 404-0600
Galloway *(G-3710)*
Christian Mssons In Many Lands ....G 732 449-8880
Wall Township *(G-11469)*
Commerce Enterprises Inc ....F 201 368-2100
Paramus *(G-7862)*
Data Cntrum Communications Inc ....F 201 391-1911
Montvale *(G-6452)*
Diversityinc Media LLC ....F 973 494-0539
Princeton *(G-9029)*
Dowden Health Media Inc ....D 201 740-6100
Montvale *(G-6453)*
E W Williams Publications ....F 201 592-7007
Fort Lee *(G-3552)*
Evergreen Information Svcs Inc ....F 973 339-9672
Little Falls *(G-5475)*
Garden State Woman Mag LLC ....G 908 879-7143
Long Valley *(G-5638)*
Golf Odyssey LLC ....G 973 564-6223
Short Hills *(G-9978)*
Haymarket Media Inc ....G 201 799-4800
Paramus *(G-7875)*
Heinrich Bauer Publishing LP ....F 201 569-6699
Englewood *(G-2902)*
Heinrich Bauer Verlag ....F 201 569-0006
Englewood Cliffs *(G-2963)*
Hobby Publications Inc ....E 732 536-5160
Freehold *(G-3659)*
Industry Publications Inc ....F 973 331-9545
Parsippany *(G-8029)*
Interntonal Med News Group LLC ....F 973 290-8237
Parsippany *(G-8032)*
Investment Casting Institute ....G 201 573-9770
Montvale *(G-6460)*
Jonas Media Group Inc ....F 973 438-1900
Newark *(G-7208)*

Jury Vrdict Rview Publications...............G 973 376-9002
Springfield *(G-10560)*
Know America Media LLC ....G 770 650-1102
Roseland *(G-9653)*
Lead Conversion Plus ....F 802 497-1557
Manalapan *(G-5853)*
Middlesex Publications ....F 732 435-0005
North Brunswick *(G-7527)*
Modern Drummer Publications ....F 973 239-4140
Fairfield *(G-3263)*
Music Trades Corp ....G 201 871-1965
Englewood *(G-2918)*
National Housing Institute ....G 973 509-1600
Montclair *(G-6424)*
New Jersey Bus & Indust Assn ....D 609 393-7707
Trenton *(G-11084)*
New Jrsey State Leag Mncplties ....G 609 695-3481
Trenton *(G-11087)*
Northstar Travel Media LLC ....C 201 902-2000
Secaucus *(G-9907)*
Npt Publishing Group Inc ....F 973 401-0202
Morris Plains *(G-6675)*
Nsgv Inc ....G 212 620-2200
Jersey City *(G-4793)*
Pillar of Fire ....D 732 356-0102
Zarephath *(G-12270)*
Recruit Co Ltd ....G 201 216-0600
Jersey City *(G-4816)*
Retail Management Pubg Inc ....F 212 981-0217
Montclair *(G-6434)*
Rodman Media Corp ....E 201 825-2552
Montvale *(G-6478)*
Schiff & Co ....F 973 227-1830
West Caldwell *(G-11805)*
Scholastic Uk Group LLC ....C 201 633-2400
Secaucus *(G-9924)*
Sports Impact Inc ....G 732 257-1451
East Brunswick *(G-2186)*
Steppin Out Magazine ....G 201 703-0911
Fair Lawn *(G-3115)*
Teg New Jersey Inc ....A 973 776-8660
Newark *(G-7338)*
Tommax Inc ....G 732 224-1046
Red Bank *(G-9347)*
Vicinity Publications Inc ....G 973 276-1688
Fairfield *(G-3343)*
Visual Impact Advertising Inc ....F 973 763-4900
Maplewood *(G-5932)*
Vitamin Retailer Magazine Inc ....G 732 432-9600
East Brunswick *(G-2197)*
Walden Mott Corp ....G 201 962-3704
Ramsey *(G-9255)*

PUBLISHERS: Maps

Columbia Marketing Corp ....G 973 275-1700
Maplewood *(G-5916)*

PUBLISHERS: Miscellaneous

Access Response Inc ....G 732 660-0770
Ocean *(G-7712)*
Action Press Park Slope ....G 718 624-3457
Holmdel *(G-4507)*
American Directory Publishing ....G 609 494-4055
Surf City *(G-10664)*
Berlitz Publishing Company Inc ....E 609 514-9650
Princeton *(G-9015)*
Better Listen LLC ....G 917 623-9834
Teaneck *(G-10744)*
Cape Publishing Inc ....G 609 898-4500
Cape May *(G-1094)*
Captivate Internationallc ....G 732 734-0403
Edison *(G-2478)*
Cariletha Company Inc ....F 609 222-3055
Mount Laurel *(G-6786)*
Central Record Publications ....E 609 654-5000
Trenton *(G-11038)*
Charles Kerr Enterprises Inc ....G 732 738-6500
Edison *(G-2482)*
Cimware USA Inc ....G 201 493-0521
Ridgewood *(G-9421)*
Cohansey Cove ....G 609 884-7726
Cape May *(G-1095)*
Consumer Graphics Inc ....G 732 469-4699
Somerset *(G-10085)*
Criterion Publishing Co ....G 732 548-8300
Metuchen *(G-6101)*
Crossfire Publications ....G 516 352-9087
Caldwell *(G-1025)*
Down Shore Publishing Corp ....G 609 978-1233
West Creek *(G-11810)*

Dune Grass Publishing LLC ....G 609 774-6562
Blackwood (G-476)

Eastside Express Corporation ....G 908 486-3300
Linden (G-5370)

Ebsco Industries Inc ....E 732 542-8600
Shrewsbury (G-9998)

Ebsco Industries Inc ....D 201 569-2500
Tinton Falls (G-10835)

Ebsco Publishing Inc ....G 201 968-9899
Hackensack (G-3908)

Eclecticism Publishing LLC ....G 212 714-4714
Robbinsville (G-9515)

Electrochemical Society Inc ....E 609 737-1902
Pennington (G-8450)

Entourage Imaging Inc ....E 888 926-6571
Princeton Junction (G-9153)

Epoch Press Inc ....E 973 357-0080
Wayne (G-11628)

Exit Zero Cookhouse Inc ....G 609 770-8479
Cape May (G-1098)

Financial Information Inc ....E 908 222-5300
South Plainfield (G-10365)

Florentine Press Inc ....G 201 386-9200
Jersey City (G-4753)

Form Lectro Inc ....G 973 777-0621
Hackensack (G-3917)

Friday Morning Quarterback ....E 856 424-6873
Cherry Hill (G-1366)

Galves Auto Price List Inc ....F 201 393-0051
Teterboro (G-10797)

Gmp Publications Inc ....G 609 859-3400
Southampton (G-10474)

Gorgias Press ....G 732 699-0343
Piscataway (G-8770)

Grafwed Internet Media Studios ....G 201 632-1771
Midland Park (G-6227)

Grey House Publishing Inc ....G 201 968-0500
Hackensack (G-3924)

Heritage Publishing ....G 732 747-7770
Colts Neck (G-1788)

Ihs Inc ....G 201 391-0084
Woodcliff Lake (G-12194)

J D M Associates Inc ....G 973 773-8699
Lodi (G-5590)

J S Paluch Co Inc ....E 732 238-2412
East Brunswick (G-2163)

Jav Latin America Express ....G 201 868-5004
West New York (G-11869)

Jem Printing Inc ....G 908 782-9986
Flemington (G-3450)

Jen Mar Graphics Inc ....E 973 256-6622
Totowa (G-10952)

Jersey Shore News Mgazines Inc ....E 609 494-5900
Surf City (G-10665)

Jigsaw Publishing LLC ....G 973 838-4838
Butler (G-1010)

John Patrick Publishing LLC ....D 609 883-2700
Ewing (G-3027)

John R Zabka Associates Inc ....F 201 405-0075
Oakland (G-7693)

JS Paluch Co Inc ....F 732 516-1900
Edison (G-2550)

Kabab & Curry Express ....G 732 416-6560
Edison (G-2551)

Laennec Publishing Inc ....G 973 882-9500
Parsippany (G-8036)

Light Inc ....G 973 777-2704
Clifton (G-1662)

Lympha Press USA ....G 732 792-9677
Freehold (G-3669)

Macie Publishing Company ....F 973 983-8700
Mendham (G-6088)

Magazinexperts LLC ....G 973 383-0888
Newton (G-7395)

Marquis - Whos Who Inc ....D 908 673-1006
New Providence (G-7047)

Media Vista Inc ....G 732 747-8060
Red Bank (G-9337)

Nanking Express ....G 732 549-7788
Iselin (G-4635)

National Home Planning Service ....G 973 376-3200
Chatham (G-1335)

Nextwave Web LLC ....F 973 742-4339
Paterson (G-8351)

Nighthawk Interactive LLC ....G 732 243-9922
Edison (G-2581)

North Jersey Media Group Inc ....E 973 569-7100
Woodland Park (G-12226)

Northern State Periodicals LLC ....G 973 782-6100
Paterson (G-8354)

Oggi Media Group LLC ....E 201 358-6582
Norwood (G-7633)

Pavexpress ....G 201 330-8300
Clifton (G-1692)

Princeton Information Center ....G 609 924-7019
Princeton (G-9095)

Princeton University Press ....D 609 258-4900
Princeton (G-9104)

Publishers Partnership Co ....D 201 689-1613
Ridgewood (G-9428)

Raphel Marketing Inc ....G 609 348-6646
Atlantic City (G-107)

Review and Judge LLC ....G 732 987-3905
Lakewood (G-5183)

Rockwood Corporation ....G 908 355-8600
Union (G-11219)

Scholastic Book Fairs Inc ....G 609 578-4142
Cranbury (G-1878)

School Publications Co Inc ....E 732 988-1100
Neptune (G-6929)

Seven Mile Pubg & Creative ....F 609 967-7707
Avalon (G-120)

Shoppe CMC Shoppers Guide ....G 609 886-4112
Villas (G-11316)

Simon & Schuster Inc ....B 856 461-6500
Delran (G-2022)

Simon & Schuster Inc ....E 973 656-6000
Parsippany (G-8087)

South Jersey Publishing Co ....G 856 692-0455
Vineland (G-11406)

Stanger Robert A & Co LP ....E 732 389-3600
Shrewsbury (G-10011)

Steven Orros ....G 732 972-1104
Monroe Township (G-6396)

Success Publishers LLC ....G 609 443-0792
Perrineville (G-8603)

Tap Into LLC ....G 908 370-1158
New Providence (G-7056)

Teckchek ....G 919 497-0136
East Brunswick (G-2193)

Thepositive Press ....G 856 266-8765
Cinnaminson (G-1492)

Thomsom Health Care Inc ....C 201 358-7300
Montvale (G-6481)

Thomson Reuters Corporation ....F 973 662-3070
Nutley (G-7655)

Token Torch Ltd Liability Co ....F 973 629-1805
East Orange (G-2272)

Treasure Chest Corp ....G 973 328-7747
Wharton (G-12001)

Triple S Express ....G 908 686-0557
Union (G-11230)

Victory Press ....G 201 729-1007
Moonachie (G-6551)

PUBLISHERS: Music Book & Sheet Music

Lead Bead Publishing Company ....G 732 246-0410
Somerset (G-10122)

Subito Music Service Inc ....G 973 857-3440
Verona (G-11311)

PUBLISHERS: Music, Book

Oasis Entertainment Group ....G 973 256-7077
Cedar Grove (G-1294)

PUBLISHERS: Music, Sheet

Clyde Otis Music Group ....G 845 425-8198
Englewood (G-2884)

Hal Leonard LLC ....C 973 337-5034
Montclair (G-6415)

Iws License Corp ....F 732 872-0014
Atlantic Highlands (G-112)

Sueta Music Ed Publications ....F 888 725-2333
Mendham (G-6091)

Trf Music Inc ....F 201 335-0005
Tinton Falls (G-10851)

PUBLISHERS: Newsletter

Excerpta Medica Inc ....D 908 547-2100
Bridgewater (G-837)

Harrison Scott Pblications Inc ....E 201 659-1700
Hoboken (G-4472)

Old Barracks Association Inc ....F 609 396-1776
Trenton (G-11092)

P O V Incorporated ....F 914 258-4361
Montclair (G-6428)

Wpi Communications Inc ....F 973 467-8700
Springfield (G-10586)

PUBLISHERS: Newspaper

21st Century Media Newsppr LLC ....D 215 504-4200
Trenton (G-11009)

50 Plus Monthly Inc ....G 973 584-7911
Succasunna (G-10618)

Alm Media LLC ....E 973 642-0075
Newark (G-7080)

Arts Weekly Inc ....E 973 812-6766
Little Falls (G-5470)

Bernardsville News ....G 908 766-3900
Bernardsville (G-448)

Binding Products Inc ....E 212 947-1192
Jersey City (G-4719)

Bloomfield Life Inc ....F 973 233-5001
Cedar Grove (G-1273)

Bloomfield News LLC ....G 973 226-2127
West Caldwell (G-11769)

Bright Hrzons Fmly Sltions LLC ....E 609 520-7501
Monmouth Junction (G-6333)

Cgw News LLC ....G 973 473-3972
Clifton (G-1581)

Coaster Inc ....F 732 775-3010
Asbury Park (G-75)

Daily News LP ....F 212 210-2100
Jersey City (G-4736)

David Sisco Jr ....G 908 454-0880
Phillipsburg (G-8646)

Dolan LLC ....G 800 451-9998
Princeton (G-9030)

Dorf Feature Service Inc ....E 908 518-1802
Mountainside (G-6878)

Epoch Times ....G 908 548-8026
South Plainfield (G-10357)

Gannett Co Inc ....E 973 428-6200
Parsippany (G-8020)

Gannett Stllite Info Ntwrk Inc ....B 973 428-6200
Parsippany (G-8021)

Gannett Stllite Info Ntwrk Inc ....G 856 691-5000
Vineland (G-11357)

Gannett Stllite Info Ntwrk LLC ....D 856 663-6000
Cherry Hill (G-1369)

Halsey News ....G 973 645-0017
Newark (G-7184)

James Kinkade ....F 856 451-1177
Bridgeton (G-787)

Jersey Beat ....G 201 864-9054
Weehawken (G-11697)

Jose Moreira ....G 201 991-9001
Kearny (G-4890)

Korean Bergen News Inc ....F 201 894-9061
Englewood Cliffs (G-2971)

Latino U S A ....G 732 870-1475
Long Branch (G-5628)

Link News ....G 732 222-4300
Long Branch (G-5629)

Mandip Inc ....G 732 752-4875
Piscataway (G-8789)

Medieval Times USA Inc ....C 201 933-2220
Lyndhurst (G-5691)

Muse Monthly LLC ....G 609 443-3509
East Windsor (G-2362)

New Jersey Jewish News ....E 973 887-3900
Whippany (G-12027)

New Satellite Network LLC ....G 908 922-0967
Scotch Plains (G-9853)

North Jersey Media Group Inc ....E 973 569-7100
Woodland Park (G-12226)

Packet Media LLC ....G 856 779-3800
Englishtown (G-2996)

Palisades Magnolia Prpts LLC ....G 201 424-7180
Palisades Park (G-7841)

Paper Dove Press LLC ....G 201 641-7938
Little Ferry (G-5513)

Paradise Publishing Group LLC ....G 609 227-7642
Willingboro (G-12122)

Penn Jersey Advance Inc ....D 201 775-6610
Secaucus (G-9909)

Philadelphia Inquirer ....G 856 779-3840
Cherry Hill (G-1413)

Recorder Newspaper ....G 973 226-4000
Caldwell (G-1033)

Recorder Publishing Co ....E 908 647-1180
Stirling (G-10605)

Red Bank Gstrntrology Assoc PA ....E 732 842-4294
Red Bank (G-9342)

Reminder Newspaper ....F 856 825-8811
Millville (G-6322)

Reporte Hispano ....G 609 933-1400
Princeton (G-9112)

Riverbend Advertiser ....G...... 908 475-3431
   Belvidere *(G-375)*
Sample Media Inc ....G...... 609 884-2021
   Cape May *(G-1104)*
Sample Media Inc ....E...... 609 399-5411
   Ocean City *(G-7757)*
School Publications Co Inc ....E...... 732 988-1100
   Neptune *(G-6929)*
Str8line Publishing Company ....G...... 919 717-6740
   Newark *(G-7331)*
Summit Professional Networks ....E...... 201 526-1230
   Hoboken *(G-4499)*
Tapintonet ....G...... 908 279-0303
   New Providence *(G-7057)*
Times of Trenton Pubg Corp ....A...... 609 989-5454
   Trenton *(G-11121)*
Ukrainian National Association ....G...... 973 292-9800
   Parsippany *(G-8106)*
Venture Info Network ....G...... 609 279-0777
   Princeton *(G-9136)*
Wilmington Trust Sp Services ....C...... 609 272-7000
   Pleasantville *(G-8918)*
Worrall Community Newspapers ....G...... 973 743-4040
   Bloomfield *(G-537)*

PUBLISHERS: Newspapers, No Printing

24 Horas Inc ....F...... 973 817-7400
   Newark *(G-7062)*
Advocate Publishing Corp ....E...... 973 497-4200
   Newark *(G-7073)*
African Telecom Inc ....G...... 973 675-9919
   East Orange *(G-2254)*
Atlantic City Week ....F...... 609 646-4848
   Pleasantville *(G-8902)*
Bayonne Community News ....E...... 201 437-2460
   Bayonne *(G-214)*
Brazilian Press & Advertising ....F...... 973 344-4555
   Newark *(G-7112)*
Cabio Newspaper ....G...... 201 902-0811
   West New York *(G-11861)*
Catholic Star Herald ....G...... 856 583-6142
   Camden *(G-1051)*
Coast Star ....E...... 732 223-0076
   Manasquan *(G-5869)*
Community News Network Inc ....G...... 856 428-3399
   Haddonfield *(G-4058)*
Cumberland News Inc ....G...... 856 691-2244
   Vineland *(G-11345)*
Current Newspaper LLC ....E...... 609 383-8994
   Pleasantville *(G-8906)*
Diocese of Camden New Jersey ....A...... 856 756-7900
   Camden *(G-1059)*
Diocese of Paterson ....F...... 973 279-8845
   Clifton *(G-1600)*
Dyer Communications Inc ....E...... 732 219-5788
   Red Bank *(G-9328)*
Elmer Times Co Inc ....G...... 856 358-6171
   Elmer *(G-2791)*
Evergreen Information Svcs Inc ....F...... 973 339-9672
   Little Falls *(G-5475)*
Gannett Stllite Info Ntwrk LLC ....F...... 609 561-2300
   Vineland *(G-11358)*
Gatehuse Media PA Holdings Inc ....E...... 732 246-7677
   New Brunswick *(G-6961)*
Greater Media Newspapers ....E...... 732 358-5200
   Englishtown *(G-2993)*
Gruppo Editoriale Oggi Inc ....E...... 201 358-6582
   Norwood *(G-7623)*
Hawthorne Press ....F...... 973 427-3330
   Hawthorne *(G-4239)*
Hudson West Publishing Co ....F...... 201 991-1600
   Kearny *(G-4882)*
La Tribuna Publication Inc ....E...... 201 617-1360
   Union City *(G-11253)*
Leader Newsgroup LLC ....E...... 201 438-6801
   Lyndhurst *(G-5685)*
Luso Americano ....E...... 973 344-3200
   Newark *(G-7227)*
Luso-Americano Co Inc ....E...... 973 344-3200
   Newark *(G-7229)*
Medianews Group Inc ....D...... 856 451-1000
   Salem *(G-9807)*
Micro Media Publications Inc ....G...... 732 657-7344
   Lakehurst *(G-5059)*
New View Media ....E...... 973 691-3002
   Budd Lake *(G-938)*
Ocean Star ....G...... 732 899-7606
   Point Pleasant Beach *(G-8925)*
Parker Publications ....F...... 908 766-3900
   Madison *(G-5730)*

Richard Rein ....F...... 609 452-7000
   Lawrence Township *(G-5247)*
South Jersey Publishing Co ....B...... 609 272-7000
   Pleasantville *(G-8916)*
Teg New Jersey Inc ....A...... 973 776-8660
   Newark *(G-7338)*
Times The Villadom Inc ....F...... 201 652-0744
   Midland Park *(G-6240)*
Tribuna Hispana ....G...... 609 646-9167
   Pleasantville *(G-8917)*
U S A Distributors Inc ....E...... 201 348-1959
   Union City *(G-11269)*
Walden Mott Corp ....G...... 201 962-3704
   Ramsey *(G-9255)*
Watthung Communications Inc ....F...... 908 232-4407
   Westfield *(G-11933)*
West Essex Tribune Inc ....F...... 973 992-1771
   Livingston *(G-5571)*

PUBLISHERS: Pamphlets, No Printing

Banquet Services International ....G...... 732 270-1188
   Toms River *(G-10867)*
Excerpta Medica Inc ....D...... 908 547-2100
   Bridgewater *(G-837)*
J S Paluch Co Inc ....E...... 732 238-2412
   East Brunswick *(G-2163)*
Shy Kramer & Associates ....F...... 609 646-2063
   Pleasantville *(G-8915)*

PUBLISHERS: Periodical Statistical Reports, No Printing

John Wiley & Sons Inc ....D...... 201 748-6000
   Hoboken *(G-4479)*
Keypoint Intelligence LLC ....G...... 201 489-6439
   Hackensack *(G-3936)*
Keypoint Intelligence LLC ....E...... 973 797-2100
   Fairfield *(G-3240)*
SMR Research Corporation ....G...... 908 852-7677
   Hackettstown *(G-4037)*

PUBLISHERS: Periodical, With Printing

Alexander Communications Group ....F...... 973 265-2300
   Mountain Lakes *(G-6854)*
Skinder-Strauss LLC ....E...... 973 642-1440
   New Providence *(G-7054)*

PUBLISHERS: Periodicals, Magazines

42 Design Square LLC ....F...... 888 272-5979
   Parsippany *(G-7937)*
Alternate Side Street Suspende ....G...... 201 291-7878
   Paramus *(G-7853)*
AM Best Company Inc ....B...... 908 439-2200
   Oldwick *(G-7804)*
Central Record Publications ....E...... 609 654-5000
   Trenton *(G-11038)*
Civic Research Institute Inc ....G...... 609 683-4450
   Kingston *(G-5027)*
Convention News Company Inc ....F...... 201 444-5075
   Midland Park *(G-6224)*
Curran & Connors Inc ....G...... 609 514-0104
   Princeton *(G-9024)*
Diversity Plus Magazine ....E...... 973 275-1405
   South Orange *(G-10303)*
Friday Morning Quarterback ....E...... 856 424-6873
   Cherry Hill *(G-1366)*
Galen Publishing LLC ....E...... 908 253-9001
   Somerville *(G-10210)*
General Commis Archives & Hstr ....G...... 973 408-3189
   Madison *(G-5723)*
Hammonton Gazette Inc ....G...... 609 704-1939
   Hammonton *(G-4138)*
Hsh Assoc Financial Publishers ....G...... 973 838-3330
   Butler *(G-1008)*
JS Paluch Co Inc ....F...... 732 516-1900
   Edison *(G-2550)*
Krystal Clear Media Group LLC ....G...... 302 715-1069
   Bloomfield *(G-517)*
Lont & Overkamp Pubg Co Inc ....E...... 973 942-2243
   Clifton *(G-1664)*
Macromedia Incorporated ....E...... 201 646-4000
   Hackensack *(G-3942)*
Medical Strategic Planning Inc ....G...... 732 219-5090
   Lincroft *(G-5339)*
Mindwise Media LLC ....G...... 973 701-0685
   Chatham *(G-1334)*
Missionary Society of St Paul ....E...... 201 825-7300
   Mahwah *(G-5792)*

N J W Magazine ....F...... 201 886-2185
   Fort Lee *(G-3571)*
Options Edge LLC ....G...... 973 701-0051
   Summit *(G-10652)*
P D Salco Inc ....F...... 973 716-0517
   Livingston *(G-5553)*
Relx Inc ....D...... 973 812-1900
   Woodland Park *(G-12232)*
School Publications Co Inc ....E...... 732 988-1100
   Neptune *(G-6929)*
Sino Monthly New Jersey Inc ....F...... 732 650-0688
   Edison *(G-2619)*
US News & World Report Inc ....F...... 212 716-6800
   Jersey City *(G-4841)*

PUBLISHERS: Periodicals, No Printing

American Foreclosures Inc ....F...... 201 501-0200
   Bergenfield *(G-380)*
Foundation For Student Comm ....E...... 609 258-1111
   Princeton *(G-9046)*
Houses Magazine Inc ....F...... 973 605-1877
   Morris Plains *(G-6669)*
Jannetti Publications ....D...... 856 256-2300
   Sewell *(G-9960)*
Lawyers Diary and Manual LLC ....E...... 973 642-1440
   New Providence *(G-7041)*
Pentacle Publishing Corp ....E...... 732 240-3000
   Toms River *(G-10901)*
Quick Frozen Foods Intl ....E...... 201 592-7007
   Fort Lee *(G-3579)*
Transaction Publishers Inc ....F...... 732 445-2280
   Piscataway *(G-8830)*
Union Institute Inc ....E...... 800 914-8138
   Mahwah *(G-5823)*
Voicings Publication Inc ....G...... 609 822-9401
   Ventnor City *(G-11294)*

PUBLISHERS: Posters

Door Center Enterprises Inc ....G...... 609 333-1233
   Hopewell *(G-4541)*

PUBLISHERS: Shopping News

Hudson West Publishing Co ....F...... 201 991-1600
   Kearny *(G-4882)*

PUBLISHERS: Technical Manuals

Franklin Electronic Publs Inc ....D...... 609 386-2500
   Burlington *(G-974)*

PUBLISHERS: Technical Manuals & Papers

American Soc of Mech Engineers ....D...... 973 244-2282
   Little Falls *(G-5468)*
Micro Logic Inc ....F...... 201 962-7510
   Mahwah *(G-5790)*

PUBLISHERS: Technical Papers

Hyman W Fisher Inc ....G...... 973 992-9155
   Livingston *(G-5534)*

PUBLISHERS: Telephone & Other Directory

Dex Media Inc ....E...... 856 988-2700
   Marlton *(G-5972)*
Sic-Naics LLC ....G...... 929 344-2633
   Red Bank *(G-9344)*

PUBLISHERS: Textbooks, No Printing

Childrens Research & Dev Co ....G...... 856 546-8814
   Haddon Heights *(G-4046)*
Gann Law Books Inc ....F...... 973 268-1200
   Newark *(G-7169)*
John Wiley & Sons Inc ....D...... 201 748-6000
   Hoboken *(G-4479)*
John Wiley & Sons Inc ....D...... 732 302-2265
   Edison *(G-2547)*
John Wiley & Sons Inc ....D...... 201 748-6000
   Hoboken *(G-4480)*
Pearson Technology Centre Inc ....E...... 201 767-5000
   Old Tappan *(G-7800)*
Peoples Education Inc ....C...... 201 712-0090
   Montvale *(G-6469)*
Wiley Subscription Services ....F...... 201 748-6000
   Hoboken *(G-4505)*
World Scientific Publishing Co ....F...... 201 487-9655
   Hackensack *(G-3992)*

PUBLISHERS: Trade journals, No Printing

Anderson Publishing Ltd ....G...... 908 301-1995
 Scotch Plains **(G-9845)**
BNP Media Inc ....G...... 201 291-9001
 Paramus **(G-7859)**
Dentistry Today Inc ....E...... 973 882-4700
 Fairfield **(G-3176)**
Excerpta Medica Inc ....D...... 908 547-2100
 Bridgewater **(G-837)**
Fellowship In Prayer Inc ....G...... 609 924-6863
 Princeton **(G-9044)**
Global Strategy Institute A ....G...... 973 615-7447
 Bloomfield **(G-513)**
Information Today Inc ....E...... 609 654-6266
 Medford **(G-6071)**
International Data Group Inc ....F...... 732 460-9404
 Eatontown **(G-2408)**
Montage Media Corporation ....E...... 201 891-3200
 Mahwah **(G-5793)**
Physicans Educatn Resource LLC ......G...... 609 378-3701
 Plainsboro **(G-8895)**
Pioneer Associates Inc ....E...... 201 592-7007
 Fort Lee **(G-3577)**
Plexus Publishing Inc ....E...... 609 654-6500
 Medford **(G-6078)**
Springer Scnce + Bus Media LLC ......D...... 201 348-4033
 Secaucus **(G-9931)**
Thomas Publishing Company LLC ......E...... 973 543-4994
 Chester **(G-1440)**
Webannuitiescom Inc ....G...... 732 521-5110
 Monroe **(G-6376)**

PUBLISHING & BROADCASTING: Internet Only

Beterrific Corp ....G...... 201 735-7711
 Fort Lee **(G-3546)**
Bitwine Inc ....F...... 888 866-9435
 Tenafly **(G-10782)**
Chryslis Data Sltons Svcs Corp ......G...... 609 375-2000
 Princeton **(G-9022)**
College Spun Media Inc ....G...... 973 945-5040
 Hoboken **(G-4465)**
Creationsrewards Net LLC ....G...... 908 526-3127
 Manville **(G-5893)**
Edge Ventures Inc ....G...... 877 841-1402
 Old Bridge **(G-7777)**
Electedface LLC ....E...... 609 924-3636
 Princeton **(G-9037)**
Go Waddle Inc ....G...... 301 452-5084
 Berkeley Heights **(G-411)**
Greetingtap ....G...... 347 731-4263
 South Plainfield **(G-10375)**
J Media LLC ....G...... 201 600-4573
 Norwood **(G-7627)**
Jersey Bound Latino LLC ....G...... 908 591-2830
 Union **(G-11197)**
Manna Group LLC ....F...... 856 881-7650
 Mount Laurel **(G-6816)**
Moscova Enterprises Inc ....F...... 848 628-4873
 Jersey City **(G-4786)**
Nonzero Foundation Inc ....G...... 609 688-0793
 Princeton **(G-9082)**
Perfect Clicks LLC ....G...... 845 323-6116
 Woodcliff Lake **(G-12199)**
Sight2site Media LLC ....G...... 856 637-2479
 Pomona **(G-8945)**
Sima S Enterprises LLC ....G...... 877 223-7639
 Wall Township **(G-11510)**
Squash Beef LLC ....G...... 917 577-8723
 Colts Neck **(G-1792)**
Tonymacx86 LLC ....G...... 973 584-5273
 Ledgewood **(G-5312)**
Wcd Enterprises Inc ....G...... 732 888-4422
 Keyport **(G-5026)**

PUBLISHING & PRINTING: Art Copy

Scafa-Tornabene Art Pubg Co ......E...... 201 842-8500
 Lyndhurst **(G-5706)**

PUBLISHING & PRINTING: Books

Avstar Publishing Corp ....G...... 908 236-6210
 Lebanon **(G-5277)**
Franklin Mint LLC ....E...... 800 843-6468
 Fort Lee **(G-3555)**
Pearson Inc ....E...... 201 236-7000
 Upper Saddle River **(G-11282)**
Pegasus Group Publishing Inc ......F...... 973 884-9100
 East Hanover **(G-2239)**

Peoples Eductl Holdings Inc ......C...... 201 712-0090
 Saddle Brook **(G-9781)**
Techsetters Inc ....E...... 856 240-7905
 Collingswood **(G-1774)**
TFH Publications Inc ....D...... 732 897-6860
 Neptune **(G-6934)**
TFH Publications Inc ....E...... 732 988-8400
 Neptune **(G-6935)**
Thomson Reuters (markets) LLC ......G...... 973 286-7200
 Newark **(G-7342)**
Truckeros News LLC ....F...... 732 340-1043
 Rahway **(G-9225)**
W G I Corp ....F...... 732 370-2900
 Lakewood **(G-5203)**
Wiley Publishing LLC ....B...... 201 748-6000
 Hoboken **(G-4504)**
Wt Media LLC ....F...... 609 921-3490
 Trenton **(G-11135)**

PUBLISHING & PRINTING: Catalogs

Rdl Marketing Group LLC ....G...... 732 446-0817
 Perrineville **(G-8602)**
Starnet Printing Inc ....G...... 201 760-2600
 Mahwah **(G-5815)**
Tommax Inc ....G...... 732 224-1046
 Red Bank **(G-9347)**

PUBLISHING & PRINTING: Directories, NEC

City Master Barbers Inc ....G...... 732 536-6400
 Morganville **(G-6640)**
Commerce Register Inc ....E...... 201 445-3000
 Midland Park **(G-6223)**
Triefeldt Studios Inc ....G...... 609 656-2380
 Trenton **(G-11128)**

PUBLISHING & PRINTING: Guides

Jersey Shore Publications ....G...... 732 892-1276
 Brick **(G-748)**
Little Fox Inc ....G...... 609 919-9691
 Englewood Cliffs **(G-2975)**

PUBLISHING & PRINTING: Magazines: publishing & printing

Advantage Business Media LLC ......D...... 973 920-7000
 Rockaway **(G-9547)**
Airbrush Action Inc ....G...... 732 223-7878
 Barnegat **(G-160)**
Amy Publications LLC ....G...... 973 235-1800
 Nutley **(G-7640)**
Area Auto Racing News Inc ....G...... 609 888-3618
 Trenton **(G-11019)**
Arts Weekly Inc ....E...... 973 812-6766
 Little Falls **(G-5470)**
Bondi Digital Publishing LLC ......G...... 212 405-1655
 Edgewater **(G-2434)**
Charter Fincl Pubg Netwrk Inc ......E...... 732 450-8866
 Shrewsbury **(G-9993)**
Drug Delivery Technology LLC ......G...... 973 299-1200
 Montville **(G-6487)**
Ensembleiq Inc ....D...... 973 252-0100
 Newark **(G-7155)**
Hyp Hair Inc ....E...... 201 843-4004
 Montclair **(G-6416)**
Innovation In Medtech LLC ....G...... 888 202-5939
 Chatham **(G-1328)**
Kicksonfirecom LLC ....G...... 718 753-4248
 South Amboy **(G-10240)**
Mod Media Ltd Liability Co ....G...... 973 249-6157
 Fairfield **(G-3262)**
Neighborhood Shoppers ....G...... 856 988-7722
 Marlton **(G-5989)**
New Jersey Business Magazine ......G...... 973 882-5004
 Fairfield **(G-3269)**
New Jersey Monthly LLC ....E...... 973 539-8230
 Morristown **(G-6730)**
Outsourcing Today LLC ....F...... 973 439-0060
 Roseland **(G-9654)**
Princeton Almni Pblications Inc ......G...... 609 258-4885
 Princeton **(G-9105)**
Renard Commmunications Inc ......E...... 973 912-8550
 Springfield **(G-10576)**
Rvs Publishing Inc ....F...... 856 810-7743
 Marlton **(G-5997)**
Sj Magazine ....F...... 856 722-9300
 Maple Shade **(G-5908)**
Sneaker Swarm LLC ....F...... 908 693-9262
 Woodbridge **(G-12153)**

Steward LLC ....G...... 609 816-8825
 Princeton **(G-9125)**
Thomas Greco Publishing Inc ......F...... 973 667-6965
 Nutley **(G-7654)**
Unisphere Media LLC ....F...... 908 795-3701
 New Providence **(G-7059)**

PUBLISHING & PRINTING: Newsletters, Business Svc

Dorado Systems LLC ....F...... 856 354-0048
 Haddonfield **(G-4059)**
M J Powers & Co Publishers ....F...... 973 898-1200
 Morristown **(G-6724)**
Sepers Countryside Nursery LLC ......G...... 856 451-0719
 Bridgeton **(G-797)**

PUBLISHING & PRINTING: Newspapers

10x Daily LLC ....G...... 732 276-6407
 Lakewood **(G-5061)**
About Our Town Inc ....G...... 732 968-1615
 Piscataway **(G-8723)**
Achievement Journal LLC ....G...... 732 297-1570
 North Brunswick **(G-7501)**
Ainsworth Media ....G...... 856 854-1400
 Collingswood **(G-1769)**
Andis Inc ....G...... 973 627-0400
 Denville **(G-2030)**
Arab Voice Newspaper ....G...... 973 523-7815
 Paterson **(G-8214)**
Area Auto Racing News Inc ....G...... 609 888-3618
 Trenton **(G-11019)**
Argo Corp ....F...... 609 652-4560
 Pomona **(G-8944)**
Aus Inc ....G...... 856 234-9200
 Mount Laurel **(G-6779)**
Bay Shore Press Inc ....G...... 732 957-0070
 Middletown **(G-6211)**
Borton Enterprises ....F...... 856 453-9221
 Bridgeton **(G-778)**
Brazilian Voice ....G...... 973 491-6200
 Newark **(G-7113)**
Casas News Publishing Co ....E...... 908 245-6767
 Roselle Park **(G-9690)**
Convention News Company Inc ......F...... 201 444-5075
 Midland Park **(G-6224)**
Daily Dish ....G...... 973 537-9700
 Wharton **(G-11983)**
Daily Dog Walker LLC ....G...... 609 755-5364
 Robbinsville **(G-9514)**
Daily Dollar LLC ....G...... 732 236-9709
 Monroe Township **(G-6381)**
Daily Plan It Executive Center ......G...... 609 514-9494
 Princeton **(G-9027)**
Direct Development LLC ....G...... 732 739-8890
 Tinton Falls **(G-10831)**
Dow Jones & Company Inc ....F...... 609 520-4000
 Cranbury **(G-1829)**
Dow Jones & Company Inc ....D...... 609 520-5238
 Monmouth Junction **(G-6341)**
Financial Information Inc ....E...... 908 222-5300
 South Plainfield **(G-10365)**
First Friday Global Inc ....G...... 201 776-6709
 Newark **(G-7162)**
Gail Gersons Wine & Dine Resta ......G...... 732 758-0888
 Shrewsbury **(G-9999)**
Gannett Co Inc ....D...... 908 243-6953
 Somerville **(G-10211)**
Glassboro News & Food Store ......G...... 856 881-1181
 Glassboro **(G-3806)**
Gloucester County Times ....G...... 856 845-7484
 Woodbury **(G-12162)**
Greater Media Newspapers ....G...... 732 254-7004
 Sayreville **(G-9822)**
Herald News ....G...... 973 569-7000
 Woodland Park **(G-12221)**
Hoboken Reporter ....G...... 201 553-0130
 North Bergen **(G-7457)**
Home News Tribune ....E...... 908 243-6600
 Somerville **(G-10214)**
Hunterdon County Democrat Inc ......G...... 908 996-4047
 Frenchtown **(G-3701)**
Jersey Shore News Mgazines Inc ......E...... 609 494-5900
 Surf City **(G-10665)**
Jewish Standard Inc ....F...... 201 837-8818
 Teaneck **(G-10758)**
Jewish Times of South Jersey ......G...... 609 646-2063
 Pleasantville **(G-8911)**
Journal News V Inc ....G...... 201 986-1458
 Paramus **(G-7879)**

PRODUCT

Levy Innovation ....G...... 908 303-4492
  Morristown *(G-6722)*
Macromedia Incorporated ....E...... 201 646-4000
  Hackensack *(G-3942)*
Monmouth Journal ....G...... 732 747-7007
  Red Bank *(G-9338)*
Montclair Local News LLC ....G...... 973 744-6243
  Montclair *(G-6423)*
Montgomery News ....G...... 908 874-0020
  Skillman *(G-10034)*
Newark Morning Ledger Co ....C...... 732 560-1560
  Piscataway *(G-8796)*
Newark Morning Ledger Co ....C...... 973 882-6120
  Pine Brook *(G-8711)*
News Inc Gloucester City ....G...... 856 456-1199
  Gloucester City *(G-3841)*
Newspaper Media Group LLC ....E...... 856 779-3800
  Cherry Hill *(G-1404)*
NJ Advance Media LLC ....D...... 732 902-4300
  Edison *(G-2582)*
NJ Press Media ....G...... 732 643-3604
  Neptune *(G-6926)*
North Jersey Media Group Inc ....A...... 201 646-4000
  Woodland Park *(G-12225)*
North Jersey Media Group Inc ....G...... 201 933-1166
  Rutherford *(G-9741)*
North Jersey Media Group Inc ....E...... 973 233-5000
  Montclair *(G-6426)*
North Jersey Media Group Inc ....C...... 201 485-7800
  Mahwah *(G-5798)*
Observer Park ....F...... 201 798-7007
  Hoboken *(G-4488)*
Oggi Media Group LLC ....E...... 201 358-6582
  Norwood *(G-7633)*
Parker Publications Inc ....E...... 908 766-3900
  Bernardsville *(G-453)*
Pascack Press ....G...... 201 664-2105
  Westwood *(G-11965)*
Philedlphia-Newspapers-Llc ....A...... 609 823-0453
  Ventnor City *(G-11293)*
Publishing Technology Inc ....G...... 732 563-9292
  New Brunswick *(G-6997)*
Redhedink LLC ....G...... 973 890-2320
  Totowa *(G-10968)*
Seawave Corp ....G...... 609 886-8600
  Rio Grande *(G-9462)*
Targum Publishing Company ....E...... 732 247-1286
  New Brunswick *(G-7006)*
Valuewalk LLC ....G...... 973 767-2181
  Passaic *(G-8188)*
Vicinity Media Group Inc ....F...... 973 276-1688
  Fairfield *(G-3342)*
Wall Street Journal ....G...... 609 520-4000
  Monmouth Junction *(G-6370)*
World Journal LLC ....F...... 732 632-8890
  Metuchen *(G-6134)*

PUBLISHING & PRINTING: Pamphlets

Bon Venture Services LLC ....D...... 973 584-5699
  Flanders *(G-3402)*
Dawn Bible Students Assn ....G...... 201 438-6421
  East Rutherford *(G-2293)*
Life Skills Education Inc ....G...... 507 645-2994
  Springfield *(G-10564)*

PUBLISHING & PRINTING: Periodical Statistical Reports

McMunn Associates ....E...... 856 858-3440
  Collingswood *(G-1772)*

PUBLISHING & PRINTING: Technical Manuals

Faulkner Information Svcs LLC ....D...... 856 662-2070
  Medford *(G-6069)*

PUBLISHING & PRINTING: Technical Papers

Sheridan Printing Company Inc ....E...... 908 454-0700
  Alpha *(G-46)*

PUBLISHING & PRINTING: Textbooks

McGraw-Hill Glbl Edctn Hldngs ....D...... 609 371-8301
  East Windsor *(G-2361)*

PUBLISHING & PRINTING: Trade Journals

Barry Urner Publications Inc ....D...... 732 240-5330
  Toms River *(G-10868)*

Frontline Med Cmmnications Inc ....C...... 973 206-2328
  Parsippany *(G-8018)*
Intellisphere LLC ....E...... 609 716-7777
  Plainsboro *(G-8892)*
M2 Communications Inc ....E...... 201 433-1746
  Jersey City *(G-4781)*
Quadrant Media Corp Inc ....G...... 973 701-8900
  Parsippany *(G-8074)*
Showcase Publications Inc ....F...... 732 349-1134
  Toms River *(G-10911)*
Sys-Con Publications Inc ....E...... 201 802-3000
  Woodcliff Lake *(G-12204)*

PULLEYS: Metal

Polytech Designs Inc ....F...... 973 340-1390
  Clifton *(G-1701)*

PULP MILLS

County of Somerset ....C...... 732 469-3363
  Bridgewater *(G-830)*
Laminated Industries Inc ....E...... 908 862-5995
  Linden *(G-5400)*
Reliable Paper Recycling Inc ....C...... 201 333-5244
  Jersey City *(G-4819)*

PUMP JACKS & OTHER PUMPING EQPT: Indl

Vanton Pump & Equipment Corp ....E...... 908 688-4120
  Hillside *(G-4450)*

PUMP SLEEVES: Rubber

C M H Hele-Shaw Inc ....F...... 201 974-0570
  Hoboken *(G-4462)*

PUMPS

Apple Air Compressor Corp ....F...... 888 222-9940
  Rutherford *(G-9725)*
Bio Compression Systems Inc ....E...... 201 939-0716
  Moonachie *(G-6508)*
Boc Group Inc ....A...... 908 665-2400
  New Providence *(G-7030)*
Callaghan Pump Controls Inc ....G...... 201 621-0505
  Hackensack *(G-3891)*
Cooper Alloy Corporation ....F...... 908 688-4120
  Hillside *(G-4403)*
Davis-Standard LLC ....E...... 908 722-6000
  Somerset *(G-10089)*
Dynaflow Engineering Inc ....G...... 732 356-9790
  Middlesex *(G-6164)*
E Wortmann Machine Works Inc ....F...... 201 288-1654
  Teterboro *(G-10793)*
Energy Beams Inc ....F...... 973 291-6555
  Bloomingdale *(G-543)*
Flowserve Corporation ....G...... 973 334-9444
  Parsippany *(G-8013)*
Hayward Industries Inc ....B...... 908 351-5400
  Elizabeth *(G-2742)*
Hhh Machine Co ....G...... 908 276-1220
  Cranford *(G-1910)*
Ingersoll-Rand Company ....E...... 856 793-7000
  Mount Laurel *(G-6803)*
Interntional Cnsld Chemex Corp ....E...... 732 828-7676
  New Brunswick *(G-6969)*
Kraissl Company Inc ....E...... 201 342-0008
  Hackensack *(G-3937)*
Leistritz Advanced Tech Corp ....E...... 201 934-8262
  Allendale *(G-11)*
Linde LLC ....C...... 908 464-8100
  Bridgewater *(G-855)*
Linde LLC ....G...... 973 579-2065
  Sparta *(G-10510)*
Linde North America Inc ....D...... 908 464-8100
  New Providence *(G-7045)*
Linde North America Inc ....B...... 908 464-8100
  Bridgewater *(G-857)*
Magnatrol Valve Corporation ....F...... 856 829-4580
  Roebling *(G-9638)*
Melville Industries Inc ....G...... 856 461-0091
  Riverside *(G-9503)*
Nes Company Inc ....G...... 973 795-1519
  Jersey City *(G-4788)*
Orion Machinery Co Ltd ....E...... 201 569-3220
  Rutherford *(G-9742)*
Science Pump Corporation ....E...... 856 963-7700
  Camden *(G-1085)*
Valcor Engineering Corporation ....C...... 973 467-8400
  Springfield *(G-10583)*
Valley Tech Inc ....G...... 908 534-5565
  Whitehouse Station *(G-12064)*

Xylem Dewatering Solutions Inc ....C...... 856 467-3636
  Bridgeport *(G-775)*

PUMPS & PARTS: Indl

C & L Machining Company Inc ....G...... 856 456-1932
  Brooklawn *(G-920)*
Flowserve Corporation ....C...... 908 859-7000
  Phillipsburg *(G-8648)*
Flowserve Corporation ....D...... 856 241-7800
  Bridgeport *(G-766)*
Flowserve Corporation ....D...... 973 227-4565
  Fairfield *(G-3198)*
Shoreway Industry ....G...... 856 307-2020
  Clayton *(G-1528)*

PUMPS & PUMPING EQPT REPAIR SVCS

Frontline Industries Inc ....F...... 973 373-7211
  Irvington *(G-4587)*
Hights Electric Motor Service ....G...... 609 448-2298
  Hightstown *(G-4312)*
Longo Elctrical-Mechanical Inc ....E...... 973 537-0400
  Linden *(G-5404)*

PUMPS & PUMPING EQPT WHOLESALERS

Apple Air Compressor Corp ....F...... 888 222-9940
  Rutherford *(G-9725)*
Arcadia Equipment Inc ....F...... 201 342-3308
  Hackensack *(G-3874)*
Cooper Alloy Corporation ....F...... 908 688-4120
  Hillside *(G-4403)*
Dynaflow Engineering Inc ....G...... 732 356-9790
  Middlesex *(G-6164)*
Flemington Precast & Sup LLC ....F...... 908 782-3246
  Flemington *(G-3442)*
Frontline Industries Inc ....F...... 973 373-7211
  Irvington *(G-4587)*
Hights Electric Motor Service ....G...... 609 448-2298
  Hightstown *(G-4312)*
Leistritz Advanced Tech Corp ....E...... 201 934-8262
  Allendale *(G-11)*
Longo Elctrical-Mechanical Inc ....D...... 973 537-0400
  Wharton *(G-11991)*
UNI-Tech Drilling Company Inc ....E...... 856 694-4200
  Franklinville *(G-3633)*
United Eqp Fabricators LLC ....G...... 973 242-2737
  Newark *(G-7353)*
Xylem Dewatering Solutions Inc ....C...... 856 467-3636
  Bridgeport *(G-775)*

PUMPS, HEAT: Electric

Bfhj Holdings Inc ....G...... 908 730-6280
  Montvale *(G-6447)*

PUMPS: Domestic, Water Or Sump

Carter Pump Inc ....G...... 201 568-9798
  Waldwick *(G-11442)*

PUMPS: Fluid Power

Neptune Products Inc ....F...... 973 366-8200
  Dover *(G-2103)*

PUMPS: Gasoline, Measuring Or Dispensing

Newton Tool & Mfg Inc ....D...... 856 241-1500
  Pennsauken *(G-8554)*

PUMPS: Vacuum, Exc Laboratory

Eagletree-Pump Aquisiton Corp ....D...... 201 569-1173
  Rutherford *(G-9730)*
Orion Machinery Co Ltd ....E...... 201 569-3220
  Rutherford *(G-9742)*
Polvac Inc ....G...... 732 828-1662
  New Brunswick *(G-6992)*
United Vacuum LLC ....F...... 973 827-1661
  Hamburg *(G-4098)*

PUNCHES: Forming & Stamping

Bonney-Vehslage Tool Co ....F...... 973 589-6975
  Springfield *(G-10544)*
Hudson Manufacturing Corp ....F...... 973 376-7070
  Millburn *(G-6252)*
Ipsco Apollo Punch & Die Corp ....G...... 973 884-0900
  East Hanover *(G-2224)*

PURCHASING SVCS

Congoleum Corporation ....D 609 584-3601
Trenton (G-11045)

PURIFICATION & DUST COLLECTION EQPT

Camfil USA Inc ....C 973 616-7300
Riverdale (G-9476)
Cross Rip Ocean Engrg LLC..........G 973 455-0005
Parsippany (G-7978)
Gpt Inc ....F 732 446-2400
Manalapan (G-5849)
Handler Manufacturing Company ....E 908 233-7796
Westfield (G-11926)

QUARTZ CRYSTALS: Electronic

Bomar Exo Ltd Liability Co ....F 732 356-7787
Middlesex (G-6152)
Solar Products Inc ....E 973 248-9370
Pompton Lakes (G-8948)

QUILTING SVC

E B R Manufacturing Inc ....E 973 263-8810
Parsippany (G-7991)

RACEWAYS

Liberty Park Raceway LLC..............G 201 333-7223
Jersey City (G-4776)
Raceway Carwash...........................G 215 886-8252
Clementon (G-1533)
Raceway Petroleum Inc ....F 908 222-2999
North Plainfield (G-7561)
Raceway Petroleum Inc ....G 732 729-7350
East Brunswick (G-2178)
Raceway Petroleum Inc ....E 732 613-4404
East Brunswick (G-2179)
Speed Raceway ....G 856 314-8264
Cinnaminson (G-1489)

RACKS: Display

Auto-Stak Systems Inc ....G 201 358-9070
Westwood (G-11956)
East Coast Storage Eqp Co Inc ....E 732 451-1316
Brick (G-742)
Gauer Metal Products Co Inc ....E 908 241-4080
Kenilworth (G-4958)
Leo Prager Inc ....G 201 266-8888
Englewood (G-2909)
Spark Wire Products Co Inc...........G 973 773-6945
Clifton (G-1729)

RACKS: Garment, Exc Wood

All Racks Industries Inc ....G 212 244-1069
Linden (G-5346)
Ted-Steel Industries Ltd ....G 212 279-3878
Linden (G-5452)

RACKS: Garment, Wood

Bga Construction Inc.....................D 973 809-9745
Pine Brook (G-8689)
East Coast Storage Eqp Co Inc ....E 732 451-1316
Brick (G-742)

RACKS: Pallet, Exc Wood

Frazier Industrial Company ....C 908 876-3001
Long Valley (G-5637)
Modern Store Equipment ....F 609 241-7438
Burlington (G-985)

RADAR SYSTEMS & EQPT

Mwt Materials Inc ....F 973 928-8300
Passaic (G-8166)

RADIO & TELEVISION COMMUNICATIONS EQUIPMENT

Anatech Microwave Company Inc.........G 973 772-7369
Garfield (G-3717)
BNS Enterprises Inc ....G 908 285-6556
Hillsborough (G-4321)
Centurum Information Tech Inc ....G 856 751-1111
Marlton (G-5967)
Comm Port Technologies Inc ....G 732 738-8780
Cranbury (G-1825)

Computeradio.................................G 973 220-0087
Montville (G-6486)
Crestron Electronics Inc ....C 201 767-3400
Rockleigh (G-9628)
Daysequerra Corporation.................F 856 719-9900
Pennsauken (G-8501)
Draztic Designs LLC ....E 609 678-4200
Columbus (G-1803)
Eclearview Technologies Inc ....G 732 695-6999
Ocean (G-7724)
Eigent Technologies Inc ....G 732 673-0402
Holmdel (G-4515)
Engility LLC ....F 703 633-8300
Princeton Junction (G-9152)
Ensync Intrctive Solutions Inc............G 732 542-4001
Freehold (G-3654)
Grass Valley Usa LLC ....E 201 818-4050
Montvale (G-6458)
Integrated Microwave Tech LLC ....D 908 852-3700
Hackettstown (G-4012)
International Telematics Corp ....F 888 887-0935
Fort Lee (G-3559)
Kef America Inc ....E 732 414-2074
Marlboro (G-5946)
L3 Technologies Inc ....A 856 338-3000
Camden (G-1074)
Lg Elctrnics Mbilecomm USA Inc ....D 201 816-2000
Englewood Cliffs (G-2972)
Linearizer Technology Inc ....G 609 584-8424
Hamilton (G-4111)
Lucent Technologies World Svcs ....C 908 582-3000
New Providence (G-7046)
Microlab/Fxr..................................C 973 386-9696
Parsippany (G-8048)
Microsignals Inc ....E 800 225-4508
Palisades Park (G-7839)
Mphase Technologies Inc ....F 973 256-3737
Clifton (G-1676)
Natural Wireless LLC ....E 201 438-2865
East Rutherford (G-2313)
Network Communications Cons...........F 201 968-0684
Hackensack (G-3953)
OSI Laser Diode Inc ....E 732 549-9001
Edison (G-2590)
Peter-Lisand Machine Corp ....G 201 943-5600
New Milford (G-7024)
Powertrunk Inc ....E 201 630-4520
Jersey City (G-4805)
Qualcomm Incorporated ....D 908 443-8000
Bridgewater (G-882)
R H A Audio Communications...........G 732 257-9180
East Brunswick (G-2177)
R&D Microwaves LLC ....E 908 212-1696
Boonton (G-580)
Radio Systems Design Inc ....E 856 467-8000
Swedesboro (G-10721)
Radwin Inc ....G 201 252-4224
Mahwah (G-5806)
Renae Telecom LLC ....D 908 362-8112
Elizabeth (G-2772)
Rigztools LLC ....G 908 361-5433
Fairfield (G-3294)
Telcontel Corp ....F 732 441-0800
Laurence Harbor (G-5235)
Telescript Inc ....G 201 767-6733
Norwood (G-7636)
Turn-Key Technologies Inc ....F 732 553-9100
Sayreville (G-9842)
Wireworks Corporation ....E 908 686-7400
Hillside (G-4451)

RADIO BROADCASTING & COMMUNICATIONS EQPT

Alcatel-Lucent USA Inc ....D 908 582-3275
New Providence (G-7026)
Blitz Safe of America Inc ....F 201 569-5000
Englewood (G-2877)
Bogen Communications Inc ....D 201 934-8500
Mahwah (G-5754)
Bogen Corporation ....G 201 934-8500
Ramsey (G-9237)
Comtron Inc ....F 732 446-7571
Springfield (G-10548)
Hbc Solutions Inc ....G 973 267-5990
Rockleigh (G-9630)
Homan Communications Inc ....G 609 654-9594
Medford (G-6070)
Major Auto Installations Inc ....E 973 252-4262
Kenvil (G-5011)

On Site Communication ....E 201 488-4123
South Hackensack (G-10285)
R F Products Inc ....E 856 365-5500
Camden (G-1083)
Techflex Inc ....E 973 300-9242
Sparta (G-10522)
Wireless Communications Inc ....F 732 926-1000
Metuchen (G-6132)
Wireless Electronics Inc.................E 856 768-4310
West Berlin (G-11761)

RADIO BROADCASTING STATIONS

Brilliant Brdcstg Concept Inc ....F 732 287-9201
Edison (G-2475)

RADIO COMMUNICATIONS: Airborne Eqpt

Lockheed Martin Corporation...........B 856 787-3104
Mount Laurel (G-6814)

RADIO MAGNETIC INSTRUMENTATION

Aeronautical Instr & Rdo Co ....E 973 473-0034
Lodi (G-5573)

RADIO PRODUCERS

Dawn Bible Students Assn ....G 201 438-6421
East Rutherford (G-2293)

RADIO REPAIR SHOP, NEC

Turn-Key Technologies Inc ....F 732 553-9100
Sayreville (G-9842)

RADIO, TELEVISION & CONSUMER ELECTRONICS STORES: Eqpt, NEC

Ecom 2000 Inc...............................F 718 504-7355
Edison (G-2507)

RADIO, TELEVISION/CONSUMER ELEC STORES: Video Cameras/Access

Flir Security Inc ....G 201 368-9700
Ridgefield Park (G-9406)

RADIO, TV & CONSUMER ELEC STORES: Automotive Sound Eqpt

Model Electronics Inc.....................D 201 961-9200
Ramsey (G-9248)

RADIO, TV & CONSUMER ELECTRONICS: VCR & Access

Comm Port Technologies Inc ....G 732 738-8780
Cranbury (G-1825)

RADIOS WHOLESALERS

Model Electronics Inc.....................D 201 961-9200
Ramsey (G-9248)

RAILINGS: Prefabricated, Metal

Construction Specialties Inc...............E 908 236-0800
Lebanon (G-5282)
Nicks Inc ....G 908 272-3739
Kenilworth (G-4981)
North Jersey Metal Fabricators ....G 973 305-9830
Wayne (G-11667)

RAILROAD CARGO LOADING & UNLOADING SVCS

Northstar Travel Media LLC ....C 201 902-2000
Secaucus (G-9907)
Romark Logistics CES LLC ....E 908 789-2800
Westfield (G-11929)

RAILROAD EQPT

Hainesport Industrial Railroad...........F 609 261-8036
Hainesport (G-4072)
Rails Company Inc..........................E 973 763-4320
Maplewood (G-5926)
Strato Inc ....D 732 981-1515
Piscataway (G-8818)

RAILROAD EQPT: Cars & Eqpt, Interurban

Bombardier Transportation..........C....... 856 580-5609
Camden (G-1045)

RAILROAD EQPT: Cars & Eqpt, Train, Freight Or Passenger

Bombardier Transportation...................G....... 201 955-5874
Kearny (G-4866)

RAILROAD EQPT: Cars, Motor

Marmon Industrial LLC......................F....... 609 655-4287
Cranbury (G-1860)

RAILROAD EQPT: Engines, Locomotive, Steam

Multipower International Inc ....G....... 973 727-0327
Towaco (G-10999)

RAILROAD EQPT: Locomotives & Parts, Electric Or Nonelectric

American Rail Company Inc ....F....... 732 785-1110
Brick (G-733)

RAILROAD MAINTENANCE & REPAIR SVCS

Harsco Corporation ....E....... 856 779-7795
Cherry Hill (G-1374)

RAILROAD RELATED EQPT

Neu Inc...G....... 281 648-9751
Hamilton (G-4119)

RAILROAD SWITCHING & TERMINAL SVCS

CMI-Promex Inc ....F....... 856 351-1000
Pedricktown (G-8433)

RAILS: Elevator, Guide

G-Tech Elevator Associates LLC..........F....... 866 658-9296
Linden (G-5378)

RAILS: Rails, rolled & drawn, aluminum

American Custom Fabricators..............G....... 732 237-0037
Bayville (G-248)

RAMPS: Prefabricated Metal

Diamond Scooters Inc ....G....... 609 646-0003
Absecon (G-2)

RAZORS, RAZOR BLADES

Art of Shaving - FI LLC ....G....... 732 410-2520
Freehold (G-3639)
Hobby Blade Specialty Inc ....G....... 908 317-9306
Scotch Plains (G-9851)
IDL Techni-Edge LLC........................C....... 908 497-9818
Kenilworth (G-4962)

REAL ESTATE AGENCIES: Rental

PCI Inc ....G....... 973 226-8007
West Caldwell (G-11796)

REAL ESTATE AGENCIES: Selling

Max Pro Services LLC ....G....... 973 396-2373
Livingston (G-5542)
Sell All Properties LLC ....F....... 856 963-8800
Camden (G-1086)

REAL ESTATE AGENTS & MANAGERS

American Foreclosures Inc..................F....... 201 501-0200
Bergenfield (G-380)

REAL ESTATE INVESTMENT TRUSTS

McQuade Enterprises LLC ....G....... 609 501-2437
Millville (G-6313)

REAL ESTATE OPERATORS, EXC DEVELOPERS: Apartment Hotel

Bellia & Sons..................................E....... 856 845-2234
Woodbury (G-12158)

REAL ESTATE OPERATORS, EXC DEVELOPERS: Commercial/Indl Bldg

Recruit Co Ltd ....E 201 216-0600
Jersey City (G-4816)
Ukrainian National Association ....E....... 973 292-9800
Parsippany (G-8106)
Valley Plastic Molding Co...................F....... 973 334-2100
Boonton (G-587)

RECLAIMED RUBBER: Reworked By Manufacturing Process

Bsrm Inc.......................................G....... 888 509-0668
Mount Laurel (G-6784)
Derv2000 ....G....... 503 470-9158
Kearny (G-4871)

RECORD BLANKS: Phonographic

Sun Plastics Co Inc ....F....... 908 490-0870
Watchung (G-11595)

RECORDERS: Sound

York Telecom Corporation ....D....... 732 413-6000
Eatontown (G-2430)

RECORDING & PLAYBACK HEADS: Magnetic

Asti Corp.......................................F....... 201 501-8900
Bergenfield (G-381)

RECORDING HEADS: Speech & Musical Eqpt

Robert Wynn ....G....... 856 435-6398
Clementon (G-1534)

RECORDING TAPE: Video, Blank

Cabletime Ltd ....G....... 973 770-8070
Mount Arlington (G-6752)

RECORDS & TAPES: Prerecorded

Maxell Corporation of America............E....... 973 653-2400
Woodland Park (G-12224)
PM Swapco Inc ....F....... 201 438-7700
Lyndhurst (G-5701)
Recorded Publications Labs.................E....... 856 963-3000
Camden (G-1084)
Sony Electronics Inc.........................A....... 201 930-1000
Woodcliff Lake (G-12203)
Sony Music Holdings Inc ....B....... 201 777-3933
Rutherford (G-9745)
United Sound Arts Inc ....F....... 732 229-4949
Eatontown (G-2428)

RECORDS OR TAPES: Masters

Masterwork Recording Inc ....G....... 267 731-7031
Pennsauken (G-8545)
Metrolpolis Mastering LP ....E....... 212 604-9433
Edgewater (G-2441)

RECOVERY SVCS: Metal

Recycling N Hensel Amer Inc ....E....... 856 753-7614
West Berlin (G-11746)

RECOVERY SVCS: Solvents

Veolia Es ....E....... 732 469-5100
Middlesex (G-6208)

RECREATIONAL SPORTING EQPT REPAIR SVCS

P & S Blizzard Corporation ....G....... 973 523-1700
Paterson (G-8358)

RECTIFIERS: Electronic, Exc Semiconductor

Kinetics Industries Inc......................E....... 609 883-9700
Ewing (G-3030)

RECYCLABLE SCRAP & WASTE MATERIALS WHOLESALERS

Khanna Paper Inc.............................G....... 201 706-8050
Hoboken (G-4482)

RECYCLING: Paper

All Amrcan Recycl Corp Clifton............C....... 201 656-3363
Jersey City (G-4701)
Garden State Recycl Edison LLC ....F....... 732 393-0200
Edison (G-2526)
Reliable Wood Products LLC................D....... 856 456-6300
Westville (G-11947)

REELS: Fiber, Textile, Made From Purchased Materials

Alvaro P Escandon Inc ....G....... 973 274-1040
Newark (G-7081)

REFINERS & SMELTERS: Aluminum

Aleris Rolled Products Inc ....C....... 856 881-3600
Clayton (G-1522)
American Aluminum Alloys LLC ....E....... 717 417-5966
Pennsauken (G-8477)

REFINERS & SMELTERS: Brass, Secondary

Kearny Smelting & Ref Corp................E....... 201 991-7276
Kearny (G-4891)

REFINERS & SMELTERS: Copper

Amrod Corp....................................D....... 973 344-3806
Newark (G-7085)

REFINERS & SMELTERS: Gold, Secondary

Reldan Metals Inc ....E....... 732 238-8550
South River (G-10464)
Reldan Metals Inc ....C....... 732 238-8550
South River (G-10465)

REFINERS & SMELTERS: Lead, Secondary

Alpha Assembly Solutions Inc ....E....... 908 561-5170
South Plainfield (G-10325)
Alpha Assembly Solutions Inc ....E....... 908 791-3000
Somerset (G-10054)

REFINERS & SMELTERS: Nonferrous Metal

County of Somerset ....C....... 732 469-3363
Bridgewater (G-830)
Cumberland Rcycl Corp S Jersey ....E....... 856 825-4153
Millville (G-6296)
Emil A Schroth Inc ....E....... 732 938-5015
Howell (G-4553)
Federal Metals & Alloys Co ....E....... 908 756-0900
South Plainfield (G-10363)
Globe Metals Inc ....E....... 973 589-2563
Newark (G-7174)
Johnson Matthey Inc ....C....... 856 384-7000
West Deptford (G-11832)
Metal MGT Pittsburgh Inc...................E....... 201 333-2902
Jersey City (G-4783)
Minmetals Inc ....F....... 201 809-1898
Leonia (G-5318)
National Electronic Alloys Inc ....E....... 201 337-9400
Oakland (G-7698)
Nedohon Inc ....G....... 302 533-5512
Wildwood Crest (G-12076)
Park Steel & Iron Co ....F....... 732 775-7500
Neptune (G-6927)
Semi Conductor Manufacturing ....E....... 973 478-2880
Clifton (G-1720)
Stainless Surplus LLC........................G....... 914 661-3800
Green Brook (G-3864)
State Metal Industries Inc...................D....... 856 964-1510
Camden (G-1087)

REFINERS & SMELTERS: Platinum Group Metal Refining, Primary

Matthey Johnson Inc ....C....... 856 384-7132
West Deptford (G-11835)

REFINERS & SMELTERS: Platinum Group Metals, Secondary

Matthey Johnson Inc ....C....... 856 384-7022
Paulsboro (G-8419)
Matthey Johnson Inc ....C....... 856 384-7132
West Deptford (G-11835)

REFINERS & SMELTERS: Silicon, Primary, Over 99% Pure

Path Silicones Inc ....F 201 796-0833
Elmwood Park (G-2841)

REFINERS & SMELTERS: Zinc, Primary, Including Slabs & Dust

L D L Technology Inc ....G 973 345-9111
Paterson (G-8315)

REFINERS & SMELTERS: Zinc, Primary, Including Zinc Residue

Perl Pigments LLC ....G...... 201 836-1212
East Brunswick (G-2172)

REFINING LUBRICATING OILS & GREASES, NEC

Bel-Ray Company Inc ....D 732 378-4000
Wall Township (G-11465)

REFINING: Petroleum

BP Corporation North Amer Inc ....G 973 633-2200
Wayne (G-11613)
BP Corporation North Amer Inc ....E 908 474-5000
Linden (G-5353)
Intertek USA Inc ....E 732 969-5200
Carteret (G-1260)
McAllister Service Company ....E 856 665-4545
Pennsauken (G-8546)
Mobil Research and Dev Corp ....A 856 224-2134
Paulsboro (G-8421)
Pbf Energy Company ....G 973 455-7500
Parsippany (G-8055)
Pbf Energy Company LLC ....D 973 455-7500
Parsippany (G-8056)
Pbf Energy Inc ....A 973 455-7500
Parsippany (G-8057)
Pbf Holding Company LLC ....B 888 661-8949
Parsippany (G-8058)
Pbf Services Company LLC ....G 973 455-7500
Parsippany (G-8059)
Pennzoil-Quaker State Company ....G 856 423-1388
Paulsboro (G-8425)
Speedway LLC ....B 732 750-7800
Port Reading (G-8990)
Total American Services Inc ....F 206 626-3500
Jersey City (G-4838)
Valero Ref Company-New Jersey ....A 856 224-6000
Paulsboro (G-8428)

REFLECTIVE ROAD MARKERS, WHOLESALE

Traffic Safety Service LLC ....E 908 561-4800
South Plainfield (G-10441)

REFRACTORIES: Clay

Harbisonwalker Intl Inc ....G 732 388-4011
Rahway (G-9195)

REFRACTORIES: Nonclay

Curran-Pfeiff Corp ....F 732 225-0555
Edison (G-2499)
Morgan Advanced Ceramics Inc ....E 973 808-1621
Fairfield (G-3264)

REFRACTORY CASTABLES

P & R Castings LLC ....E 732 302-3600
Somerset (G-10150)

REFRIGERATION & HEATING EQUIPMENT

Atomizing Systems Inc ....F 201 447-1222
Ho Ho Kus (G-4453)
Banicki Sheet Metal Inc ....G...... 201 385-5938
Bergenfield (G-382)
Comfortaire Ltd Liability Co ....G...... 856 692-5000
Vineland (G-11338)
Drytech Inc ....E 609 758-1794
Cookstown (G-1806)
Ewc Controls Inc ....E 732 446-3110
Manalapan (G-5846)
Heritage Service Solutions LLC ....F 856 845-7311
Westville (G-11942)

Hussmann Corporation ....E 800 320-3510
West Deptford (G-11828)
Ingersoll-Rand US Trane ....D 732 652-7100
Piscataway (G-8779)
ML Mettler Corp ....G 201 869-0170
North Bergen (G-7469)
On Site Manufacturing Inc ....G 812 794-6040
Flemington (G-3458)
Ryder Technology ....G 215 817-7868
Villas (G-11315)
Stamm International Corp ....G 201 947-1700
Fort Lee (G-3583)
Trane Inc ....C 732 652-7100
Piscataway (G-8828)
Trane US Inc ....C 732 652-7100
Piscataway (G-8829)
Trane US Inc ....D 609 587-3400
Trenton (G-11123)
Trane US Inc ....G 973 882-3220
Pine Brook (G-8718)
York International Corporation ....F 732 346-0606
Edison (G-2653)
Zanotti Transblock USA Corp ....G 917 584-9357
Delran (G-2025)

REFRIGERATION EQPT & SPLYS WHOLESALERS

Bar-Maid Corporation ....C 973 478-7070
Garfield (G-3722)
Icy Cools Inc ....G 609 448-0172
Roosevelt (G-9641)

REFRIGERATION EQPT: Complete

Calmac Manufacturing Corp ....E 201 797-1511
Fair Lawn (G-3085)
Cold Stat Refregiration ....F 201 251-2203
Paramus (G-7861)
Electro Impulse Laboratory Inc ....E 732 776-5800
Neptune (G-6910)
Kohlder Manufacturing Inc ....G 856 963-1801
Pennsauken (G-8540)

REFRIGERATION SVC & REPAIR

Heat-Timer Corporation ....E 212 481-2020
Fairfield (G-3219)
McAllister Service Company ....E 856 665-4545
Pennsauken (G-8546)

REFUSE SYSTEMS

Camden Iron & Metal LLC ....D 856 969-7065
Bellmawr (G-334)
Federal Lorco Petroleum LLC ....D 908 352-0542
Elizabeth (G-2731)
Federal Metals & Alloys Co ....G 908 756-0900
South Plainfield (G-10363)
Globe Metals Inc ....E 973 589-2563
Newark (G-7174)
Safety-Kleen Systems Inc ....F 609 859-2049
Southampton (G-10481)

REGULATORS: Transmission & Distribution Voltage

Somerset Cpitl Mark Tr MGT Inc ....F 848 228-0842
Chesterfield (G-1442)
Wolock & Lott Transmission Eqp ....F 908 218-9292
Branchburg (G-718)

REGULATORS: Transmission & Distribution Voltage

Zero Surge Inc ....F 908 996-7700
Frenchtown (G-3707)

REHABILITATION CENTER, OUTPATIENT TREATMENT

Venetian Care and Rehablitatn ....G 732 721-8200
South Amboy (G-10246)

REHABILITATION SVCS

Venetian Care and Rehablitatn ....G 732 721-8200
South Amboy (G-10246)

RELAYS & SWITCHES: Indl, Electric

Amperite Co Inc ....E 201 864-9503
North Bergen (G-7430)
M&L Power Systems Maint Inc ....E 732 679-1800
Old Bridge (G-7783)

RELAYS: Electric Power

Comus International Inc ....C 973 777-6900
Clifton (G-1588)

RELAYS: Electronic Usage

Panasonic Corp North America ....D 201 348-7000
Newark (G-7261)
Sealed Unit Parts Co Inc ....C 732 223-1201
Allenwood (G-37)

RELIGIOUS SPLYS WHOLESALERS

Devon Trading Corp ....E 973 812-9190
Caldwell (G-1026)

REMOVERS & CLEANERS

Ricks Cleanouts Inc ....E 973 340-7454
Garfield (G-3756)
Turquoise Chemistry Inc ....F 908 561-0002
Piscataway (G-8831)

REMOVERS: Paint

Affordable Lead Solutions LLC ....G 856 207-1348
Bridgeton (G-777)
Noopys Research Inc ....G 856 358-6001
Newfield (G-7369)

RENTAL CENTERS: Furniture

Bedding Shoppe Inc ....G 973 334-9000
Parsippany (G-7959)

RENTAL CENTERS: Party & Banquet Eqpt & Splys

Sconda Canvas Products Inc ....E 732 225-3500
Edison (G-2612)

RENTAL SVCS: Business Machine & Electronic Eqpt

Pitney Bowes Inc ....F 908 903-2870
Warren (G-11564)
Pitney Bowes Inc ....C 800 521-0080
Newark (G-7271)
Pitney Bowes Inc ....C 856 764-2240
Delran (G-2020)

RENTAL SVCS: Costume

Party City Corporation ....F 973 537-1707
Randolph (G-9294)
Party City of North Bergen ....F 201 865-0040
North Bergen (G-7473)

RENTAL SVCS: Eqpt, Theatrical

Acadia Scenic Inc ....E 201 653-8889
Jersey City (G-4697)

RENTAL SVCS: Stores & Yards Eqpt

Winslow Rental & Supply Inc ....G 856 767-5554
Berlin (G-446)

RENTAL SVCS: Tuxedo

Cozy Formal Wear Inc ....G 973 661-9781
Nutley (G-7645)

RENTAL: Passenger Car

Town Ford Inc ....D 609 298-4990
Bordentown (G-613)

RENTAL: Trucks, With Drivers

Jid Transportation LLC ....G 201 362-0841
West New York (G-11870)

REPRODUCTION SVCS: Video Tape Or Disk

Recorded Publications Labs ....E 856 963-3000
Camden (G-1084)

RESEARCH & DEVELOPMENT SVCS, COMMERCIAL: Engineering Lab

M C Technologies Inc ....E 973 839-2779
Pompton Plains (G-8961)

RESEARCH, DEV & TESTING SVCS, COMM: Chem Lab, Exc Testing

Sanofi-Synthelabo Inc ....A 908 231-2000
Bridgewater (G-891)

RESEARCH, DEVELOPMENT & TEST SVCS, COMM: Business Analysis

Wizdata Systems Inc ....F 973 975-4113
Parsippany (G-8115)

RESEARCH, DEVELOPMENT & TEST SVCS, COMM: Cmptr Hardware Dev

Able Group Technologies Inc ....G 732 591-9299
Morganville (G-6634)
Berkeley Varitronics Systems.........E 732 548-3737
Metuchen (G-6096)
Mikros Systems Corporation ....G 609 987-1513
Princeton (G-9074)

RESEARCH, DEVELOPMENT & TEST SVCS, COMM: Research, Exc Lab

Analytical Sales and Svcs Inc........F 973 616-0700
Flanders (G-3401)
Photonics Management Corp ....G 908 231-0960
Bridgewater (G-874)

RESEARCH, DEVELOPMENT & TESTING SVCS, COMM: Research Lab

Accumix Pharmaceuticals LLC ....G 609 632-2225
Old Bridge (G-7772)
Foresight Group LLC ....F 888 992-8880
Parsippany (G-8015)
Novotec Pharma LLC........................G 609 632-2239
Monroe Township (G-6386)
United Silicon Carbide Inc ....F 732 355-0550
Monmouth Junction (G-6368)

RESEARCH, DEVELOPMENT & TESTING SVCS, COMMERCIAL: Business

Pearson Technology Centre Inc ....G 201 767-5000
Old Tappan (G-7800)
Simon & Schuster Inc ....E 973 656-6000
Parsippany (G-8087)
SMR Research Corporation ....G 908 852-7677
Hackettstown (G-4037)

RESEARCH, DEVELOPMENT & TESTING SVCS, COMMERCIAL: Energy

Brilliant Light Power Inc ....E 609 490-0427
East Windsor (G-2371)
Eos Energy Storage LLC...................E 732 225-8400
Edison (G-2514)

RESEARCH, DEVELOPMENT & TESTING SVCS, COMMERCIAL: Medical

Chromak Research Inc ....G 732 560-1366
Somerset (G-10082)
Hisamitsu Phrm Co Inc....................F 973 765-0122
Florham Park (G-3506)
Immtech Pharmaceuticals Inc ....E 212 791-2911
Montclair (G-6417)
Nephros Inc ....G 201 343-5202
South Orange (G-10312)
Songbird Hearing Inc.......................E 732 422-7203
North Brunswick (G-7539)

RESEARCH, DEVELOPMENT & TESTING SVCS, COMMERCIAL: Physical

Aero TEC Laboratories Inc...............E 201 825-1400
Ramsey (G-9231)
Mondelez Global LLC ....A 201 794-4000
Fair Lawn (G-3103)

RESEARCH, DVLPMT & TESTING SVCS, COMM: Merger, Acq & Reorg

Toppan Vintage Inc ....E 201 226-9220
Saddle Brook (G-9797)

RESEARCH, DVLPT & TEST SVCS, COMM: Mkt Analysis or Research

Aus Inc ....G 856 234-9200
Mount Laurel (G-6779)
Brite Concepts Inc ....G 201 270-8544
Englewood (G-2878)
Geolytics Inc...................................G 908 707-1505
Branchburg (G-663)
Webb-Mason Inc ....G 732 747-6585
Tinton Falls (G-10854)

RESEARCH, DVLPT & TESTING SVCS, COMM: Survey, Mktg

Jersey Bound Latino LLC ....G 908 591-2830
Union (G-11197)

RESIDENTIAL REMODELERS

C G I Cstm Fiberglas & Decking ....F 609 646-5302
Pleasantville (G-8904)
EZ General Construction Corp ....G 201 223-1101
Wayne (G-11631)
Mdb Construction ....G 908 628-8010
Lebanon (G-5296)
Taylor Made Custom Cabinetry ....F 856 786-5433
Pennsauken (G-8583)

RESIDUES

Purely Organic SA LLC ....G 201 942-0400
Jersey City (G-4810)

RESINS: Custom Compound Purchased

Bayshore Recycling Corp ....E 732 738-6000
Keasbey (G-4924)
Borealis Compounds Inc..................C 908 850-6200
Port Murray (G-8976)
Diamond Sg Intl Ltd Lblty Co............G 732 861-9850
Eatontown (G-2390)
Federal Plastics Corporation ....E 908 272-5800
Cranford (G-1907)
Joyce Leslie Inc ....D 201 804-7800
Hillsborough (G-4352)
Lion Extruding Corp ....F 973 344-4648
Newark (G-7220)
Lubrizol Advanced Mtls Inc ....E 856 299-3764
Pedricktown (G-8438)
Nobel Biocare Procera LLC ....E 201 529-7100
Mahwah (G-5797)
Polymeric Resources Corp ....E 973 694-4141
Wayne (G-11674)
Recycle Inc ....D 908 756-2200
South Plainfield (G-10433)
Waste Management NJ Inc...............C 609 434-5200
Ewing (G-3069)

RESISTORS

Nte Electronics Inc.........................D 973 748-5089
Bloomfield (G-524)
State Electronics Parts Corp ....E 973 887-2550
East Hanover (G-2244)

RESTAURANT EQPT REPAIR SVCS

Taylor Products Inc.........................E 732 225-4620
Edison (G-2637)

RESTAURANT EQPT: Carts

Custom Sales & Service Inc...................E 800 257-7855
Hammonton (G-4136)

RESTAURANT EQPT: Food Wagons

Lbd Corp ....E 201 541-6760
Englewood (G-2908)

RESTAURANTS: Delicatessen

Bagel Club ....F 908 806-6022
Flemington (G-3429)
Livingston Bagel Warren Inc ....E 973 994-1915
Livingston (G-5540)

Lo Presti & Sons LLC ....E 973 523-9258
Paterson (G-8325)

RESTAURANTS:Full Svc, American

Cheesecake Factory Inc ....G 973 921-0930
Short Hills (G-9976)
S M Z Enterprises Inc ....F 908 232-1921
Westfield (G-11930)
Summerlands Inc ....E 973 729-8428
Sparta (G-10521)

RESTAURANTS:Full Svc, Diner

Amys Omelette Hse Burlington ....F 609 386-4800
Burlington (G-956)

RESTAURANTS:Full Svc, Family, Independent

Renault Winery Inc ....E 609 965-2111
Egg Harbor City (G-2669)

RESTAURANTS:Full Svc, Italian

Antonio Mozzarella Factory Inc ....F 973 353-9411
Newark (G-7087)
Antonio Mozzarella Factory Inc ....E 973 353-9411
Newark (G-7088)

RESTAURANTS:Limited Svc, Coffee Shop

Coffee Company LLC ....G 609 399-5533
Ocean City (G-7750)
Coffee Company LLC ....G 609 398-2326
Ocean City (G-7751)
Millburn Bagel Inc ....E 973 258-1334
Millburn (G-6258)
Perk & Pantry ....G 856 451-4333
Bridgeton (G-794)
Zenas Patisserie.............................E 856 303-8700
Riverton (G-9509)

RESTAURANTS:Limited Svc, Ice Cream Stands Or Dairy Bars

Agape Inc ....F 973 923-7625
Irvington (G-4570)
Bertolotti LLC..................................F 201 941-3116
Fairview (G-3358)
Confectionately Yours LLC ....E 732 821-6863
Franklin Park (G-3626)
Country Club Ice Cream ....G 973 729-5570
Sparta (G-10494)
Dairy Queen ....F 732 892-5700
Point Pleasant Boro (G-8937)
Dunkin Donuts Baskin Robbins ....G 201 692-1900
Teaneck (G-10750)
Enjou Chocolat Morristown Inc ....G 973 993-9090
Morristown (G-6707)
Guernsey Crest Ice Cream Co ....G 973 742-4620
Paterson (G-8285)
Millstone Dq Inc ....G 609 259-6733
Clarksburg (G-1521)
Rolo Systems ....E 973 627-4214
Denville (G-2056)

RESTAURANTS:Ltd Svc, Ice Cream, Soft Drink/Fountain Stands

South Jersey Pretzel Inc ....F 856 435-5055
Stratford (G-10617)

RETAIL BAKERY: Bagels

Bagel Street ....E 609 936-1755
Plainsboro (G-8875)
Branchville Bagels Inc.....................G 973 948-7077
Branchville (G-727)
Cambridge Bagels Inc ....F 973 743-5683
Bloomfield (G-505)
Danmark Enterprises Inc..................E 732 321-3366
South Plainfield (G-10352)
Delicious Bagels Inc ....G 732 892-9265
Point Pleasant Boro (G-8938)
Frell Corp ....F 201 825-2500
Ramsey (G-9240)
Livingston Bagel Warren Inc ....E 973 994-1915
Livingston (G-5540)
S M Z Enterprises Inc ....F 908 232-1921
Westfield (G-11930)

RETAIL BAKERY: Bread

Artisan Oven Inc ....G....... 201 488-6261
  Hackensack (G-3875)
Calandra Italian & French Bky ....D...... 973 484-5598
  Newark (G-7118)
Kohouts Bakery ....G....... 973 772-7270
  Garfield (G-3741)
Serranis Bakery ....F....... 973 678-1777
  Orange (G-7827)
Zinicola Baking Co ....G....... 973 667-1306
  Nutley (G-7658)

RETAIL BAKERY: Cakes

Spindlers Bake Shop ....G....... 201 288-1345
  Hasbrouck Heights (G-4198)

RETAIL BAKERY: Cookies

Fairfield Gourmet Food Corp..............D...... 973 575-4365
  Cedar Grove (G-1283)

RETAIL BAKERY: Doughnuts

9001 Corporation ....E...... 201 963-2233
  Jersey City (G-4693)
9002 Corporation ....E...... 201 792-9595
  Jersey City (G-4694)
All Madina Inc................................F....... 973 226-7772
  West Caldwell (G-11765)
G N J Inc.......................................F....... 856 786-1127
  Cinnaminson (G-1463)
J K P Donuts Inc ....G....... 856 234-9844
  Mount Laurel (G-6809)
Jay Jariwala...................................F....... 908 806-8266
  Ringoes (G-9439)
O O M Inc ....G....... 973 328-9408
  Rockaway (G-9592)

RETAIL BAKERY: Pastries

Bella Palermo Pastry Shop ....E...... 908 931-0298
  Kenilworth (G-4943)
Symphony Inc ....F....... 856 727-9596
  Moorestown (G-6626)

RETAIL BAKERY: Pretzels

Auntie Annes Hmde Sft Prtzls ....F....... 856 772-3737
  Voorhees (G-11422)
Auntie Annes Soft Pretzels ....E...... 856 845-3667
  Woodbury (G-12157)
Auntie Annes Soft Pretzels ....E...... 856 722-0433
  Moorestown (G-6561)
South Jersey Pretzel Inc ....F....... 856 435-5055
  Stratford (G-10617)

RETAIL LUMBER YARDS

Everlast Associates Inc ....G....... 609 261-1888
  Southampton (G-10472)
Palisade Lumber & Supply Inc ....G....... 201 656-4400
  Jersey City (G-4797)
Woodhaven Lumber & Millwork ....E...... 732 295-8800
  Point Pleasant Beach (G-8928)

RETAIL STORES, NEC

Jubili Bead & Yarn Shoppe ....G....... 856 858-7844
  Collingswood (G-1771)

RETAIL STORES: Artificial Limbs

Harry J Lawall & Son Inc ....G....... 856 691-7764
  Vineland (G-11369)

RETAIL STORES: Awnings

William Opdyke Awnings Inc ....G....... 732 449-5940
  Wall Township (G-11519)

RETAIL STORES: Baby Carriages & Strollers

Buy Buy Baby Inc ....F....... 908 688-0888
  Union (G-11161)

RETAIL STORES: Batteries, Non-Automotive

Hoppecke Batteries Inc ....E...... 856 616-0032
  Hainesport (G-4073)

RETAIL STORES: Communication Eqpt

Industronic Inc ....G....... 908 393-5960
  Bridgewater (G-845)
Vcom Intl Multi-Media Corp..................D...... 201 814-0405
  Fairfield (G-3337)

RETAIL STORES: Cosmetics

Bio-Nature Labs Ltd Lblty Co ....E...... 732 738-5550
  Edison (G-2474)
Cheringal Associates Inc ....D...... 201 784-8721
  Norwood (G-7618)
Fiabila USA Inc ....E...... 973 659-9510
  Mine Hill (G-6326)

RETAIL STORES: Decals

Craft Signs....................................G....... 201 656-1991
  Jersey City (G-4735)

RETAIL STORES: Electronic Parts & Eqpt

Ea Pilot Supply ....G....... 201 934-8449
  Bradley Beach (G-627)
I Trade Technology Ltd ....G....... 615 348-7233
  Mahwah (G-5785)

RETAIL STORES: Hair Care Prdts

Art of Shaving - Fl LLC ....G....... 732 410-2520
  Freehold (G-3639)

RETAIL STORES: Hearing Aids

Davis Center Inc ....G....... 862 251-4637
  Succasunna (G-10622)

RETAIL STORES: Hospital Eqpt & Splys

J J L & W Inc..................................E...... 856 854-3100
  Magnolia (G-5741)

RETAIL STORES: Infant Furnishings & Eqpt

Steico USA Inc ....F....... 732 364-6200
  Lakewood (G-5191)

RETAIL STORES: Medical Apparatus & Splys

Electric Mobility Corporation..............C...... 856 468-1000
  Sewell (G-9955)
JFK Supplies Inc ....F....... 732 985-7800
  Edison (G-2545)
Krieck Enterprises LLC ....G....... 908 789-8600
  Madison (G-5727)
Nouveau Prosthetics Ltd.....................F....... 732 739-0888
  Hazlet (G-4280)
Sensonics Inc ....F....... 856 547-7702
  Haddon Heights (G-4051)

RETAIL STORES: Monuments, Finished To Custom Order

Brewster Vaults & Monuments ....F....... 856 785-1412
  Millville (G-6290)

RETAIL STORES: Motors, Electric

Absecon Electric Motor Works............G....... 609 641-1523
  Absecon (G-1)
Lakewood Elc Mtr Sls & Svc ....G....... 732 363-2865
  Howell (G-4560)
Lockwoods Electric Motor Svc ....E...... 609 587-2333
  Trenton (G-11077)
Longo Elctrical-Mechanical Inc ....E...... 973 537-0400
  Linden (G-5404)
Motors and Drives Inc ....G....... 609 344-8058
  Atlantic City (G-103)
New Jersey Electric Motors ....G....... 908 526-5225
  Somerville (G-10221)
VS Systematics Corp..........................G....... 908 241-5110
  Kenilworth (G-5003)

RETAIL STORES: Orthopedic & Prosthesis Applications

Atlantic Prsthtic Orthotic Svc ....G....... 609 927-6330
  Linwood (G-5465)
Garden State Orthopedic Center ....G....... 973 538-4948
  Morristown (G-6709)
J C Orthopedic Inc ....G....... 732 458-7900
  Brick (G-747)

RETAIL STORES: Orthopedic...

Swiss Orthopedic Inc ....G....... 908 874-5522
  Hillsborough (G-4375)

RETAIL STORES: Perfumes & Colognes

Interntnal Flvors Frgrnces Inc ....C...... 732 264-4500
  Hazlet (G-4276)
Victory International USA LLC...............F....... 732 417-5900
  Eatontown (G-2429)

RETAIL STORES: Pet Food

Klein Distributors Inc.........................G....... 732 446-7632
  Burlington (G-982)

RETAIL STORES: Pet Splys

Tuff Mutters LLC ....G....... 973 291-6679
  Kinnelon (G-5041)

RETAIL STORES: Pets

Animals Etc Inc ....G....... 609 386-8442
  Burlington (G-957)

RETAIL STORES: Photocopy Machines

Imperial Copy Products Inc ....E...... 973 927-5500
  Randolph (G-9284)

RETAIL STORES: Plumbing & Heating Splys

Tlw Bath Ltd Liability Company ....E...... 732 942-7117
  Lakewood (G-5196)

RETAIL STORES: Police Splys

Suroma Ltd Liability Company ....G....... 908 735-7700
  Annandale (G-61)

RETAIL STORES: Rock & Stone Specimens

Stoneworld At Redbank Inc ....G....... 732 383-5110
  Red Bank (G-9345)

RETAIL STORES: Rubber Stamps

A A A Stamp and Seal Mfg Co..............G....... 201 796-1500
  Saddle Brook (G-9747)

RETAIL STORES: Safety Splys & Eqpt

Atlas Flasher & Supply Co Inc...............E...... 856 423-3333
  Mickleton (G-6136)

RETAIL STORES: Spas & Hot Tubs

Van Brill Pool & Spa Center ....G....... 856 424-4333
  Marlton (G-6002)

RETAIL STORES: Telephone Eqpt & Systems

Arose Inc.......................................E...... 856 481-4351
  Blackwood (G-471)

RETAIL STORES: Water Purification Eqpt

Bellaqua Inc...................................G....... 201 460-8379
  East Rutherford (G-2284)
Favs Corp......................................G....... 856 358-1515
  Elmer (G-2792)
South Jersey Water Cond Svc...............E...... 856 451-0620
  Bridgeton (G-798)

RETAIL STORES: Wheelchair Lifts

Adaptive Technology Entps LLC ....G....... 877 847-6272
  Medford (G-6063)

REUPHOLSTERY & FURNITURE REPAIR

Colonial Uphl & Win Treatments ....G....... 609 641-3124
  Pleasantville (G-8905)

REUPHOLSTERY SVCS

Costa Mar Cnvas Enclosures LLC ....F....... 609 965-1538
  Egg Harbor City (G-2660)
Franks Upholstery & Draperies ....G....... 856 779-8585
  Maple Shade (G-5902)
H Lauzon Furniture Co Inc ....F....... 201 837-7598
  Teaneck (G-10756)
Lawrence Custom Drapery Shop ....F....... 609 882-4007
  Ewing (G-3034)
Stessl & Neugebauer Inc ....F....... 908 277-3340
  Summit (G-10659)

REWINDING SVCS

Custom Converters Inc ....E 201 994-9000
Livingston (G-5527)

RHEOSTATS: Electronic

Interplex Nas Inc ....E 201 367-1300
Northvale (G-7586)

RIBBONS & BOWS

Circle Visual Inc ....E 212 719-5153
Carlstadt (G-1141)
Colonial - Bende Ribbons Inc ....G 973 777-8700
Passaic (G-8130)
Papillon Ribbon & Bow Inc ....G 973 928-6128
Clifton (G-1689)
Premier Ribbon Company ....G 973 589-2600
Newark (G-7273)

RIBBONS, NEC

Carson & Gebel Ribbon Co LLC ......E 973 627-4200
Rockaway (G-9556)
Cottage Lace and Ribbon Co Inc ....G 732 776-9353
Neptune (G-6905)
Denali Company LLC ....E 732 219-7771
Red Bank (G-9326)
Jrm Industries Inc ....D 973 779-9340
Passaic (G-8152)
Klein Ribbon Corp ....E 973 684-4671
Paterson (G-8310)

RIBBONS: Machine, Inked Or Carbon

Commander Imaging Products Inc .....E 973 742-9298
Paterson (G-8237)
Ricoh Prtg Systems Amer Inc ....G 973 316-6051
Mountain Lakes (G-6861)
Waste Not Computers & Supplies ....G 201 384-4444
Dumont (G-2125)

RIDING APPAREL STORES

Interntonal Riding Helmets Inc ....E 732 772-0165
Marlboro (G-5945)

RIVETS: Metal

Arrow Fastener Co LLC ....B 201 843-6900
Saddle Brook (G-9752)
Celus Fasteners Mfg Inc ....E 800 289-7483
Northvale (G-7576)
New Jersey Rivet Co LLC ....F 856 963-2237
Camden (G-1077)

ROAD CONSTRUCTION EQUIPMENT WHOLESALERS

Ransome Equipment Sales LLC ....G 856 797-8100
Lumberton (G-5663)

ROAD MATERIALS: Bituminous, Not From Refineries

Barrett Industries Corporation ....E 973 533-1001
Morristown (G-6692)
Barrett Paving Materials Inc ....E 973 533-1001
Roseland (G-9647)
Colas Inc ....G 973 290-9082
Morristown (G-6700)
Flemington Bituminous Corp ....F 908 782-2722
Flemington (G-3441)
Rosano Asphalt LLC ....G 732 620-8400
Farmingdale (G-3393)
Weldon Materials Inc ....G 201 991-3200
Kearny (G-4919)

ROBOTS, SERVICES OR NOVELTY, WHOLESALE

Five Elements Robotics LLC ....G 800 681-8514
Wall Township (G-11482)

ROLL FORMED SHAPES: Custom

Specialty Measures ....G 609 882-6071
Ewing (G-3055)

ROLLERS & FITTINGS: Window Shade

Arts Windows Inc ....G 732 905-9595
Toms River (G-10864)

ROLLING MILL EQPT: Finishing

Indemax Inc ....G 973 209-2424
Vernon (G-11298)

ROLLS & ROLL COVERINGS: Rubber

Ames Rubber Corporation ....D 973 827-9101
Hamburg (G-4088)
Kappus Plastic Company Inc ....D 908 537-2288
Hampton (G-4163)

ROLLS: Rubber, Solid Or Covered

Passaic Rubber Co ....D 973 696-9500
Wayne (G-11671)

ROOF DECKS

Bouras Industries Inc ....A 908 918-9400
Summit (G-10637)
C M C Steel Fabricators Inc ....C 908 561-3484
South Plainfield (G-10342)
Elgee Manufacturing Company ....G 908 647-4100
Warren (G-11545)
Great Railing Inc ....F 856 875-0050
Williamstown (G-12089)
Pro-Deck Supply ....G 609 771-1100
Trenton (G-11109)
Roof Deck Inc ....F 609 448-6666
East Windsor (G-2365)

ROOFING GRANULES

G Holdings Inc ....G 973 628-3000
Parsippany (G-8019)
G-I Holdings Inc ....G 973 628-3000
Wayne (G-11638)

ROOFING MATERIALS: Asphalt

Icote USA Inc ....G 908 359-7575
Hillsborough (G-4343)
Karnak Corporation ....D 732 388-0300
Clark (G-1502)
Karnak Midwest LLC ....G 732 388-0300
Clark (G-1503)
Koadings Inc ....G 732 517-0784
Allenhurst (G-26)
United Asphalt Co Inc ....E 856 753-9811
Berlin (G-444)
Vector Foiltec LLC ....G 862 702-8909
Fairfield (G-3339)

ROOFING MATERIALS: Sheet Metal

GAF Elk Materials Corporation ....C 973 628-4083
Wayne (G-11639)

ROOM COOLERS: Portable

Icy Cools Inc ....G 609 448-0172
Roosevelt (G-9641)

ROPE

Egg Harbor Rope Products Inc ....G 609 965-2435
Egg Harbor City (G-2663)
William Kenyon & Sons Inc ....E 732 985-8980
Piscataway (G-8836)

RUBBER

Ansell Healthcare Products LLC ....C 732 345-5400
Iselin (G-4611)
Dicar Inc ....E 973 575-1377
Pine Brook (G-8697)
Dicar Inc ....D 973 575-4220
Pine Brook (G-8698)
Gel United Ltd Liability Co ....G 855 435-8683
Saddle Brook (G-9766)
Harmony Elastomers LLC ....E 973 340-4000
Paterson (G-8287)
Newark Auto Top Co Inc ....F 973 677-9935
East Orange (G-2262)
Pierce-Roberts Rubber Company ....F 609 394-5245
Ewing (G-3043)
Stiles Enterprises Inc ....F 973 625-9660
Rockaway (G-9610)

RUBBER PRDTS: Appliance, Mechanical

Minor Rubber Co Inc ....E 973 338-6800
Bloomfield (G-522)

RUBBER PRDTS: Automotive, Mechanical

Tire Place LLC ....G 732 970-6667
Keyport (G-5025)

RUBBER PRDTS: Mechanical

Aarubco Rubber Co Inc ....E 973 772-8177
Saddle Brook (G-9749)
AMP Custom Rubber Inc ....F 732 888-2714
Keyport (G-5015)
Denaka Partners LP ....E 609 394-1176
Trenton (G-11053)
Eastern Molding Co Inc ....G 973 759-0220
Belleville (G-301)
Hawthorne Rubber Mfg Corp ....E 973 427-3337
Hawthorne (G-4240)
Kinnarney Rubber Co Inc ....F 856 468-1320
Mantua (G-5892)
Manville Rubber Products Inc ....E 908 526-9111
Manville (G-5896)
Monmouth Rubber Corp ....E 732 229-3444
Long Branch (G-5630)
Panova Inc ....E 973 263-1700
Towaco (G-11000)
Passaic Rubber Co ....D 973 696-9500
Wayne (G-11671)
Pierce-Roberts Rubber Company .....F 609 394-5245
Ewing (G-3043)
Reiss Corporation ....C 732 446-6100
Rumson (G-9714)
Rempac LLC ....C 201 843-4585
Rochelle Park (G-9536)
Research & Mfg Corp Amer ....F 908 862-6744
Linden (G-5433)
Rubber & Silicone Products Co ....E 973 227-2300
Fairfield (G-3298)
Shock Tech Inc ....E 845 368-8600
Mahwah (G-5812)
Stiles Enterprises Inc ....F 973 625-9660
Rockaway (G-9610)
T & B Specialties Inc ....G 732 928-4500
Jackson (G-4679)
Tbmc Inc ....E 864 288-9916
Fairfield (G-3321)
Tricomp Inc ....C 973 835-1110
Pompton Plains (G-8966)
Troy Hills Manufacturing Inc ....G 973 263-1885
Towaco (G-11005)

RUBBER PRDTS: Medical & Surgical Tubing, Extrudd & Lathe-Cut

Fermatex Vascular Tech LLC ....F 732 681-7070
Wall Township (G-11481)
Nbs Group Sup Med Pdts Div LLC ....G 732 745-9292
New Brunswick (G-6983)

RUBBER PRDTS: Oil & Gas Field Machinery, Mechanical

Mid-State Enterprises Inc ....F 973 427-6040
Hawthorne (G-4247)

RUBBER PRDTS: Sheeting

Banks Bros Corporation ....D 973 680-4488
Bloomfield (G-502)

RUBBER PRDTS: Silicone

Kini Products Inc ....G 732 299-5555
New Egypt (G-7016)
Paul Englehardt ....G 908 637-4556
Great Meadows (G-3852)
Reiss Manufacturing Inc ....C 732 446-6100
Rumson (G-9715)

RUBBER PRDTS: Sponge

Supply Plus NJ Inc ....E 973 782-5930
Paterson (G-8390)

RUBBER PRDTS: Wet Suits

Henderson Aquatic Inc ....E 856 825-4771
Millville (G-6307)

RUBBER STAMP, WHOLESALE

Magic Printing Corp ....F 732 726-0620
Avenel (G-139)

RUBBER STRUCTURES: Air-Supported

Air Cruisers Company LLC ....C 732 681-3527
Wall Township *(G-11460)*

RUGS : Tufted

Mannington Mills Inc ....A 856 935-3000
Salem *(G-9806)*

RULERS: Metal

National Steel Rule Company ....D 908 862-3366
Linden *(G-5415)*
National Steel Rule Company ....F 800 922-0885
Linden *(G-5416)*

RUST RESISTING

Por-15 Inc ....E 973 887-1999
Whippany *(G-12035)*

SAFES & VAULTS: Metal

United Hospital Supply Corp ....C 609 387-7580
Burlington *(G-993)*

SAFETY EQPT & SPLYS WHOLESALERS

Garden State Highway Pdts Inc ....E 856 692-7572
Millville *(G-6303)*
Jontol Unlimited LLC ....G 858 652-1113
Blackwood *(G-485)*
Power Hawk Technologies Inc ....F 973 627-4646
Rockaway *(G-9599)*

SAFETY INSPECTION SVCS

Forman Industries Inc ....D 732 727-8100
Old Bridge *(G-7779)*

SAILS

Linthicum Sails ....G 856 783-4288
Somerdale *(G-10041)*
North Sales ....G 732 528-8899
Manasquan *(G-5876)*

SALES PROMOTION SVCS

Angus Systems Group Inc ....E 770 521-5553
Middlesex *(G-6147)*

SALT

Saltopia Artisan Infused Sea S ....G 917 628-8433
Hackettstown *(G-4035)*

SALT & SULFUR MINING

Morton Salt Inc ....F 732 826-8414
Perth Amboy *(G-8625)*

SAMPLE BOOKS

Tomwar Corp ....E 856 740-0111
Williamstown *(G-12109)*

SAND & GRAVEL

Baer Aggregates Inc ....F 908 454-4412
Phillipsburg *(G-8641)*
Control Industries Inc ....F 201 437-3826
Bayonne *(G-221)*
County Concrete Corporation ....F 973 538-3113
Morristown *(G-6702)*
Earthwork Associates Inc ....F 609 624-9395
Ocean View *(G-7763)*
Eastern Concrete Materials Inc ....E 973 827-7625
Hamburg *(G-4091)*
Hanson Aggregates Wrp Inc ....E 972 653-5500
Wall Township *(G-11487)*
Harmony Sand & Gravel Inc ....E 908 475-4690
Phillipsburg *(G-8652)*
Intelligentproject LLC ....G 732 928-3421
Jackson *(G-4669)*
J Gennaro Trucking ....F 973 773-0805
Garfield *(G-3740)*
Mays Landing Sand & Gravel Co ....G 856 447-4294
Newport *(G-7377)*
North Church Gravel Inc ....G 201 796-1556
Oak Ridge *(G-7663)*
Orsillo & Company ....G 973 248-1833
Wayne *(G-11668)*

Pinnacle Materials Inc ....F 732 254-7676
East Brunswick *(G-2173)*

SAND MINING

Dun-Rite Sand & Gravel Co ....E 856 692-2520
Vineland *(G-11353)*
Partac Peat Corp ....F 908 637-4191
Great Meadows *(G-3850)*
Whibco of New Jersey Inc ....E 856 455-9200
Port Elizabeth *(G-8972)*

SAND: Hygrade

Covia Holdings Corporation ....E 856 785-2700
Dividing Creek *(G-2071)*
Covia Holdings Corporation ....E 856 451-6400
Bridgeton *(G-782)*
New Jersey Pulverizing Co Inc ....F 732 269-1400
Bayville *(G-259)*
Whibco Inc ....F 856 455-9200
Bridgeton *(G-804)*
Whibco of New Jersey Inc ....E 856 455-9200
Port Elizabeth *(G-8972)*

SANITARY SVC, NEC

All American Oil Recovery Co ....E 973 628-9278
Wayne *(G-11603)*

SANITARY SVCS: Chemical Detoxification

Phibro-Tech Inc ....E 201 329-7300
Teaneck *(G-10767)*

SANITARY SVCS: Environmental Cleanup

Demaio Inc ....E 609 965-4094
Egg Harbor City *(G-2661)*
Doolan Industries Incorporated ....G 856 985-1880
Marlton *(G-5973)*

SANITARY SVCS: Radioactive Waste Materials, Disposal

John J Chando Jr Inc ....F 732 793-2122
Mantoloking *(G-5890)*

SANITARY SVCS: Refuse Collection & Disposal Svcs

County of Somerset ....C 732 469-3363
Bridgewater *(G-830)*

SANITARY SVCS: Sewage Treatment Facility

Organica Water Inc ....F 609 651-8885
West Windsor *(G-11909)*

SANITARY SVCS: Waste Materials, Recycling

All Amrcan Recycl Corp Clifton ....C 201 656-3363
Jersey City *(G-4701)*
All County Recycling Inc ....F 609 393-6445
Trenton *(G-11015)*
Bayshore Recycling Corp ....E 732 738-6000
Keasbey *(G-4924)*
Cumberland Rcycl Corp S Jersey ....E 856 825-4153
Millville *(G-6296)*
EMR (usa Holdings) Inc ....E 856 365-7500
Bellmawr *(G-339)*
Glass Cycle Systems Inc ....G 973 838-0034
Riverdale *(G-9481)*
James R Macauley Inc ....G 856 767-3474
Waterford Works *(G-11598)*
Natures Choice Corporation ....F 973 969-3299
Sparta *(G-10513)*
Plastic Specialties & Tech Inc ....C 201 941-2900
Ridgefield *(G-9380)*
Pure Tech International Inc ....G 908 722-4800
Branchburg *(G-696)*
Recycle Inc ....D 908 756-2200
South Plainfield *(G-10433)*
Reliable Paper Recycling Inc ....G 201 333-5244
Jersey City *(G-4819)*
Wilenta Carting Inc ....F 201 325-0044
Secaucus *(G-9939)*
Wilenta Feed Inc ....F 201 325-0044
Secaucus *(G-9940)*

SANITARY WARE: Metal

Aero Manufacturing Co ....D 973 473-5300
Clifton *(G-1558)*

SANITATION CHEMICALS & CLEANING AGENTS

3M Company ....B 973 884-2500
Whippany *(G-12004)*
Astra Cleaners of Hazlet ....G 732 264-4144
Hazlet *(G-4270)*
Benckiser N Reckitt Amer Inc ....A 973 404-2600
Parsippany *(G-7960)*
Chemetall US Inc ....D 908 464-6900
New Providence *(G-7033)*
Ep Systems Inc ....G 570 424-0581
Hackettstown *(G-4005)*
Global Spclty Products-Usa Inc ....F 609 518-7577
Mount Holly *(G-6771)*
Harvester Inc ....F 201 445-1122
Irvington *(G-4588)*
Houghton Chemical Corporation ....F 201 460-8071
Carlstadt *(G-1170)*
International Products Corp ....F 609 386-8770
Burlington *(G-979)*
Interntonal Specialty Pdts Inc ....A 859 815-3333
Wayne *(G-11653)*
James R Macauley Inc ....G 856 767-3474
Waterford Works *(G-11598)*
Made Solutions LLC ....G 201 254-3693
Fair Lawn *(G-3101)*
Matchless United Companies ....G 908 862-7300
Linden *(G-5406)*
PQ Corporation ....E 732 750-9040
Avenel *(G-146)*
Prestige Laboratories Inc ....E 973 772-8922
East Rutherford *(G-2318)*
Reckitt Benckiser LLC ....C 973 404-2600
Montvale *(G-6471)*
Stanson Corporation ....D 973 344-8666
Kearny *(G-4916)*
Stepan Company ....E 609 298-1222
Bordentown *(G-611)*
Trap-Zap Environmental Systems ....E 201 251-9970
Wyckoff *(G-12266)*
Venus Laboratories Inc ....E 973 257-8983
Parsippany *(G-8109)*

SASHES: Door Or Window, Metal

Architectural Window Mfg Corp ....C 201 933-5094
Rutherford *(G-9726)*
RSI Woodworking Products Co ....D 609 484-1600
Egg Harbor Township *(G-2694)*

SATELLITE COMMUNICATIONS EQPT

Aphelion Orbitals Inc ....G 321 289-0872
Union City *(G-11242)*

SATELLITES: Communications

Maxentric Technologies LLC ....E 201 242-9800
Fort Lee *(G-3566)*
Modulation Sciences Inc ....F 732 302-3090
Somerset *(G-10139)*
Orbcomm LLC ....E 703 433-6300
Rochelle Park *(G-9532)*
Satellite Pros Inc ....G 908 823-9500
Whitehouse Station *(G-12062)*
SES Engineering (us) Inc ....D 609 987-4000
Princeton *(G-9117)*
Ussecurenet LLC ....G 201 447-0130
Hawthorne *(G-4262)*

SAW BLADES

Forrest Mfg Co Inc ....E 973 473-5236
Clifton *(G-1622)*
IDL Techni-Edge LLC ....C 908 497-9818
Kenilworth *(G-4962)*
National Steel Rule Company ....D 908 862-3366
Linden *(G-5415)*

SAWDUST & SHAVINGS

Landew Sawdust Co Inc ....F 973 344-5255
Newark *(G-7216)*
Sawdust Depot LLC ....F 973 344-5255
Howell *(G-4565)*

SAWING & PLANING MILLS

Boards and Beams Co LLC ....G 973 299-6100
Towaco *(G-10989)*
Mellon D P M L L C ....G 732 563-0030
Somerset *(G-10136)*

P J Murphy Forest Pdts Corp ....G...... 973 316-0800
Montville *(G-6491)*
Schairer Brothers ....G...... 609 965-0996
Egg Harbor City *(G-2670)*
Thomas Cobb & Sons ....G...... 856 451-0671
Bridgeton *(G-800)*

SAWING & PLANING MILLS: Custom

Logpowercom LLC ....G...... 732 350-9663
Whiting *(G-12068)*
Rex Lumber Company ....D...... 732 446-4200
Manalapan *(G-5861)*

SAWS & SAWING EQPT

Chatham Lawn Mowler ....G...... 973 635-8855
Chatham *(G-1327)*
Mendham Garden Center ....G...... 973 543-4178
Mendham *(G-6089)*
Precision Saw & Tool Corp ....F...... 973 773-7302
Clifton *(G-1703)*
Winslow Rental & Supply Inc...............G...... 856 767-5554
Berlin *(G-446)*

SCALES & BALANCES, EXC LABORATORY

American Garvens Corporation...............G...... 973 276-1093
Pine Brook *(G-8687)*
Coperion K-Tron Pitman Inc ....G...... 856 589-0500
Sewell *(G-9947)*
Technidyne Corporation ....G...... 732 363-1055
Toms River *(G-10917)*
W T Winter Associates Inc ....E...... 888 808-3611
Fairfield *(G-3349)*

SCALES: Indl

Empire Scale & Balance ....G...... 856 299-1651
Penns Grove *(G-8465)*
Ohaus Corporation ....D...... 973 377-9000
Parsippany *(G-8051)*

SCANNING DEVICES: Optical

Chiral Photonics Inc ....F...... 973 732-0030
Pine Brook *(G-8691)*
MRC Precision Metal Optics Inc...............E...... 941 753-8707
Northvale *(G-7592)*
Ncs Pearson Inc...............D...... 201 896-1011
Lyndhurst *(G-5695)*
Scantron Corporation...............G...... 201 666-7009
Westwood *(G-11971)*
Sqn Peripherals Inc...............E...... 609 261-5500
Rancocas *(G-9263)*

SCHOOL BUS SVC

Dealaman Enterprises Inc...............E...... 908 647-5533
Warren *(G-11544)*

SCHOOLS: Vocational, NEC

Union Institute Inc...............E...... 800 914-8138
Mahwah *(G-5823)*

SCIENTIFIC INSTRUMENTS WHOLESALERS

Daco Limited Partnership ....D...... 973 263-1100
Boonton *(G-562)*
Topcon Medical Systems Inc...............D...... 201 599-5100
Oakland *(G-7707)*

SCRAP & WASTE MATERIALS, WHOLESALE: Metal

Camden Iron & Metal LLC ....D...... 856 969-7065
Bellmawr *(G-334)*
Hugo Neu Recycling LLC ....E...... 914 530-2350
Kearny *(G-4883)*

SCRAP & WASTE MATERIALS, WHOLESALE: Nonferrous Metals Scrap

Emil A Schroth Inc ....E...... 732 938-5015
Howell *(G-4553)*
Globe Metals Inc ....E...... 973 589-2563
Newark *(G-7174)*
Metal MGT Pittsburgh Inc...............E...... 201 333-2902
Jersey City *(G-4783)*

SCRAP & WASTE MATERIALS, WHOLESALE: Paper

Reliable Paper Recycling Inc...............C...... 201 333-5244
Jersey City *(G-4819)*

SCRAP & WASTE MATERIALS, WHOLESALE: Plastics Scrap

Gdb International Inc ....D...... 732 246-3001
New Brunswick *(G-6962)*
Lion Extruding Corp ....F...... 973 344-4648
Newark *(G-7220)*
Recycle-Tech Corp ....F...... 201 475-5000
Elmwood Park *(G-2847)*

SCREENS: Window, Metal

Belleville Corp ....F...... 201 991-6222
Kearny *(G-4863)*
Verona Aluminum Products Inc...............G...... 973 857-4809
Verona *(G-11312)*

SCREENS: Window, Wood Framed

Screens Incorporated ....G...... 973 633-8558
Wayne *(G-11683)*

SCREW MACHINE PRDTS

Accurate Screw Machine Corp ....D...... 973 276-0379
Fairfield *(G-3126)*
Amark Industries Inc ....G...... 973 992-8900
Livingston *(G-5524)*
Automatic Machine Product ....G...... 973 383-9929
Newton *(G-7380)*
Bmb Machining LLC ....G...... 973 256-4010
Woodland Park *(G-12211)*
C & K Punch & Screw Mch Pdts...............G...... 201 343-6750
Hackensack *(G-3886)*
Champion Fasteners Inc ....E...... 609 267-5222
Lumberton *(G-5655)*
Chicago Pneumatic Tool ....G...... 973 276-1377
Fairfield *(G-3158)*
Congruent Machine Co Inc ....G...... 973 764-6767
Vernon *(G-11297)*
Duro Manufacturing Company ....G...... 908 810-9588
Union *(G-11175)*
Eastern Machining Corporation ....G...... 856 694-3303
Franklinville *(G-3630)*
Edston Manufacturing Company...............G...... 908 647-0116
Fairfield *(G-3182)*
Esco Precision Inc...............E...... 908 722-0800
Hillsborough *(G-4331)*
F P Schmidt Manufacturing Co...............F...... 201 343-4241
South Hackensack *(G-10267)*
Ferrum Industries Inc ....F...... 201 935-1220
Carlstadt *(G-1160)*
Form Cut Industries Inc...............F...... 973 483-5154
Newark *(G-7165)*
Gadren Machine Co Inc ....F...... 856 456-4329
Mount Ephraim *(G-6763)*
H & H Swiss Screw Machine PR ....E...... 908 688-6390
Hillside *(G-4410)*
Hi-Grade Products Mfg Co ....F...... 908 245-4133
Kenilworth *(G-4961)*
Industrial Machine & Engrg Co...............F...... 908 862-8874
Linden *(G-5386)*
International Tool & Mch LLC ....G...... 908 687-5580
Hillside *(G-4419)*
J & S Precision Products Co ....E...... 609 654-0900
Medford *(G-6072)*
Karl Neuweiler Inc...............G...... 908 464-6532
Berkeley Heights *(G-415)*
Labern Machine Products LLC...............G...... 908 722-1970
Branchburg *(G-673)*
Main Robert A & Sons Holdg Co ....E...... 201 447-3700
Wyckoff *(G-12258)*
Meltom Manufacturing Inc ....G...... 973 546-0058
Clifton *(G-1672)*
Metal Components Inc...............G...... 973 247-1204
North Haledon *(G-7551)*
Mw Industries Inc ....D...... 973 244-9200
Fairfield *(G-3265)*
Nova Precision Products Inc ....C...... 973 625-1586
Rockaway *(G-9590)*
O E M Manufacturers Ltd Inc ....E...... 201 475-8585
Elmwood Park *(G-2839)*
Orion Precision Industries ....E...... 732 247-9704
Somerset *(G-10147)*
Oroszlany Laszlo ....G...... 201 666-2101
Hillsdale *(G-4386)*

Peter Yaged ....G...... 973 427-4219
Hawthorne *(G-4253)*
S J Screw Company Inc ....E...... 908 475-2155
Belvidere *(G-376)*
Salem Manufacturing Corp ....F...... 973 751-6331
Belleville *(G-317)*
Sumatic Co Inc ....G...... 973 772-1288
Garfield *(G-3766)*
Supermatic Corp ....F...... 973 627-4433
Rockaway *(G-9611)*
Telemark Cnc LLC ....G...... 973 794-4857
Boonton *(G-586)*
Tool Shop Inc ....G...... 856 767-8077
West Berlin *(G-11758)*
Ultimate Spinning Turning Corp ....G...... 201 372-9740
Moonachie *(G-6550)*
Welton V Johnson Engineering...............F...... 908 241-3100
Kenilworth *(G-5006)*
Zago Manufacturing Company ....E...... 973 643-6700
Newark *(G-7362)*

SCREW MACHINES

High Point Precision Products ....E...... 973 875-6229
Sussex *(G-10672)*

SCREWS: Metal

Cold Headed Fasteners Inc ....G...... 856 461-3244
Delanco *(G-2004)*
P & R Fasteners Inc ....D...... 732 302-3600
Somerset *(G-10151)*

SEALANTS

Compounders Inc ....G...... 732 938-5007
Farmingdale *(G-3381)*
CR Laurence Co Inc...............F...... 856 727-1022
Moorestown *(G-6570)*
Royal Adhesives & Sealants LLC ....E...... 973 694-0845
Wayne *(G-11680)*
Sika Corporation ....C...... 201 933-8800
Lyndhurst *(G-5709)*

SEALING COMPOUNDS: Sealing, synthetic rubber or plastic

Assem - Pak Inc ....C...... 856 692-3355
Vineland *(G-11323)*
La Favorite Industries Inc ....F...... 973 279-1266
Paterson *(G-8316)*

SEALS: Hermetic

A P M Hexseal Corporation ....E...... 201 569-5700
Englewood *(G-2865)*
Aspe Inc ....E...... 973 808-1155
Fairfield *(G-3141)*
Bryan Snook ....G...... 888 747-3250
Bedminster *(G-268)*
Concept Group Inc ....E...... 856 767-5506
West Berlin *(G-11711)*
Frc Electrical Industries Inc ....E...... 908 464-3200
New Providence *(G-7036)*
Glasseal Products Inc ....C...... 732 370-9100
Lakewood *(G-5129)*
T & E Industries Inc ....E...... 973 672-5454
Orange *(G-7830)*
Zago Manufacturing Company ....E...... 973 643-6700
Newark *(G-7362)*

SEALS: Oil, Rubber

East Coast Rubber Products ....G...... 856 384-2747
Westville *(G-11938)*

SEARCH & DETECTION SYSTEMS, EXC RADAR

National Prtective Systems Inc...............F...... 732 922-3609
Eatontown *(G-2415)*

SEARCH & NAVIGATION SYSTEMS

Aeropanel Corporation ....D...... 973 335-9636
Boonton *(G-552)*
Alk Technologies Inc ....C...... 609 683-0220
Princeton *(G-9002)*
Allied-Signal China Ltd ....E...... 973 455-2000
Morristown *(G-6685)*
American Gas & Chemical Co Ltd ....E...... 201 767-7300
Northvale *(G-7572)*

Bae Systems Info & Elec Sys ....B 603 885-4321
　Totowa *(G-10933)*
Check-It Electronics Corp ....E 973 520-8435
　Elizabeth *(G-2718)*
Drs Infrared Technologies LP ....G 973 898-1500
　Parsippany *(G-7986)*
Drs Leonardo Inc ....E 973 898-1500
　Parsippany *(G-7988)*
Ferry Machine Corp ....E 201 641-9191
　Little Ferry *(G-5504)*
GE Aviation Systems LLC ....C 973 428-9898
　Whippany *(G-12021)*
Glasseal Products Inc ....C 732 370-9100
　Lakewood *(G-5129)*
Halberd Match Corp ....G 609 882-7000
　Ewing *(G-3019)*
Harris Corporation ....C 973 284-0123
　Clifton *(G-1634)*
Harris Corporation ....C 585 269-6600
　Clifton *(G-1637)*
Ho-Ho-Kus Inc ....E 973 278-2274
　Paterson *(G-8290)*
Intertek Laboratories Inc ....E 908 903-1800
　Stirling *(G-10601)*
Kearfott Corporation ....C 973 785-6000
　Woodland Park *(G-12223)*
Lockheed Martin ....C 856 762-2222
　Marlton *(G-5983)*
Lockheed Martin ....D 856 722-7782
　Marlton *(G-5984)*
Lockheed Martin ....C 856 722-2418
　Marlton *(G-5985)*
Lockheed Martin Corporation ....D 856 722-7782
　Moorestown *(G-6594)*
Lockheed Martin Corporation ....C 856 722-3336
　Moorestown *(G-6595)*
Northrop Grumman Systems Corp ......G 908 276-6677
　Cranford *(G-1918)*
Oaviation Corporation ....E 609 619-3060
　Princeton *(G-9085)*
Primacy Engineering Inc ....F 201 731-3272
　Englewood Cliffs *(G-2979)*
Sun Dial & Panel Corporation ....E 973 226-4334
　Fairfield *(G-3316)*
Transistor Devices Inc ....C 908 850-5088
　Hackettstown *(G-4041)*

SEARCH & RESCUE SVCS

Anvima Technologies LLC ....G 973 531-7077
　Brookside *(G-922)*

SEATING: Stadium

Archer Plastics Inc ....G 856 692-0242
　Elmer *(G-2789)*

SECRETARIAL SVCS

Premier Printing Solutions LLC ....G 732 525-0740
　Sayreville *(G-9836)*

SECURITY CONTROL EQPT & SYSTEMS

AAS Technologies Inc ....G 201 342-7300
　Hackensack *(G-3872)*
Blonder Tongue Labs Inc ....C 732 679-4000
　Old Bridge *(G-7775)*
Checkpoint Systems Inc ....C 800 257-5540
　West Deptford *(G-11821)*
Checkpoint Systems Inc ....C 856 848-1800
　West Deptford *(G-11822)*
Checkpoint Systems Inc ....C 856 848-1800
　West Deptford *(G-11824)*
Daq Electronics LLC ....E 732 981-0050
　Piscataway *(G-8753)*
East Coast Security Products ....F 973 625-3277
　Rockaway *(G-9562)*
Ecsi International Inc ....F 973 574-8555
　Clifton *(G-1610)*
Electronic Control SEC Inc ....F 973 574-8555
　Clifton *(G-1613)*
Engineered Security Systems ....E 973 257-0555
　Towaco *(G-10995)*
Essexusa LLC ....F 201 576-0001
　Paramus *(G-7867)*
Ifortress ....G 973 812-6400
　Woodland Park *(G-12222)*
K & A Industries Inc ....G 908 226-7000
　South Plainfield *(G-10390)*
Ketec ....F 856 778-4343
　Moorestown *(G-6591)*

LTS NJ Inc ....G 856 780-9888
　Mount Laurel *(G-6815)*
Mobile Intelligent Alerts Inc ....G 201 410-5324
　Holmdel *(G-4523)*
Multicomm Solutions Inc ....G 877 796-8480
　Toms River *(G-10898)*
Qsa Global National Corp ....G 865 888-6798
　Red Bank *(G-9341)*
Quantum Security Systems Inc ....G 609 252-0505
　Princeton *(G-9108)*
Secure System Inc ....E 732 922-3609
　Stirling *(G-10606)*
Security 21 LLC ....G 856 384-7474
　Woodbury *(G-12169)*
Specialized Fire & SEC Inc ....E 212 255-1010
　Riverdale *(G-9489)*
T F S Inc ....E 973 890-7651
　Totowa *(G-10974)*
Talon7 LLC ....F 908 595-2121
　Bridgewater *(G-901)*
Techntime Bus Sltns Ltd Lblty ....F 973 246-8153
　East Rutherford *(G-2331)*
Wickr Inc ....G 516 637-2882
　Newark *(G-7360)*

SECURITY DEVICES

Almetek Industries Inc ....E 908 850-9700
　Hackettstown *(G-3996)*
Digitize Inc ....F 973 663-1011
　Lake Hopatcong *(G-5056)*
Enterprisecc Ltd Liability Co ....G 201 266-0020
　Jersey City *(G-4749)*
Infinova Corporation ....E 732 355-9100
　Monmouth Junction *(G-6347)*
M & Z International Inc ....G 201 864-3331
　West New York *(G-11872)*
Skycam Technologies LLC ....G 908 205-5548
　Perth Amboy *(G-8631)*

SECURITY EQPT STORES

Vcom Intl Multi-Media Corp ....D 201 296-0600
　Fairfield *(G-3338)*

SECURITY PROTECTIVE DEVICES
MAINTENANCE & MONITORING SVCS

Hookway Enterprises Inc ....F 973 691-0382
　Netcong *(G-6941)*
Ketec ....F 856 778-4343
　Moorestown *(G-6591)*
Qsa Global National Corp ....G 865 888-6798
　Red Bank *(G-9341)*
Secure System Inc ....E 732 922-3609
　Stirling *(G-10606)*
Sightlogix Inc ....E 609 951-0008
　Princeton *(G-9118)*
Solar Rig Technologies LLC ....G 973 600-0500
　Carlstadt *(G-1221)*

SECURITY SYSTEMS SERVICES

National Prtective Systems Inc ....F 732 922-3609
　Eatontown *(G-2415)*
T F S Inc ....E 973 890-7651
　Totowa *(G-10974)*
Vanderbilt LLC ....E 973 316-3900
　Parsippany *(G-8108)*

SEMICONDUCTOR CIRCUIT NETWORKS

M E C Technologies Inc ....E 732 505-0308
　Toms River *(G-10894)*
Solar Rig Technologies LLC ....G 973 600-0500
　Carlstadt *(G-1221)*
Xtreme Powertech LLC ....E 201 791-5050
　Upper Saddle River *(G-11289)*

SEMICONDUCTORS & RELATED DEVICES

Aeon Corporation ....G 609 275-9003
　Princeton Junction *(G-9144)*
Akela Laser Corporation ....F 732 305-7105
　Monroe Township *(G-6377)*
Altera Corporation ....G 732 649-3477
　Somerset *(G-10055)*
American Microsemiconductor ....E 973 377-9566
　Madison *(G-5719)*
Automatic Switch Company ....A 973 966-2000
　Florham Park *(G-3489)*
Bel Fuse Inc ....C 201 432-0463
　Jersey City *(G-4715)*

Cast Inc ....G 201 391-8300
　Woodcliff Lake *(G-12185)*
Compufab Sales Inc ....G 856 786-0175
　Cinnaminson *(G-1452)*
Data Delay Devices Inc ....E 973 202-3268
　Clifton *(G-1597)*
Dialight Corporation ....D 732 919-3119
　Wall Township *(G-11477)*
Discovery Semiconductors Inc ....E 609 434-1311
　Ewing *(G-3014)*
G T Associates ....G 973 694-6040
　Wayne *(G-11637)*
Gce Market Inc ....G 856 401-8900
　Blackwood *(G-478)*
Hamamatsu Corporation ....D 908 231-0960
　Bridgewater *(G-841)*
Ii-VI Optoelectronic Dvcs Inc ....B 908 668-5000
　Warren *(G-11555)*
Infineon Tech Americas Corp ....F 732 603-5914
　Iselin *(G-4629)*
Inphot Inc ....G 609 799-7172
　Plainsboro *(G-8886)*
Intel Corporation ....G 908 894-6035
　Hampton *(G-4162)*
International Diode Corp ....G 973 482-6518
　Harrison *(G-4186)*
Jerome Industries Corp ....E 908 353-5700
　Hackettstown *(G-4013)*
Keyence Corporation America ....E 201 930-0100
　Elmwood Park *(G-2828)*
Kyocera International Inc ....D 856 691-7000
　Cherry Hill *(G-1386)*
Lucent Technologies World Svcs ....C 908 582-3000
　New Providence *(G-7046)*
Memory International Corp ....F 973 586-2653
　Denville *(G-2049)*
Micro-Tek Laboratories Inc ....G 973 779-5577
　Clifton *(G-1674)*
Microsemi Stor Solutions Inc ....G 908 953-9400
　Basking Ridge *(G-198)*
Moser Jewel Company ....G 908 454-1155
　Phillipsburg *(G-8660)*
Multi-Tech Industries Inc ....F 732 431-0550
　Marlboro *(G-5948)*
Multilink Technology Corp ....E 732 805-9355
　Somerset *(G-10142)*
Nanonex Corp ....F 732 355-1600
　Monmouth Junction *(G-6352)*
Nte Electronics Inc ....D 973 748-5089
　Bloomfield *(G-524)*
Princeton Lightwave Inc ....E 609 495-2600
　Cranbury *(G-1873)*
Renesas Electronics Amer Inc ....E 908 685-6000
　Bridgewater *(G-883)*
Richards Manufacturing Co Inc ....G 973 371-1771
　Irvington *(G-4602)*
Roxboro Holdings Inc ....D 732 919-3119
　Wall Township *(G-11506)*
Rudolph Technologies Inc ....G 973 448-4307
　Ledgewood *(G-5309)*
Sharp Electronics Corporation ....A 201 529-8200
　Mahwah *(G-5811)*
Sunlight Photonics Inc ....G 732 362-7501
　Edison *(G-2632)*
Thinfilms Inc ....F 908 359-7014
　Hillsborough *(G-4376)*
Universal Display Corporation ....C 609 671-0980
　Ewing *(G-3064)*
Viavi Solutions Inc ....C 609 632-0800
　Trenton *(G-11131)*
Vicor Industries Inc ....F 201 569-1947
　Tenafly *(G-10789)*
William Kenyon & Sons Inc ....E 732 985-8980
　Piscataway *(G-8836)*

SENSORS: Radiation

Frauscher Sensor Tech USA Inc ....F 609 285-5492
　Princeton *(G-9047)*
Itech Instruments LLC ....G 609 924-7310
　Ewing *(G-3026)*

SENSORS: Temperature For Motor Windings

NRG Bluewater Wind LLC ....G 201 748-5000
　Hoboken *(G-4487)*

SENSORS: Temperature, Exc Indl Process

Palmer Electronics Inc ....F 973 772-5900
　Garfield *(G-3744)*

P
R
O
D
U
C
T

SEPTIC TANKS: Concrete

Double Twenties Inc ....F 973 827-7563
Franklin *(G-3598)*

Flemington Precast & Sup LLC ....F 908 782-3246
Flemington *(G-3442)*

Granville Concrete Products ....G 973 584-6653
Randolph *(G-9280)*

Northeast Con Pdts & Sup Inc ......G 973 728-1667
Hewitt *(G-4291)*

Peerless Concrete Products Co ......E 973 838-3060
Butler *(G-1015)*

SEWAGE & WATER TREATMENT EQPT

Favs Corp ....G 856 358-1515
Elmer *(G-2792)*

Fin-Tek Corporation ....G 973 628-2988
Wayne *(G-11634)*

Monitoring Solutions Inc ....G 908 713-0172
Hampton *(G-4165)*

Site Drainer LLC ....C 862 225-9940
Clifton *(G-1726)*

Suez Treatment Solutions Inc ....C 201 767-9300
Paramus *(G-7907)*

U V International LLC ....G 973 993-9454
Morristown *(G-6747)*

Ugsi Chemical Feed Inc ....E 856 896-2160
Vineland *(G-11411)*

Water Resources New Jersey LLC ....G 609 268-7965
Tabernacle *(G-10739)*

SEWAGE TREATMENT SYSTEMS & EQPT

East Brunswick Sewerage Auth ....F 732 257-8313
East Brunswick *(G-2148)*

Franklin Miller Inc ....E 973 535-9200
Livingston *(G-5531)*

SEWING CONTRACTORS

A & R Sewing Company Inc ....F 201 332-0622
Jersey City *(G-4695)*

Bethel Industries Inc ....C 201 656-8222
Jersey City *(G-4717)*

Tex Spar Co Inc ....C 732 367-9439
Lakewood *(G-5194)*

SEWING MACHINES & PARTS: Indl

Clinton Industries Inc ....E 201 440-0400
Little Ferry *(G-5498)*

Imperial Sewing Machine Co ....G 973 374-3405
Irvington *(G-4591)*

John N Fehlinger Co Inc ....G 973 633-0699
Fairfield *(G-3237)*

Kansai Special Amercn Mch Corp ....G 973 470-8321
East Rutherford *(G-2301)*

SHADES: Lamp & Light, Residential

Jay-Bee Lamp & Shade Co Inc ....G 201 265-0762
Paramus *(G-7877)*

Nicholas Longo Sr ....G 856 642-1971
Riverton *(G-9508)*

SHADES: Lamp Or Candle

Natal Lamp & Shade Corp ....E 201 224-7844
Fort Lee *(G-3574)*

New Brunswick Lamp Shade Co ....E 732 545-0377
New Brunswick *(G-6986)*

SHADES: Window

A Plus Installs LLC ....G 201 255-4412
Bloomfield *(G-499)*

C & M Shade Corp ....E 201 807-1200
Fairfield *(G-3152)*

Griffith Shade Company Inc ....G 973 667-1474
Nutley *(G-7647)*

Kay Window Fashions Inc ....F 862 591-1554
Saddle Brook *(G-9771)*

RFS Commercial ....E 201 796-0006
Saddle Brook *(G-9785)*

SHAPES & PILINGS, STRUCTURAL: Steel

Bloomfield Iron Co Inc ....G 973 748-7040
Belleville *(G-296)*

McAlister Welding & Fabg ....F 856 740-3890
Glassboro *(G-3809)*

SHAPES: Extruded, Aluminum, NEC

Frameware Inc ....F 800 582-5608
Fairfield *(G-3201)*

SHAVING PREPARATIONS

Edgewell Personal Care LLC ....G 973 753-3000
Cedar Knolls *(G-1310)*

SHEET METAL SPECIALTIES, EXC STAMPED

A B Scantlebury Co Inc ....F 973 770-3000
Newton *(G-7378)*

Allmike Metal Technology Inc ....F 201 935-2306
Moonachie *(G-6502)*

Broadhurst Sheet Metal Works ....G 973 304-4001
Hawthorne *(G-4223)*

Burns Link Manufacturing Co ....F 856 429-6844
Voorhees *(G-11424)*

Cheney Flashing Company LLC ....F 609 394-8175
Trenton *(G-11039)*

Clifton Metal Products Co Inc ....F 973 777-6100
Clifton *(G-1584)*

Coronation Sheet Metal Co ....G 908 686-0930
Union *(G-11167)*

Custom Fabricators Inc ....G 908 862-4244
Linden *(G-5365)*

D&N Machine Manufacturing Inc ....E 856 456-1366
Gloucester City *(G-3835)*

Diversified Fab Pdts Ltd Lblty ....G 973 773-3189
Clifton *(G-1602)*

Edker Industries Inc ....E 856 786-1971
Cinnaminson *(G-1460)*

Elmco Two Inc ....E 856 365-2244
Camden *(G-1061)*

Franklen Sheet Metal Co Inc ....F 732 988-0808
Ocean Grove *(G-7761)*

General Aviation & Elec Mfg Co ....E 201 487-1700
Hackensack *(G-3920)*

Globe Engineering Corp ....G 609 898-0349
Cape May *(G-1101)*

International Shtmtl Plate Mfg ....E 908 722-6614
Somerville *(G-10216)*

J & E Metal Fabricators Inc ....E 732 548-9650
Metuchen *(G-6112)*

Jersey Sheet Metal & Machine ....E 973 366-8628
Dover *(G-2097)*

Kinetron Inc ....F 732 918-7777
Ocean *(G-7729)*

Lentine Sheet Metal Inc ....F 908 486-8974
Linden *(G-5402)*

Lynn Mechanical Contractors ....F 856 829-1717
Cinnaminson *(G-1474)*

Metal Specialties New Jersey ....G 609 261-9277
Mount Holly *(G-6775)*

Metalfab Inc ....E 973 764-2000
Vernon *(G-11299)*

Metalix Inc ....G 973 546-2500
Little Falls *(G-5482)*

Moreng Metal Products Inc ....D 973 256-2001
Totowa *(G-10956)*

Neumann Sheet Metal Inc ....G 908 756-0415
Plainfield *(G-8867)*

New Age Metal Fabg Co Inc ....D 973 227-9107
Fairfield *(G-3268)*

Pemberton Fabricators Inc ....A 609 267-0922
Rancocas *(G-9260)*

Pioneer Machine & Tool Co Inc ....E 856 779-8800
Maple Shade *(G-5907)*

Quality Sheet Metal & Wldg Inc ....F 732 469-7111
Piscataway *(G-8804)*

Radiation Systems Inc ....G 201 891-7515
Wyckoff *(G-12261)*

Rhoads Metal Works Inc ....E 856 486-1551
Pennsauken *(G-8573)*

S P Sheet Metal Co Inc ....F 609 698-8800
Barnegat *(G-164)*

Service Metal Fabricating Inc ....D 973 625-8882
Rockaway *(G-9608)*

Shamong Manufacturing Company ....E 609 654-2549
Shamong *(G-9971)*

Springfield Metal Pdts Co Inc ....F 973 379-4600
Springfield *(G-10578)*

Theodore E Mozer Inc ....E 856 829-1432
Palmyra *(G-7851)*

Trenton Sheet Metal Inc ....E 609 695-6328
Trenton *(G-11126)*

Unique Metal Products ....F 732 388-1888
Rahway *(G-9226)*

Vfi Fabricators Inc ....E 856 629-8786
Williamstown *(G-12113)*

Wecom Inc ....E 856 863-8400
Glassboro *(G-3813)*

Westfield Shtmtl Works Inc ....E 908 276-5500
Kenilworth *(G-5007)*

SHEETING: Laminated Plastic

Graphic Express Menu Co Inc ....G 973 685-0022
Clifton *(G-1630)*

JMJ Profile Inc ....G 856 767-3930
West Berlin *(G-11726)*

Monmouth Rubber Corp ....E 732 229-3444
Long Branch *(G-5630)*

Washington Stamp Exchange Inc ....F 973 966-0001
Florham Park *(G-3523)*

SHEETS & SHEETINGS, COTTON

Homespun Global LLC ....G 917 674-9684
Sayreville *(G-9823)*

SHEETS: Fabric, From Purchased Materials

Triangle Home Fashions LLC ....G 732 355-9800
Dayton *(G-1993)*

SHELLAC

PPG Industries Inc ....E 856 273-7870
Mount Laurel *(G-6830)*

Rust-Oleum Corporation ....E 732 469-8100
Somerset *(G-10169)*

SHELTERED WORKSHOPS

Bestwork Inds For The Blind ....D 856 424-2510
Cherry Hill *(G-1349)*

SHELVES & SHELVING: Wood

Frank & Jims Inc ....G 609 646-1655
Pleasantville *(G-8908)*

SHERARDIZING SVC: Metals Or Metal Prdts

Armadillo Metalworks Inc ....E 973 777-2105
Passaic *(G-8125)*

SHIELDS OR ENCLOSURES: Radiator, Sheet Metal

USA Industries Inc ....E 201 438-6606
Carlstadt *(G-1237)*

SHIMS: Metal

Wm Hbrewster Jr Incorporated ....G 973 227-1050
Fairfield *(G-3353)*

SHIP BLDG/RPRG: Submersible Marine Robots, Manned/Unmanned

Bishop Ascendant Inc ....G 973 210-5298
West Caldwell *(G-11768)*

SHIP BUILDING & REPAIRING: Cargo, Commercial

Ocean Power & Equipment Co ....G 973 575-5775
West Caldwell *(G-11793)*

SHIP BUILDING & REPAIRING: Dredges

Wittich Bros Marine Inc ....E 732 722-8656
Manasquan *(G-5885)*

SHIP BUILDING & REPAIRING: Fishing Vessels, Large

Allen Steel Co ....G 856 785-1171
Leesburg *(G-5314)*

SHIP BUILDING & REPAIRING: Passenger, Commercial

Island Breeze Intl Inc ....F 856 931-1505
Marlton *(G-5980)*

SHIP BUILDING & REPAIRING: Rigging, Marine

American Rigging & Repair Inc ....F 866 478-7129
Roselle *(G-9660)*

SHIPBUILDING & REPAIR

Bayonne Drydock & Repair Corp ....E..... 201 823-9295
Bayonne **(G-215)**

Conneaut Creek Ship Repr Inc ....G..... 212 863-9406
Jersey City **(G-4732)**

Kerney Service Group Inc ....E..... 908 486-2644
Linden **(G-5397)**

Maxwell McKenney Inc ....G..... 856 310-0700
Haddon Heights **(G-4048)**

Nvs International Inc ....E..... 908 523-0266
Linden **(G-5421)**

Simplex Americas LLC ....G..... 908 237-9099
Flemington **(G-3466)**

Union Dry Dock & Repair Co ....E..... 201 963-5833
Hoboken **(G-4502)**

White Marine Inc ....F..... 732 826-4491
Towaco **(G-11007)**

SHIPPING AGENTS

E C D Ventures Inc ....G..... 856 875-1100
Blackwood **(G-477)**

Hub Print & Copy Center LLC ....G..... 201 585-7887
Fort Lee **(G-3558)**

Rostek Innovations LLC ....G..... 908 996-6007
Frenchtown **(G-3705)**

SHOE MATERIALS: Counters

Cross Counter Inc ....G..... 973 677-0600
East Orange **(G-2255)**

SHOE MATERIALS: Quarters

Hair Quarters ....G..... 856 624-4072
Woodstown **(G-12238)**

Major Bs General Quarters LLC ....G..... 732 710-6088
Matawan **(G-6024)**

SHOE MATERIALS: Rands

Ingersoll-Rand Company ....G..... 973 882-0924
Pine Brook **(G-8706)**

SHOE MATERIALS: Rubber

Aerogroup Retail Holdings Inc ....D..... 732 819-9843
Edison **(G-2451)**

SHOE STORES

Ballet Makers Inc ....B..... 973 595-9000
Totowa **(G-10934)**

SHOE STORES: Athletic

Rags International Inc ....G..... 787 632-8447
Springfield **(G-10574)**

Schusters Shoes Inc ....G..... 856 885-4551
Williamstown **(G-12105)**

SHOE STORES: Children's

J T Murdoch Shoes ....F..... 973 748-6484
Bloomfield **(G-514)**

SHOE STORES: Orthopedic

Carlascio Custom & Orthopedic ....G..... 201 333-8716
Jersey City **(G-4723)**

SHOES & BOOTS WHOLESALERS

Jese Apparel LLC ....F..... 732 969-3200
Dayton **(G-1973)**

Lust For Life Footwear LLC ....F..... 631 327-2811
Teaneck **(G-10761)**

Man-How Inc ....G..... 609 392-4895
Trenton **(G-11078)**

S Goldberg & Co Inc ....C..... 201 342-1200
Hackensack **(G-3969)**

SHOES: Athletic, Exc Rubber Or Plastic

Komar Inc ....B..... 212 725-1500
Jersey City **(G-4772)**

SHOES: Ballet Slippers

Ballet Makers Inc ....B..... 973 595-9000
Totowa **(G-10934)**

SHOES: Canvas, Rubber Soled

Vans Inc ....F..... 732 493-1516
Tinton Falls **(G-10853)**

SHOES: Children's, Sandals, Exc Rubber Or Plastic

S Goldberg & Co Inc ....C..... 201 342-1200
Hackensack **(G-3969)**

SHOES: Men's

Bm USA Incorporated ....E..... 800 624-5499
Carlstadt **(G-1132)**

CB Marathon Opco LLC ....D..... 201 843-5416
Paramus **(G-7860)**

Steven Madden Ltd ....D..... 973 533-0121
Livingston **(G-5564)**

Vf Outdoor LLC ....G..... 908 352-5390
Elizabeth **(G-2781)**

SHOES: Orthopedic, Children's

Carlascio Custom & Orthopedic ....G..... 201 333-8716
Jersey City **(G-4723)**

SHOES: Orthopedic, Men's

Carlascio Custom & Orthopedic ....G..... 201 333-8716
Jersey City **(G-4723)**

SHOES: Orthopedic, Women's

Carlascio Custom & Orthopedic ....G..... 201 333-8716
Jersey City **(G-4723)**

Schusters Shoes Inc ....G..... 856 885-4551
Williamstown **(G-12105)**

SHOES: Plastic Or Rubber

Nike Inc ....E..... 732 695-0108
Tinton Falls **(G-10842)**

SHOES: Plastic Or Rubber Soles With Fabric Uppers

Bear USa Inc ....F..... 201 943-4748
Palisades Park **(G-7835)**

SHOES: Rubber Or Rubber Soled Fabric Uppers

Crocs Inc ....F..... 609 344-6300
Atlantic City **(G-94)**

SHOES: Women's, Dress

Je TAime Shoes ....G..... 201 845-7463
Paramus **(G-7878)**

SHOWCASES & DISPLAY FIXTURES: Office & Store

Acme Manufacturing Co ....G..... 732 541-2800
Port Reading **(G-8985)**

Axg Corporation ....G..... 212 213-3313
Secaucus **(G-9866)**

Clip Strip Corp ....G..... 201 342-9155
Hackensack **(G-3897)**

Display Equation LLC ....G..... 201 343-4135
Hackensack **(G-3906)**

Modern Showcase Inc ....F..... 201 935-2929
Carlstadt **(G-1190)**

National Display Group Inc ....E..... 856 661-1212
Pennsauken **(G-8553)**

Pam International Co Inc ....D..... 201 291-1200
Saddle Brook **(G-9779)**

Sk Custom Creations Inc ....E..... 973 754-9261
Totowa **(G-10972)**

Vitillo & Sons Inc ....F..... 732 886-1393
Lakewood **(G-5201)**

SHOWER STALLS: Metal

Interlink Products Intl Inc ....E..... 908 862-8090
Linden **(G-5389)**

SHREDDERS: Indl & Commercial

Autoshred LLC ....G..... 732 244-0950
Toms River **(G-10865)**

SIDING & STRUCTURAL MATERIALS: Wood

Dolan & Traynor Inc ....E..... 973 696-8700
Wayne **(G-11625)**

Global Teak Inc ....F..... 609 208-2854
Winslow **(G-12132)**

Ufp Berlin LLC ....C..... 856 767-0596
Berlin **(G-443)**

SIDING: Sheet Metal

Fairfield Metal Ltd Lblty Co ....F..... 973 276-8440
Fairfield **(G-3194)**

SIGN LETTERING & PAINTING SVCS

Kdf Reprographics Inc ....F..... 201 784-9991
South Hackensack **(G-10274)**

Lettering Plus Sign Company ....G..... 856 299-0404
Pedricktown **(G-8437)**

SIGN PAINTING & LETTERING SHOP

Ace Sign Company Inc ....G..... 732 826-3858
Perth Amboy **(G-8604)**

American Graphic Systems Inc ....G..... 201 796-0666
Fair Lawn **(G-3076)**

J Vitale Sign Co Inc ....G..... 732 388-8401
Rahway **(G-9202)**

Riedel Sign Company Inc ....G..... 201 641-9121
Little Ferry **(G-5515)**

Salmon Signs ....G..... 856 589-5600
Pitman **(G-8845)**

SIGNALING APPARATUS: Electric

Work Zone Contractors LLC ....G..... 856 845-8201
Deptford **(G-2069)**

SIGNALS: Traffic Control, Electric

A C L Equipment Corp ....G..... 973 740-9800
Livingston **(G-5521)**

Intellgent Trffic Sup Pdts LLC ....G..... 908 791-1200
South Plainfield **(G-10385)**

J C Contracting Inc ....F..... 973 748-5600
Rahway **(G-9201)**

Jen Electric Inc ....F..... 973 467-4901
Springfield **(G-10559)**

SIGNALS: Transportation

Telegenix Inc ....F..... 609 265-3910
Rancocas **(G-9264)**

SIGNS & ADVERTISING SPECIALTIES

A C Display Studios Inc ....G..... 609 345-0814
Atlantic City **(G-93)**

A Sign Company ....G..... 609 298-3388
Trenton **(G-11012)**

A Sign of Excellence Inc ....G..... 732 264-0404
Hazlet **(G-4267)**

All Colors Screen Printing LLC ....G..... 732 777-6033
Highland Park **(G-4300)**

All Nu Trophy & Screen Prtg ....F..... 201 807-0808
Ridgefield Park **(G-9396)**

Alpha 1 Studio Inc ....G..... 609 859-2200
Southampton **(G-10469)**

Alu Inc ....E..... 201 935-2213
Moonachie **(G-6503)**

American Graphic Systems Inc ....G..... 201 796-0666
Fair Lawn **(G-3076)**

American Sign Instllations LLC ....G..... 856 506-0610
Millville **(G-6283)**

American Stencyl Inc ....G..... 201 251-6460
Glen Rock **(G-3819)**

Arnold Furniture Mfrs Inc ....G..... 973 399-0505
Irvington **(G-4575)**

Astro Outdoor Advertising Inc ....F..... 856 881-4300
Glassboro **(G-3801)**

Atlas Flasher & Supply Co Inc ....E..... 856 423-3333
Mickleton **(G-6136)**

Aura Signs Inc ....G..... 866 963-7446
Hillsborough **(G-4317)**

B & A Grafx Inc ....F..... 646 302-8849
Harrison **(G-4171)**

Bamboo & Rattan Works Inc ....G..... 732 255-4239
Toms River **(G-10866)**

Bankers Pen Inc ....E..... 800 499-7367
Garfield **(G-3721)**

Banner Design Inc ....E..... 908 687-5335
Hillside **(G-4395)**

Bbk Technologies Inc..........G....... 908 231-0306
Raritan *(G-9307)*
Bergen Digital Graphics LLC..........G....... 201 825-0011
Upper Saddle River *(G-11274)*
Blanc Industries Inc..........E....... 973 537-0090
Dover *(G-2078)*
Blazing Visuals..........G....... 732 781-1401
Point Pleasant Boro *(G-8933)*
Brilliant Brdcstg Concept Inc..........F....... 732 287-9201
Edison *(G-2475)*
Brunswick Signs & Exhibit..........G....... 732 246-2500
North Brunswick *(G-7508)*
Cad Signs Nyc Corp..........E....... 201 525-5415
Hackensack *(G-3888)*
Carpenter LLC..........F....... 609 689-3090
Trenton *(G-11034)*
Copyshop..........G....... 732 721-5700
South Amboy *(G-10236)*
Creoh Trading Corp..........F....... 718 821-0570
Lakewood *(G-5098)*
Custom Graphics of Vineland..........E....... 856 691-7858
Vineland *(G-11347)*
D3 Led LLC..........G....... 201 583-9486
North Bergen *(G-7444)*
Dale Behre..........G....... 908 850-4225
Hackettstown *(G-4002)*
Davis Sign Systems Inc..........G....... 973 394-9909
Boonton *(G-563)*
Daysol Inc..........D....... 908 272-5900
Kenilworth *(G-4950)*
Delaware Valley Sign Corp..........D....... 609 386-0100
Burlington *(G-967)*
Design Productions Inc..........G....... 201 447-5656
Waldwick *(G-11444)*
Designs By James..........G....... 856 692-1316
Vineland *(G-11352)*
Digital Arts Imaging LLC..........F....... 908 237-4646
Flemington *(G-3435)*
Dimensional Communications Inc..........D....... 201 767-1500
Mahwah *(G-5766)*
Display Works LLC..........C....... 201 327-1260
Parsippany *(G-7983)*
Dpj Inc..........F....... 732 499-8600
Rahway *(G-9184)*
Et Manufacturing & Sales Inc..........E....... 973 777-6662
Passaic *(G-8138)*
Exhibit Co Inc..........E....... 732 465-1070
Piscataway *(G-8766)*
Exhibit Network Inc..........F....... 732 751-9600
Oakhurst *(G-7668)*
F & A Signs Inc..........G....... 732 442-9399
Hopelawn *(G-4540)*
Fastsigns..........G....... 973 887-6700
East Hanover *(G-2216)*
Fedex Office & Print Svcs Inc..........E....... 856 427-0099
Cherry Hill *(G-1364)*
Fioplex..........G....... 856 689-7213
Swedesboro *(G-10697)*
Franbeth Inc..........G....... 856 488-1480
Pennsauken *(G-8512)*
G & R Graphics Inc..........G....... 973 731-7438
South Orange *(G-10307)*
Garden State Highway Pdts Inc..........E....... 856 692-7572
Millville *(G-6303)*
General Sign Co Inc..........G....... 856 753-3535
West Berlin *(G-11724)*
Genesis Marketing Group Inc..........G....... 201 836-1392
Teaneck *(G-10754)*
GF Supplies LLC..........G....... 336 539-1666
Elmwood Park *(G-2821)*
Glasscare Inc..........F....... 201 943-1122
Cliffside Park *(G-1540)*
Graphic Solutions & Signs LLC..........F....... 201 343-7446
Hackensack *(G-3922)*
Heros Salute Awards Co..........G....... 973 696-5085
Wayne *(G-11648)*
Hub Sign Crane Corp..........G....... 732 252-9090
Manalapan *(G-5850)*
Identity Depot Inc..........G....... 973 584-9301
Ledgewood *(G-5305)*
Impact Displays Inc..........E....... 201 804-6262
Carlstadt *(G-1171)*
Infinite Mfg Group Inc..........E....... 973 649-9950
Kearny *(G-4885)*
Ionni Sign Inc..........G....... 973 625-3815
Rockaway *(G-9576)*
J & G Diversified..........G....... 732 543-2537
New Brunswick *(G-6970)*
J D Crew Inc..........G....... 856 665-3676
Pennsauken *(G-8534)*
J H M Communications Inc..........F....... 908 859-6668
Phillipsburg *(G-8653)*
J Vitale Sign Co Inc..........G....... 732 388-8401
Rahway *(G-9202)*
J&E Business Services LLC..........G....... 973 984-8444
Morris Plains *(G-6672)*
Jarco U S Casting Corp..........E....... 201 271-0003
Union City *(G-11250)*
JKA Specialties Mfr Inc..........F....... 609 859-2090
Southampton *(G-10476)*
L & F Graphics Ltd Lblty Co..........G....... 973 240-7033
Paterson *(G-8312)*
L&M Architectural Graphics Inc..........F....... 973 575-7665
Fairfield *(G-3245)*
Larue Manufacturing Corp..........F....... 908 534-2700
Whitehouse *(G-12046)*
M & W Franklin LLC..........G....... 609 927-0885
Egg Harbor Township *(G-2689)*
Madhouz LLC..........G....... 609 206-8009
Glassboro *(G-3808)*
Manhattan Signs & Designs Ltd..........E....... 973 278-3603
Paterson *(G-8330)*
Mashal Signs Co Inc..........G....... 201 348-8500
West New York *(G-11874)*
Mason Display Innovations Inc..........F....... 609 860-0675
Cranbury *(G-1861)*
Mc Does Inc..........G....... 856 985-8730
Marlton *(G-5986)*
McLain Studios Inc..........G....... 732 775-0271
Asbury Park *(G-81)*
Medlaurel Inc..........E....... 856 461-6600
Delanco *(G-2007)*
Mega Media Concepts Ltd Lblty..........G....... 973 919-5661
Sparta *(G-10511)*
Mej Signs Inc..........G....... 609 584-6881
Hamilton *(G-4115)*
Merchandising Display Corp..........G....... 973 299-8400
Boonton *(G-576)*
Metaline Products Company Inc..........E....... 732 721-1373
South Amboy *(G-10242)*
Michele Maddalena..........G....... 973 244-0033
Fairfield *(G-3260)*
Miller Signs LLC..........G....... 732 521-0904
Helmetta *(G-4286)*
Mr Quick Sign..........G....... 201 670-1690
Midland Park *(G-6233)*
MS Signs Inc..........G....... 973 569-1111
Paterson *(G-8345)*
Nomadic North America LLC..........G....... 703 866-9200
Fairfield *(G-3273)*
North Star Signs Inc..........G....... 973 244-1144
Highland Lakes *(G-4299)*
NW Sign Industries Inc..........D....... 856 802-1677
Moorestown *(G-6604)*
Opdyke Awnings Inc..........F....... 732 449-5940
Wall Township *(G-11501)*
Outfront Media LLC..........D....... 973 575-6900
Fairfield *(G-3278)*
Ovadia Corporation..........E....... 973 256-9200
Little Falls *(G-5483)*
Packet Media LLC..........G....... 856 779-3800
Englishtown *(G-2996)*
Pat Bry Advertising Spc..........G....... 732 591-0999
Morganville *(G-6650)*
Permalith Plastics LLC..........D....... 215 925-5659
Pennsauken *(G-8560)*
Presentation Solutions Inc..........G....... 732 961-1960
Jackson *(G-4675)*
Princeton Packet Inc..........C....... 609 924-3244
Princeton *(G-9097)*
Printing & Signs Express Inc..........G....... 201 368-1255
Mahwah *(G-5803)*
Printing Lab Ltd Liability Co..........F....... 201 305-0404
West New York *(G-11877)*
Pro-Pack Corp..........G....... 908 725-5000
Branchburg *(G-694)*
Progress Displays Inc..........G....... 908 757-6650
Edison *(G-2597)*
Rand Diversified Companies LLC..........B....... 732 985-0800
Edison *(G-2601)*
Red Feather Mktg Group LLC..........F....... 973 377-1988
Madison *(G-5732)*
Rich Designs..........G....... 908 369-5035
Hillsborough *(G-4369)*
Robden Enterprises Inc..........G....... 973 273-1200
Newark *(G-7290)*
Roxboro Holdings Inc..........D....... 732 919-3119
Wall Township *(G-11506)*
S S P Enterprises Inc..........G....... 732 602-7878
Iselin *(G-4643)*
Salmon Signs..........G....... 856 589-5600
Pitman *(G-8845)*
Sign A Rama..........G....... 609 702-1444
Hainesport *(G-4077)*
Sign A Rama..........G....... 201 489-6969
Hackensack *(G-3975)*
Sign A Rama..........G....... 973 471-5558
Clifton *(G-1724)*
Sign Engineers Inc..........G....... 732 382-4224
Colonia *(G-1778)*
Sign Shoppe Inc..........G....... 856 384-2937
Woodbury *(G-12170)*
Sign Up Inc..........G....... 201 902-8640
Secaucus *(G-9928)*
Signs & Custom Metal Inc..........F....... 201 200-0110
Jersey City *(G-4827)*
Signs of Security Inc..........E....... 973 340-8404
Garfield *(G-3762)*
Sjshore Marketing Ltd Lblty Co..........F....... 609 390-1400
Marmora *(G-6006)*
Smith Enterprises..........G....... 215 416-9881
Mount Laurel *(G-6842)*
Speedy Sign-A-Rama..........G....... 973 605-8313
Morristown *(G-6743)*
Spinningdesigns Inc..........F....... 732 775-7050
Asbury Park *(G-83)*
Stephen Swinton Studio Inc..........G....... 908 537-9135
Washington *(G-11588)*
Suburban Sign Co Inc..........E....... 908 862-7222
Linden *(G-5451)*
T L C Specialties Inc..........F....... 732 244-4225
Toms River *(G-10916)*
Tally Display Corp..........G....... 973 777-7760
Fairfield *(G-3320)*
Tdk Associates Corp..........G....... 862 210-8085
Roseland *(G-9656)*
Tech-Pak Inc..........F....... 201 935-3800
Wood Ridge *(G-12140)*
Technical Nameplate Corp..........E....... 973 773-4256
Passaic *(G-8184)*
Testrite Instrument Co Inc..........C....... 201 543-0240
Hackensack *(G-3984)*
Tlg Signs Inc..........G....... 609 912-0500
Lawrenceville *(G-5270)*
Total Image and Sign..........G....... 201 941-2307
Ridgefield *(G-9387)*
Trademarksign..........F....... 848 223-4548
Jackson *(G-4680)*
Traffic Safety Service LLC..........E....... 908 561-4800
South Plainfield *(G-10441)*
Trans World Marketing Corp..........C....... 201 935-5565
East Rutherford *(G-2334)*
Trukmanns Inc..........E....... 973 538-7718
Cedar Knolls *(G-1321)*
US Propack Inc..........G....... 732 294-4500
Freehold *(G-3690)*
Vital Signs Medcl Legl Consltn..........F....... 908 537-7857
Asbury Park *(G-74)*
Vitillo & Sons Inc..........F....... 732 886-1393
Lakewood *(G-5201)*
Winemiller Press Inc..........G....... 732 223-0100
Manasquan *(G-5884)*
Yasheel Inc..........G....... 856 275-6812
Sewell *(G-9967)*

SIGNS & ADVERTISING SPECIALTIES: Artwork, Advertising

Adiant..........F....... 800 264-8303
Somerville *(G-10199)*
I Associates LLC..........G....... 215 262-7754
Pennsauken *(G-8525)*
Nickolaos Kappatos Entps Inc..........F....... 856 939-1099
Glendora *(G-3832)*
South Shore Sign Co Inc..........F....... 718 984-5624
Matawan *(G-6032)*

SIGNS & ADVERTISING SPECIALTIES: Displays, Paint Process

Kubik Maltbie Inc..........E....... 856 234-0052
Mount Laurel *(G-6811)*
Mechtronics Corporation..........E....... 845 231-1400
Franklin Lakes *(G-3621)*

SIGNS & ADVERTISING SPECIALTIES: Novelties

Aura Badge Co..........D....... 856 881-9026
Clayton *(G-1523)*

Touch of Class Promotions LLC ....G...... 267 994-0860
 Voorhees **(G-11440)**
Two Jays Bingo Supply Inc................F...... 609 267-4542
 Hainesport **(G-4080)**

SIGNS & ADVERTISING SPECIALTIES: Signs

A Affordable Sign ....F...... 732 287-0446
 Rahway **(G-9171)**
Adco Signs of NJ Inc ....E...... 908 965-2112
 Elizabeth **(G-2705)**
Art Dmensions ....G...... 908 322-8488
 Scotch Plains **(G-9846)**
Artsign Studio ....G...... 856 546-4889
 Haddon Heights **(G-4045)**
Central Art & Enginering Inc ....G...... 609 758-5922
 Cream Ridge **(G-1932)**
Cnr Products Co ....G...... 201 384-7003
 Bergenfield **(G-384)**
Colorcraft Sign Co ....F...... 609 386-1115
 Beverly **(G-461)**
Designer Sign Systems LLC ....F...... 212 939-5577
 Carlstadt **(G-1155)**
East Trading West Inv LLC ....G...... 973 678-0800
 Orange **(G-7819)**
Em Signs ....G...... 973 300-9703
 Newton **(G-7386)**
Empro Products Co Inc ....G...... 973 302-4351
 Belleville **(G-302)**
Essex Morris Sign Co ....G...... 973 386-1755
 Whippany **(G-12019)**
G-Force River Signs LLC ....G...... 609 397-4467
 Lambertville **(G-5212)**
Griffin Signs Inc ....E...... 856 786-8517
 Cinnaminson **(G-1465)**
Infinite Sign Industries Inc ....G...... 973 649-9950
 Kearny **(G-4886)**
Kna Graphics Inc ....G...... 908 272-4232
 Kenilworth **(G-4969)**
Lettering Plus Sign Company ....G...... 856 299-0404
 Pedricktown **(G-8437)**
Lincoln Signs & Awnings Inc ....G...... 732 442-3151
 Perth Amboy **(G-8621)**
M C Signs ....G...... 609 399-7446
 Ocean City **(G-7753)**
New Dawn Inc ....G...... 732 774-1377
 Neptune **(G-6925)**
Nickel Artistic Services LLC ....G...... 973 627-0390
 Rockaway **(G-9589)**
Parrish Sign Co Inc ....G...... 856 696-4040
 Vineland **(G-11389)**
Ricztone Inc ....G...... 609 695-6263
 Trenton **(G-11112)**
Riedel Sign Company Inc ....G...... 201 641-9121
 Little Ferry **(G-5515)**
Stone Graphics ....F...... 732 919-1111
 Wall Township **(G-11511)**
Traffic Safety & Equipment Co ....F...... 201 327-6050
 Mahwah **(G-5822)**
Visual Graphic Systems Inc ....C...... 201 528-2700
 Carlstadt **(G-1240)**

SIGNS & ADVERTSG SPECIALTIES: Displays/Cutouts Window/Lobby

Azar International Inc ....E...... 845 624-8808
 Paramus **(G-7855)**
Brinker Industries ....E...... 973 678-1200
 Dover **(G-2080)**
CDI Group Inc ....F...... 908 862-1493
 Linden **(G-5356)**
Design Display Group Inc ....C...... 201 438-6000
 Carlstadt **(G-1154)**
Dublin Management Assoc of NJ ....C...... 609 387-1600
 Burlington **(G-969)**
Graphic Presentations Systems.........F...... 732 981-1120
 Piscataway **(G-8771)**
Insign Inc ....E...... 856 424-1161
 Cherry Hill **(G-1381)**
Montana Electrical Decorating ....G...... 973 344-1815
 Newark **(G-7244)**
Premier Disp & Exhibits Inc ....F...... 856 382-7497
 Pennsauken **(G-8563)**
Resources Inc In Display ....E...... 908 272-5900
 Kenilworth **(G-4992)**
Riccarr Displays Inc ....E...... 973 983-6701
 Rockaway **(G-9603)**
Sama Plastics Corp ....E...... 973 239-7200
 Cedar Grove **(G-1300)**

SIGNS, ELECTRICAL: Wholesalers

Tdk Associates Corp ....G...... 862 210-8085
 Roseland **(G-9656)**

SIGNS, EXC ELECTRIC, WHOLESALE

East Trading West Inv LLC................G...... 973 678-0800
 Orange **(G-7819)**
GF Supplies LLC ....G...... 336 539-1666
 Elmwood Park **(G-2821)**
Rich Designs ....G...... 908 369-5035
 Hillsborough **(G-4369)**
Signs & Custom Metal Inc...............F...... 201 200-0110
 Jersey City **(G-4827)**

SIGNS: Electrical

A C L Equipment Corp ....G...... 973 740-9800
 Livingston **(G-5521)**
ABC Sign Systems Inc ....F...... 856 665-0950
 Pennsauken **(G-8469)**
Ace Sign Company Inc ....G...... 732 826-3858
 Perth Amboy **(G-8604)**
Aesys Inc ....G...... 201 871-3223
 Emerson **(G-2856)**
Bruce Kindberg ....G...... 973 664-0195
 Rockaway **(G-9554)**
Cad Signs LLC ....G...... 201 267-0457
 Hackensack **(G-3887)**
Craft Signs ....G...... 201 656-1991
 Jersey City **(G-4735)**
DCI Signs & Awnings Inc ....E...... 973 350-0400
 Newark **(G-7134)**
Ervin Advertising Co Inc ....G...... 732 363-7645
 Howell **(G-4554)**
F & S Awning and Blind Co Inc ....G...... 732 738-4110
 Edison **(G-2517)**
Four Way Enterprises Inc ....F...... 973 633-5757
 Wayne **(G-11636)**
Jencks Signs Corp ....G...... 908 542-1400
 Warren **(G-11557)**
Kdf Reprographics Inc ....F...... 201 784-9991
 South Hackensack **(G-10274)**
Mag Signs ....F...... 609 747-9600
 Burlington **(G-983)**
Mark-O-Lite Sign Co Inc ....G...... 732 462-8530
 Howell **(G-4561)**
Michael Anthony Sign Dsign Inc ....E...... 732 453-6120
 Piscataway **(G-8791)**
Nes Light Inc ....G...... 201 840-0400
 Ridgefield **(G-9377)**
NW Sign Industries Inc ....E...... 856 802-1677
 Moorestown **(G-6603)**
Sign On Inc ....G...... 201 384-7714
 Dumont **(G-2124)**
Sign Spec Inc ....D...... 856 663-2292
 Elmer **(G-2798)**
Signal Sign Company LLC ....F...... 973 535-9277
 Livingston **(G-5562)**
Signs of 2000 ....F...... 973 253-1333
 Clifton **(G-1725)**
Sweet Sign Systems Inc ....G...... 732 521-9300
 Jamesburg **(G-4690)**
Urban Sign & Crane Inc ....G...... 856 691-8388
 Vineland **(G-11413)**
US Sign and Lighting Svc LLC ....G...... 973 305-8900
 Wayne **(G-11689)**
Wurz Signsystems LLC ....G...... 856 461-4397
 Pennsauken **(G-8590)**
Yates Sign Co Inc ....E...... 732 578-1818
 Farmingdale **(G-3398)**

SIGNS: Neon

A B S Sign Company Inc ....G...... 609 522-6833
 Wildwood **(G-12069)**
Bergen Sign Company Inc ....E...... 973 742-7755
 Paterson **(G-8222)**
Spectrum Neon Sign Group LLC ....G...... 856 317-9223
 Pennsauken **(G-8581)**
Sun Neon Sign and Electric Co ....G...... 856 667-6977
 Cherry Hill **(G-1422)**

SILICA MINING

James D Morrissey Inc ....F...... 609 859-2860
 Vincentown **(G-11317)**

SILICON WAFERS: Chemically Doped

Ii-VI Incorporated ....F...... 973 227-1551
 Pine Brook **(G-8704)**

SILICONES

Engineered Silicone Pdts LLC...........G...... 973 300-5120
 Newton **(G-7387)**
Talent Investment LLC....................G...... 732 931-0088
 Hazlet **(G-4284)**

SILK SCREEN DESIGN SVCS

C Q Corporation ....F...... 201 935-8488
 East Rutherford **(G-2289)**
Clarici Graphics Inc ....E...... 609 587-7204
 Trenton **(G-11041)**
Cumberland Marble & Monument ....G...... 856 691-3334
 Vineland **(G-11344)**
Flying Fish Studio ....G...... 609 884-2760
 West Cape May **(G-11808)**
Koehler Industries Inc ....G...... 732 364-2700
 Howell **(G-4559)**
Microcast Technologies Corp ....D...... 908 523-9503
 Linden **(G-5409)**
Monogram Center Inc ....E...... 732 442-1800
 Perth Amboy **(G-8624)**
University Fashions By Janet ....G...... 856 228-1615
 Williamstown **(G-12111)**
Wally Enterprises Inc ....F...... 732 329-2613
 Monmouth Junction **(G-6371)**
Z Line Beachwear ....G...... 732 793-1234
 Lavallette **(G-5238)**
Zaller Studios Inc ....G...... 973 743-5175
 Bloomfield **(G-538)**

SILVER ORES

Freeport-Mcmoran Inc ....G...... 908 558-4361
 Elizabeth **(G-2735)**

SILVERWARE & PLATED WARE

Kraftware Corporation ....E...... 732 345-7091
 Roselle **(G-9674)**
Medin Technologies Inc ....C...... 973 779-2400
 Totowa **(G-10955)**

SIMULATORS: Flight

Max Flight Corp ....E...... 732 281-2007
 Toms River **(G-10895)**

SINK TOPS, PLASTIC LAMINATED

Hawthorne Kitchens Inc ....F...... 973 427-9010
 Hawthorne **(G-4238)**

SIRENS: Vehicle, Marine, Indl & Warning

Octopus Yachts Ltd Lblty Co.............F...... 732 698-8550
 Belmar **(G-361)**

SKIN CARE PRDTS: Suntan Lotions & Oils

Aloe Science Inc ....E...... 908 231-8888
 Branchburg **(G-631)**
Merck & Co Inc ....B...... 908 740-4000
 Kenilworth **(G-4974)**
Merck & Co Inc ....D...... 908 740-4000
 Rahway **(G-9212)**

SKYLIGHTS

Fiore Skylights Inc ....F...... 856 346-0118
 Somerdale **(G-10040)**

SLAB & TILE, ROOFING: Concrete

GAF Elk Materials Corporation...........C...... 973 628-4083
 Wayne **(G-11639)**

SLAB & TILE: Precast Concrete, Floor

Construction Specialties Inc..............E...... 908 236-0800
 Lebanon **(G-5282)**

SLAB, CROSSING: Concrete

Midstate Filigree Systems Inc.............D...... 609 448-8700
 Cranbury **(G-1862)**

SLAUGHTERING & MEAT PACKING

Beef International Inc ....D...... 856 663-6763
 Pennsauken **(G-8485)**
Burger Maker Inc..........................E...... 201 939-4747
 Carlstadt **(G-1134)**

Employee Codes: A=Over 500 employees, B=251-500
C=101-250, D=51-100, E=20-50, F=10-19, G=4-9

2018 Harris New Jersey
Manufacturers Directory

961

PRODUCT

Ena Meat Packing Inc ....E 973 742-4790
Paterson (G-8264)

SLIDES & EXHIBITS: Prepared

Palumbo Associates Inc ....F 908 534-2142
Whitehouse Station (G-12060)
Springworks Group Ltd ....G 973 276-7940
Fairfield (G-3310)

SLINGS: Lifting, Made From Purchased Wire

Brown and Perkins Inc ....F 609 655-1150
Cranbury (G-1816)
Doran Sling and Assembly Corp ....G 908 355-1101
Hillside (G-4406)

SLIP RINGS

Electro-Miniatures Corp ....D 201 460-0510
Moonachie (G-6516)

SLIPCOVERS & PADS

Custom Alley ....G 609 294-1875
Ltl Egg Hbr (G-5643)

SLIPPERS: House

S Goldberg & Co Inc ....C 201 342-1200
Hackensack (G-3969)

SMOKE DETECTORS

Ea Pilot Supply ....G 201 934-8449
Bradley Beach (G-627)
Heat-Timer Corporation ....E 973 575-4004
Fairfield (G-3218)

SMOKERS' SPLYS, WHOLESALE

Nichem Co ....G 973 399-9810
Newark (G-7259)

SNOW PLOWING SVCS

All Seasons Construction Inc ....G 908 852-0955
Long Valley (G-5634)
Blades Landscaping Inc ....F 856 779-7665
Mount Laurel (G-6783)
J Gennaro Trucking ....F 973 773-0805
Garfield (G-3740)
US Outworkers LLC ....G 973 362-1458
Sussex (G-10680)

SOAPS & DETERGENTS

Americare Laboratories Ltd ....E 973 279-5100
Paterson (G-8210)
Ardmore Inc ....G 973 481-2406
Newark (G-7091)
Atlantic Associates Intl Inc ....F 856 662-1717
Pennsauken (G-8481)
Aura Detergent LLC ....E 718 824-2162
Newark (G-7099)
Cantol Inc ....G 609 846-7912
Wildwood (G-12070)
Detergent 20 LLC ....F 732 545-0200
New Brunswick (G-6954)
Ecolab Inc ....C 856 596-4845
Moorestown (G-6574)
Fiabila USA Inc ....E 973 659-9510
Mine Hill (G-6326)
Hy-Test Packaging Corp ....G 973 754-7000
Paterson (G-8291)
Inopak Ltd ....F 973 962-1121
Ringwood (G-9450)
Interntional Cnsld Chemex Corp ....E 732 828-7676
New Brunswick (G-6969)
Inventek Colloidal Clrs LLC ....E 856 206-0058
Mount Laurel (G-6808)
Kempak Industries ....F 908 687-4188
Springfield (G-10561)
Kync Design LLC ....G 201 293-4677
Secaucus (G-9900)
Made Solutions LLC ....G 201 254-3693
Fair Lawn (G-3101)
Magnuson Products ....F 973 472-9292
Clifton (G-1667)
Sanitary Soap Company ....E 973 279-8500
Paterson (G-8378)
Si Packaging LLC ....F 973 869-9920
Rutherford (G-9744)

Technick Products Inc ....F 908 791-0400
South Plainfield (G-10438)
Univerclean Ltd ....G 201 674-1563
Fair Lawn (G-3122)

SOAPS & DETERGENTS: Dishwashing Compounds

Cavalier Chemical Co Inc ....E 908 558-0110
Short Hills (G-9975)

SOAPSTONE MINING

Mteixeira Soapstone VA LLC ....G 201 757-8608
Fort Lee (G-3570)

SOCIAL SVCS: Individual & Family

Life Skills Education Inc ....G 507 645-2994
Springfield (G-10564)

SOFT DRINKS WHOLESALERS

Continental Food & Bev Inc ....F 973 815-1600
Clifton (G-1589)
Increase Beverage Intl Inc ....F 609 303-3117
Pennsauken (G-8526)
Pepsi-Cola Metro Btlg Co Inc ....C 732 922-9000
Ocean (G-7734)

SOFTWARE PUBLISHERS: Application

51maps Inc ....G 800 927-5181
Wenonah (G-11701)
Able Group Technologies Inc ....G 732 591-9299
Morganville (G-6634)
Accely Inc ....F 609 598-1882
Avenel (G-123)
Airchartercom LLC ....E 212 999-4926
West New York (G-11860)
Almond Branch Inc ....G 973 728-3479
West Milford (G-11849)
Alt Shift Creative LLC ....G 609 619-0009
Flanders (G-3400)
Amerindia Technologies Inc ....G 609 664-2224
Cranbury (G-1810)
Appex Innovation Solutions LLC ....G 215 313-3332
Princeton (G-9004)
Aptimized LLC ....G 203 733-2868
Cedar Grove (G-1270)
Avyakta It Services LLC ....F 609 790-7517
East Windsor (G-2352)
Bavelle Tech Sltions Ltd Lblty ....F 973 992-8086
East Hanover (G-2201)
Beseech Ltd Liability Company ....G 908 461-7888
Belford (G-286)
Brayniac LLC ....F 212 993-7222
Hoboken (G-4460)
Brittingham Sftwr Design Inc ....G 908 832-2691
Califon (G-1034)
Buzzboard Inc ....F 201 820-0697
Lyndhurst (G-5672)
Chisholm Technologies Inc ....G 732 859-5578
Shrewsbury (G-9994)
Coles and Blenman Network LLC ....G 973 432-7041
Bloomfield (G-507)
Computech Applications LLC ....G 201 261-5251
Oradell (G-7807)
Computer Sources ....G 201 791-9443
Elmwood Park (G-2811)
Continuity Logic LLC ....D 866 321-5079
Fairfield (G-3166)
Custom Business Software LLC ....G 732 534-9557
Freehold (G-3649)
Dial Connection LLC ....F 856 753-6620
Berlin (G-433)
Double Check ....G 973 984-2229
Morris Plains (G-6659)
Easy Analytic Software Inc ....G 856 931-5780
Bellmawr (G-338)
Enertia LLC ....G 856 330-4767
Pennsauken (G-8508)
Enforsys Inc ....E 973 515-8126
Millburn (G-6250)
Ezrirx LLC ....G 718 502-6610
Lakewood (G-5120)
Factonomy Inc ....F 201 848-7812
Wyckoff (G-12252)
Fourscsonsulting Ltd Lblty Co ....G 732 599-4324
South Plainfield (G-10367)
Fusar Technologies Inc ....G 201 563-0189
Kearny (G-4874)

Healthper Inc ....G 888 257-1804
Princeton (G-9054)
I-Exceed Tech Solutions Inc ....G 917 693-3207
Princeton (G-9056)
Idt Global Processing Svcs Inc ....G 973 438-3556
Newark (G-7195)
Innovi Mobile LLC ....F 646 588-0165
Millburn (G-6253)
Interactive Advisory Software ....E 770 951-2929
Egg Harbor Township (G-2686)
International Bus Mchs Corp ....E 201 307-5136
Park Ridge (G-7923)
J-Tech Creations Inc ....G 201 944-2968
Fort Lee (G-3561)
Kandasamy Lingeswaran ....F 978 631-7662
Bloomfield (G-516)
Kingster LLC ....G 310 951-5127
Paramus (G-7881)
Lattice Incorporated ....F 856 910-1166
Pennsauken (G-8542)
Log Storm Security Inc ....E 732 393-6000
Piscataway (G-8786)
Microsoft Corporation ....D 732 476-5600
Iselin (G-4634)
Mobilogy Inc ....F 201 848-8552
Parsippany (G-8049)
Modelware Inc ....F 732 264-3020
Holmdel (G-4524)
Mosaic Golf LLC ....G 201 906-6136
Hoboken (G-4485)
Mplayer Entertainment LLC ....G 302 229-3034
Cherry Hill (G-1402)
Munipol Systems ....F 856 985-2929
Marlton (G-5988)
Nb Ventures Inc ....G 732 382-6565
Clark (G-1509)
Netcom Systems Inc ....E 732 393-6100
Edison (G-2579)
Ngenious Solutions Inc ....G 732 873-3385
Piscataway (G-8797)
Novega Venture Partners Inc ....G 732 528-2600
Holmdel (G-4527)
Optherium Labs Ou ....G 516 253-1777
Holmdel (G-4528)
Orion Cloud Cmpt Solutions Inc ....G 732 485-8658
Bridgewater (G-870)
Pario Group LLC ....G 732 906-2302
Edison (G-2591)
Polysystems Inc ....G 312 332-5670
Cherry Hill (G-1415)
Qad Inc ....C 856 273-1717
Mount Laurel (G-6833)
Real Soft Inc ....A 609 409-3636
Monmouth Junction (G-6360)
Redstage Networks LLC ....F 888 335-2747
Jersey City (G-4817)
Relational Security Corp ....E 201 867-1330
Secaucus (G-9917)
Relatnship Capitl Partners Inc ....F 908 962-4881
Short Hills (G-9984)
Relpro Inc ....G 908 962-4881
Short Hills (G-9985)
Revelation Technologies Inc ....E 201 594-1422
Westwood (G-11969)
Robokiller LLC ....E 723 838-1901
South Amboy (G-10244)
Rx Trade Zone Inc ....G 833 933-6600
Edison (G-2608)
Scalable Systems Inc ....C 732 993-4320
Piscataway (G-8808)
Secured MBL Hlth Applctons Inc ....G 732 997-9609
Long Branch (G-5632)
Sirma Group Inc ....B 646 357-3067
Jersey City (G-4829)
Ssam Sports Inc ....G 917 553-0596
Allendale (G-17)
Ssam Sports Inc ....G 917 553-0596
Allendale (G-18)
Storis Inc ....D 888 478-6747
Mount Arlington (G-6760)
Strivr Inc ....G 973 216-7379
Livingston (G-5565)
Sybase Inc ....D 973 537-5700
Parsippany (G-8095)
T N T Information Systems ....G 609 799-9488
Plainsboro (G-8901)
Tangoe Us Inc ....C 973 257-0300
Parsippany (G-8096)
Tech Brains Solutions Inc ....E 732 952-0552
Somerset (G-10183)

Technovision Inc ....E 732 381-0200
  Lyndhurst **(G-5710)**

Total Cover It LLC ....G 973 342-4623
  South Orange **(G-10316)**

Transportation Tech Svcs Inc ....E 732 326-0700
  Woodbridge **(G-12155)**

Uniphy Health Holdings LLC ....E 866 874-8616
  Newark **(G-7352)**

Universal Business Automation ....G 973 575-3568
  Montville **(G-6496)**

US Software Group Inc ....G 732 361-4636
  South Plainfield **(G-10447)**

Vst Consulting Inc ....D 732 404-0025
  Iselin **(G-4650)**

Workwave LLC ....F 866 794-1658
  Holmdel **(G-4532)**

Xchange Software Inc ....E 732 444-6666
  Parlin **(G-7936)**

Zwivel LLC ....E 844 499-4835
  Paramus **(G-7915)**

SOFTWARE PUBLISHERS: Business & Professional

3i Infotech Financial Software ....E 732 710-4444
  Edison **(G-2444)**

3i Infotech Inc ....G 732 710-4444
  Edison **(G-2445)**

Acclivity LLC ....E 973 586-2200
  Rockaway **(G-9542)**

Acrelic Interactive LLC ....G 908 222-2900
  Warren **(G-11535)**

Adherence Solutions LLC ....G 800 521-2269
  Fairfield **(G-3127)**

Aim Computer Associates Inc ....G 201 489-3100
  Bergenfield **(G-379)**

Alloy Software Inc ....F 973 661-9700
  Bloomfield **(G-501)**

American Soft Solutions Corp ....G 732 272-0052
  Morganville **(G-6636)**

Aplnow LLC ....G 732 223-5575
  Manasquan **(G-5866)**

Ariba Inc ....E 908 333-3400
  Bridgewater **(G-814)**

Artezio LLC ....G 609 786-2435
  Princeton **(G-9011)**

Auraplayer USA Inc ....F 617 879-9013
  West Orange **(G-11887)**

Avada Software LLC ....F 973 697-1043
  Mahwah **(G-5751)**

Avaya Inc ....C 732 852-2030
  Lincroft **(G-5336)**

Bluebird Auto Rentl Systems LP ....E 973 989-2423
  Dover **(G-2079)**

C Systems LLC ....F 732 338-9347
  Edison **(G-2477)**

Catalogic Software Inc ....C 201 249-8980
  Woodcliff Lake **(G-12186)**

Clientsrver Tech Solutions LLC ....G 732 710-4495
  Iselin **(G-4621)**

Cloudageit Ltd Liability Co ....G 888 205-4128
  North Brunswick **(G-7513)**

Cognizant Tech Solutions Corp ....D 201 801-0233
  Teaneck **(G-10746)**

Comprehensive Healthcare Systm ....G 732 362-2000
  Edison **(G-2488)**

Computer Doc Associates Inc ....D 908 647-4445
  Martinsville **(G-6009)**

Daddy Donkey Labs LLC ....G 646 461-4677
  Fair Haven **(G-3071)**

Datamotion Inc ....E 973 455-1245
  Florham Park **(G-3498)**

Docbox Solutions Ltd Lblty Co ....G 201 650-0970
  Montclair **(G-6411)**

Dun & Bradstreet Inc ....E 973 921-5500
  Short Hills **(G-9977)**

E Pro Inc ....F 732 283-0499
  Iselin **(G-4624)**

Educhat Inc ....G 201 871-8649
  Englewood **(G-2889)**

Effexoft Inc ....G 732 221-3642
  Somerset **(G-10092)**

Elevate Hr Inc ....E 973 917-3230
  Parsippany **(G-8000)**

Eroomsystem Technologies Inc ....F 732 730-0116
  Lakewood **(G-5118)**

Ezcom Software Inc ....E 201 731-1800
  Englewood **(G-2895)**

Fabricated Software Inc ....G 973 857-0524
  Cedar Grove **(G-1282)**

Fis Avantgard LLC ....G 732 530-9303
  Tinton Falls **(G-10837)**

Fis Financial Systems LLC ....D 856 784-7230
  Voorhees **(G-11430)**

Foundation Software Inc ....G 908 359-0588
  Belle Mead **(G-291)**

GL Consulting Inc ....G 201 938-0200
  Jersey City **(G-4760)**

Gray Hair Software Inc ....E 856 924-2253
  Mount Laurel **(G-6801)**

Greycell Labs Inc ....E 732 444-0123
  Edison **(G-2529)**

Harms Software Inc ....D 973 402-9500
  Parsippany **(G-8027)**

Hr Acuity LLC ....F 888 598-0161
  Florham Park **(G-3507)**

I Physician Hub ....D 732 274-0155
  Monmouth Junction **(G-6346)**

Intangible Labs Inc ....F 917 375-1301
  Hoboken **(G-4476)**

Interntnal Digital Systems Inc ....E 201 983-7700
  Fort Lee **(G-3560)**

Intrinsiq Spclty Solutions Inc ....E 973 251-2039
  Livingston **(G-5536)**

Invessence Inc ....G 201 977-1955
  Chatham **(G-1329)**

Limosys LLC ....F 212 222-4433
  Englewood Cliffs **(G-2974)**

Lumeta Corporation ....E 732 357-3500
  Somerset **(G-10126)**

Machine Atomated Ctrl Tech LLC ....G 732 921-8935
  Piscataway **(G-8788)**

Markov Processes International ....E 908 608-1558
  Summit **(G-10649)**

Mentor Graphics Corporation ....C 908 604-0800
  Bedminster **(G-280)**

Moblty Inc ....E 973 535-3600
  Livingston **(G-5547)**

Montgomery Investment Tech ....G 610 688-8111
  Cinnaminson **(G-1479)**

Ms Health Software Corp ....G 908 850-5564
  Hackettstown **(G-4027)**

MSI Technologies LLC ....F 973 263-0080
  Parsippany **(G-8050)**

Nextgen It LLC ....G 908 837-9443
  Bridgewater **(G-864)**

Nicomac Systems Inc ....G 201 871-0916
  Norwood **(G-7630)**

Nogpo Inc ....F 908 642-3545
  Basking Ridge **(G-200)**

Objecutive Inc ....F 201 242-1522
  Fort Lee **(G-3575)**

Oli Systems Inc ....G 973 539-4996
  Cedar Knolls **(G-1320)**

Onco Inc ....F 732 292-7460
  Wall Township **(G-11500)**

One Source Solutions LLC ....F 732 536-0578
  Freehold **(G-3675)**

Ontimeworks LLC ....F 800 689-3568
  New Providence **(G-7051)**

Open Solutions Inc ....E 856 424-0150
  Cherry Hill **(G-1408)**

Oracle Corporation ....C 908 547-6200
  Bridgewater **(G-869)**

Oracle Corporation ....B 201 842-7000
  East Rutherford **(G-2315)**

Output Services Group Inc ....E 201 871-1100
  Ridgefield Park **(G-9412)**

Parabole LLC ....G 609 917-8479
  Monmouth Junction **(G-6353)**

Patientstar LLC ....F 856 722-0808
  Mooresttown **(G-6610)**

Pds Prclnical Data Systems Inc ....E 973 398-2800
  Mount Arlington **(G-6759)**

Pinsonault Associates LLC ....G 800 372-9009
  Parsippany **(G-8066)**

Priority-Software US LLC ....G 973 586-2200
  Rockaway **(G-9600)**

Proscape Technologies Inc ....E 215 441-0300
  Hillsborough **(G-4364)**

Qcom Inc ....E 732 772-0990
  Marlboro **(G-5955)**

Quadramed Corporation ....E 732 751-0400
  Eatontown **(G-2420)**

Relayware Inc ....F 201 433-3331
  Jersey City **(G-4818)**

Remote Landlord Systems LLC ....G 732 534-4445
  Lakewood **(G-5180)**

Scivantage Inc ....D 646 452-0001
  Jersey City **(G-4824)**

Simon & Schuster Inc ....E 973 656-6000
  Parsippany **(G-8087)**

Smartlinx Solutions LLC ....G 732 385-5507
  Edison **(G-2623)**

Spectare Systems Inc ....G 609 303-0957
  Titusville **(G-10856)**

Sunbird Software Inc ....D 732 993-4476
  Somerset **(G-10176)**

Supply Chain Technologies LLC ....G 856 206-9849
  Shrewsbury **(G-10012)**

Swapshub Company Inc ....G 732 529-4813
  Piscataway **(G-8819)**

Taptask LLC ....G 201 294-2371
  Clifton **(G-1735)**

Trendmark LLC ....G 551 226-7973
  Princeton **(G-9132)**

Tunnel Networks Inc ....G 609 414-9799
  East Windsor **(G-2369)**

Ubertesters Inc ....F 201 203-7903
  Ridgewood **(G-9434)**

Unicorn Group Inc ....D 973 360-5904
  Fairfield **(G-3333)**

Unicorn Group Inc ....E 973 360-0688
  Florham Park **(G-3522)**

Utah Intermediate Holding Corp ....C 856 787-2700
  Mount Laurel **(G-6845)**

Valuemomentum Inc ....D 908 755-0025
  Piscataway **(G-8832)**

Wizcom Corporation ....E 609 750-0601
  Princeton Junction **(G-9166)**

Zoluu LLC ....G 862 686-1774
  Fair Lawn **(G-3125)**

SOFTWARE PUBLISHERS: Computer Utilities

BMC Software Inc ....E 973 401-7700
  Parsippany **(G-7962)**

Espertech Inc ....F 973 577-6406
  Wayne **(G-11629)**

Genomesafe LLC ....G 203 676-3752
  West Orange **(G-11895)**

SOFTWARE PUBLISHERS: Education

Bandemar Networks LLC ....G 732 991-5112
  East Brunswick **(G-2136)**

Edu-Met Interactive Systems Co ....F 908 851-9394
  Union **(G-11179)**

Educloud Inc ....E 201 944-0445
  Cliffside Park **(G-1538)**

Gwf Associates LLC ....E 732 933-8780
  Eatontown **(G-2398)**

Integrate Tech Inc ....G 201 693-5625
  Ridgewood **(G-9426)**

Kittyhawk Digital LLC ....G 269 767-8399
  Emerson **(G-2860)**

Mvn Usa Inc ....G 732 817-1400
  Holmdel **(G-4526)**

Netx Information Systems Inc ....E 609 298-9118
  Long Beach Township **(G-5618)**

Nxlevel Inc ....E 609 483-6900
  Lambertville **(G-5219)**

Pearson Education Inc ....D 914 287-8000
  Hoboken **(G-4491)**

Specialneedsware Inc ....F 646 278-9959
  Newark **(G-7323)**

Sunrise Intl Educatn Inc ....D 917 525-0272
  North Brunswick **(G-7541)**

SOFTWARE PUBLISHERS: Home Entertainment

Storm City Entertainment Inc ....F 856 885-6902
  Sicklerville **(G-10027)**

Vu Sound Incorporated ....F 215 990-2864
  Lumberton **(G-5666)**

SOFTWARE PUBLISHERS: NEC

Accelerated Technologies Inc ....G 609 632-0350
  Princeton **(G-8994)**

Accession Data Systems ....G 973 992-7392
  Livingston **(G-5522)**

Ackk Studios LLC ....G 973 876-1327
  Bloomfield **(G-500)**

Acqueon Technologies Inc ....G 609 945-3139
  Princeton **(G-8995)**

Alaquest International Inc ....F 908 713-9399
  Lebanon **(G-5275)**

Alcatel-Lucent USA Inc ....D 908 582-3275
New Providence (G-7026)

Alk Technologies Inc ....C 609 683-0220
Princeton (G-9002)

Altibase Incorporated ....G 888 837-7333
Mahwah (G-5747)

Amber Road Inc ....C 201 935-8588
East Rutherford (G-2276)

Angus Systems Group Inc ....E 770 521-5553
Middlesex (G-6147)

Anju Clinplus LLC ....F 732 764-6969
Bound Brook (G-616)

Antenna Software Inc ....E 201 217-3824
Jersey City (G-4708)

Aone Touch Inc ....G 732 261-6841
Bordentown (G-590)

Applied Voice Speech Tech Inc .....E 949 699-2300
Clinton (G-1749)

Apprentice Fs Inc ....E 201 819-1575
Jersey City (G-4709)

Astrix Software Technology ....C 732 661-0400
Red Bank (G-9321)

Athletic Organizational Aids ....E 201 652-1485
Midland Park (G-6221)

Aurora Information Systems............G 856 596-4180
Cherry Hill (G-1344)

Auto Injury Solutions Inc ....F 240 245-3117
Iselin (G-4614)

Automated Office Inc ....G 888 362-7638
Cherry Hill (G-1345)

Avalon Globocare Corp ....G 646 762-4517
Freehold (G-3640)

Avaya World Services Inc ....E 908 953-6000
Morristown (G-6690)

Aztec Software Associates Inc ....E 973 258-0011
Springfield (G-10540)

Basic Commerce & Industries........E 609 482-3740
Hammonton (G-4133)

Basys Inc ....G 732 616-5276
Mount Laurel (G-6781)

Bio-Key International Inc.................E 732 359-1100
Wall Township (G-11467)

Blue Marlin Systems Inc.................D 973 722-0816
Long Valley (G-5635)

BMC Software Inc ....G 703 761-0400
Woodcliff Lake (G-12182)

Brainstorm Software Corp ....G 856 234-4945
Moorestown (G-6565)

Burgiss Group LLC ....D 201 427-9600
Hoboken (G-4461)

Business Dev Solutions Inc ....G 856 433-8005
Cherry Hill (G-1354)

Business Software Applications ......G 908 500-9980
Somerset (G-10071)

Cape Atlantic Software LLC ....G 609 442-1331
Egg Harbor Township (G-2683)

Cardinal Health Systems Inc ....B 732 537-6544
Somerset (G-10073)

Ce Tech LLC ....G 908 229-3803
Whitehouse Station (G-12050)

Cegedim Inc ....C 908 443-2000
Bedminster (G-269)

Channel Logistics LLC ....F 856 614-5441
Camden (G-1053)

Com Tek Wrkplace Solutions LLC ......F 973 927-6814
Lyndhurst (G-5678)

Commvault Americas Inc ....G 888 746-3849
Tinton Falls (G-10827)

Commvault Systems Inc ....C 732 870-4000
Tinton Falls (G-10828)

Compco Analytical Inc ....G 201 641-3936
Little Ferry (G-5499)

Corcentric.....................................F 877 790-7272
Cherry Hill (G-1357)

Corner Stone Software Inc ....G 732 938-5229
Howell (G-4549)

Criterion Software LLC ....G 908 754-1166
Freehold (G-3648)

Cybage Software Inc ....G 848 219-1221
Princeton (G-9025)

Cyberextrudercom Inc ....G 973 623-7900
Wayne (G-11622)

Cygate Sftwr & Consulting LLC ......G 732 452-1881
Edison (G-2500)

Cypher Insurance Software ....G 856 216-0575
Stratford (G-10615)

Datayog Inc ....F 714 253-6558
Jersey City (G-4737)

Dcm Group Inc ....G 732 516-1173
Newark (G-7135)

Dell Software Inc ....E 201 556-4600
Rochelle Park (G-9527)

Diacritech LLC ....A 732 238-1157
Jersey City (G-4742)

Direct Computer Resources Inc ......E 201 848-0018
Franklin Lakes (G-3614)

Dma Data Industries Inc ....G 201 444-5733
Wyckoff (G-12251)

Dymax Systems Inc ....F 732 918-2424
Neptune (G-6908)

Ebaotech Inc USA ....G 917 977-1145
Jersey City (G-4746)

Ebic Prparedness Solutions LLC ......G 719 244-6209
Leonia (G-5316)

Eclearview Technologies Inc ....G 732 695-6999
Ocean (G-7724)

Edison Design Group Inc ....G 732 993-3341
Monroe (G-6373)

Enterprise Services LLC ....D 609 259-9400
Princeton (G-9039)

First Internet Systems ....F 201 991-1889
North Arlington (G-7419)

First Mountain Consulting ....G 973 325-8480
West Orange (G-11894)

Fis Data Systems Inc ....E 201 945-1774
Ridgefield (G-9360)

Flexicious LLC ....G 646 340-5066
Jersey City (G-4752)

Forge Ahead LLC ....E 908 346-4794
Skillman (G-10031)

Four Bros Ventures Inc ....G 732 890-9469
East Brunswick (G-2155)

Freyr Inc ....C 908 483-7958
Princeton (G-9048)

Genexosome Technologies Inc ....F 646 762-4517
Freehold (G-3657)

Global IDS Inc ....D 609 683-1066
Princeton (G-9050)

Healthstar Communications Inc ......A 201 560-5370
Mahwah (G-5780)

Hozric LLC ....G 908 420-8821
Green Brook (G-3857)

Image Access Corp ....E 201 342-7878
Rockleigh (G-9631)

Indotronix International Corp ....G 609 750-0700
Plainsboro (G-8885)

Infinix Corp ....E 609 936-0101
Princeton (G-9058)

Inn-Client Server Systems LLC ....F 908 782-9500
Flemington (G-3449)

Inspire Works Inc ....F 908 730-7447
Annandale (G-59)

Integration International Inc............E 973 796-2300
Parsippany (G-8030)

Integration Partners-Ny Corp..........B 973 871-2100
Parsippany (G-8031)

Intellect Design Arena Inc ....F 732 769-1037
Piscataway (G-8782)

It Worqs LLC ....G 732 494-0009
Metuchen (G-6111)

Junganew LLC ....G 201 832-0892
Rutherford (G-9737)

Juniper Networks Inc.....................D 908 947-4436
Bridgewater (G-849)

Justice Laboratory Software............G 973 586-8551
Denville (G-2044)

Kaizen Technologies Inc ....E 732 452-9555
Edison (G-2552)

Key Software Systems LLC ....F 732 409-6068
Wall Township (G-11494)

Labvantage Solutions Inc ....E 908 707-4100
Somerset (G-10121)

Link2consult Inc...........................F 888 522-0902
Fort Lee (G-3564)

Liquid Holdings Group Inc ....D 212 293-1836
Hoboken (G-4484)

Local Wisdom Inc ....E 609 269-2320
Lambertville (G-5218)

M + P International Inc ....E 973 239-3005
Verona (G-11307)

Majesco ....G 973 461-5200
Morristown (G-6725)

Maxisit Inc...................................C 732 494-2005
Metuchen (G-6114)

Medical Transcription Billing ....F 732 873-5133
Somerset (G-10133)

Megaplex Software Inc ....G 908 647-3273
Warren (G-11559)

Melillo Consulting Inc ....E 732 563-8400
Somerset (G-10135)

Microsoft Corporation ....G 973 785-0982
Wayne (G-11665)

Microtelecom Ltd Liability Co..............G 866 676-5679
Fort Lee (G-3569)

Microwize Technology Inc ....F 800 955-0321
Paramus (G-7889)

Millennium Info Tech Inc ....D 609 750-7120
Princeton (G-9075)

Mind-Alliance Systems LLC ....G 212 920-1911
Livingston (G-5546)

Mistras Group Inc ....C 609 716-4000
Princeton Junction (G-9159)

Mtbc Health Inc ....G 732 873-5133
Somerset (G-10140)

Mtbc Practice Management Corp ......C 732 873-5133
Somerset (G-10141)

Nconnex Inc.................................G 413 658-5582
New Brunswick (G-6984)

New Venture Partners LLC ....A 908 464-8131
New Providence (G-7049)

Nexagen Networks Inc....................D 732 598-1277
Morganville (G-6649)

Nlyte Software Inc.........................E 732 395-6920
Edison (G-2583)

Nokia of America Corporation ....A 908 582-3275
New Providence (G-7050)

Northwind Ventures Inc ....G 917 509-1964
Vernon (G-11301)

Nuance Communications Inc..........C 201 252-9100
Mahwah (G-5799)

Objectif Lune LLC ....F 973 780-0100
Bloomfield (G-525)

Objectif Lune LLC ....G 203 878-7206
Bloomfield (G-526)

Onx USA LLC ....E 440 569-2417
Edison (G-2588)

Oracle America Inc ....D 732 623-4821
Edison (G-2589)

Orangehrm Inc ....E 914 458-4254
Secaucus (G-9908)

Os33 Services Corp ....G 866 796-0310
Iselin (G-4638)

Oxford Biochronometrics LLC ....G 201 755-5932
Montclair (G-6427)

Pace Business Solutions Inc ....E 908 451-0355
Manahawkin (G-5833)

Pai Services LLC ....C 856 231-4667
Mount Laurel (G-6823)

Paylocity Holding Corporation ....B 908 917-3027
Springfield (G-10570)

Picture Window Software LLC ....G 908 362-4000
Blairstown (G-498)

Pjm Software Inc ....G 973 330-0405
Clifton (G-1698)

Planet Associates Inc ....E 201 693-8700
Park Ridge (G-7927)

Plescia & Company Inc ....F 856 793-0137
Marlton (G-5994)

Polaris Consulting & Svcs Ltd.........F 732 590-8151
Jersey City (G-4803)

Predictive Analytcs Dcision ....G 973 541-7020
Parsippany (G-8071)

Premier Healthcare Exch Corp ....D 908 658-3535
Bedminster (G-283)

Primepoint LLC ....E 609 298-7373
Westampton (G-11915)

Promia Incorporated......................G 609 252-1850
Princeton (G-9106)

Ptc Inc ....F 973 631-6195
Morristown (G-6738)

Quarter Spot ....F 917 647-9170
Wayne (G-11676)

Radix M I S ....G 973 707-2121
Bloomfield (G-528)

Ramco Systems Corporation ....E 609 620-4800
Lawrence Township (G-5246)

Rbs Intrntonal Direct Mktg LLC ......G 856 663-2500
Pennsauken (G-8569)

Re Systems Group Inc....................G 201 883-1572
Westwood (G-11968)

Red Oak Software Inc ....F 973 316-6064
Mountain Lakes (G-6860)

Redi-Data Inc ....F 973 227-4380
Fairfield (G-3291)

Redi-Data Inc ....A 856 988-0551
Marlton (G-5996)

Redi-Direct Marketing Inc...............B 973 808-4500
Fairfield (G-3292)

Rey Consulting Inc ....F 201 337-0051
Oakland (G-7703)

Rhodium Software Inc ....G...... 848 248-2906
Dayton (G-1985)

RSD America Inc ....F...... 201 996-1000
Teaneck (G-10771)

Sage Software Inc ....D...... 856 231-4667
Mount Laurel (G-6837)

Saksoft Inc ....C...... 201 451-4609
Jersey City (G-4821)

Samsung SDS Globl Scl Amer Inc ....E...... 201 229-4456
Ridgefield Park (G-9413)

Saviance Technologies ....F...... 609 448-7095
Metuchen (G-6120)

Scimar Technologies LLC ....G...... 609 208-1796
Allentown (G-35)

Screendreamercom Inc ....G...... 856 702-6400
Blackwood (G-492)

Sequel Software Inc ....E...... 908 575-0252
Bridgewater (G-894)

Sfp Software Inc ....G...... 856 235-7778
Mount Laurel (G-6840)

Shiva Software Group Inc ....E...... 973 691-5475
Flanders (G-3415)

Shore Software Inc ....G...... 732 899-6878
Point Pleasant Boro (G-8940)

Sierra Communication Intl LLC ....G...... 866 462-8292
Morristown (G-6742)

Simtronics Corporation ....F...... 732 747-0322
Little Silver (G-5520)

Sitetracker Inc ....F...... 551 486-2087
Montclair (G-6435)

Software Practices and Tech ....G...... 908 464-2923
Summit (G-10658)

Software Services & Solutions ....F...... 203 630-2000
Lawrence Township (G-5248)

Solbright Group Inc ....F...... 973 339-3855
Newark (G-7319)

Specialty Systems Inc ....E...... 732 341-1011
Toms River (G-10913)

Sphinx Software Inc ....G...... 609 275-5085
Plainsboro (G-8900)

SRS Software LLC ....F...... 201 802-1300
Montvale (G-6480)

Starbeam Software Solutions ....G...... 201 384-0017
Bergenfield (G-395)

Streamserve Inc ....E...... 781 863-1510
Asbury Park (G-84)

Strikeforce Technologies Inc ....G...... 732 661-9641
Edison (G-2628)

Structured Healthcare MGT Inc ....E...... 201 569-3290
Englewood (G-2935)

Surround Technologies LLC ....G...... 973 743-1277
Bloomfield (G-534)

Swce Inc ....E...... 908 766-5695
Bernardsville (G-455)

Tab Networks ....G...... 201 746-0067
Woodcliff Lake (G-12205)

Taxstream LLC ....D...... 201 610-0390
Hoboken (G-4500)

Thomson Reuters Corporation ....F...... 973 662-3070
Nutley (G-7655)

Total Reliance LLC ....F...... 732 640-5079
Dayton (G-1992)

Tropaion Inc ....G...... 908 654-3870
Springfield (G-10580)

Turbot Hq Inc ....E...... 973 922-0297
Maplewood (G-5930)

U S Tech Solutions Inc ....D...... 201 524-9600
Jersey City (G-4840)

Uniken Inc ....G...... 917 324-0399
Chatham (G-1339)

Universal Techncl Resrce Svcs ....C...... 973 663-7930
Mount Arlington (G-6761)

Vantage Business Systems Inc ....G...... 609 625-7020
Mays Landing (G-6044)

Varsity Software Inc ....G...... 609 309-9955
Lawrenceville (G-5271)

Venture App LLC ....G...... 908 644-3985
Summit (G-10663)

Verint Systems Inc ....D...... 201 438-1429
Lyndhurst (G-5712)

Vertican Technologies Inc ....G...... 800 435-7257
Fairfield (G-3341)

Vibgyor Solutions Inc ....G...... 609 750-9158
Princeton Junction (G-9165)

Visionware Systems Inc ....F...... 609 924-0800
Skillman (G-10037)

Vyral Systems Inc ....G...... 201 321-2488
Hawthorne (G-4265)

Wizdata Systems Inc ....F...... 973 975-4113
Parsippany (G-8115)

World Software Corporation ....E...... 201 444-3228
Glen Rock (G-3831)

X-Factor Cmmnctons Hldings Inc .....G...... 877 741-3727
Northvale (G-7612)

Xanthus Inc ....G...... 973 643-0920
Newark (G-7361)

Yeghen Computer System ....F...... 732 996-5500
Ocean (G-7749)

Zycus Inc ....E...... 609 799-5664
Princeton (G-9143)

SOFTWARE PUBLISHERS: Operating Systems

Csf Corporation ....E...... 732 302-2222
Somerset (G-10087)

Innovative Sftwr Solutions Inc ....D...... 856 910-9190
Maple Shade (G-5903)

Lm Matrix Solutions LLC ....G...... 908 756-7952
Bridgewater (G-858)

Zultner & Company ....F...... 609 452-0216
Princeton (G-9142)

SOFTWARE PUBLISHERS: Publisher's

Advance Digital Inc ....C...... 201 459-2808
Jersey City (G-4699)

Automated Resource Group Inc ....D...... 201 391-8357
Montvale (G-6443)

Museami Inc ....F...... 609 917-3000
North Brunswick (G-7528)

Signify Fincl Solutions LLC ....E...... 862 930-4682
Parsippany (G-8086)

Trisys Inc ....F...... 973 360-2300
Florham Park (G-3518)

SOFTWARE TRAINING, COMPUTER

Adaptive Technology Entps LLC ....G...... 877 847-6272
Medford (G-6063)

Computer Doc Associates Inc ....D...... 908 647-4445
Martinsville (G-6009)

Pds Prclnical Data Systems Inc ....E...... 973 398-2800
Mount Arlington (G-6759)

Planet Associates Inc ....E...... 201 693-8700
Park Ridge (G-7927)

Tropaion Inc ....G...... 908 654-3870
Springfield (G-10580)

SOLAR CELLS

Ecs Energy Ltd ....G...... 201 341-5044
Jackson (G-4667)

Holistic Solar Usa Inc ....G...... 732 757-5500
Newark (G-7191)

Mc Renewable Energy LLC ....F...... 732 369-9933
Manasquan (G-5873)

Nanopv Corporation ....F...... 609 851-3666
Ewing (G-3038)

Reuge Management Group Inc ....G...... 888 306-3253
Hoboken (G-4495)

Solution and System Inc ....G...... 201 488-7770
Hackensack (G-3976)

SOLAR HEATING EQPT

Holistic Solar Usa Inc ....G...... 732 757-5500
Newark (G-7191)

Inenergy Inc ....E...... 609 466-2512
Ringoes (G-9438)

Panatech Corporation ....G...... 732 331-5692
Manalapan (G-5860)

Sun Pacific Power Corp ....F...... 888 845-0242
Manalapan (G-5864)

Trinity Heating & Air Inc ....D...... 732 780-3779
Wall Township (G-11516)

SOLDERING EQPT: Electrical, Exc Handheld

Hexacon Electric Company Inc ....E...... 908 245-6200
Roselle Park (G-9697)

SOLDERING EQPT: Electrical, Handheld

Hexacon Electric Company Inc ....E...... 908 245-6200
Roselle Park (G-9697)

SOLDERS

Alpha Assembly Solutions Inc ....E...... 908 561-5170
South Plainfield (G-10325)

Alpha Assembly Solutions Inc ....E...... 908 791-3000
Somerset (G-10054)

SOLVENTS

United Energy Corp ....G...... 732 994-5225
Howell (G-4569)

SOLVENTS: Organic

G Holdings Inc ....G...... 973 628-3000
Parsippany (G-8019)

G-I Holdings Inc ....G...... 973 628-3000
Wayne (G-11638)

SONAR SYSTEMS & EQPT

Innerspace Technology Inc ....G...... 201 933-1600
Carlstadt (G-1172)

SOUND REPRODUCING EQPT

Sdi Technologies Inc ....D...... 732 574-9000
Rahway (G-9223)

SOUVENIR SHOPS

Flying Fish Studio ....G...... 609 884-2760
West Cape May (G-11808)

SOUVENIRS, WHOLESALE

Italian Treasures ....G...... 856 770-9188
Voorhees (G-11434)

SPACE VEHICLE EQPT

Aeropanel Corporation ....D...... 973 335-9636
Boonton (G-552)

Breeze-Eastern LLC ....D...... 973 602-1001
Whippany (G-12015)

Drytech Inc ....E...... 609 758-1794
Cookstown (G-1806)

H & W Tool Co Inc ....F...... 973 366-0131
Dover (G-2088)

McWilliams Forge Company ....D...... 973 627-0200
Rockaway (G-9586)

Zenith Precision Inc ....F...... 201 933-8640
East Rutherford (G-2338)

SPACE VEHICLES

Lockheed Martin Overseas LLC ....G...... 856 787-3105
Moorestown (G-6597)

SPEAKER MONITORS

Rcf USA Inc ....G...... 732 902-6100
Edison (G-2602)

SPEAKER SYSTEMS

Apogee Sound International LLC ....E...... 201 934-8500
Ramsey (G-9234)

Gabriel Sound Ltd Liability Co ....G...... 973 831-7800
Pompton Lakes (G-8947)

Sharkk LLC ....F...... 302 377-3974
Livingston (G-5561)

SPECIAL EVENTS DECORATION SVCS

De Zaio Productions Inc ....D...... 973 423-5000
Fair Lawn (G-3089)

SPECIALTY FOOD STORES: Coffee

All Madina Inc ....F...... 973 226-7772
West Caldwell (G-11765)

SPECIALTY FOOD STORES: Health & Dietetic Food

Severino Pasta Mfg Co Inc ....E...... 856 854-3716
Collingswood (G-1773)

SPECIALTY FOOD STORES: Juices, Fruit Or Vegetable

Halo Farm Inc ....G...... 609 695-3311
Lawrenceville (G-5257)

SPECIALTY FOOD STORES: Tea

Adagio Teas Inc ....G...... 973 253-7400
Elmwood Park (G-2801)

Employee Codes: A=Over 500 employees, B=251-500
C=101-250, D=51-100, E=20-50, F=10-19, G=4-9

2018 Harris New jersey
Manufacturers Directory

965

PRODUCT

SPECIALTY FOOD STORES: Vitamin

Vitamin Shoppe Industries Inc ....A 201 868-5959
North Bergen (G-7491)

SPECIALTY OUTPATIENT CLINICS, NEC

BMA of Colonia ....E 732 382-7333
Colonia (G-1777)
Um Equity Corp..............................G 856 354-2200
Haddonfield (G-4065)

SPICE & HERB STORES

PDM Packaging Inc.........................F 201 864-1115
North Bergen (G-7474)
Weiling Yang ....G 201 440-5329
Ridgefield Park (G-9418)

SPONGES: Bleached & Dyed

Fuji Electric Corp America ....D 732 560-9410
Edison (G-2522)

SPOOLS: Fiber, Made From Purchased Materials

Union Container Corp.........................E 973 242-3600
Newark (G-7351)

SPORTING & ATHLETIC GOODS: Bowling Alleys & Access

Grill Creations.................................G 908 264-8426
Garwood (G-3778)
Holiday Bowl Inc ....E 201 337-6516
Oakland (G-7691)

SPORTING & ATHLETIC GOODS: Cases, Gun & Rod

Belleplain Supply Co Inc ....G 609 861-2345
Woodbine (G-12141)

SPORTING & ATHLETIC GOODS: Driving Ranges, Golf, Electronic

Tee-Rific Golf Center ....F 908 253-9300
Branchburg (G-709)
Willowbrook Golf Center LLC ....F 973 256-6922
Wayne (G-11693)

SPORTING & ATHLETIC GOODS: Fishing Eqpt

Julian Bait Company Inc ....G 732 291-0050
Atlantic Highlands (G-114)
Offshore Enterprises Inc ....G 609 345-9099
Atlantic City (G-105)

SPORTING & ATHLETIC GOODS: Fishing Tackle, General

Captain John Inc..............................F 609 494-2094
Barnegat Light (G-168)

SPORTING & ATHLETIC GOODS: Guards, Football, Soccer, Etc

J & S Enterprises LLC ....F 973 696-9199
Lincoln Park (G-5328)
South County Soccer League Inc..........G 908 310-9052
Lambertville (G-5221)

SPORTING & ATHLETIC GOODS: Gymnasium Eqpt

Peloton Interactive Inc.......................G 201 784-9510
Northvale (G-7601)

SPORTING & ATHLETIC GOODS: Hockey Eqpt & Splys, NEC

Ss Equipment Holdings LLC................E 732 627-0006
Bridgewater (G-900)

SPORTING & ATHLETIC GOODS: Hunting Eqpt

Big Daddys Sports Haven ....G 856 453-9009
Millville (G-6288)

International Tech Lasers..................G 201 262-4580
Emerson (G-2858)

SPORTING & ATHLETIC GOODS: Pools, Swimming, Exc Plastic

Delair LLC ....D 856 663-2900
Pennsauken (G-8502)
Kayden Manufacturing Inc ....F 201 880-9898
Hackensack (G-3935)
USA Industries Inc ....E 201 438-6606
Carlstadt (G-1237)

SPORTING & ATHLETIC GOODS: Pools, Swimming, Plastic

Aquasports Pools LLC ....F 732 247-6298
New Brunswick (G-6946)

SPORTING & ATHLETIC GOODS: Rackets/Frames, Tennis, Etc

Prince Sports Inc ....D 609 291-5800
Bordentown (G-609)

SPORTING & ATHLETIC GOODS: Rods & Rod Parts, Fishing

Fred S Burroughs North Jersey ....D 908 850-8773
Hackettstown (G-4008)

SPORTING & ATHLETIC GOODS: Shafts, Golf Club

RCM Ltd Inc ....G 201 337-3328
Oakland (G-7702)

SPORTING & ATHLETIC GOODS: Shooting Eqpt & Splys, General

Ultimate Trining Munitions Inc.............E 908 725-9000
Branchburg (G-714)

SPORTING & ATHLETIC GOODS: Skateboards

Elite Surf Snow Skateboard Sp ....G 856 427-7873
Cherry Hill (G-1362)

SPORTING & ATHLETIC GOODS: Target Shooting Eqpt

Newbold Inc...................................G 732 469-5654
Middlesex (G-6185)

SPORTING & ATHLETIC GOODS: Targets, Archery & Rifle Shooting

Reagent Chemical & RES Inc...............E 908 284-2800
Ringoes (G-9442)

SPORTING & ATHLETIC GOODS: Team Sports Eqpt

A & R Sports LLC............................E 201 941-8875
Randolph (G-9266)

SPORTING & ATHLETIC GOODS: Tennis Eqpt & Splys

Lob-Ster Inc ....G 818 764-6000
Plainfield (G-8866)

SPORTING & ATHLETIC GOODS: Track & Field Athletic Eqpt

Tri State Athc Field Svcs Sups ....G 201 760-9700
Ramsey (G-9254)

SPORTING & ATHLETIC GOODS: Treadmills

Landice Incorporated ....E 973 927-9010
Randolph (G-9286)
Um Equity Corp..............................G 856 354-2200
Haddonfield (G-4065)

SPORTING & ATHLETIC GOODS: Water Sports Eqpt

Alden - Leeds Inc ....G 973 344-7986
Kearny (G-4858)
Jersey Cover Corp ....F 732 286-6300
Toms River (G-10889)
Seaville Motorsports.........................F 609 624-0040
Ocean View (G-7766)

SPORTING & ATHLETIC GOODS: Winter Sports

Stingray Sport Pdts Ltd Lblty ....G 201 300-6482
Fair Lawn (G-3116)

SPORTING & RECREATIONAL GOODS & SPLYS WHOLESALERS

Armin Kososki ....G 908 689-0411
Washington (G-11575)
Refuel Inc ....G 917 645-2974
South Hackensack (G-10292)
Sports Stop Inc ....F 856 881-2763
Glassboro (G-3812)

SPORTING & RECREATIONAL GOODS, WHOLESALE: Athletic Goods

Akadema Inc...................................E 973 304-1470
Bloomingdale (G-540)
Gamit Force Athc Ltd Lblty Co ....F 908 675-0733
Long Branch (G-5624)

SPORTING & RECREATIONAL GOODS, WHOLESALE: Boat Access & Part

Fisher Canvas Products Inc.................G 609 239-2733
Burlington (G-972)

SPORTING & RECREATIONAL GOODS, WHOLESALE: Fishing

Julian Bait Company Inc ....G 732 291-0050
Atlantic Highlands (G-114)

SPORTING & RECREATIONAL GOODS, WHOLESALE: Fishing Tackle

Blue Claw Mfg & Supply Company ....G 856 696-4366
Richland (G-9349)

SPORTING & RECREATIONAL GOODS, WHOLESALE: Golf

Crown Products Inc ....E 732 493-0022
Ocean (G-7720)

SPORTING & RECREATIONAL GOODS, WHOLESALE: Surfing

Primal Surf.....................................G 609 264-1999
Brigantine (G-918)

SPORTING GOODS

AB Coaster LLC ....F 908 879-2713
Chester (G-1432)
Beachcarts USA..............................G 201 319-0091
Secaucus (G-9867)
Bergen Manufacturing & Supply ....E 201 854-3461
North Bergen (G-7434)
CDK Industries LLC ....G 856 488-5456
Cherry Hill (G-1356)
Cover Co Inc ....G 908 707-9797
Branchburg (G-651)
Cressi Sub USA..............................G 201 594-1450
Saddle Brook (G-9760)
Crown Products Inc ....E 732 493-0022
Ocean (G-7720)
Endurance Net Inc ....G 609 499-3450
Florence (G-3478)
G A D Inc ....G 973 383-3499
Newton (G-7390)
Gamit Force Athc Ltd Lblty Co ....F 908 675-0733
Long Branch (G-5624)
Great Socks LLC ....E 856 964-9700
Pennsauken (G-8518)
Hayward Industrial Products ....C 908 351-5400
Elizabeth (G-2741)

Hollywood Tanning Systems Inc ....E 856 302-1368
  Mahwah (G-5782)
Interntnal Globl Solutions Inc ....G 201 791-1500
  Elmwood Park (G-2826)
J and S Sporting Apparel LLC ....G 732 787-5500
  Keansburg (G-4856)
Lacrosse Republic ....G 856 853-8787
  West Deptford (G-11834)
Mulbro Manufacturing & Svc Co ....G 732 805-0290
  Middlesex (G-6182)
Pro Sports Inc ....E 732 294-5561
  Marlboro (G-5953)
Pure Soccer Academy Ltd Lblty ....G 877 945-6423
  Pine Brook (G-8714)
Rags International Inc ....G 787 632-8447
  Springfield (G-10574)
Rke Athletic Lettering ....G 732 280-1111
  Belmar (G-363)
Sterling Net & Twine Co Inc ....F 973 783-9800
  Montclair (G-6436)

SPORTING GOODS STORES, NEC

Armin Kososki ....G 908 689-0411
  Washington (G-11575)
Athletes Alley ....F 732 842-1127
  Shrewsbury (G-9990)
Bauer Sport Shop ....G 201 384-6522
  Dumont (G-2115)
Rockwood Corporation ....G 908 355-8600
  Union (G-11219)
Sports Stop Inc ....F 856 881-2763
  Glassboro (G-3812)
Way It Was Sporting Svc Inc ....G 856 231-0111
  Moorestown (G-6631)

SPORTING GOODS STORES: Ammunition

Ultimate Trining Munitions Inc ....E 908 725-9000
  Branchburg (G-714)

SPORTING GOODS STORES: Baseball Eqpt

Akadema Inc ....E 973 304-1470
  Bloomingdale (G-540)

SPORTING GOODS STORES: Camping Eqpt

Important Papers Inc ....G 856 751-4544
  Cherry Hill (G-1379)

SPORTING GOODS STORES: Firearms

Henry RAC Holding Corp ....D 201 858-4400
  Bayonne (G-231)

SPORTING GOODS STORES: Hockey Eqpt, Exc Skates

Ss Equipment Holdings LLC ....E 732 627-0006
  Bridgewater (G-900)

SPORTING GOODS STORES: Pool & Billiard Tables

Pool Tables Plus Inc ....G 732 968-8228
  Green Brook (G-3862)

SPORTING GOODS STORES: Specialty Sport Splys, NEC

Pro Sports Inc ....E 732 294-5561
  Marlboro (G-5953)

SPORTING GOODS STORES: Surfing Eqpt & Splys

Ron Jon Surf Shop Fla Inc ....F 609 494-8844
  Ship Bottom (G-9973)

SPORTING GOODS STORES: Team sports Eqpt

Bigflysports Inc ....G 201 653-4414
  Secaucus (G-9868)

SPORTING GOODS: Fishing Nets

Sterling Net & Twine Co Inc ....F 973 783-9800
  Montclair (G-6436)

SPORTING GOODS: Surfboards

Primal Surf ....G 609 264-1999
  Brigantine (G-918)
Ron Jon Surf Shop Fla Inc ....F 609 494-8844
  Ship Bottom (G-9973)

SPORTING/ATHLETIC GOODS: Gloves, Boxing, Handball, Etc

Totowa Kickboxing Ltd Lblty Co ....F 973 507-9106
  Totowa (G-10975)

SPORTS APPAREL STORES

Armin Kososki ....G 908 689-0411
  Washington (G-11575)
Athletes Alley ....F 732 842-1127
  Shrewsbury (G-9990)
Belleplain Supply Co Inc ....G 609 861-2345
  Woodbine (G-12141)
CRA-Z Works Co Inc ....G 732 390-8238
  Sayreville (G-9819)
Pioneer & Co Inc ....E 856 866-9191
  Moorestown (G-6613)
Refuel Inc ....G 917 645-2974
  South Hackensack (G-10292)

SPORTS CLUBS, MANAGERS & PROMOTERS

Totowa Kickboxing Ltd Lblty Co ....F 973 507-9106
  Totowa (G-10975)

SPOUTING: Plastic & Fiberglass Reinforced

Seal-Spout Corp ....F 908 647-0648
  Liberty Corner (G-5324)

SPOUTS: Sheet Metal

Seal-Spout Corp ....F 908 647-0648
  Liberty Corner (G-5324)

SPRAYING & DUSTING EQPT

Falcon Safety Products Inc ....D 908 707-4900
  Branchburg (G-658)
Jetstream of Houston LLP ....G 732 448-7830
  New Brunswick (G-6972)

SPRAYING EQPT: Agricultural

Tifa International LLC ....F 908 647-4570
  Hillsborough (G-4377)

SPRAYS: Artificial & Preserved

Fluid Coating Systems Inc ....G 973 767-1028
  Garfield (G-3733)

SPRINGS: Coiled Flat

Spring Eureka Co Inc ....E 973 589-4960
  Newark (G-7326)

SPRINGS: Steel

Matthew Warren Inc ....F 908 788-5800
  Ringoes (G-9440)
Sealy Mattress Co N J Inc ....C 973 345-8800
  Paterson (G-8381)

SPRINGS: Wire

Matthew Warren Inc ....F 908 788-5800
  Ringoes (G-9440)
Spring Eureka Co Inc ....E 973 589-4960
  Newark (G-7326)

SPRINKLING SYSTEMS: Fire Control

Absolute Protective Systems ....E 732 287-4500
  Edison (G-2448)
Confires Fire Prtction Svc LLC ....F 908 822-2700
  South Plainfield (G-10349)
Teneyck Inc ....D 201 939-1100
  Lyndhurst (G-5711)

SQUIBS: Electric

Mjg Technologies Incorporated ....G 856 228-6118
  Blackwood (G-488)

STAFFING, EMPLOYMENT PLACEMENT

Corporate Computer Systems ....F 732 739-5600
  Newark (G-7127)

STAINLESS STEEL

Alloy Stainless Products Co ....D 973 256-1616
  Totowa (G-10928)
Atiair Technology Inc ....G 973 334-4980
  Boonton (G-556)
Dso Fluid Handling Co Inc ....E 732 225-9100
  Edison (G-2505)
Easyflex East Inc ....G 201 853-9005
  Little Ferry (G-5503)
Faber Precision Inc ....G 973 983-1844
  Rockaway (G-9566)
Ford Fasteners Inc ....G 201 487-3151
  Hackensack (G-3915)
Stainless Metal Source Intl ....G 973 977-2200
  Clifton (G-1730)
Yarde Metals Inc ....E 973 463-1166
  East Hanover (G-2251)

STAINLESS STEEL WARE

Dynamic Metals Inc ....E 908 769-0522
  Piscataway (G-8761)

STAIRCASES & STAIRS, WOOD

Alvaro Stairs LLC ....G 201 864-6754
  North Bergen (G-7429)
American Stairs Inc ....F 732 363-3734
  Lakewood (G-5070)
Greenbrook Stairs Inc ....G 908 221-9145
  Bernardsville (G-450)
Iacovelli Stairs Incorporated ....F 609 693-3476
  Forked River (G-3538)
Kaufman Stairs Inc ....E 908 862-3579
  Rahway (G-9206)
Maranatha Ceramic Tile & Marbl ....E 609 758-1168
  Wrightstown (G-12242)
Stairworks Inc ....G 908 276-2829
  Cranford (G-1927)
Urban Millwork & Supply Corp ....G 973 278-7072
  Paterson (G-8406)
Wood Products Inc ....G 609 859-0303
  Southampton (G-10484)

STAMPINGS: Automotive

Robert Freeman ....G 973 751-0082
  Belleville (G-315)
Taurus International Corp ....E 201 825-2420
  Ramsey (G-9252)

STAMPINGS: Metal

A Plus Products Incorporated ....E 732 866-9111
  Marlboro (G-5935)
Accurate Tool & Die Co Inc ....G 201 476-9348
  Montvale (G-6440)
Aspe Inc ....E 973 808-1155
  Fairfield (G-3141)
B E C Mfg Corp ....E 201 414-0000
  Glen Rock (G-3822)
Be CU Manufacturing Co Inc ....E 908 233-3342
  Scotch Plains (G-9847)
Bel-Tech Stamping Inc ....F 973 728-8229
  West Milford (G-11851)
Bigelow Components Corp ....E 973 467-1200
  Springfield (G-10543)
Bilt Rite Tool & Die Co Inc ....G 973 227-2882
  Fairfield (G-3150)
Boyle Tool & Die Co Inc ....F 856 853-1819
  West Deptford (G-11818)
Charles E Green & Son Inc ....E 973 485-3630
  Newark (G-7120)
Contact Untd TI & Stamping Co ....D 973 256-7171
  Woodland Park (G-12216)
Eagle Systems Inc ....G 732 226-2111
  Ocean (G-7723)
Frameware Inc ....F 800 582-5608
  Fairfield (G-3201)
G Big Corp ....G 973 242-6521
  Newark (G-7167)
General Wire & Stamping Co ....F 973 366-8080
  Randolph (G-9278)
Geneva Metal Products Co Inc ....F 973 472-3073
  Passaic (G-8144)
Golden Metal Products Corp ....E 973 399-1157
  Hillside (G-4409)

PRODUCT

Heyco Molded Products Inc ....F 732 286-4336
Toms River *(G-10884)*

Ht Stamping Co LLC ....G 973 227-4858
Fairfield *(G-3224)*

Luso Machine Inc ....F 973 242-1717
Newark *(G-7228)*

Main Robert A & Sons Holdg Co ....E 201 447-3700
Wyckoff *(G-12258)*

Manutech Inc ....G 856 358-6136
Elmer *(G-2794)*

Micro Stamping Corporation ....C 732 302-0800
Somerset *(G-10138)*

Minitec Corporation ....G 973 989-1426
Dover *(G-2100)*

Mjse LLC ....F 201 791-9888
Saddle Brook *(G-9776)*

Molnar Tools Inc ....F 908 580-0671
Warren *(G-11560)*

Monroe Tool & Die Inc ....G 856 629-5164
Williamstown *(G-12092)*

Pcr Technologies Inc ....G 973 882-0017
Pine Brook *(G-8713)*

Phillips Enterprises Inc ....G 732 493-3191
Ocean *(G-7736)*

R M F Associates Inc ....C 908 687-9355
Union *(G-11218)*

S & W Precision Tool Corp ....F 908 526-6097
Bridgewater *(G-885)*

S H P C Inc ....E 973 589-5242
Newark *(G-7298)*

Sofield Manufacturing Co Inc ....G 201 931-1530
Ridgefield Park *(G-9414)*

Stampex Corp ....F 973 839-4040
Haskell *(G-4214)*

Stamping Com Inc ....G 732 493-4697
Ocean *(G-7747)*

Triform Products Inc ....E 973 278-2042
Pompton Plains *(G-8967)*

Tryco Tool & Mfg Co Inc ....G 973 674-6867
Orange *(G-7831)*

Turul Bookbindery Inc ....G 973 361-2810
Wharton *(G-12003)*

Unilite Incorporated ....G 973 667-1674
Nutley *(G-7656)*

United Industries Inc ....D 973 256-7171
Woodland Park *(G-12236)*

STAPLES

Hugo Neu Recycling LLC ....E 914 530-2350
Kearny *(G-4883)*

STAPLES: Steel, Wire Or Cut

Arrow Fastener Co LLC ....B 201 843-6900
Saddle Brook *(G-9752)*

STATIONARY & OFFICE SPLYS, WHOL: Computer/Photocopying Splys

Central Technology Inc ....F 732 431-3339
Freehold *(G-3645)*

Waste Not Computers & Supplies ....G 201 384-4444
Dumont *(G-2125)*

STATIONARY & OFFICE SPLYS, WHOLESALE: Blank Books

Nobelus LLC ....G 800 895-2747
North Brunswick *(G-7531)*

STATIONARY & OFFICE SPLYS, WHOLESALE: Inked Ribbons

GSC Imaging LLC ....F 856 317-9301
Pennsauken *(G-8519)*

STATIONARY & OFFICE SPLYS, WHOLESALE: Marking Devices

Acedepotcom ....F 800 844-0962
Northvale *(G-7568)*

STATIONARY/OFFICE SPLYS, WHOL: Soc Stationery/Greeting Cards

Jersey Printing Associates Inc ....E 732 872-9654
Atlantic Highlands *(G-113)*

STATIONERY & OFFICE SPLYS WHOLESALERS

Adler International Ltd ....G 201 843-4525
Maywood *(G-6045)*

Arrow Paper Company Inc ....G 908 756-1111
Plainfield *(G-8855)*

Commander Imaging Products Inc ....E 973 742-9298
Paterson *(G-8237)*

Gabhen Inc ....C 800 631-3572
Totowa *(G-10945)*

Nu-Plan Business Systems Inc ....G 732 231-6944
Clark *(G-1510)*

Officemate International Corp ....D 732 225-7422
Edison *(G-2587)*

Scorpio Posters Inc ....E 718 499-2001
Marlboro *(G-5957)*

Spiral Binding LLC ....C 973 256-0666
Totowa *(G-10973)*

Supplies-Supplies Inc ....F 908 272-5100
Watchung *(G-11596)*

STATIONERY ARTICLES: Pottery

Larose Industries LLC ....D 973 543-2037
Randolph *(G-9287)*

STATIONERY PRDTS

Adler International Ltd ....G 201 843-4525
Maywood *(G-6045)*

Bind-Rite Graphics Inc ....E 201 863-8100
Secaucus *(G-9869)*

Yerg Inc ....G 973 759-4041
Lakehurst *(G-5060)*

STATIONERY: Made From Purchased Materials

Officemate International Corp ....D 732 225-7422
Edison *(G-2587)*

STATUES: Nonmetal

Art Plaque Creations Inc ....F 973 482-2536
Kearny *(G-4862)*

STEEL & ALLOYS: Tool & Die

Atco Products Inc ....E 973 379-3171
Springfield *(G-10538)*

Bilt Rite Tool & Die Co Inc ....G 973 227-2882
Fairfield *(G-3150)*

STEEL FABRICATORS

Able Fab Co ....E 732 396-0600
Avenel *(G-122)*

Acrow Corporation of America ....E 973 244-0080
Parsippany *(G-7938)*

Air & Specialties Sheet Metal ....F 908 233-8306
Mountainside *(G-6866)*

Airmet Inc ....G 973 481-5550
Newark *(G-7074)*

Ajay Metal Fabricators Inc ....G 908 523-0557
Linden *(G-5345)*

All American Metal Fabricators ....G 201 567-2898
Tenafly *(G-10780)*

Alloy Welding Co ....F 908 218-1551
Branchburg *(G-630)*

American Strip Steel Inc ....F 800 526-1216
South Plainfield *(G-10327)*

American Strip Steel Inc ....E 856 461-8300
Delanco *(G-2002)*

Andrew B Duffy Inc ....E 856 845-4900
West Deptford *(G-11815)*

Arca Industrial (nj) Inc ....G 732 339-0450
Edison *(G-2463)*

Archer Day Inc ....E 732 396-0600
Avenel *(G-124)*

Architectural Metals Inc ....G 718 765-0722
Carteret *(G-1250)*

Atlantic Precision Tech LLC ....G 732 658-3060
North Brunswick *(G-7506)*

Atlas Enterprise ....F 908 561-1144
South Plainfield *(G-10333)*

B & B Iron Works ....E 862 238-7203
Clifton *(G-1571)*

B L White Welding & Steel Co ....G 973 684-4111
Paterson *(G-8218)*

Banker Steel Nj LLC ....D 732 968-6061
South Plainfield *(G-10334)*

Bouras Industries Inc ....A 908 918-9400
Summit *(G-10637)*

Brayco Inc ....F 609 758-5235
Creamridge *(G-1942)*

Brunnquell Iron Works Inc ....E 609 409-6101
Cranbury *(G-1817)*

Brunswick Waste System ....G 908 369-2223
Somerville *(G-10203)*

C M C Steel Fabricators Inc ....C 908 561-3484
South Plainfield *(G-10342)*

C W Grimmer & Sons Inc ....F 732 741-2189
Tinton Falls *(G-10825)*

Capital Steel Service LLC ....E 609 882-6983
Ewing *(G-3005)*

Cs Industrial Services LLC ....G 609 381-4380
Newfield *(G-7364)*

D S Jh LLC ....E 973 782-4086
Lincoln Park *(G-5326)*

De Jong Iron Works Inc ....G 973 684-1633
Paterson *(G-8246)*

DMJ Industrial Services LLC ....G 973 692-8406
Wayne *(G-11624)*

Eagle Steel & Iron LLC ....G 908 587-1025
Stewartsville *(G-10595)*

Equipment Distributing Corp ....G 201 641-8414
Ridgefield Park *(G-9405)*

Falstrom Company ....D 973 777-0013
Passaic *(G-8140)*

FMB Systems Inc ....D 973 485-5544
Harrison *(G-4184)*

Francis Metals Company Inc ....F 732 761-0500
Lakewood *(G-5125)*

Frazier Industrial Company ....C 908 876-3001
Long Valley *(G-5637)*

G J Oliver Inc ....G 908 454-9743
Phillipsburg *(G-8649)*

Gavan Graham Elec Pdts Corp ....E 908 729-9000
Union *(G-11188)*

Geneva Metal Products Co Inc ....F 973 472-3073
Passaic *(G-8144)*

Giant Stl Fabricators Erectors ....G 908 241-6766
Roselle *(G-9671)*

Glentech Inc ....F 908 685-2205
Somerville *(G-10212)*

Grimbilas Enterprises Corp ....E 973 686-5999
Wayne *(G-11644)*

Hackensack Steel Corp ....E 201 935-0090
Carlstadt *(G-1167)*

Harold R Henrich Inc ....D 732 370-4455
Lakewood *(G-5132)*

Harris Structural Steel Co Inc ....E 732 752-6070
South Plainfield *(G-10378)*

Harris Structural Steel Co Inc ....G 732 752-6070
South Plainfield *(G-10379)*

Helidex LLC ....G 201 636-2546
East Rutherford *(G-2299)*

I K Construction Inc ....E 908 925-5200
East Orange *(G-2256)*

Ideal Tile Fabrications LLC ....F 732 751-0074
Farmingdale *(G-3387)*

Imperial Metal Products Inc ....G 908 647-8181
Bound Brook *(G-618)*

Industrial Metal Inc ....G 908 362-0084
Blairstown *(G-497)*

Industrial Services Entps Inc ....E 973 361-6780
Rockaway *(G-9574)*

Infinite Mfg Group Inc ....E 973 649-9950
Kearny *(G-4885)*

Innovative Metal Solutions LLC ....G 609 784-8406
Mount Holly *(G-6774)*

Iron Asylum Incorporated ....F 856 228-2700
Sewell *(G-9958)*

J & M Cstm Shtmtl Ltd Lblty Co ....G 856 627-6252
Sicklerville *(G-10020)*

JC Macelroy Co Inc ....D 732 572-7100
Piscataway *(G-8784)*

Jemco Inc ....E 732 446-1112
Manalapan *(G-5852)*

Jersey Metal Works LLC ....G 732 565-1313
Somerset *(G-10117)*

John Cooper Company Inc ....F 201 487-4018
Hackensack *(G-3933)*

John F Pearce ....E 201 440-8765
Moonachie *(G-6525)*

Leets Steel Inc ....G 917 416-7977
Sayreville *(G-9828)*

Lehigh Utility Associates Inc ....F 908 561-5252
South Plainfield *(G-10397)*

Lesli Katchen Steel Cnstr Inc ....G 732 521-2600
Jamesburg *(G-4686)*

Lummus Technology Ventures LLC ......G....... 973 893-1515
Bloomfield (G-521)

M K Enterprises Inc ......G....... 201 891-4199
Wyckoff (G-12257)

Marino International Corp ......G....... 732 752-5100
South Plainfield (G-10404)

Max Gurtman & Sons Inc ......G....... 973 478-7000
Clifton (G-1671)

Metal USA Plates and Shapes ......E....... 973 242-1000
Newark (G-7241)

Metals Plus ......E....... 908 862-7677
Linden (G-5408)

Metfab Steel Works LLC ......E....... 973 675-7676
Orange (G-7822)

Napco Separation Equipment Inc ......G....... 908 862-7677
Linden (G-5414)

Newark Ironworks Inc ......F....... 973 424-9790
Newark (G-7255)

Nicks Inc ......G....... 908 272-3739
Kenilworth (G-4981)

Oeg Building Materials Inc ......E....... 732 667-3636
Sayreville (G-9834)

ONeal Flat Rolled Metals LLC ......E....... 609 395-7007
Monroe Township (G-6388)

Pabst Enterprises Equipment Co ......E....... 908 353-2880
Elizabeth (G-2764)

Paone Fabrication Inc ......G....... 856 589-3821
Sewell (G-9964)

Park Steel & Iron Co ......F....... 732 775-7500
Neptune (G-6927)

Peter Garafano & Son Inc ......E....... 973 278-0350
Paterson (G-8364)

Precision Metalcrafters Inc ......E....... 856 629-1020
Williamstown (G-12100)

Prime Rebar LLC ......E....... 908 707-1234
Bridgewater (G-877)

Priore Construction Svcs LLC ......F....... 973 785-2262
Little Falls (G-5486)

R Way Tooling & Met Works LLC ......F....... 856 692-2218
Vineland (G-11394)

Ramsey Charles Company ......F....... 845 338-1464
Swedesboro (G-10723)

RS Phillips Steel LLC ......E....... 973 827-6464
Sussex (G-10676)

Runding LLC ......G....... 973 277-8775
Oak Ridge (G-7666)

Samna Cnstrctn & Steel Fabrctn ......F....... 973 977-8400
Paterson (G-8375)

Senco Metals LLC ......G....... 973 342-1742
Edison (G-2614)

Skripak Metal Fabricators Inc ......G....... 732 364-9662
Howell (G-4566)

Southern New Jersey Stl Co Inc ......E....... 856 696-1612
Vineland (G-11407)

Springfield Metal Pdts Co Inc ......F....... 973 379-4600
Springfield (G-10578)

Squillace Stl Fabricators LLC ......G....... 908 241-6424
Roselle Park (G-9703)

Stainless Steel Fabricators ......G....... 856 464-1999
Bellmawr (G-352)

Stirrup Metal Products Corp ......F....... 973 824-7086
Newark (G-7330)

T G Manufacturing Inc ......F....... 609 561-0022
Hammonton (G-4150)

Theodore E Mozer Inc ......E....... 856 829-1432
Palmyra (G-7851)

Thomas Russo & Sons Inc ......G....... 201 332-4159
Jersey City (G-4837)

Tri-Steel Fabricators Inc ......E....... 609 392-8660
Trenton (G-11127)

Truckform Inc ......F....... 908 526-5443
Somerville (G-10231)

United Steel Products Co Inc ......G....... 609 518-9230
Lumberton (G-5665)

Victory Iron Works Inc ......G....... 201 485-7181
Wyckoff (G-12269)

Vision Railings Ltd Lblty Co ......F....... 908 310-8926
Glen Gardner (G-3817)

W W Manufacturing Co Inc ......F....... 856 451-5700
Bridgeton (G-802)

Weir Welding Company Inc ......E....... 201 939-2284
Carlstadt (G-1243)

Westfield Shtmtl Works Inc ......E....... 908 276-5500
Kenilworth (G-5007)

STEEL MILLS

Aibens Imort ......G....... 609 902-9953
Princeton Junction (G-9146)

Amrod Corp ......D....... 973 344-3806
Newark (G-7085)

Camden Iron & Metal Inc ......F....... 856 365-7500
Camden (G-1047)

Camden Iron & Metal LLC ......D....... 856 969-7065
Bellmawr (G-334)

CB&i LLC ......C....... 856 482-3000
Trenton (G-11036)

DAngelo Metal Products Inc ......F....... 908 862-8220
Linden (G-5367)

E C Electroplating Inc ......E....... 973 340-0227
Garfield (G-3731)

Fox Steel Products LLC ......G....... 856 778-4661
Mount Laurel (G-6799)

Gerdau Amrsteel Sayreville Inc ......A....... 732 721-6600
Sayreville (G-9821)

Haas Environmental Inc ......F....... 609 859-3100
Roseland (G-9652)

Hoeganaes Corporation ......B....... 856 303-0366
Cinnaminson (G-1468)

New World Stainless LLC ......E....... 732 412-7137
Somerset (G-10144)

Tms International LLC ......G....... 732 721-7477
Sayreville (G-9841)

STEEL, COLD-ROLLED: Strip NEC, From Purchased Hot-Rolled

Sandvik Inc ......C....... 201 794-5000
Fair Lawn (G-3112)

STEEL, HOT-ROLLED: Sheet Or Strip

Welded Products Co Inc ......E....... 973 589-0180
Newark (G-7358)

STEEL: Cold-Rolled

American Strip Steel Inc ......F....... 800 526-1216
South Plainfield (G-10327)

American Strip Steel Inc ......G....... 856 461-8300
Delanco (G-2002)

Bigelow Components Corp ......E....... 973 467-1200
Springfield (G-10543)

Fox Steel Products LLC ......G....... 856 778-4661
Mount Laurel (G-6799)

Leibrock Metal Products Inc ......G....... 732 695-0326
Ocean (G-7731)

STEEL: Laminated

Bozak Inc ......G....... 732 282-1556
Spring Lake (G-10532)

STENCILS

American Stencyl Inc ......G....... 201 251-6460
Glen Rock (G-3819)

Innovative Art Concepts LLC ......F....... 201 828-9146
Ramsey (G-9244)

STONE: Cast Concrete

Grinnell Con Pavingstones Inc ......D....... 973 383-9300
Sparta (G-10501)

Jersey Cast Stone Ltd Lblty Co ......F....... 856 333-6900
Pennsauken (G-8536)

STONE: Dimension, NEC

Ankur International Inc ......F....... 609 409-6009
Cranbury (G-1812)

Bedrock Granite Inc ......E....... 732 741-0010
Shrewsbury (G-9991)

Dun-Rite Sand & Gravel Co ......E....... 856 692-2520
Vineland (G-11353)

Eastern Concrete Materials Inc ......E....... 973 827-7625
Hamburg (G-4091)

Morelli Contracting LLC ......G....... 732 356-8800
Middlesex (G-6181)

S J Quarry Materials Inc ......D....... 856 691-3133
Elmer (G-2797)

STONE: Quarrying & Processing, Own Stone Prdts

Stavola Construction Mtls Inc ......E....... 732 542-2328
Tinton Falls (G-10849)

Stavola Construction Mtls Inc ......E....... 732 356-5700
Bound Brook (G-625)

STORE FIXTURES: Exc Wood

Alternative Air LLC ......G....... 609 261-5870
Willingboro (G-12116)

E J M Store Fixtures Inc ......G....... 973 372-7907
Irvington (G-4582)

Handy Store Fixtures Inc ......D....... 973 242-1600
Newark (G-7186)

LG&p Group LLC ......E....... 201 634-9099
Paramus (G-7884)

Lyle/Carlstrom Associates Inc ......E....... 908 526-2270
Branchburg (G-677)

Toltec Products LLC ......G....... 908 832-2131
Califon (G-1037)

Vira Insight LLC ......C....... 732 442-6756
Piscataway (G-8835)

STORE FIXTURES: Wood

E Berkowitz & Co Inc ......G....... 856 608-1118
Mount Laurel (G-6794)

Handy Store Fixtures Inc ......D....... 973 242-1600
Newark (G-7186)

Lyle/Carlstrom Associates Inc ......E....... 908 526-2270
Branchburg (G-677)

Paramount Fixture Corporation ......E....... 973 485-1585
Newark (G-7265)

Sawitz Studios Inc ......E....... 201 842-9444
Carlstadt (G-1214)

Universal Systems Installers ......E....... 732 656-9002
Monroe (G-6375)

STORES: Auto & Home Supply

Cervinis Inc ......F....... 856 691-1744
Vineland (G-11335)

Ida Automotive Inc ......G....... 732 591-1245
Morganville (G-6643)

STRAINERS: Line, Piping Systems

Hayward Industrial Products ......C....... 908 351-5400
Elizabeth (G-2741)

STRAPPING

Versabar Corporation ......F....... 973 279-8400
Totowa (G-10979)

STRAPS: Apparel Webbing

Brian Lenhart Interactive LLC ......G....... 610 737-5314
Berkeley Heights (G-402)

STRAPS: Bindings, Textile

Star Binding & Trimming LLC ......E....... 201 864-2220
Lodi (G-5601)

STRAPS: Braids, Textile

Carolace Embroidery Co Inc ......D....... 201 945-2151
Ridgefield (G-9354)

STRIPS: Copper & Copper Alloy

H Cross Company ......E....... 201 964-9380
Moonachie (G-6519)

STRUCTURAL SUPPORT & BUILDING MATERIAL: Concrete

Donald Mason Baker Contractor ......G....... 908 782-2115
Flemington (G-3437)

Kuiken Brothers Company ......E....... 201 796-2082
Fair Lawn (G-3100)

Ulma Form-Works Inc ......D....... 201 882-1122
Hawthorne (G-4261)

STUCCO

Bestwall LLC ......D....... 856 966-7600
Camden (G-1044)

Brambila Jorge Stucco & Stone ......G....... 856 451-2039
Bridgeton (G-779)

California Stucco Products ......G....... 201 457-1900
Hackensack (G-3890)

Mediterranean Stucco Corp ......F....... 973 491-0160
Newark (G-7239)

Perfect Shapes Inc ......E....... 856 783-3844
Elmer (G-2795)

STUDIOS: Artists & Artists' Studios

McT Dairies Inc ......F....... 973 258-9600
Millburn (G-6256)

PRODUCT

STUDS & JOISTS: Sheet Metal

Super Stud Building Pdts Inc ....D 732 662-6200
Edison (G-2633)

SUBSCRIPTION FULFILLMENT SVCS: Magazine, Newspaper, Etc

Jersey Bound Latino LLC ....G...... 908 591-2830
Union (G-11197)

SUGAR SUBSTITUTES: Organic

Farbest-Tallman Foods Corp ....D 714 897-7199
Park Ridge (G-7919)
Quality Sweets ....G...... 732 283-3799
Iselin (G-4641)
Sweet Solutions Inc ....G...... 732 512-0777
Edison (G-2635)

SUGAR SUBSTITUTES: Sorbitol

Technical Oil Products Co Inc ....G...... 973 940-8920
Newton (G-7408)

SUNDRIES & RELATED PRDTS: Medical & Laboratory, Rubber

Sxwell USA LLC ....B 732 345-5400
Iselin (G-4647)
West Phrm Svcs Lakewood Inc ....G...... 732 730-3295
Lakewood (G-5205)

SUPERMARKETS & OTHER GROCERY STORES

Paulaur Corporation ....D 609 395-8844
Cranbury (G-1868)
Porfirio Foods Inc ....G...... 609 393-4116
Trenton (G-11100)
Socio Produce Inc ....G...... 201 348-3660
Union City (G-11266)
Wakefern Food Corp ....B 732 819-0140
Edison (G-2649)

SUPPOSITORIES

G & W Laboratories Inc ....B 908 753-2000
South Plainfield (G-10369)
G & W Laboratories Inc ....D 908 753-2000
South Plainfield (G-10370)

SURFACE ACTIVE AGENTS

Agilis Chemicals Inc ....G...... 973 910-2424
Rockaway (G-9548)
Aromac Inc ....G...... 973 365-1090
Clifton (G-1566)
BASF Corporation ....D 908 689-2500
Washington (G-11576)
BASF Corporation ....B 973 245-6000
Florham Park (G-3492)
Basfin Corporation ....A 973 245-6000
Florham Park (G-3493)
G Holdings Inc ....G...... 973 628-3000
Parsippany (G-8019)
G-I Holdings Inc ....G...... 973 628-3000
Wayne (G-11638)
Interntonal Specialty Pdts Inc ....A 859 815-3333
Wayne (G-11653)
Lanxess Sybron Chemicals Inc ....C 609 893-1100
Birmingham (G-468)
Pflaumer Brothers Inc ....G...... 609 883-4610
Ewing (G-3042)
Solv-TEC Incorporated ....G...... 609 261-4242
Medford (G-6082)
Stepan Company ....D 609 298-1222
Bordentown (G-611)

SURFACE ACTIVE AGENTS: Penetrants

AIG Industrial Group Inc ....F 201 767-7300
Northvale (G-7569)
American Gas & Chemical Co Ltd.........E 201 767-7300
Northvale (G-7572)
Meson Group Inc ....G...... 201 767-7300
Northvale (G-7591)

SURFACE ACTIVE AGENTS: Softeners, Textile Assisting

Atlas Refinery Inc.................................E 973 589-2002
Newark (G-7096)
Commercial Products Co Inc.................F 973 427-6887
Hawthorne (G-4227)

SURFACE ACTIVE AGENTS: Textile Processing Assistants

Nutech Corp ....G...... 908 707-2097
Franklin Lakes (G-3622)

SURGICAL & MEDICAL INSTRUMENTS WHOLESALERS

Bbg Surgical Ltd Liability Co................G...... 551 404-7920
Lakewood (G-5082)
Dexmed LLC ....G...... 732 831-0507
Elizabeth (G-2725)
Total Tech Medical LLC ....G...... 973 980-6458
Dover (G-2113)

SURGICAL APPLIANCES & SPLYS

Brenner Metal Products ....E 973 778-2466
Wallington (G-11523)
Teleflex Incorporated ....D 856 349-7234
Gloucester City (G-3846)

SURGICAL APPLIANCES & SPLYS

Acuitive Technologies Inc ....F 973 617-7175
Allendale (G-5)
Ahs Hospital Corp ....E 908 522-2000
Summit (G-10633)
Alexander James Corp ....D 908 362-9266
Blairstown (G-494)
Ansell Healthcare Products LLC ....C 732 345-5400
Iselin (G-4611)
Bard Devices Inc ....E 908 277-8000
New Providence (G-7027)
Bard Healthcare Inc ....F 908 277-8000
New Providence (G-7028)
Bard International Inc ....D 908 277-8000
New Providence (G-7029)
Belair Instrument Company LLC ....E 973 912-8900
Springfield (G-10542)
Biomet Fair Lawn LP ....F 201 797-7300
Fair Lawn (G-3084)
Boston Scientific Corporation ....E 973 709-7000
Wayne (G-11612)
Burpee Medsystems LLC ....G...... 732 544-8900
Eatontown (G-2387)
C R Bard Inc ....C 908 277-8000
New Providence (G-7032)
Capintec Inc ....E 201 825-9500
Florham Park (G-3495)
Csus LLC ....G...... 973 298-8599
Rockaway (G-9559)
Derma Sciences Inc ....C 609 514-4744
Plainsboro (G-8880)
Ebi LLC ....A 800 526-2579
Parsippany (G-7995)
Ebi LP ....E 973 299-9022
Parsippany (G-7996)
Ebi Medical Systems LLC ....F 973 299-3330
Parsippany (G-7997)
Ethicon Inc ....E 908 253-6464
Bridgewater (G-835)
Genzyme Corporation ....G...... 973 256-2106
Totowa (G-10948)
Hanger Prsthetcs & Ortho Inc...............G...... 732 919-7774
Wall Township (G-11486)
Hanger Prsthetcs & Ortho Inc...............G...... 609 889-8447
Rio Grande (G-9458)
Healthcaredepotonlinecom Inc..............G...... 732 761-9600
Edison (G-2536)
Howmedica Osteonics Corp ....G...... 201 831-5000
Mahwah (G-5783)
Integra Lfscnces Holdings Corp.............C 609 275-0500
Plainsboro (G-8887)
Janssen Ortho LLC ....G...... 609 730-2000
New Brunswick (G-6971)
Jentec Inc ....G...... 201 784-1031
Northvale (G-7587)
Jnj International Inv LLC ....G...... 732 524-0400
New Brunswick (G-6973)
Johnson & Johnson ....G...... 908 722-9319
Raritan (G-9311)

Johnson & Johnson ....C 908 874-1000
Morris Plains (G-6673)
Johnson & Johnson ....C 732 524-0400
New Brunswick (G-6975)
Johnson & Johnson ....A 732 524-0400
New Brunswick (G-6974)
Johnson & Johnson Medical Inc ....A 908 218-0707
Somerville (G-10219)
K & S Drug & Surgical Inc ....G...... 201 886-9191
Fort Lee (G-3562)
Lightfield Llr Corporation ....G...... 732 462-9200
Freehold (G-3668)
Lumiscope Co Inc ....D 678 291-3207
East Rutherford (G-2306)
Medical Device Bus Svcs Inc ....G...... 732 524-0400
New Brunswick (G-6980)
Pacon Manufacturing Corp ....C 732 764-9070
Somerset (G-10152)
Peace Medical Inc ....F 800 537-9564
Wharton (G-11996)
Precise Cmpnents TI Design Inc ....G...... 973 928-2928
Clifton (G-1702)
Prescription Podiatry Labs ....G...... 609 695-1221
Trenton (G-11103)
Respironics Inc ....C 973 581-6000
Parsippany (G-8079)
Superior Intl Srgical Sups LLC ....F 609 695-6591
Ewing (G-3057)
Switlik Parachute Company Inc ....F 609 587-3300
Trenton (G-11119)
Tronex International Inc ....D 973 335-2888
Budd Lake (G-945)
Tyrx Inc ....E 732 246-8676
Monmouth Junction (G-6367)
Universal Tape Supply Corp ....F 609 653-3191
Somers Point (G-10048)
Zimmer Inc ....G...... 856 778-8300
Mount Laurel (G-6848)
Zounds Inc ....F 856 234-8844
Mount Laurel (G-6849)

SURGICAL EQPT: See Also Instruments

3M Company ....B 973 884-2500
Whippany (G-12004)
Acme International Inc ....G...... 973 594-4866
Clifton (G-1557)
Anderson Tool & Die Corp ....E 908 862-5550
Linden (G-5349)
Automated Medical Pdts Corp...............G...... 732 602-7717
Sewaren (G-9943)
Bbg Surgical Ltd Liability Co................G...... 551 404-7920
Lakewood (G-5082)
Cross Medical Specialties Inc................F 856 589-3288
Pitman (G-8841)
Ellis Instruments Inc ....G...... 973 593-9222
Madison (G-5722)
Haldor USA Inc ....E 856 254-2345
Cherry Hill (G-1373)
P A K Manufacturing Inc ....F 973 372-1090
Irvington (G-4599)
Pentax of America Inc ....E 973 628-6200
Montvale (G-6468)

SURGICAL IMPLANTS

Endotec Inc..F 973 762-6100
South Orange (G-10304)
Infront Medical LLC ....G...... 888 515-2532
Clifton (G-1646)
Link Bio Inc ....G...... 973 625-1333
Rockaway (G-9584)
Midlantic Medical Systems Inc ....G...... 908 432-4599
Skillman (G-10033)
Onkos Surgical Inc ....E 973 264-5400
Parsippany (G-8052)
Oticon Medical LLC ....E 732 560-0727
Somerset (G-10149)
Q-Med Scandinavia Inc ....E 609 953-8069
Edison (G-2600)
Zimmer Trabecular Met Tech Inc ....C 973 576-0032
Parsippany (G-8118)

SURVEYING & MAPPING: Land Parcels

Planet Associates Inc ....E 201 693-8700
Park Ridge (G-7927)
T O Najarian Associates ....D 732 389-0220
Eatontown (G-2424)

(G-0000) Company's Geographic Section entry number

SURVEYING SVCS: Photogrammetric Engineering

Dpk Consulting LLC ....F ... 732 764-0100
Piscataway *(G-8759)*

SVC ESTABLISH EQPT, WHOLESALE: Carpet/Rug Clean Eqpt & Sply

Stephco Sales Inc ....E ... 973 278-5454
Paterson *(G-8384)*

SVC ESTABLISHMENT EQPT & SPLYS WHOLESALERS

Confires Fire Prtction Svc LLC ....F ... 908 822-2700
South Plainfield *(G-10349)*
Morris Industries Inc ....E ... 973 835-6600
Pompton Plains *(G-8963)*

SVC ESTABLISHMENT EQPT, WHOL: Cleaning & Maint Eqpt & Splys

Trim Brush Company Inc ....G ... 973 887-2525
East Hanover *(G-2247)*

SVC ESTABLISHMENT EQPT, WHOL: Concrete Burial Vaults & Boxes

Delaware Valley Vault Co Inc ....G ... 856 227-2555
Blackwood *(G-475)*

SVC ESTABLISHMENT EQPT, WHOLESALE: Beauty Parlor Eqpt & Sply

Salon Interiors Inc...............E ... 201 488-7888
South Hackensack *(G-10295)*

SVC ESTABLISHMENT EQPT, WHOLESALE: Floor Machinery, Maint

Amano USA Holdings Inc...............G ... 973 403-1900
Roseland *(G-9643)*

SVC ESTABLISHMENT EQPT, WHOLESALE: Vacuum Cleaning Systems

Aer X Dust Corporation ....G ... 732 946-9462
Holmdel *(G-4508)*
Jetstream of Houston LLP ....G ... 732 448-7830
New Brunswick *(G-6972)*

SWEEPING COMPOUNDS

Capital Soap Products LLC...............F ... 973 333-6100
Paterson *(G-8230)*

SWIMMING POOL & HOT TUB CLEANING & MAINTENANCE SVCS

Merlin Industries Inc...............D ... 609 807-1000
Hamilton *(G-4117)*

SWIMMING POOL ACCESS: Leaf Skimmers Or Pool Rakes

Hayward Industries Inc...............B ... 908 351-5400
Elizabeth *(G-2742)*

SWIMMING POOL EQPT: Filters & Water Conditioning Systems

Aqua Products Inc ....C ... 973 857-2700
Cedar Grove *(G-1271)*
Filtrex Inc ....F ... 973 595-0400
Wayne *(G-11633)*
Hayward Industries Inc...............B ... 908 351-5400
Elizabeth *(G-2742)*
Hayward Industries Inc...............G ... 908 351-0899
Elizabeth *(G-2743)*
NMP Water Systems LLC ....G ... 201 252-8333
Mahwah *(G-5796)*
South Jersey Water Cond Svc ....E ... 856 451-0620
Bridgeton *(G-798)*

SWIMMING POOL SPLY STORES

Merlin Industries Inc...............D ... 609 807-1000
Hamilton *(G-4117)*

SWIMMING POOLS, EQPT & SPLYS: Wholesalers

Alden - Leeds Inc ....G ... 973 344-7986
Kearny *(G-4858)*
Hayward Pool Products Inc ....A ... 908 351-5400
Elizabeth *(G-2744)*
Seaboard Industries ....F ... 732 901-5700
Lakewood *(G-5187)*

SWITCHES

Asco Power Services Inc ....F ... 973 966-2000
Florham Park *(G-3485)*
Calculagraph Co ....E ... 973 887-9400
East Hanover *(G-2205)*

SWITCHES: Electric Power

Astrodyne Corporation...............D ... 908 850-5088
Hackettstown *(G-3998)*
Sigma-Netics Inc ....E ... 973 227-6372
Riverdale *(G-9488)*
Transistor Devices Inc...............C ... 908 850-5088
Hackettstown *(G-4041)*

SWITCHES: Electric Power, Exc Snap, Push Button, Etc

Comus International Inc ....C ... 973 777-6900
Clifton *(G-1588)*

SWITCHES: Electronic

Auto Remind Inc ....G ... 800 277-1299
Fair Lawn *(G-3079)*
Mennekes Electronics Inc ....E ... 973 882-8333
Fairfield *(G-3258)*
Sensigraphics Inc ....G ... 856 853-9100
Mount Laurel *(G-6839)*

SWITCHES: Electronic Applications

Asco Investment Corp ....C ... 973 966-2000
Florham Park *(G-3484)*
Fitness Technologies Inc ....E ... 201 457-0030
Hackensack *(G-3913)*
Tusa Products Inc ....G ... 609 448-8333
Ewing *(G-3063)*

SWITCHES: Time, Electrical Switchgear Apparatus

Precision Multiple Contrls Inc ....E ... 201 444-0600
Midland Park *(G-6236)*
Precision Multiple Contrls Inc ....D ... 201 444-0600
Midland Park *(G-6237)*
Techniques Inc ....E ... 973 256-0947
Woodland Park *(G-12234)*

SWITCHGEAR & SWITCHBOARD APPARATUS

Apelio Innovative Inds LLC...............F ... 973 777-8899
Kearny *(G-4861)*
Astrodyne Corporation...............D ... 908 850-5088
Hackettstown *(G-3998)*
Automatic Switch Company ....A ... 973 966-2000
Florham Park *(G-3489)*
Blackhawk Cre Corporation ....F ... 856 887-0162
Salem *(G-9803)*
Circonix Technologies LLC ....F ... 973 962-6160
Ringwood *(G-9445)*
Galaxy Switchgear Inds LLC...............E ... 914 668-8200
Kearny *(G-4876)*
Marine Electric Systems Inc ....E ... 201 531-8600
South Hackensack *(G-10278)*
Primacy Engineering Inc...............F ... 201 731-3272
Englewood Cliffs *(G-2979)*

SWITCHING EQPT: Radio & Television Communications

F S R Inc...............D ... 973 785-4347
Woodland Park *(G-12218)*

SYRUPS, DRINK

Briars Usa...............G ... 732 821-7600
Monmouth Junction *(G-6332)*
Drink A Toast Company Inc ....F ... 856 461-1000
Riverside *(G-9497)*

J & J Snack Foods Corp...............B ... 856 665-9533
Pennsauken *(G-8531)*
J & J Snack Foods Corp...............D ... 856 467-9552
Bridgeport *(G-767)*
Sea Breeze Fruit Flavors Inc...............D ... 973 334-7777
Towaco *(G-11003)*
Sodastream USA Inc...............D ... 856 755-3400
Mount Laurel *(G-6843)*

SYRUPS: Pharmaceutical

Tris Pharma Inc ....D ... 732 940-0358
Monmouth Junction *(G-6365)*

SYSTEMS ENGINEERING: Computer Related

Bavelle Tech Sltions Ltd Lblty ....F ... 973 992-8086
East Hanover *(G-2201)*
Hitechone Inc ....G ... 201 500-8864
Englewood Cliffs *(G-2964)*
International Telematics Corp...............F ... 888 887-0935
Fort Lee *(G-3559)*

SYSTEMS INTEGRATION SVCS

Automated Control Concepts Inc...............E ... 732 922-6611
Neptune *(G-6901)*
Blueclone Networks LLC...............G ... 609 944-8433
Princeton *(G-9017)*
Datamotion Inc...............E ... 973 455-1245
Florham Park *(G-3498)*
Edu-Met Interactive Systems Co ....F ... 908 851-9394
Union *(G-11179)*
Thermo Systems LLC...............D ... 609 371-3300
East Windsor *(G-2368)*
Vst Consulting Inc ....D ... 732 404-0025
Iselin *(G-4650)*

SYSTEMS INTEGRATION SVCS: Office Computer Automation

Interntnal Digital Systems Inc...............F ... 201 983-7700
Fort Lee *(G-3560)*

SYSTEMS SOFTWARE DEVELOPMENT SVCS

Amerindia Technologies Inc ....E ... 609 664-2224
Cranbury *(G-1810)*
Appex Innovation Solutions LLC ....G ... 215 313-3332
Princeton *(G-9004)*
Aurora Information Systems...............G ... 856 596-4180
Cherry Hill *(G-1344)*
Aurora Research Company Inc ....G ... 973 827-8055
Franklin *(G-3595)*
Creative Cmpt Concepts LLC ....G ... 877 919-7988
Williamstown *(G-12085)*
Emdeon Corporation ....A ... 201 703-3400
Elmwood Park *(G-2819)*
Kittyhawk Digital LLC ....G ... 269 767-8399
Emerson *(G-2860)*
Linden Group Corporation...............F ... 973 983-8809
Cedar Knolls *(G-1315)*
Smartlinx Solutions LLC...............G ... 732 385-5507
Edison *(G-2623)*
Valuemomentum Inc ....D ... 908 755-0025
Piscataway *(G-8832)*
Verint Systems Inc ....D ... 201 438-1429
Lyndhurst *(G-5712)*

TABLE OR COUNTERTOPS, PLASTIC LAMINATED

Intelco ....E ... 856 384-8562
Paulsboro *(G-8417)*
Laminetics Inc ....G ... 732 367-1116
Lakewood *(G-5144)*
Wilsonart LLC ....F ... 800 822-7613
Moorestown *(G-6633)*

TABLE TOPS: Porcelain Enameled

Bernardaud Na Inc ....G ... 973 274-3555
Kearny *(G-4864)*

TABLECLOTHS & SETTINGS

A & R Sewing Company Inc ....F ... 201 332-0622
Jersey City *(G-4695)*
A-1 Tablecloth Co Inc ....C ... 201 727-4364
South Hackensack *(G-10250)*

Employee Codes: A=Over 500 employees, B=251-500
C=101-250, D=51-100, E=20-50, F=10-19, G=4-9

2018 Harris New Jersey
Manufacturers Directory

PRODUCT

971

Ballard Collection Inc ....G 908 604-0082
Warren **(G-11538)**

TABLES: Lift, Hydraulic

Hanson & Zollinger Inc ....F 856 626-3440
Berlin **(G-434)**

Intech Powercore Corporation ....G 201 767-8066
Closter **(G-1761)**

TABLETS: Bronze Or Other Metal

Cargille-Sacher Labs Inc ....F 973 267-8888
Cedar Knolls **(G-1308)**

Research and Pvd Materials ....G 973 575-4245
Fairfield **(G-3293)**

TAGS & LABELS: Paper

Mod-Tek Converting LLC ....F 856 662-6884
Pennsauken **(G-8551)**

TAGS: Paper, Blank, Made From Purchased Paper

Arch Crown Inc ....E 973 731-6300
Hillside **(G-4390)**

Cenveo Inc ....D 201 434-2100
Jersey City **(G-4725)**

Jrm Industries Inc ....D 973 779-9340
Passaic **(G-8152)**

TANK COMPONENTS: Military, Specialized

Savit Corporation ....F 862 209-4516
Rockaway **(G-9607)**

TANK REPAIR SVCS

Jersey Tank Fabricators Inc ....E 609 758-7670
South Plainfield **(G-10388)**

JW Parr Leadburing Co ....G 973 256-8093
Little Falls **(G-5479)**

TANKS & OTHER TRACKED VEHICLE CMPNTS

ALI Envmtl & Tank Svcs LLC ....F 908 755-2962
Scotch Plains **(G-9844)**

AST Construction Inc ....E 609 277-7101
Egg Harbor Township **(G-2679)**

Clogic LLC ....G 973 934-5223
Augusta **(G-119)**

TANKS: Concrete

Mershon Concrete LLC ....E 609 298-2150
Bordentown **(G-603)**

TANKS: Cryogenic, Metal

Corban Energy Group Corp ....E 201 509-8555
Elmwood Park **(G-2812)**

TANKS: Fuel, Including Oil & Gas, Metal Plate

DI Myers Corp ....F 609 698-8800
Barnegat **(G-161)**

Harsco Corporation ....E 856 779-7795
Cherry Hill **(G-1374)**

Prospect Transportation Inc ....D 201 933-9999
Carlstadt **(G-1210)**

TANKS: Lined, Metal

Deb Maintenance Inc ....E 856 786-0440
Cinnaminson **(G-1453)**

JW Parr Leadburing Co ....G 973 256-8093
Little Falls **(G-5479)**

Russell W Anderson Inc ....G 201 825-2092
Mahwah **(G-5810)**

TANKS: Plastic & Fiberglass

Cardinal Fibreglass Industries ....G 718 625-4350
Perth Amboy **(G-8608)**

TANKS: Standard Or Custom Fabricated, Metal Plate

Arde Inc ....D 201 784-9880
Carlstadt **(G-1127)**

Central Metal Fabricators Inc...............F 732 938-6900
Farmingdale **(G-3379)**

Holler Metal Fabricators Inc ....G 732 635-9050
Metuchen **(G-6109)**

Leland Limited Inc ....F 908 561-2000
South Plainfield **(G-10398)**

Tolan Machinery Company Inc ....E 973 983-7212
Rockaway **(G-9615)**

Welded Products Co Inc ....E 973 589-0180
Newark **(G-7358)**

TANKS: Water, Metal Plate

Lobster Life Systems Inc ....F 201 398-0303
Lodi **(G-5592)**

Rosenwach Tank Co LLC ....E 732 563-4900
Somerset **(G-10167)**

TANNERIES: Leather

Myers Group LLC ....G 973 761-6414
South Orange **(G-10310)**

TANNING AGENTS: Synthetic Organic

Glamorous Glo ....G 732 361-3235
Eatontown **(G-2396)**

TANNING SALON EQPT & SPLYS, WHOLESALE

PC Marketing Inc ....E 201 943-6100
Ridgefield **(G-9379)**

TANNING SALONS

Hollywood Tanning Systems Inc ....E 856 302-1368
Mahwah **(G-5782)**

TAPE DRIVES

Pascack Data Services Inc ....F 973 304-4858
Hawthorne **(G-4251)**

TAPE STORAGE UNITS: Computer

Aurora Research Company Inc ....G 973 827-8055
Franklin **(G-3595)**

TAPES, ADHESIVE: MedicaL

Ace Box Landau Co Inc ....G 201 871-4776
Englewood Cliffs **(G-2946)**

Rep Trading Associates Inc ....F 732 591-1140
Old Bridge **(G-7792)**

TAPES: Fabric

R Tape Corporation ....C 908 753-5570
South Plainfield **(G-10431)**

Snapco Manufacturing Corp ....E 973 282-0300
Hillside **(G-4441)**

TAPES: Gummed, Cloth Or Paper Based, From Purchased Matls

Holland Manufacturing Co Inc ....C 973 584-8141
Succasunna **(G-10623)**

TAPES: Pressure Sensitive

Capital Label and Affixing Co ....G 856 786-1700
Cinnaminson **(G-1450)**

Intertape Polymer Corp ....C 201 391-3315
River Vale **(G-9470)**

Jrm Industries Inc ....D 973 779-9340
Passaic **(G-8152)**

Label Master Inc ....G 973 546-3110
Lodi **(G-5591)**

Lamart Corporation ....C 973 772-6262
Clifton **(G-1657)**

Main Tape Company Inc ....C 609 395-1704
Cranbury **(G-1859)**

Microseal Industries Inc ....F 973 523-0704
Paterson **(G-8338)**

Nitto Americas Inc ....F 732 901-7905
Lakewood **(G-5165)**

Nitto Americas Inc ....F 201 645-4950
Teaneck **(G-10763)**

Nitto Inc ....G 732 901-0035
Lakewood **(G-5166)**

Universal Tape Supply Corp ....F 609 653-3191
Somers Point **(G-10048)**

Web-Cote Ltd ....F 973 827-2299
Hamburg **(G-4099)**

TARGET DRONES

Drone Go Home LLC ....G 732 991-3605
Highlands **(G-4308)**

TELECOMMUNICATION EQPT REPAIR SVCS, EXC TELEPHONES

Abris Distribution Inc ....G 732 252-9819
Manalapan **(G-5836)**

TELECOMMUNICATION SYSTEMS & EQPT

Alcatel-Lucent USA Inc ....D 908 582-3275
New Providence **(G-7026)**

Avaya Cala Inc ....G 866 462-8292
Morristown **(G-6689)**

Avaya Inc ....B 908 953-6000
Basking Ridge **(G-181)**

Avaya Inc ....G 732 852-2030
Lincroft **(G-5336)**

Avaya World Services Inc ....E 908 953-6000
Morristown **(G-6690)**

Bogen Communications Inc ....D 201 934-8500
Mahwah **(G-5754)**

Bogen Corporation ....G 201 934-8500
Ramsey **(G-9237)**

Centurum Information Tech Inc ....G 856 751-1111
Marlton **(G-5967)**

Conair Corporation ....C 609 426-1300
East Windsor **(G-2354)**

Conolog Corporation ....F 908 722-8081
Branchburg **(G-650)**

Dataprobe Inc ....E 201 934-9944
Allendale **(G-8)**

Dialogic Inc ....C 973 967-6000
Parsippany **(G-7981)**

Inlc Technology Corporation ....F 908 834-8390
Warren **(G-11556)**

IPC Systems Inc ....C 201 253-2000
Jersey City **(G-4768)**

LAp Marketing MGT Svcs Inc ....F 609 654-9266
Cherry Hill **(G-1387)**

Lattice Incorporated ....F 856 910-1166
Pennsauken **(G-8542)**

Lucent Technologies World Svcs...........C 908 582-3000
New Providence **(G-7046)**

Packetstorm Communications Inc ....F 732 840-3871
Westwood **(G-11964)**

Quintum Technologies Inc ....D 732 460-9000
Eatontown **(G-2421)**

Sierra Communication Intl LLC ....G 866 462-8292
Morristown **(G-6742)**

Star Dynamic Corp ....D 732 257-7488
Garfield **(G-3764)**

Telcontel Corp ....F 732 441-0800
Laurence Harbor **(G-5235)**

Telecom Assistance Group Inc ....E 856 753-8585
West Berlin **(G-11756)**

TMC Corporation ....G 609 860-1830
Metuchen **(G-6128)**

Tyco Elec Sbsea Cmmnctions LLC ....B 732 578-7000
Eatontown **(G-2427)**

Vytran Corporation ....E 732 972-2880
Morganville **(G-6655)**

TELECOMMUNICATIONS CARRIERS & SVCS: Wired

360 Media Innovations LLC..................G 201 228-0941
Union **(G-11145)**

TELECOMMUNICATIONS CARRIERS & SVCS: Wireless

Centurum Information Tech Inc............G 856 751-1111
Marlton **(G-5967)**

E Group Inc ....G 856 320-9688
Mount Laurel **(G-6795)**

ID Systems Inc ....C 201 996-9000
Woodcliff Lake **(G-12193)**

TELEGRAPHS & RELATED APPARATUS

D R Tielmann Inc ....G 732 332-1860
Matawan **(G-6016)**

Lyca Tel LLC ....E 973 286-0771
Newark **(G-7231)**

TELEMARKETING BUREAUS

Hanover Direct Inc...................................B... 201 863-7300
  Weehawken *(G-11695)*

Redi-Direct Marketing Inc.....................B... 973 808-4500
  Fairfield *(G-3292)*

TELEMETERING EQPT

Iniven LLC..G... 908 722-3770
  Branchburg *(G-669)*

Zzyzx LLC...G... 908 722-3770
  Branchburg *(G-723)*

TELEPHONE ANSWERING MACHINES

J C Contracting Inc..............................F... 973 748-5600
  Rahway *(G-9201)*

TELEPHONE BOOTHS, EXC WOOD

Independent Welding Co.......................F... 973 361-9731
  Wharton *(G-11989)*

TELEPHONE CENTRAL OFFICE EQPT: Dial Or Manual

Tollgrade Communications Inc.............G... 732 743-6720
  Piscataway *(G-8827)*

TELEPHONE EQPT INSTALLATION

Arose Inc...E... 856 481-4351
  Blackwood *(G-471)*

Princeton Hosted Solutions LLC..........F... 856 470-2350
  Haddonfield *(G-4062)*

Wireless Experience of PA Inc.............G... 732 552-0050
  Toms River *(G-10922)*

TELEPHONE EQPT: NEC

Adva Optical Networking Inc................E... 201 258-8300
  Mahwah *(G-5744)*

Shore Microsystems Inc.......................G... 732 870-0800
  Long Branch *(G-5633)*

Technology Corp America Inc...............E... 866 462-8292
  Morristown *(G-6744)*

TELEPHONE STATION EQPT & PARTS: Wire

Eagle Communications Inc...................G... 973 366-6181
  Denville *(G-2038)*

TELEPHONE SWITCHING EQPT

AT&T Technologies Inc.........................A... 201 771-2000
  Berkeley Heights *(G-400)*

Vytran LLC...E... 732 972-2880
  Morganville *(G-6656)*

TELEPHONE SWITCHING EQPT: Toll Switching

Transcore LP.......................................F... 201 329-9200
  Teterboro *(G-10816)*

TELEPHONE: Automatic Dialers

Nokia Inc...F... 908 582-3149
  Murray Hill *(G-6895)*

TELEPHONE: Fiber Optic Systems

Chromis Fiberoptics Inc.......................F... 732 764-0900
  Warren *(G-11543)*

Eastern Instrumentation of.................G... 856 231-0668
  Moorestown *(G-6573)*

Fiber-Span Inc.....................................E... 908 253-9080
  Toms River *(G-10876)*

Infinova Corporation............................E... 732 355-9100
  Monmouth Junction *(G-6347)*

Iniven LLC..G... 908 722-3770
  Branchburg *(G-669)*

Innovance Inc......................................G... 732 529-2300
  Piscataway *(G-8781)*

Oe Solutions America Inc.....................F... 201 568-1188
  Ridgefield Park *(G-9411)*

Optequip Inc..G... 609 758-8609
  Cream Ridge *(G-1939)*

Response Time Incorporated...............E... 856 875-0025
  Williamstown *(G-12102)*

Vitex LLC...G... 201 296-0145
  Ridgefield Park *(G-9417)*

Zzyzx LLC...G... 908 722-3770
  Branchburg *(G-723)*

TELEPHONE: Switchboards

Ntt Electronics America Inc ....F... 201 556-1770
  Saddle Brook *(G-9778)*

TELEVISION BROADCASTING & COMMUNICATIONS EQPT

Blonder Tongue Labs Inc ....C... 732 679-4000
  Old Bridge *(G-7775)*

DMJ and Associates Inc.......................E... 732 613-7867
  Sayreville *(G-9820)*

Miranda MTI Inc...................................F... 973 376-4275
  Springfield *(G-10565)*

Panasonic Corp North America............G... 201 348-7000
  Newark *(G-7262)*

Patchamp Inc.......................................G... 201 457-1504
  Hackensack *(G-3961)*

Telemetrics Inc....................................E... 201 848-9818
  Allendale *(G-21)*

Telvue Corporation ....E... 800 885-8886
  Mount Laurel *(G-6844)*

Zaxcom Inc..F... 973 835-5000
  Pompton Plains *(G-8969)*

TELEVISION SETS

Jvc Industrial America Inc ....E... 800 247-3608
  Wayne *(G-11657)*

Sharp Electronics Corporation..............A... 201 529-8200
  Mahwah *(G-5811)*

Toshiba Amer Consmr Pdts Inc............C... 973 628-8000
  Wayne *(G-11685)*

TELEVISION SETS WHOLESALERS

Sony Corporation of America ....F... 201 930-1000
  Woodcliff Lake *(G-12202)*

TELEVISION: Closed Circuit Eqpt

Checkpoint Systems Inc ....C... 800 257-5540
  West Deptford *(G-11821)*

Checkpoint Systems Inc ....C... 856 848-1800
  West Deptford *(G-11822)*

Infinova Corporation............................E... 732 355-9100
  Monmouth Junction *(G-6347)*

L3 Mobile-Vision Inc.............................D... 973 263-1090
  Rockaway *(G-9583)*

Selway Partners LLC............................F... 201 712-7974
  Englewood *(G-2929)*

Turner Engineering Inc.........................F... 973 263-1000
  Mountain Lakes *(G-6863)*

TEMPORARY HELP SVCS

Astrix Software Technology...................C... 732 661-0400
  Red Bank *(G-9321)*

TEN PIN CENTERS

Holiday Bowl Inc ....E... 201 337-6516
  Oakland *(G-7691)*

TERMINAL BOARDS

Armel Electronics Inc...........................E... 201 869-4300
  North Bergen *(G-7433)*

TEST BORING SVCS: Nonmetallic Minerals

Jersey Boring & Drlg Co Inc ....E... 973 242-3800
  Fairfield *(G-3235)*

TEST KITS: Pregnancy

Armkel LLC...A... 609 683-5900
  Princeton *(G-9010)*

TESTERS: Battery

Btech Inc..E... 973 983-1120
  Rockaway *(G-9555)*

TESTERS: Environmental

Bios International Corp ....E... 973 492-8400
  Butler *(G-998)*

Dynatec Systems Inc............................F... 609 387-0330
  Burlington *(G-970)*

Princeton Biomeditech Corp.................D... 732 274-1000
  Monmouth Junction *(G-6356)*

Tess-Com Inc.......................................E... 412 233-5782
  Middlesex *(G-6205)*

TESTERS: Gas, Exc Indl Process

Airscan Inc...G... 908 823-9425
  Lebanon *(G-5274)*

TESTERS: Integrated Circuit

EMD Performance Materials Corp........B... 908 429-3500
  Branchburg *(G-657)*

TESTERS: Liquid, Exc Indl Process

Acustrip Co Inc....................................F... 973 299-8237
  Denville *(G-2029)*

Acustrip Co Inc....................................G... 973 299-8237
  Mountain Lakes *(G-6853)*

TESTERS: Physical Property

Fluitec International LLC.......................G... 201 946-4584
  Bayonne *(G-226)*

Marine Cont Eqp Crtfction Corp...........G... 732 938-6622
  Farmingdale *(G-3389)*

SGS UStesting Company ....F... 973 575-5252
  Fairfield *(G-3306)*

Thwing-Albert Instrument Co...............D... 856 767-1000
  West Berlin *(G-11757)*

TEXTILE & APPAREL SVCS

Safer Textile Processing Corp..............B... 973 482-6400
  Newark *(G-7300)*

TEXTILE BAGS WHOLESALERS

Alex Real LLC.......................................F... 732 730-8770
  Toms River *(G-10860)*

Alvaro P Escandon Inc ....G... 973 274-1040
  Newark *(G-7081)*

TEXTILE CONVERTERS: Knit Goods

Dollfus Mieg Company Inc ....C... 732 662-1005
  Edison *(G-2502)*

Markbilt Inc..D... 201 891-7842
  Wyckoff *(G-12259)*

TEXTILE FABRICATORS

Bright Ideas Usa LLC...........................E... 732 886-8865
  Lakewood *(G-5089)*

Covalence Spcialty Coatings LLC.........D... 732 356-2870
  Middlesex *(G-6159)*

Northcott Silk USA Inc..........................E... 201 672-9600
  Lyndhurst *(G-5696)*

TEXTILE FINISH: Chem Coat/Treat, Fire Resist, Manmade

Life Liners Inc......................................G... 973 635-9234
  Chatham *(G-1333)*

TEXTILE FINISHING: Calendering, Cotton

Finn & Emma LLC.................................G... 973 227-7770
  Fairfield *(G-3195)*

TEXTILE FINISHING: Chem Coating/Treating, Broadwoven, Cotton

Brookline Chemical Corp ....E... 301 767-1177
  Wayne *(G-11615)*

TEXTILE FINISHING: Decorative, Cotton, Broadwoven

Decorating With Fabric Inc ....G... 845 352-5064
  Park Ridge *(G-7917)*

TEXTILE FINISHING: Dyeing, Broadwoven, Cotton

Hanes Companies - NJ LLC ....F... 201 729-9100
  Edison *(G-2532)*

Keystone Dyeing and Finishing ....G... 718 482-7780
  Dayton *(G-1975)*

Martin Corporation...............................F... 856 451-0900
  Bridgeton *(G-790)*

Paul Dyeing Company...........................F... 973 484-1121
  Newark *(G-7266)*

Rebtex Inc ....C 908 722-3549
Branchburg *(G-698)*

TEXTILE FINISHING: Dyeing, Manmade Fiber & Silk, Broadwoven

Keystone Dyeing and Finishing ....G 718 482-7780
Dayton *(G-1975)*
Martin Corporation ....F 856 451-0900
Bridgeton *(G-790)*
North Jersey Skein Dyeing Co ....G 201 247-4202
Paterson *(G-8352)*
Sunbrite Dye Co Inc ....E 973 777-9830
Passaic *(G-8183)*

TEXTILE FINISHING: Embossing, Cotton, Broadwoven

Lacoa Inc ....G 973 754-1000
Elmwood Park *(G-2831)*

TEXTILE MACHINERY ACCESS, HARDWOOD

Airborne Systems N Amer Inc ....G 856 663-1275
Pennsauken *(G-8473)*

TEXTILE: Finishing, Cotton Broadwoven

E & W Piece Dye Works ....E 973 942-8718
Haledon *(G-4082)*
Manner Textile Processing Inc ....D 973 942-8718
North Haledon *(G-7550)*
Safer Textile Processing Corp ....B 973 482-6400
Newark *(G-7300)*

TEXTILE: Finishing, Raw Stock NEC

Franco Manufacturing Co Inc ....C 732 494-0500
Metuchen *(G-6104)*
Kennetex Inc ....D 610 444-0600
Paterson *(G-8308)*
Manner Textile Processing Inc ....D 973 942-8718
North Haledon *(G-7550)*
Multi-Tex Products Corp ....E 201 991-7262
Kearny *(G-4902)*

TEXTILE: Goods, NEC

Classic Silks Com I ....G 908 204-0940
Bernardsville *(G-449)*
Peribu Global Sourcing ....F 704 560-2035
Skillman *(G-10035)*

TEXTILES

Ultraflex Systems Florida Inc ....E 973 627-8608
Randolph *(G-9303)*

TEXTILES: Crash, Linen

Clean-Tex Services Inc ....B 908 912-2700
Trenton *(G-11042)*

TEXTILES: Linen Fabrics

AMD Fine Linens LLC ....G 201 568-5255
Englewood *(G-2868)*
American Dawn Inc ....G 856 467-9211
Bridgeport *(G-761)*
American Home Essentials Inc ....G 908 561-3200
South Plainfield *(G-10326)*
Sander Sales Enterprises Ltd ....E 201 808-6705
Secaucus *(G-9920)*
Something Different Linen Inc ....C 973 272-0601
Clifton *(G-1728)*
Star Linen Inc ....E 800 782-7999
Moorestown *(G-6623)*

TEXTILES: Mill Waste & Remnant

Texx Team LLC ....E 201 289-1039
Hillsdale *(G-4387)*

TEXTILES: Padding & Wadding

Elkay Products Co Inc ....F 973 376-7550
Springfield *(G-10553)*

THEATRICAL SCENERY

Acadia Scenic Inc ....E 201 653-8889
Jersey City *(G-4697)*
Joseph C Hansen Company Inc ....G 201 222-1677
Jersey City *(G-4770)*

THEOLOGICAL SEMINARIES

Pillar of Fire ....D 732 356-0102
Zarephath *(G-12270)*

THERMOMETERS: Medical, Digital

Medical Indicators Inc ....F 609 737-1600
Hamilton *(G-4114)*

THERMOPLASTIC MATERIALS

Dow Chemical Company ....D 800 258-2436
Somerset *(G-10090)*
Plastic Specialties & Tech Inc ....C 201 941-2900
Ridgefield *(G-9380)*
Pure Tech International Inc ....G 908 722-4800
Branchburg *(G-696)*

THERMOPLASTICS

Ensinger Grenloch Inc ....D 856 227-0500
Grenloch *(G-3866)*
Saint-Gobain Prfmce Plas Corp ....D 856 423-6630
Mickleton *(G-6138)*

THERMOSETTING MATERIALS

A&C Catalysts Inc ....E 908 474-9393
Linden *(G-5342)*
Anhydrides & Chemicals Inc ....G 973 465-0077
Newark *(G-7086)*

THREAD: Embroidery

5 Kids Group Ltd Liability Co ....F 732 774-5331
Neptune *(G-6896)*
Athletes Alley ....F 732 842-1127
Shrewsbury *(G-9990)*
Cobyco Inc ....G 732 446-4448
Manalapan *(G-5841)*

THYROID PREPARATIONS

Corrigan Center For Integrativ ....G 973 239-0700
Cedar Grove *(G-1276)*

TIES, FORM: Metal

Clements Industries Inc ....E 201 440-5500
South Hackensack *(G-10258)*

TILE: Asphalt, Floor

Hup & Sons ....G 908 832-7878
Glen Gardner *(G-3815)*

TILE: Brick & Structural, Clay

Glen-Gery Corporation ....E 908 359-5111
Hillsborough *(G-4336)*
Morgan Advanced Ceramics Inc ....E 973 808-1621
Fairfield *(G-3264)*

TILE: Clay, Drain & Structural

R & R Irrigation Co Inc ....F 732 271-7070
Middlesex *(G-6192)*

TILE: Mosaic, Ceramic

Industrie Bitossi Inc ....E 201 796-0722
Elmwood Park *(G-2825)*

TILE: Vinyl, Asbestos

Allied Tile Mfg Corp ....G 718 647-2200
South Plainfield *(G-10324)*

TILE: Wall & Floor, Ceramic

Andrevin Inc ....G 732 270-2794
Toms River *(G-10863)*
Best Tile of New Jersey ....G 732 390-7700
East Brunswick *(G-2137)*

TILE: Wall, Ceramic

Mannington Mills Inc ....A 856 935-3000
Salem *(G-9806)*

TIMING DEVICES: Electronic

American Teletimer Corp ....E 908 654-4200
Mountainside *(G-6869)*

Artisan Controls Corporation ....E 973 598-9400
Randolph *(G-9271)*
Swatch Group Les Btques US Inc ....G 201 271-1400
Weehawken *(G-11699)*

TIN

Times Tin Cup ....G 973 983-1095
Mountain Lakes *(G-6862)*
Tin Panda Inc ....G 973 916-0707
Clifton *(G-1737)*
Tin Sigh Stop ....G 973 691-2712
Byram Township *(G-1023)*

TIRE & INNER TUBE MATERIALS & RELATED PRDTS

Coilhose Pneumatics Inc ....E 732 432-7177
East Brunswick *(G-2142)*

TIRE & TUBE REPAIR MATERIALS, WHOLESALE

Rema Tip Top/North America Inc ....E 201 768-8100
Northvale *(G-7605)*

TIRE CORD & FABRIC

Jomel Industries Inc ....F 973 282-0300
Hillside *(G-4421)*
Jomel Seams Reasonable LLC ....G 973 282-0300
Hillside *(G-4422)*
Passaic Rubber Co ....D 973 696-9500
Wayne *(G-11671)*
Skyline Steel Corporation ....B 973 428-6100
Parsippany *(G-8088)*

TIRE DEALERS

American Tire Distributors ....G 973 646-5600
Totowa *(G-10929)*

TIRES & INNER TUBES

American Tire Distributors ....G 973 646-5600
Totowa *(G-10929)*
J G Carpenter Contractor ....G 732 271-8991
Middlesex *(G-6171)*

TIRES & TUBES, WHOLESALE: Automotive

Top Rated Shopping Bargains ....F 201 630-0770
Hasbrouck Heights *(G-4200)*

TIRES: Truck

Leopard Inc ....F 908 964-3600
Hillside *(G-4425)*

TITANIUM MILL PRDTS

Titanium Industries Inc ....G 973 428-1900
East Hanover *(G-2246)*
Titanium Smoking Kings LLC ....G 908 339-8876
Phillipsburg *(G-8673)*
Titanium Technical Services ....G 908 323-9899
Flemington *(G-3472)*

TOBACCO & PRDTS, WHOLESALE: Cigarettes

Sherman Nat Inc ....E 201 735-9000
Englewood *(G-2930)*

TOBACCO & PRDTS, WHOLESALE: Cigars

Csonka Worldwide ....E 609 514-2766
Plainsboro *(G-8879)*

TOBACCO LEAF PROCESSING

Schweitzer-Mauduit Intl Inc ....B 732 723-6100
Spotswood *(G-10530)*

TOBACCO: Cigarettes

Philip Morris USA Inc ....F 908 781-6400
Bedminster *(G-282)*
Sherman Group Holdings ....G 201 735-9000
Fort Lee *(G-3582)*
Sherman Nat Inc ....E 201 735-9000
Englewood *(G-2930)*
Shermans 1400 Brdway N Y C Ltd ....D 201 735-9000
Englewood *(G-2931)*

Urban State ....G 646 836-4311
Hillside (G-4449)

TOBACCO: Cigars

Csonka Worldwide ....E 609 514-2766
Plainsboro (G-8879)

Itg Brands LLC ....G 973 386-9087
East Hanover (G-2225)

Sherman Nat Inc ....E 201 735-9000
Englewood (G-2930)

TOILET PREPARATIONS

ADS Sales Co Inc ....E 732 591-0500
Morganville (G-6635)

Dnp Foods America Ltd Lblty Co ....G 201 654-5581
Waldwick (G-11445)

Mennen Company ....B 973 630-1500
Morristown (G-6726)

Nature Labs LLC ....G 856 839-0400
Vineland (G-11384)

Procter & Gamble Mfg Co ....D 732 602-4500
Avenel (G-148)

Reviva Labs Inc ....E 856 428-3885
Haddonfield (G-4064)

TOILET SEATS: Wood

Swiss Madison LLC ....F 434 623-4766
Dayton (G-1990)

TOILETRIES, COSMETICS & PERFUME STORES

Beauty-Fill LLC ....E 908 353-1600
Hillside (G-4397)

Health and Natural Beauty USA ....F 732 640-1830
Piscataway (G-8772)

Revlon Inc ....E 732 287-1400
Edison (G-2605)

TOILETRIES, WHOLESALE: Perfumes

Dosis Fragrance LLC ....G 718 874-0074
Newark (G-7142)

Elixens America Inc ....G 732 388-3555
Rahway (G-9187)

Intarome Fragrance Corporation ....D 201 767-8700
Norwood (G-7625)

Lvmh Fragrance Brands US LLC ....G 212 931-2668
Edison (G-2561)

Quest Intl Flvors Frgrnces Inc ....B 973 576-9500
East Hanover (G-2240)

TOILETRIES, WHOLESALE: Razor Blades

Art of Shaving - FI LLC ....G 732 410-2520
Freehold (G-3639)

TOILETRIES, WHOLESALE: Toilet Soap

Sysco Guest Supply LLC ....C 732 537-2297
Somerset (G-10177)

TOILETRIES, WHOLESALE: Toiletries

Americare Laboratories Ltd ....E 973 279-5100
Paterson (G-8210)

TOILETS: Portable Chemical, Plastics

Zirti LLC ....G 201 316-4791
Allendale (G-24)

TOOL & DIE STEEL

Atlas Copco North America LLC ....G 973 397-3400
Parsippany (G-7955)

CMI-Promex Inc ....F 856 351-1000
Pedricktown (G-8433)

Unity Steel Rule Die Co ....E 201 569-6400
Englewood (G-2941)

TOOLS: Hand

Apex Saw & Tool Co Inc ....G 201 438-8777
Lyndhurst (G-5668)

Brasscraft Manufacturing Co ....G 856 241-7700
Swedesboro (G-10685)

C T A Manufacturing Corp ....E 201 896-1000
Carlstadt (G-1136)

Cementex Products Inc ....E 609 387-1040
Burlington (G-962)

CS Osborne & Co ....D 973 483-3232
Harrison (G-4177)

DAKA Manufacturing LLC ....G 908 782-0360
Flemington (G-3433)

Dicar Diamond Tool Corp ....F 973 684-0949
Paterson (G-8250)

Dreyco Inc ....F 201 896-9000
Carlstadt (G-1158)

Excel Hobby Blades Corp ....E 973 278-4000
Paterson (G-8267)

General Tools & Instrs Co LLC ....E 212 431-6100
Secaucus (G-9888)

Grommet Mart Inc ....F 973 278-4100
Paterson (G-8284)

IDL Techni-Edge LLC ....C 908 497-9818
Kenilworth (G-4962)

Indo-US Mim TEC Private Ltd ....G 734 327-9842
Princeton (G-9057)

J R S Tool & Metal Finishing ....G 908 753-2050
South Plainfield (G-10387)

Jdv Products Inc ....F 201 794-6467
Fair Lawn (G-3098)

Jesco Iron Crafts Inc ....F 201 488-4545
Bogota (G-548)

Mastercool USA Inc ....F 973 252-9119
Randolph (G-9288)

National Steel Rule Company ....D 908 862-3366
Linden (G-5417)

Ohaus Corporation ....D 973 377-9000
Parsippany (G-8051)

Ox Group Usa LLC ....F 888 850-6710
Cranford (G-1920)

Phoenix Industrial LLC ....G 908 955-0114
Whitehouse Station (G-12061)

Power Hawk Technologies Inc ....F 973 627-4646
Rockaway (G-9599)

S & G Tool Aid Corporation ....D 973 824-7730
Newark (G-7297)

Sine Tru Tool Company Inc ....G 732 591-1100
Marlboro (G-5959)

Stanley Black & Decker Inc ....F 860 225-5111
Jersey City (G-4831)

Thirty-Three Queen Realty Inc ....F 973 824-5527
Newark (G-7341)

TOOLS: Hand, Jewelers'

Acon Watch Crown Company ....F 973 546-8585
Garfield (G-3715)

American Logistics Network LLC ....G 201 391-1054
Woodcliff Lake (G-12180)

Du-Matt Corporation ....G 201 861-4271
West New York (G-11864)

TOOLS: Hand, Power

Black & Decker (us) Inc ....G 201 475-3524
Elmwood Park (G-2806)

Colwood Electronics Inc ....G 732 938-5556
Farmingdale (G-3380)

Congruent Machine Co Inc ....G 973 764-6767
Vernon (G-11297)

Epcos Inc ....D 732 906-4300
Iselin (G-4626)

Epcos Inc ....F 732 603-5941
Lumberton (G-5657)

Ingersoll-Rand Company ....C 908 238-7000
Annandale (G-58)

Ingersoll-Rand Company ....E 856 793-7000
Mount Laurel (G-6803)

Jdv Products Inc ....F 201 794-6467
Fair Lawn (G-3098)

National Steel Rule Company ....D 908 862-3366
Linden (G-5415)

Newell Brands Inc ....B 201 610-6600
Hoboken (G-4486)

S & G Tool Aid Corporation ....D 973 824-7730
Newark (G-7297)

Singe Corporation ....G 908 289-7900
Hillside (G-4440)

William T Hutchinson Company ....F 908 688-0533
Union (G-11235)

TOOLS: Hand, Stonecutters'

Legend Stone Products ....G 973 473-7088
Clifton (G-1660)

TOOTHPASTES, GELS & TOOTHPOWDERS

Church & Dwight Co Inc ....B 609 806-1200
Ewing (G-3009)

Colgate-Palmolive Company ....B 732 878-6062
Highland Park (G-4302)

Colgate-Palmolive Company ....A 732 878-7500
Piscataway (G-8751)

Colgate-Palmolive Company ....E 609 239-6001
Burlington (G-966)

TOWELS: Fabric & Nonwoven, Made From Purchased Materials

Anchor Sales & Marketing Inc ....F 973 545-2277
West Milford (G-11850)

Asbury Towel Company Inc ....F 732 370-3908
Lakewood (G-5076)

Crown Products Inc ....E 732 493-0022
Ocean (G-7720)

Franco Manufacturing Co Inc ....C 732 494-0500
Metuchen (G-6104)

TOWELS: Indl

Jay Franco & Sons Inc ....D 732 721-0022
Sayreville (G-9825)

Material Imports ....G 201 229-1180
Moonachie (G-6531)

Sensible Collection Inc ....G 201 831-1063
Hackensack (G-3972)

TOWERS, SECTIONS: Transmission, Radio & Television

Lingo Inc ....F 856 273-6594
Mount Laurel (G-6812)

Main Robert A & Sons Holdg Co ....E 201 447-3700
Wyckoff (G-12258)

Morgan Towers Inc ....G 856 786-7200
Moorestown (G-6602)

TOWING & TUGBOAT SVC

Wittich Bros Marine Inc ....E 732 722-8656
Manasquan (G-5885)

TOYS

Ambo Consulting LLC ....G 732 663-0000
Deal (G-1997)

Amloid Corporation ....F 973 328-0654
Cedar Knolls (G-1306)

Answers In Motion LLC ....G 732 267-7792
Maple Shade (G-5899)

Atlas O LLC ....E 908 687-9590
Hillside (G-4393)

Babysmart LLC ....G 908 766-4900
Bernardsville (G-447)

Bally Technologies Inc ....F 609 641-7711
Egg Harbor Township (G-2681)

Electronics Boutique Amer Inc ....G 856 435-3900
Clementon (G-1531)

Epoch Everlasting Play LLC ....E 973 316-2500
Parsippany (G-8002)

Froyo Skyview LLC ....G 718 607-5656
Jersey City (G-4758)

Horizon Group USA Inc ....C 908 810-1111
Warren (G-11553)

Pride Products Mfg LLC ....F 908 353-1900
Elizabeth (G-2768)

Primetime Trading Corp ....E 646 580-8223
Bayonne (G-241)

Proteus Designs LLC ....G 215 519-0135
Moorestown (G-6616)

Reeves International Inc ....E 973 956-9555
Wayne (G-11678)

Steico USA Inc ....F 732 364-6200
Lakewood (G-5191)

Wecool Toys Inc ....E 856 296-9766
Medford (G-6084)

Zimpli Kids Inc ....G 732 945-5995
Neptune (G-6937)

TOYS & HOBBY GOODS & SPLYS, WHOLESALE: Amusement Goods

Two Jays Bingo Supply Inc ....F 609 267-4542
Hainesport (G-4080)

TOYS & HOBBY GOODS & SPLYS, WHOLESALE: Arts/Crafts Eqpt/Sply

Environmolds LLC ....F 908 273-5401
Summit (G-10641)

Employee Codes: A=Over 500 employees, B=251-500
C=101-250, D=51-100, E=20-50, F=10-19, G=4-9   2018 Harris New jersey
Manufacturers Directory   975

PRODUCT

Hygloss Products Inc ....E 973 458-1700
Wallington (G-11527)
Larose Industries LLC ....D 973 543-2037
Randolph (G-9287)

TOYS & HOBBY GOODS & SPLYS, WHOLESALE: Dolls

Pretty Ugly LLC ....F 908 620-0931
Green Brook (G-3863)
Reeves International Inc ....E 973 694-5006
Pequannock (G-8601)

TOYS & HOBBY GOODS & SPLYS, WHOLESALE: Toys & Games

Ambo Consulting LLC ....G 732 663-0000
Deal (G-1997)
Kiddesigns Inc ....E 732 574-9000
Rahway (G-9207)

TOYS, HOBBY GOODS & SPLYS WHOLESALERS

AMS Toy Intl Inc ....E 973 442-5790
Wharton (G-11979)
Dream Makers Inc ....G 201 248-5502
Park Ridge (G-7918)
Epoch Everlasting Play LLC ....E 973 316-2500
Parsippany (G-8002)
Kids of America Corp ....E 973 808-8242
Fairfield (G-3241)
Top Rated Shopping Bargains ....F 201 630-0770
Hasbrouck Heights (G-4200)

TOYS: Dolls, Stuffed Animals & Parts

De Zaio Productions Inc ....D 973 423-5000
Fair Lawn (G-3089)
Dream Makers Inc ....G 201 248-5502
Park Ridge (G-7918)
Homeco LLC ....E 732 802-7733
Piscataway (G-8774)
Kids of America Corp ....E 973 808-8242
Fairfield (G-3241)
New Adventures LLC ....G 973 884-8887
East Hanover (G-2231)
Pretty Ugly LLC ....F 908 620-0931
Green Brook (G-3863)
Tiffanees Toys Inc ....G 732 828-6333
North Brunswick (G-7543)

TOYS: Electronic

Kiddesigns Inc ....E 732 574-9000
Rahway (G-9207)
R & R Distributors Inc ....G 201 804-0077
Branchville (G-732)
Toysruscom Inc....................................C 973 617-3500
Wayne (G-11686)

TOYS: Rubber

Dream Makers Inc ....G 201 248-5502
Park Ridge (G-7918)

TOYS: Video Game Machines

AG&e Holdings Inc ....E 609 704-3000
Hammonton (G-4126)

TRADE SHOW ARRANGEMENT SVCS

CPB Inc ....E 856 697-2700
Buena (G-946)
Creating Your Design LLC ....G 973 357-1080
Paterson (G-8240)
Display Works LLC ....C 201 327-1260
Parsippany (G-7983)

TRADING STAMP PROMOTION & REDEMPTION

Crown Roll Leaf Inc ....E 973 684-2600
Paterson (G-8242)

TRAILERS & PARTS: Truck & Semi's

E Loc Total Logistics LLC ....G 609 685-6117
Mount Laurel (G-6796)
Hercules Enterprises LLC ....D 908 369-0000
Hillsborough (G-4340)

M W Trailer Repair Inc ....F 609 298-1113
Bordentown (G-600)
Trac Intermodal LLC ....G 609 452-8900
Princeton (G-9130)
Trac Interstar LLC ....G 609 452-8900
Princeton (G-9131)
Vanco USA LLC (de) ....C 609 499-4141
Bordentown (G-615)
Wjm Trucking Inc ....G 856 381-3635
Mullica Hill (G-6893)

TRAILERS & TRAILER EQPT

Sealion Metal Fabricators Inc ....F 856 933-3914
Bellmawr (G-350)
Steve Green Enterprises ....F 732 938-5572
Farmingdale (G-3394)

TRAILERS: Bodies

Richard Shafer ....G 856 358-3483
Elmer (G-2796)

TRAILERS: Demountable Cargo Containers

ASAP Containers NJ NY Corp ....F 732 659-4402
West Orange (G-11886)
Granco Group LLC ....G 973 515-4721
Roseland (G-9651)

TRAILERS: Semitrailers, Truck Tractors

Vanco Usa LLC ....D 609 499-4141
Bordentown (G-614)

TRAILERS: Truck, Chassis

Automann Inc ....D 201 529-4996
Somerset (G-10068)
Universal Parts New Jersey LLC ....G 732 615-0626
Middletown (G-6219)

TRANSDUCERS: Pressure

American Sensor Tech Inc ....D 973 448-1901
Budd Lake (G-924)

TRANSFORMERS: Distribution

Voltis LLC ....G 607 349-9411
Fairfield (G-3346)

TRANSFORMERS: Distribution, Electric

G & S Motor Equipment Co Inc............D 201 998-9244
Kearny (G-4875)
High Energy Group Ltd Lblty Co ....G 732 741-9099
Eatontown (G-2400)
Siemens Corporation ....D 732 590-6895
Iselin (G-4645)

TRANSFORMERS: Electric

Baltimore Transformer Company ....E 973 942-2222
Paterson (G-8220)
Cooper Power Systems LLC ....C 732 481-4630
Ocean (G-7719)
Cooper Power Systems LLC ....C 856 719-1100
West Berlin (G-11712)
Galaxy Trans & Magnetics LLC ....F 856 753-4546
West Berlin (G-11722)
Glen Magnetics Inc ....E 908 454-3717
Alpha (G-41)
Hitran Corporation ....C 908 782-5525
Flemington (G-3447)
Hunterdon Transformer Co Inc ....D 908 454-2400
Alpha (G-42)
Megatran Industries ....B 609 227-4300
Bordentown (G-601)
Nwl Inc ....B 609 298-7300
Bordentown (G-606)
Power Magnetics Inc ....E 609 695-1170
Trenton (G-11101)
Transistor Devices Inc ....E 908 850-5088
Hackettstown (G-4041)
Transistor Devices Inc ....C 908 850-5088
Hackettstown (G-4042)

TRANSFORMERS: Electronic

Baltimore Transformer Company ....E 973 942-2222
Paterson (G-8220)
Edko Electronics ....E 973 942-2222
Paterson (G-8254)

TRANSFORMERS: Machine Tool

Ivey Katrina Owner ....G 973 951-8328
Newark (G-7202)

TRANSFORMERS: Meters, Electronic

Magnetran Inc......................................F 856 768-7787
Ocean View (G-7764)
Nilsson Electrical Laboratory ....G 201 521-4860
Jersey City (G-4790)

TRANSFORMERS: Power Related

AFP Transformers Corporation ....D 732 248-0305
Edison (G-2453)
Edko Electronics ....E 973 942-2222
Paterson (G-8254)
Jerome Industries Corp ....E 908 353-5700
Hackettstown (G-4013)
KG Squared LLC ....F 973 627-0643
Rockaway (G-9581)
Mesa Veterans Power LLC ....G 856 222-1000
Moorestown (G-6601)
Microsignals Inc ....E 800 225-4508
Palisades Park (G-7839)
Pioneer Power Solutions Inc ....E 212 867-0700
Fort Lee (G-3578)
Raritan Inc ....E 732 764-8886
Somerset (G-10162)

TRANSFORMERS: Rectifier

Model Rectifier Corporation.................E 732 225-2100
Edison (G-2575)

TRANSFORMERS: Specialty

Beverly Manufacturing Co Inc ....G 856 764-7898
Riverside (G-9493)
Globtek Inc ....B 201 784-1000
Northvale (G-7582)
Hbs Electronics Inc..............................G 973 439-1147
Fairfield (G-3217)
High Gate Corp ....F 609 267-0680
Mount Holly (G-6773)

TRANSFORMERS: Tripping

Power Magne-Tech Corp ....E 732 826-4700
Perth Amboy (G-8626)

TRANSISTORS

United Silicon Carbide Inc ....F 732 355-0550
Monmouth Junction (G-6368)

TRANSLATION & INTERPRETATION SVCS

Berlitz Languages US Inc.....................D 609 759-5371
Princeton (G-9014)
Newtype Inc ....F 973 361-6000
Randolph (G-9290)

TRANSMISSIONS: Motor Vehicle

Transmission Technology Co ....G 973 305-3600
Lincoln Park (G-5334)

TRANSPORTATION EPQT & SPLYS, WHOLESALE: Marine Crafts/Splys

JC Macelroy Co Inc..............................D 732 572-7100
Piscataway (G-8784)

TRANSPORTATION EPQT/SPLYS, WHOL: Guided Missiles/Space Veh

Aphelion Orbitals Inc ....G 321 289-0872
Union City (G-11242)

TRANSPORTATION EPQT/SPLYS, WHOL: Marine Propulsn Mach/Eqpt

Ocean Power & Equipment Co ....G 973 575-5775
West Caldwell (G-11793)

TRANSPORTATION EQPT & SPLYS WHOLESALERS, NEC

Bristol-Donald Company Inc.................E 973 589-2640
Newark (G-7115)
Defense Photonics Group Inc ....F 908 822-1075
South Plainfield (G-10354)

Jet Aviation St Louis Inc ....E 201 462-4026
Teterboro (G-10800)

Steelstran Industries Inc ....E 732 574-0700
Avenel (G-152)

Taurus International Corp ....E 201 825-2420
Ramsey (G-9252)

TRANSPORTATION SVCS, WATER: Boat Cleaning

Sea Harvest Inc ....E 609 884-3000
Cape May (G-1105)

TRANSPORTATION SVCS, WATER: Intracoastal, Freight

Fornazor International Inc ....E 201 664-4000
Hillsdale (G-4382)

TRANSPORTATION SVCS, WATER: Salvaging & Surveying, Marine

T O Najarian Associates ....D 732 389-0220
Eatontown (G-2424)

TRANSPORTATION SVCS: Railroads, Belt line

Holtec Government Services LLC ....G 856 291-0600
Marlton (G-5978)

TRANSPORTATION: Deep Sea Domestic Freight

Bulkhaul (usa) Limited ....F 908 272-3100
Iselin (G-4618)

TRANSPORTATION: Deep Sea Foreign Freight

Bulkhaul (usa) Limited ....F 908 272-3100
Iselin (G-4618)

Global Commodities Exportacao ....G 201 613-1532
Newark (G-7171)

TRANSPORTATION: Local Passenger, NEC

Carry Easy Inc ....E 201 944-0042
Leonia (G-5315)

TRANSPORTATION: Monorail Transit Systems

Bombardier Transportation ....B 973 624-9300
Newark (G-7109)

TRAP ROCK: Crushed & Broken

Cedar Hill Landscaping ....E 732 469-1400
Somerset (G-10081)

Eastern Concrete Materials Inc ....C 201 797-7979
Saddle Brook (G-9763)

Emil Dipalma Inc ....G 973 477-2766
Hackettstown (G-4004)

Joseph and William Stavola ....E 609 924-0300
Kingston (G-5028)

Millington Quarry Inc ....D 908 542-0055
Basking Ridge (G-199)

Tilcon New York Inc ....B 800 789-7625
Parsippany (G-8101)

Tilcon New York Inc ....E 800 789-7625
Pompton Lakes (G-8950)

Tilcon New York Inc ....G 800 789-7625
Parsippany (G-8102)

Tilcon New York Inc ....E 800 789-7625
Oxford (G-7833)

Tilcon New York Inc ....F 973 347-2405
Stanhope (G-10590)

Trap Rock Industries Inc ....B 609 924-0300
Kingston (G-5030)

Trap Rock Industries LLC ....D 609 924-0300
Kingston (G-5031)

TRAPS: Animal & Fish, Wire

Blue Claw Mfg & Supply Company ....G 856 696-4366
Richland (G-9349)

TRAVEL AGENCIES

Northstar Travel Media LLC ....C 201 902-2000
Secaucus (G-9907)

TRAYS: Plastic

Bel-Art Products Inc ....E 973 694-0500
Wayne (G-11608)

Sabert Corporation ....C 800 722-3781
Sayreville (G-9837)

Sabert Corporation ....E 732 721-5544
Sayreville (G-9838)

TRIM: Window, Wood

Trim and Tassels LLC ....G 973 808-1566
Fairfield (G-3331)

TROPHIES, NEC

AMG International Inc ....G 404 297-9083
Parsippany (G-7945)

AMG International Inc ....D 201 475-4800
Parsippany (G-7946)

Freeman Products Inc ....F 201 475-4800
Parsippany (G-8017)

Trophy King Inc ....G 201 836-1482
Teaneck (G-10775)

TROPHIES, PLATED, ALL METALS

III Eagle Enterprises Ltd ....E 973 237-1111
Ringwood (G-9449)

Picture It Inc ....G 732 819-0420
Edison (G-2594)

TROPHIES: Metal, Exc Silver

All State Medal Co Inc ....G 973 458-1458
Lodi (G-5575)

Awards Trophy Company ....G 908 687-5775
Hillside (G-4394)

NJ Logo Wear LLC ....G 609 597-9400
Manahawkin (G-5832)

Tropar Manufacturing Co Inc ....E 973 765-0380
Florham Park (G-3519)

Tropar Trophy Manufacturing Co ....D 973 822-2400
Florham Park (G-3520)

TROPHY & PLAQUE STORES

All Nu Trophy & Screen Prtg ....F 201 807-0808
Ridgefield Park (G-9396)

All State Medal Co Inc ....G 973 458-1458
Lodi (G-5575)

Armin Kososki ....G 908 689-0411
Washington (G-11575)

Blue Ribbon Awards Inc ....G 732 560-0046
Somerset (G-10070)

Colorcraft Sign Co ....F 609 386-1115
Beverly (G-461)

Crown Trophy ....G 973 808-8400
Pine Brook (G-8696)

Heros Salute Awards Co ....G 973 696-5085
Wayne (G-11648)

Picture It Inc ....G 732 819-0420
Edison (G-2594)

Rolferrys Specialties Inc ....G 856 456-2999
Brooklawn (G-921)

Stewart-Morris Inc ....G 973 822-2777
Madison (G-5736)

Trophy King Inc ....G 201 836-1482
Teaneck (G-10775)

TRUCK & BUS BODIES: Ambulance

Waldwick Vol Amb Corps Inc ....E 201 445-8772
Waldwick (G-11457)

TRUCK & BUS BODIES: Automobile Wrecker Truck

Alexam Riverdale ....G 973 831-0065
Riverdale (G-9474)

TRUCK & BUS BODIES: Bus Bodies

American Bus & Coach LLC ....E 732 283-1982
Iselin (G-4609)

TRUCK & BUS BODIES: Dump Truck

Peter Garafano & Son Inc ....E 973 278-0350
Paterson (G-8364)

TRUCK & BUS BODIES: Tank Truck

Vacuum Sales Inc ....E 856 627-7790
Laurel Springs (G-5234)

TRUCK & BUS BODIES: Truck Cabs, Motor Vehicles

Jid Transportation LLC ....G 201 362-0841
West New York (G-11870)

TRUCK & BUS BODIES: Truck, Motor Vehicle

Columbia Industries Inc ....G 201 337-7332
Franklin Lakes (G-3612)

Custom Sales & Service Inc ....E 800 257-7855
Hammonton (G-4136)

Garden St Chasis Remanuf ....E 732 283-1910
Woodbridge (G-12149)

Transtar Truck Body & Wldg Co ....G 908 832-2688
Califon (G-1038)

TRUCK BODIES: Body Parts

Barrier Enterprises Inc ....G 973 770-3983
Andover (G-48)

Demountable Concepts Inc ....E 856 863-3081
Glassboro (G-3803)

Summit Truck Body Inc ....F 908 277-4342
Summit (G-10661)

TRUCK BODY SHOP

Cliffside Body Corporation ....E 201 945-3970
Fairview (G-3359)

Transtar Truck Body & Wldg Co ....G 908 832-2688
Califon (G-1038)

Trucktech Parts & Services ....G 973 799-0500
Newark (G-7348)

TRUCK DRIVER SVCS

Jid Transportation LLC ....G 201 362-0841
West New York (G-11870)

TRUCK GENERAL REPAIR SVC

Chizzys Service Center ....G 201 641-7222
Little Ferry (G-5496)

Fleetsource LLC ....E 732 566-4970
Cliffwood (G-1547)

R & H Spring & Truck Repair ....F 732 681-9000
Wall Township (G-11504)

Ram Hydraulics Inc ....G 732 237-0904
Shrewsbury (G-10009)

TRUCK PAINTING & LETTERING SVCS

Dux Paint LLC ....F 973 473-2376
Lodi (G-5583)

Essex Morris Sign Co ....G 973 386-1755
Whippany (G-12019)

Rich Designs ....G 908 369-5035
Hillsborough (G-4369)

Sign Shoppe Inc ....G 856 384-2937
Woodbury (G-12170)

Sign Up Inc ....G 201 902-8640
Secaucus (G-9928)

TRUCK PARTS & ACCESSORIES: Wholesalers

Automann Inc ....D 201 529-4996
Somerset (G-10068)

Cliffside Body Corporation ....E 201 945-3970
Fairview (G-3359)

Suburban Auto Seat Co Inc ....F 973 778-9227
Lodi (G-5603)

Transaxle LLC ....C 856 665-4445
Cinnaminson (G-1495)

TRUCKING & HAULING SVCS: Building Materials

Concrete On Demand Inc ....F 201 337-0005
Oakland (G-7680)

TRUCKING & HAULING SVCS: Contract Basis

Penske Truck Leasing Co LP ....E 973 575-0169
Parsippany (G-8060)

Employee Codes: A=Over 500 employees, B=251-500
C=101-250, D=51-100, E=20-50, F=10-19, G=4-9

2018 Harris New jersey
Manufacturers Directory

977

PRODUCT

Wakefern Food Corp..............................B...... 732 819-0140
Edison (G-2649)
Wakefern Food Corp..............................B...... 908 527-3300
Keasbey (G-4932)

TRUCKING & HAULING SVCS: Haulage & Cartage, Light, Local

Jlb Hauling Ltd Liability Co..................G...... 856 514-2771
Pennsville (G-8592)

TRUCKING & HAULING SVCS: Hazardous Waste

Safety-Kleen Systems Inc ....F...... 609 859-2049
Southampton (G-10481)

TRUCKING & HAULING SVCS: Machinery, Heavy

Lynn Amiee Inc ....E...... 201 840-6766
Ridgefield (G-9372)

TRUCKING & HAULING SVCS: Mail Carriers, Contract

Frontend Graphics Inc..........................G...... 856 547-1600
Cherry Hill (G-1367)

TRUCKING & HAULING SVCS: Petroleum, Local

Prospect Transportation Inc ....D...... 201 933-9999
Carlstadt (G-1210)

TRUCKING, AUTOMOBILE CARRIER

Chariot Courier & Trans Svcs ....F...... 888 532-9125
Sayreville (G-9816)

TRUCKING, DUMP

Cedar Hill Landscaping ....E...... 732 469-1400
Somerset (G-10081)
J G Carpenter Contractor......................G...... 732 271-8991
Middlesex (G-6171)
J Spinelli & Sons Inc ....E...... 856 691-3133
Elmer (G-2793)

TRUCKING, REFRIGERATED: Long-Distance

Power Pool Plus Inc..............................G...... 908 454-1124
Alpha (G-44)

TRUCKING: Except Local

Barrett Industries Corporation ....E...... 973 533-1001
Morristown (G-6692)
Barrett Paving Materials Inc.................E...... 973 533-1001
Roseland (G-9647)
Kramme Consolidated Inc.....................G...... 856 358-8151
Monroeville (G-6400)

TRUCKING: Local, With Storage

Bouras Industries Inc ....A...... 908 918-9400
Summit (G-10637)

TRUCKING: Local, Without Storage

Bouras Industries Inc ....A...... 908 918-9400
Summit (G-10637)
D Depasquale Paving LLC ....G...... 301 674-9775
Jackson (G-4661)
Fence America New Jersey Inc ....G...... 973 472-5121
Hackensack (G-3910)
L & S Contracting Inc ....G...... 609 397-1281
Hopewell (G-4542)
Mondelez Global LLC ....A...... 201 794-4080
Fair Lawn (G-3104)
Select Enterprises Inc ....G...... 732 287-8622
Edison (G-2613)
Tonys Auto Entp Ltd Lblty Co...............G...... 203 223-5776
Edison (G-2639)

TRUCKS & TRACTORS: Industrial

Excalibur Miretti Group LLC ....F...... 973 808-8399
Fairfield (G-3188)
Morse Metal Products Co Inc................G...... 732 422-3676
Princeton (G-9078)
Palfinger North America ....D...... 609 588-5400
Trenton (G-11095)

Permadur Industries Inc........................D...... 908 359-9767
Hillsborough (G-4362)
Saturn Overhead Equipments LLC ....F...... 732 560-7210
Somerset (G-10171)
Trucktech Parts & Services...................G...... 973 799-0500
Newark (G-7348)
Vanco USA LLC (de)..............................C...... 609 499-4141
Bordentown (G-615)

TRUCKS, INDL: Wholesalers

Excalibur Miretti Group LLC ....F...... 973 808-8399
Fairfield (G-3188)

TRUCKS: Forklift

Hilman Incorporated..............................D...... 732 462-6277
Marlboro (G-5943)
Prestige Forklift Maint Svc ....G...... 732 297-1001
New Brunswick (G-6993)
Rentalift Inc ....F...... 973 684-6111
Paterson (G-8368)

TRUCKS: Indl

Caravan Inc...F...... 732 590-0210
Avenel (G-128)
Global Express Freight Inc ....G...... 201 376-6613
Bergenfield (G-385)
Showtime Express ....G...... 732 238-2701
East Brunswick (G-2183)

TRUSSES & FRAMING: Prefabricated Metal

Marino Building Systems Corp..............C...... 732 968-0555
South Plainfield (G-10403)

TRUSSES: Wood, Floor

Atlantic Exterior Wall Systems ....D...... 973 646-8200
Wayne (G-11606)

TRUSSES: Wood, Roof

Truss Engineering.................................G...... 201 871-4800
Englewood (G-2938)
Woodbury Roof Truss Inc ....D...... 856 845-3848
Woodbury Heights (G-12178)

TUB CONTAINERS: Plastic

Chefler Foods LLC.................................F...... 201 596-3710
Saddle Brook (G-9757)

TUBE & TUBING FABRICATORS

Century Tube Corp................................E...... 908 534-2001
Somerville (G-10204)
G & J Steel & Tubing Inc ....D...... 908 526-4445
Hillsborough (G-4334)
Jettron Products Inc.............................E...... 973 887-0571
East Hanover (G-2226)
M P Tube Works Inc ....G...... 908 317-2500
Mountainside (G-6883)
Samstubend Inc....................................F...... 973 278-2555
Paterson (G-8376)

TUBES: Electron, NEC

Troy-Onic Inc ....E...... 973 584-6830
Kenvil (G-5014)

TUBES: Light Sensing & Emitting

Petra Systems Inc.................................C...... 908 462-5200
South Plainfield (G-10419)

TUBES: Photomultiplier

Hamamatsu Corporation ....D...... 908 231-0960
Bridgewater (G-841)

TUBES: Steel & Iron

Century Tube Corp................................E...... 908 534-2001
Somerville (G-10204)

TUBING, COLD-DRAWN: Mech Or Hypodermic Sizes, Stainless

Rathgibson North Branch LLC ....C...... 908 253-3260
Branchburg (G-697)

TUBING: Copper

250 Lackland Holding Inc......................D...... 732 469-7420
Middlesex (G-6140)
Handytube Corporation ....E...... 732 469-7420
Middlesex (G-6169)
Industrial Tube Corporation ....E...... 908 369-3737
Hillsborough (G-4345)

TUBING: Flexible, Metallic

Avony Enterprises Inc ....E...... 212 242-8144
Trenton (G-11022)
Testrite Instrument Co Inc....................C...... 201 543-0240
Hackensack (G-3984)

TUBING: Glass

Betco Glass Inc.....................................G...... 856 327-4301
Millville (G-6286)

TUBING: Plastic

Alpha Wire Corporation.........................C...... 908 925-8000
Elizabeth (G-2708)
Ber Plastics Inc ....E...... 973 839-2100
Riverdale (G-9475)
Cobon Plastics Corp.............................F...... 973 344-6330
Newark (G-7123)
Illinois Tool Works Inc ....D...... 732 968-5300
Parsippany (G-8028)
K Jabat Inc ....F...... 732 469-8177
Green Brook (G-3860)
Plastic Specialties & Tech Inc..............C...... 201 941-2900
Ridgefield (G-9380)
Pure Tech International Inc ....G...... 908 722-4800
Branchburg (G-696)
Resdel Corporation ....E...... 609 886-1111
Rio Grande (G-9461)
Tpi Partners Inc....................................G...... 908 561-3000
Stirling (G-10608)
X-L Plastics Inc ....C...... 973 777-9400
Clifton (G-1745)

TUBING: Seamless

Sandvik Inc...E...... 201 794-5000
Fair Lawn (G-3112)

TUNGSTEN MILL PRDTS

Union City Filament Corp.......................E...... 201 945-3366
Ridgefield (G-9390)

TURBINES & TURBINE GENERATOR SET UNITS, COMPLETE

Hydro-Mechanical Systems Inc.............F...... 856 848-8888
Westville (G-11943)

TURBINES & TURBINE GENERATOR SET UNITS: Gas, Complete

Solar Turbines Incorporated ....F...... 201 825-8200
Upper Saddle River (G-11285)

TURBINES & TURBINE GENERATOR SETS

Boc Group Inc.......................................A...... 908 665-2400
New Providence (G-7030)
I4 Sustainability LLC.............................G...... 732 618-3310
Springfield (G-10557)
Linde LLC ....G...... 973 579-2065
Sparta (G-10510)
Linde North America Inc ....D...... 908 464-8100
New Providence (G-7045)
Linde North America Inc ....B...... 908 464-8100
Bridgewater (G-857)
Lummus Overseas Corporation ....E...... 973 893-3000
Bloomfield (G-520)
Polaris America Ltd Lblty Co.................E...... 614 540-1710
Lakewood (G-5174)

TURBINES: Hydraulic, Complete

Micheller & Son Hydraulics Inc ....F...... 908 687-1545
Roselle (G-9677)

TURBINES: Steam

Babcock & Wilcox Company ....G...... 609 261-2424
Cinnaminson (G-1448)
Babcock & Wilcox Powr Generatn ....F...... 973 227-7008
Fairfield (G-3143)

TURKEY PROCESSING & SLAUGHTERING

Hinck Turkey Farm Inc ...... G 732 681-0508
Neptune (G-6918)

TURNKEY VENDORS: Computer Systems

Maingear Inc ...... E 888 624-6432
Kenilworth (G-4972)

TWINE

Seaboard Paper and Twine LLC ...... E 973 413-8100
Paterson (G-8380)

TWINE PRDTS

American Power Cord Corp ...... G 973 574-8301
Somerset (G-10057)

TYPESETTING SVC

Action Copy Centers Inc ...... G 973 744-5520
Montclair (G-6404)

Allegro Printing Corporation ...... G 609 641-7060
Galloway (G-3708)

American Graphic Systems Inc ...... G 201 796-0666
Fair Lawn (G-3076)

Arch Crown Inc ...... E 973 731-6300
Hillside (G-4390)

Ayr Composition Inc ...... G 908 241-8118
Roselle Park (G-9688)

Aztec Graphics Inc ...... F 609 587-1000
Trenton (G-11023)

Bar Lan Inc ...... G 856 596-2330
Brigantine (G-917)

Bartlett Printing & Graphic ...... G 609 386-1525
Burlington (G-958)

Bowmar Enterprises Inc ...... G 908 277-3000
New Providence (G-7031)

Budget Print Center ...... G 973 743-0073
Bloomfield (G-503)

Commerce Financial Prtrs Corp ...... E 908 241-9880
Roselle (G-9667)

Commercial Composition & Prtg ...... G 856 662-0557
Pennsauken (G-8496)

Comptime Inc ...... G 201 760-2400
Ramsey (G-9238)

Consumer Graphics Inc ...... G 732 469-4699
Somerset (G-10085)

Copy-Rite Printing ...... G 609 597-9182
Manahawkin (G-5830)

Cordes Printing Inc ...... G 201 652-7272
Wyckoff (G-12248)

Cornerstone Prints Imaging LLC ...... G 908 782-7966
Flemington (G-3431)

Craftsmen Photo Lithographers ...... E 973 316-5791
East Hanover (G-2211)

Creative Color Lithographers ...... F 908 789-2295
Garwood (G-3777)

D A K Office Services Inc ...... G 609 586-8222
Trenton (G-11052)

Data Communique Inc ...... E 201 508-6000
Ridgefield Park (G-9402)

Devece & Shaffer Inc ...... G 856 829-7282
Palmyra (G-7847)

Downtown Printing Center Inc ...... F 732 246-7990
New Brunswick (G-6955)

E Nevin Miller Inc ...... F 201 444-5784
Hawthorne (G-4230)

Earth Color New York Inc ...... E 973 884-1300
Parsippany (G-7992)

Fedex Office & Print Svcs Inc ...... F 732 249-9222
New Brunswick (G-6960)

Fedex Office & Print Svcs Inc ...... G 856 273-5959
Mount Laurel (G-6797)

Fedex Office & Print Svcs Inc ...... G 973 376-3966
Springfield (G-10555)

Fedex Office & Print Svcs Inc ...... E 856 427-0099
Cherry Hill (G-1364)

Gangi Graphics Inc ...... G 732 840-8680
Brick (G-744)

Hub Print & Copy Center LLC ...... G 201 585-7887
Fort Lee (G-3558)

Inserts East Incorporated ...... C 856 663-8181
Pennsauken (G-8528)

Instant Printing of Dover Inc ...... G 973 366-6855
Dover (G-2093)

J K Design Inc ...... G 908 428-4700
Hillsborough (G-4351)

Jem Printing Inc ...... G 908 782-9986
Flemington (G-3450)

Jmp Press Inc ...... G 201 444-0236
Ho Ho Kus (G-4454)

John S Swift Company Inc ...... G 201 935-2002
Teterboro (G-10801)

Johnston Letter Co Inc ...... G 973 482-7535
Flanders (G-3412)

Kirms Printing Co Inc ...... E 732 774-8000
Neptune (G-6920)

Laser Dim Graphics & Prtg Inc ...... F 732 821-9000
Colts Neck (G-1789)

Laserwave Graphics Inc ...... F 732 745-7764
New Brunswick (G-6977)

Lont & Overkamp Pubg Co Inc ...... E 973 942-2243
Clifton (G-1664)

Lunet Inc ...... G 201 261-3883
Paramus (G-7885)

Marks Management Systems Inc ...... G 856 866-0588
Maple Shade (G-5906)

McKella 2-8-0 Inc ...... D 856 813-1153
Pennsauken (G-8548)

Metro Publishing Group Inc ...... F 201 385-2000
New Milford (G-7023)

Michael Graphics Inc ...... E 732 846-8680
Branchburg (G-680)

Morgan Printing Service Inc ...... F 732 721-2959
South Amboy (G-10243)

Morris Plains Pip Inc ...... G 973 533-9330
Livingston (G-5548)

Network Typesetting Inc ...... G 732 819-0949
Piscataway (G-8795)

New Jersey Label LLC ...... F 201 880-5102
South Hackensack (G-10283)

Newtype Inc ...... F 973 361-6000
Randolph (G-9290)

Old Hights Print Shop Inc ...... G 609 443-4700
Jackson (G-4674)

OShea Services Inc ...... G 201 343-8668
Hackensack (G-3957)

Otis Graphics Inc ...... F 201 438-7120
Lyndhurst (G-5700)

Pad and Publ Assembly Corp ...... E 856 424-0158
Cherry Hill (G-1409)

Painton Studios Inc ...... G 732 752-8842
Green Brook (G-3861)

Palm Press Inc ...... G 201 767-6504
Northvale (G-7600)

Patel Printing Plus Corp ...... F 908 964-6422
Union (G-11214)

Permagraphics Inc ...... F 201 814-1200
Moonachie (G-6535)

Philip Holzer and Assoc LLC ...... E 212 691-9500
Carlstadt (G-1202)

Printing Craftsman Inc ...... F 201 943-0276
Fairview (G-3370)

Printing Delite Inc ...... G 973 676-3033
East Orange (G-2266)

Puent-Romer Communications Inc ...... G 973 509-7591
Montclair (G-6433)

Redmond Bcms Inc ...... D 973 664-2000
Denville (G-2053)

Roan Printing Inc ...... F 908 526-5990
Somerville (G-10226)

S & M Press Inc ...... F 973 546-6111
Garfield (G-3760)

Sandoval Graphics & Printing ...... G 856 435-7320
Somerdale (G-10043)

Scarlet Printing ...... G 732 560-1415
Middlesex (G-6193)

Scott Graphics Printing Co Inc ...... G 201 262-0473
New Milford (G-7025)

Sheroy Printing Inc ...... F 973 242-4040
Newark (G-7312)

Sign On Inc ...... G 201 384-7714
Dumont (G-2124)

Sonata Graphics Inc ...... G 201 866-0186
Secaucus (G-9930)

Staines Inc ...... F 856 784-2718
Somerdale (G-10044)

Standard Prtg & Mail Svcs Inc ...... F 973 790-3333
Fairfield (G-3311)

Star Promotions Inc ...... F 732 356-5959
Bound Brook (G-624)

Steb Inc ...... G 973 584-0990
Ledgewood (G-5310)

Tangent Graphics Inc ...... G 201 488-2840
Englewood (G-2936)

Tanter Inc ...... G 732 382-3555
Clark (G-1516)

Techsetters Inc ...... E 856 240-7905
Collingswood (G-1774)

Tedco Inc ...... G 609 883-0799
Ewing (G-3060)

Thewal Inc ...... F 973 635-1880
Chatham (G-1338)

Trade Thermographers Inc ...... F 201 489-2060
Rochelle Park (G-9539)

Typeline ...... F 201 251-2201
Wyckoff (G-12267)

Typen Graphics Inc ...... G 973 838-6544
Kinnelon (G-5042)

Verni Vito ...... G 732 449-1760
Wall Township (G-11517)

Wilker Graphics LLC ...... G 201 447-4800
Midland Park (G-6242)

Zwier Corp ...... G 973 748-4009
Bloomfield (G-539)

TYPESETTING SVC: Computer

B & B Press Inc ...... G 908 840-4093
Lebanon (G-5278)

Nassau Communications Inc ...... F 609 208-9099
Lawrence Township (G-5245)

TYPESETTING SVC: Hand Composition

A M Graphics Inc ...... G 201 767-5320
Harrington Park (G-4169)

Word Center Printing ...... G 609 586-5825
Trenton (G-11134)

TYPEWRITERS & PARTS

Swintec Corp ...... F 201 935-0115
Moonachie (G-6548)

TYPOGRAPHY

Newark Trade Typographers ...... F 973 674-3727
Orange (G-7823)

ULTRASONIC EQPT: Cleaning, Exc Med & Dental

Crest Group Inc ...... F 609 883-4000
Trenton (G-11049)

Crestek Inc ...... E 609 883-4000
Ewing (G-3012)

L & R Manufacturing Co Inc ...... C 201 991-5330
Kearny (G-4895)

L & R Manufacturing Co Inc ...... D 201 991-5330
Kearny (G-4894)

Zenith Mfg & Chemical Corp ...... F 201 767-1332
Norwood (G-7638)

ULTRASONIC EQPT: Dental

L & R Manufacturing Co Inc ...... D 201 991-5330
Kearny (G-4894)

South East Instruments LLC ...... G 201 569-0050
Englewood (G-2933)

UMBRELLAS & CANES

Galleria Enterprises Inc ...... G 646 416-6683
Fairfield (G-3205)

Peerless Umbrella Co Inc ...... C 973 578-4900
Newark (G-7267)

UMBRELLAS: Garden Or Wagon

Rainmen USA Incorporated ...... D 201 784-3244
Norwood (G-7634)

S Frankford & Sons Inc ...... F 856 222-4134
Mount Laurel (G-6836)

UNIFORM STORES

Somes Uniforms Inc ...... F 201 843-1199
Hackensack (G-3977)

UNSUPPORTED PLASTICS: Floor Or Wall Covering

Congoleum Corporation ...... E 609 584-3000
Trenton (G-11044)

Congoleum Corporation ...... B 609 584-3000
Trenton (G-11046)

Prestige Associates Inc ...... E 609 393-1509
Trenton (G-11105)

Zack Painting Co Inc ...... E 732 738-7900
Fords (G-3531)

Employee Codes: A=Over 500 employees; B=251-500
C=101-250; D=51-100; E=20-50; F=10-19; G=4-9   2018 Harris New Jersey
Manufacturers Directory   979

PRODUCT

UPHOLSTERY WORK SVCS

Kushner Draperies Mfg LLC ....E 856 317-9696
Pennsauken *(G-8541)*

USED BOOK STORES

Chatham Bookseller Inc ....G 973 822-1361
Madison *(G-5720)*

USED CAR DEALERS

Herald News ....G 973 569-7000
Woodland Park *(G-12221)*

USED MERCHANDISE STORES

Good As Gold Jewelers Inc ....G 732 286-1111
Toms River *(G-10881)*

USED MERCHANDISE STORES: Building Materials

Delta Procurement Inc ....G 201 623-9353
Carlstadt *(G-1153)*

USED MERCHANDISE STORES: Musical Instruments

W E Wamsley Restorations Inc ....G 856 795-4001
Haddonfield *(G-4066)*

UTENSILS: Household, Cooking & Kitchen, Metal

Sowa Corp ....G 973 297-0008
Newark *(G-7321)*

UTENSILS: Household, Cooking & Kitchen, Porcelain Enameled

Newell Brands Inc ....B 201 610-6600
Hoboken *(G-4486)*

VACUUM CLEANER STORES

Hillsborough Vacuum LLC ....G 908 904-6600
Hillsborough *(G-4341)*

VACUUM CLEANERS: Household

Hillsborough Vacuum LLC ....G 908 904-6600
Hillsborough *(G-4341)*
Metropolitan Vacuum Clr Co Inc ....D 201 405-2225
Oakland *(G-7696)*

VACUUM CLEANERS: Indl Type

Clayton Associates Inc ....F 732 363-2100
Lakewood *(G-5094)*
Dcm Clean Air Products Inc ....G 732 363-2100
Lakewood *(G-5106)*
Metropolitan Vacuum Clr Co Inc ....D 201 405-2225
Oakland *(G-7696)*
Vac-U-Max ....F 973 759-4600
Belleville *(G-323)*

VACUUM PUMPS & EQPT: Laboratory

Denton Vacuum LLC ....E 856 439-9100
Moorestown *(G-6572)*
Emse Corp ....F 973 227-9221
Fairfield *(G-3184)*
Knf Neuberger Inc ....D 609 890-8889
Trenton *(G-11074)*
Nes Company Inc ....G 973 795-1519
Jersey City *(G-4788)*

VACUUM SYSTEMS: Air Extraction, Indl

Croll-Reynolds Co Inc ....E 908 232-4200
Parsippany *(G-7976)*
Vairtec Corporation ....G 201 445-6965
Midland Park *(G-6241)*

VALUE-ADDED RESELLERS: Computer Systems

Adaptive Technology Entps LLC ....G 877 847-6272
Medford *(G-6063)*
Computer Sources ....G 201 791-9443
Elmwood Park *(G-2811)*

Essexusa LLC ....F 201 576-0001
Paramus *(G-7867)*

VALVE REPAIR SVCS, INDL

Emerson Automation Solutions ....F 856 542-5252
Bridgeport *(G-763)*

VALVES

Fujikin of America Inc ....G 201 641-1119
Hasbrouck Heights *(G-4192)*
Rotarex Inc North America ....D 724 696-3345
Hackettstown *(G-4033)*
Straval Machine Co Inc ....E 973 340-9955
Elmwood Park *(G-2851)*

VALVES & PARTS: Gas, Indl

Cavagna North America Inc ....E 732 469-2100
Somerset *(G-10080)*

VALVES & PIPE FITTINGS

Ammark Corporation ....G 973 616-2555
Pompton Plains *(G-8952)*
Ceodeux Incorporated ....E 724 696-4340
Hackettstown *(G-4000)*
CP Test & Valve Products Inc ....G 201 998-1500
Kearny *(G-4868)*
DAngelo Metal Products Inc ....F 908 862-8220
Linden *(G-5367)*
Durst Corporation Inc ....E 800 852-3906
Cranford *(G-1903)*
Everlasting Valve Company Inc ....E 908 769-0700
South Plainfield *(G-10359)*
Fluidyne Corp ....E 856 663-1818
Pennsauken *(G-8510)*
Gadren Machine Co Inc ....F 856 456-4329
Mount Ephraim *(G-6763)*
Gasflo Products Inc ....E 973 276-9011
Fairfield *(G-3207)*
Gorton Heating Corp ....G 908 276-1323
Cranford *(G-1909)*
Hayward Industries Inc ....B 908 351-5400
Elizabeth *(G-2742)*
Holby Valve Co Inc ....F 973 465-7400
Newark *(G-7190)*
Imperial Weld Ring Corp Inc ....E 908 354-0011
Elizabeth *(G-2746)*
Knickerbocker Machine Shop Inc ......D 973 256-1616
Totowa *(G-10953)*
Kraissl Company Inc ....E 201 342-0008
Hackensack *(G-3937)*
Lindstrom & King Co Inc ....G 973 279-2511
Paterson *(G-8321)*
Marotta Controls Inc ....C 973 334-7800
Montville *(G-6490)*
Newco Valves LLC ....E 732 257-0300
East Brunswick *(G-2169)*
Nippon Benkan Kagyo ....E 732 435-0777
New Brunswick *(G-6988)*
RGI Inc ....F 973 697-2624
Newfoundland *(G-7376)*
Scientific Machine and Sup Co ....E 732 356-1553
Middlesex *(G-6195)*
Sigma International Group Inc ....F 609 758-0800
Cream Ridge *(G-1941)*
Sims Pump Valve Company Inc ....E 201 792-0600
Hoboken *(G-4496)*
Symcon Inc ....G 973 728-8661
West Milford *(G-11857)*
Vac-U-Max ....E 973 759-4600
Belleville *(G-322)*
Wire Cloth Manufacturers Inc ....E 973 328-1000
Mine Hill *(G-6329)*
Wm Steinen Mfg Co ....D 973 887-6400
Parsippany *(G-8116)*
World Wide Metric Inc ....F 732 247-2300
Branchburg *(G-719)*

VALVES & REGULATORS: Pressure, Indl

Chemiquip Products Co Inc ....G 201 868-4445
Linden *(G-5359)*
Hayward Industrial Products ....C 908 351-5400
Elizabeth *(G-2741)*

VALVES Solenoid

Asco Valve LLC ....D 973 966-2437
Florham Park *(G-3488)*

Automatic Switch Company ....A 973 966-2000
Florham Park *(G-3489)*
Automatic Switch Company ....A 209 941-4111
Florham Park *(G-3490)*
Automatic Switch Company ....F 732 596-1731
Woodbridge *(G-12146)*
Bio-Chem Fluidics Inc ....D 973 263-3001
Boonton *(G-557)*
Magnatrol Valve Corporation ....F 856 829-4580
Roebling *(G-9638)*
Neptune Research & Development ......E 973 808-8811
West Caldwell *(G-11792)*
Parker-Hannifin Corporation ....E 973 575-4844
Pine Brook *(G-8712)*

VALVES: Aerosol, Metal

D K Trading Inc ....G 856 225-1130
Camden *(G-1058)*

VALVES: Aircraft, Control, Hydraulic & Pneumatic

A V Hydraulics Ltd Lblty Co ....G 973 621-6800
Newark *(G-7066)*

VALVES: Aircraft, Hydraulic

Air & Hydraulic Power Inc ....G 201 447-1589
Wyckoff *(G-12244)*

VALVES: Control, Automatic

Heat-Timer Corporation ....E 973 575-4004
Fairfield *(G-3218)*

VALVES: Fire Hydrant

Firefighter One Ltd Lblty Co ....G 973 940-3061
Sparta *(G-10499)*

VALVES: Fluid Power, Control, Hydraulic & pneumatic

Hayward Industrial Products ....C 908 351-5400
Elizabeth *(G-2741)*
Versa Products Company Inc ....C 201 291-0379
Paramus *(G-7912)*
Westlock Controls Corporation ....C 201 794-7650
Saddle Brook *(G-9800)*

VALVES: Indl

Admiral Technology LLC ....E 973 698-5920
Rockaway *(G-9544)*
American Products Company Inc ......D 908 687-4100
Union *(G-11152)*
Armadillo Automation Inc ....E 856 829-2888
Cinnaminson *(G-1447)*
Asco LP ....B 800 972-2726
Florham Park *(G-3483)*
Barworth Inc ....G 973 376-4883
Springfield *(G-10541)*
Carpathian Industries LLC ....E 201 386-5356
Hoboken *(G-4463)*
Chase Machine Co ....F 201 438-2214
Lyndhurst *(G-5677)*
Emerson Automation Solutions ....E 856 542-5252
Bridgeport *(G-763)*
Farrell Eqp & Contrls Inc ....F 732 770-4142
Roselle *(G-9669)*
Fisher Service Co ....G 609 386-5000
Burlington *(G-973)*
Flodyne Controls Inc ....E 908 464-6200
New Providence *(G-7035)*
Gadren Machine Co Inc ....F 856 456-4329
Mount Ephraim *(G-6763)*
Gasflo Products Inc ....E 973 276-9011
Fairfield *(G-3207)*
Gemco Valve Co LLC ....E 732 752-7900
Middlesex *(G-6168)*
Generant Company Inc ....C 814 337-0380
Butler *(G-1004)*
Industrial Habonim Valves & AC ......F 201 820-3184
Wayne *(G-11650)*
Instrment Vlve Svcs Burlington ....G 609 386-5000
Burlington *(G-973)*
Magnatrol Valve Corporation ....G 973 427-4341
Hawthorne *(G-4246)*
Micromat Co ....E 201 529-3738
Ringwood *(G-9452)*

O Plast Matic Valves Inc ....D 973 256-3000
Cedar Grove **(G-1293)**

Picut Industries Inc ....D 908 754-1333
Warren **(G-11562)**

Tyco International MGT Co LLC ....E 609 720-4200
Princeton **(G-9133)**

VALVES: Plumbing & Heating

Everflow Supplies Inc ....E 908 436-1100
Carteret **(G-1256)**

Primak Plumbing & Heating Inc.............G 732 270-6282
Toms River **(G-10904)**

VALVES: Regulating & Control, Automatic

Simple Home Automation Inc ....C 877 405-2397
Edison **(G-2618)**

VALVES: Regulating, Process Control

Wm Steinen Mfg Co ....D 973 887-6400
Parsippany **(G-8116)**

VALVES: Water Works

Purity Labs ....G 201 372-0236
East Rutherford **(G-2320)**

VANILLIN: Synthetic

Elan Food Laboratories Inc.................F 973 344-8014
Newark **(G-7149)**

VARNISHES, NEC

Royce Associates A Ltd Partnr ....D 201 438-5200
East Rutherford **(G-2322)**

Superior Printing Ink Co Inc ....C 201 478-5600
Teterboro **(G-10810)**

VARNISHING SVC: Metal Prdts

Superior Powder Coating Inc.................C 908 351-8707
Elizabeth **(G-2777)**

VAULTS & SAFES WHOLESALERS

Bar-Maid Corporation ....C 973 478-7070
Garfield **(G-3722)**

VEGETABLE OILS: Medicinal Grade, Refined Or Concentrated

Chefler Foods LLC...........................F 201 596-3710
Saddle Brook **(G-9757)**

VEGETABLES, FROZEN: Wholesaler

CHR International Inc ....G 201 262-8186
Oradell **(G-7806)**

VEHICLES: All Terrain

Savino Del Bene USA Inc ....D 347 960-5568
Avenel **(G-150)**

VENDING MACHINES & PARTS

Universal Vending MGT LLC.................F 908 233-4373
Westfield **(G-11932)**

VENETIAN BLIND REPAIR SHOP

Spotless Venetian Blind Servic ....G 732 548-1711
Edison **(G-2625)**

VENETIAN BLINDS & SHADES

Hudson & Bergen Company ....G 201 991-4900
Kearny **(G-4881)**

Spotless Venetian Blind Servic ....G 732 548-1711
Edison **(G-2625)**

VENTILATING EQPT: Metal

Atco Rubber Products Inc....................E 856 794-3393
Vineland **(G-11324)**

Ductworks Inc ....F 908 754-8190
Plainfield **(G-8858)**

Hays Sheet Metal Inc ....E 856 662-7722
Pennsauken **(G-8521)**

Professional Envmtl Systems.................E 201 991-3000
Kearny **(G-4911)**

Totowa Metal Fabricators Inc...............F 973 423-1943
North Haledon **(G-7555)**

VENTILATING EQPT: Sheet Metal

Bonland Industries Inc ....D 973 694-3211
Wayne **(G-11611)**

VERIFIERS: Punch Card

Symbology Enterprises Inc..................F 908 725-1699
Somerville **(G-10227)**

VESSELS: Process, Indl, Metal Plate

Dusenbery Engineering Co Inc ....G 973 539-2200
Morristown **(G-6706)**

VETERINARY PHARMACEUTICAL PREPARATIONS

Eco LLC ....G 609 683-9030
Princeton **(G-9035)**

Iron4u Inc ....G 609 514-5163
Princeton **(G-9060)**

Newmarket Pharmaceuticals LLC ....G 609 252-9600
Trenton **(G-11089)**

Nutri-Pet Research Inc ....G 732 786-8822
Manalapan **(G-5857)**

Phibro Animal Health Corp ....D 201 329-7300
Teaneck **(G-10765)**

VETERINARY PRDTS: Instruments & Apparatus

Zimmer Trabecular Met Tech Inc ....C 973 576-0032
Parsippany **(G-8118)**

VIALS: Glass

Nipro Glass Americas Corp ....F 856 825-1400
Millville **(G-6314)**

Nipro Phrmpckging Amricas Corp ....C 856 825-1400
Millville **(G-6315)**

Worldwide Glass Resources Inc ....E 856 205-1508
Vineland **(G-11418)**

VIDEO & AUDIO EQPT, WHOLESALE

Mardee Company Inc........................E 908 753-4343
South Plainfield **(G-10402)**

Sound Professionals Inc.....................G 609 267-4400
Hainesport **(G-4078)**

VIDEO EQPT

Kultur International Films Ltd...............E 732 229-2343
Red Bank **(G-9334)**

Murray Electronics Inc ....G 201 405-1158
Oakland **(G-7697)**

Peter-Lisand Machine Corp ....G 201 943-5600
New Milford **(G-7024)**

VIDEO REPAIR SVCS

Murray Electronics Inc ....G 201 405-1158
Oakland **(G-7697)**

VIDEO TAPE PRODUCTION SVCS

Kultur International Films Ltd...............E 732 229-2343
Red Bank **(G-9334)**

VISUAL COMMUNICATIONS SYSTEMS

Aurora Multimedia Corporation............E 732 591-5800
Morganville **(G-6637)**

Hope Center.................................F 201 798-1234
Jersey City **(G-4766)**

Kinly Inc ....G 973 585-3000
Cedar Knolls **(G-1314)**

Pixell Creative Group LLC....................G 609 410-3024
Burlington **(G-988)**

Sightlogix Inc ....E 609 951-0008
Princeton **(G-9118)**

York Telecom Corporation..................D 732 413-6000
Eatontown **(G-2430)**

VISUAL EFFECTS PRODUCTION SVCS

Beterrific Corp ....G 201 735-7711
Fort Lee **(G-3546)**

VITAMINS: Natural Or Synthetic, Uncompounded, Bulk

Aromac Inc ....G 973 365-1090
Clifton **(G-1566)**

Life Science Labs Mfg LLC ....F 732 367-9937
Lakewood **(G-5147)**

Mpt Delivery Systems Inc...................D 973 279-4132
Paterson **(G-8344)**

Pacifichealth Laboratories Inc...............G 732 739-2900
Parsippany **(G-8053)**

Shanghai Freemen Americas LLC ....E 732 981-1288
Piscataway **(G-8809)**

Solgar Inc....................................F 201 944-2311
Leonia **(G-5319)**

Sunflower Seed ....G 908 735-3822
Clinton **(G-1755)**

Vita-Pure Inc ....E 908 245-1212
Roselle **(G-9686)**

Vitamin Shoppe Industries Inc ....A 201 868-5959
North Bergen **(G-7491)**

VITAMINS: Pharmaceutical Preparations

Agilis Chemicals Inc.........................G 973 910-2424
Rockaway **(G-9548)**

Alteon ....G 201 934-1624
Ramsey **(G-9232)**

Ans Nutrition Inc ....E 212 235-5205
Farmingdale **(G-3377)**

Archon Vitamin LLC ....D 732 537-1220
Edison **(G-2464)**

Archon Vitamin LLC ....G 973 371-1700
Edison **(G-2465)**

Bioactive Resources LLC....................F 908 561-3114
South Plainfield **(G-10337)**

DSM Sight & Life Inc........................G 973 257-8208
Parsippany **(G-7990)**

Genavite LLC ....F 973 779-1532
Clifton **(G-1625)**

INB Manhattan Drug Company Inc........D 973 926-0816
Hillside **(G-4415)**

INB Manhattan Drug Company Inc........E 973 926-0816
Hillside **(G-4417)**

International Vitamin Corp ....C 973 371-4400
Irvington **(G-4592)**

Jamol Laboratories Inc......................G 201 262-6363
Emerson **(G-2859)**

Kwik Enterprises LLC ....G 732 663-1559
Oakhurst **(G-7670)**

Life Science Laboratories LLC ....G 732 367-1900
Lakewood **(G-5146)**

Life Scnce Labs Spplements LLC ....F 732 367-1749
Lakewood **(G-5148)**

Nutro Laboratories Inc ....C 908 755-7984
South Plainfield **(G-10416)**

Plantfusion ....G 732 537-1220
Edison **(G-2595)**

Rasi Laboratories Inc ....D 732 873-8500
Cranbury **(G-1876)**

Reliance Vitamin LLC ....C 732 537-1220
Edison **(G-2603)**

Soma Labs Inc...............................F 732 271-3444
Middlesex **(G-6199)**

Unitao Nutraceuticals LLC ....G 973 983-1121
Rockaway **(G-9620)**

Vitaquest International LLC ....G 973 575-9200
Fairfield **(G-3344)**

Vitaquest International LLC ....B 973 575-9200
West Caldwell **(G-11807)**

VOCATIONAL REHABILITATION AGENCY

Employment Horizons Inc...................B 973 538-8822
Cedar Knolls **(G-1311)**

VOCATIONAL TRAINING AGENCY

Chromak Research Inc.......................G 732 560-1366
Somerset **(G-10082)**

WALL COVERINGS: Rubber

Fidelity Industries Inc ....E 973 696-9120
Wayne **(G-11632)**

Fidelity Industries Inc ....E 973 777-2592
Clifton **(G-1619)**

WALLBOARD: Gypsum

Baruffi Bros Inc..............................F 856 692-6400
Vineland **(G-11327)**

New Ngc Inc..............................D....... 609 499-1323
  Burlington (G-986)

WALLPAPER & WALL COVERINGS

Burlington Design Center Inc ....F....... 856 778-7772
  Mount Laurel (G-6785)
Collins and Company LLC ....G....... 973 427-4068
  Hawthorne (G-4226)

WALLPAPER: Embossed Plastic, Textile Backed

J Josephson Inc...........................C....... 201 440-7000
  South Hackensack (G-10271)
J Josephson Inc...........................C....... 201 440-7000
  South Hackensack (G-10272)
J Josephson Inc...........................C....... 201 426-2646
  South Hackensack (G-10273)

WALLS: Curtain, Metal

Architectural Metal and Glass ....G....... 732 994-7575
  Lakewood (G-5075)

WAREHOUSING & STORAGE FACILITIES, NEC

Bright Lights Usa Inc ....E....... 856 546-5656
  Camden (G-1046)
Fujifilm North America Corp ....B....... 732 857-3000
  Edison (G-2523)
Kuehne Chemical Company Inc ....E....... 973 589-0700
  Kearny (G-4893)
Lockwood Boat Works Inc ....E....... 732 721-1605
  South Amboy (G-10241)
Tech-Pak Inc ....F....... 201 935-3800
  Wood Ridge (G-12140)

WAREHOUSING & STORAGE, REFRIGERATED: Cold Storage Or Refrig

United States Cold Storage Inc ....B....... 856 354-8181
  Camden (G-1088)

WAREHOUSING & STORAGE: Fur

S & H R Inc..............................G....... 908 925-3797
  Linden (G-5436)

WAREHOUSING & STORAGE: General

Gordon Terminal Service Co PA...........D....... 201 437-8300
  Bayonne (G-229)
Mondelez Global LLC ....A....... 201 794-4080
  Fair Lawn (G-3104)
Romark Logistics CES LLC ....E....... 908 789-2800
  Westfield (G-11929)
S L Enterprises Inc ....G....... 908 272-8145
  Ewing (G-3054)

WAREHOUSING & STORAGE: General

Alfred Dunner Inc ....D....... 212 944-6660
  Parsippany (G-7942)
Alu Inc ....E....... 201 935-2213
  Moonachie (G-6503)
Cei Holdings Inc ....E....... 732 888-7788
  Holmdel (G-4511)
Cosmetic Essence LLC ....C....... 732 888-7788
  Holmdel (G-4512)
Grignard Company LLC ....E....... 732 340-1111
  Rahway (G-9194)
Jan Packaging Inc........................D....... 973 361-7200
  Dover (G-2095)
Mitzi Intl Handbag & ACC Ltd ....C....... 973 483-5015
  Newark (G-7243)
Tatara Group Inc ....G....... 732 231-6031
  Avenel (G-155)
Valley Die Cutting Inc ....G....... 973 731-8884
  Randolph (G-9305)

WAREHOUSING & STORAGE: Household Goods

Vaswani Inc ....F....... 877 376-4425
  Edison (G-2642)

WAREHOUSING & STORAGE: Miniwarehouse

Bng Industries LLC.......................F....... 862 229-2414
  Harrison (G-4173)

WAREHOUSING & STORAGE: Self Storage

T Wiker Enterprises Inc ....G....... 609 261-9494
  Hainesport (G-4079)

WARFARE COUNTER-MEASURE EQPT

Dewey Electronics Corporation............E....... 201 337-4700
  Oakland (G-7685)

WARM AIR HEATING & AC EQPT & SPLYS, WHOLESALE Air Filters

Bellaqua Inc..............................G....... 201 460-8379
  East Rutherford (G-2284)
Elaine Inc ....G....... 973 345-6200
  Woodland Park (G-12217)
Filter Technologies Inc ....G....... 732 329-2500
  Monmouth Junction (G-6344)
Momentum Usa Inc ....F....... 844 300-1553
  Edison (G-2576)

WARM AIR HEATING & AC EQPT & SPLYS, WHOLESALE Furnaces

Pennington Furnace Supply Inc ....G....... 609 737-2500
  Pennington (G-8457)

WARM AIR HEATING/AC EQPT/SPLYS, WHOL Dehumidifiers, Exc Port

Csonka Worldwide.........................E....... 609 514-2766
  Plainsboro (G-8879)

WARM AIR HEATING/AC EQPT/SPLYS, WHOL Warm Air Htg Eqpt/Splys

Industrial Combustion Assn ....F....... 732 271-0300
  Somerset (G-10111)

WARP KNIT FABRIC FINISHING

Ques Aprv A R Knitwear Inc................G....... 201 869-1333
  North Bergen (G-7477)

WASHCLOTHS & BATH MITTS, FROM PURCHASED MATERIALS

Tatara Group Inc ....G....... 732 231-6031
  Avenel (G-155)

WASHERS: Metal

H K Metal Craft Mfg Corp ....E....... 973 471-7770
  Lodi (G-5585)

WASHERS: Rubber

Thomas A Caserta Inc ....F....... 609 586-2807
  Robbinsville (G-9522)

WATCH & CLOCK STORES

Dksh Luxury & Lifestyle N Amer ....G....... 609 750-8800
  Lawrence Township (G-5242)
Garrett Moore ....G....... 908 231-9231
  Bridgewater (G-840)

WATCH REPAIR SVCS

Corbo Jewelers Inc ....F....... 973 777-1635
  Clifton (G-1592)
Madhu B Goyal MD ....G....... 908 769-0307
  South Plainfield (G-10400)
Movado Group Inc ....B....... 201 267-8000
  Paramus (G-7890)

WATCHES

Acon Watch Crown Company..............F....... 973 546-8585
  Garfield (G-3715)
Belair Time Corporation ....D....... 732 905-0100
  Lakewood (G-5083)
Watchitude LLC ....G....... 732 745-2626
  New Brunswick (G-7011)

WATER HEATERS

Triangle Tube/Phase III Co Inc ....D....... 856 228-9940
  Paulsboro (G-8427)

WATER PURIFICATION EQPT: Household

Bellaqua Inc..............................G....... 201 460-8379
  East Rutherford (G-2284)
Cantel Medical Corp ....G....... 973 890-7220
  Little Falls (G-5471)
Glasco Uv LLC ....F....... 201 934-3348
  Mahwah (G-5776)
Vivreau Advanced Water Systems ....F....... 212 502-3749
  Fairfield (G-3345)

WATER PURIFICATION PRDTS: Chlorination Tablets & Kits

Foresight Group LLC ....F....... 888 992-8880
  Parsippany (G-8015)
Isdin Corp ....E....... 862 242-8129
  Morristown (G-6718)

WATER SOFTENER SVCS

NMP Water Systems LLC ....G....... 201 252-8333
  Mahwah (G-5796)
South Jersey Water Cond Svc ....E....... 856 451-0620
  Bridgeton (G-798)

WATER SPLY: Irrigation

Cutting Edge Grower Supply LLC ....G....... 732 905-9220
  Howell (G-4551)

WATER SUPPLY

Middlesex Water Company ....C....... 732 579-0290
  Edison (G-2572)
Nice Instrumentation ....F....... 732 851-4300
  Manalapan (G-5855)

WATER TREATMENT EQPT: Indl

Chem-Aqua Inc...........................F....... 972 438-0211
  Monmouth Junction (G-6336)
CP Equipment Sales Co ....F....... 908 687-9621
  Union (G-11168)
Delta Cooling Towers Inc ....G....... 973 586-2201
  Flanders (G-3404)
Dynatec Systems Inc ....F....... 609 387-0330
  Burlington (G-970)
Enpro Inc ....E....... 908 236-2137
  Lebanon (G-5285)
Envirnmntal Mgt Chem Wste Svcs........G....... 201 848-7676
  Mahwah (G-5770)
Evoqua Water Technologies LLC ....D....... 908 851-4250
  Union (G-11183)
Global Ecology Corporation ....G....... 973 655-9001
  Roseland (G-9650)
GP Jager Inc ....G....... 973 750-1180
  Kinnelon (G-5035)
Graver Water Systems LLC ....G....... 908 516-1400
  New Providence (G-7039)
Hungerford & Terry Inc ....E....... 856 881-3200
  Clayton (G-1524)
JDV Equipment Corp ....G....... 973 366-6556
  Dover (G-2096)
Metawater Usa Inc ....G....... 201 935-3436
  Rutherford (G-9740)
Middlesex Water Company ....C....... 732 579-0290
  Edison (G-2572)
Nitto Americas Inc ....F....... 732 901-7905
  Lakewood (G-5165)
Nitto Americas Inc ....F....... 201 645-4950
  Teaneck (G-10763)
Organica Water Inc ....F....... 609 651-8885
  West Windsor (G-11909)
Pure H2o Technologies Inc ....F....... 973 622-0440
  Newark (G-7279)
Waterdoctor Inc ....F....... 732 972-4510
  Ridgefield (G-9393)

WATER: Mineral, Carbonated, Canned & Bottled, Etc

J & J Snack Foods Corp ....B....... 856 665-9533
  Pennsauken (G-8531)
J & J Snack Foods Corp ....D....... 856 467-9552
  Bridgeport (G-767)
Shrem Consulting Ltd Lblty Co ....G....... 917 371-0581
  West Long Branch (G-11846)

WATER: Pasteurized & Mineral, Bottled & Canned

Gerber Products Company .... C 973 593-7500
Florham Park **(G-3504)**

WATER: Pasteurized, Canned & Bottled, Etc

Water On Time Bottled .... G 862 252-9798
East Orange **(G-2273)**

WAXES: Petroleum, Not Produced In Petroleum Refineries

Honeywell International Inc .... C 973 455-2000
Morris Plains **(G-6668)**
Honeywell Speclty Wax & Additv .... F 973 455-2000
Morristown **(G-6717)**

WEATHER STRIP: Sponge Rubber

Lamatek Inc .... E 856 599-6000
Paulsboro **(G-8418)**
Rak Foam Sales Inc .... G 908 668-1122
Plainfield **(G-8872)**
Tricomp Inc .... C 973 835-1110
Pompton Plains **(G-8966)**

WEATHER STRIPS: Metal

Tricomp Inc .... C 973 835-1110
Pompton Plains **(G-8966)**

WEDDING CONSULTING SVCS

Geislers Liquor Store .... F 856 845-0482
Thorofare **(G-10820)**

WEIGHING MACHINERY & APPARATUS

Advance Scale Company Inc .... E 856 784-4916
Lindenwold **(G-5461)**

WEIGHING SVCS: Food & Commodity

Global Commodities Exportacao .... G 201 613-1532
Newark **(G-7171)**

WELDING & CUTTING APPARATUS & ACCESS, NEC

Cni Ceramic Nozzles Inc .... G 973 276-1535
Fairfield **(G-3162)**
Cotterman Inc .... F 856 415-0800
Wenonah **(G-11703)**
Orgo-Thermit Inc .... E 732 657-5781
Manchester **(G-5887)**
Rowan Technologies Inc .... D 609 267-9000
Rancocas **(G-9262)**

WELDING EQPT

Cerbaco Ltd .... E 908 996-1333
Frenchtown **(G-3699)**
Emabond Solutions LLC .... E 201 767-7400
Norwood **(G-7621)**
Waage Electric Inc .... G 908 245-9363
Kenilworth **(G-5004)**

WELDING EQPT & SPLYS WHOLESALERS

Airgas Usa LLC .... F 609 685-4241
Cherry Hill **(G-1342)**
Airgas Usa LLC .... E 856 829-7878
Cinnaminson **(G-1445)**
Frank E Ganter Inc .... G 856 692-2218
Vineland **(G-11356)**
Linde Gas USA LLC .... C 908 464-8100
Bridgewater **(G-854)**
Matheson Tri-Gas Inc .... F 908 991-9200
Basking Ridge **(G-194)**
Matheson Tri-Gas Inc .... D 908 991-9200
Basking Ridge **(G-195)**
Matheson Tri-Gas Inc .... E 908 991-9200
Basking Ridge **(G-196)**
Praxair Distribution Inc .... F 908 862-7200
Linden **(G-5430)**
Stud Welding Co The Inc .... G 856 866-9300
Moorestown **(G-6624)**
Welding & Radiator Supply Co .... G 609 965-0433
Egg Harbor City **(G-2674)**

WELDING EQPT & SPLYS: Electrodes

Stulz-Sickles Steel Company .... E 609 531-2172
Burlington **(G-990)**

WELDING EQPT REPAIR SVCS

M K Enterprises Inc .... G 201 891-4199
Wyckoff **(G-12257)**

WELDING EQPT: Electric

Wikstrom Machines Inc .... F 732 826-4800
Perth Amboy **(G-8637)**

WELDING EQPT: Electrical

Stud Welding Co The Inc .... G 856 866-9300
Moorestown **(G-6624)**

WELDING REPAIR SVC

A 1 Fencing Inc .... F 908 527-1066
Elizabeth **(G-2702)**
Alba Translations CPA .... G 973 340-1130
Lodi **(G-5574)**
Atlas Enterprise .... F 908 561-1144
South Plainfield **(G-10333)**
Auto Tig Welding Fabricating .... G 973 839-8877
Pompton Lakes **(G-8946)**
B L White Welding & Steel Co .... G 973 684-4111
Paterson **(G-8218)**
Blue Light Welding & Fabg LLC .... G 856 629-5891
Williamstown **(G-12081)**
Bluewater Industries Inc .... F 609 427-1012
Dennisville **(G-2028)**
BR Welding Inc .... F 732 363-8253
Howell **(G-4547)**
Browns Welding Service .... G 732 988-9530
Neptune **(G-6902)**
Chizzys Service Center .... G 201 641-7222
Little Ferry **(G-5496)**
CMI-Promex Inc .... F 856 351-1000
Pedricktown **(G-8433)**
Creative Machining Systems .... F 609 586-3932
Trenton **(G-11048)**
D J B Welding Inc .... G 732 657-7478
Jackson **(G-4662)**
D K Tool & Die Welding Group .... G 908 241-7600
Roselle Park **(G-9693)**
D N D Corp .... G 908 637-4343
Great Meadows **(G-3849)**
Edward Kurth and Son Inc .... E 856 227-5252
Sewell **(G-9951)**
Elmco Two Inc .... G 856 365-2244
Camden **(G-1061)**
Eme Electrical Contractors .... G 973 228-6608
Caldwell **(G-1027)**
Ferry Machine Corp .... E 201 641-9191
Little Ferry **(G-5504)**
Folgore Mobil Welding Inc .... E 732 541-2974
Carteret **(G-1258)**
Frank E Ganter Inc .... G 856 692-2218
Vineland **(G-11356)**
Ironbound Welding Inc .... G 973 589-3128
Newark **(G-7201)**
J D Machine Parts Inc .... F 856 691-8430
Vineland **(G-11374)**
J P Rotella Co Inc .... F 973 942-2559
Haledon **(G-4083)**
John B Horay Welding .... G 856 336-2154
West Berlin **(G-11727)**
K H Machine Works .... G 201 867-2338
North Bergen **(G-7459)**
Kt Welding .... G 908 862-7370
Linden **(G-5398)**
Laurelton Welding Service Inc .... G 732 899-6348
Point Pleasant Beach **(G-8922)**
Lodi Welding Co Inc .... G 908 852-8367
Hackettstown **(G-4017)**
Louis Iron Works Inc .... G 973 624-2700
Newark **(G-7226)**
Lusotech LLC .... G 973 332-3861
Newark **(G-7230)**
M & M Welding & Steel Fabg .... G 908 647-6060
Stirling **(G-10603)**
Machine Plus Inc .... G 973 839-8884
Haskell **(G-4210)**
McAlister Welding & Fabg .... F 856 740-3890
Glassboro **(G-3809)**
Micheller & Son Hydraulics Inc .... F 908 687-1545
Roselle **(G-9677)**

WHEELCHAIRS

Oceanview Marine Welding LLC .... G 609 624-9669
Ocean View **(G-7765)**
Off-Road Welding Inc .... G 908 832-2967
Glen Gardner **(G-3816)**
Orgo-Thermit Inc .... E 732 657-5781
Manchester **(G-5887)**
P K Welding LLC .... F 908 928-1002
Garwood **(G-3783)**
Pabst Enterprises Equipment Co .... E 908 353-2880
Elizabeth **(G-2764)**
Pennetta & Sons .... E 201 420-1693
Jersey City **(G-4798)**
Peter Garafano & Son Inc .... E 973 278-0350
Paterson **(G-8364)**
Pmje Welding LLC .... G 973 685-7344
Clifton **(G-1699)**
Precision Welding Machine .... G 609 625-1465
Mays Landing **(G-6042)**
Reuther Engineering .... F 973 485-5800
Edison **(G-2604)**
Ricklyn Co Inc .... G 908 689-6770
Columbia **(G-1800)**
Serious Welding & Mech LLC .... F 732 698-7478
South River **(G-10466)**
Sine Tru Tool Company Inc .... G 732 591-1100
Marlboro **(G-5959)**
Stecher Dave Welding & Fabg Sp ...... G 856 467-3558
Swedesboro **(G-10729)**
Sulzer Pump Services (us) Inc .... F 856 542-5046
Bridgeport **(G-774)**
Union City Whirlpool Repair .... G 908 428-9146
Union City **(G-11271)**
Vep Manufacturing .... F 732 657-0666
Jackson **(G-4681)**
Vermes Machine Co Inc .... E 856 642-9300
Moorestown **(G-6630)**
W W Manufacturing Co Inc .... F 856 451-5700
Bridgeton **(G-802)**
Wel-Fab Inc .... G 609 261-1393
Rancocas **(G-9265)**
Weld Tech Fab .... G 732 919-2185
Farmingdale **(G-3396)**
Welded Products Co Inc .... E 973 589-0180
Newark **(G-7358)**
Welding & Radiator Supply Co .... G 609 965-0433
Egg Harbor City **(G-2674)**
Willow Run Construction Inc .... F 201 659-7266
Jersey City **(G-4849)**

WELDING SPLYS, EXC GASES: Wholesalers

Airgas Usa LLC .... F 609 685-4241
Cherry Hill **(G-1342)**
Airgas Usa LLC .... E 856 829-7878
Cinnaminson **(G-1445)**
Praxair Distribution Inc .... E 973 589-7895
Newark **(G-7272)**

WELDING TIPS: Heat Resistant, Metal

Cold Headed Fasteners Inc .... G 856 461-3244
Delanco **(G-2004)**

WELDMENTS

L & L Welding Contractors .... F 609 395-1600
Dayton **(G-1976)**

WET CORN MILLING

Ingredion Incorporated .... D 908 685-5000
Bridgewater **(G-846)**
National Strch Chem Holdg Corp .... A 908 685-5000
Bridgewater **(G-861)**
Unilever Bestfoods North Amer .... F 201 894-4000
Englewood Cliffs **(G-2985)**

WHEELCHAIR LIFTS

Adaptive Technology Entps LLC .... G 877 847-6272
Medford **(G-6063)**

WHEELCHAIRS

Brick City Wheelchair RPS LLC .... G 862 371-4311
Newark **(G-7114)**
Carry Easy Inc .... E 201 944-0042
Leonia **(G-5315)**
Electric Mobility Corporation .... E 856 468-1000
Sewell **(G-9954)**
Independence Technology LLC .... F 908 722-3767
Somerville **(G-10215)**

Employee Codes: A=Over 500 employees, B=251-500
C=101-250, D=51-100, E=20-50, F=10-19, G=4-9

2018 Harris New jersey
Manufacturers Directory

983

PRODUCT

WHEELS

Hands On Wheels ....G....... 609 892-4693
Atlantic City *(G-99)*

WHEELS & PARTS

Vahlco Racing Wheels LLC.................G....... 609 758-7013
New Egypt *(G-7018)*

WHEELS: Abrasive

Alpex Wheel Co Inc................F....... 201 871-1700
Tenafly *(G-10781)*

WHEELS: Buffing & Polishing

Garfield Industries Inc................E....... 973 575-3322
Fairfield *(G-3206)*

WHEELS: Water

Ocean Energy Industries Inc ....F....... 954 828-2177
Oakhurst *(G-7671)*

WHIRLPOOL BATHS: Hydrotherapy

Alliance Hand & Physical................F....... 201 822-0100
Westwood *(G-11952)*

WIG & HAIRPIECE STORES

Look of Love Wigs Inc................F....... 908 687-9502
Edison *(G-2558)*

WIGS & HAIRPIECES

Hair Depot Limited................F....... 973 251-9924
Maplewood *(G-5921)*
Look of Love Wigs Inc................F....... 908 687-9502
Edison *(G-2558)*

WIGS, DOLL: Hair

Ultimate Hair World Ltd Lblty ....F....... 973 622-6900
Bloomfield *(G-535)*

WIGS, WHOLESALE

Revlon Inc................E....... 732 287-1400
Edison *(G-2605)*

WINCHES

Breeze-Eastern LLC................G....... 973 602-1001
Whippany *(G-12014)*
Ingersoll-Rand Company ....E....... 856 793-7000
Mount Laurel *(G-6803)*

WIND TUNNELS

Wind Tunnel Inc ....G....... 201 485-7793
Mahwah *(G-5824)*

WINDINGS: Coil, Electronic

Jinpan International USA Ltd................G....... 201 460-8778
Carlstadt *(G-1174)*
KG Squared LLC................F....... 973 627-0643
Rockaway *(G-9581)*
SCI-Bore Inc ....G....... 973 414-9001
East Orange *(G-2268)*

WINDMILLS: Electric Power Generation

Fishermens Energy NJ LLC ....F....... 609 286-9650
Cape May *(G-1099)*

WINDOW & DOOR FRAMES

Champion Opco LLC................F....... 856 662-3400
West Berlin *(G-11707)*
Northern Architectural Systems...........D....... 201 943-6400
Teterboro *(G-10807)*
Royal Prime Inc................D....... 908 354-7600
Elizabeth *(G-2773)*
Thomas Erectors Inc ....G....... 908 810-0030
Hillside *(G-4444)*
Thomas Manufacturing Inc ....E....... 908 810-0030
Hillside *(G-4445)*
Winstar Windows LLC ....G....... 973 403-0574
Essex Fells *(G-3001)*

WINDOW FRAMES & SASHES: Plastic

Royal Aluminum Co Inc................D....... 973 589-8880
Newark *(G-7293)*
Superseal Manufacturing Co Inc...........E....... 908 561-5910
South Plainfield *(G-10437)*
Versatile Distributors Inc................D....... 973 773-0550
Livingston *(G-5570)*

WINDOW FRAMES, MOLDING & TRIM: Vinyl

Silver Line Building Pdts LLC................C....... 732 752-8704
Middlesex *(G-6198)*
Survivor II Inc ....E....... 908 353-1155
Hillside *(G-4442)*
Thermal Chek Inc................E....... 856 742-1200
Westville *(G-11950)*
United Window & Door Mfg Inc ....E....... 973 912-0600
Springfield *(G-10581)*
Vinylast Inc................E....... 732 367-7200
Lakewood *(G-5200)*

WINDOWS: Frames, Wood

Window Trends ....G....... 973 887-6676
Parsippany *(G-8113)*

WINE CELLARS, BONDED: Wine, Blended

Renault Winery Inc................E....... 609 965-2111
Egg Harbor City *(G-2669)*
Tomasello Winery Inc ....F....... 609 561-0567
Hammonton *(G-4151)*

WIRE

Amark Industries Inc ....G....... 973 992-8900
Livingston *(G-5524)*
Iwc................F....... 732 968-8122
Green Brook *(G-3858)*
Ninsa LLC ....G....... 609 561-7103
Hammonton *(G-4145)*
Phillips Enterprises Inc................G....... 732 493-3191
Ocean *(G-7736)*
Screentek Manufacturing Co LLC ....F....... 973 328-2121
Randolph *(G-9296)*

WIRE & CABLE: Aluminum

Lapp Holding NA Inc................E....... 973 660-9700
Florham Park *(G-3509)*
Okonite Company ....C....... 201 825-0300
Ramsey *(G-9250)*

WIRE & CABLE: Nonferrous, Aircraft

CDM Electronics Inc................C....... 856 740-1200
Turnersville *(G-11141)*

WIRE & CABLE: Nonferrous, Automotive, Exc Ignition Sets

M Parker Autoworks Inc ....E....... 856 933-0801
Bellmawr *(G-345)*

WIRE & CABLE: Nonferrous, Building

Communications Supply Corp ....E....... 732 346-1864
Edison *(G-2487)*
Prysmian Cbles Systems USA LLC.......F....... 732 469-5902
Bridgewater *(G-878)*

WIRE & WIRE PRDTS

Accent Fence Inc ....E....... 609 965-6400
Egg Harbor City *(G-2655)*
Ace Electronics Inc................D....... 732 603-9800
Metuchen *(G-6093)*
Acme Wire Forming LLC ....F....... 201 218-2912
Kinnelon *(G-5032)*
Aw Machinery LLC................F....... 973 882-3223
Fairfield *(G-3142)*
Bamboo & Rattan Works Inc................G....... 732 255-4239
Toms River *(G-10866)*
Belden Inc................F....... 908 925-8000
Elizabeth *(G-2712)*
Belleville Wire Cloth Co Inc ....E....... 973 239-0074
Cedar Grove *(G-1272)*
Belmont Whl Fence Mfg Inc ....E....... 973 472-5121
Garfield *(G-3723)*
Better Sleep Inc................F....... 908 464-2200
Branchburg *(G-643)*
Boyle Tool & Die Co Inc................F....... 856 853-1819
West Deptford *(G-11818)*
Carl Stahl Sava Industries Inc ....D....... 973 835-0882
Riverdale *(G-9477)*
Cerbaco Ltd................E....... 908 996-1333
Frenchtown *(G-3699)*
Clements Industries Inc ....E....... 201 440-5500
South Hackensack *(G-10258)*
Compass Wire Cloth & ....E....... 856 853-7616
Vineland *(G-11339)*
Compass Wire Cloth Corp ....E....... 856 853-7616
Vineland *(G-11340)*
Consoldated Stl Alum Fence Inc ....E....... 908 272-0494
Kenilworth *(G-4948)*
Dearborn A Belden Cdt Company ....D....... 908 925-8000
Elizabeth *(G-2723)*
Deborah Sales & Mfg Co ....G....... 973 344-8466
Newark *(G-7138)*
Delair LLC................D....... 856 663-2900
Pennsauken *(G-8502)*
Edwin R Burger & Son Inc ....E....... 856 468-2300
Sewell *(G-9952)*
Evergard Steel Corp ....F....... 908 925-6800
South Plainfield *(G-10358)*
Fisk Alloy Conductors Inc................C....... 973 825-8500
Hawthorne *(G-4233)*
Fisk Alloy Inc................E....... 973 427-7550
Hawthorne *(G-4234)*
Fisk Alloy Wire Incorporated ....C....... 973 949-4491
Hawthorne *(G-4235)*
Form Cut Industries Inc................E....... 973 483-5154
Newark *(G-7165)*
Gabhen Inc................G....... 973 256-0666
Totowa *(G-10946)*
General Wire & Stamping Co ....F....... 973 366-8080
Randolph *(G-9278)*
High Energy Group Ltd Lblty Co ....G....... 732 741-9099
Eatontown *(G-2400)*
Jcc Military Supply LLC ....G....... 973 341-1314
Paterson *(G-8301)*
M P M Display Inc................F....... 973 374-3477
Irvington *(G-4597)*
Main Robert A & Sons Holdg Co ....E....... 201 447-3700
Wyckoff *(G-12258)*
New Jersey Wire Cloth Co Inc ....G....... 973 340-0101
Clifton *(G-1681)*
Newark Wire Works Inc ....E....... 732 661-2001
Edison *(G-2580)*
Phillips Enterprises Inc ....G....... 732 493-3191
Ocean *(G-7736)*
Plasti-Clad Metal Products Inc ....F....... 732 449-2665
Wall Township *(G-11503)*
Precision Ball Specialties ....F....... 856 881-5646
Williamstown *(G-12099)*
Robert J Donaldson Inc................F....... 856 629-2737
Williamstown *(G-12104)*
Robert Main Sons Inc ....E....... 201 447-3700
Fair Lawn *(G-3110)*
Security Fabricators Inc................F....... 908 272-9171
Kenilworth *(G-4996)*
Seminole Wire & Cable Co Inc................F....... 856 324-2929
Pennsauken *(G-8577)*
Skorr Products LLC................F....... 973 523-2606
Paterson *(G-8383)*
Vibration Muntings Contrls Inc................D....... 800 569-8423
Bloomingdale *(G-545)*
William Kenyon & Sons Inc................E....... 732 985-8980
Piscataway *(G-8836)*
Wire Displays Inc ....F....... 973 537-0090
Dover *(G-2114)*
Wire Fabricators & Insulators................E....... 973 768-2839
Livingston *(G-5572)*
Wytech Industries Inc................D....... 732 396-3900
Rahway *(G-9228)*

WIRE CLOTH & WOVEN WIRE PRDTS, MADE FROM PURCHASED WIRE

Wire Cloth Manufacturers Inc ....E....... 973 328-1000
Mine Hill *(G-6329)*

WIRE FENCING & ACCESS WHOLESALERS

Blue Gauntlet Fencing Gear Inc ....F....... 201 797-3332
Saddle Brook *(G-9755)*
General Metal Manufacturing Co................E....... 973 386-1818
East Hanover *(G-2218)*
Wayside Fence Company Inc ....E....... 201 791-7979
Fair Lawn *(G-3124)*

WIRE MATERIALS: Copper

AT&T Technologies Inc ....A....... 201 771-2000
Berkeley Heights *(G-400)*

Little Falls Alloys Inc ....E 973 278-1666
Paterson (G-8323)

WIRE MATERIALS: Steel

Amark Wire LLC ....G 973 882-7818
Fairfield (G-3134)
Boyle Tool & Die Co Inc..............F 856 853-1819
West Deptford (G-11818)
Bushwick Metals LLC ....G 908 604-1450
South Plainfield (G-10340)
Dearborn A Belden Cdt Company ....D 908 925-8000
Elizabeth (G-2723)
Fisk Alloy Inc ....E 973 427-7550
Hawthorne (G-4234)
Fisk Alloy Wire Incorporated ....C 973 949-4491
Hawthorne (G-4235)
Jersey Specialty Co Inc ....E 413 525-2292
Pennsauken (G-8537)
Metallia USA LLC ....G 201 585-5000
Fort Lee (G-3567)
Plasma Powders & Systems Inc...........G 732 431-0992
Marlboro (G-5952)
Roll Tech Industries ....F 609 730-9500
Pennington (G-8459)

WIRE PRDTS: Ferrous Or Iron, Made In Wiredrawing Plants

C D E Inc ....D 732 297-2540
North Brunswick (G-7509)
Evergard Steel Corp ....F 908 925-6800
South Plainfield (G-10358)
Sandvik Inc ....C 201 794-5000
Fair Lawn (G-3112)
Wytech Industries Inc ....D 732 396-3900
Rahway (G-9228)

WIRE PRDTS: Steel & Iron

Equipment Distributing Corp...........G 201 641-8414
Ridgefield Park (G-9405)

WIRE: Communication

Arose Inc ....E 856 481-4351
Blackwood (G-471)

WIRE: Mesh

Metal Textiles Corporation ....D 732 287-0800
Edison (G-2569)

WIRE: Nonferrous

AFL Telecommunications LLC ....D 864 486-7303
Jersey City (G-4700)
Ambro Inc ....E 201 818-9717
Pequannock (G-8597)
Associated Plastics Inc ....F 732 574-2800
Rahway (G-9176)
Brim Electronics Inc ....F 201 796-2886
Lodi (G-5578)
Bruker Ost LLC ....C 732 541-1300
Carteret (G-1254)
Colonial Wire & Cable Co Inc ....G 732 287-1557
Edison (G-2486)
Daburn Wire & Cable Corp ....G 973 328-3200
Dover (G-2084)
Dearborn A Belden Cdt Company ....D 908 925-8000
Elizabeth (G-2723)
Esi ....E 856 629-2492
Sicklerville (G-10018)
Francis Metals Company Inc ....F 732 761-0500
Lakewood (G-5125)
Global Wire & Cable Inc ....E 973 471-1000
Passaic (G-8145)
Harris Driver Co ....G 973 267-8100
Morristown (G-6712)
Harrison Electro Mechanical...........F 732 382-6008
Rahway (G-9196)
Iboco Corp ....G 732 417-0066
Lakewood (G-5136)
Lapp Cable Works Inc ....E 973 660-9632
Florham Park (G-3508)
Micro-Tek Corporation ....G 856 829-3855
Cinnaminson (G-1477)
Molecu-Wire Corporation ....F 908 429-0300
Manville (G-5897)
National Communications Inc ....E 973 325-3151
West Orange (G-11901)
Newtech Group Corp ....G 732 355-0392
Kendall Park (G-4935)

Okonite Company ....C 201 825-0300
Ramsey (G-9250)
Okonite Company ....D 201 825-0300
Paterson (G-8355)
Okonite Company ....G 212 239-0660
Woodland Park (G-12227)
Paramount Wire Co Inc ....E 973 672-0500
East Orange (G-2264)
Seminole Wire & Cable Co Inc.........F 856 324-2929
Pennsauken (G-8577)
Te Wire & Cable LLC ....C 201 845-9400
Saddle Brook (G-9796)
Wireworks Corporation ....E 908 686-7400
Hillside (G-4451)

WIRE: Nonferrous, Appliance Fixture

Service Tech ....G 908 788-0072
Flemington (G-3465)

WIRE: Steel, Insulated Or Armored

Global Wire & Cable Inc ....E 973 471-1000
Passaic (G-8145)
Plasti-Clad Metal Products Inc ....F 732 449-2665
Wall Township (G-11503)

WIRING DEVICES WHOLESALERS

Mennekes Electronics Inc ....E 973 882-8333
Fairfield (G-3258)

WOMEN'S & CHILDREN'S CLOTHING WHOLESALERS, NEC

Attitudes In Dressing Inc...............B 908 354-7218
Elizabeth (G-2711)
Burlington Coat Factory ....D 908 994-9562
Elizabeth (G-2716)
C3 Concepts Inc ....E 212 840-1116
North Bergen (G-7437)
Cejon Inc ....E 201 437-8780
Bayonne (G-217)
Cs Apparel Inc ....G 732 906-9666
Edison (G-2498)
Handcraft Manufacturing Corp ....E 973 565-0077
Newark (G-7185)
Impact Design Inc ....E 908 289-2900
Elizabethport (G-2785)
Jasper Fashion Ltd Lblty Co ....F 917 561-4533
Elizabeth (G-2749)
Lollytogs Ltd ....F 732 438-5500
Dayton (G-1978)
New York Popular Inc ....D 718 499-2020
Carteret (G-1263)
Personality Handkerchiefs Inc...........E 973 565-0077
Newark (G-7269)
Steps Clothing Inc ....E 201 420-1496
Jersey City (G-4834)

WOMEN'S & GIRLS' SPORTSWEAR WHOLESALERS

Frenchtoastcom LLC ....F 732 438-5500
Dayton (G-1964)
Leeward International Inc...............F 201 836-8830
Teaneck (G-10760)
Lollytogs Ltd ....D 732 438-5500
Dayton (G-1979)
Monogram Center Inc ....E 732 442-1800
Perth Amboy (G-8624)

WOMEN'S CLOTHING STORES

Betsy & Adam Ltd ....F 212 302-3750
Passaic (G-8128)
Blue Fish Clothing Inc ....C 908 996-3720
Frenchtown (G-3697)
Elie Tahari Ltd ....C 973 671-6300
Millburn (G-6249)
Komar Intimates LLC ....F 212 725-1500
Jersey City (G-4773)
Ralph Lauren Corporation ....D 201 531-6000
Lyndhurst (G-5704)

WOMEN'S CLOTHING STORES: Ready-To-Wear

Janet Shops Inc ....F 973 748-4992
Bloomfield (G-515)
Pvh Corp ....F 908 788-5880
Flemington (G-3464)

WOMEN'S SPECIALTY CLOTHING STORES

Maidenform Brands Inc ....E 888 573-0299
Iselin (G-4633)
Paradise ....G 973 425-0505
Morristown (G-6732)

WOMEN'S SPORTSWEAR STORES

Sock Company Inc ....E 201 307-0675
Westwood (G-11972)

WOOD FENCING WHOLESALERS

All-State Fence Inc ....E 732 431-4944
West Orange (G-11885)
General Metal Manufacturing Co........E 973 386-1818
East Hanover (G-2218)
Hoda Inc ....F 609 695-3000
Trenton (G-11063)

WOOD PRDTS: Door Trim

Jarahian Millwork Inc...................G 732 240-5151
Whiting (G-12067)

WOOD PRDTS: Moldings, Unfinished & Prefinished

Adhisa Molding ....G 862 324-5222
West Caldwell (G-11762)
AM Wood Inc ....F 732 246-1506
East Brunswick (G-2133)
Creative Wood Products Inc ....F 732 370-0051
Jackson (G-4660)
Randall Mfg Co Inc......................E 973 482-8603
Newark (G-7284)

WOOD PRDTS: Mulch Or Sawdust

Greenway Products & Svcs LLC ....C 732 442-0200
New Brunswick (G-6965)

WOOD PRDTS: Mulch, Wood & Bark

Anthony Excavating & Dem ....G 609 926-8804
Egg Harbor Township (G-2678)

WOOD PRDTS: Poles

Steelstran Industries Inc ....G 732 566-5040
Matawan (G-6033)

WOOD PRDTS: Policemen's Clubs

Howell Township Police ....D 732 919-2805
Howell (G-4556)
Pba of West Windsor ....E 609 799-6535
Princeton Junction (G-9161)

WOOD PRDTS: Trophy Bases

Crown Trophy ....G 973 808-8400
Pine Brook (G-8696)

WOOD PRDTS: Veneer Work, Inlaid

T M Baxter Services LLC................E 908 500-9065
Washington (G-11589)

WOOD PRDTS: Yard Sticks

Color Decor Ltd Liability Co ....G 973 689-2699
Paterson (G-8235)

WOOD PRODUCTS: Reconstituted

Alcan Baltek Corporation..............D 201 767-1400
Northvale (G-7570)
AMP Custom Rubber Inc ....F 732 888-2714
Keyport (G-5015)
Building Materials Mfg Corp ....G 973 628-3000
Wayne (G-11616)
Greenbuilt Intl Bldg Co ....C 609 300-9091
Voorhees (G-11432)
Homestyle Kitchens & Baths LLC........G 908 979-9000
Hackettstown (G-4011)
Shelan Chemical Company Inc............G 732 796-1003
Monroe Township (G-6392)

WOOD TREATING: Creosoting

Atlantic Wood Industries Inc ....F 609 267-4700
Hainesport (G-4070)

PRODUCT

WOOD TREATING: Flooring, Block

Rq Floors Corp ....E 201 654-3587
  Ridgefield (G-9383)
Rq Floors Corp ....F 201 654-3587
  South Hackensack (G-10294)

WOOD TREATING: Wood Prdts, Creosoted

New England Wood Crafters ....G 856 241-9270
  Swedesboro (G-10714)

WOODWORK & TRIM: Exterior & Ornamental

Trim Factory Inc ....G 856 769-8746
  Pilesgrove (G-8677)

WOODWORK & TRIM: Interior & Ornamental

Bell arte Inc ....F 908 355-1199
  Elizabeth (G-2713)
Creative Concepts of NJ LLC ....G 732 833-1776
  Jackson (G-4659)
Designcore Ltd ....D 718 499-0337
  Secaucus (G-9877)
Katadin Inc ....G 908 526-0166
  Branchburg (G-671)
Patella Construction Corp ....D 973 916-0100
  Passaic (G-8169)
Sandkamp Woodworks LLC ....G 201 200-0101
  Jersey City (G-4822)
Vigor Inc ....G 973 851-9539
  Totowa (G-10981)
Woodhaven Lumber & Millwork ....C 732 901-0030
  Lakewood (G-5206)
Zone Defense Inc ....F 973 328-0436
  Hackettstown (G-4044)

WOODWORK: Carved & Turned

Africa Imports Inc ....E 201 457-1995
  South Hackensack (G-10253)

WOODWORK: Interior & Ornamental, NEC

Architectural Wdwkg Assoc ....G 908 996-7866
  Frenchtown (G-3696)
B & C Custom WD Handrail Corp ....G 732 530-6640
  Red Bank (G-9322)
Crincoli Woodwork Co Inc ....F 908 352-9332
  Elizabeth (G-2721)
Cwi Architectural Millwork LLC ....G 856 307-7900
  Glassboro (G-3802)
F L Feldman Associates ....F 732 776-8544
  Asbury Park (G-77)
Infinite Mfg Group Inc ....E 973 649-9950
  Kearny (G-4885)

Jeffrey Danee Inc ....G 973 872-9388
  Paterson (G-8302)
Juliali Woodwork ....G 856 225-0772
  Pennsauken (G-8538)
Kenneth Asmar Custom Interiors ....G 732 544-6137
  Tinton Falls (G-10840)
Lukach Interiors Inc ....F 973 777-1499
  Clifton (G-1666)
Midhattan Woodworking Corp ....E 732 727-3020
  Old Bridge (G-7785)
National Woodworking Co ....G 908 851-9316
  Union (G-11211)

WOOL: Glass

Fbm Galaxy Inc ....E 856 966-1105
  Camden (G-1066)

WORD PROCESSING SVCS

Word Center Printing ....G 609 586-5825
  Trenton (G-11134)

WOVEN WIRE PRDTS, NEC

Unique Wire Weaving Co Inc ....E 908 688-4600
  Hillside (G-4447)

WRENCHES

Chicago Pneumatic Tool ....F 973 928-5222
  Clifton (G-1583)
Jetyd Corporation ....F 201 512-9500
  Mahwah (G-5786)

WRITING FOR PUBLICATION SVCS

Medpen Inc ....G 973 627-8067
  Denville (G-2048)

X-RAY EQPT & TUBES

Glenbrook Technologies Inc ....F 973 361-8866
  Randolph (G-9279)
M T D Inc ....G 908 362-6807
  Hardwick (G-4168)
Security Defense Systems Corp ....G 973 235-0606
  Nutley (G-7653)
Swissray America Inc ....E 908 353-0971
  Elizabeth (G-2778)
Vision Ten Inc ....F 201 935-3000
  Carlstadt (G-1239)

YACHT BASIN OPERATIONS

Arnolds Yacht Basin Inc ....G 732 892-3000
  Point Pleasant Boro (G-8931)

YARN & YARN SPINNING

American Drawtech Company Inc ....E 973 684-1600
  Paterson (G-8207)
Kennetex Inc ....D 610 444-0600
  Paterson (G-8308)
Multi-Tex Products Corp ....E 201 991-7262
  Kearny (G-4902)
World Class Marketing Corp ....E 201 313-0022
  Fort Lee (G-3591)

YARN : Crochet, Spun

Kync Design LLC ....G 201 293-4677
  Secaucus (G-9900)

YARN MILLS: Texturizing

Brawer Bros Inc ....C 973 238-0163
  Hawthorne (G-4222)
Dillon Yarn Corporation ....E 973 684-1600
  Paterson (G-8251)

YARN MILLS: Texturizing, Throwing & Twisting

Star Narrow Fabrics Inc ....G 973 778-8600
  Lodi (G-5602)
Warp Processing Inc ....G 973 238-1800
  Hawthorne (G-4266)

YARN MILLS: Throwing

Middleburg Yarn Processing Co ....E 973 238-1800
  Hawthorne (G-4248)

YARN WHOLESALERS

Dollfus Mieg Company Inc ....C 732 662-1005
  Edison (G-2502)

YARN: Manmade & Synthetic Fiber, Twisting Or Winding

Kairos Enterprises LLC ....F 201 731-3181
  Englewood Cliffs (G-2969)

YARN: Specialty & Novelty

Jubili Bead & Yarn Shoppe ....G 856 858-7844
  Collingswood (G-1771)
Multi-Tex Products Corp ....E 201 991-7262
  Kearny (G-4902)